Dear Colleague,

My co-editors and I have worked to present both the classics of British literature and newly current works, in fresh and highly teachable ways. We view this anthology as a collaboration with all who bring it into the classroom, and I would be happy to answer any questions you may have about our selections (either as you consider adopting our text or as you teach from it). I am also very interested in your reactions, your thoughts on how to make things work in class, and suggestions for the anthology's ongoing evolution. I look forward to hearing from you at any time.

David Damrosch
dnd2@columbia.edu

Thank you for requesting
The Longman Anthology of British Literature.
Please accept this hardcover edition with our
compliments. We think you'll discover that this
comprehensive and engaging anthology is much more
than a text—it's an invaluable resource you'll
return to again and again.

When you order *The Longman Anthology of British Literature*
for your students (available only in paperback),
please use this information—

Volume I ISBN 0-321-01173-2
Volume II ISBN 0-321-01174-0

The Longman Anthology
of British Literature

VOLUME 1

David Damrosch
COLUMBIA UNIVERSITY

Christopher Baswell
BARNARD COLLEGE

Clare Carroll
QUEENS COLLEGE, CITY UNIVERSITY OF NEW YORK

Kevin J. H. Dettmar
CLEMSON UNIVERSITY

Heather Henderson
MOUNT HOLYOKE COLLEGE

Constance Jordan
CLAREMONT GRADUATE UNIVERSITY

Peter J. Manning
UNIVERSITY OF SOUTHERN CALIFORNIA

Anne Howland Schotter
WAGNER COLLEGE

William Chapman Sharpe
BARNARD COLLEGE

Stuart Sherman
FORDHAM UNIVERSITY

Jennifer Wicke
UNIVERSITY OF VIRGINIA

Susan J. Wolfson
PRINCETON UNIVERSITY

The Longman Anthology of British Literature

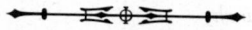

David Damrosch

General Editor

VOLUME 1

THE MIDDLE AGES
Christopher Baswell *and* Anne Howland Schotter

THE EARLY MODERN PERIOD
Constance Jordan *and* Clare Carroll

THE RESTORATION AND THE 18TH CENTURY
Stuart Sherman

An imprint of Addison Wesley Longman, Inc.

New York • Reading, Massachusetts • Menlo Park, California • Harlow, England
Don Mills, Ontario • Sydney • Mexico City • Madrid • Amsterdam

Editor-in-Chief: *Patricia Rossi*
Senior Editor: *Lisa Moore*
Development Editor: *Mark Getlein*
Senior Marketing Manager: *John Holdcroft*
Supplements Editor: *Donna Campion*
Project Coordination and Text Design: *York Production Services*
Cover Designer: *Kay Petronio*
Cover Design Manager: *Nancy Danahy*
On the Cover: *Frontispiece to* The Book of Kells, *Irish (vellum), late 8th century, MS 58 f.291v,*
  Trinity College, Dublin.
Photo Researcher: *Julie Tesser*
Full Service Production Manager: *Valerie Zaborski*
Publishing Services Manager: *Al Dorsey*
Senior Print Buyer: *Hugh Crawford*
Electronic Page Makeup: *York Production Services*
Printer and Binder: *R.R. Donnelley and Sons Company*
Cover Printer: *The Lehigh Press, Inc.*

For permission to use copyrighted material, grateful acknowledgment is made to the copyright holders on pages 2951–2953, which are hereby made part of this copyright page.

Library of Congress Cataloging-in-Publication Data

The Longman anthology of British literature / David Damrosch, general
  editor.
      p.   cm.
    Includes bibliographical references and indexes.
    Contents: v. 1. The Middle Ages / Christopher Baswell and Anne Howland
  Schotter. The early modern period / Constance Jordan and Clare
  Carroll. The Restoration and the 18th century / Stuart Sherman —
  v. 2. The romantics and their contemporaries / Susan Wolfson and Peter
  Manning. The Victorian age / Heather Henderson and William Sharpe.
  The twentieth century / Kevin Dettmar and Jennifer Wicke.
    ISBN 0-321-01173-2 (v. 1). — ISBN 0-321-01174-0 (v. 2)
    1. English literature.   2. Great Britain—Literary collections.
  I. Damrosch, David.
  PR1109.L67   1998
  820.8—dc21   98-4325
                                                            CIP

ISBN 0-321-01173-2

1234567890–DOC–01009998

CONTENTS

Preface   xxix

Acknowledgments   xxxv

The Middle Ages   2

Before the Norman Conquest

BEOWULF   27

THE TÁIN BÓ CUAILNGE   95
    The Pillow Talk   97
    The Táin Begins   103
    The Last Battle   104

JUDITH   114

THE DREAM OF THE ROOD   120

PERSPECTIVES: ETHNIC AND RELIGIOUS ENCOUNTERS   124
BEDE   126
    from An Ecclesiastical History of the English People   126
BISHOP ASSER   131
    from The Life of King Alfred   132
KING ALFRED   134
    Preface to Saint Gregory's *Pastoral Care*   134
OHTHERE'S JOURNEYS   135
THE ANGLO-SAXON CHRONICLE   138
    Stamford Bridge and Hastings   138

TALIESIN   139
    Urien Yrechwydd   140
    The Battle of Argoed Llwyfain   141
    The War-Band's Return   141
    Lament for Owain Son of Urien   143

THE WANDERER   143

WULF AND EADWACER *and* THE WIFE'S LAMENT   146

RIDDLES   149

Three Anglo-Latin Riddles by Aldhelm   150
Five Old English Riddles   150

After the Norman Conquest

PERSPECTIVES: ARTHURIAN MYTH IN THE HISTORY OF BRITAIN   152
GEOFFREY OF MONMOUTH   153
    from History of the Kings of Britain   155
GERALD OF WALES   165
    from The Instruction of Princes   165
EDWARD I   167
    Letter sent to the Papal Court   167
        COMPANION READING
        A Report to Edward I   169

Arthurian Romance   170

MARIE DE FRANCE   170

LAIS   171
Prologue   171
Lanval   172

SIR GAWAIN AND THE GREEN KNIGHT   185

SIR THOMAS MALORY   242

MORTE DARTHUR   243
from Caxton's Prologue   243
The Miracle of Galahad   245
The Poisoned Apple   252
The Day of Destiny   262

GEOFFREY CHAUCER   272

The Parliament of Fowls   276

THE CANTERBURY TALES   293
The General Prologue   293
The Miller's Tale   313
    The Introduction   314
    The Tale   315
The Wife of Bath's Prologue   329
The Wife of Bath's Tale   348
The Pardoner's Prologue   357
The Pardoner's Tale   361
The Nun's Priest's Tale   372

The Parson's Tale   387
   The Introduction   388
   from The Tale   389
     The Remedy for the Sin of Lechery   390
   Chaucer's Retraction   392

To His Scribe Adam   392
Complaint to His Purse   393

WILLIAM LANGLAND   394
  Piers Plowman   396
    Prologue   396
    Passus 2   401
    Passus 6   406
    Passus 18   414

    PIERS PLOWMAN IN CONTEXT: **The Rising of 1381**   425
    from *The Anonimalle Chronicle*   [Wat Tyler's Demands to Richard II,
      and His Death]   426
    Three Poems on the Rising of 1381   John Ball's First Letter   431 •
      John Ball's Second Letter   431 • The Course of Revolt   432
    John Gower   from The Voice of One Crying   434

Mystical Writings   437
RICHARD ROLLE   438
  The Fire of Love   438
    Prologue   438
    Chapter 2. No one attains supreme devotion quickly   440
    Chapter 12. About not judging another, but rather giving thanks   441
    Chapter 15. How and when he was urged to the solitary life   442

from **THE CLOUD OF UNKNOWING**   445

JULIAN OF NORWICH   447
  A Book of Showings   448
    [Three Graces. Illness. The First Relevation]   448
    [Christ Draws Julian in Through His Wound]   452
    [The Necessity of Sin, and of Hating Sin]   453
    [God as Father, Mother, Husband]   455
    [The Meaning of the Visions Is Love]   460

THE SECOND PLAY OF THE SHEPHERDS   461

Literature of Travel: Marvels and Pilgrimage   481

THE VOYAGE OF SAINT BRENDAN   482
    from The Voyage of Saint Brendan   483

SIR JOHN MANDEVILLE   492
    The Travels of Sir John Mandeville   493
        from Chapter 30. Of the royal estate of Prester John   493
        from Chapter 31. Of the head of the devil in the Vale Perilous   496
        Chapter 33. Of the mountains of gold, which the ants watch over   498

MARGERY KEMPE   500
    The Book of Margery Kempe   502
        The Preface   502
        [Life and Temptations, Revelation, Desire for Foreign Pilgrimage]   502
        [Visit with Julian of Norwich]   512
        [Pilgrimage to Jerusalem]   514
        [Mystic Marriage with God]   518

MIDDLE ENGLISH LYRICS   520
    The Cuckoo Song ("Sumer is icumen in")   522
    Spring ("Lenten is come with love to toune")   523
    Alisoun ("Bitwene Mersh and Averil")   523
    I Have a Noble Cock   525
    My Lefe Is Faren in a Lond   525
    Fowles in the Frith   525
    Abuse of Women ("In every place ye may well see")   525
    The Irish Dancer ("Gode sire pray ich thee")   527
    A Forsaken Maiden's Lament ("I lovede a child of this cuntree")   527
    The Wily Clerk ("This enther day I mete a clerke")   528
    Jolly Jankin ("As I went on Yol Day in our procession")   528
    Adam Lay Ibounden   530
    I Sing of a Maiden   530
    In Praise of Mary ("Edi be thu, Hevene Quene")   531
    Mary Is with Child ("Under a tree")   532
    Sweet Jesus, King of Bliss   533
    Now Goeth Sun under Wood   534
    Jesus, My Sweet Lover ("Jesu Christ, my lemmon swete")   535
    Contempt of the World ("Where beth they biforen us weren")   535

THE TALE OF TALIESIN   536

DAFYDD AP GWILYM   549
    Aubade   551
    One Saving Place   552
    The Girls of Llanbadarn   553

Tale of a Wayside Inn   554
The Hateful Husband   556
The Winter   557
The Ruin   558

Middle Scots Poets
558

WILLIAM DUNBAR
559

Lament for the Makars   559
Done Is a Battell   562
In Secreit Place This Hyndir Nycht   563

ROBERT HENRYSON
564

Robene and Makyne   565

The Early Modern Period
568

JOHN SKELTON
589

Philip Sparrow   590

SIR THOMAS WYATT
619

The Long Love, That in My Thought Doth Harbor   620
COMPANION READING
Petrarch, Sonnet 140   621
Whoso List to Hunt   621
COMPANION READING
Petrarch, Sonnet 190   622
My Galley   622
They Flee from Me   623
Some Time I Fled the Fire   623
My Lute, Awake!   623
Tagus, Farewell   624
Forget Not Yet   624
Blame Not My Lute   625
Lucks, My Fair Falcon, and Your Fellows All   626
Stand Whoso List   626
Mine Own John Poyns   627

HENRY HOWARD, EARL OF SURREY
629

Love That Doth Reign and Live within My Thought   630
Th'Assyrians' King, in Peace with Foul Desire   630
Set Me Whereas the Sun Doth Parch the Green   630
The Soote Season   631
Alas, So All Things Now Do Hold Their Peace   631
COMPANION READING
Petrarch, Sonnet 164   631
So Cruel Prison   632
London, Hast Thou Accused Me   633

Wyatt Resteth Here   635
My Radcliffe, When Thy Reckless Youth Offends   636

SIR THOMAS MORE   636

Utopia   637

PERSPECTIVES: GOVERNMENT AND SELF-GOVERNMENT   707

WILLIAM TYNDALE   708
from The Obedience of a Christian Man   708
JUAN LUIS VIVES   709
from Instruction of a Christian Woman   709
SIR THOMAS ELYOT   710
from The Book Named the Governor   711
from The Defence of Good Women   712
JOHN PONET   713
from A Short Treatise of Political Power   713
JOHN FOXE   715
from The Book of Martyrs   716
RICHARD HOOKER   718
from The Laws of Ecclesiastical Polity   718
JAMES I (JAMES VI OF SCOTLAND)   720
from The True Law of Free Monarchies   721
BALDASSARE CASTIGLIONE   722
from The Book of the Courtier   723
ROGER ASCHAM   724
from The Schoolmaster   724
RICHARD MULCASTER   726
from The First Part of the Elementary   726

GEORGE GASCOIGNE   728

Seven Sonnets to Alexander Neville   728
Woodmanship   731

EDMUND SPENSER   735

The Shepheardes Calender   736
October   736

THE FAERIE QUEENE   740
A Letter of the Authors   741
Book 1   744
Book 2, Canto 12   879
Amoretti   898
1 ("Happy ye leaves when as those lilly hands")   898
4 ("New yeare forth looking out of Janus gate")   898
13 ("In that proud port, which her so goodly graceth")   898
22 ("This holy season fit to fast and pray")   899
62 ("The weary yeare his race now having run")   899

65 ("The doubt which ye misdeeme, fayre love, is vaine") 899
66 ("To all those happy blessings which ye have") 900
68 ("The most glorious Lord of lyfe that on this day") 900
75 ("One day I wrote her name upon the strand") 901
Epithalamion 901

SIR PHILIP SIDNEY   911

The Apology for Poetry 913

THE APOLOGY IN CONTEXT: The Art of Poetry 946
Stephen Gosson from The School of Abuse 946
George Puttenham from The Art of English Poesie 948
George Gascoigne from Certain Notes of Instruction 950
Samuel Daniel from A Defense of Rhyme 952

The Arcadia 954
Book 1 954
Astrophil and Stella 987
1 ("Loving in truth, and fain in verse my love to show") 987
31 ("With how sad steps, O Moon, thou climb'st the skies") 987
39 ("Come sleep, O sleep, the certain knot of peace") 988
45 ("Stella oft sees the very face of woe") 988
60 ("When my good Angel guides me to the place") 988
71 ("Who will in fairest book of Nature know") 989
Fourth song ("Only joy, now here you are") 989
Eighth song ("In a grove most rich of shade") 990
106 ("O absent presence, Stella is not here") 993
108 ("When sorrow (using mine own fire's might)") 993

ISABELLA WHITNEY   994
I. W. To Her Unconstant Lover 994
The Admonition by the Author 998
A Careful Complaint by the Unfortunate Author 1001
The Manner of Her Will 1002

MARY HERBERT, COUNTESS OF PEMBROKE   1010
Even Now That Care 1010
To Thee Pure Sprite 1013
Psalm 71: In Te Domini Speravi ("On thee my trust is grounded") 1015
COMPANION READING
Miles Coverdale: Psalm 71 1018
Psalm 121: Levavi Oculos ("Unto the hills, I now will bend") 1018
The Doleful Lay of Clorinda 1019

ELIZABETH I   1021
Written with a Diamond on Her Window at Woodstock 1023
Written on a Wall at Woodstock 1024

The Doubt of Future Foes   1024
On Monsieur's Departure   1024
Psalm 13 ("Fools that true faith yet never had")   1025
The Metres of Boethius's *Consolation of Philosophy*   1025
    Book 1, No. 2 ("O in how headlong depth the drowned mind is dim")   1025
    Book 1, No. 7 ("Dim clouds")   1026
    Book 2, No. 3 ("In pool when Phoebus with reddy wain")   1027

SPEECHES   1027
On Marriage   1027
On Mary, Queen of Scots   1028
On Mary's Execution   1031
To the English Troops at Tilbury   1033
The Golden Speech   1034

AEMILIA LANYER   1036
The Description of Cookham   1036
Salve Deus Rex Judaeorum   1041
    To the Doubtful Reader   1041
    To the Virtuous Reader   1041
    [Invocation]   1042
    [Against Beauty Without Virtue]   1043
    [Pilate's Wife Apologizes for Eve]   1044

SIR WALTER RALEIGH   1046
Nature That Washed Her Hands in Milk   1047
To the Queen   1048
On the Life of Man   1049
The Author's Epitaph, Made by Himself   1049
As You Came from the Holy Land   1049
from The 21st and Last Book of the Ocean to Cynthia   1051
The Discovery of the Large, Rich and Beautiful Empire of Guiana   1055
    from Epistle Dedicatory   1055
    To the Reader   1057
    [The Amazons]   1060
    [The Orinoco]   1061
    [The King of Aromaia]   1062
    [The New World of Guiana]   1064

THE DISCOVERY IN CONTEXT: Voyage Literature   1066
    Arthur Barlow   from The First Voyage Made to the Coasts of America   1067
    Thomas Hariot   from A Brief and True Report of the Newfound Land
        of Virginia   1071
    René Landonnière   from A Notable History Containing Four Voyages
        Made to Florida   1074
    Michel de Montaigne   from Of Cannibals   1077

RICHARD BARNFIELD   1078
The Affectionate Shepherd   1079

Sonnets from *Cynthia*   1095
   1 ("Sporting at fancy, setting light by love")   1095
   5 ("It is reported of fair Thetis' son")   1095
   9 ("Diana (on a time) walking the wood")   1096
   11 ("Sighing, and sadly sitting by my love")   1096
   13 ("Speak, Echo, tell; how may I call my love?")   1096
   19 ("Ah no; nor I myself: though my pure love")   1097

CHRISTOPHER MARLOWE   1098

The Passionate Shepherd to His Love   1098
  COMPANION READING
  Sir Walter Raleigh: The Nymph's Reply to the Shepherd   1099
Hero and Leander   1100
The Tragical History of Dr. Faustus   1117

WILLIAM SHAKESPEARE   1166

SONNETS   1169
   1 ("From fairest creatures we desire increase")   1169
   12 ("When I do count the clock that tells the time")   1169
   15 ("When I consider every thing that grows")   1170
   18 ("Shall I compare thee to a summer's day")   1170
   20 ("A woman's face with Nature's own hand painted")   1170
   29 ("When, in disgrace with fortune and men's eyes")   1171
   31 ("Thy bosom is endearèd with all hearts")   1171
   33 ("Full many a glorious morning have I seen")   1171
   35 ("No more be grieved at that which thou hast done")   1172
   55 ("Not marble nor the gilded monuments")   1172
   60 ("Like as the waves make towards the pebbled shore")   1172
   73 ("That time of year thou mayst in me behold")   1173
   80 ("O, how I faint when I of you do write")   1173
   86 ("Was it the proud full sail of his great verse")   1173
   87 ("Farewell! Thou art too dear for my possessing")   1174
   93 ("So shall I live, supposing thou art true")   1174
   104 ("To me, fair friend, you never can be old")   1175
   106 ("When in the chronicle of wasted time")   1175
   107 ("Not mine own fears nor the prophetic soul")   1175
   116 ("Let me not to the marriage of true minds")   1176
   123 ("No, Time, thou shalt not boast that I do change")   1176
   124 ("If my dear love were but the child of state")   1176
   126 ("O thou, my lovely boy, who in thy power")   1177
   130 ("My mistress' eyes are nothing like the sun")   1177
   138 ("When my love swears that she is made of truth")   1178
   144 ("Two loves I have, of comfort and despair")   1178
   152 ("In loving thee thou know'st I am forsworn")   1178

Othello, the Moor of Venice   1179

OTHELLO IN CONTEXT: Ethnography in the Literature
of Travel and Colonization   1261
Peter Martyr   *from* Decades of the New World   1261
Pliny the Elder   *from* The History of the World   1265
Leo Africanus   *from* The History and Description of Africa   1265
Edmund Spenser   *from* A View of the Present State of Ireland   1271
Sir John Smith   *from* The General History of Virginia, New England and the
Summer Isles   1273

ELIZABETH CARY   1275
The Tragedy of Mariam, The Fair Queen of Jewry   1277

PERSPECTIVES: TRACTS ON WOMEN AND GENDER   1329
DESIDERIUS ERASMUS   1330
from In Laude and Praise of Matrimony   1331
BARNABE RICHE   1332
from My Lady's Looking Glass   1332
MARGARET TYLER   1333
from Preface to The First Part of the Mirror of Princely Deeds   1334
JOSEPH SWETNAM   1335
from The Arraignment of Lewd, Idle, Forward, and Inconstant Women   1336
RACHEL SPEGHT   1338
from A Muzzle for Melastomus   1339
ESTHER SOWERNAM   1344
from Ester Hath Hanged Haman   1344
HIC MULIER AND HAEC VIR   1347
from Hic-Mulier; or, The Man-Woman   1348
from Haec Vir; or, The Womanish Man   1350

THOMAS DEKKER and THOMAS MIDDLETON   1355
The Roaring Girl; or, Moll Cut-Purse   1357

THE ROARING GIRL IN CONTEXT: City Life   1425
Barnabe Riche   *from* My Lady's Looking Glass   1427
Robert Greene   *from* A Notable Discovery of Cosenage   1428
Thomas Dekker   *from* Lantern and Candlelight   1429
Thomas Deloney   *from* Thomas of Reading   1432
Thomas Nashe   *from* Pierce Penniless   1439
King James I   *from* A Counterblast to Tobacco   1441

BEN JONSON   1443
Volpone; or, The Fox   1444
On Something, That Walks Somewhere   1531
On My First Daughter   1531
To John Donne   1532
On My First Son   1532
Inviting a Friend to Supper   1532
To Penshurst   1533
Song to Celia   1535

Queen and Huntress   1536

To the Memory of My Beloved, the Author, Mr. William Shakespeare,
and What He Hath Left Us   1536

To the Immortal Memory, and Friendship of that Noble Pair, Sir Lucius
Cary and Sir H. Morison   1538

Pleasure Reconciled to Virtue   1541

JOHN DONNE   1549

The Good Morrow   1550

Song ("Go, and catch a falling star")   1551

The Undertaking   1552

The Sun Rising   1552

The Indifferent   1553

The Canonization   1554

Air and Angels   1555

Break of Day   1555

A Valediction: of Weeping   1556

Love's Alchemy   1557

The Flea   1557

The Bait   1558

The Apparition   1558

A Valediction: Forbidding Mourning   1559

The Ecstasy   1560

The Funeral   1562

The Relic   1562

Elegy 19: To His Mistress Going to Bed   1563

Holy Sonnets   1564

1 ("As due by many titles I resign")   1564

2 ("Oh my black soul! Now thou art summoned")   1565

3 ("This is my play's last scene, here heavens appoint")   1565

4 ("At the round earth's imagined corners, blow")   1565

5 ("If poisonous minerals, and if that tree")   1566

6 ("Death be not proud, though some have called thee")   1566

7 ("Spit in my face ye Jews, and pierce my side")   1566

8 ("Why are we by all creatures waited on?")   1567

9 ("What if this present were the world's last night?")   1567

10 ("Batter my heart, three-personed God; for, you")   1567

11 ("Wilt thou love God, as he thee? Then digest")   1568

12 ("Father, part of his double interest")   1568

Devotions Upon Emergent Occasions   1568

["For whom the bell tolls"]   1568

from A Sermon Preached to the Honorable Company
of the Virginia Plantation   1569

LADY MARY WROTH   1571

Pamphilia to Amphilanthus   1573

1 ("When night's black mantle could most darkness prove")   1573

16 ("Am I thus conquered? Have I lost the powers")   1573

17 ("Truly poor Night thou welcome art to me")   1573
26 ("When everyone to pleasing pastime hies")   1574
28. Song ("Sweetest love, return again")   1574
39 ("Take heed mine eyes, how you your looks do cast")   1575
40 ("False hope which feeds but to destroy, and spill")   1575
48 ("If ever Love had force in human breast?")   1575
68 ("My pain, still smothered in my grièved breast")   1576
74. Song ("Love a child is ever crying")   1576
from A Crown of Sonnets Dedicated to Love   1576
77 ("In this strange labyrinth how shall I turn?")   1576
83 ("How blessed be they then, who his favors prove")   1577
103 ("My muse now happy, lay thyself to rest")   1577

ROBERT HERRICK   1578

The Argument of His Book   1578
Delight in Disorder   1579
Corinna's Going A-Maying   1579
To the Virgins, to Make Much of Time   1581
The Hock-Cart, or Harvest Home   1581
His Prayer to Ben Jonson   1582
Upon Julia's Clothes   1583
Upon His Spaniel Tracie   1583

GEORGE HERBERT   1583

The Altar   1584
Redemption   1585
Easter   1585
Easter Wings   1586
Affliction (1)   1586
Prayer (1)   1588
Jordan (1)   1588
Church Monuments   1589
The Windows   1589
Denial   1590
Virtue   1591
Man   1591
Jordan (2)   1592
Time   1593
The Collar   1593
The Pulley   1594
The Forerunners   1595
Love (3)   1596

PERSPECTIVES: EMBLEM, STYLE, AND METAPHOR   1596

GEOFFREY WHITNEY   1599
The Phoenix   1599

BEN JONSON   1600
  from Timber: or Discoveries   1600
GIORDANO BRUNO   1604
  from On the Composition of Images, Signs, and Ideas   1604
CONTE EMMANUELE TESAURO   1605
  from Through the Lens of Aristotle   1606
RICHARD CRASHAW   1607
  To the Noblest and best of Ladies, the Countess of Denbigh   1608

RICHARD LOVELACE   1609
  To Lucasta, Going to the Wars   1610
  The Grasshopper   1610
  To Althea, from Prison   1612
  Love Made in the First Age: To Chloris   1612

HENRY VAUGHAN   1614
  Regeneration   1615
  The Retreat   1617
  Silence, and Stealth of Days   1618
  The World   1618
  They Are All Gone into the World of Light!   1620
  The Night   1621

ANDREW MARVELL   1622
  The Coronet   1624
  Bermudas   1624
  The Nymph Complaining for the Death of Her Fawn   1625
  To His Coy Mistress   1628
  The Definition of Love   1629
  The Mower Against Gardens   1630
  The Mower's Song   1631
  The Garden   1631
  from Upon Appleton House   1633
  An Horatian Ode Upon Cromwell's Return from Ireland   1643

KATHERINE PHILIPS   1646
  Friendship in Emblem, or the Seal   1647
  Upon the Double Murder of King Charles   1648
  On the Third of September, 1651   1649
  To the Truly Noble, and Obliging Mrs. Anne Owen   1650
  To Mrs. Mary Awbrey at Parting   1651
  To My Excellent Lucasia, on Our Friendship   1652
  The World   1653

            The Development of English Prose   1655
FRANCIS BACON   1655
  Of Truth   1656

Of Marriage and Single Life   1657
Of Superstition   1658
Of Plantations   1659
Of Studies [version of 1597]   1661
Of Studies [version of 1625]   1662

THE KING JAMES BIBLE   1663
Genesis 2-3   1663

LADY MARY WROTH   1666
from The Countess of Montgomery's Urania   1666

THOMAS HOBBES   1670
Leviathan   1670
Chapter 13. Of the Natural Condition of Mankind as Concerning
their Felicity, and Misery   1670

SIR THOMAS BROWNE   1673
Religio Medici   1674
from Part 1   1674
Pseudodoxia Epidemica   1678
Book 1, Chapter 1. Of the first Cause of Common Errors;
the common infirmity of Human Nature   1678
Hydriotaphia, Urn Burial   1680
from Chapter 1   1680
Chapter 5   1684

ROBERT BURTON   1690
The Anatomy of Melancholy   1690
[The Utopia of Democritus]   1690
Division of the Body, Humors, Spirits   1696

PERSPECTIVES: THE CIVIL WAR, OR THE WARS
OF THREE KINGDOMS   1698
JOHN GAUDEN   1701
from Eikon Basilike   1702
JOHN MILTON   1704
from Eikonoklastes   1705
THE PETITION OF THE GENTLEWOMEN AND TRADESMEN'S WIVES   1711
JOHN LILBURNE   1715
from England's New Chains Discovered   1715
OLIVER CROMWELL   1718
from Letters from Ireland   1719
JOHN O'DWYER OF THE GLENN   1722
THE STORY OF ALEXANDER AGNEW; OR, JOCK OF BROAD SCOTLAND   1724

EDWARD HYDE, EARL OF CLARENDON   1725
  from True Historical Narrative of the Rebellion   1726

JOHN MILTON   1729
  L'Allegro   1731
  Il Penseroso   1734
  Lycidas   1738
  How Soon Hath Time   1743
  On the New Forcers of Conscience Under the Long Parliament   1743
  To the Lord General Cromwell   1744
  On the Late Massacre in Piedmont   1745
  When I Consider How My Light Is Spent   1745
  Methought I Saw My Late Espoused Saint   1746
  from Areopagitica   1746

  PARADISE LOST   1755
  Book 1   1756
  Book 2   1776
  from Book 3   1799
  from Book 4   1813
  from Book 5   1832
  Book 6   1842
      The Argument   1842
  Book 7   1842
      The Argument   1842
      [The Invocation]   1843
  from Book 8   1844
  Book 9   1854
  Book 10   1879
  Book 11   1897
      The Argument   1897
  Book 12   1898

  Samson Agonistes   1905

PERSPECTIVES: SPIRITUAL SELF-RECKONINGS   1946
THE LADY FALKLAND: HER LIFE   1946
  from The Lady Falkland: Her Life, by one of Her Daughters   1947
ANNA TRAPNEL   1954
  from Anna Trapnel's Report and Plea   1954
ALICE THORNTON   1961
  from Book of Remembrances   1961
RALPH JOSSELIN   1965
  from Diary   1965
DANIEL DEFOE   1966
  from The Life and Strange and Surprizing Adventures
    of Robinson Crusoe, of York, Mariner   1967
JOHN BUNYAN   1968
  from The Pilgrim's Progress   1968

The Restoration and the Eighteenth Century   1978

SAMUEL PEPYS   2003
The Diary   2004
[First Entries]   2004
[The Coronation of Charles II]   2006
[The Plague Year]   2008
[The Fire of London]   2014
COMPANION READING
John Evelyn: *from* Kalendarium   2018
[The Royal Society]   2020
[Theater and Music]   2024
[Elizabeth Pepys and Deborah Willett]   2025

MARY CARLETON   2030
from The Case of Madam Mary Carleton   2030

PERSPECTIVES: THE ROYAL SOCIETY AND THE NEW SCIENCE   2039
THOMAS SPRAT   2041
from The History of the Royal Society of London   2042
PHILOSOPHICAL TRANSACTIONS   2044
from Philosophical Transactions   2044
ROBERT HOOKE   2047
from Micrographia   2048
JOHN AUBREY   2054
from Brief Lives   2055

MARGARET CAVENDISH, DUTCHESS OF NEWCASTLE   2058
POEMS AND FANCIES   2059
The Poetress's Hasty Resolution   2059
The Poetress's Petition   2060
An Apology for Writing So Much upon This Book   2060
The Hunting of the Hare   2060

from A True Relation of My Birth, Breeding, and Life   2063

Observations upon Experimental Philosophy   2068
Of Micrography, and of Magnifying and Multiplying Glasses   2068
The Description of a New Blazing World   2070
from To the Reader   2070
[Creating Worlds]   2071
[Empress, Duchess, Duke]   2072
Epilogue   2073

JOHN DRYDEN   2074

Absalom and Achitophel: A Poem   2076
COMPANION READING
Charles II: His Majesty's Declaration   2101
Mac Flecknoe   2103
To the Memory of Mr. Oldham   2109
To the Pious Memory of the Accomplished Young Lady
   Mrs. Anne Killigrew   2109
Alexander's Feast   2114
Fables Ancient and Modern   2119
   from the Preface   2119
   from The Cock and the Fox   2127

APHRA BEHN   2129

The Disappointment   2130
To Lysander, On Some Verses He Writ   2133
To Lysander at the Music-Meeting   2135
A Letter to Mr. Creech at Oxford   2136
To the Fair Clarinda, Who Made Love to Me, Imagined More
   than Woman   2138

   APHRA BEHN IN CONTEXT: Coterie Writing   2139
   Mary, Lady Chudleigh   To the Ladies   2139 • To Almystrea   2140
   Anne Finch, Countess of Winchilsea   The Introduction   2141 •
     Friendship Between Ephelia and Ardelia   2143 •
     A Ballad to Mrs. Catherine Fleming in London   2143
   Mary Leapor   The Headache. To Aurelia   2145 •
     Advice to Sophronia   2147 • An Essay on Woman   2147 •
     The Epistle of Deborah Dough   2149
Oroonoko   2150

JOHN WILMOT, EARL OF ROCHESTER   2193

Against Constancy   2194
The Disabled Debauchee   2195
Song ("Love a woman? You're an ass!")   2196
The Imperfect Enjoyment   2196
Upon Nothing   2198
A Satyr Against Reason and Mankind   2199

GEORGE ETHEREGE   2204

The Man of Mode; or, Sir Fopling Flutter   2205

   THE MAN OF MODE IN CONTEXT: The Collier
    Controversy   2270
   Jeremy Collier   from A Short View of the Immorality and Profaneness
   of the English Stage   2271

Richard Steele   The Spectator, No. 65   2273
John Dennis   *from* A Defense of "Sir Fopling Flutter"   2275

MARY ASTELL   2280
from Some Reflections upon Marriage   2280

DANIEL DEFOE   2289
A True Relation of the Apparition of One Mrs. Veal   2291

A TRUE RELATION IN CONTEXT: Parallel Accounts   2297
L. Lukyn   Letter to her Aunt   2298
Stephen Gray   Letter to John Flamsteed   2299
An Interview with Mrs. Bargrave   2303

A Journal of the Plague Year   2304
[At the Burial Pit]   2304
[Encounter with a Waterman]   2308

PERSPECTIVES: READING PAPERS   2311
NEWS AND COMMENT   2312
from Mercurius Publicus [Anniversary of the Regicide]   2312
from The London Gazette [The Fire of London]   2313
from Daily Courant No. 1 [Editorial Policy]   2314
Daniel Defoe: *from* A Review of the State of the British Nation, Vol. 4, No. 21
   [The New Union]   2315
from The Craftsman No. 307 [Vampires in Britain]   2317
PERIODICAL PERSONAE   2320
Richard Steele: *from* Tatler No. 1 [Introducing Mr. Bickerstaff]   2321
Joseph Addison: *from* Spectator No. 1 [Introducing Mr. Spectator]   2324
from Female Spectator No. 1 [The Author's Intent]   2326
Richard Steele: *from* Tatler No. 18 [The News Writers in Danger]   2328
Joseph Addison: *from* Tatler No. 155 [The Political Upholsterer]   2328
Joseph Addison: *from* Spectator No. 10 [The *Spectator* and Its Readers]   2330
GETTING, SPENDING, SPECULATING   2332
Joseph Addison: Spectator No. 69 [Royal Exchange]   2334
Richard Steele: Spectator No. 11 [Inkle and Yarico]   2337
Daniel Defoe: *from* A Review of the State of the British Nation, Vol. 1, No. 43
   [Weak Foundations]   2340
Advertisements from the *Spectator*   2341
A BUBBLER'S MEDLEY   2341
from Historical Register for the Year 1720   2343
Anne Finch: A Song on the South Sea   2344
Thomas D'Urfey: The Hubble Bubbles   2344
Thomas Read: *from* The Weekly Journal   2345
Nicholas Amhurst: *from* The Craftsman No. 47 [Usbeck to Rica at Ispahan]   2346
WOMEN AND MEN, MANNERS AND MARRIAGE   2347
Richard Steele: *from* Tatler No. 25 [Duellists]   2347

Daniel Defoe: *from* A Review of the State of the British Nation, Vol. 9, No. 34
  [A Duellist's Conscience]   2349
from The Athenian Mercury   2351
Richard Steele: *from* Tatler No. 104 [Jenny Distaff Newly Married]   2354
Joseph Addison: Spectator No. 128 [Variety of Temper]   2355
Eliza Haywood: *from* The Female Spectator, Vol. 1, No. 1
  [Seomanthe's Elopement]   2357
Eliza Haywood: *from* The Female Spectator, Vol. 2, No. 10
  [Women's Education]   2360

JONATHAN SWIFT   2362
  A Description of the Morning   2364
  A Description of a City Shower   2365
  Stella's Birthday, 1719   2367
  Stella's Birthday, 1727   2368
  The Lady's Dressing Room   2370
  Verses on the Death of Dr. Swift, D.S.P.D.   2374
  Journal to Stella   2387
    Letter 10   2387
  Gulliver's Travels   2391
    Part 3. A Voyage to Laputa   2392
      Chapter 5   2392
      Chapter 10   2397
    Part 4. A Voyage to the Country of the Houyhnhnms   2402
    COMPANION READINGS
    LETTERS ON *GULLIVER'S TRAVELS*
    Jonathan Swift to Alexander Pope   2447
    Alexander Pope to Jonathan Swift   2448
    John Gay to Jonathan Swift   2448
    Jonathan Swift to Alexander Pope   2450
    "The Prince of Lilliput" to Stella   2450
  A Modest Proposal   2451
    COMPANION READING
    William Petty: *from* Political Arithmetic   2457

ALEXANDER POPE   2459
  An Essay on Criticism   2461
  Windsor-Forest   2478
  The Rape of the Lock   2489
  The Iliad   2509
    from Preface [On Translation]   2509
    from Book 12 [Sarpedon's Speech]   2511
  Eloisa to Abelard   2512
  Epistle 4. To Richard Boyle, Earl of Burlington   2520
  An Essay on Man   2526
    Epistle 1   2526
      To the Reader   2526

The Design   2527
Argument   2528
An Epistle from Mr. Pope, to Dr. Arbuthnot   2535
The Dunciad   2546
Book the Fourth   2546
[The Goddess Coming in Her Majesty]   2547
[The Geniuses of the Schools]   2548
[Young Gentlemen Returned from Travel]   2549
[The Minute Philosophers and the Consummation of All]   2550

LADY MARY WORTLEY MONTAGU   2557
The Turkish Embassy Letters   2558
To Lady —— [On the Turkish Baths]   2558
To Lady Mar [On Turkish Dress]   2560
Letter to Lady Bute [On Her Granddaughter]   2563
Epistle from Mrs. Yonge to her Husband   2565
The Lover: A Ballad   2567
The Reasons That Induced Dr. S. to write a Poem called
The Lady's Dressing Room   2568

JOHN GAY   2571
The Beggar's Opera   2573

WILLIAM HOGARTH   2616
A Rake's Progress   2618

PERSPECTIVES: MIND AND GOD   2626
ISAAC NEWTON   2627
from Letter to Richard Bentley   2628
JOHN LOCKE   2630
from An Essay Concerning Human Understanding   2631
ISAAC WATTS   2635
A Prospect of Heaven Makes Death Easy   2635
The Hurry of the Spirits, in a Fever and Nervous Disorders   2636
Against Idleness and Mischief   2637
Man Frail, and God Eternal   2638
Miracles Attending Israel's Journey   2639
JOSEPH ADDISON   2640
Spectator No. 465   2640
GEORGE BERKELEY   2641
from Three Dialogues Between Hylas and Philonous   2642
DAVID HUME   2644
from A Treatise of Human Nature   2644
from An Enquiry Concerning Human Understanding   2647
CHRISTOPHER SMART   2650
from Jubilate Agno   2650

WILLIAM COWPER   2653
   Light Shining out of Darkness   2654
   from The Task   2654
   The Cast-away   2655

JAMES THOMSON   2657
   Winter. A Poem   2658
     [Autumn Evening and Night]   2658
     [Winter Night]   2661
   The Seasons   2662
     from Autumn   2662
   Rule, Britannia   2666

     THE SEASONS IN CONTEXT: Poems of Nightfall
       and Night   2667
     Anne Finch   A Nocturnal Reverie   2668
     Edward Young   *from* The Complaint   2669
     William Collins   Ode to Evening   2671 • Ode Occasioned by
       the Death of Mr. Thomson   2673
     William Cowper   *from* The Task   2674

THOMAS GRAY   2677
   LETTERS
   To Horace Walpole, 16 April 1734   2678
   To Richard West, December 1736   2679
   To Horace Walpole, 12 June 1750   2680
   To Horace Walpole, 11 February 1751   2680
   To Horace Walpole, 20 February 1751   2681

   Sonnet on the Death of Mr. Richard West   2682
   Ode on a Distant Prospect of Eton College   2682
   Ode on the Death of a Favorite Cat, Drowned in a Tub of
     Gold Fishes   2684
   Elegy Written in a Country Churchyard   2685

SAMUEL JOHNSON   2689
   The Vanity of Human Wishes   2692
   A Short Song of Congratulation   2700
   On the Death of Dr. Robert Levet   2701

   THE RAMBLER
   No. 4 [On Fiction]   2702
   No. 5 [On Spring]   2705
   No. 60 [On Biography]   2708
   No. 170 [On Misella, a Prostitute]   2711
   No. 171 [Misella Continues]   2713
   No. 207 [Beginnings, Middles, and Ends]   2716

from A Review of Soame Jenyns' *A Free Inquiry into the Nature and Origin of Evil*   2719

THE IDLER
No. 31 [On Idleness]   2724
No. 32 [On Sleep]   2725
No. 84 [On Autobiography]   2727
No. 97 [On Travel Writing]   2729

A Dictionary of the English Language   2730
    from Preface   2731
    [Some Entries]   2737
Rasselas   2744
    [The History of Imlac]   2745
The Plays of William Shakespeare   2753
    from Preface   2754
    [Selected Notes on *Othello*]   2762

TRAVEL WRITING   2765
Letter to Hester Thrale (21 September 1773)   2765
A Journey to the Western Islands of Scotland   2770
    Anoch   2770
    Glensheals   2773
    The Highlands   2774
    Glenelg   2777
    from Skye. Armidel   2778

Lives of the Poets   2778
    from The Life of Milton   2779
    from The Life of Pope   2781

from Annals [Infancy and Childhood]   2788

LETTERS
To Lord Chesterfield (7 February 1755)   2792
To Hester Thrale (19 June 1783)   2793
To Hester Thrale Piozzi (2 July 1784)   2795
To Hester Thrale Piozzi (8 July 1784)   2795

JAMES BOSWELL   2796

London Journal   2797
    [A Scot in London]   2797
    [Louisa]   2800
    [First Meeting with Johnson]   2805
An Account of My Last Interview with David Hume, Esq.   2805
from A Journal of a Tour to the Hebrides with Dr. Samuel Johnson   2809
The Life of Samuel Johnson, LL.D.   2813
    [Introduction; Boswell's Method]   2813
    [Conversations about Hume]   2815

[Dinner with Wilkes]   2817
[Conversations at Streatham and the Club]   2823

HESTER SALUSBURY THRALE PIOZZI   2829
The Family Book   2830
[On Her Daughter's Progress]   2830
[On the Death of Her Son]   2831
[On Her Marriage and Household]   2834
Thraliana   2835
[First Entries]   2835
[The Death of Henry Thrale; Marriage to Gabriel Piozzi]   2838
[The Death of Johnson]   2842

OLIVER GOLDSMITH   2843
The Deserted Village   2844
COMPANION READINGS
George Crabbe: *from* The Village   2854
George Crabbe: *from* The Parish Register   2856

PERSPECTIVES: LANDSCAPE, PLEASURE, POWER   2857
SIR JOHN DENHAM   2858
Cooper's Hill   2859
JOSEPH ADDISON   2867
from Spectator No. 412 [The Great, the Uncommon, the Beautiful]   2867
Spectator No. 414 [Nature, Art, Gardens]   2869
ALEXANDER POPE   2872
Letter to Edward Blount [Grotto and Garden]   2872
HORACE WALPOLE   2874
Letter to Sir Horace Mann [The Garden at Strawberry Hill]   2874
EDMUND BURKE   2875
from A Philosophical Enquiry into the Origin of Our Ideas of the Sublime
and the Beautiful   2875
THOMAS GRAY   2882
from A Journal-Letter to Thomas Wharton [The Sublime and the Beautiful in
the Lake District]   2882
WILLIAM GILPIN   2883
from On Picturesque Travel   2884

Political and Religious Orders   2887

Money, Weights, and Measures   2893

Glossary of Literary and Cultural Terms   2895

Bibliographies   2919

Credits   2951

Index   2955

PREFACE

This is an exciting time to be reading British literature. Literary studies are experiencing a time of transformation, involving lively debate about the nature of literature itself, its relations to the wider culture, and the best ways to read and understand it. These questions have been sharpened by the "culture wars" of recent years, in which traditionalists have debated advocates of fundamental reform, close readers have come up against cultural theorists who may seem more interested in politics than in aesthetic questions, and lovers of canonical texts have found themselves sharing the stage with multiculturalists who typically focus on ethnic and minority literatures, usually contemporary and often popular in nature, rather than on earlier and more elite literary productions.

The goal of this anthology is to present the wealth of British literature, old and new, classic and newly current, in ways that will respond creatively to these debates. We have constructed this anthology in the firm belief that it is important to attend both to aesthetic and to cultural questions as we study literature, and to continue to read the great classics even as we discover or rediscover new or neglected works. Admittedly, it is difficult to do all this at once, especially within the pages of a single anthology or the time constraints of a survey course. To work toward these goals, it has been necessary to rethink the very form of an anthology. This preface can serve as a kind of road map to the several thousand pages that follow.

A NEW LITERARY GEOGRAPHY

Let us begin by defining our basic terms: What is "British" literature? What is literature itself? And just what is the function of an anthology at the present time? The term "British" can mean many things, some of them contradictory, some of them even offensive to people on whom the name has been imposed. If the term has no ultimate essence, it does have a history. The first British were Celtic people who inhabited the British Isles and the northern coast of France (still called Brittany), before various Germanic tribes of Angles and Saxons moved onto the islands in the fifth and sixth centuries. Gradually the Angles and Saxons amalgamated into the Anglo-Saxon culture that became dominant in the southern and eastern regions of Britain and then spread outward; the old British people were pushed west, toward what became known as Cornwall, Wales, and Ireland, which remained independent kingdoms for centuries, as did Celtic Scotland to the north. By an ironic twist of linguistic fate, the Anglo-Saxons began to appropriate the term British from the Britons they had displaced, and they took as a national hero the legendary Welsh King Arthur. By the seventeenth century, English monarchs had extended their sway over Wales, Ireland, and Scotland, and they began to refer to their holdings as "Great Britain." Today, Great Britain includes England, Wales, Scotland, and Northern Ireland, but does not include the Republic of Ireland, which has been independent from England since 1922.

This anthology uses "British" in a broad sense, as a geographical term encompassing the whole of the British Isles. For all its fraught history, it seems a more satisfactory term than to speak simply of "English" literature, for two reasons. First: most speakers of English live in countries that are not the focus of this anthology; second, while the English language and its literature have long been dominant in the British Isles, other cultures in the region have always used other languages and have produced great literature in these languages. Important works by Irish, Welsh, and Scots writers appear regularly in the body of this anthology, some of them written directly in their languages and presented here in translation, others written in an English inflected by the rhythms, habits of thought, and modes of expression characteristic of these other languages and the people who use them. Important works, moreover, have often been written in the British Isles by recent arrivals, from Marie de France in the twelfth century to T. S. Eliot and Salman Rushdie in the twentieth; in a very real sense, their writings too are part of British literary production.

We use the term "literature" itself in a similarly capacious sense, to refer to a range of artistically shaped works written in a charged language, appealing to the imagination at least as much as to discursive reasoning. It is only relatively recently that creative writers have been able to make a living composing poems, plays, and novels purely "for art's sake," and only in the past hundred years or so have "belles lettres" or works of high literary art been thought of as sharply separate from other sorts of writing that the same authors would regularly produce. Sometimes, Romantic poets wrote sonnets to explore the deepest mysteries of individual perception and memory; at other times, they wrote sonnets the way a person might now write an Op-Ed piece, and such a sonnet would be published and read along with parliamentary debates and letters to the editor on the most pressing contemporary issues.

Great literature is double in nature: it is deeply rooted in its cultural moment, and yet it transcends this moment as well, speaking to new readers in distant times and places, long after the immediate circumstances of its production have been forgotten. The challenge today is to restore our awareness of cultural contexts without trapping our texts within them. Great writers create imaginative worlds that have their own compelling internal logic, built around the stories they tell using formal patterns of genre, literary reference, imagery, and style. At the same time, as Virginia Woolf says in *A Room of One's Own*, the gossamer threads of the artist's web are joined to reality "with bands of steel." To understand where a writer is taking us imaginatively, it is helpful to know where we are supposed to be starting from in reality: any writer assumes a common body of current knowledge, which this anthology attempts to fill in by means of detailed period introductions, full introductions to the individual authors, and notes and glosses to each text. Many of the greatest works of literature, moreover, have been written in response to the most sharply contested issues of the authors' own times. This anthology presents and groups selections in such a way as to suggest the literary and cultural contexts in which, and for which, they were created.

WOMEN'S WRITING, AND MEN'S

Literary culture has always involved an interplay between central and marginal regions, groups, and individuals. At a given time, some will seem dominant; in retrospect, some will remain so and others will be eclipsed, for a time or permanently, while formerly neglected writers may achieve a new currency. A major emphasis in literary study in recent years has been the recovery of writing by a range of women writers, some of them little read until recently, others major figures in their time and now again fascinating to read. Attending to the voices of such compelling writers as Margery Kempe, Elizabeth Cary, Mary Wollstonecraft, Mary Shelley, and Edith Nesbit often involves a shift in our understanding of the literary landscape, giving a new and lively perspective on much-read works. Thus, Shakespeare's *Othello* can fruitfully be read together with Elizabeth Cary's *Tragedy of Mariam, the Fair Queen of Jewry*, which tells a tale of jealousy and betrayal from a woman's point of view. On a larger scale, the first third of the nineteenth century can be defined more broadly than as a "Romantic Age" dominated by six male poets; looking closely at women's writing as well as men's, and at prose writing as well as poetry, we can deepen our understanding of the period as a whole—including the specific achievements of Blake, William Wordsworth, Coleridge, Keats, Percy Shelley, and Byron, all of whom continue to have a major presence in these pages as most of them did during the nineteenth century.

HISTORICAL PERIODS IN PERSPECTIVE

Overall, we have sought to give a varied presentation of the major periods of literary history, as customarily construed by scholars today: the Middle Ages (punctuated by the Norman Conquest in 1066); the early modern period or Renaissance; the Restoration and the eighteenth century; the era of the Romantics and their contemporaries; the Victorian age; and the twentieth century. These names mix chronology, politics, and literary movements: each period is of course a mixture of all of these elements and many others. Further, the boundaries of all these periods are fluid. Milton should be thought of in the context of Restoration politics as well as of early modern humanism; what is more, selections from *Paradise Lost* will also be found in Volume 2, in a Context section showing Milton's influence on the Romantics and their contemporaries. Reflecting the division of Thomas Hardy's literary life, Hardy appears in the Victorian section as a prose writer, and in the Twentieth Century as a poet. In general, one of the great pleasures of a survey of centuries of British literary production is the opportunity to see the ways texts speak to one another both across periods and within them, and indeed several layers of time may coexist within a single era: many writers consciously or unconsciously hearken back to earlier values (there were medievalists in the nineteenth century), while other writers cast "shadows of futurity" before them, in Percy Shelley's phrase.

Within periods, we have sought a variety of means to suggest the many linkages that make up a rich literary culture, which is something more than a sequence of individual writers all producing their separate bodies of work. In this anthology, each period includes several groupings called "Perspectives," with texts that address an important literary or social issue of the time. These Perspective sections typically illuminate underlying issues in a variety of the major works of their time, as with a section on Government and Self-Government that relates broadly to Sir Thomas More's *Utopia*, to Spenser's *Faerie Queene*, and to Milton's *Paradise Lost*. Most of the writers included in Perspective sections are important period figures, less well known today, who might be neglected if they were listed on their own with just a few pages each; grouping them together should be useful pedagogically as well as intellectually. Perspective sections may also include writing by a major author whose primary listing appears elsewhere in the period: thus, a Perspective section on the abolition of slavery and the slave trade—a hotly debated issue in England from the 1790s through the 1830s—includes poems and essays by Wordsworth, Byron, and Barbauld, so as to give a rounded presentation of the issue in ways that can inform the reading of those authors in their individual sections.

WORKS IN CONTEXT

Periodically throughout the anthology we also present major works "In Context," to show the terms of a specific debate to which an author is responding. Thus Sir Philip Sidney's great *The Apology for Poetry* is accompanied by a context section to show the controversy that was raging at the time concerning the nature and value of poetry. Similarly, Thomas Dekker and Thomas Middleton's hilarious seventeenth-century comedy *The Roaring Girl: Or, Moll Cut-Purse* is accompanied by a Context section giving several readings on the virtues and vices of city life. Some of the writers in that context section are not classically literary figures, but all have produced lively and intriguing works, from King James I's *Counterblast to Tobacco* to Thomas Deloney's satiric account of *How Simon's Wife . . . Being Wholly Bent to Pride and Pleasure, Requested Her Husband to See London*.

Additionally, we include "Companion Readings" to present specific prior texts to which a work is responding: when Sir Thomas Wyatt creates a beautiful poem, *Whoso List to Hunt,* by making a free translation of a Petrarch sonnet, we include Petrarch's original (and a more literal translation) as a companion reading. For Conrad's *Heart of Darkness,* companion texts include Conrad's diary of the Congo journey on which he based his novella, and a bizarre lecture by Sir Henry Morton Stanley, the explorer-adventurer whose travel writings Conrad parodies.

ILLUSTRATING VISUAL CULTURE

Literature has always been a product of cultures that are visual as well as verbal. We include a hundred illustrations in the body of the anthology, presenting artistic and cultural images that figured importantly for literary creation. Sometimes, a poem refers to a specific painting, or more generally emulates qualities of a school of visual art. At other times, photographs, advertisements, or political cartoons can set the stage for literary works. In some cases, visual and literary creation have merged, as in Hogarth's series *A Rake's Progress,* included in Volume 1, or Blake's engravings of his *Songs of Innocence and Experience,* several of whose plates are reproduced in Volume 2.

AIDS TO UNDERSTANDING

We have tried to contextualize our selections in a suggestive rather than an exhaustive way, wishing to enhance rather than overwhelm the experience of reading the texts themselves. Our introductions to periods and authors are intended to open up ways of reading rather than dictating a particular interpretation, and the suggestions presented here should always be seen as points of departure rather than definitive pronouncements. We have striven for clarity and ease of use in our editorial matter.

Thus, when difficult or archaic words need defining in poems, we use glosses in the margins, in all periods, so as to disrupt the reader's eye as little as possible; footnotes are intended to be concise and informative, rather than massive or interpretive. Spelling and punctuation are modernized in Volume 1, except when older forms are important for meter or rhyme, and with general exceptions for certain major writers, like Chaucer and Spenser, whose specific usages are crucial to their understanding. Important literary and social terms are defined when they are used; for convenience of reference, there is also an extensive glossary of literary and cultural terms at the end of each volume, together with useful summaries of British political and religious orders, and of money, weights, and measures. For further reading, carefully selected bibliographies for each period and for each author can be found at the end of each volume.

VARIETIES OF LITERARY EXPERIENCE

Above all, we have striven to give as full a presentation as possible to the varieties of great literature produced over the centuries in the British Isles, by women as well as by men, in outlying regions as well as in the metropolitan center of London, and in prose, drama, and verse alike. This is, in fact, the most capacious anthology of British literature ever assembled in a form suited to a survey course. We have taken particular care to do justice to prose fiction, a genre often neglected in past anthologies: we include entire novels or novellas by Mary Shelley, Charles Dickens, George Eliot, Joseph Conrad, and D. H. Lawrence, as well as a wealth of short fiction from the eighteenth century to the present. For the earlier periods, we give More's *Utopia* entire, and we devote major space to narrative poetry by Chaucer, Spenser, and Milton, among others. Throughout the anthology we give many dramatic works, from the medieval *Second Play of the Shepherds* to postwar twentieth-century works in several media: a radio play by Dylan Thomas, a stage play by Samuel Beckett, and Hanif Kureishi's film script for *My Beautiful Laundrette*—this last, an indication of the degree to which the always culturally varied British landscape is now being transformed once again by new waves of immigration. Finally, lyric poetry appears in profusion throughout the anthology, from early lyrics by anonymous Middle English poets and the trenchantly witty Dafydd ap Gwilym to the powerful contemporary voices of Philip Larkin, Seamus Heaney, Medbh McGuckian, and Derek Walcott—himself a product of colonial British education, heir of Shakespeare and James Joyce, who closes the anthology with poems about Englishness abroad and foreignness in Britain.

As topical as these contemporary writers are, we hope that this anthology will show that the great works of earlier centuries can also speak to us compellingly today, their value only increased by the resistance they offer to our views of ourselves and our world. To read and reread the full sweep of this literature is to be struck anew by the degree to which the most radically new works are rooted in centuries of prior innovation. Even this preface can close in no better way than by quoting the words written eighteen hundred years ago by Apuleius—both a consummate artist and a kind of anthologist of extraordinary tales—when he concluded the prologue to his masterpiece *The Golden Ass*: Attend, reader, and pleasure is yours.

David Damrosch

ACKNOWLEDGMENTS

Throughout the extended collaborative process that has produced these volumes, the editors have benefited enormously from advice and counsel of many kinds. Our first and greatest debt is to our editor, Lisa Moore, who inspired us to begin this project, and whose enthusiasm and good judgment have seen us through. She and her associates Roth Wilkofsky, Richard Wohl, and Patricia Rossi have supported us in every possible way throughout the process, ably assisted by Lynn Huddon and Christopher Narozny. We have also been fortunate to enjoy the constant aid of Mark Getlein, the Platonic ideal of a developmental editor, whose literary and visual sensitivity have benefited every page of this anthology.

The best table of contents in the world would be of little use without actual texts following it. For these we are first of all indebted to the eloquence and cajolery of permissions wizards Kathy Smeilis and Robert Ravas, who negotiated hundreds of permissions with often recalcitrant publishers and occasionally unbalanced heirs. Julie Tesser traced and cleared our illustrations. Kevin Bradley, Candice Carta, and the staff of York Production Services then performed miracles in producing a beautiful and highly accurate text out of incredible masses of tearsheets, sometimes involving semilegible texts of works that hadn't been republished for centuries. The canny copyediting of Stephanie Argeros-Magean and her colleagues did much to bring clarity and consistency to the work of a dozen editors across thirteen thousand pages of copyedited manuscript. Through these stages and as the book went to press, Valerie Zaborski, Paula Soloway, and Patti Brecht oversaw a production process of Joycean complexity, with an edgy good humor that kept everyone focused on a constantly endangered schedule.

At every stage of the project, our plans and our prose were thoughtfully reviewed and assessed by colleagues at institutions around the country. Their advice helped us enormously in selecting our materials and in refining our presentation of them. We owe hearty thanks to Lucien Agosta (California State University, Sacramento), Anne W. Astell (Purdue University), Derek Attridge (Rutgers University), Linda Austin (Oklahoma State University), Joseph Bartolomeo (University of Massachusetts, Amherst), Todd Bender (University of Wisconsin, Madison), Bruce Boehrer (Florida State University), Joel J. Brattin (Worcester Polytechnic Institute), James Campbell (University of Central Florida), J. Douglas Canfield (University of Arizona), Paul A. Cantor (University of Virginia), George Allan Cate (University of Maryland, College Park), Eugene R. Cunnar (New Mexico State University), Earl Dachslager (University of Houston), Elizabeth Davis (University of California, Davis), Andrew Elfenbein (University of Minnesota), Margaret Ferguson (University of California, Davis), Sandra K. Fisher (State University of New York, Albany), Allen J. Frantzen (Loyola University, Chicago), Kate Garder Frost (University of Texas), Leon Gottfried (Purdue University), Mark L. Greenberg (Drexel University), James Hala (Drew University), Wayne Hall (University of Cincinnati), Wendell Harris (Pennsylvania State University), Richard H. Haswell (Washington State University), Susan Sage Heinzelman (University of Texas, Austin), Standish Henning (University of Wisconsin, Madison), Jack W. Herring (Baylor University),

Maurice Hunt (Baylor University), Colleen Juarretche (University of California, Los Angeles), R. B. Kershner (University of Florida), Lisa Klein (Ohio State University), Rita S. Kranidis (Radford University), Elizabeth B. Loizeaux (University of Maryland), John J. Manning (University of Connecticut), Michael B. McDonald (Iowa State University), Celia Millward (Boston University), Thomas C. Moser, Jr. (University of Maryland), Jude V. Nixon (Baylor University), Violet O'Valle (Tarrant County Junior College, Texas), Richard Pearce (Wheaton College), Renée Pigeon (California State University, San Bernardino), Tadeusz Pioro (Southern Methodist University), Deborah Preston (Dekalb College), Elizabeth Robertson (University of Colorado), Deborah Rogers (University of Maine), Brian Rosenberg (Allegheny College), Charles Ross (Purdue University), Harry Rusche (Emory University), Kenneth D. Shields (Southern Methodist University), Clare A. Simmons (Ohio State University), Sally Slocum (University of Akron), Phillip Snyder (Brigham Young University), Isabel Bonnyman Stanley (East Tennessee University), Margaret Sullivan (University of California, Los Angeles), Herbert Sussmann (Northeastern University), Ronald R. Thomas (Trinity College), Theresa Tinkle (University of Michigan), William A. Ulmer (University of Alabama), Jennifer A. Wagner (University of Memphis), Anne D. Wallace (University of Southern Mississippi), Jackie Walsh (McNeese State University, Louisiana), John Watkins (University of Minnesota), Martin Wechselblatt (University of Cincinnati), Arthur Weitzman (Northeastern University), Bonnie Wheeler (Southern Methodist University), Dennis L. Williams (Central Texas College), and Paula Woods (Baylor University).

Other colleages brought our developing book into the classroom, teaching from portions of the work-in-progress while it was still in page proof. Our thanks for classroom testing to Lisa Abney (Northwestern State University), Charles Lynn Batten (University of California, Los Angeles), Brenda Riffe Brown (College of the Mainland, Texas), John Brugaletta (California State University, Fullerton), Dan Butcher (Southeastern Louisiana University), Lynn Byrd (Southern University at New Orleans), David Cowles (Brigham Young University), Sheila Drain (John Carroll University), Lawrence Frank (University of Oklahoma), Leigh Garrison (Virginia Polytechnic Institute), David Griffin (New York University), Rita Harkness (Virginia Commonwealth University), Linda Kissler (Westmoreland County Community College, Pennsylvania), Brenda Lewis (Motlow State Community College, Tennessee), Paul Lizotte (River College), Wayne Luckman (Green River Community College, Washington), Arnold Markely (Pennsylvania State University, Delaware County), James McKusick (University of Maryland, Baltimore), Eva McManus (Ohio Northern University), Manuel Moyrao (Old Dominion University), Kate Palguta (Shawnee State University, Ohio), Paul Puccio (University of Central Florida), Sarah Polito (Cape Cod Community College), Meredith Poole (Virginia Western Community College), Tracy Seeley (University of San Francisco), Clare Simmons (Ohio State University), and Paul Yoder (University of Arkansas, Little Rock).

As if all this help weren't enough, the editors also drew directly on friends and colleagues in many ways, for advice, for information, sometimes for outright contributions to headnotes and footnotes, even (in a pinch) for aid in proofreading. In particular, we wish to thank James Cain, Michael Coyle, Pat Denison, Andrew Fleck, Laurie Glover, Lisa Gordis, Joy Hayton, Jean Howard, David Kastan, Stanislas Kemper, Ron Levao, Carol Levin, David Lipscomb, Denise MacNeil, Jackie Maslowski, Richard Matlak, Anne Mellor, James McKusick, Michael North, David Paroissien, Stephen M. Parrish, Peter Platt, Cary Plotkin, Gina Renee, Alan Richardson, Esther Schor, Catherine Siemann, Glenn Simshaw, David Tresilian, Shasta Turner, Nicholas Watson, Michael Winckleman, and Gillen Wood for all their guidance and assistance.

The pages on the Restoration and the eighteenth century are the work of many collaborators, diligent and generous. Michael F. Suarez, S. J. (Campion Hall, Oxford) edited the Swift and Pope sections; Mary Bly (Washington University) edited Etherege and Sheridan; Michael Caldwell (University of Chicago) edited the portions of "Reading Papers" on *The Craftsman* and the South Sea Bubble. Steven N. Zwicker (Washington University) co-wrote the period introduction, and the head-notes for the Dryden section. Bruce Redford (Boston University) crafted the footnotes for Dryden, Gay, Johnson, and Boswell. Susan Brown, Christine Coch, and Paige Reynolds helped with texts, footnotes, and other matters throughout; William Pritchard gathered texts, wrote notes, and prepared bibliography. To all, abiding thanks.

It has been a pleasure to work with all of these colleagues, and this is, after all, only the beginning of what we hope will be a long-term collaboration with those who use this anthology, as teachers, students, and general readers. This book exists for its readers, whose reactions and suggestions we warmly welcome, as these will in turn reshape this book for later users in the years to come.

The Longman Anthology of British Literature

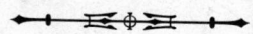

VOLUME 1

Laurence, Prior of Durham, depicted as a scribe, from a 12th-century manuscript.

The Middle Ages

> At the present time, there are five languages in Britain, just as the divine law is written in five books, all devoted to seeking out and setting forth one and the same kind of wisdom, namely the knowledge of sublime truth and of true sublimity. These are the English, British, Irish, Pictish, as well as the Latin languages; through the study of the scriptures, Latin is in general use among them all.
>
> Bede, *Ecclesiastical History of the English People*

The Venerable Bede's famous and enormously influential *Ecclesiastical History of the English People*, written in early 700s, reflects a double triumph. First, its very title acknowledges the dominance by Bede's day of the Anglo-Saxons, who, centuries earlier, had established themselves on an island already inhabited by Celtic Britons and by Picts. Second, the Latin of Bede's text and his own life as a monk point to the presence of ancient Mediterranean influences in the British Isles, earlier through Rome's military colonization of ancient Britain and later through the conversion of Bede's people to Roman Christianity.

In this first chapter of his first book, Bede shows a complex awareness of the several populations still active in Britain and often resisting or encroaching on Anglo-Saxon rule, and much of his *History* narrates the successive waves of invaders and missionaries who had brought their languages, governments, cultures, and beliefs to his island. This initial emphasis on peoples and languages should not be taken as early medieval multiculturalism, however: Bede's brief comparison to the single truth embodied in the five books of divine law also shows us his eagerness to draw his fragmented world into a coherent and transcendent system of Latin-based Christianity.

It is useful today, however, to think about medieval Britain, before and long after Bede, as a multilingual and multicultural setting, densely layered with influences and communities that divide, in quite different ways, along lines of geography, language, and ethnicity, as well as religion, gender, and class. These elements produced extraordinary cultures and artistic works, whose richness and diversity challenge the modern imagination. The medieval British Isles were a meeting place, but also a point of resistance, for wave after wave of cultural and political influences. Awareness of these multiple origins, moreover, persisted. Six hundred years after Bede we encounter a historian like Sir Thomas Gray complaining that recent disorders were "characteristic of a medley of different races. Wherefore some people are of the opinion that the diversity of spirit among the English is the cause of their revolutions" (*Scalacronica*, c. 1363).

This complex mixture sometimes resulted from systematic conquest, as with the Romans and, three centuries after Bede, the famous Norman Conquest of 1066; sometimes it was from slower, less unified movements of ethnic groups, such as the Celts, Anglo-Saxons, the Irish in Scotland, and the Vikings. Other important influences arrived more subtly: various forms of Christianity, classical Latin literature and learning, continental French culture in the thirteenth century, and an imported Italian humanism toward the close of the British Middle Ages.

3

Map of England, from Matthew Paris's *Historia Major.* Mid-13th century. A monk of Saint Albans, Matthew Paris wrote a monumental *History of England,* of which two illustrated copies in his own hand survive. Matthew's richly detailed map of England, including counties and major towns, illustrates the geographical knowledge of his day. It further suggests how alert he was to the ethnic divisions that still crossed his island and to the settlements and invasions, both mythic and actual, that had given rise to them. His inscription near the depiction of Hadrian's Wall, for example, informs us that the wall "once divided the English and the Picts." Recalling the claim that the original Britons were Trojan refugees, he writes about Wales (left center): "The people of this region are descended from the followers of Brutus." The story of Arthur's conception may have led Paris to identify Tintagel (*Tintaiol,* lower left). Matthew also links geography and racial character, as in his comment on northern Scotland (top center): "A mountainous, woody region producing an uncivilized people."

Our understanding of this long period and our very name for it also reflect a long history of multiple influences and cultural and political orders. The term "medieval" began as a condescending and monolithic label, first applied by Renaissance humanists who were eager to distinguish their revived classical scholarship from what they interpreted as a "barbarous" past. They and later readers often dismissed the Middle Ages as rigidly hierarchical, feudal, and Church-dominated. Others embraced the period for equally tendentious reasons, rosily picturing "feudal" England and Europe as a harmonious society of contented peasants, chivalrous nobles, and holy clerics. It is true that those who exercised political and religious control during the Middle Ages—the Roman church and the Anglo-Norman and then the English monarchy— sought to impose hierarchy on their world and created explicit ideologies to justify doing so. They were not unopposed, however; those who had been pushed aside continued to resist—and to contribute to Britain's multiple and dynamic literatures.

The period that we call "the Middle Ages" is vast and ungainly, spanning eight hundred years by some accounts. Scholars traditionally divide medieval English literature into the Old English period, from about 700 to 1066 (the date of the Norman Conquest), and the Middle English period, from 1066 to about 1500. Given the very different state of the English language during the two periods and given the huge impact of the Norman Conquest, this division is reasonable and is reflected in this collection under the headings "Before the Norman Conquest" and "After the Norman Conquest." There were substantial continuities, nevertheless, before and after the Conquest, especially in the Celtic areas beyond the Normans' immediate control.

THE CELTS

It is with the Celts, in fact, that the recorded history of Britain begins, and their literatures continue to the present day in Ireland and Wales. The Celts first migrated to Britain about 400 B.C., after spreading over most of Europe in the two preceding centuries. In England these "Brittonic" Celts absorbed some elements of Roman culture and social order during Rome's partial occupation of the island from the first to the fifth centuries A.D. After the conversion of the Roman emperor Constantine in the fourth century and the establishment of Christianity as the official imperial religion, many British Celts adopted Christianity. The language of these "British" to whom Bede refers gave rise to Welsh. The Celts maintained contact with their people on the Continent, who were already being squeezed toward what is now Brittany, in the west of France. The culture of the Brittonic Celts was thus not exclusively insular, and their myths and legends came to incorporate these cross-Channel memories, especially in the stories of King Arthur.

Celts also arrived in Ireland; and as one group, the "Goidelic" Celts, achieved linguistic and social dominance there, their language split off from that of the Britons. Some of these Irish Celts later established themselves in Argyll and the western isles of Scotland, "either by friendly treaty or by the sword," says Bede, and from them the Scottish branch of the Celtic languages developed. Bede mentions this language as the "Irish" that is spoken in Britain. The Irish converted to Christianity early but slowly, without the pressure of a Christianized colonizer. When the great Irish monasteries flourished in the sixth century, their extraordinary Latin scholarship seems to have developed alongside the traditional learning preserved by the rigorous schools of vernacular poetry. If anything, Irish monastic study was stimulated by these surviving institutions of a more poetic and priestly class. The Irish monasteries in turn became the impetus behind Irish and Anglo-Saxon missionaries who carried Christianity to the northern and eastern reaches of Europe. Both as missionaries and as scholars, insular Christians had great impact on continental Europe, especially in the eighth and ninth centuries.

By 597 when Pope Gregory the Great sent Augustine (later of Canterbury) to expand the Christian presence in England, there was already a flourishing Christian Celtic society, especially in Ireland. Ensuing disagreements over Celtic versus Roman ways of worship were ultimately resolved in favor of the Roman liturgy and calendar, but the cultural impact of Celts on British Christianity remained enormous. The Irish Book of Kells, shown on the cover of this volume, and the Lindisfarne Gospels, produced in England, are enlivened by the swirls, interlace, and stylized animals long evident in the work of pagan Celtic craftsmen on the continent. The monks who illuminated such magnificent gospel books also copied classical Latin texts, notably Virgil's *Aeneid* and works by Cicero and Seneca, thereby helping keep ancient Roman literature alive when much of continental Europe fell into near chaos during the Germanic invasions that led to the fall of Rome.

Included in this anthology are examples from the two great literatures written in Celtic languages, Irish and Welsh. Passages from the eighth-century Irish *Táin Bó Cuailnge* reveal a heroic spirit and an acceptance of the magical which can be compared with aspects of *Beowulf*. Like much Irish heroic narrative, though, the *Táin* also reveals a far more prominent and assertive role for women, some of whom retain resemblances to the goddess figures of Ireland's pagan era. Welsh literature is represented first by lyrics attributed to the early, shadowy poet Taliesin and second by a much later story about his accomplishments which serves to show some of the continuities of Welsh literary culture. Wales also absorbed Latin and later European influences, as represented by fourteenth-century lyrics from the marvelously sophisticated Dafydd ap Gwilym, who resembles Chaucer in his use of continental poetry.

THE GERMANIC MIGRATIONS

While Celtic culture flourished in Ireland, the British Celts and their faith suffered a series of disastrous reversals after the withdrawal of the Romans and the aggressive incursions of the pagan Angles, Saxons, and Jutes from the continent. The Picts and Scots in the north, never Romanized, had begun to harass the Britons, who responded by inviting allies from among the Germanic tribes on the continent in the mid-fifth century. These protectors soon became predators, demanding land and establishing small kingdoms of their own in roughly the eastern half of modern-day England. Uneasy and temporary settlements followed. The Britons retained a presence in the northwest, in the kingdoms of Rheged and of the Strathclyde Welsh; others were slowly pressed toward present-day Wales in the southwest.

The Angles, Saxons, and Jutes were not themselves a monolithic force, though. Divided into often warring states, they faced resistance, however diminishing, from the Britons and still had to battle the aggressive Picts and Scots, who were the original reason for their arrival. Their own culture was further changed as they converted to Christianity. The piecemeal Anglo-Saxon colonization of England in the sixth and seventh centuries and the island's conversion and later reconversion to Christianity present a complex picture, then—one that could be retold very differently depending on the perspectives of later historians. As the Angles and Saxons settled in and extended their control, the emerging "English" culture drew on new interpretations of the region's history. The most influential account of all was Bede's *Ecclesiastical History*, completed in 731. Our most reliable and eloquent source for early British history, Bede nonetheless wrote as an Anglo-Saxon. He presented his people's history from a providential perspective, seeing their role in Britain and their conversion to Christianity as a crucial part of a divine plan. King Alfred extended this world view when, in the late ninth century, he wrote of his people's struggle against the invading pagan Vikings.

Bede thus adopts an approach to history that reflects his own devout Christian faith and the disciplined religious practices of his monastic brethren in Northumberland. Nevertheless, Bede lived in a wider culture still deeply imbued with the tribal values of its Germanic and pagan past, a culture that maintained at least a nostalgic regard for the kind of individual heroic glory that rarely looks beyond this world. Even in Bede's day, most kings died young and on the battlefield. And natural disasters such as those in 664 (a plague, and the deaths of a king and an archbishop occurring on the day of an eclipse) could send the Anglo-Saxons back to pagan worship. The two worlds, one with its roots in Mediterranean Christianity and the other in Germanic paganism, overlapped and interpenetrated for generations.

The pagan culture that is the setting for the epic *Beowulf* still strongly resembled that of the Germanic "barbarians" described by the Roman historian Tacitus in the first century. The heroic code of the Germanic warrior bands—what Tacitus called the *"comitatus"*—valued courage in battle above all, followed by loyalty to the tribal leader and the warband. These formed the core of heroic identity. A warrior whose leader fell in battle was obliged to seek vengeance at any cost; it was an indelible shame to survive an unavenged leader. Family links were also profound, however, and a persistent tragic theme in Germanic and Anglo-Saxon heroic narrative pits the claims of vengeance against those of family loyalty.

Early warrior culture in the British Isles, as elsewhere, was fraught with violence, as fragile truces between warring tribes and clans were continually broken. The tone of Old English poetry (as of much of Old Irish heroic narrative) is consequently somber, often suffused with a sense of doom. Even moments of high festivity are darkened by allusions to later disasters. Humor often occurs through a kind of ironic understatement: a poet may state that a warrior strode less swiftly into battle, for example, when the warrior in fact is dead. Similarly Cet, an Irish warrior, claims that if his brother were in the house, he would overcome his opponent, Conall. Conall replies, "But he is in the house," and almost casually flings the brother's head at Cet. A lighter tone is found mostly in shorter forms, such as the playful Anglo-Saxon riddles and in some Old Irish poetry.

The Angles and Saxons had come to England as military opportunists, and they in turn faced attacks and settlement from across the Channel. Their increasingly ordered political world and their thriving monastic establishments, such as Bede's monastery of Jarrow, were plundered by Vikings in swift attacks by boat as early as the end of the eighth century. This continued for a hundred years, and eventually resulted in widespread Scandinavian settlements north of the Thames, in areas called the Danelaw. By the 890s Christian Viking kings reigned at York and in East Anglia, extending a history of independence from the southern kingdoms. The period of raids and looting was largely over by 900, but even King Alfred (d. 899) faced Viking incursions in Wessex and consciously depicted himself as a Christian hero holding the line against pagan invaders. Only his kingdom, in fact, resisted their attacks with complete success. Vikings also intermarried with Anglo-Saxons and expanded their influence by political means. Profiting from English dynastic disorder around the turn of the eleventh century, aristocrats in the Danelaw became brokers of royal power. From 1016 to 1035 the Danish Cnut (Canute) was king of both England and Denmark, briefly uniting the two in a maritime empire. The Scandinavian presence was not exclusively combative, however. They sent peaceful traders to the British Isles—among them Ohthere, whose tale of his voyages is included here. They also left their mark on literature and language, as in the early Middle English romance *Havelock the Dane*, which contains many words borrowed from Old Norse.

PAGAN AND CHRISTIAN: TENSION AND CONVERGENCE

Given that writing in the Roman alphabet was introduced to pre-Conquest England by churchmen, it is not surprising that most texts from the period are written in Latin on Christian subjects. Most writing even in the Old English language was also religious. In Anglo-Saxon England and in the Celtic cultures, vernacular literature tended at first to be orally composed and performed. The body of written vernacular Anglo-Saxon poetry that survives is thus very small indeed, although there are plenty of prose religious works. It is something of a miracle that *Beowulf*, which celebrates the exploits of a pagan hero, was deemed worthy of being copied by scribes who were almost certainly clerics. (In fact, almost all the greatest Anglo-Saxon poetry survives in only a single copy—so tenuous is our link to that past.) Yet the copying of *Beowulf* also hints at the complex interaction of the pagan and Christian traditions in Anglo-Saxon culture.

The conflict between the two traditions was characterized (and perhaps exaggerated) by Christian writers and readers as a struggle between pagan violence and Christian values of forgiveness. The old, deep-seated respect for treasure as a sign of power and achievement seemed to conflict with Christian contempt for worldly goods. In fact, however, pagan Germanic and Christian values were alike in many respects and coexisted with various degrees of mutual influence.

Old English poets explored the tensions as well as the overlap between the two sets of values in two primary poetic modes—the heroic and the elegiac. The heroic mode, of which *Beowulf* is the supreme example, celebrates the values of bravery, loyalty, vengeance, and desire for treasure. The elegiac mode, by contrast, calls the value of these things into question, as at best transient and at worst a worldly distraction from spiritual life. The elegiac speaker, usually an exile, laments the loss of earthly goods—his lord, his comrades, the joys of the mead hall—and, in the case of the short poem known as *The Wanderer*, turns his thoughts to heaven. *Beowulf*, composed most likely by a Christian poet looking back at the deeds of his pagan Scandinavian ancestors, uses elements of both the heroic and the elegiac to focus on the overlap of pagan and Christian virtues.

The goals of earthly glory and heavenly salvation that concern Old English poetry are presented primarily as they affect men. Recent scholarship, however, reveals the active roles played in society by Anglo-Saxon women, particularly aristocratic ones. One of these is Aethelflaed, daughter of King Alfred, who co-ruled the kingdom of Mercia with her brother Edward at the turn of the tenth century, taking an active military role in fighting off the Danes. Better known today is Abbess Hilda, who founded and ran the great monastery at Whitby from 657 until her death in 680; five Whitby monks became bishops across England during her rule. Nevertheless, women generally take a marginal role in Old English poetry. In secular works marriages are portrayed as being arranged to strengthen military alliances, in efforts (often doomed) to heal bloody rifts between clans. Women thus function primarily as "peace weavers," a term referring occasionally to their active diplomacy in settling disputes but more often to their passive role in marriage exchanges. This latter role was fraught with danger, for if a truce were broken between the warring groups, the woman would face tragically conflicting loyalties to husband and male kin.

The effect of the Germanic heroic code on women is explored in two tantalizingly short poems that invest the elegiac mode with women's voices: *Wulf and Eadwacer* and *The Wife's Lament*. In both, a woman speaker laments her separation from her lord, whether husband or lover, through some shadowy events of heroic warfare. More indicative of the actual power of aristocratic and religious women in Anglo-Saxon society, perhaps, is the Old English poem *Judith*, a biblical narrative which uses heroic diction reminiscent of that in *Beowulf* to celebrate the heroine's military triumph over the pagan Holofernes.

ORAL POETRY, WRITTEN MANUSCRIPTS

For all their deep linguistic differences and territorial conflicts, the Celts and Anglo-Saxons had affinities in the heroic themes and oral settings of their greatest surviving narratives and in the echoes of a pre-Christian culture that endure there. Indeed, these can be compared to conditions of authorship in oral cultures worldwide, from Homer's Greece to parts of contemporary Africa. In a culture with little or no writing, the singer of tales has an enormously important role as the conservator of the past. In *Beowulf*, for instance, the traditional content and verbal formulas of the poetry of praise are swiftly reworked to celebrate the hero's killing of the monster Grendel:

> And now and then one of Hrothgar's thanes
> who brimmed with poetry, and remembered lays,
> a man acquainted with ancient traditions
> of every kind, composed a new song
> in correct metre. Most skilfully that man
> began to sing of Beowulf's feat,
> to weave words together, and fluently
> to tell a fitting tale.

A poet of this kind (in Anglo-Saxon, a *scop* or "shaper") does not just enhance the great warrior's prestige by praising his hero's ancestors and accomplishments. He also recalls and performs the shared history and beliefs of the entire people, in great feats of memory that make the poet virtually the encyclopedia of his culture. A poet from the oral tradition might also become a singer of the new Christian cosmology, like the illiterate herdsman Caedmon, whom Bede describes as having been called to monastic vows by the Abbess Hilda, in honor of his Christian poems composed in the vernacular oral mode.

In Celtic areas, oral poets had even greater status. The ancient class of learned Irish poets were honored servants of noblemen and kings; they remained as a powerful if reduced presence after the establishment of Christianity. The legal status of such a poet (a *fili*) was similar to that of a bishop, and indeed the *fili* carried out some functions of spells and divination inherited from the pagan priestly class, the druids. The ongoing influence of these poets in Irish politics and culture is reflected in the body of surviving secular literature from medieval Ireland, which is considerably larger than that from Anglo-Saxon England. A comparable situation prevailed in Wales. Even in the quite late Welsh *Tale of Taliesin*, the poet Taliesin appears as a public performer before the king as well as a possessor of arcane wisdom, magic, and prophecy.

In a culture in which a poet has such a wide and weighty role, ranging from entertainer to purveyor of the deepest reaches of religious belief, possession of the word bestows tremendous, even magical power. In a text that describes the wonders of the Irish epic the *Táin*, we hear about the promise of "a year's protection to him to whom it is recited." Even when these tales were copied into manuscripts, their written versions were essentially scripts for later performance, or for memorization. In a twelfth-century Irish manuscript, the copyist wishes "A blessing on everyone who will memorize the *Táin* with fidelity in this form and will not put any other form on it."

This attitude of awe toward the word as used by the oral poet was only enhanced by the arrival of Christianity, a faith that attributes creation itself to an act of divine speech. Throughout the Middle Ages and long after orally composed poetry had retreated from many centers of high culture, the power of the word also inhered in its written form, as encountered in certain prized books. Chief among these were the Bible and other books of religious story, especially by such church fathers as Saints Augustine and Jerome, and books of the liturgy. Since these texts bore the authority of divine revelation, the manuscripts that contained them shared in their charisma.

The power of these manuscripts was both reflected and aided by their visual grandeur. Among the highest expressions of the fervor and discipline of early insular monasticism is its production of beautifully copied and exquisitely decorated books of the Bible. The extreme elaboration of their production and the great labor and expense lavished on them suggest their almost holy status. Figures holding a book in the Book of Kells, or writing in the Lindisfarne Gospels, indicate this importance; a fascination with the new technology is suggested by Old English riddles whose answers are "a hand writing," "a book worm," or "a bookcase."

The cost and effort of making manuscript books and their very scarcity contributed to their aura. Parchment was produced from animal skins, stretched and scraped. The training and discipline involved in copying texts, especially sacred texts, were great. The decoration of the most ambitious manuscripts involved rare colors, gold leaf, and often supreme artistry. Thus these magnificent manuscripts could become almost magical icons: Bede, for example, tells of scrapings from Irish manuscripts which mixed with water cured the bites of poisonous snakes.

Manuscripts slowly became more widely available. By the twelfth century we hear more of manuscripts in private hands and the beginning of production outside ecclesiastical settings. By the fourteenth century merchants and private scholars were buying books from shops that resembled modern booksellers. The glamour and prestige of beautiful manuscripts remained, though, even if the sense of their magic faded to a degree. Great families would donate psalters and gospels to religious foundations, with the donor carefully represented in the decoration presenting the book to the Virgin Mary or the Christ child. Spectacular books of private devotion were at once a medium for spiritual meditation and proof of great wealth. Stories of epic conquest like the *Aeneid* would sometimes feature their aristocratic owners' coat of arms.

Saint John, from the
Book of Kells. Late 8th
century.

THE NORMAN CONQUEST

By the time of these developments in book production, though, a gigantic change had occurred. In a single year, 1066, England witnessed the death of the Anglo-Saxon King Edward and the coronation of his disputed successor King Harold, the invasion and triumph of the foreigner William of Normandy, and his own coronation as King William. The Normans conquered, with relative ease, an Anglo-Saxon kingdom disordered by civil strife. The monastic movement had lost much of its earlier fervor and discipline, despite reform in the tenth century. Baronial interests had weakened severely the reign of the late King Edward "the Confessor." On an island that already perceived itself as repeatedly colonized, 1066 nonetheless represented a climactic change, experienced and registered at virtually all levels of social, religious, and cultural experience.

One sign of how great a breach had been opened in England, paradoxically, is the multifaceted effort put forth by conquerors and conquered to maintain—or invent—continuity with the pre-Conquest past. In religious institutions, in dynastic genealogies, in the intersection of history and racial myth, in the forms and records of social institutions, the generations after 1066 sought to absorb a radically changed world yet to ground their world in an increasingly mythicized Anglo-Saxon or Briton

Anne, Duchess of Bedford, kneeling before the Virgin Mary and Saint Anne, from the *Bedford Hours.* Early 15th century. A book of hours was a prayerbook used by laypersons for private devotion. The *Bedford Hours* was produced in a Paris workshop for the Duke of Bedford, a brother of King Henry V, and his wife, Anne of Burgundy. Here, Saint Anne is shown teaching her daughter, the Virgin Mary, to read; another book lies open on a lectern in front of the kneeling Anne of Burgundy.

antiquity. The Normans and their dynastic successors the Angevins eagerly took up and adapted to their own preoccupations ancient Briton political myths such as that of King Arthur and his court, and the stories of such saintly Anglo-Saxon kings as Oswald and Edward the Confessor.

They promoted narratives of their ancestors, like Wace's *Roman de Rou*, the story of the Normans' founder Rollo, commissioned by Henry II. Geoffrey of Monmouth dedicated his *History of the Kings of England* partly to Henry II's uncle, Robert Duke of Gloucester. In that work Geoffrey links the Celtic myths of King Arthur and his followers to an equally ancient myth that England was founded by descendants of the survivors of Troy; he makes his combined, largely fictive but enormously appealing work available to a Norman audience by writing it in Latin. Geoffrey's story was soon retold in "romance," the French from which vernacular texts took their name. The Angevin court also supported the "romances of antiquity," poems in French that narrate the story of Troy (the *Roman de Troie*), its background (*Roman de Thèbes*), and its aftermath (*Roman d'Eneas*), thus creating a model in the antique past for the Normans and their westward conquest of England. And the *Song of Roland,* the great crusading narrative celebrating the heroic death of Charlemagne's nephew as he protected Christendom from the Spanish Moslems, was probably written in the milieu of Henry II's court.

The Normans brought with them a new system of government, a freshly renovated Latin culture, and most important a new language. Anglo-Saxon sank into relative insignificance at the level of high culture and central government. Norman French became the language of the courts of law, of literature, and of most of the nobility. By the time English rose again to widespread cultural significance, about 250 years later, it was a hybrid that combined Romance and Germanic elements.

Latin offered a lifeline of communication at some social levels of this initially fractured society. The European clerics who arrived under the immigrant archbishops Lanfranc and Anselm brought a new and different learning, and often new and deeply unwelcome religious practices: a celibate priesthood, skepticism about local saints, and newly disciplined monasticism. Yet despite these differences and the tensions that accompanied them, clerics of European or British origin were linked by a common liturgy, a considerable body of shared reading, and most of all a common learned language. Secular as well as religious society were coming to be based more and more on the practical use of the written word: the letter, the charter, the documentary record, and the written book. Whereas Anglo-Saxon England had been governed by the word enacted and performed—a law of oral witness and a culture of oral poets—Norman England increasingly became a land of documents and books.

SOCIAL AND RELIGIOUS ORDER

The famed Domesday Book is a first instance of many of these developments. The Domesday survey was a gigantic undertaking, carried out with a speed that still astonishes between Christmas 1085 and William the Conqueror's death in September 1087. A county-by-county survey of the lands of King William and those held by his tenants-in-chief and subtenants, Domesday also records the obligations of landholders and thus reflects a new feudal system by which, increasingly, land was held in post-Conquest England.

Under the Normans a nobleman held land from the king as a fief, in exchange for which he owed the king certain military and judicial services, including the provision of armed knights. These knights in turn held land from their lord, to whom they also owed military service and other duties. Some of this land they might keep for their own farming and profit, and the rest they divided among serfs (who were obliged, in theory, to stay on the land to which they were born) and free peasantry. Both groups owed their knight or lord labor and either a portion of their agricultural produce or rents in cash. This system of land tenure was surely more complex and irregular in practice than in the theoretical model called feudalism. For instance, services at all levels were sometimes (and increasingly) commuted to cash payment, and while fiefs were theoretically held only by an individual for a lifetime, increasingly there were expectations that they would be inherited. Royal power gradually grew during the thirteenth and fourteenth centuries, yet the local basis of landholding and social order always acted as a counterbalance, even a block, to royal ambition.

The Domesday Book was only one piece of the multifaceted effort by which the Norman and later kings sought to extend and centralize royal power in their territories. William and his successors established a system of royal justices who traveled throughout the realm and reported ultimately to the king, and an organized royal bureaucracy began to appear. The most powerful and learned of these Anglo-Norman kings was William the Conqueror's great-grandson, Henry II, who ruled from 1154 to 1177. Under Henry, royal justice, bureaucracy, and record-keeping made great advances; the production of documents was centralized and took on more standardized forms, and copies of these documents (called "pipe rolls") began to be produced for later reference and proof.

Along with a stronger royal government, the Normans brought a clergy invigorated both by new learning and by the spirituality of recent monastic reforms. Saint Anselm, the second of the Norman archbishops of Canterbury, was a great prelate and the writer of beautiful and widely influential texts and prayers of private devotion. The Victorines and the Cistercians (inspired in part by Saint Bernard of Clairvaux) also brought a strong mystical streak to English monasticism. All these would bear fruit once again in the fourteenth century in a group of mystics writing in Latin and in English.

On the other hand, the Norman prelates, like their kings, brought an urge toward centralized order in the church and a belief that the church and its public justice (the "canon law") should be independent of secular power. This created frequent conflict with kings and aristocrats, who wanted to extend their judicial power and expected to wield considerable influence in the appointment of church officials.

The Murder of Thomas Becket, from Matthew Paris's *Historia Major*. Mid-13th century.

The most explosive moment in this ongoing controversy occurred in the disagreements between Henry II and Thomas Becket, who was Henry's Chancellor
and then Archbishop of Canterbury. Becket's increasingly public refusal to accommodate the king, either in the judicial sphere or the matter of clerical appoint-
ments, finally led to his murder by Henry's henchmen in 1170 at the altar of Canterbury Cathedral and his canonization very soon thereafter. A large body of
hagiography (narratives of his martyrdom and posthumous miracles) swiftly developed, adding to an already rich tradition of writing about the lives of English
saints. As Saint Thomas, Becket became a powerful focus for ecclesiastical ambition, popular devotion and pilgrimage, and religious and secular narrative. In fact,
the characters of Chaucer's *Canterbury Tales* tell their stories while making a pilgrimage to his shrine.

At least in theory, feudal tenure involved an obligation of personal loyalty
between lord and vassal that was symbolically enacted in the rituals of enfeoff-
ment, in which the lord would bestow a fief on his vassal. This belief was elaborated in a large body of secular literature in the twelfth century and after. Yet feudal
loyalty was always fragile and ideologically charged. Vassals regularly resisted the
wills of their lord or king when their interests collided, sometimes to the extent of
officially withdrawing from the feudal bond. Connected to feudal relations was
the notion of a chivalric code among the knightly class (those who fought on
horses, *chevaliers*), which involved not just loyalty to the lord but also honorable
behavior within the class, even among enemies. Chivalric literature is thus full of
stories of captured opponents being treated with the utmost politeness, as indeed
happened when Henry II's son Richard was held hostage for years in Germany,
awaiting ransom.

Similarly, although medieval theories of social order had some basis in fact,
they exercised shifting influence within a much more complex social reality. For
instance, medieval society was often analyzed by the model of the "three
estates"—those who fought (secular aristocrats), those who prayed (the clergy),
and those who worked the land (the free and servile peasantry). This model
appears more or less explicitly in the poetry of William Langland and Chaucer.
Such a system, though, did not allow for the gradual increase in manufacturing
(weaving, pottery, metalwork, even the copying of books) or for the urban merchants who traded in such products. As society became more complex, a model of
the "mystical social body" gained popularity, especially in the fourteenth century.
Here a wider range of classes and jobs was compared to limbs and other body parts.
Even this more flexible image was strictly hierarchical, though. Peasants and
laborers were the feet, knights (on the right) and merchants (on the left) were
hands, and townspeople were the heart, but the head was made up of kings,
princes, and prelates of the church.

CONTINENTAL AND INSULAR CULTURES

The arrival of the Normans, and especially the learned clerics who came then and
after, opened England to influences from a great intellectual current that was stirring
on the continent, the "renaissance of the twelfth century," which was to have a significant impact in the centuries that followed. A period of comparative political stability and economic growth made travel easier, and students and teachers were on
the move, seeking new learning in Paris and the Loire valley, in northern Italy, and
in Toledo with its Arab and Jewish cultures. Schools were expanding beyond the

monasteries and into the precincts of urban cathedrals and other religious foundations. Along with offering traditional biblical and theological study, these schools sparked a revived interest in elegant Latin writing, Neoplatonic philosophy, and science deriving from Aristotle.

Because the Normans and Angevins ruled large territories on the Continent, movement across the Channel was frequent; by the mid-twelfth century learned English culture was urbane and international. English clerics like John of Salisbury studied at Chartres and Paris, and texts by eminent speculative and scientific writers like William of Conches and Bernard Silvestris came to England. As these foreign works entered England, education became more ambitious and widely available, and its products show growing contact with the works of classical Latin writers such as Horace, Virgil, Terence, Cicero, Seneca, and Ovid in his erotic as much as in his mythological poetry.

The renewed attention to these works went along with a revival of interest in the *trivium*, the traditional division of the arts of eloquence: grammar, rhetoric, and dialectic. The most aggressive of these was dialectic, a form of logic developed by the Greeks and then rediscovered by Christian Europe from Arab scholars who had preserved and pursued Greek learning. John of Salisbury, who promoted dialectic in his *Metalogicon*, described it with metaphors of military prowess, as though it were an extension of knightly jousting. "Since dialectic is carried on between two persons," he writes, Aristotle's *Topics* "teaches the matched contestants whom it trains and provides with reasons and topics, to handle their proper weapons and engage in verbal, rather than physical conflict." Rhetoric was elaborately codified in technical manuals of poetry. Though in one sense it was merely ornamental, teaching how to flesh out a description or incident with figures of speech, rhetoric could be as coercive as dialectic, though, since it specified strategies of persuasion in a tradition deriving from ancient oratory. Rhetorical texts also instructed the student in letter-writing, increasingly important as an administrative skill and as a form of elevated composition.

The study of the *trivium* generated many Latin school texts and helped foster a high level of Latinity and a self-consciously sophisticated, classicizing literature in the second half of the twelfth century. Some school texts had great influence on vernacular literature, such as the *Poetria Nova* by Geoffrey of Vinsauf, a rhetorical handbook filled with vivid poetic examples. More intriguing is *Pamphilus*, a short Ovidian poem about a seduction, aided by Venus, which turns into a rape. It is thought to have been an exercise in *disputatio*, the oral form that dialectic assumed in the classroom. The poem was immensely popular in the next few centuries and was translated into many vernacular languages. *Pamphilus* was a conduit at once for Ovidian eroticism and for the language of debate on love. Chaucer mentions it as a model of passionate love and seems to have adapted some of its plot devices in his *Troilus and Criseyde*.

While classical Latin literature was often read with a frank interest in pagan ideas and practices, commentators also offered allegorical interpretations that drew pagan stories into the spiritual and cosmological preoccupations of medieval Christianity. Ovid's *Metamorphoses* were thus interpreted in a French poem, the *Ovide Moralisé*, that was clearly known to Chaucer, and in Latin commentaries such as the *Ovidius moralizatus* of Pierre Bersuire. For instance, Ovid describes Jupiter, in the form of a bull, carrying the Tyrian princess Europa into the sea to rape her. Bersuire interprets this as Christ taking on human flesh in order to take up the human soul he loves. Alternatively, he offers an explicitly misogynist allegory, casting Europa as young women who like to see handsome young men—bulls: "They are drawn through the stormy sea of evil temptations and are raped." Neither text is often very subtle in the extraction of Christian or moral analogies from Ovid's stories, yet both were popular and influential, if only because they also tell Ovid's tales before allegorizing them.

The allegorization of ancient secular literature was only one facet of allegorical reading, which was even more persistently applied to the Bible. Allegory became a complex and fruitful area of the medieval imagination and had profound implications for artistic production as well as reading. In its simplest sense, an allegorical text takes a metaphor and extends it into narrative, often personifying a quality as a character. Yet this practice takes a wealth of forms. In Langland's *Piers Plowman,* the reader encounters personification allegory in the character of Lady Meed, whose name can mean either "earned reward" or "bribery," suggesting the complexity of social critique that underlies such a symbolic character. Langland's narrator is named Will; short for William, the name also implies the wayward and resistant human will and verges toward moral allegory. Piers arrives on the scene as a peasant plowman, but increasingly becomes an allegorical embodiment of Saint Peter and even Christ. Langland thereby draws biblical events into analogy with everyday life, and offers the peasant as a "figure" of the savior. Later on, the patriarch Abraham appears in the poem as an allegory of Christian faith, as well as one of the fruits on the tree of charity. Such associations draw from the interpretive practice of typology, which sees Old Testament events (such as Abraham's willingness to sacrifice his son Isaac) as literally true but also symbolically predictive of and fulfilled by events in the New Testament. Typology so deeply colored the medieval reader's perceptions that we can see it operating in approaches to secular history and texts as well; we will encounter an instance of this in Geoffrey of Monmouth's *History of the Kings of Britain.*

The continent provided not only Latin but also significant vernacular influences: French was the international language of aristocratic culture and an important literary language in England, and continental French literature was crucial in the rise of courtly literature in Middle English. Many English Arthurian works, including *Sir Gawain and the Green Knight* and Sir Thomas Malory's *Morte Darthur,* are less indebted to English sources than to French romances, whether written on the continent or in England by authors such as Marie de France and Thomas of Britain. Chaucer translated into English the enormously popular allegorical dream vision the *Roman de la Rose* by Guillaume de Lorris and Jean de Meun. He also borrowed the conventions and imagery of Guillaume de Machaut and Eustache Deschamps; even the meter of his earlier poetry derives from their French octosyllabic couplet. Italian influences can be seen in Chaucer's use of Dante's *Divine Comedy* and his extensive borrowing from Petrarch and Boccaccio. Such continental vernacular literatures infiltrated even the Celtic cultures, as seen in the witty mix of Welsh and European traditions in the poems of Dafydd ap Gwilym.

If such writers and records reflect the higher achievements of education in England of the twelfth century and later, literacy was also diffusing in wider circles and new venues. In a society like England's that continued to produce considerable oral and public literature, indeed, the divide between literacy and illiteracy was always unstable and permeable. A secular aristocrat might have a clerk read to him or her; an urbanite could attend and absorb parts of public rituals that involved poems and orations; even a peasant would be able to pick up Latin tags from sermons or the liturgy. Thus a fourteenth-century writer like William Langland could expect his wide and mixed audience to recognize at least some of the Latin phrases he used along with English; and

Grotesques and a Courtly Scene, from the *Ormesby Psalter.* c. 1310–1325.

Chaucer could imagine a character like the Wife of Bath who, at best semi-literate, could still quote bits of the Latin liturgy. Access to texts and the self-awareness fostered by private reading may have helped promote the social ambitions and disruptions within the mercantile and even peasant classes during the later Middle Ages.

WOMEN, COURTLINESS, AND COURTLY LOVE

Access to books also increased the self-awareness of women. Possession of books that encouraged prayer and private devotion, such as psalters and Books of Hours, appears to have facilitated early language training in the home. The many images in manuscripts of women reading—especially the Virgin Mary and her mother, Saint Anne—have interesting implications for our understanding of women's literacy and cultural roles. A number of aristocratic Norman and Angevin women received good educations at convents. Women in the holy life possessed at least some literacy, though this often may have been minimal indeed. Even well-educated women were more likely to read English or French than Latin, with the exception of liturgical books.

The roles of women in the society and cultural imagination of post-Conquest England are complex and contradictory. No Anglo-Norman woman held ecclesiastical prestige like the Anglo-Saxon abbess Hilda or other Anglo-Saxon holy women. Women's power seems to have declined in the long term, both in worldly affairs and in the church, as the Normans consolidated their hold on England and imposed their order on society. Nevertheless, ambitious women could have great influence, especially when they siezed upon moments of disruption. In civil strife over the succession to King Henry I, the Empress Matilda organized an army, issued royal writs, and in the end guaranteed the accession of her son Henry II. If Henry II's wife, Eleanor of Aquitaine, spent the latter decades of her husband's reign under virtual house arrest, it was largely because she had conspired with her sons to raise an army against her own husband.

Despite the limitations of their actual power, women were the focus, often the worshiped focus, of much of the best imaginative literature of the twelfth and thirteenth centuries; and women were central to the social rituals we associate with

A Knight, rubbing from a funerary brass. Early 14th century. This funerary brass depicts a knight as he presented himself to eternity, sheathed in chain mail and fully armed but with his hands joined in prayer. The dog at his feet is a symbol of fidelity.

courtliness and the idea of courtly love. Despite her later imprisonment, Eleanor of Aquitaine was a crucial influence in the diffusion of courtly ideas from the continent, especially the south of France; and among the great writers of the century was Marie de France, who was probably related to Henry II. Scholars continue to debate whether the observances of "courtly love" were in fact widely practiced and whether its worship of women was empowering or restrictive: the image of the distant, adored lady implies immobility and even silence on her part. Certainly lyrics and narratives that embody courtly values are widespread, even if they often question what they celebrate; and the ideals of courtliness may have had as great an impact through these imaginative channels as through actual enactment.

The ideas and rituals of courtliness reach back to Greek and Roman models of controlled and stylized behavior in the presence of great power. In the Middle Ages, values of discretion and modesty also may have filtered into the secular world from the rigidly disciplined setting of the monasteries. As the society of western Europe took on a certain degree of order in the eleventh and twelfth centuries, courtly attainments began to converge and even compete with simple martial prowess in the achievement of worldly power. The presence of large numbers of armed and ambitious men at the great courts provided at once an opportunity for courtly behavior and the threat of its disruption.

Whatever its historical reality, courtly love as a literary concept had an immense influence. In this it adopted the vocabulary of two distinct traditions: the veneration of the Virgin Mary and the love poetry of Ovid and his heirs. Mariolatry, which has a particularly rich tradition in England, celebrates the perfection of Mary as a woman and mother, who undid the sins of Eve and now intercedes for fallen mankind. Ovid, with his celebration of sensuality and cynical instructions for achieving the lover's desire, provided medieval Europe with a whole catalog of love psychology and erotic persuasion.

The self-conscious command of fine manners, whether the proper way of hunting, dressing, addressing a superior, or wooing a lady, became a key mark of an aristocrat. Great reputations grew around courtly attainment, as in the legends that circulated about Richard I. Centuries later, the hero of *Sir Gawain and the Green Knight* is tested as much through his courtly behavior as through his martial bravery. A literature of etiquette emerged as early as the reign of Henry I in England and continued through the thirteenth century. In the court of Henry II, Daniel of Beccles wrote *Urbanus Magnus*, a verse treatise in Latin on courtesy. In this poem he offers detailed advice in many arenas of specific behavior at court: avoiding frivolity, giving brief counsel, and especially comporting oneself among the wealthy:

> Eating at the table of the rich, speak little
> Lest you be called a chatterbox among the diners.
> Be modest, make reverence your companion.

In a mildly misogynist passage, Daniel especially warns against becoming involved with the lord's wife, even if she makes an overture, as occurs in Marie de France's *Lanval*. Should this happen, Daniel offers polite evasive strategies, skills we see demonstrated in *Sir Gawain and the Green Knight*.

ROMANCE

Courtliness was expressed both in lyric poetry and in a wide range of vernacular narratives that we now loosely call "romances"—referring both to their genre and to the romance language in which they were first written. The Arthurian tradition, featured in this anthology, is only one of many romance traditions; others include the legends of Tristan and Isolde, Alexander, and Havelock the Dane. In romances that focus on courtly love, the hero's devotion to an unapproachable lady tends to elevate his character. Although many courtly romances conclude in a happy and acceptable marriage of hero and heroine, others such as Marie's *Lanval* warn of the dangers of transgressive love to the hero and his society. To the extent that they portray women as disruptive agents of erotic desire, some romances take on elements of the misogynist tradition that persisted in clerical thought alongside the adoration of the Virgin. Near the end of *Sir Gawain and the Green Knight*, even the courtly Gawain explodes in a virulent diatribe against women.

Love was not the only subject of romance, however. Stories of love and war typically lead the protagonists into encounters with the uncanny, the marvelous, the taboo. This is not so surprising when we recall the practices of medieval Christianity that brought the believer into daily contact with such miracles as the Eucharist; even chronicles of saints' lives regularly showed the divine will breaking miraculously into everyday life. We may say today that romance looses the hero and heroine onto the landscape of the private or social subconscious; a medieval writer might have stressed that nature itself is imbued with mystery both by God and by other, more shadowy, spiritual forces.

In romances, the line between the mundane and the extraordinary is often highly permeable: an episode may move swiftly from a simple ride to a meeting with a magical lady or malevolent dwarf, as often occurs in Thomas Malory. Romance also seems to be a form of imaginative literature in which medieval society could acknowledge the transgressions of its own ordering principles: adultery, incest, unmotivated martial violence. And it often revisits areas of belief and imagination that official culture long had put aside: *Sir Gawain and the Green Knight,* for instance, features a magical knight who can survive having his head cut off and a powerful aged woman who is called a goddess. Both characters reach back, however indirectly, to pre-Christian figures encountered in early Irish and Welsh stories.

THE RETURN OF ENGLISH

The romances are another of the dense points of contact among the many languages and ethnicities of the medieval British Isles. These powerful and evocative narratives often feature figures of Celtic origin like the British King Arthur and his court who came to French- and English-language culture through the Latin *History* of Geoffrey of Monmouth. Such transmission is typical of the linguistic mix in post-Conquest England. The language of the aristocracy was French, used in government and law as well as in the nascent vernacular literature. A few conservative monasteries continued the famed Anglo-Saxon Chronicle in its original language after the Conquest. But increasingly English or an evolving form of Anglo-Saxon was the working language of the peasantry. Mixed-language households must have appeared as provincial Anglo-Saxon gentry began, quite quickly, to intermarry with the Normans and their descendants. The twelfth-century satirist Nigel of Canterbury (or "Wireker"), author of the *Mirror of Fools,* came from just such a mixed family.

Few writings in Middle English survive from the late twelfth century, and very little of value besides the extraordinary *Brut* of Layamon, which retranslates much of Geoffrey of Monmouth's *History* from a French version. A manuscript containing the earliest English lyric in this collection, the thirteenth-century *sumer is ycumen in,* can suggest the linguistic complexity of the era: it contains lyrics in English and French, and instructions for performance in Latin.

English began to reenter the world of official discourse in the thirteenth century. Communications between the church and the laity took place increasingly in English, and by the late 1250s, Archbishop Sewal of York tended to reject papal candidates for bishoprics if they did not have good English. In 1258 King Henry III issued a proclamation in Latin, French, and English, though the circumstances were unusual. Teaching glossaries include a growing number of English words, as well as the French traditionally used to explain difficult Latin.

The fourteenth century inaugurated a distinct change in the status of English, however, as it became the language of parliament and a growing number of governmental activities. We hear of Latin being taught in the 1340s through English rather than

French. In 1362 a statute tried (but failed) to switch the language of law courts from French to English, and in 1363 Parliament was opened in English. The period also witnesses tremendous activity in translating a wide range of works into English, including Chaucer's version of Boethius' *Consolation of Philosophy* and the Wycliffite translations of the Bible, completed by 1396. Finally, at the close of the century, the Rolls of Parliament record in Latin the overthrow of Richard II, but they feature Henry IV (in what was probably a self-consciously symbolic gesture) claiming the throne in a brief, grave speech in English and promising to uphold "the gude lawes and custumes of the Rewme."

The reemergence of English allowed an extraordinary flowering of vernacular literature, most notably the achievements of Chaucer, Langland, and the anonymous genius who wrote *Sir Gawain and the Green Knight*. It would be more accurate, nevertheless, to speak of the reemergence of "Englishes" in the second half of the fourteenth century. The language scholars now call Middle English divides into four quite distinct major dialects in different regions of the island. These dialects were in many ways mutually unintelligible, so that Chaucer, who was from London in the Southeast Midlands, might have been hard-pressed to understand *Sir Gawain and the Green Knight*, written in the West Midlands near Lancashire. (Certainly Chaucer was aware of dialects and mimics some northern vocabulary in his *Canterbury Tales*.) London was the center of government and commerce in this era and later the place of early book printing, which served to stabilize the language. Thus Chaucer's dialect ultimately dominated and developed into modern English. Therefore English-speaking students today can read Chaucer in the original without much difficulty, whereas Langland's *Piers Plowman* is very challenging and *Sir Gawain* may seem virtually a foreign tongue. As a result, the latter two works are offered in translation in this anthology. (For a practical guide to Chaucer's Middle English, also helpful in reading lyrics and *The Second Play of the Shepherds*, see pages 274–276.)

Not only are *Piers Plowman* and *Sir Gawain* written in dialects different from that of Chaucer's London, they also employ a quite distinct poetic style which descends from the alliterative meter of Old English poetry, based on repetitions of key consonants and on general patterns of stress. By contrast, the rhymed syllabic style used by poets like Chaucer developed under the influence of medieval French poetry and its many lyric forms. Fourteenth-century alliterative poetry was part of a revival that occurred in the North and West of the country, at a time when the form would have seemed old fashioned to many readers in the South. In the next two centuries, in a region even more distant from London, alliterative poetry or its echoes persisted in the Middle Scots poetry of William Dunbar, Robert Henryson, and Gavin Douglas.

POLITICS AND SOCIETY IN THE FOURTEENTH CENTURY

The fourteenth-century authors wrote in a time of enormous ferment, culturally and politically as well as linguistically. During the second half of the fourteenth century, new social and theological movements shook past certainties about the divine right of kings, the division of society among three estates, the authority of the church, and the role of women. An optimistic backward view can see in that time the struggle of the peasantry for greater freedom, the growing power of the Commons in Parliament, and the rise of a mercantile middle class. These changes often appeared far darker at the time, though, with threatening, even apocalyptic implications, as can be seen in *Piers Plowman*.

The forces of nature also cast a shadow across the century. In a time that never produced large agricultural surpluses, poor harvests led to famine in the second and third decades of the century, and an accompanying deflation drove people off the land. In 1348 the Black Death arrived in England, killing at least 35 percent of the population by 1350. Plague struck violently three more times before 1375, emptying whole villages. Overall, as much as half the population may have died.

The kingship was already in trouble. After the consolidation of royal power under Henry II and the Angevins in the twelfth century, the regional barons began to reassert their power. In a climactic confrontation in 1215, they forced King John to sign the Magna Carta, guaranteeing (in theory at least) their traditional rights and privileges as well as due process in law and judgment by peers. In the fourteenth century the monarchy came under considerable new pressures. Edward II (1307–1327) was deposed by one of his barons, Roger de Mortimer, and with the connivance of his own queen, Isabella. His son Edward III had a long and initially brilliant reign, marked by great military triumphs in a war against France, but the conflict dragged on so long that it became known as the Hundred Years' War. Edward III's reign was marked at home by famine, deflation, and then, most horribly, plague. His later years were marked by premature senility and control by a court circle. These years were further darkened by the death of that paragon of chivalry, Edward's son and heir-apparent, Edward "The Black Prince." Edward's successor, the Black Prince's son Richard II, launched a major peace initiative in the Hundred Years' War and became a great patron of the arts, but he was also capable of great tyranny. In 1399 like his great-grandfather, he was deposed. An ancient and largely creaky royal bureaucracy had difficulty running a growing mercantile economy, and when royal justice failed to control crime in the provinces, it was increasingly replaced by local powers.

The aristocracy too experienced pressures from the increased economic power of the urban merchants and from the peasants' efforts to exploit labor shortages and win better control over their land. The aristocrats responded with fierce, though only partly successful, efforts to limit wages and with stricter and more articulate divisions within society, even between the peerage and gentry. It is not clear, however, that fourteenth-century aristocrats perceived themselves as a threatened order. If anything, events may have pressed them toward a greater class cohesion, a more self-conscious pursuit of chivalric culture and values. The reign of Edward III saw the foundation of the royal Order of the Garter, a select group of nobles honored for their chivalric accomplishments as much as their power (the order is almost certainly evoked at the close of *Sir Gawain and the Green Knight*). Edward further exploited the Arthurian myth in public rituals such as tournaments and Round Tables. The ancient basis of the feudal tie, land tenure, began to give way to contract and payment in the growing, hierarchicalized retinues of the period. These were still lifelong relationships between lord and retainer, nevertheless, and contemporary historians of aristocratic sympathies like Jean Froissart idealize an ongoing community of chivalric conduct that could reach even across combating nations.

The second estate, the church, was also troubled—in part, paradoxically, because of the growing and active piety of the laity. Encouraged by the annual confession that had been required since the Fourth Lateran Council of 1215, laymen increasingly took control of their own spiritual lives. But the new emphasis on confession also led to clerical corruption. Mendicant (begging) friars, armed with manuals of penance, spread across the countryside to confess penitents in their own homes and sometimes accepted money for absolving them. Whether or not these abuses were truly widespread, they inspired much anticlerical satire—as is reflected in the works of Chaucer and Langland—and the Church's authority diminished in the process. The traditional priesthood, if better educated, was also more worldly than in the past, increasingly pulled from parish service into governmental bureaucracy; it too faced widespread literary satire. Well aware of clerical venality, the church nevertheless fearfully resisted the criticisms and innovations of "reforming clerics" like John Wycliffe and his supporters among the gentry, the

"Lollard knights." The church's control over religious experience was further complicated and perhaps undermined by the rise of popular mysticism, among both the clergy and the laity, which was difficult to contain within the traditional ecclesiastical hierarchy. Mystical writing by people as varied as Richard Rolle, Julian of Norwich, the anonymous author of *The Cloud of Unknowing,* and the emotive Margery Kempe all promulgate the notion of an individual's direct experience of the divine. Finally, and on a much broader scale, all of Christian Europe was rocked by the Great Schism of 1378, when believers faced the disconcerting spectacle of two popes ruling simultaneously.

The third estate, the commoners, was the most problematic and rapidly evolving of the three in the fourteenth century. The traditional division of medieval society into three estates had no place for the rising mercantile bourgeoisie and grouped them with the peasants who worked the land. In fact the new urban wealthy formed a class quite of their own. Patrons and consumers of culture, they also served in the royal bureaucracy under Edward III, as is illustrated by the career of Geoffrey Chaucer who came from just such a background. Yet only the wealthiest married into the landed gentry, and poor health conditions in the cities made long mercantile dynasties uncommon. Cities in anything like a modern sense were few and retained rural features. Houses often had gardens, even orchards, and pigs (and pig dung) filled the narrow, muddy streets. Only magnates built in stone; only they and ecclesiastical institutions had the luxury of space and privacy. Otherwise, cities were crowded and dirty—the suburbs especially disreputable—and venues for communicable disease.

The peasants too had a new sense of class cohesion. Events had already loosened the traditional bond of serfs to the land on which they were born, and the plagues further shifted the relative economic power of landowning and labor. As peasants found they could demand better pay, fiercely repressive laws were passed to stop them. These and other discontents, like the arrival of foreign labor and technologies, led to the Rising of 1381 (also known as the Peasants' Revolt). Led by literate peasants and renegade priests, the rebels attacked aristocrats, foreigners, and some priests. They were swiftly and violently put down, but the event was nevertheless a watershed and haunted the minds of the English.

When one leader of the revolt, the priest John Ball, cited Langland's fictional character Piers Plowman with approval, Langland reacted with dismay and revised his poem to emphasize the proper place of peasants. Even more conservative, Chaucer's friend John Gower wrote a horrified Latin allegory on the revolt, *Vox Clamantis* (*The Voice of One Crying*), where he compared the rebels to beasts. By contrast, Chaucer virtually ignored the revolt, aside from a brief comic reference in the *Nun's Priest's Tale;* it remains unclear, though, whether Chaucer's silence reflects comfortable bourgeois indifference or stems from deep anxiety and discomfort. At the same time, these disruptions introduced a period of cultural ferment, and the mercantile middle class also provided a creative force, appearing (though not without some nervous condescension) in some of Chaucer's most enduring characters like the *Canterbury Tales'* Merchant, the Wife of Bath, and the Miller.

It is both from this new middle class and from the established upper class that wider choices in the lives of women emerged in the later Middle Ages. Their social and political power had been curtailed both by clerical antifeminism and by the increasingly centralized government during the twelfth and thirteenth centuries. Starting in the fourteenth century, however, women began to regain an increased voice and presence. Among the aristocracy, Edward II's wife Isabella was an important player in events that brought about the king's deposition. And at the end of the century, Edward III's mistress Alice Perrers was widely criticized for her avarice and her influence on the aging king (for instance by William Langland who refers to her in the allegorical figure Lady Meed).

Women were also important in the spread of lay literacy among the middle class. In France, Christine de Pizan reexamined whole areas of her culture, especially ancient and biblical narrative, from a feminist perspective; her work was known and translated in England. Important autobiographical works were composed in Middle English by Julian of Norwich and Margery Kempe. Julian was an anchoress, living a cloistered religious life but able to speak to visitors such as Margery herself; Margery was an illiterate but prosperous townswoman, daughter of a mayor, who dictated to scribes her experiences of wifehood and rebellion against it, of travel to holy places, and of spiritual growth. Still, for the representation of women's voices in this period we are largely dependent on the fictional creations of men. Chaucer's famous Wife of Bath, for instance, strikes many modern readers as an articulate voice opposing women's repression and expressing their ambitions, but for all her critique of the antifeminist stereotypes of the church, she is in many ways their supreme embodiment. And in a number of Middle English lyrics, probably by men, the woman's voice may evoke scorn rather than pity as she laments her seduction and abandonment by a smooth-talking man, usually a cleric.

THE SPREAD OF BOOK CULTURE IN THE FIFTEENTH CENTURY

Geoffrey Chaucer died in 1400, a convenient date for those who like their eras to end with round numbers. Certainly literary historians have often closed off the English Middle Ages with Chaucer and left the fifteenth century as a sort of drab and undefined waiting period before the dawn of the Renaissance. Yet parts of fifteenth-century England are sites of vital and burgeoning literary culture. Book ownership spread more and more widely. Already in the late fourteenth century, Chaucer had imagined a fictional Clerk of Oxford with a solid collection of university texts despite his relative poverty. More of the urban bourgeoisie bought books and even had appealing collections assembled for them. When printing came to England in the later fifteenth century, books became even more available, though still not cheap.

Whether in manuscript or print, a swiftly growing proportion of these books was in English. The campaigns of Henry V in the second decade of the fifteenth century and his death in 1422 mark England's last great effort to reclaim the old Norman and Angevin territories on the continent. With the loss of all but a scrap of this land and the decline of French as a language of influence, these decades consolidate a notion of cultural and nationalistic Englishness. The Lancastrian kings, Henry the Fourth, Fifth, and Sixth, seem to have adopted English as the medium for official culture and patronized translators like Lydgate. Later in the period William Caxton made a great body of French and English texts available to aristocratic and middle-class readers, both by translating and by diffusing them in the new medium of print.

Ancient aristocratic narratives continued to evolve, as in Thomas Malory's retelling of the Arthurian story in his *Morte Darthur*, one of the books printed by Caxton. Malory works mostly from French prose versions but trims back much of the exploration of love and the uncanny; the result is a recharged tale of chivalric battle and familial and political intrigue. Other continental and local traditions are revived in another courtly setting by a group of Scots poets including Dunbar and Henryson.

As more and more commoners had educational and financial access to books, they also participated in a lively public literary culture in towns and cities. The fifteenth century sees the flowering of the great dramatic "mystery cycles," sets of plays on religious themes produced and in part performed by craft guilds of larger towns in the Midlands and North. Included here is a brilliant sample, *The Second Play of the Shepherds* from the Wakefield Plays. Probably written by clerics, these plays are nonetheless dense with the preoccupations of contemporary working people and enriched by implicit analogies between the lives of their actors and the biblical events they portray. Lyrics and political poems continue to flourish. Sermons remain a popular and widespread form of religious instruction and literary production. And highly literary public rituals, such as Henry V's triumphal civic entries as he returned from his French campaigns, are part of Lancastrian royal propaganda.

By the time Caxton was editing and printing Malory in 1485 with an eye to sales and profit, over eight hundred years had passed since Caedmon is said to have composed his first Christian hymn under angelic direction. The idea of the poet had moved from a version of magician and priest to something more like a modern author; and the dominant model of literary transmission was shifting from listening to an oral performance to reading a book privately. Chaucer, that most bookish of poets, is a case in point. Many of his early poems refer to the pleasures of reading, not only for instruction but even as a mere pastime, often to avoid insomnia. He opens the dream vision *The Parliament of Fowls* with the poet reading a classical Latin text, Cicero's *Dream of Scipio*. Chaucer, of course, read his books and disseminated his own work in handwritten manuscript; in his humorous lyric *To His Scribe Adam* he expresses his frustration with copyists who might mistranscribe his words.

Despite such private bookishness, however, a more public and oral literary culture never disappeared from medieval Britain. Considerable interdependence between oral and literate modes of communication remained; poetry was both silently read and orally performed. In the *Canterbury Tales*, for instance, when the pilgrim Chaucer apologizes for the bawdiness of *The Miller's Tale*, he suggests that if the listener/reader doesn't like what he *hears*, he should simply turn the *page* and choose another tale. At the same time, literate clerics practiced what we might call learned orality, through lectures or disputations at Oxford and Cambridge or from the pulpit in a more popular setting. Langland imitates such sophisticated oral practice in the theological debates in *Piers Plowman*, and Chaucer uses the sermon form in the *Wife of Bath's Prologue*, *Pardoner's Tale*, and *Parson's Tale*. The popular orality of minstrel performance, harking back however distantly to the world of the Anglo-Saxon *scop* and the Irish *fili*, was also exploited with great self-consciousness by literate poets. Langland expresses harsh disapproval of those minstrels who were mere entertainers, undercutting the serious work of preachers. *Sir Gawain and the Green Knight* presents itself as an oral performance, based on a tale that the narrator has heard recited. By contrast, Chaucer gently twits minstrels in his marvelous parody of popular romance, *Sir Thopas*. Chaucer remains a learned poet whose greatest achievement, paradoxically, was the presentation of fictional oral performances—the tale-telling of the Canterbury pilgrims.

The speed with which communication technologies are changing in our own era has heightened our awareness of such changes in the past. We are now closing the era of the book and moving into the era of the endlessly malleable electronic text. In many ways the means by which we have come to receive and transmit information—television, radio, CD-ROM, Internet—mix orality and literacy in a fashion wholly new yet also intriguingly reminiscent of the later Middle Ages. In contrast to the seeming fixity of texts in the intervening centuries, contemporary literary culture may be recovering the sense of textual and cultural fluidity that brought such dynamism to literary creation in the Middle Ages.

Before the Norman Conquest

⊷ ⊱⊰ ⊶

Beowulf

Beowulf has come down to us as if by chance, for it is preserved only in a single manuscript, Cotton Vitellius A.XV, which almost perished in a fire in 1731. An anonymous poem transcribed in the West Saxon dialect of Old English at the end of the tenth century, it was most likely composed two centuries earlier. Although it was studied by a few antiquarians during the Renaissance, the poem remained virtually unknown until its first printing in 1815; only in this century has it achieved a place in the canon, not just as a cultural artifact or a good adventure story but as a philosophical epic of great complexity and power.

Several features of *Beowulf* make its genre a challenge for modern readers: the vivid accounts of battles with monsters link it to the folktale, and the recurring tone of sorrow for the passing of worldly things marks it as elegiac. Nevertheless, the poem is best approached as an epic. Like the *Iliad* and the *Odyssey*, it is a "primary epic," originating in oral tradition and recounting the legendary wars and exploits of great heroes from a lost heroic age.

The values of Germanic tribal society are central to *Beowulf*. A member of the *comitatus*—the band of warriors following a tribal lord—was expected to follow a code of heroic behavior stressing bravery, loyalty, and willingness to avenge his comrades and his lord at any cost. His lord rewarded him with treasure that symbolized this obligation, and he would suffer the shame of exile if he should survive his lord in battle. The values of the Germanic heroic code are invoked at the end of the poem, when Wiglaf, the hero's only loyal retainer, upbraids his comrades for having abandoned Beowulf to the dragon. He says that their prince wasted his war gear when he gave it to them at the mead hall and predicts the demise of their people, the Geats, once their ancient enemies, the Swedes, hear that Beowulf is dead.

Beowulf offers an extraordinarily double perspective, however. First, for all its acceptance of the values of pagan heroic code, it also refers to Christian concepts which in many cases conflict with them. While all characters in the poem—Danes, Swedes, and Geats, as well as the monsters—are pagan, the monster Grendel is described as descended from Cain and going to hell. Furthermore, while violence in the service of revenge is presented as the proper way for Beowulf to respond to inhuman assailants such as Grendel's mother, the narrator expresses a pacifist view, perhaps influenced by Christianity, of the unending chain of violence engaged in by feuding tribes. And although the Danish king Hrothgar uses wealth as a kind of social sacrament when he lavishly rewards Beowulf for his military aid, he simultaneously invokes God in a "sermon" warning him against excessive pride in his youthful strength. This rich division of emotional loyalty probably arises from a poet and audience of Christians who look back at their pagan Scandinavian ancestors with both pride and grief, stressing the intersection of pagen and Christian values in an effort to reconcile the two. By restricting Biblical references to events in the Old Testament, the poet shows the Germanic revenge ethic as consistent with the Old Law of retribution and plays down the New Testament injunction to forgive one's enemies.

Beowulf's style is simultaneously a challenge and a reward to the modern reader. Some of its features, such as the variation of an idea in different words—which would have been welcomed by a listening, and often illiterate, audience—can seem repetitious to a literate audience. Other features equally indebted to the poem's oral origin are admired today. For instance, like other Old English poems, *Beowulf* uses alliteration as a structural principle, beginning the first three of four stressed words in a line with the same letter, as in "wæs se grimma gǣst Grendel hāten" ("this gruesome creature was called Grendel"). Such alliterative formulas—collocations of words—were an aid to a Germanic poet reliant on memory for composing poems. The *Beowulf* poet also loves to use compound words. While these are common in Germanic languages, including modern English (e.g., "mankind," "homesick"), this poet uses them with unusual inventiveness and force. Examples in the passage below include the terms "fifelcynnes" ("of monsterkind"), "mearcstapa" ("borderland-prowler"), and "wonsaeli" ("unhappy," "cursed"). A specific type of compound that is used for powerful stylistic effects is the "kenning," a kind of compressed metaphor, as in "swan's way" for "ocean." The kennings resemble the Old English riddles in their teasing, riddling quality.

On a larger narrative level is another feature, also traceable to the poem's oral origin: the tendency to digress into stories tangential to the action of the main plot. The poet's digressions, however, actually contribute to his artistry of broad contrasts—youth and age, joy and sorrow, good and bad kingship. For instance, Hrothgar, while urging humility and generosity on the victorious Beowulf, tells the story of the proud and stingy King Heremod. Similarly, when Beowulf returns home in glory to the kingdom of the Geats, the poet praises his uncle Hygelac's young Queen Hygd by contrasting her with the bad Queen Thryth, who lost her temper and sent her suitors to death.

The poet uses digression in a subtler way to foreshadow events to come. To celebrate Beowulf's victory over Grendel, the Scop at Hrothgar's hall sings of events generations earlier, in which a feud caused the deaths of a Danish princess's brother and son. Although this story has nothing to do with the main plot of the poem, there is an implied parallel a few lines later: the original audience would have known that after Hrothgar's death, his queen would lose her own son in comparable circumstances. The poet thus applies his broad principle of comparison and contrast to complex narrative situations as well as to simpler concepts such as good and bad kings. It is the often tragic tenor of these digressions that evokes much of the dark mood that suffuses *Beowulf*, even in its moments of heroic triumph.

The following passage of *Beowulf*, describing the monster's genealogy and menacing behavior, illustrates some of the stylistic features discussed above; included is a literal translation which makes these points more clearly than the more elegant one used in this anthology.*

	Swā ðā drihtguman drēamum lifdon,
100	ēadiglice, oð ðæt ān ongan
	fyrene fre(m)man fēond on helle;
	wæs se grimma gǣst Grendel hāten,
	mǣre mearcstapa, sē þe mōras hēold,
	fen ond fæsten; fifelcynnes eard
105	wonsāeliwer weardode hwile,
	siþðan him Scyppend forscrifen haefde
	in Cāines cynne— þone cwealm gewraec
	ēce Drihten, þaes þe hē Abel slōg;

---

* The passage is taken from *Beowulf and the Fight at Finnsburg*, ed. Frederick Klaeber, 3d ed. (Boston: D. C. Heath, 1950). The translation is by Anne Schotter.

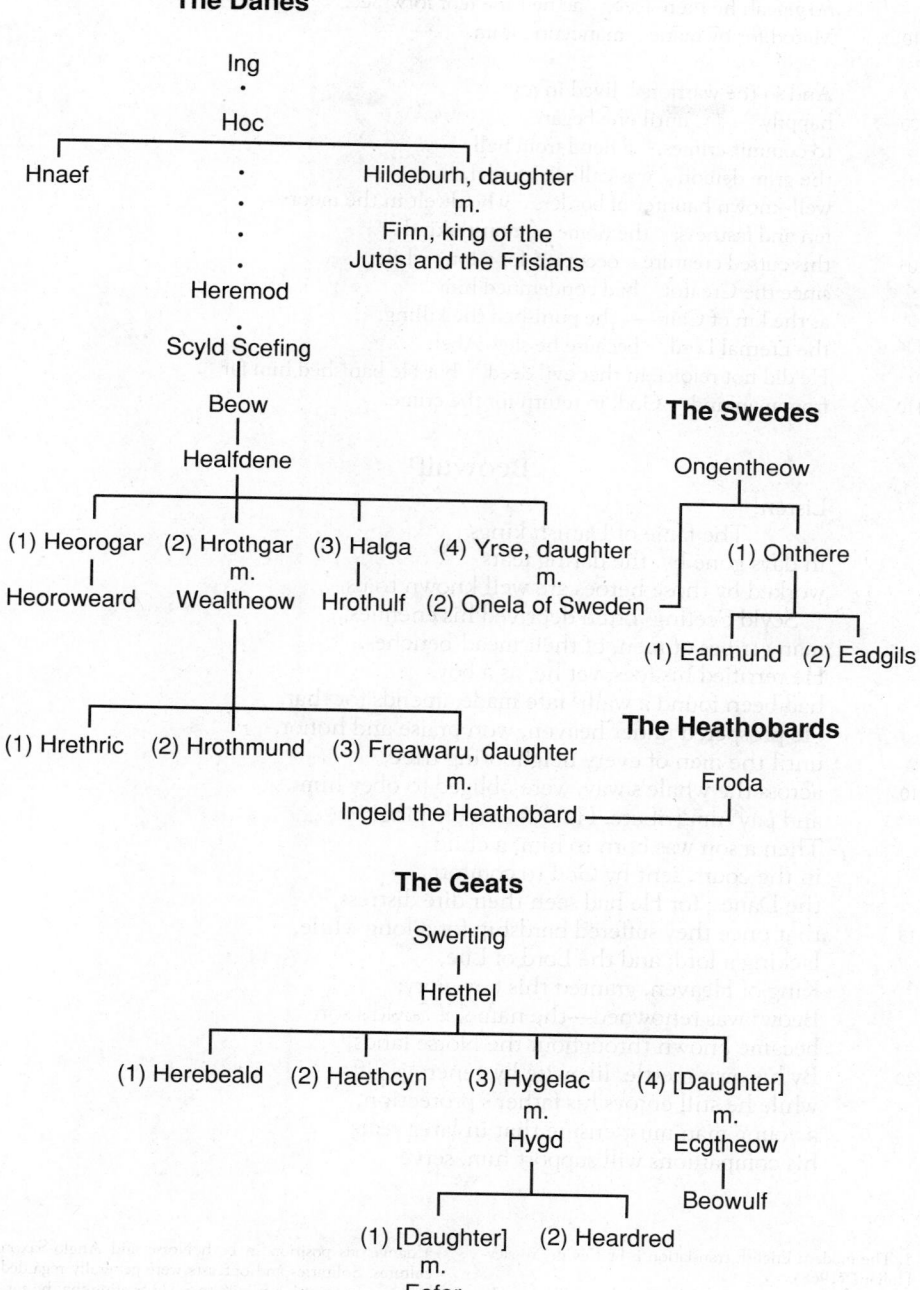

Royal genealogies of the Northern European tribes according to the *Beowulf* text.

ne gefeah hē þære fǣð,   ac hē hine feor forwraec,
110   Metod for þȳ māne   mancynne fram.

And so the warriors   lived in joy
100   happily   until one began
to commit crimes,   a fiend from hell
the grim demon   was called Grendel,
well-known haunter of borders   who dwelt in the moors
fen and fastness;   the home of monsterkind
105   this cursed creature   occupied for a long while
since the Creator   had condemned him
as the kin of Cain—   he punished the killing,
the Eternal Lord,   because he slew Abel;
He did not rejoice in that evil deed,   but He banished him far
110   from mankind,   God, in return for the crime.

Beowulf[1]

Listen!
        The fame of Danish kings
in days gone by, the daring feats
worked by those heroes are well known to us.
        Scyld Scefing[2] often deprived his enemies,
5   many tribes of men, of their mead-benches.
He terrified his foes; yet he, as a boy,
had been found a waif;[3] fate made amends for that.
He prospered under heaven, won praise and honor,
until the men of every neighboring tribe,
10   across the whale's way, were obliged to obey him
and pay him tribute. He was a noble king!
Then a son was born to him, a child
in the court, sent by God to comfort
the Danes; for He had seen their dire distress,
15   that once they suffered hardship for a long while,
lacking a lord; and the Lord of Life,
King of Heaven, granted this boy glory;
Beow[4] was renowned—the name of Scyld's son
became known throughout the Norse lands.
20   By his own mettle, likewise by generous gifts
while he still enjoys his father's protection,
a young man must ensure that in later years
his companions will support him, serve

---

1. The modern English translation is by Kevin Crossley-Holland (1968).
2. The traditional founder of the Danish royal house. His name means "shield" or "protection" of the "sheaf," suggesting an earlier association in Norse mythology with the god of vegetation. The Danes are known afterwards as "Scyldings," descendants of Scyld.
3. Scyld Scefing arrives among the Danes as a foundling, a dangerous position in both Norse and Anglo-Saxon cultures. Solitaries and outcasts were generally regarded with suspicion; it is a tribute to Scyld Scefing that he surmounted these obstacles to become the leader and organizer of the Danish people.
4. The manuscript reads "Beowulf" here, the copyist's mind having skipped ahead to the story's protagonist.

their prince in battle; a man who wins renown
25 will always prosper among any people.
        Then Scyld departed at the destined hour,
that powerful man sought the Lord's protection.
His own close companions carried him
down to the sea, as he, lord of the Danes,
30 had asked while he could still speak.
That well-loved man had ruled his land for many years.
There in harbor stood the ring-prowed ship,
the prince's vessel, icy, eager to sail;
and then they laid their dear lord,
35 the giver of rings, deep within the ship
by the mast in majesty; many treasures
and adornments from far and wide were gathered there.
I have never heard of a ship equipped
more handsomely with weapons and war-gear,
40 swords and corslets; on his breast
lay countless treasures that were to travel far
with him into the waves' domain.
They gave him great ornaments, gifts
no less magnificent than those men had given him
45 who long before had sent him alone,
child as he was, across the stretch of the seas.
Then high above his head they placed
a golden banner and let the waves bear him,
bequeathed him to the sea; their hearts were grieving,
50 their minds mourning. Mighty men
beneath the heavens, rulers in the hall,
cannot say who received that cargo.
        When his royal father had traveled from the earth,
Beow of Denmark, a beloved king,
55 ruled long in the stronghold, famed
amongst men; in the time Healfdene the brave
was born to him; who, so long as he lived,
gray-haired and redoubtable, ruled the noble Danes.
Beow's son Healfdene, leader of men,
60 was favored by fortune with four children:
Heorogar and Hrothgar and Halga the good;
Yrse, the fourth, was Onela's queen,
the beloved wife of that warlike Swedish king.
        Hrothgar[5] won honor in war,
65 glory in battle, and so ensured
his followers' support—young men
whose number multiplied into a mighty troop.
And he resolved to build a hall,
a large and noble feasting-hall
70 of whose splendors men would always speak,

---

5. Significantly, Hrothgar is not the first-born of his generation. Leadership of the tribe was customarily conferred by acclamation upon the royal candidate who showed the greatest promise and ability.

and there to distribute as gifts to old and young
all the things that God had given him—
but not men's lives or the public land.
Then I heard that tribes without number, even
75 to the ends of the earth, were given orders
to decorate the hall. And in due course
(before very long) this greatest of halls
was completed. Hrothgar, whose very word was counted
far and wide as a command, called it Heorot.[6]
80 He kept his promise, gave presents of rings
and treasure at the feasting. The hall towered high,
lofty and wide-gabled—fierce tongues of loathsome fire
had not yet attacked it, nor was the time yet near
when a mortal feud should flare between father-
85 and son-in-law, sparked off by deeds of deadly enmity.[7]
    Then the brutish demon who lived in darkness
impatiently endured a time of frustration:
day after day he heard the din of merry-making
inside the hall, and the sound of the harp
90 and the bard's clear song. He who could tell
of the origin of men from far-off times lifted his voice,
sang that the Almighty made the earth,
this radiant plain encompassed by oceans;
and that God, all powerful, ordained
95 sun and moon to shine for mankind,
adorned all regions of the world
with trees and leaves; and sang that He gave life
to every kind of creature that walks about earth.
So those warrior Danes lived joyful lives,
100 in complete harmony, until the hellish fiend
began to perpetrate base crimes.
This gruesome creature was called Grendel,
notorious prowler of the borderland, ranger of the moors,
the fen and the fastness; this cursed creature
105 lived in a monster's lair for a time
after the Creator had condemned him
as one of the seed of Cain—the Everlasting Lord
avenged Abel's murder. Cain had
no satisfaction from that feud, but the Creator
110 sent him into exile, far from mankind,
because of his crime.[8] He could no longer
approach the throne of grace, that precious place
in God's presence, nor did he feel God's love.
In him all evil-doers find their origin,

---

6. The name of Hrothgar's hall in Anglo-Saxon literally means "hart" or "stag," a male deer. The epithet "adorned with horns," which is applied to Heorot later, may further suggest its function as a hunting lodge.
7. The peace concluded between the Danes and the Heathobards through intermarriage is already doomed before it has taken place. The events foreshadowed here will occur long after the time of the poem.
8. See Genesis 4.3–16.

115   monsters and elves and spiteful spirits of the dead,
       also the giants who grappled with God
       for a long while; the Lord gave them their deserts.
           Then, under cover of night, Grendel came
       to Hrothgar's lofty hall to see how the Ring-Danes[9]
120   were disposed after drinking ale all evening;
       and he found there a band of brave warriors,
       well-feasted, fast asleep, dead to worldly sorrow,
       man's sad destiny. At once that hellish monster,
       grim and greedy, brutally cruel,
125   started forward and seized thirty thanes
       even as they slept; and then, gloating
       over his plunder, he hurried from the hall,
       made for his lair with all those slain warriors.
       Then at dawn, as day first broke,
130   Grendel's power was at once revealed;
       a great lament was lifted, after the feast
       an anguished cry at that daylight discovery.
       The famous prince, best of all men, sat apart in mourning;
       when he saw Grendel's gruesome footprints,
135   that great man grieved for his retainers.
       This enmity was utterly one-sided, too repulsive,
       too long-lasting. Nor were the Danes allowed respite,
       but the very next day Grendel committed
       violent assault, murders more atrocious than before,
140   and he had no qualms about it. He was caught up in his crimes.
       Then it was not difficult to find the man
       who preferred a more distant resting-place,
       a bed in the outbuildings, for the hatred
       of the hall-warden was quite unmistakable.
145   He who had escaped the clutches of the fiend
       kept further off, at a safe distance.
           Thus Grendel ruled, resisted justice,
       one against all, until the best of halls
       stood deserted. And so it remained:
150   for twelve long winters the lord of the Danes
       was sorely afflicted with sorrows and cares;
       then men were reminded in mournful songs
       that the monster Grendel fought with Hrothgar
       for a long time, fought with fierce hatred
155   committing crime and atrocity day after day
       in continual strife. He had no wish for peace
       with any of the Danes, would not desist
       from his deadly malice or pay *wergild*.[1]
       No! None of the counselors could hold out hope
160   Of handsome compensation at that slayer's hands.

9. "Ring-Danes" refers to the Danes' practice of giving gifts in exchange for military services.
1. A cash payment for someone's death. *Wergild* was regarded as an advance over violent revenge, and Grendel is marked as uncivilized because he refuses to acknowledge this practice.

But the cruel monster constantly terrified
young and old, the dark death-shadow
lurked in ambush; he prowled the misty moors
at the dead of night; men do not know
165   where such hell-whisperers shrithe in their wanderings.
Such were the many and outrageous injuries
that the fearful solitary, foe of all men,
endlessly inflicted; he occupied Heorot,
that hall adorned with treasures, on cloudless nights.
170   This caused the lord of the Danes deep,
heart-breaking grief. Strong men often sat
in consultation, trying in vain to devise
a good plan as to how best valiant men
could safeguard themselves against sudden attack.
175   At times they offered sacrifices to the idols
in their pagan tabernacles, and prayed aloud
to the soul-slayer[2] that he would assist them
in their dire distress. Such was the custom
and comfort of the heathen; they brooded in their hearts
180   on hellish things—for the Creator, Almighty God,
the judge of all actions, was neglected by them;
truly they did not know how to praise the Protector of Heaven,
the glorious Ruler. Woe to the man who,
in his wickedness, commits his soul to the fire's embrace;
185   he must expect neither comfort nor change.
He will be damned forever. Joy shall be his
who, when he dies, may stand before the Lord,
seek peace in the embrace of our Father.
    Thus Healfdene's son endlessly brooded
190   over the afflictions of this time; that wise warrior
was altogether helpless, for the hardship upon them—
violent visitations, evil events in the night—
was too overwhelming, loathsome, and long-lasting.
    One of Hygelac's thanes,[3] Beowulf by name,
195   renowned among the Geats[4] for his great bravery,
heard in his own country of Grendel's crimes;
he was the strongest man alive,
princely and powerful. He gave orders
that a good ship should be prepared, said he would sail
200   over the sea to assist the famous leader,
the warrior king, since he needed hardy men.
Wise men admired his spirit of adventure.
Dear to them though he was, they encouraged
the warrior and consulted the omens.
205   Beowulf searched out the bravest of the Geats,

---

2. In their fear, the Danes resume heathen practices. In Christian belief, the pagan gods were transformed into devils.
3. One of the king's principal retainers, chief among these being the earls.
4. A Germanic tribe who lived along the southwestern coast of what is now Sweden.

asked them to go with him; that seasoned sailor
led fourteen thanes to the ship at the shore.
    Days went by; the boat was on the water,
moored under the cliff. The warriors, all prepared,
210   stepped onto the prow—the water streams eddied,
stirred up sand; the men stowed
gleaming armor, noble war-gear
deep within the ship; then those warriors launched
the well-built boat and so began their journey.
215   Foaming at the prow and most like a sea-bird,
the boat sped over the waves, urged on by the wind;
until next day, at the expected time,
so far had the curved prow come
that the travelers sighted land,
220   shining cliffs, steep hills,
broad headlands. So did they cross the sea;
their journey was at its end. Then the Geats
disembarked, lost no time in tying up
the boat—their corslets clanked;
225   the warriors gave thanks to God
for their safe passage over the sea.
    Then, on the cliff-top, the Danish watchman
(whose duty it was to stand guard by the shore)
saw that the Geats carried flashing shields
230   and gleaming war-gear down the gangway,
and his mind was riddled with curiosity.
Then Hrothgar's thane leapt onto his horse
and, brandishing a spear, galloped
down to the shore; there, he asked at once:
235   "Warriors! Who are you, in your coats of mail,
who have steered your tall ship over the sea-lanes
to these shores? I've been a coastguard here
for many years, kept watch by the sea,
so that no enemy band should encroach
240   upon this Danish land and do us injury.
Never have warriors, carrying their shields,
come to this country in a more open manner.
Nor were you assured of my leaders' approval,
my kinsmen's consent. I've never set eyes
245   on a more noble man, a warrior in armor,
than one among your band; he's no mere retainer,
so ennobled by his weapons. May his looks never belie him,
and his lordly bearing. But now, before you step
one foot further on Danish land
250   like faithless spies, I must know
your lineage. Bold seafarers,
strangers from afar, mark my words
carefully: you would be best advised
quickly to tell me the cause of your coming."
255   The man of highest standing, leader of that troop,

unlocked his hoard of words, answered him:
"We are all Geats, hearth-companions of Hygelac;
my father was famed far and wide,
a noble lord, Ecgtheow by name—

260 he endured many winters before he,
in great old age, went on his way; every wise man
in this world readily recalls him.
We have sailed across the sea to seek your lord,
Healfdene's son, protector of the people,

265 with most honorable intentions; give us your guidance!
We have come on an errand of importance
to the great Danish prince; nor, I imagine, will the cause
of our coming long remain secret. You will know
whether it is true—as we have heard tell—

270 that here among the Danes a certain evil-doer,
a fearful solitary, on dark nights commits deeds
of unspeakable malice—damage
and slaughter. In all good conscience
I can counsel Hrothgar, that wise and good man,

275 how he shall overcome the fiend,
and how his anguish shall be assuaged—
if indeed his fate ordains that these foul deeds
should ever end, and be avenged;
he will suffer endless hardship otherwise,

280 dire distress, as long as Heorot, best of dwellings,
stands unshaken in its lofty place."
    Still mounted, the coastguard,
a courageous thane, gave him this reply:
"The discriminating warrior—one whose mind is keen—

285 must perceive the difference between words and deeds.
But I see you are a company well disposed
towards the Danish prince. Proceed, and bring
your weapons and armor! I shall direct you.
And I will command my companions, moreover,

290 to guard your ship with honor
against any foe—your beached vessel,
caulked so recently—until the day that timbered craft
with its curved prow shall carry back
the beloved man across the sea currents

295 to the shores of the storm-loving Geats:
he who dares deeds with such audacity and valor
shall be granted safety in the squall of battle."
    Then they hurried on. The ship lay still;
securely anchored, the spacious vessel

300 rode on its hawser. The boar crest, brightly gleaming,
stood over their helmets: superbly tempered,
plated with glowing gold, it guarded the lives
of those grim warriors. The thanes made haste,
marched along together until they could discern

305 the glorious, timbered hall, adorned with gold;

they saw there the best-known building
under heaven. The ruler lived in it;
its brilliance carried across countless lands.
Then the fearless watchman pointed out the path
310   leading to Heorot, bright home of brave men,
so that they should not miss the way;
that bold warrior turned his horse, then said:
"I must leave you here. May the Almighty Father,
of His grace, guard you in your enterprise.
315   I will go back to the sea again,
and there stand watch against marauding bands."

    The road was paved; it showed those warriors
the way. Their corslets were gleaming,
the strong links of shining chain-mail
320   clinked together. When the sea-stained travelers
had reached the hall itself in their fearsome armor,
they placed their broad shields
(worked so skillfully) against Heorot's wall.
Then they sat on a bench; the brave men's
325   armor sang. The seafarers' gear
stood all together, a gray-tipped forest
of ash spears; that armed troop was well equipped
with weapons.
    Then Wulfgar, a proud warrior,
asked the Geats about their ancestry:
330   "Where have you come from with these gold-plated shields,
these gray coats of mail, these visored helmets,

Boar, from a bas-relief carving on Saint Nicholas Church, Ipswich, England, 12th century.
Although this large and vigorous boar dates from the 12th century, it retains stylistic elements of
earlier Anglo-Saxon and Viking art. An ancient totem of power, boars were often depicted on
early medieval weapons and helmets.

and this pile of spears? I am Hrothgar's
messenger, his herald. I have never seen
so large a band of strangers of such bold bearing.
335 You must have come to Hrothgar's court
not as exiles, but from audacity and high ambition."
Then he who feared no man, the proud leader
of the Geats, stern-faced beneath his helmet,
gave him this reply: "We are Hygelac's
340 companions at the bench: my name is Beowulf.
I wish to explain to Healfdene's son,
the famous prince, your lord,
why we have come if he, in his goodness,
will give us leave to speak with him."
345 Wulfgar replied—a prince of the Vandals,
his mettle, his wisdom and prowess in battle
were widely recognized: "I will ask
the lord of the Danes, ruler of the Scyldings,
renowned prince and ring-giver,
350 just as you request, regarding your journey,
and bring back to you at once whatever answer
that gracious man thinks fit to give me."
   Then Wulfgar hurried to the place where Hrothgar sat,
grizzled and old, surrounded by his thanes;
355 the brave man moved forward until he stood
immediately before the Danish lord;
he well knew the customs of warriors.
Wulfgar addressed his friend and leader:
"Geatish men have traveled to this land,
360 come from far, across the stretch of the seas.
These warriors call their leader Beowulf;
they ask, my lord, that they should be allowed
to speak with you. Gracious Hrothgar,
do not give them *no* for answer.
365 They, in their armor, seem altogether worthy
of the highest esteem. I have no doubt of their leader's
might, he who has brought these brave men to Heorot."
Hrothgar, defender of the Danes, answered:
"I knew him when he was a boy;
370 his illustrious father was called Ecgtheow;
Hrethel the Geat gave him his only daughter
in marriage; now his son, with daring spirit,
has voyaged here to visit a loyal friend.
And moreover, I have heard seafarers say—
375 men who have carried rich gifts to the Geats
as a mark of my esteem—that in the grasp
of his hand that man renowned in battle
has the might of thirty men. I am convinced
that Holy God, of His great mercy,
380 has directed him to us West-Danes[5]

5. Hrothgar is, in fact, king of all the Danes: North, South, East, and West. The different terms merely conform to the Anglo-Saxon alliterative pattern established in each line.

and that he means to come to grips with Grendel.
I will reward this brave man with treasures.
Hurry! Tell them to come in and meet
our band of kinsmen; and make it clear, too,
385   that they are most welcome to the Danes!"
Then Wulfgar went to the hall door with Hrothgar's reply:
"My conquering lord, the leader of the East-Danes
commands me to tell you that he knows your lineage
and that you, so bold in mind, are welcome
390   to these shores from over the rolling sea.
You may see Hrothgar in your armor,
under your helmets, just as you are;
but leave your shields out here, and your deadly ashen spears,
let them await the outcome of your words."
395   Then noble Beowulf rose from the bench,
flanked by his fearless followers; some stayed behind
at the brave man's bidding, to stand guard over their armor.
Guided by Wulfgar, the rest hurried into Heorot
together; there went that hardy man, stern-faced
400   beneath his helmet, until he was standing under Heorot's roof.
Beowulf spoke—his corslet, cunningly linked
by the smith, was shining: "Greetings, Hrothgar!
I am Hygelac's kinsman and retainer. In my youth
I achieved many daring exploits. Word of Grendel's deeds
405   has come to me in my own country;
seafarers say that this hall Heorot,
best of all buildings, stands empty and useless
as soon as the evening light is hidden under the sky.
So, Lord Hrothgar, men known by my people
410   to be noble and wise advised me to visit you
because they knew of my great strength:
they saw me themselves when, stained by my enemies' blood,
I returned from the fight when I destroyed five,
a family of giants, and by night slew monsters
415   on the waves; I suffered great hardship,
avenged the affliction of the Storm-Geats and crushed
their fierce foes—they were asking for trouble.
And now, I shall crush the giant Grendel
in single combat. Lord of the mighty Danes,
420   guardian of the Scyldings, I ask one favor:
protector of warriors, lord beloved of your people,
now that I have sailed here from so far,
do not refuse my request—that I alone, with my band
of brave retainers, may cleanse Heorot.
425   I have also heard men say this monster
is so reckless he spurns the use of weapons.
Therefore (so that Hygelac, my lord,
may rest content over my conduct) I deny myself
the use of a sword and a broad yellow shield
430   in battle; but I shall grapple with this fiend
hand to hand; we shall fight for our lives,
foe against foe; and he whom death takes off

must resign himself to the judgment of God.
I know that Grendel, should he overcome me,

435   will without dread devour many Geats,
matchless warriors, in the battle-hall,
as he has often devoured Danes before. If death claims me
you will not have to cover my head,
for he already will have done so—

440   with a sheet of shining blood; he will carry off
the blood-stained corpse, meaning to savor it;
the solitary one will eat without sorrow
and stain his lair; no longer then
will you have to worry about burying my body.

445   But if battle should claim me, send this most excellent
coat of mail to Hygelac, this best of corslets
that protects my breast; it once belonged to Hrethel,
the work of Weland.[6] Fate goes ever as it must!"
    Hrothgar, protector of the Scyldings, replied:

450   "Beowulf, my friend! So you have come here,
because of past favors, to fight on our behalf!
Your father Ecgtheow, by striking a blow,
began the greatest of feuds. He slew Heatholaf of the Wylfings
with his own hand; after that, the Geats

455   dared not harbor him for fear of war.
So he sailed here, over the rolling waves,
to this land of the South-Danes, the honored Scyldings;
I was young then, had just begun to reign
over the Danes in this glorious kingdom,

460   this treasure-stronghold of heroes; my elder brother,
Heorogar, Healfdene's son, had died
not long before; he was a better man than I!
I settled your father's feud by payment;
I sent ancient treasures to the Wylfings

465   over the water's back; and Ecgtheow swore oaths to me.
It fills me with anguish to admit to all the evil
that Grendel, goaded on by his hatred,
has wreaked in Heorot with his sudden attacks
and infliction of injuries; my hall-troop is depleted,

470   my band of warriors; fate has swept them
into Grendel's ghastly clutches. Yet God can easily
prevent this reckless ravager from committing such crimes.
After quaffing beer, brave warriors of mine
have often boasted over the ale-cup

475   that they would wait in Heorot
and fight against Grendel with their fearsome swords.
Then, the next morning, when day dawned,
men could see that this great mead-hall was stained
by blood, that the floor by the benches

480   was spattered with gore; I had fewer followers,
dear warriors, for death had taken them off.

---

6. Legendary blacksmith of the Norse gods.

But first, sit down at our feast, and in due course,
as your inclination takes you, tell how warriors
have achieved greatness."

Then, in the feasting-hall,

485 a bench was cleared for the Geats all together,
and there those brave men went and sat,
delighting in their strength; a thane did his duty—
held between his hands the adorned ale-cup,
poured out gleaming liquor; now and then the poet sang,

490 raised his clear voice in Heorot; the warriors caroused,
no small company of Scyldings and Geats.
Ecglaf's son, Unferth,[7] who sat at the feet
of the lord of the Scyldings, unlocked his thoughts
with these unfriendly words—for the journey of Beowulf,

495 the brave seafarer, much displeased him
in that he was unwilling for any man
in this wide world to gain more glory than himself:
"Are you the Beowulf who competed with Breca,
vied with him at swimming in the open sea

500 when, swollen with vanity, you both braved
the waves, risked your lives on deep waters
because of a foolish boast? No one,
neither friend nor foe, could keep you
from your sad journey, when you swam out to sea,

505 clasped in your arms the water-streams,
passed over the sea-paths, swiftly moved your hands
and sped over the ocean. The sea heaved,
the winter flood; for seven nights
you both toiled in the water; but Breca outstayed you,

510 he was the stronger; and then, on the eighth morning,
the sea washed him up on the shores of the Heathoreams.
From there he sought his own country,
the land of the Brondings who loved him well;
he went to his fair stronghold where he had a hall

515 and followers and treasures. In truth, Beanstan's son
fulfilled his boast that he could swim better than you.
So I am sure you will pay a heavy price—
although you have survived countless battle storms,
savage sword-play—if you dare

520 ambush Grendel in the watches of the night."
Beowulf, the son of Ecgtheow, replied:
"Truly, Unferth my friend, all this beer
has made you talkative: you have told us much
about Breca and his exploits. But I maintain

525 I showed the greater stamina, endured
hardship without equal in the heaving water.
Some years ago when we were young men,
still in our youth, Breca and I made a boast,

7. Hrothgar's spokesman or court jester; his rude behavior toward Beowulf is consistent with other figures in epics and romances who taunt the hero before he undertakes his exploits. "Unferth" may mean "strife."

530   a solemn vow, to venture our lives
        on the open sea; and we kept our word.
        When we swam through the water, we each held
        a naked sword with which to ward off
        whales; by no means could Breca
535   swim faster than I, pull away from me
        through the press of the waves—
        I had no wish to be separated from him.
        So for five nights we stayed together in the sea,
        until the tides tore us apart,
        the foaming water, the freezing cold,
540   day darkening into night—until the north wind,
        that savage warrior, rounded against us.
        Rough were the waves; fishes in the sea
        were roused to great anger. Then my coat of mail,
        hard and hand-linked, guarded me against my enemies;
545   the woven war-garment, adorned with gold,
        covered my breast. A cruel ravager
        dragged me down to the sea-bed, a fierce monster
        held me tightly in its grasp; but it was given to me
        to bury my sword, my battle weapon,
550   in its breast; the mighty sea-beast
        was slain by my blow in the storm of battle.
        In this manner, and many times, loathsome monsters
        harassed me fiercely; with my fine sword
        I served them fittingly.
555   I did not allow those evil destroyers to enjoy
        a feast, to eat me limb by limb
        seated at a banquet on the sea-bottom;
        but the next morning they lay in the sand
        along the shore, wounded by sword strokes,
560   slain by battle-blades, and from that day on
        they could not hinder seafarers from sailing
        over deep waters. Light came from the east,
        God's bright beacon; the swell subsided,
        and I saw then great headlands,
565   cliffs swept by the wind. Fate will often spare
        an undoomed man, if his courage is good.
        As it was I slew nine sea-beasts
        with my sword. I have never heard
        of a fiercer fight by night under heaven's vault
570   nor of a man who endured more on the ocean streams.
        But I escaped with my life from the enemies' clutches,
        worn out by my venture. Then the swift current,
        the surging water, carried me
        to the land of the Lapps. I have not heard tell
575   that you have taken part in any such contests,
        in the peril of sword-play. Neither you nor Breca
        have yet dared such a deed with shining sword
        in battle—I do not boast because of this—
        though of course it is true you slew your own brothers,

580 your own close kinsmen. For that deed, however clever
you may be, you will suffer damnation in hell.
I tell you truly, son of Ecglaf,
that if you were in fact as unflinching
as you claim, the fearsome monster Grendel
585 would never have committed so many crimes
against your lord, nor created such havoc in Heorot;
but he has found he need not fear unduly
your people's enmity, fearsome assault
with swords by the victorious Scyldings.
590 So he spares none but takes his toll
of the Danish people, does as he will,
kills and destroys, expects no fight
from the Spear-Danes. But soon, quite soon,
I shall show him the strength, the spirit and skill
595 of the Geats. And thereafter, when day dawns,
when the radiant sun shines from the south
over the sons of men, he who so wishes
may enter the mead-hall without terror."
     Then the grizzled warrior, giver of gold,
600 was filled with joy; the lord of the Danes,
shepherd of his people, listened to Beowulf's
brave resolution and relied on his help.
The warriors laughed, there was a hum
of contentment. Wealhtheow came forward,[8]
605 mindful of ceremonial—she was Hrothgar's queen;
adorned with gold, that proud woman
greeted the men in the hall, then offered the cup
to the Danish king first of all.
She begged him, beloved of his people,
610 to enjoy the feast; the king, famed
for victory, ate and drank in happiness.
Then the lady of the Helmings walked about the hall,
offering the precious, ornamented cup
to old and young alike, until at last
615 the queen, excellent in mind, adorned with rings,
moved with the mead-cup towards Beowulf.
She welcomed the Geatish prince and with wise words
thanked God that her wish was granted
that she might depend on some warrior for help
620 against such attacks. The courageous warrior
took the cup from Wealhtheow's hands
and, eager for battle, made a speech:
Beowulf, the son of Ecgtheow, said:
"When I put to sea, sailed
625 through the breakers with my band of men,
I resolved to fulfill the desire

8. "Wealhtheow" means "foreign slave," and she may be British or Celtic in origin. Even after her marriage to Hrothgar, she continues to maintain her identity as the "lady of the Helmings," an epithet recalling her father Helm.

of your people, or suffer the pangs of death,
caught fast in Grendel's clutches.
Here, in Heorot, I shall either work a deed
630   of great daring, or lay down my life."
Beowulf's brave boast delighted Wealhtheow:
adorned with gold, the noble Danish queen
went to sit beside her lord.
    Then again, as of old, fine words were spoken
635   in the hall, the company rejoiced,
a conquering people, until in due course
the son of Healfdene wanted to retire
and take his rest. He realized the monster
meant to attack Heorot after the blue hour,
640   when black night has settled over all—
when shadowy shapes come shrithing
dark beneath the clouds. All the company rose.
Then the heroes Hrothgar and Beowulf saluted
one another; Hrothgar wished him luck
645   and control of Heorot, and confessed:
"Never since I could lift hand and shield,
have I entrusted this glorious Danish hall
to any man as I do now to you.
Take and guard this greatest of halls.
650   Make known your strength, remember your might,
stand watch against your enemy. You shall have
all you desire if you survive this enterprise."
    Then Hrothgar, defender of the Danes,
withdrew from the hall with his band of warriors.
655   The warlike leader wanted to sleep with Wealhtheow,
his queen. It was said the mighty king
had appointed a hall-guard—a man who undertook
a dangerous duty for the Danish king,
elected to stand watch against the monster.
660   Truly, the leader of the Geats fervently trusted
in his own great strength and in God's grace.
Then he took off his helmet and his corslet
of iron, and gave them to his servant,
with his superb, adorned sword,
665   telling him to guard them carefully.
And then, before he went to his bed,
the brave Geat, Beowulf, made his boast:
"I count myself no less active in battle,
no less brave than Grendel himself:
670   thus, I will not send him to sleep with my sword,
so deprive him of life, though certainly I could.
Despite his fame for deadly deeds,
he is ignorant of these noble arts, that he might strike
at me, and hew my shield; but we, this night,
675   shall forgo the use of weapons, if he dares fight
without them; and then may wise God,
the holy Lord, give glory in battle

to whichever of us He should think fitting."
Then the brave prince leaned back, put his head
680   on the pillow while, around him,
many a proud seafarer lay back on his bed.
Not one of them believed he would see
day dawn, or ever return to his family
and friends, and the place where he was born;
685   they well knew that in recent days
far too many Danish men had come to bloody ends
in that hall. But the Lord wove the webs of destiny,
gave the Geats success in their struggle,
help and support, in such a way
690   that all were enabled to overcome their enemy
through the strength of one man. We cannot doubt
that mighty God has always ruled
over mankind.[9]
                    Then the night prowler
came shrithing through the shadows. All the Geats
695   guarding Heorot had fallen asleep—
all except one. Men well knew that the evil enemy
could not drag them down into the shadows
when it was against the Creator's wishes,
but Beowulf, watching grimly for his adversary Grendel,
700   awaited the ordeal with increasing anger.
Then, under night's shroud, Grendel walked down
from the moors; he shouldered God's anger.
The evil plunderer intended to ensnare
one of the race of men in the high hall.
705   He strode under the skies, until he stood
before the feasting-hall, in front of the gift-building
gleaming with gold. And this night was not the first
on which he had so honored Hrothgar's home.
But never in his life did he find hall-wardens
710   more greatly to his detriment. Then the joyless warrior
journeyed to Heorot. The outer door, bolted
with iron bands, burst open at a touch from his hands:
with evil in his mind, and overriding anger,
Grendel swung open the hall's mouth itself. At once,
715   seething with fury, the fiend stepped onto
the tessellated floor; a horrible light,
like a lurid flame, flickered in his eyes.
He saw many men, a group of warriors,
a knot of kinsmen, sleeping in the hall.
720   His spirits leapt, his heart laughed;
the savage monster planned to sever,
before daybreak, the life of every warrior
from his body—he fully expected to eat

9. This interpolation of Christian belief into what is essentially a pagan tradition has been taken as evidence of a conscious rewriting of much earlier material. The narrative assures its reader that Christian beliefs were still valid, regardless of what the characters in the story may have believed.

his fill at the feast. But after that night
725   fate decreed that he should no longer feed off
human flesh. Hygelac's kinsman,
the mighty man, watched the wicked ravager
to see how he would make his sudden attacks.
The monster was not disposed to delay;
730   but, for a start, he hungrily seized
a sleeping warrior, greedily wrenched him,
bit into his body, drank the blood
from his veins, devoured huge pieces;
until, in no time, he had swallowed the whole man,
735   even his feet and hands. Now Grendel stepped forward,
nearer and nearer, made to grasp the valiant Geat
stretched out on his bed—the fiend reached towards him
with his open hand; at once Beowulf perceived
his evil plan, sat up and stayed Grendel's outstretched arm.
740   Instantly that monster, hardened by crime,
realized that never had he met any man
in the regions of earth, in the whole world,
with so strong a grip. He was seized with terror.
But, for all that, he was unable to break away.
745   He was eager to escape to his lair, seek the company
of devils, but he was restrained as never before.
Then Hygelac's brave kinsman bore in mind
his boast: he rose from the bed and gripped
Grendel fiercely. The fiend tried to break free,
750   his fingers were bursting. Beowulf kept with him.
The evil giant was desperate to escape,
if indeed he could, and head for his lair
in the fens; he could feel his fingers cracking
in his adversary's grip; that was a bitter journey
755   that Grendel made to the ring-hall Heorot.
The great room boomed; all the proud warriors—
each and every Dane living in the stronghold—
were stricken with panic. The two hall-wardens
were enraged. The building rang with their blows.
760   It was a wonder the wine-hall withstood
two so fierce in battle, that the fair building
did not fall to earth; but it stood firm,
braced inside and out with hammered
iron bands. I have heard tell that there,
765   where they fought, many a mead-bench,
studded with gold, started from the floor.
Until that time, elders of the Scyldings
were of the opinion that no man could wreck
the great hall Heorot, adorned with horns,
770   nor by any means destroy it unless it were gutted
by greedy tongues of flame. Again and again
clang and clatter shattered the night's silence;
dread numbed the North-Danes, seized all
who heard the shrieking from the wall,

775   the enemy of God's grisly lay of terror,
his song of defeat, heard hell's captive
keening over his wound. Beowulf held him fast,
he who was the strongest of all men
ever to have seen the light of life on earth.

780   By no means did the defender of thanes
allow the murderous caller to escape with his life;
he reckoned that the rest of Grendel's days
were useless to anyone. Then, time and again,
Beowulf's band brandished their ancestral swords;

785   they longed to save the life, if they
so could, of their lord, the mighty leader.
When they did battle on Beowulf's behalf,
struck at the monster from every side,
eager for his end, those courageous warriors

790   were unaware that no war-sword,
not even the finest iron on earth,
could wound their evil enemy,
for he had woven a secret spell
against every kind of weapon, every battle blade.

795   Grendel's death, his departure from this world,
was destined to be wretched, his migrating spirit
was fated to travel far into the power of fiends.
Then he who for years had committed crimes
against mankind, murderous in mind,

800   and had warred with God, discovered
that the strength of his body could not save him,
that Hygelac's brave kinsman held his hand
in a vicelike grip; each was a mortal enemy
to the other. The horrible monster

805   suffered grievous pain; a gaping wound
opened on his shoulder; the sinews sprang apart,
the muscles were bursting. Glory in battle
was given to Beowulf; fatally wounded,
Grendel was obliged to make for the marshes,

810   head for his joyless lair. He was
well aware that his life's days were done,
come to an end. After that deadly encounter
the desire of every Dane was at last accomplished.
    In this way did the wise and fearless man

815   who had traveled from far cleanse Hrothgar's hall,
release it from affliction. He rejoiced in his night's work,
his glorious achievement. The leader of the Geats
made good his boast to the East-Danes;
he had removed the cause of their distress,

820   put an end to the sorrow every Dane had shared,
the bitter grief that they had been constrained
to suffer. When Beowulf, brave in battle,
placed hand, arm and shoulder—Grendel's
entire grasp—under Heorot's spacious roof,

825   that was evidence enough of victory.

Then I have heard that next morning
many warriors gathered round the gift-hall;
leaders of men came from every region,
from remote parts, to look on the wonder,
830   the tracks of the monster. Grendel's death
seemed no grievous loss to any of the men
who set eyes on the spoor of the defeated one,
saw how he, weary in spirit, overcome in combat,
fated and put to flight, had made for the lake
835   of water-demons—leaving tracks of life-blood.
    There the water boiled because of the blood;
the fearful swirling waves reared up,
mingled with hot blood, battle gore;
fated, he hid himself, then joyless
840   laid aside his life, his heathen spirit,
in the fen lair; hell received him there.
    After this, the old retainers left the lake
and so did the company of young men too;
brave warriors rode back on their gleaming horses
845   from this joyful journey. Then Beowulf's exploit
was acclaimed; many a man asserted
time and again that there was no better
shield-bearer in the whole world, to north or south
between the two seas, under the sky's expanse,
850   no man more worthy of his own kingdom.
Yet they found no fault at all with their friendly lord,
gracious Hrothgar—he was a great king.
    At times the brave warriors spurred their bays,
horses renowned for their speed and stamina,
855   and raced each other where the track was suitable.
And now and then one of Hrothgar's thanes
who brimmed with poetry, and remembered lays,
a man acquainted with ancient traditions
of every kind, composed a new song
860   in correct meter. Most skillfully that man
began to sing of Beowulf's feat,
to weave words together, and fluently
to tell a fitting tale.
            He recounted all he knew
of Sigemund, the son of Waels;[1] many a strange story
865   about his exploits, his endurance, and his journeys
to earth's ends; many an episode
unknown or half-known to the sons of men, songs
of feud and treachery. Only Fitela knew of these things,
had heard them from Sigemund who liked to talk
870   of this and that, for he and his nephew
had been companions in countless battles—

---

1. The story of Sigemund is also told in the Old Norse *Volsunga Saga* and with major variations in the Middle High German *Niebelungenlied*. The scop's comparison of Sigemund with Beowulf is ironic in that the order and the outcome of Beowulf's later encounter with a dragon will be reversed.

they slew many monsters with their swords.
After his death, no little fame attached to Sigemund's name,
that courageous man who had killed the dragon,
875 guardian of the hoard. Under the gray rock
the son of the prince braved that dangerous deed
alone; Fitela was not with him;
for all that, as fate had it, he impaled
the wondrous serpent, pinned it to the rock face
880 with his patterned sword; the dragon was slain.
Through his own bravery, that warrior ensured
that he could enjoy the treasure hoard
at will; the son of Waels loaded it all
onto a boat, stowed the shining treasure
885 into the ship; the serpent burned in its own flames.
Because of all his exploits, Sigemund,
guardian of strong men, was the best known
warrior in the world—so greatly had he prospered—
after Heremod's prowess, strength and daring
890 had been brought to an end, when, battling with giants,
he fell into the power of fiends, and was at once
done to death. He had long endured
surging sorrows, had become a source
of grief to his people, and to all his retainers.
895 And indeed, in those times now almost forgotten,
many wise men often mourned that great warrior,
for they had looked to him to remedy their miseries;
they thought that the prince's son would prosper
and attain his father's rank, would protect his people,
900 their heirlooms and their citadel, the heroes' kingdom,
land of the Scyldings. Beowulf, Hygelac's kinsman,
was much loved by all who knew him,
by his friends; but Heremod was stained by sin.[2]
      Now and then the brave men raced their horses,
905 ate up the sandy tracks—and they were so absorbed
that the hours passed easily. Stout-hearted warriors
without number traveled to the high hall
to inspect that wonder; the king himself, too,
glorious Hrothgar, guardian of ring-hoards,
910 came from his quarters with a great company, escorted
his queen and her retinue of maidens into the mead-hall.
Hrothgar spoke—he approached Heorot,
stood on the steps, stared at the high roof
adorned with gold, and at Grendel's hand:
915 "Let us give thanks at once to God Almighty
for this sight. I have undergone many afflictions,
grievous outrages at Grendel's hands; but God,
Guardian of heaven, can work wonder upon wonder.
Until now, I had been resigned,

---

2. Heremod, an earlier Danish king, was the stock illustration of the unjust and unwise ruler. After bringing bloodshed upon his own house, Heremod took refuge among the Jutes, who eventually put him to death.

920   had no longer believed that my afflictions
       would ever end: this finest of buildings
       stood stained with battle blood,
       a source of sorrow to my counselors;
       they all despaired of regaining this hall
925   for many years to come, of guarding it from foes,
       from devils and demons. Yet now one warrior
       alone, through the Almighty's power, has succeeded
       where we failed for all our fine plans.
       Indeed, if she is still alive,
930   that woman (whoever she was) who gave birth
       to such a son, to be one of humankind,
       may claim that the Creator was gracious to her
       in her childbearing. Now, Beowulf,
       best of men, I will love you in my heart
935   like a son; keep to our new kinship
       from this day on. You shall lack
       no earthly riches I can offer you.
       Most often I have honored a man for less,
       given treasure to a poorer warrior,
940   more sluggish in the fight. Through your deeds
       you have ensured that your glorious name
       will endure forever. May the Almighty grant you
       good fortune, as He has always done before!"
       Beowulf, the son of Ecgtheow, answered:
945   "We performed that dangerous deed
       with good will; at peril we pitted ourselves
       against the unknown. I wish so much
       that you could have seen him for yourself,
       that fiend in his trappings, in the throes of death.
950   I meant to throttle him on that bed of slaughter
       as swiftly as possible, with savage grips,
       to hear death rattle in his throat
       because of my grasp, unless he should escape me.
       But I could not detain him, the Lord
955   did not ordain it—I did not hold my deadly enemy
       firm enough for that; the fiend jerked free
       with immense power. Yet, so as to save
       his life, he left behind his hand,
       his arm and shoulder; but the wretched monster
960   has bought himself scant respite;
       the evil marauder, tortured by his sins,
       will not live the longer, but agony
       embraces him in its deadly bonds,
       squeezes life out of his lungs; and now this creature,
965   stained with crime, must await the day of judgment
       and his just deserts from the glorious Creator."
          After this, the son of Ecglaf[3] boasted less
       about his prowess in battle—when all the warriors,

---

3. Unferth is referred to by his father's name. This may be ironic, since Unferth has killed members of his own family.

through Beowulf's might, had been enabled
970 to examine that hand, the fiend's fingers,
nailed up on the gables. Seen from in front,
each nail, each claw of that warlike,
heathen monster looked like steel—
a terrifying spike. Everyone said
975 that no weapon whatsoever, no proven sword
could possibly harm it, could damage
that battle-hardened, blood-stained hand.
      Then orders were quickly given for the inside of Heorot
to be decorated; many servants, both men and women,
980 bustled about that wine-hall, adorned that building
of retainers. Tapestries, worked in gold,
glittered on the walls, many a fine sight
for those who have eyes to see such things.
That beautiful building, braced within
985 by iron bands, was badly damaged;
the door's hinges were wrenched; when the monster,
damned by all his crimes, turned in flight,
despairing of his life, the hall roof only
remained untouched. Death is not easy
990 to escape, let him who will attempt it.
Man must go to the grave that awaits him—
fate has ordained this for all who have souls,
children of men, earth's inhabitants—
and his body, rigid on its clay bed,
995 will sleep there after the banquet.   Then it was time
for Healfdene's son to proceed to the hall,
the king himself was eager to attend the feast.
I have never heard of a greater band of kinsmen
gathered with such dignity around their ring-giver.
1000 Then the glorious warriors sat on the benches,
rejoicing in the feast. Courteously
their kinsmen, Hrothgar and Hrothulf,
quaffed many a mead-cup, confident warriors
in the high hall. Heorot was packed
1005 with feasters who were friends; the time was not yet come
when the Scyldings practiced wrongful deeds.[4]
Then Hrothgar gave Beowulf Healfdene's sword,
and a battle banner, woven with gold,
and a helmet and a corslet, as rewards for victory;
1010 many men watched while the priceless, renowned sword
was presented to the hero. Beowulf emptied
the ale-cup in the hall; he had no cause
to be ashamed at those precious gifts.
There are few men, as far as I have heard,
1015 who have given four such treasures, gleaming with gold,
to another on the mead-bench with equal generosity.
A jutting ridge, wound about with metal wires,

4. Possibly an allusion to the later usurpation of the Danish throne by Hrothgar's nephew Hrothulf.

ran over the helmet's crown, protecting the skull,
so that well-ground swords, proven in battle,
1020   could not injure the well-shielded warrior
when he advanced against his foes.
Then the guardian of thanes ordered
that eight horses with gold-plated bridles
be led into the courtyard; onto one was strapped
1025   a saddle, inlaid with jewels, skillfully made.
That was the war-seat of the great king,
Healfdene's son, whenever he wanted
to join in the sword-play. That famous man
never lacked bravery at the front in battle,
1030   when men about him were cut down like corn.
Then the king of the Danes, Ing's[5] descendants,
presented the horses and weapons to Beowulf,
bade him use them well and enjoy them.
Thus the renowned prince, the retainers' gold-warden,
1035   rewarded those fierce sallies in full measure,
with horses and treasure, so that no man
would ever find reason to reproach him fairly.
Furthermore, the guardian of warriors gave
a treasure, an heirloom at the mead-bench,
1040   to each of those men who had crossed the sea
with Beowulf; and he ordered that gold
be paid for that warrior Grendel slew
so wickedly—as he would have slain many another,
had not foreseeing God and the warrior's courage
1045   together forestalled him. The Creator ruled over
all humankind, even as He does today.
Wherefore a wise man will value forethought
and understanding. Whoever lives long
on earth, endures the unrest of these times,
1050   will be involved in much good and much evil.
    Then Hrothgar, leader in battle, was entertained
with music—harp and voice in harmony.
The strings were plucked, many a song rehearsed,
when it was the turn of Hrothgar's poet
1055   to please men at the mead-bench, perform in the hall.
He sang of Finn's troop,[6] victims of surprise attack,
and of how that Danish hero, Hnaef of the Scyldings,
was destined to die among the Frisian slain.
    Hildeburh, indeed, could hardly recommend
1060   the honor of the Jutes; that innocent woman
lost her loved ones, son and brother,
in the shield-play; they fell, as fate ordained,

---

5. Another, earlier king of the Danes.
6. The following episode is one of the most obscure in *Beowulf*. It seems that Hnaef and Hildeburh are both children of an earlier Danish king named Hoc and that Hildeburh has been sent to marry Finn, the son of Folcwalda and king of the Jutes and Frisians, in order to conclude a marriage alliance and thus settle a prior blood feud between the two tribes. Upon going to visit his sister and her husband, Hnaef is treacherously ambushed and killed by Finn's men; Hildeburh's son by Finn is also killed. In her role as peace-weaver, Hildeburh, is torn by conflicting allegiances, foreshadowing the fate of Hrothgar's own daughter Freawaru in her marriage to Ingeld.

stricken by spears; and she was stricken with grief.
Not without cause did Hoc's daughter

1065 mourn the shaft of fate, for in the light of morning
she saw that her kin lay slain under the sky,
the men who had been her endless pride
and joy. That encounter laid claim
to all but a few of Finn's thanes,

1070 and he was unable to finish that fight
with Hnaef's retainer, with Hengest in the hall,
unable to dislodge the miserable survivors;
indeed, terms for a truce were agreed:
that Finn should give up to them another hall,

1075 with its high seat, in its entirety,
which the Danes should own in common with the Jutes;
and that at the treasure-giving the son of Folcwalda
should honor the Danes day by day,
should distribute rings and gold-adorned gifts

1080 to Hengest's band and his own people in equal measure.
Both sides pledged themselves to this peaceful
settlement. Finn swore Hengest solemn oaths
that he would respect the sad survivors
as his counselors ordained, and that no man there

1085 must violate the covenant with word or deed,
or complain about it, although they
would be serving the slayer of their lord
(as fate had forced those lordless men to do);
and he warned the Frisians that if, in provocation,

1090 they should mention the murderous feud,
the sword's edge should settle things.
The funeral fire was prepared, glorious gold
was brought up from the hoard: the best of Scyldings,
that race of warriors, lay ready on the pyre.

1095 Blood-stained corslets, and images of boars
(cast in iron and covered in gold)
were plentiful on that pyre, and likewise the bodies
of many retainers, ravaged by wounds;
renowned men fell in that slaughter.

1100 Then Hildeburh asked that her own son
be committed to the flames at her brother's funeral,
that his body be consumed on Hnaef's pyre.
That grief-stricken woman keened over his corpse,
sang doleful dirges. The warriors' voices

1105 soared towards heaven. And so did the smoke
from the great funeral fire that roared
before the barrow; heads sizzled,
wounds split open, blood burst out
from battle scars. The ravenous flames

1110 swallowed those men whole, made no distinction
between Frisians and Danes; the finest men departed.
Then those warriors, their friends lost to them,
went to view their homes, revisit the stronghold
and survey the Frisian land. But Hengest

1115   stayed with Finn, in utter dejection, all through
that blood-stained winter. And he dreamed
of his own country, but he was unable to steer
his ship homeward, for the storm-beaten sea
wrestled with the wind; winter sheathed the waves
1120   in ice—until once again spring made its sign
(as still it does) among the houses of men:
clear days, warm weather, in accordance as always
with the law of the seasons. Then winter was over,
the face of the earth was fair; the exile
1125   was anxious to leave that foreign people
and the Frisian land. And yet he brooded
more about vengeance than about a voyage,
and wondered whether he could bring about a clash
so as to repay the sons of the Jutes.
1130   Thus Hengest did not shrink from the duty of vengeance
after Hunlafing had placed the flashing sword,
finest of all weapons, on his lap;
this sword's edges had scarred many Jutes.
And so it was that cruel death by the sword later
1135   cut down the brave warrior Finn in his own hall,
after Guthlaf and Oslaf, arrived from a sea-journey,
had fiercely complained of that first attack,
condemned the Frisians on many scores:
the Scyldings' restless spirits could no longer
1140   be restrained. Then the hall ran red with the blood
of the enemy—Finn himself was slain,
the king with his troop, and Hildeburh was taken.
The Scylding warriors carried that king's
heirlooms down to their ship,
1145   all the jewels and necklaces they discovered
at Finn's hall. They sailed over the sea-paths,
brought that noble lady back to Denmark
and her own people.
                        Thus was the lay sung,
the song of the poet. The hall echoed with joy,
1150   waves of noise broke out along the benches;
cup-bearers carried wine in glorious vessels.
Then Wealhtheow, wearing her golden collar, walked
to where Hrothgar and Hrothulf were sitting side by side,
uncle and nephew, still friends together, true to one another.
1155   And the spokesman Unferth sat at the feet
of the Danish lord; all men admired
his spirit and audacity, although he had deceived
his own kinsmen in a feud. Then the lady of the Scyldings
spoke these words: "Accept this cup, my loved lord,
1160   treasure-giver; O gold-friend of men,
learn the meaning of joy again, and speak words
of gratitude to the Geats, for so one ought to do.
And be generous to them too, mindful of gifts
which you have now amassed from far and wide.
1165   I am told you intend to adopt this warrior,

take him for your son. This resplendent ring-hall,
Heorot, has been cleansed; give many rewards
while you may, but leave this land and the Danish people
to your own descendants when the day comes
1170   for you to die. I am convinced
that gracious Hrothulf will guard our children
justly, should he outlive you, lord of the Scyldings,
in this world; I believe he will repay our sons
most generously if he remembers all we did
1175   for his benefit and enjoyment when he was a boy."
Then Wealhtheow walked to the bench where her sons,
Hrethric and Hrothmund, sat with the sons of thanes,
fledgling warriors; where also that brave man,
Beowulf of the Geats, sat beside the brothers.
1180   To him she carried the cup, and asked in gracious words
if he would care to drink; and to him she presented
twisted gold with courtly ceremonial—
two armlets, a corslet and many rings,
and the most handsome collar in the world.
1185   I have never heard that any hero had a jewel
to equal that, not since Hama made off
for his fortress with the Brosings' necklace,[7] that pendant
in its precious setting; he fled from the enmity
of underhand Eormenric, he chose long-lasting gain.
1190   Hygelac the Geat, grandson of Swerting,
wore that necklace on his last raid
when he fought beneath his banner to defend his treasure,
his battle spoils; fate claimed him then,
when he, foolhardy, courted disaster,
1195   a feud with the Frisians. On that occasion the famous prince
had carried the treasure, the priceless stones,
over the cup of the waves; he crumpled under his shield.
Then the king's body fell into the hands of Franks,
his coat of mail and the collar also;
1200   after that battle, weaker warriors picked at
and plundered the slain; many a Geat lay dead, guarding
that place of corpses.
                    Applause echoed in the hall.
Wealhtheow spoke these words before the company:
"May you, Beowulf, beloved youth, enjoy
1205   with all good fortune this necklace and corslet,
treasures of the people; may you always prosper;
win renown through courage, and be kind in your counsel
to these boys; for that, I will reward you further.
You have ensured that men will always sing
1210   your praises, even to the ends of the world,
as far as oceans still surround cliffs,
home of the winds. May you thrive, O prince,

---

7. The narrative jumps ahead beyond Beowulf's return home to the Geats. His uncle, Hygelac, the king, will not only receive the necklace from Beowulf but will die with it in battle among the Frisians. The necklace thus connects different events at different times.

all your life. I hope you will amass
a shining hoard of treasure. O happy Beowulf,
1215 be gracious in your dealing with my sons.
Here, each warrior is true to the others,
gentle of mind, loyal to his lord;
the thanes are as one, the people all alert,
the warriors have drunk well. They will do as I ask."
1220   Then Wealhtheow retired to her seat
beside her lord. That was the best of banquets,
men drank their fill of wine; they had not tasted
bitter destiny, the fate that had come and claimed
many of the heroes at the end of dark evenings,
1225 when Hrothgar the warrior had withdrawn
to take his rest. Countless retainers
defended Heorot as they had often done before;
benches were pushed back; the floor was padded
with beds and pillows. But one of the feasters
1230 lying on his bed was doomed, and soon to die.
They set their bright battle-shields
at their heads. Placed on the bench
above each retainer, his crested helmet,
his linked corslet and sturdy spear-shaft
1235 were plainly to be seen. It was their habit,
both at home and in the field,
to be prepared for battle always,
for any occasion their lord might need
assistance; that was a loyal band of retainers.
1240   And so they slept. One man paid a heavy price
for his night's rest, as often happened
after Grendel first held the gold-hall
and worked his evil in it, until he met his doom,
death for his crimes. For afterwards it became clear,
1245 and well known to the Scyldings, that some avenger
had survived the evil-doer, still lived after
that grievous, mortal combat.
                            Grendel's mother
was a monster of a woman; she mourned her fate—
she who had to live in the terrible lake,
1250 the cold water streams, after Cain slew
his own brother, his father's son,
with a sword; he was outlawed after that;
a branded man, he abandoned human joys,
wandered in the wilderness. Many spirits, sent
1255 by fate, issued from his seed; one of them, Grendel,
that hateful outcast, was surprised in the hall
by a vigilant warrior spoiling for a fight.
Grendel gripped and grabbed him there,
but the Geat remembered his vast strength,
1260 that glorious gift given him of God,
and put his trust for support and assistance
in the grace of the Lord; thus he overcame

the envoy of hell, humbled his evil adversary.
So the joyless enemy of mankind journeyed
1265   to the house of the dead. And then Grendel's mother,
mournful and ravenous, resolved to go
on a grievous journey to avenge her son's death.
    Thus she reached Heorot; Ring-Danes, snoring,
were sprawled about the floor. The thanes suffered
1270   a serious reverse as soon as Grendel's mother
entered the hall. The terror she caused,
compared to her son, equaled the terror
a warrior woman[8] inspires as opposed to a man,
when the ornamented sword, forged on the anvil,
1275   the razor-sharp blade stained with blood,
shears through the boar-crested helmets of the enemy.
Then swords were snatched from benches, blades
drawn from scabbards, many a broad shield
was held firmly in the hall; none could don helmet
1280   or spacious corslet—that horror caught them by surprise.
The monster wanted to make off for the moors,
fly for her life, as soon as she was found out.
Firmly she grasped one of the thanes
and made for the fens as fast as she could.
1285   That man whom she murdered even as he slept
was a brave shield-warrior, a well-known thane,
most beloved by Hrothgar of all his hall retainers
between the two seas. Beowulf was not there;
the noble Geat had been allotted another lodging
1290   after the giving of treasure earlier that evening.
Heorot was in uproar; she seized her son's
blood-crusted hand; anguish once again
had returned to the hall. What kind of bargain
was that, in which both sides forfeited
1295   the lives of friends?
                    Then the old king,
the grizzled warrior, was convulsed with grief
when he heard of the death of his dearest retainer.
    Immediately Beowulf, that man blessed with victory,
was called to the chamber of the king. At dawn
1300   the noble warrior and his friends, his followers,
hurried to the room where the wise man was waiting,
waiting and wondering whether the Almighty
would ever allow an end to their adversity.
Then Beowulf, brave in battle, crossed
1305   the floor with his band—the timbers thundered—
and greeted the wise king, overlord of Ing's
descendants; he asked if the night had passed off
peacefully, since his summons was so urgent.
    Hrothgar, guardian of the Scyldings, said:
1310   "Do not speak of peace; grief once again

8. This term may have the sense of the fierce war-brides of Germanic legend, the *Walkyrie.*

afflicts the Danish people. Yrmenlaf's
elder brother, Aeschere, is dead,
my closest counselor and my comrade,
my shoulder-companion when we shielded
1315   our heads in the fight, when soldiers clashed on foot,
slashed at boar-crests. Aeschere was all
that a noble man, a warrior should be.
The wandering, murderous monster slew him
in Heorot; and I do not know where that ghoul,
1320   drooling at her feast of flesh and blood,
made off afterwards. She has avenged her son
whom you savaged yesterday with vicelike holds
because he had impoverished and killed my people
for many long years. He fell in mortal combat,
1325   forfeit of his life; and now another mighty
evil ravager has come to avenge her kinsman;
and many a thane, mournful in his mind
for his treasure-giver, may feel she has avenged
that feud already, indeed more than amply;
1330   now that hand lies still which once sustained you.
       "I have heard my people say,
men of this country, counselors in the hall,
that they have seen *two* such beings,
equally monstrous, rangers of the fell-country,
1335   rulers of the moors; and these men assert
that so far as they can see one bears
a likeness to a woman; grotesque though he was,
the other who trod the paths of exile looked like a man,
though greater in height and build than a goliath;
1340   he was christened *Grendel* by my people
many years ago; men do not know if he
had a father, a fiend once begotten
by mysterious spirits. These two live
in a little-known country, wolf-slopes, windswept headlands,
1345   perilous paths across the boggy moors, where a mountain stream
plunges under the mist-covered cliffs,
rushes through a fissure. It is not far from here,
if measured in miles, that the lake stands
shadowed by trees stiff with hoar-frost.
1350   A wood, firmly-rooted, frowns over the water.
There, night after night, a fearful wonder may be seen—
fire on the water; no man alive
is so wise as to know the nature of its depths.
Although the moor-stalker, the stag with strong horns,
1355   when harried by hounds will make for the wood,
pursued from afar, he will succumb
to the hounds on the brink, rather than plunge in
and save his head. That is not a pleasant place.
When the wind arouses the wrath of the storm,
1360   whipped waves rear up black from the lake,
reach for the skies, until the air becomes misty,

the heavens weep. Now, once again, help may be had
from you alone. As yet, you have not seen the haunt,
the perilous place where you may meet this most evil monster
1365   face to face. Do you dare set eyes on it?
If you return unscathed, I will reward you
for your audacity, as I did before,
with ancient treasures and twisted gold."
    Beowulf, the son of Ecgtheow, answered:
1370   "Do not grieve, wise Hrothgar! Better each man
should avenge his friend than deeply mourn.
The days on earth for every one of us
are numbered; he who may should win renown
before his death; that is a warrior's
1375   best memorial when he has departed from this world.
Come, O guardian of the kingdom, let us lose
no time but track down Grendel's kinswoman.
I promise you that wherever she turns—
to honeycomb caves, to mountain woods,
1380   to the bottom of the lake she shall find no refuge.
Shoulder your sorrows with patience
this day; this is what I expect of you."
    Then the old king leapt up, poured out his gratitude
to God Almighty for the Geat's words.
1385   Hrothgar's horse, his stallion with plaited mane,
was saddled and bridled; the wise ruler
set out in full array; his troop of shield-bearers
fell into step. They followed the tracks
along forest paths and over open hill-country
1390   for mile after mile; the monster had made
for the dark moors directly, carrying the corpse
of the foremost thane of all those
who, with Hrothgar, had guarded the hall.
Then the man of noble lineage left Heorot far behind,
1395   followed narrow tracks, string-thin paths
over steep, rocky slopes—remote parts
with beetling crags and many lakes
where water-demons lived. He went ahead
with a handful of scouts to explore the place;
1400   all at once he came upon a dismal wood,
mountain trees standing on the edge
of a gray precipice; the lake lay beneath,
blood-stained and turbulent. The Danish retainers
were utterly appalled when they came upon
1405   the severed head of their comrade Aeschere
on the steep slope leading down to the lake;
all the thanes were deeply distressed.
    The water boiled with blood, with hot gore;
the warriors gaped at it. At times the horn sang
1410   an eager battle-song. The brave men all sat down;
then they saw many serpents in the water,
strange sea-dragons swimming in the lake,

and also water-demons, lying on cliff-ledges,
monsters and serpents of the same kind
1415 as often, in the morning, molest ships
on the sail-road. They plunged to the lake bottom,
bitter and resentful, rather than listen
to the song of the horn. The leader of the Geats
1420 picked off one with his bow and arrow,
ended its life; the metal tip
stuck in its vitals; it swam more sluggishly
after that, as the life-blood ebbed from its body;
in no time this strange sea-dragon
1425 bristled with barbed boar-spears, was subdued
and drawn up onto the cliff; men examined
that disgusting enemy.   Beowulf donned
his coat of mail, did not fear for his own life.
His massive corslet, linked by hand
1430 and skillfully adorned, was to essay the lake—
it knew how to guard the body, the bone-chamber,
so that his foe's grasp, in its malicious fury,
could not crush his chest, squeeze out his life;
and his head was guarded by the gleaming helmet
1435 which was to explore the churning waters,
stir their very depths; gold decorated it,
and it was hung with chain-mail, as the weapon smith
had wrought it long before, wondrously shaped it
and beset it with boar-images, so that
1440 afterwards no battle-blade could do it damage.
Not least among his mighty aids was Hrunting,
the long-hilted sword Unferth lent him in his need;
it was one of the finest of heirlooms; the iron blade
was engraved with deadly, twiglike patterning,
1445 tempered with battle blood. It had not failed
any of those men who had held it in their hands,
risked themselves on hazardous exploits,
pitted themselves against foes. That was not
the first time it had to do a hard day's work.
1450 Truly, when Ecglaf's son, himself so strong,
lent that weapon to his better as a swordsman,
he had forgotten all those taunts he flung
when tipsy with wine; he dared not chance
his own arm under the breakers, dared not
1455 risk his life; at the lake he lost
his renown for bravery. It was not so with Beowulf
once he had armed himself for battle.
    The Geat, son of Ecgtheow, spoke:
"Great son of Healfdene, gracious ruler,
1460 gold-friend of men, remember now—
for I am now ready to go—
what we agreed if I, fighting on your behalf,
should fail to return: that you would always

be like a father to me after I had gone.
1465 Guard my followers, my dear friends,
if I die in battle; and, beloved Hrothgar,
send to Hygelac the treasures you gave me.
When the lord of the Geats, Hrethel's son,
sees those gifts of gold, he will know
1470 that I found a noble giver of rings
and enjoyed his favor for as long as I lived.
And, O Hrothgar, let renowned Unferth
have the ancient treasure, the razor sharp
ornamented sword; and I will make my name
1475 with Hrunting, or death will destroy me."
      After these words the leader of the Geats
dived bravely from the bank, did not even
wait for an answer; the seething water
received the warrior. A full day elapsed
1480 before he could perceive the bottom of the lake.
      She who had guarded the lake's length and breadth
for fifty years, vindictive, fiercely ravenous for blood,
soon realized that one of the race of men
was looking down into the monsters' lair.
1485 Then she grasped him, clutched the Geat
in her ghastly claws; and yet she did not
so much as scratch his skin; his coat of mail
protected him; she could not penetrate
the linked metal rings with her loathsome fingers.
1490 Then the sea-wolf dived to the bottom-most depths,
swept the prince to the place where she lived,
so that he, for all his courage, could not
wield a weapon; too many wondrous creatures
harassed him as he swam; many sea-serpents
1495 with savage tusks tried to bore through his corslet,
the monsters molested him. Then the hero saw
that he had entered some loathsome hall
in which there was no water to impede him,
a vaulted chamber where the floodrush
1500 could not touch him. A light caught his eye,
a lurid flame flickering brightly.
      Then the brave man saw the sea-monster,
fearsome, infernal; he whirled his blade,
swung his arm with all his strength,
1505 and the ring-hilted sword sang a greedy war-song
on the monster's head. Then that guest realized
that his gleaming blade could not bite into her flesh,
break open her bone-chamber; its edge failed Beowulf
when he needed it; yet it had endured
1510 many a combat, sheared often through the helmet,
split the corslet of a fated man; for the first time
that precious sword failed to live up to its name.
      Then, resolute, Hygelac's kinsman took his courage
in both hands, trusted in his own strength.

1515 Angrily the warrior hurled Hrunting away,
the damascened sword with serpent patterns on its hilt;
tempered and steel-edged, it lay useless on the earth.
Beowulf trusted in his own strength,
the might of his hand. So must any man
1520 who hopes to gain long-lasting fame
in battle; he must risk his life, regardless.
Then the prince of the Geats seized the shoulder
of Grendel's mother—he did not mourn their feud;
when they grappled, that brave man in his fury
1525 flung his mortal foe to the ground.
Quickly she came back at him, locked him
in clinches and clutched at him fearsomely.
Then the greatest of warriors stumbled and fell.
She dropped on her hall-guest, drew her dagger,
1530 broad and gleaming; she wanted to avenge her son,
her only offspring. The woven corslet
that covered his shoulders saved Beowulf's life,
denied access to both point and edge.
Then Ecgtheow's son, leader of the Geats,
1535 would have died far under the wide earth
had not his corslet, his mighty chain-mail,
guarded him, and had not holy God
granted him victory; the wise Lord,
Ruler of the Heavens, settled the issue
1540 easily after the hero had scrambled to his feet.
   Then Beowulf saw among weapons an invincible sword
wrought by the giants, massive and double-edged,
the joy of many warriors; that sword was matchless,
well-tempered and adorned, forged in a finer age,
1545 only it was so huge that no man but Beowulf
could hope to handle it in the quick of combat.
Ferocious in battle, the defender of the Scyldings
grasped the ringed hilt, swung the ornamented sword
despairing of his life—he struck such a savage blow
1550 that the sharp blade slashed through her neck,
smashed the vertebrae; it severed her head
from the fated body; she fell at his feet.
The sword was bloodstained; Beowulf rejoiced.
   A light gleamed; the chamber was illumined
1555 as if the sky's bright candle were shining
from heaven. Hygelac's thane inspected
the vaulted room, then walked round the walls,
fierce and resolute, holding the weapon firmly
by the hilt. The sword was not too large
1560 for the hero's grasp, but he was eager to avenge
at once all Grendel's atrocities,
all the many visits the monster had inflicted
on the West-Danes—which began with the time
he slew Hrothgar's sleeping hearth-companions,
1565 devoured fifteen of the Danish warriors

even as they slept, and carried off as many more,
a monstrous prize. But the resolute warrior
had already repaid him to such a degree
that he now saw Grendel lying on his death-bed,
1570   his life's-blood drained because of the wound
he had sustained in battle at Heorot. Then Grendel's corpse
received a savage blow at the hero's hands,
his body burst open: Beowulf lopped off his head.
        At once the wise men, anxiously gazing at
1575   the lake with Hrothgar, saw that the water
had begun to chop and churn, that the waves
were stained with blood. The gray-haired Scyldings
discussed that bold man's fate, agreed
there was no hope of seeing that brave thane again—
1580   no chance that he would come, rejoicing in victory,
before their renowned king; it seemed certain
to all but a few that the sea-wolf had destroyed him.
        Then the ninth hour came. The noble Scyldings
left the headland; the gold-friend of men
1585   returned to Heorot; the Geats, sick at heart,
sat down and stared at the lake.
Hopeless, they yet hoped to set eyes
on their dear lord.
                Then the battle-sword
began to melt like a gory icicle
1590   because of the monster's blood. Indeed,
it was a miracle to see it thaw entirely,
as does ice when the Father (He who ordains
all times and seasons) breaks the bonds of frost,
unwinds the flood fetters; He is the true Lord.
1595   The leader of the Geats took none of the treasures
away from the chamber—though he saw many there—
except the monster's head and the gold-adorned
sword-hilt; the blade itself had melted,
the patterned sword had burned, so hot was that blood,
1600   so poisonous the monster who had died in the cave.
He who had survived the onslaught of his enemies
was soon on his way, swimming up through the water;
when the evil monster ended his days on earth,
left this transitory life, the troubled water
1605   and all the lake's expanse was purged of its impurity.
        Then the fearless leader of the seafarers
swam to the shore, exulting in his plunder,
the heavy burdens he had brought with him.
The intrepid band of thanes hurried towards him,
1610   giving thanks to God, rejoicing
to see their lord safe and sound of limb.
The brave man was quickly relieved of his helmet
and corslet.
                The angry water under the clouds,
the lake stained with battle-blood, at last became calm.

1615   Then they left the lake with songs on their lips,
        retraced their steps along the winding paths
        and narrow tracks; it was no easy matter
        for those courageous men, bold as kings,
        to carry the head away from the cliff
1620   overlooking the lake. With utmost difficulty
        four of the thanes bore Grendel's head
        to the gold-hall on a battle-pole;
        thus the fourteen Geats, unbroken
        in spirit and eager in battle, very soon
1625   drew near to Heorot; with them, that bravest
        of brave men crossed the plain towards the mead-hall.
        Then the fearless leader of the thanes,
        covered with glory, matchless in battle,
        once more entered Heorot to greet Hrothgar.
1630   Grendel's head was carried by the hair
        onto the floor where the warriors were drinking,
        a ghastly thing paraded before the heroes and the queen.
        Men stared at that wondrous spectacle.
        Beowulf, the son of Ecgtheow, said:
1635   "So, son of Healfdene, lord of the Scyldings,
        we proudly lay before you plunder from the lake;
        this head you look at proves our success.
        I barely escaped with my life from that combat
        under the water, the risk was enormous;
1640   our encounter would have ended at once if God
        had not guarded me. Mighty though it is,
        Hrunting was no use at all in the battle;
        but the Ruler of men—how often He guides
        the friendless one—granted that I
1645   should see a huge ancestral sword hanging,
        shining, on the wall; I unsheathed it.
        Then, at the time destiny decreed, I slew
        the warden of the hall. And when the blood,
        the boiling battle-blood burst from her body,
1650   that sword burnt, the damascened blade
        was destroyed. I deprived my enemies
        of that hilt; I repaid them as they deserved
        for their outrages, murderous slaughter of the Danes.
        I promise, then, O prince of the Scyldings,
1655   that you can sleep in Heorot without anxiety,
        rest with your retainers, with all the thanes
        among your people—experienced warriors
        and striplings together—without further fear
        of death's shadow skulking near the hall."
1660   Then the golden hilt, age-old work of giants,
        was given to Hrothgar, the grizzled warrior,
        the warlike lord; wrought by master-smiths,
        it passed into the hands of the Danish prince
        once the demons died; for that embittered fiend,
1665   enemy of God, guilty of murder
        had abandoned this world—and so had his mother.

Thus the hilt was possessed by the best
of earthly kings between the two seas,
the best of those who bestowed gold on Norse men.
1670   Hrothgar spoke, first examining the hilt,
the ancient heirloom. On it was engraved
the origins of strife in time immemorial,
when the tide of rising water drowned
the race of giants; their end was horrible;
1675   they were opposed to the Eternal Lord,
and their reward was the downpour and the flood.
Also, on the sword-guards of pure gold,
it was recorded in runic letters, as is the custom,
for whom that sword, finest of blades,
1680   with twisted hilt and serpentine patterning
had first been made.
                    Then Healfdene's wise son
lifted his voice—everyone listened:
"This land's grizzled guardian, who promotes truth
and justice among his people, and forgets nothing
1685   though the years pass, can say for certain that this man
is much favored by fate! Beowulf my friend,
your name is echoed in every country
to earth's end. You wear your enormous might
with wisdom and with dignity. I shall keep
1690   my promise made when last we spoke. You will
beyond doubt be the shield of the Geats
for days without number, and a source
of strength to warriors.
                    "Heremod was hardly that
to Ecgwala's sons, the glorious Scyldings;
1695   he grew to spread slaughter and destruction
rather than happiness among the Danish people.
In mad rage he murdered his table-companions,
his most loyal followers; it came about
that the great prince cut himself off
1700   from all earthly pleasures, though God had endowed him
with strength and power above all other men,
and had sustained him. For all that, his heart
was filled with savage blood-lust. He never gave
gifts to the Danes, to gain glory. He lived joyless,
1705   agony racked him; he was long an affliction
to his people. Be warned, Beowulf,
learn the nature of nobility. I who tell you
this story am many winters old.
                    "It is a miracle
how the mighty Lord in his generosity
1710   gives wisdom and land and high estate
to people on earth; all things are in His power.
At times he allows a noble man's mind to experience
happiness, grants he should rule over a pleasant,
prosperous country, a stronghold of men,
1715   makes subject to him regions of earth,

a wide kingdom, until in his stupidity
there is no end to his ambition.
His life is unruffled—neither old age
nor illness afflict him, no unhappiness
1720 gnaws at his heart, in his land no hatred
flares up in mortal feuds, but all the world
bends to his will. He suffers no setbacks
until the seed of arrogance is sown and grows
within him, while still the watchman slumbers;
1725 how deeply the soul's guardian sleeps
when a man is enmeshed in matters of this world;
the evil archer stands close with his drawn bow,
his bristling quiver. Then the poisoned shaft
pierces his mind under his helmet
1730 and he does not know how to resist
the devil's insidious, secret temptations.
What had long contented him now seems insufficient;
he becomes embittered, begins to hoard
his treasures, never parts with gold rings
1735 in ceremonial splendor; he soon forgets
his destiny and disregards the honors
given him of God, the Ruler of Glory.
In time his transient body wizens and withers,
and dies as fate decrees; then another man
1740 succeeds to his throne who gives treasures and heirlooms
with great generosity; *he* is not obsessed with suspicions.
Arm yourself, dear Beowulf, best of men,
against such diseased thinking; always swallow pride;
remember, renowned warrior, what is more worthwhile—
1745 gain everlasting. Today and tomorrow
you will be in your prime; but soon you will die,
in battle or in bed; either fire or water,
the fearsome elements, will embrace you,
or you will succumb to the sword's flashing edge,
1750 or to the arrow's flight, or to extreme old age;
then your eyes, once bright, will be clouded over;
all too soon, O warrior, death will destroy you.
     "I have ruled the Ring-Danes under the skies
for fifty years, shielded them in war
1755 from many tribes of men in this world,
from swords and from ash-spears, and the time had come
when I thought I had no enemies left on earth.
All was changed utterly, gladness
became grief, after Grendel,
1760 my deadly adversary, invaded Heorot.
His visitations caused me continual pain.
Thus I thank the Creator, the Eternal Lord,
that after our afflictions I have lived to see,
to see with my own eyes this blood-stained head.
1765 Now, Beowulf, brave in battle,
go to your seat and enjoy the feast;
tomorrow we shall share many treasures."

The Geat, full of joy, straightway went
to find his seat as Hrothgar had suggested.
1770 Then, once again, as so often before,
a great feast was prepared for the brave warriors
sitting in the hall.
                    The shadows of night
settled over the retainers. The company arose;
the gray-haired man, the old Scylding,
1775 wanted to retire. And the Geat, the shield-warrior,
was utterly exhausted, his bones ached for sleep.
At once the chamberlain—he who courteously
saw to all such needs as a thane,
a traveling warrior, had in those days—
1780 showed him, so limb-weary, to his lodging.
    Then Beowulf rested; the building soared,
spacious and adorned with gold; the guest
slept within until the black raven gaily
proclaimed sunrise. Bright light
1785 chased away the shadows of night.
                            Then the warriors
hastened, the thanes were eager to return
to their own people; the brave seafarer
longed to see his ship, so far from that place.
Then the bold Geat ordered that Hrunting,
1790 that sword beyond price, be brought before Unferth;
he begged him to take it back and thanked him
for the loan of it; he spoke of it as an ally
in battle, and assured Unferth he did not
underrate it: what a brave man he was!
1795 After this the warriors, wearing their chain-mail,
were eager to be off; their leader,
so dear to the Danes, walked to the dais
where Hrothgar was sitting, and greeted him.
    Beowulf, the son of Ecgtheow, spoke:
1800 "Now we seafarers, who have sailed here from far,
beg to tell you we are eager
to return to Hygelac. We have been happy here,
hospitably entertained; you have treated us kindly.
If I can in any way win more of your affection,
1805 O ruler of men, than I have done already,
I will come at once, eager for combat.
If news reaches me over the seas
that you are threatened by those around you
(just as before enemies endangered you)
1810 I will bring thousands of thanes,
all heroes, to help you. I know that Hygelac,
lord of the Geats, guardian of his people,
will advance me in word and deed
although he is young, so that I can back
1815 these promises with spear shafts, and serve you
with all my strength where you need men.
Should Hrethric, Hrothgar's son, wish

to visit the court of the Geatish king,
he will be warmly welcomed. Strong men
1820 should seek fame in far-off lands."
    Hrothgar replied: "The wise Lord put these words
into your mind; I have never heard a warrior
speak more sagely while still so young.
You are very strong and very shrewd,
1825 you speak with discerning. If your leader,
Hrethel's son, guardian of the people,
were to lose his life by illness or by iron,
by spear or grim swordplay, and if you survived him,
it seems to me that the Geats could not choose
1830 a better man for king, should you wish to rule
the land of your kinsmen. Beloved Beowulf,
the longer I know you, the more I like your spirit.
Because of your exploit, your act of friendship,
there will be an end to the gross outrages,
1835 the old enmity between Geats and Danes;
they will learn to live in peace.
For as long as I rule this spacious land,
heirlooms will be exchanged; many men
will greet their friends with gifts, send them
1840 over the seas where gannets swoop and rise;
the ring-prowed ship will take tokens of esteem,
treasures across the waters. I know the Geats
are honorable to friend and foe alike,
always faithful to their ancient code."
1845   Then Healfdene's son, guardian of thanes,
gave him twelve treasures in the hall,
told him to go safely with those gifts
to his own dear kinsmen, and to come back soon.
That king, descendant of kings,
1850 leader of the Scyldings, kissed and embraced
the best of thanes; tears streamed down
the old man's face. The more that warrior thought,
wise and old, the more it seemed
improbable that they would meet again,
1855 brave men in council. He so loved Beowulf
that he could not conceal his sense of loss;
but in his heart and in his head,
in his very blood, a deep love burned
for that dear man.
                            Then Beowulf the warrior,
1860 proudly adorned with gold, crossed the plain,
exulting in his treasure. The ship
rode at anchor, waiting for its owner.
Then, as they walked, they often praised
Hrothgar's generosity. He was an altogether
1865 faultless king, until old age deprived him
of his strength, as it does most men.
    Then that troop of brave young retainers
came to the water's edge; they wore ring-mail,

woven corslets. And the same watchman
1870 who had seen them arrive saw them now returning.
He did not insult them, ask for explanations,
but galloped from the cliff-top to greet the guests;
he said that those warriors in gleaming armor,
so eager to embark, would be welcomed home.
1875 Then the spacious ship, with its curved prow,
standing ready on the shore, was laden with armor,
with horses and treasure. The mast towered
over Hrothgar's precious heirlooms.
    Beowulf gave a sword bound round with gold
1880 to the ship's watchman—a man who thereafter
was honored on the mead-bench that much the more
on account of this heirloom.   The ship surged forward,
butted the waves in deep waters;
it drew away from the shores of the Scyldings.
1885 Then a sail, a great sea-garment, was fastened
with guys to the mast; the timbers groaned;
the boat was not blown off its course
by the stiff sea-breezes. The ship swept
over the waves; foaming at the bows,
1890 the boat with its well-wrought prow sped
over the waters, until at last the Geats
set eyes on the cliffs of their own country,
the familiar headlands; the vessel pressed forward,
pursued by the wind—it ran up onto dry land.
1895 The harbor guardian hurried down to the shore;
for many days he had scanned the horizon,
anxious to see those dear warriors once more.
He tethered the spacious sea-steed with ropes
(it rode on its painter restlessly)
1900 so that the rolling waves could not wrench it away.
Then Beowulf commanded that the peerless treasures,
the jewels and plated gold, be carried up from the shore.
He had not to go far to find the treasure-giver,
Hygelac son of Hrethel, for his house and the hall
1905 for his companions stood quite close to the sea-wall.
That high hall was a handsome building;
it became the valiant king.   Hygd, his queen,
Haereth's daughter, was very young; but she
was discerning, and versed in courtly customs,
1910 though she had lived a short time only
in that citadel; and she was not too thrifty,
not ungenerous with gifts of precious treasures
to the Geatish thanes.   Queen Thryth[9] was proud
and perverse, pernicious to her people.

---

9. The name "Thryth" may simply mean "arrogant"; it may be a reference to an arrogant woman rather than a proper name.

1915 No hero but her husband, however bold,
dared by day so much as turn his head
in her direction—that was far too dangerous;
but, if he did, he could bargain on being cruelly
bound with hand-plaited ropes; soon
1920 after his seizure, the blade was brought into play,
the damascened sword to settle the issue,
to inflict death. It is not right for a queen,
compelling though her beauty, to behave like this,
for a peace-weaver to deprive a dear man of his life
1925 because she fancies she has been insulted.
But Offa,[1] Hemming's kinsman, put an end to that.
Ale-drinking men in the hall have said
that she was no longer perfidious to her people,
and committed no crimes, once she had been given,
1930 adorned with gold, to that young warrior
of noble descent—once she had sailed,
at her father's command, to Offa's court
beyond the pale gold sea. After that,
reformed, she turned her life to good account;
1935 renowned for virtue, she reigned with vision;
and she loved the lord of warriors in the high way
of love—he who was, as I have heard,
the best of all men, the mighty human race,
between the two seas. Offa the brave
1940 was widely esteemed both for his gifts
and his skill in battle; he ruled his land
wisely. He fathered Eomer, guardian
of thanes, who was Hemming's kinsman,
grandson of Garmund, great in battle.
1945 	Then Beowulf and his warrior band walked
across the sand, tramped over
the wide foreshore; the world's candle shone,
the sun hastening from the south. The men hurried too
when they were told that the guardian of thanes,
1950 Ongentheow's slayer, the excellent young king,
held court in the hall, distributing rings.
Hygelac was informed at once of Beowulf's arrival—
that the shield of warriors, his comrade in battle,
had come back alive to the fortified enclosure,
1955 was heading for the hall unscathed after combat.
Space on the benches for Beowulf and his band
was hastily arranged, as Hygelac ordered.
	The guardian of thanes formally greeted
that loyal man; then they sat down—
1960 the unfated hero opposite the king,
kinsman facing kinsman. Haereth's daughter
carried mead-cups round the hall,

---

1. The reference to Offa may suggest that the poem was composed in the kingdom of Mercia in central England, since the Mercian king Offa II claimed descent from this king, Offa the Great.

spoke kindly to the warriors, handed the stoups
of wine to the thanes. Hygelac began
1965 to ask his companion courteous questions
in the high hall; he was anxious to hear
all that had happened to the seafaring Geats:
"Beloved Beowulf, tell me what became of you
after the day you so hurriedly decided
1970 to do battle far from here over the salt waters,
to fight at Heorot. And were you able
to assuage the grief, the well-known sorrow
of glorious Hrothgar? Your undertaking
deeply troubled me; I despaired, dear Beowulf,
1975 of your return. I pleaded with you
not on any account to provoke that monster,
but to let the South-Danes settle their feud
with Grendel themselves. God be praised
that I am permitted to see you safe and home."
1980 Then Beowulf, the son of Ecgtheow, said:
"Half the world, lord Hygelac, has heard
of my encounter, my great combat
hand to hand with Grendel in that hall
where he had harrowed and long humiliated
1985 the glorious Scyldings. I avenged it all;
none of Grendel's brood, however long
the last of that hateful race survives,
steeped in crime, has any cause to boast about
that dawn combat.
                    "First of all,
1990 I went to the ring-hall to greet Hrothgar;
once Healfdene's great son knew of my intentions,
he assigned me a seat beside his own sons.
Then there was revelry; never in my life,
under heaven's vault, have I seen men
1995 happier in the mead-hall. From time to time
the famous queen, the peace-weaver, walked across the floor,
exhorting the young warriors; often she gave
some man a twisted ring before returning to her seat.
At times Hrothgar's daughter, whom I heard
2000 men call Freawaru, carried the ale-horn
right round the hall in front of that brave company,
offered that vessel adorned with precious metals
to the thirsty warriors.
                    "Young, and decorated
with gold ornaments, she is promised to Froda's noble son,
2005 Ingeld of the Heathobards; that match was arranged
by the lord of the Scyldings, guardian of the kingdom;
he believes that it is an excellent plan
to use her as a peace-weaver to bury old antagonisms,
mortal feuds. But the deadly spear rarely sleeps
2010 for long after a prince lies dead in the dust,
however exceptional the bride may be!

"For Ingeld, leader of the Heathobards, and all
his retainers will later be displeased when he
and Freawaru walk on the floor—man and wife—
2015   and when Danish warriors are being entertained.
For the guests will gleam with Heathobard heirlooms,
iron-hard, adorned with rings,
precious possessions that had belonged
to their hosts' fathers for as long as they
2020   could wield their weapons, until in the shield-play
they and their dear friends forfeited their lives.
Then, while men are drinking, an old
warrior will speak; a sword he has seen,
marvelously adorned, stirs his memory
2025   of how Heathobards were slain by spears;
he seethes with fury; sad in his heart,
he begins to taunt a young Heathobard,
incites him to action with these words:
    "'Do you not recognize that sword, my friend,
2030   the sword your father, fully armed, bore into battle
that last time, when he was slain by Danes,
killed by brave Scyldings who carried the field
when Withergyld fell and many warriors beside him?
See how the son of one of those
2035   who slew him struts about the hall;
he sports the sword; he crows about that slaughter,
and carries that heirloom which is yours by right!'
In this way, with acid words, he will endlessly
provoke him and rake up the past,
2040   until the time will come when a Danish warrior,
Freawaru's thane, sleeps blood-stained,
slashed by the sword, punished by death
for the deeds of his father; and the Heathobard
will escape, well-acquainted with the country.
2045   Then both sides will break the solemn oath
sworn by their leaders; and Ingeld will come
to hate the Scyldings, and his love for his wife
will no longer be the same after such anguish and grief.
Thus I have little faith in friendship with Heathobards;
2050   they will fail to keep their side of the promise,
friendship with the Danes.[2]
                    "I have digressed;
Grendel is my subject. Now you must hear,
O treasure-giver, what the outcome was
of that hand-to-hand encounter. When the jewel of heaven
2055   had journeyed over the earth, the angry one,
the terrible night-prowler paid us a visit—
unscathed warriors watching over Heorot.
A fight awaited Hondscio, a horrible end

---

2. Beowulf seems to know of events that have not taken place yet, perhaps on the basis of what he knows from the Finns-
burgh story.

for that fated man; he was the first to fall;
2060 Grendel tore that famous young retainer to bits
between his teeth, and swallowed the whole body
of that dear man, that girded warrior.
And even then that murderer, mindful of evil,
his mouth caked with blood, was not content
2065 to leave the gold-hall empty-handed
but, famed for his strength, he tackled me,
gripped me with his outstretched hand.
A huge unearthly glove swung at his side,
firmly secured with subtle straps;
2070 it had been made with great ingenuity,
with devils' craft and dragons' skins.
Innocent as I was, the demon monster
meant to shove me in it, and many another
innocent besides; that was beyond him
2075 after I leapt up, filled with fury.
It would take too long to tell you how I repaid
that enemy of men for all his outrages;
but there, my prince, I ennobled your people
with my deeds. Grendel escaped,
2080 and lived a little longer; but he left
behind at Heorot his right hand; and, in utter
wretchedness, sank to the bottom of the lake.
        "The sun rose; we sat down together
to feast, then the leader of the Scyldings
2085 paid a good price for the bloody battle,
gave me many a gold-plated treasure.
There was talk and song; the gray-haired Scylding
opened his immense hoard of memories;
now and then a happy warrior touched
2090 the wooden harp, reciting some story,
mournful and true; at times the generous king
recalled in proper detail some strange incident;
and as the shadows lengthened, an aged thane,
cramped and rheumatic, raised his voice
2095 time and again, lamenting his lost youth,
his prowess in battle; worn with winters,
his heart quickened to the call of the past.
        "In these ways we relaxed agreeably
throughout the long day until darkness closed in,
2100 another night for men. Then, in her grief,
bent on vengeance, Grendel's mother
hastened to the hall where death had lain
in wait for her son—the battle-hatred
of the Geats. The horrible harridan avenged
2105 her offspring, slew a warrior brazenly.
Aeschere, the wise old counselor, lost
his life. And when morning came,
the Danes were unable to cremate him,
to place the body of that dear man

2110 on the funeral pyre; for Grendel's mother
had carried it off in her gruesome grasp,
taken it under the mountain lake.
Of all the grievous sorrows Hrothgar
long sustained, none was more terrible.
2115 Then the king in his anger called upon your name
and entreated me to risk my life,
to accomplish deeds of utmost daring
in the tumult of waves; he promised me rewards.
And so, as men now know all over the earth,
2120 I found the grim guardian of the lake-bottom.
For a while we grappled; the water boiled
with blood; then in that battle-hall,
I lopped off Grendel's mother's head
with the mighty sword. I barely escaped
2125 with my life; but I was not fated.
    "And afterwards the guardian of thanes,
Healfdene's son, gave me many treasures.
Thus the king observed excellent tradition:
in no wise did I feel unrewarded
2130 for all my efforts, but Healfdene's son
offered me gifts of my own choosing;
gifts, O noble king, I wish now
to give to you in friendship. I still depend
entirely on your favors; I have few
2135 close kinsmen but you, O Hygelac!"
    Then Beowulf caused to be brought in
a standard bearing the image of a boar,
together with a helmet towering in battle,
a gray corslet, and a noble sword; he said:
2140 "Hrothgar, the wise king, gave me
these trappings and purposely asked me
to tell you their history: he said that Heorogar,
lord of the Scyldings, long owned them.
Yet he has not endowed his own brave son,
2145 Heoroweard, with this armor, much as
he loves him. Make good use of everything!"
    I heard that four bays, apple-brown,
were brought into the hall after the armor—
swift as the wind, identical. Beowulf gave them
2150 as he gave the treasures. So should a kinsman do,
and never weave nets with underhand subtlety
to ensnare others, never have designs
on a close comrade's life. His nephew,
brave in battle, was loyal to Hygelac;
2155 each man was mindful of the other's pleasure.
    I heard that he gave Hygd the collar,
the wondrous ornament with which Wealhtheow,
daughter of the prince, had presented him,
and gave her three horses also, graceful creatures
2160 with brightly-colored saddles; Hygd

wore that collar, her breast was adorned.

    Thus Ecgtheow's son, feared in combat,
confirmed his courage with noble deeds;
he lived a life of honor, he never slew
2165   companions at the feast; savagery was
alien to him, but he, so brave in battle,
made the best use of those ample talents
with which God endowed him.

                 He had been despised
for a long while, for the Geats saw no spark
2170   of bravery in him, nor did their king deem him
worthy of much attention on the mead-bench;
people thought that he was a sluggard,
a feeble princeling. How fate changed,
changed completely for that glorious man!

2175   Then the guardian of thanes, the famous king,
ordered that Hrethel's gold-adorned heirloom
be brought in; no sword was so treasured
in all Geatland; he laid it in Beowulf's lap,
and gave him seven thousand hides of land,
2180   a hall and princely throne. Both men
had inherited land and possessions
in that country; but the more spacious kingdom
had fallen to Hygelac, who was of higher rank.

    In later days, after much turmoil,
2185   things happened in this way: when Hygelac lay dead
and murderous battle-blades had beaten down
the shield of his son Heardred,
and when the warlike Swedes, savage warriors,
had hunted him down among his glorious people,
2190   attacked Hereric's nephew with hatred,
the great kingdom of the Geats passed
into Beowulf's hands. He had ruled it well
for fifty winters—he was a wise king,
a grizzled guardian of the land—when, on dark nights,
2195   a dragon began to terrify the Geats:
he lived on a cliff, kept watch over a hoard
in a high stone barrow; below, there was
a secret path; a man strayed
into this barrow by chance, seized
2200   some of the pagan treasures, stole drinking vessels.
At first the sleeping dragon was deceived
by the thief's skill, but afterwards he avenged
this theft of gleaming gold; people far and wide
bands of retainers, became aware of his wrath.
2205   That man did not intrude upon the hoard
deliberately, he who robbed the dragon;
but it was some slave, a wanderer in distress
escaping from men's anger who entered there,
seeking refuge. He stood guilty of some sin.

2210 As soon as he peered in, the outsider
stiffened with horror. Unhappy as he was,
he stole the vessel, the precious cup.
There were countless heirlooms in that earth-cave,
the enormous legacy of a noble people,
2215 ancient treasures which some man or other
had cautiously concealed there many years
before. Death laid claim to all that people
in days long past, and then that retainer
who outlived the rest, a gold-guardian
2220 mourning his friends, expected the same fate—
thought he would enjoy those assembled heirlooms
a little while only. A newly built barrow
stood ready on a headland which overlooked
the sea, protected by the hazards of access.
2225 To this barrow the protector of rings brought the heirlooms,
the plated gold, all that part of the precious treasure
worthy of hoarding; then he spoke a few words:
"Hold now, O earth, since heroes could not,
these treasures owned by nobles! Indeed, strong men
2230 first quarried them from you. Death in battle,
ghastly carnage, has claimed all my people—
men who once made merry in the hall
have laid down their lives; I have no one
to carry the sword, to polish the plated vessel,
2235 this precious drinking-cup; all the retainers
have hurried elsewhere. The iron helmet
adorned with gold shall lose its ornaments;
men who should polish battle-masks are sleeping;
the coat of mail, too, that once withstood
2240 the bite of swords in battle, after shields were shattered,
decays like the warriors; the linked mail may no longer
range far and wide with the warrior,
stand side by side with heroes. Gone is the pleasure
of plucking the harp, no fierce hawk
2245 swoops about the hall, nor does the swift stallion
strike sparks in the courtyard. Cruel death
has claimed hundreds of this human race."
     Thus the last survivor mourned time passing,
and roamed about by day and night,
2250 sad and aimless, until death's lightning
struck at his heart.
                    The aged dragon of darkness
discovered that glorious hoard unguarded,
he who sought out barrows, smooth-scaled
and evil, and flew by night, breathing
2255 fire; the Geats feared him greatly.
He was destined to find the hoard
in that cave and, old in winters, guard
the heathen gold; much good it did him!
     Thus the huge serpent who harassed men

2260   guarded that great stronghold under the earth
        for three hundred winters, until
        a man enraged him; the wanderer carried
        the inlaid vessel to his lord, and begged him
        for a bond of peace. Then the hoard was raided
2265   and plundered, and that unhappy man
        was granted his prayer. His lord examined
        the ancient work of smiths for the first time.
           There was conflict once more after the dragon
        awoke; intrepid, he slid swiftly
2270   along by the rock, and found the footprints
        of the intruder; that man had skillfully
        picked his way right past the dragon's head.
        Thus he who is undoomed will easily survive
        anguish and exile provided he enjoys
2275   the grace of God. The warden of the hoard
        prowled up and down, anxious to find
        the man who had pillaged it while he slept.
        Breathing fire and filled with fury,
        he circled the outside of the earth mound
2280   again and again; but there was no one
        in that barren place; yet he exulted at the thought
        of battle, bloody conflict; at times he wheeled back
        into the barrow, hunting for the priceless heirloom.
        He realized at once that one of the race of men
2285   had discovered the gold, the glorious treasure.
        Restlessly the dragon waited for darkness;
        the guardian of the hoard was bursting with rage,
        he meant to avenge the vessel's theft
        with fire.
                 Then daylight failed
2290   as the dragon desired; he could no longer
        confine himself to the cave but flew in a ball
        of flame, burning for vengeance. The Geats
        were filled with dread as he began his flight;
        it swiftly ended in disaster for their lord.
2295   Then the dragon began to breathe forth fire,
        to burn fine buildings; flame tongues flickered,
        terrifying men; the loathsome winged creature
        meant to leave the whole place lifeless.
        Everywhere the violence of the dragon, the venom
2300   of that hostile one, was clearly to be seen—
        how he had wrought havoc, hated and humiliated
        the Geatish people. Then, before dawn he rushed back
        to his hidden lair and the treasure hoard.
        He had girdled the Geats with fire,
2305   with ravening flames; he relied on his own strength,
        and on the barrow and the cliff; his trust played him false.
           Then news of that terror was quickly brought
        to Beowulf, that flames enveloped
        his own hall, best of buildings,

2310 and the gift-throne of the Geats. That good man
was choked with intolerable grief.
Wise that he was, he imagined
he must have angered God, the Lord Eternal,
by ignoring some ancient law; he was seldom
2315 dispirited, but now his heart was like lead.
  The fire dragon had destroyed the fortified hall,
the people's stronghold, and laid waste with flames
the land by the sea. The warlike king,
prince of the Geats, planned to avenge this.
2320 The protector of warriors, leader of men,
instructed the smith to forge a curious shield
made entirely of iron; he well knew
that a linden shield would not last long
against the flames. The eminent prince
2325 was doomed to reach the end of his days on earth,
his life in this world. So too was the dragon,
though he had guarded the hoard for generations.
  Then the giver of gold disdained
to track the dragon with a troop
2330 of warlike men; he did not shrink
from single combat, nor did he set much store
by the fearless dragon's power, for had he not before
experienced danger, again and again
survived the storm of battle, beginning with that time
2335 when, blessed with success, he cleansed
Hrothgar's hall, and crushed in battle
the monster and his vile mother?
                    That grim combat
in which Hygelac was slain—Hrethel's son,
leader of the Geats, dear lord of his people,
2340 struck down by swords in the bloodbath
in Frisia—was far from the least
of his encounters. Beowulf escaped
because of his skill and stamina at swimming;
he waded into the water, bearing no fewer
2345 than thirty corslets, a deadweight on his arms.
But the Frankish warriors who shouldered
their shields against him had no cause to boast
about that combat; a handful only
eluded that hero and returned home.
2350 Then the son of Ecgtheow, saddened and alone,
rode with the white horses to his own people.
Hygd offered him heirlooms there, and even
the kingdom, the ancestral throne itself; for she feared
that her son would be unable to defend it
2355 from foreign invaders now that Hygelac was gone.
But the Geats, for all their anguish, failed
to prevail upon the prince—he declined
absolutely to become Heardred's lord,
or to taste the pleasures of royal power.

2360 But he stood at his right hand,
ready with advice, always friendly,
and respectful, until the boy came of age
and could rule the Geats himself.
Two exiles,
Ohthere's sons, sailed to Heardred's court;
2365 they had rebelled against the ruler of the Swedes,
a renowned man, the best of sea-kings,
gold-givers in Sweden. By receiving them,
Heardred rationed the days of his life;
in return for his hospitality, Hygelac's son
2370 was mortally wounded, slashed by swords.
Once Heardred lay lifeless in the dust,
Onela, son of Ongentheow, sailed home again;
he allowed Beowulf to inherit the throne
and rule the Geats; he was a noble king!
2375 But Beowulf did not fail with help
after the death of the prince, although years passed;
he befriended unhappy Eadgils, Ohthere's son,
and supplied him with weapons and warriors
beyond the wide seas. Eadgils afterwards
2380 avenged Eanmund, he ravaged and savaged
the Swedes, and killed the king, Onela himself.
Thus the son of Ecgtheow had survived
these feuds, these fearful battles, these acts
of single combat, up to that day
2385 when he was destined to fight against the dragon.
Then in fury the leader of the Geats set out
with eleven to search for the winged serpent.
By then Beowulf knew the cause of the feud,
bane of men; the famous cup
2390 had come to him through the hands of its finder.
The unfortunate slave who first brought about
such strife made the thirteenth man
in that company—cowed and disconsolate,
he had to be their guide. Much against his will,
2395 he conducted them to the entrance of the cave,
an earth-hall full of filigree work
and fine adornments close by the sea,
the fretting waters. The vile guardian,
the serpent who had long lived under the earth,
2400 watched over the gold, alert; he who hoped
to gain it bargained with his own life.
Then the brave king sat on the headland,
the gold-friend of the Geats wished success
to his retainers. His mind was most mournful,
2405 angry, eager for slaughter; fate hovered
over him, so soon to fall on that old man,
to seek out his hidden spirit, to split
life and body; flesh was to confine
the soul of the king only a little longer.

2410   Beowulf, the son of Ecgtheow, spoke:
"Often and often in my youth I plunged
into the battle maelstrom; how well I remember it.
I was seven winters old when the treasure guardian,
ruler of men, received me from my father.[3]

2415   King Hrethel took me into his ward, reared me,
fed me, gave me gold, mindful of our kinship;
for as long as he lived, he loved me no less
than his own three sons, warriors with me
in the citadel, Herebeald, Haethcyn, and my dear Hygelac.

2420   A death-bed for the firstborn was unrolled
most undeservedly by the action of his kinsman—
Haethcyn drew his horn-tipped bow
and killed his lord-to-be; he missed his mark,
his arrow was stained with his brother's blood.

2425   That deed was a dark sin, sickening
to think of, not to be settled by payment of *wergild*;
yet Herebeald's death could not be requited.

"Thus the old king, Hrethel, is agonized
to see his son, so young, swing

2430   from the gallows.[4] He sings a dirge, a song
dark with sorrow, while his son hangs,
raven's carrion, and he cannot help him
in any way, wise and old as he is.
He wakes each dawn to the ache

2435   of his son's death; he has no desire
for a second son, to be his heir
in the stronghold, now that his firstborn
has finished his days and deeds on earth.
Grieving, he wanders through his son's dwelling,

2440   sees the wine-hall now deserted, joyless,
home of the winds; the riders, the warriors,
sleep in their graves. No longer is the harp
plucked, no longer is there happiness in that place.
Then Hrethel takes to his bed, and intones

2445   dirges for his dead son, Herebeald;
his house and his lands seem empty now,
and far too large. Thus the lord of the Geats
endured in his heart the ebb and flow
of sorrow for his firstborn; but he could not

2450   avenge that feud on the slayer—his own son;
although Hrethel had no love for Haethcyn,
he could no more readily requite death
with death. Such was his sorrow that he lost
all joy in life, chose the light of God;

2455   he bequeathed to his sons, as a wealthy man does,
his citadel and land, when he left this life.

---

3. It was customary for nephews to be brought up in the house of their maternal uncles as foster-children.
4. Even in cases of involuntary manslaughter, punish-ment was required to avenge the dead. In this instance, it seems that a ritual, sacrificial hanging was performed to spare Haethcyn for murdering his brother Herebeald.

"Then there was strife, savage conflict
between Swedes and Geats; after Hrethel's death
the feud we shared, the fierce hatred
2460   flared up across the wide water.
The sons of Ongentheow, Onela and Ohthere,
were brave and battle-hungry; they had no wish
for peace over the sea but several times,
and wantonly, butchered the people of the Geats
2465   on the slopes of Slaughter Hill. As is well known,
my kinsmen requited that hatred, those crimes;
but one of them paid with his own life—
a bitter bargain; that fight was fatal
to Haethcyn, ruler of the Geats.
2470   Then I heard that in the morning
one kinsman avenged another, repaid
Haethcyn's slayer with the battle-blade,
when Ongentheow attacked the Geat Eofor;
the helmet split, the old Swede fell,
2475   pale in death; Eofor remembered
that feud well enough, his hand and sword
spared nothing in their death-swing.
"I repaid Hygelac for his gifts of heirlooms
with my gleaming blade, repaid him in battle,
2480   as was granted to me; he gave me land
and property, a happy home. He had
no need to hunt out and hire mercenaries—
inferior warriors from the Gepidae,
from the Spear-Danes or from tribes in Sweden;
2485   but I was always at the head of his host,
alone in the van; and I shall still fight
for as long as I live and this sword lasts,
that has often served me early and late
since I became the daring slayer
2490   of Daeghrefn, champion of the Franks.
He was unable to bring adornments,
breast-decorations to the Frisian king,
but fell in the fight bearing the standard,
a brave warrior; it was my battle-grip,
2495   not the sharp blade, that shattered his bones,
silenced his heartbeat. Now the shining edge,
hand and tempered sword, shall engage in battle
for the treasure hoard. I fought many battles
when I was young; yet I will fight again,
2500   the old guardian of my people, and achieve
a mighty exploit if the evil dragon dares
confront me, dares come out of the earth-cave!"
Then he addressed each of the warriors,
the brave heroes, his dear companions,
2505   a last time: "I would not wield a sword
against the dragon if I could grasp this hideous being
with my hands (and thus make good my boast),

as once I grasped the monster Grendel;
but I anticipate blistering battle-fire,
2510 venomous breath; therefore I have with me
my shield and corslet. I will not give an inch
to the guardian of the mound, but at that barrow
it will befall us both as fate ordains,
every man's master. My spirit is bold,
2515 I will not boast further against the fierce flier.
Watch from the barrow, warriors in armor,
guarded by corslets, which of us will better
weather his wounds after the combat.
This is not your undertaking, nor is it
2520 possible for any man but me alone
to pit his strength against the gruesome one,
and perform great deeds. I will gain the gold
by daring, or else battle, dread destroyer
of life, will lay claim to your lord."
2525   Then the bold warrior, stern-faced beneath his helmet,
stood up with his shield; sure of his own strength,
he walked in his corslet towards the cliff;
the way of the coward is not thus!
Then that man endowed with noble qualities,
2530 he who had braved countless battles, weathered
the thunder when warrior troops clashed together,
saw a stone arch set in the cliff
through which a stream spurted; steam rose
from the boiling water; he could not stay long
2535 in the hollow near the hoard for fear
of being scorched by the dragon's flames.
Then, such was his fury, the leader of the Geats
threw out his chest and gave a great roar,
the brave man bellowed; his voice, renowned
2540 in battle, hammered the gray rock's anvil.
The guardian of the hoard knew the voice for human;
violent hatred stirred within him. Now no time
remained to entreat for peace. At once
the monster's breath, burning battle vapor,
2545 issued from the barrow; the earth itself snarled.
The lord of the Geats, standing under the cliff,
raised his shield against the fearsome stranger;
then that sinuous creature spoiled
for the fight. The brave and warlike king
2550 had already drawn his keen-edged sword,
(it was an ancient heirloom); a terror of each other
lurked in the hearts of the two antagonists.
While the winged creature coiled himself up,
the friend and lord of men stood unflinching
2555 by his shield; Beowulf waited ready armed.
    Then, fiery and twisted, the dragon swiftly
shrithed towards its fate. The shield protected
the life and body of the famous prince
for far less time than he had looked for.

2560	It was the first occasion in all his life
	that fate did not decree triumph for him
	in battle. The lord of the Geats raised
	his arm, and struck the mottled monster
	with his vast ancestral sword; but the bright blade's
2565	edge was blunted by the bone, bit
	less keenly than the desperate king required.
	The defender of the barrow bristled with anger
	at the blow, spouted murderous fire, so that flames
	leapt through the air. The gold-friend of the Geats
2570	did not boast of famous victories; his proven sword,
	the blade bared in battle, had failed him
	as it ought not to have done. That great Ecgtheow's
	greater son had to journey on from this world
	was no pleasant matter; much against his will,
2575	he was obliged to make his dwelling
	elsewhere—sooner or later every man must leave
	this transitory life. It was not long
	before the fearsome ones closed again.
	The guardian of the hoard was filled with fresh hope,
2580	his breast was heaving; he who had ruled a nation
	suffered agony, surrounded by flame.
	And Beowulf's companions, sons of nobles—
	so far from protecting him in a troop together,
	unflinching in the fright—shrank back into the forest
2585	scared for their own lives. One man alone
	obeyed his conscience. The claims of kinship
	can never be ignored by a right-minded man.
	His name was Wiglaf, a noble warrior,
	Weohstan's son, kinsman of Aelfhere,
2590	a leader of the Swedes; he saw that his lord,
	helmeted, was tormented by the intense heat.
	Then he recalled the honors Beowulf had bestowed
	on him—the wealthy citadel of the Waegmundings,
	the rights to land his father owned before him.
2595	He could not hold back then; he grasped the round,
	yellow shield; he drew his ancient sword,
	reputed to be the legacy of Eanmund,
	Ohthere's son.
	Weohstan had slain him
	in a skirmish while Eanmund was a wanderer,
2600	a friendless man, and then had carried off
	to his own kinsmen the gleaming helmet,
	the linked corslet, the ancient sword
	forged by giants. It was Onela,
	Eanmund's uncle, who gave him that armor,
2605	ready for use; but Onela did not refer to the feud,
	though Weohstan had slain his brother's son.
	For many years Weohstan owned that war-gear,
	sword and corslet, until his son was old enough
	to achieve great feats as he himself had done.
2610	Then, when Weohstan journeyed on from the earth,

an old man, he left Wiglaf—who was
with the Geats—a great legacy of armor
of every kind.
          This was the first time
the young warrior had weathered the battle storm,
2615   standing at the shoulder of his lord.
His courage did not melt, nor did his kinsman's sword
fail him in the fight. The dragon found that out
when they met in mortal combat.
    Wiglaf spoke, constantly reminding
2620   his companions of their duty—he was mournful.
"I think of that evening we emptied the mead-cup
in the feasting-hall, partook and pledged our lord,
who presented us with rings, that we would repay him
for his gifts of armor, helmets and hard swords,
2625   if ever the need, need such as this, arose.
For this very reason he asked us
to join with him in this journey, deemed us
worthy of renown, and gave me these treasures;
he looked on us as loyal warriors,
2630   brave in battle; even so, our lord,
guardian of the Geats, intended to perform
this feat alone, because of all men
he had achieved the greatest exploits,
daring deeds. Now the day has come
2635   when our lord needs support, the might
of strong men; let us hurry forward
and help our leader as long as fire remains,
fearsome, searing flames. God knows
I would rather that fire embraced my body
2640   beside the charred body of my gold-giver;
it seems wrong to me that we should shoulder
our shields, carry them home afterwards,
unless we can first kill the venomous foe,
guard the prince of the Geats. I know
2645   in my heart his feats of old were such
that he should not now be the only Geat to suffer
and fall in combat; in common we shall share
sword, helmet, corslet, the trappings of war."
    Then that man fought his way through the fumes,
2650   went helmeted to help his lord. He shouted out:
"Brave Beowulf, may success attend you—
for in the days when you were young, you swore
that so long as you lived you would never allow
your fame to decay; now, O resolute king,
2655   renowned for your exploits, you must guard your life
with all your skill. I shall assist you."
    At this the seething dragon attacked a second time;
shimmering with fire the venomous visitor fell on his foes,
the men he loathed. With waves of flame, he burned
2660   the shield right up to its boss; Wiglaf's
corslet afforded him no protection whatsoever.

But the young warrior still fought bravely, sheltered
behind his kinsman's shield after his own
was consumed by flames. Still the battle-king
2665   set his mind on deeds of glory; with prodigious strength
he struck a blow so violent that his sword stuck
in the dragon's skull. But Naegling snapped!
Beowulf's old gray-hued sword
failed him in the fight. Fate did not ordain
2670   that the iron edge should assist him
in that struggle; Beowulf's hand was too strong.
Indeed I have been told that he overtaxed
each and every weapon, hardened by blood, that he bore
into battle; his own great strength betrayed him.
2675   Then the dangerous dragon, scourge of the Geats,
was intent a third time upon attack; he rushed
at the renowned man when he saw an opening:
fiery, battle-grim, he gripped the hero's neck
between his sharp teeth; Beowulf was bathed
2680   in blood; it spurted out in streams.
Then, I have heard, the loyal thane
alongside the Geatish king displayed great courage,
strength and daring, as was his nature.
To assist his kinsman, that man in mail
2685   aimed not for the head but lunged at the belly
of their vile enemy (in so doing his hand
was badly burned); his sword, gleaming and adorned,
sank in up to the hilt and at once the flames
began to abate. The king still had control then
2690   over his senses; he drew the deadly knife,
keen-edged in battle, that he wore on his corslet;
then the lord of the Geats dispatched the dragon.
Thus they had killed their enemy—their courage
enabled them—the brave kinsmen together
2695   had destroyed him. Such should a man,
a thane, be in time of necessity!
                                    That was the last
of all the king's achievements, his last
exploit in the world. Then the wound
the earth-dragon had inflicted with his teeth
2700   began to burn and swell; very soon he
was suffering intolerable pain as the poison
boiled within him. Then the wise leader
tottered forward and slumped on a seat
by the barrow; he gazed at the work of giants,
2705   saw how the ancient earthwork contained
stone arches supported by columns.
Then, with his own hands, the best of thanes
refreshed the renowned prince with water,
washed his friend and lord, blood-stained
2710   and battle-weary, and unfastened his helmet.
    Beowulf began to speak, he defied
his mortal injury; he was well aware

that his life's course, with all its delights,
had come to an end; his days on earth
2715 were exhausted, death drew very close:
"It would have made me happy, at this time,
to pass on war-gear to my son, had I
been granted an heir to succeed me,
sprung of my seed. I have ruled the Geats
2720 for fifty winters; no king of any
neighboring tribe has dared to attack me
with swords, or sought to cow and subdue me.
But in my own home I have awaited
my destiny, cared well for my dependents,
2725 and I have not sought trouble, or sworn
any oaths unjustly. Because of all these things
I can rejoice, drained now by death-wounds;
for the Ruler of Men will have no cause to blame me
after I have died on the count that I deprived
2730 other kinsmen of their lives. Now hurry,
dear Wiglaf; rummage the hoard
under the gray rock, for the dragon sleeps,
riddled with wounds, robbed of his treasure.
Be as quick as you can so that I may see
2735 the age-old golden treasure, and examine
all the priceless, shimmering stones; once I
have set eyes on such a store, it will be
more easy for me to die, to abandon
the life and land that have so long been mine."
2740   Then, I have been told, as soon as he heard
the words of his lord, wounded in battle,
Wiglaf hastened into the earth-cavern,
still wearing his corslet, his woven coat of mail.
After the fierce warrior, flushed with victory,
2745 had walked past a dais, he came upon
the hoard—a hillock of precious stones,
and gold treasure glowing on the ground;
he saw wondrous wall-hangings; the lair
of the serpent, the aged twilight-flier;
2750 and the stoups and vessels of a people
long dead, now lacking a polisher,
deprived of adornments. There were many old,
rusty helmets, and many an armlet
cunningly wrought. A treasure hoard,
2755 gold in the ground, will survive its owner
easily, whosoever hides it!
And he saw also hanging high
over the hoard a standard fashioned with gold strands,
a miracle of handiwork; a light shone from it,
2760 by which he was able to distinguish the earth
and look at the adornments. There was no sign
of the serpent, the sword had savaged and slain him.
Then I heard that Wiglaf rifled the hoard
in the barrow, the antique work of giants—

2765 he chose and carried off as many cups and salvers
as he could; and he also took the standard,
the incomparable banner; Beowulf's sword,
iron-edged, had injured
the guardian of the hoard, he who had held it
2770 through the ages and fought to defend it
with flames—terrifying, blistering,
ravening at midnight—until he was slain.
Wiglaf hurried on his errand, eager to return,
spurred on by the treasures; in his heart he was troubled
2775 whether he would find the prince of the Geats,
so grievously wounded, still alive
in the place where he had left him.
Then at last he came, carrying the treasures,
to the renowned king; his lord's life-blood
2780 was ebbing; once more he splashed him
with water, until Beowulf revived a little,
began to frame his thoughts.
                          Gazing at the gold,
the warrior, the sorrowing king, said:
"With these words I thank
2785 the King of Glory, the Eternal Lord,
the Ruler, for all the treasures here before me,
that in my lifetime I have been able
to gain them for the Geats.
And now that I have bartered my old life
2790 for this treasure hoard, you must serve
and inspire our people. I will not long be with you.
Command the battle-warriors, after the funeral fire,
to build a fine barrow overlooking the sea;
let it tower high on Whaleness
2795 as a reminder to my people.
And let it be known as *Beowulf's barrow*
to all seafarers, to men who steer their ships
from far over the swell and the saltspray."
     Then the prince, bold of mind, detached
2800 his golden collar and gave it to Wiglaf,
the young spear-warrior, and also his helmet
adorned with gold, his ring and his corslet,
and enjoined him to use them well;
"You are the last survivor of our family,
2805 the Waegmundings; fate has swept
all my kinsmen, those courageous warriors,
to their doom. I must follow them."
     Those were the warrior's last words
before he succumbed to the raging flames
2810 on the pyre; his soul migrated from his breast
to meet the judgment of righteous men.
     Then it was harrowing for the young hero
that he should have to see that beloved man
lying on the earth at his life's end,
2815 wracked by pain. His slayer lay

there too, himself slain, the terrible
cave-dragon. That serpent, coiled evilly,
could no longer guard the gold-hoard,
but blades of iron, beaten and tempered
2820 by smiths, notched in battle, had taken him off;
his wings were clipped now, he lay
mortally wounded, motionless on the earth
at the mound's entrance. No more did he fly
through the night sky, or spread his wings,
2825 proud of his possessions; but he lay prostrate
because of the power of Beowulf, their leader.
Truly, I have heard that no hero of the Geats,
no fire-eater, however daring, could quell
the scorching blast of that venomous one
2830 and lay his hands on the hoard in the lair,
should he find its sentinel waiting there,
watching over the barrow. Beowulf paid
the price of death for that mighty hoard;
both he and the dragon had traveled to the end
2835 of this transitory life.
                    Not long after that
the lily-livered ones slunk out of the wood;
ten cowardly oath-breakers, who had lacked
the courage to let fly with their spears
as their lord so needed, came forward together;
2840 overcome with shame, they carried their shields
and weapons to where their leader lay;
they gazed at Wiglaf. That warrior, bone-weary,
knelt beside the shoulders of his lord; he tried
to rouse him with water; it was all in vain.
2845 For all his efforts, his longing, he could not
detain the life of his leader on earth,
or alter anything the Ruler ordained.
God in His wisdom governed the deeds
of all men, as He does now.
2850   Then the young warrior was not at a loss
for well-earned, angry words for those cowards.
Wiglaf, Weohstan's son, sick at heart,
eyed those faithless men and said:
"He who does not wish to disguise the truth
2855 can indeed say that—when it was a question
not of words but war—our lord completely wasted
the treasures he gave you, the same war-gear
you stand in over there, helmets and corslets
the prince presented often to his thanes on the ale-bench
2860 in the feasting-hall, the very finest weapons
he could secure from far and wide.
The king of the Geats had no need to bother
with boasts about his battle-companions;
yet God, Giver of victories, granted
2865 that he should avenge himself with his sword
single-handed, when all his courage was called for.

I could hardly begin to guard his life
in the fight; but all the same I attempted
to help my kinsman beyond my power.
2870 Each time I slashed at that deadly enemy,
he was a little weaker, the flames leaped
less fiercely from his jaws. Too few defenders
rallied round our prince when he was most pressed.
Now you and your dependents can no longer delight
2875 in gifts of swords, or take pleasure in property,
a happy home; but, after thanes from far and wide
have heard of your flight, your shameful cowardice,
each of your male kinsmen will be condemned
to become a wanderer, an exile deprived
2880 of the land he owns. For every warrior
death is better than dark days of disgrace."
    Then Wiglaf ordered that Beowulf's great feat
be proclaimed in the stronghold, up along the cliff-edge,
where a troop of shield-warriors had waited all morning,
2885 wondering sadly if their dear lord was dead,
or if he would return.
                    The man who galloped
to the headland gave them the news at once;
he kept back nothing but called out:
"The lord of the Geats, he who gave joy
2890 to all our people, lies rigid on his death-bed;
slaughtered by the dragon, he now sleeps;
and his deadly enemy, slashed by the knife,
sleeps beside him; he was quite unable
to wound the serpent with a sword. Wiglaf,
2895 son of Weohstan, sits by Beowulf,
the quick and the dead—both brave men—
side by side; weary in his heart
he watches over friend and foe alike.
    "Now the Geats must make ready for a time
2900 of war, for the Franks and the Frisians,
in far-off regions, will hear soon
of the king's death. Our feud with the Franks
grew worse when Hygelac sailed with his fleet
to the shores of Frisia. Frankish warriors
2905 attacked him there, and outfought him,
bravely forced the king in his corslet
to give ground; he fell, surrounded
by his retainers; that prince presented
not one ornament to his followers. Since then,
2910 the king of the Franks has been no friend of ours.
    "Nor would I in the least rely on peace
or honesty from the Swedish people; everyone
remembers how Ongentheow slew Haethcyn,
Hrethel's son, in battle near Ravenswood
2915 when, rashly, the Geats first attacked the Swedes.
At once Ongentheow, Ohthere's father,
old but formidable, retaliated; he killed

Haethcyn, and released his wife from captivity,
set free the mother of Onela and Ohthere,
2920   an aged woman bereft of all her ornaments;
and then he pursued his mortal enemies
until, lordless, with utmost difficulty,
they reached and found refuge in Ravenswood.
Then Ongentheow, with a huge army, penned in
2925   those warriors, exhausted by wounds,
who had escaped the sword; all night long
he shouted fearsome threats at those shivering thanes,
swore that in the morning he and his men would let
their blood in streams with sharp-edged swords,
2930   and string some up on gallows-trees
as sport for birds. Just as day dawned
those despairing men were afforded relief;
they heard the joyful song of Hygelac's
horn and trumpet as that hero came,
2935   hurrying to their rescue with a band of retainers.
after that savage, running battle, the soil
was blood-stained, scuffled—a sign of how
the Swedes and the Geats fomented their feud.
Then Ongentheow, old and heavy-hearted,
2940   headed for his stronghold with his retainers,
that resolute man retreated; he realized
how spirit and skill combined in the person
of proud Hygelac; he had no confidence
about the outcome of an open fight with the seafarers,
2945   the Geatish warriors, in defense of his hoard,
his wife and children; the old man thus withdrew
behind an earth-wall. Then the Swedes were pursued,
Hygelac's banner was hoisted over that earth-work
after the Geats, sons of Hrethel, had stormed
2950   the stronghold. Then gray-haired Ongentheow
was cornered by swords, the king of the Swedes
was constrained to face and suffer his fate
as Eofor willed it. Wulf, the son
of Wonred, slashed angrily at Ongentheow
2955   with his sword, so that blood spurted
from the veins under his hair. The old Swede,
king of his people, was not afraid
but as soon as he had regained his balance
repaid that murderous blow with interest.
2960   Then Wonred's daring son could no longer
lift his hand against the aged warrior
but, with that stroke, Ongentheow had sheared
right through his helmet so that Wulf, blood-stained,
was thrown to the ground; he was not yet doomed to die
2965   but later recovered from that grievous wound.
When Wulf collapsed, his brother Eofor,
Hygelac's brave thane, swung his broad sword,
made by giants, shattered the massive helmet
above the raised shield; Ongentheow fell,

2970   the guardian of the people was fatally wounded.
Then many warriors quickly rescued Wulf,
and bandaged his wounds, once they had won control
(as fate decreed) of that field of corpses.
Meanwhile Eofor stripped Ongentheow's body
2975   of its iron corslet, wrenched the helmet
from his head, the mighty sword from his hands;
he carried the old man's armor to Hygelac.
He received those battle adornments, honorably
promised to reward Eofor above other men;
2980   he kept his word; the king of the Geats,
Hrethel's son, repaid Eofor and Wulf
for all they had accomplished with outstanding gifts
when he had returned home; he gave each of them
land and interlocked rings to the value
2985   of a hundred thousand pence—no man on earth
had cause to blame the brothers for accepting
such wealth, they had earned it by sheer audacity.
Then, as a pledge of friendship, Hygelac gave
Eofor his only daughter to grace his home.
2990   "That is the history of hatred and feud
and deadly enmity; and because of it,
I expect the Swedes to attack us
as soon as they hear our lord is lifeless—
he who in earlier days defended a land
2995   and its treasure against two monstrous enemies
after the death of its heroes, daring Scyldings,
he who protected the people, and achieved feats
all but impossible.
           "Let us lose no time now
but go and gaze there upon our king
3000   and carry him, who gave us rings,
to the funeral pyre. And let us not grudge gold
to melt with that bold man, for we have a mighty hoard,
a mint of precious metal, bought with pain;
and now, from this last exploit, a harvest
3005   he paid for with his own life; these the fire
shall devour, the ravening flames embrace.
No thane shall wear or carry these treasures
in his memory, no fair maiden shall hang
an ornament of interlinked rings at her throat,
3010   but often and again, desolate, deprived of gold,
they must tread the paths of exile,
now that their lord has laid aside laughter,
festivity, happiness. Henceforth, fingers must grasp,
hands must hold, many a spear
3015   chill with the cold of morning; no sound of the harp
shall rouse the warriors but, craving for carrion,
the dark raven shall have its say
and tell the eagle how it fared at the feast
when, competing with the wolf, it laid bare the bones of corpses."
3020   Thus the brave messenger told of and foretold

harrowing times; and he was not far wrong.
Those events were fated. Every man in the troop
stood up, stained with tears, and set out
for Eagleness to see that strange spectacle.

3025 There they found him lifeless on the sand,
the soft bed where he slept, who often before
had given them rings; that good man's days
on earth were ended; the warrior-king,
lord of the Geats, had died a wondrous death.

3030 But first they saw a strange creature
there, a loathsome serpent lying
nearby; the fire-dragon, fierce
and mottled, was scorched by its own flames.
It measured fifty paces from head to tail;

3035 sometimes it had soared at night
through the cool air, then dived
to its dark lair; now it lay rigid in death,
no longer to haunt caverns under the earth.
Goblets and vessels stood by it,

3040 salvers and valuable swords, eaten through
by rust, as if they had lain
for a thousand winters in the earth's embrace.
That mighty legacy, gold of men long dead,
lay under a curse; it was enchanted

3045 so that no human might enter
the cavern save him to whom God,
the true Giver of Victories, Guardian of Men,
granted permission to plunder the hoard—
whichever warrior seemed worthy to Him.

3050 Then it was clear that, whoever devised it,
the evil scheme of hiding the hoard under the rock
had come to nothing; the guardian had killed
a brave and famous man; that feud
was violently avenged. The day that a warrior,

3055 renowned for his courage, will reach the end
(as fate ordains) of his life on earth,
that hour when a man may feast in the hall
with his friends no longer, is always unpredictable.
It was thus with Beowulf when he tracked down

3060 and attacked the barrow's guardian; he himself
was not aware how he would leave this world.
The glorious princes who first placed that gold there
had solemnly pronounced that until domesday
any man attempting to plunder the hoard

3065 should be guilty of wickedness, confined,
tormented and tortured by the devil himself.
Never before had Beowulf been granted
such a wealth of gold by the gracious Lord.
Wiglaf, the son of Weohstan, said:

3070 "Many thanes must often suffer
because of the will of one, as we do now.
We could not dissuade the king we loved,

or in any way restrain the lord of our land
from drawing his sword against the gold-warden,
3075   from letting him lie where he had long lain
and remain in his lair until the world's end;
but he fulfilled his high destiny. The hoard,
so grimly gained, is now easy of access;
our king was driven there by too harsh a fate.
3080   I took the path under the earth-wall,
entered the hall and examined all
the treasures after the dragon deserted it;
I was hardly invited there. Hurriedly
I grasped as many treasures as I could,
3085   a huge burden, and carried them here
to my king; he was still alive then,
conscious and aware of this world around him.
He found words for his thronging thoughts,
born of sorrow, asked me to salute you,
3090   said that as a monument to your lord's exploits
you should build a great and glorious barrow
over his pyre, for he of all men
was the most famous warrior on the wide earth
for as long as he lived, happy in his stronghold.
3095   Now let us hurry once more together
and see the hoard of priceless stones,
that wonder under the wall; I will lead you
so that you will come sufficiently close
to the rings, the solid gold. After we
3100   get back, let us quickly build the bier,
and then let us carry our king,
the man we loved, to where he must
long remain in the Lord's protection."
        Then the brave warrior, Weohstan's son,
3105   directed that orders be given to many men
(to all who owned houses, elders of the people)
to fetch wood from far to place beneath
their prince on the funeral pyre:
                                "Now flames,
the blazing fire, must devour the lord of warriors
3110   who often endured the iron-tipped arrow-shower,
when the dark cloud loosed by bow strings
broke above the shield-wall, quivering;
when the eager shaft, with its feather garb,
discharged its duty to the barb."
3115   I have heard that Weohstan's wise son
summoned from Beowulf's band his seven
best thanes, and went with those warriors
into the evil grotto; the man leading
the way grasped a brand. Then those retainers
3120   were not hesitant about rifling the hoard
as soon as they set eyes on any part of it,
lying unguarded, gradually rusting,
in that rock cavern; no man was conscience-stricken

about carrying out those priceless treasures
3125   as quickly as he could. Also, they pushed the dragon,
the serpent over the precipice; they let the waves take him,
the dark waters embrace the warden of the hoard.
Then the wagon was laden with twisted gold,
with treasures of every kind, and the king,
3130   the old battle-warrior, was borne to Whaleness.
     Then, on the headland, the Geats prepared a mighty pyre
for Beowulf, hung round with helmets and shields
and shining mail, in accordance with his wishes;
and then the mourning warriors laid
3135   their dear lord, the famous prince, upon it.
     And there on Whaleness, the heroes kindled
the most mighty of pyres; the dark wood-smoke
soared over the fire, the roaring flames
mingled with weeping—the winds' tumult subsided—
3140   until the body became ash, consumed even
to its core. The heart's cup overflowed;
they mourned their loss, the death of their lord.
And, likewise, a maiden of the Geats,
with her tresses swept up, intoned
3145   a dirge for Beowulf time after time,
declared she lived in dread of days to come
dark with carnage and keening, terror of the enemy,
humiliation and captivity.
                          Heaven swallowed the smoke.
     Then the Geats built a barrow on the headland—
3150   it was high and broad, visible from far
to all seafarers; in ten days they built the beacon
for that courageous man; and they constructed
as noble an enclosure as wise men
could devise, to enshrine the ashes.
3155   They buried rings and brooches in the barrow,
all those adornments that brave men
had brought out from the hoard after Beowulf died.
They bequeathed the gleaming gold, treasure of men,
to the earth, and there it still remains
3160   as useless to men as it was before.
     Then twelve brave warriors, sons of heroes,
rode round the barrow, sorrowing;
they mourned their king, chanted
an elegy, spoke about that great man:
3165   they exalted his heroic life, lauded
his daring deeds; it is fitting for a man,
when his lord and friend must leave this life,
to mouth words in his praise
and to cherish his memory.
3170   Thus the Geats, his hearth-companions,
grieved over the death of their lord;
they said that of all kings on earth
he was the kindest, the most gentle,
the most just to his people, the most eager for fame.

The Táin Bó Cuailnge

The Táin Bó Cuailnge (The Cattle Raid of Colley, pronounced "Toin Bow Coo-ling-e"), the chief work in the "Ulster Cycle" of Irish heroic narratives, was already a famed and ancient story by the twelfth century, when it was copied into the manuscript now called the Book of Leinster. That manuscript also contains a legend about the recovery of the whole *Táin* by the poets of Ireland, who knew it only in fragments. Followers of the chief poet set out for Brittany, the story reports, where a complete copy had been carried. In the course of their journey, though, they pass the grave of Fergus mac Roich (guttural "ch"), an earlier poet and a hero in the events of the *Táin*. Alone at the grave, the chief poet's son calls up the spirit of Fergus, who recites to him the tale in its entirety.

This legend offers a window on Irish literary culture and its sense of the past at the time when the *Táin* was written down. The legend comes from a world of written books that could be sought out and copied; yet it also recalls the prestige and priority of an oral tradition in which the ghost of Fergus might chant the work across three days and nights. The rigorous education of Irish poets, and their habits of composition in the vernacular, remained largely oral for centuries after a usable alphabet and books had come into circulation. Further, the story evokes the aura of magic surrounding poets in medieval Ireland and the poets' own sense of themselves as spiritual and even genealogical heirs of an ancient calling which stretched back into the mythic past. Ireland had developed a deeply Christian culture yet celebrated pagan stories and did so with a vigor that has little of the elegiac nostalgia and biblical echoes seen in *Beowulf*. The highest class of poets, the *filid* (singular *fili*), also inherited practices like divination which had been the work of other learned classes, such as the druids, in the pagan era. Poets were advisors to great men, at once honored for their arcane learning and feared for the satires in which they might reproach and humiliate even the most powerful king.

If the Book of Leinster thus displays a lively but complicated connection to a rich literary past, the *Táin* itself looks backward to a still more ancient world of warring heroes, magical weapons, shape-shifters, and wondrous beasts, in which the line between mortals and gods was blurry and often crossed. The earliest version of the *Táin* stems from an oral tradition perhaps as early as the fourth century, but the society it depicts—with warriors riding in battle chariots,

The Ardagh Chalice. Early 8th century. This exquisite communion vessel has the names of the apostles engraved in a ring below the lip. The chalice represents a high point in the revival of the fine metalwork which had been part of Celtic culture for centuries.

fighting naked, and taking the heads of conquered enemies—mirrors what we know of Celtic peoples on the Continent as early as the second century B.C. The Roman geographer Strabo called the "whole race . . . madly fond of war, high-spirited and quick to battle." Some of their habits persisted in Ireland but were long over by the sixth century A.D. Other social practices—such as clientship, rigid standards of hospitality, and the obligation to safeguard anyone taken under protection—continued late into the medieval period.

Four great stories converge in the *Táin*. It draws, first, on the history of the bulls Finnbennach the White Horned and Donn Cuailnge the Brown Bull of Cooley, who originated as two pig-keepers and passed through a series of animal forms before the moment of the main narrative. Second, the immediate occasion of the cattle raid emerges from a debate between Ailill (*Al-il*), king of Connacht, and his wife, Medb (Maive). Medb's quest to match the wealth of Ailill leads her into an armed attempt to take Donn Cuailnge from its owner on the borderlands of Ulster. To achieve this end, third, Medb and Ailill gather an army to march against Ulster. Finally, the hero Cú Chulainn (coo-*chull*-in, guttural "ch") single-handedly protects Ulster's borders until the men of Ulster can recover from a seasonal debility with which they have been long cursed.

The debate of Ailill and Medb introduces one of the most powerful women in medieval Irish literature, stemming partly from a pagan goddess of sovereignty. Medb and similar women reflect a persistent aspect of mythic and literary imagination in the Irish heroic narratives, although in medieval Irish law women actually had fewer rights than their Anglo-Saxon counterparts. The story acknowledges Medb's power as a wealthy woman, leader of armies, and queen, but constantly places that power in question. Indeed, several important men are openly hostile to Medb's strong will; even the bull Finnbennach is in Ailill's herds because he refused to be owned by a woman. Yet Medb's role is emphasized in the version of the *Táin* translated here, which transfers to her a number of key actions that other versions attribute to her husband. Medb's power is explicitly sexual. Far from the passive object of desire that we often meet elsewhere in the period, she uses her sexuality as an active force, often frankly used for political gain. Yet Medb is much more than a cunning body; she exploits her wealth and is willing to debate and even to battle with her own ally and husband over issues of military strategy.

The armies that gather against the Ulstermen are replete with heroic fighters and complex allegiances, and the *Táin*'s emotional weight lies in the passionate devotion and divided loyalties of its warriors. There is particular sadness in the plight of a group of Ulstermen, among them Fergus mac Roich, whose own king Conchobor had killed men taken under their protection; they have fled his court and placed themselves in the service of Ailill. Even more personal is the repeated clash between political fidelity and the quasi-familial link of fosterage in the story.

These issues press hard on the *Táin*'s heroic center, Cú Chulainn, the preeminent hero of the Ulster Cycle. The line between the heroic, the superhuman, and the monstrous can be fluid in the *Táin*, as it is in the curious links between Beowulf and Grendel. Cú Chulainn is of divine birth, and has performed a series of wondrous boyhood exploits, before the events of the *Táin*. Even within the *Táin*, he is persistently boyish in appearance and often distracted by activities that approach play. We witness Cú Chulainn coming into his maturity as he fights an exhausting series of border combats single-handedly and unwaveringly, and as he finally must face and defeat his foster-brother Ferdia (Fer-*di*-a). Despite this poignant humanity, Cú Chulainn possesses godlike strength and skill with weapons; yet his heroic rage works a physical distortion on him that is almost monstrous, eliciting comparisons with a giant or "a man from the sea-kingdom."

Geography is as important as heroism in the *Táin*. Battles, wonders, and other events repeatedly lead to the naming of a locale, so that the story virtually maps the mythic significance of place in the northern parts of Ireland. It also enfolds much of the genealogy of its legendary heroes. In style and theme, too, the *Táin* counterbalances the wonders of superhuman force by the works of human skill, with elaborate descriptions of clothing, ornament, and decorated weaponry. It narrates the physical beauty of men and women alike with an exquisite attention not found in *Beowulf*. Like much narrative that derives closely from its oral background, the *Táin* is as much the encyclopedia of a people's beliefs and values—or a commemoration of its past beliefs and their impact on current values—as it is a single story of heroic action.

from **The Táin**[1]

[THE PILLOW TALK]

Once when their royal bed had been prepared for them in Ráth Crúachain[2] in Connacht, Ailill and Medb spoke together as they lay on their pillow. "In truth, woman," said Ailill, "she is a well-off woman who is the wife of a nobleman." "She is indeed," said the woman; "why do you think so?" "I think so," said Ailill, "because you are better off today than when I married you." "I was well-off before marrying you," said Medb. "It was wealth that we had not heard of and did not know of," said Ailill, "but you were a woman of property, and foes from lands next to you were carrying off spoils and booty from you."

"I was not so," said Medb, "but my father was in the high-kingship of Ireland:[3] Eochu Feidlech mac Find meic Findomain meic Findeoin meic Findguill meic Rotha meic Rigéoin meic Blathachta meic Beothechta meic Enna Agnig meic Óengusa Turbig. He had six daughters: Derbriu, Ethne and Éle, Clothru, Mugain and Medb. I was the noblest and worthiest of them. I was the most generous of them in bounty and the bestowal of gifts. I was best of them in battle and fight and combat.[4] I had fifteen hundred royal mercenaries of the sons of strangers exiled from their own land and as many of the sons of native freemen within the province. And there were ten men for each mercenary of these, and nine men for every mercenary and eight men for every mercenary, and seven for every mercenary, and six for every mercenary, and five for every mercenary, and four for every mercenary, and three for every mercenary, and two for every mercenary, and one mercenary for every mercenary. I had these as my standing household," said Medb, "and for that reason my father gave me one of the provinces of Ireland, the province of Crúachu. So I am called Medb Chrúachna.

"Messengers came from Find mac Rosa Rúaid, the King of Leinster, to court me, and from Cairbre Nia Fer mac Rosa, the King of Tara, and they came from Conchobor mac Fachtna, the King of Ulster, and they came from Eochu Bec. But I did not consent, for I demanded a strange bride-gift such as no woman before me had asked of a man of the men of Ireland: a husband without miserliness, without jealousy, without fear. If my husband should be miserly, it would not be fitting for us to be together, for I am generous in largesse and the bestowal of gifts and it would be a reproach for my husband that I should be better than he in generosity, but it would be no reproach if we were equal, provided that both of us were generous. Nor would it be fitting for us

---

1. Translated by Cecile O'Rahilly, in a translation accompanying her scholarly edition of *The Táin* for the Irish Texts Society (1967). As given here, some phrasings have been modified to improve its readability as a freestanding text.
2. Ráth Crúachain (*Croo-a-chan*, guttural "ch"), the royal fortress of Connacht. Like many fortress towns in Irish legend, it was founded by a woman (Cruacha) and retained traces of its ancient role as a sacred place.
3. Early Ireland was ruled by a shifting company of petty kings, some of whom entered into clientship, a relationship of dependence and service, with "high kings." The idea of a high king of all Ireland was pure legend until long after the era of the *Táin*. The genealogy that follows (both "mac" and "meic" mean "son of") grounds the claim to kingship.
4. Medb's wealth and military resources probably derive from her namesake, the goddess of sovereignty on whose assent (and sometimes sexual favors) the kingship depended.

to be together if my husband were timorous, for single-handed I am victorious in battles and contests and combats, and it would be a reproach to my husband that his wife should be more courageous than he, but it is no reproach if they are equal, provided that both are courageous. Nor would it be fitting if the man with whom I should be were jealous, for I was never without one lover quickly succeeding another.

Now I have just such a husband: you, Ailill mac Rosa Rúaid of Leinster. You are not miserly, you are not jealous, you are not inactive. I gave you a contract and a bride-price as befits a woman: the raiment of twelve men, a chariot worth thrice seven *cumala*,[5] the breadth of your face in red gold, the weight of your left arm in white bronze. Whoever brings shame and annoyance and confusion on you, you have no claim for compensation or for honor-price for it except what claim I have," said Medb, "for you are a man dependent on a woman's marriage-portion."

"I was not so," said Ailill, "but I had two brothers, one of them reigning over Tara, the other over Leinster, Find over Leinster and Cairbre over Tara. I left the rule to them because of their seniority but they were no better in bounty and the bestowal of gifts than I. And I heard of no province in Ireland dependent on a woman except this province alone, so I came and assumed the kingship here in virtue of my mother's rights, for Máta Muirisc the daughter of Mága was my mother. And what better queen could I have than you, for you are the daughter of the high-king of Ireland." "Nevertheless," said Medb, "my property is greater than yours." "I marvel at that," said Ailill, "for there is none who has greater possessions and riches and wealth than I, and I know that there is not."

They had brought to them what was least valuable among their possessions that they might know which of them had more goods and riches and wealth. They had brought to them their wooden cups and their vats and their iron vessels, their cans, their washing-basins and their tubs. They had brought to them their rings and their bracelets and their thumb-rings, their treasures of gold and their garments, purple as well as blue and black and green, yellow and vari-colored and gray, dun and checkered and striped.

Their great flocks of sheep were brought from fields and lawns and open plains. They were counted and reckoned and it was recognized that they were equal, of the same size and of the same number. Among Medb's sheep there was a splendid ram which was the equivalent of a *cumal* in value, but among Ailill's sheep was a ram corresponding to him. From grazing lands and paddocks were brought their horses and steeds. In Medb's horse-herd there was a splendid horse which might be valued at a *cumal*. Ailill had a horse to match him. Then their great herds of swine were brought from woods and sloping glens and solitary places. They were counted and reckoned and recognized. Medb had a special boar and Ailill had another. Then their herds of cows, their cattle and their droves were brought to them from the woods and waste places of the province. They were counted and reckoned and recognized, and they were of equal size and equal number.

But among Ailill's cows there was a special bull. He had been a calf of one of Medb's cows, and his name was Findbennach.[6] But he deemed it unworthy of him to be counted as a woman's property, so he went and took his place among the king's cows. It seemed to Medb as if she owned not a penny of possessions since she had not a bull as great as that among her kine.

---

5. An amount usually set at the value of three milch cows.

6. "Finn-ven-ach," a gigantic, blood-red bull with white head and feet. He and Donn Cúailgne, the Brown Bull of Cooley, are the final incarnation of two pig-keepers who fought over their supernatural powers in a series of animal and human shapes.

Then Mac Roth the herald was summoned to Medb and she asked him to find out where in any province of Ireland there might be a bull such as he. "I know indeed," said Mac Roth, "where there is a bull even better and more excellent than he, in the province of Ulster in the cantred of Cúailnge[7] in the house of Dáire mac Fiachna. Donn Cúailnge is his name." "Go you there, Mac Roth, and ask of Dáire for me a year's loan of Donn Cúailnge. At the year's end he will get the fee for the bull's loan, namely, fifty heifers, and Donn Cúailnge himself returned. And take another offer with you, Mac Roth: if the people of that land and country object to giving that precious possession Donn Cúailnge, let Dáire himself come with his bull and he shall have the extent of his own lands in the level plain of Mag Aí and a chariot worth thrice seven *cumala*, and he shall have my own intimate friendship."

Then the messengers proceeded to the house of Dáire mac Fiachna. The number of Mac Roth's embassy was nine messengers. Mac Roth was welcomed in the house of Dáire. That was only right for Mac Roth was the chief herald of all. Dáire asked Mac Roth what was the cause of his journey and why he had come. The herald told why he had come and related the contention between Medb and Ailill. "So I have come to ask for a loan of the Donn Cúailnge to match the Findbennach," he he said, "and you shall get the fee for his loan, fifty heifers and the return of Donn Cúailnge him-self. And there is something more: come yourself with your bull and you shall get an area equal to your own lands in the level plain of Mag Aí and a chariot worth thrice seven *cumala* and Medb's intimate friendship to boot." Dáire was well pleased with that and in his pleasure he shook himself so that the seams of the flock-bed cushions beneath him burst asunder, and he said: "By the truth of my conscience, even if the Ulstermen object, this precious possession Donn Cúailnge, will now be taken to Ailill and Medb in the land of Connacht." Mac Roth was pleased to hear what Mac Fiachna said.

Then they were attended to and straw and fresh rushes were strewn underfoot for them. The choicest food was served to them and a drinking feast provided until they were merry. And a conversation took place between two of the messengers. "Truly," said one messenger, "our host is generous." "Generous indeed," said the other. "Is there any Ulsterman who is more generous than he?" said the first messenger. "There is indeed," said the second. "More generous is Conchobor[8] whose vassal Dáire is, and it would be no shame if all Ulstermen should rally round Conchobor." "A great act of generosity it is indeed for Dáire to have given Donn Cúailnge to us nine messengers! It would have been the work of the four great provinces of Ireland to carry him off from the land of Ulster." Then a third messenger joined their conversation. "And what are you saying?" he asked. "That messenger says that the man in whose house we are is a generous man." "He is generous indeed," says another. "Is there any Ulsterman who is more generous than he?" asks the first messenger. "There is indeed," says the second. "Conchobor, whose vassal Dáire is, is more generous, and if all Ulstermen adhered to him it would indeed be no shame for them. It was generous of Dáire to give to us nine messengers what only the four great provinces of Ireland could carry off from the land of Ulster." "I should like to see a gush of blood and gore from the mouth that says that, for if the bull were not given willingly, he would be given perforce."

---

7. An outlying district on the east coast of Ireland.

8. "Con-chov-or" (guttural "ch"), high king of Ulster and the husband of Medb before her marriage to Ailill.

Then Dáire mac Fiachna's butler came into the house with a man carrying liquor and another carrying meat, and he heard what the messengers said. He flew into a passion and laid down the meat and drink for them; he did not invite them to consume it, nor did he tell them not to consume it. He went to the house where Dáire mac Fiachna was and said: "Was it you who gave that excellent treasure, the Donn Cúailnge, to the messengers?" "It was I indeed", said Dáire. "Where he was given may there be no proper rule, for they rightly say that if you do not give him of your own free will, you will give him by force, thanks to the armies of Ailill and Medb and the guidance of Fergus mac Róig."[9] "I swear by the gods whom I worship,"[1] Dáire replied, "unless they take him by force, they shall not take him by fair means." They spent the night talking until morning.

Early next day the messengers arose and went into the house where Dáire was. "Guide us, noble sir, to the spot where Donn Cúailnge is." "Not so indeed," said Dáire, "but if it were my custom to deal treacherously with messengers or travelers or voyagers not one of you should escape alive." "What is this?" said Mac Roth. "There is great cause for it," said Dáire. "You said that if I did not give the bull willingly, then I should give him under compulsion from the army of Ailill and Medb and the sure guidance of Fergus." "Nay," said Mac Roth, "whatever messengers might say as a result of indulging in your meat and drink, it should not be heeded or noticed nor accounted as a reproach to Ailill and Medb." "Yet I shall not give my bull, Mac Roth, on this occasion."

The messengers went on their way home and reached Ráth Crúachan in Connacht. Medb asked tidings of them. Mac Roth told her that they had not brought back his bull from Dáire. "What was the cause of that?" asked Medb. Mac Roth told her the reason. "There is no necessity to 'smooth the knots,' Mac Roth, for it was certain," said Medb, "that he would not be given freely if he were not given by force. So he shall be given by force."

Messengers went from Medb to the Maines[2] to bid them come to Crúachu, the seven Maines with their seven divisions of three thousand, namely, Maine Máithremail, Maine Aithremail, Maine Condagaib Uile, Maine Míngor, Maine Mórgor and Maine Conda Mó Epert. Other messengers went to the sons of Mágu,[3] namely Cet mac Mágach, Anlúan mac Mágach, Mac Corb mac Mágach, Baiscell mac Mágach, Én mac Mágach, Dóche mac Mágach and Scannal mac Mágach. These arrived, in number three thousand armed men. Other messengers went from them to Cormac Cond Longas mac Conchobuir[4] and to Fergus mac Róig, and they too came, in number three thousand.

The first band of all had shorn heads of hair. Green cloaks about them with silver brooches in them. Next to their skin they wore shirts of gold thread with insertions of red gold. They carried swords with white grips and handles of silver. "Is that Cormac yonder?" they all asked. "It is not indeed," said Medb.

The second band had newly shorn heads of hair. They wore gray cloaks and pure white shirts next to their skins. They carried swords with round guards of gold and silver handles. "Is that Cormac yonder?" they all asked. "It is not he indeed," said Medb.

9. Fergus mac Róig (or mac Roich) warrior, poet, and prophet—had been king of Ulster before Conchobor took the throne from him. Conchobor had further violated Fergus's honor by arranging the murder of men who were under his protection, after which Fergus and Ulstermen loyal to him fled into Connacht. He became an advisor to Ailill and one of Medb's many lovers.
1. A conscious historicizing reference to the polytheism of the era of the Táin.

2. The seven sons of Medb and Ailill. Only six are listed here: their names mean the Motherlike, the Fatherlike, he of All the Qualities, the Sweetly Dutiful, the Strongly Dutiful, and Above Description.
3. Another group of Connacht warriors; Cet ultimately kills Conchobor.
4. Cormac, "Leader of the Exiles," is a son of Conchobor who had fled with Fergus and entered the service of Ailill and Medb.

The last band had flowing hair, fair-yellow, golden, streaming manes. They wore purple embroidered cloaks with golden inset brooches over their breasts. They had smooth, long, silken shirts reaching to their insteps. All together they would lift their feet and set them down again. "Is that Cormac yonder?" they all asked. "It is he indeed," said Medb.

That night they pitched their camp and stronghold and there was a dense mass of smoke and fire from their camp-fires between the four fords of Aí, Áth Moga, Áth mBercna, Áth Slissen and Áth Coltna. And they stayed for a full fortnight in Ráth Crúachan of Connacht drinking and feasting and merrymaking so that their journey and hosting should be the lighter for them. And then Medb bade her charioteer harness her horses for her that she might go to speak with her druid[5] to seek foreknowledge and prophecy from him.

When Medb came to where her druid was, she asked foreknowledge and prophecy of him. "There are many who part here today from comrades and friends," said Medb, "from land and territory, from father and mother, and if not all return safe and sound, it is on me their grumbles and their curses will fall. Yet none goes forth and none stays here who is any dearer to us than we ourselves. And find out for us whether we shall come back or not." And the druid said: "Whoever comes or comes not back, you yourself will come."

The driver turned the chariot and Medb returned. She saw something that she deemed wonderful, a woman coming towards her by the shaft of the chariot. The girl was weaving a fringe, holding a weaver's beam of white bronze in her right hand with seven strips of red gold on its points. She wore a spotted, green-speckled cloak, with a round, heavy-headed brooch in the cloak above her breast. She had a crimson, rich-blooded countenance, a bright, laughing eye, thin, red lips. She had shining pearly teeth; you would have thought they were showers of fair pearls which were displayed in her head. Like new *partaing* [crimson] were her lips. The sweet sound of her voice and speech was as melodious as the strings of harps plucked by the hands of masters. As white as snow falling at night was the luster of her skin and body shining through her garments. She had long and very white feet with pink, even, round and sharp nails. She had long, fair-yellow, golden hair; three tresses of her hair wound round her head, another tress falling behind which touched the calves of her legs.

Medb gazed at her. "And what are you doing here now, girl?" said Medb. "I am promoting your interest and your prosperity, gathering and mustering the four great provinces of Ireland with you to go into Ulster for Táin Bó Cúailnge." "Why do you do that for me?" said Medb. "I have good reason to do so. I am a bondmaid of your people." "Who of my people are you?" said Medb. "That is not hard to tell. I am Feidelm the prophetess from Síd Chrúachna."[6] "Well then, Feidelm Prophetess, how do you see our army?" "I see red on them. I see crimson."

"Conchobor is suffering in his debility in Emain,"[7] said Medb. "My messengers have gone to him. There is nothing we fear from the Ulstermen. But tell the truth, Feidelm. O Feidelm Prophetess, how do you see our army?" "I see red on them. I see crimson."

---

5. Another archaizing touch. The Druids had been a pagan priestly class, expert in prophecy.

6. The *Síd* (pronounced "sheeth") was a fairy mound or underground dwelling of the superhuman races who preceded men in Ireland; Feidelm claims to come from one near Medb's capital. Her weaving may be a part of prophetic ritual.

7. Macha, a goddess of war, had come among the Ulstermen in human guise. Conchobor forced her to race with his horses even though she was pregnant. She won but gave birth just over the finish line; she cursed the Ulstermen to suffer in times of danger a period of weakness like that of a woman in labor. Only women, children, and Cú Chulainn were exempt. Emain is Conchobor's capital.

"Cuscraid Mend Macha mac Conchobuir is in Inis Cuscraid in his debility.[8] My messengers have gone to him. There is nothing we fear from the Ulstermen. But speak truth, Feidelm. O Feidelm Prophetess, how do you see our army?" "I see red upon them. I see crimson."

"Eogan mac Durthacht is at Ráth Airthir in his debility. My messengers have gone to him. There is nothing we fear from the Ulstermen. But speak truth to us, Feidelm. O Feidelm Prophetess, how do you see our army?" "I see red on them. I see crimson."

"Celtchair mac Cuthechair is in his fortress in his debility. My messengers have reached him. There is nothing we fear from the Ulstermen. But speak truth, Feidelm. O Feidelm Prophetess, how do you see our army?" "I see red on them. I see crimson."

"I care not for your reasoning, for when the men of Ireland[9] gather in one place, among them will be strife and battle and broils and affrays, in dispute as to who shall lead the van or bring up the rear or first cross ford or river or first kill swine or cow or stag or game. But speak truth to us, Feidelm. O Feidelm Prophetess, how do you see our army?" "I see red on them. I see crimson."

And Feidelm began to prophesy and foretell Cú Chulainn[1] to the men of Ireland, and she chanted a lay:

"I see a fair man who will perform weapon-feats,
with many a wound in his fair flesh.
The hero's light is on his brow,
his forehead is the meeting-place of many virtues.

"Seven gems of a hero are in his eyes.
His spear-heads are unsheathed.
He wears a red mantle with clasps.

"His face is the fairest. He amazes womenfolk,
a young lad of handsome countenance;
yet in battle he shows a dragon's form.

"His strength is that of Cú Chulainn of Muirtheimne;
I know not who is this Cú Chulainn from Murtheimne,
but this I know:
this army will be bloodstained from him.

"Four excellent daggers he has in each hand;
he will manage to ply them on the host.
Each weapon has its own special use.

"When he carries his *ga bulga*[2]
and his sword and spear,
this man wrapped in red
sets his foot on every battle-field.

---

8. Cuscraid is a son of Conchobor, suffering at his island fort.
9. The alliance of armies grouped against Ulster, sometimes specifically those allies who are not men of Connacht. In legendary times, Ulster had been the dominant province, and the *Táin* may reflect early conflicts that reduced Ulster's power and size.

1. Cú Chulainn, the "hound of Culann," so named for a boyhood feat in which he killed the savage guard dog of Culann the Smith, then offered to guard Culann's house in the dog's place.
2. The "belly spear" is one of Cú Chulainn's magical weapons, the gift of the woman warrior who trained him in arms. Once it enters the body, it opens into 30 barbs.

"His two spears across his chariot's wheel-rim,
high above valor is the distorted one.[3]
So he has appeared to me before,
but he will change his appearance again.

"He has moved forward to the battle.
If he is not warded off, there will be destruction.
It is he who seeks you in combat:
Cú Chulainn mac Sualtaim.

"He will lay low your entire army,
and he will slaughter you in dense crowds.
Ye shall leave with him all your heads—
the prophetess Feidelm conceals it not.

"Blood will flow from heroes' bodies.
Long will it be remembered:
Men's bodies will be hacked, women will lament,
through the Hound of the Smith that I see."

This has been the prophecy and augury, and the prelude to the tale, the basis of its invention and composition, and the pillow-talk held by Ailill and Medb in Crúachu.

[THE TÁIN BEGINS]

This is the route of the Táin and the beginning of the army's march together with the names of the roads on which the men of the four great provinces of Ireland traveled into the land of Ulster:[1]

To Mag Cruinn, by way of Tuaim Móna, by Turloch Teóra Crích, by Cúl Sílinne, by Dubfid, by Badbna, by Coltan, across the river Shannon, by Glúine Gabur, by Mag Trega, by northern Tethba, by southern Tethba, by Cúil, by Ochain, by Uata northwards, by Tiarthechta eastwards, by Ord, by Slass, across the river Inneoin, by Carn, across Meath, by Ortrach, by Findglassa Asail, by Drong, by Delt, by Duelt, by Deland, by Selach, by Slabra, by Slechta which was cleared by swords for Medb and Ailill's passage, by Cúil Siblinne, by Dub, by Ochan, by Catha, by Cromma, by Tromma, by Fodromma, by Sláine by Gort Sláine, by Druimm Licci, by Áth nGabla, by Ardachad, by Feoraind, by Findabair, by Aisse, by Airne, by Aurthaile, by Druimm Salaind, by Druimm Caín, by Druimm Caimthechta, by Druimm mac nDega, by Eódond Bec, by Eódond Mór, by Méide in Togmaill, by Méide ind Eoin, by Baile, by Aile, by Dall Scena, by Ball Scena, by Ros Mór, by Scúap, by Timscúap, by Cend Ferna, by Ammag, by Fid Mór in Crannach Cúailnge, by Druimm Caín to Slige Midlúachra.

After the first day's march, the armies spent that night in Cúil Silinne and Ailill mac Rosa's tent was pitched for him. Fergus mac Róich's tent was on his right hand. Cormac Cond Longas mac Conchobuir was beside Fergus. Íth mac Étgaíth was next, then Fiachu mac Fir Aba, then Goibnend mac Lurgnig. Such was the placing of

---

3. In his battle frenzy Cú Chulainn undergoes a monstrous distortion or "warp-spasm," one eye swelling over his cheek, a beam of light leaping from his forehead, and blood erupting from his skull.

1. The following catalog of place-names, along with genealogies elsewhere, is typical of the encyclopedic impulse in the Táin. Much of the list can be traced on a map, though it diverges from the armies' route in the narrative that follows.

Ailill's tent on his right during that hosting, and thus were the thirty hundred men of Ulster at his right hand so that the confidential talk and discourse and the choicest portions of food and drink might be nearer to them. Medb Chrúachna was on Ailill's left with Findabair[2] beside her. Then came Flidais Fholtchaín, the wife of Ailill Find, who had slept with Fergus on Táin Bó Cúailnge, and it was she who every seventh night on that hosting quenched with milk the thirst of all the men of Ireland, king and queen and prince, poet and learner. Medb was the last of the hosts that day for she had been seeking foreknowledge and prophecy and tidings, to learn who was loath and who was eager to go on the expedition. Medb did not permit her chariot to be let down or her horses to be unyoked until she had made a circuit of the encampment.

[THE LAST BATTLE][1]

In the same night Dubthach Dáel Ulad spoke these words among the men of Ireland in Slemain Mide: *Móra maitne*. . . .[2]

Then Dubthach awoke from his sleep and the Nemain[3] brought confusion on the host so that they made a clangor of arms with the points of their spears and their swords, and a hundred warriors of them died on the floor of their encampment through the fearsomeness of the shout they had raised. This was not the most peaceful night ever experienced by the men of Ireland, because of the prophecies and the predictions and because of the specters and visions which appeared to them.

Then said Ailill: "I have succeeded in laying waste Ulster and the land of the Picts from the Monday at the beginning of Samain until the beginning of spring.[4] We have carried off their women-folk, their sons and their youths, their horses and steeds, their flocks and herds and cattle. We have leveled their hills behind them into lowlands, so that they might be of equal height. So I shall not wait here for them any longer, but let them give me battle on Mag Aí if they like. And yet though we say this, let some one go forth to reconnoiter the broad plain of Meath to see whether the Ulstermen come there, and if they do, I shall not retreat, for it is not the good custom of a king ever to retreat." "Who should go there?" everyone said: "Who but Mac Roth, the chief messenger yonder."

Mac Roth went out to reconnoiter the great plain of Meath. Soon he heard a noise and a tumult and a clamor. It seemed to him almost as if the sky had fallen onto the surface of the earth, or as if the fish-abounding, blue-bordered sea had swept across the face of the world, or as if the earth had split in an earthquake, or as if the

2. "Fin-av-ir," the daughter of Medb and Ailill, used more than once by Medb as a sexual pawn.

1. In the intervening episodes, the men of Ireland do succeed in seizing the Brown Bull of Cooley. The armies of Medb and Ailill also move around a large part of central and northern Ireland, trying to penetrate the borders of Ulster. Cú Chulainn repeatedly prevents this, despite the continuing weakness of the Ulstermen. He first places impassable taboo signs along their route, then stages night raids on the armies, and finally conducts an exhausting series of single combats, mostly at fords, which climax in a three-day battle with his beloved foster-brother Ferdia. In the face of his onslaught and the gathering army of the now-strong Ulstermen, the men of Ireland have retreated into Meath, moving back toward Connacht. Near collapse, Cú Chulainn is guarded by his

father the god Lug and tied down with wooden hoops lest he return to battle and injure himself mortally.

2. "Duv-thach" the black-tongued, another Ulster warrior, appears to have a prophetic vision in his sleep and calls out to the men around him. His words are in a form and vocabulary of virtually untranslatable obscurity, called "rosc." A series of such archaic and obscure prophecies punctuates the later parts of the story (see pp. 108–109) and is left untranslated here.

3. "Ne-van," or Panic, one of a group of war goddesses and wife of the war god, Net.

4. Samain is a pre-Christian festival in late fall. The Ulstermen have suffered from their debility for most of the time from then until spring, which may link their weakness and returning strength to seasonal cycles and even vegetation ritual.

trees of the forest had all fallen into each other's forked trunks and branches. The wild beasts were fleeing across the plain in such numbers that the surface of the plain of Meath was not visible beneath them.

Mac Roth went to where Ailill was with Medb and Fergus and the nobles of the men of Ireland. He related those tidings to them. "What was that, Fergus?" asked Ailill. "Not difficult to tell," said Fergus. "The noise and clamor and tumult that he heard, the din and the thunder and the uproar, were the Ulstermen attacking the wood, the throng of champions and warriors cutting down the trees with their swords in front of their chariots. It was that which scattered the wild beasts across the plain so that the surface of the plain of Meath is not visible beneath them."

Once more Mac Roth scanned the plain. He saw a great gray mist which filled the void between heaven and earth. He seemed to see islands in lakes above the slopes of the mist. He seemed to see yawning caverns in the forefront of the mist itself. It seemed to him that pure-white linen cloths or sifted snow dropping down appeared through a rift in the same mist. He seemed to see a large flock of varied, wonderful, birds, or the shimmering of shining stars on a bright, frosty night, or the sparks of a blazing fire. He heard a noise and a tumult, a din and thunder, a clamor and uproar. He went to tell those tidings to Ailill and Medb and Fergus and the nobles of the men of Ireland. He told them these things.

"What was that, Fergus?" asked Ailill. "Not difficult to tell," said Fergus. "The gray mist he saw which filled the void between earth and sky was the breathing of horses and heroes, and the cloud of dust from the ground and from the roads which rises above them driven by the wind so that it becomes a heavy, deep-gray mist in the clouds and in the air.

"The islands in lakes which he saw there, and the tops of hills and mounds rising above the valleys of the mist, were the heads of the heroes and warriors above their chariots and the chariots themselves. The yawning caverns he saw there in the fore-front of the same mist were the mouths and nostrils of horses and heroes, exhaling and inhaling the sun and the wind with the swiftness of the host.

"The pure-white linen cloths he saw there or the sifted snow dropping down were the foam and froth that the bits of the reins cast from the mouths of the strong, stout steeds with the fierce rush of the host. The large flock of varied, wonderful birds which he saw there was the dust of the ground and the surface of the earth which the horses flung up from their feet and their hooves and which rose above them with the driving of the wind.

"The noise and the tumult, the din and the thunder, the clamor and the outcry which he heard there was the shock of shields and the smiting of spears and the loud striking of swords, the clashing of helmets, the clangor of breastplates, the friction of the weapons and the vehemence of the feats of arms, the straining of ropes, the rattle of wheels, the trampling of the horses' hoofs and the creaking of chariots, and the loud voices of heroes and warriors coming towards us here.

"The shimmering of shining stars on a bright night that he saw there, or the sparks of a blazing fire, were the fierce, fearsome eyes of the warriors and heroes from the beautiful, shapely, ornamented helmets, eyes full of the fury and anger with which they came, against which neither equal combat nor overwhelming number prevailed at any time and against which none will ever prevail until the day of doom."

"We make little account of it," said Medb. "Goodly warriors and goodly soldiers will be found among us to oppose them." "I do not count on that, Medb," said Fergus, "for I pledge my word that you will not find in Ireland or in Alba a host which could oppose the Ulstermen when once their fits of wrath come upon them."

The four great provinces of Ireland made their encampment at Clártha that night. They left a band to keep watch and guard against the Ulstermen lest they should come upon them unawares.

Conchobor and Celtchair set forth with thirty hundred chariot-fighters armed with spears and halted in Slemain Mide[5] in the rear of the host. But though we say "halted," they did not halt completely, but soon came forward to the encampment of Medb and Ailill in an attempt to be the first to shed blood. * * *[6]

"Come now, men of Ireland," said Ailill, "let someone go to reconnoiter the broad plain of Meath to find out how the Ulstermen come to the hill in Slemain Mide and to give us an account of their arms and equipment, their heroes and soldiers and their battle-champions and the people of their land. It will be all the more pleasant for us to listen to him now." "Who should go there?" asked they all. "Who but Mac Roth, the chief messenger," said Ailill.

Mac Roth came forward and took up his station in Slemain Mide to await the Ulstermen. The Ulstermen began to muster on that hill and continued doing so from the twilight of early morning until sunset. In all that time the ground was hardly bare of them as they came with every division round its king, every band round its leader, and every king and every leader and every lord with the full number of his own forces and his army, his muster and his gathering. Before the hour of evening sunset all the Ulstermen had reached that hill in Slemain Mide.

Mac Roth went to Ailill and Medb and Fergus and the nobles of the men of Ireland, bringing an account of the first band. Ailill and Medb asked tidings of him on his arrival. "Well now, O Mac Roth," said Ailill, "in what guise and fashion do the men of Ulster come to the hill in Slemain Mide?"

"This is all I know," said Mac Roth. "There came a fierce, powerful, well-favored band onto that hill in Slemain Mide. It seems, if one looks at it, as if it numbered thirty hundred. They all cast off their garments and dug up a mound of turf as a seat for their leader. A warrior, slender, very tall, of great stature and of proud mien, at the head of that band. Finest of the princes of the world was he among his troops, in fearsomeness and horror, in battle and in contention. Fair yellow hair he had, curled, well-arranged, ringletted, cut short. His countenance was comely and clear crimson. An eager gray eye in his head, fierce and awe-inspiring. A forked beard, yellow and curly, on his chin. A purple mantle fringed, five-folded, about him and a golden brooch in the mantle over his breast. A pure-white, hooded shirt with inserts of red gold he wore next to his white skin. He carried a white shield ornamented with animal designs in red gold. In one hand he had a gold-hilted, ornamented sword, in the other a broad, gray spear. That warrior took up position at the top of the hill and everyone came to him and his company took their places around him.

"There came also another band to the same hill in Slemain Mide," said Mac Roth. "It numbered almost thirty hundred. A handsome man in the forefront of that same band. Fair yellow hair he had. A bright and very curly beard on his chin. A green mantle wrapped around him. A pure silver brooch in the mantle over his breast. A dark-red, soldierly tunic with insertion of red gold next to his fair skin and reaching to his knees. A spear like the torch of a royal palace in his hand, with bands of silver and rings of gold. Wonderful are the feats and games performed by that spear in the warrior's hand. The silver bands revolve round the golden rings alternately

5. In Meath, between Ulster and Connacht. The men of Ulster are now pursuing Medb and Ailill.

6. At this point more Ulster warriors assemble to oppose Medb and Ailill.

from butt to socket, and the golden rings revolve round the silver bands from socket to thong. He bore a smiting shield with scalloped rim. On his left side a sword with guards of ivory and ornament of gold thread. That warrior sat on the left hand of the warrior who had first come to the hill, and his company sat around him. But though we say that they sat, yet they did not really do so, but knelt on the ground with the rim of their shields at their chins, in their eagerness to be let at us. And yet it seemed to me that the tall, fierce warrior who led that company stammered greatly.

"Yet another company came to the same hill in Slemain Mide," said Mac Roth, "very like the preceding one in number and appearance and apparel. A handsome, broad-headed warrior in the van of that company. Thick, dark-yellow hair he had. An eager, dark-blue, restless eye in his head. A bright and very curly beard, forked and tapering, on his chin. A dark-gray, fringed cloak wrapped about him. A leaf-shaped brooch of white bronze in the cloak over his breast. A white-hooded shirt next to his skin. A white shield with animal ornaments of silver he carried. A sword with rounded hilt of bright silver in a warlike scabbard at his waist. A spear like the pillar of a palace on his back. This warrior sat on the turfy mound in front of the warrior who had come first to the hill, and his company took up their positions around him. But sweeter I thought than the sound of lutes in the hands of expert players was the melodious tone of the voice and speech of that warrior as he addressed the warrior who had come first to the hill and gave him counsel."

"Who are those?" asked Ailill of Fergus. "We know them indeed," said Fergus. "The first warrior for whom the sodded mound was cast up on the top of the hill until they all came to him was Conchobor mac Fachtna Fáthaig meic Rosa Rúaid meic Rudraige, the high-king of Ulster and the son of the high-king of Ireland. The great stammering hero who took up his position on the left of Conchobor was Causcraid Mend Macha, the son of Conchobar, with the sons of the Ulster princes around him and the sons of the kings of Ireland who are with him. The spear with silver bands and rings of gold that Mac Roth saw in his hand is called the Torch of Causcraid. With that spear, the silver bands do not revolve around the golden rings except shortly before some victory, and not at any other time, and it is likely that they are now revolving just before victory.

"The handsome, broad-headed warrior who sat on the mound in front of the warrior who had first come to the hill was Sencha mac Ailella meic Máilchló, the eloquent speaker of Ulster, the man who appeases the armies of the men of Ireland. But I pledge my word that he is not giving his lord counsel of cowardice or fear in this day of battle, but counsel to act with valor and bravery, courage and might. And I pledge my word too," said Fergus, "that those who rose up around Conchobor in the early morning today are fine men who can carry out such deeds." "We care little for them," said Medb. "There will be found among us fine heroes and fine warriors to answer them." "I don't count on that," said Fergus, "but I swear that you will not find in Ireland or in Alba an army which can answer the Ulstermen when once their fits of wrath have come upon them."[7] * * *

"Yet another company came to the same hill in Slemain Mide," said Mac Roth, "which numbered no less than thirty hundred. Fierce, bloodstained warrior bands. Fair, clear, blue and crimson men. They had long, fair-yellow hair, beautiful, brilliant countenances, clear kingly eyes. Shining, beautiful garments they wore. Wonderful,

7. In the following section, omitted here, Mac Roth continues with a catalog of sixteen more war bands and their leaders, coming to support Conchobor.

golden brooches on their bright-hued arms. Silken, fine-textured shirts. Shining, blue spears they carried. Yellow, smiting shields. Gold-hilted ornamented swords are set on their thighs. Loud-voiced care has come to them. Sad are all the horsemen. Sorrowful are the royal leaders. Orphaned the bright company without their protecting lord who used to defend their borders." "Who are these?" asked Ailill of Fergus. "We know them indeed," said Fergus. "They are fierce lions. They are champions of battle. They are the thirty hundred from Mag Muirtheimne. The reason they are downcast, sorrowful and joyless, is because their territorial king is not among them—Cú Chulainn, the restraining, victorious, red-sworded, triumphant one." "They have good cause," said Medb, "to be downcast, sorrowful and joyless, for there is no evil we have not wrought on them. We have plundered them and we have ravaged them from the Monday at the beginning of Samain until the beginning of spring. We have carried off their women and their sons and their youths, their horses and their steeds, their herds and their flocks and their cattle. We have cast down their hills behind them on to their slopes until they were of equal height." "You have no reason to boast over them, Medb," said Fergus, "for you did no harm or wrong to them that the leader of that fine band yonder has not avenged on you, since every mound and every grave, every tombstone and every tomb from here to the eastern part of Ireland is a mound and a grave, a tombstone and a tomb for some fine hero or for some brave warrior slain by the valiant leader of yonder band. Fortunate is he whom they will uphold! Woe to him whom they will oppose! They alone will be as much as half an army against the men of Ireland when they defend their lord in the battle tomorrow morning."

"I heard a great outcry there," said Mac Roth, "to the west of the battle or to the east of the battle." "What outcry was that?" asked Ailill of Fergus. "We know it indeed," said Fergus. "That was Cú Chulainn trying to come to the battle when he was being laid prostrate on his sick-bed in Fert Sciach, with wooden hoops and restraining bands and ropes holding him down, for the Ulstermen do not allow him to come because of his wounds and gashes, for he is unfit for battle and combat after his fight with Fer Diad."

It was as Fergus said. That was Cú Chulainn being laid prostrate on his sick-bed in Fert Sciach, held down with hoops and restraining bands and ropes.

Then two female satirists called Fethan and Collach came out of the encampment of the men of Ireland. They pretended to weep and lament over Cú Chulainn, telling him that the Ulstermen had been routed and that Conchobor had been killed and that Fergus had fallen in the fight against them.

It was on that night that the Morrígu daughter of Ernmas[8] came and sowed strife and dissension between the two encampments on either side, and she spoke these words: Crennait brain. . . . She whispered to the Érainn[9] that they will not fight the battle which lies ahead.

Then said Cú Chulainn to Láeg mac Riangabra[1]: "Alas for you, my friend Láeg, if anything happens today between the two battle-forces that you don't find out for me." "Whatever I find out, little Cú," said Láeg, "shall be told to you. But see a little flock coming from the west out of the encampment now onto the plain. There is a

---

8. Morrígu (or Morrigan, later Morgan), Great Queen or Queen of Demons, the major goddess of war, a shape-shifter and sower of discord.
9. The men of Ireland, that is the allies of Medb and

Ailill from outside Connacht, who now begin to withdraw their allegiance.
1. Láeg ("Loyg") is Cú Chulainn's charioteer and trusted advisor.

band of youths after them to check and hold them. See too a band of youths coming from the east out of the encampment to seize them." "That is true indeed," said Cú Chulainn. "It is the omen of a mighty combat and a cause of great strife. The little flock will go across the plain and the youths from the east will encounter those from the west." It was as Cú Chulainn said: The little flock went across the plain and the youths met. "Who gives battle now, my friend Láeg?" asked Cú Chulainn. "The people of Ulster," said Láeg, "that is, the youths."[2] "How do they fight?" asked Cú Chulainn. "Bravely," said Láeg. "The champions who come from the east will make a breach through the battle-line to the west. The champions from the west will make a breach through the battle-line to the east." "Alas that I am not strong enough to go afoot among them! For if I were, my breach too would be clearly seen there today like that of the rest." "Nay then, little Cú," said Láeg, "it is no disgrace to your valor and no reproach to your honor. You have done bravely before and you will do bravely again." "Well now, friend Láeg," said Cú Chulainn, "rouse the Ulstermen to the battle now; it is time for them to go."

Láeg came and roused the Ulstermen to the battle, and he spoke these words: Coméirget ríg Macha. . . .

Then all the Ulstermen rose up at the call of their king and at the behest of their lord and to answer the summons of Láeg mac Riangabra. They all arose stark naked except for their weapons which they bore in their hands. Each man whose tent door faced east would break westwards through his tent westwards, thinking it too long to go around.

"How do the men of Ulster rise for battle now, friend Láeg?" asked Cú Chulainn. "Bravely," answered Láeg. "All are stark naked. Each man whose tent-door faces east rushed westwards through his tent, thinking it too long to go around." "I pledge my word," said Cú Chulainn, "that their early rising around Conchobor is speedy help in answer to a call of alarm."

Then Conchobor said to Sencha mac Ailella: "Good master Sencha, hold back the men of Ulster, and do not let them come to the battle until omens and auguries are strongly in their favor and until the sun rises into the vaults of heaven and fills the glens and slopes, the hills and mounds of Ireland." There they remained until a good omen was strengthened and sunshine filled the glens and slopes and hills and mounds of the province.

"Good master Sencha," said Conchobor, "rouse the men of Ulster for battle; it is time for them to go." Sencha roused the men of Ulster for the fight, and he spoke the words: Coméirget ríg Macha. . . .

Láeg had not been there long when he saw all the men of Ireland rising together and taking up their shields and their spears and their swords and their helmets, and driving the troops before them to the battle. All the men of Ireland began to strike and smite, to hew and cut, to slay and slaughter the others for a long while. Then Cú Chulainn asked Láeg, his charioteer, when a bright cloud covered the sun: "How are they fighting the battle now, my friend Láeg?" "Bravely," said Láeg. "If we were to mount, I into my chariot and Conall's charioteer Én into his, and if we were to go in two chariots from one wing of the army to the other along the tips of their weapons, not a hoof nor a wheel nor an axle nor a shaft of those chariots would touch the

---

2. These are probably the three boy troops who train in mock battles around Conchobor's capital. Cú Chulainn, when still a boy and untutored in the ways of court, had first challenged and then joined them. Because of their age they are untouched by the debility of the Ulstermen and rush into battle before their elders.

ground, so densely, so firmly and so strongly are their weapons held in the hands of the soldiers." "Alas that I have not the strength to be among them!" said Cú Chulainn, "for if I had, my attack would be clearly seen there today like that of the rest." "Nay then, little Cú," said Láeg, "it is no disgrace to your valor and no reproach to your honor. You have done bravely before and you will do bravely again."

Then the men of Ireland began again to strike and smite, to hew and cut, to slay and slaughter the others for a long while. The nine chariot-fighters of the warriors of Irúad arrived and three men on foot together with them, and the nine chariot-riders were no swifter than the three on foot.

Then came also the *ferchuitredaig*, the triads of the men of Ireland, and their sole function in the battle was to slay Conchobor if he should be defeated and to rescue Ailill and Medb if it were they who were overcome. * * * [3]

Then said Medb to Fergus: "It would be fitting for you to aid us unstintingly in fighting today, for you were banished from your territory and your land, and we gave you territory and land and property and showed you much kindness." "If I had my sword today," said Fergus, "I would cut them down so that the trunks of men would be piled high on the trunks of men and arms of men piled high on arms of men and the crowns of men's heads piled on the crowns of men's heads and men's heads piled on the edges of shields, and all the Ulstermen's limbs I would scatter to the east and to the west would be as numerous as pebbles between two dry fields along which a king's horses drive: if only I had my sword." Then Ailill said to his own charioteer, Fer Loga: "Bring me quickly the sword that wounds men's flesh, O fellow. I pledge my word that if you take worse care of it today than on the day when I gave it to you on the hillside at Crúachna Aí, even if the men of Ireland and of Alba are protecting you against me today, not all of them will save you."[4] Fer Loga came forward and brought the sword in all the beauty of its fair condition, shining bright as a torch, and the sword was given into Ailill's hand. Ailill gave the sword to Fergus and Fergus welcomed the sword: "Welcome to you, O Caladbolg, the sword of Leite," he said. "The champions of the war-goddess are weary. On whom shall I ply this sword?" asked Fergus. "On the hosts that surround you on all sides," said Medb. "Let none receive mercy or quarter from you today except a true friend."

Then Fergus seized his weapons and went forward to the battle. Ailill seized his weapons. Medb seized her weapons and came to the battle. Three times they were victorious in the battle northwards, until a phalanx of spears and swords forced them to retreat again. Conchobor heard from his place in the battle-line that the battle had three times gone against him in the north. Then he said to his people, the intimate household of the Cráebrúad: "Take my place a while, my men, so I can go and see who is victorious three times to the north of us." Then his household said: "We shall do so, for heaven is above us and earth beneath us and the sea all around us, and unless the firmament with its showers of stars fall upon the surface of the earth, or unless the blue-bordered fish-abounding sea come over the face of the world, or unless the earth quake, we shall never retreat one inch from this spot until you come back to us again."

Conchobor went where he had heard the rout of battle against him three times in the north, and against the shield of Fergus mac Róig he raised his shield, the Óchaín Conchobuir, with its four golden corners and its four coverings of red gold.

3. There follows a catalog of these triads of warriors.
4. Ailill's charioteer had taken the sword when he spotted Fergus having sex with Medb, and Fergus was reduced to carrying a wooden sword. Ailill here reminds Fergus that he knows of the affair and leaves a hint of threat if Fergus does not use it well.

Then Fergus gave three strong, warlike blows on the Óchaín Conchobuir and Conchobor's shield groaned. Whenever Conchobor's shield groaned, the shields of all the Ulstermen groaned. Strongly and violently as Fergus struck Conchobor's shield, just as stoutly and as bravely did Conchobor hold the shield, so that the corner of the shield did not even touch Conchobor's ear.

"Alas, my men!" said Fergus, "who is it who holds his shield against me today, in this day of conflict where the four great provinces of Ireland meet at Gáirech and Ilgáirech in the battle of the Foray of Cúailnge?" "There is a man here younger and mightier than you, whose father and mother were nobler, one who banished you from your land and territory and estate, one who drove you to dwell with deer and hare and fox, one who did not permit you to hold even the length of your own stride in your land and territory, one who made you dependent on a woman of property, one who once outraged you by slaying the three sons of Usnech despite your safeguard, one who today will ward you off in the presence of the men of Ireland: Conchobor mac Fachtna Fáthaig meic Rossa Rúaid meic Rudraigi, the high king of Ulster and the son of the high king of Ireland."

"That is indeed what has happened," said Fergus. And Fergus grasped the Caladbolg in both hands and swung it back behind him so that its point touched the ground, and his intent was to strike three terrible and warlike blows on the Ulstermen so that their dead might outnumber their living. Cormac Cond Longas, the son of Conchobor, saw him; he rushed towards Fergus and clasped his arms about him. "Ready, yet not ready, my master Fergus. This is hostile and not friendly, my master Fergus. Ungentle but thoughtless, my master Fergus. Do not slay and destroy the Ulsterman with your mighty blows, but take thought for their honor on this day of battle." "Begone from me, lad," said Fergus, "for I shall not live if I do not strike my three mighty, warlike blows upon the Ulstermen today so that their living outnumber their dead."

"Turn your hand level," said Cormac Cond Longas, "and strike off the tops of the hills over the heads of the hosts; that will appease your anger." "Tell Conchobor to come then into his battle-position," Fergus replied. Conchobor came to his place in the battle.

Now that sword, the sword of Fergus, was the sword of Leite from the elf-mounds. When one wished to strike with it, it was as big as a rainbow in the air. Then Fergus turned his hand level above the heads of the hosts and cut off the tops of the three hills which are still there in the marshy plain as evidence. Those are the three Máela of Meath.

Now as for Cú Chulainn, when he heard the Óchaín Conchobuir being struck by Fergus mac Róig, he said: "Come now, my friend Láeg, who dares to smite the Óchaín of Conchobor my master while I am alive?" "This huge sword, as big as a rainbow, sheds blood, increase of slaughter," said Láeg. "It is the hero Fergus mac Róig. The chariot sword was hidden in the fairy mounds. The horsemen of my master Conchobor have reached the battlefield."

"Quick, loosen the wooden hoops over my wounds, fellow," said Cú Chulainn. Then Cú Chulainn gave a mighty spring and the wooden hoops flew from him to Mag Túaga in Connacht. The bindings of his wounds went from him to Bacca in Corco M'ruad.[5] The dry wisps of tow which plugged his wounds soared into the

5. Mag Tuaga, the Plain of Hoops, named for the hazel hoops that had held Cú Chulainn. Corco M'ruad, modern Corcomroe in County Clare.

uppermost air as high as larks soar on a day of fair weather when there is no wind. His wounds broke out afresh and the trenches and furrows in the earth were filled with his blood and the plugs from his wounds.

The first exploit which Cú Chulainn performed after rising from his sickbed was against the two female satirists, Fethan and Colla, who had been feigning to weep and lament over him. He dashed their two heads together so that he was red with their blood and gray with their brains. None of his weapons had been left beside him apart from his chariot. And he took his chariot on his back and came towards the men of Ireland, and with his chariot he smote them until he reached the spot where Fergus mac Róig stood. "Turn this way, my master Fergus," said Cú Chulainn. Fergus did not answer for he did not hear him. Cú Chulainn said again: "Turn this way, my master Fergus, or if you do not, I shall grind you as a mill grinds fine grain, I shall belabor you as flax-heads are belabored in a pool, I shall entwine you as a vine entwines trees, I shall swoop on you as a hawk swoops on little birds." "That is indeed what has happened," said Fergus. "Who dares to speak those proud, warlike words to me here where the four great provinces of Ireland meet at Gáirech and Ilgáirech in the battle of the Foray of Cúailnge?" "Your own fosterson," said Cú Chulainn, "and the fosterson of Conchobor and of the rest of the men of Ulster, Cú Chulainn mac Sualtaim. You promised that you would flee before me when I should be wounded, bloody and pierced with stabs in the battle of the Táin, for I fled before you in your own battle on the Táin."

Fergus heard that, and he turned and took three mighty, heroic strides, and when he turned, all the men of Ireland turned and were routed westwards over the hill. The conflict was centred against the men of Connacht. At midday Cú Chulainn had come to the battle. It was sunset in the evening when the last band of the men of Connacht fled westwards over the hill. By that time there remained in Cú Chulainn's hand only a fistful of the spokes around the wheel and a handful of shafts around the body of the chariot, but he kept on slaying and slaughtering the four great provinces of Ireland during all that time.

Then Medb covered the retreat of the men of Ireland and she sent the Donn Cúailnge around to Crúachu together with fifty of his heifers and eight of Medb's messengers, so that whoever might reach Crúachu or whoever might not, at least the Donn Cúailnge would arrive there as she had promised. Then her issue of blood came upon Medb and she said: "O Fergus, cover the retreat of the men of Ireland that I may pass my water." "By my conscience," said Fergus, "It is ill-timed and it is not right to do so." "Yet I must," said Medb, "for I shall not live unless I do." Fergus came then and covered the retreat of the men of Ireland. Medb passed her water and it made three great trenches in each of which a household can fit. Hence the place is called Fúal Medba.[6]

Cú Chulainn came upon her thus engaged but he did not wound her for he would not strike her from behind. "Grant me a favor today, Cú Chulainn," said Medb. "What favor do you ask?" said Cú Chulainn. "That this army may be under your protection and safeguard till they have gone westwards past Áth Mór."[7] "I grant it," said Cú Chulainn. Cú Chulainn came around the men of Ireland and covered their retreat on one side to protect them. The triads of the men of Ireland came on the other side, and Medb came into her own position and covered their retreat in the rear. In that fashion they took the men of Ireland westwards past Áth Mór.

6. The Foul Place of Medb.
7. The Ford of Mor, also called Áth Luain (modern Athlone), on the River Shannon at the border of Con-nacht. Medb is asking Cú Chulainn to spare her army in its retreat.

Then Cú Chulainn's sword was given to him and he smote a blow on the three blunt-topped hills at Áth Luain, as a counterblast to the three Máela Mide, and cut off their three tops.

Fergus began to survey the host as they went westwards from Áth Mór. "This day was indeed a fitting one for those who were led by a woman," said Fergus . . . .[8] said Medb to Fergus. "This host has been plundered and despoiled today. As when a mare goes before her band of foals into unknown territory, with none to lead or counsel them, so this host has perished today."

As for Medb, she gathered and assembled the men of Ireland to Crúachu that they might see the combat of the bulls.

When the Donn Cúailnge saw the beautiful strange land, he bellowed loudly three times. The Findbennach of Aí heard him. Because of the Findbennach no male animal between the four fords of all Mag Aí, (Áth Moga and Áth Coltna, Áth Slissen and Áth mBercha) dared utter a sound louder than the lowing of a cow. The Findbennach tossed his head violently and came forward to Crúachu to meet the Donn Cúailnge.

The men of Ireland asked who should be an eye-witness for the bulls, and they all decided that it should be Bricriu mac Garbada.[9] A year before these events in the Foray of Cúailnge, Bricriu had come from one province to another begging from Fergus, and Fergus had retained him in his service waiting for his chattels and wealth. And a quarrel arose between him and Fergus as they were playing chess, and Bricriu spoke very insultingly to Fergus. Fergus struck him with his fist and with the chessman that he held in his hand and drove the chessman into his head and broke a bone in his skull. While the men of Ireland were on the hosting of the Táin, Bricriu was being cured in Crúachu, and the day they returned from the hosting was the day Bricriu rose from his sickness. The reason they chose Bricriu in this manner was because he was no fairer to his friend than to his enemy. So Bricriu was brought to a gap in front of the bulls.

Each of the bulls caught sight of the other and they pawed the ground and cast the earth over them. They dug up the ground and threw it over their shoulders and their withers, and their eyes blazed in their heads like distended balls of fire. Their cheeks and nostrils swelled like smith's bellows in a forge. And each collided with the other with a crashing noise. Each of them began to gore and to pierce and to slay and slaughter the other. Then the Findbennach Aí took advantage of the confusion of the Donn Cúailnge's journeying and wandering and traveling, and thrust his horn into his side and visited his rage on him. Their violent rush took them to where Bricriu stood and the bulls' hooves trampled him a man's length into the ground after they had killed him.

Hence that is called the Tragical Death of Bricriu.

Cormac Cond Longas, the son of Conchobor, saw this happening and he took a spear which filled his grasp and struck three blows on the Donn Cúailnge from his ear to his tail. "This beast will be no wonderful, lasting possession for us," said Cormac, "since he cannot repel a calf of his own age." Donn Cúailnge heard this for he had human understanding, and he attacked the Findbennach, and for a long while they fought together until night fell on the men of Ireland. And when night fell, all the men of Ireland could do was to listen to their noise and their uproar. That night the bulls traversed the whole of Ireland.

8. There is a gap in the manuscript text here.   9. Bricriu "of the Poison Tongue," often a troublemaker among the heroes of the Ulster Cycle.

Not long after the men of Ireland arrived early the next day, they saw the Donn Cúailnge coming past Crúachu from the west with the Findbennach Aí a mangled mass on his antlers and horns. The men of Ireland arose and they did not know which of the bulls was there. "Well now, men," said Fergus, "leave him alone if it is the Findbennach Aí, and if it is Donn Cúailnge, leave him his triumph. I swear that what has been done concerning the bulls is but little in comparison with what will be done now."

The Donn Cúailnge arrived. He turned his right side to Crúachu and left there a heap of the liver of the Findbennach. Whence the name Crúachna Áe. He came forward to the brink of Áth Mór and there he left the loin of the Findbennach. Whence the name Áth Luain. He came eastwards into the land of Meath to Áth Troim and there he left the liver of the Findbennach. He tossed his head fiercely and shook off the Findbennach over Ireland. He threw his thigh as far as Port Lárge. He threw his rib-cage as far as Dublin which is called Áth Clíath. After that he faced towards the north and recognized the land of Cúailnge and came towards it. There there were women and boys and children lamenting the Donn Cúailnge. They saw the forehead of the Donn Cúailnge coming towards them. "A bull's forehead comes to us!" they cried. Hence the name Taul Tairb ever since.

Then the Donn Cúailnge attacked the women and boys and children of the territory of Cúailnge and inflicted great slaughter on them. After that he turned his back to the hill and his heart broke like a nut in his breast.

So far the account and the story and the end of the Táin.

A blessing on every one who shall faithfully memorize the Táin as it is written here and shall not add any other form to it.

But I who have written this story, or rather this fable, give no credence to the various incidents related in it. For some things in it are the deceptions of demons, others poetic figments; some are probable, others improbable; while still others are intended for the delectation of foolish men.

⊫◆⊠⊨

Judith

The Old English poem *Judith*, concerning the legendary beheader of the Assyrian general Holofernes, has been seen most often as a heroic poem, like *Beowulf*, which it immediately follows in the same unique manuscript. It expresses the same fierce love of battle, and uses the same heroic poetic conventions—archaic diction, formulas, and themes. *Judith* achieves ironic effects, however, by placing these conventions in unexpected contexts, for instance calling Holofernes a "brave man" as he hides behind a net to spy on his retainers. Similarly, it presents his raucous feast as an antifeast—a symbol of misrule rather than of social harmony—and his henchmen as a parody of the traditional band of loyal retainers, as they flee in terror to save their lives.

In addition to *Beowulf*, *Judith* has affinities with Old English poems based on the Old Testament, like *Exodus* and *Daniel*, whose heroes devote their military zeal to the glory of God. Like them, it assumes the timeless perspective of Christian salvation history, so that the apparent anachronisms of Judith's praying to the Trinity or Christ's abhorring Holofernes are entirely appropriate. Based on the Book of Judith in the Latin Bible, which the Anglo-Saxons considered canonical, this poem, like many others in Old English, exists only in fragmentary form.

The original audience would have known that Holofernes had entered Judea to besiege the Hebrew city of Bethulia. At the point where the Old English poem begins, the "wickedly promiscuous" general, after his drunken feast, orders the beautiful Hebrew maiden Judith to be brought to his bed. Finding him stretched out in a drunken stupor, she first prays for help and then decapitates him. She thereupon returns to her camp, brandishing the head and exhorting the Hebrews to battle with a stirring speech, which inspires them to victory over the leaderless Assyrians.

The poem does not simply express the timeless Christian theme of the struggle of God's people against the pagans, but also comments on the immediate social and historical context of its time. It seems to reflect the resistance of the Christian Anglo-Saxons against the pagan Danes during the ninth-century invasions, perhaps exaggerating the Assyrians' drunkenness in order to comment on the notorious Danish drinking habits. Furthermore, Holofernes' plan to rape Judith may evoke the rape of Anglo-Saxon women by Danish soldiers in the presence of their husbands and fathers.

Judith's identity as a woman warrior also puts the poem in the social context of the time. The poem's emphasis on her power, in contrast to the biblical source's emphasis on God's power to operate through the hand of a mere woman, reflects the relatively strong role of aristocratic women in England before the Norman Conquest. (Other Old English poems that reflect this strength include *Juliana*, a typical saint's legend whose heroine is martyred while resisting a Roman general's advances, and *Elene*, whose heroine—Constantine's mother Saint Helen—was believed to have discovered the true cross.) Finally, Judith's heroic action has been seen as an inversion of the rape which Holofernes himself intends to commit upon her, as, seeing him unconscious on his bed, she "took the heathen man by the hair, dragged him ignominiously towards her with her hands, and carefully laid out the debauched and odious man."

Judith[1]

. . . She was suspicious of gifts in this wide world. So she readily met with a helping hand from the glorious Prince when she had most need of the supreme Judge's support and that he, the Prime Mover, should protect her against this supreme danger. The illustrious Father in the skies granted her request in this because she always had firm faith in the Almighty.

I have heard, then, that Holofernes cordially issued invitations to a banquet and had dishes splendidly prepared with all sorts of wonderful things, and to it this lord over men summoned all the most senior functionaries. With great alacrity those shield-wielders complied and came wending to the puissant prince, the nation's chief person. That was on the fourth day after Judith, shrewd of purpose, the woman of elfin beauty first visited him.

So they went and settled down to the feasting, insolent men to the wine-drinking, all those brash armored warriors, his confederates in evil. Deep bowls were borne continually along the benches there and brimming goblets and pitchers as well to the hall-guests. They drank it down as doomed men, those celebrated shield-wielders—though the great man, the awesome lord over evils, did not foresee it. Then Holofernes, the bountiful lord of his men, grew merry with tippling. He laughed and bawled and roared and made a racket so that the children of men could hear from far away how the stern-minded man bellowed and yelled, insolent and flown with mead, and frequently exhorted the guests on the benches to enjoy themselves well. So the

1. Translated by S. A. J. Bradley.

whole day long the villain, the stern-minded dispenser of treasure, plied his retainers with wine until they lay unconscious, the whole of his retinue drunk as though they had been struck dead, drained of every faculty.

Thus the men's elder commanded the hall-guests to be ministered to until the dark night closed in on the children of men. Then, being wickedly promiscuous, he commanded the blessed virgin, decked with bracelets and adorned with rings, to be fetched in a hurry to his bed. The attendants promptly did as their master, the ruler of armored warriors, required them. They went upon the instant to the guest-hall where they found the astute Judith, and then the shield-wielding warriors speedily conducted the noble virgin to the lofty pavilion where the great man always rested of a night, Holofernes, abhorrent to the Savior.

There was an elegant all-golden fly-net there, hung about the commandant's bed so that the debauched hero of his soldiers could spy through on every one of the sons of men who came in there, but no one of humankind on him, unless, brave man, he summoned one of his evilly renowned soldiers to go nearer to him for a confidential talk.

Hastily, then, they brought the shrewd lady to bed. Then they went, stout-hearted heroes, to inform their master that the holy woman had been brought to his pavilion. The man of mark, lord over cities, then grew jovial of mood: he meant to defile the noble lady with filth and with pollution. To that heaven's Judge, Shepherd of the celestial multitude, would not consent but rather he, the Lord, Ruler of the hosts, prevented him from the act.

So this species of fiend, licentious, debauched, went with a crowd of his men to seek his bed—where he was to lose his life, swiftly, within the one night: he had then come to his violent end upon earth, such as he had previously deserved, the stern-minded prince over men, while he lived in this world under the roof of the skies.

Then the great man collapsed in the midst of his bed, so drunk with wine that he was oblivious in mind of any of his designs. The soldiers stepped out of his quarters with great alacrity, wine-glutted men who had put the perjurer, the odious persecutor, to bed for the last time.

Then the glorious handmaid of the Savior was sorely preoccupied as to how she might most easily deprive the monster of his life before the sordid fellow, full of corruption, awoke. Then the ringletted girl, the Maker's maiden, grasped a sharp sword, hardy in the storms of battle, and drew it from its sheath with her right hand. Then she called by name upon the Guardian of heaven, the Savior of all the world's inhabitants, and spoke these words:

"God of beginnings, Spirit of comfort, Son of the universal Ruler, I desire to entreat you for your grace upon me in my need, Majesty of the Trinity. My heart is now sorely anguished and my mind troubled and much afflicted with anxieties. Give me, Lord of heaven, victory and true faith so that with this sword I may hew down this dispenser of violent death. Grant me my safe deliverance, stern-minded Prince over men. Never have I had greater need of your grace. Avenge now, mighty Lord, illustrious Dispenser of glory, that which is so bitter to my mind, so burning in my breast."

Then the supreme Judge at once inspired her with courage—as he does every single man dwelling here who looks to him for help with resolve and with true faith. So hope was abundantly renewed in the holy woman's heart. She then took the heathen man firmly by his hair, dragged him ignominiously towards her with her hands and carefully laid out the debauched and odious man so as she could most easily manage the wretch efficiently. Then the ringletted woman struck the malignant-minded enemy with the gleaming sword so that she sliced through half his neck, so that he lay unconscious, drunk and mutilated.

He was not then yet dead, not quite lifeless. In earnest then the courageous woman struck the heathen dog a second time so that his head flew off on to the floor. His foul carcass lay behind, dead; his spirit departed elsewhere beneath the deep ground and was there prostrated and chained in torment ever after, coiled about by snakes, trussed up in tortures and cruelly prisoned in hellfire after his going hence. Never would he have cause to hope, engulfed in darkness, that he might get out of that snake-infested prison, but there he shall remain forever to eternity henceforth without end in that murky abode, deprived of the joys of hope.

Judith then had won outstanding glory in the struggle according as God the Lord of heaven, who gave her the victory, granted her. Then the clever woman swiftly put the harrier's head, all bloody, into the bag in which her attendant, a pale-cheeked woman, one proved excellent in her ways, had brought food there for them both; and then Judith put it, all gory, into her hands for her discreet servant to carry home. From there the two women then proceeded onwards, emboldened by courage, until they had escaped, brave, triumphant virgins, from among the army, so that they could clearly see the walls of the beautiful city, Bethulia, shining. Then the ring-adorned women hurried forward on their way until, cheered at heart, they had reached the rampart gate.

There were soldiers, vigilant men, sitting and keeping watch in the fortress just as Judith the artful-minded virgin had enjoined the despondent folk when she set out on her mission, courageous lady. Now she had returned, their darling, to her people, and quickly then the shrewd woman summoned one of the men to come out from the spacious city to meet her and speedily to let them in through the gate of the rampart; and to the victorious people she spoke these words:

"I can tell you something worthy of thanksgiving: that you need no longer grieve in spirit. The ordaining Lord, the Glory of kings, is gracious to you. It has been revealed abroad through the world that dazzling and glorious success is impending for you and triumph is granted you over those injuries which you long have suffered."

Then the citizens were merry when they heard how the saintly woman spoke across the high rampart. The army was in ecstasies and the people rushed towards the fortress gate, men and women together, in flocks and droves; in throngs and troops they surged forward and ran towards the handmaid of the Lord, both old and young in their thousands. The heart of each person in that city of mead-halls was exhilarated when they realized that Judith had returned home; and then with humility they hastily let her in.

Then the clever woman ornamented with gold directed her attentive servant-girl to unwrap the harrier's head and to display the bloody object to the citizens as proof of how she had fared in the struggle. The noble lady then spoke to the whole populace:

"Victorious heroes, leaders of the people; here you may openly gaze upon the head of that most odious heathen warrior, the dead Holofernes, who perpetrated upon us the utmost number of violent killings of men and painful miseries, and who intended to add to it even further, but God did not grant him longer life so that he might plague us with afflictions. I took his life, with God's help. Now I want to urge each man among these citizens, each shield-wielding soldier, that you immediately get yourselves ready for battle. Once the God of beginnings, the steadfastly gracious King, has sent the radiant light from the east, go forth bearing shields, bucklers in front of your breasts and mail-coats and shining helmets into the ravagers' midst; cut down the commanders, the doomed leaders, with gleaming swords. Your enemies are sentenced to death and you shall have honor and glory in the fight according as the mighty Lord has signified to you by my hand."

Then an army of brave and keen men was quickly got ready for the battle. Renowned nobles and their companions advanced; they carried victory-banners; beneath their helms the heroes issued forth straight into battle from out of the holy city upon the very dawning of the day. Shields clattered, loudly resonated. At that, the lean wolf in the wood rejoiced, and that bird greedy for carrion, the black raven. Both knew that the men of that nation meant to procure them their fill among those doomed to die; but in their wake flew the eagle, eager for food, speckled-winged; the dark-feathered, hook-beaked bird sang a battle-chant.

On marched the soldiers, warriors to the warfare, protected by their shields, hollowed linden bucklers, they who a while previously had been suffering the abuse of aliens, the blasphemy of heathens. This was strictly repaid to all the Assyrians in the spear-fight once the Israelites under their battle-ensigns had reached the camp. Firmly entrenched, they vigorously let fly from the curved bow showers of darts, arrows, the serpents of battle. Loudly the fierce fighting-men roared and sent spears into their cruel enemies' midst. The heroes, the in-dwellers of the land, were enraged against the odious race. Stern of mood they advanced; hardened of heart they roughly roused their drink-stupefied enemies of old. With their hands, retainers unsheathed from scabbards bright-ornamented swords, proved of edge, and set about the Assyrian warriors in earnest, intending to smite them. Of that army they spared not one of the men alive, neither the lowly nor the mighty, whom they could overpower.

Thus in the hour of morn those comrades in arms the whole time harried the aliens until those who were their adversaries, the chief sentries of the army, acknowledged that the Hebrew people were showing them very intensive sword-play. They went to inform the most senior officers of this by word of mouth and they roused those warriors and fearfully announced to them in their drunken stupor the dreadful news, the terror of the morning, the frightful sword-encounter.

Then, I have heard, those death-doomed heroes quickly shook off their sleep and thronged in flocks, demoralized men, to the pavilion of the debauched Holofernes. They meant to give their lord warning of battle at once, before the terror and the force of the Hebrews descended upon him; all supposed that the men's leader and that beautiful woman were together in the handsome tent, the noble Judith and the lecher, fearsome and ferocious. Yet there was not one of the nobles who dared awaken the warrior to inquire how it had turned out for the soldier with the holy virgin, the woman of the Lord.

The might of the Hebrews, their army, was drawing closer; vehemently they fought with tough and bloody weapons and violently they indemnified with gleaming swords their former quarrels and old insults: in that day's work the Assyrians' repute was withered, their arrogance abased. The men stood around their lord's tent, extremely agitated and growing gloomier in spirit. Then all together they began to cough and loudly make noises and, having no success, to chew the grist with their teeth, suffering agonies. The time of their glory, good fortune and valorous doings was at an end. The nobles thought to awaken their lord and friend; they succeeded not at all.

Then one of the soldiers belatedly and tardily grew so bold that he ventured pluckily into the pavilion as necessity compelled him. Then he found his lord lying pallid on the bed, deprived of his spirit, dispossessed of life. Straightway then he fell chilled to the ground, and distraught in mind he began to tear his hair and his clothing alike and he uttered these words to the soldiers who were waiting there miserably outside:

"Here is made manifest our own perdition, and here it is imminently signalled that the time is drawn near, along with its tribulations, when we must perish and be destroyed together in the strife. Here, hacked by the sword, decapitated, lies our lord."

Then distraught in mind they threw down their weapons; demoralized they went scurrying away in flight. The nation magnified in strength attacked them in the rear until the greatest part of the army lay on the field of victory levelled by battle, hacked by swords, as a treat for the wolves and a joy to the carrion-greedy birds. Those who survived fled from the linden spears of their foes. In their wake advanced the troop of Hebrews, honoured with the victory and glorified in the judgment: the Lord God, the almighty Lord, had come handsomely to their aid. Swiftly then with their gleaming swords those valiant heroes made an inroad through the thick of their foes; they hacked at targes and sheared through the shield-wall. The Hebrew spear-throwers were wrought up to the fray; the soldiers lusted mightily after a spear-contest on that occasion. There in the dust fell the main part of the muster-roll of the Assyrian nobility, of that odious race. Few survivors reached their native land.

The soldiers of royal renown turned back in retirement amidst carnage and reeking corpses. That was the opportunity for the land's in-dwellers to seize from those most odious foes, their old dead enemies, bloodied booty, resplendent accoutrements, shield and broad sword, burnished helmets, costly treasures. The guardians of their homeland had honorably conquered their enemies on the battlefield and destroyed with swords their old persecutors. In their trail lay dead those who of living peoples had been most inimical to their existence.

Then the whole nation, most famous of races, proud, curled-locked, for the duration of one month were carrying and conveying into the beautiful city, Bethulia, helmets and hip-swords, gray mail-coats, and men's battle-dress ornamented with gold, more glorious treasures than any man among ingenious men can tell. All that the people splendidly gained, brave beneath their banners in the fray, through the shrewd advice of Judith, the courageous woman. As a reward the celebrated spearmen brought back for her from the expedition the sword and the bloodied helmet of Holofernes as well as his huge mail-coat adorned with red gold; and everything the ruthless lord of the warriors owned of riches or personal wealth, of rings and of beautiful treasures, they gave it to that beautiful and resourceful lady.

For all this Judith gave glory to the Lord of hosts who granted her esteem and renown in the realm of earth and likewise too a reward in heaven, the prize of victory in the glory of the sky because she always had true faith in the Almighty. Certainly at the end she did not doubt the reward for which she long had yearned.

For this be glory into eternity to the dear Lord who created the wind and the clouds, the skies and the spacious plains and likewise the cruel seas and the joys of heaven, through his peculiar mercy.

The Dream of the Rood

The Dream of the Rood is a remarkable tenth-century poem, a mystical dream vision whose narrator tells of his dream that the rood—Christ's cross—appeared to him and told the story of its unwilling role in the crucifixion. The poem is an excellent illustration of how the conventions of Old English heroic poems like *Beowulf* were adapted to the doctrines of Christianity. Christ's Passion is converted into a heroic sacrifice as the cross reports that it watched him— the young hero—strip himself naked, as if preparing for battle, and bravely ascend it. In the same vein, the cross presents itself as a thane (retainer) forced into disloyalty, as it watches— and participates in—the crucifixion, unable to avenge its beloved Lord.

In addition to heroic poetry, *The Dream of the Rood* recalls Old English genres such as the riddle and the elegy. In riddle fashion, the cross asks, "What am I?"—that started as a tree, became an instrument of torture, and am now a beacon of victory, resplendent with jewels. In the manner of elegies like *The Wanderer,* the speaker, stained with sin, presents himself as a lonely exile whose companions have left him and gone to heaven. After his vision, he resolves seek the fellowship of his heavenly Lord and his former companions, which he pictures as taking place in a celestial mead hall: "the home of joy and happiness, / where the people of God are seated at the feast / in eternal bliss."

One of the most striking poetic effects of *The Dream of the Rood* is its focus on the Incarnation, God's taking on human flesh. The poet often juxtaposes references to Christ's humanity and divinity in the same line, thereby achieving a powerful effect of paradox, as when he tells of the approach of "the young warrior, God Almighty." It is noteworthy that the aspect of Christ's humanity which the poet stresses is the heroism rather than the pathos which was to become so prominent in later medieval poetry and art. This heroism provides a context for a cryptic passage at the end of the poem, where the dreamer refers to Christ's "journey" to bring "those who before suffered burning" victoriously to heaven. In *The Harrowing of Hell* (based on the apocryphal Gospel of Nicodemus), Christ heroically freed the virtuous Old Testament patriarchs from damnation and led them to eternal bliss.

The fame of *The Dream of the Rood* appears to have been widespread in its own time. Our knowledge of it comes from three sources: the huge stone Ruthwell Cross in southern Scotland built in the eighth century (on which a short version is inscribed in runic letters); the silver Brussels Cross, made in England in the tenth century; and the manuscript found written in Vercelli in northern Italy, also written in the tenth century—the only complete version of the poem. These varied locations are a testament to the wide influence of Anglo-Saxon scholars, not only in the British Isles but on the Continent as well.

The Dream of the Rood[1]

> Listen! I will describe the best of dreams
> which I dreamed in the middle of the night
> when, far and wide, all men slept.
> It seemed that I saw a wondrous tree
> 5   soaring into the air, surrounded by light,
> the brightest of crosses; that emblem was entirely
> cased in gold; beautiful jewels
> were strewn around its foot, just as five
> studded the cross-beam. All the angels of God,

---

1. Translated by Kevin Crossley-Holland.

The Ruthwell Cross, north side, top section. 7th–8th century. Preserved in a church in southern Scotland, this 18-foot stone cross is carved with many Christian scenes, including this depiction of Saint John the Baptist, bearded and holding the Lamb of God. The Latin inscription beneath the saint is written in runes—the traditional Germanic alphabet, used for ritualistic purposes. Runic inscriptions elsewhere on the cross reproduce portions of the *Dream of the Rood* in Old English. Still other inscriptions are in Latin and employ the Roman alphabet. Thus, like the *Dream of the Rood* itself, whose Christlike hero resembles a Germanic warrior, the Ruthwell Cross illustrates the fusion of Mediterranean and Germanic traditions in Anglo-Saxon Christian culture.

10   fair creations, guarded it. That was no cross
of a criminal, but holy spirits and men on earth
watched over it there—the whole glorious universe.

Wondrous was the tree of victory, and I was stained
by sin, stricken by guilt. I saw this glorious tree
15   joyfully gleaming, adorned with garments,
decked in gold; the tree of the Ruler
was rightly adorned with rich stones;
yet through that gold I could see the agony
once suffered by wretches, for it had bled
20   down the right hand side. Then I was afflicted,
frightened at this sight; I saw that sign often change
its clothing and hue, at times dewy with moisture,
stained by flowing blood, at times adorned with treasure.
Yet I lay there for a long while
25   and gazed sadly at the Savior's cross

until I heard it utter words;
the finest of trees began to speak:
"I remember the morning a long time ago
that I was felled at the edge of the forest

30   and severed from my roots. Strong enemies seized me,
bade me hold up their felons on high,
made me a spectacle. Men shifted me
on their shoulders and set me on a hill.

35   Many enemies fastened me there. I saw the Lord of Mankind
hasten with such courage to climb upon me.
I dared not bow or break there
against my Lord's wish, when I saw the surface
of the earth tremble. I could have felled

40   all my foes, yet I stood firm.
Then the young warrior, God Almighty,
stripped Himself, firm and unflinching. He climbed
upon the cross, brave before many, to redeem mankind.
I quivered when the hero clasped me,

45   yet I dared not bow to the ground,
fall to the earth. I had to stand firm.
A rood was I raised up; I bore aloft the mighty King,
the Lord of Heaven. I dared not stoop.
They drove dark nails into me; dire wounds are there to see,

50   the gaping gashes of malice; I dared not injure them.
They insulted us both together; I was drenched in the blood
that streamed from the Man's side after He set His spirit free.

"On that hill I endured many grievous trials;
I saw the God of Hosts stretched

55   on the rack; darkness covered the corpse
of the Ruler with clouds, His shining radiance.
Shadows swept across the land, dark shapes
under the clouds. All creation wept,
wailed for the death of the King; Christ was on the cross.

60   Yet men hurried eagerly to the Prince
from afar; I witnessed all that too.
I was oppressed with sorrow, yet humbly bowed to the hands of men,
and willingly. There they lifted Him from His heavy torment,
they took Almighty God away. The warriors left me standing there,

65   stained with blood; sorely was I wounded by the sharpness of spear-shafts.
They laid Him down, limb-weary; they stood at the corpse's head,
they beheld there the Lord of Heaven; and there He rested for a while,
worn-out after battle. And then they began to build a sepulchre;
under his slayers' eyes, they carved it from the gleaming stone,

70   and laid therein the Lord of Victories. Then, sorrowful at dusk,
they sang a dirge before they went, weary,
from their glorious Prince; He rested in the grave alone.
But we still stood there, weeping blood,
long after the song of the warriors

75   had soared to heaven; the corpse grew cold,
the fair human house of the soul. Then our enemies

began to fell us; that was a terrible fate.
They buried us in a deep pit; but friends
and followers of the Lord found me there
80   and girded me with gold and shimmering silver.

"Now, my loved man, you have heard
how I endured bitter anguish
at the hands of evil men. Now the time is come
when men far and wide in this world,
85   and all this bright creation, bow before me;
they pray to this sign. On me the Son of God
suffered for a time; wherefore I now stand on high,
glorious under heaven; and I can heal
all those who stand in awe of me.
90   Long ago I became the worst of tortures,
hated by men, until I opened
to them the true way of life.
Lo! The Lord of Heaven, the Prince of Glory,
honored me over any other tree
95   just as He, Almighty God, for the sake of mankind
honored Mary, His own mother,
before all other women in the world.
Now I command you, my loved man,
to describe your vision to all men;
100   tell them with words this is the tree of glory
on which the Son of God suffered once
for the many sins committed by mankind,
and for Adam's wickedness long ago.
He sipped the drink of death. Yet the Lord rose
105   with His great strength to deliver man.
Then He ascended into heaven. The Lord Himself,
Almighty God, with His host of angels,
will come to the middle-world again
on Domesday to reckon with each man.
110   Then He who has the power of judgment
will judge each man just as he deserves
for the way in which he lived this fleeting life.
No-one then will be unafraid
as to what words the Lord will utter.
115   Before the assembly, He will ask where that man is
who, in God's name, would undergo the pangs of death,
just as He did formerly upon the cross.
Then men will be fearful and give
scant thought to what they say to Christ.
120   But no-one need be numbed by fear
who has carried the best of all signs in his breast;
each soul that has longings to live with the Lord
must search for a kingdom far beyond the frontiers of this world."

Then I prayed to the cross, eager
125   and light-hearted, although I was alone
with my own poor company. My soul

longed for a journey, great yearnings
always tugged at me. Now my hope in this life
is that I can turn to that tree of victory
130   alone and more often than any other man
and honor it fully. These longings master
my heart and mind, and my help comes
from holy cross itself. I have not many friends
of influence on earth; they have journeyed on
135   from the joys of this world to find the King of Glory,
they live in heaven with the High Father,
dwell in splendor. Now I look day by day
for that time when the cross of the Lord,
which once I saw in a dream here on earth,
140   will fetch me away from this fleeting life
and lift me to the home of joy and happiness
where the people of God are seated at the feast
in eternal bliss, and set me down
where I may live in glory unending and share
145   the joy of the saints. May the Lord be a friend to me,
He who suffered once for the sins of men
here on earth on the gallows-tree.
He has redeemed us; He has given life to us,
and a home in heaven.   Hope was renewed,
150   blessed and blissful, for those who before suffered burning.
On that journey the Son was victorious,
strong and successful. When He, Almighty Ruler,
returned with a thronging host of spirits
to God's kingdom, to joy among the angels
155   and all the saints who lived already
in heaven in glory, then their King,
Almighty God, entered His own country.

PERSPECTIVES

Ethnic and Religious Encounters

In the centuries of their insurgency and the consolidation of their influence in Britain, the Angles and Saxons negotiated a series of encounters that left them, and England, profoundly transformed. They arrived from the distant coasts of northwest continental Europe as self-conscious foreigners, divided into large tribal groups and often warring among themselves. They were pagans and masters of a great but essentially oral culture. By the end of their dominance, in 1066, they were long-Christianized and increasingly had come to perceive themselves as a single people. Moreover, their conversion involved a new commitment to the practical uses of writing and the talismanic power of the written book, as well as a heightened sense of the conflicting claims and uses of their ancient vernacular and of Latin. They now experienced England as their native place and registered their ancestral geography on the Continent as an area of nostalgic exploration or, equally, the source of hostile invasion.

All this was the work of centuries. It was not an unconscious or "natural" development, however. The passages in this section, in their different ways, offer key moments in the lengthy and complex process by which the Germanic newcomers encountered other peoples, religions, textual cultures, and geographies.

The initial contact between the Germanic invaders and the prior inhabitants of England—Britons, the "Irish" of the northwest, and the Picts—was based on military service which turned into military aggression. Relatively soon, though, and even as their territorial ambitions continued, the Angles and Saxons developed other contacts, especially with the Britons. The British were already Christian, and the Angles and Saxons first came to Christianity through British models if not by British hands. Later, the Anglo-Saxons themselves would face invasion by Vikings, who ultimately settled north of the Humber in the "Danelaw." Much of Asser's *Life of King Alfred* documents Alfred's struggle against Viking raiders.

Though he celebrated Alfred's West Saxon kingship and culture, Asser was himself a Welshman. His presence at Alfred's court is a sign of how Latin learning had declined in the disordered era of Viking incursions; Alfred was obliged to turn to other peoples to restore education in his own realm. The Norwegian trader Ohthere, too, came to Alfred's court even while the king was fending off Viking raiders. Ohthere seems to have sparked lively interest in his own people and their social order, as well as in his visits to what the Anglo-Saxons knew was their ancestral home.

Christianization was also a slow, complex, and incomplete process of acculturation. Bede recounts a number of moments when the differing responses to a single event register the encounters of pagan and Christian, literate and illiterate, and Latin and Germanic traditions. The conversion of King Edwin, for instance, involved not just the king fulfilling a promise made in a vision but also his nobles learning to imagine a new spiritual geography which went far beyond the brief joys of their warrior cohort. In the story of Imma, the magical loosing of a prisoner's chains is seen by some as the effect of an ancient pagan "loosing spell," but by Imma (and Bede's Christian readers) as the effect of masses said for his soul.

Language and literacy equally figure in the conversion of the Angles and Saxons and in the slow emergence of the idea of an "English" people. Imma is freed by the uncanny (and somewhat misdirected) power of the Latin mass. The high level of Bede's own Latin suggests how that language was becoming a cohesive force, at least among clerics. Yet in one of his tenderest stories, Bede tells about the illiterate Caedmon who learned, by divine intervention, to tell biblical stories in vernacular poetry. Bede admits that his Latin version of *Caedmon's Hymn* is inadequte, which suggests that Anglo-Saxon could assume its own place in the operations of the sacred. And Asser celebrates Alfred's childhood love of Saxon poems, laments Alfred's illiteracy, yet tells how the illiterate prince competed for the gift of a book he valued almost as a talisman. Alfred's acquisition of literacy and of Latin is part of his rise to successful kingship, and he caps his own reign with the series of translations that bring crucial texts of Latin Christianity into an Anglo-Saxon that Alfred now seems to see as a unifying national tongue.

Finally, even as some Anglo-Saxons aspire to nationhood, they do so by nostalgic memories of their foreign past, as seen in the information they draw from the Norwegian visitor Ohthere. At the same time, though, they mark themselves off from this geography and see themselves as the sinning victims of invasions that will end their power, just as their own successful invasions had punished and subdued the earlier Britons. This is repeatedly made explicit in the *Táin*, the *Anglo-Saxon Chronicle*'s report of the twin battles fought by King Harold against Norwegian aggressors in the North and then against the triumphant Normans in the South. Their sense of nationhood and of being folded into processes of Christian history is clearest as the Chronicler witnesses the close of Anglo-Saxon dominance.

Bede
672–735

Bede was born on lands belonging to the abbey of Wearmouth-Jarrow. He entered that monastery at the age of seven and never traveled more than seventy-five miles away. Bede is the most enduring product of the golden age of Northumbrian monasticism. In the generations just preceding his, a series of learned abbots had brought Roman liturgical practices and monastic habits to Wearmouth-Jarrow, as well as establishing there the best library in England. Out of this settled life and disciplined religious culture Bede created a diverse body of writings which are learned both in scholarly research and in the purity of their Latin. They include biblical commentaries, school texts from spelling to metrics, treatises on the liturgical calendar, hymns, and lives of saints.

Bede's *An Ecclesiastical History of the English People*, completed in 731, marks the apex of his achievement. Given the localism of his life, Bede's grasp of English history is extraordinary, not just in terms of his eager pursuit of information, but equally in his balanced and complex sense of the broad movement of history. Bede registers a persistent concern about his sources and their reliability. He prefers written and especially documentary evidence, but he will use oral reports if they come from several sources and are close enough to the original event.

The *Ecclesiastical History* suggests the contours of a national history, even a providential history, in the arrival of the Angles and Saxons, and in the island's uneven conversion to Christianity. Despite his frequent stories of battles among the Germanic peoples in Britain, Bede speaks of the English people emphatically in the singular. Nevertheless, Bede is delicately aware of the historical layering brought about by colonization and the ongoing resistance of earlier inhabitants. Further, he is always alert to profoundly transformative influences, aside from ethnicity, that color his time: the process of conversion to Christianity, and the variable coexistence of Christian and pagan instincts in individual minds; the interplay of oral and written culture; the status in religious and official life of Latin and the Anglo-Saxon vernaculars.

from An Ecclesiastical History of the English People[1]
[THE CONVERSION OF KING EDWIN][2]

King Edwin hesitated to accept the word of God which Paulinus[3] preached but, as we have said, used to sit alone for hours at a time, earnestly debating within himself what he ought to do and what religion he should follow. One day Paulinus came to him and, placing his right hand on the king's head, asked him if he recognized this sign. The king began to tremble and would have thrown himself at the bishop's feet but Paulinus raised him up and said in a voice that seemed familiar, "First you have escaped with God's help from the hands of the foes you feared; secondly you have acquired by His gift the kingdom you desired; now, in the third place, remember your own promise; do not delay in fulfilling it but receive the faith and keep the commandments of Him who rescued you from your earthly foes and raised you to the

---

1. Edited and translated by Bertram Colgrave and R.A.B. Mynors.
2. From Book 2, chs. 12–14. Edwin became king of Northumbria in 616, aided by Raedwald, king of the East Angles. Exiled at Raedwald's court, Edwin had a vision wherein he promised a shadowy visitor he would convert

if he achieved the crown. The visitor laid his right hand on Edwin's head as a sign to remember that promise when the gesture was repeated.
3. Later archbishop of York, Paulinus had been sent to Northumbria from Kent with Edwin's Christian wife after Edwin had promised tolerance of Christian worship.

honor of an earthly kingdom. If from henceforth you are willing to follow His will which is made known to you through me, He will also rescue you from the everlasting torments of the wicked and make you a partaker with Him of His eternal kingdom in heaven."

When the king had heard his words, he answered that he was both willing and bound to accept the faith which Paulinus taught. He said, however, that he would confer about this with his loyal chief men and his counselors so that, if they agreed with him, they might all be consecrated together in the waters of life. Paulinus agreed and the king did as he had said. A meeting of his council was held and each one was asked in turn what he thought of this doctrine hitherto unknown to them and this new worship of God which was being proclaimed.

Coifi, the chief of the priests, answered at once, "Notice carefully, King, this doctrine which is now being expounded to us. I frankly admit that, for my part, I have found that the religion which we have hitherto held has no virtue nor profit in it. None of your followers has devoted himself more earnestly than I have to the worship of our gods, but nevertheless there are many who receive greater benefits and greater honor from you than I do and are more successful in all their undertakings. If the gods had any power they would have helped me more readily, seeing that I have always served them with greater zeal. So it follows that if, on examination, these new doctrines which have now been explained to us are found to be better and more effectual, let us accept them at once without any delay."

Another of the king's chief men agreed with this advice and with these wise words and then added, "This is how the present life of man on earth, King, appears to me in comparison with that time which is unknown to us. You are sitting feasting with your ealdormen and thegns in winter time; the fire is burning on the hearth in the middle of the hall and all inside is warm, while outside the wintry storms of rain and snow are raging; and a sparrow flies swiftly through the hall. It enters in at one door and quickly flies out through the other. For the few moments it is inside, the storm and wintry tempest cannot touch it, but after the briefest moment of calm, it flits from your sight, out of the wintry storm and into it again. So this life of man appears but for a moment; what follows or indeed what went before, we know not at all. If this new doctrine brings us more certain information, it seems right that we should accept it."[4] Other elders and counselors of the king continued in the same manner, being divinely prompted to do so.

Coifi added that he would like to listen still more carefully to what Paulinus himself had to say about God. The king ordered Paulinus to speak, and when he had said his say, Coifi exclaimed, "For a long time now I have realized that our religion is worthless; for the more diligently I sought the truth in our cult, the less I found it. Now I confess openly that the truth shines out clearly in this teaching which can bestow on us the gift of life, salvation, and eternal happiness. Therefore I advise your Majesty that we should promptly abandon and commit to the flames the temples and the altars which we have held sacred without reaping any benefit." Why need I say more? The king publicly accepted the gospel which Paulinus preached, renounced idolatry, and confessed his faith in Christ. When he asked the high priest of their religion which of them should be the first to profane the altars and the shrines of the idols, together with their precincts, Coifi answered, "I will; for through the wisdom

---

4. This famous simile is put in the mouth of a lay nobleman, not the pagan priest Coifi whose argument for conversion was based on disappointed self-interest.

the true God has given me no one can more suitably destroy those things which I once foolishly worshiped, and so set an example to all." And at once, casting aside his vain superstitions, he asked the king to provide him with arms and a stallion; and mounting it he set out to destroy the idols. Now a high priest of their religion was not allowed to carry arms or to ride except on a mare. So, girded with a sword, he took a spear in his hand and mounting the king's stallion he set off to where the idols were. The common people who saw him thought he was mad. But as soon as he approached the shrine, without any hesitation he profaned it by casting the spear which he held into it; and greatly rejoicing in the knowledge of the worship of the true God, he ordered his companions to destroy and set fire to the shrine and all the enclosures. The place where the idols once stood is still shown, not far from York, to the east, over the river Derwent. Today it is called Goodmanham, the place where the high priest, through the inspiration of the true God, profaned and destroyed the altars which he himself had consecrated.[5]

So King Edwin, with all the nobles of his race and a vast number of the common people, received the faith and regeneration by holy baptism in the eleventh year of his reign, that is in the year of our Lord 627 and about 180 years after the coming of the English to Britain. He was baptized at York on Easter Day, 12 April, in the church of Saint Peter the Apostle, which he had hastily built of wood while he was a catechumen and under instruction before he received baptism. He established an episcopal see for Paulinus, his instructor and bishop, in the same city.

[THE STORY OF IMMA][6]

In this battle in which King Aelfwine[7] was killed, a remarkable incident is known to have happened which in my opinion should certainly not be passed over in silence, since the story may lead to the salvation of many. During the battle one of the king's retainers, a young man named Imma was struck down among others; he lay all that day and the following night as though dead, among the bodies of the slain, but at last he recovered consciousness, sat up, and bandaged his wounds as best he could; then, having rested for a short time, he rose and set out to find friends to take care of him. But as he was doing so, he was found and captured by men of the enemy army and taken to their lord, who was a *gesith*[8] of King Aethelred. On being asked who he was, he was afraid to admit that he was a thegn; but he answered instead that he was a poor peasant and married; and he declared that he had come to the army in company with other peasants to bring food to the soldiers. The *gesith* took him and had his wounds attended to. But when Imma began to get better, he ordered him to be bound at night to prevent his escape. However, it proved impossible to bind him, for no sooner had those who chained him gone, than his fetters were loosed.

Now he had a brother whose name was Tunna, a priest and abbot of a monastery in a city which is still called *Tunnacaestir* after him. When Tunna heard that his brother had perished in the fight, he went to see if he could find his body; having found another very like him in all respects, he concluded that it must be his brother's body. So he carried it to the monastery, buried it with honor, and took care to offer many masses for the absolution of his soul. It was on account of these celebrations

---

5. This detail is typical of Bede's liking for textual or archeological authentication.
6. Book 4, ch. 22.
7. A battle in 679, between King Ecgfrith of Northumbria and Aethelred king of the Mercians caused the death of

this under-king and brother of Ecgfrith.
8. A nobleman, serving a king but having his own household of retainers and servants. A thegn is a noble warrior still serving within the king's household.

that, as I have said, no one could bind Imma because his fetters were at once loosed. Meanwhile the *gesith* who kept him captive grew amazed and asked him why he could not be bound and whether he had about him any loosing spells such as are described in stories. But Imma answered that he knew nothing of such arts. "However," said he, "I have a brother in my country who is a priest and I know he believes me to be dead and offers frequent masses on my behalf; so if I had now been in another world, my soul would have been loosed from its punishment by his intercessions." When he had been a prisoner with the *gesith* for some time, those who watched him closely realized by his appearance, his bearing, and his speech that he was not of common stock as he had said, but of noble family. Then the *gesith* called him aside and asked him very earnestly to declare his origin, promising that no harm should come to him, provided that he told him plainly who he was. The prisoner did so, revealing that he had been one of the king's thegns. The *gesith* answered, "I realized by every one of your answers that you were not a peasant, and now you ought to die because all my brothers and kinsmen were killed in the battle: but I will not kill you for I do not intend to break my promise."

As soon as Imma had recovered, the *gesith* sold him to a Frisian in London; but he could neither be bound on his way there nor by the Frisian. So after his enemies had put every kind of bond on him and as his new master realized that he could not be bound, he gave him leave to ransom himself if he could. Now the bonds were most frequently loosed from about nine in the morning, the time when masses were usually said. So having sworn that he would either return or send his master the money for his ransom, he went to King Hlothhere of Kent, who was the son of Queen Aethelthryth's sister already mentioned, because he had once been one of Aethelthryth's thegns; he asked for and received the money from him for his ransom and sent it to his master as he had promised.[9]

He afterwards returned to his own country, where he met his brother and gave him a full account of all his troubles and the comfort that had come to him in those adversities; and from what his brother told him, he realized that his bonds had generally been loosed at the time when masses were being celebrated on his behalf; so he perceived that the other comforts and blessings which he had experienced during his time of danger had been bestowed by heaven, through the intercession of his brother and the offering up of the saving Victim. Many who heard about this from Imma were inspired to greater faith and devotion, to prayer and almsgiving and to the offering up of sacrifices to God in the holy oblation, for the deliverance of their kinsfolk who had departed from the world; for they realized that the saving sacrifice availed for the everlasting redemption of both body and soul.

This story was told me by some of those who heard it from the very man to whom these things happened; therefore since I had so clear an account of the incident, I thought that it should undoubtedly be inserted into this *History*.

[CAEDMON'S HYMN][1]

In the monastery of this abbess[2] there was a certain brother who was specially marked out by the grace of God, so that he used to compose godly and religious songs; thus, whatever he learned from the holy Scriptures by means of interpreters, he quickly

9. Imma had been thegn to Aethelthryth, wife of King Ecgfrith, before he entered Aelfwine's service. He now turns to her nephew, implicitly invoking obligations of kinship, for help with his ransom.

1. Book 4, ch. 24.
2. Hild, an aristocratic woman famed for her piety, who had founded and ruled the abbey of Whitby.

turned into extremely delightful and moving poetry, in English, which was his own tongue. By his songs the minds of many were often inspired to despise the world and to long for the heavenly life. It is true that after him other Englishmen attempted to compose religious poems, but none could compare with him. For he did not learn the art of poetry from men nor through a man but he received the gift of song freely by the grace of God. Hence he could never compose any foolish or trivial poem but only those which were concerned with devotion and so were fitting for his devout tongue to utter. He had lived in the secular habit until he was well advanced in years and had never learned any songs.[3] Hence sometimes at a feast, when for the sake of providing entertainment, it had been decided that they should all sing in turn, when he saw the harp approaching him, he would rise up in the middle of the feasting, go out, and return home.

On one such occasion when he did so, he left the place of feasting and went to the cattle byre, as it was his turn to take charge of them that night. In due time he stretched himself out and went to sleep, whereupon he dreamed that someone stood by him, saluted him, and called him by name: "Caedmon," he said, "sing me something." Caedmon answered, "I cannot sing; that is why I left the feast and came here because I could not sing." Once again the speaker said, "Nevertheless you must sing to me." "What must I sing?" said Caedmon. "Sing," he said, "about the beginning of created things." Thereupon Caedmon began to sing verses which he had never heard before in praise of God the Creator, of which this is the general sense: "Now we must praise the Maker of the heavenly kingdom, the power of the Creator and his counsel, the deeds of the Father of glory and how He, since he is the eternal God, was the Author of all marvels and first created the heavens as a roof for the children of men and then, the almighty Guardian of the human race, created the earth." This is the sense but not the order of the words which he sang as he slept. For it is not possible to translate verse, however well composed, literally from one language to another without some loss of beauty and dignity. When he awoke, he remembered all that he had sung while asleep and soon added more verses in the same manner, praising God in fitting style.

In the morning he went to the reeve[4] who was his master, telling him of the gift he had received, and the reeve took him to the abbess. He was then bidden to describe his dream in the presence of a number of the more learned men and also to recite his song so that they might all examine him and decide upon the nature and origin of the gift of which he spoke; and it seemed clear to all of them that the Lord had granted him heavenly grace. They then read to him a passage of sacred history or doctrine, bidding him make a song out of it, if he could, in metrical form. He undertook the task and went away; on returning next morning he repeated the passage he had been given, which he had put into excellent verse. The abbess, who recognized the grace of God which the man had received, instructed him to renounce his secular habit and to take monastic vows. She and all her people received him into the community of the brothers and ordered that he should be instructed in the whole course of sacred history. He learned all he could by listening to them and then, memorizing it and ruminating over it, like some clean animal chewing the cud, he turned it into the most melodious verse: and it sounded so sweet as he recited it that his teachers

3. Monks, who devoted their lives to prayer and the celebration of the liturgy, needed to be literate in Latin. Caedmon was one of the lay brothers, who performed

menial tasks and were often uneducated.
4. Person responsible for running the monastery's estates.

became in turn his audience. He sang about the creation of the world, the origin of the human race, and the whole history of Genesis, of the departure of Israel from Egypt and the entry into the promised land and of many other of the stories taken from the sacred Scriptures: of the incarnation, passion, and resurrection of the Lord, of His ascension into heaven, of the coming of the Holy Spirit and the teaching of the apostles. He also made songs about the terrors of future judgment, the horrors of the pains of hell, and the joys of the heavenly kingdom. In addition he composed many other songs about the divine mercies and judgments, in all of which he sought to turn his hearers away from delight in sin and arouse in them the love and practice of good works. He was a most religious man, humbly submitting himself to the discipline of the Rule; and he opposed all those who wished to act otherwise with a flaming and fervent zeal. It was for this reason that his life had a beautiful ending.

When the hour of his departure drew near he was afflicted, fourteen days before, by bodily weakness, yet so slight that he was able to walk about and talk the whole time. There was close by a building to which they used to take those who were infirm or who seemed to be at the point of death. On the night on which he was to die, as evening fell, he asked his attendant to prepare a place in this building where he could rest. The attendant did as Caedmon said though he wondered why he asked, for he did not seem to be by any means at the point of death. They had settled down in the house and were talking and joking cheerfully with each of those who were already there and it was past midnight, when he asked whether they had the Eucharist in the house. They answered, "What need have you of the Eucharist? You are not likely to die, since you are talking as cheerfully with us as if you were in perfect health." "Nevertheless," he repeated, "bring me the Eucharist." When he had taken it in his hand he asked if they were all charitably disposed towards him and had no complaint nor any quarrel nor grudge against him. They answered that they were all in charity with him and without the slightest feeling of anger; then they asked him in turn whether he was charitably disposed towards them. He answered at once, "My sons, I am in charity with all the servants of God." So, fortifying himself with the heavenly viaticum, he prepared for his entrance into the next life. Thereupon he asked them how near it was to the time when the brothers had to awake to sing their nightly praises to God. They answered, "It will not be long." And he answered, "Good, let us wait until then." And so, signing himself with the sign of the holy cross, he laid his head on the pillow, fell asleep for a little while, and so ended his life quietly. Thus it came about that, as he had served the Lord with a simple and pure mind and with quiet devotion, so he departed into His presence and left the world by a quiet death; and his tongue which had uttered so many good words in praise of the Creator also uttered its last words in His praise, as he signed himself with the sign of the cross and commended his spirit into God's hands; and from what has been said, it would seem that he had foreknowledge of his death.

✦✦✦

Bishop Asser
?–c. 909

When Bede died in 735, he left an island that was very unstable in its political geography but apparently ever more stable and accomplished in its religion and learning. By the end of the century that world was shattered. In 793 Vikings sacked the monastery of Lindisfarne, not far from Wearmouth-Jarrow. Waves of raiders and then settlers followed. Monastic communities fled inland, and some shifted for generations before resettling finally. However sporadic and temporary may have been the worldly impact of these Viking raiders, however quickly they became peaceful settlers, they had a disastrous effect on the kind of disciplined learning witnessed by the life of Bede. By the time of Asser, Latin learning in most of England was fragmented and in decline, though not so bad as it suits Alfred to claim. Asser, a Welsh monk and later bishop of Sherborne, was summoned to Wessex by King Alfred as part of a project to revive learning and extend its audience beyond those who read Latin. Alfred accomplished this, in part, by looking to men like Asser, from areas such as Wales which had preserved some traditions of classical learning.

Asser's worshipful and disorganized but lively *Life of King Alfred* was written in Latin during the king's life, about 893. It depicts the origins of the king's scholarly ambitions, interwoven with the struggles by which Alfred established and extended his rule and resisted renewed Viking incursions. Asser thus offers a double narrative of texts and conquests which make one another possible and worthy. The diffusion of learning and revival of religious discipline become enmeshed in a logic that also includes Alfred's ambitions to rule all the Anglo-Saxons.

from The Life of King Alfred[1]

[ALFRED'S BOYHOOD]

Now he was greatly cherished above all his brothers by the united and ardent love of his father and mother, and indeed of all people; and he was ever brought up entirely at the royal court. As he passed through his infancy and boyhood he surpassed all his brothers in beauty, and was more pleasing in his appearance, in his speech, and in his manners. From his earliest childhood the noble character of his mind gave him a desire for all things useful in this present life, and, above all, a longing for wisdom; but, alas! the culpable negligence of his relations, and of those who had care of him, allowed him to remain ignorant of letters until his twelfth year, or even to a later age. Albeit, day and night did he listen attentively to the Saxon poems, which he often heard others repeating, and his retentive mind enabled him to remember them.

An ardent hunter, he toiled persistently at every form of that art, and not in vain. For in his skill and success at this pursuit he surpassed all, as in all other gifts of God. And this skill we have ourselves seen on many occasions.

Now it chanced on a certain day that his mother showed to him and to his brothers a book of Saxon poetry, which she had in her hand, and said, "I will give this book to that one among you who shall the most quickly learn it." Then, moved at these words, or rather by the inspiration of God, and being carried away by the beauty of the initial letter in that book, anticipating his brothers who surpassed him in years but not in grace, he answered his mother, and said, "Will you of a truth give that book to one of us? To him who shall soonest understand it and repeat it to you?" And at this she smiled and was pleased, and affirmed it, saying, "I will give it to him." Then forthwith he took the book from her hand and went to his master, and read it; and when he had read it he brought it back to his mother and repeated it to her.

After this he learnt the Daily Course, that is, the services for each hour, and then some psalms and many prayers. These were collected in one book, which, as we have ourselves seen, he constantly carried about with him everywhere in the fold of his cloak, for the sake of prayer amid all the passing events of this present

---

1. Translated by L.C. Jane.

life. But, alas! the art of reading which he most earnestly desired he did not acquire in accordance with his wish, because, as he was wont himself to say, in those days there were no men really skilled in reading in the whole realm of the West Saxons.

With many complaints, and with heartfelt regrets, he used to declare that among all the difficulties and trials of this life this was the greatest. For at the time when he was of an age to learn, and had leisure and ability for it, he had no masters; but when he was older, and indeed to a certain extent had anxious masters and writers, he could not read. For he was occupied day and night without ceasing both with illnesses unknown to all the physicians of that island, and with the cares of the royal office both at home and abroad, and with the assaults of the heathen by land and sea.[2] None the less, amid the difficulties of this life, from his infancy to the present day, he has not in the past faltered in his earnest pursuit of knowledge, nor does he even now cease to long for it, nor, as I think, will he ever do so until the end of his life.

[ALFRED'S KINGSHIP]

Yet amid the wars and many hindrances of this present life, and amid the assaults of the pagans, and his daily illness, the king ceased not from the governance of the kingdom and from the pursuit of every form of hunting. Nor did he omit to instruct also his goldsmiths and all his artificers, his falconers and his huntsmen and the keepers of his dogs; nor to make according to new designs of his own articles of goldsmiths' work, more venerable and more precious than had been the wont of all his predecessors. He was constant in the reading of books in the Saxon tongue, and more especially in committing to memory the Saxon poems, and in commanding others to do so. And he by himself labored most zealously with all his might.

Moreover he heard the divine offices daily, the Mass, and certain psalms and prayers. He observed the services of the hours by day and by night, and oftentimes was he wont, as we have said, without the knowledge of his men, to go in the night-time to the churches for the sake of prayer. He was zealous in the giving of alms, and generous towards his own people and to those who came from all nations. He was especially and wonderfully kindly towards all men, and merry. And to the searching out of things not known did he apply himself with all his heart.

Moreover many Franks, Frisians and Gauls, pagans, Britons, Scots and Armoricans, of their own free will, submitted them to his rule, both nobles and persons of low degree. All these he ruled, according to his excellent goodness, as he did his own people, and loved them and honored them, and enriched them with money and with power.

He was eager and anxious to hear the Holy Scripture read to him by his own folk, but he would also as readily pray with strangers, if by any chance one had come from any place. Moreover he loved with wonderful affection his bishops and all the clergy, his ealdormen and nobles, his servants and all his household. And cherishing their sons, who were brought up in the royal household, with no less love than he bore towards his own children, he ceased not day and night, among other things, himself to teach them all virtue and to make them well acquainted with letters.

---

2. Alfred's patient suffering in illness is one of several patterns by which Asser implies analogies with the lives of saints.

But it was as though he found no comfort in all these things. For, as if he suffered no other care from within or without, in anxious sorrow, day and night, he would make complaint to the Lord and to all who were joined to him in close affection, lamenting with many sighs for that Almighty God had not made him skilled in divine wisdom and in the liberal arts.

+⧻ ⧻⧻⧻ ⧻+

King Alfred
849–899

Alfred, king of the West Saxons, had ambitions to be king of all England, at least south of the Humber. He spent much of his reign in a series of campaigns against Viking raiders. After a decisive victory at the battle of Edington in 878, Alfred negotiated a peace that included the departure of the Danes from Wessex and the baptism of their king Guthrum. In the later years of his reign, starting about 890, he embarked on a quite different, but ultimately more influential, campaign of conquest and Christian conversion, through the series of Anglo-Saxon translations from Latin produced by his own hand and under his patronage. Pope Gregory the Great's *Pastoral Care* (c. 591), a handbook for bishops, was the first. This effort assuredly had charitable and scholarly motivations, but it also takes on interesting national overtones when it assumes that Anglo-Saxon is one language and known by all, and even more when it is linked to earlier translations and the westward movement of ancient power.

Preface to Saint Gregory's *Pastoral Care*[1]

King Alfred bids greet Bishop Waerferth[2] with his words lovingly and with friendship; and I let it be known to thee that it has very often come into my mind what wise men there formerly were throughout England, both of sacred and secular orders; and what happy times there were then throughout England; and how the kings who had power over the nation in those days obeyed God and His ministers; how they preserved peace, morality, and order at home, and at the same time enlarged their territory abroad; and how they prospered both with war and with wisdom; and also how zealous the sacred orders were both in teaching and learning, and in all the services they owed to God; and how foreigners came to this land in search of wisdom and instruction, and how we should now have to get them from abroad if we were to have them. So general was its decay in England that there were very few on this side of the Humber who could understand their rituals in English, or translate a letter from Latin into English; and I believe that there were not many beyond the Humber. There were so few of them that I cannot remember a single one south of the Thames when I came to the throne. Thanks be to Almighty God that we have any teachers among us now. And therefore I command thee to do as I believe thou art willing, to disengage thyself from worldly matters as often as thou canst, that thou mayest apply the wisdom which God has given thee wherever thou canst. Consider what punishments would come upon us on account of this world, if we neither loved it [wisdom] ourselves nor suffered other men to obtain it: we should love the name only of Christian, and very few the virtues. When I considered all this, I remembered also that I saw, before it had been all ravaged and burned, how the churches throughout the whole of England stood filled with treasures and books; and there was also a great

1. Translated by Kevin Crossley-Holland.
2. Waerferth, bishop of Worcester, had earlier translated

Gregory's *Dialogues* for Alfred and perhaps inspired the king's more ambitious program.

multitude of God's servants, but they had very little knowledge of the books, for they could not understand anything of them, because they were not written in their own language. As if they had said: "Our forefathers, who formerly held these places, loved wisdom, and through it they obtained wealth and bequeathed it to us. In this we can still see their tracks, but we cannot follow them, and therefore we have lost both the wealth and the wisdom, because we would not incline our hearts after their example." When I remembered all this, I wondered extremely that the good and wise men who were formerly all over England, and had perfectly learned all the books, had not wished to translate them into their own language. But again I soon answered myself and said: "They did not think that men would ever be so careless, and that learning would so decay; through that desire they abstained from it, since they wished that the wisdom in this land might increase with our knowledge of languages." Then I remembered how the law was first known in Hebrew, and again, when the Greeks had learned it, they translated the whole of it into their own language, and all other books besides. And again the Romans, when they had learned them, translated the whole of them by learned interpreters into their own language. And also all other Christian nations translated a part of them into their own language.[3] Therefore it seems better to me, if you think so, for us also to translate some books which are most needful for all men to know into the language which we can all understand, and for you to do as we very easily can if we have tranquility enough, that is, that all the youth now in England of free men, who are rich enough to be able to devote themselves to it, be set to learn as long as they are not fit for any other occupation, until they are able to read English writing well: and let those be afterwards taught more in the Latin language who are to continue in learning, and be promoted to a higher rank. When I remembered how the knowledge of Latin had formerly decayed throughout England, and yet many could read English writing, I began, among other various and manifold troubles of this kingdom, to translate into English the book which is called in Latin *Pastoralis*, and in English *Shepherd's Book*, sometimes word by word, and sometimes according to the sense, as I had learned it from Plegmund my archbishop, and Asser my bishop, and Grimbald my mass-priest, and John my mass-priest. And when I had learned it as I could best understand it, and as I could most clearly interpret it, I translated it into English; and I will send a copy to every bishopric in my kingdom; and in each there is a book-mark worth fifty mancuses.[4] And I command in God's name that no man take the book-mark from the book, or the book from the monastery. It is uncertain how long there may be such learned bishops as now, thanks be to God, there are nearly everywhere; therefore I wish them always to remain in their places unless the bishop wish to take them with him, or they be lent out anywhere, or any one be making a copy from them.

⊷ ⊰◆⊱ ⊶

Ohthere's Journeys

Along with religious and speculative works like *Pastoral Care* and Boethius' *Consolation of Philosophy*, Alfred also sponsored the translation of histories, both Bede's *Ecclesiastical History of the English People* and the early fifth-century *Seven Books of History against the Pagans*, of Paulus

---

3. An early statement of the widespread medieval idea of the persistent westward movement of learning, *translatio studii*, in parallel with the westward movement of power, *translatio imperii*. If Alfred will now revive learning in

England, he may imply, should he not also consolidate power?
4. Gold coins.

Orosius. In the latter, Orosius' opening survey of geography is expanded to include lands north of the Alps, and the translator inserts the following account of two northern voyages by the Norwegian trader Ohthere, who later came to Alfred's court.

Ohthere describes two journeys, one made largely for curiosity (but also for walrus tusks) and the other mostly for trade. In the first, he heads north along the west coast of Norway, around the north edge of modern Sweden and Finland, and into the White Sea—a little-known area, inhabited only by hunters and fishermen. In the second he goes to the main trading town of his nation, Sciringes-heal (on the south coast of modern Norway), and then to a large town and trading center, Hedeby (modern Schleswig in northern Germany). Along with keen details of fauna and almost anthropological observation of local tribes, Ohthere notes the great exports of his area: furs, amber, and ivory—some of which he has brought to King Alfred. Throughout the passage, an implicit, curious interlocutor mediates between the interests (and ignorance) of the English audience and the foreign traveler.

Ohthere's Journeys[1]

Ohthere told his lord, King Alfred,[2] that he lived the furthest north of all Norwegians. He said that he lived in the north of Norway on the coast of the Atlantic. He also said that the land extends very far north beyond that point, but it is all uninhabited, except for a few places here and there where the *Finnas*[3] have their camps, hunting in winter, and in summer fishing in the sea.

He told how he once wished to find out how far the land extended due north, or whether anyone lived to the north of the unpopulated area. He went due north along the coast, keeping the uninhabited land to starboard and the open sea to port continuously for three days. He was then as far north as the whale hunters go at their furthest. He then continued due north as far as he could reach in the second three days. There the land turned due east, or the sea penetrated the land he did not know which—but he knew that he waited there for a west-northwest wind, and then sailed east along the coast as far as he could sail in four days. There he had to wait for a due northern wind, because there the land turned due south, or the sea penetrated the land he did not know which. Then from there he sailed due south along the coast as far as he could sail in five days. A great river went up into the land there. They turned up into the river, not daring to sail beyond it without permission, since the land on the far side of the river was fully settled. He had not previously come across any settled district since he left his own home, but had, the whole way, land to starboard that was uninhabited apart from fishers and bird-catchers and hunters, and they were all *Finnas*. To port he always had the open sea. The *Beormas* had extensive settlements in their country but the Norwegians did not dare to venture there. But the land of the *Terfinnas* was totally uninhabited except where hunters made camp, or fishermen or bird-catchers.

The *Beormas* told him many stories both about their own country and about the lands which surrounded them, but he did not know how much of it was true because he had not seen it for himself. It seemed to him that the *Finnas* and the *Beormas* spoke almost the same language. His main reason for going there, apart from exploring the land, was for the walruses, because they have very fine ivory in their tusks—

---

1. Translated by Christine E. Fell.
2. As a foreign visitor, Ohthere would need the official protection of the king, who is thus "his lord."
3. The *Finnas* (modern Lapps) are a nomadic people who give tribute to the Norwegians. They herd deer, hunt, and fish. They are not the peoples we now call Finns, whom Ohthere called *Beormas* and *Cwenas*.

they brought some of these tusks to the king—and their hide is very good for ship-ropes. This whale [i.e., walrus] is much smaller than other whales; it is no more than seven ells long. The best whale-hunting is in his own country; those are forty-eight ells long, the biggest fifty ells long; of these he said that he, one of six, killed sixty in two days.

He was a very rich man in those possessions which their riches consist of, that is in wild deer. He had still, when he came to see the king, six hundred unsold tame deer. These deer they call "reindeer." Six of these were decoy-reindeer. These are very valuable among the *Finnas* because they use them to catch the wild reindeer. He was among the chief men in that country, but he had not more than twenty cattle, twenty sheep and twenty pigs, and the little that he plowed he plowed with horses. Their wealth, however, is mostly in the tribute which the *Finnas* pay them. That tribute consists of the skins of beasts, the feathers of birds, whale-bone, and ship-ropes made from whale-hide and sealskin. Each pays according to his rank. The highest in rank has to pay fifteen marten skins, five reindeer skins, one bear skin and ten measures of feathers, and a jacket of bearskin or otterskin and two ship-ropes. Each of these must be sixty ells long, one made from whale-hide the other from seal.

He said that the land of the Norwegians is very long and narrow. All of it that can be used for grazing or plowing lies along the coast and even that is in some places very rocky. Wild mountains lie to the east, above and alongside the cultivated land. In these mountains live the *Finnas*. The cultivated land is broadest in the south, and the further north it goes the narrower it becomes. In the south it is perhaps sixty miles broad or a little broader; and in the middle, thirty or broader; and to the north, he said, where it is narrowest, it might be three miles across to the mountains. The mountains beyond are in some places of a width that takes two weeks to cross, in others of a width that can be crossed in six days.

Beyond the mountains Sweden borders the southern part of the land as far as the north, and the country of the *Cwenas* borders the land in the north. Sometimes the *Cwenas* make raids on the Norwegians across the mountains, and sometimes the Norwegians make raids on them. There are very large fresh-water lakes throughout these mountains, and the *Cwenas* carry their boats overland onto the lakes and from there make raids on the Norwegians. They have very small, very light boats.

Ohthere said that the district where he lived is called *Halgoland*.[4] He said no-one lived to the north of him. In the south part of Norway there is a trading-town which is called *Sciringes heal*. He said that a man could scarcely sail there in a month, assuming he made camp at night, and each day had a favorable wind. He would sail by the coast the whole way. To starboard is first of all *Iraland*[5] and then those islands which are between *Iraland* and this land, and then this land until he comes to *Sciringes heal*, and Norway is on the port side the whole way. To the south of *Sciringes heal* a great sea penetrates the land; it is too wide to see across. Jutland is on the far side and after that *Sillende*.[6] This sea flows into the land for many hundred miles.

From *Sciringes heal* he said that he sailed in five days to the trading-town called Hedeby, which is situated among Wends, Saxons and Angles and belongs to the Danes. When he sailed there from *Sciringes heal* he had Denmark to port and the open sea to starboard for three days. Then two days before he arrived at Hedeby he

---

4. The northernmost province of Norway, much of it within the polar circle.

5. Possibly a corruption of Iceland.

6. Probably southern Jutland, modern North Schleswig.

had Jutland and *Sillende* and many islands to starboard. The Angles lived in these districts before they came to this land. On the port side he had, for two days, those islands which belong to Denmark.

—•—✠—•—

The Anglo-Saxon Chronicle

The Anglo-Saxon Chronicle began to be assembled in the 890s at Winchester, in the heart of King Alfred's Wessex and at the high point of his reign. The decision to use Anglo-Saxon in this originally monastic product reflects the influence of Alfred's translation projects. The original version of the *Chronicle* was distributed to a number of monasteries, which made their own additions sometimes as late as the mid-twelfth century. If the *Chronicles* began as a gesture of common language and shared history, though, their later entries—like the one below—increasingly record dynastic struggle and civil strife. And the *Chronicles* themselves, in their extensions after the Conquest, emblematize the fate of the Anglo-Saxon vernacular and culture: increasingly isolated, fragmentary, and recorded in a disappearing tongue.

from The Anglo-Saxon Chronicle[1]
STAMFORD BRIDGE AND HASTINGS

1066   In this year King Harold came from York to Westminster at the Easter following the Christmas that the king died,[2] and Easter was then on 16 April. Then over all England there was seen a sign in the skies such as had never been seen before. Some said it was the star "comet" which some call the long-haired star; and it first appeared on the eve of the Greater Litany, that is 24 April, and so shone all the week. And soon after this Earl Tosti came from overseas into the Isle of Wight with as large a fleet as he could muster and both money and provisions were given him.[3] And King Harold his brother assembled a naval force and a land force larger than any king had assembled before in this country, because he had been told that William the Bastard[4] meant to come here and conquer this country. This was exactly what happened afterwards. Meanwhile Earl Tosti came into the Humber with sixty ships and Earl Edwin came with a land force and drove him out, and the sailors deserted him. And he went to Scotland with twelve small vessels, and there Harold, king of Norway, met him with three hundred ships, and Tosti submitted to him and became his vassal; and they both went up the Humber until they reached York. And there Earl Edwin and Morcar his brother fought against them; but the Norwegians had the victory. Harold, king of the English, was informed that things had gone thus; and the fight was on the Vigil of Saint Matthew. Then Harold our king came upon the Norwegians by surprise and met them beyond York at Stamford Bridge with a large force of the English people; and that day there was a very fierce fight on both sides. There was killed Harold Fairhair and Earl Tosti, and the Norwegians who survived took to flight; and the English attacked them fiercely as they pursued them until some got to the ships. Some were drowned, and some burned, and some destroyed in various ways so that few survived and the English remained in command of the field. The king gave quarter to Olaf, son

---

1. Translated by Kevin Crossley-Holland.
2. Edward "the Confessor" ruled 1042–1066. Harold claims the throne through his sister Edith, Edward's widow.

3. Tosti was Harold's estranged brother, and now supported the rival claim of Harold Fairhair, king of Norway.
4. William of Normandy, "the Conqueror."

of the Norse king, and their bishop and the earl of Orkney and all those who survived on the ships, and they went up to our king and swore oaths that they would always keep peace and friendship with this country; and the king let them go home with twenty-four ships. These two pitched battles were fought within five nights.

Then Count William came from Normandy to Pevensey on Michaelmas Eve, and as soon as they were able to move on they built a castle at Hastings. King Harold was informed of this and he assembled a large army and came against him at the hoary apple-tree. And William came against him by surprise before his army was drawn up in battle array. But the king nevertheless fought hard against him, with the men who were willing to support him, and there were heavy casualties on both sides. There King Harold was killed and Earl Leofwine his brother, and Earl Gyrth his brother, and many good men, and the French remained masters of the field, even as God granted it to them because of the sins of the people. Archbishop Aldred and the citizens of London wanted to have Edgar Cild[5] as king, as was his proper due; and Edwin and Morcar promised him that they would fight on his side; but always the more it ought to have been forward the more it got behind, and the worse it grew from day to day, exactly as everything came to be at the end. The battle took place on the festival of Calixtus the pope. And Count William went back to Hastings, and waited there to see whether submission would be made to him. But when he understood that no one meant to come to him, he went inland with all his army that was left to him, and that came to him afterwards from overseas, and ravaged all the region that he overran until he reached Berkhamstead. There he was met by Archbishop Aldred and Edgar Cild, and Earl Edwin and Earl Morcar, and all the chief men from London. And they submitted out of necessity after most damage had been done—and it was a great piece of folly that they had not done it earlier, since God would not make things better, because of our sins. And they gave hostages and swore oaths to him, and he promised them that he would be a gracious liege lord, and yet in the meantime they ravaged all that they overran. Then on Christmas Day, Archbishop Aldred consecrated him king at Westminster. And he promised Aldred on Christ's book and swore moreover (before Aldred would place the crown on his head) that he would rule all this people as well as the best of the kings before him, if they would be loyal to him. All the same he laid taxes on people very severely, and then went in spring overseas to Normandy, and took with him Archbishop Stigand, and Aethelnoth, abbot of Glastonbury, and Edgar Cild and Earl Edwin and Earl Morcar, and Earl Waltheof, and many other good men from England. And Bishop Odo and Earl William stayed behind and built castles far and wide throughout this country, and distressed the wretched folk, and always after that it grew much worse. May the end be good when God wills!

[END OF PERSPECTIVES: ETHNIC AND RELIGIOUS ENCOUNTERS]

——— ⊫◊⊨ ———

Taliesin

The name of Taliesin resonated through Welsh literary imagination for more than a millennium, from the late sixth century until the end of the Middle Ages. Only a small cluster of about a dozen poems can be securely identified with him, all of them praise poems and elegies for

---

5. Son of Edgar the Exile, grandson and great-grandson of kings; his great-uncle King Edward had titled him "Aetheling," or "throne-worthy." He was still a minor in 1066 and would have had to rule through a regent.

contemporary kings. These must have circulated for generations in oral form. They appear in their earliest surviving manuscript, the late thirteenth-century Book of Taliesin, already embedded within a nimbus of intriguing legends and falsely attributed works that had been attached to the prestige of his name across the centuries. (For one such legend, see *The Tale of Taliesin*, page 536.)

Despite this central role, Taliesin was not a poet of "Wales" in anything like its modern geography. In the later sixth century when he was active, Welsh-speaking kingdoms survived in the north and west of Britain and into modern Scotland. They were embattled, pressured by the expanding Anglo-Saxon kingdoms to the east and south, by Picts in the north, and by Irish Celts in the kingdom of Dalriada to the far northwest. Among these unstable Welsh kingdoms, especially Rheged around the Solway Firth, Taliesin became an important court poet.

The warrior kings in the Welsh north, such as Taliesin's chief patrons Urien king of Rheged and his son Owain, were extolled in a poetic culture that celebrated treasure and heroic violence, yet did so in forms of considerable intricacy and language of dramatic spareness. Taliesin's poems use ambitious meters and stanzas involving internal rhyme, end rhyme, and alliteration. They do not merely glory in armed bloodshed but also explore the boasts and emotions leading up to battle; they often display a haunting visual sense of its grisly aftermath. Taliesin further celebrates the generosity and gaiety of the triumphant court: in ways reminiscent of the Anglo-Saxon *Wanderer*, one poem here registers the poet's terror at the thought of losing his patron and protector. In an elegy for Owain ap Urien, Taliesin combines all these elements, yet brackets them with a suddenly broadened and suggestively discordant perspective, a Christian plea for the needs of Owain's soul.

Urien Yrechwydd[1]

	Urien of Yrechwydd	most generous of Christian men,
	much do you give	to the people of your land;
	as you gather	so also you scatter,
	the poets of Christendom	rejoice while you stand.
5	More is the gaiety	and more is the glory
	that Urien and his heirs	are for riches renowned,
	and he is the chieftain,	the paramount ruler,
	the far-flung refuge,	first of fighters found.
	The Lloegrians[2] know it	when they count their numbers,
10	death have they suffered	and many a shame,
	their homesteads a-burning,	stripped their bedding,
	and many a loss	and many a blame,
	and never a respite	from Urien of Rheged.
	Rheged's defender,	famed lord, your land's anchor,
15	all that is told of you	has my acclaim.
	Intense is your spear-play	when you hear ploy of battle,
	when to battle you come	'tis a killing you can,
	fire in their houses ere day	in the lord of Yrechwydd's way,
	Yrechwydd the beautiful	and its generous clan.
20	The Angles are succorless.	Around the fierce king
	are his fierce offspring.	Of those dead, of those living,
	of those yet to come,	you head the column.
	To gaze upon him	is a widespread fear;

---

1. "I-rech-ooeed" (guttural "ch"), or Rheged. Like many Anglo-Saxon poems, this poem uses a break (caesura) in mid-line. Translated by Saunders Lewis.

2. The Angles and Saxons.

25   Gaiety clothes him,   the ribald ruler,
      gaiety clothes him   and riches abounding,
      gold king of the Northland   and of kings king.

The Battle of Argoed Llwyfain[1]

There was a great battle Saturday morning
From when the sun rose until it grew dark.
The fourfold hosts of Fflamddwyn[2] invaded,
Goddau and Rheged gathered in arms,
5   Summoned from Argoed as far as Arfynydd[3]—
They might not delay by as much as a day.

With a great blustering din, Fflamddwyn shouted,
"Have these the hostages come? Are they ready?"[4]
To him then Owain, scourge of the eastlands,
10   "They've not come, no! they're not, nor shall they be ready."
And a whelp of Coel would indeed be afflicted
Did he have to give any man as a hostage!

And Urien, lord of Erechwydd, shouted,
"If they would meet us now for a treaty,
15   High on the hilltop let's raise our ramparts,
Carry our faces over the shield rims,
Raise up our spears, men, over our heads
And set upon Fflamddwyn in the midst of his hosts
And slaughter him, ay, and all that go with him!"

20   There was many a corpse beside Argoed Llwyfain;
From warriors ravens grew red
And with their leader a host attacked.
For a whole year I shall sing to their triumph.

The War-Band's Return[1]

Through a single year
This man has poured out
Wine, bragget, and mead,
Reward for valor.
5   A host of singers,
A swarm about spits,
Their torques round their heads,
Their places splendid.
Each went on campaign,
10   Eager in combat,
His steed beneath him,
Set to raid Manaw
For the sake of wealth,

---

1. "Ar-goid Lloo-ee-vine, the Welsh "ll" rather like "tl"
pronounced quickly as a single sound. Translated by
Anthony Conran.
2. "Flom-thoo-een," the Flame-bearer, identity uncertain.
3. "Goddau ("Go-thy,") and Arfynydd ("Ar-vi-nith")

British territories.
4. Fflamddwyn arrogantly demands hostages, guarantees
of submission, before the battle. The use of direct quotation is unique among Taliesin's poems.
1. Translated by Joseph P. Clancy.

Profit in plenty,
15 Eight herds alike
Of calves and cattle,
Milch cows and oxen,
And each one worthy.

I could have no joy
20 Should Urien be slain,
So loved before he left,
Brandishing his lance,
And his white hair soaked,
And a bier his fate,
25 And gory his cheek
With the stain of blood,
A strong, steadfast man,
His wife made a widow,
My faithful king,
30 My faithful trust,
My bulwark, my chief,
Before savage pain.

Go, lad, to the door:
What is that clamor?
35 Is the earth shaking?
Is the sea in flood?
The chant grows stronger
From marching men!

Were a foe in hill,
40 Urien will stab him;
Were a foe in dale,
Urien has pierced him;
Were foe in mountain,
Urien conquers him;
45 Were foe on hillside,
Urien will wound him;
Were foe on rampart,
Urien will smite him:
Foe on path, foe on peak,
50 Foe at every bend,
Not one sneeze or two
He permits before death.
No famine can come,
Plunder about him.
55 Like death his spear
Piercing a foeman.
And until I die, old,
By death's strict demand,
I shall not be joyful
60 Unless I praise Urien.

Lament for Owain Son of Urien[1]

God, consider the soul's need
    Of Owain son of Urien!
Rheged's prince, secret in loam:
    No shallow work to praise him.

5   A straight° grave, a man much praised,   *narrow*
    His whetted spear the wings of dawn:
That lord of bright Llwyfenydd,
    Where is his peer?

Reaper of enemies; strong of grip;
10   One kind with his fathers;
Owain, to slay Fflamddwyn,
    Thought it no more than sleep.

Sleepeth the wide host of England
    With light in their eyes,
15   And those that had not fled
    Were braver than were wise.

Owain dealt them doom
    As the wolves devour sheep;
That warrior, bright of harness,
20   Gave stallions for the bard.

Though he hoarded wealth like a miser
    For his soul's sake he gave it.
God, consider the soul's need
    Of Owain son of Urien!

━►◄━♦━►◄━

The Wanderer

In the Exeter Book, a manuscript copied about 975 and donated to the Bishop of Exeter, are preserved some of the greatest short poems in Old English, including a number of poems referred to as elegies—laments which contrast past happiness with present sorrow and remark on how fleeting is the former. Along with *The Wanderer*, the elegies include its companion piece *The Seafarer*; *The Ruin*; *The Husband's Message*; *The Wife's Lament*; and *Wulf and Eadwacer*. While the last two are exceptional in dealing with female experience, elegies for the most part focus on male bonds and companionship, particularly the joys of the mead hall. Old English poetry as a whole is almost entirely devoid of interest in romantic love between men and women and focuses instead on the bond between lord and retainer; elegiac poems such as *The Wanderer* have in fact been called "the love poetry of a heroic society."

    The Wanderer opens with an appeal to a Christian concept, as the third-person narrator speaks of the wanderer's request for God's mercy. The body of the poem, however—primarily a first-person account in the wanderer's voice—reflects more pagan values in its regret for the

1. Translated by Saunders Lewis.

loss of earthly joys. Though the poem's structure is somewhat confusing, one can discern two major parts. In the first, the wanderer laments his personal situation: he was once a member of a warrior band, but his lord—his beloved "gold-friend"—has died, leaving him a homeless exile. He dreams that he "clasps and kisses" his lord, but he then wakes to see only the dark waves, the snow, and the sea birds.

The second part of the poem turns from personal narrative to a more general statement of the transitoriness of all earthly things. The speaker (possibly someone other than the wanderer at this point), looking at the ruin of ancient buildings, is moved to express the ancient Roman motif known as *ubi sunt* (Latin for "where are"): "Where has the horse gone? Where the man? Where the giver of gold? / Where is the feasting place? And where the pleasures of the hall?" In the concluding five lines, the reader is urged to seek comfort in heaven.

There has been much debate about the degrees of Christianity and paganism in this tenth-century poem. The positions range from the view that the Christian opening and closing are totally extraneous to the poem and have been tacked on by a monkish copyist, to the view that the poem is a Christian allegory about a soul exiled from his heavenly home, longing for his lord Jesus Christ. It is now generally held that the poem is authentically Christian, in a literal rather than an allegorical way, but that the values of pagan society still exert a powerful pull in it.

The Wanderer[1]

Often the wanderer pleads for pity
and mercy from the Lord; but for a long time,
sad in mind, he must dip his oars
into icy waters, the lanes of the sea;
5 he must follow the paths of exile: fate is inflexible.

Mindful of hardships, grievous slaughter,
the ruin of kinsmen, the wanderer said:
"Time and again at the day's dawning
I must mourn all my afflictions alone.
10 There is no one still living to whom I dare open
the doors of my heart. I have no doubt
that it is a noble habit for a man
to bind fast all his heart's feelings,
guard his thoughts, whatever he is thinking.
15 The weary in spirit cannot withstand fate,
a troubled mind finds no relief:
wherefore those eager for glory often
hold some ache imprisoned in their hearts.
Thus I had to bind my feelings in fetters,
20 often sad at heart, cut off from my country,
far from my kinsmen, after, long ago,
dark clods of earth covered my gold-friend;
I left that place in wretchedness,
plowed the icy waves with winter in my heart;
25 in sadness I sought far and wide
for a treasure-giver, for a man
who would welcome me into his mead-hall,

---

1. Translated by Kevin Crossley-Holland.

give me good cheer (for I boasted no friends),
entertain me with delights. He who has experienced it

30 knows how cruel a comrade sorrow can be
to any man who has few loyal friends:
for him are the ways of exile, in no wise twisted gold;
for him is a frozen body, in no wise the fruits of the earth.
He remembers hall-retainers and treasure

35 and how, in his youth, his gold-friend
entertained him. Those joys have all vanished.
A man who lacks advice for a long while
from his loved lord understands this,
that when sorrow and sleep together

40 hold the wretched wanderer in their grip,
it seems that he clasps and kisses
his lord, and lays hands and head
upon his lord's knee as he had sometimes done
when he enjoyed the gift-throne in earlier days.

45 Then the friendless man wakes again
and sees the dark waves surging around him,
the sea-birds bathing, spreading their feathers,
frost and snow falling mingled with hail.

"Then his wounds lie more heavy in his heart,

50 aching for his lord. His sorrow is renewed;
the memory of kinsmen sweeps through his mind;
joyfully he welcomes them, eagerly scans
his comrade warriors. Then they swim away again.
Their drifting spirits do not bring many old songs

55 to his lips. Sorrow upon sorrow attend
the man who must send time and again
his weary heart over the frozen waves.

"And thus I cannot think why in the world
my mind does not darken when I brood on the fate

60 of brave warriors, how they have suddenly
had to leave the mead-hall, the bold followers.
So this world dwindles day by day,
and passes away; for a man will not be wise
before he has weathered his share of winters

65 in the world. A wise man must be patient,
neither too passionate nor too hasty of speech,
neither too irresolute nor too rash in battle;
not too anxious, too content, nor too grasping,
and never too eager to boast before he knows himself.

70 When he boasts a man must bide his time
until he has no doubt in his brave heart
that he has fully made up his mind.
A wise man must fathom how eerie it will be
when all the riches of the world stand waste,

75 as now in diverse places in this middle-earth
old walls stand, tugged at by winds
and hung with hoar-frost, buildings in decay.

The wine-halls crumble, lords lie dead,
deprived of joy, all the proud followers
80   have fallen by the wall: battle carried off some,
led them on journeys; the bird carried one
over the welling waters; one the gray wolf
devoured; a warrior with downcast face
hid one in an earth-cave.
85   Thus the Maker of Men laid this world waste
until the ancient works of the giants stood idle,
hushed without the hubbub of inhabitants.
Then he who has brooded over these noble ruins,
and who deeply ponders this dark life,
90   wise in his mind, often remembers
the many slaughters of the past and speaks these words:
Where has the horse gone? Where the man? Where the giver of gold?
Where is the feasting-place? And where the pleasures of the hall?
I mourn the gleaming cup, the warrior in his corselet,
95   the glory of the prince. How that time has passed away,
darkened under the shadow of night as if it had never been.
Where the loved warriors were, there now stands a wall
of wondrous height, carved with serpent forms.
The savage ash-spears, avid for slaughter,
100   have claimed all the warriors—a glorious fate!
Storms crash against these rocky slopes,
sleet and snow fall and fetter the world,
winter howls, then darkness draws on,
the night-shadow casts gloom and brings
105   fierce hailstorms from the north to frighten men.
Nothing is ever easy in the kingdom of earth,
the world beneath the heavens is in the hands of fate.
Here possessions are fleeting, here friends are fleeting,
here man is fleeting, here kinsman is fleeting,
110   the whole world becomes a wilderness."
So spoke the wise man in his heart as he sat apart in thought.
Brave is the man who holds to his beliefs; nor shall he ever
show the sorrow in his heart before he knows how he
can hope to heal it. It is best for a man to seek
115   mercy and comfort from the Father in heaven, the safe home that awaits us all.

Wulf and Eadwacer *and* The Wife's Lament

Old English literature focuses largely on masculine and military concerns and lacks a concept of romantic love—what the twelfth-century French would later call *"fine amour."* Against this backdrop *Wulf and Eadwacer* and *The Wife's Lament* stand out, first, by their use of woman's voice and second, by their treatment of the sorrows of love.

Though the exact genre of these poems is problematic, some scholars classifying them as riddles and others as religious allegories, most group them with a class of Old English poems known as elegies, with which they are preserved in the same manuscript, the Exeter Book. The elegies lament the loss of earthly goods, comradeship, and the "hall joys," often, as in *The Wanderer* and *The Seafarer*, by a speaker in exile. *The Wife's Lament* and *Wulf and Eadwacer* differ from the other elegies in that the speakers, as women, had no experience of comradeship to lose, as their main function was to be exchanged in marriage to cement relationships between feuding tribes. They are in a sense twice exiled, first from the noble brotherhood by their gender, and second from their beloved by their personal history. Furthermore, unlike the speakers in *The Wanderer* and *The Seafarer*, they do not look forward to the consolation of a heavenly kingdom imagined as a warlord with his group of retainers.

Although the two elegies in woman's voice are unique in the Old English corpus, they have analogues within the larger tradition of continental woman's song, which flourished in medieval Latin and the vernaculars from the eleventh century on. (More humorous examples of this genre in Middle English can be found later in this volume.) Their composition was so early—990 at the latest—that this tradition could not have influenced them, although the Roman poet Ovid's *Heroides* (verse letters of abandoned heroines to their faithless lovers) could have done so. One critic has raised the question of female authorship, on the grounds that continental nuns in the eighth century were criticized for writing romantic songs. As the critic Marilynn Desmond has suggested, perhaps Virginia Woolf's speculation that "anonymous was a woman" is true of these poems.

Though scholars agree that *Wulf and Eadwacer* is "heart-rending" and "haunting," they cannot agree on the dramatic situation—each translation is an act of interpretation. The present translator, Kevin Crossley-Holland, sees the poem as involving the female speaker; her husband (Eadwacer); her lover (Wulf), from whom she is separated; and her child (a "cub"). Although what transpired before is unclear, she wistfully concludes, "men easily savage what was never secure, our song together." The dramatic setting of *The Wife's Lament* is similary ambiguous; it is not clear whether the woman's anger is directed toward her husband or to a third person who plotted to separate them.

Wulf and Eadwacer

Prey, it's as if my people have been handed prey.
They'll tear him to pieces if he comes with a troop.

O, we are apart.

Wulf is on one island, I on another,
5   a fastness that island, a fen-prison.
Fierce men roam there, on that island;
they'll tear him to pieces if he comes with a troop.

O, we are apart.

How I have grieved for my Wulf's wide wanderings.
10   When rain slapped the earth and I sat apart weeping,
when the bold warrior wrapped his arms about me,
I seethed with desire and yet with such hatred.
Wulf, my Wulf, my yearning for you
and your seldom coming have caused my sickness,
15   my mourning heart, not mere starvation.
Can you heart, Eadwacer? Wulf will spirit
our pitiful whelp to the woods.
Men easily savage what was never secure,
our song together.

The Wife's Lament[1]

I draw these words from my deep sadness,
my sorrowful lot. I can say that,
since I grew up, I have not suffered
such hardships as now, old or new.
5   I am tortured by the anguish of exile.

First my lord forsook his family
for the tossing waves; I fretted at dawn
as to where in the world my lord might be.
In my sorrow I set out then,
10   a friendless wanderer, to search for my man.
But that man's kinsmen laid secret plans
to part us, so that we should live
most wretchedly, far from each other
in this wide world; I was seized with longings.

15   My lord asked me to live with him here;
I had few loved ones, loyal friends
in this country; that is reason for grief.
Then I found my own husband was ill-starred,
sad at heart, pretending, plotting
20   murder behind a smiling face. How often
we swore that nothing but death should ever
divide us; that is all changed now;
our friendship is as if it had never been.
Early and late, I must undergo hardship
25   because of the feud of my own dearest loved one.
Men forced me to live in a forest grove,
under an oak tree in the earth-cave.
This cavern is age-old; I am choked with longings.
Gloomy are the valleys, too high the hills,
30   harsh strongholds overgrown with briars:
a joyless abode. The journey of my lord so often
cruelly seizes me. There are lovers on earth,
lovers alive who lie in bed,
when I pass through this earth-cave alone
35   and out under the oak tree at dawn;
there I must sit through the long summer's day
and there I mourn my miseries,
my many hardships; for I am never able
to quiet the cares of my sorrowful mind,
40   all the longings that are my life's lot.

Young men must always be serious in mind
and stout-hearted; they must hide
their heartaches, that host of constant sorrows,
behind a smiling face.

Whether he is master
45   of his own fate or is exiled in a far-off land—

1. Translated by Kevin Crossley-Holland.

sitting under rocky storm-cliffs, chilled
with hoar-frost, weary in mind,
surrounded by the sea in some sad place—
my husband is caught in the clutches of anguish;
over and again he recalls a happier home.
50 Grief goes side by side with those
who suffer longing for a loved one.

Riddles

Riddles were a popular genre in Anglo-Saxon England, appealing to a taste for intellectual puzzles, which we also see in *Beowulf*, with its kennings; *The Dream of the Rood*, with its speaking cross; and *Wulf and Eadwacer*, with its cryptic dramatic situation. In the Exeter Book, one of the four major manuscripts containing Anglo-Saxon poetry (including *The Wanderer*, *The Wife's Lament*, and *Wulf and Eadwacer*) there are nearly a hundred riddles in Old English, dating from the seventh to the tenth centuries. They were in some cases modeled on collections of a hundred Latin riddles by the seventh-century Anglo-Saxon scholar Aldhelm, but they also derive in large part from indigenous folk tradition. In fact, they mark an important point of intersection between literate and oral culture in Anglo-Saxon England: though designed to be recited, they are written and sometimes focus on the technology of writing.

The three Anglo-Latin riddles of Aldhelm included here reveal an attitude of awe toward writing, conceived as an almost magical act, partly because of its novelty in a recently oral culture, but more because of its ownership by a priestly class in control of Christianity, the religion of "the Book." Aldhelm gives a sense of the tremendous effort that went into book-making—scratching treated animal skins with a quill pen or cutting into tablets made of wax, wood, and leather—and the resultant splendid object, adorned with "artful windings," cut into a "fair design." In the *Alphabet*, he makes the personified letters express their pride in the paradox of writing as voiceless speech: "We / in silence quickly bring out hoarded words." The pen in the riddle of that name speaks of its origin as a bird's feather and of its ability, despite its present earthbound state, to help lead the virtuous to heaven.

Of the Old English riddles included here, four also have to do with writing, an activity important in the daily life of priests. Old English Riddle 2 traces the making of a book by speaking as a sheep slain for its skin to make parchment, describing the "bird's feather" leaving tracks on its surface, and concluding in the person of the Bible itself, decorated with "the wondrous work of smiths," sacred and useful at the same time. Old English Riddle 5 similarly traces a tool from its origin in nature to its status as a manufactured thing. The narrator speaks of its life growing by the water (as a plant), the paradox that, though "mouthless," it should "sing / to men sitting at the mead-bench" (as a flute), and the "miracle" by which it can send a private message (as a pen).

In contrast to those Old English riddles concerned with writing, the majority deal with aspects of Anglo-Saxon secular life, with answers such as a shield, a storm, an iceberg, or a ship. The poem of this sort included here, Old English Riddle 1, explores areas of experience usually ignored by Old English epic, elegiac, and religious poetry. Beginning traditionally, "I'm a strange creature," it treats domestic activity—the storage and preparation of food—by a lower-class woman, a churl's daughter. One of several sexual riddles in the Exeter Book, it is a finely sustained *double entendre*, showing that there was indeed humor in Old English poetry.

(Following the manuscripts, Aldhelm's riddles are printed with the titles that state their solutions, while those from the Exeter Book—which offers no solutions—are followed by solutions given by modern editors).

Three Anglo-Latin Riddles by Aldhelm[1]

Alphabet

We seventeen sisters, voiceless all, declare
Six others bastards are, and not of us.
Of iron we are born, and find our death
Again by iron; or at times we come
From pinion of a lofty-flying bird.
Three brothers got us of an unknown mother.
To him who thirsts for instant counsel, we
In silence quickly bring out hoarded words.

Writing Tablets

Of honey-laden bees I first was born,
But in the forest grew my outer coat;
My tough backs came from shoes. An iron point
In artful windings cuts a fair design,
And leaves long, twisted furrows, like a plow.
From heaven unto that field is borne the seed
Or nourishment, which brings forth generous sheaves
A thousandfold. Alas, that such a crop,
A holy harvest, falls before grim war.

Pen

The shining pelican, whose yawning throat
Gulps down the waters of the sea, long since
Produced me, white as he. Through snowy fields
I keep a straight road, leaving deep-blue tracks
Upon the gleaming way, and darkening
The fair champaign with black and tortuous paths;
Yet one way through the plain suffices not,
For with a thousand bypaths runs the road,
And them who stray not from it, leads to heaven.

Five Old English Riddles[2]

1

I'm a strange creature, for I satisfy women,
a service to the neighbors! No one suffers
at my hands except for my slayer.
I grow very tall, erect in a bed,
5   I'm hairy underneath. From time to time
a good-looking girl, the doughty daughter
of some churl dares to hold me,
grips my russet skin, robs me of my head
and puts me in the pantry. At once that girl
10   with plaited hair who has confined me
remembers our meeting. Her eye moistens.

1. Translated by James Hall Pitman.   2. Translated by Kevin Crossley-Holland.

2

An enemy ended my life, took away
of my bodily strength; then he dipped me
in water and drew me out again,
15   and put me in the sun where I soon shed
all my hair. The knife's sharp edge
bit into me once my blemishes had been scraped away;
fingers folded me and the bird's feather
often moved across my brown surface,
20   sprinkling useful drops; it swallowed the wood-dye
(part of the stream) and again traveled over me
leaving black tracks. Then a man bound me,
he stretched skin over me and adorned me
with gold; thus I am enriched by the wondrous work
25   of smiths, wound about with shining metal.
Now my clasp and my red dye
and these glorious adornments bring fame far and wide
to the Protector of Men, and not to the pains of hell.
If the sons of men would make use of me
30   they would be the safer and more sure of victory,
their hearts would be bolder, their minds more at ease,
their thoughts wiser, they would have more friends,
companions and kinsmen (true and honorable,
brave and kind) who would gladly increase
35   their honor and prosperity, and heap
benefits upon them, holding them fast
in love's embraces. Ask what I am called,
of such use to men. My name is famous,
of service to men and sacred in itself.

3

A moth devoured words. When I heard
of that wonder it struck me as a strange event
that a worm should swallow the song of some man,
a thief gorge in the darkness on fine phrases
and their firm foundation. The thievish stranger
was not a whit the wiser for swallowing words.

4

I watched four curious creatures
traveling together; their tracks were swart,
each imprint very black. The birds' support
moved swiftly; it flew in the air,
dived under the wave. The toiling warrior
worked without pause, pointing the paths
to all four over the beaten gold.

5

I sank roots first of all, stood
near the shore, close by the dyke

and dash of waves; few men
saw my home in that wilderness,
5   but each dawn, each dusk,
the tawny waves surged and swirled
around me. Little did I think
that I, mouthless, should ever sing
to men sitting at the mead-bench,
10   varying my pitch. It is rather puzzling,
a miracle to men ignorant of such arts,
how a knife's point and a right hand
(mind and implement moving as one)
could cut and carve me—so that I
15   can send you a message without fear,
and no one else can overhear
or noise abroad the words we share.

Solutions: 1. Penis or onion; 2. Bible; 3. Book worm; 4. Pen and fingers; 5. Reed.

After the Norman Conquest

PERSPECTIVES

Arthurian Myth in the History of Britain

Almost since it first appeared, the story of King Arthur has occupied a contested zone between myth and history. Far from diminishing the Arthurian tradition, though, this ambiguity has lent it a tremendous and protean impact on the political and cultural imagination of Europe, from the Middle Ages to the present. Probably no other body of medieval legend remains today as widely known and as often revisited as the Arthurian story.

One measure of Arthur's undiminished importance is the eager debate, eight centuries old and going strong, about his historical status. Whether or not a specific "Arthur" ever existed, legends and attributes gathered around his name from a very early date, mostly in texts of Welsh background. Around 600 a Welsh poem refers briefly to Arthur's armed might, and by about 1000, the story *Culhwch and Olwen*, from the Mabinogion, assumes knowledge of Arthur as a royal warlord. Other early Welsh texts begin to give him more-than-mortal attributes, associating Arthur with such marvels as an underworld quest and a mysterious tomb. In the ninth century, the Latin *History of the Britons* by the Welshman Nennius confidently speaks of Arthur as a great leader and lists his twelve victories ending with that at Mount Badon.

Some of this at least fits with better-documented history and with less-shadowy commanders who might have been models for an Arthurian figure, even if they were not "Arthur." When the Romans withdrew in 410, the romanized Britons soon faced territorial aggression from the Saxons and Picts. In the decades after midcentury, the Britons mounted a successful defense, led in part by Aurelius Ambrosius and culminating, it appears, with the battle of Badon in roughly 500, after which Saxon incursions paused for a time. In those same years of territorial threat, some Britons had emigrated to what is now Brittany, and in the 460s or 470s a warlord named Riothamus led an army, probably from Britain, and fought successfully in Gaul in alliance with local rulers sympathetic to Rome. His name was latinized from a British title meaning "supreme king." Both Riothamus and Aurelius Ambrosius correspond to parts of the later narratives of Arthur: his role as high king, his triumphs against the Saxons, his links to Rome (both friendly and hostile), and his campaigns on the continent.

Whether the origins of Arthur's story lie in fact or in an urge among the Welsh to imagine a great leader who once restored their power against the ever-expanding Anglo-Saxons, he was clearly an established figure in Welsh oral and written literature by the ninth century. Arthur, however, also held a broader appeal for other peoples of England. The British Isles were felt to lie at the outer edge of world geography, but the story of Arthur and his ancestor Brutus served to create a Britain with other kinds of centrality. The legend of Brutus made Britain the end point of an inexorable westward movement of Trojan imperial power, the *translatio imperii*, and Arthur's forebears became linked to Roman imperial dynasties. Finally, the general movement of Arthur's continental campaigns neatly reversed the patterns of Roman and then Norman colonization.

In the later Middle Ages and after, Arthur and his court are most often encountered in works that lay little claim to historical accuracy. Rather, they exploit the very uncertainty of Arthurian narrative to explore the highest (if sometimes self-deceiving) yearnings of private emotion and social order. These Arthurian romances also probe, often in tragic terms, the limits and taboos that both define and subvert such ideals, including the mutual threats posed by private emotion and social order.

Nevertheless, the Arthurian tradition has also been pulled persistently into the realm of the real. It was presented as serious historical writing from the twelfth century through the end of the Middle Ages. Political agents have used Arthur's kingship as a model or precedent for their own aspirations, as seen in the Kennedy administration's portrayal as a version of Camelot. Even elements of the Christian church wrote their doctrines into Arthurian narrative or claimed Arthur as a patron.

The texts in this section present three illuminating moments of Arthur's emergence into history and politics. Geoffrey of Monmouth's *History of the Kings of Britain*, finished around 1138, was the fullest version yet of Arthur's origin and career. Geoffrey was the first to make Arthur such a central figure in British history, and it was largely through Geoffrey's Latin "history" that Arthur became so widespread a feature of cultural imagination in the Middle Ages and beyond. Writing at the close of the twelfth century, Gerald of Wales narrates an occasion, possibly orchestrated by Henry II, in which Arthurian tradition was slightly altered and folded into emergent Norman versions of British antiquity. The section ends with two politically charged versions of national origin, English and Scottish, proposed in 1301 as part of Edward I's efforts to influence royal succession in Scotland.

━━━ ⫯◈⫯ ━━━

Geoffrey of Monmouth
c. 1100–1155

From the perspective of surviving British peoples in Wales and Cornwall, the Norman Conquest of 1066 was only the last among successive waves of invasion by Romans, Picts, Anglo-Saxons, and Vikings. The Celtic Britons had long been pushed into the far southwest by the time the Normans arrived, where they continued to resist colonization. The Welsh maintained a vital language, culture, and ethnic mythology, including a memory of their fellow Celts in Brittany and a divided nostalgia for the long-departed Romans. Thus a whole Celtic linguistic and political world offered an alternative to the languages and legends of the Normans, much of which derived ultimately from Mediterranean antiquity. Arthur, king of the Britons, emerged as a key figure as these peoples and cultures began to articulate the complex new forms of political and private identity precipitated by the Conquest.

No one was more important in this process than Geoffrey of Monmouth. He was prior of the Abbey of Monmouth in Wales and later was named bishop of Saint Asaph, though civil disorder prevented his taking the post. Yet he was also active in the emerging schools of Oxford, he was patronized by Norman nobles and bishops, and he wrote in Latin. Geoffrey's learning reflects this double allegiance. Well schooled in the Latin curriculum that embraced ancient Roman and Christian literature, he was also deeply versed in the oral and written culture of Wales. As a creative negotiater between Welsh and Anglo-Norman legends and languages, his influence was without parallel.

Both of Geoffrey's surviving prose works, the *Prophecies of Merlin* (finished around 1135) and the *History of the Kings of Britain* (about 1138) present themselves as translations of ancient texts from Wales or Brittany. Geoffrey also wrote a *Life of Merlin* in Latin verse. He probably synthesized a number of sources and added material of his own in his "translations." It was a pointed gesture, nevertheless, to posit a Celtic text whose authority rivaled the Latin culture and legends that had underwritten later Anglo-Saxon and then Norman power in England. Geoffrey daringly inverted the general hierarchy of Latin and vernaculars in his time; instead, he offered "British" as the ancient tongue that he wanted to make more broadly accessible for Latin-reading newcomers.

Geoffrey's central heroes are Brutus, the exiled Trojan descendant who colonized and named Britain, and Arthur, who reunified England after Saxon and Pictish attacks, and repulsed Roman efforts to re-establish power there. Geoffrey's own purposes in the *History* were complex but he was responding in part to contemporary events. The 1130s were a decade of civil strife in England, as nobles shifted their allegiances between King Stephen and the other claimant to the throne, the future Henry II. Welsh nobles took advantage of this disorder to rebel and set up their own principalities. Scholars remain divided as to whether Geoffrey was more interested in a return to strong and unified rule in Norman England, or wanted rather to encourage the Welsh princes with the story of a great predecessor who might one day return.

Geoffrey's narrative carefully presents itself as history, in a century of great historical writing. He uses the typical armature of documentary and other written records, archeological evidence, and claims to well-founded witness. Casting the story of Arthur into this respected form allows Geoffrey to employ but also to counter the dominant master-narrative of Christian history in England, which was Bede's. Rather than a story of Anglo-Saxon arrival and conversion, Geoffrey offers a story of an earlier foundation and a prior conversion; he thus creates imaginative space for a convergence between Norman power and the culture and ambitions of people and languages at its edges. Moreover, the *History* generates an exterior (if now conveniently absent) common enemy in the imperial Romans. Geoffrey pulls in yet more ancient models by frequently echoing Virgil's *Aeneid* and its story of exile and refoundation, and by placing his story within biblical, Trojan, and Roman chronologies. And he points forward to his own time by inserting the earlier *Prophecies of Merlin* in the midst of the *History*.

The continued influence of Geoffrey's *History* on later literature is testimony to the powerful themes he folded into his story. Much that is developed in later romance explorations of the Arthurian world is already here: the tragedy of a people bravely battling its own decline; the danger and overwhelming attraction of illicit sexual desire; the ambivalent position of Mordred as cousin or nephew; the Arthurian realm brought down, ultimately, by the treachery of the king's own kin and by a transgression of the marriage bed that echoes Arthur's own conception.

The following selections from Geoffrey's *History* feature the Trojan background of Britain and the birth and early kingship of Arthur. Other texts in this section and following trace later episodes in his evolving legend: the development of Arthur's court, the celebration and tragedy of romantic desire, and the death of the king.

from **History of the Kings of Britain**[1]
Dedication

Whenever I have chanced to think about the history of the kings of Britain, on those occasions when I have been turning over a great many such matters in my mind, it has seemed a remarkable thing to me that, apart from such mention of them as Gildas and Bede had each made in a brilliant book on the subject, I have not been able to discover anything at all on the kings who lived here before the Incarnation of Christ, or indeed about Arthur and all the others who followed on after the Incarnation. Yet the deeds of these men were such that they deserve to be praised for all time. What is more, these deeds were handed joyfully down in oral tradition, just as if they had been committed to writing, by many peoples who had only their memory to rely on.

At a time when I was giving a good deal of attention to such matters, Walter, Archdeacon of Oxford, a man skilled in the art of public speaking and well-informed about the history of foreign countries, presented me with a certain very ancient book written in the British language.[2] This book, attractively composed to form a consecutive and orderly narrative, set out all the deeds of these men, from Brutus, the first King of the Britons, down to Cadwallader, the son of Cadwallo.[3] At Walter's request I have taken the trouble to translate the book into Latin, although, indeed, I have been content with my own expressions and my own homely style and I have gathered no gaudy flowers of speech in other men's gardens. If I had adorned my page with high-flown rhetorical figures, I should have bored my readers, for they would have been forced to spend more time in discovering the meaning of my words than in following the story.

I ask you, Robert, Earl of Gloucester,[4] to do my little book this favor. Let it be so emended by your knowledge and your advice that it must no longer be considered as the product of Geoffrey of Monmouth's small talent. Rather, with the support of your wit and wisdom, let it be accepted as the work of one descended from Henry, the famous King of the English; of one whom learning has nurtured in the liberal arts and whom his innate talent in military affairs has put in charge of our soldiers, with the result that now, in our own lifetime, our island of Britain hails you with heartfelt affection, as if it had been granted a second Henry.

You too, Waleran, Count of Mellent, second pillar of our kingdom, give me your support, so that, with the guidance provided by the two of you, my work may appear all the more attractive when it is offered to its public.[5] For indeed, sprung as you are from the race of the most renowned King Charles, Mother Philosophy has taken you to her bosom, and to you she has taught the subtlety of her sciences. What is more, so that you might become famous in the military affairs of our army, she has led you to the camp of kings, and there, having surpassed your fellow-warriors in bravery, you have learned, under your father's guidance, to be a terror to your enemies and a protection to your own folk. Faithful defender as you are of those dependent on you, accept under your patronage this book which is published for your pleasure. Accept

---

1. Translated by Lewis Thorpe (1966).
2. Walter and Geoffrey were both associated with an early Oxford college, and their names appear together on several legal documents. In two of these, Geoffrey calls himself a *magister*, a teacher at an advanced level.
3. Bede's *Ecclesiastical History of the English People* was the source most used by 12th-century historians, but it has little to say about England before the coming of the Angles and Saxons. Geoffrey offers a (perhaps fictive)

source for a more ancient history of the people who preceded the Saxons.
4. An illegitimate son of King Henry I. He had a hand in the education of the future Henry II, his nephew.
5. Waleran de Beaumont, Count of Meulan (1104–1166) moved in the same circles as the Earl of Gloucester, and was patron of the Norman Abbey of Bec, a great center of learning. Geoffrey's fulsome tone is typical of dedications to great magnates in the period.

me, too, as your writer, so that, reclining in the shade of a tree which spreads so wide, and sheltered from envious and malicious enemies, I may be able in peaceful harmony to make music on the reed-pipe of a muse who really belongs to you.

[TROY, AENEAS, BRUTUS' EXILE][6]

After the Trojan war, Aeneas fled from the ruined city with his son Ascanius and came by boat to Italy. He was honorably received there by King Latinus, but Turnus, King of the Rutuli, became jealous of him and attacked him. In the battle between them Aeneas was victorious. Turnus was killed and Aeneas seized both the kingdom of Italy and the person of Lavinia, who was the daughter of Latinus.[7]

When Aeneas' last day came, Ascanius was elected King. He founded the town of Alba on the bank of the Tiber and became the father of a son called Silvius. This Silvius was involved in a secret love-affair with a certain niece of Lavinia's; he married her and made her pregnant. When this came to the knowledge of his father Ascanius, the latter ordered his soothsayers to discover the sex of the child which the girl had conceived. As soon as they had made sure of the truth of the matter, the soothsayers said that she would give birth to a boy, who would cause the death of both his father and his mother; and that after he had wandered in exile through many lands this boy would eventually rise to the highest honor.

The soothsayers were not wrong in their forecast. When the day came for her to have her child, the mother bore a son and died in childbirth. The boy was handed over to the midwife and was given the name Brutus. At last, when fifteen years had passed, the young man killed his father by an unlucky shot with an arrow, when they were out hunting together. Their beaters drove some stags into their path and Brutus, who was under the impression that he was aiming his weapon at these stags, hit his own father below the breast. As the result of this death Brutus was expelled from Italy by his relations, who were angry with him for having committed such a crime. He went in exile to certain parts of Greece; and there he discovered the descendants of Helenus, Priam's son, who were held captive in the power of Pandrasus, King of the Greeks. After the fall of Troy, Pyrrhus, the son of Achilles, had dragged this man Helenus off with him in chains, and a number of other Trojans, too. He had ordered them to be kept in slavery, so that he might take vengeance on them for the death of his father.

When Brutus realized that these people were of the same race as his ancestors, he stayed some time with them. However, he soon gained such fame for his military skill and prowess that he was esteemed by the kings and princes more than any young man in the country.

[THE NAMING OF BRITAIN][8]

[Brutus conquers the Greek king (reversing the Greek conquest of his ancestral Troy), marries the king's daughter Ignoge, and leads the Trojan descendants off to seek a new land. They pass through continental Europe, where they do battle with the Gauls.]

In their pursuit the Trojans continued to slaughter the Gauls, and they did not abandon the bloodshed until they had gained victory.

---

6. From book 1, ch. 3.
7. This summarizes the political narrative of Virgil's *Aeneid*, a text Geoffrey knew well and echoed frequently

throughout his *History*.
8. From book 1, ch. 15–18 and book 2, ch. 1.

Although this signal triumph brought him great joy, Brutus was nevertheless filled with anxiety, for the number of his men became smaller every day, while that of the Gauls was constantly increasing. Brutus was in doubt as to whether he could oppose the Gauls any longer; and he finally chose to return to his ships in the full glory of his victory while the greater part of his comrades were still safe, and then to seek out the island which divine prophecy had promised would be his. Nothing else was done. With the approval of his men Brutus returned to his fleet. He loaded his ships with all the riches which he had acquired and then went on board. So, with the winds behind him, he sought the promised island, and came ashore at Totnes.

At this time the island of Britain was called Albion. It was uninhabited except for a few giants. It was, however, most attractive, because of the delightful situation of its various regions, its forests and the great number of its rivers, which teemed with fish; and it filled Brutus and his comrades with a great desire to live there. When they had explored the different districts, they drove the giants whom they had discovered into the caves in the mountains. With the approval of their leader they divided the land among themselves. They began to cultivate the fields and to build houses, so that in a short time you would have thought that the land had always been inhabited.

Brutus then called the island Britain from his own name, and his companions he called Britons. His intention was that his memory should be perpetuated by the derivation of the name. A little later the language of the people, which had up to then been known as Trojan or Crooked Greek, was called British, for the same reason.[9]

[BRUTUS BUILDS NEW TROY]

Once he had divided up his kingdom, Brutus decided to build a capital. In pursuit of this plan, he visited every part of the land in search of a suitable spot. He came at length to the River Thames, walked up and down its banks and so chose a site suited to his purpose. There then he built his city and called it Troia Nova. It was known by this name for long ages after, but finally by a corruption of the word it came to be called Trinovantum. * * *

When the above-named leader Brutus had built the city about which I have told you, he presented it to the citizens by right of inheritance, and gave them a code of laws by which they might live peacefully together. At that time the priest Eli was ruling in Judea and the Ark of the Covenant was captured by the Philistines. The sons of Hector reigned in Troy, for the descendants of Antenor had been driven out. In Italy reigned Aeneas Silvius, son of Aeneas and uncle of Brutus, the third of the Latin Kings. * * * [1]

In the meantime Brutus had consummated his marriage with his wife Ignoge. By her he had three sons called Locrinus, Kamber and Albanactus, all of whom were to become famous. When their father finally died, in the twenty-third year after his landing, these three sons buried him inside the walls of the town which he had founded. They divided the kingdom of Britain between them in such a way that each succeeded to Brutus in one particular district. Locrinus, who was the first-born, inherited the part of the island which was afterwards called Loegria after him. Kamber received the region which is on the further bank of the River Severn, the part which is now

---

9. With this detail, Geoffrey creates a linguistic history in which early Welsh is as ancient as classical Latin, and more purely "Trojan."

1. Medieval historians often made such parallels between biblical and secular chronologies.

known as Wales but which was for a long time after his death called Kambria from his name. As a result the people of that country still call themselves Kambri today in the Welsh tongue. Albanactus, the youngest, took the region which is nowadays called Scotland in our language. He called it Albany, after his own name.

[MERLIN AND THE FIRST CONQUEST OF IRELAND][2]

[*The descendants of Brutus' three sons include Leir (Shakespeare's King Lear), the brothers Brennius and Belinus who conquer Rome, and Lud who rebuilds New Troy and names it Kaerlud after himself (whence "London"). In the reign of Lud's brother, Julius Caesar invades England; generations of Britons resist, until King Coel makes peace with the Roman legate Constantius. The latter succeeds Coel, marries Coel's daughter, and sires Constantine who becomes emperor of Rome. The Romans tire of defending Britain against invaders and withdraw from the island. Vortigern usurps the throne from the Briton line, then holds it in alliance with the Saxons Hengist and Horsa. The Saxons become aggressors, and Vortigern flees them but is overcome by the brothers Aurelius Ambrosius and Utherpendragon, who restore the Briton royal line and drive the Saxons into the north. Aurelius reigns, restoring churches and the rule of law; he wants to commemorate the Britons who died fighting off the Saxons.*]

Aurelius collected carpenters and stone-masons together from every region and ordered them to use their skill to contrive some novel building which would stand forever in memory of such distinguished men. The whole band racked their brains and then confessed themselves beaten. Then Tremorinus, Archbishop of the City of the Legions,[3] went to the King and said: "If there is anyone anywhere who has the ability to execute your plan, then Merlin, the prophet of Vortigern, is the man to do it.[4] In my opinion, there is no one else in your kingdom who has greater skill, either in the foretelling of the future or in mechanical contrivances. Order Merlin to come and use his ability, so that the monument for which you are asking can be put up."

Aurelius asked many questions about Merlin; then he sent a number of messengers through the various regions of the country to find him and fetch him. They traveled through the provinces and finally located Merlin in the territory of the Gewissei, at the Galabes Springs, where he often went. They explained to him what they wanted of him and then conducted him to the King. The King received Merlin gaily and ordered him to prophesy the future, for he wanted to hear some marvels from him. "Mysteries of that sort cannot be revealed," answered Merlin, "except where there is the most urgent need for them. If I were to utter them as an entertainment, or where there was no need at all, then the spirit which controls me would forsake me in the moment of need."

He gave the same refusal to everyone present. The King had no wish to press him about the future, but he spoke to him about the monument which he was planning. "If you want to grace the burial-place of these men with some lasting monument," replied Merlin, "send for the Giants' Ring which is on Mount Killaraus in Ireland. In that place there is a stone construction which no man of this period could ever erect,

---

2. From book 8, ch. 10–13.
3. Also called Caerusk or Caerleon; Geoffrey mentions it often and may have had some connection with it.
4. Merlin, son of a Briton princess and a demonic spirit, has already appeared; he triumphed over Vortigern's

magicians and uttered a series of prophecies. Merlin's roles as a royal advisor, a prophet, and even a shape-shifter can be compared to those of poets in early Celtic cultures.

unless he combined great skill and artistry. The stones are enormous and there is no one alive strong enough to move them. If they are placed in position round this site, in the way in which they are erected over there, they will stand forever."

At these words of Merlin's Aurelius burst out laughing. "How can such large stones be moved from so far-distant a country?" he asked. "It is hardly as if Britain itself is lacking in stones big enough for the job!" "Try not to laugh in a foolish way, your Majesty," answered Merlin. "What I am suggesting has nothing ludicrous about it. These stones are connected with certain secret religious rites and they have various properties which are medicinally important. Many years ago the Giants transported them from the remotest confines of Africa and set them up in Ireland at a time when they inhabited that country. Their plan was that, whenever they felt ill, baths should be prepared at the foot of the stones; for they used to pour water over them and to run this water into baths in which their sick were cured. What is more, they mixed the water with herbal concoctions and so healed their wounds. There is not a single stone among them which hasn't some medicinal virtue."

When the Britons heard all this, they made up their minds to send for the stones and to make war on the people of Ireland if they tried to hold them back. In the end the King's brother, Utherpendragon, and fifteen thousand men, were chosen to carry out the task. Merlin, too, was co-opted, so that all the problems which had to be met could have the benefit of his knowledge and advice. They made ready their ships and they put to sea. The winds were favorable and they arrived in Ireland.

At that time there reigned in Ireland a young man of remarkable valor called Gillomanius. As soon as he heard that the Britons had landed in the country, he collected a huge army together and hurried to meet them. When he learned the reason of their coming, Gillomanius laughed out loud at those standing round him. "I am not surprised that a race of cowards has been able to devastate the island of the Britons," said he, "for the Britons are dolts and fools. Who ever heard of such folly? Surely the stones of Ireland aren't so much better than those of Britain that our realm has to be invaded for their sake! Arm yourselves, men, and defend your fatherland, for as long as life remains in my body they shall not steal from us the minutest fragment of the Ring."

When he saw that the Irish were spoiling for a fight, Uther hurriedly drew up his own line of battle and charged at them. The Britons were successful almost immediately. The Irish were either mangled or killed outright, and Gillomanius was forced to flee. Having won the day, the Britons made their way to Mount Killaraus. When they came to the stone structure, they were filled with joy and wonder. Merlin came up to them as they stood round in a group. "Try your strength, young men," said he, "and see whether skill can do more than brute strength, or strength more than skill, when it comes to dismantling these stones!"

At his bidding they all set to with every conceivable kind of mechanism and strove their hardest to take the Ring down. They rigged up hawsers and ropes and they propped up scaling-ladders, each preparing what he thought most useful, but none of these things advanced them an inch. When he saw what a mess they were making of it, Merlin burst out laughing. He placed in position all the gear which he considered necessary and dismantled the stones more easily than you could ever believe. Once he had pulled them down, he had them carried to the ships and stored on board, and they all set sail once more for Britain with joy in their hearts.

The winds were fair. They came to the shore and then set off with the stones for the spot where the heroes had been buried. The moment that this was reported to him, Aurelius dispatched messengers to all the different regions of Britain, ordering the clergy and the people to assemble and, as they gathered, to converge on Mount Ambrius, where they were with due ceremony and rejoicing to re-dedicate the burial-place which I have described. At the summons from Aurelius the bishops and abbots duly assembled with men from every rank and file under the King's command. All came together on the appointed day. Aurelius placed the crown on his head and celebrated the feast of Whitsun in right royal fashion, devoting the next three days to one long festival. * * *

Once he had settled these matters, and others of a similar nature, Aurelius ordered Merlin to erect round the burial-place the stones which he had brought from Ireland. Merlin obeyed the King's orders and put the stones up in a circle round the sepulchre, in exactly the same way as they had been arranged on Mount Killa-raus in Ireland, thus proving that his artistry was worth more than any brute strength.

[UTHERPENDRAGON SIRES ARTHUR][5]

[*Vortigern's son attacks Aurelius Ambrosius and Utherpendragon. They drive him off, though Aurelius is poisoned through Saxon treachery. A miraculous star appears, which Merlin interprets as a sign of Uther's destined kingship, the coming of Arthur, and the rule of Uther's dynasty. At the same time, however, Merlin prophesies the decline of the Britons. As king, Uther fights off more Saxon incursions.*]

The next Eastertide Uther told the nobles of his kingdom to assemble in that same town of London, so that he could wear his crown and celebrate so important a feast-day with proper ceremony. They all obeyed, traveling in from their various cities and assembling on the eve of the feast. The King was thus able to celebrate the feast as he had intended and to enjoy himself in the company of his leaders. They, too, were all happy, seeing that he had received them with such affability. A great many nobles had gathered there, men worthy of taking part in such a gay festivity, together with their wives and daughters.

Among the others there was present Gorlois, Duke of Cornwall, with his wife Ygerna, who was the most beautiful woman in Britain. When the King saw her there among the other women, he was immediately filled with desire for her, with the result that he took no notice of anything else, but devoted all his attention to her. To her and to no one else he kept ordering plates of food to be passed and to her, too, he kept sending his own personal attendants with golden goblets of wine. He kept smiling at her and engaging her in sprightly conversation. When Ygerna's husband saw what was happening, he was so annoyed that he withdrew from the court without taking leave. No one present could persuade him to return, for he was afraid of losing the one object that he loved better than anything else. Uther lost his temper and ordered Gorlois to come back to court, so that he, the King, could seek satisfaction for the way in which he had been insulted. Gorlois refused to obey. The King was furious and swore an oath that he would ravage Gorlois' lands, unless the latter gave him immediate satisfaction.

Without more ado, while the bad blood remained between the two of them, the King collected a huge army together and hurried off to the Duchy of Cornwall, where he set fire to towns and castles. Gorlois' army was the smaller of the two and he did not dare to meet the King in battle. He preferred instead to garrison his cas-

5. From book 8, ch. 19–24.

tles and to bide his time until he could receive help from Ireland. As he was more worried about his wife than he was about himself, he left her in the castle of Tintagel,[6] on the sea-coast, which he thought was the safest place under his control. He himself took refuge in a fortified camp called Dimilioc,[7] so that, if disaster overtook them, they should not both be endangered together. When the King heard of this, he went to the encampment where Gorlois was, besieged it and cut off every line of approach.

Finally, after a week had gone by, the King's passion for Ygerna became more than he could bear. He called to him Ulfin of Ridcaradoch, one of his soldiers and a familiar friend, and told him what was on his mind. "I am desperately in love with Ygerna," said Uther, "and if I cannot have her I am convinced that I shall suffer a physical breakdown. You must tell me how I can satisfy my desire for her, for otherwise I shall die of the passion which is consuming me." "Who can possibly give you useful advice," answered Ulfin, "when no power on earth can enable us to come to her where she is inside the fortress of Tintagel? The castle is built high above the sea, which surrounds it on all sides, and there is no other way in except that offered by a narrow isthmus of rock. Three armed soldiers could hold it against you, even if you stood there with the whole kingdom of Britain at your side. If only the prophet Merlin would give his mind to the problem, then with his help I think you might be able to obtain what you want." The King believed Ulfin and ordered Merlin to be sent for, for he, too, had come to the siege.

Merlin was summoned immediately. When he appeared in the King's presence, he was ordered to suggest how the King could have his way with Ygerna. When Merlin saw the torment which the King was suffering because of this woman, he was amazed at the strength of his passion. "If you are to have your wish," he said, "you must make use of methods which are quite new and until now unheard-of in your day. By my drugs I know how to give you the precise appearance of Gorlois, so that you will resemble him in every respect. If you do what I say, I will make you exactly like him, and Ulfin exactly like Gorlois' companion, Jordan of Tintagel. I will change my own appearance, too, and come with you. In this way you will be able to go safely to Ygerna in her castle and be admitted."

The King agreed and listened carefully to what he had to do. In the end he handed the siege over to his subordinates, took Merlin's drugs, and was changed into the likeness of Gorlois. Ulfin was changed into Jordan and Merlin into a man called Britaelis, so that no one could tell what they had previously looked like. They then set off for Tintagel and came to the Castle in the twilight. The moment the guard was told that his leader was approaching, he opened the gates and the men were let in. Who, indeed, could possibly have suspected anything, once it was thought that Gorlois himself had come? The King spent that night with Ygerna and satisfied his desire by making love with her. He had deceived her by the disguise which he had taken. He had deceived her, too, by the lying things that he said to her, things which he planned with great skill. He said that he had come out secretly from his besieged encampment so that he might make sure that all was well with her, whom he loved so dearly, and with his castle, too. She naturally believed all that he said and refused him nothing that he asked. That night she conceived

---

6. Tin-*ta*-jel, on the rocky northwestern coast of Cornwall.

7. Di-*mi*-li-oc, perhaps a site roughly five miles from Tintagel.

Arthur, the most famous of men, who subsequently won great renown by his out-standing bravery.

Meanwhile, when it was discovered at the siege of Dimilioc that the King was no longer present, his army, acting without his instructions, tried to breach the walls and challenge the beleaguered Duke to battle. The Duke, equally ill-advisedly, sallied forth with his men, imagining apparently that he could resist such a host of armed men with his own tiny band. As the struggle between them swayed this way and that, Gorlois was among the first to be killed. His men were scattered and the besieged camp was captured. The treasure which had been deposited there was shared out in the most inequitable way, for each man seized in his greedy fist whatever good luck and his own brute strength threw in his way.[8]

Not until the outrages which followed this daring act had finally subsided did messengers come to Ygerna to announce the death of the Duke and the end of the siege. When they saw the King sitting beside Ygerna in the likeness of their leader, they blushed red with astonishment to see that the man whom they had left behind dead in the siege had in effect arrived there safely before them. Of course, they did not know of the drugs prepared by Merlin. The King put his arms round the Duchess and laughed aloud to hear these reports. "I am not dead," he said. "Indeed, as you see, I am very much alive! However, the destruction of my camp saddens me very much and so does the slaughter of my comrades. What is more, there is great danger that the King may come this way and capture us in this castle. I will go out to meet him and make peace with him, lest even worse should befall us."

The King set out and made his way towards his own army, abandoning his disguise as Gorlois and becoming Utherpendragon once more. When he learned all that had happened, he mourned for the death of Gorlois; but he was happy, all the same, that Ygerna was freed from her marital obligations. He returned to Tintagel Castle, captured it and seized Ygerna at the same time, she being what he really wanted. From that day on they lived together as equals, united by their great love for each other; and they had a son and a daughter. The boy was called Arthur and the girl Anna.

[ANGLO-SAXON INVASION]

As the days passed and lengthened into years, the King fell ill with a malady which affected him for a long time. Meanwhile the prison warders who guarded Octa and Eosa,[9] as I have explained above, led a weary life. In the end they escaped with their prisoners to Germany and in doing so terrified the kingdom: for rumor had it that they had already stirred up Germany, and had fitted out a huge fleet in order to return to the island and destroy it. This, indeed, actually happened. They came back with an immense fleet and more men than could ever be counted. They invaded certain parts of Albany[1] and busied themselves in burning the cities there and the

8. Geoffrey emphasizes the destructive potential of private greed, private ambition, and brute force, even in the rule of a strong king like Uther. This becomes a dominant theme in Geoffrey and later Arthurian narratives.
9. A son and a kinsman of the Saxon Hengist; Uther had

imprisoned them in London. Geoffrey closely connects the resurgence of the Saxon invaders with Uther's adultery and the disorder within his own army.
1. That is, Scotland, named for Brutus' son Albanactus.

citizens inside them. The British army was put under the command of Loth of Lodonesia, with orders that he should keep the enemy at a distance. This man was one of the leaders, a valiant soldier, mature both in wisdom and age. As a reward for his prowess, the King had given him his daughter Anna and put him in charge of the kingdom while he himself was ill. When Loth moved forward against the enemy he was frequently driven back again by them, so that he had to take refuge inside the cities. On other occasions he routed and dispersed them, forcing them to fly either into the forests or to their ships. Between the two sides the outcome of each battle was always in doubt, it being hard to tell which of them was victorious. Their own arrogance was a handicap to the Britons, for they were unwilling to obey the orders of their leaders. This undermined their strength and they were unable to beat the enemy in the field.

Almost all the island was laid waste. When this was made known to the King, he fell into a greater rage than he could really bear in his weakened state. He told all his leaders to appear before him, so that he could rebuke them for their overweening pride and their feebleness. As soon as he saw them all assembled in his presence, he reproached them bitterly and swore that he himself would lead them against the enemy. He ordered a litter to be built, so that he could be carried in it; for his weakness made any other form of progress impossible. Then he instructed them all to be in a state of preparedness, so that they could advance against the enemy as soon as the opportunity offered. The litter was constructed immediately, the men were made ready to start and the opportunity duly came.

They put the King in his litter and set out for Saint Albans, where the Saxons I have told you about were maltreating all the local population * * *

[*Despite his illness, Uther prevails. Octa and Eosa are killed.*]

Once the Saxons had been defeated, as I have explained above, they did not for that reason abandon their evil behavior. On the contrary, they went off to the northern provinces and preyed relentlessly upon the people there. King Uther was keen to pursue them, as he had proposed, but his princes dissuaded him from it, for after his victory his illness had taken an even more serious turn. As a result the enemy became bolder still in their enterprises, striving by every means in their power to take complete control of the realm. Having recourse, as usual, to treachery, they plotted to see how they could destroy the King by cunning. When every other approach failed, they made up their minds to kill him with poison. This they did: for while Uther lay ill in the town of St. Albans, they sent spies disguised as beggars, who were to discover how things stood at court. When the spies had obtained all the information that they wanted, they discovered one additional fact which they chose to use as a means of betraying Uther. Near the royal residence there was a spring of very limpid water which the King used to drink when he could not keep down any other liquids because of his illness. These evil traitors went to the spring and polluted it completely with poison, so that all the water which welled up was infected. When the King drank some of it, he died immediately. Some hundred men died after him, until the villainy was finally discovered. Then they filled the well in with earth. As soon as the death of the King was made known, the bishops of the land came with their clergy and bore his body to the monastery of Ambrius and buried it with royal honors at the side of Aurelius Ambrosius, inside the Giants' Ring.

[ARTHUR OF BRITAIN][2]

After the death of Utherpendragon, the leaders of the Britons assembled from their various provinces in the town of Silchester and there suggested to Dubricius, the Archbishop of the City of the Legions, that as their King he should crown Arthur, the son of Uther. Necessity urged them on, for as soon as the Saxons heard of the death of King Uther, they invited their own countrymen over from Germany, appointed Colgrin as their leader and began to do their utmost to exterminate the Britons. They had already over-run all that section of the island which stretches from the River Humber to the sea named Caithness.[3]

Dubricius lamented the sad state of his country. He called the other bishops to him and bestowed the crown of the kingdom upon Arthur. Arthur was a young man only fifteen years old; but he was of outstanding courage and generosity, and his inborn goodness gave him such grace that he was loved by almost all the people. Once he had been invested with the royal insignia, he observed the normal custom of giving gifts freely to everyone. Such a great crown of soldiers flocked to him that he came to an end of what he had to distribute. However, the man to whom openhandedness and bravery both come naturally may indeed find himself momentarily in need, but poverty will never harass him for long. In Arthur courage was closely linked with generosity, and he made up his mind to harry the Saxons, so that with their wealth he might reward the retainers who served his own household. The justness of his cause encouraged him, for he had a claim by rightful inheritance to the kingship of the whole island. He therefore called together all the young men whom I have just mentioned and marched on York.

* * *[4]

[Arthur and his followers attack Colgrin and ultimately subdue the Saxons; then they repel armies of Scots, Picts, and Irish. Arthur restores Briton dynasties throughout England, marries Guinevere, and establishes a stable peace.]

Arthur then began to increase his personal entourage by inviting very distinguished men from far-distant kingdoms to join it. In this way he developed such a code of courtliness in his household that he inspired peoples living far away to imitate him. The result was that even the man of noblest birth, once he was roused to rivalry, thought nothing at all of himself unless he wore his arms and dressed in the same way as Arthur's knights. At last the fame of Arthur's generosity and bravery spread to the very ends of the earth; and the kings of countries far across the sea trembled at the thought that they might be attacked and invaded by him, and so lose control of the lands under their dominion. They were so harassed by these tormenting anxieties that they rebuilt their towns and the towers in their towns, and then went so far as to construct castles on carefully chosen sites, so that, if invasion should bring Arthur against them, they might have a refuge in their time of need.

All this was reported to Arthur. The fact that he was dreaded by all encouraged him to conceive the idea of conquering the whole of Europe.

---

2. From book 9, ch. 1–11.
3. That is, Northumberland and Scotland.
4. Geoffrey links the ancient practice of a king's largesse to his warrior band together with the claim of dynastic genealogy. Arthur will again use the latter claim when he decides to invade Gaul and then march toward Rome.

Gerald of Wales
c. 1146–1222

Geoffrey of Monmouth's *History of the Kings of Britain* was soon translated into French, early Middle English, and Welsh, and it reappears in other languages for centuries. Contemporary historians, especially those interested in pre-Saxon history, were enthusiastic about this new story. Others were skeptical. Nevertheless, Geoffrey's narrative was soon accepted widely as fact, adopted, and revised to serve the interests of the Angevin dynasty.

The discovery of Arthur's bones at Glastonbury Abbey in 1191, as reported by the prolific writer Gerald of Wales, is a particularly rich instance of this habit, benefiting both the status of Henry II and the prestige of the abbey. Glastonbury faced a crisis common among Anglo-Saxon monastic foundations after the Norman Conquest. It was, in fact, probably the earliest Christian community in Britain; nonetheless, the oral tradition of its antiquity was weakened as the Normans took power, bringing with them a new insistence on written documentation. Glastonbury had little proof of its claims to ancient privilege, either by way of charters (and those mostly spurious) or the related prestige of holy relics. At the same time, Henry II was interested in ancient narratives that might legitimize his imperial aims.

Gerald's version of events both suggests Henry's almost wondrous wisdom in identifying the very spot of Arthur's burial and implies the existence of early written records at Glastonbury. To have Arthur as a patron, authenticated by King Henry himself, greatly substantiated the abbey's other claims. At the same time, Henry's knowledge mysteriously linked him to Arthur, and the corpse itself neatly altered Arthurian tradition, certifying Arthur's actual death and perhaps damping Welsh hopes for a messianic return.

from The Instruction of Princes[1]

The memory of Arthur, that most renowned King of the Britons, will endure forever. In his own day he was a munificent patron of the famous Abbey at Glastonbury, giving many donations to the monks and always supporting them strongly, and he is highly praised in their records. More than any other place of worship in his kingdom he loved the church of the Blessed Mary, Mother of God, in Glastonbury, and he fostered its interests with much greater loving care than that of any of the others. When he went out to fight, he had a full-length portrait of the Blessed Virgin painted on the front of his shield, so that in the heat of battle he could always gaze upon her; and whenever he was about to make contact with the enemy he would kiss her feet with great devoutness.

In our lifetime Arthur's body was discovered at Glastonbury, although the legends had always encouraged us to believe that there was something otherworldly about his ending, that he had resisted death and had been spirited away to some far-distant spot.[2] The body was hidden deep in the earth in a hollowed-out oak-bole and between two stone pyramids which had been set up long ago in the churchyard there. They carried it into the church with every mark of honor and buried it decently there in a marble tomb. It had been provided with most unusual indications which were, indeed, little short of miraculous, for beneath it—and not on top,

---

1. Translated by Lewis Thorpe. Gerald reports the same events again in a later text, the *Speculum Ecclesiae*.
2. In his other version (the *Speculum Ecclesiae*) Gerald is more nervously dismissive: "In their stupidity the British

people maintain that he is still alive. . . . According to them, once he has recovered from his wounds this strong and all-powerful King will return to rule over the Britons in the normal way" (page 285).

as would be the custom nowadays—there was a stone slab, with a leaden cross attached to its underside. I have seen this cross myself and I have traced the lettering which was cut into it on the side turned towards the stone, instead of being on the outer side and immediately visible. The inscription read as follows: HERE IN THE ISLE OF AVALON LIES BURIED THE RENOWNED KING ARTHUR, WITH GUINEVERE, HIS SECOND WIFE.

There are many remarkable deductions to be made from this discovery. Arthur obviously had two wives, and the second one was buried with him. Her bones were found with those of her husband, but they were separate from his. Two-thirds of the coffin, the part towards the top end, held the husband's bones, and the other section, at his feet, contained those of his wife. A tress of woman's hair, blond, and still fresh and bright in color, was found in the coffin. One of the monks snatched it up and it immediately disintegrated into dust. There had been some indications in the Abbey records that the body would be discovered on this spot, and another clue was provided by lettering carved on the pyramids, but this had been almost completely erased by the passage of the years. The holy monks and other religious had seen visions and revelations. However, it was Henry II, King of England, who had told the monks that, according to a story which he had heard from some old British soothsayer,[3] they would find Arthur's body buried at least sixteen feet in the ground, not in a stone coffin but in a hollowed-out oak-bole. It had been sunk as deep as that, and carefully concealed, so that it could never be discovered by the Saxons, whom Arthur had attacked relentlessly as long as he lived and whom, indeed, he had almost wiped out, but who occupied the island [of Britain] after his death. That was why the inscription, which was eventually to reveal the truth, had been cut into the inside of the cross and turned inwards towards the stone. For many a long year this inscription was to keep the secret of what the coffin contained, but eventually, when time and circumstance were both opportune, the lettering revealed what it had so long concealed.

What is now known as Glastonbury used in ancient times to be called the Isle of Avalon. It is virtually an island, for it is completely surrounded by marshlands. In Welsh it is called "Ynys Avallon," which means the Island of Apples. "Aval" is the Welsh word for apple, and this fruit used to grow there in great abundance.[4] After the Battle of Camlann,[5] a noblewoman called Morgan, who was the ruler and patroness of these parts as well as being a close blood-relation of King Arthur, carried him off to the island now known as Glastonbury, so that his wounds could be cared for. Years ago the district had also been called "Ynys Gutrin" in Welsh, that is the Island of Glass, and from these words the invading Saxons later coined the place-name "Glastingebury." The word "glass" in their language means "vitrum" in Latin, and "bury" means "castrum" [camp] or "civitas" [city].

You must know that the bones of Arthur's body which were discovered there were so big that in them the poet's words seem to be fulfilled:

> All men will exclaim at the size of the bones they've exhumed.[6]

The Abbot showed me one of the shin-bones. He held it upright on the ground against the foot of the tallest man he could find, and it stretched a good three inches above the man's knee. The skull was so large and capacious that it seemed a veritable

---

3. In the *Speculum Ecclesiae*, Gerald says that Henry learned this "from the historical accounts of the Britons and from their bards" (page 286).
4. Citing and explaining words from the various British vernaculars is a widespread habit in Latin historical writing as early as Bede.
5. Arthur's last battle, fought against the rebel army of his kinsman Mordred. Arthur kills Mordred but is himself mortally wounded.
6. Virgil, *Georgics*, 1.497.

prodigy of nature, for the space between the eyebrows and the eye-sockets was as broad as the palm of a man's hand. Ten or more wounds could clearly be seen, but they had all mended except one. This was larger than the others and it had made an immense gash. Apparently it was this wound which had caused Arthur's death.

1193

‧‧‧ ⚔ ‧‧‧

Edward I
1239–1307

Beginning in 1291, King Edward I of England revived an ancient claim to be feudal over-lord of Scotland and thereby sought to control a disputed succession to its throne. By 1293 the Scottish king John Balliol had become Edward's vassal, but rebelled and was forced to abdicate in 1296. The military and diplomatic struggle (later called the "Great Cause") stretched across the decade. By the turn of the fourteenth century, in an extraordinary move, both the English and Scots had turned to the court of Pope Boniface VIII for a legal decision. In pursuing Edward's claim, his agents ransacked chronicles—including Geoffrey of Monmouth's *History*—as well as ancient charters, to compile a dossier of historical and legal precedents. Despite his own bureaucratic reforms requiring documentary proof for most legal claims, Edward was ready to invoke common memory and ancient legends to support his position regarding Scotland. Knowing that such chronicle material would have no status in court, in May of 1301 Edward resorted to the following letter before Pope Boniface ruled in the matter.

The written letter was a highly developed and self-conscious genre during the Middle Ages. Letters were often meant to be public and could carry the force of law. Indeed, the form of many legal documents had developed from royal letters. Letter writing became an area for textbooks and school study, the *ars dictaminis*. Elaborate formulas of salutation and closing, and other rhetorical figures, were taught and used for important correspondence as a way of establishing the sender's learning and prestige. The papal curia employed a particularly chal-lenging system of prose rhythm called the *cursus*, which was imitated in some royal chanceries and is found in the Latin of Edward's letter.

King Edward I
Letter sent to the Papal Court of Rome concerning the king's rights in the realm of Scotland.[1]

To the most Holy Father in Christ lord Boniface, by divine providence the supreme pontiff of the Holy Roman and Universal Church, Edward, by grace of the same providence king of England, lord of Ireland, and duke of Aquitaine offers his hum-blest devotion to the blessed saints.[2] What follows we send to you not to be treated in the form or manner of a legal plea, but altogether extrajudicially, in order to set the mind of your Holiness at rest. The All-Highest, to whom all hearts are open, will tes-tify how it is graven upon the tablets of our memory with an indelible mark, that our predecessors and progenitors, the kings of England, by right of lordship and domin-ion, possessed, from the most ancient times, the suzerainty of the realm of Scotland

1. Translated by E. L. G. Stones (1965). Although sent in the name of the king, a Latin letter of such formality would have been written by notaries in his chancery. A French draft also survives, which might have been used by Edward himself.

2. A flowery opening formula was typical of formal letters between persons of power; it also provided a place for Edward to make ambitious (and in the case of Aquitaine, highly optimistic) territorial claims.

and its kings in temporal matters, and the things annexed thereto, and that they received from the self-same kings, and from such magnates of the realm as they so desired, liege homage and oaths of fealty. We, continuing in the possession of that very right and dominion, have received the same acknowledgments in our time, both from the king of Scotland, and from the magnates of that realm; and indeed such prerogatives of right and dominion did the kings of England enjoy over the realm of Scotland and its kings, that they have even granted to their faithful folk the realm itself, removed its kings for just causes, and constituted others to rule in their place under themselves. Beyond doubt these matters have been familiar from times long past and still are, though perchance it has been suggested otherwise to your Holiness' ears by foes of peace and sons of rebellion, whose elaborate and empty fabrications your wisdom, we trust, will treat with contempt.

Thus, in the days of Eli and of Samuel the prophet, after the destruction of the city of Troy, a certain valiant and illustrious man of the Trojan race called Brutus, landed with many noble Trojans, upon a certain island called, at that time, Albion.[3] It was then inhabited by giants, and after he had defeated and slain them, by his might and that of his followers, he called it, after his own name, Britain, and his people Britons, and built a city which he called Trinovant, now known as London. Afterwards he divided his realm among his three sons, that is he gave to his first born, Locrine, that part of Britain now called England, to the second, Albanact, that part then known as Albany, after the name of Albanact, but now as Scotland, and to Camber, his youngest son, the part then known by his son's name as Cambria and now called Wales, the royal dignity being reserved for Locrine, the eldest. Two years after the death of Brutus there landed in Albany a certain king of the Huns, called Humber, and he slew Albanact, the brother of Locrine. Hearing this, Locrine, the king of the Britons, pursued him, and he fled and was drowned in the river which from his name is called Humber, and thus Albany reverted to Locrine. * * * Again, Arthur, king of the Britons, a prince most renowned, subjected to himself a rebellious Scotland, destroyed almost the whole nation, and afterwards installed as king of Scotland one Angusel by name. Afterwards, when King Arthur held a most famous feast at Caerleon, there were present there all the kings subject to him, and among them Angusel, king of Scotland, who manifested the service due for the realm of Scotland by bearing the sword of King Arthur before him; and in succession all the kings of Scotland have been subject to all the kings of the Britons. Succeeding kings of England enjoyed both monarchy and dominion in the island, and subsequently Edward, known as the elder, son of Alfred, king of England, had subject and subordinate to him, as lord superior, the kings of the Scots, the Cumbrians, and the Strathclyde Welsh. * * *

Since, indeed, from what has been said already, and from other evidence, it is perfectly clear and well-known that the realm of Scotland belongs to us of full right, by reason of property and of possession, and that we have not done and have not dared to do anything, as indeed we could not do, in writing or in action, by which any prejudice may be implied to our right or possession, we humbly beseech your Holiness to weigh all this with careful meditation, and to condescend to keep it all in mind when making your decision, setting no store, if you please, by the adverse assertions which come to you on this subject from our enemies, but, on the contrary,

---

3. Here the letter borrows closely from Geoffrey of Monmouth's foundation narrative; see page 157.

retaining our welfare and our royal rights, if it so please you, in your fatherly regard. May the Most High preserve you, to rule his Holy Church through many years of prosperity.

Kempsey, 7 May 1301, the twenty-ninth year of our reign.

COMPANION READING

A Report to Edward I[1]

Sir, seeing that you have lately sent a statement to the pope concerning your right to Scotland, the Scots are making efforts to nullify that statement by certain objections which are given below. * * * They say that in that letter you ground your right on old chronicles, which contain various falsehoods and lies, and are abrogated and made void by the subsequent contrary actions of your predecessors and of yourself, which vitiate all the remaining part of your letter, and therefore one should give no credence to such a document. And they say further, that with only this unworthy and feeble case to rely upon, you are striving to evade the cognizance of your true judge, and to suppress the truth, and unlawfully, by force of arms, to repel your weaker neighbors, and to prevent the pope from pursuing the examination of this case. * * *

Again, they say that the old chronicles that you use as evidence of your right could not assist you, even if they were authenticated, as is not the case, they say, because it is notorious that these same old chronicles are utterly made naught and of no avail by other subsequent documents of greater significance, by contrary agreements and actions, and by papal privileges. * * * Then, sir, in order that credence be not given to the documents, histories, and deeds described in your statement, they say that allegations like those recounted in your narrative are put out of court by the true facts, and they endeavor to demonstrate their assertion by chronicles and narratives of a contrary purport. Brutus divided between his three sons the island once called Britain, and now England, and gave to one son Loegria, to another Wales, and to the third what is now called Scotland, and made them peers, so that none of them was subject to another. Afterwards came a woman named Scota, daughter of Pharaoh of Egypt, who came via Spain and occupied Ireland, and afterwards conquered the land of Albany, which she had called, after her name, *Scotland*,[2] and one place in that land she had called after the names of her son Erk and her husband Gayl, wherefore that district was called *Ergaill* [Argyll], and they drove out the Britons, and from that time the Scots, as a new race and possessing a new name, had nothing to do with the Britons, but pursued them daily as their enemies, and were distinguished from them by different ranks and customs, and by a different language. Afterwards they joined company with the Picts, by whose strength they destroyed the Britons, and the land which is now called England, and for this reason the Britons gave tribute to the Romans, to obtain the help of the Roman emperor, whose name was Severus,

---

1. The Scots learned about Edward's letter and made their own response to the pope; this report to Edward, written in the French he would actually have used with his counselors, specifies the Scots' rebuttal. The Scots carefully assert the superior force of later charters and other legal instruments, and dismiss Edward's reliance on unauthenticated legends. In case Edward's story should carry weight with Boniface, however, they also provide a counternarrative of their own national foundation by Scota, daughter of the Pharaoh, and how she expelled

British influence from her land. The English and Scots diplomats thus tell opposing prehistories that underwrite their current claims. Just as important, though, they are negotiating around an unusually articulate moment in the contest between different forms of textuality—legendary and chronicle tradition versus legal documents—in the creation of contemporary political power.

2. This neatly replicates Brutus' trajectory from the eastern Mediterranean, across part of continental Europe, and thence to the British Isles.

against the Scots, and by his help the Britons made a wall between themselves and the Scots, having a length of 130 leagues in length from one sea to the other, and they say that by this it appears that Scotland was not at any time under the lordship of the Britons.[3] But they do not deny that King Arthur by his prowess conquered Denmark, France, Norway and also Scotland, and held them until he and Mordred were slain in battle, and from that time the realm of Scotland returned to its free status. They say that the Britons were then expelled by the Saxons, and then the Saxons by the Danes, and then the Danes by the Saxons, and that in the whole period of the Saxon kings the Scots remained free without being subject to them, and at that time, by the relics of Saint Andrew which came from Greece, they were converted to the faith five hundred years before the English became Christians, and from that time the realm of Scotland, with the king and the realm (sic), were under the lordship of the Roman church without any intermediary, and by it were they defended against all their enemies. * * *

Arthurian Romance

▸✦◈✦◂

Marie de France

In a famous line from the prologue to her *Lais*, Marie de France suggested that serious readers could approach an obscure old book and "supply its significance from their own wisdom." The original French text, "*de lur sen le surplus mettre*," implies that such readers add on something that is missing. In part a gesture of respect toward the study of pagan Latin literature in a Christian setting, this statement also seems to permit Marie herself a dramatically new perspective when she encounters the long-established Arthurian story, in *Lanval*. Starting with a scene of war that readers of Geoffrey of Monmouth might recognize, Marie swiftly brings into play elements that had been largely absent in the historicizing stories of Arthur: bodily desire and its dangers, romantic longing, the realm of the uncanny, the power of women, the force of wealth and influence in even the noblest courts.

Marie's specific identity remains obscure, but it is clear that she was a woman of French origin writing in England in the later decades of the twelfth century, widely educated, and in touch with the royal court. She dedicates her book of *Lais* to a "noble King" who was probably Henry II, and she may have been his kinswoman, possibly an illegitimate half-sister. Marie's works draw into that courtly culture the languages and traditions of the English and Celtic past. She rewrote a Latin narrative about the origin of "Saint Patrick's Purgatory" and the adventure of an Irish knight there; and she retold the fables of Aesop using an English translation that she attributed to King Alfred. The *Lais*, she says, came to her through oral transmission, and she connects them with the Bretons. Indeed, the best early copy of the *Lais*, Harley manuscript 978 in the British Library, is itself a multilingual compilation that includes the early Middle English poem *The Cuckoo Song* ("Sumer is icumen in"; see page 522).

Writing a generation after Geoffrey of Monmouth and not long before Gerald of Wales, Marie brings a quite different and rather critical set of preoccupations to her Arthurian story. She opens her tale with a realistic and admirable occasion of male power and strong kingship:

---

3. The Scots artfully shift the emphasis found in Geoffrey of Monmouth. Roman colonization and Hadrian's wall become evidence of an ancient ethnic division and Scots independence both from the Britons and from the Britons' later invaders.

Arthur's battle for territory and his reward of faithful vassals. A bleaker side of that courtly world, and perhaps of Marie's own, is also implicit, however. With a terseness and indirection typical of her *lais*, Marie shows women as property in the king's gift, knights forgotten when their wealth runs out, and the perversion of judicial process.

Marvels and erotic desire dominate her tale, though, and women's power, for good or ill, is its primary motivating force. Guinevere, in a hostile portrait of adulterous aggression and vengeful dishonesty, nonetheless manages to manipulate Arthur and his legal codes when Lanval rejects her advances. The queen is countered by Lanval's supernatural mistress, who commands luxurious riches that dwarf Arthur's; she rescues Lanval by being an unimpeachable legal witness in his defense. Indeed, she arrives on her white palfrey as the moment of judgment nears, almost like a knightly champion in a trial by battle. Lanval vanishes into a timeless world of fulfilled desire and limitless wealth that has analogies in much older Celtic tradition. This closing scene defies the reintegration of male courtly order that is typical even in the erotic romances of Marie's contemporary Chrétien de Troyes.

The realm of eroticism and women's power in *Lanval*, though, is not automatically any more virtuous or stable than the ostentatious wealth and corruptible law of the world of Arthurian men. If Lanval's mysterious lady is beautiful and generous, she also takes his knightliness from him. Lanval is last seen riding behind the lady, and not on a warhorse but on a palfrey. Guinevere swiftly reduces Arthur to a weak and temporizing king. And in her initial explosion after Lanval rejects her, Guinevere accuses him of homosexuality. For all its absurdity, the moment articulates unnerving implications of the profound bonds among men in the Arthurian world, implications that could interrupt genealogical transmission of wealth and power. Marie's Guinevere again voices fears the tradition has left unsaid.

Marie de France may be trying less to propound a critique of the received stories of Arthur than to recall her readers' attention to elements that tradition has left aside, as she suggests in her prologue. Some of this is no more troubling than a delightful fantasy of wealth and pleasure, outside time and without consequences. Other elements imply, with startling economy, forces that (in the hands of later romancers) tear the Arthurian world to pieces.

from LAIS[1]
Prologue

Whoever has received knowledge
and eloquence in speech from God
should not be silent or secretive
but demonstrate it willingly.
5   When a great good is widely heard of,
then, and only then, does it bloom,
and when that good is praised by many,
it has spread its blossoms.
The custom among the ancients—
10   as Priscian[2] testifies—
was to speak quite obscurely
in the books they wrote,
so that those who were to come after
and study them
15   might gloss the letter

---

1. Translated by Robert Hanning and Joan Ferrante.
2. A famed grammarian of the late Roman empire,

Priscian remained widely influential in the study of Latin language and literature in the 12th century.

and supply its significance from their own wisdom.[3]
Philosophers knew this,
they understood among themselves
that the more time they spent,
20   the more subtle their minds would become
and the better they would know how to keep themselves
from whatever was to be avoided.
He who would guard himself from vice
should study and understand
25   and begin a weighty work
by which he might keep vice at a distance,
and free himself from great sorrow.
That's why I began to think
about composing some good stories
30   and translating from Latin to Romance;[4]
but that was not to bring me fame:
too many others have done it.
Then I thought of the *lais* I'd heard.[5]
I did not doubt, indeed I knew well,
35   that those who first began them
and sent them forth
composed them in order to preserve
adventures they had heard.
I have heard many told;
40   and I don't want to neglect or forget them.
To put them into word and rhyme
I've often stayed awake.

In your honor, noble King,[6]
who are so brave and courteous,
45   repository of all joys
in whose heart all goodness takes root,
I undertook to assemble these *lais*
to compose and recount them in rhyme.
In my heart I thought and determined,
50   sire, that I would present them to you.
If it pleases you to receive them,
you will give me great joy;
I shall be happy forever.
Do not think me presumptuous
55   if I dare present them to you.
Now hear how they begin.

Lanval

I shall tell you the adventure of another *lai*,
just as it happened:

---

3. Marie refers to the practice of supplying glosses—
explanatory notes such as this one—to school texts; she
also implies that later readers bring their own perspective
to earlier works, a point relevant to her own free adaptation of earlier Arthurian stories.
4. That is, to French.

5. A *lai* was typically a short verse narrative, meant for
oral performance with music. A particular group of these,
often including Arthurian tales, was especially connected
with Brittany.
6. Probably Henry II.

it was composed about a very noble vassal;
in Breton, they call him Lanval.[1]

5   Arthur, the brave and the courtly king,
       was staying at Cardoel,[2]
       because the Scots and the Picts
       were destroying the land.[3]
       They invaded Logres°   England
10   and laid it waste.
       At Pentecost, in summer,[4]
       the king stayed there.
       He gave out many rich gifts:
       to counts and barons,
15   members of the Round Table—
       such a company had no equal in all the world—
       he distributed wives and lands,
       to all but one who had served him.
       That was Lanval; Arthur forgot him,
20   and none of his men favored him either.
       For his valor, for his generosity,
       his beauty and his bravery,
       most men envied him;
       some feigned the appearance of love
25   who, if something unpleasant happened to him,
       would not have been at all disturbed.
       He was the son of a king of high degree
       but he was far from his heritage.
       He was of the king's household
30   but he had spent all his wealth,
       for the king gave him nothing
       nor did Lanval ask.
       Now Lanval was in difficulty,
       depressed and very worried.
35   My lords, don't be surprised:
       a strange man, without friends,
       is very sad in another land,
       when he doesn't know where to look for help.
       The knight of whom I speak,
40   who had served the king so long,
       one day mounted his horse
       and went off to amuse himself.
       He left the city
       and came, all alone, to a field;
45   he dismounted by a running stream
       but his horse trembled badly.
       He removed the saddle and went off,
       leaving the horse to roll around in the meadow.

1. Marie seems to imply knowledge of Breton, a Celtic language related to Welsh. In other works, she shows knowledge of English as well, and excellent Latin.
2. Carlisle, in the north of England.
3. Scots and Picts were Arthur's traditional enemies.

4. "Summer" here refers to late spring. The feast of Pentecost commemorates the descent of the Holy Spirit among Christ's apostles; it is often the occasion of Arthurian stories, especially those that involve marvels.

	He folded his cloak beneath his head
50	and lay down.
	He worried about his difficulty,
	he could see nothing that pleased him.
	As he lay there
	he looked down along the bank
55	and saw two girls approaching;
	he had never seen any lovelier.
	They were richly dressed,
	tightly laced,
	in tunics of dark purple;
60	their faces were very lovely.
	The older one carried basins,
	golden, well made, and fine;
	I shall tell you the truth about it, without fail.
	The other carried a towel.
65	They went straight
	to where the knight was lying.
	Lanval, who was very well bred,
	got up to meet them.
	They greeted him first
70	and gave him their message:
	"Sir Lanval, my lady,
	who is worthy and wise and beautiful,
	sent us for you.
	Come with us now.
75	We shall guide you there safely.
	See, her pavilion is nearby!"
	The knight went with them;
	giving no thought to his horse
	who was feeding before him in the meadow.
80	They led him up to the tent,[5]
	which was quite beautiful and well placed.
	Queen Semiramis,
	however much more wealth,
	power, or knowledge she had,
85	or the emperor Octavian[6]
	could not have paid for one of the flaps.
	There was a golden eagle on top of it,
	whose value I could not tell,
	nor could I judge the value of the cords or the poles
90	that held up the sides of the tent;
	there is no king on earth who could buy it,
	no matter what wealth he offered.
	The girl was inside the tent:
	the lily and the young rose
95	when they appear in the summer
	are surpassed by her beauty.

---

5. Elaborate tents are often found in contemporary narratives of kings going out to battle.
6. Semiramis, legendary queen of Assyria and builder of Babylon, led armies of conquest; she is also a conventional figure of uncontrolled sexual desire. She is interestingly placed here as a female counterpart to Octavian (Augustus Caesar), the first Roman emperor.

She lay on a beautiful bed—
the bedclothes were worth a castle—
dressed only in her shift.
100 Her body was well shaped and elegant;
for the heat, she had thrown over herself,
a precious cloak of white ermine,
covered with purple alexandrine,°   *embroidery*
but her whole side was uncovered,
105 her face, her neck and her bosom;
she was whiter than the hawthorn flower.
The knight went forward
and the girl addressed him.
He sat before the bed.
110 "Lanval," she said, "sweet love,
because of you I have come from my land;
I came to seek you from far away.
If you are brave and courtly,
no emperor or count or king
115 will ever have known such joy or good;
for I love you more than anything."
He looked at her and saw that she was beautiful;
Love stung him with a spark
that burned and set fire to his heart.
120 He answered her in a suitable way.
"Lovely one," he said, "if it pleased you,
if such joy might be mine
that you would love me,
there is nothing you might command,
125 within my power, that I would not do,
whether foolish or wise.
I shall obey your command;
for you, I shall abandon everyone.
I want never to leave you.
130 That is what I most desire."
When the girl heard the words
of the man who could love her so,
she granted him her love and her body.
Now Lanval was on the right road!
135 Afterward, she gave him a gift:
he would never again want anything,
he would receive as he desired;
however generously he might give and spend,
she would provide what he needed.
140 Now Lanval is well cared for.
The more lavishly he spends,
the more gold and silver he will have.
"Love," she said, "I admonish you now,
I command and beg you,
145 do not let any man know about this.
I shall tell you why:
you would lose me for good
if this love were known;

you would never see me again
150   or possess my body."
He answered that he would do
exactly as she commanded.
He lay beside her on the bed;
now Lanval is well cared for.
155   He remained with her
that afternoon, until evening
and would have stayed longer, if he could,
and if his love had consented.
"Love," she said, "get up.
160   You cannot stay any longer.
Go away now; I shall remain
but I will tell you one thing:
when you want to talk to me
there is no place you can think of
165   where a man might have his mistress
without reproach or shame,
that I shall not be there with you
to satisfy all your desires.
No man but you will see me
170   or hear my words."
When he heard her, he was very happy,
he kissed her, and then got up.
The girls who had brought him to the tent
dressed him in rich clothes;
175   when he was dressed anew,
there wasn't a more handsome youth in all the world;
he was no fool, no boor.
They gave him water for his hands
and a towel to dry them,
180   and they brought him food.
He took supper with his love;
it was not to be refused.
He was served with great courtesy,
he received it with great joy.
185   There was an entremet°   side dish
that vastly pleased the knight
for he kissed his lady often
and held her close.
When they finished dinner,
190   his horse was brought to him.
The horse had been well saddled;
Lanval was very richly served.
The knight took his leave, mounted,
and rode toward the city,
195   often looking behind him.
Lanval was very disturbed;
he wondered about his adventure
and was doubtful in his heart;
he was amazed, not knowing what to believe;
200   he didn't expect ever to see her again.

He came to his lodging
and found his men well dressed.
That night, his accommodations were rich
but no one knew where it came from.

205   There was no knight in the city
who really needed a place to stay
whom he didn't invite to join him
to be well and richly served.
Lanval gave rich gifts,

210   Lanval released prisoners,
Lanval dressed jongleurs,°   *performers*
Lanval offered great honors.
There was no stranger or friend
to whom Lanval didn't give.

215   Lanval's joy and pleasure were intense;
in the daytime or at night,
he could see his love often;
she was completely at his command.

In that same year, it seems to me,
220   after the feast of Saint John,
about thirty knights
were amusing themselves
in an orchard beneath the tower
where the queen was staying.

225   Gawain was with them
and his cousin, the handsome Yvain;[7]
Gawain, the noble, the brave,
who was so loved by all, said:
"By God, my lords, we wronged

230   our companion Lanval,
who is so generous and courtly,
and whose father is a rich king,
when we didn't bring him with us."
They immediately turned back,

235   went to his lodging
and prevailed on Lanval to come along with them.
At a sculpted window
the queen was looking out;
she had three ladies with her.

240   She saw the king's retinue,
recognized Lanval and looked at him.
Then she told one of her ladies
to send for her maidens,
the loveliest and the most refined;

245   together they went to amuse themselves
in the orchard where the others were.
She brought thirty or more with her;
they descended the steps.

---

7. Gawain and Yvain serve to place Marie's hero in the context of more famous Arthurian episodes. Gawain, nephew of
Arthur and distinguished both for bravery and courtesy, increasingly acts as Lanval's sponsor in the rest of the *lai*.

The knights came to meet them,
250   because they were delighted to see them.
The knights took them by the hand;
their conversation was in no way vulgar.
Lanval went off to one side,
far from the others; he was impatient
255   to hold his love,
to kiss and embrace and touch her;
he thought little of others' joys
if he could not have his pleasure.
When the queen saw him alone,
260   she went straight to the knight.
She sat beside him and spoke,
revealing her whole heart:
"Lanval, I have shown you much honor,
I have cherished you, and loved you.
265   You may have all my love;
just tell me your desire.
I promise you my affection.
You should be very happy with me."
"My lady," he said, "let me be!
270   I have no desire to love you.
I've served the king a long time;
I don't want to betray my faith to him.
Never, for you or for your love,
will I do anything to harm my lord."
275   The queen got angry;
in her wrath, she insulted him:
"Lanval," she said, "I am sure
you don't care for such pleasure;
people have often told me
280   that you have no interest in women.
You have fine-looking boys
with whom you enjoy yourself.
Base coward, lousy cripple,
my lord made a bad mistake
285   when he let you stay with him.
For all I know, he'll lose God because of it."
When Lanval heard her, he was quite disturbed;
he was not slow to answer.
He said something out of spite
290   that he would later regret.
"Lady," he said, "of that activity
I know nothing,
but I love and I am loved
by one who should have the prize
295   over all the women I know.
And I shall tell you one thing;
you might as well know all:
any one of those who serve her,
the poorest girl of all,
300   is better than you, my lady queen,

in body, face, and beauty,
in breeding and in goodness."
The queen left him
and went, weeping, to her chamber.
305   She was upset and angry
because he had insulted her.
She went to bed sick;
never, she said, would she get up
unless the king gave her satisfaction
310   for the offense against her.
The king returned from the woods,
he'd had a very good day.
He entered the queen's chambers.
When she saw him, she began to complain.
315   She fell at his feet, asked his mercy,
saying that Lanval had dishonored her;
he had asked for her love,
and because she refused him
he insulted and offended her:
320   he boasted of a love
who was so refined and noble and proud
that her chambermaid,
the poorest one who served her,
was better than the queen.
325   The king got very angry;
he swore an oath:
if Lanval could not defend himself in court
he would have him burned or hanged.
The king left her chamber
330   and called for three of his barons;
he sent them for Lanval
who was feeling great sorrow and distress.
He had come back to his dwelling,
knowing very well
335   that he'd lost his love,
he had betrayed their affair.
He was all alone in a room,
disturbed and troubled;
he called on his love, again and again,
340   but it did him no good.
He complained and sighed,
from time to time he fainted;
then he cried a hundred times for her to have mercy
and speak to her love.
345   He cursed his heart and his mouth;
it's a wonder he didn't kill himself.
No matter how much he cried and shouted,
ranted and raged,
she would not have mercy on him,
350   not even let him see her.
How will he ever contain himself?
The men the king sent

arrived and told him
to appear in court without delay:
355   the king had summoned him
because the queen had accused him.
Lanval went with his great sorrow;
they could have killed him, for all he cared.
He came before the king;
360   he was very sad, thoughtful, silent;
his face revealed great suffering.
In anger the king told him:
"Vassal, you have done me a great wrong!
This was a base undertaking,
365   to shame and disgrace me
and to insult the queen.
You have made a foolish boast:
your love is much too noble
if her maid is more beautiful,
370   more worthy, than the queen."
Lanval denied that he'd dishonored
or shamed his lord,
word for word, as the king spoke:
he had not made advances to the queen;
375   but of what he had said,
he acknowledged the truth,
about the love he had boasted of,
that now made him sad because he'd lost her.
About that he said he would do
380   whatever the court decided.
The king was very angry with him;
he sent for all his men
to determine exactly what he ought to do
so that no one could find fault with his decision.
385   They did as he commanded,
whether they liked it or not.
They assembled,
judged, and decided,
that Lanval should have his day;
390   but he must find pledges for his lord
to guarantee that he would await the judgment,
return, and be present at it.[8]
Then the court would be increased,
for now there were none but the king's household.
395   The barons came back to the king
and announced their decision.
The king demanded pledges.
Lanval was alone and forlorn,
he had no relative, no friend.
400   Gawain went and pledged himself for him,
and all his companions followed.

8. Marie introduces judicial procedures that may have recalled those in Henry's reign: summons and accusation, setting a day for judgment, the rise of royal jurisdiction, the possibility of a champion, and trial by battle.

The king addressed them: "I release him to you
on forfeit of whatever you hold from me,
lands and fiefs, each one for himself."
405   When Lanval was pledged, there was nothing else to do.
He returned to his lodging.
The knights accompanied him,
they reproached and admonished him
that he give up his great sorrow;
410   they cursed his foolish love.
Each day they went to see him,
because they wanted to know
whether he was drinking and eating;
they were afraid that he'd kill himself.
415   On the day that they had named,
the barons assembled.
The king and the queen were there
and the pledges brought Lanval back.
They were all very sad for him:
420   I think there were a hundred
who would have done all they could
to set him free without a trial
where he would be wrongly accused.
The king demanded a verdict
425   according to the charge and rebuttal.
Now it all fell to the barons.
They went to the judgment,
worried and distressed
for the noble man from another land
430   who'd gotten into such trouble in their midst.
Many wanted to condemn him
in order to satisfy their lord.
The Duke of Cornwall said:
"No one can blame us;
435   whether it makes you weep or sing
justice must be carried out.
The king spoke against his vassal
whom I have heard named Lanval;
he accused him of felony,
440   charged him with a misdeed—
a love that he had boasted of,
which made the queen angry.
No one but the king accused him:
by the faith I owe you,
445   if one were to speak the truth,
there should have been no need for defense,
except that a man owes his lord honor
in every circumstance.
He will be bound by his oath,
450   and the king will forgive us our pledges
if he can produce proof;
if his love would come forward,

if what he said,
what upset the queen, is true,
455   then he will be acquitted,
because he did not say it out of malice.
But if he cannot get his proof,
we must make it clear to him
that he will forfeit his service to the king;
460   he must take his leave."
They sent to the knight,
told and announced to him
that he should have his love come
to defend and stand surety for him.
465   He told them that he could not do it:
he would never receive help from her.
They went back to the judges,
not expecting any help from Lanval.
The king pressed them hard
470   because of the queen who was waiting.
When they were ready to give their verdict
they saw two girls approaching,
riding handsome palfreys.
They were very attractive,
475   dressed in purple taffeta,
over their bare skin.
The men looked at them with pleasure.
Gawain, taking three knights with him,
went to Lanval and told him;
480   he pointed out the two girls.
Gawain was extremely happy, and begged him
to tell if his love were one of them.
Lanval said he didn't know who they were,
where they came from or where they were going.
485   The girls proceeded
still on horseback;
they dismounted before the high table
at which Arthur, the king, sat.
They were of great beauty,
490   and spoke in a courtly manner:
"King, clear your chambers,
have them hung with silk
where my lady may dismount;
she wishes to take shelter with you."
495   He promised it willingly
and called two knights
to guide them up to the chambers.
On that subject no more was said.
The king asked his barons
500   for their judgment and decision;
he said they had angered him very much
with their long delay.
"Sire," they said, "we have decided.
Because of the ladies we have just seen

505   we have made no judgment.
       Let us reconvene the trial."
       Then they assembled, everyone was worried;
       there was much noise and strife.
       While they were in that confusion,
510   two girls in noble array,
       dressed in Phrygian silks
       and riding Spanish mules,
       were seen coming down the street.
       This gave the vassals great joy;
515   to each other they said that now
       Lanval, the brave and bold, was saved.
       Gawain went up to him,
       bringing his companions along.
       "Sire," he said, "take heart.
520   For the love of God, speak to us.
       Here come two maidens,
       well adorned and very beautiful;
       one must certainly be your love."
       Lanval answered quickly
525   that he did not recognize them,
       he didn't know them or love them.
       Meanwhile they'd arrived,
       and dismounted before the king.
       Most of those who saw them praised them
530   for their bodies, their faces, their coloring;
       each was more impressive
       than the queen had ever been.
       The older one was courtly and wise,
       she spoke her message fittingly:
535   "King, have chambers prepared for us
       to lodge my lady according to her need;
       she is coming here to speak with you."
       He ordered them to be taken
       to the others who had preceded them.
540   There was no problem with the mules.
       When he had seen to the girls,
       he summoned all his barons
       to render their judgment;
       it had already dragged out too much.
545   The queen was getting angry
       because she had fasted so long.
       They were about to give their judgment
       when through the city came riding
       a girl on horseback:
550   there was none more beautiful in the world.
       She rode a white palfrey,
       who carried her handsomely and smoothly:
       he was well apportioned in the neck and head,
       no finer beast in the world.
555   The palfrey's trappings were rich;
       under heaven there was no count or king

who could have afforded them all
without selling or mortgaging lands.
She was dressed in this fashion:
560   in a white linen shift
that revealed both her sides
since the lacing was along the side.
Her body was elegant, her hips slim,
her neck whiter than snow on a branch,
565   her eyes bright, her face white,
a beautiful mouth, a well-set nose,
dark eyebrows and an elegant forehead,
her hair curly and rather blond;
golden wire does not shine
570   like her hair in the light.
Her cloak, which she had wrapped around her,
was dark purple.
On her wrist she held a sparrow hawk,
a greyhound followed her.
575   In the town, no one, small or big,
old man or child,
failed to come look.
As they watched her pass,
there was no joking about her beauty.
580   She proceeded at a slow pace.
The judges who saw her
marveled at the sight;
no one who looked at her
was not warmed with joy.
585   Those who loved the knight
came to him and told him
of the girl who was approaching,
if God pleased, to rescue him.
"Sir companion, here comes one
590   neither tawny nor dark;
this is, of all who exist,
the most beautiful woman in the world."
Lanval heard them and lifted his head;
he recognized her and sighed.
595   The blood rose to his face;
he was quick to speak.
"By my faith," he said, "that is my love.
Now I don't care if I am killed,
if only she forgives me.
600   For I am restored, now that I see her."
The lady entered the palace;
no one so beautiful had ever been there.
She dismounted before the king
so that she was well seen by all.
605   And she let her cloak fall
so they could see her better.
The king, who was well bred,
rose and went to meet her;

all the others honored her
610   and offered to serve her.
When they had looked at her well,
when they had greatly praised her beauty,
she spoke in this way,
she didn't want to wait:
615   "I have loved one of your vassals:
you see him before you—Lanval.
He has been accused in your court—
I don't want him to suffer
for what he said; you should know
620   that the queen was in the wrong.
He never made advances to her.
And for the boast that he made,
if he can be acquitted through me,
let him be set free by your barons."
625   Whatever the barons judged by law
the king promised would prevail.
To the last man they agreed
that Lanval had successfully answered the charge.
He was set free by their decision
630   and the girl departed.
The king could not detain her,
though there were enough people to serve her.
Outside the hall stood
a great stone of dark marble
635   where heavy men mounted
when they left the king's court;
Lanval climbed on it.
When the girl came through the gate
Lanval leapt, in one bound,
640   onto the palfrey, behind her.
With her he went to Avalun,[9]
so the Bretons tell us,
to a very beautiful island;
there the youth was carried off.
645   No man heard of him again,
and I have no more to tell.

Sir Gawain and the Green Knight

As a subject of literary romance, Arthurian tradition never had the centrality in later
medieval England it had gained in France. It was only one of a wide range of popular topics
like Havelok the Dane, King Horn, and the Troy story. Nevertheless Arthur and his court
played an ongoing role in English society, written into histories and emulated by aristocrats

---

9. Avalon is the mysterious island to which Arthur is also carried, mortally wounded, after his final battle. Marie's contemporary Gerald of Wales expresses far older associations of Avalon with powerful women (see page 166).

and kings. And in the later fourteenth or early fifteenth century, several very distinguished Arthurian poems appeared, such as the alliterative *Morte Arthure* and the *Awntyrs* (Adventures) *off Arthure*.

Sir Gawain and the Green Knight is the greatest of the Arthurian romances produced in England. The poem embraces the highest aspirations of the late medieval aristocratic world, both courtly and religious, even while it eloquently admits the human failings that threaten those values. A knight's troth and word, a Christian's election and covenant, the breaking point of a person's or a society's virtues, all come in for celebration and painful scrutiny during Gawain's adventure.

Like *Beowulf*, *Sir Gawain and the Green Knight* comes down to us by the thread of a single copy. Its manuscript contains a group of poems (*Sir Gawain*, *Pearl*, *Purity*, and *Patience*) that mark their anonymous author as a poet whose range approaches that of his contemporary Chaucer, and whose formal craft is in some ways more ambitious than Chaucer's.

Gawain is the work of a highly sophisticated provincial court poet (likely in the northwest Midlands), working in a form and narrative tradition that is conservative in comparison with Chaucer's. The poet uses the alliterative long line, a meter with its roots in Anglo-Saxon poetry; the unrhymed alliterative stanzas, of irregular length, each end with five shorter rhymed lines often called a "bob-and-wheel" stanza. (For a further discussion of the alliterative style, see the introduction to Langland, pages 395–396.) Within these traditional constraints, however, the poem achieves an apex of medieval courtly literature, as a superlatively crafted and stylized version of quest romance.

The romance never aims to detach itself from society or history, though. It opens and closes by referring to Troy, the ancient, fallen empire whose survivors were legendary founders of Britain, a connection well known through Geoffrey of Monmouth. Arthur, their ultimate heir, went on later in his myth to pursue imperial ambitions that, like those of Troy, were foiled by adulterous desire and political infidelity. *Sir Gawain* also echoes its contemporary world in the technical language of architecture, crafts, and arms. This helps draw in the kind of conservative, aristocratic court for which the poem seems to have been written, probably in Cheshire or Lancashire, a somewhat backward region whose nobles remained loyal to Richard II. Along with the pleasure it takes in fine armor and courtly ritual, the poem seems to enfold anxieties about the economic pressures of maintaining chivalric display in a period of costly new technology, inflation, and declining income from land.

By the time this poem was written, toward the close of the fourteenth century, Gawain was a famous Arthurian hero. His reputation was ambiguous, though; he was both Arthur's faithful retainer and nephew, but also a suave seducer. Which side of Gawain would dominate in this particular poem? Would he stand for a civilization of Christian chivalry or one of cynical sophistication?

The test that begins to answer this question occurs during Arthur's ritual celebrations of Christmas and the New Year, and within the civilized practices of Eucharist and secular feast. A gigantic green knight interrupts Arthur's banquet to offer a deadly game of exchanged ax-blows, to be resolved in one year's time. Although the Green Knight, with his ball of holly leaves, seems at first to come from the tradition of the Wild Man—a giant force of nature itself—he is also a sophisticated knight, gorgeously attired. He knows, too, just how to taunt a young king without quite overstepping the bounds of courtly behavior. Gawain takes up the challenge, but a still greater marvel ensues.

As the term of the agreement approaches, Gawain rides off, elaborately armed, to find the Green Knight and fulfill his obligation, even if that means his death. What Gawain encounters first, though, are temptations of character and sexuality even trickier and more crucial than they at first seem.

Sir Gawain and the Green Knight is remarkable not only for the intricacy of its plot but also for the virtuosity of its descriptions, such as the almost elegiac review of the passing seasons ("And so the year moves on in yesterdays many"). The poem rejoices in the masterful exercise of skill as the mark of civilization. Beautifully crafted knots appear everywhere, and we encounter artisanal craft as well in narrative elements like the Green Knight's dress (a dazzling mixture of leafy green and jeweler's gold), Gawain's decorated shield and arms, and the expertise of the master of the hunt who carves up the prey of Gawain's host with ritual precision. Even Gawain's exquisite courtly manners appear as a civilizing artifice.

The ambition of the poem's own craft is equally evident in its extraordinary range of formal devices. Preeminent among these is the symbolic register of number. The poem can be seen as a single unit, circling back to the Trojan scene with which it begins. It has a double structure, too, as it shifts between the courts of Arthur and Gawain's mysterious host. In the manuscript it is divided into four parts ("fits") that respond to the seasonal description at the opening of Part 2. The narrative proper ends by echoing the very start of the poem, at line 2525, itself a multiple of fives that recalls the pentangle on Gawain's shield symbolizing his virtues. The final rhyming stanza, with its formula of grace and salvation, brings the line total to 2530, whose individual digits add up to ten, a number associated with the divine in medieval numerology.

This symbolic structure can seem sometimes overdetermined. A range of elements, however, invites the reader to come at the poem from other perspectives. The poem's very circularity, narrative and formal, allows it to be viewed from beginning or ending. From the front it is a poem of male accomplishment, largely celebrating *men's* courts and *men's* virtues (even men's horses). At the other end, however, it focuses on a court presided over by an old woman (later called a goddess), a court whose irruption into the Arthurian world is explained as the playing out of an old and mysterious rivalry between two queens. Male, even patriarchal from one direction, the poem seems matriarchal, almost pagan, from the other. For all its formal cohesion and celebration of craft, the poem also pulls the reader back and keeps its mysteries intact by leaving many narrative loose ends and unanswered questions.

Unresolvable ambiguities reside most clearly in the pentangle on Gawain's shield and in the "green girdle" whose true owner remains uncertain. For all their differences, both are figures that insist on repetition, end where they begin, and possess a geometry that can be traced forward or backward. Yet the static perfection of the pentangle is subtly set against the protean green girdle, which passes through so many hands, alters its shape (being untied and retied repeatedly), and connects with so many issues in the poem: mortality, women's power, Gawain's fault and the acceptance of that fault by the whole Arthurian court. The girdle becomes an image both of flaw and triumph and of all the loose ends in this early episode of the Arthurian myth.

The girdle also serves to link *Sir Gawain* to political and social issues of the poet's own time, particularly efforts to revalidate a declining system of chivalry. After the last line in the manuscript, a later medieval hand has added "Hony Soyt Qui Mal Pence" ("shamed be he who thinks ill thereof"), the motto of the royal Order of the Garter, founded by Edward III in 1349 to promote a revival of knighthood. The Arthurian myth had already been redeployed to buttress royal power when Edward III refounded a Round Table in 1344. King Arthur's wisdom at the close of Gawain's adventure lies in transforming Gawain's shame, rage, and humiliated sense of sin into an emblem at once of mortal humanity and aristocratic cohesion. This is the place—back with the king and ritually connected with the Order of the Garter—where the closed circle of the poem opens to the social, historical world of empire, court, and kingship.

Sir Gawain and the Green Knight[1]
Part 1

Since the siege and the assault was ceased at Troy,
The walls breached and burnt down to brands and ashes,

---

1. This translation, remarkably faithful to the original alliterative meter and stanza form, is by Marie Borroff (1967).

The knight that had knotted the nets of deceit
Was impeached for his perfidy, proven most true.
5   It was high-born Aeneas[2] and his haughty race
That since prevailed over provinces, and proudly reigned
Over well-nigh all the wealth of the West Isles.[3]
Great Romulus to Rome repairs in haste;
With boast and with bravery builds he that city
10   And names it with his own name, that it now bears.
Ticius to Tuscany,[4] and towers raises,
Langobard[5] in Lombardy lays out homes,
And far over the French Sea, Felix Brutus[6]
On many broad hills and high Britain he sets,
15   most fair.
        Where war and wrack and wonder
        By shifts have sojourned there,
        And bliss by turns with blunder
        In that land's lot had share.

20   And since this Britain was built by this baron great,
Bold boys bred there, in broils delighting,
That did in their day many a deed most dire.
More marvels have happened in this merry land
Than in any other I know, since that olden time,
25   But of those that here built, of British kings,
King Arthur was counted most courteous of all,
Wherefore an adventure I aim to unfold,
That a marvel of might some men think it,
And one unmatched among Arthur's wonders.
30   If you will listen to my lay but a little while,
As I heard it in hall, I shall hasten to tell
                              anew.
        As it was fashioned featly
        In tale of derring-do,
35   And linked in measures meetly
        By letters tried and true.

This king lay at Camelot[7] at Christmastide;
Many good knights and gay his guests were there,
Arrayed of the Round Table[8] rightful brothers,
40   With feasting and fellowship and carefree mirth.
There true men contended in tournaments many,
Joined there in jousting these gentle knights,

2. Aeneas led the survivors of Troy to Italy, after a series of ambiguous omens and misadventures. In medieval tradition, he was also said to have plotted to betray his own city. "The knight" in line 3, though, may refer to the Trojan Antenor, also said to have betrayed Troy.
3. Perhaps Europe, or just the British Isles. Many royal houses traced their ancestry to Rome and Troy.
4. Possibly Titus Tatius, ancient king of the Sabines.
5. Ancestor of the Lombards, and a nephew of Brutus.
6. According to Geoffrey of Monmouth and others, a great-grandson of Aeneas, exiled after accidentally killing his father and later the founder of Britain.
7. Arthur's capital; its location is uncertain, probably in Wales, and perhaps it is to be connected with Caerleon-on-Usk where Arthur had been crowned. Knights were expected to gather at his court, in celebration and homage, on the five liturgical holidays on which Arthur wore his crown: Easter, Ascension, Pentecost, All Saints' Day, and Christmas.
8. Its shape symbolized the unity of Arthur's knights but also avoided disputes over precedence.

Then came to the court for carol-dancing,
For the feast was in force full fifteen days,
45 With all the meat and the mirth that men could devise,
Such gaiety and glee, glorious to hear,
Brave din by day, dancing by night.
High were their hearts in halls and chambers,
These lords and these ladies, for life was sweet.
50 In peerless pleasures passed they their days,
The most noble knights known under Christ,
And the loveliest ladies that lived on earth ever,
And he the comeliest king, that that court holds,
For all this fair folk in their first age[9]
55   were still.
          Happiest of mortal kind,
          King noblest famed of will;
          You would now go far to find
          So hardy a host on hill.

60 While the New Year was new, but yesternight come,
This fair folk at feast two-fold was served,
When the king and his company were come in together,
The chanting in chapel achieved and ended.
Clerics and all the court acclaimed the glad season,
65 Cried Noel anew, good news to men;
Then gallants gather gaily, hand-gifts to make,
Called them out clearly, claimed them by hand,
Bickered long and busily about those gifts.
Ladies laughed aloud, though losers they were,
70 And he that won was not angered, as well you will know.[1]
All this mirth they made until meat was served;
When they had washed them worthily, they went to their seats,
The best seated above, as best it beseemed,
Guenevere the goodly queen gay in the midst
75 On a dais[2] well-decked and duly arrayed
With costly silk curtains, a canopy over,
Of Toulouse and Turkestan tapestries rich,
All broidered and bordered with the best gems
Ever brought into Britain, with bright pennies
80   to pay.
          Fair queen, without a flaw,
          She glanced with eyes of gray.
          A seemlier that once he saw,
          In truth, no man could say.

85 But Arthur would not eat till all were served;
So light was his lordly heart, and a little boyish;
His life he liked lively—the less he cared

---

9. Arthur is emphatically a young king here, even "boy-ish." The phrase may also recall the Golden Age, an era of uncorrupted happiness.
1. The distribution of gifts at New Year, displayed the king's wealth and power; it was also the occasion here of

some courtly game of exchange, in which the loser per-haps gave up a kiss.
2. A medieval nobleman's hall typically had a raised platform at one end, on which the "high table" stood.

To be lying for long, or long to sit,
So busy his young blood, his brain so wild.
90   And also a point of pride pricked him in heart,
For he nobly had willed, he would never eat
On so high a holiday, till he had heard first
Of some fair feat or fray some far-borne tale,
Of some marvel of might, that he might trust,
95   By champions of chivalry achieved in arms,
Or some suppliant came seeking some single knight
To join with him in jousting, in jeopardy each
To lay life for life, and leave it to fortune
To afford him on field fair hap or other.
100   Such is the king's custom, when his court he holds
At each far-famed feast amid his fair host
                    so dear.
              The stout king stands in state
              Till a wonder shall appear;
105   He leads, with heart elate,
              High mirth in the New Year.

So he stands there in state, the stout young king,
Talking before the high table of trifles fair.
There Gawain the good knight by Guenevere sits,
110   With Agravain à la dure main on her other side,
Both knights of renown, and nephews of the king.
Bishop Baldwin above begins the table,
And Yvain,[3] son of Urien, ate with him there.
These few with the fair queen were fittingly served;
115   At the side-tables sat many stalwart knights.
Then the first course comes, with clamor of trumpets
That were bravely bedecked with bannerets bright,
With noise of new drums and the noble pipes.[4]
Wild were the warbles that wakened that day
120   In strains that stirred many strong men's hearts.
There dainties were dealt out, dishes rare,
Choice fare to choose, on chargers so many
That scarce was there space to set before the people
The service of silver, with sundry meats,
                    on cloth.
125   Each fair guest freely there
              Partakes, and nothing loth;
              Twelve dishes before each pair;
              Good beer and bright wine both.

130   Of the service itself I need say no more,
For well you will know no tittle was wanting.
Another noise and a new was well-nigh at hand,
That the lord might have leave his life to nourish;

3. Another nephew of Arthur. The relationship of uncle
and nephew is close in many Arthurian romances, and
noble youths were often sent to be raised by an uncle on
the mother's side.
4. Holiday banquets were formalized, almost theatrical.

For scarce were the sweet strains still in the hall,
135 And the first course come to that company fair,
There hurtles in at the hall-door an unknown rider,
One the greatest on ground in growth of his frame:
From broad neck to buttocks so bulky and thick,
And his loins and his legs so long and so great,
140 Half a giant on earth I hold him to be,
But believe him no less than the largest of men,
And that the seemliest in his stature to see, as he rides,
For in back and in breast though his body was grim,
His waist in its width was worthily small,
145 And formed with every feature in fair accord
                              was he.
          Great wonder grew in hall
          At his hue most strange to see,
          For man and gear and all
150   Were green as green could be.

And in guise all of green, the gear and the man:
A coat cut close, that clung to his sides,
And a mantle to match, made with a lining
Of furs cut and fitted—the fabric was noble,
155 Embellished all with ermine, and his hood beside,
That was loosed from his locks, and laid on his shoulders.
With trim hose and tight, the same tint of green,
His great calves were girt, and gold spurs under
He bore on silk bands that embellished his heels,
160 And footgear well-fashioned, for riding most fit.
And all his vesture verily was verdant green;
Both the bosses on his belt and other bright gems
That were richly ranged on his raiment noble
About himself and his saddle, set upon silk,
165 That to tell half the trifles would tax my wits,
The butterflies and birds embroidered thereon
In green of the gayest, with many a gold thread.
The pendants of the breast-band, the princely crupper,
And the bars of the bit were brightly enameled;
170 The stout stirrups were green, that steadied his feet,
And the bows of the saddle and the side-panels both,
That gleamed all and glinted with green gems about.
The steed he bestrides of that same green
                              so bright.
175   A green horse great and thick;
          A headstrong steed of might;
          In broidered bridle quick,
          Mount matched man aright.

Gay was this goodly man in guise all of green,
180 And the hair of his head to his horse suited;
Fair flowing tresses enfold his shoulders;
A beard big as a bush on his breast hangs,
That with his heavy hair, that from his head falls,

Was evened all about above both his elbows,

185 That half his arms thereunder were hid in the fashion
Of a king's cap-à-dos,[5] that covers his throat.
The mane of that mighty horse much to it like,
Well curled and becombed, and cunningly knotted
With filaments of fine gold amid the fair green,

190 Here a strand of the hair, here one of gold;
His tail and his foretop twin in their hue,
And bound both with a band of a bright green
That was decked adown the dock with dazzling stones
And tied tight at the top with a triple knot

195 Where many bells well burnished rang bright and clear.
Such a mount in his might, nor man on him riding,
None had seen, I dare swear, with sight in that hall
                        so grand.
             As lightning quick and light

200   He looked to all at hand;
             It seemed that no man might
             His deadly dints withstand.

Yet had he no helm, nor hauberk[6] neither,
Nor plate, nor appurtenance appending to arms,

205 Nor shaft pointed sharp, nor shield for defense,
But in his one hand he had a holly bob
That is goodliest in green when groves are bare,
And an ax in his other, a huge and immense,
A wicked piece of work in words to expound:

210 The head on its haft was an ell long;
The spike of green steel, resplendent with gold;
The blade burnished bright, with a broad edge,
As well shaped to shear as a sharp razor;
Stout was the stave in the strong man's gripe,

215 That was wound all with iron to the weapon's end,
With engravings in green of goodliest work.
A lace lightly about, that led to a knot,
Was looped in by lengths along the fair haft,
And tassels thereto attached in a row,

220 With buttons of bright green, brave to behold.
This horseman hurtles in, and the hall enters;
Riding to the high dais, recked he no danger;
Not a greeting he gave as the guests he o'erlooked,
Nor wasted his words, but "Where is," he said,

225 "The captain of this crowd? Keenly I wish
To see that sire with sight, and to himself say
                        my say."
             He swaggered all about
             To scan the host so gay;

230   He halted, as if in doubt
             Who in that hall held sway.

---

5. Probably a hooded cape, fastened under the chin.   6. A tunic of chain mail.

There were stares on all sides as the stranger spoke,
For much did they marvel what it might mean
That a horseman and a horse should have such a hue,
235 Grow green as the grass, and greener, it seemed,
Than green fused on gold more glorious by far.
All the onlookers eyed him, and edged nearer,
And awaited in wonder what he would do,
For many sights had they seen, but such a one never,
240 So that phantom and faerie the folk there deemed it,
Therefore chary of answer was many a champion bold,
And stunned at his strong words stone-still they sat
In a swooning silence in the stately hall.
As all were slipped into sleep, so slackened their speech
245   apace.
                    Not all, I think, for dread,
                    But some of courteous grace
                    Let him who was their head
                    Be spokesman in that place.

250 Then Arthur before the high dais that entrance beholds,
And hailed him, as behooved, for he had no fear,
And said "Fellow, in faith you have found fair welcome;
The head of this hostelry Arthur am I;
Leap lightly down, and linger, I pray,
255 And the tale of your intent you shall tell us after."
"Nay, so help me," said the other, "He that on high sits,
To tarry here any time, 'twas not mine errand;
But as the praise of you, prince, is puffed up so high,
And your court and your company are counted the best,
260 Stoutest under steel-gear on steeds to ride,
Worthiest of their works the wide world over,
And peerless to prove in passages of arms,
And courtesy here is carried to its height,
And so at this season I have sought you out.
265 You may be certain by the branch that I bear in hand
That I pass here in peace,[7] and would part friends,
For had I come to this court on combat bent,
I have a hauberk at home, and a helm beside,
A shield and a sharp spear, shining bright,
270 And other weapons to wield, I ween well, to boot,
But as I willed no war, I wore no metal.
But if you be so bold as all men believe,
You will graciously grant the game that I ask
                          by right."
275   Arthur answer gave
                    And said, "Sir courteous knight,
                    If contest here you crave,
                    You shall not fail to fight."

---

7. A holly branch could symbolize peace and was used in games of the Christmas season.

"Nay, to fight, in good faith, is far from my thought;
280   There are about on these benches but beardless children,
Were I here in full arms on a haughty steed,
For measured against mine, their might is puny.
And so I call in this court for a Christmas game,
For 'tis Yule and New Year, and many young bloods about;
285   If any in this house such hardihood claims,
Be so bold in his blood, his brain so wild,
As stoutly to strike one stroke for another,
I shall give him as my gift this gisarme[8] noble,
This ax, that is heavy enough, to handle as he likes,
290   And I shall bide the first blow, as bare as I sit.
If there be one so willful my words to assay,
Let him leap hither lightly, lay hold of this weapon;
I quitclaim it forever, keep it as his own,
And I shall stand him a stroke, steady on this floor,
295   So you grant me the guerdon to give him another,
                          sans blame.
              In a twelvemonth and a day
              He shall have of me the same;
              Now be it seen straightway
300   Who dares take up the game."

If he astonished them at first, stiller were then
All that household in hall, the high and the low;
The stranger on his green steed stirred in the saddle,
And roisterously his red eyes he rolled all about,
305   Bent his bristling brows, that were bright green,
Wagged his beard as he watched who would arise.
When the court kept its counsel he coughed aloud,
And cleared his throat coolly, the clearer to speak:
"What, is this Arthur's house," said that horseman then,
310   "Whose fame is so fair in far realms and wide?
Where is now your arrogance and your awesome deeds,
Your valor and your victories and your vaunting words?
Now are the revel and renown of the Round Table
Overwhelmed with a word of one man's speech,
315   For all cower and quake, and no cut felt!"
With this he laughs so loud that the lord grieved;
The blood for sheer shame shot to his face,
                          and pride.
              With rage his face flushed red,
320   And so did all beside.
              Then the king as bold man bred
              Toward the stranger took a stride.

And said "Sir, now we see you will say but folly,
Which whoso has sought, it suits that he find.
325   No guest here is aghast of your great words.
Give to me your gisarme, in God's own name,

---

8. A long-handled ax with a spike at the end.

And the boon you have begged shall straight be granted."
He leaps to him lightly, lays hold of his weapon;
The green fellow on foot fiercely alights.
330 Now has Arthur his ax, and the haft grips,
And sternly stirs it about, on striking bent.
The stranger before him stood there erect,
Higher than any in the house by a head and more;
With stern look as he stood, he stroked his beard,
335 And with undaunted countenance drew down his coat,
No more moved nor dismayed for his mighty dints
Than any bold man on bench had brought him a drink
                    of wine.
                Gawain by Guenevere
340   Toward the king doth now incline:
               "I beseech, before all here,
               That this melee may be mine."

"Would you grant me the grace," said Gawain to the king,
"To be gone from this bench and stand by you there,
345 If I without discourtesy might quit this board,
And if my liege lady misliked it not,
I would come to your counsel before your court noble.
For I find it not fit, as in faith it is known,
When such a boon is begged before all these knights,
350 Though you be tempted thereto, to take it on yourself
While so bold men about upon benches sit,
That no host under heaven is hardier of will,
Nor better brothers-in-arms where battle is joined;
I am the weakest, well I know, and of wit feeblest;
355 And the loss of my life would be least of any;
That I have you for uncle is my only praise;
My body, but for your blood, is barren of worth;
And for that this folly befits not a king,
And 'tis I that have asked it, it ought to be mine,
360 And if my claim be not comely let all this court judge,
                    in sight."
               The court assays the claim,
               And in counsel all unite
               To give Gawain the game
365   And release the king outright.

Then the king called the knight to come to his side,
And he rose up readily, and reached him with speed,
Bows low to his lord, lays hold of the weapon,
And he releases it lightly, and lifts up his hand,
370 And gives him God's blessing, and graciously prays
That his heart and his hand may be hardy both.
"Keep, cousin," said the king, "what you cut with this day,
And if you rule it aright, then readily, I know,
You shall stand the stroke it will strike after."
375 Gawain goes to the guest with gisarme in hand,
And boldly he bides there, abashed not a whit.

Then hails he Sir Gawain, the horseman in green:
"Recount we our contract, ere you come further.
First I ask and adjure you, how you are called
380 That you tell me true, so that trust it I may."
"In good faith," said the good knight, "Gawain am I
Whose buffet befalls you, whate'er betide after,
And at this time twelvemonth take from you another
With what weapon you will, and with no man else
385   alive."
          The other nods assent:
          "Sir Gawain, as I may thrive,
          I am wondrous well content
          That you this dint shall drive."

390 "Sir Gawain," said the Green Knight, "By God, I rejoice
That your fist shall fetch this favor I seek,
And you have readily rehearsed, and in right terms,
Each clause of my covenant with the king your lord,
Save that you shall assure me, sir, upon oath,
395 That you shall seek me yourself, wheresoever you deem
My lodgings may lie, and look for such wages
As you have offered me here before all this host."
"What is the way there?" said Gawain, "Where do you dwell?
I heard never of your house, by Him that made me,
400 Nor I know you not, knight, your name nor your court.
But tell me truly thereof, and teach me your name,
And I shall fare forth to find you, so far as I may,
And this I say in good certain, and swear upon oath."
"That is enough in New Year, you need say no more,"
405 Said the knight in the green to Gawain the noble,
"If I tell you true, when I have taken your knock,
And if you handily have hit, you shall hear straightway
Of my house and my home and my own name;
Then follow in my footsteps by faithful accord.
410 And if I spend no speech, you shall speed the better:
You can feast with your friends, nor further trace
                              my tracks.
          Now hold your grim tool steady
          And show us how it hacks."
415   "Gladly, sir; all ready,"
          Says Gawain; he strokes the ax.

The Green Knight upon ground girds him with care:
Bows a bit with his head, and bares his flesh:
His long lovely locks he laid over his crown,
420 Let the naked nape for the need be shown.
Gawain grips to his ax and gathers it aloft—
The left foot on the floor before him he set—
Brought it down deftly upon the bare neck,
That the shock of the sharp blow shivered the bones
425 And cut the flesh cleanly and clove it in twain,
That the blade of bright steel bit into the ground.

The head was hewn off and fell to the floor;
Many found it at their feet, as forth it rolled;
The blood gushed from the body, bright on the green,
430   Yet fell not the fellow, nor faltered a whit,
But stoutly he starts forth upon stiff shanks,
And as all stood staring he stretched forth his hand,
Laid hold of his head and heaved it aloft,
Then goes to the green steed, grasps the bridle,
435   Steps into the stirrup, bestrides his mount,
And his head by the hair in his hand holds,
And as steady he sits in the stately saddle
As he had met with no mishap, nor missing were
                   his head.
440   His bulk about he haled,
           That fearsome body that bled;
           There were many in the court that quailed
           Before all his say was said.

For the head in his hand he holds right up;
445   Toward the first on the dais directs he the face,
And it lifted up its lids, and looked with wide eyes,
And said as much with its mouth as now you may hear:
"Sir Gawain, forget not to go as agreed,
And cease not to seek till me, sir, you find,
450   As you promised in the presence of these proud knights.
To the Green Chapel come, I charge you, to take
Such a dint as you have dealt—you have well deserved
That your neck should have a knock on New Year's morn.
The Knight of the Green Chapel I am well-known to many,
455   Wherefore you cannot fail to find me at last;
Therefore come, or be counted a recreant knight."
With a roisterous rush he flings round the reins,
Hurtles out at the hall-door, his head in his hand,
That the flint-fire flew from the flashing hooves.
460   Which way he went, not one of them knew
Nor whence he was come in the wide world
                   so fair.
           The king and Gawain gay
           Make game of the Green Knight there,
465   Yet all who saw it say
           'Twas a wonder past compare.

Though high-born Arthur at heart had wonder,
He let no sign be seen, but said aloud
To the comely queen, with courteous speech,
470   "Dear dame, on this day dismay you no whit;
Such crafts are becoming at Christmastide,
Laughing at interludes,[9] light songs and mirth,
Amid dancing of damsels with doughty knights.
Nevertheless of my meat now let me partake,

---

9. Brief performances between the courses of the banquet.

475 For I have met with a marvel, I may not deny."
He glanced at Sir Gawain, and gaily he said,
"Now, sir, hang up your ax,[1] that has hewn enough,"
And over the high dais it was hung on the wall
That men in amazement might on it look,
480 And tell in true terms the tale of the wonder.
Then they turned toward the table, these two together,
The good king and Gawain, and made great feast,
With all dainties double, dishes rare,
With all manner of meat and minstrelsy both,
485 Such happiness wholly had they that day
                    in hold.
          Now take care, Sir Gawain,
          That your courage wax not cold
          When you must turn again
490   To your enterprise foretold.

Part 2

This adventure had Arthur of handsels[2] first
When young was the year, for he yearned to hear tales;
Though they wanted for words when they went to sup,
Now are fierce deeds to follow, their fists stuffed full.
495 Gawain was glad to begin those games in hall,
But if the end be harsher, hold it no wonder,
For though men are merry in mind after much drink,
A year passes apace, and proves ever new:
First things and final conform but seldom.
500 And so this Yule to the young year yielded place,
And each season ensued at its set time;[3]
After Christmas there came the cold cheer of Lent,
When with fish and plainer fare our flesh we reprove;
But then the world's weather with winter contends:
505 The keen cold lessens, the low clouds lift;
Fresh falls the rain in fostering showers
On the face of the fields; flowers appear.
The ground and the groves wear gowns of green;
Birds build their nests, and blithely sing
510 That solace of all sorrow with summer comes
                    ere long.
          And blossoms day by day
          Bloom rich and rife in throng;
          Then every grove so gay
515   Of the greenwood rings with song.

And then the season of summer with the soft winds,
When Zephyr sighs low over seeds and shoots;

---

1. A literal suggestion, but also an invitation to put the matter aside.
2. New Year's gifts.
3. This famous passage on the cycle of seasons draws both on Germanic conventions of the battle of Winter and Summer, and on Romance springtime lyrics, the *reverdies*.

Glad is the green plant growing abroad,
When the dew at dawn drops from the leaves,
520 To get a gracious glance from the golden sun.
But harvest with harsher winds follows hard after,
Warns him to ripen well ere winter comes;
Drives forth the dust in the droughty season,
From the face of the fields to fly high in air.
525 Wroth winds in the welkin wrestle with the sun,
The leaves launch from the linden and light on the ground,
And the grass turns to gray, that once grew green.
Then all ripens and rots that rose up at first,
And so the year moves on in yesterdays many,
530 And winter once more, by the world's law,
               draws nigh.
          At Michaelmas the moon[4]
          Hangs wintry pale in sky;
          Sir Gawain girds him soon
535   For travails yet to try.

Till All-Hallows' Day[5] with Arthur he dwells,
And he held a high feast to honor that knight
With great revels and rich, of the Round Table.
Then ladies lovely and lords debonair
540 With sorrow for Sir Gawain were sore at heart;
Yet they covered their care with countenance glad:
Many a mournful man made mirth for his sake.
So after supper soberly he speaks to his uncle
Of the hard hour at hand, and openly says,
545 "Now, liege lord of my life, my leave I take;
The terms of this task too well you know—
To count the cost over concerns me nothing.
But I am bound forth betimes to bear a stroke
From the grim man in green, as God may direct."
550 Then the first and foremost came forth in throng:[6]
Yvain and Eric and others of note,
Sir Dodinal le Sauvage, the Duke of Clarence,
Lionel and Lancelot and Lucan the good,
Sir Bors and Sir Bedivere, big men both,
555 And many manly knights more, with Mador de la Porte.
All this courtly company comes to the king
To counsel their comrade, with care in their hearts;
There was much secret sorrow suffered that day
That one so good as Gawain must go in such wise
560 To bear a bitter blow, and his bright sword
               lay by.
          He said, "Why should I tarry?"
          And smiled with tranquil eye;

---

4. The harvest moon at Michaelmas, on September 29.
5. All Saints' Day, on November 1, another holiday on which Arthur presided, crowned, over his court.
6. The following list would have recalled, especially to readers of French romances, other great quests and chal-lenges encountered by Arthur's knights. The list's order may also suggest later and more tragic episodes in the Arthurian narrative, ending with Bedivere who throws Excalibur into a lake after Arthur is mortally wounded.

"In destinies sad or merry,
565   True men can but try."

He dwelt there all that day, and dressed in the morning;
Asked early for his arms, and all were brought.
First a carpet of rare cost was cast on the floor
Where much goodly gear gleamed golden bright;
570   He takes his place promptly and picks up the steel,
Attired in a tight coat of Turkestan silk
And a kingly cap-à-dos, closed at the throat,
That was lavishly lined with a lustrous fur.
Then they set the steel shoes on his sturdy feet
575   And clad his calves about with comely greaves,
And plate well-polished protected his knees,
Affixed with fastenings of the finest gold.
Fair cuisses enclosed, that were cunningly wrought,
His thick-thewed thighs, with thongs bound fast,
580   And massy chain-mail of many a steel ring
He bore on his body, above the best cloth,
With brace burnished bright upon both his arms,
Good couters[7] and gay, and gloves of plate,
And all the goodly gear to grace him well
                                        that tide.
585   His surcoat blazoned bold;
           Sharp spurs to prick with pride;
           And a brave silk band to hold
           The broadsword at his side.

590   When he had on his arms, his harness was rich,
The least latchet or loop laden with gold;
So armored as he was, he heard a mass,
Honored God humbly at the high altar.
Then he comes to the king and his comrades-in-arms,
595   Takes his leave at last of lords and ladies,
And they clasped and kissed him, commending him to Christ.
By then Gringolet was girt with a great saddle
That was gaily agleam with fine gilt fringe,
New-furbished for the need with nail-heads bright;
600   The bridle and the bars bedecked all with gold;
The breast-plate, the saddlebow, the side-panels both,
The caparison and the crupper accorded in hue,
And all ranged on the red the resplendent studs
That glittered and glowed like the glorious sun.
605   His helm now he holds up and hastily kisses,
Well-closed with iron clinches, and cushioned within;
It was high on his head, with a hasp behind,
And a covering of cloth to encase the visor,
All bound and embroidered[8] with the best gems
610   On broad bands of silk, and bordered with birds,

---

7. Elbow-pieces.
8. The preceding technical language of armor is now

joined by an equally technical description of needlework,
for which English women were famous.

Parrots and popinjays preening their wings,
Lovebirds and love-knots as lavishly wrought
As many women had worked seven winters thereon,
                            entire.
615   The diadem costlier yet
            That crowned that comely sire,
            With diamonds richly set,
            That flashed as if on fire.

        Then they showed forth the shield, that shone all red,
620   With the pentangle portrayed in purest gold.
        About his broad neck by the baldric he casts it,
        That was meet for the man, and matched him well.
        And why the pentangle[9] is proper to that peerless prince
        I intend now to tell, though detain me it must.
625   It is a sign by Solomon sagely devised
        To be a token of truth, by its title of old,
        For it is a figure formed of five points,
        And each line is linked and locked with the next
        For ever and ever, and hence it is called
630   In all England, as I hear, the endless knot.
        And well may he wear it on his worthy arms,
        For ever faithful five-fold in five-fold fashion
        Was Gawain in good works, as gold unalloyed,
        Devoid of all villainy, with virtues adorned
635   in sight.
            On shield and coat in view
            He bore that emblem bright,
            As to his word most true
            And in speech most courteous knight.

640   And first, he was faultless in his five senses,
        Nor found ever to fail in his five fingers,
        And all his fealty was fixed upon the five wounds
        That Christ got on the cross, as the creed tells;
        And wherever this man in melee took part,
645   His one thought was of this, past all things else,
        That all his force was founded on the five joys
        That the high Queen of heaven had in her child.[1]
        And therefore, as I find, he fittingly had
        On the inner part of his shield her image portrayed,
650   That when his look on it lighted, he never lost heart.
        The fifth of the five fives followed by this knight
        Were beneficence boundless and brotherly love
        And pure mind and manners, that none might impeach,
        And compassion most precious—these peerless five
655   Were forged and made fast in him, foremost of men.
        Now all these five fives were confirmed in this knight,

---

9. A five-pointed star and symbol of perfection and eternity, since it can be drawn with an uninterrupted line ending at the point of the star where it begins. Inscribed within a circle, it was called Solomon's seal.

1. Poems and meditations on the Virgin's joys and sorrows were widespread. Her five joys were the Annunciation, Nativity, Resurrection, Ascension, and Assumption.

And each linked in other, that end there was none,
And fixed to five points, whose force never failed,
Nor assembled all on a side, nor asunder either,
660   Nor anywhere at an end, but whole and entire
However the pattern proceeded or played out its course.
And so on his shining shield shaped was the knot
Royally in red gold against red gules,
That is the peerless pentangle, prized of old
665   in lore.
               Now armed is Gawain gay,
               And bears his lance before,
               And soberly said good day,
               He thought forevermore.

670   He struck his steed with the spurs and sped on his way
So fast that the flint-fire flashed from the stones.
When they saw him set forth they were sore aggrieved,
And all sighed softly, and said to each other,
Fearing for their fellow, "Ill fortune it is
675   That you, man, must be marred, that most are worthy!
His equal on this earth can hardly be found;
To have dealt more discreetly had done less harm,
And have dubbed him a duke, with all due honor.
A great leader of lords he was like to become,
680   And better so to have been than battered to bits,
Beheaded by an elf-man, for empty pride!
Who would credit that a king could be counseled so,
And caught in a cavil in a Christmas game?"
Many were the warm tears they wept from their eyes
685   When goodly Sir Gawain was gone from the court
                              that day.
               No longer he abode,
               But speedily went his way
               Over many a wandering road,
690   As I heard my author say.

Now he rides in his array through the realm of Logres,[2]
Sir Gawain, God knows, though it gave him small joy!
All alone must he lodge through many a long night
Where the food that he fancied was far from his plate;
695   He had no mate but his mount, over mountain and plain,
Nor man to say his mind to but almighty God,
Till he had wandered well-nigh into North Wales.
All the islands of Anglesey he holds on his left,
And follows, as he fares, the fords by the coast,
700   Comes over at Holy Head, and enters next
The Wilderness of Wirral—few were within
That had great good will toward God or man.

2. Identified with England in Geoffrey of Monmouth, elsewhere a vaguer term for Arthur's kingdom. Here, Gawain is heading northward through Wales, then along the coast of the Irish Sea and into the forest of Wirral in Cheshire—a wild area and resort of outlaws in the 14th century. Gawain thus moves into the area around Chester, where the poem may well have been written.

And earnestly he asked of each mortal he met
If he had ever heard aught of a knight all green,
705   Or of a Green Chapel, on ground thereabouts,
And all said the same, and solemnly swore
They saw no such knight all solely green
        in hue.
      Over country wild and strange
710   The knight sets off anew;
      Often his course must change
      Ere the Chapel comes in view.

Many a cliff must he climb in country wild;
Far off from all his friends, forlorn must he ride;
715   At each strand or stream where the stalwart passed
'Twere a marvel if he met not some monstrous foe,
And that so fierce and forbidding that fight he must.
So many were the wonders he wandered among
That to tell but the tenth part would tax my wits.
720   Now with serpents he wars, now with savage wolves,
Now with wild men of the woods, that watched from the rocks,
Both with bulls and with bears, and with boars besides,
And giants that came gibbering from the jagged steeps.
Had he not borne himself bravely, and been on God's side,
725   He had met with many mishaps and mortal harms.
And if the wars were unwelcome, the winter was worse,
When the cold clear rains rushed from the clouds
And froze before they could fall to the frosty earth.
Near slain by the sleet he sleeps in his irons
730   More nights than enough, among naked rocks,
Where clattering from the crest the cold stream ran
And hung in hard icicles high overhead.
Thus in peril and pain and predicaments dire
He rides across country till Christmas Eve,
735   our knight.
      And at that holy tide
      He prays with all his might
      That Mary may be his guide
      Till a dwelling comes in sight.

740   By a mountain next morning he makes his way
Into a forest fastness, fearsome and wild;
High hills on either hand, with hoar woods below,
Oaks old and huge by the hundred together.
The hazel and the hawthorn were all intertwined
745   With rough raveled moss, that raggedly hung,
With many birds unblithe upon bare twigs
That peeped most piteously for pain of the cold.
The good knight on Gringolet glides thereunder
Through many a marsh and mire, a man all alone;
750   He feared for his default, should he fail to see
The service of that Sire that on that same night
Was born of a bright maid, to bring us His peace.

And therefore sighing he said, "I beseech of Thee, Lord,
And Mary, thou mildest mother so dear,
755 Some harborage where haply I might hear mass
And Thy matins[3] tomorrow—meekly I ask it,
And thereto proffer and pray my pater and ave
                                    and creed."[4]
        He said his prayer with sighs,
760   Lamenting his misdeed;
        He crosses himself, and cries
        On Christ in his great need.

No sooner had Sir Gawain signed himself thrice
Than he was ware, in the wood, of a wondrous dwelling,
765 Within a moat, on a mound, bright amid boughs
Of many a tree great of girth that grew by the water—
A castle as comely as a knight could own,
On grounds fair and green, in a goodly park
With a palisade of palings planted about
770 For two miles and more, round many a fair tree.
The stout knight stared at that stronghold great
As it shimmered and shone amid shining leaves,
Then with helmet in hand he offers his thanks
To Jesus and Saint Julian,[5] that are gentle both,
775 That in courteous accord had inclined to his prayer;
"Now fair harbor," said he, "I humbly beseech!"
Then he pricks his proud steed with the plated spurs,
And by chance he has chosen the chief path
That brought the bold knight to the bridge's end
                                    in haste.
780   The bridge hung high in air;
        The gates were bolted fast;
        The walls well-framed to bear
        The fury of the blast.

785 The man on his mount remained on the bank
Of the deep double moat that defended the place.
The wall went in the water wondrous deep,
And a long way aloft it loomed overhead.
It was built of stone blocks to the battlements' height,
790 With corbels under cornices in comeliest style;
Watch-towers trusty protected the gate,
With many a lean loophole, to look from within:
A better-made barbican the knight beheld never.[6]
And behind it there hoved a great hall and fair:
795 Turrets rising in tiers, with tines[7] at their tops,
Spires set beside them, splendidly long,

---

3. First of the canonical hours of prayer and praise in monastic tradition, observed between midnight and dawn.
4. The Paternoster ("Our Father . . ."), Ave Maria ("Hail Mary . . ."), and Creed (the articles of the Christian faith).
5. Patron saint of hospitality.
6. The poet again revels in technical vocabulary, here architectural; this is a fashionable (if exaggerated) building of the 14th century.
7. Pinnacles.

With finials well-fashioned, as filigree fine.
Chalk-white chimneys over chambers high
Gleamed in gay array upon gables and roofs;
800   The pinnacles in panoply, pointing in air,
So vied there for his view that verily it seemed
A castle cut of paper for a king's feast.[8]
The good knight on Gringolet thought it great luck
If he could but contrive to come there within
805   To keep the Christmas feast in that castle fair
                and bright.
        There answered to his call
        A porter most polite;
        From his station on the wall
810   He greets the errant knight.

"Good sir," said Gawain, "Wouldst go to inquire
If your lord would allow me to lodge here a space?"
"Peter!"[9] said the porter, "For my part, I think
So noble a knight will not want for a welcome!"
815   Then he bustles off briskly, and comes back straight,
And many servants beside, to receive him the better.
They let down the drawbridge and duly went forth
And kneeled down on their knees on the naked earth
To welcome this warrior as best they were able.
820   They proffered him passage—the portals stood wide—
And he beckoned them to rise, and rode over the bridge.
Men steadied his saddle as he stepped to the ground,
And there stabled his steed many stalwart folk.
Now come the knights and the noble squires
825   To bring him with bliss into the bright hall.
When his high helm was off, there hied forth a throng
Of attendants to take it, and see to its care;
They bore away his brand and his blazoned shield;
Then graciously he greeted those gallants each one,
830   And many a noble drew near, to do the knight honor.
All in his armor into hall he was led,
Where fire on a fair hearth fiercely blazed.
And soon the lord himself descends from his chamber
To meet with good manners the man on his floor.
835   He said, "To this house you are heartily welcome:
What is here is wholly yours, to have in your power
            and sway."
        "Many thanks," said Sir Gawain;
        "May Christ your pains repay!"
840   The two embrace amain
        As men well met that day.

Gawain gazed on the host that greeted him there,
And a lusty fellow he looked, the lord of that place:

8. Models in cut paper sometimes decorated elaborate feasts such as that at the beginning of the poem.

9. Swearing by Saint Peter, keeper of the keys to heaven.

A man of massive mold, and of middle age;
845 Broad, bright was his beard, of a beaver's hue,
Strong, steady his stance, upon stalwart shanks,
His face fierce as fire, fair-spoken withal,
And well-suited he seemed in Sir Gawain's sight
To be a master of men in a mighty keep.
850 They pass into a parlor, where promptly the host
Has a servant assigned him to see to his needs,
And there came upon his call many courteous folk
That brought him to a bower where bedding was noble,
With heavy silk hangings hemmed all in gold,
855 Coverlets and counterpanes curiously wrought,
A canopy over the couch, clad all with fur,
Curtains running on cords, caught to gold rings,
Woven rugs on the walls of eastern work,
And the floor, under foot, well-furnished with the same.
860 With light talk and laughter they loosed from him then
His war-dress of weight and his worthy clothes.
Robes richly wrought they brought him right soon,
To change there in chamber and choose what he would.
When he had found one he fancied, and flung it about,
865 Well-fashioned for his frame, with flowing skirts,
His face fair and fresh as the flowers of spring,
All the good folk agreed, that gazed on him then,
His limbs arrayed royally in radiant hues,
That so comely a mortal never Christ made
870   as he.
            Whatever his place of birth,
            It seemed he well might be
            Without a peer on earth
            In martial rivalry.

875 A couch before the fire, where fresh coals burned,
They spread for Sir Gawain splendidly now
With quilts quaintly stitched, and cushions beside,
And then a costly cloak they cast on his shoulders
Of bright silk, embroidered on borders and hems,
880 With furs of the finest well-furnished within,
And bound about with ermine, both mantle and hood;
And he sat at that fireside in sumptuous estate
And warmed himself well, and soon he waxed merry.
Then attendants set a table upon trestles[1] broad,
885 And lustrous white linen they laid thereupon,
A saltcellar of silver, spoons of the same.
He washed himself well and went to his place,
Men set his fare before him in fashion most fit.
There were soups of all sorts, seasoned with skill,
890 Double-sized servings, and sundry fish,
Some baked, some breaded, some broiled on the coals,

---

1. A castle's great hall had many uses; tables were set up for dining and then put aside or hung.

Some simmered, some in stews, steaming with spice,
And with sauces to sup that suited his taste.
He confesses it a feast with free words and fair;
895 They requite him as kindly with courteous jests,
                    well-sped.
          "Tonight you fast and pray;
          Tomorrow we'll see you fed."[2]
          The knight grows wondrous gay
900   As the wine goes to his head.

Then at times and by turns, as at table he sat,
They questioned him quietly, with queries discreet,
And he courteously confessed that he comes from the court,
And owns him of the brotherhood of high-famed Arthur,
905 The right royal ruler of the Round Table,
And the guest by their fireside is Gawain himself,
Who has happened on their house at that holy feast.
When the name of the knight was made known to the lord,
Then loudly he laughed, so elated he was,
910 And the men in that household made haste with joy
To appear in his presence promptly that day,
That of courage ever-constant, and customs pure,
Is pattern and paragon, and praised without end:
Of all knights on earth most honored is he.
915 Each said solemnly aside to his brother,
"Now displays of deportment shall dazzle our eyes
And the polished pearls of impeccable speech;
The high art of eloquence is ours to pursue
Since the father of fine manners is found in our midst.
920 Great is God's grace, and goodly indeed,
That a guest such as Gawain he guides to us here
When men sit and sing of their Savior's birth
                    in view.
          With command of manners pure
925   He shall each heart imbue;
          Who shares his converse, sure,
          Shall learn love's language true."[3]

When the knight had done dining and duly arose,
The dark was drawing on; the day nigh ended.
930 Chaplains in chapels and churches about
Rang the bells aright, reminding all men
Of the holy evensong of the high feast.
The lord attends alone; his fair lady sits
In a comely closet, secluded from sight.
935 Gawain in gay attire goes thither soon;
The lord catches his coat, and calls him by name,
And has him sit beside him, and says in good faith

---

2. An exchange of graceful courtesies. Gawain has politely praised the many fish dishes; his hosts demur, remind
him that Christmas Eve is a fast day, and promise him
better meals later.

3. Though Gawain is engaged on a serious quest, his reputation as a graceful courtier and master in the arts of love
has preceded him.

No guest on God's earth would be gladlier greet.
For that Gawain thanked him; the two then embraced
940 And sat together soberly the service through.
Then the lady, that longed to look on the knight,
Came forth from her closet with her comely maids.
The fair hues of her flesh, her face and her hair
And her body and her bearing were beyond praise,
945 And excelled the queen herself, as Sir Gawain thought.
He goes forth to greet her with gracious intent;
Another lady led her by the left hand
That was older than she—an ancient, it seemed,
And held in high honor by all men about.
950 But unlike to look upon, those ladies were,
For if the one was fresh, the other was faded:
Bedecked in bright red was the body of one;
Flesh hung in folds on the face of the other;
On one a high headdress, hung all with pearls;
955 Her bright throat and bosom fair to behold,
Fresh as the first snow fallen upon hills;
A wimple the other one wore round her throat;
Her swart chin well swaddled, swathed all in white,
Her forehead enfolded in flounces of silk
960 That framed a fair fillet, of fashion ornate,
And nothing bare beneath save the black brows,
The two eyes and the nose, the naked lips,
And they unsightly to see, and sorrily bleared.
A beldame, by God, she may well be deemed,
965   of pride!
          She was short and thick of waist,
          Her buttocks round and wide;
          More toothsome, to his taste,
          Was the beauty by her side.

970 When Gawain had gazed on that gay lady,
With leave of her lord, he politely approached;
To the elder in homage he humbly bows;
The lovelier he salutes with a light embrace.
He claims a comely kiss, and courteously he speaks;
975 They welcome him warmly, and straightway he asks
To be received as their servant, if they so desire.
They take him between them; with talking they bring him
Beside a bright fire; bade then that spices
Be freely fetched forth, to refresh them the better,
980 And the good wine therewith, to warm their hearts.
The lord leaps about in light-hearted mood;
Contrives entertainments and timely sports;
Takes his hood from his head and hangs it on a spear,
And offers him openly the honor thereof
985 Who should promote the most mirth at that Christmas feast;
"And I shall try for it, trust me—contend with the best,
Ere I go without my headgear by grace of my friends!"

Thus with light talk and laughter the lord makes merry
To gladden the guest he had greeted in hall

990   that day.
      At the last he called for light
      The company to convey;
      Gawain says goodnight
      And retires to bed straightway.

995 On the morn when each man is mindful in heart
That God's son was sent down to suffer our death,
No household but is blithe for His blessed sake;
So was it there on that day, with many delights.
Both at larger meals and less they were lavishly served

1000 By doughty lads on dais, with delicate fare;
The old ancient lady, highest she sits;
The lord at her left hand leaned, as I hear;
Sir Gawain in the center, beside the gay lady,
Where the food was brought first to that festive board,

1005 And thence throughout the hall, as they held most fit,
To each man was offered in order of rank.
There was meat, there was mirth, there was much joy,
That to tell all the tale would tax my wits,
Though I pained me, perchance, to paint it with care;

1010 But yet I know that our knight and the noble lady
Were accorded so closely in company there,
With the seemly solace of their secret words,
With speeches well-sped, spotless and pure,
That each prince's pastime their pleasures far

1015   outshone.
      Sweet pipes beguile their cares,
      And the trumpet of martial tone;
      Each tends his affairs
      And those two tend their own.

1020 That day and all the next, their disport was noble,
And the third day, I think, pleased them no less;
The joys of Saint John's Day[4] were justly praised,
And were the last of their like for those lords and ladies;
Then guests were to go in the gray morning,

1025 Wherefore they whiled the night away with wine and with mirth,
Moved to the measures of many a blithe carol;[5]
At last, when it was late, took leave of each other,
Each one of those worthies, to wend his way.
Gawain bids goodbye to his goodly host

1030 Who brings him to his chamber, the chimney beside,
And detains him in talk, and tenders his thanks
And holds it an honor to him and his people
That he has harbored in his house at that holy time
And embellished his abode with his inborn grace.

---

4. December 27, traditionally given over to drinking and celebration.

5. A ring dance.

1035 "As long as I may live, my luck is the better
That Gawain was my guest at God's own feast!"
"Noble sir," said the knight, "I cannot but think
All the honor is your own—may heaven requite it!
And your man to command I account myself here
1040 As I am bound and beholden, and shall be, come
what may."
The lord with all his might
Entreats his guest to stay;
Brief answer makes the knight:
1045 Next morning he must away.

Then the lord of that land politely inquired
What dire affair had forced him, at that festive time,
So far from the king's court to fare forth alone
Ere the holidays wholly had ended in hall.
1050 "In good faith," said Gawain, "you have guessed the truth:
On a high errand and urgent I hastened away,
For I am summoned by myself to seek for a place—
I would I knew whither, or where it might be!
Far rather would I find it before the New Year
1055 Than own the land of Logres, so help me our Lord!
Wherefore, sir, in friendship this favor I ask,
That you say in sober earnest, if something you know
Of the Green Chapel, on ground far or near,
Or the lone knight that lives there, of like hue of green.
1060 A certain day was set by assent of us both
To meet at that landmark, if I might last,
And from now to the New Year is nothing too long,
And I would greet the Green Knight there, would God but allow,
More gladly, by God's son, than gain the world's wealth!
1065 And I must set forth to search, as soon as I may;
To be about the business I have but three days
And would as soon sink down dead as desist from my errand."
Then smiling said the lord, "Your search, sir, is done,
For we shall see you to that site by the set time.
1070 Let Gawain grieve no more over the Green Chapel;
You shall be in your own bed, in blissful ease,
All the forenoon, and fare forth the first of the year,
And make the goal by midmorn, to mind your affairs,
no fear!
1075 Tarry till the fourth day
And ride on the first of the year.
We shall set you on your way;
It is not two miles from here."

Then Gawain was glad, and gleefully he laughed:
1080 "Now I thank you for this, past all things else!
Now my goal is here at hand! With a glad heart I shall
Both tarry, and undertake any task you devise."
Then the host seized his arm and seated him there;
Let the ladies be brought, to delight him the better,

1085 And in fellowship fair by the fireside they sit;
So gay waxed the good host, so giddy his words,
All waited in wonder what next he would say.
Then he stares on the stout knight, and sternly he speaks:
"You have bound yourself boldly my bidding to do—
1090 Will you stand by that boast, and obey me this once?"
"I shall do so indeed," said the doughty knight;
While I lie in your lodging, your laws will I follow."
"As you have had," said the host, "many hardships abroad
And little sleep of late, you are lacking, I judge,
1095 Both in nourishment needful and nightly rest;
You shall lie abed late in your lofty chamber
Tomorrow until mass, and meet then to dine
When you will, with my wife, who will sit by your side
And talk with you at table, the better to cheer
1100   our guest.
        A-hunting I will go
        While you lie late and rest."
        The knight, inclining low,
        Assents to each behest.

1105 "And Gawain," said the good host, "agree now to this:
Whatever I win in the woods I will give you at eve,
And all you have earned you must offer to me;
Swear now, sweet friend, to swap as I say,
Whether hands, in the end, be empty or better."
1110 "By God," said Sir Gawain, "I grant it forthwith!
If you find the game good, I shall gladly take part."
"Let the bright wine be brought, and our bargain is done,"
Said the lord of that land—the two laughed together.
Then they drank and they dallied and doffed all constraint,
1115 These lords and these ladies, as late as they chose,
And then with gaiety and gallantries and graceful adieux
They talked in low tones, and tarried at parting.
With compliments comely they kiss at the last;
There were brisk lads about with blazing torches
1120 To see them safe to bed, for soft repose
        long due.
        Their covenants, yet awhile,
        They repeat, and pledge anew;
        That lord could well beguile
1125   Men's hearts, with mirth in view.

Part 3

Long before daylight they left their beds;
Guests that wished to go gave word to their grooms,
And they set about briskly to bind on saddles,
Tend to their tackle, tie up trunks.
1130 The proud lords appear, appareled to ride,
Leap lightly astride, lay hold of their bridles,
Each one on his way to his worthy house.

Courtly Women Hunting and Dancing, from the *Taymouth Hours.* 14th century. Above, women in courtly dress dismember a stag, usually the work of aristocratic men. On the opposite page, women reenact another famous male moment, tying an inverted Christ to a cross.

	The liege lord of the land was not the last
	Arrayed there to ride, with retainers many;
1135	He had a bite to eat when he had heard mass;
	With horn to the hills he hastens amain.[6]
	By the dawn of that day over the dim earth,
	Master and men were mounted and ready.
	Then they harnessed in couples the keen-scented hounds,
1140	Cast wide the kennel-door and called them forth,
	Blew upon their bugles bold blasts three;
	The dogs began to bay with a deafening din,
	And they quieted them quickly and called them to heel,
	A hundred brave huntsmen, as I have heard tell,
1145	together.
	Men at stations meet;
	From the hounds they slip the tether;
	The echoing horns repeat,
	Clear in the merry weather.

| 1150 | At the clamor of the quest, the quarry trembled; |
| | Deer dashed through the dale, dazed with dread; |

6. The hunts that follow, for all their violent energy, are as ritualized in their procedure as the earlier feasts and games. The poet delights in describing still another area of knightly lore. A number of contemporary treatises on hunting survive.

Hastened to the high ground, only to be
Turned back by the beaters, who boldly shouted.
They harmed not the harts, with their high heads,
1155   Let the bucks go by, with their broad antlers,
For it was counted a crime, in the close season,
If a man of that demesne should molest the male deer.
The hinds were headed up, with "Hey!" and "Ware!"
The does with great din were driven to the valleys.
1160   Then you were ware, as they went, of the whistling of arrows;
At each bend under boughs the bright shafts flew
That tore the tawny hide with their tapered heads.
Ah! they bray and they bleed, on banks they die,
And ever the pack pell-mell comes panting behind;
1165   Hunters with shrill horns hot on their heels—
Like the cracking of cliffs their cries resounded.
What game got away from the gallant archers
Was promptly picked off at the posts below
When they were harried on the heights and herded to the streams:
1170   The watchers were so wary at the waiting-stations,
And the greyhounds so huge, that eagerly snatched,
And finished them off as fast as folk could see
                    with sight.
            The lord, now here, now there,
1175   Spurs forth in sheer delight.

And drives, with pleasures rare,
The day to the dark night.

So the lord in the linden-wood leads the hunt
And Gawain the good knight in gay bed lies,
1180   Lingered late alone, till daylight gleamed,
Under coverlet costly, curtained about.
And as he slips into slumber, slyly there comes
A little din at his door, and the latch lifted,
And he holds up his heavy head out of the clothes;
1185   A corner of the curtain he caught back a little
And waited there warily, to see what befell.
Lo! it was the lady, loveliest to behold,
That drew the door behind her deftly and still
And was bound for his bed—abashed was the knight,
1190   And laid his head low again in likeness of sleep;
And she stepped stealthily, and stole to his bed,
Cast aside the curtain and came within,
And set herself softly on the bedside there,
And lingered at her leisure, to look on his waking.
1195   The fair knight lay feigning for a long while,
Conning in his conscience what his case might
Mean or amount to—a marvel he thought it.
But yet he said within himself, "More seemly it were
To try her intent by talking a little."
1200   So he started and stretched, as startled from sleep,
Lifts wide his lids in likeness of wonder,
And signs himself swiftly, as safer to be,
                              with art.
                    Sweetly does she speak
                    And kindling glances dart,
1205   Blent white and red on cheek
                    And laughing lips apart.

"Good morning, Sir Gawain," said that gay lady,
"A slack sleeper you are, to let one slip in!
1210   Now you are taken in a trice—a truce we must make,
Or I shall bind you in your bed, of that be assured."
Thus laughing lightly that lady jested.
"Good morning, good lady," said Gawain the blithe,
"Be it with me as you will; I am well content!
1215   For I surrender myself, and sue for your grace,
And that is best, I believe, and behooves me now."
Thus jested in answer that gentle knight.
"But if, lovely lady, you misliked it not,
And were pleased to permit your prisoner to rise,
1220   I should quit this couch and accoutre me better,
And be clad in more comfort for converse here."
"Nay, not so, sweet sir," said the smiling lady;
"You shall not rise from your bed; I direct you better:
I shall hem and hold you on either hand,
1225   And keep company awhile with my captive knight.

For as certain as I sit here, Sir Gawain you are,
Whom all the world worships, whereso you ride;
Your honor, your courtesy are highest acclaimed
By lords and by ladies, by all living men;

1230 And lo! we are alone here, and left to ourselves:
My lord and his liegemen are long departed,
The household asleep, my handmaids too,
The door drawn, and held by a well-driven bolt,
And since I have in this house him whom all love,

1235 I shall while the time away with mirthful speech
                    at will.
          My body is here at hand,
          Your each wish to fulfill;
          Your servant to command
1240   I am, and shall be still."

"In good faith," said Gawain, "my gain is the greater,
Though I am not he of whom you have heard;
To arrive at such reverence as you recount here
I am one all unworthy, and well do I know it.

1245 By heaven, I would hold me the happiest of men
If by word or by work I once might aspire
To the prize of your praise—'twere a pure joy!"
"In good faith, Sir Gawain," said that gay lady,
"The well-proven prowess that pleases all others,

1250 Did I scant or scout it, 'twere scarce becoming.
But there are ladies, believe me, that had liefer far
Have thee here in their hold, as I have today,
To pass an hour in pastime with pleasant words,
Assuage all their sorrows and solace their hearts,

1255 Than much of the goodly gems and gold they possess.
But laud be to the Lord of the lofty skies,
For here in my hands all hearts' desire
                    doth lie."
          Great welcome got he there
1260   From the lady who sat him by;
          With fitting speech and fair
          The good knight makes reply.

"Madame," said the merry man, "Mary reward you!
For in good faith, I find your beneficence noble.

1265 And the fame of fair deeds runs far and wide,
But the praise you report pertains not to me,
But comes of your courtesy and kindness of heart."
"By the high Queen of heaven" (said she) "I count it not so,
For were I worth all the women in this world alive,

1270 And all wealth and all worship were in my hands,
And I should hunt high and low, a husband to take,
For the nurture I have noted in thee, knight, here,
The comeliness and courtesies and courtly mirth—
And so I had ever heard, and now hold it true—

1275 No other on this earth should have me for wife."

"You are bound to a better man," the bold knight said,
"Yet I prize the praise you have proffered me here,
And soberly your servant, my sovereign I hold you,
And acknowledge me your knight, in the name of Christ."
1280   So they talked of this and that until 'twas nigh noon,
And ever the lady languishing in likeness of love.
With feat words and fair he framed his defense,
For were she never so winsome, the warrior had
The less will to woo, for the wound that his bane
1285   must be.
            He must bear the blinding blow,
            For such is fate's decree;
            The lady asks leave to go;
            He grants it full and free.

1290   Then she gaily said goodbye, and glanced at him, laughing,
And as she stood, she astonished him with a stern speech:
"Now may the Giver of all good words these glad hours repay!
But our guest is not Gawain—forgot is that thought."
"How so?" said the other, and asks in some haste,
1295   For he feared he had been at fault in the forms of his speech.
But she held up her hand, and made answer thus:
"So good a knight as Gawain is given out to be,
And the model of fair demeanor and manners pure,
Had he lain so long at a lady's side,
1300   Would have claimed a kiss, by his courtesy,
Through some touch or trick of phrase at some tale's end."
Said Gawain, "Good lady, I grant it at once!
I shall kiss at your command, as becomes a knight,
And more, lest you mislike, so let be, I pray."
1305   With that she turns toward him, takes him in her arms,
Leans down her lovely head, and lo! he is kissed.
They commend each other to Christ with comely words,
He sees her forth safely, in silence they part,
And then he lies no later in his lofty bed,
1310   But calls to his chamberlain, chooses his clothes,
Goes in those garments gladly to mass,
Then takes his way to table, where attendants wait,
And made merry all day, till the moon rose
                           in view
1315   Was never knight beset
                'Twixt worthier ladies two:
                The crone and the coquette;
                Fair pastimes they pursue.

And the lord of the land rides late and long,
1320   Hunting the barren hind over the broad heath.
He had slain such a sum, when the sun sank low,
Of does and other deer, as would dizzy one's wits.
Then they trooped in together in triumph at last,
And the count of the quarry quickly they take.
1325   The lords lent a hand with their liegemen many,

Picked out the plumpest and put them together
And duly dressed the deer, as the deed requires.
Some were assigned the assay of the fat:
Two fingers'-width fully they found on the leanest.
1330 Then they slit the slot open and searched out the paunch,
Trimmed it with trencher-knives and tied it up tight.
They flayed the fair hide from the legs and trunk,
Then broke open the belly and laid bare the bowels,
Deftly detaching and drawing them forth.
1335 And next at the neck they neatly parted
The weasand[7] from the windpipe, and cast away the guts.
At the shoulders with sharp blades they showed their skill,
Boning them from beneath, lest the sides be marred;
They breached the broad breast and broke it in twain,
1340 And again at the gullet they begin with their knives,
Cleave down the carcass clear to the breach;
Two tender morsels they take from the throat,
Then round the inner ribs they rid off a layer
And carve out the kidney-fat, close to the spine,
1345 Hewing down to the haunch, that all hung together,
And held it up whole, and hacked it free,
And this they named the numbles,[8] that knew such terms
                    of art.
              They divide the crotch in two,
1350   And straightway then they start
              To cut the backbone through
              And cleave the trunk apart.

With hard strokes they hewed off the head and the neck,
Then swiftly from the sides they severed the chine,
1355 And the corbie's bone[9] they cast on a branch.
Then they pierced the plump sides, impaled either one
With the hock of the hind foot, and hung it aloft,
To each person his portion most proper and fit.
On a hide of a hind the hounds they fed
1360 With the liver and the lights,[1] the leathery paunches,
And bread soaked in blood well blended therewith.
High horns and shrill set hounds a-baying,
Then merrily with their meat they make their way home,
Blowing on their bugles many a brave blast.
1365 Ere dark had descended, that doughty band
Was come within the walls where Gawain waits
                    at leisure.
              Bliss and hearth-fire bright
              Await the master's pleasure;
1370   When the two men met that night,
              Joy surpassed all measure.

---

7. The esophagus.
8. Internal organs such as heart, liver, lungs.
9. The gristle at the end of the breastbone was left for the

ravens ("corbies"), still another of the prescribed rituals
of the hunt.
1. Lungs.

Then the host in the hall his household assembles,
With the dames of high degree and their damsels fair.
In the presence of the people, a party he sends
1375   To convey him his venison in view of the knight.
And in high good-humor he hails him then,
Counts over the kill, the cuts on the tallies,
Holds high the hewn ribs, heavy with fat.
"What think you, sir, of this? Have I thriven well?
1380   Have I won with my woodcraft a worthy prize?"
"In good earnest," said Gawain, "this game is the finest
I have seen in seven years in the season of winter."
"And I give it to you, Gawain," said the goodly host,
"For according to our covenant, you claim it as your own."
1385   "That is so," said Sir Gawain, "the same say I:
What I worthily have won within these fair walls,
Herewith I as willingly award it to you."
He embraces his broad neck with both his arms,
And confers on him a kiss in the comeliest style.
1390   "Have here my profit, it proved no better;
Ungrudging do I grant it, were it greater far."
"Such a gift," said the good host, "I gladly accept—
Yet it might be all the better, would you but say
Where you won this same award, by your wits alone."
1395   "That was no part of the pact; press me no further,
For you have had what behooves; all other claims
                 forbear."
         With jest and compliment
         They conversed, and cast off care;
1400   To the table soon they went;
         Fresh dainties wait them there.

And then by the chimney-side they chat at their ease;
The best wine was brought them, and bounteously served;
And after in their jesting they jointly accord
1405   To do on the second day the deeds of the first:
That the two men should trade, betide as it may,
What each had taken in, at eve when they met.
They seal the pact solemnly in sight of the court;
Their cups were filled afresh to confirm the jest;
1410   Then at last they took their leave, for late was the hour,
Each to his own bed hastening away.
Before the barnyard cock had crowed but thrice
The lord had leapt from his rest, his liegemen as well.
Both of mass and their meal they made short work:
1415   By the dim light of dawn they were deep in the woods
                 away.
         With huntsmen and with horns
         Over plains they pass that day;
         They release, amid the thorns,
1420   Swift hounds that run and bay.

Soon some were on a scent by the side of a marsh;
When the hounds opened cry, the head of the hunt

Rallied them with rough words, raised a great noise.
The hounds that had heard it came hurrying straight
1425 And followed along with their fellows, forty together.
Then such a clamor and cry of coursing hounds
Arose, that the rocks resounded again.
Hunters exhorted them with horn and with voice;
Then all in a body bore off together
1430 Between a mere in the marsh and a menacing crag,
To a rise where the rock stood rugged and steep,
And boulders lay about, that blocked their approach.
Then the company in consort closed on their prey:
They surrounded the rise and the rocks both,
1435 For well they were aware that it waited within,
The beast that the bloodhounds boldly proclaimed.
Then they beat on the bushes and bade him appear,
And he made a murderous rush in the midst of them all;
The best of all boars broke from his cover,
1440 That had ranged long unrivaled, a renegade old,
For of tough-brawned boars he was biggest far,
Most grim when he grunted—then grieved were many,
For three at the first thrust he threw to the earth,
And dashed away at once without more damage.
1445 With "Hi!" "Hi!" and "Hey!" "Hey!" the others followed,
Had horns at their lips, blew high and clear.
Merry was the music of men and of hounds
That were bound after this boar, his bloodthirsty heart
           to quell.
1450   Often he stands at bay,
    Then scatters the pack pell-mell;
    He hurts the hounds, and they
    Most dolefully yowl and yell.

Men then with mighty bows moved in to shoot,
1455 Aimed at him with their arrows and often hit,
But the points had no power to pierce through his hide,
And the barbs were brushed aside by his bristly brow;
Though the shank of the shaft shivered in pieces,
The head hopped away, wheresoever it struck.
1460 But when their stubborn strokes had stung him at last,
Then, foaming in his frenzy, fiercely he charges,
Hies at them headlong that hindered his flight,
And many feared for their lives, and fell back a little.
But the lord on a lively horse leads the chase;
1465 As a high-mettled huntsman his horn he blows;
He sounds the assembly and sweeps through the brush,
Pursuing this wild swine till the sunlight slanted.
All day with this deed they drive forth the time
While our lone knight so lovesome lies in his bed
1470 Sir Gawain safe at home, in silken bower
           so gay.
    The lady, with guile in heart,
    Came early where he lay;

She was at him with all her art
To turn his mind her way.

1475

She comes to the curtain and coyly peeps in;
Gawain thought it good to greet her at once,
And she richly repays him with her ready words,
Settles softly at his side, and suddenly she laughs,

1480   And with a gracious glance, she begins on him thus:
"Sir, if you be Gawain, it seems a great wonder—
A man so well-meaning, and mannerly disposed,
And cannot act in company as courtesy bids,
And if one takes the trouble to teach him, 'tis all in vain.

1485   That lesson learned lately is lightly forgot,
Though I painted it as plain as my poor wit allowed."
"What lesson, dear lady?" he asked all alarmed;
"I have been much to blame, if your story be true."
"Yet my counsel was of kissing," came her answer then,

1490   "Where favor has been found, freely to claim
As accords with the conduct of courteous knights."
"My dear," said the doughty man, "dismiss that thought;
Such freedom, I fear, might offend you much;
It were rude to request if the right were denied."

1495   "But none can deny you," said the noble dame,
"You are stout enough to constrain with strength, if you choose,
Were any so ungracious as to grudge you aught."
"By heaven," said he, "you have answered well,
But threats never throve among those of my land,

1500   Nor any gift not freely given, good though it be.
I am yours to command, to kiss when you please;
You may lay on as you like, and leave off at will."
With this,
The lady lightly bends
And graciously gives him a kiss;
1505   The two converse as friends
Of true love's trials and bliss.

"I should like, by your leave," said the lovely lady,
"If it did not annoy you, to know for what cause
1510   So brisk and so bold a young blood as you,
And acclaimed for all courtesies becoming a knight—
And name what knight you will, they are noblest esteemed
For loyal faith in love, in life as in story;[2]
For to tell the tribulations of these true hearts,
1515   Why, 'tis the very title and text of their deeds,
How bold knights for beauty have braved many a foe,
Suffered heavy sorrows out of secret love,
And then valorously avenged them on villainous churls
And made happy ever after the hearts of their ladies.
1520   And you are the noblest knight known in your time;

---

2. The lady compares Gawain's behavior to descriptions of courtly love in romances; the poem is mirrored within itself.

No household under heaven but has heard of your fame,
And here by your side I have sat for two days
Yet never has a fair phrase fallen from your lips
Of the language of love, not one little word!
1525 And you, that with sweet vows sway women's hearts,
Should show your winsome ways, and woo a young thing,
And teach by some tokens the craft of true love.
How! are you artless, whom all men praise?
Or do you deem me so dull, or deaf to such words?
1530   Fie! Fie!
                    In hope of pastimes new
                    I have come where none can spy;
                    Instruct me a little, do,
                    While my husband is not nearby."

1535 "God love you, gracious lady!" said Gawain then;
"It is a pleasure surpassing, and a peerless joy,
That one so worthy as you would willingly come
And take the time and trouble to talk with your knight
And content you with his company—it comforts my heart.
1540 But to take to myself the task of telling of love,
And touch upon its texts, and treat of its themes
To one that, I know well, wields more power
In that art, by a half, than a hundred such
As I am where I live, or am like to become,
1545 It were folly, fair dame, in the first degree!
In all that I am able, my aim is to please,
As in honor behooves me, and am evermore
Your servant heart and soul, so save me our Lord!"
Thus she tested his temper and tried many a time,
1550 Whatever her true intent, to entice him to sin,
But so fair was his defense that no fault appeared,
Nor evil on either hand, but only bliss
                          they knew.
                    They linger and laugh awhile;
1555   She kisses the knight so true,
                    Takes leave in comeliest style
                    And departs without more ado.

Then he rose from his rest and made ready for mass,
And then a meal was set and served, in sumptuous style;
1560 He dallied at home all day with the dear ladies,
But the lord lingered late at his lusty sport;
Pursued his sorry swine, that swerved as he fled,
And bit asunder the backs of the best of his hounds
When they brought him to bay, till the bowmen appeared
1565 And soon forced him forth, though he fought for dear life,
So sharp were the shafts they shot at him there.
But yet the boldest drew back from his battering head,
Till at last he was so tired he could travel no more,
But in as much haste as he might, he makes his retreat
1570 To a rise on rocky ground, by a rushing stream.

With the bank at his back he scrapes the bare earth,
The froth foams at his jaws, frightful to see.
He whets his white tusks—then weary were all
Those hunters so hardy that hoved round about
1575   Of aiming from afar, but ever they mistrust
                his mood.
        He had hurt so many by then
        That none had hardihood
        To be torn by his tusks again,
1580   That was brainsick, and out for blood.

Till the lord came at last on his lofty steed,
Beheld him there at bay before all his folk;
Lightly he leaps down, leaves his courser,
Bares his bright sword, and boldly advances;
1585   Straight into the stream he strides towards his foe.
The wild thing was wary of weapon and man;
His hackles rose high; so hotly he snorts
That many watched with alarm, lest the worst befall.
The boar makes for the man with a mighty bound
1590   So that he and his hunter came headlong together
Where the water ran wildest—the worse for the beast,
For the man, when they first met, marked him with care,
Sights well the slot, slips in the blade,
Shoves it home to the hilt, and the heart shattered,
1595   And he falls in his fury and floats down the water,
                ill-sped.
        Hounds hasten by the score
        To maul him, hide and head;
        Men drag him in to shore
1600   And dogs pronounce him dead.

With many a brave blast they boast of their prize,
All hallooed in high glee, that had their wind;
The hounds bayed their best, as the bold men bade
That were charged with chief rank in that chase of renown.
1605   Then one wise in woodcraft, and worthily skilled,
Began to dress the boar in becoming style:
He severs the savage head and sets it aloft,
Then rends the body roughly right down the spine;
Takes the bowels from the belly, broils them on coals,
1610   Blends them well with bread to bestow on the hounds.
Then he breaks out the brawn in fair broad flitches,
And the innards to be eaten in order he takes.
The two sides, attached to each other all whole,
He suspended from a spar that was springy and tough;
1615   And so with this swine they set out for home;
The boar's head was borne before the same man
That had stabbed him in the stream with his strong arm,
                right through.
        He thought it long indeed
1620   Till he had the knight in view;

At his call, he comes with speed
To claim his payment due.

The lord laughed aloud, with many a light word,
When he greeted Sir Gawain—with good cheer he speaks.
1625 They fetch the fair dames and the folk of the house;
He brings forth the brawn, and begins the tale
Of the great length and girth, the grim rage as well,
Of the battle of the boar they beset in the wood.
The other man meetly commended his deeds
1630 And praised well the prize of his princely sport,
For the brawn of that boar, the bold knight said,
And the sides of that swine surpassed all others.
Then they handled the huge head; he owns it a wonder,
And eyes it with abhorrence, to heighten his praise.
1635 "Now, Gawain," said the good man, "this game becomes yours
By those fair terms we fixed, as you know full well."
"That is true," returned the knight, "and trust me, fair friend,
All my gains, as agreed, I shall give you forthwith."
He clasps him and kisses him in courteous style,
1640 Then serves him with the same fare a second time.
"Now we are even," said he, "at this evening feast,
And clear is every claim incurred here to date,
                    and debt."
          "By Saint Giles!"[3] the host replies,
1645   "You're the best I ever met!
          If your profits are all this size,
          We'll see you wealthy yet!"

Then attendants set tables on trestles about,
And laid them with linen; light shone forth,
1650 Wakened along the walls in waxen torches.
The service was set and the supper brought;
Royal were the revels that rose then in hall
At that feast by the fire, with many fair sports:
Amid the meal and after, melody sweet,
1655 Carol-dances comely and Christmas songs,
With all the mannerly mirth my tongue may describe.
And ever our gallant knight beside the gay lady;
So uncommonly kind and complaisant was she,
With sweet stolen glances, that stirred his stout heart,
1660 That he was at his wits' end, and wondrous vexed;
But he could not in conscience her courtship repay,
Yet took pains to please her, though the plan might
                    go wrong.
          When they to heart's delight
1665   Had reveled there in throng,
          To his chamber he calls the knight,
          And thither they go along.

---

3. A hermit and patron saint of woodlands.

And there they dallied and drank, and deemed it good sport
To enact their play anew on New Year's Eve,
1670   But Gawain asked again to go on the morrow,
For the time until his tryst was not two days.
The host hindered that, and urged him to stay,
And said, "On my honor, my oath here I take
That you shall get to the Green Chapel to begin your chores
1675   By dawn on New Year's Day, if you so desire.
Wherefore lie at your leisure in your lofty bed,
And I shall hunt hereabouts, and hold to our terms,
And we shall trade winnings when once more we meet,
For I have tested you twice, and true have I found you;
1680   Now think this tomorrow: the third pays for all;
Be we merry while we may, and mindful of joy,
For heaviness of heart can be had for the asking."
This is gravely agreed on and Gawain will stay.
They drink a last draught and with torches depart
1685   to rest.
          To bed Sir Gawain went;
          His sleep was of the best;
          The lord, on his craft intent,
          Was early up and dressed.

1690   After mass, with his men, a morsel he takes;
Clear and crisp the morning; he calls for his mount;
The folk that were to follow him afield that day
Were high astride their horses before the hall gates.
Wondrous fair were the fields, for the frost was light;
1695   The sun rises red amid radiant clouds,
Sails into the sky, and sends forth his beams.
They let loose the hounds by a leafy wood;
The rocks all around re-echo to their horns;
Soon some have set off in pursuit of the fox,
1700   Cast about with craft for a clearer scent;
A young dog yaps, and is yelled at in turn;
His fellows fall to sniffing, and follow his lead,
Running in a rabble on the right track,
And he scampers all before; they discover him soon,
1705   And when they see him with sight they pursue him the faster,
Railing at him rudely with a wrathful din.
Often he reverses over rough terrain,
Or loops back to listen in the lee of a hedge;
At last, by a little ditch, he leaps over the brush,
1710   Comes into a clearing at a cautious pace,
Then he thought through his wiles to have thrown off the hounds
Till he was ware, as he went, of a waiting-station
Where three athwart his path threatened him at once,
                              all gray.
1715   Quick as a flash he wheels
                And darts off in dismay;
                With hard luck at his heels
                He is off to the wood away.

Then it was heaven on earth to hark to the hounds
1720 When they had come on their quarry, coursing together!
Such harsh cries and howls they hurled at his head
As all the cliffs with a crash had come down at once.
Here he was hailed, when huntsmen met him;
Yonder they yelled at him, yapping and snarling;
1725 There they cried "Thief!" and threatened his life,
And ever the harriers at his heels, that he had no rest.
Often he was menaced when he made for the open,
And often rushed in again, for Reynard was wily;
And so he leads them a merry chase, the lord and his men,
1730 In this manner on the mountains, till midday or near,
While our hero lies at home in wholesome sleep
Within the comely curtains on the cold morning.
But the lady, as love would allow her no rest,
And pursuing ever the purpose that pricked her heart,
1735 Was awake with the dawn, and went to his chamber
In a fair flowing mantle that fell to the earth,
All edged and embellished with ermines fine;
No hood on her head, but heavy with gems
Were her fillet and the fret[4] that confined her tresses;
1740 Her face and her fair throat freely displayed;
Her bosom all but bare, and her back as well.
She comes in at the chamber-door, and closes it with care,
Throws wide a window—then waits no longer,
But hails him thus airily with her artful words,
1745   with cheer:
      "Ah, man, how can you sleep?
      The morning is so clear!"
      Though dreams have drowned him deep,
      He cannot choose but hear.

1750 Deep in his dreams he darkly mutters
As a man may that mourns, with many grim thoughts
Of that day when destiny shall deal him his doom
When he greets his grim host at the Green Chapel
And must bow to his buffet, bating all strife.
1755 But when he sees her at his side he summons his wits,
Breaks from the black dreams, and blithely answers.
That lovely lady comes laughing sweet,
Sinks down at his side, and salutes him with a kiss.
He accords her fair welcome in courtliest style;
1760 He sees her so glorious, so gaily attired,
So faultless her features, so fair and so bright,
His heart swelled swiftly with surging joys.
They melt into mirth with many a fond smile,
And there was bliss beyond telling between those two,
1765   at height.
      Good were their words of greeting;
      Each joyed in other's sight;

---

4. Ornamental hairnet.

Great peril attends that meeting
Should Mary forget her knight.

1770   For that high-born beauty so hemmed him about,
Made so plain her meaning, the man must needs
Either take her tendered love or distastefully refuse.
His courtesy concerned him, lest crass he appear,
But more his soul's mischief, should he commit sin

1775   And belie his loyal oath to the lord of that house.
"God forbid!" said the bold knight, "That shall not befall!"
With a little fond laughter he lightly let pass
All the words of special weight that were sped his way;
"I find you much at fault," the fair one said,

1780   "Who can be cold toward a creature so close by your side,
Of all women in this world most wounded in heart,
Unless you have a sweetheart, one you hold dearer,
And allegiance to that lady so loyally knit
That you will never love another, as now I believe.

1785   And, sir, if it be so, then say it, I beg you;
By all your heart holds dear, hide it no longer
                    with guile."
            "Lady, by Saint John,"
            He answers with a smile,

1790   "Lover have I none,
            Nor will have, yet awhile."

"Those words," said the woman, "are the worst of all,
But I have had my answer, and hard do I find it!
Kiss me now kindly; I can but go hence

1795   To lament my life long like a maid lovelorn."
She inclines her head quickly and kisses the knight,
Then straightens with a sigh, and says as she stands,
"Now, dear, ere I depart, do me this pleasure:
Give me some little gift, your glove or the like,

1800   That I may think on you, man, and mourn the less."
"Now by heaven," said he, "I wish I had here
My most precious possession, to put it in your hands,
For your deeds, beyond doubt, have often deserved
A repayment far passing my power to bestow.

1805   But a love-token, lady, were of little avail;
It is not to your honor to have at this time
A glove as a guerdon from Gawain's hand,
And I am here on an errand in unknown realms
And have no bearers with baggage with becoming gifts,

1810   Which distresses me, madame, for your dear sake.
A man must keep within his compass: account it neither grief
                    nor slight."
            "Nay, noblest knight alive,"
            Said that beauty of body white,

1815   "Though you be loath to give,
            Yet you shall take, by right."

She reached out a rich ring, wrought all of gold,
With a splendid stone displayed on the band

That flashed before his eyes like a fiery sun;
1820 It was worth a king's wealth, you may well believe.
But he waved it away with these ready words:
"Before God, good lady, I forgo all gifts;
None have I to offer, nor any will I take."
And she urged it on him eagerly, and ever he refused,
1825 And vowed in very earnest, prevail she would not.
And she sad to find it so, and said to him then,
"If my ring is refused for its rich cost—
You would not be my debtor for so dear a thing—
I shall give you my girdle; you gain less thereby."
1830 She released a knot lightly, and loosened a belt
That was caught about her kirtle, the bright cloak beneath,
Of a gay green silk, with gold overwrought,
And the borders all bound with embroidery fine,
And this she presses upon him, and pleads with a smile,
1835 Unworthy though it were, that it would not be scorned.
But the man still maintains that he means to accept
Neither gold nor any gift, till by God's grace
The fate that lay before him was fully achieved.
"And be not offended, fair lady, I beg,
1840 And give over your offer, for ever I must
                    decline.
          I am grateful for favor shown
          Past all deserts of mine,
          And ever shall be your own
1845   True servant, rain or shine."

"Now does my present displease you," she promptly inquired,
"Because it seems in your sight so simple a thing?
And belike, as it is little, it is less to praise,
But if the virtue that invests it were verily known,
1850 It would be held, I hope, in higher esteem.
For the man that possesses this piece of silk,
If he bore it on his body, belted about,
There is no hand under heaven that could hew him down,
For he could not be killed by any craft on earth."
1855 Then the man began to muse, and mainly he thought
It was a pearl for his plight, the peril to come
When he gains the Green Chapel to get his reward:
Could he escape unscathed, the scheme were noble!
Then he bore with her words and withstood them no more,
1860 And she repeated her petition and pleaded anew,
And he granted it, and gladly she gave him the belt,
And besought him for her sake to conceal it well,
Lest the noble lord should know—and the knight agrees
That not a soul save themselves shall see it thenceforth
1865   with sight.
          He thanked her with fervent heart,
          As often as ever he might;
          Three times, before they part,
          She has kissed the stalwart knight.

1870 Then the lady took her leave, and left him there,
     For more mirth with that man she might not have.
     When she was gone, Sir Gawain got from his bed,
     Arose and arrayed him in his rich attire;
     Tucked away the token the temptress had left,
1875 Laid it reliably where he looked for it after.
     And then with good cheer to the chapel he goes,
     Approached a priest in private, and prayed to be taught
     To lead a better life and lift up his mind,
     Lest he be among the lost when he must leave this world.
1880 And shamefaced at shrift he showed his misdeeds
     From the largest to the least, and asked the Lord's mercy,
     And called on his confessor to cleanse his soul,
     And he absolved him of his sins as safe and as clean
     As if the dread Day of Judgment should dawn on the morrow.[5]
1885 And then he made merry amid the fine ladies
     With deft-footed dances and dalliance light,
     As never until now, while the afternoon wore
                    away.
          He delighted all around him,
1890   And all agreed, that day,
          They never before had found him
          So gracious and so gay.

     Now peaceful be his pasture, and love play him fair!
     The host is on horseback, hunting afield;
1895 He has finished off this fox that he followed so long:
     As he leapt a low hedge to look for the villain
     Where he heard all the hounds in hot pursuit,
     Reynard comes racing out of a rough thicket,
     And all the rabble in a rush, right at his heels.
1900 The man beholds the beast, and bides his time,
     And bares his bright sword, and brings it down hard,
     And he blenches from the blade, and backward he starts;
     A hound hurries up and hinders that move,
     And before the horse's feet they fell on him at once
1905 And ripped the rascal's throat with a wrathful din.
     The lord soon alighted and lifted him free,
     Swiftly snatched him up from the snapping jaws,
     Holds him over his head, halloos with a will,
     And the dogs bayed the dirge, that had done him to death.
1910 Hunters hastened thither with horns at their lips,
     Sounding the assembly till they saw him at last.
     When that comely company was come in together,
     All that bore bugles blew them at once,
     And the others all hallooed, that had no horns.
1915 It was the merriest medley that ever a man heard,
     The racket that they raised for Sir Reynard's soul
                    that died.

---

5. Gawain's confession and absolution are problematic, since he has just accepted the green girdle and resolved to break the covenant of exchange with his host.

Their hounds they praised and fed,
Fondling their heads with pride,
1920   And they took Reynard the Red
And stripped away his hide.

And then they headed homeward, for evening had come,
Blowing many a blast on their bugles bright.
The lord at long last alights at his house,
1925   Finds fire on the hearth where the fair knight waits,
Sir Gawain the good, that was glad in heart.
With the ladies, that loved him, he lingered at ease;
He wore a rich robe of blue, that reached to the earth
And a surcoat lined softly with sumptuous furs;
1930   A hood of the same hue hung on his shoulders;
With bands of bright ermine embellished were both.
He comes to meet the man amid all the folk,
And greets him good-humoredly, and gaily he says,
"I shall follow forthwith the form of our pledge
1935   That we framed to good effect amid fresh-filled cups."
He clasps him accordingly and kisses him thrice,
As amiably and as earnestly as ever he could.
"By heaven," said the host, "you have had some luck
Since you took up this trade, if the terms were good."
1940   "Never trouble about the terms," he returned at once,
"Since all that I owe here is openly paid."
"Marry!" said the other man, "mine is much less,
For I have hunted all day, and nought have I got
But this foul fox pelt, the fiend take the goods!
1945   Which but poorly repays those precious things
That you have cordially conferred, those kisses three
                    so good."
            "Enough!" said Sir Gawain;
            "I thank you, by the rood!"
1950   And how the fox was slain
            He told him, as they stood.

With minstrelsy and mirth, with all manner of meats,
They made as much merriment as any men might
(Amid laughing of ladies and light-hearted girls,
1955   So gay grew Sir Gawain and the goodly host)
Unless they had been besotted, or brainless fools.
The knight joined in jesting with that joyous folk,
Until at last it was late; ere long they must part,
And be off to their beds, as behooved them each one.
1960   Then politely his leave of the lord of the house
Our noble knight takes, and renews his thanks:[6]
"The courtesies countless accorded me here,
Your kindness at this Christmas, may heaven's King repay!
Henceforth, if you will have me, I hold you my liege,

6. Gawain's highly stylized leave-taking is typical of courtly romance and again emphasizes his command of fine manners.

1965 And so, as I have said, I must set forth tomorrow,
If I may take some trusty man to teach, as you promised,
The way to the Green Chapel, that as God allows
I shall see my fate fulfilled on the first of the year."
"In good faith," said the good man, "with a good will
1970 Every promise on my part shall be fully performed."
He assigns him a servant to set him on the path,
To see him safe and sound over the snowy hills,
To follow the fastest way through forest green
                              and grove.
1975   Gawain thanks him again,
             So kind his favors prove,
             And of the ladies then
             He takes his leave, with love.

Courteously he kissed them, with care in his heart,
1980 And often wished them well, with warmest thanks,
Which they for their part were prompt to repay.
They commend him to Christ with disconsolate sighs;
And then in that hall with the household he parts—
Each man that he met, he remembered to thank
1985 For his deeds of devotion and diligent pains,
And the trouble he had taken to tend to his needs;
And each one as woeful, that watched him depart,
As he had lived with him loyally all his life long.
By lads bearing lights he was led to his chamber
1990 And blithely brought to his bed, to be at his rest.
How soundly he slept, I presume not to say,
For there were matters of moment his thoughts might well
                              pursue.
             Let him lie and wait;
1995   He has little more to do,
             Then listen, while I relate
             How they kept their rendezvous.

Part 4

Now the New Year draws near, and the night passes,
The day dispels the dark, by the Lord's decree;
2000 But wild weather awoke in the world without:
The clouds in the cold sky cast down their snow
With great gusts from the north, grievous to bear.
Sleet showered aslant upon shivering beasts;
The wind warbled wild as it whipped from aloft,
2005 And drove the drifts deep in the dales below.
Long and well he listens, that lies in his bed;
Though he lifts not his eyelids, little he sleeps;
Each crow of the cock he counts without fail.
Readily from his rest he rose before dawn,
2010 For a lamp had been left him, that lighted his chamber.
He called to his chamberlain, who quickly appeared,
And bade him get him his gear, and gird his good steed,

And he sets about briskly to bring in his arms,
And makes ready his master in manner most fit.
2015 First he clad him in his clothes, to keep out the cold,
And then his other harness, made handsome anew,
His plate-armor of proof, polished with pains,
The rings of his rich mail rid of their rust,
And all was fresh as at first, and for this he gave thanks
2020   indeed.
          With pride he wears each piece,
          New-furbished for his need:
          No gayer from here to Greece;
          He bids them bring his steed.

2025 In his richest raiment he robed himself then:
His crested coat-armor, close-stitched with craft,
With stones of strange virtue on silk velvet set;
All bound with embroidery on borders and seams
And lined warmly and well with furs of the best.
2030 Yet he left not his love-gift, the lady's girdle;
Gawain, for his own good, forgot not that:
When the bright sword was belted and bound on his haunches,
Then twice with that token he twined him about.
Sweetly did he swathe him in that swatch of silk,
2035 That girdle of green so goodly to see,
That against the gay red showed gorgeous bright.
Yet he wore not for its wealth that wondrous girdle,
Nor pride in its pendants, though polished they were,
Though glittering gold gleamed at the tips,
2040 But to keep himself safe when consent he must
To endure a deadly dint, and all defense
                    denied.
          And now the bold knight came
          Into the courtyard wide;
2045   That folk of worthy fame
          He thanks on every side.

Then was Gringolet girt, that was great and huge,
And had sojourned safe and sound, and savored his fare;
He pawed the earth in his pride, that princely steed.
2050 The good knight draws near him and notes well his look,
And says sagely to himself, and soberly swears,
"Here is a household in hall that upholds the right!
The man that maintains it, may happiness be his!
Likewise the dear lady, may love betide her!
2055 If thus they in charity cherish a guest
That are honored here on earth, may they have His reward
That reigns high in heaven—and also you all;
And were I to live in this land but a little while,
I should willingly reward you, and well, if I might."
2060 Then he steps into the stirrup and bestrides his mount;
His shield is shown forth; on his shoulder he casts it;

Strikes the side of his steed with his steel spurs,
And he starts across the stones, nor stands any longer
                    to prance.
2065   On horseback was the swain
            That bore his spear and lance;
            "May Christ this house maintain
            And guard it from mischance!"

The bridge was brought down, and the broad gates
2070   Unbarred and carried back upon both sides;
He commended him to Christ, and crossed over the planks;
Praised the noble porter, who prayed on his knees
That God save Sir Gawain, and bade him good day,
And went on his way alone with the man
2075   That was to lead him ere long to that luckless place
Where the dolorous dint must be dealt him at last.
Under bare boughs they ride, where steep banks rise,[7]
Over high cliffs they climb, where cold snow clings;
The heavens held aloof, but heavy thereunder
2080   Mist mantled the moors, moved on the slopes.
Each hill had a hat, a huge cape of cloud;
Brooks bubbled and broke over broken rocks,
Flashing in freshets that waterfalls fed.
Roundabout was the road that ran through the wood
2085   Till the sun at that season was soon to rise,
                    that day.
            They were on a hilltop high;
            The white snow round them lay;
            The man that rode nearby
2090   Now bade his master stay.

"For I have seen you here safe at the set time,
And now you are not far from that notable place
That you have sought for so long with such special pains.
But this I say for certain, since I know you, sir knight,
2095   And have your good at heart, and hold you dear—
Would you heed well my words, it were worth your while—
You are rushing into risks that you reck not of:
There is a villain in yon valley, the veriest on earth,
For he is rugged and rude, and ready with his fists,
2100   And most immense in his mold of mortals alive,
And his body bigger than the best four
That are in Arthur's house, Hector[8] or any.
He gets his grim way at the Green Chapel;
None passes by that place so proud in his arms
2105   That he does not dash him down with his deadly blows,
For he is heartless wholly, and heedless of right,
For be it chaplain or churl that by the Chapel rides,

7. The grimness of this landscape, reminiscent of wastelands in Anglo-Saxon poetry, swiftly returns the poem
from the courtly world to the elemental challenge
Gawain now faces.

8. Chief hero among the defenders of Troy and, like
Arthur, one of the "Nine Worthies" celebrated for their
heroic valor; or perhaps Arthur's knight Hector De Maris.

Monk or mass-priest or any man else,
He would as soon strike him dead as stand on two feet.
2110 Wherefore I say, just as certain as you sit there astride,
You cannot but be killed, if his counsel holds,
For he would trounce you in a trice, had you twenty lives
               for sale.
      He has lived long in this land
2115   And dealt out deadly bale;
      Against his heavy hand
      Your power cannot prevail.

"And so, good Sir Gawain, let the grim man be;
Go off by some other road, in God's own name!
2120 Leave by some other land, for the love of Christ,
And I shall get me home again, and give you my word
That I shall swear by God's self and the saints above,
By heaven and by my halidom[9] and other oaths more,
To conceal this day's deed, nor say to a soul
2125 That ever you fled for fear from any that I knew."
"Many thanks!" said the other man—and demurring he speaks—
"Fair fortune befall you for your friendly words!
And conceal this day's deed I doubt not you would,
But though you never told the tale, if I turned back now,
2130 Forsook this place for fear, and fled, as you say,
I were a caitiff coward; I could not be excused.
But I must to the Chapel to chance my luck
And say to that same man such words as I please,
Befall what may befall through Fortune's will
2135   or whim.
      Though he be a quarrelsome knave
      With a cudgel great and grim,
      The Lord is strong to save:
      His servants trust in Him."

2140 "Marry," said the man, "since you tell me so much,
And I see you are set to seek your own harm,
If you crave a quick death, let me keep you no longer!
Put your helm on your head, your hand on your lance,
And ride the narrow road down yon rocky slope
2145 Till it brings you to the bottom of the broad valley.
Then look a little ahead, on your left hand,
And you will soon see before you that self-same Chapel,
And the man of great might that is master there.
Now goodbye in God's name, Gawain the noble!
2150 For all the world's wealth I would not stay here,
Or go with you in this wood one footstep further!"
He tarried no more to talk, but turned his bridle,
Hit his horse with his heels as hard as he might,
Leaves the knight alone, and off like the wind
2155   goes leaping.

9. "By my holy relics."

"By God," said Gawain then,
"I shall not give way to weeping;
God's will be done, amen!
I commend me to His keeping."

2160 He puts his heels to his horse, and picks up the path;
Goes in beside a grove where the ground is steep,
Rides down the rough slope right to the valley;
And then he looked a little about him—the landscape was wild,
And not a soul to be seen, nor sign of a dwelling,
2165 But high banks on either hand hemmed it about,
With many a ragged rock and rough-hewn crag;
The skies seemed scored by the scowling peaks.
Then he halted his horse, and hoved there a space,
And sought on every side for a sight of the Chapel,
2170 But no such place appeared, which puzzled him sore,
Yet he saw some way off what seemed like a mound,[1]
A hillock high and broad, hard by the water,
Where the stream fell in foam down the face of the steep
And bubbled as if it boiled on its bed below.
2175 The knight urges his horse, and heads for the knoll;
Leaps lightly to earth; loops well the rein
Of his steed to a stout branch, and stations him there.
He strides straight to the mound, and strolls all about,
Much wondering what it was, but no whit the wiser;
2180 It had a hole at one end, and on either side,
And was covered with coarse grass in clumps all without,
And hollow all within, like some old cave,
Or a crevice of an old crag—he could not discern
                              aright.
2185   "Can this be the Chapel Green?
              Alack!" said the man, "Here might
              The devil himself be seen
              Saying matins at black midnight!"

"Now by heaven," said he, "it is bleak hereabouts;
2190 This prayer-house is hideous, half-covered with grass!
Well may the grim man mantled in green
Hold here his orisons, in hell's own style!
Now I feel it is the Fiend, in my five wits,
That has tempted me to this tryst, to take my life;
2195 This is a Chapel of mischance, may the mischief take it!
As accursed a country church as I came upon ever!"
With his helm on his head, his lance in his hand,
He stalks toward the steep wall of that strange house.
Then he heard, on the hill, behind a hard rock,
2200 Beyond the brook, from the bank, a most barbarous din:
Lord! it clattered in the cliff fit to cleave it in two,
As one upon a grindstone ground a great scythe!
Lord! it whirred like a mill-wheel whirling about!

---

1. The barrow, perhaps a burial mound, seems to link the moment to ancient, probably pagan, inhabitants.

Lord! it echoed loud and long, lamentable to hear!
2205   Then "By heaven," said the bold knight, "That business up there
Is arranged for my arrival, or else I am much
                            misled.
            Let God work! Ah me!
            All hope of help has fled!
2210   Forfeit my life may be
            But noise I do not dread."

Then he listened no longer, but loudly he called,
"Who has power in this place, high parley to hold?
For none greets Sir Gawain, or gives him good day;
2215   If any would a word with him, let him walk forth
And speak now or never, to speed his affairs."
"Abide," said one on the bank above over his head,
"And what I promised you once shall straightway be given."
Yet he stayed not his grindstone, nor stinted its noise,
2220   But worked awhile at his whetting before he would rest,
And then he comes around a crag, from a cave in the rocks,
Hurtling out of hiding with a hateful weapon,
A Danish ax[2] devised for that day's deed,
With a broad blade and bright, bent in a curve,
2225   Filed to a fine edge—four feet it measured
By the length of the lace that was looped round the haft.
And in form as at first, the fellow all green,
His lordly face and his legs, his locks and his beard,
Save that firm upon two feet forward he strides,
2230   Sets a hand on the ax-head, the haft to the earth;
When he came to the cold stream, and cared not to wade,
He vaults over on his ax, and advances amain
On a broad bank of snow, overbearing and brisk
                            of mood.
2235   Little did the knight incline
            When face to face they stood;
            Said the other man, "Friend mine,
            It seems your word holds good!"

"God love you, Sir Gawain!" said the Green Knight then,
2240   "And well met this morning, man, at my place!
And you have followed me faithfully and found me betimes,
And on the business between us we both are agreed:
Twelve months ago today you took what was yours,
And you at this New Year must yield me the same.
2245   And we have met in these mountains, remote from all eyes:
There is none here to halt us or hinder our sport;
Unhasp your high helm, and have here your wages;
Make no more demur than I did myself
When you hacked off my head with one hard blow."
2250   "No, by God," said Sir Gawain, "that granted me life,
I shall grudge not the guerdon, grim though it prove;

2. A long-bladed ax, associated with Viking raiders.

Bestow but one stroke, and I shall stand still,
And you may lay on as you like till the last of my part
                              be paid.

2255   He proffered, with good grace,
                       His bare neck to the blade,
                       And feigned a cheerful face:
                       He scorned to seem afraid.

Then the grim man in green gathers his strength,
2260   Heaves high the heavy ax to hit him the blow.
With all the force in his frame he fetches it aloft,
With a grimace as grim as he would grind him to bits;
Had the blow he bestowed been as big as he threatened,
A good knight and gallant had gone to his grave.
2265   But Gawain at the great ax glanced up aside
As down it descended with death-dealing force,
And his shoulders shrank a little from the sharp iron.
Abruptly the brawny man breaks off the stroke,
And then reproved with proud words that prince among knights.
2270   "You are not Gawain the glorious," the green man said,
"That never fell back on field in the face of the foe,
And now you flee for fear, and have felt no harm:
Such news of that knight I never heard yet!
I moved not a muscle when you made to strike,
2275   Nor caviled at the cut in King Arthur's house;
My head fell to my feet, yet steadfast I stood,
And you, all unharmed, are wholly dismayed—
Wherefore the better man I, by all odds,
                              must be."

2280   Said Gawain, "Strike once more;
                       I shall neither flinch nor flee;
                       But if my head falls to the floor
                       There is no mending me!"

"But go on, man, in God's name, and get to the point!
2285   Deliver me my destiny, and do it out of hand,
For I shall stand to the stroke and stir not an inch
Till your ax has hit home—on my honor I swear it!"
"Have at thee then!" said the other, and heaves it aloft,
And glares down as grimly as he had gone mad.
2290   He made a mighty feint, but marred not his hide;
Withdrew the ax adroitly before it did damage.
Gawain gave no ground, nor glanced up aside,
But stood still as a stone, or else a stout stump
That is held in hard earth by a hundred roots.
2295   Then merrily does he mock him, the man all in green:
"So now you have your nerve again, I needs must strike;
Uphold the high knighthood that Arthur bestowed,
And keep your neck-bone clear, if this cut allows!"
Then was Gawain gripped with rage, and grimly he said,
2300   "Why, thrash away, tyrant, I tire of your threats;
You make such a scene, you must frighten yourself."

Said the green fellow, "In faith, so fiercely you speak
That I shall finish this affair, nor further grace
            allow."

2305
       He stands prepared to strike
       And scowls with both lip and brow;
       No marvel if the man mislike
       Who can hope no rescue now.

He gathered up the grim ax and guided it well:
2310
Let the barb at the blade's end brush the bare throat;
He hammered down hard, yet harmed him no whit
Save a scratch on one side, that severed the skin;
The end of the hooked edge entered the flesh,
And a little blood lightly leapt to the earth.
2315
And when the man beheld his own blood bright on the snow,
He sprang a spear's length with feet spread wide,
Seized his high helm, and set it on his head,
Shoved before his shoulders the shield at his back,[3]
Bares his trusty blade, and boldly he speaks—
2320
Not since he was a babe born of his mother
Was he once in this world one-half so blithe—
"Have done with your hacking—harry me no more!
I have borne, as behooved, one blow in this place;
If you make another move I shall meet it midway
2325
And promptly, I promise you, pay back each blow
            with brand.
       One stroke acquits me here;
       So did our covenant stand
       In Arthur's court last year—
2330
       Wherefore, sir, hold your hand!"

He lowers the long ax and leans on it there,
Sets his arms on the head, the haft on the earth,
And beholds the bold knight that bides there afoot,
How he faces him fearless, fierce in full arms,
2335
And plies him with proud words—it pleases him well.
Then once again gaily to Gawain he calls,
And in a loud voice and lusty, delivers these words:
"Bold fellow, on this field your anger forbear!
No man has made demands here in manner uncouth,
2340
Nor done, save as duly determined at court.
I owed you a hit and you have it; be happy therewith!
The rest of my rights here I freely resign.
Had I been a bit busier, a buffet, perhaps,
I could have dealt more directly, and done you some harm.
2345
First I flourished with a feint, in frolicsome mood,
And left your hide unhurt—and here I did well
By the fair terms we fixed on the first night;
And fully and faithfully you followed accord:

---

3. Gawain, who has displayed so much courtly refinement and religious emotion, now shows himself a practiced fighter, swiftly pulling his armor into place.

Gave over all your gains as a good man should.
2350   A second feint, sir, I assigned for the morning
You kissed my comely wife—each kiss you restored.
For both of these there behooved but two feigned blows
by right.
True men pay what they owe;
2355   No danger then in sight.
You failed at the third throw,
So take my tap, sir knight.

"For that is my belt about you, that same braided girdle,
My wife it was that wore it; I know well the tale,
2360   And the count of your kisses and your conduct too,
And the wooing of my wife—it was all my scheme!
She made trial of a man most faultless by far
Of all that ever walked over the wide earth;
As pearls to white peas, more precious and prized,
2365   So is Gawain, in good faith, to other gay knights.
Yet you lacked, sir, a little in loyalty there,
But the cause was not cunning, nor courtship either,
But that you loved your own life; the less, then, to blame."
The other stout knight in a study stood a long while,
2370   So gripped with grim rage that his great heart shook.
All the blood of his body burned in his face
As he shrank back in shame from the man's sharp speech.
The first words that fell from the fair knight's lips:
"Accursed be a cowardly and covetous heart!
2375   In you is villainy and vice, and virtue laid low!"
Then he grasps the green girdle and lets go the knot,
Hands it over in haste, and hotly he says:
"Behold there my falsehood, ill hap betide it!
Your cut taught me cowardice, care for my life,
2380   And coveting came after, contrary both
To largesse and loyalty belonging to knights.
Now am I faulty and false, that fearful was ever
Of disloyalty and lies, bad luck to them both!
and greed.
2385   I confess, knight, in this place,
Most dire is my misdeed;
Let me gain back your good grace,
And thereafter I shall take heed."

Then the other laughed aloud, and lightly he said,
2390   "Such harm as I have had, I hold it quite healed.
You are so fully confessed, your failings made known,
And bear the plain penance of the point of my blade,
I hold you polished as a pearl, as pure and as bright
As you had lived free of fault since first you were born.
2395   And I give you, sir, this girdle that is gold-hemmed
And green as my garments, that, Gawain, you may
Be mindful of this meeting when you mingle in throng

With nobles of renown—and known by this token
How it chanced at the Green Chapel, to chivalrous knights.
2400 And you shall in this New Year come yet again
And we shall finish out our feast in my fair hall,
                    with cheer."
          He urged the knight to stay,
          And said, "With my wife so dear
2405   We shall see you friends this day,
          Whose enmity touched you near."

"Indeed," said the doughty knight, and doffed his high helm,
And held it in his hands as he offered his thanks,
"I have lingered long enough—may good luck be yours,
2410 And He reward you well that all worship bestows!
And commend me to that comely one, your courteous wife,
Both herself and that other, my honored ladies,
That have trapped their true knight in their trammels so quaint.
But if a dullard should dote, deem it no wonder,
2415 And through the wiles of a woman be wooed into sorrow,
For so was Adam by one, when the world began,
And Solomon by many more, and Samson the mighty—
Delilah was his doom, and David thereafter
Was beguiled by Bathsheba, and bore much distress;[4]
2420 Now these were vexed by their devices—'twere a very joy
Could one but learn to love, and believe them not.
For these were proud princes, most prosperous of old,
Past all lovers lucky, that languished under heaven,
                    bemused.
2425   And one and all fell prey
          To women that they had used;
          If I be led astray,
          Methinks I may be excused.

"But your girdle, God love you! I gladly shall take
2430 And be pleased to possess, not for the pure gold,
Nor the bright belt itself, nor the beauteous pendants,
Nor for wealth, nor worldly state, nor workmanship fine,
But a sign of excess it shall seem oftentimes
When I ride in renown, and remember with shame
2435 The faults and the frailty of the flesh perverse,
How its tenderness entices the foul taint of sin;
And so when praise and high prowess have pleased my heart,
A look at this love-lace will lower my pride,
But one thing would I learn, if you were not loath,
2440 Since you are lord of yonder land where I have long sojourned
With honor in your house—may you have His reward
That upholds all the heavens, highest on throne!

---

4. Gawain suddenly erupts in a brief but fierce diatribe, including this list of treacherous women recognizable from contemporary misogynist texts.

How runs your right name?—and let the rest go."
"That shall I give you gladly," said the Green Knight then;
2445 "Bercilak de Hautdesert this barony I hold,
Through the might of Morgan le Fay,[5] that lodges at my house,
By subtleties of science and sorcerers' arts,
The mistress of Merlin, she has caught many a man,
For sweet love in secret she shared sometime
2450 With that wizard, that knows well each one of your knights
                              and you.
              Morgan the Goddess, she,
              So styled by title true;
              None holds so high degree
2455   That her arts cannot subdue.

"She guided me in this guise to your glorious hall,
To assay, if such it were, the surfeit of pride
That is rumored of the retinue of the Round Table.
She put this shape upon me to puzzle your wits,
2460 To afflict the fair queen, and frighten her to death
With awe of that elvish man that eerily spoke
With his head in his hand before the high table.
She was with my wife at home, that old withered lady,
Your own aunt is she, Arthur's half-sister,
2465 The Duchess' daughter of Tintagel, that dear King Uther
Got Arthur on after, that honored is now.[6]
And therefore, good friend, come feast with your aunt;
Make merry in my house; my men hold you dear,
And I wish you as well, sir, with all my heart,
2470 As any mortal man, for your matchless faith."
But the knight said him nay, that he might by no means.
They clasped then and kissed, and commended each other
To the Prince of Paradise, and parted with one
                              assent.
2475   Gawain sets out anew;
              Toward the court his course is bent;
              And the knight all green in hue,
              Wheresoever he wished, he went.

Wild ways in the world our worthy knight rides
2480 On Gringolet, that by grace had been granted his life.
He harbored often in houses, and often abroad,
And with many valiant adventures verily he met
That I shall not take time to tell in this story.
The hurt was whole that he had had in his neck,

---

5. Morgan is Arthur's half-sister and ruler of the mysterious Avalon; she learned magical arts from Merlin. Her presence can bode good or ill. In some stories she holds a deep grudge against Guinevere, yet she carries off the wounded Arthur after his final battle, perhaps to heal him. The earlier Celtic Morrigan, possibly related, is queen of demons, sower of discord, and goddess of war.

6. The poem now recalls an earlier transgression of guest–host obligations, when Uther began to lust for Ygerne while her husband, Gorlois, was at his court; he later killed Gorlois and married Ygerne. See Geoffrey of Monmouth, pages 160–162.

2485 And the bright green belt on his body he bore,
Oblique, like a baldric, bound at his side,
Below his left shoulder, laced in a knot,
In betokening of the blame he had borne for his fault;
And so to court in due course he comes safe and sound.
2490 Bliss abounded in hall when the high-born heard
That good Gawain was come, glad tidings they thought it.
The king kisses the knight, and the queen as well,
And many a comrade came to clasp him in arms,
And eagerly they asked, and awesomely he told,
2495 Confessed all his cares and discomfitures many,
How it chanced at the Chapel, what cheer made the knight,
The love of the lady, the green lace at last.
The nick on his neck he naked displayed
That he got in his disgrace at the Green Knight's hands,
2500   alone.
    With rage in heart he speaks,
    And grieves with many a groan;
    The blood burns in his cheeks
    For shame at what must be shown.

2505 "Behold, sir," said he, and handles the belt,
"This is the blazon of the blemish that I bear on my neck;
This is the sign of sore loss that I have suffered there
For the cowardice and coveting that I came to there;
This is the badge of false faith that I was found in there,
2510 And I must bear it on my body till I breathe my last.
For one may keep a deed dark, but undo it no whit,
For where a fault is made fast, it is fixed evermore."
The king comforts the knight, and the court all together
Agree with gay laughter and gracious intent
2515 That the lords and the ladies belonging to the Table,
Each brother of that band, a baldric should have,
A belt oblique, of a bright green,
To be worn with one accord for that worthy's sake.
So that was taken as a token by the Table Round,
2520 And he honored that had it, evermore after,
As the best book of knighthood bids it be known.
In the old days of Arthur this happening befell;
The books of Brutus' deeds bear witness thereto
Since Brutus, the bold knight, embarked for this land
2525 After the siege ceased at Troy and the city fared
          amiss.
    Many such, ere we were born,
    Have befallen here, ere this.
    May He that was crowned with thorn
2530   Bring all men to His bliss! Amen.

Hony Soyt Qui Mal Pence

Sir Thomas Malory
c. 1410–1471

The full identity of Sir Thomas Malory shimmers just beyond our grasp. In several of his colophons—those closing formulas to texts—the author of the *Morte Darthur* says he is "a knyght presoner, sir Thomas Malleorré," and prays that "God sende hym good delyveraunce sone and hastely." Scholars have traced a number of such names in the era, among whom two seem particularly likely: Sir Thomas Malory of Newbold Revell, and Thomas Malory of Papworth. The former Thomas Malory had a scabrous criminal record and was long kept prisoner awaiting trial, while the latter had links to a rich collection of Arthurian books.

Another colophon provides the more useful information that "the hoole book of kyng Arthur and of his noble knyghtes of the Rounde Table" was completed in the ninth year of King Edward IV, that is 1469 or 1470. So whichever Malory wrote the *Morte Darthur*, he was certainly working in the unsettled years of the War of the Roses, in which the great ducal families of York and Lancaster battled for control of the English throne. As one family gained dominance, adherents of the other were often jailed on flimsy charges. The spectacle of a nation threatening to crumble into clan warfare provides much of the thematic weight of the *Morte Darthur*, while the declining chivalric order of the later fifteenth century underlies Malory's increasingly elegiac tone.

Whether he gained his remarkable knowledge of French and English Arthurian tradition in or out of jail, Malory infused his version of these stories with a darkening perspective very much his own. Malory sensed the high aspirations, especially the bonds of honor and fellowship in battle, that held together Arthur's realm. Yet he was also bleakly aware of how tenuous those bonds were and how easily undone by tragically competing pressures. These include the centuries-old Arthurian preoccupation with transgressive love, but Malory is more concerned with the conflicting claims of loyalty to clan or king, the urge to avenge the death of a fellow knight, and the resulting alienation even among the best of knights. Still more unnerving, agents of a virtually unmotivated or unexplained malice have ever more impact as the *Morte Darthur* progresses.

For all his initial energy and control, Malory's Arthur is increasingly a king forced to suppress knightly grievances, to deplore religious quest, even to overlook the adultery of his wife and his greatest knight, all in the interest of his fading hopes for chivalric honor and unity. Arthur's commitment to courtesy finally undoes his honor in the eyes of his own knights. As the Round Table is broken (an image Malory uses repeatedly) Arthur is put in the agonizing position of acting as judge in his wife's trial, making war on his early companion Lancelot, and finally engaging in single combat with his own treacherous son Mordred.

Malory would have found many of these themes in his sources. Twelfth-century Arthurian romances in French verse had explored the elevation and danger of courtly eroticism, and the theme was extended in the enormous French prose versions of the thirteenth century that Malory had read in great detail. In these prose romances, too, religious and chivalric themes converged around the story of the Grail. Malory also knew the alliterative *Morte Arthur* poems of fourteenth-century England, with their emphases on conquest, treachery, and the military details of Arthur's final battles.

Malory regularly acknowledges these sources, but his powers of synthesis and the stamp of his style make his *Morte Darthur* unique. While he occasionally writes a complex, reflective sentence, Malory's prose is typically composed of simple, idiomatic narrative statements, and speeches so brief as to be almost gnomic. On hearing of his brother's death, Gawain faints, then rises and says only "Alas!" Yet the grief of his cry resonates across the closing episodes of the work. Malory's imagery is similarly resonant. He tends to strip it of the explanations that had become frequent in the French prose works, and he concentrates its impact by an almost obsessive repetition. The later episodes of the work become almost an incantation of breakage and dispersal, blood and wounds, each image cluster reaching alternately toward religious experience or secular destruction.

These versions of chivalric ambition, sacred or secular, do not divide easily in the *Morte Darthur*. The saintly Galahad and the scheming Mordred may represent extremes of contrary ambition, but Malory is more preoccupied by the sadly mixed motives of Lancelot or Arthur himself. In three late episodes offered below, the reader is drawn into the perspective of lesser knights like Bors and Bedivere, who witness great moments while affecting them only marginally. They bring back to the world of lesser men stories of uncanny experience and oversee their conversion from verbal rumor to written form, whether in books or on tombs. Much of Malory's power and his continuing appeal come from his unresolved doubleness of perspective. Whether by way of his characters or his style, resonant and mysterious elements emerge from a narrative of gritty realism.

from MORTE DARTHUR
from Caxton's Prologue[1]

After that I had accomplysshed and fynysshed dyuers hystoryes as wel of° contemplacyon as of other hystoryal and worldly actes of *[both about]* grete conquerours and prynces, and also certeyn bookes of ensaumples° and doctryne, many noble and dyuers gentylmen of *[moral tales]* thys royame° of Englond camen and demaunded me many and *[realm]* oftymes, wherefore that I haue not do made and enprynte the noble hystorye of the Sayntgreal° and of the moost renomed° Crysten *[Holy Grail / famed]* kyng, fyrst and chyef of the thre best Crysten[2] and worthy, Kyng Arthur, whyche ought moost to be remembred emonge vs Englysshemen tofore° al other Crysten kynges. * * * *[before]*

To whome I answerd that dyuers men holde oppynyon that there was no suche Arthur, and that alle suche bookes as been maad of hym ben° but fayned and fables, bycause that somme cronycles *[are]* make of hym no mencyon ne° remembre hym noothynge ne of his *[nor]* knyghtes.

Wherto they answerd, and one in specyal sayd, that in hym that shold say or thynke that there was neuer suche a kyng callyd Arthur myght wel be aretted° grete folye and blyndenesse; for he sayd that *[presumed]* there were many euydences of the contrarye. Fyrst ye may see his sepulture° in the monasterye of Glastyngburye. And also in Poly- *[tomb]* cronycon,[3] * * * where his body was buryed and after founden and translated into the sayd monasterye. Ye shal se also in th'ystory of Bochas, in his book De Casu Principum,[4] parte of his noble actes and also of his falle; also Galfrydus in his Brutysshe book[5] recounteth his lyf. And in dyuers places of Englond many remembraunces ben yet

---

1. The first English printer, William Caxton exerted a major literary influence through his translations of French works and his pioneering editions of English writers, including Chaucer and Gower. In 1485 he published a version of *Le Morte Darthur*, probably based on a revision by Malory himself but different from the text edited by Vinaver (1947, 1975) and used here. Caxton's *Prologue* is interesting in its own right as an early response to Malory, even as Caxton takes the opportunity to promote interest in his book. To give a sense of early printed English, the passages from Caxton's *Prologue* are presented in unaltered spelling.

2. Arthur appears in the traditional list of "nine worthies," three heroes each from pagan, Jewish, and Christian narratives.

3. The *Polychronicon*, a universal history by the monk Ranulph Higden (d. 1364).

4. Boccaccio's *On the Fall of Princes*.

5. Geoffrey of Monmouth, *History of the Kings of Britain*, whose later versions were often called simply *Brut*.

of hym and shall remayne perpetuelly, and also of his knyghtes. Fyrst in the Abbey of Westmestre at Saynt Edwardes Shryne remayneth the prynte of his seal in reed waxe closed in beryll, in which is wryton, PATRICIUS ARTHURUS BRITANNIE GALLIE GERMANIE DACIE IMPERATOR.[6] Item° in the Castel of Douer ye may see Gauwayns skulle and Cradoks mantel; at Wynchester, the Round Table; in other places, Launcelottes swerde, and many other thynges.

Thenne, al these thynges consydered, there can no man resonably gaynsaye but there was a kyng of thys lande named Arthur.

** Thenne al these thynges forsayd aledged, I coude not wel denye but that there was suche a noble kynge named Arthur, and reputed one of the ix worthy, and fyrst and chyef of the Cristen men. And many noble volumes be made of hym and of his noble knyghtes in Frensshe, which I haue seen and redde beyonde the see, which been not had in our maternal tongue. But in Walsshe ben many, and also in Frensshe, and somme in Englysshe, but nowher nygh alle. Wherfore suche as haue late ben drawen oute bryefly° into Englysshe, I haue, after the symple connyng° that God hath sente to me, vnder the fauour and correctyon of al noble lordes and gentylmen, enprysed° to enprynte a book of the noble hystoryes of the sayd Kynge Arthur and of certeyn of his knyghtes, after a copye vnto me delyuerd, whyche copye Syr Thomas Malorye dyd take oute of certeyn bookes of Frensshe and reduced it into Englysshe. And I, accordyng to my copye, haue doon sette it in enprynte, to the entente° that noble men may see and lerne the noble actes of chyualrye, the ientyl° and vertuous dedes that somme knyghtes used in tho° dayes, by whyche they came to honour, and how they that were vycious were punysshed and ofte put to shame and rebuke. Humbly bysechyng al noble lordes and ladyes, wyth al other estates° of what estate or degree they been of, that shal see and rede in this sayd book and werke, that they take the good and honest actes in their remembraunce and to folowe the same, wherin they shalle fynde many ioyous and playsaunt hystoryes and noble and renomed actes of humanyte, gentylnesss, and chyualryes. For herein may be seen noble chyualrye, curtosye, humanyte, frendlynesse, hardynesse, loue, frendshyp, cowardyse, murdre, hate, vertue, and synne. Doo after the good and leue the euyl, and it shal brynge you to good fame and renommee.°

And for to passe the tyme thys book shal be plesaunte to rede in, but for to gyue fayth and byleue that al is trewe that is conteyned herin, ye be at your lyberte. But al is wryton for our doctryne and for to beware that we falle not to vyce ne synne, but t'excersyse° and folowe vertu, by whyche we may come and atteyne to good fame and renomme in thys lyf, and after thys shorte and transytorye lyf to come vnto euerlastyng blysse in heuen, the whyche He graunte vs that reygneth in heuen, the Blessyd Trynyte. Amen.

---

6. The Noble Arthur, Emperor of Britain, Gaul, Germany, Dacia.

Marginal glosses:

also

abridged
wit

undertaken

with the aim
noble
those

ranks

renown

to practice

The Miracle of Galahad[1]

Now saith the tale that Sir Galahad rode many journeys in vain, and at last he came to the abbey where King Mordrains was. And when he heard that, he thought he would abide to see him.

And so upon the morn, when he had heard mass, Sir Galahad came unto King Mordrains. And anon the king saw him, which had lain blind of long time, and then he dressed him against° him and said,

rose to meet

"Sir Galahad, the servant of Jesu Christ and very° knight, whose coming I have abiden° long, now embrace me and let me rest on thy breast, so that I may rest° between thine arms! For thou art a clean virgin above all knights, as the flower of the lily in whom virginity is signified. And thou art the rose which is the flower of all good virtue, and in colour of fire.[2] For the fire of the Holy Ghost is taken so in thee that my flesh, which was all dead of oldness, is become again young."

true
awaited
die

When Galahad heard these words, then he embraced him and all his body. Then said he,°

"Fair Lord Jesu Christ, now I have my will! Now I require Thee, in this point° that I am in, that Thou come and visit me."

Mordrains

state

And anon Our Lord heard his prayer, and therewith the soul departed from the body. And then Sir Galahad put him in the earth as a king ought to be, and so departed and came into a perilous forest where he found the well which boiled with great waves, as the tale telleth tofore.°

earlier

And as soon as Sir Galahad set his hand thereto it ceased, so that it brent° no more, and anon the heat departed away. And cause why it brent, it was a sign of lechery that was that time much used. But that heat might not abide his pure virginity. And so this was taken in the country for a miracle, and so ever after was it called Galahad's Well.

burned

So by adventure he came unto the country of Gore, and into the abbey where Sir Lancelot had been toforehand and found the tomb of King Bagdemagus; but he was founder thereof.[3] For there was the tomb of Joseph of Arimathea's son and the tomb of Simeon, where Lancelot had failed.[4] Then he looked into a croft° under the minster,° and there he saw a tomb which brent full marvellously. Then asked he the brethren what it was.

crypt
church

---

1. From *The Holy Grail,* in *King Arthur and His Knights,* ed. Eugène Vinaver (1975). Earlier in the text, Lancelot's saintly son Galahad had come to the Round Table and precipitated a brief apparition of the Holy Grail (the cup with which Christ had celebrated the Last Supper). One hundred fifty of Arthur's knights then took a vow to seek a fuller vision of the Grail, but in the mysterious adventures that followed, many died or despaired. Malory's attention now narrows to Lancelot and his partial vision of the Grail, and the continuing quest of Galahad, Perceval, and Bors. The blind King Mordrains is one of several maimed or aged kings cured by Galahad's presence.

2. Galahad's physical and spiritual purity are shown in a number of earlier episodes.

3. Gore, the mysterious realm of Bagdemagus, who had been gravely wounded when he presumed to take a shield intended for Galahad. Words may be missing from the final phrase.

4. In Arthurian tradition, Joseph of Arimathea was keeper of the Grail and used it to catch Christ's blood at the Crucifixion. His son Joseph was the first Christian bishop and carried both the faith and the Grail to England. Galahad is the last of their lineage. Lancelot's failure refers to an episode in the French source that Malory never tells, either inadvertently or because he assumed that many readers would know the story.

"Sir," said they, "a marvellous adventure that may not be brought to an end but by him that passeth of bounty and of knighthood all them of the Round Table."

"I would," said Sir Galahad, "that ye would bring me thereto."

"Gladly," said they, and so led him till° a cave. And he went down upon greses° and came unto the tomb. And so the flaming failed, and the fire staunched° which many a day had been great. *to* *steps* *was quenched*

Then came there a voice which said,

"Much are ye beholden to thank God which hath given you a good hour,° that ye may draw out the souls of earthly pain and to put them into the joys of Paradise. Sir, I am of your kindred, which hath dwelled in this heat this three hundred winter and four-and-fifty to be purged of the sin that I did against Arimathea Joseph." *good luck*

Then Sir Galahad took the body in his arms and bare it into the minster. And that night lay Sir Galahad in the abbey; and on the morn he gave him his service and put him in the earth before the high altar.

So departed he from thence, and commended the brethren to God, and so he rode five days till that he came to the Maimed King. And ever followed Perceval the five days asking where he had been, and so one told him how the adventures of Logres were achieved.[5] So on a day it befell that he came out of a great forest, and there they met at traverse with Sir Bors[6] which rode alone. It is no need to ask if they were glad! And so he salewed them, and they yielded to him° honour and good adventure, and everych told other how they had sped. Then said Sir Bors, *wished him*

"It is more than a year and a half that I ne lay° ten times where men dwelled, but in wild forests and in mountains. But God was ever my comfort." *have not slept*

Then rode they a great while till they came to the castle of Corbenic. And when they were entered within, King Pelles knew them. So there was great joy, for he wist well by their coming that they had fulfilled the Sankgreall.[7]

Then Eliazar, King Pelles' son, brought tofore them the broken sword wherewith Joseph was stricken through the thigh.[8] Then Bors set his hand thereto to essay if he might have sowded° it again; but it would not be. Then he took it to Perceval, but he had no more power thereto than he. *joined*

"Now have ye it again," said Sir Perceval unto Sir Galahad, "for an° it be ever achieved by any bodily man, ye must do it." *if*

And then he took the pieces and set them together, and seemed to them as it had never be broken, and as well as it was first forged. And when they within espied that the adventure of the sword was achieved, then they gave the sword to Sir Bors, for it might no better be set,° for he was so good a knight and a worthy man. *used*

5. Perceval has followed Galahad's movements. Malory reduces a five-year period in his source to five days and omits the two knights' meeting.
6. Sir Bors has also been wandering in search of the Grail.
7. Pelles is the maimed king and keeper of Corbenic, the Grail Castle. The past tense looks forward to events not yet achieved.
8. This sword had wounded Joseph of Arimathea; joining its broken havles is part of the Grail quest.

And a little before even the sword[9] arose, great and marvellous, and was full of great heat, that many men fell for dread. And anon alight a voice among them and said, "They that ought not to sit at the table of Our Lord Jesu Christ, avoid° hence! For now there shall very° knights be fed."

withdraw
true

So they went thence, all save King Pelles and Eliazar, his son, which were holy men, and a maid which was his niece. And so there abode these three knights and these three; else were no more. And anon they saw knights all armed come in at the hall door, and did off their helms and their arms, and said unto Sir Galahad,

"Sir, we have hied° right much for to be with you at this table where the holy meat shall be departed."°

hastened
distributed

Then said he, "Ye be welcome! But of whence be ye?"

So three of them said they were of Gaul, and other three said they were of Ireland, and other three said they were of Denmark.

And so as they sat thus, there came out a bed of tree° of° a chamber, which four gentlewomen brought; and in the bed lay a good man sick, and had a crown of gold upon his head. And there, in the midst of the palace, they set him down and went again. Then he lift up his head and said,

wood / from

"Sir Galahad, good knight, ye be right welcome, for much have I desired your coming! For in such pain and in such anguish as I have no man else° might have suffered long. But now I trust to God the term is come that my pain shall be allayed, and so I shall pass out of this world, so as it was promised me long ago."

no other man

And therewith a voice said, "There be two among you that be not in the quest of the Sankgreall, and therefore departeth!"

Then King Pelles and his son departed. And therewithal beseemed them° that there came an old man and four angels from heaven, clothed in likeness of a bishop, and had a cross in his hand. And these four angels bare him up in a chair and set him down before the table of silver whereupon the Sankgreall was. And it seemed that he had in midst of his forehead letters which said: "See ye here Joseph, the first bishop of Christendom, the same which Our Lord succoured[1] in the city of Sarras in the spiritual palace." Then the knights marvelled, for that bishop was dead more than three hundred year tofore.

it seemed

"Ah, knights," said he, "marvel not, for I was sometime an earthly man."

So with that they heard the chamber door open, and there they saw angels; and two bare candles of wax, and the third bare a towel,[2] and the fourth a spear which bled marvellously, that the drops fell within a box which he held with his other hand. And anon they set the candles upon the table, and the third the towel upon the vessel, and the fourth the holy spear even° upright upon the vessel.

straight

---

9. Malory misconstrues a phrase meaning "a wind."
1. Joseph of Arimathea was blessed by Christ.
2. In the French source, a veil of samite.

And then the bishop made semblaunt as though he would have gone to the sacring° of a mass, and then he took an ubblie° which was made in likeness of bread. And at the lifting up there came a figure in likeness of a child, and the visage was as red and as bright as any fire, and smote himself° into the bread, that all they saw it that the bread was formed of a fleshly man. And then he put it into the holy vessel again, and then he did that longed° to a priest to do mass.

consecration/
wafer

impressed itself

what was right

And then he went to Sir Galahad and kissed him and bade him go and kiss his fellows. And so he did anon.

"Now," said he, "the servants of Jesu Christ, ye shall be fed afore this table with sweet meats that never knights yet tasted."

And when he had said he vanished away. And they set them at the table in great dread and made their prayers. Then looked they and saw a Man come out of the holy vessel that had all the signs of the Passion of Jesu Christ, bleeding all openly, and said,

"My knights and my servants and my true children which be come out of deadly life into the spiritual life, I will no longer cover me from you, but ye shall see now a part of my secrets and of my hid things. Now holdeth and receiveth the high order and meat which ye have so much desired."

Then took He himself the holy vessel and came to Sir Galahad. And he kneeled down and received his Saviour. And after him so received all his fellows, and they thought it so sweet that it was marvellous to tell. Then said He to Sir Galahad,

"Son, wotest thou what I hold betwixt my hands?"

"Nay," said he, "but if ye tell me."

"This is," said He, "the holy dish wherein I ate the lamb on Easter Day, and now hast thou seen that thou most desired to see. But yet hast thou not seen it so openly as thou shalt see it in the city of Sarras, in the spiritual palace. Therefore thou must go hence and bear with thee this holy vessel, for this night it shall depart from the realm of Logres, and it shall nevermore be seen here. And knowest thou wherefore? For he° is not served nother worshipped to his right° by them of this land, for they be turned to evil living, and therefore I shall disinherit them of the honour which I have done them. And therefore go ye three to-morn unto the sea, where ye shall find your ship ready, and with you take the sword with the strange girdles,° and no more with you but Sir Perceval and Sir Bors. Also I will that ye take with you of this blood of this spear for to anoint the Maimed King, both his legs and his body, and he shall have his heal."

it
properly

belts

"Sir," said Galahad, "why shall not these other fellows go with us?"

"For this cause: for right as I depart° my apostles one here and another there, so I will that ye depart. And two of you shall die in my service, and one of you shall come again and tell tidings."

separate

Then gave He them His blessing and vanished away.

And Sir Galahad went anon to the spear which lay upon the table and touched the blood with his fingers, and came after to the maimed knight and anointed his legs and his body. And therwith he clothed him anon, and start upon his feet out of his bed as an whole man, and thanked God that He had healed him. And anon he left the world and yielded himself to a place of religion of white monks,[3] and was a full holy man.

And that same night, about midnight, came a voice among them which said,

"My sons, and not my chief sons,[4] my friends, and not mine enemies, go ye hence where ye hope best to do, and as I bade you do."

"Ah, thanked be Thou, Lord, that Thou wilt whightsauf° to call us Thy sons! Now may we well prove that we have not lost our pains."

And anon in all haste they took their harness and departed; but the three knights of Gaul (one of them hight Claudine, King Claudas' son, and the other two were great gentlemen) then prayed° Sir Galahad to everych of them, that an° they come to King Arthur's court, "to salew my lord Sir Lancelot, my father and them all of the Round Table"; and prayed them, an they came on that party,° not to forget it.

Right so departed Sir Galahad, and Sir Perceval and Sir Bors with him, and so they rode three days. And then they came to a rivage° and found the ship whereof the tale speaketh of tofore. And when they came to the board° they found in the midst of the bed the table of silver which they had left with the Maimed King, and the Sankgreall which was covered with red samite.° Then were they glad to have such things in their fellowship; and so they entered and made great reverence thereto, and Sir Galahad fell on his knees and prayed long time to Our Lord, that at what time he asked he might pass out of this world. And so long he prayed till a voice said,

"Sir Galahad, thou shalt have thy request, and when thou asketh the death of thy body thou shalt have it, and then shalt thou have the life of thy soul."

Then Sir Perceval heard him a little, and prayed him of° fellowship that was between them wherefore he asked such things.

"Sir, that shall I tell you," said Sir Galahad. "This other day, when we saw a part of the adventures of the Sankgreall, I was in such a joy of heart that I trow° never man was that was earthly. And therefore I wot° well, when my body is dead, my soul shall be in great joy to see the Blessed Trinity every day, and the majesty of Our Lord, Jesu Christ."

And so long were they in the ship that they said to Galahad,

"Sir, in this bed ye ought to lie, for so saith the letters."°

And so he laid him down, and slept a great while. And when he awaked he looked tofore him and saw the city of Sarras. And as they would have landed they saw the ship wherein Sir Perceval had put his sister in.

vouchsafe

asked
if

to that region

shore
on board

silk

for the sake of

believe
know

writings

---

3. The white monks were Cistercians, whose spirituality had some role in Malory's French sources.   4. A confusing phrase, perhaps in error for "stepsons."

"Truly," said Sir Perceval, "in the name of God, well hath my sister holden us covenant."[5]

Then they took out of the ship the table of silver, and he took it to Sir Perceval and to Sir Bors to go tofore, and Sir Galahad came behind, and right so they went into the city. And at the gate of the city they saw an old man crooked, and anon Sir Galahad called him and bade him help "to bear this heavy thing."

"Truly," said the old man, "it is ten year ago that I might not go but with crutches."

"Care thou not," said Galahad, "and arise up and show thy good will!"

And so he essayed, and found himself as whole as ever he was.   beside
Then ran he to the table and took one part against° Galahad.

Anon arose there a great noise in the city that a cripple was made whole by knights marvellous that entered into the city. Then anon after the three knights went to the water and brought up into the palace Sir Perceval's sister, and buried her as richly as them ought a king's daughter.

And when the king of that country knew that and saw that fellowship (whose name was Estorause), he asked them of whence they were, and what thing it was that they had brought upon the table of silver. And they told him the truth of the Sankgreall, and the power which God hath set there.

Then this king was a tyrant, and was come of the line of paynims,° and took them and put them in prison in a deep hole. But as   pagans
soon as they were there Our Lord sent them the Sankgreall, through whose grace they were alway fulfilled° while that they were   fed
in prison.

So at the year's end it befell that this king lay sick and felt that he should die. Then he sent for the three knights, and they came afore him, and he cried them mercy of that he had done to them, and they forgave it him goodly, and he died anon.

When the king was dead all the city stood dismayed and wist°   knew
not who might be their king. Right so as they were in council there came a voice among them, and made them choose the youngest knight of three to be their king, "for he shall well maintain you and all yours."

So they made Sir Galahad king by all the assent of the whole city, and else they would have slain him. And when he was come to behold his land he let make° above the table of silver a chest of   had made
gold and of precious stones that covered the holy vessel, and every day early the three knights would come before it and make their prayers.

Now at the year's end, and the self Sunday after that Sir Galahad had borne the crown of gold, he arose up early and his fellows, and came to the palace, and saw tofore them the holy vessel and a man

---

5. Kept her promise to us. In an earlier episode Perceval's sister died after giving a basin of her blood to heal a leper woman.

kneeling on his knees in likeness of a bishop that had about him a great fellowship of angels, as it had been Jesu Christ himself. And then he arose and began a mass of Our Lady. And so he came to the sacring, and anon made an end. He called Sir Galahad unto him and said,

"Come forth, the servant of Jesu Christ, and thou shalt see that thou hast much desired to see."

And then he began to tremble right hard when the deadly° flesh began to behold the spiritual things. Then he held up his hands toward heaven and said,   *mortal*

"Lord, I thank Thee, for now I see that that hath been my desire many a day. Now, my Blessed Lord, I would not live in this wretched world no longer, if it might please Thee, Lord."

And therewith the good man took Our Lord's Body[6] betwixt his hands, proffered it to Sir Galahad, and he received it right gladly and meekly.

"Now wotest thou what I am?" said the good man.

"Nay, Sir," said Sir Galahad.

"I am Joseph, the son of Joseph of Arimathea, which Our Lord hath sent to thee to bear thee fellowship. And wotest thou wherefore He hath sent me more than any other? For thou hast resembled me in two things: that thou hast seen, that is the marvels of the Sankgreall, and for thou hast been a clean maiden° as I have been and am."   *chaste virgin*

And when he had said these words Sir Galahad went to Sir Perceval and kissed him and commended him to God. And so he went to Sir Bors and kissed him and commended him to God, and said,

"My fair lord, salew me° unto my lord Sir Lancelot, my father, and as soon as ye see him bid him remember of this world unstable."   *give my greeting*

And therewith he kneeled down tofore the table and made his prayers. And so suddenly departed his soul to Jesu Christ, and a great multitude of angels bare it up to heaven, even in the sight of his two fellows.

Also these two knights saw come from heaven an hand, but they saw not the body, and so it came right to the vessel, and took it, and the spear, and so bare it up to heaven. And sithen° was there never man so hardy to say that he had seen the Sankgreall.   *since then*

So when Sir Perceval and Sir Bors saw Sir Galahad dead they made as much sorrow as ever did men. And if they had not been good men they might lightly° have fallen in despair. And so people of the country and city, they were right heavy. But so he was buried, and soon as he was buried Sir Perceval yielded him to an hermitage out of the city and took religious clothing. And Sir Bors was alway with him, but he changed never his secular clothing, for that he purposed him to go again into the realm of Logres.   *easily*

Thus a year and two months lived Sir Perceval in the hermitage a full holy life, and then passed out of the world. Then Sir Bors let bury him by[7] his sister and by Sir Galahad in the spiritualities.°   *consecrated ground*

---

6. The wafer of the Eucharist.   7. Had him buried next to.

So when Bors saw that he was in so far° countries as in the parts   *remote*
of Babylon, he departed from the city of Sarras and armed him and
came to the sea, and entered into a ship. And so it befell him, by
good adventure, he came unto the realm of Logres, and so he rode a
pace° till he came to Camelot where the king was.   *swiftly*

And then was there made great joy of him in all the court, for
they weened all he had been lost forasmuch as he had been so long
out of the country. And when they had eaten, the king made great
clerks to come before him, for cause they should chronicle of° the   *record*
high adventures of the good knights. So when Sir Bors had told him
of the high adventures of the Sankgreall such as had befallen him
and his three fellows, which were Sir Lancelot, Perceval, Sir Galahad and himself, then Sir Lancelot told the adventures of the
Sankgreall that he had seen. All this was made in great books and
put up in almeries° at Salisbury.   *libraries*

And anon Sir Bors said to Sir Lancelot,

"Sir Galahad, your own son, salewed you by me, and after you
my lord King Arthur and all the whole court, and so did Sir Perceval.
For I buried them with both mine own hands in the city of Sarras.
Also, Sir Lancelot, Sir Galahad prayed you to remember of this
unsiker° world, as ye behight him° when ye were together more than   *uncertain /*
half a year."   *promised*

"This is true," said Sir Lancelot; "now I trust to God his prayer
shall avail me."

Then Sir Lancelot took Sir Bors in his arms and said,

"Cousin, ye are right welcome to me! For all that ever I may do
for you and for yours, ye shall find my poor body ready at all times
while the spirit is in it, and that I promise you faithfully, and never
to fail. And wit ye well, gentle cousin Sir Bors, ye and I shall never
depart in sunder while our lives may last."

"Sir," said he, "as ye will, so will I."

THUS ENDETH THE TALE OF THE SANKGREALL THAT WAS BRIEFLY
DRAWN OUT OF FRENCH, WHICH IS A TALE CHRONICLED FOR ONE OF
THE TRUEST AND OF THE HOLIEST THAT IS IN THIS WORLD, BY SIR
THOMAS MALEORRÉ, KNIGHT.

O BLESSED JESU HELP HIM THROUGH HIS MIGHT! AMEN.

The Poisoned Apple[1]

So after the quest of the Sankgreall was fulfilled, and all knights that
were left on live were come home again unto the Table Round, as
The Book of the Sankgreall maketh mention, then was there great joy
in the court, and in especial King Arthur and Queen Guinevere
made great joy of the remnant that were come home. And passing
glad was the king and the queen of Sir Lancelot and of Sir Bors, for
they had been passing long away in the quest of the Sankgreall.

---

1. From the section titled *The Book of Sir Launcelot and Queen Guinevere*, in *King Arthur and His Knights*, ed. Eugène Vinaver (1975).

Then, as the book saith, Sir Lancelot began to resort unto Queen Guinevere again and forgat the promise and the perfection° that he made in the quest; for, as the book saith, had not Sir Lancelot been in his privy° thoughts and in his mind so set inwardly to the queen as he was in seeming outward to God, there had no knight passed him in the quest of the Sankgreall. But ever his thoughts privily were on the queen, and so they loved together more hotter than they did to forehand, and had many such privy draughts° together that many in the court spake of it, and in especial Sir Agravain, Sir Gawain's brother, for he was ever open-mouthed. *of perfection* *secret* *meetings*

So it befell that Sir Lancelot had many resorts of° ladies and damsels which daily resorted unto him, that besought him to be their champion. In all such matters of right Sir Lancelot applied him daily to do for the pleasure of Our Lord Jesu Christ, and ever as much as he might he withdrew him from the company of Queen Guinevere for to eschew the slander and noise.° Wherefore the queen waxed wroth with Sir Lancelot. *entreaties from* *rumor*

So on a day she called him unto her chamber and said thus:

"Sir Lancelot, I see and feel daily that your love beginneth to slake,° for ye have no joy to be in my presence, but ever ye are out of this court, and quarrels and matters ye have nowadays for ladies, maidens and gentlewomen, more than ever ye were wont to have beforehand." *cool*

"Ah, madam," said Sir Lancelot, "in this ye must hold me excused for divers causes. One is, I was but late in the quest of the Sankgreall, and I thank God of His great mercy, and never of my deserving, that I saw in that my quest as much as ever saw any sinful man living, and so was it told me. And if that I had not had my privy thoughts to return to your love again as I do, I had° seen as great mysteries as ever saw my son, Sir Galahad, Perceval, other Sir Bors. And therefore, madam, I was but late in that quest, and wit you well, madam, it may not be yet lightly forgotten, the high service in whom I did my diligent labour. *should have*

"Also, madam, wit you well that there be many men speaketh of our love in this court, and have you and me greatly in await,° as this Sir Agravain and Sir Mordred.[2] And, madam, wit you well I dread them more for your sake than for any fear I have of them myself, for I may happen to escape and rid myself in a great need where, madam, ye must abide all that will be said unto you. And then, if that ye fall in any distress throughout° wilful folly, then is there none other help but by me and my blood.° *suspicion* *through* *kinsmen*

"And wit you well, madam, the boldness of you and me will bring us to shame and slander; and that were me loath to see you dishonoured. And that is the cause I take upon me more for to do for damsels and maidens than ever I did toforn:° that men should understand my joy and my delight is my pleasure to have ado for damsels and maidens." *before*

---

2. Mordred was Arthur's illegitimate son, by an incestuous encounter with his half-sister Morgause (or in some versions, Morgan le Fay).

All this while the queen stood still and let Sir Lancelot say what he would; and when he had all said she brast out of weeping, and so she sobbed and wept a great while. And when she might speak she said,

"Sir Lancelot, now I well understand that thou art a false, recreant° knight and a common lecher, and lovest and holdest other *cowardly* ladies, and of me thou hast disdain and scorn. For wit thou well, now I understand thy falsehood I shall never love thee more, and look thou be never so hardy° to come in my sight. And right here I dis- *bold* charge thee this court, that thou never come within it, and I forfend° thee my fellowship, and upon pain° of thy head that thou *forbid / at the risk* see me nevermore!"

Right so Sir Lancelot departed with great heaviness that unneth° he might sustain himself for great dole-making. *scarcely*

Then he called Sir Bors, Ector de Maris and Sir Lionel, and told them how the queen had forfended him the court, and so he was in will to depart into his own country.

"Fair sir," said Bors de Ganis, "ye shall not depart out of this land by mine advice, for ye must remember you what ye are, and renowned the most noblest knight of the world, and many great matters ye have in hand. And women in their hastiness will do oftentimes that after them sore repenteth. And therefore, by mine advice, ye shall take your horse and ride to the good hermit here beside Windsor, that sometime was a good knight; his name is Sir Brastias. And there shall ye abide till that I send you word of better tidings."

"Brother," said Sir Lancelot, "wit you well I am full loath to depart out of this realm, but the queen hath defended° me so *dismissed* highly,° that meseemeth she will never be my good lady as she *angrily* hath been."

"Say ye never so," said Sir Bors, "for many times or° this time *before* she hath been wroth with you, and after that she was the first that repented it."

"Ye say well," said Sir Lancelot, "for now will I do by your counsel and take mine horse and mine harness and ride to the hermit Sir Brastias, and there will I repose me till I hear some manner of tidings from you. But, fair brother, in that° ye can get me the love of my *so far as* lady, Queen Guinevere."

"Sir," said Sir Bors, "ye need not to move° me of such matters, *persuade* for well ye wot I will do what I may to please you."

And then Sir Lancelot departed suddenly, and no creature wist where he was become° but Sir Bors. So when Sir Lancelot was *had gone* departed the queen outward made no manner of sorrow in showing to none of his blood nor to none other, but wit ye well, inwardly, as the book saith, she took great thought;° but she bare it out with a *grief* proud countenance, as though she felt no thought nother danger.° *fear*

So the queen let make° a privy dinner in London unto the *had made* knights of the Round Table, and all was for to show outward that she had as great joy in all other knights of the Round Table as she had in

Sir Lancelot. So there was all only at that dinner Sir Gawain and his brethren, that is for to say Sir Agravain, Sir Gaheris, Sir Gareth and Sir Mordred, also there was Sir Bors de Ganis, Sir Blamore de Ganis, Sir Bleoberis de Ganis, Sir Galihad, Sir Eliodin, Sir Ector de Maris, Sir Lionel, Sir Palomides, Sir Safir, his brother, Sir La Cote Male Tayle, Sir Persaunt, Sir Ironside, Sir Braundiles, Sir Kay le Seneschal, Sir Mador de la Porte, Sir Patrise, a knight of Ireland, Sir Aliduke, Sir Ascamore, and Sir Pinel le Savage, which was cousin to Sir Lamorak de Galis, the good knight that Sir Gawain and his brethren slew by treason.[3]

And so these four-and-twenty knights should dine with the queen in a privy place by themselves, and there was made a great feast of all manner of dainties. But Sir Gawain had a custom that he used daily at meat and at supper, that he loved well all manner of fruit, and in especial apples and pears. And therefore whosomever dined other° feasted Sir Gawain would commonly purvey for° good fruit for him. And so did the queen; for to please Sir Gawain she let purvey for him all manner of fruit. For Sir Gawain was a passing hot° knight of nature, and this Sir Pinel hated Sir Gawain because of his kinsman Sir Lamorak's death, and therefore, for pure envy and hate, Sir Pinel enpoisoned certain apples for to enpoison Sir Gawain.

So this was well yet unto° the end of meat, and so it befell by misfortune a good knight Sir Patrise, which was cousin unto Sir Mador de la Porte, took an apple, for he was enchafed° with heat of wine. And it mishapped him to take a poisoned apple. And when he had eaten it he swall° sore till he brast,° and there Sir Patrise fell down suddenly° dead among them.

Then every knight leap from the board ashamed, and araged for° wrath out of their wits, for they wist not what to say; considering Queen Guinevere made the feast and dinner they had all suspicion unto her.

"My lady the queen!" said Sir Gawain. "Madam, wit you that this dinner was made for me and my fellows, for all folks that knoweth my condition understand that I love well fruit. And now I see well I had near been slain. Therefore, madam, I dread me lest ye will be shamed."

Then the queen stood still and was so sore abashed that she wist not what to say.

"This shall not so be ended," said Sir Mador de la Porte, "for here have I lost a full noble knight of my blood, and therefore upon this shame and despite° I will be revenged to the utterance!"°

And there openly Sir Mador appealed° the queen of the death of his cousin Sir Patrise.

Then stood they all still, that° none would speak a word against him, for they all had great suspicion unto the queen because she let make that dinner. And the queen was so abashed that she could none otherways do but wept so heartily that she fell on a swough. So with

---

or/provide

hot-tempered

toward

inflamed

swelled/burst
instantly
enraged with

wrong/utmost
accused

for

---

3. This catalog draws together most of the Round Table knights who survived the Grail quest, except for Sir Bors, absent perhaps because his kinsman Lancelot is in disgrace with the queen.

this noise and cry came to them King Arthur, and when he wist of the trouble he was a passing heavy° man. And ever Sir Mador stood still before the king, and appealed the queen of treason. (For the custom was such at that time that all manner of shameful death was called treason.)

"Fair lords," said King Arthur, "me repenteth of this trouble, but the case is so I may not have ado° in this matter, for I must be a rightful judge. And that repenteth me that I may not do battle[4] for my wife, for, as I deem, this deed came never by her.° And therefore I suppose she shall not be all disdained° but that some good knight shall put his body in jeopardy for my queen rather than she should be brent° in a wrong quarrel.° And therefore, Sir Mador, be not so hasty; for, perdy,° it may happen she shall not be all friendless. And therefore desire thou thy day of battle, and she shall purvey her of° some good knight that shall answer you, other else it were to me great shame and to all my court."

"My gracious lord," said Sir Mador, "ye must hold me excused, for though ye be our king, in that degree° ye are but a knight as we are, and ye are sworn unto knighthood as well as we be. And therefore I beseech you that ye be not displeased, for there is none of all these four-and-twenty knights that were bidden to this dinner but all they have great suspicion unto the queen. What say ye all, my lords?" said Sir Mador.

Then they answered by and by and said they could not excuse the queen for why she made the dinner, and other it must come by her other by her servants.

"Alas," said the queen, "I made this dinner for a good intent and never for none evil, so Almighty Jesu help me in my right,° as I was never purposed to do such evil deeds, and that I report me unto God."[5]

"My lord the king," said Sir Mador, "I require you as ye be a righteous king, give me my day that I may have justice."

"Well," said the king, "this day fifteen days look thou be ready armed on horseback in the meadow beside Winchester. And if it so fall° that there be any knight to encounter against you, there may you do your best, and God speed the right. And if so befall that there be no knight ready at that day, then must my queen be brent, and there she shall be ready to have her judgment."

"I am answered," said Sir Mador.

And every knight yode° where him liked.

So when the king and the queen were together the king asked the queen how this case° befell. Then the queen said,

"Sir, as Jesu be my help!" She wist not how nother° in what manner.

"Where is Sir Lancelot?" said King Arthur. "An° he were here he would not grudge to do battle for you."

"Sir," said the queen, "I wot not where he is, but his brother and his kinsmen deem that he be not within this realm."

Margin glosses: sad; intervene; by her doing; dishonored; burned/unjustly; by God; find herself; rank; just cause; happens; went; misfortune; nor; if

4. Malory refers to a procedure in law, archaic in his day, wherein an armed champion could vindicate a person's innocence in a "trial by battle."
5. I appeal to God to confirm.

"That me repenteth," said King Arthur, "for an he were here he would soon stint° this strife. Well, then I will counsel you," said the king, "that ye go unto Sir Bors, and pray him for to do battle for you for Sir Lancelot's sake, and upon my life he will not refuse you. For well I see," said the king, "that none of the four-and-twenty knights that were at your dinner where Sir Patrise was slain that will do battle for you, nother none of them will say well of you, and that shall be great slander to you in this court."

"Alas," said the queen, "an I may not do withall,[6] but now I miss Sir Lancelot, for an he were here he would soon put me in my heart's ease."

"What aileth you," said the king, "that ye cannot keep Sir Lancelot upon your side? For wit you well," said the king, "who hath Sir Lancelot upon his party° hath the most man of worship in this world upon his side. Now go your way," said the king unto the queen, "and require Sir Bors to do battle for you for Sir Lancelot's sake."

So the queen departed from the king and sent for Sir Bors into the chamber. And when he came she besought him of succour.

"Madam," said he, "what would ye that I did? For I may not with my worship° have ado in this matter, because I was at the same dinner, for dread of any of those knights would have you in suspicion. Also Madam," said Sir Bors, "now miss ye Sir Lancelot, for he would not a failed you in your right nother in your wrong, for when ye have been in right great dangers he hath succoured you. And now ye have driven him out of this country, by whom ye and all we were daily worshipped° by. Therefore, madam, I marvel how ye dare for shame to require me to do anything for you, insomuch ye have enchased out of your court by whom° we were upborne and honoured."

"Alas, fair knight," said the queen, "I put me wholly in your grace, and all that is amiss I will amend as ye will counsel me." And therewith she kneeled down upon both her knees, and besought Sir Bors to have mercy upon her, "other else I shall have a shameful death, and thereto I never offended."°

Right so came King Arthur and found the queen kneeling. And then Sir Bors took her up, and said,

"Madam, ye do me great dishonour."

"Ah, gentle knight," said the king, "have mercy upon my queen, courteous knight, for I am now in certain she is untruly defamed! And therefore, courteous knight," the king said, "promise her to do battle for her, I require you for the love ye owe unto Sir Lancelot."

"My lord," said Sir Bors, "ye require me the greatest thing that any man may require me. And wit you well, if I grant to do battle for the queen I shall wrath° many of my fellowship of the Table Round. But as for that," said Sir Bors, "I will grant° for my lord Sir Lancelot's

stop

faction

with honor

honored

the man by whom

did wrong

enrage

consent

6. If I cannot help it.

sake, and for your sake: I will at that day be the queen's champion unless that there come by adventures a better knight than I am to do battle for her."

"Will ye promise me this," said the king, "by your faith?"

"Yea sir," said Sir Bors, "of that I shall not fail you, nother her; but if there come a better knight than I am, then shall he have the battle."

Then was the king and the queen passing glad, and so departed, and thanked him heartily.

Then Sir Bors departed secretly upon a day, and rode unto Sir Lancelot thereas he was with Sir Brastias, and told him of all this adventure.

"Ah Jesu," Sir Lancelot said, "this is come happily as I would have it. And therefore I pray you make you ready to do battle, but look that ye tarry till ye see me come as long as ye may. For I am sure Sir Mador is an hot knight when he is enchafed for the more ye suffer him the hastier will he be to battle."

"Sir," said Sir Bors, "let me deal with him. Doubt ye not ye shall have all your will."

So departed Sir Bors from him and came to the court again. Then it was noised° in all the court that Sir Bors should do battle for the queen, wherefore many knights were displeased with him that he would take upon him to do battle in the queen's quarrel; for there were but few knights in all the court but they deemed the queen was in the wrong and that she had done that treason. So Sir Bors answered thus to his fellows of the Table Round.

"Wit you well, my fair lords, it were shame to us all an we suffered to see the most noble queen of the world to be shamed openly, considering her lord and our lord is the man of most worship christened, and he hath ever worshipped° us all in all places."

Many answered him again: "As for our most noble King Arthur, we love him and honour him as well as ye do, but as for Queen Guinevere we love her not, because she is a destroyer of good knights."

"Fair lords," said Sir Bors, "meseemeth ye say not as ye should say, for never yet in my days knew I never ne° heard say that ever she was a destroyer of good knights, but at all times as far as ever I could know, she was a maintainer of good knights; and ever she hath been large° and free of her goods to all good knights, and the most bounteous lady of her gifts and her good grace that ever I saw other heard speak of. And therefore it were shame to us all and to our most noble king's wife whom we serve an we suffered her to be shamefully slain. And wit ye well," said Sir Bors, "I will not suffer it, for I dare say so much, for the queen is not guilty of Sir Patrise's death: for she owed° him never none evil will nother none of the four-and-twenty knights that were at that dinner, for I dare say for good love she bade us to dinner, and not for no mal engine.° And that, I doubt not, shall be proved hereafter, for howsomever the game goeth, there was treason among us."

rumored

honored

nor

generous

felt towards

evil intent

Then some said to Bors, "We may well believe your words." And so some were well pleased and some were not.

So the day came on fast until the even that° the battle should be. Then the queen sent for Sir Bors and asked him how he was disposed.°

evening before

resolved

"Truly, madam," said he, "I am disposed in like wise as I promised you, that is to say I shall not fail you unless there by adventure come a better knight than I am to do battle for you. Then, madam, I am of° you discharged° of my promise."

by/released

"Will ye," said the queen, "that I tell my lord the king thus?"

"Do as it pleaseth you, madam."

Then the queen yode° unto the king and told the answer of Sir Bors.

went

'Well, have ye no doubt," said the king, "of Sir Bors, for I call him now that is living° one of the noblest knights of the world, and most perfectest man."

of those now alive

And thus it passed on till the morn, and so the king and the queen and all manner of knights that were there at that time drew° them unto the meadow beside Winchester where the battle should be. And so when the king was come with the queen and many knights of the Table Round, so the queen was then put in the constable's award,° and a great fire made about an iron stake, that an Sir Mador de le Porte had the better, she should there be brent; for such custom was used in those days: for favour, love, nother affinity° there should be none other but righteous judgment, as well upon a king as upon a knight, and as well upon a queen as upon another° poor lady.

gathered

custody

kinship

any

So this meanwhile came in Sir Mador de la Porte, and took his oath before the king, how that the queen did this treason until° his cousin Sir Patrise, "and unto mine oath I will prove it with my body, hand for hand, who that will say the contrary."

toward

Right so came in Sir Bors de Ganis and said that as for Queen Guinevere, "she is in the right, and that will I make good that she is not culpable of this treason that is put upon her."

"Then make thee ready," said Sir Mador, "and we shall prove whether thou be in the right or I."

"Sir Mador," said Sir Bors, "wit you well, I know you for a good knight. Notforthen° I shall not fear you so greatly but I trust to God I shall be able to withstand your malice. But thus much have I promised my lord Arthur and my lady the queen, that I shall do battle for her in this cause to the utterest, unless that there come a better knight than I am and discharge° me."

nevertheless

release

"Is that all?" said Sir Mador. "Other come thou off and do battle with me, other else say nay!"

"Take your horse," said Sir Bors, "and, as I suppose, I shall not tarry long but ye shall be answered."

Then either departed to their tents and made them ready to horseback° as they thought best. And anon Sir Mador came into the field with his shield on his shoulder and his spear in his hand, and so rode about the place crying unto King Arthur,

to mount

"Bid your champion come forth an he dare!"

Then was Sir Bors ashamed, and took his horse and came to the lists'° end. And then was he ware° where came from a wood there fast by a knight all armed upon a white horse with a strange shield of strange arms, and he came driving all that° his horse might run. And so he came to Sir Bors and said thus:

jousting field's/
noticed

as fast as

"Fair knight, I pray you be not displeased, for here must a better knight than ye are have this battle. Therefore I pray you withdraw you, for wit you well I have had this day a right great journey and this battle ought to be mine. And so I promised you when I spake with you last, and with all my heart I thank you of your good will."

Then Sir Bors rode unto King Arthur and told him how there was a knight come that would have the battle to fight for the queen.

"What knight is he?" said the king.

"I wot not," said Sir Bors, "but such covenant he made with me to be here this day. Now, my lord," said Sir Bors, "here I am discharged."

Then the king called to that knight, and asked him if he would fight for the queen. Then he answered and said,

"Sir, therefore come I hither. And therefore, sir king, tarry° me no longer, for anon as I have finished this battle I must depart hence, for I have to do many battles elsewhere. For wit you well," said the knight, "this is dishonour to you and to all knights of the Round Table to see and know so noble a lady and so courteous as Queen Guinevere is, thus to be rebuked and shamed amongst you."

delay

Then they all marvelled what knight that might be that so took the battle upon him, for there was not one that knew him but if it were Sir Bors. Then said Sir Mador de la Porte unto the king:

"Now let me wit with whom I shall have ado."

And then they rode to the lists' end, and there they couched° their spears and ran together with all their mights. And anon Sir Mador's spear brake all to pieces, but the other's spear held and bare Sir Mador's horse and all backwards to the earth a great fall. But mightily and deliverly he avoided his horse from him and put his shield before him and drew his sword and bade the other knight alight and do battle with him on foot.

lowered

Then that knight descended down from his horse and put his shield before him and drew his sword. And so they came eagerly unto battle, and either gave other many sad° strokes, tracing and traversing and foining° together with their swords as it were wild boars, thus fighting nigh an hour; for this Sir Mador was a strong knight, and mightily proved in many strong battles. But at the last this knight smote Sir Mador grovelling upon the earth, and the knight stepped near him to have pulled Sir Mador flatling° upon the ground; and therewith Sir Mador arose, and in his rising he smote that knight through the thick of the thighs, that the blood brast out fiercely.

grievous
thrusting

at full length

And when he felt himself so wounded and saw his blood, he let him arise upon his feet, and then he gave him such a buffet upon the helm that he fell to the earth flatling. And therewith he strode to

him to have pulled off his helm off his head. And so Sir Mador
prayed that knight to save his life. And so he yielded him as overcome, and released the queen of his quarrel.°   *accusation*

"I will not grant thee thy life," said the knight, "only that° thou *unless*
freely release the queen forever, and that no mention be made upon
Sir Patrise's tomb that ever Queen Guinevere consented to that
treason."

"All this shall be done," said Sir Mador, "I clearly discharge my
quarrel forever."

Then the knights parters° of the lists took up Sir Mador and led *stewards*
him till his tent. And the other knight went straight to the stairfoot
where sat King Arthur. And by that time was the queen came to the
king, and either kissed other heartily.

And when the king saw that knight he stooped down to him and
thanked him, and in like wise did the queen. And the king prayed
him put off his helmet and to repose him and to take a sop of wine.

And then he put off his helm to drink, and then every knight
knew him that it was Sir Lancelot. And anon as the king wist
that, he took the queen in his hand and yode unto Sir Lancelot
and said,

"Sir, gramercy of your great travail° that ye have had this day for *labor*
me and for my queen."

"My lord," said Sir Lancelot, "wit you well I ought of right ever
to be in your quarrel,° and my lady the queen's quarrel, to do battle; *on your side*
for ye are the man that gave me the high Order of Knighthood, and
that day my lady, your queen, did me worship.° And else I had been *honor*
shamed, for that same day that ye made me knight through my hastiness I lost my sword, and my lady, your queen, found it, and lapped° *wrapped*
it in her train, and gave me my sword when I had need thereto; and
else had I been shamed among all knights. And therefore, my lord
Arthur, I promised her at that day ever to be her knight in right other in wrong."

"Gramercy," said the king, "for this journey. And wit you well,"
said the king, "I shall acquit° your goodness." *reward*

And evermore the queen beheld Sir Lancelot and wept so
tenderly that she sank almost to the ground for sorrow, that he
had done to her so great kindness where she showed him great
unkindness. Then the knights of his blood drew unto him, and
there either of them made great joy of other. And so came all the
knights of the Table Round that were there at that time and welcomed him.

And then Sir Mador was healed of his leechcraft,° and Sir *by surgery*
Lancelot was healed of his play.° And so there was made great joy *wound*
and many mirths there was made in that court.

And so it befell that the Damsel of the Lake that hight Ninive,
which wedded the good knight Sir Pelleas, and so she came to the
court, for ever she did great goodness unto King Arthur and to all his
knights through her sorcery and enchantments. And so when she
heard how the queen was grieved° for the death of Sir Patrise, then she *blamed*

told it openly that she was never guilty, and there she disclosed by whom it was done, and named him Sir Pinel, and for what cause he did it. There it was openly known and disclosed, and so the queen was excused. And this knight Sir Pinel fled into his country, and was openly known that he enpoisoned the apples at that feast to that intent to have destroyed Sir Gawain, because Sir Gawain and his breathren destroyed Sir Lamorak de Galis which Sir Pinel was cousin unto.

Then was Sir Patrise buried in the church of Westminster in a tomb, and thereupon was written: "Here lieth Sir Patrise of Ireland, slain by Sir Pinel le Savage, that enpoisoned apples to have slain Sir Gawain, and by misfortune Sir Patrise ate one of the apples, and then suddenly he brast." Also there was written upon the tomb that Queen Guinevere was appealed° of treason of° the death of Sir Patrise by Sir Mador de la Porte, and there was made the mention how Sir Lancelot fought with him for Queen Guinevere and overcame him in plain battle. All this was written upon the tomb of Sir Patrise in excusing of the queen. *accused/for*

And then Sir Mador sued daily and long to have the queen's good grace, and so by the means of Sir Lancelot he caused him to stand in the queen's good grace, and all was forgiven.

[In intervening episodes, Agravain and Mordred, nursing long-held grudges, connive to expose the adultery of Lancelot and Guinevere. Their brother, Gawain, reluctantly joins their plot. Mordred traps Lancelot at night in Guinevere's chamber, and in escaping Lancelot kills Agravain. Rescuing Guinevere as she is about to be burned at the stake, Lancelot kills another of Gawain's brothers, Gareth, thereby earning Gawain's implacable enmity. Arthur must now make war on Lancelot and, pressed by Gawain, repeats his siege even after Guinevere is returned to him. Arthur thus besieges Lancelot in his French domain, leaving Mordred as regent.]

The Day of Destiny[1]

As Sir Mordred was ruler of all England, he let make° letters as though that they had come from beyond the sea, and the letters specified that King Arthur was slain in battle with Sir Lancelot. Wherefore Sir Mordred made a parliament, and called the lords together, and there he made them to choose him king. And so was he crowned at Canterbury, and held a feast there fifteen days. *commissioned*

And afterward he drew him unto Winchester, and there he took Queen Guinevere, and said plainly that he would wed her (which was his uncle's wife and his father's wife). And so he made ready for the feast, and a day prefixed that they should be wedded; wherefore Queen Guinevere was passing heavy,° but spake fair, and agreed to Sir Mordred's will. *sad*

And anon she desired of Sir Mordred to go to London to buy all manner things that longed to the bridal. And because of her fair

1. From the section titled *The Most Piteous Tale of the Morte Arthur Saunz Guerdon,* in *King Arthur and His Knights,* ed. Eugène Vinaver (1975).

speech Sir Mordred trusted her and gave her leave; and so when she came to London she took the Tower of London and suddenly in all haste possible she stuffed it with all manner of victual, and well garnished° it with men, and so kept it. *garrisoned*

And when Sir Mordred wist this he was passing wroth out of measure. And short tale to make, he laid a mighty siege about the Tower and made many assaults, and threw engines° unto them, and shot great guns. But all might not prevail, for Queen Guinevere would never, for fair speech neither for foul, never to trust unto Sir Mordred to come in his hands again. *siege machines*

Then came the Bishop of Canterbury, which was a noble clerk and an holy man, and thus he said unto Sir Mordred:

"Sir, what will ye do? Will you first displease God and sithen° shame yourself and all knighthood? For is not King Arthur your uncle, and no farther but your mother's brother, and upon her he himself begat you, upon his own sister? Therefore how may you wed your own father's wife? And therefore, sir," said the Bishop, "leave this opinion,° other else I shall curse you with book, bell and candle." *then* *intention*

"Do thou thy worst," said Sir Mordred, "and I defy thee!"

"Sir," said the Bishop, "and wit you well I shall not fear me to do that me ought to do. And also ye noise° that my lord Arthur is slain, and that is not so, and therefore ye will make a foul work in this land!" *spread rumors*

"Peace, thou false priest!" said Sir Mordred, "for an thou chafe° me any more, I shall strike off thy head." *anger*

So the Bishop departed, and did the cursing in the most orgulust° wise that might be done. And then Sir Mordred sought the Bishop of Canterbury for to have slain him. Then the Bishop fled, and took part of his goods with him, and went nigh unto Glastonbury. And there he was a priest-hermit in a chapel, and lived in poverty and in holy prayers; for well he understood that mischievous war was at hand. *defiant*

Then Sir Mordred sought upon Queen Guinevere by letters and sonds,° and by fair means and foul means, to have her to come out of the Tower of London; but all this availed nought, for she answered him shortly, openly and privily,[2] that she had liefer° slay herself than be married with him. *messengers* *rather*

Then came there word unto Sir Mordred that King Arthur had araised the siege from Sir Lancelot and was coming homeward with a great host to be avenged upon Sir Mordred; wherefore Sir Mordred made write writs° unto all the barony of this land, and much people drew unto him. For then was the common voice among them that with King Arthur was never other life but war and strife, and with Sir Mordred was great joy and bliss. Thus was King Arthur depraved° and evil said of; and many there were that King Arthur had brought up of nought, and given them lands, that might not then say him a good word. *summonses* *disparaged*

Lo ye Englishmen, see ye not what a mischief° here was? For he that was the most kind and noblest knight of the world, and most loved *evil*

2. At once, publicly and privately.

the fellowship of noble knights, and by him they all were upholden, and
yet might not these Englishmen hold them content with him. Lo thus
was the old custom and the usages of this land, and men say that we of
this land have not yet lost that custom. Alas! this is a great default of us
Englishmen, for there may no thing us please no term.° *length of time*

And so fared the people at that time: they were better pleased
with Sir Mordred than they were with the noble King Arthur, and
much people drew unto Sir Mordred and said they would abide with
him for better and for worse. And so Sir Mordred drew with a great
host to Dover, for there he heard say that King Arthur would arrive,
and so he thought to beat his own father from his own lands. And
the most party of all England held with Sir Mordred, for the people
were so new-fangle.° *fond of new things*

And so as Sir Mordred was at Dover with his host, so came King
Arthur with a great navy of ships and galleys and carracks, and there
was Sir Mordred ready awaiting upon his landing, to let° his own *stop*
father to land° upon the land that he was king over. *from landing*

Then there was launching of great boats and small, and full of
noble men of arms; and there was much slaughter of gentle knights,
and many a full bold baron was laid full low, on both parties. But
King Arthur was so courageous that there might no manner of
knight let him to land, and his knights fiercely followed him. And so
they landed maugre° Sir Mordred's head° and all his power, and put *against/will*
Sir Mordred aback, that he fled and all his people.

So when this battle was done King Arthur let search his people[3]
that were hurt and dead. And then was noble Sir Gawain found in a
great boat, lying more than half dead. When King Arthur knew that
he was laid so low he went unto him and so found him. And there
the king made great sorrow out of measure, and took Sir Gawain in
his arms, and thrice he there swooned. And then when he was
waked, King Arthur said,

"Alas! Sir Gawain, my sister son, here now thou liest, the man
in the world that I loved most. And now is my joy gone! For now,
my nephew, Sir Gawain, I will discover me unto° you, that in your *disclose*
person and in Sir Lancelot I most had my joy and my affiance.° And *trust*
now have I lost my joy of you both, wherefore all mine earthly joy is
gone from me!"

"Ah, mine uncle," said Sir Gawain, "now I will that ye wit that
my death-days be come! And all I may wite° mine own hastiness° *blame/rashness*
and my wilfulness, for through my wilfulness I was causer of mine
own death; for I was this day hurt and smitten upon mine old wound
that Sir Lancelot gave me, and I feel myself that I must needs be
dead by the hour of noon. And through me and my pride ye have all
this shame and disease,° for had that noble knight, Sir Lancelot, *sorrow*
been with you, as he was and would have been, this unhappy war
had never been begun; for he, through his noble knighthood and his
noble blood, held all your cankered° enemies in subjection and dan- *malignant*

3. Had his people searched for.

ger.° And now," said Sir Gawain, "ye shall miss Sir Lancelot. But °control
alas that I would not accord° with him! And therefore, fair uncle, I °make peace
pray you that I may have paper, pen and ink, that I may write unto
Sir Lancelot a letter written with mine own hand."

So when paper, pen and ink was brought, then Sir Gawain was set
up weakly° by King Arthur, for he was shriven a little afore. And then °gently
he took his pen and wrote thus, as the French book maketh mention:

"Unto thee, Sir Lancelot, flower of all noble knights that ever I
heard of or saw by my days, I, Sir Gawain, King Lot's son of Orkney,
and sister's son unto the noble King Arthur, send thee greeting, letting thee to have knowledge that the tenth day of May I was smitten upon the old wound that thou gave me afore the city of Ben-
wick, and through that wound I am come to my death-day. And I
will that all the world wit that I, Sir Gawain, knight of the Table
Round, sought my death, and not through thy deserving, but mine
own seeking. Wherefore I beseech thee, Sir Lancelot, to return
again unto this realm and see my tomb and pray some prayer more
other less for my soul. And this same day that I wrote the same
cedle° I was hurt to the death, which wound was first given of thine °letter
hand, Sir Lancelot; for of a more nobler man might I not be slain.

"Also, Sir Lancelot, for all the love that ever was betwixt us, make
no tarrying, but come over the sea in all the goodly haste that ye may,
with your noble knights, and rescue that noble king that made thee
knight, for he is full straitly bestead with° a false traitor which is my half- °hard pressed by
brother, Sir Mordred. For he hath crowned himself king and would have
wedded my lady, Queen Guinevere; and so had he done, had she not
kept the Tower of London with strong hand. And so the tenth day of
May last past my lord King Arthur and we all landed upon them at
Dover, and there he put that false traitor, Sir Mordred, to flight. And so
it misfortuned me to be smitten upon the stroke that ye gave me of old.

"And the date of this letter was written but two hours and a half
before my death, written with mine own hand and subscribed with
part of my heart blood. And therefore I require thee, most famous
knight of the world, that thou wilt see my tomb."

And then he wept and King Arthur both, and swooned. And
when they were awaked both, the king made Sir Gawain to receive
his sacrament, and then Sir Gawain prayed the king for to send for
Sir Lancelot and to cherish him above all other knights.

And so at the hour of noon Sir Gawain yielded up the ghost.
And then the king let inter him° in a chapel within Dover Castle. °had him buried
And there yet all men may see the skull of him, and the same wound
is seen that Sir Lancelot gave in battle.

Then was it told the king that Sir Mordred had pight a new field
upon Barham Down.[4] And so upon the morn King Arthur rode
thither to him, and there was a great battle betwixt them, and much
people were slain on both parties. But at the last King Arthur's party
stood best, and Sir Mordred and his party fled unto Canterbury.

4. Set up a new battleground at Barham Down (southeast of Canterbury).

And there the king let search all the downs for his knights that were slain and interred them; and salved them with soft salves° that full sore were wounded. Then much people drew unto King Arthur, and then they said that Sir Mordred warred upon King Arthur with wrong.

ointments

And anon King Arthur drew him with his host down by the seaside westward, toward Salisbury. And there was a day assigned betwixt King Arthur and Sir Mordred, that they should meet upon a down beside Salisbury, and not far from the seaside. And this day was assigned on Monday after Trinity Sunday, whereof King Arthur was passing glad that he might be avenged upon Sir Mordred.

Then Sir Mordred araised much people about London, for they of Kent, Sussex and Surrey, Essex, Suffolk and Norfolk held the most party with Sir Mordred. And many a full noble knight drew unto him and also to the king; but they that loved Sir Lancelot drew unto Sir Mordred.

So upon Trinity Sunday at night King Arthur dreamed a wonderful dream, and in his dream him seemed that he saw upon a chafflet° a chair, and the chair was fast to a wheel, and thereupon sat King Arthur in the richest cloth of gold that might be made. And the king thought there was under him, far from him, an hideous deep black water, and therein was all manner of serpents and worms° and wild beasts, foul and horrible. And suddenly the king thought that the wheel turned up-so-down, and he fell among the serpents, and every beast took him by a limb. And then the king cried as he lay in his bed, "Help! help!"

platform

dragons

And then knights, squires and yeomen awaked the king, and then he was so amazed that he wist not where he was. And then so he awaked until it was nigh day, and then he fell on slumbering again, not sleeping nor thoroughly waking. So° the king seemed verily that there came Sir Gawain unto him with a number of fair ladies with him. So when King Arthur saw him he said,

to

"Welcome, my sister's son, I weened° ye had been dead. And now I see thee on live, much am I beholden unto Almighty Jesu. Ah, fair nephew, what been these ladies that hither be come with you?"

thought

"Sir," said Sir Gawain, "all these be ladies for whom I have foughten for, when I was man living. And all these are those that I did battle for in righteous quarrels, and God hath given them that grace at their great prayer, because I did battle for them for their right, that they should bring me hither unto you. Thus much hath given me leave God for to warn you of your death: for an ye fight as to-morn with Sir Mordred, as ye both have assigned, doubt ye not ye shall be slain, and the most party of your people on both parties. And for the great grace and goodness that Almighty Jesu hath unto you, and for pity of you and many more other good men there shall be slain, God hath sent me to you of His especial grace to give you warning that in no wise ye do battle as to-morn, but that ye take a treatise for a month-day.[5] And proffer you largely,° so that to-morn ye put in a delay. For within a month shall come Sir Lancelot with

generously

5. Make a compact for a month from today.

all his noble knights, and rescue you worshipfully, and slay Sir Mordred and all that ever will hold with him."

Then Sir Gawain and all the ladies vanished, and anon the king called upon his knights, squires, and yeomen, and charged° them *ordered* mightly to fetch his noble lords and wise bishops unto him. And when they were come the king told them of his avision: that Sir Gawain had told him and warned him that an he fought on the morn he should be slain. Then the king commanded Sir Lucan the Butler and his brother Sir Bedivere the Bold, with two bishops with them, and charged them in any wise to take a treatise for a month-day with Sir Mordred:

"And spare not, proffer him lands and goods as much as you think reasonable."

So then they departed and came to Sir Mordred where he had a grim° host of an hundred thousand. And there they entreated Sir *fierce* Mordred long time, and at the last Sir Mordred was agreed for to have Cornwall and Kent by° King Arthur's days;° and after that all *during / lifetime* England, after the days of King Arthur. Then were they condescended° that King Arthur and Sir Mordred should meet betwixt both *agreed* their hosts, and every each of them should bring fourteen persons. And so they came with this word unto Arthur. Then said he,

"I am glad that this is done," and so he went into the field.

And when King Arthur should depart he warned all his host that an they see any sword drawn, "look ye come on fiercely and slay that traitor, Sir Mordred, for I in no wise trust him." In like wise Sir Mordred warned his host that "an ye see any manner of sword drawn look that ye come on fiercely and so slay all that ever before you standeth, for in no wise I will not trust for this treatise." And in the same wise said Sir Mordred unto his host: "for I know well my father will be avenged upon me."

And so they met as their pointment was, and were agreed and accorded thoroughly. And wine was fette,° and they drank together. *fetched* Right so came out an adder of a little heath-bush, and it stang a knight in the foot. And so when the knight felt him so stung, he looked down and saw the adder; and anon he drew his sword to slay the adder, and thought none other harm. And when the host on both parties saw that sword drawn, then they blew beams,° trumpets, and *bugles* horns, and shouted grimly, and so both hosts dressed them together.° *confronted each* And King Arthur took his horse and said, "Alas, this unhappy day!" *other* And so rode to his party, and Sir Mordred in like wise.

And never since was there seen a more dolefuller battle in no Christian land, for there was but rushing and riding, foining° and *thrusting* striking, and many a grim word was there spoken of either to other, and many a deadly stroke. But ever King Arthur rode throughout the battle° of Sir Mordred many times and did full nobly, as a noble king *battle formation* should do, and at all times he fainted never. And Sir Mordred did his devour° that day and put himself in great peril. *utmost effort*

And thus they fought all the long day, and never stinted° till the *ceased* noble knights were laid to the cold earth. And ever they fought still till it was near night, and by then was there an hundred thousand laid dead upon the earth. Then was King Arthur wood wroth° out of measure, when he saw his people so slain from him. *wild with rage*

And so he looked about him and could see no mo° of all his host, and good knights left no mo on live but two knights: the tone° was Sir Lucan de Butler and his brother, Sir Bedivere; and yet they were full sore wounded. *more / one*

"Jesu mercy!" said the king, "where are all my noble knights become? Alas, that ever I should see this doleful day! For now," said King Arthur, "I am come to mine end. But would to God," said he, "that I wist now where were that traitor Sir Mordred that hath caused all this mischief."° *evil*

Then King Arthur looked about and was ware where stood Sir Mordred leaning upon his sword among a great heap of dead men.

"Now, give me my spear," said King Arthur unto Sir Lucan, "for yonder I have espied the traitor that all this woe hath wrought."

"Sir, let him be," said Sir Lucan, "for he is unhappy.° And if ye pass this unhappy day ye shall be right well revenged. And, good lord, remember ye of your night's dream and what the spirit of Sir Gawain told you to-night, and yet God of His great goodness hath preserved you hitherto. And for God's sake, my lord, leave off this, for, blessed be God, ye have won the field: for yet we been here three on live, and with Sir Mordred is not one of live. And therefore if ye leave off now, this wicked day of Destiny is past!" *unlucky*

"Now tide° me death, tide me life," said the king, "now I see him yonder alone, he shall never escape mine hands! For at a better avail° shall I never have him." *befall / advantage*

"God speed you well!" said Sir Bedivere.

Then the king gat his spear in both his hands, and ran toward Sir Mordred, crying and saying,

"Traitor, now is thy death-day come!"

And when Sir Mordred saw King Arthur he ran until° him with his sword drawn in his hand, and there King Arthur smote Sir Mordred under the shield with a foin° of his spear throughout the body more than a fathom. And when Sir Mordred felt that he had his death wound he thrust himself with the might that he had up to the burr° of King Arthur's spear, and right so he smote his father, King Arthur, with his sword holding in both his hands, upon the side of the head, that the sword pierced the helmet and the tay° of the brain. And therewith Mordred dashed down stark dead to the earth. *toward / thrust / hand guard / lining*

And noble King Arthur fell in a swough to the earth, and there he swooned oftentimes, and Sir Lucan and Sir Bedivere oftentimes hove° him up. And so weakly° betwixt them they led him to a little chapel not far from the sea, and when the king was there, him thought him reasonably eased. *lifted/gently*

Then heard they people cry in the field.

"Now go thou, Sir Lucan," said the king, "and do me to wit° what betokens that noise in the field." *let me know*

So Sir Lucan departed, for he was grievously wounded in many places; and so as he rode he saw and harkened by the moonlight how that pillers° and robbers were come into the field to pille and to rob *plunderers*

many a full noble knight of brooches and bees° and of many a good ring   *bracelets*
and many a rich jewel. And who that were not dead all out, there they
slew them for their harness° and their riches.   *armor*

When Sir Lucan understood his work he came to the king as
soon as he might, and told him all what he had heard and seen.

"Therefore by my rede,"° said Sir Lucan, "it is best that we bring   *advice*
you to some town."

"I would it were so," said the king, "but I may not stand, my head
works° so. . . . Ah, Sir Lancelot!" said King Arthur, "this day have I   *aches*
sore missed thee! And alas, that ever I was against thee! For now
have I my death, whereof Sir Gawain me warned in my dream."

Then Sir Lucan took up the king the tone party° and Sir Bedi-   *on one side*
vere the other party, and in the lifting up the king swooned, and in
the lifting Sir Lucan fell in a swoon, that part of his guts fell out of
his body; and therewith the noble knight his heart brast. And when
the king awoke he beheld Sir Lucan, how he lay foaming at the
mouth and part of his guts lay at his feet.

"Alas," said the king, "this is to me a full heavy sight, to see this
noble duke so die for my sake, for he would have holpen° me that had   *helped*
more need of help than I! Alas, that he would not complain him, for his
heart was so set to help me. Now Jesu have mercy upon his soul!"

Then Sir Bedivere wept for the death of his brother.

"Now leave this mourning and weeping, gentle knight," said the
king, "for all this will not avail° me. For wit thou well an I might live   *aid*
myself, the death of Sir Lucan would grieve me evermore. But my
time passeth on fast," said the king. "Therefore," said King Arthur
unto Sir Bedivere, "take thou here Excalibur, my good sword, and go
with it to yonder water's side; and when thou comest there, I charge
thee throw my sword in that water, and come again and tell me what
thou seest there."

"My lord," said Sir Bedivere, "your commandment shall be
done, and lightly° bring you word again."   *I will quickly*

So Sir Bedivere departed. And by the way he beheld that noble
sword, and the pomell° and the haft° was all precious stones. And   *hand guard/*
then he said to himself, "If I throw this rich sword in the water,   *handle*
thereof shall never come good, but harm and loss." And then Sir
Bedivere hid Excalibur under a tree, and so soon as he might he
came again unto the king and said he had been at the water and
thrown the sword into the water.

"What saw thou there?" said the king.

"Sir," he said, "I saw nothing but waves and winds."

"That is untruly said of thee," said the king. "And therefore go
thou lightly again, and do my commandment as thou art to me lief°   *beloved*
and dear: spare not but throw it in."

Then Sir Bedivere returned again and took the sword in his
hand; and yet him thought sin and shame to throw away that noble
sword. And so eft° he hid the sword and returned again and told the   *again*
king that he had been at the water and done his commandment.

"What sawest thou there?" said the king.

"Sir," he said, "I saw nothing but waters wap° and waves wan."°   *lapping/dark*

"Ah, traitor unto me and untrue," said King Arthur, "now hast thou betrayed me twice! Who would ween° that thou who has been to me so lief and dear, and also named so noble a knight, that thou would betray me for the riches of this sword? But now go again lightly; for thy long tarrying putteth me in great jeopardy of my life, for I have taken cold. And but if° thou do now as I bid thee, if ever I may see thee, I shall slay thee mine own hands, for thou wouldest for my rich sword see me dead." — *believe* / *unless*

Then Sir Bedivere departed and went to the sword and lightly took it up, and so he went unto the water's side. And there he bound the girdle about the hilt, and threw the sword as far into the water as he might. And there came an arm and an hand above the water, and took it and cleight° it, and shook it thrice and brandished, and then vanished with the sword into the water. — *clutched*

So Sir Bedivere came again to the king and told him what he saw.

"Alas!" said the king, "help me hence, for I dread me I have tarried over long."

Then Sir Bedivere took the king upon his back and so went with him to the water's side. And when they were there, even fast by° the bank hoved° a little barge with many fair ladies in it, and among them all was a queen, and all they had black hoods. And all they wept and shrieked when they saw King Arthur. — *next to/floated*

"Now put me into that barge," said the king.

And so he did softly, and there received him three ladies with great mourning. And so they set him down, and in one of their laps King Arthur laid his head. And then the queen said,

"Ah, my dear brother!⁶ Why have you tarried so long from me? Alas, this wound on your head hath caught overmuch cold!"

And anon they rowed fromward° the land, and Sir Bedivere beheld all those ladies go fromward him. Then Sir Bedivere cried and said, — *away from*

"Ah, my lord Arthur, what shall become of me, now ye go from me and leave me here alone among mine enemies?"

"Comfort thyself," said the king, "and do as well as thou mayst, for in me is no trust for to trust in. For I must into the vale of Avalon to heal me of my grievous wound. And if thou hear nevermore of me, pray for my soul!"

But ever the queen and ladies wept and shrieked, that it was pity to hear. And as soon as Sir Bedivere had lost sight of the barge he wept and wailed, and so took° the forest and went all that night. — *went into*

And in the morning he was ware, betwixt two holts hoar°, of a chapel and an hermitage. Then was Sir Bedivere fain°, and thither he went, and when he came into the chapel he saw where lay an hermit grovelling° on all fours, fast thereby a tomb was new graven.° When the hermit saw Sir Bedivere he knew him well, for he was but little tofore Bishop of Canterbury, that Sir Mordred fleamed.° — *gray woods* / *glad* / *face down/freshly dug* / *put to flight*

"Sir," said Sir Bedivere, "what man is there here interred that you pray so fast° for?" — *intently*

6. The queen is thus revealed as Morgan le Fay, in whose story magical healing powers mixed with inveterate hostility to Guinevere and sometimes to Arthur himself.

"Fair son," said the hermit, "I wot not verily but by deeming.° *guessing*
But this same night, at midnight, here came a number of ladies and
brought here a dead corse and prayed me to inter him. And here they
offered an hundred tapers, and gave me a thousand besants."° *gold coins*

"Alas," said Sir Bedivere, "that was my lord King Arthur, which
lieth here graven° in this chapel." *buried*

Then Sir Bedivere swooned, and when he awoke he prayed the
hermit that he might abide with him still, there to live with fasting
and prayers:

"For from hence will I never go," said Sir Bedivere, "by my will,
but all the days of my life here to pray for my lord Arthur."

"Sir, ye are welcome to me," said the hermit, "for I know you
better than ye ween that I do: for ye are Sir Bedivere the Bold, and
the full noble duke Sir Lucan de Butler was your brother."

Then Sir Bedivere told the hermit all as you have heard
tofore, and so he beleft° with the hermit that was beforehand *remained*
Bishop of Canterbury. And there Sir Bedivere put upon him poor
clothes, and served the hermit full lowly in fasting and in prayers.

Thus of Arthur I find no more written in books that been
authorised, neither more of the very certainty of his death heard I
never read, but thus was he led away in a ship wherein were three
queens; that one was King Arthur's sister, Queen Morgan le Fay, the
tother was the Queen of North Galis, and the third was the Queen
of the Waste Lands.

Now more of the death of King Arthur could I never find, but
that these ladies brought him to his grave, and such one was interred
there which the hermit bare witness that sometime° Bishop of Can- *was once*
terbury. But yet the hermit knew not in certain that he was verily
the body of King Arthur; for this tale Sir Bedivere, a knight of the
Table Round, made it to be written.

Yet some men say in many parts of England that King Arthur is
not dead, but had° by the will of our Lord Jesu into another place; *was carried*
and men say that he shall come again, and he shall win the Holy
Cross. Yet I will not say that it shall be so, but rather I would say:
here in this world he changed his life. And many men say that there
is written upon the tomb this:

HIC IACET ARTHURUS REX QUONDAM REXQUE FUTURUS[7]

And thus leave I here Sir Bedivere with the hermit that dwelled
that time in a chapel beside Glastonbury, and there was his hermitage.
And so they lived in prayers and fastings and great abstinence.

And when Queen Guinevere understood that King Arthur was
dead and all the noble knights, Sir Mordred and all the remnant,
then she stole away with five ladies with her, and so she went to
Amesbury. And there she let make herself° a nun, and weared white *became*
clothes and black, and great penance she took upon her, as ever did
sinful woman in this land. And never creature could make her merry, but ever she lived in fasting, prayers and alms-deeds, that all
manner of people marvelled how virtuously she was changed.

---

7. Here lies Arthur, once and future king.

Geoffrey Chaucer
c. 1340–1400

On Easter weekend 1300, the Italian poet Dante Alighieri had a vision in which he descended to hell, climbed painfully through purgatory, and then attained a transcendent experience of paradise. He tells his tale in his visionary, passionately judgmental *Divine Comedy*. One hundred years later, on 25 October 1400, Geoffrey Chaucer—the least judgmental of poets—died quietly in his house at the outskirts of London. By a nice accident of history, these two great writers bracket the last great century of the Middle Ages.

Of Chaucer's own life our information is abundant but often frustrating. Many documents record the important and sensitive posts he held in government, but there are only faint hints of his career as a poet. During his lifetime, he was frequently in France and made at least two trips to Italy, which proved crucial for his own growth as a writer and indeed for the history of English literature. He also served under three kings: the aging Edward III, his brilliant and sometimes tyrannical grandson Richard II, and—at the very end of his life—Richard's usurper Henry IV.

Chaucer was born into a rising mercantile family, part of the growing bourgeois class that brought so much wealth to England even while it challenged medieval theories of social order. Chaucer's family fit nowhere easily in the old model of the three estates: those who pray (the clergy), those who fight (the aristocracy), and those who work the land (the peasants). Yet like many of their class, they aspired to a role among the aristocracy, and in fact Chaucer's parents succeeded in holding minor court positions. Chaucer himself became a major player in the cultural and bureaucratic life of the court, and Thomas Chaucer (who was very probably his son) was ultimately knighted.

Geoffrey was superbly but typically educated. He probably went to one of London's fine grammar schools, and as a young man he very likely followed a gentlemanly study of law at one of the Inns of Court. He shows signs of knowing and appreciating the topics debated in the university life of his time. His poems reflect a vast reading in classical Latin, French, and Italian (of which he was among the earliest English readers). *The Parliament of Fowls*, for instance, reveals the influence not only of French court poetry but also of Dante's *Divine Comedy*; and the frame-story structure of *The Canterbury Tales* may have been inspired by Boccaccio's *Decameron*.

By 1366 Chaucer had married Philippa de Roet, a minor Flemish noblewoman, and a considerable step up the social hierarchy. Her sister later became the mistress and ultimately the wife of Chaucer's great patron, John of Gaunt. Thus, when John's son Henry Bolingbroke seized the throne from Richard II, the elderly Geoffrey Chaucer found himself a distant in-law of his king. Chaucer had been associated with Richard II and suffered reverses when Richard's power was restricted by the magnates. But he was enough of a cultural figure that Henry IV continued (perhaps with some prompting) the old man's earlier annuities. Whatever western literature owes to Chaucer (and its debts are profound), in his own life his writing made a place in the world for him and his heirs.

Despite his lifelong productivity as a writer, and despite the slightly obtuse narrative voice he consistently uses, Geoffrey Chaucer was a canny and ambitious player in the world of his time. He was a soldier, courtier, diplomat, and government official in a wide range of jobs. These included controller of the customs on wool and other animal products, a lucrative post, and later controller of the Petty Custom that taxed wine and other goods. Chaucer's frequent work overseas extended his contacts with French and particularly Italian literature. He was ward of estates for several minors, a job that also benefited the guardian. Chaucer began to accumulate property in Kent, where he served as justice of the peace (an important judicial post) and then Member of Parliament in the mid-1380s.

Despite the comfortable worldly progress suggested by such activities, these were troubled years in the nation and in Chaucer's private life. Chaucer's personal fortunes were affected by the frequent struggles between King Richard and his magnates over control of the government. From another direction, the Peasants' Revolt exploded in 1381, rocking all of English society. The year before that, Chaucer had been accused of *raptus* by Cecilia Chaumpaigne, daughter of a baker in London. A great deal of nervous scholarship has been exercised over this case, but it becomes increasingly clear that in legal language *raptus* meant some form of rape. The case was settled, and there are signs of efforts to hush it up at quite high levels of government. The somewhat bland and bumbling quality of Chaucer's narrative persona would probably have seemed more artificially constructed and more ironic to Chaucer's contemporaries than it does at first glance today.

Chaucer was a Janus-faced poet, truly innovative at the levels of language and theme yet deeply involved with literary and intellectual styles that stretched back to Latin antiquity and twelfth- and thirteenth-century France. His early poems—the dream visions such as *The Parliament of Fowls* and the great romance *Troilus and Criseyde*—derive from essentially medieval genres and continental traditions: the French poets Deschamps and Machaut and the Italians Dante, Boccaccio, and Petrarch. Yet in his reliance on the English vernacular, Chaucer was in a vanguard generation along with the *Gawain* poet and William Langland. English was indeed gaining importance in other parts of this world, such as in Parliament, some areas of education, and in the "Wycliffite" translations of the Bible. Chaucer's own exclusive use of English was particularly ambitious, though, for a poet whose patronage came from the court of the francophile Richard II.

The major work of Chaucer's maturity, *The Canterbury Tales*, founds an indisputably English tradition. While he still uses the craft and allusions he learned from his continental

Portrait of Geoffrey the Canterbury Pilgrim, from an early 15th-century manuscript.

masters, he also experiments with the subject matter of everyday English life and the vocabularies of the newly valorized English vernacular. Moreover, starting with traditional forms and largely traditional models of society and the cosmos, Chaucer found spaces for new and sometimes disruptive perspectives, especially those of women and the rising mercantile class into which he had been born. Though always a court poet, Chaucer increasingly wrote in ways that reflected both the richness and the uncertainties of his entire social world. The *Tales* include a Knight who could have stepped from a twelfth-century *chanson de geste;* yet they also offer the spectacle of the Knight's caste being aped, almost parodied, and virtually shouted down by a sword-carrying peasant, the Miller. And the entire notion of old writings as sources of authoritative wisdom is powerfully challenged by the illiterate or only minimally literate Wife of Bath.

The *Canterbury Tales* also differ from the work of many of Chaucer's continental predecessors in their deep hesitation to cast straightforward judgment, either socially or spiritually. Here we may return to Chaucer's connection with Dante. His *Divine Comedy* presented mortal life as a pilgrimage and an overt test in stable dogma, a journey along a dangerous road toward certain damnation or the reward of the heavenly Jerusalem. The *Canterbury Tales* are literally about a pilgrimage, and Chaucer presents the road as beautiful and fascinating in its own right. The greatness of the poem lies in its exploration of the variousness of the journey and that journey's reflection of a world pressured by spiritual and moral fractures. In depicting a mixed company of English men and women traveling England's most famous pilgrimage route and telling one another stories, Chaucer shows us not only the spiritual meaning of humankind's earthly pilgrimage, but also its overflowing beauties and attractions as well as the evils and temptations that lie along the way. The vision of the serious future, the day of judgment, is constantly attended in *The Canterbury Tales* by the troubling yet hilarious and distracting present.

Unlike Dante, Chaucer almost never takes it upon himself to judge, at least not openly. He records his characters with dizzying immediacy, but he never tells his reader quite what to think of them, leaving the gaps for us as readers to fill. He does end the *Tales* with a kind of sermon, the Parson's long prose treatise on the Christian vices and virtues. That coda by no means erases the humor and seriousness, sentiment and ribaldry, high spiritual love and unmasked carnal desire, profound religious belief and squalid clerical corruption that have been encountered along the way. Indeed, Chaucer's genius is to transmute the disorder of his world almost into an aesthetic of plenitude: "foyson" in Middle English. His poem overflows constantly with rich detail, from exquisite visions to squabbling pilgrims. His language overflows with its multiple vocabularies, Anglo-Saxon, Latin, and French. And finally, the tales themselves are notable for the range of genres used by the pilgrims: the Miller's bawdy fabliau, the Wife of Bath's romance, the Nun's Priest's beast fable, the Pardoner's hypocritical cautionary tale, as well as the Parson's sermon. *The Canterbury Tales* are an anthology embracing almost every important literary type of Chaucer's day.

None of this celebratory richness, however, fully masks the unresolved social and spiritual tensions that underlie the *Tales*. The notion of spiritual pilgrimage is deeply challenged by the very density of characterization and worldly detail that so enlivens the work. And the model of a competitive game, which provides the fictional pretext for the tales themselves, is only one version of what the critic Peggy Knapp has called Chaucer's "social contest" in the work as a whole. The traditional estates such as knight and peasant openly clash during the pilgrimage, and the estate of the clergy is more widely represented by its corrupt than by its virtuous members. Women, merchants, common landowners, and others from outside the traditional three estates bulk large in the tales. And their stories cast doubt upon such fundamental religious institutions as penance and such social institutions as marriage. For all their pleasures, *The Canterbury Tales* have survived, in part, because they are so riven by challenge and doubt.

CHAUCER'S MIDDLE ENGLISH
Grammar

The English of Chaucer's London, and particularly the English of government bureaucracy, became the source for the more standardized vernacular that emerged in the era of print at the close of the Middle Ages. As a result, Chaucer's English is easier to understand today than the dialect of many of his great contemporaries such as the *Gawain* poet, who worked far to the north. The text that follows preserves Chaucer's language, with some spellings slightly modernized and regularized by its editor, E. Talbot Donaldson.

The marginal glosses in the readings are intended to help the nonspecialist reader through Chaucer's language without elaborate prior study. It will be helpful, though, to explain a few key differences from Modern English.

Nouns: The possessive is sometimes formed without a final *-s*.

Pronouns: Readers will recognize the archaic *thou, thine, thee* of second-person singular, and *ye* of the plural. Occasional confusion can arise from the form *hir*, which can mean "her" or "their." *Hem* is Chaucer's spelling for "them," and *tho* for "those." Chaucer uses *who* to mean "whoever."

Adverbs: Formed, as today, with *-ly*, but also with *-liche*. Sometimes an adverb is unchanged from its adjective form: *fairly, fairliche, faire* can all be adverbs.

Verbs: Second-person singular is formed with *-est* (*thou lovest*, past tense *thou lovedest*); thirdperson singular often with *-eth* (*he loveth*); plurals often with *-n* (*we loven*); and infinitive with *-n* (*loven*).

Strong verbs/impersonal verbs: Middle English has many "strong verbs," which form the past and perfect by changing a vowel in their stem; these are usually recognizable by analogy with surviving forms in Modern English (*go, went, gone; sing, sang, sung;* etc.). Middle English also often uses "impersonal verbs" (*liketh*, "it pleases"; *as me thinketh*, "as I think"), in which case sometimes no obvious subject noun or pronoun occurs.

Pronunciation

A few guidelines will help approximate the sound of Chaucer's English and the richness of his versification. For fuller discussion, consult sources listed in the bibliography.

Pronounce all consonants: *knight* is "k/neecht" with a guttural *ch*, not "nite"; *gnaw* is "g/naw." Middle English consonants preserve many of the sounds of the language's Germanic roots: guttural *gh*; sounded *l* and *w* in words like *folk* or *write*. (Exceptions occur in some words that derive from French, like *honour* whose *h* is silent.)

Final *-e* was sounded in early Middle English. Such pronunciation was becoming archaic by Chaucer's time, but was available to aid meter in the stylized context of poetry.

The distinction between short and long vowels was greater in Middle English than today. Middle English short vowels have mostly remained short in Modern English, with some shift in pronunciation: short *a* sounds like the *o* in *hot*, short *o* like a quick version of the *aw* in *law*, short *u* like the *u* in *full*.

Long vowels in Middle English are close to long vowels in modern Romance languages. The chart shows some differences in Middle English long vowels.

Middle English	pronounced as in	Modern English
a (as in *name*)		*father*
open *e* (*deel*)		*swear, bread*
close *e* (*sweet*)		*fame*
i (*whit*)		*feet*
open *o* (*holy*)		*law*
close *o* (*roote*)		*note*
u (as in *town, aboute*)		*root*
u (*Vertu*)		*few*

Open and close long vowels are a challenge for modern readers. Generally, open long *e* in Middle English (*deel*) has become Modern English spelling with *ea* (*deal*); close long *e* (*sweet*) has become Modern English spelling with *ee* (*sweet*). Open long *o* in Middle English has come to be pronounced as in *note*; close long *o* in Middle English has come to be pronounced *root*. This latter case illustrates the idea of "vowel shift," in which some long vowels have moved forward in the throat and palate across the centuries.

Versification

All of Chaucer's poetry presented here is in a loosely iambic pentameter line, which Chaucer was greatly responsible for bringing into prominence in England. He is a fluid versifier, though, and often shifts stress, producing metrical effects that have come to be called trochees and spondees. Final *-e* is often pronounced within lines to provide an unstressed syllable and is typically pronounced at the end of each line. Yet final *-e* may also elide with a following word that begins with a vowel. The following lines from *The Nun's Priest's Tale* have a proposed scansion, but the reader will see that alternate scansions are possible at several places.

> "Ăvoi," quod she, "fy on you, hertelees!
> Ăllas," quod she, "for by that God above,
> Now han ye lost myn herte and al my love!
> Ĭ can nat love a coward, by my faith.
> For certes, what so any womman saith,
> We alle desiren, if it mighte be,
> To han housbondes hardy, wise, and free,
> And secree, and no nigard, ne no fool,
> Ne him that is agast of every tool,
> Ne noon avauntour. By that God above,
> How dorste ye sayn for shame unto youre love
> That any thing mighte make you aferd?
> Have ye no mannes herte and han a beerd?

The Parliament of Fowls

The Parliament of Fowls initially seems to be a rather conventional poem of dream and courtly love. Yet it swiftly draws into play a surprising exploration of cosmic harmony and social order, and then a delightful critique of aristocratic courtliness in the voice of other classes. This multiplication of challenging perspectives is especially daring in a poem that may well have at its core a sophisticated allegory of Richard II's negotiations to wed Anne of Bohemia, in which (like Chaucer's tercel eagle) he faced vocal competitors. Certainly Chaucer employs and may have helped initiate the courtly convention of love play and love poems on Saint Valentine's day. For all its nerve and range, the *Parliament* (written in the late 1370s or early 1380s) is the work of a court poet, attentive to his patrons and audience.

Chaucer extends a pattern he had established in earlier dream-vision poems, in which the worlds of books, dreams, and experience interpenetrate and question one another. The narrator is presented as a feckless, unsuccessful lover who hesitates before tough choices. (His dream guide finally has to shove him into the garden.) He reads Cicero's famed survey of social order and the cosmos, *The Dream of Scipio*, then falls into a dream of his own that seems to derive instead from the literary conventions of the enclosed garden of love. The worlds of book and dream are surrounded by the narrator's own limited waking experience, and the garden of the dream erupts, in the parliament of birds, into a class-specific debate about love and procreation. In this, Chaucer's audience would have recognized echoes of the divisive English Parliaments of their own time.

The convention of dream vision in an enclosed garden draws upon French love poetry of the thirteenth and fourteenth centuries. Equally, the summary of Cicero's *Dream*, as well as the poem's broader reference to number and harmony, engage a tradition of cosmological and natural speculation important in late antiquity and the twelfth century. This includes texts like Alan of Lille's *Complaint of Nature* (specifically mentioned in the poem) and numerous commentaries on *The Dream of Scipio* itself, beginning with that by Macrobius. One way the poem reflects these neoplatonic concerns is its elaborate numerical structure. Cosmic symbolism linked the number seven to the created world and ten to the divine. The poem is written in "rime royal" (seven-line stanzas rhyming ABABBCC) and totals 699 or 700 lines and 100 or 101 stanzas, depending on how the closing roundel is presented. At a more local level, the seven chapters of *The Dream of Scipio* are summarized in seven stanzas; and the nine spheres and their harmony are first mentioned in stanza nine. The platonic notion of creation as an expression of divine love and plenitude emerges in the poem's exuberant catalogs of trees and birds.

Together these elements lead the narrator through multiple versions of love. The poem's numerological structure encloses a dream that includes, on the one hand, the erotic servitude and superheated frustration of Venus's temple, and on the other hand the eagerly fecund birds gathered to mate on the goddess Nature's hill. Yet these persistently mix, too, as early as the double message of the garden gate and as late as the courtly debate of the tercel eagles. Both versions of desire occupy the same garden.

In the parliament of birds the poem fully breaks out of its inherited conventions. While love debates often focus on an arcane issue of love-service, the *"demande d'amours,"* Chaucer's birds move swiftly past such gestures, even parodying them. These birds mimic a range of human social classes; and even while Chaucer allows his reader space to condescend to lower classes (like the worm-fowl), their perspectives also result in a lively critique of courtly love. The parliament also raises wider, more immediate issues of social order, public good, and simple propagation of the species.

Each order of birds chooses a spokesman, and each speaker is wonderfully characterized, as seen in the slightly fussy traditionalism of the tercel eagles, the dismissive tone of the duck, and the cuckoo's indifference to the rest so long as he gets his own mate. Yet the *Parliament* finally returns, by now from a far different angle, to the issues of social harmony and "commune profit" raised in the opening cosmological journey. The notions of a circular cosmos whose concentric spheres generate a musical harmony returns, too, in the form of the lyric rondel that closes the poem.

The Parliament of Fowls

The lif so short, the craft° so long to lerne,	skill
Th'assay° so sharp, so hard the conqueringe,	attempt
The dredful joye alway that slit° so yerne,°	slides away / quickly
Al this mene I by Love, that my feelinge	
5 Astonieth[1] with his wonderful werkinge	
So sore, ywis,° that whan I on him thinke,	certainly
Nat woot° I wel wher° that I flete° or sinke.	know / whether / float

For al be that I knowe nat Love in deede,	
Ne woot how that he quiteth° folk hir hire,°	repays / their wages
10 Yit happeth me ful ofte in bookes rede	

---

1. Turns to stone, is astonished.

Of his miracles and his cruel ire;
That rede I wel, he wol be lord and sire:
I dar nat sayn—his strokes been so sore—
But° "God save swich° a lord!"—I saye namore.   *except / such*

15   Of usage, what for lust and what for lore,[2]
On bookes rede I ofte, as I you tolde;
But wherfore° that I speke al this: nat yore°   *why / long*
Agoon it happed me for to biholde
Upon a book, was write with lettres olde;
20   And therupon, a certain thing to lerne,
The longe day ful faste I redde and yerne.°   *eagerly*

For out of olde feeldes, as men saith,
Cometh al this newe corn from yeer to yere;
And out of olde bookes, in good faith,
25   Cometh al this newe science that men lere.°   *learn*
But now to purpos as of this matere:
To rede forth so gan me to delite
That al that day me thoughte but a lite.°   *little while*

This book of which I make of mencioun
30   Entitled was al thus, as I shal telle:
"Tullius of the Dreem of Scipioun."[3]
Chapitres sevene it hadde, of hevene and helle
And erthe, and soules that therinne dwelle;
Of which as shortly as I can it trete,
35   Of his sentence° I wol you sayn the grete:°   *meaning / major part*

First telleth it when Scipion was come
In Affrike, how he meeteth Massinisse,[4]
That him for joye in armes hath ynome;[5]
Thanne telleth he[6] hir speeche, and of the blisse
40   That was bitwixe hem til that day gan misse;°   *disappeared*
And how his auncestre Affrican[7] so dere
Gan in his sleep that night to him appere.

Thanne telleth it that from a sterry place
How Affrican hath him Cartage shewed,
45   And warned him biforn of al his grace,°   *destiny*
And saide what man, lered other lewed,°   *learned or unlearned*
That loved commune profit,° wel ythewed,[8]   *public good*
He sholde into a blisful place wende,°   *go*
Ther as joye is° that last withouten ende.   *where there is joy*

50   Thanne axed he if folk that now been dede
Han lif and dwelling in another place;
And Affrican saide, "Ye, withouten drede,°   *doubt*
And that oure present worldes lives space

2. By habit, both for pleasure and for learning.
3. Macrobius' 4th- to 5th-century allegorical commentary
on Marcus Tullius Cicero's *Dream of Scipio*.
4. Masinissa, King of Numidia.
5. Took him in his arms, embraced him.

6. Cicero, in the book.
7. Scipio's ancestor, Scipio Africanus, who fought against
Hannibal in the Punic Wars.
8. Endowed with good qualities.

Nis but a manere deeth, what way we trace.[9]
55   And rightful folk shul goon after they die
To hevene"; and shewed him the Galaxye.

Thanne shewed he him the litel erthe that here is,
At regard of° the hevenes quantitee;   *in comparison to*
And after shewed he him the nine speres;[1]
60   And after that the melodye herde he
That cometh of thilke° speres thries three,   *such*
That welle° is of musik and melodye   *source*
In this world here, and cause of armonye.°   *harmony*

Thanne bad he him, sin erthe was so lite,°   *small*
65   And deceivable,° and ful of harde grace,   *deceiving*
That he ne sholde him in the world delite.
Thanne tolde he him in certain yeres space
That every sterre sholde come into his place,
Ther it was first, and al sholde out of minde
70   That in this world is doon of al mankinde.

Thanne prayed him Scipion to telle him al
The way to come into that hevene blisse;
And he saide, "Know thyself first immortal,
And looke ay bisily thou werke and wisse°   *instruct*
75   To commune profit, and thou shalt nat misse
To comen swiftly to this place dere,
That ful of blisse is, and of soules clere.°   *pure*

"But brekeres of the lawe, sooth° to sayne,   *truth*
And likerous° folk, after that they been dede   *lecherous*
80   Shul whirle aboute th'erthe alway in paine,
Til many a world be passed, out of drede,
And that° foryiven is hir wikked deede: *until*
Thanne shal they comen into this blisful place,
To which to comen, God sende thee his grace."

85   The day gan folwen° and the derke night,   *to follow*
That reveth° beestes from hir bisinesse,   *steals*
Birafte me my book for lak of light,
And to my bed I gan me for to dresse,
Fulfild of thought and bisy hevinesse:
90   For bothe I hadde thing which that I nolde,°   *did not want*
And eek I ne hadde that thing that I wolde.

But finally my spirit at the laste,
Forwery° of my labour al the day,   *exhausted*
Took reste, that made me to sleepe faste;
95   And in my sleep I mette,° as that I lay,   *dreamed*
How Affrican, right in the same array
That Scipion him saw bifore that tide,°   *time*
Was come, and stood right at my beddes side.

---

9. And that the length of our life in the present world / Is just a type of death, whatever path we take.
1. The seven planets, the sun, and the moon, thought to generate music through their revolutions around the earth.

The wery hunter, sleeping in his bed,
100   To wode ayain his minde gooth anoon;
The juge dremeth how his plees been sped;
The cartere dremeth how his carte is goon;
The riche, of gold; the knight fight with his foon;°   foes
The sike met he drinketh of the tonne;°.   cask
105   The lovere met he hath his lady wonne.

Can I nat sayn if that the cause were
For I hadde red of Affrican biforn,
That made me to mete that he stood there:
But thus saide he: "Thou hast thee so wel born
110   In looking of myn olde book totorn,°   tattered
Of which Macrobie roughte° nat a lite,   reckoned
That somdeel° of thy labour wolde I quite."°   somewhat /repay

Cytherea,° thou blisful lady sweete,   Venus
That with thy firbrand dauntest whom thee lest,°   it pleases
115   And madest me this swevene° for to mete,   dream
Be thou myn help in this, for thou maist best;
As wisly° as I sawgh thee north-north-west   certainly
Whan I bigan my swevene for to write,
So yif° me might to ryme and eek t'endite.   give

120   This forsaide Affrican me hente° anoon,   seized
And forth with him unto a gate broughte,
Right of a park walled with greene stoon,
And over the gates with lettres large ywroughte°   worked
Ther were vers ywriten, as me thoughte,
125   On either side, of ful greet difference,
Of which I shal now sayn the plein sentence:

"Thurgh me men goon into that blisful place
Of hertes hele° and deedly woundes cure;   health
Thurgh me men goon unto the welle of grace,
130   Ther greene and lusty May shal evere endure:
This is the way to al good aventure;
Be glad, thou redere, and thy sorwe of-caste;°   cast off
Al open am I: passe in, and speed thee faste."

"Thurgh me men goon," thanne spak that other side,
135   "Unto the mortal strokes of the spere
Of which Desdain and Daunger° is the gide,   Haughtiness
That nevere yit shal fruit ne leves bere;
This streem you ledeth to the sorweful were°   net
Ther as the fissh in prison is al drye:
140   Th'eschewing° is only the remedye."   avoiding

Thise vers of gold and blak ywriten were,
Of whiche I gan astonied to biholde,
Forwhy° that oon encreessed ay my fere,°   because/fear
And with that other gan myn herte bolde.
145   That oon me hette,° that other dide me colde: heated me up

No wit hadde I, for errour, for to chese°   choose
To entre or fleen, or me to save or lese.°   lose

Right as bitwixen adamantes° two   magnets
Of evene might, a pece of iren set
150   Ne hath no might to meve to ne fro—
For what that oon may hale,° that other let°—   welcome/stop
Ferde° I, that niste° whether me was bet   acted/did not know
To entre or leve, til Affrican my gide
Me hente, and shoof° in at the gates wide,   shoved

155   And saide, "It stant writen in thy face
Thyn errour, though thou telle it nat to me;
But dreed thee nat to come into this place,
For this writing nis no thing ment by thee,
Ne by noon but he Loves servant be;
160   For thou of love hast lost thy tast, I gesse,
As sik man hath of sweete and bitternesse.

"But nathelees, although that thou be dul,
Yit that thou canst nat do, yit maist thou see;
For many a man that may nat stonde a pul,[2]
165   It liketh him at wrastling for to be,
And deemen° yit wher he do bet or he.   judge
And ther, if thou haddest conning for t'endite,°   compose
I shal thee shewe matere for to write."

With that myn hand he took in his anoon,
170   Of which I confort caughte, and that as faste;
But Lord, so I was glad and wel bigoon,°   in a good situation
For overal wher that I mine yën° caste   eyes
Were trees clad with leves that ay° shal laste,   forever
Eech in his kinde, of colour fressh and greene
175   As emeraude, that joye was to seene.

The bildere ook,° and eek the hardy assh;   oak for building
The pilere elm, the cofre unto caraine;[3]
The boxtree pipere;° holm to whippes lassh;   for flutes
The sailing firre;[4] the cypres, deeth to plaine;°   to lament death
180   The shetere ew;[5] the asp° for shaftes plaine;°   aspen/smooth arrows
The olive of pees;° and eek the dronke° vine;   peace/drunken
The victour palm; the laurer to divine.[6]

A gardin saw I ful of blosmy boughes
Upon a river in a greene mede,°   meadow
185   Ther as the swetnesse everemore ynough is,
With flowres white, blewe, and yelowe, and rede,
And colde welle-stremes no thing dede,
That swimmen ful of smale fisshes lighte,
With finnes rede, and scales silver-brighte.

2. Withstand a fall (at wrestling).
3. The elm for making pillars, boxwood for corpses.
4. Fir tree for sailing (shipbuilding).
5. Yew for shooting (bows and arrows).
6. Laurel for divining oracles.

190   On every bough the briddes° herde I singe   *birds*
         With vois of angel in hir armonye;
         Some bisied hem hir briddes forth to bringe.
         The litel conies° to hir play gonne hie;   *rabbits*
         And ferther al aboute I gan espye
195   The dredful ro, the buk, the hert, the hinde,[7]
         Squireles, and beestes smale of gentil kinde.°   *noble nature*

         Of instruments of stringes in accord
         Herde I so playe a ravisshing swetnesse
         That God, that Makere is of al and Lord,
200   Ne herde nevere bettre, as I gesse.
         Therwith a wind, unnethe° it mighte be lesse,   *scarcely*
         Made in the leves greene a noise softe
         Accordant to the briddes song alofte.

         The air of that place so attempre° was   *temperate*
205   That nevere was grevance of hoot ne cold;
         Ther weex° eek every hoolsom spice and gras: *grew*
         No man may there waxe sik ne old.
         Yit was ther joye more than a thousandfold
         Than man can telle; ne nevere wolde it nighte,
210   But ay cleer day to any mannes sighte.

         Under a tree biside a welle I sey°   *saw*
         Cupide oure lord his arwes forge and file;
         And at his feet his bowe al redy lay,
         And Wil his doughter tempered al this while
215   The hevedes° in the welle, and with hir wile°   *(arrow)heads/skill*
         She couched° hem after they sholde serve,   *laid out*
         Some for to slee, and some to wounde and kerve.°   *cut*

         Tho was I war of Plesance anoon right,[8]
         And of Array, and Lust,° and Curteisye,   *Desire*
220   And of the Craft that can and hath the might
         To doon by force a wight to doon folye:
         Disfigurat was she, I nil nat lie.
         And by hemself under an ook, I gesse,
         Saw I Delit that stood by Gentilesse.°   *Nobility*

225   I saw Beautee withouten any attir,
         And Youthe ful of game and jolitee,
         Foolhardinesse, and Flaterye, and Desir,
         Messagerye,[9] and Meede,° and othere three—   *Bribery, Reward*
         Hir names shal nat here be told for me;
230   And upon pileres grete of jasper longe
         I saw a temple of bras yfounded stronge.

         Aboute that temple daunceden alway
         Wommen ynowe,° of whiche some ther were   *enough*

---

7. The timid female deer, the hart, the male red deer, the
female red deer.
8. The 19 virtues that follow are allegorical figures com-

mon in the Garden of Earthly Delights since the time of
The Romance of the Rose.
9. Sending of messengers between lovers.

235 Faire of hemself, and some of hem were gay;
In kirteles° al dischevele[1] wente they there: *frocks*
That was hir office° alway, yeer by yere.   *duty, business*
And on the temple of douves° white and faire   *doves*
Saw I sittinge many an hundred paire.

240 Bifore the temple-dore ful sobrely
Dame Pees sat with a curtin in hir hond,[2]
And by hir side, wonder discreetly,
Dame Pacience sitting ther I foond,
With face pale, upon an hil of sond;°   *sand*
245 And aldernext° withinne and eek withoute   *next of all*
Biheeste and Art, and of hir folk a route.[3]

Within the temple of sikes° hote as fir   *sighs*
I herde a swough° that gan aboute renne,   *groan*
Whiche sikes were engendred with desir,
250 That maden every auter° for to brenne   *altar*
Of newe flaumbe; and wel espied I thenne
That al the cause of sorwes that they drie°   *suffered*
Cometh of the bittre goddesse Jalousye.

The god Priapus[4] saw I, as I wente,
255 Within the temple in soverein place stonde,
In swich array as whan the asse him shente°[5]   *ruined*
With cry by night, and with his sceptre in honde;
Ful bisily men gonne assaye and fonde°   *attempt and strive*
Upon his heed to sette, of sondry hewe,
Gerlandes ful of flowres fresshe and newe.

260 And in a privee corner in disport
Foond I Venus and hir porter Richesse,
That was ful noble and hautain of hir port;°   *haughty in bearing*
Derk was the place, but afterward lightnesse
I saw a lite—unnethe it mighte be lesse;
265 And on a bed of gold she lay to reste,
Til that the hote sonne gan to weste.

Hire gilte heres° with a golden threed   *hairs*
Ybounden were, untressed° as she lay;   *unbraided*
And naked from the brest up to the heed
270 Men mighte hire seen; and soothly for to say,
The remenant was wel covered to my pay°   *pleasure*
Right with a subtil coverchief of Valence:[6]
Ther nas no thikker cloth of no defence.°   *of any protection*

The place yaf a thousand savours soote,°   *sweet smells*
275 And Bacus, god of win, sat hire biside,

---

1. With hair hanging loose.
2. The "curtin" may be a royal emblem of peace or mercy, the *cortina* or short sword used at the coronation of English kings, or alternately, the curtain in front of the Old Testament tabernacle.
3. Promise and Craft, and a crowd of their folk.

4. Roman god of gardens and of fertility, often depicted with an enormous phallus.
5. In Ovid's *Fasti* (1.415–40), the braying of an ass awakens the nymph whom Priapus was preparing to deflower.
6. Valencia was a center for producing finely woven textiles.

And Ceres next that dooth of hunger boote,°   *remedy*
And as I saide, amiddes lay Cypride,°   *Venus*
To whom on knees two yonge folk ther cride
To been hir help; but thus I leet hire lie,
280   And ferther in the temple I gan espye,

That, in despit of Diane the chaste,
Ful many a bowe ybroke heeng on the wal,
Of maidenes swiche as gonne hir times waste
In hir service; and painted overal
285   Ful many a storye, of which I touche shal
A fewe, as of Caliste and Atalante,[7]
And many a maide of which the name I wante.°   *lack*

Semiramis,[8] Candace, and Ercules,
Biblis, Dido, Thisbe, and Pyramus,
290   Tristam, Isoude, Paris, and Achilles,
Elaine, Cleopatre, and Troilus,
Sylla, and eek the moder of Romulus:
Alle thise were painted on that other side,
And al hir love, and in what plit they dyde.

295   Whan I was come ayain unto the place
That I of spak, that was so soote and greene,
Forth welk° I tho° myselven to solace;   *walked/then*
Tho was I war wher that ther sat a queene,
That as of light the someres sonne sheene
300   Passeth the sterre, right so over mesure
She fairer was than any creature.

And in a launde° upon an hil of flowres   *meadow*
Was set this noble goddesse Nature;
Of braunches were hir halles and hir bowres,
305   Ywrought after hir cast° and hir mesure;   *design*
Ne was ther fowl that cometh of engendrure°   *procreation*
That they ne were alle prest° in hir presence   *ready*
To take hir doom,° and yive hire audience.   *pass judgment*

For this was on Saint Valentines[9] day,
310   Whan every brid cometh ther to chese his make,°   *mate*
Of every kinde that men thinke may;
And that so huge a noise gan they make,
That erthe and air and tree and every lake

7. Callisto and Atalanta, two of the virgins dedicated to the cult of Diana, who later became famous lovers.
8. Semiramis, queen of Babylon and wife of King Ninus, conceived an incestuous passion for her own son; Candace, queen of India, fell in love with Alexander the Great and was the cause of his death by poisoning; Ercules (Hercules) was inadvertently slain by his jealous wife, Deianira; Biblis fell in love with her brother Caunus; Dido, queen of Carthage, was abandoned by her lover Aeneas, a Trojan prince and ancestor of the Romans; Thisbe and Piramus were lovers who met their deaths during a secret tryst in ancient Babylon; Tristram

and Isaude (Isolde) were adulterous lovers in Arthurian legend; Paris' abduction of Helen of Troy ("Elaine" in line 291) started the Trojan War; Achilles died in battle for love of Polyxena; Cleopatra lost her life and her kingdom in Egypt because of her love for Antony; Troilus died unhappily after his lover Criseyde left him; Sylla (Scylla), daughter of King Nisus of Athens, betrayed her city to her father's enemy, Minos, king of Crete, with whom she had fallen in love; the mother of Romulus was Rhea Silvia, a priestess of Diana.
9. This is the first mention of Valentine's Day in English literature.

So ful was that unnethe was ther space
315 For me to stonde, so ful was al the place.

And right as Alain in the "Plainte of Kinde"[1]
Deviseth° Nature in array and face,   *describes*
In swich array men mighte hire there finde.
This noble emperesse, ful of grace,
320 Bad every fowl to take his owene place,
As they were wont alway, from yeer to yere,
Saint Valentines day, to stonden there.

That is to sayn, the fowles of ravine°   *birds of prey*
Were hyest set, and thanne the fowles smale
325 That eten as hem Nature wolde encline.
As worm, or thing of which I telle no tale;
And waterfowl sat lowest in the dale;
But fowl that liveth by seed sat on the greene,
And that so fele° that wonder was to seene.   *many*

330 Ther mighte men the royal egle finde,
That with his sharpe look perceth the sonne;[2]
And othere egles of a lower kinde
Of whiche that clerkes wel devise conne;
Ther was the tyrant with his fetheres donne°   *brown*
335 And greye—I mene the goshawk—that dooth pine°   *cause pain*
To briddes for his outrageous ravine.

The gentil faucon that with his feet distraineth°   *seizes*
The kinges hand; the hardy sperhawk[3] eke,°   *also*
The quailes fo; the merlion[4] that paineth
340 Himself ful ofte the larke for to seeke;
Ther was the douve with hir yën meeke;
The jalous swan, ayains° his deeth that singeth;   *at the point of*
The owle eek that of deeth the bode° bringeth;   *foreboding*

The crane, geant with his trompes soun;
345 The theef, the chough,° and eek the jangling pie;[5]   *crow*
The scorning jay; the eeles fo, heroun;
The false lapwing, ful of trecherye;
The starling that the conseil can biwrye;°   *reveal (secrets)*
The tame rodok, and the coward kite;[6]
350 The cok, that orlogge is of thropes lite;[7]

The sparwe, Venus sone; the nightingale,
That clepeth° forth the greene leves newe;   *calls*
The swalwe, mortherere of the fowles smale°   *killer of bees*

---

1. *De Planctu Naturae* (*The Complaint of Nature*) was a
12th-century Latin allegorical poem by Alan of Lille, in
which the figure of Nature laments the irregularity of
human sexual practices. Within the text, all other creatures are shown to obey her laws, including the birds, the
"concilium avium" (the parliament of fowls), from which
Chaucer derives the title of his work.
2. The eagle was believed to be able to look directly

into the sun.
3. Sparrowhawk, a smaller member of the falcon species.
4. Merlin, another type of falcon.
5. The chattering magpie.
6. The ruddock is a European robin; the kite is another
kind of crow.
7. The rooster, that is the clock for little villages.

That maken hony of flowres fresshe of hewe;
355   The wedded turtel,° with hir herte trewe;   *turtledove*
The pecok, with his angeles clothes brighte;
The fesant, scornere of the cok by nighte;[8]

The wakere goos;[9] the cokkou evere unkinde;
The popinjay° ful of delicasye;   *parrot*
360   The drake, stroyere of his owene kinde;[1]
The stork,[2] the wrekere of avouterye;°   *adultery*
The hote cormerant of glotonye;
The raven wis; the crowe with vois of care;
The throstel° old; the frosty feeldefare.[3]   *thrush*

365   What sholde I sayn? Of fowles every kinde
That in this world hath fetheres and stature,
Men mighten in that place assembled finde,
Bifore the noble goddesse Nature;
And everich of hem dide his bisy cure°   *business*
370   Benignely to chese or for to take,
By hir accord, his formel or his make.

But to the point: Nature heeld on hir hond
A formel° egle, of shap the gentileste   *female*
That evere she among hir werkes foond,
375   The most benigne and the goodlieste:
In hire was every vertu at his reste,
So ferforth that Nature hirself hadde blisse
To looke on hire, and ofte hir beek to kisse.

Nature, vicarye° of the Almighty Lord   *deputy*
380   That hoot, cold, hevy, light, and moist and dreye
Hath knit with evene nombres of accord,
In esy vois gan for to speke and saye,
"Fowles, take heede of my sentence, I praye;
And for youre ese, in forthering of youre neede,
385   As faste as I may speke, I wol you speede.

"Ye knowe wel how, Saint Valentines Day,
By my statut and thurgh my governaunce,
Ye come for to chese—and flee youre way—
Youre makes as I prike° you with plesaunce.   *goad*
390   But nathelees, my rightful ordinaunce
May I nat breke, for al this world to winne,
That he that most is worthy shal biginne.

"The tercelet° egle, as that ye knowe ful weel,   *young male*
The fowl royal aboven every degree,
395   The wise and worthy, secree,° trewe as steel,   *discreet*
Which I have formed, as ye may wel see,

8. The pheasant was thought to mate with chickens during the night.
9. Geese were reputed to have wakened Rome against barbarian attack; the cuckoo was thought unnatural because it left its eggs in the nests of other birds.

1. Male ducks were thought to destroy their own offspring.
2. Storks were thought to kill their adulterous rivals.
3. Fieldfare, another kind of thrush.

In every part as it best liketh me—
It needeth nat his shap you to devise—
He shal first chese and speken in his gise.°   *manner*

400   "And after him by ordre shul ye chese,
After youre kinde, everich as you liketh,
And as youre hap is shul ye winne or lese—
But which of you that love most entriketh,°   *entraps*
God sende him hire that sorest for him siketh."

405   And therwithal the tercel gan she calle,
And saide, "My sone, the chois is to you falle.

"But nathelees, in this condicioun
Moot° be the chois of everich that is here: *must*
That she agree to his eleccioun,

410   What so he be that sholde be hir fere.°   *companion*
This is oure usage alway, from yeer to yere:
And who so may at this time have his grace,
In blisful time he cam into this place."

With heed enclined and with humble cheere°   *expression*

415   This royal tercel spak and taried nought:
"Unto my soverein lady, and nat my fere,°   *equal*
I chese, and chese with wil and herte and thought,
The formel on your hand, so wel ywrought,
Whos I am al, and evere wil hire serve,

420   Do what hire list to do me live or sterve;°   *die*

"Biseeking hire of mercy and of grace,
As she that is my lady sovereine—
Or lat me die present in this place:
For certes, longe I may nat live in paine,

425   For in myn herte is corven° every veine;   *cut*
And having reward° only to my trouthe,°   *regard/faithfulness*
My dere herte, have of my wo som routhe.°   *pity*

"And if that I to hire be founde untrewe,
Disobeisant, or wilful necligent,

430   Avauntour,° or in proces⁴ love a newe,   *boaster*
I praye to you, this be my juggement:
That with thise fowles be I al torent°   *torn apart*
That ilke day that evere she me finde
To hire untrewe, or in my gilt unkinde.

435   "And sin that hire loveth noon so wel as I—
Al be that she me nevere of love bihette°—   *promised*
Thanne oughte she be myn thurgh hir mercy,
For other bond can I noon on hire knette;°   *tie*
Ne nevere for no wo ne shal I lette°   *stop*

440   To serven hire, how fer so that she wende;
Saye what you list: my tale is at an ende."

4. The course of time.

Right as the fresshe, rede rose newe
Ayain the somer sonne coloured is,
Right so for shame al waxen gan the hewe
445   Of this formel, whan she herde al this.
She neither answerde wel, ne saide amis,
So sore abasshed° was she, til that Nature   *embarrassed*
Saide, "Doughter, drede you nought, I you assure."

Another tercel egle spak anoon,
450   Of lower kinde,° and saide, "That shal nat be!   *nature, lineage*
I love hire bet than ye doon, by saint John,
Or at the leeste I love as wel as ye,
And lenger have served hire in my degree:
And if she sholde have loved for long loving,
455   To me ful longe° hadde be the guerdoning.°   *long ago/reward*

"I dar eek sayn, if she me finde fals,
Unkinde,° or janglere,° or rebel in any wise,   *unnatural/gossip*
Or jalous, do me hangen by the hals;°   *neck*
And but I bere me in hir servise
460   As wel as that my wit can me suffise,
From point to point, hir honour for to save,
Take ye my lif, and al the good I have."

The thridde tercel egle answerde tho:
"Now, sires, ye seen the litel leiser here,
465   For every fowl crieth out to been ago
Forth with his make, or with his lady dere;
And eek Nature hirself ne wol nat heere,
For tarying here, nat half that I wolde saye;
And but I speke, I moot for sorwe deye:

470   "Of long service avaunte I me no thing—
But as possible is me to die today
For wo, as he that hath been languisshing
This twenty yeer; and as wel happen may
A man may serven bet, and more to pay,
475   In half a yeer, although it were no more,
Than som man dooth that hath served ful yore.

"I saye nat this by me, for I ne can
Doon no service that may my lady plese;
But I dar sayn I am hir trewest man,
480   As to my doom,° and fainest° wolde hire ese;   *judgment/gladly*
At shorte wordes, til that deeth me sese,°   *seize*
I wil been hires, whether I wake or winke,°   *sleep*
And trewe in al that herte may bithinke."

Of al my lif, sin that day I was born,
485   So gentil plee in love or other thing
Ne herde nevere no man me biforn,
Who that hadde leiser and conning
For to reherce hir cheere and hir speking:

And from the morwe gan this speeche laste,
490 Til downward drow the sonne wonder faste.

The noise of fowles for to been delivered
So loude roong: "Have doon, and lat us wende!"°   *go*
That wel wende° I the wode hadde al toslivered.[5]   *thought*
"Come of!" they criden, "allas, ye wole us shende.°   *ruin*
495 Whan shal youre cursed pleting° have an ende?   *pleading*
How sholde a juge either partye leve,°   *believe*
For ye or nay, withouten other preve?"

The goos, the cokkou, and the doke also
So cride, "Kek kek, cokkou, quek quek," hye
500 That thurgh mine eres the noise wente tho.
The goos saide, "Al this nis nat worth a flye!
But I can shape° herof a remedye: *arrange*
And I wol saye my verdit° faire and swithe°   *verdict/quickly*
For waterfowl, who so be wroth or blithe."°   *angry or happy*

505 "And I for wormfowl," quod the fool cokkou.
"And I wol of myn owene auctoritee,
For commune speed,° take on me the charge now: *profit*
For to delivere us is greet charitee."
"Ye may abide a while yit, pardee,"°   *by God*
510 Quod the turtel, "if it be youre wille:
A wight may speke him were as fair been stille.[6]

"I am a seedfowl, oon the unworthieste,
That woot° I wel, and litel of conninge;°   *know/understanding*
But bet is that a wightes tonge reste
515 Than entremetten° him of swich doinge   *interfere*
Of which he neither rede° can ne singe.   *advise*
And who so dooth, ful foule himself accloyeth:°   *overburdens*
For office uncommitted° ofte anoyeth."   *unassigned*

Nature, which that alway hadde an ere
520 To murmur of the lewednesse° bihinde,   *the uneducated*
With facound° vois saide, "Holde youre tonges there,   *eloquent*
And I shal soone, I hope, a conseil finde
You to delivere, and from this noise unbinde;
I jugge of every folk men shul oon calle
525 To sayn the verdit for you fowles alle."

Assented was to this conclusioun
The briddes alle; and fowles of ravine
Han chosen first, by plain eleccioun,
The tercelet of the faucon to diffine°   *state*
530 Al hir sentence,° as hem liste to termine;°   *opinion/conclude*
And to Nature him gonne to presente,
And she accepteth him with glad entente.°   *intention*

---

5. Broken into slivers.

6. "A creature may express himself, though he would have done better to keep quiet."

The tercelet saide thanne, "In this manere
Ful hard were it to preve by resoun
535 Who loveth best this gentil formel here,
For everich hath swich replicacioun,°   reply
That noon by skiles° may been brought adown.   arguments
I can nat see that arguments availe:
Thanne seemeth it ther moste be bataile."

540 "Al redy," quod thise egles tercels tho.
"Nay, sires," quod he, "if that I dorste it saye,
Ye doon me wrong, my tale is nat ydo.
For sires, ne taketh nat agrief, I praye,
It may nat goon as ye wolde in this waye:
545 Oure⁷ is the vois that han the charge on honde,
And to the juges doom ye moten stonde.

"And therfore, pees; I saye, as to my wit,
Me wolde thinke how that the worthieste
Of knighthood, and lengest hath used it,
550 Most of estaat, of blood the gentileste,
Were sittingest° for hire, if that hire leste;   most suitable
And of thise three she woot hirself, I trowe,
Which that he be, for hire is light° to knowe."   easy

The waterfowles han hir hedes laid
555 Togidre; and of a short avisement,°   deliberation
Whan everich hadde his large golee° said,   mouthful
They saiden soothly, alle by oon assent,
How that the goos, with hir facounde gent,°   noble eloquence
"That so desireth to pronounce oure neede
560 Shal telle oure tale," and prayed God hire speede.

As for thise waterfowles tho bigan
The goos to speke, and in hir cakelinge
She saide, "Pees, now take keep,° every man,   heed
And herkneth which a reson I shal bringe:
565 My wit is sharp, I love no taryinge.
I saye, I rede° him, though he were my brother,   counsel
But° she wil love him, lat him take another."   unless

"Lo, here a parfit° reson of a goos,"   perfect
Quod the sperhawk. "Nevere mote she thee!°   thrive
570 Lo, swich it is to have a tonge loos!
Now pardee, fool, now were it bet for thee
Han holde thy pees than shewe thy nicetee.°   simpleness
It lith nat in his might ne in his wille,
But sooth is said, a fool can nat be stille."

575 The laughtre aroos of gentil fowles alle,
And right anoon the seedfowl chosen hadde
The turtel trewe, and gonne hire to hem calle,
And prayed hire for to sayn the soothe sadde°   earnest

7. Royal "we," indicating the tercelet.

Of this matere, and axed what she radde:°   *advised*
580 And she answerde that plainly hir entente
She wolde it shewe, and soothly what she mente.

"Nay, God forbede a lovere sholde chaunge,"
The turtel saide, and weex for shame al reed.
"Though that his lady everemore be straunge,°   *reserved*
585 Yit lat him serve hire til that he be deed.
Forsoothe, I praise nat the gooses reed.°   *advice*
For though she dyde, I wolde noon other make:
I wil been hires til that the deeth me take."

"Wel bourded,"° quod the doke, "by myn hat!   *joked*
590 That men shal loven alway causelees—
Who can a reson finde or wit in that?
Daunceth he merye that is mirthelees?
What sholde I rekke° of him that is recchelees?   *care for*
Ye, queke," yit said the doke, ful wel and faire:
595 "Ther been mo sterres, God woot, than a paire."

"Now fy, cherl,"° quod the gentil° tercelet: *commoner/noble*
"Out of the donghil cam that word ful right.
Thou canst nat seen what thing is wel biset;°   *arranged*
Thou farest° by love as owles doon by light: *go about*
600 The day hem blent,° but wel they seen by night.   *blinds*
Thy kinde is of so lowe a wrecchednesse
That what love is thou canst nat seen ne gesse."

Tho gan the cokkou putte him forth in prees°   *in the midst*
For fowl that eteth worm, and saide blive,°   *quickly*
605 "So I," quod he, "may have my make in pees,
I recche nat how longe that ye strive.
Lat eech of hem be solein° al hir live,   *single*
This is my reed, sin they may nat accorde:
This shorte lesson needeth nat recorde."°   *repeat*

610 "Ye, have the gloton fild ynough his paunche,
Thanne are we wel," saide thanne a merlioun.
"Thou mortherere of the haysoge° on the braunche   *hedge sparrow*
That broughte thee forth, thou reweful° glotoun,   *pitiful*
Live thou solein, wormes corrupcioun,
615 For no fors is of lak of thy nature:[8]
Go, lewed° be thou whil that the world may dure."°   *ignorant/endure*

"Now pees," quod Nature, "I comande heer,
For I have herd al youre opinioun,
And in effect yit be we nevere the neer.°   *no closer*
620 But finally, this is my conclusioun:
That she hirself shal han the eleccioun
Of whom hire list; and who be wroth or blithe,
Him that she cheseth he shal hire have as swithe.°   *at once*

8. For it is no matter if your nature (lineage) disappears.

"For sin it may nat here discussed be

625 Who loveth hire best, as saith the tercelet,
Thanne wol I doon hire this favour, that she
Shal have right him on whom hir herte is set,
And he hire that his herte hath on hire knet.°   *joined*

630 Thus jugge I, Nature, for I may nat lie:
To noon estaat have I noon other yë.

"But as for conseil for to chese a make,
If I were Reson, certes thanne wolde I
Conseile you the royal tercel take—
As saide the tercelet ful skilfully—

635 As for the gentileste and most worthy,
Which I have wrought so wel to my pleasaunce
That to you oughte it been a suffisaunce."°   *sufficient*

With dredful° vois the formel tho answerde,   *timid*
"Myn rightful lady, goddesse of Nature,

640 Sooth is that I am evere under youre yerde,°   *rod, authority*
As is another lives creature,
And moot been youre whil that my lif may dure;
And therfore, graunteth me my firste boone,°   *request*
And myn entente you wol I sayn wel soone."

645 "I graunte it you," quod she. And right anoon
This formel egle spak in this degree:
"Almighty queene, unto° this yeer be goon,   *until*
I axe respit for to avise me,
And after that to have my chois al free:

650 This al and som that I wol speke and saye;
Ye gete namore although ye do me deye.°   *kill me*

"I wol nat serve Venus ne Cupide
Forsoothe, as yit, by no manere waye."
"Now, sin it may noon otherwise bitide,"

655 Quod tho Nature, "here is namore to saye.
Thanne wolde I that thise fowles were awaye,
Eech with his make, for tarying° lenger here,"   *to avoid delaying*
And saide hem thus, as ye shul after heere.

"To you speke I, you tercelets," quod Nature.

660 "Beeth of good herte, and serveth alle three:
A yeer is nat so longe to endure,
And eech of you paine him in his degree
For to do wel; for God woot, quit° is she   *released*
Fro you this yeer, what after so bifalle:

665 This entremes⁹ is dressed° for you alle."   *prepared*

And whan this werk al brought was to an ende,
To every fowl Nature yaf his make
By evene accord,° and on hir way they wende.   *mutual agreement*
But Lord, the blisse and joye that they make,

---

9. Either food or an entertainment given in between main courses.

670 For eech gan other in his winges take,
And with hir nekkes eech gan other winde,
Thanking alway the noble queene of Kinde.°   *Nature*

But first were chosen fowles for to singe—
As yeer by yere was alway the usaunce—
675 To singe a roundel[1] at hir departinge,
To doon to Nature honour and plesaunce.
The note, I trowe, ymaked was in Fraunce;
The wordes were swiche as ye may here finde
The nexte vers, as I now have in minde.

680 "Now welcome, somer, with thy sonne softe,
That hast thise wintres wedres° overshake,   *storms*
And driven away the large nightes blake.
Saint Valentin, that art ful heigh on lofte,
Thus singen smale fowles for thy sake:
685 Now welcome, somer, with thy sonne softe,
That hast thise wintres wedres overshake,
And driven away the large nightes blake.

"Wel han they cause for to gladen ofte,
Sith° eech of hem recovered hath his make;   *since*
Ful blisful mowe° they singe whan they wake;   *may*
Now welcome, somer, with thy sonne softe,
That hast thise wintres wedres overshake,
And driven away the large nightes blake."

And with the shouting, whan the song was do,
695 That fowles maden at hir flight away,
I wook, and othere bookes took me to
To rede upon, and yit I rede alway,
In hope, ywis, to rede so somday,
That I shal mete° somthing for to fare   *dream*
700 The bet, and thus to rede I nil nat spare.

FROM **THE CANTERBURY TALES**
The General Prologue

The twenty-nine "sondry folke" of the Canterbury company gather at the Tabard Inn, ostensibly with the pious intent of making a pilgrimage to England's holiest shrine, the tomb of Saint Thomas Becket at Canterbury. From the start in the raffish and worldly London suburb of Southwerk, though, the pilgrims' attentions and energy veer wildly between the sacred and the profane. The mild story-telling competition proposed by the Host also slides swiftly into a contest among social classes. Set in Chaucer's own time and place, *The Canterbury Tales* reflect both the dynamism and the uncertainties of a society still nostalgic for archaic models of church and state, yet riven by such crises as plague, economic disruption, and the new claims of peasants and mercantile bourgeois—claims expressed and repressed most violently in the recent Rising, or "Peasants' Revolt," of 1381.

Chaucer's *Prologue* has roots in the genre known as "estates satire." Such writings criticized the failure of the members of the three traditional "estates" of medieval society—the aristocracy, the clergy, and the commons—to fulfill their ordained function of fighting, praying, and working the

---

1. Rondo, a song with repeating refrain which originated in France.

land, respectively. From the beginning the pilgrims' portraits are couched in language fraught with class connotations. The Knight, the idealized (if archaic) representative of the aristocracy, is called *gentil* (that is, "noble, aristocratic") and is said never to have uttered any *vileynye*—speech characteristic of peasants or *villeyns*. Many of the pilgrims in the other two estates display aristocratic manners, among the clergy notably the Prioress, with her "cheere of court," and the Monk, who lives like a country gentleman, hunting with greyhounds and a stable full of fine horses. Both pilgrims contrast with the ideal of their estate, the Parson, who, though "*povre*" is "rich" in holy works.

The commons are traditionally the last of the "three estates," yet they bulk largest in the Canterbury company and fit least well in that model of social order. There are old-fashioned laborers on the pilgrimage, but many more characters from the emerging and disruptive world of small industry and commerce. They are commoners, but hate ambitions that lend them both to envy and to mock the powers held by their aristocratic and clerical companions.

Among the group that traditionally comprised the commons, the peasants, Chaucer singles out one ideal, the Plowman, who is, significantly, the Parson's brother. He is characterized as a diligent *swynkere* (worker), in implicit contrast to the lazy peasants castigated in estates satire. Most of the rest of the commons, however, such as the Miller and the Cook, are presented as "churlish," and their tales have a coarse vigor that Chaucer clearly relishes even as he disassociates himself from their vulgarity.

In theory, women were treated as a separate category, defined by their sexual nature and marital role rather than by their class. Nevertheless, the Prioress and the Wife of Bath are both satirized as much for their social ambition as for the failings of their gender. The Prioress prides herself on her courtesy, and the commoner Wife of Bath aspires to the same social recognition as the guildsmen's upwardly mobile wives. Her portrait is complex, however, for she is simultaneously satirized and admired for challenging the expected roles of women at the time, with her economic independence (as a rich widow and a cloth-maker) and her resultant freedom to travel. The narrator's suggestion that she goes on many pilgrimages in order to find a sixth husband bears out the stereotype of unbridled female sexuality familiar from estates satire, as her fondness of talking and laughing bears out the stereotype of female garrulousness.

Chaucer's satire is pointed but also exceptionally subtle, largely because of the irony achieved through his use of the narrator, seemingly naive and a little dense. His deadpan narration leaves the readers themselves to supply the judgment.

FROM THE CANTERBURY TALES
The General Prologue

	Whan that April with his showres soote°	*sweet*
	The droughte of March hath perced to the roote,	
	And bathed every veine in swich licour,°	*such liquid*
	Of which vertu° engendred is the flowr;	*by whose strength*
5	Whan Zephyrus[1] eek° with his sweete breeth	*also*
	Inspired hath in every holt and heeth°	*wood and field*
	The tendre croppes, and the yonge sonne	
	Hath in the Ram° his halve cours yronne,	*the zodiac sign Aries*
	And smale fowles maken melodye	
10	That sleepen al the night with open yë°—	*eye*
	So priketh hem Nature in hir corages°—	*hearts, spirits*
	Thanne longen folk to goon on pilgrimages,	
	And palmeres[2] for to seeken straunge strondes°	*shores*
	To ferne halwes,° couthe° in sondry londes;	*far-off shrines / known*
15	And specially from every shires ende	

1. In Roman mythology Zephyrus was the demigod of the west wind, herald of warmer weather.   2. Pilgrims who had traveled to the Holy Land.

Of Engelond to Canterbury they wende,
The holy blisful martyr[3] for to seeke
That hem hath holpen° whan that they were seke.°   *helped/sick*
   Bifel that in that seson on a day,
20   In Southwerk[4] at the Tabard as I lay,
Redy to wenden on my pilgrimage
To Canterbury with ful devout corage,
At night was come into that hostelrye
Wel nine and twenty in a compaignye
25   Of sondry folk, by aventure yfalle
In felaweshipe, and pilgrimes were they alle
That toward Canterbury wolden ride.
The chambres° and the stables weren wide,   *guestrooms*
And wel we weren esed° at the beste.   *accommodated*
30   And shortly, whan the sonne was to reste,
So hadde I spoken with hem everichoon
That I was of hir felaweshipe anoon,
And made forward° erly for to rise,   *agreed*
To take oure way ther as I you devise.°   *relate*
35   But nathelees, whil I have time and space,°   *opportunity*
Er that I ferther in this tale pace,°   *proceed*
Me thinketh it accordant to resoun
To telle you al the condicioun°   *circumstances*
Of eech of hem, so as it seemed me,
40   And whiche they were, and of what degree,°   *social status*
And eek in what array that they were inne:
And at a knight thanne wol I first biginne.
   A Knight ther was, and that a worthy man,
That fro the time that he first bigan
45   To riden out, he loved chivalrye,
Trouthe and honour, freedom and curteisye.[5]
Ful worthy was he in his lordes werre,°   *war*
And therto hadde he riden, no man ferre,°   *farther*
As wel in Cristendom as hethenesse,°   *heathen lands*
50   And evere honoured for his worthinesse.
   At Alisandre[6] he was whan it was wonne;
Ful ofte time he hadde the boord bigonne[7]
Aboven alle nacions in Pruce;
In Lettou had he reised,° and in Ruce,   *campaigned*
55   No Cristen man so ofte of his degree;
In Gernade at the sege eek hadde he be
Of Algezir, and riden in Belmarye;
At Lyeis was he, and at Satalye,

---

3. St. Thomas Becket, murdered in Canterbury Cathedral in 1170.
4. Southwark, a suburb of London south of the Thames and the traditional starting point for the pilgrimage to Canterbury in Kent, was notorious as a center of gambling and prostitution. The Tabard Inn was an actual public house at the time, named for the shape of its sign which resembled the coarse, sleeveless outergarment worn by members of the lower classes, monks, and footsoldiers alike.
5. Fidelity and good reputation, generosity and courtliness.

6. The place-names Chaucer lists over the next 15 lines were primarily associated with 14th-century Crusades against both Moslems and Eastern Orthodox Christians. Alisandre: Alexandria in Egypt; Pruce: Prussia; Lettou: Lithuania; Ruce: Russia; Gernade and Algezir: Granada and Algeciras in Spain; Belmarye: Ben-Marin near Morocco; Lyeis: Ayash in Turkey; Satalye: Atalia in Turkey; Grete See: Mediterranean; Tramissene: Tlemcen near Morocco; Palatye: Balat in Turkey.
7. Held the place of honor at feasts.

Whan they were wonne; and in the Grete See

60 At many a noble arivee° hadde he be.   *military landing*

At mortal batailes[8] hadde he been fifteene,

And foughten for oure faith at Tramissene

In listes° thries, and ay° slain his fo.   *duels/always*

This ilke° worthy Knight hadde been also   *same*

65 Somtime with the lord of Palatye

Again° another hethen in Turkye;   *against*

And everemore he hadde a soverein pris.°   *reputation*

And though that he were worthy, he was wis,

And of his port° as meeke as is a maide.   *bearing*

70 He nevere yit no vilainye° ne saide   *rudeness*

In al his lif unto no manere wight:

He was a verray,° parfit,° gentil° knight.   *true/perfect/noble*

But for to tellen you of his array,°   *equipment*

His hors were goode, but he was nat gay.°   *gaily attired*

75 Of fustian° he wered a gipoun°   *coarse cloth/tunic*

Al bismotered with his haubergeoun,[9]

For he was late come from his viage,°   *expedition*

And wente for to doon his pilgrimage.

With him ther was his sone, a yong Squier,

80 A lovere and a lusty bacheler,[1]

With lokkes crulle° as they were laid in presse.   *curled*

Of twenty yeer of age he was, I gesse.

Of his stature he was of evene° lengthe,   *average*

And wonderly delivere,° and of greet strengthe.   *agile*

85 And he hadde been som time in chivachye°   *cavalry expedition*

In Flandres, in Artois, and Picardye,[2]

And born him wel as of so litel space,°   *time*

In hope to stonden in his lady grace.°   *lady's favor*

Embrouded° was he as it were a mede,°   *embroidered/meadow*

90 Al ful of fresshe flowres, white and rede;

Singing he was, or floiting,° al the day: *playing the flute*

He was as fressh as is the month of May.

Short was his gowne, with sleeves longe and wide.

Wel coude he sitte on hors, and faire ride;

95 He coude songes make, and wel endite,°   *compose*

Juste° and eek daunce, and wel portraye° and write.   *joust/draw*

So hote he loved that by nightertale°   *nighttime*

He slepte namore than dooth a nightingale.

Curteis he was, lowely,° and servisable,°   *humble/attentive*

100 And carf° biforn his fader at the table   *carved*

A Yeman[3] hadde he° and servants namo   *(the Knight)*

At that time, for him liste° ride so;   *he liked*

And he was clad in cote and hood of greene.

A sheef of pecok arwes,° bright and keene,   *peacock arrows*

---

8. Tournaments waged to the death.
9. Rust-stained from his coat of mail.
1. An unmarried and unpropertied younger knight.
2. Regions in the north of France and in what is now Belgium, where the English and the French were fighting out

the Hundred Years' War.
3. A yeoman was a freeborn servant (not a peasant), who
looked after the affairs of the gentry. This particular yeoman was a forester and gamekeeper for the Knight.

105   Under his belt he bar ful thriftily;
       Wel coude he dresse° his takel° yemanly: *arrange/gear*
       His arwes drouped nought with fetheres lowe.
       And in his hand he bar a mighty bowe.
       A not-heed° hadde he with a brown visage.°   *short haircut/face*
110   Of wodecraft° wel coude he al the usage.   *forestry*
       Upon his arm he bar a gay bracer,°   *archer's armguard*
       And by his side a swerd and a bokeler,°   *small shield*
       And on that other side a gay daggere,
       Harneised wel and sharp as point of spere;
115   A Cristophre[4] on his brest of silver sheene;
       An horn he bar, the baudrik° was of greene.   *shoulder strap*
       A forster° was he soothly, as I gesse.   *gamekeeper*
          Ther was also a Nonne, a Prioresse,
       That of hir smiling was ful simple and coy.°   *quiet, shy*
120   Hir gretteste ooth was but by Sainte Loy![5]
       And she was cleped° Madame Eglantine.°   *called/Briar-rose*
       Ful wel she soong the service divine,
       Entuned in hir nose ful semely;
       And Frenssh she spak ful faire and fetisly,°   *elegantly*
125   After the scole of Stratford at the Bowe[6]—
       For Frenssh of Paris was to hire unknowe.
       At mete° wel ytaught was she withalle: *meals*
       She leet no morsel from hir lippes falle,
       Ne wette hir fingres in hir sauce deepe;
130   Wel coude she carye a morsel, and wel keepe°   *safeguard*
       That no drope ne fille upon hir brest.
       In curteisye was set ful muchel hir lest.°   *her great pleasure*
       Hir over-lippe° wiped she so clene   *upper lip*
       That in hir coppe ther was no ferthing[7] seene
135   Of grece,° whan she dronken hadde hir draughte;   *grease*
       Ful semely after hir mete she raughte.°   *reached for her food*
       And sikerly° she was of greet disport,°   *certainly/good cheer*
       And ful plesant, and amiable of port,
       And pained hire to countrefete cheere°   *appearance*
140   Of court, and to been estatlich° of manere,   *stately*
       And to been holden digne° of reverence.   *worthy*
       But, for to speken of hir conscience,
       She was so charitable and so pitous
       She wolde weepe if that she saw a mous
145   Caught in a trappe, if it were deed or bledde.
       Of smale houndes hadde she that she fedde
       With rosted flessh,° or milk and wastelbreed;[8]   *meat*
       But sore wepte she if oon of hem were deed,
       Or if men smoot° it with a yerde° smerte;°   *hit/rod/painfully*
150   And al was conscience and tendre herte.

4. Medal of St. Christopher, patron saint of travelers.
5. St. Eligius, patron saint of metalworkers, believed never to have sworn an oath in his life.
6. From the school (i.e., after the manner) of Stratford, a suburb of London where the prosperous convent of St.

Leonard's was located; her French is Anglo-Norman as opposed to the French spoken on the Continent.
7. Spot the size of a farthing.
8. Bread of the finest quality.

Ful semely hir wimpel[9] pinched was,
Hir nose tretis,° hir yën greye as glas,   *shapely*
Hir mouth ful smal, and therto softe and reed—
But sikerly she hadde a fair forheed:
155 It was almost a spanne[1] brood, I trowe,°   *believe*
For hardily,° she was nat undergrowe.°   *assuredly/short*
Ful fetis° was hir cloke, as I was war;   *elegant*
Of smal coral aboute hir arm she bar
A paire of bedes, gauded al with greene,[2]
160 And theron heeng a brooch of gold ful sheene,
On which ther was first writen a crowned A.[3]
And after, *Amor vincit omnia*.[4]
    Another Nonne with hire hadde she
That was hir chapelaine,° and preestes three.   *secretary*
165   A Monk ther was, a fair for the maistrye,°   *very good-looking*
An outridere[5] that loved venerye,°   *hunting*
A manly° man, to been an abbot able.   *courageous*
Ful many a daintee° hors hadde he in stable,   *fine*
And whan he rood, men mighte his bridel heere
170 Ginglen° in a whistling wind as clere   *jingling*
And eek as loude as dooth the chapel belle
Ther as this lord was kepere of the celle.[6]
The rule of Saint Maure or of Saint Beneit,[7]
By cause that it was old and somdeel strait°—   *somewhat strict*
175 This ilke Monk leet olde thinges pace,
And heeld after the newe world the space.°   *the times (customs)*
He yaf nought of that text° a pulled° hen   *regulation/plucked*
That saith that hunteres been nought holy men,
Ne that a monk, whan he is recchelees,°   *careless*
180 Is likned til a fissh that is waterlees—
This is to sayn, a monk out of his cloistre;
But thilke° text heeld he nat worth an oystre.   *that same*
And I saide his opinion was good:
What sholde he studye and make himselven wood°   *crazy*
185 Upon a book in cloistre alway to poure,
Or swinke° with his handes and laboure,   *work*
As Austin[8] bit?° How shal the world be served?   *orders*
Lat Austin have his swink to him reserved!
Therfore he was a prikasour° aright.   *hunter on horseback*
190 Grehoundes he hadde as swift as fowl in flight.
Of priking and of hunting for the hare
Was al his lust,° for no cost wolde he spare.   *pleasure*
I sawgh his sleeves purfiled° at the hand   *fur-lined*

9. A pleated headdress covering all but the face, such as nuns and married women wore.
1. A hand's width, 7 to 9 inches.
2. A set of rosary beads, marked off by larger beads (gauds) to indicate where the Paternosters should be said.
3. The letter "A" with a crown on top.
4. Love conquers all (Virgil, *Eclogues*, 10.69). Though pagan and secular in origin, the phrase was often used to refer to divine love as well.

5. A monk who worked outside the confines of the monastery.
6. Supervisor of the outlying cell of the monastery.
7. St. Benedict (Beneit) was the founder of Western monasticism, and his Rule prohibited monks from leaving the grounds of the monastery without special permission. St. Maurus introduced the Benedictine order into France.
8. St. Augustine recommended that monks perform manual labor.

With gris,° and that the fineste of a land;   *gray fur*
195 And for to festne his hood under his chin
He hadde of gold wrought a ful curious° pin: *elaborate*
A love-knotte[9] in the grettere° ende ther was.   *larger*
His heed was balled,° that shoon as any glas,   *bald*
And eek his face, as he hadde been anoint:
200 He was a lord ful fat and in good point;°   *in good shape*
His yën steepe,° and rolling in his heed,   *bright*
That stemed as a furnais of a leed;[1]
His bootes souple,° his hors in greet estat[2]—   *supple*
Now certainly he was a fair prelat.[3]
205 He was nat pale as a forpined° gost: *tormented*
A fat swan loved he best of any rost.
His palfrey° was as brown as is a berye.   *saddle horse*
    A Frere° ther was, a wantoune[4] and a merye,   *Friar*
A limitour,[5] a ful solempne man.
210 In alle the ordres foure[6] is noon that can°   *knows*
So muche of daliaunce° and fair langage: *flirtation*
He hadde maad ful many a mariage
Of yonge wommen at his owene cost;
Unto his ordre he was a noble post.°   *pillar*
215 Ful wel biloved and familier was he
With frankelains[7] over al in his contree,
And with worthy wommen of the town—
For he hadde power of confessioun,
As saide himself, more than a curat,°   *parish priest*
220 For of his ordre he was licenciat.[8]
Ful swetely herde he confessioun,
And plesant was his absolucioun.
He was an esy man to yive penaunce
Ther as he wiste to have a good pitaunce;[9]
225 For unto a poore ordre for to yive
Is signe that a man is wel yshrive;°   *absolved*
For if he yaf, he dorste make avaunt°   *boast*
He wiste that a man was repentaunt;
For many a man so hard is of his herte
230 He may nat weepe though him sore smerte:°   *hurts*
Therfore, in stede of weeping and prayeres,
Men mote yive silver to the poore freres.
    His tipet° was ay farsed° ful of knives   *scarf/packed*
And pinnes, for to yiven faire wives;
235 And certainly he hadde a merye note;
Wel coude he singe and playen on a rote;°   *fiddle*
Of yeddinges° he bar outrely the pris;[1]   *singing ballads*
His nekke whit was as the flowr-de-lis;[2]

9. An elaborate knot.
1. Glowed like a furnace under a cauldron.
2. Excellent condition.
3. Prelate, important churchman.
4. Jovial, pleasure-seeking.
5. Friar licensed by his order to beg for alms within a given district.

6. The four orders of friars were the Carmelites, Augustinians, Dominicans, and Franciscans.
7. Franklins, important property holders.
8. Licensed by the Church to hear confessions.
9. Where he knew he would get a good donation.
1. Utterly took the prize.
2. Lily, emblem of the royal house of France.

Therto he strong was as a champioun.

240   He knew the tavernes wel in every town,
And every hostiler and tappestere,°   *innkeeper and barmaid*
Bet than a lazar or a beggestere.°   *a leper or a beggar*
For unto swich a worthy man as he
Accorded nat, as by his facultee,°3   *official position*

245   To have with sike lazars aquaintaunce:
It is nat honeste,° it may nought avaunce,°   *dignified/profit*
For to delen with no swich poraile,°   *poor people*
But al with riche, and selleres of vitaile;°   *food*
And over al ther as profit sholde arise,

250   Curteis he was, and lowely° of servise.   *humble*
Ther was no man nowher so vertuous:°   *capable*
He was the beste beggere in his hous.
And yaf a certain ferme for the graunt:4
Noon of his bretheren cam ther in his haunt.°   *territory*

255   For though a widwe hadde nought a sho,
So plesant was his *In principio*5
Yit wolde he have a ferthing er he wente;
His purchas° was wel bettre than his rente.°   *income/expense*
And rage° he coude as it were right a whelpe;°   *flirt/puppy*

260   In love-dayes6 ther coude he muchel helpe,
For ther he was nat lik a cloisterer,
With a thredbare cope, as is a poore scoler,
But he was lik a maister° or a pope.   *professor*
Of double worstede was his semicope,°7   *short cloak*

265   And rounded as a belle out of the presse.°   *bell-mold*
Somwhat he lipsed for his wantounesse
To make his Englissh sweete upon his tonge;
And in his harping, whan that he hadde songe,
His yën twinkled in his heed aright

270   As doon the sterres in the frosty night.
This worthy limitour was cleped Huberd.

    A Marchant was ther with a forked beerd,
In motlee,° and hye on hors he sat,   *multicolored fabric*
Upon his heed a Flandrissh° bevere hat,   *Flemish*

275   His bootes clasped faire and fetisly.°   *elegantly*
His resons° he spak ful solempnely,   *opinions*
Souning° alway th'encrees of his winning.   *announcing*
He wolde the see were kept for any thing°   *protected at all costs*
Bitwixen Middelburgh and Orewelle.8

280   Wel coude he in eschaunge sheeldes9 selle.
This worthy man ful wel his wit bisette:°   *employed*
Ther wiste° no wight that he was in dette,   *knew*
So estatly° was he of his governaunce,°   *dignified/management*
With his bargaines, and with his chevissaunce.°   *borrowing*

---

3. It was unbecoming to his official post.
4. And gave a certain fee for the license to beg.
5. "In the beginning," the opening line in Genesis and the Gospel of John, popular for devotions.
6. Holidays for settling disputes out of court.

7. His short cloak was made of thick woolen cloth.
8. Middleburgh in the Netherlands and Orwell in Suffolk were major ports for the wool trade.
9. Unit of exchange, a credit instrument for foreign merchants.

285   Forsoothe he was a worthy man withalle;
        But, sooth to sayn, I noot° how men him calle.   *do not know*
          A Clerk ther was of Oxenforde also
        That unto logik hadde longe ygo.
        As lene was his hors as is a rake,
290   And he was nought right fat, I undertake,
        But looked holwe, and therto sobrely.
        Ful thredbare was his overeste courtepy,°   *outer cloak*
        For he hadde geten him yit no benefice,°   *church income*
        Ne was so worldly for to have office.°   *secular employment*
295   For him was levere° have at his beddes heed   *rather*
        Twenty bookes, clad in blak or reed,
        Of Aristotle and his philosophye,
        Than robes riche, or fithele,° or gay sautrye.°   *fiddle / harp*
        But al be that he was a philosophre[1]
300   Yit hadde he but litel gold in cofre;
        But al that he mighte of his freendes hente,°   *get*
        On bookes and on lerning he it spente,
        And bisily gan for the soules praye
        Of hem that yaf him wherwith to scoleye.°   *study*
305   Of studye took he most cure° and most heede.   *care*
        Nought oo° word spak he more than was neede,   *one*
        And that was said in forme° and reverence,   *formally*
        And short and quik, and ful of heigh sentence:°   *lofty meaning*
        Souning in° moral vertu was his speeche,   *consonant with*
310   And gladly wolde he lerne, and gladly teche.
          A Sergeant of the Lawe,[2] war and wis,
        That often hadde been at the Parvis[3]
        Ther was also, ful riche of excellence.
        Discreet he was, and of greet reverence—
315   He seemed swich, his wordes weren so wise.
        Justice he was ful often in assise[4]
        By patente and by plein commissioun.[5]
        For his science° and for his heigh renown   *knowledge*
        Of fees and robes hadde he many oon.
320   So greet a purchasour° was nowher noon;   *buyer of land*
        Al was fee simple[6] to him in effect—
        His purchasing mighte nat been infect.°   *invalidated*
        Nowher so bisy a man as he ther nas;
        And yit he seemed bisier than he was.
325   In termes hadde he caas and doomes° alle   *lawsuits and judgments*
        That from the time of King William[7] were falle.
        Therto he coude endite and make a thing,[8]
        Ther coude no wight° pinchen° at his writing;   *person / find fault with*
        And every statut coude he plein by rote.[9]

---

1. A philosopher could be a scientist or alchemist.
2. A lawyer of the highest rank.
3. The porch of St. Paul's Cathedral, a meeting place for lawyers.
4. He was often judge in the court of assizes (civil court).
5. By letter of appointment from the king and by full jurisdiction.
6. Owned outright with no legal impediments.
7. Since the introduction of Norman law in England under William the Conqueror.
8. Compose and draw up a deed.
9. He knew entirely from memory.

330 He rood but hoomly° in a medlee° cote,   *simply/multicolored*
    Girt with a ceint° of silk, with barres° smale.   *belt/stripes*
    Of his array telle I no lenger tale.
        A Frankelain[1] was in his compaignye:
    Whit was his beerd as is the dayesye;°   *daisy*
335 Of his complexion he was sanguin.[2]
    Wel loved he by the morwe a sop in win.[3]
    To liven in delit° was evere his wone,°   *pleasure/custom*
    For he was Epicurus owene sone,
    That heeld opinion that plein° delit   *complete*
340 Was verray felicitee parfit.[4]
    An housholdere and that a greet was he:
    Saint Julian[5] he was in his contree.
    His breed, his ale, was always after oon;°   *just as good*
    A bettre envined° man was nevere noon.   *stocked with wine*
345 Withouten bake mete was nevere his hous,
    Of fissh and flessh, and that so plentevous°   *plentiful*
    It snewed° in his hous of mete and drinke,   *snowed*
    Of alle daintees that men coude thinke.
    After the sondry sesons of the yeer
350 So chaunged he his mete and his soper.[6]
    Ful many a fat partrich° hadde he in mewe,°   *partridge/cage*
    And many a breem,° and many a luce° in stewe.°   *carp/pike/pond*
    Wo was his cook but if his sauce were
    Poinant° and sharp, and redy al his gere.   *pungent*
355 His table dormant[7] in his halle alway
    Stood redy covered al the longe day.
    At sessions[8] ther was he lord and sire.
    Ful ofte time he was Knight of the Shire.[9]
    An anlaas° and a gipser° al of silk   *dagger/purse*
360 Heeng at his girdel, whit as morne milk.
    A shirreve hadde he been, and countour.[1]
    Was nowher swich a worthy vavasour.[2]
        An Haberdasshere° and a Carpenter,   *hat-maker*
    A Webbe, a Dyere, and a Tapicer[3]—
365 And they were clothed alle in oo liveree°   *in the same uniform*
    Of a solempne and a greet fraternitee.°   *parish guild*
    Ful fresshe and newe hir gere apiked was;[4]
    Hir knives were chaped° nought with bras,   *mounted*
    But al with silver; wrought ful clene and weel
370 Hir girdles and hir pouches everydeel.
    Wel seemed eech of hem a fair burgeis°   *townsperson*
    To sitten in a yeldehalle° on a dais.   *guildhall*

---

1. A large landholder, freeborn but not belonging to the nobility.
2. In temperament he was sanguine (optimistic, governed by blood as his chief humor).
3. In the morning a sop of bread soaked in wine.
4. True and perfect happiness.
5. Patron saint of hospitality.
6. For health he changed his diet according to the different seasons.

7. Left standing rather than dismantled between meals.
8. Meetings of the justices of the peace.
9. A representative of the district at Parliament.
1. He had been sheriff and auditor of the county finances.
2. Lower member of the feudal elite.
3. A weaver, dyer, and tapestry-maker, all members of the same commercial guild.
4. Their gear was decorated.

Everich, for the wisdom that he can,°   knows
Was shaply° for to been an alderman.°   fit/mayor
375   For catel° hadde they ynough and rente,°   property/income
And eek hir wives wolde it wel assente—
And elles certain were they to blame:
It is ful fair to been ycleped° "Madame,"   called
And goon to vigilies⁵ al bifore,
380   And have a mantel royalliche ybore.
        A Cook they hadde with hem for the nones,°   for the occasion
To boile the chiknes with the marybones,°   marrowbones
And powdre-marchant tart and galingale.°   aromatic spices
Wel coude he knowe a draughte of London ale.
385   He coude roste, and seethe,° and broile, and frye,   boil
Maken mortreux,° and wel bake a pie.   stews
But greet harm was it, as it thoughte me,
That on his shine a mormal° hadde he.   ulcer
For blankmanger,° that made he with the beste.   thick stew
390   A Shipman was ther, woning° fer by weste—   dwelling
For ought I woot, he was of Dertemouthe.⁶
He rood upon a rouncy° as he couthe,   nag
In a gowne of falding° to the knee.   coarse brown cloth
A daggere hanging on a laas° hadde he   strap
395   Aboute his nekke, under his arm adown.
The hote somer hadde maad his hewe al brown;
And certainly he was a good felawe.
Ful many a draughte of win hadde he drawe
Fro Burdeuxward, whil that the chapman° sleep⁷: merchant
400   Of nice° conscience took he no keep;   scrupulous
If that he faught and hadde the hyer hand,
By water he sente hem hoom to every land.
But of his craft, to rekene wel his tides,
His stremes° and his daungers° him bisides,   currents/hazards
405   His herberwe° and his moone, his lodemenage,°   harboring/navigation
Ther was noon swich from Hulle to Cartage.⁸
Hardy he was and wis to undertake;
With many a tempest hadde his beerd been shake;
He knew alle the havenes as they were
410   Fro Gotlond to the Cape of Finistere,⁹
And every crike° in Britaine° and in Spaine.   inlet/Brittany
His barge ycleped was the Maudelaine.
        With us ther was a Doctour of Physik:°   Medicine
In al this world ne was ther noon him lik
415   To speken of physik and of surgerye.
For he was grounded in astronomye,°   astrology
He kepte his pacient a ful greet deel
In houres° by his magik naturel.   astronomical hours

---

5. Feasts held the night before a holy day.
6. Dartmouth, a port on the southwestern coast.
7. On the trip back from Bordeaux while the merchant
slept.
8. Hull, on the northeastern coast in Yorkshire; Cartage:

Carthage in North Africa or Cartagena on the Mediterranean coast of Spain.
9. Gotland in the Baltic Sea; Finistere: Land's End in
western Spain.

Wel coude he fortunen the ascendent[1]
420 Of his images° for his pacient.   *talismans*
He knew the cause of every maladye,
Were it of hoot or cold or moiste or drye,[2]
And where engendred° and of what humour:[3]   *originated*
He was a verray parfit praktisour.°   *practitioner*
425 The cause yknowe, and of his harm the roote,
Anoon he yaf the sike man his boote.°   *remedy*
     Ful redy hadde he his apothecaries
To senden him drogges and his letuaries,°   *medicines*
For eech of hem made other for to winne:
430 Hir frendshipe was nought newe to biginne.
Wel knew he the olde Esculapius,[4]
And Deiscorides and eek Rufus,
Olde Ipocras, Hali, and Galien,
Serapion, Razis, and Avicen,
435 Averrois, Damascien, and Constantin,
Bernard, and Gatesden, and Gilbertin.
Of his diete mesurable° was he,   *moderate*
For it was of no superfluitee,
But of greet norissing and digestible.
440 His studye was but litel on the Bible.
In sanguin° and in pers° he clad was al,   *red/Persian blue*
Lined with taffata and with sendal;°   *silks*
And yit he was but esy of dispence;°   *thrifty*
He kepte that he wan in pestilence.
445 For gold in physik is a cordial,°   *tonic*
Therfore he loved gold in special.
     A good Wif was ther of biside Bathe,
But she was somdeel deef, and that was scathe.°   *a pity*
Of cloth-making she hadde swich an haunt,°   *practice*
450 She passed hem of Ypres and of Gaunt.[5]
In al the parissh wif ne was ther noon
That to the offring[6] bifore hire sholde goon,
And if ther dide, certain so wroth° was she   *angry*
That she was out of alle charitee.
455 Hir coverchiefs ful fine were of ground[7]—
I dorste swere they weyeden° ten pound   *weighed*
That on a Sonday weren upon hir heed.
Hir hosen° weren of fin scarlet reed,   *stockings*
Ful straite yteyd,° and shoes ful moiste° and newe.   *tightly laced/supple*
460 Bold was hir face and fair and reed of hewe.

---

1. Calculate the ascendent (propitious moment).
2. The qualities of the four natural elements, corresponding to the humors of the body and the composition of the
universe, needed to be kept in perfect balance.
3. Bodily fluids, or "humors," thought to govern moods
(blood, phlegm, black bile, yellow bile).
4. The Physician is acquainted with a full range of medical
authorities from among the ancient Greeks (Aesculapius,
Dioscorides, Rufus, Hippocrates, Galen, and Serapion),
the Persians (Hali and Rhazes), the Arabs (Avicenna and

Averroes), the Mediterranean transmitters of Eastern science to the West (John of Damascus, Constantine the
African), and later medical school professors (Bernard of
Gordon, who taught at Montpellier; John of Gaddesden,
who taught at Merton College; and Gilbertus Anglicus,
an early contemporary of Chaucer's).
5. Centers of Flemish cloth-making.
6. The collection of gifts at the consecration of the Mass.
7. Her linen kerchiefs were fine in texture.

She was a worthy womman al hir live:
Housbondes at chirche dore she hadde five,
Withouten other compaignye in youthe—
But therof needeth nought to speke as nouthe.°   *for now*

465 And thries hadde she been at Jerusalem;
She hadde passed many a straunge streem;
At Rome she hadde been, and at Boloigne,[8]
In Galice at Saint Jame, and at Coloigne:
She coude° muchel of wandring by the waye.   *knew*

470 Gat-toothed° was she, soothly for to saye.   *gap-toothed*
Upon an amblere[9] esily she sat,
Ywimpled[1] wel, and on hir heed an hat
As brood as is a bokeler or a targe,°   *small shields*
A foot-mantel° aboute hir hipes large,   *riding skirt*

475 And on hir feet a paire of spores° sharpe.   *spurs*
In felaweshipe wel coude she laughe and carpe:
Of remedies of love she knew parchaunce,[2]
For she coude of that art the olde daunce.°   *tricks*

A good man was ther of religioun,

480 And was a poore Person° of a town,   *parson*
But riche he was of holy thought and werk.
He was also a lerned man, a clerk,
That Cristes gospel trewely wolde preche;
His parisshens° devoutly wolde he teche.   *parishioners*

485 Benigne he was, and wonder diligent,
And in adversitee ful pacient,
And swich he was preved ofte sithes.
Ful loth were him to cursen for his tithes,[3]
But rather wolde he yiven, out of doute,

490 Unto his poore parisshens aboute
Of his offring and eek of his substaunce:°   *possessions*
He coude in litel thing have suffisaunce.
Wid was his parissh, and houses fer asonder,
But he ne lafte nought for rain ne thonder,

495 In siknesse nor in meschief, to visite
The ferreste in his parissh, muche and lite,[4]
Upon his feet, and in his hand a staf.
This noble ensample° to his sheep he yaf   *example*
That first he wroughte,° and afterward he taughte.   *did*

500 Out of the Gospel he tho wordes caughte,
And this figure° he added eek therto: *saying*
That if gold ruste, what shal iren do?
For if a preest be foul, on whom we truste,
No wonder is a lewed° man to ruste.   *uneducated*

505 And shame it is, if a preest take keep,°   *is concerned*
A shiten° shepherde and a clene sheep.   *shit-covered*

---

8. Rome, Boulogne, Santiago Compostela, and Cologne
were major European pilgrimage sites.
9. A horse with a gentle pace.
1. Wearing a large headdress that covers all but the face.
2. She knew cures for lovesickness, as it happened.

3. And so was he shown to be many times. / He was most
unwilling to curse parishioners (with excommunication)
if they failed to pay his tithes (a tenth of their income due
to the Church).
4. The furthest away in his parish, great and small.

Wel oughte a preest ensample for to yive
By his clennesse how that his sheep sholde live.
He sette nought his benefice to hire[5]

510   And leet his sheep encombred in the mire
And ran to London, unto Sainte Poules,
To seeken him a chaunterye for soules,
Or with a bretherhede to been withholde,
But dwelte at hoom and kepte wel his folde,

515   So that the wolf ne made it nought miscarye:
He was a shepherde and nought a mercenarye.
And though he holy were and vertuous,
He was to sinful men nought despitous,°   scornful
Ne of his speeche daungerous ne digne,°   haughty

520   But in his teching discreet and benigne,
To drawen folk to hevene by fairnesse
By good ensample—this was his bisinesse.
But it were any persone obstinat,
What so he were, of heigh or lowe estat,

525   Him wolde he snibben° sharply for the nones:°   rebuke / on the spot
A bettre preest I trowe° ther nowher noon is.   believe
He waited after° no pompe and reverence,   expected
Ne maked him a spiced° conscience,   overly critical
But Cristes lore° and his Apostles twelve   teaching

530   He taughte, but first he folwed it himselve.
    With him ther was a Plowman, was his brother,
That hadde ylad of dong ful many a fother.[6]
A trewe swinkere° and a good was he,   worker
Living in pees° and parfit charitee.   peace

535   God loved he best with al his hoole herte
At alle times, though him gamed or smerte,[7]
And thanne his neighebor right as himselve.
He wolde thresshe, and therto dike and delve,°   make ditches and dig
For Cristes sake, for every poore wight,

540   Withouten hire,° if it laye in his might.   pay
His tithes payed he ful faire and wel,
Bothe of his propre swink[8] and his catel.°   possessions
In a tabard°rood upon a mere.°   smock / mare
    Ther was also a Reeve° and a Millere,   estate manager

545   A Somnour, and a Pardoner[9] also,
A Manciple,° and myself—ther were namo.   Steward
    The Millere was a stout carl° for the nones.   fellow
Ful big he was of brawn and eek of bones—
That preved wel, for overal ther he cam

550   At wrastling he wolde have alway the ram.[1]
He was short-shuldred, brood, a thikke knarre.°   bully

5. The priest did not rent out his parish to another in
order to take a more profitable position saying masses for
the dead at the chantries of St. Paul's in London or to
serve as chaplain to a wealthy guild (bretherhede).
6. That had carried many a cartload of manure.

7. Enjoyed himself or suffered pain.
8. Money earned from his own work.
9. A Summoner, a server of summonses for the ecclesiastical courts; Pardoner: a seller of indulgences.
1. Awarded as a prize for wrestling.

Ther was no dore that he nolde heve of harre,°   *off its hinges*
Or breke it at a renning with his heed.
His beerd as any sowe or fox was reed,
555   And therto brood, as though it were a spade;
Upon the cop° right of his nose he hade   *tip*
A werte, and theron stood a tuft of heres,
Rede as the bristles of a sowes eres;
His nosethirles° blake were and wide.   *nostrils*
560   A swerd and a bokeler bar he by his side.
His mouth as greet was as a greet furnais.
He was a janglere and a Goliardais,[2]
And that was most of sinne and harlotries.°   *obscenities*
Wel coude he stelen corn and tollen thries[3]—
565   And yit he hadde a thombe of gold,[4] pardee.
A whit cote and a blew hood wered he.
A baggepipe wel coude he blowe and soune,
And therwithal he broughte us out of towne.
      A gentil Manciple was ther of a temple,°   *law school*
570   Of which achatours° mighte take exemple   *buyers*
For to been wise in bying of vitaile;°   *food*
For wheither that he paide or took by taile,°   *on credit*
Algate he waited so in his achat[5]
That he was ay biforn° and in good stat.°   *ahead/well off*
575   Now is nat that of God a ful fair grace°   *blessing*
That swich a lewed° mannes wit shal pace°   *uneducated/surpass*
The wisdom of an heep of lerned men?
Of maistres hadde he mo than thries ten
That weren of lawe expert and curious,°   *skillful*
580   Of whiche ther were a dozeine in that house
Worthy to been stiwardes of rente° and lond   *managers of revenues*
Of any lord that is in Engelond,
To make him live by his propre good°   *own wealth*
In honour dettelees but if he were wood,°   *unless he were crazy*
585   Or live as scarsly° as him list° desire,   *thriftily/pleases*
And able for to helpen al a shire
In any caas° that mighte falle° or happe,   *event/befall*
And yit this Manciple sette hir aller cappe!°   *made fools of them all*
      The Reeve was a sclendre° colerik° man;   *lean/ill-tempered*
590   His beerd was shave as neigh° as evere he can;   *close*
His heer was by his eres ful round yshorn;
His top was dokked° lik a preest biforn;°   *clipped/in front*
Ful longe were his legges and ful lene,
Ylik a staf, ther was no calf yseene.
595   Wel coude he keepe a gerner° a binne—   *granary*
Ther was noon auditour coude on him winne.[6]
Wel wiste he by the droughte and by the rain

---

2. He was a teller of dirty stories and a reveller.
3. Collect three times as much tax as was due.
4. It was proverbial that millers were dishonest and that an honest miller was as rare as one who had a golden thumb. The statement is meant ironically.
5. He was always so watchful for his opportunities to purchase.
6. Gain anything (by catching him out).

The yeelding of his seed and of his grain.
His lordes sheep, his neet,° his dayerye,°   *cattle/dairy cattle*
600   His swim, his hors, his stoor,° and his pultrye   *livestock*
Was hoolly in this Reeves governinge,
And by his covenant° yaf the rekeninge,°   *contract/gave account*
Sin that his lord was twenty yeer of age.
Ther coude no man bringe him in arrerage.°   *financial arrears*
605   Ther nas baillif, hierde, nor other hine,[7]
That he ne knew his sleighte° and his covine°—   *tricks/plotting*
They were adrad of him as of the deeth.
His woning° was ful faire upon an heeth;°   *dwelling/meadow*
With greene trees shadwed was his place.
610   He coude bettre than his lord purchace.°   *buy property*
Ful riche he was astored prively.°   *stocked in secret*
His lord wel coude he plesen subtilly,
To yive and lene° him of his owene good,°   *lend/possessions*
And have a thank, and yit a cote and hood.
615   In youthe he hadde lerned a good mister:°   *profession*
He was a wel good wrighte, a carpenter.
This Reeve sat upon a ful good stot°   *stallion*
That was a pomely° grey and highte° Scot.   *dappled/named*
A long surcote° of pers° upon he hade,   *overcoat/blue*
620   And by his side he bar a rusty blade.
Of Northfolk[8] was this Reeve of which I telle,
Biside a town men clepen Baldeswelle.
Tukked[9] he was as is a frere aboute,
And evere he rood the hindreste° of oure route.°   *hindmost/group*
625   A Somnour was ther with us in that place
That hadde a fir-reed° cherubinnes° face,   *fire-red/cherub's*
For saucefleem° he was, with yën narwe,   *pimply*
And hoot he was, and lecherous as a sparwe,°   *sparrow*
With scaled° browes blake and piled[1] beerd: *scabby*
630   Of his visage children were aferd.°   *frightened*
Ther nas quiksilver, litarge, ne brimstoon,
Boras, ceruce, ne oile of tartre noon,[2]
Ne oinement that wolde clense and bite,
That him mighte helpen of his whelkes° white,   *blotches*
635   Nor of the knobbes° sitting on his cheekes.   *lumps*
Wel loved he garlek, oinons, and eek leekes,
And for to drinke strong win reed as blood.
Thanne wolde he speke and crye as he were wood;°   *crazy*
And whan that he wel dronken hadde the win,
640   Thanne wolde he speke no word but Latin:
A fewe termes hadde he, two or three,
That he hadde lerned out of som decree;

---

7. There was no foreman, herdsman, or other farm-
hand.
8. Norfolk in the north of England. The Reeve is notable
for his northern dialect and regionalisms.
9. He wore his clothes tucked up with a cinch as friars did.

1. With hair falling out.
2. There was not mercury, lead ointment, or sulphur, /
Borax, white lead, nor any oil of tartar that could clean
him.

No wonder is—he herde it al the day,
And eek ye knowe wel how that a jay°   *parrot*
645 Can clepen "Watte"° as wel as can the Pope—   *call "Walter"*
But whoso coude in other thing him grope,°   *examine*
Thanne hadde he spent all his philosophye;
Ay *Questio quid juris*[3] wolde he crye.
     He was a gentil harlot° and a kinde;   *rascal*
650 A bettre felawe sholde men nought finde:
He wolde suffre,° for a quart of win,   *allow*
A good felawe to have his concubin°   *mistress*
A twelfmonth, and excusen him at the fulle;
Ful prively a finch eek coude he pulle.[4]
655 And if he foond owher° a good felawe   *anywhere*
He wolde techen him to have noon awe
In swich caas of the Ercedekenes curs,[5]
But if a mannes soule were in his purs,°   *wallet*
For in his purs he sholde ypunisshed be.
660 "Purs is the Ercedekenes helle," saide he.
     But wel I woot he lied right in deede:
Of cursing° oughte eech gilty man him drede,°   *excommunication / fear*
For curs wol slee right as assoiling° savith—   *absolving*
And also war him of a *significavit*.[6]
665   In daunger hadde he at his owene gise[7]
The yonge girles of the diocise,
And knew hir conseil,° and was al hir reed.°   *secrets / advice*
A gerland hadde he set upon his heed
As greet as it were for an ale-stake;°   *tavern sign*
670 A bokeler hadde he maad him of a cake.°   *loaf of bread*
     With him ther rood a gentil Pardoner
Of Rouncival,[8] his freend and his compeer,°   *companion*
That straight was comen fro the Court of Rome.
Ful loude he soong, "Com hider, love, to me."[9]
675 This Somnour bar to him a stif burdoun:°   *a strong baritone*
Was nevere trompe° of half so greet a soun.   *trumpet*
     This Pardoner hadde heer as yelow as wex,
But smoothe it heeng as dooth a strike of flex;°   *clump of flax*
By ounces° heenge his lokkes that he hadde,   *thin strands*
680 And therwith he his shuldres overspradde,
But thinne it lay, by colpons,° oon by oon;   *strands*
But hood for jolitee° wered he noon,   *fanciness*
For it was trussed up in his walet:°   *pack*
Him thoughte he rood al of the newe jet.°   *fashion*
685 Dischevelee° save his cappe he rood al bare.   *loose-haired*
Swiche glaring yën hadde he as an hare.
A vernicle[1] hadde he sowed upon his cappe,

---

3. "The question as to what point of law (applies)"; often used in ecclesiastical courts.
4. And secretly he also knew how to fool around.
5. In case of excommunication by the archdeacon.
6. Order of transfer from ecclesiastical to secular courts.

7. Under his control he had at his disposal.
8. A hospital at Charing Cross in London.
9. A popular ballad.
1. A pilgrim badge, reproducing St. Veronica's veil bearing the imprint of Christ's face.

His walet biforn him in his lappe,
Bretful of pardon,[2] comen from Rome al hoot.

690 A vois he hadde as smal° as hath a goot;°   *high-pitched/goat*
No beerd hadde he, ne nevere sholde have;
As smoothe it was as it were late yshave:
I trowe he were a gelding or a mare.[3]
But of his craft,° fro Berwik into Ware,[4]   *skill*

695 Ne was ther swich another pardoner;
For in his male° he hadde a pilwe-beer°   *bag/pillowcase*
Which that he saide was Oure Lady veil;
He saide he hadde a gobet° of the sail   *chunk*
That Sainte Peter hadde whan that he wente

700 Upon the see, til Jesu Crist him hente.°   *grabbed*
He hadde a crois of laton,° ful of stones,   *brass cross*
And in a glas he hadde pigges bones,
But with thise relikes whan that he foond
A poore person° dwelling upon lond,   *parson*

705 Upon a day he gat him more moneye
Than that the person gat in monthes twaye;
And thus with feined flaterye and japes°   *tricks*
He made the person and the peple his apes.°   *dupes*
But trewely to tellen at the laste,

710 He was in chirche a noble ecclesiaste;
Wel coude he rede a lesson and a storye,°   *liturgical texts*
But alderbest° he soong an offertorye,   *best of all*
For wel he wiste whan that song was songe,
He moste preche and wel affile° his tonge   *sharpen*

715 To winne silver, as he ful wel coude—
Therfore he soong the merierly and loude.
     Now have I told you soothly in a clause°   *briefly*
Th'estaat, th'array, the nombre, and eek the cause
Why that assembled was this compaignye

720 In Southwerk at this gentil hostelrye
That highte the Tabard, faste by the Belle;[5]
But now is time to you for to telle
How that we baren us that ilke° night   *same*
Whan we were in that hostelrye alight;

725 And after wol I telle of oure viage,°   *trip*
And al the remenant of oure pilgrimage.
     But first I praye you of youre curteisye
That ye n'arette° it nought my vilainye°   *consider/rudeness*
Though that I plainly speke in this matere

730 To telle you hir wordes and hir cheere,°   *comportment*
Ne though I speke hir wordes proprely;°   *accurately*
For this ye knowen also wel as I:
Who so shal telle a tale after a man
He moot reherce,° as neigh as evere he can,   *must repeat*

735	Everich a word, if it be in his charge,	
	Al speke he nevere so rudeliche° and large,°	*crudely/freely*
	Or elles he moot telle his tale untrewe,	
	Or feine° thing, or finde wordes newe;	*invent, falsify*
	He may nought spare although he were his brother:	
740	He moot as wel saye oo word as another.	
	Crist spak himself ful brode° in Holy Writ,	*plainly*
	And wel ye woot no vilainye is it;	
	Eek Plato saith, who so can him rede,	
	The wordes mote be cosin° to the deede.	*closely related*
745	Also I praye you to foryive it me	
	Al° have I nat set folk in hir degree°	*although/rank*
	Here in this tale as that they sholde stonde:	
	My wit is short, ye may wel understonde.	
	Greet cheere made oure Host us everichoon,	
750	And to the soper sette he us anoon.	
	He served us with vitaile at the beste.	
	Strong was the win, and wel to drinke us leste.°	*it pleased*
	A semely man oure Hoste was withalle	
	For to been a marchal° in an halle;	*master of ceremonies*
755	A large man he was, with yën steepe;	
	A fairer burgeis was ther noon in Chepe°—	*Cheapside (in London)*
	Bold of his speeche, and wis, and wel ytaught,	
	And of manhood him lakkede right naught.	
	Eek therto he was right a merye man,	
760	And after soper playen he bigan,	
	And spak of mirthe amonges othere thinges—	
	Whan that we hadde maad oure rekeninges°—	*paid the bill*
	And saide thus, "Now, lordinges, trewely,	
	Ye been to me right welcome, hertely.	
765	For by my trouthe, if that I shal nat lie,	
	I sawgh nat this yeer so merye a compaignye	
	At ones in this herberwe° as is now.	*inn*
	Fain wolde I doon you mirthe, wiste I how.	
	And of a mirthe I am right now bithought,	
770	To doon you ese, and it shal coste nought.	
	Ye goon to Canterbury—God you speede;	
	The blisful martyr quite° you youre meede.°	*repay/reward*
	And wel I woot as ye goon by the waye	
	Ye shapen° you to talen° and to playe,	*intend/tell tales*
775	For trewely, confort ne mirthe is noon	
	To ride by the waye domb as stoon;	
	And therfore wol I maken you disport	
	As I saide erst,° and doon you som confort;	*before*
	And if you liketh alle, by oon assent,	
780	For to stonden at my juggement,	
	And for to werken as I shal you saye,	
	Tomorwe whan ye riden by the waye—	
	Now by my fader soule that is deed,	
	But° ye be merye I wol yive you myn heed!	*unless*
785	Holde up youre handes withouten more speeche."	

Oure conseil was nat longe for to seeche;°   seek
Us thoughte it was nat worth to make it wis,°   deliberate
And graunted him withouten more avis,°   opinions
And bade him saye his voirdit° as him leste.   verdict
790 "Lordinges," quod he, "now herkneth for the beste;
But taketh it nought, I praye you, in desdain.
This is the point, to speken short and plain,
That eech of you, to shorte with oure waye
In this viage, shal tellen tales twaye°—   two
795 To Canterburyward, I mene it so,
And hoomward he shal tellen othere two,
Of aventures that whilom° have bifalle;   long ago
And which of you that bereth him best of alle—
That is to sayn, that telleth in this cas
800 Tales of best sentence° and most solas°—   substance/pleasure
Shal have a soper at oure aller cost,
Here in this place, sitting by this post,
Whan that we come again fro Canterbury.
And for to make you the more mury
805 I wol myself goodly° with you ride—   gladly
Right at myn owene cost—and be youre gide.
And who so wol my juggement withsaye°   contradict
Shal paye al that we spende by the waye.
And if ye vouche sauf° that it be so,   grant
810 Telle me anoon, withouten wordes mo,
And I wol erly shape° me therfore."   prepare
       This thing was graunted and oure othes swore
With ful glad herte, and prayden him also
That he wolde vouche sauf for to do so,
815 And that he wolde been oure governour,
And of oure tales juge° and reportour,°   judge/recordkeeper
And sette a soper at a certain pris,°   price
And we wol ruled been at his devis,°   plan
In heigh and lowe; and thus by oon assent
820 We been accorded to his juggement.
And therupon the win was fet° anoon;   fetched
We dronken and to reste wente eechoon
Withouten any lenger taryinge.
       Amorwe° whan that day bigan to springe   next morning
825 Up roos oure Host and was oure aller cok,°   cock, wake-up call
And gadred us togidres in a flok,
And forth we riden, a litel more than pas,°   slow walk
Unto the watering of Saint Thomas;[6]
And ther oure Host bigan his hors arreste,°   stop
830 And saide, "Lordes, herkneth if you leste:
       "Ye woot youre forward° and it you recorde:°   agreement/remember
If evensong and morwesong accorde,
Lat see now who shal telle the firste tale.
As evere mote I drinken win or ale,

---

6. A brook two miles from London.

835 Who so be rebel to my juggement
Shal paye for al that by the way is spent.
Now draweth cut° er that we ferrer twinne:°   *lots/separate furthur*
He which that hath the shorteste shal biginne.
"Sire Knight," quod he, "my maister and my lord,
840 Now draweth cut, for that is myn accord.°   *wish*
Cometh neer," quod he, "my lady Prioresse,
And ye, sire Clerk, lat be youre shamefastnesse°—   *modesty*
Ne studieth nought. Lay hand to, every man!"
Anoon to drawen every wight bigan,
845 And shortly for to tellen as it was,
Were it by aventure, or sort, or cas,°   *luck, fate or chance*
The soothe is this, the cut fil° to the Knight;   *fell*
Of which ful blithe° and glad was every wight,   *happy*
And telle he moste his tale, as was resoun,
850 By forward and by composicioun,°   *agreement*
As ye han herd. What needeth wordes mo?
And whan this goode man sawgh that it was so,
As he that wis was and obedient
To keepe his forward by his free assent,
855 He saide, "Sin I shal biginne the game,
What, welcome be the cut, in Goddes name!
Now lat us ride, and herkneth what I saye."
And with that word we riden forth oure waye,
And he bigan with right a merye cheere°   *expression*
860 His tale anoon, and saide as ye may heere.

The Miller's Tale

The Miller's Tale both answers and parodies *The Knight's Tale*, a long aristocratic romance about two knights in rivalry for the hand of a lady. While the Miller tells a neatly analogous story of erotic competition, his tale is radically shorter and explicitly sexual. Such brevity and physicality fit his tale's genre—a fabliau, or short comic tale, usually bawdy and often involving a clerk, a wife, and a cuckolded husband. Following the convention (if not the reality) that romances were written by and for the nobility and fabliaux by and for the commons, Chaucer suits *The Miller's Tale* to its teller as aptly as he does the Knight's. Slyly disclaiming responsibility for the tale, he explains its bawdiness by the Miller's class status: "the Millere is a cherle" and like his peer the Reeve who follows and "requites" him, tells "harlotrye."

The drunken Miller's insistence on telling his tale to requite the Knight's tale has been called a "literary peasants' revolt." Although the Miller, a free man, was not actually a peasant, yeomen of his status were active in the Rising of 1381, and millers in particular played a symbolic role in it (see the letters of John Ball, page 432). In fact, this tale is highly literate, with its echoes of the Song of Songs and its parody of the language of courtly love: an actual miller would have had neither the education nor the social sophistication to tell it. Yet a parody implies some degree of attachment to the very model being ridiculed, and *The Miller's Tale* is as much as claim upon the Knight's world as a repudiation of it. The Miller wants to "quiten" the Knight's tale, he says, using a word that can mean to repay or avenge, but also to fulfill. The tale's several plots converge brilliantly upon a single cry: "Water!" The tale's impact derives as well from its plenitude of pleasures (sexual, comic, even religious) after the austere and rigid desires of *The Knight's Tale.*

The Miller's Tale
The Introduction

Whan that the Knight hadde thus his tale ytold,
In al the route° nas ther yong ne old   *group*
That he ne saide it was a noble storye,
And worthy for to drawen° to memorye,   *recall*
5   And namely the gentils° everichoon.   *upper class*
　　　Oure Hoste lough° and swoor, "So mote I goon,[1]   *laughed*
This gooth aright: unbokeled is the male.[2]
Lat see now who shal telle another tale.
For trewely the game is wel bigonne.
10   Now telleth ye, sire Monk, if that ye conne,°   *know*
Somwhat to quite° with the Knightes tale."   *repay*
　　　The Millere, that for dronken was al pale,
So that unnethe° upon his hors he sat,   *barely*
He nolde avalen° neither hood ne hat,   *remove*
15   Ne abiden no man for his curteisye,
But in Pilates[3] vois he gan to crye,
And swoor, "By armes and by blood and bones,°   *(of Christ)*
I can° a noble tale for the nones,   *know*
With which I wol now quite the Knightes tale."
20   　　　Oure Hoste sawgh that he was dronke of ale,
And saide, "Abide,° Robin, leve° brother,   *wait/dear*
Som bettre man shal telle us first another.
Abide, and lat us werken thriftily."°   *properly*
　　　"By Goddes soule," quod he, "that wol nat I,
25   For I wol speke or elles go my way."
　　　Oure Host answerde, "Tel on, a devele way!°   *in the devil's name*
Thou art a fool; thy wit is overcome."
　　　"Now herkneth," quod the Millere, "alle and some.°   *one and all*
But first I make a protestacioun
30   That I am dronke: I knowe it by my soun.°   *sound*
And therfore if that I mis speke or saye,
Wite it° the ale of Southwerk, I you praye;   *blame it on*
For I wol telle a legende and a lif[4]
Bothe of a carpenter and of his wif,
35   How that a clerk hath set the wrightes cappe."[5]
　　　The Reeve answerde and saide, "Stint thy clappe!°   *hold your tongue*
Lat be thy lewed° dronken harlotrye.°   *unlearned/obscenity*
It is a sinne and eek a greet folye
To apairen° any man or him defame,   *injure*
40   And eek to bringen wives in swich fame.
Thou maist ynough of othere thinges sayn."
　　　This dronken Millere spak ful soone again,
And saide, "Leve brother Osewold,
Who hath no wif, he is no cokewold."°   *cuckold*

1. Thus I may proceed.
2. The bag is opened (i.e., the games are begun).
3. The role of Pilate was traditionally played in a loud

and raucous voice in the mystery plays.
4. The story of a saint's life.
5. Made a fool of the carpenter.

45 But I saye nat therfore that thou art oon.
Ther ben ful goode wives many oon,
And evere a thousand goode ayains oon badde.
That knowestou wel thyself but if thou madde.°   *go insane*
Why artou angry with my tale now?
50 I have a wif, pardee,° as wel as thou,   *by God*
Yet nolde I, for the oxen in my plough,[6]
Take upon me more than ynough
As deemen° of myself that I were oon:°   *judge / one (a cuckold)*
I wol bileve wel that I am noon.
55 An housbonde shal nought been inquisitif
Of Goddes privetee,° nor of his wif.   *secrets*
So he may finde Goddes foison° there,   *plenty*
Of the remenant needeth nought enquere."
        What sholde I more sayn but this Millere
60 He nolde his wordes for no man forbere,
But tolde his cherles° tale in his manere.   *commoner's*
M'athinketh° that I shal reherce° it here,   *I regret / repeat*
And therfore every gentil wight I praye,
Deemeth nought, for Goddes love, that I saye
65 Of yvel entente, but for° I moot reherse   *because*
Hir tales alle, be they bet or werse,
Or elles falsen som of my matere.
And therfore, whoso list it nought yheere
Turne over the leef,° and chese° another tale,   *page / choose*
70 For he shal finde ynowe,° grete and smale,   *enough*
Of storial° thing that toucheth gentilesse,°   *historical / nobility*
And eek moralitee and holinesse:
Blameth nought me if that ye chese amis.
The Millere is a cherl, ye knowe wel this,
75 So was the Reeve eek, and othere mo,
And harlotrye they tolden bothe two.
Aviseth you,° and putte me out of blame: *be warned*
And eek men shal nought maken ernest of game.°   *treat jokes seriously*

The Tale

        Whilom° ther was dwelling at Oxenforde   *long ago*
80 A riche gnof° that gestes heeld to boorde,°   *fool / took in boarders*
And of his craft he was a carpenter.
With him ther was dwelling a poore scoler,
Hadde lerned art,[7] but al his fantasye°   *fancy*
Was turned for to lere° astrologye,   *learn*
85 And coude a certain of conclusiouns,°   *predictions*
To deemen by interrogaciouns,[8]
If that men axed° him in certain houres   *asked*
Whan that men sholde have droughte or elles showres,
Or if men axed him what shal bifalle

6. Yet I wouldn't, not even (in wager) for the oxen in my plough.

7. The arts curriculum (trivium).
8. To estimate by consulting (the stars).

90   Of every thing—I may nat rekene hem alle.
      This clerk was cleped° hende[9] Nicholas.   *called*
    Of derne° love he coude, and of solas,[1]   *secret*
    And therto he was sly and ful privee,°   *secretive*
    And lik a maide meeke for to see.
95   A chambre hadde he in that hostelrye°   *inn*
    Allone, withouten any compaignye,
    Ful fetisly ydight with herbes swoote,[2]
    And he himself as sweete as is the roote
    Of licoris or any setewale.[3]
100   His Almageste[4] and bookes grete and smale,
    His astrelabye,[5] longing for° his art,   *belonging to*
    His augrim stones,° layen faire apart   *abacus beads*
    On shelves couched° at his beddes heed;   *arranged*
    His presse° ycovered with a falding° reed; *dresser/coarse cloth*
105   And al above ther lay a gay sautrye,°   *harp*
    On which he made a-nightes melodye
    So swetely that al the chambre roong,
    And *Angelus ad Virginem*[6] he soong,
    And after that he soong the *Kinges Note:*[7]
110   Ful often blessed was his merye throte.
    And thus this sweete clerk his time spente
    After his freendes finding and his rente.[8]
      This carpenter hadde wedded newe a wif
    Which that he loved more than his lif.
115   Of eighteteene yeer she was of age;
    Jalous he was, and heeld hire narwe in cage,
    For she was wilde and yong, and he was old,
    And deemed himself been lik a cokewold.
    He knew nat Caton,[9] for his wit was rude,
120   That bad men sholde wedde his similitude:° *equal in age*
    Men sholde wedden after hir estat,°   *station in life*
    For youthe and elde is often at debat.
    But sith that he was fallen in the snare,
    He moste endure, as other folk, his care.
125   Fair was this yonge wif, and therwithal
    As any wesele hir body gent and smal.[1]
    A ceint° she wered, barred° al of silk;   *belt/striped*
    A barmcloth° as whit as morne milk   *apron*
    Upon hir lendes,° ful of many a gore;° *loins/flounce*
130   Whit was hir smok,° and broiden° al bifore *slip/embroidered*
    And eek bihinde, on hir coler aboute,° *around her collar*
    Of col-blak silk, withinne and eek withoute;
    The tapes° of hir white voluper°   *ribbons/cap*

9. Handsome, courteous, handy.
1. Pleasure, (sexual) comforts.
2. Elegantly decked out with sweet herbs.
3. Setwall, a gingerlike spice used as a stimulant.
4. An astrological treatise by Ptolemy.
5. Astrolabe, an astrological instrument.
6. A prayer commemorating the Annunciation.

7. A popular song.
8. According to what his friends gave him and his income.
9. Cato, Latin author of a book of maxims used in elementary education.
1. Her body as delicate and slender as any weasel.

	Were of the same suite° of hir coler;	*pattern*
135	Hir filet° brood° of silk and set ful hye;	*headband/broad*
	And sikerly she hadde a likerous yë;[2]	
	Ful smale ypulled° were hir browes two,	*plucked*
	And tho were bent, and blake as any slo.°	*plum*
	She was ful more blisful on to see	
140	Than is the newe perejonette° tree,	*pear*
	And softer than the wolle is of a wether;°	*ram*
	And by hir girdel° heeng a purs of lether,	*belt*
	Tasseled with silk and perled° with latoun.°	*decorated/brass*
	In al this world, to seeken up and down,	
145	Ther nis no man so wis that coude thenche°	*imagine*
	So gay a popelote° or swich a wenche.[3]	*doll*
	Ful brighter was the shining of hir hewe	
	Than in the Towr the noble° yforged newe.[4]	*gold coin*
	But of hir song, it was as loud and yerne°	*lively*
150	As any swalwe sitting on a berne.	
	Therto she coude skippe and make game	
	As any kide or calf folwing his dame.°	*mother*
	Hir mouth was sweete as bragot or the meeth,°	*honey drinks*
	Or hoord of apples laid in hay or heeth.°	*heather*
155	Winsing° she was as is a joly° colt,	*skittish/spirited*
	Long as a mast, and upright° as a bolt.°	*strait/arrow*
	A brooch she bar upon hir lowe coler	
	As brood as is the boos° of a bokeler;°	*boss/shield*
	Hir shoes were laced on hir legges hye.	
160	She was a primerole,° a piggesnye,[5]	*primrose*
	For any lord to leggen in his bedde,	
	Or yet for any good yeman to wedde.	
	Now sire, and eft° sire, so bifel the cas	*again*
	That on a day this hende Nicholas	
165	Fil with this yonge wif to rage° and playe,	*sport*
	Whil that hir housbonde was at Oseneye°	*Osney, near Oxford*
	(As clerkes been ful subtil and ful quainte),°	*clever*
	And prively he caughte hire by the queinte,[6]	
	And saide, "Ywis,° but if ich have my wille,	*certainly*
170	For derne° love of thee, lemman,° I spille,"°	*secret/sweetheart/die*
	And heeld hire harde by the haunche-bones,	
	And saide, "Lemman, love me al atones,°	*at once*
	Or I wol dien, also° God me save."	*so*
	And she sproong as a colt dooth in a trave,[7]	
175	And with hir heed she wried° faste away;	*twisted*
	She saide, "I wol nat kisse thee, by my fay.°	*faith*
	Why, lat be," quod she, "lat be, Nicholas!	
	Or I wol crye "Out, harrow, and allas!'	
	Do way youre handes, for your curteisye!"	

2. And certainly she had a wanton eye.
3. Woman of the working class.
4. Than the new-forged gold coin in the Tower (of London, the royal mint).
5. Pig's eye, a flower.
6. Literally "dainty part," slang for the female genitals.
7. A restraint for horses when they are being shod.

180   This Nicholas gan mercy for to crye,
        And spak so faire, and profred him° so faste,   *pressed his case*
        That she hir love him graunted atte laste,
        And swoor hir ooth by Saint Thomas of Kent
        That she wolde been at his comandement,
185   Whan that she may hir leiser° wel espye.   *opportunity*
        "Myn housbonde is so ful of jalousye
        That but ye waite wel and been privee,[8]
        I woot right wel I nam but deed," quod she.
        "Ye moste been ful derne as in this cas."
190   "Nay, therof care thee nought," quod Nicholas.
        "A clerk hadde litherly biset his while,°   *wasted his time*
        But if he coude a carpenter bigile."
        And thus they been accorded and ysworn
        To waite a time, as I have told biforn.
195   Whan Nicholas hadde doon this everydeel,
        And thakked° hire upon the lendes° weel,   *patted/loins*
        He kiste hire sweete, and taketh his sautrye,
        And playeth faste, and maketh melodye.
            Thanne fil it thus, that to the parissh chirche,
200   Cristes owene werkes for to wirche,
        This goode wif wente on an haliday:°   *holy day*
        Hir forheed shoon as bright as any day,
        So was it wasshen whan she leet° hir werk.   *left off*
            Now was ther of that chirche a parissh clerk,
205   The which that was ycleped° Absolon: *called*
        Crul° was his heer, and as the gold it shoon,   *curly*
        And strouted as a fanne[9] large and brode;
        Ful straight and evene lay his joly shode.°   *part in his hair*
        His rode° was reed, his y'n greye as goos.   *complexion*
210   With Poules window[1] corven° on his shoos,   *carved*
        In hoses rede he wente fetisly.°   *elegantly*
        Yclad he was ful smale° and proprely,   *fine*
        Al in a kirtel° of a light waget°—   *tunic/blue*
        Ful faire and thikke been the pointes° set—   *laces*
215   And therupon he hadde a gay surplis,°   *clerical robe*
        As whit as is the blosme upon the ris.°   *twig*
        A merye child° he was, so God me save.   *lad*
        Wel coude he laten blood,[2] and clippe,° and shave, *cut hair*
        And maken a chartre of land, or acquitaunce;°   *legal release*
220   In twenty manere coude he trippe and daunce
        After the scole of Oxenforde tho,
        And with his legges casten to and fro,
        And playen songes on a smal rubible;°   *fiddle*
        Therto he soong somtime a loud quinible,°   *high treble*
225   And as wel coude he playe on a giterne:°   *guitar*
        In al the town nas brewhous ne taverne

---

8. That unless you're very cautious and discreet.
9. And spread out like a winnowing fan (for separating wheat from chaff).

1. The windows of St. Paul's Chapel were intricately patterned.
2. Let blood (a medical treatment performed by barbers).

That he ne visited with his solas,[3]
Ther any gailard tappestere° was.   *saucy barmaid*
But sooth to sayn, he was somdeel squaimous°   *somewhat squeamish*
230 Of farting, and of speeche daungerous.°   *haughty*
   This Absolon, that joly was and gay,
Gooth with a cencer° on the haliday,   *incense bowl*
Cencing the wives of the parissh faste,
And many a lovely look on hem he caste,
235 And namely on this carpenteres wif:
To looke on hire him thoughte a merye lif.
She was so propre and sweete and likerous,
I dar wel sayn, if she hadde been a mous,
And he a cat, he wolde hire hente° anoon.   *catch*
240 This parissh clerk, this joly Absolon,
Hath in his herte swich a love-longinge
That of no wif ne took he noon offringe—
For curteisye he saide he wolde noon.
The moone, whan it was night, ful brighte shoon,
245 And Absolon his giterne hath ytake—
For paramours he thoughte for to wake—[4]
And forth he gooth, jolif° and amorous,   *pretty*
Til he cam to the carpenteres hous,
A litel after cokkes hadde ycrowe,
250 And dressed° him up by a shot-windowe°   *placed/hinged window*
That was upon the carpenteres wal.
He singeth in his vois gentil and smal,°   *high*
"Now dere lady, if thy wille be,
I praye you that ye wol rewe° on me,"   *take pity*
255 Ful wel accordant° to his giterninge.   *harmonizing*
This carpenter awook and herde him singe,
And spak unto his wif, and saide anoon,
"What, Alison, heerestou nought Absolon
That chaunteth thus under oure bowres° wal?"   *bedroom's*
260 And she answerde hir housbonde therwithal,
"Yis, God woot, John, I heere it everydeel."°   *every bit*
   This passeth forth. What wol ye bet than weel?[5]
Fro day to day this joly Absolon
So woweth° hire that him is wo-bigoon: *woos*
265 He waketh al the night and al the day;
He kembed° his lokkes brode° and made him gay;   *combed/wide-spreading*
He woweth hire by menes and brocage,[6]
And swoor he wolde been hir owene page;°   *attendant*
He singeth, brokking° as a nightingale;   *trilling*
270 He sente hire piment,° meeth,° and spiced ale, *spiced wine/mead*
And wafres° piping hoot out of the gleede;°   *pastries/coals*
And for she was of towne, he profred meede°—   *bribes*
For som folk wol be wonnen for richesse,
And som for strokes,° and som for gentilesse.   *by force*

<hr>

3. Entertainment (also with sexual connotations).
4. For the sake of love he thought to keep a vigil.
5. What more would you want?
6. He woos her with go-betweens and mediation.

275   Somtime to shewe his lightnesse° and maistrye,°   *agility/skill*
    He playeth Herodes[7] upon a scaffold° hye.   *platform*
    But what availeth him as in this cas?
    She loveth so this hende Nicholas
    That Absolon may blowe the bukkes horn;[8]
280   He ne hadde for his labour but a scorn.
    And thus she maketh Absolon hir ape,°   *fool*
    And al his ernest turneth til a jape.°   *joke*
    Ful sooth is this proverbe, it is no lie;
    Men saith right thus: "Alway the nye slye°   *sly one nearby*
285   Maketh the ferre leve to be loth."[9]
    For though that Absolon be wood° or wroth,   *crazy*
    By cause that he fer was from hir sighte,
    This nye Nicholas stood in his lighte.°   *in the way*
      Now beer thee wel, thou hende Nicholas,
290   For Absolon may waile and singe allas.
      And so bifel it on a Saterday
    This carpenter was goon til Oseney,
    And hende Nicholas and Alisoun
    Accorded been to this conclusioun,
295   That Nicholas shal shapen hem a wile°   *devise them a trick*
    This sely° jalous housbonde to bigile,   *innocent*
    And if so be this game wente aright,
    She sholden sleepen in his arm al night—
    For this was his desir and hire also.
300   And right anoon, withouten wordes mo,
    This Nicholas no lenger wolde tarye,
    But dooth ful softe unto his chambre carye
    Bothe mete and drinke for a day or twaye,
    And to hir housbonde bad hire for to saye,
305   If that he axed after Nicholas,
    She sholde saye she niste° wher he was—   *did not know*
    Of al that day she sawgh him nought with yë:
    She trowed° that he was in maladye,   *believed*
    For for no cry hir maide coude him calle,
310   He nolde answere for no thing that mighte falle.°   *happen*
      This passeth forth al thilke Saterday
    That Nicholas stille in his chambre lay,
    And eet, and sleep, or dide what him leste,°   *he liked*
    Til Sonday that the sonne gooth to reste.
315   This sely carpenter hath greet mervaile
    Of Nicholas, or what thing mighte him aile,
    And saide, "I am adrad,° by Saint Thomas,   *afraid*
    It stondeth nat aright with Nicholas.
    God shilde° that he deide sodeinly!   *forbid*
320   This world is now ful tikel,° sikerly: *changeable*
    I sawgh today a corps yborn to chirche
    That now a Monday last I sawgh him wirche.°   *working*

---

7. In the English mystery plays, Herod was often portrayed as a bully.

8. Undertake a useless endeavor.
9. Makes the distant beloved seem hateful.

Go up," quod he unto his knave° anoon,　　　　　　*manservant*
"Clepe° at his dore or knokke with a stoon.　　　　　*call*
325　Looke how it is and tel me boldely."
　　　This knave gooth him up ful sturdily,
And at the chambre dore whil that he stood
He cride and knokked as that he were wood,
"What? How? What do ye, maister Nicholay?
330　How may ye sleepen al the longe day?".
But al for nought: he herde nat a word.
An hole he foond ful lowe upon a boord,
Ther as the cat was wont in for to creepe,
And at that hole he looked in ful deepe,
335　And atte laste he hadde of him a sighte.
　　　This Nicholas sat evere caping° uprighte　　　　*staring*
As he hadde kiked° on the newe moone.　　　　　　*gazed*
Adown he gooth and tolde his maister soone
In what array° he saw this ilke man.　　　　　　　*condition*
340　This carpenter to blessen him[1] bigan,
And saide, "Help us, Sainte Frideswide![2]
A man woot litel what him shal bitide.
This man is falle, with his astromye,
In som woodnesse or in som agonye.°　　　　　　　*fit*
345　I thoughte ay wel how that it sholde be:
Men sholde nought knowe of Goddes privetee.
Ye, blessed be alway a lewed° man　　　　　　　　*unlearned*
That nought but only his bileve can.°　　　　　　*knows his creed*
So ferde° another clerk with astromye:　　　　　　*fared*
350　He walked in the feeldes for to prye°　　　　　　*gaze*
Upon the sterres, what ther sholde bifalle,
Til he was in a marle-pit° yfalle—　　　　　　　*clay-pit*
He saw nat that. But yet, by Saint Thomas,
Me reweth sore° for hende Nicholas.　　　　　　　*feel sorry*
355　He shal be rated° of his studying,　　　　　　　*scolded*
If that I may, by Jesus, hevene king!
Get me a staf that I may underspore,°　　　　　　*pry upward*
Whil that thou, Robin, hevest up the dore.
He shal out of his studying, as I gesse."
360　And to the chambre dore he gan him dresse.°　　　*placed himself*
His knave was a strong carl° for the nones,°　　　　*fellow/purpose*
And by the haspe° he haaf° it up atones:　　　　　*hinge/heaved*
Into the floor the dore fil anoon.
This Nicholas sat ay as stille as stoon,
365　And evere caped up into the air.
This carpenter wende° he were in despair,　　　　　*thought*
And hente° him by the shuldres mightily,　　　　　*grabbed*
And shook him harde, and cride spitously,°　　　　　*vigorously*
"What, Nicholay, what, how! What! Looke adown!
370　Awaak and thenk on Cristes passioun![3]

---

1. Bless himself (with the sign of the cross).
2. A saint venerated for her healing powers.

3. Thinking about Christ's death and resurrection was supposed to ward off evil spells.

I crouche° thee from elves and fro wightes."°   *bless/evil spirits*
Therwith the nightspel° saide he anoonrightes   *charm*
On foure halves° of the hous aboute,   *sides*
And on the thresshfold on the dore withoute:
375   "Jesu Crist and Sainte Benedight,[4]
Blesse this hous from every wikked wight!
For nightes nerye° the White Pater Noster.[5]   *protect*
Where wentestou, thou Sainte Petres soster?"°   *sister*
And at the laste this hende Nicholas
380   Gan for to sike° sore, and saide, "Allas,   *sigh*
Shal al the world be lost eftsoones° now?"   *immediately*
This carpenter answerde, "What saistou?
What, thenk on God as we doon, men that swinke."°   *work*
This Nicholas answerde, "Fecche me drinke,
385   And after wol I speke in privetee
Of certain thing that toucheth me and thee.
I wol telle it noon other man, certain."
This carpenter gooth down and comth again,
And broughte of mighty ale a large quart,
390   And whan that eech of hem hadde dronke his part,
This Nicholas his dore faste shette,°   *shut*
And down the carpenter by him he sette,
And saide, "John, myn hoste lief° and dere,   *beloved*
Thou shalt upon thy trouthe° swere me here   *word of honor*
395   That to no wight thou shalt this conseil° wraye;°   *advice/disclose*
For it is Cristes conseil that I saye,
And if thou telle it man, thou art forlore,°   *lost*
For this vengeance thou shalt have therfore,
That if thou wraye me, thou shalt be wood."
400   "Nay, Crist forbede it, for his holy blood,"
Quod tho this sely man. "I nam no labbe,°   *blabbermouth*
And though I saye, I nam nat lief to gabbe.
Say what thou wilt, I shal it nevere telle
To child ne wif, by him that harwed helle."[6]
405   "Now John," quod Nicholas, "I wol nought lie.
I have yfounde in myn astrologye,
As I have looked in the moone bright,
That now a Monday next, at quarter night,°   *near dawn*
Shal falle a rain, and that so wilde and wood,°   *furious*
410   That half so greet was nevere Noees° flood.   *Noah's*
This world," he saide, "in lasse than an hour
Shal al be dreint,° so hidous is the showr.   *drowned*
Thus shal mankinde drenche° and lese hir lif."°   *drown/lose their lives*
This carpenter answerde, "Allas, my wif!
415   And shal she drenche? Allas, myn Alisoun!"
For sorwe of this he fil almost adown,
And saide, "Is there no remedye in this cas?"
"Why yis, for Gode," quod hende Nicholas,

---

4. St. Benedict, founder of western monasticism.
5. The Lord's Prayer, used as a charm.

6. Christ, who harrowed hell upon his resurrection, releasing captive souls.

	"If thou wolt werken° after lore° and reed°—	*act/learning/advice*
420	Thou maist nought werken after thyn owene heed;	
	For thus saith Salomon that was ful trewe,	
	'Werk al by conseil and thou shalt nought rewe.'°	*regret*
	And if thou werken wolt by good conseil,	
	I undertake, withouten mast or sail,	
425	Yet shal I save hire and thee and me.	
	Hastou nat herd how saved was Noee	
	Whan that Oure Lord hadde warned him biforn	
	That al the world with water sholde be lorn?"°	*lost*
	"Yis," quod this carpenter, "ful yore ago."	
430	"Hastou nat herd," quod Nicholas, "also	
	The sorwe° of Noee with his felaweshipe?°	*sorrow/companions*
	Er that he mighte gete his wif to shipe,	
	Him hadde levere,° I dar wel undertake,	*would have preferred*
	At thilke time than alle his wetheres° blake	*rams*
435	That she hadde had a ship hirself allone.[7]	
	And therfore woostou° what is best to doone?	*do you know*
	This axeth haste, and of an hastif° thing	*urgent*
	Men may nought preche or maken tarying.	
	Anoon go gete us faste into this in°	*inn*
440	A kneeding trough or elles a kimelin°	*brewing trough*
	For eech of us, but looke that they be large,	
	In whiche we mowen swimme as in a barge,	
	And han therinne vitaile suffisaunt°	*enough food*
	But for a day—fy on the remenaunt!	
445	The water shal aslake° and goon away	*recede*
	Aboute prime° upon the nexte day.	*6 a.m.*
	But Robin may nat wite° of this, thy knave,	*know*
	Ne eek thy maide Gille I may nat save.	
	Axe nought why, for though thou axe me,	
450	I wol nought tellen Goddes privetee.	
	Suffiseth thee, but if thy wittes madde,°	*go mad*
	To han° as greet a grace as Noee hadde.	*have*
	Thy wif shal I wel saven, out of doute.	
	Go now thy way, and speed thee heraboute.	
455	But whan thou hast for hire and thee and me	
	Ygeten° us thise kneeding-tubbes three,	*gotten*
	Thanne shaltou hangen hem in the roof ful hye,	
	That no man of oure purveyance° espye.	*preparations*
	And whan thou thus hast doon as I have said,	
460	And hast oure vitaile faire in hem ylaid,	
	And eek an ax to smite the corde atwo,	
	Whan that the water comth that we may go,	
	And broke an hole an heigh° upon the gable	*on high*
	Unto the gardinward,° over the stable,	*toward the garden*
465	That we may freely passen forth oure way,	
	Whan that the grete showr is goon away,	
	Thanne shaltou swimme as merye, I undertake,	

7. Noah's wife was traditionally portrayed in the mystery plays as a complaining wife who resisted boarding the ark.

As dooth the white doke° after hir drake.   *female duck*
Thanne wol I clepe, 'How, Alison? How, John?
470 Be merye, for the flood wol passe anoon.'
And thou wolt sayn, 'Hail, maister Nicholay!
Good morwe, I see thee wel, for it is day!'
And thanne shal we be lordes al oure lif
Of al the world, as Noee and his wif.
475 But of oo thing I warne thee ful right:
Be wel avised on that ilke night
That we been entred into shippes boord
That noon of us ne speke nought a word,
Ne clepe, ne crye, but been in his prayere,
480 For it is Goddes owene heeste° dere.   *commandment*
Thy wif and thou mote hange fer atwinne,°   *apart*
For that bitwixe you shal be no sinne—
Namore in looking than ther shal in deede.
This ordinance is said: go, God thee speede.
485 Tomorwe at night whan men been alle asleepe,
Into oure kneeding-tubbes wol we creepe,
And sitten there, abiding Goddes grace.
Go now thy way, I have no lenger space°   *time*
To make of this no lenger sermoning.
490 Men sayn thus: 'Send the wise and say no thing.'
Thou art so wis it needeth thee nat teche:
Go save oure lif, and that I thee biseeche."
     This sely carpenter gooth forth his way:
Ful ofte he saide allas and wailaway,
495 And to his wif he tolde his privetee,
And she was war,° and knew it bet° than he,   *aware/better*
What al this quainte cast° was for to saye.°   *clever trick/mean*
But nathelees she ferde° as she wolde deye,   *acted*
And saide, "Allas, go forth thy way anoon.
500 Help us to scape,° or we been dede eechoon.   *escape*
I am thy trewe verray wedded wif:
Go, dere spouse, and help to save oure lif."
     Lo, which a greet thing is affeccioun!°   *emotion*
Men may dien° of imaginacioun,°   *die/fantasy*
505 So deepe may impression be take.
This sely carpenter biginneth quake;
Him thinketh verrailiche° that he may see   *truly*
Noees flood come walwing° as the see   *rolling in*
To drenchen Alison, his hony dere.
510 He weepeth, waileth, maketh sory cheere;°   *expression*
He siketh° with ful many a sory swough,°   *sighs/breath*
And gooth and geteth him a kneeding-trough,
And after a tubbe and a kimelin,
And prively he sente hem to his in,
515 And heeng hem in the roof in privetee;
His owene hand he made laddres three,
To climben by the ronges and the stalkes°   *uprights*
Unto the tubbes hanging in the balkes,°   *rafters*

	And hem vitailed, bothe trough and tubbe,	
520	With breed and cheese and good ale in a jubbe,°	jug
	Suffising right ynough as for a day.	
	But er that he hadde maad al this array,	
	He sente his knave, and eek his wenche also,	
	Upon his neede° to London for to go.	errand
525	And on the Monday whan it drow to nighte,	
	He shette his dore withouten candel-lighte,	
	And dressed° alle thing as it sholde be,	arranged
	And shortly up they clomben alle three.	
	They seten stille wel a furlong way.[8]	
530	"Now, Pater Noster, clum,"[9] saide Nicholay,	
	And "Clum" quod John, and "Clum" saide Alisoun.	
	This carpenter saide his devocioun,	
	And stille he sit and biddeth his prayere,	
	Awaiting on the rain, if he it heere.	
535	The dede sleep, for wery bisinesse,	
	Fil on this carpenter right as I gesse	
	Aboute corfew time,° or litel more.	dusk
	For travailing of his gost° he groneth sore,	spirit
	And eft he routeth,° for his heed mislay.	snores
540	Down of the laddre stalketh Nicholay,	
	And Alison ful softe adown she spedde:	
	Withouten wordes mo they goon to bedde	
	Ther as the carpenter is wont to lie.	
	Ther was the revel and the melodye,	
545	And thus lith Alison and Nicholas	
	In bisinesse of mirthe and of solas,	
	Til that the belle of Laudes[1] gan to ringe,	
	And freres° in the chauncel° gonne singe.	friars/chapel
550	This parissh clerk, this amorous Absolon,	
	That is for love alway so wo-bigoon,	
	Upon the Monday was at Oseneye,	
	With compaignye him to disporte and playe,	
	And axed upon caas° a cloisterer[2]	by chance
555	Ful prively after John the carpenter;	
	And he drow him apart out of the chirche,	
	And saide, "I noot:° I sawgh him here nought wirche°	don't know/working
	Sith Saterday. I trowe that he be went	
	For timber ther oure abbot hath him sent.	
560	For he is wont for timber for to go,	
	And dwellen atte grange° a day or two.	outlying farm
	Or elles he is at his hous, certain.	
	Where that he be I can nought soothly sayn."	
	This Absolon ful jolif was and light,°	amorous and happy
565	And thoughte, "Now is time to wake al night,	
	For sikerly,° I sawgh him nought stiringe	surely
	Aboute his dore sin day bigan to springe.	

8. The length of time to travel a furlong.
9. Say the Lord's Prayer and hush.
1. Lauds, daily church service before sunrise.
2. Member of the monastery.

So mote I thrive,° I shal at cokkes crowe   *may I prosper*
Ful prively knokken at his windowe
That stant ful lowe upon his bowres° wal.   *bedroom's*
570   To Alison now wol I tellen al
My love-longing, for yet I shal nat misse
That at the leeste way I shal hire kisse.
Som manere confort shal I have, parfay.°   *indeed*
My mouth hath icched° al this longe day: *itched*
575   That is a signe of kissing at the leeste.
Al night me mette° eek I was at a feeste.   *dreamed*
Therfore I wol go sleepe an hour or twaye,
And al the night thanne wol I wake and playe."
       Whan that the firste cok hath crowe, anoon
580   Up rist this joly lovere Absolon,
And him arrayeth gay at point devis.°   *fastidiously*
But first he cheweth grain³ and licoris,
To smellen sweete, er he hadde kembd his heer.
Under his tonge a trewe-love⁴ he beer,
585   For therby wende° he to be gracious.°   *supposed/attractive*
He rometh to the carpenteres hous,
And stille he stant under the shot-windowe—
Unto his brest it raughte,° it was so lowe—   *reached*
And ofte he cougheth with a semisoun.°   *soft noise*
590   "What do ye, hony-comb, sweete Alisoun,
My faire brid,° my sweete cinamome?   *bird or bride*
Awaketh, lemman° myn, and speketh to me.   *sweetheart*
Wel litel thinken ye upon my wo
That for your love I swete° ther I go.   *dissolve*
595   No wonder is though that I swelte and swete:
I moorne as dooth a lamb after the tete.
Ywis,° lemman, I have swich love-longinge,   *certainly*
That lik a turtle° trewe is my moorninge: *turtle-dove*
I may nat ete namore than a maide."
600   "Go fro the windowe, Jakke fool," she saide.
"As help me God, it wol nat be com-pa-me.°   *come kiss me*
I love another, and elles I were to blame,
Wel bet than thee, by Jesu, Absolon.
Go forth thy way or I wol caste a stoon,
605   And lat me sleepe, a twenty devele way."⁵
       "Allas," quod Absolon, "and wailaway,
That trewe love was evere so yvele biset.°   *badly done to*
Thanne kis me, sin that it may be no bet,
For Jesus love and for the love of me."
610   "Woltou thanne go thy way therwith?" quod she.
"Ye, certes, lemman," quod this Absolon.
"Thanne maak thee redy," quod she. "I come anoon."
And unto Nicholas she said stille,
"Now hust,° and thou shalt laughen al thy fille."   *hush*
615   This Absolon down sette him on his knees,

---

3. Grain of paradise, an aromatic spice.   5. In the name of twenty devils.
4. Four-leafed herb in the shape of a love knot.

And saide, "I am a lord at alle degrees,°   *in every way*
For after this I hope ther cometh more.
Lemman, thy grace, and sweete brid, thyn ore!"°   *mercy*
   The windowe she undooth, and that in haste.
620   "Have do," quod she, "com of and speed thee faste,
Lest that oure neighebores thee espye."
   This Absolon gan wipe his mouth ful drye:
Derk was the night as pich or as the cole,
And at the windowe out she putte hir hole,
625   And Absolon, him fil no bet ne wers,
But with his mouth he kiste hir naked ers,
Ful savourly,° er he were war of this.   *enthusiastically*
Abak he sterte, and thoughte it was amis,
For wel he wiste a womman hath no beerd.
630   He felte a thing al rough and longe yherd,°   *haird*
And saide, "Fy, allas, what have I do?"
"Teehee," quod she, and clapte the windowe to.
And Absolon gooth forth a sory pas.°   *with downcast step*
"A beerd, a beerd!" quod hende Nicholas,
635   "By Goddes corpus,° this gooth faire and weel."   *body*
   This sely Absolon herde everydeel,
And on his lippe he gan for anger bite,
And to himself he saide, "I shal thee quite."°   *repay*
   Who rubbeth now, who froteth now his lippes
640   With dust, with sond, with straw, with cloth, with chippes,
But Absolon, that saith ful ofte allas?
"My soule bitake° I unto Satanas,   *hand over*
But me were levere than⁶ all this town," quod he,
"Of this despit° awroken° for to be.   *insult/avenged*
645   Allas," quod he, "allas I ne hadde ybleint!"°   *turned aside*
His hote love was cold and al yqueint,°   *quenched*
For fro that time that he hadde kist hir ers
Of paramours he sette nought a kers,⁷
For he was heled of his maladye.
650   Ful ofte paramours he gan defye,°   *renounce*
And weep as dooth a child that is ybete.°   *beaten*
A softe paas he wente over the streete
Until a smith men clepen daun° Gervais,   *Sir*
That in his forge smithed plough harneis:°   *equipment*
655   He sharpeth shaar° and cultour° bisily.   *plowshare/plough-blade*
This Absolon knokketh al esily,°   *softly*
And saide, "Undo,° Gervais, and that anoon."   *open up*
   "What, who artou?" "It am I, Absolon."
"What, Absolon? What, Cristes sweete tree!
660   Why rise ye so rathe?° Ey, benedicite,°   *early/bless me*
What aileth you? Som gay girl, God it woot,
Hath brought you thus upon the viritoot.°   *on the prowl*
By Sainte Note,⁸ ye woot wel what I mene."
   This Absolon ne roughte nat a bene°   *did not care a bean*

---

6. I would rather than (have).
7. Did not value as much as a piece of cress.

8. St. Noet, a ninth-century saint, with possible pun on Noah.

665 Of al his play. No word again he yaf:
     He hadde more tow on his distaf[9]
     Than Gervais knew, and saide, "Freend so dere,
     This hote cultour in the chimenee° here,   *fireplace*
     As lene it me:[1] I have therwith to doone.
670 I wol bringe it thee again ful soone."
         Gervais answerde, "Certes, were it gold,
     Or in a poke nobles alle untold,[2]
     Thou sholdest have, as I am trewe smith.
     Ey, Cristes fo,[3] what wol ye do therwith?"
675   "Therof," quod Absolon, "be as be may.
     I shal wel telle it thee another day,"
     And caughte the cultour by the colde stele.°   *handle*
     Ful softe out at the dore he gan to stele,
     And wente unto the carpenteres wal:
680 He cougheth first and knokketh therwithal
     Upon the windowe, right as he dide er.°   *before*
         This Alison answerde, "Who is ther
     That knokketh so? I warante° it a thief."   *bet*
         "Why, nay," quod he, "God woot, my sweete lief,°   *dear*
685 I am thyn Absolon, my dereling.
     Of gold," quod he, "I have thee brought a ring—
     My moder yaf it me, so God me save;
     Ful fin it is and therto wel ygrave:°   *engraved*
     This wol I yiven thee if thou me kisse."
690   This Nicholas was risen for to pisse,
     And thoughte he wolde amenden al the jape:[4]
     He sholde kisse his ers er that he scape.
     And up the windowe dide he hastily,
     And out his ers he putteth prively,
695 Over the buttok to the haunche-boon.°   *thigh*
         And therwith spak this clerk, this Absolon,
     "Speek, sweete brid, I noot nought wher thou art."
     This Nicholas anoon leet flee° a fart   *let fly*
     As greet as it hadde been a thonder-dent°   *thunderbolt*
700 That with the strook he was almost yblent,°   *blinded*
     And he was redy with his iren hoot,
     And Nicholas amiddle the ers he smoot:
     Of gooth the skin an hande-brede° aboute;   *hand's width*
     The hote cultour brende so his toute°   *backside*
705 That for the smert° he wende° for to die;   *pain/thought*
     As he were wood for wo he gan to crye,
     "Help! Water! Water! Help, for Goddes herte!"
         This carpenter out of his slomber sterte,
     And herde oon cryen "Water!" as he were wood,
710 And thoughte, "Allas, now cometh Noweles° flood!"   *Noah's*
     He sette him up withoute wordes mo,

9. Flax on his distaff (i.e., cares on his mind).   3. By Christ's foe (i.e., the Devil).
1. Be so good as to lend it to me.   4. Make the joke even better.
2. Or in a pouch of uncounted gold coins.

And with his ax he smooth the corde atwo,
And down gooth al: he foond neither to selle
Ne breed ne ale til he cam to the celle,[5]
715 Upon the floor, and ther aswoune° he lay.   *stunned*
        Up sterte hire Alison and Nicholay,
And criden "Out" and "Harrow" in the streete.
The neighebores, bothe smale and grete,[6]
In ronnen for to gauren° on this man   *stare*
720 That aswoune lay bothe pale and wan,
For with the fal he brosten° hadde his arm;   *broken*
But stonde he moste unto his owene harm,
For whan he spak he was anoon bore down°   *restrained*
With° hende Nicholas and Alisoun: *by*
725 They tolden every man that he was wood—
He was agast° so of Noweles flood,   *afraid*
Thurgh fantasye, that of his vanitee°   *folly*
He hadde ybought him kneeding-tubbes three,
And hadde hem hanged in the roof above,
730 And that he prayed hem, for Goddes love,
To sitten in the roof, *par compaignye.*°   *for fellowship*
        The folk gan laughen at his fantasye.
Into the roof they kiken° and they cape,°   *peer/gape*
And turned al his harm unto a jape,
735 For what so that this carpenter answerde,
It was for nought: no man his reson herde;
With othes grete he was so sworn adown,°   *refuted by oaths*
That he was holden wood in al the town,
For every clerk anoonright heeld with other:
740 They saide, "The man was wood, my leve brother,"
And every wight gan laughen at this strif.
Thus swived° was the carpenteres wif   *screwed*
For al his keeping and his jalousye,
And Absolon hath kist hir nether° yë,   *lower*
745 And Nicholas is scalded in the toute:
This tale is doon, and God save al the route!

The Wife of Bath's Prologue and Tale

Dame Alison, the Wife of Bath, is Chaucer's greatest contribution to the stock characters of
western culture. She has a long literary ancestry, most immediately in the Duenna of the thirteenth-century French poem, *The Romance of the Rose,* and stretching back to the Roman poet
Ovid. Dame Alison stands out in bold relief, even among the vivid Canterbury pilgrims, partly
because Chaucer gives her so rebellious and explicitly self-created a biography. She has outlived five husbands, accumulated wealth from the first three, and made herself rich in the
growing textile industry of her time. At once a great companion and greatly unnerving, Alison
lives in constant battle with a secular and religious world mostly controlled by men and yet has
a keen appetite both for the men and for the battle.
        The Wife of Bath's *Prologue* and *Tale* seem only the current installments of a multifaceted
struggle in which she has long been engaged, at first through her body and social role and now,

5. He found no time to sell either bread or ale until he   be aware of what was happening).
reached the floor (i.e., he fell to the ground too quickly to   6. Lower- and upper-class people alike.

in the face of advancing years, through the remaining agency of retrospective storytelling. Dame Alison battles a society in which many young women are almost chattels in a marital market, as was the twelve-year-old version of herself who first was married off to a wealthier, much older man. She battles him and later husbands for power within the marriage, and her ambition to social dominance, as the *General Prologue* reports, extends to life in her urban parish.

By the moment of the Canterbury pilgrimage, though, the Wife's adversaries are more daunting, less easily conquered. The Wife's *Prologue*, for all its autobiographical energy, is primarily a debate with the clergy and with "auctoritee"—the whole armature of learning and literacy by which the clergy (like her clerically educated fifth husband, Jankyn) seeks to silence her.

The Wife of Bath's Tale, too, can be seen as an angry riposte to the secular fantasies of Arthurian chivalry and genetic nobility. The Wife's well-born Arthurian knight is a common rapist, who finds himself at the mercy of a queen and then in the arms of a crone. The tale turns Arthurian conventions on their head, lays sexual violence in the open, and puts legal and magical power in the hands of women. It is explicitly a fantasy, but a powerful one.

Alison's final enemy, mortality itself, is what makes her both most desperate and most sympathetic. The husbands are gone. Even the fondly recalled Jankyn slips into a rosy glow and the past tense; so does her own best friend and "gossip," the odd mirror-double "Alisoun." The Wife of Bath keeps addressing other "wives" in her *Prologue*, but there are no others on the pilgrimage. Her very argument with the institutionalized church distances her from its comforts, and she is deeply aware that time is stealing her beauty as it has taken away the companions who made up her earlier life. If Alison's *Tale* closes with a delicious fantasy of restored youth, it is only a pendant to the much longer *Prologue* and its cheerful yet poignant acceptance of age.

The Wife of Bath's Prologue

Experience, though noon auctoritee[1]
Were in this world, is right ynough for me
To speke of wo that is in mariage:
For lordinges,° sith I twelf yeer was of age—   *gentlemen*
5   Thanked be God that is eterne on live—
Housbondes at chirche dore I have had five
(If I so ofte mighte han wedded be),
And alle were worthy men in hir° degree.   *their*
But me was told, certain, nat longe agoon is,
10   That sith that Crist ne wente nevere but ones°   *once*
To wedding in the Cane of Galilee,[2]
That by the same ensample taughte he me
That I ne sholde wedded be but ones.
Herke eek, lo, which a sharp word for the nones,°   *for the purpose*
15   Biside a welle, Jesus, God and man,
Spak in repreve° of the Samaritan:[3]   *reproof*
"Thou hast yhad five housbondes," quod he,
"And that ilke° man that now hath thee   *same*
Is nat thyn housbonde." Thus saide he certain.
20   What that he mente therby I can nat sayn,
But that I axe why that the fifthe man
Was noon housbonde to the Samaritan?

---

1. Even if no authority, textual precedent.
2. Cana, where Jesus performed his first miracle at a wedding feast (John 2.1).
3. The story of Jesus and the Samaritan woman is related in John 4.6ff.

How manye mighte she han in mariage?
Yit herde I nevere tellen in myn age
25 Upon this nombre diffinicioun.
Men may divine° and glosen° up and down, *guess/interpret*
But wel I woot,° expres,° withouten lie, *know/manifestly*
God bad us for to wexe° and multiplye: *increase*
That gentil text can I wel understonde.
30 Eek wel I woot he saide that myn housbonde
Sholde lete° fader and moder and take to me, *leave*
But of no nombre mencion made he—
Of bigamye or of octogamye:
Why sholde men thanne speke of it vilainye?° *as churlish*
35 Lo, here the wise king daun° Salomon: *Lord*
I trowe° he hadde wives many oon, *believe*
As wolde God it leveful° were to me *lawful*
To be refresshed half so ofte as he.
Which yifte° of God hadde he for alle his wives! *what a gift*
40 No man hath swich that in this world alive is.
God woot this noble king, as to my wit,° *understanding*
The firste night hadde many a merye fit
With eech of hem, so wel was him on live.
Blessed be God that I have wedded five,
45 Of whiche I have piked° out the beste, *picked*
Bothe of hir nether purs and of hir cheste.[4]
Diverse° scoles maken parfit° clerkes, *different/accomplished*
And diverse practikes in sondry werkes
Maken the werkman° parfit sikerly: *craftsman*
50 Of five housbondes scoleying° am I. *studying*
Welcome the sixte whan that evere he shal!
For sith I wol nat keepe me chast in al,
Whan myn housbonde is fro the world agoon,
Som Cristen man shal wedde me anoon.
55 For thanne th'Apostle[5] saith that I am free
To wedde, a Goddes half,[6] where it liketh° me. *please*
He said that to be wedded is no sinne:
Bet° is to be wedded than to brinne.° *better/burn (in hell)*
What rekketh° me though folk saye vilainye *do I care*
60 Of shrewed° Lamech[7] and his bigamye? *cursed*
I woot wel Abraham was an holy man,
And Jacob eek, as fer as evere I can,° *know*
And eech of hem hadde wives mo than two,
And many another holy man also.
65 Where can ye saye in any manere age
That hye God defended° mariage *prohibited*
By expres word? I praye you, telleth me.
Or where comanded he virginitee?
I woot as wel as ye, it is no drede,° *doubt*
70 Th'Apostle, whan he speketh of maidenhede,° *virginity*

4. Money chest, with a pun on body parts.
5. St. Paul, in Romans 7.2.
6. From God's perspective.
7. The earliest bigamist in the Bible (Genesis 4.19).

He saide that precept therof hadde he noon:
Men may conseile a womman to be oon,°   *single*
But conseiling nis no comandement.
He putte it in oure owene juggement.
75   For hadde God comanded maidenhede,
Thanne hadde he dampned° wedding with the deede;   *condemned*
And certes, if ther were no seed ysowe,
Virginitee, thanne wherof sholde it growe?
Paul dorste nat comanden at the leeste
80   A thing of which his maister yaf no heeste.°   *commandment*
The dart° is set up for virginitee: *prize*
Cacche whoso may, who renneth° best lat see.   *runs*
But this word is nought take° of every wight,   *required*
But ther as God list° yive it of his might.   *pleases*
85   I woot wel that th'Apostle was a maide,°   *virgin*
But nathelees, though that he wroot or saide
He wolde that every wight were swich as he,
Al nis but° conseil to virginitee;   *it is only*
And for to been a wif he yaf me leve
90   Of indulgence; so nis it no repreve
To wedde me if that my make° die,   *mate*
Withouten excepcion° of bigamye—   *legal objection*
Al were it good no womman for to touche
(He mente as in his bed or in his couche,
95   For peril is bothe fir and tow t'assemble[8]—
Ye knowe what this ensample may resemble).
This al and som,° he heeld virginitee   *all told*
More parfit than wedding in freletee.°   *due to weakness*
(Freletee clepe° I but if° that he and she   *call/except*
100 Wolde leden al hir lif in chastitee).
I graunte it wel, I have noon envye
Though maidenhede preferre° bigamye: *surpasses*
It liketh hem to be clene in body and gost.°   *soul*
Of myn estaat° ne wol I make no boost;   *condition*
105 For wel ye knowe, a lord in his houshold
Ne hath nat every vessel al of gold:
Some been of tree,° and doon hir lord servise.   *wood*
God clepeth folk to him in sondry wise,
And everich hath of God a propre yifte,
110 Som this, som that, as him liketh shifte.[9]
Virginitee is greet perfeccioun,
And continence eek with devocioun,
But Crist, that of perfeccion is welle,°   *source*
Bad nat every wight he sholde go selle
115 Al that he hadde and yive it to the poore,
And in swich wise folwe him and his fore:°   *footsteps*
He spak to hem that wolde live parfitly°—   *perfectly*
And lordinges, by youre leve, that am nat I.
I wol bistowe the flour of al myn age

8. To bring together fire and flax.   9. As it pleases him to provide.

120 In th'actes and in fruit of mariage.
      Telle me also, to what conclusioun°   *end*
    Were membres maad of generacioun
    And of so parfit wis a wrighte ywrought?[1]
    Trusteth right wel, they were nat maad for nought.
125 Glose whoso wol, and saye bothe up and down
    That they were maked for purgacioun
    Of urine, and oure bothe thinges smale
    Was eek to knowe a femele from a male,
    And for noon other cause—saye ye no?
130 Th'experience woot wel it is nought so.
    So that the clerkes be nat with me wrothe,
    I saye this, that they maked been for bothe,
    That is to sayn, for office° and for ese°   *use/pleasure*
    Of engendrure,° ther we nat God displese.   *procreation*
135 Why sholde men elles in hir bookes sette
    That man shal yeelde° to his wif hir dette?°   *pay/marriage debt*
    Now wherwith sholde he make his payement
    If he ne used his sely° instrument?   *innocent*
    Thanne were they maad upon a creature
140 To purge urine, and eek for engendrure.
      But I saye nought that every wight is holde,°   *bound*
    That hath swich harneis° as I to you tolde,   *equipment*
    To goon and usen hem in engendrure:
    Thanne sholde men take of chastitee no cure.°   *heed*
145 Crist was a maide and shapen as a man,
    And many a saint sith that the world bigan,
    Yit lived they evere in parfit chastitee.
    I nil envye no virginitee:
    Lat hem be breed° of pured° whete seed,   *bread/refined*
150 And lat us wives hote° barly breed—   *be called*
    And yit with barly breed, Mark telle can,
    Oure Lord Jesu refresshed many a man.
    In swich estaat as God hath cleped us
    I wol persevere: I nam nat precious.°   *fussy*
155 In wifhood wol I use myn instrument
    As freely° as my Makere hath it sent.   *generously*
    If I be daungerous,° God yive me sorwe: *withholding*
    Myn housbonde shal it han both eve and morwe,°   *morning*
    Whan that him list come forth and paye his dette.
160 An housbonde wol I have, I wol nat lette,°   *forgo*
    Which shal be bothe my dettour and my thral,°   *slave*
    And have his tribulacion withal
    Upon his flessh whil that I am his wif.
    I have the power during al my lif
165 Upon his propre° body, and nat he: *own*
    Right thus th'Apostle tolde it unto me,
    And bad oure housbondes for to love us weel.
    Al this sentence° me liketh everydeel.   *interpretation*

1. And created by so perfectly wise a Creator?

An Interlude

	Up sterte° the Pardoner and that anoon:	*started*
170	"Now dame," quod he, "by God and by Saint John,	
	Ye been a noble prechour° in this cas.	*preacher*
	I was aboute to wedde a wif: allas,	
	What° sholde I bye° it on my flessh so dere?	*why/buy*
	Yit hadde I levere° wedde no wif toyere."°	*rather/this year*
175	"Abid," quod she, "my tale is nat bigonne.	
	Nay, thou shalt drinken of another tonne,°	*barrel*
	Er that I go, shal savoure wors than ale.	
	And whan that I have told thee forth my tale	
	Of tribulacion in mariage,	
180	Of which I am expert in al myn age—	
	This is to saye, myself hath been the whippe—	
	Thanne maistou chese° wheither thou wolt sippe	*may you choose*
	Of thilke tonne that I shal abroche:°	*open*
	Be war of it, er thou too neigh approche,	
185	For I shal telle ensamples mo than ten.	
	'Whoso that nile° be war by othere men,	*will not*
	By him shal othere men corrected be.'	
	Thise same wordes writeth Ptolomee:[2]	
	Rede in his *Almageste* and take it there."	
190	"Dame, I wolde praye you if youre wil it were,"	
	Saide this Pardoner, "as ye bigan,	
	Telle forth youre tale; spareth for no man,	
	And teche us yonge men of youre practike."	
	"Gladly," quod she, "sith it may you like;	
195	But that I praye to al this compaignye,	
	If that I speke after my fantasye,°	*fancy*
	As taketh nat agrief° of that I saye,	*amiss*
	For myn entente nis but for to playe."	

The Wife Continues

	Now sire, thanne wol I telle you forth my tale.	
200	As evere mote I drinke win or ale,	
	I shal saye sooth: tho housbondes that I hadde,	
	As three of hem were goode, and two were badde.	
	The three men were goode, and riche, and olde;	
	Unnethe° mighte they the statut holde	*scarcely*
205	In which they were bounden unto me—	
	Ye woot wel what I mene of this, pardee.	
	As help me God, I laughe whan I thinke	
	How pitously anight I made hem swinke;°	*work*
	And by my fay, I tolde of it no stoor:°	*gave it no heed*
210	They hadde me yiven hir land and hir tresor;	
	Me needed nat do lenger diligence	
	To winne hir love or doon hem reverence.	
	They loved me so wel, by God above,	

---

2. Ptolemy, ancient Greek astronomer and author of the *Almageste*.

That I ne tolde no daintee° of hir love.   *set no value on*
215 A wis womman wol bisye hire evere in oon°   *constantly*
To gete hire love, ye, ther as she hath noon.
But sith I hadde hem hoolly in myn hand,
And sith that they hadde yiven me al hir land,
What sholde I take keep° hem for to plese,   *care*
220 But it were for my profit and myn ese?
I sette hem so awerke, by my fay,°   *faith*
That many a night they songen wailaway.
The bacon was nat fet° for hem, I trowe,   *collected*
That some men han in Essexe at Dunmowe.[3]
225 I governed hem so wel after my lawe
That eech of hem ful blisful was and fawe°   *glad*
To bringe me gaye thinges fro the faire;
They were ful glade whan I spak to hem faire,
For God it woot, I chidde° hem spitously.°   *scolded/cruelly*
230   Now herkneth how I bar me proprely:
Ye wise wives, that conne understonde,
Thus sholde ye speke and bere him wrong on honde°—   *wrongly accuse*
For half so boldely can ther no man
Swere and lie as a woman can.
235 I saye nat this by wives that been wise,
But if it be whan they hem misavise.°   *err*
A wis wif, if that she can hir good,[4]
Shal bere him on hande the cow is wood,[5]
And take witnesse of hir owene maide
240 Of hir assent.° But herkneth how I saide: *as her accomplice*
"Sire olde cainard,° is this thyn array?   *dotard*
Why is my neighebores wif so gay?
She is honoured overal ther she gooth:
I sitte at hoom; I have no thrifty° cloth.   *decent*
245 What doostou at my neighebores hous?
Is she so fair? Artou so amorous?
What roune° ye with oure maide, benedicite?°   *whisper/bless us*
Sire olde lechour, lat thy japes° be.   *tricks*
And if I have a gossib° or a freend,   *confidante*
250 Withouten gilt ye chiden as a feend,
If that I walke or playe unto his hous.
Thou comest hoom as dronken as a mous,
And prechest on thy bench, with yvel preef.°   *bad luck to you*
Thou saist to me, it is a greet meschief
255 To wedde a poore womman for costage.°   *expense*
And if that she be riche, of heigh parage,°   *breeding*
Thanne saistou that it is a tormentrye
To suffre hir pride and hir malencolye.
And if that she be fair, thou verray knave,
260 Thou saist that every holour° wol hire have: *whoremonger*
She may no while in chastitee abide

3. At Dunmowe, spouses who had spent a year without
quarrelling were awarded a side of bacon.
4. Knows what's good for her.

5. Shall convince him the chough is mad. The chough, a
crow-like bird, was fabled to reveal wives' infidelities.

That is assailed upon eech a side.
　"Thou saist som folk desiren us for richesse,
Som for oure shap, and som for oure fairnesse,

265 And som for she can outher° singe or daunce,　　　　*either*
And som for gentilesse and daliaunce,°　　　　*conversation*
Som for hir handes and hir armes smale—
Thus gooth al to the devel by thy tale!⁶
Thou saist men may nat keepe a castel wal,

270 It may so longe assailed been overal.
And if that she be foul, thou saist that she
Coveiteth° every man that she may see;　　　　*desires*
For as a spaniel she wol on him lepe,
Til that she finde som man hire to chepe.°　　　　*take*

275 Ne noon so grey goos gooth ther in the lake,
As, saistou, wol be withoute make;
And saist it is an hard thing for to weelde°　　　　*control*
A thing that no man wol, his thankes,° heelde.°　　　*willingly/hold*
Thus saistou, lorel,° whan thou goost to bedde,　　　*scoundrel*

280 And that no wis man needeth for to wedde,
Ne no man that entendeth° unto hevene—　　　　*expects (to go)*
With wilde thonder-dint° and firy levene°　　　*thunderclap/lightning*
Mote° thy welked° nekke be tobroke!°　　　*may/withered/broken*
Thou saist that dropping° houses and eek smoke　　　*leaking*

285 And chiding wives maken men to flee
Out of hir owene houses: a, benedicite,
What aileth swich an old man for to chide?
Thou saist we wives wil oure vices hide
Til we be fast,° and thanne we wol hem shewe—　　　*bound (in marriage)*

290 Wel may that be a proverbe of a shrewe!°　　　*scoundrel*
Thou saist that oxen, asses, hors, and houndes,
They been assayed at diverse stoundes;
Bacins, lavours, er that men hem bye,
Spoones, stooles, and al swich housbondrye,

295 And so be pottes, clothes, and array—
But folk of wives maken noon assay
Til they be wedded—olde dotard shrewe!
And thanne, saistou, we wil oure vices shewe.
Thou saist also that it displeseth me

300 But if that thou wolt praise my beautee,
And but thou poure alway upon my face,
And clepe me 'Faire Dame' in every place,
And but thou make a feeste on thilke day
That I was born, and make me fressh and gay,

305 And but thou do to my norice° honour,　　　　*nurse*
And to my chamberere° within my bowr,°　　　*chambermaid/bedroom*
And to my fadres folk, and his allies°—　　　*kinsmen*
Thus saistou, olde barel-ful of lies.
And yit of our apprentice Janekin,

310 For his crispe heer,° shining as gold so fin,　　　*curly hair*

---

6. According to what you say.

And for he squiereth° me bothe up and down,   *chaperones*
Yit hastou caught a fals suspecioun;
I wil° him nat though thou were deed tomorwe.   *desire*
        "But tel me this, why hidestou with sorwe
315 The keyes of thy cheste away fro me?
It is my good as wel as thyn, pardee.
What, weenestou° make an idiot of oure dame?   *do you suppose*
Now by that lord that called is Saint Jame,[7]
Thou shalt nought bothe, though that thou were wood,°   *enraged*
320 Be maister of my body and of my good:
That oon thou shalt forgo, maugree thine yën.[8]
        "What helpeth it of me enquere and spyen?
I trowe thou woldest loke° me in thy cheste.   *lock*
Thou sholdest saye, 'Wif, go wher thee leste.
325 Taak youre disport. I nil leve° no tales: *believe*
I knowe you for a trewe wif, dame Alis.'
We love no man that taketh keep° or charge   *notice*
Wher that we goon: we wol been at oure large.°   *liberty*
Of alle men yblessed mote he be
330 The wise astrologen daun Ptolomee,
That saith this proverbe in his Almageste:
'Of alle men his wisdom is the hyeste
That rekketh° nat who hath the world in honde.'   *cares*
By this proverbe thou shalt understonde,
335 Have thou ynough, what thar° thee rekke or care   *need*
How merily that othere folkes fare?
For certes, olde dotard, by youre leve,
Ye shal han queinte° right ynough at eve: *sex*
He is too greet a nigard that wil werne°   *refuse*
340 A man to lighte a candle at his lanterne;
He shal han nevere the lasse lighte, pardee.°   *by God*
Have thou ynough, thee thar nat plaine thee.°   *complain*
        "Thou saist also that if we make us gay
With clothing and with precious array,
345 That it is peril of oure chastitee,
And yit with sorwe thou moste enforce thee,[9]
And saye thise wordes in th'Apostles name:
'In habit° maad with chastitee and shame   *clothing*
Ye wommen shal apparaile you,' quod he,
350 'And nat in tressed heer° and gay perree,°   *styled hair / jewels*
As perles ne with gold ne clothes riche.'
After thy text, ne after thy rubriche,[1]
I wol nat werke as muchel as a gnat.
Thou saidest this, that I was lik a cat:
355 For whoso wolde senge° a cattes skin,   *singe*
Thanne wolde the cat wel dwellen in his in;°   *inn*
And if the cattes skin be slik° and gay,   *sleek*
She wol nat dwelle in house half a day,

---

7. Santiago de Compostela, whose shrine in Spain the Wife of Bath has already made a pilgrimage to visit.
8. In spite of your eyes (an oath).
9. Reinforce (your position).
1. Rubric, interpretive heading on a text.

	But forth she wol, er any day be dawed,°	*dawned*
360	To shewe her skin and goon a-caterwawed.°	*caterwauling*
	This is to saye, if I be gay, sire shrewe,	
	I wol renne out, my borel° for to shewe.	*coarse cloth*
	Sire olde fool, what helpeth thee t'espyen?	
	Though thou praye Argus[2] with his hundred yën	
365	To be my wardecors,° as he can best,	*bodyguard*
	In faith, he shal nat keepe me but me lest:	
	Yit coude I make his beerd,[3] so mote I thee.°	*so may I prosper*
	"Thou saidest eek that ther been thinges three,	
	The whiche thinges troublen al this erthe,	
370	And that no wight may endure the ferthe.°	*fourth*
	O leve sire shrewe, Jesu shorte thy lif!	
	Yit prechestou and saist an hateful wif	
	Yrekened° is for oon of thise meschaunces.	*accounted*
	Been ther nat none othere resemblaunces	
375	That ye may likne youre parables to,	
	But if a sely° wif be oon of tho?	*innocent*
	"Thou liknest eek wommanes love to helle,	
	To bareine land ther water may nat dwelle;	
	Thou liknest it also to wilde fir—	
380	The more it brenneth,° the more it hath desir	*burns*
	To consumen every thing that brent wol be;	
	Thou saist right as wormes shende° a tree,	*destroy*
	Right so a wif destroyeth hir housbonde—	
	This knowen they that been to wives bonde."	
385	Lordinges, right thus, as ye han understonde,	
	Bar I stifly° mine olde housbondes on honde°	*firmly/swore*
	That thus they saiden in hir dronkenesse—	
	And al was fals, but that I took witnesse	
	On Janekin and on my nece° also.	*kinswoman*
390	O Lord, the paine I dide hem and the wo,	
	Ful giltelees, by Goddes sweete pine!°	*suffering*
	For as an hors I coude bite and whine;	
	I coude plaine and° I was in the gilt,°	*when/wrong*
	Or elles often time I hadde been spilt.°	*ruined*
395	Whoso that first to mille comth first grint.°	*grinds*
	I plained first: so was oure werre° stint.°	*war/stopped*
	They were ful glad to excusen hem ful blive°	*quickly*
	Of thing of which they nevere agilte° hir live.	*offended (in)*
	Of wenches wolde I beren hem on honde,	
400	Whan that for sik they mighte unnethe° stonde,	*barely*
	Yit tikled I his herte for that he	
	Wende° I hadde had of him so greet cheertee.°	*supposed/fondness*
	I swoor that al my walking out by nighte	
	Was for to espye wenches that he dighte.°	*had sex with*
405	Under that colour° hadde I many a mirthe.	*pretense*

---

2. Mythical hundred-eyed monster employed by Juno to guard over Io, one of Jove's many lovers, whom the god- dess turned into a cow.
3. Deceive him.

For al swich wit is yiven us in oure birthe:
Deceite, weeping, spinning God hath yive
To wommen kindely° whil they may live.   by nature
And thus of oo thing I avaunte° me: boast
410   At ende I hadde the bet in eech degree,
By sleighte° or force, or by som manere thing,   deception
As by continuel murmur° or grucching;°   complaining/grumbling
Namely abedde° hadden they meschaunce:°   in bed/misfortune
Ther wolde I chide and do hem no plesaunce;
415   I wolde no lenger in the bed abide
If that I felte his arm over my side,
Til he hadde maad his raunson° unto me;   amends
Thanne wolde I suffre him do his nicetee.°   lust
And therfore every man this tale I telle:
420   Winne whoso may, for al is for to selle;
With empty hand men may no hawkes lure.
For winning° wolde I al his lust endure,   profit
And make me a feined appetit—
And yit in bacon° hadde I nevere delit.   old meat
425   That made me that evere I wolde hem chide;
For though the Pope hadde seten° hem biside,   sat
I wolde nought spare hem at hir owene boord.°   table
For by my trouthe, I quitte° hem word for word.   repaid
As help me verray God omnipotent,
430   Though I right now sholde make my testament,
I ne owe hem nat a word that it nis quit.
I broughte it so aboute by my wit
That they moste yive it up as for the beste,
Or elles hadde we nevere been in reste;
435   For though he looked as a wood leoun,
Yit sholde he faile of his conclusion.°   purpose
        Thanne wolde I saye, "Goodelief,° taak keep,   Sweetheart
How mekely looketh Wilekin, oure sheep!
Com neer my spouse, lat me ba° thy cheeke—   kiss
440   Ye sholden be al pacient and meeke,
And han a sweete-spiced conscience,
Sith ye so preche of Jobes⁴ pacience;
Suffreth alway, sin ye so wel can preche;
And but ye do, certain, we shal you teche
445   That it is fair to han a wif in pees.
Oon of us two moste bowen, doutelees,
And sith a man is more resonable
Than womman is, ye mosten been suffrable.°   patient
What aileth you to grucche thus and grone?
450   Is it for ye wolde have my queinte allone?
Why, taak it al—lo, have it everydeel.
Peter,° I shrewe° you but ye love it weel.   by St. Peter/curse
For if I wolde selle my bele chose,⁵

---

4. The Biblical Job, who suffers patiently the trials imposed by God.   5. "Beautiful thing," a euphemism for female genitals.

I coude walke as fressh as is a rose;

455   But I wol keepe it for youre owene tooth.°   *taste*

Ye be to blame. By God, I saye you sooth!"

Swiche manere wordes hadde we on honde.

Now wol I speke of my ferthe housbonde.

    My ferthe housbonde was a revelour—

460   This is to sayn, he hadde a paramour°—   *lover*

And I was yong and ful of ragerye,°   *wantonness*

Stibourne° and strong and joly as a pie:°   *stubborn/magpie*

How coude I daunce to an harpe smale,°   *gracefully*

And singe, ywis, as any nightingale,

465   Whan I hadde dronke a draughte of sweete win.

Metellius,[6] the foule cherl,° the swin,   *ruffian*

That with a staf birafte his wif hir lif

For she drank win, though I hadde been his wif,

Ne sholde nat han daunted me fro drinke;

470   And after win on Venus moste I thinke,

For also siker° as cold engendreth hail,   *certainly*

A likerous° mouth moste han a likerous° tail: *gluttonous/lecherous*

In womman vinolent° is no defence—   *drunken*

This knowen lechours by experience.

475   But Lord Crist, whan that it remembreth me

Upon my youthe and on my jolitee,

It tikleth me aboute myn herte roote°—   *bottom of my heart*

Unto this day it dooth myn herte boote°   *good*

That I have had my world as in my time.

480   But age, allas, that al wol envenime,°   *poison*

Hath me biraft my beautee and my pith°—   *vigor*

Lat go, farewel, the devel go therwith!

The flour is goon, ther is namore to telle:

The bren° as I best can now moste I selle;   *bran*

485   But yit to be right merye wol I fonde.°   *try*

Now wol I tellen of my ferthe housbonde.

    I saye I hadde in herte greet despit

That he of any other hadde delit,

But he was quit,° by God and by Saint Joce:° *repaid/St. Judocus*

490   I made him of the same wode a croce°—   *cross*

Nat of my body in no foul manere—

But, certainly, I made folk swich cheere

That in his owene grece° I made him frye,   *grease*

For angre and for verray jalousye.

495   By God, in erthe I was his purgatorye,

For which I hope his soule be in glorye.

For God it woot, he sat ful ofte and soong

Whan that his sho° ful bitterly him wroong.°   *shoe/pinched*

Ther was no wight save God and he that wiste

500   In many wise how sore I him twiste.

He deide whan I cam fro Jerusalem,

And lith ygrave° under the roode-beem,°   *buried/crossbeam*

---

6. Egnatius Metellius, whose actions are described in Valerius Maximus' *Facta et dicta memorabilia*, 6.3.

Al is his tombe nought so curious°   *carefully made*
As was the sepulcre of him Darius,[7]
505 Which that Appelles wroughte subtilly:
It nis but wast to burye him preciously.°   *expensively*
Lat him fare wel, God yive his soule reste;
He is now in his grave and in his cheste.
      Now of my fifthe housbonde wol I telle—
510 God lete his soule nevere come in helle—
And yit he was to me the moste shrewe:
That feele I on my ribbes al by rewe,°   *in a row*
And evere shal unto myn ending day.
But in oure bed he was so fressh and gay,
515 And therwithal so wel coude he me glose°   *flatter*
Whan that he wolde han my bele chose,
That though he hadde me bet° on every boon,°   *beaten/bone*
He coude winne again my love anoon.
I trowe I loved him best for that he
520 Was of his love daungerous° to me.   *hard to get*
We wommen han, if that I shal nat lie,
In this matere a quainte fantasye:
Waite° what thing we may nat lightly° have,   *note that/easily*
Therafter wol we crye al day and crave;
525 Forbede us thing, and that desiren we;
Presse on us faste, and thanne wol we flee.
With daunger oute we al oure chaffare:[8]
Greet prees° at market maketh dere ware,°   *crowd/costly goods*
And too greet chepe° is holden at litel pris.   *bargain*
530 This knoweth every womman that is wis.
      My fifthe housbonde—God his soule blesse!—
Which that I took for love and no richesse,
He somtime was a clerk of Oxenforde,
And hadde laft scole and wente at hoom to boorde
535 With my gossib,° dwelling in oure town—   *close friend*
God have hir soule!—hir name was Alisoun;
She knew myn herte and eek my privetee°   *secrets*
Bet than oure parissh preest, as mote I thee.
To hire biwrayed° I my conseil° al,   *revealed/thoughts*
540 For hadde myn housbonde pissed on a wal,
Or doon a thing that sholde han cost his lif,
To hire, and to another worthy wif,
And to my nece which that I loved weel,
I wolde han told his conseil everydeel;
545 And so I dide ful often, God it woot,
That made his face often reed° and hoot°   *red/hot*
For verray shame, and blamed himself for he
Hadde told to me so greet a privetee.
      And so bifel that ones in a Lente—
550 So often times I to my gossib wente,

---

7. Persian Emperor defeated by Alexander the Great, whose tomb was elaborately designed by the Jewish craftsman Apelles.
8. With coyness we spread out all our merchandise.

For evere yit I loved to be gay,
And for to walke in March, Averil, and May,
From hous to hous, to heere sondry tales—
That Janekin clerk and my gossib dame Alis
555   And I myself into the feeldes wente.
Myn housbonde was at London al that Lente:
I hadde the better leiser° for to playe,   *opportunity*
And for to see, and eek for to be seye°   *seen*
Of lusty° folk—what wiste I wher my grace°   *merry/luck*
560   Was shapen° for to be, or in what place?   *destined*
Therfore I made my visitaciouns
To vigilies[9] and to processiouns,
To preching eek, and to thise pilgrimages,
To playes of miracles and to mariages,
565   And wered upon my gaye scarlet gites°—   *robes*
Thise wormes ne thise motthes ne thise mites,
Upon my peril, frete° hem neveradeel: *devoured*
And woostou why? For they were used weel.
    Now wol I tellen forth what happed me.
570   I saye that in the feeldes walked we,
Til trewely we hadde swich daliaunce,°   *flirtation*
This clerk and I, that of my purveyaunce°   *providence*
I spak to him and saide him how that he,
If I were widwe, sholde wedde me.
575   For certainly, I saye for no bobaunce°   *boast*
Yit was I nevere withouten purveyaunce
Of mariage n'of othere thinges eek:
I holde a mouses herte nought worth a leek
That hath but oon hole for to sterte° to,   *flee*
580   And if that faile thanne is al ydo.
I bar him on hand he hadde enchaunted me
(My dame taughte me that subtiltee);
And eek I saide I mette° of him al night: *dreamed*
He wolde han slain me as I lay upright,°   *facing up*
585   And al my bed was ful of verray blood—
"But yit I hope that ye shul do me good;
For blood bitokeneth gold, as me was taught."
And al was fals, I dremed of it right naught,
But as I folwed ay my dames lore°   *teaching*
590   As wel of that as of othere thinges more.
But now sire—lat me see, what shal I sayn?
Aha, by God, I have my tale again.
    Whan that my ferthe housbonde was on beere,°   *funeral bier*
I weep algate,° and made sory cheere,   *constantly*
595   As wives moten, for it is usage,°   *custom*
And with my coverchief covered my visage;
But for that I was purveyed° of a make,°   *provided/mate*
I wepte but smale, and that I undertake.°   *vouch*
    To chirche was myn housbonde born amorwe°   *next morning*

600	With neighebores that for him maden sorwe,	
	And Janekin oure clerk was oon of tho.	
	As help me God, whan that I saw him go	
	After the beere, me thoughte he hadde a paire	
	Of legges and of feet so clene and faire,	
605	That al myn herte I yaf unto his hold.°	possession
	He was, I trowe, twenty winter old,	
	And I was fourty, if I shal saye sooth—	
	But yit I hadde alway a coltes tooth:°	youthful tastes
	Gat-toothed° was I, and that bicam me weel;	gap-toothed
610	I hadde the prente° of Sainte Venus seel.°	imprint/beauty mark
	As help me God, I was a lusty oon,	
	And fair and riche and yong and wel-bigoon,°	well situated
	And trewely, as mine housbondes tolde me,	
	I hadde the beste quoniam° mighte be.	you-know-what
615	For certes I am al Venerien[1]	
	In feeling, and myn herte is Marcien:°	governed by Mars
	Venus me yaf my lust, my likerousnesse,	
	And Mars yaf me my sturdy hardinesse.	
	Myn ascendent° was Taur° and Mars therinne—	zodiac sign/Taurus
620	Allas, allas, that evere love was sinne!	
	I folwed ay my inclinacioun;	
	By vertu of my constellacioun;	
	That made me I coude nought withdrawe°	withhold
	My chambre of Venus from a good felawe.	
625	Yit have I Martes° merk upon my face,	Mars's
	And also in another privee place.	
	For God so wis° be my savacioun,°	surely/salvation
	I loved nevere by no discrecioun,	
	But evere folwede myn appetit,	
630	Al were he short or long or blak or whit;	
	I took no keep, so that he liked° me,	pleased
	How poore he was, ne eek of what degree.	
	What sholde I saye but at the monthes ende	
	This joly clerk Janekin that was so hende°	courteous
635	Hath wedded me with greet solempnitee,	
	And to him yaf I al the land and fee°	property
	That evere was me yiven therbifore—	
	But afterward repented me ful sore:	
	He nolde suffre no thing of my list.°	pleasure
640	By God, he smoot° me ones on the list°	struck/ear
	For that I rente° out of his book a leef,°	tore/page
	That of the strook myn ere weex° al deef.	grew, became
	Stibourne I was as is a leonesse,	
	And of my tonge a verray jangleresse,°	chatterbox
645	And walke I wolde, as I hadde doon biforn,	
	From hous to hous, although he hadde it sworn;°	prohibited
	For which he often times wolde preche,	
	And me of olde Romain geestes° teche,	Latin stories

1. Governed by Venus, the planet.

How he Simplicius Gallus[2] lafte his wif,
And hire forsook for terme of al his lif,
Nought but for open-heveded° he hire sey°   *bare-headed/saw*
Looking out at his dore upon a day.
    Another Romain[3] tolde he me by name
That, for his wif was at a someres° game   *summer's*
Withouten his witing,° he forsook hire eke;   *knowledge*
And thanne wolde he upon his Bible seeke
That ilke proverbe of Ecclesiaste[4]
Where he comandeth and forbedeth faste
Man shal nat suffre his wif go roule° aboute;   *roam*
Thanne wolde he saye right thus withouten doute:
"Whoso that buildeth his hous al of salwes,°   *willow branches*
And priketh° his blinde hors over the falwes,°   *rides/open fields*
And suffreth his wif to go seeken halwes,°   *shrines*
Is worthy to be hanged on the galwes."
But al for nought—I sette nought an hawe[5]
Of his proverbes n'of his olde sawe;
N'I wolde nat of him corrected be:
I hate him that my vices telleth me,
And so doon mo, God woot, of us than I.
This made him with me wood al outrely:°   *utterly*
I nolde nought forbere° him in no cas.   *submit*
    Now wol I saye you sooth, by Saint Thomas,
Why that I rente out of his book a leef,
For which he smoot me so that I was deef.
He hadde a book that gladly night and day
For his disport° he wolde rede alway.   *amusement*
He cleped° it Valerie and Theofraste,[6]   *called*
At which book he lough° alway ful faste;   *laughed*
And eek ther was somtime a clerk at Rome,
A cardinal, that highte Saint Jerome,
That made a book again Jovinian;
In which book eek ther was Tertulan,
Crysippus, Trotula, and Helouis,
That was abbesse nat fer fro Paris;
And eek the Parables of Salomon,
Ovides Art, and bookes many oon—
And alle thise were bounden in oo volume.
And every night and day was his custume,°   *custom*
Whan he hadde leiser and vacacioun
From other worldly occupacioun,

650
655
660
665
670
675
680
685
690

---

2. Narrated in Valerius Maximus' *Facta et dicta memorabilia*, 6.3.
3. P. Sempronius Sophus, as related in Valerius Maximus' *Facta*, 6.3.
4. Ecclesiasticus 25.25.
5. Hawthorn berry (i.e., little value).
6. Janekin's book is a collection of different works, nearly all of which are directed against women: Walter Map's fictitious letter entitled Valerius' *Dissuasion of Rufinus from Marrying* (Valerius); Theophrastus' *Golden Book on*

Marriage (Theofraste); Saint Jerome's *Against Jovinian*; Tertullian's misogynist tracts on sexual continence (Tertulan); Crysippus' writings, mentioned by Jerome but otherwise unknown; *The Sufferings of Women*, an 11th-century book on gynecology by Trotula di Ruggiero, a female physician from Sicily (Trotula); the letters of the abbess Heloise to her lover Abelard (Helouis); the biblical Book of Proverbs (Parables of Salomon), and Ovid's *Art of Love*.

To reden in this book of wikked wives.
He knew of hem mo legendes and lives
Than been of goode wives in the Bible.
For trusteth wel, it is an impossible°   *impossibility*
695 That any clerk wol speke good of wives,
But if it be of holy saintes lives,
N'of noon other womman nevere the mo—
Who painted the leon, tel me who?[7]
By God, if wommen hadden writen stories,
700 As clerkes han within hir oratories,
They wolde han writen of men more wikkednesse
Than al the merk of° Adam may redresse.   *mark, sex*
The children of Mercurye and Venus[8]
Been in hir werking° ful contrarious:°   *deeds/contradictory*
705 Mercurye loveth wisdom and science,
And Venus loveth riot° and dispence;°   *celebration/expense*
And for hir diverse disposicioun
Each falleth in otheres exaltacioun,[9]
And thus, God woot, Mercurye is desolat°   *powerless*
710 In Pisces wher Venus is exaltat,
And Venus falleth ther Mercurye is raised:
Therfore no womman of no clerk is praised.
The clerk, whan he is old and may nought do
Of Venus werkes worth his olde sho,°   *shoe*
715 Thanne sit he down and writ in his dotage
That wommen can nat keepe hir mariage.
     But now to purpos why I tolde thee
That I was beten for a book, pardee:
Upon a night Janekin, that was oure sire,°   *master of our house*
720 Redde on his book as he sat by the fire
Of Eva[1] first, that for hir wikkednesse
Was al mankinde brought to wrecchednesse,
For which that Jesu Crist himself was slain
That boughte° us with his herte blood again—   *redeemed*
725 Lo, heer expres of wommen may ye finde
That womman was the los° of al mankinde.   *ruin*
     Tho redde he me how Sampson loste his heres:
Sleeping his lemman° kitte° it with hir sheres, *lover/cut*
Thurgh which treson loste he both his yën.
730 Tho redde he me, if that I shal nat lien,
Of Ercules and of his Dianire,[2]
That caused him to sette himself afire.
     No thing forgat he the sorwe and wo
That Socrates hadde with his wives two—

---

7. In one of Aesop's fables, a lion asked this question when confronted by a painting of a man killing a lion, indicating that if a lion had painted the picture, the scene would have been very different.
8. Followers of Mercury, the god of rhetoric (scholars, poets, orators); followers of Venus (lovers).
9. Astrologically, one planet diminishes in influence as the other ascends.
1. Eve's temptation by the serpent was blamed for humanity's fall from grace and thus required Christ's incarnation to redeem the world.
2. Deianira gave her husband, Hercules, a robe which she believed was charmed with a love potion, but once he put it on, it burned his flesh so badly that he died.

735 How Xantippa³ caste pisse upon his heed:
     This sely man sat stille as he were deed;
     He wiped his heed, namore dorste he sayn
     But "Er° that thonder stinte,° comth a rain."   *before/stops*
        Of Phasipha⁴ that was the queene of Crete—
740 For shrewednesse° him thoughte the tale sweete—   *wickedness*
     Fy, speek namore, it is a grisly thing
     Of hir horrible lust and hir liking.
        Of Clytermistra⁵ for hir lecherye
     That falsly made hir housbonde for to die,
745 He redde it with ful good devocioun.
        He tolde me eek for what occasioun
     Amphiorax⁶ at Thebes loste his lif:
     Myn housbonde hadde a legende of his wif
     Eriphylem, that for an ouche° of gold   *trinket*
750 Hath prively unto the Greekes told
     Wher that hir housbonde hidde him in a place,
     For which he hadde at Thebes sory grace.
        Of Livia⁷ tolde he me and of Lucie:
     They bothe made hir housbondes for to die,
755 That oon for love, that other was for hate;
     Livia hir housbonde on an even late
     Empoisoned hath for that she was his fo;
     Lucia likerous loved hir housbonde so
     That for he sholde alway upon hire thinke,
760 She yaf him swich a manere love-drinke
     That he was deed er it were by the morwe.
     And thus algates° housbondes han sorwe.   *continually*
        Thanne tolde he me how oon Latumius
     Complained unto his felawe Arrius
765 That in his gardin growed swich a tree,
     On which he saide how that his wives three
     Hanged hemself for herte despitous.°   *cruel*
        "O leve brother," quod this Arrius,
     "Yif me a plante of thilke blessed tree,
770 And in my gardin planted shal it be."
        Of latter date of wives hath he red
     That some han slain hir housbondes in hir bed
     And lete hir lechour dighte° hire al the night,   *screw*
     Whan that the cors° lay in the floor upright;°   *corpse/face up*
775 And some han driven nailes in hir brain
     Whil that they sleepe, and thus they han hem slain;
     Some han hem yiven poison in hir drinke.
     He spak more harm than herte may bithinke,
     And therwithal he knew of mo proverbes

---

3. Xanthippe was famous for nagging her husband, the philosopher Socrates.
4. Pasiphae, wife of Minos, became enamored of a bull, engendering the Minotaur.
5. Clytemnestra, queen of Mycenae, slew her husband Agamemnon when he returned from the Trojan War.

6. Amphiaraus died at the Siege of Thebes after listening to the advice of his wife, Eriphyle.
7. Livia poisoned her husband, Drusus, to satisfy her lover Sejanus; Lucia unwittingly poisoned her husband, the poet Lucretius, with a potion meant to keep him faithful.

780   Than in this world ther growen gras or herbes:
"Bet is," quod he, "thyn habitacioun
Be with a leon or a foul dragoun
Than with a wommman using° for to chide."   *accustomed*
"Bet is," quod he, "hye in the roof abide
785   Than with an angry wif down in the hous:
They been so wikked and contrarious,
They haten that hir housbondes loveth ay."
He saide, "A womman cast hir shame away
Whan she cast of hir smok,"° and ferthermo,   *slip*
790   "A fair womman, but she be chast also,
Is lik a gold ring in a sowes nose."
Who wolde weene, or who wolde suppose
The wo that in myn herte was and pine?
      And whan I sawgh he wolde nevere fine°   *end*
795   To reden on this cursed book al night,
Al sodeinly three leves have I plight°   *plucked*
Out of his book right as he redde, and eke
I with my fist so took° him on the cheeke   *struck*
That in oure fir he fil bakward adown.
800   And up he sterte as dooth a wood° leoun,   *enraged*
And with his fist he smoot me on the heed
That in the floor I lay as I were deed.
And whan he sawgh how stille that I lay,
He was agast,° and wolde have fled his way,   *afraid*
805   Til atte laste out of my swough° I braide:°   *faint/arose*
"O hastou slain me, false thief?" I saide,
"And for my land thus hastou mordred me?
Er I be deed yit wol I kisse thee."
      And neer he cam and kneeled faire adown,
810   And saide, "Dere suster Alisoun,
As help me God, I shal thee nevere smite.
That I have doon, it is thyself to wite.°   *blame*
Foryif it me, and that I thee biseeke."
And yit eftsoones° I hitte him on the cheeke,   *immediately*
815   And saide, "Thief, thus muchel am I wreke.°   *avenged*
Now wol I die: I may no lenger speke."
      But at the laste with muchel care and wo
We fille accorded by us selven two.
He yaf me al the bridel° in myn hand,
820   To han the governance of hous and land,   *bridle, control*
And of his tonge and his hand also;
And made him brenne his book anoonright tho.
And whan that I hadde geten unto me
By maistrye° al the sovereinetee,°   *skill/dominance*
825   And that he saide, "Myn owene trewe wif,
Do as thee lust° the terme of al thy lif,   *please*
Keep thyn honour, and keep eek myn estat,"
After that day we hadde nevere debat.
God help me so, I was to him as kinde
830   As any wif from Denmark unto Inde,

And also trewe, and so was he to me.
I praye to God that sit in majestee,
So blesse his soule for his mercy dere.
Now wol I saye my tale if ye wol heere.

Another Interruption

835 The Frere lough whan he hadde herd al this:
"Now dame," quod he, "so have I joye or blis,
This is a long preamble of a tale."
And whan the Somnour herde the Frere gale,°   exclaim
"Lo," quod the Somnour, "Goddes armes two,
840 A frere wol entremette him° everemo!   interfere
Lo, goode men, a flye and eek a frere
Wol falle in every dissh and eek matere.
What spekestou of preambulacioun?
What, amble or trotte or pisse or go sitte down!
845 Thou lettest oure disport in this manere."
    "Ye, woltou so, sire Somnour?" quod the Frere.
"Now by my faith, I shal er that I go
Telle of a somnour swich a tale or two
That al the folk shal laughen in this place."
850   "Now elles, Frere, I wol bishrewe thy face,"
Quod this Somnour, "and I bishrewe me,
But if I telle tales two or three
Of freres, er I come to Sidingborne,[8]
That I shal make thyn herte for to moorne—
855 For wel I woot thy pacience is goon."
    Oure Hoste cride, "Pees, and that anoon!"
And saide, "Lat the womman telle hir tale:
Ye fare as folk that dronken been of ale.
Do, dame, tel forth youre tale, and that is best."
860   "Al redy, sire," quod she, "right as you lest—
If I have licence of this worthy Frere."
"Yis, dame," quod he, "tel forth and I wol heere."

The Wife of Bath's Tale

In th'olde dayes of the King Arthour,
Of which that Britouns° speken greet honour,   Bretons
865 Al was this land fulfild° of faïrye: filled
The elf-queene° with hir joly compaignye   fairy queen
Daunced ful ofte in many a greene mede°—   meadow
This was the olde opinion as I rede;
I speke of many hundred yeres ago.
870 But now can no man see none elves mo,
For now the grete charitee and prayeres
Of limitours,[9] and othere holy freres,
That serchen every land and every streem,
As thikke as motes° in the sonne-beem,   dust particles

---

8. Sittingbourne, a town about 40 miles from London.   9. Friars licensed to beg within set districts.

875 Blessing halles, chambres, kichenes, bowres,°   *bedrooms*
    Citees, burghes,° castels, hye towres,   *boroughs*
    Thropes,° bernes,° shipnes,° dayeries—   *villages/barns/stables*
    This maketh that ther been no faïries.
    For ther as wont° to walken was an elf   *where there used*
880 Ther walketh now the limitour himself,
    In undermeles° and in morweninges,°   *afternoons/mornings*
    And saith his Matins° and his holy thinges,   *morning prayers*
    As he gooth in his limitacioun.°   *prescribed district*
    Wommen may go saufly° up and down: *safely*
885 In every bussh or under every tree
    Ther is noon other incubus² but he,
    And he ne wol doon hem but dishonour.
        And so bifel it that this King Arthour
    Hadde in his hous a lusty bacheler,°   *young knight*
890 That on a day cam riding fro river,°   *hunting waterfowl*
    And happed that, allone as he was born,
    He sawgh a maide walking him biforn;
    Of which maide anoon, maugree hir heed,°   *against her will*
    By verray force he rafte° hir maidenheed;   *stole*
895 For which oppression was swich clamour,
    And swich pursuite° unto the King Arthour,   *petitioning*
    That dampned° was this knight for to be deed   *condemned*
    By cours of lawe, and sholde han lost his heed—
    Paraventure° swich was the statut tho°—   *as it happens/then*
900 But that the queene and othere ladies mo
    So longe prayeden the king of grace,
    Til he his lif him graunted in the place,
    And yaf him to the queene, al at hir wille,
    To chese° wheither she wolde him save or spille.°   *decide/destroy*
905 The queene thanked the king with al hir might,
    And after this thus spak she to the knight,
    Whan that she saw hir time upon a day:
    "Thou standest yit," quod she, "in swich array°   *situation*
    That of thy lif yit hastou no suretee.°   *guarantee*
910 I graunte thee lif if thou canst tellen me
    What thing it is that wommen most desiren:
    Be war and keep thy nekke boon° from iren.°   *bone/iron*
    And if thou canst nat tellen me anoon,
    Yit wol I yive thee leve for to goon
915 A twelfmonth and a day to seeche° and lere°   *seek out/learn*
    An answere suffisant° in this matere,   *satisfactory*
    And suretee° wol I han er that thou pace,°   *pledge/pass*
    Thy body for to yeelden° in this place."   *surrender*
        Wo was this knight, and sorwefully he siketh.°   *sighs*
920 But what, he may nat doon al as him liketh,
    And atte laste he chees him° for to wende,°   *decided/travel*
    And come again right at the yeres ende,
    With swich answere as God wolde him purveye,°   *provide*

---

1. Demon who fornicates with women.

And taketh his leve and wendeth forth his waye.
925 He seeketh every hous and every place
Wher as he hopeth for to finde grace,
To lerne what thing wommen love most.
But he ne coude arriven in no coost°   *country*
Wher as he mighte finde in this matere
930 Two creatures according in fere.°   *agreeing together*
      Some saiden wommen loven best richesse;
Some saide honour, some saide jolinesse;°   *pleasure*
Some riche array, some saiden lust abedde,
And ofte time to be widwe and wedde.
935 Some saide that oure herte is most esed
Whan that we been yflatered and yplesed—
He gooth ful neigh the soothe,° I wol nat lie: *near the truth*
A man shal winne us best with flaterye,
And with attendance and with bisinesse°   *attentive service*
940 Been we ylimed,° bothe more and lesse.   *ensnared*
      And some sayen that we loven best
For to be free, and do right as us lest,°   *pleases*
And that no man repreve° us of oure vice,   *scold*
But saye that we be wise and no thing nice.°   *foolish*
945 For trewely, ther is noon of us alle,
If any wight wol clawe us on the galle,°   *rub a sore spot*
That we nil kike for he saith us sooth:
Assaye° and he shal finde it that so dooth.   *try*
For be we nevere so vicious withinne,
950 We wol be holden° wise and clene of sinne.   *considered*
      And some sayn that greet delit han we
For to be holden stable° and eek secree,°   *constant/discreet*
And in oo purpos stedefastly to dwelle,
And nat biwraye° thing that men us telle—   *reveal*
955 But that tale is nat worth a rake-stele.°   *rake handle*
Pardee, we wommen conne no thing hele:°   *conceal*
Witnesse on Mida.² Wol ye heere the tale?
      Ovide, amonges othere thinges smale,
Saide Mida hadde under his longe heres,
960 Growing upon his heed, two asses eres,
The whiche vice° he hidde as he best mighte   *fault*
Ful subtilly from every mannes sighte,
That save his wif ther wiste of it namo.°   *no one else know*
He loved hire most and trusted hire also.
965 He prayed hire that to no creature
She sholde tellen of his disfigure.°   *deformity*
      She swoor him nay, for al this world to winne,
She nolde° do that vilainye or sinne   *would not*
To make hir housbonde han so foul a name:
970 She nolde nat telle it for hir owene shame.
But nathelees, hir thoughte that she dyde°   *would die*
That she so longe sholde a conseil° hide;   *secret*

---

2. Midas' story is recounted in Ovid's *Metamorphoses,* 9.

Hire thoughte it swal so sore aboute hir herte
That nedely° som word hire moste asterte,°   *surely/come out*
975   And sith she dorste nat telle it to no man,
Down to a mareis° faste° by she ran—   *marsh/close*
Til she cam there hir herte was afire—
And as a bitore° bombleth° in the mire,   *heron/squawks*
She laide hir mouth unto the water down:
980   "Biwray° me nat, thou water, with thy soun,"°   *betray/sound*
Quod she. "To thee I telle it and namo:
Myn housbonde hath longe asses eres two.
Now is myn herte al hool, now is it oute.
I mighte no lenger keepe it, out of doute."
985   Here may ye see, though we a time abide,
Yit oute it moot:° we can no conseil hide.   *must*
The remenant of the tale if ye wol heere,
Redeth Ovide, and ther ye may it lere.°   *learn*
    This knight of which my tale is specially,
990   Whan that he sawgh he mighte nat come therby—
This is to saye what wommen loven most—
Within his brest ful sorweful was his gost,°   *spirit*
But hoom he gooth, he mighte nat sojurne:°   *linger*
The day was come that hoomward moste he turne.
995   And in his way it happed him to ride
In al this care under a forest side,
Wher as he sawgh upon a daunce go
Of ladies foure and twenty and yit mo;
Toward the whiche daunce he drow° ful yerne,°   *drew/gladly*
1000   In hope that som wisdom sholde he lerne.
But certainly, er he cam fully there,
Vanisshed was this daunce, he niste° where.   *did not know*
No creature sawgh he that bar lif,
Save on the greene he sawgh sitting a wif—
1005   A fouler wight ther may no man devise.°   *imagine*
Again the knight this olde wif gan rise,
And saide, "Sire knight, heer forth lith no way.°   *road*
Telle me what ye seeken, by youre fay.°   *faith*
Paraventure it may the better be:
1010   Thise olde folk conne° muchel thing," quod she.   *know*
    "My leve moder," quod this knight, "certain,
I nam but deed but if that I can sayn
What thing it is that wommen most desire.
Coude ye me wisse,° I wolde wel quite youre hire."°   *inform/repay you*
1015   "Plight° me thy trouthe° here in myn hand," quod she,   *pledge/promise*
"The nexte thing that I require thee,
Thou shalt it do, if it lie in thy might,
And I wol telle it you er it be night."
    "Have heer my trouthe," quod the knight. "I graunte."
1020   "Thanne," quod she, "I dar me wel avaunte°   *brag*
Thy lif is sauf, for I wol stande therby.
Upon my lif the queene wol saye as I.
Lat see which is the pruddeste° of hem alle   *proudest*

That wereth on a coverchief or a calle°   *headdress*
1025 That dar saye nay of that I shal thee teche.
Lat us go forth withouten lenger speeche."
Tho rouned° she a pistel° in his ere,   *whispered/message*
And bad him to be glad and have no fere.
Whan they be comen to the court, this knight
1030 Saide he hadde holde his day as he hadde hight,°   *promised*
And redy was his answere, as he saide.
Ful many a noble wif, and many a maide,
And many a widwe—for that they been wise—
The queene hirself sitting as justise,°   *judge*
1035 Assembled been this answere for to heere,
And afterward this knight was bode appere.
To every wight comanded was silence,
And that the knight sholde telle in audience
What thing that worldly wommen loven best.
1040 This knight ne stood nat stille° as dooth a best,°   *silent/beast*
But to his question anoon answerde
With manly vois that al the court it herde.
"My lige° lady, generally," quod he,   *liege*
"Wommen desire to have sovereinetee
1045 As wel over hir housbonde as hir love,
And for to been in maistrye him above.
This is youre moste desir though ye me kille.
Dooth as you list: I am here at youre wille."
In al the court ne was ther wif ne maide
1050 Ne widwe that contraried that he saide,
But saiden he was worthy han his lif.
And with that word up sterte that olde wif,
Which that the knight sawgh sitting on the greene;
"Mercy," quod she, "my soverein lady queene,
1055 Er that youre court departe, do me right.
I taughte this answere unto the knight,
For which he plighte me his trouthe there
The firste thing I wolde him requere
He wolde it do, if it laye in his might.
1060 Bifore the court thanne praye I thee, sire knight,"
Quod she, "that thou me take unto thy wif,
For wel thou woost° that I have kept° thy lif.   *know/saved*
If I saye fals, say nay, upon thy fay."
This knight answerde, "Allas and wailaway,
1065 I woot right wel that swich was my biheeste.°   *promise*
For Goddes love, as chees° a newe requeste: *choose*
Taak al my good and lat my body go."
"Nay thanne," quod she, "I shrewe° us bothe two.   *curse*
For though that I be foul and old and poore,
1070 I nolde for al the metal ne for ore
That under erthe is grave° or lith above,   *buried*
But if thy wif I were and eek thy love."
"My love," quod he. "Nay, my dampnacioun!
Allas, that any of my nacioun°   *lineage*

1075 Sholde evere so foule disparaged° be."   *degraded*
But al for nought, th'ende is this, that he
Constrained was: he needes moste hire wedde,
And taketh his olde wif and gooth to bedde.
    Now wolden some men saye, paraventure,
1080 That for my necligence I do no cure
To tellen you the joy and al th'array
That at the feeste was that ilke day.
To which thing shortly answere I shal:
I saye ther nas no joye ne feeste at al;
1085 Ther nas but hevinesse and muche sorwe.
For prively he wedded hire on morwe,
And al day after hidde him as an owle,
So wo was him, his wif looked so foule.
    Greet was the wo the knight hadde in his thought:
1090 Whan he was with his wif abedde brought,
He walweth° and he turneth to and fro.   *rolls over*
His olde wif lay smiling everemo,
And saide, "O dere housbonde, benedicite,°   *bless us*
Fareth° every knight thus with his wif as ye?   *behaves*
1095 Is this the lawe of King Arthures hous?
Is every knight of his thus daungerous?°   *reserved*
I am youre owene love and youre wif;
I am she which that saved hath youre lif;
And certes yit ne dide I you nevere unright.°   *injustice*
1100 Why fare ye thus with me this firste night?
Ye faren like a man hadde lost his wit.
What is my gilt? For Goddes love, telle it,
And it shal been amended if I may."
    "Amended!" quod this knight. "Allas, nay, nay,
1105 It wol nat been amended neveremo.
Thou art so lothly° and so old also,   *loathsome*
And therto comen of so lowe a kinde,°   *breeding*
That litel wonder is though I walwe and winde.°   *turn*
So wolde God myn herte wolde breste!"°   *burst*
1110   "Is this," quod she, "the cause of youre unreste?"
"Ye, certainly," quod he. "No wonder is."
"Now sire," quod she, "I coude amende al this,
If that me liste, er it were dayes three,
So° wel ye mighte bere you° unto me.   *provided that / behave*
1115   "But for ye speken of swich gentilesse°   *nobility*
As is descended out of old richesse—
That therfore sholden ye be gentilmen—
Swich arrogance is nat worth an hen.
Looke who that is most vertuous alway,
1120 Privee and apert,° and most entendeth ay   *privately and publicly*
To do the gentil deedes that he can,
Taak him for the gretteste gentilman.
Crist wol° we claime of him oure gentilesse,   *wishes*
Nat of oure eldres for hir 'old richesse.'
1125 For though they yive us al hir heritage,

For which we claime to been of heigh parage,°   *noble lineage*
Yit may they nat biquethe for no thing
To noon of us hir vertuous living,
That made hem gentilmen ycalled be,
1130   And bad us folwen hem in swich degree.
      "Wel can the wise poete of Florence,
That highte° Dant,[3] speken in this sentence;°   *was called /opinion*
Lo, in swich manere rym is Dantes tale:
'Ful selde° up riseth by his braunches[4] smale   *seldom*
1135   Prowesse° of man, for God of his prowesse   *excellence*
Wol that of him we claime oure gentilesse.'
For of oure eldres may we no thing claime
But temporel thing that man may hurte and maime.
Eek every wight woot this as wel as I,
1140   If gentilesse were planted natureelly
Unto a certain linage down the line,
Privee and apert, thanne wolde they nevere fine°   *end*
To doon of gentilesse the faire office°—   *duty*
They mighte do no vilainye or vice.
1145   "Taak fir and beer° it in the derkeste hous   *bring*
Bitwixe this and the Mount of Caucasus,
And lat men shette° the dores and go thenne,°   *shut /thence*
Yit wol the fir as faire lie and brenne
As twenty thousand men mighte it biholde:
1150   His° office natureel ay wol it holde,   *its*
Up peril of my lif, til that it die.
Heer may ye see wel how that genterye°   *gentility*
Is nat annexed° to possessioun,   *connected*
Sith folk ne doon hir operacioun
1155   Alway, as dooth the fir, lo, in his kinde.°   *nature*
For God it woot, men may wel often finde
A lordes sone do shame and vilainye;
And he that wol han pris° of his gentrye,°   *esteem /noble birth*
For he was boren of a gentil hous,
1160   And hadde his eldres noble and vertuous,
And nil° himselven do no gentil deedes,   *will not*
Ne folwen his gentil auncestre that deed is,
He nis nat gentil, be he duc or erl—
For vilaines sinful deedes maken a cherl.°   *ruffian*
1165   Thy gentilesse nis but renomee°   *reputation*
Of thine auncestres for hir heigh bountee,°   *generosity*
Which is a straunge° thing for thy persone.   *foreign*
For gentilesse cometh fro God allone.
Thanne comth oure verray gentilesse of grace:
1170   It was no thing biquethe us with oure place.
Thenketh how noble, as saith Valerius,[5]

---

3. Dante Alighieri, the 13th-century Italian poet, expressed similar views in his *Convivio*.
4. Branches (of his family tree).

5. The Roman historian Valerius Maximus, in his *Facta et dicta memorabilia*, 3.4.

Was thilke Tullius Hostilius[6]
That out of poverte roos to heigh noblesse.
Redeth Senek,[7] and redeth eek Boece:
1175 Ther shul ye seen expres that no drede° is   *doubt*
That he is gentil that dooth gentil deedes.
And therfore, leve housbonde, I thus conclude:
Al were it that mine auncestres weren rude,°   *low born*
Yit may the hye God—and so hope I—
1180 Graunte me grace to liven vertuously.
Thanne am I gentil whan that I biginne
To liven vertuously and waive° sinne.   *avoid*
    "And ther as ye of poverte me repreve,
The hye God, on whom that we bileve,
1185 In wilful poverte chees to live his lif;
And certes every man, maiden, or wif
May understonde that Jesus, hevene king,
Ne wolde nat chese a vicious living.
Glad poverte is an honeste° thing, certain;   *honorable*
1190 This wol Senek and othere clerkes sayn.
Whoso that halt him paid of his poverte,[8]
I holde him riche al° hadde he nat a sherte.°   *although/shirt*
He that coveiteth is a poore wight,
For he wolde han that is nat in his might;
1195 But he that nought hath, ne coveiteth have,
Is riche, although we holde him but a knave.°   *servant*
Verray poverte it singeth proprely.
Juvenal[9] saith of poverte, 'Merily
The poore man, whan he gooth by the waye,
1200 Biforn the theves he may singe and playe.'
Poverte is hateful good, and as I gesse,
A ful greet bringere out of bisinesse;°   *wordly cares*
A greet amendere eek of sapience°   *wisdom*
To him that taketh it in pacience;
1205 Poverte is thing, although it seeme elenge,°   *miserable*
Possession that no wight wol chalenge;
Poverte ful often, whan a man is lowe,
Maketh his God and eek himself to knowe;
Poverte a spectacle° is, as thinketh me,   *eyeglass*
1210 Thurgh which he may his verray freendes see.
And therfore, sire, sin that I nought you greve,
Of my poverte namore ye me repreve.
    "Now sire, of elde° ye repreve me: *old age*
And certes sire, though noon auctoritee
1215 Were in no book, ye gentils of honour
Sayn that men sholde an old wight doon favour,
And clepe him fader for youre gentilesse—
And auctours° shal I finden, as I gesse.   *authorities*

6. The legendary third king of Rome who started as a shepherd.
7. Seneca, the Stoic author, in his *Epistle* 44; Boece: Boethius in his *Consolation of Philosophy*.
8. Whoever is satisfied with poverty.
9. The misogynist Roman poet in his *Satires* 10.21, 22.

"Now ther ye saye that I am foul and old:

1220 Thanne drede you nought to been a cokewold,° *cuckold*
For filthe and elde, also mote I thee,
Been grete wardeins° upon chastitee. *guardians*
But nathelees, sin I knowe your delit,
I shal fulfille youre worldly appetit.

1225 "Chees now," quod she, "oon of thise thinges twaye:
To han me foul and old til that I deye
And be to you a trewe humble wif,
And nevere you displese in al my lif,
Or elles ye wol han me yong and fair,

1230 And take youre aventure° of the repair° *chances/visits*
That shal be to youre hous by cause of me—
Or in som other place, wel may be.
Now chees youreselven wheither° that you liketh." *whichever*
This knight aviseth him° and sore siketh;° *considers/sighs*

1335 But atte laste he saide in this manere:
"My lady and my love, and wif so dere,
I putte me in youre wise governaunce:
Cheseth youreself which may be most plesaunce
And most honour to you and me also.

1240 I do no fors° the wheither of the two, *do not care*
For as you liketh it suffiseth° me." *satisfies*
"Thanne have I gete of you maistrye," quod she,
"Sin I may chese and governe as me lest?"
"Ye, certes, wif," quod he. "I holde it best."

1245 "Kisse me," quod she. "We be no lenger wrothe.° *opposed*
For by my trouthe, I wol be to you bothe—
This is to sayn, ye, bothe fair and good.
I praye to God that I mote sterven wood,° *die mad*
But I to you be al so good and trewe

1250 As evere was wif sin that the world was newe.
And but I be tomorn° as fair to seene *in the morning*
As any lady, emperisse, or queene,
That is bitwixe the eest and eek the west,
Do with my lif and deeth right as you lest:

1255 Caste up the curtin, looke how that it is."
And whan the knight sawgh verraily al this,
That she so fair was and so yong therto,
For joye he hente° hire in his armes two; *seized*
His herte bathed in a bath of blisse;

1260 A thousand time arewe° he gan hire kisse, *in a row*
And she obeyed him in every thing
That mighte do him plesance or liking.
And thus they live unto hir lives ende
In parfit joye. And Jesu Crist us sende

1265 Housbondes meeke, yonge, and fresshe abedde—
And grace t'overbide° hem that we wedde. *outlive*
And eek I praye Jesu shorte hir lives
That nought wol be governed by hir wives,
And olde and angry nigardes of dispence°— *misers in spending*

1270 God sende hem soone a verray pestilence!

The Pardoner's Prologue and Tale

There is something in Chaucer's Pardoner to unnerve practically everyone. The Pardoner's physiology blurs gender itself, his apparent homosexuality challenges the dominant heterosexual ordering of medieval society, his *Prologue* subverts the notion that the intent and effect of words are connected, and his willingness to convert religious discourse into cash undermines the very bases of faith. He initiates a sequence of moments in the later tales that threaten to puncture or tear the social fabric of the Canterbury company.

The Pardoner and "his freend and his compeer," the Summoner, are the last two pilgrims described in *The General Prologue*, reflecting the distaste with which such marginal clergy were often regarded in the period. Summoners were the policing branch of the ecclesiastical courts, paid to bring in transgressors against the canon law. Pardoners had the job, criticized even within the church, of exchanging indulgences for cash. The sufferings of Christ and saintly martyrs, it was thought, had left the church with a legacy of goodness. This could be transferred to sinners, freeing them from a period in Purgatory, if they proved their penitence (among other ways) by gifts to support good works such as the hospital for which the Pardoner worked.

The Pardoner has turned this part of the structure of penitence into a profit center. In his own *Prologue*, the Pardoner is boastfully explicit about this:

> For myn entente is nat but for to winne,
> And no thing for correccion of sinne . . .

This merciless equation of his verbal power with cash profit deeply subverts the logic of Christian language and the priestly role in salvation. These are replaced by language working in a strange self-consuming circle: the Pardoner brilliantly achieves the very sin his sermon most vituperates.

The Pardoner's physiology—he has either lost his testicles or never had them—may emblematize this exploitation of language emptied of spiritual intention. His uncertain or incomplete gender, though, also challenges the fundamental distinctions of the body within the medieval social economy, as does his apparent homosexuality. The Pardoner's theatrical self-presentation, abetted by rhetorical techniques he lovingly describes, draws the fascinated if queasy attention of his audience and seems to provide him a monstrous though (as it turns out) fragile power.

The Pardoner's tale of three rioters and their encounter with death is actually folded into his Prologue as an exemplum, an illustrative story, in the sermon against cupidity he proposes to offer as a sample of his skills. Yet the Pardoner's obsession with bodies in extremity, seeking or denying death, skeletal or gorged, pulls against his tale as a parable of greed. The tale draws toward its close in a scene of rage, exposure, and angry silence, which threatens to undo the pilgrim society, rather as the Pardoner and his discourse have threatened so much of the broader social contract. The Knight steps in, though, and almost bullies the Host and the Pardoner into a kiss of peace. This ritual gesture, nearly as empty of real goodwill as any of the Pardoner's most cynical words, does allow the shaken group to continue on their way, even as it hints at the emptiness that may hide in other, less openly challenged systems of value in the tales and their world.

The Pardoner's Prologue
The Introduction

Oure Hoste gan to swere as he were wood;°   *mad*
"Harrow," quod he, "by nailes[1] and by blood,

---

1. Nails (of Christ's cross).

This was a fals cherl° and a fals justice.°[2]   *villain/judge*
As shameful deeth as herte may devise
5   Come to thise juges and hir advocats.°   *lawyers*
Algate° this sely° maide is slain, allas!   *anyway/innocent*
Allas, too dere boughte she beautee!
Wherfore I saye alday° that men may see   *always*
The yiftes of Fortune and of Nature
10 Been cause of deeth to many a creature.
As bothe yiftes that I speke of now,
Men han ful ofte more for harm than prow.°   *profit*
    "But trewely, myn owene maister dere,
This is a pitous tale for to heere.
15 But nathelees, passe over, is no fors:°   *concern*
I praye to God so save thy gentil° cors,°   *noble/body*
And eek thine urinals[3] and thy jurdones,°   *chamberpots*
Thyn ipocras and eek thy galiones,[4]
And every boiste° ful of thy letuarye°—   *box/medicine*
20 God blesse hem, and oure lady Sainte Marye.
So mote I theen,° thou art a propre man,   *so may I prosper*
And lik a prelat,° by Saint Ronian![5]   *Church officer*
Saide I nat wel? I can nat speke in terme.°   *jargon*
But wel I woot, thou doost myn herte to erme°   *grieve*
25 That I almost have caught a cardinacle.°   *heart condition*
By corpus bones,[6] but if I have triacle,°   *medicine*
Or elles a draughte of moiste° and corny° ale,   *fresh/malted*
Or but I heere anoon a merye tale,
Myn herte is lost for pitee of this maide.
30 "Thou bel ami,[7] thou Pardoner," he saide,
"Tel us som mirthe or japes° right anoon."   *joke*
    "It shal be doon," quod he, "by Saint Ronian.
But first," quod he, "here at this ale-stake°   *tavern marker*
I wol bothe drinke and eten of a cake."°   *loaf of bread*
35   And right anoon thise gentils gan to crye,
"Nay, lat him telle us of no ribaudye.°   *obscenity*
Tel us som moral thing that we may lere,°   *learn*
Som wit, and thanne wol we gladly heere."
    "I graunte, ywis," quod he, "but I moot thinke
40 Upon som honeste° thing whil that I drinke."   *honorable*

The Prologue

Lordinges—quod he—in chirches whan I preche,
I paine me to han an hautein° speeche,   *loud*
And ringe it out as round as gooth a belle,
For I can al by rote° that I telle.   *know it all by heart*

---

2. Harry Baily, the host, is responding to *The Physician's Tale* and the story of a young woman named Virginia whose father kills her rather than surrender her to a wicked judge and his accomplice.
3. Physician's vessels for analyzing urine samples.
4. Medicines named after the ancient Greek physicians

Hypocrates and Galen.
5. Saint Ronan, a Scottish saint, with a possible pun on "runnions," the male sexual organs.
6. A confused oath mixing God's body and God's bones.
7. Fair friend (French, affected).

45 My theme is alway oon,° and evere was: *the same*
Radix malorum est cupiditas.[8]
First I pronounce whennes that I come,
And thanne my bulles° shewe I alle and some: *indulgences*
Oure lige lordes seel[9] on my patente;°   *license*
50 That shewe I first, my body to warente,°   *safeguard*
That no man be so bold, ne preest ne clerk,
Me to destourbe of Cristes holy werk.
And after that thanne telle I forth my tales—
Bulles of popes and of cardinales,
55 Of patriarkes and bisshopes I shewe,
And in Latin I speke a wordes fewe,
To saffron° with my predicacioun,°   *season/preaching*
And for to stire hem to devocioun.
   Thanne shewe I forth my longe crystal stones,°   *jars*
60 Ycrammed ful of cloutes° and of bones—   *rags*
Relikes been they, as weenen° they eechoon.   *suppose*
Thanne have I in laton° a shulder-boon   *brazened*
Which that was of an holy Jewes sheep.
"Goode men," I saye, "take of my wordes keep:°   *notice*
65 If that this boon be wasshe in any welle,
If cow, or calf, or sheep, or oxe swelle,
That any worm° hath ete or worm ystonge,   *snake*
Take water of that welle and wassh his tonge,
And it is hool° anoon. And ferthermoor,   *healthy*
70 Of pokkes° and of scabbe and every soor   *pox*
Shal every sheep be hool that of this welle
Drinketh a draughte. Take keep eek that I telle:
If that the goode man that the beestes oweth°   *owns*
Wol every wike,° er that the cok him croweth,   *week*
75 Fasting drinken of this welle a draughte—
As thilke holy Jew oure eldres taughte—
His beestes and his stoor° shal multiplye.   *stock*
   "And sire, also it heleth jalousye:
For though a man be falle in jalous rage,
80 Lat maken with this water his potage,°   *soup*
And nevere shal he more his wif mistriste,
Though he the soothe° of hir defaute wiste,°   *truth/knows*
Al hadde she taken preestes two or three.
   "Here is a mitein° eek that ye may see: *mitten*
85 He that his hand wol putte in this mitein
He shal have multiplying of his grain,
Whan he hath sowen, be it whete or otes—
So that he offre pens° or elles grotes.°   *pennies/silver coins*
   "Goode men and wommen, oo thing warne I you:
90 If any wight° be in this chirche now   *person*
That hath doon sinne horrible, that he
Dar nat for shame of it yshriven° be,   *confessed*
Or any womman, be she yong or old,

8. Greed is the root of all evil.   9. Seal of our liege lord (i.e., the Pope).

That hath ymaked hir housbonde cokewold,°   *cuckold*
95   Swich folk shal have no power ne no grace
To offren to my relikes in this place;
And whoso findeth him out of swich blame,
He wol come up and offre in Goddes name,
And I assoile° him by the auctoritee   *absolve*
100   Which that by bulle ygraunted was to me."
        By this gaude° have I wonne, yeer by yeer,   *trick*
An hundred mark[1] sith I was pardoner.
I stonde lik a clerk in my pulpet,
And whan the lewed° peple is down yset,   *ignorant*
105   I preche so as ye han herd bifore,
And telle an hundred false japes° more.   *tricks*
Thanne paine I me to strecche forth the nekke,
And eest and west upon the peple I bekke°   *nod*
As dooth a douve,° sitting on a berne;°   *dove/barn*
110   Mine handes and my tonge goon so yerne°   *fast*
That it is joye to see my bisinesse.
Of avarice and of swich cursednesse
Is al my preching, for to make hem free°   *generous*
To yiven hir pens, and namely unto me,
115   For myn entente is nat but for to winne,°   *profit*
And no thing for correccion of sinne:
I rekke° nevere whan that they been beried°   *care/buried*
Though that hir soules goon a-blakeberied.[2]
For certes, many a predicacioun
120   Comth ofte time of yvel entencioun:
Som for plesance of folk and flaterye,
To been avaunced by ypocrisye,
And som for vaine glorye, and som for hate;
For whan I dar noon otherways debate,
125   Thanne wol I stinge him with my tonge smerte°   *hurting*
In preching, so that he shal nat asterte°   *escape*
To been defamed falsly, if that he
Hath trespassed to my bretheren or to me.
For though I telle nought his propre name,
130   Men shal wel knowe that it is the same
By signes and by othere circumstaunces.
Thus quite° I folk that doon us displesaunces;°   *repay/trouble*
Thus spete I out my venim under hewe°   *color*
Of holinesse, to seeme holy and trewe.
135   But shortly myn entente I wol devise:°   *describe*
I preche of no thing but for coveitise;°   *greed*
Therfore my theme is yit and evere was
Radix malorum est cupiditas.
        Thus can I preche again that same vice
140   Which that I use, and that is avarice.
But though myself be gilty in that sinne,
Yit can I make other folk to twinne°   *separate*
From avarice, and sore to repente—

---

1. About 66 pounds.   2. Looking for blackberries.

But that is nat my principal entente:
145 I preche no thing but for coveitise.
Of this matere it oughte ynough suffise.
   Thanne telle I hem ensamples° many oon   *exemplary tales*
Of olde stories longe time agoon,
For lewed peple loven tales olde—
150 Swiche thinges can they wel reporte° and holde.°   *repeat/remember*
What, trowe° ye that whiles I may preche,   *believe*
And winne gold and silver for I teche,
That I wol live in poverte wilfully?
Nay, nay, I thoughte it nevere, trewely,
155 For I wol preche and begge in sondry landes;
I wol nat do no labour with mine handes,
Ne make baskettes and live therby,
By cause I wol nat beggen idelly.°   *in vain*
I wol none of the Apostles countrefete:°   *imitate*
160 I wol have moneye, wolle,° cheese, and whete,   *wool*
Al were it yiven of the pooreste page,°   *servant*
Or of the pooreste widwe in a village—
Al sholde hir children sterve° for famine.   *die*
Nay, I wol drinke licour of the vine
165 And have a joly wenche in every town.
But herkneth, lordinges, in conclusioun:
Youre liking is that I shal telle a tale:
Now have I dronke a draughte of corny ale,
By God, I hope I shal you telle a thing
170 That shal by reson been at youre liking;
For though myself be a ful vicious man,
A moral tale yit I you telle can,
Which I am wont to preche for to winne.
Now holde youre pees, my tale I wol biginne.

The Pardoner's Tale

175 In Flandres whilom° was a compaignye   *once*
Of yonge folk that haunteden° folye—   *practiced*
As riot, hasard, stewes,[1] and tavernes,
Wher as with harpes, lutes, and giternes°   *guitars*
They daunce and playen at dees° bothe day and night, *dice*
180 And ete also and drinke over hir might,
Thurgh which they doon the devel sacrifise
Withinne that develes temple in cursed wise
By superfluitee° abhominable.   *overindulgence*
Hir othes been so grete and so dampnable
185 That it is grisly for to heere hem swere:
Oure blessed Lordes body they totere°—   *rip apart*
Hem thoughte that Jewes rente° him nought ynough. *tore*
And eech of hem at otheres sinne lough.°   *laughed*
And right anoon thanne comen tombesteres,° *dancing girls*
190 Fetis° and smale,° and yonge frutesteres,[2] *elegant/slender*

---

1. Such as carousing, gambling, brothels.   2. Girls selling fruit.

Singeres with harpes, bawdes, wafereres°—   *cake sellers*
Whiche been the verray develes officeres,
To kindle and blowe the fir of lecherye
That is annexed° unto glotonye:°   *connected/gluttony*
195   The Holy Writ take I to my witnesse
That luxure° is in win and dronkenesse.   *lechery*
Lo, how that dronken Lot[3] unkindely°   *against nature*
Lay by his doughtres two unwitingly:
So dronke he was he niste what he wroughte.°   *knew not what he did*
200   Herodes,[4] who so wel the stories soughte,
Whan he of win was repleet at his feeste,
Right at his owene table he yaf his heeste°   *command*
To sleen° the Baptist John, ful giltelees.   *slay*
    Senek[5] saith a good word doutelees:
205   He saith he can no difference finde
Bitwixe a man that is out of his minde
And a man which that is dronkelewe,°   *drunk*
But that woodnesse, yfallen in a shrewe,[6]
Persevereth lenger than dooth dronkenesse.
210   O glotonye, ful of cursednesse!
O cause first of oure confusioun!°   *ruin*
O original of oure dampnacioun,
Til Crist hadde bought° us with his blood again!   *redeemed*
Lo, how dere, shortly for to sayn,
215   Abought was thilke cursed vilainye;
Corrupt was al this world for glotonye:
Adam oure fader and his wif also
Fro Paradis to labour and to wo
Were driven for that vice, it is no drede.°   *doubt*
220   For whil that Adam fasted, as I rede,
He was in Paradis; and whan that he
Eet of the fruit defended° on a tree,   *forbidden*
Anoon he was out cast to wo and paine.
O glotonye, on thee wel oughte us plaine!°   *lament*
225   O, wiste a man how manye maladies
Folwen of excesse and of glotonies,
He wolde been the more mesurable°   *moderate*
Of his diete, sitting at his table.
Allas, the shorte throte, the tendre mouth,
230   Maketh that eest and west and north and south,
In erthe, in air, in water, men to swinke,°   *labor*
To gete a gloton daintee mete and drinke.
Of this matere, O Paul, wel canstou trete:°   *discuss*
"Mete unto wombe, and wombe° eek unto mete,   *belly*
235   Shal God destroyen bothe," as Paulus saith.[7]
Allas, a foul thing is it, by my faith,
To saye this word, and fouler is the deede

3. Lot, the nephew of Abraham, whose story is told in Genesis 19.30–38.
4. King Herod, who was enticed by Salome into bringing her the head of John the Baptist (Mark 6.17–29,

Matthew 14.1–12).
5. The stoic author Seneca in his *Epistle* 83.18. 493–97.
6. Madness, occurring in a wicked person.
7. St. Paul in 1 Corinthians 6.13.

Whan man so drinketh of the white and rede°   *white and red wines*
That of his throte he maketh his privee°   *toilet*
240 Thurgh thilke cursed superfluitee.
　　The Apostle[8] weeping saith ful pitously,
"Ther walken manye of which you told have I—
I saye it now weeping with pitous vois—
They been enemies of Cristes crois,°   *cross*
245 Of whiche the ende is deeth—wombe is hir god!"
O wombe, O bely, O stinking cod,°   *bag*
Fulfilled of dong and of corrupcioun!
At either ende of thee foul is the soun.°   *sound*
How greet labour and cost is thee to finde!°   *provide for*
250 Thise cookes, how they stampe and straine and grinde,
And turnen substance into accident[9]
To fulfillen al thy likerous talent!°   *greedy desire*
Out of the harde bones knokke they
The mary,° for they caste nought away   *marrow*
255 That may go thurgh the golet° softe and soote.°   *gullet/sweet*
Of spicerye of leef and bark and roote
Shal been his sauce ymaked by delit,
To make him yit a newer appetit.
But certes, he that haunteth swiche delices°   *delicacies*
260 Is deed whil that he liveth in tho vices.
　　A lecherous thing is win, and dronkenesse
Is ful of striving° and of wrecchednesse.   *quarreling*
O dronke man, disfigured is thy face!
Sour is thy breeth, foul artou to embrace!
265 And thurgh thy dronke nose seemeth the soun
As though thou saidest ay "Sampsoun, Sampsoun."
And yit, God woot, Sampson drank nevere win.
Thou fallest as it were a stiked swin;°   *stuck pig*
Thy tonge is lost, and al thyn honeste cure,°   *care for honor*
270 For dronkenesse is verray sepulture°   *grave*
Of mannes wit and his discrecioun.
In whom that drinke hath dominacioun
He can no conseil keepe, it is no drede.
Now keepe you fro the white and fro the rede—
275 And namely fro the white win of Lepe[1]
That is to selle in Fisshstreete or in Chepe:[2]
The win of Spaine creepeth subtilly[3]
In othere wines growing faste° by,   *close*
Of which ther riseth swich fumositee°   *vapors*
280 That whan a man hath dronken draughtes three
And weeneth that he be at hoom in Chepe,
He is in Spaine, right at the town of Lepe,
Nat at The Rochele ne at Burdeux town;

8. St. Paul, in Philippians 3.18–19.
9. A philosophical joke playing on the transubstantiation of bread and wine into the holy Eucharist, according to Catholic doctrine, where matter (substance) is transformed in its qualities (accident).
1. Wine-growing region in Spain.
2. Commercial districts in London.
3. Chaucer is referring to the illegal practice of using cheap wine (here, Spanish wine from Lepe) to dilute more-expensive wines (from the neighoring French provinces of La Rochelle and Bourdeaux).

And thanne wol he sayn "Sampsoun, Sampsoun."

285   But herkneth, lordinges, oo word I you praye,
That alle the soverein actes,° dar I saye,   *excellent deeds*
Of victories in the Olde Testament,
Thurgh verray God that is omnipotent,
Were doon in abstinence and in prayere:
290   Looketh the Bible and ther ye may it lere.°   *learn*

    Looke Attilla, the grete conquerour,[4]
Deide in his sleep with shame and dishonour,
Bleeding at his nose in dronkenesse:
A capitain sholde live in sobrenesse.

295   And overal this, aviseth you right wel
What was comanded unto Lamuel[5]—
Nat Samuel, but Lamuel, saye I—
Redeth the Bible and finde it expresly,
Of win-yiving° to hem that han° justise: *wine-serving/dispense*
300   Namore of this, for it may wel suffise.

    And now that I have spoken of glotonye,
Now wol I you defende hasardrye:°   *gambling*
Hasard is verray moder of lesinges,°   *lies*
And of deceite and cursed forsweringes,
305   Blaspheme of Crist, manslaughtre, and wast° also   *waste*
Of catel° and of time; and ferthermo,   *property*
It is repreve° and contrarye of honour   *reprobate*
For to been holden a commune hasardour,
And evere the hyer he is of estat
310   The more is he holden desolat.°   *dissolute*
If that a prince useth hasardrye,
In alle governance and policye
He is, as by commune opinioun,
Yholde the lasse in reputacioun.

315   Stilbon,[6] that was a wis embassadour,
Was sent to Corinthe in ful greet honour
Fro Lacedomye° to make hir alliaunce,   *Sparta*
And whan he cam him happede parchaunce
That alle the gretteste that were of that lond
320   Playing at the hasard he hem foond,
For which as soone as it mighte be
He stal him hoom again to his contree,
And saide, "Ther wol I nat lese my name,
N'I wol nat take on me so greet defame
325   You to allye unto none hasardours:
Sendeth othere wise embassadours,
For by my trouthe, me were levere° die   *I would rather*
Than I you sholde to hasardours allye.
For ye that been so glorious in honours
330   Shal nat allye you with hasardours
As by my wil, ne as by my tretee."

---

4. Attila the Hun died on his wedding night from excessive drinking.
5. Biblical king of Massa, warned against drinking in

Proverbs 31.4.
6. Possibly referring to the Greek philosopher Stilbo or
Chilon.

This wise philosophre, thus saide he.
    Looke eek that to the king Demetrius
The King of Parthes,[7] as the book saith us,
335   Sente him a paire of dees of gold in scorn,
For he hadde used hasard therbiforn,
For which he heeld his glorye or his renown
At no value or reputacioun.
Lordes may finden other manere play
340   Honeste ynough to drive the day away.
    Now wol I speke of othes false and grete
A word or two, as olde bookes trete:
    Greet swering is a thing abhominable,
And fals swering is yit more reprevable.°   *reprehensible*
345   The hye God forbad swering at al—
Witnesse on Mathew. But in special
Of swering saith the holy Jeremie,[8]
"Thou shalt swere sooth thine othes and nat lie,
And swere in doom° and eek in rightwisnesse,   *judgment*
350   But idel swering is a cursednesse."
    Biholde and see that in the firste Table°   *tablet*
Of hye Goddes heestes° honorable   *commandments*
How that the seconde heeste of him is this:
"Take nat my name in idel or amis."
355   Lo, rather° he forbedeth swich swering   *sooner*
Than homicide, or many a cursed thing.
I saye that as by ordre thus it stondeth—
This knoweth that° his heestes understondeth   *he who*
How that the seconde heeste of God is that.
360   And fertherover, I wol thee telle al plat°   *flatly*
That vengeance shal nat parten from his hous
That of his othes is too outrageous.
"By Goddes precious herte!" and "By his nailes!"
And "By the blood of Crist that is in Hailes,[9]
365   Sevene is my chaunce, and thyn is cink and traye!"°   *five and three*
"By Goddes armes, if thou falsly playe
This daggere shal thurghout thyn herte go!"
This fruit cometh of the bicche bones° two—   *cursed dice*
Forswering, ire, falsnesse, homicide.
370   Now for the love of Crist that for us dyde,
Lete° youre othes bothe grete and smale.   *leave off*
But sires, now wol I telle forth my tale.
    Thise riotoures° three of whiche I telle,   *revelers*
Longe erst er° prime° ronge of any belle,   *before/6 a.m.*
375   Were set hem in a taverne to drinke,
And as they sat they herde a belle clinke
Biforn a cors° was caried to his grave.   *corpse*
That oon of hem gan callen to his knave:°   *servant*
"Go bet,"° quod he, "and axe redily   *quickly*
380   What cors is this that passeth heer forby,

---

7. Parthia in northern Persia.
8. The prophet Jeremiah (4.2).

9. Hales Abbey in Gloucestershire owned a relic of Christ's blood.

And looke that thou reporte his name weel."

"Sire," quod this boy, "it needeth neveradeel:[1]

It was me told er ye cam heer two houres.

He was, pardee, an old felawe of youres,

385   And sodeinly he was yslain tonight,

Fordronke° as he sat on his bench upright;   *very drunk*

Ther cam a privee° thief men clepeth° Deeth,   *stealthy/call*

That in this contree al the peple sleeth,

And with his spere he smoot his herte atwo,

390   And wente his way withouten wordes mo.

He hath a thousand slain this pestilence.°   *during this plague*

And maister, er ye come in his presence,

Me thinketh that it were necessarye

For to be war of swich an adversarye;

395   Beeth redy for to meete him everemore:

Thus taughte me my dame.° I saye namore."   *mother*

    "By Sainte Marye," saide this taverner,

"The child saith sooth, for he hath slain this yeer,

Henne° over a mile, within a greet village,   *from here*

400   Bothe man and womman, child and hine° and page.°   *farmhand/servant*

I trowe his habitacion be there.

To been avised° greet wisdom it were   *warned*

Er that he dide a man a dishonour."

    "Ye, Goddes armes," quod this riotour,

405   "Is it swich peril with him for to meete?

I shal him seeke by way and eek by streete,

I make avow to Goddes digne° bones.   *worthy*

Herkneth, felawes, we three been alle ones:

Lat eech of us holde up his hand to other

410   And eech of us bicome otheres brother,

And we wol sleen this false traitour Deeth.

He shal be slain, he that so manye sleeth,

By Goddess dignitee, er it be night."

    Togidres han thise three hir trouthes° plight°   *words of honor/pledged*

415   To live and dien eech of hem with other,

As though he were his owene ybore° brother.   *born*

And up they sterte, al dronken in this rage,

And forth they goon towardes that village

Of which the taverner hadde spoke biforn.

420   And many a grisly ooth thanne han they sworn,

And Cristes blessed body they torente:°   *tore apart*

Deeth shal be deed if that they may him hente.°   *capture*

    Whan they han goon nat fully half a mile,

Right as they wolde han treden° over a stile,   *stepped*

425   An old man and a poore with hem mette;

This olde man ful mekely hem grette,°   *greeted*

And saide thus, "Now lordes, God you see."°   *look after*

    The pruddeste° of thise riotoures three   *proudest*

Answerde again, "What, carl with sory grace,°   *unlucky fellow*

---

1. Is not necessary in the least.

430 Why artou al forwrapped° save thy face?   *bundled up*
    Why livestou so longe in so greet age?"
        This olde man gan looke in his visage,
    And saide thus, "For I ne can nat finde
    A man, though that I walked into Inde,
435 Neither in citee ne in no village,
    That wolde chaunge his youthe for myn age;
    And therfore moot I han myn age stille,
    As longe time as it is Goddes wille.
        "Ne Deeth, allas, ne wol nat have my lif.
440 Thus walke I lik a restelees caitif,°   *wretch*
    And on the ground which is my modres° gate   *mother's*
    I knokke with my staf bothe erly and late,
    And saye, 'Leve° moder, leet me in: *dear*
    Lo, how I vanisshe, flessh and blood and skin.
445 Allas, whan shal my bones been at reste?
    Moder, with you wolde I chaunge° my cheste°   *exchange/strongbox*
    That in my chambre longe time hath be,
    Ye, for an haire-clout° to wrappe me.'   *winding sheet*
    But yit to me she wol nat do that grace,
450 For which ful pale and welked° is my face.   *withered*
    But sires, to you it is no curteisye
    To speken to an old man vilainye,°   *discourtesy*
    But he trespasse in word or elles in deede.
    In Holy Writ ye may yourself wel rede,
455 'Agains an old man, hoor upon his heed,
    Ye shal arise.' Wherfore I yive you reed,°   *advice*
    Ne dooth unto an old man noon harm now,
    Namore than that ye wolde men dide to you
    In age, if that ye so longe abide.
460 And God be with you wher ye go or ride:
    I moot go thider as I have to go."
        "Nay, olde cherl, by God thou shalt nat so,"
    Saide this other hasardour anoon.
    "Thou partest nat so lightly,° by Saint John!   *easily*
465 Thou speke right now of thilke traitour Deeth,
    That in this contree alle oure freendes sleeth:
    Have here my trouthe, as thou art his espye,
    Tel wher he is, or thou shalt it abye,°   *pay for*
    By God and by the holy sacrament!
470 For soothly thou art oon of his assent°   *in league with him*
    To sleen us yonge folk, thou false thief."
        "Now sires," quod he, "if that ye be so lief°   *eager*
    To finde Deeth, turne up this crooked way,
    For in that grove I lafte him, by my fay,
475 Under a tree, and ther he wol abide:
    Nat for youre boost he wol him no thing hide.
    See ye that ook?° Right ther ye shal him finde.   *oak*
    God save you, that boughte again° mankinde,   *redeemed*
    And you amende." Thus saide this olde man.
480   And everich of thise riotoures ran

Til he cam to that tree, and ther they founde
Of florins° fine of gold ycoined rounde   *gold coins*
Wel neigh an eighte busshels as hem thoughte—
Ne lenger thanne after Deeth they soughte,
485 But eech of hem so glad was of the sighte,
For that the florins been so faire and brighte,
That down they sette hem by this precious hoord.
The worste of hem he spak the firste word:
     "Bretheren," quod he, "take keep what that I saye:
490 My wit is greet though that I bourde° and playe.   *joke*
This tresor hath Fortune unto us yiven
In mirthe and jolitee oure lif to liven,
And lightly as it cometh so wol we spende.
Ey, Goddes precious dignitee, who wende°   *would suppose*
495 Today that we sholde han so fair a grace?
But mighte this gold be caried fro this place
Hoom to myn hous—or elles unto youres—
For wel ye woot that al this gold is oures—
Thanne were we in heigh felicitee.
500 But trewely, by daye it mighte nat be:
Men wolde sayn that we were theves stronge,°   *flagrant*
And for oure owene tresor doon us honge.°   *have us hanged*
This tresor moste ycaried be by nighte,
As wisely and as slyly as it mighte.
505 Therfore I rede that cut° amonges us alle   *lots*
Be drawe, and lat see wher the cut wol falle;
And he that hath the cut with herte blithe°   *happy*
Shal renne to the town, and that ful swithe,°   *swiftly*
And bringe us breed and win ful prively;
510 And two of us shal keepen subtilly
This tresor wel, and if he wol nat tarye,
Whan it is night we wol this tresor carye
By oon assent wher as us thinketh best."
That oon of hem the cut broughte in his fest°   *fist*
515 And bad hem drawe and looke wher it wol falle;
And it fil on the yongeste of hem alle,
And forth toward the town he wente anoon.
And also soone as that he was agoon,
That oon of hem spak thus unto that other:
520 "Thou knowest wel thou art my sworen brother;
Thy profit wol I telle thee anoon:
Thou woost wel that oure felawe is agoon,
And here is gold, and that ful greet plentee,
That shal departed° been among us three.   *divided*
525 But nathelees, if I can shape° it so   *arrange*
That it departed were among us two,
Hadde I nat doon a freendes turn to thee?"
     That other answerde, "I noot° how that may be: *do not know*
He woot that the gold is with us twaye.
530 What shal we doon? What shal we to him saye?"
     "Shal it be conseil?"° saide the firste shrewe.°   *secret/villain*

"And I shal telle in a wordes fewe
What we shul doon, and bringe it wel aboute."
   "I graunte," quod that other, "out of doute,
535   That by my trouthe I wol thee nat biwraye."°   *betray*
   "Now," quod the firste, "thou woost wel we be twaye,
And two of us shal strenger be than oon:
Looke whan that he is set that right anoon
Aris as though thou woldest with him playe,
540   And I shal rive° him thurgh the sides twaye,   *stab*
Whil that thou strugelest with him as in game,
And with thy daggere looke thou do the same;
And thanne shal al this gold departed be,
My dere freend, bitwixe thee and me.
545   Thanne we may bothe oure lustes° al fulfille,   *desires*
And playe at dees right at oure owene wille."
And thus accorded been thise shrewes twaye
To sleen the thridde, as ye han herd me saye.
   This yongeste, which that wente to the town,
550   Ful ofte in herte he rolleth up and down
The beautee of thise florins newe and brighte.
"O Lord," quod he, "if so were that I mighte
Have al this tresor to myself allone,
Ther is no man that liveth under the trone°   *throne*
555   Of God that sholde live so merye as I."
And at the laste the feend oure enemy
Putte in his thought that he sholde poison beye,°   *buy*
With which he mighte sleen his felawes twaye—
Forwhy° the feend foond him in swich livinge   *wherefore*
560   That he hadde leve° him to sorwe bringe: *permission*
For this was outrely his fulle entente,
To sleen hem bothe, and nevere to repente.
   And forth he gooth—no lenger wolde he tarye—
Into the town unto a pothecarye,°   *druggist*
565   And prayed him that he him wolde selle
Som poison that he mighte his rattes quelle,°   *kill*
And eek ther was a polcat° in his hawe°   *weasel/yard*
That, as he saide, his capons° hadde yslawe,°   *chickens/slain*
And fain° he wolde wreke° him if he mighte   *gladly/avenge*
570   On vermin that destroyed him by nighte.
   The pothecarye answerde, "And thou shalt have
A thing that, also° God my soule save,   *so*
In al this world ther is no creature
That ete or dronke hath of this confiture°—   *concoction*
575   Nat but the mountance° of a corn° of whete—   *amount/grain*
That he ne shal his lif anoon forlete.°   *lose*
Ye, sterve° he shal, and that in lasse while   *die*
Than thou wolt goon a paas° nat but a mile,   *walking*
The poison is so strong and violent."
580   This cursed man hath in his hand yhent°   *taken*
This poison in a box and sith he ran
Into the nexte streete unto a man

And borwed of him large botels three,
And in the two his poison poured he—
585   The thridde he kepte clene for his drinke,
For al the night he shoop° him for to swinke°   prepared/work
In carying of the gold out of that place.
And whan this riotour with sory grace
Hadde filled with win his grete botels three,
590   To his felawes again repaireth he.
        What needeth it to sermone of it more?
For right as they had cast his deeth bifore,
Right so they han him slain, and that anoon.
And whan that this was doon, thus spak that oon:
595   "Now lat us sitte and drinke and make us merye,
And afterward we wol his body berye."
And with that word it happed him par cas°   by chance
To take the botel ther the poison was,
And drank, and yaf his felawe drinke also,
600   For which anoon they storven bothe two.
        But certes I suppose that Avicen[2]
Wroot nevere in no canon ne in no *fen*
Mo wonder signes of empoisoning
Than hadde thise wrecches two er hir ending:
605   Thus ended been thise homicides two,
And eek the false empoisonere also.
        O cursed sinne of alle cursednesse!
O traitours homicide, O wikkednesse!
O glotonye, luxure,° and hasardrye!   lechery
610   Thou balsphemour of Crist with vilainye
And othes grete of usage° and of pride!   habit
Allas, mankinde, how may it bitide
That to thy Creatour which that thee wroughte,
And with his precious herte blood thee boughte,
615   Thou art so fals and so unkinde,° allas?   unnatural
        Now goode men, God foryive you youre trespas,
And ware° you fro the sinne of avarice: guard
Myn holy pardon may you alle warice°—   save
So that ye offre nobles or sterlinges,°   gold or silver coins
620   Or elles silver brooches, spoones, ringes.
Boweth your heed under this holy bulle!
Cometh up, ye wives, offreth of youre wolle!°   wool
Youre name I entre here in my rolle: anoon
Into the blisse of hevene shul ye goon.
625   I you assoile° by myn heigh power—   absolve
Ye that wol offre—as clene and eek as cleer°   pure
As ye were born.—And lo, sires, thus I preche.
And Jesu Crist that is oure soules leeche°   physician
So graunte you his pardon to receive,
630   For that is best—I wol you nat deceive.

2. The 12th-century Arab philosopher Avicenna composed a *Canon of Medicine*, divided into sections called fens.

The Epilogue

"But sires, oo word forgat I in my tale:
I have relikes and pardon in my male°   bag
As faire as any man in Engelond,
Whiche were me yiven by the Popes hond.
635   If any of you wol of devocioun
Offren and han myn absolucioun,
Come forth anoon, and kneeleth here adown,
And mekely receiveth my pardoun,
Or elles taketh pardon as ye wende,
640   Al newe and fressh at every miles ende—
So that ye offre alway newe and newe°   over and over
Nobles or pens whiche that be goode and trewe.
It is an honour to everich that is heer
That ye mowe have a suffisant° pardoner   competent
645   T'assoile you in contrees as ye ride,
For aventures whiche that may bitide:
Paraventure ther may falle oon or two
Down of his hors and breke his nekke atwo;
Looke which a suretee° is it to you alle   safeguard
650   That I am in youre felaweshipe yfalle
That may assoile you, bothe more and lasse,
Whan that the soule shal fro the body passe.
I rede° that oure Hoste shal biginne,   advise
For he is most envoluped in sinne.
655   Com forth, sire Host, and offre first anoon,
And thou shalt kisse the relikes everichoon,
Ye, for a grote:° unbokele anoon thy purs."   fourpence coin
"Nay, nay," quod he, "thanne have I Cristes curs!
Lat be," quod he, "it shal nat be, so theech!°   may I prosper
660   Thou woldest make me kisse thyn olde breech
And swere it were a relik of a saint,
Though it were with thy fundament° depeint.°   bowels/stained
But, by the crois° which that Sainte Elaine[3] foond,   cross
I wolde I hadde thy coilons° in myn hond,   testicles
665   In stede of relikes or of saintuarye.°   container of relics
Lat cutte hem of: I wol thee helpe hem carye.
They shal be shrined in an hogges tord."°   turd
This Pardoner answerde nat a word:
So wroth he was no word ne wolde he saye.
670   "Now," quod oure Host, "I wol no lenger playe
With thee, ne with noon other angry man."
But right anoon the worthy Knight bigan,
Whan that he sawgh that al the peple lough,
"Namore of this, for it is right ynough.
675   Sire Pardoner, be glad and merye of cheere,
And ye, sire Host that been to me so dere,
I praye you that ye kisse the Pardoner,

3. St. Helen, who was said to have found the True Cross on which Jesus was crucified.

And Pardoner, I praye thee, draw thee neer,
And as we diden lat us laughe and playe."
680   Anoon they kiste and riden forth hir waye.

The Nun's Priest's Prologue and Tale

Of all his varied and ambitious output, *The Nun's Priest's Tale* may be Chaucer's most impressive tour de force. At its core is a wonderful animal fable, free of the conventionality and sometimes easy moralities this ancient form had taken on by the fourteenth century. The fable of Chauntecleer and Pertelote achieves quite extraordinary density, further, because of the multiple frames—structural and thematic—that surround it.

As part of the Canterbury tale-telling competition, the priest's fable plays a role in that broadest contest of classes and literary genres. More locally, it is one of many moments in which the Host, Harry Bailey, demands a tale from a male pilgrim in a style that also suggests a sexual challenge, and then adjusts his estimate of the teller's virility (even his social position) to suit. The fable itself is surrounded by an intimate portrait of Chauntecleer's peasant owner and her simple life, content with "hertes suffisaunce," a marked contrast to courtly values.

The central story of Chauntecleer's dream, danger, and escape works within a subtle and funny exploration of relations between the sexes. This is conditioned by courtly love conventions, literacy and education, and even the vocabulary of Pertelote's mostly Saxon diction and Chauntecleer's love of French. This linguistic competition has its high point when Chauntecleer condescendingly mistranslates a misogynist Latin tag. Linguistic vanity, though, is exactly what puts Chauntecleer most in jeopardy. It is not the destiny Chauntecleer thinks he glimpses in his dream that almost costs his life, but rather another verbal competition, and an almost Oedipal challenge to his father.

Much of the story's energy, however, derives not from its frames but from the explosion of those frames—literary, spatial, even social—enacted and recalled at the heart of the tale. The chickens are simultaneously, and hilariously, both courtly lovers and very realistic fowl. When Chauntecleer is carried off, the whole world of the tale—widow, daughters, dogs, even bees—bursts outward in pursuit. In the midst of mock-epic and mock-romance comparisons to this joyful disorder, Chaucer even inserts one of his very few direct references to the greatest disorder of his time, the Rising of 1381.

The Nun's Priest's Tale is a comedy as well as a fable, reversing a lugubrious series of tragedies in the preceding *Monk's Tale*. In the end, it is a story of canniness, acquired self-knowledge, and self-salvation. Woven into the priest's humor are a gentle satire and a quiet assertion that free will is the final resource of any agent, avian or human.

The Nun's Priest's Tale
The Introduction

"Ho!" quod the Knight, "good sire, namore of this:
That ye han said is right ynough, ywis,°   *indeed*
And muchel more, for litel hevinesse
Is right ynough to muche folk° I gesse:[1]   *for most folks*
5   I saye for me it is a greet disese,
Wher as men han been in greet welthe and ese,

1. The Monk has just told a series of stark and repetitive "tragedies"—the falls of men both ancient and modern.

To heeren of hir sodein° fal, allas;   *sudden*
And the contrarye is joye and greet solas,°   *comfort*
As whan a man hath been in poore estat,
10 And climbeth up and wexeth° fortunat,   *becomes*
And there abideth in prosperitee:
Swich thing is gladsom, as it thinketh° me,   *seems to*
And of swich thing were goodly for to telle."
   "Ye," quod oure Host, "by Sainte Poules° belle,   *Paul's*
15 Ye saye right sooth: this Monk he clappeth° loude.   *chatters*
He spak how Fortune covered with a cloude—
I noot nevere what.° And als of a tragedye   *I don't know what*
Right now ye herde, and pardee,° no remedye   *by God*
It is for to biwaile ne complaine
20 That that is doon, and als° it is a paine,   *also*
As ye han said, to heere of hevinesse.
   "Sire Monk, namore of this, so God you blesse:
Youre tale anoyeth al this compaignye;
Swich talking is nat worth a boterflye,
25 For therinne is ther no disport ne game.
Wherfore, sire Monk, or daun° Piers by youre name,   *Master*
I praye you hertely telle us somwhat elles:
For sikerly, nere clinking of youre belles,[2]
That on youre bridel hange on every side,
30 By hevene king that for us alle dyde,
I sholde er this have fallen down for sleep,
Although the slough° hadde nevere been so deep.   *mud*
Thanne hadde youre tale al be told in vain;
For certainly, as that thise clerkes sayn,
35 Wher as a man may have noon audience,
Nought helpeth it to tellen his sentence;°   *statement*
And wel I woot the substance is in me,
If any thing shal wel reported be.
Sire, saye somwhat of hunting, I you praye."
40   "Nay," quod this Monk, "I have no lust° to playe.   *wish*
Now lat another telle, as I have told."
   Thanne spak oure Host with rude speeche and bold,
And saide unto the Nonnes Preest anoon,
"Com neer, thou Preest,[3] com hider, thou sire John:
45 Tel us swich thing as may oure hertes glade.°   *gladden our hearts*
Be blithe,° though thou ride upon a jade!°   *happy/nag*
What though thyn hors be bothe foul and lene?
If he wol serve thee, rekke nat a bene.°   *don't care a bean*
Looke that thyn herte be merye everemo."
50   "Yis, sire," quod he, "yis, Host, so mote I go,
But I be merye, ywis, I wol be blamed."
And right anoon his tale he hath attamed,°   *begun*
And thus he saide unto us everichoon,
This sweete Preest, this goodly man sire John.

---

2. For truly, were it not for the jingling of your bells.
3. The Host uses the familiar, somewhat condescending   "thou," then contemptuously calls the priest "Sir John."

The Tale

55	A poore widwe somdeel stape° in age *well along*
	Was whilom° dwelling in a narwe cotage, *once upon a time*
	Biside a grove, stonding in a dale:
	This widwe of which I telle you my tale,
	Sin° thilke° day that she was last a wif, *since/that*
60	In pacience ladde a ful simple lif.
	For litel was hir catel° and hir rente,° *property/income*
	By housbondrye° of swich as God hire sente *management*
	She foond° hirself and eek hir doughtren two. *provided for*
	Three large sowes hadde she and namo,
65	Three kin,° and eek a sheep that highte° Malle. *cows/was named*
	Ful sooty was hir bowr° and eek hir halle, *bedroom*
	In which she eet ful many a sclendre meel;
	Of poinant° sauce hire needed neveradeel: *pungent*
	No daintee morsel passed thurgh hir throte—
70	Hir diete was accordant to hir cote.° *cottage*
	Repleccioun° ne made hire nevere sik: *gluttony*
	Attempre° diete was al hir physik, *moderate*
	And exercise and hertes suffisaunce.
	The goute lette hire nothing for to daunce,[4]
75	N'apoplexye shente° nat hir heed. *hurt*
	No win ne drank she, neither whit ne reed:
	Hir boord° was served most with whit and blak, *table*
	Milk and brown breed, in which she foond no lak;° *fault*
	Seind° bacon, and somtime an ey° or twaye,° *singed/egg/two*
80	For she was as it were a manere daye.° *dairy maid*
	A yeerd° she hadde, enclosed al withoute *yard*
	With stikkes, and a drye dich aboute,
	In which she hadde a cok heet° Chauntecleer: *called*
	In al the land of crowing nas his peer.
85	His vois was merier than the merye orgon
	On massedayes that in the chirche goon;° *is played*
	Wel sikerer° was his crowing in his logge° *surer/dwelling*
	Than is a clok or an abbeye orlogge;° *timepiece*
	By nature he knew eech ascensioun
90	Of th'equinoxial[5] in thilke town:
	For whan degrees fifteene were ascended,
	Thanne crew he that it mighte nat been amended.° *surpassed*
	His comb was redder than the fin coral,
	And batailed° as it were a castel wal; *crenellated*
95	His bile° was blak, and as the jeet it shoon; *beak*
	Like asure° were his legges and his toon;° *azure/toes*
	His nailes whitter than the lilye flowr,
	And lik the burned° gold was his colour. *burnished*
	This gentil cok hadde in his governaunce
100	Sevene hennes for to doon al his plesaunce,

4. Did not keep her from dancing.   5. The points marking the celestial hours.

Whiche were his sustres and his paramours,°   *lovers*
And wonder like to him as of colours;
Of whiche the faireste hewed° on hir throte   *colored*
Was cleped° faire damoisele Pertelote: *called*
105   Curteis she was, discreet, and debonaire,°   *gracious*
And compaignable,° and bar hirself so faire,   *sociable*
Sin thilke day that she was seven night old,
That trewely she hath the herte in hold
Of Chauntecleer, loken in every lith.[6]
110   He loved hire so that wel was him therwith.
But swich a joye was it to heere hem singe,
Whan that the brighte sonne gan to springe,
In sweete accord "My Lief is Faren in Londe"[7]—
For thilke time, as I have understonde,
115   Beestes and briddes couden speke and singe.
     And so bifel that in a daweninge,
As Chauntecleer among his wives alle
Sat on his perche that was in the halle,
And next him sat this faire Pertelote,
120   This Chauntecleer gan gronen in his throte,
As man that in his dreem is drecched° sore.   *disturbed*
     And whan that Pertelote thus herde him rore,
She was agast, and saide, "Herte dere,
What aileth you to grone in this manere?
125   Ye been a verray° slepere, fy, for shame!"   *true*
     And he answerde and saide thus, "Madame,
I praye you that ye take it nat agrief.°   *amiss*
By God, me mette° I was in swich meschief   *I dreamed*
Right now, that yit myn herte is sore afright.
130   Now God," quod he, "my swevene recche aright,[8]
And keepe my body out of foul prisoun!
Me mette how that I romed up and down
Within oure yeerd, wher as I sawgh a beest,
Was lik an hound and wolde han maad arrest°   *taken captive*
135   Upon my body, and han had me deed.
His colour was bitwixe yelow and reed,
And tipped was his tail and bothe his eres
With blak, unlik the remenant of his heres;°   *the rest of his hair*
His snoute smal, with glowing yën twaye.
140   Yit of his look for fere almost I deye:
This caused me my groning, doutelees."
     "Avoi,'"° quod she, "fy on you, hertelees!°   *Have done!/coward*
Allas," quod she, "for by that God above,
Now han ye lost myn herte and al my love!
145   I can nat love a coward, by my faith.
For certes, what so any womman saith,
We alle desiren, if it mighte be,

6. Locked in every limb (i.e., thoroughly).
7. A popular ballad, "My Love Has Gone to the Country."
8. Intepret my dream correctly.

To han housbondes hardy, wise, and free,°   *generous*
And secree,° and no nigard, ne no fool,   *discreet*
150 Ne him that is agast° of every tool,°   *afraid/weapon*
Ne noon avauntour.° By that God above,   *braggart*
How dorste ye sayn for shame unto youre love
That any thing mighte make you aferd?
Have ye no mannes herte and han a beerd?
155 Allas, and conne ye been agast of swevenes?
No thing, God woot, but vanitee° in swevene is!   *illusion*
Swevenes engendren of replexiouns,
And ofte of fume° and of complexiouns,°   *gas/bodily humors*
Whan humours been too habundant in a wight.°   *creature*
160 Certes, this dreem which ye han met tonight
Comth of the grete superfluitee
Of youre rede colera,[9] pardee,°   *by God*
Which causeth folk to dreden in hir dremes
Of arwes,° and of fir with rede lemes,°   *arrows/flames*
165 Of rede beestes, that they wol hem bite,
Of contek,° and of whelpes° grete and lite—   *strife/dogs*
Right as the humour of malencolye[1]
Causeth ful many a man in sleep to crye
For fere of blake beres or boles° blake,   *bulls*
170 Or elles blake develes wol hem take.
Of othere humours coude I telle also
That werken many a man in sleep ful wo,
But I wol passe as lightly as I can.
Lo, Caton,[2] which that was so wis a man,
175 Saide he nat thus? 'Ne do no fors° of dremes.'   *pay no attention to*
Now, sire," quod she, "whan we flee° fro the bemes,°   *fly/rafters*
For Goddes love, as take som laxatif.
Up° peril of my soule and of my lif,   *upon*
I conseile you the beste, I wol nat lie,
180 That bothe of colere and of malencolye
Ye purge you; and for ye shal nat tarye,
Though in this town is noon apothecarye,
I shal myself to herbes techen you,
That shal been for youre hele° and for youre prow,°   *health/profit*
185 And in oure yeerd tho° herbes shal I finde,   *then*
The whiche han of hir propretee by kinde°   *nature*
To purge you binethe and eek above.
Foryet nat this, for Goddes owene love.
Ye been ful colerik of complexioun;
190 Ware° the sonne in his ascencioun   *beware lest*
Ne finde you nat repleet° of humours hote;°   *full/hot*
And if it do, I dar wel laye[3] a grote°   *fourpence*
That ye shul have a fevere terciane,[4]

---

9. Coleric bile, thought to overheat the body.
1. Black bile, thought to produce dark thoughts.
2. Marcus Porcius Cato, ancient author of a book of

proverbs used by school children.
3. Bet (with a pun on egg-laying).
4. Recurring fever.

	Or an agu° that may be youre bane.°	*fever/death*
195	A day or two ye shul han digestives	
	Of wormes, er ye take youre laxatives	
	Of lauriol, centaure, and fumetere,⁵	
	Or elles of ellebor that groweth there,	
	Of catapuce, or of gaitres beries,	
200	Of herbe-ive growing in oure yeerd ther merye is.°	*where it is pleasant*
	Pekke hem right up as they growe and ete hem in.	
	Be merye, housbonde, for youre fader kin!	
	Dredeth no dreem: I can saye you namore."	
	"Madame," quod he, "graunt mercy of youre lore.°	*learning*
205	But nathelees, as touching daun Catoun,	
	That hath of wisdom swich a greet renown,	
	Though that he bad no dremes for to drede,	
	By God, men may in olde bookes rede	
	Of many a man more of auctoritee	
210	Than evere Caton was, so mote I thee,°	*so may I prosper*
	That al the revers sayn of his sentence,°	*opinion*
	And han wel founden by experience	
	That dremes been significaciouns	
	As wel of joye as tribulaciouns	
215	That folk enduren in this lif present.	
	Ther needeth make of this noon argument:	
	The verray preve° sheweth it in deede.	*proof*
	"Oon of the gretteste auctour that men rede	
	Saith thus, that whilom two felawes wente	
220	On pilgrimage in a ful good entente,	
	And happed so they comen in a town,	
	Wher as ther was swich congregacioun	
	Of peple, and eek so strait of herbergage,°	*short of lodging*
	That they ne founde as muche as oo° cotage	*one*
225	In which they bothe mighte ylogged be;	
	Wherfore they mosten of necessitee	
	As for that night departe compaignye.	
	And eech of hem gooth to his hostelrye,	
	And took his logging as it wolde falle.	
230	That oon of hem was logged in a stalle,	
	Fer in a yeerd, with oxen of the plough;	
	That other man was logged wel ynough,	
	As was his aventure or his fortune,	
	That us governeth alle as in commune.	
235	And so bifel that longe er it were day,	
	This man mette in his bed, ther as he lay,	
	How that his felawe gan upon him calle,	
	And saide, 'Allas, for in an oxes stalle	
	This night I shal be mordred° ther I lie!	*murdered*
240	Now help me, dere brother, or I die!	
	In alle haste com to me,' he saide.	

5. These and the following are bitter herbs that produce hot and dry sensations and lead to purging.

"This man out of his sleep for fere abraide,°   *bolted up*
But whan that he was wakened of his sleep,
He turned him and took of this no keep:°   *heed*
245   Him thoughte his dreem nas° but a vanitee.   *was not*
Thus twies in his sleeping dremed he,
And atte thridde time yit his felawe
Cam, as him thoughte, and saide, 'I am now slawe:°   *slain*
Bihold my bloody woundes deepe and wide.
250   Aris up erly in the morwe tide°   *morning time*
And atte west gate of the town,' quod he,
'A carte ful of dong° ther shaltou see,   *dung*
In which my body is hid ful prively:
Do thilke carte arresten° boldely.   *have seized*
255   My gold caused my mordre, sooth° to sayn'—   *truth*
And tolde him every point how he was slain,
With a ful pitous face, pale of hewe.
And truste wel, his dreem he foond ful trewe,
For on the morwe as soone as it was day,
260   To his felawes in he took the way,
And whan that he cam to this oxes stalle,
After his felawe he bigan to calle.
     "The hostiler° answerde him anoon,   *innkeeper*
And saide, 'Sire, youre felawe is agoon:
265   As soone as day he wente out of the town.'
     "This man gan fallen in suspecioun,
Remembring on his dremes that he mette;
And forth he gooth, no lenger wolde he lette,°   *delay*
Unto the west gate of the town, and foond
270   A dong carte, wente as it were to donge° lond,   *spread manure on*
That was arrayed in that same wise
As ye han herd the dede man devise;
And with an hardy herte he gan to crye,
'Vengeance and justice of this felonye!
275   My felawe mordred is this same night,
And in this carte he lith gaping upright!°   *facing up*
I crye out on the ministres,'° quod he,   *magistrates*
'That sholde keepe and rulen this citee.
Harrow, allas, here lith my felawe slain!'
280   What sholde I more unto this tale sayn?
The peple up sterte and caste the carte to grounde,
And in the middel of the dong they founde
The dede man that mordred was al newe.°   *just recently*
     "O blisful God that art so just and trewe,
285   Lo, how that thou biwrayest° mordre alway!   *reveal*
Mordre wol out, that see we day by day:
Mordre is so wlatsom° and abhominable   *loathsome*
To God that is so just and resonable,
That he ne wol nat suffre it heled° be,   *concealed*
290   Though it abide a yeer or two or three.
Mordre wol out: this my conclusioun.
And right anoon ministres of that town

Han hent° the cartere and so sore him pined,°   *seized/tortured*
And eek the hostiler so sore engined,
295 That they biknewe° hir wikkednesse anoon,   *confessed*
And were anhanged by the nekke boon.
Here may men seen that dremes been to drede.
    "And certes, in the same book I rede—
Right in the nexte chapitre after this—
300 I gabbe° nat, so have I joye or blis—   *lie*
Two men that wolde han passed over see
For certain cause into a fer contree,
If that the wind ne hadde been contrarye
That made hem in a citee for to tarye,
305 That stood ful merye upon an haven° side—   *harbor*
But on a day again° the even tide   *toward*
The wind gan chaunge, and blewe right as hem leste:°   *they wanted*
Jolif° and glad they wenten unto reste,   *merry*
And casten hem° ful erly for to saile.   *decided*
310   "But to that oo man fil a greet mervaile;
That oon of hem, in sleeping as he lay,
Him mette a wonder dreem again the day:
Him thoughte a man stood by his beddes side,
And him comanded that he sholde abide,
315 And saide him thus, 'If thou tomorwe wende,°   *travel*
Thou shalt be dreint:° my tale is at an ende.'   *drowned*
    "He wook and tolde his felawe what he mette,
And prayed him his viage to lette;°   *put off his journey*
As for that day he prayed him to bide.
320   "His felawe that lay by his beddes side
Gan for to laughe, and scorned him ful faste.
'No dreem,' quod he, 'may so myn herte agaste
That I wol lette for to do my thinges.°   *business*
I sette nat a straw by thy dreminges,
325 For swevenes been but vanitees and japes:°   *tricks*
Men dreme alday° of owles or of apes,   *constantly*
And of many a maze° therwithal—   *delusion*
Men dreme of thing that nevere was ne shal.
But sith° I see that thou wolt here abide,   *since*
330 And thus forsleuthen° wilfully thy tide,   *waste due to sloth*
Good woot, it reweth me; and have good day.'
And thus he took his leve and wente his way.
But er that he hadde half his cours ysailed—
Noot° I nat why ne what meschaunce it ailed°—   *know/went wrong*
335 But casuelly° the shippes botme rente,°   *by accident/split apart*
And ship and man under the water wente,
In sighte of othere shippes it biside,
That with hem sailed at the same tide.
And therfore, faire Pertelote so dere,
340 By swiche ensamples olde maistou lere°   *may you learn*
That no man sholde been too recchelees°   *careless*
Of dremes, for I saye thee doutelees
That many a dreem ful sore is for to drede.

　　　　"Lo, in the lif of Saint Kenelm[6] I rede—
345　That was Kenulphus sone, the noble king
　　　　Of Mercenrike—how Kenelm mette a thing
　　　　A lite er he was mordred on a day.
　　　　His mordre in his avision° he sey.°　　　　　　　*dream/saw*
　　　　His norice° him expounded everydeel　　　　　　*nurse*
350　His swevene, and bad him for to keepe him° weel　*guard against*
　　　　For traison, but he nas but seven yeer old,
　　　　And therfore litel tale hath he told°　　　　　*he cared little for*
　　　　Of any dreem, so holy was his herte.
　　　　By God, I hadde levere than my sherte°　　　　*would give my shirt*
355　That ye hadde rad his legende as have I.
　　　　"Dame Pertelote, I saye you trewely,
　　　　Macrobeus,[7] that writ the Avisioun
　　　　In Affrike of the worthy Scipioun,
　　　　Affermeth° dremes, and saith that they been　*confirms*
360　Warning of thinges that men after seen.
　　　　"And ferthermore, I praye you looketh wel
　　　　In the Olde Testament of Daniel,
　　　　If he heeld dremes any vanitee.[8]
　　　　"Rede eek of Joseph and ther shul ye see
365　Wher° dremes be somtime—I saye nat alle—　*whether*
　　　　Warning of thinges that shul after falle.
　　　　"Looke of Egypte the king daun Pharao,
　　　　His bakere and his botelere° also,　　　　　*butler*
　　　　Wher they ne felte noon effect in dremes.[9]
370　Whoso wol seeke actes of sondry remes°　　　*various kingdoms*
　　　　May rede of dremes many a wonder thing.
　　　　"Lo Cresus, which that was of Lyde° king,　*Lydia*
　　　　Mette he nat that he sat upon a tree,
　　　　Which signified he sholde anhanged be?
375　"Lo here Andromacha, Ectores° wif,　　　*Hector of Troy*
　　　　That day that Ector sholde lese° his lif,　*lose*
　　　　She dremed on the same night biforn
　　　　How that the lif of Ector sholde be lorn,
　　　　If thilke day he wente into bataile;
380　She warned him, but it mighte nat availe:
　　　　He wente for to fighte nathelees,
　　　　But he was slain anoon of Achilles.
　　　　But thilke tale is al too long to telle,
　　　　And eek it is neigh day, I may nat dwelle.
385　Shortly I saye, as for conclusioun,
　　　　That I shal han of this avisioun
　　　　Adversitee, and I saye ferthermoor
　　　　That I ne telle of laxatives no stoor,°　　*hold no regard for*
　　　　For they been venimes,° I woot it weel:　*poisons*
390　I hem defye, I love hem neveradeel.

6. St. Cenhelm, son of Cenwulf, a 9th-century child-king
in Mercia who was murdered at his sister's orders.
7. Macrobius, a 4th-century author, wrote an extensive
commentary on Cicero's *Dream of Scipio*.

8. Daniel interprets the pagan King Nebuchadnezzar's
dream, which foretells his downfall (Daniel 4).
9. Joseph interpreted dreams for the pharaoh's chief baker
and butler (Genesis 40–41).

"Now lat us speke of mirthe and stinte° al this.   *stop*
Madame Pertelote, so have I blis,
Of oo thing God hath sente me large grace:
For whan I see the beautee of youre face—
395   Ye been so scarlet reed aboute youre yën—
It maketh al my drede for to dien.
For also siker° as *In principio*,[1]   *certain*
Mulier est hominis confusio.[2]
Madame, the sentence° of this Latin is,   *meaning*
400   'Womman is mannes joye and al his blis.'
For whan I feele anight youre softe side—
Al be it that I may nat on you ride,
For that oure perche is maad so narwe, allas—
I am so ful of joye and of solas°   *delight*
405   That I defye bothe swevene and dreem."
And with that word he fleigh down fro the beem,
For it was day, and eek° his hennes alle,   *also*
And with a "chuk" he gan hem for to calle,
For he hadde founde a corn lay in the yeerd.
410   Real° he was, he was namore aferd:°   *regal/afraid*
He fethered Pertelote twenty time,
And trad° hire as ofte er it was prime.[3]   *mounted*
He looketh as it were a grim leoun,°   *lion*
And on his toes he rometh up and down:
415   Him deined nat to sette his foot to grounde.
He chukketh whan he hath a corn yfounde,
And to him rennen thanne his wives alle.
Thus royal, as a prince is in his halle,
Leve I this Chauntecleer in his pasture,
420   And after wol I telle his aventure.
        Whan that the month in which the world bigan,
That highte March, whan God first maked man,
Was compleet, and passed were also,
Sin March biran,° thritty days and two,[4]   *finished*
425   Bifel that Chauntecleer in al his pride,
His sevene wives walking him biside,
Caste up his yën to the brighte sonne,
That in the signe of Taurus hadde yronne
Twenty degrees and oon and somwhat more,
430   And knew by kinde,° and by noon other lore,   *nature*
That it was prime, and crew with blisful stevene.°   *voice*
"The sonne," he saide, "is clomben up on hevene
Fourty degrees and oon and more, ywis.
Madame Pertelote, my worldes blis,
435   Herkneth thise blisful briddes° how they singe,   *birds*
And see the fresshe flowres how they springe:
Ful is myn herte of revel and solas."
But sodeinly him fil a sorweful cas,°   *event*

1. "In the beginning," the opening verse of the Book of
Genesis and the Gospel of John.
2. "Woman is the ruination of mankind."

3. First hour of the day.
4. The date is thus May 3.

For evere the latter ende of joye is wo—

440 God woot that worldly joye is soone ago,
And if a rethor° coude faire endite,°   *rhetorician/compose*
He in a cronicle saufly° mighte it write,   *safely*
As for a soverein notabilitee.
Now every wis man lat him herkne me:

445 This storye is also° trewe, I undertake,   *as*
As is the book of Launcelot de Lake,[5]
That wommen holde in ful greet reverence.
Now wol I turne again to my sentence.
    A colfox° ful of sly iniquitee,   *black fox*

450 That in the grove° hadde woned° yeres three,   *woods/lived*
By heigh imaginacion forncast,[6]
The same night thurghout the hegges brast
Into the yeerd ther Chauntecleer the faire
Was wont, and eek his wives, to repaire;

455 And in a bed of wortes° stille he lay   *cabbages*
Til it was passed undren° of the day,   *midmorning*
Waiting his time on Chauntecleer to falle,
As gladly doon thise homicides alle,
That in await liggen to mordre men.

460 O false mordrour, lurking in thy den!
O newe Scariot! Newe Geniloun![7]
False dissimilour!° O Greek Sinoun,[8]   *dissembler*
That broughtest Troye al outrely° to sorwe!   *entirely*
O Chauntecleer, accursed be that morwe

465 That thou into the yeerd flaugh fro the bemes!
Thou were ful wel ywarned by thy dremes
That thilke day was perilous to thee;
But what that God forwoot° moot needes be,   *foreknows*
After the opinion of certain clerkes:

470 Witnesse on him that any parfit° clerk is   *accomplished*
That in scole is greet altercacioun
In this matere, and greet disputisoun,
And hath been of an hundred thousand men.
But I ne can nat bulte it to the bren,[9]

475 As can the holy doctour Augustin,
Or Boece, or the bisshop Bradwardin[1]—
Wheither that Goddes worthy forwiting°   *foreknowledge*
Straineth° me nedely for to doon a thing   *compels*
("Nedely" clepe I simple necessitee),

480 Or elles if free chois be graunted me
To do that same thing or do it nought,
Though God forwoot it er that I was wrought;°   *made*

---

5. The adventures of the Arthurian knight.
6. Predicted (in Chauntecleer's dream).
7. Judas Iscariot, who handed Jesus over to the Roman authorities for execution; Ganelon, a medieval traitor who betrayed the hero Roland to his Saracen enemies.
8. The Greek who tricked the Trojans into accepting the Trojan horse behind the city walls.

9. Sift it from the husks (i.e., discriminate).
1. St. Augustine, the ancient writer Boethius, and the 14th-century Archbishop of Canterbury Thomas Bradwardine attempted to explain how God's predestination of events still allowed for humans to have free will.

Or if his witing straineth neveradeel,
But by necessitee condicionel[2]—
485   I wol nat han to do of swich matere:
My tale is of a cok, as ye may heere,
That took his conseil of his wif with sorwe,
To walken in the yeerd upon that morwe
That he hadde met the dreem that I you tolde.
490   Wommenes conseils been ful ofte colde,°   *disastrous*
Wommanes conseil broughte us first to wo,
And made Adam fro Paradis to go,
Ther as he was ful merye and wel at ese.
But for I noot° to whom it mighte displese   *do not know*
495   If I conseil of wommen wolde blame,
Passe over, for I saide it in my game—
Rede auctours where they trete of swich matere,
And what they sayn of wommen ye may heere—
Thise been the cokkes wordes and nat mine:
500   I can noon harm of no womman divine.°   *guess at*
   Faire in the sond° to bathe hire merily   *sand*
Lith° Pertelote, and alle hir sustres by,   *lies*
Again the sonne, and Chauntecleer so free
Soong merier than the mermaide in the see—
505   For Physiologus[3] saith sikerly
How that they singen wel and merily.
   And so bifel that as he caste his yë
Among the wortes on a boterflye,°   *butterfly*
He was war of this fox that lay ful lowe.
510   No thing ne liste him° thanne for to crowe,   *he wanted*
But cride anoon "Cok cok!" and up he sterte,
As man that was affrayed in his herte—
For naturelly a beest desireth flee
Fro his contrarye° if he may it see,   *natural enemy*
515   Though he nevere erst° hadde seen it with his yë.   *before*
This Chauntecleer, whan he gan him espye,
He wolde han fled, but that the fox anoon
Saide, "Gentil sire, allas, wher wol ye goon?
Be ye afraid of me that am youre freend?
520   Now certes, I were worse than a feend°   *devil*
If I to you wolde harm or vilainye.
I am nat come youre conseil for t'espye,
But trewely the cause of my cominge
Was only for to herkne how that ye singe:
525   For trewely, ye han as merye a stevene°   *voice*
As any angel hath that is in hevene.
Therwith ye han in musik more feelinge
Than hadde Boece,[4] or any that can singe.
My lord your fader—God his soule blesse!—

2. Boethius argued only for conditional necessity, which still permitted for much exercise of free will.
3. Said to have written a bestiary.

4. In addition to theology, Boethius also wrote a music textbook.

530	And eek youre moder, of hir gentilesse,°	*gentility*
	Han in myn hous ybeen, to my grete ese.	
	And certes sire, ful fain° wolde I you plese.	*gladly*
	But for men speke of singing, I wol saye,	
	So mote I brouke° wel mine yën twaye,	*use*
535	Save ye, I herde nevere man so singe	
	As dide youre fader in the morweninge.	
	Certes, it was of herte° al that he soong.	*heartfelt*
	And for to make his vois the more strong,	
	He wolde so paine him that with bothe his yën	
540	He moste winke,° so loude wolde he cryen;	*shut his eyes*
	And stonden on his tiptoon therwithal,	
	And strecche forth his nekke long and smal;	
	And eek he was of swich discrecioun	
	That ther nas no man in no regioun	
545	That him in song or wisdom mighte passe.°	*surpass*
	I have wel rad in Daun Burnel the Asse⁵	
	Among his vers how that ther was a cok,	
	For° a preestes sone yaf him a knok	*because*
	Upon his leg whil he was yong and nice,°	*foolish*
550	He made him for to lese his benefice.⁶	
	But certain, ther nis no comparisoun	
	Bitwixe the wisdom and discrecioun	
	Of youre fader and of his subtiltee.	
	Now singeth, sire, for sainte° charitee!	*holy*
555	Lat see, conne ye youre fader countrefete?"°	*imitate*
	This Chauntecleer his winges gan to bete,	
	As man that coude his traison nat espye,	
	So was he ravisshed with his flaterye.	
	Allas, ye lordes, many a fals flatour	
560	Is in youre court, and many a losengeour,°	*deceiver*
	That plesen you wel more, by my faith,	
	Than he that soothfastnesse° unto you saith!	*truth*
	Redeth Ecclesiaste⁷ of flaterye.	
	Beeth war, ye lordes, of hir trecherye.	
565	This Chauntecleer stood hye upon his toos,	
	Strecching his nekke, and heeld his yën cloos,	
	And gan to crowe loude for the nones;°	*for the purpose*
	And daun Russel the fox sterte up atones,	
	And by the gargat° hente° Chauntecleer,	*throat/seized*
570	And on his bak toward the wode him beer,	
	For yit ne was ther no man that him sued.	
	O destinee that maist nat been eschued!°	*avoided*
	Allas that Chauntecleer fleigh fro the bemes!	
	Allas his wif ne roughte° nat of dremes!	*cared*
575	And on a Friday⁸ fil al this meschaunce!	
	O Venus that art goddesse of plesaunce,	
	Sin that thy servant was this Chauntecleer,	

---

5. The hero of a 12th-century satirical poem, *Speculum Stultorum*, by Nigel Wirecker, Brunellus was a donkey who traveled around Europe trying to educate himself.

6. Lose his commission (because he overslept).
7. The Book of Ecclesiasticus.
8. Venus' day, but also an ominous day of the week.

And in thy service dide al his power—
More for delit than world° to multiplye—   *population*
580   Why woldestou suffre him on thy day to die?
    O Gaufred,[9] dere maister soverein,
That, whan thy worthy king Richard was slain
With shot,° complainedest his deeth so sore,   *(of an arrow)*
Why ne hadde I now thy sentence and thy lore,
585   The Friday for to chide as diden ye?
For on a Friday soothly slain was he.
Thanne wolde I shewe you how that I coude plaine°   *lament*
For Chauntecleres drede and for his paine.
    Certes, swich cry ne lamentacioun
590   Was nevere of ladies maad whan Ilioun°   *Troy*
Was wonne, and Pyrrus[1] with his straite° swerd,   *drawn*
Whan he hadde hent King Priam by the beerd
And slain him, as saith us Eneidos,°   *Virgil's Aeneid*
As maden alle the hennes in the cloos,°   *yard*
595   Whan they hadde seen of Chauntecleer the sighte.
But sovereinly Dame Pertelote shrighte°   *shrieked*
Ful louder than dide Hasdrubales wif[2]
Whan that hir housbonde hadde lost his lif,
And that the Romains hadden brend Cartage:
600   She was so ful of torment and of rage
That wilfully unto the fir she sterte,
And brende hirselven with a stedefast herte.
    O woful hennes, right so criden ye
As, whan that Nero[3] brende the citee
605   Of Rome, criden senatoures wives
For that hir housbondes losten alle hir lives:
Withouten gilt this Nero hath hem slain.
Now wol I turne to my tale again.
    The sely° widwe and eek hir doughtres two   *innocent*
610   Herden thise hennes crye and maken wo,
And out at dores sterten they anoon,
And sien° the fox toward the grove goon,   *saw*
And bar upon his bak the cok away,
And criden, "Out, harrow, and wailaway,
615   Ha, ha, the fox," and after him they ran,
And eek with staves many another man;
Ran Colle oure dogge, and Talbot and Gerland,[4]
And Malkin with a distaf in hir hand,
Ran cow and calf, and eek the verray hogges,
620   Sore aferd for berking of the dogges
And shouting of the men and wommen eke.
They ronne so hem thoughte hir herte breke;
They yelleden as feendes doon in helle;
The dokes criden as men wolde hem quelle;°   *kill*

9. Geoffrey of Vinsauf, who wrote a poem when King
Richard the Lion-Hearted died, cursing the day of the
week on which he died, a Friday.
1. Pyrrhus, the son of Achilles, who slew Troy's king Priam.

2. Hasdrubal was king of Carthage when it was defeated
by the Romans during the Punic Wars.
3. The Emperor Nero set fire to Rome, killing many of his
senators.
4. Common names for dogs.

625 The gees for fere flowen over the trees;
     Out of the hive cam the swarm of bees;
     So hidous was the noise, a, benedicite,
     Certes, he Jakke Straw[5] and his meinee
     Ne made nevere shoutes half so shrille
630 Whan that they wolden any Fleming kille,
     As thilke day was maad upon the fox:
     Of bras they broughten bemes° and of box,°   *trumpets/boxwood*
     Of horn, of boon, in whiche they blewe and pouped,°   *puffed*
     And therwithal they skriked and they houped—
635 It seemed as that hevene sholde falle.
          Now goode men, I praye you herkneth alle:
     Lo, how Fortune turneth sodeinly
     The hope and pride eek of hir enemy.
     This cok that lay upon the foxes bak,
640 In al his drede unto the fox he spak,
     And saide, "Sire, if that I were as ye,
     Yit sholde I sayn, as wis° God helpe me,   *certainly*
     'Turneth ayain, ye proude cherles° alle!   *ruffians*
     A verray pestilence upon you falle!
645 Now am I come unto this wodes side,
     Maugree° your heed,° the cok shal here abide.   *despite/planning*
     I wol him ete, in faith, and that anoon.'"
          The fox answerde, "In faith, it shal be doon."
     And as he spak that word, al sodeinly
650 The cok brak from his mouth deliverly,°   *nimbly*
     And hye upon a tree he fleigh anoon.
          And whan the fox sawgh that he was agoon,
     "Allas," quod he, "O Chauntecleer, allas!
     I have to you," quod he, "ydoon trespas,
655 In as muche as I maked you aferd
     Whan I you hente and broughte out of the yeerd.
     But sire, I dide it in no wikke° entente: *wicked*
     Come down, and I shal telle you what I mente.
     I shal saye sooth to you, God help me so."
660   "Nay thanne," quod he, "I shrewe° us bothe two: *curse*
     But first I shrewe myself, bothe blood and bones,
     If thou bigile me ofter than ones;
     Thou shalt namore thurgh thy flaterye
     Do° me to singe and winken with myn yë.   *make*
665 For he that winketh whan he sholde see,
     Al wilfully, God lat him nevere thee."°   *prosper*
          "Nay," quod the fox, "but God yive him meschaunce
     That is so undiscreet of governaunce
     That jangleth° whan he sholde holde his pees."   *chatters*
670   Lo, swich it is for to be recchelees°   *careless*
     And necligent and truste on flaterye.
     But ye that holden this tale a folye
     As of a fox, or of a cok and hen,

5. Jack Straw was one of the leaders of the Peasants' Revolt of 1381, which was directed in part against the Flemish traders in London.

Taketh the moralitee, goode men.
675   For Saint Paul saith that al that writen is
To oure doctrine° it is ywrit, ywis: *instruction*
Taketh the fruit, and lat the chaf be stille.
Now goode God, if that it be thy wille,
As saith my lord, so make us alle goode men,
680   And bringe us to his hye blisse. Amen.

The Epilogue

"Sire Nonnes Preest," oure Hoste saide anoon,
"Yblessed be thy breech° and every stoon:°   *buttocks / testicle*
This was a merye tale of Chauntecleer.
But by my trouthe, if thou were seculer°   *a layman*
685   Thou woldest been a tredefowl° aright: *a cock*
For if thou have corage° as thou hast might   *desire*
Thee were neede of hennes, as I weene,°   *suppose*
Ye, mo than sevene times seventeene.
See whiche brawnes° hath this gentil preest—   *muscles*
690   So greet a nekke and swich a large breest.
He looketh as a sperhawk° with his yën;   *sparrowhawk*
Him needeth nat his colour for to dyen
With brasil ne with grain of Portingale.[6]
Now sire, faire falle you for youre tale."
695   And after that he with ful merye cheere
Saide unto another as ye shul heere.

The Parson's Tale

Although *The Canterbury Tales* remain unfinished and even the order of the tales is unclear, we know that Chaucer's plan was to end them with *The Parson's Tale*, just as it was to begin them with the pilgrimage to Canterbury in *The General Prologue*. Thus, when the Parson responds to the Host's request for a final tale by praying Jesus to show the way to the "glorious pilgrimage" called "Jerusalem celestial," there is a sense of closure in his return to an idea that has been obscured during the tale-telling. His shift of the destination from Canterbury to the heavenly city, however, gives us pause. The view that life on earth is a pilgrimage to heaven was a Christian commonplace, but was it Chaucer's view? The three parts of *The Parson's Tale* included here raise questions about how Chaucer's religious beliefs relate to his art. What is his final judgment of the artful, but often sinful, tales he has been telling?

In the introduction, the Parson rejects the idea of poetry entirely, scornfully refusing to tell a "fable" or to adorn his tale with alliteration or rhyme; instead, he will tell what he refers to as a "merye tale in prose," which turns out to be a forty-page treatise on penitence. Thus Chaucer specifically attributes to him an ascetic view of art which is hard to reconcile with his own extraordinary poetry. Does the Parson speak for Chaucer? Although he has a measure of authority as the only exemplary member of the clergy on the pilgrimage, he is nevertheless a fictional character. Since, however, Chaucer is thought to have written the introduction to this tale as well as the *Retraction* at the end of his life, perhaps he could have come to share the Parson's aesthetic views.

The Parson begins his tale proper with a second reference to celestial Jerusalem, stating that the route to it is through penitence. The tale, which Chaucer had translated at an earlier period, belongs to a common type of manuals of confession for either clergy or laity. Included in it is an analysis of the seven deadly sins—pride, envy, anger, sloth, avarice, gluttony, and

6. Two types of red dye, the latter from Portugal.

lechery—in an order that suggests that Chaucer, like Dante, considered the last to be the least serious, although still worthy of damnation. The passage on lechery excerpted here offers an opportunity to measure *The Parson's Tale* against the tales that have gone before, particularly such "sinful" works as *The Miller's Tale* and *The Wife of Bath's Prologue*.

Whatever conclusion we draw about the relevance of *The Parson's Tale* to the tales preceding, the *Retraction* appended to it is troubling yet intriguing. In it Chaucer repudiates much of the work for which he is most loved and admired, such "worldly vanitees" as *Troilus and Criseyde, The Parliament of Fowls,* and those *Canterbury Tales* that "sounen [lead] into sinne." On the other hand, he thanks God for his works of "moralitee," including his translation of Boethius and his saints' legends, works that are seldom read today. He himself is engaged in penance—repentance, confession, and satisfaction—thus connecting his own spiritual experience with the manual he has translated. However disappointing it is to read this rejection of his most artistically satisfying tales, we must remember that a concept of art for art's sake would have been historically unavailable to him. Perhaps his last tale was indeed his last word.

from The Parson's Tale
The Introduction

	By that° the Manciple hadde his tale al ended,	*by that time*
	The sonne fro the south line[1] was descended	
	So lowe, that he nas nat to my sighte	
	Degrees nine and twenty as in highte.	
5	Four of the clokke it was, so as I gesse,	
	For elevene foot, or litel more or lesse,	
	My shadwe was at thilke time as there,	
	Of swich feet as my lengthe parted were	
	In sixe feet equal of proporcioun.	
10	Therwith the moones exaltacioun°—	*dominant influence*
	I mene Libra[2]—alway gan ascende,	
	As we were entring at a thropes ende.°	*village boundary*
	For which oure Host, as he was wont to gie°	*lead*
	As in this caas oure joly compaignye,	
15	Saide in this wise, "Lordinges everichoon,	
	Now lakketh us no tales mo than oon:	
	Fulfild is my sentence° and my decree;	*design*
	I trowe° that we han herd of eech degree;	*believe*
	Almost fulfild is al myn ordinaunce.	
20	I praye to God, so yive him right good chaunce	
	That telleth this tale to us lustily.	
	Sire preest," quod he, "artou a vicary,°	*vicar*
	Or arte a Person?° Say sooth, by thy fay.°	*parish priest/faith*
	Be what thou be, ne breek thou nat oure play,	
25	For every man save thou hath told his tale.	
	Unbokele and shew us what is in thy male!°	*bag*
	For trewely, me thinketh by thy cheere°	*expression*
	Thou sholdest knitte up wel a greet matere.	
	Tel us a fable anoon, for cokkes bones!"[3]	
30	This Person answerde al atones,	
	"Thou getest fable noon ytold for me,	
	For Paul, that writeth unto Timothee,[4]	

---

1. Astronomical marking parallel to the celestial equator.
2. Seventh sign in the Zodiac, the Scales.

3. Cock's bones, a euphemism for God's bones.
4. St. Paul's Epistle to Timothy.

Repreveth hem that waiven soothfastnesse,°   *truth*
And tellen fables and swich wrecchednesse.
35   Why sholde I sowen draf° out of my fest,°   *chaff/fist*
Whan I may sowen whete if that me lest?
For which I saye that if you list to heere
Moralitee and vertuous matere,
And thanne that ye wol yive me audience,
40   I wol ful fain,° at Cristes reverence,   *gladly*
Do you plesance leveful° as I can.   *lawfully*
But trusteth wel, I am a southren man:[5]
I can nat geeste° Rum-Ram-Ruf by lettre—   *tell stories*
Ne, God woot, rym holde° I but litel bettre.   *appreciate*
45   And therfore, if you list, I wol nat glose;°   *adorn my speech*
I wol you telle a merye tale in prose,
To knitte up al this feeste and make an ende.
And Jesu for his grace wit me sende
To shewe you the way in this viage°   *journey*
50   Of thilke parfit glorious pilgrimage
That highte Jerusalem celestial.
And if ye vouche sauf, anoon I shal
Biginne upon my tale, for which I praye
Telle youre avis:° I can no bettre saye.   *opinion*
55   But nathelees, this meditacioun
I putte it ay under correccioun
Of clerkes, for I am nat textuel:°   *a literalist*
I take but the sentence,° trusteth wel.   *sense*
Therfore I make protestacioun
60   That I wol stonde to correccioun."
Upon this word we han assented soone,
For, as it seemed, it was for to doone
To enden in som vertuous sentence,
And for to yive him space° and audience;   *time*
65   And bede oure Host he sholde to him saye
That alle we to telle his tale him praye.
Oure Hoste hadde the wordes for us alle:
"Sire preest," quod he, "now faire you bifalle:
Telleth," quod he, "youre meditacioun.
70   But hasteth you, the sonne wol adown.
Beeth fructuous, and that in litel space,
And to do wel God sende you his grace.
Saye what you list, and we wol gladly heere."
And with that word he saide in this manere.

from *The Tale*

Oure sweete Lord God of Hevene, that no man wol perisse[1] but wol
that we comen alle to the knowliche of him and to the blisful lif that is
perdurable,° amonesteth° us by the prophete Jeremie[2] that saith in   *enduring/warns*
this wise: "Stondeth upon the wayes and seeth and axeth of olde

---

5. The parson, like Chaucer himself, comes from the
south of England and so is not accustomed to telling stories in the alliterative meter used traditionally in the

north. Rum-Ram-Raf is an example of alliteration.
1. Who wishes no man to perish.
2. Jeremiah 6.16.

pathes (that is to sayn, of olde sentences)° which is the goode way, and
walketh in that way, and ye shul finde refresshing for youre soules."   *opinions*

Manye been the wayes espirituels that leden folk to oure Lord
Jesu Crist and to the regne of glorye: of whiche wayes ther is a ful
noble way and a ful covenable° which may nat faile to man ne to   *suitable*
womman that thurgh sinne hath misgoon fro the righte way of
Jerusalem celestial; and this way is cleped° Penitence. * * *   *called*

THE REMEDY FOR THE SIN OF LECHERY

Now cometh the remedye agains Lecherye, and that is generally
Chastitee and Continence that restraineth alle the desordainee
mevinges° that comen of flesshly talents.° And evere the gretter   *impulses/desires*
merite shal he han that most restraineth the wikkede eschaufinges°   *inflammations*
of the ardure of this sinne. And this is in two maneres: that is to
sayn, chastitee in mariage and chastitee of widwehood.

Now shaltou understonde that matrimoine is leeful° assembling   *lawful*
of man and of womman that receiven by vertu of the sacrement the
bond thurgh which they may nat be departed in al hir life—that is to
sayn, whil that they liven bothe. This, as saith the book, is a ful greet
sacrement: God maked it, as I have said, in Paradis, and wolde himself be born in mariage. And for to halwen° mariage, he was at a wed-   *bless*
ding where as he turned water into win, which was the firste miracle
that he wroughte in erthe biforn his disciples. Trewe effect of
mariage clenseth fornicacion and replenisseth Holy Chirche of good
linage° (for that is the ende of mariage), and it chaungeth deedly   *offspring*
sinne³ into venial sinne bitwixe hem that been ywedded, and maketh
the hertes al oon° of hem that been ywedded, as wel as the bodies.   *united*

This is verray mariage that was establissed by God er that sinne
bigan, whan naturel lawe was in his right point° in Paradis; and it was   *order*
ordained that oo man sholde have but oo womman, and oo womman
but oo man (as saith Saint Augustine) by manye resons: First, for
mariage is figured° bitwixe Crist and Holy Chirche; and that other is for   *represented*
a man is heved° of a womman—algate,° by ordinance it sholde be so.   *head/at least*
For if a womman hadde mo men than oon, thanne sholde she have mo
hevedes than oon, and that were an horrible thing biforn God; and eek
a womman ne mighte nat plese to many folk at ones. And also ther ne
sholde nevere be pees ne reste amonges hem, for everich wolde axen his
owene thing. And fortherover, no man sholde knowe his owene engendrure,° ne who sholde have his heritage, and the womman sholde been   *offspring*
the lesse biloved fro the time that she were conjoint to manye men.

Now cometh how that a man sholde bere him with his wif, and
namely in two thinges, that is to sayn, in suffrance° and in rever-   *obedience*
ence, as shewed Crist when he made first womman. For he ne made
hire nat of the heved of Adam for she sholde nat claime too greet
lorshipe: for ther as womman hath the maistrye she maketh too greet
desray° (ther needen none ensamples of this: the experience of day   *disorder*
by day oughte suffise). Also, certes, God ne made nat womman of
the foot of Adam, for she ne sholde nat be holden too lowe, for she

---

3. Sex remains a minor sin even within marriage, but it is a more serious sin outside of marriage.

can nat paciently suffre. But God made womman of the rib of Adam for womman sholde be felawe unto man. Man sholde bere him to his wif in faith, in trouthe, and in love, as saith Sainte Paul, that a man sholde loven his wif as Crist loved Holy Chirche, that loved it so wel that he deide for it. So sholde a man for his wif, if it were neede.

Now how that a womman sholde be subjet to hir housbonde, that telleth Sainte Peter: First, in obedience. And eek, as saith the decree, a womman that is a wif, as longe as she is a wif, she hath noon auctoritee to swere ne to bere witnesse withoute leve of hir housbonde that is hir lord—algate, he sholde be so by reson. She sholde eek serven him in alle honestee, and been attempree° of hir array; I woot wel that they sholde setten hir entente° to plesen hir housbondes, but nat by hir quaintise of array:° Saint Jerome saith that wives that been apparailed in silk and in precious purpre ne mowe nat clothen hem in Jesu Crist. What saith Saint John eek in this matere? Saint Gregorye eek saith that no wight seeketh precious array but only for vaine glorye to been honoured the more biforn the peple. It is a greet folye a womman to have a fair array outward and in hireself be foul inward. A wif sholde eek be mesurable° in looking and in bering and in laughing, and discreet in alle hir wordes and hir deedes. And aboven alle worldly thinges she sholde loven hir housbonde with al hir herte, and to him be trewe of hir body (so sholde an housbonde eek be to his wif): for sith that° al the body is the housbondes, so sholde hir herte been, or elles ther is bitwixe hem two as in that no parfit mariage.

Thanne shul men understonde that for three thinges a man and his wif flesshly mowen° assemble. The firste is in entente of engendrure of children to the service of God: for certes, that is the cause final of matrimoine. Another cause is to yeelden everich° of hem to other the dette of hir bodies, for neither of hem hath power of his owene body. The thridde is for to eschewe lecherye and vilainye. The ferthe is, for soothe, deedly sinne. As to the firste, it is meritorye; the seconde also, for, as saith the decree, that she hath merite of chastitee that yeeldeth to hir housbonde the dette of hir body, ye, though it be again hir liking and the lust of hir herte. The thridde manere is venial sinne—and, trewely, scarsly may any of thise be withoute venial sinne, for the corrupcion and for the delit. The ferthe manere is for to understonde if they assemble only for amorous love and for noon of the forsaide causes, but for to accomplice thilke brenning delit—they rekke° nevere how ofte—soothly, it is deedly sinne. And yit with sorwe some folk wol painen hem° more to doon than to hir appetit suffiseth. * * *

Another remedye agains lecherye is specially to withdrawen swiche thinges as yive occasion to thilke vilainye, as ese,° eting, and drinking: for certes, whan the pot boileth strongly, the beste remedye is to withdrawe the fir. Sleeping longe in greet quiete is eek a greet norice° to lecherye. Another remedye agains lecherye is that a man or a womman eschewe the compaignye of hem by whiche he douteth° to be tempted: for al be it so that the deede be withstonden, yit is ther greet temptacion. Soothly, a whit wal,° although it ne brenne nought fully by stiking of a candele, yit is the wal blak of the leit.° Ful ofte

moderate
purpose
flamboyant attire

modest

since

may

each

care

trouble themselves
leisure

nurse
suspects

wall
from the flame

time I rede that no man truste in his owene perfeccion but he be stronger than Sampson, holier than David, and wiser than Salomon.

Chaucer's Retraction

HERE TAKETH THE MAKERE OF THIS BOOK HIS LEVE

Now praye I to hem alle that herkne this litel tretis° or rede,° that if ther be any thing in it that liketh° hem, that therof they thanken oure Lord Jesu Crist, of whom proceedeth al wit and al goodnesse. And if ther be any thing that displese hem, I praye hem also that they arrette° it to the defaute of myn unconning,° and nat to my wil, that wolde ful fain have said bettre if I hadde had conning. For oure book saith, "Al that is writen is writen for oure doctrine," and that is myn entente. Wherfore I biseeke you mekely, for the mercy of God, that ye praye for me that Crist have mercy on me and foryive me my giltes,° and namely of my translacions and enditinges° of worldly vanitees, the whiche I revoke in my retraccions:[4] as is the book of Troilus; the book also of Fame; the book of the five and twenty Ladies; the book of the Duchesse; the book of Saint Valentines Day of the Parlement of Briddes; the tales of Canterbury, thilke that sounen° into sinne; the book of the Leon; and many another book, if they were in my remembrance, and many a song and many a leccherous lay: that Crist for his grete mercy foryive me the sinne. But of the translacion of Boece *de Consolatione*, and othere bookes of legendes of saintes, and omelies, and moralitee, and devocion, that thanke I oure Lord Jesu Crist and his blisful Moder and alle the saintes of hevene, biseeking hem that they from hennes forth unto my lives ende sende me grace to biwaile° my giltes and to studye to the salvacion of my soule, and graunte me grace of verray penitence, confession, and satisfaccion to doon in this present lif, thurgh the benigne grace of him that is king of kinges and preest over alle preestes, that boughte° us with the precious blood of his herte, so that I may been oon of hem at the day of doom that shulle be saved. *Qui cum patre et Spiritu Sancto vivis et regnas Deus per omnia saecula. Amen.*[5]

treatise/advice
pleases

attribute
inability

sins
writings

lead

repent

redeemed

To His Scribe Adam[1]

Adam scrivain,° if evere it thee bifalle   *copyist*
Boece[2] or Troilus for to writen newe,

4. Here Chaucer repents having written most of his major works: *Troilus and Criseyde, The Book* (or *House*) *of Fame, The Legend of Good Women, The Book of the Duchess, The Parliament of Fowls,* and various of *The Canterbury Tales. The Book of the Lion* has not been preserved. Chaucer's translation of Boethius' *Consolation of Philosophy* is excepted.
5. You who live with the Father and the Holy Spirit and reign as God through all the centuries. Amen.
1. Given his position at court, Chaucer was asked to write many lyrics and occasional poems, such as this poem and the one that follows. In both, he wittily bemoans the conditions of authorship under which he was forced to work, depending on scribes to reproduce his poetry and on patrons to support it. In *To His Scribe Adam,* he strikes a

pose of affectionate raillery toward his scribe, whose occupation writers widely scorned. Perhaps he sees it as fitting to curse Adam with a skin disease which will make him scratch his scalp, just as Chaucer has had to scratch out the errors from his manuscripts. However, the poem has a serious undertone too. In fearing that Adam will miscopy his great romance, *Troilus and Criseyde,* he echoes a concern for the accurate reproduction of his work, which he voiced at the end of *Troilus* itself: he prays God that, in view of the great dialectal "diversitee/ in Englissh, and in writing of oure tonge," no one "miswrite" his book (5.1793–94).
2. Chaucer's translation of Boethius' *Consolation of Philosophy.*

Under thy longe lokkes thou moste have° the scalle,°   *may you get/mange*
But after my making thou write more trewe,[3]
So ofte a day I moot° thy werk renewe,   *must*
It to correcte, and eek to rubbe and scrape:
And al is thurgh thy necligence and rape.°   *haste*

Complaint to His Purse[1]

To you, my purs, and to noon other wight,°   *creature*
Complaine I, for ye be my lady dere.
I am so sory, now that ye be light,°   *empty, wanton*
For certes, but if° ye make me hevy cheere,[2]   *unless*
5   Me were as lief° be laid upon my beere;°   *I would prefer/bier*
For which unto youre mercy thus I crye:
Beeth hevy again, or elles moot° I die.   *must*

Now voucheth sauf this day er it be night
That I of you the blisful soun may heere,
10   Or see youre colour, lik the sonne bright,
That of yelownesse hadde nevere peere.
Ye be my lif, ye be myn hertes steere,°   *guide*
Queene of confort and of good compaignye:
Beeth hevy again, or elles moot I die.

15   Ye purs, that been to me my lives light
And saviour, as in this world down here,
Out of this tonne° helpe me thurgh your might,   *dark situation*
Sith that ye wol nat be my tresorere;
For I am shave as neigh° as any frere.[3]   *close*
20   But yit I praye unto youre curteisye:
Beeth hevy again, or elles moot I die.

Envoy to Henry IV[4]

O conquerour of Brutus Albioun,[5]
Which that by line° and free eleccioun   *inheritance*
Been verray king, this song to you I sende,
25   And ye, that mowen° alle oure harmes amende,   *may*
Have minde upon my supplicacioun.

3. Unless you make a more reliable copy of what I have composed.
1. This is a traditional "begging" poem, based on French models. The request for money is presented humorously, as a parody of a courtly love complaint to a cruel mistress. The parallel takes on ironic force when one recalls Chaucer's presentation of himself, in such early poems as *The Parliament of Fowls*, as a failed lover. This is one of Chaucer's last poems, written a year before his death. It was addressed to Henry IV when he took the throne in 1399, to request a renewal of the annuity Chaucer had received from the deposed Richard II. The flattering "envoy" to Henry at the end alludes to the tradition dating from Geoffrey of Monmouth that Britain was founded by Brutus, the grandson of Aeneas, the exiled prince of Troy and founder of Rome.
2. Serious expression (in a person); full weight (in a purse).
3. Friar (with a bald tonsure).
4. The "envoy" is the traditional close of a ballade, usually directed to its addressee.
5. According to legend, Brutus conquered the kingdom of Albion and renamed it "Britain," after himself.

✦ ᛞ✦᛬ ✦

William Langland

c. 1330–1387

Little is known of William Langland. On the basis of evidence in his best-known work, *Piers Plowman*, he is thought to have been a clerk in minor orders whose career in the church was curtailed by his marriage. He may have come from the Malvern Hills in the west of England, but he spent much of his professional life in London. He was clearly learned, using many Latin quotations from the Bible (given below primarily in English translation and designated by italics), and the style of his poem in many ways resembles sermon rhetoric.

Piers Plowman is an ambitious and multilayered allegory, an attempt to combine Christian history, social satire, and an account of the individual soul's quest for salvation. It is presented as a dream vision whose hero is a humble plowman, and whose narrator, the naive dreamer named Will, may only be a convenient fiction. Even its first audience sometimes reacted to this mysterious poem in surprising ways. *Piers Plowman* was so inspiring to the leaders of the peasants who led the Rising of 1381 that they saw Piers not as a fictional character but as an actual seditious person, as can be seen in the letter of radical priest John Ball in the "In Context" section following the poem. This interpretation of the poem is remarkable given Langland's profound conservatism; despite his scathing social satire, he offers no program for social change. In fact, he supports the model of the three estates, whereby the king and knights protect the body politic, the clergy prays for it, and the commons provide its food. Although he was sympathetic toward the poor and scornful of the rich and powerful, he felt that what ailed society was that *none* of the three estates was performing its proper role.

Piers Plowman survives in many manuscripts, a fact that suggests a large audience, which most likely included secular readers in the government and law as well as the clergy. Most of John Ball's followers would have been unable to read it. The poem exists in three versions— known as the A-, B-, and C-texts—and their history throws light on the poem's role in the Rising of 1381. The short A-text was expanded into the B-text some time between 1377 and 1381, when John Ball and other rebel leaders referred to it, while the C-text is generally agreed to reflect Langland's attempt to distance himself from the radical beliefs of the rebels. Nevertheless, the poem remained popular for the next two centuries as a document of social protest and was ultimately regarded as a prophecy of the English Reformation. Langland's social criticism, however, is only part of his project, for he considered individual salvation to be equally important. A strictly political reading of *Piers Plowman*—whether in the fourteenth century or the twentieth—misses a great deal of its originality and its power.

Piers Plowman is a challenge to read: it is almost surrealistic in its rapid and unexplained transitions, its many dreams, and its complex use of allegory. It is as confusing to people reading it in its entirety as to those reading it in excerpts, as here. Nevertheless, the poem does have a kind of unity, of a thematic rather than a narrative sort. It is held together by the dreamer's vision of the corruption of society and his personal quest to save his own soul. This quest is loosely structured by the metaphor of the journey, which is reflected in the poem's subdivision into parts called *passūs*—Latin for "steps." The poem is further unified by the allegorical character of Piers the plowman: a literal fourteenth-century English farmer when we first meet him, in the course of the poem he becomes a figural representation of Saint Peter, the first pope and founder of the church, and of Christ himself.

The four passages included here suggest the connection between the social and spiritual aspects of the poem. In the *Prologue*, the dreamer has a vision of a tower on a hill (later explained as the seat of Truth, i.e., God), a hellish dungeon beneath, and between them, a "field full of folk," representing various professions from the three estates, who are later said to be more concerned with their material than their spiritual welfare. A final fable of rats trying to bell a cat shows great dissatisfaction with the king's governance but simultaneously express-es skepticism about the ability of the commons to govern themselves.

Passus 2 is the first of three on the Marriage of Lady Meed, an ambiguous allegorical figure whose name can mean "just reward," "bribery," or the profit motive generally, the last being a cause for anxiety as England moved from a barter economy to one based on money. The dreamer is invited by Lady Holy Church to Meed's marriage to "False Fickle Tongue." Mem-bers of all three estates approve this event (a sign of corruption on every social level), except for the king, who arrests Lady Meed and her fiancé, who then run away.

Langland discusses the issues of poverty and work most directly in Passus 6, where Piers Plowman insists that the assembled people help him plow his half-acre before he will agree to lead them on a pilgrimage to Truth. Piers supports the traditional division of labor, explicitly exempting the knight from producing food, as long as he protects the commons and clergy from "wasters"—lazy shirkers. He insists, however, that the knight treat peasants well—in part because roles may be reversed in heaven, and earthly underlings can become heavenly masters. Yet Langland is not simply taking the workers' side. The knight turns out to be too courteous to control wasters, and Hunger must be called in to offer an incentive to work. When Piers takes pity on the poor and sends Hunger away, Waster refuses to work and the laborers demand more money, cursing the king for the statutes that have instituted wage freezes.

The spiritual climax of the poem takes place in Passus 18, which depicts Christ's crucifix-ion, harrowing of hell (release of the souls of Adam and other Old Testament figures), and res-urrection. After many passūs of theological debate about his own salvation, the dreamer falls asleep on Palm Sunday and dreams of a man entering Jerusalem on a donkey. The dreamer thinks the man looks like Piers the Plowman, until he recognizes him as Jesus. This man is pre-sented as a young knight going to be dubbed: he will joust against the devil in Piers's armor ("human nature") for the "fruit of Piers the Plowman" (human souls).

Before Christ can release the souls from hell, a lively debate takes place among the "four daughters of God"—Mercy and Truth, Righteousness and Peace—homely "wenches" who embody the words of Psalm 84.11: "Mercy and Truth have met together, Righteousness and Peace have kissed each other." They concede that forgiveness can take precedence over retri-bution, whereupon Jesus, having "jousted well," leads out the patriarchs and prophets in victo-ry. As church bells ring to signal the resurrection, the dreamer awakes and calls his wife and daughter to church to celebrate Easter with him, thus connecting the grand scheme of salva-tion history to his personal experience.

The remainder of the poem, Passūs 19–20, which are not included here, recount the foun-dation of the church (by Piers as Saint Peter), and offer an apocalyptic vision of its subsequent corruption by the friars and its attack by Antichrist. There are no answers: the poem ends inconclusively with the allegorical figure of Conscience setting out on a pilgrimage in search of Piers Plowman.

Langland did not write French-inspired rhymed poetry, which was fashionable in London and used by Chaucer; instead, he composed old-fashioned alliterative poetry, which survived from Old English. The so-called Alliterative Revival was divided into two traditions, one based in the north of England and featuring romances in the alliterative "high" style, such as Sir Gawain and the Green Knight, and the other based in the south and west, and tending to social protest poems in a plain style. Langland's subject matter and style link him to the latter tradi-tion, which includes satirical poems such as Richard the Redeless, Mum and the Sothsegger, and Jack Upland. In Middle English alliterative poetry, each line contains at least four major stressed syllables, with the first three usually beginning with the same sound. The translations of alliter-ative poems in this anthology—including Beowulf and Sir Gawain, as well as Piers Plowman—all sufficiently retain the alliteration to convey its flavor in modern English. The following passage from Piers Plowman in Middle English, the description of Lady Meed in her gaudy clothes, makes the point more clearly. The dreamer, with naive admiration, reports that he

> . . . was war of a womman wonderliche yclothed,
> Purfiled with Pelure, the pureste on erthe,
> Ycorouned in a coroune, the kyng hath noon bettre.
> Fetisliche hire fyngres were fretted with gold wyr
> And theron riche Rubyes as rede as any gleede,
> And Diamaundes of derrest pris and double manere saphires,
> Orientals and Ewages enuenymes to destroye.
> Hire Robe ful riche, of reed scarlet engreyned,
> With Ribanes of reed gold and of riche stones.
> Hire array me rauysshed; swich richesse saugh I neuere.*
>
> (B 2. 8–17)

Although Langland generally uses the plainer alliterative style of southern protest poetry, here he uses the high style of northern alliterative romances, for satirical purposes. Meed's dress recalls that of Bercilak's lady in *Sir Gawain*, in "rich red rayled" (line 952), as well as the elegant clothing of the Green Knight, "with pelure pured apert, the pane ful clene" (154). In contrast to the clothing of Lady Holy Church, whom Langland introduces in *Passus* 1 simply as "a lady lovely of look, clothed in linen," the robes of lady Meed seem dangerously seductive, thus underscoring a sexual metaphor for bribery which Langland consistently develops. Thus, in a more subtle fashion than some of his followers, such as the Wycliffite author of *Pierce the Ploughman's Crede*, Langland was able to use the specialized language of alliterative poetry in the service of social criticism.

from Piers Plowman[1]
Prologue

> In a summer season when the sun was mild
> I clad myself in clothes as I'd become a sheep;
> In the habit of a hermit unholy of works
> Walked wide in this world, watching for wonders.
5 > And on a May morning, on Malvern Hills,[2]
> There befell me as by magic a marvelous thing:
> I was weary of wandering and went to rest
> At the bottom of a broad bank by a brook's side,
> And as I lay lazily looking in the water
10 > I slipped into a slumber, it sounded so pleasant.
> There came to me reclining there a most curious dream
> That I was in a wilderness, nowhere that I knew;
> But as I looked into the east, up high toward the sun,
> I saw a tower on a hill-top, trimly built,
15 > A deep dale beneath, a dungeon tower in it,
> With ditches deep and dark and dreadful to look at.
> A fair field full of folk I found between them,
> Of human beings of all sorts, the high and the low,
> Working and wandering as the world requires.
20 >   Some applied themselves to plowing, played very rarely,
> Sowing seeds and setting plants worked very hard;

---

* The passage is taken from *Piers Plowman: The B-Text*, ed. George Kane and E. Talbot Donaldson (1975).
1. Translated by E. Talbot Donaldson.

2. These hills in the west of England were probably Langland's original home.

Won what wasters gluttonously consume.
And some pursued pride, put on proud clothing,
Came all got up in garments garish to see.
25   To prayers and penance many put themselves,
All for love of our Lord lived hard lives,
Hoping thereafter to have Heaven's bliss—
Such as hermits and anchorites[3] hold to their cells,
Don't care to go cavorting about the countryside,
30   With some lush livelihood delighting their bodies.
And some made themselves merchants—they managed better,
As it seems to our sight that such men prosper.
And some make mirth as minstrels can
And get gold for their music, guiltless, I think.
35   But jokers and word jugglers, Judas' children,
Invent fantasies to tell about and make fools of themselves,
And have whatever wits they need to work if they wanted.
What Paul preaches of them I don't dare repeat here:
Qui loquitur turpiloquium[4] is Lucifer's henchman.
40   Beadsmen[5] and beggars bustled about
Till both their bellies and their bags were crammed to the brim;
Staged flytings° for their food, fought over beer.   *insult contests*
In gluttony, God knows, they go to bed.
And rise up with ribaldry, those Robert's boys.°   *robbers*
45   Sleep and sloth pursue them always.
    Pilgrims and palmers[6] made pacts with each other
To seek out Saint James[7] and saints at Rome.
They went on their way with many wise stories,
And had leave to lie all their lives after.
50   I saw some that said they'd sought after saints:
In every tale they told their tongues were tuned to lie
More than to tell the truth—such talk was theirs.
A heap of hermits with hooked staffs
Went off to Walsingham,[8] with their wenches behind them.
55   Great long lubbers that don't like to work
Dressed up in cleric's dress to look different from other men
And behaved as they were hermits, to have an easy life.
I found friars there—all four of the orders[9]—
Preaching to the people for their own paunches' welfare,
60   Making glosses of the Gospel that would look good for themselves;
Coveting copes,° they construed it as they pleased.   *monk's capes*
Many of these Masters° may clothe themselves richly,   *Divinity*
For their money and their merchandise march hand in hand.
Since Charity has proved a peddler and principally shrives[1] lords,

---

3. Both were vowed to a religious life of solitude, hermits in the wilderness and anchorites walled in a tiny dwelling.
4. Who speaks filthy language; not Paul, though (cf. Ephesians 5.3–4).
5. People who said prayers, often counting on rosary beads, for the souls of those who gave them alms.
6. "Professional" pilgrims who took advantage of the hospitality offered them in order to travel.

7. That is, his shrine at Compostela, in Spain.
8. English town, site of a famous shrine to the Virgin Mary.
9. The four orders of friars—Franciscans, Dominicans, Carmelites, and Augustinians. In 14th-century England they were much satirized for their corruption (cf. the friar in the *General Prologue* to Chaucer's *Canterbury Tales*).
1. Confesses. Confession and the remission of sins (shrift) is the "merchandise" cynically sold by the friars.

65	Many marvels have been manifest within a few years.
	Unless Holy Church and friars' orders hold together better,
	The worst misfortune in the world will be welling up soon.
	A pardoner[2] preached there as if he had priest's rights,
	Brought out a bull° with bishop's seals,	*papal license*
70	And said he himself could absolve them all
	Of failure to fast, of vows they'd broken.
	Unlearned men believed him and liked his words,
	Came crowding up on knees to kiss his bulls.
	He banged them with his brevet° and bleared their eyes,	*pardoner's license*
75	And raked in with his parchment-roll rings and brooches.
	Thus you give your gold for gluttons' well-being,
	And squander it on scoundrels schooled in lechery.
	If the bishop were blessed and worth both his ears,
	His seal should not be sent out to deceive the people.
80	—It's nothing to the bishop that the blackguard preaches,
	And the parish priest and the pardoner split the money
	That the poor people of the parish would have but for them.
	Parsons and parish priests complained to the bishop
	That their parishes were poor since the pestilence-time,[3]
85	Asked for license and leave to live in London,
	And sing Masses there for simony,[4] for silver is sweet.
	Bishops and Bachelors, both Masters and Doctors,[5]
	Who have cures under Christ and their crowns shaven
	As a sign that they should shrive their parishioners,
90	Preach and pray for them, and provide for the poor,
	Take lodging in London in Lent and other seasons.
	Some serve the king and oversee his treasury,
	In the Exchequer and in Chancery[6] press charges for debts
	Involving wards' estates and city-wards, waifs and strays.
95	And some like servants serve lords and ladies
	And in the stead of stewards° sit and make judgments.	*estate managers*
	Their Masses and their matins and many of their Hours[7]
	Are done undevoutly: there's dread that in the end
	Christ in his consistory will condemn full many.
100	I pondered on the power that Peter had in keeping
	To bind and unbind as the Book tells,[8]
	How he left it with love as our Lord commanded
	Among four virtues, most virtuous of all,
	That are called "cardinals"—and closing gates
105	Of the kingdom of Christ, who may close and lock them,
	Or else open them up and show Heaven's bliss.
	But as for the cardinals at court that thus acquired their name
	And presumed they had the power to appoint a pope

2. An official empowered to pass on from the pope absolution for the sins of people who had given money to charity.

3. Since 1349 England had suffered a number of epidemics of the "Black Death."

4. Buying and selling church offices or spiritual functions.

5. Bachelors and Doctors of Divinity.

6. The Exchequer was a royal commission that received revenue and audited accounts; Chancery dealt with petitions addressed to the king.

7. Clerics organized their day around seven canonical "hours," of which matins was the first.

8. Matthew 16.18–20 recounts Christ's giving Peter and the succeeding popes the authority to make pronouncements on earth that will also be binding in Heaven.

Who should have the power that Peter had—well I'll not impugn them,
110   For the election belongs to love and to learning:
Therefore I can and cannot speak of court further.
    Then there came a king, knighthood accompanied him,
Might of the community made him a ruler.
And then came Kind Wit, and he created clerks
115   To counsel the king and keep the commons safe.
The king in concert with knighthood and with clergy as well
Contrived that the commons should provide their commons⁹ for them.
The commons with Kind Wit contrived various crafts,
And for profit of all the people appointed plowmen
120   To till and to toil as true life requires.
The king and the commons and Kind Wit the third
Defined law and lewte°—for every kind of life, known limits.   justice
Then a lunatic looked up—a lean one at that—
And counseled the king with clerkly words, kneeling before him:
125   "Christ keep you, sir King, and the kingdom you rule
And grant you to lead your land so that Lewte loves you,
And for your righteous ruling be rewarded in Heaven."
And after in the air on high an angel of Heaven
Came low to speak in Latin, for illiterate men lacked
130   The jargon or the judgment to justify themselves,
But can only suffer and serve; therefore said the angel:
"'I'm a king. I'm a prince!'—Neither perhaps when you've gone hence.
You, King, who're here to save the special laws that King Christ gave.
To do this better you will find it's well to be less just than kind.
135   *By you law's naked truth wants to be clothed in ruth.°*   mercy
Such seeds as you sow, such a crop will grow.
If you strip law bare, bare law will be your share.
If you sow pity, you'll be sitting pretty."
Then a Goliard¹ grew angry, a glutton of words,
140   And to the angel on high answered after:
"Since the name of king, rex, comes from regere, 'to rule,'
Unless he law directs, he's a wright without a tool."
Then all the commons commenced to cry in Latin verse
To the king's council—let who will construe it:
145   *"What the king ordains is to us the law's chains."*
With that there ran a rabble of rats together,
And little mice along with them, no less than a thousand,
Came to a council for their common profit;
For a cat of court came when he pleased
150   And leapt lightly over them and when he liked seized them,
And played with them perilously, and pushed them about.
"For dread of various deeds we hardly dare move,
And if we grumble at his games he will grieve us all,
Scratch us or claw us or catch us in his clutches.
155   So that we'll loathe life before he lets us go.

9. The first occurrence of "commons" in this line means "the common people"; the second, "food."
1. A wandering student or cleric. Goliards were known for satirical songs and poetry that attacked the clerical establishment.

If by any wit we might withstand his will
We could be lofty as lords and live at our ease."
A rat of renown, most ready of tongue,
Said as a sovereign salve for them all:
160   "I've seen creatures," he said, "in the city of London
Bear chains full bright about their necks,
And collars of fine craftsmanship; they come and go without leashes
Both in warren and in wasteland, wherever they please;
And at other times they are in other places, as I hear tell.
165   If there were a bell to clink on their collars, by Christ, I think
We could tell where they went and keep well out of their way.
And right so," said the rat, "reason tells me
To buy a bell of brass or of bright silver
And clip it on a collar for our common profit
170   And hang it over the cat's head; then we'd be able to hear
Whether he's riding or resting or roving out to play.
And if he desires sport we can step out
And appear in his presence while he's pleased to play.
And if he's angry we'll take heed and stay out of his way."
175   This whole convention of vermin was convinced by this advice,
But when the bell was brought and bound to the collar
There was no rat in the rabble, for all the realm of France,
That dared bind the bell about the cat's neck
Or hang it over his head to win all England;
180   But they held themselves faint-hearted and their whole plan foolish,
And allowed all their labor lost, and all their long scheming.
A mouse that knew much good, as it seemed to me then,
Strode forth sternly and stood before them all,
And to the rats arrayed there recited these words:
185   "Though we killed the cat, yet there would come another
To scratch us and all our kind though we crept under benches.
Therefore I counsel all the commons to let the cat alone,
And let's never be so bold as to show the bell to him.
While he's catching conies° he doesn't crave our flesh,   *rabbits*
190   But feeds himself on rich food—let's not defame him.
For a little loss is better than a long sorrow:
We'd all be muddling through a maze though we'd removed one foe.
For I heard my sire say, seven years ago,
Where the cat is a kitten, the court is wholly wretched.
195   That's how Holy Writ reads, whoever wants to look:
Woe to the land where the king is a child![2]
For no creature may rest quiet because of rats at night,
And many a man's malt we mice would destroy,
And also you rabble of rats would ruin men's clothing
200   If it weren't for the court-cat that can outleap you.
For if you rats held the reins, you couldn't rule yourselves.
I speak for myself," said the mouse, "I foresee such trouble later,
That by my counsel neither cat nor kitten shall be grieved—
And let's have no carping of this collar, that cost me nothing.

---

2. Ecclesiastes 10.16. A reference to the boy-king Richard II.

205 And though it had cost me money, I'd not admit it had—
But suffer as himself wishes to slay what he pleases,
Coupled and uncoupled let them catch what they will.
Therefore I warn every wise creature to stick to what's his own."
—What this dream may mean, you men that are merry,
210 You divine, for I don't dare, by dear God in Heaven.
       Yet scores of men stood there in silken coifs
Who seemed to be law-sergeants[3] that served at the bar,
Pleaded cases for pennies and impounded the law,
And not for love of our Lord once unloosed their lips:
215 You might better measure mist on Malvern Hills
Than get a "mum" from their mouths till money's on the table.
Barons and burgesses and bondmen[4] also
I saw in this assemblage, as you shall hear later;
Bakers and brewers and butchers aplenty,
220 Weavers of wool and weavers of linen,
Tailors, tinkers, tax-collectors in markets,
Masons, miners, many other craftsmen.
Of all living laborers there leapt forth some,
Such as diggers of ditches that do their jobs badly,
225 And dawdle away the long day with *Dieu save dame Emme.*[5]
Cooks and their kitchen-boys kept crying, "Hot pies, hot!
Good geese and pork! Let's go and dine!"
Tavern-keepers told them a tale of the same sort:
"White wine of Alsace and wine of Gascony,
230 Of the Rhine and of La Rochelle, to wash the roast down with."
All this I saw sleeping, and seven times more.

Passus 2
[THE MARRIAGE OF LADY MEAD]

       Still kneeling on my knees I renewed my plea for grace
And said, "Mercy, madam, for Mary's love in heaven,
Who bore the blissful babe that bought° us on the Cross,   redeemed
Teach me some talent to distinguish the false."
5 "Look on your left side, and lo, where he stands,
Both False and Favel[1] and lots of fellows of theirs."
I looked on my left side as the lady told me
And was aware of a woman wonderfully dressed.
Her gown was faced with fur, the finest on earth;
10 Crowned with a coronet—the king has none better.
Her fingers were filigreed fancifully with gold,
And rich rubies on them, as red as hot coals,
And diamonds most dear of cost, and two different kinds of sapphires,
Pearls and precious water-stones to repel poisons.

3. Important lawyers; a silk scarf, or "coif," was a lawyer's
badge of office.
4. Barons were members of the higher aristocracy;
burgesses were town-dwellers with full rights as citizens;
and bondmen were peasants who held their land from a

lord in return for services or rent.
5. Presumably a popular song.
1. "Lying"; the name of characters representing deceit in
Old French literature.

15　Her robe was most rich, dyed with red-scarlet,
　　With ribbons of red gold and with rich stones.
　　Her array ravished me—I'd seen such riches nowhere.
　　I wondered who she was and whose wife she might be.
　　　"Who is this woman," said I, "so worthily attired?"
20　"That is Meed[2] the maid who has harmed me very often
　　And maligned my lover—Lewte° is his name—　　　　　　　　　*Justice*
　　And has told lords who enforce laws lies about him.
　　In the Pope's palace she's as privileged as I am,
　　But Soothness[3] would not have it so, for she is a bastard,
25　And her father was false—he has a fickle tongue
　　And never told the truth since the time he came to earth.
　　And Meed has manners like his, as men say is natural:
　　　　Like father, like son. A good tree brings forth good fruit.
　　I ought to be higher than she: I came of better parentage.
　　My father is the great God, the giver of all graces,
30　One God without beginning, and I'm his good daughter.
　　And he's granted me that I might marry Mercy as my own,
　　And any man who's merciful and loves me truly
　　Shall be my lord and I his love, aloft in Heaven;
　　And the man who takes Meed—I'll bet my head on it—
35　Shall lose for her love a lump of *caritatis*.[4]
　　What does David the King declare of men that crave meed
　　And of the others on earth who uphold truth,
　　And how you shall save yourselves? The Psalter[5] bears witness:
　　　Lord, who shall dwell in thy tabernacle? etc.
40　And now this Meed is being married to a most accursed wretch,
　　To one False Fickle-Tongue—a fiend begot him.
　　Favel through his fair speech has these folk under enchantment,
　　And it's all by Liar's leadership that this lady is thus wedded.
　　Tomorrow will be made the maiden's bridal,
45　If you wish you may witness there who they all are
　　That belong to that lordship, the lesser and the greater.
　　Acquaint yourself with them if you can, and keep clear of them all,
　　And don't malign them but let them be until Lewte becomes justice
　　And has power to punish them—then put forth your evidence.
50　Now I commend you to Christ," said she, "and to Christ's pure mother,
　　And don't let your conscience be overcome by coveting Meed."
　　　Thus that lady left me lying asleep,
　　And how Meed was married was shown me in a dream—
　　How all the rich retinue that rule with False
55　Were bidden to the bridal for both sides of the match,
　　Of all manner of men, the moneyless and the rich;
　　To marry off this maiden many men were assembled,
　　Including knights and clerks and other common people,
　　Such as assizers and summoners, sheriffs and their clerks,
60　Beadles and bailiffs and brokers of merchandise,

---

2. A richly ambiguous word referring to a wide variety of "reward," both positive and negative, including just reward, heavenly salvation, recompense, the profit motive, graft, and bribery.

3. Truth, truthfulness, fidelity.
4. Of love (Latin).
5. The book of Psalms.

Harbingers and hostelers and advocates of the Arches[6]—
I can't reckon the rabble that ran about Meed.
But Simony and Civil[7] and assizers of courts
Were most intimate with Meed of any men, I thought.
65   But Favel was the first that fetched her from her bedroom
And like a broker brought her to be joined to False.
    When Simony and Civil saw the couple's wish
They assented for silver to say as both wanted.
Then Liar leaped forth and said, "Lo, here's a charter
70   That Guile with his great oaths has given them jointly."
And he prayed Simony to inspect it and Civil to read it.
Simony and Civil both stand forth
And unfold the conveyance that False has made;
Then these characters commence to cry on high:
    Let men now living and those to come after know, etc.[8]
75   "Let all who are on earth hear and bear witness
That Meed is married more for her property
Than for any goodness or grace or any goodly parentage.
Falseness fancies her for he knows she's rich,
And Favel with his fickle speech enfeoffs[9] them by this charter
80   That they may be princes in pride and despise Poverty,
Backbite and boast and bear false witness,
Scorn and scold and speak slander,
Disobedient and bold break the Ten Commandments;
And the Earldom of Envy and Ire together,
85   With the Castelet[1] of Quarreling and uncurbed Gossip,
The County of Covetousness and the countryside about,
That is Usury and Avarice—all I grant them
In bargainings and brokerings with the Borough of Theft,
With all the Lordship of Lechery in length and in breadth,
90   As in works and in words and with watching of eyes,
And in wild wishes and fantasies and with idle thoughts,
When to do what their wills would they want° the strength."   *lack*
Gluttony he gave them too and great oaths together,
And to drink all day at diverse taverns,
95   And to jabber there, and joke, and judge their fellow-Christians;
And to gobble food on fasting days before the fitting time,
And then to sit supping till sleep assails them,
And grow portly as town-pigs, and repose in soft beds,
Till sloth and sleep sleek their sides;
100   And then they'll wake up with Wanhope,[2] with no wish to amend,
For he believes he's lost—this is their last fortune.
"And they to have and to hold and their heirs after them
A dwelling with the Devil, and be damned forever,
With all the appurtenances of Purgatory, into the pain of hell,

---

6. The officials in this and the two preceding lines had jobs that made them particularly open to bribery.
7. Simony is the buying and selling of church offices or spiritual functions; Civil is civil as opposed to criminal law (especially noted for its bribery and corruption).
8. The formula for the beginning of a charter, a legal document often conveying rights or property.

9. Grants them territory in the manner of a feudal lord, to be specifically held by them as his liegemen, in return for military and other service.
1. Little castle.
2. Despair, considered the ultimate development of sloth, one of the Seven Deadly Sins.

105   Yielding for this thing at some year's end
    Their souls to Satan, to suffer pain with him,
    And to live with him in woe while God is in Heaven."
    To witness which thing Wrong was the first,
    And Piers the pardoner of Pauline doctrine,
110   Bart the beadle of Buckinghamshire,
    Reynold the reeve of Rutland district,
    Mund the miller and many more besides.
    "In the date of the Devil this deed is sealed
    In sight of Sir Simony and with Civil's approval."
115   Then Theology grew angry when he heard all this talk,
    And said to Civil, "Now sorrow on your books,
    To permit such a marriage to make Truth angry;
    And before this wedding is performed, may it befall you foul!
    Since Meed is *mulier*[3]—Amends is her parent—
120   God granted to give Meed to truth,
    And you've bestowed her on a deceiver, now God send you sorrow!
    The text does not tell you so, Truth knows what's true,
    For *dignus est operarius*[4] to have his hire.
    And you've fastened her to False—fie on your law!
125   For you live wholly by lies and by lecherous acts.
    Simony and yourself are sullying Holy Church;
    The notaries[5] and you are noxious to the people.
    You shall both make amends for it, by God that made me!
    You know well, you wastrels, unless your wits are failing,
130   That False is unflaggingly fickle in his deeds,
    And like a bastard born of Beëlzebub's° kindred.   *Satan's*
    And Meed is *mulier*, a maiden of property:
    She could kiss the king for cousin if she wished.
    Work with wisdom and with your wit as well:
135   Lead her to London where law is determined—
    If it's legally allowable for them to lie together.
    And if the Justice judges it's right to join her with False,
    Yet be wary of the wedding, for Truth is wise and discerning,
    And Conscience is of his council and knows all your characters,
140   And if he finds that you've offended and are one of False's followers,
    It shall beset your soul most sourly in the end."
      Civil assents to this, but Simony was unwilling
    Till he had silver for his seal and the stamps of the notaries.
    Then Favel fetched forth florins° enough   *gold coins*
145   And bade Guile, "Go give gold all about,
    And don't neglect the notaries, see that they need nothing.
    And fee False Witness with florins enough,
    For he may overmaster Meed and make her obey me."
    When this gold had been given, there was great thanking
150   To False and Favel for their fair gifts.
    And they all came to comfort False from the care that afflicted him,
    And said, "Be sure we shall never cease our efforts

---

3. Literally, "woman"; technically, a woman of legitimate birth.
4. Worthy is the laborer (Luke 10.7).

5. Officials charged with drawing up important documents; also the clerks or secretaries of important persons.

Till Meed is your wedded wife through wit of us all,
For we've overmastered Meed with our merry speech
155 So that she grants to go with a good will
To London to learn whether law would
Judge you jointly in joy forever."
Then False felt well pleased and Favel was glad,
And they sent to summon all men in shires about,
160 And bade them all be ready, beggars and others,
To go with them to Westminster to witness this deed.
And then they had to have horses to haul them thither;
Then Favel fetched foals of the best;
Set Meed on a sheriff shod all new;
165 And False sat on an assizer that softly trotted,
And Favel on Fair Speech, clad in feigning clothes.
Then notaries had no horses, and were annoyed also
Because Simony and Civil should walk on foot.
But then Simony swore and Civil as well
170 That summoners[6] should be saddled and serve them all:
"And let these provisors[7] be put into palfrey's harness;
Sir Simony himself shall sit on their backs.
Deans and subdeans,[8] you draw together,
Archdeacons and officials and all your registrars,
175 Let them be saddled with silver to suffer our sins
Such as adultery and divorce and clandestine usury,[9]
To bear bishops about, abroad on visitations.
Pauline's people, for complaints in the consistory,[1]
Shall serve myself, Civil is my name.
180 And let the commissary[2] be cart-saddled and our cart pulled by him,
And he must fetch us victuals from *fornicatores*.°   fornicators
And make a long cart of Liar, loaded with all the rest,
Such as twisters and tricksters that trot on their feet."
False and Favel fare forth together,
185 And Meed in the midst and her serving men behind.
I've no opportunity to tell of the tail of the procession,
Of many manner of men that move over this earth.
But Guile was foregoer and guided them all.
    Soothness saw them well and said but a little,
190 And pressed ahead on his palfrey and passed them all
And came to the King's court and told Conscience about it,
And Conscience recounted it to the King afterward.
"By Christ!" said the King, "if I can catch
False or Favel or any of his fellows,
195 I'll be avenged on those villains that act so viciously,
And have them hanged by the neck, and all who support them.
Shall no bondsman be allowed to go bail for the least,

---

6. Officials who served summons to the ecclesiastical courts, which dealt with matters of private morality. They were much feared because of their power to blackmail and demand bribes.
7. Clerics nominated to their benefices directly by the pope; petitions for such offices were regularly accompanied by bribes.

8. Clerics in charge of a body of priests generally attached to a cathedral; thought to be open to bribery.
9. Lending money for interest.
1. A bishop's court.
2. The bishop's official representative in part of his diocese.

But whatever law will allot, let it fall on them all."
And he commanded a constable that came straightway
200 To "detain those tyrants, despite their treasure, I say;
Fetter Falseness fast no matter what he gives you,
And get Guile's head off at once—let him go no farther;
And bring Meed to me no matter what they do.
Simony and Civil, I send to warn them
205 That their actions will hurt Holy Church forever.
And if you lay hand on Liar, don't let him escape
Before he's put in the pillory, for any prayer he makes."
     Dread stood at the door and heard this declaration,
How the King commanded constables and sergeants
210 That Falseness and his fellowship should be fettered and bound.
Then Dread came away quickly and cautioned the False
And bade him flee for fear and his fellows too.
Then Falseness for fear fled to the friars;
And Guile in dread of death dashed away fast.
215 But merchants met with him and made him stay
And shut him up in their shop to show their wares,
Appareled him as an apprentice to wait on purchasers.
Lightly Liar leapt away then,
Lurking through lanes, belabored by many:
220 Nowhere was he welcome for his many tales,
Everywhere hunted out and ordered to pack,
Till pardoners took pity and pulled him indoors;
Washed him and wiped him and wound him in cloths,
And sent him on Sundays with seals[3] to church,
225 Where he gave pardon for pennies by the pound about.
Then doctors were indignant and drafted letters to him
That he should come and stay with them to examine urine.
Apothecaries wanted to employ him to appraise their wares,
For he was trained in their trade and could distinguish many gums.[4]
230 But minstrels and messengers met with him once
And had him with them half a year and eleven days.
Friars with fair speech fetched him thence;
To keep him safe from the curious they coped him as a friar
But he has leave to leap out as often as he pleases,
235 And is welcome to come when he wants, and he stays with them often.
All fled for fear and flew into corners;
Except for Meed the maid none remained there.
But truly to tell she trembled for dread
And twisted about tearfully when she was taken into custody.

Passus 6
[Piers Plowing the Half-Acre]

"This would be a bewildering way unless we had a guide
Who could trace our way foot by foot": thus these folk complained.

---

3. A pardoner needed the bishop's seal on the document that gave him license to preach and collect money for indulgences in a particular diocese or district.
4. Gums used as perfumes, spices, and medicines.

Plowmen, from the *Luttrell Psalter*. Early 14th century.

Said Perkin[1] the Plowman, "By Saint Peter of Rome!
I have a half-acre to plow by the highway;
5 If I had plowed this half-acre and afterwards sowed it,
I would walk along with you and show you the way to go."
"That would be a long delay," said a lady in a veil.
"What ought we women to work at meanwhile?"
"Some shall sew sacks to stop the wheat from spilling.
10 And you lovely ladies, with your long fingers,
See that you have silk and sendal[2] to sew when you've time
Chasubles° for chaplains for the Church's honor.   *robes*
Wives and widows, spin wool and flax;
Make cloth, I counsel you, and teach the craft to your daughters.
15 The needy and the naked, take note how they fare:
Keep them from cold with clothing, for so Truth wishes.
For I shall supply their sustenance unless the soil fails
As long as I live, for the Lord's love in Heaven.
And all sorts of folk that feed on farm products,
20 Busily abet him who brings forth your food."
"By Christ!" exclaimed a knight then, "your counsel is the best.
But truly, how to drive a team has never been taught me.
But show me," said the knight, "and I shall study plowing."
"By Saint Paul," said Perkin, "since you proffer help so humbly,
25 I shall sweat and strain and sow for us both,
And also labor for your love all my lifetime,
In exchange for your championing Holy Church and me
Against wasters and wicked men who would destroy me.
And go hunt hardily hares and foxes,
30 Boars and bucks that break down my hedges,
And have falcons at hand to hunt down the birds
That come to my croft° and crop my wheat."   *field*
Thoughtfully the knight then spoke these words:
"By my power, Piers, I pledge you my word
35 To uphold this obligation though I have to fight.
As long as I live I shall look after you."

---

1. A nickname for Piers, or Peter.   2. A thin, rich form of silk.

"Yes, and yet another point," said Piers, "I pray you further:
See that you trouble no tenant unless Truth approves,
And though you may amerce° him, let Mercy set the fine,   *fine*
40   And Meekness be your master no matter what Meed does.
And though poor men proffer you presents and gifts,
Don't accept them for it's uncertain that you deserve to have them.
For at some set time you'll have to restore them
In a most perilous place called purgatory.
45   And treat no bondman badly—you'll be the better for it;
Though here he is your underling, it could happen in Heaven
That he'll be awarded a worthier place, one with more bliss:
         Friend, go up higher.[3]
For in the charnelhouse[4] at church churls are hard to distinguish,
Or a knight from a knave: know this in your heart.
50   And see that you're true of your tongue, and as for tales—hate them
Unless they have wisdom and wit for your workmen's instruction.
Avoid foul-mouthed fellows and don't be friendly to their stories,
And especially at your repasts shun people like them,
For they tell the Fiend's fables—be very sure of that."
55   "I assent, by Saint James," said the knight then,
"To work by your word while my life lasts."
"And I shall apparel myself," said Perkin, "in pilgrims' fashion
And walk along the way with you till we find Truth."
He donned his working-dress, some darned, some whole,
60   His gaiters and his gloves to guard his limbs from cold,
And hung his seed-holder behind his back instead of a knapsack:
"Bring a bushel of bread-wheat for me to put in it,
For I shall sow it myself and set out afterwards
On a pilgrimage as palmers[5] do to procure pardon.
65   And whoever helps me plow or work in any way
Shall have leave, by our Lord, to glean my land in harvest-time,
And make merry with what he gets, no matter who grumbles.
And all kinds of craftsmen that can live in truth,
I shall provide food for those that faithfully live,
70   Except for Jack the juggler and Jonette from the brothel,
And Daniel the dice-player and Denot the pimp,
And Friar Faker and folk of his order,
And Robin the ribald for his rotten speech.
Truth told me once and bade me tell it abroad:
75   *Deleantur de libro viventium:*[6] I should have no dealings with them,
For Holy Church is under orders to ask no tithes[7] of them.
         For let them not be written with the righteous.[8]
Their good luck has left them, the Lord amend them now."
Dame-Work-When-It's-Time-To was Piers's wife's name;
His daughter was called Do-Just-So-Or-Your-Dame-Will-Beat-You;
80   His son was named Suffer-Your-Sovereigns-To-Have-Their-Will-

---

3. Luke 14.10.
4. Crypt for dead bodies.
5. "Professional" pilgrims.
6. Let them be blotted out of the book of the living.
(Psalms 68.29).

7. Because the money they make is illegitimate, they do
not owe the church the customary tithes, or ten percent
of their income.
8. Psalms 68.29.

Condemn-Them-Not-For-If-You-Do-You'll-Pay-A-Dear-Price-
Let-God-Have-His-Way-With-All-Things-For-So-His-Word-Teaches.
"For now I am old and hoary and have something of my own,
To penance and to pilgrimage I'll depart with these others;
85   Therefore I will, before I go away, have my will written:
"*In Dei nomine, amen,*[9] I make this myself.
He shall have my soul that has deserved it best,
And defend it from the Fiend—for so I believe—
Till I come to his accounting, as my Creed teaches me—
90   To have release and remission I trust in his rent book.
The kirk° shall have my corpse and keep my bones,   church
For of my corn and cattle it craved the tithe:
I paid it promptly for peril of my soul;
It is obligated, I hope, to have me in mind
95   And commemorate me in its prayers among all Christians.
My wife shall have what I won with truth, and nothing else,
And parcel it out among my friends and my dear children.
For though I die today, my debts are paid;
I took back what I borrowed before I went to bed.'
100   As for the residue and the remnant, by the Rood of Lucca,[1]
I will worship Truth with it all my lifetime,
And be his pilgrim at the plow for poor men's sake.
My plowstaff shall be my pikestaff and push at the roots
And help my coulter° to cut and cleanse the furrows."   slow blade
105   Now Perkin and the pilgrims have put themselves to plowing.
Many there helped him to plow his half-acre.
Ditchers and diggers dug up the ridges;
Perkin was pleased by this and praised them warmly.
There were other workmen who worked very hard:
110   Each man in his manner made himself a laborer,
And some to please Perkin pulled up the weeds.
At high prime[2] Piers let the plow stand
To oversee them himself; whoever worked best
Should be hired afterward, when harvest-time came.
115   Then some sat down and sang over ale
And helped plow the half-acre with "Ho! trolly-lolly!"[3]
"Now by the peril of my soul!" said Piers in pure wrath,
"Unless you get up again and begin working now,
No grain that grows here will gladden you at need,
120   And though once off the dole you die let the Devil care!"
Then fakers were afraid and feigned to be blind;
Some set their legs askew as such loafers can
And made their moan to Piers, how they might not work:
    "We have no limbs to labor with, Lord, we thank you;
125   But we pray for you, Piers, and for your plow as well,
That God of his grace make your grain multiply,
And reward you for whatever alms you will give us here,

9. In the name of God, amen; customary beginning of a will.
1. Ornate crucifix in the Italian city of Lucca, which was a popular object of pilgrimage.
2. Nine in the morning, after a substantial amount of work has been done.
3. Probably the refrain of a popular song.

For we can't strain and sweat, such sickness afflicts us."
"If what you say is so," said Piers, "I'll soon find out.
130   I know you're ne'er-do-wells, and Truth knows what's right,
And I'm his sworn servant and so should warn him
Which ones they are in this world that do his workmen harm.
You waste what men win with toil and trouble.
But Truth shall teach you how his team should be driven,
135   Or you'll eat barley bread and use the brook for drink;
Unless you're blind or broken-legged, or bolted° with iron—   braced
Those shall eat as well as I do, so God help me,
Till God of his goodness gives them strength to arise.
But you could work as Truth wants you to and earn wages and bread
140   By keeping cows in the field, the corn from the cattle,
Making ditches or dikes or dinging° on sheaves,   beating
Or helping make mortar, or spreading muck afield.
You live in lies and lechery and in sloth too,
And it's only for suffrance that vengeance has not fallen on you.
145   But anchorites and hermits that eat only at noon
And nothing more before the morrow, they shall have my alms,
And buy copes at my cost—those that have cloisters and churches.
But Robert Runabout shall have no rag from me,
Nor 'Apostles' unless they can preach and have the bishop's permission.
150   They shall have bread and boiled greens and a bit extra besides,
For it's an unreasonable religious life that has no regular meals."
        Then Waster waxed angry and wanted to fight;
To Piers the Plowman he proffered his glove.
A Breton, a braggart, he bullied Piers too,
155   And told him to go piss with his plow, peevish wretch.
"Whether you're willing or unwilling, we will have our will
With your flour and your flesh, fetch it when we please,
And make merry with it, no matter what you do."
Then Piers the Plowman complained to the knight
160   To keep him safe, as their covenant was, from cursed rogues,
"And from these wolfish wasters that lay waste the world,
For they waste and win nothing, and there will never be
Plenty among the people while my plow stands idle."
Because he was born a courteous man the knight spoke kindly to Waster
165   And warned him he would have to behave himself better:
"Or you'll pay the penalty at law, I promise, by my order!"
"It's not my way to work," said Waster, "I won't begin now!"
And made light of the law and lighter of the knight,
And said Piers wasn't worth a pea or his plow either,
170   And menaced him and his men if they met again.
        "Now by the peril of my soul!" said Piers, "I'll punish you all."
And he whooped after Hunger who heard him at once.
"Avenge me on these vagabonds," said he, "that vex the whole world."
Then Hunger in haste took hold of Waster by the belly
175   And gripped him so about the guts that his eyes gushed water.
He buffeted the Breton about the cheeks
That he looked like a lantern all his life after.
He beat them both so that he almost broke their guts.

Had not Piers with a pease loaf prayed him to leave off
180 They'd have been dead and buried deep, have no doubt about it.
"Let them live," he said, "and let them feed with hogs,
Or else on beans and bran baked together."
Fakers for fear fled into barns
And flogged sheaves with flails from morning till evening,
185 So that Hunger wouldn't be eager to cast his eye on them.
For a potful of peas that Piers had cooked
A heap of hermits laid hands on spades
And cut off their copes and made short coats of them
And went like workmen to weed and to mow,
190 And dug dirt and dung to drive off Hunger.
Blind and bedridden got better by the thousand;
Those who sat to beg silver were soon healed,
For what had been baked for Bayard[4] was boon to many hungry,
And many a beggar for beans obediently labored,
195 And every poor man was well pleased to have peas for his wages,
And what Piers prayed them to do they did as sprightly as sparrowhawks.
And Piers was proud of this and put them to work,
And gave them meals and money as they might deserve.
      Then Piers had pity and prayed Hunger to take his way
200 Off to his own home and hold there forever.
"I'm well avenged on vagabonds by virtue of you.
But I pray you, before you part," said Piers to Hunger,
"With beggars and street-beadsmen[5] what's best to be done?
For well I know that once you're away, they will work badly;
205 Misfortune makes them so meek now,
And it's for lack of food that these folk obey me.
And they're my blood brothers, for God bought us all.
Truth taught me once to love them every one
And help them with everything after their needs.
210 Now I'd like to learn, if you know, what line I should take
And how I might overmaster them and make them work."
      "Hear now," said Hunger, "and hold it for wisdom:
Big bold beggars that can earn their bread,
With hounds' bread and horses' bread hold up their hearts,
215 And keep their bellies from swelling by stuffing them with beans—
And if they begin to grumble, tell them to get to work,
And they'll have sweeter suppers once they've deserved them.
And if you find any fellow-man that fortune has harmed
Through fire or through false men, befriend him if you can.
220 Comfort such at your own cost, for the love of Christ in Heaven;
Love them and relieve them—so the law of Kind[6] directs.
      Bear ye one another's burdens.[7]
And all manner of men that you may find
That are needy or naked and have nothing to spend,
With meals or with money make them the better.

---

4. A generic name for a horse; a bread made of beans and
bran was fed to horses.
5. Paid prayer-sayers.

6. Nature (an aspect of God).
7. Galatians 6.2.

225 Love them and don't malign them; let God take vengeance.
Though they behave ill, leave it all up to God
Vengeance is mine and I will repay.[8]
And if you want to gratify God, do as the Gospel teaches,
And get yourself loved by lowly men: so you'll unloose his grace."
Make to yourselves friends of the mammon of unrighteousness.[9]
"I would not grieve God," said Piers, "for all the goods on earth!
230 Might I do as you say without sin?" said Piers then.
"Yes, I give you my oath," said Hunger, "or else the Bible lies:
Go to Genesis the giant, engenderer of us all:
In sudore[1] and slaving you shall bring forth your food
And labor for your livelihood, and so our Lord commanded.
235 And Sapience says the same—I saw it in the Bible.
Piger propter frigus[2] would plow no field;
He shall be a beggar and none abate his hunger.
Matthew with man's[3] face mouths these words:
'Entrusted with a talent, *servus nequam*[4] didn't try to use it,
240 And earned his master's ill-will for evermore after,
And he took away his talent who was too lazy to work,
And gave it to him in haste that had ten already;
And after he said so that his servants heard it,
He that has shall have, and help when he needs it,
245 And he that nothing has shall nothing have and no man help him,
And what he trusts he's entitled to I shall take away.'
Kind Wit wants each one to work,
Either in teaching or tallying or toiling with his hands,
Contemplative life or active life; Christ wants it too.
250 The Psalter says in the Psalm of *Beati omnes*,[5]
The fellow that feeds himself with his faithful labor,
He is blessed by the Book in body and in soul."
The labors of thy hands, etc.[6]
"Yet I pray you," said Piers, "*pour charité*,[7] if you know
Any modicum of medicine, teach me it, dear sir.
255 For some of my servants and myself as well
For a whole week do not work, we've such aches in our stomachs."
"I'm certain," said Hunger, "what sickness ails you.
You've munched down too much: that's what makes you groan,
But I assure you," said Hunger, "if you'd preserve your health,
260 You must not drink any day before you've dined on something.
Never eat, I urge you, ere Hunger comes upon you
And sends you some of his sauce to add savor to the food;
And keep some till suppertime, and don't sit too long;
Arise up ere Appetite has eaten his fill.
265 Let not Sir Surfeit sit at your table;

---

8. Romans 12.19.
9. Luke 16.9.
1. In the sweat [of thy brow thou shalt eat bread] (Genesis 3.19).
2. The sluggard [will not plow] by reason of the cold (Proverbs 20.4).
3. Each of the four Evangelists was represented by a different symbol; Matthew was represented by a man.
4. The wicked servant (Luke 19.22); a talent is a unit of money.
5. Blessed [are] all [who] (Psalms 127.1).
6. Psalms 127.2.
7. For charity.

Love him not for he's a lecher whose delight is his tongue,
And for all sorts of seasoned stuff his stomach yearns.
And if you adopt this diet, I dare bet my arms
That Physic for his food will sell his furred hood
270 And his Calabrian cloak with its clasps of gold,
And be content, by my troth, to retire from medicine
And learn to labor on the land lest livelihood fail him.
There are fewer physicians than frauds—reform them, Lord!—
Their drinks make men die before destiny ordains."
275 "By Saint Parnel," said Piers, "these are profitable words.
This is a lovely lesson; the Lord reward you for it!
Take your way when you will—may things be well with you always!"
"My oath to God!" said Hunger, "I will not go away
Till I've dined this day and drunk as well."
280 "I've no penny," said Piers, "to purchase pullets,
And I can't get goose or pork; but I've got two green cheeses,
A few curds and cream and a cake of oatmeal,
A loaf of beans and bran baked for my children.
And yet I say, by my soul, I have no salt bacon
285 Nor any hen's egg, by Christ, to make ham and eggs,
But scallions aren't scarce, nor parsley, and I've scores of cabbages,
And also a cow and a calf, and a cart-mare
To draw dung to the field while the dry weather lasts.
By this livelihood I must live till Lammass[8] time
290 When I hope to have harvest in my garden.
Then I can manage a meal that will make you happy."
All the poor people fetched peasepods;
Beans and baked apples they brought in their skirts,
Chives and chervils and ripe cherries aplenty,
295 And offered Piers this present to please Hunger with.
Hunger ate this in haste and asked for more.
Then poor folk for fear fed Hunger fast,
Proffering leeks and peas, thinking to appease him.
And now harvest drew near and new grain came to market.
300 Then poor people were pleased and plied Hunger with the best;
With good ale as Glutton taught they got him to sleep.
Then Waster wouldn't work but wandered about,
And no beggar would eat bread that had beans in it,
But the best bread or the next best, or baked from pure wheat,
305 Nor drink any half-penny ale in any circumstances,
But of the best and the brownest that barmaids sell.
Laborers that have no land to live on but their hands
Deign not to dine today on last night's cabbage.
No penny-ale can please them, nor any piece of bacon,
310 But it must be fresh flesh or else fried fish,
And that *chaud* or *plus chaud*[9] so it won't chill their bellies.
Unless he's hired at high wages he will otherwise complain;
That he was born to be a workman he'll blame the time.

8. The harvest festival, August 1, when a loaf made from   9. Hot or very hot.
the first wheat of the season was offered at mass.

Against Cato's counsel he commences to murmur:

315   *Remember to bear your burden of poverty patiently.*[1]

He grows angry at God and grumbles against Reason,

And then curses the king and all the council after

Because they legislate laws that punish laboring men.

But while Hunger was their master there would none of them complain

320   Or strive against the statute,[2] so sternly he looked.

But I warn you workmen, earn wages while you may,

For Hunger is hurrying hitherward fast.

With waters he'll awaken Waster's chastisement;

Before five years are fulfilled such famine shall arise.

325   Through flood and foul weather fruits shall fail,

And so Saturn[3] says and has sent to warn you:

When you see the moon amiss and two monks' heads,

And a maid have the mastery, and multiply by eight,

Then shall Death withdraw and Dearth be justice,

330   And Daw the diker° die for hunger,   *ditch-digger*

Unless God of his goodness grants us a truce.

Passus 18

[THE CRUCIFIXION AND THE HARROWING OF HELL]

Wool-chafed and wet-shoed I went forth after

Like a careless creature unconscious of woe,

And trudged forth like a tramp, all the time of my life,

Till I grew weary of the world and wished to sleep again,

5   And lay down till Lent, and slept a long time,

Rested there, snoring roundly, till *Ramis-Palmarum.*[1]

I dreamed chiefly of children and cheers of "*Gloria, laus!*"[2]

And how old folk to an organ sang "*Hosanna!*"

And of Christ's passion and pain for the people he had reached for.

10   One resembling the Samaritan and somewhat Piers the Plowman

Barefoot on an ass's back bootless came riding

Without spurs or spear: sprightly was his look,

As is the nature of a knight that draws near to be dubbed,

To get himself gilt spurs and engraved jousting shoes.

15   Then was Faith watching from a window and cried, "*A, fili David!*"[3]

As does a herald of arms when armed men come to joust.

Old Jews of Jerusalem joyfully sang,

      "*Blessed is he who cometh in the name of the Lord.*"[4]

And I asked Faith to reveal what all this affair meant,

And who was to joust in Jerusalem. "Jesus," he said,

20   "And fetch what the Fiend claims, the fruit of Piers the Plowman."

"Is Piers in this place?" said I; and he pierced me with his look:

---

1. From Cato's *Distichs*, a collection of phrases used to teach Latin to beginning students.
2. The Statutes of Laborers, passed after 1351, when the Black Death depopulated the countryside and a labor shortage ensued. They were intended to control the mobility and the wages of laborers.
3. Planet thought to influence the weather, generally perceived to be hostile.

1. Palm Sunday (literally, "branches of palms"): this part of the poem reflects the biblical account of Christ's entry into Jerusalem.
2. "Glory, praise [and honor]": the first words of an anthem sung by children on Palm Sunday.
3. On the first Palm Sunday, crowds greeted Christ crying "Hosanna [l. 8] to the son of David."
4. Matthew 21.9.

Passion Scenes, from the *Winchester Psalter.* 12th century. These crowded, agitated scenes depict the betrayal and scourging of Christ. The artist depicts Christ's tormentors as grotesques but also employs a stereotyped iconography of Semitic and African Features. This unlikely enthnic geography suggests how foreignness itself could be used as a marker of moral degeneracy in some medieval art.

"This Jesus for his gentleness will joust in Piers's arms,
In his helmet and in his hauberk, *humana natura*,[5]
So that Christ be not disclosed here as *consummatus Deus*.[6]
25   In the plate armor of Piers the Plowman this jouster will ride,
For no dint will do him injury as in *deitate Patris*.[7]
"Who shall joust with Jesus," said I, "Jews or Scribes?"[8]
"No," said Faith, "but the Fiend and False-Doom-To-Die.
Death says he will undo and drag down low
30   All that live or look upon land or water.
Life says that he lies, and lays his life in pledge
That for all that Death can do, within three days he'll walk
And fetch from the Fiend the fruit of Piers the Plowman,
And place it where he pleases, and put Lucifer in bonds,
35   And beat and bring down burning death forever.

---

5. A hauberk is a coat of mail; in the Incarnation Christ assumed human nature, to redeem humankind.
6. The perfect (triune) God.
7. In the godhead of the Father: as God Christ could not suffer, but as man he could.
8. Scribes were persons who made a strict literal interpretation of the Old Law and hence rejected Christ's teaching of the New.

O *death, I will be thy death.*"[9]
    Then Pilate came with many people, *sedens pro tribunali,*[1]
To see how doughtily Death should do, and judge the rights of both.
The Jews and the justice were joined against Jesus,
And all the court cried upon him, *"Crucifige!"*[2] loud.

40   Then a plaintiff appeared before Pilate and said,
"This Jesus made jokes about Jerusalem's temple,
To have it down in one day and in three days after
Put it up again all new—here he stands who said it—
And yet build it every bit as big in all dimensions,

45   As long and as broad both, above and below."
"Crucifige!" said a sergeant, "he knows sorcerer's tricks."
"Tolle! tolle!"[3] said another, and took sharp thorns
And began to make a garland out of green thorn,
And set it sorely on his head and spoke in hatred,

50   *"Ave, Rabbi,"*[4] said that wretch, and shot reeds° at him;   *arrows*
They nailed him with three nails naked on a Cross,
And with a pole put a potion up to his lips
And bade him drink to delay his death and lengthen his days,
And said, "If you're subtle, let's see you help yourself.

55   If you are Christ and a king's son, come down from the Cross!
Then we'll believe that Life loves you and will not let you die."
"Consummatum est,"[5] said Christ and started to swoon,
Piteously and pale like a prisoner dying.
The Lord of Life and of Light then laid his eyelids together.

60   The day withdrew for dread and darkness covered the sun;
The wall wavered and split and the whole world quaked.
Dead men for that din came out of deep graves
And spoke of why that storm lasted so long:
"For a bitter battle," the dead body said;

65   "Life and Death in this darkness, one destroys the other.
No one will surely know which shall have the victory
Before Sunday about sunrise"; and sank with that to earth.
Some said that he was God's son that died so fairly:
    Truly this was the Son of God.[6]
    And some said he was a sorcerer: "We should see first

70   Whether he's dead or not dead before we dare take him down."
Two thieves were there that suffered death that time
Upon crosses beside Christ; such was the common law.
A constable came forth and cracked both their legs
And the arms afterward of each of those thieves.

75   But no bastard was so bold as to touch God's body there;
Because he was a knight and a king's son, Nature decreed that time
That no knave should have the hardiness to lay hand on him.
But a knight with a sharp spear was sent forth there
Named Longeus[7] as the legend tells, who had long since lost his sight;

9. Hosea 13.14.
1. Sitting as a judge (Matthew 27.19).
2. Crucify! (John 19.6).
3. "Away with him! Away with him!" (John 19.15).
4. "Hail, Rabbi [i.e., Master]" (Matthew 26.49): the words Judas spoke when he kissed Christ to identify him

to the arresting officers.
5. "It is finished" (John 19.30).
6. Matthew 27.54.
7. Longeus (usually Longinus) appears in the apocryphal Gospel of Nicodemus, which was the principal source of this account of Christ's harrowing of hell.

80	Before Pilate and the other people in that place he waited on his horse.
	For all that he might demur, he was made that time
	To joust with Jesus, that blind Jew Longeus.
	For all who watched there were unwilling, whether mounted or afoot,
	To touch him or tamper with him or take him down from the cross,
85	Except this blind bachelor that bore him through the heart.
	The blood sprang down the spear and unsparred° his eyes. *opened*
	The knight knelt down on his knees and begged Jesus for mercy.
	"It was against my will, Lord, to wound you so sorely."
	He sighed and said, "Sorely I repent it.
90	For what I here have done, I ask only your grace.
	Have mercy on me, rightful Jesu!" and thus lamenting wept.
	Then Faith began fiercely to scorn the false Jews,[8]
	Called them cowards, accursed forever.
	"For this foul villainy, may vengeance fall on you!
95	To make the blind beat the dead, it was a bully's thought.
	Cursed cowards, no kind of knighthood was it
	To beat a dead body with any bright weapon.
	Yet he's won the victory in the fight for all his vast wound,
	For your champion jouster, the chief knight of you all,
100	Weeping admits himself worsted and at the will of Jesus.
	For when this darkness is done, Death will be vanquished,
	And you louts have lost, for Life shall have the victory;
	And your unfettered freedom has fallen into servitude;
	And you churls and your children shall achieve no prosperity,
105	Nor have lordship over land or have land to till,
	But be all barren and live by usury,° *money-lending*
	Which is a life that every law of our Lord curses.
	Now your good days are done as Daniel prophesied;
	When Christ came their kingdom's crown should be lost:
	When the Holy of Holies comes your anointing shall cease.[9]
110	What for fear of this adventure and of the false Jews
	I withdrew in that darkness to *Descendit-ad-Inferna*[1]
	And there I saw surely *Secundum Scripturas*[2]
	Where out of the west a wench, as I thought,
	Came walking on the way—she looked toward hell.
115	Mercy was that maid's name, a meek thing withal,
	A most gracious girl, and goodly of speech.
	Her sister as it seemed came softly walking
	Out of the east, opposite, and she looked westward,
	A comely creature and cleanly: Truth was her name.
120	Because of the virtue that followed her, she was afraid of nothing.
	When these maidens met, Mercy and Truth,
	Each of them asked the other about this great wonder,
	And of the din and of the darkness, and how the day lowered,
	And what a gleam and a glint glowed before hell.
125	"I marvel at this matter, by my faith," said Truth,
	"And am coming to discover what this queer affair means."

---

8. This and the next eighteen lines are an example of late medieval antisemitism.
9. Compare with Daniel 9.24.

1. He descended into hell (from the Apostles' Creed).
2. According to the Scriptures.

"Do not marvel," said Mercy, "it means only mirth.
A maiden named Mary, and mother without touching
By any kind of creature, conceived through speech
130 And grace of the Holy Ghost; grew great with child;
With no blemish to her woman's body brought him into this world.
And that my tale is true, I take God to witness,
Since this baby was born it has been thirty winters,
Who died and suffered death this day about midday.
135 And that is the cause of this eclipse that is closing off the sun,
In meaning that man shall be removed from darkness
While this gleam and this glow go to blind Lucifer.
For patriarchs and prophets have preached of this often
That man shall save man through a maiden's help,
140 And what a tree took away a tree shall restore,[3]
And what Death brought down a death shall raise up."
"What you're telling," said Truth, "is just a tale of nonsense.
For Adam and Eve and Abraham and the rest,
Patriarchs and prophets imprisoned in pain,
145 Never believe that yonder light will lift them up,
Or have them out of hell—hold your tongue, Mercy!
Your talk is mere trifling. I, Truth, know the truth,
For whatever is once in hell, it comes out never.
Job the perfect patriarch disproves what you say:
Since in hell there is no redemption."[4]
150   Then Mercy most mildly uttered these words:
"From observation," she said, "I suppose they shall be saved,
Because venom destroys venom, and in that I find evidence
That Adam and Eve shall have relief.
For of all venoms the foulest is the scorpion's:
155 No medicine may amend the place where it stings
Till it's dead and placed upon it—the poison is destroyed,
The first effect of the venom, through the virtue it possesses.
So shall this death destroy—I dare bet my life—
All that Death did first through the Devil's tempting.
160 And just as the beguiler with guile beguiled man first,
So shall grace that began everything make a good end
And beguile the beguiler—and that's a good trick:
A trick by which to trick trickery."
"Now let's be silent," said Truth. "It seems to me I see
Out of the nip° of the north, not far from here,   *chill*
165 Righteousness come running—let's wait right here,
For she knows far more than we—she was here before us both."
"That is so," said Mercy, "and I see here to the south
Where Peace clothed in patience comes sportively this way.
Love has desired her long: I believe surely
170 That Love has sent her some letter, what this light means
That hangs over hell thus: she will tell us what it means."

---

3. The first tree bore the fruit that Adam and Eve ate, thereby damaging humankind; the second tree is the cross on which Christ was crucified, thereby redeeming humankind. 4. Compare with Job 7.9.

When Peace clothed in patience approached near them both,
Righteousness did her reverence for her rich clothing
And prayed Peace to tell her to what place she was going,
175   And whom she was going to greet in her gay garments.
"My wish is to take my way," said she, "and welcome them all
Whom many a day I might not see for murk of sin.
Adam and Eve and the many others in hell,
Moses and many more will merrily sing,
180   And I shall dance to their song: sister, do the same.
Because Jesus jousted well, joy begins to dawn.
    Weeping may endure for a night, but joy cometh in the morning.[5]
Love who is my lover sent letters to tell me
That my sister Mercy and I shall save mankind,
And that God has forgiven and granted me, Peace, and Mercy
185   To make bail for mankind for evermore after.
Look, here's the patent,"[6] said Peace: "*In pace in idipsum:*
And that this deed shall endure, *dormiam et requiescam.*"[7]
"What? You're raving," said Righteousness. "You must be really drunk.
Do you believe that yonder light might unlock hell
190   And save man's soul? Sister, don't suppose it.
At the beginning God gave the judgment himself
That Adam and Eve and all that followed them
Should die downright and dwell in torment after
If they touched a tree and ate the tree's fruit.
195   Adam afterwards against his forbidding
Fed on that fruit and forsook as it were
The love of our Lord and his lore too,
And followed what the Fiend taught and his flesh's will
Against Reason. I, Righteousness, record this with Truth,
200   That their pain should be perpetual and no prayer should help them,
Therefore let them chew as they chose, and let us not chide, sisters,
For it's misery without amendment, the morsel they ate."
"And I shall prove," said Peace, "that their pain must end,
And in time trouble must turn into well-being;
205   For had they known no woe, they'd not have known well-being;
For no one knows what well-being is who was never in woe,
Nor what is hot hunger who has never lacked food.
If there were no night, no man, I believe,
Could be really well aware of what day means.
210   Never should a really rich man who lives in rest and ease
Know what woe is if it weren't for natural death.
So God, who began everything, of his good will
Became man by a maid for mankind's salvation
And allowed himself to be sold to see the sorrow of dying.
215   And that cures all care and is the first cause of rest,
For until we meet *modicum*,° I may well avow it,   *a little*
No man knows, I suppose, what 'enough' means.
Therefore God of his goodness gave the first man Adam

---

5. Psalms 29.6.
6. Document conferring authority.

7. In peace in the self-same: . . . I will find rest (Psalms 4.9).

A place of supreme ease and of perfect joy,
220   And then he suffered him to sin so that he might know sorrow,
And thus know what well-being is—to be aware of it naturally.
And afterward God offered himself, and took Adam's nature,
To see what he had suffered in three separate places,
Both in Heaven and on earth, and now he heads for hell,
225   To learn what all woe is like who has learned of all joy.
So it shall fare with these folk: their folly and their sin
Shall show them what sickness is—and succor from all pain.
No one knows what war is where peace prevails,
Nor what is true well-being till 'Woe, alas!' teaches him."
230   Then was there a wight° with two broad eyes: *creature*
Book was that beaupere's[8] name, a bold man of speech.
"By God's body," said this Book, "I will bear witness
That when this baby was born there blazed a star
So that all the wise men in the world agreed with one opinion
235   That such a baby was born in Bethlehem city
Who should save man's soul and destroy sin.
And all the elements," said the Book, "hereof bore witness.
The sky first revealed that he was God who formed all things:
The hosts in Heaven took *stella comata*[9]
240   And tended her like a torch to reverence his birth.
The light followed the Lord into the low earth.
The water witnessed that he was God for he walked on it;
Peter the Apostle perceived his walking
And as he went on the water knew him well and said,
       'Bid me come unto thee on the water.'[1]
245   And lo, how the sun locked her light in herself
When she saw him suffer that made sun and sea.
The earth for heavy heart because he would suffer
Quaked like a quick thing, and the rock cracked all to pieces.
Lo, hell might not hold, but opened when God suffered,
250   And let out Simeon's sons[2] to see him hang on Cross.
And now shall Lucifer believe it, loath though he is,
For Jesus like a giant with an engine[3] comes yonder
To break and beat down all that may be against him,
And to have out of hell every one he pleases.
255   And I, Book, will be burnt unless Jesus rises to life
In all the mights of a man and brings his mother joy,
And comforts all his kin, and takes their cares away,
And all the joy of the Jews disjoins and disperses;
And unless they reverence his Rood° and his resurrection   *cross*
260   And believe on a new law be lost body and soul."
      "Let's be silent," said Truth, "I hear and see both
A spirit speaks to hell and bids the portals be opened."
            Lift up your gates.[4]

---

8. Fine fellow; Book's two broad eyes suggest the Old and New Testaments.
9. Hairy star (i.e., comet).
1. Matthew 14.28.
2. According to the apocryphal Gospel of Nicodemus, Simeon's sons were raised from the dead at the time of Christ's crucifixion.
3. A military device, perhaps like a giant slingshot.
4. The first words from Psalms 23.9, which reads in the Latin Bible, "Lift up your gates, O princes, and be ye lifted up, ye everlasting doors, and the King of Glory shall come in."

A voice loud in that light cried to Lucifer,
"Princes of this place, unpin and unlock,
265 For he comes here with crown who is King of Glory."
Then Satan[5] sighed and said to hell,
"Without our leave such a light fetched Lazarus away:[6]
Care and calamity have come upon us all.
If this King comes in he will carry off mankind
270 And lead it to where Lazarus is, and with small labor bind me.
Patriarchs and prophets have long prated of this,
That such a lord and a light should lead them all hence."
"Listen," said Lucifer, "for this lord is one I know;
Both this lord and this light, it's long ago I knew him.
275 No death may do this lord harm, nor any devil's trickery,
And his way is where he wishes—but let him beware of the perils.
If he bereaves me of my right he robs me by force.
For by right and by reason the race that is here
Body and soul belongs to me, both good and evil.
280 For he himself said it who is Sire of Heaven,
If Adam ate the apple, all should die
And dwell with us devils: the Lord laid down that threat.
And since he who is Truth himself said these words,
And since I've possessed them seven thousand winters,
285 I don't believe law will allow him the least of them."
"That is so," said Satan, "but I'm sore afraid
Because you took them by trickery and trespassed in his garden,
And in the semblance of a serpent sat upon the apple tree
And egged them to eat, Eve by herself,
290 And told her a tale with treasonous words;
And so you had them out, and hither at the last."
"It's an ill-gotten gain where guile is at the root,
For God will not be beguiled," said Goblin, "nor tricked.
We have no true title to them, for it was by treason they were damned."
295 "Certainly I fear," said the Fiend, "lest Truth fetch them out.
These thirty winters, as I think, he's gone here and there and preached.
I've assailed him with sin, and sometimes asked
Whether he was God or God's son: he gave me short answer.
And thus he's traveled about like a true man these two and thirty winters.
300 And when I saw it was so, while she slept I went
to warn Pilate's wife what sort of man was Jesus,
For some hated him and have put him to death.
I would have lengthened his life, for I believed if he died
That his soul would suffer no sin in his sight.
305 For the body, while it walked on its bones, was busy always
To save men from sin if they themselves wished.
And now I see where a soul comes descending hitherward
With glory and with great light; God it is, I'm sure.
My advice is we all flee," said the Fiend, "fast away from here.
310 For we had better not be at all than abide in his sight.
For your lies, Lucifer, we've lost all our prey.

---

5. Satan pictures hell as populated by a number of devils: 6. Compare with John 11.
Satan, Lucifer, Goblin, Belial, and Astoreth.

Through you we fell first from Heaven so high:
Because we believed your lies we all leapt out.
And now for your latest lie we have lost Adam,
315   And all our lordship, I believe, on land and in hell."
        Now shall the prince of this world be cast out.[7]
    Again the light bade them unlock, and Lucifer answered,
        "Who is that?"[8]
What lord are you?" said Lucifer. The light at once replied,
        "The King of Glory.
The Lord of might and of main and all manner of powers:
        The Lord of Powers.
Dukes of this dim place, at once undo these gates
320   That Christ may come in, the Heaven-King's son."
And with that breath hell broke along with Belial's bars;
For any warrior or watchman the gates wide opened.
Patriarchs and prophets, *populus in tenebris,*[9]
Sang Saint John's song, *Ecce agnus Dei.*[1]
325   Lucifer could not look, the light so blinded him.
And those that the Lord loved his light caught away,
And he said to Satan, "Lo, here's my soul in payment
For all sinful souls, to save those that are worthy.
Mine they are and of me—I may the better claim them.
330   Although Reason records, and right of myself,
That if they ate the apple all should die,
I did not hold out to them hell here forever.
For the deed that they did, your deceit caused it;
You got them with guile against all reason.
335   For in my palace Paradise, in the person of an adder,
You stole by stealth something I loved.
Thus like a lizard with a lady's face
Falsely you filched from me; the Old Law confirms
That guilers be beguiled, and that is good logic:
        A tooth for a tooth and an eye for an eye.[2]
340   *Ergo*[3] soul shall requite soul and sin revert to sin,
And all that man has done amiss, I, man, will amend.
Member for member was amends in the Old Law,
And life for life also, and by that law I claim
Adam and all his issue at my will hereafter.
345   And what Death destroyed in them, my death shall restore
And both quicken[4] and requite what was quenched through sin.
And that grace destroy guile is what good faith requires.
So don't believe it, Lucifer, against the law I fetch them,
But by right and by reason here ransom my liegemen.
        I have not come to destroy the law but to fulfill it.[5]
350   You fetched mine in my place unmindful of all reason
Falsely and feloniously; good faith taught me

---

7. John 12.31; "prince of this world" is a title of the devil.
8. This phrase and the next two translated from Latin come from Psalms 23.8.
9. People in darkness (Matthew 4.16, citing Isaiah 9.2).
1. Behold the Lamb of God (John 1.36).

2. Matthew 5.38, citing Exodus 21.14.
3. "Therefore," a central term in scholastic argument, used to introduce the logical conclusion to an argument.
4. Bring to life.
5. Matthew 5.17.

To recover them by reason and rely on nothing else.
So what you got with guile through grace is won back.
You, Lucifer, in likeness of a loathsome adder
355   Got by guile those whom God loved;
And I, in likeness of a mortal man, who am master of Heaven,
Have graciously requited your guile: let guile go against guile!
And as Adam and all died through a tree
Adam and all through a tree return to life,
360   And guile is beguiled and grief has come to his guile:
         And he is fallen into the ditch which he made.[6]
And now your guile begins to turn against you,
And my grace to grow ever greater and wider.
The bitterness that you have brewed, imbibe it yourself
365   Who are doctor of death, the drink you made.
     "For I who am Lord of Life, love is my drink
And for that drink today I died upon earth.
I struggled so I'm thirsty still for man's soul's sake.
No drink may moisten me or slake my thirst
370   Till vintage time befall in the Vale of Jehoshaphat,[7]
When I shall drink really ripe wine, *Resurrectio mortuorum.*[8]
And then I shall come as a king crowned with angels
And have out of hell all men's souls.
Fiends and fiendkins shall stand before me
And be at my bidding, where best it pleases me.
375   But to be merciful to man then, my nature requires it.
For we are brothers of one blood, but not in baptism all.
And all that are both in blood and in baptism my whole brothers
Shall not be damned to the death that endures without end.
         Against thee only have I sinned, etc.[9]
It is not the custom on earth to hang a felon
380   Oftener than once, even though he were a traitor.
And if the king of the kingdom comes at that time
When a felon should suffer death or other such punishment,
Law would he give him life if he looks upon him.
And I who am King of Kings shall come in such a time
385   Where doom to death damns all wicked,
And if law wills I look on them, it lies in my grace
Whether they die or do not die because they did evil.
And if it be any bit paid for, the boldness of their sins,
I may grant mercy through my righteousness and all my true words;
390   And though Holy Writ wills that I wreak vengeance on those that
         wrought evil,
         No evil unpunished, etc.[1]
They shall be cleansed and made clear and cured of their sins
In my prison purgatory till *Parce!*° says 'Stop!'   *spare*
And my mercy shall be shown to many of my half-brothers,

---

6. Psalms 7.16.
7. On the evidence of Joel 3.2, 12, the Last Judgment was to take place at the Vale of Jehosaphat.
8. The Resurrection of the dead (from the Nicene Creed).

9. Psalms 50.6.
1. [He is a just judge who leaves] no evil unpunished [and no good unrewarded] (from Pope Innocent III's tract *Of Contempt for the World;* see 4.143–44).

For blood-kin may see blood-kin both hungry and cold,

395   But blood-kin may not see blood-kin bleed without his pity:

I heard unspeakable words which it is not lawful for a man to utter.[2]

But my righteousness and right shall rule all hell

And mercy rule all mankind before me in Heaven.

For I'd be an unkind king unless I gave my kin help,

And particularly at such a time when help was truly needed.

Enter not into judgment with thy servant.[3]

400   Thus by law," said our Lord, "I will lead from here

Those I looked on with love who believed in my coming;

And for your lie, Lucifer, that you lied to Eve,

You shall buy it back in bitterness"—and bound him with chains.

Ashtoreth and all the gang hid themselves in corners;

405   They dared not look at our Lord, the least of them all,

But let him lead away what he liked and leave what he wished.

Many hundreds of angels harped and sang,

Flesh sins, flesh redeems, flesh reigns as God of God.[4]

Then Peace piped a note of poetry:

As a rule the sun is brighter after the biggest cloud; After hostilities
love is brighter.[5]

"After sharp showers," said Peace, "the sun shines brightest;

410   No weather is warmer than after watery clouds;

Nor any love lovelier, or more loving friends,

Than after war and woe when Love and peace are masters.

There was never war in this world nor wickedness so sharp

That Love, if he liked, might not make a laughing matter.

415   And peace through patience puts an end to all perils."

"Truce!" said Truth, "you tell the truth, by Jesus!

Let's kiss in covenant and each of us clasp other."

"And let no people," said Peace, "perceive that we argued;

For nothing is impossible to him that is almighty."

420   "You speak the truth," said Righteousness, and reverently kissed her,

Peace, and Peace her, *per saecula saeculorum:*[6]

Mercy and Truth have met together; Righteousness and Peace
have kissed each other.[7]

Truth sounded a trumpet then and sang *Te Deum Laudamus,*[8]

And then Love strummed a lute with a loud note:

Behold how good and how pleasant, etc.[9]

Till the day dawned these damsels caroled.

425   When bells rang for the Resurrection, and right then I awoke

And called Kit my wife and Calote my daughter:

"Arise and go reverence God's resurrection,

And creep to the Cross on knees, and kiss it as a jewel,

For God's blessed body it bore for our good,

And it frightens the Fiend, for such is its power

430   That no grisly ghost may glide in its shadow."

---

2. In 2 Corinthians 12.4, Saint Paul tells of how in a mystical vision he was caught up to heaven, where he saw things that cannot be repeated.
3. Psalms 142.2.
4. From a medieval Latin hymn.

5. From Alain de Lille, a 12th-century poet and philosopher.
6. Forever and ever (the liturgical formula).
7. Psalms 84.11.
8. We praise thee, God (a celebrated Latin hymn).
9. Psalms 132.1.

PIERS PLOWMAN IN CONTEXT
The Rising of 1381

The event previously known as the "Peasants' Revolt" is generally referred to by today's historians as the "Rising of 1381," since it is now recognized that it included many members of the commons who were not peasants but rather middle-class landholders, artisans, and so forth. William Langland had a rather ambiguous relation to the rising, for while deploring the conditions that caused it, he refused to endorse its radical social program. When the rebels invoked his character Piers as a cultural hero, he revised *Piers Plowman* for a second time (the so-called C-text), thus disassociating himself from them. This section brings together a number of documents that record the events of the rising, and more importantly, reveal the subjective responses of contemporary writers to it.

The causes of the rising were varied. Among them was the "Statute of Laborers" enacted by Parliament in 1351 to freeze wages and restrict laborers' mobility, both of which had been increasing as a result of the depopulation caused by the Black Death. The more immediate catalyst, however, was a flat poll tax enacted in 1380, which hurt the poor disproportionately and which the government collected in a particularly ruthless way.

The rising itself was astonishingly brief, beginning at the end of May 1381 and collapsing by the end of July. From the prosperous southern counties of Essex and Kent the rebels marched to London, swearing loyalty to one another and to Richard II. Their hostility was directed against the church hierarchy and the feudal lords rather than against the monarchy. In London they burned the Savoy Palace, the local residence of the powerful John of Gaunt, Duke of Lancaster and uncle of King Richard. The king, then only fourteen years old, found his advisers ineffectual, and so retreated with them to the Tower of London.

Having agreed to meet the Essex contingent outside the city, at Mile End, the king acceded to their demands of an end to villeinage (serfdom), and ordered his office of chancery to make multiple copies of charters to that effect. During this meeting, some rebels broke into the Tower of London and beheaded two of the most hated men in the kingdom, Simon Sudbury (the king's chancellor and Archbishop of Canterbury) and Robert Hales (his treasurer). Afterward, they displayed their heads on London Bridge, as a sign that they were traitors to the commons.

The next day the king met with the Kentish rebels, again outside the city, at Smithfield. Here their captain Wat Tyler demanded not only the abolition of villeinage but fixed rents, partial disendowment of the church and dispersal of its goods to the poor, and punishment of all "traitors" held to be responsible for the poll tax. In the course of a scuffle, the Lord Mayor of London, William Walworth, stabbed Tyler and mortally wounded him; thereupon, the king rode before the rebels and declared himself their new captain, successfully leading them off the field.

Tyler's death broke the will of the rebels, and the king promptly revoked the charters freeing the serfs. In a series of trials, he prosecuted the instigators, among them John Ball, the priest who had shortly before preached to the rebels at Blackheath the famous sermon challenging the division of society into three estates: "Whan Adam dalf and Eve span, / who was thanne a gentilman?" Ball was found guilty of treason, and drawn, hanged, and quartered. Aside from such punishments, there were few apparent effects of the rising, although the nobles and the clergy relented in their treatment of the commons, and in the long run, the institution of villeinage declined. For the ruling class itself, the rising caused intense anxiety. John Gower, in his allegorized account, *The Voice of One Crying*, reports hiding in the woods to escape the peasants. Like him, the monastic chroniclers like Thomas of Walsingham generally present the rebels as mad beasts.

What is perhaps most significant about the written reception of the rising is the languages—Latin, French, and English—in which it occurs. Like Gower's *Voice of One Crying,* the chronicles are generally written in Latin, although the *Anonimalle Chronicle,* from which a passage is included here, is in French. Langland and Chaucer wrote in English, while the short poem below, *The Course of the Revolt,* is macaronic, alternating English lines with Latin ones. Although there is little written evidence in the voice of the rebels themselves (who were generally illiterate), there are two tantalizing scraps identified as John Ball's letters, written in English although embedded in hostile Latin chronicle accounts of Ball's trial and execution. It has been suggested recently that the most important fact about the rebel speeches and writings is their "vernacularity"—the fact that they appear in a language that the common people could understand.

from *The Anonimalle Chronicle*[1]
[Wat Tyler's Demands to Richard II, and His Death]

At this time a great body of the commons[2] went to the Tower of London to speak with the king. As they could not get a hearing from him, they laid siege to the Tower from the side of Saint Katherine's, towards the south. Another group of the commons, who were within the city, went to the Hospital of Saint John, Clerkenwell, and on their way they burned the place and houses of Roger Legett, questmonger,[3] who had been beheaded in Cheapside, as well as all the rented property and tenements of the Hospital of Saint John they could find. Afterwards they came to the beautiful priory of the said hospital, and set on fire several fine and pleasant buildings within it—a great and horrible piece of damage to the priory for all time to come. They then returned to London to rest or to do more mischief.

At this time the king was in a turret of the great Tower of London, and saw the manor of the Savoy[4] and the Hospital of Clerkenwell, and the houses of Simon Hosteler near Newgate, and John Butterwick's place, all in flames. He called all the lords about him into a chamber, and asked their counsel as to what should be done in such a crisis. But none of them could or would give him any counsel; and so the young king said that he would order the mayor of the city to command the sheriffs and aldermen to have it cried within their wards that everyone between the age of fifteen and sixty, on pain of life and limb, should go next morning (which was Friday) to Mile End, and meet him there at seven of the bell. He did this in order that all the commons who were stationed around the Tower would be persuaded to abandon the siege, and come to Mile End to see him and hear him, so that those who were in the Tower could leave safely at their will and save themselves as they wished. But it came to nothing, for some of them did not have the good fortune to be saved.

Later that Thursday, the said feast of Corpus Christi, the king, remaining anxiously and sadly in the Tower, climbed on to a little turret facing Saint Katherine's, where a large number of the commons were lying. He had it proclaimed to them that they should all go peaceably to their homes, and he would pardon them all their different offenses. But all cried with one voice that they would not go before they had captured the traitors within the Tower, and obtained charters to free them from all manner of serfdom, and certain other points which they wished to demand. The king

---

1. This gripping account describes the rebel Wat (Walter) Tyler's confrontation with the king. Written in French rather than Latin, *The Anonimalle Chronicle* is considered to be more contemporary and more balanced than judgmental Latin accounts like that of Thomas of Walsingham. Translated by R. B. Dobson.

2. The common people as opposed to the nobility or the clergy; the third estate.
3. One who made a business of conducting inquests.
4. The beautiful palace of John of Gaunt, the king's powerful uncle.

benevolently granted their requests and made a clerk write a bill in their presence in these terms: "Richard, king of England and France, gives great thanks to his good commons, for that they have so great a desire to see and maintain their king; and he grants them pardon for all manner of trespasses and misprisions and felonies done up to this hour, and wills and commands that every one should now quickly return to his own home: He wills and commands that everyone should put his grievances in writing, and have them sent to him; and he will provide, with the aid of his loyal lords and his good council, such remedy as shall be profitable both to him and to them, and to the kingdom." He put his signet seal to this document in their presence and then sent the said bill by the hands of two of his knights to the people around Saint Katherine's. And he caused it to be read to them, the man who read it standing up on an old chair above the others so that all could hear. All this time the king remained in the Tower in great distress of mind. And when the commons had heard the bill, they said that it was nothing but a trifle and mockery. Therefore they returned to London and had it cried around the city that all lawyers, all the men of the Chancery and the Exchequer and everyone who could write a writ or a letter should be beheaded,[5] wherever they could be found. At this time they burnt several more houses within the city. The king himself ascended to a high garret of the Tower to watch the fires; then he came down again, and sent for the lords to have their counsel. But they did not know how to advise him, and were surprisingly abashed.

On the next day, Friday, the commons of the country and the commons of London assembled in fearful strength, to the number of a hundred thousand or more, besides some four score who remained on Tower Hill to watch those who were within the Tower. Some went to Mile End, on the way to Brentwood, to wait for the king's arrival, because of the proclamation that he had made. But others came to Tower Hill, and when the king knew that they were there, he sent them orders by a messenger to join their companions at Mile End, saying that he would come to them very soon. And at this time of the morning he advised the archbishop of Canterbury and the others who were in the Tower, to go down to the little water-gate, and take a boat and save themselves. And the archbishop proceeded to do this; but a wicked woman raised a cry against him, and he had to turn back to the Tower, to his own confusion.

And by seven of the bell the king himself came to Mile End, and with him his mother in a carriage, and also the earls of Buckingham, Kent, Warwick and Oxford, as well as Sir Thomas Percy, Sir Robert Knolles, the mayor of London and many knights and squires; and Sir Aubrey de Vere carried the royal sword. And when the king arrived and the commons saw him, they knelt down to him, saying "Welcome our Lord King Richard, if it pleases you, and we will not have any other king but you." And Wat Teghler, their master and leader, prayed on behalf of the commons that the king would suffer them to take and deal with all the traitors against him and the law. The king granted that they should freely seize all who were traitors and could be proved to be such by process of law. The said Walter and the commons were carrying two banners as well as pennons and pennoncels[6] while they made their petition to the king. And they required that henceforward no man should be a serf nor make homage or any type of service to any lord, but should give four pence for an

---

5. Chancery held the archives of public, record and the Exchequer dealt with the collection of revenue. The Latin chroniclers saw the rising as a threat to writing itself; Thomas of Walsingham, for example, reports that the rebels gleefully burned records they saw as guaranteeing the lords' legal power over them.
6. Small flags and streamers borne on a lance.

acre of land. They asked also that no one should serve any man except at his own will and by means of regular covenant. And at this time the king had the commons arrayed in two lines, and had it proclaimed before them that he would confirm and grant that they should be free, and generally should have their will; and that they could go through all the realm of England and catch all traitors and bring them to him in safety, and then he would deal with them as the law demanded.

Because of this grant Wat Tyghler and the commons took their way to the Tower, to seize the archbishop and the others while the king remained at Mile End. Meanwhile the archbishop had sung his mass devoutly in the Tower, and confessed the prior of the Hospital of Clerkenwell and others; and then he heard two or three masses and chanted the *Commendatio*, and the *Placebo* and *Dirige*, and the Seven Psalms, and the Litany; and when he was at the words "*Omnes sancti orate pro nobis*" [All saints pray for us], the commons entered and dragged him out of the chapel of the Tower, and struck and hustled him roughly, as they did also the others who were with him, and led them to Tower Hill. There they cut off the heads of Master Simon of Sudbury, archbishop of Canterbury, of Sir Robert Hales,[7] High Prior of the Hospital of Saint John's of Clerkenwell, Treasurer of England, of Brother William of Appleton, a great physician and surgeon, and one who had much influence with the king and the duke of Lancaster. And some time after they beheaded John Legge, the king's serjeant-at-arms, and with him a certain juror. At the same time the commons had it proclaimed that whoever could catch any Fleming[8] or other aliens of any nation, might cut off their heads; and so they did accordingly. Then they took the heads of the archbishop and of the others and put them on wooden poles, and carried them before them in procession through all the city as far as the shrine of Westminster Abbey, to the contempt of themselves, of God and of Holy Church: for which reason vengeance descended on them shortly afterwards. Then they returned to London Bridge and set the head of the archbishop above the gate, with the heads of eight others they had executed, so that all who passed over the bridge could see them. This done, they went to the church of Saint Martin's in the Vintry, and found therein thirty-five Flemings, whom they dragged outside and beheaded in the street. On that day there were beheaded 140 or 160 persons. Then they took their way to the places of Lombards and other aliens, and broke into their houses, and robbed them of all their goods that they could discover. So it went on for all that day and the night following with hideous cries and horrible tumult.

At this time, because the Chancellor had been beheaded, the king made the earl of Arundel Chancellor for the day, and entrusted him with the Great Seal; and all that day he caused various clerks to write out charters, patents, and letters of protection, granted to the commons in consequence of the matters before mentioned, without taking any fines for the sealing or transcription.

On the next day, Saturday, great numbers of the commons came into Westminster Abbey at the hour of Tierce,[9] and there they found John Imworth, Marshal of the Marshalsea and warden of the prisoners, a tormentor without pity; he was near the shrine of Saint Edward, embracing a marble pillar, hoping for aid and succor from the saint to preserve him from his enemies. But the commons wrenched his arms away from the pillar of the shrine, and dragged him into Cheap, and there beheaded

---

7. Sudbury and Hales were especially hated by the rebels—the former, as chancellor of England, for instituting the poll tax, and the latter, as treasurer, for collecting it.
8. Immigrants from Flanders, who had become wealthy in

the London wool trade; they were particular targets of the rebels (see Chaucer, *The Nun's Priest's Tale*, line 576).
9. The third of seven canonical "hours" around which clerics organized their day; usually, the third hour after sunrise.

him. And at the same time they took from Bread Street a valet named John of Greenfield, merely because he had spoken well of Brother William Appleton and the other murdered persons; and they brought him into Cheap and beheaded him. All this time the king was having it cried through the city that every one should go peaceably to his own country and his own house, without doing more mischief; but to this the commons would not agree.

And on this same day, at three hours after noon, the king came to Westminster Abbey and about two hundred persons with him. The abbot and convent of the said abbey, and the canons and vicars of Saint Stephen's Chapel, came to meet him in procession, clothed in their copes and their feet bare, halfway to Charing Cross; and they brought him to the abbey, and then to the high altar of the church. The king made his prayers devoutly, and left an offering for the altar and the relics. Afterwards he spoke with the anchorite,[1] and confessed to him, and remained with him some time. Then the king caused a proclamation to be made that all the commons of the country who were still within the city should come to Smithfield[2] to meet him there; and so they did.

And when the king with his retinue arrived there, he turned to the east, in a place before Saint Bartholomew's a house of canons: and the commons arrayed themselves in bands of great size on the west side. At this moment the mayor of London, William of Walworth, came up, and the king ordered him to approach the commons, and make their chieftain come to him. And when he was called by the mayor, this chieftain, Wat Tyghler of Maidstone by name, approached the king with great confidence, mounted on a little horse so that the commons might see him. And he dismounted, holding in his hand a dagger which he had taken from another man; and when he had dismounted he half bent his knee and took the king by the hand, shaking his arm forcefully and roughly, saying to him, "Brother, be of good comfort and joyful, for you shall have, in the fortnight that is to come, forty thousand more commons than you have at present, and we shall be good companions." And the king said to Walter, "Why will you not go back to your own country?" But the other answered, with a great oath, that neither he nor his fellows would leave until they had got their charter as they wished to have it with the inclusion of certain points which they wished to demand. Tyghler threatened that the lords of the realm would rue it bitterly if these points were not settled at the commons' will. Then the king asked him what were the points which he wished to have considered, and he should have them freely and without contradiction, written out and sealed. Thereupon the said Wat rehearsed the points which were to be demanded; and he asked that there should be no law except for the law of Winchester[3] and that henceforward there should be no outlawry[4] in any process of law, and that no lord should have lordship in future, but it should be divided among all men, except for the king's own lordship. He also asked that the goods of Holy Church should not remain in the hands of the religious, nor of parsons and vicars, and other churchmen; but that clergy already in possession should have a sufficient sustenance and the rest of their goods should be divided among the people of the parish. And he demanded that there should be only one bishop in England and only one prelate, and all the lands and tenements of the possessioners should be taken from them and divided among the commons, only reserving for them a reasonable sustenance. And he demanded that there should be no more villeins[5] in

---

1. A religious recluse who lived enclosed in a tiny dwelling.
2. An area outside the walls of the city of London.
3. The reference is unclear; it may refer to a claim by the

rebels to the rights of tenants on royal lands.
4. Condition of being outside traditional legal protection.
5. Serfs tied to the land; bondmen.

England, and no serfdom nor villeinage but that all men should be free and of one condition. To this the king gave an easy answer, and said that Wat should have all that he could fairly grant, reserving only for himself the regality of his crown. And then he ordered him to go back to his own home, without causing further delay.

During all the time that the king was speaking, no lord or counselor dared or wished to give answer to the commons in any place except for the king himself. Presently Wat Tyghler, in the presence of the king, sent for a jug of water to rinse his mouth, because of the great heat that he felt; and as soon as the water was brought he rinsed out his mouth in a very rude and villainous manner before the king. And then he made them bring him a jug of ale, and drank a great draught, and then, in the presence of the king, climbed on his horse again. At that time a certain valet from Kent, who was among the king's retinue, asked to see the said Wat, chieftain of the commons. And when he saw him, he said aloud that he was the greatest thief and robber in all Kent. Wat heard these words, and commanded the valet to come out to him, shaking his head at him as a sign of malice; but Wat himself refused to go to him for fear that he had of the others there. But at last the lords made the valet go out to Wat, to see what the latter would do before the king. And when Wat saw him he ordered one of his followers, who was mounted on horseback and carrying a banner displayed, to dismount and behead the said valet. But the valet answered that he had done nothing worthy of death, for what he had said was true, and he would not deny it, although he could not lawfully debate the issue in the presence of his liege lord, without leave, except in his own defense: but that he could do without reproof, for whoever struck him would be struck in return. For these words Wat wanted to strike the valet with his dagger, and would have slain him in the king's presence; but because he tried to do so, the mayor of London, William of Walworth, reasoned with the said Wat for his violent behavior and contempt, done in the king's presence, and arrested him. And because he arrested him, the said Wat stabbed the mayor with his dagger in the body in great anger. But, as it pleased God, the mayor was wearing armor and took no harm, but like a hardy and vigorous man drew his dagger and struck back at the said Wat, giving him a deep cut in the neck, and then a great blow on the head. And during this scuffle a valet of the king's household drew his sword, and ran Wat two or three times through the body, mortally wounding him. Wat spurred his horse, crying to the commons to avenge him, and the horse carried him some four score paces, and then he fell to the ground half dead. And when the commons saw him fall, and did not know for certain how it happened, they began to bend their bows and to shoot. Therefore the king himself spurred his horse, and rode out to them, commanding them that they should all come to him at the field of Saint John of Clerkenwell.

Meanwhile the mayor of London rode as hastily as he could back to the city, and commanded those who were in charge of the twenty-four wards to have it cried round their wards, that every man should arm himself as quickly as he could, and come to the king's aid in Saint John's Fields, where the commons were, for he was in great trouble and necessity. But at this time almost all of the knights and squires of the king's household, and many others, were so frightened of the affray that they left their liege lord and went each his own way.

Afterwards, when the king had reached the open fields, he made the commons array themselves on the west side. And presently the aldermen came to him in a body, bringing with them the keepers of the wards arrayed in several bands, a fine company of well-armed men in great strength. And they enveloped the commons like sheep within a pen. Meanwhile, after the mayor had sent the keepers of the town on their way to the king, he returned with a good company of lances to Smithfield in order to make an end of the captain of the commons. And when he came to Smithfield he failed to find there the said captain Wat Tyghler, at which he marveled much, and asked what had become of the traitor. And he was told that Wat had been carried by a group of the commons to the hospital for the poor near Saint Bartholomew's, and put to bed in the chamber of the master of the hospital. The mayor went there and found him, and had him carried out to the middle of Smithfield, in the presence of his companions, and had him beheaded. And so ended his wretched life. But the mayor had his head set on a pole and carried before him to the king, who still remained in the field. And when the king saw the head he had it brought near him to subdue the commons, and thanked the mayor greatly for what he had done. And when the commons saw that their chieftain, Wat Tyghler, was dead in such a manner, they fell to the ground there among the corn, like beaten men, imploring the king for mercy for their misdeeds. And the king benevolently granted them mercy, and most of them took to flight.

Three Poems on the Rising of 1381
John Ball's First Letter[1]

John Ball Saint Mary Priest, greeteth well all manner of men, and biddeth them in name of the Trinitie, Father, Sonne, & holy Ghost, stand manlike together in truth, & helpe truth, and truth shall helpe you:

> now raygneth pride in price,
> couetise° is holden° wise   *greed/held*
> lechery without shame,
> gluttonie without blame,
> enuye raygneth° with reason,   *reigns*
> and sloath is taken in great season,
> God doe boote° for nowe is time.   Amen.   *make amends*

John Ball's Second Letter[2]

LITTERA IOHANNIS BALLE MISSA COMMUNIBUS ESTSEXIE
[THE LETTER OF JOHN BALL TO THE ESSEX COMMONS]

Iohan schep, som-tyme seynte marie prest of york, and now of colchestre, Greteth wel Iohan nameles & Iohn the mullere and Iohon cartere, and biddeth hem thei bee

1. This and the piece following can only provisionally be called "poems," despite their rhymed couplets and sporadic alliteration. The court that tried and convicted Ball regarded them as actual directions to his followers, and modern scholarship has tended to concur. If so they are directions in code, for they are, in the words of one chronicler, "full of enigmas." In this poem the complaint about the Seven Deadly Sins running rampant is conventional, but the conclusion, "God do bote for neow is time" (God make amends, for now is the time) is highly unusual in its call to action. Significantly, the sin of anger is absent from the list.

2. According to the chronicle from which this "letter" was taken, Ball sent it to "the leaders of the commons in Essex . . . in order to urge them to finish what they had begun," and it was "afterwards found in the sleeve of a man about to be hanged for disturbing the peace." It appears in Thomas Walsingham's Latin *Historia Anglicana*, where it is included as evidence of the treason for which Ball was hanged. In the prose introduction to the poem, John the "shep," priest of Colchester, is the assumed name of John Ball (as "pastor"), while John Carter and John the Miller are both generic occupational names often ascribed to the leaders of the rebels. The reference to "Pers Ploughman" in the poem's introduction indicates that the rebels interpreted Langland's conservative poem for their own purposes. It presents Piers not as Langland's patient laborer, but as one who should get to his "work" of punishing "robbers," perhaps "Hobbe" (Robert) Hales, the treasurer of the king, beheaded by the rebels for his role in collecting the poll tax.

war of gyle [treachery] in borugh, and stondeth to-gidere in godes name, and biddeth
Pers ploughman / go to his werk and chastise wel hobbe the robbere; and taketh with
yow Iohan Trewman and alle hijs felawes and no mo, and loke schappe you to on
heued[3] and no mo.

> Iohan the mullere hath y-grounde smal, smal, smal.
> The kynges sone of heuene schal paye for al.
> be war or the be wo.°   *beware or be sorry*
> knoweth your freend fro your foo.
> haueth y-now & seith hoo!
> and do wel and bettre and fleth° synne,   *flee*
> and seketh pees and hold yow ther-inne.
> and so biddeth Iohan trewaman and alle his felawes.

*Hanc litteram Idem Iohannes balle confessus est scripsisse, et communibus transmisisse,
et plura alia fatebatur et fecit; propter-que, ut diximus, traitus, suspensus, et decollatus
apud sanctum albanum Idibus Iulij, presente rege, et cadauer eius quadripertitum
quatuor regni cuntatibus missum est.* [John Ball confessed that he wrote this letter
and sent it to the commons, and said and did many other things. For which reason, as we have said, he was drawn, hanged, and beheaded before the king at Saint
Albans, on the ides of July; and his body was quartered and sent to four cities in
the kingdom.]

The Course of Revolt[4]

	The taxe hath tened° vs alle,	*harmed*
	probat hoc mors tot validorum;°	*this death tests so many of the strong[?]*
	The Kyng therof had small,	
	ffuit in manibus cupidorum.°[5]	*it was in the hands of the greedy ones*
5	yt had ful hard hansell,°	*bad omen*
	dans causam fine dolorum;°	*giving cause to an end of sorrows*
	vengeaunce nedes most° fall,	*must*
	propter peccata malorum.°	*on account of the sins of the wicked*
	In Kent care° be-gan,[6]	*troubles*
10	*mox infestando potentes;*°	*soon attacking the rulers*
	On rowtes° tho Rebawdes° they ran,	*crowds / rascals*
	Sua turpida arma ferentes.°	*bearing their shameful weapons*
	ffoles° they dred no man,	*fools*
	Regni Regem, neque gentes;°	*neither king of the realm, nor the people*

3. Take one head for yourself; possibly a reference to the rebels' loyalty to Richard II as opposed to the nobles.

4. Unlike the two preceding letters, there is no doubt that this piece is a poem: it is written in six- or eight-line stanzas of English alternating with Latin, with a rhyme scheme ababab (ab). The masculine rhymes of the English (alle, small, etc.) contrast with the feminine rhymes

of the Latin (validorum, cupidorum, etc.) to give it a lilt-ing quality. The poem laments the violence of the rising, although it opens with a recognition of the rebels' griev-ances: the poll tax of 1377, 1379, and 1380–1381 "hath tened [harmed] vs alle."

5. Much of the tax revenue was diverted to collectors rather than returned to the king.

6. The rising actually began in Essex and spread to Kent.

15 laddes° they were there Cheveteyns,°	*churls/captains*
Sine iure fere superantes.°	*lawlessly rising above their station*
laddes° lowde they lowght,°	*churls/laughed*
Clamantes voce sonora,°	*shouting in a loud voice*
The bischop[7] wan they slowght,°	*slew*
20 Et corpora plura decora.°	*and many handsome people*
Maners down they drowght,°	*they threw down manor houses*
In regno non meliora;°	*there were none better in the kingdom*
Harmes they dyde y-nowght;°	*enough*
habuerunt libera lora.°	*they had free rein*
25 Iak strawe[8] made yt stowte°	*swaggered*
Cum profusa comitiua,°	*with a captain's munificence*
And seyd al schuld hem lowte,°	*bow down to them*
Anglorum corpora viua.°	*the living community of Englishmen*
Sadly° can they schowte,°	*vigorously/shouted*
30 pulsant pietatis oliua,°	*they beat the olive branch of pity*
The wycche were wont to lowte,°	*those who used to skulk*
aratrum traducere stiua.°	*disgrace the plough and plough handle*
Hales,[9] that dowghty° knyght,	*brave*
quo splenduit Anglia tota,°	*in whom all England shone*
35 dolefully° he was dyght,°	*pitiably/cut down*
Cum stultis pace remota.°	*when removed from peace by fools*
There he myght not fyght,	
nec Christo soluere vota.°	*nor say his prayers to Christ*
Savoy[1] semely set°	*beautifully built*
40 heu! funditus igne cadebat.°	*alas, it was given over to the fire*
Arcan don there they bett,[2]	
Et eos virtute premebat.°	*and threatened them with force*
deth was ther dewe dett,	
qui captum quisque ferebat.°	*whoever carried off stolen goods*
45 Oure kyng myght have no rest,	
Alii latuere cauerna;°	*others hid in caves*
To ride he was ful prest,	
recolendo gesta paterna.°	*remembering his father's deeds*
Iak straw dovn they cast[3]	
50 Smethefeld virtute superna.°	*at Smithfield with superior strength*
god, as thou may best,	
Regem defende, guberna.°	*defend the kingdom and govern it*

---

7. Simon Sudbury, Archbishop of Canterbury.
8. Jack Straw was a fictional character believed to have been a leader of the Rising; see Chaucer, *Nun's Priest's Tale*, lines 574–75.
9. Sir Robert Hales, treasurer of England and therefore closely associated with the collection of the poll tax. He was beheaded at the Tower of London during the rising.

1. John of Gaunt's London residence.
2. A reference to Achan (Joshua 7), who transgressed the law of God by stealing valuables from Jericho. Several chronicles mention the rebels' restraint in not looting the houses of the nobles.
3. It was not (the fictional) Jack Straw, but Wat Tyler who was mortally wounded at Smithfield.

John Gower

from *The Voice of One Crying*[1]

FROM PROLOGUE

In the beginning of this work, the author intends to describe how the lowly peasants violently revolted against the freemen and nobles of the realm. And since an event of this kind was as loathsome and horrible as a monster, he reports that in a dream he saw different throngs of the rabble transformed into different kinds of domestic animals. He says, moreover, that those domestic animals deviated from their true nature and took on the barbarousness of wild beasts. In accordance with the separate divisions of this book, which is divided into seven parts (as will appear more clearly below in its headings), he treats furthermore of the causes for such outrages taking place among men. * * *

[WAT TYLER AS A JACKDAW INCITING THE PEASANTS TO RIOT][2]

> Here he says that in his dream he saw that when all the aforementioned madmen stood herded together, a certain Jackdaw (in English a Jay, which is commonly called Wat) assumed the rank of command over the others. And to tell the truth of the matter, this Wat was their leader.

When this great multitude of monsters like wild beasts stood united, a multitude like the sands of the sea, there appeared a Jackdaw, well instructed in the art of speaking, which no cage could keep at home. While all were looking on, this bird spread his wings and claimed to have top rank, although he was unworthy. Just as the Devil was placed in command over the army of the lower world, so this scoundrel was in charge of the wicked mob. A harsh voice, a fierce expression, a very faithful likeness to a death's head—these things gave token of his appearance. He checked the murmuring and all kept silent so that the sound from his mouth might be better heard. He ascended to the top of a tree, and with the voice from his open mouth he uttered such words as these to his compeers:

"O you low sort of wretches, which the world has subjugated for a long time by its law, look, now the day has come when the peasantry will triumph and will force the freemen to get off their lands. Let all honor come to an end, let justice perish, and let no virtue that once existed endure further in the world. Let the law give over which used to hold us in check with its justice, and from here on let our court rule."

1. Gower grew up in Kent (one of the counties where the Rising of 1381 started), in a well-connected family, and both Richard II and Henry IV were his patrons. He was a friend of Chaucer, who refers to him as "moral Gower." The immorality of contemporary society, particularly the refusal of the three estates to work together, is in fact the unifying theme of Gower's work. Of his three long poems (written in the three languages of the period, English, Anglo-Norman, and Latin), the Middle English *Lover's Confession* (*Confessio amantis*), though primarily a dream vision exploring the frustrations and folly of human divine love, is set a framing complaint about the three estates, and the Anglo-Norman *Mirror of Man* (*Mirour de l'Omme*) is based on such a complaint.

Gower's Latin *Voice of One Crying* (*Vox Clamantis*) laments the failure of the three estates in a more prophet-ic way: the speaker identifies himself with John the Baptist, crying in the wilderness of 14th-century England. Like *Piers Plowman*, the poem takes the form of an allegorical dream vision. Like Langland, Gower revised his work in response to the revolt. He had written Books 2–7 by 1378 as a general complaint about the three estates, though he blamed the peasants in particular. Their refusal to produce food "by the sweat of their brow" as God decreed shows their laziness, and their demand of higher wages shows their wickedness and greed (Bk. 5.9). After the Rising of 1381 occurred, he composed what is now Book 1 to decry the violence, which he saw as led by the devil; in it, he casts the peasants as beasts lacking reason, and their leader, Wat Tyler, as a rabble-rousing jackdaw, or jay (Bk. 1.9). Translated by Eric W. Stockton.
2. From Book 1.

The whole mob was silent and took note of the speaker's words, and they liked every command he delivered from his mouth. The rabble lent a deluded ear to his fickle talk, and it saw none of the future things that would result. For when he had been honored in this way by the people, he quickly grabbed all the land for himself. Indeed, when the people had unadvisedly given themselves into servitude, he called the populace together and gave orders. Just as a billow usually grows calm after a stiff breeze, and just as a wave swells by the blast of a whirlwind, so the Jackdaw stirred up all the others with his outrageous shouting, and he drew the people's minds toward war. The stupid portion of the people did not know what its "court" might be, but he ordered them to adopt the laws of force. He said, "Strike," and one man struck. He said, "Kill," and another killed. He said, "Commit crime"; everyone committed it, and did not oppose his will. Everyone he called to in his madness listened with ears pricked up, and once aroused to his voice, pursued the [prescribed] course. Thus many an unfortunate man, driven by his persuasive raving, stuck his hand into the fire again and again. All proclaimed in a loud voice, "So be it," so that the sound was like the din of the sea. Stunned by the great noise of their voice, I now could scarcely lift my trembling feet. Yet from a distance I observed how they made their mutual arrangements by clasping their hands. For they said this, that the mob from the country would destroy whatever was left of the noble class in the world.

With these words, they all marched together in the same fashion, and the wicked ruler of hell led the way. A black cloud mingled with the furies of hell approached, and every wickedness poured into their hearts rained down. The earth was so thoroughly soaked with the dew of hell that no virtue could flourish from that time forth. But every vice that a worthy man abhors flourished and filled men's hearts from that time on. Then at midday the Devil attacked and his hard-shot arrow flew during that painful day. Satan himself was freed and on hand, together with all the sinful band of servile hell. Behold, the untutored heart's sense of shame was lost, and it no longer feared the terrors of crime or punishment. And so when I saw the leaders of hell ruling the world, the rights of heaven were worth nothing. The more I saw them, the more I judged I ought to be afraid of them, not knowing what sort of end would be bound to come.

[THE LAZINESS AND GREED OF PLOUGHMEN][3]

Now that he has spoken of those of knightly rank who ought
to keep the state unharmed, it is necessary to speak of those
who are under obligation to enter into the labors of agriculture, which are necessary for obtaining food and drink for the
sustenance of the human race.

Now you have heard what knighthood is, and I shall speak in addition of what the guiding principle for other men ought to be. For after knighthood there remains only the peasant rank; the rustics in it cultivate the grains and vineyards. They are the men who seek food for us by the sweat of their heavy toil, as God Himself has decreed. The guiding principle of our first father Adam, which he received from the

3. From Book 5.

mouth of God on high, is rightly theirs. For God said to him, when he fell from the glories of Paradise, "O sinner, the sweat and toil of the world be thine; in them shalt thou eat thy bread."[4] So if God's peasant pays attention to the plowshare as it goes along, and if he thus carries on the work of cultivation with his hand, then the fruit which in due course the fertile field will bear and the grape will stand abundant in their due seasons. Now, however, scarcely a farmer wishes to do such work; instead, he wickedly loafs everywhere.

An evil disposition is widespread among the common people, and I suspect that the servants of the plow are often responsible for it. For they are sluggish, they are scarce, and they are grasping. For the very little they do they demand the highest pay. Now that this practice has come about, see how one peasant insists upon more than two demanded in days gone by. Yet a short time ago one performed more service than three do now, as those maintain who are well acquainted with the facts. For just as the fox seeks his hole and enters it while the woods are echoing on every side of the hole, so does the servant of the plow, contrary to the law of the land, seek to make a fool of the land. They desire the leisures of great men, but they have nothing to feed themselves with, nor will they be servants. God and Nature have ordained that they shall serve, but neither knows how to keep them within bounds. Everyone owning land complains in his turn about these people; each stands in need of them and none has control over them. The peasants of old did not scorn God with impunity or usurp a noble worldly rank. Rather, God imposed servile work upon them, so that the peasantry might subdue its proud feelings; and liberty, which remained secure for freemen, ruled over the serfs and subjected them to its law.

The experience of yesterday makes us better informed as to what perfidy the unruly serf possesses. As the teasel[5] harmfully thins out the standing crops if it is not thinned out itself, so does the unruly peasant weigh heavily upon the well-behaved ones. The peasant strikes at the subservient and soothes the troublesome, yet the principle which the old order of things teaches is not wrong: let the law accordingly cut down the harmful teasels of rabble, lest they uproot the nobler grain with their stinging. Unless it is struck down first, the peasant race strikes against freemen, no matter what nobility or worth they possess. Its actions outwardly show that the peasantry is base, and it esteems the nobles the less because of their very virtues. Just as lopsided ships begin to sink without the right load, so does the wild peasantry, unless it is held in check.

God and our toil confer and bestow everything upon us. Without toil, man's advantages are nothing. The peasant should therefore put his limbs to work, as is proper for him to do. Just as a barren field cultivated by the plowshare fails the granaries and brings home no crop in autumn, so does the worthless churl, the more he is cherished by your love, fail you and bring on your ruin. The serfs perform none of their servile duties voluntarily and have no respect for the law. Whatever the serf's body suffers patiently under compulsion, inwardly his mind ever turns toward utter wickedness. Miracles happen only contrary to nature; only the divinity of nature can go against its own powers. It is not for man's estate that anyone from the class of serfs should try to set things right.

---

4. Genesis 3.19.   5. A bristly plant like a thistle.

Mystical Writings

Throughout the Middle Ages, religious belief was communally expressed in the great public liturgies: the mass and the Divine Office—those prayers, hymns, and readings performed, especially by monastic communities, at the eight liturgical "hours" from dawn until dark. Private devotion, however, also had a continuous place in medieval Christianity. The British Isles enjoyed a particularly rich and ancient tradition of lives led in holy solitude and of texts and collections intended for private devotion by both clergy and laity. Such early works were enriched in the late eleventh century by the influential *Prayers or Meditations* of Anselm, Archbishop of Canterbury.

Anselm's prayers and related works were collected into portable books. Beginning in the thirteenth century, England also produced distinguished, sometimes elaborately decorated psalters—collections of psalms and other prayers—that were often privately owned. Toward the middle of the thirteenth century, an Oxford workshop produced the earliest of the decorated books of hours, a form that was to prove enormously popular across Europe for the rest of the Middle Ages.

Books of Hours typically contained the "Little Hours of the Virgin," an abbreviated version of the Divine Office that allowed for private commemoration of the holy hours, as well as other prayers, extracts from the gospels, and the "seven penitential psalms." Psalters and Books of Hours both featured texts devoted to the Virgin Mary, only one manifestation of a widespread English tradition. Many were explicitly intended for use by women, both lay and clerical, and emphasize female readership in their illustrations, as in the scene of women reading from the Bedford Hours (see page 12). Indeed, psalters and especially Books of Hours played a key role in the growth of lay literacy during the later Middle Ages.

By the fourteenth century, then, England had an ancient tradition of private religious devotion and varied books created especially for that purpose as well as a growing readership, lay and clerical. Two further, related elements added to the growth in that century of works that have been grouped, largely retrospectively, as "mystical." First, across Europe there was a renewed expression of "affective spirituality," the emotionally, even physically empathetic contemplation of the crises of salvation, especially the crucifixion of Christ and the sufferings of the Virgin Mary. This is reflected in the vision of the crucifixion in *Passus* 18 of Langland's *Piers Plowman,* and in many lyrics. Second, widespread dissatisfaction with the established church—or a more diffuse sense of spiritual needs left unfulfilled there—led a growing number of Christians to explore more immediate and often private avenues of religious experience. The quest for a mystical union with Christ or God the Father is a particularly ambitious aspect of such exploration.

This search was often exercised, particularly in the lay community and among religious women, in the recently invigorated vernacular, which (whether French or English) had long had a place along with Latin in Books of Hours. Among these expressions were the "Wycliffite" translations of the Bible into Middle English, as well as texts intended for religious recluses and for people seeking mystical experience even as they remained active in the mundane world.

Some of this religious fervor, of course, could be folded easily into existing structures and habits of the church, such as the very popular activity of pilgrimage as illustrated in Chaucer's *Canterbury Tales.* Yet the rising quest for more-direct religious experience could unnerve a clergy accustomed to mediating, even controlling, lay access to the divine. Given the dense interweaving of royal and ecclesiastical power in the period, too, this tension extended beyond the church, especially when the seekers of renewed religious experience were also people of secular power, as were the "Lollard knights" who were influenced by the ideas of John Wycliffe. Hostility to these movements, from both clerical and lay officials, was exacerbated by the social disorders of the second half of the fourteenth century.

These emergent religious aspirations, as well as some of their accompanying fears and tensions, are expressed in the three fourteenth-century "mystical" works that follow.*

* The editors express their gratitude to Professor Nicholas Watson for assistance with this section.

⊶ ⧆ ⊷

Richard Rolle
ca. 1300–1349

Richard Rolle was born around the turn of the fourteenth century, and perhaps died in one of the plagues that swept over England at midcentury. He studied at Oxford and then spent part of his life as a hermit but also acted as spiritual director for women engaged in solitary contemplation. The energy of his writing reflects an eager, sometimes aggressive personality, warm but capable of lifelong grudges, as he displays against certain women and patrons. Impassioned descriptions of the sensible experience of divinity are interspersed with angry memories of humiliations and betrayals. Rolle never fully leaves the public world from which he seeks exile.

Like others who wrote about mystical experience, Rolle faced the challenge of using the world and worldly language to express and draw his readers toward the ineffable experience of the divine that they sought. He made particularly intensive use of the imagery of bodily sensation and bodily action—warmth, sweetness, and song—to explore experiences of the divine. Rolle could assume his readers' knowledge of the Song of Songs and of an ancient tradition of allegorical interpretation, in which the songs of the two lovers are interpreted as the individual souls' longing for contact with the divine. Further, Rolle draws on the Book of Revelation, with its report of the heavenly New Jerusalem, and the perpetual singing there of an angelic host surrounding the risen and enthroned Christ.

These widely known biblical expressions of desire through the imagery of the body and of song provide both a precedent and a language for Rolle's exploration and preaching of the mortal quest and experience of divinity. Unlike more-rigorous mystics, Rolle presents at least the earlier stages of the mystical ascent as an almost spontaneous, if also conflict-ridden, rising of the soul like a spark toward God. Rolle wrote a number of English lyrics and meditations; the following passages are from his most famous Latin treatise.

from The Fire of Love[1]
Prologue

I cannot tell you how surprised I was the first time I felt my heart begin to warm. It was real warmth too, not imaginary, and it felt as if it were actually on fire. I was astonished at the way the heat surged up, and how this new sensation brought great and unexpected comfort. I had to keep feeling my breast to make sure there was no physical reason for it! But once I realized that it came entirely from within, that this fire of love had no cause, material or sinful, but was the gift of my Maker, I was absolutely delighted, and wanted my love to be even greater. And this longing was all the more urgent because of the delightful effect and the interior sweetness which this spiritual flame fed into my soul. Before the infusion of this comfort I had never thought that we exiles could possibly have known such warmth, so sweet was the devotion it kindled. It set my soul aglow as if a real fire was burning there.

Yet as some may well remind us, there are people on fire with love for Christ, for we can see how utterly they despise the world, and how wholly they are given over to the service of God. If we put our finger near a fire we feel the heat; in much the same way a soul on fire with love feels, I say, a genuine warmth. Sometimes it is more, sometimes less: it depends on our particular capacity.

---

1. Translated by Clifton Wolters.

What mortal man could survive that heat at its peak—as we can know it, even here—if it persisted? He must inevitably wilt before the vastness and sweetness of love so perfervid, and heat so indescribable. Yet at the same time he is bound to long eagerly for just this to happen: to breathe his soul out, with all its superb endowment of mind, in this honeyed flame, and, quit of this world, be held in thrall with those who sing their Maker's praise.

But some things are opposed to charity: carnal, sordid things which beguile a mind at peace. And sometimes in this bitter exile physical need and strong human affection obtrude into this warmth, to disturb and quench this flame (which metaphorically I call "fire," because it burns and enlightens). They cannot take away what is irremovable, of course, because this is something which has taken hold of my heart. Yet because of these things this cheering warmth is for a while absent. It will reappear in time, though until it does I am going to be spiritually frozen, and because I am missing what I have become accustomed to, will feel myself bereft. It is then that I want to recapture that awareness of inner fire which my whole being, physical as well as spiritual, so much approves; with it it knows itself to be secure.

Nowadays I find that even sleep ranges itself against me! The only spare time I have is that which I am obliged to give to slumber. When I am awake I can try to warm my soul up, though it is numb with cold. For I know how to kindle it when the soul is settled in devotion and how to raise it above earthly things with overwhelming desire. But this eternal and overflowing love does not come when I am relaxing, nor do I feel this spiritual ardor when I am tired out after, say, traveling; nor is it when I am absorbed with worldly interests, or engrossed in never-ending arguments. At times like these I catch myself growing cold: cold until once again I put away all things external, and make a real effort to stand in my Savior's presence: only then do I abide in this inner warmth.

I offer, therefore, this book for the attention, not of the philosophers and sages of this world, not of great theologians bogged down in their interminable questionings, but of the simple and unlearned, who are seeking rather to love God than to amass knowledge. For he is not known by argument, but by what we do and how we love. I think that while the matters contained in such questionings are the most demanding of all intellectually, they are much less important when the love of Christ is under consideration. Anyhow they are impossible to understand! So I have not written for the experts, unless they have forgotten and put behind them all those things that belong to the world; unless now they are eager to surrender to a longing for God.

To achieve this however they must, first, fly from every worldly honor; they must hate all vainglory and the parade of knowledge. And then, conditioned by great poverty, through prayer and meditation they can devote themselves to the love of God. It will not be surprising if then an inner spark of the uncreated charity should appear to them and prepare their hearts for the fire which consumes everything that is dark, and raises them to that pitch of ardor which is so lovely and pleasant. Then will they pass beyond the things of time, and sit enthroned in infinite peace. The more learned they are, the more ability they naturally have for loving, always provided of course that they both despise themselves, and rejoice to be despised by others. And so, because I would stir up by these means every man to love God, and because I am trying to make plain the ardent nature of love and how it is supernatural, the title selected for this book will be *The Fire of Love*.

Chapter 2

No One Attains Supreme Devotion Quickly, or is Refreshed by the Sweetness of Contemplation.

It is obvious to those who are in love that no one attains the heights of devotion at once, or is ravished with contemplative sweetness. In fact it is only very occasionally—and then only momentarily—that they are allowed to experience heavenly things; their progress to spiritual strength is a gradual one. When they have attained the gravity of behavior so necessary and have achieved a certain stability of mind—as much as changing circumstances permit—a certain perfection is acquired after great labor. It is then that they can feel some joy in loving God.

Notwithstanding, it appears that all those who are mighty performers in virtue immediately and genuinely experience the warmth of uncreated or created charity, melt in the immense fire of love, and sing within their hearts the song of divine praise. For this mystery is hidden from the many, and is revealed to the few, and those the most special. So the more sublime such a level is, the fewer—in this world—are those who find it. Rarely in fact have we found a man who is so holy or even perfect in this earthly life endowed with love so great as to be raised up to contemplation to the level of jubilant song. This would mean that he would receive within himself the sound that is sung in heaven, and that he would echo back the praises of God as it were in harmony, pouring forth sweet notes of music and composing spiritual songs as he offers his heavenly praises, and that he would truly experience in his heart the genuine fire of the love of God. It would be surprising if anyone without such experience should claim the name of contemplative when the psalmist, speaking in character as the typical contemplative, exclaims, *I will go into the house of the Lord, with the voice of praise and thanksgiving.*[2] The praise, of course, is the praise offered by the banqueter, one who is feeding on heavenly sweetness.

Further, perfect souls who have been caught up into this friendship—surpassing, abundant, and eternal!—discover that life is suffused with imperishable sweetness from the glittering chalice of sweet charity. In holy happy wisdom they inhale joyful heat into their souls, and as a result are much cheered by the indescribable comfort of God's healing medicine. Here at all events is refreshment for those who love their high and eternal heritage, even though in their earthly exile distress befell them. However they think it not unfitting to endure a few years' hardship in order to be raised to heavenly thrones, and never leave them. They have been selected out of all mankind to be the beloved of their Maker and to be crowned with glory, since, like the seraphim in highest heaven, they have been inflamed with the same love. Physically they may have sat in solitary state, but in mind they have companied with angels, and have yearned for their Beloved. Now they sing most sweetly a prayer of love everlasting as they rejoice in Jesus:

O honeyed flame, sweeter than all sweet, delightful beyond all creation!
My God, my Love, surge over me, pierce me by your love, wound me with your
  beauty.
Surge over me, I say, who am longing for your comfort.
Reveal your healing medicine to your poor lover.
See, my one desire is for you; it is you my heart is seeking.
My soul pants for you; my whole being is athirst for you.
  Yet you will not show yourself to me; you look away;

2. Psalms 42.4.

you bar the door, shun me, pass me over;
You even laugh at my innocent sufferings.
And yet you snatch your lovers away from all earthly things.
You lift them above every desire for worldly matters.
You make them capable of loving you—
    and love you they do indeed.
So they offer you their praise in spiritual song
    which bursts out from that inner fire;
    they know in truth the sweetness of the dart of love.
Ah, eternal and most lovable of all joys,
    you raise us from the very depths,
    and entrance us with the sight of divine majesty so often!
Come into me, Beloved!
All ever I had I have given up for you;
    I have spurned all that was to be mine,
    that you might make your home in my heart,
    and I your comfort.
Do not forsake me now, smitten with such great longing,
    whose consuming desire is to be amongst those who love you.
Grant me to love you, to rest in you, that in your kingdom I may be worthy
    to appear before you world without end.

Chapter 12

ABOUT NOT JUDGING ANOTHER, BUT RATHER GIVING THANKS;
THE EIGHT RESULTS OF LOVING GOD; ABOUT AVOIDING THE COMPANY OF WOMEN.

The man who lives a holy and righteous life is not going to despise sinners, however bad. Those who are tempted fall because they have not the grace to resist—though it was through their own sinfulness that they turned from good to evil. No one can do good, or love God, or be chaste, unless God enables him to do so. So if you get puffed up because you have done well, or have kept off carnal pleasures, or have endured hard penance (and consequently have received the praise of human lips!) you should remember that unless Christ in his kindness had protected you, you would have fallen into similar evils as did the bad man—or worse. You have no power to resist of your own, but only his power of whom it is said, *I will love you, Lord, my strength*.[3] If therefore you have nothing that in the first place you did not receive, *why do you boast as if you had not received it?*[4] I thank my God, who not for any merit of mine but solely for my good and his own glory so chastised me his child, and so frightened me his servant, that to me it seemed sweet to flee from the "delights" of the world (which in any case are few and fleeting) and to escape the many, never-ending pains of hell. Moreover this was the way he taught me, and through that teaching endowed me with such strength that I can now gladly put up with present, difficult, penance, especially since I am to come so easily to eternal delight and full reward. For if we want to, even in this life and without undue hardship, we can repent completely and purge ourselves of our sins, so long as we destroy all those sins to the best of our ability. If in fact we are not cleansed here, in time to come we shall find the Apostle speaks the truth when he says, *It is a fearful thing to fall into the hands of the living God*.[5]

3. Psalms 18.1.
4. 1 Corinthians 4.7.

5. Hebrews 10.31.

Lord God, pity me: my infancy was stupid,
my boyhood vain, my adolescence unclean.
But now, Lord Jesus, my heart has been set on fire with holy love,
and my disposition has been changed,
so that my soul has no wish to touch those bitter things
which once were meat and drink to me.

Such are my affections now that it is nothing but sin I hate, none but God I fear to offend, nothing but God in which I rejoice. My only grief is for sin, my only love is God, my only hope is in him. Nothing saddens me except wrong, nothing pleases me except Christ.

Yet there was a time when I was rebuked, quite properly, by three different women. One rebuked me because in my eagerness to restrain the feminine craze for dressy and suggestive clothes I inspected too closely their extravagant ornamentation. She said I ought not to notice them so as to know whether they were wearing horned headdresses or not. I think she was right to reprove me. Another rebuked me because I spoke of her great bosom as if it pleased me. She said, "What business is it of yours whether it is big or little?" She too was right. The third jokingly took me up when I appeared to be going to touch her somewhat rudely, and perhaps had already done so, by saying, "Calm down, brother!" It was as if she had said, "It doesn't go with your office of hermit to be fooling with women." She too deservedly made me feel uncomfortable. I ought to have held off rather than to have behaved this way. When I came to myself[6] I thanked God for teaching me what was right through their words, and for showing me a more pleasant way than my previous one, so that I might cooperate more fully with Christ's grace. I am not going to put myself in the wrong with women henceforward.

A fourth woman with whom I was in some way familiar did not so much rebuke me as despise me when she said "You are no more than a beautiful face and a lovely voice: you have *done* nothing." I think it better therefore to dispense with whatever their particular contribution to life is, rather than to fall into their hands, hands which know no moderation whether loving or despising! Yet these things happened because I was seeking their salvation, and not because I was after anything improper. What is more, they were the very people from whom I had for a while received physical sustenance!

Chapter 15

HOW AND WHEN HE WAS URGED TO THE SOLITARY LIFE, AND THE SONG OF LOVE; ABOUT THE CHANGE OF PLACE.

As adolescence dawned in my unhappy youth, present too was the grace of my Maker. It was he who curbed my youthful lust and transformed it into a longing for spiritual embrace. He lifted and transferred my soul from the depths up to the heights, so that I ardently longed for the pleasures of heaven more than I had ever delighted in physical embrace or worldly corruption. The way all this worked out, if I were minded to publish it, obliges me to preach the solitary life. For the inbreathing Spirit meant me to follow this life, and love its purpose. And this, from that moment, with all my limitations, I have sought to do. Yet I was still living amongst those who flourished in the world, and it was their food I used to eat. And I used to listen to that

6. Compare with Luke 15.17.

kind of flattery which all too often can drag the most doughty warriors from their heights down to hell itself. But when I rejected everything of this sort to set myself to one purpose, my soul was absorbed with love for my Maker. I longed for the sweet delights of eternity, and I gave my soul over to love Christ with every ounce of my power. And this she has received from the Beloved, so that now it is solitude that seems most sweet, and those comforts which in their madness men treasure are counted nothing.

From then on I continually sought quiet, and that although I went from one place to another. For to desert one's cell for reasonable cause does a hermit no harm any more than does its recovery if that seems right. Some of the holy Fathers were accustomed to do this, and thereby incurred criticism—but not from good men! For evil men spoke evil things, and would have gone on to do them if they had continued in the same place, for that is the way of them. Lift the lid of the pan, and there is only stink! Those who speak evil speak out of the abundance of their heart, and there lurks the poison of asps! I know this: the more men have been furious with me with their denigrations, the more have I advanced in spiritual growth. My worst detractors have been those I once counted my faithful friends. Yet I did not give up the things which helped my soul because of them, but got on with my study, always with the favor of God. I recalled the scripture which said, *They may curse, but you bless.*[7] And in the course of time I was granted growth in spiritual joy.

From the time my conversion of life and mind began until the day the door of Heaven swung back and his Face was revealed, so that my inner eye could contemplate the things that are above, and see by what way it might find the Beloved and cling to him, three years passed, all but three or four months. But the door remained open for nearly a year longer before I could really feel in my heart the warmth of eternal love.

I was sitting in a certain chapel, delighting in the sweetness of prayer or meditation, when suddenly I felt within myself an unusually pleasant heat. At first I wondered where it came from, but it was not long before I realized that it was from none of his creatures but from the Creator himself. It was, I found, more fervent and pleasant than I had ever known. But it was just over nine months before a conscious and incredibly sweet warmth kindled me, and I knew the infusion and understanding of heavenly, spiritual sounds, sounds which pertain to the song of eternal praise, and to the sweetness of unheard melody; sounds which cannot be known or heard save by him who has received it, and who himself must be clean and separate from the things of earth.

While I was sitting in that same chapel, and repeating as best I could the night-psalms before I went in to supper, I heard, above my head it seemed, the joyful ring of psalmody, or perhaps I should say, the singing. In my prayer I was reaching out to heaven with heartfelt longing when I became aware, in a way I cannot explain, of a symphony of song, and in myself I sensed a corresponding harmony at once wholly delectable and heavenly, which persisted in my mind. Then and there my thinking itself turned into melodious song, and my meditation became a poem, and my very prayers and psalms took up the same sound. The effect of this inner sweetness was that I began to sing what previously I had spoken; only I sang inwardly, and that for my Creator. But it was not suspected by those who saw me, for if they had known they would have honored me beyond all measure, and I should have lost part of this

7. Psalms 109.28.

most lovely flower, and have fallen into desolation. Meantime wonder seized me that I should be caught up into such joy while I was still an exile, and that God should give me gifts, the like of which I did not know I could ask for, and such that I thought that not even the most holy could have received in this life. From which I deduce that they are not given for merit, but freely to whomsoever Christ wills. All the same I fancy that no one will receive them unless he has a special love for the Name of Jesus, and so honors it that he never lets it out of his mind, except in sleep. Anyone to whom this is given will, I think, achieve this very thing.

From the time my conversion began until, by the help of God, I was able to reach the heights of loving Christ, there passed four years and three months. When I had attained this high degree I could praise God with joyful song indeed! And here that blessed state has remained since that initial impetus: and so it will continue to the end. In fact it will be more perfect after death, for though it is here that joyful love and burning charity begin, it is there, in the kingdom of heaven, that it will receive its most glorious fulfillment. But a man who has passed through these stages in his life profits to no small degree, yet he does not ascend to a higher stage, for he is one who has been confirmed in grace as it were, and so far as mortal man can be, is at rest.

I thank God that this is so, and I want to give him unceasing praise. In tribulations, in troubles, in persecutions, he has given me comfort; and in prosperity and success he makes me await in confidence his everlasting crown.

> So, Jesus, I want to be praising you always, such is my joy.
> When I was down and out you stooped to me,
> > and associated me with those sweet ministers
> > who through the Spirit give out those lovely and heavenly melodies.
> I will express my joy and gratitude
> > because you have made me like one of those
> > whose superb song springs from a clear conscience.
> Their soul burns with their unending love.
> And your servant too, when he sits in prayer,
> > glows and loves in his fervor.
> His mind is transformed: he burns with fire;
> > indeed, he expands in the vehemence of his longing.
> And virtue, beautiful, true, lovely and faultless,
> > flourishes before the face of his Creator.
> His song suffuses his whole being,
> > and with its glad melody
> > lightens his burden,
> > and brightens his labour.

God's gifts to us are manifold, wonderful and great, but none of them in this life can be compared with this one, which so perfectly confirms our hope in the beauty of the unseen life in the loving soul, and comforts him with its sweetness as he sits in prayer, and catches him up to the heights of contemplation, and to the sound of angels' praise.

And now, my brothers, I have told you how I came to the fire of love: not in order that you should praise me, but rather that you might glorify God. From him I have received whatever I have had of good. It is so that you who are aware that everything under the sun is vanity[8] might be moved to imitate, not denigrate.

---

8. Ecclesiastes 1.14 (and elsewhere).

The Cloud of Unknowing

The anonymous author of *The Cloud of Unknowing* wrote toward the end of the fourteenth century, and comes from a much more self-consciously learned tradition of spiritual reflection than did Richard Rolle. *The Cloud of Unknowing* draws upon an influential tradition of neopla-tonic Christianity. One strand of this tradition extolled the *"via negativa"*: the approach to union with God by completely emptying the mind of worldly consciousness, and entering instead a dark place of uncertainty, a "cloud of unknowing."

Even with its very private notion of disciplined spiritual quest, though, the *Cloud* insists that the mystic's work serves the salvation of all the faithful. At the same time, the *Cloud of Unknowing* also betrays a considerable anxiety about, even hostility to, the spread of an undi-rected and body-oriented spirituality in its time. The text particularly warns against the danger of demonic influence in those seeking too eagerly some bodily sign of the divine. It mentions the sensation of heat and other enthusiastic bodily manifestations, which may recall the high-ly affective imagery of Rolle.

from The Cloud of Unknowing[1]
CHAPTER 3

Lift up your heart to God with humble love: and mean God himself, and not what you get out of him. Indeed, hate to think of anything but God himself, so that noth-ing occupies your mind or will but only God. Try to forget all created things that he ever made, and the purpose behind them, so that your thought and longing do not turn or reach out to them either in general or in particular. Let them go, and pay no attention to them. It is the work of the soul that pleases God most. All saints and angels rejoice over it, and hasten to help it on with all their might. All the fiends, however, are furious at what you are doing, and try to defeat it in every conceivable way. Moreover, the whole of mankind is wonderfully helped by what you are doing, in ways you do not understand. Yes, the very souls in purgatory find their pain eased by virtue of your work. And in no better way can you yourself be made clean or virtu-ous than by attending to this. Yet it is the easiest work of all when the soul is helped by grace and has a conscious longing. And it can be achieved very quickly. Otherwise it is hard and beyond your powers.

Do not give up then, but work away at it till you have this longing. When you first begin, you find only darkness, and as it were a cloud of unknowing. You don't know what this means except that in your will you feel a simple steadfast inten-tion reaching out towards God. Do what you will, this darkness and this cloud remain between you and God, and stop you both from seeing him in the clear light of rational understanding, and from experiencing his loving sweetness in your affection. Reconcile yourself to wait in this darkness as long as is necessary, but still go on longing after him whom you love. For if you are to feel him or to see him in this life, it must always be in this cloud, in this darkness. And if you will work hard at what I tell you, I believe that through God's mercy you will achieve this very thing.

1. Translated by Clifton Wolters.

FROM CHAPTER 4

So that you may make no mistake, or go wrong in this matter, let me tell you a little more about it as I see it. This work does not need a long time for its completion. Indeed, it is the shortest work that can be imagined! It is no longer, no shorter, than one atom, which as a philosopher of astronomy will tell you is the smallest division of time. It is so small that it cannot be analyzed: it is almost beyond our grasp. Yet it is as long as the time of which it has been written, "All the time that is given to thee, it shall be asked of thee how thou hast spent it." And it is quite right that you should have to give account of it. It is neither shorter nor longer than a single impulse of your will, the chief part of your soul. * * *

So pay great attention to this marvelous work of grace within your soul. It is always a sudden impulse and comes without warning, springing up to God like some spark from the fire. An incredible number of such impulses arise in one brief hour in the soul who has a will to this work! In one such flash the soul may completely forget the created world outside. Yet almost as quickly it may relapse back to thoughts and memories of things done and undone—all because of our fallen nature. And as fast again it may rekindle.

This then, in brief, is how it works. It is obviously not make-believe, nor wrong thinking, nor fanciful opinion. These would not be the product of a devout and humble love, but the outcome of the pride and inventiveness of the imagination. If this work of grace is to be truly and genuinely understood, all such proud imaginings must ruthlessly be stamped out!

For whoever hears or reads about all this, and thinks that it is fundamentally an activity of the mind, and proceeds then to work it all out along these lines, is on quite the wrong track. He manufactures an experience that is neither spiritual nor physical. He is dangerously misled and in real peril. So much so, that unless God in his great goodness intervenes with a miracle of mercy and makes him stop and submit to the advice of those who really know, he will go mad, or suffer some other dreadful form of spiritual mischief and devilish deceit. Indeed, almost casually as it were, he may be lost eternally, body and soul. So for the love of God be careful, and do not attempt to achieve this experience intellectually. I tell you truly it cannot come this way. So leave it alone.

Do not think that because I call it a "darkness" or a "cloud" it is the sort of cloud you see in the sky, or the kind of darkness you know at home when the light is out. That kind of darkness or cloud you can picture in your mind's eye in the height of summer, just as in the depth of a winter's night you can picture a clear and shining light. I do not mean this at all. By "darkness" I mean "a lack of knowing"—just as anything that you do not know or may have forgotten may be said to be "dark" to you, for you cannot see it with your inward eye. For this reason it is called "a cloud," not of the sky, of course, but "of unknowing," a cloud of unknowing between you and your God.

CHAPTER 52

The madness I speak of is effected like this: they read and hear it said that they should stop the "exterior" working with their mind, and work interiorly. And because they do not know what this "interior" work means, they do it wrong. For they turn their actual physical minds inwards to their bodies, which is an unnatural thing, and they strain as if to see spiritually with their physical eyes, and to hear within with their outward ears, and to smell and taste and feel and so on inwardly in the same way. So they pervert the natural order, and with this false ingenuity they put their minds to such unnecessary strains that ultimately their brains are turned. And at once the devil is able to deceive them with false lights and sounds, sweet odors and wonderful tastes, glowing and burning in their hearts or stomachs, backs or loins or limbs.

In all this make-believe they imagine they are peacefully contemplating their God, unhindered by vain thoughts. So they are, in a fashion, for they are so stuffed with falsehood that a little extra vanity cannot disturb them. Why? Because it is the same devil that is working on them now as would be tempting them if they were on the right road. You know very well that he will not get in his own way. He does not remove all thought of God from them, lest they should become suspicious.

✦ ✛ ✦

Julian of Norwich
1342–c.1420

Dame Julian of Norwich was an anchoress, a woman devoted to God who lived separate from the world, literally enclosed in a modest residence. Yet Julian also lived in the midst of the world, since her anchorhold was in the busy market town of Norwich. Dame Julian's lifelong stability as an anchoress and her persistent rhetoric of humility (she most often speaks of herself only as a "creature") may have masked or softened the daring of her theology. This she developed from decades of meditation on a sequence of sixteen visions of the crucifixion—"showings"—which she received in extreme illness at age thirty.

The urban space and domestic arrangements of Julian's anchorhold serve as an emblem for her theology and her place in the spiritual world. She received and spoke to guests, and some of those encounters were reported—as for example by Margery Kempe from nearby Lynne, whose own work appears later in this anthology. Julian brought eminence to the churches of Norwich without threatening their hierarchy; she lived under the direction of a priestly confessor and made no claim to worldly power. Yet a visitor like Margery Kempe could use Julian's approval as a defense for her own more mobile and subversive quest for holiness. Further, Dame Julian used her own background of household and family as images to create a domestic theology of the Trinity and especially of the sacrifice of Christ.

Julian probably dictated the two versions of her *Book of Showings*. The earlier is largely focused on the visions themselves, while the very much longer version (selections from which follow) enfolds the decades of theological speculations to which Julian's visions led her. She will often expound a statement by Christ in one of her visions with all the nuance that contemporary theologians would apply to a line from the Bible. In an extraordinary series of reflections, Julian at once returns to key moments in her initial visions and explores the role of Christ in mankind and in the Trinity through the multifaceted image of the Lord as mother. Julian exploits all the moments of motherhood—conception, labor, breast-feeding, and child-rearing—to articulate the place of Christ in the scheme of salvation and the necessity of sin. At the same time, other aspects of motherhood also serve Julian to explore the other persons of the Trinity, God the Father and the Holy Spirit, as well as the sufferings and joys of the Virgin Mary.

Like Rolle and *The Cloud of Unknowing*, Julian is explicitly concerned with the love and salvation of all the faithful, not just private communion with the divine. She addresses herself, more broadly than her predecessors, to the entire community of the faithful. She explicitly does not privilege herself above those of simple belief and again uses the imagery of a nurturing mother to urge the sinful soul's recourse to Holy Church.

from **A Book of Showings**[1]
[THREE GRACES. ILLNESS. THE FIRST REVELATION]
CHAPTER 2

This revelation was made to a simple, unlettered creature, living in this mortal flesh, the year of our Lord one thousand, three hundred and seventy-three, on the thirteenth day of May;[2] and before this the creature had desired three graces by the gift of God. The first was recollection of the Passion. The second was bodily sickness. The third was to have, of God's gift, three wounds. As to the first, it seemed to me that I had some feeling for the Passion of Christ, but still I desired to have more by the grace of God. I thought that I wished that I had been at that time with Magdalen and with the others who were Christ's lovers, so that I might have seen with my own eyes the Passion which our Lord suffered for me, so that I might have suffered with him as others did who loved him. Therefore I desired a bodily sight, in which I might have more knowledge of our savior's bodily pains, and of the compassion of our Lady and of all his true lovers who were living at that time and saw his pains, for I would have been one of them and have suffered with them. I never desired any other sight of God or revelation, until my soul would be separated from the body, for I believed that I should be saved by the mercy of God. This was my intention, because I wished afterwards, because of that revelation, to have truer recollection of Christ's Passion. As to the second grace, there came into my mind with contrition—a free gift which I did not seek—a desire of my will to have by God's gift a bodily sickness. I wished that sickness to be so severe that it might seem mortal, so that I might in it receive all the rites which Holy Church has to give me, whilst I myself should think that I was dying, and everyone who saw me would think the same; for I wanted no comfort from any human, earthly life in that sickness. I wanted to have every kind of pain, bodily and spiritual, which I should have if I had died, every fear and temptation from devils, and every other kind of pain except the departure of the spirit. I intended this because I wanted to be purged by God's mercy, and afterwards live more to his glory because of that sickness; because I hoped that this would be to my reward when I should die, because I desired soon to be with my God and my Creator.

These two desires about the Passion and the sickness which I desired from him were with a condition, for it seemed to me that this was not the ordinary practice of prayer; therefore I said: Lord, you know what I want, if it be your will that I have it, and if it be not your will, good Lord, do not be displeased, for I want nothing which you do not want. When I was young I desired to have this sickness when I would be thirty years old. As to the third, by the grace of God and the teaching of Holy Church I conceived a great desire to receive three wounds in my life, that is, the wound of true contrition, the wound of loving compassion, and the wound of longing with my will for God. Just as I asked for the other two conditionally, so I asked urgently for this third without any condition. The two desires which I mentioned first passed from my mind, and the third remained there continually.

CHAPTER 3

And when I was thirty and a half years old, God sent me a bodily sickness in which I lay for three days and three nights, and on the third night I received all the rites of Holy Church, and did not expect to live until day. And after this I lay for two days and

---

1. Translated by Edmund Colledge and James Walsh.
2. Julian provides the biographical setting of her visions

in this chapter. By "unlettered" she may mean that she was not formally schooled; it is clear she was literate.

two nights, and on the third night I often thought that I was on the point of death, and those who were with me often thought so. And yet in this I felt a great reluctance to die, not that there was anything on earth which it pleased me to live for, or any pain of which I was afraid, for I trusted in the mercy of God. But it was because I wanted to live to love God better and longer, so that I might through the grace of that living have more knowledge and love of God in the bliss of heaven. Because it seemed to me that all the time that I had lived here was very little and short in comparison with the bliss which is everlasting, I thought: Good Lord, can my living no longer be to your glory? And I understood by my reason and the sensation of my pains that I should die; and with all the will of my heart I assented to be wholly as was God's will.

So I lasted until day, and by then my body was dead from the middle downwards, as it felt to me. Then I was helped to sit upright and supported, so that my heart might be more free to be at God's will, and so that I could think of him whilst my life would last. My curate was sent for to be present at my end; and before he came my eyes were fixed upwards, and I could not speak. He set the cross before my face, and said: I have brought the image of your savior; look at it and take comfort from it. It seemed to me that I was well, for my eyes were set upwards towards heaven, where I trusted that I by God's mercy was going; but nevertheless I agreed to fix my eyes on the face of the crucifix if I could, and so I did, for it seemed to me that I would hold out longer with my eyes set in front of me rather than upwards. After this my sight began to fail. It grew as dark around me in the room as if it had been night, except that there was ordinary light trained upon the image of the cross, I did not know how. Everything around the cross was ugly and terrifying to me, as if it were occupied by a great crowd of devils.

After this the upper part of my body began to die, until I could scarcely feel anything. My greatest pain was my shortness of breath and the ebbing of my life. Then truly I believed that I was at the point of death. And suddenly at that moment all my pain was taken from me, and I was as sound, particularly in the upper part of my body, as ever I was before. I was astonished by this sudden change, for it seemed to me that it was by God's secret doing and not natural; and even so, in this ease which I felt, I had no more confidence that I should live, nor was the ease I felt complete for me, for I thought that I would rather have been delivered of this world, because that was what my heart longed for.

Then suddenly it came into my mind that I ought to wish for the second wound as a gift and a grace from our Lord, that my body might be filled full of recollection and feeling of his blessed Passion, as I had prayed before, for I wished that his pains might be my pains, with compassion which would lead to longing for God. So it seemed to me that I might with his grace have the wounds which I had before desired; but in this I never wanted any bodily vision or any kind of revelation from God, but the compassion which I thought a loving soul could have for our Lord Jesus, who for love was willing to become a mortal man. I desired to suffer with him, living in my mortal body, as God would give me grace.

Chapter 4

And at this, suddenly I saw the red blood running down from under the crown, hot and flowing freely and copiously, a living stream, just as it was at the time when the crown of thorns was pressed on his blessed head.[3] I perceived, truly and powerfully, that it was he who just so, both God and man, himself suffered for me, who showed it to me without any intermediary.

---

3. This begins the first of Julian's sixteen revelations.

And in the same revelation, suddenly the Trinity filled my heart full of the greatest joy, and I understood that it will be so in heaven without end to all who will come there. For the Trinity is God, God is the Trinity. The Trinity is our maker, the Trinity is our protector, the Trinity is our everlasting lover, the Trinity is our endless joy and our bliss, by our Lord Jesus Christ and in our Lord Jesus Christ. And this was revealed in the first vision and in them all, for where Jesus appears the blessed Trinity is understood, as I see it. And I said: Blessed be the Lord! This I said with a reverent intention and in a loud voice, and I was greatly astonished by this wonder and marvel, that he who is so to be revered and feared would be so familiar with a sinful creature living in this wretched flesh.

I accepted it that at that time our Lord Jesus wanted, out of his courteous love, to show me comfort before my temptations began; for it seemed to me that I might well be tempted by devils, by God's permission and with his protection, before I would die. With this sight of his blessed Passion, with the divinity which I saw in my understanding, I knew well that this was strength enough for me, yes, and for all living creatures who were to be saved, against all the devils of hell and against all their spiritual enemies.

In this he brought our Lady Saint Mary to my understanding. I saw her spiritually in her bodily likeness, a simple, humble maiden, young in years, grown a little taller than a child, of the stature which she had when she conceived.[4] Also God showed me part of the wisdom and the truth of her soul, and in this I understood the reverent contemplation with which she beheld her God, who is her Creator, marveling with great reverence that he was willing to be born of her who was a simple creature created by him. And this wisdom and truth, this knowledge of her Creator's greatness and of her own created littleness, made her say very meekly to Gabriel: Behold me here, God's handmaiden. In this sight I understood truly that she is greater, more worthy and more fulfilled, than everything else which God has created, and which is inferior to her. Above her is no created thing, except the blessed humanity of Christ, as I saw.

CHAPTER 5

At the same time as I saw this sight of the head bleeding, our good Lord showed a spiritual sight of his familiar love. I saw that he is to us everything which is good and comforting for our help. He is our clothing, who wraps and enfolds us for love, embraces us and shelters us, surrounds us for his love, which is so tender that he may never desert us. And so in this sight I saw that he is everything which is good, as I understand.

And in this he showed me something small, no bigger than a hazelnut, lying in the palm of my hand, as it seemed to me, and it was as round as a ball. I looked at it with the eye of my understanding and thought: What can this be? I was amazed that it could last, for I thought that because of its littleness it would suddenly have fallen into nothing. And I was answered in my understanding: It lasts and always will, because God loves it; and thus everything has being through the love of God.

In this little thing I saw three properties. The first is that God made it, the second is that God loves it, the third is that God preserves it. But what did I see in it? It is that God is the Creator and the protector and the lover. For until I am

---

4. Julian will have two further visions of the Virgin Mary in different manifestations: as mother mourning at the crucifixion and as ascended saint.

substantially united to him, I can never have perfect rest or true happiness, until, that is, I am so attached to him that there can be no created thing between my God and me.

This little thing which is created seemed to me as if it could have fallen into nothing because of its littleness. We need to have knowledge of this, so that we may delight in despising as nothing everything created, so as to love and have uncreated God. For this is the reason why our hearts and souls are not in perfect ease, because here we seek rest in this thing which is so little, in which there is no rest, and we do not know our God who is almighty, all wise and all good, for he is true rest. God wishes to be known, and it pleases him that we should rest in him; for everything which is beneath him is not sufficient for us. And this is the reason why no soul is at rest until it has despised as nothing all things which are created. When it by its will has become nothing for love, to have him who is everything, then is it able to receive spiritual rest.

And also our good Lord revealed that it is very greatly pleasing to him that a simple soul should come naked, openly and familiarly. For this is the loving yearning of the soul through the touch of the Holy Spirit, from the understanding which I have in this revelation: God, of your goodness give me yourself, for you are enough for me, and I can ask for nothing which is less which can pay you full worship. And if I ask anything which is less, always I am in want; but only in you do I have everything.

And these words of the goodness of God are very dear to the soul, and very close to touching our Lord's will, for his goodness fills all his creatures and all his blessed works full, and endlessly overflows in them. For he is everlastingness, and he made us only for himself, and restored us by his precious Passion and always preserves us in his blessed love; and all this is of his goodness.

CHAPTER 9

I am not good because of the revelations, but only if I love God better; and inasmuch as you love God better, it is more to you than to me. I do not say this to those who are wise, because they know it well. But I say it to you who are simple, to give you comfort and strength; for we are all one in love, for truly it was not revealed to me that God loves me better than the humblest soul who is in a state of grace. For I am sure that there are many who never had revelations or visions, but only the common teaching of Holy Church, who love God better than I. If I pay special attention to myself, I am nothing at all; but in general I am, I hope, in the unity of love with all my fellow Christians. For it is in this unity that the life of all men consists who will be saved. For God is everything that is good, as I see; and God has made everything that is made, and God loves everything that he has made. And he who has general love for all his fellow Christians in God has love towards everything that is. For in mankind which will be saved is comprehended all, that is to say all that is made and the maker of all. For God is in man and in God is all. And he who loves thus loves all. And I hope by the grace of God that he who may see it so will be taught the truth and greatly comforted, if he has need of comfort.

I speak of those who will be saved, for at this time God showed me no one else. But in everything I believe as Holy Church preaches and teaches. For the faith of Holy Church, which I had before I had understanding, and which, as I hope by the grace of God, I intend to preserve whole and to practice, was always in my sight, and I wished and intended never to accept anything which might be contrary to it. And to this end and with this intention I contemplated the revelation with all diligence, for throughout this blessed revelation I contemplated it as God intended.

All this was shown in three parts,[5] that is to say, by bodily vision and by words formed in my understanding and by spiritual vision. But I may not and cannot show the spiritual visions as plainly and fully as I should wish. But I trust in our Lord God almighty that he will, out of his goodness and for love of you, make you accept it more spiritually and more sweetly than I can or may tell it.

[CHRIST DRAWS JULIAN IN THROUGH HIS WOUND]

CHAPTER 24[6]

With a kindly countenance our good Lord looked into his side, and he gazed with joy, and with his sweet regard he drew his creature's understanding into his side by the same wound;[7] and there he revealed a fair and delectable place, large enough for all mankind that will be saved and will rest in peace and in love. And with that he brought to mind the dear and precious blood and water which he suffered to be shed for love. And in this sweet sight he showed his blessed heart split in two, and as he rejoiced he showed to my understanding a part of his blessed divinity, as much as was his will at that time, strengthening my poor soul to understand what can be said, that is the endless love which was without beginning and is and always shall be.

And with this our good Lord said most joyfully: See how I love you, as if he had said, my darling, behold and see your Lord, your God, who is your Creator and your endless joy; see your own brother, your savior; my child, behold and see what delight and bliss I have in your salvation, and for my love rejoice with me.

And for my greater understanding, these blessed words were said: See how I love you, as if he had said, behold and see that I loved you so much, before I died for you, that I wanted to die for you. And now I have died for you, and willingly suffered what I could. And now all my bitter pain and my hard labor is turned into everlasting joy and bliss for me and for you. How could it now be that you would pray to me for anything pleasing to me which I would not very gladly grant to you? For my delight is in your holiness and in your endless joy and bliss in me.

This is the understanding, as simply as I can say it, of these blessed words: See how I loved you. Our Lord revealed this to make us glad and joyful.

CHAPTER 25[8]

And with this same appearance of mirth and joy our good Lord looked down on his right, and brought to my mind where our Lady stood at the time of his Passion, and he said: Do you wish to see her? And these sweet words were as if he had said, I know well that you wish to see my blessed mother, for after myself she is the greatest joy that I could show you, and the greatest delight and honor to me, and she is what all my blessed creatures most desire to see. And because of the wonderful, exalted and singular love that he has for this sweet maiden, his blessed mother, our Lady Saint Mary, he reveals her bliss and joy through the sense of these sweet words, as if he said, do you wish to see how I love her, so that you could rejoice with me in the love which I have in her and she has in me?

---

5. Or three ways of perception.
6. This chapter recounts Julian's tenth revelation.

7. The spear wound in Christ's side.
8. The eleventh revelation.

And for greater understanding of these sweet words our good Lord speaks in love to all mankind who will be saved, addressing them all as one person, as if he said, do you wish to see in her how you are loved? It is for love of you that I have made her so exalted, so noble, so honorable; and this delights me. And I wish it to delight you. For next to him, she is the most blissful to be seen. But in this matter I was not taught to long to see her bodily presence whilst I am here, but the virtues of her blessed soul, her truth, her wisdom, her love, through which I am taught to know myself and reverently to fear my God.

And when our good Lord had revealed this, and said these words: Do you wish to see her? I answered and said: Yes, good Lord, great thanks, yes, good Lord, if it be your will. Often times I had prayed for this, and I had expected to see her in a bodily likeness; but I did not see her so. And Jesus, saying this, showed me a spiritual vision of her. Just as before I had seen her small and simple, now he showed her high and noble and glorious and more pleasing to him than all creatures. And so he wishes it to be known that all who take delight in him should take delight in her, and in the delight that he has in her and she in him.

And for greater understanding he showed this example, as if, when a man loves some creature particularly, more than all other creatures, he will make all other creatures to love and delight in that creature whom he loves so much. And in these words which Jesus said: Do you wish to see her? it seemed to me that these were the most delectable words which he could give me in this spiritual vision of her which he gave me. For our Lord showed me no particular person except our Lady Saint Mary, and he showed her on three occasions. The first was as she conceived, the second was as she had been under the Cross, and the third was as she is now, in delight, honor and joy.

CHAPTER 26[9]

And after this our Lord showed himself to me, and he appeared to me more glorified than I had seen him before, in which I was taught that our soul will never have rest till it comes into him, acknowledging that he is full of joy, familiar and courteous and blissful and true life. Again and again our Lord said: I am he, I am he, I am he who is highest. I am he whom you love. I am he in whom you delight. I am he whom you serve. I am he for whom you long. I am he whom you desire. I am he whom you intend. I am he who is all. I am he whom Holy Church preaches and teaches to you. I am he who showed himself before to you. The number of the words surpasses my intelligence and my understanding and all my powers, for they were the most exalted, as I see it, for in them is comprehended I cannot tell what; but the joy which I saw when they were revealed surpasses all that the heart can think or the soul may desire. And therefore these words are not explained here, but let every man accept them as our Lord intended them, according to the grace God gives him in understanding and love.

[THE NECESSITY OF SIN, AND OF HATING SIN]

CHAPTER 27[1]

And after this our Lord brought to my mind the longing that I had for him before, and I saw that nothing hindered me but sin, and I saw that this is true of us all in general, and it seemed to me that if there had been no sin, we should all have

---

9. The twelfth revelation.   1. The thirteenth revelation.

been pure and as like our Lord as he created us. And so in my folly before this time I often wondered why, through the great prescient wisdom of God, the beginning of sin was not prevented. For then it seemed to me that all would have been well.

The impulse to think this was greatly to be shunned; and nevertheless I mourned and sorrowed on this account, unreasonably, lacking discretion. But Jesus, who in this vision informed me about everything needful to me, answered with these words and said: Sin is necessary, but all will be well, and all will be well, and every kind of thing will be well. In this naked word "sin," our Lord brought generally to my mind all which is not good, and the shameful contempt and the direst tribulation which he endured for us in this life, and his death and all his pains, and the passions, spiritual and bodily, of all his creatures. For we are all in part troubled, and we shall be troubled, following our master Jesus until we are fully purged of our mortal flesh and all our inward affections which are not very good.

And with the beholding of this, with all the pains that ever were or ever will be, I understood Christ's Passion for the greatest and surpassing pain. And yet this was shown to me in an instant, and it quickly turned into consolation. For our good Lord would not have the soul frightened by this ugly sight. But I did not see sin, for I believe that it has no kind of substance, no share in being, nor can it be recognized except by the pain caused by it. And it seems to me that this pain is something for a time, for it purges and makes us know ourselves and ask for mercy; for the Passion of our Lord is comfort to us against all this, and that is his blessed will. And because of the tender love which our good Lord has for all who will be saved, he comforts readily and sweetly, meaning this: It is true that sin is the cause of all this pain, but all will be well, and every kind of thing will be well.

These works were revealed most tenderly, showing no kind of blame to me or to anyone who will be saved. So it would be most unkind of me to blame God or marvel at him on account of my sins, since he does not blame me for sin.

And in these same words I saw hidden in God an exalted and wonderful mystery, which he will make plain and we shall know in heaven. In this knowledge we shall truly see the cause why he allowed sin to come, and in this sight we shall rejoice forever.

CHAPTER 40

And this is a supreme friendship of our courteous Lord, that he protects us so tenderly whilst we are in our sins; and furthermore he touches us most secretly, and shows us our sins by the sweet light of mercy and grace. But when we see ourselves so foul, then we believe that God may be angry with us because of our sins. Then we are moved by the Holy Spirit through contrition to prayer, and we desire with all our might an amendment of ourselves to appease God's anger, until the time that we find rest of soul and ease of conscience. And then we hope that God has forgiven us our sin; and this is true. And then our courteous Lord shows himself to the soul, happily and with the gladdest countenance, welcoming it as a friend, as if it had been in pain and in prison, saying: My dear darling, I am glad that you have come to me in all your woe. I have always been with you, and now you see me loving, and we are made one in bliss.

So sins are forgiven by grace and mercy, and our soul is honorably received in joy, as it will be when it comes into heaven, as often as it comes by the operation of grace of the Holy Spirit and the power of Christ's Passion.

Here I truly understood that every kind of thing is made available to us by God's great goodness, so much so that when we ourselves are at peace and in charity we are truly safe. But because we cannot have this completely whilst we are here, therefore it is fitting for us to live always in sweet prayer and in loving longing with our Lord Jesus. For he always longs to bring us to the fullness of joy, as has been said before, where he reveals his spiritual thirst. But now, because of all this spiritual consolation which has been described, if any man or woman be moved by folly to say or to think "If this be true, then it would be well to sin so as to have the greater reward, or else to think sin less important," beware of this impulse, for truly, should it come, it is untrue and from the fiend.

For the same true love which touches us all by its blessed strength, that same blessed love teaches us that we must hate sin only because of love. And I am sure by what I feel that the more that each loving soul sees this in the courteous love of our Lord God, the greater is his hatred of sinning and the more he is ashamed. For if it were laid in front of us, all the pain there is in hell and in purgatory and on earth, death and all the rest, we should choose all that pain rather than sin. For sin is so vile and so much to be hated that it can be compared with no pain which is not itself sin. And no more cruel hell than sin was revealed to me, for a loving soul hates no pain but sin; for everything is good except sin, and nothing is evil except sin. And when by the operation of mercy and grace we set our intention on mercy and grace, we are made all fair and spotless.

And God is as willing as he is powerful and wise to save man. And Christ himself is the foundation of all the laws of Christian men, and he taught us to do good in return for evil. Here we may see that he is himself this love, and does to us as he teaches us to do; for he wishes us to be like him in undiminished, everlasting love towards ourselves and our fellow Christians. No more than his love towards us is withdrawn because of our sin does he wish our love to be withdrawn from ourselves or from our fellow Christians; but we must unreservedly hate sin and endlessly love the soul as God loves it. Then we should hate sin just as God hates it, and love the soul as God loves it. For these words which God said are an endless strength: I protect you most truly.

[GOD AS FATHER, MOTHER, HUSBAND]

CHAPTER 58

God the blessed Trinity, who is everlasting being, just as he is eternal from without beginning, just so was it in his eternal purpose to create human nature, which fair nature was first prepared for his own Son, the second person; and when he wished, by full agreement of the whole Trinity he created us all once. And in our creating he joined and united us to himself, and through this union we are kept as pure and as noble as we were created. By the power of that same precious union we love our Creator and delight in him, praise him and thank him and endlessly rejoice in him. And this is the work which is constantly performed in every soul which will be saved, and this is the godly will mentioned before.

And so in our making, God almighty is our loving Father, and God all wisdom is our loving Mother,[2] with the love and the goodness of the Holy Spirit, which is all one God, one Lord. And in the joining and the union he is our very

---

2. The image of God as a wise woman draws from an ancient tradition of the female Sophia, Holy Wisdom, who figures in the apocryphal book of Ecclesiasticus, chapter 24.

true spouse and we his beloved wife and his fair maiden, with which wife he was never displeased; for he says: I love you and you love me, and our love will never divide in two.

I contemplated the work of all the blessed Trinity, in which contemplation I saw and understood these three properties: the property of the fatherhood, and the property of the motherhood, and the property of the lordship in one God. In our almighty Father we have our protection and our bliss, as regards our natural substance, which is ours by our creation from without beginning; and in the second person, in knowledge and wisdom we have our perfection, as regards our sensuality, our restoration and our salvation, for he is our Mother, brother and savior; and in our good Lord the Holy Spirit we have our reward and our gift for our living and our labor, endlessly surpassing all that we desire in his marvelous courtesy, out of his great plentiful grace. For all our life consists of three: In the first we have our being, and in the second we have our increasing, and in the third we have our fulfillment. The first is nature, the second is mercy, the third is grace.

As to the first, I saw and understood that the high might of the Trinity is our Father, and the deep wisdom of the Trinity is our Mother, and the great love of the Trinity is our Lord; and all these we have in nature and in our substantial creation. And furthermore I saw that the second person, who is our Mother, substantially the same beloved person, has now become our mother sensually, because we are double by God's creating, that is to say substantial and sensual. Our substance is the higher part, which we have in our Father, God almighty; and the second person of the Trinity is our Mother in nature in our substantial creation, in whom we are founded and rooted, and he is our Mother of mercy in taking our sensuality. And so our Mother is working on us in various ways, in whom our parts are kept undivided; for in our Mother Christ we profit and increase, and in mercy he reforms and restores us, and by the power of his Passion, his death and his Resurrection he unites us to our substance. So our Mother works in mercy on all his beloved children who are docile and obedient to him, and grace works with mercy, and especially in two properties, as it was shown, which working belongs to the third person, the Holy Spirit. He works, rewarding and giving. Rewarding is a gift for our confidence which the Lord makes to those who have labored; and giving is a courteous act which he does freely, by grace, fulfilling and surpassing all that creatures deserve.

Thus in our Father, God almighty, we have our being, and in our Mother of mercy we have our reforming and our restoring, in whom our parts are united and all made perfect man, and through the rewards and the gifts of grace of the Holy Spirit we are fulfilled. And our substance is in our Father, God almighty, and our substance is in our Mother, God all wisdom, and our substance is in our Lord God, the Holy Spirit, all goodness, for our substance is whole in each person of the Trinity, who is one God. And our sensuality is only in the second person, Christ Jesus, in whom is the Father and the Holy Spirit; and in him and by him we are powerfully taken out of hell and out of the wretchedness on earth, and gloriously brought up into heaven, and blessedly united to our substance, increased in riches and nobility by all the power of Christ and by the grace and operation of the Holy Spirit.

Chapter 59

And we have all this bliss by mercy and grace, and this kind of bliss we never could have had and known, unless that property of goodness which is in God had been opposed, through which we have this bliss. For wickedness has been suffered to rise in opposition to that goodness; and the goodness of mercy and grace opposed that wickedness, and turned everything to goodness and honor for all who will be saved. For this is that property in God which opposes good to evil. So Jesus Christ, who opposes good to evil, is our true Mother. We have our being from him, where the foundation of motherhood begins, with all the sweet protection of love which endlessly follows.

As truly as God is our Father, so truly is God our Mother, and he revealed that in everything, and especially in these sweet words where he says: I am he; that is to say: I am he, the power and goodness of fatherhood; I am he, the wisdom and the lovingness of motherhood; I am he, the light and the grace which is all blessed love; I am he, the Trinity; I am he, the unity; I am he, the great supreme goodness of every kind of thing; I am he who makes you to love; I am he who makes you to long; I am he, the endless fulfilling of all true desires. For where the soul is highest, noblest, most honorable, still it is lowest, meekest and mildest.

And from this foundation in substance we have all the powers of our sensuality by the gift of nature, and by the help and the furthering of mercy and grace, without which we cannot profit. Our great Father, almighty God, who is being, knows us and loved us before time began. Out of this knowledge, in his most wonderful deep love, by the prescient eternal counsel of all the blessed Trinity, he wanted the second person to become our Mother, our brother and our savior. From this it follows that as truly as God is our Father, so truly is God our Mother. Our Father wills, our Mother works, our good Lord the Holy Spirit confirms. And therefore it is our part to love our God in whom we have our being, reverently thanking and praising him for our creation, mightily praying to our Mother for mercy and pity, and to our Lord the Holy Spirit for help and grace. For in these three is all our life: nature, mercy and grace, of which we have mildness, patience and pity, and hatred of sin and wickedness; for the virtues must of themselves hate sin and wickedness.

And so Jesus is our true Mother in nature by our first creation, and he is our true Mother in grace by his taking our created nature. All the lovely works and all the sweet loving offices of beloved motherhood are appropriated to the second person, for in him we have this godly will, whole and safe forever, both in nature and in grace, from his own goodness proper to him.

I understand three ways of contemplating motherhood in God. The first is the foundation of our nature's creation; the second is his taking of our nature, where the motherhood of grace begins; the third is the motherhood at work. And in that, by the same grace, everything is penetrated, in length and in breadth, in height and in depth without end; and it is all one love.

CHAPTER 60

But now I should say a little more about this penetration, as I understood our Lord to mean: How we are brought back by the motherhood of mercy and grace into our natural place, in which we were created by the motherhood of love, a mother's love which never leaves us.

Our Mother in nature, our Mother in grace, because he wanted altogether to become our Mother in all things, made the foundation of his work most humbly and most mildly in the maiden's womb. And he revealed that in the first revelation, when he brought that meek maiden before the eye of my understanding in the simple stature which she had when she conceived; that is to say that our great God, the supreme wisdom of all things, arrayed and prepared himself in this humble place, all ready in our poor flesh, himself to do the service and the office of motherhood in everything. The mother's service is nearest, readiest and surest: nearest because it is most natural, readiest because it is most loving, and surest because it is truest. No one ever might or could perform this office fully, except only him. We know that all our mothers bear us for pain and for death. O, what is that? But our true Mother Jesus, he alone bears us for joy and for endless life, blessed may he be. So he carries us within him in love and travail, until the full time when he wanted to suffer the sharpest thorns and cruel pains that ever were or will be, and at the last he died. And when he had finished, and had borne us so for bliss, still all this could not satisfy his wonderful love. And he revealed this in these great surpassing words of love: If I could suffer more, I would suffer more. He could not die any more, but he did not want to cease working; therefore he must needs nourish us, for the precious love of motherhood has made him our debtor.

The mother can give her child to suck of her milk, but our precious Mother Jesus can feed us with himself, and does, most courteously and most tenderly, with the blessed sacrament, which is the precious food of true life; and with all the sweet sacraments he sustains us most mercifully and graciously, and so he meant in these blessed words, where he said: I am he whom Holy Church preaches and teaches to you. That is to say: All the health and the life of the sacraments, all the power and the grace of my word, all the goodness which is ordained in Holy Church for you, I am he.

The mother can lay her child tenderly to her breast, but our tender Mother Jesus can lead us easily into his blessed breast through his sweet open side, and show us there a part of the godhead and of the joys of heaven, with inner certainty of endless bliss. And that he revealed in the tenth revelation, giving us the same understanding in these sweet words which he says: See, how I love you, looking into his blessed side, rejoicing.

This fair lovely word "mother" is so sweet and so kind in itself that it cannot truly be said of anyone or to anyone except of him and to him who is the true Mother of life and of all things. To the property of motherhood belong nature, love, wisdom and knowledge, and this is God. For though it may be so that our bodily bringing to birth is only little, humble and simple in comparison with our spiritual bringing to birth, still it is he who does it in the creatures by whom it is done. The kind, loving mother who knows and sees the need of her child guards it very tenderly, as the nature and condition of motherhood will have. And always as the child grows in age and in stature, she acts differently, but she does not change her love. And when it is even older, she allows it to be chastised to destroy its faults, so as to make the child receive virtues and grace. This work, with everything which is lovely and good, our Lord performs in those by whom it is done. So he is our Mother in nature by the operation of grace in the lower part, for love of the higher part. And he wants us to know it, for he wants to have all our love attached to him; and in this I saw that every debt which we owe by God's command to fatherhood and motherhood is fulfilled in truly loving God, which blessed love Christ works in us. And this was revealed in everything, and especially in the great bounteous words when he says: I am he whom you love.

CHAPTER 61

And in our spiritual bringing to birth he uses more tenderness, without any comparison, in protecting us. By so much as our soul is more precious in his sight, he kindles our understanding, he prepares our ways, he eases our conscience, he comforts our soul, he illumines our heart and gives us partial knowledge and love of his blessed divinity, with gracious memory of his sweet humanity and his blessed Passion, with courteous wonder over his great surpassing goodness, and makes us to love everything which he loves for love of him, and to be well satisfied with him and with all his works. And when we fall, quickly he raises us up with his loving embrace and his gracious touch. And when we are strengthened by his sweet working, then we willingly choose him by his grace, that we shall be his servants and his lovers, constantly and forever.

And yet after this he allows some of us to fall more heavily and more grievously than ever we did before, as it seems to us. And then we who are not all wise think that everything which we have undertaken was all nothing. But it is not so, for we need to fall, and we need to see it; for if we did not fall, we should not know how feeble and how wretched we are in ourelves, nor, too, should we know so completely the wonderful love of our Creator.

For we shall truly see in heaven without end that we have sinned grievously in this life; and notwithstanding this, we shall truly see that we were never hurt in his love, nor were we ever of less value in his sight. And by the experience of this falling we shall have a great and marvelous knowledge of love in God without end; for enduring and marvelous is that love which cannot and will not be broken because of offenses.

And this was one profitable understanding; another is the humility and meekness which we shall obtain by the sight of our fall, for by that we shall be raised high in heaven, to which raising we might never have come without that meekness. And therefore we need to see it; and if we do not see it, though we fell, that would not profit us. And commonly we first fall and then see it; and both are from the mercy of God.

The mother may sometimes suffer the child to fall and to be distressed in various ways, for its own benefit, but she can never suffer any kind of peril to come to her child, because of her love. And though our earthly mother may suffer her child to perish, our heavenly Mother Jesus may never suffer us who are his children to perish, for he is almighty, all wisdom and all love, and so is none but he, blessed may he be.

But often when our falling and our wretchedness are shown to us, we are so much afraid and so greatly ashamed of ourselves that we scarcely know where we can put ourselves. But then our courteous Mother does not wish us to flee away, for nothing would be less pleasing to him; but he then wants us to behave like a child. For when it is distressed and frightened, it runs quickly to its mother; and if it can do no more, it calls to the mother for help with all its might. So he wants us to act as a meek child, saying: My kind Mother, my gracious Mother, my beloved Mother, have mercy on me. I have made myself filthy and unlike you, and I may not and cannot make it right except with your help and grace.

And if we do not then feel ourselves eased, let us at once be sure that he is behaving as a wise Mother. For if he sees that it is profitable to us to mourn and to weep, with compassion and pity he suffers that until the right time has come, out of his love. And then he wants us to show a child's characteristics, which always naturally trusts in its mother's love in well-being and in woe. And he wants us to commit ourselves fervently to the faith of Holy Church, and find there our beloved Mother in consolation and true understanding, with all the company of the blessed. For one single person may often be broken, as it seems to him, but the entire body of Holy Church was never broken, nor ever will be without end. And therefore it is a certain thing, and good and gracious to will, meekly and fervently, to be fastened and united to our mother Holy Church, who is Christ Jesus. For the flood of mercy which is his dear blood and precious water is plentiful to make us fair and clean. The blessed wounds of our savior are open and rejoice to heal us. The sweet gracious hands of our Mother are ready and diligent about us; for he in all this work exercises the true office of a kind nurse, who has nothing else to do but attend to the safety of her child. And when we fall quickly he raises us up with his loving call.

It is his office to save us, it is his glory to do it, and it is his will that we know it; for he wants us to love him sweetly and trust in him meekly and greatly. And he revealed this in these gracious words: I protect you very safely.

CHAPTER 62

For at that time he revealed our frailty and our falling, our trespasses and our humiliations, our chagrins and our burdens and all our woe, as much as it seemed to me could happen in this life. And with that he revealed his blessed power, his blessed wisdom, his blessed love, and that he protects us at such times, as tenderly and as sweetly, to his glory, and as surely to our salvation as he does when we are in the greatest consolation and comfort, and raises us to this in spirit, on high in heaven, and turns everything to his glory and to our joy without end. For his precious love, he never allows us to lose time; and all this is of the natural goodness of God by the operation of grace.

God is essence in his very nature; that is to say, that goodness which is natural is God. He is the ground, his is the substance, he is very essence or nature, and he is the true Father and the true Mother of natures. And all natures which he has made to flow out of him to work his will, they will be restored and brought back into him by the salvation of man through the operation of grace. For all natures which he has put separately in different creatures are all in man, wholly, in fullness and power, in beauty and in goodness, in kingliness and in nobility, in every manner of stateliness, preciousness and honor.

Here we can see that we are all bound to God by nature, and we are bound to God by grace. Here we can see that we do not need to seek far afield so as to know various natures, but to go to Holy Church, into our Mother's breast, that is to say into our own soul, where our Lord dwells. And there we should find everything, now in faith and understanding, anad afterwards truly, in himself, clearly, in bliss.

But let no man or woman apply this particularly to himself, because it is not so. It is general, because it is our precious Mother Christ, and for him was this fair nature prepared for the honor and the nobility of man's creation, and for the joy and the bliss of man's salvation, just as he saw, knew and recognized from without beginning.

[THE MEANING OF THE VISIONS IS LOVE]

CHAPTER 86

This book is begun by God's gift and his grace, but it is not yet performed, as I see it. For charity, let us all join with God's working in prayer, thanking, trusting, rejoicing, for so will our good Lord be entreated, by the understanding which I took in all his own intention, and in the sweet words where he says most happily: I am the foundation of your beseeching. For truly I saw and understood in our Lord's meaning that he revealed it because he wants to have it better known than it is. In which knowledge he wants to give us grace to love him and to cleave to him, for he beholds his heavenly treasure with so great love on earth that he will give us more light and solace in heavenly joy, by drawing our hearts from the sorrow and the darkness which we are in.

And from the time that it was revealed, I desired many times to know in what was our Lord's meaning. And fifteen years after and more, I was answered in spiritual understanding, and it was said: What, do you wish to know your Lord's meaning in this thing? Know it well, love was his meaning. Who reveals it to you? Love. What did he reveal to you? Love. Why does he reveal it to you? For love. Remain in this, and you will know more of the same. But you will never know different, without end.

So I was taught that love is our Lord's meaning. And I saw very certainly in this and in everything that before God made us he loved us, which love was never abated and never will be. And in this love he has done all his works, and in this love he has made all things profitable to us, and in this love our life is everlasting. In our creation we had beginning, but the love in which he created us was in him from without beginning. In this love we have our beginning, and all this shall we see in God without end.

> Thanks be to God. Here ends the book of revelations of Julian the anchorite of Norwich, on whose soul may God have mercy.[3]

May Jesus grant us this. Amen. So ends the revelation of love of the blessed Trinity, shown by our savior Jesus Christ for our endless comfort and solace, and also that we may rejoice in him in the passing journey of this life. Amen. Jesus. Amen. I pray almighty God that this book may not come except into the hands of those who wish to be his faithful lovers, and those who will submit themselves to the faith of Holy Church and obey the wholesome understanding and teaching of men who are of virtuous life, settled age and profound learning; for this revelation is exalted divinity and wisdom, and therefore it cannot remain with him who is a slave to sin and to the devil. And beware that you do not accept one thing which is according to your pleasure and liking, and reject another, for that is the disposition of heretics. But accept it all together, and understand it truly; it all agrees with Holy Scripture, and is founded upon it, and Jesus, our true love and light and truth, will show this to all pure souls who meekly and perseveringly ask this wisdom from him. And you to whom this book will come, give our savior Christ Jesus great and hearty thanks that he made these showings and revelations for you and to you out of his endless love, mercy and goodness, for a safe guide and conduct for you and us to everlasting bliss, which may Jesus grant us. Amen. Here end the sublime and wonderful revelations of the unutterable love of God, in Jesus Christ vouchsafed to a dear lover of his, and in her to all his dear friends and lovers whose hearts like hers do flame in the love of our dearest Jesus.

⊷ ⊱◈⊰ ⊶

The Second Play of the Shepherds

Medieval drama is marvelously entertaining, but it was meant to instruct as well. It developed not from classical drama, which virtually died out in the Middle Ages, but from the church liturgy. Although it originated on the Continent, its greatest flowering was in England, in the plays of the Corpus Christi cycle performed from the end of the fourteenth to

---

3. What follows is a lengthy version of the traditional "colophon" in which the author takes leave of the work and its audience; expressions of inadequacy and appeals to God are common elements.

the end of the sixteenth century. So called because they were put on at the feast of Corpus Christi in midsummer, these plays portray the entire cycle of sacred history from Creation to the Last Judgment, including such events as the Fall of Lucifer, Noah's flood, the Nativity, and Christ's Passion and Resurrection. The plays are given coherence by a pattern of typology whereby Satan's deception and Adam's sin are redeemed by Christ's sacrifice. Old Testament events and characters predict and are fulfilled by New Testament ones: Isaac and Moses are types of Christ, and Cain, Pharaoh, and Herod, usually played as comic tyrants, are types of Satan.

The Corpus Christi plays exist in four nearly complete versions, primarily from the north of England: the Chester, N-Town, York, and Wakefield (or Towneley) cycles. They were generally performed outdoors, in partnership with the Church, by craft guilds—associations of tradesmen who made up a newly prosperous mercantile class. Often these guilds sponsored plays whose subject matter was specifically appropriate to their craft—for instance, the Butchers putting on the killing of Abel, and the Water-drawers the story of Noah.

The popularity of the plays—as well as their function as a surrogate Bible for the poor—can be seen in Chaucer's *Miller's Tale*. The Miller himself insists on telling his tale out of turn, speaking in "Pilate's voice," the ranting manner of Pontius Pilate in the passion plays, and the foppish Absolon woos his beloved Alison by playing the role of the tyrant Herod on a scaffold. More importantly, the chief trick of this fabliau—the clerk Nicholas's arranging to be alone with Alison by frightening her husband with the threat of a second flood—relies on the old man's dim memory of the play of Noah.

Nicholas's invocation of a sacred story to pursue a profane goal walks a thin line between comedy and blasphemy. So too did many of the Corpus Christi plays, but for a more obviously sacred purpose. The Wakefield Annunciation, for instance, presents Joseph in fabliau fashion as an old man fearing that he has been cuckolded when he discovers that Mary, his young bride-to-be, is pregnant. Only at the end does he come to understand the divine purpose at work.

Nowhere are the sacred and profane paired as brilliantly as in the nativity play known as *The Second Play of the Shepherds*, one of the Wakefield plays, named after the prosperous Yorkshire town in which they were performed. It was written or revised by an artist of great imagination and skill, no doubt a cleric, known as the Wakefield master. His great achievement is his ability to relate biblical stories to fifteenth-century England in such a way that daily life takes on typological significance: a stolen sheep, hidden in swaddling clothes in a cradle, prefigures the newborn Christ child whom the shepherds visit at the end of the play. The shepherds show mercy to the thief by tossing him in a blanket rather than delivering him to be hanged, prefiguring the mercy that the Christ child will bring into the world.

No matter how neatly the typological scheme works, however, the author does not present the birth of Christ as entirely nullifying the dissatisfactions of the characters in the play. The thief Mak may be a type of the devil, with his guileful assault on the sheep fold and his concealment of a "horned lad" swaddled in a cradle, but his complaints of poverty (he stole the sheep to feed his rapidly expanding family) are real. So too are the lengthy opening complaints of the shepherds against taxes, lords and their condescending servants, and wives who produce too many mouths to feed. Their frustration reflects actual social and economic conditions stemming from the wool and cloth trade that enriched landowners but impoverished laborers in the fourteenth and fifteenth centuries, and thus cannot be dismissed as the grumbling of fallen men who fail to understand their need for divine grace. Similarly, the complaints of Mak's wife Gill about the burden of women's work should not be seen as simply setting her up as a foil to the Virgin Mary: the play gives vivid expression to pressing daily concerns.

The Second Play of the Shepherds

[Scene: Field near Bethlehem.]

I PASTOR Lord, what these weathers are cold!   And I am ill happed.[1]

    I am near hand dold,°   so long have I napped;   *almost numb*

    My legs they fold,   my fingers are chapped.

    It is not as I would,   for I am all lapped°   *tied up*

5   In sorrow.

    In storms and tempest,

    Now in the east, now in the west,

    Woe is him has never rest

    Mid-day nor morrow!

10   But we sely° shepherds   that walks on the moor,   *poor*

    In faith we are near hands   out of the door.

    No wonder, as it stands,   if we be poor,

    For the tilthe of our lands   lies fallow as the floor,

    As ye ken.°   *know*

15   We are so hamed,°   *hamstrung*

    For-taxed° and ramed,°   *overburdened/oppressed*

    We are made hand tamed

    With these gentlery men.°   *gentry, aristocrats*

    Thus they reave° us our rest,   our Lady them wary!°   *rob/curse*

20   These men that are lord-fest,[2]   they cause the plow tarry.

    That men say is for the best,   we find it contrary.

    Thus are husbandys° opprest,   in point to miscarry   *farmhands*

    On live.

    Thus hold they us hunder;°   *under*

25   Thus they bring us in blonder;°   *trouble*

    It were great wonder

    And ever should we thrive.

    For may he get a paint slefe°   or a broche now on days,   *painted sleeve*

    Woe is him that him grefe°   or once again says!   *troubles*

30   Dare noman him reprefe,°   what mastry° he mays,   *reprove/power*

    And yet may noman lefe°   one word that he says,   *believe*

    No letter.

    He can make purveance°   *provision*

    With boast and bragance,

35   And all is through maintenance

    Of men that are greater.

    There shall come a swane   as proud as a po,[3]

    He must borrow my wane,°   my plow also,   *wagon*

    Then I am full fane°   to grant or he go.   *pleased*

40   Thus live we in pain,   anger, and woe,

    By night and day.

    He must have if he langed,°   *desired*

    If I should forgang° it;   *forgo*

    I were better be hanged

45   Then once say him nay.

1. Clothed.
2. Bound to their lords.

3. A servant as proud as a peacock.

It does me good, as I walk   thus by mine one,
Of this world for to talk   in manner of moan.
To my sheep will I stalk,   and hearken anone,°   *awhile*
There abide on a balk,°   or sit on a stone,   *ridge*
50   Full soon.
For I trowe,° perde,°   *believe/by God*
True men if they be,
We get more company
Or° it be noon.   *before*

[*The Second Shepherd enters without noticing the First.*]
II PASTOR   Benste and Dominus!⁴   What may this bemean?
Why fares this world thus?   Oft have we not seen?
Lord, these weathers are spytus,°   and the winds full keen,   *spiteful*
And the frosts so hideous   they water my eyes—
No lie.
60   Now in dry, now in wete,
Now in snow, now in sleet;
When my shoen° freeze to my feet,   *shoes*
It is not all easy.

But as far as I ken,   or yet as I go,
65   We sely wedmen   dre mekyll woe;⁵
We have sorrow then and then: it falls oft so.
Sely Copple,⁶ our hen,   both to and fro
She cackles;
But begin she to croak,
70   To groan or to cluck,
Woe is him is of our cock,
For he is in the shackels.

These men that are wed   have not all their will;
When they are full hard sted,°   they sigh full still;   *placed*
75   God wayte° they are led   full hard and full ill;   *knows*
In bower° nor in bed   they say nought there till,°   *bedroom/thereto*
This tide.°   *time*
My part have I fun;°   *found*
I know my lesson.
80   Woe is him that is bun,°   *bound in marriage*
For he must abide.

But now late in our lives   a marvel to me,
That I think my heart rives°   such wonders to see.   *breaks*
What that destiny drives   it should so be;
85   Some men will have two wives   and some men three,
In store;
Some are woe that has any,
But so far can I,

---

4. Corruption of a Latin blessing, *Benedicite ad Dominum*.   6. A copple is the crest on a bird's head.
5. We poor, innocent married men suffer much.

Woe is him that has many,
90   For he felys° sore.   *suffers*

But young men of a-wooing,   for God that you bought,°   *redeemed*
Be well ware of wedding,   and think in your thought,
"Had I wist"° is a thing   it serves of nought;   *known*
Mekyll° still° mourning   has wedding home brought,   *much/constant*
95   And griefs,
With many a sharp shower;
For thou may catch in an hour
That shall savour fulle sour
As long as thou lives.

100   For, as ever read I pistill[7]   I have one to my fere,°   *mate*
As sharp as a thistle,   as rough as a brere;
She is browed like a bristle   with a sour-loten cheer;[8]
Had she once wet her whistle   she could sing full clear
Her *Paternoster*.°   *Lord's Prayer*
105   She is as great as a whale;
She has a gallon of gall.
By him that died for us all,
I would I had run to°   I had lost her.   *until*

I PASTOR God look over the raw![9]   Full deafly ye stand.
II PASTOR Yea, the devil in thy maw,°   so tariand.°   *mouth/slow*
Saw thou awre° of Daw?[1]   *anywhere*
I PASTOR   Yea, on a ley land°   *fallow ground*
Hard I him blaw.[2]   He comes here at hand,
Not far.
Stand still.
II PASTOR   Why?
I PASTOR For he comes, hope I.
II PASTOR He will make us both a lie
But if° we beware.   *unless*

[*Enter Third Shepherd.*]
III PASTOR Christ's cross me speed,   and Saint Nicholas!
There of had I need;   it is worse than it was.
120   Whoso could take heed   and let the world pass,
It is ever in dread   and brekill° as glass,   *brittle*
And slithes.°   *slides away*
This world fowre°   never so,   *fared*
With marvels mo and mo,
125   Now in weal, now in woe,
And all thing writhes.°   *turns about*

Was never sin° Noah's flood   such floods seen;   *since*
Winds and rains so rude,   and storms so keen;
Some stammerd, some stood   in doubt,° as I ween;   *fear*

7. [St.Paul's] Epistle.
8. Sour-looking face.
9. Let God pay attention to his audience (row), i.e., God
attend me.
1. The Third Shepherd.
2. I just blew by him.

130   Now God turn all to good!   I say as I mean,
        For° ponder.   *to*
        These floods so they drown,
        Both fields and in town,
        And bears all down,
135   And that is a wonder.

        We that walk on the nights,   our cattle to keep,
        We see sudden sights   when other men sleep.
        Yet me think my heart lights;   I see shrews peep;[3]
        Ye are two ill wights.   I will give my sheep
140   A turn.
        But full ill have I meant;
        As I walk on this bent,
        I may lightly repent,
        My toes if I spurn.

145   Ah, sir, God you save,   and master mine!
        A drink fain would I have,   and somewhat to dine.
I PASTOR   Christ's curse, my knave,   thou art a leder hine!°   *lazy servant*
II PASTOR   What, the boy list rave!   Abide unto sine;[4]
        We have made it.[5]
150   Ill thrift on thy pate!
        Though the shrew came late,
        Yet is he in state
        To dine, if he had it.

III PASTOR   Such servants as I,   that sweats and swinks,°   *works*
155   Eats our bread full dry,   and that me forthinks;°   *upsets*
        We are oft wet and weary   when master-men winks;°   *sleeps*
        Yet comes full lately   both diners and drinks,
        But nately.°   *thoroughly*
        Both our dame and our sire,
160   When we have run in the mire,
        They can nip° at our hire,°   *trim/wages*
        And pay us full lately.

        But here my troth, master: for the fare that ye make,
        I shall do therafter,   work as I take;
165   I shall do a little, sir,   and emang ever lake,[6]
        For yet lay my supper   never on my stomach
        In fields.
        Whereto should I threpe?°   *wrangle*
        With my staff can I leap,
170   And men say "Light cheap°   *little cost*
        Letherly for-yields."°   *poorly yields*

I PASTOR   Thou were an ill lad   to ride a-wooing
        With a man that had   but little of spending.
II PASTOR   Peace, boy, I bade.   No more jangling,°   *chattering*

---

3. I see villains peeping out.   5. We have already eaten.
4. The boy is crazy; wait a while.   6. Keep playing besides.

175   Or I shall make there full rad,° by the heavens king!   *quickly*
    With thy gauds°—   *tricks*
    Where are our sheep, boy?—we scorn.°   *despise*
III PASTOR Sir, this same day at morn
    I them left in the corn,
180   When they rang lauds.[7]

    They have pasture good, they cannot go wrong.
I PASTOR That is right, by the roode![8] these nights are long,
    Yet I would, or we yode,° one gave us a song.   *went*
II PASTOR So I thought as I stood, to mirth us among.
III PASTOR I grant.
I PASTOR Let me sing the tenory.
II PASTOR And I treble so hee.
III PASTOR Then the meyne° falls to me: *middle*
    Let see how ye chant.
   [*They sing.*]
   Tunc intrat Mak in clamide se super togam vestitus.[9]

MAK Now, Lord, for thy names vii,[1] that made both moon and starns° *stars*
    Well mo then can I neven° thy will, Lord, of me tharns;[2] *say*
    I am all uneven, that moves oft my harness.
    Now would God I were in heaven, for there weep no barnes° *babies*
    So still.
I PASTOR Who is that pipes so poor?
MAK Would God ye wist how I foor!°   *fared*
    Lo, a man that walks on the moor,
    And has not all his will!

II PASTOR Mak, where has thou gone? Tell us tiding.
III PASTOR Is he comme? Then ylkon° take heed to his thing. *everyone*
   Et accipit clamidem ab ipso.[3]
MAK What! Ich be a yoman,[4] I tell you, of the king;
    The self and the same, sond° from a great lording, *messenger*
    And sich.°   *such like*
    Fy on you! Goeth hence
205   Out of my presence!
    I must have reverence;
    Why, who be ich?
I PASTOR Why make ye it so quaint?[5] Mak, ye do wrang.
II PASTOR But, Mak, list ye saint? I trow that ye lang.[6]
III PASTOR I trow the shrew can paint, the devill might him hang!
MAK Ich shall make complaint, and make you all to thwang[7]
    At a word,
    And tell even how ye doth.

---

7. Lauds; first church service of the day.
8. Cross: The humor here, as with the other oaths, is based on the anachronism that Jesus has not yet been born, much less crucified.
9. Then Mak enters, wearing a cloak over his garment.
1. Seven (written by the copyist as the roman numeral).

2. Is lacking.
3. And he takes his cloak from him.
4. Free-born property-holder.
5. Why act so elegant?
6. Do you want to be a saint? I think you long to be.
7. Be beaten.

I PASTOR But, Mak, is that sooth?
215   Now take out that southren tooth,°   *accent*
        And set in a turd!

II PASTOR Mak, the devil in your eye!   A stroke would I lean° you.   *lend*
III PASTOR Mak, know ye not me?   By God, I could teen° you.   *rage at*
MAK   God look you all three!   Me thought I had seen you;
220   Ye are a fair company.
I PASTOR   Can ye now mean you?
II PASTOR Shrew, pepe!⁸
        Thus late as thou goes,
        What will men suppose?
        And thou has an ill nose°   *reputation*
225   Of steeling of sheep.

MAK   And I am true as steel,   all men waytt,°   *know*
        But a sickness I feel   that holds me full haytt;°   *hot*
        My belly fares not weel;   it is out of estate.
III PASTOR Seldom lies the devil   dead by the gate.⁹
MAK   Therfore
        Full sore am I and ill,
        If I stand stone still;
        I eat not an nedill°   *scrap*
        This month and more.

I PASTOR How fares thy wife? By my hood,   how fares sho?°   *she*
MAK   Lies waltering,° by the rood,   by the fire, lo!   *collapsed*
        And a house full of brood.°   She drinks well, too;   *children*
        Ill spede° other good   that she will do!   *success*
        But sho
240   Eats as fast as she can,
        And ilk° year that comes to man   *each*
        She brings forth a lakan,°   *baby*
        And some years two.

        But were I not more gracious   and richer by far;
245   I were eaten out of house   and of harbar;°   *home*
        Yet is she a foul dowse,°   if ye come nar;   *wench*
        There is none that trowse°   nor knows a war°   *imagines/worse*
        Than ken I.
        Now will ye see what I proffer,
250   To give all in my coffer
        To morn at next to offer
        Her hed mas-penny.¹

II PASTOR I wote so forwaked°   is none in this shire: *sleepless*
        I would sleep if I taked   less to my hire.
III PASTOR I am cold and naked,   and would have a fire.
I PASTOR I am weary, for-rakyd,°   and run in the mire.   *exhausted*

---

8. Villain, look around!.
9. Proverbial: The devil seldom lies dead by the wayside;
i.e., the devil is not often an innocent victim.
1. Penny offering for a mass for the dead.

Wake thou!

II PASTOR Nay, I will lyg° down by,   *lie*
    For I must sleep truly.

III PASTOR As good a man's son was I
    As any of you.

   But, Mak, come hither! Between shall thou lyg down.

[*Mak lies down with the Shepherds.*]

MAK Then might I let you bedene of that ye would rowne,[2]
    No drede.
265 From my top to my toe,
    Manus tuas commendo,
    Poncio Pilato;[3]
    Christ cross me speed!

Tunc surgit, pastoribus dormientibus, et dicit[4]

   Now were time for a man that lacks what he would
270 To stalk privily than unto a fold,
   And nimbly to work than, and be not too bold,
   For he might aby the bargain, if it were told
   At the ending.
   Now were time for to reyll;°   *revel*
275 But he needs good counsel
   That fain would fare well,
   And has but little spending.

   But about you a circle, as round as a moon,
   Too I have done that I will, till° that it be noon,[5]   *until*
280 That ye lyg stone still to that I have done,
   And I shall say theretill of good words a foyne.°   *a few*
   "On hight
   Over your heads my hand I lift;
   Out go your eyes! Fordo° your sight!"   *ruin*
285 But yet I must make better shift,
   And it be right.

   Lord, what they sleep hard! That may ye all here;
   Was I never a shepherd, but now will I lere.°   *learn*
   If the flock be scared, yet shall I nip near.
290 How, drawes° hitherward! Now mends our cheer   *come*
   From sorrow:
   A fat sheep, I dare say,
   A good fleece, dare I lay,
   Eft-whyte when I may,[6]
295 But this will I borrow.

[*Mak goes home to his wife.*]

2. That way I can readily prevent you from whispering together.
3. An amusing corruption of two Bible verses: "Into your hands I commend my soul" and "I wash my hands of this man."
4. Then Mak arises, while the shepherds are sleeping, and speaks.
5. Mak is casting a spell on the shepherds in the form of a fairy circle to keep them from waking.
6. I will pay it back when I can.

How, GIll, art thou in?   Get us some light.

UXOR EIUS[7] Who makes such din   this time of the night?
I am set for to spin;   I hope not[8] I might
Rise a penny to win,°   I shrew° them on height!   *gain/curse*

300   So fares
A housewife that has been
To be raised° thus between: *disturbed*
Here may no note° be seen   *scrap*
For such small chares.°   *chores*

MAK   Good wife, open the hek!°   Sees thou not what I bring?   *inner door*
UXOR   I may thole the dray the snek.[9]   Ah, come in, my sweeting!
MAK   Yea, thou thar not rek°   of my long standing.   *care*
UXOR   By the naked neck   art thou like for to hing.
MAK   Do way:
310   I am worthy my meat,°   *supper*
For in a strait° can I get   *tight spot*
More than they that swink° and sweat   *work*
All the long day.

Thus it fell to my lot,   Gill, I had such grace.
UXOR   It were a foul blot   to be hanged for the case.
MAK   I have skaped, Jelot,[1]   oft as hard a glase.°   *blow*
UXOR   But so long goes the pot   to the water, men says,
At last
Comes it home broken.
MAK   Well know I the token,
But let it never be spoken;
But come and help fast.

I would he were flayn;°   I lyst° well eat: *skinned/wish*
This twelvemonth was I not   so fain of one sheep mete.
UXOR   Come they or° he be slain,   and hear the sheep bleat—   *before*
MAK   Then might I be tane.°   That were a cold sweat!   *taken*
Go spar°   *lock*
The gate-door.
UXOR   Yes, Mak,
For and° they come at thy back—   *if*
MAK   Then might I buy, for all the pack,[2]
The devil of the war.

UXOR   A good bowrde° have I spied,   sin thou can none.   *trick*
Here shall we him hide   to° they be gone;   *until*
335   In my cradle abide.   Let me alone,
And I shall lyg beside   in childbed, and groan.
MAK   Thou red;°   *get ready*
And I shall say thou was light°   *delivered*

---

7. His wife.
8. I don't expect that.
9. I will let you draw the latch.

1. Affectionate nickname for "Gill."
2. Then I may have the worse, for there are such a pack of them.

Of a knave child this night.

UXOR   Now well is me day bright,
340   That ever was I bred.

This is a good gise°   and a far cast;   *way*
Yet a woman avise   helps at the last.
I wote° never who spies,   agane° go thou fast.   *know/back*
MAK   But I come or they rise, else blows a cold blast!
345   I will go sleep.

[*Mak returns to the Shepherds and lies down.*]

Yet sleeps all this meneye,°   *household*
And I shall go stalk privily
As it had never been I
That carried there sheep.

I PASTOR   Resurrex a mortruis!³   Have hold my hand.
           Iudas carnas dominus!⁴   I may not well stand:
           My foot sleeps, by Jesus,   and I water fastand.⁵
           I thought that we had laid us   full near England.

II PASTOR Ah ye!
355   Lord, what I have slept well;
           As fresh as an eel,
           As light I me feel
           As leaf on a tree.

III PASTOR Benste° be here in!   So my heart quakes,   *a blessing*
360   My heart is out of skin,°   what so it makes.   *(body)*
           Who makes all this din?   So my brows blakes°   *darkens*
           To the door will I win.   Hark, fellows, wakes!
           We were four:
           See ye awre° of Mak now?   *anywhere*

I PASTOR   We were up or thou.

II PASTOR Man, I give God a vow,
           Yet yede° he nawre.°   *went/nowhere*

III PASTOR Me thought he was lapt,°   in a wolf skin.   *clothed*
I PASTOR   So are many hapt°   now namely within.   *covered*
II PASTOR When we had long napped,   me thought with a gyn°   *trap*
           A fat sheep he trapped,   but he made no din.

III PASTOR Be still:
           Thy dream makes thee woode:°   *mad*
           It is but phantom, by the roode.°   *cross*

I PASTOR   Now God turn all to good,
           If it be his will.

II PASTOR Rise, Mak, for shame!   Thou lies right long.

MAK   Now Christ's holy name   be us among!
           What is this? For Saint Jame,   I may not well gang!

---

3. Corruption from the Latin Bible of "He rose from the dead."

4. A corruption into Latin gibberish, "Judas lord of the flesh."
5. Stagger from lack of food.

380	I trow I be the same. Ah, my neck has lain wrong	
	Enough.	
	Mekill,° thanks syn° yister even,	*many/since*
	Now, by Saint Steven,	
	I was flayd° with a sweven,°	*frightened/dream*
385	My heart out of slough.°	*skin*

	I thought Gill began to croak and travail° full sad,	*struggle*
	Welner° at the first cock, of a young lad	*nearly*
	For to mend our flock. Then be I never glad;	
	I have tow° on my rock° more then ever I had.	*flax/distaff*
390	Ah, my head!	
	A house full of young tharms;°	*children*
	The devil knock out their harns!°	*brains*
	Woe is him has many barns,	
	And thereto little bread!	

395	I must go home, by your leave, to Gill, as I thought.	
	I pray you looke,° my sleeve that I steal nought:	*inspect*
	I am loath you to grieve, or from you take ought.	
	III PASTOR Go forth, ill might thou chefe!° Now would I we sought,	*fare*
	This morn,	
400	That we had all our store.	
	I PASTOR But I will go before;	
	Let us meet.	
	II PASTOR Whore?	
	III PASTOR At the crooked thorn.	
	[*The Shepherds leave. Mak knocks at his door.*]	
	MAK Undo this door! Who is here? How long shall I stand?	
	UXOR EIUS Who makes such a bere?° Now walk in the wenyand.[6]	*noise*
	MAK Ah Gill, what cheer? It is I, Mak, your husband.	
	UXOR Then may we be here the devil in a band,	
	Sir Gyle:[7]	
	Lo, he comes with a lote°	*noise*
410	As he were holden° in the throat.	*held*
	I may not sit at my note,°	*work*
	A hand-lang° while.	*little*

	MAK Will ye hear what fare she makes to get her a glose?[8]	
	And does nought but lakes° and claws her toes.	*plays*
	UXOR Why, who wanders, who wakes? Who commes, who goes?	
	Who brews, who bakes? What makes me thus hose?°	*hoarse*
	And than,	
	It is rewthe° to behold,	*pitiful*
	Now in hot, now in cold,	
420	Full woeful is the household	
	That wants a woman.	

---

6. Waning hour, unlucky time.   8. Make up an excuse.
7. Mister Deceiver (the Devil).

But what end has thou made   with the herds, Mak?

MAK   The last word that thay said   when I turned my back,
      They would look that they had   their sheep, all the pack.
425   I hope⁹ they will not be well paid   when they their sheep lack,
      Perde!
      But how so the game goes,
      To me they will suppose,
      And make a foul noise,
430   And cry out upon me.

      But thou must do as thou hight.°   *said*

UXOR   I accord me there till.
      I shall swaddle him right   in my cradle;
      If it were a greater sleight,°   yet could I help till.   *trick*
      I will lyg down straight.   Come hap me.

MAK   I will.

UXOR   Behind!
      Come Coll¹ and his maroo,°   *mate*
      They will nyp° us full naroo.°   *pinch/hard*

MAK   But I may cry out "Haroo!"
      The sheep if they find.

UXOR   Harken ay when they call;   they will come onone.°   *soon*
      Come and make ready all   and sing by thine one;
      Sing "lullay" thou shall,   for I must groan,
      And cry out by the wall   on Mary and John,
      For sore.
445   Sing "lullay" on fast
      When thou hears at the last;
      And but I play a false cast,°   *trick*
      Trust me no more.

    [*At the crooked thorn.*]

III PASTOR   Ah, Coll, good morn.   Why sleeps thou not?

I PASTOR   Alas, that ever was I born!   We have a foul blot.
      A fat wether° have we lorne.°   *ram/lost*

III PASTOR   Mary, God's forbot!

II PASTOR   Who should do us that scorn?°   That were a foul spot.   *harm*

I PASTOR   Some shrewe.°   *villain*
      I have sought with my dogs
455   All Horbury² shrogs,°   *hedges*
      And of xv° hogs   *fifteen*
      Found I but one ewe.

III PASTOR   Now trow me, if ye will,   by Saint Thomas of Kent,
      Either Mak or Gill   was at that assent.°   *affair*

I PASTOR   Peace, man, be still!   I saw when he went;
      Thou slanders him ill;   thou ought to repent,

---

9. Expect.   2. A town south of Wakefield.
1. The First Shepherd.

Good speed.

II PASTOR Now as ever might I the,°   *thrive*
  If I should even here die,
465 I would say it were he,
  That did that same deed.

III PASTOR Go we thither, I read, and run on our feet.
  Shall I never eat bread the sothe to I wytt.[3]
I PASTOR Nor drink in my head with him till I meet.
II PASTOR I will rest in no stead till that I him greet,
  My brother.
  One I will hight:°   *promise*
  Till I see him in sight
  Shall I never sleep one night
475 There I do another.

  [They approach Mak's house.]
III PASTOR Will ye hear how they hack?[4] Our sire list croon.
I PASTOR Heard I never none crack so clear out of toon;
  Call on him.
II PASTOR   Mak, undo your door soon.
MAK Who is that spake, as it were noon
480 On loft?
  Who is that, I say?
III PASTOR Good felows, were it day.
MAK As far as ye may,
  Good, speaks soft,

485 Over a sick woman's head that is at malaise;
  I had lever° be dead or she had any disease.   *rather*
UXOR Go to another stead! I may not well qweasse.° *breathe*
  Each foot that ye tread goes through my nese,° *nose*
  So hee!°   *loudly*
I PASTOR Tell us, Mak, if ye may,
  How fare ye, I say?
MAK But are ye in this town to-day?
  Now how fare ye?

  Ye have run in the mire, and are wet yit:
495 I shall make you a fire, if you will sit.
  A nurse would I hire. Think ye on yit,
  Well quit is my hire—[5] my dream this is it—
  A season.
  I have barns, if ye knew,
500 Well mo then enewe,
  But we must drink as we brew,
  And that is but reason.

3. Until I know the truth.   5. My wages are paid; i.e., his dream has been fulfilled.
4. Sing (badly).

        I would ye dined or ye yode.[6] | Me think that ye sweat.

II PASTOR Nay, neither mends our mood   drink nor meat.

MAK   Why, sir, ails you ought but good?

III PASTOR   Yea, our sheep that we get,
        Are stolen as they yode.   Our loss is great.

MAK   Sirs, drinks!
        Had I been there,
        Some should have bought it full sore.

I PASTOR Mary, some men trowes° that ye wore,   *believes*
        And that us forthinks.°   *disturbs*

II PASTOR Mak, some men trowys   that it should be ye.

III PASTOR Either ye or your spouse,   so say we.

MAK   Now if ye have suspowse°   to Gill or to me,   *suspicion*
515   Come and ripe° our house,   and then may ye see   *search*
        Who had her;
        If I any sheep fot,°   *took*
        Either cow or stot;°   *heifer*
        And Gill, my wife, rose not
520   Here sin she laid her.

        As I am true and leal,°   to God here I pray,   *loyal*
        That this be the first meal   that I shall eat this day.

I PASTOR Mak, as have I ceyll,°   advise thee, I say;   *heaven*
        He learned timely to steal   that could not say nay.

UXOR   I swelt!°   *die*
        Out, thieves, from my wonys!°   *home*
        Ye come to rob us for the nonys.°   *for the purpose*

MAK   Here ye not how she groans?
        Your hearts should melt.

UXOR   Out, thieves, from my barn!   Nigh him not thor!°   *there*
MAK   Wist ye how she had farn,°   your hearts would be sore.   *fared*
        Ye do wrong, I you warn,   that thus comes before
        To a woman that has farn—   but I say no more.

UXOR   Ah, my medill!°   *middle*
535   I pray to God so mild,
        If ever I you beguiled,
        That I eat this child
        That lies in this cradle.

MAK   Peace, woman, for God's pain,   and cry not so:
540   Thou spills thy brain,   and makes me full woe.

II PASTOR I trow our sheep be slain.   What find ye two?

III PASTOR All work we in vain;   as well may we go.
        But hatters,°   *(an oath)*
        I can find no flesh,
545   Hard nor nesh,°   *soft*
        Salt nor fresh,
        But two tome° platters.   *empty*

---

6. I would like you to eat before you go.

Whik° cattle but this,   tame nor wild,   *living*
None, as have I bliss,   as loud as he smiled.°   *smelled*

UXOR No, so God me bliss,   and give me joy of my child!

I PASTOR We have marked amiss;   I hold us beguiled.

II PASTOR Sir, don,°   *it is done*
Sir, our Lady him save,
Is your child a knave?[7]

MAK   Any lord might him have
This child to his son.

When he wakens he kips,°   that joy is to see.   *snatches*

III PASTOR In good time to his hips,   and in cele.°   *heaven*
But who was his gossips°,   so soon rede?°   *godparents/ready*

MAK   So fair fall their lips!

I PASTOR   Hark now, a le.°   *lie*

MAK   So God them thank,
Parkin, and Gibon Waller, I say,
And gentle John Horne,[8] in good fay,
He made all the garray,°   *noise*
565   With the great shank.°   *leg*

II PASTOR Mak, friends will we be,   for we are all one.

MAK   We? Now I hold for me,   for mends° get I none.   *profit*
Farewell all three!   All glad were ye gone.

[*The Shepherds depart.*]

III PASTOR Fair words may there be,   but love is there none
570   This year.

I PASTOR Gave ye the child anything?

II PASTOR I trow not one farthing.

III PASTOR Fast again will I fling,°   *hurry*
Abide ye me there.

[*Returns to the house.*]

575   Mak, take it to no grief   if I come to thy barn.°   *baby*

MAK   Nay, thou does me great reproof,   and foul has thou farn.° *done*

III PASTOR The child will it not grief,   that little daystarn.[9]
Mak, with your leaf,   let me give your barn
But vi° pence.   *six*

MAK   Nay, do way: he sleeps.

III PASTOR Me think he peeps.

MAK   When he wakens he weeps.
I pray you go hence.

[*The other Shepherds return.*]

III PASTOR Give me leave him to kiss,   and lift up the clout.°   *cloth*
585   What the devil is this?   He has a long snout.

I PASTOR He is marked amiss.   We wat° ill about.   *watch*

II PASTOR Ill-spun weft, iwys,   ay comes foul out.[1]
Aye, so!

---

7. Boy-child (of the serving-class).
8. Parkin, Gibon Waller, and John Horne are the names of the shepherds in the First Play of the Shepherds, possibly referring to actual townspeople.

9. Little day star; a term also used of the Christ child later in the play, indicating a parallel with Mak's baby.
1. Badly spun thread always makes poor cloth.

He is like to our sheep!

III PASTOR How, Gyb,° may I peep?   *the Second Shepherd*

I PASTOR I trow kind° will creep   *Nature*

    Where it may not go.°   *walk*

II PASTOR This was a quaint gawde,°   and a far cast.   *clever trick*

    It was a high fraud.

III PASTOR   Yea, sirs, was't.

595   Let bren° this bawd,   and bind her fast.   *burn*

    A false skawd°   hang at the last;   *scold*

    So shall thou.

    Will ye see how they swaddle

    His four feet in the middle?

600   Saw I never in a cradle

    A horned lad[2] or° now.   *before*

MAK   Peace bid I. What,   let be youre fare;

    I am he that him gat,°   and yond woman him bare.   *begat*

I PASTOR What devil shall he hat,°   Mak? Lo, God, Mak's heir.   *be called*

II PASTOR Let be all that.   Now God give him care,

    I sagh.°   *saw*

UXOR   A pretty child is he

    As sits on a woman's knee;

    A dillydown,° perde,   *darling*

610   To gar° a man laugh.   *make*

III PASTOR I know him by the earn mark: that is a good token.

MAK   I tell you, sirs, hark!—   his nose was broken.

    Sithen° told me a clerk   that he was forspoken.°   *since/bewitched*

I PASTOR This is a false work;   I would fain be wroken.°   *avenged*

615   Get wepyn.

UXOR   He was taken with° an elf;   *by*

    I saw it myself.

    When the clock struck twelve

    Was he forshapen.°   *changed*

II PASTOR Ye two are well feft°   sam° in a stead.   *endowed/together*

III PASTOR Sin they maintain their theft,   let do them to dead.

MAK   If I trespass eft,°   gird° off my head.   *again/cut*

    With you will I be left.

I PASTOR   Sirs, do my read.°   *advice*

    For this trespass,

625   We will neither ban ne flite,°   *curse nor quarrel*

    Fight nor chite,°   *chide*

    But have done as tite,°   *quickly*

    And cast him in canvas.

    [They toss Mak in a sheet.]

    Lord, what I am sore,   in point for to brist.

630   In faith I may no more;   therefore will I rist.

II PASTOR As a sheep of vii score[3]   he weighed in my fist.

    For to sleep ay-whore°   me think that I list.   *anywhere*

2. A horned child (devil).   3. Seven score pounds (140 lbs).

III PASTOR Now I pray you,
      Lyg down on this green.
I PASTOR On these thieves yet I mene.°   *speak*
III PASTOR Whereto should ye tene?°   *be angry*
      Do as I say you.
      [The Shepherds sleep.]
      Angelus cantat "Gloria in excelsis"; postea dicat[4]

ANGELUS Rise, herd-men heynd! For now is he born
      That shall take fro the fiend   that Adam had lorn;°   *lost*
640   That warloo° to shend,°   this night is he born.   *devil/destroy*
      God is made your friend   now at this morn.
      He behestys°   *orders*
      At Bedlem° go see: *Bethlehem*
      There lies that fre°   *lord*
645   In a crib full poorly,
      Betwyx two bestys.

I PASTOR This was a quaint steven°   that ever yet I heard.   *voice*
      It is a marvel to neven,°   thus to be scared.   *mention*
II PASTOR Of God's son of heaven   he spake upward.°   *on high*
650   All the wood on a leven   me thought that he gard
      Appear.[5]
III PASTOR He spake of a barn
      In Bedlem, I you warn.
I PASTOR That betokens yond starn.°   *star*
655   Let us seek him there.

II PASTOR Say, what was his song?   Heard ye not how he cracked° it?   *roared*
      Three breves to a long.[6]
III PASTOR   Yea, marry, he hakt° it.   *sang*
      Was no crochett° wrong,   nor nothing that lacked it.   *note*
I PASTOR For to sing us among   right as he knacked° it,   *sang*
660   I can.
II PASTOR Let se how ye croon.
      Can ye bark at the moon?
III PASTOR Hold your tongues, have done!
I PASTOR Hark after than.
      [Sings.]

II PASTOR To Bedlem he bade   that we should gang:
      I am full fard°   that we tarry too lang.   *afraid*
III PASTOR Be merry and not sad;   of mirth is our sang;
      Ever-lasting glad   to mede° may we fang,°   *reward/get*
      Without noise.
I PASTOR Hie we thither for-thy;°   *therefore*
      If we be wet and weary,
      To that child and that lady,
      We have it not to lose.

II PASTOR We find by the prophecy—   let be your din—
675   Of David and Isay,[7]   and mo than I min,

---

4. The Angel sings "Glory to God in the highest," and
afterwards says.
5. I thought he lit up the woods like lightning.

6. Three short notes to one long.
7. The prophet Isaiah.

Pro patribus tuis nati sunt ti

The Magi with Shepherds, from the *Luttrel Psalter.* Early 14th century.

They prophesied by clergy   that in a virgin
Should he light and lie,   to sloken° our sin   *remove*
And slake it,
Our kynd° from woe;   *humankind*
680   For Isay said so,
Ecce virgo
Concipiet[8] a child that is naked.

III PASTOR Full glad may we be,   and abide that day
That lovely to see,   that all mights may.
685   Lord, well were me,   for once and for ay,
Might I kneel on my knee,   some word for to say
To that child.
But the angel said
In a crib was he laid;
690   He was poorly arrayed,
Both mener° and milde.   *poor*

I PASTOR Patriarchs that has been,   and prophets beforn,
They desired to have seen   this child that is born.
They are gone full clean,°   that have they lorn.°   *entirely/lost*
695   We shall see him, I ween,   or it be morn,
To token.°   *as proof*
When I see him and feel,
Then wot I full weel
It is true as steel
700   That prophets have spoken:

To so poore as we are   that he would appear,
First find, and declare   by his messenger.
II PASTOR Go we now, let us fare;   the place is us near.
III PASTOR I am ready and yare;°   go we in fere°   *prepared/together*
705   To that bright.
Lord, if thy wills be,
We are lewde° all three,   *unschooled*
Thou grant us somkyns glee°   *some kind of joy*
To comfort thy wight.°   *creature*
[*They enter the stable.*]

8. Behold, a virgin conceives (Isaiah 7.14).

I PASTOR Hail, comely and clean!   Hail, young child!
    Hail, maker, as I mean,   of a maiden so mild!
    Thou has waryd,° I ween,   the warlo° so wild;   *cursed/devil*
    The false gyler° of teen°   now goes he beguiled.   *deceiver/anger*
    Lo, he merries!
715   Lo, he laughs, my sweeting!
    A well fair meeting!
    I have holden my heting;°   *kept my promise*
    Have a bob° of cherries.   *bunch*

II PASTOR Hail, sovereign saviour,   for thou has us sought!
720   Hail, freely food and flour,[9]   that all thing has wrought!
    Hail, full of favour,   that made all of nought!
    Hail! I kneel and I cower.   A bird have I brought
    To my barn.
    Hail, little tyne mop!°   *tiny baby*
725   Of our creed thou art crop:°   *fruit, fulfillment*
    I would drink on thy cop,°   *cup*
    Little day starn.°   *star*

III PASTOR Hail, darling dear,   full of Godhede!
    I pray thee be near   when that I have need.
730   Hail, sweet is thy cheer!   My heart would bleed
    To see thee sit here   in so poor weed,°   *clothing*
    With no pennies.
    Hail, put forth thy dall!°   *hand*
    I bring thee but a ball:
735   Have and play thee with all,
    And go to the tenys.°   *tennis*

MARIA The Father of heaven,   God omnipotent,
    That set all on seven,[1]   his son has he sent.
    My name could he neven,°   and light or he went. *name*
740   I conceived him full even   through might, as he ment,° *intended*
    And now is he born.
    He keep you from woe!
    I shall pray him so.
    Tell forth as ye go,
745   And myn° on this morn.   *remember*

I PASTOR Farewell, lady,   so fair to behold,
    With thy child on thy knee.
II PASTOR   But he lies full cold.
    Lord, well is me!   Now we go, thou behold.
III PASTOR Forsooth already   it seems to be told
750   Full oft.
I PASTOR What grace we have fun!°   *found*
II PASTOR Come forth: now are we won.
III PASTOR To sing are we bun:°   *bound*
    Let take on loft![2]
    [*They go out singing.*]
                Explicit pagina Pastorum.[3]

9. Noble child and flower.   2. Let us sing on high
1. Made everything in seven days.   3. The play of the Shepherds is finished.

Literature of Travel: Marvels and Pilgrimage

Medieval travel was far more frequent and ambitious than is usually thought. Even under the constraints of travel by foot, horse, or sailing ship, medieval men and women regularly crossed all of Europe, and some adventurers went far beyond. Royal courts and their agents were constantly on the move, for purposes of war or administration; diplomats had no choice but to negotiate in person, often for extended periods. Merchants traveled along with their goods, and minstrels and other entertainers roved between courts and cities. The church was international: local representatives went to the papal curia at Rome or Avignon, and papal legates were sent to every major city.

Equally important, distant places exercised people's imaginations, perhaps more than today because so much geography was still unknown or scarcely known. The natural and social marvels of foreign lands helped define ethnic, religious, even human identity. The same boundaries that marked the edge of the known also tended to mark the edge of the human, so that a demon in the *Voyage of Saint Brendan* is represented as an Ethiopian boy. Despite the terrors that hovered at the edge of known geography, though, medieval travelers like Ohthere (see page 135) and Sir John Mandeville were also pressed by pure *curiositas*, for all the moral ambiguity of that emotion.

If travel had an almost anthropological valence, it also had moral and spiritual associations, for good or ill. Stability was highly valued, especially for those religious orders (like monks and anchorites) who sought to renounce this world and pray for the salvation of mankind. Yet travel could also be a part of religious virtue, in crusades, missionary work, or pilgrimages. Christians viewed each pilgrimage—to a local shrine, the tomb of a national saint like Thomas Becket, or the holy city of Jerusalem—as an anticipatory enactment of the soul's quest for Paradise, the "New Jerusalem" of the Book of Revelation (21.10–22.5). Yet because

A Norman-Style Boat, detail from the *Bayeux Tapestry.* Late 11th century. Embroidered on linen in a continuous frieze some 230 feet long, the Bayeux Tapestry narrates events leading up to the Battle of Hastings and the triumph of William the Conqueror over the English, led by King Harold. The boat with a cross on its mast depicted here may be the Conqueror's. Housed today in a museum in Bayeux, France, the tapestry was probably made by English women, who were famed for their needlework.

pilgrimage was an effort of worldly souls to improve or even transcend their fallen state, the trip was always at least symbolically incomplete. Geoffrey Chaucer's story of pilgrimage ends not at the tomb of Saint Thomas, but at the edge of a hamlet outside Canterbury. In the *Voyage of Saint Brendan*, the holy abbot and his companions arrive briefly at the "Land of Promise of the Saints," but their exploration is blocked by a river they cannot cross. Mandeville hesitantly describes the earthly paradise, but (uncharacteristically) insists that he has not seen it and that he reports only from hearsay. And Margery Kempe's very need to repeat her many pilgrimages suggests that no one such experience was spiritually sufficient.

These many kinds of travel were sometimes recorded, in a wide variety of texts: reports by merchant voyagers, practical travelers' guides, pious accounts of pilgrimage, descriptions of the Holy Land, and wonder books of marvels further to the east. From this perspective, the Book of Revelation is at once the most fantastic and most authoritative travel story circulating in the Middle Ages. Its evocation of paradise as a "New Jerusalem," brimming with precious stones and giving rise to four great rivers which flow outward into the fallen world, resonated in works as diverse as pilgrimage narratives and stories of the wonders of the East. Taken together, the following texts dramatize the pervasive interweaving of sacred and secular in medieval culture, as travel to distant places links other physical worlds with spiritual otherworldliness, at the same time providing new venues to explore and express the traveler's—and the reader's—home concerns.

━━◆☰◆━━

The Voyage of Saint Brendan

Saint Brendan "the Navigator" flourished in the sixth century (c. 486–575). Like many early Irish Christians, such as his contemporary Saint Columba, Brendan was an active traveler and missionary and founded several monasteries. He ranged widely across Ireland and Gaelic Scotland and may have visited Wales and Brittany, though he was most active in western Ireland. Written first in Latin, *The Voyage of Saint Brendan* was probably composed in the tenth century by an Irish expatriate in Europe, one of many Irish *peregrini* who pursued voluntary exile and found their way to continental monasteries. The *Voyage* became enormously popular, and survives in over 120 Latin manuscripts and in translations into most medieval European languages.

The stories that grew up around the life of Brendan exemplify the rich and persistent synthesis of native and Christian elements in early medieval Irish culture. The historical if hazy events of Saint Brendan's life engendered a narrative that took its structure and many details from the *immrana*, native tales of wondrous voyages to otherworldly islands. The most famous of these is *The Voyage of Bran*.

Despite its analogies with the magical islands and fairy world of some of the *immrana*, *The Voyage of Saint Brendan* is distinctly an exploration of Christian fall and salvation, set within Brendan's quest for a glimpse of paradise, the "Land of Promise of the Saints." Movements in the *Voyage* are linked to the liturgical calendar; and the sequence of islands Brendan visits displays the gamut of spiritual conditions, from death in a state of sin, through souls in limbo, to saintly hermits living in almost superhuman grace.

In Brendan's adventures, both holiness and time work along a logic of distance. The Land of Promise of the Saints appears to be the most distant of the islands Brendan visits, yet arriving there equally involves testing the travelers' faith during seven years of quest. Conversely, though, as they encounter greater sanctity of life and location, Brendan and his companions experience a stretching of time itself. Years are experienced as days, and holy hermits live for decades on water alone.

Narrative is as important as travel in the *Voyage*. Brendan is inspired to undertake his own quest by another monk's report of a visit to the Land of Promise. Within the story, Brendan prophesies the fate of some of his followers, and other characters predict the time and trajectory of Brendan's journey. Knowledge and language become more transparent with distance, so that the saintly Paul the Hermit knows the names of Brendan's companions at the moment they arrive. Finally, Brendan's own report of his journey, upon his return, generates still another impulse toward holiness among his monks. If *The Voyage of Saint Brendan* is a fantasy of holy travel, it equally emphasizes the efficacy of missionary language.

from The Voyage of Saint Brendan[1]

Saint Brendan, the son of Findlug, great-grandson of Alta of the line of Eogen, was born in the marshy region of Munster.[2] He led a very ascetical life, was renowned for his powers as a miracle worker, and was spiritual father to almost three thousand monks.

One evening, while he was engaged in spiritual warfare[3] in the place known as Brendan's Meadow of Miracles, a monk called Barinthus, one of Brendan's own kinsmen, came to visit him. Brendan questioned him at length and, when the interrogation was over, Barinthus began to weep. He threw himself full-length on the ground, and remained there a long time in prayer until Brendan lifted him to his feet, kissed him, and said, "Father, your visit ought to be filling us with joy, not sadness. Surely you came with the intention of cheering us up, so preach the word of God to us and then regale our spirits with an account of the wonders you have seen on your voyage over the sea."

In answer to this request Barinthus started to tell them about an island he had visited:

"My son Mernoc, the steward of Christ's poor," he began, "fled from my sight in order to live the life of a hermit. He discovered an island called the Island of Delights,[4] situated near a rocky mountain. A long while later I received news that there were many other monks with him on the island, and that God had worked numerous miracles through him. So I went to visit him myself.

"After a three days' journey I reached the island and found Mernoc and his brethren hurrying down to the shore to meet me—the Lord had revealed to him that I was coming. As we went round the island monks poured from their cells like a swarm of bees to look at us. The cells were scattered far and wide over the island, but the monks lived in close spiritual union with each other, bound together in faith, hope, and charity; they all ate at the same table and always sang the Divine Office[5] in common. Their diet was made up of apples, nuts, roots, green vegetables, and nothing else. At night, when compline[6] was over, each monk had to go to his cell and remain there till cockcrow or until the rising bell was rung. My son Mernoc and I stayed awake to wander round the island during the night. He led me to the western shore where there was a small boat moored. 'Father,' he said, 'let us embark and row away westwards to the isle which is called the Land of Promise of the Saints, that land which God will give to us and our successors on the last day.' We boarded ship and sailed away.

"Clouds came down and covered us on all sides, so completely that we could scarcely make out the prow or stern of the vessel, but after we had sailed an hour or two a brilliant light shone round us and a country appeared before us, spacious,

1. Translated by J.F. Webb. From chapters 1–11 and 26–29.
2. This lineage connects Brendan with the Eoganachta clan which ruled Munster, the southwestern province of Ireland, in legendary times. In early myth Munster is a paradoxical place of death (the world of the dead lies off its west coast) and of origin (several invading gods arrive through Munster). Wizards occupy its offshore islands.
3. Private religious observance or struggle. The work of

faith was often compared to battle; St. Brendan later calls his monks "co-warriors."
4. This isle, near the terrestrial paradise but not identical to it, has analogs in many Irish *immrana*.
5. The prayers, hymns, and readings that mark the eight liturgical "hours" of the day; especially observed in monastic communities. Their communal life contrasts with the more strenuous life of hermits later in the voyage.
6. The last of the daily hours.

green, and exceedingly fruitful. The ship put in to land and we disembarked to make a tour of the island. We walked for fifteen days and still did not reach the farther shore. All the plants we saw were flowering plants and every tree was a fruit tree; the very stones beneath our feet were precious.[7] On the fifteenth day we came to a river flowing from east to west. We stood and thought of all the marvels we had seen and wondered what direction we should take: we were eager to cross the river but were waiting for God to show us His will in the matter. Our ponderings were interrupted by the sudden appearance of a man surrounded by an aura of shining light. He greeted us by name and said: 'Be of good cheer, brethren. The Lord has shown you this land which is intended for His saints. The river you see before you divides the island in two. You may not cross it; go back, therefore, the way you came.' I asked him where he came from and what was his name. 'Why do you ask me where I come from or what is my name?' he answered. 'Why do you not rather question me about the island itself? From the very beginning of the world it has remained exactly as you see it now. Do you need any food, drink, or clothing? You have been here a whole year already without tasting food or drink. You have never felt the need for sleep, for it has been daylight all the time. Here there is no obscuring darkness but only perpetual day, the Lord Jesus Christ being Himself our light.'

"We set out at once and the man accompanied us as far as our boat. He disappeared from sight when we boarded the vessel, and we sailed back through the same dense cloud as before and arrived at the Island of Delights. When the brethren caught sight of us they rejoiced greatly and expressed their sorrow over our prolonged absence. 'Why, fathers,' they complained, 'did you leave your sheep to wander about in a wood without their shepherd to tend them? We are becoming accustomed to our abbot's leaving us quite frequently to go we know not where and to stay there for perhaps a week, a fortnight, or even a month.' I tried to comfort them. 'Brethren,' I said, 'please do not think ill of us. You are living before the gate of Paradise. Not far from here is that island which is called the Land of Promise of the Saints, where night never falls and day knows no ending. It is to this place that Mernoc, your abbot, so often goes. Have no fear, for an angel guards him on his journey. Can you not tell by the smell of our garments that we have been in Paradise?'

"'Father,' they answered, 'we know that you have been to God's Paradise over the sea, but exactly where it is we do not know. We have often been able to smell the fragrance issuing from our abbot's garments for forty days after his return.'

"I had stayed with my son for two full weeks on the Island of Promise without eating a bite or drinking a mouthful, yet we felt so replete that anyone might well have thought we were full of new wine. After forty days on the Island of Delights I received the blessing of the abbot and his monks and left with my companions to return to my own cell—I shall arrive there tomorrow."

Saint Brendan and his whole community prostrated themselves, glorifying God and saying "The Lord is righteous in all his ways: and holy in all his works." When they had finished praying, Brendan said: "Let us take some refreshment and carry out the Lord's 'new commandment'."[8] The following morning Saint Barinthus received the brethren's blessing and set off for his own cell.

7. This setting derives ultimately from the New Jerusalem in Revelation 21–22.
8. To be a loving community—which Jesus commands in place of following him on his journey to death and resur-

rection: "Where I am going you cannot come. A new commandment I give to you, that you love one another" (John 13.33–34).

Saint Brendan chose out fourteen monks from the community, shut himself up with them in an oratory, and addressed them thus: "My most beloved co-warriors in spiritual conflict, I beg you to help me with your advice, for I am consumed with a desire so ardent that it casts every other thought and desire out of my heart. I have resolved, if it be God's will, to seek out that Land of Promise of the Saints which our father Barinthus described. What do you think of my plan? Have you any advice to offer?"

As soon as their father in God had made known his intention, they all replied, as with one voice: "Father, your will is ours too. Have we not left our parents and set aside our earthly inheritance in order to put ourselves completely in your hands?[9] We are prepared to come with you, no matter what the consequences may be. We seek to do one thing alone—the will of God."

Saint Brendan and his companions observed a series of three-day fasts, to cover the period of forty days before they were due to set out. At the end of forty days, Brendan bade farewell to the body of his community, commended them to the prior's care (this prior later succeeded Brendan as abbot), and set out westwards with his group of fourteen monks to the island of a holy monk called Enda. There they remained for three days and nights.

At the end of their stay Brendan received the blessing of Enda and of all his monks and set out to the most distant part of the region, where his parents lived. He did not wish to visit them, but, rather, pitched his tent on the top of a mountain that extended far out to sea, in the place that is called Brendan's seat. Below, at the water's edge, there was room for only one boat to put in. Brendan and his companions made a coracle, using iron tools.[1] The ribs and frame were of wood, as is the custom in those parts, and the covering was tanned ox-hide stretched over oak bark. They greased all the seams on the outer surface of the skin with fat and stored away spare skins inside the coracle, together with forty days' supplies, fat for waterproofing the skins, tools and utensils. A mast, a sail, and various pieces of equipment for steering were fitted into the vessel; then Brendan commanded his brethren in the name of the Father, Son, and Holy Spirit to go aboard.

As Brendan was standing alone on the shore blessing the harbor, three of his own monks, who left the monastery in search of him, approached. They fell down in front of their abbot's feet. "Father," they begged, "let us go with you. If you refuse we will remain here and die of hunger and thirst, for we are determined to go with you as pilgrims all the days of our life." Seeing their plight he ordered them aboard: "Your will be done, my sons, though I know what you have come for. One of you has done well and God will reward him with the place he deserves. The other two have a terrible judgment awaiting them."

Then he stepped aboard, the sails were hoisted and they set off towards the summer solstice; the wind was fair and they needed to do no more than steady the sails. After fifteen days' sailing the wind fell and they rowed and rowed until their strength failed. "Have no fear," said Brendan, losing no time in encouraging the brethren, "for God is our helper. He is our captain and guide and will steer us out of danger. Just leave the sails and let Him do as He will with His servants and their boat." They ate every day about the time for vespers, and from time to time the wind would fill their sails, though they knew neither whence it came nor whither it was taking them.

---

9. As Jesus' 12 disciples did in following him.
1. The construction of the boat is a conventional ele-

ment in the *immrana*. Brendan's "iron tools" may suggest technological sophistication.

Forty days passed and they found themselves without food. Then one day an island came in sight towards the south. It looked very high and rocky, and as they drew in to the shore they saw a bank, built high like a wall, and several streams gushing down from the crest of the island into the sea. They could find no harbor at which to put in. Being sorely tormented with hunger and thirst, some of the monks picked up their flasks to fill them from the streams. The saint reproved them for this: "Stop, brethren! What a foolish thing to do! Since God does not intend to show us a way in just yet, why must you start assaulting the place? In three days' time Our Lord Jesus Christ will show us a harbor and a place in which to stay and refresh our weary bodies." They circled round the island for three days and on the third, about the ninth hour, found a harbor just big enough for one ship. Brendan at once stood up and blessed it. On each side loomed a rock, cut away sheer like a wall and tremendously high. When they had all disembarked and were standing on dry land, Saint Brendan forbade them to bring any gear out of the boat. While they were wandering along the shore, a dog ran towards them down a path and sat at Brendan's feet as though he were its master. "You must admit," said Brendan, "that God has sent us a trustworthy messenger. Let us follow him." He and his monks followed the dog till it led them to a group of buildings.

They entered and saw before them a vast hall, well furnished with seats and couches. Jugs of water had been put out for them to wash their feet. When they had sat down, Saint Brendan charged them: "Be on your guard, brethren, lest Satan lead you into temptation. I can see him persuading one of those three brethren who followed us to commit an awful theft. Pray for his soul, for his body is given over to the power of the devil." The walls of the room were hung with vases of various kinds of metal and bridles and drinking horns chased with silver.

Brendan told the monk who normally served their food to prepare supper. This monk found a table already laid, with cloths, rolls of extraordinarily white bread, and fishes. When everything was set out, Brendan blessed the food, praying thus: "Let us praise the God of Heaven who gives every creature its food." There was also plenty to drink. When the meal was over and they had finished the canonical hours for the day, the saint told them to sleep. "Take your rest," he said, "for there is a good, well-covered bed here for each of you. You need rest; you are worn out with over-exertion."

After they had fallen asleep, Saint Brendan witnessed the machinations of the evil one. He saw a little Ethiopian boy[2] holding out a silver necklace and juggling with it in front of the monk. At once the saint arose and persevered in prayer till dawn. At daybreak they went briskly about their business of singing the divine office, so that they might be able to get down to their boat in good time. When they had finished singing, a table appeared before them, already laid for a meal, just as had happened on the previous day. For three days and nights God provided for His servants in this way.

Then they set out on their voyage with this warning from Brendan: "Take care, brethren, not to take anything with you from this island."

"Far be it from us," they rejoined, "to mar our journey with theft."

"What I forecast yesterday has now come to pass. That brother of ours is hiding a silver necklace in his bosom; a devil handed it to him last night."

---

2. The demon as a black boy is common in the Middles Ages; it reflects associations between darkness and demons but equally connects boys and tricksters. This case, further, plays on a geography of morality and the uncanny: what is strange and distant can also be dangerous.

At this the monk flung the necklace from him, fell at Brendan's feet, and cried: "Father, I have sinned. Pardon me and pray for me lest I perish."

The rest of the monks cast themselves to the ground and begged the Lord to save their brother's soul. Brendan lifted the culprit to his feet and the rest of the monks stood up—to see a little Ethiopian boy pop out of the culprit's breast and cry out: "Man of God, why are you expelling me from the home I have lived in these past seven years? You are casting me off from my inheritance."

"In the name of Our Lord Jesus Christ," Brendan replied, "I forbid you to harm any man from now till the Day of Judgment." Then, turning to the monk, "You must receive the Body and Blood of the Lord, for your body and soul are soon to part company. You will be buried here, but that brother of yours who accompanied you out of the monastery will rest only in hell."

The monk received Communion, his soul left his body and was borne heavenwards by angels of light, as the brethren stood looking on. Brendan buried him where he had died.

Saint Brendan and his monks reached the shore of the island where the boat was moored and, just as they were embarking, a young man arrived carrying a basket full of bread and a large jug of water. He greeted them, saying: "Accept a blessing from the hand of your servant. You have a long journey ahead of you before you will find the fulfillment of your desires, but at least you will not lack food and water between now and Easter." They received his blessing and sailed out into the open sea, where they refreshed themselves with food and drink every two days, while their bark was borne hither and thither over the face of the deep.

One day they sighted an island close at hand. A fair wind sprang up after they had set course for it and saved them from being overtaxed by the effort of rowing. On arrival, the man of God ordered them all out, but was himself the last to disembark. A tour of the island led to the discovery of springs gushing forth to form vast streams teeming with fish. "Let us sing the divine office here," said Brendan, "and offer to God the spotless victim of the Cross, for today is Maundy Thursday." They stayed there till Holy Saturday.

In their walks round the island they came across several flocks of sheep, all the same color, white, and so enormous that their great bulky forms quite blotted out the ground from view. Saint Brendan called his brethren together and told them: "Take as many sheep as we shall need for the coming feast." They hurried away to carry out his order. One animal was singled out and its horns were tied. One of the monks took the cord attached to its horns and the sheep trotted along behind him, like a domestic pet. On their return Brendan repeated his command to one of the monks, saying: "Take an unspotted lamb from among the flock." The monk hastily did as he was bidden.

When all preparations had been made for the following day, a man suddenly appeared before them, carrying a basket full of bread baked in hot ashes, and other victuals. He put these down in front of Brendan and fell down three times full length on the ground at the saint's feet, crying out: "What have I done, you pearl of God, to deserve the honor of providing meat and drink for you by the sweat of my brow during this holy season?" Brendan raised him up and kissed him. "My son," he said, "Our Lord Jesus Christ Himself has indicated the place in which we are to celebrate His holy Resurrection."

"Father," the man replied, "you will celebrate Holy Saturday here, but God has decided that you will celebrate the Easter Vigil and tomorrow's masses on the island you can now catch a glimpse of." Then the man began to wait on the servants of God and started collecting together whatever they would need the next day. He packed these supplies and carried them down to the coracle, then said to Brendan: "The boat can hold no more, but in eight days' time I shall bring across to you everything you will need in the way of food and drink, sufficient to last you till Pentecost."

"And how," asked Brendan, "do you know where we will be in eight days from now?"

"By tonight," the man rejoined, "you will be on that island you see close by and you will remain there till the sixth hour tomorrow. Then you will sail westwards to another island, called the Paradise of Birds. There you will remain till the octave of Pentecost."

Saint Brendan asked him how the sheep could possibly grow to so great a size— they were as big as bulls.

"There is nobody on the island to milk them, and since there is no winter to make them go thin they stay out at pasture and feed the whole year round. That is why they are bigger than sheep in your country."

They blessed each other, then Saint Brendan and his monks set out for their boat and were soon rowing away.

Before reaching the neighboring island, their vessel came to a standstill and the monks, on their master's advice, jumped into the shallows and fixed ropes to either side of the boat to enable them to drag it in to the shore. The island was rocky and bare, there was hardly a grain of sand on the beach and only an occasional tree here and there. The monks landed and passed the whole night in prayer in the open, but Brendan stayed on board. He knew perfectly well what kind of an island it was but refrained from telling the others, lest they should take fright.

When morning came, he told the monks who were priests each to say his own mass, and this they did. After Brendan had sung mass in the boat, the monks took out of the coracle joints of raw meat and fish which they had brought over with them from the other island, and sprinkled them with salt. Then they lighted a fire and put a cooking pot on it. When they had built the fire up with sticks and the pot began to boil, the island started to heave like a wave. The monks ran towards the boat, imploring their abbot to protect them. He dragged them in one by one and they set off, leaving behind all the things they had taken ashore. The island moved away across the sea, and when it had gone two miles and more the monks could still see their fire burning brightly. Brendan explained the situation: "Brethren, does the island's behavior surprise you?"

"Indeed it does! We are almost petrified with fright."

"Have no fear, my sons. Last night God revealed to me the meaning of this wonder in a vision. It was no island that we landed on, but that animal which is the greatest of all creatures that swim in the sea. It is called Jasconius."[3]

They rowed towards the island on which they had previously made a three days' stay. They climbed its summit, which faces westwards across the sea, and from there they espied another island close at hand. It was grassy, covered with flowers, full of glades, and separated from the island they were on by only a narrow strait. They sailed round it, looking for a harbor, and put in at the mouth of a stream on the southern shore. This stream was about as wide as the coracle. The monks disembarked, and Brendan instructed them to fix ropes to the sides of the coracle and pull it, with himself on board, as hard as they could, against the current. He was conveyed about a mile upstream to the source. "Our Lord Jesus Christ," he said, "has led us to a

---

3. The most widely known episode in the *Voyage*; "Jasconius" derives from *iasc*, Irish for fish, and may have connections to giant fish of northern mythology.

place in which to stay and celebrate his Resurrection." Then he added: "I think that, even if we had brought no supplies at all, this spring would provide us with all the nourishment we need."

Beyond the spring, on higher ground, there was an exceptionally tall tree growing, with a trunk of colossal girth. This tree was full of pure white birds; so thickly had they settled on it that there was hardly a branch, or even a leaf, to be seen.[4] Brendan wondered why so vast a number of birds should have flocked together. So keenly did he long to unravel the mystery that he threw himself on his knees in tears and prayed silently: "O God, to whom nothing is unknown and who can bring to light every hidden fact, you see how anxious I am. I beseech your infinite majesty to deign to make known to me, a sinner, this secret design of yours which I see before me. I presume to ask, not because of any merit or dignity of my own, but solely on account of your boundless clemency."

He sat down in the boat and one of the birds flew down from the tree towards him. The flapping of its wings sounded like a bell. It settled on the prow, spread out its wings as a sign of joy, and looked placidly at Brendan. He realized at once that God had paid heed to his prayer. "If you are God's messenger," he said to the bird, "tell me where these birds come from and why they are gathered together."

"We are fallen angels," the bird replied, "part of the host which was banished from Heaven through the sin of man's ancient foe. Our sin lay in approving the sin of Lucifer; when he and his band fell, we fell with them. Our God is faithful and just and, by His great justice, we were placed here. Thanks to His mercy, we suffer no torment: our only punishment is to have no part in the vision of His glory which those who stand before His throne in Heaven enjoy. Like the other messengers of God, we wander through the air, over the bowl of Heaven, and upon the earth, but on Sundays and holy days we take on this physical form and tarry here to sing the praises of our creator. You and your companions have completed one year of your journey; six more years remain. Every year you will celebrate Easter in the same place as you are going to spend it today, and at the end of your travels you will achieve your heart's desire—you will find the Land of Promise of the Saints." With that the bird flew away from the prow of the boat and rejoined the flock.

When it was almost time for vespers, the birds all began to sing in unison: "*Thou, O God, art praised in Sion: and unto thee shall the vow be performed in Jerusalem*—,"[5] beating their wings against their sides, and they continued singing the verse antiphonally for a whole hour. To the man of God and his companions the rhythm of the melody combined with the sound of their beating wings seemed as sweet and moving as a plaintive song of lament.

* * *

Saint Brendan and his co-warriors in Christ sailed away in a southerly direction, glorifying God in all things. The appearance of a small island in the distance towards the south made them row more spiritedly. "Do not row too fast," Brendan advised them, as they were approaching it. "You will soon tire yourselves out. You have toiled quite enough—this coming Easter will mark the seventh anniversary of our leaving our homeland. In a short time you will meet Paul the Hermit, a very holy man.[6] He has lived on that island for the past sixty years without a mouthful of food. For thirty years before that an animal used to bring him food."

---

4. Souls of the dead often appear as birds in Irish folklore, and early Celtic Christians thought some fallen angels had a limited knowledge of God.

5. Psalm 64.1.
6. Probably recalling the desert hermit Paul in early Christian Egypt, also called the "first hermit."

The cliffs were so sheer that it was impossible to find a landing place. The island itself was small and round, about a furlong in circumference and as high as it was wide. On top of the cliffs there was no soil, only bare, jagged flint. They sailed round and round and came upon a narrow harbor, barely wide enough to let the prow of the boat pass through. They had difficulty in clambering out of the boat. "Wait here," Brendan instructed them, "till I return. You may not have access to the island without first obtaining permission from the servant of God who dwells here."

He climbed up to the summit and saw two caves with their mouths facing each other, on the eastern side of the isle, and a tiny spring gushing out from a rock in front of the mouth of the cave where the soldier of Christ was sitting. The spring water, as it fell, was at once absorbed by the rock. While Brendan was peering into the mouth of one cave, the old hermit emerged from the cave opposite, saying: "Behold how good and joyful it is for brethren to dwell together in unity."[7] Paul told Brendan to call the monks up from the coracle, kissed them when they arrived, and addressed them each by name. This prophetic gift of knowing their names added to their astonishment at his attire: he wore no clothes at all, yet only his face and eyes were visible, the rest of his body being covered from head to foot with his hair, beard and body hair—all of which was snow white on account of his age. Brendan felt sad within himself at the sight: "How ashamed I feel, I who wear the habit of a monk and have jurisdiction over many monks in our order, when I see this mortal man living like an angel and wholly free from the sins of the flesh."

"Venerable father," the hermit replied, "God has worked many astounding miracles on your behalf, such as have never been vouchsafed to any of the holy fathers. You say you are not worthy to wear the habit of a monk, yet you are higher than any monk. A monk has to support himself by the sweat of his brow, but, for the past seven years, God has secretly fed and clothed you and your family of monks."

In answer to Brendan's questions where he had come from, how he had come and how long he had borne so hard a life, Paul replied: "For forty years I was brought up in Saint Patrick's monastery, where I was caretaker of the cemetery. One day the prior told me to dig a grave in a certain spot for one of the monks. As I was digging, an old man, whom I did not recognize, came up to me and said: 'Do not dig the grave there, brother. That plot of ground is for someone else.'

"'Who are you, father?' I asked.

"'What! Do you not know me? Do you not recognize your abbot?'

"'St. Patrick is my abbot,' I answered.[8]

"'I am he,' the apparition replied. 'Yesterday I departed this life and here I am to be buried.' He pointed to another spot. 'Dig a grave here for the brother who has died recently, and do not repeat what I have told you. Go down to the shore tomorrow and you will find a small boat waiting. Step into it and it will take you to the place where you are to await the day of your death.'

"The following morning I went down to the shore and found a boat, just as Saint Patrick had said. I boarded it and sailed for three days and nights. From the fourth day onward I let myself sail with the wind and on the seventh day I sighted this island and the vessel came straight towards it. Once landed I pushed the boat off with my foot and back it went to my native land, furrowing swiftly through the waves. And here I have remained. Every third day, at the ninth hour, a sea-otter would emerge from the water on its hind legs, with a fish for my dinner in its mouth and a small bundle of twigs between its front paws for kindling a fire. It put down the fish

---

7. Psalm 132.1.

8. Patron saint of Ireland, said to have prophesied Brendan's birth.

and the bundle of twigs and returned to the sea. I lit a fire with flint and iron and cooked the fish. For thirty years the otter fed me. I ate a third part of the fish each day and, thank God, never experienced thirst, for on Sundays a trickle of water flowed from a rock. This provided me with drink there and then and I used to fill a flask to last me for the rest of the week. I did not discover these two caves nor the spring until I had been here thirty years. From then on I lived—indeed am still living—on spring water and nothing else. I have lived ninety years on this island—for thirty of which I lived on fish, and the remaining sixty on water from this spring—and I was fifty when I left my own country; so I am now one hundred and forty years old. And here, in this mortal flesh, I shall soon see my judgment day dawn. Away you go now, and fill your bottles at the spring. You will need water: you have a forty-day journey ahead of you between now and Holy Saturday. You will celebrate Holy Saturday and Easter Sunday and its octave in the same places as you have done these past six years. But this time, when you have received your steward's blessing, you will journey to the Land of Promise of the Saints, and after forty days spent there the God of your fathers will bring you back safe and sound to the land of your birth."

Saint Brendan and his monks received the old man's blessing and set off southwards. During the whole of Lent their little bark was carried hither and thither over the ocean and their only source of nourishment was the water they had brought with them from Paul the Hermit's isle. Yet they were quite content: one drink every three days perfectly satisfied their appetite for food and drink.

On Holy Saturday they arrived at the island where their steward was waiting for them. He was so overjoyed to see them that he lifted them bodily out of the coracle, one by one. When the office of the day was over, he set before them a meal, and on the evening of that same day they put to sea again, taking the steward with them.

They found Jasconius in the usual place, climbed out on to his back, and sang to the Lord the whole night, and said their masses the next morning. After the last mass, the whale swam away and all the brethren called out: "Hear us, O God of our salvation, thou that art the hope of all the ends of the earth, and of them that remain in the broad sea."[9]

"Have no fear," said Brendan, trying to comfort them. "The beast will not harm you; it is helping us on our way."

The whale swam in a straight line towards the Island of Birds, and there they stayed till the octave of Pentecost.

When the solemn season had ended, the steward said to Brendan: "Fill your waterbottles from this spring here and go back on board. This time I shall be your guide and companion, for without me you will never find the Land of Promise of the Saints." As they left, all the birds called out: "May the God of our salvation grant you a safe journey!"

The steward took them back to his island and stocked up the coracle with all they would need on the forty days' journey east which they were about to undertake. He led the way, sailing on in front of them. On the evening of the fortieth day they were enveloped in darkness, so thick that they could hardly see each other. "Do you know what this darkness is?" the steward asked.

"No," said Brendan.

"It swirls round that island which you have been seeking these seven long years." An hour later a brilliant light shone round them—their boat had reached the shore. Before them lay open country covered with apple trees laden with fruit. The monks ate as much as they wanted and drank deeply from the springs. The island was so wide that forty days' wandering still did not bring them to the farther shore. One day

9. Psalm 64.6.

they came upon a vast river flowing through the middle of the country. "What are we to do?" asked Brendan. "We have no idea of the size of the country and we cannot cross this river." While he was standing pondering, a young man approached, kissed the monks joyfully, called them each by name, and said: "Blessed are they that dwell in thy house, O Lord. They shall praise thee for ever and ever."[1]

He turned to Brendan. "Now, at last, you have found the land you have been seeking all these years. The Lord Jesus Christ did not allow you to find it immediately, because first He wished to show you the richness of His wonders in the deep. Fill your ship brim-full with precious stones and return to the land of your birth. The day of your final journey is at hand; you shall soon be laid to rest with your fathers. After many more years have rolled by, this island will be revealed to your successors at the time when Christians will be undergoing persecution. This river divides the island in two. You must be thinking that it is autumn and the fruit has just ripened—it is like this the whole year round; dusk and darkness are unknown, for Christ Himself is our light."

They gathered fruit and all kinds of gems, bade the young man farewell, dismissed their steward with a blessing, and sailed away into the belt of darkness. Once they had passed beyond it, they soon came to the Island of Delights. After a three days' stay they set off, with the abbot's blessing, on a direct route for their own monastery.

Brendan's community was rapturous with joy at his return, and glorified God for His kindness in letting them once more enjoy the sight of their father from whom they had been separated so long. Saint Brendan returned their affection and recounted everything he remembered of the voyage and all the wonders God had deigned to show him. Finally he informed them of the prophecy made by the young man on the Island of Promise, assuring them that he had not long to live. Events proved him right; he put all his affairs in order, and very shortly afterwards, fortified with the sacraments of the Church, lay back in the arms of his disciples and gave up his illustrious spirit to the Lord, to whom be honor and glory, world without end. Amen.

THE END

----+⩺⫯⩹+----

Sir John Mandeville

Mandeville's Travels is a work of fiction that turned into fact, a hoax of such skill that it came to be taken seriously. Scholars have shown how this appealing "eyewitness" travel account—full of sights, sounds, smells, and tastes—is in fact entirely drawn from earlier texts about eastern travel and exotic lands. Yet serious navigators like Columbus and Walter Raleigh carried copies on their voyages. Sir John Mandeville, supposedly a knight from Saint Albans in England, is probably as much an assembled fiction as the work that bears his name. The *Travels* were first written in the mid-fourteenth century, in French, and were quickly translated into most European languages. Over 250 medieval copies survive, a testimony to the work's enormous popularity.

Mandeville's Travels shifts its generic tone as geographical distance increases. "Mandeville" offers an itinerary on the model of many earlier pilgrims' guides, until his story reaches Jerusalem. Beyond that point his narrative becomes ever more fabulous and increasingly is informed by an associative and densely thematic logic, converging ever more with the geography and imagery of the Book of Revelation. It also shifts backward across time, from the site of the Crucifixion to the Earthly Paradise and the first fall of humankind.

1. Psalm 83.5.

Mandeville's exotic geography is filled with marvels and monsters that still delight his readers, but it is equally a space for a loose and associative deployment of social as well as spiritual concerns. Cathay and the empire of Prester John occupy contrary poles of mercantilism and spiritual fervor. Dark deserts and beautiful places are virtually embodiments of the temptation to sin and the desire for salvation. The land of Prester John possesses an idealized feudal order and a humble yet powerful Christian prince. The institution of the "fools of despair" enfolds sexuality and its terrors, which in turn are seen as a journey into the unknown.

Mandeville's narrative moves always roughly eastward, but its cohesion and verisimilitude do not emerge from any precise itinerary. Rather, as the critic Mary Campbell has pointed out, Mandeville invites the reader's trust through a series of strategies we now associate with fiction: appeals to all the senses, assertions of the narrator's personal presence, and complex internal resonance at the level of theme and imagery. Yet, also like fiction, Mandeville's narrative voice sometimes pushes to a level of self-assertion that approaches irony or parody, and thus invites the reader to question its authenticity.

from The Travels of Sir John Mandeville[1]

from Chapter 30: Of the royal estate of Prester John; and of a rich man who built a wonderful castle and called it Paradise

This Emperor, Prester John, has many different countries under his rule, in which are many noble cities and fair towns, and many isles great and broad. For this land of India is divided into isles on account of the great rivers which flow out of Paradise and run through and divide up his land. He also has many great isles in the sea. The principal city of the isle of Pentoxere is called Nise; the Emperor's seat is there, and so it is a noble and rich city. Prester John has under him many kings and many different peoples; and his land is good and wealthy, but not so rich as the land of the Great Khan of Cathay.[2] For merchants do not travel so much to that land as to the land of Cathay, for it is too long a journey. And also merchants can get all they need in the isle of Cathay—spices, golden cloth, and other rich things; and they are reluctant to go to Pentoxere because of the long way and the dangers of the sea. For there are in many places in that sea great rocks of the stone called adamant, which of its nature draws iron to itself. And because no ships that have iron nails in them can sail that way because of these rocks, which would attract the ships to them, men dare not sail there. The ships of that part of the world are all made of wood with no iron. I was once in that sea, and I saw what looked like an island of trees and growing bushes; and the seamen told me that it was all great ships that the rock of adamant had attracted and caught there, and that all these trees and bushes had grown from the things that were in the ships. So because of these dangers and others like them, and because of the distance, they go to Cathay. And yet Cathay is not so near that those who set out from Venice or Genoa or other places in Lombardy do not spend eleven or twelve months traveling by land and sea before they arrive in Cathay. The land of Prester John is many days' journey further. Merchants who do go there go through the land of Persia and come to a city called Hermes,[3] because a philosopher called Hermes founded it. Then they cross an arm of the sea and come to another city

---

1. Translated by C. W. R. D. Moseley. The opening selection reflects widespread belief that a Christian king, Prester John, reigned in an Asian empire beyond the Islamic lands. Mandeville locates Prester John's land beyond "Cathay" (China).
2. Marco Polo (c. 1254–1324) had reported a journey to

the Chinese court of Kublai Khan and the wonders of his realm.
3. Hormuz, on the Persian Gulf, appropriately corrupted to Hermes, who in Greek myth was the gods' messenger and the protector of travelers.

called Soboth or Colach;[4] there they get all kinds of goods, and as great plenty of parrots as there is of larks in our country. In this country there is little wheat or barley, and therefore they eat millet and rice, honey and milk and cheese and all sorts of fruits. Merchants can travel safely enough from there if they wish to. In that land are many parrots, which in their language they call *psitakes*; of their nature they talk just like a man. Those that talk well have long broad tongues, and five toes on each foot; those that do not talk at all—or not much—have only three toes.

This same royal King Prester John and the Great Khan of Tartary are always allied through marriage; for each of them marries the other's daughter or sister. In the land of Prester John there is a great plenty of precious stones of different sorts, some so big that they make from them dishes, bowls, cups and many other things too numerous to mention.

Now I shall speak of some of the principal isles of Prester John's land, and of the royalty of his state and of what religion and creed he and his people follow. This Emperor Prester John is a Christian, and so is the greater part of his land, even if they do not have all the articles of the faith as clearly as we do.[5] Nevertheless they believe in God as Father, Son and Holy Ghost; they are a very devout people, faithful to each other, and there is neither fraud nor guile among them. This Emperor has under his rule seventy-two provinces, each one ruled by a king. These kings have other kings under them, and all are tributary to Prester John. In the land of Prester John there are many marvels. Among others there is a vast sea of gravel and sand, and no drop of water is in it. It ebbs and flows as the ocean itself does in other countries, and there are great waves on it; it never stays still and unmoving. No man can cross that sea by ship or in any other way; and so it is unknown what kind of land or country is on the far side. And though there is no water in that sea, yet is there great plenty of good fish caught on its shores; they are very tasty to eat, but they are of different shape to the fish in other waters. I, John Mandeville, ate of them, and so believe it, for it is true.

And three days' journey from that sea are great mountains, from which flows a large river that comes from Paradise. It is full of precious stones, without a drop of water. It runs with great waves through the wilderness into the Gravelly Sea, and then it disappears. Each week for three days this river runs so fast that no man dare enter it; but on the other days people go into it when they like and gather the precious stones. Beyond that river towards the wilderness is a great plain, set among the hills, all sandy and gravelly, in which there are, as it seems, trees which at the rising of the sun begin to grow, and a fruit grows on them; they grow until midday, and then they begin to dwindle and return back into the earth, so that by sunset nothing is seen of them; this happens each day. No man dare eat of this fruit, or go near it, for it looks like a deceptive phantom. That is accounted a marvelous thing, as well it may be.

In this wilderness are many wild men with horns on their heads; they dwell in woods and speak not, only grunting like pigs. And in some woods in that land are wild dogs, that will never come near to man, any more than foxes do in this country. There are birds, too, that of their own nature speak and call out to men who are crossing the desert, speaking as clearly as if they were men. These birds have large tongues and five claws on each foot. There are others that have only three claws on each foot, and they do not speak so well or clearly. These birds are called parrots, as I said before.

4. Cambay, on an arm of the Arabian Sea.
5. Belief in the land of Prester John involved a yearning for a Christian ally beyond the military and religious threat of Islam.

This same King and Emperor Prester John, when he goes to battle against his enemies, has no banner borne before him; instead there are carried before him three crosses, of fine gold, which are very large and tall and encrusted with precious stones. Ten thousand men at arms and more than a hundred thousand foot soldiers are detailed to look after each cross, in the same way as men guard a banner or standard in battle or wherever. And this number of men is always assigned to the guarding of these crosses whenever the Emperor goes to battle; this is not counting the main army, or certain lords and their men who are ordered to be in the Emperor's own division, and also not counting certain wings whose job it is to forage. And when he rides with his private company in time of peace, there is carried before him a wooden cross, without gold or painting or precious stones, in remembrance of the Passion of Christ who died on a wooden cross. He also has carried in front of him a golden plate full of earth, as a token that notwithstanding his great nobleness and power he came from the earth and to the earth shall he return. And there is carried before him another vessel full of gold and jewels and precious stones, like rubies, diamonds, sapphires, emeralds, topazes, chrysolites and many others, as a token of his nobility, power and might.

I shall now tell you of the arrangement of Prester John's palace, which is usually at the city of Susa. That palace is so wealthy, so noble, so full of delights that it is a marvel to tell of. For on top of the main tower are two balls of gold, in each of which are two great fair carbuncles, which shine very brightly in the night. The chief gates of the palace are of precious stones, which men call sardonyx, and the bars are of ivory. The windows of the hall and the chambers are of crystal. All the tables they eat off are of emeralds, amethysts and, some, of gold, set with precious stones; the pedestals that support the tables are, in the same way, of precious stone. The steps up which the Emperor goes to his throne where he sits at meals are, in turn, onyx, crystal, jasper, amethyst, sardonyx, and coral; and the highest step, which he rests his feet on when at meat, is chrysolite. All the steps are bordered with fine gold, set full of pearls and other precious stones on the sides and edges. The sides of his throne are of emerald, edged in fine gold set with precious stones. The pillars in his chamber are of gold set with precious stones, many of which are carbuncles to give light at night. Nevertheless every night he has burning in his chamber twelve vessels of crystal full of balm, to give a good sweet smell and drive away noxious airs. The frame of his bed is of sapphire, well set in gold, to make him sleep well and to destroy lustful thoughts—for he only lies with his wives on four set occasions in the year, and even then for the sole purpose of engendering children.

This Emperor also has another palace, rich and noble, in the city of Nise, and he sojourns there when it pleases him; but the air is not so good there nor as healthy as it is at Susa. Throughout all Prester John's lands men eat only once a day, as they do in the court of the Great Khan. You must know that every day in his court Prester John has more than thirty thousand people eating, not counting those who come and go; but thirty thousand people neither there nor in the court of the Great Khan consume as much in one day as would twelve thousand in our country. This Emperor always has seven kings in his court to serve him; and when they have served for a month, they go home and another seven kings come and serve for another month. And with those kings there always serve seventy-two dukes and 360 earls and many other lords and knights. And each day in his court twelve archbishops and twenty bishops dine. The Patriarch of Saint Thomas[6] is there rather like a Pope. All the archbishops and

6. St. Thomas was thought to have converted India to Christianity.

bishops and abbots there are kings and lords of great fiefs. Each one of them has some office in the Emperor's court; for one king is porter, another steward, another chamberlain, another steward of the household, another butler, another server, another marshal—and so on, through all the positions that there are in his court. So he is very richly and honorably served. His land is four months' journey in breadth; in length it is without measure. Believe all this, for truly I saw it with my own eyes, and much more than I have told you. For my companions and I lived with him a long time and saw all I have told you, and much more than I have leisure to tell. * * *

from *Chapter 31: Of the head of the devil in the Vale Perilous; and of the customs of the peoples in different isles round there*

A little way from that place towards the River Phison[7] is a great marvel. For there is a valley between two hills, about four miles long; some men call it the Vale of Enchantment, some the Vale of Devils, and some the Vale Perilous. In this valley there are often heard tempests, and ugly, hideous noises, both by day and by night. And sometimes noises are heard as if of trumpets and tabors and drums, like at the feasts of great lords. This valley is full of devils and always has been, and men of those parts say it is an entrance to Hell. There is much gold and silver in this valley, and to get it many men—Christian and heathen—come and go into that valley. But very few come out again—least of all unbelievers—for all who go therein out of covetousness are strangled by devils and lost. In the middle of the valley under a rock one can clearly see the head and face of a devil, very hideous and dreadful to see; nothing else is seen of it except from the shoulders up. There is no man in this world, Christian or anyone else, who would not be very terrified to see it, it is so horrible and foul. He looks at each man so keenly and so cruelly, and his eyes are rolling so fast and sparkling like fire, and he changes his expression so often, and out of his nose and mouth comes so much fire of different colors with such an awful stench, that no man can bear it. But good Christian men, however, who are firm in the faith, can enter that valley without great harm if they are cleanly confessed and absolved and bless themselves with the sign of the Cross; then devils will not harm them. Even if they do get out without bodily hurt, they will not escape without great fear; for devils appear openly to them, menace them, and fly up and down in the air with great thunders and lightnings and awful tempests. Good men as well as evil will have great fear when they pass through, thinking that perhaps God will take vengeance on them for their past sins. My companions and I, when we came near that valley and heard all about it, wondered in our hearts whether to trust ourselves totally to the mercy of God and pass through it; some turned aside and said they would not put themselves in that danger. There were in our company two Friars Minor of Lombardy, who said they would go through that valley if we would go with them; so what with their encouragement and the comfort of their words, we confessed cleanly and heard Mass and took Communion and went into the valley, fourteen of us together. But when we came out we were only nine. We never knew what became of the remainder, whether they were lost or turned back, but we never saw them again. Two of them were Greeks and three Spaniards. Our other companions, who would not cross the Vale Perilous, went round by another way to meet us. And my companions and I went through the valley, and saw many marvelous things, and gold and silver and precious

7. Ganges.

stones and many other jewels on each side of us—so it seemed to us. But whether it really was as it seemed, or was merely illusion, I do not know. But because of the fear that we were in, and also so as not to hinder our devotion, we would touch nothing we saw: for we were more devout then than we ever were before or after, because of the fear we had on account of devils appearing to us in different guises and of the multitude of dead men's bodies that lay in our path. For if two kings with their armies had fought together and the greater part of both sides been slain, there would not have been a greater number of dead bodies than we saw. And when I saw so many bodies lying there, I was very astonished that they were so healthy, without corruption, as fresh as if they had been newly dead. But I dare not affirm that they were all true bodies that I saw in that valley; I believe that devils made so many bodies appear so as to frighten us; for it is not likely that so great a multitude of folk should have really been dead there so freshly that there was no smell or corruption. Many of those bodies I saw seemed to be wearing the clothing of Christian men; but I well believe they came there from covetousness of the gold and other jewels in that valley, or because false hearts cannot stand the great fear and dread that they had on account of the horrible sights they saw. And I assure you that we were often struck to the earth by terrible great blasts of wind, thunder and tempests; but through the grace of Almighty God we passed through safe and sound.

Beyond that valley is a great isle where the folk are as big in stature as giants of twenty-eight or thirty feet tall. They have no clothes to wear except the skins of beasts, which they cover their bodies with. They eat no bread; but they eat raw flesh and drink milk, for there is an abundance of animals. They have no houses to live in, and they will more readily eat human flesh than any other. Thanks to them no pilgrim dare enter this isle; for if they see a ship in the sea with men aboard, they will wade into the sea to take the men. We were told that there is another isle beyond that where there are giants much bigger than these, for some are fifty or sixty feet tall. I had no desire to see them, for no man can go to that isle without being promptly strangled by those monsters. In these isles among these giants are sheep as big as oxen, but their wool is thick and coarse. I have often seen those sheep; and some men have often seen those giants catch people in the sea and go back to the land with two in one hand and two in the other, eating their flesh raw.

There is another fair and good isle, full of people, where the custom is that when a woman is newly married, she shall not sleep the first night with her husband, but with another young man, who shall have ado with her that night and take her maidenhead, taking in the morning a certain sum of money for his trouble. In each town there are certain young men set apart to do that service, which are called *gadlibiriens*, which is to say "fools of despair." They say, and affirm as a truth, that it is a very dangerous thing to take the maidenhead of a virgin; for, so they say, whoever does puts himself in peril of death. And if the husband of the woman find her still virgin on the next night following (perchance because the man who should have had her maidenhead was drunk, or for any other reason did not perform properly to her), then shall he have an action at law against the young man before the justices of the land—as serious as if the young man had intended to kill him. But after the first night, when those women are so defiled, they are kept so strictly that they shall not speak to or even come into the company of those men. I asked them what the cause and reason was for such a custom there. They told me that in ancient times some men had died in that land in deflowering maidens, for the latter had snakes within them, which stung the husbands on their penises inside the women's bodies; and thus many men were slain, and so they follow that custom there to make other men test out the route before they themselves set out on that adventure.

Another isle is to the southwards in the Great Sea Ocean where there are wicked and cruel women, who have precious stones growing in their eyes. They are such a nature that if they look upon a man with an angry intention, the power of those stones slays him with a look, as the basilisk does.

Near there is another isle, where the women make great sorrow when their children are born and great joy when they are dead. They call their friends together and make a feast and take the dead child and throw it into a great fire and burn it. And women who loved their husbands well, when they are dead, throw themselves with their children into the fire to be burned. It is their opinion there that they are purged by the fire, so that no corruption shall ever after come by them, and, purged of all vice and all deformity, they will pass to their husbands in the next world. The cause why they weep and sorrow at the birth of their children and rejoice when they die is that when they are born into this world they come to sorrow and trouble, and when they die, they go to the joy of Paradise, where rivers of milk and honey and plenty of all kinds of good things are, and a life without sorrow. In this isle the King is always elected; they do not choose the richest or noblest man, but him who has the best character and is the most just and true, they make their King. They also ensure that he is an old man and not young. In that isle too are very righteous judges; for they do justice and right to every man, to poor as to rich, and judge every man according to his guilt and not according to his state or degree. The King also may not put anyone to death without the assent and advice of all his barons. If the King himself commits a trespass, like killing a man or some other such notable thing, he shall be killed for it. But he will not be killed by a man's hand; rather they shall forbid any man to be so bold as to keep company with him, or speak to him, come to him, or give him food or drink. And so he dies for pure need, hunger, thirst, and the sorrow in his heart. No one who is convicted of a trespass is spared, neither for riches, high estate, dignity, high birth, nor for any kind of gift; every man shall have according to his deeds. * * *

Chapter 33: Of the mountains of gold, which the ants watch over; and of the four rivers that come from the Earthly Paradise

East from the land of Prester John is a large fertile land called Taprobane.[8] There is a rich and noble King in that isle, subject to Prester John. He is chosen by election. Here there are two summers and two winters in a single year, and harvest also twice in a year. And at all times of the year their gardens are full of flowers and their meadows green. Good and rational people dwell in this isle; there are many good Christian men among them who are so rich that they do not know the total of their goods. In former times, when people sailed there from the land of Prester John, they used ships of such a type that they needed twenty days to sail thither; but in the ships we use now they can do it in seven days. And as they sail they can often see the bottom of the sea in several places, for it is not very deep.

On the east there are two isles near this one, of which one is called Oriell and the other Arget;[9] in those two isles the earth is full of gold and silver ore. And they are near the Red Sea, where it enters the Great Sea Ocean. And in those isles no

---

8. Sri Lanka, formerly called Ceylon.
9. In the *Etymologies* of Isidore of Seville (c. 560–636), these islands are called Chryse and Argyre, for their production of gold and silver.

stars can clearly be seen shining, except for one they call Canapos;[1] nor can the moon be seen there except in the second quarter. In this isle of Ceylon are great hills of gold, which ants busily look after, purifying the gold and separating the fine from the unfine. Those ants are as big as dogs are here, so that no man dare go near those hills for fear that the ants might attack them; however, men win that gold by a trick. For the nature of the ants is that when the weather is hot, they will hide in the earth from mid-morning till after noon; and then the men of that country come with camels and dromedaries and horses, load them up with that gold, and go away before the ants come out of their holes. At other times of the year, when the weather is not hot and the ants do not hide in the earth, they use another trick to get this gold. They take mares who have young foals, and hang on each side of each mare an empty container with the mouth of it uppermost, trailing near to the ground, and then send them forth early in the morning to pasture round the hills where the gold is, keeping the foals at home. Then these ants, when they see these empty containers, go and fill them with gold; for it is the nature of the ant to leave nothing empty near them—there is no hole or cranny or anything else that they will not fill. And when it is thought that the mares are fully laden with gold, the men let the foals out, and they neigh after their dams. Then the mares hear their foals neighing and hurry quickly to them, laden with gold. And in this way men get a great deal of gold; for the ants easily tolerate all sorts of animals, man excepted.

Beyond these isles I have told you of, beyond the deserts in the empire of Prester John, going still east, there is no inhabited land, as I said earlier; only wastes and wilderness and great crags and mountains and a dark land, where no man can see by night or day, as we were told. That dark land and those deserts last right to the Earthly Paradise, in which Adam and Eve were put; but they were only there a little while. And in the east of that place the earth begins. But that is not our east, where the sun rises for us; for when the sun rises in those countries, it is midnight in our land, because of the roundness of the earth. For, as I said before, God made the earth quite round, in the middle of the firmament. The hills and the valleys that are now on the earth are the result only of Noah's flood, by which soft earth was moved from its place leaving a valley, and the hard ground stayed still and became a hill.

Of Paradise I cannot speak properly, for I have not been there; and that I regret. But I shall tell you as much as I have heard from wise men and trustworthy authorities in those countries. The Earthly Paradise, so men say, is the highest land on earth; it is so high it touches the sphere of the moon. For it is so high that Noah's flood could not reach it, though it covered all the rest of the earth. Paradise is encircled by a wall; but no man can say what the wall is made of. It is all grown over with moss and with bushes so that no stone can be seen, nor anything else a wall might be made of. The wall of Paradise stretches from the south to the north; there is no way into it open because of ever burning fire, which is the flaming sword that God set up before the entrance so that no man should enter.

In the middle of Paradise is a spring from which come four rivers, which run through different lands. These rivers sink down into the earth inside Paradise and then run many a mile underground; afterwards they rise up out of the earth again in distant lands. The first of these rivers is called Phison or Ganges; it rises in India

1. Canopus, the second-brightest star in the sky.

below the hills of Orcobares,[2] and runs eastwards through India into the Great Sea Ocean. In that river are many precious stones and plenty of the wood called *lignum aloes,*[3] and much gold in the gravel. This river is called the Phison because many waters collect and join it, for "Phison" means roughly "gathering." It is also called Ganges after a king who was in India, whom men called Gangaras; because it runs through his land it was called Ganges. This river is clear in some places, disturbed in others, in some places hot, in others cold. The second river is called Nile or Gyon; it rises out of the earth a little way from Mount Atlant.[4] Not far thence it sinks down again into the earth and runs underground until it comes to the shore of the Red Sea, and there it rises again out of the earth and runs all round Ethiopia, and so through Egypt until it comes to Alexandria the Great; there it enters the Mediterranean. This river is always disturbed and is therefore called Gyon; for "Gyon" means the same as "troubled." The third river is called the Tigris, that is, "fast running"; for it is one of the swiftest rivers of the world. It is called Tigris after an animal of the same name, which is the fastest animal on foot in the world. This river rises in Armenia under the Mount Parchoatra and runs through Armenia and Asia to the south, and then turns into the Mediterranean Sea. The fourth river is called Euphrates, which is as much as to say "bearing well"; for many good things grow along that river. That river runs through Media, Armenia and Persia. And men say that all the fresh rivers of the world have their beginning in the spring that wells up in Paradise.

You should realize that no living man can go to Paradise. By land no man can go thither because of the wild beasts in the wilderness, and because of the hills and rocks, which no one can cross; and also because of the many dark places that are there. No one can go there by water either, for those rivers flow with so strong a current, with such a rush and such waves that no boat can sail against them. There is also such a great noise of waters that one man cannot hear another, shout he never so loudly. Many great lords have tried at different times to travel by those rivers to Paradise, but they could not prosper in their journeys; some of them died through exhaustion from rowing and excessive labor, some went blind and deaf through the noise of the waters, and some were drowned through the violence of the waves. And so no man, as I said, can get there except through the special grace of God. And so of that place I can tell you no more; so I shall go back and tell you of things that I have seen in the isles and lands of the empire of Prester John, which, relative to us, are below the earth.

→+ ⌖ +←

Margery Kempe
c. 1373–after 1439

Spiritual quest and literal travel converge in *The Book of Margery Kempe*. Daughter of a mayor in the prosperous market town of Lynn, Margery began her adult life quite traditionally, married to the burger John Kempe. A mental and religious crisis followed the birth of her first child, influencing Margery to take up a holier form of life. Her highly expressive spirituality

---

2. Perhaps the Himalayas.
3. A precious, fragrant wood, used in incense, mentioned

in the Bible.
4. Mount Atlas.

annoyed and unnerved many of her contemporaries, as Kempe was aware. Yet her visions and warmly physical imagery, which verged on the erotic, her weeping and noisy mourning for the sufferings of Christ, were recurrent elements of later medieval affective piety. Nonetheless, Kempe sometimes enraged political and ecclesiastical authorities and later alienated her fellow pilgrims. Despite her admiration for Julian of Norwich and the similarity of their religious yearnings, Margery took a very different path. Julian had prospered, in part at least, because of her physical enclosure, her self-deprecating rhetoric, and her carefully managed status within ecclesiastical structures. Margery Kempe, by contrast, continued to live in the world, spoke without clerical mediation, and frequently traveled into areas where her habits were unknown. She was repeatedly accused and taken into custody for being a Lollard heretic, although doctrinally quite conservative as she ably and repeatedly proved under hostile examination.

Kempe both defended and explored her spirituality in a series of journeys to ecclesiastical authorities and to pilgrimage sites as distant as Jerusalem, Rome, and Santiago de Compostela in Spain. On such journeys she typically was most sorely tempted, but also most rewarded by visionary encounters. Kempe's pilgrimage toward Jerusalem becomes a kind of literal *imitatio Christi* or retracing of Christ's life. Her abandonment by companions, ridicule as a holy fool, and persecution all echo events of the Passion, especially as it was depicted in the mystery plays she had probably attended. This imitation had its climax on Mount Calvary, where Margery received a vision of the crucifixion, and fell in agony "spreading her arms out wide."

Margery Kempe's travel, dress, and frankly uncontrolled expressivity invited repeated criticism in her own time. The wayward structure of her book, ordered as events came into her memory, has encouraged a dismissive attitude among many modern readers. Yet Margery's sobs and roars did no more than exaggerate the religious modes of her era, and the book's recursive structure has analogies in mystical meditation. Kempe was keenly aware of the pressure her faith placed on the social fabric, and her book is by turns apologetic and articulate in her own defense. Kempe knew she was heir to an established spiritual tradition. She visited with Julian of Norwich and mentions that she heard readings from the works of Richard Rolle and Walter Hilton. Just as important, Kempe had biographical and religious models in a series of women from the continent who had disengaged themselves (with difficulty) from their secular lives as wives and mothers and embraced a life of religious quest, among them Mary of Oignies, Bridget of Sweden, and Angela of Foligno.

Margery Kempe had to struggle and negotiate with forms of male authority that only began with her husband. By canon law, John Kempe could demand the rights of the marriage bed, and did so for many years. Only a bishop could allow the weekly Eucharist for which Margery yearned. Hostile officials and clerics repeatedly attempted to silence or misrepresent her. And her very book depended on a sequence of inadequate and unreliable male amanuenses. Yet it is possible to exaggerate Margery's struggle against the hierarchies of male power. She was warmly supported by a number of holy men, including the Bishop of Lincoln. For all the conflicts within her marriage, Margery often expresses a wry and affectionate sense of John Kempe's indulgence, and sympathy for his weakness. Much of the domestic imagery of *The Book of Margery Kempe* derives from her fractious but loving relationship with her husband.

Perhaps the most appealing aspects of Margery's religious imagery derive, in fact, from domestic life. If Jesus becomes her lover, he does so very much as a husband, and when Margery has a vision of Christ's birth she bustles about like a midwife. Margery's concentration on the Eucharist is continuous with her experience of meals in the family and in society. Indeed, a long negotiation with her husband, crucial to Margery's pursuit of chastity, centers around the heat and thirst of travel, a cake and a bottle of beer. Yet the humble meal that caps their agreement has clear eucharistic implications. Whatever the spectacle of her religious expression, and the struggle to maintain and record it, Margery Kempe's religion and sense of her own limits are grounded in the very life she was eager to abjure.

from The Book of Margery Kempe[1]
The Preface

A short treatise of a creature set in great pomp and pride of the world, who later was drawn to our Lord by great poverty, sickness, shame, and great reproofs in many diverse countries and places, of which tribulations some shall be shown hereafter, not in the order in which they befell, but as the creature could remember them when they were written.

For it was twenty years and more from the time when this creature had forsaken the world and busily cleaved to our Lord before this book was written, notwithstanding that this creature had much advice to have her tribulations and her feelings written down, and a White Friar[2] freely offered to write for her if she wished. And she was warned in her spirit that she should not write so soon. And many years later she was bidden in her spirit to write.

And then it was written first by a man who could neither write English nor German well, so that it could not be read except by special grace alone, for there was so much obloquy and slander of this creature that few men would believe her.

And so at last a priest was greatly moved to write this treatise, and he could not read it for four years together. And afterwards, at the request of this creature, and compelled by his own conscience, he tried again to read it, and it was much easier than it was before. And so he began to write in the year of our Lord 1436, on the next day after Mary Magdalene,[3] after the information of this creature.

[LIFE AND TEMPTATIONS, REVELATION, DESIRE FOR FOREIGN PILGRIMAGE]
CHAPTER 1

When this creature was twenty years of age, or somewhat more, she was married to a worshipful burgess and was with child within a short time, as nature would have it. And after she had conceived, she was troubled with severe attacks of sickness until the child was born. And then, what with the labor-pains she had in childbirth and the sickness that had gone before, she despaired of her life, believing she might not live. Then she sent for her confessor, for she had a thing on her conscience which she had never revealed before that time in all her life. For she was continually hindered by her enemy—the devil—always saying to her while she was in good health that she didn't need to confess but to do penance by herself alone, and all should be forgiven, for God is merciful enough. And therefore this creature often did great penance in fasting on bread and water, and performed other acts of charity with devout prayers, but she would not reveal that one thing in confession.

And when she was at any time sick or troubled, the devil said in her mind that she should be damned, for she was not shriven of that fault.[4] Therefore, after her child was born, and not believing she would live, she sent for her confessor, as said before, fully wishing to be shriven of her whole lifetime, as near as she could. And when she came to the point of saying that thing which she had so long concealed, her confessor was a little too hasty and began sharply to reprove her before she had fully said what she meant, and so she would say no more in spite of anything he

1. Translated by B. A. Windeatt.
2. Alan of Lynne, a Carmelite.
3. July 23.
4. Margery had not completed the stages of penance: contrition, confession, restitution (or other act of repentance), absolution. She never says openly what her unconfessed sin was.

might do. And soon after, because of the dread she had of damnation on the one hand, and his sharp reproving of her on the other, this creature went out of her mind and was amazingly disturbed and tormented with spirits for half a year, eight weeks and odd days.

And in this time she saw, as she thought, devils opening their mouths all alight with burning flames of fire, as if they would have swallowed her in, sometimes pawing at her, sometimes threatening her, sometimes pulling her and hauling her about both night and day during the said time. And also the devils called out to her with great threats, and bade her that she should forsake her Christian faith and belief, and deny her God, his mother, and all the saints in heaven, her good works and all good virtues, her father, her mother, and all her friends. And so she did. She slandered her husband, her friends, and her own self. She spoke many sharp and reproving words; she recognized no virtue nor goodness; she desired all wickedness; just as the spirits tempted her to say and do, so she said and did. She would have killed herself many a time as they stirred her to, and would have been damned with them in hell,[5] and in witness of this she bit her own hand so violently that the mark could be seen for the rest of her life. And also she pitilessly tore the skin on her body near her heart with her nails, for she had no other implement, and she would have done something worse, except that she was tied up and forcibly restrained both day and night so that she could not do as she wanted.

And when she had long been troubled by these and many other temptations, so that people thought she should never have escaped from them alive, then one time as she lay by herself and her keepers were not with her, our merciful Lord Christ Jesus—ever to be trusted, worshiped be his name, never forsaking his servant in time of need—appeared to his creature who had forsaken him, in the likeness of a man, the most seemly, most beauteous, and most amiable that ever might be seen with man's eye, clad in a mantle of purple silk, sitting upon her bedside, looking upon her with so blessed a countenance that she was strengthened in all her spirits, and he said to her these words: "Daughter, why have you forsaken me, and I never forsook you?"

And as soon as he had said these words, she saw truly how the air opened as bright as any lightning, and he ascended up into the air, not hastily and quickly, but beautifully and gradually, so that she could clearly behold him in the air until it closed up again.

And presently the creature grew as calm in her wits and her reason as she ever was before, and asked her husband, as soon as he came to her, if she could have the keys of the buttery to get her food and drink as she had done before. Her maids and her keepers advised him that he should not deliver up any keys to her, for they said she would only give away such goods as there were, because she did not know what she was saying, as they believed.

Nevertheless, her husband, who always had tenderness and compassion for her, ordered that they should give her the keys. And she took food and drink as her bodily strength would allow her, and she once again recognized her friends and her household, and everybody else who came to her in order to see how our Lord Jesus Christ had worked his grace in her—blessed may he be, who is ever near in tribulation. When people think he is far away from them he is very near through his grace. Afterwards this creature performed all her responsibilities wisely and soberly enough, except that she did not truly know our Lord's power to draw us to him.

---

5. Suicide was considered a mortal sin.

CHAPTER 2

And when this creature had thus through grace come again to her right mind, she thought she was bound to God and that she would be his servant. Nevertheless, she would not leave her pride or her showy manner of dressing, which she had previously been used to, either for her husband, or for any other person's advice. And yet she knew full well that people made many adverse comments about her, because she wore gold pipes on her head,[6] and her hoods with the tippets were fashionably slashed. Her cloaks were also modishly slashed and underlaid with various colors between the slashes, so that she would be all the more stared at, and all the more esteemed.

And when her husband used to try and speak to her, to urge her to leave her proud ways, she answered sharply and shortly, and said that she was come of worthy kindred—he should never have married her—for her father was sometime mayor of the town of N., and afterwards he was alderman of the High Guild of the Trinity in N.[7] And therefore she would keep up the honor of her kindred, whatever anyone said.

She was enormously envious of her neighbors if they were dressed as well as she was. Her whole desire was to be respected by people. She would not learn her lesson from a single chastening experience, nor be content with the worldly goods that God had sent her—as her husband was—but always craved more and more.

And then, out of pure covetousness, and in order to maintain her pride, she took up brewing, and was one of the greatest brewers in the town of N. for three or four years until she lost a great deal of money, for she had never had any experience in that business. For however good her servants were and however knowledgeable in brewing, things would never go successfully for them. For when the ale had as fine a head of froth on it as anyone might see, suddenly the froth would go flat, and all the ale was lost in one brewing after another, so that her servants were ashamed and would not stay with her. Then this creature thought how God had punished her before—and she could not take heed—and now again by the loss of her goods; and then she left off and did no more brewing.

And then she asked her husband's pardon because she would not follow his advice previously, and she said that her pride and sin were the cause of all her punishing, and that she would willingly put right all her wrongdoing. But yet she did not entirely give up the world, for she now thought up a new enterprise for herself. She had a horse-mill. She got herself two good horses and a man to grind people's corn, and thus she was confident of making her living. This business venture did not last long, for shortly afterwards, on the eve of Corpus Christi,[8] the following marvel happened. The man was in good health, and his two horses were strong and in good condition and had drawn well in the mill previously, but now, when he took one of those horses and put him in the mill as he had done before, this horse would not pull in the mill in spite of anything the man might do. The man was sorry, and tried everything he could think of to make his horse pull. Sometimes he led him by the head, sometimes he beat him, and sometimes he made a fuss of him, but nothing did any good, for the horse would rather go backwards than forwards. Then this man set a pair of sharp spurs on his heels and rode on the horse's back to make him pull, but it was no

---

6. Margery wore the fashionable *crespine*, a horned head-dress of wire, often in gold or silver.

7. Margery here uses an initial for her town; later she openly calls it Lynn.

8. A feast day toward midsummer commemorating the Eucharist; marked by the performance of mystery plays in major mercantile towns such as York.

better. When this man saw it was no use, he put the horse back in his stable, and gave him food, and the horse ate well and freshly. And afterwards he took the other horse and put him in the mill. And just as his fellow had done so did he, for he would not pull for anything the man might do. And then this man gave up his job and would not stay any longer with the said creature.[9]

Then it was noised about in the town of N. that neither man nor beast would serve the said creature, and some said she was accursed; some said God openly took vengeance on her; some said one thing and some said another. And some wise men, whose minds were more grounded in the love of our Lord, said it was the high mercy of our Lord Jesus Christ that called her from the pride and vanity of this wretched world.

And then this creature, seeing all these adversities coming on every side, thought they were the scourges of our Lord that would chastise her for her sin. Then she asked God for mercy, and forsook her pride, her covetousness, and the desire that she had for worldly dignity, and did great bodily penance, and began to enter the way of everlasting life as shall be told hereafter.

CHAPTER 3

One night, as this creature lay in bed with her husband, she heard a melodious sound so sweet and delectable that she thought she had been in paradise.[1] And immediately she jumped out of bed and said, "Alas that ever I sinned! It is full merry in heaven." This melody was so sweet that it surpassed all the melody that might be heard in this world, without any comparison, and it caused this creature when she afterwards heard any mirth or melody to shed very plentiful and abundant tears of high devotion, with great sobbings and sighings for the bliss of heaven, not fearing the shames and contempt of this wretched world. And ever after her being drawn towards God in this way, she kept in mind the joy and the melody that there was in heaven, so much so that she could not very well restrain herself from speaking of it. For when she was in company with any people she would often say, "It is full merry in heaven!"

And those who knew of her behavior previously and now heard her talk so much of the bliss of heaven said to her, "Why do you talk so of the joy that is in heaven? You don't know it, and you haven't been there any more than we have." And they were angry with her because she would not hear or talk of worldly things as they did, and as she did previously.

And after this time she never had any desire to have sexual intercourse with her husband, for paying the debt of matrimony was so abominable to her that she would rather, she thought, have eaten and drunk the ooze and muck in the gutter than consent to intercourse, except out of obedience.

And so she said to her husband, "I may not deny you my body, but all the love and affection of my heart is withdrawn from all earthly creatures and set on God alone." But he would have his will with her, and she obeyed with much weeping and sorrowing because she could not live in chastity. And often this creature advised her husband to live chaste and said that they had often (she well knew) displeased God by their inordinate love, and the great delight that each of them had in using the other's body, and now it would be a good thing if by mutual consent they punished and chastised themselves by abstaining from the lust of their bodies. Her husband

---

9. Popular superstition can be glimpsed behind the failure in brewing and milling, and the servants' refusal to stay with Margery thereafter.

1. Compare Richard Rolle's discussion of heavenly music, page 440.

said it was good to do so, but he might not yet—he would do so when God willed. And so he used her as he had done before, he would not desist. And all the time she prayed to God that she might live chaste, and three or four years afterwards, when it pleased our Lord, her husband made a vow of chastity, as shall be written afterwards, by Jesus's leave.

And also, after this creature heard this heavenly melody, she did great bodily penance. She was sometimes shriven two or three times on the same day, especially of that sin which she had so long concealed and covered up, as is written at the beginning of this book. She gave herself up to much fasting and keeping of vigils; she rose at two or three of the clock and went to church, and was there at her prayers until midday and also the whole afternoon. And then she was slandered and reproved by many people because she led so strict a life. She got herself a hair-cloth from a kiln—the sort that malt is dried on—and put it inside her gown as discreetly and secretly as she could, so that her husband should not notice it. And nor did he, although she lay beside him every night in bed and wore the hair-shirt every day, and bore him children during that time.

Then she had three years of great difficulty with temptations, which she bore as meekly as she could, thanking our Lord for all his gifts, and she was as merry when she was reproved, scorned or ridiculed for our Lord's love, and much more merry than she was before amongst the dignities of this world. For she knew very well that she had sinned greatly against God and that she deserved far more shame and sorrow than any man could cause her, and contempt in this world was the right way heavenwards, for Christ himself chose that way. All his apostles, martyrs, confessors and virgins, and all those who ever came to heaven, passed by the way of tribulation, and she desired nothing as much as heaven. Then she was glad in her conscience when she believed that she was entering upon the way which would lead her to the place that she most desired.

And this creature had contrition and great compunction, with plentiful tears and much loud and violent sobbing, for her sins and for her unkindness towards her maker. She reflected on her unkindness since her childhood, as our Lord would put it into her mind, very many times. And then when she contemplated her own wickedness, she could only sorrow and weep and ever pray for mercy and forgiveness. Her weeping was so plentiful and so continual that many people thought that she could weep and leave off when she wanted, and therefore many people said she was a false hypocrite, and wept when in company for advantage and profit. And then very many people who loved her before while she was in the world abandoned her and would not know her, and all the while she thanked God for everything, desiring nothing but mercy and forgiveness of sin.

CHAPTER 4

For the first two years when this creature was thus drawn to our Lord she had great quiet of spirit from any temptations. She could well endure fasting—it did not trouble her. She hated the joys of the world. She felt no rebellion in her flesh. She was so strong—as she thought—that she feared no devil in hell, for she performed such great bodily penance. She thought that she loved God more than he loved her. She was smitten with the deadly wound of vainglory and felt it not, for she desired many times that the crucifix should loosen his hands from the cross and embrace her in token of love. Our merciful Lord Christ Jesus, seeing this creature's presumption, sent her—as is written before—three years of great temptations, of one of the hardest of which I intend to write, as an example to those who come after that they should not trust in themselves nor have joy in themselves as this creature had—for undoubtedly our spiritual enemy does not sleep but busily probes our temperament and attitudes, and wherever he finds us most frail, there, by our Lord's sufferance, he lays his snare, which no one may escape by his own power.

And so he laid before this creature the snare of lechery, when she thought that all physical desire had been wholly quenched in her, and so she was tempted for a long time with the sin of lechery, in spite of anything she might do. Yet she was often shriven, she wore her hair-shirt, and did great bodily penance and wept many a bitter tear, and often prayed to our Lord that he should preserve her and keep her so that she should not fall into temptation, for she thought she would rather have been dead than consent to that. And in all this time she had no desire to have intercourse with her husband, and it was very painful and horrible to her.

In the second year of her temptations it so happened that a man whom she liked said to her on Saint Margaret's Eve before evensong that, for anything, he would sleep with her and enjoy the lust of his body, and that she should not withstand him, for if he might not have his desire that time, he said, he would have it another time instead—she should not choose. And he did it to test what she would do, but she imagined that he meant it in earnest and said very little in reply. So they parted then and both went to hear evensong, for her church was dedicated to Saint Margaret. This woman was so troubled with the man's words that she could not listen to evensong, nor say her paternoster, nor think any other good thought, but was more troubled than she ever was before.

The devil put it into her mind that God had forsaken her, or else she would not be so tempted. She believed the devil's persuasions, and began to consent because she could not think any good thought. Therefore she believe that God had forsaken her. And when evensong was over, she went to the said man, in order that he should have his will of her, as she believed he desired, but he put forward such a pretence that she could not understand his intent, and so they parted for that night. This creature was so troubled and vexed all that night that she did not know what she could do. She lay beside her husband, and to have intercourse with him was so abominable to her that she could not bear it, and yet it was permissible for her and at a rightful time if she had wished it. But all the time she was tormented to sin with the other man because he had spoken to her. At last—through the importunings of temptation and a lack of discretion—she was overcome and consented in her mind, and went to the man to know if he would then consent to have her. And he said he would not for all the wealth in this world; he would rather be chopped up as small as meat for the pot.

She went away all ashamed and confused in herself, seeing his steadfastness and her own instability. Then she thought about the grace that God had given her before, of how she had two years of great quiet in her soul, of repentance for her sins with many bitter tears of compunction, and a perfect will never again to turn to sin but rather, she thought, to be dead. And now she saw how she had consented in her will to sin. Then she half fell into despair. She thought herself in hell, such was the sorrow that she had. She thought she was worthy of no mercy because her consenting to sin was so wilfully done, nor ever worthy to serve God, because she was so false to him.

Nevertheless she was shriven many times and often, and did whatever penance her confessor would enjoin her to do, and was governed according to the rules of the Church. That grace God gave this creature—blessed may he be—but he did not withdraw her temptation, but rather increased it, as she thought.

And therefore she thought that he had forsaken her, and dared not trust to his mercy, but was troubled with horrible temptations to lechery and despair nearly all the following year, except that our Lord in his mercy, as she said to herself, gave her every day for the most part two hours of compunction for her sins, with many bitter tears. And afterwards she was troubled with temptations to despair as she was before, and was as far from feelings of grace as those who never felt any. And that she could not bear, and so she continued to despair. Except for the time that she felt grace, her trials were so amazing that she could not cope very well with them, but always mourned and sorrowed as though God had forsaken her.

CHAPTER 5

Then on a Friday before Christmas Day, as this creature was kneeling in a chapel of Saint John, within a church of Saint Margaret in N., weeping a very great deal and asking mercy and forgiveness for her sins and her trespasses, our merciful Lord Christ Jesus—blessed may he be—ravished her spirit and said to her, "Daughter, why are you weeping so sorely? I have come to you, Jesus Christ, who died on the cross suffering bitter pains and passion for you. I, the same God, forgive you your sins to the uttermost point. And you shall never come into hell nor into purgatory, but when you pass out of this world, within the twinkling of an eye, you shall have the bliss of heaven, for I am the same God who has brought your sins to your mind and caused you to be shriven of them. And I grant you contrition until your life's end.

"Therefore, I command you, boldly call me Jesus, your love, for I am your love and shall be your love without end. And, daughter, you have a hair-shirt on your back. I want you to leave off wearing it, and I shall give you a hair-shirt in your heart which shall please me much more than all the hair-shirts in the world. But also, my beloved daughter, you must give up that which you love best in this world, and that is the eating of meat. And instead of meat you shall eat my flesh and my blood, that is the true body of Christ in the sacrament of the altar. This is my will, daughter, that you receive my body every Sunday, and I shall cause so much grace to flow into you that everyone shall marvel at it.[2]

"You shall be eaten and gnawed by the people of the world just as any rat gnaws the stockfish.[3] Don't be afraid, daughter, for you shall be victorious over all your enemies. I shall give you grace enough to answer every cleric in the love of God. I swear to you by my majesty that I shall never forsake you whether in happiness or in sorrow. I shall help you and protect you, so that no devil in hell shall ever part you from me, nor angel in heaven, nor man on earth—for devils in hell may not, nor angels in heaven will not, nor man on earth shall not.

"And daughter, I want you to give up your praying of many beads, and think such thoughts as I shall put into your mind. I shall give you leave to pray until six o'clock to say what you wish. Then you shall lie still and speak to me in thought, and I shall give you high meditation and true contemplation.[4] And I command you to go to the anchorite at the Preaching Friars and tell him my confidences and counsels which I reveal to you, and do as he advises, for my spirit shall speak in him to you."

---

2. Weekly communion was uncommon, and required special ecclesiastical permission. Margery may have known that an admired predecessor, St. Bridget of Sweden, took weekly communion.

3. Dried cod.

4. Christ thus promises Margery the mystic way, without the ecclesiastical mediation of set prayers.

Then this creature went off to see the anchorite as she was commanded, and revealed to him the revelations that had been shown to her. Then the anchorite, with great reverence and weeping, thanking God, said, "Daughter, you are sucking even at Christ's breast, and you have received a pledge of paradise.[5] I charge you to receive such thoughts—when God will give them—as meekly and devoutly as you can, and then come and tell me what they are, and I shall, by the leave of our Lord Jesus Christ, tell you whether they are from the Holy Ghost or else from your enemy the devil."

CHAPTER 11

It happened one Friday, Midsummer Eve,[6] in very hot weather—as this creature was coming from York carrying a bottle of beer in her hand, and her husband a cake tucked inside his clothes against his chest—that her husband asked his wife this question: "Margery, if there came a man with a sword who would strike off my head unless I made love with you as I used to do before, tell me on your conscience—for you say you will not lie—whether you would allow my head to be cut off, or else allow me to make love with you again, as I did at one time?"

"Alas, sir," she said, "why are you raising this matter, when we have been chaste for these past eight weeks?"

"Because I want to know the truth of your heart."

And then she said with great sorrow, "Truly, I would rather see you being killed, than that we should turn back to our uncleanness."

And he replied, "You are no good wife."

And then she asked her husband what was the reason that he had not made love to her for the last eight weeks, since she lay with him every night in his bed. And he said that he was made so afraid when he would have touched her, that he dared do no more.

"Now, good sir, mend your ways and ask God's mercy, for I told you nearly three years ago that your desire would suddenly be slain—and this is now the third year, and I hope yet that I shall have my wish. Good sir, I pray you to grant what I shall ask, and I shall pray for you to be saved through the mercy of our Lord Jesus Christ, and you shall have more reward in heaven than if you wore a hair-shirt or wore a coat of mail as a penance. I pray you, allow me to make a vow of chastity at whichever bishop's hand that God wills."

"No," he said, "I won't allow you to do that, because now I can make love to you without mortal sin, and then I wouldn't be able to."

Then she replied, "If it be the will of the Holy Ghost to fulfill what I have said, I pray God that you may consent to this; and if it be not the will of the Holy Ghost, I pray God that you never consent."

Then they went on towards Bridlington[7] and the weather was extremely hot, this creature all the time having great sorrow and great fear for her chastity. And as they came by a cross her husband sat down under the cross, calling his wife to him and saying these words to her: "Margery, grant me my desire, and I shall grant you your desire. My first desire is that we shall still lie together in one bed as we have done before; the second, that you shall pay my debts before you go to Jerusalem; and the third, that you shall eat and drink with me on Fridays as you used to do."

---

5. The image of Christ as mother particularly recalls Julian of Norwich, whom Margery later visits.
6. Probably 23 June 1413. The feast of Corpus Christi fell on the previous day, and it is likely that Margery and her husband had seen the great cycle of mystery plays traditionally performed in York on that day.
7. On the coast, east of York.

"No, sir," she said, "I will never agree to break my Friday fast as long as I live."

"Well," he said, "then I'm going to have sex with you again."

She begged him to allow her to say her prayers, and he kindly allowed it. Then she knelt down beside a cross in the field and prayed in this way, with a great abundance of tears: "Lord God, you know all things. You know what sorrow I have had to be chaste for you in my body all these three years, and now I might have my will and I dare not, for love of you. For if I were to break that custom of fasting from meat and drink on Fridays which you commanded me, I should now have my desire. But, blessed Lord, you know I will not go against your will, and great is my sorrow now unless I find comfort in you. Now, blessed Jesus, make your will known to my unworthy self, so that I may afterwards follow and fulfill it with all my might."

And then our Lord Jesus Christ with great sweetness spoke to this creature, commanding her to go again to her husband and pray him to grant her what she desired: "And he shall have what he desires. For, my beloved daughter, this was the reason why I ordered you to fast, so that you should the sooner obtain your desire, and now it is granted to you. I no longer wish you to fast, and therefore I command you in the name of Jesus to eat and drink as your husband does."

Then this creature thanked our Lord Jesus Christ for his grace and his goodness, and afterwards got up and went to her husband, saying to him, "Sir, if you please, you shall grant me my desire, and you shall have your desire. Grant me that you will not come into my bed, and I grant you that I will pay your debts before I go to Jerusalem. And make my body free to God, so that you never make any claim on me requesting any conjugal debt after this day as long as you live—and I shall eat and drink on Fridays at your bidding."[8]

Then her husband replied to her, "May your body be as freely available to God as it has been to me."

This creature thanked God greatly, rejoicing that she had her desire, praying her husband that they should say three paternosters in worship of the Trinity for the great grace that had been granted them. And so they did, kneeling under a cross, and afterwards they ate and drank together in great gladness of spirit. This was on a Friday, on Midsummer's Eve.

Then they went on to Bridlington and also to many other places, and spoke with God's servants, both anchorites and recluses, and many other of our Lord's lovers, with many worthy clerics, doctors and bachelors of divinity as well, in many different places. And to various people amongst them this creature revealed her feelings and her contemplations, as she was commanded to do, to find out if there were any deception in her feelings.

CHAPTER 15

This creature, when our Lord had forgiven her her sin (as has been written before), had a desire to see those places where he was born, and where he suffered his Passion and where he died, together with other holy places where he was during his life, and also after his resurrection.

While she was feeling these desires, our Lord commanded her in her mind—two years before she went[9]—that she should go to Rome, to Jerusalem, and to Santiago de Compostela, and she would gladly have gone, but she had no money to go with.

---

8. Margery may have received an inheritance from her father by now, giving her the financial leverage to strike a deal, in effect, for her chastity.

9. Probably 1411.

And then she said to our Lord, "Where shall I get the money to go to these holy places with?"

Our Lord replied to her, "I shall send you enough friends in different parts of England to help you. And, daughter, I shall go with you in every country and provide for you. I shall lead you there and bring you back again in safety, and no Englishman shall die in the ship that you are in. I shall keep you from all wicked men's power. And, daughter, I say to you that I want you to wear white clothes and no other color, for you shall dress according to my will."[1]

"Ah, dear Lord, if I go around dressed differently from how other chaste women dress, I fear people will slander me. They will say I am a hypocrite and ridicule me."

"Yes, daughter, the more ridicule that you have for love of me, the more you please me."

Then this creature dared not do otherwise than as she was commanded in her soul. And so she set off on her travels with her husband, for he was always a good and easygoing man with her. Although he sometimes—out of groundless fear—left her on her own for a while, yet he always came back to her again, and felt sorry for her, and spoke up for her as much as he dared for fear of other people. But all others that went along with her forsook her, and they most falsely accused her—through temptation of the devil—of things that she was never guilty of.

And so did one man in whom she greatly trusted, and who offered to travel with her, at which she was very pleased, believing he would give her support and help her when she needed it, for he had been staying a long time with an anchorite, a doctor of divinity and a holy man, and that anchorite was this woman's confessor.

And so his servant—at his own inward stirring—took his leave to travel with this creature; and her own maidservant went with her too, for as long as things went well with them and nobody said anything against them.

But as soon as people—through the enticing of our spiritual enemy, and by permission of our Lord—spoke against this creature because she wept so grievously, and said she was a false hypocrite and deceived people, and threatened her with burning, then this man, who was held to be so holy, and in whom she trusted so much, rebuked her with the utmost force and scorned her most foully, and would not go any further with her. Her maidservant, seeing discomfort on every side, grew obstreperous with her mistress. She would not do as she was told, or follow her mistress's advice. She let her mistress go alone into many fine towns and would not go with her.

And always, her husband was ready when everybody else let her down, and he went with her where our Lord would send her, always believing that all was for the best, and would end well when God willed.

And at this time, he took her to speak with the Bishop of Lincoln, who was called Philip,[2] and they stayed for three weeks before they could speak to him, for he was not at home at his palace. When the Bishop came home, and heard tell of how such a woman had waited so long to speak to him, he then sent for her in great haste to find out what she wanted. And then she came into his presence and greeted him, and he warmly welcomed her and said he had long wanted to speak with her, and he was very glad she had come. And so she asked him if she might speak with him in private and confide in him the secrets of her soul, and he appointed a convenient time for this.

---

1. White dress implied special holiness or virginity.
2. Philip Repyngdon, Bishop of Lincoln 1405–1419. This journey occurred after their private agreement of chastity in June 1413.

When the time came, she told him all about her meditations and high contemplations, and other secret things, both of the living and the dead, as our Lord revealed to her soul.[3] He was very glad to hear them, and graciously allowed her to say what she pleased, and greatly commended her feelings and her contemplations, saying they were high matters and most devout matters, and inspired by the Holy Ghost, advising her seriously that her feelings should be written down.

And she said that it was not God's will that they should be written so soon, nor were they written for twenty years afterwards and more.

And then she said furthermore, "My Lord, if it please you, I am commanded in my soul that you shall give me the mantle and the ring, and clothe me all in white clothes. And if you clothe me on earth, our Lord Jesus Christ shall clothe you in heaven, as I understand through revelation."[4]

Then the Bishop said to her, "I will fulfill your desire if your husband will consent to it."

Then she said to the Bishop, "I pray you, let my husband come into your presence, and you shall hear what he will say."

And so her husband came before the Bishop, and the Bishop asked him, "John, is it your will that your wife shall take the mantle and the ring and that you live chaste, the two of you?"

"Yes, my lord," he said, "and in token that we both vow to live chaste I here offer my hands into yours," and he put his hands between the Bishop's hands.

And the Bishop did no more with us on that day, except that he treated us very warmly and said we were most welcome. * * *

[VISIT WITH JULIAN OF NORWICH]

CHAPTER 18

This creature was charged and commanded in her soul that she should go to a White Friar in the same city of Norwich, who was called William Southfield, a good man who lived a holy life, to reveal to him the grace that God had wrought in her, as she had done to the good Vicar before. She did as she was commanded and came to the friar one morning, and was with him in a chapel for a long time, and told him her meditations and what God had wrought in her soul, in order to know if she were deceived by any delusions or not.[5]

This good man, the White Friar, all the time that she told him of her feelings, held up his hands and said, "Jesus, mercy, and thanks be to Jesus."

"Sister," he said, "have no fear about your manner of life, for it is the Holy Ghost plentifully working his grace in your soul. Thank him highly of his goodness, for we are all bound to thank him for you, who now in our times inspires you with his grace, to the help and comfort of all of us who are supported by your prayers and by others such as you. And we are preserved from many misfortunes and troubles which we should deservedly suffer for our trespasses, were there not such good creatures among us. Blessed be Almighty God for his goodness.

---

3. Margery had some prophetic visions, though on a smaller scale than those of her predecessor St. Bridget of Sweden.
4. By clothing her, the bishop would acknowledge Margery and John's vow of chastity. In the Book if Revelation (ch.

7), the saints in heaven and clothed in white robes.
5. Southfield was a Carmelite friar who received visions of the Virgin Mary. Many mystical texts warn against the possibility that visions may be of demonic origin; see selections from *The Cloud of Unknowing*, pages 445–447.

"And therefore, sister, I advise you to dispose yourself to receive the gifts of God as lowly and meekly as you can, and put up no obstacle or objections against the goodness of the Holy Ghost, for he may give his gifts where he will, and the unworthy he makes worthy, the sinful he makes righteous. His mercy is always ready for us unless the fault be in ourselves, for he does not dwell in a body subject to sin. He flies from all false pretense and falsehood; he asks of us a low, a meek, and a contrite heart, with a good will.[6] Our Lord says himself, 'My spirit shall rest upon a meek man, a contrite man, and one who fears my words.'[7]

"Sister, I trust to our Lord that you have these conditions either in your will or in your affections or else in both, and I do not consider that our Lord allows to be endlessly deceived those who place their trust in him, and seek and desire nothing but him only, as I hope you do. And therefore believe fully that our Lord loves you and is working his grace in you. I pray God increase it and continue it to his everlasting worship, for his mercy."

The said creature was much comforted both in body and in soul by this good man's words, and greatly strengthened in her faith.

And then she was commanded by our Lord to go to an anchoress in the same city who was called Dame Julian.[8] And so she did, and told her about the grace, that God had put into her soul, of compunction, contrition, sweetness and devotion, compassion with holy meditation and high contemplation, and very many holy speeches and converse that our Lord spoke to her soul, and also many wonderful revelations, which she described to the anchoress to find out if there were any deception in them, for the anchoress was expert in such things and could give good advice.

The anchoress, hearing the marvelous goodness of our Lord, highly thanked God with all her heart for his visitation, advising this creature to be obedient to the will of our Lord and fulfill with all her might whatever he put into her soul, if it were not against the worship of God and the profit of her fellow Christians.[9] For if it were, then it were not the influence of a good spirit, but rather of an evil spirit. "The Holy Ghost never urges a thing against charity, and if he did, he would be contrary to his own self, for he is all charity. Also he moves a soul to all chasteness, for chaste livers are called the temple of the Holy Ghost,[1] and the Holy Ghost makes a soul stable and steadfast in the right faith and the right belief.

"And a double man in soul is always unstable and unsteadfast in all his ways.[2] He that is forever doubting is like the wave of the sea which is moved and borne about with the wind, and that man is not likely to receive the gifts of God.[3]

"Any creature that has these tokens may steadfastly believe that the Holy Ghost dwells in his soul. And much more, when God visits a creature with tears of contrition, devotion or compassion, he may and ought to believe that the Holy Ghost is in his soul. Saint Paul says that the Holy Ghost asks for us with mourning and weeping unspeakable;[4] that is to say, he causes us to ask and pray with mourning and weeping so plentifully that the tears may not be numbered. No evil spirit may give these

6. Psalm 51.17.
7. Isaiah 66.2.
8. Dame Julian of Norwich; see selections from her *Showings*, pages 448–61.
9. This concern with the whole community of the faithful, a new note in Kempe's book, is highly characteristic of Julian's spirituality.
1. 1 Corinthians 6.19. The density of biblical reference in

this passage suggests not only Dame Julian's learning but also Kempe's powerful memory for Scripture and theology. It is important that such biblical justification comes to Kempe through another holy woman.
2. James 1.8.
3. James 1.6–7.
4. Romans 8.26.

tokens, for Saint Jerome says that tears torment the devil more than do the pains of hell. God and the devil are always at odds, and they shall never dwell together in one place, and the devil has no power in a man's soul.

"Holy Writ says that the soul of a righteous man is the seat of God,[5] and so I trust, sister, that you are. I pray God grant you perseverance. Set all your trust in God and do not fear the talk of the world, for the more contempt, shame and reproof that you have in this world, the more is your merit in the sight of God.[6] Patience is necessary for you, for in that shall you keep your soul."[7]

Great was the holy conversation that the anchoress and this creature had through talking of the love of our Lord Jesus Christ for the many days that they were together.

This creature revealed her manner of life to many a worthy clerk, to honored doctors of divinity, both religious men and others of secular habit, and they said that God wrought great grace in her and bade her not to be afraid—there was no delusion in her manner of living. They counseled her to be persevering, for their greatest fear was that she would turn aside and not keep her perfection. She had so many enemies and so much slander, that it seemed to them that she might not bear it without great grace and a mighty faith. * * *

[PILGRIMAGE TO JERUSALEM]
CHAPTER 26

When the time came that this creature should visit those holy places where our Lord lived and died, as she had seen by revelation years before, she asked the parish priest of the town where she was living to say on her behalf from the pulpit that, if there were any man or woman who claimed any debt against her husband or her, they should come and speak with her before she went, and she, with God's help, would settle up with each of them so that they would hold themselves content. And so she did.[8]

Afterwards, she took leave of her husband and of the holy anchorite, who had told her before the sequence of her going and the great distress that she would suffer along the way and, when all her companions abandoned her, how a broken-backed man would escort her on her way in safety, through the help of our Lord. And so it happened indeed, as it shall be written afterwards.

Then she took her leave of Master Robert and asked him for his blessing, and so took leave of other friends. And then she went on her way to Norwich, and offered at the Trinity, and afterwards she went to Yarmouth, and offered at an image of our Lady, and there she boarded her ship.

And next day they came to a large town called Zierikzee, where our Lord in his high goodness visited this creature with abundant tears of contrition for her own sins, and sometimes for other people's sins as well. And especially, she had tears of compassion at the memory of our Lord's Passion. And she received communion every Sunday, when time and place were convenient for it, with much weeping and violent sobbing, so that many people marveled and wondered at the great grace that God worked in his creature.

---

5. 2 Corinthians 6.16, Revelation 21.3.
6. Luke 6.22–23.
7. Luke 21.19.
8. A trip to the Holy Land was arduous, and Kempe puts

her affairs in order before her departure in the fall of 1413. Equally, though, a pilgrimage to Jerusalem imitated the soul's journey to paradise, the "New Jerusalem," and Kempe is symbolically departing the secular world.

This creature had eaten no meat and drunk no wine for four years before she left England, and now her confessor directed her, by virtue of obedience, that she should both eat meat and drink wine, and so she did for a little while. Afterwards, she prayed to her confessor to excuse her if she ate no meat, and allow her to do as she wished for what time he pleased.

And soon after, because of prompting by some of her companions, her confessor was displeased because she ate no meat, and so were many of the company. And they were most annoyed because she wept so much and spoke all the time about the love and goodness of our Lord, as much at table as in other places. And so they rebuked her shamefully and chided her harshly, and said they would not put up with her as her husband did when she was at home in England.

And she replied meekly to them, "Our Lord, Almighty God, is as great a lord here as in England, and I have as great cause to love him here as there—blessed may he be."

At these words her companions were angrier than they were before, and their anger and unkindness were a matter of great unhappiness to this creature, for they were considered very good men, and she greatly desired their love, if she might have had it to the pleasure of God. And then she said to one of them specially, "You cause me much shame and hurt."

He replied, "I pray God that the devil's death may overtake you soon and quickly," and he said many more cruel words to her than she could repeat. And soon after, some of the company she trusted best, and also her own maidservant, said she should not accompany them any longer, and they said they would take her maidservant away from her so that she would not be prostituted in her company. And then one of them, who was looking after her money, very angrily left her a noble to go where she liked and shift for herself as well as she could—for with them, they said, she could stay no longer, and they abandoned her that night.

Then, on the next morning, one of her company came to her, a man who got on with her well, who asked her to go to his fellow pilgrims and behave meekly to them, and ask them if she might still travel with them until she came to Constance.

And so she did, and went on with them until she came to Constance with great distress and trouble, for they caused her much shame and reproof as they went along, in various places. They cut her gown so short that it only came a little below her knee, and made her put on some white canvas in a kind of sacking apron, so that she would be taken for a fool, and people would not make much of her or hold her in any repute. They made her sit at the end of the table below all the others, so that she scarcely dared speak a word.

And notwithstanding all their malice, she was held in more esteem than they were, wherever they went. And the good man of the house where they were staying, even though she sat at the end of the table, would always do whatever he could to cheer her up before them all and sent her what he had from his own meal, and that annoyed her companions terribly.

As they traveled towards Constance, they were told they would be harmed and have great trouble unless they had great grace. Then this creature came to a church and went in to pray, and she prayed with all her heart, with much weeping and many tears, for help and succor against their enemies.

Then our Lord said to her mind, "Don't be afraid, daughter, your party will come to no harm while you are in their company."

And so—blessed may our Lord be in all his works—they went on in safety to Constance.

CHAPTER 28

Also this company, which had excluded the said creature from their table so that she should no longer eat amongst them, arranged a ship for themselves to sail in.[9] They bought containers for their wine and arranged bedding for themselves, but nothing for her. Then she, seeing their unkindness, went to the man they had been to and provided herself with bedding as they had done, and came where they were and showed them what she had done, intending to sail with them in that ship which they had engaged.

Afterwards, as this creature was in contemplation, our Lord warned her in her mind that she should not sail in that ship, and he assigned her another ship, a galley, that she should sail in. Then she told this to some of the company, and they told it to others of their party, and then they dared not sail in the ship which they had arranged. And so they sold off the containers which they had got for their wines, and were very glad to come to the galley where she was, and so, though it was against her will, she went on with them in their company, for they did not dare do otherwise.

When it was time to make their beds they locked up her bedclothes, and a priest who was in her party took a sheet away from this creature, and said it was his. She took God to witness that it was her sheet. Then the priest swore a great oath, by the book in his hand, that she was as false as she might be, and despised her and severely rebuked her.

And so she had great and continual tribulation until she came to Jerusalem.[1] And before she arrived there, she said to them that she supposed they were annoyed with her. "I pray you, sirs, be in charity with me, for I am in charity with you, and forgive me if I have annoyed you along the way. And if any of you have in any way trespassed against me, God forgive you for it, as I do."

And so they went on into the Holy Land until they could see Jerusalem. And when this creature saw Jerusalem—she was riding on an ass—she thanked God with all her heart, praying him for his mercy that, just as he had brought her to see this earthly city of Jerusalem, he would grant her grace to see the blissful city of Jerusalem above, the city of heaven. Our Lord Jesus Christ, answering her thought, granted her her desire.

Then for the joy that she had and the sweetness that she felt in the conversation of our Lord, she was on the point of falling off her ass, for she could not bear the sweetness and grace that God wrought in her soul. Then two German pilgrims went up to her and kept her from falling—one of them was a priest, and he put spices in her mouth to comfort her, thinking she was ill. And so they helped her onwards to Jerusalem, and when she arrived there she said, "Sirs, I beg you, don't be annoyed though I weep bitterly in this holy place where our Lord Jesus Christ lived and died."

Then they went to the Church of the Holy Sepulchre in Jerusalem, and they were let in on the one day at evensong time, and remained until evensong time on the next day. Then the friars lifted up a cross and led the pilgrims about from one place to another where our Lord had suffered his pains and his Passion, every man and woman carrying a wax candle in one hand.[2] And the friars always, as they went about, told them what our Lord suffered in every place. And this creature wept and sobbed as plenteously as though she had seen our Lord with her bodily eyes suffering his Passion at that time. Before her in her soul she saw him in truth by contempla-

9. In ch. 27 the party of pilgrims repudiates Margery, and she is helped by the Papal legate at Constance, an English friar. She continues her travel toward Italy with an elderly Englishman, William Wever. She rejoins the English pilgrims at Bologna.

1. Accommodation for Christian pilgrims was very mea-

ger, and their movements were restricted and chaperoned by Moslem officials.

2. Although Jerusalem was under Islamic control, Franciscan friars had negotiated permission to keep a convent next to the Church of the Holy Sepulchre and to guide pilgrims around a number of holy sites.

tion, and that caused her to have compassion. And when they came up on to the Mount of Calvary, she fell down because she could not stand or kneel, but writhed and wrestled with her body, spreading her arms out wide, and cried with a loud voice as though her heart would have burst apart, for in the city of her soul she saw truly and freshly how our Lord was crucified. Before her face she heard and saw in her spiritual sight the mourning of our Lady, of Saint John and Mary Magdalene, and of many others that loved our Lord.

And she had such great compassion and such great pain to see our Lord's pain, that she could not keep herself from crying and roaring though she should have died for it. And this was the first crying that she ever cried in any contemplation. And this kind of crying lasted for many years after this time, despite anything that anyone might do, and she suffered much contempt and much reproof for it. The crying was so loud and so amazing that it astounded people, unless they had heard it before, or else knew the reason for the cryings. And she had them so often that they made her very weak in her bodily strength, and specially if she heard of our Lord's Passion.

And sometimes, when she saw the crucifix, or if she saw a man had a wound, or a beast, whichever it were, or if a man beat a child before her or hit a horse or other beast with a whip, if she saw or heard it, she thought she saw our Lord being beaten or wounded, just as she saw it in the man or in the beast, either in the fields or in the town, and alone by herself as well as among people.

When she first had her cryings at Jerusalem, she had them often, and in Rome also. And when she first came home to England her cryings came but seldom, perhaps once a month, then once a week, afterwards daily, and once she had fourteen in one day, and another day she had seven, just as God would visit her with them, sometimes in church, sometimes in the street, sometimes in her chamber, sometimes in the fields, when God would send them, for she never knew the time nor hour when they would come. And they never came without surpassingly great sweetness of devotion and high contemplation.

And as soon as she perceived that she was going to cry, she would hold it in as much as she could, so that people would not hear it and get annoyed. For some said it was a wicked spirit tormented her; some said it was an illness; some said she had drunk too much wine; some cursed her; some wished she was in the harbor; some wished she was on the sea in a bottomless boat; and so each man as he thought. Other, spiritually inclined men loved her and esteemed her all the more. Some great clerks said our Lady never cried so, nor any saint in heaven, but they knew very little what she felt, nor would they believe that she could not stop herself from crying if she wanted.

And therefore, when she knew that she was going to cry, she held it in as long as she could, and did all that she could to withstand it or else to suppress it, until she turned the color of lead, and all the time it would be seething more and more in her mind until such time as it burst out. And when the body might no longer endure the spiritual effort, but was overcome with the unspeakable love that worked so fervently in her soul, then she fell down and cried astonishingly loud. And the more that she labored to keep it in or to suppress it, so much the more would she cry, and the louder.

And thus she did on the Mount of Calvary, as it is written before: she had as true contemplation in the sight of her soul as if Christ had hung before her bodily eye in his manhood.[3] And when through dispensation of the high mercy of our sovereign

---

3. The detailed rendering of Christ's suffering corresponds to Julian of Norwich's visions and to depictions of the Crucifixion in later medieval art. Margery's gestures reinforce the pattern of imitation of Christ seen throughout her book.

savior, Christ Jesus, it was granted to this creature to behold so truly his precious tender body, all rent and torn with scourges, more full of wounds than a dovecote ever was of holes, hanging upon the cross with the crown of thorns upon his head, his blessed hands, his tender feet nailed to the hard wood, the rivers of blood flowing out plenteously from every limb, the grisly and grievous wound in his precious side shedding out blood and water for her love and her salvation, then she fell down and cried with a loud voice, twisting and turning her body amazingly on every side, spreading her arms out wide as if she would have died, and could not keep herself from crying and these physical movements, because of the fire of love that burned so fervently in her soul with pure pity and compassion.[4]

It is not to be wondered at if this creature cried out and made astonishing expressions, when we may see every day with our own eyes both men and women—some for loss of worldly wealth, some for love of their family or for worldly friendships, through overmuch study and earthly affection, and most of all for inordinate love and physical feeling, if their friends are parted from them—who will cry and roar and wring their hands as if they were out of their wits and minds, and yet they know well enough that they displease God.

And if anybody advises them to leave off their weeping and crying, they will say that they cannot; they loved their friend so much and he was so gentle and kind to them that they may in no way forget him. How much more might they weep, cry and roar, if their most beloved friends were violently seized in front of their eyes and brought with every kind of reproof before the judge, wrongfully condemned to death, and especially so shameful a death as our merciful Lord suffered for our sake. How would they bear it? No doubt they would both cry and roar and avenge themselves if they could, or else people would say they were no friends.

Alas, alas for sorrow, that the death of a creature who has often sinned and trespassed against his Maker should be so immeasurably mourned and sorrowed over. It is an offence to God and a hindrance to other souls.

And the compassionate death of our Savior, by which we are all restored to life, is not kept in mind by us unworthy and unkind wretches, nor will we support those whom our Lord has entrusted with his secrets and endued with love, but rather disparage and hinder them as much as we may.

[MYSTIC MARRIAGE WITH GOD]
CHAPTER 35[5]

As this creature was in the church of the Holy Apostles at Rome on Saint Lateran's Day, the Father of Heaven said to her, "Daughter, I am well pleased with you, inasmuch as you believe in all the sacraments of Holy Church and in all faith involved in that, and especially because you believe in the manhood of my son, and because of the great compassion that you have for his bitter Passion."

The Father also said to this creature, "Daughter, I will have you wedded to my Godhead, because I shall show you my secrets and my counsels, for you shall live with me without end."

---

4. Margery's images of the dovecote and the fire of love echo Richard Rolle.

5. After seeing other sites in the Holy Land, Margery received a visionary command to visit Rome on her journey homeward late in 1414. There she dresses in white clothes, fulfilling a command from years earlier. She is protected by a German priest with whom she enjoys miraculous communication; at his order she wears black clothes and acts as servant to an elderly woman.

Then this creature kept silence in her soul and did not answer to this, because she was very much afraid of the Godhead; and she had no knowledge of the conversation of the Godhead, for all her love and affection were fixed on the manhood of Christ, and of that she did have knowledge and would not be parted from that for anything.

She had so much feeling for the manhood of Christ, that when she saw women in Rome carrying children in their arms, if she could discover that any were boys, she would cry, roar and weep as if she had seen Christ in his childhood. And if she could have had her way, she would often have taken the children out of their mothers' arms and kissed them instead of Christ. And if she saw a handsome man, she had great pain to look at him, lest she might see him who was both God and man. And therefore she cried many times and often when she met a handsome man, and wept and sobbed bitterly for the manhood of Christ as she went about the streets of Rome, so that those who saw her were greatly astonished at her, because they did not know the reason.

Therefore it was not surprising if she was still and did not answer the Father of Heaven, when he told her that she should be wedded to his Godhead. Then the Second Person, Christ Jesus, whose manhood she loved so much, said to her, "What do you say to my Father, Margery, daughter, about these words that he speaks to you? Are you well pleased that it should be so?"

And then she would not answer the Second Person, but wept amazingly much, desiring to have himself still, and in no way to be parted from him. Then the Second Person in Trinity answered his Father for her, and said, "Father, excuse her, for she is still only young and has not completely learned how she should answer."

And then the Father took her by the hand [spiritually] in her soul, before the Son and the Holy Ghost, and the Mother of Jesus, and all the twelve apostles, and Saint Katherine and Saint Margaret[6] and many other saints and holy virgins, with a great multitude of angels, saying to her soul, "I take you, Margery, for my wedded wife, for fairer, for fouler, for richer, for poorer, provided that you are humble and meek in doing what I command you to do. For, daughter, there was never a child so kind to its mother as I shall be to you, both in joy and sorrow, to help you and comfort you. And that I pledge to you."

And then the Mother of God and all the saints that were present there in her soul prayed that they might have much joy together. Then this creature with high devotion, with great abundance of tears, thanked God for this spiritual comfort, holding herself in her own feeling very unworthy of any such grace as she felt, for she felt many great comforts, both spiritual comforts and bodily comforts. Sometimes she sensed sweet smells in her nose; they were sweeter, she thought, than any earthly sweet thing ever was that she smelled before, nor could she ever tell how sweet they were, for she thought she might have lived on them if they had lasted.

Sometimes she heard with her bodily ears such sounds and melodies that she could not hear what anyone said to her at that time unless he spoke louder. These sounds and melodies she had heard nearly every day for twenty-five years when this book was written, and especially when she was in devout prayer, also many times while she was at Rome, and in England too.

---

6. St. Catherine of Alexandria and St. Margaret of Antioch (patron saint of childbirth) were both popular in medieval England. Both had resisted seduction and marriage.

She saw with her bodily eyes many white things flying all about her on all sides, as thickly in a way as specks in a sunbeam; they were very delicate and comforting, and the brighter the sun shone, the better she could see them. She saw them at many different times and in many different places, both in church and in her chamber, at her meals and at her prayers, in the fields and in town, both walking and sitting. And many times she was afraid what they might be, for she saw them at night in darkness as well as in daylight. Then when she was afraid of them, our Lord said to her, "By this token, daughter, believe it is God who speaks in you, for wherever God is, heaven is, and where God is, there are many angels, and God is in you and you are in him. And therefore, don't be afraid, daughter, for these betoken that you have many angels around you, to keep you both day and night so that no devil shall have power over you, nor evil men harm you."[7]

Then from that time forward she used to say when she saw them coming: "*Benedictus qui venit in nomine Domini.*"[8]

Our Lord also gave her another token which lasted about sixteen years, and increased ever more and more, and that was a flame of fire of love—marvelously hot and delectable and very comforting, never diminishing but ever increasing; for though the weather were never so cold she felt the heat burning in her breast and at her heart, as veritably as a man would feel the material fire if he put his hand or his finger into it.[9]

When she first felt the fire of love burning in her breast she was afraid of it, and then our Lord answered in her mind and said, "Daughter, don't be afraid, because this heat is the heat of the Holy Ghost, which will burn away all your sins, for the fire of love quenches all sins. And you shall understand by this token that the Holy Ghost is in you, and you know very well that wherever the Holy Ghost is, there is the Father, and where the Father is, there is the Son, and so you have fully in your soul all of the Holy Trinity. Therefore you have great cause to love me well, and yet you shall have greater cause than you ever had to love me, for you shall hear what you never heard, and you shall see what you never saw, and you shall feel what you never felt.

"For, daughter, you are as sure of the love of God, as God is God. Your soul is more sure of the love of God than of your own body, for your soul will part from your body, but God shall never part from your soul, for they are united together without end. Therefore, daughter, you have as great reason to be merry as any lady in this world; and if you knew, daughter, how much you please me when you willingly allow me to speak in you, you would never do otherwise, for this is a holy life and the time is very well spent. For, daughter, this life pleases me more than wearing the coat of mail for penance, or the hair-shirt, or fasting on bread and water; for if you said a thousand *paternosters* every day you would not please me as much as you do when you are in silence and allow me to speak in your soul."

----- ✦◆✦ -----

Middle English Lyrics

Although many Middle English lyrics have a beguilingly fresh and unselfconscious tone, they owe much to learned and sophisticated continental sources—the medieval Latin lyrics of the "Goliard poets" and the Provençal and French lyrics of the Troubadours and Trouvères.

7. Echoing Psalm 91.11.
8. "Blessed is he that comes in the name of the Lord."

9. This experience of heat, like the angelic music above, is in the tradition of Richard Rolle; see page 438.

Most authors were clerics, aware of the similarities between earthly and divine love, and fond of punning in Latin or English.

The anonymity of the Middle English lyrics prevents us from seeing them as part of a single poet's *oeuvre*, as we can, for instance, with the poems of Chaucer, Dunbar, and Dafydd ap Gwilym. Rather, we must rely on more general contexts, such as genre, to establish relationships among poems. One of the most popular genres among the secular lyrics was the *reverdie*, or poem celebrating the return of spring. The early thirteenth-century *Cuckoo Song* ("Sumer is icumen in") joyfully invokes the bird's song, and revels in the blossoming of the countryside and the calls of the animals to their young. More typical examples of the *reverdie* are *Alisoun* and *Spring*, whose male speakers ruefully contrast the burgeoning of nature with the stinginess of their beloveds; in *Spring*, flowers bloom, birds sing, animals mate—but one woman remains unmoved. In the genre of the love complaint, *My Lief Is Faren in a Lond* and *Fowls in the Frith* express erotic loss and frustration with great succinctness.

Frustration was not the only attitude in Middle English love lyrics, however. A stance more boasting than adoring or despairing is taken in the witty lyric *I Have a Noble Cock*. Furthermore, clerical misogyny is expressed in *Abuse of Women*, which ostensibly praises women by absolving them of the vices—gossip, infidelity, shrewishness—typically attributed to them in satires against women; yet the refrain first praises women as the best of creatures but then undercuts this claim in Latin, which few women would have been able to understand.

Although most of the Middle English lyrics are in the male voice, there are a few "women's songs"—most likely written by men—which convey female experience. Occasionally these songs are invitations (for instance, the enigmatic *Irish Dancer*), but more often they are laments by an abandoned, and often pregnant, woman. *A Forsaken Maiden's Lament* is punctuated by the regretful refrain: "Were it undo that is ido, / I wolde bewar." Two of the women's songs, while concluding with laments about pregnancy, stress the cleverness and charm of the clerical seducers, perhaps suggesting that churchmen were their audience as well as their authors. *The Wily Clerk* attributes a young man's skill at deception to his scholarly training, as does *Jolly Jankin*, whose clerk engages in multilingual word play, turning the "Kyrie Eleison" into a request for mercy from the woman herself, "Alison."

The majority of Middle English lyrics were not secular but religious. Songs in praise of the Virgin Mary or Christ, however, employ the same erotic language as the secular lyrics, often in conjunction with typological figures linking events in the Old Testament to those in the New. In *Adam Lay Ibounden*, for instance, the poet follows a statement of the "fortunate Fall"—that Adam's sin was necessary to permit Christ's redemption—with a courtly compliment to the Virgin Mary. Similarly, *I Sing of a Maiden* draws on the typological significance of Gideon's fleece in Judges 6 (the soaking of the fleece by dew figuring Mary's impregnation by the Holy Spirit) while also employing the courtly imagery of a poet "singing of a maiden" who "chooses" Christ as her son, as if he were a lover. In a much longer poem in praise of the Virgin, the poet—casting himself as Mary's "knight" caught in the bonds of love—begs her mercy and also compliments her by contrasting her with her antitype, Eve.

Occasionally the Middle English religious lyric uses secular motifs and genres in a way that approaches parody. For instance, the second stanza of the Nativity poem *Mary Is with Child* resembles a pregnancy lament by a young girl. Mary, however, explains that her condition will be a source of joy rather than shame, when she will sing a lullaby to her "darling." This Middle English poet, far from blaspheming, was trying to humanize the mystery of the Nativity and relate it to daily life.

Other religious poems either celebrate Christ or reject the world. The poems to Christ, in their tenderness and immediacy, resemble those to Mary. In only four lines, *Now Goeth Sun Under Wood* evokes nature's oneness with Christ (the setting sun figuring the crucifixion) and the poet's empathy with the Virgin mother. Poets used erotic language in poems to Christ as well as those to Mary, as in *Sweet Jesus, King of Bliss* and *Jesus, My Sweet Lover*. Finally, in a

This page contains the words and music to one of the earliest and best loved of Middle English lyrics, *The Cuckoo Song* ("Summer is icumen in"). The lyric is a *reverdie,* or spring song, but its joyful description of nature's rebirth is given a more sober allegorical interpretation by the interlinear Latin gloss, apparently to be sung to the same tune. The gloss parallels the lyric's celebration of the reawakening landscape with an account of the "heavenly farmer" *(celicus agricola)* whom "rot on the vine" *(vitis vicio)* leads to sacrifice his Son. The fact that the manuscript was copied at a monastery reminds us that this song, like much other early English secular poetry, survives only because it was seen to have religious relevance.

different vein, the *Contempt of the World* questions the values of courtly life, with the *"ubi sunt"* ("where are") motif. "Where beth they biforen us weren?" it asks, evoking the lovely women who enjoyed their paradise on earth and now suffer the eternal fires of hell.

The Cuckoo Song

Sumer is icumen in,°   *spring has come in*
Lhude° sing, cuccu!°   *loudly/cuckoo*
Groweth sed° and bloweth° med°   *seed/blooms/meadow*
And springth° the wude° nu.°   *grows/forest/now*
5   Sing, cuccu!

Awe° bleteth after lomb,   *ewe*
Lhouth° after calve° cu,°   *lows/calf/cow*
Bulluc sterteth,° bucke ferteth.°   *leaps/farts*
Murie° sing, cuccu!   *merrily*
10   Cuccu, cuccu,
Wel singes thu, cuccu.
Ne swik° thu naver° nu!   *cease/never*

Sing cuccu nu, sing cuccu!
Sing cuccu, sing cuccu nu!

Spring

Lenten° is come with love to toune,°   *spring/town*
With blosmen° and with briddes° roune,°   *flowers/birds'/song*
  That all this blisse bringeth.
Dayeseyes° in this° dales,   *daisies/these*
5 Notes swete of nightegales—
  Uch° foul° song singeth.   *each/bird*
The threstelcok him threteth o;[1]
Away is here° winter wo their   *their*
When woderove° springeth.°   *woodruff/grows*
10 This foules° singeth ferly fele,°   *birds/wonderfully much*
And wliteth on here winne wele,[2]
  That all the wode ringeth.

The rose raileth hire rode,°   *puts on her rosy hue*
The leves on the lighte° wode   *bright*
15 Waxen° all with wille.°   *grow/pleasure*
The mone mandeth hire bleo,[3]
The lilie is lossom° to seo,°   *lovely/see*
  The fenil° and the fille.°   *fennel/chervil*
Wowes° this° wilde drakes;   *woo/these*
20 Miles murgeth here makes,[4]
  Ase strem that striketh° stille.°   *flows/softly*
Mody meneth, so doth mo;[5]
Ichot° ich° am one of tho,°   *I know/I/those*
  For love that likes° ille.   *pleases*

25 The mone mandeth hire light;
So doth the semly,° sonne bright,   *lovely*
  When briddes singeth breme.°   *loudly*
Deawes donketh the dounes;[6]
Deores with here derne rounes,[7]
30 Domes for to deme;[8]
Wormes woweth under cloude,°   *the soil*
Wimmen waxeth° wounder° proude,   *become/wondrously*
  So well it wol hem° seme.°   *to them/appear*
If me shall wonte wille of on,[9]
35 This wunne weole° I wole forgon   *wealth of joys*
  And wight° in wode be fleme.°   *quickly/exile*

Alisoun

Bitwene Mersh° and Averil°   *March/April*
When spray° biginneth to springe,°   *twig/grow*
The lutel° fowl° hath hire° will   *little/bird/her*
On° hire lud° to singe.   *in/language*

---

1. The song thrush contends always.
2. And chirp their wealth of joys.
3. The moon sends forth her light.
4. Beasts gladden their mates.
5. The high-spirited man mourns, so do others.
6. Dew moistens the downs (hills).
7. Animals with their secret whispers.
8. Speak their opinions.
9. If I shall lack the pleasure of one.

5   Ich° libbe° in love-longinge *I/live*
     For semlokest° of alle thinge: *fairest*
     He° may me blisse bringe; *she*
     Ich° am in hire baundoun.° *I/power*
       An hendy hap ich habbe ihent![1]
10   *Ichot°* from hevene it is me sent; *I know*
     From alle wimmen my love is lent,°, *taken away*
     And light° on Alisoun.[2] *settled*

    On hew° hire her° is fair inogh, *color/hair*
     Hire browe browne, hire eye blake;
15   With lossum chere he on me logh,[3]
     With middel° small and well imake.° *waist/made*
     Bote° he me wolle° to hire take *unless/will*
     For to ben hire° owen° make,° *her/own/mate*
     Longe to liven ichulle° forsake,° *I will/refuse*
20   And feye° fallen adoun. *doomed*
       An hendy hap ich habbe ihent!
       Ichot from hevene it is me sent;
       From alle wimmen my love is lent,
       And light on Alisoun.

25   Nightes° when I wende° and wake— *at night/turn*
     Forthy min wonges waxeth won[4]—
     Levedy,° all for thine sake *lady*
     Longinge is ilent° me on. *come*
     In world nis non so witer° mon *wise*
30   That all hire° bounte° telle con: *her/excellence*
     Hire swire° is whittore° then the swon, *neck/whiter*
     And feirest may° in toune. *maiden*
       An hendy hap ich habbe ihent!
       Ichot from hevene it is me sent;
35   *From alle wimmen my love is lent,*
       And light on Alisoun.

    Ich am for wowing all forwake,[5]
     Wery so water in wore[6]
     Lest eny reve° me my make° *steal/mate*
40   Ich habbe iyerned yore.[7]
     Betere is tholien while sore[8]
     Then mournen evermore.
     Geynest° under gore,° *kindest/petticoat*
     Herkne to my roun!° *song*
45   *An hendy hap ich habbe ihent!*
       Ichot from hevene it is me sent;
       From alle wimmen my love is lent,
       And light on Alisoun.

1. A fair destiny I have received.
2. Alison is a stock name for a country woman, shared by the wife in Chaucer's *Miller's Tale* and by his Wife of Bath.
3. With lovely manner she laughed at me.
4. Therefore my cheeks become pale.
5. I am for wooing all sleepless.
6. Weary as water in a troubled pool.
7. (For whom) I have long yearned.
8. It is better to suffer sorely for a time.

I Have a Noble Cock

I have a gentil° cok,   *noble*
  Croweth° me day;   *who crows*
He doth° me risen erly,   *makes*
  My matins for to say.

5 I have a gentil cok,
  Comen he is of gret;°   *a great family*
  His comb is of red corel,
    His tayel is of jet.

I have a gentil cok,
10 Comen he is of kinde;°   *good lineage*
  His comb is of red corel,
    His tail is of inde.°   *indigo*

His legges ben of asor,°   *azure*
  So gentil and so smale;
15 His spores° arn of silver white,   *spurs*
    Into the worte-wale.°   *root of cock's spur*

His eynen° arn of cristal,   *eyes*
  Loken° all in aumber;   *set*
And every night he percheth him
20   In min ladyes chaumber.

My Lefe Is Faren in a Lond[9]

My lefe is faren in a lond[1]—
Alas! why is she so?
And I am so sore bound
  I may nat com her to.
She hath my hert in hold,°   *imprisoned*
Where-ever she ride or go,
With trew love a thousandfold.

Fowls in the Frith

Foweles° in the frith,°   *birds/wood*
The fisses° in the flod,°   *fishes/river*
And I mon° waxe° wod.°   *must/become/mad*
Mulch° sorw° I walke with   *much/sorrow*
For beste[2] of bon° and blod.°   *bone/blood*

Abuse of Women

Of all creatures women be best:
Cuius contrarium verum est.[3]

In every place ye may well see
That women be trewe as tirtil° on tree,   *turtle-dove*

---

9. Chaucer alludes to this poem in the *Nun's Priest's Tale*,
line 112.
1. My beloved has gone away.

2. Either "beast" or "best."
3. Latin for "The opposite of this is true."

5   Not liberal° in langage, but ever in secree,°   *licentious/secrecy*
      And gret joye amonge them is for to be.

     Of all creatures women be best:
     Cuius contrarium verum est.

      The stedfastnes of women will never be don,
10   So jentil, so curtes they be everychon,[4]
      Meke as a lambe, still as a stone,
      Croked° nor crabbed find ye none!   *perverse*

     Of all creatures women be best:
     Cuius contrarium verum est.

15   Men be more cumbers° a thousand fold,   *troublesome*
      And I mervail how they dare be so bold
      Against women for to hold,
      Seeing them so pacient, softe, and cold.

     Of all creatures women be best:
20   *Cuius contrarium verum est.*

      For tell a woman all your counsaile,
      And she can kepe it wonderly well;
      She had lever go quik° to hell,   *alive*
      Than to her neighbour she wold it tell!

25   *Of all creatures women be best:*
           Cuius contrarium verum est.

      For by women men be reconsiled,
      For by women was never man begiled,
      For they be of the condicion of curtes Grisell,[5]
30   For they be so meke and milde.

     Of all creatures women be best:
     Cuius contrarium verum est.

      Now say well by° women or elles be still,   *about*
      For they never displesed man by ther will;
35   To be angry or wroth they can° no skill,   *have*
      For I dare say they think non ill.

     Of all creatures women be best:
     Cuius contrarium verum est.

      Trow° ye that women list° to smater,°   *think/like/chatter*
40   Or against ther husbondes for to clater?
      Nay, they had lever° fast bred and water,   *rather*
      Then for to dele in suche a mater.

     Of all creatures women be best:
     Cuius contrarium verum est.

---

4. So well-bred, so courteous is each one.
5. Griselda, the long-suffering wife of Chaucer's *Clerk's*

Tale; the tale ends with the observation that there are no
more Griseldas left.

45   Though all the paciens in the world were drownd,
        And non were lefte here on the ground,
        Again in a woman it might be found,
        Suche vertu in them dothe abound!

50   *Of all creatures women be best:*
            Cuius contrarium verum est.

        To the tavern they will not go,
        Nor to the alehous never the mo,°   more
        For, God wot,° ther hartes wold be wo,   knows
        To spende ther husbondes money so.

55   *Of all creatures women be best:*
            Cuius contrarium verum est.

        If here were a woman or a maid,
        That list for to go freshely arayed,
        Or with fine kirchers° to go displayed,   kerchiefs
60   Ye wold say, "They be proude": it is ill said.

            Of all creatures women be best:
            Cuius contrarium verum est.

The Irish Dancer

        Ich° am of Irlaunde,   *I*
        And of the holy londe
        Of Irlande.
        Gode° sire, pray ich thee,   *good*
        For of sainte° charitee,°   *holy/charity*
        Come and daunce wit me
        In Irlaunde.

A Forsaken Maiden's Lament

        Were it undo° that is ido,°   *undone/done*
        I wolde bewar.

        I lovede a child° of this cuntree,   *young man*
        And so I wende° he had do me;   *thought*
5   Now myself the sothe° I see,   *truth*
            That he is far.

        Were it undo that is ido,
        I wolde bewar.

        He seide to me he wolde be trewe,
10   And change me for non other newe;
        Now I sikke° and am pale of hewe,   *sigh*
            For he is far.

        Were it undo that is ido,
        I wolde bewar.

15   He seide his sawes° he wolde fulfille: *promises*
        Therfore I lat him have all his wille;

Now I sikke and morne stille,°   *quietly*
    For he is far.

Were it undo that is ido,
20   *I wolde bewar.*

The Wily Clerk

A, dere God, what I am fayn,
For I am madyn now gane![6]

This enther° day I mete a clerke,°   *other/cleric*
And he was wily in his werke;
5   He prayd me with° him to herke,°   *to/listen*
    And his counsel all for to layne.°   *conceal*

A, dere God, what I am fayn,
For I am madyn now gane!

I trow° he coud° of gramery;[7]   *believe/knew*
10   I shall now telle a good skill° why: *reason*
For what I hade siccurly,°   *certainly*
    To warne° his will had I no mayn.°   *resist/strength*

A, dere God, what I am fayn,
For I am madyn now gane!

15   Whan he and me brout° un° us the schete,°   *brought/on/sheet*
Of all his will I him lete;°   *permitted*
Now will not my girdil met—°   *meet*
    A, dere God, what shall I sayn?

A, dere God, what I am fayn,
20   *For I am madyn now gane!*

I shall sey to man and page°   *youth*
That I have bene of pilgrimage.
Now will I not lete° for no rage°   *permit/lust*
    With me a clerk for to pleyn.°   *play*

25   *A, dere God, what I am fayn,*
   For I am madyn now gane!

Jolly Jankin

"Kyrie,"° so "Kyrie,"   *Lord*
Jankin[8] *singeth merie,°*   *merrily*
With "aleison."[9]

As I went on Yol° Day in our procession,   *Yule (Christmas)*

---

6. Ah, dear God, how worthless I am, / For I am no longer a virgin.

7. Latin, learning, or magic—indicates the magical power which the speaker attributes to the clergy, who could read Latin.

8. "Johnny," a stock name. Also the name of Chaucer's Wife of Bath's fifth husband, who was a clerk.

9. "Kyrie eleison," Greek for "Lord have mercy upon us" (an early part of the mass). The poem puns on "Alison," supposedly the speaker's name (a stock female name).

5   Knew I joly Jankin be° his mery ton.°   *by*/*tone*
        Kyrieleison.

    "Kyrie," so "Kyrie,"
    Jankin singeth merie,
    With "aleison."

10 Jankin began the offis° on the Yol Day,   *church service*
    And yet me thinketh[1] it dos me good, so merie gan he say
        Kyrieleison.

    "Kyrie," so "Kyrie,"
    Jankin singeth merie,
15 *With "aleison."*

    Jankin red the pistil° full fair and full well,   *Epistle*
    And yet me thinketh it dos me good, as evere have I sell.° *luck*
        Kyrieleison.

20 *"Kyrie," so "Kyrie,"*
    Jankin singeth merie,
    With "aleison."

    Jankin at the *Sanctus* craked° a merie note,   *uttered*
    And yet me thinketh it dos me good—I payed for his cote.
        Kyrieleison.

25 *"Kyrie," so "Kyrie,"*
    Jankin singeth merie,
    With "aleison."

    Jankin craked notes an hundered on a knot,°   *at once*
    And yet he hakked hem smaller than wortes[2] to the pot.
30   *Kyrieleison.*

    "Kyrie," so "Kyrie,"
    Jankin singeth merie,
    With "aleison."

    Jankin at the *Angnus* bered the *pax-brede;*[3]
35 He twinkeled, but said nout, and on min fot he trede.[4]
        Kyrieleison.

    "Kyrie," so "Kyrie,"
    Jankin singeth merie,
    With "aleison."

40 *Benedicamus Domino,*[5] Crist fro° schame me schilde.° *from*/*shield*
    Deo gracias,[6] therto—alas, I go with childe!
        Kyrieleison.

---

1. It seems to me.
2. Vegetables.
3. At the *Agnus Dei* (at the later part of the Mass), Jankin carried the *pax-brede,* an article signalling the exchanging of the kiss of pence.

4. He winked, but said nothing, and on my foot he stepped.
5. Let us bless the Lord.
6. Thanks be to God.

"Kyrie," so "Kyrie,"
Jankin singeth merie,
45   *With "aleison."*

Adam Lay Ibounden

Adam lay ibounden,°   bound
Bounden in a bond;
Foure thousand winter
Thowt° he not too long.   thought
5   And all was for an appil,
An appil that he took,
As clerkes finden wreten
In here° book.   their

Ne° hadde the appil take° ben,   if not/taken
10   The appil taken ben,
Ne° hadde never our lady   not
A ben hevene quen.[7]
Blissed be the time
That appil take was!
15   Therfore we moun° singen   may
"Deo gracias!"°   Thanks be to God!

I Sing of a Maiden

I sing of a maiden
That is makeles,[8]
King of alle kinges
To° here° sone she ches.°   for/her/chose

5   He cam also° stille°   as/quietly
Ther° his moder was   where
As dew in Aprille
That falleth on the gras.

He cam also stille
10   To his moderes bowr
As dew in Aprille
That falleth on the flour.

He cam also stille
Ther his moder lay
15   As dew in Aprille
That falleth on the spray.°   twigs

Moder and maiden
Was never non but she:
Well may swich° a lady   such
20   Godes moder be.

---

7. Have been heaven's queen.   8. Spotless, matchless, and mateless.

In Praise of Mary

Edi° be thu, Hevene Quene, — *blessed*
Folkes froure° and engles° blis, — *comfort/angels'*
Moder unwemmed° and maiden clene, — *unspotted*
Swich° in world non other nis.° — *such/is*

5 On thee it is well eth° sene° — *easily/seen*
Of alle wimmen thu havest that pris.° — *prize*
My swete Levedy,° her my bene,° — *Lady/prayer*
And rew° of me yif° thy wille is. — *take pity/if*

Thu asteye° so° the dais-rewe° — *climb/as/dawn's ray*
10 The° deleth° from the derke night; — *that/separates*
Of thee sprong a leme° newe light — *light*
That all this world haveth ilight.° — *illuminated*
Nis non maide of thine hewe
So fair, so shene,° so rudy, so bright. — *beautiful*
15 Swete Levedy, of me thu rewe,
And have mercy of thine knight.

Spronge° blostme° of one rote,° — *sprung/blossom/root*
The Holy Ghost thee reste upon;
That wes for monkunnes° bote,° — *mankind's/healing*
20 And here° soule to alesen° for on. — *their/deliver*
Levedy milde, softe and swote,° — *sweet*
Ic° crye thee mercy: ic am thy mon,° — *I/man*
Bothe to honde and to fote,
On alle wise° that ic con.° — *way/can*

25 Thu ert° erthe° to° gode sede; — *art/earth/for*
On thee lighte° the Hevene° dews; — *came down/of heaven*
Of thee sprong the edi° blede—° — *blessed/fruit*
The Holy Ghost hire on thee sews.° — *sowed it*
Thu bring us ut of care, of drede,° — *fear*
30 That Eve bitterliche us brews.
Thu shalt us into Hevene lede—
Welle° swete is the ilke° dews. — *most/same*

Moder, full of thewes° hende,° — *virtues/gracious*
Maide, dreigh° and well itaught,° — *patient/taught*
35 Ic em in thine lovebende,° — *bonds of love*
And to thee is all my draught.° — *leaning*
Thu me shilde° from the Fende,° — *shield/Fiend*
Ase thu ert fre,° and wilt° and maught:° — *noble/will/can*
Help me to my lives ende,
40 And make me with thine sone isaught.° — *reconciled*

Thu ert icumen° of heghe° cunne,° — *come/high/lineage*
Of David the riche king.
Nis non maiden under sunne
The° mey be thine evening,° — *that/equal*
45 Ne that so derne° loviye cunne,° — *secretly/can*
Ne non so trewe of alle thing.

Thy love us broughte eche° wunne:°   eternal/bliss
Ihered° ibe° thu, swete thing!   praised/be

Selcudliche ure Louerd it dighte[9]
50   That thu, maide, withute were,°   mate
That all this world bicluppe ne mighte,°   could not encompass
Thu sholdest of thine boseme° bere.°   womb/bear
Thee ne stighte,° ne thee ne prighte,°   stabbing/pricking
In side, in lende° ne elleswhere:°   loins/elleswhere
55   That wes° with full muchel° righte,   was/much
For thu bere° thine Helere.°   bore/Savior

Tho° Godes sune alighte wolde°   when/wished
On erthe, all for ure° sake,   our
Herre° teyen° he him nolde   higher/servant
60   Thene° that maide to ben° his make:°   than/be/mate
Betere ne mighte he, thaigh° he wolde,   though
Ne swetture thing on erthe take.
Levedy,° bring us to thine bolde°   Lady/abode
And shild° us from helle wrake.°   shield/vengeance
                                   Amen.

Mary Is with Child

Nowel! nowel! nowel!
Sing we with mirth!
Christ is come well
With us to dwell,
5   By his most noble birth.

Under a tree
In sporting me,
Alone by a wod-side,°   side of a wood
I hard° a maid[1]   heard
10   That swetly said,
"I am with child this tide.°   time

"Graciously
Conceived have I
The Son of God so swete:
15   His gracious will
I put me till,
As moder him to kepe.

"Both night and day
I will him pray,
20   And her° his lawes taught,   hear
And every dell°   in every way
His trewe gospell
In his apostles fraught.°   carried

9. Marvellously our Lord arranged it.
1. A poem that opens with the speaker in the countryside
overhearing a woman's lament raises expectations that

we will hear a *chanson d'aventure*, with erotic connotations.

	"This ghostly° case°	*spiritual/act*
25	Doth me embrace,	
	Without despite or mock;	
	With my derling,	
	'Lullay,'° to sing,	*lullabye*
	And lovely him to rock.	

	"Without distress	
30	In grete lightness	
	I am both night and day.	
	This hevenly fod°	*child*
	In his childhod	
35	Shall daily with me play.	

	"Soone must I sing	
	With rejoicing,	
	For the time is all ronne°	*run out*
	That I shall child,°	*give birth to*
40	All undefil'd,	
	The King of Heven's Sonne."	

Sweet Jesus, King of Bliss

	Swete Jesu, king of blisse,	
	Min herte° love, min herte lisse,°	*heart's/joy*
	Thou art swete mid iwisse.°	*certainly*
	Wo is him that thee shall misse!	

5	Swete Jesu, min herte light,	
	Thou art day withoute night,	
	Thou geve° me streinthe and eke° might	*may you give/also*
	For to lovien thee aright.	

	Swete Jesu, min herte bote,°	*remedy*
10	In min herte thou sete° a rote°	*may you set/root*
	Of thy love, that is so swote,°	*sweet*
	And leve° that it springe mote.°	*grant/may grow*

	Swete Jesu, min herte gleem,°	*light*
	Brightore then the sonnebeem,	
15	Ibore° thou were in Bedleheem;	*born*
	Thou make me here thy swete dreem.[2]	

	Swete Jesu, thy love is swete;	
	Wo is him that thee shall lete!°	*abandon*
	Gif me grace for to grete°	*cry*
20	For my sinnes teres° wete.°	*with tears/wet*

	Swete Jesu, king of londe,	
	Thou make me fer° understonde	*to*
	That min herte mote° fonde°	*may/experience*
	How swete beth° thy love-bonde.	*is*

2. May thou make me hear thy sweet melody.

25   Swete Jesu, Louerd° min,   *Lord*
        My lif, min herte, all is thin;°   *yours*
        Undo° min herte and light° therin,   *open/alight*
        And wite° me from fendes° engin.°   *guard/the Devil's/trick*

        Swete Jesu, my soule° fode,   *soul's*
30   Thin werkes beth° bo° swete and gode;   *are/both*
        Thou boghtest° me upon the rode;°   *redeemed/cross*
        For me thou sheddest thy blode.

        Swete Jesu, me reoweth° sore I regret   *I regret*
        Gultes that I ha wroght yore;[3]
35   Tharefore I bidde° thin milse° and ore;° *beg/mercy/grace*
        Mercy, Lord, I nul° namore.   *will not*

        Swete Jesu, Louerd God,
        Thou me boghtest with thy blod;
        Out of thin herte orn° the flod;   *ran*
40   Thy moder° it segh° that thee by stod.   *mother/saw*

        Swete Jesu, bright and shene,°   *beautiful*
        I preye thee thou here my bene°   *prayer*
        Thourgh ernding° of the hevene quene, *intercession*
        That thy love on me be sene.°   *seen*

45   Swete Jesu, berne° best,   *of men*
        With thee ich hope habbe° rest;   *to have*
        Whether I be south other° west,   *or*
        The help of thee be me nest.°   *nearest*

        Swete Jesu, well may him be
50   That thee may in blisse see.
        With love-cordes drawe thou me
        That I may comen and wone° with thee.   *dwell*

        Swete Jesu, hevene king,
        Feir and best of alle thing,
55   Thou bring me of° this longing   *out of*
        To come to thee at min ending.

        Swete Jesu, all folkes reed,°   *counsel*
        Graunte us er we buen° ded   *are*
        Thee underfonge° in fourme of bred,   *to receive*
60   And sethe° to heovene thou us led.°   *later/may lead*

Now Goeth Sun under Wood

        Now goth° sonne under wod:°   *goes/forest*
        Me reweth,[4] Marye, thy faire rode.°   *face*
        Now goth sonne under tree:
        Me reweth, Marye, thy sone and thee.

---

3. The sins that I have committed in the past.   4. I feel pity for.

Jesus, My Sweet Lover

Jesu Christ, my lemmon° swete,   *lover*
That diyedest on the Rode° Tree,   *Cross*
With all my might I thee beseche,
For thy woundes two and three,
That also° faste mot° thy love   *as/may*
Into mine herte fitched° be   *fixed*
As was the spere into thine herte,
Whon thou soffredest deth for me.

Contempt of the World

Where beth° they biforen us weren?   *are*
Houndes ladden° and hawkes beren,°   *led/bore*
And hadden feld and wode;
The riche levedies° in here° bour,°   *ladies/their/bower*
5   That wereden° gold in here tressour,°   *wore/head-dress*
With here° brighte rode:°   *their/face*

Eten and drounken and maden hem° glad;   *themselves*
Here lif was all with gamen° ilad.°   *sport/spent*
Men keneleden° hem° biforen;   *kneeled/them*
10   They beren hem well swithe° heye—°   *very/high*
And in a twinkling of an eye
Here soules weren forloren.°   *lost*

Where is that laughing and that song,
That trailing⁵ and that proude gong,°   *gait*
15   Tho hawkes and tho° houndes?   *those*
All that joye is went away,
That wele° is comen to weylaway,°   *prosperity/woe*
To manye harde stoundes.°   *times*

Here° paradis hy° nomen° here,   *their/they/took*
20   And now they lien° in helle ifere;°   *lie/together*
The fuir° it brennes° evere.   *fire/burns*
Long is "ah!" and long is "oh!"
Long is "wy!" and long is "wo!"
Thennes° ne cometh they nevere.   *thence*

25   Drey° here, man, thenne, if thou wilt,   *suffer*
A litel pine that me thee bit;⁶
Withdraw thine eyses° ofte.   *comforts*
They° thy pine° be unrede,°   *though/pain/severe*
And° thou thenke° on thy mede,°   *if/think/reward*
30   It shall thee thinken° softe.   *seem*

If that fend,° that foule thing,   *the Devil*
Thorou wikke roun, thorou fals egging,°   *counsel*
Nethere° thee haveth icast, down   *down*

---

5. Walking with trailing garments.   6. A little pain that one enjoins.

Up and be good chaunpioun!
35   Stond, ne fall namore adoun
For a litel blast.

Thou tak the rode° to° thy staf,   *cross/as*
And thenk on him that thereonne gaf°   *gave*
His lif that wes so lef.°   *dear*
40   He it gaf for thee; thou yelde° it him;   *give back*
Agein° his fo that staf thou nim°   *against/take*
And wrek° him of that thef.°   *avenge/thief*

Of righte bileve° thou nim that sheld,   *belief*
The whiles that thou best° in that feld,   *are*
45   Thin hond to strengthen fonde;°   *try*
And kep thy fo with° staves° ord,°   *at/staff's/point*
And do° that traitre seyen that word.   *make*
Biget° that murie° londe.   *win/happy*

Thereinne is day withouten night,
50   Withouten ende strengthe and might,
And wreche° of everich fo;   *punishment*
Mid° God himselven eche° lif,   *with/eternal*
And pes° and rest withoute strif,   *peace*
Wele° withouten wo.   *happiness*

55   Maiden moder,° hevene° quene,   *mother/heaven's*
Thou might and const and owest to bene[7]
Oure sheld agein the fende;°   *Devil*
Help us sunne° for to flen,°   *sin/flee*
That we moten° they sone° iseen°   *may/Son/see*
60   In joye withouten ende.

—◆—

The Tale of Taliesin

The Tale of Taliesin extends a series of very ancient legends about the great bard Taliesin, placing him about a generation after the time of King Arthur. Yet this version was not written down until the sixteenth century, by the antiquarian Elis Grufydd, who expresses occasional doubt about the truth and orthodoxy of his story. Nonetheless, the tale's coherence, its references to pagan Welsh myth, and its depiction of bardic practice at royal courts all reflect the extraordinary continuity of ancient and medieval Welsh culture. Like Celtic culture in Ireland, Welsh literature and art display remarkable tenacity as well as flexibility. The Britons and their Welsh successors absorbed wave after wave of cultural, religious, and ethnic influence: Latin, Christian, Roman, Saxon, and Norman. Yet they folded these elements into cultural expressions that remained distinctive in style and structure. As a people, too, the Welsh clung to beliefs that they were as ancient as the Trojans, and to prophecies that they would one day reconquer the Anglo-Saxon and Norman parvenus.

Especially in its reverence for the nearly supernatural role of the poet-prophet, *The Tale of Taliesin* is a genuine survival of medieval, even pagan, Welsh culture. Taliesin was regarded as the founder of Welsh poetry (for poems attributed to him, see pages 139–143), and as his repu-

7. You may and can and ought to be.

tation grew, so did his image. In this story Taliesin is a magician, trickster, shape-shifter, and prophet, an incarnation of bards and wise men from both the Celtic and Mediterranean past. Miraculously reborn, he is more the product of the elements than the child of mortal parents, and his consciousness crosses both time and space. He has the poetic learning of his ancestors, yet knows what is happening to his patron Elphin at a distant royal court. He can loose chains and render other bards dumb; and his keen powers of observation enable him to solve the mystery of a severed finger.

At the same time, the story deftly extends Taliesin's wisdom to encompass Old Testament prophecy, Roman myth, Christian practices such as the Eucharist, and the major languages of late medieval England. All this is done with lightness and wit, and the occasional (if still delighted) demur of the copyist. The tale also registers historical developments throughout Britain, though—not only by listing the competitor languages (Latin, French, and English) but also by acknowledging wryly that French is now the language of royal largesse.

The Tale of Taliesin[1]

In the days when Maelgwn Gwynedd[2] was holding court in Castell Deganwy, there was a holy man named Cybi living in Môn.[3] Also in that time there lived a wealthy squire near Caer Deganwy, and the story says he was called Gwyddno Garanhir[4] (he was a lord). The text says that he had a weir on the shore of the Conway adjacent to the sea, in which was caught as much as ten pounds[5] worth of salmon every eve of All Hallows. The tale also says that Gwyddno had a son called Elphin son of Gwyddno, who was in service in the court of King Maelgwn. The text says that he was a noble and generous man, much loved among his companions, but that he was an incorrigible spendthrift—as are the majority of courtiers. As long as Gwyddno's wealth lasted, Elphin did not lack for money to spend among his friends. But as Gwyddno's riches began to dwindle, he stopped lavishing money on his son. The latter regretfully informed his friends that he was no longer able to maintain a social life and keep company with them in the manner he had been accustomed to in the past, because his father had fallen on hard times. But as before, he asked some of the men of the court to request the fish from the weir as a gift to him on the next All Hallow's eve; they did that and Gwyddno granted their petition.

And so when the day and the time arrived, Elphin took some servants with him, and came to set up and watch the weir, which he tended from high tide until the ebb.

When Elphin and his people came within the arms of the weir, they saw there neither head nor tail of a single young salmon; its sides were usually full of such on that night. But the story says that on this occasion he saw nothing but some dark hulk within the enclosure. On account of that, he lowered his head and began to protest his ill-fortune, saying as he turned homeward that his misery and misfortune were greater than those of any man in the world. Then it occurred to him to turn around and see what the thing in the weir was. Immediately, he found a coracle or hide-covered basket, wrapped from above as well as from below. Without delay, he took his knife and cut a slit in the hide, revealing a human forehead.

---

1. From *The Mabinogi and Other Medieval Welsh Tales*, translated by Patrick K. Ford.
2. "*Mael-goon Gwi-neth*," a 6th-century king of Gwynedd, in northwestern Wales.
3. Pronounced "moan," the island of Anglesey, off northwestern Wales.
4. "*Gwith-*no Ga-*ron-*hir."
5. A great deal of money at the time.

As soon as Elphin saw the forehead, he said, "behold the radiant forehead!"[6] To those words the child replied from the coracle, "Tal-iesin he is!" People suppose that this was the spirit of Gwion Bach, who had been in the womb of Ceridwen;[7] after she was delivered of him, she had cast him into fresh water or into the sea, as the present work shows above. He had been in the pouch, floating about in the sea, from the beginning of Arthur's time until about the beginning of Maelgwn's time—and that was approximately forty years.

Indeed, this is far from reason and sense. But as before, I will keep to the story, which says that Elphin took the bundle and placed it in a basket upon one of the horses. Thereupon, Taliesin sang the stanzas known as *Dehuddiant Elphin*, or, *Elphin's Consolation*, saying as follows:

> Fair Elphin, cease your weeping!
>> Despair brings no profit.
> No catch in Gwyddno's weir
> Was ever as good as tonight's.
> Let no one revile what is his.
> Man sees not what nurtures him;
> Gwyddno's prayers shall not be in vain.
> God breaks not his promises.

> Fair Elphin, dry your cheeks!
>> It does not become you to be sad.
> Though you think you got no gain
> Undue grief will bring you nothing—
> Nor will doubting the miracles of the Lord.
> Though I am small, I am gifted.
> From the sea and the mountain, from rivers' depths
> God sends bounty to the blessed.

> Elphin of the cheerful disposition—
>> Meek is your mind—
> You must not lament so heavily.
> Better God than gloomy foreboding.
> Though I am frail and little
> And wet with the spume of Dylan's sea,
> I shall earn in a day of contention
> Riches better than three score for you.

> Elphin of the remarkable qualities.
>> Grieve not for your catch.
> Though I am frail here in my bunting,
> There are wonders on my tongue.
> You must not fear greatly
> While I am watching over you.
> By remembering the name of the Trinity
> None can overcome you.

6. In Welsh, *tal iesin*. This is only one of the legends that cluster around Taliesin; see page 140.
7. Gwion Bach ("Little Gwion") gained three magical drops, conferring wisdom, which the magician Ceridwen had intended for her son. Enraged, she pursued Gwion; when he took the form of a grain of wheat, she became a hen, swallowed him, and nine months later gave birth to him. Unwilling to kill the infant, she launched him in a small boat—a coracle.

Together with various other stanzas which he sang to cheer Elphin along the path from there toward home, where Elphin turned over his catch to his wife. She raised him lovingly and dearly.

From that moment on, Elphin's wealth increased more and more each succeeding day, as well as his favor and acceptance with the king. Some while after this, at the feast of Christmas, the king was holding open court at Deganwy Castle, and all his lords—both spiritual and temporal—were there, with a multitude of knights and squires. Their conversation grew, as they queried one another, saying:

"Is there in the entire world a man as powerful as Maelgwn? Or one to whom the heavenly father has given as many spiritual gifts as God has given him: beauty, shape, nobility, and strength, besides all the powers of the soul?" And with these gifts, they proclaimed that the Father had given him an excellent gift, one that surpassed all of the others, namely, the beauty, appearance, demeanor, wisdom, and faithfulness of his queen. In these virtues, she excelled all the ladies and daughters of the nobility in the entire land. Beside that, they asked themselves: "whose men are more valiant? Whose horses and hounds are swifter and fairer? Whose bards more proficient and wiser than Maelgwn's?"

At that time poets were received with great esteem among the eminent ones of the realm. And in those days, none of whom we now call "heralds" were appointed to that office, unless they were learned men, and not only in the proper service of kings and princes, but steeped and skilled in pedigrees, arms, the deeds of kings and princes of foreign kingdoms as well as the ancestors of this kingdom, especially in the history of the chief nobility. Furthermore, each of these bards had to have their responses readily prepared in various languages, such as Latin, French, Welsh, and English, and in addition, be a great historian and good chronicler, be skilled in the composition of poetry and ready to compose metrical stanzas in each of these languages. On this feast, there was in the court of Maelgwn no less than twenty-four of these; chief among them was the one called Heinin Fardd the Poet.

And so after everyone had spoken in praise of the king and his blessings, Elphin happened to say this: "Indeed, no one can compete with a king except another king; but, truly, were he not a king, I would surely say that I had a wife as chaste as any lady in the kingdom. Furthermore, I have a bard who is more proficient than all the king's bards."

Some time later, the king's companions told him the extent of Elphin's boast, and the king commanded that he be put into a secure prison until he could get confirmation of his wife's chastity and his poet's knowledge. And after putting Elphin in one of the castle towers with a heavy chain on his feet (some people say that it was a silver chain that was put upon him, because he was of the king's blood), the story says that the king sent his son Rhun to test the continence of Elphin's wife. It says that Rhun was one of the lustiest men in the world, and that neither woman nor maiden with whom he had spent a diverting moment came away with her reputation intact.

As Rhun was hastening toward Elphin's residence, fully intending to despoil Elphin's wife, Taliesin was explaining to her how the king had thrown his master into prison and how Rhun was hurrying there with the intention of corrupting her virtue. Because of that he had his mistress dress one of the scullery maids in her own garb. The lady did this cheerfully and unstintingly, adorning the maid's fingers with the finest rings that she and her husband possessed. In this guise, Taliesin had his mistress seat the girl in her own chamber to sup at her own table and in her own place; Taliesin had made the girl look like his mistress, his mistress like the girl.

As they sat most handsomely at their supper in the manner described above, Rhun appeared suddenly at the court of Elphin. He was received cheerfully, for all the servants knew him well. They escorted him without delay to their mistress's chamber. The girl disguised as the mistress rose from her supper and greeted him pleasantly, then sat back down to her meal, and Rhun with her. He began to beguile the girl with seductive talk, while she preserved the mien of her mistress.

The story says that the maiden got so inebriated that she fell asleep. It says that Rhun had put a powder in her drink that made her sleep so heavily—if the tale can be believed—that she didn't even feel him cutting off her little finger, around which was Elphin's signet ring that he had sent to his wife as a token a short time before. In this way he did his will with the maiden, and afterwards, he took the finger—with the ring on it—to the king as proof. He told him that he had violated her chastity, explaining how he had cut off her finger as he left, without her awakening.

The king took great delight in this news, and, because of it, summoned his council, to whom he explained the whole affair from one end to the other. Then he had Elphin brought from the prison to taunt him for his boast, and said to him as follows: "It should be clear to you, Elphin, and beyond doubt, that it is nothing but foolishness for any man in the world to trust his wife in the matter of chastity any farther than he can see her. And so that you may harbor no doubts that your wife broke her marriage vows last night, here is her finger as evidence for you, with your own signet ring on it; the one who lay with her cut it off her hand while she slept. So that there is no way that you can argue that she did not violate her fidelity."

To this Elphin replied, "with your permission, honorable king, indeed, there is no way I can deny my ring, for a number of people know it. But, indeed, I do deny vehemently that the finger encircled by my ring was ever on my wife's hand, for one sees there three peculiar things not one of which ever characterized a single finger of my wife's hands. The first of these is that—with your grace's permission—wherever my wife is at this moment, whether she is sitting, standing, or lying down, this ring will not even fit her thumb! And you can easily see that it was difficult to force the ring over the knuckle of the little finger of the hand from which it was cut. The second thing is that my wife has never gone a single Saturday since I have known her without paring her nails before going to bed. And you can see clearly that the nail of this finger has not been cut for a month. And the third thing, indeed, is that the hand from which this finger was cut kneaded rye dough within the past three days, and I assure you, your graciousness, that my wife has not kneaded rye dough since she became my wife."

The story says that the king became more outraged at Elphin for standing so firmly against him in the matter of his wife's fidelity. As a result, the king ordered him to be imprisoned again, saying that he would not gain release from there until he proved true his boast about the wisdom of his bard as well as about the fidelity of his wife.

Those two, meanwhile, were in Elphin's palace, taking their ease. Then Taliesin related to his mistress how Elphin was in prison on account of them. But he exhorted her to be of good cheer, explaining to her how he would go to the court of Maelgwn to free his master. She asked him how he could set his master free, and he replied as follows:

> I shall set out on foot,
>   Come to the gate,
>   And make for the hall.
>   I shall sing my song
>   And proclaim my verse,
>   And the lord's bards I shall inhibit:

> Before the chief one
> I shall make demands,
> And I shall overcome them.
>
> And when the contention comes
> In the presence of the chieftains,
> And a summons to the minstrels
> For precise and harmonious songs
> In the court of the scions of nobles,
> Companion to Gwion,
> There are some who assumed the appearance
> Of anguish and great pains.
>
> They shall fall silent by rough words,
> If it grows ever worse, like Arthur, Chief of givers,
> With his blades long and red
> From the blood of nobles;
> The king's battle against his enemies,
> Whose gentles' blood flows
> From the battle of the woods in the distant North.
>
> May there be neither blessing nor beauty
> On Maelgwn Gwynedd,
> But let the wrong be avenged—
> And the violence and the arrogance—finally,
> For the act of Rhun his offspring:
> Let his lands be desolate,
> Let his life be short,
> Let the punishment last long
> On Maelgwn Gwynedd.

And after that he took leave of his mistress, and came at last to the court of Maelgwn Gwynedd. The latter, in his royal dignity, was going to sit in his hall at supper, as kings and princes were accustomed to do on every high feast in those days. And as soon as Taliesin came into the hall, he saw a place for himself to sit in an inconspicuous corner, beside the place where the poets and minstrels had to pass to pay their respects and duty to the king—as is still customary in proclaiming largess in the courts on high holidays, except that they are proclaimed now in French. And so the time came for the bards or the heralds to come and proclaim the *largesse*, power, and might of the king. They came past the spot where Taliesin sat hunched over in the corner, and as they went by, he puckered his lips and with his finger made a sound like *blerum blerum*. Those going past paid no attention to him, but continued on until they stood before the king. They performed their customary curtsy as they were obliged to do; not a single word came from their mouths, but they puckered up, made faces at the king, and made the *blerum blerum* sound on their lips with their fingers as they had seen the lad do it earlier. The sight astonished the king, and he wondered to himself whether they had had too much to drink. So he ordered one of the lords who was administering to his table to go to them and ask them to summon their wits and reflect upon where they were standing and what they were obliged to do. The lord complied.

But they did not stop their nonsense directly, so he sent to them again, and a third time, ordering them to leave the hall; finally, the king asked one of the squires to clout their chief, the one called Heinin Fardd. The squire seized a platter and struck him over the head with it until he fell back on his rump. From that spot, he rose up onto his knees whence he begged the king's mercy and leave to show him that it was neither of the two failings on them—neither lack of intelligence nor drunkenness—but due to some spirit that was inside the hall. And then Heinin said as follows: "O glorious king! Let it be known to your grace, that it is not from the pickling effect of a surfeit of spirits that we stand here dumb, unable to speak properly, like drunkards, but because of a spirit, who sits in the corner yonder, in the guise of a little man."

Whereupon, the king ordered a squire to fetch him. He went to the corner where Taliesin sat, and brought him thence before the king, who asked him what sort of thing he was and whence he came. He answered the king in verse, and spoke as follows:

> Official chief-poet
> > to Elphin am I,
> And my native abode
> > is the land of the Cherubim.

Then the king asked him what he was called, and he answered him saying this:

> Johannes the prophet
> > called me Merlin,[8]
> But now all kings
> > call me Taliesin.

Then the king asked him where he had been, and thereupon he recited his history to the king, as follows here in this work:

> I was with my lord
> > in the heavens
> When Lucifer fell
> > into the depths of hell;
> I carried a banner
> > before Alexander;
> I know the stars' names
> > from the North to the South
> I was in the fort of Gwydion,[9]
> > in the Tetragramaton;[1]
> I was in the canon
> > when Absalon was killed;
> I brought seed down
> > to the vale of Hebron;
> I was in the court of Dôn
> > before the birth of Gwydion;
> I was patriarch
> > to Elijah and Enoch;
> I was head keeper
> > on the work of Nimrod's tower;
> I was atop the cross

---

8. Taliesin claims still another poetic incarnation as Merlin, and links him in turn to John the Baptist.
9. The magician Gwydion, son of the goddess Dôn.

1. The four Hebrew letters that spell God's name, Yahweh. The text continues its playful combination of ancient Celtic and Christian references.

of the merciful son of God;
I was three times
    in the prison of Arianrhod;[2]
I was in the ark
    with Noah and Alpha;
I witnessed the destruction
    of Sodom and Gomorrah;
I was in Africa
    before the building of Rome;
I came here
    to the survivors of Troy.[3]

And I was with my lord
    in the manger of oxen and asses;
I upheld Moses
    through the water of Jordan;
I was in the sky
    with Mary Magdalen;
I got poetic inspiration
    from the cauldron of Ceridwen;[4]
I was poet-harper
    to Lleon Llychlyn;
I was in Gwynfryn
    in the court of Cynfelyn;
In stock and fetters
    a day and a year.

I was revealed
    in the land of the Trinity;
And I was moved
    through the entire universe;
And I shall remain till doomsday,
    upon the face of the earth.
And no one knows what my flesh is—
    whether meat or fish.

And I was nearly nine months
    in the womb of the witch Ceridwen;
I was formerly Gwion Bach,
    but now I am Taliesin.

And the story says that this song amazed the king and his court greatly. Then he sang a song to explain to the king and his people why he had come there and what he was attempting to do, as the following poem sets forth.

Provincial bards! I am contending!
    To refrain I am unable.
    I shall proclaim in prophetic song
    To those that will listen.

2. A daughter of the goddess Dôn.
3. As descendants of the ancient Britons (founded by Brutus), the Welsh claimed Trojan lineage and an antiquity as great as the Romans.

4. Ceridwen prepared the three drops conferring wisdom in a great cauldron; it cried out and burst when the drops fell on Gwion Bach.

And I seek that loss
That I suffer:
Elphin, from the punishment
Of Caer Deganwy.

And from him, my lord will pull
The binding chain.
The Chair of Caer Deganwy—
Mighty is my pride—
Three hundred songs and more
Are the songs I shall sing;
No bard that knows them not
Shall merit spear
Nor stone nor ring,
Nor remain about me.

Elphin son of Gwyddno
Suffers torment now,
'Neath thirteen locks
For praising his master-bard.

And I am Taliesin,
Chief-poet of the West,
And I shall release Elphin
From the gilded fetters.

After this, as the text shows, he sang a song of succor, and they say that instantly a tempestuous wind arose, until the king and his people felt that the castle would fall upon them. Because of that, the king had Elphin fetched from prison in a hurry, and brought to the side of Taliesin. He is said to have sung a song at that moment that resulted in the opening of the fetters from around his feet—indeed, in my opinion, it is very difficult for anyone to believe that this tale is true. But I will continue the story with as many of the poems by him as I have seen written down.

Following this, he sang the verses called "Interrogation of the Bards," which follows herewith.

What being first
Made Alpha?
What is the fairest refined language
Designed by the Lord?

What food? What drink?
Whose raiment prudent?
Who endured rejection
From a deceitful land?

Why is a stone hard?
Why is a thorn sharp?
Who is hard as a stone,
And as salty as salt?

Why is the nose like a ridge?
Why is the wheel round?

Why does the tongue articulate
More than any one organ?

Then he sang a series of verses called "The Rebuke of the Bards," and it begins like this:

If you are a fierce bard
Of spirited poetic-inspiration,
Be not testy
In your king's court,
Unless you know the name for *rimin*,
And the name for *ramin*,
And the name for *rimiad*,
And the name for *ramiad*,
And the name of your forefather
Before his baptism.

And the name of the firmament,
And the name of the element,
And the name of your language,
And the name of your district.

Company of poets above,
Company of poets below;
My darling is below
'Neath the fetters of Aranrhod.
You certainly do not know
The meaning of what my lips sing,
Nor the true distinction
Between the true and the false.
Bards of limited horizons,
Why do you not flee?
The bard who cannot shut me up
Shall have no quiet
Till he come to rest
Beneath a gravelly grave.
And those who listen to me,
Let God listen to them.

And after this follows the verses called "The Satire on the Bards."

Minstrels of malfeasance make
Impious lyrics; in their praise
They sing vain and evanescent song,
Ever exercising lies.
They mock guileless men
They corrupt married women,
They despoil Mary's chaste maidens.
Their lives and times they waste in vain,
They scorn the frail and the guileless,
They drink by night, sleep by day,
Idly, lazily, making their way.
They despise the Church
Lurch toward the taverns;
In harmony with thieves and lechers,

They seek out courts and feasts,
Extol every idiotic utterance,
Praise every deadly sin.
They lead every manner of base life,
Roam every village, town, and land.
The distresses of death concern them not,
Never do they give lodging or alms.
Excessive food they consume.
They rehearse neither the psalms nor prayer,
Pay neither tithes nor offerings to God,
Worship not on Holy Days nor the Lord's day,
Fast on neither Holy Days nor ember days.
    Birds fly,
    Fish swim,
    Bees gather honey,
    Vermin crawl;
    Everything bustles
    To earn its keep
    Except minstrels and thieves, the lazy and worthless.

I do not revile your minstrelsy,
For God gave that to ward off evil blasphemy;
But he who practices it in perfidy
Reviles Jesus and his worship.

After Taliesin had freed his master from prison, verified the chastity of his mistress, and silenced the bards so that none of them dared say a single word, he asked Elphin to wager the king that he had a horse faster and swifter than all the king's horses. Elphin did that.

On the day, time, and place determined—the place known today as Morfa Rhianedd—the king arrived with his people and twenty-four of the swiftest horses he owned. Then, after a long while, the course was set, and a place for the horses to run. Taliesin came there with twenty-four sticks of holly, burnt black. He had the lad who was riding his master's horse put them under his belt, instructing him to let all the king's horses go ahead of him, and as he caught up with each of them in turn, to take one of the rods and whip the horse across his rump, and then throw it to the ground. Then take another rod and do in the same manner to each of the horses as he overtook them. And he instructed the rider to observe carefully the spot where his horse finished, and throw down his cap on that spot.

The lad accomplished all of this, both the whipping of each of the king's horses as well as throwing down his cap in the place where the horse finished. Taliesin brought his master there after his horse won the race, and he and Elphin set men to work to dig a hole. When they had dug the earth to a certain depth, they found a huge cauldron of gold, and therewith Taliesin said, "Elphin, here is payment and reward for you for having brought me from the weir and raising me from that day to this." In that very place there stands a pool of water, which from that day to this is called "Cauldon's Pool."

After that, the king had Taliesin brought before him, and asked for information concerning the origin of the human race. Forthwith, he sang the verses that follow here below, and that are known today as one of the four pillars of song. They begin as follows:

Here begin the prophecies of Taliesin.

> The Lord made
> In the midst of Glen Hebron
> With his blessed hands,
>> I know, the shape of Adam.

5 He made the beautiful;
> In the court of paradise,
> From a rib, he put together
>> Fair woman.

> Seven hours they
10 Tended the Orchard
> Before Satan's strife,
>> Most insistent suitor.

> Thence they were driven
> Through cold and chill
15 To lead their lives
>> In this world.

> To bear in affliction
> Sons and daughters,
> To get tribute
20 From the land of Asia.

> One hundred and eight
> Was she fertile,
> Bearing a mixed brood,
>> Masculine and feminine.

25 And then, openly,
> When she bore Abel
> And Cain, unconcealable,
>> Most unredeemable.

> To Adam and his mate
30 Was given a digging shovel
> To break the earth
>> To gain bread.

> And shining white wheat
> To sow, the instrument
35 To feed all men
>> Until the great feast.

> Angels sent
> From God Almighty
> Brought the seed of growth
40 To Eve.

> She hid
> A tenth of the gift
> So that not all did
>> The whole garden enclose.

45   But black rye was had
      In place of the fine wheat,
      Showing the evil
            For stealing.

      Because of that treacherous turn,
50   It is necessary, says Sattwrn,
      For each to give his tithe
            To God first.

      From crimson red wine
      Planted on a sunny day,
55   And the moon's night prevails
            Over white wine.

      From wheat of true privilege,
      From red wine generous and privileged.
      Is made the finely molded body
60   Of Christ son of Alpha.

      From the wafer is the flesh.
      From the wine is the flow of blood.
      And the words of the Trinity
            Consecrated him.

65   Every sort of mystical book
      Of Emmanuel's work
      Rafael brought
            To give to Adam.

      When he was in ferment,
70   Above his two jaws
      Within the Jordan River
            Fasting.

      Moses found,
      To guard against great need,
75   The secret of the three
            Most famous rods.

      Samson got
      Within the tower of Babylon
      All the magical arts
80   Of Asia land.

      I got, indeed,
      In my bardic song,
      All the magical arts
            Of Europe and Africa.

85   And I know whence she emanates
      And her home and her hospitality,
      Her fate and her destiny
            Till Doomsday.

      Alas, God, how wretched,
90   Through excessive plaint,

Comes the prophecy
　　To the race of Troy.

A coiled serpent,
Proud and merciless,
95　With golden wings
　　Out of Germany.

It shall conquer
England and Scotland,
From the shore of the Scandinavian Sea
100　　To the Severn.

Then shall the Britons be
Like prisoners,
With status of aliens,
　　To the Saxons.

105　Their lord they shall praise.
Their language preserve,
And their land they will lose—
　　Save wild Wales.

Until comes a certain period
110　After long servitude,
When shall be of equal duration
　　The two proud ones.

Then will the Britons gain
Their land and their crown,
115　And the foreigners
　　Will disappear.

And the words of the angels
On peace and war
Will be true
120　　Concerning Britain.

And after this he proclaimed to the king various prophecies in verse, concerning the world that would come hereafter.

━━━◄━◆━►━━━

Dafydd ap Gwilym

Widely regarded as the greatest Welsh poet, Dafydd ap Gwilym flourished in the fourteenth century, during a period of relative peace between two failed rebellions—that of Llywelyn, the last native prince of Wales, in 1282, and that of Owain Glyn Dwr (Owen Glendower), in 1400. A member of an upper-class family whose ancestors had served the English king, he wrote for a sophisticated audience of poets and patrons.

Dafydd drew inspiration from both continental and Welsh poetry but not, significantly, from English. (Influence, if any, went the other way, for the Middle English Harley lyrics, composed near the Welsh border, may owe their intricate rhyme scheme and ornamental alliteration to Welsh poetry; see *Spring* and *Alisoun*, pages 523–524). Among continental poets, the Roman Ovid is the greatest influence, whether directly or through twelfth-century Latin adaptations. He is the only foreign poet whom Dafydd mentions by name (*One Saving Place*, line 39). Dafydd is also indebted to medieval French and Provençal lyric genres—the *aubade* (dawn song), and the *reverdie* (spring song)—as well as to the *fabliau*.

Much of Dafydd's charm comes from his undercutting and transforming inherited poetic conventions through his personal revelations. His most endearing device, the self-deprecating persona, has been compared to that of his younger contemporary, Geoffrey Chaucer. There is an important difference, however, for while Chaucer in early love poems like *The Parliament of Fowls* presents himself as a failed lover, Dafydd often boasts of his success. Although he gives comic accounts of romantic failures in such anecdotal poems as *The Girls of Llanbadarn* (in which the women he ogles in church scornfully dismiss him) and the *Tale of a Wayside Inn* (in which a tryst ends in disaster when he goes to the wrong room), these are as often due to external obstacles as to his own inadequacy. In fact, Dafydd's persona is much more akin to Ovid's than to Chaucer's, with *The Hateful Husband* echoing the exasperated and scheming lover of *Amores* 1.4 and 1.6. In *The Ruin*, Dafydd gives an erotic twist to the ascetic Christian motif of the impermanence of worldly pleasures (as in the Old English *Wanderer*, page 144, and the Middle English *Contempt of the World*, page 535) by recalling that he once made love in a cottage that is now abandoned. He concludes his complaint *The Winter* with the observation that he would not venture out in such snowy weather for the sake of any girl.

Dafydd's poetry owes an equal debt to the rich poetic tradition of Wales. He shows familiarity with characters from the Arthurian tradition, which was originally Celtic although transformed by French adaptations by the time it reached him (see *The Tale of Taliesin*, page 536). In the poems included here, he often emphasizes the local Welsh setting. In *One Saving Place*, for instance, he lists all the locales where he sought his beloved Morvith, or she refused him—places with names like Meirch, Eleirch, Rhiw, and Cwcwll hollow. In *The Winter*, it is specifically in north Wales that he is assailed by snow. Finally, part of the humor in the *Tale of a Wayside Inn* derives from Dafydd's self-presentation as a "Welshman" whose accidental presence in their bedroom is discovered by three coarse Englishmen.

Dafydd's work is also distinguished by the poetic techniques of Welsh poetry, which are extraordinarily complex. His *cywyddau* (lyric poems) are written in the traditional lines of seven syllables, which rhyme in couplets, with the rhyming syllables alternately stressed and unstressed. He applies further ornamentation with a technique called *cynghanned*—internal alliteration or rhyme, which he sometimes extends over many lines. Although such an intricate style is impossible to capture in English, Rolfe Humphries has tried to approximate it in the translations given here. Easier to reproduce are Daffyd's *dyfalu*— strings of fanciful comparisons, such as the metaphors for snow used in *The Winter*:

> The snowflakes wander,
> A swarm of white bees.
> Over the woods
> A cold veil lies.
> A load of chalk
> Bows down the trees,
>
> * * *
>
> Will someone tell me
> What angels lift
> Planks in the flour-loft
> Floor of heaven
> Shaking down dust?
> An angel's cloak
> Is cold quicksilver.

In extending the virtuoso techniques of the native tradition, Dafydd set the standard for Welsh poets for the next two centuries.

Aubade[1]

It seemed as if we did not sleep
One wink that night; I was sighing deep.
The cruellest judge in the costliest court
Could not condemn a night so short.

5   We had the light out, but I know,
Each time I turned, a radiant glow
Suffused the room, and shining snow
Alit from Heaven's candle-fires
Illuminated our desires.

10   But the last time I held her, strong,
Excited, closest, very long,
Something started going wrong.
The edge of dawn's despotic veil
Showed at the eastern window-pale
15   And there it was,—the morning light!
Gwen[2] was seized with a fearful fright,
Became an apparition, cried,
"Get up, go now with God, go hide!

"Love is a salt, a gall, a rue,
20   A vinegar-vintage. Dos y Ddw,
Vaya con Dios,[3], quickly, too!"
"Ah, not yet, never yet, my love;
The stars and moon still shine above."
"Then why do the raucous ravens talk
25   With such a loud insistent squawk?"
"Crows always cry like that, when fleas
Nibble their ankles, nip their knees."

"And why do the dogs yip, yammer, yell?"
"They think they've caught a fox's smell."
30   "Poet, the wisdom of a fool
Offers poor counsel as a rule.
Open the door, open it wide
As fast as you can, and leap outside.
The dogs are fierce when they get untied."
35   "The woods are only a bound from here,
And I can outjump a deer, my dear!"

"But tell me, best beloved of men,
Will you come again? Will you come again?"
"Gwen, you know I'm your nightingale,
40   And I'll be with you, without fail,

---

1. The aubade or dawn song is a genre of love lyric with a long European tradition, in which two lovers lament the necessity of parting at dawn. Chaucer uses the aubade, as later do Shakespeare (in *Romeo and Juliet*) and John Donne in *The Sun Rising*.

2. Along with Morvith and Dovekie, a woman's name which recurs in many of Dafydd's love poems.
3. "Go with God"; this Spanish phrase represents license, on the part of the translator, in the spirit of Dafydd's playfulness.

When the cloud is cloak, and the dark is sky,
And when the night comes, so will I."

One Saving Place

What wooer ever walked through frost and snow,
Through rain and wind, as I in sorrow?
My two feet took me to a tryst in Meirch[1]
No luck; I swam and waded the Eleirch,
5   No golden loveliness, no glimpse of her;
Night or day, I came no nearer
Except in Bleddyn's arbors, where I sighed
When she refused me, as she did beside
Maesalga's murmuring water-tide.
10   I crossed the river, Bergul, and went on
Beyond its threatening voices; I have gone
Through the mountain-pass of Meibion,
Came to Camallt, dark in my despair,
For one vision of her golden hair.
15   All for nothing. I've looked down from Rhiw,
All for nothing but a valley view,
Kept on going, on my journey through
Cyfylfaen's gorge, with rock and boulder,
Where I had thought to ermine-cloak her shoulder.
20   Never; not here, there, thither, thence,
Could I ever find her presence.
Eagerly on summer days I'd go
Brushing my way through Cwcwll hollow,
Never stopped, continued, skirting
25   Gastell Gwrgan and its ring
Where the red-winged blackbirds sing,
Tramped across fields where goslings feed
Below the cat-tail and the reed.
I have limped my way, a weary hound,
30   In shadow of the walls that bound
Adail Heilyn's broken ground.
I have hidden, like a friar,
In Ifor's Court, among the choir,
Sought to seek my sweet one there,
35   But there was no sign of her.
On both sides of Nant-y-glo
There's no vale, no valley, no
Stick or stump where I failed to go,
Only Gwynn of the Mist for guide,
40   Without Ovid[2] at my side.

Gwenn-y-Talwrn!—there I found
My hand close on hers, on ground
Where no grass was ever green,

---

1. This and other Welsh place names are listed by Dafydd
in his account of his search for his beloved, Morvith.

2. See introduction for Dafydd's indebtedness to the
Roman love poet.

45 Where not even a shrub was seen,
There at last I made the bed
For my Morvith,[3] my moon-maid,
Underneath the dark leaf-cloak
Woven by saplings of an oak.
50 Bitter, if a man must move
On his journeys without love.
Bitter, if soul's pilgrimage
Must be like the body's rage,
Must go down the desolate road
Midway through the darkling wood.

The Girls of Llanbadarn[1]

I am one of passion's asses,
Plague on all these parish lasses!
Though I long for them like mad,
Not one female have I had,
5 Not a one in all my life,
Virgin, damsel, hag, or wife.
What maliciousness, what lack,
What does make them turn their back?
Would it be a shame to be
10 In a bower of leaves with me?
No one's ever been so bitched,
So bewildered, so bewitched
Saving Garwy's[2] lunatics
By their foul fantastic tricks.
15 So I fall in love, I do,
Every day, with one or two,
Get no closer, any day,
Than an arrow's length away.
Every single Sunday, I,
20 Llanbadarn can testify,
Go to church and take my stand
With my plumed hat in my hand,
Make my reverence to the altar,
Find the right page in my psalter,
25 Turn my back on holy God,
Face the girls, and wink, and nod
For a long, long time, and look
Over feather, at the folk.
Suddenly, what do I hear?
30 A stage whisper, all too clear,
A girl's voice, and her companion
Isn't slow at catching on?
"See that simple fellow there,
Pale and with his sister's hair

---

3. The lady most frequently mentioned in Dafydd's love poems, apparently married.

1. A village near the busy Welsh market town of Aberystwyth.
2. A legendary lover.

35   Giving me those leering looks
Wickeder than any crook's?"
"Don't you think that he's sincere?"
Asks the other in her ear.

"All I'll give him is *Get out!*
40   Let the Devil take the lout!"
Pretty payment, in return
For the love with which I burn.
Burn for what? The bright girl's gift
Offers me the shortest shrift.
45   I must give them up, resign
These fear-troubled hopes of mine:
Better be a hermit, thief,
Anything, to bring relief.
Oh, strange lesson, that I must
50   Go companionless and lost,
Go because I looked too long,
I, who loved the power of song.

Tale of a Wayside Inn

With one servant, I went down
To a sportive sort of town
Where a Welshman might secure
Comely welcome, and pleasure.
5   There we found the book to sign
In the inn, and ordered wine.

But whatever did I see
But the loveliest lady
Blooming beautiful and bright,
10   Blossom stemming from sunlight,
Graceful as the gossamer.
I said, "Let me banquet her!"
Feasting's a fine way, it seems,
For fulfilling young men's dreams.

15   So, unshy, she took her seat
At my side, and we did eat,
Sipped our wine, and smiled and dallied
Like a man and maid, new-married.
Bold I was, but whispering,
20   And the others heard nothing.

Troth and tryst we pledged, to keep
When the others were asleep.
I should find my way, and come
Through the darkness to her room.
25   Love would haul my steps aright
Down the hallways of the night;
Love would steer my steps,—alas,
This was not what came to pass.

For, by some outrageous miss,
30 What I got was not a kiss,
But a stubble-whiskered cheek
And a triple whiskey-reek,
Not one Englishman, but three,
(What a Holy Trinity!)
35 Diccon, 'Enry, Jerk-off Jack,
Each one pillowed on his pack.

One of them let out a yell,
"What's that thing I think I smell?
There's a Welshman must have hid
40 In the closet or under t' bed,
Come to cut our throats with knives,
Guard your wallets and your lives,
They're all thieves, beyond all doubt,
Throw the bloody bugger out!"

45 None too nimble for my need,
First I found how shins will bleed
When you bark them in your haste
On a stool that's been misplaced
By some ostler-stupid fool,
50 Then the sawney of a stool
Squealed its pig-stuck tattle-tale
After my departing trail.

By good luck, I never got
Wet-foot from the chamber-pot.
55 That was all I saved myself,
Knocked my noggin on a shelf,
Overturned the table-trestles,
Down came all the pans and kettles.
As I dove to outer dark,
60 All the dogs began to bark.

Asses bray, and scullions rouse
Every sleeper in the house.
I could hear the hunt come round me,
Scowl-faced scoundrels, till they found me.
65 I could feel their stones and sticks,
So I clasped my crucifix,
Jesu, Jesu, Jesu dear,
Don't let people catch me here!

Since my prayer was strong, I came
70 Through the mercy of His name
Safely to my room at last,
All my perils over-passed.
No girl's love to ease my plight,
Only God's that dreadful night,
75 To the saints be brought the praise,
And the Good Lord mend my wicked ways.

The Hateful Husband

'Tis sorrow and pain,
'Tis endless chagrin
For Dafydd to gain
His dark-haired girl.
5   Her house is a jail,
Her turnkey a vile,
Sour, yellow-eyed, pale,
Odious churl.

She cannot go out
10   Unless he's about,
The blackguard, the lout,
The stingy boor.
The look in her eye
Of fondness for me—
15   God bless her bounty!—
He can't endure.

I know he hates play:
The greenwood in May,
The birds' roundelay
20   Are not for him.
The cuckoo, I know,
He'd never allow
To sing on his bough,
Light on his limb

25   The flash of the wing,
The swell of the song,
Harp-music playing
Draw his black looks.
The hounds in full cry,
30   A race-horse of bay,
He cannot enjoy
More than the pox.

My heart would be glad
At seeing him laid
35   All gray in his shroud;
How could I grieve?
Should he die this year,
I'd give him with cheer
Good oak for his bier,
40   Sods for his grave.

O starling, O swift,
Go soaring aloft,
Come down to the croft
By Dovekie's home.
45   This message give her,
Tell her I love her,

And I will have her,
All in good time.

The Winter

Across North Wales
The snowflakes wander,
A swarm of white bees.
Over the woods
5   A cold veil lies.
A load of chalk
Bows down the trees.

No undergrowth
Without its wool,
10   No field unsheeted;
No path is left
Through any field;
On every stump
White flour is milled.

15   Will someone tell me
What angels lift
Planks in the flour-loft
Floor of heaven
Shaking down dust?
20   An angel's cloak
Is cold quicksilver.

And here below
The big drifts blow,
Blow and billow
25   Across the heather
Like swollen bellies.
The frozen foam
Falls in fleeces.

Out of my house
30   I will not stir
For any girl
To have my coat
Look like a miller's
Or stuck with feathers
35   Of eider down.

What a great fall
Lies on my country!
A wide wall, stretching
One sea to the other,
40   Greater and graver
Than the sea's graveyard.
When will rain come?

The Ruin

Nothing but a hovel now
Between moorland and meadow,
Once the owners saw in you
A comely cottage, bright, new,
5   Now roof, rafters, ridge-pole, all
Broken down by a broken wall.

A day of delight was once there
For me, long ago, no care
When I had a glimpse of her
10   Fair in an ingle-corner.
Beside each other we lay
In the delight of that day.

Her forearm, snowflake-lovely,
Softly white, pillowing me,
15   proferred a pleasant pattern
For me to give in my turn,
And that was our blessing for
The new-cut lintel and door.

"Now the wild wind, wailing by,
20   Crashes with curse and with cry
Against my stones, a tempest
Born and bred in the East,
Or south ram-batterers break
The shelter that folk forsake."

25   Life is illusion and grief;
A tile whirls off, as a leaf
Or a lath goes sailing, high
In the keening of kite-kill cry.
Could it be, our couch once stood
30   Sturdily under that wood?

"Pillar and post, it would seem
Now you are less than a dream.
Are you that, or only the lost
Wreck of a riddle, rune-ghost?"

35   "Dafydd, the cross on their graves
Marks what little it saves,
Says, *They did well in their lives.*"

Middle Scots Poets

In the late fifteenth and early sixteenth centuries, Scotland enjoyed a brief flowering of poetry centered in a sophisticated court society. Relations with England were fraught with irony, marked, on the one hand, by royal alliance (James IV married Margaret Tudor, daughter of England's Henry VII in 1503) and on the other by disastrous warfare (James IV also, in alliance with France, invaded England and perished with most of the Scottish nobility at the

Battle of Flodden in 1513). The poets of this period have been variously known as the "Scottish Chaucerians," the "Middle Scots Poets," and the "Makars"—each term privileging a significant, though only partial, aspect of their work. The first conveys the debt that William Dunbar, Robert Henryson, and Gavin Douglas (to name the three most famous) owed to Chaucer's subject matter, rhetorical style, and techniques of parody. The second suggests their equal debt to a native Scottish tradition, which includes such overtly nationalist works as Barbour's *Bruce* and Blind Harry's *Wallace*. The best term to describe these poets is perhaps the one used by Dunbar himself—"Makars" (makers)—for it suggests their powerful and self-conscious artistry.

William Dunbar

Of all the Makars, Dunbar is the greatest virtuoso, intoxicated with language, whether it be the elevated vocabulary borrowed from Latin, or the Germanic diction of alliterative poetry, whose tradition was kept alive in Scotland a century after it had died out in England. He was versatile in his choice of genres, writing occasional poems (such an an allegory in celebration of the marriage of James IV and Princess Margaret), divine poems, and parodies such as *The Tretis of Two Mariit Wemen and the Wedo*, a bawdy satire on the morals of court ladies written in the traditional alliterative long line. Included here are a meditation on death (*Lament for the Makars*), an Easter hymn (*Done Is a Battell*) and a parody of the courtly genre of the *chanson d'aventure* (*In Secreit Place This Hyndir Nycht*).

Lament for the Makars[1]

	I that in heill° wes° and gladnes	*health/was*
	Am trublit now with gret seiknes	
	And feblit with infermite:	
	Timor mortis conturbat me.[2]	
5	Our plesance heir is all vane glory,	
	This fals warld is bot transitory,	
	The flesche is brukle,° the Fend° is sle:°	*frail/Devil/sly*
	Timor mortis conturbat me.	
	The stait of man dois change and vary,	
10	Now sound, now seik, now blith, now sary,	
	Now dansand mery, now like to dee:°	*die*
	Timor mortis conturbat me.	
	No stait in erd° heir standis sickir;°	*on earth/secure*
	As with the wynd wavis the wickir,	
15	Wavis this warldis vanite:	
	Timor mortis conturbat me.	

---

1. This poem reflects the late medieval fascination with death. The speaker wistfully observes that beautiful ladies, brave knights, and wise clerks have had their lives cut short but gives most of his attention to poets. He lists 23 of these—three English (Chaucer, Gower, and Lydgate) and 20 Scots, only half of whom modern scholars can identify. Since Death has taken all his "brothers," he regards himself as next and resolves to prepare himself for the next world. The poem was printed in 1508 by Walter Chepman and Andrew Myllar, who introduced the printing press to Scotland.

2. Fear of death shakes me (from the liturgical Office of the Dead).

On to the ded gois all estatis,
Princis, prelotis,° and potestatis,°   *prelates/rulers*
Baith riche and pur of al degre:
20   *Timor mortis conturbat me.*

He takis the knychtis° in to feild,°   *knights/the field*
Anarmit° under helme and scheild;   armed   *armed*
Victour he is at all mellie:°.   *battles*
Timor mortis conturbat me.

25   That strang unmercifull tyrand
Takis, on the moderis° breist sowkand,°   *mother's/sucking*
The bab full of benignite:
Timor mortis conturbat me.

He takis the campion° in the stour,°   *champion/conflict*
30   The capitane closit in the tour,
The lady in bour° full of bewte: *bower*
Timor mortis conturbat me.

He sparis no lord for his piscence,°   *power*
Na clerk for his intelligence;
35   His awfull strak° may no man fle: *stroke*
Timor mortis conturbat me.

Art magicianis and astrologgis,
Rethoris,° logicianis and theologgis,   *rhetoricians*
Thame helpis no conclusionis sle:°   *clever*
40   *Timor mortis conturbat me.*

In medicyne the most practicianis,
Lechis,° surrigianis,° and phisicianis,   *doctors/surgeons*
Thame self fra ded° may not supple:°   *death/deliver*
Timor mortis conturbat me.

45   I se that makaris° amang the laif°   *poets/remainder*
Playis heir ther pageant, syne gois to graif;°   *grave*
Sparit° is nocht ther faculte: *spared*
Timor mortis conturbat me.

He hes done petuously devour
50   The noble Chaucer of makaris flour,°   *flower of poets*
The Monk of Bery,[3] and Gower, all thre:
Timor mortis conturbat me.

The gude Syr Hew of Eglintoun,[4]
And eik Heryot, and Wyntoun,[5]
55   He hes tane out of this cuntre:
Timor mortis conturbat me.

3. John Lydgate, monk of Bury St. Edmunds, a minor poet
who was an imitator of Chaucer. He also used the "*timor
mortis*" refrain in a poem on the same subject.

4. Brother-in-law of Robert II and not otherwise known
as a poet.
5. Andrew of Wyntoun, author of the *Oryginale Chrony-
kil of Scotland.*

That scorpion fell° hes done infek°   *fierce/infect*
Maister Johne Clerk and James Afflek[6]
Fra ballat making and tragidie:
60 *Timor mortis conturbat me.*

Holland and Barbour[7] he hes berevit;
Allace,° that he nocht with us levit   *alas*
Schir Mungo Lokert of the Le:[8]
 Timor mortis conturbat me.

65 Clerk of Tranent eik he hes tane,
That maid the Anteris° of Gawane;   *adventures*
Schir Gilbert Hay endit hes he:[9]
 Timor mortis conturbat me.

He hes Blind Hary and Sandy Traill
70 Slaine with his schour° of mortall haill,   *shower*
Quhilk Patrik Johnestoun[1] myght nocht fle:
 Timor mortis conturbat me.

He hes reft° Merseir his endite°   *taken from/talent*
That did in luf so lifly° write,   *in a lively manner*
75 So schort, so quyk, of sentence hie:
 Timor mortis conturbat me.

He hes tane Roull of Aberdene
And gentill Roull of Corstorphin;
Two bettir fallowis did no man se:
80 *Timor mortis conturbat me.*

In Dunfermelyne he hes done roune°   *held conversation*
With Maister Robert Henrisoun.[2]
Schir Johne the Ros enbrast° hes he: *embraced*
 Timor mortis conturbat me.

85 And he hes now tane last of aw
Gud gentill Stobo and Quintyne Schaw,[3]
Of quham all wichtis hes pete:[4]
 Timor mortis conturbat me.

Gud Maister Walter Kennedy[5]
90 In° poynt of dede° lyis veraly;°   *on/death/truly*
Gret reuth° it wer that so suld be: *pity*
 Timor mortis conturbat me.

---

6. These two are unknown, as are the other poets in this list not identified.
7. Sir Richard Holland, author of the allegorical *Buke of the Howlat* (c. 1450), and John Barbour, author of the patriotic *Actes and Life . . . of Robert Bruce* (1376).
8. This Scotsman (d. 1489?) is not otherwise known as a poet.
9. The "clerk of Tranent" is unknown, but Arthurian romances focusing on Gawain were popular in Scotland; Sir Gilbert Hay (d. 1456) translated the poem *The Buik of Alexander* from French.

1. Blind Harry is credited with writing the Scots epic *Wallace* (c. 1475); Patrick Johnstoune was a producer of stage entertainments at court in the late 1400s.
2. Henryson was a major Middle Scots poet; see his *Robene and Makyne*, page 565.
3. John Reid, known as Stobo, was priest and secretary to James II, James III, and James IV; Schaw was a minor Scots poet.
4. On whom all people have pity.
5. Known for his *Flyting* (poem of ritual insult) with Dunbar.

Sen he hes all my brether tane
He will nocht lat me lif alane;
95   On forse° I man his nyxt pray be: *of necessity*
    Timor mortis conturbat me.

Sen for the deid remeid° is none,   *remedy*
Best is that we for dede dispone°   *prepare*
Eftir our deid that lif may we:
    Timor mortis conturbat me.

Done Is a Battell[1]

Done is a battell on° the dragon blak,   *with*
Our campioun° Chryst confountet hes his force;   *champion*
The yettis° of hell ar brokin with a crak,   *gates*
The signe triumphall rasit is of the croce,°   *cross*
5   The divillis trymmillis° with hiddous voce,   *trembles*
The saulis° ar borrowit° and to the blis can go,   *souls/redeemed*
Chryst with his blud our ransonis dois indoce:°   *endorse*
Surrexit dominus de sepulchro.[2]

Dungin° is the deidly dragon Lucifer,   *beaten*
10   The crewall° serpent with the mortall stang,°   *cruel/sting*
The auld kene tegir with his teith on char°   *ajar*
Quhilk° in a wait hes lyne° for us so lang, which/ lain   *which/lain*
Thinking to grip us in his clowis strang:
The mercifull lord wald° nocht that it wer so,   *would*
15   He maid him for to felye° of that fang:°   *fail/booty*
Surrexit dominus de sepulchro.

He for our saik that sufferit to be slane
And lyk a lamb in sacrifice wes dicht,°   *prepared*
Is lyk a lyone° rissin up agane,   *lion*
20   And as a gyane raxit him on hicht:[3]
Sprungin° is Aurora radius° and bricht,   *arisen/radiant*
On loft° is gone the glorius Appollo,[4]   *aloft*
The blisfull day depairtit° fro the nycht: *separated*
Surrexit dominus de sepulchro.

25   The grit victour agane is rissin on hicht
That for our querrell to the deth wes woundit;
The sone that wox° all paill now schynis bricht,   *became*
And, dirknes clerit, our fayth is now refoundit:°   *reestablished*
The knell of mercy fra the hevin is soundit,[5]
30   The Cristin ar deliverit of thair wo,
The Jowis° and thair errour ar confoundit: *Jews*
Surrexit dominus de sepulchro.

---

1. This Easter hymn heroically portrays Christ's Resurrection as a battle with the devil, drawing on the account of the harrowing of hell in the apocryphal Gospel of Nicodemus, in which Christ journeys to hell to release worthy souls who had been born before his coming. It gains much of its power from the juxtaposition of alliterative diction from the Scots tradition with Latinate vocabulary. As in the *Lament for the Makars*, the Latin refrain fits within the overall English rhyme scheme.

2. The Lord is risen from the tomb. From the opening of the service for matins on Easter Sunday.
3. And like a giant stretched himself on high. A reference to Sampson, who in bearing off the gates of Gaza was seen as a type of Christ breaking the gates of hell.
4. Christ, the sun (and Son) of righteousness, is identified with Apollo, the sun god, which explains the reference to Aurora, goddess of the dawn.
5. An allusion to the ringing of the bells on Easter morning.

The fo is chasit, the battell is done ceis,°   *ceased*
The presone brokin, the jevellouris fleit and flemit⁶,
35   The weir° is gon, confermit is the peis,°   *war/peace*
The fetteris lowsit° and the dungeoun temit,°   *loosed/emptied*
The ransoun maid, the presoneris° redemit,°   *prisoners/redeemed*
The feild is win,° ourcummin° is the fo,   *won/overcome*
Dispulit° of the tresur that he yemit:°   *despoiled/kept*
Surrexit dominus de sepulchro.

In Secreit Place This Hyndir Nycht¹

In secreit place this hyndir° nycht   *last*
I hard ane beyrne° say till ane bricht,°   *man/fair lady*
"My huny, my hart, my hoip, my heill,²
I have bene lang° your luifar° leill°   *long/lover/loyal*
5   And can of yow get confort nane:°   *none*
How lang will ye with danger deill?³
Ye brek my hart, my bony ane."°   *pretty one*

His bony beird was kemmit and croppit,⁴
Bot all with cale° it was bedroppit,°   *soup/smeared*
10 And he wes townysche, peirt and gukit.⁵
He clappit fast, he kist and chukkit⁶
As with the glaikis° he wer ouirgane;°   *lust/overcome*
Yit be his feirris° he wald have fukkit: *manner*
"Ye brek my hart, my bony ane."

15 Quod he, "My hairt, sweit° as the hunye,   *sweet*
Sen that I borne wes of my mynnye°   *mother*
I never wowit° weycht° bot yow;   *wooed/creature*
My wambe° is of your luif sa fow°   *belly/full*
That as ane gaist° I glour° and grane,°   *ghost/glower/groan*
20 I trymble° sa, ye will not trow:°   *tremble/believe*
Ye brek my hart, my bony ane."

"Tehe,"° quod scho, and gaif ane gawfe;°   *Teehee/guffaw*
"Be still my tuchan⁷ and my calfe,
My new spanit howffing fra the sowk,⁸
25 And all the blythnes° of my bowk;°   *joy/body*
My sweit swanking,° saif yow allane   *fine fellow*
Na leid° I luiffit° all this owk:°   *no man/loved/week*
Full leifis° me° your graceles gane."°   *dear/to me/face*

Quod he, "My claver° and my curldodie,°   *clover/a plant*
30 My huny soppis, my sweit possodie,°   *sheep's head broth*
Be not oure bosteous° to your billie,°   *rough/sweetheart*
Be warme hairtit° and not evill willie;°   *hearted/ill-willed*

6. The prison broken, the jailers fled and banished.
1. This comic account of the wooing of a kitchen maid by a boorish man parodies the *chanson d'aventure*, a genre in which the speaker overhears a dialogue between two lovers. Dunbar undercuts the poem's courtly language, which he has used seriously elsewhere, with overtly sexual references. In addition to words familiar to modern readers, the poem features terms of endearment from colloquial Scots which have long since been lost.

2. My honey, my heart, my hope, my salvation.
3. Ladies were expected to be "dangerous" (reluctant) in a courtship situation.
4. His handsome beard was combed and trimmed.
5. And he was townish (uncourtly), pert, and foolish.
6. He fondled fast, kissed and chucked her under the chin.
7. Calf skin stuffed with straw, to encourage a cow to give milk.
8. My clumsy fellow newly weaned from nursing.

Your heylis quhyt as quhalis bane,[9]
Garris ryis° on loft my quhillelillie:°   *makes rise/penis*
35   Ye brek my hart, my bony ane."

Quod scho, "My clype, my unspaynit gyane[1]
With moderis° mylk yit in your mychane,°   *mother's/mouth*
My belly huddrun,° my swete hurle bawsy,[2]   *big-bellied glutton*
My huny gukkis,° my slawsy gawsy,   *sweet fool*
40   Your musing waild perse° ane hart of stane: *would pierce*
Tak gud confort, my grit heidit° slawsy,   *great-headed*
Full leifis me your graceles gane."

Quod he, "My kid, my capirculyoun,°   *woodgrouse*
My bony baib° with the ruch° brylyoun,   *babe/rough*
45   My tendir gyrle, my wallie gowdye,°   *pretty goldfinch*
My tyrlie myrlie, my crowdie mowdie,°   *milky porridge*
Quhone° that oure mouthis dois meit° at ane   *when/do meet*
My stang dois storkyn with your towdie:[3]
Ye brek my hairt, my bony ane."

50   Quod scho, "Now tak me be the hand,
Welcum, my golk° of Marie° land,   *cuckoo/fairy*
My chirrie and my maikles munyoun,[4]
My sowklar° sweit as ony unyoun,°   *suckling/any onion*
My strumill stirk yit new to spane,[5]
55   I am applyit° to your opunyoun:°   *inclined/opinion*
I luif rycht weill° your graceles gane."   *love right well*

He gaiff to hir ane apill rubye;°   *apple red*
Quod scho, "Gramercye,° my sweit cowhubye.°"   *thanks/fool*
And thai tway to ane play began
60   Quhilk° men dois call the dery dan,[6]   *which*
Quhill° that thair myrthis° met baythe in ane: *while/pleasure*
"Wo is me," quod scho, "Quhair will ye,° man?   *where will you go*
Best now I luif° that graceles gane."   *love*

Robert Henryson

We know little about Robert Henryson, although he is said to have been a schoolmaster at the
town of Dumferline, and Dunbar implies that he was dead by 1506, when he mentions him in
the *Lament for the Makars*. Unlike Dunbar, he wrote not for the Scottish court but for the literate
middle class, which gives his poetry a more moralistic and less witty tone. Henryson is a "Scottish
Chaucerian" with a somber cast, for his major work, the *Testament of Crisseid*, picks up where
Chaucer's great romance, *Troilus and Criseide*, leaves off, depicting the faithless heroine as punished with leprosy, achieving redemption, and entering a nunnery. *Robene and Makyne*, however,
is a much more lighthearted poem. Like Dunbar's *In Secret Place*, it is a *chanson d'aventure* which
parodies the language of courtly love, though its shepherd and shepherdess are far more appealing
than Dunbar's grimy lovers. The roles are comically reversed, with the shepherdess Makyne,

---

9. Your neck white as whale's bone; a common alliterative phrase in the conventional love poetry.
1. Said she, "My big soft fellow, my unweaned giant."
2. An obscure term of endearment, as are several other
phrases in the following lines.

3. My pole does stiffen by your thing.
4. My cherry and my matchless darling.
5. My stumbling bullock still newly weaned.
6. A dance (i.e., copulation).

offering to instruct the shepherd Robene in the "ABCs" of love's lore, while he, in his ignorance, resists. After Robene dutifully departs with his sheep, he has regrets and returns, only to have Makyne tell him that he has delayed too long. She states the poem's moral, *carpe diem*:

> The man that will nocht quhen he may
> Sall haif nocht quhen he wald.

Robyn is thus left to repeat in vain courtly love sentiments that he learned from her.

Robene and Makyne[1]

	Robene sat on gud grene hill	
	Kepand° a flok of fe;°	*keeping/sheep*
	Mirry Makyne said him till:°	*to*
	"Robene, thow rew° on me!	*have pity*
5	I haif the luvit lowd and still[2]	
	Thir yeiris° two or thre;	*these years*
	My dule in dern bot gif thow dill,[3]	
	Dowtless but dreid° I de."	*surely*
	Robene ansuerit: "Be the Rude,°	*by the Cross*
10	Nathing of lufe I knaw,	
	Bot keipis my scheip under yone° wude—	*yonder*
	Lo quhair thay raik on raw![4]	
	Quhat° hes marrit° the in thy mude,°	*what/harmed/mind*
	Makyne, to me thow schaw:°	*declare*
15	Or quhat is lufe, or to be lude?°	*loved*
	Fane °wald I leir° that law."	*gladly/learn*
	"At luvis lair gife thow will leir,[5]	
	Tak thair ane ABC:	
	Be heynd, courtas and fair of feir,[6]	
20	Wyse, hardy° and fre;°	*brave/generous*
	So that no denger° do the deir,°	*disdain/do harm*
	Quhat dule in dern thow dre,[7]	
	Preiss° the with pane at all poweir°—	*strive/effort*
	Be patient and previe."°	*discreet*
25	Robene anserit hir agane:	
	"I wait° nocht quhat is luve,	*know*
	Bot I haif mervell° in certane	*wonder*
	Quhat makis the this wanrufe;°	*restless*
	The weddir is fair and I am fane,°	*happy*
30	My scheip gois haill aboif;[8]	
	And we wald play° us in this plane°	*disport/valley*
	Thay wald us bayth reproif."	
	"Robene, tak tent° unto my taill,°	*heed/advice*
	And wirk° all as I reid,°	*do/advise*
35	And thow sall haif my hairt all haill,°	*entirely*
	Eik° and my madinheid:	*also*
	Sen God sendis bute° for baill°	*cure/pain*

---

1. In Scots, as in Middle English poetry, Makyn (or Malkin) was a conventional name for a rustic girl, as Robin was for a boy.
2. I have loved thee openly and secretly.
3. Unless you relieve my secret pain.
4. See how they wander afield!

5. Of love's learning if you would learn.
6. Be gentle, courteous, and fair of manners (these and the qualities that follow are conventional attributes of the courtly lover; cf. Chaucer's *Num's Priest's Tale*, page 372).
7. What sorrow in secret you suffer.
8. Are all around me on this hill.

	And for murnyng° remeid,°	*sorrow/remedy*
	I dern with the bot gif I daill,[9]	
40	Dowtles I am bot deid.[1]	

	"Makyne, tomorne this ilka° tyde,°	*same/time*
	And° ye will meit me heir,	*if*
	Peraventure my scheip ma gang besyd°	*fend for themselves*
	Quhill we haif liggit full neir[2]—	
45	Bot mawgre haif I and I byd,[3]	
	Fra° thay begin to steir;°	*when/stray*
	Quhat lyis on hairt° I will nocht hyd;°	*lies in my heart/not*
	Makyn, than mak gud cheir."	

	"Robene, thow reivis° me roif° and rest—	*rob/tranquility*
50	I luve bot the allone."	
	"Makyne, adew; the sone gois west,	
	The day is neir-hand gone."	
	"Robene, in dule° I am so drest°	*to pain/resigned*
	That lufe wil be my bone."°	*bane*
55	"Ga lufe, Makyne, quhairever thow list,[4]	
	For lemman° I lue° none."	*lover/love*
	"Robene, I stand in sic a styll;°	*such a plight*
	I sicht°—and that full sair."°	*sigh/painfully*
	"Makyne, I haif bene heir this quhyle;°	*while*
60	At hame God gif I wair![5]	
	"My huny Robene, talk ane quhill,°	*a while*
	Gif thow will do na mair."	
	"Makyne, sum uthir man begyle,[6]	
	For hamewart° I will fair."°	*homeward/go*

65	Robene on his wayis went	
	Als licht as leif of tre;[7]	
	Mawkin murnit° in hir intent	*mourned*
	And trowd° him nevir to se;°	*expected/see*
	Robene brayd attour the bent;[8]	
70	Than Mawkyne cryit on hie:°	*loudly*
	"Now ma thow sing, for I am schent!°	*ruined*
	Quhat alis° lufe at me?"	*ails*

	Mawkyne went hame withowttin faill;	
	Full wery eftir cowth weip[9]:	
75	Than Robene in a ful fair daill°	*very neat order*
	Assemblit all his scheip.	
	Be that, sum pairte of Mawkynis aill°	*pain*
	Outthrow his hairt cowd creip;[1]	
	He fallowit fast thair till assaill,[2]	
80	And till hir tuke gude keip.°	*paid good heed*

| | "Abyd, abyd, thow fair Makyne! | |
| | A word for ony thing! | |

---

9. Unless in secret I deal (i.e., have sex) with you.
1. Conventionally, the courtly lover threatens to die unless his lady takes pity on him.
2. While we have lain nearby.
3. But yet I am uneasy if I wait.
4. Go love, Makyn, wherever you wish.
5. I wish to God I were at home!

6. Seduce some other man.
7. As light as a leaf on a tree.
8. Bounded across the field.
9. Wearily afterward wept.
1. Entered his heart.
2. He went back to accost her there.

For all my luve it sal be thyne,
Withowttin depairting.°   *wholly*
85   All haill° thy harte for till haif myne   *whole*
Is all my cuvating;
My scheip tomorne quhill houris nyne°   *until nine o'clock*
Will neid of no keiping."

"Robene, thow hes hard° soung and say   *hast heard*
90   In gestis° and storeis auld,   *legends*
The man that will nocht quhen° he may   *when*
Sall haif nocht quhen he wald.°   *would*
I pray to Jesu every day
Mot eik thair cairis cauld[3]
95   That first preiss° with the to play   *strives*
Be firth,° forrest or fawld."°   *wood/sheepfold*

"Makyne, the nicht° is soft and dry,   *night*
The wedder° is warme and fair,   *weather*
And the grene woid° rycht° neir us by   *wood/right*
100   To walk attour° allquhair;°   *across/everywhere*
Thair ma na janglour[4] us espy,
That is to lufe contrair;
Thairin, Makyne, bath ye and I
Unsene we ma repair."

105   "Robene, that warld is all away
And quyt° brocht° till ane end,   *entirely/brought*
And nevir agane thairto perfay,°   *by my faith*
Sall it be as thow wend:°   *think*
For of my pane thow maid it play,[5]
110   And all in vane I spend:°   *made an effort*
As thow hes done, sa sall I say:
Murne° on! I think to mend."   *grieve*

"Mawkyne, the howp° of all my heill°,[6]   *hope/salvation*
My hairt on the° is sett,   *thee*
115   And evirmair to the be leill,°   *loyal*
Quhill I may leif but lett;[7]
Nevir to faill—as utheris feill—
Quhat grace° that evir I gett."   *favor*
"Robene, with the I will nocht deill;[8]
120   Adew!° For thus we mett."   *adieu*

Malkyne went hame blyth annewche°   *blithe enough*
Attour the holttis hair:[9]
Robene murnit, and Malkyne lewche,°   *laughed*
Scho sang,° he sichit sair°—   *sang/sighed sorely*
125   And so left him bayth wo° and wrewche,°   *sad/troubled*
In dolour° and in cair,   *sorrow*
Kepand his hird under a huche,°   *hovel*
Amangis° the holtis hair.   *among*

---

3. That he might make them too suffer.
4. Gossip; "janglours" were a stock threat to courtly lovers.
5. For you made fun of my pain.
6. Robene uses the religious metaphors of courtly love.
7. Unceasingly, while I live.
8. Robene, I will not have dealings (i.e., sex) with you.
9. Across the woods gray (a traditional alliterative phrase).

Frontispiece from Saxton's *Atlas*. 1579.

The Early Modern Period

━━━◆━━━

We see the past through lenses that show us something of the world we are living in. How we mark periods in history depends less on an objective evaluation of evidence than on our sense of its relation to our own present. The centuries between 1500 and 1700 have been termed the "Renaissance" and, more recently, "the early modern period." What do these two names mean and what do they tell us about our understanding of this single and continuous stretch of time?

However we describe these centuries, they encompassed events that changed profoundly the way people lived and thought. In 1500, the English church was part of a united Western Christendom led by the Pope, and people around the country prayed according to a common liturgy. It was understood that the earth was the center of the universe; that the human body was a balance of the four elements—earth, air, fire, and water; and that nature, read like a book, could reveal a moral order. English men and women had a deep respect for law, which they assumed would protect them from tyranny as well as anarchy. These beliefs had been challenged in the preceding century and a half by the natural calamities of plague and famine, by the political upheaval of the Rising of 1381, and more generally by the growth of towns, trade, and a degree of social mobility. Yet for most people in 1500 the old beliefs held fast, as did the traditional way of life that sustained them. And outside the growing merchant class, a person's place tended to be fixed at birth; the majority of folk lived in country villages, worked the land, and traded in regional markets.

By the end of the seventeenth century, much of this way of life had vanished. England had broken away from Roman religious authority; in addition to the Church of England and the Presbyterian churches of Scotland, Protestantism had created a variety of sects: Anabaptists, Puritans, and Quakers. Worship was conducted in English, not in the Latin that had been used for centuries. Catholics, suspected of subversive intentions, were barely tolerated. A natural philosophy based on experimental methods had begun to reshape the disciplines of physics, medicine, and biology; such ancient authorities as Aristotle, Galen, and Pliny were no longer unquestioned. Sketched in principle by Sir Francis Bacon in his treatise on scientific inquiry, *Novum Organum* (literally, "the new instrument"), published in 1620, a systematic investigation of nature had not begun before the restoration of the Stuart monarchy in 1660. But the world view it would help to confirm was already evident early in the seventeenth century: the work of the Italian physicist Galileo Galilei on gravitational force had demonstrated that the most elementary laws of nature were mathematical; the German astronomer Johannes Kepler had confirmed that the universe was heliocentric; and in England, William Harvey had established that the body was energized not by the eccentric flow of "humors" but by a circulation of blood to and from the heart. Scientists would consolidate their status as intellectuals by forming the Royal Society for the Advancement of Science in 1660—a foundation that was vigorously supported by the new Stuart king, Charles II.

Political life had taken a new direction as well. A civil war, interrupting the peace of over a century, had created a new kind of monarchy. The war had been fought over social and economic issues but also over a matter of principle: England was to be governed by a monarch whose authority and power were not absolute but limited by law and the actions of Parliament, a legislative assembly representing his subjects. The cities, enjoying a prosperity created by international commerce, became crowded even as they expanded with new streets, marketplaces, and buildings for private as well as public use. Country folk flocked to these burgeoning urban centers. Succumbing to diseases spread by filth and overcrowding, they often died younger than did their rural relatives. But England was becoming a nation of city dwellers, and everyone knew of "citizens" who had gained wealth and station in these exciting, if also terrifying, cities.

THE HUMANIST RENAISSANCE AND EARLY MODERN SOCIETY

The tumultuous character of the age has been described as a "renaissance"—literally a "rebirth." Nineteenth-century historians attributed the intellectual and social energy that initiated the reform of the medieval world to a revival of interest in the classical past. By 1400, Italian scholars had begun to reread the works of Greek and Roman authors—Plato and Aristotle, Virgil, Ovid, and Horace—and to look with fresh eyes at the physical monuments of the ancient world that were still so prominent in their landscapes. Their movement traveled north and west to France, the Low Countries, Germany, the Iberian peninsula, and eventually England. What was "reborn" as a result was a sense of the meanings to be discovered in the here and now, in the social, political and economic everyday world. Writing about the intellectual vitality of the age, the French humanist François Rabelais had his amiable giant Gargantua confess that his own education had been "darksome, obscured with clouds of ignorance." Gargantua knows, however, that his son will be taught differently:

> Good literature has been restored unto its former light and dignity, and with such amendment and increase of knowledge, that now hardly should I be admitted unto the first form of the little grammar-school boys . . . I see robbers, hangmen, freebooters, tapsters, ostlers, and such like, of the very rubbish of the people, more learned now than the doctors and preachers were in my time.

These comically overstated remarks nevertheless convey the spirit of the Renaissance: learning was no longer only to be devoted to securing salvation, but should address the conditions of ordinary life as well. The pre-Christian cultures of the ancient Mediterranean had introduced Europeans to philosophies that valued human society and its future generations; studying classical texts afresh, thinkers began to attend in new ways to the world around them. The writers and scholars responsible for the rebirth of a secular culture have been known as "humanists," because they read "humane" as well as "sacred" letters; and their intellectual and artistic practices have been termed "humanism."

The humanists cultivated certain habits of thought that became widely adopted by early modern thinkers of all kinds: skill in using language analytically, attentiveness to public and political affairs as well as private and moral ones, and an acute appreciation for differences between peoples, regions, and times. It was, after all, the humanists who began to realize that the classical past required *understanding*; they recognized the past as unfamiliar, neither Christian nor European, and they knew, therefore, that it had to be studied, interpreted, and, in a sense, reborn.

At the same time, changes were occurring for which there were no precedents. During these years, the modern world was born as much as an older world was reborn, and for this reason the sixteenth and seventeenth centuries have also been called the "early modern period." Its modernity was registered in many ways. Instruments for measuring time and space provided a knowledge of physical nature, a mapping of land, sea, and even the sky that began to permit global travel. Means had to be designed to compute the wealth that was being created by manufacture and trade, and new methods were employed by a people keen to exploit all kinds of resources, including the labor of individuals. Money was used in new and complex ways, its flow managed through such innovations as double-entry bookkeeping and letters of exchange that registered debt and credit in interregional markets. The capital that accumulated as a result of these kinds of transactions fueled merchant banks, joint-stock companies, and—notably in England—trading companies that sponsored colonies abroad. In England especially, wealth was increasingly based on money, not land, and the change encouraged a social mobility that reflected but also exploited the old hierarchy. Riches could and did make it possible for an artisan's son to purchase a coat of arms and become a gentleman, as William Shakespeare did. More important, moneyed wealth supported the artistic and scholarly institutions that allowed the stepson of a bricklayer to go to the best school in London, to profit from the business of the theater, and to compose literary works of sufficient brilliance to make him poet laureate, as Ben Jonson did. "Ambition is like choler," warned Francis Bacon; it makes men "active, earnest, full of alacrity and stirring." But if ambition "be stopped and cannot have his way, it becommeth adust, and thereby maligne and venomous." Early modern society was certainly both active and stirring; but the very energy that gave it momentum could also lead to hardship, distress, and personal tragedy.

Urban life flourished in conditions that were increasingly hospitable to commerce; rural existence became precarious as small farms failed. During the fifteenth century the nobility had begun to enlarge their estates by the incorporation or "enclosing" of what had formerly been public or common land. They sought to profit from a new activity: sheep farming. Thousands of men and women who had worked the land on modest estates lost their livelihoods as a result. Many came to the cities, particularly London; others traveled through the country, looking for odd work, begging, and thieving. The situation got worse when Henry VIII broke England's tie to the Catholic Church, for Henry added to the property of the very rich by giving them the land he had confiscated from the church. On the other hand, the great centers of commerce—Bristol, Norwich, and London—sustained not only trade but also many kinds of manufacture. One of the most important was printing. The invention of movable type in 1436 by a German printer, Johann Gutenberg, revolutionized the dissemination of texts. A single illuminated manuscript took years to produce and provided what was often a unique version of a text, an item that might cost as much as a small farm; a printing press could quickly produce multiple copies of identical versions of a text for as little as a few shillings.

Both the mentality of the "Renaissance" and the more comprehensive culture of the early modern period are illustrated by the history of the most frequently disseminated and contested text of these centuries: the Bible. It was the work of humanists to establish what that text was (after centuries of corrupted versions) and then to translate it into the vernacular languages. Desiderius Erasmus provided accurate Hebrew and Greek texts and translated them into Latin. Printed English translations

Hans Holbein. *The Ambassadors*. 1533. National Portrait Gallery, London.

begin with William Tyndale's New Testament, introduced to England in the 1520s. Later versions included the Geneva Bible with its Calvinist commentary; the Bishops' Bible, repudiating much of that commentary; and the King James Bible, or "Authorized Version," a work by forty-seven translators that was published in 1611. Protestant doctrine emphasized the importance of reading Scripture as a means to spiritual enlightenment, and the preface to the King James Bible insists that for this purpose a translation is as good as the original: "No cause why the word translated should be denied to be the word." But the importance of the Bible went beyond its status as the basis for religious belief.

People from various walks of life, not only humanists, found the Bible a source of inspiration for social reform, a means to link together religious conviction and political practice. Drawing on the Bible to justify their ideas of government, writers as different as the radical Bishop of Winchester, John Ponet, and the scholarly King James VI of Scotland, eventually James I of England, presented arguments for distinctive kinds of monarchy. Ponet insisted that a monarch was obliged to obey the law of the land and thus to adhere to a "constitution"; James thought that a monarch should respect only divine law and be considered "absolute." Other writers, inspired by their

SCVLPTVRA IN ÆS.

Sculptor noua arte, bracteata in lamina   Scalpit figuras, atque prælis imprimit.

Hans Collaert, after Jan van der Straet, called Stradanus. *The Printmaker's Workshop* (detail).

own understanding of God's word, forged new concepts of the state, the subject, and sovereignty that would continue to shape political philosophy to the American War of Independence.

The Bible and the attitudes it prompted were also factors in the establishment of an English church. The English people had been forced to break formally and definitively from the Catholic Church because their king, Henry VIII, wished to be independent of the papacy and its government in Rome. His reasons were many and complex. Certainly responsive to the demand for changes in church government, doctrine, and liturgy, Henry was motivated by personal and political interests as well. In love with a lady of the court, Anne Boleyn, he was persuaded that his marriage to Catherine of Aragon, the widow of his older brother, Prince Arthur, violated divine law. Catherine, mother of the girl who would become Mary I, had failed to give Henry a son, and he saw in his frustrated hopes for the dynastic stability that would come from having a male heir a sign that God was displeased with his marriage. He sought a divorce from the Pope and was refused. In 1533, however, his pliable Archbishop of Canterbury, Thomas Cranmer, defying the Pope out of loyalty to his king, pronounced Henry's marriage to Catherine invalid. The following year, Parliament passed the Act of Supremacy; besides making the monarch of England head of an English church, it made Henry immediately free from the Pope's jurisdiction. English clergy who had promoted the idea of a reformation began to institute the changes they had envisaged. But the socially destabilizing effects of the English reformation, far from abating, grew more profound as time went on.

Huge numbers of the faithful would suffer, Protestants as well as Catholics. The creation of an English church not only separated England from most of the continent, it disturbed the religious peace that had prevailed for centuries. The story is a grim one: Catholics in the north of England unsuccessfully resisted Henry's imposition of Protestantism in their Pilgrimage of Grace in 1536; Protestants were in turn persecuted by Mary I throughout her reign; Catholics were suppressed by Elizabeth I; and sectarians of various denominations were required to adhere to Anglican forms of worship and obey episcopal power under the Stuarts.

The prodigiously revolutionary changes in early modern England were vividly reflected in its profuse and varied literature. Topics and issues that for centuries had been considered by relatively small numbers of literate people were now registered in general debate. New and evolving conditions of religious, intellectual, and political life provided writers with a vast subject matter, and their work shed light on the world that they saw unfolding before them. They showed its potential for prosperous development through all kinds of human activity; they represented its long and varied history as proof of providential direction; and they praised its myriad forms as the expression of a divine and beneficent artificer.

As late twentieth-century readers, we come to the literature of this period with our own perspectives on what is modern and what we understand as postmodern. Many features of early modern culture are again in transition today: the printed book, which once superseded the manuscript, is now being challenged by computer-generated hypertext; the nation-state, which once eclipsed the feudal domain and divided "Christendom," is now qualified by an international economy; and the belief in human progress, which was once applauded as an advance over the medieval faith in divine providence, is now subject to criticism, in large part because of such kinds of injustice and inequity as slavery, colonialism, and the exploitation of wage labor—all factors in the growth of early modern England and of other states in Europe. As modern and postmodern readers, we have a special affinity with our early modern counterparts. Like them, we study change.

HISTORY AND EPIC

The political life of the sixteenth century was dominated by the genius of a single dynasty: the Tudors. Its founder was Owen Tudor, a squire of an ancient Welsh family who was employed at the court of Henry V and eventually married his widow, Catherine of Valois. Its first monarch was Owen Tudor's grandson, Henry, Earl of Richmond, who defeated Richard III at Bosworth Field in 1485 to become Henry VII. He married Elizabeth, daughter of Edward IV, whom Richard III had succeeded—a fortunate event for the people of England, as it united the two parties by whom the crown had been disputed for many decades. Once Henry, who represented the House of Lancaster (whose emblem was a white rose), was joined to Elizabeth, a member of the House of York (signified by a red rose), the "Wars of the Roses" were at an end. Henry VII's bureaucratic skills then settled the kingdom in ways that allowed it to grow and become identified as a single nation, however much it also comprised different peoples: the midlands and the north were distinguished from the more populous south by dialectal forms of speech; and to the west, in Cornwall and Wales, many English subjects still spoke Gaelic. More thoroughly Gaelic were Scotland to the north and Ireland across the sea to the west. Although the Anglo-Normans had invaded Ireland in the twelfth century, it was not until the reign of Elizabeth that the English pursued the subjugation of Ireland by establishing colonizing plantations and conducting a brutal military campaign that produced famine, massacres, and the forced relocation of people. But this supposed English fiefdom remained rebellious and effectively unconquered for Elizabeth's entire reign. Its resistance to English rule was crushed only in 1603, an event that marked the end of an independent Ireland for three hundred years. Scotland, to the far north, was a separate and generally unfriendly kingdom with strong ties to France until James VI of Scotland became James I of England. His accession to the English throne in 1603 began a process that would end with the complete union of the two kingdoms in 1707. There were also more remote regions to consider: England's colonization of the Americas began under Elizabeth I, progressed under James I, and allowed the English to think of themselves as an imperial power.

Writing history offered a way to reinforce the developing sense of nationhood, a project that was all the more appealing after the creation of an English church and the beginnings of a British empire. Medieval historians had concentrated on the actions of ambitious men and women whose lives reflected their good or bad qualities; early modern historians wrote about events and their manifold causes. William Camden's *Britannia* and Raphael Holinshed's *Chronicles of England, Scotland, and Ireland* (the source for many of Shakespeare's plays) celebrate the deeds and the character of the early peoples of the British Isles, including the ancient origins of the English kingdom, its exemplars of heroism and villainy, its struggle for unity realized under the Tudors, and the sturdy resistance of its subjects to absolute monarchic power. The land itself became the subject of comment: William Harrison wrote a description of the English counties (included in Holinshed), and John Stow surveyed the neighborhoods of London; Michael Drayton, a Stuart poet, wrote a mythopoetic account of England's towns and countryside entitled *Poly-Olbion*; and Richard Hakluyt's collection of travel histories, *The Principal Navigations, Voyages and Discoveries of the English Nation*, reported in magnificent detail the exploration of the New World. Accounts of this wild and fruitful land fired the imaginations of English readers, who, it was hoped, would decide to promote and even participate in the laborious task of colonization. Describing landfall on the coast of Virginia, Arthur Barlow wrote:

> we found shoal water, where we smelled so sweet and so strong a smell as if we had been in the midst of some delicate garden abounding with all kind of odoriferous flowers. . . . I think in all the world the like abundance is not to be found. And my selfe having seen those parts of Europe that most abound, find such difference as were incredible to be written.

All these works comprising history, the description of various regions, and reports of travel have been loosely described as *epic*, but none of them conforms to the genre as contemporary poetics represented it—expressing heroic grandeur not only in action but also in the musical verse form and elevated language of the epic tradition.

The masterpieces of the early modern English epic are Edmund Spenser's *The Faerie Queene* and John Milton's *Paradise Lost*. Spenser imitated continental models to create an English Protestant epic-romance, an optimistic projection of Elizabethan culture. The realities of Elizabeth I's reign, though far from the poet's vision of things, were nonetheless very impressive. England's cities had grown to be centers of commerce, her navy controlled the principal routes of trade, and her people pursued lucrative interests in Europe and the Americas, successfully resisting Spanish efforts to dominate world settlement and trade. The defeat of the Spanish Armada in 1588 and the bold explorations of such men as Sir Francis Drake and Sir Walter Raleigh testified to the nation's seafaring power. In the figures of his poem, Spenser embodied the energies producing this expansive growth. His virtuous knights overcome monstrous threats to order, peace, and tranquillity. Aspects of the queen's own genius are reflected in his heroines. Like the warrior maiden Britomart, Elizabeth I assumed a martial character when England was in danger from abroad; like his Queen Mercilla, she could be gracious to her enemies; like the virgin Una, she stood for what the poet and most of his readers believed was the one true faith: Protestantism. And like Spenser's enigmatic and distant Queen Gloriana, the Faerie Queene of the title, Elizabeth exercised her authority and power in unpredictable ways: secrecy and dissimulation were her stock in trade. To her subjects, her majesty was awful and sometimes terrifying. But she was also mortal, and at her death, few could have foreseen the new and divided nation that came into being with the accession of James I. The new king was greeted with mixed feelings: on the one hand, his claim to the throne was not disputed; on the other hand, he came from Scotland, long an enemy of England and always the source of anxiety to those who sought dominion over the British Isles as a whole. Although he was educated by the humanist George Buchanan, whose treatises praising republican government were widely known and read, James favored absolute rule and believed that a monarch should be *lex loquens,* the living spirit of the law, beyond the control of Parliament and indifferent to the rights of his subjects. His personal conduct appeared to be dubious: his critics represented him as frequently unkempt and claimed that he preferred to hunt deer rather than to take charge of matters of state. Disputes with the House of Commons over money to support the Crown's activities were frequent. Reports of intrigue with Catholic Spain shattered the nation's sense of security; an attempt in 1605 to blow up the Houses of Parliament, revealed as the Gunpowder Plot, caused a near panic. These and other kinds of unrest grew more intense when James's heir, Charles I, proved to be even more autocratic than his father. Charles's queen, Henrietta Maria, the daughter of Henry IV of France, was a Catholic, and it was rumored that she was treacherous. Religious controversy raged throughout the British Isles, and the struggle over the authority and power of the monarch culminated in a series of bloody civil wars. Across England and Scotland, forces loyal the king fought the army of Parliament, led by Oliver Cromwell, a Puritan Member of the Commons. The war, which lasted from 1642 to 1651, ended with the defeat of the royalists.

In 1649, Charles I was captured and executed by order of Parliament, and England began to be governed as a republic. She was no longer a kingdom but a Commonwealth, and this period in her history is known as the Interregnum, the period between kingdoms. The long-advocated change, now a reality, could hardly have begun in a more shocking way. The monarchy had always been regarded as a sacred office and institution, as Shakespeare's Richard II had said:

> Not all the water in the rough rude sea
> Can wash the balm off from an anointed king;
> The breath of worldly men cannot depose
> The deputy elected by the Lord.

But in the course of half a century, the people had proved themselves to be a sovereign power, and it was politically irrelevant that Charles, on the block, exemplified regal self-control. As the Parliamentarian poet Andrew Marvell later wrote of the king's execution:

> He nothing common did or mean
> Upon that memorable scene,
>   But with his keener eye
> The ax's edge did try,

> Nor called the gods with vulgar spite
> To vindicate his helpless right;
>   But bowed his comely head
>   Down as upon a bed.

The conflict itself, its causes, and its outcome have been variously interpreted. As a revolution in government, it was defined by common lawyers, energized by Puritan enthusiasm, and motivated by widespread hatred of Stuart autocracy. As a religious and cultural struggle, it has been described as the War of Three Kingdoms, comprising the resistance of Scots Presbyterians and Irish Catholics to the centralizing control of the English church and government. But whatever its historical character, the Civil War marked England's transition to a society in which the absolute rule of a monarch was no longer a possibility. The people themselves had acquired a political voice. To some extent, this was a religious voice: Puritans who professed a belief in congregational church government were generally proponents of republican rule. Their dedication to the ideal of a society of equals under the law was shared by men and women of other sects: the Levellers, led by John Lilburne, who argued for a written constitution, universal manhood suffrage, and religious toleration; the Diggers, led by Gerrard Winstanley, who proposed to institute a communistic society in the wastelands they were ploughing and cultivating; the Quakers, led by George Fox, who rejected all forms of church order in deference to the inner light of an individual conscience and, insisting on social equality, refused to take off their hats before gentry or nobility; and the Ranters, who denied the authority of Scripture and saw God everywhere in nature. Without widespread acceptance of the egalitarian concept that had initiated the Protestant reformation—all believers are members of a real though invisible priesthood—it is hard to see how the move from a monarchy to a representative and republican government could have taken place.

The most comprehensive contemporary history of the Civil War, *The True Historical Narrative of the Rebellion and Civil Wars in England,* by Edward Hyde, Earl of Clarendon, was not published before 1704, but the troubled period found an oblique commentary in what is arguably England's greatest and certainly most humanistic epic poem: Milton's *Paradise Lost,* in print by 1667. Milton's career was inextricably bound up with the fate of the Commonwealth. Educated at Cambridge and with his reputation as a poet well established, Milton had begun to contribute to a defense of Puritanism and the creation of a republican government by 1649. Despite worsening eyesight, he published *The Tenure of Kings and Magistrates,* a sustained and eloquent apology for tyrannicide, after the execution of Charles I; and in his *Eikonoklastes* ("image-breaker"), written after he was made Latin secretary to the new executive, the Council of State, Milton derided attempts by royalists to celebrate Charles I in their pamphlet *Eikon Basilike* ("image of a king"). In 1660, disturbed by the proposed restoration of Charles Stuart, soon to be Charles II, Milton—now completely blind—published his last political treatise, *The Ready and Easy Way to Establish a Commonwealth.* It represented the case for a republicanism that had already lost most of its popularity: the government of the Commonwealth had adopted measures that resembled the autocratic rule of the monarchy it had overthrown. Meanwhile, the composition of *Paradise Lost* was underway. Indebted to many of Spenser's themes in *The Faerie Queene,* Milton infused his subject—the fall of the rebellious angels and the exile from paradise of the disobedient Adam and Eve—with the spirit of the account in Genesis. His poem is the product of a doubly dark vision of life. Sightless and suffering again what he felt were the constraints of a monarchy, Milton shaped his story of exile from Paradise to speak of his own and England's loss of innocence and painful acquisition of the knowledge of good and evil during the Civil War, the Interregnum, and the Restoration. His *Paradise Lost* and its sequel, *Paradise Regained*, are poems that express the most provocative ambiguities of contemporary English culture; they were—and still are—praised as rivaling the epics of Homer, Virgil, and Dante in their power and scope.

DRAMA AND SOCIAL SATIRE

Drama provided another perspective on English life. While epic depicted the grander aspirations of the nation, its human character was expressed in stage plays, masques or speaking pageants, and dramatic processions. These forms exploited the material of chronicle so that it illustrated not only the virtues of heroes, but also their foibles and limitations; history's villains warned viewers that evil was punished, if not by civil authority then by providence. Writing tragedy based on history and legend, Christopher Marlowe and Shakespeare complicated the direct moralism of medieval drama. Rather than portraying characters who became victims of their own misdoings, rising to power only to fall to disgrace, the early modern stage showed virtue and vice as intertwined—a hero's tragic error could also be at the heart of his greatness. The origins of evil were seen to be mysterious, even obscure. Some sense of this moral ambiguity can be traced to the tragedies of the Roman philosopher Seneca, which were translated into English and published in 1581. English drama reproduced many of their features: the five-act structure; rapid-fire dialogue punctuated by pithy maxims; and images of tyranny, revenge, and fate illustrated by haunting dreams and echoing curses. Shakespeare's *Richard III*, the most frequently performed of his plays in his own time, and Elizabeth Cary's *Tragedy of Mariam*, the first tragedy in English by a woman, powerfully exemplify the qualities of early modern tragedy.

If tragedy turned away from straightforward piety, so did comedy. The medieval drama of Christian salvation, in which the hero's struggle against sin was ended by his acknowledgment of grace, was replaced with plays about the wars between the sexes and between parents and children. Much of this material was modeled on the comedies of Plautus, a Roman playwright, and on the tales or *novellas* of contemporary Italian writers. Playwrights such as Ben Jonson also found a wealth of material in the improvisatory Italian *commedia dell'arte*, with its stock characters of the old dotard, the cuckolded husband, the damsel in distress, and the mountebank or quack. An even more topical form of comedy combined some of these continental traditions with themes and figures specifically drawn from London life: Thomas Dekker and Thomas Middleton's *The Roaring Girl* dramatizes the urban culture of guildsmen, shopkeepers, city wives, and coney-catchers (con artists) as they encounter the city gentry and their servants. The social critique implicit in these plays was, of course, one reason why they were so popular; their pointed criticisms of various kinds of behaviors, including religious practices, appeared in various genres from city presses, and their popularity showed just how ready audiences were to imagine a reform of their society. The end of the century saw a brilliant example of satire in a series of pamphlets secretly published by an anonymous author, known as Martin Marprelate, who disparaged all aspects of the episcopacy and promoted in its place a frankly Presbyterian church, in which authority would reside in Scripture and in congregations rather than in a church hierarchy. These expressions of a new kind of self-consciousness revealed an understanding of the whole social order that appeared anarchic to some, particularly moralists opposed to stage plays. As Stephen Gosson wrote in *Plays Confuted in Five Actions*:

> If private men be suffered to forsake their calling because they desire to talk gentlemen-like in satin & velvet, with a buckler at their heels, proportion is so broken, unity dissolved, harmony confounded, that the whole body must be dismembered, and the prince or head cannot choose but sicken.

The fear was not only that the tricksters of drama would be the objects of emulation rather than scorn, but also that the actors' masquerade of identities would spur social instability in the public theater's audience from the "groundlings of the pit" (crowded in front of the stage) to the gentry in the higher-priced seats. Only in 1633 did Parliament repeal the strict sumptuary laws that determined which styles and fabrics were allowed to nobility but denied to everyone else. Although some, like the playwright Thomas Heywood, praised plays as a form of instruction of the unschooled, others, like the Puritan pamphleteer Philip Stubbes, asserted that plays "maintain bawdry, insinuate foolery, and revive the remembrance of heathen idolatry."

Londoners enjoyed two kinds of theater: public and private. The public theaters were open to all audiences for a fee and were generally immune from oversight because they were located outside the City of London in an area referred to as the Liberties, notorious for prostitution and the sport of bearbaiting. London's two biggest theaters were located there: the Fortune and the more famous Globe, home to Shakespeare's company. Private theaters—open only to invited guests—were located in the large houses of the gentry, the Inns of Court (the schools of common law), and the guildhalls; the best-known, Blackfriars, was housed in an old monastery. Their performances were acted almost exclusively by boy actors. The popularity of these companies was short-lived; James I, annoyed by the send-up of the Scots court in *Eastward Ho!*, a play that Ben Jonson had a part in writing, dissolved his queen's own company, known as the Queen's Revels Children. The most private and prestigious stage of all remained the royal court. Shakespeare's *Othello* was first acted at James's court in 1604. Of exclusive interest to this audience was the masque, a speaking pageant accompanied by music and dancing, staged with elaborate sets and costumes, and acted by members of the court, including the Queens Anne (wife of James I) and Henrietta Maria (wife of Charles I). But in 1649 a Puritan Parliament, disgusted by what it considered the immorality of the drama, banned all stage plays, and the theaters remained closed until the Restoration in 1660.

LYRIC POETRY AND ROMANCE

In early modern England, epic narratives, stage plays, and satire in all forms were genres designed for audiences and readers the writer did not know, a general public with varied tastes and background. Lyric poetry, prose romances, and tales were more often written for a closed circle of friends. Circulated in manuscript, works in these genres allowed a writer's wit to play on personal or coterie matters. Here writers could speak of the pain of love or the thrill of ambition, and both reveal and, in a sense, create their own identities in and through language. By imitating and at the same time changing the conventions of lyric, particularly as they were illustrated by the Italian poet Francesco Petrarch, English poets were able to represent a persona or fictive self that became, in turn, a model for others. Unlike Petrarch, who saw his

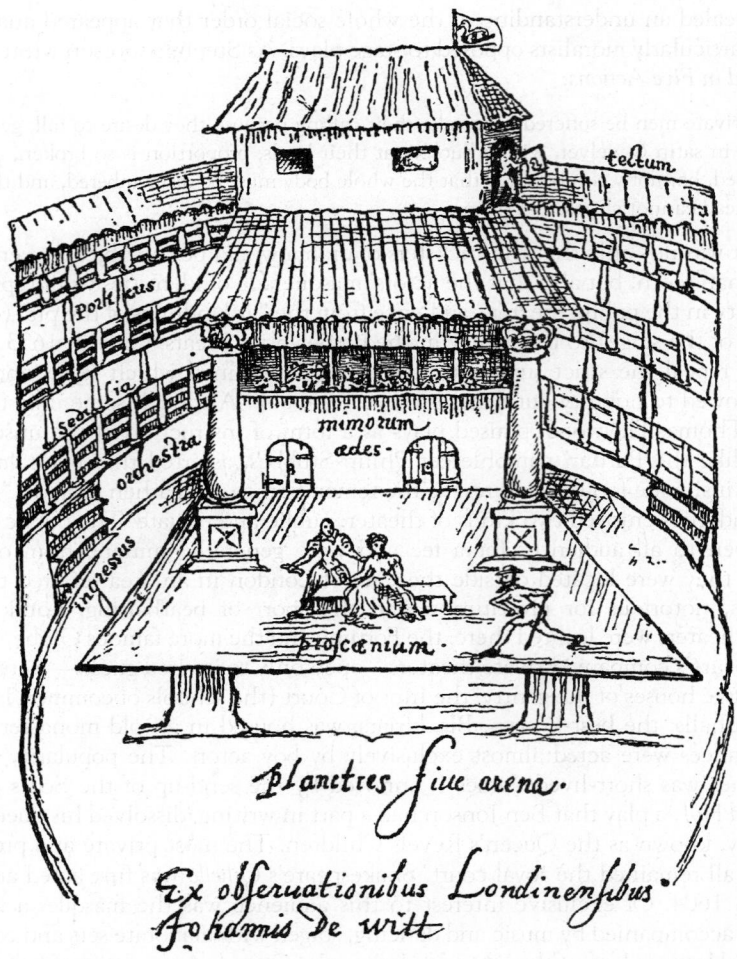

planities sive arena.

Ex observationibus Londinensibus
Johannis de witt

Arend von Buchell. *The Swan Theater,* after Johannes de Witt. c. 1596. The only extant drawing of a public theater in 1590s London, this sketch shows what Shakespeare's Globe must have looked like. The round playhouse centered on the curtainless platform of the stage (*proscenium*), which projected into the yard (*planities sive arena*). Raised above the stage by two pillars, the roof (*tectum*) stored machinery. At the back of the stage, the tiring house (*mimorum aedes*), where the actors dressed, contained two doors for entrances and exit. There were no stage sets and only moveable props such as thrones, tables, beds, and benches, like the one shown here. Other documents on the early modern stage are the contract of the Fortune Theatre, where *The Roaring Girl* was performed, and stage directions in the plays themselves. Modelled on The Globe, although square in shape, The Fortune featured a stage forty-three feet broad and twenty-seven and a half feet deep. Stage directions include further clues: sometimes a curtained booth made "discovery" scenes possible; trapdoors allowed descents; and a space "aloft," such as the gallery above the stage doors, represented a room above the street. Eyewitness accounts fill out the picture. In the yard stood the groundlings who paid a penny for standing room, exposed to the sky, which provided natural lighting. For those willing to pay a penny or two more, three galleries (*orchestra, sedilia, and porticulus*) provided seats—the most expensive of which were cushioned. Spectators could buy food and drink during the performance. The early modern theater held an audience of roughly eight hundred standing in the yard, and fifteen hundred more seated in the galleries. According to Thomas Platter, who had seen Shakespeare's *Julius Caesar* in 1599, "everyone has a good view."

lady as imbued with numinous power before which he could only submit, such poets as Sir Thomas Wyatt, Sir Philip Sidney, Shakespeare, Ben Jonson, John Donne, and Andrew Marvell imagined love in social and very human terms; in the struggle to gain affection and power, their subjectivity took strength from their conquests as well as their resistance to defeat. Women poets, such as Mary Herbert, Amelia Lanyer, Lady Mary Wroth, and Katherine Philips reworked the conventions of love lyric to encompass a feminine perspective on passion and, equally important, on friendship. Sonnet sequences were popular and, reflecting a taste for narrative romance, often dramatized a conflict between lovers. Shakespeare wrote the best-known sonnets of the period; his cast of characters, including the poet as principal speaker, his beloved male friend, a rival poet, and a fickle lady, appear as protagonists in a drama of love, betrayal, devotion, and despair. Some poets embedded their love poetry in prose narratives that told a story, as the Italian poet Dante Alighieri had in his sequence of songs and sonnets to the lady Beatrice, entitled *The New Life*. A brilliant tale of seduction frames George Gascoigne's lyrics in his *Adventures of Master F.J.*, and Sidney's eclogues or pastoral poems punctuate the long and complicated narrative of his romance *Arcadia*.

Prose romances also provided images of new kinds of identity. Stories of marvels surrounded the lives of the powerful and exotic—such as Robert Greene's *Pandosto* (the source for Shakespeare's *The Winter's Tale*) and Thomas Lodge's *Rosalind*—while the tales of lower-class artisan-adventurers illustrate the enthusiasm with which early modern writers and readers embraced a freedom to reinvent themselves. The romantic notion of the "marvelous" gained a new meaning in the tales of tricksters as well as of sturdy entrepreneurs who survived against all odds—they illustrated the creative energies possessed by plain folk. The short fiction of Thomas Nashe, Thomas Deloney, and the hilarious (and anonymous) *Life and Pranks of Long Meg of Westminster* conclusively broke with the delicate sentimentality of pure romance and, appealing to a taste for the ordinarily wonderful, pointed the way for such later novelists as Daniel Defoe, Henry Fielding, and Charles Dickens. Finally, the spirit of romance infused narratives of travel, many of which made little distinction between fact and fantasy.

Sir John Mandeville's fifteenth-century *Travels*, in print throughout the sixteenth century, responded to Europeans' growing curiosity about the wonders of nature in distant lands, which harbored whole peoples who were pictured as utterly different from anything known at home. The wonders reported in popular collections of travel narratives—such as Richard Hakluyt's *Principal Navigations, Voyages, and Discoveries of the English Nation* (1589) and Samuel Purchas's *Purchas his Pilgrimage, or Relations of the World and the Religions observed in all Ages* (1613)—were designed to attract not repel readers, but a horror of "the other" was nevertheless implied in many of these accounts. Shakespeare's Othello both embodies foreignness himself and shares the European love of the exotic: confusing fact with fantasy, he tells the Venetian senate that parts of the globe are inhabited by "Cannibals that each other eat, / The Anthropophagi," as well as "men whose heads / Do grow beneath their shoulders." But the lure of distant lands could also attract the social critic who sought to devise images of an ideal world in order to better the real world. Sir Thomas More's *Utopia* projects a fantasy of a communal state that does double duty by pointing to both the inequities of English society and the absurdities of reforms that assume men and women can be consistently reasonable. Literally describing a *utopia*, or a "nowhere," More's treatise is effectively also a "dystopia," or a work describing a "bad place." Neither Sir Francis Bacon's *New Atlantis* (1627) nor James Harrington's *Commonwealth of Oceana* (1656)—true utopias suggesting a radical reform of political and intellectual life—emulates More's embrace of both utopian and dystopian perspectives. But the dystopias of later writers, such as Jonathan Swift's *Gulliver's Travels* (1726), Samuel Butler's *Erewhon*, an anagram for "nowhere" (1872), and George Orwell's *Nineteen-Eighty-Four* (1949) impressively illustrate the hazards of idealistic and visionary social thought.

The situation for women was somewhat different. Ancient philosophy and medieval theology had insisted that womankind was essentially and naturally different from *mankind*, distinguished by physical weakness, intellectual passivity, and an aptitude for housework, childcare, and the minor decorative arts. The fact that women had distinguished themselves in occupations traditionally reserved for men was understood to signal an exception, and in general social doctrine imposed rigid codes of behavior on men and women. But early modern life was changing in this respect, too. Contemporary treatises devoted to pro-woman argument or the defense of womankind drew on evidence that supported a revolution in ideas of sex and gender. The Bible, they pointed out, stated that woman, like man, was made in the image of God and therefore had the same degree of reason as man; history, they insisted, revealed that women had undertaken all kinds of activity and therefore had same range of talents as man. In short, they maintained that the absolute difference between man and woman was not naturally part of things, but rather was conventional and subject to modification. Social practice reflected and substantiated some of this argument. Early modern women who were classified as legally independent or *femes soles* (literally, women alone) could own and manage property and businesses as men did; educated women, such as Mary Herbert, Aemilia Lanyer, and Katherine Philips, contributed to all the literary genres and got their work published; and during the Civil War, sectarian women registered political protest in public places, including the House of Commons.

These novel ways of understanding women found corresponding changes in attitudes toward men. Departing from medieval social norms, humanists had stressed that men should be educated in the arts as well as arms, and writers such as Sir Philip Sidney, illustrating the sensitivity of men to emotional life, devised characters whose masculinity was amplified by attributes that were conventionally associated with women: passion, sympathy, and an aptitude for creative deception. The central figure in Sidney's *Arcadia* is the prince Pyrocles who appears as an Amazonian warrior through most of the narrative; as the androgynous Cleophila, he is always referred to as "she." Flexibility with respect to categories of gender is also a feature of much lyric poetry; the male poet's beloved is sometimes another man. Shakespeare's sonnets include striking examples of homoerotic verse in this period, and homoerotic innuendo, often suggested as a feature of a love triangle, is common in all genres of writing. In Marlowe's poem *Hero and Leander* the youth Leander loves the girl Hero, and Leander attracts the sexual attentions of the sea-god Neptune.

Ideas as well as social forms and practices were also changing. The repeated shifts in religious practice, from medieval Catholicism to Henrician Protestantism back to the Catholicism dictated by Queen Mary I and then on to the Anglican Church of Queen Elizabeth I, revealed that divine worship could alter its form without bringing on the apocalypse. More subtly, the emerging capitalist economy produced a conceptual model for cultural exchange. Just as material goods flowed through regional and national markets, entering a particular locale to move elsewhere, sometimes great distances, so might ideas, styles, and artistic sensibilities. Drama especially conveyed how fluid were the customs, codes, and practices that gave society its sense of identity. The enthusiasm for stage plays was motivated, in part, by an interest in role-playing: If an actor who in real life might have been born a servant could perform the part of a king in a play, then might he not also perform the part of a king indeed? Was there more to being than performing? This mutability was both liberating and dangerous, as Shakespeare showed by dramatizing the protean powers of Othello's false friend, Iago, who chillingly boasts: "I am not what I am."

THE BUSINESS OF LITERATURE

It was the business of early modern literature to ask these questions. The idea that social convention was established on a natural order of things was no longer accepted. As Shakespeare's bastard Edmund declares, rejecting the customary inferiority of a person who is born out of wedlock, "Why bastard, Wherefore base? / When my dimensions are as well compact . . . As honest madam's issue." Writers were certainly supposed to educate their readers in virtuous ways. Spenser intended that his epic would "fashion a gentleman or noble person in vertuous and gentle discipline." And Sidney believed that poetry, at its finest, could "take naughtiness away and plant goodness even in the secretest cabinet of our souls." But literature also questioned matters of being and identity because writers themselves were in the forefront of a class that was in the process of changing its way of life and its means of support.

During the early modern period an educated man who sought employment as a writer was the object of patronage by the gentry or nobility, often functioning as a tutor or secretary in a prosperous household. The poet John Skelton taught the future Henry VIII; John Donne accompanied his patron Sir William Drury on his European journeys and dedicated his *Anniversaries* to Drury's deceased daughter Elizabeth; and Andrew Marvell educated Lord Fairfax's daughter Mary. Men who were employed in other ways—in diplomacy, law, or some aspect of commerce—might be rewarded for their writing by stipends from the rich. Elizabeth I gave Spenser, one of her administrators in Ireland, a single grant of fifty pounds for *The Faerie Queene*; and Ben Jonson, thanks to the generosity of James I, was able to make a successful career for himself as a poet. As a young man, Milton was patronized by the noble Egerton family, for whom he wrote a masque called *Comus*. But as the seventeeth century progressed, writers discovered that they could be supported by a broader public; after the Restoration the talented playwright Aphra Behn gained a living by selling her literary work to producers and printers. Increasingly, the forces of the market had moved to include the business of printing and thus to both liberate and captivate the energies of the nation's writers.

It was obvious to those in power and authority that the printing press was an agent of change; the question they had to answer was how to control it. Under Elizabeth I, all printing was regulated (in effect, subject to censorship) by the Stationer's Company, which had the exclusive right to print and sell literary work. The theater was also controlled. From 1574, all plays had to be licensed by the Master of Revels, a servant and appointee of the monarch, before they could be produced. These conditions bound writers to observe royal and ecclesiastical policy, at least in their direct statements. Some resorted to coded critique; others openly defied custom. In 1579 John Stubbs wrote a pamphlet against the Queen's proposed marriage to the French king's brother, the Duke of Alençon, entitled *The Discoverie of a Gaping Gulf wherein-to England is like to be Swallowed*; he was arrested and had his hand cut off as punishment. This situation, in which publication was officially regulated, was altered early in the seventeenth century by the development of a new institution: journalism.

By the middle of James I's reign, there was a market for a periodical news pamphlet known as a "coranto," or current of news, which contained foreign intelligence taken from foreign papers: the first was actually printed in Amsterdam and shipped to England. Within a short time, English printers were publishing their own news in the form of sixteen-page "newsbooks" or Diurnalls, and by 1646, Londoners could read fourteen different papers in English. The rapid growth of the news industry promoted a public readership increasingly informed of political affairs. Parliament grew alarmed and discussed imposing stringent forms of licensing; in 1649 it approved the publication of only two newspapers, both dedicated to printing official news. Underground presses continued to publish on current affairs, however; some of them took a royalist point of view and others endorsed Parliament's position. Their writers enjoyed a risky freedom, but it was still a freedom. The boldest of them was Marchamont Nedham, a supporter of Parliament and the chief author of the *Mercurius Britanicus* (still an important source of information about the Civil War and the Interregnum); he had to flee to Holland at the Restoration, although he subsequently was pardoned and returned to England. But journalism did more than provide news; it also created a basis for the freedom of writers in general. The most eloquent attack on a state-controlled press was by Milton, whose *Areopagitica* protested the practice of licensing books before their publication—that is, before readers had a chance to make up their minds about what these books contained. Milton drew on ideas of democracy from ancient Athens and on the Puritan notion that good emerges only in contact with evil: "I cannot praise a fugitive and cloistered virtue," he announced; no true virtue is untested, unchallenged, unexamined—it is valid only when it has deliberately and consciously rejected what is false. The journalistic enterprise of this period fostered the right to free speech and a free press that is now the bedrock of modern democracies.

THE LANGUAGES OF LITERATURE:
THE NEW SCIENCE AND THE OLD NATURE

Changing ideas of identity, both personal and political, were reflected in changes in the English language, which responded to popular as well as learned culture. An accomplished classicist, Ben Jonson closely modeled his verses on Latin poems and their syntax; at the same time the language of his poetry and plays often echoes the cadences of the English spoken by ordinary folk. Authors of popular comic pamphlets, such as Dekker and Robert Greene, conveyed the lively language of London rogues and vagabonds, combining local slang with parodic Latin. The writing of English prose was further changed by the study of Latin grammar and rhetoric in the humanist curriculum that was inspired by the pedagogical reforms of Erasmus and his English followers, John Colet, Roger Ascham (tutor to Elizabeth I), and Richard Mulcaster. Many words of Latin origin were introduced into English vocabulary; many writers experimented with analytic prose by adapting Latin syntax, which allowed them to show relations of cause and effect by resorting to clauses beginning with "if," "when," "because," and so forth. The first Latin-English dictionary on humanist principles was compiled by Sir Thomas Elyot; and one of the most important English grammars, Ascham's *The Schoolmaster* (1570), instructed readers in the merits of an eloquent style.

This enrichment of language from various sources inevitably caused debate. Prose composition was especially affected. Proponents of the so-called Ciceronian style (after the Roman orator Cicero) liked long sentences of many clauses exhibiting variation and restatement. Practitioners of the Senecan style favored short, direct, and uncomplicated sentences. Francis Bacon in particular criticized Ciceronian rhetoric for its emphasis on decorative "tropes and figures" rather than descriptive substance or "weight of matter"; he argued for a language that would accurately denote what he considered "scientific" data: the measures of the physical world. Bacon's reforms influenced English pedagogy and were further realized in the enterprise of the Royal Academy of Science, founded in 1660 by Charles II, who was determined to give his monarchy a new look and a new purpose. The terse, clear, pointed language of Bacon's *Essays* (1597) resembles more what we might think of as modern than does, for example, the florid style that Robert Burton used a quarter of a century later for his mythological-historical, medical discourse *The Anatomy of Melancholy*.

Language and style were changing notions of the world and God's design in creating it. Habits of thought that had prevailed during the medieval period now seemed to be incompatible with knowledge that derived from experience of nature. Europeans had inherited from classical philosophy an idea of creation as a vast aggregate of layered systems or spheres, supposedly centered on the densest matter at the earth's core, that emanated out and up to end, finally, in the sphere of pure spirit or the ethereal presence of divinity. The entities in these layered spheres had assigned places that determined their natures both within their particular sphere and in relation to other spheres. Thus gold, the most precious metal, was superior to silver, but it was at the same time analogous to a lion, a king, and the sun, each also representing the peak of perfection within its particular class of beings. Human nature was also systematized, the body and personality alike being regulated by a balanced set of "humors," each of which consisted of a primary element. The earth, water, air, and fire that made up the great world, or macrocosm, of nature also composed the small universe, or microcosm, of the individual man or woman, whose personality was ideally balanced between impulses that were melancholic (caused by a kind of bile), phlegmatic (brought on by a watery substance), sanguine or bloody, and choleric or hot-tempered. Excessive learning, the contemplation of death, the darkness of night, and isolation were all associated with melancholia, a diseased condition that in more or less severe form is represented in such disparate texts as Marlowe's *Dr. Faustus*, Milton's *Il Penseroso*, and Sir Thomas Browne's *Religio Medici* (literally, "the religion of a doctor").

This view of creation was important for artists and writers because it gave them a symbolic language of correspondences by which they could refer to creatures in widely differing settings and conditions. In a sense, it made nature hospitable to poetry by seeing creation as a divine work of art, designed to inspire awe but also a kind of familiarity. Things were the likenesses of other things. In the poetry of Donne, Herbert, Henry Vaughan, and Marvell, human emotional experience is compared to the realms of astronomy, geography, medicine, Neoplatonic philosophy, and Christian theology. These correspondences are created through strikingly unusual metaphors, which some have called metaphysical conceits, from the Italian *concetto* ("concept"). The result is a pervasive sense of a universal harmony in all human experience.

Such analogies were not always respected, however; increasingly, they were questioned by proponents of a kind of vision that depended on a quantitative or denotative sense of identity or difference. Poetic metaphor might not be able to account for creation in all its complexity; instead, nature had to be understood through the abstractions of science. By the seventeenth century it was becoming difficult to regard creation as a single and comprehensive whole; natural philosophers and scientists in the making wanted to analyze it piece by individual piece. As John Donne wrote of the phenomenon of uniqueness in his elegy for Elizabeth Drury, *The First Anniversary*:

> The element of fire is quite put out;
> The Sun is lost, and th' earth, and no man's wit
> Can well direct him, where to look for it.
> And freely men confess, that this world's spent,
> When in the Planets, and the Firmament
> They seek so many new; they see that this
> Is crumbled out again to his Atomies.
> Tis all in pieces, all coherence gone;
> All just supply, and all Relation:
> Prince, Subject, Father, Son, are things forgot,
> For every man alone thinks he has got
> To be a Phoenix, and that there can be
> None of that kind, of which he is, but he.

The earth had been decentered by the insights of the astronomer Nicholas Copernicus, who in the 1520s deduced that the earth orbits the sun. This "Copernican revolution" was confirmed by the calculations of Tycho Brahe and Johannes Kepler, and our solar system itself was revealed as one among many. With traditional understandings of the natural order profoundly shaken, many thinkers feared for the survival of the human capacity to order and understand society as well. Ironically, Donne complains of radical individualism by invoking the emblem of the phoenix, the very sort of traditional metaphor that constituted the coherence that he claims has "gone." But whereas the symbol in a devotional book would carry with it the myth of the bird's Christlike death and rebirth, the image of the rare bird takes on a newly skeptical and even satirical meaning in *The Anniversary*: it becomes the sign of a dangerous fragmentation within nature's order. Donne's audience would have been familiar with such symbols from emblem books, which presented images along with poems and mottoes, as well as in interior decoration, clothing, coats of arms, and the printers' marks on title pages of books. They were also featured on the standards or flags carried in the Civil War—antique signs in a decidedly modern conflict.

THE CIVIL WAR AND THE MODERN ORDER OF THINGS

The Civil War, or the War of Three Kingdoms, ended with the restoration of the Stuart monarchy, but the society to which Charles II was heir in 1660 was very different from the one his grandfather, James I, had come from Scotland to rule in 1603. The terms of modern life were formulated during this period, even though they were only partially and inconsistently realized. They helped to shape these essentially modern institutions: a representative government under law, a market economy fueled by concentrations of capital, and a class system determined by wealth and the power it conferred. They supported a culture in which extreme and opposing points of view were usual. Milton's republican *Tenure of Kings and Magistrates* (1649) was followed by Thomas Hobbes's defense of absolute rule, *The Leviathan, or the Matter, Form, and Power of a Commonwealth, Ecclesiastical and Civil* (1651). Hobbes rejected

The Souldiers in their passage to York turn unto reformers pull down Popish pictures, break down rayles, turn altars into Tables

Wenceslaus Hollar. *Parliamentarian soldiers in Yorkshire destroying "Popish" paintings, etc.* Illustration to *Sight of the Transactions of these latter yeares,* by John Vicars. 1646.

the assumption that had determined all previous political thought—based on Aristotle's idea that man was naturally sociable—by characterizing the natural condition of human life as "solitary, poor, nasty, brutish and short." A civil state, said Hobbes, depended on the willingness of each and every citizen to relinquish all his or her rights to the sovereign, which is the Commonwealth. The vigorous language of Puritan sermons, preached and published during the 1640s and 1650s, underlay such topical writing as Oliver Cromwell's letters from his campaign to subdue Ireland on behalf of Parliament, the Leveller John Lilburne's pamphlets supporting the common man (for God, he wrote, "doth not choose many rich, nor many wise"), and the corantoes, newsbooks, and Diurnalls of the period. These new forms would eventually lead to the sophisticated commentary of eighteenth-century journalism. Nationalism, however problematic, was registered in history and epic, as well as in attempts to colonize the Americas and to subdue the Gaelic peoples to the west and the north. Irish poems supporting the Stuarts and lamenting the losses of the Cromwellian wars would become rallying cries in the late seventeenth- and eighteenth-century nationalist risings against English control, eventually to result in Ireland's inclusion in the 1801 Union of Great Britain.

Intellectual thought, mental attitudes, religious practices, and the customs of the people fostered new relations to the past and a new sense of self. While Milton was perhaps the greatest humanist of his time, able to read and write Hebrew, Greek, Latin, Italian, and French, his contemporaries witnessed the disappearance of the culture of Petrarch, Erasmus, and More—humanists who had fashioned the disciplines of humanism. Much seventeenth-century literature reflected personal experience; the diary of Ralph Josselin, a prosperous country squire, and the printed testimony of the trial of Anna Trapnel, a Quaker woman accused of witchcraft, convey the details of social life with an immediacy that avoids the studied figures of earlier

Renaissance prose. Such personal reckonings are comparable to the spiritual interiority revealed in John Bunyan's allegorical novel about his conversion to faith in God, *The Pilgrim's Progress*, and the first-person narrative of Daniel Defoe's *Robinson Crusoe*, the story of a sailor shipwrecked on an island somewhere off the coast of South America, which was actually modeled on the history of a Scotsman, Alexander Selkirk, who was similarly marooned.

As more particularized portraits of individual life emerged, new philosophical trends promoted abstract figurations of the world. The modern organization of Europe was based on new modes of representation, such as schematic outlines of arguments, the grids sectioning the world maps of Gerardus Mercator (facilitating the circumnavigation of the globe), and the discourses of political economy characterized by an interest in quantitative analysis. Shortly after the Restoration of Charles II, the Royal Academy of Science would form "a committee for improving the English language," an attempt to design a universal grammar and an ideal philosophical language. This project, inspired by the intellectual reforms of Francis Bacon, would have been uncongenial to the skeptical casts of mind exhibited by Erasmus and More. The abstract rationalism of the new science, the growth of an empire overseas, a burgeoning industry and commerce at home, and a print culture spreading news throughout Europe and across the Atlantic would continue to be features of life in the British Isles through the eighteenth century.

John Skelton
1460?–1529

The first great Tudor satirist, John Skelton illustrates the appeal of the unorthodox. When he took holy orders at the age of thirty-eight, Skelton already enjoyed an impressive reputation as a writer of satire and love lyrics. His poems must have appealed to Henry VII, who made him responsible for the education of his second son, the future Henry VIII, and they would eventually prompt Erasmus to call Skelton "a light and ornament of British literature." In 1502, following the death of Henry's older brother Arthur, Skelton lost his employment as royal tutor; Henry, now heir apparent to the English throne, was obliged to trade Skelton's gentle instruction in humane and sacred letters for practical training in statecraft and the art of war. At forty-two already an old man (by contemporary reckoning), Skelton undertook pastoral duties, although he lived away from his rectory for much of the rest of his life. His satires of the clergy in *Colin Clout* and of Cardinal Wolsey in *Why Come Ye Not to Court* may have placed him in some jeopardy; it is said that a threat from the Cardinal forced Skelton to take refuge on the grounds of Westminster Abbey in London. Skelton never got the satisfaction of witnessing Wolsey's disgrace; he died just a few months before Wolsey lost the office of Lord Chancellor for failing to procure a divorce for the king.

Skelton's poetry is as unusual as was his career. His favorite verse form has become known as "skeltonics"; it consists of a series of lines of two or three stresses whose end rhyme repeats itself for an unspecified number of lines. The lines themselves show alliteration and move at a headlong pace. In *Colin Clout*, Skelton excused his practice by noting the "pith" or substance it conveys:

> For though my rhyme be ragged,
> Tattered and jagged,
> Rudely rain-beaten,
> Rusty and moth-eaten,
> If ye take well therewith,
> It hath in it some pith.

Skelton's satires poke fun at the pretensions that characterize all forms of public life, including the ways of courtiers and vagabonds. His dream poem, *The Bowge of Court*, and his morality play about wealth and power, *Magnificence*, provide a witty view of court corruption. His elegy *Philip Sparrow*, on a pet sparrow mauled and eaten by its young mistress's cat, weaves themes and figures from liturgy and the Office of the Dead to create an extraordinary burlesque of sacred elegy that manages to be at once tender and cutting.

The poem falls into three parts. Between passages of prayer for the soul of Philip, assumed to be in a Christian heaven, the bereaved girl, Jane Scrope, expresses her grief in terms that recall the lamentations of women who mourn dead lovers in classical legend. Jane addresses her sparrow as her beloved, even while she defends the propriety of her affection for him. A thematics of erotic love—announced by the poet speaking in his own voice—features in the second part of the poem. It transforms Jane into the unattainable lady of courtly lyric, and in an apparent allusion to Dante's angelic Beatrice, the beloved lady of his sonnet sequence, *The New Life*, compares her to a divine creature. The poem ends with *The Addition*, which instructs the reader to overlook Jane's innocently frivolous devotion to Philip and defends (in Latin) the poet's own celebration of her grief on the death of her pet.

Philip Sparrow[1]

Pla ce bo,[2]
Who is there, who?
Di le xi,
Dame Margery;
5   Fa, re, mi, mi,°   *notes of the musical scale*
Wherefore and why, why?
For the soul of Philip Sparrow,
That was late slain at Carrow,[3]
Among the Nuns Black,
10 For that sweet soul's sake,
And for all sparrows' souls,
Set in our beadrolls,[4]
Pater noster qui,°   *Our Father who*
With an *Ave Marie*,°   *Hail Mary*
15 And with the corner of a Creed,
The more shall be your meed.°   *reward*
     When I remember again
How my Philip was slain,
Never half the pain
20 Was between you twain,
Pyramus and Thisbe,[5]
As then befell to me:
I wept and I wailed,
The tears down hailed;
25 But nothing it availed
To call Philip again,
Whom Gib our cat hath slain.
     Gib, I say, our cat
Worried her on that
30 Which I loved best:
It cannot be expressed
My sorrowful heaviness,
But all without redress;
For within that stound,°   *moment*
35 Half slumbering, in a sound
I fell down to the ground.
     Unneth° I cast mine eyes   *scarcely*
Toward the cloudy skies:
But whan I did behold
40 My sparrow dead and cold,
No creature but that wold°   *would*
Have rued° upon me,   *taken pity*
To behold and see

---

1. This poem, usually dated 1505–1507, echoes phrases
from the funeral liturgy known as Office for the Dead and
its sequel, the Order for Commendations (lines 1–844 and
845–1268, respectively). It is spoken by Skelton's character, Jane Scrope, but closes with an "Addition" in Skelton's own voice (in print in 1523), his response to the criticism of Alexander Barclay, a contemporary Scots poet.
2. *Placebo*: "I shall please"; *Dilexi*: "I have loved" (Psalm

114.9 and 1).
3. Carrow Abbey, a Benedictine nunnery. Benedictines,
who wore black habits, followed the rule of St. Benedict,
the first of the monastic orders.
4. Lists of souls for whom prayers, signified by the beads of
the rosary, were offered.
5. Unfortunate lovers who die in each other's arms
(Ovid, *Metamorphoses* 4.55ff.).

What heaviness did me pang;
45 Wherewith my hands I wrang,°   *wrung*
That my sinews cracked,
As though I had been racked,
So pained and so strained,
That no life wellnigh° remained.   *nearly*
50   I sighed and I sobbed,
For that I was robbed
Of my sparrow's life.
O maiden, widow, and wife,
Of what estate you be,
55 Of high or low degree,
Great sorrow than you might see,
And learn to weep at me!
Such pains did me fret,
That mine heart did beat,
60 My visage pale and dead,
Wan, and blue as lead;
The pangs of hateful death
Wellnigh had stopped my breath.
    Heu, heu, me,
65 That I am woe for thee!
Ad Dominum, cum tribularer, clamavi:[6]
Of God nothing else crave I
But Philip's soul to keep
From the marees° deep   *marshes*
70 Of Acherontes well,[7]
That is a flood of hell;
And from the great Pluto,
The prince of endless woe;
And from foul Alecto,
75 With visage black and blo;°   *blue*
And from Medusa, that mare,°   *specter*
That like a fiend doth stare;
And from Megaera's udders,
For ruffling of Philip's feathers,
80 And from her fiery sparklings,
For burning of his wings;
And from the smokes sour
Of Proserpina's bower;
And from the dens dark,
85 Where Cerberus doth bark,
Whom Theseus did affray,°   *frighten*
Whom Hercules did outray,°   *overcome*
As famous poets say;
From that hell hound,

6. "I cried out to the Lord when I suffered" (Psalm 119.1).
7. The well of Acheron, source of one of the mythical rivers of hell. In the following lines, Skelton names mythological figures associated with hell: Pluto, god of the underworld; Alecto, a fury or spirit of wrathful revenge; Medusa, a monster who turns whoever looks at her to stone; Megaera, another Fury, whose hair (like Medusa's) is composed of adders or poisonous snakes; Proserpina, goddess of spring who descends to the underworld every autumn; Cerberus, the three-headed dog who guards the gates of hell; Theseus, the legendary hero who frightened Cerberus as he descended to hell to rescue his friend, Pirithous; Hercules, the legendary hero who dragged Cerberus out of hell.

90   That lieth in chains bound,
      With ghastly heads three,
      To Jupiter° pray we   *king of the gods*
      That Philip preserved may be!
      Amen, say you with me!
95   *Do mi nus,°*   *Lord*
      Help now, sweet Jesus!
      Levavi oculos meos in montes:[8]
      Would God I had Zenophontes,[9]
      Or Socrates the wise,
100   To show me their devise,°   *instruction*
      Moderately to take
      This sorrow that I make
      For Philip Sparrow's sake!
      So fervently I shake,
105   I feel my body quake;
      So urgently I am brought
      Into careful thought.
      Like Andromach, Hector's wife,[1]
      Was weary of her life,
110   When she had lost her joy,
      Noble Hector of Troy;
      In like manner also
      Encreaseth my deadly woe,
      For my sparrow is go.
115   It was so pretty a fool,
      It would sit on a stool,
      And learned after my school
      For to keep his cut,°   *place*
      With, Philip, keep your cut!
120   It had a velvet cap,
      And would sit upon my lap,
      And seek after small worms,
      And sometime white bread crumbs;
      And many times and oft
125   Between my breasts soft
      It would lie and rest;
      It was proper and pressed.°   *lively*
          Sometimes he would gasp
      When he saw a wasp;
130   A fly or a gnat,
      He would fly at that;
      And prettily he would pant
      When he saw an ant;
      Lord, how he would pry
135   After the butterfly!
      Lord, how he would hop
      After the gressop!°   *grasshopper*

8. "I lifted my eyes to the mountains" (Psalm 120.1).
9. Xenophon, a Greek historian; Socrates: a Greek philosopher whose teaching is represented in the dialogues of the philosopher Plato.

1. Homer decribes Andromache's grief when Achilles, the Greek hero, kills her husband, the principal defender of Troy (*Iliad* 24.725ff.).

And when I said, Phip, Phip,
Than he would leap and skip,
140 And take me by the lip.
Alas, it will me slo,°   slay
That Philip is gone me fro!°   from
    Si in i qui ta tes,[2]
Alas, I was evil at ease!
145 *De pro fun dis cla ma vi,*[3]
When I saw my sparrow die!
    Now, after my dome,°   judgment
Dame Sulpicia at Rome,[4]
Whose name registered was
150 For ever in tables of brass,
Because that she did pass
In poesy to endite,°   write
And eloquently to write,
Though she would pretend
155 My sparrow to commend,
I trowe° she could not amend   trust
Reporting the virtues all
Of my sparrow royal.
    For it would come and go,
160 And fly so to and fro;
And on me it would leap
When I was asleep,
And his feathers shake,
Wherewith he would make
165 Me often for to wake,
And for to take him in
Upon my naked skin;
God wot,° we thought no sin: knows
What though he crept so low?
170 It was no hurt, I trowe,
He did nothing perde°   indeed
But sit upon my knee:
Philip, though he were nice,°   wanton, fresh
In him it was no vice;
175 Philip had leave to go
To pick my little toe;
Philip might be bold
And do what he would;
Philip would seek and take
180 All the fleas black
That he could there espy
With his wanton eye.
    O pe ra,[5]
La, sol, fa, fa,

2. "If iniquities" (Psalm 129.3).
3. "Out of the depths I have cried" (Psalm 129.1).
4. There were two women poets in ancient Rome who were named Sulpicia; Skelton has combined them in a single figure.
5. Works; i.e., "works of your hand I have not despised" (Psalm 137.8).

185	*Confitebor tibi, Domine, in toto corde meo.*[6]
	Alas, I would ride and go
	A thousand mile of ground!
	If any such might be found,
	It were worth an hundred pound
190	Of king Croesus's gold,
	Or of Attalus the old,
	The rich prince of Pargame,[7]
	Who so list° the story to see. *wishes*
	Cadmus, that his sister sought,[8]
195	And he should be bought
	For gold and fee,
	He should over the sea,
	To weet° if he could bring *know*
	Any of the offspring,
200	Or any of the blood.
	But whoso understood
	Of Medea's art,[9]
	I would I had a part
	Of her crafty magic!
205	My sparrow then should be quick
	With a charm or twain,
	And play with me again.
	But all this is in vain
	Thus for to complain.
210	I took my sampler once,
	Of purpose, for the nonce,° *occasion*
	To sew with stitches of silk
	My sparrow white as milk,
	That by representation
215	Of his image and fashion,
	To me it might import
	Some pleasure and comfort
	For my solace and sport:
	But when I was sewing his beak,
220	Methought, my sparrow did speak,
	And opened his pretty bill,
	Saying, Maid, you are in will
	Again me for to kill,
	You prick me in the head!
225	With that my needle waxed red,
	Methought, of Philip's blood;
	Mine hair right upstood,
	And was in such a fray,° *fright*
	My speech was taken away.
230	I cast down that there was,
	And said, Alas, alas,

6. "I shall confess to you, Lord, with all my heart" (Psalm 137.1).

7. Croesus, king of Lydia, 560–546 B.C.; Attalus, ancient king of Pergamum in Asia Minor, known for extraordinary wealth. Jane emphasizes how valuable Philip was.

8. Cadmus, son of Agenor, mythological king of Tyre, was sent to find his sister Europa; she had been carried off by Jupiter, who had taken the form of a bull (Ovid, *Metamorphoses* 3.1ff.).

9. Medea, a mythological sorceress, restored youth to Jason, the hero who secured the golden fleece.

How cometh this to pass?
My fingers, dead and cold,
Could not my sampler hold;
235 My needle and thread
I threw away for dread.
The best now that I may,
Is for his soul to pray:
A *porta inferi*,[1]
240 Good Lord, have mercy
Upon my sparrow's soul,
Written in my beadroll!
   Au di vi vo cem,[2]
Japhet, Cam, and Sem,
245 *Mag gni fi cat*,
Show me the right path
To the hills of Armony,[3]
Wherefore the boards yet cry
Of your father's boat,
250 That was sometime afloat,
And now they lie and rot;
Let some poets write
Deucalion's flood[4] it hight:°   *was called*
But as verily as you be
255 The natural sons three
Of Noah the patriarch,
That made that great ark,
Wherein he had apes and owls,
Beasts, birds, and fowls,
260 That if you can find
Any of my sparrow's kind,
God send the soul good rest!
I would have yet a nest
As pretty and as pressed
265 As my sparrow was.
But my sparrow did pass
All sparrows of the wood
That were since Noah's flood,
Was never none so good;
270 King Philip of Macedony[5]
Had no such Philip as I,
No, no, sir, hardly.
   That vengeance I ask and cry,
By way of exclamation,
275 On all the whole nation
Of cats wild and tame;
God send them sorrow and shame!
That cat specially

---

1. From the gates of hell; Jane Scrope prays that Philip's soul be delivered from the underworld.
2. "I have heard a voice" (Revelation 14.13). Jane Scrope, calling on the sons of Noah—Shem, Ham, and Japhet—concludes with the first word of the *Magnificat*, "My soul magnifies the Lord," Mary's hymn of thanks when God makes her pregnant with Jesus (Luke 1.46).
3. Armenia, where Noah's ark ("your father's boat") was said to have come to rest after the flood.
4. Deucalion was the survivor of the flood according to Greek mythology.
5. Father of the Emperor Alexander the Great.

That slew so cruelly
280   My little pretty sparrow
That I brought up at Carrow.
    O cat of carlish° kind,   *churlish*
The fiend was in thy mind
When thou my bird untwined!°   *destroyed*
285   I would thou hadst been blind!
The leopards savage,
The lions in their rage,
Might catch thee in their paws,
And gnaw thee in their jaws!
290   The serpents of Lybany°   *Libya*
Might sting thee venomously!
The dragons with their tongues
Might poison thy liver and lungs!
The manticors of the mountains°   *monsters*
295   Might feed them on thy brains!
    Melanchates,[6] that hound
That plucked Actaeon to the ground,
Gave him his mortal wound,
Changed to a deer,
300   The story doth appear,
Was changed to an hart:
So thou, foul cat that thou art,
The selfsame hound
Might thee confound,
305   That his own lord bote,°   *bit*
Might bite assunder thy throat!
    Of Inde° the greedy gripes°   *India/griffins*
Might tear out all thy tripes!
Of Arcady the bears
310   Might pluck away thine ears!
The wild wolf Lycaon
Bite asunder thy back bone!
Of Etna the brennyng° hill,   *burning*
That day and night brenneth still,
315   Set in thy tail ablaze,
That all the world may gaze
And wonder upon thee,
From Occya° the great sea   *Ocean*
Unto the Iles of Orchady,°   *Orkney*
320   From Tilbury[7] ferry
To the plain of Salisbury!
So traiterously my bird to kill
That never ought° thee evil will!   *showed*
    Was never bird in cage
325   More gentle of corage°   *spirit*
In doing his homage

---

6. A hound that devoured his master, Actaeon, who had been turned into a deer by the goddess Diana. Jane Scrope continues to inveigh against her cat by citing animals that attack human beings: griffins (mythical birds) of India; bears of Arcady, a region in Greece; Lycaon, a king who was turned into a wolf.

7. A town on the Channel coast, near London.

Unto his sovereign.
Alas, I say again,
Death hath departed us twain!
330   The false cat hath thee slain:
Farewell, Philip, adieu!
Our Lord thy soul rescue!
Farewell without restore,
Farewell for evermore!
335   And it were a Jew,
It would make one rue,°   *pity*
To see my sorrow new.
These villainous false cats
Were made for mice and rats,
340   And not for birds small.
Alas, my face waxeth° pale,   *grows*
Telling this piteous tale,
How my bird so fair,
That was wont to repair,
345   And go in at my spare,°   *pocket*
And creep in at my gore°   *opening*
Of my gown before,
Flickering with his wings!
Alas, my heart it stings,
350   Remembering pretty things!
Alas, mine heart is sleth°   *slain*
My Philip's doleful death,
When I remember it,
How prettily it would sit,
355   Many times and oft,
Upon my finger aloft!
I played with him tittle tattle,
And fed him with my spittle,
With his bill between my lips;
360   It was my pretty Phips!
Many a pretty kusse°   *kiss*
Had I of his sweet musse;°   *mouth*
And now the cause is thus,
That he is slain me fro,
365   To my great pain and woe.
        Of fortune this the chance
Standeth on variance:
Oft time after pleasance
Trouble and grievance;
370   No man can be sure
Allway° to have pleasure: *always*
As well perceive you may
How my disport and play
From me was taken away
375   By Gib, our cat savage,
That in a furious rage
Caught Philip by the head,
And slew him there stark dead.

Kyrie, eleison,
Christe, eleison,
380   *Christe, eleison,*
        Kyrie, eleison![8]
        For Philip Sparrow's soul,
        Set in our beadroll,
        Let us now whisper
385   A *Pater noster*.
        Lauda, anima mea, Dominum![9]
        To weep with me look that you come,
        All manner of birds in your kind;
        See none be left behind.
390   To mourning look that you fall
        With dolorous songs funeral,
        Some to sing, and some to say,
        Some to weep, and some to pray,
        Every bird in his lay.°   own voice
395   The goldfinch, the wagtail;
        The jangling jay to rail,
        The flecked pie° to chatter   magpie
        Of this dolorous matter;
        And robin redbreast,
400   He shall be the priest
        The requiem mass to sing,
        Softly warbling,
        With help of the red sparrow,
        And the chattering swallow,
405   This hearse for to hallow;
        The lark with his long toe;
        The spink,° and the martinet also;   finch
        The shovelar° with his broad beak;   spoonbill
        The doterel,° that foolish peak,°   plover / silly bird
410   And also the mad coot,
        With a bald face to toot;°   look carefully
        The feldefare,° and the snite;°   thrush / snipe
        The crow, and the kite;°   hawk
        The raven, called Rolf,
415   His plain song to solfe;°   sing
        The partridge, the quail;
        The plover with us to wail;
        The woodhack,° that singeth "chur"   woodpecker
        Hoarsely, as he had the mur;°   a cold
420   The lusty chanting nightingale;
        The popingay° to tell her tale,   parrot
        That toteth° oft in a glass,   looks
        Shall read the Gospel at mass;
        The mavys° with her whistle   thrush
425   Shall read there the 'pistle.
        But with a large and a long°   correct rhythm
        To keep just plain song,

8. Lord have mercy, Christ have mercy; phrases from the Mass.
9. Jane Scrope intends to say "Our Father," i.e., the Lord's Prayer. But she continues with "Praise the Lord, my soul" (Psalm 145.1).

Our chanters° shall be the cuckoo,   *singers*
The culver, the stockdove,
430 With "peewit," the lapwing
The versicles shall sing.
    The bitter° with his "bump,"   *bittern*
The crane with his "trump,"
The swan of Menander,
435 The goose and the gander,
The duck and the drake,
Shall watch at this wake;
The peacock so proud,
Because his voice is loud,
440 And hath a glorious tail,
He shall sing the grail;[1]
The owl, that is so foul,
Must help us to howl;
The heron so gaunce,°   *gaunt, thin*
445 And the cormoraunce,°   *cormorant*
With the pheasant,
And the gagling gaunte,°   *goose*
And the churlish chough;°   *crow*
The knoute° and the rough;°   *kinds of sandpipers*
450 The barnacle,° the buzzard,   *goose*
With the wild mallard;
The dyvendop° to sleep;   *waterbird*
The water hen to weep;
The puffin and the teal°   *a duck*
455 Money they shall deal
To poor folk at large,
That shall be their charge;
The seamew and the titmouse;
The woodcock with the longe nose;
460 The threstle° with her warbling;   *thrush*
The starling with her brabbling;
The rook, with the osprey
That putteth fishes to a fraye;°   *fright*
And the dainty curlew,
465 With the turtle most true.
    At this *Placebo*
We may not well forgo
The countering of the coe:[2]
The stork also,
470 That maketh his nest
In chimneys to rest;
Within those walls
No broken galls°   *sores*
May there abide
475 Of cuckoldry side,
Or else philosophy

---

1. A book of prayers to be used on the church steps, also known as the gradual.

2. The accompaniment of the jackdaw.

Maketh a great lie.[3]
   The estrige,° that will eat   *ostrich*
An horseshoe so great,
480 In the stead of meat,
Such fervent heat
His stomach doth freat;°   *consume*
He cannot well fly,
Nor sing tunably,
485 Yet at a braid°   *in an outburst*
He hath well assayed
To solfe above ela,[4]
Fa, lorell, fa, fa;
Ne quando
490 *Male cantando*,[5]
The best that we can,
To make him our bellman,
And let him ring the bells;
He can do nothing else.
495   Chaunteclere, our cock,
Must tell what is of the clock
By the astrology
That he hath naturally
Conceived and caught,
500 And was never taught
By Albumazar[6]
The astronomer,
Nor by Ptolomy
Prince of astronomy,
505 Nor yet by Haly;
And yet he croweth daily
And nightly the tides
That no man abides,
With Partlot his hen,
510 Whom now and then
He plucketh by the head
When he doth her tread.°   *mate with her*
   The bird of Araby,
That potentially
515 May never die,
And yet there is none
But one alone;[7]
A phoenix it is
This hearse that must blys°   *bless*
520 With armatycke° gums   *aromatic*
That cost great sums,
The way of thurifycation°   *burning incense*
To make a fumigation,

---

3. Jane Scrope believes that the stork protects a household from cuckoldry, according to "philosophy," if it does not lie.
4. The ostrich, in a sudden burst of energy, has tried to sing fa, a note above ela.
5. Lest when, singing badly. This makes no literal sense; Jane Scrope suggests that the ostrich, because he sings badly, can only be employed as a bell ringer.
6. Jane Scrope mentions several famous astronomers: Albumazar, Ptolemy, and Haly Aben Ragel.
7. The phoenix, a mythical bird, was as Jane Scrope describes it: unique in the world, both self-consuming and self-regenerating.

	Sweet of reflayre,°	*smell*
525	And redolent of air,	
	This corse° for to cense°,	*body/perfume*
	With great reverence,	
	As patriarch or pope	
	In a black cope;°	*cape*
530	Whiles he censeth the hearse,	
	He shall sing the verse,	
	Libera me,[8]	
	In de, la, sol, re,	
	Softly bemole[9]	
535	For my sparrow's soul.	
	Pliny[1] showeth all	
	In his story natural,	
	What he doth find	
	Of the phoenix kind;	
540	Of whose incineration	
	There riseth a new creation	
	Of the same fashion	
	Without alteration,	
	Saving that old age	
545	Is turned into corage	
	Of fresh youth again;	
	This matter true and plain,	
	Plain matter indeed,	
	Who so list to read.	
550	But for the eagle doth fly	
	Highest in the sky,	
	He shall be the sedeane,°	*subdean*
	The choir to demean,	
	As provost principal,	
555	To teach them their ordinal;°	*order of service*
	Also the noble falcon,[2]	
	With the gyrfalcon,	
	The tarsel° gentle,	*small falcon*
	They shall mourn soft and still	
560	In their amysse° of gray;	*robe*
	The sacre° with them shall say	*large falcon*
	Dirige[3] for Philip's soul;	
	The goshawk shall have a role	
	The choristers to control;	
565	The lanners° and the marlyons°	*falcons/merlin*
	Shall stand in their mourning gowns;	
	The hobby° and the muskette°	*falcon/hawk*
	The censers° and the cross shall fet;°	*incense holders/fetch*
	The kestrel in all this work,	
570	Shall be holy water clerk.	

8. Free me; the first words of the response in the service of the Mass.
9. I.e., sing softly the notes indicated in the preceding line.
1. Roman philosopher who wrote *Historia Naturalis*, an account of the natural world.

2. Jane lists different kinds of falcon—the gyrfalcon, the tarsel, the sacre, the lanner, and the hobby (lines 556–567)—all of which participate in Philip's funeral.
3. Proceed; a word indicating the beginning of the service for the dead.

And now the dark cloudy night
Chaseth away Phoebus° bright,   *the sun*
Taking his course toward the west,
God send my sparrow's soul good rest!
575   *Requiem aeternam dona eis, Domine!*[4]
Fa, fa, fa, mi, re,
A por ta in fe ri,
Fa, fa, fa, mi, mi.
　　Credo videre bona Domini,
580   I pray God, Philip to heaven may fly!
Domine, exaudi orationem meam!
To heaven he shall, from heaven he came!
　　Do mi nus vo bis cum!
Of all good prayers God send him some!
585   　　　*Oremus:*
Deus, cui proprium est misereri et parcere,
On Philip's soul have pity!
For he was a pretty cock,
And came of a gentle stock,
590   And wrapped in a maiden's smock,
And cherished full daintily,
Till cruel fate made him to die:
Alas, for doleful destiny!
But whereto should I
595   Longer mourn or cry?
To Jupiter I call,
Of heaven imperial,
That Philip may fly
Above the starry sky,
600   To tread the pretty wren,
That is our Lady's hen:
Amen, amen, amen!
　　Yet one thing is behind,
That now cometh to mind;
605   An epitaph I would have
For Philip's grave:
But for I am a maid,
Timorous, half afraid,
That never yet assayed
610   Of Elyconys well,
Where the Muses dwell;[5]
Though I can read and spell,
Recount, report, and tell
Of the Tales of Canterbury,[6]
615   Some sad stories, some merry;
As Palamon and Arcet,°   *Arcite*
Duke Theseus, and Partelet;°   *Pertelot*
And of the Wife of Bath,

---

4. Lord, grant them eternal rest. Translations of subsequent lines follow: I believe I shall see the good things of the Lord (line 579); Lord, hear my prayer (line 581); The Lord be with you (line 583); Let us pray; O Lord, who alone can pity and pardon (lines 585–586).

5. The Muses were said to live on Mount Helicon in Greece.
6. Jane Scrope, having said she is unlearned, states that she knows Geoffrey Chaucer's *Canterbury Tales;* she names characters from *The Knight's Tale, The Nun's Priest's Tale,* and *The Wife of Bath's Tale.*

	That worketh much scath°	*harm*
620	When her tale is told	
	Among huswives° bold,	*wives*
	How she controlled	
	Her husbands as she wolde,°	*would*
	And them to despise	
625	In the homeliest wise,	
	Bring other wives in thought	
	Their husbands to set at nought:	
	And though that read have I	
	Of Gawain and sir Guy,[7]	
630	And tell can a great piece	
	Of the Golden Fleece,	
	How Jason it wan,°	*won*
	Like a valiant man;	
	Of Arthur's round table,	
635	With his knights commendable,	
	And dame Gaynour,° his queen,	*Guinevere*
	Was somewhat wanton, I ween;°	*think*
	How sir Launcelot de Lake	
	Many a spear brake°	*broke*
640	For his ladies' sake;	
	Of Tristram, and king Mark,	
	And all the whole warke°	*work*
	Of Belle Isold his wife,	
	For whom was much strife;	
645	Some say she was light,	
	And made her husband knight	
	Of the common hall,	
	That cuckolds men call;	
	And of sir Libius,	
650	Named Desconius;	
	Of Quater Fylz Amund,°	*Four Sons of Aymon*
	And how they were summoned	
	To Rome, to Charlemagne,	
	Upon a great pain,	
655	And how they rode each one	
	On Bayard Mountalbon;	
	Men see him now and then	
	In the forest of Arden:	
	What though I can frame	
660	The stories[8] by name	

7. Jane Scrope lists the romances she has read: the stories of Gawain; Guy of Warwick; Jason and the Golden Fleece; King Arthur and his Round Table; Lancelot and Queen Guinevere; Tristram and Isolde, wife of King Mark; Libius or Libaeus Desconus, son of Gawain; the four sons of Aymon, who rode on the " bayard" or horse called Montalbon; see lines 628–658.

8. Jane Scrope also knows stories from classical epic and history: She cites accounts of Judas Maccabeus and Julius Caesar (two of nine "worthies"); Paris and Helen (Vyene); Hannibal, the Carthaginian general who invaded Rome by crossing the Alps from France; Scipio Africanus Minor, who sacked Carthage in 146 B.C.; Hector and Achilles, the great warriors of the Trojan War; the Trojan Troilus, who, through the mediation of Pandarus, fell in love with Cressida, who eventually sided with the Greeks; Penelope, who waited years for the return of Ulysses; Marcus Marcellus, the Roman consul who triumphed in Gaul and fought Hannibal in Sicily; Antiochus, King of Antioch and ally of Hannibal. She has also read Josephus's *Jewish Antiquities*; The Book of Esther (Hester) telling of Mordecai (Mardocheus), Ahasuerus (Assuerus), and Vashti (Vesca); the histories of Alexander the Great; King Evander who ruled the region that would become Rome before Aeneas arrived (*Aeneid* 8.126ff.); and King Porsena, King of Etruria; see lines 659–748.

	Of Judas Maccabeus,	
	And of Caesar Julius;	
	And of the love between	
	Paris and Vyene;	
665	And of the duke Hannibal,	
	What made the Romans all	
	Fordrede° and to quake;	fear
	How Scipio did wake	
	The city of Carthage,	
670	Which by his merciful rage	
	He beat down to the ground:	
	And though I can expound	
	Of Hector of Troy,	
	That was all their joy,	
675	Whom Achilles slew,	
	Wherefore all Troy did rue;	
	And of the love so hote°	hot
	That made Troilus to dote	
	Upon fair Cresseyde,	
680	And what they wrote and said,	
	And of their wanton wills	
	Pandar bare the bills°	letters
	From one to the other;	
	His master's love to further,	
685	Sometimes a precious thing,	
	An ouche,° or else a ring;	brooch
	From her to him again	
	Sometimes a pretty chain,	
	Or a bracelet of her hair,	
690	Prayed Troilus for to wear	
	That token for her sake;	
	How hartely° he did it take,	lovingly
	And much thereof did make;	
	And all that was in vain,	
695	For she did but feign;	
	The story telleth plain,	
	He could not obtain,	
	Though his father were a king,	
	Yet there was a thing	
700	That made the male to wring;[9]	
	She made him to sing	
	The song of lovers' lay;°	story
	Musing night and day,	
	Mourning all alone,	
705	Comfort had he none,	
	For she was quite gone;	
	Thus in conclusion,	
	She brought him in abusion;°	deception
	In earnest and in game	
710	She was much to blame;	

9. An obscure phrase that seems to mean "to bring about trouble."

Disparaged is her fame,
And blemished is her name,
In manner half with shame;
Troilus also hath lost
715 On her much love and cost,
And now must kiss the post;°   *pay the price*
Pandara, that went between,
Hath won nothing, I ween,°   *think*
But light° for summer green;   *light clothing*
720 Yet for a special laud°   *praise*
He is named Troilus's bawd,
Of that name he is sure
While the world shall dure:°   *last*
    Though I remember the fable
725 Of Penelope most stable,
To her husband most true,
Yet long time she ne knew°   *did not know*
Whether he were on live or dead;
Her wit stood her in stead,[1]
730 That she was true and just
For any bodily lust
To Ulysses her make,°   *mate*
And never would him forsake:
    Of Marcus Marcellus
735 A process I could tell us;
And of Antiochus;
And of Josephus
De Antiquitatibus;
And of Mardocheus,
740 And of great Assuerus,
And of Vesca his queen,
Whom he forsook with teen,°   *anger*
And of Hester his other wife,
With whom he led a pleasant life;
745 Of King Alexander;
And of King Evander;
And of Porsena the great,
That made the Romans to sweat:
    Though I have enrolled
750 A thousand new and old
Of these historious tales,
To fill bougets° and males°   *bags/trunks*
With books that I have read,
Yet I am nothing sped,
755 And can but little skill
Of Ovid or Virgil,[2]
Or of Plutarch,
Or Francis Petrarch,
Alcaeus or Sappho,

---

1. I.e., her wit informed her.
2. Jane Scrope confesses that she is not skilled in Latin, Greek, or Italian (despite having referred to classical mythol-ogy and history). Among Greek authors whom she mentions she does not know are Alcaeus, Sappho, Linus, Euphorion, Arion, Philemon, Simonides, Philistion, and Phorocides.

760	Or such other poets mo,°	*more*
	As Linus and Homerus,	
	Euphorion and Theocritus,	
	Anacreon and Arion,	
	Sophocles and Philemon,	
765	Pindarus and Simonides,	
	Philistion and Phorocides;	
	These poets of auncyente,°	*antiquity*
	They are too diffuse for me:	
	For, as I tofore° have said,	*before*
770	I am but a young maid,	
	And cannot in effect	
	My style as yet direct	
	With English words elect:	
	Our natural tongue is rude,	
775	And hard to be enneude°	*revived*
	With polished terms lusty;	
	Our language is so rusty,	
	So cankered, and so full	
	Of frowards,° and so dull,	*addities*
780	That if I would apply	
	To write ornately,	
	I wot not where to find	
	Terms to serve my mind.	
	Gower's³ English is old,	
785	And of no value told;	
	His matter° is worth gold,	*content*
	And worthy to be enrolled.	
	In Chaucer I am sped,°	*acquainted*
	His tales I have read:	
790	His matter is delectable,	
	Solacious,° and commendable;	*salacious*
	His English well allowed,	
	So as it is enprowed,⁴	
	For as it is employed,	
795	There is no English void,	
	At those days much commended;	
	And now men would have amended	
	His English, whereat they bark,	
	And mar all they warke:°	*write*
800	Chaucer, that famous clerk,	
	His terms were not dark,	
	But pleasant, easy, and plain;	
	Ne word he wrote in vain.	
	Also John Lydgate	
805	Writeth after an higher rate;	
	It is diffuse° to find	*difficult*

---

3. Jane refers to the poet John Gower, who wrote a popular collection of love stories, the *Confessio Amantis* (literally, "the confession of lovers"); to Chaucer and later to John Lydgate who wrote (among many other works) an English translation of Giovanni Boccaccio's *Concerning*

the Fall of Famous Men, entitled *The Fall of Princes*; see lines 784–812.
4. I.e., as long as it is used to advantage. Jane Scrope praises Chaucer's English, which is not "void" (empty) and was much commended in his own time.

	The sentence° of his mind,	*meaning*
	Yet writeth he in his kind,	
	No man that can amend	
810	Those matters that he hath penned;	
	Yet some men find a faute,°	*fault*
	And say he writeth too haute.°	*abstractly*
	Wherefore hold me excused	
	If I have not well perused	
815	Mine English half abused;	
	Though it be refused,	
	In worth I shall it take,	
	And fewer words make.	
	But, for my sparrow's sake,	
820	Yet as a woman may,	
	My wit I shall assay	
	An epitaph to write	
	In Latin plain and light,	
	Whereof the elegy	
825	Followeth by and by:	

Flos volucrum formose, vale![5]
Philippe, sub isto
Marmore jam recubas,
Qui mihi carus eras.

830 *Semper erunt nitido*
Radiantia sidera cœlo;
Impressusque meo
Pectore semper eris.
Per me laurigerum

835 *Britonum Skeltonida vatem*
Hæc cecinisse licet
Ficta sub imagine texta.
Cujus eris volucris,
Præstanti corpore virgo:

840 *Candida Nais erat,*
Formosior ista Joanna est;
Docta Corinna fuit,
Sed magis ista sapit.
Bien m'en souvient.

THE COMMENDATIONS

845 *Beati im ma cu la ti in via,*
O gloriosa foemina![6]
Now mine whole imagination

---

5. The following Latin elegy is represented up to line 833 as being by Jane Scrope. The remaining lines disclose that their actual author is Skelton, writing in the persona of Jane, who nevertheless continues to mourn for Philip. "O flower of birds, fair one, farewell! Philip, now you lie under this marble, you who were dear to me. The shining stars will always be in the bright sky; you will always be held in my heart. By me, Skelton, the British poet laureate, it has been permitted to sing these things, composed in the guise of her whose bird you were; [she is] a maiden with a lovely body: Nais was fair, but this Joanna is more beautiful; Corinna was learned, but this girl knows more." Skelton concludes with a French phrase: "I remember it well."

6. Skelton continues the remainder of the poem in his own voice, commending Jane Scrope for her devotion to Philip: "Blessed are the pure, in the course [of this life], O glorious woman."

And studious meditation
Is to take this commendation
850   In this consideration;
And under patient toleration
Of that most goodly maid
That *Placebo* hath said,
And for her sparrow prayed
855   In lamentable wise,
Now will I enterprise,°   *undertake*
Through the grace divine
Of the Muses nine,
Her beauty to commend,
860   If Arethusa° will send   *a fountain in Sicily*
Me influence to endite,
And with my pen to write;
If Apollo° will promise   *god of music*
Melodiously it to devise
865   His tunable harp strings
With harmony that sings
Of princes and of kings
And of all pleasant things,
Of lust° and of delight,   *pleasure*
870   Through his godly might;
To whom be the laud° ascribed   *praise*
That my pen hath imbibed
With the aureat° drops,   *golden*
As verily my hope is,
875   Of Tagus,⁷ that golden flood,
That passeth all earthly good;
And as that flood doth pass
All floods that ever was
With his golden sands,
880   Who so that understands
Cosmography, and the stremes°   *rivers*
And the floods in strange remes,°   *kingdoms*
Right so she doth exceed
All other of whom we read,
885   Whose fame by me shall spread
Into Perce° and Mede,°   *Persia/Medea*
From Britons' Albion°   *British Isles*
To the Tower of Babylon.
I trust it is no shame,
890   And no man will me blame,
Though I register her name
In the court of Fame;
For this most goodly flower,⁸
This blossom of fresh color,

7. A river in Spain whose sands were apparently golden.
8. "For this most goodly flower . . . In beauty and virtue": a refrain throughout the rest of the poem. In subsequent lines, Skelton renders "flower" as "floure"; the words were probably pronounced the same, rhyming with "colór" (accented on second syllable).

895 So Jupiter me succor,°   *help*
She flourisheth new and new
In beauty and virtue:
Hac claritate gemina[9]
O gloriosa fœmina,
900 *Retribue servo tuo, vivifica me!*
Labia mea laudabunt te.
     But enforced am I
Openly to askry,°   *protest*
And to make an outcry
905 Against odious Envy,
That evermore will lie,
And say cursedly;
With his ledder° eye,   *leather*
And cheeks dry;
910 With visage wan,
As swart° as tan;   *dark*
His bones crake,°   *crack*
Lean as a rake;
His gums rusty
915 Are full unlusty;°   *useless*
His heart withal
Bitter as gall;
His liver, his lung
With anger is wrung;
920 His serpent's tongue
That many one hath stung;
He frowneth ever;
He laugheth never,
Even nor morrow,
925 But other men's sorrow
Causeth him to grin
And rejoice therein;
No sleep can him catch,
But ever doth watch,
930 He is so bete°   *agitated*
With malice, and frete°   *worn out*
With anger and ire,
His foul desire
Will suffer no sleep
935 In his head to creep;
His foul semblaunt°   *appearance*
All displeasaunt;
When other are glad,
Then is he sad;
940 Frantic and mad;
His tongue never still
For to say ill,

9. "With this twin brightness, O glorious woman, deal bountifully with your servant, give me life! My lips will praise you" (Psalm 62.3).

Writing and wringing,
Biting and stinging;
945   And thus this elf
Consumeth himself,
Himself doth slo°   slay
With pain and woe.
This false Envy
950   Sayeth that I
Use great folly
For to endite,
And for to write,
And spend my time
955   In prose and rhyme,
For to express
The nobleness
Of my mistress,
That causeth me
960   Studious to be
To make a relation
Of her commendation;
And there again
Envy doth complain,
965   And hath disdain;
But yet certain
I will be plain,
And my style dress°   suit
To this process.
970   Now Phoebus° me ken°   Apollo/teach
To sharp my pen,
And lead my fist
As him best list,
That I may say
975   Honor alway
Of womankind!
Truth doth me bind
And loyalty
Ever to be
980   Their true bedell,°   herald
To write and tell
How women excel
In nobleness;
As my mistress,
985   Of whom I think
With pen and ink
For to compile
Some goodly style;
For this most goodly floure,
990   This blossom of fresh color,
So Jupiter me succor,
She flourisheth new and new
In beauty and virtue:

Hac claritate gemina
995 *O gloriosa fœmina,*
Legem pone mihi, domina, in viam justificationum tuarum!
Quemadmodum desiderat cervus ad fontes aquarum.[1]
　　How shall I report
　　All the goodly sort
1000 　　Of her features clear,
　　That hath none earthly peer?
　　Her favor of her face
　　Ennewed° all with grace,　　　　　　　　　　*enlivened*
　　Comfort, pleasure, and solace,
1005 　　Mine heart doth so embrace,
　　And so hath ravished me
　　Her to behold and see,
　　That in words plain
　　I cannot me refrain
1010 　　To look on her again:
　　Alas, what should I fain?°　　　　　　　　　*desire*
　　It were a pleasant pain
　　With her aye to remain.
　　　　Her eyen gray and stepe°　　　　　　　*arched*
1015 　　Causeth mine heart to leap;
　　With her brows bent
　　She may well represent
　　Fair Lucres,[2] as I ween,
　　Or else fair Polexene,
1020 　　Or else Calliope,
　　Or else Penelope;
　　For this most goodly floure,
　　This blossom of fresh color,
　　So Jupiter me succor,
1025 　　She flourisheth new and new
　　In beauty and virtue:
　　Hac claritate gemina
　　O gloriosa fœmina,
　　Memor esto verbi tui servo tuo!
1030 　　*Servus tuus sum ego.*[3]
　　　　The Indy° sapphire blue　　　　　　　　*India*
　　Her veins doth ennew;°　　　　　　　　　　*ornament*
　　The orient pearl so clear,
　　The whiteness of her lere;°　　　　　　　　*face*
1035 　　The lusty ruby ruddes°　　　　　　　　　*complexion*
　　Resemble the rose buds;
　　Her lips soft and merry
　　Emblomed° like the cherry,　　　　　　　　*blooming*
　　It were an heavenly bliss

1. "Teach me the law, O my lady, the way of your statutes! As the deer pants after the water brooks" (Psalm 41.2). Scripture addresses a *dominus* or lord, not a *domina* or lady.
2. Skelton compares Jane to Lucrece, i.e., Lucretia and

Polyxena (both legendary heroines); Caliope: the muse of epic poetry.
3. "Remember thy word to thy servant; I am your servant" (Psalm 118.49 and 125).

1040   Her sugared mouth to kiss.
           Her beauty to augment,
        Dame Nature hath her lent
        A wart upon her cheek,
        Whoso list to seek
1045   In her visage a scar,
        That seemeth from afar
        Like to the radiant star,
        All with favor fret,°   *beauty adorned*
        So properly it is set:
1050   She is the violet,
        The daisy delectable,
        The columbine commendable,
        The jelofer° amiable;   *gilly flower*
        For this most goodly floure,
1055   This blossom of fresh color,
        So Jupiter me succor,
        She flourisheth new and new
        In beauty and virtue:
        Hac claritate gemina
1060   *O gloriosa fœmina,*
        Bonitatem fecisti cum servo tuo, domina,
        Et ex praecordiis sonant praeconia![4]
           And when I perceived
        Her wart and conceived,
1065   It cannot be denayd°   *denied*
        But it was well conveyed,
        And set so womanly,
        And nothing wantonly,
        But right conveniently,
1070   And full congruently,
        As Nature could devise,
        In most goodly wise;
        Whoso list, behold,
        It maketh lovers bold
1075   To her to sue for grace,
        Her favor to purchase;
        The scar upon her chin,
        Enhached° on her fair skin,   *inlaid*
        Whiter than the swan,
1080   It would make any man
        To forget deadly sin
        Her favor to win;
        For this most goodly floure,
        This blossom of fresh color,
1085   So Jupiter me succor,
        She flourisheth new and new
        In beauty and virtue:
        Hac claritate gemina

---

4. "Thou hast dealt bountifully with thy servant, O Lady, and from the heart praises sound" (Psalm 118).

O gloriosa fœmina,
1090   *Defecit in salutatione tua anima mea;*
       Quid petis filio, mater dulcissima? babae![5]
           Soft, and make no din,
       For now I will begin
       To have in remembrance
1095   Her goodly dalliance,
       And her goodly pastaunce:°   pastime
       So sad and so demure,
       Behaving her so sure,
       With words of pleasure
1100   She would make to the lure°   draw to her
       And any man convert
       To give her his whole heart.
       She made me sore amazed
       Upon her whan I gazed,
1105   Me thought mine heart was crazed,
       My eyne° were so dazed;   eyes
       For this most goodly floure,
       This blossom of fresh color,
       So Jupiter me succor,
1110   She flourisheth new and new
       In beauty and virtue:
       Hac claritate gemina
       O gloriosa fœmina,
       Quomodo dilexi legem tuam, domina!
1115   *Recedant vetera, nova sint omnia.*[6]
           And to amend her tale,
       When she list to avale,[7]
       And with her fingers small,
       And hands soft as silk,
1120   Whiter than the milk,
       That are so quickly veined,
       Wherewith my hand she strained,
       Lord, how I was pained!
       Unneth° I me refrained,   unless
1125   How she me had reclaimed,
       And me to her retained,
       Embracing therewithal
       Her goodly middle small
       With sides long and straight;
1130   To tell you what conceit
       I had then in a trice,
       The matter were too nice,
       And yet there was no vice,
       Nor yet no villainy,

---

5. "My soul faints as it greets you; what do you ask for
your son, sweetest mother?" (Psalm 118.81).
6. "How I loved thy law, O Lady; old things pass away,
everything is new" (Psalm 118.97 and 2 Corinthians
5.17).

7. Skelton proposes to "amend" or improve upon her
"tale" or the account of her excellence. He states that
when she desires to "avale" or condescend to take his
hand, he suffers pain.

1135	But only fantasy;	
	For this most goodly floure,	
	This blossom of fresh color,	
	So Jupiter me succor,	
	She flourisheth new and new	
1140	In beauty and virtue:	
	Hac claritate gemina	
	O gloriosa fœmina,	
	Iniquos odio habui!	
	Non calumnientur me superbi.[8]	
1145	But whereto should I note	
	How often did I tote	
	Upon her pretty fote?°	foot
	It raised mine heart rote°	root
	To see her tread the ground	
1150	With heels short and round.	
	She is plainly express°	exactly
	Egeria,[9] the goddess,	
	And like to her image,	
	Emportured° with corage,	painted(?)
1155	A lover's pilgrimage;	
	There is no beast savage,	
	Nor no tiger so wood,°	furious
	But she would change his mood,	
	Such relucent grace	
1160	Is formed in her face;	
	For this most goodly floure,	
	This blossom of fresh color,	
	So Jupiter me succor,	
	She flourisheth new and new	
1165	In beauty and virtue:	
	Hac claritate gemina	
	O gloriosa fœmina,	
	Mirabilia testimonia tua!	
	Sicut novellæ plantationes in juventute sua.[1]	
1170	So goodly as she dresses,	
	So properly she presses	
	The bright golden tresses	
	Of her hair so fine,	
	Like Phoebus beams shine.	
1175	Whereto should I disclose	
	The gartering of her hose?	
	It is for to suppose	
	How that she can were°	wear
	Gorgeously her gere;°	garments
1180	Her fresh habiliments°	clothes
	With other implements	

8. "I hate vain thoughts; let not the proud oppress me" (Psalm 118.113 and 122).
9. A nymph who counseled the legendary King Numa Pompilius, the successor to Romulus, supposed to be the first king of Rome.
1. "Wonderful are thy testimonies; that our sons may be as plants grown up in their youth" (Psalms 118.129 and 143.12).

To serve for all intents,
Like dame Flora,° queen   *goddess of spring*
Of lusty summer green;
1185   For this most goodly floure,
This blossom of fresh color,
So Jupiter me succor,
She flourisheth new and new
In beauty and virtue:
1190   *Hac claritate gemina*
O gloriosa fœmina,
Clamavi in toto corde, exaudi me!
Misericordia tua magna est super me.[2]
Her kirtle° so goodly laced,   *skirt*
1195   And under that is braced
Such pleasures that I may
Neither write nor say;
Yet though I write not with ink,
No man can let me think,
1200   For thought hath liberty,
Thought is frank and free;
To think a merry thought
It cost me little nor nought.
Would God mine homely style
1205   Were polished with the file
Of Cicero's eloquence,
To praise her excellence!
For this most goodly floure,
This blossom of fresh color,
1210   So Jupiter me succor,
She flourisheth new and new
In beauty and virtue:
Hæ claritate gemina
O gloriosa fœmina,
1215   *Principes persecuti sunt me gratis!*
Omnibus consideratis,
Paradisus voluptatis
Hæc virgo est dulcissima.[3]
        My pen it is unable,
1220   My hand it is unstable,
My reason rude and dull
To praise her at the full;
Goodly mistress Jane,
Sober, demure Diane;[4]
1225   Jane this mistress hight
The lode star of delight,
Dame Venus of all pleasure,
The well of worldly treasure;

2. "I have cried with all my heart, hear me; great is thy mercy toward me" (Psalms 118.145 and 85.13).
3. "Princes have persecuted me unjustly" (Psalm 118.161); "All things considered, this girl is the sweetest of heavenly pleasures."
4. By naming Jane Scrope "Diane" here and "Venus" and "Pallas" (Athena) later, Skelton transforms her into a composite of goddesses.

	She doth exceed and pass	
1230	In prudence dame Pallas;	
	For this most goodly floure,	
	This blossom of fresh color,	
	So Jupiter me succor,	
	She flourisheth new and new	
1235	In beauty and virtue:	
	Hac claritate gemina	
	O gloriosa foemina!	
	Requiem aeternam dona eis, Domine![5]	
	With this psalm, *Domine, probasti me,*[6]	
1240	Shall° sail over the sea,	*I shall*
	With *Tibi, Domine, commendamus,*[7]	
	On pilgrimage to saint James,[8]	
	For shrimps, and for pranys,°	*prawns*
	And for stalking cranys;°	*cranes*
1245	And where my pen hath offended,	
	I pray you it may be amended	
	By discrete consideration	
	Of your wise reformation;	
	I have not offended, I trust,	
1250	If it be sadly discussed.	
	It were no gentle guise°	*fashion*
	This treatise to despise	
	Because I have written and said	
	Honor of this fair maid;	
1255	Wherefore should I be blamed,	
	That I Jane have named,	
	And famously proclaimed?	
	She is worthy to be enrolled	
	With letters of gold.	
1260	*Car elle vault.*[9]	
	Per me laurigerum Britonum Skeltonida vatem[1]	
	Laudibus eximiis merito hæc redimita puella est:	
	Formosam cecini, qua non formosior ulla est;	
	Formosam potius quam commendaret Homerus.	
1265	*Sic juvat interdum rigidos recreare labores,*	
	Nec minus hoc titulo tersa Minerva mea est:	
	Rien que playsere.	

Thus endeth the boke of Philip Sparow, and here followeth an addition made by master Skelton.

	The guise nowadays	
1270	Of some jangling jays°	*i.e., raucous critics*
	Is to discommend	

5. Grant them eternal rest, O Lord.
6. Lord, you have tested me.
7. We commend ourselves to thee, O Lord.
8. The shrine of St. James was in Compostela, in northern Spain.
9. Because she is deserving.
1. Through me, Skelton, laureate poet of Britain, this girl is honored with praise for her merit; I have sung of her beauty, she of whom none is more beautiful; Homer would praise no beauty more. Thus it is delightful to recreate demanding labor now and then. Nor is my Minerva [i.e., my art] less free from error than this title: Nothing but to please.

          That they cannot amend,
          Though they would spend
1275   All the wits they have.
              What ail them to deprave°   *vilify*
          Philip Sparrow's grave?
          His *Dirige,* her Commendation
          Can be no derogation,
1280   But mirth and consolation
          Made by protestation,
          No man to miscontent
          With Philip's interment.
              Alas, that goodly maid,
1285   Why should she be afraid?
          Why should she take shame
          That her goodly name,
          Honorably reported,
          Should be set and sorted,
1290   To be matriculate°   *enrolled*
          With ladies of estate?
              I conjure thee, Philip Sparrow,
          By Hercules that hell did harrow,[2]
          And with a venomous arrow
1295   Slew of the Epidaures[3]
          One of the Centaurs,°   *half man, half horse*
          Or Onocentaurs,°   *half man, half ass*
          Or Hippocentaurs;°   *centaur*
          By whose might and main
1300   An heart was slain
          With horns twain
          Of glittering gold;
          And the apples of gold
          Of Hesperides[4] withhold,
1305   And with a dragon kept
          That never more slept,
          By martial strength
          He won at length;
          And slew Gerion[5]
1310   With three bodies in one;
          With mighty corage
          Adauntid° the rage   *subdued*
          Of a lion savage;
          Of Diomedes' stable[6]
1315   He brought out a rabble
          Of coursers° and rounces°   *war horses/riding horses*
          With leaps and bounces;
          And with mighty lugging,

2. Skelton describes the labors of Hercules; see lines
1291–1322.
3. Men of the region in Greece known as Epidaurus.
4. Mythical daughters of the evening, who lived far to the
west.

5. A three-headed monster who owned oxen that Hercules was required to steal.
6. Diomedes, a mythical king of Thrace whose horses ate
human flesh.

Wrestling and tugging,
1320   He plucked the bull
By the horned skull,
And offered to Cornucopia;°   *horn of plenty*
And so forth *per cetera:*
Also by Ecate's⁷ bower
1325   In Pluto's ghastly tower;
By the ugly Eumenides,
That never have rest nor ease;
By the venomous serpent,
That in hell is never brent,°   *burned*
1330   In Lerna, the Greeks' fen,
That was engendered then;
By Chimera's flames,
And all the deadly names
Of infernal posty,°   *power*
1335   Where souls fry and rousty;°   *roast*
By the Stygyal° flood,   *of Styx*
And the streams wood°   *mad waters*
Of Cocytus's bottomless well;
By the ferryman of hell,
1340   Charon with his beard hoar,°   *white, frosted*
That roweth with a rude oar
And with his frounced foretop°   *wrinkled forehead*
Guideth his boat with a prop:°   *pole*
I conjure Philip, and call
1345   In the name of king Saul,⁸
Primo Regum express;°   *specifically*
He bad the Phitoness°   *Pythoness*
To witchcraft her to dress,
And by her abusions,°   *abusive actions*
1350   And damnable illusions
Of marvelous conclusions,
And by her superstitions
Of wonderful conditions,
She raised up in that stead
1355   Samuel that was dead;
But whether it were so,
He were *idem in numero,*°   *in the same body*
The selfsame Samuel,
How be it to Saul did he tell
1360   The Philistines should him ascry,°   *assail*
And the next day he should die,
I will myself discharge

7. Skelton invokes mythological figures associated with the underworld. "Ecate," or Hecate, and Pluto were deities who presided over the underworld; the Eumenides were the Furies, who tormented the dead as well as the living; Lerna was the home of the many-headed Hydra; the Chimera was a fire-breathing beast. The Styx and Cocytus were rivers in the underworld; Charon was the boatman who ferried souls across the Styx.
8. Skelton refers to passages in 1 Samuel (or the book that was known as *Primum Regum,* or First Kings) in which King Saul orders the Pythoness, a witch, to raise King Samuel from the dead; Samuel then prophecies the death of Saul at the hands of the Philistines.

To lettered men at large:
    But, Philip, I conjure thee
1365   Now by these names three,
    Diana⁹ in the woods green,
    Luna that so bright doth shene,°   *shine*
    Proserpina in hell,
    That thou shortly tell,
1370   And show now unto me
    What the cause may be
    Of this perplexity!

Inferias, Philippe, tuas Scroupe pulchra Joanna
Instanter petiit: cur nostri carminis illam
1375   *Nunc pudet? est sero; minor est infamia vero.*¹

    Than such as have disdained
    And of this work complained,
    I pray God they be pained
    No worse than is contained
1380   In verses two or three
    That follow as you may see.
    Luride, cur, livor, volucris pia funera damnas?
    Talia te rapiant rapiunt quæ fata volucrem!
    *Est tamen invidia mors tibi continua.*²

Sir Thomas Wyatt
1503–1542

A gifted poet and diplomat, Sir Thomas Wyatt exemplified the ambitious mixture of social and artistic skills that later ages would see as the ideal of the "Renaissance man." Having entered the household of King Henry VIII immediately after his education at Cambridge, Wyatt promoted English interests on missions to France, Venice, Rome, Spain, and the Low Countries. His career was to prove more precarious at home, where he became involved in court politics. He was deeply attached to the Lady Anne Boleyn, who, by 1527, was the object of Henry's affections and a probable pretext for the King's divorce from Catherine of Aragon and England's break from the Roman Catholic Church. Made Henry's queen in 1533 but out of favor by 1536, Anne implicated by association those who were supposed to have been her lovers. Wyatt was lucky to suffer no more than imprisonment; the Queen's other favorites were executed. Wyatt subsequently regained political status both at home and abroad, although not without periods of disappointment: his verse letter *Mine Own John Poyns* praises the security of a country life away from London and its intrigues. Wyatt's most protracted mission was from 1537 to 1539, as the King's ambassador to the court of the Holy Roman Emperor in Spain: he tells of his anticipated return to England in the hauntingly brief lyric *Tagus, Farewell*. Despite

---

9. Luna (or Lucina), Proserpina: the two other aspects of Diana who, as the goddess of the moon, also represents the cycles of life: virginity, procreation, and death.
1. "O Philip, the beautiful Joanna Scrope urgently desires your obsequies. Why is she ashamed of our song? It is too late. Shame is less than truth."
2. "Why, ghastly envy, do you condemn the sacred funeral of a bird? May such fates seize you as seized the bird. Yet envy is a continual death to you."

the execution of his powerful patron Sir Thomas Cromwell and a second prison term in 1541 for suspected treason, Wyatt obtained Henry's goodwill at the end of his short life. He died from a fever at the age of thirty-nine while on a diplomatic mission for the king.

By any poetic reckoning, Wyatt is to be valued as a pioneer of English verse. Although many of his poems exhibit irregular meters, they have been praised for their remarkable texture and sense of surprise. His translations of Francesco Petrarch's sonnets established the principal forms of English lyric, the rhyming sonnet with its pentameter line and the more loosely configured song derived from the Italian *canzone*. Wyatt's own poems change the spirit of their Petrarchan themes by giving erotic subjects a satirical and even bitter twist, and political topics an inward and personal reference. In one of his best-known sonnets, *Whoso List to Hunt*, he writes of vainly pursuing a "hind" or "deer" (a dear or beloved lady) belonging to "Caesar" (King Henry VIII). Long understood to be a reference to Anne Boleyn, Wyatt's "deer" is quite a different figure than the "deer" in his source, Petrarch's sonnet to a "white doe," who represents his lady, Laura, whom he met in 1327 and loved from a distance until her death in 1350. While Petrarch's lady is imagined as chastely devoted to a heavenly Caesar or God, and therefore as inspiring a religious awe, Wyatt's beloved is the possession of an earthly Caesar, King Henry VIII, and thus the cause of his immediate frustration.

Wyatt's verse was circulated in manuscript during his lifetime and probably read only by his friends and his acquaintances at court. A few poems were published in 1540, in a collection entitled *The Court of Venus*, but the majority—ninety-seven poems in all—appeared in 1557, in a massive anthology called *Songs and Sonnets*, published by the printer Richard Tottel. This volume, which includes poems by Henry Howard, Earl of Surrey and others, was a milestone in the history of literature. Unlike the earlier sixteenth-century poetry of the British Isles, which remained relatively simple in its genres and diction, *Tottel's Miscellany* (as it has come to be known), exhibited a range of new forms and meters: the sonnet, the song (or *canzone*), the epigram, and rhyming and blank verse. Familiar to writers and readers of Italian and French, these forms allowed poets (now writing a recognizably modern English) to develop a stylistic flexibility and thematic richness previously achieved only by the Middle English poet Geoffrey Chaucer. Before presenting his anthology to the public, however, Tottel did some fairly drastic editing: smoothing out metrical irregularities by adding, subtracting, or changing words, he obviously sought to impress readers with what he judged to be the elegant and up-to-date styles represented by the works in his collection. The poems reprinted here are based not on the *Songs and Sonnets* but on Wyatt's original texts.

The Long Love, That in My Thought Doth Harbor

The long love, that in my thought doth harbor
And in mine heart doth keep his residence,
Into my face presseth with bold pretence,
And therein campeth, spreading his banner.
5   She that me learneth° to love and suffer,   *teaches*
And will that my trust and lust's negligence
Be reined by reason, shame and reverence,
With his hardiness° taketh displeasure.   *boldness*
Wherewithal, unto the heart's forest he fleeth,
10   Leaving his enterprise with pain and cry,
And there him hideth and not appeareth.
What may I do when my master feareth
But in the field with him to live and die?
For good is the life, ending faithfully.

Petrarch, Sonnet 140[1]

Amor, che nel penser mio vive et regna
e 'l suo seggio maggior nel mio cor tene,
talor armato ne la fronte vene;
ivi si loca et ivi pon sua insegna.
5   Quella ch' amare et sofferir ne 'nsegna
e vol che 'l gran desio, l'accesa spene
ragion, vergogna, et reverenza affrene,
di nostro ardir fra se stessa si sdegna.
Onde Amor paventoso fugge al core,
10   lasciando ogni sua impresa, et piange et trema;
ivi s'asconde et non appar più fore.
Che poss' io far, temendo il mio signore,
se non star seco infin a l'ora estrema?
ché bel fin fa chi ben amando more.

Petrarch, Sonnet 140: A Translation

Love, who lives and reigns in my thought and keeps his principal seat in my heart, sometimes comes forth all in armor into my forehead, there camps, and there sets up his banner.

    She who teaches us to love and to be patient, and wishes my great desire, my kindled hope, to be reined in by reason, shame, and reverence, at our boldness is angry within herself.

    Wherefore Love flees terrified to my heart, abandoning his every enterprise, and weeps and trembles; there he hides and no more appears outside.

    What can I do, when my lord is afraid, except stay with him until the last hour? For he makes a good end who dies loving well.

Whoso List to Hunt

Who so list° to hunt, I know where is an hind,°   *wishes/doe*
But as for me, helas, I may no more:
The vain travail° hath wearied me so sore.   *idle labor*
I am of them that farthest cometh behind.
5   Yet may I by no means my wearied mind
Draw from° the deer: but as she fleeth afore,   *forget*
Fainting I follow. I leave off therefore,
Since in a net I seek to hold the wind.
Who list her hunt I put him out of doubt,
10   As well as I may spend his time in vain:
And, graven° with diamonds, in letters plain   *engraved*
There is written her fair neck round about:

1. Petrarch (1304–1374), known to his fellow Italians as Francesco Petrarca, was the virtual inventor of modern lyric poetry. Comprising sonnets, songs (*canzone*), and odes, his *Rime sparse* or "various poems"—widely circulated during and after his lifetime—were translated and imitated by poets throughout Europe. Petrarch's verse demonstrated to his early modern readers that a lyric poet could invest subjects with a spirituality and a seriousness previously attributed to the epic, the ode, and to philosophical poems. Translations by Robert M. Durling.

Noli me tangere,[1] for Caesar's I am,
And wild for to hold though I seem tame.

COMPANION READING

Petrarch, Sonnet 190

Una candida cerva sopra l'erba
verde m'apparve con duo corna d'oro,
fra due riviere all' ombra d'un alloro,
Levando 'l sole a la stagione acerba.
5   Era sua vista sì dolce superba
ch' i'lasciai per seguirla ogni lavoro,
come l'avaro che 'n cercar tesoro
con diletto l'affanno disacerba.
"Nessun mi tocchi," al bel collo d'intorno
10   scritto avea di diamanti et di topazi.
"Libera farmi al mio Cesare parve."
Et era 'l sol già vòlto al mezzo giorno,
gli occhi miei stanchi di mirar, non sazi,
quand' io caddi ne l'acqua et ella sparve.

Petrarch, Sonnet 190: A Translation

A white doe on the green grass appeared to me, with two golden horns, between two rivers, in the shade of a laurel, when the sun was rising in the unripe season.

Her look was so sweet and proud that to follow her I left every task, like the miser who as he seeks treasure sweetens his trouble with delight.

"Let no one touch me," she bore written with diamonds and topazes around her lovely neck. "It has pleased my Caesar to make me free."

And the sun had already turned at midday; my eyes were tired by looking but not sated, when I fell into the water, and she disappeared.

My Galley

My galley charged° with forgetfulness	*loaded*
Through sharp seas in winter nights doth pass	
'Tween rock and rock; and eke° mine enemy, alas,	*also*
That is my lord, steereth with cruelness;	
5 And every hour a thought in readiness,	
As though that death were light° in such a case.	*easy*
An endless wind doth tear the sail apace.	
Of forced sights and trusty fearfulness.	
A rain of tears, a cloud of dark disdain	
10 Hath done the wearied cords° great hindrance,	*worn rigging*
Wreathed with error and eke with ignorance.	
The stars be hid that led me to this pain,	
Drowned is reason that should me comfort,	
And I remain despairing of the port.	

---

1. "Touch me not," the words the resurrected but not yet risen Christ spoke to Mary Magdalene before his tomb (John 20.17). The "deer" of the poem has often been identified with Anne Boleyn and "Caesar" with Henry VIII.

They Flee from Me

They flee from me that sometime did me seek
With naked foot stalking in my chamber.
I have seen them gentle tame and meek
That now are wild and do not remember
5   That sometime they put themself in danger
To take bread at my hand; and now they range
Busily seeking with a continual change.
Thanked be fortune, it hath been otherwise
Twenty times better; but once in special,
10   In thine array after a pleasant guise,°   *manner*
When her loose gown from her shoulders did fall,
And she me caught in her arms long and small;
Therewithal sweetly did me kiss,
And softly said, "dear heart, how like you this?"
15   It was no dream: I lay broad waking.
But all is turned through my gentleness
Into a strange fashion of forsaking;
And I have leave to go of her goodness,
And she also to use new fangledness.
20   But since that I so kindly am served,
I would fain° know what she hath deserved.   *wish to*

Some Time I Fled the Fire[1]

Some time I fled the fire that me brent°   *burned*
By sea, by land, by water and by wind;
And now I follow the coals that be quent°   *quenched*
From Dover to Calais against my mind.
5   Lo! how desire is both sprung and spent!
And he may see that whilom° was so blind;   *formerly*
And all his labor now he laugh to scorn,
Mashed in the breers° that erst° was all to torn.°   *briars/once/torn up*

My Lute, Awake!

My lute, awake! perform the last
Labor that thou and I shall waste
   And end that I have now begun,
For when this song is sung and past,
5   My lute be still, for I have done.

As to be heard where ere is none,°   *there is no one*
As lead to grave in marble stone,
   My song may pierce her heart as sone;°   *soon*
Should we then sigh, or sing, or moan?
10   No, no, my lute, for I have done.

1. This poem appears to record Wyatt's attitude as he attended Anne Boleyn on her way to Calais in October 1532. Having been burned by her "fire" (a possible reference to a love affair), he now follows the dead coals of that fire against his will.

The rocks do not so cruelly
Repulse the waves continually,
   As she my suit and affection,
So that I am past remedy,
15   Whereby my lute and I have done.

Proud of the spoil that thou hast got
Of simple hearts through love's shot,
   By whom, unkind, thou has them won,
Think not he hath his bow forgot,
20   Although my lute and I have done.

Vengeance shall fall on thy disdain,
That makest but game on earnest pain;
   Think not alone under the sun
Unquit° to cause thy lover's plain,°   *freely / lament*
25   Although my lute and I have done.

Perchance thee lie weathered and old,
The winter nights that are so cold,
   Plaining in vain unto the mone;°   *moon*
Thy wishes then dare not be told,
30   Care then who list,° for I have done.   *wishes*

And then may chance thee to repent
The time that thou hast lost and spent
   To cause thy lover's sigh and swoon;
Then shalt thou know beauty but lent
35   And wish and want as I have done.

Now cease, my lute, this is the last
Labor that thou and I shall wast,°   *waste*
   And ended is that we begun;
Now is this song both sung and past,
40   My lute be still, for I have done.

Tagus, Farewell

Tagus,[1] farewell, that westward with thy streams
Turns up the grains of gold already tried:
With spur and sail for I go seek the Thames,
Gainward° the sun that showeth her wealthy pride;   *toward*
5 And to the town which Brutus[2] sought by dreams
Like bended moon doth lend her lusty side.
My King, my country, alone for whom I live,
Of mighty love the wings for this me give.

Forget Not Yet

Forget not yet the tried° intent   *proven*
Of such a truth as I have meant,

---

1. The Tagus, or Tajo, River is the longest on the Iberian peninsula and empties into the Atlantic at Portugal. Wyatt was sent to Spain as a diplomat but returned to England in 1539.

2. The legendary Trojan hero Brutus was supposed to have settled the British Isles and founded London, to which he was led by a series of dreams sent to him by the goddess Diana.

My great travail° so gladly spent   *effort*
　　　Forget not yet.

5　Forget not yet when first began
　The weary life ye know since whan,°   *when*
　The suit, the service none tell can,
　　　Forget not yet.

　Forget not yet the great assays,°   *trials*
10　The cruel wrong, the scornful ways,
　The painful patience in denays,°   *denials*
　　　Forget not yet.

　Forget not yet, forget not this,
　How long ago hath been and is
15　The mind that never meant amiss,
　　　Forget not yet.

　Forget not then thine own aprovyd,[1]
　The which so long hath thee so lovyd,
　Whose steadfast faith yet never movyd,
20　　　Forget not this.

Blame Not My Lute

Blame not my lute for he must sound
　　Of this or that as liketh me,
For lack of wit the lute is bound
　　To give such tunes as pleaseth me:
5　Though my songs be somewhat strange,
And speaks such words as touch thy change,[1]
　　Blame not my lute.

My lute, alas, doth not offend,
　　Though that perforce he must agree
10　To sound such tunes as I intend
　　To sing to them that heareth me;
Then though my songs be somewhat plain,
And toucheth some that used to fain,[2]
　　Blame not my lute.

15　My lute and strings may not deny,
　　But as I strike they must obey;
Break not them then so wrongfully,
　　But wreak° thyself some wiser way: *revenge*
And though the songs which I endite°   *write*
20　Do quit° thy change with rightful spite,   *discharge, answer*
　　Blame not my lute.

Spite asketh spite and changing change,
　　And falsed° faith must needs be known;   *betrayed*

---

1. The poet himself, her "approved" lover.
1. I.e., the lady's change of heart, probably also to be signified by a change of tone in the music to which this lyric
was supposedly set.
2. Who used to be desirous or who used to feign desire.

The fault so great, the case so strange,
25   Of right it must abroad be blown:
Then since that by thine own desert°   *desert*
My songs do tell how true thou art,
          Blame not my lute.

Blame but the self that hast misdone
30   And well deserved to have blame;
Change thou thy way, so evil begun,
          And then my lute shall sound that same:
But if till then my fingers play
By thy desert their wonted way,
35   Blame not my lute.

Farewell, unknown, for though thou break
          My strings in spite with great disdain,
Yet have I found out for thy sake
          Strings for to string my lute again;
40   And if perchance this folys° rhyme   *foolish*
Do make thee blush at any time,
          Blame not my lute.

Lucks, My Fair Falcon, and Your Fellows All

Lucks, my fair falcon, and your fellows all,
How well pleasant it were your liberty!
Ye not forsake me that fair might ye befall.[1]
But they that sometime liked my company,
5   Like lice away from dead bodies they crawl:
Lo, what a proof in light adversity![2]
But ye my birds I swear by all your bells,
Ye be my friends, and so be but few else.

Stand Whoso List

Stand whoso list° upon the slipper° top   *wishes/slippery*
Of courts' estates, and let me here rejoice;
And use me° quiet without let° or stop,   *my/hindrance*
Unknown in court, that hath such brackish joys:
5   In hidden place, so let my days forth pass,
That when my years be done, withouten noise,
I may die aged after the common trace.[1]
For him death greep' the° right hard by the crop°   *grips/throat*
That is much known of other; and of himself alas,
10   Doth die unknown, dazed with dreadful face.

---

1. I.e., "You do not forsake me so that good luck may come your way." Wyatt states that despite the falcon's name, which suggests that he seeks good fortune, Lucks is loyal to his master.
2. Wyatt may have written this poem during one of his imprisonments; in any event, he complains here that in prison only his falcons visit and befriend him. Falcons wore bells on their legs to let their masters know where they were.

1. In the common or usual manner; from age and sickness rather than murder. Wyatt alludes to the perilous existence of a man in public life.

Mine Own John Poyns

Mine own John Poyns,[1] since ye delight to know
   The cause why that homeward I me draw,
   And flee the press of courts[2] where so they° go,   *courtiers*
Rather then to live thrall° under the awe   *enslaved*
5   Of lordly looks, wrapped within my cloak,
   To will and lust learning to set a law;
It is not for because I scorn or mock
   The power of them to whom fortune hath lent
   Charge over us, of right, to strike the stroke.
10 But true it is that I have always meant
   Less to esteem them than the common sort
   Of outward things that judge in their intent
Without regard what doth inward resort.
   I grant sometime that of glory the fire
15   Doth touch my heart: me list° not to report   *wish*
Blame by honor and honor to desire.
   But how may I this honor now attain
   That cannot dye the color black a liar?[3]
My Poyns, I cannot frame my tongue to feign,
20   To cloak the truth for praise, without desert,
   Of them that list all vice for to retain.[4]
I cannot honor them that sets their part
   With Venus and Bacchus[5] all their life long;
   Nor hold my piece of them although I smart.
25 I cannot crouch nor kneel nor do so great a wrong,
   To worship them like God on earth alone,
   That are as wolves these sely° lambs among.   *innocent*
I cannot with my words complain and moan
   And suffer nought, nor smart without complaint,
30   Nor turn the word that from my mouth is gone.
I cannot speak and look like a saint,
   Use wiles for wit and make deceit a pleasure,
   And call craft counsel, for profit still to paint.[6]
I cannot wrest the law to fill the coffer,
35   With innocent blood to feed myself fat,
   And do most hurt where most help I offer.
I am not he that can allow the state
   Of high Caesar and damn Cato to die,[7]
   That with his death did scape out of the gate
40 From Caesar's hands, if Livy do not lie,

1. John Poyns, or Poynz, a friend of Wyatt, spent time at court in the 1520s.
2. Here Wyatt's posing as a retired courtier critical of the court may illustrate his attitude during one of the periods in which he was out of favor with Henry VIII. He had extensive holdings in Kent, to which he could retire and from which he was elected to Parliament shortly before his death.
3. I.e., who cannot change (dye) black another color and hence call black a liar.
4. I.e., to lie by praising those who wish to retain vicious ways and therefore do not deserve praise.
5. Venus: the goddess of love; Bacchus: the god of wine (also known as Dionysius). Together they represented lust and excess.
6. I.e., to represent a falsehood as the truth for profit.
7. I.e., I cannot condone the rule of Caesar and damn Cato. Livy: a Roman historian of the republican period; he records the story of Cato of Utica, who opposed the tyrannical impulses of Julius Caesar and committed suicide rather than live under tyranny.

And would not live where liberty was lost:
    So did his heart the common weal° apply.°   *state/value*
I am not he such eloquence to boast,
    To make the crow singing as the swan,
45   Nor call the lion of coward beasts the most
That cannot take a mouse as the cat can:
    And he that dieth for hunger of the gold
    Call him Alessaundre;[8] and say that Pan
Passeth Apollo in music manifold;°   *many times*
50   Praise Sir Thopas[9] for a noble tale,
    And scorn the story that the knight told.
Praise him for counsel that is drunk of ale;
    Grin when he laugheth that beareth all the sway,
    Frown when he frowneth and groan when he is pale;
55   On others lust to hang both night and day:
    None of these points would ever frame in me;
    My wit is nought, I cannot learn the way.
And much the less of things that greater be,
    That asken help of colors of device°   *kinds of deception*
60   To join the mean with each extremity,
With the nearest virtue to cloak alway the vice:
    And as to purpose likewise it shall fall,[1]
    To press° the virtue that it may not rise;   *suppress*
As drunkenness good fellowship to call;
65   The friendly foe with his double face
    Say he is gentle and courteous therewithal;
And say that Favel° hath a goodly grace   *Flattery, a character*
    In eloquence, and cruelty to name
    Zeal of justice and change in time and place;
70   And he that suffereth offence without blame
    Call him pitiful; and him true and plain
    That raileth reckless° to every man's shame.   *carelessly criticizes*
Say he is rude that cannot lie and feign,
    The lecher a lover, and tyranny
75   To be the right of a prince's reign.
I cannot, I. No, no, it will not be.
    This is the cause that I could never yet
    Hang on their sleeves that weigh as thou mayst see
A chip of chance more than a pound of wit.[2]
80   This maketh me at home to hunt and to hawk
    And in foul weather at my book to sit.
In frost and snow then with my bow to stalk;
    No man doth mark whereso I ride or go;
    In lusty lees at liberty I walk,
85   And of these news I feel nor weal° nor woe,   *happiness*

---

8. I.e., flatter as Alexander the Great a man so greedy for gold that he dies of hunger. Wyatt continues to list the flattery he cannot give: Pan—half-man, half-goat—was god of shepherds and famous for his music on his reed pipe, but the undisputed god of music was Apollo.
9. *The Tale of Sir Thopas*, one of Chaucer's *Canterbury*

Tales, was composed to illustrate how not to tell a story; *The Knight's Tale*, by contrast, exemplified the high style of poetic narrative.
1. Also, when occasion permits.
2. I.e., follow those who value a little good fortune more than a lot of intelligence.

Sauf° that a clog doth hang yet at my heel: *except*
   No force for that, for it is ordered so
That I may leap both hedge and dike full well.
   I am not now in France to judge the wine,
90   With saffry° sauce the delicates to feel;   *saffron*
Nor yet in Spain where one must him incline
   Rather than to be, outwardly to seem.
   I meddle not with wits that be so fine,
Nor Flanders' cheer[3] letteth° not my sight to deem°   *hinders/judge*
95   Of black and white, nor taketh my wit away
With beastliness, they beasts do so esteem;[4]
   Nor I am not where Christ is given in prey°   *in exchange*
   For money, poison and treason at Rome,
   A common practice used night and day:
100 But here I am in Kent and Christendom
   Among the muses where I read and rhyme;
   Where if thou list, my Poyns, for to come,
Thou shalt be judge how I do spend my time.

•—▪◆▪—•

Henry Howard, Earl of Surrey
1517?–1545

To belong to a rich and powerful family was no guarantee of a secure and prosperous life. Henry Howard, son of the Duke of Norfolk, was one of the most gifted young men in the court of King Henry VIII, yet he was embroiled in factionalism from a very early age. As a boy, he was the companion of Henry Fitzroy, Duke of Richmond, the king's illegitimate son. They spent a year together as guests of the King of France and, after their return to England, continued their friendship at Windsor Castle. After Richmond's death in 1536, Surrey apparently ran afoul of the law and found himself again at Windsor Castle, this time the king's prisoner. Playing up the irony of his situation in *So Cruel Prison*, he memorializes Windsor, formerly a "place of bliss" but now the site of his sorrow at the loss of his freedom and the greater loss of his friend. Surrey was imprisoned again five years later in London, ostensibly for breaking windows. This punishment occasioned a satire, *London, Thou Hast Accused Me*, on the real corruption in the city. At twenty-seven, Surrey took part in the war against the French, was wounded, and, a year later, was made commander of Boulogne. But he fell from favor when he opposed his sister's marriage to the brother of his rival, Edward Seymour, Lord Hertford, and denounced Seymour as guardian of Prince Edward, Henry's heir. Angered beyond all reconciliation, Henry had Surrey tried and executed for treason in 1545.

As a poet, Surrey is often coupled with Wyatt, who was actually a generation older. Many of his poems (like Wyatt's) emulated Petrarchan forms, themes, and imagery, and were published initially by Richard Tottel in 1557 in a volume entitled *Songs and Sonnets*. But Surrey's own accomplishments were unique. He perfected English blank or unrhymed verse, characterized by the pentameter or five-stress line, and he was the likely inventor of the form that became the standard for the English sonnet: three quatrains followed by a couplet, rhyming *ababcdcdefefgg*. Some of his poems on social subjects adopt a satirical tone and convey his vigorous rejection of contemporary manners and morals.

---

3. The Flemish were reputed to love drinking.   4. The Flemish esteem beasts, i.e., drunks.

Love That Doth Reign and Live within My Thought

Love that doth reign and live within my thought,
And built his seat within my captive breast,
Clad in the arms wherein with me he fought
Oft in my face he doth his banner rest.
5   But she that taught me love and suffer pain,
My doubtful hope and eke° my hot desire   *also*
With shamefast° cloak to shadow and refrain,   *ashamed*
Her smiling grace converteth straight to ire.
And coward love then to the heart apace
10   Taketh his flight, where he doth lurk and plain°   *complain*
His purpose lost, and dare not show his face.
For my lord's guilt thus faultless bide° I pain;   *suffer*
Yet from my lord shall not foot remove:
Sweet is the death that taketh end by love.

Th'Assyrians' King, in Peace with Foul Desire

Th'Assyrian's king,[1] in peace with foul desire
And filthy lusts that stained his regal heart,
In war that should set princely hearts afire
Vanquished did yield for want of martial art.
5   The dent of swords from kisses seemed strange,[2]
And harder than his lady's side his targe;°   *shield*
From glutton feasts to soldiers' fare a change,
His helmet, far above a garland's charge.[3]
Who scarce the name of manhood did retain,
10   Drenched in sloth and womanish delight;
Feeble of sprite,° unpatient of pain,   *spirit*
When he had lost his honor and his right—
Proud time of wealth, in storms appalled with dread—
Murdered himself to show some manful deed.

Set Me Whereas the Sun Doth Parch the Green

Set me whereas the sun doth parch the green,
Or where his beams may not dissolve the ice,
In temperate heat where he is felt and seen;
With proud people, in presence sad and wise;
5   Set me in base, or yet in high degree,
In the long night or in the shortest day,
In clear weather or where mists thickest be,
In lusty youth, or when my hairs be grey;
Set me in earth, in heaven, or yet in hell,
10   In hill, in dale, or in the foaming flood;
Thrall,° or at large, alive whereso I dwell,   *captive*
Sick, or in health, in ill fame or in good:

---

1. The king was Sardanapalus, often regarded as dissolute. He committed suicide by self-immolation.

2. I.e., the dent of swords seemed distasteful compared to kisses.

3. I.e., his helmet was a greater burden than a garland.

Yours will I be, and with that only thought
Comfort myself when that my hap° is nought.   *fortune*

The Soote Season

The soote° season, that bud and bloom forth brings,   *sweet*
With green hath clad the hill and eke the vale:
The nightingale with feathers new she sings:
The turtle to her make° hath told her tale: *mate*
5   Summer is come, for every spray now springs,
The hart° hath hung his old head° on the pale:°   *stag / horns / stake*
The buck in brake° his winter coat he flings: *thicket*
The fishes float with new repaired scale:
The adder all her slough away she slings:
10 The swift swallow pursueth the flies small:
The busy bee her honey now she minges:°   *remembers*
Winter is worn° that was the flowers' bale:°   *passed / evil*
And thus I see among these pleasant things
Each care decays, and yet my sorrow springs.

Alas, So All Things Now Do Hold Their Peace

Alas, so all things now do hold their peace.
Heaven and earth disturbed in nothing:
The beasts, the air, the birds their song do cease:
The night's chair° the stars about doth bring: *Ursa Major*
5   Calm is the sea, the waves work less and less:
So am not I, whom love alas doth wring,
Bringing before my face the great increase
Of my desires, whereat I weep and sing
In joy and woe as in a doubtful ease.
10 For my sweet thoughts sometime do pleasure bring:
But by and by the cause of my disease
Gives me a pang, that inwardly doth sting,
When that I think what grief it is again,
To live and lack the thing should rid my pain.

COMPANION READING

Petrarch, Sonnet 164

Or che 'l ciel et la terra e 'l vento tace
et le fere e gli augelli il sonno affrena,
notte il carro stellato in giro mena
et nel suo letto il mar senz' onda giace,

5   vegghio, penso, ardo, piango; et chi mi sface
sempre m'è inanzi per mia dolce pena:
guerra è 'l mio stato, d'ira e di duol piena,
et sol di lei pensando ò qualche pace.

Così sol d'una chiara fonte viva
10 move 'l dolce et l'amaro ond' io mi pasco,

una man sola mi risana et punge;
et perché 'l mio martir non giunga a riva,
mille volte il dì moro et mille nasco,
tanto da la salute mia son lunge.

Petrarch, Sonnet 164: A Translation[1]

Now that the heavens and the earth and the wind are silent, and sleep reins in the beasts and the birds, Night drives her starry car about, and in its bed the sea lies without a wave,

I am awake, I think, I burn, I weep; and she who destroys me is always before me, to my sweet pain: war is my state, full of sorrow and suffering, and only thinking of her do I have any peace.

Thus from one clear living fountain alone spring the sweet and the bitter on which I feed; one hand alone heals me and pierces me.

And that my suffering may not reach an end, a thousand times a day I die and a thousand am born, so distant am I from health.

So Cruel Prison

So cruel prison, how could betide,° alas,   *it happen*
As proud Windsor,[1] where I in lust and joy
With a king's son my childish years did pass,
In greater feast than Priam's sons of Troy;[2]

5   Where° each sweet place returns a taste full sour.   *that*
The large green courts, where we were wont to hove,°   *accustomed to linger*
With eyes cast up unto the maidens' tower,
And easy sighs, such as folk draw in love.

The stately sales,° the ladies bright of hue,   *halls*
10 The dances short, long tales of great delight,
With words and looks that tigers could but rue,
Where each of us did plead the other's right.

The palm play,[3] where, despoiled for the game,
With dazed eyes oft we by gleams of love
15 Have missed the ball and got sight of our dame
To bait her eyes which kept the leads° above.   *roofs*

The graveled ground,° with sleeves tied on the helm,[4]   *jousting arena*
On foaming horse, with swords and friendly hearts,
With cheer,° as° though the one should overwhelm,   *joyfully/even*
20 Where we have fought and chased oft with darts.

With silver drops the meads yet spread for ruth,°   *pity*
In active games of nimbleness and strength
Where we did strain, trailed by swarms of youth,
Our tender limbs, that yet shot up in length.

---

1. For Petrarch, see the introductory footnote to the Wyatt companion reading, page 621. This translation is also by Durling.
1. Surrey was imprisoned in Windsor Castle in 1537; in this poem his distress at his imprisonment is augmented by his memories of Henry Fitzroy, the Earl of Richmond and bastard son of Henry VIII, with whom he spent time at Windsor when they were young. Richmond married Surrey's sister in 1533; he died in 1536.

2. Priam, King of Troy, was defeated by the Greeks in the Trojan War.
3. Surrey refers to court tennis, a game resembling modern tennis but played against the walls of a court; he remembers that as players, he and Fitzroy watched the ladies who followed the game from the "leads," sheets of metal used to cover roofs.
4. When jousting, a man would tie the sleeve of a lady's garment to his helmet as a sign of her favor.

25	The secret groves, which oft we made resound	
	Of pleasant plaint° and of our ladies' praise,	*complaint*
	Recording soft what grace each one had found,	
	What hope of speed, what dread of long delays.	

25 The secret groves, which oft we made resound
Of pleasant plaint° and of our ladies' praise,   *complaint*
Recording soft what grace each one had found,
What hope of speed, what dread of long delays.

30 The wild forest, the clothed holts° with green,   *woods*
With reins avaled° and swift ybreathed° horse,   *slackened/panting*
With cry of hounds and merry blasts between,
Where we did chase the fearful hart a force.°   *ran it down*

The void° walls eke, that harbored us each night;   *empty*
Wherewith, alas, revive within my breast
35 The sweet accord, such sleeps as yet delight,
The pleasant dreams, the quiet bed of rest,

The secret thoughts imparted with such trust,
The wanton talk, the divers change of play,
The friendship sworn, each promise kept so just,
40 Wherewith we passed the winter nights away.

And with this thought the blood forsakes my face,
The tears berain my cheeks of deadly hue;
The which, as soon as sobbing sighs, alas,
Upsupped° have, thus I my plaint renew: *absorbed*

45 O place of bliss! renewer of my woes!
Give me accompt where is my noble fere,°   *companion*
Whom in thy walls thou didst each night enclose,
To other lief,° but unto me most dear.   *dear*

Each wall, alas, that doth my sorrow rue,
50 Returns thereto a hollow sound of plaint.
Thus I, alone, where all my freedom grew,
In prison pine with bondage and restraint,

And with remembrance of the greater grief,
To banish the less, I find my chief relief.

London, Hast Thou Accused Me

London, hast thou accused me
Of breach of laws, the root of strife?[1]
Within whose breast did boil to see,
(So fervent hot) thy dissolute life,
5 That even the hate of sins, that grow
Within thy wicked walls so rife,
For to break forth did convert so
That terror could it not repress.
The which, by words, since preachers know
10 What hope is left for to redress,
By unknown means it liked me
My hidden burden to express,

---

1. Surrey was accused of breaking windows with his bow in the city of London in 1543. He states that he was moved to this action by his hatred of the dissolute life within the city (line 4) and that he was responding to an idea of Justice (line 15).

Whereby it might appear to thee
That secret sin hath secret spite;
15 From Justice° rod no fault is free;   *Justice's*
But that all such as works unright
In most quiet are next ill rest.²
In secret silence of the night
This made me, with a reckless breast,
20 To wake thy sluggards with my bow;
A figure of the Lord's behest,³
Whose scourge for sin the scriptures show.
That, as the fearful thunder clap
By sudden flame at hand we know,
25 Of pebble stones the soundless rap,
The dreadful plage° might make thee see   *shore*
Of God's wrath, that doth thee enwrap;⁴
That pride might know, from conscience free,
How lofty works may her defend;⁵
30 And envy find, as he hath sought,
How other seek him to offend;
And wrath taste of each cruel thought
The just shapp hire in the end;⁶
And idle sloth, that never wrought,
35 To heaven his spirit lift° may begin;   *to lift*
And greedy lucre live in dread
To see what hate ill-got goods win;
The lechers, ye that lusts do feed,
Perceive what secrecy is in sin;
40 And gluttons' hearts for sorrow bleed,
Awaked when their fault they find.
In loathsome vice, each drunken wight°   *man*
To stir to God, this was my mind.
Thy windows had done me no spite;
45 But proud people that dread no fall,
Clothed with falsehed° and unright   *falsehood*
Bred in the closures of thy wall,
But wrested to wrath in fervent zeal
Thou hast to strife my secret call.⁷
50 Endured° hearts no warning feel.   *hardened*
Oh shameless whore! is dread then gone
By such thy foes as meant thy weal?⁸
Oh member of false Babylon!
The shop of craft! the den of ire!

2. I.e., all those who act wrongly, if they are resting quietly, are nearest to being disturbed.
3. Surrey imagines that he is like a prophet who does the
Lord's command (cf. Isaiah 47.11).
4. The phrase is obscure: "just as we know lightening by
thunder, so the soundless rap of pebble stones might
make you see the dreadful shore of God's wrath, that surrounds you."
5. Surrey becomes ironic: "Pride, free from conscience,
might know how lofty works may defend her"—i.e.,

important or prodigious works do not defend from punishment the proud, who are (by definition) without a
conscience.
6. I.e., wrath receives, for each of its cruel thoughts, the
justly shaped or appointed hire or payment in the end.
7. I.e., you have heard my secret call to strife or struggle.
8. Surrey addresses London as the whore of Babylon, the
epitome of iniquity, and asks, "Do you no longer fear
those enemies that complain of your happiness?"

55   Thy dreadful dome° draws fast upon;   *judgment*
        Thy martyrs' blood, by sword and fire,
        In heaven and earth for Justice call.
        The Lord shall hear their just desire;
        The flame of wrath shall on thee fall;
60   With famine and pest lamentably
        Stricken shall be thy lechers all;
        Thy proud towers and turrets high,
        Enemies to God, beat° stone from stone;   *beaten*
        Thine idols burnt that wrought iniquity.
65   When none thy ruin shall bemoan,
        But render unto the right wise Lord,
        That so hath judged Babylon,
        Immortal praise with one accord.

Wyatt Resteth Here

        Wyatt resteth here, that quick° could never rest;[1]   *alive*
        Whose heavenly gifts increased by disdain
        And virtue sank the deeper in his breast:
        Such profit he of envy could obtain.

5   A head, where wisdom mysteries did frame;
        Whose hammers beat still in that lively brain
        As on a stith,° where some work of fame   *anvil*
        Was daily wrought, to turn to Britain's gain.

        A visage, stern and mild; where both did grow,
10   Vice to condemn, in virtues to rejoice;
        Amid great storms whom grace assured so
        To live upright and smile at fortune's choice.

        A hand that taught what might be said in rhyme;
        That reft° Chaucer the glory of his wit;   *took from*
15   A mark the which (unperfited, for time)[2]—
        Some may approach, but never none shall hit.

        A tongue that served in foreign realms his king;
        Whose courteous talk to virtue did enflame
        Each noble heart, a worthy guide to bring
20   Our English youth, by travail[3] unto fame.

        An eye whose judgment no affect° could blind,   *feeling*
        Friends to allure, and foes to reconcile;
        Whose piercing look did represent a mind
        With virtue fraught, reposed, void of guile.

25   A heart where dread yet never so impressed
        To hide the thought that might the truth avaunce;°   *advance*

---

1. This elegy for the poet Thomas Wyatt was published in
1542, shortly after his death.
2. I.e., was left unperfected for lack of time.

3. Work, but also travel, in that Surrey describes Wyatt as
a "guide."

In neither fortune lift, nor so repressed,[4]
To swell in wealth, or yield unto mischance.

A valiant corps,° where force and beauty met,   *body*
30   Happy, alas! too happy, but for foes,
Lived, and ran the race that nature set;
Of manhood's shape, where she the mold did lose.

But to the heavens that simple soul is fled;
Which left with such, as covet° Christ to know   *desire*
35   Witness to faith that never shall be dead:
Sent for our wealth, but not received so.

Thus, for our guilt, this jewel have we lost;
The earth his bones, the heavens possess his ghost.
                                           Amen.

My Radcliffe, When Thy Reckless Youth Offends

My Radcliffe,[1] when thy reckless youth offends:
Receive thy scourge by others' chastisement.
For such calling, when it works none° amends: *no*
Then plagues are sent without advertisement.
5   Yet Salomon[2] said, the wronged shall recure:°   *recover*
But Wyatt said true, the scar doth aye endure.

Sir Thomas More
1477?–1535

After fifteen years of loyal and distinguished service as a government minister and finally Lord Chancellor, Sir Thomas More refused to do the King's bidding. He declined to take the Oath of Allegiance that Henry VIII required of all his subjects, a token of their repudiation of the Pope and recognition of the king as "Defender of the Faith" in England. More's stubborn fidelity to the only church he had ever known drove Henry to extreme measures. He ordered More to the Tower of London and, a year later, had him executed for treason. More may not have been surprised by the decision; he once observed that "If my head should win [Henry] a castle in France, it should not fail to go." It is reported that More's parboiled severed head was fastened to a pole on London Bridge for all to see. By displaying this pathetic remnant of the most conspicuously brilliant man in England, Henry signaled his iron determination to control not only the religious destiny of his kingdom but also its intellectual life.

More's beginnings were auspicious. The son of Agnes and John More, a barrister, he was sent to be a page in the household of Thomas Morton, Archbishop of Canterbury and Lord Chancellor, and then to Oxford, where he met John Colet (1467?–1519), who became, in More's words, "the director of my life." Colet was in many respects a paradoxical source of

---

4. I.e., neither raised up by fortune to get rich, nor so depressed (by ill fortune) as to yield to a temptation that will lead to misfortune.
1. This epigram is probably addressed to Thomas Rad-

cliffe, third Earl of Essex.
2. Surrey concludes by contrasting an optimistic sentence of King Solomon, which he probably associated with the book of Ecclesiasticus, with the dour reflection of Wyatt.

inspiration for More. A schoolmaster and later a university don, Colet was identified with the scholarship of a Christian humanism that had as its purpose a return to the practices of the primitive and apostolic church. More would end his life professing the authority of the Pope and affirming the Catholic faith as the only true way to salvation.

More was called to the bar and, in 1504, was elected to Parliament. Married that year to Jane Colte and soon the father of four, More organized his household in Chelsea as a center of intellectual activity; there his guests included Desiderius Erasmus and even the King himself. In 1526 the painter Holbein began the first of several visits; his portrait of Thomas More surrounded by numerous family members, including More's gifted daughter Margaret, testifies to the highly conscientious civility that More cultivated in domestic life.

Busy with state and diplomatic affairs from 1504 on, More was knighted and made subtreasurer to the king in 1521. As Lord Chancellor from 1529 to 1532, More was known for his wit, his judicial acumen, and his deft treatment of parties to a case. A popular jingle suggests how swiftly he saw justice done:

> When More some time had Chancellor been,
> No more suits did remain;
> The like will never more be seen,
> Till More be there again.

Perhaps More's dispatch in matters of law gave him some leisure for literature. In any case his talent as a writer was obvious in his first works: Latin translations of Lucian's dialogues, the *Life of Johan Picus, Earl of Mirandula, Utopia* (in Latin), and the *History of Richard III*. Later works reflect the passion for religious orthodoxy that drove him to oppose reforms proposed by Luther, Calvin, and their followers. In 1528 he published *A Dialogue of Sir Thomas More* against the opinions of the English reformer William Tyndale, whose "Englishing" of the Bible had resolved many of its readers to espouse the new faith. *Supplication of Souls* and *The Confutation of Tyndale's Answer*—similarly directed against the reformation—appeared in 1529 and 1532. More's religious enthusiasm was also expressed in punitive action against those he decided were enemies of the church. John Foxe, whose *Acts and Monuments of These Latter Perilous Days* chronicles the persecution of Christians from the earliest days of the church to his present moment, described More as "blinded in the zeal of popery to all humane considerations." Blinded More was not, however, when he cast an eye to the future. Foreseeing the consequences of Henry's divorce from Catherine of Aragon and his intention to marry again, More resigned his chancellorship in 1532, the year that Parliament published the *Supplication Against the Ordinaries,* a list of grievances against the Catholic Church, and the English church accepted the king as its head. More wrote two more works, the first while still a free (although suspect) man and the second as the King's prisoner: *The Apology of Sir Thomas More* (1533) denounces the reformation, and *A Dialogue of Comfort Against Tribulation* (1533) testifies to the courage that faith could instill in a man who, once possessed of great authority and power, finally found himself in desperate circumstances.

Utopia

When More published his account of a hitherto unknown island republic in 1516, Europeans were still largely ignorant of the world beyond their continent. The exploration that would open up so much of the globe was just getting underway, and accounts of voyages to places hardly dreamed of were yet to constitute a literary genre. What travel writing there was catered to readers who loved reports of "marvels" and had no clear appreciation for what later centuries would call a "fact." Sir John Mandeville, whose still popular account of his travels was first circulated in 1356, described the peoples, customs, and wild life of lands in the East in utterly fantastic terms. But when More called his newly discovered land *Utopia*, literally "nowhere" in Greek, he did so only half in fun. Although his island republic was clearly a figment of More's imagination, the political order that he gave it challenged many of the ideals and practices of contemporary monarchies in Europe, especially in England. His *Utopia* is therefore deceptive: apparently a report of a new people and their society, it was also a critique of the habits of thought and the government that had sustained European and English society for centuries. More composed this work, in Latin, between late September 1515 and September 3, 1516, when he sent it to Erasmus, who helped arrange for the book's first publication in Holland; the first English translation, by Ralph Robinson, appeared in 1551. *Utopia*'s text reflects the international scope of its own production. In fact, More the author did, like "More" the character, visit Peter Giles in Antwerp while on a diplomatic mission; and John Clement was More's "pupil-servant"—a tutor to his children and eventually one of the king's physicians.

The second book of the *Utopia*, written before the first, describes a government in which administrative and legal authority rotates among the elders of the society, a society in which all property is common, and a culture supported by citizens who have identical tastes, aspirations, and outlooks on life. In the words of the aged philosopher and world traveler, a character More names Hythlodaeus (literally "learned in nonsense"), Utopian society is populated entirely by rational beings. Each citizen is trained in a trade, is guaranteed employment, and will get what he or she needs from cradle to grave. The economy is one in which exchange is by barter, not money; clothing is uniform; education and medical care are free to everyone; and defense is conducted by foreigners whom the Utopians hire to protect them. Utopians who protest or rebel against these policies and practices are seen as unreasonable. The first book, evidently an afterthought, establishes a perspective by which to view the extraordinary claims of the second; it shows why Hythlodaeus can be considered an idealistic dreamer as well as an acute critic. Here More prefaces the praise he will have Hythlodaeus give Utopian society by having the philosopher point out the social ills of contemporary England. Refusing to compromise the ideals he says were practiced in Utopia, Hythlodaeus maintains that he must withdraw from societies like those in England and Europe because he can do them no good. His critique of governments is supported by his denunciation of enclosures and capital punishment for minor felonies and of kings and magistrates who are driven by greed and a lust for power.

More's account of Utopia, as reported by his character Hythlodaeus, has convinced some readers that he meant his treatise to be taken as a model for the future. Others have given more weight to its elaborate framing as a report from "nowhere" and have seen it rather as a satire on the idea of a wholly rational society. Whatever balance the reader finds in More's brilliant distinctions, his images of an ideal and imaginary society find analogues in those later represented by Jonathan Swift in *Gulliver's Travels*, Samuel Butler in *Erewhon*, and William Morris in *News from Nowhere*.

Utopia[1]

The Best State of a Commonwealth and the New Island Of Utopia

A Truly Golden Handbook, No Less Beneficial Than Entertaining, by the Distinguished and Eloquent Author

1. Translated by Edward Surtz, S. J.

THOMAS MORE
Citizen and Sheriff of the Famous City
of London

Thomas More to Peter Giles,[2]
Greetings.

I am almost ashamed, my dear Peter Giles, to send you this little book about the state of Utopia after almost a year, when I am sure you looked for it within a month and a half. Certainly you know that I was relieved of all the labor of gathering materials for the work and that I had to give no thought at all to their arrangement. I had only to repeat what in your company I heard Raphael[3] relate. Hence there was no reason for me to take trouble about the style of the narrative, seeing that his language could not be polished. It was, first of all, hurried and impromptu and, secondly, the product of a person who, as you know, was not so well acquainted with Latin as with Greek. Therefore the nearer my style came to his careless simplicity the closer it would be to the truth, for which alone I am bound to care under the circumstances and actually do care.

I confess, my dear Peter, that all these preparations relieved me of so much trouble that scarcely anything remained for me to do. Otherwise the gathering or the arrangement of the materials could have required a good deal of both time and application even from a talent neither the meanest nor the most ignorant. If it had been required that the matter be written down not only accurately but eloquently, I could not have performed the task with any amount of time or application. But, as it was, those cares over which I should have had to perspire so hard had been removed. Since it remained for me only to write out simply what I had heard, there was no difficulty about it.

Yet even to carry through this trifling task, my other tasks left me practically no leisure at all. I am constantly engaged in legal business, either pleading or hearing, either giving an award as arbiter or deciding a case as judge. I pay a visit of courtesy to one man and go on business to another. I devote almost the whole day in public to other men's affairs and the remainder to my own. I leave to myself, that is to learning, nothing at all.

When I have returned home, I must talk with my wife, chat with my children, and confer with my servants. All this activity I count as business when it must be done—and it must be unless you want to be a stranger in your own home. Besides, one must take care to be as agreeable as possible to those whom nature has supplied, or chance has made, or you yourself have chosen, to be the companions of your life, provided you do not spoil them by kindness, or through indulgence make masters out of your servants.

Amid these occupations that I have named, the day, the month, the year slip away. When, then, can we find time to write? Nor have I spoken a word about sleep, nor even of food, which for many people takes up as much time as sleep—and sleep takes up almost half a man's life! So I get for myself only the time I filch from sleep and food. Slowly, therefore, because this time is but little, yet finally, because this time *is* something, I have finished *Utopia* and sent it to you, my dear Peter, to read—and to remind me of anything that has escaped me.

---

2. More was made undersheriff of London in 1510, sitting as judge and representing the sheriff's cases in the city court. His friend Peter Giles (c. 1486–1533) was a classical scholar, a member of Erasmus's circle, and city clerk of Antwerp, where he oversaw commercial business.

3. Raphael Hythlodaeus, the fictional traveler who tells the character Sir Thomas More about Utopia.

In this respect I do not entirely distrust myself. (I only wish I were as good in intelligence and learning as I am not altogether deficient in memory!) Nevertheless, I am not so confident as to believe that I have forgotten nothing. As you know, John Clement,[4] my pupil-servant, was also present at the conversation. Indeed I do not allow him to absent himself from any talk which can be somewhat profitable, for from this young plant, seeing that it has begun to put forth green shoots in Greek and Latin literature, I expect no mean harvest some day. He has caused me to feel very doubtful on one point.

According to my own recollection, Hythlodaeus[5] declared that the bridge which spans the river Anydrus at Amaurotum is five hundred paces in length. But my John says that two hundred must be taken off, for the river there is not more than three hundred paces in breadth. Please recall the matter to mind. If you agree with him, I shall adopt the same view and think myself mistaken. If you do not remember, I shall put down, as I have actually done, what I myself seem to remember. Just as I shall take great pains to have nothing incorrect in the book, so, if there is doubt about anything, I shall rather tell an objective falsehood than an intentional lie—for I would rather be honest than wise.

Nevertheless, it would be easy for you to remedy this defect if you ask Raphael himself by word of mouth or by letter. You must do so on account of another doubt which has cropped up, whether more through my fault or through yours or Raphael's I do not know. We forgot to ask, and he forgot to say, in what part of the new world Utopia lies. I am sorry that point was omitted, and I would be willing to pay a considerable sum to purchase that information, partly because I am rather ashamed to be ignorant in what sea lies the island of which I am saying so much, partly because there are several among us, and one in particular, a devout man and a theologian by profession, burning with an extraordinary desire to visit Utopia. He does so not from an idle and curious lust for sight-seeing in new places but for the purpose of fostering and promoting our religion, begun there so felicitously.

To carry out his plan properly, he has made up his mind to arrange to be sent by the pope and, what is more, to be named bishop for the Utopians. He is in no way deterred by any scruple that he must sue for this prelacy, for he considers it a holy suit which proceeds not from any consideration of honor or gain but from motives of piety.

Therefore I beg you, my dear Peter, either by word of mouth if you conveniently can or by letter if he has gone, to reach Hythlodaeus and to make sure that my work includes nothing false and omits nothing true. I am inclined to think that it would be better to show him the book itself. No one else is so well able to correct any mistake, nor can he do this favor at all unless he reads through what I have written. In addition, in this way you will find out whether he accepts with pleasure or suffers with annoyance the fact that I have composed this work. If he himself has decided to put down in writing his own adventures, perhaps he may not want me to do so. By making known the commonwealth of Utopia, I should certainly dislike to forestall him and to rob his narrative of the flower and charm of novelty.

Nevertheless, to tell the truth, I myself have not yet made up my mind whether I shall publish it at all. So varied are the tastes of mortals, so peevish the characters of some, so ungrateful their dispositions, so wrongheaded their judgments, that those

---

4. John Clement (d. 1572), who tutored More's children, was also a distinguished humanist: a Reader at Oxford; co-editor of the first Greek edition of Galen (c. 130–200), a celebrated physician whose works on medicine remained authoritative through the early modern period; and physician to Henry VIII.

5. This reference introduces the play on Greek words that will characterize the description of Utopia in Book II. Hythlodaeus means "learned in nonsense"; the river Anydrus and the city Amaurotum mean "waterless" and "made dark or dim," respectively.

persons who pleasantly and blithely indulge their inclinations seem to be very much better off than those who torment themselves with anxiety in order to publish something that may bring profit or pleasure to others, who nevertheless receive it with disdain or ingratitude.

Very many men are ignorant of learning; many despise it. The barbarian rejects as harsh whatever is not positively barbarian. The smatterers despise as trite whatever is not packed with obsolete expressions. Some persons approve only of what is old; very many admire only their own work. This fellow is so grim that he will not hear of a joke; that fellow is so insipid that he cannot endure wit. Some are so dull-minded that they fear all satire as much as a man bitten by a mad dog fears water. Others are so fickle that sitting they praise one thing and standing another thing.

These persons sit in taverns, and over their cups criticize the talents of authors. With much pontificating, just as they please, they condemn each author by his writings, plucking each one, as it were, by the hair. They themselves remain under cover and, as the proverb goes, out of shot. They are so smooth and shaven that they present not even a hair of an honest man by which they might be caught.

Besides, others are so ungrateful that, though extremely delighted with the work, they do not love the author any the more. They are not unlike discourteous guests who, after they have been freely entertained at a rich banquet, finally go home well filled without thanking the host who invited them. Go now and provide a feast at your own expense for men of such dainty palate, of such varied taste, and of such unforgetful and grateful natures!

At any rate, my dear Peter, conduct with Hythlodaeus the business which I mentioned. Afterwards I shall be fully free to take fresh counsel on the subject. However, since I have gone through the labor of writing, it is too late for me to be wise now. Therefore, provided it be done with the consent of Hythlodaeus, in the matter of publishing which remains I shall follow my friends' advice, and yours first and foremost. Good-by, my sweetest friend, with your excellent wife. Love me as you have ever done, for I love you even more than I have ever done.

The Best State of a Commonwealth,
The Discourse of the Extraordinary
Character, Raphael Hythlodaeus, as
Reported by the Renowned Figure,
THOMAS MORE,
Citizen and Sheriff
of the Famous City of
Great Britain,
London

BOOK 1

The most invincible King of England, Henry, the eighth of that name, who is distinguished by all the accomplishments of a model monarch, had certain weighty matters[6] recently in dispute with His Serene Highness, Charles, Prince of Castile.[7] With

---

6. The "weighty matters" that took More to Flanders concerned the payment of tolls to Flemish ports by the English merchant fleet.
7. The future Charles I of Spain and Charles V, Holy

Roman emperor; he ruled the Spanish kingdoms, Spanish America, Naples, Sicily, the Low Countries, and parts of Austria.

a view to their discussion and settlement, he sent me as a commissioner to Flanders—as a companion and associate of the peerless Cuthbert Tunstal, whom he has just created Master of the Rolls[8] to everyone's immense satisfaction. Of the latter's praises I shall say nothing, not because I fear that the testimony of a friend should be given little credit but because his integrity and learning are too great for it to be possible, and too well-known for it to be necessary, for me to extol them—unless I should wish to give the impression, as the proverb goes, of displaying the sun with a lamp!

We were met at Bruges, according to previous arrangement, by those men put in charge of the affair by the Prince—all outstanding persons. Their leader and head was the Burgomaster[9] of Bruges, a figure of magnificence, but their chief speaker and guiding spirit was Georges de Themsecke,[1] Provost of Cassel, a man not only trained in eloquence but a natural orator—most learned, too, in the law and consummately skillful in diplomacy by native ability as well as by long experience. When after one or two meetings there were certain points on which we could not agree sufficiently, they bade farewell to us for some days and left for Brussels to seek an official pronouncement from the Prince.

Meanwhile, as my business led me, I made my way to Antwerp. While I stayed there, among my other visitors, but of all of them the most welcome, was Peter Giles, a native of Antwerp, an honorable man of high position in his home town yet worthy of the very highest position, being a young man distinguished equally by learning and character; for he is most virtuous and most cultured, to all most courteous, but to his friends so open-hearted, affectionate, loyal, and sincere that you can hardly find one or two anywhere to compare with him as the perfect friend on every score. His modesty is uncommon; no one is less given to deceit, and none has a wiser simplicity of nature. Besides, in conversation he is so polished and so witty without offense that his delightful society and charming discourse largely took away my nostalgia and made me less conscious than before of the separation from my home, wife, and children to whom I was exceedingly anxious to get back, for I had then been more than four months away.

One day I had been at divine service in Notre Dame, the finest church in the city and the most crowded with worshippers. Mass being over, I was about to return to my lodging when I happened to see him in conversation with a stranger, a man of advanced years, with sunburnt countenance and long beard and cloak hanging carelessly from his shoulder, while his appearance and dress seemed to me to be those of a ship's captain.

When Peter had espied me, he came up and greeted me. As I tried to return his salutation, he drew me a little aside and, pointing to the man I had seen him talking with, said:

"Do you see this fellow? I was on the point of taking him straight to you."

"He would have been very welcome," said I, "for your sake."

"No," said he, "for his own, if you knew him. There is no mortal alive today who can give you such an account of unknown peoples and lands, a subject about which I know you are always most greedy to hear."

"Well, then," said I, "my guess was not a bad one. The moment I saw him, I was sure he was a ship's captain."

---

8. The principal clerk of the Chancery Court, a court of appeals from decisions by the common-law courts.
9. Mayor.

1. A Flemish diplomat, employed on numerous missions, who died in 1536.

"But you are quite mistaken," said he, "for his sailing has not been like that of Palinurus but that of Ulysses or, rather, of Plato.[2] Now this Raphael—for such is his personal name, with Hythlodaeus as his family name—is no bad Latin scholar, and most learned in Greek. He had studied that language more than Latin because he had devoted himself unreservedly to philosophy, and in that subject he found that there is nothing valuable in Latin except certain treatises of Seneca and Cicero.[3] He left his patrimony at home—he is a Portuguese—to his brothers, and, being eager to see the world, joined Amerigo Vespucci[4] and was his constant companion in the last three of those four voyages which are now universally read of, but on the final voyage he did not return with him. He importuned and even wrested from Amerigo permission to be one of the twenty-four who at the farthest point of the last voyage were left behind in the fort. And so he was left behind that he might have his way, being more anxious for travel than about the grave. These two sayings are constantly on his lips: 'He who has no grave is covered by the sky,' and 'From all places it is the same distance to heaven.' This attitude of his, but for the favor of God, would have cost him dear.[5] However, when after Vespucci's departure he had traveled through many countries with five companions from the fort, by strange chance he was carried to Ceylon, whence he reached Calicut.[6] There he conveniently found some Portuguese ships, and at length arrived home again, beyond all expectation."

When Peter had rendered this account, I thanked him for his kindness in taking such pains that I might have a talk with one whose conversation he hoped would give me pleasure; then I turned to Raphael. After we had greeted each other and exchanged the civilities which commonly pass at the first meeting of strangers, we went off to my house. There in the garden, on a bench covered with turfs of grass, we sat down to talk together.

He recounted how, after the departure of Vespucci, he and his friends who had stayed behind in the fort began by degrees through continued meetings and civilities to ingratiate themselves with the natives till they not only stood in no danger from them but were actually on friendly terms and, moreover, were in good repute and favor with a ruler (whose name and country I have forgotten). Through the latter's generosity, he and his five companions were supplied with ample provision and travel resources and, moreover, with a trusty guide on their journey (which was partly by water on rafts and partly over land by wagon) to take them to other rulers with careful recommendations to their favor. For, after traveling many days, he said, they found towns and cities and very populous commonwealths with excellent institutions.

To be sure, under the equator and on both sides of the line nearly as far as the sun's orbit extends, there lie waste deserts scorched with continual heat. A gloomy and dismal region looms in all directions without cultivation or attractiveness, inhabited by wild beasts and snakes or, indeed, men no less savage and harmful than

---

2. Palinurus: the pilot of the ship sailed by Aeneas from Troy to Italy in Virgil's *Aeneid;* he fell overboard while sleeping at the helm. Ulysses: the Latin name for Odysseus, the hero of Homer's epic poem, the *Odyssey,* who returns to his kingdom, Ithaka, after years of wandering. Plato: the Greek philosopher who is said to have traveled throughout the Mediterranean world.
3. Two Roman writers who composed works on moral and political philosophy.
4. Florentine merchant adventurer (1451–1512), whose accounts of his voyages to the New World were reprinted in many editions.
5. More's paraphrases of two classical authors indicate his humanist training. From Lucan's epic *Pharsalia* he takes: "Mother Earth has room for all her children, and he who lacks an urn has the sky to cover him" (8.819); and from Cicero's *Tusculan Disputations* he takes: "There is a fine remark of Anaxagoras. He was dying at Lampasacus, and his friends asked if he wanted to be taken home.... 'There's no need,' he said, 'it's the same distance from anywhere to the underworld'" (1.43.104).
6. Seaport on the west coast of India.

are the beasts. But when you have gone a little farther, the country gradually assumes a milder aspect, the climate is less fierce, the ground is covered with a pleasant green herbage, and the nature of living creatures becomes less wild. At length you reach peoples, cities, and towns which maintain a continual traffic by sea and land not only with each other and their neighbors but also with far-off countries.

Then they had opportunity of visiting many countries in all directions, for every ship which was got ready for any voyage made him and his companions welcome as passengers. The ships they saw in the parts first traveled were flat-bottomed and moved under sails made of papyrus or osiers[7] stitched together and sometimes under sails made of leather. Afterwards they found ships with pointed keels and canvas sails, in fact, like our own in all respects.

Their mariners were skilled in adapting themselves to sea and weather. But he reported that he won their extraordinary favor by showing them the use of the magnetic needle[8] of which they had hitherto been quite ignorant so that they had hesitated to trust themselves to the sea and had boldly done so in the summer only. Now, trusting to the magnet, they do not fear wintry weather, being dangerously confident. Thus, there is a risk that what was thought likely to be a great benefit to them may, through their imprudence, cause them great mischief.

What he said he saw in each place would be a long tale to unfold and is not the purpose of this work. Perhaps on another occasion we shall tell his story, particularly whatever facts would be useful to readers, above all, those wise and prudent provisions which he noticed anywhere among nations living together in a civilized way. For on these subjects we eagerly inquired of him, and he no less readily discoursed; but about stale travelers' wonders we were not curious. Scyllas and greedy Celaenos and folk-devouring Laestrygones[9] and similar frightful monsters are common enough, but well and wisely trained citizens are not everywhere to be found.

To be sure, just as he called attention to many ill-advised customs among these new nations, so he rehearsed not a few points from which our own cities, nations, races, and kingdoms may take example for the correction of their errors. These instances, as I said, I must mention on another occasion. Now I intend to relate merely what he told us of the manners and customs of the Utopians, first, however, giving the talk which drew and led him on to mention that commonwealth.

Raphael had touched with much wisdom on faults in this hemisphere and that, of which he found very many in both, and had compared the wiser measures which had been taken among us as well as among them; for he remembered the manners and customs of each nation as if he had lived all his life in places which he had only visited. Peter expressed his surprise at the man as follows:

"Why, my dear Raphael, I wonder that you do not attach yourself to some king. I am sure there is none of them to whom you would not be very welcome because you are capable not only of entertaining a king with this learning and experience of men and places but also of furnishing him with examples and of assisting him with counsel. Thus, you would not only serve your own interests excellently but be of great assistance in the advancement of all your relatives and friends."

"As for my relatives and friends," he replied, "I am not greatly troubled about them, for I think I have fairly well performed my duty to them already. The possessions, which other men do not resign unless they are old and sick and even then

---

7. Papyrus: reed paper. Osiers: willow twigs.
8. Compass.
9. Fabulous monsters from the *Odyssey* and the *Aeneid*:

Scylla is a six-headed sea monster; Celaeno, a harpy, is a bird with a woman's face; the Lestrygonians were gigantic cannibals.

resign unwillingly when incapable of retention, I divided among my relatives and friends when I was not merely hale and hearty but actually young. I think they ought to be satisfied with this generosity from me and not to require or expect additionally that I should, for their sakes, enter into servitude to kings."

"Fine words!" declared Peter. "I meant not that you should be in servitude but in service to kings."

"The one is only one syllable less than the other," he observed.

"But my conviction is," continued Peter, "whatever name you give to this mode of life, that it is the very way by which you can not only profit people both as private individuals and as members of the commonwealth but also render your own condition more prosperous."

"Should I," said Raphael, "make it more prosperous by a way which my soul abhors? As it is, I now live as I please, which I surely fancy is very seldom the case with your grand courtiers. Nay, there are plenty of persons who court the friendship of the great, and so you need not think it a great loss if they have to do without me and one or two others like me."

"Well," I then said, "it is plain that you, my dear Raphael, are desirous neither of riches nor of power. Assuredly, I reverence and look up to a man of your mind no whit less than to any of those who are most high and mighty. But it seems to me you will do what is worthy of you and of this generous and truly philosophic spirit of yours if you so order your life as to apply your talent and industry to the public interest, even if it involves some personal disadvantages to yourself. This you can never do with as great profit as if you are councilor to some great monarch and make him follow, as I am sure you will, straightforward and honorable courses. From the monarch, as from a never-failing spring, flows a stream of all that is good or evil over the whole nation. You possess such complete learning that, even had you no great experience of affairs, and such great experience of affairs that, even had you no learning, you would make an excellent member of any king's council."

"You are twice mistaken, my dear More," said he, "first in me and then in the matter in question. I have no such ability as you ascribe to me and, if I had ever so much, still, in disturbing my own peace and quiet, I should not promote the public interest. In the first place almost all monarchs prefer to occupy themselves in the pursuits of war—with which I neither have nor desire any acquaintance—rather than in the honorable activities of peace, and they care much more how, by hook or by crook, they may win fresh kingdoms than how they may administer well what they have got.

"In the second place, among royal councilors everyone is actually so wise as to have no need of profiting by another's counsel, or everyone seems so wise in his own eyes as not to condescend to profit by it, save that they agree with the most absurd sayings of, and play the parasite to, the chief royal favorites whose friendliness they strive to win by flattery. To be sure, it is but human nature that each man favor his own discoveries most—just as the crow and the monkey like their own off-spring best.

"If anyone, when in the company of people who are jealous of others' discoveries or prefer their own, should propose something which he either has read of as done in other times or has seen done in other places, the listeners behave as if their whole reputation for wisdom were jeopardized and as if afterwards they would deserve to be thought plain blockheads unless they could lay hold of something to find fault with in the discoveries of others. When all other attempts fail, their last resource is a remark such as this: 'Our forefathers were happy with that sort of thing, and would to heaven we had their wisdom.' And then, as if that comment were a brilliant conclusion to the whole business, they take their seats—implying, of course, that it would be a dangerous thing to be found with more wisdom on any point than our forefathers. And yet, no matter what excellent ideas our forefathers may have had, we very serenely bid them a curt farewell. But if in any situation they failed to take the wiser course, that defect gives us a handle which we greedily grab and never let go. Such proud, ridiculous, and obstinate prejudices I have encountered often in other places and once in England too."

"What," I asked, "were you ever in our country?"

"Yes," he answered, "I spent several months there, not long after the disastrous end of the insurrection of western Englishmen against the king, which was put down with their pitiful slaughter.[1] During that time I was much indebted to the Right Reverend Father, John Cardinal Morton, Archbishop of Canterbury, and then also Lord Chancellor of England.[2] He was a man, my dear Peter (for More knows about him and needs no information from me), who deserved respect as much for his prudence and virtue as for his authority. He was of middle stature and showed no sign of his advanced age. His countenance inspired respect rather than fear. In conversation he was agreeable, though serious and dignified. Of those who made suit to him he enjoyed making trial by rough address, but in a harmless way, to see what mettle and what presence of mind a person would manifest. Provided it did not amount to impudence, such behavior gave him pleasure as being akin to his own disposition and excited his admiration as being suited to those holding public office. His speech was polished and pointed. His knowledge of law was profound, his ability incomparable, and his memory astonishingly retentive, for he had improved his extraordinary natural qualities by learning and practice.

"The king placed the greatest confidence in his advice, and the commonwealth seemed much to depend upon him when I was there. As one might expect, almost in earliest youth he had been taken straight from school to court, had spent his whole life in important public affairs, and had sustained numerous and varied vicissitudes of fortune, so that by many and great dangers he had acquired a statesman's sagacity which, when thus learned, is not easily forgotten.

"It happened one day that I was at his table when a layman, learned in the laws of your country, was present. Availing himself of some opportunity or other, he began to speak punctiliously of the strict justice which was then dealt out to thieves. They were everywhere executed, he reported, as many as twenty at a time being hanged on one gallows, and added that he wondered all the more, though so few escaped execution, by what bad luck the whole country was still infested with them. I dared be free in expressing my opinions without reserve at the Cardinal's table, so I said to him:

"'You need not wonder, for this manner of punishing thieves goes beyond justice and is not for the public good. It is too harsh a penalty for theft and yet is not a sufficient deterrent. Theft alone is not a grave offense that ought to be punished with death, and no penalty that can be devised is sufficient to restrain from acts of robbery those who have no other means of getting a livelihood. In this respect not your country alone but a great part of our world resembles bad schoolmasters, who would rather

---

1. In 1497 the people of Cornwall rebelled against taxation by the crown; they were defeated by the king's army outside London, in the Battle of Blackheath.

2. More served for two years as a page in the household of Cardinal Morton (1420–1500).

beat than teach their scholars. You ordain grievous and terrible punishments for a thief when it would have been much better to provide some means of getting a living, that no one should be under this terrible necessity first of stealing and then of dying for it.'

"'We have,' said the fellow, 'made sufficient provision for this situation. There are manual crafts. There is farming. They might maintain themselves by these pursuits if they did not voluntarily prefer to be rascals.'

"'No,' I countered, 'you shall not escape so easily. We shall say nothing of those who often come home crippled from foreign or civil wars, as recently with you Englishmen from the battle with the Cornishmen and not long ago from the war in France.[3] They lose their limbs in the service of the commonwealth or of the king, and their disability prevents them from exercising their own crafts, and their age from learning a new one. Of these men, I say, we shall take no account because wars come sporadically, but let us consider what happens every day.

"'Now there is the great number of noblemen who not only live idle themselves like drones on the labors of others, as for instance the tenants of their estates whom they fleece to the utmost by increasing the returns[4] (for that is the only economy they know of, being otherwise so extravagant as to bring themselves to beggary!) but who also carry about with them a huge crowd of idle attendants who have never learned a trade for a livelihood. As soon as their master dies or they themselves fall sick, these men are turned out at once, for the idle are maintained more readily than the sick, and often the heir is not able to support as large a household as his father did, at any rate at first.

"'In the meantime the fellows devote all their energies to starving, if they do not to robbing. Indeed what can they do? When by a wandering life they have worn out their clothes a little, and their health to boot, sickly and ragged as they are, no gentleman deigns to engage them and the farmers dare not do so either. The latter know full well that a man who has been softly brought up in idleness and luxury and has been wont[5] in sword and buckler to look down with a swaggering face on the whole neighborhood and to think himself far above everybody will hardly be fit to render honest service to a poor man with spade and hoe, for a scanty wage, and on frugal fare.'

"'But this,' the fellow retorted, 'is just the sort of man we ought to encourage most. On them, being men of a loftier and nobler spirit than craftsmen and farmers, depend the strength and sinews of our army when we have to wage war.'

"'Of course,' said I, 'you might as well say that for the sake of war we must foster thieves. As long as you have these men, you will certainly never be without thieves. Nay, robbers do not make the least active soldiers, nor do soldiers make the most listless robbers, so well do these two pursuits agree. But this defect, though frequent with you, is not peculiar to you, for it is common to almost all peoples.

"'France in particular is troubled with another more grievous plague. Even in peacetime (if you can call it peacetime) the whole country is crowded and beset with mercenaries hired because the French follow the train of thought you Englishmen take in judging it a good thing to keep idle retainers. These wiseacres think that the public safety depends on having always in readiness a strong and reliable garrison, chiefly of veterans, for they have not the least confidence in tyros.[6] This attitude

---

3. Hythlodaeus refers to actual battles at Dixmude in 1489 and in Boulogne in 1492.
4. Rents.

5. Accustomed.
6. Raw recruits.

obliges them always to be seeking for a pretext for war just so they may not have soldiers without experience, and men's throats must be cut without cause lest, to use Sallust's witty saying, "the hand or the mind through lack of practice become dulled." Yet how dangerous it is to rear such wild beasts France has learned to its cost, and the examples of Rome, Carthage, Syria, and many other nations show.[7] Not only the supreme authority of the latter countries but their land and even their cities have been more than once destroyed by their own standing armies.

"'Now, how unnecessary it is to maintain them is clearly proved by this consideration: not even the French soldiers, assiduously trained in arms from infancy, can boast that they have very often got the better of it face to face with your draftees.[8] Let me say no more for fear of seeming to flatter you barefacedly. At any rate, your town-bred craftsmen or your rough and clodhopper farmers are not supposed to be much afraid of those idle attendants on gentlemen, except those of the former whose build of body is unfitted for strength and bravery or those whose stalwart spirit is broken by lack of support for their family. Consequently there is no danger that those attendants whose bodies, once strong and vigorous (for it is only the picked men that gentlemen deign to corrupt), are now either weakened by idleness or softened by almost womanish occupations, should become unmanned if trained to earn their living in honest trades and exercised in virile labors!

"'However the case may be, it seems to me by no means profitable to the common weal to keep for the emergency of a war a vast multitude of such people as trouble and disturb the peace. You never have war unless you choose it, and you ought to take far more account of peace than of war. Yet this is not the only situation that makes thieving necessary. There is another which, as I believe, is more special to you Englishmen.'

"'What is that?' asked the Cardinal.

"'Your sheep,' I answered, 'which are usually so tame and so cheaply fed, begin now, according to report, to be so greedy and wild that they devour human beings themselves and devastate and depopulate fields, houses, and towns.[9] In all those parts of the realm where the finest and therefore costliest wool is produced, there are noblemen, gentlemen, and even some abbots, though otherwise holy men, who are not satisfied with the annual revenues and profits which their predecessors used to derive from their estates. They are not content, by leading an idle and sumptuous life, to do no good to their country; they must also do it positive harm. They leave no ground to be tilled; they enclose every bit of land for pasture; they pull down houses and destroy towns, leaving only the church to pen the sheep in. And, as if enough of your land were not wasted on ranges and preserves of game, those good fellows turn all human habitations and all cultivated land into a wilderness.

"'Consequently, in order that one insatiable glutton and accursed plague of his native land may join field to field and surround many thousand acres with one fence, tenants are evicted. Some of them, either circumvented by fraud or overwhelmed by violence, are stripped even of their own property, or else, wearied by unjust acts, are driven to sell. By hook or by crook the poor wretches are compelled to leave their

7. The Romans, Carthaginians, and Syrians used mercenary armies but suffered mutinies as a result.

8. Hythlodaeus refers to English soldiers who won victories over French forces in such battles as Crecy (1346), Poitiers (1356), and Agincourt (1415).

9. Hythlodaeus criticizes the management of the English wool trade. The potential for profit from sheep's wool led landlords to fence off or enclose vast open spaces that had previously been shared in common and farmed by peasants. Many of these displaced people sought work in the cities or became migrant day-laborers throughout the country.

homes—men and women, husbands and wives, orphans and widows, parents with lit-tle children and a household not rich but numerous, since farm work requires many hands. Away they must go, I say, from the only homes familiar and known to them, and they find no shelter to go to. All their household goods which would not fetch a great price if they could wait for a purchaser, since they must be thrust out, they sell for a trifle.

"After they have soon spent that trifle in wandering from place to place, what remains for them but to steal and be hanged—justly, you may say!—or to wander and beg. And yet even in the latter case they are cast into prison as vagrants for going about idle when, though they most eagerly offer their labor, there is no one to hire them. For there is no farm work, to which they have been trained, to be had, when there is no land for plowing left. A single shepherd or herdsman is sufficient for grazing livestock on that land for whose cultivation many hands were once required to make it raise crops.

"A result of this situation is that the price of food has risen steeply in many localities. Indeed, the price of raw wools has climbed so high that your poor people who used to make cloth cannot possibly buy them, and so great numbers are driven from work into idleness. One reason is that, after the great increase in pasture land, a plague carried off a vast multitude of sheep as though God were punishing greed by sending upon the sheep a murrain[1]—which should have fallen on the owners' heads more justly! But, however much the number of sheep increases, their price does not decrease a farthing because, though you cannot brand that a monopoly which is a sale by more than one person, yet their sale is certainly an oligopoly,[2] for all sheep have come into the hands of a few men, and those already rich, who are not obligat-ed to sell before they wish and who do not wish until they get the price they ask.

"By this time all other kinds of livestock are equally high-priced on the same account and still more so, for the reason that, with the pulling down of farmsteads and the lessening of farming, none are left to devote themselves to the breeding of stock. These rich men will not rear young cattle as they do lambs, but they buy them lean and cheap abroad and then, after they are fattened in their pastures, sell them again at a high price. In my estimation, the whole mischief of this system has not yet been felt. Thus far, the dealers raise the prices only where the cattle are sold, but when, for some time, they have been removing them from other localities faster than they can be bred there, then, as the supply gradually diminishes in the markets where they are purchased, great scarcity must needs be here.

"Thus, the unscrupulous greed of a few is ruining the very thing by virtue of which your island was once counted fortunate in the extreme. For the high price of food is causing everyone to get rid of as many of his household as possible, and what, I ask, have they to do but to beg, or—a course more readily embraced by men of met-tle—to become robbers?

"In addition, alongside this wretched need and poverty you find wanton luxury. Not only the servants of noblemen but the craftsmen and almost the clodhoppers themselves, in fact all classes alike, are given to much ostentatious sumptuousness of dress and to excessive indulgence at table. Do not dives, brothels, and those other places as bad as brothels, to wit, taverns, wine shops and ale-houses—do not all those crooked games of chance, dice, cards, backgammon, ball, bowling, and quoits, soon drain the purses of their votaries[3] and send them off to rob someone?

---

1. A disease of livestock.
2. Control of a commercial market by a small number of companies or merchants.
3. Devotees.

"'Cast out these ruinous plagues. Make laws that the destroyers of farmsteads and country villages should either restore them or hand them over to people who will restore them and who are ready to build. Restrict this right of rich individuals to buy up everything and this license to exercise a kind of monopoly for themselves. Let fewer be brought up in idleness. Let farming be resumed and let cloth-working be restored once more that there may be honest jobs to employ usefully that idle throng, whether those whom hitherto pauperism has made thieves or those who, now being vagrants or lazy servants, in either case are likely to turn out thieves. Assuredly, unless you remedy these evils, it is useless for you to boast of the justice you execute in the punishment of theft. Such justice is more showy than really just or beneficial. When you allow your youths to be badly brought up and their characters, even from early years, to become more and more corrupt, to be punished, of course, when, as grown-up men, they commit the crimes which from boyhood they have shown every prospect of committing, what else, I ask, do you do but first create thieves and then become the very agents of their punishment?'

"Even while I was saying these things, the lawyer had been busily preparing himself to reply and had determined to adopt the usual method of disputants who are more careful to repeat what has been said than to answer it, so highly do they regard their memory.

"'Certainly, sir,' he began, 'you have spoken well, considering that you are but a stranger who could hear something of these matters rather than get exact knowledge of them—a statement which I shall make plain in a few words. First, I shall repeat, in order, what you have said; then I shall show in what respects ignorance of our conditions has deceived you; finally I shall demolish and destroy all your arguments. So, to begin with what I promised first, on four points you seemed to me—'

"'Hold your peace,' interrupted the Cardinal, 'for you hardly seem about to reply in a few words if you begin thus. So we shall relieve you of the trouble of making your answer now, but we shall reserve your right unimpaired till your next meeting, which I should like to set for tomorrow, provided neither you nor Raphael here is hindered by other business.

"'But now I am eager to have you tell me, my dear Raphael, why you think that theft ought not to be punished with the extreme penalty, or what other penalty you yourself would fix, which would be more beneficial to the public. I am sure that not even you think it ought to go unpunished. Even as it is, with death as the penalty, men still rush into stealing. What force and what fear, if they once were sure of their lives, could deter the criminals? They would regard themselves as much invited to crime by the mitigation of the penalty as if a reward were offered.'

"'Certainly,' I answered, 'most reverend and kind Father, I think it altogether unjust that a man should suffer the loss of his life for the loss of someone's money. In my opinion, not all the goods that fortune can bestow on us can be set in the scale against a man's life. If they say that this penalty is attached to the offense against justice and the breaking of the laws, hardly to the money stolen, one may well characterize this extreme justice as extreme wrong. For we ought not to approve such stern Manlian rules of law[4] as would justify the immediate drawing of the sword when they

4. Manlius Torquatus, a Roman general of the 4th century B.C., who, having made a law against single encounters, executed his own son for fighting and defeating an enemy warrior.

are disobeyed in trifles nor such Stoical[5] ordinances as count all offenses equal so that there is no difference between killing a man and robbing him of a coin when, if equity has any meaning, there is no similarity or connection between the two cases.[6]

"'God has said, "Thou shalt not kill," and shall we so lightly kill a man for taking a bit of small change? But if the divine command against killing be held not to apply where human law justifies killing, what prevents men equally from arranging with one another how far rape, adultery, and perjury are admissible? God has withdrawn from man the right to take not only another's life but his own. Now, men by mutual consent agree on definite cases where they may take the life of one another. But if this agreement among men is to have such force as to exempt their henchmen from the obligation of the commandment, although without any precedent set by God they take the life of those who have been ordered by human enactment to be put to death, will not the law of God then be valid only so far as the law of man permits? The result will be that in the same way men will determine in everything how far it suits them that God's commandments should be obeyed.

"'Finally, the law of Moses,[7] though severe and harsh—being intended for slaves, and those a stubborn breed—nevertheless punished theft by fine and not by death. Let us not suppose that God, in the new law of mercy in which He gives commands as a father to his sons, has allowed us greater license to be cruel to one another.

"'These are the reasons why I think this punishment unlawful. Besides, surely everyone knows how absurd and even dangerous to the commonwealth it is that a thief and a murderer should receive the same punishment. Since the robber sees that he is in as great danger if merely condemned for theft as if he were convicted of murder as well, this single consideration impels him to murder the man whom otherwise he would only have robbed. In addition to the fact that he is in no greater danger if caught, there is greater safety in putting the man out of the way and greater hope of covering up the crime if he leaves no one left to tell the tale. Thus, while we endeavor to terrify thieves with excessive cruelty, we urge them on to the destruction of honest citizens.

"'As to the repeated question about a more advisable form of punishment, in my judgment it is much easier to find a better than a worse. Why should we doubt that a good way of punishing crimes is the one which we know long found favor of old with the Romans, the greatest experts in managing the commonwealth? When men were convicted of atrocious crimes they condemned them for life to stone quarries and to digging in metal mines, and kept them constantly in chains.

"'Yet, as concerns this matter, I can find no better system in any country than that which, in the course of my travels, I observed in Persia among the people commonly called the Polylerites,[8] a nation that is large and well-governed and, except that it pays an annual tribute to the Persian padishah [emperor], otherwise free and autonomous in its laws. They are far from the sea, almost ringed round by mountains, and satisfied with the products of their own land, which is in no way infertile. In consequence they rarely pay visits to other countries or receive them. In accordance with their long-standing national policy, they do not try to enlarge their territory and easily protect what they have from all aggression by their mountains and by the tribute

---

5. Austere.

6. Hythlodaeus alludes to an important feature of the law: Cases in which the law invoked to cover them is too general to do justice to their complexity are decided by addressing the circumstances in which the alleged violation was committed, the condition of the dis-

putants, and the remedies apart from the law that might serve to settle the case. Such a mitigated justice was known as equity.

7. The Decalogue or Ten Commandments, one of which is "Thou shalt not kill" (Exodus 20.13).

8. "People of Much Nonsense."

paid to their overlord. Being completely free from militarism, they live a life more comfortable than splendid and more happy than renowned or famous, for even their name, I think, is hardly known except to their immediate neighbors.

"'Now, in their land, persons who are convicted of theft repay to the owner what they have taken from him, not, as is usual elsewhere, to the prince, who, they consider, has as little right to the thing stolen as the thief himself. But if the object is lost, the value is made up out of the thieves' goods, and the balance is then paid intact to their wives and children. They themselves are condemned to hard labor. Unless the theft is outrageous, they neither are confined to prison nor wear shackles about their feet but, without any bonds or restraints, are set to public works. Convicts who refuse to labor or are slack are not put in chains but urged on by the lash. If they do a good day's work, they need fear no insult or injury. The only check is that every night, after their names are called over, they are locked in their sleeping quarters.

"'Except for the constant toil, their life has no hardship. For example, as serviceable to the common weal, they are fed well at the public's expense, the mode varying from place to place. In some parts, what is spent on them is raised by almsgiving. Though this method is precarious, the Polylerite people are so kindhearted that no other is found to supply the need more plentifully. In other parts, fixed public revenues are set aside to defray the cost. Elsewhere, all pay a specified personal tax for these purposes. Yes, and in some localities the convicts do no work for the community, but, whenever a private person needs a hired laborer, he secures in the market place a convict's service for that day at a fixed wage, a bit lower than what he would have paid for free labor. Moreover, the employer is permitted to chastise with stripes a hired man if he be lazy. The result is that they are never out of work and that each one, besides earning his own living, brings in something every day to the public treasury.

"'All of them wear clothes of a color not worn by anyone else. Their hair is not shaved but cropped a little above the ears, from one of which the tip is cut off. Food and drink and clothes of the proper color may be given them by their friends. The gift of money is a capital offense, both for the donor and the receiver. It is no less dangerous for a free man to receive a penny for any reason from a condemned person, or for slaves (which is the name borne by the convicts) to touch weapons. The slaves of each district are distinguished by a special badge, which it is a capital offense to throw away, as it is to appear beyond their own bounds or to talk to a slave from another district. Further, it is no safer to plot escape than actually to run away. Yes, and the punishment for connivance in such a plan is death for the slave and slavery for the free man. On the other hand, rewards are appointed for an informer: money for a free man, liberty for a slave, and pardon and immunity for both for their complicity. The purpose is never to make it safer to follow out an evil plan than to repent of it.

"'This is the law and this the procedure in the matter, as I have described it to you. You can easily see how humane and advantageous it is. The object of public anger is to destroy the vices but to save the persons and so to treat them that they necessarily become good and that, for the rest of their lives, they repair all the damage done before.

"'Further, so little is it to be feared that they may sink back into their old evil ways, even travelers who have to go on a journey think themselves most safe if they secure as guides these slaves, who are changed with each new district. For the latter have nothing suitable with which to commit robbery. They bear no arms; money would merely insure the detection of the crime; punishment awaits the man who is caught; and there is absolutely no hope of escaping to a safe place. How could a man so cover his flight as to elude observation when he resembles ordinary people in no part of his attire—unless he were to run away naked? Even then his ear would betray him in his flight!

"'But, of course, would there not at least be risk of their taking counsel together and conspiring against the commonwealth? As if any district could conceive a hope of success without having first sounded and seduced the slave gangs of many other districts! The latter are so little able to conspire together that they may not even meet and converse or greet one another. Much less will they boldly divulge to their own fellow slaves the plot, which they know is dangerous to those concealing it and very profitable to those betraying it. On the other hand, no one is quite without hope of gaining his freedom eventually if he accepts his punishment in a spirit of obedience and resignation and gives evidence of reforming his future life; indeed, every year a number of them are granted their liberty which they have merited by their submissive behavior.'

"When I had finished this speech, I added that I saw no reason why this method might not be adopted even in England and be far more beneficial in its working than the justice which my legal opponent had praised so highly. The lawyer replied: 'Never could that system be established in England without involving the commonwealth in a very serious crisis.' In the act of making this statement, he shook his head and made a wry face and so fell silent. And all who were present gave him their assent.

"Then the Cardinal remarked: 'It is not easy to guess whether it would turn out well or ill inasmuch as absolutely no experiment has been made. If, after pronouncement of the sentence of death, the king were to order the postponement of its execution and, after limitation of the privileges of sanctuary,[9] were to try this system, then, if success proved its usefulness, it would be right to make the system law. In case of failure, then and there to put to death those previously condemned would be no less for the public good and no more unjust than if execution were done here and now. In the meantime no danger can come of the experiment. Furthermore, I am sure that vagrants might very well be treated in the same way for, in spite of repeated legislation against them, we have made no progress.'

"When the Cardinal had finished speaking, they all vied in praising what they all had received with contempt when suggested by me, but especially the part relating to vagrants because this was the Cardinal's addition.

"I am at a loss as to whether it were better to suppress what followed next, for it was quite absurd. But I shall relate it since it was not evil in itself and had some bearing on the matter in question.

"There happened to be present a hanger-on, who wanted to give the impression of imitating a jester but whose imitation was too close to the real thing. His ill-timed witticisms were meant to raise a laugh, but he himself was more often the object of laughter than his jests. The fellow, however, sometimes let fall observations which were to the point, thus proving the proverb true, that if a man throws the dice often he will sooner or later make a lucky throw. One of the guests happened to say:

"'Raphael's proposal has made good provision for thieves. The Cardinal has taken precautions also for vagrants. It only remains now that public measures be devised for persons whom sickness or old age has brought to want and made unable to work for their living.'

9. From the 7th century until the Reformation, English churches and sometimes their surrounding precincts provided limited asylum for fugitives from judicial authority.

"'Give me leave,' volunteered the hanger-on. 'I shall see that this situation, too, be set right. I am exceedingly anxious to get this sort of person out of my sight. They have often harassed me with their pitiful whinings in begging for money—though they never could pitch a tune which would get a coin out of my pocket. For one of two things always happens: either I do not want to give or I cannot, since I have nothing to give. Now they have begun to be wise. When they see me pass by, they say nothing and spare their pains. They no longer expect anything from me—no more, by heaven, than if I were a secular priest! As for me, I should have a law passed that all those beggars be distributed and divided among the Benedictine monasteries and that the men be made so-called lay brothers.[1] The women I should order to become nuns.'

"The Cardinal smiled and passed it off in jest, but the rest took it in earnest. Now a certain theologian who was a friar[2] was so delighted by this jest at the expense of secular priests and of monks that he also began to make merry, though generally he was serious almost to the point of being dour.

"'Nay,' said he, 'not even so will you be rid of mendicants unless you make provision for us friars too.'

"'But this has been taken care of already,' retorted the hanger-on. 'His Eminence made excellent provision for you when he determined that tramps should be confined and made to work, for you are the worst tramps of all.'

"When the company, looking at the Cardinal, saw that he did not think this jest any more amiss than the other, they all proceeded to take it up with vigor—but not the friar. He—and I do not wonder—deluged by these taunts, began to be so furious and enraged that he could not hold back even from abusing the joker. He called him a rascal, a slanderer, and a 'son of perdition,' quoting the while terrible denunciations out of Holy Scripture. Now the scoffer began to scoff in earnest and was quite in his element:

"'Be not angry, good friar. It is written: "In your patience shall you possess your souls."'[3]

"Then the friar rejoined—I shall repeat his very words: 'I am not angry, you gallows bird, or at least I do not sin, for the psalmist says: "Be angry, and sin not."'[4]

"At this point the Cardinal gently admonished the friar to calm his emotions, but he replied:

"'No, my lord, I speak motivated only by a good zeal—as I should. For holy men have had a good zeal; wherefore Scripture says, "The zeal of Thy house has eaten me up,"[5] and churches resound with the hymn: "The mockers of Eliseus[6] as he went up to the house of God felt the zeal of the baldhead"—just as this mocking, scorning, ribald fellow will perhaps feel it.'

"'Maybe,' said the Cardinal, 'you behave with proper feeling, but I think that you would act, if not more holily, at any rate more wisely, if you would not set your wits against those of a silly fellow and provoke a foolish duel with a fool.'

---

1. Members of the regular religious orders who performed manual labor and sometimes administrative or temporal functions within the monastery. They were distinct from those men who had taken monastic vows and devoted their lives entirely to following the word of God.
2. Friars were members of the mendicant orders who lived solely off alms in return for their prayers and preaching.
3. Luke 21.19.
4. Psalms 4.4.

5. Psalms 69.9.
6. Elisha, the son of the prophet Elijah. Hythlodaeus refers to a hymn ascribed to the medieval writer Adam of St. Victor. It alludes to the story of Elisha, who, when mocked by children for his baldness, curses them "in the name of the Lord"; this causes two bears to emerge from the woods and rip forty-two of the children to pieces (2 Kings 2.23–4).

"'No, my lord,' he replied, 'I should not do more wisely. Solomon himself, the wisest of men, says: "Answer a fool according to his folly"[7]—as I do now. I am showing him the pit into which he will fall if he does not take good heed, for, if many scorners of Eliseus, who numbered only one baldhead, felt the zeal of the baldhead, how much more will one scorner of many friars, among whom are numbered many baldheads! And, besides, we have a papal bull[8] by which all who scoff at us are excommunicated!'

"When the Cardinal realized there was no making an end, he sent away the hanger-on by a motion of his head and tactfully turned the conversation to another subject. Soon afterwards he rose from the table and, going to hear the petitions of his suitors, dismissed us.

"Look, my dear More, with how lengthy a tale I have burdened you. I should have been quite ashamed to protract it if you had not eagerly called for it and seemed to listen as if you did not want any part of the conversation to be left out. Though I ought to have related this conversation more concisely, still I felt bound to tell it to exhibit the attitude of those who had rejected what I had said first yet who, immediately afterward, when the Cardinal did not disapprove of it, also gave their approval, flattering him so much that they even smiled on and almost allowed in earnest the fancies of the hanger-on, which his master in jest did not reject. From this reaction you may judge what little regard courtiers would pay to me and my advice."

"To be sure, my dear Raphael," I commented, "you have given me great pleasure, for everything you have said has been both wise and witty. Besides, while listening to you, I felt not only as if I were at home in my native land but as if I were become a boy again, by being pleasantly reminded of the very Cardinal in whose court I was brought up as a lad. Since you are strongly devoted to his memory, you cannot believe how much more attached I feel to you on that account, attached exceedingly as I have been to you already. Even now, nevertheless, I cannot change my mind but must needs think that, if you could persuade yourself not to shun the courts of kings, you could do the greatest good to the common weal by your advice. The latter is the most important part of your duty as it is the duty of every good man. Your favorite author, Plato, is of opinion that commonwealths will finally be happy only if either philosophers become kings or kings turn to philosophy.[9] What a distant prospect of happiness there will be if philosophers will not condescend even to impart their counsel to kings!"

"They are not so ungracious," he rejoined, "that they would not gladly do it—in fact, many have already done it in published books—if the rulers would be ready to take good advice. But, doubtless, Plato was right in foreseeing that if kings themselves did not turn to philosophy, they would never approve of the advice of real philosophers because they have been from their youth saturated and infected with wrong ideas. This truth he found from his own experience with Dionysius.[1] If I proposed beneficial measures to some king and tried to uproot from his soul the seeds of evil and corruption, do you not suppose that I should be forthwith banished or treated with ridicule?

"Come now, suppose I were at the court of the French king and sitting in his privy council. In a most secret meeting, a circle of his most astute councilors over which he personally presides is setting its wits to work to consider by what crafty

---

7. Proverbs 26.5.
8. Edict.
9. *Republic*, 5.473d.

1. Having tried to instruct Dionysius II, King of Syracuse, in the art of ruling as a philosopher, Plato became a virtual prisoner of the court.

machinations he may keep his hold on Milan and bring back into his power the Naples which has been eluding his grasp; then overwhelm Venice and subjugate the whole of Italy; next bring under his sway Flanders, Brabant, and finally, the whole of Burgundy—and other nations, too, whose territory he has already conceived the idea of usurping.

"At this meeting, one advises that a treaty should be made with the Venetians to last just as long as the king will find it convenient, that he should communicate his intentions to them, and that he should even deposit in their keeping part of the booty, which, when all has gone according to his mind, he may reclaim. Another recommends the hiring of German *Landsknechte* [infantry], and another the mollification of the Swiss with money, and another the propitiation of the offended majesty of the emperor with gold as an acceptable offering. Another thinks that a settlement should be made with the King of Aragon and that, as a guarantee of peace, someone else's kingdom of Navarre should be ceded him! Another proposes that the Prince of Castile be caught by the prospect of a marriage alliance and that some nobles of his court be drawn to the French side by a fixed pension.

"Meanwhile the most perplexing question of all comes up: what is to be done with England? They agree that negotiations for peace should be undertaken, that an alliance always weak at best should be strengthened with the strongest bonds, and that the English should be called friends but suspected as enemies. The Scots therefore must be posted in readiness, prepared for any opportunity to be let loose on the English if they make the slightest movement. Moreover, some exiled noble must be fostered secretly—for treaties prevent it being done openly—to maintain a claim to the throne, that by this handle France may keep in check a king in whom it has no confidence.

"In such a meeting, I say, when such efforts are being made, when so many distinguished persons are vying with each other in proposals of a warlike nature, what if an insignificant fellow like myself were to get up and advise going on another tack? Suppose I expressed the opinion that Italy should be left alone. Suppose I argued that we should stay at home because the single kingdom of France by itself was almost too large to be governed well by a single man so that the king should not dream of adding other dominions under his sway. Suppose, then, I put before them the decisions made by the people called the Achorians[2] who live on the mainland to the south-southeast of the island of Utopia.

"Once upon a time they had gone to war to win for their king another kingdom to which he claimed to be the rightful heir by virtue of an old tie by marriage. After they had secured it, they saw they would have no less trouble in keeping it than they had suffered in obtaining it. The seeds of rebellion from within or of invasion from without were always springing up in the people thus acquired. They realized they would have to fight constantly for them or against them and to keep an army in continual readiness. In the meantime they were being plundered, their money was being taken out of the country, they were shedding their blood for the little glory of someone else, peace was no more secure than before, their morals at home were being corrupted by war, the lust for robbery was becoming second nature, criminal recklessness was emboldened by killings in war, and the laws were held in contempt—all because the king, being distracted with the charge of two kingdoms, could not properly attend to either.

2. A people "without place, region, or district."

"At length, seeing that in no other way would there be any end to all this mischief, they took counsel together and most courteously offered their king his choice of retaining whichever of the two kingdoms he preferred. He could not keep both because there were too many of them to be ruled by half a king, just as no one would care to engage even a muleteer whom he had to share with someone else. The worthy king was obliged to be content with his own realm and to turn over the new one to one of his friends, who was driven out soon afterwards.

"Furthermore, suppose I proved that all this war-mongering, by which so many nations were kept in a turmoil on the French king's account, would, after draining his resources and destroying his people, at length by some mischance end in naught and that therefore he had better look after his ancestral kingdom and make it as prosperous and flourishing as possible, love his subjects and be loved by them, live with them and rule them gently, and have no designs upon other kingdoms since what he already possessed was more than enough for him. What reception from my listeners, my dear More, do you think this speech of mine would find?"

"To be sure, not a very favorable one," I granted.

"Well, then, let us proceed," he continued. "Picture the councilors of some king or other debating with him and devising by what schemes they may heap up treasure for him. One advises crying up the value of money when he has to pay any and crying down its value below the just rate when he has to receive any—with the double result that he may discharge a large debt with a small sum and, when only a small sum is due to him, may receive a large one. Another suggests a make-believe war under pretext of which he would raise money and then, when he saw fit, make peace with solemn ceremonies to throw dust in his simple people's eyes because their loving monarch in compassion would fain avoid human bloodshed.

"Another councilor reminds him of certain old and moth-eaten laws, annulled by long non-enforcement, which no one remembers being made and therefore everyone has transgressed. The king should exact fines for their transgression, there being no richer source of profit nor any more honorable than such as has an outward mask of justice! Another recommends that under heavy penalties he prohibit many things and especially such as it is to the people's advantage not to allow. Afterwards for money he should give a dispensation to those with whose interests the prohibition has interfered. Thus favor is won with the people and a double profit is made: first, by exacting fines from those whose greed of gain has entangled them in the snare and, second, by selling privileges to others—and, to be sure, the higher the price the better the king, since he hates to give any private citizen a privilege which is contrary to the public welfare and will not do so except at a great price!

"Another persuades him that he must bind to himself the judges, who will in every case decide in favor of the king's side. In addition, he must summon them to the palace and invite them to debate his affairs in his presence. There will be no cause of his so patently unjust in which one of them will not, either from a desire to contradict or from shame at repeating another's view or to curry favor, find some loophole whereby the law can be perverted. When through the opposite opinions of the judges a thing in itself as clear as daylight has been made a subject of debate, and when truth has become a matter of doubt, the king is opportunely furnished a handle to interpret the law in his own interest. Everyone else will acquiesce from shame or from fear. Afterwards the decision is boldly pronounced from the Bench. Then, too, a pretext can never be wanting for deciding on the king's side. For such a judge it is enough that either equity be on his side or the letter of the law or the twisted meaning of the written word or, what finally outweighs all law with conscientious judges, the indisputable royal prerogative![3]

"All the councilors agree and consent to the famous statement of Crassus:[4] no amount of gold is enough for the ruler who has to keep an army. Further, the king, however much he wishes, can do no wrong; for all that all men possess is his, as they themselves are, and so much is a man's own as the king's kindness has not taken away from him. It is much to the king's interest that the latter be as little as possible, seeing that his safeguard lies in the fact that the people do not grow insolent with wealth and freedom. These things make them less patient to endure harsh and unjust commands, while, on the other hand, poverty and need blunt their spirits, make them patient, and take away from the oppressed the lofty spirit of rebellion.

"At this point, suppose I were again to rise and maintain that these counsels are both dishonorable and dangerous for the king, whose very safety, not merely his honor, rests on the people's resources rather than his own. Suppose I should show that they choose a king for their own sake and not for his—to be plain, that by his labor and effort they may live well and safe from injustice and wrong. For this very reason, it belongs to the king to take more care for the welfare of his people than for his own, just as it is the duty of a shepherd, insofar as he is a shepherd, to feed his sheep rather than himself.[5]

"The blunt facts reveal that they are completely wrong in thinking that the poverty of the people is the safeguard of peace. Where will you find more quarreling than among beggars? Who is more eager for revolution than he who is discontented with his present state of life? Who is more reckless in the endeavor to upset everything, in the hope of getting profit from some source or other, than he who has nothing to lose? Now if there were any king who was either so despicable or so hateful to his subjects that he could not keep them in subjection otherwise than by ill usage, plundering, and confiscation and by reducing them to beggary, it would surely be better for him to resign his throne than to keep it by such means—means by which, though he retain the name of authority, he loses its majesty. It is not consistent with the dignity of a king to exercise authority over beggars but over prosperous and happy subjects. This was certainly the sentiment of that noble and lofty spirit, Fabricius,[6] who replied that he would rather be a ruler of rich people than be rich himself.

"To be sure, to have a single person enjoy a life of pleasure and self-indulgence amid the groans and lamentations of all around him is to be the keeper, not of a kingdom, but of a jail. In fine, as he is an incompetent physician who cannot cure one

---

3. Conditions in which the principle of equity is subverted: The law, rather than being applied in such a way as to respect the conditions and circumstances of a particular case, is bent or twisted to suit the interest of a particular party. In England the courts of equity were often devoted to matters of state and were susceptible to corruption in the interest of promoting royal business. The prerogative was the absolute power of the monarch only in special categories of activity (i.e., the import and export trade), and it was exempt from any legal restrictions.
4. Marcus Licinius Crassus (d. 53 B.C.), a man of great wealth who, together with Julius Caesar and Pompey,

formed a coalition known as the first triumvirate.
5. A king who did not care for the welfare of his people was usually identified as a tyrant. As Aristotle stated, a tyranny is a perversion of a monarchy and it is characterized by "irresponsible rule over subjects . . . with a view to its own private interest and not in the interest of the persons ruled" (Politics, 4.8.3).
6. Roman commander of the republican period; whether he actually made the statement attributed to him is unclear. In any case it outlines a critique of monarchy common in antityrannical literature of the early modern period.

disease except by creating another, so he who cannot reform the lives of citizens in any other way than by depriving them of the good things of life must admit that he does not know how to rule free men.

"Yea, the king had better amend his own indolence or arrogance, for these two vices generally cause his people either to despise him or to hate him. Let him live harmlessly on what is his own. Let him adjust his expenses to his revenues. Let him check mischief and crime, and, by training his subjects rightly, let him prevent rather than allow the spread of activities which he will have to punish afterwards. Let him not be hasty in enforcing laws fallen into disuse, especially those which, long given up, have never been missed. Let him never take in compensation for violation anything that a private person would be forbidden in court to appropriate for the reason that such would be an act of crooked craftiness.

"What if then I were to put before them the law of the Macarians,[7] a people not very far distant from Utopia? Their king, on the day he first enters into office, is bound by an oath at solemn sacrifices that he will never have at one time in his coffer more than a thousand pounds of gold or its equivalent in silver. They report that this law was instituted by a very good king, who cared more for his country's interest than his own wealth, to be a barrier against hoarding so much money as would cause a lack of it among his people. He saw that this treasure would be sufficient for the king to put down rebellion and for his kingdom to meet hostile invasions. It was not large enough, however, to tempt him to encroach on the possessions of others. The prevention of the latter was the primary purpose of his legislation. His secondary consideration was that provision was thus made to forestall any shortage of the money needed in the daily business transactions of the citizens. He felt, too, that since the king had to pay out whatever came into his treasury beyond the limit prescribed by law, he would not seek occasion to commit injustice. Such a king will be both a terror to the evil and beloved by the good. To sum it all up, if I tried to obtrude these and like ideas on men strongly inclined to the opposite way of thinking, to what deaf ears should I tell the tale!"

"Deaf indeed, without doubt," I agreed, "and, by heaven, I am not surprised. Neither, to tell the truth, do I think that such ideas should be thrust on people, or such advice given, as you are positive will never be listened to. What good could such novel ideas do, or how could they enter the minds of individuals who are already taken up and possessed by the opposite conviction? In the private conversation of close friends this academic philosophy is not without its charm, but in the councils of kings, where great matters are debated with great authority, there is no room for these notions."

"That is just what I meant," he rejoined, "by saying there is no room for philosophy with rulers."

"Right," I declared, "that is true—not for this academic philosophy which thinks that everything is suitable to every place. But there is another philosophy, more practical for statesmen, which knows its stage, adapts itself to the play in hand, and performs its role neatly and appropriately. This is the philosophy which you must employ. Otherwise we have the situation in which a comedy of Plautus is being performed and the household slaves are making trivial jokes at one another and then you come on the stage in a philosopher's attire and recite the passage

7. "Happy Ones."

from the *Octavia* where Seneca is disputing with Nero.[8] Would it not have been preferable to take a part without words than by reciting something inappropriate to make a hodgepodge of comedy and tragedy? You would have spoiled and upset the actual play by bringing in irrelevant matter—even if your contribution would have been superior in itself. Whatever play is being performed, perform it as best you can, and do not upset it all simply because you think of another which has more interest.

"So it is in the commonwealth. So it is in the deliberations of monarchs. If you cannot pluck up wrongheaded opinions by the root, if you cannot cure according to your heart's desire vices of long standing, yet you must not on that account desert the commonwealth. You must not abandon the ship in a storm because you cannot control the winds.

"On the other hand, you must not force upon people new and strange ideas which you realize will carry no weight with persons of opposite conviction. On the contrary, by the indirect approach you must seek and strive to the best of your power to handle matters tactfully. What you cannot turn to good you must at least make as little bad as you can. For it is impossible that all should be well unless all men were good, a situation which I do not expect for a great many years to come!"

"By this approach," he commented, "I should accomplish nothing else than to share the madness of others as I tried to cure their lunacy. If I would stick to the truth, I must needs speak in the manner I have described. To speak falsehoods, for all I know, may be the part of a philosopher, but it is certainly not for me. Although that speech of mine might perhaps be unwelcome and disagreeable to those councilors, yet I cannot see why it should seem odd even to the point of folly. What if I told them the kind of things which Plato creates in his republic or which the Utopians actually put in practice in theirs? Though such institutions were superior (as, to be sure, they are), yet they might appear odd because here individuals have the right of private property, there all things are common.

"To persons who had made up their minds to go headlong by the opposite road, the man who beckons them back and points out dangers ahead can hardly be welcome. But, apart from this aspect, what did my speech contain that would not be appropriate or obligatory to have propounded everywhere? Truly, if all the things which by the perverse morals of men have come to seem odd are to be dropped as unusual and absurd, we must dissemble among Christians almost all the doctrines of Christ. Yet He forbade us to dissemble them to the extent that what He had whispered in the ears of His disciples He commanded to be preached openly from the housetops.[9] The greater part of His teaching is far more different from the morals of mankind than was my discourse. But preachers, crafty men that they are, finding that men grievously disliked to have their morals adjusted to the rule of Christ and following I suppose your advice, accommodated His teaching to men's morals as if it

---

8. More's character "More" illustrates the poor social skills of the philosopher by imagining a situation in which the philosopher quotes lines from Seneca's tragedy while everyone else is enjoying a comedy by Plautus. "More" asks not only that the philosopher observe conditions of time and place, but also that—in political situations in which the philosopher might like to instruct his people in moral action but finds that they do not want to listen to him—he not give up his civic obligations and go

into retirement. The predicament was one that More and many of his contemporary humanist statesmen actually confronted when they attempted to give advice to their political superiors.

9. Hythlodaeus paraphrases Matthew 10.27 and Luke 12.3; he proposes that the practical and accommodating flexibility that "More" advocates finds its limits in the absolute moral doctrine preached by Jesus Christ and therefore to be followed by Christians.

were a rule of soft lead that at least in some way or other the two might be made to correspond.[1] By this method I cannot see what they have gained, except that men may be bad in greater comfort.

"And certainly I should make as little progress in the councils of princes. For I should hold either a different opinion, which would amount to having none at all, or else the same, and then I should, as Mitio says in Terence, help their madness.[2] As to that indirect approach of yours, I cannot see its relevancy; I mean your advice to use my endeavors, if all things cannot be made good, at least to handle them tactfully and, as far as one may, to make them as little bad as possible. At court there is no room for dissembling, nor may one shut one's eyes to things. One must openly approve the worst counsels and subscribe to the most ruinous decrees. He would be counted a spy and almost a traitor, who gives only faint praise to evil counsels.

"Moreover, there is no chance for you to do any good because you are brought among colleagues who would easily corrupt even the best of men before being reformed themselves. By their evil companionship, either you will be seduced yourself or, keeping your own integrity and innocence, you will be made a screen for the wickedness and folly of others. Thus you are far from being able to make anything better by that indirect approach of yours.

"For this reason, Plato by a very fine comparison shows why philosophers are right in abstaining from administration of the commonwealth. They observe the people rushing out into the streets and being soaked by constant showers and cannot induce them to go indoors and escape the rain. They know that, if they go out, they can do no good but will only get wet with the rest. Therefore, being content if they themselves at least are safe, they keep at home, since they cannot remedy the folly of others.[3]

"Yet surely, my dear More, to tell you candidly my heart's sentiments, it appears to me that wherever you have private property and all men measure all things by cash values, there it is scarcely possible for a commonwealth to have justice or prosperity—unless you think justice exists where all the best things flow into the hands of the worst citizens or prosperity prevails where all is divided among very few—and even they are not altogether well off, while the rest are downright wretched.

"As a result, when in my heart I ponder on the extremely wise and holy institutions of the Utopians, among whom, with very few laws, affairs are ordered so aptly that virtue has its reward, and yet, with equality of distribution, all men have abundance of all things, and then when I contrast with their policies the many nations elsewhere ever making ordinances and yet never one of them achieving good order—nations where whatever a man has acquired he calls his own private property, but where all these laws daily framed are not enough for a man to secure or to defend or

1. The "rule of soft lead," or the Lesbian rule (after the leaden measure used in architecture on the island of Lesbos in the Aegean), is the figure Aristotle uses to illustrate the concept of equity. The measure, supposedly a rule or an absolute, corresponds to the idea of a written law; but because it is flexible, it is also a written law that is always interpreted in such a way as to fit the particulars of a case.
2. Hythlodaeus insists that for a philosopher to cross a person in authority and with power will only make the philosopher appear nonsensical and therefore render the ruler less reasonable than he was at first; that is, both philosopher and ruler will appear to be madmen. He instances Mitio, a character in Terence's play *The Brothers*, who declares: "Still, if I inflamed or even fell in with his passionate temper, I should surely give him another madman for company" (1.145–147).
3. Cf. *Republic* 6.496d: "he keeps quiet and minds his own business—as a man in a storm . . . stands aside under a little wall. Seeing others filled with lawlessness, he is content if somehow he himself can live his life here pure of injustice and unholy deeds."

even to distinguish from someone else's the goods which each in turn calls his own, a predicament readily attested by the numberless and ever new and interminable lawsuits—when I consider, I repeat, all these facts, I become more partial to Plato and less surprised at his refusal to make laws for those who rejected that legislation which gave to all an equal share in all goods.

"This wise sage, to be sure, easily foresaw that the one and only road to the general welfare lies in the maintenance of equality in all respects. I have my doubts that the latter could ever be preserved where the individual's possessions are his private property. When every man aims at absolute ownership of all the property he can get, be there never so great abundance of goods, it is all shared by a handful who leave the rest in poverty. It generally happens that the one class preeminently deserves the lot of the other, for the rich are greedy, unscrupulous, and useless, while the poor are well-behaved, simple, and by their daily industry more beneficial to the commonwealth than to themselves. I am fully persuaded that no just and even distribution of goods can be made and that no happiness can be found in human affairs unless private property is utterly abolished.[4] While it lasts, there will always remain a heavy and inescapable burden of poverty and misfortunes for by far the greatest and by far the best part of mankind.

"I admit that this burden can be lightened to some extent, but I contend that it cannot be removed entirely. A statute might be made that no person should hold more than a certain amount of land and that no person should have a monetary income beyond that permitted by law. Special legislation might be passed to prevent the monarch from being overmighty and the people overweening; likewise, that public offices should not be solicited with gifts, nor be put up for sale, nor require lavish personal expenditures. Otherwise, there arise, first, the temptation to recoup one's expenses by acts of fraud and plunder and, secondly, the necessity of appointing rich men to offices which ought rather to have been administered by wise men. By this type of legislation, I maintain, as sick bodies which are past cure can be kept up by repeated medical treatments, so these evils, too, can be alleviated and made less acute. There is no hope, however, of a cure and a return to a healthy condition as long as each individual is master of his own property. Nay, while you are intent upon the cure of one part, you make worse the malady of the other parts. Thus, the healing of the one member reciprocally breeds the disease of the other as long as nothing can so be added to one as not to be taken away from another."[5]

"But," I ventured, "I am of the contrary opinion. Life cannot be satisfactory where all things are common. How can there be a sufficient supply of goods when each withdraws himself from the labor of production? For the individual does not have the motive of personal gain and he is rendered slothful by trusting to the indus-

---

4. It was thought that primordial humans did not understand that property could be private and belong to one party only. With the congregation of men and women into tribes, however, private property was established by markers: boundary lines, signs and emblems, and distinctive styles of manufacture. This moment also saw the institution of a civil society characterized by religion and law. By advocating a state in which there is no private property, Hythlodaeus posits a political and economic situation that his contemporaries would have recognized in such limited societies as those under monastic or some other kind of religious rule.

5. The trope of the body politic is ubiquitous in early modern political thought. In *The Education of a Christian Prince*, Erasmus argues: "[A monarch] should consider his kingdom as a great body of which he is the most outstanding member and remember that they who have entrusted all their fortunes and their very safety to the good faith of one man are deserving of consideration. He should keep constantly in mind the example of those rulers to whom the welfare of their people was dearer than their own lives; for it is obviously impossible for a prince to do violence to the state without injuring himself." See also Plato's *Republic*, 5.462.

try of others. Moreover, when people are goaded by want and yet the individual cannot legally keep as his own what he has gained, must there not be trouble from continual bloodshed and riot? This holds true especially since the authority of magistrates and respect for their office have been eliminated, for how there can be any place for these among men who are all on the same level I cannot even conceive."

"I do not wonder," he rejoined, "that it looks this way to you, being a person who has no picture at all, or else a false one, of the situation I mean. But you should have been with me in Utopia and personally seen their manners and customs as I did, for I lived there more than five years and would never have wished to leave except to make known that new world. In that case you unabashedly would admit that you had never seen a well-ordered people anywhere but there."

"Yet surely," objected Peter Giles, "it would be hard for you to convince me that a better-ordered people is to be found in that new world than in the one known to us. In the latter I imagine there are equally excellent minds, as well as commonwealths which are older than those in the new world. In these commonwealths long experience has come upon very many advantages for human life—not to mention also the chance discoveries made among us, which no human mind could have devised."

"As for the antiquity of commonwealths," he countered, "you could give a sounder opinion if you had read the historical accounts of that world. If we must believe them, there were cities among them before there were men among us. Furthermore, whatever either brains have invented or chance has discovered hitherto could have happened equally in both places. But I hold for certain that, even though we may surpass them in brains, we are far inferior to them in application and industry.

"According to their chronicles, up to the time of our landing they had never heard anything about our activities (they call us the Ultra-equinoctials) except that twelve hundred years ago a ship driven by a tempest was wrecked on the island of Utopia. Some Romans and Egyptians were cast on shore and remained on the island without ever leaving it. Now mark what good advantage their industry took of this one opportunity. The Roman empire possessed no art capable of any use which they did not either learn from the shipwrecked strangers or discover for themselves after receiving the hints for investigation—so great a gain was it to them that on a single occasion some persons were carried to their shores from ours.

"But if any like fortune has ever driven anyone from their shores to ours, the event is as completely forgotten as future generations will perhaps forget that I had once been there. And, just as they immediately at one meeting appropriated to themselves every good discovery of ours, so I suppose it will be long before we adopt anything that is better arranged with them than with us. This trait, I judge, is the chief reason why, though we are inferior to them neither in brains nor in resources, their commonwealth is more wisely governed and more happily flourishing than ours."

"If so, my dear Raphael," said I, "I beg and beseech you, give us a description of the island. Do not be brief, but set forth in order the terrain, the rivers, the cities, the inhabitants, the traditions, the customs, the laws, and, in fact, everything which you think we should like to know. And you must think we wish to know everything of which we are still ignorant."

"There is nothing," he declared, "I shall be more pleased to do, for I have the facts ready to hand. But the description will take time."

"In that case," I suggested, "let us go in to dine. Afterwards we shall take up as much time as we like."

"Agreed," he replied.

So we went in and dined. We then returned to the same place, sat down on the same bench, and gave orders to the servants that we should not be interrupted. Peter Giles and I urged Raphael to fulfill his promise. As for him, when he saw us intent and eager to listen, after sitting in silent thought for a time, he began his tale as follows.

THE END OF BOOK ONE

BOOK 2

The island of the Utopians extends in the center (where it is broadest) for two hundred miles and is not much narrower for the greater part of the island, but toward both ends it begins gradually to taper. These ends form a circle five hundred miles in circumference and so make the island look like a new moon, the horns of which are divided by straits about eleven miles across. The straits then unfold into a wide expanse. As the winds are kept off by the land which everywhere surrounds it, the bay is like a huge lake, smooth rather than rough, and thus converts almost the whole center of the country into a harbor which lets ships cross in every direction to the great convenience of the inhabitants.

The mouth of this bay is rendered perilous here by shallows and there by reefs. Almost in the center of the gap stands one great crag which, being visible, is not dangerous. A tower built on it is occupied by a garrison. The other rocks are hidden and therefore treacherous. The channels are known only to the natives, and so it does not easily happen that any foreigner enters the bay except with a Utopian pilot. In fact, the entrance is hardly safe even for themselves, unless they guide themselves by landmarks on the shore. If these were removed to other positions, they could easily lure an enemy's fleet, however numerous, to destruction.

On the outer side of the island, harbors are many. Everywhere, however, the landing is so well defended by nature or by engineering that a few defenders can prevent strong forces from coming ashore.

As the report goes and as the appearance of the ground shows, the island once was not surrounded by sea. But Utopus,[6] who as conqueror gave the island its name (up to then it had been called Abraxa[7]) and who brought the rude and rustic people to such a perfection of culture and humanity as makes them now superior to almost all other mortals, gained a victory at his very first landing. He then ordered the excavation of fifteen miles on the side where the land was connected with the continent and caused the sea to flow around the land. He set to the task not only the natives but, to prevent them from thinking the labor a disgrace, his own soldiers also. With the work divided among so many hands, the enterprise was finished with incredible speed and struck the neighboring peoples, who at first had derided the project as vain, with wonder and terror at its success.

The island contains fifty-four city-states,[8] all spacious and magnificent, identical in language, traditions, customs, and laws. They are similar also in layout and everywhere, as far as the nature of the ground permits, similar even in appearance. None of them is separated by less than twenty-four miles from the nearest, but none is so isolated that a person cannot go from it to another in a day's journey on foot. From each

---

6. Ruler over no place.
7. The name for the highest of 365 heavens, according to the Gnostic philosopher Basilides.
8. When More wrote *Utopia*, England consisted of fifty-three counties and the City of London, its principal

urban center. This allusion to England establishes a connection between Books 1 and 2 and suggests that More intended aspects of Utopia to be understood in relation to life in England.

city three old and experienced citizens meet to discuss the affairs of common interest to the island once a year at Amaurotum, for this city, being in the very center of the country, is situated most conveniently for the representatives of all sections. It is considered the chief as well as the capital city.

The lands are so well assigned to the cities that each has at least twelve miles of country on every side, and on some sides even much more, to wit, the side on which the cities are farther apart. No city has any desire to extend its territory, for they consider themselves the tenants rather than the masters of what they hold.

Everywhere in the rural districts they have, at suitable distances from one another, farmhouses well equipped with agricultural implements. They are inhabited by citizens who come in succession to live there. No rural household numbers less than forty men and women, besides two serfs attached to the soil.[9] Over them are set a master and a mistress, serious in mind and ripe in years. Over every group of thirty households rules a phylarch.[1]

Twenty from each household return every year to the city, namely, those having completed two years in the country. As substitutes in their place, the same number are sent from the city. They are to be trained by those who have been there a year and who therefore are more expert in farming; they themselves will teach others in the following years. There is thus no danger of anything going wrong with the annual food supply through want of skill, as might happen if all at one time were newcomers and novices at farming. Though this system of changing farmers is the rule, to prevent any individual's being forced against his will to continue too long in a life of rather hard work, yet many men who take a natural pleasure in agricultural pursuits obtain leave to stay several years.

The occupation of the farmers is to cultivate the soil, to feed the animals, and to get wood and convey it to the city either by land or by water, whichever way is more convenient. They breed a vast quantity of poultry by a wonderful contrivance. The hens do not brood over the eggs, but the farmers, by keeping a great number of them at a uniform heat, bring them to life and hatch them. As soon as they come out of the shell, the chicks follow and acknowledge humans as their mothers!

They rear very few horses, and these only high-spirited ones, which they use for no other purpose than for exercising their young men in horsemanship. All the labor of cultivation and transportation is performed by oxen, which they admit are inferior to horses in a sudden spurt but which are far superior to them in staying power and endurance and not liable to as many diseases. Moreover, it requires less trouble and expense to feed them. When they are past work, they finally are of use for food.

They sow grain only for bread. Their drink is wine or cider or perry,[2] or it is even water. The latter is sometimes plain and often that in which they have boiled honey or licorice, whereof they have a great abundance.

Though they are more than sure how much food the city with its adjacent territory consumes, they produce far more grain and cattle than they require for their own use: they distribute the surplus among their neighbors. Whenever they need things

---

9. According to feudal practice in medieval Europe, a serf was a person who was in servitude for life and could not leave the land whose lord he served. Unlike most slaves, however, who were generally men or women taken captive in the course of a war and who could buy their freedom, a serf was never freed from his connection to an estate. Hythlodaeaus refers to other kinds of Utopian slaves later in his account of how Utopians organize their society.
1. Chief.
2. Pear liqueur.

not found in the country, they send for all the materials from the city and, having to give nothing in exchange, obtain it from the municipal officials without the bother of bargaining. For very many go there every single month to observe the holyday.

When the time of harvest is at hand, the agricultural phylarchs inform the municipal officials what number of citizens they require to be sent. The crowd of harvesters, coming promptly at the appointed time, dispatch the whole task of harvesting almost in a single day of fine weather.

THE CITIES, ESPECIALLY AMAUROTUM

The person who knows one of the cities will know them all, since they are exactly alike insofar as the terrain permits. I shall therefore picture one or other (nor does it matter which), but which should I describe rather than Amaurotum? First, none is worthier, the rest deferring to it as the meeting place of the national senate; and, secondly, none is better known to me, as being one in which I had lived for five whole years.

To proceed. Amaurotum is situated on the gentle slope of a hill and is almost four-square in outline. Its breadth is about two miles starting just below the crest of the hill and running down to the river Anydrus; its length along the river is somewhat more than its breadth.

The Anydrus rises eighty miles above Amaurotum from a spring not very large; but, being increased in size by several tributaries, two of which are of fair size, it is half a mile broad in front of the city. After soon becoming still broader and after running farther for sixty miles, it falls into the ocean. Through the whole distance between the city and the sea, and even above the city for some miles, the tide alternately flows in for six whole hours and then ebbs with an equally speedy current. When the sea comes in, it fills the whole bed of the Anydrus with its water for a distance of thirty miles, driving the river back. At such times it turns the water salt for some distance farther, but above that point the river grows gradually fresh and passes the city uncontaminated. When the ebb comes, the fresh and pure water extends down almost to the mouth of the river.[3]

The city is joined to the opposite bank of the river not by a bridge built on wooden pillars or piles but by one magnificently arched with stonework. It is situated in the quarter which is farthest from the sea so that ships may pass along the whole of that side of the city without hindrance.

They have also another river, not very large, but very gentle and pleasant, which rises out of the same hill whereon the city is built and runs down through its middle into the river Anydrus. The head and source of this river just outside the city has been connected with it by outworks, lest in case of hostile attack the water might be cut off and diverted or polluted. From this point the water is distributed by conduits made of baked clay into various parts of the lower town. Where the ground makes that course impossible, the rain water collected in capacious cisterns is just as useful.

The city is surrounded by a high and broad wall with towers and ravelins at frequent intervals. A moat, dry but deep and wide and made impassable by thorn hedges, surrounds the fortifications on three sides; on the fourth the river itself takes the place of the moat.

The streets are well laid out both for traffic and for protection against the winds. The buildings, which are far from mean, are set together in a long row, continuous through the block and faced by a corresponding one. The house fronts of the respec-

---

3. These features of the Anydrus resemble those of London's Thames River.

tive blocks are divided by an avenue twenty feet broad. On the rear of the houses, through the whole length of the block, lies a broad garden enclosed on all sides by the backs of the blocks. Every home has not only a door into the street but a back door into the garden. What is more, folding doors, easily opened by hand and then closing of themselves, give admission to anyone. As a result, nothing is private property anywhere. Every ten years they actually exchange their very homes by lot.

The Utopians are very fond of their gardens. In them they have vines, fruits, herbs, flowers, so well kept and flourishing that I never saw anything more fruitful and more tasteful anywhere. Their zest in keeping them is increased not merely by the pleasure afforded them but by the keen competition between blocks as to which will have the best kept garden. Certainly you cannot readily find anything in the whole city more productive of profit and pleasure to the citizens. Therefore it would seem their founder attached the greatest importance to these gardens.

In fact, they report that the whole plan of the city had been sketched at the very beginning by Utopus himself. He left to posterity, however, to add the adornment and other improvements for which he saw one lifetime would hardly suffice. Their annals, embracing the history of 1760 years, are preserved carefully and conscientiously in writing. Here they find stated that at first the houses were low, mere cabins and huts, haphazardly made with any wood to hand, with mud-plastered walls. They had thatched the ridged roofs with straw.

But now all the homes are of handsome appearance with three stories. The exposed faces of the walls are made of stone or cement or brick, rubble being used as filling for the empty space between the walls. The roofs are flat and covered with a kind of cement which is cheap but so well mixed that it is impervious to fire and superior to lead in defying the damage caused by storms. They keep the winds out of their windows by glass (which is in very common use in Utopia) or sometimes by thin linen smeared with translucent oil or amber. The advantage is twofold: the device results in letting more light in and keeping more wind out.

THE OFFICIALS

Every thirty families choose annually an official whom in their ancient language they call a syphogrant[4] but in their newer a phylarch. Over ten syphogrants with their families is set a person once called a tranibor but now a protophylarch.[5] The whole body of syphogrants, in number two hundred, having sworn to choose the man whom they judge most useful, by secret balloting appoint a governor, specifically one of the four candidates named to them by the people, for one is selected out of each of the four quarter of the city to be commended to the senate.

The governor holds office for life, unless ousted on suspicion of aiming at a tyranny. The tranibors are elected annually but are not changed without good reason. The other officials all hold their posts for one year.

The tranibors enter into consultation with the governor every other day and sometimes, if need arises, oftener. They take counsel about the commonwealth. If there are any disputes between private persons—there are very few—they settle them without loss of time. They always admit to the senate chamber two syphogrants, and different ones every day. It is provided that nothing concerning the commonwealth be ratified if it has not been discussed in the senate three days before the passing of the decree. To take counsel on matters of common interest outside the senate or the

4. Wise old man.   5. Tranibor: glutton; protophylarch: principal chief.

popular assembly is considered a capital offense. The object of these measures, they say, is to prevent it from being easy, by a conspiracy between the governor and the tranibors and by tyrannous oppression of the people, to change the order of the commonwealth. Therefore whatever is considered important is laid before the assembly of the syphogrants who, after informing their groups of families, take counsel together and report their decision to the senate. Sometimes the matter is laid before the council of the whole island.

In addition, the senate has the custom of debating nothing on the same day on which it is first proposed but of putting it off till the next meeting. This is their rule lest anyone, after hastily blurting out the first thought that popped into his head, should afterwards give more thought to defending his opinion than to supporting what is for the good of the commonwealth, and should prefer to jeopardize the public welfare rather than to risk his reputation through a wrongheaded and misplaced shame, fearing he might be thought to have shown too little foresight at the first—though he should have been enough foresighted at the first to speak with prudence rather than with haste!

OCCUPATIONS

Agriculture is the one pursuit which is common to all, both men and women, without exception. They are all instructed in it from childhood, partly by principles taught in school, partly by field trips to the farms closer to the city as if for recreation. Here they do not merely look on, but, as opportunity arises for bodily exercise, they do the actual work.

Besides agriculture (which is, as I said, common to all), each is taught one particular craft as his own. This is generally either wool-working or linen-making or masonry or metal-working or carpentry. There is no other pursuit which occupies any number worth mentioning. As for clothes, these are of one and the same pattern throughout the island and down the centuries, though there is a distinction between the sexes and between the single and married. The garments are comely to the eye, convenient for bodily movement, and fit for wear in heat and cold. Each family, I say, does its own tailoring.

Of the other crafts, one is learned by each person, and not the men only, but the women too. The latter as the weaker sex have the lighter occupations and generally work wool and flax. To the men are committed the remaining more laborious crafts. For the most part, each is brought up in his father's craft, for which most have a natural inclination. But if anyone is attracted to another occupation, he is transferred by adoption to a family pursuing that craft for which he has a liking. Care is taken not only by his father but by the authorities, too, that he will be assigned to a grave and honorable householder. Moreover, if anyone after being thoroughly taught one craft desires another also, the same permission is given. Having acquired both, he practices his choice unless the city has more need of the one than of the other.

The chief and almost the only function of the syphogrants is to manage and provide that no one sit idle, but that each apply himself industriously to his trade, and yet that he be not wearied like a beast of burden with constant toil from early morning till late at night. Such wretchedness is worse than the lot of slaves, and yet it is almost everywhere the life of workingmen—except for the Utopians. The latter divide the day and night into twenty-four equal hours and assign only six to work. There are three before noon, after which they go to dinner. After dinner, when they have rested for two hours in the afternoon, they again give three to work and finish up with supper. Counting one o'clock as the first hour after noon, they go to bed about eight o'clock, and sleep claims eight hours.

The intervals between the hours of work, sleep, and food are left to every man's discretion, not to waste in revelry or idleness, but to devote the time free from work to some other occupation according to taste. These periods are commonly devoted to intellectual pursuits. For it is their custom that public lectures are daily delivered in the hours before daybreak. Attendance is compulsory only for those who have been specially chosen to devote themselves to learning. A great number of all classes, however, both males and females, flock to hear the lectures, some to one and some to another, according to their natural inclination. But if anyone should prefer to devote this time to his trade, as is the case with many minds which do not reach the level for any of the higher intellectual disciplines, he is not hindered; in fact, he is even praised as useful to the commonwealth.

After supper they spend one hour in recreation, in summer in the gardens, in winter in the common halls in which they have their meals. There they either play music or entertain themselves with conversation. Dice and that kind of foolish and ruinous game they are not acquainted with. They do play two games not unlike chess. The first is a battle of numbers in which one number plunders another. The second is a game in which the vices fight a pitched battle with the virtues. In the latter is exhibited very cleverly, to begin with, both the strife of the vices with one another and their concerted opposition to the virtues; then, what vices are opposed to what virtues, by what forces they assail them openly, by what stratagems they attack them indirectly, by what safeguards the virtues check the power of the vices, by what arts they frustrate their designs; and, finally, by what means the one side gains the victory.

But here, lest you be mistaken, there is one point you must examine more closely. Since they devote but six hours to work, you might possibly think the consequence to be some scarcity of necessities. But so far is this from being the case that the aforesaid time is not only enough but more than enough for a supply of all that is requisite for either the necessity or the convenience of living. This phenomenon you too will understand if you consider how large a part of the population in other countries exists without working. First, there are almost all the women, who constitute half the whole; or, where the women are busy, there as a rule the men are snoring in their stead. Besides, how great and how lazy is the crowd of priests and so-called religious! Add to them all the rich, especially the masters of estates, who are commonly termed gentlemen and noblemen. Reckon with them their retainers—I mean, that whole rabble of good-for-nothing swashbucklers. Finally, join in the lusty and sturdy beggars who make some disease an excuse for idleness. You will certainly find far less numerous than you had supposed those whose labor produces all the articles that mortals require for daily use.

Now estimate how few of those who do work are occupied in essential trades. For, in a society where we make money the standard of everything, it is necessary to practice many crafts which are quite vain and superfluous, ministering only to luxury and licentiousness. Suppose the host of those who now toil were distributed over only as few crafts as natural needs and conveniences require. In the great abundance of commodities which must then arise, the prices set on them would be too low for the craftsmen to earn their livelihood by their work. But suppose all those fellows who are now busied with unprofitable crafts, as well as all the lazy and idle throng, any one of whom now consumes as much of the fruits of other men's labors as any two of the workingmen, were all set to work and indeed to useful work. You can easily see how small an allowance of time would be enough and to spare for the production of all that is required by necessity or comfort (or even pleasure, provided it be genuine and natural).

The very experience of Utopia makes the latter clear. In the whole city and its neighborhood, exemption from work is granted to hardly five hundred of the total of men and women whose age and strength make them fit for work. Among them the syphogrants, though legally exempted from work, yet take no advantage of this privilege so that by their example they may the more readily attract the others to work. The same exemption is enjoyed by those whom the people, persuaded by the recommendation of the priests, have given perpetual freedom from labor through the secret vote of the syphogrants so that they may learn thoroughly the various branches of knowledge. But if any of these scholars falsifies the hopes entertained of him, he is reduced to the rank of workingman. On the other hand, not seldom does it happen that a craftsman so industriously employs his spare hours on learning and makes such progress by his diligence that he is relieved of his manual labor and advanced into the class of men of learning. It is out of this company of scholars that they choose ambassadors, priests, tranibors, and finally the governor himself, whom they call in their ancient tongue Barzanes but in their more modern language Ademus.[6]

Nearly all the remaining populace being neither idle nor busied with useless occupations, it is easy to calculate how much good work can be produced in a very few hours. Besides the points mentioned, there is this further convenience that in most of the necessary crafts they do not require as much work as other nations. In the first place the erection or repair of buildings requires the constant labor of so many men elsewhere because what a father has built, his extravagant heir allows gradually to fall into ruin. As a result, what might have been kept up at small cost, his successor is obliged to erect anew at great expense. Further, often even when a house has cost one man a large sum, another is so fastidious that he thinks little of it. When it is neglected and therefore soon becomes dilapidated, he builds a second elsewhere at no less cost. But in the land of the Utopians, now that everything has been settled and the commonwealth established, a new home on a new site is a rare event, for not only do they promptly repair any damage, but they even take care to prevent damage. What is the result? With the minimum of labor, buildings last very long, and masons and carpenters sometimes have scarcely anything to do, except that they are set to hew out timber at home and to square and prepare stone meantime so that, if any work be required, a building may the sooner be erected.

In the matter of clothing, too, see how little toil and labor is needed. First, while at work, they are dressed unpretentiously in leather or hide, which lasts for seven years. When they go out in public, they put on a cape to hide their comparatively rough working clothes. This garment is of one color throughout the island and that the natural color. Consequently not only is much less woolen cloth needed than elsewhere, but what they have is much less expensive. On the other hand, since linen cloth is made with less labor, it is more used. In linen cloth only whiteness, in woolen cloth only cleanliness, is considered. No value is set on fineness of thread. So it comes about that, whereas elsewhere one man is not satisfied with four or five woolen coats of different colors and as many silk shirts, and the more fastidious not even with ten, in Utopia a man is content with a single cape, lasting generally for two years. There is no reason, of course, why he should desire more, for if he had them he would not be better fortified against the cold nor appear better dressed in the least.

---

6. Barzanes: "son of Zeus"; Ademus, "peopleless." These names indicate that the governor of Utopia, although considered a divinity in the primitive period of the state, is so impartial in his efforts to rule that he seems to belong to no family, region, or people.

Wherefore, seeing that they are all busied with useful trades and are satisfied with fewer products from them, it even happens that when there is an abundance of all commodities, they sometimes take out a countless number of people to repair whatever public roads are in bad order. Often, too, when there is nothing even of this kind of work to be done, they announce publicly that there will be fewer hours of work. For the authorities do not keep the citizens against their will at superfluous labor since the constitution of their commonwealth looks in the first place to this sole object: that for all the citizens, as far as the public needs permit, as much time as possible should be withdrawn from the service of the body and devoted to the freedom and culture of the mind. It is in the latter that they deem the happiness of life to consist.

Social Relations

But now, it seems, I must explain the behavior of the citizens toward one another, the nature of their social relations, and the method of distribution of goods. Since the city consists of households, households as a rule are made up of those related by blood. Girls, upon reaching womanhood and upon being settled in marriage, go to their husbands' domiciles. On the other hand, male children and then grandchildren remain in the family and are subject to the oldest parent, unless he has become a dotard with old age. In the latter case the next oldest is put in his place.

But that the city neither be depopulated nor grow beyond measure, provision is made that no household shall have fewer than ten or more than sixteen adults; there are six thousand such households in each city, apart from its surrounding territory. Of children under age, of course, no number can be fixed.[7] This limit is easily observed by transferring those who exceed the number in larger families into those that are under the prescribed number. Whenever all the families of a city reach their full quota, the extra persons help to make up the deficient population of other cities.

And if the population throughout the island should happen to swell above the fixed quotas, they enroll citizens out of every city and, on the mainland nearest them, wherever the natives have much unoccupied and uncultivated land, they found a colony under their own laws. They join with themselves the natives if they are willing to dwell with them. When such a union takes place, the two parties gradually and easily merge and together absorb the same way of life and the same customs, much to the great advantage of both peoples. By their procedures they make the land sufficient for both, which previously seemed poor and barren to the natives. The inhabitants who refuse to live according to their laws, they drive from the territory which they carve out for themselves. If they resist, they wage war against them. They consider it a most just cause for war when a people which does not use its soil but keeps it idle and waste nevertheless forbids the use and possession of it to others who by the rule of nature ought to be maintained by it.

If ever any misfortune so diminishes the number in any of their cities that it cannot be made up out of other parts of the island without bringing other cities below their proper strength (this has happened, they say, only twice in all the ages on account of the raging of a fierce pestilence), they are filled up by citizens returning from colonial territory. They would rather that the colonies should perish than that any of the cities of the island should be enfeebled.

---

7. In England, women came of age at 18, men at 22.

But to return to the dealings of the citizens. The oldest, as I have said, rules the household. Wives wait on their husbands, children on their parents, and generally the younger on their elders.

Every city is divided into four equal districts. In the middle of each quarter is a market of all kinds of commodities. To designated market buildings the products of each family are conveyed. Each kind of goods is arranged separately in storehouses. From the latter any head of a household seeks what he and his require and, without money or any kind of compensation, carries off what he seeks. Why should anything be refused? First, there is a plentiful supply of all things and, secondly, there is no underlying fear that anyone will demand more than he needs. Why should there be any suspicion that someone may demand an excessive amount when he is certain of never being in want? No doubt about it, avarice and greed are aroused in every kind of living creature by the fear of want, but only in man are they motivated by pride alone—pride which counts it a personal glory to excel others by superfluous display of possessions. The latter vice can have no place at all in the Utopian scheme of things.

Next to the market place that I have mentioned are the food markets. Here are brought not only different kinds of vegetables, fruit, and bread but also fish and whatever is edible of bird and four-footed beast. Outside the city are designated places where all gore and offal may be washed away in running water. From these places they transport the carcasses of the animals slaughtered and cleaned by the hands of slaves. They do not allow their citizens to accustom themselves to the butchering of animals, by the practice of which they think that mercy, the finest feeling of our human nature, is gradually killed off. In addition, they do not permit to be brought inside the city anything filthy or unclean for fear that the air, tainted by putrefaction, should engender disease.

To continue, each street has spacious halls, located at equal distance from one another, each being known by a special name of its own. In these halls live the syphogrants. To each hall are assigned thirty families, fifteen on either side, to take their meals in common. The managers of each hall meet at a fixed time in the market and get food according to the number of person in their individual charge.

Special care is first taken of the sick who are looked after in public hospitals. They have four at the city limits, a little outside the walls. These are so roomy as to be comparable to as many small towns. The purpose is twofold: first, that the sick, however numerous, should not be packed too close together in consequent discomfort and, second, that those who have a contagious disease likely to pass from one to another may be isolated as much as possible from the rest.[8] These hospitals are very well furnished and equipped with everything conducive to health. Besides, such tender and careful treatment and such constant attendance of expert physicians are provided that, though no one is sent to them against his will, there is hardly anybody in the whole city who, when suffering from illness, does not prefer to be nursed there rather than at home.

After the supervisor for the sick has received food as prescribed by the physicians, then the finest of everything is distributed equally among the halls according to the number in each, except that special regard is paid to the governor, the high

8. The germ theory of disease dates from the 19th century and the work of Louis Pasteur. Here More seems to be basing his idea of contagion on the experience of the bubonic plague, or Black Death, a major 14th-century European epidemic that killed roughly three-quarters of the population in 20 years.

priest, and the tranibors, as well as to ambassadors and all foreigners (if there are any, but they are few and far between). Yet the latter, too, when they are in Utopia, have definite homes got ready for them.

To these halls, at the hours fixed for dinner and supper, the entire syphograncy assembles, summoned by the blast of a brazen trumpet, excepting persons who are taking their meals either in the hospitals or at home. No one is forbidden, after the halls have been served, to fetch food from the market to his home: they realize that no one would do it without good reason. For, though nobody is forbidden to dine at home, yet no one does it willingly since the practice is considered not decent and since it is foolish to take the trouble of preparing an inferior dinner when an excellent and sumptuous one is ready at hand in the hall nearby.

In this hall all menial offices which to some degree involve heavy labor or soil the hands are performed by slaves. But the duty of cooking and preparing the food and, in fine, of arranging the whole meal is carried out by the women alone, taking turns for each family. Persons sit down at three or more tables according to the number of the company. The men sit with their backs to the wall, the women on the outside, so that if they have any sudden pain or sickness, such as sometimes happens to women with child, they may rise without disturbing the arrangements and go to the nurses.

The nurses sit separately with the infants in a dining room assigned for the purpose, never without a fire and a supply of clean water nor without cradles. Thus they can both lay the infants down and, when they wish, undo their wrappings and let them play freely by the fire. Each woman nurses her own offspring, unless prevented by either death or disease. When that happens, the wives of the syphogrants quickly provide a nurse and find no difficulty in doing so. The reason is that women who can do the service offer themselves with the greatest readiness since everybody praises this kind of pity and since the child who is thus fostered looks on his nurse as his natural mother. In the nurses' quarters are all children up to five years of age. All other minors, among whom they include all of both sexes below the age of marriage, either wait at table on the diners or, if they are not old and strong enough, stand by—and that in absolute silence. Both groups eat what is handed them from the table and have no other separate time for dining.

The syphogrant and his wife sit in the middle of the first table, which is the highest place and which allows them to have the whole company in view, for it stands crosswise at the farthest end of the dining room. Alongside them are two of the eldest, for they always sit four by four at all tables. But if there is a temple in the syphograncy, the priest and his wife so sit with the syphogrant as to preside. On both sides of them sit younger people, and next to them old people again, and so through the house those of the same age sit together and yet mingle with those of a different age. The reason for this practice, they say, is that the grave and reverend behavior of the old may restrain the younger people from mischievous freedom in word and gesture, since nothing can be done or said at table which escapes the notice of the old present on every side.

The trays of food are not served in order from the first place and so on, but all the old men, who are seated in conspicuous places, are served first with the best food, and then equal portions are given to the rest. The old men at their discretion give a share of their delicacies to their neighbors when there is not enough to go around to everybody in the house. Thus, due respect is paid to seniority, and yet all have an equal advantage.

They begin every dinner and supper with some reading which is conducive to morality but which is brief so as not to be tiresome. Taking their cue from the reading, the elders introduce approved subjects of conversation, neither somber nor dull. But they do not monopolize the whole dinner with long speeches: they are ready to hear the young men too, and indeed deliberately draw them out that they may test each one's ability and character, which are revealed in the relaxed atmosphere of a feast.

Their dinners are somewhat short, their suppers more prolonged, because the former are followed by labor, the latter by sleep and a night's rest. They think the night's rest to be more efficacious to wholesome digestion. No supper passes without music, nor does the dessert course lack delicacies. They burn spices and scatter perfumes and omit nothing that may cheer the company. For they are somewhat more inclined to this attitude of mind: that no kind of pleasure is forbidden, provided no harm comes of it.

This is the common life they live in the city. In the country, however, since they are rather far removed from their neighbors, all take their meals in their own homes. No family lacks any kind of edible inasmuch as all the food eaten by the city dwellers comes from those who live in the country.

UTOPIAN TRAVEL, [ETC.]

Now if any citizens conceive a desire either to visit their friends who reside in another city or to see the place itself, they easily obtain leave from their syphogrants and tranibors, unless some good reason prevents them. Accordingly a party is made up and dispatched carrying a letter from the governor which bears witness to the granting of leave to travel and fixes the day of their return. A wagon is granted them with a public slave to conduct and see to the oxen, but, unless they have women in their company, they dispense with the wagon, regarding it as a burden and hindrance. Throughout their journey, though they carry nothing with them, yet nothing is lacking, for they are at home everywhere. If they stay longer than a day in any place, each practices his trade there and is entertained very courteously by workers in the same trade.

If any person gives himself leave to stray out of his territorial limits and is caught without the governor's certificate, he is treated with contempt, brought back as a runaway, and severely punished. If he dares to repeat the offense, he is punished with slavery.

If anyone is seized with the desire of exploring the country belonging to his own city, he is not forbidden to do so, provided he obtain his father's leave and his wife's consent. In any district of the country to which he comes, he receives no food until he has finished the morning share of the day's work or the labor that is usually performed there before supper. If he keep to this condition, he may go where he pleases within the territory belonging to his city. In this way he will be just as useful to the city as if he were in it.

Now you can see how nowhere is there any license to waste time, nowhere any pretext to evade work—no wine shop, no alehouse, no brothel anywhere, no opportunity for corruption, no lurking hole, no secret meeting place. On the contrary, being under the eyes of all, people are bound either to be performing the usual labor or to be enjoying their leisure in a fashion not without decency. This universal behavior must of necessity lead to an abundance of all commodities. Since the latter are distributed evenly among all, it follows, of course, that no one can be reduced to poverty or beggary.

In the senate at Amaurotum (to which, as I said before, three are sent annually from every city), they first determine what commodity is in plenty in each particular place and again where on the island the crops have been meager. They at once fill up the scarcity of one place by the surplus of another. This service they perform without payment, receiving nothing in return from those to whom they give. Those who have given out of their stock to any particular city without requiring any return from it receive what they lack from another to which they have given nothing. Thus, the whole island is like a single family.

But when they have made sufficient provision for themselves (which they do not consider complete until they have provided for two years to come, on account of the next year's uncertain crop), then they export into other countries, out of their surplus, a great quantity of grain, honey, wool, linen, timber, scarlet and purple dyestuffs, hides, wax, tallow, leather, as well as livestock. Of all these commodities they bestow the seventh part on the poor of the district and sell the rest at a moderate price.

By this trade they bring into their country not only such articles as they lack themselves—and practically the only thing lacking is iron—but also a great quantity of silver and gold. This exchange has gone on day by day so long that now they have everywhere an abundance of these metals, more than would be believed. In consequence, they now care little whether they sell for ready cash or appoint a future day for payment, and in fact have by far the greatest amount out on credit. In all transactions on credit, however, they never trust private citizens but the municipal government, the legal documents being drawn up as usual. When the day for payment comes, the city collects the money due from private debtors and puts it into the treasury and enjoys the use of it until the Utopians claim payment.

The Utopians never claim payment of most of the money. They think it hardly fair to take away a thing useful to other people when it is useless to themselves. But if circumstances require that they should lend some part of it to another nation, then they call in their debts—or when they must wage war. It is for that single purpose that they keep all the treasure they possess at home: to be their bulwark in extreme peril or in sudden emergency. They use it above all to hire at sky-high rates of pay foreign mercenaries (whom they would jeopardize rather than their own citizens), being well aware that by large sums of money even their enemies themselves may be bought and set to fight one another either by treachery or by open warfare.

For these military reasons they keep a vast treasure, but not as a treasure. They keep it in a way which I am really quite ashamed to reveal for fear that my words will not be believed. My fears are all the more justified because I am conscious that, had I not been there and witnessed the phenomenon, I myself should have been with difficulty induced to believe it from another's account. It needs must be almost always the rule that, as far as a thing is unlike the ways of the hearers, so far is it from obtaining their credence. An impartial judge of things, however, seeing that the rest of their institutions are so unlike ours, will perhaps wonder less that their use of silver and gold should be adapted to their way of life rather than to ours. As stated, they do not use money themselves but keep it only for an emergency, which may actually occur, yet possibly may never happen.

Meanwhile, gold and silver, of which money is made, are so treated by them that no one values them more highly than their true nature deserves. Who does not see that they are far inferior to iron in usefulness since without iron mortals cannot live any more than without fire and water? To gold and silver, however, nature has given no use that we cannot dispense with, if the folly of men had not made them valuable because they are rare. On the other hand, like a most kind and indulgent mother, she has exposed to view all that is best, like air and water and earth itself, but has removed as far as possible from us all vain and unprofitable things.

If in Utopia these metals were kept locked up in a tower, it might be suspected that the governor and the senate—for such is the foolish imagination of the common folk—were deceiving the people by the scheme and they themselves were deriving some benefit therefrom. Moreover, if they made them into drinking vessels and other such skillful handiwork, then if occasion arose for them all to be melted down again and applied to the pay of soldiers, they realize that people would be unwilling to be deprived of what they had once begun to treasure.

To avoid these dangers, they have devised a means which, as it is consonant with the rest of their institutions, so it is extremely unlike our own—seeing that we value gold so much and are so careful in safeguarding it—and therefore incredible except to those who have experience of it. While they eat and drink from earthenware and glassware of fine workmanship but of little value, from gold and silver they make chamber pots and all the humblest vessels for use everywhere, not only in the common halls but in private homes also. Moreover, they employ the same metals to make the chains and solid fetters which they put on their slaves. Finally, as for those who bear the stigma of disgrace on account of some crime, they have gold ornaments hanging from their ears, gold rings encircling their fingers, gold chains thrown around their necks, and, as a last touch, a gold crown binding their temples. Thus by every means in their power they make gold and silver a mark of ill fame. In this way, too, it happens that, while all other nations bear the loss of these metals with as great grief as if they were losing their very vitals, if circumstances in Utopia ever required the removal of all gold and silver, no one would feel that he were losing as much as a penny.[9]

They also gather pearls by the seashore and diamonds and rubies on certain cliffs. They do not look for them purposely, but they polish them when found by chance. With them they adorn little children, who in their earliest years are proud and delighted with such decorations. When they have grown somewhat older and perceive that only children use such toys, they lay them aside, not by any order of their parents, but through their own feeling of shame, just as our own children, when they grow up, throw away their marbles, rattles, and dolls.

What opposite ideas and feelings are created by customs so different from those of other people came home to me never more clearly than in the case of the Anemolian ambassadors. They arrived in Amaurotum during my stay there. Because they came to treat of important matters, the three representatives of each city had assembled before their appearance. Now all the ambassadors of neighboring nations, who had previously visited the land, were well acquainted with the manners of the Utopians and knew that they paid no respect to costly clothes but looked with contempt on silk and regarded gold as a badge of disgrace. These persons usually came in the simplest possible dress. But the Anemolians, living farther off and having had fewer dealings with them, since they heard that in Utopia all were dressed alike, and in a homespun fashion at that, felt sure that they did not possess what they made no use of. Being more proud than wise, they determined by the grandeur of their apparel to represent the gods themselves and by their splendid adornment to dazzle the eyes of the poor Utopians.

---

9. Hythlodaeus distinguishes first between the use value and the exchange value of an object: Gold, a soft metal, is useless except as decoration; but as a scarce commodity, it can be exchanged for other objects that do have a use value. He then places a moral construction on precious (or scarce) metals because they are used to indicate wealth and promote ostentation.

Consequently the three ambassadors made a grand entry with a suite of a hundred followers, all in parti-colored clothes and most in silk. The ambassadors themselves, being noblemen at home, were arrayed in cloth of gold, with heavy gold necklaces and earrings, with gold rings on their fingers, and with strings of gleaming pearls and gems upon their caps; in fact, they were decked out with all those articles which in Utopia are used to punish slaves, to stigmatize evil-doers, or to amuse children. It was a sight worth seeing to behold their cockiness when they compared their grand clothing with that of the Utopians, who had poured out into the street to see them pass. On the other hand, it was no less delightful to notice how much they were mistaken in their sanguine[1] expectations and how far they were from obtaining the consideration which they had hoped to get. To the eyes of all the Utopians, with the exception of the very few who for a good reason had visited foreign countries, all this gay show appeared disgraceful. They therefore bowed to the lowest of the party as to the masters but took the ambassadors themselves to be slaves because they were wearing gold chains, and passed them over without any deference whatever.

Why, you might have seen also the children who had themselves discarded gems and pearls, when they saw them attached to the caps of the ambassadors, poke and nudge their mothers and say to them:

"Look, mother, that big rascal is still wearing pearls and jewels as if he were yet a little boy!"

But the mother, also in earnest, would say:

"Hush, son, I think it is one of the ambassadors' fools."

Others found fault with the golden chains as useless, being so slender that a slave could easily break them or, again, so loose that at his pleasure he could throw them off and escape anywhere scot-free.

After spending one or more days there, the ambassadors saw an immense quantity of gold held as cheaply and in as great contempt there as in honor among themselves. They saw, too, that more gold and silver were amassed to make the chains and fetters of one runaway slave than had made up the whole array of the three of them. They then were crestfallen and for shame put away all the finery with which they had made themselves haughtily conspicuous, especially when, after familiar talk with the Utopians, they had learned their ways and opinions.

The Utopians wonder that any mortal takes pleasure in the uncertain sparkle of a tiny jewel or precious stone when he can look at a star or even the sun itself. They wonder that anyone can be so mad as to think himself more noble on account of the texture of a finer wool, since, however fine the texture is, a sheep once wore the wool and yet all the time was nothing more than a sheep.

They wonder, too, that gold, which by its very nature is so useless, is now everywhere in the world valued so highly that man himself, through whose agency and for whose use it got this value, is priced much cheaper than gold itself. This is true to such an extent that a blockhead who has no more intelligence than a log and who is as dishonest as he is foolish keeps in bondage many wise men and good men merely for the reason that a great heap of gold coins happens to be his. Yet if some chance or some legal trick (which is as apt as chance to confound high and low) transfers it from this master to the lowest rascal in his entire household, he will surely very soon pass into the service of his former servant—as if he were a mere appendage of and

1. Optimistic.

addition to the coins! But much more do they wonder at and abominate the madness of persons who pay almost divine honors to the rich, to whom they neither owe anything nor are obligated in any other respect than that they are rich. Yet they know them to be so mean and miserly that they are more than sure that of all that great pile of cash, as long as the rich men live, not a single penny will ever come their way.

These and similar opinions they have conceived partly from their upbringing, being reared in a commonwealth whose institutions are far removed from follies of the kind mentioned, and partly from instruction and reading good books. Though there are not many in each city who are relieved from all other tasks and assigned to scholarship alone, that is to say, the individuals in whom they have detected from childhood an outstanding personality, a first-rate intelligence, and an inclination of mind toward learning, yet all children are introduced to good literature. A large part of the people, too, men and women alike, throughout their lives, devote to learning the hours which, as we said, are free from manual labor.

They learn the various branches of knowledge in their native tongue. The latter is copious in vocabulary and pleasant to the ear and a very faithful exponent of thought. It is almost the same as that current in a great part of that side of the world, only that everywhere else its form is more corrupt, to different degrees in different regions.

Of all those philosophers whose names are famous in the part of the world known to us, the reputation of not even a single one had reached them before our arrival. Yet in music, dialectic, arithmetic, and geometry they have made almost the same discoveries as those predecessors of ours in the classical world. But while they measure up to the ancients in almost all other subjects, still they are far from being a match for the inventions of our modern logicians. In fact, they have discovered not even a single one of those very ingeniously devised rules about restrictions, amplifications, and suppositions which our own children everywhere learn in the *Small Logicals*. In addition, so far are they from ability to speculate on second intentions that not one of them could see even man himself as a so-called universal—though he was, as you know, colossal and greater than any giant, as well as pointed out by us with our finger.[2]

They are most expert, however, in the courses of the stars and the movements of the celestial bodies. Moreover, they have ingeniously devised instruments in different shapes, by which they have most exactly comprehended the movements and positions of the sun and moon and all the other stars which are visible in their horizon. But of the agreements and discords of the planets and, in sum, of all that infamous and deceitful divination by the stars, they do not even dream.

They forecast rains, winds, and all the other changes in weather by definite signs which they have ascertained by long practice. But as to the causes of all these phenomena, and of the flow of the sea and its saltiness, and, in fine, of the origin and nature of the heavens and the universe, they partly treat of them in the same way as our ancient philosophers and partly, as the latter differ from one another, they, too, in introducing new theories disagree with them all and yet do not in all respects agree with fellow Utopians.

In that part of philosophy which deals with morals, they carry on the same debates as we do. They inquire into the good: of the soul and of the body and of external gifts. They ask also whether the name of good may be applied to all three or

---

2. In logic a first intention is the conception gained from the apprehension of an object as a whole; a second intention is the abstracted conception gained by generalizing upon a first intention and as such exists only in the mind. The Utopians cannot conceive of second intentions because they are themselves second intentions; they are the product of More's reflection upon the particular European governments he has studied.

simply belongs to the endowments of the soul. They discuss virtue and pleasure, but their principal and chief debate is in what thing or things, one or more, they are to hold that happiness consists. In this matter they seem to lean more than they should to the school that espouses pleasure as the object by which to define either the whole or the chief part of human happiness.

What is more astonishing is that they seek a defense for this soft doctrine from their religion, which is serious and strict, almost solemn and hard. They never have a discussion of happiness without uniting certain principles taken from religion as well as from philosophy, which uses rational arguments. Without these principles they think reason insufficient and weak by itself for the investigation of true happiness. The following are examples of these principles. The soul is immortal and by the goodness of God born for happiness. After this life rewards are appointed for our virtues and good deeds, punishment for our crimes. Though these principles belong to religion, yet they hold that reason leads men to believe and to admit them.[3]

Once the principles are eliminated, the Utopians have no hesitation in maintaining that a person would be stupid not to realize that he ought to seek pleasure by fair means or foul, but that he should only take care not to let a lesser pleasure interfere with a greater nor to follow after a pleasure which would bring pain in retaliation. To pursue hard and painful virtue and not only to banish the sweetness of life but even voluntarily to suffer pain from which you expect no profit (for what profit can there be if after death you gain nothing for having passed the whole present life unpleasantly, that is, wretchedly?)—this policy they declare to be the extreme of madness.

As it is, they hold happiness rests not in every kind of pleasure but only in good and decent pleasure. To such, as to the supreme good, our nature is drawn by virtue itself, to which the opposite school alone attributes happiness. The Utopians define virtue as living according to nature since to this end we were created by God. That individual, they say, is following the guidance of nature who, in desiring one thing and avoiding another, obeys the dictates of reason.[4]

Now reason first of all inflames men to a love and veneration of the divine majesty, to whom we owe both our existence and our capacity for happiness. Secondly, it admonishes and urges us to lead a life as free from care and as full of joy as possible and, because of our natural fellowship, to help all other men, too, to attain that end. No one was ever so solemn and severe a follower of virtue and hater of pleasure that he, while imposing on you labors, watchings, and discomforts, would not at the same time bid you do your best to relieve the poverty and misfortunes of others. He would bid you regard as praiseworthy in humanity's name that one man should provide for another man's welfare and comfort—if it is especially humane (and humanity is the virtue most peculiar to man) to relieve the misery of others and, by taking away all sadness from their life, restore them to enjoyment, that is, to pleasure. If so, why should not nature urge everyone to do the same for himself also?

---

3. By believing in the immortality of the soul, an afterlife of rewards or punishments, and the goodness of God, the Utopians show that they are aware of "natural law," held to be apprehensible by reason.

4. The Utopians represent a people for whom religion is manifest in nature, as it was for the Greeks and the Romans, rather than revealed by God, as it was for the ancient Israelites and, after them, the disciples of Christ.

The Utopian is typically reasonable, follows the dictates of reason, and is guided by a beneficent nature that has not been revealed as fallen from an Edenic state of purity and excellence. Hence in Utopia there is no harm in seeking and enjoying pleasure. Nothing in this conception of human nature admits that humankind is inherently corrupted by original sin, a point of doctrine for Christians.

For either a joyous life, that is, a pleasurable life, is evil, in which case not only ought you to help no one to it but, as far as you can, should take it away from everyone as being harmful and deadly, or else, if you not only are permitted but are obliged to win it for others as being good, why should you not do so first of all for yourself, to whom you should show no less favor than to others? When nature bids you to be good to others, she does not command you conversely to be cruel and merciless to yourself. So nature herself, they maintain, prescribes to us a joyous life or, in other words, pleasure, as the end of all our operations. Living according to her prescription they define as virtue.

To pursue this line. Nature calls all men to help one another to a merrier life. (This she certainly does with good reason, for no one is raised so far above the common lot of mankind as to have his sole person the object of nature's care, seeing that she equally favors all whom she endows with the same form.) Consequently nature surely bids you take constant care not so to further your own advantages as to cause disadvantages to your fellows.[5]

Therefore they hold that not only ought contracts between private persons to be observed but also public laws for the distribution of vital commodities, that is to say, the matter of pleasure, provided they have been justly promulgated by a good king or ratified by the common consent of a people neither oppressed by tyranny nor deceived by fraud. As long as such laws are not broken, it is prudence to look after your own interests, and to look after those of the public in addition is a mark of devotion. But to deprive others of their pleasure to secure your own, this is surely an injustice. On the contrary, to take away something from yourself and to give it to others is a duty of humanity and kindness which never takes away as much advantage as it brings back. It is compensated by the return of benefits as well as by the actual consciousness of the good deed. Remembrance of the love and good will of those whom you have benefited gives the mind a greater amount of pleasure than the bodily pleasure which you have forgone would have afforded. Finally—and religion easily brings this home to a mind which readily assents—God repays, in place of a brief and tiny pleasure, immense and never-ending gladness. And so they maintain, having carefully considered and weighed the matter, that all our actions, and even the very virtues exercised in them, look at last to pleasure as their end and happiness.

By pleasure they understand every movement and state of body or mind in which, under the guidance of nature, man delights to dwell. They are right in including man's natural inclinations. For just as the senses as well as right reason aim at whatever is pleasant by nature—whatever is not striven after through wrong-doing, nor involves the loss of something more pleasant, nor is followed by pain—so they hold that whatever things mortals imagine by a futile consensus to be sweet to them in spite of being against nature (as though they had the power to change the nature of things as they do their names) are all so far from making for happiness that they are even a great hindrance to it. The reason is that they possess the minds of persons in whom they have once become deep-seated with a false idea of pleasure so that no room is left anywhere for true and genuine delights. In fact, very many are the things which, though of their own nature they contain no sweetness, nay, a good part of

---

5. Hythlodaeus describes the classical notion of a benefit, an action that furthers the welfare of a community of persons rather than that of a particular person. The logic of a benefit dictates that an individual can act to confer an advantage not only to himself but also to the community of which he is a part; correspondingly, an action that is to the disadvantage of another individual or his community may not be beneficial to him, however profitable it may seem in the short run.

them very much bitterness, still are, through the perverse attraction of evil desires, not only regarded as the highest pleasures but also counted among the chief reasons that make life worth living.

In the class that follow this spurious pleasure, they put those whom I mentioned before, who think themselves the better men, the better the coat they wear. In this one thing they make a twofold mistake: they are no less deceived in thinking their coat better than in thinking themselves better. If you consider the use of the garment, why is wool of finer thread superior to that of thicker? Yet, as if it were by nature and not by their own mistake that they had the advantage, they hold their heads high and believe some extra worth attaches to themselves thereby. Thus, the honor which, if ill-clad, they would not have ventured to hope for, they require as if of right for a smarter coat. If passed by with some neglect, they are indignant.

Again, does it not show the same stupidity to think so much of empty and unprofitable honors? What natural and true pleasure can another's bared head or bent knees afford you? Will this behavior cure the pain in your own knees or relieve the lunacy in your own head? In this conception of counterfeit pleasure, a strange and sweet madness is displayed by men who imagine themselves to be noble and plume themselves on it and applaud themselves because their fortune has been to be born of certain ancestors of whom the long succession has been counted rich—for that is now the only nobility—and especially rich in landed estates. They consider themselves not a whit less noble even if their ancestors have not left them a square foot or if they themselves have consumed in extravagant living what was left them.

With these persons they class those who, as I said, dote on jewels and gems and who think they become a species of god if ever they secure a fine specimen, especially of the sort which at the period is regarded as of the highest value in their country. It is not everywhere or always that one kind of stone is prized. They will not purchase it unless taken out of its gold setting and exposed to view, and not even then unless the seller takes an oath and gives security that it is a true gem and a true stone, so anxious are they lest a spurious stone in place of a genuine one deceive their eyes. But why should a counterfeited one give less pleasure to your sight when your eye cannot distinguish it from the true article? Both should be of equal value to you, even as they would be, by heaven, to a blind man!

What can be said of those who keep superfluous wealth to please themselves, not with putting the heap to any use but merely with looking at it?[6] Do they feel true pleasure, or are they not rather cheated by false pleasure? Or, what of those who have the opposite failing and hide the gold, which they will never use and perhaps never see again, and who, in their anxiety not to lose it, thereby do lose it? What else but loss is it to deprive yourself of its use, and perhaps all other men too, and to put it back in the ground? And yet you joyfully exult over your hidden treasure as though your mind were now free from all anxiety. Suppose that someone removed it by stealing it and that you died ten years afterwards knowing nothing of the theft. During the whole decade which you lived after the money was stolen, what did it matter to you whether it was stolen or safe? In either case it was of just as little use to you.

Among those who indulge such senseless delights they reckon dicers (whose madness they know not by experience but by hearsay only), as well as hunters and hawkers. What pleasure is there, they ask, in shooting dice upon a table? You have

---

6. Hythlodaeus implies that money is useful because it can be exchanged for goods in a market. Money exchange is more efficient than barter, as it can always find a commensurable value.

shot them so often that, even if some pleasure had been in it, weariness by now could have arisen from the habitual practice. Or what sweetness can there be, and not rather disgust, in hearing the barking and howling of dogs? Or what greater sensation of pleasure is there when a dog chases a hare than when a dog chases a dog? The same thing happens in both cases: there is racing in both if speed gives you delight.

But if you are attracted by the hope of slaughter and the expectation of a creature being mangled under your eyes, it ought rather to inspire pity when you behold a weak, fugitive, timid, and innocent little hare torn to pieces by a strong, fierce, and cruel dog. In consequence the Utopians have imposed the whole activity of hunting, as unworthy of free men, upon their butchers—a craft, as I explained before, they exercise through their slaves. They regard hunting as the meanest part of the butcher's trade and its other functions as more useful and more honorable, seeing that they do much more positive good and kill animals only from necessity, whereas the hunter seeks nothing but pleasure from the killing and mangling of a poor animal. Even in the case of brute beasts, this desire of looking on bloodshed, in their estimation, either arises from a cruel disposition or degenerates finally into cruelty through the constant practice of such brutal pleasure.

Although the mob of mortals regards these and all similar pursuits—and they are countless—as pleasures, yet the Utopians positively hold them to have nothing to do with true pleasure since there is nothing sweet in them by nature. The fact that for the mob they inspire in the senses a feeling of enjoyment—which seems to be the function of pleasure—does not make them alter their opinion. The enjoyment does not arise from the nature of the thing itself but from their own perverse habit. The latter failing makes them take what is bitter for sweet, just as pregnant women by their vitiated taste suppose pitch and tallow sweeter than honey. Yet it is impossible for any man's judgment, depraved either by disease or by habit, to change the nature of pleasure any more than that of anything else.

The pleasures which they admit as genuine they divide into various classes, some pleasures being attributed to the soul and others to the body. To the soul they ascribe intelligence and the sweetness which is bred of contemplation of truth. To these two are joined the pleasant recollection of a well-spent life and the sure hope of happiness to come.

Bodily pleasure they divide into two kinds. The first is that which fills the sense with clearly perceptible sweetness. Sometimes it comes from the renewal of those organs which have been weakened by our natural heat. These organs are then restored by food and drink. Sometimes it comes from the elimination of things which overload the body. This agreeable sensation occurs when we discharge feces from our bowels or perform the activity generative of children or relieve the itching of some part by rubbing or scratching. Now and then, however, pleasure arises, not in process of restoring anything that our members lack, nor in process of eliminating anything that causes distress, but from something that tickles and affects our senses with a secret but remarkable moving force and so draws them to itself. Such is that pleasure which is engendered by music.

The second kind of bodily pleasure they claim to be that which consists in a calm and harmonious state of the body. This is nothing else than each man's health undisturbed by any disorder. Health, if assailed by no pain, gives delight of itself, though there be no motion arising from pleasure applied from without. Even though it is less obvious and less perceptible by the sense than that overblown craving for eating and drinking, yet none the less many hold it to be the greatest of pleasures. Almost all the Utopians regard it as great and as practically the foundation and basis of all pleasures. Even by itself it can make the state of life peaceful and desirable, whereas without it absolutely no place is left for any pleasure. The absence of pain without the presence of health they regard as insensibility rather than pleasure.

They long ago rejected the position of those who held that a state of stable and tranquil health (for this question, too, had been actively discussed among them) was not to be counted as a pleasure because its presence, they said, could not be felt except through some motion from without. But on the other hand now they almost all agree that health is above all things conducive to pleasure. Since in disease, they query, there is pain, which is the bitter enemy of pleasure no less than disease is of health, why should not pleasure in turn be found in the tranquillity of health? They think that it is of no importance in the discussion whether you say that disease is pain or that disease is accompanied with pain, for it comes to the same thing either way. To be sure, if you hold that health is either a pleasure or the necessary cause of pleasure, as fire is of heat, in both ways the conclusion is that those who have permanent health cannot be without pleasure.

Besides, while we eat, say they, what is that but health, which has begun to be impaired, fighting against hunger, with food as its comrade in arms? While it gradually gains strength, the very progress to the usual vigor supplies the pleasure by which we are thus restored. Shall the health which delights in conflict not rejoice when it has gained the victory? When at length it has successfully acquired its former strength, which was its sole object through the conflict, shall it immediately become insensible and not recognize and embrace its own good? The assertion that health cannot be felt they think to be far wide of the truth. Who in a waking state, ask they, does not feel that he is in good health—except the man who is not? Who is bound fast by such insensibility or lethargy that he does not confess that health is agreeable and delightful to him? And what is delightful except pleasure under another name?

To sum up, they cling above all to mental pleasures, which they value as the first and foremost of all pleasures. Of these the principal part they hold to arise from the practice of the virtues and the consciousness of a good life. Of these pleasures which the body supplies, they give the palm to health. The delight of eating and drinking, and anything that gives the same sort of enjoyment, they think desirable, but only for the sake of health. Such things are not pleasant in themselves but only in so far as they resist the secret encroachment of ill health. Just as a wise man should pray that he may escape disease rather than crave a remedy for it and that he may drive pain off rather than seek relief from it, so it would be better not to need this kind of pleasure rather than to be soothed by it.

If a person thinks that his felicity consists in this kind of pleasure, he must admit that he will be in the greatest happiness if his lot happens to be a life which is spent in perpetual hunger, thirst, itching, eating, drinking, scratching, and rubbing. Who does not see that such a life is not only disgusting but wretched? These pleasures are surely the lowest of all as being most adulterated, for they never occur unless they are coupled with the pains which are their opposites. For example, with the pleasure of eating is united hunger—and on no fair terms, for the pain is the stronger and lasts the longer. It comes into existence before the pleasure and does not end until the pleasure dies with it. Such pleasures they hold should not be highly valued and only insofar as they are necessary. Yet they enjoy even these pleasures and gratefully acknowledge the kindness of mother nature who, with alluring sweetness, coaxes her offspring to that which of necessity they must constantly do. In what discomfort should we have to live if, like all other sicknesses which less frequently assail us, so also these daily diseases of hunger and thirst had to be expelled by bitter poisons and drugs?

Beauty, strength, and nimbleness—these as special and pleasant gifts of nature they gladly cherish. Nay, even those pleasures entering by the ears, eyes, or nostrils, which nature intended to be peculiarly characteristic of man (for no other species of living creature either takes in the form and fairness of the world or is affected by the pleasantness of smell, except in choice of food, or distinguishes harmonious and dissonant intervals of sound)—these, too, I say, they follow after as pleasant seasonings of life.[7] But in all they make this limitation: that the lesser is not to interfere with the greater and that pleasure is not to produce pain in aftermath. Pain they think a necessary consequence if the pleasure is base.

But to despise the beauty of form, to impair the strength of the body, to turn nimbleness into sluggishness, to exhaust the body by fasts, to injure one's health, and to reject all the other favors of nature, unless a man neglects these advantages to himself in providing more zealously for the pleasure of other persons or of the public, in return for which sacrifice he expects a greater pleasure from God—but otherwise to deal harshly with oneself for a vain and shadowy reputation of virtue to no man's profit or for preparing oneself more easily to bear adversities which may never come—this attitude they think is extreme madness and the sign of a mind which is both cruel to itself and ungrateful to nature, to whom it disdains to be indebted and therefore renounces all her benefits.

This is their view of virtue and pleasure. They believe that human reason can attain to no truer view, unless a heaven-sent religion inspire man with something more holy. Whether in this stand they are right or wrong, time does not permit us to examine—nor is it necessary. We have taken upon ourselves only to describe their principles, and not also to defend them. But of this I am sure, that whatever you think of their ideas, there is nowhere in the world a more excellent people nor a happier commonwealth. They are nimble and active of body, and stronger than you would expect from their stature. The latter, however, is not dwarfish. Though they have not a very fertile soil or a very wholesome climate, they protect themselves against the atmosphere by temperate living and make up for the defects of the land by diligent labor. Consequently, nowhere in the world is there a more plentiful supply of grain and cattle, nowhere are men's bodies more vigorous and subject to fewer diseases. Not only may you behold the usual agricultural tasks carefully administered there, whereby the naturally barren soil is improved by art and industry, but you may also see how a whole forest has been uprooted in one place by the hands of the people and planted in another. Herein they were thinking not so much of abundance as of transport, that they might have wood closer to the sea or the rivers or the cities themselves. For it takes less labor to convey grain than timber to a distance by land.

The people in general are easygoing, good-tempered, ingenious, and leisure-loving. They patiently do their share of manual labor when occasion demands, though otherwise they are by no means fond of it. In their devotion to mental study they are unwearied. When they had heard from us about the literature and learning of the

---

7. Just as the Utopians imagine humankind without original sin, so they cannot imagine any point in ascetic discipline of the body for the sake of curbing or controlling its inherent tendency to sin.

Greeks (for in Latin there was nothing, apart from history and poetry, which seemed likely to gain their great approval), it was wonderful to see their extreme desire for permission to master them through our instruction.

We began, therefore, to give them public lessons, more at first that we should not seem to refuse the trouble than that we expected any success. But after a little progress, their diligence made us at once feel sure that our own diligence would not be bestowed in vain. They began so easily to imitate the shapes of the letters, so readily to pronounce the words, so quickly to learn by heart, and so faithfully to reproduce what they had learned that it was a perfect wonder to us. The explanation was that most of them were scholars picked for their ability and mature in years, who undertook to learn their tasks not only fired by their own free will but acting under orders of the senate. In less than three years they were perfect in the language and able to peruse good authors without any difficulty unless the text had faulty readings. According to my conjecture, they got hold of Greek literature more easily because it was somewhat related to their own. I suspect that their race was derived from the Greek because their language, which in almost all other respects resembles the Persian, retains some traces of Greek in the names of their cities and officials.

When about to go on the fourth voyage, I put on board, in place of wares to sell, a fairly large package of books,[8] having made up my mind never to return rather than to come back soon. They received from me most of Plato's works, several of Aristotle's, as well as Theophrastus on plants, which I regret to say was mutilated in parts. During the voyage an ape found the book, left lying carelessly about, and in wanton sport tore out and destroyed several pages in various sections. Of grammarians they have only Lascaris, for I did not take Theodore with me. They have no dictionaries except those of Hesychius and Dioscorides. They are very fond of the works of Plutarch and captivated by the wit and pleasantry of Lucian. Of the poets they have Aristophanes, Homer, and Euripides, together with Sophocles in the small Aldine type. Of the historians they possess Thucydides and Herodotus, as well as Herodian.

In medicine, moreover, my companion Tricius Apinatus had carried with him some small treatises of Hippocrates and the *Ars medica* of Galen, to which books they attribute great value. Even though there is scarcely a nation in the whole world that needs medicine less, yet nowhere is it held in greater honor—and this for the reason that they regard the knowledge of it as one of the finest and most useful branches of philosophy. When by the help of this philosophy they explore the secrets of nature, they appear to themselves not only to get great pleasure in doing so but also to win

---

8. Hythlodaeus has given the Utopians only works in Greek, even though they cover topics in the history of Rome. By this, More clearly intended to emphasize what he thought was the intellectual superiority of Greek over Roman culture. Beyond the works of Plato and Aristotle, Hythlodaeus's library contains the works of Theophrastus (3rd century B.C.), who wrote a history of plants; Constantine Lascaris and Theodore of Gaza, both grammarians of the 15th century; Hesychius, a Greek lexicographer of the 4th century B.C.; Dioscurides, a Greek physician of the 1st century, who wrote a medical textbook, known and used through the early modern period; Plutarch, a Greek biographer and moralist of the 2nd century; Lucian, a Greek rhetorician of the 2nd century, who wrote satirical dialogues; Aristophanes, a Greek dramatist of the 4th century B.C., who wrote comic drama; Homer, the name given the author or authors of the Greek epics,

the *Iliad* and the *Odyssey*, committed to writing about 800 B.C.; and Euripides and Sophocles, both Greek tragedians of the 5th century B.C.. Herodotus and Thucydides lived during the 5th century B.C.; Herodotus wrote of the wars between the kingdoms of the near east and the Greek states in his *Histories*, Thucydides of the tragic fall of the Athenian state in his *Peloponnesian Wars*. Herodian, a Syrian historian, wrote, in Greek, of the Roman emperors from the death of Marcus Aurelius in A.D. 180 to 238. "Tricius Apinatus" is a fictitious author, but Hippocrates and Galen were Greek physicians of the 5th century B.C. and the 2nd century, respectively, whose medical treatises were popular until the end of the 17th century. "Aldine type" was the particular typeface used by the early 16-century Venetian printer Aldus Manutius, who was famous for his publication of fine editions of Greek authors.

the highest approbation of the Author and Maker of nature. They presume that, like all other artificers, He has set forth the visible mechanism of the world as a spectacle for man, whom alone He has made capable of appreciating such a wonderful thing. Therefore He prefers a careful and diligent beholder and admirer of His work to one who like an unreasoning brute beast passes by so great and so wonderful a spectacle stupidly and stolidly.

Thus, trained in all learning, the minds of the Utopians are exceedingly apt in the invention of the arts which promote the advantage and convenience of life. Two, however, they owe to us, the art of printing and the manufacture of paper—though not entirely to us but to a great extent also to themselves. When we showed them the Aldine printing in paper books, we talked about the material of which paper is made and the art of printing without giving a detailed explanation, for none of us was expert in either art. With the greatest acuteness they promptly guessed how it was done. Though previously they wrote only on parchment, bark, and papyrus, from this time they tried to manufacture paper and print letters. Their first attempts were not very successful, but by frequent experiment they soon mastered both. So great was their success that if they had copies of Greek authors, they would have no lack of books. But at present they have no more than I have mentioned, but by printing books they have increased their stock by many thousands of copies.

Whoever, coming to their land on a sight-seeing tour, is recommended by any special intellectual endowment or is acquainted with many countries through long travel, is sure of a hearty welcome, for they delight in hearing what is happening in the whole world. On this score our own landing was pleasing to them. Few persons, however, come to them in the way of trade. What could they bring except iron, or what everybody would rather take back home with him—gold and silver! And as to articles of export, the Utopians think it wiser to carry them out of the country themselves than to let strangers come to fetch them. By this policy they get more information about foreign nations and do not forget by disuse their skill in navigation.

SLAVERY, [ETC.]

Prisoners of war are not enslaved unless captured in wars fought by the Utopians themselves; nor are the sons of slaves,[9] nor anyone who was in slavery when acquired of slaves, nor anyone whom they could acquire from slavery in other countries. Their slaves are either such or such as have been condemned to death elsewhere for some offense. The greater number are of this latter kind. They carry away many of them; sometimes they buy them cheaply; but often they ask for them and get them for nothing. These classes of slaves they keep not only continually at work but also in chains. Their own countrymen are dealt with more harshly, since their conduct is regarded as all the more regrettable and deserving a more severe punishment as an object lesson because, having had an excellent rearing to a virtuous life, they still could not be restrained from crime.

There is yet another class of slaves, for sometimes a hard-working and poverty-stricken drudge of another country voluntarily chooses slavery in Utopia. These individuals are well treated and, except that they have a little more work assigned to

---

9. More uses the Latin word *servus*, which means servant, slave, and serf. Most commonly captives in war, slaves were also persons punished for crime, as in Utopia. Voluntary slavery, aside from indentured servitude (for a term), was rare except in theory; presumably such persons chose to work as slaves in exchange for a subsistence living.

them as being used to it, are dealt with almost as leniently as citizens. If anyone wishes to depart, which seldom happens, they do not detain him against his will nor send him away empty-handed.

The sick, as I said, are very lovingly cared for, nothing being omitted which may restore them to health, whether in the way of medicine or diet. They console the incurable diseased by sitting and conversing with them and by applying all possible alleviations. But if a disease is not only incurable but also distressing and agonizing without any cessation, then the priests and the public officials exhort the man, since he is now unequal to all life's duties, a burden to himself, and a trouble to others, and is living beyond the time of his death, to make up his mind not to foster the pest and plague any longer nor to hesitate to die now that life is torture to him but, relying on good hope, to free himself from this bitter life as from prison and the rack, or else voluntarily to permit others to free him.[1] In this course he will act wisely, since by death he will put an end not to enjoyment but to torture. Because in doing so he will be obeying the counsels of the priests, who are God's interpreters, it will be a pious and holy action.

Those who have been persuaded by these arguments either starve themselves to death or, being put to sleep, are set free without the sensation of dying. But they do not make away with anyone against his will, nor in such a case do they relax in the least their attendance upon him. They do believe that death counseled by authority is honorific. But if anyone commits suicide without having obtained the approval of priests and senate, they deem him unworthy of either fire or earth and cast his body ignominiously into a marsh without proper burial.

Women do not marry till eighteen, men not till they are four years older. If before marriage a man or woman is convicted of secret intercourse, he or she is severely punished, and they are forbidden to marry altogether unless the governor's pardon remits their guilt. In addition, both father and mother of the family in whose house the offense was committed incur great disgrace as having been neglectful in doing their duties. The reason why they punish this offence so severely is their foreknowledge that, unless persons are carefully restrained from promiscuous intercourse, few will contract the tie of marriage, in which a whole life must be spent with one companion and all the troubles incidental to it must be patiently borne.

In choosing mates, they seriously and strictly espouse a custom which seemed to us very foolish and extremely ridiculous. The woman, whether maiden or widow, is shown naked to the suitor by a worthy and respectable matron, and similarly the suitor is presented naked before the maiden by a discreet man. We laughed at this custom and condemned it as foolish. They, on the other hand, marvelled at the remarkable folly of all other nations. In buying a colt, where there is question of only a little money, persons are so cautious that though it is almost bare they will not buy until they have taken off the saddle and removed all the trappings for fear some sore lies concealed under these coverings. Yet in the choice of a wife, an action which will cause either pleasure or disgust to follow them the rest of their lives, they are so careless that, while the rest of her body is covered with clothes, they estimate the value of the whole woman from hardly a single handbreadth of her, only the face being visible, and clasp her to themselves not without great danger of their agreeing ill together if something afterwards gives them offense.

---

1. Neither suicide nor euthanasia was considered immoral in Greek and Roman society.

All are not so wise as to regard only the character of the spouse, and even in the marriages of the wise, bodily attractions also are no small enhancement to the virtues of the mind. Certainly such foul deformity may be hidden beneath these coverings that it may quite alienate a man's mind from his wife when bodily separation is no longer lawful. If such a deformity arises by chance after the marriage has been contracted, each person must bear his own fate, but beforehand the laws ought to protect him from being entrapped by guile.

This provision was the more necessary because the Utopians are the only people in those parts of the world who are satisfied with one spouse and because matrimony there is seldom broken except by death, unless it be for adultery or for intolerable offensiveness of character. When husband or wife is thus offended, leave is granted by the senate to take another mate.[2] The other party perpetually lives a life of disgrace as well as of celibacy. But they cannot endure the repudiation of an unwilling wife, who is in no way to blame, because some bodily calamity has befallen her. They judge it cruel that a person should be abandoned when most in need of comfort and that old age, since it both entails disease and is a disease itself, should have only an unreliable and weak fidelity.

It sometimes happens, however, that when a married couple agree insufficiently in their dispositions and both find others with whom they hope to live more agreeably, they separate by mutual consent and contract fresh unions, but not without the sanction of the senate. The latter allows of no divorce until its members and their wives have carefully gone into the case. Even then they do not readily give consent because they know that it is a very great drawback to cementing the affection between husband and wife if they have before them the easy hope of a fresh union.

Violators of the conjugal tie are punished by the strictest form of slavery. If both parties are married, the injured parties, provided they consent, are divorced from their adulterous mates and couple together, or else are allowed to marry whom they like. But if one of the injured parties continues to feel affection for so undeserving a mate, it is not forbidden to have the marriage continue in force on condition that the party is willing to accompany and share the labor of the other who has been condemned to slavery. Now and then it happens that the penance of the one and the dutiful assiduity of the other move the compassion of the governor and win back their liberty. Relapse into the same offense, however, involves the penalty of death.

For all other crimes there is no law prescribing any fixed penalty, but the punishment is assigned by the senate according to the atrocity, or veniality, of the individual crime. Husbands correct their wives, and parents their children, unless the offense is so serious that it is to the advantage of public morality to have it punished openly. Generally the worst offenses are punished by the sentence of slavery since this prospect, they think, is no less formidable to the criminal and more advantageous to the state than if they make haste to put the offenders to death and get them out of the way at once. Their labor is more profitable than their death, and their example lasts longer to deter others from like crimes. But if they rebel and kick against this treatment, they are thereupon put to death like untameable beasts that cannot be restrained by prison or chain. If they are patient, however, they are not entirely deprived of all hope. When tamed by long and hard punishment, if they

2. In England, divorce was granted only on the grounds of adultery. By contrast, the Utopians grant divorce for incompatibility and extend the privilege to the wife as well as the husband. Adultery, however, is punished with slavery.

show such repentance as testifies that they are more sorry for their sin than for their punishment, then sometimes by the prerogative of the governor and sometimes by the vote of the people their slavery is either lightened or remitted altogether.

To tempt another to an impure act is no less punishable than the commission of that impure act. In every crime the deliberate and avowed attempt is counted equal to the deed, for they think that failure ought not to benefit one who did everything in his power not to fail.

They are very fond of fools.[3] It is a great disgrace to treat them with insult, but there is no prohibition against deriving pleasure from their foolery. The latter, they think, is of the greatest benefit to the fools themselves. If anyone is so stern and morose that he is not amused with anything they either do or say, they do not entrust him with the care of a fool. They fear that he may not treat him with sufficient indulgence since he would find in him neither use nor even amusement, which is his sole faculty.

To deride a man for a disfigurement or the loss of a limb is counted as base and disfiguring, not to the man who is laughed at but to him who laughs, for foolishly upbraiding a man with something as if it were a fault which he was powerless to avoid. While they consider it a sign of a sluggish and feeble mind not to preserve natural beauty, it is, in their judgment, disgraceful affectation to help it out by cosmetics. Experience itself shows them how no elegance of outward form recommends wives to husbands as much as probity and reverence. Some men are attracted only by a handsome shape, but no man's love is kept permanently except by virtue and obedience.

Not merely do they discourage crime by punishment but they offer honors to invite men to virtue. Hence, to great men who have done conspicuous service to their country they set up in the market place statues to stand as a record of noble exploits and, at the same time, to have the glory of forefathers serve their descendants as a spur and stimulus to virtue.

The man who solicits votes to obtain any office is deprived completely of the hope of holding any office at all. They live together in affection and good will. No official is haughty or formidable. They are called fathers and show that character. Honor is paid them willingly, as it should be, and is not exacted from the reluctant. The governor himself is distinguished from citizens not by a robe or a crown but by the carrying of a handful of grain, just as the mark of the high priest is a wax candle borne before him.

They have very few laws because very few are needed for persons so educated. The chief fault they find with other peoples is that almost innumerable books of laws and commentaries are not sufficient. They themselves think it most unfair that any group of men should be bound by laws which are either too numerous to be read through or too obscure to be understood by anyone.

Moreover, they absolutely banish from their country all lawyers, who cleverly manipulate cases and cunningly argue legal points. They consider it a good thing that every man should plead his own cause and say the same to the judge as he would tell his counsel. Thus there is less ambiguity and the truth is more easily elicited when a man, uncoached in deception by a lawyer, conducts his own case and the judge skillfully weighs each statement and helps untutored minds to defeat the false accusations of the crafty. To secure these advantages in other countries is difficult, owing to the

---

3. In early modern Europe, a "fool" could be a professional jester; usually, he was employed at a royal or noble court and had special license to amuse and even criticize his master.

immense mass of extremely complicated laws. But with the Utopians each man is expert in law. First, they have, as I said, very few laws and, secondly, they regard the most obvious interpretation of the law as the most fair interpretation.

This policy follows from their reasoning that, since all laws are promulgated to remind every man of his duty, the more recondite interpretation reminds only very few (for there are few who can arrive at it) whereas the more simple and obvious sense of the laws is open to all. Otherwise, what difference would it make for the common people, who are the most numerous and also most in need of instruction, whether you framed no law at all or whether the interpretation of the law you framed was such that no one could elicit it except by great ingenuity and long argument? Now, the untrained judgment of the common people cannot attain to the meaning of such an interpretation nor can their lives be long enough, seeing that they are wholly taken up with getting a living.

These virtues of the Utopians have spurred their neighbors (who are free and independent since many of them were long ago delivered from tyrants by the Utopians) to obtain officials from them, some for one year and others for five years. On the expiration of their office they escort them home with honor and praise and bring back successors with them to their own country. Certainly these peoples make very good and wholesome provision for the commonwealth. Seeing that the latter's prosperity or ruin depends on the character of officials, of whom could they have made a wiser choice than of those who cannot be drawn from the path of honor by any bribe since it is no good to them as they will shortly return home, nor influenced by crooked partiality or animosity toward any since they are strangers to the citizens? These two evils, favoritism and avarice, wherever they have settled in men's judgments, instantly destroy all justice, the strongest sinew of the commonwealth. The nations who seek their administrators from Utopia are called allies by them; the name of friend is reserved for all the others whom they have benefited.

Treaties which all other nations so often conclude among themselves, break, and renew, they never make with any nation. "What is the use of a treaty," they ask, "as though nature of herself did not sufficiently bind one man to another? If a person does not regard nature, do you suppose he will care anything about words?"

They are led to this opinion chiefly because in those parts of the world treaties and alliances between kings are not observed with much good faith. In Europe, however, and especially in those parts where the faith and religion of Christ prevails, the majesty of treaties is everywhere holy and inviolable, partly through the justice and goodness of kings, partly through the reverence and fear of the Sovereign Pontiffs. Just as the latter themselves undertake nothing which they do not most conscientiously perform, so they command all other rulers to abide by their promises in every way and compel the recalcitrant by pastoral censure and severe reproof.[4] Popes are perfectly right, of course, in thinking it a most disgraceful thing that those who are specially called the faithful should not faithfully adhere to their commitments.

But in that new world, which is almost as far removed from ours by the equator as their life and character are different from ours, there is no trust in treaties. The more numerous and holy the ceremonies with which a treaty is struck the more quickly is it broken. They find some defect in the wording, which sometimes they cunningly devise of set purpose, so that they can never be held by such strong bonds

---

4. More is being ironic in extolling the faithful observance of treaties by the papacy. Pope Julius II, who died a few years before the publication of More's treatise, was notorious for breaking his word.

as not somehow to escape from them and break both the treaty and their faith. If this cunning, nay fraud and deceit, were found to have occurred in the contracts of private persons, the treaty-makers with great disdain would exclaim against it as sacrilegious and meriting the gallows—though the very same men plume themselves on being the authors of such advice when given to kings.

In consequence men think either that all justice is only a plebeian and low virtue which is far below the majesty of kings or that there are at least two forms of it: the one which goes on foot and creeps on the ground, fit only for the common sort and bound by many chains so that it can never overstep its barriers; the other a virtue of kings, which, as it is more august than that of ordinary folk, is also far freer so that everything is permissible to it—except what it finds disagreeable.

This behavior, as I said, of rulers there who keep their treaties so badly is, I suppose, the reason why the Utopians make none; if they lived here, they would perhaps change their minds. Nevertheless they believe that, though treaties are faithfully observed, it is a pity that the custom of making them at all had grown up. The result (as though peoples which are divided by the slight interval of a hill or a river were joined by no bond of nature) is men's persuasion that they are born one another's adversaries and enemies and that they are right in aiming at one another's destruction except in so far as treaties prevent it. What is more, even when treaties are made, friendship does not grow up but the license of freebooting continues to the extent that, for lack of skill in drawing up the treaty, no sufficient precaution to prevent this activity has been included in the articles. But the Utopians, on the contrary, think that nobody who has done you no harm should be accounted an enemy, that the fellowship created by nature takes the place of a treaty, and that men are better and more firmly joined together by good will than by pacts, by spirit than by words.

Military Affairs

War, as an activity fit only for beasts and yet practiced by no kind of beast so constantly as by man, they regard with utter loathing. Against the usage of almost all nations they count nothing so inglorious as glory sought in war. Nevertheless men and women alike assiduously exercise themselves in military training on fixed days lest they should be unfit for war when need requires. Yet they do not lightly go to war. They do so only to protect their own territory or to drive an invading enemy out of their friends' lands or, in pity for a people oppressed by tyranny, to deliver them by force of arms from the yoke and slavery of the tyrant, a course prompted by human sympathy.

They oblige their friends with help, not always indeed to defend them merely but sometimes also to requite and avenge injuries previously done to them. They act, however, only if they themselves are consulted before any step is taken and if they themselves initiate the war after they have approved the cause and demanded restitution in vain. They take the final step of war not only when a hostile inroad has carried off booty but also much more fiercely when the merchants among their friends undergo unjust persecution under the color of justice in any other country, either on the pretext of laws in themselves unjust or by the distortion of laws in themselves good.

Such was the origin of the war which the Utopians had waged a little before our time on behalf of the Nephelogetes[5] against the Alaopolitans. The Nephelogetic traders suffered a wrong, as they thought, under pretence of law, but whether right or

---

5. "Cloud born" (insubstantial) people; the Alaopolitans are "citizens without a people or a country"—that is, stateless.

wrong, it was avenged by a fierce war. Into this war the neighboring nations brought their energies and resources to assist the power and to intensify the rancor of both sides. Most flourishing nations were either shaken to their foundations or grievously afflicted. The troubles upon troubles that arose were ended only by the enslavement and surrender of the Alaopolitans. Since the Utopians were not fighting in their own interest, they yielded them into the power of the Nephelogetes, a people who, when the Alaopolitans were prosperous, were not in the least comparable to them.

So severely do the Utopians punish wrong done to their friends, even in money matters—but not wrongs done to themselves. When they lose their goods anywhere through fraud, but without personal violence, their anger goes no further than abstention from trade with that nation until satisfaction is made. The reason is not that they care less for their citizens than their allies. They are more grieved at their allies' pecuniary loss than their own because their friends' merchants suffer severely by the loss as it falls on their private property, but their own citizens lose nothing but what comes from the common stock and what was plentiful and, as it were, superfluous at home—or else it would not have been exported. As a result, the loss is not felt by any individual. They consider it excessively cruel to avenge such a loss by the death of many when the disadvantage of the loss affects neither the life nor the subsistence of any of their own people.

If a Utopian citizen, however, is wrongfully disabled or killed anywhere, whether the plot is due to the government or to a private citizen, they first ascertain the facts by an embassy and then, if the guilty persons are not surrendered, they cannot be appeased but forthwith declare war. If the guilty persons are surrendered, they are punished either with death or with enslavement.

They not only regret but blush at a victory that has cost much bloodshed, thinking it folly to purchase wares, however precious, too dear. If they overcome and crush the enemy by stratagem and cunning, they feel great pride and celebrate a public triumph over the victory and put up a trophy as for a strenuous exploit. They boast themselves as having acted with valor and heroism whenever their victory is such as no animal except man could have won, that is, by strength of intellect; for, by strength of body, say they, bears, lions, boars, wolves, dogs, and other wild beasts are wont to fight. Most of them are superior to us in brawn and fierceness, but they are all inferior in cleverness and calculation.

Their one and only object in war is to secure that which, had it been obtained beforehand, would have prevented the declaration of war. If that is out of the question, they require such severe punishment of those on whom they lay the blame that for the future they may be afraid to attempt anything of the same sort. These are their chief interests in the enterprise, which they set about promptly to secure, yet taking more care to avoid danger than to win praise or fame.

The moment war is declared, they arrange that simultaneously a great number of placards, made more effective by bearing their public seal, should be set up secretly in the most prominent spots of enemy territory. Herein they promise huge rewards to anyone who will kill the enemy king. Further, they offer smaller sums, but those considerable, for the heads of the individuals whose names they specify in the same proclamations. These are the men whom, next to the king himself, they regard as responsible for the hostile measures taken against them. Whatever reward they fix for an assassin, they double for the man who brings any of the denounced parties alive to them. They actually offer the same rewards, with a guarantee of personal safety, to the persons proscribed, if they will turn against their fellows.

So it swiftly comes about that their enemies suspect all outsiders and, in addition, neither trust nor are loyal to one another. They are in a state of utter panic and no less peril. It is well known that it has often happened that many of them, and especially the king himself, have been betrayed by those in whom they had placed the greatest trust, so easily do bribes incite men to commit every kind of crime. They are boundless in their offers of reward. Remembering, however, what a risk they invite the man to run, they take care that the greatness of the peril is balanced by the extent of the rewards. In consequence they promise and faithfully pay down not only an immense amount of gold but also landed property with high income in very secure places in the territory of friends.

This habit of bidding for and purchasing an enemy, which is elsewhere condemned as the cruel deed of a degenerate nature, they think reflects great credit, first on their wisdom because they thus bring to a conclusion great wars without any battle at all, and secondly on their humanity and mercy because by the death of a few guilty people they purchase the lives of many harmless persons who would have fallen in battle, both on their own side and that of the enemy. They are almost as sorry for the throng and mass of the enemy as for their own citizens. They know that the common folk do not go to war of their own accord but are driven to it by the madness of kings.

If this plan does not succeed, they sow the seeds of dissension broadcast and foster strife by leading a brother of the king or one of the noblemen to hope that he may obtain the throne. If internal strife dies down, then they stir up and involve the neighbors of their enemies by reviving some forgotten claims to dominion such as kings have always at their disposal. Promising their own assistance for the war, they supply money liberally but are very chary of sending their own citizens. They hold them so singularly dear and regard one another of such value that they would not care to exchange any of their own people for the king of the opposite party. As to gold and silver, since they keep it all for this one use, they pay it out without any reluctance, for they would live just as well if they spent it all. Moreover, in addition to the riches which they keep at home, they have also a vast treasure abroad in that many nations, as I said before, are in their debt.

With the riches, they hire and send to war soldiers from all parts, but especially from among the Zapoletans.[6] These people live five hundred miles to the east of Utopia and are fearsome, rough, and wild. They prefer their own rugged woods and mountains among which they are bred. They are a hard race, capable of enduring heat, cold, and toil, lacking all refinements, engaging in no farming, careless about the houses they live in and the clothes they wear, and occupied only with their flocks and herds. To a great extent they live by hunting and plundering. They are born for warfare and zealously seek an opportunity for fighting. When they find it, they eagerly embrace it. Leaving the country in great force, they offer themselves at a cheap rate to anyone who needs fighting men. The only trade they know in life is that by which they seek their death.

They fight with ardor and incorruptible loyalty for those from whom they receive their pay. Yet they bind themselves for no fixed period but take sides on such terms that the next day when higher pay is offered them, even by the enemy, they take his side, and then the day after, if a trifle more is offered to tempt them back, return to the side they took at first.

6. "Busy sellers," that is, of their services.

In almost every war that breaks out there are many of them in both armies. It is a daily occurrence that men connected by ties of blood, who were hired on the same side and so became intimate with one another, soon afterward are separated into two hostile forces and meet in battle. Forgetting both kinship and friendship, they run one another through with the utmost ferocity. They are driven to mutual destruction for no other reason than that they are hired by opposing kings for a tiny sum of which they take such careful account that they are readily induced to change sides by the addition of a penny to their daily rate of pay. So have they speedily acquired a habit of avarice which nevertheless profits them not one whit. What they get by exposing their lives they spend instantly in debauchery and that of a dreary sort.

This people will battle for the Utopians against any mortals whatsoever because their service is hired at a rate higher than they could get anywhere else. The Utopians, just as they seek good men to use them, so enlist these villains to abuse them. When need requires, they thrust them under the tempting bait of great promises into greatest perils. Generally a large proportion never returns to claim payment, but the survivors are honestly paid what has been promised them to incite them again to like deeds of daring. The Utopians do not care in the least how many Zapoletans they lose, thinking that they would be the greatest benefactors to the human race if they could relieve the world of all the dregs of this abominable and impious people.

Next to them they employ the forces of the people for whom they are fighting and then auxiliary squadrons of all their other friends. Last of all they add a contingent of their own citizens out of which they appoint some man of tried valor to command the whole army. For him they have two substitutes who hold no rank as long as he is safe. But if he is captured or killed, the first of the two becomes as it were his heir and successor, and he, if events require, is succeeded by the third. They thus avoid the disorganization of the whole army through the endangering of the commander, the fortunes of war being always incalculable.

In each city a choice is made among those who volunteer. No one is driven to fight abroad against his will because they are convinced that if anyone is somewhat timorous by nature, he not only will not acquit himself manfully but will throw fear into his companions. Should any war, however, assail their own country, they put the fainthearted, if physically fit, on shipboard mixed among the braver sort or put them here and there to man the walls where they cannot run away. Thus, shame at being seen to flinch by their own side, the close quarters with the enemy, and the withdrawal of hope of escape combine to overpower their timidity, and often they make a virtue of extreme necessity.

Just as no one of the men is made to go to a foreign war against his will, so if the women are anxious to accompany their husbands on military service, not only do they not forbid them but actually encourage them and incite them by expressions of praise. When they have gone out, they are placed alongside their husbands on the battle front. Each man is surrounded by his own children and relations by marriage and blood so that those may be closest and lend one another mutual assistance whom nature most impels to help one another. It is the greatest reproach for one spouse to return without the other or for a son to come back having lost his parent. The result is that, when it comes to hand-to-hand fighting, if the enemy stands his ground, the battle is long and anguished and ends with mutual extermination.

As I have said, they take every care not to be obliged to fight in person as long as they can finish the war by the assistance of hired substitutes. When personal service is inevitable, they are as courageous in fighting as they were ingenious in avoiding it as long as they might. They are not fierce in the first onslaught, but their strength increases by degrees through their slow and hard resistance. Their spirit is so stubborn that they would rather be cut to pieces than give way. The absence of anxiety about livelihood at home, as well as the removal of that worry which troubles men about the future of their families (for such solicitude everywhere breaks the highest courage), makes their spirit exalted and disdainful of defeat.

Moreover, their expert training in military discipline gives them confidence. Finally, their good and sound opinions, in which they have been trained from childhood both by teaching and by the good institutions of their country, give them additional courage. So they do not hold their life so cheap as recklessly to throw it away and not so immoderately dear as greedily and shamefully to hold fast to it when honor bids them give it up.

While the battle is everywhere most hot, a band of picked youths who have taken an oath to devote themselves to the task hunt out the opposing general. They openly attack him; they secretly ambush him. They assail him both from far and from near. A long and continuous wedge of men, fresh comers constantly taking the place of those exhausted, keeps up the attack. It seldom happens, unless he look to his safety by running away, that he is not killed or does not fall alive into the enemy's hands.

If the victory rests with them, there is no indiscriminate carnage, for they would rather take the routed as prisoners than kill them. They never pursue the fleeing enemy without keeping one division all the time drawn up ready for engagement under their banners. To such an extent is this the case that if, after the rest of the army has been beaten, they win the victory by this last reserve force, they prefer to let all their enemies escape rather than get into the habit of pursuing them with their own ranks in disorder. They remember that more than once it has happened to themselves that, when the great bulk of their army has been beaten and routed and when the enemy, flushed with victory, has been chasing the fugitives in all directions, a few of their number, held in reserve and ready for emergencies, have suddenly attacked the scattered and straying enemy who, feeling themselves quite safe, were off their guard. Thereby they have changed the whole fortune of the battle and, wresting out of the enemy's hands a certain and undoubted victory, have, though conquered, conquered their conquerors in turn.

It is not easy to say whether they are more cunning in laying ambushes or more cautious in avoiding them. You would think they contemplated flight when that is the very last thing intended; but, on the other hand, when they do determine to flee, you would imagine that they were thinking of anything but that. If they feel themselves to be inferior in number or in position, either by night they noiselessly march and move their camp or evade the enemy by some stratagem, or else by day they retire so imperceptibly and in such regular order that it is as dangerous to attack them in retreat as it would be in advance. They protect their camp most carefully by a deep and broad ditch, the earth taken out of it being thrown inside. They do not utilize the labor of the lowest workmen for the purpose, but the soldiers do it with their own hands. The whole army is set at work, except those who watch under arms in front of the rampart in case of emergencies. Thus, through the efforts of so many, they complete great fortifications, enclosing a large space, with incredible speed.

They wear armor strong enough to turn blows but easily adapted to all motions and gestures of the body. They do not feel any awkwardness even in swimming, for they practice swimming under arms as part of their apprenticeship in military discipline. The weapons they use at a distance are arrows, which they shoot with great strength and sureness of aim not only on foot but also on horseback. At close quarters they use not swords but battle-axes which, because of their sharp point and great weight, are deadly weapons, whether employed for thrusting or hacking. They are very clever in inventing war machines. They hide them, when made, with the greatest care lest, if made known before required by circumstances, they be rather a laughingstock than an instrument of war. In making them, their first object is to have them easy to carry and handy to pivot.

If a truce is made with the enemy, they keep it so religiously as not to break it even under provocation. They do not ravage the enemy's territory nor burn his crops. Rather, they do not even allow them to be trodden down by the feet of men or horses, as far as can be, thinking that they grow for their own benefit. They injure no noncombatant unless he is a spy. When cities are surrendered to them, they keep them intact. They do not plunder even those which they have stormed but put to death the men who prevented surrender and make slaves of the rest of the defenders. They leave unharmed the crowd of noncombatants. If they find out that any persons recommended the surrender of the town, they give them a share of the property of the condemned. They present their auxiliaries with the rest of the confiscated goods, but not a single one of their own men gets any of the booty.

When the war is over, they do not charge the expense against their friends, for whom they have borne the cost, but against the conquered. Under this head they make them not only pay money, which they lay aside for similar warlike purposes, but also surrender estates, from which they may enjoy forever a large annual income. In many countries they have such revenues which, coming little by little from various sources, have grown to the sum of over seven hundred thousand ducats a year.[7] To these estates they dispatch some of their own citizens under the title of Financial Agents to live there in great style and to play the part of magnates. Yet much is left over to put into the public treasury, unless they prefer to give the conquered nation credit. They often do the latter until they need to use the money, and even then it scarcely ever happens that they call in the whole sum. From these estates they confer a share on those who at their request undertake the dangerous mission which I have previously described.

If any king takes up arms against them and prepares to invade their territory, they at once meet him in great strength beyond their borders. They never lightly make war in their own country nor is any emergency so pressing as to compel them to admit foreign auxiliaries into their island.

Utopian Religions

There are different kinds of religion not only on the island as a whole but also in each city. Some worship as god the sun, others the moon, others one of the planets. There are some who reverence a man conspicuous for either virtue or glory in the past not only as god but even as the supreme god. But by far the majority, and those by far the wiser, believe in nothing of the kind but in a certain single being, unknown, eternal, immense, inexplicable, far above the reach of the human mind, diffused throughout the universe not in mass but in power. Him they call father. To him alone they attribute the beginnings, the growth, the increase, the changes, and the ends of all things as they have perceived them. To no other do they give divine honors.

In addition, all the other Utopians too, though varying in their beliefs, agree with them in this respect that they hold there is one supreme being, to whom are due both the creation and the providential government of the whole world. All alike call him Mithras[8] in their native language, but in this respect they disagree, that he is

---

7. A vast sum of money; by today's reckoning, the amount would equal several million dollars.

8. Persian sun god.

looked on differently by different persons. Each professes that whatever that is which he regards as supreme is that very same nature to whose unique power and majesty the sum of all things is attributed by the common consent of all nations. But gradually they are all beginning to depart from this medley of superstitions and are coming to unite in that one religion which seems to surpass the rest in reasonableness. Nor is there any doubt that the other beliefs would all have disappeared long ago had not whatever untoward event, that happened to anyone when he was deliberating on a change of religion, been construed by fear as not having happened by chance but as having been sent from heaven as if the deity whose worship he was forsaking were thus avenging an intention so impious against himself.

But after they had heard from us the name of Christ, His teaching, His character, His miracles, and the no less wonderful constancy of the many martyrs whose blood freely shed had drawn so many nations far and wide into their fellowship, you would not believe how readily disposed they, too, were to join it, whether through the rather mysterious inspiration of God or because they thought it nearest to that belief which has the widest prevalence among them. But I think that this factor, too, was of no small weight, that they had heard that His disciples' common way of life had been pleasing to Christ and that it is still in use among the truest societies of Christians. But whatever it was that influenced them, not a few joined our religion and were cleansed by the holy water of baptism.

But because among us four (for that was all that was left, two of our group having succumbed to fate) there was, I am sorry to say, no priest, they were initiated in all other matters, but so far they lack those sacraments which with us only priests administer. They understand, however, what they are, and desire them with the greatest eagerness. Moreover, they are even debating earnestly among themselves whether, without the dispatch of a Christian bishop, one chosen out of their own number might receive the sacerdotal character. It seemed that they would choose a candidate, but by the time of my departure they had not yet done so.

Even those who do not agree with the religion of Christ do not try to deter others from it. They do not attack any who have made their profession. Only one of our company, while I was there, was interfered with. As soon as he was baptized, in spite of our advice to the contrary, he spoke publicly of Christ's religion with more zeal than discretion. He began to grow so warm in his preaching that not only did he prefer our worship to any other but he condemned all the rest outright. He proclaimed them to be profane in themselves and their followers to be impious and sacrilegious and worthy of everlasting fire. When he had long been preaching in this style, they arrested him, tried him, and convicted him not for despising their religion but for stirring up a riot among the people. His sentence after the verdict of guilty was exile. Actually, they count this principle among their most ancient institutions, that no one should suffer for his religion.

Utopus had heard that before his arrival the inhabitants had been continually quarreling among themselves about religion. He had observed that the universal dissensions between the individual sects who were fighting for their country had given him the opportunity of overcoming them all. From the very beginning, therefore, after he had gained the victory, he especially ordained that it should be lawful for every man to follow the religion of his choice, that each might strive to bring others over to his own, provided that he quietly and modestly supported his own by reasons nor bitterly demolished all others if his persuasions were not successful nor used any violence and refrained from abuse. If a person contends too vehemently in expressing his views, he is punished with exile or enslavement.

Utopus laid down these regulations not merely from regard for peace, which he saw to be utterly destroyed by constant wrangling and implacable hatred, but because he thought that this method of settlement was in the interest of religion itself. On religion he did not venture rashly to dogmatize. He was uncertain whether God did not desire a varied and manifold worship and therefore did not inspire different people with different views. But he was certain in thinking it both insolence and folly to demand by violence and threats that all should think to be true what you believe to be true. Moreover, even if it should be the case that one single religion is true and all the rest are false, he readily foresaw that, provided the matter was handled reasonably and moderately, truth by its own natural force would finally emerge sooner or later and stand forth conspicuously. But if the struggle were decided by arms and riots, since the worst men are always the most unyielding, the best and holiest religion would be overwhelmed because of the conflicting false religions, like grain choked by thorns and underbrush.

So he made the whole matter of religion an open question and left each one free to choose what he should believe. By way of exception, he conscientiously and strictly gave injunction that no one should fall so far below the dignity of human nature as to believe that souls likewise perish with the body or that the world is the mere sport of chance and not governed by any divine providence. After this life, accordingly, vices are ordained to be punished and virtue rewarded. Such is their belief, and if anyone thinks otherwise, they do not regard him even as a member of mankind, seeing that he has lowered the lofty nature of his soul to the level of a beast's miserable body—so far are they from classing him among their citizens whose laws and customs he would treat as worthless if it were not for fear. Who can doubt that he will strive either to evade by craft the public laws of his country or to break them by violence in order to serve his own private desires when he has nothing to fear but laws and no hope beyond the body?

Therefore an individual of this mind is tendered no honor, is entrusted with no office, and is put in charge of no function. He is universally regarded as of a sluggish and low disposition. But they do not punish him in any way, being convinced that it is in no man's power to believe what he chooses, nor do they compel him by threats to disguise his views, nor do they allow in the matter any deceptions or lies which they hate exceedingly as being next door to calculated malice. They forbid him to argue in support of his opinion in the presence of the common people, but in private before the priests and important personages they not only permit but also encourage it, being sure that such madness will in the end give way to reason.

There are others, too, and these not a few, who are not interfered with because they do not altogether lack reason for their view and because they are not evil men. By a much different error, these believe that brute animals also have immortal souls, but not comparable to ours in dignity or destined to equal felicity. Almost all Utopians are absolutely certain and convinced that human bliss will be so immense that, while they lament every man's illness, they regret the death of no one but him whom they see torn from life anxiously and unwillingly. This behavior they take to be a very bad omen as though the soul, being without hope and having a guilty conscience, dreaded its departure through a secret premonition of impending punishment. Besides, they suppose that God will not be pleased with the coming of one who, when summoned, does not gladly hasten to obey but is reluctantly drawn against his will. Persons who behold this kind of death are filled with horror and therefore carry the dead out to burial in melancholy silence. Then, after praying God to be merciful to their shades and graciously to pardon their infirmities, they cover the corpse with earth.

On the other hand, when men have died cheerfully and full of good hope, no one mourns for them, but they accompany their funerals with song, with great affection commending their souls to God. Then, with reverence rather than with sorrow, they cremate the bodies. On the spot they erect a pillar on which are inscribed the good points of the deceased. On returning home they recount his character and his deeds. No part of his life is more frequently or more gladly spoken of than his cheerful death.

They judge that this remembrance of uprightness is not only a most efficacious means of stimulating the living to good deeds but also a most acceptable form of attention to the dead. The latter they think are present when they are talked about, though invisible to the dull sight of mortals. It would be inconsistent with the lot of the blessed not to be able to travel freely where they please, and it would be ungrateful of them to reject absolutely all desire of revisiting their friends to whom they were bound during their lives by mutual love and charity. Charity, like all other good things, they conjecture to be increased after death rather than diminished in all good men. Consequently they believe that the dead move about among the living and are witnesses of their words and actions. Hence they go about their business with more confidence because of reliance on such protection. The belief, moreover, in the personal presence of their forefathers keeps men from any secret dishonorable deed.

They utterly despise and deride auguries and all other divinations of vain superstition, to which great attention is paid in other countries. But miracles, which occur without the assistance of nature, they venerate as operations and witnesses of the divine power at work.[9] In their country, too, they say, miracles often occur. Sometimes in great and critical affairs they pray publicly for a miracle, which they very confidently look for and obtain.

They think that the investigation of nature, with the praise arising from it, is an act of worship acceptable to God. There are persons, however, and these not so very few, who for religious motives eschew learning and scientific pursuit and yet allow themselves no leisure. It is only by keeping busy and by all good offices that they are determined to merit the happiness coming after death. Some tend the sick. Others repair roads, clean out ditches, rebuild bridges, dig turf and sand and stone, fell and cut up trees, and transport wood, grain, and other things into the cities in carts. Not only for the public but also for private persons they behave as servants and as more than slaves.

If anywhere there is a task so rough, hard, and filthy that most are deterred from it by the toil, disgust, and despair involved, they gladly and cheerfully claim it all for themselves. While perpetually engaged in hard work themselves, they secure leisure for the others and yet claim no credit for it. They neither belittle insultingly the life of others nor extol their own. The more that these men put themselves in the position of slaves the more are they honored by all.

Of these persons there are two schools. The one is composed of celibates who not only eschew all sexual activity but also abstain from eating flesh meat and in

9. Christian doctrine held that a miracle was an intervention by God into the natural order of things. God can perform miracles among non-Christians as well as Christians.

some cases from eating all animal food. They entirely reject the pleasures of this life as harmful. They long only for the future life by means of their watching and sweat. Hoping to obtain it very soon, they are cheerful and active in the meantime.

The other school is just as fond of hard labor, but regards matrimony as preferable, not despising the comfort which it brings and thinking that their duty to nature requires them to perform the marital act and their duty to the country to beget children. They avoid no pleasure unless it interferes with their labor. They like flesh meat just because they think that this fare makes them stronger for any work whatsoever. The Utopians regard these men as the saner but the first-named as the holier. If the latter based upon arguments from reason their preference of celibacy to matrimony and of a hard life to a comfortable one, they would laugh them to scorn. Now, however, since they say they are prompted by religion, they look up to and reverence them. For there is nothing about which they are more careful than not lightly to dogmatize on any point of religion. Such, then, are the men whom in their language they call by a special name of their own, Buthrescae, a word which may be translated as "religious par excellence."

They have priests of extraordinary holiness, and therefore very few. They have no more than thirteen in each city—with a like number of churches—except when they go to war. In that case, seven go forth with the army, and the same number of substitutes is appointed for the interval. When the regular priests come back, everyone returns to his former duties. Then those who are above the number of thirteen, until they succeed to the places of those who die, attend upon the high priest in the meantime. One, you see, is appointed to preside over the rest. They are elected by the people, just as all the other officials are, by secret ballot to avoid party spirit. When elected, they are ordained by their own group.

They preside over divine worship, order religious rites, and are censors of morals. It is counted a great disgrace for a man to be summoned or rebuked by them as not being of upright life. It is their function to give advice and admonition, but to check and punish offenders belongs to the governor and the other civil officials. The priests, however, do exclude from divine services persons whom they find to be unusually bad. There is almost no punishment which is more dreaded: they incur very great disgrace and are tortured by a secret fear of religion. Even their bodies will not long go scot-free. If they do not demonstrate to the priests their speedy repentance, they are seized and punished by the senate for their impiety.

To the priests is entrusted the education of children and youths. They regard concern for their morals and virtue as no less important than for their advancement in learning. They take the greatest pains from the very first to instill into children's minds, while still tender and pliable, good opinions, which are also useful for the preservation of their commonwealth. When once they are firmly implanted in children, they accompany them all through their adult lives and are of great help in watching over the condition of the commonwealth. The latter never decays except through vices which arise from wrong attitudes.

The feminine sex[1] is not debarred from the priesthood, but only a widow advanced in years is ever chosen, and that rather rarely. Unless they are women, the priests have for their wives the very finest women of the country.

---

1. In Greek and Roman religious practice, women could perform priestly functions. As these were the peoples whom More identified as understanding natural law, he must have thought that natural law did not limit a woman's role in religion.

To no other office in Utopia is more honor given, so much so that, even if they have committed any crime, they are subjected to no tribunal, but left only to God and to themselves. They judge it wrong to lay human hands upon one, however guilty, who has been consecrated to God in a singular manner as a holy offering. It is easier for them to observe this custom because their priests are very few and very carefully chosen.

Besides, it does not easily happen that one who is elevated to such dignity for being the very best among the good, nothing but virtue being taken into account, should fall into corruption and wickedness. Even if it does happen, human nature being ever prone to change, yet since they are but few and are invested with no power except the influence of honor, it need not be feared that they will cause any great harm to the state. In fact, the reason for having but few and exceptional priests is to prevent the dignity of the order, which they now reverence very high-ly, from being cheapened by communicating the honor to many. This is especially true since they think it hard to find many men so good as to be fit for so honorable a position for the filling of which it is not enough to be endowed with ordinary virtues.

They are not more esteemed among their own people than among foreign nations. This can easily be seen from a fact which, I think, is its cause. When the armies are fighting in battle, the priests are to be found separate but not very far off, settled on their knees, dressed in their sacred vestments. With hands out-stretched to heaven, they pray first of all for peace, next for a victory to their own side—but without much bloodshed on either side. When their side is winning, they run among the combatants, and restrain the fury of their own men against the rout-ed enemy. Merely to see and to appeal to them suffices to save one's life; to touch their flowing garments protects one's remaining goods from every harm arising from war.

This conduct has brought them such veneration among all nations every-where and has given them so real a majesty that they have saved their own citi-zens from the enemy as often as they have protected the enemy from their own men. The following is well known. Sometimes their own side had given way, their case had been desperate, they were taking to flight, and the enemy was rush-ing on to kill and to plunder. Then the carnage had been averted by the interven-tion of the priests. After the armies had been parted from each other, peace had been concluded and settled on just terms. Never had there been any nation so savage, cruel, and barbarous that it had not regarded their persons as sacred and inviolable.

They celebrate as holydays the first and the last day of each month and likewise of each year. The latter they divide into months, measured by the orbit of the moon just as the course of the sun rounds out the year. In their language they call the first days Cynemerni and the last days Trapemerni. These names have the same meaning as if they were rendered "First-Feasts" and "Final-Feasts."

Their temples are fine sights, not only elaborate in workmanship but also capa-ble of holding a vast throng, and necessarily so, since there are so few of them. The temples are all rather dark. This feature, they report, is due not to an ignorance of architecture but to the deliberate intention of the priests. They think that excessive light makes the thoughts wander, whereas scantier and uncertain light concentrates the mind and conduces to devotion.

In Utopia, as has been seen, the religion of all is not the same, and yet all its manifestations, though varied and manifold, by different roads as it were, tend to the same end, the worship of the divine nature. Therefore nothing is seen or heard in the temples which does not seem to agree with all in common. If any sect has a rite of its own, it is performed within the walls of each man's home. Public worship is conducted according to a ritual which does not at all detract from any of the private devotions. Therefore no image of the gods is seen in the temple so that the individual may be free to conceive of God with the most ardent devotion in any form he pleases. They invoke God by no special name except that of Mithras. By this word they agree to represent the one nature of the divine majesty whatever it be. The prayers formulated are such as every man may utter without offense to his own belief.

On the evening of the Final-Feasts, they gather in the temple, still fasting. They thank God for the prosperity they have enjoyed in the month or year of which that holyday is the last day. Next day, which is the First-Feast, they flock to the temples in the morning. They pray for good luck and prosperity in the ensuing year or month, of which this holyday is the auspicious beginning.

On the Final-Feasts, before they go to the temple, wives fall down at the feet of their husbands, children at the feet of their parents. They confess that they have erred, either by committing some fault or by performing some duty carelessly, and beg pardon for their offense. Hence, if any cloud of quarrel in the family has arisen, it is dispelled by this satisfaction so that with pure and clear minds they may be present at the sacrifices, for they are too scrupulous to attend with a troubled conscience. If they are aware of hatred or anger against anyone they do not assist at the sacrifices until they have been reconciled and have cleansed their hearts, for fear of swift and great punishment.

When they reach the temple, they part, the men going to the right side and the women to the left. Then they arrange their places so that the males in each home sit in front of the head of the household and the womenfolk are in front of the mother of the family. They thus take care that every gesture of everyone abroad is observed by those whose authority and discipline govern them at home. They also carefully see to it that everywhere the younger are placed in the company of the elder. If children were trusted to children, they might spend in childish foolery the time in which they ought to be conceiving a religious fear toward the gods, the greatest and almost the only stimulus to the practice of virtues.

They slay no animal in their sacrifices. They do not believe that the divine clemency delights in bloodshed and slaughter, seeing that it has imparted life to animate creatures that they might enjoy life. They burn incense and other fragrant substances and also offer a great number of candles. They are not unaware that these things add nothing to the divine nature, any more than do human prayers, but they like this harmless kind of worship. Men feel that, by these sweet smells and lights, as well as the other ceremonies, they somehow are uplifted and rise with livelier devotion to the worship of God.

The people are clothed in white garments in the temple. The priest wears vestments of various colors, of wonderful design and shape, but not of material as costly as one would expect. They are not interwoven with gold or set with precious stones but wrought with the different feathers of birds so cleverly and artistically that no costly material could equal the value of the handiwork. Moreover, in these birds' feathers and plumes and the definite order and plan by which they are set off on the priest's vestment, they say certain hidden mysteries are contained. By knowing the meaning as it is carefully handed down by the priests, they are reminded of God's benefits toward them and, in turn, of their own piety toward God and their duty toward one another.

As soon as the priest thus arrayed appears from the vestibule, all immediately fall on the ground in reverence. The silence all around is so deep that the very appearance of the congregation strikes one with awe as if some divine power were really present. After remaining a while on the ground, at a signal from the priest they rise.

At this point they sing praises to God, which they diversify with musical instruments, largely different in shape from those seen in our part of the world. Very many of them surpass in sweetness those in use with us, but some are not even comparable with ours. But in one respect undoubtedly they are far ahead of us. All their music, whether played on instruments or sung by the human voice, so renders and expresses the natural feelings, so suits the sound to the matter (whether the words be supplicatory, or joyful, or propitiatory, or troubled, or mournful, or angry), and so represents the meaning by the form of the melody that it wonderfully affects, penetrates, and inflames the souls of the hearers.

At the end, the priest and the people together repeat solemn prayers fixed in form, so drawn up that each individual may apply to himself personally what all recite together. In these prayers every man recognizes God to be the author of creation and governance and all other blessings besides. He thanks Him for all the benefits received, particularly that by the divine favor he has chanced on that commonwealth which is the happiest and has received that religion which he hopes to be the truest. If he errs in these matters or if there is anything better and more approved by God than that commonwealth or that religion, he prays that He will, of His goodness, bring him to the knowledge of it, for he is ready to follow in whatever path He may lead him. But if this form of a commonwealth be the best and his religion the truest, he prays that then He may give him steadfastness and bring all other mortals to the same way of living and the same opinion of God—unless there be something in this variety of religions which delights His inscrutable will.

Finally, he prays that God will take him to Himself by an easy death, how soon or late he does not venture to determine. However, if it might be without offense to His Majesty, it would be much more welcome to him to die a very hard death and go to God than to be kept longer away from Him even by a very prosperous career in life.[2]

After this prayer has been said, they prostrate themselves on the ground again. Then shortly they rise and go away to dinner. The rest of the day they pass in games and in exercises of military training.

Now I have described to you, as exactly as I could, the structure of that commonwealth which I judge not merely the best but the only one which can rightly claim the name of a commonwealth. Outside Utopia, to be sure, men talk freely of the public welfare—but look after their private interests only. In Utopia, where nothing is

---

2. The Utopians do not pray for forgiveness of the sins they have committed in the past, although they do pray for divine guidance in avoiding the errors they may commit in the future.

private, they seriously concern themselves with public affairs. Assuredly in both cases they act reasonably. For, outside Utopia, how many are there who do not realize that, unless they make some separate provision for themselves, however flourishing the commonwealth, they will themselves starve? For this reason, necessity compels them to hold that they must take account of themselves rather than of the people, that is, of others.

On the other hand, in Utopia, where everything belongs to everybody, no one doubts, provided only that the public granaries are well filled, that the individual will lack nothing for his private use. The reason is that the distribution of goods is not niggardly. In Utopia there is no poor man and no beggar. Though no man has anything, yet all are rich.

For what can be greater riches for a man than to live with a joyful and peaceful mind, free of all worries—not troubled about his food or harassed by the querulous demands of his wife or fearing poverty for his son or worrying about his daughter's dowry, but feeling secure about the livelihood and happiness of himself and his family: wife, sons, grandsons, great-grandsons, great-great-grandsons, and all the long line of their descendants that gentlefolk anticipate? Then take into account the fact that there is no less provision for those who are now helpless but once worked than for those who are still working.

At this point I should like anyone to be so bold as to compare this fairness with the so-called justice prevalent in other nations, among which, upon my soul, I cannot discover the slightest trace of justice and fairness. What brand of justice is it that any nobleman whatsoever or goldsmith-banker or moneylender or, in fact, anyone else from among those who either do no work at all or whose work is of a kind not very essential to the commonwealth, should attain a life of luxury and grandeur on the basis of his idleness or his nonessential work? In the meantime, the common laborer, the carter, the carpenter, and the farmer perform work so hard and continuous that beasts of burden could scarcely endure it and work so essential that no commonwealth could last even one year without it. Yet they earn such scanty fare and lead such a miserable life that the condition of beasts of burden might seem far preferable. The latter do not have to work so incessantly nor is their food much worse (in fact, sweeter to their taste) nor do they entertain any fear for the future. The workmen, on the other hand, not only have to toil and suffer without return or profit in the present but agonize over the thought of an indigent old age. Their daily wage is too scanty to suffice even for the day: much less is there an excess and surplus that daily can be laid by for their needs in old age.

Now is not this an unjust and ungrateful commonwealth? It lavishes great rewards on so-called gentlefolk and banking goldsmiths and the rest of that kind, who are either idle or mere parasites and purveyors of empty pleasures. On the contrary, it makes no benevolent provision for farmers, colliers, common laborers, carters, and carpenters without whom there would be no commonwealth at all. After it has misused the labor of their prime and after they are weighed down with age and disease and are in utter want, it forgets all their sleepless nights and all the great benefits received at their hands and most ungratefully requites them with a most miserable death.

What is worse, the rich every day extort a part of their daily allowance from the poor not only by private fraud but by public law. Even before they did so it seemed unjust that persons deserving best of the commonwealth should have the worst return. Now they have further distorted and debased the right and, finally, by making laws, have palmed it off as justice. Consequently, when I consider and turn over in my mind the state of all commonwealths flourishing anywhere today, so help me God, I can see nothing else than a kind of conspiracy of the rich, who are aiming at their own interests under the name and title of the commonwealth.[3] They invent and devise all ways and means by which, first, they may keep without fear of loss all that they have amassed by evil practices and, secondly, they may then purchase as cheaply as possible and abuse the toil and labor of all the poor. These devices become law as soon as the rich have once decreed their observance in the name of the public—that is, of the poor also!

Yet when these evil men with insatiable greed have divided up among themselves all the goods which would have been enough for all the people, how far they are from the happiness of the Utopian commonwealth! In Utopia all greed for money was entirely removed with the use of money. What a mass of troubles was then cut away! What a crop of crimes was then pulled up by the roots! Who does not know that fraud, theft, rapine, quarrels, disorders, brawls, seditions, murders, treasons, poisonings, which are avenged rather than restrained by daily executions, die out with the destruction of money? Who does not know that fear, anxiety, worries, toils, and sleepless nights will also perish at the same time as money? What is more, poverty, which alone money seemed to make poor, forthwith would itself dwindle and disappear if money were entirely done away with everywhere.

To make this assertion clearer, consider in your thoughts some barren and unfruitful year in which many thousands of men have been carried off by famine. I emphatically contend that at the end of that scarcity, if rich men's granaries had been searched, as much grain could have been found as, if it had been divided among the people killed off by starvation and disease, would have prevented anyone from feeling that meager return from soil and climate. So easily might men get the necessities of life if that blessed money, supposedly a grand invention to ease access to those necessities, was not in fact the only barrier to our getting what we need.

Even the rich, I doubt not, have such feelings. They are not unaware that it would be a much better state of affairs to lack no necessity than to have abundance of superfluities—to be snatched from such numerous troubles rather than to be hemmed in by great riches. Nor does it occur to me to doubt that a man's regard for his own interests or the authority of Christ our Savior—who in His wisdom could not fail to know what was best and who in His goodness would not fail to counsel what He knew to be best—would long ago have brought the whole world to adopt the laws of the Utopian commonwealth, had not one single monster, the chief and progenitor of all plagues, striven against it—I mean, Pride.

Pride measures prosperity not by her own advantages but by others' disadvantages.[4] Pride would not consent to be made even a goddess if no poor wretches were left for her to domineer over and scoff at, if her good fortune might not dazzle by

---

3. Hythlodaeus condemns practices associated with the accumulation of wealth as capital and the corresponding exploitation of workers in the interest of increasing capital. This goal is promoted by various legal "devices," particularly involving estates, that preserve capital within the upper ranks of society. But capital cannot be accumulated in a barter economy, where goods are exchanged for goods rather than for money. Hence Hythlodaeus eliminates money as a way of preventing the formation of capital. 4. Pride therefore prevents a society based on benefits, which typically redound to the welfare of a community rather than to that of particular individuals.

comparison with their miseries, if the display of her riches did not torment and intensify their poverty. This serpent from hell entwines itself around the hearts of men and acts like the suckfish in preventing and hindering them from entering on a better way of life.

Pride is too deeply fixed in men to be easily plucked out. For this reason, the fact that this form of a commonwealth—which I should gladly desire for all—has been the good fortune of the Utopians at least, fills me with joy. They have adopted such institutions of life as have laid the foundations of the commonwealth not only most happily, but also to last forever, as far as human prescience can forecast. At home they have extirpated the roots of ambition and factionalism, along with all the other vices. Hence there is no danger of trouble from domestic discord, which has been the only cause of ruin to the well-established prosperity of many cities. As long as harmony is preserved at home and its institutions are in a healthy state, not all the envy of neighboring rulers, though it has rather often attempted it and has always been repelled, can avail to shatter or to shake that nation.

When Raphael had finished his story, many things came to my mind which seemed very absurdly established in the customs and laws of the people described—not only in their method of waging war, their ceremonies and religion, as well as their other institutions, but most of all in that feature which is the principal foundation of their whole structure. I mean their common life and subsistence—without any exchange of money. This latter alone utterly overthrows all the nobility, magnificence, splendor, and majesty which are, in the estimation of the common people, the true glories and ornaments of the commonwealth.

I knew, however, that he was wearied with his tale, and I was not quite certain that he could brook any opposition to his views, particularly when I recalled his censure of others on account of their fear that they might not appear to be wise enough, unless they found some fault to criticize in other men's discoveries. I therefore praised their way of life and his speech and, taking him by the hand, led him in to supper. I first said, nevertheless, that there would be another chance to think about these matters more deeply and to talk them over with him more fully. If only this were some day possible!

Meanwhile, though in other respects he is a man of the most undoubted learning as well as of the greatest knowledge of human affairs, I cannot agree with all that he said. But I readily admit that there are very many features in the Utopian commonwealth which it is easier for me to wish for in our countries than to have any hope of seeing realized.

END OF BOOK TWO

THE END OF THE AFTERNOON DISCOURSE OF
RAPHAEL HYTHLODAEUS ON THE LAWS
AND CUSTOMS OF THE ISLAND OF
UTOPIA, HITHERTO KNOWN BUT
TO FEW, AS REPORTED BY THE
MOST DISTINGUISHED AND
MOST LEARNED MAN,
MR. THOMAS MORE,
CITIZEN AND SHERIFF OF LONDON
FINIS

PERSPECTIVES

Government and Self-Government

In a period marked by an increasingly centralized monarchy and a corresponding resistance to its bureaucratic reforms, ideas on government were debated in a variety of discourses. Political philosophers, such as More, described ideal forms of rule; historians reported events that actually happened and attempted to explain what followed as a result. A writer's point of view was clearly important; philosophers constructed models of order that reflected their belief in a certain kind of creation and the deity overseeing its development, while historians tried to interpret the actions of a person or a group in relation to the social interests they judged were at stake. Inevitably, the practice of government demonstrated the limits of a theory, while theory suggested the implications of a practice.

The selections included here reveal how comprehensive were these concerns, understood both in theory and in relation to daily life. Political thinkers sought to determine the proper business of state and also the conduct required of individual persons. Of course, they identified men and women as particular characters, each with his or her habits of mind and behavior, but they also recognized that every person had a specific office, a place and a role in life that was governed by expectations created by custom and, to a lesser extent, by common law. A man

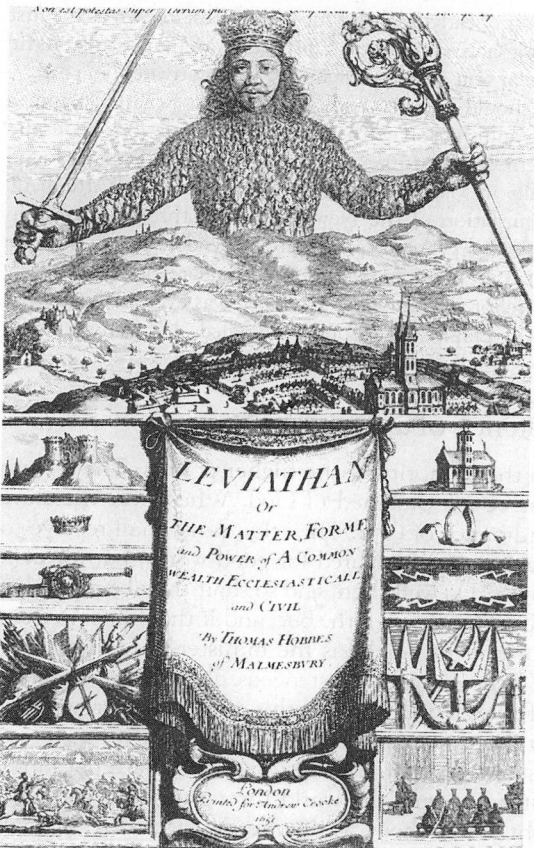

Frontispiece to *Leviathan,* by Thomas Hobbes. 1651. This engraving illustrates the author's idea of government in a "commonwealth." Rising above the countryside is the mystical figure of the body politic. It consists of a crowned head—perhaps a dictator, perhaps a monarch—who has sovereign authority, and a body comprising the people, his subjects. The sovereign wields two powers: a civil power, symbolized by the sword in his right hand, and an ecclesiastical power, symbolized by the crozier in his left. Cells in the lower register of the engraving depict the mechanisms that support these powers, with scenes and symbols of the military on the left and of the church on the right. Published in 1651, *Leviathan* attempted to articulate conditions of rule proclaimed two years earlier, after the execution of Charles I. Hobbes believed that government was created by men who, rejecting the warlike state of nature in which they had originated, had handed over their natural rights to a sovereign in a kind of "contract" which traded their obedience for his protection. The idea of a body politic regularly was featured in early modern political thought and was discussed by writers as different as Bishop John Ponet and James I.

was primarily understood in terms of his work—as servant, artisan, yeoman, merchant, magistrate, or lord. A woman had fewer options and was usually identified according to her marital status—as a maid, a mother, or a widow. Over the course of the century, these categories became subject to challenge. Controversy grew as to the very basis of social order, the fundamental authority and power of the superior (whatever the office) over his or her subordinates. Protestant notions of the primacy of the individual conscience over collective authority were particularly effective in upsetting customary hierarchies of rule. On the one hand, they were used to justify individual rights; on the other, they supplied a rationale for those claiming such rights to protest as a group or a social body. There was a general agreement that states and persons should be governed by rules, but what these rules ought to be was becoming a contentious topic. Discussions of the power and authority of monarchs and magistrates generally emphasized that their power and authority were not absolute but limited by divine, natural, and positive law or the law of the land. This emphasis is matched by a pervasive fear of the tyrant—the ruler who not only makes and unmakes the law but does so in his own interest rather than for his people's welfare.

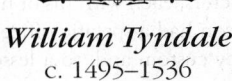

William Tyndale
c. 1495–1536

William Tyndale was perhaps the foremost of early English Protestants. Best known as the first translator of the Bible into English, he was active in political disputes as well, insisting on the absolute authority and power of the secular arm of government. He was motivated, in part, by his belief that no European monarch should have to obey the Pope in Rome. To him a monarch and his magistrates were God's ministers on earth. In its later formulations under the Stuarts, this view of government was criticized for its toleration of tyranny. Tyndale found allies in Protestant Europe, and especially in Martin Luther whom he visited in Wittenberg. He travelled extensively, seeing his translation of the New Testament through presses in Cologne and Worms, settling finally in Antwerp. As the popularity of Tyndale's work grew, he became increasingly the target of criticism. Denounced by bishops in England and particularly by Sir Thomas More, then a privy counsellor to Henry VIII, Tyndale was eventually arrested for heresy by officers of the Holy Roman Empire, imprisoned, strangled, and burned at the stake at Vilvorde in 1535.

from The Obedience of a Christian Man

Let every soul submit himself unto the authority of the higher powers. There is no power but of God; the powers that be are ordained of God. Whosoever therefore resisteth the power, resisteth the ordinance of God. They that resist shall receive to themselves damnation. For rulers are not to be feared for good works, but for evil. Wilt thou be without fear of the power? Do well then, and so shalt thou be praised of the same, for he is the minister of God for thy wealth. But, and if thou do evil, then fear, for he beareth not a sword for nought, for he is the minister of God, to take vengeance on them that do evil. Wherefore ye must needs obey, not for fear of vengeance only, but also because of conscience. Even for this cause pay ye tribute: for they are God's ministers serving for the same purpose. * * *

God therefore hath given laws unto all nations, and in all lands hath put kings, governors, and rulers in his own stead, to rule the world through them. And hath commanded all causes to be brought before them, as thou readest (Exod. 22). In all causes (saith he) of injury or wrong, whether it be ox, ass, sheep, or vesture, or any lost thing which another challengeth, let the cause of both parties be brought unto the gods; whom the gods condemn, the same shall pay double unto his neighbor. Mark, the judges are called gods in the Scriptures, because they are in God's room,[1] and execute the commandments of God. And in another place of the said chapter, Moses chargeth saying, See that thou rail not on[2] the gods, neither speak evil of the ruler of thy people. Whosoever therefore resisteth them, resisteth God (for they are in the room of God) and they that resist shall receive the damnation.

Such obedience unto father and mother, master, husband, emperor, king, lords, and rulers, requireth God of all nations, yea of the very Turks and infidels. * * *

Neither may the inferior person avenge himself upon the superior, or violently resist him for whatsoever wrong it be. If he do, he is condemned in the deed doing, inasmuch as he taketh upon him that which belongeth to God only, which saith, Vengeance is mine, and I will reward (Deut. 32). And Christ sayeth (Mat. 26), All they that take the sword shall perish with the sword. Taketh thou a sword to avenge thyself? So givest thou not room unto God to avenge thee, but robbest him of his most high honor, in that thou wilt not let him be judge over thee.

1528

━━◆◆◆◆━━

Juan Luis Vives
1492–1540

A Spanish philosopher educated in Valencia, Paris, and Bruges, Vives lectured at Oxford and attended the court of Henry VIII between 1523 and 1528. His treatise on the education of women was composed for Mary Tudor while she was still a child, at the request of her mother, Catherine of Aragon, wife of Henry VIII. It was published in Latin in 1523; the English translation, by Richard Hyrde, was published in 1540. It illustrates the way in which the idea of government comprised doctrine on matters of individual conduct. Vives clearly believed that the subordination of a wife to a husband was an expression of the natural order of things, not a social convention; he thought it depended on the innate characteristics of the female in contrast to the male.

from Instruction of a Christian Woman

Chastity is the principal virtue of a woman, and counterepayseth with[1] all the rest. If she have that, no man will look for any other, and if she lack that, no man will regard other. * * * She that is chaste is fair, well-favored, rich, fruitful, noble, and all best things that can be named, and contrary, she that is unchaste is a sea and treasure of all illness. Now shamefastness[2] and soberness be the inseparable companions of chastity, insomuch that she cannot be chaste that is not ashamed.[3] * * *

Of shamefastness cometh demureness and measureableness, that whether she think ought, or say, or do, nothing shall be outrageous, neither in passions of mind, nor words, nor deeds; nor presumptuous; nor nice,[4] wanton, pert; nor boasting; nor ambitious; and as for honors she will neither think herself worthy nor desire them but rather flee them, and if they chance unto her, she will be ashamed of them, as of a

---

1. Place.
2. Complain against.
1. Outweighs.
2. Modesty.

3. I.e., good manners and temperance derive from modesty.
4. Fastidious.

thing not deserved; nor be for nothing high-minded, neither for beauty, nor properness,[5] nor kindred, nor riches, being sure that they shall soon perish and that pride shall have everlasting pain.

The man getteth, that woman saveth and keepeth. Therefore he hath stomach given to him to gather lustily,[6] and she hath it taken from her, that she may warily keep.[7] And of this soberness of body cometh soberness of mind. * * * Let her apply herself to virtue and be content with a little, and take in worth that[8] she hath nor seek for other that she hath not, nor for [the wealth of] other folks, whereof riseth envy, hate, or curiosity of other folks' matters.

Forth she must go sometimes, but I would it should be as seldom as may be for many causes. Principally because as often as a maid goeth forth among people, so often she cometh in judgment and extreme peril of her beauty, honesty, demureness, wit, shamefastness, and virtue. For nothing is more tender than is the fame and estimation of women, nor nothing more in danger of wrong, insomuch that it hath been said, and not without a cause, to hang by a cobweb.

Let the woman understand that if she will not spend all her substance to save her husband from never so little harms, she is not worthy to bear the name neither of a good nor Christian woman, nor once to be called wife. * * * I will that she shall give him great worship, reverence, great obedience, and service also, which thing not only the example of the old world teacheth us, but also all laws, both spiritual and temporal, and nature herself cryeth and commandeth that the woman shall be subject and obedient to the man. And in all kinds of beasts the females obey the males and wait upon them and fawn upon them and suffer themselves to be corrected of them, which thing nature showeth must be and is convenient[9] to be done. * * * Nature showeth that the male's duty is to succor and defend, and the female's to follow and wait upon the male and to creep under his aid and obey him, that she may live the better.

Let the authority and rule be reserved unto thy husband and be thou an example to all thine house what sovereignty they owe unto him. Do thou prove him to be lord by thine obedience, and make him great with thine humility, for the more honor thou givest unto him, the [more] honorable thou shalt be thyself.

That thou mayest better obey thy husband and do all things after his mind, first thou must learn all his manners and consider well his dispositions and state, for there be many kinds of husbands and all ought to be loved, honored and worshipped and obeyed, but all must not be entreated under one manner. * * * If thou have one after thine appetite, thou mayest be glad, * * * but if he be ill, either find some craft to make him good or at the leastwise better to deal with.

+ ⊰⊱ +

Sir Thomas Elyot
c. 1490–1546

To support his defense of monarchy in his treatise on government, Sir Thomas Elyot—a humanist and Henry VIII's ambassador to Emperor Charles V—drew on popular analogies with what he saw as the hierarchical order of the heavens and the natural world. He also insisted that a monarchy—in which the king (or queen) held a patriarchal kind of power—

---

5. Station in life.
6. Energetically.
7. Carefully conserve.

8. Value what.
9. Appropriate.

preserved security within society and yet, by observing custom and established law, avoided tyranny or anarchy. His later work continued to engage political topics. His dialogue supporting women's rule may have been composed in the anticipation of Mary Tudor's queenship; its argument drew on a literature debating the nature of womankind as it was represented in both the medieval *querelle des femmes*, or "controversy on the subject of womankind," and the classical and humanist histories of famous women. His character Candidus ("honest and open-minded") represents the affirmative case; Caninius ("snarling and spiteful") states his objections to it.

from The Book Named the Governor

Like as to a castle or fortress sufficeth one owner or sovereign, and where any more be of like power and authority seldom cometh the work to perfection; or being already made, where the one diligently overseeth and the other neglecteth, in that contention all is subverted and cometh to ruin, in semblable wise[1] doth a public weal[2] that hath more chief governors than one. Example we may take of the Greeks, among whom in divers cities were divers forms of public weals governed by multitudes. Wherein one was most tolerable where the governance and rule was always permitted to them which excelled in virtue, and was in the Greek tongue called *Aristocratia*, in Latin *Optimorum Potentia*, in the English rule of men of best disposition, which the Thebans of long time observed.

Another public weal was among the Athenians, where equality was of estate among[3] the people, and only by their whole consent their city and dominions were governed: which might well be called a monster with many heads. Nor never was it certain nor stable, and often times they banished or slew the best citizens, which by their virtue and wisdom had most profited to the public weal. This manner of governance was called in Greek *Democratia*, in Latin *Popularis Potentia*, in English the rule of the commonalty. Of these two governances none of them may be sufficient. For in the first, which consisteth of good men, virtue is not so constant in a multitude, but that some, being once in authority be incensed with a glory, some with ambition, other with covetousness and desire of treasure or possessions. Whereby they fall into contention, and finally, where any achieveth the superiority, the whole government is reduced unto a few in number, which fearing the multitude and their mutability, to the intent to keep them in dread to rebel, ruleth by terror and cruelty, thinking thereby to keep themselves in surety.[4] Notwithstanding, rancour, coarcted[5] and long detained in a narrow room, at the last bursteth out with intolerable violence and bringeth all to confusion. For the power that is practised to the hurt of many cannot continue. The popular estate,[6] if it anything do vary from equality of substance or estimation, or that the multitude of people have overmuch liberty, of necessity one of these inconveniences must happen: either tyranny, where he that is too much in favor would be elevate and suffer none equality, or else into the rage of a commonalty,[7] which of all rules is most to be feared. For like as the commons, if they feel some severity, they do humbly serve and obey, so where they embracing a license refuse to be bridled, they fling[8] and plunge. And if they once throw down their governor, they order everything without justice, only with vengeance and cruelty, and

---

1. The same way.
2. State.
3. Endorsed by.
4. Elyot argues against democracy because he believes that it leads to various forms of tyranny: Among the many, a few will gain ascendancy and, to keep their fellow citizens from rebelling, will rule by terror and think themselves secure.

5. Confined.
6. Common people.
7. Democracy also leads to the tyranny of a single man or of the mob: either the single man manages to take charge and allows no "equality" among the ruled, or the many degenerate into a mob.
8. Rear.

with incomparable difficulty and unneth[9] by any wisdom [can they] be pacified and brought again into order. Wherefore undoubtedly the best and most sure governance is by one king or prince, which ruleth only for the weal[1] of his people to him subject; and that manner of governance is best approved, and hath longest continued, and is most ancient. For who can deny but that all thing in heaven and earth is governed by one God, by one perpetual order, by one providence? One sun ruleth over the day, and one moon over the night. And to descend down to the earth, in a little beast, which of all other is most to be marveled at, I mean the bee, is left to man by nature, as it seemeth, a perpetual figure of a just governance or rule, who hath among them one principal bee for their governor, who excelleth all other in greatness, yet hath he no prick or sting, but in him is more knowledge than in the residue.[2] For if the day following shall be fair and dry, and that the bees may issue out of their stalls without peril of rain or vehement wind, in the morning early he calleth them, making a noise as it were the sound of the horn or a trumpet; and with that all the residue prepare them to labor, and flyeth abroad, gathering nothing but that shall be sweet and profitable, although they sit often times on herbs and other things that be venomous and stinking.

The captain himself laboreth not for his sustenance, but all the other for him; he only seeth that if any drone or other unprofitable bee entereth into the hive and consumeth the honey gathered by other, that he be immediately expelled from that company. And when there is another number of bees increased, they semblably[3] have also a captain, which be not suffered to continue with the other. Wherefore this new company gathered into a swarm, having their captain among them and environing[4] him to preserve him from harm, they issue forth seeking a new habitation, which they find in some tree, except with some pleasant noise they be lured and conveyed unto another hive. I suppose who seriously beholdeth this example, and hath any commendable wit, shall thereof gather much matter to the forming of a public weal.

1531

from The Defence of Good Women

CANDIDUS   [to Caninius, detractor of women] And so ye conclude,[1] that the power of reason is more in the prudent and diligent keeping than in the valiant or politic getting, and that discretion, election, and prudence, which is all and in every part reason, do excel strength, wit, and hardiness.[2] And consequently, they in whom be those virtues, in that, that they have them, do excel in just estimation them that be strong, hardy, or politic in getting of anything.

CANINIUS   Ye have well gathered together all that conclusion.

CANDIDUS   Behold Caninius, where ye be now: ye have so much extolled reason, that in the respect thereof bodily strength remaineth as nothing. Forasmuch as the corporal powers with powers of the soul can make no comparison. And ye have

9. Scarcely.
1. Good.
2. Elyot did not realize that the bee that ruled the hive was in fact female.
3. Similarly.
4. Surrounding.
1. Candidus reminds Caninius that they have reached a conclusion: Reason is more manifest in the arts that conserve resources than in those that acquire them. The effect of this conclusion will then prove decisive to the

debate between the two men: By putting reason above any other attribute, Caninius has unwittingly established a basis for Candidus's claim that women, conventionally held to excel in virtues associated with introspection, are superior to men, who were rather praised for excelling in virtues associated with physical strength. The notion of a woman's function as conservative is expressed in treatises on domestic economy by Xenophon and Aristotle.
2. Courage.

not denied but that this word *Man*, unto whom reason pertaineth, doth imply in it both man and woman.[3] And agreeing unto Aristotle's saying ye have confirmed that prudence which in effect is more aptly applied to the woman, whereby she is more circumspect in keeping, as strength is to the man, that he may be more valiant in getting. And likewise ye have preferred the prudence in keeping, for the utility thereof, before the valiantness in getting, and seemingly them which be prudent in keeping before them that be only strong and hardy in getting. And so ye have concluded that women, which are prudent in keeping, be more excellent than men in reason, which be only strong and valiant in getting. And where excellency is, there is most perfection. Wherefore a woman is not a creature unperfect, but as it seemeth is more perfect than man.

CANINIUS   Why, have ye dallied herefore with me all this long season?

CANDIDUS   Surely I have used neither dalliance nor sophistry, but if ye consider it well, ye shall find it but a natural induction, and plain to all them that have any capacity. But yet have I somewhat more to say to you. Ye said moreover Caninius, that the wits of women were apt only to trifles and shrewdness and not to wisdom and civil policy. I will be plain to you, I am sorry to find in your words such manner of lewdness, I cry you mercy, I would have said so much ungentleness, and in your own words so much forgetfulness.

CANINIUS   What mean ye thereby?

CANDIDUS   Ye have twice granted that natural reason is in women as well as in men.

CANINIUS   Yes and what then?

CANDIDUS   Then have women also discretion, election, and prudence, which do make that wisdom which pertaineth to governance. And perdy,[4] many arts and necessary occupations have been invented by women, as I will bring now some unto your remembrance.

                                                                                    1540

John Ponet
1514–1556

Ponet was among the most articulate and thoughtful of the Protestants who wrote against tyranny. Made Bishop of Winchester under Henry VIII, he fled to Frankfurt after the accession of Mary I; his treatise on government was composed in 1556 while he was abroad and is one of several such works produced during this period by writers who have been called the Marian exiles. Ponet's argument supporting tyrannicide is grounded in his belief that the monarch has authority and power by virtue of his office not his person; once he fails to rule according to the requirements of office, he is no longer a monarch and therefore can be deposed and even tried for crimes like any other subject. Many of the points in Ponet's treatise were rehearsed in arguments against the rule of Charles I.

from A Short Treatise of Political Power

Forasmuch as those that be the rulers in the world and would be taken for gods (that is, the ministers and images of God here in earth, the examples and mirrors of all godliness, justice, equity, and other virtues) claim and exercise an absolute power, which

3. A reminder that man and woman were alike in being   4. Indeed.
made in the image of God (Genesis 1.27).

also they call a fullness of power, or prerogative to do what they lust, and none may gainsay them; to dispense with the laws as pleaseth them, and freely and without correction or offence do contrary to the law of nature, and other [of] God's laws and the positive laws and customs of their countries, or break them; and use their subjects as men do their beasts, and as lords do their villeins and bondmen, getting their goods from them by hook and by crook, with *Sic voio, Sic jubeo* [As I wish, so I command], and spending it to the destruction of their subjects, the misery of this time requireth to examine whether they do it rightfully or wrongfully; that if it be rightful, the people may the more willingly obey and receive the same; if it be wrongful, that then those that use it may the rather for the fear of God leave it. For (no doubt) God will come, and judge the world with equity, and revenge the cause of the oppressed. * * *

True it is, that in matters indifferent, that is, that of themselves be neither good nor evil, hurtful, or profitable, but for a decent order, kings and princes (to whom the people have given their authority) may make such laws, and dispense with them. But in matters not indifferent, but godly and profitably ordained for the commonwealth, there can they not (for all their authority) break them or dispense with them. For princes are ordained to do good, not to do evil; to take away evil, not to increase it; to give example of well doing, not to be procurers of evil; to procure the wealth and benefit of their subjects, and not to work their hurt or undoing. * * *

Antiochus the third, King of Syria, wrote thus to all the cities of his dominion, that if he did command anything that should be contrary to the laws, they should not pass thereon, but that rather they should think it was stolen or forged without his knowledge, considering that the prince or governor is nothing else but the minister of the laws. And this same saying of this most noble king seemed to be so just and reasonable that it is taken for a common principle, how subjects should know when they should do that they be commanded, and when they ought not.

Likewise a bishop of Rome, called Alexander the third,[1] wrote to an archbishop to do a thing which seemed to the archbishop to be unreasonable and contrary to the laws. The pope perceiving that the archbishop was offended with his writing and would not do that he required, desired him not to be offended, but that if there were cause why he thought he should not do that he required, he would advertise him and therewith would be satisfied.[2]

This is a pope's saying, which who is so hardy daring to deny to be of less authority than a law? Yea, not below, but above God's word?[3] Whereupon this is a general rule, that the pope is not to be obeyed, but in lawful and honest things, and so by good argument from the more to the less, that princes (being but footstools and stirrup holders to popes) commanding their subjects [to do] that [which] is not godly, not just, not lawful, or hurtful to their country, ought not to be obeyed, but withstood. For the subjects ought not (against nature) to further their own destruction, but to seek their own salvation, not to maintain evil but to suppress evil. For not only the doers but also the consentors to evil shall be punished, say both God's and man's laws. And men ought to have more respect to their country, than to their prince; to the commonwealth, than to any one person. For the country and commonwealth is a degree above the king. Next unto God, men ought to love their country, and the

---

1. I.e., Pope Alexander III. As a Protestant, Ponet could not consider that the Pope was anything more than the Bishop of Rome.
2. The Pope would reconsider his order to determine whether it was lawful.

3. The law is above not only the word of the Pope but even the word of God expressed in Scripture. Ponet understands the law as positive law, the aggregate of the common law and statute; it is, in other words, law made by the people.

whole commonwealth before any member of it, as kings and princes (be they never so great) are but members, and commonwealths may stand well enough and flourish, albeit there be no kings, but contrarywise, without a commonwealth there can be no king. Commonwealths and realms may live when the head is cut off, and may put on a new head, that is, make them a new governor, when they see their old head seek too much his own will and not the wealth of the whole body, for the which he was only ordained. And by that justice and law that lately hath been executed in England (if it may be called justice and law), it should appear that the ministers of civil power do sometimes command that, that the subjects ought not to do.

When the innocent Lady Jane, contrary to her will, yea by force, with tears dropping down her cheeks, suffered herself to be called Queen of England, yet ye see, because she consented to that which was not by civil justice lawful, she and her husband for company suffered the pains of traitors, both headless, buried in one pit. * * *

But thou wilt say, whereof cometh this common saying: all things be the kaiser's, all things be the king's?[4] It cannot come of nothing. But by that that is already said, ye see that every man may keep his own and none may take it from him, so that it cannot be interpreted that all things be the kaiser's or king's, as his own proper,[5] or that they may take them from their subjects at their pleasure, but it is thus to be expounded, that they ought to defend that[6] every man hath, that he may quietly enjoy his own, and to see that they be not robbed or spoiled thereof. For as in a great man's house all things be said to be the steward's, because it is committed to his charge to see that every man in the house behave himself honestly and do his duty to see that all things be well kept and preserved; and may take nothing away from any man, nor misspend, or waste; and of his doings he must render account to his lord for all, so in a realm or other dominion, the realm and country are God's. He is the lord, the people are his servants, and the king or governor is but God's minister or steward, ordained not to misuse the servants, that is the people, neither to spoil them of what they have, but to see the people do their duty to their lord God, that the goods of this world be not abused but spent to God's glory, to the maintenance and defense of the commonwealth, and not to the destruction of it. The prince's watch ought to defend the poor man's house, his labor the subject's ease, his diligence the subject's pleasure, his trouble the subject's quietness. And as the sun never standeth still but continually goeth about the world, doing his office, with his heat refreshing and comforting all natural things in the world, so ought a good prince to be continually occupied in his ministry, not seeking his own profit, but the wealth of those that be committed to his charge.

John Foxe
1516–1587

Like John Ponet, Foxe was a Protestant scholar who left England after the accession of Mary I. He went to live in Basel, where he (barely) supported himself as a proofreader. In Basel he began the work that would eventually result in his major history of the Christian church and its martyrs. He returned to London after the Protestant Queen Elizabeth ascended the throne, and in 1563 published his book under the title *Acts and Monuments of these latter and perilous*

---

4. Cf. Matthew 22.21: "Render unto Caesar the things which are Caesar's, and unto God the things that are God's."

5. Property.
6. That which.

days; it soon became known as *The Book of Martyrs.* Like many of his fellow Marian exiles, Foxe believed that the authority and power of the monarchy should be limited, especially with respect to church doctrine and matters of faith. His accounts of martyrs to Catholicism testify not only to the gruesome persecutions the state enacted and the formidable courage of those who resisted the power of the secular arm of government, but also to his own skillful use of images, reported speech, and descriptive detail, as he shapes the reader's sympathies toward his cause. His book was enormously popular, a fact that illustrates how ready contemporary readers were to take sides in religious conflict and how effectively historical narrative, however polemical and one-sided, could be used to advance or discredit a particular political or religious position.

from The Book of Martyrs

There was a certain act of parliament made in the government of the lord Hamilton, earl of Arran, and governor of Scotland, giving privilege to all men of the realm of Scotland, to read the Scriptures in their mother tongue and language, secluding nevertheless all reasoning, conference, convocation of people to hear the Scriptures read or expounded. Which liberty of private reading being granted by public proclamation, lacked not its own fruit, so that in sundry parts of Scotland thereby were opened the eyes of the elect of God to see the truth, and abhor the papistical abominations, amongst whom were certain persons in St. John's-town, as after is declared.

At this time there was a sermon made by friar Spence, in St. John's-town, otherwise called Perth, affirming prayer made to saints to be so necessary that without it there could be no hope of salvation to man. This blasphemous doctrine a burgess of the said town, called Robert Lamb, could not abide, but accused him in open audience of erroneous doctrine, and adjured[1] him, in God's name, to utter the truth. This the friar, being stricken with fear, promised to do; but the trouble, tumult, and stir of the people increased so, that the friar could have no audience, and yet the said Robert, with great danger of his life, escaped the hands of the multitude, namely of the women who, contrary to nature, addressed them to extreme cruelty against him.

At this time, A.D. 1543, the enemies of the truth procured John Charterhouse, who favored the truth and was provost of the said city and town of Perth, to be deposed from his office by the said governor's authority, and a papist, called Master Alexander Marbeck, to be chosen in his room, that they might bring the more easily their wicked and ungodly enterprise to an end.

After the deposing of the former provost and election of the other, in the month of January the year aforesaid, on St. Paul's day came to St. John's-town the governor, the cardinal, the Earl of Argyle, Justice Sir John Campbell of Lundie, knight, and Justice Defort, the Lord Borthwicke, the bishops of Dunblane and Orkney, with certain other of the nobility. And although there were many accused for the crime of heresy (as they term it), yet these persons only were apprehended upon the said St. Paul's day: Robert Lamb, William Anderson, James Hunter, James Raveleson, James Finlason, and Helen Stirke his wife, and were cast that night in the Spay Tower of the said city, the morrow after to abide judgment.

Upon the morrow, when they appeared and were brought forth to judgment in the town, were laid in general to all their charge the violating of the act of parliament before expressed and their conference and assemblies in hearing and expounding of Scripture against the tenor of the said act. Robert Lamb was accused, in spe-

1. Charged.

cial, for interrupting of the friar in the pulpit; which he not only confessed, but also affirmed constantly, that it was the duty of no man who understood and knew the truth to hear the same impugned without contradiction, and therefore sundry who were there present in judgment, who hid the knowledge of the truth, should bear the burden in God's presence for consenting to the same.

The said Robert also, with William Anderson and James Raveleson, were accused for hanging up the image of St. Francis in a cord, nailing of rams' horns to his head, and a cow's rump to his tail, and for eating of a goose on Allhallow-even.

James Hunter, being a simple man and without learning, and a flesher[2] by occupation, so that he could be charged with no great knowledge in the doctrine, yet because he often used that suspected company of the rest, he was accused.

The woman Helen Stirke was accused, for that in her childbed she was not accustomed to call on the name of the Virgin Mary, being exorted thereto by her neighbors, but only on God for Jesus Christ's sake; and because she said, in like manner, that if she herself had been in the time of the Virgin Mary, God might have looked to her humility and base estate as he did to the Virgin's in making her the mother of Christ, thereby meaning that there were no merits in the Virgin which procured her that honor, to be made the Mother of Christ and to be preferred before other women, but that only God's free mercy exalted her to that estate, which words were counted most execrable in the face of the clergy, and of the whole multitude.

James Raveleson aforesaid, building a house, set upon the round of his fourth stair the three-crowned diadem of Peter carved out of tree, which the cardinal took as done in mockage of his cardinal's hat; and this procured no favor to the said James at their hands.

These aforesaid persons, upon the morrow after St. Paul's day, were condemned and judged to death, and that by an assize, for violating (as was alleged) the act of parliament, in reasoning and conferring upon Scripture, for eating flesh upon days forbidden, for interrupting the holy friar in the pulpit, for dishonoring of images, and for blaspheming of the Virgin Mary, as they alleged.

After sentence was given, their hands were bound and the men cruelly treated, which thing the woman beholding, desired likewise to be bound by the sergeants with her husband for Christ's sake.

There was great intercession made by the town in the mean season, for the life of these persons aforenamed, to the governor, who of himself was willing so to have done that they might have been delivered, but the governor was so subject to the appetite of the cruel priests that he could not do that which he would. Yea, they menaced to assist his enemies and to depose him, except that he assisted their cruelty.[3]

There were certain priests in the city, who did eat and drink before these honest men's houses, to whom the priests were much bounden. These priests were earnestly desired to entreat for their hosts at the cardinal's hands, but they altogether refused, desiring rather their death than their preservation.[4] So cruel are these beasts, from the lowest to the highest.

Then after, they were carried by a great band of armed men (for they feared rebellion in the town except they had their men of war) to the place of execution, which was common to all thieves, and that to make their cause appear more odious to the people.

---

2. Butcher.
3. If the governor did not agree with the priests, they would turn to his enemies and attempt to depose him.

4. I.e., the priests discounted the hospitality they had enjoyed and agreed to the persecution of their hosts.

Robert Lamb, at the gallows' foot, made his exortation to the people, desiring them to fear God, and leave the leaven of papistical abominations,[5] and manifestly there prophesied of the ruin and plague which came upon the cardinal thereafter. So every one comforting another, and assuring themselves they should sup together in the kingdom of heaven that night, they commended themselves to God, and died constantly in the Lord.

The woman desired earnestly to die with her husband, but she was not suffered; yet, following him to the place of execution, she gave him comfort, exorting him to perseverance and patience for Christ's sake, and, parting from him with a kiss, said on this manner, "Husband, rejoice, for we have lived together many joyful days; but this day, in which we must die, ought to be most joyful unto us both, because we must have joy forever. Therefore I will not bid you good night, for we shall suddenly meet with joy in the kingdom of heaven." The woman, after that, was taken to a place to be drowned, and albeit she had a child sucking on her breast, yet this moved nothing the unmerciful hearts of the enemies. So, after she had commended her children to the neighbors of the town for God's sake, and the sucking bairn was given to the nurse, she sealed up the truth by her death.

⊶ ⚎ ⊷

Richard Hooker
1554–1600

Richard Hooker was a theologian and a professor of Hebrew at Oxford whose *Laws of Ecclesiastical Polity* embraced a wide range of topics as it explored on the moral and political foundations of the Church of England. One of the great masters of English prose, Hooker began his book as a final reply to a controversy that had been stirred up by *An Admonition to the Parliament*, which had been secretly published in 1572 by Puritans who denied Queen Elizabeth's right to lead a national church. Hooker worked on his book from 1591 to the end of his life; it was published in sections from 1593 through 1614. In his work, he defended the newly established church against both Roman Catholics and Puritans, arguing for a middle position that would give weight both to the individual reading of Scripture and to the authority of a national church, headed by the monarch rather than the Pope. His discussions of national and church governance entailed probing basic concepts of law itself. Hooker distinguished between natural law—unwritten, universally recognized, and discoverable by reason—on the one hand, and positive law or "laws politic"—the written law of a particular people or state—on the other. He valued human reason and its capacity to discern "goodness" and natural law, but he also believed that human beings harbored a "wild beast" within themselves which had to be controlled by positive law. The first selection is from Book 1; the second is from Book 8.

from The Laws of Ecclesiastical Polity

Signs and tokens to know good by are of sundry kinds; some more certain and some less. The most certain token of evident goodness is if the general persuasion of all men do so account it. And therefore a common received error is never utterly overthrown, till such time as we go from signs unto causes, and show some manifest root or fountain thereof common unto all, whereby it may clearly appear how it hath come to pass that so many have been overseen. In which case surmises and slight

---

5. Lamb imagines that Catholic doctrine is the "leaven" or corruption (as in fermentation) of Christianity.

probabilities will not serve, because the universal consent of men is the perfectest and strongest in this kind, which comprehendeth only the signs and tokens of goodness. Things casual do vary, and that which a man doth but chance to think well of cannot still have the like hap.[1] Wherefore although we know not the cause, yet thus much we may know; that some necessary cause there is, whensoever the judgments of all men generally or for the most part run one and the same way, especially in matters of natural discourse. For of things necessarily and naturally done there is no more affirmed but this, "They keep either always or for the most part one tenure."[2] The general and perpetual voice of men is as the sentence of God himself.[3] For that which all men have at all times learned, nature herself must needs have taught; and God being the author of nature, her voice is but his instrument. By her from Him we receive whatsoever in such sort we learn. Infinite duties there are, the goodness whereof is by this rule sufficiently manifested, although we had no other warrant besides to approve them. The Apostle St. Paul having speech concerning the heathen saith of them, "They are a law unto themselves" (Rom. 2:14). His meaning is, that by force of the light of reason, wherewith God illuminateth every one which cometh into the world, men being enabled to know truth from falsehood and good from evil, do thereby learn in many things what the will of God is; which will, himself not revealing by any extraordinary means unto them, but they by natural discourse attaining the knowledge thereof, seem the makers of those laws which indeed are his, and they but only the finders of them out. * * *

We see then how nature itself teacheth laws and statutes to live by. The laws which have been hitherto mentioned do bind men absolutely even as they are men, although they have never any settled fellowship, never any solemn agreement amongst themselves what to do or not to do. But forasmuch as we are not by ourselves sufficient to furnish ourselves with competent store of things needful for such a life as our nature doth desire, a life fit for the dignity of man; therefore to supply those defects and imperfections which are in us living single and solely by ourselves, we are naturally induced to seek communion and fellowship with others.[4] This was the cause of men's uniting themselves at the first in politic societies, which societies could not be without government, nor government without a distinct kind of law from that which hath been already declared. Two foundations there are which bear up public societies; the one, a natural inclination, whereby all men desire sociable life and fellowship; the other, an order expressly or secretly agreed upon touching the manner of their union in living together. The latter is that which we call the law of a commonweal, the very soul of a politic body, the parts whereof are by law animated, held together, and set on work in such actions as the common good requireth. Laws politic, ordained for external order and regiment amongst men, are never framed as they should be, unless presuming the will of man to be inwardly obstinate, rebellious, and adverse from all obedience unto the sacred laws of his nature; in a word, unless presuming man to be in regard of his depraved mind little better than a wild beast, they do accordingly provide notwithstanding so to frame his outward actions, that they be no hindrance unto the common good for which societies are instituted. Unless they do this, they are not perfect.

---

1. Cannot always have the same outcome.
2. Condition.
3. Hooker identifies the law of nature in human beings, the law they know by virtue of being human, with the law of God. He further identifies the source of this law as reason.

4. The following sentences describe the origins of government in man's natural instinct to gather into societies. The classic statement of this idea of a political society is Aristotle's; see *Politics*, 1.1252b1–1253a1.

[THE RULE OF LAW]

Many of the ancients in their writings do speak of kings with such high and ample terms, as if universality of power, even in regard of things and not of persons only, did appertain[5] to the very being of a king. The reason is because their speech concerning kings they frame according to the state of those monarchs to whom unlimited authority was given, which some not observing imagine that all kings, even in that they are kings, ought to have whatsoever power they find any sovereign ruler lawfully to have enjoyed. But that most judicious philosopher,[6] whose eye scarce anything did escape which was to be found in the bosom of nature, he considering how far the power of one sovereign ruler may be different from another regal authority, noteth in Spartan kings, "that of all others they were most tied to law, and so had the most restrained power." A king which hath not supreme power in the greatest things, is rather entitled a king, than invested with real sovereignty. We cannot properly term him a king, of whom it may not be said, at the leastwise as touching certain the very chiefest affairs of state, "his right in them is to have rule, not subject to any other predominant."[7] I am not of opinion that simply always in kings the most, but the best limited power is best. The most limited is that which may deal in fewest things; the best, that which in dealing is tied unto the soundest, perfectest, and most indifferent rule, which rule is the law.[8] I mean not only the law of nature and of God, but very national or municipal law consonant thereunto. Happier that people whose law is their king in the greatest of things, than that whose king is himself their law. Where the king doth guide the state, and the law the king, that commonwealth is like an harp or melodious instrument, the strings whereof are tuned and handled all by one hand, following as laws the rules and canons of musical science. Most divinely therefore Archytas[9] maketh unto public felicity these four steps, every later whereof doth spring from the former, as from a mother cause: "The king ruling by law, the magistrate following, the subject free, and the whole society happy"; adding on the contrary side, that "where this order is not, it cometh by transgression thereof to pass that the king grows a tyrant; he that ruleth under him abhorreth to be guided and commanded by him; the people subject under both, have freedom under neither; and the whole community is wretched."

—— ✠ ——

James I (James VI of Scotland)
1567–1625

James VI of Scotland, eventually James I of England, wrote his treatise on monarchy to curb the enthusiasm of his subjects for a government under the law rather than by an all-powerful ruler. He had ascended his throne in highly uncertain circumstances. His father died when James was eight months old; a few months later his mother Mary was forced from the throne, and James became king of Scotland in 1567 at the age of one. Mary left the kingdom the following year; James never saw her again. He grew up reading widely, writing poetry, harrassed

5. Belong.
6. Aristotle; see *Politics*, 3.1284b–1285b.
7. Power.
8. Hooker states that a king's "best" power is not the most power but rather the "best limited" power; that is, it is limited not because it deals with only a few things, but

rather it is limited by law—it therefore comprehends what law does, the workings of the entire body politic. Hooker goes on to argue for a monarchy under positive law, much as Ponet did.
9. A mathematician and friend of Plato, to whom is attributed the treatise *On Law and Justice*. (c. 400 B.C.)

by fears of the devil but enjoying the fellowship of a few trusted Scottish lords. He published a work on devils entitled *Daemonologie* in 1597; *The True Law of Free Monarchies* was published the next year, following conflicts with the Scottish parliament and church authorities. In his book, James insisted that the people had no rights of resistance, even against monarchs who broke divine and natural law; at the same time, he acknowledged that a good king, obeying the law, would not give his subjects a reason to dispute his rule. In theory, James was unequivocally committed to the proposition that Scripture and moral law justified absolute monarchy; in practice, however, he conceded authority and power to Parliament and the common law.

from The True Law of Free Monarchies

Kings are called gods by the prophetical King David, because they sit upon God's Throne in the earth and have the count of their administration to give unto him. Their office is to minister justice and judgment to the people, as the same David saith; to advance the good and punish the evil, as he likewise saith; to establish good laws to his people, and procure obedience to the same, as divers good kings of Judah did; to procure the peace of the people, as the same David saith; to decide all controversies that can arise among them, as Solomon did; to be the minister of God for the weal[1] of them that do well, and as the minister of God, to take vengeance upon them that do evil, as St. Paul saith. And finally, as a good pastor, to go out and in before his people as is said in the first of Samuel; that through the prince's prosperity, the people's peace may be procured, as Jeremy saith. * * *

By the law of nature the king becomes a natural father to all his lieges at his coronation and as the father, of his fatherly duty, is bound to care for the nourishing, education, and virtuous government of his children, even so is the king bound to care for all his subjects.[2] As all the toil and pain that the father can take for his children will be thought light and well-bestowed by him, so that the effect thereof redound to their profit and weal, so ought the prince to do towards his people. As the kindly father ought to foresee all inconveniences and dangers that may arise towards his children, and though with the hazard of his own person press to prevent the same, so ought the king towards his people. As the father's wrath and correction upon any of his children that offendeth ought to be by a fatherly chastisement seasoned with pity, as long as there is any hope of amendment in them, so ought the king towards any of his lieges that offend in that measure. * * *

The kings therefore in Scotland were before any estates or ranks of men within the same, before any Parliaments were holden or laws made, and by them was the land distributed (which at the first was wholly theirs), states erected and discerned, and forms of government devised and established. And so it follows of necessity that the kings were the authors and makers of the laws and not the laws of the kings. And to prove this my assertion more clearly, it is evident by the rolls of our chancellery (which contain our eldest and fundamental Laws) that the king is *Dominus omnium honorum*, and *Dominus directus totius Dominii*,[3] the whole subjects being but his vassals and from him holding all their lands as their overlord, who according to good services done unto him, changeth their holdings from tack to fee, from ward to blanch,[4]

---

1. Benefit.
2. James's identification of royal with paternal or patriarchal power—that is, the power of the father over his children, or the head of the family over its members—is modeled after what was thought to be Roman law and custom, in which the male head of the household ruled absolutely over it.

3. The lord of the manor, the first lord of all lords.
4. These are legal terms relating to the conditions of feudal tenure. James notes that the king can change what is required of his tenants from knightly service to the payment of rent and can change the nature of the rent his tenants pay from goods to coin.

erecteth new baronies and uniteth old, without advice or authority of either Parliament or any other subaltern judicial seat. So as if wrong might be admitted in play (albeit I grant wrong should be wrong in all persons), the king might have a better color for his pleasure, without further reason, to take the land from his lieges,[5] as overlord of the whole, and do with it as pleaseth him, since all that they hold is of him, then, as foolish writers say, the people might unmake the king and put in another in his room; but either of them, as unlawful and against the ordinance of God, ought to be alike odious to be thought, much less put in practice. * * *

The king is overlord of the whole land, so is he master over every person that inhabiteth the same, having power over the life and death of every one of them. For although a just prince will not take the life of any of his subjects without a clear law, yet the same laws whereby he taketh them are made by himself, or his predecessors, and so the power flows always from himself; as by daily experience we see, good and just princes will from time to time make new laws and statutes, adjoining the penalties to the breakers thereof, which before the law was made, had been no crime to the subject to have committed. Not that I deny the old definition of a king, and of a law, which makes the king to be a speaking law, and the law a dumb king, for certainly a king that governs not by his law can neither be countable to God for his administration nor have a happy and established reign. For albeit be true that I have at length proved that the king is above the law, as both the author and giver of strength thereto, yet a good king will not only delight to rule his subjects by the law, but even will conform himself in his own actions thereto, always keeping that ground that the health of the commonwealth be his chief law. And where he sees the law doubtsome or rigorous, he may interpret or mitigate the same, lest otherwise *Summum jus be summa injuria.*[6] And therefore general laws, made publicly in Parliament, may upon known respects to the king by his authority be mitigated and suspended upon causes only known to him.

Baldassare Castiglione
1478–1529

A courtier at Urbino, the ducal seat of the Gonzaga family, Castiglione wrote his book of advice for men and women seeking advancement in court society. Published in 1528, it proved popular not only with Italian readers but throughout Europe. It was translated into English in 1561 by the diplomat Sir Thomas Hoby. One of the most influential prose stylists of his generation. Hoby belonged to a group of writers who sought to create a clear and forceful English prose free of ornate Latinisms. Written in dialogue form, *The Book of the Courtier* sketched the principles of self-government as they applied to those who sought favor and patronage from rich and powerful nobility; chiefly, it specified how a courtier could gain and keep his lord's attention. One of Castiglione's best-known directives concerns the manner in which the courtier should perform his duties: it will only be impressive, Castiglione insists, if it seems to be completely unlearned, unrehearsed, and natural. Castiglione's arguments influenced many writers, including Shakespeare; the courtier and writer Sir Philip Sidney "never stirred abroad without a copy in his pocket."

---

5. Lords.
6. The most exacting enforcement of the law may be an injustice. Here James invokes the principle of equity, which allows a magistrate discretion to moderate the effect of the law in certain cases.

from The Book of the Courtier

Whoso mindeth to be gracious or to have a good grace in the exercises of the body (presupposing first that he be not of nature unapt) ought to begin betimes and to learn his principles of cunning men. The which thing how necessary a matter Philip King of Macedonia thought it, a man may gather in that his will was that Aristotle, so famous a philosopher and perhaps the greatest that hath ever been in the world, should be the man that should instruct Alexander his son in the first principles of letters. * * *

He therefore that will be a good scholar, beside the practicing of good things must evermore set all his diligence to be like his master, and (if it were possible) change himself into him. And when he hath had some entry, it profiteth him much to behold sundry men of that profession, and governing himself with that good judgment that must always be his guide, go about to pick out, sometime of one and sometime of another, sundry matters. And even as the bee in the green meadows fleeth always about the grass choosing out flowers, so shall our courtier steal this grace from them that to his seeming have it, and from each one that parcel that shall be most worthy praise. And not do, as a friend of ours, whom you all know, that thought he resembled much King Ferdinand the younger of Aragon, and regarded not to resemble him in any other point but in the often lifting up his head, wrying therewithall a part of his mouth, the which custom the king had gotten by infirmity. And many such there are that think they do much, so they resemble a great man in somewhat, and take many times the thing in him that worst becometh him. But I, imagining with myself oftentimes how this grace cometh, leaving apart such as have it from above, find one rule that is most general which in this part (methink) taketh place in all things belonging to man in word or deed above all other. And that is to eschew as much as a man may, and as a sharp and dangerous rock, affectation or curiosity and (to speak a new word) to use in everything a certain recklessness, to cover art withall, and seem whatsoever he doth and sayeth to do it without pain and (as it were) not minding it. And of this do I believe grace is much derived, for in rare matters and well brought to pass every man knoweth the hardness[1] of them, so that a readiness therein maketh great wonder. And contrariwise to use force, and (as they say) to haul by the hair, giveth a great disgrace, and maketh every thing how great soever it be, to be little esteemed. Therefore that may be said to be a very art that appeareth not to be art, neither ought a man to put more diligence in anything than in covering it, for in case it be open, it loseth credit clean, and maketh a man little set by. And I remember that I have read in my days that there were some most excellent orators, which among other their cares, enforced themselves to make every man believe that they had no sight in letters, and dissembling their cunning, made semblant[2] their orations to be made very simply, and rather as nature and truth lead them than study and art, the which if it had been openly known would have put a doubt in the people's mind, for fear least he beguiled them. You may see then how to show art and such bent[3] study taketh away the grace of every thing.

1. Difficulty.
2. Made it apparent that.
3. Dedicated.

Roger Ascham
1515–1568

Secretary to both Queen Mary and Queen Elizabeth, Ascham was convinced that the education of children was crucial to the prosperity of the state; for him, education was not a private concern but a public matter. Adopting humanist methods of instruction, teachers in this period had become increasingly committed to preparing students not only to understand what they read but also why it was important. In short, the value of rote learning, which depends on a quick memory and a willing acceptance of authority, had become debatable. Ascham favored an education based on discussion, questioning, and criticism, and he preferred teaching in English rather than Latin. In 1545 he had published the first book written in English on the subject of archery; *The Schoolmaster,* published posthumously in 1570, embodies Ascham's ideals in a lively and emphatic style. In the following excerpt, he defends a "hard-witted" student, one who learns slowly but thoroughly, thereby highlighting the importance of character in the process of learning; by stressing character, Ascham turns the attention of the reader from the formal aspects of education and toward its role in the formation of the individual citizen.

from The Schoolmaster

If your scholar do miss sometimes in marking rightly these foresaid six things, chide not hastily, for that shall both dull his wit and discourage his diligence; but monish[1] him gently, which shall make him both willing to amend and glad to go forward in love and hope of learning.

I have now wished, twice or thrice, this gentle nature to be in a schoolmaster, and that I have done so neither by chance nor without some reason I will now declare at large, why, in mine opinion, love is fitter than fear, gentleness better than beating, to bring up a child rightly in learning.

With the common use of teaching and beating in common schools of England I will not greatly contend, which if I did, it were but a small grammatical controversy, neither belonging to heresy nor treason, nor greatly touching God nor the prince; although in very deed, in the end the good or ill bringing up of children doth as much serve to the good or ill service of God, our prince, and our whole country, as any one thing doth beside.

I do gladly agree with all good schoolmasters in these points: to have children brought to good perfectness in learning, to all honesty in manners, to have all faults rightly amended, to have every vice severally corrected; but for the order and way that leadeth rightly to these points, we somewhat differ. For commonly, many schoolmasters, some, as I have seen, more, as I have heard tell, be of so crooked a nature as when they meet with a hard-witted scholar, they rather break him than bow him, rather mar him than mend him. For when the schoolmaster is angry with some other matter, then will he soonest fall to beat his scholar, and though he himself should be punished for his folly, yet must he beat some scholar for his pleasure though there be no cause for him to do so nor yet fault in the scholar to deserve so. These will ye say be fond schoolmasters, and few they be

---

1. Admonish.

that be found to be such. They be found indeed, but surely over-many such be found everywhere. But this will I say, that even the wisest of your great beaters do as oft punish nature as they do correct faults. Yea, many times, the better nature is sorer punished, for if one by quickness of wit take his lesson readily, another, by hardness of wit taketh it not so speedily; the first is always commended, the other is commonly punished, when a wise schoolmaster should rather discreetly consider the right disposition of both their natures and not so much weigh what either of them is able to do now, as what either of them is likely to do hereafter. For this I know, not only by reading of books in my study, but also by experience of life abroad in the world, that those which be commonly the wisest, the best learned and best men also, when they be old, were never commonly the quickest of wit when they were young. The causes why, amongst other, which be many, that move me thus to think be these few which I will reckon. Quick wits commonly be apt to take, unapt to keep; soon hot and desirous of this and that; as cold and soon weary of the same again; more quick to enter speedily than able to pierce far; even like some over-sharp tools, whose edges be very soon turned. Such wits delight themselves in easy and pleasant studies and never pass far forward in high and hard sciences. And therefore the quickest wits commonly may prove the best poets, but not the wisest orators; ready of tongue to speak boldly, not deep of judgment, either for good counsel or wise writing. Also, for manners and life, quick wits commonly be in desire newfangled; in purpose, unconstant; light to promise anything, ready to forget everything, both benefit and injury; and thereby neither fast to friend nor fearful to foe; inquisitive of every trifle, not secret in greatest affairs; bold with any person; busy in any matter; soothing such as be present, nipping any that is absent; of nature also, always flattering their betters, envying their equals, despising their inferiors; and by quickness of wit, very quick and ready to like none so well as themselves.

Moreover, commonly, men very quick of wit be also very light of conditions, and thereby very ready of disposition, to be carried over quickly by any light company to any riot and unthriftiness when they be young, and therefore seldom either honest of life or rich in living when they be old. For, quick in wit and light in manners be either seldom troubled or very soon weary in carrying a heavy purse. Quick wits also be, in most part of all their doings, over-quick, hasty, rash, heady, and brainsick. These last two words, heady and brainsick, be fit and proper words, rising naturally of the matter and termed aptly by the condition of overmuch quickness of wit. In youth also they be ready scoffers, privy mockers, and ever over-light and merry. In age, soon testy, very waspish, and always over-miserable, and yet few of them come to any great age, by reason of their misordered life when they were young; but a great deal fewer of them come to show any great countenance or bear any great authority abroad in the world, but either live obscurely, men know not how, or die obscurely, men mark not when. They be like trees that show forth fair blossoms and broad leaves in springtime, but bring out small and not long lasting fruit in harvest time; and that only such as fall and rot before they be ripe and so never or seldom come to any good at all. For this ye shall find most true by experience, that amongst a number of quick wits in youth, few be found in the end either very fortunate for themselves or very profitable to serve the commonwealth, but decay and vanish men know not which way, except a very few, to whom peradventure blood and happy parentage may perchance purchase a long standing upon the stage. The which felicity, because it cometh by others' procuring, not by their own deserving, and stand by other men's feet, and not by their own, what outward brag so ever is born by them, is indeed, of itself and in wise men's eyes, of no great estimation. * * *

Contrariwise, a wit in youth, that is not over dull, heavy, knotty, and lumpish, but hard, rough and though somewhat staffish, as Tully wisheth *otium, quietum, non languidum,* and *negotium cum labore, non cum periculo,*[2] such a wit, I say, if it be first well handled by the mother and rightly smoothed and wrought as it should, not over-thwartly and against the wood by the schoolmaster, both for learning and whole course of living, proveth always the best. In wood and stone, not the softest, but hardest be always aptest for portraiture, both fairest for pleasure and most durable for profit. Hard wits be hard to receive, but sure to keep; painful without weariness, heedful without wavering, constant without newfangledness; bearing heavy things, though not lightly, yet willingly; entering hard things, though not easily, yet deeply; and so come to that perfectness of learning in the end that quick wits seem in hope, but do not in deed, or else very seldom ever attain unto. Also, for manners and life, hard wits commonly are hardly carried either to desire every new thing or else to marvel at every strange thing, and therefore they be careful and diligent in their own matters, not curious or busy in other men's affairs; and so they become wise them-selves and also are counted honest by others. They be grave, steadfast, silent of tongue, secret of heart; not hasty in making, but constant in keeping any promise; not rash in uttering, but wary in considering every matter; and thereby, not quick in speaking, but deep of judgment, whether they write or give counsel in all weighty affairs. And these be the men that become in the end both most happy for them-selves and always best esteemed abroad in the world.

⊷ ⊨◊⊨ ⊶

Richard Mulcaster
1530–1611

One of the best-known humanists of the early Tudor period, Mulcaster remained a schoolteacher all his life, first at Merchant Taylors' School and then at Saint Paul's, both in London. Like Ascham, he rejected methods of teaching that did not result in a thoughtful and open-minded student. Early in the second of his two treatises on education, *The Elementary* (1582), he identi-fies ignorance and prejudice as impediments to learning; of the two, he insists, prejudice is worse.

from The First Part of the Elementary

What greater enemies hath learning even in nature than prejudice and ignorance? Whence is there more open show of implacable hostility to knowledge than from prejudice and ignorance? Ignorance knoweth nothing, and therefore is no friend to an unknown good, prejudice knoweth and will not, and therefore is a great foe to a not-favored good. Ignorance yet in part deserveth some excuse for all her disfriend-ship, because infirmity is her fault, not bolstered with ill will, and the worst is her own, an ordinary case, where even enmity pitieth.[1] But prejudice is a poison to any commonweal, so far as it stretcheth, which being at the first infected with the incur-

---

2. Ascham refers to Cicero, who desires "a quiet not a languid leisure" and "an occupation that entails work not danger."

1. I.e., ignorance does not imply ill will; its effects are limited by its own failure to seek knowledge; even his enemies pity the ignorant man.

able disease of a cankered and a corrupt opinion gathered by confluence of sundry ill humors, will neither itself yield to a right judgment, nor will suffer any other, where her persuasion can take place. For by yielding herself she feareth the impairing of her misconceived estimation, and by suffering other to yield, she feareth the increase of knowledge's friends, whereby herself shall come in danger to be oppressed, both with truth of matter and number of patrons. Wherefore she opposeth herself, she bendeth all her eloquence, she mureth up[2] all passages, so much as she may, both by persuasion and entreaty, that none shall judge right which will hear her speak and regard her authority, but shall take that music to sound the sweetest which cometh from her, though she be but a mermaid, which by offering of delight endeavoreth to destroy.

Ignorance is violent and like unto a lion, when it encountereth with knowledge, still in fury without feeling, in rage without reason, and riseth of two causes, either infirmity in nature or negligence in labor. Whereof the one could not, the other would not conceive at the first when knowledge was in dealing. Both enemies to knowledge, but negligence the greater,[3] which, either fearing disdain for her first refusal or envying him which loveth where she left, will not seem to favor where she once forsook and stomacheth[4] him which embraceth her leavings, wreaking her malice in show upon knowledge, indeed upon folly. Which folly, being lodged within her own breast beside that negligent ignorance, useth to call in a dangerous opinion the contempt of that good, which she ought to commend, rather than she will by change of opinion and altering her hue, bewray her own error, which all men see saving she that should.[5] Being at defiance with knowledge, not by simplicity of nature, which offered, but by naughtiness of choice, which refused the attaining thereof.

Now natural infirmity the other and more gentle mean of ignorance would perhaps, nay would indeed change her blind opinion, if she could once change her ingenerate heaviness. She would reverence learning if she might see her beauty wherewith to be ravished, being enemy unto her, not of malice but of weakness. * * *

But that same perverse prejudice is a subtle foe to knowledge like a many-headed hydra, and as the venom of his authority is gathered of diverse grounds, so the sting of his poison infecteth diverse ways. The person himself which is thus carried away by a peevish opinion is commonly no heavy head,[6] but either superfically learned and yet loath to seem so, or enviously affected and still carping at[7] his better; or ambitiously given and presumeth upon countenance;[8] or he measureth knowledge by gain, and setteth naught by any more than he himself shall need to compass that [which] he coveteth, where a little cunning will compass much more than reason thinks enough in corruption of minds.[9] * * * The party so corrupted will seek by all means to continue his credit, so much the more a deadly enemy to knowledge, because prejudice must give place if knowledge come in place, and therefore that it may not come, he employeth all his forces, by all cunning and all well-colored shifts[1] to shoulder it out: a professed foe, and so much the shrewder, because he supplanteth knowledge under the opinion of knowledge.

[END OF PERSPECTIVES: GOVERNMENT AND SELF-GOVERNMENT]

---

2. Walls up.
3. Negligence is a greater enemy to knowledge than "infirmity in nature" because it will not seem to favor the knowledge it has rejected or to tolerate the person who picks up that knowledge; negligence acts with malice toward knowledge, acting foolishly.
4. Will not tolerate.
5. Folly persists in condemning what is good lest others see her error—as they do anyway.
6. Slow learner.
7. Criticizing.
8. Appearance.
9. I.e., cleverness will do more than reason thinks is necessary to corrupt minds.
1. Persuasive arguments.

·→· ≤✦≥· ←·

George Gascoigne
c. 1534–1577

Satire may produce ambiguous results, particularly when it is directed at the author's own life and work. To judge from his candidly witty self-portraits in *Alexander Neville's Theme* and *Woodmanship*, Gascoigne saw a good subject in his own career. The events of his life indicate that whatever ventures he attempted, he failed "to hit the whites [bulls-eyes] which live with all good luck." Educated at Cambridge and trained as a lawyer at Gray's Inn, Gascoigne went into debt trying to keep up with fashionable life in London. His election to Parliament was voided by the claims of his creditors, and in 1561 he compounded his legal difficulties by a bigamous marriage to Elizabeth Boyes, the widow of Willam Breton and the estranged wife of Edward Boyes. His service in the Low Countries was no more successful. He commanded English troops against the Spanish but, after several miscalculated maneuvers, surrendered to the Spanish at Leiden and spent four months as a prisoner of Spain. Upon returning to England he found himself under yet another kind of attack, this time for poetry that was supposed to report the scandalous behavior of certain figures at court. It had been published in 1573 in his absence (and perhaps without his knowledge) in a volume entitled *A Hundreth Sundrie Flowres*. After augmenting the collection—and reworking much of its material so that it conformed to more conventional standards of propriety, he reissued the volume as *The Posies of George Gascoigne* (1575), the version used here. The same volume also contains a prose romance, *The Adventures of Master F.J.*, a racy account of seduction and betrayal, opportunistic lovers, and resourceful ladies.

As Sir Thomas Wyatt had shown, the conventions that had dictated modes of self-expression in lyric poetry were capable of great transformation. Professions of virtuous love and devotion to patriotic ideals in the manner of Petrarch and his followers were no longer the only topics a poet was supposed to address, and Gascoigne, like Wyatt and such later poets as Sir Philip Sidney and John Donne, retuned the lyric voice so that it became capable of illustrating a sense of self charged not only with desire, but also with chagrin, dismay, bitterness, and even revulsion. At the same time, Gascoigne's vision of society remained essentially humorous; throughout his verse he is more committed to castigating himself than those who may have exploited him. Rarely has an author plagued by so many reversals represented as mellow a vision of society. As a rule, satire flattens its subjects to achieve pointed and deliberate effects; Gascoigne's satire gives his subjects a complexity that makes them seem less outrageous than familiar.

Seven Sonnets to Alexander Neville

Alexander Neville delivered him this theme, *Sat cito, si sat bene*, whereupon he compiled these seven sonnets in sequence, therein bewraying his own *Nimis cito*, and therewith his *Vix bene*, as followeth.[1]

1

In haste, post haste, when first my wand'ring mind,
Beheld the glist'ring court with gazing eye,

---

1. Gascoigne states that he composed these sonnets at the request of Alexander Neville (a poet, translator of Seneca, and secretary to Archbishop Matthew Parker). He was given a theme, *sat cito, si sat bene*, "if it be [done] well, let it be quickly," which he developed to satirize his own fault of acting too quickly: *nimis cito, vix bene*, or "if it be [done] very quickly, it is hardly well."

Such deep delights I seemed therein to find,
As might beguile a graver guest than I.
5   The stately pomp of princes and their peers,
Did seem to swim in floods of beaten gold,
The wanton world of young delightful years,
Was not unlike a heaven for to behold.
Wherin did swarm (for every saint) a dame,
10   So fair of hue, so fresh of their attire,
As might excel dame Cynthia[2] for fame,
Or conquer Cupid with his own desire.
These and such like were baits that blazed still
Before mine eye to feed my greedy will.

2

15   Before mine eye to feed my greedy will,
'Gan° muster eke° mine old acquainted mates,   *began to / also*
Who helped the dish (of vain delight) to fill
My empty mouth with dainty delicates:
And foolish boldness took the whip in hand,
20   To lash my life into this trustless trace,°   *harness*
Till all in haste I leaped aloof° from land,   *aloft*
And hoist° up sail to catch a courtly grace: *hoisted*
Each ling'ring day did seem a world of woe,
Till in that hapless haven my head was brought:
25   Waves of wanhope° so tossed me to and fro,   *discouragement*
In deep despair to drown my dreadful thought:
Each hour a day, each day a year did seem,
And every year a world my will did deem.

3

And every year a world my will did deem,
30   Till lo, at last, to court now am I come,
A seemly swaine, that might the place beseem,
A gladsome guest embraced of all and some:
Not there content with common dignity,
My wand'ring eye in haste, (yea post post haste)
35   Beheld the blazing badge of bravery,
For want whereof, I thought myself disgraced:
Then peevish pride puffed up my swelling heart,
To further forth so hot an enterprise:
And comely cost began to play his part,
40   In praising patterns of mine own devise.°   *devising*
Thus all was good that might be got in haste,
To prink° me up, and make me higher placed.   *dress*

4

To prink me up and make me higher placed,
All came too late that taried any time,
45   Pill of provision[3] pleased not my taste,
They made my heels too heavy for to climb:
Me thought it best that boughs of boist'rous oak,

2. The goddess of the moon, an aspect of the goddess
Diana, the goddess of chastity.
3. The property his family had provided him as his inheritance. Requiring greater wealth, he began to cut the
trees on his estate.

Should first be shred to make my feathers gay.
Till at the last a deadly dinting stroke,
50   Brought down the bulk with edgetools of decay:
Of every farm I then let fly a lease,
To feed the purse that paid for peevishness,
Till rent and all were fall'n in such disease,
As scarce could serve to maintain cleanliness:
55   They bought the body, fine,° farm, lease, and land,   *recorded grant*
All were too little for the merchant's hand.[4]

5

All were too little for the merchant's hand,
And yet my bravery bigger than his book:
But when this hot accompt° was coldly scanned,   *account*
60   I thought high time about me for to look:
With heavy cheer I cast my head aback,
To see the fountain of my furious race.
Compared my loss, my living, and my lack,
In equal balance with my jolly grace.
65   And saw expenses grating on the ground
Like lumps of lead to press my purse full oft,
When light reward and recompense were found,
Fleeting like feathers in the wind aloft:
These thus compared, I left the court at large,
70   For why? the gains doth seldom quit° the charge.   *compensate for*

6

For why? the gains doth seldom quit the charge,
And so say I, by proof too dearly bought,
My haste made waste, my brave and brainsick barge,
Did float too fast, to catch a thing of naught:
75   With leisure, measure, mean, and many mo,°   *more*
I mought° have kept a chair of quiet state,   *might*
But hasty heads cannot be settled so,
Till crooked Fortune give a crabbed mate:[5]
As busy brains must beat on tickle° toys,   *fickle*
80   As rash invention breeds a raw device,
So sudden falls do hinder hasty joys,
And as swift baits do fleetest fish entice.
So haste makes waste, and therefore now I say,
No haste but good, where wisdom makes the way.

7

85   No haste but good, where wisdom makes the way,
For proof whereof, behold the simple snail,
(Who sees the soldier's carcass cast away,
With hot assault the castle to assail,)
By line and leisure climbs the lofty wall,

---

4. Having leased his farms, he could no longer sell what
they produced; in all, none of the financial arrangements
he made to acquire more money proved adequate to meet
what the merchant charged for his apparel and upkeep.
5. Fortune will give those who act in haste an outcome
that is unsatisfactory.

90 And wins the turret's top more cunningly,
Than doughty Dick, who lost his life and all,
With hoisting up his head too hastily.
The swiftest bitch brings forth the blindest whelps,
The hottest fevers coldest cramps ensue,
95 The naked'st need hath over latest helps:[6]
With Neville then I find this proverb true,
That haste makes waste, and therefore still I say,
No haste but good, where wisdom makes the way.

Sic tuli[7]

Woodmanship[1]

Gascoigne's woodmanship written to the Lord Grey of Wilton upon this occasion, the said Lord Grey delighting (amongst many other good qualities) in choosing of his winter deer, and killing the same with his bow, did furnish the author with a crossbow *cum pertinenciis* [with accessories] and vouchsafed to use his company in the said exercise, calling him one of his woodmen. Now the author shooting very often, could never hit any deer, yea and oftentimes he let the herd pass by as though he had not seen them. Whereat when this noble lord took some pastime, and had often put him in remembrance of his good skill in choosing, and readiness in killing of a winter deer, he thought good thus to excuse it in verse.

My worthy Lord, I pray you wonder not,
To see your woodman shoot so oft awry,
Nor that he stands amazed like a sot,
And lets the harmless deer (unhurt) go by.
5 Or if he strike a doe which is but carren,°   *pregnant*
Laugh not good Lord, but favor such a fault,
Take will in worth, he would fain hit the barren,
But though his heart be good, his hap is naught:
And therefore now I crave your Lordship's leave,
10 To tell you plain what is the cause of this:
First, if it please your honour to perceive,
What makes your woodman shoot so oft amiss,
Believe me, Lord, the case is nothing strange,
He shoots awry almost at every mark,
15 His eyes have been so used for to range,
That now, God knows, they be both dim and dark.
For proof, he bears the note of folly now,
Who shot sometimes to hit philosophy,[2]
And ask you why? forsooth I make avow,
20 Because his wanton wit went all awry.
Next that, he shot to be a man of law,

And spent sometime with learned Littleton,[3]
Yet in the end, he proved but a daw,°   *fool*
For law was dark and he had quickly done.
25   Then could he with Fitzherbert[4] such a brain,
As Tully had, to write the law by art,
So that with pleasure or with little pain,
He might perhaps have caught a truant's part.
But all to late, he most misliked the thing,
30   Which most might help to guide his arrow straight:
He winked° wrong, and so let slip the string,   *aimed*
Which cast him wide, for all his quaint conceit.°   *foolish fancy*
From thence he shot to catch a courtly grace,
And thought even there to wield the world at will,
35   But out, alas, he much mistook the place,
And shot awrie at every rover° still.   *random mark*
The blazing baits which draw the gazing eye,
Unfeathered there his first affection,
No wonder then although° he shot awry,   *that*
40   Wanting the feathers of discretion.
Yet more than them, the marks of dignity,
He much mistook and shot the wronger way,
Thinking the purse of prodigality,
Had been best mean to purchase such a prey.
45   He thought the flatt'ring face which fleareth° still,   *smiles*
Had been full fraught with all fidelity,
And that such words as courtiers use at will,
Could not have varied from the verity.
But when his bonnet buttoned with gold,
50   His comely cape beguarded all with gay,°   *lavishly decorated*
His bombast hose,° with linings manifold,   *upper stockings*
His knit silk stocks° and all his quaint array,   *lower stockings*
Had picked his purse of all the Peter pence,[5]
Which might have paid for his promotion,
55   Then (all to late) he found that light expense,
Had quite quenched out the court's devotion.
So that since then the taste of misery,
Hath been always full bitter in his bit,
And why? forsooth because he shot awry,
60   Mistaking still the marks which others hit.
But now behold what mark the man doth find,
He shoots to be a soldier in his age,
Mistrusting all the virtues of the mind,
He trusts the power of his personage.

---

3. Written by Sir Thomas Littleton in the 15th century and always referred to as "Littleton," this was the principal text used in the practice of common law.
4. Sir Anthony Fitzherbert wrote an abridgment of the common law in 1514; Gascoigne states that if he had had a brain like that of Fitzherbert or "Tully" (Cicero), he would have been able to reduce the law to a set of basic principles and to play truant at law school. As it happened, he took aim badly and missed the mark by a wide margin.
5. An annual tax paid to Rome before the Reformation. Gascoigne alludes to it as a symbol of bribery, what was needed to pay for his advancement.

65	As though long limbs led by a lusty heart,	
	Might yet suffice to make him rich again;	
	But Flushing frays° have taught him such a part,[6]	*battles*
	That now he thinks the war yield no such gain.	
	And sure I fear, unless your Lordship deign,	
70	To train him yet into some better trade,	
	It will be long before he hit the vein,	
	Whereby he may a richer man be made.	
	He cannot climb as other catchers can,	
	To lead a charge before himself be led;	
75	He cannot spoil the simple sakeless° man,	*innocent*
	Which is content to feed him with his bread.	
	He cannot pinch the painful soldier's pay,	
	And shear° him out his share in ragged sheets,	*dole*
	He cannot stoop to take a greedy pray	
80	Upon his fellows groveling in the streets.	
	He cannot pull the spoil from such as pill,°	*steal*
	And seem full angry at such foul offence,	
	Although the gain content his greedy will,	
	Under the cloak of contrary pretense:	
85	And nowadays, the man that shoots not so,	
	May shoot amiss, even as your woodman doth:	
	But then you marvel why I let them go,	
	And never shoot, but say farewell forsooth:	
	Alas my Lord, while I do muse hereon,	
90	And call to mind my youthful years misspent,	
	They give me such a bone to gnaw upon,	
	That all my senses are in silence pent.	
	My mind is rapt in contemplation,	
	Wherein my dazzled eyes only behold,	
95	The black hour of my constellation,[7]	
	Which framed me so luckless on the mold:°	*on earth*
	Yet therewithal I cannot but confess,	
	That vain presumption makes my heart to swell,	
	For thus I think, not all the world (I guess)	
100	Shoots bet° than I, nay some shoots not so well.[8]	*better*
	In Aristotle somewhat did I learn,	
	To guide my manners all by comeliness,	
	And Tully taught me somewhat to discern	
	Between sweet speech and barbarous rudeness.	
105	Old Parkins, Rastell, and Dan Bracton's books,[9]	
	Did lend me somewhat of the lawless law;	
	The crafty courtiers with their guileful looks,	

---

6. Gascoigne was deployed as a soldier in Flushing in 1572.

7. I.e., the unfortunate alignment of the stars at his birth.

8. Gascoigne's argument is complex and somewhat ironic; he states he cannot cheat (lines 73ff.) as if to establish his moral rectitude, but then he declares that his behavior is the result of a poor configuration of the stars at his

birth (lines 95ff.) as if to denigrate that moral rectitude. Finally, he asserts that he is not the worst shot; some hunters are even less able to exploit others than he is.

9. Gascoigne lists various moral and legal authorities, including the lawyers John Parkins, John Rastell, and Henry Bracton, all of whom published books on the common law. None has made him a successful shot.

Must needs put some experience in my maw:°   *stomach*
Yet cannot these with many maistries mo,°   *more skills*
110   Make me shoot straight at any gainful prick,°   *point on a target*
Where some that never handled such a bow,
Can hit the white,° or touch it near the quick,°   *center/heart*
Who can nor speak, nor write in pleasant wise,
Nor lead their life by Aristotle's rule,[1]
115   Nor argue well on questions that arise,
Nor plead a case more than my Lord Mayor's mule;
Yet can they hit the marks that I do miss,
And win the mean which may the man maintain.
Now when my mind doth mumble upon this,
120   No wonder then although I pine for pain:
And whiles mine eyes behold this mirror thus,
The herd goeth by, and farewell gentle does:
So that your Lordship quickly may discuss
What blinds mine eyes so oft (as I suppose).
125   But since my Muse can to my Lord rehearse
What makes me miss, and why I do not shoot,
Let me imagine in this worthless verse,
If right before me, at my standing's foot°   *hunting position*
There stood a doe, and I should strike her dead,
130   And then she prove a carrion carcass too,
What figure might I find within my head,
To 'scuse the rage which ruled me so to do?
Some might interpret by plain paraphrase,
That lack of skill or fortune led the chance,
135   But I must otherwise expound the case.
I say Jehovah did this doe advance,
And made her bold to stand before me so,
Till I had thrust mine arrow to her heart
That by the sudden of her overthrow,
140   I might endeavor to amend my part,
And turn mine eyes that they no more behold,
Such guileful markes as seem more than they be:
And though they glister° outwardly like gold,   *glisten*
Are inwardly but brass, as men may see:
145   And when I see the milk hang in her teat,
Methinks it saith: old babe, now learn to suck,
Who in thy youth couldst never learn the feat
To hit the whites which live with all good luck.[2]
Thus have I told my Lord, (God grant in season)
150   A tedious tale in rhyme, but little reason.
                    Haud ictus sapio[3]

---

1. Probably the rule of the virtuous mean between behavioral extremes.
2. Gascoigne extracts an ironic moral from his suppositious story of yet another failure: Jehovah or God sent him this pregnant doe not to warn him against hunting or hoping to get lucky, but rather to teach him to "suck," to take advantage of the circumstances in which he finds

himself, however unlucky they may appear to be. With this reflection, Gascoigne avoids the temptation to attribute his lack of success to a superior morality and instead admits that he wants to be like everyone else: interested in his own advancement.
3. Not having been completely defeated, I [now] know.

Edmund Spenser
1552?–1599

A man whose poetry has come to be known as a monument to Queen Elizabeth's England began life modestly enough. Attending Cambridge as a "sizar," or "poor scholar," he worked as a servant to pay for his fees. Allegiance to the English church was expected of all subjects, and Spenser showed his support of the faith while still a student by contributing anti-Catholic verses to the first emblem book published in England. The genre, consisting of emblems or symbolic scenes explained by clever captions, acquainted the aspiring poet with elements of the mode he was later to master: allegory. Literally a writing that conveys "other" (from the Greek *allos*, "other") than literal meanings, the allegory that Spenser would eventually perfect for his epic poem *The Faerie Queene* produced narrative verse of great flexibility and verve. Building on powerful images, his verse allegories of education in a "virtuous" chivalry convey the challenges he saw attending the creation of a civil society in early modern England.

Shortly after leaving Cambridge in 1576, Spenser found employment as a secretary in the London household of the rich and influential Earl of Leicester, a favorite courtier of Queen Elizabeth and an ardent defender of international Protestantism. There he met Leicester's already famous nephew, Sir Philip Sidney, to whom Spenser dedicated his first work, the deliberately archaic, neo-Chaucerian *The Shepheardes Calendar,* a sequence of twelve eclogues or poems on pastoral subjects, one for each month of the year. A work of a paradoxically innovative style, *The Shepheardes Calendar* demonstrated a range of metrical forms that had yet to be seen in English poetry; probably more compelling to the general reader was Spenser's use of pastoral motifs and settings to represent opinions on love, poetry, and social order. Sidney's response to the poem was, nevertheless, somewhat ambivalent. While recognizing that Spenser's eclogues had "much poetry" in them, he stated that he disliked verse composed in an "old rustic language"; among earlier and model poets of pastoral, "neither Theocritus in Greek, Virgil in Latin, nor Sannazaro in Italian did affect it." But precisely because this "old rustic language" could be recognized as purely English and independent of European traditions, Spenser would use a modified form of it in *The Faerie Queene;* in this way he hoped to demonstrate that English literature had as rich a past as any in Europe. He probably began the poem while in Leicester's service; the seventeenth-century biographer John Aubrey reported the discovery of "an abundance of cards, with stanzas of the *Faerie Queene* written on them" in the wainscoting of Spenser's London lodging.

From 1580 to the end of his life, Spenser lived in Ireland, serving as secretary to the Lord Deputy of Ireland, Arthur Grey. At such a distance from Queen Elizabeth's court, Spenser could not have secured royal favor. He was rescued from obscurity in 1589 by Sir Walter Raleigh, who, impressed with the first three books of *The Faerie Queene,* invited Spenser to present his poem to the queen. Beside the gallant and charismatic Raleigh, the poet—said to have been a "little man, who wore short hair, little bands (collars) and little cuffs"—must have cut a poor figure. But the queen liked the poem that illustrated her majesty in so many ways, "desired at timely hours to hear" it, and rewarded Spenser with a life pension of £50 a year. When Spenser returned to Ireland in 1590, he met and fell in love with Elizabeth Boyle, a woman much his junior. They were married in 1594, and Spenser celebrated their courtship and wedding in the *Amoretti,* a sonnet sequence describing the poet's quest for his "deer" or dear, and *Epithalamion,* a hymn to each of the twenty-four hours of their wedding day. The second three books of *The Faerie Queene,* published in 1596, proved as popular with readers as the first three, although James VI of Scotland (later James I of England) thought slanderous its portrait of the evil queen Duessa, whom he identified as his mother, Mary, Queen of Scots. He demanded that Spenser be "duly tried and punished"; fortunately, however, Spenser's friends at court intervened, and nothing came of the king's displeasure.

The last years of the poet's life were full of grief and bitter disappointment. In 1598 the Irish in the province of Munster, rebelling against the English colonial authorities, burned the castle in which Spenser lived. The poet and his wife fled; their newborn child was reported to have perished in the flames. In December of that year, Spenser went to London to deliver letters to the queen from the Governor of Ireland concerning the uprising. He included a note describing his own assessment of the situation—a note that may have included material in a treatise entitled A *View of the Present State of Ireland*, supporting a militaristic policy to colonize the people of Ireland, which he is supposed to have written. He died a month after arriving in London in January of 1599 and was buried in Westminster Abbey near Geoffrey Chaucer, whose poetry had meant so much to him. The monument placed on his grave is inscribed with these words: "Prince of poets in his time, whose Divine Spirit needs no other witness than the works which he left behind."

Consciously aspiring both to Chaucer's humane dignity and to his vividly colloquial style, Spenser saw himself as fashioning and refashioning a tradition of English and possibly British poetry. As he made a point of using older terms and spelling, his poems are presented here unmodernized. Spenser's choice of language parallels his use of the motifs of knightly romance: turning to the past, he sought a vital perspective on the present. John Milton would later describe him as a "sage and serious" poet, who, in *The Faerie Queene*, wrote of the struggle of good against evil and the triumph of faith over falsehood. The subject, treated by weaving different story lines together to form a vast tapestry, interested not only Milton, who was clearly inspired by Spenser's complex understanding of human psychology, but also the next generation of poets in England, especially Ben Jonson, John Donne, and George Herbert, who turned to Spenser for a poetry of satirical vigor and spiritual insight. Yet other readers have been moved by Spenser's lyrics. His shorter poems and occasional verse show his skillful use of repetitive sounds or verbal echoes and reveal his unerring sense of language as a musical medium.

The Shepheardes Calender

The genre of pastoral, which originated with Greek and Latin poets, especially Virgil, was popular with early modern writers of lyric verse. Because the genre represents its subjects from the idealized perspectives of rural life, it gave writers who were critical of the more sophisticated manners of the city a chance to praise the virtues of simplicity and artlessness. In fact, Spenser's eclogues are rhetorically complex. Composed as dialogues, they exhibit a consciously archaic diction and a demanding rhyme scheme. *October* is "eclogue the tenth" (*aegloga decima*) in a series of twelve eclogues or pastoral poems, published in 1579. Each eclogue was composed for a month of the year and as a whole they formed a "calendar." The subject of *October* is the poet's craft; it presents an argument between Cuddie, a shepherd and also a piper who wants to renounce his art as unremunerative, and Piers, a shepherd who tells Cuddie that the purpose of his music is to lead its listeners in better ways.

from The Shepheardes Calender
October
AEGLOGA DECIMA
Argument[1]

In Cuddie is set out the perfecte paterne of a Poete, whiche finding no maintenaunce of his state and studies, complayneth of the contempte of Poetrie, and the causes

---

1. This "Argument" is a prose synopsis of the following dialogue and was written by "E.K.," thought to be Edward Kirke, a friend of Spenser.

thereof: Specially having bene in all ages, and even amongst the most barbarous alwayes of singular accounpt and honor, and being indede so worthy and commendable an arte: or rather no arte, but a divine gift and heavenly instinct not to bee gotten by laboure and learning, but adorned with both: and poured into the witte by a certaine ἐνθουσιασμὸς [enthusiasm] and celestiall inspiration, as the Author hereof els where at large discourseth, in his booke called the English Poete, which booke being lately come to my hands, I mynde also by Gods grace upon further advisement to publish.

PIERS

Cuddie, for shame hold up thy heavye head,
And let us cast with what delight to chace,
And weary thys long lingring Phoebus race.[2]
Whilome° thou wont the shepheards laddes to leade,   *formerly*
5 In rymes, in ridles, and in bydding base:°   *simple requests*
Now they in thee, and thou in sleepe art dead.

CUDDIE

Piers, I have pyped erst° so long with payne,   *first*
That all mine Oten reedes° bene rent and wore: *shepherd's pipe*
And my poore Muse hath spent her spared store,
10 Yet little good hath got, and much lesse gayne.
Such pleasaunce makes the Grashopper so poore,
And ligge so layd,[3] when Winter doth her straine:

The dapper ditties, that I wont devise,
To feede youthes fancie, and the flocking fry,°   *children*
15 Delighten much: what I the bett for thy?[4]
They han the pleasure, I a sclender prise.
I beate the bush, the byrds to them doe flye:[5]
What good thereof to Cuddie can arise?

PIERS

Cuddie, the prayse is better, then the price,°   *prize*
20 The glory eke° much greater then the gayne: *also*
O what an honor is it, to restraine
The lust of lawlesse youth with good advice:
Or pricke them forth with pleasaunce of thy vaine,°   *poetic vein*
Whereto thou list° their trayned willes entice.[6]   *wish*

25 Soone as thou gynst to sette thy notes in frame,
O how the rurall routes° to thee doe cleave: *crowds*
Seemeth thou dost their soule of sence bereave,
All as the shepheard, that did fetch his dame
From Plutoes balefull bowre withouten leave:
30 His musicks might the hellish hound did tame.[7]

2. The race of Apollo, god of the sun, through the day.
3. Having sung all summer, the grasshopper lies in poverty when winter comes.
4. What am I the better for this?
5. I rouse game that flies to others.
6. Piers advises Cuddie that a poet must entice the educated wills of his readers by the pleasure his subject matter gives them.
7. Orpheus, mythic father of poetry, rescued his wife from hell, kingdom of the underworld god Pluto, using his music to charm Pluto's savage guard dog Cerberus.

CUDDIE

So praysen babes the Peacoks spotted traine,
And wondren at bright Argus[8] blazing eye:
But who rewards him ere° the more for thy?°   *ever/this*
Or feedes him once the fuller by a graine?
35   Sike° prayse is smoke, that sheddeth in the skye,   *such*
Sike words bene wynd, and wasten soone in vayne.

PIERS

Abandon then the base and viler clowne,°   *bumpkin*
Lyft up thy selfe out of the lowly dust:
And sing of bloody Mars,° of wars, of giusts,°   *god of war/jousts*
40   Turne thee to those, that weld° the awful crowne.   *wield*
To doubted° Knights, whose woundlesse armour rusts,   *undefeated*
And helmes unbruzed wexen° dayly browne.   *grow*

There may thy Muse display her fluttryng wing,
And stretch her selfe at large from East to West:
45   Whither thou list in fayre Elisa[9] rest,
Or if thee please in bigger notes to sing,
Advaunce the worthy whome shee loveth best,
That first the white beare to the stake did bring.[1]

And when the stubborne stroke of stronger stounds,°   *times*
50   Has somewhat slackt the tenor of thy string:
Of love and lustihead tho° mayst thou sing,   *then*
And carrol lowde, and leade the Myllers rownde,
All° were Elisa one of thilke° same ring.   *although/that*
So mought° our Cuddies name to Heaven sownde.   *might*

CUDDIE

55   Indeede the Romish Tityrus, I heare,
Through his Mecoenas left his Oaten reede,[2]
Whereon he earst had taught his flocks to feede,
And laboured lands to yield the timely eare,
And eft° did sing of warres and deadly drede,   *often*
60   So as the Heavens did quake his verse to here.

But ah Mecoenas is yclad in claye,
And great Augustus long ygoe is dead:
And all the worthies liggen° wrapt in leade,   *lie*
That matter made for Poets on to play:
65   For ever, who in derring doe° were dreade,°   *bold action/feared*
The loftie verse of hem° was loved aye.°   *about them/ever*

But after vertue gan for age to stoupe,
And mighty manhode brought a bedde of ease:
The vaunting Poets found nought worth a pease,
70   To put in preace° emong the learned troupe.   *public*

8. Mythical herdsman who had eyes all over his body.
9. Queen Elizabeth. Piers suggests that Cuddie may wish
to take the queen for his poetic subject.
1. "He meaneth (as I guesse) the most honorable and
renowned the Erle of Leycester" (E.K.). Leicester's
emblem was a bear and staff.

2. Cuddie explains that when Tityrus (the name the poet
Virgil assumes in his *Eclogues*) was patronized by
Mecoenas, or Maecenas, a liberal patron of letters during
the reign of the Roman Emperor Augustus, he could
afford to write epic, that is, a long verse narrative that
describes a heroic action.

Tho gan the streames of flowing wittes to cease,
And sonnebright honour pend in shamefull coupe.°   *pen*

And if that any buddes of Poesie,
Yet of the old stocke gan to shoote agayne:
75   Or it° mens follies mote be forst to fayne,°   *poetry/represent*
And rolle with rest in rymes of rybaudrye:
Or as it sprong, it wither must agayne:
Tom Piper makes us better melodie.³

PIERS

O pierlesse Poesye, where is then thy place?
80   If nor° in Princes pallace thou doe sitt: *neither*
(And yet is Princes pallace the most fitt)
Ne° brest of baser birth doth thee embrace.   *nor*
Then make thee winges of thine aspyring wit,
And, whence thou camst, flye backe to heaven apace.

CUDDIE

85   Ah Percy it is all to weake and wanne,
So high to sore, and make so large a flight:
Her peeced pyneons bene not so in plight,⁴
For Colin⁵ fittes° such famous flight to scanne: *it suits*
He, were he not with love so ill bedight,°   *afflicted*
90   Would mount as high, and sing as soote° as Swanne.   *sweet*

PIERS

Ah fon,° for love does teach him climbe so hie,   *fool*
And lyftes him up out of the loathsome myre:
Such immortall mirrhor, as he doth admire,
Would rayse ones mynd above the starry skie.
95   And cause a caytive° corage to aspire,   *cowardly*
For lofty love doth loath a lowly eye.

CUDDIE

All otherwise the state of Poet stands,
For lordly love is such a Tyranne fell:°   *terrible*
That where he rules, all power he doth expell.
100   The vaunted verse a vacant head demaundes,
Ne wont° with crabbed care the Muses dwell.   *used*
Unwisely weaves, that takes two webbes in hand.

Who ever casts to compasse° weightye prise,   *gain*
And thinks to throwe out thondring words of threate:
105   Let powre in lavish cups and thriftie° bitts of meate,   *good*
For Bacchus° fruite is frend to Phoebus wise.   *god of wine*
And when with Wine the braine begins to sweate,
The nombers flowe as fast as spring doth ryse.

Thou kenst not Percie howe the ryme should rage.
110   O if my temples were distaind with wine,
And girt in girlonds of wild Yvie twine,

3. Cuddie states that because the present age has no virtuous subjects, such poetry as epic is no longer written.
To be revived, it must either represent the folly of the
present time or wither again for lack of a subject; for the
present, a "Tom Piper" or popular singer will produce better songs than poets can.
4. I.e., the mended wings of Poetry are not in such a condition.
5. Another of the shepherds who participate in the
eclogues' dialogues.

How I could reare the Muse on stately stage,
And teache her tread aloft in bus-kin° fine,   *high boots*
With queint Bellona° in her equipage.   *gooddess of war*

115   But ah my corage cooles ere it be warme,
For thy,° content us in thys humble shade: *now*
Where no such troublous tydes han us assayde,°   *tried*
Here we our slender pipes may safely charme.

                          PIERS
And when my Gates° shall han their bellies layd:°   *she-goats / borne kids*
120   Cuddie shall have a Kidde to store° his farme.   *enrich*
                    Cuddies Embleme
            Agitante calescimus illo &c.[6]

THE FAERIE QUEENE

In 1583 Spenser told guests at a dinner he was attending that he proposed to write a poem in which he would "represent all the moral virtues, assigning to every virtue a knight in whose actions and chivalry the operations of that virtue are to be expressed, and the vices and unruly appetites that oppose themselves to be beaten down." The project, obviously ambitious, recalls the great epics of classical antiquity: the twenty-four books of Homer's *Iliad*, the twelve books of Virgil's *Aeneid*. Spenser must have believed he was prepared for such an undertaking; like Virgil, he had served his apprenticeship by writing pastoral poetry, with the composition of *The Shepheardes Calendar*. But whatever his intention, he realized his great work only in part. He depicted the first six virtues in the "legends" of Holiness, Temperance, Chastity, Friendship, Justice, and Courtesy, in which each virtue is perfected by the trials of a particular knight fighting the evil that most threatens his character. He published the first three books in 1590, adding the next three in a second edition in 1596. His plan for a second set of six books resulted in only two cantos—on the virtue of Constancy.

Spenser's moral chivalry is sponsored and sustained by the court of Gloriana, the Faerie Queene, in whom is reflected the imposing figure of Queen Elizabeth. Gloriana's story is illustrated by the actions of a character called Prince Arthur, who intervenes at crucial moments to assist Gloriana's knights and is otherwise bent on seeking out Gloriana herself, the bride he has chosen in a dream. In the mythical genealogy of the Tudors, King Arthur (known to Spenser's readers through Sir Thomas Malory's *Morte Darthur*) was identified as the dynasty's progenitor; thus, in the allegorical schema of the poem, the prospective marriage of the Faerie Queene and Prince Arthur, also the champion of Magnificence, signifies the perfect union of monarch and state.

Book 1 relates the adventures of the knight of Holiness, known as the Redcrosse Knight from the sign on his shield and identified as Saint George, England's patron saint. His mission is to overcome the machinations of spiritual error menacing the English church and to deliver the parents of Una, his lady, who is the Truth, from the demons of false faith. The foes of the Redcrosse Knight are many: the fiendish wizard Archimago, who stands for corrupt doctrine; the cunning queen Duessa, who, as the embodiment of duplicity, is never what she seems; the bloated giant Orgoglio, or Pride; and the loathsome many-headed dragon who is supposed to wield the institutional power of the Catholic Church. The Redcrosse Knight kills Pride and the dragon but, although he at last understands that they are thoroughly sinister, fails to capture Duessa and Archimago. They return in later books to trouble Gloriana's other knights.

Book 2 tells of the adventures of the knight of Temperance, Sir Guyon, who must destroy a garden of surpassing beauty, known as the Bower of Bliss, presided over by a brilliantly seductive witch called Acrasia. He is accompanied on his quest by the Palmer, who as the embodi-

---

6. "When he stirs, we glow, etc." From Ovid's *Fasti* 6.5, referring to "Deus in nobis," (the god [of poetry] within us).

ment of reason, informs and guides him in achieving the perfection of his virtue. In Canto 12, perhaps the best-known canto in the entire poem, Guyon sails to Acrasia's island garden in the company of the Palmer, is tempted by the illusionistic pleasures Acrasia provides her suitors, but finally rejects her in a massive act of defiance, tearing down all the beguiling structures of her island in a salutary rage.

The verse form of *The Faerie Queene* is virtually unique to Spenser. It features a sequence of stanzas each (known to later readers as "Spenserian") comprising nine lines, of which the first eight contain five feet or accented syllables and the last contains six feet. They are rhymed in a pattern—*ababbcbcc*—particularly difficult for poets writing in English. Unlike the Romance languages (French, Italian, and Spanish), English has relatively few words ending in vowel sounds, which are easily rhymed. Spenser's ear for the sound of English allowed him to compose verse of a musicality comparable to what was possible in the Romance languages, itself an extraordinary accomplishment. The narrative units of Spenser's epic poem achieve a dramatic coherence by his constructive use of imagery in particular story lines that continuously develop new contexts for their subjects. In other words, a character signifying a special quality in one canto will not signify precisely that quality in another canto: Spenser will change his or her role with the setting the story demands. This gives the reader an active role in the poem's interpretation; in a sense, the reader finds the meaning of the poem in the process of reading it.

FROM THE FAERIE QUEENE
A Letter of the Authors[1]

A letter of the Authors expounding his whole intention in the course of this worke: which for that it giveth great light to the Reader, for the better understanding is hereunto annexed.

To the Right noble, and Valorous, Sir Walter Raleigh knight, Lo. Wardein of the Stanneryes, and her Majesties liefetenaunt of the County of Cornewayll.

Sir knowing how doubtfully all Allegories may be construed, and this booke of mine, which I have entituled the Faery Queene, being a continued Allegory, or darke conceit,[2] I have thought good aswell for avoyding of gealous opinions and misconstructions, as also for your better light in reading thereof, (being so by you commanded,) to discover unto you the general intention and meaning, which in the whole course thereof I have fashioned, without expressing of any particular purposes or by-accidents therein occasioned. The generall end therefore of all the booke is to fashion a gentleman or noble person in vertuous and gentle discipline: Which for that I conceived shoulde be most plausible and pleasing, being coloured with an historicall fiction, the which the most part of men delight to read, rather for variety of matter, then for profite of the ensample:[3] I chose the historye of king Arthure,[4] as most fitte for the excellency of his person, being made famous by many mens former workes, and also furthest from

1. Spenser addressed this letter explaining the purpose and plot of *The Faerie Queene* to Sir Walter Raleigh, who had agreed to bring the poem to the attention of Elizabeth I.
2. In Spenser's poetics a series of images or figures that are to be interpreted as metaphor. The narrative understood literally thus implies a second level whose meaning or meanings the reader is to infer.
3. Example.
4. Spenser states that he chose material from the legendary past of Britain: the story of King Arthur and his knights. In fact, apart from a few characters such as Prince Arthur and the magician Merlin, Spenser repre-

sented virtually nothing of the Arthurian cycle, known to his readers from Sir Thomas Malory's prose narrative *Morte Darthur*. More important in a structural and thematic sense were the poets mentioned subsequently: Homer and Virgil; Lodovico Ariosto (1474–1533), who wrote *Orlando Furioso;* and Torquato Tasso (1544–1595), who wrote *Jerusalem Delivered*. From these models, Spenser derived the idea of a hero in whom a particular virtue would be exemplified. His division of virtues into moral or ethical on the one hand and political on the other is indebted to Aristotle, who considered the actions of a private person in his *Ethics* and the organization of a whole society in his *Politics*.

the daunger of envy, and suspition of present time. In which I have followed all the antique Poets historicall, first Homere, who in the Persons of Agamemnon and Ulysses hath ensampled a good governour and a vertuous man, the one in his Ilias, the other in his Odysseis: then Virgil, whose like intention was to doe in the person of Aeneas: after him Ariosto comprised them both in his Orlando: and lately Tasso dissevered[5] them againe, and formed both parts in two persons, namely that part which they in Philosophy call Ethice, or vertues of a private man, coloured in his Rinaldo: The other named Politice in his Godfredo. By ensample of which excellente Poets, I labour to pourtraict in Arthure, before he was king, the image of a brave knight, perfected in the twelve private morall vertues, as Aristotle hath devised, the which is the purpose of these first twelve bookes: which if I finde to be well accepted, I may be perhaps encoraged, to frame the other part of polliticke vertues in his person, after that hee came to be king. To some I know this Methode will seeme displeasaunt, which had rather have good discipline delivered plainly in way of precepts, or sermoned at large, as they use,[6] then thus clowdily enwrapped in Allegoricall devises.[7] But such, me seeme, should be satisfide with the use of these dayes, seeing all things accounted by their showes, and nothing esteemed of, that is not delightfull and pleasing to commune sence. For this cause is Xenophon preferred before Plato,[8] for that the one in the exquisite depth of his judgement, formed a Commune welth such as it should be, but the other in the person of Cyrus and the Persians fashioned a governement such as might best be: So much more profitable and gratious is doctrine by ensample, then by rule. So have I laboured to doe in the person of Arthure: whome I conceive after his long education by Timon, to whom he was by Merlin delivered to be brought up, so soone as he was borne of the Lady Igrayne, to have seene in a dream or vision the Faery Queen, with whose excellent beauty ravished,[9] he awaking resolved to seeke her out, and so being by Merlin armed, and by Timon throughly instructed, he went to seeke her forth in Faerye land. In that Faery Queene I meane glory in my generall intention,[1] but in my particular I conceive the most excellent and glorious person of our soveraine the Queene, and her kingdome in Faery land. And yet in some places els, I doe otherwise shadow her.[2] For considering she beareth two persons, the one of a most royall Queene or Empresse, the other of a most vertuous and beautifull Lady, this latter part in some places I doe expresse in Belphoebe, fashioning her name according to your owne excellent conceipt of Cynthia, (Phoebe and Cynthia being both names of Diana.) So in the person of Prince Arthure[3] I sette forth magnificence in particular, which vertue for that (according to Aristotle and the rest) it is the perfection of all the rest, and conteineth in it them all, therefore in the whole course I mention the deedes of Arthure applyable to that vertue, which I write of in that booke. But of the xii. other vertues, I make xii. other knights the patrones, for the more variety of the history: Of which these three

---

5. Revealed.
6. Are accustomed to.
7. Figures.
8. Xenophon: the Greek historian (c. 430–355 B.C.), whose account of the Persian king Cyrus creates memorable characters for the reader to emulate; Plato: the Greek philosopher (c. 427–348 B.C.), whose works comprise ethics, politics, and metaphysics. Spenser repeats a conventional excuse for fiction or poetic representation in contrast to philosophy.
9. Overcome.
1. I.e., in the figure of the Faerie Queene Spenser intends to represent glory in general and Queen Elizabeth in par-

ticular. He goes on to say that the queen is also represented by the figure of Belphoebe, a nymph who has attributes of Cynthia, or the goddess of the moon, who is herself an aspect of Diana, also the goddess of chastity and the hunt.
2. Represent.
3. Legendary king of the Britons. Spenser's character is to represent "magnificence," i.e, a splendid and comprehensive generosity, traditionally the virtue most appropriate to royalty. The remaining characters Spenser mentions—the Redcrosse Knight, Sir Guyon, and Britomartis (or Britomart)—represent other virtues and are his own creations.

bookes contayn three, The first of the knight of the Redcrosse, in whome I expresse Holynes: The seconde of Sir Guyon, in whome I sette forth Temperaunce: The third of Britomartis a Lady knight, in whome I picture Chastity. But because the beginning of the whole worke seemeth abrupte and as depending upon other antecedents, it needs that ye know the occasion of these three knights severall adventures. For the Methode of a Poet historical is not such, as of an Historiographer.[4] For an Historiographer discourseth of affayres orderly as they were donne, accounting as well the times as the actions, but a Poet thrusteth into the middest, even where it most concerneth him, and there recoursing[5] to the thinges forepaste,[6] and divining of things to come, maketh a pleasing Analysis of all. The beginning therefore of my history, if it were to be told by an Historiographer should be the twelfth booke, which is the last, where I devise[7] that the Faery Queene kept her Annuall feaste xii. dayes, upon which xii. severall dayes, the occasions of the xii. severall adventures hapned, which being undertaken by xii. severall knights, are in these xii books severally handled and discoursed. The first was this. In the beginning of the feast, there presented him selfe a tall clownishe[8] younge man, who falling before the Queen of Faries desired a boone[9] (as the manner then was) which during that feast she might not refuse: which was that hee might have the atchievement of any adventure, which during that feaste should happen, that being graunted, he rested him on the floore, unfitte through his rusticity for a better place. Soone after entred a faire Ladye in mourning weedes,[1] riding on a white Asse, with a dwarfe behind her leading a warlike steed, that bore the Armes of a knight, and his speare in the dwarfes hand. Shee falling before the Queene of Faeries, complayned that her father and mother an ancient King and Queene, had bene by an huge dragon many years shut up in a brasen[2] Castle, who thence suffred them not to yssew:[3] and therefore besought the Faery Queene to assygne her some one of her knights to take on him that exployt. Presently that clownish person upstarting, desired that adventure: whereat the Queene much wondering, and the Lady much gainesaying,[4] yet he earnestly importuned[5] his desire. In the end the Lady told him that unlesse that armour which she brought, would serve him (that is the armour of a Christian man specified by Saint Paul v. Ephes.)[6] that he could not succeed in that enterprise, which being forthwith put upon him with dewe furnitures[7] thereunto, he seemed the goodliest man in al that company, and was well liked of the Lady. And eftesoones[8] taking on him knighthood, and mounting on that straunge Courser,[9] he went forth with her on that adventure: where beginneth the first booke, vz.

A gentle knight was pricking on the playne. &c.

4. History represents sequential narratives of real events revealing relations of cause and effect; by contrast, poetry constructs narratives governed by the poet's wish to pick and choose among a variety of sources and to speculate on outcomes that may or may not ever come to pass.
5. Having recourse.
6. Passed.
7. Imagine.
8. Countrified.
9. Wish.
1. Clothes.
2. Brass.
3. Get out.
4. Protesting.
5. Begged for.
6. St. Paul's Letter to the Ephesians, often used to justify the spiritual symbolism that from the late Middle Ages had become associated with the practices of chivalry. "Wherefore take unto you the whole armour of God, that ye may be able to withstand in the evil day, and having done all, to stand. Stand therefore, having your loins girt about with truth, and having on the breastplate of righteousness; And your feet shod with the preparation of the gospel of peace; Above all, taking the shield of faith, wherewith ye shall be able to quench all the fiery darts of the wicked. And take the helmet of salvation, and the sword of the Spirit, which is the word of God" (Ephesians 6.13–17).
7. Equipment.
8. Immediately.
9. Warhorse.

The second day ther came in a Palmer[1] bearing an Infant with bloody hands, whose Parents he complained to have bene slayn by an Enchaunteresse called Acrasia: and therfore craved of the Faery Queene, to appoint him some knight, to performe that adventure, which being assigned to Sir Guyon, he presently went forth with that same Palmer: which is the beginning of the second booke and the whole subject thereof. The third day there came in, a Groome who complained before the Faery Queene, that a vile Enchaunter called Busirane had in hand a most faire Lady called Amoretta, whom he kept in most grievous torment, because she would not yield him the pleasure of her body. Whereupon Sir Scudamour the lover of that Lady presently tooke on him that adventure. But being unable to performe it by reason of the hard Enchauntments, after long sorrow, in the end met with Britomartis, who succoured[2] him, and reskewed his love.

But by occasion hereof, many other adventures are intermedled, but rather as Accidents, then intendments.[3] As the love of Britomart, the overthrow of Marinell, the misery of Florimell, the vertuousnes of Belphoebe, the lasciviousnes of Hellenora, and many the like.

Thus much Sir, I have briefly overronne[4] to direct your understanding to the welhead[5] of the History, that from thence gathering the whole intention of the conceit, ye may as in a handfull gripe[6] al the discourse, which otherwise may happily seeme tedious and confused. So humbly craving the continuaunce of your honorable favour towards me, and th'eternall establishment of your happines, I humbly take leave.

23. January, 1589.

Yours most humbly affectionate.

ED. SPENSER.

The First Booke of the Faerie Queene
Contayning The Legende of the Knight of the Red Crosse,
or
Of Holinesse.

1

Lo I the man, whose Muse whilome° did maske,[1]   *formerly*
   As time her taught, in lowly Shepheards weeds,°   *clothing*
   Am now enforst a far unfitter taske,
   For trumpets sterne to chaunge mine Oaten reeds,
5   And sing of Knights and Ladies gentle deeds;
   Whose prayses having slept in silence long,
   Me, all too meane,° the sacred Muse areeds°   *lowly/commands*
   To blazon broad° emongst her learned throng: *proclaim abroad*
Fierce warres and faithfull loves shall moralize my song.

2

10   Helpe then, O holy Virgin chiefe of nine,[2]
   Thy weaker Novice to performe thy will,

1. A pilgrim who carries a palm leaf signifying that he has been to the Holy Land; hence any pilgrim.
2. Helped.
3. I.e., they are not central to the principal development of the allegory.
4. Outlined.
5. Source.
6. Gather
1. In this stanza and in the rest of the Proem (introduction), Spenser is announcing his intention to write an epic poem. His earlier Shepheardes Calender had been written in the more modest pastoral style, characterized

by the "oaten reed" of the shepherd's pipe. Here, he casts off the guise of the shepherd to undertake the lofty subject of The Faerie Queene.
2. Spenser calls on a muse to inspire him; he may be referring to Clio, the muse of history, or to Calliope, the muse of epic poetry. Tanaquill was a Roman woman famous for her chaste and noble character; here Spenser establishes a symbolic relation between Tanaquill, the Faerie Queene (whom Arthur seeks in the poem), and Queen Elizabeth I, much as he will later refer to other characters—most prominently, Britomart, Gloriana, and Mercilla—as figuring aspects of the queen, her power and attributes.

Lay forth out of thine everlasting scryne°   *treasure chest*
The antique rolles,° which there lye hidden still,   *scrolls*
Of Faerie knights and fairest Tanaquill,
15   Whom that most noble Briton Prince° so long   *Arthur*
Sought through the world, and suffered so much ill,
That I must rue° his undeserved wrong: *regret*
O helpe thou my weake wit, and sharpen my dull tong.

3

And thou most dreaded impe° of highest Jove,[3]   *child*
20   Faire Venus sonne,° that with thy cruell dart   *Cupid, god of love*
At that good knight° so cunningly didst rove,°   *Arthur*
That glorious fire it kindled in his hart,
Lay now thy deadly Heben° bow apart,   *ebony*
And with thy mother milde come to mine ayde:[4]
25   Come both, and with you bring triumphant Mart,°   *Mars*
In loves and gentle jollities arrayd,
After his murdrous spoiles and bloudy rage allayd.°   *quelled*

4

And with them eke, O Goddesse heavenly bright,[5]
Mirrour of grace and Majestie divine,
30   Great Lady of the greatest Isle, whose light
Like Phoebus lampe throughout the world doth shine,
Shed thy faire beames into my feeble eyne,
And raise my thoughts too humble and too vile,
To thinke of that true glorious type° of thine,   *the Faerie Queene*
35   The argument of mine afflicted stile:
The which to heare, vouchsafe,° O dearest dread° a-while.   *grant/power*

Canto 1

The Patron of true Holinesse,
Foule Errour doth defeate:
Hypocrisie him to entrapp;
Doth to his home entreate.

1

A Gentle Knight[6] was pricking° on the plaine,   *riding*
Y cladd in mightie armes and silver shielde,
Wherein old dints of deepe wounds did remaine,
The cruell markes of many a bloudy fielde;
5   Yet armes till that time did he never wield:
His angry steede did chide his foming bitt,
As much disdayning to the curbe to yield:
Full jolly knight he seemd, and faire did sitt,
As one for knightly giusts° and fierce encounters fitt.   *joust*

---

3. The king of the pagan gods. Like all the poets of the period who were not writing religious verse, Spenser refers to the classical pantheon as a way of alluding to God and to his various expressions of power.
4. Spenser also invokes Cupid, who combines the loving nature of Venus and the warlike spirit of Mars, to illustrate the mood of his poem.
5. Spenser celebrates the nature of Elizabeth I in grandiose terms: She is a "goddess" whose eyes, like the

lamp of Phoebus Apollo (the sun), shine throughout the world and must now illuminate the poet's mind.
6. This gentle or well-born knight, soon to be identified as the Redcrosse Knight from the sign on his shield, wears the armor of Christianity. The armor itself has been worn by many who fought for the faith, but the Redcrosse Knight is new to the spiritual battlefield and will have to prove himself.

2

10 But on his brest a bloudie Crosse[7] he bore,
      The deare remembrance of his dying Lord,
      For whose sweete sake that glorious badge he wore,
      And dead as living ever him ador'd:
      Upon his shield the like was also scor'd,°   *represented*
15   For soveraine hope, which in his° helpe he had: *his Lord's*
      Right faithfull true he was in deede and word,
      But of his cheere° did seeme too solemne sad;   *demeanor*
      Yet nothing did he dread,° but ever was ydrad.°   *fear/feared*

3

      Upon a great adventure he was bond,
20   That greatest Gloriana[8] to him gave,
      That greatest Glorious Queene of Faerie lond,
      To winne him worship, and her grace to have,
      Which of all earthly things he most did crave;
      And ever as he rode, his hart did earne
25   To prove his puissance° in battell brave   *power*
      Upon his foe, and his new force to learne;
      Upon his foe, a Dragon horrible and stearne.

4

      A lovely Ladie[9] rode him faire beside,
      Upon a lowly Asse more white then snow,
30   Yet she much whiter, but the same did hide
      Under a vele, that wimpled° was full low,   *gathered*
      And over all a blacke stole she did throw,
      As one that inly mournd: so was she sad,
      And heavie sat upon her palfrey[1] slow:
35   Seemed in heart some hidden care she had,
      And by her in a line a milke white lambe she lad.

5

      So pure an innocent, as that same lambe,
      She was in life and every vertuous lore,
      And by descent from Royall lynage came
40   Of ancient Kings and Queenes, that had of yore
      Their scepters stretcht from East to Westerne shore,
      And all the world in their subjection held;[2]
      Till that infernall feend with foule uprore
      Forwasted all their land, and them expeld:
45   Whom to avenge, she had this Knight from far compeld.

---

7. The red cross is Spenser's figure for the salvation offered by Christ to humankind through his death on the cross, the sacrifice of his blood, and his resurrection. It was also the badge traditionally worn by St. George, the patron saint of England, with whom the Redcrosse Knight will later be identified.
8. The character Spenser most frequently invokes when he alludes to Elizabeth I. Gloriana presides over the action of the poem, although she does not take part in it herself.
9. Later revealed to be Una or ("one"). The undivided truth (as opposed to "two," that is, doubleness or duplicity), she is associated with the one true Church. The snow-white ass she rides signifies Christ's humility; her veil is emblematic of the veil that stands between Truth and fallen humanity; and the lamb symbolizes innocence and Christian sacrifice. The mourning garb she wears suggests her sorrow over the captivity of her parents, later understood to be Adam and Eve, trapped by the dragon that embodies the forces of evil that have conspired to corrupt the true Church.
1. A horse suitable for a woman.
2. The Lady traces her lineage to Adam and Eve, who held dominion over Eden before the Fall. The "infernall feend," or Satan, is represented as the destroyer of their realm, which stretched from East to West and was therefore truly universal, unlike the regions dominated by Rome or by the Catholic Church. By designating the Knight as the avenger of Adam and Eve, Spenser identifies him with Christ.

6

Behind her farre away a Dwarfe³ did lag,
　That lasie seemd in being ever last,
　Or wearied with bearing of her bag
　Of needments at his backe. Thus as they past,
50　The day with cloudes was suddeine overcast,
　And angry Jove an hideous storme of raine
　Did poure into his Lemans⁴ lap so fast,
　That every wight to shrowd° it did constrain,° ..... *shelter/impel*
And this faire couple eke° to shroud themselves were fain.° ..... *also/desirous*

7

55　Enforst to seeke some covert° nigh at hand, ... *hiding place*
　A shadie grove not far away they spide,
　That promist ayde the tempest to withstand:
　Whose loftie trees yclad with sommers pride,
　Did spred so broad, that heavens light did hide,
60　Not perceable with power of any starre:
　And all within were pathes and alleies wide,
　With footing worne, and leading inward farre:
Faire harbour that them seemes; so in they entred arre.

8

And foorth they passe, with pleasure forward led,
65　Joying to heare the birdes sweete harmony,
　Which therein shrouded from the tempest dred,
　Seemd in their song to scorne the cruell sky.
　Much can they prayse the trees so straight and hy,
　The sayling° Pine, the Cedar proud and tall, ... *soaring*
70　The vine-prop Elme, the Poplar never dry,
　The builder Oake, sole king of forrests all,
The Aspine good for staves,° the Cypresse funerall. ..... *poles*

9

　The Laurell, meed° of mightie Conquerours ..... *reward*
　And Poets sage, the Firre that weepeth still,
75　The Willow worne of forlorne Paramours,° ..... *forsaken lovers*
　The Eugh obedient to the benders will,
　The Birch for shaftes, the Sallow° for the mill, ... *willow*
　The Mirrhe sweete bleeding in the bitter wound,
　The warlike Beech, the Ash for nothing ill,
80　The fruitfull Olive, and the Platane° round, ... *sycamore*
The carver Holme,° the Maple seeldom inward sound. ..... *holly*

10

Led with delight, they thus beguile° the way, ... *make pleasant*
　Untill the blustring storme is overblowne;
　When weening° to returne, whence they did stray, ... *thinking*
85　They cannot finde that path, which first was showne,
　But wander too and fro in wayes unknowne,
　Furthest from end then, when they neerest weene,
　That makes them doubt, their wits be not their owne:

3. The servant who serves the Lady, a source of prudence,　　4. I.e., his lady love's, or the earth's.
common sense, and wariness.

So many pathes, so many turnings seene,
90   That which of them to take, in diverse doubt they been.

11

At last resolving forward still to fare,
    Till that some end° they finde or° in or out,   way/either
    That path they take, that beaten seemd most bare,
    And like to lead the labyrinth about;
95   Which when by tract they hunted had throughout,
    At length it brought them to a hollow cave,
    Amid the thickest woods. The Champion stout
    Eftsoones dismounted from his courser brave,
And to the Dwarfe a while his needlesse spere he gave.

12

100   Be well aware, quoth then that Ladie milde,
    Least suddaine mischiefe ye too rash provoke:
    The danger hid, the place unknowne and wilde,
    Breedes dreadful doubts: Oft fire is without smoke,
    And perill without show: therefore your stroke
105   Sir knight with-hold, till further triall made.
    Ah Ladie (said he) shame were to revoke
    The forward footing for an hidden shade:
Vertue gives her selfe light, through darkenesse for to wade.[5]

13

Yea but (quoth she) the perill of this place
110   I better wot° then you, though now too late   know
    To wish you backe returne with foule disgrace,
    Yet wisedome warnes, whilest foot is in the gate,
    To stay° the steppe, ere forced to retrate.°   halt/retreat
    This is the wandring wood, this Errours den,
115   A monster vile, whom God and man does hate:
    Therefore I read beware. Fly fly (quoth then
The fearefull Dwarfe:) this is no place for living men.

14

But full of fire and greedy hardiment,
    The youthfull knight could not for ought° be staide,   anything
120   But forth unto the darksome hole he went,
    And looked in: his glistring armor made
    A litle glooming light, much like a shade,
    By which he saw the ugly monster plaine,
    Halfe like a serpent horribly displaide,
125   But th'other halfe did womans shape retaine,[6]
Most lothsom, filthie, foule, and full of vile disdaine.

15

And as she lay upon the durtie ground,
    Her huge long taile her den all overspred,

5. Lacking humility and overly confident of his own virtue, the Redcrosse Knight believes he is strong enough to withstand the dangers of the wood. In fact, as we learn in the next stanza, he has stepped into the den of a monster who personifies Error, one of Satan's many manifestations in the poem.
6. Spenser follows traditional treatments of Error in giving her a woman's face and a serpent's body.

Yet was in knots and many boughtes° upwound,   *coils*
130   Pointed with mortall sting. Of her there bred
A thousand yong ones, which she dayly fed,
Sucking upon her poisonous dugs, eachone
Of sundry shapes, yet all ill favored:
Soone as that uncouth° light upon them shone,   *strange*
135   Into her mouth they crept, and suddain all were gone.

16
Their dam upstart, out of her den effraide,
And rushed forth, hurling her hideous taile
About her cursed head, whose folds displaid
Were stretcht now forth at length without entraile.°   *coiling*
140   She lookt about, and seeing one in mayle°   *armor*
Armed to point, sought backe to turne againe;
For light she hated as the deadly bale,°   *injury*
Ay wont° in desert darknesse to remaine,   *ever used*
Where plaine° none might her see, nor she see any plaine.   *plainly*

17
145   Which when the valiant Elfe° perceiv'd, he lept   *Redcrosse Knight*
As Lyon fierce upon the flying pray,
And with his trenchand blade her boldly kept
From turning backe, and forced her to stay:
Therewith enrag'd she loudly gan to bray,
150   And turning fierce, her speckled taile advaunst,
Threatning her angry sting, him to dismay:
Who nought aghast, his mightie hand enhaunst:°   *raised up*
The stroke down from her head unto her shoulder glaunst.

18
Much daunted with that dint, her sence was dazd,
155   Yet kindling rage, her selfe she gathered round,
And all attonce her beastly body raizd
With doubled forces high above the ground:
Tho wrapping up her wrethed sterne° arownd,   *tail*
Lept fierce upon his shield, and her huge traine°   *tail*
160   All suddenly about his body wound,
That hand or foot to stirre he strove in vaine:
God helpe the man so wrapt in Errours endlesse traine.

19
His Lady sad to see his sore constraint,°   *predicament*
Cride out, Now now Sir knight, shew what ye bee,
165   Add faith unto your force, and be not faint:
Strangle her, else she sure will strangle thee.
That when he heard, in great perplexitie,
His gall did grate° for griefe and high disdaine,   *anger was aroused*
And knitting all his force got one hand free,
170   Wherewith he grypt her gorge with so great paine,
That soone to loose her wicked bands did her constraine.

20
Therewith she spewd out of her filthy maw°   *stomach*
A floud of poyson horrible and blacke,
Full of great lumpes of flesh and gobbets raw,

175   Which stunck so vildly, that it forst him slacke
       His grasping hold, and from her turne him backe:
       Her vomit full of bookes and papers was,[7]
       With loathly frogs and toades, which eyes did lacke,
       And creeping sought way in the weedy gras:
180   Her filthy parbreake° all the place defiled has.   *vomit*

                              21
       As when old father Nilus° gins to swell   *the river Nile*
          With timely pride aboue the Aegyptian vale,
          His fattie° waves do fertile slime outwell,°   *fertile/pour forth*
          And overflow each plaine and lowly dale:
185   But when his later spring° gins to avale,°   *last waters/subside*
          Huge heapes of mudd he leaves, wherein there breed
          Ten thousand kindes of creatures, partly male
          And partly female of his fruitfull seed;
       Such ugly monstrous shapes elswhere may no man reed.°   *know*

                              22
190   The same so sore annoyed has the knight,
          That welnigh choked with the deadly stinke,
          His forces faile, ne can no longer fight.
          Whose corage when the feend perceiv'd to shrinke,
          She poured forth out of her hellish sinke°   *womb*
195   Her fruitfull cursed spawne° of serpents small,   *offspring*
          Deformed monsters, fowle, and blacke as inke,
          Which swarming all about his legs did crall,
       And him encombred sore, but could not hurt at all.

                              23
       As gentle Shepheard in sweete even-tide,
200   When ruddy Phoebus gins to welke° in west,   *sink*
          High on an hill, his flocke to vewen wide,
          Markes which do byte their hasty supper best;
          A cloud of combrous gnattes do him molest,
          All striving to infixe their feeble stings,
205   That from their noyance he no where can rest,
          But with his clownish hands their tender wings
       He brusheth oft, and oft doth mar their murmurings.

                              24
       Thus ill bestedd,° and fearefull more of shame,   *situated*
          Then of the certaine perill he stood in,
210   Halfe furious unto his foe he came,
          Resolv'd in minde all suddenly to win,
          Or soone to lose, before he once would lin;°   *surrender*
          And strooke at her with more then manly force,
          That from her body full of filthie sin
215   He raft° her hatefull head without remorse;   *cut off*
       A streame of cole black bloud forth gushed from her corse.

                              25
       Her scattred brood, soone as their Parent deare
          They saw so rudely° falling to the ground,   *violently*

---

7. Error's vomit is a figurative depiction of the falsehoods that corrupt religion. The vehicles of such lies are both the spoken and written word; hence the material issuing from Error's mouth includes books as well as other poisonous things.

Groning full deadly, all with troublous feare,
220   Gathred themselves about her body round,
    Weening their wonted entrance to have found
    At her wide mouth: but being there withstood
    They flocked all about her bleeding wound,
    And sucked up their dying mothers blood,
225 Making her death their life, and eke her hurt their good.

26

That detestable sight him much amazde,
    To see th'unkindly Impes° of heaven accurst,   *unnatural offspring*
    Devoure their dam; on whom while so he gazd,
    Having all satisfide their bloudy thurst,
230   Their bellies swolne he saw with fulnesse burst,
    And bowels gushing forth: well worthy end
    Of such as drunke her life, the which them nurst;
    Now needeth him no lenger labour spend,
His foes have slaine themselves, with whom he should contend.

27

235 His Ladie seeing all, that chaunst, from farre
    Approcht in hast to greet his victorie,
    And said, Faire knight, borne under happy starre,
    Who see your vanquisht foes before you lye:
    Well worthy be you of that Armorie,[8]
240   Wherein ye have great glory wonne this day,
    And proov'd your strength on a strong enimie,
    Your first adventure: many such I pray,
And henceforth ever wish, that like succeed it may.

28

Then mounted he upon his Steede againe,
245   And with the Lady backward sought to wend;
    That path he kept, which beaten was most plaine,
    Ne ever would to any by-way bend,
    But still did follow one unto the end,
    The which at last out of the wood them brought.
250   So forward on his way (with God to frend)
    He passed forth, and new adventure sought;
Long way he travelled, before he heard of ought.

29

At length they chaunst to meet upon the way
    An aged Sire, in long blacke weedes yclad,
255   His feete all bare, his beard all hoarie gray,
    And by his belt his booke he hanging had;
    Sober he seemde, and very sagely sad,
    And to the ground his eyes were lowly bent,
    Simple in shew, and voyde of malice bad,
260   And all the way he prayed, as he went,
And often knockt his brest, as one that did repent.

---

8. The Lady is proclaiming that by conquering Error, the Redcrosse Knight has become worthy to wear the armor of Christ; the episode foreshadows the knight's final triumph over the many-headed dragon that represents false faith.

30

He faire the knight saluted, louting° low,   *bowing*
   Who faire him quited,° as that courteous was: *answered*
   And after asked him, if he did know
265   Of straunge adventures, which abroad did pas.
   Ah my deare Sonne (quoth he) how should, alas,
   Silly° old man, that lives in hidden cell,   *simple*
   Bidding° his beades all day for his trespas,   *telling*
   Tydings of warre and worldly trouble tell?
270 With holy father sits not with such things to mell.°   *meddle*

31

But if of daunger which hereby doth dwell,
   And homebred evill ye desire to heare,
   Of a straunge man I can you tidings tell,
   That wasteth° all this countrey farre and neare.   *destroys*
275   Of such (said he)° I chiefly do inquere,   *Redcrosse Knight*
   And shall you well reward to shew the place,
   In which that wicked wight his dayes doth weare°:   *spend*
   For to all knighthood it is foule disgrace,
That such a cursed creature lives so long a space.

32

280 Far hence (quoth he)° in wastfull wildernesse   *the aged Sire*
   His dwelling is, by which no living wight
   May ever passe, but thorough° great distresse.   *through*
   Now (sayd the Lady) draweth toward night,
   And well I wote,° that of your later fight   *know*
285   Ye all forwearied° be: for what so strong,   *exhausted*
   But wanting rest will also want of might?
   The Sunne that measures heaven all day long,
At night doth baite° his steedes the Ocean waves emong.   *nourish*

33

Then with the Sunne take Sir, your timely rest,
290   And with new day new worke at once begin:
   Untroubled night they say gives counsell best.
   Right well Sir knight ye have advised bin,
   (Quoth then that aged man;) the way to win
   Is wisely to advise: now day is spent;
295 Therefore with me ye may take up your In
   For this same night. The knight was well content:
So with that godly father to his home they went.

34

A little lowly Hermitage it was,[9]
   Downe in a dale, hard by° a forests side,   *next to*
300 Far from resort of people, that did pas
   In travell to and froe: a little wyde
   There was an holy Chappell edifyde,°   *built*

9. This stanza illustrates the use of symbol in allegory; taken as a whole, its imagery suggests that the Redcrosse Knight has met the hermit because he suffers from a failing that the hermit will exploit. The hermitage is down in a dale, or valley, because the knight has begun to descend into a false faith; it is isolated because he is traveling in a strange and unusual direction; and it is by a fountain that appears to be sacred but that will be revealed as the antithesis of the Well of Life that will later restore him.

Wherein the Hermite dewly wont to say
His holy things each morne and eventyde:
305 Thereby a Christall streame did gently play,
Which from a sacred fountaine welled forth alway.

35

Arrived there, the little house they fill,
Ne looke for entertainement, where none was:
Rest is their feast, and all things at their will;
310 The noblest mind the best contentment has.
With faire discourse the evening so they pas:
For that old man of pleasing wordes had store,
And well could file his tongue as smooth as glas;
He told of Saintes and Popes, and evermore
315 He strowd° an Ave-Mary after and before.[1] — *recited*

36

The drouping Night thus creepeth on them fast,
And the sad humour° loading their eye liddes, — *moisture*
As messenger of Morpheus° on them cast — *god of sleep*
Sweet slombring deaw, the which to sleepe them biddes.
320 Unto their lodgings then his guestes he° riddes: — *the aged Sire*
Where when all drownd in deadly sleepe he findes,
He to his study goes, and there amiddes
His Magick bookes and artes of sundry kindes,
He seekes out mighty charmes, to trouble sleepy mindes.

37

325 Then choosing out few wordes most horrible,
(Let none them read) thereof did verses frame,° — *compose*
With which and other spelles like terrible,
He bad awake blacke Plutoes griesly Dame,[2]
And cursed heaven, and spake reprochfull shame
330 Of highest God, the Lord of life and light;
A bold bad man, that dar'd to call by name
Great Gorgon,[3] Prince of darknesse and dead night,
At which Cocytus quakes, and Styx is put to flight.[4]

38

And forth he cald out of deepe darknesse dred
335 Legions of Sprights,° the which like little flyes — *spirits*
Fluttring about his ever damned hed,
A-waite whereto their service he applyes,
To aide his friends, or fray° his enimies: — *frighten*
Of those he chose out two, the falsest twoo,
340 And fittest for to forge true-seeming lyes;
The one of them he gave a message too,
The other by him selfe staide other worke to doo.

---

1. Despite his pious demeanor, the old man's discourse of saints and popes and his recital of Ave Marias indicate his affiliation with Catholicism; they are therefore intended to signal his corrupt and duplicitous character. The Redcrosse Knight is intended to represent English Protestantism and the true Church; by contrast, Spenser rejects Catholicism as a corruption of that Church.

2. Persephone, Pluto's wife and sometimes goddess of the underworld.
3. One of a family of monsters, daughters of the primitive gods of antiquity; Spenser, making her male, identifies the Gorgon with Pluto and also Satan.
4. The Cocytus and the Styx were rivers in the classical underworld.

39

He making speedy way through spersed° ayre,   *empty*
  And through the world of waters wide and deepe,
345 To Morpheus⁵ house doth hastily repaire.
  Amid the bowels of the earth full steepe,
  And low, where dawning day doth never peepe,
  His dwelling is; there Tethys his wet bed
350 Doth ever wash, and Cynthia still doth steepe
  In silver deaw his ever-drouping hed,
Whiles sad Night over him her mantle black doth spred.

40

Whose double gates he findeth locked fast,
  The one faire fram'd of burnisht Yvory,
  The other all with silver overcast;
355 And wakefull dogges before them farre do lye,
  Watching to banish Care their enimy,
  Who oft is wont to trouble gentle Sleepe.
  By them the Sprite doth passe in quietly,
  And unto Morpheus comes, whom drowned deepe
360 In drowsie fit° he findes: of nothing he takes keepe.°   *stupor/notice*

41

And more, to lulle him in his slumber soft,
  A trickling streame from high rocke tumbling downe
  And ever-drizling raine upon the loft,
  Mixt with a murmuring winde, much like the sowne
365 Of swarming Bees, did cast him in a swowne°:   *faint*
  No other noyse, nor peoples troublous cryes,
  As still are wont t'annoy the walled towne,
  Might there be heard: but carelesse Quiet lyes,
Wrapt in eternall silence farre from enemyes.

42

370 The messenger approching to him spake,
  But his wast wordes returnd to him in vaine:
  So sound he° slept, that nought mought him awake.   *Morpheus*
  Then rudely he him thrust, and pusht with paine,
  Whereat he gan to stretch: but he againe
375 Shooke him so hard, that forced him to speake.
  As one then in a dreame, whose dryer braine
  Is tost with troubled sights and fancies weake,
He mumbled soft, but would not all his silence breake.

43

The Sprite then gan more boldly him to wake,
380 And threatned unto him the dreaded name
  Of Hecate:⁶ whereat he gan to quake,
  And lifting up his lumpish head, with blame
  Halfe angry asked him, for what he came.

---

5. God of sleep, who lives in the depths of the dark earth:
Tethus or the sea washes him; Cynthia or the moon
bedews him, and Night covers him.

6. The dark aspect of Cynthia, the moon, and thus also of
Diana; Hecate figures the underworld, death, and darkness.

385
Hither (quoth he) me Archimago[7] sent,
He that the stubborne Sprites can wisely tame,
He bids thee to him send for his intent
A fit false dreame, that can delude the sleepers sent.°   *senses*

44

390
The God obayde, and calling forth straight way
A diverse dreame out of his prison darke,
Delivered it to him, and downe did lay
His heavie head, devoide of carefull carke,°   *sorrowful anxiety*
Whose sences all were straight benumbd and starke.°   *paralyzed*
He backe returning by the Yvorie dore,
395
Remounted up as light as chearefull Larke,
And on his litle winges the dreame he bore
In hast unto his Lord, where he him left afore.

45

Who all this while with charmes and hidden artes,
Had made a Lady of that other Spright,
And fram'd of liquid ayre her tender partes
400
So lively, and so like in all mens sight,
That weaker sence it° could have ravisht quight: *the spright*
The maker selfe for all his wondrous witt,
Was nigh beguiled with so goodly sight:
Her all in white he clad, and over it
405
Cast a blacke stole, most like to seeme for Una[8] fit.

46

Now when that ydle dreame was to him brought,
Unto that Elfin knight he° bad him° fly,   *Archimago/the spright*
Where he slept soundly void of evill thought,
And with false shewes abuse his fantasy,
410
In sort as he him schooled privily:
And that new creature borne without her dew,°   *unnaturally*
Full of the makers guile, with usage sly
He taught to imitate that Lady trew,
Whose semblance she did carrie under feigned hew.

47

415
Thus well instructed, to their worke they hast,
And comming where the knight in slomber lay,
The one upon his hardy head him plast,
And made him dreame of loves and lustfull play,
That nigh his manly hart did melt away,
420
Bathed in wanton blis and wicked joy:
Then seemed him his Lady by him lay,
And to him playnd, how that false winged boy°   *Cupid*
Her chast hart had subdewd, to learne Dame pleasures toy.

---

7. The sage Sire is named Archimago, an "arch (or chief) magus (or magician)" and hence a forger or architect of images rather than real things. Because these images are clever and deceptive imitations of reality, Archimago is associated with hypocrisy and magic, an art that Chris-tians were forbidden to practice.

8. Here the Lady is named Una; she is to symbolize the ideal unity of Truth and the Church whose faith the Red-crosse Knight defends. She is named only when her false double appears.

48

And she her selfe of beautie soveraigne Queene,
425   Faire Venus seemde unto his bed to bring
Her,[9] whom he waking evermore did weene
To be the chastest flowre, that ay did spring
On earthly braunch, the daughter of a king,
430   And eke the Graces seemed all to sing,
Hymen iō Hymen,[1] dauncing all around,
Whilst freshest Flora her with Yvie girlond crownd.

49

In this great passion of unwonted lust,
Or wonted feare of doing ought amis,
435   He° started up, as seeming to mistrust   *Redcrosse Knight*
Some secret ill, or hidden foe of his:
Lo there before his face his Lady is,
Under blake stole hyding her bayted hooke,
And as halfe blushing offred him to kis,
440   With gentle blandishment and lovely looke,
Most like that virgin true, which for her knight him took.

50

All cleane° dismayd to see so uncouth sight,   *fully*
And halfe enraged at her shamelesse guise,
He thought have slaine her in his fierce despight:°   *indignation*
445   But hasty heat tempring with sufferance° wise,   *patience*
He stayde his hand, and gan himselfe advise
To prove his sense,° and tempt° her faigned truth.[2]   *what he saw/test*
Wringing her hands in wemens pitteous wise,
Tho° can she weepe, to stirre up gentle ruth,   *then*
450   Both for her noble bloud, and for her tender youth.

51

And said, Ah Sir, my liege Lord and my love,
Shall I accuse the hidden cruell fate,
And mightie causes wrought in heaven above,
Or the blind God, that doth me thus amate,°   *dismay*
455   For hoped love to winne me certaine hate?
Yet thus perforce he bids me do, or die.
Die is my dew:° yet rew° my wretched state   *due/pity*
You, whom my hard avenging destinie
Hath made judge of my life or death indifferently.

52

460   Your owne deare sake forst me at first to leave
My Fathers kingdome, There she stopt with teares;

9. I.e., she, impersonating Una, seemed also a Venus; this composite queen of beauty appears to the Redcrosse Knight to have come into his bed.
1. A Roman chant praising Hymen, the god of marriage, sung here by the Graces, handmaids of Venus, who personify the arts of courtesy and courtship. The union they celebrate in this case is not, however, a lawful Christian marriage but rather one provoked by lust and sexuality. In Roman mythology, Flora is the goddess of flowers, but early modern poets often gave her the role of a harlot.

This entire scene uses the imagery of the Roman Bacchanalia (celebration of the god Bacchus) to suggest the mood of an orgy.
2. The Redcrosse Knight unwisely tests his senses rather than his faith. In doing so, he succumbs to the sensuality of the false Una and thus proves himself false to the true Una. The episode illustrates the danger inherent in powerful illusion; in such cases the false and the true may be indistinguishable.

Her swollen hart her speach seemd to bereave,
And then againe begun, My weaker yeares
Captiv'd to fortune and frayle worldly feares,
465   Fly to your faith for succour and sure ayde:
Let me not dye in languor and long teares.
Why Dame (quoth he) what hath ye thus dismayd?
What frayes° ye, that were wont to comfort me affrayd?   *frightens*

53

Love of your selfe, she said, and deare° constraint°   *dire / danger*
470   Lets me not sleepe, but wast the wearie night
In secret anguish and unpittied plaint,
Whiles you in carelesse sleepe are drowned quight.
Her doubtfull words made that redoubted knight
Suspect her truth: yet since no'untruth he knew,
475   Her fawning love with foule disdainefull spight
He would not shend,° but said, Deare dame I rew,   *reproach*
That for my sake unknowne such griefe unto you grew.

54

Assure your selfe, it fell not all to ground;
For all so deare as life is to my hart,
480   I deeme your love, and hold me to you bound;
Ne let vaine feares procure your needlesse smart,°   *pain*
Where cause is none, but to your rest depart.
Not all content, yet seemd she to appease
Her mournefull plaintes, beguiled of her art,
485   And fed with words, that could not chuse but please,
So slyding softly forth, she turnd as to her ease.

55

Long after lay he musing at her mood,
Much griev'd to thinke that gentle Dame so light,
For whose defence he was to shed his blood.
490   At last dull wearinesse of former fight
Having yrockt a sleepe his irkesome spright,
That troublous dreame gan freshly tosse his braine,
With bowres, and beds, and Ladies deare delight:
But when he saw his labour all was vaine,
495   With that misformed spright he backe returnd againe.

Canto 2

The guilefull great Enchaunter parts
The Redcrosse Knight from Truth:
Into whose stead faire falshood steps,
And workes him wofull ruth.

1

By this the Northerne wagoner had set
His sevenfold teme behind the stedfast starre,[1]

---

1. Spenser is referring to a constellation that includes Ursa Major, which contemporary English readers envisioned as a ploughman drawing a wagon. The "stedfast starre" is the Pole Star; it remains at the center of the stars in Ursa Major, which revolve around it and is "never wet" because it never sets into the ocean. The brightest star in this constellation is Arcturus, which the English associated with the mythical King Arthur.

That was in Ocean waves yet never wet,
But firme is fixt, and sendeth light from farre
5   To all, that in the wide deepe wandring arre:
And chearefull Chauntic1ere° with his note shrill   *a rooster*
Had warned once, that Phoebus fiery carre°   *chariot*
In hast was climbing up the Easterne hill,
Full envious that night so long his roome° did fill.   *the sky*

2

10   When those accursed messengers of hell,
That feigning dreame, and that faire-forged Spright
Came to their wicked maister, and gan° tell   *did*
Their bootelesse paines,° and ill succeeding night: *fruitless efforts*
Who all in rage to see his skilfull might
15   Deluded so, gan threaten hellish paine
And sad Proserpines wrath, them to affright.
But when he saw his threatning was but vaine,
He cast about, and searcht his balefull° bookes againe.   *evil*

3

Eftsoones° he tooke that miscreated faire,   *soon after*
20   And that false other Spright, on whom he spred
A seeming body of the subtile aire,
Like a young Squire, in loves and lusty-hed°   *lechery*
His wanton dayes that ever loosely led,
Without regard of armes and dreaded fight:
25   Those two he tooke, and in a secret bed,
Covered with darknesse and misdeeming° night,   *deceiving*
Them both together laid, to joy in vaine delight.

4

Forthwith he runnes with feigned faithfull hast
Unto his guest, who after troublous sights
30   And dreames, gan° now to take more sound repast,   *began*
Whom suddenly he wakes with fearefull frights,
As one aghast with feends or damned sprights,
And to him cals, Rise rise unhappy Swaine,°   *youth*
That here wex old in sleepe, whiles wicked wights
35   Have knit themselves in Venus shamefull chaine;
Come see, where your false Lady doth her honour staine.

5

All in amaze he suddenly up start
With sword in hand, and with the old man went;
Who soone him brought into a secret part,
40   Where that false couple were full closely ment°   *joined*
In wanton lust and lewd embracement:
Which when he saw, he burnt with gealous fire,
The eye of reason was with rage yblent,°   *blinded*
And would have slaine them in his furious ire,
45   But hardly was restreined of that aged sire.

6

Returning to his bed in torment great,
And bitter anguish of his guiltie sight,

He could not rest, but did his stout heart eat,
And wast his inward gall° with deepe despight,°   *irritation/malice*
50   Yrkesome° of life, and too long lingring night.   *tired*
At last faire Hesperus[2] in highest skie
Had spent his lampe, and brought forth dawning light,
Then up he rose, and clad him hastily;
The Dwarfe him brought his steed: so both away do fly.

7

55   Now when the rosy-fingred Morning faire,
Weary of aged Tithones[3] saffron bed,
Had spred her purple robe through deawy aire,
And the high hils Titan[4] discovered,
The royall virgin shooke off drowsy-hed,
60   And rising forth out of her baser bowre,
Lookt for her knight, who far away was fled,
And for her Dwarfe, that wont to wait° each houre;   *used to attend*
Then gan she waile and weepe, to see that woefull stowre.°   *plight*

8

And after him she rode with so much speede
65   As her slow beast could make; but all in vaine:
For him so far had borne his light-foot steede,
Pricked with wrath and fiery fierce disdaine,
That him to follow was but fruitlesse paine;
Yet she her weary limbes would never rest,
70   But every hill and dale, each wood and plaine
Did search, sore grieved in her gentle brest,
He so ungently left her, whom she loved best.

9

But subtill Archimago, when his guests
He saw divided into double parts,
75   And Una wandring in woods and forrests,
Th'end of his drift,° he praisd his divelish arts,   *intention*
That had such might over true meaning harts;
Yet rests not so, but other meanes doth make,
How he may worke unto her further smarts:
80   For her he hated as the hissing snake,
And in her many troubles did most pleasure take.

10

He then devisde himselfe how to disguise;
For by his mightie science he could take
As many formes and shapes in seeming wise,
85   As ever Proteus[5] to himselfe could make:
Sometime a fowle, sometime a fish in lake,
Now like a foxe, now like a dragon fell,°   *deadly*
That of himselfe he oft for feare would quake,

2. The evening and morning star, the planet Venus.   5. A sea-god, son of two other deities of the sea, Oceanus
3. Husband of the dawn.   and Tethys; Proteus could change his shape at will.
4. The sun. I.e., when the sun revealed the high hills.

And oft would flie away. O who can tell
90   The hidden power of herbes, and might of Magicke spell?

11

But now seemde best, the person to put on
Of that good knight, his late beguiled° guest: *deceived*
In mighty armes he was yclad anon,°   *presently*
And silver shield: upon his coward brest
95   A bloudy crosse, and on his craven crest°   *cowardly head*
A bounch of haires discolourd diversly:
Full jolly knight he seemde, and well addrest,
And when he sate upon his courser free,
Saint George himself ye would have deemed him to be.[6]

12

100   But he the knight, whose semblaunt° he did beare,   *likeness*
The true Saint George was wandred far away,
Still flying from his thoughts and gealous feare;
Will was his guide, and griefe led him astray.
At last him chaunst to meete upon the way
105   A faithlesse Sarazin[7] all arm'd to point,
In whose great shield was writ with letters gay
Sans-Foy:° full large of limbe and every joint   *faithless*
He was, and cared not for God or man a point.°   *bit*

13

He had a faire companion of his way,
110   A goodly Lady[8] clad in scarlot° red,   *a royal cloth*
Purfled with gold and pearle of rich assay,°   *quality*
And like a Persian mitre° on her hed   *papal hat*
She wore, with crownes and owches° garnished,   *jewels*
The which her lavish lovers to her gave;
115   Her wanton palfrey all was overspred
With tinsell trappings, woven like a wave,
Whose bridle rung with golden bels and bosses brave.°   *splendid ornaments*

14

With faire disport° and courting dalliaunce°   *teasing/play*
She intertainde her lover all the way:
120   But when she saw the knight his speare advaunce,
She soone left off her mirth and wanton play,
And bad her knight addresse him to the fray:°   *face the challenge*
His foe was nigh at hand. He prickt° with pride   *spurred on*
And hope to winne his Ladies heart that day,
125   Forth spurred fast: adowne his coursers side
The red bloud trickling staind the way, as he did ride.

---

6. Here, Archimago assumes the appearance of the Redcrosse Knight; incidentally, he reveals that the true
knight is actually Saint George.
7. A Saracen, or follower of Islam. Early modern Europeans commonly represented believers in a non-Christ-
ian faith as infidels or nonbelievers. Sans-Foy (as this
knight is later named—literally, "without faith") is there-

fore not actually without a faith, but he is a Saracen and
not a Christian.
8. The description of this Lady associates her with the
Whore of Babylon (Revelation 17.4), who was identified
by 16th-century Protestants with the Antichrist, i.e., the
Pope and his retinue.

15

The knight of the Redcrosse when him he spide,
  Spurring so hote with rage dispiteous,°   *cruel*
  Gan fairely couch his speare, and towards ride:
130   Soone meete they both, both fell and furious,
  That daunted° with their forces hideous,   *dazed*
  Their steeds do stagger, and amazed stand,
  And eke themselves too rudely rigorous,
  Astonied° with the stroke of their owne hand,   *stunned*
135 Do backe rebut,° and each to other yeeldeth land. *recoil*

16

As when two rams stird with ambitious pride,
  Fight for the rule of the rich fleeced flocke,
  Their horned fronts so fierce on either side
  Do meete, that with the terrour of the shocke
140 Astonied both, stand sencelesse as a blocke,
  Forgetfull of the hanging victory:
  So stood these twaine, unmoved as a rocke,
  Both staring fierce, and holding idely
The broken reliques of their former cruelty.

17

145 The Sarazin sore daunted with the buffe°   *blow*
  Snatcheth his sword, and fiercely to him flies;
  Who well it wards, and quyteth° cuff° with cuff: *repays/blow*
  Each others equall puissaunce° envies,   *power*
  And through their iron sides with cruell spies
150 Does seeke to perce: repining° courage yields *exhausted*
  No foote to foe. The flashing fier flies
  As from a forge out of their burning shields,
And streames of purple bloud new dies the verdant fields.

18

Curse on that Crosse (quoth then the Sarazin)
155 That keepes thy body from the bitter fit;° *pangs of death*
  Dead long ygoe I wote thou haddest bin,
  Had not that charme from thee forwarned° it: *prevented*
  But yet I warne thee now assured sitt,
  And hide thy head. Therewith upon his crest
160 With rigour so outrageous he smitt,°   *struck*
  That a large share it hewd out of the rest,
And glauncing downe his shield, from blame° him fairely blest.° *injury/protected*

19

Who thereat wondrous wroth,° the sleeping spark *angry*
  Of native vertue gan eftsoones revive,
165 And at his haughtie helmet making mark,
  So hugely stroke, that it the steele did rive,° *cut*
  And cleft his head. He tumbling downe alive,
  With bloudy mouth his mother earth did kis,
  Greeting his grave: his grudging ghost did strive
170 With the fraile flesh; at last it flitted is,
Whither the soules do fly of men, that live amis.

20

The Lady when she saw her champion fall,
  Like the old ruines of a broken towre,
  Staid not to waile his woefull funerall,
175   But from him° fled away with all her powre;   *Redcrosse Knight*
  Who after her as hastily gan scowre,°   *pursue*
  Bidding the Dwarfe with him to bring away
  The Sarazins shield, signe of the conqueroure.
  Her soone he overtooke, and bad° to stay,   *commanded*
180 For present cause was none of dread her to dismay.[9]

21

She turning backe with ruefull° countenaunce,   *pitiful*
  Cride, Mercy mercy Sir vouchsafe to show
  On silly Dame, subject to hard mischaunce,
  And to your mighty will. Her humblesse low
185   In so ritch weedes and seeming glorious show,
  Did much emmove his stout heroïcke heart,
  And said, Deare dame, your suddein overthrow
  Much rueth me;° but now put feare apart,   *I regret*
And tell, both who ye be, and who that tooke your part.

22

190 Melting in teares, then gan she thus lament;
  The wretched woman, whom unhappy howre
  Hath now made thrall to your commandement,
  Before that angry heavens list to lowre,°   *scowl*
  And fortune false betraide me to your powre,
195   Was, (O what now availeth° that I was!)   *does it help*
  Borne the sole daughter of an Emperour,
  He that the wide West under his rule has,[1]
And high hath set his throne, where Tiberis° doth pas.   *Tiber River, in Rome*

23

He in the first flowre of my freshest age,
200   Betrothed me unto the onely haire
  Of a most mighty king, most rich and sage;
  Was never Prince so faithfull and so faire,
  Was never Prince so meeke and debonaire;°   *gentle*
  But ere my hoped day of spousall° shone,   *marriage*
205   My dearest Lord fell from high honours staire,
  Into the hands of his accursed fone,°   *foe*
And cruelly was slaine, that shall I ever mone.

24

His blessed body spoild of lively breath,
  Was afterward, I know not how, convaid
210   And fro me hid: of whose most innocent death
  When tidings came to me unhappy maid,

---

9. I.e., he did not mean to frighten her.
1. The Lady's story in this and the next two stanzas allegorically describes the corruption of the Holy Roman Empire and its separation from true Christianity. The Lady's father, an emperor, reigned in Rome, the seat of Catholicism (cf. Una's father, who is Adam), and the prince she was to marry was Christ. The Lady's quest to find his corpse suggests that she denies the doctrine of the resurrection of the body. In any case, Protestants in this period were critical of the Catholic emphasis on Christ's dead body in religious art and literature and contrasted it to the Protestant celebration of his resurrection.

O how great sorrow my sad soule assaid.°   *afflicted*
Then forth I went his woefull corse to find,
And many yeares throughout the world I straid,
215   A virgin widow, whose deepe wounded mind
With love, long time did languish as the striken hind.°   *doe*

25

At last it chaunced this proud Sarazin
To meete me wandring, who perforce° me led   *forcibly*
With him away, but yet could never win
220   The Fort, that Ladies hold in soveraigne dread.
There lies he now with foule dishonour dead,
Who whiles he liv'de, was called proud Sans-Foy,
The eldest of three brethren, all three bred
Of one bad sire, whose youngest is Sans-Joy,
225   And twixt them both was borne the bloudy bold Sans-Loy.[2]

26

In this sad plight, friendlesse, unfortunate,
Now miserable I Fidessa[3] dwell,
Craving of you in pitty of my state,
To do none ill, if please ye not do well.
230   He in great passion all this while did dwell,
More busying his quicke eyes, her face to view,
Then his dull eares, to heare what she did tell;
And said, Faire Lady hart of flint would rew
The undeserved woes and sorrowes, which ye shew.

27

235   Henceforth in safe assuraunce may ye rest,
Having both found a new friend you to aid,
And lost an old foe, that did you molest:
Better new friend then an old foe is said.
With chaunge of cheare the seeming simple maid
240   Let fall her eyen,° as shamefast to the earth,   *eyes*
And yeelding soft, in that she nought gain-said,°   *denied*
So forth they rode, he feining seemely merth,
And she coy lookes: so dainty they say maketh derth.[4]

28

Long time they thus together traveiled,
245   Till weary of their way, they came at last,
Where grew two goodly trees, that faire did spred
Their armes abroad, with gray mosse overcast,
And their greene leaves trembling with every blast,
Made a calme shadow far in compasse round:
250   The fearefull Shepheard often there aghast°   *frightened*
Under them never sat, ne wont there sound
His mery oaten pipe, but shund th'unlucky ground.

---

2. Sans-Loy ("without law") and Sans-Joy ("without joy") illustrate other aspects of the infidel attacking the spiritual well-being of the Redcrosse Knight. Spenser draws on Galatians 5.22–23: "But the fruit of the spirit is love, joy . . . faith . . . temperance; against such there is no Law."
3. The Lady in Persian dress calls herself Fidessa, a name

that can mean "faithful" in a corrupted kind of Latin. From her association with Sans-Foy, however, the reader knows that she is not representative of the true faith and so only puts on the appearance of fidelity.
4. I.e., such daintiness is costly.

29

But this good knight soone as he them can spie,
　For the coole shade him thither hastly got:
255　For golden Phoebus now ymounted hie,
　From fiery wheeles of his faire chariot
　Hurled his beame so scorching cruell hot,
　That living creature mote° it not abide;　　*might*
　And his new Lady it endured not.
260　There they alight, in hope themselves to hide
From the fierce heat, and rest their weary limbs a tide.°　　*while*

30

Faire seemely pleasaunce each to other makes,
　With goodly purposes there as they sit:
　And in his falsed fancy he her takes
265　To be the fairest wight,° that lived yit;　　*creature*
　Which to expresse, he bends his gentle wit,
　And thinking of those braunches greene to frame
　A girlond for her dainty forehead fit,
　He pluckt a bough; out of whose rift there came
270　Small drops of gory bloud, that trickled downe the same.[5]

31

Therewith a piteous yelling voyce was heard,
　Crying, O spare with guilty hands to teare
　My tender sides in this rough rynd embard,°　　*enclosed*
　But fly, ah fly far hence away, for feare
275　Least to you hap, that happened to me heare,
　And to this wretched Lady, my deare love,
　O too deare love, love bought with death too deare.
　Astond he stood, and up his haire did hove,
And with that suddein horror could no member move.

32

280　At last whenas the dreadfull passion
　Was overpast, and manhood well awake,
　Yet musing at the straunge occasion,
　And doubting much his sence, he thus bespake;
　What voyce of damned Ghost from Limbo lake,°　　*the pit of hell*
285　Or guilefull spright wandring in empty aire,
　Both which fraile men do oftentimes mistake,
　Sends to my doubtfull eares these speaches rare,
And ruefull plaints, me bidding guiltlesse bloud to spare?

33

Then groning deepe, Nor damned Ghost, (quoth he,)
290　Nor guilefull sprite to thee these wordes doth speake,
　But once a man Fradubio,[6] now a tree,
　Wretched man, wretched tree; whose nature weake,

---

5. Following Dante and Ariosto, Spenser imitates a well-known episode in Virgil's *Aeneid* in which the hero Aeneas, thinking he might have reached the country in which he was to found a new Troy, is warned by a bleeding bush that he must continue his quest. Spenser probably expected that his readers would take pleasure in his own inventive transformation of this powerful image.
6. Brother Doubt (Italian). Since loss of faith through doubt is dehumanizing, Fradubio is cast into the form of a plant. He is intended to convey to the Redcrosse Knight how dangerous a creature Fidessa is.

A cruell witch her cursed will to wreake,
Hath thus transformd, and plast in open plaines,
295 Where Boreas° doth blow full bitter bleake, *the north wind*
And scorching Sunne does dry my secret vaines:
For though a tree I seeme, yet cold and heat me paines.

34

Say on Fradubio then, or man, or tree,
Quoth then the knight, by whose mischievous arts
300 Art thou misshaped thus, as now I see?
He oft finds med'cine, who his griefe imparts;
But double griefs afflict concealing harts,
As raging flames who striveth to suppresse.
The author then (said he) of all my smarts,° *pains*
305 Is one Duessa[7] a false sorceresse,
That many errant knights hath brought to wretchednesse.

35

In prime of youthly yeares, when corage° hot *spirit*
The fire of love and joy of chevalree° *chivalry*
First kindled in my brest, it was my lot
310 To love this gentle Lady, whom ye see,
Now not a Lady, but a seeming tree;
With whom as once I rode accompanyde,
Me chaunced of a knight encountred bee,
That had a like faire Lady by his syde,
315 Like a faire Lady, but did fowle Duessa hyde.

36

Whose forged° beauty he did take in hand, *artificial*
All other Dames to have exceeded farre;
I in defence of mine did likewise stand,
Mine, that did then shine as the Morning starre:
320 So both to battell fierce arraunged° arre, *engaged*
In which his harder fortune was to fall
Under my speare: such is the dye° of warre: *hazard*
His Lady left as a prise martiall,
Did yield her comely person, to be at my call.

37

325 So doubly lov'd of Ladies unlike° faire, *differently*
Th'one seeming such, the other such indeede,
One day in doubt I cast° for to compare, *sought*
Whether in beauties glorie did exceede;
A Rosy girlond was the victors meede:
330 Both seemde to win, and both seemde won to bee,
So hard the discord was to be agreede.
Fraelissa[8] was as faire, as faire mote bee,
And ever false Duessa seemde as faire as shee.

---

7. Double-being (Italian), i.e., two-faced or duplicitous. The name contrasts with Una, or the undivided truth. Duessa wears a mask of beauty, although she is actually hideous and evil. Spenser places Duessa, who is not what she appears to be, in opposition to Una, whose beauty is hidden beneath a veil but who signifies wholeness or integrity.

8. Fradubio's lady is Fraelissa, "frail nature" (Italian); she, like Fradubio, is Duessa's victim.

38

The wicked witch now seeing all this while
335   The doubtfull ballaunce equally to sway,
     What not by right, she cast to win by guile,
     And by her hellish science raisd streight way
     A foggy mist, that overcast the day,
     And a dull blast, that breathing on her face,
340   Dimmed her° former beauties shining ray,   *Fraelissa's*
     And with foule ugly forme did her disgrace:°   *disfigure*
Then was she faire alone, when none was faire in place.

39

Then cride she out, Fye, fye, deformed wight,
     Whose borrowed beautie now appeareth plaine
345   To have before bewitched all mens sight;
     O leave her soone, or let her soone be slaine.[9]
     Her loathly visage viewing with disdaine,
     Eftsoones I thought her such, as she me told,
     And would have kild her; but with faigned paine,
350   The false witch did my wrathfull hand with-hold;
So left her, where she now is turnd to treen mould.°   *a treelike shape*

40

Thens forth I tooke Duessa for my Dame,
     And in the witch unweeting° joyd long time,   *without knowing*
     Ne ever wist, but that she was the same,
355   Till on a day (that day is every Prime,°   *first (of the month)*
     When Witches wont do penance for their crime)
     I chaunst to see her in her proper hew,
     Bathing her selfe in origane° and thyme: *oregano*
     A filthy foule old woman I did vew,
360 That ever to have toucht her, I did deadly rew.

41

Her neather° partes misshapen, monstruous,   *lower*
     Were hidd in water, that I could not see,
     But they did seeme more foule and hideous,
     Then womans shape man would beleeve to bee.
365   Thens forth from her most beastly companie
     I gan refraine, in minde to slip away,
     Soone as appeard safe opportunitie:
     For danger great, if not assur'd decay
I saw before mine eyes, if I were knowne to stray.

42

370 The divelish hag by chaunges of my cheare
     Perceiv'd my thought, and drownd in sleepie night,
     With wicked herbes and ointments did besmeare
     My bodie all, through charmes and magicke might,
     That all my senses were bereaved° quight: *departed*
375   Then brought she me into this desert waste,
     And by my wretched lovers side me pight,°   *planted*

---

9. Duessa ironically condemns Fraelissa as a witch and tells Fradubio to abandon her.

Where now enclosd in wooden wals full faste,
Banisht from living wights, our wearie dayes we waste.

43

But how long time, said then the Elfin knight,
380   Are you in this misformed house to dwell?
We may not chaunge (quoth he) this evil plight,
Till we be bathed in a living well;[1]
That is the terme prescribed by the spell.
O how, said he, mote I that well out find,
385   That may restore you to your wonted well?
Time and suffised fates to former kynd
Shall us restore, none else from hence may us unbynd.

44

The false Duessa, now Fidessa hight,°   *called*
Heard how in vaine Fradubio did lament,
390   And knew well all was true. But the good knight
Full of sad feare and ghastly dreriment,°   *terror*
When all this speech the living tree had spent,° *finished*
The bleeding bough did thrust into the ground,
That from the bloud he might be innocent,
395   And with fresh clay did close the wooden wound:
Then turning to his Lady, dead with feare her found.

45

Her seeming dead he found with feigned feare,
As all unweeting of that well she knew,
And paynd himselfe with busie care to reare
400   Her out of carelesse° swowne. Her eylids blew   *unconscious*
And dimmed sight with pale and deadly hew°   *color*
At last she up gan lift: with trembling cheare
Her up he tooke, too simple and too trew,[2]
And oft her kist. At length all passed feare,
405   He set her on her steede, and forward forth did beare.

Canto 3

Forsaken Truth long seekes her love,
And makes the Lyon mylde,
Marres blind Devotions mart, and fals
In hand of leachour vylde.

1

Nought is there under heav'ns wide hollownesse,
That moves more deare compassion of mind,
Then beautie brought t'unworthy wretchednesse
Through envies snares or fortunes freakes unkind:
5   I, whether lately through her brightnesse blind,

---

1. The Well of Life: a spring of constantly flowing water, figured in the water of baptism that promises eternal life to the faithful (John 4.14).
2. The Redcrosse Knight fails to connect Fradubio's story to his own; he does not follow the model presented by Virgil's Aeneas, and therefore he remains deceived and on the wrong course.

Or through alleageance and fast fealtie,°   *loyalty*
Which I do owe unto all woman kind,
Feele my heart perst° with so great agonie,   *pierced*
When such I see, that all for pittie I could die.

2

10   And now it is empassioned° so deepe,   *moved*
For fairest Unaes sake, of whom I sing,
That my fraile eyes these lines with teares do steepe,°   *soak*
To thinke how she through guilefull handeling,
Though true as touch, though daughter of a king,
15·   Though faire as ever living wight was faire,
Though nor in word nor deede ill meriting,
Is from her knight divorced° in despaire   *separated*
And her due loves° deriv'd to that vile witches share.   *the love due her*

3

Yet she most faithfull Ladie all this while
20   Forsaken, wofull, solitarie mayd
Farre from all peoples prease,° as in exile,   *crowds*
In wildernesse and wastfull deserts strayd,
To seeke her knight; who subtilly betrayd
Through that late vision, which th'Enchaunter wrought,
25   Had her abandond. She of nought affrayd,
Through woods and wastnesse wide him daily sought;
Yet wished tydings none of him unto her brought.

4

One day nigh wearie of the yrkesome way,
From her unhastie beast she did alight,
30   And on the grasse her daintie limbes did lay
In secret shadow, farre from all mens sight:
From her faire head her fillet she undight,
And laid her stole aside. Her angels face
As the great eye of heaven shyned bright,
35   And made a sunshine in the shadie place;
Did never mortall eye behold such heavenly grace.

5

It fortuned out of the thickest wood
A ramping Lyon[1] rushed suddainly,
Hunting full greedie after salvage° blood;   *savage*
40   Soone as the royall virgin he did spy,
With gaping mouth at her ran greedily,
To have attonce devour'd her tender corse:
But to the pray when as he drew more ny,
His bloudie rage asswaged with remorse,
45   And with the sight amazd, forgat his furious forse.

6

In stead thereof he kist her wearie feet,
And lickt her lilly hands with fawning tong,
As° he her wronged innocence did weet.   *as if*

1. This is the typical heraldic posture of the lion: standing on its hind legs with its paws in the air. A symbol of royal power, the lion was believed to protect virgins and weary pilgrims.

O how can beautie maister the most strong,
50   And simple truth subdue avenging wrong?
Whose yeelded pride and proud submission,
Still dreading death, when she had marked long,
Her hart gan melt in great compassion,
And drizling teares did shed for pure affection.

7

55   The Lyon Lord of everie beast in field,
Quoth she, his princely puissance° doth abate,   *strength*
And mightie proud to humble weake does yield,
Forgetfull of the hungry rage, which late
Him prickt, in pittie of my sad estate:
60   But he° my Lyon, and my noble Lord,   *Redcrosse Knight*
How does he find in cruell hart to hate
Her that him lov'd, and ever most adord,
As the God of my life? why hath he me abhord?

8

Redounding teares did choke th'end of her plaint,
65   Which softly ecchoed from the neighbour wood;
And sad to see her sorrowfull constraint
The kingly beast upon her gazing stood;
With pittie calmd, downe fell his angry mood.
At last in close hart shutting up her paine,
70   Arose the virgin borne of heavenly brood,
And to her snowy Palfrey got againe,
To seeke her strayed Champion, if she might attaine.°   *overtake him*

9

The Lyon would not leave her desolate,
But with her went along, as a strong gard
75   Of her chast person, and a faithfull mate
Of her sad troubles and misfortunes hard:
Still when she slept, he kept both watch and ward,
And when she wakt, he waited diligent,
With humble service to her will prepard:
80   From her faire eyes he tooke commaundement,
And ever by her lookes conceived° her intent.   *understood*

10

Long she thus traveiled through deserts wyde,
By which she thought her wandring knight shold pas,
Yet never shew of living wight espyde;
85   Till that at length she found the troden gras,
In which the tract° of peoples footing was,   *trace*
Under the steepe foot of a mountaine hore;°   *barren*
The same she followes, till at last she has
A damzell spyde slow footing her before,
90   That on her shoulders sad a pot of water bore.

11

To whom approching she to her gan call,
To weet, if dwelling place were nigh at hand;
But the rude wench her answer'd nought at all,
She could not heare, nor speake, nor understand;

95 Till seeing by her side the Lyon stand,
    With suddaine feare her pitcher downe she threw,
    And fled away: for never in that land
    Face of faire Ladie she before did vew,
    And that dread Lyons looke her cast in deadly hew.

12

100 Full fast she fled, ne° ever lookt behynd,   nor
    As if her life upon the wager lay,
    And home she came, whereas her mother blynd
    Sate in eternall night: nought could she say,
    But suddaine catching hold, did her dismay
105 With quaking hands, and other signes of feare:
    Who full of ghastly fright and cold affray,°   terror
    Gan shut the dore. By this arrived there
    Dame Una, wearie Dame, and entrance did requere.°   request

13

    Which when none yeelded, her unruly Page
110 With his rude clawes the wicket° open rent,   small gate
    And let her in; where of his cruell rage
    Nigh dead with feare, and faint astonishment,
    She found them both in darkesome corner pent;
    Where that old woman day and night did pray
115 Upon her beades devoutly penitent;
    Nine hundred *Pater nosters* every day,
    And thrise nine hundred *Aves* she was wont to say.[2]

14

    And to augment her painefull pennance more,
    Thrise every weeke in ashes she did sit,
120 And next her wrinkled skin rough sackcloth wore,
    And thrise three times did fast from any bit:°   bit of food
    But now for feare her beads she did forget.
    Whose needlesse dread for to remove away,
    Faire Una framed words and count'nance fit:
125 Which hardly doen,° at length she gan them pray,   done
    That in their cotage small, that night she rest her may.

15

    The day is spent, and commeth drowsie night,
    When every creature shrowded is in sleepe;
    Sad Una downe her laies in wearie plight,
130 And at her feet the Lyon watch doth keepe:
    In stead of rest, she does lament, and weepe
    For the late losse of her deare loved knight,
    And sighes, and grones, and evermore does steepe
    Her tender brest in bitter teares all night,
135 All night she thinks too long, and often lookes for light.

16

    Now when Aldeboran was mounted hie
    Above the shynie Cassiopeias chaire,[3]

---

2. Spenser's readers would have identified Pater Nosters
and Ave Marias as Catholic prayers.
3. Aldeboran and Cassiopeia are stars that appear at mid-

night during the winter solstice; the references to winter
and midnight reflect Una's distress.

And all in deadly sleepe did drowned lie,
One knocked at the dore, and in would fare;
140 ·   He knocked fast, and often curst, and sware,
That readie entrance was not at his call:
For on his backe a heavy load he bare
Of nightly stelths° and pillage severall,   *thefts*
Which he had got abroad by purchase criminall.

17

145   He was to weete° a stout and sturdie thiefe,[4]   *wit*
Wont to robbe Churches of their ornaments,
And poore mens boxes of their due reliefe,
Which given was to them for good intents;
The holy Saints of their rich vestiments
150   He did disrobe, when all men carelesse slept,
And spoild the Priests of their habiliments,°   *holy things*
Whiles none the holy things in safety kept;
Then he by cunning sleights° in at the window crept.   *tricks*

18

And all that he by right or wrong could find,
155   Unto this house he brought, and did bestow
Upon the daughter of this woman blind,
Abessa daughter of Corceca slow,[5]
With whom he whoredome usd, that few did know,
And fed her fat with feast of offerings,
160   And plentie, which in all the land did grow;
Ne spared he to give her gold and rings:
And now he to her brought part of his stolen things.

19

Thus long the dore with rage and threats he bet,
Yet of those fearefull women none durst rize,
165   The Lyon frayed° them, him in to let: *frightened*
He would no longer stay him to advize,°   *consider*
But open breakes the dore in furious wize,
And entring is; when that disdainfull° beast   *indignant*
Encountring fierce, him suddaine doth surprize,
170   And seizing cruell clawes on trembling brest,
Under his Lordly foot him proudly hath supprest.

20

Him booteth not° resist, nor succour call,   *it did no good to*
His bleeding hart is in the vengers hand,
Who streight him rent° in thousand peeces small,   *tore*
175   And quite dismembred hath: the thirstie land
Drunke up his life; his corse left on the strand.[6]
His fearefull friends weare out the wofull night,
Ne dare to weepe, nor seeme to understand

---

4. This thief is later named Kirkrapine, literally "church robber" (see stanza 22). Spenser's Protestant contemporaries complained that the Roman Catholic Church had used English abbeys and monasteries as a means of amassing wealth at the expense of the spiritual well-being of the people that they were supposed to serve.
5. Corceca means "blind of heart"; her daughter, Abessa,

who is both deaf and mute, is the offspring of ignorant superstition. Through her name, Spenser associates Abessa with Catholic abbeys and monasteries, which he criticizes in this and the previous two stanzas.
6. Kirkrapine's death signifies a step toward the purification of the Church and thereby an approach to the true Church, which Una represents.

The heavie hap,° which on them is alight,   *event*
180 Affraid, least to themselves the like mishappen might.

21

Now when broad day the world discovered has,
    Up Una rose, up rose the Lyon eke,
    And on their former journey forward pas,
    In wayes unknowne, her wandring knight to seeke,
185   With paines farre passing that long wandring Greeke,[7]
    That for his love refused deitie;
    Such were the labours of this Lady meeke,
    Still seeking him, that from her still did flie,
Then furthest from her hope, when most she weened nie.

22

190 Soone as she parted thence, the fearefull twaine,
    That blind old woman and her daughter deare
    Came forth, and finding Kirkrapine° there slaine,   *church-robber*
    For anguish great they gan to rend their heare,
    And beat their brests, and naked flesh to teare.
195   And when they both had wept and wayld their fill,
    Then forth they ranne like two amazed deare,
    Halfe mad through malice, and revenging will,°   *desire to revenge*
To follow her, that was the causer of their ill.

23

Whom overtaking, they gan loudly bray,
200   With hollow howling, and lamenting cry,
    Shamefully at her rayling° all the way,   *accusing*
    And her accusing of dishonesty,
    That was the flowre of faith and chastity;
    And still amidst her rayling, she did pray,
205   That plagues, and mischiefs, and long misery
    Might fall on her, and follow all the way,
And that in endlesse error she might ever stray.

24

But when she saw her prayers nought prevaile,
    She backe returned with some labour lost;
210   And in° the way as she did weepe and waile,   *along*
    A knight her met in mighty armes embost,
    Yet knight was not for all his bragging bost,°   *display*
    But subtill Archimag, that Una sought
    By traynes° into new troubles to have tost: *tricks*
215   Of that old woman tydings he besought,
If that of such a Ladie she could tellen ought.

25

Therewith she gan her passion to renew,
    And cry, and curse, and raile,° and rend her heare,   *accuse*
    Saying, that harlot she too lately knew,
220   That causd her shed so many a bitter teare,
    And so forth told the story of her feare:
    Much seemed he to mone her haplesse chaunce,

7. Una is compared to Ulysses, whose love for his wife Penelope caused him to reject the goddess Calypso and the promise of immortality she offered him.

And after for that Ladie did inquere;°   *inquire*
  Which being taught, he forward gan advance
225 His fair enchaunted steed, and eke his charmed launce.

26

Ere long he came, where Una traveild slow,
  And that wilde Champion wayting her besyde:
  Whom seeing such, for dread he° durst not show   *Archimago*
  Himselfe too nigh at hand, but turned wyde
230 Unto an hill; from whence when she him spyde,
  By his like seeming shield, her knight by name
  She weend it was, and towards him gan ryde:[8]
  Approching nigh, she wist it was the same,
And with faire fearefull humblesse towards him shee came.

27

235 And weeping said, Ah my long lacked° Lord,   *lost*
  Where have ye bene thus long out of my sight?
  Much feared I to have bene quite abhord,
  Or ought have done, that ye displeasen might,
  That should as death unto my deare hart light:°   *come*
240 For since mine eye your joyous sight did mis,
  My chearefull day is turnd to chearelesse night,
  And eke my night of death the shadow is;
But welcome now my light, and shining lampe of blis.

28

He thereto meeting said, My dearest Dame,
245 Farre be it from your thought, and fro° my will,   *from*
  To thinke that knighthood I so much should shame,
  As you to leave,° that have me loved still,   *lose*
  And chose in Faery court of meere goodwill,
  Where noblest knights were to be found on earth:
250 The earth shall sooner leave her kindly skill°   *natural art*
  To bring forth fruit, and make eternall derth,°   *famine*
Then I leave you, my liefe, yborne of heavenly berth.

29

And sooth° to say, why I left you so long,   *truly*
  Was for to seeke adventure in strange place,
255 Where Archimago said a felon strong
  To many knights did daily worke disgrace;
  But knight he now shall never more deface:
  Good cause of mine excuse; that mote° ye please   *might*
  Well to accept, and evermore embrace
260 My faithfull service, that by land and seas
Have vowd you to defend, now then your plaint appease.

30

His lovely words her seemd due recompence
  Of all her passed paines: one loving howre
  For many yeares of sorrow can dispence:°   *compensate*
265 A dram of sweet is worth a pound of sowre:
  She has forgot, how many a wofull stowre°   *hardship*

8. Una recognizes the arms of the Redcrosse Knight but is deceived by appearances; she is actually greeting Archima-go.

For him she late endur'd; she speakes no more
Of past: true is, that true love hath no powre
To looken backe; his eyes be fixt before.

270   Before her stands her knight, for whom she toyld so sore.

31

Much like, as when the beaten marinere,
That long hath wandred in the Ocean wide,
Oft soust° in swelling Tethys° saltish teare,   *drenched/a sea-goddess*
And long time having tand his tawney hide
275   With blustring breath of heaven, that none can bide,
And scorching flames of fierce Orions hound,[9]
Soone as the port from farre he has espide,
His chearefull whistle merrily doth sound,
And Nereus° crownes with cups;° his mates him pledg around.   *a sea-god/of wine*

32

280   Such joy made Una, when her knight she found;
And eke th'enchaunter joyous seemd no lesse,
Then° the glad marchant, that does vew from ground   *than*
His ship farre come from watrie wildernesse,
He hurles out vowes,° and Neptune oft doth blesse: *makes promises*
285   So forth they past, and all the way they spent
Discoursing of her dreadfull late distresse,
In which he askt her, what the Lyon ment:
Who° told her all that fell° in journey as she went.   *Una/had happened*

33

They had not ridden farre, when they might see
290   One pricking towards them with hastie heat,
Full strongly armd, and on a courser free,
That through his fiercenesse fomed all with sweat,
And the sharpe yron° did for anger eat,   *iron bit*
When his hot ryder spurd his chauffed side;
295   His looke was sterne, and seemed still to threat
Cruell revenge, which he in hart did hyde,
And on his shield Sans-Loy in bloudie lines was dyde.

34

When nigh he drew unto this gentle payre
And saw the Red-crosse, which the knight did beare,
300   He burnt in fire, and gan eftsoones prepare
Himselfe to battell with his couched° speare.   *lowered*
Loth was that other,° and did faint through feare,   *Archimago*
To taste th'vntryed dint of deadly steele;
But yet his Lady did so well him cheare,
305   That hope of new good hap he gan to feele;
So bent his speare, and spurnd° his horse with yron heele.   *spurred*

35

But that proud Paynim° forward came so fierce,[1]   *pagan*
And full of wrath, that with his sharp-head speare

9. Sirius, the Dog Star, which marks the hottest days of the year. Nereus is the eldest child of Tethys, a sea-goddess.
1. The double deception registered in this episode is characteristic of Spenser's complex allegories: mistaken in his sense of identity, Sans-Loy attacks the very person who is best able to protect him. Archimago, having assumed the guise of the Redcrosse Knight, finds that the cross that should protect him from harm does not in fact do so. In this instance his shield is "vainely crossed."

Through vainely crossed shield he quite did pierce,
310　And had his staggering steede not shrunke for feare,
Through shield and bodie eke he should him beare:
Yet so great was the puissance of his push,
That from his saddle quite he did him beare:
He tombling rudely downe to ground did rush,
315　And from his gored wound a well of bloud did gush.

36

Dismounting lightly from his loftie steed,
He to him lept, in mind to reave° his life,　　　　　*take*
And proudly said, Lo there the worthie meed
Of him, that slew Sans-Foy with bloudie knife;
320　Henceforth his ghost freed from repining° strife,　　*fretting*
In peace may passen° over Lethe lake,[2]　　　　　　*pass*
When morning altars° purgd with enemies life,　*altars of mourning*
The blacke infernall Furies doen aslake:°　　　　　*satisfy*
Life from Sans-Foy thou tookst, Sans-Loy shall from thee take.

37

325　Therewith in haste his helmet gan unlace,
Till Una cride, O hold that heavie hand,
Deare Sir, what ever that thou be in place:
Enough is, that thy foe doth vanquisht stand
Now at thy mercy: Mercie not withstand:°　　　　　*oppose*
330　For he is one the truest° knight alive,　　　　*the one truest*
Though conquered now he lie on lowly land,
And whilest him fortune favour, faire did thrive
In bloudie field: therefore of life him not deprive.

38

Her piteous words might not abate his rage,
335　But rudely° rending up his helmet, would　　　　*violently*
Have slaine him straight: but when he sees his age,
And hoarie head of Archimago old,
His hastie hand he doth amazed hold,
And halfe ashamed, wondred at the sight:
340　For the old man well knew he, though untold,°　　*i.e., by sight*
In charmes and magicke to have wondrous might,
Ne ever wont in field, ne in round lists° to fight.　*tournament arenas*

39

And said, Why Archimago, lucklesse syre,
What doe I see? what hard mishap is this,
345　That hath thee hither brought to taste mine yre?
Or thine the fault, or mine the error is,
In stead of foe to wound my friend amis?
He answered nought, but in a traunce still lay,
And on those guilefull dazed eyes of his
350　The cloud of death did sit. Which doen away,°　*having passed*
He left him lying so, ne would no lenger stay.

40

But to the virgin comes, who all this while
Amased stands, her selfe so mockt to see

2. The lake of forgetfulness in the underworld.

By him, who has the guerdon° of his guile,   reward
For so misfeigning her true knight to bee:
355
Yet is she now in more perplexitie,°   distress
Left in the hand of that same Paynim bold,
From whom her booteth° not at all to flie;   it helped her
Who by her cleanly° garment catching hold,   pure
360   Her from her Palfrey pluckt, her visage to behold.

41

But her fierce servant full of kingly awe
And high disdaine, whenas his soveraine Dame
So rudely handled by her foe he sawe,
With gaping jawes full greedy at him came,
365   And ramping on° his shield, did weene the same   charging at
Have reft away with his sharpe rending clawes:
But he was stout, and lust did now inflame
His corage more, that from his griping pawes
He hath his shield redeem'd,° and foorth his swerd he drawes.   retained

42

370   O then too weake and feeble was the forse
Of salvage beast, his puissance to withstand:
For he was strong, and of so mightie corse,
As ever wielded speare in warlike hand,
And feates of armes did wisely understand.
375   Eftsoones he perced through his chaufed° chest   angered
With thrilling° point of deadly yron brand,   piercing
And launcht° his Lordly hart: with death opprest   pierced
He roar'd aloud, whiles life forsooke his stubborne brest.

43

Who now is left to keepe the forlorne maid
380   From raging spoile of lawlesse victors will?[3]
Her faithful gard remov'd, her hope dismaid,°   thwarted
Her selfe a yeelded pray to save or spill.°   destroy
He now Lord of the field, his pride to fill,
With foule reproches, and disdainfull spight
385   Her vildly entertaines,° and will or nill,   treats
Beares her away upon his courser light:
Her prayers nought prevaile, his rage is more of might.

44

And all the way, with great lamenting paine,
And piteous plaints she filleth his dull eares,
390   That stony hart could riven have in twaine,
And all the way she wets with flowing teares:
But he enrag'd with rancor, nothing heares.
Her servile beast yet would not leave her so,
But followes her farre off, ne ought he feares,
395   To be partaker of her wandring woe,
More mild in beastly kind,° then that her beastly foe.   animal nature

3. I.e., who will now protect Una from becoming the spoil or booty of the lawless victor's raging will?

Canto 4

To sinfull house of Pride,[1] Duessa
guides the faithfull knight,
Where brothers death to wreak° Sans-Joy   avenge
doth chalenge him to fight.

1

Young knight, what ever° that dost armes professe,	whoever
And through long labours huntest after fame,	
Beware of fraud, beware of ficklenesse,	
In choice, and change of thy deare loved Dame,	
Least° thou of her beleeve° too lightly blame,	lest / faith
And rash misweening° doe thy hart remove:	rashly mistrusting
For unto knight there is no greater shame,	
Then lightnesse and inconstancie in love;	
That doth this Redcrosse knights ensample° plainly prove.	example

2

Who after that he had faire Una lorne,°	lost
Through light misdeeming of her loialtie,	
And false Duessa in her sted had borne,	
Called Fidess', and so supposd to bee;	
Long with her traveild, till at last they see	
A goodly building, bravely garnished,	
The house of mightie Prince it seemd to bee:	
And towards it a broad high way that led,	
All bare° through peoples feet, which thither traveiled.	worn bare

3

Great troupes of people traveild thitherward	
Both day and night, of each degree and place,	
But few returned, having scaped hard,	
With balefull° beggerie, or foule disgrace,	wretched
Which ever after in most wretched case,	
Like loathsome lazars,° by the hedges lay.	lepers
Thither Duessa bad him bend° his pace:	direct
For she is wearie of the toilesome way,	
And also nigh consumed is the lingring day.	

4

A stately Pallace built of squared bricke,[2]	
Which cunningly was without morter laid,	
Whose wals were high, but nothing strong, nor thick,	
And golden foile all over them displaid,	
That purest skye with brightnesse they dismaid:°	shamed
High lifted up were many loftie towres,	
And goodly galleries farre over laid,°	built high above
Full of faire windowes, and delightfull bowres;°	chambers
And on the top a Diall° told the timely howres.	sundial

1. An extended metaphor for the consequences of the sin of Pride. Like the Tower of Babel, which Spenser invokes in this passage, the house of Pride is the product of humanity's art, ambition, and vanity but is devoid of Christian values.

2. The house of Pride offers a dazzling facade, but its construction is weak, much like the sin of Pride itself, which places outward appearances over inner substance. It is surmounted by a sundial to tell the hours, a sign that Pride has no sense of eternity but lives only for the moment.

5

It was a goodly heape° for to behould,   *structure*
    And spake the praises of the workmans wit;
    But full great pittie, that so faire a mould
40 Did on so weake foundation ever sit:
    For on a sandie hill, that still did flit,°   *shift*
    And fall away, it mounted was full hie,
    That every breath of heaven shaked it:
    And all the hinder° parts, that few could spie,   *rear*
45 Were ruinous and old, but painted cunningly.

6

Arrived there they passed in forth right;
    For still° to all the gates stood open wide,   *always*
    Yet charge of them was to a Porter hight°   *called*
    Cald Malvenù,° who entrance none denide: *welcome to evil*
50 Thence to the hall, which was on every side
    With rich array and costly arras dight:°   *furnished*
    Infinite sorts of people did abide
    There waiting long, to win the wished sight
Of her, that was the Lady of that Pallace bright.

7

55 By them they passe, all gazing on them round,
    And to the Presence mount; whose glorious vew
    Their frayle amazed senses did confound:°   *confuse*
    In living Princes court none ever knew
    Such endlesse richesse, and so sumptuous shew;
60 Ne° Persia selfe, the nourse° of pompous pride   *not even / nurse*
    Like ever saw. And there a noble crew
    Of Lordes and Ladies stood on every side,
Which with their presence faire, the place much beautifide.

8

High above all a cloth of State was spred,
65 And a rich throne, as bright as sunny day,
    On which there sate most brave embellished
    With royall robes and gorgeous array,
    A mayden Queene,[3] that shone as Titans ray,
    In glistring gold, and peerelesse pretious stone:
70 Yet her bright blazing beautie did assay°   *strive*
    To dim the brightnesse of her glorious throne,
As envying her selfe, that too exceeding shone.

9

Exceeding shone, like Phoebus fairest childe,[4]
    That did presume his fathers firie wayne,
75 And flaming mouthes of steedes unwonted° wilde   *unaccustomed*
    Through highest heaven with weaker hand to rayne;°   *guide*
    Proud of such glory and advancement vaine,
    While flashing beames do daze his feeble eyen,
He leaves the welkin° way most beaten plaine,   *well-known*

---

3. "The maiden queen": a reference to the "virgin daughter of Babylon" (Isaiah 47.1). She is later identified as Lucifera, a feminine form of Lucifer, literally "light bringer," but also Satan's name when he was still an angel. Hence the queen shines as brightly as the sun (Titan).
4. Phaeton (son of the sun god Apollo), who stole his father's chariot and perished because he could not manage the horses. He is a figure for the sin of Pride.

80 And rapt with whirling wheeles, inflames the skyen,
With fire not made to burne, but fairely for to shyne.

10

So proud she shyned in her Princely state,
Looking to heaven; for earth she did disdayne,
And sitting high; for lowly she did hate:
85 Lo underneath her scornefull feete, was layne
A dreadfull Dragon with an hideous trayne,
And in her hand she held a mirrhour bright,
Wherein her face she often vewed fayne,
And in her selfe-lov'd semblance° tooke delight;   *image*
90 For she was wondrous faire, as any living wight.

11

Of griesly Pluto she the daughter was,[5]
And sad Proserpina the Queene of hell;
Yet did she thinke her pearelesse° worth to pas   *unequaled*
That parentage, with pride so did she swell,
95 And thundring Jove, that high in heaven doth dwell,
And wield the world, she claymed for her syre,
Or if that any else did Jove excell:
For to the highest she did still aspyre,
Or if ought higher were then° that, did it desyre.   *than*

12

100 And proud Lucifera men did her call,
That made her selfe a Queene, and crownd to be,
Yet rightfull kingdome she had none at all,
Ne heritage° of native° soveraintie,   *inheritance / rightful*
But did ysurpe° with wrong and tyrannie   *usurp*
105 Upon the scepter, which she now did hold:
Ne ruld her Realmes with lawes, but pollicie,°   *political cunning*
And strong advizement of six wisards old,
That with their counsels bad her kingdome did uphold.

13

Soone as the Elfin knight in presence came,
110 And false Duessa seeming Lady faire,
A gentle Husher,° Vanitie by name   *usher*
Made rowme, and passage for them did prepaire:
So goodly brought them to the lowest staire
Of her high throne, where they on humble knee
115 Making obeyssance,° did the cause declare,   *submissive bows*
Why they were come, her royall state to see,
To prove° the wide report of her great Majestee.   *confirm*

14

With loftie eyes, halfe loth° to looke so low,   *disdaining*
She thanked them in her disdainefull wise,
120 Ne other grace vouchsafed° them to show   *condescended*
Of Princesse worthy, scarse them bad arise.
Her Lordes and Ladies all this while devise

5. Lucifera is identified as the daughter of Pluto, king of the underworld, and Proserpina, goddess of the seasons, who is obliged to spend half the year underground with her husband Pluto. The conflation of mythologies represented in this description
of Lucifera is characteristic of Spenser's allegory; here he associates the biblical figure of the daughter of Babylon with the
pagan figures of Pluto and Proserpina. Their "daughter" Lucifera is his own invention.

Themselves to setten forth to straungers sight:
Some frounce° their curled haire in courtly guise,   *arrange*
125   Some prancke° their ruffes, and others trimly dight   *adjust*
Their gay attire: each others greater pride does spight.

15

Goodly they all that knight do entertaine,
Right glad with him to have increast their crew:
But to Duess' each one himselfe did paine
130   All kindnesse and faire courtesie to shew;
For in that court whylome° her well they knew: *previously*
Yet the stout Faerie[6] mongst the middest crowd
Thought all their glorie vaine in knightly vew,
And that great Princesse too exceeding prowd,
135   That to strange knight no better countenance° allowd.   *reception*

16

Suddein upriseth from her stately place
The royall Dame, and for her coche doth call:
All hurtlen° forth, and she with Princely pace,   *rush*
As faire Aurora° in her purple pall,   *goddess of the dawn*
140   Out of the East the dawning day doth call:
So forth she comes: her brightnesse brode° doth blaze;   *abroad*
The heapes of people thronging in the hall,
Do ride each other, upon her to gaze:
Her glorious glitterand° light doth all mens eyes amaze.   *glittering*

17

145   So forth she comes, and to her coche does clyme,
Adorned all with gold, and girlonds gay,
That seemd as fresh as Flora° in her prime,   *goddess of spring*
And strove to match, in royall rich array,
Great Junoes golden chaire, the which they say
150   The Gods stand gazing on, when she does ride
To Joves high house through heavens bras-paved way
Drawne of faire Pecocks, that excell in pride,
And full of Argus[7] eyes their tailes dispredden° wide.   *spread out*

18

But this was drawne of six unequall beasts,
155   On which her six sage Counsellours[8] did ryde,
Taught to obay their bestiall beheasts,°   *urges*
With like conditions to their kinds° applyde: *natures*
Of which the first, that all the rest did guyde,
Was sluggish Idlenesse the nourse of sin;
160   Upon a slouthfull Asse he chose to ryde,
Arayd in habit blacke, and amis° thin,   *monk's hood*
Like to an holy Monck, the service to begin.

19

And in his hand his Portesse° still he bare,   *prayer book*
That much was worne, but therein little red,

---

6. The Redcrosse Knight. He is designated as a faerie because he is an inhabitant of Faerie Land but also to distinguish him from the inhabitants of the house of Pride.
7. A mythical herdsman with 100 eyes. When Argus died, Juno—goddess of marriage and wife to Jupiter or Jove,

king of the gods—set his eyes in the tail of a peacock.
8. The following stanzas describe the procession of Lucifer's wise counsellors, actually the Seven Deadly Sins: Pride (in the person of Lucifera), Idleness, Gluttony, Lechery, Avarice (greed), Envy, and Wrath.

165   For of devotion he had little care,
           Still drownd in sleepe, and most of his dayes ded;
           Scarse could he once uphold his heavie hed,
           To looken, whether it were night or day:
170   May seeme° the wayne was very evill led,   *it may seem that*
           When such an one had guiding of the way,
      That knew not, whether right he went, or else astray.

20

     From worldly cares himselfe he did esloyne,°   *withdraw*
           And greatly shunned manly exercise,
           From every worke he chalenged essoyne,°   *claimed exception*
175   For contemplation sake: yet otherwise,
           His life he led in lawlesse riotise;°   *unruly conduct*
           By which he grew to grievous malady;
           For in his lustlesse limbs through evill guise
           A shaking fever raignd° continually: *ruled*
180   Such one was Idlenesse, first of this company.

21

    And by his side rode loathsome Gluttony,
           Deformed creature, on a filthie swyne,
           His belly was up-blowne with luxury,
           And eke with fatnesse swollen were his eyne,°   *eyes*
185   And like a Crane his necke was long and fyne,
           With which he swallowd up excessive feast,
           For want whereof poore people oft did pyne;
           And all the way, most like a brutish beast,
    He spued up his gorge,° that all did him deteast.   *vomited his food*

22

190   In greene vine leaves he was right fitly clad;
           For other clothes he could not weare for heat,
           And on his head an ivie girland had,
           From under which fast trickled downe the sweat:
           Still as he rode, he somewhat still did eat,
195   And in his hand did beare a bouzing° can,   *drinking*
           Of which he supt so oft, that on his seat
           His dronken corse he scarse upholden can,
    In shape and life more like a monster, then a man.

23

    Unfit he was for any worldly thing,
200   And eke unhable once to stirre or go,
           Not meet to be of counsell to a king,
           Whose mind in meat and drinke was drowned so,
           That from his friend he seldome knew his fo:
           Full of diseases was his carcas blew,
205   And a dry dropsie[9] through his flesh did flow:
           Which by misdiet daily greater grew:
    Such one was Gluttony, the second of that crew.

24

    And next to him rode lustfull Lechery,
           Upon a bearded Goat, whose rugged haire,

---

9. A disease characterized by bloating.

210   And whally° eyes (the signe of gelosy,)   *glaring*
       Was like the person selfe,° whom he did beare: *himself*
       Who rough, and blacke, and filthy did appeare,
       Unseemely man to please faire Ladies eye;
       Yet he of Ladies oft was loved deare,
215   When fairer faces were bid standen by:
    O who does know the bent of womens fantasy?

                        25
    In a greene gowne he clothed was full faire,
       Which underneath did hide his filthinesse,
       And in his hand a burning hart he bare,
220   Full of vaine follies, and new fanglenesse:
       For he was false, and fraught with ficklenesse,
       And learned had to love with secret lookes,
       And well could daunce, and sing with ruefulnesse,°   *melancholy*
       And fortunes tell, and read in loving bookes,°   *books of love*
225   And thousand other wayes, to bait his fleshly hookes.

                        26
    Inconstant man, that loved all he saw,
       And lusted after all, that he did love,
       Ne would his looser life be tide to law,
       But joyd weake wemens hearts to tempt and prove°   *test*
230   If from their loyall loves he might them move;
       Which lewdnesse fild him with reprochfull paine
       Of that fowle evill, which all men reprove,
       That rots the marrow, and consumes the braine:
    Such one was Lecherie, the third of all this traine.

                        27
235   And greedy Avarice by him did ride,
       Upon a Camell loaden all with gold;
       Two iron coffers hong on either side,
       With precious mettall full, as they might hold,
       And in his lap an heape of coine he told;°   *counted*
240   For of his wicked pelfe° his God he made,   *profits*
       And unto hell him selfe for money sold;
       Accursed usurie was all his trade,[1]
    And right and wrong ylike in equall ballaunce waide.

                        28
    His life was nigh unto deaths doore yplast,°   *i.e., nearly over*
245   And thred-bare cote, and cobled° shoes he ware,   *patched*
       Ne scarse good morsell all his life did tast,
       But both from backe and belly still did spare,
       To fill his bags, and richesse to compare;[2]
       Yet chylde ne kinsman living had he none
250   To leave them to; but thorough daily care

---

1. Usury (lending money for profit) was forbidden by Scripture but was nevertheless practiced—with certain restrictions—in early modern Europe and England. High rates of interest were generally forbidden, but loans could be made as forms of investment in commerce or industry.
2. I.e., he wore rags and starved himself.

To get, and nightly feare to lose his owne,°   *his own wealth*
He led a wretched life unto him selfe unknowne.

29

Most wretched wight, whom nothing might suffise,
   Whose greedy lust did lacke in greatest store,
255   Whose need had end, but no end covetise,°   *coveteousness*
   Whose wealth was want, whose plenty made him pore,
   Who had enough, yet wished ever more;
   A vile disease, and eke in foote and hand
   A grievous gout tormented him full sore,
260   That well he could not touch, nor go, nor stand:
Such one was Avarice, the fourth of this faire band.

30

And next to him malicious Envie rode,
   Upon a ravenous wolfe, and still did chaw°   *chew*
   Betweene his cankred° teeth a venemous tode,   *infected*
265   That all the poison ran about his chaw;°   *mouth*
   But inwardly he chawed his owne maw°   *guts*
   At neighbours wealth, that made him ever sad;
   For death it was, when any good he saw,
   And wept, that cause of weeping none he had,
270 But when he heard of harme, he wexed° wondrous glad.   *grew*

31

All in a kirtle° of discolourd say°   *gown/fine cloth*
   He clothed was, ypainted full of eyes;
   And in his bosome secretly there lay
   An hatefull Snake, the which his taile uptyes
275   In many folds, and mortall sting implyes.[3]
   Still as he rode, he gnasht his teeth, to see
   Those heapes of gold with griple Covetyse,[4]
   And grudged at the great felicitie
Of proud Lucifera, and his owne companie.

32

280 He hated all good workes and vertuous deeds,
   And him no lesse, that any like did use,°   *perform*
   And who with gracious bread the hungry feeds,
   His almes for want of faith he doth accuse;°   *misrepresent*
   So every good to bad he doth abuse:[5]
285   And eke the verse of famous Poets witt
   He does backebite, and spightfull poison spues
From leprous mouth on all, that ever writt:
Such one vile Envie was, that fifte in row did sitt.

---

3. Envy's clothing symbolically displays the envious and covetous eyes with which he views the world. The snake he carries in his bosom was a traditional symbol of envy; its "mortall sting" is deadly to Envy himself as well as to others.
4. Grasping Avarice; Envy is envious of Avarice's gold.

5. Envy believes that good deeds reveal a lack of faith. Here Spenser attacks doctrine associated with radical Protestant sects that, rejecting Catholic belief in the merit of good works as a means to salvation, insist that it is only through faith and God's grace that a Christian is saved.

33

And him beside rides fierce revenging Wrath,
    Upon a Lion, loth for° to be led;   *reluctant*
    And in his hand a burning brond° he hath,   *brand*
    The which he brandisheth about his hed;
    His eyes did hurle forth sparkles fiery red,
    And stared sterne on all, that him beheld,
    As ashes pale of hew and seeming ded;
    And on his dagger still his hand he held,
Trembling through hasty rage, when choler° in him sweld.   *anger*

34

His ruffin° raiment all was staind with blood,   *ruffianly*
    Which he had spilt, and all to rags yrent,
    Through unadvized rashnesse woxen wood;°   *grown mad*
    For of his hands he had no governement,°   *control*
    Ne car'd for bloud in his avengement:
    But when the furious fit was overpast,
    His cruell facts° he often would repent;   *deeds*
    Yet wilfull man he never would forecast,°   *foresee*
How many mischieves° should ensue his heedlesse hast.   *evil consequences*

35

Full many mischiefes follow cruell Wrath;
    Abhorred bloudshed, and tumultuous strife,
    Unmanly murder, and unthrifty scath,°   *wasteful harm*
    Bitter despight,° with rancours rusty knife,   *malice*
    And fretting griefe the enemy of life;
    All these, and many evils moe haunt ire,
    The swelling Splene,° and Frenzy raging rife,   *temper*
    The shaking Palsey, and Saint Fraunces fire:[6]
Such one was Wrath, the last of this ungodly tire.°   *procession*

36

And after all, upon the wagon beame°   *shaft*
    Rode Sathan, with a smarting whip in hand,
    With which he forward lasht the laesie teme,
    So oft as Slowth still in the mire did stand.
    Huge routs of people did about them band,
    Showting for joy, and still° before their way   *always*
    A foggy mist had covered all the land;
    And underneath their feet, all scattered lay
Dead sculs and bones of men, whose life had gone astray.

37

So forth they marchen in this goodly sort,
    To take the solace of the open aire,
    And in fresh flowring fields themselves to sport;
    Emongst the rest rode that false Lady faire,

---

6. Erysipelas or, as it was actually known, St. Anthony's fire. A common disease of the period, it was characterized by a disfiguring and painful skin rash.

330 The fowle Duessa, next unto the chaire
   Of proud Lucifera, as one of the traine:
   But that good knight would not so nigh repaire,°   *follow*
   Him selfe estraunging from their joyaunce vaine,
  Whose fellowship seemd far unfit for warlike swaine.

38

  So having solaced themselves a space
335   With pleasaunce of the breathing fields yfed,[7]
   They backe returned to the Princely Place;
   Whereas° an errant° knight in armes ycled, *where / wandering*
   And heathnish shield, wherein with letters red
340   Was writ Sans-Joy, they new arrived find:
   Enflam'd with fury and fiers hardy-hed,°   *boldness*
   He seemd in hart to harbour thoughts unkind,
  And nourish bloudy vengeaunce in his bitter mind.

39

  Who when the shamed shield of slaine Sans-Foy
   He spide with that same Faery champions page,
345   Bewraying° him, that did of late destroy   *revealing*
   His eldest brother, burning all with rage
   He to him leapt, and that same envious gage° *envious token*
   Of victors glory from him snatcht away:
   But th'Elfin knight, which ought° that warlike wage, *owned*
350   Disdaind to loose° the meed° he wonne in fray, *give up / reward*
  And him recountring° fierce, reskewd the noble pray.[8] *combatting*

40

  Therewith they gan to hurtlen° greedily,   *fight*
   Redoubted battaile ready to darrayne,°   *wage*
   And clash their shields, and shake their swords on hy,
355   That with their sturre they troubled all the traine;
   Till that great Queene upon eternall paine
   Of high displeasure, that ensewen° might,   *follow*
   Commaunded them their fury to refraine,
   And if that either to that shield had right,
360 In equall lists° they should the morrow next it fight. *tournament*

41

  Ah dearest Dame, (quoth then the Paynim bold,)
   Pardon the errour of enraged wight,
   Whom great griefe made forget the raines° to hold *reins*
   Of reasons rule, to see this recreant° knight, *cowardly*
365   No knight, but treachour full of false despight° *indignation*
   And shamefull treason, who through guile hath slayn
   The prowest knight, that ever field did fight,

---

7. I.e., having fed themselves with fresh air from the fields, where they momentarily escape the stench of sin.

8. By striving to recover Sans-Foy's shield instead of pursuing his quest to free Una's parents, the Redcrosse Knight exhibits pride and exemplifies a false chivalry.

Even stout Sans-Foy (O who can then refrayn?)
Whose shield he beares renverst,° the more to heape disdayn.   *upside down*

42

370   And to augment the glorie of his guile,
      His dearest love the faire Fidessa loe°   *look*
      Is there possessed of° the traytour vile,[9]   *by*
      Who reapes the harvest sowen by his foe,
      Sowen in bloudy field, and bought with woe:
375   That brothers hand shall dearely well requight°   *repay*
      So be, O Queene, you equall favour showe.
      Him litle answerd th'angry Elfin knight;
He never meant with words, but swords to plead his right.°   *cause*

43

But threw his gauntlet° as a sacred pledge,   *glove*
380   His cause in combat the next day to try:
      So been they parted both, with harts on edge,
      To be aveng'd each on his enimy.
      That night they pas in joy and jollity,
      Feasting and courting both in bowre and hall;
385   For Steward was excessive Gluttonie,
      That of his plenty poured forth to all;
Which doen, the Chamberlain° Slowth did to rest them call.   *master of bedchambers*

44

Now whenas° darkesome night had all displayd   *when*
      Her coleblacke curtein over brightest skye,
390   The warlike youthes on dayntie couches layd,
      Did chace away sweet sleepe from sluggish eye,
      To muse on meanes of hoped victory.
      But whenas Morpheus had with leaden mace
      Arrested° all that courtly company,   *i.e., put to sleep*
395   Up-rose Duessa from her resting place,
And to the Paynims lodging comes with silent pace.

45

Whom broad awake she finds, in troublous fit,
      Forecasting, how his foe he might annoy,°   *injure*
      And him amoves° with speaches seeming fit: *arouses*
400   Ah deare Sans-Joy, next dearest to Sans-Foy,
      Cause of my new griefe, cause of my new joy,
      Joyous, to see his ymage in mine eye,
      And greev'd, to thinke how foe did him destroy,
      That was the flowre of grace and chevalrye;
405   Lo his Fidessa to thy secret faith I flye.

46

With gentle wordes he can° her fairely greet,   *did*
      And bad° say on the secret of her hart.   *commanded*
      Then sighing soft, I learne that little sweet
      Oft tempred is (quoth she) with muchell smart:°   *much pain*

---

9. Sans-Joy accused the Redcrosse Knight of absconding with Fidessa (i.e., Duessa), who actually belonged to his brother, Sans-Foy.

410   For since my brest was launcht° with lovely dart   *pierced*
Of deare Sans-Foy, I never joyed howre,
But in eternall woes my weaker hart
Have wasted, loving him with all my powre,
And for his sake have felt full many an heavie stowre.°   *sorrowful time*

47

415   At last when perils all I weened past,
And hop'd to reape the crop of all my care,
Into new woes unweeting I was cast,
By this false faytor,° who unworthy ware°   *deceiver/wore*
His° worthy shield, whom he with guilefull snare   *Sans-Foy's*
420   Entrapped slew, and brought to shamefull grave.
Me silly maid away with him he bare,
And ever since hath kept in darksome cave,
For that° I would not yeeld, that to Sans-Foy I gave.   *that which*

48

But since faire Sunne hath sperst° that lowring° clowd,   *dispersed/threatening*
425   And to my loathed life now shewes some light,
Under your beames I will me safely shroud,°   *take shelter*
From dreaded storme of his° disdainfull spight: *Redcrosse Knight's*
To you th'inheritance belongs by right
Of brothers prayse, to you eke longs his love.
430   Let not his love, let not his restlesse spright
Be unreveng'd, that calles to you above
From wandring Stygian° shores, where it doth endlesse move.   *underworld*

49

Thereto said he, Faire Dame be nought dismaid
For sorrowes past; their griefe is with them gone:
435   Ne yet of present perill be affraid;
For needlesse feare did never vantage none,°   *benefit anyone*
And helplesse hap it booteth° not to mone.   *helps*
Dead is Sans-Foy, his vitall paines° are past,   *troubles in life*
Though greeved ghost for vengeance deepe do grone:
440   He lives, that shall him pay his dewties last,°   *final debts*
And guiltie Elfin bloud shall sacrifice in hast.

50

O but I feare the fickle freakes° (quoth shee)   *accidents*
Of fortune false, and oddes of armes in field.
Why dame (quoth he) what oddes can ever bee,
445   Where both do fight alike, to win or yield?
Yea but (quoth she) he beares a charmed shield,
And eke enchaunted armes, that none can perce,
Ne none can wound the man, that does them wield.
Charmd or enchaunted (answerd he then ferce)
450   I no whit reck,° ne you the like need to reherce.°   *care nothing/mention*

51

But faire Fidessa, sithens° fortunes guile,   *since*
Or enimies powre hath now captived you,
Returne from whence ye came, and rest a while
Till morrow next, that I the Elfe subdew,
455   And with Sans-Foyes dead dowry you endew.°   *give*

Ay me, that is a double death (she said)
With proud foes sight my sorrow to renew:
Where ever yet I be, my secrete aid
Shall follow you. So passing forth she him obaid.

Canto 5

*The faithfull knight in equall field
subdewes his faithlesse foe,
Whom false Duessa saves, and for
his cure to hell does goe.*

1

The noble hart, that harbours vertuous thought,
    And is with child° of glorious great intent,   pregnant
    Can never rest, untill it forth have brought
    Th'eternall brood of glorie excellent:
5   Such restlesse passion did all night torment
    The flaming corage of that Faery knight,
    Devizing, how that doughtie° turnament   worthy
    With greatest honour he atchieven might;
Still did he wake, and still did he watch for dawning light.

2

10 At last the golden Orientall° gate   eastern
    Of greatest heaven gan to open faire,
    And Phoebus fresh, as bridegrome to his mate,
    Came dauncing forth, shaking his deawie haire:
    And hurld his glistring° beames through gloomy aire.   glistening
15 Which when the wakeful Elfe perceiv'd, streight way
    He started up, and did him selfe prepaire,
    In sun-bright armes, and battailous° array: warlike
For with that Pagan proud he combat will that day.

3

    And forth he comes into the commune hall,
20 Where earely waite him many a gazing eye,
    To weet° what end to straunger knights may fall.   know
    There many Minstrales maken melody,
    To drive away the dull melancholy,
    And many Bardes, that to the trembling chord
25 Can tune their timely voyces cunningly,
    And many Chroniclers, that can record
Old loves, and warres for Ladies doen by many a Lord.

4

    Soone after comes the cruell Sarazin,
    In woven maile all armed warily,°   carefully
30 And sternly lookes at him, who not a pin
    Does care for looke of living creatures eye.
    They bring them wines of Greece and Araby,°   Arabia
    And daintie spices fetcht from furthest Ynd,°   India
    To kindle heat of corage privily:°   internally
35 And in the wine a solemne oth they bynd
T'observe the sacred lawes of armes, that are assynd.

5

At last forth comes that far renowmed° Queene,   *famed*
    With royall pomp and Princely majestie;
    She is ybrought unto a paled greene,°   *enclosed field*
40   And placed under stately canapee,
    The warlike feates of both those knights to see.
    On th'other side in all mens open vew
    Duessa placed is, and on a tree
    Sans-Foy his shield is hangd with bloudy hew:
45 Both those the lawrell girlonds to the victor dew.[1]

6

A shrilling trompet sownded from on hye,
    And unto battaill bad them selves addresse:
    Their shining shieldes about their wrestes they tye,
    And burning blades about their heads do blesse,[2]
50   The instruments of wrath and heavinesse:
    With greedy force each other doth assayle,
    And strike so fiercely, that they do impresse
    Deepe dinted furrowes in the battred mayle;
 The yron walles° to ward their blowes are weake and fraile.   *of the armor*

7

55 The Sarazin was stout, and wondrous strong,
    And heaped blowes like yron hammers great:
    For after bloud and vengeance he did long.
    The knight was fiers, and full of youthly heat:
    And doubled strokes, like dreaded thunders threat:
60   For all for prayse and honour he did fight.
    Both stricken strike, and beaten both do beat,
    That from their shields forth flyeth firie light,
 And helmets hewen deepe,° shew marks of eithers might.   *deeply cut*

8

So th'one for wrong, the other strives for right:
65   As when a Gryfon[3] seized of his pray,
    A Dragon fiers encountreth in his flight,
    Through widest ayre making his ydle way,
    That would his rightfull ravine° rend away: *spoil*
    With hideous horrour both together smight,
70   And souce° so sore, that they the heavens affray: *attack*
    The wise Southsayer seeing so sad sight,
 Th'amazed vulgar tels of warres and mortall fight.

9

So th'one for wrong, the other strives for right,
    And each to deadly shame would drive his foe:
75   The cruell steele so greedily doth bight
    In tender flesh, that streames of bloud down flow,

---

1. I.e., the victor will receive both Sans-Foy's shield and
Duessa as his prize.
2. Brandish: they make the sign of the cross in the air
with their swords.
3. A lion with eagle's wings. Dante used the gryfon as a
symbol for the dual nature of Christ, as both spirit and
flesh. However, in traditional iconography the gryfon
also appeared as a creature who guarded gold and was
thus emblematic of greed. The image suggests that the
Redcrosse Knight is foolish to engage in a contest for
material prizes.

With which the armes, that earst° so bright did show,   *first*
Into a pure vermillion now are dyde:
Great ruth° in all the gazers harts did grow,   *pity*
80   Seeing the gored woundes to gape so wyde,
That victory they dare not wish to either side.

10

At last the Paynim chaunst to cast his eye,
His suddein eye, flaming with wrathfull fyre,
Upon his brothers shield, which hong thereby:
85   Therewith redoubled was his raging yre,
And said, Ah wretched sonne of wofull syre,°   *Sans-Foy*
Doest thou sit wayling by black Stygian° lake,   *by the river Styx*
Whilest here thy shield is hangd for victors hyre,
And sluggish german° doest thy forces slake,   *kinsman*
90   To after-send his foe, that him may overtake?[4]

11

Goe caytive Elfe,[5] him quickly overtake,
And soone redeeme from his long wandring woe;
Goe guiltie ghost, to him my message make,
That I his shield have quit° from dying foe.   *recovered*
95   Therewith upon his crest he stroke him so,
That twise he reeled, readie twise to fall;
End of the doubtfull battell deemed tho
The lookers on, and lowd to him gan call
The false Duessa, Thine the shield, and I, and all.[6]

12

100   Soone as the Faerie heard his Ladie speake,
Out of his swowning dreame he gan awake,
And quickning faith, that earst was woxen° weake,   *had grown*
The creeping deadly cold away did shake:
Tho mou'd with wrath, and shame, and Ladies sake,
105   Of all attonce he cast avengd to bee,
And with so'exceeding furie at him strake,°   *struck*
That forced him to stoupe upon his knee;
Had he not stouped so, he should have cloven° bee.   *cut in half*

13

And to him said, Goe now proud Miscreant,°   *heathen*
110   Thy selfe thy message doe to german deare,
Alone he wandring thee too long doth want:°   *lack*
Goe say, his foe thy shield with his doth beare.
Therewith his heavie hand he high gan reare,°   *began to raise*
Him to have slaine; when loe a darkesome clowd
115   Upon him fell: he no where doth appeare,
But vanisht is. The Elfe him cals alowd,
But answer none receiues: the darknes him does shrowd.

---

4. Sans-Joy is addressing the dead Sans-Foy, asking if
Sans-Foy grieves because his shield is a prize and the
strength of his brother, Sans-Joy, which should be wielded to dispatch the Redcrosse Knight to the shores of the
Styx, is actually slackening, growing weak.
5. Sans-Joy addresses the Redcrosse Knight. The epithet

"caytive," meaning "servile," was especially insulting in
the context of chivalry, since it implied weakness and
lack of valor.
6. Duessa is calling to Sans-Joy; however, the Redcrosse
Knight assumes that she is cheering him on and therefore
redoubles his force.

14

    In haste Duessa from her place arose,
        And to him running said, O prowest° knight,   *most valiant*
120   That ever Ladie to her love did chose,
        Let now abate the terror of your might,
        And quench the flame of furious despight,
        And bloudie vengeance; lo th'infernall powres
        Covering your foe with cloud of deadly night,
125   Have borne him hence to Plutoes balefull° bowres.   *deadly*
    The conquest yours, I yours, the shield, and glory yours.

15

    Not all so satisfide, with greedie eye
        He sought all round about, his thirstie blade
        To bath in bloud of faithlesse enemy;
130   Who all that while lay hid in secret shade:
        He standes amazed, how he thence should fade.
        At last the trumpets Triumph sound on hie,
        And running Heralds humble homage made,
        Greeting him goodly with new victorie,
135   And to him brought the shield, the cause of enmitie.

16

    Wherewith he goeth to that soveraine Queene,
        And falling her before on lowly knee,
        To her makes present of his service seene:
        Which she accepts, with thankes, and goodly gree,°   *courteous goodwill*
140   Greatly advauncing his gay chevalree.
        So marcheth home, and by her takes the knight,
        Whom all the people follow with great glee,
        Shouting, and clapping all their hands on hight,°   *high*
    That all the aire it fils, and flyes to heaven bright.

17

145   Home is he brought, and laid in sumptuous bed:
        Where many skilfull leaches° him abide,   *doctors*
        To salve° his hurts, that yet still freshly bled.   *dress*
        In wine and oyle they wash his woundes wide,
        And softly can embalme on every side.
150   And all the while, most heavenly melody
        About the bed sweet musicke did divide,°   *modulate*
        Him to beguile of griefe and agony:
    And all the while Duessa wept full bitterly.

18

    As when a wearie traveller that strayes
155   By muddy shore of broad seven-mouthed Nile,
        Unweeting of the perillous wandring wayes,
        Doth meet a cruell craftie Crocodile,
        Which in false griefe hyding his harmefull guile,
        Doth weepe full sore, and sheddeth tender teares:
160   The foolish man, that pitties all this while
        His mournefull plight, is swallowd up unwares,
    Forgetfull of his owne, that mindes° anothers cares.   *attends to*

19

So wept Duessa untill eventide,
   That shyning lampes in Joves high house were light:
165 Then forth she rose, ne lenger° would abide,   *no longer*
   But comes unto the place, where th'Hethen knight
   In slombring swownd nigh voyd of vitall spright,°   *living spirit*
   Lay cover'd with inchaunted cloud all day:
   Whom when she found, as she him left in plight,
170 To wayle his woefull case she would not stay,
But to the easterne coast of heaven makes speedy way.

20

Where griesly Night, with visage deadly sad,
   That Phoebus chearefull face durst never vew,
   And in a foule blacke pitchie mantle clad,
175 She findes forth comming from her darkesome mew,° *den*
   Where she all day did hide her hated hew.
   Before the dore her yron charet stood,
   Alreadie harnessed for journey new;
   And coleblacke steedes yborne of hellish brood,
180 That on their rustie bits did champ, as they were wood.° *mad*

21

Who when she saw Duessa sunny bright,
   Adornd with gold and jewels shining cleare,
   She greatly grew amazed at the sight,
   And th'unacquainted light began to feare:
185 For never did such brightnesse there appeare,
   And would have backe retyred to her cave,
   Untill the witches speech she gan to heare,
   Saying, Yet O thou dreaded Dame, I crave
Abide,° till I have told the message, which I have.   *wait*

22

190 She stayd, and foorth Duessa gan proceede,
   O thou most auncient Grandmother of all,[7]
   More old then Jove, whom thou at first didst breede,
   Or that great house of Gods caelestiall,
   Which wast begot in Daemogorgons° hall,   *chaos's*
195 And sawst the secrets of the world unmade,° *not yet made*
   Why suffredst thou thy Nephewes deare to fall
   With Elfin sword, most shamefully betrade?
Lo where the stout° Sans-Joy doth sleepe in deadly shade. *sturdy*

23

And him before, I saw with bitter eyes
200 The bold Sans-Foy shrinke underneath his speare;
   And now the pray of fowles in field he lyes,
   Nor wayld of friends, nor laid on groning beare,° *bier*
   That whylome was to me too dearely deare.
   O what of Gods then boots° it to be borne,   *benefits*
205 If old Aveugles[8] sonnes so evill heare?

---

7. Invoking Night, Duessa recalls that Jove was raised in a dark cave to escape being eaten by his father, Saturn; here, Spenser is implying that darkness gave birth to Jove.

8. Blind (French). Duessa uses the name "Aveugle" to refer to either Night herself or her husband; "Aveugles sonne" is Sans-Joy.

Or who shall not great Nightes children scorne,
When two of three her Nephews are so fowle forlorne?°   *foully abandoned*

24

Up then, up dreary Dame, of darknesse Queene,
  Go gather up the reliques° of thy race,   *remains*
  Or else goe them avenge, and let be seene,
  That dreaded Night in brightest day hath place,°   *highest rank*
  And can the children of faire light deface.
Her feeling speeches some compassion moved
  In hart, and chaunge in that great mothers face:
  Yet pittie in her hart was never proved°   *experienced*
Till then: for evermore she hated, never loved.

25

And said, Deare daughter rightly may I rew
  The fall of famous children borne of mee,
  And good successes, which their foes ensew:
  But who can turne the streame of destinee,
  Or breake the chayne of strong necessitee,
Which fast is tyde to Joves eternall seat?⁹
  The sonnes of Day he favoureth, I see,
  And by my ruines thinkes to make them great:
To make one great by others losse, is bad excheat.°   *exchange*

26

Yet shall they not escape so freely all;
  For some shall pay the price of° others guilt: *for*
  And he the man that made Sans-Foy to fall,
  Shall with his owne bloud price that he hath spilt.
  But what art thou, that telst of Nephews kilt?°   *killed*
I that do seeme not I, Duessa am,
  (Quoth she) how ever now in garments gilt,
  And gorgeous gold arayd I to thee came;
Duessa I, the daughter of Deceipt and Shame.

27

Then bowing downe her aged backe, she kist
  The wicked witch, saying; In that faire face
  The false resemblance of Deceipt, I wist
  Did closely° lurke; yet so true-seeming grace   *secretly*
  It carried, that I scarse in darkesome place
Could it discerne, though I the mother bee
  Of falshood, and root of Duessaes race.
  O welcome child, whom I have longd to see,
And now have seene unwares.° Lo now I go with thee.   *unknowingly*

28

Then to her yron wagon she betakes,
  And with her beares the fowle welfavourd witch:¹
  Through mirkesome° aire her readie way she makes.   *murky*
  Her twyfold° Teme, of which two blacke as pitch,   *twofold*
  And two were browne, yet each to each unlich,°   *unlike*
Did softly swim away, ne ever stampe,

---

9. Night reveals her fatalism and therefore her ignorance of Christian grace. God can forgive a repentant sinner; hence for Christians there is no "chain of necessity" prior to God's decision to send the sinner to eternal damnation.
1. Duessa is a foul creature disguised as a beautiful woman.

250   Unlesse she chaunst their stubborne mouths to twitch;
       Then foming tarre, their bridles they would champe,
       And trampling the fine element,° would fiercely rampe.°   *air/rear up*

29

    So well they sped, that they be come at length
       Unto the place, whereas the Paynim lay,
255   Devoid of outward sense, and native° strength,   *natural*
       Coverd with charmed cloud from vew of day,
       And sight of men, since his late luckelesse fray.°   *fight*
       His cruell wounds with cruddy bloud congealed,
       They binden up so wisely, as they may,
260   And handle softly, till they can be healed:
    So lay him in her charet, close° in night concealed.   *hidden*

30

    And all the while she stood upon the ground,
       The wakefull dogs did never cease to bay,°   *howl*
       As giving warning of th'unwonted° sound,   *unaccustomed*
265   With which her yron wheeles did them affray,
       And her darke griesly looke them much dismay;
       The messenger of death, the ghastly Owle
       With drearie shriekes did also her bewray;°   *expose*
       And hungry Wolves continually did howle,
270   At her abhorred face, so filthy and so fowle.

31

    Thence turning backe in silence soft they stole,
       And brought the heavie corse with easie pace
       To yawning gulfe of deepe Avernus° hole.   *a lake in hell*
       By that same hole an entrance darke and bace°   *low*
275   With smoake and sulphure hiding all the place,
       Descends to hell: there creature never past,
       That backe returned without heavenly grace;
       But dreadfull Furies,[2] which their chaines have brast,
    And damned sprights sent forth to make ill° men aghast.   *bad*

32

280   By that same way the direfull° dames doe drive   *dreadful*
       Their mournefull charet, fild° with rusty blood,   *defiled*
       And downe to Plutoes house are come bilive:°   *quickly*
       Which passing through, on every side them stood
       The trembling ghosts with sad amazed mood,
285   Chattring their yron teeth, and staring wide
       With stonie eyes; and all the hellish brood
       Of feends infernall flockt on every side,
    To gaze on earthly wight, that with the Night durst° ride.   *dared*

33

    They pas the bitter waves of Acheron,[3]
290   Where many soules sit wailing woefully,
       And come to fiery flood of Phlegeton,
       Whereas the damned ghosts in torments fry,

---

2. The three mythical female spirits who live in the underworld and punish people for their crimes; they personified the forces of revenge.

3. Acheron and Phlegeton are two of the four rivers of the underworld.

And with sharpe shrilling shrieks doe bootlesse° cry,   *futilely*
Cursing high Jove, the which them thither sent.
295   The house of endlesse paine is built thereby,
In which ten thousand sorts of punishment
The cursed creatures doe eternally torment.

34

Before the threshold dreadfull Cerberus[4]
His three deformed heads did lay along,
300   Curled with thousand adders venemous,
And lilled forth° his bloudie flaming tong: *stuck out*
At them he gan to reare his bristles strong,
And felly gnarre,° untill dayes enemy   *deadly snarl*
Did him appease; then downe his taile he hong
305   And suffered them to passen quietly:
For she in hell and heaven had power equally.

35

There was Ixion[5] turned on a wheele,
For daring tempt the Queene of heaven to sin;
And Sisyphus an huge round stone did reele
310   Against an hill, ne might from labour lin;
There thirstie Tantalus hong by the chin;
And Tityus fed a vulture on his maw;
Typhoeus joynts were stretched on a gin,
Theseus condemned to endlesse slouth by law,
315   And fifty sisters water in leake vessels draw.

36

They all beholding worldly wights in place,
Leave off their worke, unmindfull of their smart,°   *pain*
To gaze on them; who forth by them doe pace,
Till they be come unto the furthest part:
320   Where was a Cave ywrought° by wondrous art,   *built*
Deepe, darke, uneasie, dolefull, comfortlesse,
In which sad Aesculapius[6] farre a part
Emprisond was in chaines remedilesse,
For that Hippolytus rent corse he did redresse.°   *restore*

37

325   Hippolytus a jolly huntsman was,
That wont° in charet chace the foming Bore;   *often*
He all his Peeres in beautie did surpas,
But Ladies love as losse of time forbore:°   *abstained from*
His wanton stepdame° loved him the more,   *stepmother*
330   But when she saw her offred sweets refused
Her love she turnd to hate, and him before

---

4. The fierce, three-headed dog who guards the entrance to the underworld.

5. This stanza describes various mythological figures who suffer in the underworld. Ixion, king of Thessaly, sought the love of Juno and was punished by being bound forever on a revolving wheel. Sisyphus, a greedy king of Corinth, was condemned forever to roll up a hill a heavy stone, which always rolled back down again. Tantalus was doomed to stand up to his neck in water with fruit hanging at his fingertips, yet could never reach the fruit or drink the water. Tityus's punishment was to have a vulture constantly feed on his liver, which grew back as soon as it was devoured. Theseus, hero and eventually king of Athens, was famous for a multitude of exploits and adventures; he was condemned to sit forever in the chair of forgetfulness. The 50 sisters were the daughters of Danaus, king of Argos; they were condemned to collect water in leaky pots because they had murdered their husbands on their wedding night.

6. The god of medicine. In the following stanzas, Spenser tells the story of how Aesculapius revived the corpse of Hippolytus and was punished for exceeding the limits of medical art.

His father fierce of treason false accused,
And with her gealous termes his open eares abused.

38

Who ail in rage his Sea-god syre besought,
335   Some cursed vengeance on his sonne to cast:
    From surging gulf two monsters straight were brought,
    With dread whereof his chasing steedes aghast,°   *terrified*
    Both charet swift and huntsman overcast.
    His goodly corps on ragged cliffs yrent,
340   Was quite dismembred, and his members chast°   *virgin, virtuous*
    Scattered on every mountaine, as he went,
That of Hippolytus was left no moniment.°   *trace*

39

His cruell stepdame seeing what was donne,
    Her wicked dayes with wretched knife did end,
345   In death avowing th'innocence of her sonne.
    Which hearing his rash Syre, began to rend°   *tear*
    His haire, and hastie tongue, that did offend:
    Tho gathering up the relicks of his smart°   *pain*
    By Dianes° meanes, who was Hippolyts frend,   *goddess of the hunt*
350   Them brought to Aesculape, that by his art
Did heale them all againe, and joyned every part.

40

Such wondrous science in mans wit to raine°   *rule*
    When Jove avizd,° that could the dead revive,   *found out*
    And fates expired could renew againe,
355   Of endlesse life he might him not deprive,
    But unto hell did thrust him downe alive,
    With flashing thunderbolt ywounded sore:
    Where long remaining, he did alwaies strive
    Himselfe with salves to health for to restore,
360 And slake° the heavenly fire, that raged evermore.   *put out*

41

There auncient Night arriving, did alight
    From her nigh wearie waine, and in her armes
    To Aesculapius brought the wounded knight:
    Whom having softly disarayd of armes,
365   Tho gan to him discover all his harmes,°   *injuries*
    Beseeching him with prayer, and with praise,
    If either salves, or oyles, or herbes, or charmes
    A fordonne° wight from dore of death mote raise,   *dying*
He would at her request prolong her nephews daies.

42

370 Ah Dame (quoth he) thou temptest me in vaine,
    To dare the thing, which daily yet I rew,
    And the old cause of my continued paine
    With like attempt to like end to renew.[7]
    Is not enough, that thrust from heaven dew
375   Here endlesse penance for one fault I pay,
    But that redoubled crime with vengeance new

---

7. I.e., to repeat the actions which caused his punishment in the first place and thus to renew the punishment itself.

Thou biddest me to eeke?° Can Night defray°   *increase/appease*
The wrath of thundring Jove, that rules both night and day?

43

Not so (quoth she) but sith that heavens king
380   From hope of heaven hath thee excluded quight,
     Why fearest thou, that canst not hope for thing,°   *anything*
     And fearest not, that more thee hurten might,
     Now in the powre of everlasting Night?
     Goe to then, O thou farre renowmed sonne
385   Of great Apollo, shew thy famous might
     In medicine, that else hath to thee wonne
Great paines, and greater praise, both never to be donne.°   *surpassed*

44

Her words prevaild: And then the learned leach°   *doctor*
     His cunning hand gan to his wounds to lay,
390   And all things else, the which his art did teach:
     Which having seene, from thence arose away
     The mother of dread darknesse, and let stay
     Aveugles sonne there in the leaches cure,
     And backe returning tooke her wonted way,
395   To runne her timely race, whilst Phoebus pure
In westerne waves his wearie wagon did recure.°   *renew*

45

The false Duessa leaving noyous° Night,   *noxious*
     Returnd to stately pallace of dame Pride;
     Where when she came, she found the Faery knight
400   Departed thence, albe° his woundes wide   *although*
     Not throughly heald, unreadie were to ride.
     Good cause he had to hasten thence away;
     For on a day his wary Dwarfe had spide,
     Where in a dongeon deepe huge numbers lay
405 Of caytive wretched thrals,° that wayled night and day.   *prisoners*

46

A ruefull sight, as could be seene with eie;
     Of whom he learned had in secret wise°   *manner*
     The hidden cause of their captivitie,
     How mortgaging their lives to Covetise,°   *greed*
410   Through wastfull Pride, and wanton Riotise,°   *idle abandon*
     They were by law of that proud Tyrannesse
     Provokt with Wrath, and Envies false surmise,°   *suspicion*
     Condemned to that Dongeon mercilesse,
Where they should live in woe, and die in wretchednesse.[8]

47

415 There was that great proud king of Babylon,°   *Nebuchadnezzar*
     That would compell all nations to adore,
     And him as onely° God to call upon,   *the only*

8. Spenser lists some of the inhabitants of the underworld, the domain of Night, implying that they were damned for their evil deeds and were therefore in a Christian hell. The theology supporting this image is problematic: While Spenser names individuals who were considered to have been proud and malicious, they were also not people who could have known the salutary message of Christianity. Nebuchadnezzar, king of Babylon, set up a golden image to be worshipped as God and was transformed into an ox as a punishment (Daniel 3–6); Croesus was the vastly rich king of Lydia; Antiochus, king of Antioch, was supposed scornfully to have danced on an altar; Nimrod was the first tyrant to emerge after the Flood; Ninus, the founder of Ninevah, conquered India and was the first to make war. "That mightie Monarch" was Alexander the Great, who rejected his father to claim descent from Jove or Jupiter, sometimes called Jupiter Ammon.

Till through celestiall doome° throwne out of dore,   *heavenly judgment*
Into an Oxe he was transform'd of yore:°   *in ancient times*
420   There also was king Croesus, that enhaunst
His heart too high through his great riches store;
And proud Antiochus, the which advaunst
His cursed hand gainst God, and on his altars daunst.

48

And them long time before, great Nimrod was,
425   That first the world with sword and fire warrayd;°   *ravaged*
And after him old Ninus farre did pas
In princely pompe, of all the world obayd;
There also was that mightie Monarch layd
Low under all, yet above all in pride,
430   That name of native syre° did fowle upbrayd,°   *natural father/denounce*
And would as Ammons sonne be magnifide,
Till scornd of God and man a shamefull death he dide.

49

All these together in one heape were throwne,
Like carkases of beasts in butchers stall.
435   And in another corner wide were strowne°   *strewn*
The antique ruines of the Romaines fall:[9]
Great Romulus the Grandsyre of them all,
Proud Tarquin, and too lordly Lentulus,
Stout Scipio, and stubborne Hanniball,
440   Ambitious Sylla, and sterne Marius,
High Caesar, great Pompey, and fierce Antonius.

50

Amongst these mighty men were wemen mixt,[1]
Proud wemen, vaine, forgetfull of their yoke:°   *place*
The bold Semiramis, whose sides transfixt
445   With sonnes owne blade, her fowle reproches spoke;
Faire Sthenoboea, that her selfe did choke
With wilfull cord, for wanting of her will;
High minded Cleopatra, that with stroke
Of Aspes° sting her selfe did stoutly kill: *snakes'*
450   And thousands moe the like, that did that dongeon fill.

51

Besides the endlesse routs° of wretched thralles,   *crowds*
Which thither were assembled day by day,
From all the world after their wofull falles,
Through wicked pride, and wasted wealthes decay.°   *loss*
455   But most of all, which in that Dongeon lay
Fell from high Princes courts, or Ladies bowres,

9. Spenser lists men who figured prominently in the history of ancient Rome; some were heroes, others were tyrants or wrongdoers. Romulus was the founder and first king of Rome; Tarquin was the last king of Rome before it became a republic; Lentulus attempted to set fire to Rome; Scipio was a Roman general who conquered Africa; Hannibal constantly waged war against Rome; Sylla was a Roman dictator who was engaged in civil war with Marius; Caesar, Pompey, and Antonius fought among themselves for rulership of Rome and its colonies, Caesar eventually winning the office only to be assassinated shortly thereafter.

1. The women in the underworld, like the men, were figures from ancient history and mythology; those that are listed were judged to have been evil. After the death of her husband, King Ninus, Semiramis disguised herself as her son to gain the throne. Her son killed her when she tried to sleep with him. Sthenoboea lusted after her brother-in-law, Bellerophon, and committed suicide when he refused her advances. After Egypt had been defeated by the Roman forces of Octavius (later the Emperor Augustus), Cleopatra, the queen of Egypt, committed suicide by allowing herself to be bitten by asps, a kind of poisonous snake.

Where they in idle pompe, or wanton play,
Consumed had their goods, and thriftlesse howres,
And lastly throwne themselves into these heavy stowres.°   *afflictions*

52

460 Whose case when as the carefull Dwarfe had tould,
And made ensample° of their mournefull sight   *description*
Unto his maister, he no lenger° would   *longer*
There dwell in perill of like° painefull plight,   *similar*
But early rose, and ere that dawning light
465 Discovered had the world to heaven wyde,
He by a privie Posterne° tooke his flight,   *secret back door*
That of no envious eyes he mote he spyde:
For doubtlesse death ensewd, if any him descryde.°   *discovered*

53

Scarse could he footing find in that fowle way,
470 For° many corses, like a great Lay-stall°   *because of/open grave*
Of murdred men which therein strowed lay,°   *lay strewn*
Without remorse, or decent funerall:
Which all through that great Princesse pride did fall
And came to shamefull end. And them beside
475 Forth ryding underneath the castell wall,
A donghill° of dead carkases he spide,   *garbage heap*
The dreadfull spectacle of that sad house of Pride.

Canto 6

From lawlesse lust by wondrous grace
fayre Una is releast:
Whom salvage nation does adore,
and learnes her wise beheast.°   *teaching*

1

As when a ship, that flyes faire under saile,
An hidden rocke escaped hath unwares,
That lay in waite her wrack° for to bewaile,   *destruction*
The Marriner° yet halfe amazed stares   *sailor*
5 At perill past, and yet in doubt ne dares°   *dares not*
To joy at his foole-happie° oversight: *lucky*
So doubly is distrest twixt joy and cares
The dreadlesse courage of this Elfin knight,
Having escapt so sad ensamples° in his sight.   *warnings*

2

10 Yet sad he was that his too hastie speed
The faire Duess' had forst him leave behind;
And yet more sad, that Una his deare dreed°   *revered one*
Her truth had staind with treason so unkind;°   *unnatural*
Yet crime in her could never creature find,
15 But for his love, and for her owne selfe sake,
She wandred had from one to other Ynd,°   *throughout the world*
Him for to seeke, ne ever would forsake,
Till her unwares the fierce Sans-Loy did overtake.

3

Who after Archimagoes fowle defeat,
20   Led her away into a forrest wilde,
        And turning wrathfull fire to lustfull heat,
        With beastly sin thought° her to have defilde,   decided
        And made the vassall° of his pleasures vilde.   slave
        Yet first he cast by treatie,° and by traynes,°   treaty/tricks
25   Her to perswade, that stubborne fort° to yilde: i.e., her chastity
        For greater conquest of hard love he gaynes,
That workes it to his will, then he that it constraines.°   forces

4

With fawning wordes he courted her a while,
        And looking lovely,° and oft sighing sore,   amorously
30   Her constant hart did tempt with diverse guile:°   various deceits
        But wordes, and lookes, and sighes she did abhore,
        As rocke of Diamond stedfast evermore.
        Yet for to feed his fyrie lustfull eye,
        He snatcht the vele, that hong her face before;
35   Then gan her beautie shine, as brightest skye,
And burnt his beastly hart t'efforce° her chastitye.   to force

5

So when he saw his flatt'ring arts to fayle,
        And subtile engines bet from batteree,[1]
        With greedy force he gan the fort assayle,°   attack
40   Whereof he weend° possessed soone to bee,   believed
        And win rich spoile of ransackt chastetee.
        Ah heavens, that do this hideous act behold,
        And heavenly virgin thus outraged° see,   violated
        How can ye vengeance just so long withhold,
45   And hurle not flashing flames upon that Paynim bold?

6

The pitteous maiden carefull° comfortlesse,   grief-stricken
        Does throw out thrilling° shriekes, and shrieking cryes,   piercing
        The last vaine helpe of womens great distresse,
        And with loud plaints° importuneth the skyes,   laments
50   That molten° starres do drop like weeping eyes;   melting
        And Phoebus flying so most shamefull sight,
        His blushing face in foggy cloud implyes,°   hides
        And hides for shame. What wit of mortall wight
Can now devise to quit a thrall from such a plight?

7

55   Eternall providence exceeding thought,
        Where none appeares can make her selfe a way:
        A wondrous way it for this Lady wrought,
        From Lyons clawes to pluck the griped° pray.   trapped
        Her shrill outcryes and shriekes so loud did bray,
60   That all the woodes and forestes did resownd;
        A troupe of Faunes and Satyres° far away   woodland deities

1. I.e., Sans-Loy's clever devices are overcome by the success of Una's "battery" or repulses.

Within the wood were dauncing in a rownd,°   circle
Whiles old Sylvanus° slept in shady arber sownd.°   a wood god/soundly

                                        8

Who when they heard that pitteous strained voice,
65   In hast forsooke° their rurall meriment,   abandoned
        And ran towards the far rebownded° noyce,   reverberating
        To weet,° what wight so loudly did lament.   discover
        Unto the place they come incontinent:°   headlong
        Whom when the raging Sarazin espide,
70   A rude, misshapen, monstrous rablement,
        Whose like he never saw, he durst° not bide,°   dared/stay
But got his ready steed, and fast away gan ride.

                                        9

The wyld woodgods arrived in the place,
        There find the virgin dolefull desolate,
75   With ruffled rayments, and faire blubbred° face,   tear-stained
        As her outrageous foe had left her late,°   recently
        And trembling yet through feare of former hate;
        All stand amazed at so uncouth° sight,   strange
        And gin to pittie her unhappie state,
80   All stand astonied° at her beautie bright,   amazed
In their rude eyes unworthie of so wofull plight.

                                       10

She more amaz'd, in double dread doth dwell;
        And every tender part for feare does shake:
        As when a greedie Wolfe through hunger fell°   deadly
85   A seely° Lambe farre from the flocke does take,   innocent
        Of whom he meanes his bloudie feast to make,
        A Lyon spyes fast running towards him,
        The innocent pray in hast he does forsake,
        Which quit° from death yet quakes in every lim°   rescued/limb
90 With chaunge of feare, to see the Lyon looke so grim.

                                       11

Such fearefull fit assaid° her trembling hart,   assailed
        Ne word to speake, ne joynt to move she had:
        The salvage° nation² feele her secret smart,   wild
        And read her sorrow in her count'nance sad;
95   Their frowning forheads with rough hornes yclad,
        And rusticke horror all a side doe lay,°   put away
        And gently grenning,° shew a semblance° glad   grinning/expression
        To comfort her, and feare to put away,
Their backward bent knees teach her humbly to obay.³

                                       12

100   The doubtfull Damzell dare not yet commit
        Her single person to their barbarous truth,°   allegiance
        But still twixt feare and hope amazd does sit,

2. I.e., the wood gods.
3. The fauns and satyrs have goat legs, so when they
kneel before Una, their legs bend backward. It is not clear
who teaches whom to obey in this line: their own act of

kneeling may be teaching the fauns and satyrs to obey
Una, or their awkward gestures may be teaching Una to
obey them and put away her fear.

Late° learnd what harme to hastie trust ensu'th,°   *recently/follows*
They in compassion of her tender youth,
105   And wonder of her beautie soveraine,
Are wonne with pitty and unwonted° ruth,   *unaccustomed*
And all prostrate upon the lowly plaine,°   *ground*
Do kisse her feete, and fawne on her with count'nance faine.°   *glad expressions*

13

Their harts she ghesseth by their humble guise,
110   And yieldes her to extremitie of time;[4]
So from the ground she fearelesse doth arise,
And walketh forth without suspect° of crime:°   *fear/evil*
They all as glad, as birdes of joyous Prime,°   *spring*
Thence lead her forth, about her dauncing round,
115   Shouting, and singing all a shepheards ryme,
And with greene braunches strowing° all the ground,   *strewing*
Do worship her, as Queene, with olive girlond cround.

14

And all the way their merry pipes they sound,
That all the woods with doubled Eccho ring,
120   And with their horned feet do weare° the ground,   *tread*
Leaping like wanton° kids in pleasant Spring.   *playful*
So towards old Sylvanus they her bring;
Who with the noyse awaked, commeth out,
To weet° the cause, his weake steps governing,°   *discover/guiding*
125   And aged limbs on Cypresse stadle stout,[5]
And with an yvie twyne° his wast is girt° about.   *vine/wrapped*

15

Far off he wonders, what them makes so glad,
Or° Bacchus[6] merry fruit° they did inuent,   *whether/grapes*
Or Cybeles[7] franticke rites have made them mad;
130   They drawing nigh, unto their God° present   *Sylvanus*
That flowre of faith and beautie excellent.
The God himselfe vewing that mirrhour rare,
Stood long amazd, and burnt in his intent;
His owne faire Dryope[8] now he thinkes not faire,
135   And Pholoe fowle, when her to this he doth compaire.

16

The woodborne° people fall before her flat,   *born of the woods*
And worship her as Goddesse of the wood;
And old Sylvanus selfe bethinkes not,° what   *cannot tell*
To thinke of wight so faire, but gazing stood,
140   In doubt to deeme° her borne of earthly brood;   *believe*
Sometimes Dame Venus selfe he seemes to see,

4. I.e., she submits to the necessities imposed on her by circumstances and loses her fear of the fauns and satyrs.
5. Sylvanus uses a cane made from the trunk of a cypress tree.
6. The Roman god of wine; he is associated with both riot and fertility. Sylvanus suspects the fauns and satyrs of having discovered and drunk too much wine.
7. The goddess of grain and the harvest; the spring festi-
val held in her honor was a fertility rite that resembled a bacchanalia.
8. At this point, Una is still unveiled from her encounter with Sans-Loy. When Sylvanus views her, he sees a mirror reflecting heavenly faith and beauty and hence considers his beloved nymphs, Dryope and Pholoe, ugly by comparison.

But Venus never had so sober° mood;   *serious*
Sometimes Diana he her takes to bee,
But misseth bow, and shaftes,° and buskins° to her knee.   *arrows/boots*

17

145   By vew of her he ginneth to revive
His ancient love, and dearest Cyparisse,[9]
And calles to mind his pourtraiture aliue,°   *living image*
How faire he was, and yet not faire to this,
And how he slew with glauncing dart amisse
150   A gentle Hynd, the which the lovely boy
Did love as life, above all worldly blisse;
For griefe whereof the lad n'ould after° joy,   *would never afterward*
But pynd° away in anguish and selfe-wild° annoy.   *wasted/self-willed*

18

The wooddy Nymphes, faire Hamadryades°   *tree spirits*
155   Her to behold do thither runne apace,
And all the troupe of light-foot Naiades,°   *water nymphs*
Flocke all about to see her lovely face:
But° when they vewed have her heavenly grace,   *except for*
They envie her in their malitious mind,
160   And fly away for feare of fowle disgrace:
But all the Satyres scorne their woody kind,
And henceforth nothing faire, but her on earth they find.

19

Glad of such lucke, the luckelesse lucky maid,
Did her content to please their feeble eyes,
165   And long time with that salvage people staid,
To gather breath in many miseries.
During which time her gentle wit she plyes,°   *employs*
To teach them truth, which worshipt her in vaine,
And made her th'Image of Idolatryes;
170   But when their bootlesse° zeale she did restraine   *misguided*
From her own worship, they her Asse would worship fayn.°   *gladly*

20

It fortuned° a noble warlike knight   *happened*
By just occasion to that forrest came,
To seeke his kindred, and the lignage right,°   *proper lineage*
175   From whence he tooke his well deserved name:
He had in armes abroad wonne muchell° fame,   *much*
And fild far landes with glorie of his might,
Plaine, faithfull, true, and enimy of shame,
And ever lou'd to fight for Ladies right,
180   But in vaine glorious frayes° he litle did delight.   *battles*

21

A Satyres sonne yborne in forrest wyld,
By straunge adventure as it did betyde,°   *happen*

---

9. Cyparisse was a boy whom Sylvanus loved. Here Spenser recounts how Sylvanus accidentally killed Cyparisse's doe, after which the boy became so sad that Apollo turned him into a cypress to relieve his distress.

And there begotten of a Lady myld,
Faire Thyamis the daughter of Labryde,[1]
185 That was in sacred bands of wedlocke tyde
To Therion, a loose unruly swayne;°   *fellow*
Who had more joy to raunge the forrest wyde,
And chase the salvage beast with busie payne,°   *painstakingly*
Then° serve his Ladies love, and wast in pleasures vayne.   *than*

22

190 The forlone mayd did with loves longing burne,
And could not lacke° her lovers company,   *do without*
But to the wood she goes, to serve her turne,°   *satisfy her desire*
And seeke her spouse, that from her still° does fly,   *always*
And followes other game and venery:
195 A Satyre chaunst her wandring for to find,
And kindling coles of lust in brutish eye,
The loyall links of wedlocke did unbind,
And made her person thrall° unto his beastly kind.   *prisoner*

23

So long in secret cabin there he held
200 Her captive to his sensuall desire,
Till that with timely fruit her belly sweld,
And bore a boy unto that salvage sire:
Then home he suffred her for to retire,°   *return*
For ransome leaving him the late borne childe;
205 Whom till to ryper yeares he gan aspire,°   *began to grow*
He noursled up° in life and manners wilde,   *raised*
Emongst wild beasts and woods, from lawes of men exilde.

24

For all he taught the tender ymp,° was but   *child*
To banish cowardize and bastard feare;
210 His trembling hand he would him force to put
Upon the Lyon and the rugged Beare,
And from the she Beares teats her whelps° to teare;   *cubs*
And eke wyld roring Buls he would him make
To tame, and ryde their backes not made to beare;°   *be ridden*
215 And the Robuckes° in flight to overtake,   *bucks*
That every beast for feare of him did fly and quake.

25

Thereby so fearelesse, and so fell° he grew,   *deadly*
That his owne sire and maister of his guise°   *behavior*
Did often tremble at his horrid vew,
220 And oft for dread of hurt would him advise,
The angry beasts not rashly to despise,
Nor too much to provoke; for he would learne°   *teach*
The Lyon stoup° to him in lowly wise,   *to bow*
(A lesson hard) and make the Libbard° sterne   *leopard*
225 Leave roaring, when in rage he for revenge did earne.° *yearn*

---

1. The Greek names reveal the natures of these characters: Thyamis means "passion"; Labryde means "turbulence" or "greed"; and Therion means "wild beast."

26

And for to make his powre approved° more,   *apparent*
  Wyld beasts in yron yokes he would compell;°   *command*
  The spotted Panther, and the tusked Bore,
  The Pardale° swift, and the Tigre cruell;   *female leopard*
230 The Antelope, and Wolfe both fierce and fell;
  And them constraine in equall teme to draw.°   *harness together*
  Such joy he had, their stubborne harts to quell,°   *subdue*
And sturdie courage tame with dreadfull aw,
That his beheast° they feared, as a tyrans° law.   *command/tyrant's*

27

235 His loving mother came upon a day
  Unto the woods, to see her little sonne;
  And chaunst unwares to meet him in the way,
  After his sportes, and cruell pastime donne,
  When after him a Lyonesse did runne,
240 That roaring all with rage, did lowd requere°   *demand*
  Her children deare, whom he away had wonne:°   *taken*
  The Lyon whelpes she saw how he did beare,
And lull° in rugged° armes, withouten childish feare.   *cradle/hairy*

28

The fearefull Dame° all quaked at the sight,   *his mother*
245 And turning backe, gan fast to fly away,
  Untill with love revokt° from vaine affright,   *restrained*
  She hardly yet perswaded was to stay,
  And then to him these womanish words gan say;
  Ah Satyrane,[2] my dearling, and my joy,
250 For love of me leave off° this dreadfull play;   *stop*
  To dally thus with death, is no fit toy,°   *pastime*
Go find some other play-fellowes, mine own sweet boy.

29

In these and like delights of bloudy game
255 He trayned was, till ryper yeares he raught,°   *reached*
  And there abode,° whilst any beast of name°   *lived/known*
  Walkt in that forest, whom he had not taught
  To feare his force: and then his courage haught°   *haughty*
  Desird of forreine foemen to be knowne,
260 And far abroad for straunge° adventures sought: *foreign*
  In which his might was never overthrowne,
But through all Faery lond his famous worth was blown.°   *broadcast*

30

Yet evermore it was his manner faire,
  After long labours and adventures spent,
  Unto those native woods for to repaire,
265 To see his sire and ofspring auncient.
  And now he thither came for like intent;
  Where he unwares the fairest Una found,
  Straunge Lady, in so straunge habiliment,°   *surroundings*

2. Like a satyr.

Teaching the Satyres, which her sat around,
270   Trew sacred lore, which from her sweet lips did redound.

                              31

He wondred at her wisedome heavenly rare,
      Whose like in womens wit he never knew;
      And when her curteous deeds he did compare,
      Gan her admire, and her sad sorrowes rew,
275   Blaming of Fortune, which such troubles threw,
      And joyd to make proofe of° her° crueltie   test / Fortune's
      On gentle Dame, so hurtlesse, and so trew:
      Thenceforth he kept her goodly company,
And learnd her discipline of faith and veritie.

                              32

280   But she all vowd unto the Redcrosse knight,
      His wandring perill closely did lament,
      Ne in this new acquaintaunce could delight,
      But her deare heart with anguish did torment,
      And all her wit in secret counsels spent,
285   How to escape. At last in privie wise°   secretly
      To Satyrane she shewed her intent;
      Who glad to gain such favour, gan devise,
How with that pensive Maid he best might thence arise.°   depart

                              33

So on a day when Satyres all were gone,
290   To do their service to Sylvanus old,
      The gentle virgin left behind alone
      He led away with courage stout and bold.
      Too late it was, to Satyres to be told,
      Or ever hope recover her againe:
295   In vaine he seekes that having cannot hold.
      So fast he carried her with carefull paine,°   skill
That they the woods are past, and come now to the plaine.

                              34

The better part now of the lingring day,
      They traveild had, when as they farre espide
300   A wearie wight forwandring° by the way,   wandering
      And towards him they gan in hast to ride,
      To weet° of newes, that did abroad betide,°   learn / occur
      Or tydings of her knight of the Redcrosse.
      But he them spying, gan to turne aside,
305   For feare as seemd, or for some feigned losse;
More greedy they of newes, fast towards him do crosse.

                              35

A silly° man, in simple weedes forworne,°   simple / old clothes
      And soild with dust of the long dried way;
      His sandales were with toilesome travell torne,
310   And face all tand with scorching sunny ray,
      As he had traveild many a sommers day,
      Through boyling sands of Arabie and Ynde;°   India
      And in his hand a Iacobs staffe,° to stay   pilgrim's staff

His wearie limbes upon: and eke behind,
315   His scrip° did hang, in which his needments he did bind.   *bag*

36

The knight approching nigh, of him inquerd°   *asked*
    Tydings of warre, and of adventures new;
    But warres, nor new adventures none he herd.
    Then Una gan to aske, if ought he knew,
320   Or heard abroad of that her champion trew,
    That in his armour bare a croslet° red.   *small cross*
    Aye me, Deare dame (quoth he) well may I rew
    To tell the sad sight, which mine eies have red:°   *seen*
These eyes did see that knight both living and eke ded.

37

325   That cruell word her tender hart so thrild,°   *pierced*
    That suddein cold did runne through every vaine,
    And stony horrour all her sences fild
    With dying fit,° that downe she fell for paine.   *deathlike swoon*
    The knight her lightly° reared° up againe,   *quickly/lifted*
330   And comforted with curteous kind reliefe:
    Then wonne° from death,[3] she bad° him tellen plaine   *brought back/ordered*
    The further processe of her hidden griefe;
The lesser pangs can beare, who hath endur'd the chiefe.°   *greater*

38

Then gan the Pilgrim thus, I chaunst this day,
335   This fatall day, that shall I ever rew,
    To see two knights in travell° on my way   *traveling*
    (A sory sight) arraung'd° in battell new,[4]   *engaged*
    Both breathing vengeaunce, both of wrathfull hew:
    My fearefull flesh did tremble at their strife,
340   To see their blades so greedily imbrew,°   *stain themselves*
    That drunke with bloud, yet thristed after life:
What more? the Redcrosse knight was slaine with Paynim knife.

39

Ah dearest Lord (quoth she) how might that bee,
    And he the stoutest° knight, that ever wonne?   *sturdiest*
345   Ah dearest dame (quoth he) how might° I see   *could*
    The thing, that might not be, and yet was donne?
    Where is (said Satyrane) that Paynims sonne,
    That him of life, and us of joy hath reft?°   *deprived*
    Not far away (quoth he) he hence doth wonne°   *stay*
350   Foreby° a fountaine, where I late him left   *nearly*
Washing his bloudy wounds, that through° the steele were cleft.°   *by/cut*

40

Therewith the knight thence marched forth in hast,
    Whiles Una with huge heavinesse opprest,°   *overcome*

---

3. Recovered from her swoon, Una asks the old man to continue telling her the details of the tale as yet unknown to her that will cause her further grief.

4. The old man (who is, in fact, Archimago) is telling the story of Archimago's battle with Sans-Loy; however, he fabricates a second round of the battle here.

Could not for sorrow follow him so fast;
355 And soone he came, as he the place had ghest,°   *guessed*
Whereas° that Pagan proud him selfe did rest,   *where*
In secret shadow by a fountaine side:
Even he it was, that earst° would have supprest   *previously*
Faire Una: whom when Satyrane espide,
360 With fowle reprochfull words he boldly him defide.°   *challenged*

                        41
And said, Arise thou cursed Miscreaunt,°   *heathen*
That hast with knightlesse guile and trecherous train°   *tricks*
Faire knighthood fowly shamed, and doest vaunt°   *boast*
That good knight of the Redcrosse to have slain:
365 Arise, and with like treason° now maintain°   *treachery/defend*
Thy guilty wrong, or else thee guilty yield.°   *admit*
The Sarazin this hearing, rose amain,°   *at once*
And catching up in hast his three square° shield,   *triangular*
And shining helmet, soone him buckled° to the field.   *prepared*

                        42
370 And drawing nigh him said, Ah misborne Elfe,
In evill houre thy foes thee hither sent,
Anothers wrongs to wreake upon° thy selfe: *bring down*
Yet ill° thou blamest me, for having blent°   *wrongly/defiled*
My name with guile and traiterous intent;
375 That Redcrosse knight, perdie,° I never slew,   *by God*
But had he beene, where earst° his armes were lent,°   *previously/borrowed*
Th'enchaunter vaine his errour should not rew:
But thou his errour shalt, I hope now proven trew.[5]

                        43
Therewith they gan, both furious and fell,
380 To thunder blowes, and fiersly to assaile
Each other bent° his enimy to quell,°   *intending/subdue*
That with their force they perst both plate and maile,°   *types of armor*
And made wide furrowes in their fleshes fraile,
That it would pitty° any living eie.   *inspire pity in*
385 Large floods of bloud adowne their sides did raile;°   *pour*
But floods of bloud could not them satisfie:
Both hungred after death: both chose to win, or die.

                        44
So long they fight, and fell revenge pursue,
That fainting each, themselves to breathen let,°   *to catch their breath*
390 And oft refreshed, battell oft renue:
As when two Bores with rancling malice met,
Their gory° sides fresh bleeding fiercely fret,°   *gored/wound*
Til breathlesse both them selves aside retire,
Where foming wrath, their cruell tuskes they whet,°   *sharpen*
395 And trample th'earth, the whiles they may respire;°   *so they can breathe*
Then backe to fight againe, new breathed and entire.°   *refreshed*

5. Sans-Loy refers to the action in 3.33–39. He denies killing the Redcrosse Knight, but he also states that had the Redcrosse
Knight, and not Archimago, been wearing his own armor, then Sans-Loy would have killed him, and Archimago would not
have to regret his, Sans-Loy's, error. But Sans-Loy will make good this error by engaging in judicial combat with Satyrane.

45

So fiersly, when these knights had breathed° once,   *rested*
  They gan to fight returne, increasing more
  Their puissant° force, and cruell rage attonce,°   *powerful/at once*
  With heaped° strokes more hugely, then before,   *increased*
  That with their drerie° wounds and bloudy gore   *bloody*
  They both deformed,° scarsely could be known.   *disfigured*
  By this sad Una fraught° with anguish sore,   *afflicted*
  Led with their noise, which through the aire was thrown,
Arriv'd, where they in erth° their fruitles° bloud had sown.   *on the ground/futile*

46

Whom all so soone as that proud Sarazin
  Espide, he gan revive the memory
  Of his lewd lusts, and late attempted sin,
  And left the doubtfull° battell hastily,   *undecided*
  To catch her, newly offred to his eie:
  But Satyrane with strokes him turning, staid,
  And sternely bad him other businesse plie,°   *attend*
  Then hunt the steps of pure unspotted Maid:
Wherewith he° all enrag'd, these bitter speaches said.   *Sans-Loy*

47

O foolish faeries sonne, what furie mad
  Hath thee incenst,° to hast thy dolefull fate?   *enraged*
  Were it not better, I that Lady had,
  Then that thou hadst repented° it too late?   *regretted*
  Most sencelesse man he, that himselfe doth hate,
  To love another. Lo then for thine ayd
  Here take thy lovers token on thy pate.°   *head*
  So they to fight; the whiles the royall Mayd
Fled farre away, of that proud Paynim sore afrayd.

48

But that false Pilgrim, which that leasing° told,   *lie*
  Being in deed old Archimage, did stay
  In secret shadow, all this to behold,
  And much rejoyced in their bloudy fray:
  But when he saw the Damsell passe away
  He left his stond,° and her pursewd apace,°   *place/awhile*
  In hope to bring her to her last decay.°   *death*
  But for to tell her lamentable cace,°   *situation*
And eke this battels end, will need another place.

Canto 7

The Redcrosse knight is captive made
By Gyaunt proud opprest,
Prince Arthur meets with Una greatly
with those newes distrest.

1

What man so wise, what earthly wit so ware,°   *alert*
  As to descry° the crafty cunning traine,°   *perceive/guile*
  By which deceipt doth maske in visour° faire,   *mask*

And cast her colours dyed deepe in graine,
5   To seeme like Truth, whose shape she well can faine,
And fitting gestures to her purpose frame,°   suit
The guiltlesse man with guile to entertaine?
Great maistresse of her art was that false Dame,
The false Duessa, cloked with Fidessaes name.[1]

2

10 Who when returning from the drery Night,
She fownd not in that perilous house of Pryde,
Where she had left, the noble Redcrosse knight,
Her hoped pray,° she would no lenger bide,°   victim/stay
But forth she went, to seeke him far and wide.
15   Ere long she fownd, whereas he wearie sate,
To rest him selfe, foreby a fountaine side,
Disarmed all of yron-coted Plate,°   armor
And by his side his steed the grassy forage ate.

3

He feedes upon the cooling shade, and bayes°   bathes
20   His sweatie forehead in the breathing wind,
Which through the trembling leaves full gently playes
Wherein the cherefull birds of sundry kind
Do chaunt sweet musick, to delight his mind:
The Witch approching gan him fairely greet,
25   And with reproch of carelesnesse unkind
Upbrayd,° for leaving her in place unmeet,   accused
With fowle words tempring faire, soure gall° with hony sweet.   anger

4

Unkindnesse past, they gan of solace treat,°   speak of pleasure
And bathe in pleasaunce of the joyous shade,
30   Which shielded them against the boyling heat,
And with greene boughes decking a gloomy glade,
About the fountaine like a girlond made;
Whose bubbling wave did ever freshly well,
Ne ever would through fervent sommer fade:°   dry up
35   The sacred Nymph, which therein wont to dwell,
Was out of Dianes favour, as it then befell.°   so happened

5

The cause was this: one day when Phoebe[2] fayre
With all her band was following the chace,
This Nymph, quite tyr'd with heat of scorching ayre
40   Sat downe to rest in middest of the race:
The goddesse wroth gan fowly her disgrace,
And bad the waters, which from her did flow,
Be such as she her selfe was then in place.
Thenceforth her waters waxed dull and slow,
45   And all that drunke thereof, did faint and feeble grow.[3]

---

1. Duessa (duplicity) falsely bears the name Fidessa (fidelity).
2. An aspect or persona of Diana. As Diana, she is goddess of the hunt, but as Phoebe she is also goddess of the moon.
3. The nymph is transformed into a fountain whose waters cause fatigue rather than rejuvenation; paradoxically, this is a fountain that is never dry.

6

Hereof° this gentle knight unweeting was,   *of this*
    And lying downe upon the sandie graile,°   *gravel*
    Drunke of the streame, as cleare as cristall glas;
    Eftsoones his manly forces gan to faile,
50   And mightie strong was turnd to feeble fraile.
    His chaunged powres at first them selves not felt,
    Till crudled° cold his corage° gan assaile,   *congealing/vital powers*
    And chearefull bloud in faintnesse chill did melt,
Which like a fever fit[4] through all his body swelt.°   *raged*

7

55 Yet goodly court° he made still to his Dame,   *advances*
    Pourd out in loosnesse° on the grassy grownd,   *licentiousness*
    Both carelesse of his health, and of his fame:
    Till at the last he heard a dreadfull sownd,
    Which through the wood loud bellowing, did rebownd,
60   That all the earth for terrour seemd to shake,
    And trees did tremble. Th'Elfe therewith astownd,
    Upstarted lightly from his looser make,°   *mate*
And his unready weapons gan in hand to take.

8

But ere he could his armour on him dight,°   *put*
65   Or get his shield, his monstrous enimy
    With sturdie steps came stalking in his sight,
    An hideous Geant horrible and hye,°   *tall*
    That with his talnesse seemd to threat the skye,
    The ground eke groned under him for dreed;
70   His living like saw never living eye,
    Ne durst° behold:[5] his stature did exceed   *nor dared*
The hight of three the tallest sonnes of mortall seed.°   *men*

9

The greatest Earth his uncouth° mother was,   *unnatural*
    And blustring Aeolus° his boasted sire,   *god of the winds*
75   Who with his breath, which through the world doth pas,
    Her hollow womb did secretly inspire,°   *impregnate*
    And fild her hidden caues with stormie yre,
    That she conceiv'd; and trebling° the dew time,   *tripling*
    In which the wombes of women do expire,°   *give birth*
80   Brought forth this monstrous masse of earthly slime,
Puft up with emptie wind, and fild with sinfull crime.

10

So growen great through arrogant delight
    Of th'high descent, whereof he was yborne,
    And through presumption of his matchlesse might,
85   All other powres and knighthood he did scorne.[6]

---

4. Heat is usually associated with strength, but here, the weakening effect of the fountain, associated with coldness, turns its forces against the Knight's strength, causing him to suffer both chill and fever.
5. I.e., no living person had ever seen anything like the giant nor would even have dared to look at such a creature.
6. I.e., the giant's ancestry has caused him to grow both extremely tall and extremely proud.

Such now he marcheth to this man forlorne,
And left to losse: his stalking steps are stayde°   *supported*
Upon a snaggy Oke, which he had torne
Out of his mothers bowelles, and it made
90   His mortall° mace,° wherewith his foemen he dismayde.   *deadly/club*

11

That when the knight he spide, he gan advance
With huge force and insupportable° mayne,°   *irresistible/force*
And towardes him with dreadfull fury praunce;
Who haplesse, and eke hopelesse, all in vaine
95   Did to him pace, sad battaile to darrayne,°   *engage*
Disarmd, disgrast, and inwardly dismayde,
And eke so faint in every joynt and vaine,
Through that fraile fountaine, which him feeble made,
That scarsely could he weeld° his bootlesse° single blade.   *raise/useless*

12

100   The Geaunt strooke so maynly° mercilesse,   *forcefully*
That could have overthrowne a stony towre,
And were not heavenly grace, that him did blesse,°   *preserve*
He had beene pouldred° all, as thin as flowre:°   *pulverized/flour*
But he was wary of that deadly stowre,°   *attack*
105   And lightly lept from underneath the blow:
Yet so exceeding was the villeins powre,
That with the wind it did him overthrow,
And all his sences stound,° that still he lay full low.   *stunned*

13

As when that divelish yron Engin° wrought   *the cannon*
110   In deepest Hell, and framd by Furies skill,[7]
With windy Nitre and quick Sulphur fraught,
And ramd with bullet round, ordaind to kill,
Conceiveth° fire, the heavens it doth fill   *catches*
With thundring noyse, and all the ayre doth choke,
115   That none can breath, nor see, nor heare at will,
Through smouldry cloud of duskish° stincking smoke,   *dusky*
That th'onely breath him daunts, who hath escapt the stroke.[8]

14

So daunted when the Geaunt saw the knight,[9]
His heavie hand he heaved up on hye,
120   And him to dust thought to have battred quight,
Untill Duessa loud to him gan crye;
O great Orgoglio,[1] greatest under skye,
O hold° thy mortall hand for Ladies sake,   *stop*
Hold for my sake, and do him not to dye,

---

7. According to Renaissance tradition, the cannon was
invented by the devil in hell. "Nitre" (potassium nitrate)
and sulfur are the main ingredients of gunpowder; they
are "windy" because they produce the blast that propels
the cannonball through the air.
8. I.e., those who are not struck by the cannonball are
overcome by the smoke.
9. I.e., when the Giant saw that the Knight was overcome
by the smoke, he raised his heavy hand to beat him down
completely.
1. Pride, haughtiness, disdain (Italian).

125   But vanquisht thine eternall bondslave make,
             And me thy worthy meed unto° thy Leman° take.   *as/beloved*

                              15
             He hearkned, and did stay from further harmes,
             To gayne so goodly guerdon,° as she spake: *prize*
             So willingly she came into his armes,
130   Who her as willingly to grace did take,
             And was possessed of his new found make.
             Then up he tooke the slombred sencelesse corse,
             And ere he could out of his swowne° awake,   *swoon*
             Him to his castle brought with hastie forse,
135   And in a Dongeon deepe him threw without remorse.

                              16
             From that day forth Duessa was his deare,
             And highly honourd in his haughtie° eye,   *proud*
             He gave her gold and purple pall° to weare,   *robe*
             And triple crowne set on her head full hye,
140   And her endowd with royall majestye:
             Then for to make her dreaded more of men,
             And peoples harts with awfull terrour tye,°   *enthrall*
             A monstrous beast ybred° in filthy fen°   *born/swamp*
      He chose, which he had kept long time in darksome den.

                              17
145   Such one it was, as that renowmed° Snake   *famous*
             Which great Alcides in Stremona slew,[2]
             Long fostred in the filth of Lerna lake,
             Whose many heads out budding ever new,
             Did breed him endlesse labour to subdew:
150   But this same Monster much more ugly was;
             For seven great heads out of his body grew,
             An yron brest, and backe of scaly bras,
      And all embrewd° in bloud, his eyes did shine as glas.   *stained*

                              18
             His tayle was stretched out in wondrous length,
155   That to the house of heavenly gods it raught,°   *reached*
             And with extorted° powre, and borrow'd strength,   *wrongfully obtained*
             The ever-burning lamps from thence it brought,
             And prowdly threw to ground, as things of nought;°   *worthless*
             And underneath his filthy feet did tread
160   The sacred things, and holy heasts foretaught.°   *previously taught*
             Upon this dreadfull Beast with sevenfold head
             He set the false Duessa, for more aw and dread.[3]

---

2. The "snake" Spenser is referring to is the hydra, a creature from Greek mythology with a hundred heads, that
lived in the lake of Lerna and was killed by Hercules
(Alcides) as one of his 12 labors. The hydra was particularly difficult for Hercules to kill because each time he cut
off one of its heads, several new ones grew in its place.
Hercules eventually burnt the hydra's neck after each
decapitation, thus preventing new heads from sprouting
up. Stremona is a river in Thrace.

3. Spenser compares the hydra with the Roman Catholic
Church. The seven heads of this monster refer to the sev-
en hills on which Rome was built, as well as the seven
deadly sins. Orgoglo mounts Duessa upon the seven-
headed monster to make her more dreaded and awe-
inspiring. This gesture also associates Duessa with the
corrupt Roman Catholic Church, which, represented by
the monster, has gained its power through tyranny and
defiles true Christian doctrine.

19

The wofull Dwarfe, which saw his maisters fall,
  Whiles he had keeping of his grasing steed,
165 And valiant knight become a caytive thrall,
  When all was past, tooke up his forlorne weed,°   *abandoned armor*
  His mightie armour, missing most at need;
  His silver shield, now idle maisterlesse;
  His poynant° speare, that many made to bleed,   *sharp*
170 The ruefull moniments of heavinesse,°   *tokens of grief*
And with them all departes, to tell his great distresse.

20

He had not travaild° long, when on the way   *traveled*
  He wofull Ladie, wofull Una met,
  Fast flying from the Paynims greedy pray,[4]
175 Whilest Satyrane him from pursuit did let:°   *hinder*
  Who when her eyes she on the Dwarfe had set,
  And saw the signes, that deadly tydings spake,
  She fell to ground for sorrowfull regret,
  And lively breath° her sad brest did forsake,   *breath of life*
180 Yet might her pitteous hart be seene to pant and quake.

21

The messenger of so unhappie newes
  Would faine° have dyde: dead was his hart within,   *rather*
  Yet outwardly some little comfort shewes:
  At last recovering hart, he does begin
185 To rub her temples, and to chaufe° her chin,   *rub*
  And every tender part does tosse and turne:
  So hardly° he the flitted life does win,   *with difficulty*
  Unto her native prison to retourne:[5]
Then gins° her grieved ghost thus to lament and mourne.   *begins*

22

190 Ye dreary instruments of dolefull° sight,[6]   *sorrowful*
  That doe this deadly spectacle behold,
  Why do ye lenger° feed on loathed light,   *longer*
  Or liking find to gaze on earthly mould,°   *shapes*
  Sith cruell fates[7] the carefull threeds° unfould,   *threads*
195 The which my life and love together tyde?
  Now let the stony dart of senselesse cold
  Perce to my hart, and pas through every side,
And let eternall night so sad sight fro° me hide.   *from*

23

O lightsome day, the lampe of highest Jove,
200 First made by him, mens wandring wayes to guyde,
  When darknesse he in deepest dongeon drove,
  Henceforth thy hated face for ever hyde,

---

4. I.e., Una is flying from Sans-Loy, who greedily has made her his prey or victim (see 6.42–47). The Dwarf meets Una at this point, while Satyrane is distracting Sans-Loy from his pursuit of her.
5. The native prison of Una's spirit is her body.

6. Here Una is addressing her eyes.
7. Mythical arbiters of human life, who measure out the life (or fate) of every individual in threads mounted on spinning wheels.

And shut up heavens windowes shyning wyde:
  For earthly sight can nought but sorrow breed,
205 And late repentance, which shall long abyde.°   *persist*
  Mine eyes no more on vanitie shall feed,
  But seeled up with death, shall have their deadly meed.°   *reward of death*

24

  Then downe againe she fell unto the ground;
    But he her quickly reared° up againe: *raised*
210 Thrise did she sinke adowne in deadly swownd,
    And thrise he her reviv'd with busie paine:
    At last when life recover'd had the raine,°   *rein, control*
    And over-wrestled his strong enemie,
    With foltring tong,° and trembling every vaine,   *faltering tongue*
215 Tell on (quoth she) the wofull Tragedie,
  The which these reliques sad present unto mine eie.

25

  Tempestuous fortune hath spent all her spight,
    And thrilling sorrow throwne his utmost dart;
    Thy sad tongue cannot tell more heavy plight,
220 Then that I feele, and harbour in mine hart:
    Who hath endur'd the whole, can beare each part.
    If death it be, it is not the first wound,[8]
    That launched° hath my brest with bleeding smart.°   *pierced/wound*
    Begin, and end the bitter balefull stound;°   *wretched situation*
225 If lesse, then° that I feare, more favour I have found.[9]   *than*

26

  Then gan the Dwarfe the whole discourse° declare,   *story*
    The subtill traines° of Archimago old;   *tricks*
    The wanton loves of false Fidessa faire,
    Bought with the bloud of vanquisht Paynim bold:
230 The wretched payre° transform'd to treen mould;°   *pair/tree shape*
    The house of Pride, and perils round about;
    The combat, which he with Sans-Joy did hould;
    The lucklesse conflict with the Gyant stout,°   *sturdy*
  Wherein captiv'd, of life or death he stood in doubt.

27

235 She heard with patience all unto the end,
    And strove to maister sorrowfull assay,°   *grief*
    Which greater grew, the more she did contend,°   *struggle*
    And almost rent her tender hart in tway;°   *two*
    And love fresh coles unto her fire did lay:
240 For greater love, the greater is the losse.
    Was never Ladie loved dearer day,
    Then she did love the knight of the Redcrosse;[1]
  For whose deare sake so many troubles her did tosse.°   *suffer*

---

8. I.e., if the Redcrosse Knight has met his death, this
would not be the first knight who died attempting to help
Una with her quest, and therefore this would not be the
first time that Una has felt the pain of learning of such a
death.

9. I.e., if what the Dwarf has to tell is less terrible than
Una fears, she will consider herself lucky.
1. I.e., there was never a lady who loved life itself more
than Una loved the Redcrosse Knight.

28

28

245

At last when fervent° sorrow slaked° was,   *burning/quenched*
   She up arose, resolving him to find
   A live or dead: and forward forth doth pas,°   *proceed*
   All as the Dwarfe the way to her assynd:°   *indicated*
   And evermore in constant carefull mind
   She fed her wound with fresh renewed bale;°   *bitterness*
   Long tost with stormes, and bet° with bitter wind,   *beat*
   High over hils, and low adowne the dale,°   *valley*
That she wandred many a wood, and measurd° many a vale.°   *crossed/valley*

29

250

At last she chaunced by good hap° to meet   *luck*
   A goodly knight, faire marching by the way
255
   Together with his Squire, arayed meet:°   *well-dressed*
   His glitterand armour shined farre away,
   Like glauncing° light of Phoebus brightest ray;   *dazzling*
   From top to toe no place appeared bare,
   That deadly dint° of steele endanger may: *stroke*
260
   Athwart° his brest a bauldrick brave° he ware,   *across/splendid belt*
That shynd, like twinkling stars, with stons most pretious rare.

30

And in the midst thereof one pretious stone
   Of wondrous worth, and eke of wondrous mights,°   *powers*
   Shapt like a Ladies head, exceeding shone,
265
   Like Hesperus[2] emongst the lesser lights,
   And strove for to amaze° the weaker sights;   *dazzle*
   Thereby his mortall° blade full comely hong   *deadly*
   In yvory sheath, ycarv'd with curious slights;°   *strange designs*
   Whose hilts were burnisht° gold, and handle strong   *polished*
270
Of mother pearle, and buckled with a golden tong.°   *pin*

31

His haughtie° helmet, horrid° all with gold,   *tall/encrusted*
   Both glorious brightnesse, and great terrour bred;
   For all the crest a Dragon did enfold
   With greedie pawes, and over all did spred
275
   His golden wings: his dreadfull hideous hed
   Close couched° on the bever,° seem'd to throw   *crouched/visor*
   From flaming mouth bright sparkles fierie red,
   That suddeine horror to faint° harts did show;   *weak*
And scaly tayle was stretcht adowne his backe full low.

32

280

Upon the top of all his loftie crest,
   A bunch of haires discolourd diversly,°   *of many colors*
   With sprincled pearle, and gold full richly drest,
   Did shake, and seem'd to daunce for jollity,
   Like to an Almond tree ymounted hye
285
   On top of greene Selinis[3] all alone,

---

2. The evening star, associated with Venus. The comparison of the stone on Arthur's breast to Venus suggests that love is central in his quest.
3. From *palmosa Selinis* ("palmy Selinis"), a town in Italy. Spenser suggests that the knight's helmet is topped with palms, signifying victory in battle. This helmet, decorated with a dragon, identifies the knight as Prince Arthur, whose father, Uther Pendragon, was so named because he carried a golden dragon to war with him. "Pendragon" literally means "dragon's head."

With blossomes brave bedecked° daintily;   *splendidly ornamented*
Whose tender locks do tremble every one
At every little breath, that under heaven is blowne.

33

His warlike shield all closely cover'd° was,   *hidden*
290   Ne might of mortall eye be ever seene;
Not made of steele, nor of enduring bras,
Such earthly mettals soone consumed bene:[4]
But all of Diamond perfect pure and cleene
It framed was, one massie entire mould,°   *solid piece*
295   Hewen° out of Adamant° rocke with engines keene,°   *cut / diamond / sharp*
That point of speare it never percen could,
Ne dint° of direfull° sword divide the substance would.   *stroke / dreadful*

34

The same to wight° he never wont disclose,[5]   *creature*
But when as monsters huge he would dismay,
300   Or daunt° unequall armies of his foes,   *vanquish*
Or when the flying heavens he would affray;°   *frighten*
For so exceeding shone his glistring ray,
That Phoebus golden face it did attaint,
As when a cloud his beames doth over-lay;
305   And silver Cynthia wexed pale and faint,
As when her face is staynd with magicke arts° constraint.   *witchcraft*

35

No magicke arts hereof had any might,
Nor bloudie wordes of bold Enchaunters call,
But all that was not such, as seemd in sight,
310   Before that shield did fade, and suddeine fall:[6]
And when him list the raskall routes appall,[7]
Men into stones therewith he could transmew,°   *transform*
And stones to dust, and dust to nought at all;
And when him list the prouder lookes subdew,
315   He would them gazing blind, or turne to other hew.[8]

36

Ne let it seeme, that credence this exceedes,[9]
For he that made the same, was knowne right well
To have done much more admirable deedes.
It Merlin[1] was, which whylome° did excell   *formerly*
320   All living wightes in might° of magicke spell: *power*
Both shield, and sword, and armour all he wrought
For this young Prince, when first to armes he fell;

---

4. I.e., steel or brass would soon have been destroyed or disintegrated. The diamond will last forever.
5. Arthur never shows his diamond to anyone except when he uses it to overcome his enemies, since it is too dazzling. In this respect, Arthur's diamond functions much like Una's face, whose truth and beauty are so brilliant that she wears a veil to cover it.
6. All that was false, i.e., that was not what it appeared to be, was vanquished in the presence of Arthur's shield.
7. When Arthur wished to subdue vulgar mobs, he would

turn them to stone.
8. When Arthur wished to subdue his more elevated opponents, he would blind them.
9. Let it not be thought that this is beyond belief.
1. A magician and prophet in the court of Arthur's father. He created the shield, sword, and armor worn by the young Prince Arthur. By commenting that Arthur's armor still exists in Faerie Land, Spenser suggests that Arthur's virtue lives on in England and may be discovered through faith.

But when he dyde, the Faerie Queene it brought
To Faerie lond, where yet it may be seene, if sought.

37

325 A gentle youth, his dearely loved Squire
His speare of heben wood° behind him bare,   *ebony*
Whose harmefull head,° thrice heated in the fire,   *point*
Had riven many a brest with pikehead° square;°   *spear tip/accurately*
A goodly person, and could menage° faire   *manage a horse*
330 His stubborne steed with curbed canon° bit,   *a kind of bit*
Who under him did trample as the aire,
And chauft,° that any on his backe should sit;   *annoyed*
The yron rowels° into frothy fome he bit.   *part of the bit*

38

When as this knight nigh to the Ladie drew,
335 With lovely court° he gan her entertaine;   *attention*
But when he heard her answeres loth,° he knew   *reluctant*
Some secret sorrow did her heart distraine:°   *afflict*
Which to allay,° and calme her storming paine,   *sooth*
Faire feeling words he wisely gan display,
340 And for her humour fitting purpose faine,[2]
To tempt the cause it selfe for to bewray;°   *reveal*
Wherewith emmou'd, these bleeding words she gan to say.

39

What worlds delight, or joy of living speach
Can heart, so plung'd in sea of sorrowes deepe,
345 And heaped with so huge misfortunes, reach?
The carefull cold beginneth for to creepe,
And in my heart his yron arrow steepe,°   *immerse*
Soone as I thinke upon my bitter bale:°   *sorrows*
Such helplesse harmes yts° better hidden keepe,   *it is*
350 Then rip up griefe, where it may not availe,°   *avail*
My last left comfort is, my woes to weepe and waile.

40

Ah Ladie deare, quoth then the gentle knight,
Well may I weene,° your griefe is wondrous great;   *know*
For wondrous great griefe groneth in my spright,
355 Whiles thus I heare you of your sorrowes treat.°   *tell*
But wofull Ladie let me you intrete,°   *entreat*
For to unfold the anguish of your hart:
Mishaps are maistred° by advice discrete,   *mastered*
And counsell° mittigates the greatest smart;   *advice*
360 Found never helpe, who never would his hurts impart.[3]

41

O but (quoth she) great griefe will not be tould,
And can more easily be thought, then said.
Right so; (quoth he) but he, that never would,
Could never: will to might gives greatest aid.[4]
365 But griefe (quoth she) does greater grow displaid,°   *when displayed*

2. Arthur chooses words more appropriate to Una's sadness.

3. He who never tells his woes will never find a remedy.

4. Desire to overcome adversity is the greatest help. Arthur is preventing Una from falling into a state of hopeless despair and helping her to reaffirm her faith.

If then it find not helpe, and breedes despaire.
 Despaire breedes not (quoth he) where faith is staid.°   *strong*
 No faith so fast° (quoth she) but flesh does paire.°   *firm/weaken*
Flesh may empaire° (quoth he) but reason can repaire.   *impair*

42

370 His goodly reason, and well guided speach
  So deepe did settle in her gratious thought,
  That her perswaded to disclose the breach,°   *wound*
  Which love and fortune in her heart had wrought,
  And said; Faire Sir, I hope good hap° hath brought   *luck*
375   You to inquire the secrets of my griefe,
  Or that your wisedome will direct my thought,
  Or that your prowesse° can me yield reliefe: *valor*
 Then heare the storie sad, which I shall tell you briefe.

43

 The forlorne Maiden, whom your eyes have seene
380   The laughing stocke of fortunes mockeries,
  Am th'only daughter of a King and Queene,
  Whose parents deare, whilest equall° destinies   *impartial*
  Did runne about,° and their felicities   *run their course*
  The favourable heavens did not envy,
385   Did spread their rule through all the territories,
  Which Phison and Euphrates floweth by,
 And Gehons golden waves doe wash continually.[5]

44

 Till that their cruell cursed enemy,
  An huge great Dragon[6] horrible in sight,
390   Bred in the loathly lakes of Tartary,°   *Hell*
  With murdrous ravine,° and devouring might   *violence*
  Their kingdome spoild, and countrey wasted quight:
  Themselves, for feare into his jawes to fall,
  He forst to castle strong to take their flight,
395   Where fast embard° in mightie brasen° wall,   *imprisoned/brass*
 He has them now foure yeres besiegd to make them thrall.

45

 Full many knights adventurous and stout
  Have enterprizd° that Monster to subdew;   *undertaken*
  From every coast that heaven walks about,
400   Have thither come the noble Martiall[7] crew,
  That famous hard atchievements still pursew,
  Yet never any could that girlond win,
  But all still shronke, and still he greater grew:
  All they for want of faith, or guilt of sin,
405 The pitteous pray of his fierce crueltie have bin.[8]

---

5. Una's parents are Adam and Eve, and the territory that they govern is Eden. The Phison, Euphrates, and Gehon are three of the four rivers surrounding Eden and were thought to water the entire world.
6. The dragon is Satan. After the Fall, Adam and Eve were exiled from Eden. The "four years" that Spenser refers to may figuratively represent the 4,000 years that, according to the Geneva Bible, passed between the Fall

and the birth of Christ.
7. This stanza refers to the many knights ("the noble Martiall crew") who have undertaken to assist Una in her quest to overcome the Dragon and rescue her parents.
8. Until now, the knights have all failed in their quest because they have lacked faith or have succumbed to sin and have thus become victims of the Dragon's cruelty.

46

At last yledd° with farre reported praise,   *led by*
   Which flying fame throughout the world had spred,
   Of doughtie° knights, whom Faery land did raise,   *worthy*
   That noble order hight of Maidenhed,°   *virginity*
410   Forthwith to court of Gloriane I sped,
   Of Gloriane great Queene of glory bright,
   Whose kingdomes seat Cleopolis⁹ is red,°   *named*
   There to obtaine some such redoubted° knight,   *formidable*
That Parents deare from tyrants powre deliver might.

47

415 It was my chance (my chance was faire and good)
   There for to find a fresh unproved° knight,   *untried in battle*
   Whose manly hands imbrew'd° in guiltie blood   *stained*
   Had never bene, ne ever by his might
   Had throwne to ground the unregarded right:¹
420   Yet of his prowesse° proofe he since hath made   *virtue*
   (I witnesse am) in many a cruell fight;
   The groning ghosts of many one dismaide°   *defeated*
Have felt the bitter dint of his avenging blade.

48

And ye² the forlorne reliques of his powre,
425   His byting sword, and his devouring speare,
   Which have endured many a dreadfull stowre,°   *conflict*
   Can speake his prowesse, that did earst° you beare,   *formerly*
   And well could rule: now he hath left you heare,
   To be the record of his ruefull losse,
430   And of my dolefull disaventurous° deare: *unfortunate*
   O heavie record of the good Redcrosse,
Where have you left your Lord, that could so well you tosse?°   *brandish*

49

Well hoped I, and faire beginnings had,
   That he my captive langour³ should redeeme,
435   Till all unweeting,° an Enchaunter bad   *unknown to the knight*
   His sence abusd,° and made him to misdeeme°   *distorted/misjudge*
   My loyalty, not such as it did seeme;⁴
   That rather death desire, then° such despight.°   *than/outrage*
   Be judge ye heavens, that all things right esteeme,
440   How I him lov'd, and love with all my might,
So thought I eke of him, and thinke I thought aright.

50

Thenceforth me desolate he quite forsooke,
   To wander, where wilde fortune would me lead,
   And other bywaies he himselfe betooke,
445   Where never foot of living wight did tread,

---

9. The city of fame or glory where the Faerie Queene lives. The knights of her court belong to the order of the "Maidenhed," or virginity, an order that reflects the Faerie Queene's own virtue as well as that of Queen Elizabeth I, who was known as the "virgin queen."
1. The right for which he had no regard or respect; on the contrary, the Redcrosse Knight promotes and pro-tects the right.
2. Here Una is addressing the Redcrosse Knight's armor.
3. Una is referring to her parents' languishment in captiv-ity but also the symbolic captivity of humankind whom the Redcrosse Knight, as a figure of Christ, will redeem.
4. The Redcrosse Knight misjudged Una's loyalty, think-ing that it was not what it appeared to be.

That brought not backe the balefull° body dead;   *wretched*
In which him chaunced false Duessa meete,
Mine onely foe, mine onely deadly dread,
Who with her witchcraft and misseeming sweete,
450   Inveigled° him to follow her desires unmeete.°   *tricked/unsuitable*

51

At last by subtill sleights° she him betraid   *tricks*
Unto his foe, a Gyant huge and tall,
Who him disarmed, dissolute,° dismaid,°   *weakened/vanquished*
Unwares surprised, and with mightie mall°   *weapon*
455   The monster mercilesse him made to fall,
Whose fall did never foe before behold;⁵
And now in darkesome dungeon, wretched thrall,
Remedilesse,° for aie° he doth him hold;   *helpless/ever*
This is my cause of griefe, more great, then° may be told.   *than*

52

460   Ere she had ended all, she gan° to faint: *began*
But he her comforted and faire bespake,
Certes,° Madame, ye have great cause of plaint,   *certainly*
That stoutest heart, I weene,° could cause to quake.   *believe*
But be of cheare, and comfort to you take:
465   For till I have acquit° your captive knight,   *avenged*
Assure your selfe, I will you not forsake.
His chearefull words reviv'd her chearelesse spright,
So forth they went, the Dwarfe them guiding ever right.

Canto 8

Faire virgin to reedeme her deare
brings Arthur to the fight:
Who slayes the Gyant, wounds the beast,
and strips Duessa quight.

1

Ay me, how many perils doe enfold
The righteous man, to make him daily fall?
Were not,° that heavenly grace doth him uphold,¹   *were it not*
And stedfast truth acquite° him out of all.   *absolve*
5   Her love is firme, her care continuall,
So oft as he through his owne foolish pride,
Or weaknesse is to sinfull bands made thrall:
Else° should this Redcrosse knight in bands have dyde,   *otherwise*
For whose deliverance she this Prince doth thither guide.

2

10   They sadly traveild thus, untill they came
Nigh to a castle builded strong and hie:
Then cryde the Dwarfe, lo yonder is the same,
In which my Lord my liege° doth lucklesse lie,   *master*
Thrall to that Gyants hatefull tyrannie:

---

5. The Redcrosse Knight had never yet been defeated in battle.
1. In this stanza, Una is overtly equated with heavenly grace. The Redcrosse Knight originally undertook the quest to help Una redeem her parents, but in this canto it is she who delivers the Redcrosse Knight from captivity.

15   Therefore, deare Sir, your mightie powres assay.°   *prove*
         The noble knight alighted by and by
         From loftie steede, and bad the Ladie stay,
To see what end of fight should him befall that day.

              3

So with the Squire, th'admirer of his might,
20   He marched forth towards that castle wall;
         Whose gates he found fast shut, ne living wight
         To ward° the same, nor answere commers° call.   *guard/visitor's*
         Then tooke that Squire an horne of bugle small,
         Which hong adowne his side in twisted gold,
25   And tassels gay. Wyde wonders over all
         Of that same hornes great vertues weren told,[2]
Which had approved bene in uses manifold.°   *many*

              4

Was never wight, that heard that shrilling sound,
         But trembling feare did feele in every vaine;
30   Three miles it might be easie heard around,
         And Ecchoes three answerd it selfe againe:
         No false enchauntment, nor deceiptfull traine°   *deception*
         Might once abide° the terror of that blast,   *tolerate*
         But presently was voide and wholly vaine:°   *ineffectual*
35   No gate so strong, no locke so firme and fast,
But with that percing noise flew open quite, or brast.°   *burst*

              5

The same before the Geants gate he blew,
         That all the castle quaked from the ground,
         And every dore of freewill° open flew.   *itself*
40   The Gyant selfe dismaied with that sownd,
         Where he with his Duessa dalliance fownd,[3]
         In hast came rushing forth from inner bowre,°   *chamber*
         With staring° countenance sterne, as one astownd,°   *glaring/confused*
         And staggering steps, to weet, what suddein stowre°   *uproar*
45   Had wrought that horror strange, and dar'd° his dreaded powre. *defied*

              6

And after him the proud Duessa came,
         High mounted on her manyheaded beast,
         And every head with fyrie tongue did flame,
         And every head was crowned on his creast,[4]
50   And bloudie mouthed with late cruell feast.
         That when the knight beheld, his mightie shild
         Upon his manly arme he soone addrest,°   *made ready*
         And at him fiercely flew, with courage fild,
And eger greedinesse through every member thrild.

              7

55   Therewith the Gyant buckled° him to fight,   *engaged*
         Inflam'd with scornefull wrath and high disdaine,
         And lifting up his dreadfull club on hight,

---

2. Wonderful stories of the horn's powers were told everywhere.
3. The sound of the horn reached the chamber where the Giant and Duessa were engaged in lovemaking.
4. Each head of Duessa's many-headed beast had a crown on it.

All arm'd° with ragged snubbes° and knottie graine,   *covered/roots*
Him thought at first encounter to have slaine.
60 But wise and warie was that noble Pere,
And lightly leaping from so monstrous maine,°   *force*
Did faire° avoide the violence him nere;   *easily*
It booted nought,° to thinke, such thunderbolts to beare.   *it was useless*

8

Ne shame° he thought to shunne so hideous might: *not shameful*
65 The idle stroke, enforcing furious way,
Missing the marke of his misaymed sight
Did fall to ground, and with his heavie sway°   *force*
So deeply dinted° in the driven° clay,   *struck/packed*
That three yardes deepe a furrow up did throw:
70 The sad earth wounded with so sore assay,°   *attack*
Did grone full grievous underneath the blow,
And trembling with strange feare, did like an earthquake show.

9

As when almightie Jove in wrathfull mood,
To wreake the guilt of mortall sins is bent,°   *determined*
75 Hurles forth his thundring dart with deadly food,°   *hatred*
Enrold° in flames, and smouldring dreriment,   *engulfed*
Through riven cloudes and molten firmament;°   *sky*
The fierce threeforked engin° making way,   *the thunderbolt*
Both loftie towres and highest trees hath rent,
80 And all that might his angrie passage stay,°   *hinder*
And shooting in the earth, casts up a mount° of clay.   *mountain*

10

His boystrous° club, so buried in the ground,   *enormous*
He could not rearen° up againe so light,°   *raise/easily*
But° that the knight him at avantage found,   *so*
85 And whiles he strove his combred° clubbe to quight°   *encumbered/free*
Out of the earth, with blade all burning bright
He smote° off his left arme, which like a blocke   *struck*
Did fall to ground, depriv'd of native might;
Large streames of bloud out of the truncked stocke°   *truncated stump*
90 Forth gushed, like fresh water streame from riven rocke.

11

Dismaied with so desperate deadly wound,
And eke impatient of unwonted paine,
He loudly brayd with beastly yelling sound,
That all the fields rebellowed° againe;   *echoed his bellows*
95 As great a noyse, as when in Cymbrian plaine⁵
An heard of Bulles, whom kindly rage doth sting,
Do for the milkie mothers want° complaine,   *absence*
And fill the fields with troublous bellowing,
The neighbour woods around with hollow murmur ring.

12

100 That when his deare Duessa heard, and saw
The evill stownd°, that daungerd her estate,°   *peril/situation*
Unto his aide she hastily did draw

5. The Cimbri were a savage tribe that invaded Europe in the first century B.C.

Her dreadfull beast, who swolne with bloud of late
Came ramping° forth with proud presumpteous gate,   *bounding*
105   And threatned all his heads like flaming brands.
But him the Squire made quickly to retrate,°   *retreat*
Encountring fierce with single sword in hand,
And twixt° him and his Lord did like a bulwarke° stand.   *between / barrier*

13

The proud Duessa full of wrathfull spight,
110   And fierce disdaine, to be affronted so,
Enforst° her purple beast with all her might   *spurred on*
That stop° out of the way to overthroe,   *obstacle*
Scorning the let° of so unequall° foe: *hindrance / inferior*
But nathemore° would that courageous swayne°   *not at all / fellow*
115   To her yeeld passage, gainst his Lord to goe,
But with outrageous strokes did him restraine,
And with his bodie bard° the way atwixt them twaine.°   *barred / between*

14

Then tooke the angrie witch her golden cup,
Which still she bore, replete° with magick artes;   *filled*
120   Death and despeyre did many thereof sup,°   *drink*
And secret poyson through their inner parts,
Th'eternall bale° of heavie wounded harts;   *destruction*
Which after charmes and some enchauntments said,
She lightly sprinkled on his weaker parts;
125   Therewith his sturdie courage soone was quayd,°   *quelled*
And all his senses were with suddeine dread dismayd.°   *overcome*

15

So downe he fell before the cruell beast,
Who on his necke his bloudie clawes did seize,
That life nigh crusht out of his panting brest:
130   No powre he had to stirre, nor will to rize.
That when the carefull knight gan well avise,°   *notice*
He lightly left the foe, with whom he fought,
And to the beast gan turne his enterprise;°   *attack*
For wondrous anguish in his hart it wrought,
135   To see his loved Squire into such thraldome brought.

16

And high advauncing° his bloud-thirstie blade,   *lifting up*
Stroke one of those deformed heads so sore,
That of his puissance° proud ensample made;   *strength*
His monstrous scalpe downe to his teeth it tore,
140   And that misformed shape mis-shaped more:
A sea of bloud gusht from the gaping wound,
That her gay garments staynd with filthy gore,
And overflowed all the field around;
That over shoes in bloud he waded on the ground.[6]

17

145   Thereat he roared for exceeding paine,
That to have heard, great horror would have bred,[7]

---

6. The pool of blood is so deep that it reaches over Arthur's shoes.

7. The beast roars so loudly from the pain that anyone who heard it would have been struck with horror.

And scourging° th'emptie ayre with his long traine,°   *tearing / tail*
Through great impatience of his grieved hed
His gorgeous ryder from her loftie sted°   *place*
150   Would have cast downe, and trod in durtie myre,
Had not the Gyant soone her succoured;°   *rescued*
Who all enrag'd with smart° and franticke yre,   *pain*
Came hurtling in full fierce, and forst the knight retyre.°   *to back off*

                                18
The force, which wont° in two to be disperst,   *usually*
155   In one alone left hand he now unites,[8]
Which is through rage more strong then both were erst;°   *before*
With which his hideous club aloft he dites,°   *raises*
And at his foe with furious rigour° smites,   *violence*
That strongest Oake might seeme to ouerthrow:
160   The stroke upon his shield so heavie lites,°   *falls*
That to the ground it doubleth° him full low: *collapse*
What mortall wight could ever beare so monstrous blow?

                                19
And in his fall his shield, that covered was,
Did loose his vele° by chaunce, and open flew: *its covering*
165   The light whereof, that heavens light did pas,°   *surpass*
Such blazing brightnesse through the aier threw,
That eye mote° not the same endure to vew.   *could*
Which when the Gyaunt spyde with staring eye,
He downe let fall his arme, and soft withdrew
170   His weapon huge, that heaved° was on hye   *raised*
For to have slaine the man, that on the ground did lye.

                                20
And eke the fruitfull-headed° beast, amaz'd   *many-headed*
At flashing beames of that sunshiny shield,
Became starke blind, and all his senses daz'd,
175   That downe he tumbled on the durtie field,
And seem'd himselfe as conquered to yield.[9]
Whom when his maistresse proud perceiv'd to fall,
Whiles yet his feeble feet for faintnesse reeld,
Unto the Gyant loudly she gan call,
180   O helpe Orgoglio, helpe, or else we perish all.

                                21
At her so pitteous cry was much amoov'd
Her champion stout, and for to ayde his frend,
Againe his wonted° angry weapon proov'd:°   *usual / tried*
But all in vaine: for he has read his end°   *death*
185   In that bright shield, and all their forces spend
Themselves in vaine: for since that glauncing° sight,   *dazzling*
He hath no powre to hurt, nor to defend;
As where th'Almighties lightning brond° does light,   *bolt*
It dimmes the dazed eyen, and daunts° the senses quight.   *stuns*

8. The strength that has been divided in the Giant's two
hands is now concentrated in his remaining hand.

9. By falling down, the beast seems not only to be conquered, but also to submit himself ("yield") to Arthur.

22

190 Whom when the Prince, to battell new addrest,
      And threatning high his dreadfull stroke did see,[1]
      His sparkling blade about his head he blest,°   *brandished*
      And smote off quite his right leg by the knee,
      That downe he tombled; as an aged tree,
195   High growing on the top of rocky clift,
      Whose hartstrings with keene steele nigh hewen be,°   *are nearly cut off*
      The mightie trunck halfe rent, with ragged rift°   *splitting*
      Doth roll adowne the rocks, and fall with fearefull drift.° *force*

23

      Or as a Castle reared° high and round,   *built*
200   By subtile° engins and malitious slight   *clever*
      Is undermined from the lowest ground,
      And her° foundation forst,° and feebled quight,   *the castle's / broken*
      At last downe falles, and with her heaped hight
      Her hastie ruine does more heavie make,
205   And yields it selfe unto the victours might;
      Such was this Gyaunts fall, that seemd to shake
      The stedfast globe of earth, as it for feare did quake.

24

      The knight then lightly leaping to the pray,°   *victim*
      With mortall steele him smot° againe so sore,   *struck*
210   That headlesse his unweldy bodie lay,
      All wallowd in his owne fowle bloudy gore,
      Which flowed from his wounds in wondrous store.°   *amounts*
      But soone as breath out of his breast did pas,
      That huge great body, which the Gyaunt bore,
215   Was vanisht quite,° and of that monstrous mas   *completely*
      Was nothing left, but like an emptie bladder was.[2]

25

      Whose grievous fall, when false Duessa spide,
      Her golden cup she cast unto the ground,
      And crowned mitre° rudely threw aside;   *papal crown*
220   Such percing griefe her stubborne hart did wound,
      That she could not endure that dolefull stound,°   *dismal situation*
      But leaving all behind her, fled away:
      The light-foot Squire her quickly turnd around,
      And by hard meanes enforcing her to stay,
225   So brought unto his Lord, as his deserved pray.

26

      The royall Virgin, which beheld from farre,
      In pensive plight, and sad perplexitie,
      The whole atchievement° of this doubtfull° warre,   *progress / fearful*
      Came running fast to greet his victorie,
230   With sober gladnesse, and myld modestie,
      And with sweet joyous cheare him thus bespake;
      Faire braunch of noblesse, flowre of chevalrie,

---

1. The Giant is already overcome by the sight of Arthur's
shield, but when Arthur sees him raising his weapon to
defend Duessa, Arthur renews the battle.

2. A bladder or balloon can be blown up to a great size,
although it is actually empty, that is, full of hot air.

That with your worth the world amazed make,
How shall I quite° the paines, ye suffer for my sake?   *repay*

27

235 And you fresh bud of vertue springing fast,
Whom these sad eyes saw nigh unto deaths dore,
What hath poore Virgin for such perill past,
Wherewith you to reward? Accept therefore
My simple selfe, and service evermore;
240 And he that high does sit, and all things see
With equall° eyes, their merites to restore,   *impartial*
Behold what ye this day have done for mee,
And what I cannot quite, requite with usuree.³

28

But sith° the heavens, and your faire handeling°   *since/skill*
245 Have made you maister of the field this day,
Your fortune maister eke with governing,
And well begun end all so well, I pray,⁴
Ne let that wicked woman scape° away;   *escape*
For she it is, that did my Lord bethrall,°   *seduce, enslave*
250 My dearest Lord, and deepe in dongeon lay,
Where he his better dayes hath wasted all.
O heare, how piteous he to you for ayd does call.

29

Forthwith he gave in charge unto his Squire,
That scarlot whore to keepen carefully;
255 Whiles he himselfe with greedie° great desire   *eager*
Into the Castle entred forcibly,
Where living creature none he did espye;
Then gan he lowdly through the house to call:
But no man car'd to answere to his crye.
260 There raignd a solemne silence over all,
Nor voice was heard, nor wight was seene in bowre or hall.

30

At last with creeping crooked pace forth came
An old old man, with beard as white as snow,
That on a staffe his feeble steps did frame,°   *support*
265 And guide his wearie gate° both too and fro: *steps*
For his eye sight him failed long ygo,°   *ago*
And on his arme a bounch of keyes he bore,
The which unused rust did overgrow:
Those were the keyes of every inner dore,
270 But he could not them use, but kept them still in store.°   *handy*

31

But very uncouth° sight was to behold,   *strange*
How he did fashion his untoward° pace,   *awkward*
For as he forward moov'd his footing old,

---

3. What Una cannot completely repay, God will repay with interest. Unlike Duessa, who offers herself as a mistress to those who are victorious in battle, Una, a virgin, can offer only her loyalty and service. She goes on to call on God to restore her champions to a state of grace, with "merites" referring to all that was lost through the Fall of humankind.

4. While the heavens and skill have made you the "maister of the field this day," now you must also master your fortune through governance, and I pray that what has begun well will also end well.

So backward still was turnd his wrincled face,
275   Unlike to men, who ever as they trace,
Both feet and face one way are wont to lead.[5]
This was the auncient keeper of that place,
And foster father of the Gyant dead;
His name Ignaro did his nature right aread.

32

280   His reverend haires and holy grauitie
The knight much honord, as beseemed well,[6]
And gently askt, where all the people bee,
Which in that stately building wont° to dwell.   *accustomed*
Who answerd him full soft, he could not tell.
285   Againe he askt, where that same knight was layd,
Whom great Orgoglio with his puissaunce fell°   *deadly strength*
Had made his caytive thrall;° againe he sayde,   *wretched prisoner*
He could not tell: ne ever other answere made.

33

Then asked he, which way he in might pas:°   *enter*
290   He could not tell, againe he answered.
Thereat the curteous knight displeased was,
And said, Old sire, it seemes thou hast not red°   *perceived*
How ill it sits° with that same silver hed   *unsuitable*
In vaine to mocke, or mockt in vaine to bee:
295   But if thou be, as thou art pourtrahed
With natures pen, in ages grave degree,
Aread° in graver wise, what I demaund of thee.[7]   *declare*

34

His answere likewise was, he could not tell.
Whose sencelesse speach, and doted° ignorance   *stupid*
300   When as the noble Prince had marked well,
He ghest° his nature by his countenance,°   *guessed/behavior*
And calmd his wrath with goodly temperance.
Then to him stepping, from his arme did reach
Those keyes, and made himselfe free enterance.
305   Each dore he opened without any breach;°   *breaking in*
There was no barre to stop, nor foe him to empeach.°   *hinder*

35

There all within full rich arayd he found,
With royall arras and resplendent gold.
And did with store of every thing abound,
310   That greatest Princes presence might behold.[8]
But all the floore (too filthy to be told)
With bloud of guiltlesse babes, and innocents trew,
Which there were slaine, as sheepe out of the fold,
Defiled was, that dreadfull was to vew,
315   And sacred ashes[9] over it was strowed new.°   *newly scattered*

---

5. The steward and doorkeeper of Orgoglio's castle, Ignaro (Ignorance), walks forward but keeps his face turned backward, unlike humans, who look where they go.
6. Arthur treats Ignaro with the respect that his appearance of advanced age warrants.
7. If you are as old and wise as you appear, respond more seriously to what I ask of you.

8. The castle is equipped with everything worthy of the greatest prince.
9. The ashes of martyred saints used here to soak up the blood of innocent Christians. The newly strewn ashes appear to be evidence of a recently performed pagan ritual, as is suggested by the altar in the next stanza.

36

And there beside of marble stone was built
An Altare, carv'd with cunning imagery,
On which true Christians bloud was often spilt,
And holy Martyrs often doen to dye,
320 With cruell malice and strong tyranny:
Whose blessed sprites from underneath the stone
To God for vengeance cryde continually,
And with great griefe were often heard to grone,
That hardest heart would bleede, to heare their piteous mone.

37

325 Through every rowme he sought, and every bowr,
But no where could he find that wofull thrall:°   *Redcrosse Knight*
At last he came unto an yron doore,
That fast was lockt, but key found not at all
Emongst that bounch, to open it withall;
330 But in the same a little grate was pight,°   *placed*
Through which he sent his voyce, and lowd did call
With all his powre, to weet, if living wight
Were housed therewithin, whom he enlargen° might.   *release*

38

Therewith an hollow, dreary, murmuring voyce
335 These piteous plaints and dolours° did resound;   *laments*
O who is that, which brings me happy choyce
Of death, that here lye dying every stound,°   *moment*
Yet live perforce° in balefull° darkenesse bound?   *constrained/wretched*
For now three Moones have changed thrice their hew,°   *shape*
340 And have beene thrice hid underneath the ground,
Since I the heavens chearefull face did vew,
O welcome thou, that doest of death bring tydings trew.[1]

39

Which when that Champion heard, with percing point
Of pitty deare his hart was thrilled° sore,   *pierced*
345 And trembling horrour ran through every joynt,
For ruth of gentle knight so fowle forlore:°   *forlorn*
Which shaking off, he rent that yron dore,
With furious force, and indignation fell;°   *deadly*
Where entred in, his foot could find no flore,
350 But all a deepe descent, as darke as hell,
That breathed ever forth a filthie banefull° smell.   *poisonous*

40

But neither darkenesse fowle, nor filthy bands,
Nor noyous° smell his purpose could withhold,   *noxious*
(Entire affection hateth nicer hands)[2]
355 But that with constant zeale, and courage bold,
After long paines and labours manifold,
He found the meanes that Prisoner up to reare;[3]

---

1. Three moons have changed their shape three times; in other words, nine months have passed. The voice they hear rings with despair, wishing for death rather than rescue or salvation.
2. A perfect love disdains great fastidiousness; Prince

Arthur could overlook the filth of Orgoglio's prison because he cares so much for the Redcrosse Knight.
3. The Prisoner's legs are too weak to hold him up, so Arthur has to lift him out of the dungeon. The "light" is also a reference to Una.

	Whose feeble thighes, unhable° to uphold	unable
	His pined corse,° him scarse to light could beare,	wasted body
360	A ruefull spectacle of death and ghastly drere.°	misery

41

	His sad dull eyes deepe sunck in hollow pits,	
	Could not endure th'unwonted° sunne to view;	unaccustomed
	His bare thin cheekes for want° of better bits,°	lack / food
	And empty sides deceived° of their dew,	deprived
365	Could make a stony hart his hap° to rew;	situation
	His rawbone° armes, whose mighty brawned bowrs°	thin / brawny muscles
	Were wont to rive steele plates, and helmets hew,	
	Were cleane consum'd, and all his vitall powres	
	Decayd, and all his flesh shrank up like withered flowres.	

42

	Whom when his Lady saw,[4] to him she ran	
370	With hasty joy: to see him made her glad,	
	And sad to view his visage pale and wan,°	thin
	Who earst in flowres of freshest youth was clad.°	dressed
	Tho when her well of teares she wasted had,	
375	She said, Ah dearest Lord, what evill starre	
	On you hath found, and pourd his influence bad,[5]	
	That of your selfe ye thus berobbed arre,	
	And this misseeming hew° your manly looks doth marre?	appearance

43

	But welcome now my Lord, in wele° or woe,	prosperity
380	Whose presence I have lackt too long a day;	
	And fie° on Fortune mine avowed foe,	shame
	Whose wrathfull wreakes° them selves do now alay.°	vengeances / abate
	And for these wrongs shall treble penaunce° pay	penance
	Of treble good: good growes of evils priefe.°	trial
385	The chearelesse man, whom sorrow did dismay,°	overcome
	Had no delight to treaten° of his griefe;	tell
	His long endured famine needed more reliefe.	

44

	Faire Lady, then said that victorious knight,	
	The things, that grievous were to do, or beare,	
390	Them to renew,° I wote, breeds no delight;	repeat
	Best musicke breeds delight in loathing eare:	
	But th'onely good, that growes of passed feare,	
	Is to be wise, and ware° of like agein.	wary
	This dayes ensample° hath this lesson deare°	example / dire
395	Deepe written in my heart with yron pen,	
	That blisse may not abide in state of mortall men.	

45

	Henceforth sir knight, take to you wonted strength,	
	And maister these mishaps° with patient might;	misfortunes
	Loe where your foe lyes stretcht in monstrous length,	
400	And loe that wicked woman in your sight,	

4. Una recognizes the Prisoner as the Redcrosse Knight.
5. The Redcrosse Knight has ended up in the dungeon through his own folly; however, Una insists here that it must have been an "evill starre," i.e., misfortune, that was responsible for his imprisonment.

The roote of all your care,° and wretched plight,   *trouble*
  Now in your powre, to let her live, or dye.
  To do her dye (quoth Una) were despight,°   *malice*
  And shame t'avenge so weake an enemy;
405 But spoile her of her scarlot robe, and let her fly.[6]

46

So as she bad,° that witch they disaraid,°   *commanded / undressed*
  And robd of royall robes, and purple pall,°   *cloak*
  And ornaments that richly were displaid;
  Ne spared they to strip her naked all.
410 Then when they had despoild her tire and call,°   *attire and headdress*
  Such as she was, their eyes might her behold,
  That her misshaped parts did them appall,
  A loathly, wrinckled hag, ill favoured, old,
  Whose secret filth good manners biddeth not be told.

47

415 Her craftie head was altogether bald,
  And as in hate of honorable eld,[7]
  Was overgrowne with scurfe° and filthy scald;[8]   *scabs*
  Her teeth out of her rotten gummes were feld,°   *fallen*
  And her sowre breath abhominably smeld;
420 Her dried dugs,° like bladders lacking wind,   *breasts*
  Hong downe, and filthy matter from them weld;°   *oozed*
  Her wrizled° skin as rough, as maple rind,[9]   *wrinkled*
  So scabby was, that would have loathd all womankind.

48

Her neather° parts, the shame of all her kind,   *lower*
425 My chaster Muse for shame doth blush to write;
  But at her rompe° she growing had behind   *rump*
  A foxes taile, with dong all fowly dight;
  And eke her feete most monstrous were in sight;
  For one of them was like an Eagles claw,
430 With griping talaunts° armd to greedy fight,   *talons*
  The other like a Beares uneven° paw: *rough*
  More ugly shape yet never living creature saw.

49

Which when the knights beheld, amazd they were,
  And wondred at so fowle deformed wight.
435 Such then (said Una) as she seemeth here,
  Such is the face of falshood, such the sight
  Of fowle Duessa, when her borrowed light
  Is laid away, and counterfesaunce° knowne.   *falsity*
  Thus when they had the witch disrobed quight,
440 And all her filthy feature° open showne,   *body*
  They let her goe at will, and wander wayes unknowne.

6. Like Christ, who seeks to destroy the works of the devil rather than the devil himself (1 John 3.8), Una seeks to
destroy Duessa's ability to do evil.
7. I.e., Duessa's ugly head is a hateful mockery of old people
whose baldness is usually a sign of honorable "eld" or old age.

8. Scall, a disease that causes scabs to form on the scalp.
9. Maples were often thought to be hard on the outside
but rotten inside. Duessa's diseased appearance also suggests syphilis.

50

She flying fast from heavens hated face,
   And from the world that her discovered wide,
   Fled to the wastfull° wildernesse apace,   *desolate*
445   From living eyes her open shame to hide,
   And lurkt in rocks and caves long unespide.
   But that faire crew of knights, and Una faire
   Did in that castle afterwards abide,
   To rest them selves, and weary powres repaire,
450 Where store° they found of all, that dainty was and rare.   *supplies*

Canto 9

His loves and lignage Arthur tells:
The knights knit friendly bands:
Sir Trevisan flies from Despayre,
Whom Redcrosse knight withstands.

1

O Goodly golden chaine, wherewith yfere°   *together*
   The vertues linked are in lovely wize:
   And noble minds of yore allyed were,
   In brave poursuit of chevalrous emprize,°   *adventure*
5   That none did others safety despize,°   *disregard*
   Nor aid envy to him, in need that stands,
   But friendly each did others prayse devize
   How to advaunce with favourable hands,
As this good Prince redeemd the Redcrosse knight from bands.° *captivity*

2

10 Who when their powres, empaird° through labour long, *weakened*
   With dew° repast they had recured° well,   *suitable/recovered*
   And that weake captive wight now wexed° strong,   *grown*
   Them list no lenger there at leasure dwell,
   But forward fare, as their adventures fell,
15   But ere they parted, Una faire besought
   That straunger knight his name and nation tell;
   Least so great good, as he for her had wrought,
Should die unknown, and buried be in thanklesse thought.

3

Faire virgin (said the Prince) ye me require
20   A thing without the compas of my wit:[1]
   For both the lignage° and the certain Sire,   *lineage*
   From which I sprong, from me are hidden yit.
   For all so soone as life did me admit
   Into this world, and shewed heavens light,
25   From mothers pap° I taken was unfit: *breast*
   And streight delivered to a Faery knight,
To be upbrought in gentle thewes° and martiall might. *manners*

---

1. I.e., your question is beyond my ability to answer.

4

	Unto old Timon[2] he me brought bylive,°	*immediately*
30	Old Timon, who in youthly yeares hath beene	
	In warlike feates th'expertest man alive,	
	And is the wisest now on earth I weene;°	*believe*
	His dwelling is low in a valley greene,	
	Under the foot of Rauran[3] mossy hore,	
35	From whence the river Dee[4] as silver cleene	
	His tombling billowes rolls with gentle rore:	
	There all my dayes he traind me up in vertuous lore.	

5

	Thither the great Magicien Merlin came,	
	As was his use,° ofttimes to visit me:	*custom*
	For he had charge my discipline to frame,[5]	
40	And Tutours nouriture to oversee.	
	Him oft and oft I askt in privitie,°	*privately*
	Of what loines and what lignage I did spring:	
	Whose aunswere bad me still assured bee,	
	That I was sonne and heire unto a king,	
45	As time in her just terme° the truth to light should bring.	*due course*

6

	Well worthy impe,° said then the Lady gent,°	*offspring/noble*
	And Pupill fit for such a Tutours hand.	
	But what adventure, or what high intent	
	Hath brought you hither into Faery land,	
50	Aread° Prince Arthur, crowne of Martiall band?[6]	*declare*
	Full hard it is (quoth he) to read aright	
	The course of heavenly cause, or understand	
	The secret meaning of th'eternall might,	
	That rules mens wayes, and rules the thoughts of living wight.	

7

55	For whither° he through fatall deepe foresight	*whether*
	Me hither sent, for cause to me unghest,°	*unguessed*
	Or that fresh bleeding wound, which day and night	
	Whilome° doth rancle in my riven° brest,	*constantly/wounded*
	With forced° fury following his behest,°	*forceful/command*
60	Me hither brought by wayes yet never found,	
	You to have helpt I hold my selfe yet blest.	
	Ah curteous knight (quoth she) what secret wound	
	Could ever find, to grieve the gentlest hart on ground?[7]	

8

	Deare Dame (quoth he) you sleeping sparkes awake,	
65	Which troubled once, into huge flames will grow,[8]	
	Ne ever will their fervent fury slake,°	*cease*
	Till living moysture[9] into smoke do flow,	

2. Honor (Greek).

3. A hill in Wales, hoary with moss.

4. A river marking the boundary between England and Wales.

5. Merlin was in charge of Arthur's education and made sure Arthur's tutor was properly recompensed.

6. Although Arthur does not declare his name, Una is able to recognize him.

7. I.e., what injury could ever find a way to hurt the gentlest heart "on ground" (in the world)?

8. Prince Arthur addresses Una; she reminds him of his hidden pain, which once reawakened will continue to grow.

9. A reference to the Renaissance medical theory of the humors that compose the human body.

And wasted life do lye in ashes low.
Yet sithens° silence lesseneth not my fire,   *since*
70   But told it flames, and hidden it does glow,
I will revele, what ye so much desire:
Ah Love, lay downe thy bow,[1] the whiles I may respire.°   *breathe*

9

It was in freshest flowre of youthly yeares,
When courage first does creepe in manly chest,
75   Then first the coale of kindly heat appeares
To kindle love in every living brest;
But me had warnd old Timons wise behest,°   *warning*
Those creeping flames° by reason to subdew,   *of love*
Before their rage grew to so great unrest,
80   As miserable lovers use to rew,
Which still wex old in woe, whiles woe still wexeth new.[2]

10

That idle name of love, and lovers life,
As losse of time, and vertues enimy
I ever scornd, and joyd to stirre up strife,
85   In middest of° their mournfull Tragedy,   *in the midst of*
Ay wont to laugh, when them I heard to cry,
And blow the fire, which them to ashes brent:°   *burned*
Their God himselfe,° griev'd at my libertie,   *Cupid*
Shot many a dart at me with fiers intent,
90   But I them warded all with wary government.°   *cautious self-control*

11

But all in vaine: no fort can be so strong,
Ne fleshly brest can armed be so sound,°   *completely*
But will at last be wonne with battrie° long,   *battery*
Or unawares at disavantage found;[3]
95   Nothing is sure, that growes on earthly ground:
And who most trustes in arme of fleshly might,
And boasts, in beauties chaine not to be bound,
Doth soonest fall in disaventrous° fight,   *unfortunate*
And yeeldes his caytive° neck to victours most despight.°   *servile / malice*

12

100   Ensampel° make of him your haplesse joy,   *example*
And of my selfe now mated,° as ye see;   *checked*
Whose prouder vaunt° that proud avenging boy   *boast*
Did soone pluck downe, and curbd my libertie.
For on a day prickt forth with jollitie
105   Of looser life, and heat of hardiment,[4]
Raunging the forest wide on courser° free,   *horse*
The fields, the floods, the heavens with one consent
Did seeme to laugh on me, and favour mine intent.

1. Cupid shoots arrows of love at people and causes them
to fall in love with the first person they see.
2. Sorrow makes lovers grow old while their sorrow
remains forever young.

3. No fort is so strong, or flesh so well protected, that it
cannot be overcome by continual battering.
4. Inspired by the joy of a life of freedom and the heat of
boldness.

13

13

For-wearied° with my sports, I did alight   *tired*
110   From loftie steed, and downe to sleepe me layd;
       The verdant° gras my couch did goodly dight,°   *green/adorn*
       And pillow was my helmet faire displayd:
       Whiles every sence the humour° sweet embayd,°   *dew of sleep/bathed*
       And slombring soft my hart did steale away,
115   Me seemed,° by my side a royall Mayd   *it seemed to me*
       Her daintie limbes full softly down did lay:
So faire a creature yet saw never sunny day.

14

Most goodly glee° and lovely blandishment   *entertainment*
       She to me made, and bad me love her deare,
120   For dearely sure her love was to me bent,
       As when just time expired should appeare.[5]
       But whether dreames delude, or true it were,
       Was never hart so ravisht with delight,
       Ne living man like° words did ever heare,   *similar*
125   As she to me delivered all that night;
And at her parting said, She Queene of Faeries hight.°   *was called*

15

When I awoke, and found her place devoyd,°   *empty*
       And nought° but pressed gras, where she had lyen,°   *nothing/lain*
       I sorrowed all so much, as earst° I joyd,   *at first*
130   And washed all her place with watry eyen.
       From that day forth I lov'd that face divine;
       From that day forth I cast° in carefull mind,   *resolved*
       To seeke her out with labour, and long tyne,°   *suffering*
       And never vow to rest, till her I find,
135 Nine monethes I seeke in vaine yet ni'll° that vow unbind.   *never will*

16

Thus as he spake, his visage wexed pale,
       And chaunge of hew great passion did bewray;°   *betray*
       Yet still he strove to cloke his inward bale,°   *sorrow*
       And hide the smoke, that did his fire display,
140   Till gentle Una thus to him gan° say;   *did*
       O happy Queene of Faeries, that hast found
       Mongst many, one that with his prowesse may
       Defend thine honour, and thy foes confound:
True Loves are often sown, but seldom grow on ground.°   *on this earth*

17

145 Thine, O then, said the gentle Redcrosse knight,
       Next to that Ladies love, shalbe the place,
       O fairest virgin, full of heavenly light,
       Whose wondrous faith, exceeding earthly race,°   *people*
       Was firmest fixt in mine extremest case.
150   And you, my Lord, the Patrone° of my life,   *protector*
       Of that great Queene may well gaine worthy grace:

---

5. Her love was directed as it would appear in the due course of time. Arthur's dream is both lifelike and prophetic.

For onely worthy you through prowes priefe[6]
If living man mote° worthy be, to be her liefe.°   *might / beloved*

18

So diversly° discoursing of their loves,   *variously*
155   The golden Sunne his glistring head gan shew,
And sad remembraunce now the Prince amoves,°   *compels*
With fresh desire his voyage to pursew:
Als Una earnd her traveill° to renew.   *quest*
Then those two knights, fast° friendship for to bynd,   *firm*
160   And love establish each to other trew,
Gave goodly gifts, the signes of gratefull mynd,
And eke° as pledges firme, right hands together joynd.   *also*

19

Prince Arthur gave a boxe of Diamond sure,
Embowd° with gold and gorgeous ornament,   *encircled*
165   Wherein were closd few drops of liquor pure,[7]
Of wondrous worth, and vertue excellent,
That any wound could heale incontinent:°   *immediately*
Which to requite, the Redcrosse knight him gave
A booke, wherein his Saveours testament°   *the Gospels*
170   Was writ with golden letters rich and brave;
A worke of wondrous grace, and able soules to save.

20

Thus beene they parted, Arthur on his way
To seeke his love, and th'other for to fight
With Unaes foe, that all her realme did pray.°   *molest*
175   But she now weighing the decayed plight,
And shrunken synewes of her chosen knight,
Would not a while her forward course pursew,
Ne bring him forth in face of dreadfull fight,
Till he recovered had his former hew:
180   For him to be yet weake and wearie well she knew.

21

So as they traveild, lo they gan espy
An armed knight towards them gallop fast,
That seemed from some feared foe to fly,
Or other griesly thing, that him agast.
185   Still as he fled, his eye was backward cast,
As if his feare still followed him behind;
Als flew his steed, as he his bands had brast,°   *burst*
And with his winged heeles did tread the wind,
As he had beene a fole° of Pegasus[8] his kind.   *foal*

22

190   Nigh as he drew, they might perceive his head
To be unarmd, and curld uncombed heares
Upstaring° stiffe, dismayd with uncouth° dread;   *standing / unknown*
Nor drop of bloud in all his face appeares

---

6. The test of your valor shows that you are the only one   8. A winged horse, belonging to the mythological hero
worthy of her grace.   Perseus.
7. The blood of Christ, the wine of the Eucharist.

Nor life in limbe: and to increase his feares,
195   In fowle reproch of knighthoods faire degree,
About his neck an hempen rope he weares,
That with his glistring armes° does ill agree;   *armor*
But he of rope or armes has now no memoree.

23

The Redcrosse knight toward him crossed fast,
200   To weet,° what mister° wight was so dismayd: *know/manner of*
There him he finds all sencelesse and aghast,
That of him selfe he seemd to be afrayd;
Whom hardly he from flying forward stayd,[9]
Till he these wordes to him deliver might;
205   Sir knight, aread who hath ye thus arayd,°   *clothed*
And eke from whom make ye this hasty flight:
For never knight I saw in such misseeming° plight.   *unseemly*

24

He answerd nought° at all, but adding new   *not*
Feare to his first amazment, staring wide
210   With stony° eyes, and hartlesse hollow hew,   *staring*
Astonisht stood, as one that had aspide
Infernall furies, with their chaines untide.
Him yet againe, and yet againe bespake
The gentle knight; who nought to him replide,
215   But trembling every joynt did inly quake,
And foltring° tongue at last these words seemd forth to shake.   *stammering*

25

For Gods deare love, Sir knight, do me not stay;°   *detain*
For loe° he comes, he comes fast after mee.   *here*
Eft° looking backe would faine° have runne away;   *again/rather*
220   But he him forst to stay, and tellen free°   *freely tell*
The secret cause of his perplexitie:
Yet nathemore° by his bold hartie speach,   *not at all*
Could his bloud-frosen hart emboldned bee,[1]
But through his boldnesse rather feare did reach,
225   Yet forst, at last he made through silence suddein breach.°   *break*

26

And am I now in safetie sure (quoth he)
From him, that would have forced me to dye?
And is the point of death now turnd fro° mee,   *from*
That I may tell this haplesse° history?   *unlucky*
230   Feare nought: (quoth he) no daunger now is nye.
Then shall I you recount a ruefull cace,°   *sad situation*
(Said he) the which with this unlucky eye
I late beheld, and had not greater grace
Me reft° from it, had bene partaker of the place.[2]   *torn*

---

9. The Redcrosse Knight could hardly keep the frightened knight (earlier identified as Sir Trevisan) from trying to flee.
1. The Redcrosse Knight's bold words do not encourage Sir Trevisan; in the end, however, the Redcrosse Knight

forces him to speak.
2. Had not greater grace torn me from the unfortunate events I beheld, I would have been a victim of those events myself.

27

235 I lately chaunst (Would I had never chaunst)
     With a faire knight to keepen companee,
     Sir Terwin hight, that well himselfe advaunst
     In all affaires, and was both bold and free,
     But not so happie as mote happie bee:
240 He lov'd, as was his lot, a Ladie gent,°   *gentle*
     That him againe° lov'd in the least degree: *in return*
     For she was proud, and of too high intent,°   *ambition*
     And joyd to see her lover languish and lament.

28

     From whom° returning sad and comfortlesse,   *Terwin's lady*
245 As on the way together we did fare,°   *travel*
     We met that villen (God from him me blesse)
     That cursed wight, from whom I scapt° whyleare,°   *escaped/earlier*
     A man of hell, that cals himselfe Despaire:
     Who first us greets, and after faire areedes°   *tells*
250 Of tydings strange, and of adventures rare:
     So creeping close, as Snake in hidden weedes,
     Inquireth of our states, and of our knightly deedes.

29

     Which when he knew, and felt our feeble harts
     Embost° with bale,° and bitter byting griefe,   *encrusted/sorrow*
255 Which love had launched with his deadly darts,
     With wounding words and termes of foule repriefe°   *scorn*
     He pluckt from us all hope of due reliefe,
     That earst° us held in love of lingring life;   *recently*
     Then hopelesse hartlesse, gan the cunning thiefe
260 Perswade us die, to stint° all further strife: *stop*
     To me he lent this rope, to him a rustie knife.

30

     With which sad instrument of hastie death,
     That wofull lover, loathing lenger° light,   *longer*
     A wide way° made to let forth living breath.   *cut*
265 But I more fearefull, or more luckie wight,°   *creature*
     Dismayd with that deformed dismall sight,
     Fled fast away, halfe dead with dying feare:°   *fear of dying*
     Ne yet assur'd of life by you, Sir knight,
     Whose like infirmitie like chaunce may beare:
270 But God you never let his charmed speeches heare.[3]

31

     How may a man (said he) with idle speach
     Be wonne,° to spoyle the Castle of his health?   *convinced*
     I wote° (quoth he) whom triall late did teach,   *would not*
     That like would not for all this worldes wealth:[4]
275 His subtill tongue, like dropping honny, mealt'th°   *melteth*
     Into the hart, and searcheth every vaine,

3. May God prevent you from hearing his seductive   4. I would not undergo such a test for all the wealth in
speeches.   the world.

That ere° one be aware, by secret stealth   *before*
His powre is reft,° and weaknesse doth remaine.   *broken*
O never Sir desire to try° his guilefull traine.°   *test/trickery*

32

280 Certes° (said he) hence shall I never rest,   *indeed*
Till I that treachours° art have heard and tride;° *traitor's/tested*
And you Sir knight, whose name mote I request,
Of grace do me unto his cabin° guide.   *cave*
I that hight° Trevisan (quoth he) will ride   *am called*
285 Against my liking backe, to doe you grace:°   *a favor*
But nor for gold nor glee will I abide
By you, when ye arrive in that same place;
For lever° had I die, then° see his deadly face.   *rather/than*

33

Ere long they come, where that same wicked wight
290 His dwelling has, low in an hollow cave,
Farre underneath a craggie clift ypight,°   *pitched*
Darke, dolefull, drearie, like a greedie grave,
That still° for carrion carcases doth crave: *always*
On top whereof aye° dwelt the ghastly Owle,   *ever*
295 Shrieking his balefull° note, which ever drave   *sorrowful*
Farre from that haunt all other chearefull fowle;
And all about it wandring ghostes did waile and howle.

34

And all about old stockes and stubs of trees,
Whereon nor fruit, nor leafe was ever seene,
300 Did hang upon the ragged rocky knees;°   *hillsides*
On which had many wretches hanged beene,
Whose carcases were scattered on the greene,
And throwne about the cliffs. Arrived there,
That bare-head knight for dread and dolefull teene,°   *grief*
305 Would faine have fled, ne durst° approchen neare,   *dared*
But th'other forst him stay, and comforted in feare.

35

That darkesome cave they enter, where they find
That cursed man, low sitting on the ground,
Musing full sadly in his sullein mind;
310 His griesie lockes, long growen, and unbound,
Disordred hong about his shoulders round,
And hid his face; through which his hollow eyne
Lookt deadly dull, and stared as astound;
His raw-bone cheekes through penurie° and pine,° *poverty/starvation*
315 Were shronke into his jawes, as he did never dine.

36

His garment nought but many ragged clouts,°   *rags*
With thornes together pind and patched was,
The which his naked sides he wrapt abouts;
And him beside there lay upon the gras
320 A drearie° corse,° whose life away did pas,   *gory/body*
All wallowd in his owne yet luke-warme blood,

That from his wound yet welled fresh alas;
   In which a rustie knife fast fixed stood,
   And made an open passage for the gushing flood.

37

325 Which piteous spectacle, approving° trew   *proving*
   The wofull tale that Trevisan had told,
   When as the gentle Redcrosse knight did vew,
   With firie zeale he burnt in courage bold,
   Him to avenge, before his bloud were cold,
330   And to the villein said, Thou damned wight,
   The author of this fact, we here behold,
   What justice can but judge against thee right,
With thine owne bloud to price° his bloud, here shed in sight?   *pay for*

38

What franticke fit (quoth he) hath thus distraught
335   Thee, foolish man, so rash a doome° to give?   *judgment*
   What justice ever other judgement taught,
   But he should die, who merites not to live?
   None° else to death this man despayring drive,° *nothing/drove*
   But his owne guiltie mind deserving death.
340   Is then unjust to each his due to give?
   Or let him die, that loatheth living breath?
Or let him die at ease, that liveth here uneath?°   *unhappily*

39

Who travels by the wearie wandring way,
   To come unto his wished home in haste,
345   And meetes a flood, that doth his passage stay,
   Is not great grace to helpe him over past,
   Or free his feet, that in the myre sticke fast?
   Most envious man, that grieves at neighbours good,
   And fond,° that joyest in the woe thou hast,   *foolish*
350   Why wilt not let him passe, that long hath stood
Upon the banke, yet wilt thy selfe not passe the flood?

40

He there does now enjoy eternall rest
   And happie ease, which thou doest want and crave,
   And further from it daily wanderest:
355   What if some litle paine the passage have,
   That makes fraile flesh to feare the bitter wave?
   Is not short paine well borne, that brings long ease,
   And layes the soule to sleepe in quiet grave?
   Sleepe after toyle, port after stormie seas,
360 Ease after warre, death after life does greatly please.

41

The knight much wondred at his suddeine wit,
   And said, The terme of life is limited,
   Ne may a man prolong, nor shorten it;
   The souldier may not move from watchfull sted,°   *post*
365   Nor leave his stand, untill his Captaine bed.°   *command*
   Who life did limit by almightie doome,
   (Quoth he) knowes best the termes established;

And he, that points the Centonell his roome,
Doth license him depart at sound of morning droome.°   *drum*

42

370 Is not his deed, what ever thing is donne,
         In heaven and earth? did not he all create
         To die againe? all ends that was begonne.
         Their times in his eternall booke of fate
         Are written sure, and have their certaine date.
375   Who then can strive with strong necessitie,
         That holds the world in his still chaunging state,
         Or shunne the death ordaynd by destinie?
When houre of death is come, let none aske whence, nor why.

43

         The lenger life, I wote the greater sin,[5]
380   The greater sin, the greater punishment:
         All those great battels, which thou boasts to win,
         Through strife, and bloud-shed, and avengement,
         Now praysd, hereafter deare° thou shalt repent: *dearly*
         For life must life, and bloud must bloud repay.
385   Is not enough thy evill life forespent?°   *wasted*
         For he, that once hath missed the right way,
The further he doth goe, the further he doth stray.

44

         Then do no further goe, no further stray,
         But here lie downe, and to thy rest betake,
390   Th'ill° to prevent, that life ensewen° may.   *evil/continue*
         For what hath life, that may it loved make,
         And gives not rather cause it to forsake?°   *leave*
         Feare, sicknesse, age, losse, labour, sorrow, strife,
         Paine, hunger, cold, that makes the hart to quake;
395   And ever fickle fortune rageth rife
         All which, and thousands mo° do make a loathsome life.   *more*

45

         Thou wretched man, of death hast greatest need,
         If in true ballance thou wilt weigh thy state:°   *condition*
         For never knight, that dared warlike deede,
400   More lucklesse disaventures did amate:°   *meet*
         Witnesse the dongeon deepe, wherein of late
         Thy life shut up, for death so oft did call;
         And though good lucke prolonged hath thy date,
         Yet death then, would the like mishaps forestall,
405 Into the which hereafter thou maiest happen fall.[6]

46

         Why then doest thou, O man of sin, desire
         To draw thy dayes forth to their last degree?
         Is not the measure of thy sinfull hire°   *employment*
         High heaped up with huge iniquitie,°   *sinfulness*
410   Against the day of wrath, to burden thee?

---

5. The longer the life, the greater the sin.

6. If death had come when you called for it, then the misfortunes that await you might have been prevented.

      Is not enough, that to this Ladie milde
      Thou falsed° hast thy faith with perjurie,   *violated*
      And sold thy selfe to serve Duessa vilde,°   *vile*
With whom in all abuse thou hast thy selfe defilde?

48 [47]

415   Is not he just, that all this doth behold
      From highest heaven, and beares an equall eye?
      Shall he thy sins up in his knowledge fold,
      And guiltie be of thine impietie?
      Is not his law, Let every sinner die:
420   Die shall all flesh? what then must needs be donne,
      Is it not better to doe willinglie,
      Then° linger, till the glasse be all out ronne?   *than*
Death is the end of woes: die soone, O faeries sonne.

48

      The knight was much enmoved° with his speach,   *moved*
425   That as a swords point through his hard did perse,°   *pierce*
      And in his conscience made a secret breach,[7]
      Well knowing true all, that he did reherse,
      And to his fresh remembrance did reverse°   *recall*
      The ugly vew of his deformed crimes,
430   That all his manly powres it did disperse,
      As° he were charmed with inchaunted rimes,   *as if*
That oftentimes he quakt, and fainted oftentimes.

49

      In which amazement, when the Miscreant°   *misbeliever (Despair)*
      Perceived him to waver weake and fraile,
435   Whiles trembling horror did his conscience dant,°   *overcome*
      And hellish anguish did his soule assaile,
      To drive him to despaire, and quite to quaile,
      He shew'd him painted in a table° plaine,°   *picture / clearly*
      The damned ghosts, that doe in torments waile,
440   And thousand feends that doe them endlesse paine
With fire and brimstone, which for ever shall remaine.

50

      The sight whereof so throughly him dismaid,
      That nought° but death before his eyes he saw,   *nothing*
      And ever burning wrath before him laid,
445   By righteous sentence of th'Almighties law:
      Then gan the villein him to overcraw,°   *triumph over*
      And brought unto him swords, ropes, poison, fire,
      And all that might him to perdition draw;
      And bad him choose, what death he would desire:
450   For death was due to him, that had provokt Gods ire.

51

      But when as none of them he saw him take,
      He to him raught° a dagger sharpe and keene,   *handed*
      And gave it him in hand: his hand did quake,
      And tremble like a leafe of Aspin greene,

---

7. Despair's words disrupt the Redcrosse Knight's inner knowledge of God's grace.

455 And troubled bloud through his pale face was seene
        To come, and goe with tydings from the hart,
        As it a running messenger had beene.
        At last resolv'd to worke his finall smart,°   *pain*
        He lifted up his hand, that backe againe did start.

52

460 Which when as Una saw, through every vaine
        The crudled cold ran to her well of life,°   *her heart*
        As in a swowne: but soone reliv'd° againe,   *revived*
        Out of his hand she snatcht the cursed knife,
        And threw it to the ground, enraged rife,°   *uncontrollably*
465 And to him said, Fie, fie,° faint harted knight,   *shame*
        What meanest thou by this reprochfull strife?
        Is this the battell, which thou vauntst° to fight   *boast*
   With that fire-mouthed Dragon, horrible and bright?

53

   Come, come away, fraile, feeble, fleshly wight,
470 Ne let vaine words bewitch thy manly hart,
        Ne divelish thoughts dismay thy constant spright.
        In heavenly mercies hast thou not a part?
        Why shouldst thou then despeire, that chosen art?
        Where justice growes, there grows eke greater grace,
475 The which doth quench the brond of hellish smart,
        And that accurst hand-writing doth deface.[8]
   Arise, Sir knight arise, and leave this cursed place.

54

   So up he rose, and thence amounted streight.°   *immediately*
        Which when the carle° beheld, and saw his guest   *villain*
480 Would safe depart, for all his subtill sleight,°   *trickery*
        He chose an halter° from among the rest,   *noose*
        And with it hung himselfe, unbid unblest.
        But death he could not worke himselfe thereby;
        For thousand times he so himselfe had drest,
485 Yet nathelesse° it could not doe° him die,   *nevertheless/make*
   Till he should die his last, that is eternally.

Canto 10

Her faithfull knight faire Una brings
to house of Holinesse,
Where he is taught repentance, and
the way to heavenly blesse.

1

   What man is he, that boasts of fleshly might,
        And vaine° assurance of mortality,   *empty*
        Which all so soone, as it doth come to fight,
        Against spirituall foes, yeelds by and by,
5   Or from the field most cowardly doth fly?

---

8. Una alludes to heavenly grace and God's mercy toward repentent sinners—an allowance that Despair had omitted from his argument.

Ne let the man ascribe it to his skill,
That thorough° grace hath gained victory.   *through*
If any strength we have, it is to ill,
But all the good is Gods, both power and eke will.

2

10   By that, which lately hapned, Una saw,
That this her knight was feeble, and too faint;
And all his sinews woxen° weake and raw,   *grown*
Through long enprisonment, and hard constraint,
Which he endured in his late restraint,
15   That yet he was unfit for bloudie fight:
Therefore to cherish° him with diets daint,°   *nourish/dainty foods*
She cast to bring him, where he chearen° might,   *be cheered*
Till he recovered had his late decayed plight.

3

There was an auntient° house not farre away,   *ancient*
20   Renowmd throughout the world for sacred lore,°   *wisdom*
And pure unspotted life: so well they say
It governd was, and guided evermore,
Through wisedome of a matrone grave and hore;°   *venerable*
Whose onely joy was to relieve the needes
25   Of wretched soules, and helpe the helpelesse pore:
All night she spent in bidding of her bedes,°   *saying prayers*
And all the day in doing good and godly deedes.

4

Dame Caelia° men did her call, as thought   *heavenly*
From heaven to come, or thither to arise,
30   The mother of three daughters, well upbrought
In goodly thewes,° and godly exercise: *manners*
The eldest two most sober, chast, and wise,
Fidelia° and Speranza° virgins were,   *Faith/Hope*
Though spousd, yet wanting wedlocks solemnize;[1]
35   But faire Charissa° to a lovely fere°   *Charity/loving husband*
Was lincked, and by him had many pledges° dere.   *children*

5

Arrived there, the dore they find fast° lockt;   *tightly*
For it was warely° watched night and day,   *carefully*
For feare of many foes: but when they knockt,
40   The Porter opened unto them streight way:°   *right away*
He was an aged syre, all hory gray,
With lookes full lowly cast,[2] and gate° full slow,   *pace*
Wont on a staffe his feeble steps to stay,°   *support*
Hight Humiltá.° They passe in stouping low;   *named Humility*
45   For streight and narrow was the way, which he did show.

6

Each goodly thing is hardest to begin,
But entred in a spacious court they see,

---

1. Faith and Hope are each engaged to be married, but their marriages have not yet taken place. The implication is that Faith and Hope are not fulfilled in this life but will be fulfilled in the hereafter through God's promise of salvation.

2. The porter casts his eyes down in an expression of humility.

Both plaine, and pleasant to be walked in,
Where them does meete a francklin[3] faire and free,
And entertaines with comely° courteous glee,   *appropriate*
His name was Zele,[4] that him right well became,
For in his speeches and behaviour hee
Did labour lively to expresse the same,
And gladly did them guide, till to the Hall they came.

50

7

There fairely them receives a gentle Squire,
Of milde demeanure,° and rare courtesie,   *manner*
Right cleanly clad in comely sad attire;
In word and deede that shew'd great modestie,
And knew his good to all of each degree,[5]
Hight Reverence. He them with speeches meet
Does faire entreat; no courting nicetie,°   *flattery*
But simple true, and eke unfained° sweet,   *honest*
As might become a Squire so great persons to greet.

55

60

8

And afterwards them to his Dame he leades,
That aged Dame, the Ladie of the place:
Who all this while was busie at her beades:
Which doen,° she up arose with seemely grace,   *done*
And toward them full matronely did pace.°   *walk*
Where when that fairest Una she beheld,
Whom well she knew to spring from heavenly race,
Her hart with joy unwonted inly° sweld,   *inwardly*
As feeling wondrous comfort in her weaker eld.°   *age*

65

70

9

And her embracing said, O happie earth,
Whereon thy innocent feet doe ever tread,
Most vertuous virgin borne of heavenly berth,
That to redeeme thy woeful parents head,
From tyrans° rage, and ever-dying dread,   *tyrant's*
Hast wandred through the world now long a day;
Yet ceasest not thy wearie soles° to lead,   *feet, souls*
What grace hath thee now hither brought this way?
Or doen° thy feeble feet unweeting hither stray?   *do*

75

80

10

Strange thing it is an errant° knight to see   *wandering*
Here in this place, or any other wight,
That hither turnes his steps. So few there bee,
That chose the narrow path, or seeke the right:
All keepe the broad high way, and take delight
With many rather for to go astray,
And be partakers of their evill plight,
Then with a few to walke the rightest° way;   *righteous*
O foolish men, why haste ye to your owne decay?

85

90

3. A person who owns his own land and is therefore his own master.
4. The franklin's zeal or enthusiasm is an attribute of his

Christian freedom.
5. He knows how to behave courteously toward members of each social rank.

11

Thy selfe to see, and tyred limbs to rest,
    O matrone sage° (quoth she) I hither came,   *wise*
    And this good knight his way with me addrest,°   *directed*
    Led with thy prayses and broad-blazed° fame,   *widely reported*
95 That up to heaven is blowne. The aunccient Dame
    Him goodly greeted in her modest guise,
    And entertaynd them both, as best became,
    With all the court'sies, that she could devise,°   *think of*
Ne wanted ought, to shew her bounteous° or wise.   *generous*

12

100 Thus as they gan of sundry things devise,
    Loe two most goodly virgins came in place,
    Ylinked° arme in arme in lovely wise,[6]   *linked*
    With countenance° demure,° and modest grace,   *expression /modest*
    They numbred even steps and equall pace:
105 Of which the eldest, that Fidelia hight,
    Like sunny beames threw from her Christall face,
    That could have dazd the rash° beholders sight,   *foolish*
And round about her head did shine like heavens light.

13

She was araied° all in lilly white,   *dressed*
110 And in her right hand bore a cup of gold,[7]
    With wine and water fild up to the hight,°   *brim*
    In which a Serpent did himselfe enfold,°   *coil*
    That horrour made to all, that did behold;
    But she no whit° did chaunge her constant mood: *not a bit*
115 And in her other hand she fast° did hold   *tightly*
    A booke, that was both signd and seald with blood,
Wherein darke things were writ, hard to be understood.

14

Her younger sister, that Speranza hight,°   *was called*
    Was clad in blew,[8] that her beseemed° well;   *suited*
120 Not all so chearefull seemed she of sight,
    As was her sister; whether dread° did dwell,   *fear*
    Or anguish in her hart, is hard to tell:
    Upon her arme a silver anchor lay,[9]
    Whereon she leaned ever, as befell:°   *it happened*
125 And ever up to heaven, as she did pray,
Her stedfast eyes were bent, ne swarved° other way.   *turned*

15

They seeing Una, towards her gan wend,
    Who them encounters° with like courtesie;   *greets*
    Many kind speeches they betwene them spend,
130 And greatly joy each other well to see:

---

6. Faith and Hope enter the room harmoniously linked,
unlike in the House of Pride, where the inhabitants are
joined by a yoke of servitude.
7. The sacramental cup of the Holy Communion; it contains the healing blood and baptismal water that poured
from Christ's wounds when he was crucified. The serpent
here is a symbol of healing and redemption, and the book

Fidelia holds is the New Testament, which is sealed with
Christ's blood in the sense that Christ's crucifixion
assures salvation for all humankind.
8. Blue is the color of the Virgin Mary.
9. Cf. Hebrews 6.19: "which hope we have as an anchor
of the soul, both sure and steadfast." Silver is a symbol of
purity.

Then to the knight with shamefast° modestie   humble
They turne themselves, at Unaes meeke request,
And him salute with well beseeming glee;
Who faire them quites,° as him beseemed best,   greets
135   And goodly gan discourse° of many a noble gest.°   speak/deed
                        16
Then Una thus; But she your sister deare,
    The deare Charissa where is she become?[1]
    Or wants° she health, or busie is elsewhere?   lacks
    Ah no, said they, but forth she may not come:
140   For she of late is lightned of her wombe,°   recently gave birth
    And hath encreast° the world with one sonne more,   increased
    That her to see should be but troublesome.
    Indeede (quoth she) that should her trouble sore,
But thankt be God, and her encrease so evermore.[2]
                        17
145   Then said the aged Caelia, Deare dame,
    And you good Sir, I wote° that of your toyle,   believe
    And labours long, through which ye hither came,
    Ye both forwearied° be: therefore a whyle   tired
    I read you rest, and to your bowres recoyle.°   retire
150   Then called she a Groome, that forth him led
    Into a goodly lodge, and gan despoile°   remove
    Of puissant armes, and laid in easie bed;
His name was meeke Obedience rightfully ared.°   understood
                        18
Now when their wearie limbes with kindly rest,
155   And bodies were refresht with due repast,
    Faire Una gan Fidelia faire request,
    To have her knight into her schoolehouse plaste,
    That of her heavenly learning he might taste,
    And heare the wisedome of her words divine.
160   She graunted, and that knight so much agraste,°   graced
    That she him taught celestiall discipline,
And opened his dull eyes, that light mote° in them shine.   might
                        19
And that her sacred Booke, with bloud ywrit,°   written
    That none could read, except° she did them teach,   unless
165   She unto him disclosed every whit,°   bit
    And heavenly documents thereout did preach,
    That weaker wit of man could never reach,
    Of God, of grace, of justice, of free will,
    That wonder was to heare her goodly speach:
170   For she was able, with her words to kill,
And raise againe to life the hart,[3] that she did thrill.°   pierce
                        20
And when she list° poure out her larger spright,   chose to
    She would commaund the hastie Sunne to stay,°   stop

---

1. What has become of her?
2. May God give her more children.
3. Cf. 2 Corinthians 3.6: "for the letter killeth, but the Spirit giveth life."

Or backward turne his course from heavens hight;
175 Sometimes great hostes of men she could dismay,°   *defeat*
Dry-shod to passe, she parts the flouds in tway;°   *two*
And eke huge mountaines from their native seat
She would commaund, themselves to beare away,
And throw in raging sea with roaring threat.°   *threatening roar*
180 Almightie God her gave such powre, and puissance great.[4]

21

The faithfull knight now grew in litle space,
By hearing her, and by her sisters lore,
To such perfection of all heavenly grace,
That wretched world he gan for to abhore,
185 And mortall life gan loath,° as thing forlore,°   *despise / lost*
Greev'd with remembrance of his wicked wayes,
And prickt° with anguish of his sinnes so sore,   *wounded*
That he desirde to end his wretched dayes:
So much the dart of sinfull guilt the soule dismayes.°   *overwhelms*

22

190 But wise Speranza gave him comfort sweet,
And taught him how to take assured hold
Upon her silver anchor, as was meet;
Else had his sinnes so great, and manifold
Made him forget all that Fidelia told.
195 In this distressed doubtfull agonie,
When him his dearest Una did behold,
Disdeining life, desiring leave° to die,   *permission*
She found her selfe assayld with great perplexitie.

23

And came to Caelia to declare her smart,°   *pain*
200 Who well acquainted with that commune plight,
Which sinfull horror workes in wounded hart,
Her wisely comforted all that she might,
With goodly counsell and advisement° right;   *advice*
And streightway sent with carefull diligence,
205 To fetch a Leach,° the which had great insight   *doctor*
In that disease of grieved conscience,
And well could cure the same; His name was Patience.

24

Who comming to that soule-diseased knight,
Could hardly him intreat,° to tell his griefe:[5]   *convince*
210 Which knowne, and all that noyd° his heavie spright   *troubled*
Well searcht,° eftsoones he gan apply reliefe   *explored*
Of salves and med'cines, which had passing priefe,°   *surpassing efficacy*
And thereto added words of wondrous might:
By which to ease he him recured briefe,°   *quickly cured*
215 And much asswag'd° the passion° of his plight,   *soothed / suffering*
That he his paine endur'd, as seeming now more light.

---

4. These miracles were attested in Scripture: stopping the sun, Joshua 10.12–13; turning back the sun, 2 Kings 20.10–11; defeating great hosts, Judges 1.21; parting the sea, Exodus 14.22; and moving mountains, Matthew 21.21.
5. Confession is a necessary element of the Redcrosse Knight's recovery.

25

But yet the cause and root of all his ill,
  Inward corruption, and infected sin,
  Not purg'd° nor heald, behind remained still,   *cleansed*
220 And festring sore did rankle yet within,
  Close creeping twixt the marrow° and the skin.   *bone*
  Which to extirpe,° he laid him privily°   *remove / privately*
  Downe in a darkesome lowly place farre in,
  Whereas he meant his corrosives to apply,
225 And with streight° diet tame his stubborne malady.[6]   *strict*

26

In ashes and sackcloth he did array°   *dress*
  His daintie corse,[7] proud humors to abate,[8]
  And dieted with fasting every day,
  The swelling of his wounds to mitigate,
230 And made him pray both earely and eke late:
  And ever as superfluous flesh did rot
  Amendment readie still at hand did wayt,
  To pluck it out with pincers firie whot,°   *not*
That soone in him was left no one corrupted jot.°   *bit*

27

235 And bitter Penance with an yron whip,
  Was wont him once to disple° every day: *discipline*
  And sharpe Remorse his hart did pricke° and nip,   *pierce*
  That drops of bloud thence° like a well did play;   *from his heart*
  And sad Repentance used to embay°   *drench*
240 His bodie in salt water smarting sore,
  The filthy blots of sinne to wash away.
  So in short space they did to health restore
The man that would not live, but earst lay at deathes dore.

28

In which his torment often was so great,
245 That like a Lyon he would cry and rore,
  And rend his flesh, and his owne synewes° eat.   *muscles*
  His owne deare Una hearing evermore
  His ruefull shriekes and gronings, often tore
  Her guiltlesse garments, and her golden heare,
250 For pitty of his paine and anguish sore;
  Yet all with patience wisely she did beare;
For well she wist, his crime could else be never cleare.°   *cleansed*

29

Whom thus recover'd by wise Patience,
  And trew Repentance they to Una brought:
255 Who joyous of his cured conscience,
  Him dearely kist, and fairely eke besought
  Himselfe to chearish, and consuming thought

---

6. To heal the Redcrosse Knight, Patience returns him to Orgoglio's dungeon. Patience intends to use corrosive medication to remove his "inward corruption."
7. Patience has the Redcrosse Knight assume the role of a penitent.
8. According to Renaissance medicine, the humors, or bodily fluids, must be in balance to achieve good health; here Patience wants to "abate" or diminish them. The Redcrosse Knight's adventure in the House of Pride has left him with an excess of pride, which the doctor seeks to remove through penance and prayer.

To put away out of his carefull° brest.   *worried*
By this Charissa, late in child-bed brought,[9]
260 Was woxen strong, and left her fruitfull nest;
To her faire Una brought this unacquainted guest.

                              30

She was a woman in her freshest age,
   Of wondrous beauty, and of bountie° rare,   *generosity*
   With goodly grace and comely° personage,   *attractive*
265 That was on earth not easie to compare;
   Full of great love, but Cupids wanton snare
   As hell she hated, chast in worke and will;
   Her necke and breasts were ever open bare,
   That ay° thereof her babes might sucke their fill;   *always*
270 The rest was all in yellow robes arayed still.°   *always*

                              31

A multitude of babes about her hong,
   Playing their sports, that joyd her to behold,
   Whom still° she fed, whiles they were weake and young,   *always*
   But thrust them forth still, as they wexed° old: *grew*
275 And on her head she wore a tyre° of gold,   *crown*
   Adornd with gemmes and owches° wondrous faire,   *jewels*
   Whose passing price uneath° was to be told;[1]   *scarcely*
   And by her side there sate a gentle paire
Of turtle doves, she sitting in an yvorie chaire.

                              32

280 The knight and Una entring, faire her greet,
   And bid her joy of that her happie brood;
   Who them requites° with court'sies seeming meet,°   *repays/suitable*
   And entertaines with friendly chearefull mood.
   Then Una her besought,° to be so good,   *requested*
285 As in her vertuous rules to schoole her knight,
   Now after all his torment well withstood,
   In that sad house of Penaunce, where his spright
Had past the paines of hell, and long enduring night.

                              33

She was right joyous of her just° request,   *reasonable*
290 And taking by the hand that Faeries sonne,
   Gan him instruct in every good behest,°   *command*
   Of love, and righteousnesse, and well to donne,°   *good deeds*
   And wrath, and hatred warely° to shonne,   *carefully*
   That drew on men Gods hatred, and his wrath,
295 And many soules in dolours had fordonne:°   *overcome*
   In which when him she well instructed hath,
From thence to heaven she teacheth him the ready° path.   *direct*

                              34

Wherein his weaker wandring steps to guide,
   An auncient matrone she to her does call,
300 Whose sober lookes her wisedome well descride:°   *revealed*

---

9. Charissa, who had recently given birth.   1. Whose surpassing value was incalculable.

Her name was Mercie, well knowne over all,
To be both gratious, and eke liberall:
To whom the carefull charge of him she gave,
To lead aright, that he should never fall
305   In all his wayes through this wide worldes wave,°   *currents*
That Mercy in the end his righteous soule might save.

35

The godly Matrone by the hand him beares°   *leads*
Forth from her presence, by a narrow way,
Scattred with bushy thornes, and ragged breares,°   *briars*
310   Which still° before him she remov'd away,   *ever*
That nothing might his ready° passage stay:°   *direct/stop*
And ever when his feet encombred were,
Or gan to shrinke,° or from the right to stray,   *pull back*
She held him fast,° and firmely did upbeare,°   *firmly/support*
315   As carefull Nourse her child from falling oft does reare.°   *raise*

36

Eftsoones unto an holy Hospitall,°   *hostel*
That was fore° by the way, she did him bring,   *close*
In which seven Bead-men° that had vowed all   *men of prayer*
Their life to service of high heavens king
320   Did spend their dayes in doing godly thing:
Their gates to all were open evermore,°   *always*
That by the wearie way were traveiling,
And one sate° wayting ever them before,   *sat*
To call in commers-by,° that needy were and pore.   *passers-by*

37

325   The first of them that eldest was, and best,
Of all the house had charge and governement,
As Guardian and Steward of the rest:
His office° was to give entertainment°   *duty/provisions*
And lodging, unto all that came, and went:
330   Not unto such, as could him feast againe,
And double quite,° for that he on them spent,   *repay*
But such, as want° of harbour did constraine:[2]   *lack*
Those for Gods sake his dewty was to entertaine.

38

The second was as Almner[3] of the place,
335   His office was, the hungry for to feed,
And thristy give to drinke, a worke of grace:
He feard not once him selfe to be in need,
Ne car'd to hoord° for those, whom he did breede:°   *hoard/his children*
The grace of God he layd up still in store,
340   Which as a stocke he left unto his seede;
He had enough, what need him care for more?
And had he lesse, yet some he would give to the pore.[4]

---

2. He did not provide for those who could return the favor with an even more lavish reception, but provided only for those who were destitute.

3. One who provides charitable relief to the poor.

4. He did not accumulate worldly goods for the wealth of his family, but gave to the poor, which made him rich in the virtue of charity.

39

The third had of their wardrobe custodie,
  In which were not rich tyres,° nor garments gay,°   *clothes/trashy*
345 The plumes of pride, and wings of vanitie,
  But clothes meet to keepe keene could° away,   *sharp cold*
  And naked nature seemely° to aray;   *suitably*
  With which bare wretched wights he dayly clad,
  The images of God in earthly clay;
350 And if that no spare cloths to give he had,
His owne coate he would cut, and it distribute glad.

40

The fourth appointed by his office was,
  Poore prisoners to relieve with gratious ayd,°   *aid*
  And captives to redeeme° with price of bras,   *ransom*
355 From Turkes and Sarazins, which them had stayd;°   *imprisoned*
  And though they faultie were,[5] yet well he wayd,°   *judged*
  That God to us forgiveth every howre
  Much more then that, why° they in bands° were layd,   *for which/chains*
  And he that harrowd hell with heavie stowre,°   *sorrow*
360 The faultie soules from thence brought to his heavenly bowre.[6]

41

The fift had charge sicke persons to attend,
  And comfort those, in point° of death which lay;   *at the brink*
  For them most needeth comfort in the end,
  When sin, and hell, and death do most dismay
365 The feeble soule departing hence away.
  All is but lost, that living we bestow,
  If not well ended at our dying day.[7]
  O man have mind of that last bitter throw;°   *agony*
For as the tree does fall, so lyes it ever low.

42

370 The sixt had charge of them now being dead,
  In seemely sort their corses to engrave,°   *bury*
  And deck with dainty flowres their bridall bed,
  That to their heavenly spouse[8] both sweet and brave
  They might appeare, when he their soules shall save.
375 The wondrous workemanship of Gods owne mould,°   *image*
  Whose face he made, all beasts to feare, and gave
  All in his hand, even dead we honour should.
Ah dearest God me graunt, I dead be not defould.°   *defiled*

43

The seventh now after death and buriall done,
380 Had charge the tender Orphans of the dead
  And widowes ayd, least° they should be undone:°   *lest/ruined*
  In face of judgement he their right would plead,

5. Christian prisoners of pagans were "faultie" if they had given up their faith, even if they had been tortured in the process. But although succumbing to pagan force was strictly speaking a sin, the fourth Beadman considers that God forgives much greater sins all the time.
6. According to a medieval story, after his crucifixion Christ descended into Hell to release good people who had lived before him and thus had not been able to enter heaven.
7. A lifetime of faith is lost if one gives in to despair at the time of death.
8. In Revelation 21.2, the redeemed are "prepared as a bride adorned for her husband."

Ne ought° the powre of mighty men did dread   *not at all*
  In their defence,[9] nor would for gold or fee
Be wonne° their rightfull causes downe to tread: *bribed*
  And when they stood in most necessitee,
He did supply their want, and gave them° ever° free.   *to them / always*

44

There when the Elfin knight arrived was,
  The first and chiefest of the seven, whose care°   *duty*
Was guests to welcome, towardes him did pas:°   *go*
  Where seeing Mercie, that his steps up bare,°   *supported*
  And always led, to her with reverence rare
He humbly louted° in meeke lowlinesse,   *bowed*
  And seemely° welcome for her did prepare: *suitable*
For of their order she was Patronesse,°   *protector*
  Albe° Charissa were their chiefest founderesse.   *although*

45

There she awhile him stayes, him selfe to rest,
  That to the rest° more able he might bee: *remainder*
During which time, in every good behest°   *deed*
  And godly worke of Almes and charitee
She him instructed with great industree;
  Shortly therein so perfect he became,
That from the first unto the last degree,
  His mortall life he learned had to frame°   *conduct*
In holy righteousnesse,[1] without rebuke or blame.

46

Thence forward by that painfull way they pas,°   *go*
  Forth to an hill, that was both steepe and hy;
On top whereof a sacred chappell was,
  And eke a litle Hermitage thereby,
Wherein an aged holy man did lye,
  That day and night said his devotion,
Ne other worldly busines did apply;°   *conduct*
  His name was heavenly Contemplation;
Of God and goodnesse was his meditation.

47

Great grace that old man to him given had;
  For God he often saw from heavens hight,°   *height*
All were his earthly eyen both blunt° and bad,   *blurred*
  And through great age had lost their kindly° sight,   *natural*
Yet wondrous quick and persant° was his spright,   *piercing*
  As Eagles eye, that can behold the Sunne:
That hill they scale° with all their powre and might,   *climb*
  That his frayle thighes nigh° wearie and fordonne   *all but*
Gan faile, but by her° helpe the top at last he wonne.°   *Mercy's / reached*

48

There they do finde that godly aged Sire,
  With snowy lockes adowne his shoulders shed,

---

9. He would plead their causes in court and did not fear the power of mighty men.

1. Spenser emphasizes that holy righteousness is not just an inner moral state but is achieved through the active practice of charity.

As hoarie frost with spangles° doth attire   *icicles*
   The mossy braunches of an Oke halfe ded.
   Each bone might through his body well be red,°   *seen*
   And every sinew° seene through his long fast: *muscle*
430   For nought he car'd his carcas long unfed;[2]
   His mind was full of spirituall repast,
And pyn'd° his flesh, to keepe his body low and chast.   *starred*

49

Who when these two approching he aspide,°   *saw*
   At their first presence grew agrieved sore,°   *very upset*
435   That forst him lay his heavenly thoughts aside;
   And had he not that Dame respected more,
   Whom highly he did reverence and adore,
   He would not once have moved for the knight.
   They him saluted standing far afore;°   *at a distance*
440   Who well them greeting, humbly did requight,°   *return the greeting*
And asked, to what end they clomb that tedious height.

50

What end (quoth° she) should cause us take such paine,   *said*
   But that same end, which every living wight
   Should make his marke,° high heaven to attaine?   *aim*
445   Is not from hence the way, that leadeth right
   To that most glorious house, that glistreth° bright   *shines*
   With burning starres, and everliuing fire,
   Whereof the keyes[3] are to thy hand behight°   *delivered*
   By wise Fidelia? she doth thee require,
450 To shew it to this knight, according° his desire.   *granting*

51

Thrise° happy man, said then the father grave,   *thrice*
   Whose staggering steps thy steady hand doth lead,
   And shewes the way, his sinfull soule to save.
   Who better can the way to heaven aread,°   *show*
455   Then thou thy selfe, that was both borne and bred
   In heavenly throne, where thousand Angels shine?
   Thou doest the prayers of the righteous sead°   *the redeemed*
   Present before the majestie divine,
And his avenging wrath to clemencie incline.[4]

52

460 Yet since thou bidst, thy pleasure shalbe donne.
   Then come thou man of earth, and see the way,
   That never yet was seene of Faeries sonne,
   That never leads the traveiler astray,
   But after labours long, and sad delay,
465   Brings them to joyous rest and endlesse blis.
   But first thou must a season fast and pray,
   Till from her bands° the spright assoiled° is,[5]   *bonds/released*
And have her strength recur'd° from fraile infirmitis.   *restored*

---

2. He did not care about the hunger of his body.   Almighty's wrath into forgiveness.
3. The keys to the kingdom of heaven.   5. The bonds that Contemplation is referring to are the
4. Contemplation is addressing Mercy, who turns the   bonds of the flesh.

53

470 That done, he leads him to the highest Mount;[6]
Such one,[7] as that same mighty man of God,
That bloud-red billowes[8] like a walled front
On either side disparted with his rod,
Till that his army dry-foot through them yod,°   *went*
475 Dwelt fortie dayes upon; where writ in stone
With bloudy letters by the hand of God,
The bitter doome of death and balefull mone°   *moan*
He did receive, whiles flashing fire about him shone.[9]

54

Or like that sacred hill, whose head full hie,
Adornd with fruitfull Olives all arownd,[1]
480 Is, as it were for endlesse memory
Of that deare Lord, who oft thereon was fownd,
For ever with a flowring girlond crownd:
Or like that pleasaunt Mount, that is for ay
Through famous Poets verse each where renownd,[2]
485 On which the thrise three learned Ladies[3] play
Their heavenly notes, and make full many a lovely lay.

55

From thence, far off he unto him did shew
A litle path, that was both steepe and long,
Which to a goodly Citie[4] led his vew;
490 Whose wals and towres were builded high and strong
Of perle and precious stone, that earthly tong
Cannot describe, nor wit of man can tell;
Too high a ditty for my simple song;
The Citie of the great king hight it well,°   *it is well named*
495 Wherein eternall peace and happinesse doth dwell.[5]

56

As he thereon stood gazing, he might see
The blessed Angels to and fro descend[6]
From highest heaven, in gladsome° companee,°   *happy/friendship*
And with great joy into that Citie wend,
500 As commonly as friend does with his frend,
Whereat he wondred much, and gan enquere,°   *asked*
What stately building durst° so high extend   *dared*
Her loftie towres unto the starry sphere,°   *heavens*
And what unknowen nation there empeopled were.°   *inhabited it*

6. This is the "great and high mountain" of Revelation 21.10, from which God showed John the New Jerusalem.
7. Such a mountain—Sinai—Moses climbed to spend 40 days before receiving the Ten Commandments.
8. Spenser is referring to the Red Sea, which Moses parted to allow the Israelites to escape from Egypt without drowning.
9. Referring to the burning bush through which God appeared to Moses (Deuteronomy 4.11).
1. The Mount of Olives, where Jesus taught.

2. Parnassus, the home of the Greek gods and celebrated by the Greek poets.
3. The nine Muses, goddesses of the arts and sciences.
4. The New Jerusalem, the promised home of the faithful in eternity (Revelation 20.10–21).
5. Cf. Psalms 48.2: "the joy of the whole earth is Mount Zion . . . the city of the great king."
6. The image recalls Jacob's vision of the ladder that extended from earth to heaven (Genesis 28.12).

57

505 Faire knight (quoth he) Hierusalem that is,
The new Hierusalem, that God has built
For those to dwell in, that are chosen his,
His chosen people purg'd from sinfull guilt,
With pretious bloud,[7] which cruelly was spilt
510 On cursed tree, of that unspotted lam,°   *lamb*
That for the sinnes of all the world was kilt:
Now are they Saints all in that Citie sam,°   *same*
More deare unto their God, then younglings to their dam.

58

Till now, said then the knight, I weened well,
515 That great Cleopolis,[8] where I have beene,
In which that fairest Faerie Queene doth dwell,
The fairest Citie was, that might be seene;
And that bright towre all built of christall cleene,
Panthea, seemd the brightest thing, that was:
520 But now by proofe all otherwise I weene;
For this great Citie that does far surpas,
And this bright Angels towre quite dims that towre of glas.

59

Most trew, then said the holy aged man;
Yet is Cleopolis for earthly frame,[9]
525 The fairest peece, that eye beholden can:
And well beseemes all knights of noble name,
That covet in th'immortall booke of fame
To be eternized, that same to haunt,
And doen their service to that soveraigne Dame,[1]
530 That glorie does to them for guerdon° graunt: *reward*
For she is heavenly borne, and heaven may justly vaunt.[2]

60

And thou faire ymp,° sprong out from English race,   *child*
How ever now accompted° Elfins sonne,   *considered*
Well worthy doest thy service for her grace,
535 To aide a virgin desolate foredonne.°   *in distress*
But when thou famous victorie hast wonne,
And high emongst all knights hast hong thy shield,
Thenceforth the suit° of earthly conquest shonne,°   *pursuit/shun*
And wash thy hands from guilt of bloudy field:
540 For bloud can nought but sin, and wars but sorrowes yield.

61

Then seeke this path, that I to thee presage,°   *foretell*
Which after all to heaven shall thee send;
Then peaceably thy painefull pilgrimage

---

7. The blood spilled by Christ when he was crucified and
by which the faithful are redeemed from sin.
8. The Redcrosse Knight compares the New Jerusalem
with Cleopolis, the city ruled by the Faerie Queene and
Panthea—literally, in Greek, all sights or the best of
sights—each a perfect representation of a political state
(as realized by Spenser and perhaps by Plato and others in
their political treatises). He finds that the transcendent

brilliance of the angels' city surpasses that of the other
cities of "glass," that is, products of a merely human power of reflection.
9. As an earthly as opposed to a heavenly structure.
1. It is fitting that noble knights who seek glory serve in
the Faerie Queene's court.
2. Since the Faerie Queene was born in Heaven, Heaven
may rightfully boast ("vaunt") that it is her home.

To yonder same Hierusalem do bend,°   *go*
545   Where is for thee ordaind a blessed end:
For thou emongst those Saints, whom thou doest see,
Shalt be a Saint, and thine owne nations frend
And Patrone: thou Saint George shalt called bee,
Saint George of mery England, the signe of victoree.

62

550   Unworthy wretch (quoth he°) of so great grace,   *Redcrosse Knight*
How dare I thinke such glory to attaine?
These that have it attaind, were in like cace
(Quoth he°) as wretched, and liv'd in like paine.   *Contemplation*
But deeds of armes must I³ at last be faine,°   *willing*
555   And Ladies love to leave so dearely bought?
What need of armes, where peace doth ay° remaine,   *ever*
(Said he) and battailes none are to be fought?
As for loose loves are vaine,° and vanish into nought.   *false*

63

O let me not (quoth he) then turne againe
560   Backe to the world, whose joyes so fruitlesse are;
But let me here for aye° in peace remaine,   *ever*
Or streight way° on that last long voyage fare,⁴   *immediately*
That nothing may my present hope empare.°   *diminish*
That may not be (said he) ne maist thou yit
565   Forgo° that royall maides bequeathed care,   *give up*
Who did her cause into thy hand commit,⁵
Till from her cursed foe thou have her freely quit.

64

Then shall I soone, (quoth he) so God me grace,
Abet° that virgins cause disconsolate,   *assist*
570   And shortly backe returne unto this place,
To walke this way in Pilgrims poore estate.°   *condition*
But now aread,° old father, why of late°   *tell me / just now*
Didst thou behight° me borne of English blood,   *call*
Whom all a Faeries sonne doen nominate?⁶
575   That word shall I (said he) avouchen° good,   *prove*
Sith to thee is unknowne the cradle of thy brood.°   *girth*

65

For well I wote, thou springst from ancient race
Of Saxon kings, that have with mightie hand
And many bloudie battailes fought in place°   *in that place*
580   High reard° their royall throne in Britane land,   *erected*
And vanquisht them,° unable to withstand: *the Britons*
From thence a Faerie thee unweeting reft,°   *took*
There as thou slepst in tender swadling band,

---

3. The Redcrosse Knight asks himself whether he can abandon chivalry and then understands that in the New Jerusalem there are neither wars nor loves.
4. The Redcrosse Knight is referring to death.
5. He may not yet give up Una's quest to which he is committed; he must avenge and free her from her enemy.
6. The Redcrosse Knight believes he is an inhabitant of

Faerie Land, the fictional ground of the poem as Spenser names it to his readers. When Contemplation tells the Redcrosse Knight that he is actually English, Spenser is alerting readers to the fact that Saint George (as Spenser apparently believed) was a historical figure, represented in historical record, and not merely a figment of the poet's imagination.

   And her base Elfin brood° there for thee left.[7]   *child*

585 Such men do Chaungelings° call, so chaungd° by Faeries theft. *changelings/*
                                  switched

            66

   Thence° she thee brought into this Faerie lond,   *from there*
   And in an heaped furrow did thee hyde,
   Where thee a Ploughman all unweeting fond,
   As he his toylesome teme° that way did guyde,   *toiling oxen*

590 And brought thee up in ploughmans state to byde,
   Whereof Georgos° he thee gave to name;   *farmer*
   Till prickt° with courage, and thy forces pryde, *moved*
   To Faery court thou cam'st to seeke for fame,
   And prove thy puissaunt armes, as seemes thee best became.[8]

            67

595 O holy Sire (quoth he) how shall I quight°   *repay*
   The many favours I with thee have found,
   That hast my name and nation red aright,°   *correctly*
   And taught the way that does to heaven bound?
   This said, adowne he looked to the ground,

600 To have returnd, but dazed were his eyne,
   Through passing brightnesse, which did quite confound° *bewilder*
   His feeble sence, and too exceeding shyne.[9]
  So darke are earthly things compard to things divine.

            68

   At last whenas himselfe he gan to find,

605 To Una back he cast him° to retire;   *decided*
   Who him awaited still with pensive mind.
   Great thankes and goodly meed° to that good syre, *reward*
   He thence departing gave for his paines hyre.[1]
   So came to Una, who him joyd to see,

610 And after litle rest, gan him desire,
   Of her adventure° mindfull for to bee.   *quest*
  So leave they take of Caelia, and her daughters three.

Canto 11

The knight with that old Dragon fights
two dayes incessantly:
The third him overthrowes, and gayns
most glorious victory.

            1

   High time now gan it wex° for Una faire,   *grow*
   To thinke of those her captive Parents deare,
   And their forwasted° kingdome to repaire: *desolated*

---

7. I.e., unknown to you, a fairy took you from your cradle
and put its own child in your place.
8. The qualities that prompted the Redcrosse Knight to
leave the farm—i.e., pride in his chivalric skill—are qualities his faith will have had to modify to conform to a

Christian mode of life.
9. The Redcrosse Knight glances down, intending to look
back up, but the force of revelation overwhelms him.
1. The hire of his pains, the trouble Contemplation took
to instruct the Redcrosse Knight.

Whereto whenas they now approched neare,
5 With hartie words her knight she gan to cheare,
And in her modest manner thus bespake;°   *said*
Deare knight, as deare, as ever knight was deare,
That all these sorrowes suffer for my sake,
High heaven behold the tedious toyle, ye for me take.[1]

2

10 Now are we come unto my native soyle,
And to the place, where all our perils dwell;
Here haunts° that feend, and does his dayly spoyle,°   *lurks/evil*
Therefore henceforth be at your keeping well,°   *on your guard*
And ever ready for your foeman fell.°   *dangerous enemy*
15 The sparke of noble courage now awake,
And strive your excellent selfe to excell;°   *outdo yourself*
That shall ye evermore renowmed make,
Above all knights on earth, that batteill undertake.

3

And pointing forth, lo yonder is (said she)
20 The brasen towre in which my parents deare
For dread of that huge feend emprisond be,
Whom I from far see on the walles appeare,
Whose sight my feeble soule doth greatly cheare:
And on the top of all I do espye
25 The watchman wayting tydings glad to heare,[2]
That O my parents might I happily
Unto you bring, to ease you of your misery.

4

With that they heard a roaring hideous sound,
That all the ayre with terrour filled wide,
30 And seemd uneath° to shake the stedfast ground.   *almost*
Eftsoones that dreadfull Dragon they espide,
Where stretcht he lay upon the sunny side
Of a great hill, himselfe like a great hill.
But all so soone, as he from far descride°   *saw*
35 Those glistring armes, that heaven with light did fill,
He rousd himselfe full blith,° and hastned them untill.°   *joyfully/toward them*

5

Then bad the knight his Lady yede aloofe,°   *stand aside*
And to an hill her selfe with draw aside,
From whence she might behold that battailles proof
40 And eke be safe from daunger far descryde:°   *seen from a distance*
She him obayd, and turnd a little wyde.°   *moved aside*
Now O thou sacred Muse, most learned Dame,[3]
Faire ympe of Phoebus, and his aged bride,
The Nourse of time, and everlasting fame,
45 That warlike hands ennoblest with immortall name;

---

1. Una asks the heavens to witness the difficult task that the Redcrosse Knight undertakes for her.
2. Waiting to hear good news. In the next line, Una addresses her parents, expressing her wish to bring them the good news of their rescue herself.
3. Spenser is calling upon Clio, the muse of history, who preserves great events and records glorious deeds.

6

O gently come into my feeble brest,
 Come gently, but not with that mighty rage,
 Wherewith the martiall troupes thou doest infest,°   *inspire*
 And harts of great Heroës doest enrage,
50 That nought their kindled courage may aswage,°   *diminish*
 Soone as they dreadfull trompe° begins to sownd;   *trumpet*
 The God of warre with his fiers equipage°   *weapons*
 Thou doest awake, sleepe never he so sownd,
And scared nations doest with horrour sterne astownd.°   *astonish*

7

55 Faire Goddesse lay that furious fit aside,[4]
 Till I of warres and bloudy Mars do sing,
 And Briton fields with Sarazin bloud bedyde,
 Twixt that great faery Queene and Paynim king,
 That with their horrour heaven and earth did ring,
60 A worke of labour long, and endlesse prayse:[5]
 But now a while let downe that haughtie string,
 And to my tunes thy second tenor° rayse,   *accompaniment*
That I this man of God his godly armes may blaze.°   *proclaim*

8

By this the dreadful Beast drew nigh to hand,°   *near*
65 Halfe flying, and halfe footing in his hast,
 That with his largenesse measured much land,
 And made wide shadow under his huge wast;°   *bulk*
 As mountaine doth the valley overcast.
 Approching nigh, he reared high afore
70 His body monstrous, horrible, and vast,
 Which to increase his wondrous greatnesse more,
Was swolne with wrath, and poyson, and with bloudy gore.

9

And over, all with brasen scales was armd,
 Like plated coate of steele, so couched neare,°   *closely set*
75 That nought mote perce, ne might his corse be harmd
 With dint of sword, nor push of pointed speare;
 Which as an Eagle, seeing pray appeare,
 His aery plumes doth rouze, full rudely dight,°   *violently arranged*
 So shaked he, that horrour was to heare,
80 For as the clashing of an Armour bright,
Such noyse his rouzed scales did send unto the knight.

10

His flaggy° wings when forth he did display,   *drooping*
 Were like two sayles, in which the hollow wynd
 Is gathered full,[6] and worketh speedy way:
85 And eke the pennes,[7] that did his pineons° bynd,   *feathers*
 Were like mayne-yards,° with flying canvas lynd,   *mainsail ropes*
 With which whenas him list the ayre to beat,

---

4. The muse's "furious fit" is music that rouses men to war.
5. The song of war that Spenser refers to here may be some part of the poem he plans to write in the future.

6. The force of the wind fills the sails and makes them billow out.
7. The bones in the Dragon's wings.

And there by force unwonted passage find,[8]
The cloudes before him fled for terrour great,
90   And all the heavens stood still amazed with his threat.

11

His huge long tayle wound up in hundred foldes,
Does overspred his long bras-scaly backe,
Whose wreathed boughts° when ever he unfoldes,   wound-up coils
And thicke entangled knots adown does slacke,
95   Bespotted as with shields of red and blacke,
It sweepeth all the land behind him farre,
And of three furlongs does but litle lacke;[9]
And at the point two stings in-fixed arre,
Both deadly sharpe, that sharpest steele exceeden farre.

12

100 But stings and sharpest steele did far exceed
The sharpnesse of his cruell rending clawes;
Dead was it sure, as sure as death in deed,
What ever thing does touch his ravenous pawes,
Or what within his reach he ever drawes.
105 But his most hideous head my toung to tell
Does tremble: for his deepe devouring jawes
Wide gaped, like the griesly mouth of hell,
Through which into his darke abisse° all ravin° fell.   pit/prey

13

And that more wondrous was, in either jaw
110 Three ranckes of yron teeth enraunged were,
In which yet trickling bloud and gobbets° raw   chunks
Of late devoured bodies did appeare,
That sight thereof bred cold congealed feare:
Which to increase, and all atonce° to kill,   suddenly
115 A cloud of smoothering smoke and sulphur seare°   burning
Out of his stinking gorge forth steemed still,
That all the ayre about with smoke and stench did fill.

14

His blazing eyes, like two bright shining shields,
Did burne with wrath, and sparkled living fyre;
120 As two broad Beacons, set in open fields,
Send forth their flames farre off to every shyre,°   district
And warning give, that enemies conspyre,
With fire and sword the region to invade;
So flam'd his eyne with rage and rancorous yre:
125 But farre within, as in a hollow glade,
Those glaring lampes were set, that made a dreadfull shade.

15

So dreadfully he towards him did pas,
Forelifting° up aloft his speckled brest,   raising
And often bounding on the brused gras,
130 As for great joyance of his newcome guest.

---

8. Although the Dragon cannot fly normally, he does so
through the sheer force with which he beats his wings.

9. The Dragon's tail measures nearly three furlongs, 660
yards, a third of a mile.

Eftsoones he gan advance his haughtie crest,
   As chauffed Bore° his bristles doth upreare,   *angry boar*
   And shoke his scales to battell readie drest;[1]
   That made the Redcrosse knight nigh quake for feare,
135   As bidding° bold defiance to his foeman neare.   *inciting*

16

The knight gan fairely couch his steadie speare,
   And fiercely ran at him with rigorous might:
   The pointed steele arriving rudely theare,
   His harder hide would neither perce, nor bight,
140   But glauncing by forth passed forward right;
   Yet sore amoved with so puissant push,
   The wrathfull beast about him turned light,°   *quickly*
   And him so rudely passing by, did brush
With his long tayle, that° horse and man to ground did rush.°   *so that/fall*

17

145 Both horse and man up lightly rose againe,
   And fresh encounter towards him addrest:
   But th'idle stroke° yet backe recoyld in vaine,   *futile swordstroke*
   And found no place his deadly point to rest.
   Exceeding rage enflam'd the furious beast,
150   To be avenged of so great despight;
   For never felt his imperceable brest
   So wondrous force, from hand of living wight;
Yet had he prov'd° the powre of many a puissant knight.   *tested*

18

Then with his waving wings displayed wyde,
155   Himselfe up high he lifted from the ground,
   And with strong flight did forcibly divide
   The yielding aire, which nigh° too feeble found   *almost*
   Her flitting partes, and element unsound,
   To beare so great a weight:[2] he cutting way
160   With his broad sayles, about him soared round:
   At last low stouping with unweldie sway,°   *awkward force*
Snatcht up both horse and man, to beare them quite away.

19

Long he them bore above the subject plaine,
   So farre as Ewghen° bow a shaft may send,   *made of yew*
165   Till struggling strong did him at last constraine,
   To let them downe before his flightes end:
   As hagard hauke° presuming to contend   *untamed hawk*
   With hardie fowle, above his hable° might,   *natural*
   His wearie pounces° all in vaine doth spend,   *claws*
170   To trusse° the pray too heavie for his flight;   *carry off*
Which comming downe to ground, does free it selfe by fight.

20

He so disseized° of his gryping grosse,°   *freed/heavy grasp*
   The knight his thrillant speare againe assayd

---

1. He shook his scales into position for battle.
2. The air is almost too weak to support the Dragon; in
other words, the Dragon is almost too heavy to fly, given
the strength of his wings in relation to his overall weight.

In his bras-plated body to embosse,°   *embed*
175   And three mens strength unto the stroke he layd;
       Wherewith the stiffe beame° quaked, as affrayd,   *shaft*
       And glauncing from his scaly necke, did glyde
       Close under his left wing, then broad displayd.
       The percing steele there wrought a wound full wyde,
180   That with the uncouth smart° the Monster lowdly cryde.   *pain*

21

       He cryde, as raging seas are wont to rore,
          When wintry storme his wrathfull wreck does threat,
          The rolling billowes beat the ragged shore,
          As they the earth would shoulder from her seat,
185   And greedie gulfe does gape, as he would eat
          His neighbour element° in his revenge: *the earth*
          Then gin the blustring brethren boldly threat,
          To move the world from off his stedfast henge,°   *hinge*
       And boystrous battell make, each other to avenge.

22

190   The steely head stucke fast° still in his flesh,   *firmly*
          Till with his cruell clawes he snatcht the wood,°   *shaft*
          And quite a sunder broke. Forth flowed fresh
          A gushing river of blacke goarie blood,
          That drowned all the land, whereon he stood;
195   The streame thereof would drive a water-mill.
          Trebly augmented was his furious mood
          With bitter sense of his deepe rooted ill,
       That flames of fire he threw forth from his large nosethrill.°   *nostril*

23

       His hideous tayle then hurled he about,
200   And therewith all enwrapt the nimble thyes°   *thighs*
          Of his froth-fomy steed, whose courage stout
          Striving to loose the knot, that fast him tyes,
          Himselfe in streighter bandes° too rash implyes,   *tighter bondage*
          That to the ground he is perforce° constraynd   *thereby*
205   To throw his rider: who can quickly ryse
          From off the earth, with durty bloud distaynd,°   *stained*
       For that reprochfull fall right fowly he disdaynd.

24

       And fiercely tooke his trenchand° blade in hand,   *sharp*
          With which he stroke so furious and so fell,
210   That nothing seemd the puissance could withstand:
          Upon his crest the hardned yron fell,
          But his more hardned crest was armd so well,
          That deeper dint therein it would not make;
          Yet so extremely did the buffe° him quell,°   *blow/overwhelm*
215   That from thenceforth he shund the like to take,
       But when he saw them come, he did them still forsake.°   *avoid*

25

       The knight was wrath to see his stroke beguyld,°   *foiled*
          And smote againe with more outrageous might;
          But backe againe the sparckling steele recoyld,
220   And left not any marke, where it did light;°   *land*

As if in Adamant° rocke it had bene pight.   *hardest*
The beast impatient of his smarting wound,
And of so fierce and forcible despight,°   *injury*
Thought with his wings to stye° above the ground;   *fly*
225   But his late wounded wing unserviceable found.

26

Then full of griefe and anguish vehement,
He lowdly brayd, that like was never heard,
And from his wide devouring oven° sent   *mouth*
A flake of fire, that flashing in his° beard,   *Redcrosse Knight's*
230   Him all amazd, and almost made affeard:
The scorching flame sore swinged° all his face,   *singed*
And through his armour all his bodie seard,°   *burned*
That he could not endure so cruell cace,°   *situation*
But thought his armes to leave, and helmet to unlace.

27

235   Not that great Champion[3] of the antique world,
Whom famous Poetes verse so much doth vaunt,°   *celebrate*
And hath for twelve huge labours high extold,°   *praised*
So many furies and sharpe fits did haunt,
When him the poysoned garment did enchaunt
240   With Centaures bloud, and bloudie verses charm'd,
As did this knight twelve thousand dolours daunt,°   *defy*
Whom fyrie steele now burnt, that earst° him arm'd,   *recently*
That erst° him goodly arm'd, now most of all him harm'd.   *at first*

28

Faint, wearie, sore, emboyled, grieved, brent
245   With heat, toyle, wounds, armes, smart, and inward fire
That never man such mischiefes did torment;
Death better were, death did he oft desire,
But death will never come, when needes require.
Whom so dismayd when that his foe° beheld,   *the Dragon*
250   He cast to suffer him no more respire,[4]
But gan his sturdie sterne° about to weld,   *tail*
And him° so strongly stroke, that to the ground him feld.   *Redcrosse Knight*

29

It fortuned (as faire it then befell)
Behind his backe unweeting, where he stood,
255   Of auncient time there was a springing well,
From which fast trickled forth a silver flood,
Full of great vertues, and for med'cine good.
Whylome, before that cursed Dragon got
That happie land, and all with innocent blood
260   Defyld those sacred waves, it rightly hot
The well of life, ne yet his vertues had forgot.

30

For unto life the dead it could restore,
And guilt of sinfull crimes cleane wash away,

3. Hercules. After successfully completing his 12 impossible labors, the hero was plagued ("haunted") by "furies": his wife gave him a tunic soaked in the poison blood of a centaur. The blood was meant to work as a love charm but instead burned Hercules' flesh, and he died in agony.
4. The Dragon, seeing how desperate the Redcrosse Knight is, determines to kill him.

Those that with sicknesse were infected sore,

265   It could recure,° and aged long decay   *cure*
    Renew, as one were borne that very day.
    Both Silo this,[5] and Jordan did excell,
    And th'English Bath, and eke the german Spau,
    Ne can Cephise, nor Hebrus match this well:
270 Into the same the knight backe overthrowen, fell.

31

Now gan the golden Phoebus for to steepe
    His fierie face in billowes of the west,
    And his faint steedes watred in Ocean deepe,
    Whiles from their journall° labours they did rest,   *daily*
275 When that infernall Monster, having kest°   *cast*
    His wearie foe into that living well,
    Can high advance his broad discoloured brest,
    Above his wonted pitch, with countenance fell,
    And clapt his yron wings, as victor he did dwell.°   *remain*

32

280 Which when his pensive° Ladie saw from farre,   *worried*
    Great woe and sorrow did her soule assay,
    As weening that the sad end of the warre,
    And gan to highest God entirely pray,
    That feared chance from her to turne away;[6]
285 With folded hands and knees full lowly bent
    All night she watcht, ne once adowne would lay
    Her daintie limbs in her sad dreriment,°   *plight*
    But praying still did wake, and waking did lament.

33

The morrow next gan early to appeare,
290 That Titan rose to runne his daily race;
    But early ere the morrow next gan reare
    Out of the sea faire Titans deawy face,
    Up rose the gentle virgin from her place,
    And looked all about, if she might spy
295 Her loved knight to move his manly pace:
    For she had great doubt° of his safety,   *fear*
    Since late she saw him fall before his enemy.

34

At last she saw, where he upstarted brave
    Out of the well, wherein he drenched lay;
300 As Eagle fresh out of the Ocean wave,
    Where he hath left his plumes all hoary gray,
    And deckt himselfe with feathers youthly gay,
    Like Eyas hauke[7] up mounts unto the skies,
    His newly budded pineons° to assay,   *wings*

---

5. Silo, Jordan, Bath, Spau, Cephise, and Hebrus: all waters reputed to have healing powers. The blind man is cured by bathing in the waters of Siloam (John 9.7), and John baptized Christ in the River Jordan (Matthew 3.16). Cephise and Hebrus are mentioned in classical mythology. Spenser probably wanted his readers to associate the water from "the well of life" with baptism, as in John 4.14.

6. She prayed to God to prevent the event she fears, the death of the Redcrosse Knight.

7. A young, untamed hawk; a symbol of victory.

305   And marveiles at himselfe, still as he flies:
        So new this new-borne knight to battell new did rise.

                    35

        Whom when the damned feend so fresh did spy,
            No wonder if he wondred at the sight,
            And doubted, whether his late enemy
310   It were, or other new supplied knight.
            He,° now to prove his late renewed might,   *Redcrosse Knight*
            High brandishing his bright deaw-burning blade,[8]
            Upon his crested scalpe so sore did smite,
            That to the scull a yawning wound it made:
315   The deadly dint his dulled senses all dismaid.

                    36

        I wote not, whether the revenging steele
            Were hardned with that holy water dew,
            Wherein he fell, or sharper edge did feele,
            Or his baptized hands now greater grew;
320   Or other secret vertue did ensew;°   *result*
            Else never could the force of fleshly arme,
            Ne molten mettall in his° bloud embrew:°   *the Dragon's/soak*
            For till that stownd° could never wight him harme,[9]   *moment*
        By subtilty, nor slight, nor might, nor mighty charme.

                    37

325   The cruell wound enraged him so sore,
            That loud he yelded for exceeding paine;
            As hundred ramping Lyons seem'd to rore,
            Whom ravenous hunger did thereto constraine:°   *torment*
            Then gan he tosse aloft his stretched traine,
330   And therewith scourge the buxome° aire so sore,   *yielding*
            That to his force to yeelden it was faine;
            Ne ought° his sturdie strokes might stand afore,°   *nor anything/before*
        That high trees overthrew, and rocks in peeces tore.

                    38

        The same° advancing high above his head,   *the Dragon*
335   With sharpe intended sting so rude him smot,
            That to the earth him drove, as stricken dead,
            Ne living wight would have him life behot:°   *predicted*
            The mortall sting his angry needle shot
            Quite through his shield, and in his shoulder seasd,°   *pierced*
340   Where fast it stucke, ne would there out be got:
            The griefe thereof him wondrous sore diseasd,
        Ne might hisranckling paine with patience be appeasd.

                    39

        But yet more mindfull of his honour deare,
            Then of the grievous smart, which him did wring,°   *afflict*
345   From loathed soile he can° him lightly reare,   *did*
            And strove to loose the farre infixed sting:
            Which when in vaine he tryde with struggeling,
            Inflam'd with wrath, his raging blade he heft,°   *lifted*
            And strooke so strongly, that the knotty string

8. The Redcrosse Knight's sword is like the sun, which
burns up the dew.

9. Until that moment, neither human strength nor human
weapons could succeed in piercing the Dragon's flesh.

350   Of his huge taile he quite a sunder cleft,
        Five joynts thereof he hewd,° and but the stump him left.   *cut*

                              40
        Hart cannot thinke, what outrage, and what cryes,
          With foule enfouldred[1] smoake and flashing fire,
          The hell-bred beast threw forth unto the skyes,
355   That all was covered with darknesse dire:
          Then fraught with rancour,° and engorged ire,   *malice*
          He cast at once him to avenge for all,
          And gathering up himselfe out of the mire,
          With his uneven wings did fiercely fall
360   Upon his sunne-bright shield, and gript it fast withall.°   *as well*

                              41
        Much was the man encombred with his hold,
          In feare to lose his weapon in his paw,
          Ne wist yet, how his talants to unfold;
          Nor harder was from Cerberus[2] greedie jaw
365   To plucke a bone, then from his cruell claw
          To reave°by strength the griped gage[3] away: *pry*
          Thrise he assayd it from his foot to draw,
          And thrise in vaine to draw it did assay,
        It booted nought to thinke, to robbe him of his pray.

                              42
370   Tho when he saw no power might prevaile,
          His trustie sword he cald to his last aid,
          Wherewith he fiercely did his foe assaile,
          And double blowes about him stoutly laid,
          That glauncing fire out of the yron plaid;°   *leaped*
375   As sparckles from the Anduile° use to fly,   *anvil*
          When heavie hammers on the wedge° are swaid;°   *metal / struck*
          Therewith at last he forst him to unty
        One of his grasping feete, him° to defend thereby.   *himself*

                              43
        The other foot, fast fixed on his shield,
380   Whenas no strength, nor stroks mote him° constraine   *the Dragon*
          To loose, ne yet the warlike pledge to yield,
          He° smot thereat with all his might and maine,   *Redcrosse Knight*
          That nought° so wondrous puissance might sustaine;   *nothing*
          Upon the joynt the lucky steele did light,
385   And made such way, that hewd it quite in twaine;
          The paw yet missed not his minisht might,°   *diminished strength*
        But hong still on the shield, as it at first was pight.°   *fixed*

                              44
        For griefe thereof, and divelish despight,
          From his infernall fournace forth he threw
390   Huge flames, that dimmed all the heavens light,
          Enrold in duskish smoke and brimstone[4] blew;
          As burning Aetna° from his boyling stew   *a volcano in Sicily*
          Doth belch out flames, and rockes in peeces broke,

---

1. Like a thundercloud filled with lightning bolts.
2. The mythological three-headed dog guarding the gates of Hell.
3. The prize over which a battle is fought; here, the Redcrosse Knight's shield.
4. Sulfur, which burns blue.

And ragged ribs of mountaines molten new,°   *newly molten*
395   Enwrapt in coleblacke clouds and filthy smoke,
That all the land with stench, and heaven with horror choke.

45

The heate whereof, and harmefull pestilence°   *destruction*
So sore him noyd,° that forst him to retire   *injured*
A little backward for his best defence,
400   To save his bodie from the scorching fire,
Which he° from hellish entrailes did expire.   *the Dragon*
It chaunst (eternall God that chaunce did guide)
As he recoyled° backward, in the mire   *shrank*
His nigh forwearied° feeble feet did slide,   *tired*
405   And downe he fell, with dread of shame sore terrifide.

46

There grew a goodly tree him faire beside,
Loaden with fruit and apples rosie red,
As they in pure vermilion had beene dide,
Whereof great vertues over all were red:
410   For happie life to all, which thereon fed,
And life eke everlasting did befall:
Great God it planted in that blessed sted°   *place*
With his almightie hand, and did it call
The tree of life,[5] the crime of our first fathers fall.

47

415   In all the world like was not to be found,
Save in that soile, where all good things did grow,
And freely sprong out of the fruitfull ground,
As incorrupted Nature did them sow,
Till that dread Dragon° all did overthrow.   *Satan, the serpent*
420   Another like faire tree eke grew thereby,[6]
Whereof who so did eat, eftsoones did know
Both good and ill: O mornefull memory:
That tree through one mans fault hath doen us all to dy.

48

From that first tree forth flowd, as from a well,
425   A trickling streame of Balme, most soveraine
And daintie deare,° which on the ground still fell, *very precious*
And overflowed all the fertill plaine,
As it had deawed° bene with timely raine: *sprinkled*
Life and long health that gratious ointment gave,
430   And deadly woundes could heale, and reare againe
The senseless corse appointed for the grave.[7]
Into that same he fell: which did from death him save.

49

For nigh thereto the ever damned beast
Durst° not approch, for he was deadly made,[8]   *dared*
435   And all that life preserved, did detest:

5. The tree of life was denied to Adam for his "crime"—his
defiance of God's commandment not to eat the fruit of the
tree of knowledge of good and evil. As a result, God expelled
him from the Garden of Eden where the tree of life grew.
6. The tree of knowledge of good and evil.
7. The balm from the tree of life heals the Redcrosse

Knight; its function follows that of the water in baptism.
Having been freed of the consequences of original sin in
baptism, the baptized are constantly open to restorations of
faith in pursuit of good works. Cf. Revelation 22.2: "The
leaves of the tree [of life] served to heale the nations."
8. He was allied with Death, not Life.

    Yet he it° oft adventur'd° to invade.°   *the tree / tried / destroy*
    By this the drouping day-light gan to fade,
    And yeeld his roome° to sad succeeding night,   *place*
    Who with her sable mantle gan to shade
440   The face of earth, and wayes of living wight,
And high her burning torch set up in heaven bright.

50

And gentle Una saw the second fall
    Of her deare knight, who wearie of long fight,
    And faint through losse of bloud, mov'd not at all,
445   But lay as in a dreame of deepe delight,
    Besmeard with pretious Balme, whose vertuous might
    Did heale his wounds, and scorching heat alay,
    Againe she stricken was with sore affright,
    And for his safetie gan devoutly pray;
450 And watch the noyous° night, and wait for joyous day.   *sorrowful*

51

The joyous day gan early to appeare,
    And faire Aurora[9] from the deawy bed
    Of aged Tithone gan her selfe to reare,
    With rosie cheekes, for shame as blushing red;
455   Her golden lockes for haste were loosely shed
    About her eares, when Una her did marke
    Clymbe to her charet, all with flowers spred,
    From heaven high to chase the chearelesse darke;
With merry note her° loud salutes the mounting larke.   *Una*

52

460 Then freshly up arose the doughtie knight,
    All healed of his hurts and woundes wide,
    And did himselfe to battell readie dight;
    Whose early foe awaiting him beside
    To have devourd, so soone as day he spyde,
465   When now he saw himselfe so freshly reare,
    As if late fight had nought him damnifyde,°   *harmed*
    He woxe° dismayd, and gan his fate to feare;   *grew*
Nathlesse° with wonted rage he him advaunced neare.   *nonetheless*

53

And in his first encounter, gaping wide,
470   He thought attonce° him to have swallowd quight,   *at once*
    And rusht upon him with outragious pride;
    Who him r'encountring fierce, as hauke in flight,
    Perforce° rebutted° backe. The weapon bright   *necessarily / attacked*
    Taking advantage of his open jaw,
475   Ran through his mouth with so importune° might,   *violent*
    That deepe emperst his darksome hollow maw,°   *mouth*
And back retyrd,° his life bloud forth with all did draw.   *retracted*

54

So downe he fell, and forth his life did breath,[1]
    That vanisht into smoke and cloudes swift;
480   So downe he fell, that th'earth him underneath

---

9. The goddess of the dawn, married to Tithone or Tithonus.

1. The blood that flows from the Dragon takes his life with it.

Did grone, as feeble so great load to lift;
So downe he fell, as an huge rockie clift,
Whose false foundation waves have washt away,
With dreadfull poyse° is from the mayneland rift,   *force*
485   And rolling downe, great Neptune doth dismay;
So downe he fell, and like an heaped mountaine lay.

55

The knight himselfe even trembled at his fall,
So huge and horrible a masse it seem'd;
And his deare Ladie, that beheld it all,
490   Durst not approch for dread, which she misdeem'd,
But yet at last, when as the direfull feend
She saw not stirre, off-shaking vaine affright,°   *empty fear*
She nigher drew, and saw that joyous end:
Then God she praysd, and thankt her faithfull knight,
495   That had atchiev'd so great a conquest by his might.

Canto 12

Faire Una to the Redcrosse knight
betrouthed is with joy:
Though false Duessa it to barre°   *prevent*
her false sleights doe imploy.

1

Behold I see the haven° nigh at hand,   *harbor*
To which I meane my wearie course to bend;
Vere° the maine shete, and beare up with° the land,   *loosen/steer toward*
The which afore is fairely to be kend,°   *recognized*
5   And seemeth safe from stormes, that may offend;
There this faire virgin wearie of her way
Must landed be, now at her journeyes end:
There eke my feeble barke° a while may stay,   *ship*
Till merry wind and weather call her thence away.

2

10   Scarsely had Phoebus in the glooming° East   *glowing*
Yet harnessed his firie-footed teeme,
Ne reard above the earth his flaming creast,
When the last deadly smoke aloft did steeme,
That signe of last outbreathed life did seeme
15   Unto the watchman on the castle wall;
Who thereby dead that balefull Beast did deeme,
And to his Lord and Ladie lowd gan call,
To tell, how he had seene the Dragons fatall fall.

3

Uprose with hastie joy, and feeble speed
20   That aged Sire,° the Lord of all that land,   *Una's father*
And looked forth, to weet, if true indeede
Those tydings were, as he did understand,
Which whenas true by tryall° he out fond,   *investigation*
He bad to open wyde his brazen gate,
25   Which long time had bene shut, and out of hond°   *immediately*

Proclaymed joy and peace through all his state;
For dead now was their foe, which them forrayed° late.°   *plundered/lately*

4

Then gan triumphant Trompets sound on hie,
   That sent to heaven the ecchoed report
30   Of their new joy, and happie victorie
   Gainst him, that had them long opprest with tort,°   *wrong*
   And fast imprisoned in sieged fort.
   Then all the people, as in solemne feast,
   To him assembled with one full consort,°   *in unison*
35   Rejoycing at the fall of that great beast,
From whose eternall bondage now they were releast.

5

Forth came that auncient Lord and aged Queene,
   Arayd° in antique robes downe to the ground,   *dressed*
   And sad habiliments right well beseene;[1]
40   A noble crew° about them waited round   *crowd*
   Of sage and sober Peres, all gravely gownd;
   Whom farre before did march a goodly band
   Of tall young men, all hable° armes to sownd,°   *able/wield*
   But now they laurell braunches bore in hand;
45 Glad signe of victorie and peace in all their land.

6

Unto that doughtie° Conquerour they came,   *worthy*
   And him before themselves prostrating low,
   Their Lord and Patrone loud did him proclame,
   And at his feet their laurell boughes did throw.
50   Soone after them all dauncing on a row
   The comely virgins came, with girlands dight,°   *prepared*
   As fresh as flowres in medow greene do grow,
   When morning deaw upon their leaves doth light:°   *land*
And in their hands sweet Timbrels° all upheld on hight.   *tambourines*

7

55 And them before, the fry° of children young   *group*
   Their wanton sports and childish mirth did play,
   And to the Maydens sounding tymbrels sung
   In well attuned notes, a joyous lay,
   And made delightfull musicke all the way,
60   Untill they came, where that faire virgin stood;
   As faire Diana in fresh sommers day
   Beholds her Nymphes, enraung'd° in shadie wood,   *spread out*
Some wrestle, some do run, some bathe in christall flood.°   *clear waters*

8

So she beheld those maydens meriment
65   With chearefull vew; who when to her they came,
   Themselves to ground with gratious humblesse bent,
   And her ador'd by honorable name,
   Lifting to heaven her everlasting fame:
   Then on her head they set a girland greene,

1. Their somber clothes were appropriate.

70   And crowned her twixt earnest and twixt game;[2]
        Who in her selfe-resemblance well beseene,[3]
        Did seeme such, as she was, a goodly maiden Queene.

                            9

        And after, all the raskall many° ran,   *playful crowd*
        Heaped together in rude rablement,°   *confusion*
75   To see the face of that victorious man:°   *Redcrosse Knight*
        Whom all admired, as from heaven sent,
        And gazd upon with gaping wonderment.
        But when they came, where that dead Dragon lay,
        Stretcht on the ground in monstrous large extent,
80   The sight with idle feare did them dismay,
        Ne durst° approch him nigh, to touch, or once assay.[4]   *nor dared*

                            10

        Some feard, and fled; some feard and well it faynd;°   *hid it well*
        One that would wiser seeme, then° all the rest,   *than*
        Warnd him not touch, for yet perhaps remaynd
85   Some lingring life within his hollow brest,
        Or in his wombe might lurke some hidden nest
        Of many Dragonets, his fruitfull seed;
        Another said, that in his eyes did rest
        Yet sparckling fire, and bad thereof take heed;°   *care*
90   Another said, he saw him move his eyes indeed.

                            11

        One mother, when as her foolehardie chyld
        Did come too neare, and with his talants° play,   *claws*
        Halfe dead through feare, her litle babe revyld,
        And to her gossips gan in counsell say;
95   How can I tell, but that his talants may
        Yet scratch my sonne, or rend his tender hand?
        So diversly themselves in vaine they fray;°   *frighten*
        Whiles some more bold, to measure him nigh stand,
        To prove how many acres he did spread of land.

                            12

100   Thus flocked all the folke him round about,
        The whiles that hoarie° king, with all his traine,   *aged*
        Being arrived, where that champion stout
        After his foes defeasance° did remaine,   *defeat*
        Him goodly greetes, and faire does entertaine,
105   With princely gifts of yvorie and gold,
        And thousand thankes him yeelds° for all his paine.   *gives*
        Then when his daughter deare he does behold,
        Her dearely doth imbrace, and kisseth manifold.°   *many times*

                            13

        And after to his Pallace he them brings,
110   With shaumes,° and trompets, and with Clarions° sweet;   *oboes/trumpets*
        And all the way the joyous people sings,
        And with their garments strowes the paved street:
        Whence mounting up, they find purveyance meet°   *suitable refreshment*

---

2. Half seriously, half playfully.
3. Una appears appropriately like herself (unlike Duessa, for instance, who appeared to be something other than what she was).
4. They did not dare to approach the dragon, to touch it, or even to try to touch it.

Of all, that royall Princes court became,
115   And all the floore was underneath their feet
      Bespred with costly scarlot° of great name,   *cloth*
      On which they lowly sit, and fitting purpose frame.°   *converse nicely*

14

      What needs me tell their feast and goodly guize,°   *behavior*
      In which was nothing riotous nor vaine?
120   What needs of daintie dishes to devize,°   *describe*
      Of comely services, or courtly trayne?
      My narrow leaves cannot in them containe
      The large discourse of royall Princes state.
      Yet was their manner then but bare° and plaine: *simple*
125   For th'antique world excesse and pride did hate;
      Such proud luxurious pompe is swollen up but late.°   *only recently*

15

      Then when with meates and drinkes of every kinde
      Their fervent appetites they quenched had,
      That auncient Lord gan fit occasion finde,
130   Of straunge adventures, and of perils sad,
      Which in his travell him befallen had,
      For to demaund of his renowmed° guest: *renowned*
      Who then with utt'rance° grave, and count'nance sad,   *expression*
      From point to point, as is before exprest,
135   Discourst° his voyage long, according his request.   *related*

16

      Great pleasure mixt with pittifull regard,°   *compassion*
      That godly King and Queene did passionate,°   *empathize*
      Whiles they his pittifull adventures heard,
      That oft they did lament his lucklesse state,
140   And often blame the too importune° fate,   *cruel*
      That heapd on him so many wrathfull wreakes:°   *injuries*
      For never gentle knight, as he of late,°   *recently*
      So tossed was in fortunes cruell freakes;°   *accidents*
      And all the while salt teares bedeawd° the hearers cheaks.   *wetted*

17

145   Then said that royall Pere in sober wise;
      Deare Sonne, great beene the evils, which ye bore
      From first to last in your late enterprise,
      That I note, whether prayse, or pitty more:
      For never living man, I weene, so sore
150   In sea of deadly daungers was distrest;
      But since now safe ye seised° have the shore,   *reached*
      And well arrived are, (high God be blest)
      Let us devize° of ease and everlasting rest.   *speak*

18

      Ah dearest Lord, said then that doughty° knight,   *worthy*
155   Of ease or rest I may not yet devize;
      For by the faith, which I to armes have plight,
      I bounden am streight after this emprize,°   *enterprise*
      As that your daughter can ye well advize,
      Backe to returne to that great Faerie Queene,
160   And her to serve six yeares in warlike wize,°   *manner*

Gainst that proud Paynim king, that workes her teene:°   *sorrow*
Therefore I ought crave pardon, till I there have beene.

19

Unhappie falles that hard necessitie,
   (Quoth he) the troubler of my happie peace,
165   And vowed foe of my felicitie;
   Ne I against the same can justly preace:°   *argue*
   But since that band° ye cannot now release,   *bond*
   Nor doen undo; (for vowes may not be vaine)
   Soone as the terme of those six yeares shall cease,
170   Ye then shall hither backe returne againe,
The marriage to accomplish vowd° betwixt you twain.   *promised*

20

Which for my part I covet° to performe,   *desire*
   In sort as through the world I did proclame,
   That who so kild that monster most deforme,
175   And him in hardy battaile overcame,
   Should have mine onely daughter to his Dame,
   And of my kingdome heire apparaunt bee:
   Therefore since now to thee perteines the same,
   By dew desert of noble chevalree,
180 Both daughter and eke kingdome, lo I yield to thee.

21

Then forth he called that his daughter faire,
   The fairest Un' his onely daughter deare,
   His onely daughter, and his onely heyre;
   Who forth proceeding with sad sober cheare,
185   As bright as doth the morning starre appeare
   Out of the East, with flaming lockes bedight,
   To tell that dawning day is drawing neare,
   And to the world does bring long wished light;
So faire and fresh that Lady shewd her selfe in sight.

22

190 So faire and fresh, as freshest flowre in May;
   For she had layd her mournefull stole° aside,   *dark cloak*
   And widow-like sad wimple throwne away,
   Wherewith her heavenly beautie she did hide,
   Whiles on her wearie journey she did ride;
195   And on her now a garment she did weare,
   All lilly white, withoutten° spot, or pride,   *without a*
   That seemd like silke and silver woven neare,
But neither silke nor silver therein did appeare.

23

The blazing brightnesse of her beauties beame,
200   And glorious light of her sunshyny face
   To tell, were as to strive against the streame.
   My ragged rimes° are all too rude and bace,   *rhymes*
   Her heavenly lineaments° for to enchace.°   *features/display*
   Ne wonder; for her owne deare loved knight,
205   All were she dayly with himselfe in place,°   *by his side*
   Did wonder much at her celestiall sight:
Oft had he seene her faire, but never so faire dight.

24

So fairely dight, when she in presence came,
   She to her Sire made humble reverence,
210   And bowed low, that her right well became,
   And added grace unto her excellence:
   Who with great wisedome, and grave eloquence
   Thus gan to say. But eare he thus had said,
   With flying speede, and seeming great pretence,°   *purpose*
215   Came running in, much like a man dismaid,°   *overwhelmed*
A Messenger with letters, which his message said.

25

All in the open hall amazed stood,
   At suddeinnesse of that unwarie° sight,   *unexpected*
   And wondred at his breathlesse hastie mood.
220   But he for nought would stay his passage right,°   *stop*
   Till fast before° the king he did alight;°   *in front of/arrive*
   Where falling flat, great humblesse he did make,
   And kist the ground, whereon his foot was pight;°   *placed*
   Then to his hands that writ° he did betake,°   *message/deliver*
225 Which he disclosing,° red thus, as the paper spake.°   *unfolding/said*

26

To thee, most mighty king of Eden faire,
   Her greeting sends in these sad lines addrest,
   The wofull daughter, and forsaken heire
   Of that great Emperour of all the West;
230   And bids thee be advized for the best,
   Ere thou thy daughter linck° in holy band   *join*
   Of wedlocke to that new unknowen guest:
   For he already plighted° his right hand   *promised*
Unto another love, and to another land.

27

235 To me sad mayd, or rather widow sad,
   He was affiaunced° long time before,   *engaged*
   And sacred pledges he both gave, and had,
   False erraunt° knight, infamous, and forswore:°   *erring/lying*
   Witnesse the burning Altars, which° he swore,[5]   *by which*
240   And guiltie heavens of his bold perjury,°   *lie*
   Which though he hath polluted oft of yore,
   Yet I to them for judgement just do fly,
And them conjure° t'avenge this shamefull injury.[6]   *implore*

28

Therefore since mine he is, or free or bond,
245   Or false or trew, or living or else dead,
   Withhold, O soveraine Prince, your hasty hond
   From knitting league with him, I you aread;°   *advise*
   Ne weene my right with strength adowne to tread,[7]
   Through weakenesse of my widowhed,° or woe: *widowhood*
250   For truth is strong, her rightfull cause to plead,

---

5. Referring to a pagan marriage ritual in which sacrifices
are burned on an altar to confirm the marriage vows.
6. Although the Redcrosse Knight has polluted the heav-

ens with his lies, the author of the message nonetheless
looks to them for judgment against him.
7. Do not try to overcome my rights by force.

And shall find friends, if need requireth soe,
So bids thee well to fare,° Thy neither friend, nor foe.   *farewell*

29

When he° these bitter byting words had red,°   *the king / heard*
 The tydings° straunge did him abashed make,   *news*
255 That still he sate long time astonished
 As in great muse,° ne word to creature spake.   *astonishment*
 At last his solemne silence thus he brake,
 With doubtfull eyes fast fixed on his guest;
 Redoubted° knight, that for mine onely sake   *formidable*
260 Thy life and honour late adventurest,
Let nought be hid from me, that ought to be exprest.

30

What meane these bloudy vowes, and idle threats,
 Throwne out from womanish impatient mind?
 What heavens? what altars? what enraged heates°   *rantings*
265 Here heaped up with termes of love unkind,
 My conscience cleare with guilty bands would bind?
 High God be witnesse, that I guiltlesse ame.
 But if your selfe, Sir knight, ye faultie° find,   *guilty*
 Or wrapped be in loves of former Dame,
270 With crime° do not it cover, but disclose the same.   *lies*

31

To whom the Redcrosse knight this answere sent,
 My Lord, my King, be nought hereat dismayd,
 Till well ye wote by grave intendiment,°   *careful consideration*
 What woman, and wherefore° doth me upbrayd   *why*
275 With breach of love, and loyalty betrayd.
 It was in my mishaps, as hitherward°   *on my way here*
 I lately traveild, that unwares I strayd
 Out of my way, through perils straunge and hard;
That day should faile me, ere I had them all declard.

32

280 There did I find, or rather I was found
 Of this false woman, that Fidessa hight,
 Fidessa hight the falsest Dame on ground,
 Most false Duessa, royall richly dight,
 That easie° was t'invegle° weaker sight: *eager / blind*
285 Who by her wicked arts, and wylie skill,
 Too false and strong for earthly skill or might,
 Unwares° me wrought unto her wicked will,   *unknowingly*
And to my foe betrayd, when least I feared ill.

33

Then stepped forth the goodly royall Mayd,
290 And on the ground her selfe prostrating° low,   *bowing*
 With sober countenaunce thus to him sayd;
 O pardon me, my soveraigne Lord, to show
 The secret treasons, which of late° I know   *recently*
 To have bene wroght° by that false sorceresse.   *committed*
295 She onely she it is, that earst did throw

This gentle knight into so great distresse,
That death him did awaite in dayly wretchednesse.

34

And now it seemes, that she suborned° hath   *bribed*
  This craftie messenger with letters vaine,°   *false*
To worke new woe and improvided° scath,   *unforeseen*
  By breaking of the band betwixt us twaine;
  Wherein she used hath the practicke paine°   *crafty labor*
Of this false footman, clokt° with simplenesse,   *cloaked*
  Whom if ye please for° to discover plaine,   *wish*
Ye shall him Archimago find, I ghesse,
The falsest man alive; who° tries shall find no lesse.   *whoever*

35

The king was greatly moved at her speach,
  And all with suddein indignation fraight,°   *filled*
Bad on that Messenger rude hands to reach.
  Eftsoones the Gard, which on his state did wait,
Attacht° that faitor false, and bound him strait: *seized*
  Who seeming sorely chauffed° at his band,   *annoyed*
As chained Beare, whom cruell dogs do bait,
  With idle force did faine° them to withstand,   *attempt*
And often semblaunce made° to scape out of their hand.[8]   *pretended*

36

But they him layd full low in dungeon deepe,
  And bound him hand and foote with yron chains.
And with continuall watch did warely° keepe;   *carefully*
  Who then would thinke, that by his subtile trains
He could escape fowle death or deadly paines?
  Thus when that Princes wrath was pacifide,
He gan renew the late forbidden banes,°   *banns*
  And to the knight his daughter deare he tyde,
With sacred rites and vowes for ever to abyde.[9]

37

His owne two hands the holy knots did knit,
  That none but death for ever can devide;
His owne two hands, for such a turne most fit,
  The housling° fire[1] did kindle and provide,   *domestic*
And holy water thereon sprinckled wide;
  At which the bushy Teade° a groome did light,   *torch*
And sacred lampe in secret chamber hide,
  Where it should not be quenched day nor night,
For feare of evill fates, but burnen ever bright.

38

Then gan they sprinckle all the posts with wine,[2]
  And made great feast to solemnize that day;

---

8. Since Archimago himself is false, his efforts to escape are also false.
9. The King recommences the announcement of marriage that had been recently forbidden by Duessa's false charges against the Redcrosse Knight.

1. Originally Roman marriage rituals, the fire and water used by the King here also suggest baptism and the sanctification of married love.
2. Roman brides sprinkled the doorposts of their new homes with wine in a ritual symbolizing joy and fertility.

They all perfumde with frankincense divine,
And precious odours fetcht from far away,
That all the house did sweat with great aray:°   *ceremony*
And all the while sweete Musicke did apply
340   Her curious skill, the warbling notes to play,
To drive away the dull Melancholy;
The whiles one sung a song of love and jollity.

39

During the which there was an heavenly noise
Heard sound through all the Pallace pleasantly,
345   Like as it had bene many an Angels voice,
Singing before th'eternall majesty,
In their trinall triplicities[3] on hye;
Yet wist no creature, whence that heavenly sweet
Proceeded, yet eachone felt secretly
350   Himselfe thereby reft of his sences meet,°   *ordinary*
And ravished with rare impression in his sprite.

40

Great joy was made that day of young and old,
And solemne feast proclaimd throughout the land,
That their exceeding merth° may not be told: *joy*
355   Suffice it heare by signes to understand[4]
The usuall joyes at knitting of loves band.
Thrise° happy man the knight himselfe did hold,   *thrice*
Possessed of his Ladies hart and hand,
And ever, when his eye did her behold,
360   His heart did seeme to melt in pleasures manifold.

41

Her joyous presence and sweet company
In full content he there did long enjoy,
Ne wicked envie, ne vile gealosy
His deare delights were able to annoy:
365   Yet swimming in that sea of blisfull joy,
He nought forgot, how he whilome had sworne,
In case he could that monstrous beast destroy,
Unto his Faerie Queene backe to returne:
The which he shortly did, and Una left to mourne.

42

370   Now strike your sailes ye jolly Mariners,
For we be come unto a quiet rode,°   *haven*
Where we must land some of our passengers,
And light this wearie vessell of her lode.
Here she a while may make her safe abode,
375   Till she repaired have her tackles spent,°   *worn out fittings*
And wants supplide. And then againe abroad
On the long voyage whereto she is bent:
Well may she speede° and fairely finish her intent.   *continue*

---

3. The triple triad or the nine orders of angels. The music
that they play is the music of the spheres, which
humankind had been unable to hear since the Fall.

4. Since the happiness of the occasion is beyond the ability of words to express, let it be sufficient to understand it
through symbols.

from The Second Booke of the Faerie Queene

Contayning The Legend of Sir Guyon
or
Temperaunce

Canto 12

Guyon, by Palmers governance,
passing through perils great,
Doth overthrow the Bowre of blisse,
and Acrasie defeat.

1

Now gins° this goodly frame of Temperance   *begins*
  Fairely to rise, and her adorned hed
  To pricke of highest praise forth to advance,
  Formerly° grounded, and fast setteled   *previously*
5   On firme foundation of true bountihed;[1]
  And this brave knight, that for that vertue fights,
  Now comes to point of that same perilous sted,°   *dangerous place*
  Where Pleasure dwelles in sensuall delights,
Mongst thousand dangers, and ten thousand magick mights.°   *powers*

2

10 Two dayes now in that sea he sayled has,
  Ne ever land beheld, ne living wight,
  Ne ought° save perill, still as he did pas: *nor anything*
  Tho when appeared the third Morrow bright,
  Upon the waves to spred her trembling light,
15   An hideous roaring farre away they heard,
  That all their senses filled with affright,
  And streight they saw the raging surges reard
Up to the skyes, that them of drowning made affeard.

3

Said then the Boteman, Palmer stere aright,
20   And keepe an even course; for yonder way
  We needes must passe (God do us well acquight,)°   *deliver*
  That is the Gulfe° of Greedinesse, they say,   *whirlpool*
  That deepe engorgeth° all this worldes pray: *swallows*
  Which having swallowd up excessively,
25   He soone in vomit up againe doth lay,
  And belcheth forth his superfluity,°   *excess*
That all the seas for feare do seeme away to fly.

4

On th'other side an hideous Rocke is pight,°   *placed*
  Of mightie Magnes° stone, whose craggie clift   *magnet*
30   Depending from on high, dreadfull to sight,
  Over the waves his rugged armes doth lift,
  And threatneth downe to throw his ragged rift°   *rocks*
On who so commeth nigh; yet nigh it drawes

---

1. The spirit of temperance begins to be inspired to celebrate and highly praise temperance, now that this virtue is established on goodness ("bountihed").

All passengers, that none from it can shift:

35
For whiles they fly that Gulfes devouring jawes,
They on this rock are rent, and sunck in helplesse waves.°   *waves*

5

Forward they passe, and strongly he them rowes,
   Untill they nigh unto that Gulfe arrive,
   Where streame more violent and greedy growes:
40
   Then he with all his puissance° doth strive   *power*
   To strike his oares, and mightily doth drive
   The hollow vessell through the threatfull wave,
   Which gaping wide, to swallow them alive,
   In th'huge abysse of his engulfing grave,
45
Doth rore at them in vaine, and with great terror rave.

6

They passing by, that griesly mouth did see,
   Sucking the seas into his entralles° deepe,   *bowels*
   That seem'd more horrible then hell to bee,
   Or that darke dreadfull hole of Tartare² steepe,
50
   Through which the damned ghosts doen often creepe
   Backe to the world, bad livers to torment:
   But nought that falles into this direfull deepe,
   Ne that approcheth nigh the wide descent,
May backe returne, but is condemned to be drent.°   *drowned*

7

55
On th'other side, they saw that perilous Rocke,
   Threatning it selfe on them to ruinate,°   *fall*
   On whose sharpe clifts the ribs of vessels broke,
   And shivered ships, which had bene wrecked late,
   Yet stuck, with carkasses exanimate°   *dead*
60
   Of such, as having all their substance spent
   In wanton joyes, and lustes intemperate,
   Did afterwards make shipwracke violent,
Both of their life, and fame for ever fowly blent.°   *destroyed*

8

For thy,° this hight The Rocke of vile Reproch,   *therefore*
65
   A daungerous and detestable place,
   To which nor fish nor fowle did once approch,
   But yelling Meawes,° with Seagulles hoarse and bace,   *gulls*
   And Cormoyrants, with birds of ravenous race,
   Which still sate waiting on that wastfull clift,
70
   For spoyle of wretches, whose unhappie cace,
   After lost credite and consumed thrift,°   *savings*
At last them driven hath to this despairefull drift.°   *end*

9

The Palmer seeing them in safetie past,
   Thus said; Behold th'ensamples° in our sights,   *examples*
75
   Of lustfull luxurie and thriftlesse wast:
   What now is left of miserable wights,
   Which spent their looser daies in lewd delights,

---

2. Tartarus, the lowest region of hell in Greek mythology.

But shame and sad reproch, here to be red,°   *seen*
By these rent reliques, speaking their ill plights?
80   Let all that live, hereby be counselled,
To shunne Rocke of Reproch, and it as death to dred.

10

So forth they rowed, and that Ferryman
  With his stiffe oares did brush the sea so strong,
  That the hoare° waters from his frigot° ran,   *foaming / boat*
85   And the light bubbles daunced all along,
  Whiles the salt brine out of the billowes sprong.
  At last farre off they many Islands spy,
  On every side floting the floods emong:°   *in the water*
  Then said the knight, Loe I the land descry,°   *see*
90 Therefore old Syre thy course do thereunto apply.°   *steer*

11

That may not be, said then the Ferryman
  Least° we unweeting hap to be fordonne:°   *lest / destroyed*
  For those same Islands, seeming now and than,°   *then*
  Are not firme lande, nor any certein wonne,°   *dwelling place*
95   But straggling plots, which to and fro do ronne
  In the wide waters: therefore are they hight
  The wandring Islands. Therefore doe them shonne;
  For they have oft drawne many a wandring wight
Into most deadly daunger and distressed plight.

12

100 Yet well they seeme to him,° that farre° doth vew,   *Guyon / afar*
  Both faire and fruitfull, and the ground dispred°   *covered*
  With grassie greene of delectable hew,
  And the tall trees with leaves apparelled,
  Are deckt with blossomes dyde in white and red,
105   That mote the passengers thereto allure;
  But whosoever once hath fastened
  His foot thereon, may never it recure,°   *recover*
But wandreth ever more uncertein and unsure.

13

As th'Isle of Delos[3] whylome men report
110 Amid th' Aegaean sea long time did stray,
  Ne made for shipping any certaine port,
  Till that Latona traveiling that way,
  Flying from Junoes wrath and hard assay,
  Of her faire twins was there delivered,°   *gave birth*
115   Which afterwards did rule the night and day;
  Thenceforth it firmely was established,
And for Apolloes honor highly herried.°   *praised*

14

They to him hearken,° as beseemeth meete,   *listen*
  And passe on forward: so their way does ly,
120 That one of those same Islands, which doe fleet°   *float*

---

3. An island in the Aegean Sea that was associated with Eden. Latona, or Leda, after being impregnated by Zeus in the form of a swan, fled Juno's wrath to the island of Delos and there gave birth to Apollo and Artemis.

In the wide sea, they needes must passen by,
Which seemd so sweet and pleasant to the eye,
That it would tempt a man to touchen there:
Upon the banck they sitting did espy

125 A daintie damzell, dressing of her heare,°   *hair*
By whom a little skippet,° floting did appeare.   *small boat*

15

She them espying, loud to them can call,
Bidding them nigher draw unto the shore;
For she had cause to busie them withall;[4]

130 And therewith loudly laught: But nathemore
Would they once turne, but kept on as afore:
Which when she saw, she left her lockes undight,°   *undone*
And running to her boat withouten ore
From the departing land[5] it launched light,°   *quickly*

135 And after them did drive with all her power and might.

16

Whom overtaking, she in merry sort°   *manner*
Them gan to bord,° and purpose diversly,[6]   *confront*
Now faining dalliance° and wanton sport,°   *flirting/sexual play*
Now throwing forth lewd words immodestly;

140 Till that the Palmer gan full bitterly
Her to rebuke, for being loose and light:
Which not abiding, but more scornefully
Scoffing at him, that did her justly wite,°   *rightfully accuse*
She turnd her bote about, and from them rowed quite.°   *away*

17

145 That was the wanton Phaedria,[7] which late
Did ferry him over the Idle lake:
Whom nought regarding, they kept on their gate,°   *way*
And all her vaine allurements did forsake,
When them the wary Boateman thus bespake;

150 Here now behoveth° us well to avyse,°   *profits/consider*
And of our safetie good heede° to take;   *care*
For here before a perlous passage lyes,
Where many Mermayds haunt,° making false melodies.   *live*

18

But by the way, there is a great Quicksand,

155 And a whirlepoole of hidden jeopardy,
Therefore, Sir Palmer, keepe an even hand;
For twixt them both the narrow way doth ly.
Scarse had he said, when hard at hand they spy
That quicksand nigh with water covered;

160 But by the checked wave they did descry
It plaine, and by the sea discoloured:
It called was the quicksand of Unthriftyhed.°   *extravagance*

---

4. She had a reason to cause them to be interested in her. The phrase may have a double meaning: "cause" is a pun on the word "case," which was Elizabethan slang for "vagina."
5. She launched her boat from the island that was floating away.

6. Intentionally to behave in various ways.
7. Glittering one (Greek). This character was identified in Book 2, Canto 6, as beguilingly licentious; on that occasion, Guyon managed to escape from her island.

19

They passing by, a goodly Ship did see,
   Laden from far with precious merchandize,
165   And bravely° furnished, as ship might bee,   *splendidly*
   Which through great disaventure,° or mesprize,°   *bad luck/poor judgment*
   Her selfe had runne into that hazardize;°   *hazard*
   Whose mariners and merchants with much toyle,
   Labour'd in vaine, to have recur'd° their prize,   *recovered*
170   And the rich wares to save from pitteous spoyle,°   *ruin*
But neither toyle nor travell might her backe recoyle.°   *retrieve*

20

On th'other side they see that perilous Poole,
   That called was the Whirlepoole of decay,
   In which full many had with haplesse doole°   *grief*
175   Beene suncke, of whom no memorie did stay:
   Whose circled waters rapt° with whirling sway,   *caught*
   Like to a restlesse wheele, still running round,
   Did covet,° as they passed by that way,   *desire*
   To draw their boate within the utmost bound
180 Of his wide Labyrinth, and then to have them dround.

21

But th'heedfull Boateman strongly forth did stretch
   His brawnie armes, and all his body straine,
   That th'utmost sandy breach° they shortly fetch,°   *beach/reach*
   Whiles the dred daunger does behind remaine.
185   Suddeine they see from midst of all the Maine,°   *sea*
   The surging waters like a mountaine rise,[8]
   And the great sea puft up with proud disdaine,
   To swell above the measure of his guise,°   *custom*
As threatning to devoure all, that his powre despise.

22

190 The waves come rolling, and the billowes rore
   Outragiously, as they enraged were,
   Or wrathfull Neptune did them drive before
   His whirling charet, for exceeding feare:
   For not one puffe of wind there did appeare,
195   That all the three thereat woxe much afrayd,
   Unweeting, what such horrour straunge did reare.
   Eftsoones they saw an hideous hoast° arrayd,   *army*
Of huge Sea monsters, such as living sence dismayd.°   *overwhelmed*

23

Most ugly shapes, and horrible aspects,°   *appearances*
200 Such as Dame Nature selfe mote feare to see,
   Or shame, that ever should so fowle defects
   From her most cunning hand escaped bee;
   All dreadfull pourtraicts° of deformitee: *portraits*
   Spring-headed Hydraes,[9] and sea-shouldring Whales,[1]

---

8. They encounter a tidal wave. This is later described as full of sea monsters.
9. In Greek mythology, sea monsters with many heads. When one head is cut off, another one springs back in its place.
1. The whale "shoulders" or raises up the sea by exhaling a spout of water up into the air and creating whirlpools.

205   Great whirlpooles, which all fishes make to flee,
    Bright Scolopendraes,[2] arm'd with silver scales,
    Mighty Monoceroses,[3] with immeasured tayles.

24

    The dreadfull Fish,[4] that hath deserv'd the name
    Of Death, and like him lookes in dreadfull hew,
210   The griesly Wasserman,° that makes his game   *merman*
    The flying ships with swiftnesse to pursew,
    The horrible Sea-satyre, that doth shew
    His fearefull face in time of greatest storme,
    Huge Ziffius,° whom Mariners eschew   *swordfish*
215   No lesse, then rockes, (as travellers informe,)
    And greedy Rosmarines° with visages deforme.   *seahorses*

25

    All these, and thousand thousands many more,
    And more deformed Monsters thousand fold,
    With dreadfull noise, and hollow rombling rore,
220   Came rushing in the fomy waves enrold,°   *rolling*
    Which seem'd to fly for feare, them to behold:
    Ne wonder, if these did the knight appall;
    For all that here on earth we dreadfull hold,
    Be but as bugs° to fearen babes withall,   *bugaboos*
225   Compared to the creatures in the seas entrall.°   *depths*

26

    Feare nought, (then said the Palmer well aviz'd;)
    For these same Monsters are not these in deed,
    But are into these fearefull shapes disguiz'd
    By that same wicked witch,[5] to worke us dreed,
230   And draw from on this journey to proceede.
    Tho lifting up his vertuous staffe[6] on hye,
    He smote the sea, which calmed was with speed,
    And all that dreadfull Armie fast gan flye
    Into great Tethys° bosome, where they hidden lye.   *goddess of the sea*

27

235   Quit° from that daunger, forth their course they kept,   *free*
    And as they went, they heard a ruefull cry
    Of one, that wayld and pittifully wept,
    That through the sea the resounding plaints did fly:
    At last they in an Island did espy
240   A seemely Maiden, sitting by the shore,
    That with great sorrow and sad agony,
    Seemed some great misfortune to deplore,°   *lament*
    And lowd° to them for succour° called evermore.   *loudly/help*

28

    Which Guyon hearing, streight° his Palmer bad,   *immediately*
245   To stere the boate towards that dolefull Mayd,

---

2. Fantastic fish.
3. Literally, one-horned fish, narwhales.
4. A walrus or "morse" (from the Latin *mors*, "death").
5. Acrasia, the spirit presiding over the Bower of Bliss, which Guyon must destroy to be perfect in temperance.

6. The Palmer calms the sea with his powerful or "vertuous" staff, which resembles both the herald's staff or caduceus of Hermes or Mercury, which was given to him by Zeus or Jupiter as a sign of power and respect, and Moses' rod, which divided the Red Sea (Exodus 14.16).

the Palmer

That he might know, and ease her sorrow sad:
Who° him avizing better, to him sayd;
Faire Sir, be not displeasd, if disobayd:
For ill it were to hearken to her cry;
250　　　For she is inly nothing ill apayd,[7]
But onely womanish fine forgery,°　　　　　　　*deceit, trick*
Your stubborne hart t'affect with fraile infirmity.

29

To which when she your courage hath inclind
Through foolish pitty, then her guilefull bayt
255　　　She will embosome° deeper in your mind,　　　*bury*
And for your ruine at the last° awayt.　　　　　*in the end*
The knight was ruled,° and the Boateman strayt　*convinced*
Held on his course with stayed° stedfastnesse,　*constant*
Ne ever shruncke, ne ever sought to bayt°　　　*rest*
260　　　His tyred armes for toylesome wearinesse,
But with his oares did sweepe the watry wildernesse.

30

And now they nigh approched to the sted,°　　　*place*
Where as those Mermayds[8] dwelt: it was a still
And calmy bay, on th'one side sheltered
265　　　With the brode shadow of an hoarie° hill,　　*mossy*
On th'other side an high rocke toured° still,　*towered*
That twixt them both a pleasaunt port they made,
And did like an halfe Theatre[9] fulfill:
There those five sisters had continuall trade,°　*residence*
270　　　And usd to bath themselves in that deceiptfull shade.

31

They were faire Ladies, till they fondly striv'd
With th'Heliconian maides[1] for maistery;
Of whom they over-comen, were depriv'd
Of their proud beautie, and th'one moyity
275　　　Transform'd to fish, for their bold surquedry,°　*arrogance*
But th'upper halfe their hew° retained still,　　*shape*
And their sweet skill in wonted melody;
Which ever after they abusd to ill,
T'allure weake travellers, whom gotten they did kill.

32

280　　So now to Guyon, as he passed by,
Their pleasant tunes they sweetly thus applide;
O thou faire sonne of gentle Faery,
That art in mighty armes most magnifide
Above all knights, that ever battell tride,
285　　　O turne thy rudder hither-ward a while:

---

7. Inwardly she is not at all distressed; the fact that she seems to be complaining about something illustrates her feminine guile, designed to induce you to lose your sense of yourself and so become ineffectual.
8. The Sirens from Homer's *Odyssey* whose beautiful songs tempt sailors to throw themselves overboard. Guyon, like Odysseus before him, does not succumb to the sirens' music. Traditionally only three in number,

Spenser's sirens are five, corresponding to the five senses.
9. The bay is in the shape of a semicircle, like half of an amphitheater.
1. The nine Muses. In Greek mythology the Sirens engaged in a contest with the Muses to see who could sing the best. The Sirens lost and were punished by being turned into sea creatures.

Here may thy storme-bet° vessell safely ride;   *storm-beaten*
This is the Port of rest from troublous toyle,
The worlds sweet In,° from paine and wearisome turmoyle.   *inn*

33

290   With that the rolling sea resounding soft,
In his big base them fitly answered,
And on the rocke the waves breaking aloft,
A solemne Meane unto them measured,
The whiles sweet Zephirus° lowd whisteled   *the west wind*
His treble, a straunge kinde of harmony;[2]
295   Which Guyons senses softly tickeled,°   *enticed*
That he the boateman bad row easily,°   *slowly*
And let him heare some part of their rare melody.

34

But him the Palmer from that vanity,°   *folly*
With temperate advice discounselled,°   *counseled*
300   That they it past, and shortly gan descry°   *see*
The land, to which their course they leveled;
When suddeinly a grosse fog over spred
With his dull vapour all that desert has,
And heavens chearefull face enveloped,°   *covered*
305   That all things one, and one as nothing was,
And this great Universe seemd one confused mas.

35

Thereat they greatly were dismayd, ne wist
How to direct their way in darkenesse wide,
But feard to wander in that wastfull mist,
310   For tombling into mischiefe unespide.
Worse is the daunger hidden, then descride.°   *exposed*
Suddeinly an innumerable flight
Of harmefull fowles° about them fluttering, cride,   *birds*
And with their wicked wings them oft did smight,
315   And sore annoyed, groping in that griesly night.

36

Even all the nation° of unfortunate   *every type*
And fatall birds about them flocked were,
Such as by nature men abhorre and hate,
The ill-faste° Owle, deaths dreadfull messengere,   *evil-faced*
320   The hoars Night-raven, trump° of dolefull drere,°   *trumpet/misery*
The lether-winged Bat, dayes enimy,
The ruefull Strich,° still waiting on the bere,   *screech-owl*
The Whistler° shrill, that who so heares, doth dy,   *a nocturnal bird*
The hellish Harpies,[3] prophets of sad destiny.

37

325   All those, and all that else does horrour breed,
About them flew, and fild their sayles with feare:
Yet stayd they not, but forward did proceed,

---

2. This forms a four-part harmony: the sirens take the alto part, the sea provides the bass, the waves the mean or tenor, and the West Wind the treble or soprano.

3. Fictional creatures—half vulture, half woman—who defile and consume food set out for human consumption.

Whiles th'one did row, and th'other stifly° steare;[4]   *steadily*
    Till that at last the weather gan to cleare,
330   And the faire land it selfe did plainly show.
    Said then the Palmer, Lo where does appeare
    The sacred soile, where all our perils grow;
Therefore, Sir knight, your ready armes about you throw.°   *put on*

38

He hearkned, and his armes about him tooke,
335   The whiles the nimble boate so well her sped,
    That with her crooked keele° the land she strooke,°   *curved prow/struck*
    Then forth the noble Guyon sallied,°   *leaped*
    And his sage Palmer, that him gouerned;
    But th'other by his boate behind did stay.
340   They marched fairly forth, of nought ydred,°   *afraid*
    Both firmely armd for every hard assay,°   *trial*
With constancy and care, gainst daunger and dismay.

39

Ere long they heard an hideous bellowing
    Of many beasts,[5] that roard outrageously,
345   As if that hungers point, or Venus sting°   *i.e., sexual desire*
    Had them enraged with fell surquedry;°   *dangerous arrogance*
    Yet nought they feard, but past on hardily,
    Untill they came in vew of those wild beasts:
    Who all attonce, gaping full greedily,
350   And rearing fiercely their upstarting crests,
Ran towards, to devoure those unexpected guests.

40

But soone as they approcht with deadly threat,
    The Palmer over them his staffe upheld,
    His mighty staffe, that could all charmes defeat:
355   Eftsoones their stubborne courages° were queld,   *spirits*
    And high advaunced crests downe meekely feld,
    In stead of fraying,° they them selves did feare,   *frightening*
    And trembled, as them passing they beheld:
    Such wondrous powre did in that staffe appeare,
360 All monsters to subdew to him, that did it beare.

41

Of that same wood it fram'd was cunningly,
    Of which Caduceus[6] whilome° was made,   *formerly*
    Caduceus the rod of Mercury,
    With which he wonts the Stygian° realmes invade,   *underworld*
365   Through ghastly horrour, and eternall shade;
    Th' infernall feends with it he can asswage,
    And Orcus° tame, whom nothing can perswade,   *Pluto, hell's ruler*

---

4. The Boatman rowed; the Palmer steered.
5. These beasts are the creatures of Acrasia, the lady governor of the Bower of Bliss; they resemble the beasts ruled
by Circe on her island, Aeaea, as depicted in the *Odyssey*.

Formerly men, they had been transformed by Circe's
witchcraft.
6. The winged staff carried by Hermes or Mercury, the
messenger god; see line 231.

And rule the Furyes,[7] when they most do rage:
Such vertue in his staffe had eke this Palmer sage.

42

370   Thence passing forth, they shortly do arrive,
    Whereas the Bowre of Blisse was situate;
    A place pickt out by choice of best alive,
    That natures worke by art can imitate
375   In which what ever in this worldly state
    Is sweet, and pleasing unto living sense,
    Or that may dayntiest fantasie aggrate,°   *please*
    Was poured forth with plentifull dispence,°   *abundance*
    And made there to abound with lavish affluence.°   *extravagance*

43

    Goodly it was enclosed round about,
380   Aswell their entred° guestes to keepe within,   *entered*
    As those unruly beasts to hold without;°   *keep out*
    Yet was the fence thereof but weake and thin;
    Nought° feard their force, that fortilage° to win, *nothing/fortress*
    But wisedomes powre, and temperaunces might,
385   By which the mightiest things efforced bin:[8]
    And eke the gate was wrought of substaunce light,
    Rather for pleasure, then for battery° or fight.   *physical assault*

44

    Yt framed was of precious yvory,
    That seemd a worke of admirable wit;°   *skill*
390   And therein all the famous history
    Of Jason and Medaea[9] was ywrit;
    Her mighty charmes, her furious loving fit,
    His goodly conquest of the golden fleece,
    His falsed° faith, and love too lightly flit,° *violated/fickle*
395   The wondred Argo, which in venturous peece° *adventurous ship*
    First through the Euxine seas bore all the flowr of Greece.

45

    Ye might have seene the frothy billowes fry
    Under the ship,° as thorough them she went,   *the Argo*
    That seemd the waves were into yvory,
400   Or yvory into the waves were sent;
    And other where° the snowy substaunce sprent° *elsewhere/sprinkled*
    With vermell, like the boyes bloud therein shed,[1]
    A piteous spectacle did represent,
    And otherwhiles° with gold besprinkeled;   *elsewhere*
405   Yt seemd th'enchaunted flame, which did Creüsa[2] wed.

---

7. Spirits of vengeance, traditionally imagined as female, who pursue the victims of crime to compel them to take revenge.

8. Acrasia did not fear beasts but only the power of wisdom and temperance, which can control the mightiest things.

9. Jason sailed in the Argo, the first oceangoing ship, to capture the golden fleece, a Greek treasure, which belonged to King Aeetes of Colchis. The king's daughter, Medea, assisted Jason with her magical powers. When

Jason abandoned her, betraying the fidelity he had promised her, Medea took revenge. Medea was said to have inherited her magical powers from Circe, her aunt.

1. A reference to Medea's murder of her brother, whose body she threw into the sea to distract her father as she and Jason fled from Colchis with the golden fleece.

2. The woman for whom Jason abandoned Medea. In revenge, Medea sent Creüsa an enchanted dress, which burned her to death with its own fire; hence Creüsa could be said to have wed a flame.

46

All this, and more might in that goodly gate
   Be red;° that ever open stood to all,   *seen*
   Which thither came: but in the Porch there sate
   A comely personage of stature tall,
410   And semblaunce pleasing, more then naturall,
   That travellers to him seemd to entize;°   *entice*
   His looser garment to the ground did fall,
   And flew about his heeles in wanton wize,°   *manner*
Not fit for speedy pace, or manly exercize.

47

415 They in that place him Genius[3] did call:
   Not that celestiall powre, to whom the care
   Of life, and generation of all
   That lives, pertaines in charge particulare,°   *as a special charge*
   Who wondrous things concerning our welfare,
420   And straunge phantomes° doth let us oft forsee,   *images*
   And oft of secret ill bids us beware:
   That is our Selfe, whom though we do not see,
Yet each doth in him selfe it well perceive to bee.

48

Therefore a God him sage Antiquity
425   Did wisely make, and good Agdistes call:
   But this same was to that quite contrary,
   The foe of life, that good envyes to all,
   That secretly doth us procure° to fall,   *cause*
   Through guilefull semblaunts,° which he makes us see. *deceitful images*
430   He of this Gardin had the governall,°   *management*
   And Pleasures porter was devizd° to bee,   *appointed*
Holding a staffe in hand for more formalitee.

49

With diverse flowres he daintily was deekt,
   And strowed° round about, and by his side   *strewn*
435   A mighty Mazer° bowle of wine was set,   *maple*
   As if it had to him bene sacrifide;[4]
   Wherewith all new-come guests he gratifide:
   So did he eke Sir Guyon passing by:
   But he his idle curtesie defide,
440   And overthrew his bowle disdainfully;
And broke his staffe, with which he charmed semblants sly.

50

Thus being entred, they behold around
   A large and spacious plaine, on every side
   Strowed with pleasauns,° whose faire grassy ground *small parks*
445   Mantled° with greene, and goodly beautifide   *cloaked*
   With all the ornaments of Floraes° pride,   *goddess of flowers*

---

3. Not what he is traditionally, that is, the spirit, associated with heavenly power, who has a specific duty to care for each individual man or woman. Identified as a "self" or ego, genius also has the force of a moral consciousness. Although we do not see this genius, each of us has a sense of it. Spenser specifies that genius is called Agdistes. However, the figure at Acrasia's gate is his diabolical double.

4. As if it were a sacrificial offering.

Wherewith her mother Art, as halfe in scorne
Of niggard Nature, like a pompous bride
Did decke her, and too lavishly adorne,[5]

450   When forth from virgin bowre she comes in th'early morne.

51

There to the Heavens alwayes Joviall,°   *joyful*
Lookt on them lovely, still° in stedfast° state,   *always/constant*
Ne suffred° storme nor frost on them to fall,   *allowed*
Their tender buds or leaves to violate,

455   Nor scorching heat, nor cold intemperate
T'afflict the creatures, which therein did dwell,
But the milde aire with season moderate
Gently attempred,° and disposd so well,   *temperate*
That still it breathed forth sweet spirit and holesome smell.

52

460   More sweet and holesome, then the pleasaunt hill
Of Rhodope,[6] on which the Nimphe, that bore
A gyaunt babe, her selfe for griefe did kill;
Or the Thessalian Tempe, where of yore
Faire Daphne Phoebus hart with love did gore;

465   Or Ida, where the Gods lov'd to repaire,°   *retire*
When ever they their heavenly bowres forlore;
Or sweet Parnasse, the haunt of Muses faire;
Or Eden selfe, if ought° with Eden mote compaire.   *anything*

53

Much wondred Guyon at the faire aspect°   *appearance*
470   Of that sweet place, yet suffred° no delight   *allowed*
To sincke into his sence, nor mind affect,
But passed forth, and lookt still forward right,°   *straight ahead*
Bridling his will, and maistering his might:
Till that he came unto another gate;

475   No gate, but like one, being goodly dight°   *decorated*
With boughes and braunches, which did broad dilate° *extend*
Their clasping armes, in wanton wreathings intricate.

54

So fashioned a Porch[7] with rare device,°   *design*
Archt over head with an embracing vine,
480   Whose bounches° hanging downe, seemed to entice   *bunches*
All passers by, to tast their lushious wine,
And did themselves into their hands incline,°   *hang*
As freely offering to be gathered:
Some deepe empurpled as the Hyacint,[8]
485   Some as the Rubine,° laughing sweetly red,   *ruby*
Some like faire Emeraudes,° not yet well ripened.   *emeralds*

---

5. Flora's mother, Art, scorns the simplicity of Nature and dresses Flora in showy clothing.
6. Spenser compares the Bower of Bliss with five Greek landscapes, all of which (except for Parnassus) were also the scenes of montrosity and tragedy. Rhodope was the hill where Orpheus sang and was torn to pieces by the Maenads, also the name of a nymph who gave birth to a giant child whose father was Neptune. Daphne was the

first love of Phoebus or Apollo, who could be said to have wounded his heart by her disdain of him; Mount Ida was the site of the beauty contest between Hera (Juno), Aphrodite (Venus), and Athena (Minerva) that led to the Trojan War.
7. The branches created a sort of porch.
8. Hyacinth or jacinth, a blue stone.

55

And them° amongst, some were of burnisht gold,   *the grapes*
   So made by art, to beautifie the rest,
   Which did themselves emongst the leaves enfold,
490   As lurking from the vew of covetous° guest,   *greedy*
   That the weake bowes,° with so rich load opprest,   *boughs*
   Did bow adowne, as over-burdened.
   Under that Porch a comely dame did rest,
   Clad in faire weedes, but fowle disordered,°   *sloppy*
495 And garments loose, that seemd unmeet for womanhed.⁹

56

In her left hand a Cup of gold she held,
   And with her right the riper fruit did reach,
   Whose sappy liquor, that with fulnesse sweld,
   Into her cup she scruzd,° with daintie breach°   *squeezed/crushing*
500   Of her fine fingers, without fowle empeach,¹
   That so faire wine-presse made the wine more sweet:
   Thereof she usd to give to drinke to each,
   Whom passing by she happened to meet:
It was her guise, all Straungers goodly so to greet.

57

505 So she to Guyon offred it to tast;
   Who taking it out of her tender hond,
   The cup to ground did violently cast,
   That all in peeces it was broken fond,
   And with the liquor stained all the lond:
510   Whereat Excesse² exceedingly was wroth,
   Yet no'te° the same amend, ne yet withstond,°   *could not/prevent*
   But suffered him to passe, all were she loth;°   *reluctant*
Who nought regarding her displeasure forward goth.

58

There the most daintie Paradise on ground,
515   It selfe doth offer to his sober eye,
   In which all pleasures plenteously abound,
   And none does others happinesse envye:
   The painted flowres, the trees upshooting hye,
   The dales for shade, the hilles for breathing space,
520   The trembling groves, the Christall running by;
   And that, which all faire workes doth most aggrace,°   *add grace to*
The art, which all that wrought, appeared in no place.³

59

One would have thought, (so cunningly, the rude,
   And scorned parts were mingled with the fine,)
525   That nature had for wantonesse ensude°   *imitated*
   Art, and that Art at nature did repine;°   *fret*
   So striving each th'other to undermine,
   Each did the others worke more beautifie;
So diff'ring both in willes, agreed in fine:

---

9. Unsuitable for womanhood.
1. She used her own fingers to squeeze the grapes without soiling her fingers or ruining the grapes.

2. The lady at the Porch.
3. The scene appears natural, and the art that created it is invisible.

530   So all agreed through sweete diversitie,°   *disagreement*
        This Gardin to adorne with all varietie.
                            60
        And in the midst of all, a fountaine stood,
            Of richest substaunce, that on earth might bee,
            So pure and shiny, that the silver flood
535   Through every channell running one might see;
            Most goodly it with curious imageree
            Was over-wrought, and shapes of naked boyes,
            Of which some seemd with lively jollitee,
            To fly about, playing their wanton toyes,
540   Whilest others did them selves embay° in liquid joyes.   *bathe*
                            61
        And over all, of purest gold was spred,
            A trayle° of yvie in his native hew: *vine*
            For the rich mettall was so coloured,
            That wight, who did not well avis'd° it vew,   *carefully*
545   Would surely deeme it to be yvie trew:
            Low his° lascivious armes adown did creepe,   *the ivy's*
            That themselves dipping in the silver dew,
            Their fleecy flowres they tenderly did steepe,
        Which drops of Christall seemd for wantones to weepe.
                            62
550   Infinit streames continually did well
            Out of this fountaine, sweet and faire to see,
            The which into an ample laver° fell,   *basin*
            And shortly grew to so great quantitie,
            That like a little lake it seemd to bee;
555   Whose depth exceeded not three cubits° hight,   *about four feet*
            That through the waves one might the bottom see,
            All pav'd beneath with Jaspar° shining bright,   *green stone*
        That seemd the fountaine in that sea did sayle upright.[4]
                            63
        And all the margent° round about was set,   *edge*
560   With shady Laurell trees, thence to defend
            The sunny beames, which on the billowes bet,°   *beat*
            And those which therein bathed, mote offend.[5]
            As Guyon hapned by the same to wend,
            Two naked Damzelles he therein espyde,
565   Which therein bathing, seemed to contend,
            And wrestle wantonly,° ne car'd to hyde,   *lewdly*
        Their dainty parts from vew of any, which them eyde.
                            64
        Sometimes the one would lift the other quight
            Above the waters, and then downe againe
570   Her plong,° as over maistered by might,   *plunge*
            Where both awhile would covered remaine,
            And each the other from to rise restraine;

4. The jet of water rose up in the fountain so that it   5. The beams of the sun might bother bathers.
resembled a ship sailing on the sea.

The whiles their snowy limbes, as through a vele,
So through the Christall waves appeared plaine:
575   Then suddeinly both would themselves unhele,°   *release*
And th'amarous sweet spoiles to greedy eyes revele.

65

As that faire Starre, the messenger of morne,
His deawy face out of the sea doth reare:
Or as the Cyprian goddesse, newly borne
580   Of th'Oceans fruitfull froth, did first appeare:[6]
Such seemed they, and so their yellow heare
Christalline humour° dropped downe apace.   *water of the fountain*
Whom such when Guyon saw, he drew him neare,
And somewhat gan relent his earnest° pace,   *brisk*
585   His stubborn brest gan secret pleasaunce° to embrace.   *pleasure*

66

The wanton Maidens him espying, stood
Gazing a while at his unwonted° guise;°   *unfamiliar / manner*
Then th'one her selfe low ducked in the flood,
Abasht, that her a straunger did a vise:°   *view*
590   But th'other rather higher did arise,
And her two lilly paps° aloft displayd,   *breasts*
And all, that might his melting hart entise
To her delights, she unto him bewrayd:°   *revealed*
The rest hid underneath, him more desirous made.

67

595   With that, the other likewise up arose,
And her faire lockes,° which formerly were bownd   *hair*
Up in one knot, she low adowne did lose:
Which flowing long and thick, her cloth'd arownd,
And th'yvorie in golden mantle gownd:°   *draped*
600   So that faire spectacle from him was reft,°   *taken*
Yet that, which reft it, no lesse faire was fownd:
So hid in lockes and waves from lookers theft,
Nought but her lovely face she for his looking left.

68

Withall she laughed, and she blusht withall,
605   That blushing to her laughter gave more grace,
And laughter to her blushing, as did fall:
Now when they spide the knight to slacke his pace,
Them to behold, and in his sparkling face
The secret signes of kindled lust appeare,
610   Their wanton meriments they did encreace,
And to him beckned, to approch more neare,
And shewd him many sights, that courage cold could reare.[7]

69

On which when gazing him the Palmer saw,
He much rebukt those wandring eyes of his,
615   And counseld well, him forward thence did draw.°   *move*

---

6. Both star and the Cyprian goddess signify Venus.   7. They showed Guyon many things that could arouse his
lust.

Now are they come nigh to the Bowre of blis
Of° her° fond favorites so nam'd amis:°   *by/Acrasia's/wrongly*
When thus° the Palmer; Now Sir, well avise;   *thus spoke*
For here the end of all our travell is:
620   Here wonnes° Acrasia,[8] whom we must surprise,   *dwells*
Else she will slip away, and all our drift° despise.   *purpose*

70

Eftsoones they heard a most melodious sound,
Of all° that mote delight a daintie eare,   *everything*
Such as attonce might not on living ground,
625   Save in this Paradise, be heard elswhere:
Right hard it was, for wight, which did it heare,
To read,° what manner musicke that mote bee: *understand*
For all that pleasing is to living eare,
Was there consorted° in one harmonee,   *joined*
630   Birdes, voyces, instruments, windes, waters, all agree.

71

The joyous birdes shrouded° in chearefull shade,   *hidden*
Their notes unto the voyce° attempred° sweet,   *harmony/attuned*
Th'Angelicall soft trembling voyces made
To th'instruments° divine respondence° meet: *of the Bower/answer*
635   The silver sounding instruments did meet
With the base murmure of the waters fall:
The waters fall with difference discreet,
Now soft, now loud, unto the wind did call:
The gentle warbling wind low answered to all.

72

640   There, whence that Musick seemed heard to bee,
Was the faire Witch her selfe now solacing,°   *relaxing*
With a new Lover, whom through sorceree
And witchcraft, she from farre did thither bring:
There she had him now layd a slombering,
645   In secret shade, after long wanton joyes:
Whilst round about them pleasauntly did sing
Many faire Ladies, and lascivious boyes,
That ever mixt their song with light licentious toyes.°   *pastimes*

73

And all that while, right over him she hong,
650   With her false eyes fast fixed in his sight,
As seeking medicine, whence she was stong,
Or greedily depasturing° delight: *grazing on*
And oft inclining downe with kisses light,
For feare of waking him, his lips bedewd,°   *wet*
655   And through his humid eyes did sucke his spright,
Quite molten° into lust and pleasure lewd;   *melted*
Wherewith she sighed soft, as if his case she rewd.

74

The whiles some one did chaunt° this lovely lay;°   *sing/song*
Ah see, who so faire thing doest faine° to see,   *wish*

8. Ill-temper, incontinence, impotence (medieval Latin).

660 In springing flowre the image of thy day;°   *life*
   Ah see the Virgin Rose, how sweetly shee
   Doth first peepe forth with bashfull modestee,
   That fairer seemes, the lesse ye see her may;⁹
   Lo see soone after, how more bold and free
665 Her bared bosome she doth broad° display;   *openly*
   Loe see soone after, how she fades, and falles away.

        75
   So passeth,° in the passing of a day,   *passes*
   Of mortall life the leafe, the bud, the flowre,
   Ne more doth flourish after first decay,°   *withering*
670 That earst was sought to decke° both bed and bowre,   *adorn*
   Of many a Ladie, and many a Paramowre:°   *lover*
   Gather therefore the Rose, whilest yet is prime,¹
   For soone comes age, that will her pride deflowre:
   Gather the Rose of love, whilest yet is time,
675 Whilest loving thou mayst loved be with equall crime.

        76
   He ceast, and then gan all the quire° of birdes   *choir*
   Their diverse notes t'attune unto his lay,
   As in approvance° of his pleasing words.   *as if approving*
   The constant paire heard all, that he did say,
680 Yet swarved,° but kept their forward way,   *turned*
   Through many covert groves, and thickets close,
   In which they creeping did at last display°   *discover*
   That wanton Ladie, with her lover lose,
   Whose sleepie head she in her lap did soft dispose.°   *lay*

        77
685 Upon a bed of Roses she was layd,
   As faint through heat, or dight to° pleasant sin,   *prepared for*
   And was arayd, or rather disarayd,
   All in a vele of silke and silver thin,
   That hid no whit her alablaster° skin,   *white*
690 But rather shewd more white, if more might bee:
   More subtile web Arachne² cannot spin,
   Nor the fine nets, which oft we woven see
   Of scorched° deaw, do not in th'aire more lightly flee.°   *dried/float*

        78
   Her snowy brest was bare to readie spoyle°   *easy view*
695 Of hungry eies, which n'ote° therewith be fild,   *could not*
   And yet through languour° of her late sweet toyle,   *weariness*
   Few drops, more cleare then Nectar, forth distild,°   *gathered*
   That like pure Orient perles adowne it trild,°   *trickled*
   And her faire eyes sweet smyling in delight,
700 Moystened their fierie beames, with which she thrild°   *pierced*

9. The less you see of her, the fairer she seems.
1. A figure common in love lyrics; the woman is compared to a flower that is to be picked just as it is about to bloom—an argument against moderation and temperance and for gratification and pleasure. Spenser concludes his version of the figure uncharacteristically, with a reminder that in the life of a temperate man or woman this kind of passion is a "crime."
2. A princess whose skill in the art of weaving surpassed that of the goddess Athena, who became jealous and transformed Arachne into a spider.

Fraile harts, yet quenched not; like starry light
Which sparckling on the silent waves, does seeme more bright.

79

The young man sleeping by her, seemd to bee
    Some goodly swayne of honorable place,
705   That certes it great pittie was to see
    Him his nobilitie so foule deface;°   *horribly disgrace*
    A sweet regard, and amiable grace,
    Mixed with manly sternnesse did appeare
    Yet sleeping, in his well proportiond face,
710   And on his tender lips the downy heare°   *hair*
Did now but freshly spring, and silken blossomes beare.

80

His warlike armes,° the idle instruments   *armor*
    Of sleeping praise, were hong upon a tree,
    And his brave shield, full of old moniments,°   *marks of battle*
715   Was fowly ra'st,° that none the signes might see;   *erased*
    Ne for them, ne for honour cared hee,
    Ne ought, that did to his advauncement tend,
    But in lewd loves, and wastfull luxuree,
    His dayes, his goods, his bodie he did spend:
720   O horrible enchantment, that him so did blend.°   *blind*

81

The noble Elfe, and carefull Palmer drew
    So nigh them, minding nought, but lustfull game,°   *pleasures*
    That suddein° forth they on them rusht, and threw   *suddenly*
    A subtile net, which onely for the same
725   The skilfull Palmer formally° did frame.   *especially*
    So held them under fast, the whiles the rest[3]
    Fled all away for feare of fowler° shame.   *fouler*
    The faire Enchauntresse, so unwares opprest,
Tryde all her arts, and all her sleights, thence out to wrest.°   *escape*

82

730   And eke her lover strove: but all in vaine;
    For that same net so cunningly was wound,°   *woven*
    That neither guile, nor force might it distraine.°   *destroy*
    They tooke them both, and both them strongly bound
    In captive bandes, which there they readie found:
735   But her in chaines of adamant° he tyde;   *hard stone*
    For nothing else might keepe her safe and sound;
    But Verdant[4] (so he hight) he soone untyde,
And counsell sage in steed° thereof to him applyde.   *stead*

83

But all those pleasant bowres and Pallace brave,
740   Guyon broke downe, with rigour° pittilesse;   *violence*
    Ne ought their goodly workmanship might save
    Them from the tempest of his wrathfulnesse,
    But that their blisse he turn'd to balefulnesse:°   *misery*

---

3. The Bower's other inhabitants.

4. Greening, growing green; here, one who is young and at the beginning of his maturity.

Their groves he feld, their gardins did deface,
745   Their arbers spoyle, their Cabinets° suppresse,   *bowers*
    Their banket° houses burne, their buildings race,°   *banquet/raze*
    And of the fairest late, now made the fowlest place.

84

Then led they her away, and eke that knight
    They with them led, both sorrowfull and sad:
750   The way they came, the same retourn'd they right,
    Till they arrived, where they lately had
    Charm'd those wild-beasts, that rag'd with furie mad.
    Which now awaking, fierce at them gan fly,
    As in their mistresse reskew, whom they lad;[5]
755   But them the Palmer soone did pacify.
Then Guyon askt, what meant those beastes, which there did ly.

85

Said he, These seeming beasts are men indeed,
    Whom this Enchauntresse hath transformed thus,
    Whylome° her lovers, which her lusts did feed,   *formerly*
760   Now turned into figures hideous,
    According to their mindes like monstruous.
    Sad end (quoth he) of life intemperate,
    And mournefull meed of joyes delicious:
    But Palmer, if it mote thee so aggrate,°   *please*
765 Let them returned be unto their former state.

86

Streight way he with his vertuous staffe them strooke,
    And streight of beasts they comely men became;
    Yet being men they did unmanly looke,
    And stared ghastly, some for inward shame,
770   And some for wrath, to see their captive Dame:
    But one above the rest in speciall,
    That had an hog beene late, hight Grille[6] by name,
    Repined° greatly, and did him miscall,°   *raged/insult*
That had from hoggish forme him brought to naturall.

87

775 Said Guyon, See the mind of beastly man,
    That hath so soone forgot the excellence
    Of his creation, when he life began,
    That now he chooseth, with vile difference,
    To be a beast, and lacke intelligence.
780   To whom the Palmer thus, The donghill kind
    Delights in filth and foule incontinence:
    Let Grill be Grill, and have his hoggish mind,
But let us hence depart, whilest wether serves and wind.[7]

---

5. The beasts attack Guyon and the Palmer as if to rescue their mistress, whom Guyon and the Palmer are leading.
6. Hog (Greek). Here Spenser follows the Odyssey: Grille is one of Ulysses's men whom Circe had transformed into a hog; he later refused to be returned to his human state.
7. While the weather and the wind are in our favor.

from **Amoretti**[1]

1

Happy ye leaves° when as those lilly hands,   *of the book*
Which hold my life in their dead doing° might,   *death-dealing*
Shall handle you and hold in loves soft bands,°   *bonds*
Lyke captives trembling at the victors sight.
5   And happy lines, on which with starry light,
Those lamping° eyes will deigne sometimes to look   *flashing*
And reade the sorrowes of my dying spright,°   *spirit*
Written with teares in harts close bleeding book.
And happy rymes bath'd in the sacred brooke,[2]
10 Of Helicon whence she derived is,
When ye behold that Angels blessed looke,
My soules long lacked foode, my heavens blis.
Leaves, lines, and rymes, seeke her to please alone,
Whom if ye please, I care for other none.

4

New yeare forth looking out of Janus[3] gate,
Doth seeme to promise hope of new delight:
And bidding th'old Adieu, his passed date
Bids all old thoughts to die in dumpish spright°   *low spirits*
5   And calling forth out of sad Winters night,
Fresh love, that long hath slept in cheerlesse bower:
Wils him awake, and soone about him dight
His wanton wings and darts of deadly power.
For lusty spring now in his timely howre,
10 Is ready to come forth him to receive:
And warnes the Earth with divers colord flowre,
To decke hir selfe, and her faire mantle weave.
Then you faire flowre, in whom fresh youth doth raine,°   *reign*
Prepare your selfe new love to entertaine.

13

In that proud port,° which her so goodly graceth,[4]   *bearing*
Whiles her faire face she reares up to the skie:
And to the ground her eie lids low embaseth°   *casts down*
Most goodly temperature° ye may descry,°   *temperament/perceive*

1. "Little loves," a sonnet sequence apparently written for Elizabeth Boyle, whom Spenser married in 1594, though he may have written some of the sonnets much earlier and for another woman. The *Amoretti* were published in 1595 together with the *Epithalamion*, Spenser's marriage hymn upon his wedding. Both the sonnets and the hymn, each referring to regular moments in the passage of time, can be read as one continuous narrative.
2. Aganippe, which rises (or is "derived") from Helicon, a mountain that is home to the Muses, goddesses of all the arts but known especially for their inspiration of poets.
3. A Roman god of the new year who has two faces; one

looks back at December, the other ahead to January. For Christians the liturgical new year began on March 25, the Feast of the Annunciation, when the Angel Gabriel was thought to have announced the coming of Jesus Christ to the Virgin Mary. Throughout the sequence, Spenser plays with these two concepts of the year, juxtaposing the time dictated by nature, figured by the Roman calendar, with time according to Christian history and celebrated by the fasts and feasts of the church.
4. Spenser describes the lady to whom the sonnet is addressed.

₅   Myld humblesse° mixt with awfull° majesty,   *humility / awesome*
For looking on the earth whence she was borne:
Her minde remembreth her mortalitie,
What so is fayrest shall to earth returne.
But that same lofty countenance seemes to scorne
₁₀   Base thing, and thinke how she to heaven may clime:
Treading downe earth as lothsome and forlorne,
That hinders heavenly thoughts with drossy° slime.   *heavy*
Yet lowly still vouchsafe° to looke on me,   *condescend*
Such lowlinesse shall make you lofty be.

22

This holy season fit to fast and pray,[5]
Men to devotion ought to be inclynd:
Therefore, I lykewise on so holy day,
For my sweet Saynt some service fit will find.
₅   Her temple fayre is built within my mind,
In which her glorious ymage placed is,
On which my thoughts doo day and night attend
Lyke sacred priests that never thinke amisse.
There I to her as th'author of my blisse,
₁₀   Will builde an altar to appease her yre:°   *anger*
And on the same my hart will sacrifise,
Burning in flames of pure and chast desyre:
The which vouchsafe O goddesse to accept,
Amongst thy deerest relicks to be kept.

62

The weary yeare his race now having run,
The new[6] begins his compast° course anew: *encompassed*
With shew of morning mylde he hath begun,
Betokening peace and plenty to ensew.
₅   So let us, which this chaunge of weather vew,
Chaunge eeke° our mynds and former lives amend,   *also*
The old yeares sinnes forepast° let us eschew,°   *gone by / avoid*
And fly the faults with which we did offend.
Then shall the new yeares joy forth freshly send,
₁₀   Into the glooming° world his gladsome ray: *gloomy*
And all these stormes which now his beauty blend,°   *dim*
Shall turne to caulmes and tymely cleare away.
So likewise love cheare you your heavy spright,
And chaunge old yeares annoy° to new delight.   *grief*

65

The doubt° which ye misdeeme,° fayre love, is vaine,   *fear / misconceive*
That fondly° feare to loose° your liberty,   *foolishly / lose*

5. The holy season is Lent; the holy day is Ash Wednesday. The sonnet celebrates the poet's admission that his
love has a spiritual dimension; complimenting his heart's
desire is the worship he gives to his lady's image in the
temple of his mind.

6. The Christian new year, the Feast of the Annunciation.

When loosing one, two liberties ye gayne,
And make him bond that bondage earst dyd fly.
Sweet be the bands, the which true love doth tye,
Without constraynt or dread of any ill:
The gentle birde feeles no captivity
Within her cage, but singes and feeds her fill.
There pride dare not approch, nor discord spill
The league twixt them, that loyal love hath bound:
But simple truth and mutuall good will,
Seekes with sweet peace to salve° each others wound: heal
There fayth doth fearlesse dwell in brasen towre,
And spotlesse pleasure builds her sacred bowre.

66

To all those happy blessings which ye have,
With plenteous hand by heaven upon you thrown:
This one disparagement they to you gave,
That ye your love lent to so meane a one.[7]
Yee whose high worths surpassing paragon,
Could not on earth have found one fit for mate,
Ne but in heaven matchable to none,
Why did ye stoup unto so lowly state.
But ye thereby much greater glory gate,°   got
Then° had ye sorted° with a princes pere:°   than/consorted/peer
For now your light doth more it selfe dilate,°   spread
And in my darknesse greater doth appeare.
Yet since your light hath once enlumind° me,   illuminated
With my reflex° yours shall encreased be.   reflected light

68

Most glorious Lord of lyfe that on this day,[8]
Didst make thy triumph over death and sin:
And having harrowd hell, didst bring away
Captivity thence captive us to win.[9]
This joyous day, deare Lord, with joy begin,
And grant that we for whom thou diddest dye
Being with thy deare blood clene washt from sin,
May live for ever in felicity.
And that thy love we weighing worthily,
May likewise love thee for the same againe:
And for thy sake that all lyke deare° didst buy,   at the same cost
With love may one another entertayne.
So let us love, deare love, lyke as we ought,
Love is the lesson which the Lord us taught.

---

7. Working forward from Sonnet 62 and counting each sonnet as representing a day of love and devotion, Sonnet 66 corresponds to Good Friday. Spenser exploits the idea of humility, consistent with the passion of Christ, to express his own sense of devotion to his lady's virtue.
8. The sonnet addresses the "dear Lord" of the Passion on Easter Day to harmonize the poet's love for his lady and his obligation to follow the lesson of Christ.
9. Christians believed that after his Resurrection, Christ descended into hell to rescue Adam and Eve and the patriarchs and prophets of the Hebrew Bible. The event is often described as the harrowing of hell.

75

One day I wrote her name upon the strand,°   beach
But came the waves and washed it away:
Agayne I wrote it with a second hand,
But came the tyde, and made my paynes his pray.
5 Vayne man, sayd she, that doest in vaine assay,°   attempt
A mortall thing so to immortalize.
For I my selve shall lyke to this decay,
And eek my name bee wyped out lykewize.
Not so, (quod I) let baser things devize,°   consent
10 To dy in dust, but you shall live by fame:
My verse your vertues rare shall eternize,°   make eternal
And in the hevens wryte your glorious name:
Where whenas death shall all the world subdew,
Our love shall live, and later life renew.

Epithalamion[1]

Ye learned sisters[2] which have oftentimes
Beene to me ayding, others to adorne:
Whom ye thought worthy of your gracefull rymes,
That even the greatest did not greatly scorne
5 To heare theyr names sung in your simple layes,°   verses
But joyed° in theyr prayse.   took pleasure
And when ye list° your owne mishaps to mourne,   wish
Which death, or love, or fortunes wreck did rayse,
Your string could soone to sadder tenor turne,
10 And teach the woods and waters to lament
Your dolefull dreriment.°   misfortune
Now lay those sorrowfull complaints aside,
And having all your heads with girland° crownd,   garlands
Helpe me mine owne loves prayses to resound,
15 Ne let the same of any be envide:
So Orpheus[3] did for his owne bride,
So I unto my selfe alone will sing,
The woods shall to me answer and my Eccho ring.

Early before the worlds light giving lampe,
20 His golden beame upon the hils doth spred,
Having disperst the nights unchearefull dampe,
Doe ye awake and with fresh lusty hed,°   merriment
Go to the bowre of my beloved love,
My truest turtle dove

---

1. An epithalamion (meaning "at the bedroom" in Greek) was a poem written in celebration of a marriage. Spenser's epithalamion is unusual in that he wrote it for his own marriage to the lady of the *Amoretti*, Elizabeth Boyle; epithalamia (the plural form of the word) were usually written by a professional for a family with whom he had no personal connection. Each of the 24 sections of Spenser's poem describes a hour in the wedding day, which begins at one in the morning and continues to 12 midnight. The temporal structure of the *Epithalamion* recalls the calendrical structure of the *Amoretti*.
2. The nine Muses, the creative spirits presiding over the arts and sciences. The "others" Spenser refers to include Queen Elizabeth, whom he celebrates in various figures throughout *The Faerie Queene*.
3. The founder of poetry, according to Greek mythology; he was often invoked as a model by lyric poets of the early modern period.

25	Bid her awake; for Hymen° is awake,	*god of marriage*
	And long since ready forth his maske° to move,	*masque*
	With his bright Tead° that flames with many a flake,	*torch*
	And many a bachelor to waite on him,	
	In theyr fresh garments trim.	
30	Bid her awake therefore and soone her dight,°	*dress*
	For lo the wished day is come at last,	
	That shall for al the paynes and sorrowes past,	
	Pay to her usury of long delight,	
	And whylest she doth her dight,	
35	Doe ye to her joy and solace sing,	
	That all the woods may answer and your eccho ring.	

Bring with you all the Nymphes[4] that you can heare°   *here*
Both of the rivers and the forrests greene:
And of the sea that neighbours to her neare,
40   Al with gay girlands goodly wel beseene.°   *appearing*
And let them also with them bring in hand,
Another gay girland
For my fayre love of lillyes and of roses,
Bound truelove wize with a blew silke riband.
45   And let them make great store of bridale poses,°   *posies*
And let them eeke bring store of other flowers
To deck the bridale bowers.
And let the ground whereas her foot shall tread,
For feare the stones her tender foot should wrong
50   Be strewed with fragrant flowers all along,
And diapred lyke the discolored mead.[5]
Which done, doe at her chamber dore awayt,
For she will waken strayt,°   *immediately*
The whiles doe ye this song unto her sing,
55   The woods shall to you answer and your Eccho ring.

Ye Nymphes of Mulla[6] which with carefull heed,°   *attention*
The silver scaly trouts doe tend full well,
And greedy pikes which use therein to feed,
(Those trouts and pikes all others doo excell)
60   And ye likewise which keepe the rushy lake,
Where none doo fishes take,
Bynd up the locks° the which hang scatterd light,   *of the nymphs*
And in his waters which your mirror make,
Behold your faces as the christall bright,
65   That when you come whereas my love doth lie,
No blemish she may spie.
And eke ye lightfoot mayds which keepe the deere,
That on the hoary mountayne use to towre,°   *soar*
And the wylde wolves which seeke them to devoure,
70   With your steele darts doo chace from comming neer

---

4. The spirits in nature, generally associated with trees and streams.
5. Variegated like the many-colored fields.
6. Spenser's name for the Awbeg, a river in the county of Munster in Ireland, where he was serving as a deputy for the English crown at the time of his marriage to Elizabeth Boyle.

Be also present heere,
To helpe to decke her and to help to sing,
That all the woods may answer and your eccho ring.

75 Wake now my love, awake; for it is time,
The Rosy Morne long since left Tithones[7] bed,
All ready to her silver coche° to clyme,   *coach*
And Phoebus[8] gins to shew his glorious hed.
Hark how the cheerefull birds do chaunt° theyr laies°   *sing/songs*
And carroll of loves praise.
80 The merry Larke hir mattins sings aloft,
The thrush replyes, the Mavis° descant° playes,   *thrush/accompaniment*
The Ouzell° shrills, the Ruddock° warbles soft,   *blackbird/redbreast*
So goodly all agree with sweet consent,
To this dayes merriment.
85 Ah my deere love why doe ye sleepe thus long,
When meeter° were that ye should now awake,   *more fitting*
T'awayt the comming of your joyous make,°   *mate*
And hearken to the birds lovelearned song,
The deawy leaves among.
90 For they of joy and pleasance to you sing,
That all the woods them answer and theyr eccho ring.

My love is now awake out of her dreame,
And her fayre eyes like stars that dimmed were
With darksome cloud, now shew theyr goodly beams
95 More bright then Hesperus[9] his head doth rere.
Come now ye damzels, daughters of delight,
Helpe quickly her to dight,
But first come ye fayre houres which were begot
In loves sweet paradice, of Day and Night,
100 Which doe the seasons of the yeare allot,
And al that ever in this world is fayre
Doe make and still° repayre.[1]   *forever*
And ye three handmayds of the Cyprian Queene,[2]
The which doe still adorne her beauties pride,
105 Helpe to addorne my beautifullest bride.
And as ye her array, still throw betweene
Some graces to be seene,
And as ye use to Venus, to her sing,
The whiles the woods shal answer and your eccho ring.

110 Now is my love all ready forth to come,
Let all the virgins therefore well awayt,
And ye fresh boyes that tend upon her groome
Prepare your selves; for he is comming strayt.
Set all your things in seemly good aray
115 Fit for so joyfull day,

7. The mythical lover of the goddess of the dawn.
8. Apollo, the god of the sun.
9. Venus, the evening or morning star.
1. The hours or time both create and recreate everything

in the world.
2. Venus, whose handmaids are the Graces, attributes of courtesy and artistic expression.

The joyfulst day that ever sunne did see.
Faire Sun, shew forth thy favourable ray,
And let thy lifull° heat not fervent be   *full of life*
For feare of burning her sunshyny face,
120 Her beauty to disgrace.
O fayrest Phoebus,[3] father of the Muse,
If ever I did honour thee aright,
Or sing the thing, that mote° thy mind delight,   *could*
Doe not thy servants simple boone° refuse,   *favor*
125 But let this day let this one day be myne,
Let all the rest be thine.
Then I thy soverayne prayses loud wil sing,
That all the woods shal answer and theyr eccho ring.

Harke how the Minstrels gin to shrill aloud
130 Their merry Musick that resounds from far,
The pipe, the tabor, and the trembling Croud,°   *violin*
That well agree withouten breach° or jar.   *discord*
But most of all the Damzels doe delite,
When they their tymbrels° smyte,   *tambourines*
135 And thereunto doe daunce and carrol sweet,
That all the sences they doe ravish quite,
The whyles the boyes run up and downe the street,
Crying aloud with strong confused noyce,
As if it were one voyce.
140 Hymen[4] io Hymen, Hymen they do shout,
That even to the heavens theyr shouting shrill
Doth reach, and all the firmament doth fill,
To which the people standing all about,
As in approvance° doe thereto applaud   *approval*
145 And loud advaunce her laud,°   *praise*
And evermore they Hymen Hymen sing,
That al the woods them answer and theyr eccho ring.

Loe where she comes along with portly° pace,   *dignified*
Lyke Phoebe[5] from her chamber of the East,
150 Arysing forth to run her mighty race,
Clad all in white, that seemes a virgin best.
So well it her beseemes° that ye would weene°   *befits/think*
Some angell she had beene.
Her long loose yellow locks lyke golden wyre,
155 Sprinckled with perle, and perling° flowres a tweene,°   *rippling/between*
Doe lyke a golden mantle her attyre,
And being crowned with a girland greene,
Seeme lyke some mayden Queene.
Her modest eyes abashed to behold
160 So many gazers, as on her do stare,
Upon the lowly ground affixed are.

---

3. Apollo, god of the sun and music, hence the father of   marriage ceremony.
the Muses and the muse of lyric poetry.   5. Diana, goddess of the moon.
4. The god of marriage who was invoked as part of the

Ne dare lift up her countenance too bold,
But blush to heare her prayses sung so loud,
So farre from being proud.
165 Nathlesse° doe ye still loud her prayses sing,   *nevertheless*
That all the woods may answer and your eccho ring.

Tell me ye merchants daughters did ye see
So fayre a creature in your towne before,
So sweet, so lovely, and so mild as she,
170 Adornd with beautyes grace and vertues store,
Her goodly eyes lyke Saphyres shining bright,
Her forehead yvory white,
Her cheekes lyke apples which the sun hath rudded,°   *reddened*
Her lips lyke cherryes charming men to byte,
175 Her brest like to a bowle of creame uncrudded,°   *uncurdled*
Her paps lyke lyllies budded,
Her snowie necke lyke to a marble towre,
And all her body like a pallace fayre,
Ascending uppe with many a stately stayre,
180 To honors seat and chastities sweet bowre.
Why stand ye still ye virgins in amaze,
Upon her so to gaze,
Whiles ye forget your former lay to sing,
To which the woods did answer and your eccho ring.

185 But if ye saw that which no eyes can see,
The inward beauty of her lively spright,
Garnisht with heavenly guifts of high degree,
Much more then would ye wonder at that sight,
And stand astonisht lyke to those which red°   *looked at*
190 Medusaes[6] mazeful hed.
There dwels sweet love and constant chastity,
Unspotted fayth and comely womanhood,
Regard of honour and mild modesty,
There vertue raynes as Queene in royal throne,
195 And giveth lawes alone.
The which the base affections doe obay,
And yeeld theyr services unto her will,
Ne thought of thing uncomely° ever may   *improper*
Thereto approch to tempt her mind to ill.
200 Had ye once seene these her celestial threasures,
And unrevealed pleasures,
Then would ye wonder and her prayses sing,
That al the woods should answer and your echo ring.

Open the temple gates unto my love,
205 Open them wide that she may enter in,
And all the postes adorne as doth behove,
And all the pillours deck with girlands trim,

6. One of three mythological monstrous women, the Gorgons; Medusa, whose hair consisted of snakes (hence her head is "mazeful"), turned anyone who looked at her to stone.

For to recyve° this Saynt with honour dew,　　　　*receive*
That commeth in to you.
210　With trembling steps and humble reverence,
She commeth in, before th'almighties vew,
Of her ye virgins learne obedience,
When so ye come into those holy places,
To humble your proud faces:
215　Bring her up to th'high altar that she may,
The sacred ceremonies there partake,
The which do endlesse matrimony make,
And let the roring Organs loudly play;
The praises of the Lord in lively notes,
220　The whiles with hollow throates
The Choristers the joyous Antheme sing,
That al the woods may answere and their eccho ring.

Behold whiles she before the altar stands
Hearing the holy priest that to her speakes
225　And blesseth her with his two happy hands,
How the red roses flush up in her cheekes,
And the pure snow with goodly vermill° stayne,　　*vermilion*
Like crimsin dyde in grayne,°　　　　　　　　　*fast dyed*
That even th'Angels which continually,
230　About the sacred Altare doe remaine,
Forget their service and about her fly,
Ofte peeping in her face that seemes more fayre,
The more they on it stare.
But her sad eyes still fastened on the ground,
235　Are governed with goodly modesty,
That suffers not one looke to glaunce awry,
Which may let in a little thought unsownd.°　　　*suspicions*
Why blush ye love to give to me your hand,
The pledge of all our band?
240　Sing ye sweet Angels, Alleluya sing,
That all the woods may answere and your eccho ring.

Now al is done; bring home the bride againe,
Bring home the triumph of our victory,
Bring home with you the glory of her gaine,
245　With joyance bring her and with jollity.°　　　*merriment*
Never had man more joyfull day then this,
Whom heaven would heape with blis.
Make feast therefore now all this live long day,
This day for ever to me holy is,
250　Poure out the wine without restraint or stay,
Poure not by cups, but by the belly full,
Poure out to all that wull,°　　　　　　　　　*will*
And sprinkle all the postes and wals with wine,
That they may sweat, and drunken be withall.
255　Crowne ye God Bacchus[7] with a coronall,°　　*garland*

---

7. The god of wine.

And Hymen also crowne with wreathes of vine,
And let the Graces daunce unto the rest;
For they can doo it best:
The whiles the maydens doe theyr carroll sing,
260   To which the woods shal answer and theyr eccho ring.

Ring ye the bels, ye yong men of the towne,
And leave your wonted labors for this day:
This day is holy; doe ye write it downe,
That ye for ever it remember may.
265   This day the sunne is in his chiefest hight,
With Barnaby the bright,[8]
From whence declining daily by degrees,
He somewhat loseth of his heat and light,
When once the Crab[9] behind his back he sees.
270   But for this time it ill ordained was,
To chose the longest day in all the yeare,
And shortest night, when longest fitter weare:°   *were*
Yet never day so long, but late would passe.
Ring ye the bels, to make it weare away,
275   And bonefiers° make all day,   *bonfires*
And daunce about them, and about them sing:
That all the woods may answer, and your eccho ring.

Ah when will this long weary day have end,
And lende me leave to come unto my love?
280   How slowly do the houres theyr numbers spend?
How slowly does sad Time his feathers° move?   *wings*
Hast thee O fayrest Planet[1] to thy home
Within the Westerne fome:°   *the sea*
Thy tyred steedes long since have need of rest.
285   Long though it be, at last I see it gloome,
And the bright evening star with golden creast
Appeare out of the East.
Fayre childe of beauty, glorious lampe of love
That all the host of heaven in rankes doost lead,
290   And guydest lovers through the nightes dread,
How chearefully thou lookest from above,
And seemst to laugh atweene° thy twinkling light   *between*
As joying in the sight
Of these glad many which for joy doe sing,
295   That all the woods them answer and their echo ring.

Now ceasse ye damsels your delights forepast;
Enough is it, that all the lay was youres:
Now day is doen, and night is nighing° fast: *approaching*
Now bring the Bryde into the brydall boures.°   *chambers*

8. Spenser's wedding took place on St. Barnabas day, June 11, the solstice or longest day of the year in the Elizabethan calendar.

9. The constellation Cancer, through which the sun passes in late July.

1. The sun, according to Ptolomaic astronomy.

300 Now night is come, now soone her disaray,°   *undress*
    And in her bed her lay;
    Lay her in lillies and in violets,
    And silken courteins over her display,
    And odour sheetes, and Arras[2] coverlets.
305 Behold how goodly my faire love does ly
    In proud humility;
    Like unto Maia,[3] when as Jove her tooke,
    In Tempe, lying on the flowry gras,
    Twixt sleepe and wake, after she weary was,
310 With bathing in the Acidalian brooke.
    Now it is night, ye damsels may be gon,
    And leave my love alone,
    And leave likewise your former lay to sing:
    The woods no more shal answere, nor your echo ring.

315 Now welcome night, thou night so long expected,
    That long daies labour doest at last defray,°   *repay*
    And all my cares, which cruell love collected,
    Hast sumd in one, and cancelled for aye:°   *ever*
    Spread thy broad wing over my love and me,
320 That no man may us see,
    And in thy sable mantle us enwrap,
    From feare of perrill and foule horror free.
    Let no false treason seeke us to entrap,
    Nor any dread disquiet once annoy
325 The safety of our joy:
    But let the night be calme and quietsome,
    Without tempestuous storms or sad afray:
    Lyke as when Jove with fayre Alcmena[4] lay,
    When he begot the great Tirynthian groome:
330 Or lyke as when he with thy selfe did lie,
    And begot Majesty.
    And let the mayds and yongmen cease to sing:
    Ne let the woods them answer, nor theyr eccho ring.

    Let no lamenting cryes, nor dolefull teares,
335 Be heard all night within nor yet without:
    Ne let false whispers breeding hidden feares,
    Breake gentle sleepe with misconceived dout.
    Let no deluding dreames, nor dreadful sights
    Make sudden sad affrights;
340 Ne let housefyres, nor lightnings helpelesse harmes,
    Ne let the Pouke,° nor other evill sprights,   *a house fairy*
    Ne let mischivous witches with theyr charmes,
    Ne let hob Goblins, names whose sence we see not,

---

2. A town in France, famous for its textiles.
3. The daughter of Atlas and the mother of Mercury by Jupiter, i.e., Jove.

4. The mother of Hercules, the "Tirynthian groom," who was supposed to have taken three nights to beget.

Fray° us with things that be not.   *frighten*
345 Let not the shriech Oule,° nor the Storke be heard: *screech owl*
     Nor the night Raven that still deadly yels,
     Nor damned ghosts cald up with mighty spels,
     Nor griesly vultures make us once affeard:
     Ne let th'unpleasant Quyre° of Frogs still croking   *choir*
350 Make us to wish theyr choking.
     Let none of these theyr drery accents sing;
     Ne let the woods them answer, nor theyr eccho ring.

     But let stil Silence trew night watches keepe,
     That sacred peace may in assurance rayne,
355 And tymely sleep, when it is tyme to sleepe,
     May poure his limbs forth on your pleasant playne,°   *complaint of love*
     The whiles an hundred little winged loves,
     Like divers° fethered doves,   *many*
     Shall fly and flutter round about your bed,
360 And in the secret darke, that none reproves,
     Their prety stealthes shal worke, and snares shal spread
     To filch away sweet snatches of delight,
     Conceald through covert night.
     Ye sonnes of Venus, play your sports at will,
365 For greedy pleasure, carelesse of your toyes,
     Thinks more upon her paradise of joyes,
     Then what ye do, albe it good or ill.
     All night therefore attend your merry play,
     For it will soone be day:
370 Now none doth hinder you, that say or sing,
     Ne will the woods now answer, nor your Eccho ring.

     Who is the same, which at my window peepes?
     Or whose is that faire face, that shines so bright,
     Is it not Cinthia,° she that never sleepes,   *the moon*
375 But walkes about high heaven al the night?
     O fayrest goddesse, do thou not envy
     My love with me to spy:
     For thou likewise didst love, though now unthought,
     And for a fleece of woll, which privily,
380 The Latmian shephard⁵ once unto thee brought,
     His pleasures with thee wrought.
     Therefore to us be favorable now;
     And sith of wemens labours thou hast charge,
     And generation goodly dost enlarge,
385 Encline thy will t'effect our wishfull vow,
     And the chast wombe informe° with timely seed,   *implant*
     That may our comfort breed:

5. Endymion, beloved of Diana, goddess of the moon, chastity, and childbirth, also known as Cynthia.

Till which we cease our hopefull hap° to sing,　　　　　*condition*
Ne let the woods us answere, nor our Eccho ring.

390　And thou great Juno,[6] which with awful might
The lawes of wedlock still dost patronize,
And the religion of the faith first plight
With sacred rites hast taught to solemnize:
And eeke for comfort often called art
395　Of women in their smart,
Eternally bind thou this lovely band,
And all thy blessings unto us impart.
And thou glad Genius,[7] in whose gentle hand,
The bridale bowre and geniall° bed remaine,　　　　　*generative*
400　Without blemish or staine,
And the sweet pleasures of theyr loves delight
With secret ayde doest succour and supply,
Till they bring forth the fruitfull progeny,
Send us the timely fruit of this same night.
405　And thou fayre Hebe,[8] and thou Hymen free,
Grant that it may so be.
Til which we cease your further prayse to sing,
Ne any woods shal answer, nor your Eccho ring.

And ye high heavens, the temple of the gods,
410　In which a thousand torches flaming bright
Doe burne, that to us wretched earthly clods:
In dreadful darknesse lend desired light;
And all ye powers which in the same remayne,
More than we men can fayne,°　　　　　*represent*
415　Poure out your blessing on us plentiously,
And happy influence upon us raine,
That we may raise a large posterity,
Which from the earth, which they may long possesse,
With lasting happinesse,
420　Up to your haughty° pallaces may mount,　　　　　*high*
And for the guerdon° of theyr glorious merit　　　　　*reward*
May heavenly tabernacles there inherit,
Of blessed Saints for to increase the count.
So let us rest, sweet love, in hope of this,
425　And cease till then our tymely joyes to sing,
The woods no more us answer, nor our eccho ring.

Song made in lieu of many ornaments,
With which my love should duly have bene dect,°　　　　　*bedecked*
Which cutting off through hasty accidents,
430　Ye would not stay your dew time to expect,
But promist both to recompens,
Be unto her a goodly ornament,
And for short time an endlesse moniment.

---

6. Wife of Jupiter, goddess of marriage.
7. In Roman religion, the spirit of paternity who protected the family.
8. Handmaid to the gods, daughter of Jupiter and Juno.

Sir Philip Sidney
1554–1586

Reality is often stranger but hardly ever more perfect than fiction. As Sir Philip Sidney tells us, the poets bring forth a "golden world." Exempt from judgments about its truth or falsehood, "poetry" (by which Sidney meant fiction) should construct forms of the ideal to mitigate our suffering and move us to good action. Sidney's own work comments brilliantly on contemporary moral and political issues: his sonnet sequence *Astrophil and Stella* illustrates the lover's paradox (love may require chastity); his prose romance *The Arcadia* describes the politics of love and sexuality; and his *Apology for Poetry* defends poetic and dramatic art from critics who would dismiss it in favor of philosophy and history. Yet to his countrymen, Sidney's most important achievement may have been a life dedicated to a public heroism and shaped by a sense of personal honor.

History has portrayed him as a prodigy. As his friend Fulke Greville wrote, "though I knew him from a child, yet I never knew him other than a man, . . . his very play tending to enrich his mind, so that even his teachers found something in him to observe and learn above that which they had usually read or taught." Play—understood in the Renaissance manner as "serious play"—took up much of Sidney's early career. Leaving Oxford at the age of seventeen but without a degree, Sidney embarked on what in later centuries was known as the Grand Tour. He visited Europe's major cities, seeking men and women who were fashioning the political goals and aesthetic sensibilities of the age. They included the philosopher Hubert Languet, whose Protestantism was linked to a fiercely antityrannical politics; the artists Tintoretto and Paolo Veronese, whose luminous realism was to determine painterly style for more than a generation; and, finally, Henry of Navarre (later King Henry IV of France) and his wife, Margaret of Valois, whose reign would see the worst of the religious wars in Europe. Back in England by 1575, Sidney espoused a politics that challenged authority. Siding with his father, Henry Sidney, Queen Elizabeth's Lord Deputy Governor of Ireland, he argued for imposing a land tax on the Anglo-Irish nobility, citing their "unreasonable and arrogant pretensions" as a cause of civil unrest. And in 1580, seeking to protect the monarchy from foreign influences, he wrote to the Queen cautioning her against a match with Francis, Duke of Alençon and brother to the French king, Henry III. She was furious at his temerity and ordered him to the country, where he was to remain out of touch with court affairs. By 1584 she had relented, sending Sidney to the Netherlands to assess the Protestant resistance to Spanish rule. There, in 1586, fighting for the Queen's interest and the Protestant cause she championed, he died of an abscessed bullet wound in his thigh.

Sidney's first literary work was a brief pastoral masque entitled *The Lady of May*, composed in honor of the Queen in 1578. His subsequent exile from court provided him with extensive time to write. He was often at Wilton, the estate of his sister, Mary Herbert, Countess of Pembroke; it was there that he wrote the first two of his major works, in all likelihood with his sister and her circle as his first readers and critics. *The Apology for Poetry*, a work defending what Sidney called his "unelected vocation," answers attacks on art, poetry, and the theater by such censorious writers as Stephen Gosson. But its argument exceeds the limits of antitheatrical debate to embrace questions about the uses of history and the effectiveness of philosophy—a subject that bears comparison with the poetics of Aristotle and Horace. Readers have remembered most its insistence that "poetry" goes beyond nature to fashion an ideal; it works "not only to make a Cyrus, which had been but a particular excellency as nature might have done, but to bestow a Cyrus upon the world to make many Cyruses." Poetry's creatures—whether heroes, heroines, or villains—cannot misrepresent fact because they exist only in the imagination of readers and listeners: "for the poet," Sidney declared, "he nothing affirms, and therefore never lieth."

The marvelous world of Sidney's *Arcadia* vividly dramatizes the chief points of his poetics. An early version of this satirical pastoral, written during Sidney's exile from Elizabeth's court and finished in 1581, depicts the willfulness of a superstitious and lazy duke, Basilius, who sequesters his marriageable daughters, Pamela and Philoclea, in the country where no suitor can meet them. His plans are foiled by two foreign princes, Pyrocles and Musidorus, who, disguised as a woman and a shepherd, manage to court and win the love of these ladies. Sidney's treatment of sex and gender is provocative: Pyrocles, disguised as a woman, attracts the interest of Basilius, who thinks "she" is female; at the same time, Pyrocles causes Gynecia, Basilius's wife, who senses that "she" is male, to fall in love with "her." Philoclea also falls in love with the disguised Pyrocles but represses that love because she thinks that Pyrocles is female. The encounters that follow challenge customary assumptions of sex as strictly linked to gender and suggest the extent to which social behavior between men and women is conventional. Interspersed throughout the prose narrative of these events are poems, termed *eclogues*, expressing the joys and sorrows of pastoral life, one of which, *As I my little flock on Ister bank*, has persuaded many readers that Sidney was arguing for a radical, essentially republican politics.

A second version of the *Arcadia*, apparently written two or three years later, very explicitly introduces politics to the plot: Sidney sketches the characters of several rulers, magnificent and tyrannical; includes arguments for resistance and rebellion; and illustrates the nature of justice and equity. This version, revised and readied for publication after Sidney's death by his sister, Mary Herbert, Countess of Pembroke, contains splendid portraits of queens both good and bad. Especially memorable is the wicked Cecropia, who plots to capture and kill the Arcadian princesses. The mother of Amphialus, who is a kind of moving target for misfortune's arrows, Cecropia has sometimes been understood to figure Catherine de'Medici, the powerful French queen, who many maintained had helped plan the massacre of hundreds of Protestants on Saint Bartholomew's Day, 1572.

Sidney's last work, *Astrophil and Stella*, has often been understood as self-satire. Its principal character, the young Astrophil, is frustrated by the marriage of his beloved Stella to a man who is characterized as "rich," an apparent reference to Sidney's disappointment when Penelope Devereux, whom he had courted for several years, married Lord Rich. Sidney mocks the young lover's passionate complaints while at the same time transforming the courtly figure of the distant yet beloved lady to reveal a paradox: as "absent," Stella may be present to Astrophil in spirit; as "present," she can only deny him her intimate friendship. The sequence is a marvelously witty reconceptualization of the principal themes of English Petrarchanism, a style that by the 1580s had become rather trite. Addressing his Stella, Sidney's Astrophil ends a sonnet with these lines:

> And not content to be Perfection's heir
> Thyself, doest strive all minds that way to move:
> Who mark in thee what is in thee most fair.
> So while thy beauty draws the heart to love,
> As fast thy virtue bends that love to good:
> But ah, Desire still cries, give me some food.

Conventionally Petrarchan in his depiction of the lady as a model and inspiration to a moral virtue that would seem to rule out any physical expressions of love, Sidney is at last very unconventional: he refuses to renounce "Desire" and its "food," or sexual gratification. A more imitative poet would not have so rejected Petrarch's idealistic asceticism. But just as Sidney had challenged the authority of church and state to promote better government (as he saw it), so did he exploit the process of "invention," the discovery of new meaning in old matter, to revitalize literary forms and expression.

The Apology for Poetry

When the right virtuous Edward Wotton[1] and I were at the Emperor's court together, we gave ourselves to learn horsemanship of John Pietro Pugliano, one that with great commendation had the place of an esquire in his stable. And he, according to the fertileness of the Italian wit, did not only afford us the demonstration of his practice, but sought to enrich our minds with the contemplations therein, which he thought most precious. But with none I remember mine ears were at that time more laden, than when (either angered with slow payment, or moved with our learner-like admiration) he exercised his speech in the praise of his faculty. He said soldiers were the noblest estate of mankind, and horsemen the noblest of soldiers. He said they were the masters of war and ornaments of peace, speedy goers and strong abiders, triumphers both in camps and courts. Nay, to so unbelieved a point he proceeded as that no earthly thing bred such wonder to a prince as to be a good horseman—skill of government was but a *pedanteria* [pedantry] in comparison. Then would he add certain praises, by telling what a peerless beast the horse was, the only serviceable courtier without flattery, the beast of most beauty, faithfulness, courage, and such more, that if I had not been a piece of a logician before I came to him, I think he would have persuaded me to have wished myself a horse. But thus much at least with his no few words he drave into me, that self-love is better than any gilding to make that seem gorgeous wherein ourselves be parties. Wherein, if Pugliano's strong affection and weak arguments will not satisfy you, I will give you a nearer example of myself, who (I know not by what mischance) in these my not old years and idlest times having slipped into the title of a poet, am provoked to say something unto you in the defense of that my unelected vocation,[2] which if I handle with more good will than good reasons, bear with me, since the scholar is to be pardoned that followeth the steps of his master. And yet I must say that, as I have more just cause to make a pitiful defense of poor poetry, which from almost the highest estimation of learning is fallen to be the laughingstock of children, so have I need to bring some more available proofs: since the former is by no man barred of his deserved credit, the silly latter hath had even the names of philosophers used to the defacing of it, with great danger of civil war among the Muses.[3]

And first, truly, to all them that, professing learning, inveigh against poetry may justly be objected that they go very near to ungratefulness, to seek to deface that which, in the noblest nations and languages that are known, hath been the first light-giver to ignorance, and first nurse, whose milk by little and little enabled them to feed afterwards of tougher knowledges. And will they now play the hedgehog that, being received into the den, drive out his host? Or rather the vipers, that with their birth kill their parents?

Let learned Greece in any of his manifold sciences be able to show me one book before Musaeus, Homer, and Hesiod, all three nothing else but poets.[4] Nay, let any history be brought that can say any writers were there before them, if they were not

---

1. Edward Wotton (1548–1626), half-brother of Henry Wotton who saw diplomatic service under James I. Edward Wotton and Sidney undertook a mission to the court of the Emperor Maximilian at Vienna in 1574–1575.
2. Sidney refers to writing poetry as his "unelected vocation" because he would have readers believe that he undertook it only after Elizabeth I had exiled him from court.
3. Mythological figures who were thought to inspire the liberal arts.
4. Musaeus was in fact a poet of the 5th century A.D.,

reported to be a pupil of the mythical Orpheus, the first musician. Homer was the legendary author of the *Iliad*, an epic poem telling of the seige of Troy by the army of the Greeks led by the hero, Achilles; and of the *Odyssey*, recounting the return of the hero, Odysseus, from Troy to his homeland in Ithaka. Hesiod is known as the poet of the *Theogony*, which tells the story of the gods in Greece; and of *Works and Days*, which describes the rituals and practices of the agricultural year. Both Homer and Hesiod lived in the 8th century B.C.

men of the same skill, as Orpheus, Linus,[5] and some other are named, who, having been the first of that country that made pens deliverers of their knowledge to the posterity, may justly challenge to be called their fathers in learning: for not only in time they had this priority (although in itself antiquity be venerable) but went before them, as causes to draw with their charming sweetness the wild untamed wits to an admiration of knowledge. So, as Amphion[6] was said to move stones with his poetry to build Thebes, and Orpheus to be listened to by beasts—indeed stony and beastly people—so among the Romans were Livius Andronicus and Ennius. So in the Italian language the first that made it aspire to be a treasure-house of science were the poets Dante, Boccaccio, and Petrarch. So in our English were Gower and Chaucer, after whom, encouraged and delighted with their excellent fore-going,[7] others have followed, to beautify our mother tongue, as well in the same kind as in other arts.

This did so notably show itself, that the philosophers of Greece durst not a long time appear to the world but under the masks of poets. So Thales, Empedocles, and Parmenides[8] sang their natural philosophy in verses; so did Pythagoras and Phocylides their moral counsels; so did Tyrtaeus in war matters, and Solon in matters of policy: or rather they, being poets, did exercise their delightful vein in those points of highest knowledge, which before them lay hid to the world. For that wise Solon was directly a poet it is manifest, having written in verse the notable fable of the Atlantic Island, which was continued by Plato. And truly even Plato[9] whosoever well considereth shall find that in the body of his work, though the inside and strength were philosophy, the skin, as it were, and beauty depended most of[1] poetry: for all standeth upon dialogues, wherein he feigneth many honest burgesses of Athens to speak of such matters, that, if they had been set on the rack, they would never have confessed them, besides his poetical describing the circumstances of their meetings, as the well ordering of a banquet,[2] the delicacy of a walk, with interlacing mere tales, as Gyges' ring and others, which who knoweth not to be flowers of poetry did never walk into Apollo's garden.[3]

And even historiographers (although their lips sound of things done, and verity[4] be written in their foreheads) have been glad to borrow both fashion and, perchance, weight of the poets. So Herodotus entitled his History by the name of the nine Muses;[5] and both he and all the rest that followed him either stale[6] or usurped of poetry

5. Supposed to have been the teacher of Orpheus.

6. Sidney lists historical and legendary poets to illustrate his claim that they were the founders of civilization and culture. Amphion was supposed to have moved stones by playing his music and thus to have built the walls of Troy; Livius Andronicus (c. 284–204 B.C.) was believed to have been the first Latin poet; Ennius (c. 239–169 B.C.) was traditionally regarded as the greatest of the early Latin poets. Dante, Boccaccio, and Petrarch were the first of the great Italian poets of the early Renaissance; Chaucer and Gower were the most important of the late medieval poets who wrote in English.

7. Example.

8. Sidney lists the best-known of the Greek philosophers before Plato: Thales, a geometrician; Empedocles, who studied the concepts of change and permanence; Parmeneides, who investigated the nature of being; Pythagoras, a mathematician and astronomer; Phocylides, a moralist; and Tyrtaeus, a poet. Solon (c. 640–558 B.C.) was an Athenian statesman, poet, and constitutional reformer. No trace remains of a poem by Solon telling of Atlantis, an island beyond the pillars of Hercules that vanishes beneath the sea; Sidney recalls Plato's dialogue (Timaeus, 21–24), in which Critias tells Socrates that the story of Atlantis originates in an unfinished poem of Solon.

9. Author of many works of philosophy in dialogue form, notably The Republic, on the construction of an ideal state, and The Symposium, on the nature of love and its association with beauty and truth. He was a key influence on Renaissance thinkers.

1. On.

2. A banquet is the setting of The Symposium; speakers take a walk in the The Phaedrus; and the story of Gyges' ring is told in The Republic.

3. Apollo was the god of poetry.

4. Truth.

5. Herodotus, a Greek historian (480–425) B.C.), wrote about the struggle between Asia and Greece; later classical editors divided his work, which he entitled simply History, into nine books named after the nine Muses: Calliope, Clio, Euterpe, Melpomene, Terpsichore, Erato, Polyhymnia, Urania, and Thalia.

6. Stole.

their passionate describing of passions, the many particularities of battles, which no man could affirm; or, if that be denied me, long orations put in the mouths of great kings and captains, which it is certain they never pronounced.

So that truly neither philosopher nor historiographer could at the first have entered into the gates of popular judgments, if they had not taken a great passport of poetry, which in all nations at this day where learning flourisheth not, is plain to be seen; in all which they have some feeling of poetry.

In Turkey, besides their law-giving divines, they have no other writers but poets. In our neighbor country Ireland, where truly learning goeth very bare, yet are their poets held in a devout reverence. Even among the most barbarous and simple Indians where no writing is, yet have they their poets who make and sing songs, which they call *areytos*,[7] both of their ancestors' deeds and praises of their gods: a sufficient probability that, if ever learning come among them, it must be by having their hard dull wits softened and sharpened with the sweet delights of poetry—for until they find a pleasure in the exercises of the mind, great promises of much knowledge will little persuade them that know not the fruits of knowledge. In Wales, the true remnant of the ancient Britons, as there are good authorities to show the long time they had poets, which they called bards, so through all the conquests of Romans, Saxons, Danes, and Normans, some of whom did seek to ruin all memory of learning from among them, yet do their poets even to this day last; so as it is not more notable in soon beginning than in long continuing.

But since the authors of most of our sciences[8] were the Romans, and before them the Greeks, let us a little stand upon their authorities, but even so far as to see what names they have given unto this now scorned skill.

Among the Romans a poet was called *vates*, which is as much as a diviner, foreseer, or prophet, as by his conjoined words *vaticinium* [prediction] and *vaticinari* [to foretell] is manifest: so heavenly a title did that excellent people bestow upon this heart-ravishing knowledge. And so far were they carried into the admiration thereof, that they thought in the chanceable hitting upon any such verses great foretokens of their following fortunes were placed. Whereupon grew the word of *Sortes Virgilianae*,[9] when by sudden opening Virgil's book they lighted upon any verse of his making, whereof the histories of the emperors' lives are full: as of Albinus, the governor of our island, who in his childhood met with this verse

Arma amens capio nec sat rationis in armis[1]

and in his age performed it. Which, although it were a very vain and godless superstition, as also it was to think spirits were commanded by such verses—whereupon this word charms, derived of *carmina* [songs], cometh—so yet serveth it to show the great reverence those wits were held in; and altogether not without ground, since both the oracles of Delphos and Sibylla's prophecies were wholly delivered in verses.[2] For that same exquisite observing of number and measure[3] in the words, and that high flying liberty of conceit proper to the poet, did seem to have some divine force in it.

---

7. A West Indian dance, recorded by José de Acosta in his *Natural and Moral History of the West Indies* (translated into English in 1604).
8. Any body of knowledge, typically natural philosophy and also including ethics and politics.
9. The Virgilian lots, or fortune as it is implied in lines from the *Aeneid*, which the reader chose at random and then subjects to interpretation.

1. "I seize arms madly, nor is there reason in arming" (2.314).
2. The shrine of Apollo at Delphi was presided over by a priestess who was believed to know the god's thoughts about the future; the Sibyls were supposed to be ancient prophetesses whose words were collected in the *Sibylline Books*.
3. Meter and rhythm.

And may not I presume a little further, to show the reasonableness of this word *vates*, and say that the holy David's Psalms are a divine poem? If I do, I shall not do it without the testimony of great learned men, both ancient and modern. But even the name of Psalms will speak for me, which being interpreted, is nothing but songs; then that it is fully written in meter, as all learned Hebricians agree, although the rules be not yet fully found; lastly and principally, his handling his prophecy, which is merely poetical: for what else is the awaking his musical instruments, the often and free changing of persons, his notable *prosopopoeias* [personifications], when he maketh you, as it were, see God coming in His majesty, his telling of the beasts' joyfulness and hills leaping,[4] but a heavenly poesy, wherein almost he showeth himself a passionate lover of that unspeakable and everlasting beauty to be seen by the eyes of the mind, only cleared by faith? But truly now having named him, I fear me I seem to profane that holy name, applying it to poetry, which is among us thrown down to so ridiculous an estimation. But they that with quiet judgments will look a little deeper into it, shall find the end and working of it such as, being rightly applied, deserveth not to be scourged out of the Church of God.

But now let us see how the Greeks named it, and how they deemed of it. The Greeks called him a "poet," which name hath, as the most excellent, gone through other languages. It cometh of this word ποιεῖν, which is, to make: wherein, I know not whether by luck or wisdom, we Englishmen have met with the Greeks in calling him a maker: which name, how high and incomparable a title it is, I had rather were known by marking the scope of other sciences than by any partial allegation.

There is no art delivered to mankind that hath not the works of nature for his principal object, without which they could not consist, and on which they so depend, as they become actors and players, as it were, of what nature will have set forth. So doth the astronomer look upon the stars, and, by that he seeth, set down what order nature hath taken therein. So doth the geometrician and arithmetician in their diverse sorts of quantities. So doth the musicians in time tell you which by nature agree, which not. The natural philosopher thereon hath his name, and the moral philosopher standeth upon the natural virtues, vices, or passions of man; and follow nature (saith he) therein, and thou shalt not err. The lawyer saith what men have determined; the historian what men have done. The grammarian speaketh only of the rules of speech; and the rhetorician and logician, considering what in nature will soonest prove and persuade, thereon give artificial rules, which still are compassed within the circle of a question according to the proposed matter. The physician weigheth the nature of man's body, and the nature of things helpful or hurtful unto it. And the metaphysic,[5] though it be in the second and abstract notions, and therefore be counted supernatural, yet doth he indeed build upon the depth of nature. Only the poet, disdaining to be tied to any such subjection, lifted up with the vigor of his own invention, doth grow in effect another nature, in making things either better than nature bringeth forth, or, quite anew, forms such as never were in nature, as the Heroes, Demigods, Cyclops, Chimeras, Furies,[6] and such like: so as he

---

4. Psalm 29.
5. A philosopher who considered abstractions and aspects of mental and spiritual life entertained in a state of contemplation rather than of action.
6. Furies: supernatural forces figured as mad goddesses pursuing revenge; demigods: male offspring of a god and a mortal, having some divine powers; cyclops: a one-eyed giant; chimeras: imaginary monsters made up of grotesquely disparate parts.

goeth hand in hand with nature, not enclosed within the narrow warrant[7] of her gifts, but freely ranging only within the zodiac of his own wit. Nature never set forth the earth in so rich tapestry as divers poets have done; neither with so pleasant rivers, fruitful trees, sweet-smelling flowers, nor whatsoever else may make the too much loved earth more lovely. Her world is brazen, the poets only deliver a golden.

But let those things alone, and go to man—for whom as the other things are, so it seemeth in him her uttermost cunning is employed—and know whether she have brought forth so true a lover as Theagenes, so constant a friend as Pylades, so valiant a man as Orlando, so right a prince as Xenophon's Cyrus, so excellent a man every way as Virgil's Aeneas.[8] Neither let this be jestingly conceived, because the works of the one be essential, the other in imitation or fiction; for any understanding knoweth the skill of each artificer standeth in that *idea* or fore-conceit[9] of the work, and not in the work itself. And that the poet hath that *idea* is manifest, by delivering them forth in such excellency as he had imagined them. Which delivering forth also is not wholly imaginative, as we are wont to say by them that build castles in the air; but so far substantially it worketh, not only to make a Cyrus, which had been but a particular excellency as nature might have done, but to bestow a Cyrus upon the world to make many Cyruses, if they will learn aright why and how that maker made him.

Neither let it be deemed too saucy a comparison to balance the highest point of man's wit with the efficacy of nature; but rather give right honor to the heavenly Maker of that maker, who having made man to His own likeness, set him beyond and over all the works of that second nature: which in nothing he showeth so much as in poetry, when with the force of a divine breath he bringeth things forth surpassing her doings—with no small arguments to the credulous of that first accursed fall of Adam, since our erected wit maketh us know what perfection is, and yet our infected will keepeth us from reaching unto it. But these arguments will by few be understood, and by fewer granted. This much (I hope) will be given me, that the Greeks with some probability of reason gave him the name above all names of learning.

Now let us go to a more ordinary opening of him, that the truth may be the more palpable: and so I hope, though we get not so unmatched a praise as the etymology of his names will grant, yet his very description, which no man will deny, shall not justly be barred from a principal commendation.

Poesy therefore is an art of imitation,[1] for so Aristotle termeth it in the word μίμησις—that is to say, a representing, counterfeiting, or figuring forth—to speak metaphorically, a speaking picture—with this end, to teach and delight.

7. Authority.
8. Sidney cites men recognized for their virtues. Theagenes exemplifies the true lover in Heliodorus's romance, the *Aethiopica*; Pylades, who helped Orestes avenge his father Agamemnon's murder, was cited by Renaissance commentators as a perfect friend; Orlando (modeled on Roland, the knight who fought for Charlemagne against the Basques at the battle of Roncesvalles, A.D. 778) was the hero of Ariosto's *Orlando Furioso* and illustrated the Renaissance idea of valor. The *Anabasis* of Xenophon (himself a general in Cyrus's army) relates how Cyrus the Younger, a Persian prince, helped the Peloponnesians resist the army of Athens and then died in an attempt to take the Persian throne from his brother

Artaxerxes in the fifth century B.C. Aeneas, the hero of Virgil's *Aeneid* and the mythical founder of the Roman Empire, was generally considered to be the epitome of the statesman.
9. The element of the literary work that determines how and to what end its subject is conveyed. Sidney later states that an *Idea* works "substantially" because it makes readers want to imitate the virtuous characters represented in a literary work.
1. Aristotle stated that poetry was a mimetic (from *mimesis*) or imitative art; Sidney (following Horace, who sees that poetry is like painting) adds that this imitation is (in some sense) pictorial.

Of this have been three general kinds. The chief, both in antiquity and excellency, were they that did imitate the unconceivable excellencies of God. Such were David in his Psalms; Solomon in his Song of Songs, in his Ecclesiastes, and Proverbs; Moses and Deborah in their Hymns; and the writer of Job: which, beside other, the learned Emanuel Tremellius and Franciscus Junius[2] do entitle the poetical part of the Scripture. Against these none will speak that hath the Holy Ghost in due holy reverence. (In this kind, though in a full wrong divinity, were Orpheus, Amphion, Homer in his Hymns, and many other, both Greeks and Romans.)[3] And this poesy must be used by whosoever will follow St. James's counsel in singing psalms when they are merry, and I know is used with the fruit of comfort by some, when, in sorrowful pangs of their death-bringing sins, they find the consolation of the never-leaving goodness.

The second kind is of them that deal with matters philosophical, either moral, as Tyrtaeus,[4] Phocylides, Cato, or natural, as Lucretius and Virgil's *Georgics*; or astronomical, as Manilius and Pontanus; or historical, as Lucan: which who mislike, the fault is in their judgment quite out of taste, and not in the sweet food of sweetly uttered knowledge.

But because this second sort is wrapped within the fold of the proposed subject, and takes not the course of his own invention, whether they properly be poets or no let grammarians dispute, and go to the third, indeed right poets, of whom chiefly this question ariseth: betwixt whom and these second is such a kind of difference as betwixt the meaner sort of painters, who counterfeit only such faces as are set before them, and the more excellent, who having no law but wit, bestow that in colors upon you which is fittest for the eye to see: as the constant though lamenting look of Lucretia,[5] when she punished in herself another's fault, wherein he painteth not Lucretia whom he never saw, but painteth the outward beauty of such a virtue. For these third be they which most properly do imitate to teach and delight, and to imitate borrow nothing of what is, hath been, or shall be; but range, only reined with learned discretion, into the divine consideration of what may be and should be. These be they that, as the first and most noble sort may justly be termed *vates*, so these are waited on in the excellentest languages and best understandings with the fore-described name of poets. For these indeed do merely make to imitate, and imitate both to delight and teach; and delight, to move men to take that goodness in hand, which without delight they would fly as from a stranger; and teach, to make them know that goodness whereunto they are moved—which being the noblest scope to which ever any learning was directed, yet want there not idle tongues to bark at them.

2. Sixteenth-century translators of the Hebrew and Greek Bible into Latin who considered the books here mentioned (all in the Hebrew Bible) to be poetry.

3. Sidney distinguishes the mystical works of Hellenic antiquity as erroneous in their depiction and understanding of divinity.

4. Sidney lists poets who he considers wrote some kind of philosophy and are not altogether "right," that is, pure poets. Tyrtaeus: mid-7th century B.C. Greek poet known for his praise of valor; Phocylides: a moralist of the 6th century B.C.; Cato: Dionysius Cato (c. A.D. 300), a moralist of whom little is known, who wrote a collection of moral sayings in verse couplets, published by Erasmus for use in schools; Lucretius: the Roman poet of the first century B.C. who wrote about the creation of the physical world; Virgil: the poet who stated the principles of farming in his *Georgics*; Manilius: the poet of the first century A.D. who wrote a versified treatise on astronomy; Pontanus: Joannes Jovius Pontanus, a late 15th-century poet who wrote a work on astronomy; and Lucan: the Roman poet of the first century A.D. who wrote the epic *Pharsalia*, which describes the events in the civil war between Caesar and Pompey up to Caesar's seduction of the Egyptian queen, Cleopatra.

5. Legendary heroine of the ancient Roman republic who committed suicide rather than live in shame after being raped by the tyrant Sextus Tarquinius. Her story was told in versions by Ovid, Livy, Chaucer, Christine de Pisan, Shakespeare, and others.

These be subdivided into sundry more special denominations. The most notable be the heroic, lyric, tragic, comic, satiric, iambic, elegiac, pastoral,[6] and certain others, some of these being termed according to the matter they deal with, some by the sorts of verses they liked best to write in; for indeed the greatest part of poets have apparelled their poetical inventions in that numbrous kind of writing which is called verse—indeed but apparelled, verse being but an ornament and no cause to poetry, since there have been many most excellent poets that never versified, and now swarm many versifiers that need never answer to the name of poets. For Xenophon, who did imitate so excellently as to give us *effigiem iusti imperii*, the portraiture of a just empire, under the name of Cyrus (as Cicero saith of him), made therein an absolute heroical poem.[7] So did Heliodorus in his sugared invention of that picture of love in Theagenes and Chariclea;[8] and yet both these wrote in prose: which I speak to show that it is not rhyming and versing that maketh a poet—no more than a long gown maketh an advocate, who though he pleaded in armor should be an advocate and no soldier. But it is that feigning notable images of virtues, vices, or what else, with that delightful teaching, which must be the right describing note to know a poet by; although indeed the senate of poets hath chosen verse as their fittest raiment, meaning, as in matter they passed all in all, so in manner to go beyond them: not speaking (table-talk fashion or like men in a dream) words as they chanceably fall from the mouth, but peising[9] each syllable of each word by just proportion according to the dignity of the subject.

Now therefore it shall not be amiss first to weigh this latter sort of poetry by his works, and then by his parts; and if in neither of these anatomies he be condemnable, I hope we shall obtain a more favorable sentence.

This purifying of wit—this enriching of memory, enabling of judgment, and enlarging of conceit—which commonly we call learning, under what name soever it come forth, or to what immediate end soever it be directed, the final end is to lead and draw us to as high a perfection as our degenerate souls, made worse by their clayey lodgings, can be capable of.

This, according to the inclination of the man, bred many-formed impressions. For some that thought this felicity principally to be gotten by knowledge, and no knowledge to be so high or heavenly as acquaintance with the stars, gave themselves to astronomy; others, persuading themselves to be demigods if they knew the causes of things, became natural and supernatural philosophers; some an admirable delight drew to music; and some the certainty of demonstration to the mathematics. But all, one and other, having this scope: to know, and by knowledge to lift up the mind from the dungeon of the body to the enjoying his own divine essence.

But when by the balance of experience it was found that the astronomer, looking to the stars, might fall in a ditch, that the inquiring philosopher might be blind in himself, and the mathematician might draw forth a straight line with a crooked heart, then lo, did proof, the overruler of opinions, make manifest that all these are but serving sciences, which, as they have each a private end in themselves, so yet are they all directed to the highest end of the mistress-knowledge, by the Greeks

---

6. Sidney lists the eight genres of poetry; "iambic" was a kind of satiric verse written in iambics, a meter made up of units or feet, each of which consists of a lightly stressed syllable followed by a heavily stressed syllable.
7. Sidney refers to Xenophon's *Cyropaedia*, his history of

Cyrus, the emperor of Persia, a work that he thinks has a heroic quality because it deals with the fate of an empire.
8. Characters in Heliodorus's romance, *Aethiopica*.
9. Weighing.

called ἀρχιτεκτονική, which stands (as I think) in the knowledge of a man's self, in the ethic and politic consideration, with the end of well-doing and not of well-knowing only—even as the saddler's next end is to make a good saddle, but his further end to serve a nobler faculty, which is horsemanship, so the horseman's to soldiery, and the soldier not only to have the skill, but to perform the practice of a soldier. So that, the ending end of all earthly learning being virtuous action, those skills that most serve to bring forth that have a most just title to be princes over all the rest.

Wherein, if we can, show we the poet's nobleness, by setting him before his other competitors. Among whom as principal challengers step forth the moral philosophers, whom, me thinketh, I see coming towards me with a sullen gravity, as though they could not abide vice by daylight, rudely clothed for to witness outwardly their contempt of outward things, with books in their hands against glory, whereto they set their names, sophistically speaking against subtlety, and angry with any man in whom they see the foul fault of anger. These men casting largess as they go, of definitions, divisions, and distinctions, with a scornful interrogative do soberly ask whether it be possible to find any path so ready to lead a man to virtue as that which teacheth what virtue is; and teach it not only by delivering forth his very being, his causes and effects, but also by making known his enemy, vice, which must be destroyed, and his cumbersome servant, passion, which must be mastered; by showing the generalities that containeth it, and the specialities that are derived from it; lastly, by plain setting down how it extendeth itself out of the limits of a man's own little world to the government of families and maintaining of public societies.

The historian scarcely giveth leisure to the moralist to say so much, but that he, laden with old mouse-eaten records, authorizing himself (for the most part) upon other histories, whose greatest authorities are built upon the notable foundation of hearsay; having much ado to accord differing writers and to pick truth out of their partiality; better acquainted with a thousand years ago than with the present age, and yet better knowing how this world goeth than how his own wit runneth; curious for antiquities and inquisitive of novelties; a wonder to young folks and a tyrant in table talk, denieth, in a great chafe,[1] that any man for teaching of virtue, and virtuous actions is comparable to him. "I am *testis temporum, lux veritatis, vita memoriae, magistra vitae, nuntia vetustatis*.[2] The philosopher," saith he, "teacheth a disputative virtue, but I do an active. His virtue is excellent in the dangerless Academy of Plato,[3] but mine showeth forth her honorable face in the battles of Marathon, Pharsalia, Poitiers, and Agincourt.[4] He teacheth virtue by certain abstract considerations, but I only bid you follow the footing of them that have gone before you. Old-aged experience goeth beyond the fine-witted philosopher, but I give the experience of many ages. Lastly, if he make the songbook, I put the learner's hand to the lute; and if he be the guide, I am the light." Then would he allege you innumerable examples, confirming story by stories, how much the wisest senators and princes have been directed by

---

1. Heat, fury.
2. Sidney quotes Cicero in his *De Oratore* (*Concerning the Orator*): "I am the witness of time, the light of truth, the life of memory, the governess of life, the herald of antiquity."
3. The olive grove near Athens, where Plato and his successors taught philosophy.
4. Sidney mentions some memorable battles: The Athe-

nians defeated the invading Persians at Marathon in 490 B.C.; Caesar defeated Pompey at Pharsalus in 48 B.C.; the Franks, under Charles Martel, defeated the Moors, led by Spanish emir Abd al-Rahman Ghafiqi in 732; the English, under Edward, the Black Prince, overcame the French army and captured their king, John II in 1356, each time at Poitiers; finally, Henry V defeated the French in 1415 at Agincourt.

the credit of history, as Brutus, Alphonsus of Aragon,[5] and who not, if need be? At length the long line of their disputation maketh a point in this, that the one giveth the precept, and the other the example.

Now whom shall we find (since the question standeth for the highest form in the school of learning) to be moderator? Truly, as me seemeth, the poet; and if not a moderator, even the man that ought to carry the title from them both, and much more from all other serving sciences. Therefore compare we the poet with the historian and with the moral philosopher; and if he go beyond them both, no other human skill can match him. For as for the divine, with all reverence it is ever to be excepted, not only for having his scope as far beyond any of these as eternity exceedeth a moment, but even for passing each of these in themselves. And for the lawyer, though *Ius* [Right] be the daughter of Justice, and justice the chief of virtues, yet because he seeketh to make men good rather *formidine poenae* than *virtutis amore;*[6] or, to say righter, doth not endeavor to make men good, but that their evil hurt not others; having no care, so he be a good citizen, how bad a man he be: therefore as our wickedness maketh him necessary, and necessity maketh him honorable, so is he not in the deepest truth to stand in rank with these who all endeavor to take naughtiness away and plant goodness even in the secretest cabinet of our souls. And these four are all that any way deal in that consideration of men's manners, which being the supreme knowledge, they that best breed it deserve the best commendation.

The philosopher, therefore, and the historian are they which would win the goal, the one by precept, the other by example. But both, not having both, do both halt.[7] For the philosopher, setting down with thorny arguments the bare rule, is so hard of utterance and so misty to be conceived, that one that hath no other guide but him shall wade in him till he be old before he shall find sufficient cause to be honest. For his knowledge standeth so upon the abstract and general, that happy is that man who may understand him, and more happy that can apply what he doth understand. On the other side, the historian, wanting the precept, is so tied, not to what should be but to what is, to the particular truth of things and not to the general reason of things, that his example draweth no necessary consequence, and therefore a less fruitful doctrine.

Now doth the peerless poet perform both: for whatsoever the philosopher saith should be done, he giveth a perfect picture of it in someone by whom he presupposeth it was done, so as he coupleth the general notion with the particular example. A perfect picture I say, for he yieldeth to the powers of the mind an image of that whereof the philosopher bestoweth but a wordish description, which doth neither strike, pierce, nor possess the sight of the soul so much as that other doth. For as in outward things, to a man that had never seen an elephant or a rhinoceros, who should tell him most exquisitely all their shapes, color, bigness, and particular marks, or of a gorgeous palace, an *architector* [architect], with declaring the full beauties, might well make the hearer able to repeat, as it were by rote, all he had heard, yet should never satisfy his inward conceit[8] with being witness to itself of a true lively

---

5. Brutus: Roman statesman, one of Caesar's assassins, who is said to have spent the night before the battle of Pharsalus reading history; Alphonsus: King of Aragon and Sicily who encouraged his soldiers to seize the libraries of those they conquered and to bring their books to him.

6. I.e., rather "from fear of punishment" than "from love of virtue" (Horace, *Epistles* 1.2.62). Sidney distinguishes between staying within the law and moral behavior.
7. Limp.
8. The listener's mental picture or image.

knowledge; but the same man, as soon as he might see those beasts well painted, or the house well in model, should straightways grow, without need of any description, to a judicial comprehending of them: so no doubt the philosopher with his learned definitions—be it of virtue, vices, matters of public policy or private government—replenisheth the memory with many infallible grounds of wisdom, which, notwithstanding, lie dark before the imaginative and judging power, if they be not illuminated or figured forth by the speaking picture of poesy.

Tully[9] taketh much pains, and many times not without poetical helps, to make us know the force love of our country hath in us. Let us but hear old Anchises speaking in the midst of Troy's flames,[1] or see Ulysses in the fullness of all Calypso's delights bewail his absence from barren and beggarly Ithaca. Anger, the Stoics said, was a short madness: let but Sophocles bring you Ajax on a stage, killing or whipping sheep and oxen, thinking them the army of Greeks, with their chieftains Agamemnon and Menelaus, and tell me if you have not a more familiar insight into anger than finding in the schoolmen his *genus* [race] and difference.[2] See whether wisdom and temperance in Ulysses and Diomedes, valor in Achilles, friendship in Nisus and Euryalus, even to an ignorant man carry not an apparent shining; and, contrarily, the remorse of conscience in Oedipus, the soon repenting pride in Agamemnon, the self-devouring cruelty in his father Atreus, the violence of ambition in the two Theban brothers, the sour-sweetness of revenge in Medea; and, to fall lower, the Terentian Gnatho and our Chaucer's Pandar so expressed that we now use their names to signify their trades:[3] and finally, all virtues, vices, and passions so in their own natural seats laid to the view, that we seem not to hear of them, but clearly to see through them.

But even in the most excellent determination of goodness, what philosopher's counsel can so readily direct a prince, as the feigned Cyrus in Xenophon; or a virtuous man in all fortunes, as Aeneas in Virgil; or a whole commonwealth, as the way of Sir Thomas More's *Utopia*? I say the way, because where Sir Thomas More erred, it was the fault of the man and not of the poet, for that way of patterning a commonwealth was most absolute, though he perchance hath not so absolutely performed it. For the question is, whether the feigned image of poetry or the regular instruction of philosophy hath the more force in teaching: wherein if the philosophers have more rightly showed themselves philosophers than the poets have attained to the high top of their profession, as in truth

> *Mediocribus esse poetis,*
> *Non dii, non homines, non concessere columnae;*[4]

it is, I say again, not the fault of the art, but that by few men that art can be accomplished.

Certainly, even our Savior Christ could as well have given the moral commonplaces of uncharitableness and humbleness as the divine narration of Dives and Lazarus;[5] or of disobedience and mercy, as that heavenly discourse of the lost child

9. Cicero.
1. In the remainder of this paragraph, Sidney refers to exemplary moments in the lives of mythical figures as illustrated in the literature of antiquity, especially the works of Virgil, Homer, and the Greek and Roman dramatists.
2. Species.
3. Gnatho: a parasite and flatterer in the Roman playwright Terence's *Eunuchus*; Pandar: the go-between for the lovers in Chaucer's *Troilus and Creseyde*.

4. Neither gods, nor men, nor booksellers permit poets to be mediocre; a statement adapted from Horace's *Art of Poetry*.
5. Sidney cites several parables from scripture. The rich man, Dives, refused to help the beggar Lazarus; Dives was condemned to hell, Lazarus went to heaven (Luke 16.19–31). He then cites the story of the Prodigal Son, welcomed home by his father after a period of dissolution (Luke 15.11–32).

and the gracious father; but that His through-searching wisdom knew the estate of Dives burning in hell, and of Lazarus in Abraham's bosom, would more constantly (as it were) inhabit both the memory and judgment. Truly, for myself, meseems I see before mine eyes the lost child's disdainful prodigality, turned to envy a swine's dinner: which by the learned divines[6] are thought not historical acts, but instructing parables.

For conclusion, I say the philosopher teacheth, but he teacheth obscurely, so as the learned only can understand him, that is to say, he teacheth them that are already taught; but the poet is the food for the tenderest stomachs, the poet is indeed the right popular philosopher, whereof Aesop's tales[7] give good proof: whose pretty allegories, stealing under the formal tales of beasts, make many, more beastly than beasts, begin to hear the sound of virtue from these dumb speakers.

But now may it be alleged that if this imagining of matters be so fit for the imagination, then must the historian needs surpass, who bringeth you images of true matters, such as indeed were done, and not such as fantastically or falsely may be suggested to have been done. Truly, Aristotle himself, in his discourse of poesy, plainly determineth this question, saying that poetry is φιλοσοφώτερον and σπουδαιότερον, that is to say, it is more philosophical and more studiously serious than history. His reason is, because poesy dealeth with καθόλου, that is to say, with the universal consideration, and the history with καθέκαστον, the particular: now, saith he, the universal weighs what is fit to be said or done, either in likelihood or necessity (which the poesy considereth in his imposed names), and the particular only marks whether Alcibiades did, or suffered, this or that.[8] Thus far Aristotle: which reason of his (as all his) is most full of reason. For indeed, if the question were whether it were better to have a particular act truly or falsely set down, there is no doubt which is to be chosen, no more than whether you had rather have Vespasian's picture[9] right as he was, or, at the painter's pleasure, nothing resembling. But if the question be for your own use and learning, whether it be better to have it set down as it should be, or as it was, then certainly is more doctrinable the feigned Cyrus in Xenophon than the true Cyrus in Justin, and the feigned Aeneas in Virgil than the right Aeneas in Dares Phrygius:[1] as to a lady that desired to fashion her countenance to the best grace, a painter should more benefit her to portrait a most sweet face, writing Canidia upon it, than to paint Canidia as she was, who, Horace sweareth, was full ill-favored.[2]

If the poet do his part aright, he will show you in Tantalus, Atreus, and such like,[3] nothing that is not to be shunned; in Cyrus, Aeneas, Ulysses, each thing to be followed; where the historian, bound to tell things as things were, cannot be liberal (without he will be poetical) of a perfect pattern, but, as in Alexander or Scipio himself, show doings, some to be liked, some to be misliked. And then how will you discern what to follow but by your own discretion, which you had without reading

6. Theologians.
7. Moralistic fables reputedly by a Greek slave who lived about 570 B.C.; numerous translations into English of his work were available in the 16th century.
8. Sidney paraphrases Aristotle's *Poetics* (9, 1451b). Alcibiades was a talented if unscrupulous Greek statesman.
9. A Roman emperor (A.D. 70–79) who was described by the historian Suetonius as very ugly.

1. Justinus (c. 4th century A.D.), and Dares Phrygius (5th century) wrote histories that some readers thought were more accurate than the more literary accounts by Xenophon, Homer, and Virgil.
2. Canidia was a prostitute who jilted the Roman poet, Horace; he then attacked her in his poems.
3. Evil figures (Tantalus served the flesh of his son, Pelops, to the gods; Atreus served his nephews' flesh to their father Thyestes).

Quintus Curtius?[4] And whereas a man may say, though in universal consideration of doctrine the poet prevaileth, yet that the history, in his saying such a thing was done, doth warrant a man more in that he shall follow—the answer is manifest: that, if he stand upon that[5] was (as if he should argue, because it rained yesterday, therefore it should rain today), then indeed hath it some advantage to a gross conceit; but if he know an example only informs a conjectured likelihood, and so go by reason, the poet doth so far exceed him as he is to frame his example to that which is most reasonable (be it in warlike, politic, or private matters), where the historian in his bare *Was* hath many times that which we call fortune to overrule the best wisdom. Many times he must tell events whereof he can yield no cause; or, if he do, it must be poetically.

For that a feigned example hath as much force to teach as a true example (for as for to move, it is clear, since the feigned may be tuned to the highest key of passion), let us take one example wherein an historian and a poet did concur. Herodotus and Justin do both testify that Zopyrus, King Darius's faithful servant, seeing his master long resisted by the rebellious Babylonians, feigned himself in extreme disgrace of his king: for verifying of which, he caused his own nose and ears to be cut off, and so flying to the Babylonians, was received, and for his known valor so sure credited, that he did find means to deliver them over to Darius.[6] Much like matter doth Livy record of Tarquinius and his son. Xenophon excellently feigneth such another stratagem performed by Abradatas in Cyrus's behalf.[7] Now would I fain know, if occasion be presented unto you to serve your prince by such an honest dissimulation, why you do not as well learn it of Xenophon's fiction as of the other's verity; and truly so much the better, as you shall save your nose by the bargain: for Abradatas did not counterfeit so far. So then the best of the historian is subject to the poet; for whatsoever action, or faction, whatsoever counsel, policy, or war stratagem the historian is bound to recite, that may the poet (if he list[8]) with his imitation make his own, beautifying it both for further teaching, and more delighting, as it please him: having all, from Dante's heaven to his hell, under the authority of his pen.[9] Which if I be asked what poets have done so, as I might well name some, so yet say I, and say again, I speak of the art, and not of the artificer.

Now, to that which commonly is attributed to the praise of history, in respect of the notable learning is got by marking the success, as though therein a man should see virtue exalted and vice punished—truly that commendation is particular to poetry, and far off from history. For indeed poetry ever sets virtue so out in her best colors, making Fortune her well-waiting handmaid, that one must needs be enamored of her. Well may you see Ulysses in a storm, and in other hard plights; but they are but exercises of patience and magnanimity, to make them shine the more in the near-following prosperity. And of the contrary part, if evil men come to the stage, they ever go out (as the tragedy writer answered to one that misliked the show of such persons) so manacled as they little animate folks to follow them. But the history, being captived to the truth of a foolish world, is many times a terror from well-doing, and an encour-

---

4. Quintus Curtius (1st century A.D.) wrote a history of Alexander the Great.
5. What.
6. The story of Zopyrus is told in Herodotus's *Histories* (3.153–58) and in Justin's *Histories* (1.10.15–22).
7. Tarquinius Superbus was the last of the Roman kings: his son, Sextus Tarquinius, passed himself off as an ally of the Gabians to spy for Rome (Livy, *Histories* 1, 3–4). Abradates (actually Araspes), acted in the same way for the Persian king, Cyrus (Xenophon, *Cyropaedia* 6.1.39).
8. Wishes.
9. Dante's *Divine Comedy* describes his journey through hell, purgatory, and paradise.

agement to unbridled wickedness. For see we not valiant Miltiades rot in his fetters?[1] The just Phocion and the accomplished Socrates put to death like traitors? The cruel Severus live prosperously? The excellent Severus miserably murdered? Sulla and Marius dying in their beds? Pompey and Cicero slain then when they would have thought exile a happiness? See we not virtuous Cato driven to kill himself, and rebel Caesar so advanced that his name yet, after 1600 years, lasteth in the highest honor? And mark but even Caesar's own words of the aforenamed Sulla (who in that only did honestly, to put down his dishonest tyranny), *literas nescivit*,[2] as if want of learning caused him to do well. He meant it not by poetry, which, not content with earthly plagues, deviseth new punishments in hell for tyrants, nor yet by philosophy, which teacheth *occidendos esse*; but no doubt by skill in history, for that indeed can afford you Cypselus, Periander, Phalaris, Dionysius, and I know not how many more of the same kennel, that speed well enough in their abominable injustice of usurpation.

I conclude, therefore, that he excelleth history, not only in furnishing the mind with knowledge, but in setting it forward to that which deserveth to be called and accounted good: which setting forward, and moving to well-doing, indeed setteth the laurel crown upon the poets as victorious, not only of the historian, but over the philosopher, howsoever in teaching it may be questionable.

For suppose it be granted (that which I suppose with great reason may be denied) that the philosopher, in respect of his methodical proceeding, doth teach more perfectly than the poet, yet do I think that no man is so much φιλοφιλόσοφος [a lover of philosophy] as to compare the philosopher in moving with the poet. And that moving is of a higher degree than teaching, it may by this appear, that it is well nigh both the cause and effect of teaching. For who will be taught, if he be not moved with desire to be taught? And what so much good doth that teaching bring forth (I speak still of moral doctrine) as that it moveth one to do that which it doth teach? For, as Aristotle saith, it is not γνῶσις [knowing] but πρᾶξις [doing] must be the fruit. And how πρᾶξις can be, without being moved to practice, it is no hard matter to consider.[3]

The philosopher showeth you the way, he informeth you of the particularities, as well of the tediousness of the way, as of the pleasant lodging you shall have when your journey is ended, as of the many by-turnings that may divert you from your way. But this is to no man but to him that will read him, and read him with attentive studious painfulness; which constant desire whosoever hath in him, hath already passed

---

1. Sidney demonstrates that the study of history is not conducive to good morals because it does not show virtue rewarded or vice punished. Miltiades: unsuccessful against the Persians in his seige of Paros, he was imprisoned by his own people, the Athenians (Herodotus, *Histories* 6, 136). Phocion: an Athenian statesman wrongly put to death for a supposed conspiracy (Plutarch, *Phocion* 38). Plato's teacher Socrates had been put to death for supposed impiety. Lucius Septimius Severus, Emperor of Rome (193–211), was able but termed "most cruel" by his biographer, Aelius Spartianus; by contrast, his virtuous successor Marcus Aurelius Alexander Severus was murdered by mutinous soldiers. Lucius Cornelius Sulla was a dictator of Rome, who tyrannized his subjects and yet died peacefully in his bed in 78 B.C.; Caius Marius was also a tyrant and never punished. Pompey opposed Caesar and was murdered after his defeat at Pharsalus; Marcus Tullius Cicero, the most accomplished of Roman lawyers and orators, was murdered by the order of Marcus Antonius in 43 B.C. Marcus Portius Cato committed suicide after his defeat at the battle of Thapsus rather than be captured by Caesar. Sidney calls Caesar a "rebel" because he invaded the territory of the Roman state (crossing the river Rubicon) without permission from the Roman Senate.

2. He knew no literature. Sidney indicates that the learning Sulla lacked was not of poetry, which reveals the punishments of hell; or of philosophy, which teaches *occidendum esse*—that is, when someone should be put to death, or the punishments inflicted by the state. Sidney argues that Sulla learned his misgovernment from history, which instructed him in the profitable ways of tyrants: Cipselus and Periander, both tyrants of Corinth; Phalaris, tyrant of Agrigentum; and Dionysius, tyrant of Syracuse.

3. *Nicomachean Ethics*, 1.1.

half the hardness of the way, and therefore is beholding to the philosopher but[4] for the other half. Nay truly, learned men have learnedly thought that where once reason hath so much overmastered passion as that the mind hath a free desire to do well, the inward light each mind hath in itself is as good as a philosopher's book; since in nature we know it is well to do well, and what is well, and what is evil, although not in the words of art which philosophers bestow upon us; for out of natural conceit the philosophers drew it. But to be moved to do that which we know, or to be moved with desire to know, *hoc opus, hic labor est*.[5]

Now therein of all sciences (I speak still of human, and according to the human conceit[6]) is our poet the monarch. For he doth not only show the way, but giveth so sweet a prospect into the way, as will entice any man to enter into it. Nay, he doth, as if your journey should lie through a fair vineyard, at the first give you a cluster of grapes, that full of that taste, you may long to pass further. He beginneth not with obscure definitions, which must blur the margin with interpretations, and load the memory with doubtfulness; but he cometh to you with words set in delightful proportion, either accompanied with, or prepared for, the well enchanting skill of music; and with a tale forsooth he cometh unto you, with a tale which holdeth children from play, and old men from the chimney corner. And, pretending no more, doth intend the winning of the mind from wickedness to virtue—even as the child is often brought to take most wholesome things by hiding them in such other as have a pleasant taste, which, if one should begin to tell them the nature of *aloes* or *rhabarbarum*[7] they should receive, would sooner take their physic at their ears than at their mouth. So is it in men (most of which are childish in the best things, till they be cradled in their graves): glad they will be to hear the tales of Hercules, Achilles, Cyrus, Aeneas; and, hearing them, must needs hear the right description of wisdom, valor, and justice; which, if they had been barely, that is to say philosophically, set out, they would swear they be brought to school again.

That imitation whereof poetry is, hath the most conveniency to nature of all other, insomuch that, as Aristotle saith, those things which in themselves are horrible, as cruel battles, unnatural monsters, are made in poetical imitation delightful.[8] Truly, I have known men that even with reading *Amadis de Gaule*[9] (which God knoweth wanteth much of a perfect poesy) have found their hearts moved to the exercise of courtesy, liberality, and especially courage. Who readeth Aeneas carrying old Anchises on his back, that wisheth not it were his fortune to perform so excellent an act? Whom doth not these words of Turnus move, the tale of Turnus having planted his image in the imagination,

> *Fugientem haec terra videbit?*
> *Usque adeone mori miserum est?*[1]

Where the philosophers, as they scorn to delight, so must they be content little to move—saving wrangling whether *virtus* [virtue] be the chief or the only good, whether the contemplative or the active life do excel—which Plato and Boethius well knew, and therefore made mistress Philosophy very often borrow the masking

---

4. Merely.
5. "This is the task, this the work"; the words of the Cumaean sybil to the hero Aeneas, who intends to return to earth from the underworld (*Aeneid* 6.128).
6. Way of thinking.
7. Medicines.
8. *Poetics*, 4.14486.

9. Chivalric romance in Spanish by Vasco de Lobeyra, c. 1325. It appeared in English translation in 1567.
1. In Virgil, Turnus unsuccessfully defended his native Latium (the region around Rome) against the invading Trojans led by Aeneas. Taking his last stand, Turnus cries: "Shall this ground see [Turnus] fleeing? Is it so hard, then, to die?" (*Aeneid* 12.645–46).

raiment of poesy.[2] For even those hard-hearted evil men who think virtue a school name, and know no other good but *indulgere genio* [self-indulgence], and therefore despise the austere admonitions of the philosopher, and feel not the inward reason they stand upon, yet will be content to be delighted—which is all the good-fellow poet seemeth to promise—and so steal to see the form of goodness (which seen they cannot but love) ere themselves be aware, as if they took a medicine of cherries.

Infinite proofs of the strange effects of this poetical invention might be alleged; only two shall serve, which are so often remembered as I think all men know them. The one of Menenius Agrippa,[3] who, when the whole people of Rome had resolutely divided themselves from the senate, with apparent show of utter ruin, though he were (for that time) an excellent orator, came not among them upon trust of figurative speeches or cunning insinuations, and much less with far-fet[4] maxims of philosophy, which (especially if they were Platonic) they must have learned geometry before they could well have conceived; but forsooth he behaves himself like a homely and familiar poet. He telleth them a tale, that there was a time when all the parts of the body made a mutinous conspiracy against the belly, which they thought devoured the fruits of each other's labor; they concluded they would let so unprofitable a spender starve. In the end, to be short (for the tale is notorious, and as notorious that it was a tale), with punishing the belly they plagued themselves. This applied by him wrought such effect in the people, as I never read that only words brought forth but then so sudden and so good an alteration; for upon reasonable conditions a perfect reconcilement ensued. The other is of Nathan the prophet,[5] who, when the holy David had so far forsaken God as to confirm adultery with murder, when he was to do the tenderest office of a friend in laying his own shame before his eyes, sent by God to call again so chosen a servant, how doth he it but by telling of a man whose beloved lamb was ungratefully taken from his bosom: the application most divinely true, but the discourse itself feigned; which made David (I speak of the second and instrumental cause) as in a glass see his own filthiness, as that heavenly psalm of mercy well testifieth.

By these, therefore, examples and reasons, I think it may be manifest that the poet, with that same hand of delight, doth draw the mind more effectually than any other art doth. And so a conclusion not unfitly ensue: that, as virtue is the most excellent resting place for all worldly learning to make his end of, so poetry, being the most familiar to teach it, and most princely to move towards it, in the most excellent work is the most excellent workman.

But I am content not only to decipher him[6] by his works (although works, in commendation or dispraise, must ever hold a high authority), but more narrowly will examine his parts; so that (as in a man) though all together may carry a presence full of majesty and beauty, perchance in some one defectuous piece we may find blemish.

Now in his parts, kinds, or species (as you list to term them), it is to be noted that some poesies have coupled together two or three kinds, as the tragical and comical, whereupon is risen the tragicomical. Some, in the manner, have mingled prose and verse, as Sannazaro and Boethius.[7] Some have mingled matters heroical and pastoral. But that cometh all to one in this question, for, if severed they be good, the

---

2. The philosophers Plato and Boethius both argued that a retired and contemplative life was superior to the active life or the life in public service. By contrast, the Roman orator Cicero asserted the value of prudence and the importance of contributing to the public good.

3. Roman consul who calmed rebellious commoners in 494 B.C. (Livy, *Histories* 2.32).

4. Far-fetched.

5. 2 Samuel 12.1–7.

6. Poetry.

7. Sannazaro: Italian poet (1458–1530) whose pastoral of mixed prose and verse, the *Arcadia*, influenced Sidney's work of the same name. Boethius (480?–524?): the Roman and Christian philosopher whose work *The Consolation of Philosophy* contains passages of prose and poetry.

conjunction cannot be hurtful. Therefore, perchance forgetting some and leaving some as needless to be remembered, it shall not be amiss in a word to cite the special kinds, to see what faults may be found in the right use of them.

Is it then the Pastoral poem which is misliked? (For perchance where the hedge is lowest they will soonest leap over.) Is the poor pipe disdained, which sometime out of Meliboeus's mouth can show the misery of people under hard lords or ravening soldiers, and again, by Tityrus, what blessedness is derived to them that lie lowest from the goodness of them that sit highest;[8] sometimes, under the pretty tales of wolves and sheep, can include the whole considerations of wrongdoing and patience; sometimes show that contentions for trifles can get but a trifling victory: where perchance a man may see that even Alexander and Darius, when they strave who should be cock of this world's dunghill, the benefit they got was that the after-livers may say

> *Haec memini et victum frustra contendere Thirsin:*
> *Ex illo Corydon, Corydon est tempore nobis.*[9]

Or is it the lamenting Elegiac;[1] which in a kind heart would move rather pity than blame; who bewails with the great philosopher Heraclitus, the weakness of mankind and the wretchedness of the world; who surely is to be praised, either for compassionate accompanying just causes of lamentations, or for rightly painting out how weak be the passions of woefulness? Is it the bitter but wholesome Iambic,[2] who rubs the galled mind, in making shame the trumpet of villainy, with bold and open crying out against naughtiness? Or the Satiric, who

> *Omne vafer vitium ridenti tangit amico;*[3]

who sportingly never leaveth till he make a man laugh at folly, and at length shamed, to laugh at himself, which he cannot avoid without avoiding the folly; who, while

> *circum praecordia ludit,*[4]

giveth us to feel how many headaches a passionate life bringeth us to; how, when all is done,

> *Est Ulubris, animus si nos non deficit aequus?*[5]

No, perchance it is the Comic, whom naughty playmakers and stage-keepers have justly made odious. To the arguments of abuse I will answer after. Only this much now is to be said, that the comedy is an imitation of the common errors of our life, which he representeth in the most ridiculous and scornful sort that may be, so as it is impossible that any beholder can be content to be such a one. Now, as in geometry the oblique must be known as well as the right, and in arithmetic the odd as well as the even, so in the actions of our life who seeth not the filthiness of evil wanteth a great foil to perceive the beauty of virtue. This doth the comedy handle so in our private and domestical matters as with hearing it we get as it were an experience what is

---

8. Meliboeus and Tityrus are characters in Virgil's *Eclogues*. Sidney responds to the idea that pastoral is the least elevated of the poetic genres; here he declares that it is capable of conveying political and moral ideas.

9. "These things I remember, how vanquished Thrysis tried in vain. Since then it has been Coridon, only Coridon, with us" (Virgil, *Eclogues*, 7.69–70). These lines suggest the futility of ambition.

1. A kind of poetry lamenting loss or remembering what

no longer exists. Heraclitus: a philosopher of conflict and flux, who lived about 500 B.C.

2. A verse form used in satire.

3. "The sly man probes every one of his friend's faults while making his friend laugh" (Persius, *Satires*, 1.116–17).

4. "He plays around the heart" (Persius, *Satires* 1.117).

5. "[Contentment] is at Ulubrae, if a well-balanced mind doesn't fail us" (Horace, *Epistles*, 1.11.30). Ulubrae was a notoriously disagreeable small town.

to be looked for of a niggardly Demea, of a crafty Davus, of a flattering Gnatho, of a vainglorious Thraso;[6] and not only to know what effects are to be expected, but to know who be such, by the signifying badge given them by the comedian. And little reason hath any man to say that men learn the evil by seeing it so set out, since, as I said before, there is no man living but, by the force truth hath in nature, no sooner seeth these men play their parts, but wisheth them *in pistrinum*;[7] although perchance the sack of his own faults lie so hidden behind his back that he seeth not himself dance the same measure; whereto yet nothing can more open his eyes than to find his own actions contemptibly set forth.

So that the right use of comedy will (I think) by nobody be blamed; and much less of the high and excellent Tragedy, that openeth the greatest wounds, and showeth forth the ulcers that are covered with tissue; that maketh kings fear to be tyrants, and tyrants manifest their tyrannical humors; that, with stirring the affects of admiration and commiseration, teacheth the uncertainty of this world, and upon how weak foundations gilden roofs are builded; that maketh us know

> *Qui sceptra saevus duro imperio regit*
> *Timet timentes; metus in auctorem redit.*[8]

But how much it can move, Plutarch yieldeth a notable testimony of the abominable tyrant Alexander Phaeraeus,[9] from whose eyes a tragedy, well made and represented, drew abundance of tears, who without all pity had murdered infinite numbers, and some of his own blood: so as he, that was not ashamed to make matters for tragedies, yet could not resist the sweet violence of a tragedy. And if it wrought no further good in him, it was that he, in despite of himself, withdrew himself from hearkening to that which might mollify his hardened heart. But it is not the tragedy they do mislike; for it were too absurd to cast out so excellent a representation of whatsoever is most worthy to be learned.

Is it the Lyric that most displeaseth, who with his tuned lyre and well-accorded voice, giveth praise, the reward of virtue, to virtuous acts; who gives moral precepts, and natural problems; who sometimes raiseth up his voice to the height of the heavens, in singing the lauds of the immortal God? Certainly, I must confess my own barbarousness, I never heard the old song of Percy and Douglas[1] that I found not my heart moved more than with a trumpet; and yet is it sung but by some blind crowder,[2] with no rougher voice than rude style; which, being so evil apparelled in the dust and cobwebs of that uncivil age, what would it work trimmed in the gorgeous eloquence of Pindar?[3] In Hungary I have seen it the manner at all feasts, and other such meetings, to have songs of their ancestors' valor, which that right soldierlike nation think one of the chiefest kindlers of brave courage. The incomparable Lacedemonians[4] did not only carry that kind of musicever with them to the field, but even at home, as such songs were made, so were they all content to be singers of them—when the lusty men were to tell what they did, the old men what they had done, and the young what they would do. And where a man may say that Pindar many times praiseth highly

---

6. Stock characters from the Roman comedies of Terence.
7. At a mill; a customary punishment for criminals and unruly slaves.
8. "The cruel man (i.e., the tyrant) who rules his people with a harsh government fears his fearful people; terror returns to its author" (Seneca, *Oedipus*, 3.705–6).
9. Tyrant of Pherae in Thessaly (369–357), described by Plutarch in his *Life of Pelopidas*.

1. Sidney refers to the ballad *Chevy Chase*, which describes the conflict between the Earls of Percy and Douglas.
2. Fiddler.
3. The most famous of Greek lyric poets (c. 522–402 B.C.), whose metrically complex odes celebrate victories in the Panhellenic games, the most famous of which was held every four years at Olympia.
4. Spartans.

victories of small moment, matters rather of sport than virtue; as it may be answered, it was the fault of the poet, and not of the poetry, so indeed the chief fault was in the time and custom of the Greeks, who set those toys at so high a price that Philip of Macedon[5] reckoned a horserace won at Olympus among his three fearful[6] felicities. But as the unimitable Pindar often did, so is that kind most capable and most fit to awake the thoughts from the sleep of idleness to embrace honorable enterprises.

There rests the Heroical—whose very name (I think) should daunt all back-biters: for by what conceit can a tongue be directed to speak evil of that which draweth with him no less champions than Achilles, Cyrus, Aeneas, Turnus, Tydeus, and Rinaldo?[7]—who doth not only teach and move to a truth, but teacheth and moveth to the most high and excellent truth; who maketh magnanimity and justice shine through all misty fearfulness and foggy desires; who, if the saying of Plato and Tully be true, that who could see virtue would be wonderfully ravished with the love of her beauty—this man sets her out to make her more lovely in her holiday apparel, to the eye of any that will deign not to disdain until they understand. But if anything be already said in the defense of sweet poetry, all concurreth to the maintaining the heroical, which is not only a kind, but the best and most accomplished kind of poetry. For as the image of each action stirreth and instructeth the mind, so the lofty image of such worthies most inflameth the mind with desire to be worthy, and informs with counsel how to be worthy. Only let Aeneas be worn in the tablet of your memory, how he governeth himself in the ruin of his country; in the preserving his old father, and carrying away his religious ceremonies; in obeying God's com-mandment to leave Dido, though not only all passionate kindness, but even the human consideration of virtuous gratefulness, would have craved other of him; how in storms, how in sports, how in war, how in peace, how a fugitive, how victorious, how besieged, how besieging, how to strangers, how to allies, how to enemies, how to his own; lastly, how in his inward self, and how in his outward government—and I think, in a mind not prejudiced with a prejudicating humor, he will be found in excellency fruitful, yea, even as Horace saith,

> *melius Chrysippo et Crantore.*[8]

But truly I imagine it falleth out with these poet-whippers, as with some good women, who often are sick, but in faith they cannot tell where; so the name of poet-ry is odious to them, but neither his cause nor effects, neither the sum that contains him, nor the particularities descending from him, give any fast handle to their carp-ing dispraise.

Since then poetry is of all human learning the most ancient and of most fatherly antiquity, as from whence other learnings have taken their beginnings; since it is so universal that no learned nation doth despise it, nor barbarous nation is without it; since both Roman and Greek gave such divine names unto it, the one of prophesy-ing, the other of making, and that indeed that name of making is fit for him, consid-ering that where all other arts retain themselves within their subject, and receive, as

---

5. Father of Alexander the Great, himself a conquering general and hero. Olympus: Sidney's error for Olympia, site of the Olympian Games.
6. Wonderful.
7. Epic heroes and moral exemplars. Tydeus fought to bring Polyneices, the son of Oedipus, to the throne of

Thebes (see Statius's *Thebaid*); Rinaldo was one of the French king Charlemagne's knights who fought against the Saracens in Italy (see Ludovico Ariosto's *Orlando Furioso* and Torquato Tasso's *Jerusalem Delivered*).
8. "Better than [the philosophers] Chrysippus and Cran-tor" (Horace, *Epistles*, 1.4).

it were, their being from it, the poet only bringeth his own stuff, and doth not learn a conceit out of a matter,[9] but maketh matter for a conceit; since neither his description nor end containing any evil, the thing described cannot be evil; since his effects be so good as to teach goodness and to delight the learners; since therein (namely in moral doctrine, the chief of all knowledges) he doth not only far pass the historian, but, for instructing, is well nigh comparable to the philosopher, for moving leaves him behind him; since the Holy Scripture (wherein there is no uncleanness) hath whole parts in it poetical, and that even our Savior Christ vouchsafed to use the flowers of it; since all his kinds are not only in their united forms but in their severed dissections fully commendable; I think (and think I think rightly) the laurel crown appointed for triumphant captains doth worthily (of all other learnings) honor the poet's triumph.

But because we have ears as well as tongues, and that the lightest reasons that may be will seem to weigh greatly, if nothing be put in the counterbalance, let us hear, and, as well as we can, ponder what objections be made against this art, which may be worthy either of yielding or answering.

First, truly I note not only in these μισόμουσοι, poet-haters, but in all that kind of people who seek a praise by dispraising others, that they do prodigally spend a great many wandering words in quips and scoffs, carping and taunting at each thing which, by stirring the spleen, may stay the brain from a through-beholding the worthiness of the subject. Those kind of objections, as they are full of a very idle easiness, since there is nothing of so sacred a majesty but that an itching tongue may rub itself upon it, so deserve they no other answer, but, instead of laughing at the jest, to laugh at the jester. We know a playing wit can praise the discretion of an ass, the comfortableness of being in debt, and the jolly commodities of being sick of the plague. So of the contrary side, if we will turn Ovid's verse

Ut lateat virtus proximitate mali,[1]

that good lie hid in nearness of the evil, Agrippa will be as merry in showing the vanity of science as Erasmus was in the commending of folly. Neither shall any man or matter escape some touch of these smiling railers. But for Erasmus and Agrippa,[2] they had another foundation than the superficial part would promise. Marry, these other pleasant faultfinders, who will correct the verb before they understand the noun, and confute others' knowledge before they confirm their own—I would have them only remember that scoffing cometh not of wisdom. So as the best title in true English they get with their merriments is to be called good fools; for so have our grave forefathers ever termed that humorous kind of jesters.

But that which giveth greatest scope to their scorning humor is rhyming and versing. It is already said (and, as I think, truly said), it is not rhyming and versing that maketh poesy. One may be a poet without versing, and a versifier without poetry. But yet, presuppose it were inseparable (as indeed it seemeth Scaliger[3] judgeth), truly it were an inseparable commendation. For if *oratio* next to *ratio*, speech next to

---

9. Does not take his theme from his material.
1. "That virtue may lie next to evil" (Cf. Ovid, *The Art of Love*, 2.662).
2. Henry Cornelius Agrippa of Nettesheim (1486–1533), a German philosopher, and Desiderius Erasmus of Rotterdam (1467–1536), the greatest humanist scholar of the

early modern period. Sidney refers to their most popular works, *The Uncertainty and Vanity of Knowledge* and *The Praise of Folly*, respectively, both written to satirize human pretensions.
3. Julius Caesar Scaliger (1484–1558), an Italian scholar who wrote a treatise, *Seven Books on Poetry*.

reason, be the greatest gift bestowed upon mortality, that cannot be praiseless which doth most polish that blessing of speech; which considers each word, not only (as a man may say) by his most forcible quality, but by his best measured quantity, carrying even in themselves a harmony—without, perchance, number, measure, order, proportion be in our time grown odious. But lay aside the just praise it hath, by being the only fit speech for music (music, I say, the most divine striker of the senses), thus much is undoubtedly true, that if reading be foolish without remembering, memory being the only treasure of knowledge, those words which are fittest for memory are likewise most convenient for knowledge. Now, that verse far exceedeth prose in the knitting up of memory, the reason is manifest: the words (besides their delight, which hath a great affinity to memory) being so set as one cannot be lost but the whole work fails; which accusing itself, calleth the remembrance back to itself, and so most strongly confirmeth it. Besides, one word so, as it were, begetting another, as, be it in rhyme or measured verse, by the former a man shall have a near guess to the follower. Lastly, even they that have taught the art of memory have showed nothing so apt for it as a certain room divided into many places well and thoroughly known. Now, that hath the verse in effect perfectly, every word having his natural seat, which seat must needs make the word remembered. But what needeth more in a thing so known to all men? Who is it that ever was a scholar that doth not carry away some verses of Virgil, Horace, or Cato, which in his youth he learned, and even to his old age serve him for hourly lessons? But the fitness it hath for memory is notably proved by all delivery of arts: wherein for the most part, from grammar to logic, mathematics, physic, and the rest, the rules chiefly necessary to be borne away are compiled in verses. So that, verse being in itself sweet and orderly, and being best for memory, the only handle of knowledge, it must be in jest that any man can speak against it.

Now then go we to the most important imputations laid to the poor poets. For aught I can yet learn, they are these. First, that there being many other more fruitful knowledges, a man might better spend his time in them than in this. Secondly, that it is the mother of lies. Thirdly, that it is the nurse of abuse, infecting us with many pestilent desires; with a siren's sweetness drawing the mind to the serpent's tail of sinful fancies (and herein, especially, comedies give the largest field to ear,[4] as Chaucer saith); how, both in other nations and in ours, before poets did soften us, we were full of courage, given to martial exercises, the pillars of manlike liberty, and not lulled asleep in shady idleness with poets' pastimes. And lastly, and chiefly, they cry out with open mouth as if they had overshot Robin Hood,[5] that Plato banished them out of his commonwealth. Truly, this is much, if there be much truth in it.

First, to the first. That a man might better spend his time, is a reason indeed; but it doth (as they say) but *petere principium* [beg the question]. For if it be as I affirm, that no learning is so good as that which teacheth and moveth to virtue; and that none can both teach and move thereto so much as poetry: then is the conclusion manifest that ink and paper cannot be to a more profitable purpose employed. And certainly, though a man should grant their first assumption, it should follow (methinks) very unwillingly, that good is not good, because better is better. But I still and utterly deny that there is sprong out of earth a more fruitful knowledge.

---

4. Sidney refers to an expression in Chaucer's *Canterbury Tales*: "a large feeld to ere," *The Knight's Tale*, 1.28.

5. The medieval folk hero, who is said to have lived in Sherwood Forest. Plato banishes poets in his treatise on the ideal state (*The Republic* 3.392).

To the second, therefore, that they should be the principal liars, I answer paradoxically, but truly, I think truly, that of all writers under the sun the poet is the least liar, and, though he would, as a poet can scarcely be a liar. The astronomer, with his cousin the geometrician, can hardly escape, when they take upon them to measure the height of the stars. How often, think you, do the physicians lie, when they aver things good for sicknesses, which afterwards send Charon[6] a great number of souls drowned in a potion before they come to his ferry? And no less of the rest, which take upon them to affirm. Now, for the poet, he nothing affirms, and therefore never lieth. For, as I take it, to lie is to affirm that to be true which is false. So as the other artists, and especially the historian, affirming many things, can, in the cloudy knowledge of mankind, hardly escape from many lies. But the poet (as I said before) never affirmeth. The poet never maketh any circles about your imagination, to conjure you to believe for true what he writes. He citeth not authorities of other histories, but even for his entry calleth the sweet Muses to inspire into him a good invention; in truth, not laboring to tell you what is or is not, but what should or should not be. And therefore, though he recount things not true, yet because he telleth them not for true, he lieth not—without we will say that Nathan lied in his speech beforealleged to David; which as a wicked man durst scarce say, so think I none so simple would say that Aesop lied in the tales of his beasts; for who thinks that Aesop wrote it for actually true were well worthy to have his name chronicled among the beasts he writeth of. What child is there, that, coming to a play, and seeing *Thebes* written in great letters upon an old door, doth believe that it is Thebes? If then a man can arrive to that child's age to know that the poets' persons and doings are but pictures what should be, and not stories what have been, they will never give the lie to things not affirmatively but allegorically and figuratively written. And therefore, as in history, looking for truth, they may go away full fraught with falsehood, so in poesy, looking but for fiction, they shall use the narration but as an imaginative ground-plot of a profitable invention. But hereto is replied, that the poets give names to men they write of, which argueth a conceit of an actual truth, and so, not being true, proves a falsehood. And doth the lawyer lie then, when under the names of *John-a-stiles* and *John-a-nokes*[7] he puts his case? But that is easily answered. Their naming of men is but to make their picture the more lively, and not to build any history: painting men, they cannot leave men nameless. We see we cannot play at chess but that we must give names to our chessmen; and yet, methinks, he were a very partial champion of truth that would say we lied for giving a piece of wood the reverend title of a bishop. The poet nameth Cyrus or Aeneas no other way than to show what men of their fames, fortunes, and estates should do.

Their third is, how much it abuseth men's wit, training it to wanton sinfulness and lustful love: for indeed that is the principal, if not only, abuse I can hear alleged.[8] They say, the comedies rather teach than reprehend amorous conceits. They say the lyric is larded with passionate sonnets; the elegiac weeps the want of his mistress; and that even to the heroical, Cupid hath ambitiously climbed. Alas, Love, I would thou couldst as well defend thyself as thou canst offend others. I would those on whom thou dost attend could either put thee away, or yield good reason why they keep thee. But grant love of beauty to be a beastly fault (although it be very hard, since

---

6. According to Greek myth, Charon ferries souls across the River Styx to the underworld.

7. I.e., John Doe, or John Roe of ancient law courts.

8. Sidney refers to contemporary criticism of the drama, the best known of which was Stephen Gosson's *School of Abuse* (1579); see page 946.

only man, and no beast, hath that gift to discern beauty); grant that lovely name of Love to deserve all hateful reproaches (although even some of my masters the philosophers spent a good deal of their lamp-oil in setting forth the excellency of it); grant, I say, whatsoever they will have granted, that not only love, but lust, but vanity, but (if they list) scurrility, possesseth many leaves of the poets' books; yet think I, when this is granted, they will find their sentence may with good manners put the last words foremost, and not say that poetry abuseth man's wit, but that man's wit abuseth poetry.

For I will not deny but that man's wit may make poesy, which should be εἰκαστική [representing real things] (which some learned have defined: figuring forth good things), to be φανταστική [representing imaginary things] (which doth, contrariwise, infect the fancy with unworthy objects), as the painter, that should give to the eye either some excellent perspective, or some fine picture, fit for building or fortification, or containing in it some notable example (as Abraham sacrificing his son Isaac, Judith killing Holofernes, David fighting with Goliath),[9] may leave those, and please an ill-pleased eye with wanton shows of better hidden matters. But what, shall the abuse of a thing make the right use odious? Nay truly, though I yield that poesy may not only be abused, but that being abused, by the reason of his sweet charming force, it can do more hurt than any other army of words: yet shall it be so far from concluding that the abuse should give reproach to the abused, that, contrariwise, it is a good reason that whatsoever, being abused, doth most harm, being rightly used (and upon the right use each thing conceiveth his title), doth most good. Do we not see the skill of physic, the best rampire[1] to our often-assaulted bodies, being abused, teach poison, the most violent destroyer? Doth not knowledge of law, whose end is to even and right all things, being abused, grow the crooked fosterer of horrible injuries? Doth not (to go to the highest) God's word abused breed heresy, and His name abused become blasphemy? Truly, a needle cannot do much hurt, and as truly (with leave of ladies be it spoken) it cannot do much good: with a sword thou mayst kill thy father, and with a sword thou mayst defend thy prince and country. So that, as in their calling poets fathers of lies they said nothing, so in this their argument of abuse they prove the commendation.

They allege herewith, that before poets began to be in price our nation had set their hearts' delight upon action, and not imagination: rather doing things worthy to be written, than writing things fit to be done. What that before-time was, I think scarcely Sphinx[2] can tell, since no memory is so ancient that hath not the precedent of poetry. And certain it is that, in our plainest homeliness, yet never was the Albion[3] nation without poetry. Marry, this argument, though it be levelled against poetry, yet is it indeed a chainshot[4] against all learning, or bookishness as they commonly term it. Of such mind were certain Goths,[5] of whom it is written that, having in the spoil of a famous city taken a fair library, one hangman (belike fit to execute the fruits of their wits) who had murdered a great number of bodies, would have set fire in it: no, said another very gravely, take heed what you do, for while they are busy about these toys, we shall with more leisure conquer their countries. This indeed is the ordinary doctrine of ignorance, and many words sometimes I have heard spent in

9. Sidney refers to episodes in the Bible (Genesis 22, 1 Samuel 17, Judith 2–14).
1. Rampart.
2. In Greek mythology a monster with a woman's head and a lion's body who posed riddles to human beings.
3. British.

4. Two cannonballs joined by a chain; it was deployed in naval warfare, usually against the rigging on enemy ships.
5. Northern European tribes, often described as uncivilized by ancient historians. The fate of "a fair library" is told by Michel de Montaigne in his essay Of Pedantry (Essays 1.24.)

it. But because this reason is generally against all learning as well as poetry, or rather, all learning but poetry; because it were too large a digression to handle it, or at least too superfluous (since it is manifest that all government of action is to be gotten by knowledge, and knowledge best by gathering many knowledges, which is reading), I only, with Horace, to him that is of that opinion

> *jubeo stultum esse libenter;*[6]

for as for poetry itself, it is the freest from this objection.

For poetry is the companion of camps. I dare undertake, Orlando Furioso, or honest King Arthur, will never displease a soldier; but the quiddity of *ens* and *prima materia* will hardly agree with a corselet;[7] and therefore, as I said in the beginning, even Turks and Tartars are delighted with poets. Homer, a Greek, flourished before Greece flourished. And if to a slight conjecture a conjecture may be opposed, truly it may seem, that as by him their learned men took almost their first light of knowledge, so their active men received their first motions of courage. Only Alexander's example may serve, who by Plutarch is accounted of such virtue, that Fortune was not his guide but his footstool; whose acts speak for him, though Plutarch did not: indeed the phoenix of warlike princes.[8] This Alexander left his schoolmaster, living Aristotle, behind him, but took dead Homer with him. He put the philosopher Callisthenes to death for his seeming philosophical, indeed mutinous, stubbornness, but the chief thing he was ever heard to wish for was that Homer had been alive. He well found he received more bravery of mind by the pattern of Achilles than by hearing the definition of fortitude. And therefore, if Cato misliked Fulvius for carrying Ennius with him to the field,[9] it may be answered that, if Cato misliked it, the noble Fulvius liked it, or else he had not done it; for it was not the excellent Cato Uticensis (whose authority I would much more have reverenced), but it was the former, in truth a bitter punisher of faults (but else a man that had never well sacrificed to the Graces: he misliked and cried out against all Greek learning, and yet, being eighty years old, began to learn it, belike fearing that Pluto understood not Latin). Indeed, the Roman laws allowed no person to be carried to the wars but he that was in the soldiers' roll; and therefore, though Cato misliked his unmustered person, he misliked not his work.[1] And if he had, Scipio Nasica, judged by common consent the best Roman, loved him. Both the other Scipio brothers, who had by their virtues no less surnames than of Asia and Afric, so loved him that they caused his body to be buried in their sepulture. So as Cato's authority, being but against his person, and that answered with so far greater than himself, is herein of no validity.

But now indeed my burden is great; now Plato's name is laid upon me, whom, I must confess, of all philosophers I have ever esteemed most worthy of reverence, and with good reason: since of all philosophers he is the most poetical. Yet if he will

6. "I order [him] to be stupid cheerfully" (Horace, *Satires,* 1.1.63).

7. Soldiers will enjoy reading about knights like Ariosto's Orlando Furioso or Malory's King Arthur, but will balk at philosophers' concerns with "quiddities" (subtleties), "*ens*" (being), and " *prima materia*" (the original matter of the universe).

8. Sidney cites various episodes from Plutarch's accounts of Alexander the Great in his *Lives* (c. A.D. 100), which was translated into English by Sir Thomas North in 1579. The phoenix was a mythic bird thought to be eternally reborn in the ashes of its own funeral pyre.

9. Marcus Portius Cato the Censor (234–184 B.C.), criticized the general Marcus Flavius Nobilior for carrying the poetry of Quintus Ennius (239–169 B.C.) on a battle campaign. Sidney goes on to distinguish Cato the Censor from his great-grandson, Marcus Porcius Cato, the chief political antagonist of Julius Caesar.

1. In fact, as Sidney states, the poet Ennius in person actually accompanied Flavius; he was "unmustered" in that he was not on the army payroll. Sidney continues to praise Ennius by saying that he was loved by various Scipios: Publius Cornelius Scipio Nasica, Publius Cornelius Scipio Africanus, and Lucius Cornelius Scipio Asiaticus, all notable patriots and generals.

defile the fountain out of which his flowing streams have proceeded, let us boldly examine with what reasons he did it. First, truly, a man might maliciously object that Plato, being a philosopher, was a natural enemy of poets. For indeed, after the philosophers had picked out of the sweet mysteries of poetry the right discerning true points of knowledge, they forthwith putting it in method, and making a school-art of that which the poets did only teach by a divine delightfulness, beginning to spurn at their guides, like ungrateful prentices, were not content to set up shops for themselves, but sought by all means to discredit their masters; which by the force of delight being barred them, the less they could overthrow them, the more they hated them. For indeed, they found for Homer seven cities strave who should have him for their citizen; where many cities banished philosophers as not fit members to live among them. For only repeating certain of Euripides' verses,[2] many Athenians had their lives saved of the Syracusans, where the Athenians themselves thought many philosophers unworthy to live. Certain poets, as Simonides and Pindar, had so prevailed with Hiero the First,[3] that of a tyrant they made him a just king; where Plato could do so little with Dionysius, that he himself of a philosopher was made a slave. But who should do thus, I confess, should requite the objections made against poets with like cavillations[4] against philosophers; as likewise one should do that should bid one read *Phaedrus* or *Symposium* in Plato, or the discourse of love in Plutarch, and see whether any poet do authorize abominable filthiness, as they do. Again, a man might ask out of what commonwealth Plato did banish them:[5] in sooth, thence where he himself alloweth community of women—so as belike this banishment grew not for effeminate wantonness, since little should poetical sonnets be hurtful when a man might have what woman he listed.[6] But I honor philosophical instructions, and bless the wits which bred them: so as they be not abused, which is likewise stretched to poetry.

St. Paul himself (who yet, for the credit of poets, twice citeth poets, and one of them by the name of "their prophet") setteth a watchword upon philosophy—indeed upon the abuse.[7] So doth Plato upon the abuse, not upon poetry. Plato found fault that the poets of his time filled the world with wrong opinions of the gods, making light tales of that unspotted essence, and therefore would not have the youth depraved with such opinions. Herein may much be said. Let this suffice: the poets did not induce such opinions, but did imitate those opinions already induced. For all the Greek stories can well testify that the very religion of that time stood upon many and many-fashioned gods, not taught so by the poets, but followed according to their nature of imitation. Who list may read in Plutarch the discourses of Isis and Osiris,[8] of the cause why oracles ceased, of the divine providence, and see whether the theology of that nation stood not upon such dreams

---

2. Plutarch states that Greek slaves living outside Greece had won their release by teaching their masters the poetry of Euripides (*Life of Nicias*, c. 29).

3. Tyrant of Syracuse (478–476 B.C.), who patronized Greek poets. Aeschylus was a playwright; Bacchylides a lyric poet; and Simonides a writer of satire. Dionysius the Elder of Syracuse was said to have sold Plato to the Spartan ambassador Pollis as a slave, a situation from which he was later liberated.

4. Objections.

5. I.e., poets. Plato argued that in his ideal republic, all women should be common, that is, not married to a sin-

gle man but sexually available to all men (*Republic* 5, 449–462). Sidney observes that Plato banishes poets not because poetry makes men licentious, an impossibility in a state in which women are readily available, but for some other reason.

6. Desired.

7. Paul rejects the assessment of poets by philosophers (Acts 17.18, Colossians 2.8); and he castigates false prophets (Titus 1.12).

8. Isis, the Egyptian goddess of fertility, was sister and wife of Osiris, civilizer of Egypt, god of the dead, and source of life.

which the poets indeed superstitiously observed—and truly (since they had not the light of Christ) did much better in it than the philosophers, who, shaking off superstition, brought in atheism. Plato therefore (whose authority I had much rather justly construe than unjustly resist) meant not in general of poets, in those words of which Julius Scaliger saith *Qua authoritate barbari quidam atque hispidi abuti velint ad poetas e republica exigendos;*[9] but only meant to drive out those wrong opinions of the Deity (whereof now, without further law, Christianity hath taken away all the hurtful belief) perchance (as he thought) nourished by the then esteemed poets. And a man need go no further than to Plato himself to know his meaning: who, in his dialogue called *Ion*, giveth high and rightly divine commendation unto poetry. So as Plato, banishing the abuse, not the thing, not banishing it, but giving due honor unto it, shall be our patron, and not our adversary. For indeed I had much rather (since truly I may do it) show their mistaking of Plato (under whose lion's skin they would make an ass-like braying against poesy) than go about to overthrow his authority; whom, the wiser a man is, the more just cause he shall find to have in admiration; especially since he attributeth unto poesy more than myself do, namely, to be a very inspiring of a divine force, far above man's wit, as in the forenamed dialogue is apparent.

Of the other side, who would show the honors have been by the best sort of judgments granted them, a whole sea of examples would present themselves: Alexanders, Caesars, Scipios, all favorers of poets; Laelius, called the Roman Socrates, himself a poet, so as part of *Heautontimorumenos*[1] in Terence was supposed to be made by him; and even the Greek Socrates, whom Apollo confirmed to be the only wise man, is said to have spent part of his old time in putting Aesop's fables into verses. And therefore, full evil should it become his scholar Plato to put such words in his master's mouth against poets. But what need more? Aristotle writes the Art of Poesy;[2] and why, if it should not be written? Plutarch teacheth the use to be gathered of them; and how, if they should not be read? And who reads Plutarch's either history or philosophy, shall find he trimmeth both their garments with guards of poesy. But I list not to defend poesy with the help of his underling historiography. Let it suffice to have showed it is a fit soil for praise to dwell upon; and what dispraise may be set upon it, is either easily overcome, or transformed into just commendation.

So that, since the excellencies of it may be so easily and so justly confirmed, and the low-creeping objections so soon trodden down: it not being an art of lies, but of true doctrine; not of effeminateness, but of notable stirring of courage; not of abusing man's wit, but of strengthening man's wit; not banished, but honored by Plato: let us rather plant more laurels for to engarland the poets' heads (which honor of being laureate, whereas besides them only triumphant captains were, is a sufficient authority to show the price they ought to be held in) than suffer the ill-favored breath of such wrong-speakers once to blow upon the clear springs of poesy.

9. By abuse of whose authority, barbarous and crude men wish to expel poets from the Republic; Scaliger is commenting on Plato's expulsion of poets from an ideal republic in his own treatise on poetry.
1. Gaius Laelius was said to have written parts of a play called *Heautontimorumenos* (*The Self-Tormenter*), reputed to be by the Roman playwright Terence. Plato reports that Socrates turned Aesop's fables into verse.
2. Sidney refers to Aristotle's *Poetics*.

But since I have run so long a career in this matter, methinks, before I give my pen a full stop, it shall be but a little more lost time to inquire why England, the mother of excellent minds, should be grown so hard a stepmother to poets, who certainly in wit ought to pass all other, since all only proceedeth from their wit, being indeed makers of themselves, not takers of others. How can I but exclaim

Musa, mihi causas memora, quo numine laeso?[3]

Sweet poesy, that hath anciently had kings, emperors, senators, great captains, such as, besides a thousand others, David, Adrian, Sophocles, Germanicus, not only to favor poets, but to be poets;[4] and of our nearer times can present for her patrons a Robert, king of Sicily, the great King Francis of France, King James of Scotland; such cardinals as Bembus and Bibbiena; such famous preachers and teachers as Beza and Melanchthon; so learned philosophers as Fracastorius and Scaliger; so great orators as Pontanus and Muretus; so piercing wits as George Buchanan; so grave counselors as, beside many, but before all, that Hospital of France,[5] than whom (I think) that realm never brought forth a more accomplished judgment, more firmly builded upon virtue: I say these, with numbers of others, not only to read others' poesies, but to poetize for others' reading—that poesy, thus embraced in all other places, should only find in our time a hard welcome in England, I think the very earth lamenteth it, and therefore decketh our soil with fewer laurels than it was accustomed. For heretofore poets have in England also flourished, and, which is to be noted, even in those times when the trumpet of Mars[6] did sound loudest. And now that an overfaint quietness should seem to strew[7] the house for poets, they are almost in as good reputation as the mountebanks[8] at Venice. Truly even that, as of the one side it giveth great praise to poesy, which like Venus (but to better purpose) had rather be troubled in the net with Mars than enjoy the homely quiet of Vulcan:[9] so serves it for a piece of a reason why they are less grateful to idle England, which now can scarce endure the pain of a pen.

Upon this necessarily followeth, that base men with servile wits undertake it, who think it enough if they can be rewarded of the printer. And so as Epaminondas[1] is said with the honor of his virtue to have made an office, by his exercising it, which before was contemptible, to become highly respected; so these men, no more but setting their names to it, by their own disgracefulness disgrace the most graceful poesy. For now, as if all the Muses were got with child to bring forth bastard poets, without any commission they do post over the banks of Helicon,[2] till they make the readers more weary than post-horses; while, in the meantime, they

Queis meliore luto finxit praecordia Titan

---

3. "Muse, tell me the cause, by what wounded divinity. . . ." (*Aeneid* 1.8).
4. King David of Israel composed psalms; the emperor Adrian (i.e., Hadrian) wrote verse and prose; Germanicus Caesar, conqueror of Germany, is supposed to have written poetry and plays. Sidney goes on to list a range of modern statesmen-poets.
5. Michel de L'Hôpital (1505–1573), a statesman who favored religious toleration, wrote Latin poems.
6. God of war.
7. Be scattered over.
8. Itinerant quacks peddling fake medicines.
9. Roman god of fire and smiths who caught his adulterous wife, Venus, and Mars, the god of war, in a net he had forged.

1. Theban general (4th century B.C.).
2. Not a very clear paragraph. The mountain named Helicon is sacred to the muses. Here it represents the inspirational springs that are being "post[ed] over," that is, bypassed, by contemporary "bastard poets" eager to publish, while better writers "whose hearts the Titan [Prometheus] molded out of better clays" (Juvenal, *Satires* 14.36) keep their works private rather than be lumped in with their inferiors. Sidney himself claims, perhaps with false modesty, that as a poet he is classed with the mediocrities, and declares that the reason for poets low esteem is "want of desert" or lack of worth: They have not been helped by Pallas Athena, goddess of wisdom.

are better content to suppress the outflowings of their wit, than, by publishing them, to be accounted knights of the same order. But I that, before ever I durst aspire unto the dignity, am admitted into the company of the paper-blurrers, do find the very true cause of our wanting estimation is want of desert—taking upon us to be poets in despite of Pallas.

Now, wherein we want desert were a thankworthy labor to express; but if I knew, I should have mended myself. But I, as I never desired the title, so have I neglected the means to come by it. Only, overmastered by some thoughts, I yielded an inky tribute unto them. Marry, they that delight in poesy itself should seek to know what they do, and how they do; and especially look themselves in an unflattering glass of reason, if they be inclinable unto it. For poesy must not be drawn by the ears; it must be gently led, or rather it must lead—which was partly the cause that made the ancient-learned affirm it was a divine gift, and no human skill: since all other knowledges lie ready for any that hath strength of wit. A poet no industry can make, if his own genius be not carried into it; and therefore it is an old proverb, *orator fit, poeta nascitur* [the orator is made, the poet born].

Yet confess I always that as the fertilest ground must be manured, so must the highest-flying wit have a Daedalus to guide him.[3] That Daedalus, they say, both in this and in other, hath three wings to bear itself up into the air of due commendation: that is, art, imitation, and exercise. But these, neither artificial rules nor imitative patterns, we much cumber ourselves withal. Exercise indeed we do, but that very fore-backwardly: for where we should exercise to know, we exercise as having known; and so is our brain delivered of much matter which never was begotten by knowledge. For there being two principal parts, matter to be expressed by words and words to express the matter, in neither we use art or imitation rightly. Our matter is *quodlibet* [what you will] indeed, though wrongly performing Ovid's verse,

> *Quicquid conabor dicere, versus erit;*[4]

never marshalling it into any assured rank, that almost the readers cannot tell where to find themselves.

Chaucer, undoubtedly, did excellently in his *Troilus and Criseyde;*[5] of whom, truly, I know not whether to marvel more, either that he in that misty time could see so clearly, or that we in this clear age go so stumblingly after him. Yet had he great wants, fit to be forgiven in so reverent an antiquity. I account the *Mirror of Magistrates* meetly furnished of beautiful parts, and in the Earl of Surrey's lyrics many things tasting of a noble birth, and worthy of a noble mind. The *Shepherds' Calendar* hath much poetry in his eclogues, indeed worthy the reading, if I be not deceived. (That same framing of his style to an old rustic language I dare not allow, since neither Theocritus in Greek, Virgil in Latin, nor Sannazaro in Italian did affect it.) Besides these I do not remember to have seen but few (to speak boldly) printed that have poetical sinews in them; for proof whereof, let but most of the

3. The mythical artisan Daedalus built wings so that he and his son Icarus could escape from Crete, where Minos had confined him in the maze of his own making; but Icarus flew too near the sun, the wax in his wings melted, and he fell into the Aegean Sea and drowned. He is often cited as a figure of ambition.
4. "Whatever I shall try to say shall become verse" (*Tristia* 4.10.26).
5. Sidney gives grudging praise to a number of poets of

the early modern period: Chaucer's romance *Troilus and Creseyde* relates the unhappy love affair of two Trojans; the *Mirror of* [i.e., for] *Magistrates,* a poem by various authors and added to at intervals during the 16th century, illustrated exemplary tragedies; the Earl of Surrey is Henry Howard; *The Shepherd's Calendar* was written by Edmund Spenser. Theocritus, Virgil, and Sannazzaro were poets of pastoral.

verses be put in prose, and then ask the meaning, and it will be found that one verse did but beget another, without ordering at the first what should be at the last; which becomes a confused mass of words, with a tingling sound of rhyme, barely accompanied with reason.

Our tragedies and comedies (not without cause cried out against), observing rules neither of honest civility nor skilful poetry—excepting Gorboduc[6] (again, I say, of those that I have seen), which notwithstanding as it is full of stately speeches and well-sounding phrases, climbing to the height of Seneca's style, and as full of notable morality, which it doth most delightfully teach, and so obtain the very end of poesy, yet in truth it is very defectuous[7] in the circumstances, which grieveth me, because it might not remain as an exact model of all tragedies. For it is faulty both in place and time, the two necessary companions of all corporal actions. For where the stage should always represent but one place, and the uttermost time presupposed in it should be, both by Aristotle's precept and common reason, but one day, there is both many days, and many places, inartificially[8] imagined.

But if it be so in Gorboduc, how much more in all the rest, where you shall have Asia of the one side, and Afric of the other, and so many other under-kingdoms, that the player, when he cometh in, must ever begin with telling where he is, or else the tale will not be conceived? Now you shall have three ladies walk to gather flowers: and then we must believe the stage to be a garden. By and by we hear news of shipwreck in the same place: and then we are to blame if we accept it not for a rock. Upon the back of that comes out a hideous monster with fire and smoke: and then the miserable beholders are bound to take it for a cave. While in the meantime two armies fly in, represented with four swords and bucklers: and then what hard heart will not receive it for a pitched field?

Now, of time they are much more liberal: for ordinary it is that two young princes fall in love; after many traverses, she is got with child, delivered of a fair boy; he is lost, groweth a man, falls in love, and is ready to get another child; and all this in two hours' space: which, how absurd it is in sense, even sense may imagine, and art hath taught, and all ancient examples justified—and at this day, the ordinary players in Italy will not err in. Yet will some bring in an example of Eunuchus in Terence, that containeth matter of two days, yet far short of twenty years. True it is, and so was it to be played in two days, and so fitted to the time it set forth. And though Plautus have in one place done amiss, let us hit with him, and not miss with him.[9]

But they will say: How then shall we set forth a story which containeth both many places and many times? And do they not know that a tragedy is tied to the laws of poesy, and not of history; not bound to follow the story, but having liberty either to feign a quite new matter or to frame the history to the most tragical conveniency? Again, many things may be told which cannot be showed, if they know the difference betwixt reporting and representing. As, for example, I may speak (though I am here) of Peru, and in speech digress from that to the description of Calicut;[1] but in action I cannot represent it without Pacolet's horse;[2] and so was the manner the ancients took, by some Nuntius [messenger] to recount things done in former time or

---

6. A tragedy by Thomas Sackville and Thomas Norton (1561).
7. Defective.
8. Inartistically.
9. Terence, Plautus: two well-known writers of Roman comedies who influenced the drama in early modern Eng-

land; Shakespeare took the plot of The Comedy of Errors from Plautus's Menaechmi.
1. Seaport on the west coast of India.
2. A magic horse in the French romance Valentine and Orson.

other place. Lastly, if they will represent a history, they must not (as Horace saith) begin *ab ovo* [from the beginning], but they must come to the principal point of that one action which they will represent.

By example this will be best expressed. I have a story of young Polydorus,[3] delivered for safety's sake, with great riches, by his father Priam to Polymnestor, king of Thrace, in the Trojan war time; he, after some years, hearing the overthrow of Priam, for to make the treasure his own, murdereth the child; the body of the child is taken up by Hecuba; she, the same day, findeth a sleight to be revenged most cruelly of the tyrant. Where now would one of our tragedy writers begin, but with the delivery of the child? Then should he sail over into Thrace, and so spend I know not how many years, and travel numbers of places. But where doth Euripides? Even with the finding of the body, leaving the rest to be told by the spirit of Polydorus. This need no further to be enlarged; the dullest wit may conceive it.

But besides these gross absurdities, how all their plays be neither right tragedies, nor right comedies, mingling kings and clowns, not because the matter so carrieth it, but thrust in the clown by head and shoulders to play a part in majestical matters with neither decency nor discretion, so as neither the admiration and commiseration, nor the right sportfulness, is by their mongrel tragicomedy obtained. I know Apuleius did somewhat so,[4] but that is a thing recounted with space of time, not represented in one moment; and I know the ancients have one or two examples of tragicomedies, as Plautus hath *Amphitryo*;[5] but, if we mark them well, we shall find that they never, or very daintily, match hornpipes and funerals. So falleth it out that, having indeed no right comedy, in that comical part of our tragedy, we have nothing but scurrility, unworthy of any chaste ears, or some extreme show of doltishness, indeed fit to lift up a loud laughter, and nothing else: where the whole tract of a comedy should be full of delight, as the tragedy should be still maintained in a well-raised admiration.

But our comedians think there is no delight without laughter; which is very wrong, for though laughter may come with delight, yet cometh it not of delight, as though delight should be the cause of laughter; but well may one thing breed both together. Nay, rather in themselves they have, as it were, a kind of contrariety: for delight we scarcely do but in things that have a conveniency to ourselves or to the general nature; laughter almost ever cometh of things most disproportioned to ourselves and nature. Delight hath a joy in it, either permanent or present. Laughter hath only a scornful tickling.

For example, we are ravished with delight to see a fair woman, and yet are far from being moved to laughter; we laugh at deformed creatures, wherein certainly we cannot delight. We delight in good chances, we laugh at mischances: we delight to hear the happiness of our friends, or country, at which he were worthy to be laughed at that would laugh; we shall, contrarily, laugh sometimes to find a matter quite mistaken and go down the hill against the bias in the mouth of some such men—as for the respect of them one shall be heartily sorry, he cannot choose but laugh, and so is rather pained than delighted with laughter.

---

3. Sidney praises the narrative of the hero Polydorus as told by Euripides, who avoids a lengthy plot in his play on the subject, *Hecuba*.
4. In his prose romance *The Golden Ass* (c. 155 A.D.); William Adlington translated the work into English in the 16th century.

5. In this play the tragic element is represented by the heroine Alcmena, tricked into sleeping with the god Jupiter, who is disguised as her husband Amphitrion, and the comic element by the burlesque behavior of the gods who arrange the deception.

Yet deny I not but that they may go well together. For as in Alexander's picture well set out we delight without laughter,[6] and in twenty mad antics we laugh without delight; so in Hercules, painted with his great beard and furious countenance, in a woman's attire, spinning at Omphale's commandment, it breedeth both delight and laughter: for the representing of so strange a power in love procureth delight, and the scornfulness of the action stirreth laughter. But I speak to this purpose, that all the end of the comical part be not upon such scornful matters as stir laughter only, but, mixed with it, that delightful teaching which is the end of poesy. And the great fault even in that point of laughter, and forbidden plainly by Aristotle, is that they stir laughter in sinful things, which are rather execrable than ridiculous, or in miserable, which are rather to be pitied than scorned. For what is it to make folks gape at a wretched beggar and a beggarly clown; or, against law of hospitality, to jest at strangers, because they speak not English so well as we do? What do we learn, since it is certain

> Nil habet infelix paupertas durius in se,
> Quam quod ridiculos homines facit?[7]

But rather, a busy loving courtier and a heartless threatening Thraso;[8] a self-wise-seeming schoolmaster; an awry-transformed traveler. These if we saw walk in stage names, which we play naturally, therein were delightful laughter, and teaching delightfulness—as in the other, the tragedies of Buchanan[9] do justly bring forth a divine admiration.

But I have lavished out too many words of this play matter. I do it because, as they are excelling parts of poesy, so is there none so much used in England, and none can be more pitifully abused; which, like an unmannerly daughter showing a bad education, causeth her mother Poesy's honesty to be called in question.

Other sort of poetry almost have we none, but that lyrical kind of songs and sonnets: which, Lord, if He gave us so good minds, how well it might be employed, and with how heavenly fruit, both private and public, in singing the praises of the immortal beauty: the immortal goodness of that God who giveth us hands to write and wits to conceive; of which we might well want words, but never matter; of which we could turn our eyes to nothing, but we should ever have new-budding occasions. But truly many of such writings as come under the banner of unresistible love, if I were a mistress, would never persuade me they were in love: so coldly they apply fiery speeches, as men that had rather read lovers' writings—and so caught up certain swelling phrases which hang together like a man that once told my father that the wind was at northwest and by south, because he would be sure to name winds enough—than that in truth they feel those passions, which easily (as I think) may be bewrayed by that same forcibleness or energia (as the Greeks call it) of the writer. But let this be a sufficient though short note, that we miss the right use of the material point of poesy.

Now, for the outside of it, which is words, or (as I may term it) diction, it is even well worse. So is that honey-flowing matron Eloquence appareled, or rather disguised, in a courtesan-like painted affectation: one time, with so far-fet words that

---

6. Sidney distinguishes reactions to different kinds of descriptions: Alexander's portrait delights; mad antics provoke laughter; Hercules, captive and dressed as a woman by Queen Omphale of Lydia, both delights and provokes laughter.
7. "Unfortunate poverty has nothing in itself harder to bear than that it makes men ridiculous" (Juvenal, Satires 3.152–3).
8. The braggart soldier of Terence's comedy Eunuchus.
9. A Scots humanist (1506—1582) who wrote four tragedies on biblical and classical themes.

may seem monsters but must seem strangers to any poor Englishman; another time, with coursing[1] of a letter, as if they were bound to follow the method of a dictionary; another time, with figures and flowers, extremely winter-starved. But I would this fault were only peculiar to versifiers, and had not as large possession among prose-printers; and (which is to be marveled) among many scholars; and (which is to be pitied) among some preachers. Truly I could wish, if at least I might be so bold to wish in a thing beyond the reach of my capacity, the diligent imitators of Tully and Demosthenes[2] (most worthy to be imitated) did not so much keep Nizolian paper-books[3] of their figures and phrases, as by attentive translation (as it were) devour them whole, and make them wholly theirs: for now they cast sugar and spice upon every dish that is served to the table—like those Indians, not content to wear ear-rings at the fit and natural place of the ears, but they will thrust jewels through their nose and lips, because they will be sure to be fine. Tully, when he was to drive out Catiline, as it were with a thunderbolt of eloquence, often used the figure of repetition, as *Vivit. Vivit? Imo in senatum venit, & c.*[4] Indeed, inflamed with a well-grounded rage, he would have his words (as it were) double out of his mouth, and so do that artificially which we see men in choler do naturally. And we, having noted the grace of those words, hale them in sometimes to a familiar epistle, when it were too too much choler to be choleric. How well store of *similiter cadences* [similar cadences] doth sound with the gravity of the pulpit, I would but invoke Demosthenes' soul to tell, who with a rare daintiness useth them. Truly they have made me think of the sophister[5] that with too much subtlety would prove two eggs three, and though he might be counted a sophister, had none for his labor. So these men bringing in such a kind of eloquence, well may they obtain an opinion of a seeming finesse, but persuade few—which should be the end of their finesse. Now for similitudes, in certain printed discourses, I think all herbarists, all stories of beasts, fowls, and fishes are rifled up,[6] that they come in multitudes to wait upon any of our conceits; which certainly is as absurd a surfeit to the ears as is possible. For the force of a similitude not being to prove anything to a contrary disputer, but only to explain to a willing hearer, when that is done, the rest is a most tedious prattling, rather over-swaying the memory from the purpose whereto they were applied, than any whit informing the judgment, already either satisfied, or by similitudes not to be satisfied. For my part, I do not doubt, when Antonius and Crassus,[7] the great forefathers of Cicero in eloquence, the one (as Cicero testifieth of them) pretended not to know art, the other not to set by it, because with a plain sensibleness they might win credit of popular ears (which credit is the nearest step to persuasion, which persuasion is the chief mark of oratory), I do not doubt (I say) but that they used these knacks very sparingly; which who doth generally use, any man may see doth dance to his own music, and so be noted by the audience more careful to speak curiously than to speak truly. Undoubtedly (at least to my opinion undoubtedly), I have found in divers smally

---

1. Alliteration.
2. Athenian statesman and orator (383–322 B.C.).
3. Marius Nizolius, a 16th-century Italian rhetorician and lexicographer, published a collection of phrases by Cicero (i.e., Tully). Sidney complains that contemporary writers use them too often. Cicero, when he prosecuted the traitor Catiline, employed repetition skillfully to heighten the effect of his argument, but writers in Sidney's time are not as discriminating.
4. "He lives. He lives? He still comes into the Senate.

. . ." The sentences paraphrase the opening of Cicero's first oration against Catiline.
5. One who argues by specious reasons.
6. Sidney suggests that the figures in beast fables are all "rifled" or taken by many writers; hence they have become trite.
7. Antonius: Marcus Antonius, consul in 99 B.C.; Crassus: Publius Licinius Crassus Dives Mucianus, consul in 175 B.C. Both men were famous orators.

learned courtiers a more sound style than in some professors of learning; of which I can guess no other cause, but that the courtier, following that which by practice he findeth fittest to nature, therein (though he know it not) doth according to art, though not by art: where the other, using art to show art, and not to hide art (as in these cases he should do), flieth from nature, and indeed abuseth art.

But what? Methinks I deserve to be pounded for straying from poetry to oratory. But both have such an affinity in the wordish consideration, that I think this digression will make my meaning receive the fuller understanding: which is not to take upon me to teach poets how they should do, but only, finding myself sick among the rest, to show some one or two spots of the common infection grown among the most part of writers, that, acknowledging ourselves somewhat awry, we may bend to the right use both of matter and manner: whereto our language giveth us great occasion, being indeed capable of any excellent exercising of it. I know some will say it is a mingled language.[8] And why not so much the better, taking the best of both the other? Another will say it wanteth grammar. Nay truly, it hath that praise, that it wants not grammar: for grammar it might have, but it needs it not, being so easy in itself, and so void of those cumbersome differences of cases, genders, moods, and tenses, which I think was a piece of the Tower of Babylon's curse,[9] that a man should be put to school to learn his mother-tongue. But for the uttering sweetly and properly the conceits of the mind (which is the end of speech), that hath it equally with any other tongue in the world; and is particularly happy in compositions of two or three words together, near the Greek, far beyond the Latin, which is one of the greatest beauties can be in a language.

Now of versifying there are two sorts, the one ancient, the other modern: the ancient marked the quantity of each syllable, and according to that framed his verse; the modern, observing only number (with some regard of the accent), the chief life of it standeth in that like sounding of the words, which we call rhyme. Whether of these be the more excellent, would bear many speeches: the ancient (no doubt) more fit for music, both words and time observing quantity, and more fit lively to express diverse passions, by the low or lofty sound of the well-weighed syllable; the latter likewise, with his rhyme, striketh a certain music to the ear, and, in fine, since it doth delight, though by another way, it obtains the same purpose: there being in either sweetness, and wanting in neither majesty. Truly the English, before any vulgar language I know, is fit for both sorts. For, for the ancient, the Italian is so full of vowels that it must ever be cumbered with elisions;[1] the Dutch so, of the other side, with consonants, that they cannot yield the sweet sliding, fit for a verse; the French in his whole language hath not one word that hath his accent in the last syllable saving two, called *antepenultima* [third from last]; and little more hath the Spanish, and therefore very gracelessly may they use dactyls.[2] The English is subject to none of these defects. Now for the rhyme, though we do not observe quantity, yet we observe the accent very precisely, which other languages either cannot do, or will not do so absolutely. That *caesura*, or breathing place in the midst of the verse, neither Italian nor Spanish have, the French and we never almost fail of. Lastly, even the very

8. Sidney describes English as a "mingled" language because it is derived from Anglo-Saxon, brought over by the invading Germanic tribes during the 6th century, and Norman-French, introduced by William the Conqueror in 1066.
9. Early modern writers identified Babylon with Babel

(see Genesis 10.10).
1. The suppression of a vowel at the end of a word when the next word begins with a vowel.
2. A metric foot in classical poetry, consisting of one long and two short syllables, as in the words "murmuring," "sensible."

rhyme itself, the Italian cannot put it in the last syllable, by the French named the masculine rhyme, but still in the next to the last, which the French call the female, or the next before that, which the Italian term *sdrucciola* [three-syllable rhyme]. The example of the former is *buono: suono*, of the *sdrucciola* is *femina: semina*. The French, of the other side, hath both the male, as *bon: son*, and the female, as *plaise: taise*, but the *sdrucciola* he hath not: where the English hath all three, as *due: true, father: rather, motion: potion*[3]—with much more which might be said, but that already I find the triflingness of this discourse is much too much enlarged.

So that since the ever-praiseworthy Poesy is full of virtue-breeding delightfulness, and void of no gift that ought to be in the noble name of learning; since the blames laid against it are either false or feeble; since the cause why it is not esteemed in England is the fault of poet-apes, not poets; since, lastly, our tongue is most fit to honor poesy, and to be honored by poesy; I conjure you all that have had the evil luck to read this ink-wasting toy of mine, even in the name of the nine Muses, no more to scorn the sacred mysteries of poesy; no more to laugh at the name of poets, as though they were next inheritors to fools; no more to jest at the reverent title of a rhymer; but to believe, with Aristotle, that they were the ancient treasurers of the Grecians' divinity; to believe, with Bembus, that they were first bringers-in of all civility; to believe, with Scaliger, that no philosopher's precepts can sooner make you an honest man than the reading of Virgil; to believe, with Clauserus,[4] the translator of Cornutus, that it pleased the heavenly Deity, by Hesiod and Homer, under the veil of fables, to give us all knowledge, logic, rhetoric, philosophy natural and moral, and *quid non?* [what not]; to believe, with me, that there are many mysteries contained in poetry, which of purpose were written darkly, lest by profane wits it should be abused; to believe, with Landino,[5] that they are so beloved of the gods that whatsoever they write proceeds of a divine fury; lastly, to believe themselves, when they tell you they will make you immortal by their verses. Thus doing, your name shall flourish in the printers' shops; thus doing, you shall be of kin to many a poetical preface; thus doing, you shall be most fair, most rich, most wise, most all, you shall dwell upon superlatives; thus doing, though you be *libertino patre natus* [son of freed slave], you shall suddenly grow *Herculea proles* [a descendant of Hercules],

> *Si quid mea carmina possunt;*[6]

thus doing, your soul shall be placed with Dante's Beatrice, or Virgil's Anchises. But if (fie of such a but) you be born so near the dull-making cataract of Nilus[7] that you cannot hear the planet-like music of poetry; if you have so earth-creeping a mind that it cannot lift itself up to look to the sky of poetry, or rather, by a certain rustical disdain, will become such a mome as to be a Momus[8] of poetry; then, though I will not wish unto you the ass's ears of Midas, nor to be driven by a poet's verses, as

---

3. *Motion* and *potion* presumably retained three syllables, as the Middle English spelling "mocioun" reveals.
4. Conrad Clauser, a 16th-century German scholar who translated the works of Lucius Annaeus Cornutus, a first-century Greek slave who wrote commentaries on Aristotle and Virgil.
5. Cristofor Landino (1424–1504), an Italian humanist who wrote moral dialogues.
6. "If my songs can do anything" (*Aeneid*, 9.446).

7. Cicero claimed that hearing the sound of the cataracts of the Nile river in Egypt caused deafness; the Neoplatonists thought the movement of the planets produced heavenly music, the music of the spheres.
8. Momus personified the faultfinder in Greek literature; a mome is a blockhead. Apollo changed Midas's ears to those of an ass to signal his stupidity after Midas judged Pan's flute playing to be superior to Apollo's (Ovid, *Metamorphosis* 11.146).

Bubonax[9] was, to hang himself, nor to be rhymed to death, as is said to be done in Ireland; yet thus much curse I must send you, in the behalf of all poets, that while you live, you live in love, and never get favor for lacking skill of a sonnet; and, when you die, your memory die from the earth for want of an epitaph.

1579–80   1595

THE APOLOGY IN CONTEXT
The Art of Poetry

After the spread of Reformation doctrine on the importance of moral discipline, English readers often encountered denunciations of poetry and especially drama. The issues that Sidney took up when he defended poetry were the subject of sharp dispute. Stephen Gosson represented the opinions of many of poetry's detractors. As he declares in *The School of Abuse,* published shortly before Sidney wrote his *Apology,* poetry provides frivolous distraction from the serious business of life and, what is worse, temptations to godlessness. But others, like Sidney, took a more optimistic view of the subject. In *The Art of English Poesy,* George Puttenham states that poets were the first lawgivers (as Sidney had) and focuses particularly on epic poetry, which, he says, give readers images of a truth beyond history as well as consistently inspiring models of action to imitate. His popular treatise contains a wealth of practical advice for aspiring writers and even today remains a useful sourcebook for information on rhetorical figures of thought and speech.

In addition to the challenge posed by moralists such as Gosson, defenders of English poetry also had to confront purely practical problems. Unlike the Romance languages—Italian, French, and Spanish—sixteenth-century English had lost almost all its feminine endings, the accented vowel sounds that made rhyming fairly easy. English was also a language in which words of one syllable were quite common, and poets had trouble creating the metrical harmonies usual in poetry written in languages rich in polysyllables. George Gascoigne's brief treatise *Certain Notes of Instruction concerning the making of verse or rhyme in English* deals with these conditions directly. He warns against trying to achieve euphony or a musical quality by "rolling in pleasant words," as in the sequence "Rim, Ram, Ruff," and he insists that the "truer Englishman" uses words of one syllable. Critics could differ in what they valued, of course; in *A Defence of Rhyme,* Samuel Daniel justified rhyme as "pleasing to nature," which desires form and closures, not chaos and infinity. More important, he defended English writers against the claim that they could never match their classical precursors. He reminded readers that imputations of barbarism and ignorance are based on relative, not absolute, judgments.

Stephen Gosson
from *The School of Abuse*[1]

The Syracusans used such variety of dishes in their banquets that when they were set and their boards furnished,[2] they were many times in doubt which they should touch first or taste last. And in my opinion the world giveth every writer so large a field to walk in that before he set pen to the book, he shall find himself feasted at Syracuse,

---

9. Sidney conflates Hipp*onax,* a Greek poet, with B*u*palus, a sculptor. The latter had made an unflattering portrait of the former, who took revenge with deadly verses. Irish poets claimed their verses could kill man or beast.

1. Stephen Gosson was a playwright who turned against the stage, and then wrote Puritanical critiques of what he considered its immorality. His *School of Abuse* was published in 1579.
2. Tables set.

uncertain where to begin or when to end. This caused Pindarus[3] to question with his Muse whether he were better with his art to decipher the life of Nimpe Melia, or Cadmus's encounter with the dragon, or the wars of Hercules at the walls of Thebes, or Bacchus's cups, or Venus's juggling? He saw so many turnings laid open to his feet, that he knew not which way to bend his pace.

Therefore, as I cannot but commend his wisdom which in banqueting feeds most upon that that doth nourish best, so must I dispraise his method in writing which, following the course of amorous poets, dwelleth longest on those points that profit least, and like a wanton whelp,[4] leaveth the game[5] to run riot. The scarab flies over many a sweet flower and lights in a cowsherd.[6] It is the custom of the fly to leave the sound places of the horse and suck at the botch,[7] the nature of colloquintida[8] to draw the worst humors to itself, the manner of swine to forsake the fair fields and wallow in the mire, and the whole practice of poets, either with fables to show their abuses or with plain terms to unfold their mischief, discover their shame, discredit themselves, and disperse their poison through the world. Virgil sweats in describing his gnat, Ovid bestirreth him to paint out his flea; the one shows his art in the lust of Dido, the other his cunning in the incest of Myrrha and that trumpet of bawdry, the craft of love.[9]

I must confess that poets are the whetstones of wit, notwithstanding that wit is dearly bought. Where honey and gall are mixed, it will be hard to sever the one from the other. The deceitful physician giveth sweet syrups to make his poison go down the smoother, the juggler casteth a mist to work the closer, the siren's song is the sailor's wrack,[1] the fowler's whistle the bird's death, the wholesome bait the fish's bane. The Harpies[2] have virgin faces, and the vultures, talents; Hyena speaks like a friend and devours like a foe; the calmest seas hide dangerous rocks; the wolf jets in wether's fells.[3] Many good sentences are spoken by David to shadow his knavery,[4] and written by poets as ornaments to beautify their works and set their trumpery to sale without suspect.

But if you look well to Epaeus's horse,[5] you shall find in his bowels the destruction of Troy; open the sepulchre of Semiramis,[6] whose title promiseth such wealth to the kings of Persia, you shall see nothing but dead bones; rip up the golden ball that Nero consecrated to Jupiter Capitolinus,[7] you shall [find] it stuffed with the shavings of his beard; pull off the visor that poets mask in, you shall disclose their reproach, bewray[8] their vanity, loathe their wantonness, lament their folly, and perceive their

---

3. Pindar, the most difficult and obscure of Greek poets, famous for his odes. The story of Cadmus's encounter with the dragon is a fragment of a cycle of legends about the city of Thebes; the legendary hero Hercules delivered the city of Thebes from the burden of paying tribute to the foreign king Orchomenus; Bacchus was the Roman god of wine; and Venus's "juggling" refers to her erotic escapades.

4. Unruly puppy.

5. Hunt.

6. Cow dung.

7. Ulcer.

8. A wild cucumber, used as an herbal medicine.

9. Dido, Queen of Carthage, with whom the legendary Trojan hero Aeneas stayed on his way to founding Rome; Virgil's *Aeneid* provides the best-known account of this episode. According to legend, Myrrha was the mother of the Greek god of vegetation, Adonis, by her father, King Cinyras, who, when he learned of his incest, changed her

into a myrtle; the story is told by Ovid in his *Metamorphoses*, a poem describing erotic transformations. Gosson condemns Ovid's poem *Ars Amatoria*, or "the craft (or art) of love," as an immoral work ("bawdry" is licentiousness).

1. The mermaid's song is the sailor's shipwreck.

2. Monstrous and filthy birds whom Aeneas and his companions encounter.

3. The wolf strolls in sheep's clothing.

4. King of the ancient Israelites and poet of the psalms, David was guilty of adulterous love for Bathsheba, whose husband he murdered.

5. The Trojan horse.

6. Mythical queen of Assyria, who is supposed to have built the city of Babylon.

7. The Emperor Nero is said to have consecrated a golden ball to Jupiter in his temple on the Capitoline Hill in Rome.

8. Expose.

sharp sayings to be placed as pearls in dunghills, fresh pictures on rotten walls, chaste matrons' apparel on common courtesans. These are the cups of Circe,[9] that turn reasonable creatures into brute beasts; the balls of Hippomenes,[1] that hinder the course of Atalanta; and the blocks of the Devil, that are cast in our ways to cut off the race of toward wits. No marvel though Plato shut them out of his school and banished them quite from his commonwealth as effeminate writers,[2] unprofitable members, and utter enemies to virtue.

George Puttenham
from *The Art of English Poesie*[1]

How Poets were the first Philosophers, the first Astronomers and Historiographers, and Orators and Musicians of the world.[2]

Utterance also and language is given by nature to man for persuasion of others and aid of themselves, I mean the first ability to speak. For speech itself is artificial and made by man, and the more pleasing it is, the more it prevaileth to such purpose as it is intended for. But speech by meter is a kind of utterance more cleanly couched and more delicate to the ear than prose is, because it is more current and slipper upon the tongue and withal tunable and melodious as a kind of music and therefore may be termed a musical speech or utterance which cannot but please the hearer very well. Another cause is for that[3] is briefer and more compendious and easier to bear away and be retained in memory than that which is contained in multitude of words and full of tedious ambage and long periods.[4] It is beside a manner of utterance more eloquent and rhetorical than the ordinary proof which we use in our daily talk, because it is decked and set out with all manner of fresh colors and figures, which maketh that it sooner inveigleth[5] the judgment of man and carryeth his opinion this way and that, whither soever the heart by impression of the ear shall be most affectionately bent and directed. The utterance in prose is not of so great efficacy because not only it is daily used, and by that occasion the care is over-glutted with it, but is also not so voluble and slipper on the tongue, being wide and loose, and nothing numerous nor contrived into measures and founded with so gallant and harmonical accents, nor in fine allowed that figurative conveyance[6] nor so great license in choice of words and phrases as meter is. So as the poets were also from the beginning the best persuaders and their eloquence the first rhetoric of the world, even so it became[7] that the high mysteries of the gods should be revealed and taught by a manner of utterance and language of extraordinary phrase and brief and compendious and above all others sweet and civil as the metrical is. The same also was meetest to register the lives and noble gifts of princes, and of the great monarchs of the world and all other memo-

9. In Homer's *Odyssey*, the goddess who transformed the companions of Odysseus into swine.
1. The legendary suitor of Atalanta, who refused to marry anyone she could defeat in a footrace. Hippomenes won the race by dropping golden apples on the race track. Atalanta could not resist stopping to pick them up, and her delay allowed Hippomenes victory.
2. Plato exiles poets from his ideal republic (see *The Republic* 3, 398A).
1. George Puttenham has always been assumed to be the author of *The Art of English Poesy*, a critical treatise that appeared in 1589. Dividing his work into three books: *Of Poets and Poesy*, *Of Proportion*, and *Of Ornament*, Putten-

ham discusses the works of English poets, poetic forms and genres, and figures of speech and thought respectively. The work as a whole is a compendium of contemporary ideas and practices illustrating the proper way to compose and appreciate poetry.
2. In his *Apology for Poetry*, Sidney also claims that poets were the first human beings to express feeling, thought, and a sense of the higher purposes of life.
3. I.e., poetry.
4. Dull indirection and long sentences.
5. Appeals to.
6. Expression.
7. Was appropriate.

rable accidents of time, so as the poet was also the first historiographer. Then forasmuch as they were the first observers of all natural causes and effects in the things generable and corruptable, and from thence mounted up to search after the celestial courses and influences and yet penetrated further to know the divine essences and substances separate,[8] as is said before, they were the first astronomers and philosophists and metaphysics. Finally, because they did altogether endeavor themselves to reduce[9] the life of man to a certain method of good manners, and made the first differences between virtue and vice, and then tempered all these knowledges and skills with the exercise of a delectable music by melodious instruments, which withall served them to delight their hearers and to call the people together by admiration to a plausible and virtuous conversation, therefore were they the first philosophers ethic[1] and the first artificial musicians of the world. Such was Linus, Orpheus, Amphion, and Musaeus,[2] the most ancient poets and philosophers, of whom there is left any memory by the profane writers. King David also and Solomon his son and many other of the holy prophets wrote in meters and used to sing them to the harp,[3] although to many of us ignorant of the Hebrew language and phrase and not observing it, the same seem but a prose. It cannot be therefore that any scorn or indignity should justly be offered to so noble, profitable, ancient, and divine a science as Poesie is. * * *

Of historical poesie,[4] by which the famous acts of Princes and the virtuous and worthy lives of our forefathers were reported.

There is nothing in man of all the potential parts of his mind (reason and will excepted) more noble or more necessary to the active life than memory. Because it maketh[5] most to a sound judgment and perfect worldly wisdom, examining and comparing the times past with the present and by them both considering the time to come, [it] concludeth with a steadfast resolution what is the best course to be taken in all his actions and advices in this world. It came upon this reason: experience [is] to be so highly commended in all consultations of importance and preferred before any learning or science, and yet experience is no more than a mass of memories assembled, that is, such trials as man hath made in time before. Right so, no kind of argument in all the oratory craft doth better persuade and more universally satisfy than example, which is but the representation of old memories and like successes [that have] happened in times past. For these regards, the poesie historical is of all other, next[6] the divine, most honorable and worthy, as well for the common benefit as for the special comfort every man receiveth by it. No one thing in the world with more delectation [is] reviving our spirits than to behold, as it were in a glass, the lively image of our dear forefathers, their noble and virtuous manner of life, with other things authentic, which because we are not able otherwise to attain to the knowledge of by any of our fences,[7] we apprehend them by memory, whereas the present time and things so swiftly pass away [so] as they give us no leisure almost to look into them

---

8. I.e., to know the divine essences and the particular objects present in the heavens.
9. Abstract.
1. I.e., philosophers who consider ethics.
2. Puttenham names legendary figures who were thought to be among the first poets: Linus, a poet and the teacher of Hercules, who later killed him with his own lyre; Orpheus, commonly considered the first poet, whose music charmed even the animals; Amphion, the poet

whose music moved stones to build Thebes; and Musaeus, said to have been a pupil of Orpheus.
3. Scripture provides accounts of King David, supposed to be the author of the psalms, and Solomon, to whom the Song of Songs is attributed.
4. Epic poetry.
5. Benefits.
6. After.
7. Ways of arguing.

and much less to know and consider of them thoroughly. The things future, being also events very uncertain, and such as cannot possibly be known because they be not yet, cannot be used for example nor for delight otherwise than by hope, though many promise the contrary, by vain and deceitful arts taking upon them to reveal the truth of accidents to come, which if it were so as they surmise, are yet but sciences merely conjectural and not of any benefit to man or to the commonwealth where they be used or professed. Therefore the good and exemplary things and actions of the former ages were reserved only to the historical reports of wise and grave men; those of the present time [were] left to the fruition and judgment of our senses; the future as hazards and uncertain events [were] utterly neglected and laid aside for magicians and mockers to get their livings by, such manner of men as by negligence of magistrates and remisses of laws every country breedeth great store of. These historical men nevertheless used not the matter so precisely to wish that all they wrote should be accounted true,[8] for that was not needful nor expedient to the purpose, namely to be used either for example or for the pleasure, considering that many times it is seen a feigned matter or altogether fabulous, besides that it maketh more mirth than any other, works no less good conclusions for example than the most true and veritable, but oftentimes more, because the poet hath the handling of them[9] to fashion at his pleasure, but not so of the other[1] which must go according to their verity and none otherwise without the writers' great blame. Again as ye know, more and more excellent examples may be feigned in one day by a good wit than many ages through man's frailty are able to put in ure,[2] which made the learned and witty men of those times to devise many historical matters of no verity at all, but with purpose to do good and no hurt, as using them for a manner of discipline and precedent of commendable life. Such was the commonwealth of Plato, and Sir Thomas More's *Utopia*, resting all in device,[3] but never [to be] put in execution and easier wished than to be performed. And you shall perceive that histories were of three sorts, wholly true and wholly false, and a third holding part of either, but for honest recreation and good example they were all of them.[4]

George Gascoigne
from *Certain Notes of Instruction*[1]

The first and most necessary point that ever I found meet to be considered in making of a delectable poem is this, to ground it upon some fine invention.[2] For it is not enough to roll in pleasant words, nor yet to thunder in Rim, Ram, Ruff, by letter (quoth my master Chaucer) nor yet to abound in apt vocables or epithets, unless the invention have in it also *aliquid salis* [something salty]. By this *aliquid salis* I mean some good and fine device, showing the quick capacity of a writer, and where I say some good and fine invention, I mean that I would have it both fine and good. For many inventions are so superfine that they are *Vix* [scarcely] good. And again many

8. Puttenham identifies epic poets as historical, in that they represent the past, but not as historians, in that they do not represent it entirely truthfully.
9. His poetic subjects.
1. I.e., the historian who must try to discover the factual truth of the past.
2. Use.
3. Conception.
4. I.e., they were all equally good for recreation and good moral example.

1. George Gascoigne's *Certain Notes* was published in 1575 as part of his second work, containing both poetry and prose, entitled *The Posies of George Gascoigne*. Gascoigne's principal listing begins on page 728.
2. In early modern treatises on the art of writing poetry, "invention" meant the discovery and development of "matter," the topics and ideas that the poet will then represent. After "invention," he draws on a knowledge of rhetoric, the techniques by which "matter" is made interesting and memorable.

inventions are good, and yet not finely handled. And for a general forewarning: what theme soever you do take in hand, if you do handle it but *tanquam in oratione perpetua* [as a perpetual sermon], and never study for some depth of device in your invention and some figures also in the handling thereof, it will appear to the skillful reader but a tale of a tub. To deliver unto you general examples it were almost impossible, since the occasions of inventions are (as it were) infinite. Nevertheless, take in worth mine opinion and perceive my further meaning in these few points. If I should undertake to write in praise of a gentlewoman, I would neither praise her crystal eye nor her cherry lip, etc., for these things are *trita et obvia* [trite and obvious]. But I would either find some supernatural cause whereby my pen might walk in superlative degree, or else I would undertake to answer for any imperfection that she hath, and thereupon raise the praise of her commendation.[3] Likewise, if I should disclose my pretense in[4] love, I would either make a strange discourse of some intolerable passion, or find occasion to plead by the example of some history, or discover[5] my disquiet in shadows *per allegoriam* [through allegory], or use the covertest mean that I could to avoid the uncomely customs of common writers. Thus much I adventure to deliver unto you (my friend) upon [the] rule of invention, which of all other rules is most to be marked and hardest to be prescribed in certain and infallible rules. Nevertheless, to conclude therein, I would have you stand most upon the excellency of your invention and stick[6] not to study deeply for some fine device. For that being found, pleasant words will follow well enough and fast enough.

Your invention being once devised, take heed that neither pleasure of rhyme nor variety of device do carry you from it. For as to use obscure and dark phrases in a pleasant[7] sonnet is nothing delectable, so to intermingle merry jests in a serious matter is an indecorum.[8]

I will next advise you that you hold the just measure wherewith you begin your verse. I will not deny but this may seem a preposterous order, but because I covet rather to satisfy you particularly than to undertake a general tradition, I will not so much stand upon the manner as the matter of my precepts. I say then, remember to hold the same measure wherewith you begin, whether it be in a verse of six syllables, eight, ten, twelve, etc., and though this precept might seem ridiculous unto you, since every young scholar can conceive that he ought to continue in the same measure wherewith he beginneth, yet do I see and read many men's poems nowadays which beginning with the measure of twelve in the first line and fourteen in the second (which is the common kind of verse), they will yet (by that time they have passed over a few verses) fall into fourteen and fourteen and *sic de similibus* [so on], the which is either forgetfulness or carelessness. * * *

I think it not amiss to forewarn you that you thrust as few words of many syllables into your verse as may be, and hereunto I might allege many reasons. First, the most ancient English words are of one syllable, so that the more monosyllables that you use, the truer Englishman you shall seem, and the less you shall smell of the inkhorn.[9] Also, words of many syllables do cloy a verse and make it unpleasant, whereas words of one syllable will more easily fall to be short or long as occasion requireth, or will be adapted to become circumflex[1] or of an indifferent[2] sound.

3. My compliment to her.
4. Profession of.
5. Reveal.
6. Hesitate.
7. Lighthearted.

8. Improper act.
9. Inkpot.
1. Accentuated.
2. Soft.

I would exhort you also to beware of rhyme without reason. My meaning is hereby that your rhyme lead you not from your first invention, for many writers when they have laid the platform of their invention are yet drawn sometimes (by rhyme) to forget it or at least to alter it, as when they cannot readily find out a word which may rhyme to the first (and yet continue their determinate invention) they do then either botch it up with a word that will rhyme (how small reason soever it carry with it) or else they alter their first word and so perhaps decline or trouble their former invention. But do you always hold your first determined invention, and do rather search the bottom of your brains for apt words than change good reason for rumbling rhyme.

* * *

Also as much as may be, eschew strange words or *obsoleta et inusitata* [obsolete and rare], unless the theme do give just occasion. Marry, in some places a strange word doth draw attentive reading, but yet I would have you therein to use discretion.

And as much as you may, frame your style to perspicuity and to be sensible, for the haughty obscure verse doth not much delight and the verse that is too easy is like a tale of a rusted[3] horse. But let your poem be such as may both delight and draw attentive reading and therewithal may deliver such matter as be worth the marking.

Samuel Daniel
from *A Defense of Rhyme*[1]

Such affliction doth laborsome curiosity[2] still lay upon our best delights (which ever must be made strange and variable) as if art were ordained to afflict nature and that we could not go but in fetters. Every science, every profession, must be so wrapped up in unnecessary intrications, as if it were not to fashion but to confound the understanding, which makes me much to distrust man and fear that our presumption goes beyond our ability and our curiosity is more than our judgment, laboring ever to seem to be more than we are or laying greater burdens upon our minds than they are well able to bear, because we would not appear like other men.

And indeed I have wished there were not that multiplicity of rhymes as is used by many in sonnets, which yet we see in some so happily to succeed and hath been so far from hindering their inventions as it hath begot conceit[3] beyond expectation and comparable to the best inventions of the world. For sure in an eminent spirit whom nature hath fitted for that mystery, rhyme is no impediment to his conceit, but rather gives him wings to mount and carries him, not out of his course, but as it were beyond his power to a far happier flight. All excellencies being sold us at the hard price of labor, it follows, where we bestow most thereof, we buy the best success, and rhyme being far more laborious than loose measures (whatsoever is objected), must needs, meeting with wit and industry, breed greater and worthier effects in our language. So that if our labors have wrought out a manumission[4] from bondage and that we go at liberty, notwithstanding these ties, we are no longer the slaves of rhyme but we make it a most excellent instrument to serve us. Nor is this certain limit observed in sonnets any tyrannical bounding of the conceit,[5] but rather a reducing it in *girum*

---

3. Restless.

1. Samuel Daniel, a poet and playwright, published a variety of works throughout his long career, notably: a collection of sonnets, *Delia* (1592); two tragedies, *Cleopatra* (1594) and *Philotas* (1604); an epic poem of the Wars of the Roses, *Civil Wars* (1595, 1609); and several masques. His essay on poetry, *A Defence of Rhyme*, was

published in 1603.
2. Daniel's criticism of "laborsome curiosity" is comparable to Gascoigne's criticism of an "inkhorn" style: both poets reject pedantry.
3. Created conceptions.
4. Release.
5. I.e., the conception informing the poem.

[in bounds], and a just form, neither too long for the shortest project nor too short for the longest, being but only employed for a present passion. For the body of our imagination, being as an unformed chaos without fashion, without day, if by the divine power of the spirit it be wrought into an orb of order and form, is it not more pleasing to nature that desires a certainty and comports not with that which is infinite, to have these closes[6] rather than not to know where to end or how far to go, especially seeing our passions are often without measure. And we find in the best of the Latins many times either not concluding or else otherwise in the end than they began. Besides, is it not most delightful to see much excellently ordered in a small room, or little gallantly disposed and made to fill up a space of like capacity, in such sort that the one would not appear so beautiful in a larger circuit nor the other do well in a less, which often we find to be so, according to the powers of nature, in the workman. And these limited proportions and rests of stanzas, consisting of six, seven, or eight lines, are of that happiness, both for the disposition of the matter, the apt planting the sentence where it may best stand to hit, the certain close of delight with the full body of a just period well-carried,[7] is such as neither the Greeks or Latins ever attained unto. For their boundless running on often so confounds the reader that having once lost himself must either give off unsatisfied or certainly cast back to retrieve the escaped sense and to find way again into his matter.

Methinks we should not so soon yield our consents captive to the authority of antiquity unless we saw more reason. All our understandings are not to be built by the square of Greece and Italy. We are the children of nature as well as they, we are not so placed out of the way of judgment but that the same sun of discretion shineth upon us, we have our portion of the same virtues as well as of the same vices. * * *

It is not the observing of trochaics nor their iambics[8] that will make our writings aught the wiser. All their poesie, all their philosophy is nothing unless we bring the discerning light of conceit[9] with us to apply it to use. It is not books, but only that great book of the world and the all-overspreading grace of heaven that makes men truly judicial.[1] Nor can it be but a touch of arrogant ignorance to hold this or that nation barbarous, these or those times gross, considering how this manifold creature man, wheresoever he stand in the world, hath always some disposition of worth, entertains the order of society, affects that which is most in use, and is eminent in some one thing or other that fits his humor and the times. The Grecians held all other nations barbarous but themselves, yet Pyrrhus when he saw the well-ordered marching of the Romans, which made them see their presumptuous error, could say it was no barbarous manner of preceding. The Goths, Vandals, and Longobards,[2] whose coming down like an innundation overwhelmed, as they say, all the glory of learning in Europe, have yet left us still their laws and customs as the originals of most of the provincial constitutions of Christendom, which well-considered with their other course of government may serve to clear them from this imputation of ignorance. And though the vanquished never yet spoke well of the conqueror,[3] yet even through the unsound coverings of malediction appear those monuments of truth as argue well their worth and proves them not without judgment, though without Greek and Latin.

---

6. Endings, as in rhyme.
7. A well-constructed sentence.
8. Meters used in classical poetry.
9. Imagination.
1. Discriminating.
2. Lombards.

3. Daniels refers to the culture of conquered peoples without specifying which conquests or peoples he has in mind. But he acknowledges that even in the curses of these peoples, as they complain about their conquerors, there are "monuments of truth" that reveal worth and judgment.

from **The Arcadia**

Book 1

To My Dear Lady and Sister
The Countess of Pembroke[1]

Here now have you (most dear, and most worthy to be most dear, lady) this idle work of mine, which I fear (like the spider's web) will be thought fitter to be swept away than worn to any other purpose. For my part, in very truth (as the cruel fathers among the Greeks were wont to do to the babes they would not foster) I could well find in my heart to cast out in some desert of forgetfulness this child which I am loath to father. But you desired me to do it, and your desire to my heart is an absolute commandment. Now it is done only for you, only to you; if you keep it to yourself, or to such friends who will weigh errors in the balance of goodwill, I hope, for the father's sake, it will be pardoned, perchance made much of, though in itself it have deformities. For indeed, for severer eyes it is not, being but a trifle, and that triflingly handled. Your dear self can best witness the manner, being done in loose sheets of paper, most of it in your presence, the rest by sheets sent unto you as fast as they were done. In sum, a young head not so well stayed[2] as I would it were (and shall be when God will) having many many fancies begotten in it, if it had not been in some way delivered, would have grown a monster, and more sorry might I be that they came in than that they gat[3] out. But his chief safety shall be the not walking abroad; and his chief protection the bearing the livery of your name which (if much much goodwill do not deceive me) is worthy to be a sanctuary for a greater offender.[4] This say I because I know the virtue so; and this say I because it may be ever so; or, to say better, because it will be ever so. Read it then at your idle times, and the follies your good judgment will find in it, blame not, but laugh at. And so, looking for no better stuff than, as in a haberdasher's shop, glasses or feathers, you will continue to love the writer who doth exceedingly love you, and most most heartily prays you may long live to be a principal ornament to the family of the Sidneys.

Your loving brother,
Philip Sidney

THE FIRST BOOK OR ACT OF
THE COUNTESS OF PEMBROKE'S ARCADIA

Arcadia[5] among all the provinces of Greece was ever had in singular reputation, partly for the sweetness of the air and other natural benefits, but principally for the moderate and well tempered minds of the people who (finding how true a contentation[6] is gotten by following the course of nature, and how the shining title of glory, so much affected by other nations, doth indeed help little to the happiness of life) were the only people which, as by their justice and providence gave neither cause nor

---

1. Sidney originally composed the *Arcadia* for his sister, Mary Herbert, the Countess of Pembroke. The work was begun about 1580, at Wilton, the Pembroke estate. Sidney completed a first version in 1581; he began but did not complete a revision in 1583–1584. His sister published the unfinished revision in 1590, then published a new edition in 1593, completing the work by adding in the last two books of the first version.
2. Balanced.

3. Got.
4. Sidney indicates that he wants his romance to be circulated privately and not published; additionally, it is protected from criticism by being dedicated to his sister.
5. A region located in the middle of the Peloponnesian peninsula, surrounded by mountains and very fertile; it was considered to be the place in which pastoral poetry originated.
6. Contentment.

hope to their neighbors to annoy them, so were they not stirred with false praise to trouble others' quiet, thinking it a small reward for the wasting of their own lives in ravening[7] that their posterity should long after say they had done so. Even the muses seemed to approve their good determination by choosing that country as their chiefest repairing place, and by bestowing their perfections so largely there that the very shepherds themselves had their fancies opened to so high conceits[8] as the most learned of other nations have been long time since content both to borrow their names and imitate their cunning. In this place some time there dwelled a mighty duke named Basilius,[9] a prince of sufficient skill to govern so quiet a country where the good minds of the former princes had set down good laws, and the well bringing up of the people did serve as a most sure bond to keep them. He married Gynecia,[1] the daughter of the king of Cyprus; a lady worthy enough to have had her name in continual remembrance if her latter time had not blotted her well governed youth, although the wound fell more to her own conscience than to the knowledge of the world, fortune something supplying her want of virtue. Of her the duke had two fair daughters, the elder Pamela,[2] the younger Philoclea,[3] both so excellent in all those gifts which are allotted to reasonable creatures as they seemed to be born for a sufficient proof that nature is no stepmother to that sex, how much soever the rugged disposition of some men, sharp-witted only in evil speaking, hath sought to disgrace them. And thus grew they on in each good increase till Pamela, a year older than Philoclea, came to the point of seventeen years of age. At which time the duke Basilius—not so much stirred with the care for his country and children as with the vanity which possesseth many who, making a perpetual mansion of this poor baiting place of man's life,[4] are desirous to know the certainty of things to come, wherein there is nothing so certain as our continual uncertainty—Basilius, I say, would needs undertake a journey to Delphos,[5] there by the oracle to inform himself whether the rest of his life should be continued in like tenor of happiness as thitherunto it had been, accompanied with the wellbeing of his wife and children, whereupon he had placed greatest part of his own felicity. Neither did he long stay; but the woman appointed to that impiety, furiously inspired, gave him in verse this answer:

> Thy elder care shall from thy careful face
> By princely mean be stolen and yet not lost;
> Thy younger shall with nature's bliss embrace
> An uncouth love, which nature hateth most.
> Thou with thy wife adult'ry shalt commit,
> And in thy throne a foreign state shall sit.
> All this on thee this fatal year shall hit.

Which, as in part it was more obscure than he could understand, so did the whole bear such manifest threatenings, that his amazement was greater than his fore[6] curiosity—both passions proceeding out of one weakness: in vain to desire to know that of which in vain thou shalt be sorry after thou hast known it. But thus the duke answered though not satisfied, he returned into his country with a countenance well

---

7. Plundering.
8. Conceptions.
9. "King."
1. "Womanly."
2. "All sweetness."
3. "Lover of glory."

4. A place in which human beings are "baited" or tempted by the prospect of learning the future.
5. A town in Greece famous for its oracle of Apollo. Its priestess, called the Pythia, uttered obscure prophecies, which were interpreted by a priest.
6. Earlier.

witnessing the dismayedness of his heart; which notwithstanding upon good considerations he thought not good to disclose, but only to one chosen friend of his named
Philanax, whom he had ever found a friend not only in affection but judgment, and
no less of the duke than dukedom[7]—a rare temper, whilst most men either servilely
yield to all appetites, or with an obstinate austerity, looking to that they fancy good,
wholly neglect the prince's person. But such was this man; and in such a man had
Basilius been happy if his mind, corrupted with a prince's fortune, had not resolved to
use a friend's secrecy rather for confirmation of fancies than correcting of errors,
which in this weighty matter he well showed. For having with many words discovered unto him both the cause and success of his Delphos journey, in the end he told
him that, to prevent all these inconveniences of the loss of his crown and children
(for as for the point of his wife, he could no way understand it), he was resolved for
this fatal year to retire himself with his wife and daughters into a solitary place where,
being two lodges built of purpose, he would in the one of them recommend his
daughter Pamela to his principal herdman—a place in that world, not so far gone
into painted vanities, of some credit—by name Dametas, in whose blunt truth he had
great confidence, thinking it a contrary salve against the destiny threatening her
mishap by a prince to place her with a shepherd. In the other lodge he and his wife
would keep their younger jewel, Philoclea; and because the oracle touched some
strange love of hers, have the more care of her, in especial keeping away her nearest
kinsmen, whom he deemed chiefly understood, and therewithal all other likely to
move any such humor.[8] And so for himself, being so cruelly menaced by fortune, he
would draw himself out of her way by this loneliness, which he thought was the surest
mean to avoid her blows; where for his pleasure he would be recreated with all those
sports and eclogues[9] wherein the shepherds of that country did much excel. As for
the government of the country, and in especial manning of his frontiers (for that
only way he thought a foreign prince might endanger his crown), he would leave the
charge to certain selected persons; the superintendence of all which he would commit to Philanax. And so ended he his speech, for fashion's sake asking him his counsel. But Philanax, having forthwith taken into the depth of his consideration both
what the duke said and with what mind he spake it, with a true heart and humble
countenance in this sort answered:

"Most redoubted[1] and beloved prince, if as well it had pleased you at your going
to Delphos, as now, to have used my humble service, both I should in better season
and to better purpose have spoken, and you perhaps at this time should have been, as
no way more in danger, so undoubtedly much more in quietness. I would then have
said unto you that wisdom and virtue be the only destinies appointed to man to follow, wherein one ought to place all his knowledge, since they be such guides as cannot fail which, besides their inward comfort, do make a man see so direct a way of
proceeding as prosperity must necessarily ensue. And, although the wickedness of the
world should oppress it, yet could it not be said that evil happened to him who
should fall accompanied with virtue; so that, either standing or falling with virtue, a
man is never in evil case. I would then have said the heavenly powers to be reverenced and not searched into, and their mercy rather by prayers to be sought than
their hidden counsels by curiosity; these kinds of soothsaying sorceries (since the

---

7. Philanax ("lover of lordship") was a friend not only to
the duke, Basilius, but also to Basilius's dukedom, the
province of Arcadia.

8. Mood.
9. Pastoral poems.
1. Dreaded.

heavens have left us in ourselves sufficient guides) to be nothing but fancies wherein there must either be vanity or infallibleness, and so either not to be respected or not to be prevented. But since it is weakness too much to remember what should have been done, and that your commandment stretcheth to know what shall be done, I do, most dear lord, with humble boldness say that the manner of your determination doth in no sort better please me than the cause of your going.[2] These thirty years past have you so governed this realm that neither your subjects have wanted justice in you, nor you obedience in them; and your neighbors have found you so hurtlessly strong that they thought it better to rest in your friendship than make new trial of your enmity. If this, then, have proceeded out of the good constitution of your state, and out of a wise providence generally to prevent all those things which might encumber your happiness, why should you now seek new courses, since your own example comforts you to continue on, and that it is most certain no destiny nor influence whatsoever can bring man's wit to a higher point than wisdom and goodness? Why should you deprive yourself of governing your dukedom for fear of losing your dukedom, like one that should kill himself for fear of death? Nay rather, if this oracle be to be accounted of, arm up your courage the more against it; for who will stick to him that abandons himself? Let your subjects have you in their eyes, let them see the benefits of your justice daily more and more; and so must they needs rather like of present sureties[3] than uncertain changes. Lastly, whether your time call you to live or die, do both like a prince. And even the same mind hold I as touching my ladies, your daughters, in whom nature promiseth nothing but goodness, and their education by your fatherly care hath been hitherto such as hath been most fit to restrain all evil, giving their minds virtuous delights, and not grieving them for want of well ruled liberty: now to fall to a sudden straitening them, what can it do but argue suspicion, the most venomous gall to virtue? Leave women's minds, the most untamed that way of any; see whether any cage can please a bird, or whether a dog grow not fiercer with tying. What doth jealousy else but stir up the mind to think what it is from which they are restrained? For they are treasures or things of great delight which men use to hide for the aptness they have to catch men's fancies; and the thoughts once awaked to that, harder sure it is to keep those thoughts from accomplishment than it had been before to have kept the mind (which, being the chief part, by this means is defiled) from thinking. Now, for the recommending so principal a charge of her, whose mind goes beyond the governing of many hundreds of such, to such a person as Dametas is, besides that the thing in itself is strange, it comes of a very ill ground that ignorance should be the mother of faithfulness. O no, he cannot be good that knows not why he is good, but stands so far good as his fortune may keep him unassayed. But coming to that, his rude[4] simplicity is either easily changed or easily deceived; and so grows that to be the last excuse of his fault which seemed to have been the first foundation of his faith.[5] Thus far hath your commandment and my zeal drawn me to speak; which I, like a man in a valley may discern hills, or like a poor passenger may spy a rock, so humbly submit to your gracious consideration, beseeching you to stand wholly upon your own virtue as the surest way to maintain you in that you are, and to avoid any evil which may be imagined."

---

2. Philanax advises Basilius that he should neither be curious to know the future nor abandon his dukedom for a new way of life, in this case, in the country and away from his subjects.
3. Certainties.

4. Rural.
5. Dametas has been chosen to guard Pamela because he is simple; but he may fail to guard her well because he is simple.

Whilst Philanax used these words, a man might see in the duke's face that, as he was wholly wedded to his own opinion, so was he grieved to have any man say that which he had not seen. Yet did the goodwill he bare to Philanax so far prevail with him that he passed into no further choler,[6] but with short manner asked him: "And would you, then," said he, "that in change of fortune I shall not change my determination,[7] as we do our apparel according to the air, and as the ship doth her course with the wind?"

"Truly sir," answered he, "neither do I as yet see any change; and though I did, yet would I think a constant virtue,[8] settled, little subject unto it. And, as in great necessity I would allow a well proportioned change,[9] so in the sight of an enemy to arm himself the lighter, or at every puff of wind to strike sail, is such a change as either will breed ill success or no success."

"To give place to blows", said the duke, "is thought no small wisdom."

"That is true," said Philanax, "but to give place before they come takes away the occasion, when they come, to give place."

"Yet the reeds stand with yielding," said the duke.

"And so are they but reeds, most worthy prince," said Philanax, "but the rocks stand still and are rocks."

But the duke, having used thus much dukely sophistry to deceive himself, and making his will wisdom, told him resolutely he stood upon his own determination; and therefore willed him, with certain other he named, to take the government of the state, and especially to keep narrow watch of the frontiers. Philanax, acknowledging himself much honored by so great trust, went with as much care to perform his commandment as before he had with faith yielded his counsel, which in the latter short disputations he had rather proportioned to Basilius's words than to any towardness[1] of argument. And Basilius, according to his determination, retired himself into the solitary place of the two lodges, where he was daily delighted with the eclogues and pastimes of shepherds. In the one of which lodges he himself remained with his wife and the beauty of the world, Philoclea; in the other, near unto him, he placed his daughter Pamela with Dametas, whose wife was Miso and daughter Mopsa, unfit company for so excellent a creature, but to exercise her patience and to serve for a foil to her perfections.

Now, newly after that the duke had begun this solitary life, there came (following the train their virtues led them) into this country two young princes: the younger, but chiefer, named Pyrocles, only son to Euarchus, king of Macedon; the other his cousin german,[2] Musidorus, duke of Thessalia;[3] both like in virtues, near in years, near in blood, but nearest of all in friendship. And because this matter runs principally of them, a few more words how they came hither will not be superfluous. Euarchus, king of Macedon, a prince of such justice that he never thought himself privileged by being a prince, nor did measure greatness by anything but by goodness; as he did thereby root an awful[4] love in his subjects towards him, so yet could he not avoid the assaults of envy—the enemy and yet the honor of virtue. For the kings of Thrace, Pannonia, and Epirus,[5] not being able to attain his perfections, thought in their base

6. Anger.
7. Way of life.
8. Resolute mind.
9. I.e., a change in a way of life must suit the challenge that confronts it.
1. Aptness.
2. First cousin.

3. Pyrocles: first glory; Euarchus: good ruler; Musidorus: gift of the Muses. Macedon and Thessalia, or Thessaly, were regions in northern Greece.
4. Full of awe.
5. Regions in Greece to the north and west of Arcadia; their kings do not wish to be compared unfavorably to Euarchus.

wickedness best to take away so odious a comparison, lest his virtues, joined now to the fame and force of the Macedonians, might in time both conquer the bodies and win the minds of their subjects. And thus conspiring together, they did three sundry ways enter into his kingdom at one time. Which sudden and dangerous invasions, although they did nothing astonish Euarchus, who carried a heart prepared for all extremities (as a man that knew both what ill might happen to a man never so prosperous, and withal[6] what the uttermost of that ill was), yet were they cause that Euarchus did send away his young son Pyrocles, at that time but six years old, to his sister, the dowager and regent of Thessalia, there to be brought up with her son Musidorus. Which, though it proceeded of necessity, yet was not the counsel in itself unwise, the sweet emulation that grew being an excellent nurse of the good parts in these two princes, two princes indeed born to the exercise of virtue. For they, accompanying the increase of their years with the increase of all good inward and outward qualities, and taking very timely into their minds that the divine part of man was not enclosed in this body for nothing, gave themselves wholly over to those knowledges which might in the course of their life be ministers to well doing. And so grew they on till Pyrocles came to be seventeen and Musidorus eighteen years of age; at which time Euarchus, having after ten years' war conquered the kingdom of Thrace and brought the other two to be his tributaries, lived in the principal city of Thrace called at that time Byzantium,[7] whither he sent for his son and nephew to delight his aged eyes in them and to make them enjoy the fruits of his victories. But so pleased it God, who reserved them to greater traverses,[8] both of good and evil fortune, that the sea, to which they committed themselves, stirred with terrible tempest, forced them to fall far from their course upon the coast of Lydia[9] where, what befell unto them, what valiant acts they did, passing in one year's space through the lesser Asia, Syria, and Egypt, how many ladies they defended from wrongs, and disinherited persons restored to their rights, it is a work for a higher style than mine. This only shall suffice: that their fame returned so fast before them into Greece that the king of Macedon received that as the comfort of their absence, although accompanied with so much more longing as he found the manifestation of their worthiness greater. But they, desirous more and more to exercise their virtues and increase their experience, took their journey from Egypt towards Greece. Which they did, they two alone, because, that being their native country they might have the most perfect knowledge of it; wherein they that hold the countenances of princes have their eyes most dazzled.

And so, taking Arcadia in their way, for the fame of the country, they came thither newly after that this strange solitariness had possessed Basilius. Now so fell it unto them that they, lodging in the house of Kerxenus, a principal gentleman in Mantinea, so was the city called, near to the solitary dwelling of the duke, it was Pyrocles' either evil or good fortune walking with his host in a fair gallery that he perceived a picture, newly made by an excellent artificer, which contained the duke and duchess with their younger daughter Philoclea, with such countenance and fashion as the manner of their life held them in, both the parents' eyes cast with a loving care upon their beautiful child, she drawn as well as it was possible art should counterfeit so perfect a workmanship of nature. For therein, besides the show of her beauties, a man might judge even the nature of her countenance, full of bashfulness, love, and reverence—and all by the cast of her eye—, mixed with a sweet grief to find her

6. Also.
7. A city on the Bosporus, today the site of Istanbul.
8. Adventures.
9. Western Asia Minor.

virtue suspected. This moved Pyrocles to fall into questions of her; wherein being answered by the gentleman as much as he understood, which was of her strange kind of captivity; neither was it known how long it should last; and there was a general opinion grown the duke would grant his daughters in marriage to nobody. As the most noble heart is most subject unto it,[1] from questions grew to pity; and when with pity once his heart was made tender, according to the aptness of the humor, it received straight a cruel impression of that wonderful passion which to be defined is impossible, by reason no words reach near to the strange nature of it. They only know it which inwardly feel it. It is called love. Yet did not the poor youth at first know his disease, thinking it only such a kind of desire as he was wont to have to see unwonted sights, and his pity to be no other but the fruits of his gentle nature. But even this arguing with himself came of a further thought; and the more he argued, the more his thought increased. Desirous he was to see the place where she remained, as though the architecture of the lodges would have been much for his learning; but more desirous to see herself, to be judge, forsooth, of the painter's cunning—for thus at the first did he flatter himself, as though his wound had been no deeper. But when within short time he came to the degree of uncertain wishes, and that those wishes grew to unquiet longings; when he could fix his thoughts upon nothing but that, within a little varying, they should end with Philoclea; when each thing he saw seemed to figure out some part of his passions, and that he heard no word spoken but that he imagined it carried the sound of Philoclea's name; then did poor Pyrocles yield to the burden, finding himself prisoner before he had leisure to arm himself, and that he might well, like the spaniel, gnaw upon the chain that ties him, but he should sooner mar his teeth than procure liberty. Then was his chief delight secretly to draw his dear friend a-walking to the desert[2] of the two lodges where he saw no grass upon which he thought Philoclea might hap to tread but that he envied the happiness of it; and yet, with a contrary folly, would sometimes recommend his whole estate unto it. Till at length love, the refiner of invention, put in his head a way how to come to the sight of his Philoclea; for which he with great speed and secrecy prepared everything that was necessary for his purpose, but yet would not put it in execution till he had disclosed it to Musidorus, both to perform the true laws of friendship and withal to have his counsel and allowance. And yet, out of the sweetness of his disposition, was bashfully afraid to break it with him to whom (besides other bonds), because he was his elder, he bare a kind of reverence, until some fit opportunity might, as it were, draw it from him. Which occasion time shortly presented unto him.

For Musidorus, having informed himself fully of the strength and riches of the country; of the nature of the people, and of the manner of their laws; and seeing the duke's court could not be visited, and that they came not without danger to that place, prohibited to all men but to certain shepherds, grew no less weary of his abode there than marvelled of the great delight Pyrocles took in that place. Whereupon one day, at Pyrocles' earnest request being walked thither again, began in this manner to say unto him:

"A mind well trained and long exercised in virtue, my sweet and worthy cousin, doth not easily change any course it once undertakes but upon well grounded and well weighed causes; for being witness to itself of his own inward good, it finds nothing without it of so high a price for which it should be altered. Even the very countenance and behavior of such a man doth show forth images of the same constancy by

---

1. I.e., pity.   2. Barren countryside.

maintaining a right harmony betwixt it and the inward good in yielding itself suitable to the virtuous resolutions of the mind. This speech I direct to you, noble friend Pyrocles, the excellency of whose mind and well chosen course in virtue, if I do not sufficiently know, having seen such rare demonstrations of it, it is my weakness and not your unworthiness. But as indeed I do know it, and knowing it, most dearly love both it and him that hath it, so must I needs say that since our late[3] coming into this country I have marked in you, I will not say an alteration, but a relenting, truly, and slacking of the main career you had so notably begun and almost performed; and that, in such sort as I cannot find sufficient reasons in my great love towards you how to allow it. For, to leave off other secreter arguments which my acquaintance with you makes me easily find, this in effect to any man may be manifest: that, whereas you were wont, in all the places you came, to give yourself vehemently to knowledge of those things which might better your mind; to seek the familiarity of excellent men in learning and soldiery; and lastly, to put all these things in practice both by continual wise proceeding and worthy enterprises, as occasions fell for them; you now leave all these things undone; you let your mind fall asleep, besides your countenance troubled (which surely comes not out of virtue; for virtue, like the clear heaven, is without clouds); and lastly, which seemeth strangest unto me, you haunt greatly this place, wherein, besides the disgrace that might fall of it (which, that it hath not already fallen upon you, is rather luck than providence, this duke having sharply forbidden it), you subject yourself to solitariness, the sly enemy that doth most separate a man from well doing."

These words, spoken vehemently and proceeding from so dearly an esteemed friend as Musidorus, did so pierce poor Pyrocles that his blushing cheeks did witness with him he rather could not help, than did not know, his fault. Yet, desirous by degrees to bring his friend to a gentler consideration of him, and beginning with two or three broken sighs, answered him to this

"Excellent Musidorus, in the praises you gave me in the beginning of your speech, I easily acknowledge the force of your goodwill unto me; for neither could you have thought so well of me if extremity of love had not something[4] dazzled your eyes, nor you could have loved me so entirely if you had not been apt to make so great, though undeserved, judgment of me. And even so must I say of those imperfections, to which though I have ever through weakness been subject, yet you by the daily mending of your mind have of late been able to look into them, which before you could not discern; so that the change you spake of falls not out by my impairing but by your bettering. And yet, under the leave of your better judgment, I must needs say thus much, my dear cousin, that I find not myself wholly to be condemned because I do not with a continual vehemency follow those knowledges which you call the bettering of my mind; for both the mind itself must, like other things, sometimes be unbent, or else it will be either weakened or broken, and these knowledges, as they are of good use, so are they not all the mind may stretch itself unto. Who knows whether I feed not my mind with higher thoughts? Truly, as I know not all the particularities, so yet see I the bounds of all those knowledges; but the workings of the mind, I find, much more infinite than can be led unto by the eye or imagined by any that distract their thoughts without[5] themselves. And in such contemplations, or, as I think, more excellent, I enjoy my solitariness; and my solitariness, perchance,

---

is the nurse of these contemplations. Eagles, we see, fly alone; and they are but sheep which always herd together. Condemn not, therefore, my mind sometimes to enjoy itself, nor blame not the taking of such times as serve most fit for it!"

And here Pyrocles suddenly stopped, like a man unsatisfied in himself, though his wit might well have served to have satisfied another. And so, looking with a countenance as though he desired he should know his mind without hearing him speak, and yet desirous to speak to breathe out some part of his inward evil, sending again new blood to his face, he continued his speech in this manner:

"And lord! dear cousin," said he, "doth not the pleasantness of this place carry in itself sufficient reward for any time lost in it, or for any such danger that might ensue? Do you not see how everything conspires together to make this place a heavenly dwelling? Do you not see the grass, how in color they excel the emeralds, everyone striving to pass his fellow—and yet they are all kept in an equal height? And see you not the rest of all these beautiful flowers, each of which would require a man's wit to know, and his life to express? Do not these stately trees seem to maintain their flourishing old age with the only happiness of their seat, being clothed with a continual spring because no beauty here should ever fade? Doth not the air breathe health, which the birds, delightful both to the ear and eye, do daily solemnize with the sweet concent of their voices? Is not every echo here a perfect music? And these fresh and delightful brooks, how slowly they slide away, as loath to leave the company of so many things united in perfection! And with how sweet a murmur they lament their forced departure! Certainly, certainly, cousin, it must needs be that some goddess this desert belongs unto, who is the soul of this soil; for neither is any less than a goddess worthy to be shrined in such a heap of pleasures, nor any less than a goddess could have made it so perfect a model of the heavenly dwellings."

And so he ended, with a deep sigh, ruefully casting his eye upon Musidorus, as more desirous of pity than pleading. But Musidorus had all this while held his look fixed upon Pyrocles' countenance, and with no less loving attention marked how his words proceeded from him. But in both these he perceived such strange diversities that they rather increased new doubts than gave him ground to settle any judgment; for, besides his eyes sometimes even great with tears, the oft changing of his color, with a kind of shaking unstaidness[6] over all his body, he might see in his countenance some great determination mixed with fear, and might perceive in him store of thoughts rather stirred than digested, his words interrupted continually with sighs which served as a burden to each sentence, and the tenor of his speech (though of his wonted phrase) not knit together to one constant end but rather dissolved in itself, as the vehemency of the inward passion prevailed: which made Musidorus frame his answer nearest to that humor which should soonest put out the secret. For, having in the beginning of Pyrocles' speech which defended his solitariness framed in his mind a reply against it in the praise of honorable action (in showing that such kind of contemplation is but a glorious title to idleness; that in action a man did not only better himself but benefit others; that the gods would not have delivered a soul into the body which hath arms and legs (only instruments of doing) but that it were intended the mind should employ them; and that the mind should best know his own good or evil by practice; which knowledge was the only way to increase the one and correct the other; besides many other better arguments which the plentifulness of the matter yielded to the sharpness of his wit), when he found Pyrocles leave that, and fall to

6. Unsteadiness.

such an affected praising of the place, he left it likewise, and joined therein with him because he found him in that humor utter most store of passion.[7] And even thus, kindly embracing him, he said:

"Your words are such, noble cousin, so sweetly and strongly handled in the praise of solitariness, as they would make me likewise yield myself up unto it, but that the same words make me know it is more pleasant to enjoy the company of him that can speak such words than by such words to be persuaded to follow solitariness. And even so do I give you leave, sweet Pyrocles, ever to defend solitariness so long as, to defend it, you ever keep company. But I marvel at the excessive praises you give to this desert. In truth, it is not unpleasant; but yet, if you would return into Macedon, you should see either many heavens or find this no more than earthly. And even Tempe[8], in my Thessalia, where you and I (to my great happiness) were brought up together, is nothing inferior unto it. But I think you will make me see that the vigor of your wit can show itself in any subject; or else you feed sometimes your solitariness with the conceits[9] of the poets whose liberal pens can as easily travel over mountains as mole-hills, and so (like well disposed men) set up everything to the highest note[1]—espe-cially when they put such words in the mouth of one of these fantastical mind-infect-ed people that children and musicians call lovers."

This word of "lover" did no less pierce poor Pyrocles than the right tune of music toucheth him that is sick of the tarantula.[2] There was not one part of his body that did not feel a sudden motion, the heart drawing unto itself the life of every part to help it, distressed with the sound of that word. Yet, after some pause, lifting up his eyes a little from the ground, and yet not daring to place them in the face of Musi-dorus, armed with the very countenance of the poor prisoner at the bar[3] whose answer is nothing but "guilty," with much ado he brought forth this question:

"And alas," said he, "dear cousin, what if I be not so much the poet, the freedom of whose pen can exercise itself in anything, as even that very miserable subject of his cunning whereof you speak?"

"Now the eternal gods forbid," mainly[4] cried out Musidorus. But Pyrocles, hav-ing broken the ice, pursued on in this manner:

"And yet such a one am I," said he, "and in such extremity as no man can feel but myself, nor no man believe; since no man ever could taste the hundredth part of that which lies in the inwardmost part of my soul. For since it was the fatal overthrow of all my liberty to see in the gallery of Mantinea the only Philoclea's picture, that beauty did pierce so through mine eyes to my heart that the impression of it doth not lie but live there, in such sort as the question is not now whether I shall love or no, but whether loving, I shall live or die."

Musidorus was no less astonished with these words of his friend than if, thinking him in health, he had suddenly told him that he felt the pangs of death oppress him. So that, amazedly looking upon him (even as Apollo is painted when he saw Daphne suddenly turned to a laurel),[5] he was not able to say one word; but gave Pyrocles occasion, having already made the breach, to pass on in this sort:

---

7. Musidorus stops reasoning with Pyrocles because he realizes that Pyrocles' mood is such that he can express only passion.

8. A valley in Thessaly known for its abundant vegeta-tion and mild climate.

9. Images.

1. Musidorus remarks that poets, who describe their sub-jects in exaggerated terms, can provoke a desire for soli-tude in impressionable audiences, such as lovers and chil-dren.

2. Poisonous spider.

3. On trial.

4. Vigorously.

5. Apollo loved the nymph Daphne, who, rejecting his attentions, fled from him; just before he caught up with her, the gods turned her into a laurel tree.

"And because I have laid open my wound, noble cousin," said he, "I will show you what my melancholy hath brought forth for the preparation at least of a salve, if it be not in itself a medicine. I am resolved, because all direct ways are barred me of opening my suit to the duke, to take upon me the estate of an Amazon lady[6] going about the world to practise feats of chivalry and to seek myself a worthy husband. I have already provided all furniture[7] necessary for it; and my face, you see, will not easily discover[8] me. And hereabout will I haunt till, by the help of this disguising, I may come to the presence of her whose imprisonment darkens the world, that my own eyes may be witnesses to my heart it is great reason why he should be thus captived. And then, as I shall have attained to the first degree of my happiness, so will fortune, occasion, and mine own industry put forward the rest. For the principal point is to set in a good way the thing we desire; for then will time itself daily discover new secret helps. As for my name, it shall be Cleophila,[9] turning Philoclea to myself, as my mind is wholly turned and transformed into her. Now therefore do I submit myself to your counsel, dear cousin, and crave your help."

And thus he ended, as who should say, "I have told you all, have pity on me." But Musidorus had by this time gathered his spirits together, dismayed to see him he loved more than himself plunged in such a course of misery. And so, when Pyrocles had ended, casting a ghastful[1] countenance upon him, as if he would conjure some strange spirit he saw possess him, with great vehemency uttered these words:

"And is it possible that this is Pyrocles, the only young prince in the world, formed by nature and framed by education to the true exercise of virtue? Or is it, indeed, some Amazon Cleophila that hath counterfeited the face of my friend in this sort to vex me? For likelier, sure, I would have thought it that any outward face might have been disguised than that the face of so excellent a mind could have been thus blemished. O sweet Pyrocles, separate yourself a little, if it be possible, from yourself, and let your own mind look upon your own proceedings; so shall my words be needless, and you best instructed. See with yourself how fit it will be for you in this your tender youth (born so great a prince, of so rare, not only expectation, but proof, desired of your old father, and wanted of your native country, now so near your home) to divert your thoughts from the way of goodness to lose, nay to abuse, your time; lastly, to overthrow all the excellent things you have done, which have filled the world with your fame (as if you should drown your ship in the long-desired haven, or like an ill player should mar the last act of his tragedy). Remember (for I know you know it) that, if we will be men, the reasonable part of our soul is to have absolute commandment, against which if any sensual weakness arise, we are to yield all our sound forces to the overthrowing of so unnatural a rebellion; wherein, how can we want courage, since we are to deal against so weak an adversary that in itself is nothing but weakness? Nay, we are to resolve that if reason direct it, we must do it; and if we must do it, we will do it; for to say I cannot is childish, and I will not womanish. And see how extremely every way you endanger your mind; for to take this woman's habit, without you frame your behavior accordingly, is wholly vain; your behavior can never come kindly[2] from you but as the mind is proportioned unto it. So that you must resolve, if you will play your part to any purpose, whatsoever peevish imperfections are in that sex, to soften your heart to receive them—the very first

---

6. A race of female warriors alleged to exist in ancient Scythia (now in Russia); hence any female warrior.
7. Equipment.
8. Identify.

9. "Glory of love."
1. Ghostlike.
2. Naturally.

down step to all wickedness. For do not deceive yourself, my dear cousin; there is no man suddenly either excellently good or extremely evil, but grows either as he holds himself up in virtue or lets himself slide to viciousness. And let us see what power is the author of all these troubles: forsooth, love; love, a passion, and the basest and fruitlessest of all passions. Fear breedeth wit; anger is the cradle of courage; joy openeth and enableth the heart; sorrow, as it closeth it, so yet draweth it inward to look to the correcting of itself. And so all of them generally have power towards some good, by the direction of reason. But this bastard love (for, indeed, the name of love is unworthily applied to so hateful a humor as it is, engendered betwixt lust and idleness), as the matter it works upon is nothing but a certain base weakness, which some gentle fools call a gentle heart; as his adjoined companions be unquietness, longings, fond comforts, faint discomforts, hopes, jealousies, ungrounded rages, causeless yieldings; so is the highest end it aspires unto a little pleasure, with much pain before, and great repentance after. But that end, how endlessly it runs to infinite evils, were fit enough for the matter we speak of; but not for your ears, in whom, indeed, there is so much true disposition to virtue. Yet thus much of his worthy effects in yourself is to be seen: that it utterly subverts the course of nature in making reason give place to sense, and man to woman. And truly, I think, hereupon it first gat the name of love. For, indeed, the true love hath that excellent nature in it, that it doth transform the very essence of the lover into the thing loved, uniting and, as it were, incorporating it with a secret and inward working. And herein do these kinds of love imitate the excellent; for, as the love of heaven makes one heavenly, the love of virtue, virtuous, so doth the love of the world make one become worldly. And this effeminate love of a woman doth so womanize a man that, if you yield to it, it will not only make you a famous Amazon, but a launder, a distaff-spinner,[3] or whatsoever other vile occupation their idle heads can imagine and their weak hands perform. Therefore, to trouble you no longer with my tedious but loving words, if either you remember what you are, what you have been, or what you must be; if you consider what it is that moves you, or for what kind of creature you are moved, you shall find the cause so small, the effects so dangerous, yourself so unworthy to run into the one or to be driven by the other, that I doubt not I shall quickly have occasion rather to praise you for having conquered it than to give you any further counsel how to do it."

Pyrocles' mind was all this while so fixed upon another devotion that he no more attentively marked his friend's discourse than the child that hath leave to play marks the last part of his lesson, or the diligent pilot in a dangerous tempest doth attend to the unskillful words of the passenger. Yet, the very sound having left the general points of his speech in his mind, the respect he bare to his friend brought forth this answer, having first paid up his late-accustomed tribute of sighs:

"Dear and worthy friend, whatsoever good disposition nature hath bestowed on me, or howsoever that disposition hath been by bringing up confirmed, this must I confess: that I am not yet come to that degree of wisdom to think lightly of the sex of whom I have my life; since, if I be anything (which your friendship rather finds than I acknowledge), I was to come to it born of a woman and nursed of a woman.[4] And certainly (for this point of your speech doth nearest touch me) it is strange to see the unmanlike cruelty of mankind who, not content with their tyrannous ambition to have brought the others' virtuous patience under them, like childish masters, think

---

3. A person who washes clothes or spins thread—occupations usually reserved for women.
4. In the speech that follows, Pyrocles rehearses many of the arguments proposed in contemporary defenses of women.

their masterhood nothing without doing injury to them who (if we will argue by reason) are framed of nature with the same parts of the mind for the exercise of virtue as we are. And, for example, even this estate[5] of Amazons, which I now for my greatest honor do seek to counterfeit, doth well witness that, if generally the sweetness of their disposition did not make them see the vainness of these things which we account glorious, they neither want[6] valor of mind, nor yet doth their fairness take away their force. And truly, we men and praisers of men should remember that, if we have such excellencies, it is reason to think them excellent creatures of whom we are, since a kite[7] never brought forth a good flying hawk. But to tell you true, I do both disdain to use any more words of such a subject which is so praised in itself as it needs no praises; and withal fear lest my conceit (not able to reach unto them) bring forth words which for their unworthiness may be a disgrace to them I so inwardly honor. Let this suffice: that they are capable of virtue. And virtue, you yourself say, is to be loved; and I, too, truly. But this I willingly confess: that it likes me much better when I find virtue in a fair lodging than when I am bound to seek it in an ill-favored creature, like a pearl in a dunghill."

And here Pyrocles stayed as to breathe himself, having been transported with a little vehemency because it seemed him Musidorus had over bitterly glanced against the reputation of womankind. But then quieting his countenance, as well as out of an unquiet mind it might be, he thus proceeded on:

"And poor love," said he, "dear cousin, is little beholding unto you, since you are not contented to spoil it of the honor of the highest power of the mind (which notable men have attributed unto it), but you deject it below all other passions—in truth, something strangely since, if love receive any disgrace, it is by the company of those passions you prefer unto it. For those kinds of bitter objections (as that lust, idleness, and a weak heart should be, as it were, the matter and form of love), rather touch me, dear Musidorus, than love. But I am good witness of mine own imperfections, and therefore will not defend myself. But herein, I must say, you deal contrary to yourself; for, if I be so weak, then can you not with reason stir me up, as you did, by the remembrance of mine own virtue. Or if indeed I be virtuous, then must you confess that love hath his working in a virtuous heart. And so no doubt hath it, whatsoever I be.[8] For, if we love virtue, in whom shall we love it but in virtuous creatures?— Without[9] your meaning be I should love this word of virtue when I see it written in a book. Those troublesome effects you say it breeds be not the fault of love, but of him that loves, as an unable vessel to bear such a power—like ill eyes, not able to look on the sun, or like a weak brain, soonest overthrown with the best wine. Even that heavenly love you speak of is accompanied in some hearts with hopes, griefs, longings, and despairs. And in that heavenly love, since there are two parts (the one, the love itself; the other, the excellency of the thing loved), I (not able at the first leap to frame both in myself) do now, like a diligent workman, make ready the chief instrument and first part of that great work, which is love itself. Which, when I have a while practised in this sort, then you shall see me turn it to greater matters. And thus gently you may, if it please you, think of me. Neither doubt you, because I wear a woman's apparel, I will be the more womanish; since, I assure you, for all my apparel, there is nothing I desire more than fully to prove myself a man in this enterprise.

---

5. Condition.
6. Lack.
7. Small hawk.
8. Pyrocles asserts if love had filled him with vice, Musi-

dorus would have converted him to reason; as he is virtuous, the cause is love, for virtue acquires its character by loving virtue in another person.
9. Unless.

Much might be said in my defence, much more for love, and most of all for that divine creature which hath joined me and love together. But these disputations are fitter for quiet schools than my troubled brains, which are bent rather in deeds to perform, than in words to defend, the noble desire that possesseth me."

"O lord," said Musidorus, "how sharp-witted you are to hurt yourself!"

"No," answered he, "but it is the hurt you speak of which makes me so sharp-witted."

"Even so," said Musidorus, "as every base occupation makes one sharp in that practice and foolish in all the rest."

"Nay rather," answered Pyrocles, "as each excellent thing, once well learned, serves for a measure of all other knowledges."

"And is that become," said Musidorus, "a measure for other things, which never received measure in itself?"

"It is counted without measure," answered Pyrocles, "because the workings of it are without measure; but otherwise in nature it hath measure, since it hath an end allotted unto it."

"The beginning being so excellent, I would gladly know the end."

"Enjoying," answered Pyrocles, with a deep sigh.

"O," said Musidorus, "now set you forth the baseness of it since, if it end in enjoying, it shows all the rest was nothing."

"You mistake me," answered Pyrocles, "I spake of the end to which it is directed; which end ends not no sooner than the life."

"Alas! Let your own brain disenchant you," said Musidorus.

"My heart is too far possessed," said Pyrocles.

"But the head gives you direction."

"And the heart gives me life," answered Pyrocles.

But Musidorus was so grieved to see his beloved friend obstinate, as he thought to his own destruction, that it forced him, with more than accustomed vehemency, to speak these words:

"Well, well," said he, "you list[1] to abuse yourself. It was a very white and red virtue which you could pick out by the sight of a picture. Confess the truth, and you shall find the uttermost was but beauty; a thing which, though it be in as great excellency in yourself as may be in any, yet am I sure you make no further reckoning of it than of an outward fading benefit nature bestowed upon you. And yet, such is your want of a true-grounded virtue (which must be like itself in all points) that what you wisely count a trifle in yourself, you fondly become a slave unto in another. For my part, I now protest I have left nothing unsaid which my wit could make me know, or my most entire friendship to you requires of me. I do now beseech you, even for the love betwixt us (if this other love have left any in you towards me), and for the remembrance of your old careful father (if you can remember him, that forgets yourself), lastly, for Pyrocles' own sake (who is now upon the point of falling or rising), to purge your head of this vile infection. Otherwise, give me leave rather in absence to bewail your mishap than to bide the continual pang of seeing your danger with mine eyes."

The length of these speeches before had not so much cloyed Pyrocles (though he were very impatient of long deliberations) as this last farewell of him he loved as his own life did wound his soul—as, indeed, they that think themselves afflicted are apt to conceive unkindness deeply—; insomuch that, shaking his head, and delivering some show of tears, he thus uttered his griefs:

1. Wish.

"Alas," said he, "Prince Musidorus, how cruelly you deal with me! If you seek the victory, take it; and if you list, triumph. Have you all the reason of the world, and with me remain all the imperfections; yet such as I can no more lay from me than the crow can be persuaded by the swan to cast off his blackness. But truly, you deal with me like a physician that, seeing his patient in a pestilent fever, should chide him instead of ministering help, and bid him be sick no more; or rather, like such a friend that, visiting his friend condemned to perpetual prison and loaden with grievous fetters, should will him to shake off his fetters, or he would leave him. I am sick, and sick to the death. I am prisoner; neither is there any redress but by her to whom I am slave. Now, if you list, leave him that loves you in the highest degree; but remember ever to carry this with you: that you abandon your friend in his greatest need."

And herewith, the deep wound of his love being rubbed afresh with this new unkindness, began, as it were, to bleed again, in such sort that he was unable to bear it any longer; but, gushing out abundance of tears and crossing his arms over his woeful heart, he sank down to the ground. Which sudden trance went so to the heart of Musidorus that, falling down by him, and kissing the weeping eyes of his friend, he besought him not to make account of his speech which, if it had been over vehement, yet was it to be borne withal, because it came out of a love much more vehement; that he had never thought fancy could have received so deep a wound, but now finding in him the force of it, he would no further contrary it, but employ all his service to medicine it in such sort as the nature of it required. But even this kindness made Pyrocles the more melt in the former unkindness, which his manlike tears well showed, with a silent look upon Musidorus, as who should say, "and is it possible that Musidorus should threaten to leave me?" And this strook Musidorus's mind and senses so dumb, too, that for grief not being able to say anything, they rested with their eyes placed one upon another, in such sort as might well paint out the true passion of unkindness, which is never aright but betwixt them that most dearly love.

And thus remained they a time, till at length Musidorus, embracing him, said, "And will you thus shake off your friend?"

"It is you that shake off me," said Pyrocles, "being, for my unperfectness, unworthy of your friendship."

"But this," said Musidorus, "shows you much more unperfect, to be cruel to him that submits himself unto you. But since you are unperfect," said he, smiling, "it is reason you be governed by us wise and perfect men. And that authority will I begin to take upon me with three absolute commandments: the first, that you increase not your evil with further griefs; the second, that you love Philoclea with all the powers of your mind; and the last commandment shall be that you command me to do you what service I can towards the attaining of your desires."

Pyrocles' heart was not so oppressed with the two mighty passions of love and unkindness but that it yielded to some mirth at this commandment of Musidorus that he should love Philoclea. So that, something clearing his face from his former shows of grief, "Well," said he, "dear cousin, I see by the well choosing of your commandments that you are far fitter to be a prince than a councillor. And therefore I am resolved to employ all my endeavor to obey you, with this condition: that the commandments you command me to lay upon you shall only be that you continue to love me, and look upon my imperfections with more affection than judgment."

"Love you," said he, "alas, how can my heart be separated from the true embracing of it without it burst by being too full of it? But," said he, "let us leave off these flowers of new-begun friendship; and since you have found out that way as your readiest remedy, let us go put on your transforming apparel. For my part, I will ever remain hereabouts, either to help you in any necessity or, at least, to be partaker of any evil may fall unto you."

Pyrocles, accepting this as a most notable testimony of his long-approved friendship, and returning to Mantinea where, having taken leave of their host (who, though he knew them not, was in love with their virtue), and leaving with him some apparel and jewels, with opinion they would return after some time unto him, they departed thence to the place where he had left his womanish apparel which, with the help of his friend, he had quickly put on in such sort as it might seem love had not only sharpened his wits but nimbled his hands in anything which might serve to his service. And to begin with his head, thus was he dressed: his hair (which the young men of Greece ware[2] very long, accounting them most beautiful that had that in fairest quantity) lay upon the upper part of his forehead in locks, some curled and some, as it were, forgotten, with such a careless care, and with an art so hiding art, that he seemed he would lay them for a paragon whether nature simply, or nature helped by cunning, be the more excellent. The rest whereof was drawn into a coronet of gold, richly set with pearls, and so joined all over with gold wires, and covered with feathers of divers colors, that it was not unlike to a helmet, such a glittering show it bare, and so bravely it was held up from the head. Upon his body he ware a kind of doublet[3] of sky-color satin, so plated over with plates of massy gold that he seemed armed in it; his sleeves of the same, instead of plates, was covered with purled[4] lace. And such was the nether part of his garment; but that made so full of stuff, and cut after such a fashion that, though the length fell under his ankles, yet in his going one might well perceive the small of the leg which, with the foot, was covered with a little short pair of crimson velvet buskins,[5] in some places open (as the ancient manner was) to show the fairness of the skin. Over all this he ware a certain mantle of like stuff, made in such manner that, coming under his right arm, and covering most part of that side, it touched not the left side but upon the top of the shoulder where the two ends met, and were fastened together with a very rich jewel, the device[6] whereof was this: an eagle covered with the feathers of a dove, and yet lying under another dove, in such sort as it seemed the dove preyed upon the eagle, the eagle casting up such a look as though the state he was in liked[7] him, though the pain grieved him. Upon the same side, upon his thigh he ware a sword (such as we now call scimitars), the pommel whereof was so richly set with precious stones as they were sufficient testimony it could be no mean personage that bare it. Such was this Amazon's attire: and thus did Pyrocles become Cleophila—which name for a time hereafter I will use, for I myself feel such compassion of his passion that I find even part of his fear lest his name should be uttered before fit time were for it; which you, fair ladies that vouchsafe to read this, I doubt not will account excusable.[8] But Musidorus, that had helped to dress his friend, could not satisfy himself with looking upon him, so did he find his excellent beauty set out with this new change, like a diamond set in a more advantageous sort. Insomuch that he could not choose, but smiling said unto him:

2. Wore.
3. Jacket.
4. Embroidered.
5. Boots.
6. Emblem.

7. Pleased.
8. The narrator declares he will rename Pyrocles Cleophila, because he shares "her" fear that she will be unmasked before she has had time to court and win Philoclea.

"Well," said he, "sweet cousin, since you are framed of such a loving mettle, I pray you, take heed of looking yourself in a glass lest Narcissus's[9] fortune fall unto you. For my part, I promise you, if I were not fully resolved never to submit my heart to these fancies, I were like enough while I dressed you to become a young Pygmalion."[1]

"Alas," answered Cleophila, "if my beauty be anything, then will it help me to some part of my desires; otherwise I am no more to set by it than the orator by his eloquence that persuades nobody."

"She is a very invincible creature, then," said he, "for I doubt me much, under your patience, whether my mistress, your mistress, have a greater portion of beauty."

"Speak not that blasphemy, dear friend," said Cleophila, "for if I have any beauty, it is the beauty which the imagination of her strikes into my fancies, which in part shines through my face into your eyes."

"Truly," said Musidorus, "you are grown a notable philosopher of fancies."

"Astronomer," answered Cleophila, "for they are heavenly fancies."

In such friendly speeches they returned again to the desert of the two lodges, where Cleophila desired Musidorus he would hide himself in a little grove where he might see how she could play her part; for there, she said, she was resolved to remain till, by some good favor of fortune, she might obtain the sight of her whom she bare continually in the eyes of her mind. Musidorus obeyed her request, full of extreme grief to see so worthy a mind thus infected; besides he could see no hope of success, but great appearance of danger. Yet, finding it so deeply grounded that striving against it did rather anger than heal the wound, and rather call his friendship in question than give place to any friendly counsel, he was content to yield to the force of the present stream, with hope afterwards, as occasion fell out, to prevail better with him; or at least to adventure his life in preserving him from any injury might be offered him. And with the beating of those thoughts, remained he in the grove till, with a new fullness, he was emptied of them—as you shall after hear.

In the mean time, Cleophila walking up and down in that solitary place, with many intricate determinations, at last wearied both in mind and body, sat her down, and beginning to tune her voice, with many sobs and tears, sang this song which she had made since her first determination thus to change her estate:

> Transformed in show, but more transformed in mind,
> I cease to strive, with double conquest foiled;
> For (woe is me) my powers all I find
> With outward force and inward treason spoiled.
>
> For from without came to mine eyes the blow,
> Whereto mine inward thoughts did faintly yield;
> Both these conspired poor reason's overthrow;
> False in myself, thus have I lost the field.
>
> And thus mine eyes are placed still in one sight,
> And thus my thoughts can think but one thing still;
> Thus reason to his servants gives his right;

---

9. A youth who fell in love with his own reflection in a pool and pined away; finally, he was changed into the flower that bears his name.

1. A king of Cyprus who fell in love with a statue of a beautiful young woman he had sculpted; subsequently, Venus brought her to life.

Thus is my power transformed to your will.
What marvel, then, I take a woman's hue,
Since what I see, think, know, is all but you?

I might entertain you, fair ladies, a great while, if I should make as many inter-
ruptions in the repeating as she did in the singing. For no verse did pass out of her
mouth but that it was waited on with such abundance of sighs, and, as it were, witnessed with her flowing tears, that, though the words were few, yet the time was long
she employed in uttering them; although her pauses chose so fit times that they rather
strengthened a sweeter passion than hindered the harmony. Musidorus himself (that
lay so as he might see and hear these things) was yet more moved to pity by the manner of Cleophila's singing than with anything he had ever seen—so lively an action
doth the mind, truly touched, bring forth. But so fell it out that, as with her sweet
voice she recorded once or twice the last verse of her song, it awakened the shepherd
Dametas, who at that time had laid his sleepy back upon a sunny bank not far thence,
gaping as far as his jaws would suffer him. But being troubled out of his sleep (the best
thing his life could bring forth) his dull senses could not convey the pleasure of the
excellent music to his rude mind, but that he fell into a notable rage. Insomuch that,
taking a hedging bill[2] lay by him, he guided himself by the voice till he came to the
place where he saw Cleophila sitting, wringing her hands, and with some few words
to herself, breathing out part of the vehemency of that passion which she had not fully declared in her song. But no more were his eyes taken with her beauty than his ears
with her music. But beginning to swear by the pantable[3] of Pallas, Venus's waistcoat,
and such other oaths as his rustical bravery could imagine, leaning his hands upon his
bill, and his chin upon his hands, he fell to mutter such railings and cursings against
her as a man might well see he had passed through the discipline of an alehouse. And
because you may take the better into your fancies his mannerliness, the manner of the
man shall in few words be described. He was a short lean fellow, of black hair, and
notably backed for a burden, one of his eyes out, his nose turned up to take more air, a
seven or eight long black hairs upon his chin, which he called his beard; his breast he
ware always unbuttoned for heat, and yet a stomacher[4] before it for cold; ever
untrussed, yet points[5] hanging down, because he might be trussed if he list; ill gartered
for a courtlike carelessness; only well shod for his father's sake, who had upon his
death bed charged him to take heed of going wet. He had for love chosen his wife
Miso, yet so handsome a beldam[6] that she was counted a witch only for her face and
her splay foot. Neither inwardly nor outwardly was there anything good in her but
that she observed decorum, having in a wretched body a froward[7] mind. Neither was
there any humor in which her husband and she could ever agree, but in disagreeing.
Betwixt these two issued forth mistress Mopsa, a fit woman to participate of both
their perfections. But because Alethes, an honest man of that time, did her praises in
verse, I will only repeat them and spare mine own pen, because she bare the sex of a
woman; and these they were:

What length of verse can serve brave Mopsa's good to show,
Whose virtues strange, and beauties such, as no man them may know?
Thus shrewdly burdened then, how can my muse escape?
The gods must help and precious things must serve to show her shape.

---

2. Pruning tool.
3. From the French *pantofle*, slipper.
4. Waistcoat.

5. Cords for attaching stockings to a doublet.
6. Hag.
7. Perverse.

Like great god Saturn[8] fair, and like fair Venus chaste;
As smooth as Pan, as Juno mild, like goddess Iris fast.
With Cupid she foresees, and goes god Vulcan's pace;
And for a taste of all these gifts, she borrows Momus' grace.
    Her forehead jacinth[9] like, her cheeks of opal hue,
Her twinkling eyes bedecked with pearl, her lips of sapphire blue;
Her hair pure crapal[1] stone; her mouth O heav'nly wide;
Her skin like burnished gold, her hands like silver ore untried.
    As for those parts unknown, which hidden sure are best,
Happy be they which will believe, and never seek the rest.

The beginning of this Dametas's credit with Basilius was by the duke's straying out of his way one time a-hunting where, meeting this fellow, and asking him the way, and so falling into other questions, he found some of his answers touching husbandry[2] matters (as a dog sure, if he could speak, had wit enough to describe his kennel) not unsensible; and all uttered with such a rudeness, which the duke interpreted plainness (although there be great difference betwixt them), that the duke, conceiving a sudden delight in his entertainment, took him to his court, with apparent show of his good opinion; where the flattering courtier had no sooner taken the prince's mind but that there were straight reasons to confirm the duke's doing, and shadows of virtues found for Dametas. His silence grew wit, his bluntness integrity, his beastly ignorance virtuous simplicity; and the duke (according to the nature of great persons, in love with that he had done himself) fancied that the weakness was in him, with his presence, would grow wisdom. And so, like a creature of his own making, he liked him more and more. And thus gave he him first the office of principal herdman. And thus lastly did he put his life into his hands—although he grounded upon a great error; for his quality was not to make men, but to use men according as men were, no more than an ass will be taught to manage, a horse to hunt, or a hound to bear a saddle, but each to be used according to the force of his own nature.

But Dametas, as I said, suddenly awaked, remembering the duke's commandment, and glad he might use his authority in chiding, came swearing to the place where Cleophila was, with a voice like him that plays Hercules[3] in a play and, God knows, never had Hercules' fancy in his head. The first word he spake, after his railing oaths, was "Am not I Dametas? Why, am not I Dametas?"

These words made Cleophila lift up her eyes upon him, and seeing what manner of man he was, the height of her thoughts would not suffer her to yield any answer to so base a creature; but casting again down her eyes, leaning upon the ground, and putting her cheek in the palm of her hand, fetched a great sigh, as if she had answered him, "my head is troubled with greater matters." Which Dametas (as all persons witnesses of their own unworthiness are apt to think they are contemned[4]) took in so heinous a chafe that, standing upon his tiptoes, and staring as if he would have had a mote[5] pulled out of his eye, "Why," said he, "thou woman or boy, or both, or whatsoever thou be, I tell thee, here is no place for thee; get thee gone, I tell thee, it is the duke's pleasure. I tell thee, it is master Dametas's pleasure."

8. Saturn: god of agriculture, remarkable for his ugliness; Venus: goddess of love (and not at all chaste); Pan: god of shepherds and flocks, whose lower body is that of a goat; Juno: goddess of marriage, Jupiter's Queen, and notoriously given to jealousy; Iris: messenger of the gods, identified as a rainbow and thus subject to change or not "fast," i.e., steadfast; Cupid: the blind god of love; Vulcan: the lame god of fire and metalworking; Momus: the god of ridicule and criticism; hence not one who exhibits grace or overlooks the faults of others.
9. Orange.
1. Tortoise shell.
2. Agricultural.
3. Legendary hero known for his prodigious feats of strength and daring.
4. Scorned.
5. Speck of dust.

Cleophila could not choose but smile at him, and yet, taking herself with the manner, spake these words to herself:

"O spirit," said she, "of mine, how canst thou receive any mirth in the midst of thine agonies? And thou, mirth, how darest thou enter into a mind so grown of late thy professed enemy?"

"Thy spirit," said Dametas, "dost thou think me a spirit? I tell thee I am the duke's officer, and have the charge of him and his daughters."

"O pearl," said sobbing Cleophila, "that so vile an oyster should keep thee!"

"By the combcase of Diana!" sware Dametas, "this woman is mad; oysters and pearls; dost thou think I will buy oysters? I tell thee, get thee packing, or else I must needs be offended."

"O sun," said Cleophila, "how long shall this cloud live to darken thee, and the poor creatures that live only by thee be deprived of thee?"

These speeches to herself put Dametas out of all patience; so that, hitting her upon the breast with the blunt end of his bill, "Maid Marian,"[6] said he, "am not I a personage to be answered?"

But Cleophila no sooner felt the blow but that, the fire sparkling out of her eyes, and rising up with a right Pyrocles countenance in a Cleophila face, "Vile creature," said she, laying her hand upon her sword, "force me not to defile this sword in thy base blood!"

Dametas, that from his childhood had ever feared the blade of a sword, ran back backwards, with his hands above his head, at least twenty paces, gaping and staring with the very countenance of those clownish churls that by Latona's[7] prayer were turned into frogs. At length staying, he came a little nearer her again, but still without the compass of blows, holding one leg, as it were, ready to run away; and then fell to scolding and railing, swearing it was but a little bashfulness in him that had made him go back; and that if she stayed any longer he would make her see his blood came out of the eldest shepherd's house in that country. But seeing her walk up and down without marking what he said, he went for more help to his own lodge where, knocking a good while, at length he cried to his wife Miso that in a whore's name she should come out to him. But instead of that, he might hear a hollow rotten voice that bid him let her alone, like a knave as he was, for she was busy about my lady Pamela. This dashed poor Dametas more than anything, for old acquaintance had taught him to fear that place; and therefore, calling with a more pitiful voice to his daughter, he might see a face look out of a window, enough to have made any blind man in love. It was mistress Mopsa that, instead of answer, asked him whether he were mad to forget his duty to her mother. Dametas shrunk down his shoulders, like the poor ass that lays down his ears when he must needs yield to the burden; and yet his tongue, the valiantest part of him, could not forbear to say these words: "Here is foreign wars abroad, and uncivil wars at home—and all with women. Now," said he, "the black jaundice and the red flix[8] take all the warbled kind of you!"

And with this prayer, he went to the other lodge where the duke lay at that time sleeping, as it was in the heat of the day. And there he whistled, and stamped, and knocked, crying "Ho! my liege!" with such faces as might well show what a deformity a passion can bring a man unto when it is not governed with reason; till at length the

---

6. The companion of Robin Hood, legendary outlaw of medieval England.
7. The goddess and daughter of the Titans, primeval gods in the Greek pantheon, who turned into frogs the fools who insulted her.
8. Dametas wishes that all warbling or babbling women would sicken with jaundice (darkening the skin) or severe (bloody) dysentery.

fair Philoclea came down in such loose apparel as was enough to have bound any man's fancies, and with a sweet look asking him what he would have. Dametas, without any reverence, commanded her in the duke's name she should tell the duke he was to speak with the duke, for he forsooth[9] had things to tell the duke that pertained to the duke's service. She answered him he should be obeyed, since such was the fortune of her and her sister. And so went she to tell her father of Dametas's being there, leaving him chafing at the door and whetting his bill, swearing if he met her again neither she nor the tallest woman in the parish should make him run away any more.

But the duke, understanding by his jewel Philoclea that something there was which greatly troubled Dametas's conscience, came presently down unto him to know the matter; where he found Dametas, talking to himself, and making faces like an ape that had newly taken a purgation,[1] pale, shaking, and foaming at the mouth. And a great while it was before the duke could get any word of him. At length, putting his leg before him (which was the manner of his curtsy), he told the duke that, saving the reverence of his duty, he should keep himself from thenceforward, he would take no more charge of him. The duke, accustomed to take all well at his hands, did but laugh to see his rage, and, stroking his head, desired him of fellowship to let him know the matter.

"I tell you," saith Dametas, "it is not for me to be an officer without I may be obeyed."

"But what troubles thee, my good Dametas?" said the duke.

"I tell you," said Dametas, "I have been a man in my days, whatsoever I be now."

"And reason," answered the duke, "but let me know that I may redress thy wrongs."

"Nay," says Dametas, "no wrongs neither. But thus falls out the case, my liege; I met with such a mankind creature yonder, with her sword by her hip, and with such a visage as, if it had not been for me and this bill, God save it, she had come hither and killed you and all your house."

"What, strike a woman!" said the duke.

"Indeed," said Dametas, "I made her but a little weep, and after I had pity of her."

"It was well and wisely done," said the duke, "but I pray thee show me her."

"I pray you," said Dametas, "first call for more company to hold me from hurting her; for my stomach riseth against her."

"Let me but see the place," said the duke, "and then you shall know whether my words or your bill be the better weapon."

Dametas went stalking on before the duke as if he had been afraid to wake his child; and then, pointing with his bill towards her, was not hasty to make any nearer approaches. But the duke no sooner saw Cleophila but that he remained amazed at the goodliness of her stature and the stateliness of her march (for at that time she was walking with a countenance well setting forth an extreme distraction of her mind), and, as he came nearer her, at the excellent perfection of her beauty; insomuch that, forgetting any anger he conceived in Dametas's behalf, and doing reverence to her, as to a lady in whom he saw much worthy of great respect, "Fair lady," said he "it is nothing strange that such a solitary place as this should receive solitary persons; but much do I marvel how such a beauty as yours is could be suffered to be thus alone."

She, looking with a grave majesty upon him, as if she found in herself cause why she should be reverenced, "They are never alone," said she, "that are accompanied with noble thoughts."

---

9. Truly.   1. Emetic.

"But those thoughts," said the duke (replying for the delight he had to speak further with her), "cannot in this your loneliness neither warrant you from suspicion in others nor defend you from melancholy in yourself."

Cleophila, looking upon him as though he pressed her further than needed, "I seek no better warrant," said she, "than mine own conscience, nor no greater pleasure than mine own contentation."[2]

"Yet virtue seeks to satisfy others," said Basilius.

"Those that be good," answered Cleophila, "and they will be satisfied as long as they see no evil."

"Yet will the best in this country," said the duke, "suspect[3] so excellent a beauty, being so weakly guarded."

"Then are the best but stark naught," answered Cleophila, "for open suspecting others comes of secret condemning themselves. But in my country," said she, continuing her speech with a brave vehemency, "whose manners I am in all places to maintain and reverence, the general goodness which is nourished in our hearts makes everyone think that strength of virtue in another whereof they find the assured foundation in themselves."

But Basilius, who began to feel the sparkles of those flames which shortly after burned all other thoughts out of his heart, felt such a music, as he thought, in her voice, and such an eye-pleasing in her face, that he thought his retiring into this solitary place was well employed if it had been only to have met with such a guest. And therefore, desirous to enter into nearer points with her, "Excellent lady," said he, "you praise so greatly, and yet so wisely, your country that I must needs desire to know what the nest is out of which such birds do fly."

"You must first deserve that knowledge," said she, "before you obtain it."

"And by what means," said Basilius, "shall I deserve to know your estate?"

"By letting me first know yours," answered she.

"To obey you," said he, "I will do it; although it were so much more reason yours should be known first, as you do deserve in all points to be preferred. Know you, fair lady," said he, "that my name is Basilius, unworthy duke of this country; the rest, either fame hath already brought to your ears, or, if it please you to make this place happy by your presence, at more leisure you shall understand of me."

Cleophila (who had from the beginning suspected it should be he, but would not seem she did so, to keep her majesty the better), making some reverence unto him, "Mighty prince," said she, "let my not knowing of you serve for the excuse of my boldness, and the little reverence I do you, impute it to the manner of my country, which is the invincible land of the Amazons, myself niece to Senicia, queen thereof, lineally descended of the famous Penthesilea,[4] slain before Troy by the bloody hand of Pyrrhus. I, having in this my youth determined to make the world see the Amazons' excellencies, as well in private as in public virtues, have passed many dangerous adventures in divers countries, till the unmerciful sea deprived me of all my company; so that shipwrack brought me to this realm, and uncertain wandering guided me to this place."

Whoever saw a man to whom a beloved child long lost did, unlooked for, return might easily figure unto his fancy the very fashion of Basilius's countenance—so far had love become his master. And so had this young siren[5] charmed his old ears, insomuch that, with more vehement importunancy than any greedy host would use to

---

2. Contentment.
3. Mistrust.
4. An Amazon killed by Phyrrus or Neoptolemus, son of

Achilles, in the Trojan War.
5. A mythical sea-nymph or mermaid whose singing enchanted sailors.

well acquainted passengers, he fell to entreat her abode there for some time. She, although nothing could come fitter to the very point of her desire, yet had she already learned that womanish quality to counterfeit backwardness in that she most wished; so that he, desirous to prove whether intercession coming out of fitter mouths might better prevail, called to Dametas, and commanded him to bring forth his wife and two daughters—three ladies, although of diverse, yet all of excellent beauty: the duchess Gynecia, in grave matronlike attire, with a countenance and behaviour far unlike to fall into those inconveniences she afterwards tasted of. The fair Pamela, whose noble heart had long disdained to find the trust of her virtue reposed in the hands of a shepherd, had yet, to show an obedience, taken on a shepherdish apparel, which was of russet velvet, cut after their fashion, with a straight body, open breasted, the nether part full of pleats, with wide open sleeves, hanging down very low; her hair at the full length, only wound about with gold lace—by the comparison to show how far her hair did excel in colour; betwixt her breasts, which sweetly rase up like two fair mountainets in the pleasant vale of Tempe, there hanged down a jewel which she had devised as a picture of her own estate.[6] It was a perfect white lamb tied at a stake with a great number of chains, as it had been feared lest the silly creature should do some great harm; neither had she added any word unto it, but even took silence as the word of the poor lamb, showing such humbleness as not to use her own voice for complaint of her misery.

But when the ornament of the earth, young Philoclea, appeared in her nymphlike apparel, so near nakedness as one might well discern part of her perfections, and yet so apparelled as did show she kept the best store of her beauties to herself; her excellent fair hair drawn up into a net made only of itself (a net indeed to have caught the wildest disposition); her body covered with a light taffeta garment, so cut as the wrought smock came through it in many places (enough to have made a very restrained imagination have thought what was under it); with the sweet cast of her black eye which seemed to make a contention whether that in perfect blackness, or her skin in perfect whiteness, were the most excellent; then, I say, the very clouds seemed to give place to make the heaven more fair. At least, the clouds of Cleophila's thoughts quite vanished, and so was her brain fixed withal that her sight seemed more forcible and clear than ever before or since she found it, with such strange delight unto her (for still, fair ladies, you remember that I use the she-title to Pyrocles, since so he would have it) that she stood like a well wrought image, with show of life, but without all exercise of life, so forcibly had love transferred all her spirits into the present contemplation of the lovely Philoclea. And so had it been like enough she would have stayed long time but that by chance Gynecia stepped betwixt her sight and the lady Philoclea, and the change of the object made her recover her senses; so that she could with good manner receive the salutation of the duchess and the princess Pamela, doing them yet no further reverence than one princess useth to another. But when she came to the lady Philoclea, she fell down on her knees, taking by force her fair hands and kissing them with great show of extreme affection, and with a bowed-down countenance began this speech unto her: "Divine lady," said she, "let not the world nor these great princes marvel to see me contrary to my manner do this especial honour unto you, since all, both men and women, owe this homage to the perfection of your beauty."

---

6. Situation.

Philoclea's blushing cheeks quickly witnessed how much she was abashed to see this singularity used to herself; and therefore, causing Cleophila to rise, "Noble lady," said she, "it is no marvel to see your judgment much mistaken in my beauty, since you begin with so great an error as to do more honor unto me than to them to whom I myself owe all service."

"Rather," answered Cleophila, "that shows the power of your beauty which hath forced me to fall into such an error, if it were an error."

"You are so acquainted," said Philoclea, sweetly smiling, "with your own beauty that it makes you easily fall into the discourse of beauty."

"Beauty in me!" said Cleophila, deeply sighing, "Alas! if there be any, it is in mine eyes, which your happy presence hath imparted unto them."

Basilius was even transported with delight to hear these speeches betwixt his well beloved daughter and his better loved lady; and so made a sign to Philoclea that she should entreat her to remain with them; which she willingly obeyed, for already she conceived delight in Cleophila's presence, and therefore said unto her: "It is a great happiness, I must confess, to be praised of them that are themselves most praiseworthy. And well I find you are an invincible Amazon, since you will overcome in a wrong matter. But if my beauty be anything," said she, "then let it obtain thus much of you: that you will remain in this company some time, to ease your own travail, and our solitariness."

"First let me die," said Cleophila, "before any word spoken by such a mouth should come in vain. I yield wholly to your commandment, fearing nothing but that you command that which may be troublesome to yourself."

Thus, with some other words of entertaining, her staying was concluded, to the unspeakable joy of the duke—although, perchance, with some little envy in the other ladies, to see young Philoclea's beauty so greatly advanced. You ladies know best whether sometimes you feel impression of that passion; for my part, I would hardly think that the affection of a mother and the noble mind of Pamela could be overthrown with so base a thing as envy is—especially Pamela, to whom fortune had already framed another, who no less was dedicated to her excellencies than Cleophila was to Philoclea's perfections, as you shall shortly hear. For the duke going into the lodge with his wife and daughters, Cleophila desired them to excuse her for a while, for that she had thoughts to pass over with herself; and that shortly after she would come in to them—indeed meaning to find her friend Musidorus, and to glory with him of the happiness of her choice. But when she looked in the grove and could nowhere find him, marveling something at it, she gave herself to feed those sweet thoughts which now had the full possession of her heart, sometimes thinking how far Philoclea herself passed her picture, sometimes fore-imagining with herself how happy she should be if she could obtain her desires; till, having spent thus an hour or two, she might perceive afar off one coming towards her, in the apparel of a shepherd, with his arms hanging down, going a kind of languishing pace, with his eyes sometimes cast up to heaven as though his fancies strave to mount up higher, sometimes thrown down to the ground as if the earth could not bear the burden of his pains. At length she heard him, with a lamentable tune, sing these few verses:

> Come shepherd's weeds,° become your master's mind: *garments*
> Yield outward show, what inward change he tries:
> Nor be abashed, since such a guest you find,
> Whose strongest hope in your weak comfort lies.

> Come shepherd's weeds, attend my woeful cries:
> Disuse yourselves from sweet Menalcas'° voice: *a shepherd*
> For other be those tunes which sorrow ties
> From those clear notes which freely may rejoice.
>   Then pour out plaint,° and in one word say this: *complaint*
>   Helpless his plaint who spoils° himself of bliss.   *robs*

And having ended, she might see him strike himself upon the breast, uttering these words: "O miserable wretch, whither do thy destinies guide thee?"

It seemed to Cleophila that she knew the voice; and therefore drawing nearer, that her sight might receive a perfect discerning, she saw plainly, to her great amazement, it was her dear friend Musidorus. And now having named him, methinks it reason I should tell you what chance brought him to this change. I left him lately, if you remember, fair ladies, in the grove by the two lodges, there to see what should befall to his dear new-transformed friend. There heard he all the complaints (not without great compassion) that his friend made to himself; and there (not without some laughter) did he see what passed betwixt him and Dametas, and how stately he played the part of Cleophila at the duke's first coming. And falling into many kind fancies towards him, sometimes pitying his case, sometimes praising his behavior, he would often say to himself: "O sweet Pyrocles, how art thou bewitched! Where is thy virtue? Where is the use of thy reason? Much am I inferior to thee in all the powers of the mind; and yet know I that all the heavens cannot bring me to such a thraldom."

Scarcely, think I, he had spoken those words but that the duchess, being sent for to entertain Cleophila, came out with her two daughters; where the beams of the princess Pamela's beauty had no sooner stricken into his eyes but that he was wounded with more sudden violence of love than ever Pyrocles was. Whether indeed it were that this strange power would be bravely revenged of him for the bitter words he had used, or that his very resisting made the wound the crueler (as we see the harquebus[7] doth most endamage the stiffest metal), or rather that the continual healthfulness of his mind made this sudden ill the more incurable (as the soundest bodies, once infected, are most mortally endangered); but howsoever the cause was, such was the effect that, not being able to bear the vehement pain, he ran away through the grove, like a madman, hoping perchance (as the fever-sick folks do) that the change of places might ease his grief. But therein was his luck indeed better than his providence; for he had not gone a little but that he met with a shepherd (according to his estate, handsomely appareled) who was as then going to meet with other shepherds (as upon certain days they had accustomed) to do exercises of activity and to play new-invented eclogues before the duke. Which, when Musidorus had learned of him (for love is full of desire, and desire is always inquisitive), it came straight into his head that there were no better way for him to come by the often enjoying of the princess Pamela's sight than to take the apparel of this shepherd upon him. Which he quickly did, giving him his own much richer; and withal, lest the matter by him might be discovered, hired him to go without stay into Thessalia, writing two or three words by him, in a pair of tables[8] well closed up, to a servant of his that he should, upon the receipt, arrest and keep him in good order till he heard his further pleasure. Yet before Menalcas departed (for so was his name), he learned of him both his own estate and the manner of their pastimes and eclogues. And thus furnished, he

---

7. Gun.   8. Writing tablets.

returned again to the place where his heart was pledged, so oppressed in mind that it seemed to him his legs were uneath[9] able to bear him. Which grief he uttered in the doleful song I told you of before, and was cause that his dear he-she friend, Cleophila, came unto him; who, when she was assured it was he (with wonted entireness embracing him), demanded of him what sudden thing had thus suddenly changed him; whether the goddess of those woods had such a power to transform everybody; or whether, indeed, as he had always in all enterprises most faithfully accompanied her, so he would continue to match her in this new metamorphosis. But Musidorus, looking dolefully upon her, wringing his hands, and pouring out abundance of tears, began to recount unto her all this I have already told you, but with such passionate dilating of it that, for my part, I have not a feeling insight enough into the matter to be able lively to express it. Sufficeth it that whatsoever a possessed heart with a good tongue, to a dear friend, could utter was at that time largely set forth. The perfect friendship Cleophila bare him, and the great pity she (by good experience) had of his case could not keep her from smiling at him, remembering how vehemently he had cried out against the folly of lovers; so that she thought good a little to punish him, playing with him in this manner: "Why, how now, dear cousin," said she, "you that were even now so high in the pulpit against love, are you now become so mean an auditor?[1] Remember that love is a passion, and that a worthy man's reason must ever have the masterhood."

"I recant, I recant!" cried Musidorus, and withal falling down prostrate, "O thou celestial, or infernal, spirit of love," said he, "or what other heavenly or hellish title thou list to have, for both those effects I find in myself, have compassion of me, and let thy glory be as great in pardoning them that be submitted to thee as in conquering those that were rebellious!"

"No, no!" said Cleophila, yet further to urge him, "I see you well enough; you make but an interlude of my mishaps, and do but counterfeit thus to make me see the deformity of my passions. But take heed," said she, "cousin, that this jest do not one day turn into earnest."

"Now I beseech thee," said Musidorus, taking her fast by the hand, "even by the truth of our friendship (of which, if I be not altogether an unhappy man, thou hast some remembrance), and by those sacred flames (which I know have likewise nearly touched thee), make no jest of that which hath so earnestly pierced me through; nor let that be light to thee which is to me so burdenous that I am not able to bear it."

Musidorus did so lively deliver out his inward griefs that Cleophila's friendly heart felt a great impression of pity withal—as certainly all persons that find themselves afflicted easily fall to compassion of them who taste of like misery, partly led by the common course of humanity, but principally because, under the image of them, they lament their own mishaps; and so the complaints the others make seem to touch the right tune of their own woes. Which did mutually work so in these two young princes that, looking ruefully one upon the other, they made their speech a great while nothing but doleful sighs. Yet sometimes they would yield out suchlike lamentations: "Alas! What further evil hath fortune reserved for us, or what shall be the end of this our tragical pilgrimage? Shipwrecks, daily dangers, absence from our country, have at length brought forth this captiving of us within ourselves which hath transformed the one in sex, and the other in state, as much as the uttermost work of changeable fortune can be extended unto."

---

9. Scarcely.   1. Listener.

And then would they kiss one another, vowing to continue partakers of all either good or evil fortune. And thus perchance would they have forgotten themselves some longer time, but that Basilius, whose heart was now set on fire with his new mistress, finding her absence long, sent out Dametas to her to know if she would command anything, and to invite her to go with his wife and daughters to a fair meadow thereby to see the sports and hear the eclogues of his country shepherds. Dametas came out with two or three swords about him, his hedging bill on his neck, and a chopping knife under his girdle,[2] armed only behind, as fearing most the blows that might fall upon the reins of his back; for, indeed, Cleophila had put such a sudden fear into his head that from thenceforth he was resolved never to come out any more ill provided. Yet had his blunt brains perceived some favor the duke bare to this new-come lady; and so framing himself thereunto (as without doubt the most servile flattery is most easy to be lodged in the most gross capacity; for their ordinary conceit draws a yielding to their greatness, and then have they not wit to discern right degrees of goodness),[3] he no sooner saw her but, with head and arms, he laid his reverence before her, enough to have made a man forswear all courtesy. And then, in the duke's name, did he require her she would take pains to see their pastorals (for so their sports were termed); but when he spied Musidorus standing by her (for his eye had been placed all this while upon her), not knowing him, he would fain have persuaded himself to have been angry but that he durst not. Yet, muttering and champing as though his cud troubled him, he gave occasion to Musidorus to come nearer him, and to feign a tale of his own life: that he was a younger brother of the shepherd Menalcas, by name Dorus,[4] sent by his father in his tender age to Athens, there to learn some cunning more than ordinary for to excel his fellow shepherds in their eclogues; and that his brother Menalcas, lately gone thither to fetch him home, was deceased; where, upon his deathbed, he had charged him to seek the service of Dametas, and to be wholly and only guided by his counsel, as one in whose judgement and integrity the duke had singular confidence; for token whereof he gave him a sum of gold in ready coin which Menalcas had bequeathed him upon condition he should receive this poor Dorus into his service, that his mind and manners might grow the better by his daily example. Dametas no sooner saw the gold but that his heart was presently infected with the self-conceit he took of it; which, being helped with the tickling of Musidorus's praises, so turned the brain of good Dametas that he became slave to that which he that would be his servant bestowed on him, and gave in himself an example for ever that the fool can never be honest since, not being able to balance what points virtue stands upon, every present occasion catches his senses, and his senses are masters of his silly mind. Yet, for countenance's sake, he seemed very squeamish, in respect he had the charge of the princess Pamela, to accept any new servant into his house. But such was the secret operation of the gold, helped with the persuasions of the Amazon Cleophila, who said it was pity so proper a young man should be anywhere else than with so good a master, that in the end he agreed to receive him for his servant, so as that day in their pastorals he proved himself active in mind and body.

And thus went they to the lodge, with greater joy to Musidorus (now only poor shepherd Dorus) than all his life before had ever brought forth unto him—so manifest it is that the greatest point outward things can bring a man unto is the content-

2. Belt.
3. Those who, like Dametas, have poor powers of reason flatter the great, for their ordinary powers of conception

make them inclined to yield to the great, and they do not have the intelligence to see any degrees of goodness.
4. "Gift."

ment of the mind, which once obtained, no state is miserable; and without that, no prince's seat restful. There found they Gynecia, with her two daughters, ready to go to the meadow; whither also they went. For, as for Basilius, he desired to stay behind them to debate a little with himself of this new guest that had entered and possessed his brains. There, it is said, the poor old Basilius, now alone (for, as I said, the rest were gone to see the pastorals), had a sufficient eclogue in his own head betwixt honor, with the long experience he had had of the world, on the one side, and this new assault of Cleophila's beauty on the other side. There hard by the lodge walked he, carrying this unquiet contention about him. But passion ere long had gotten the absolute masterhood, bringing with it the show of present pleasure, fortified with the authority of a prince whose power might easily satisfy his will against the far-fet[5] (though true) reasons of the spirit—which, in a man not trained in the way of virtue, have but slender working. So that ere long he utterly gave himself over to the longing desire to enjoy Cleophila, which finding an old broken vessel of him, had the more power in him than, perchance, it would have had in a younger man. And so, as all vice is foolish, it wrought in him the more absurd follies. But thus, as I say, in a number of intermixed imaginations, he stayed solitary by the lodge, waiting for the return of his company from the pastorals, some good space of time, till he was suddenly stirred out of his deep muses[6] by the hasty and fearful running unto him of most part of the shepherds who came flying from the pastoral sports, crying to one another to stay and save the duchess and young ladies. But even whilst they cried so they ran away as fast as they could; so that the one tumbled over the other, each one showing he would be glad his fellow should do valiantly, but his own heart served him not. The duke, amazed to see such extreme shows of fear, asked the matter of them. But fear had so possessed their inward parts that their breath would not serve to tell it him, but after such a broken manner that I think it best not to trouble you, fair ladies, with their panting speeches; but to make a full declaration of it myself. And thus it was: Gynecia, with her two daughters, Cleophila, the shepherds Dorus and Dametas, being parted from the duke whom they left solitary at the lodge, came into the fair meadow appointed for their shepherdish pastimes. It was, indeed, a place of great delight, for through the midst of it there ran a sweet brook which did both hold the eye open with her beautiful streams and close the eye with the sweet purling[7] noise it made upon the pebble-stones it ran over; the meadow itself yielding so liberally all sorts of flowers that it seemed to nourish a contention betwixt the colour and the smell whether in his kind were the more delightful. Round about the meadow, as if it had been to enclose a theater, grew all such sorts of trees as either excellency of fruit, stateliness of growth, continual greenness, or poetical fancies have made at any time famous. In most part of which trees there had been framed by art such pleasant arbors that it became a gallery aloft, from one tree to the other, almost round about, which below yielded a perfect shadow, in those hot countries counted a great pleasure.

In this place, under one of the trees, the ladies sat down, inquiring many questions of young Dorus (now newly perceived of them), whilst the other shepherds made them ready to the pastimes. Dorus, keeping his eye still upon the princess Pamela, answered with such a trembling voice and abashed countenance, and oftentimes so far from the matter, that it was some sport to the ladies, thinking it had been want of education which made him so discountenanced with unwonted presence. But Cleophila (that saw in him the glass[8] of her own misery), taking the fair hand of

5. Far-fetched.
6. Musings.

7. Murmurings.
8. Mirror.

Philoclea, and with more than womanish ardency kissing it, began to say these words: "O love, since thou art so changeable in men's estates, how art thou so constant in their torments?"—when suddenly there came out of the wood a monstrous lion, with a she-bear of little less fierceness, which, having been hunted in forests far off, had by chance come to this place where such beasts had never before been seen. Which, when the shepherds saw, like silly wretches that think all evil is ever next themselves, ran away in such sort as I told you till they came to the duke's presence. There might one have seen at one instant all sorts of passions lively painted out in the young lovers' faces—an extremity of love shining in their eyes; fear for their mistresses; assured hope in their own virtue; anger against the beasts; joy that occasion employed their service; sorrow to see their ladies in agony. For, indeed, the sweet Philoclea no sooner espied the ravenous lion but that, opening her arms, she fell so right upon the breast of Cleophila, sitting by her, that their faces at unawares closed together, which so transported all whatsoever Cleophila was that she gave leisure to the lion to come very near them before she rid herself from the dear arms of Philoclea. But necessity, the only overruler of affections, did force her then gently to unfold herself from those sweet embracements; and so drawing her sword, waited the present assault of the lion who, seeing Philoclea fly away, suddenly turned after her. For, as soon as she had risen up with Cleophila, she ran as fast as her delicate legs would carry her towards the lodge after the fugitive shepherds. But Cleophila, seeing how greedily the lion went after the prey she herself so much desired, it seemed all her spirits were kindled with an unwonted fire; so that, equaling the lion in swiftness, she overtook him as he was ready to have seized himself of his beautiful chase, and disdainfully saying "are you become my competitor?"—strake him so great a blow upon the shoulder that she almost cleaved him asunder. Yet the valiant beast turned withal so far upon the weapon, that with his paw he did hurt a little the left shoulder of Cleophila; and mortal it would have been had not the death wound Cleophila, with a new thrust, gave unto him taken away the effect of his force. But therewithal he fell down, and gave Cleophila leisure to take off his head to carry it for a present to her lady Philoclea, who all this while, not knowing what was done behind her, kept on her course, as Arethusa when she ran from Alpheus,[9] her light nymphlike apparel being carried up with the wind, that much of those beauties she would at another time have willingly hidden were presented to the eye of the twice-wounded Cleophila; which made Cleophila not follow her over hastily lest she should too soon deprive herself of that pleasure. But, carrying the lion's head in her hand, did not fully overtake her till they came both into the presence of Basilius, at that time examining the shepherds of what was passed, and preparing himself to come to their succor. Neither were they long there but that Gynecia came to them; whose look had all this while been upon the combat, eyeing so fixedly Cleophila's manner of fighting that no fear did prevail over her but, as soon as Cleophila had cut off his head, and ran after Philoclea, she could not find in her heart but to run likewise after Cleophila. So that it was a new sight fortune had prepared to those woods, to see these three great personages thus run one after the other, each carried away with the violence of an inward evil: the sweet Philoclea, with such fear that she thought she was still in the lion's mouth; Cleophila, with a painful delight she had to see without hope of enjoying; Gynecia, not so much with the love she bare to her best beloved daughter as with a new wonderful passionate love had possessed her heart of the goodly Cleophi-

---

9. The nymph Arethusa, pursued by the river-god Alpheus, was metamorphosed into a fountain.

la. For so the truth is that, at the first sight she had of Cleophila, her heart gave her she was a man thus for some strange cause disguised, which now this combat did in effect assure her of, because she measured the possibility of all women's hearts out of her own. And this doubt framed in her a desire to know, and desire to know brought forth shortly such longing to enjoy that it reduced her whole mind to an extreme and unfortunate slavery—pitifully, truly, considering her beauty and estate; but for a perfect mark of the triumph of love who could in one moment overthrow the heart of a wise lady, so that neither honor long maintained, nor love of husband and children, could withstand it. But of that you shall after hear; for now, they being come before the duke, and the fair Philoclea scarcely then stayed from her fear, Cleophila, kneeling down, presented the head of the lion unto her with these words: "Only lady," said she, "here see you the punishment of that unnatural beast which, contrary to his own kind, would have wronged prince's blood; neither were his eyes vanquished with the duty all eyes bear to your beauty."

"Happy am I and my beauty both," answered the fair Philoclea (the blood coming again to her cheeks, pale before for fear), "that you, excellent Amazon, were there to teach him good manners."

"And even thank that beauty," said Cleophila, "which forceth all noble swords to be ready to serve it."

Having finished these words, the lady Philoclea perceived the blood that ran abundantly down upon Cleophila's shoulder; so that starting aside, with a countenance full of sweet pity, "Alas," said she, "now perceive I my good hap[1] is waited on with great misfortune, since my safety is wrought with the danger of a much more worthy person."

"Noble lady," answered she, "if your inward eyes could discern the wounds of my soul, you should have a plentifuller cause to exercise your compassion."

But it was sport to see how in one instant both Basilius and Gynecia (like a father and mother to a beloved child) came running to see the wound of Cleophila; into what rages Basilius grew, and what tears Gynecia spent—for so it seemed that love had purposed to make in those solitary woods a perfect demonstration of his unresistible force, to show that no desert place can avoid his dart. He must fly from himself that will shun his evil. But so wonderful and in effect incredible was the passion which reigned as well in Gynecia as Basilius (and all for the poor Cleophila, dedicated another way) that it seems to myself I use not words enough to make you see how they could in one moment be so overtaken. But you, worthy ladies, that have at any time feelingly known what it means, will easily believe the possibility of it. Let the ignorant sort of people give credit to them that have passed the doleful passage, and daily find that quickly is the infection gotten which in long time is hardly cured. Basilius sometimes would kiss her forehead, blessing the destinies that had joined such beauty and valour together. Gynecia would kiss her more boldly, by the liberty of her womanish show, although her heart were set of nothing less; for already was she fallen into a jealous envy against her daughter Philoclea, because she found Cleophila showed such extraordinary dutiful favor unto her; and even that settled her opinion the more of her manhood. And this doubtful jealousy served as a bellows to kindle the violent coals of her passion. But as the over kind nurse may sometimes with kissing forget to give the child suck so had they, with too much kindness, unkindly forgotten the wound of Cleophila, had not Philoclea, whose heart had not

1. Fortune.

yet gone beyond the limits of a right goodwill, advised herself, and desired her mother to help her to dress the wound of Cleophila. For both those great ladies were excellently seen in that part of surgery—an art in that age greatly esteemed because it served as a minister to virtuous courage, which in those worthy days was even by ladies more beloved than any outward beauty. So to the great comfort of Cleophila, more to feel the delicate hands of Philoclea than for the care she had of her wound, these two ladies had quickly dressed it, applying so precious a balm as all the heat and pain was presently assuaged, with apparent hope of soon amendment. In which doing, I know not whether Gynecia took some greater conjectures of Cleophila's sex. But even then, and not before, did Cleophila remember herself of her dear friend Musidorus; for having only had care of the excellent Philoclea, she never missed neither her friend nor the princess Pamela—not so much to be marveled at in her, since both the duke and duchess had forgotten their daughter, so were all their thoughts plunged in one place. Besides Cleophila had not seen any danger was like to fall unto him, for her eye had been still fixed upon Philoclea, and that made her the more careless. But now, with a kind of rising in her heart, lest some evil should be fallen to her chosen friend, she hastily asked what was become of the princess Pamela, with the two shepherds, Dametas and Dorus. And then the duke and Gynecia remembered their forgetfulness, and with great astonishment made like[2] inquiry for her. But of all the company of the shepherds (so had the lion's sight put them from themselves), there was but one could say anything of her; and all he said was this: that as he ran away he might perceive a great bear run directly towards her. Cleophila (whose courage was always ready without deliberation) took up the sword lying by her, with mind to bestow her life for the succor or revenge of her Musidorus and the gracious Pamela. But as she had run two or three steps, they might all see Pamela coming betwixt Dametas and Dorus, Pamela having in her hand the paw of the bear which the shepherd Dorus had newly presented unto her, desiring her to keep it, as of such a beast which, though she was to be punished for her over great cruelty, yet was her wit to be esteemed, since she could make so sweet a choice. Dametas for his part came piping and dancing, the merriest man of a parish; but when he came so near as he might be heard of the duke, he sang this song for joy of their success:

> Now thanked be the great god Pan
> That thus preserves my loved life:
> Thanked be I that keep a man
> Who ended hath this fearful strife:
>   So if my man must praises have,
>   What then must I that keep the knave?
>
> For as the moon the eye doth please
> With gentle beams not hurting sight,
> Yet hath sir sun the greatest praise,
> Because from him doth come her light:
>   So if my man must praises have,
>   What then must I that keep the knave?

It were a very superfluous thing to tell you how glad each party was of the happy returning from these dangers, and doubt you not, fair ladies, there wanted no questioning how things had passed; but because I will have the thanks myself, it shall be I

---

2. Similar.

you shall hear it of. And thus the ancient records of Arcadia say it fell out: the lion's presence had no sooner driven away the heartless shepherds, and followed, as I told you, the excellent Philoclea, but that there came out of the same woods a monstrous she-bear which, fearing to deal with the lion's prey, came furiously towards the princess Pamela who, whether it were she had heard that such was the best refuge against that beast, or that fear (as it fell out most likely) brought forth the effects of wisdom, she no sooner saw the bear coming towards her but she fell down flat upon her face. Which when the prince Musidorus saw (whom, because such was his pleasure, I am bold to call the shepherd Dorus), with a true resolved magnanimity, although he had no other weapon but a great shepherd's knife, he leaped before the head of his dear lady, and saying these words unto her, "Receive here the sacrifice of that heart which is only vowed to your service," attended with a quiet courage the coming of the bear which, according to the manner of that beast's fight, especially against a man that resists them, rase up upon her hinder feet, so to take him in her ugly paws. But, as she was ready to give him a mortal³ embracement, the shepherd Dorus, with a lusty strength and good fortune, thrust his knife so right into the heart of the beast that she fell down dead without ever being able to touch him. Which being done, he turned to his lady Pamela (at that time in a swoon with extremity of fear), and softly taking her in his arms, he took the advantage to kiss and re-kiss her a hundred times, with such exceeding delight that he would often after say he thought the joy would have carried his life from him, had not the grief he conceived to see her in such case something diminished it. But long in that delightful agony he was not; for the lady Pamela, being come out of her swoon, opened her fair eyes, and seeing herself in the hands of this new-come shepherd, with great disdain put him from her. But when she saw the ugly bear lying hard by her, starting aside (for fear gave not reason leave to determine whether it were dead or no), she forgot her anger, and cried to Dorus to help her. Wherefore he, cutting off the forepaw of the bear, and showing unto her the bloody knife, told her she might well by this perceive that there was no heart so base, nor weapon so feeble, but that the force of her beauty was well able to enable them for the performance of great matters. She, inquiring the manner, and whether himself were hurt, gave him great thanks for his pains, with promise of reward. But being ashamed to find herself so alone with this young shepherd, looked round about if she could see anybody; and at length they both perceived the gentle Dametas, lying with his head and breast as far as he could thrust himself into a bush, drawing up his legs as close unto him as he could. For, indeed, as soon as he saw the bear coming towards him (like a man that was very apt to take pity of himself), he ran headlong into this bush, with full resolution that, at the worst hand, he would not see his own death. And when Dorus pushed him, bidding him be of good courage, it was a great while before they could persuade him that Dorus was not the bear; so that he was fain to pull him out by the heels, and show him her as dead as he could wish her—which, you may believe me, was a very joyful sight unto him. And yet, like a man of a revengeful spirit, he gave the dead body many a wound, swearing by much it was pity such beasts should be suffered in a commonwealth. And then, with as immoderate joy as before with fear (for his heart was framed never to be without a passion), he went by his fair charge, dancing, piping, and singing; till they all came to the presence of the careful company, as before I told you. Thus now this little, but noble, company united again together, the first thing was done was the

---

3. Deadly.

yielding of great thanks and praises of all sides to the virtuous Cleophila. The duke told with what a gallant grace she ran after Philoclea with the lion's head in her hand, like another Pallas with the spoils of Gorgon.[4] Gynecia sware she saw the very face of young Hercules killing the Nemean lion;[5] and all, with a grateful assent, confirmed the same praises. Only poor Dorus, though of equal desert,[6] yet not proceeding from equal estate, should have been left forgotten, had not Cleophila (partly to put by the occasion of her own excessive praises, but principally for the true remembrance she had of her professed friend), with great admiration, spoken of his hazardous act, asking afresh (as if she had never before known him) what he was, and whether he had haunted that place before, protesting that, upon her conscience, she could not think but that he came of some very noble blood—so noble a countenance he bare, and so worthy an act he had performed. This Basilius took (as the lover's heart is apt to receive all sudden sorts of impression) as though his mistress had given him a secret reprehension that he had not showed more gratefulness to the valiant Dorus. And therefore, as nimbly as he could, began forthwith to inquire of his estate, adding promise of great rewards—among the rest offering to him that, if he would exercise his valor in soldiery, he would commit some charge[7] unto him under Philanax, governor of his frontiers. But Dorus, whose ambition stretched a quite other way, having first answered (touching his estate) that he was brother to the shepherd Menalcas whom the duke had well known, and excused his going to soldiery by the unaptness he found in himself that way, told the duke that his brother, in his last testament, had commanded him to dedicate his service to Dametas; and therefore, as well for due obedience thereto as for the satisfaction of his own mind (which was wholly set upon pastoral affairs), he would think his service greatly rewarded if he might obtain by that means to live in the sight of the duke more than the rest of his fellows, and yet practise that his chosen vocation. The duke, liking well of his modest manner, charged Dametas to receive him like a son in his house, telling him, because of his tried valor, he would have him be as a guard to his daughter Pamela, to whom likewise he recommended him, sticking not to say such men were to be cherished since she was in danger of some secret misadventure.

All this while Pamela said little of him, and even as little did Philoclea of Cleophila; although everybody else filled their mouths with their praises. Whereof seeking the cause that they which were most bound said least, I note this to myself, fair ladies, that even at this time they did begin to find they themselves could not tell what kind of inclination towards them; whereof feeling a secret accusation in themselves, and in their simplicity not able to warrant it, closed up all such motion in secret, without daring scarcely to breathe out the names of them who already began to breed unwonted war in their spirits. For, indeed, fortune had framed a very stage-play of love among these few folks, making the old age of Basilius, the virtue of Gynecia, and the simplicity of Philoclea, all affected to one; but by a three-headed kind of passion: Basilius assuring himself she was, as she pretended, a young lady, but greatly despairing for his own unworthiness's sake; Gynecia hoping her judgment to be right of his disguising, but therein fearing a greater sore if already his heart were pledged to

---

4. One of three mythical monsters, with snakes for hair, who turned those who looked at them to stone; the most famous of the Gorgons was Medusa. After she was decapitated by the hero Perseus, she was flayed by Pallas, that is, Pallas Athene, the goddess of wisdom, who carried her skin about as a breastplate.

5. This lion had a skin that could not be penetrated, so Hercules choked him to death—the first of his twelve prodigious labors.

6. Merit.

7. Basilius promises that Dorus will have command of a unit of soldiers in an army led by Philanax.

her daughter. But sweet Philoclea grew shortly after of all other into worst terms; for taking her to be such as she professed, desire she did, but she knew not what; and she longed to obtain that whereof she herself could not imagine the mean, but full of unquiet imaginations rested only unhappy because she knew not her good hap. Cleophila hath (I think) said enough for herself to make you know, fair ladies, that she was not a little enchanted; and as for Dorus, a shepherd's apparel upon a duke of Thessalia will answer for him. Pamela was the only lady that would needs make open war upon herself, and obtain the victory; for, indeed, even now find she did a certain working of a new-come inclination to Dorus. But when she found perfectly in herself whither it must draw her, she did overmaster it with the consideration of his meanness. But how therein Dorus sought to satisfy her you shall after hear; for now the day being closed up in darkness the duke would fain have had Cleophila gone to rest, because of her late-received wound. But she (that found no better salve than Philoclea's presence) desired first that by torchlight they might see some of the pastorals the lion's coming had disordered. Which accordingly was done; whereof I will repeat you a few to ease you, fair ladies, of the tediousness of this long discourse.

Here ends the first book or act.

from Astrophil and Stella[1]

1

Loving in truth, and fain° in verse my love to show,   *wishing*
That she (dear she) might take some pleasure of my pain:
Pleasure might cause her read, reading might make her know,
Knowledge might pity win, and pity grace obtain,
5 I sought fit words to paint the blackest face of woe,
Studying inventions[2] fine, her wits to entertain:
Oft turning others' leaves, to see if thence would flow
Some fresh and fruitfull showers upon my sun-burned brain.
But words came halting forth, wanting Invention's stay,°   *support*
10 Invention Nature's child, fled step-dame Study's blows,
And others' feet still seemed but strangers in my way.
Thus great with child to speak, and helpless in my throes,°   *agonies*
Biting my trewand° pen, beating my self for spite,   *truant*
Fool, said my Muse to me, look in thy heart and write.

31

With how sad steps, O Moon, thou climb'st the skies,
How silently, and with how wan° a face,   *pale*
What may it be, that even in heavenly place
That busy archer° his sharp arrows tries?   *Cupid*
5 Sure if° that long with Love acquainted eyes   *surely if those*
Can judge of Love, thou feel'st a lover's case;
I read it in thy looks, thy languished grace
To me that feel the like, thy state descries.°   *reveals*
Then ev'n of fellowship, O Moon, tell me

---

1. This sonnet sequence was composed in 1582, published in 1591.
2. "Invention" was the term early modern rhetoricians used to designate the choice of a literary subject and its development as an argument, in contrast to the forms of expression, figures of thought and speech, and imagery by which that subject was conveyed. As Sidney suggests, "invention" depended on the writer's imaginative intelligence, not on his literary education.

10   Is constant Love deemed there but want of wit?
      Are Beauties there as proud as here they be?
      Do they above love to be loved, and yet
      Those lovers scorn whom that Love doth possess?
      Do they call Virtue there ungratefulness?

39

      Come sleep, O sleep, the certain knot of peace,
      The baiting° place of wit, the balm of woe,   *resting*
      The poor man's wealth, the prisoner's release,
      Th'indifferent judge between the high and low;
5   With shield of proof° shield me from out the prease°   *proven shield / throng*
      Of those fierce darts, despair at me doth throw:
      O make in me those civil wars to cease;
      I will good tribute pay if thou do so.
      Take thou of me smooth pillows, sweetest bed,
10   A chamber deaf to noise, and blind to light:
      A rosy garland, and a weary head:
      And if these things, as being thine by right,
      Move not thy heavy grace, thou shalt in me
      Livelier then elsewhere Stella's image see.

45

      Stella oft sees the very face of woe
      Painted in my beclouded stormy face:
      But cannot skill° to pity my disgrace,   *does not know how*
      Not though thereof the cause herself she know:
5   Yet hearing late a fable, which did show
      Of Lovers never known, a grievous case,°   *situation*
      Pity thereof gate° in her breast such place,   *got*
      That from that sea derived tears' spring did flow.[3]
      Alas, if Fancy drawn by imag'd° things,   *imagined*
10   Though false, yet with free scope more grace doth breed
      Than servants' wrack, where new doubts honor brings;[4]
      Then think my dear, that you in me do read
      Of Lovers' ruin some sad Tragedy:
      I am not I, pity the tale of me.

60

      When my good Angel guides me to the place,
      Where all my good I do in Stella see,
      That heav'n of joys throws only down on me
      Thundered disdains and lightnings of disgrace:
5   But when the ruggedst step of Fortune's race°   *course*
      Makes me fall from her sight, then sweetly she
      With words, wherein the Muses' treasures be,
      Shows love and pity to my absent case.[5]
      Now I wit-beaten long by hardest Fate,

3. I.e., derived from that sea [of pity], a spring of tears did
flow.
4. I.e., Fancy with free scope breeds more grace or sympathy than the actual destruction of a servant, a situation in
which a sense of honor provokes new doubts about that

person's worth.
5. I.e., when a good angel or good fortune guides the poet
to Stella, heaven throws at him only the "joys" of disdain
and disgrace. On the other hand, when he is away from
her, she shows him love and pity.

10 So dull am, that I cannot look into
    The ground of this fierce Love and lovely hate:
    Then some good body tell me how I do,
    Whose presence, absence, absence presence is;[6]
    Blist° in my curse, and cursed in my bliss.   *blessed*

71

Who will in fairest book of Nature[7] know,
How Virtue may best lodged in beauty be,
Let him but learn of Love to read in thee
Stella, those fair lines, which true goodness show.
5   There shall he find all vices overthrow,°   *overthrown*
    Not by rude force, but sweetest sovereignty
    Of reason, from whose light those night-birds fly;
    That inward sun in thine eyes shineth so.
    And not content to be Perfection's heir
10 Thyself, doest strive all minds that way to move:
    Who mark in thee what is in thee most fair.
    So while thy beauty draws the heart to love,
    As fast thy Virtue bends that love to good:
    But ah, Desire still cries, give me some food.

Fourth song

Only joy, now here you° are,   *Stella*
Fit to hear and ease my care:
Let my whispering voice obtain,
Sweet reward for sharpest pain:
5   Take me to thee, and thee to me.
    No, no, no, no, my Dear, let be.[8]

Night hath closed all in her cloak,
Twinkling stars Love-thoughts provoke:
Danger hence good care doth keep,[9]
10 Jealousy itself doth sleep:
    Take me to thee, and thee to me.
    No, no, no, no, my Dear, let be.

Better place no wit can find,
Cupid's yoke to loose or bind:
15 These sweet flowers on fine bed too,
    Us in their best language woo:
    Take me to thee, and thee to me.
    No, no, no, no, my Dear, let be.

This small light the Moon bestows,
20 Serves thy beams but to disclose,

---

6. This paradox is repeated in stanzas 106 and 108.
7. All of creation, in effect the second "book" of God and a supplement to the Bible. It was a philosophical commonplace that Nature was the repository of natural law, which all human beings could discover through reason, just as the Bible held divine law, which was revealed to the faithful through grace.

8. The last line of each stanza is Stella's reply to Astrophil's entreaties in the preceding five lines. An earlier sonnet has suggested that logically two negatives are the same as a positive; thus it is possible to read a certain ambiguity into Stella's rejection of Astrophil here.
9. I.e., good care keeps danger away.

So to raise my hap more high;[1]
Fear not else, none can us spy:
Take me to thee, and thee to me.
No, no, no, no, my Dear, let be.

25 That you heard was but a mouse,
Dumb sleep holdeth all the house:
Yet a sleep, me thinks they say,
Young folks, take time while you may:
Take me to thee, and thee to me.
30 No, no, no, no, my Dear, let be.

Niggard° Time threats, if we miss   *miserly*
This large offer of our bliss:
Long stay ere[2] he grant the same:
Sweet then, while each thing doth frame:°   *suit*
35 Take me to thee, and thee to me.
No, no, no, no, my Dear, let be.

Your fair mother is abed,
Candles out, and curtains spread:
She thinks you do letters write:
40 Write, but let me first endite:°   *speak*
Take me to thee, and thee to me.
No, no, no, no, my Dear, let be.

Sweet alas, why strive you thus?
Concord better fitteth us:
45 Leave to Mars the force of hands,
Your power in your beauty stands:
Take thee to me, and me to thee.
No, no, no, no, my Dear, let be.

Woe to me, and do you swear
50 Me to hate, but I forbear,
Cursed be my destines° all,   *destinies*
That brought me so high to fall:
Soon with my death I will please thee.
No, no, no, no, my Dear, let be.

Eighth song

In a grove most rich of shade,
Where birds wanton music made,
May then young his pied weeds showing,[3]
New perfumed with flowers fresh growing,

5 Astrophil with Stella sweet,
Did for mutual comfort meet,

1. Astrophil states that the moon reveals Stella's beauty and thus raises his fortune. Writers and artists in this period imagined fortune as a goddess or as a kind of fatal force that turned a wheel to which a person's prosperity was tied; when one was at the top of Fortune's wheel, pleasure and power were within one's grasp. In the last stanza, Astrophil declares that Stella's hate will signal his fall and foresees his death. The images of rising and dying also have a sexual meaning.
2. I.e., it will be long before Time will give us another chance.
3. I.e., May, young then, showed his many-colored garments.

Both within themselves oppressed,
But each in the other blessed.

Him great harms had taught much care,
10   Her fair neck a foul yoke[4] bare,
But her sight his cares did banish,
In his sight her yoke did vanish.

Wept they had, alas the while,
But now tears themselves did smile,
15   While their eyes by love directed,
Interchangeably reflected.

Sigh they did, but now betwixt°   *between*
Sighs of woes were glad sighs mixed,
With arms crossed, yet testifying
20   Restless rest, and living dying.

Their ears hungry of each word,
Which the dear tongue would afford,
But their tongues restrained from walking,
Till their hearts had ended talking.

25   But when their tongues could not speak,
Love itself did silence break;
Love did set his lips asunder,
Thus to speak in love and wonder:

Stella, sovereign of my joy,
30   Fair triumpher of° annoy,°   *over/despair*
Stella, star of heavenly fire,
Stella, loadstar° of desier.   *magnet*

Stella, in whose shining eyes,
Are the lights of Cupid's skies,
35   Whose beams where they once are darted,
Love therewith is straight imparted.

Stella, whose voice when it speaks,
Senses all asunder breaks;
Stella, whose voice when it singeth,
40   Angels to acquaintance bringeth.

Stella, in whose body is
Writ° each character of bliss,   *written*
Whose face all, all beauty passeth,
Save thy mind which yet surpasseth.

45   Grant, O grant, but speech alas,
Fails me fearing on to pass,
Grant, O me, what am I saying?
But no fault there is in praying.

4. The "yoke" Stella wears is her marriage to Lord Rich; it is "foul" to Astrophil, since it means that he can no longer court her, at least openly.

Grant, O dear, on knees I pray,
50   (Knees on ground he then did stay)
That not I but since I love you,
Time and place for me may move you.

Never season was more fit,
Never room more apt for it;
55   Smiling air allows my reason,
These birds sing; now use the season.

This small wind which so sweet is,
See how it the leaves doth kiss,
Each tree in his best attiring,
60   Sense of love to love inspiring.

Love makes earth the water drink,
Love to earth makes water sink;
And if dumb things be so witty,
Shall a heavenly grace want pity?

65   There his hands in their speech fain
Would have made tongue's language plain;[5]
But her hands his hands repelling,
Gave repulse all grace excelling.[6]

Then she spake; her speech was such,
70   As not ears but heart did touch:
While such wise she love denied,
As yet love she signified.

Astrophil said she, my love
Cease in these effects to prove:
75   Now be still, yet still believe me,
Thy grief more than death would grieve me.

If that any thought in me,
Can taste comfort but of thee,°   except from you
Let me feed with hellish anguish,
80   Joyless, hopeless, endless languish.

If those eyes you praised, be
Half so dear as you to me,
Let me home return, stark blinded
Of those eyes, and blinder minded.[7]

85   If to secret° of my heart,   the secrets
I do any wish impart,
Where thou art not foremost placed,
Be both wish and I defaced.

If more may be said, I say,
90   All my bliss in thee I lay;

5. I.e., he would have had the language of his hands make plain what he had spoken.
6. I.e., she rejected him in a way that excelled all the

grace that would have accompanied her acceptance of him.
7. I.e., even blinder in my mind.

If thou love, my love content thee,
For all love, all faith is meant thee,

Trust me while I thee deny,
In myself the smart° I try,°   *pain / feel*
95   Tyran° honor doth thus use thee,   *tyrant*
Stella's self might not refuse thee.

Therefore, Dear, this no more move,
Lest, though I leave not thy love,
Which too deep in me is framed,
100   I should blush when thou art named.

Therewithal away she went,
Leaving him so passion rent,
With what she had done and spoken,
That therewith my song is broken.

106

O absent presence, Stella is not here;
False flattering hope, that with so fair a face,
Bare° me in hand, that in this orphan place,   *took*
Stella, I say my Stella, should appear.
5   What sayest thou now, where is that dainty cheer,°   *food*
Thou toldst mine eyes should help their famist° case?   *famished*
But thou art gone now that self felt disgrace,
Doth make me most to wish thy comfort near.[8]
But here I do store of fair ladies meet,
10   Who may with charm of conversation sweet,
Make in my heavy mold new thoughts to grow:
Sure they prevail as much with me, as he
That bad his friend but then new maimed,° to be   *wounded*
Merry with him, and not think of his woe.

108

When sorrow (using mine own fire's might)
Melts down his lead into my boiling breast,
Through that dark furnace to heart oppressed,
There shines a joy from thee my only light;
5   But soon as thought of thee breeds my delight,
And my young soul flutters to thee his nest,
Most rude despair my daily unbidden guest,
Clips straight my wings, straight wraps me in his night,
And makes me then bow down my head, and say,
10   Ah what doth Phoebus' gold that wretch avail,
Whom iron doors do keep from use of day?
So strangely (alas) thy works[9] in me prevail,
That in my woes for thee thou art my joy,
And in my joys for thee my only annoy.

8. I.e., you are gone now that that self (my own self) has felt the disgrace of rejection; this makes me wish you here.

9. I.e., "your works," what you have done and meant, affect me strangely.

Isabella Whitney

fl. 1567–1573

Little is known about the life of Isabella Whitney. Biographers agree that she was the sister of Geoffrey Whitney, the author of the first emblem book in England, and that, like him, she was born in Cheshire. The rest is to be deduced from her poetry, which points to an author with little formal education, a sharp eye for the details of urban life, and some knowledge of classical mythology. The modesty of Whitney's literary background sets her off from such later and accomplished poets as Mary Herbert and Aemilia Lanyer, and her poems on the challenges of love, friendship, and survival in a large city distinguish her from women who wrote devotional verse. Her poems follow the form and conventions of broadside ballads, a feature that may have made them popular with readers who were drawn to stories that gave advice on affairs of the heart and matters of the purse. Of "the middling sort," Whitney probably came to London for employment and diversion, but she seems to have had difficulty supporting herself. In any case, after publishing two collections of verse, *The Copy of a Letter* (c. 1567) and *A Sweet Nosegay* (1573), she left the city, having lived out the dreams as well as the disappointments of many English villagers who went to London to find work. Poems like *The Manner of Her Will* provide a detailed sketch of the delights and horrors of urban life as it was experienced by a talented woman of limited means.

I.W. To Her Unconstant Lover

    As close° as you your wedding[1] kept   *quiet*
        yet now the truth I hear,
    Which you (ere now) might me have told
        what need you nay to swear?

5   You know I always wished you well,
        so will I during life,
    But since you shall a husband be,
        God send you a good wife.

    And this (whereso you shall become)
10   full boldly may you boast:
    That once you had as true a love
        as dwelt in any coast.

    Whose constantness had never quailed
        if you had not begun,
15   And yet it is not so far past,
        but might again be won.

    If you so would; yea and not change
        so long as life should last,
    But if that needs you marry must?
20   then farewell, hope is past.

    And if you cannot be content
        to lead a single life?

1. The formal announcement of an impending marriage; he is not yet actually married.

(Although the same right quiet be)
    then take me to your wife.

25   So shall the promises be kept,
        that you so firmly made;
Now choose whether ye will be true,
    or be of Sinon's trade.[2]

Whose trade if that you long shall use,
30   it shall your kindred stain;
Example take by many a one
    whose falsehood now is plain.

As by Aeneas[3] first of all,
    who did poor Dido leave,
35   Causing the Queen by his untruth
    with sword her heart to cleave.

Also I find that Theseus did
    his faithful love forsake,
Stealing away within the night,
40   before she did awake.

Jason that came of noble race
    two ladies did beguile;
I muse how he durst show his face
    to them that knew his wile.°   *cunning*

45   For when he by Medea's art
      had got the fleece of gold
And also had of her that time
    all kind of things he would,

He took his ship and fled away
50   regarding not the vows,
That he did make so faithfully
    unto his loving spouse.

How durst he trust the surging seas
    knowing himself forsworn?
55   Why did he scape safe to the land
    before the ship was torn?

I think King Aeolus° stayed the winds   *god of the winds*
    and Neptune° ruled the sea;   *god of the sea*
Then might he boldly pass the waves
60   no perils could him slay.

But if his falsehood had to them
    been manifest before,

2. Posing as a deserter from the Greek army, Sinon persuaded the beseiged Trojans to open the city gates to him and a large wooden horse that he pretended was a gift from Athena but in fact hid Greek warriors in its belly.
3. Whitney lists unfaithful lovers recorded in myth: Aeneas, the Trojan hero and founder of Rome, who deserted Dido, queen of Carthage, after expressing love for her; Theseus, the hero and king of Athens, who left Ariadne, the daughter of Minos, king of Crete, on a island in the sea, even though she had saved him from the monster, Minotaur; Jason, the leader of the Argonauts who captured the golden fleece—a Greek treasure—with the help of Medea, and then abandoned her in favor of Glauce, daughter of Creon, king of Corinth.

They would have rent the ship as soon
    as he had gone from shore.

65   Now may you hear how falseness is
    made manifest in time,
Although they that commit the same
    think it a venial crime.

For they, for their unfaithfulness,
70   did get perpetual fame.
Fame? Wherefore did I term it so?
    I should have called it shame.

Let Theseus be, let Jason pass,
    let Paris[4] also 'scape,°   *escape*
75   That brought destruction unto Troy
    all through the Grecian rape,

And unto me a Troilus[5] be,
    if not you may compare,
With any of these persons that
80   above expressed are.

But if I cannot please your mind,
    for wants that rest in me,
Wed whom you list,° I am content,   *wish*
    your refuse for to be.

85   It shall suffice me simple soul
    of thee to be forsaken,
And it may chance, although not yet,
    you wish you had me taken.

But rather than you should have cause
90   to wish this through° your wife,   *because of*
I wish to her, ere her you have,
    no more but loss of life.

For she that shall so happy be,
    of thee to be elect,
95   I wish her virtues to be such,
    she need not be suspect.

I rather wish her Helen's face,
    than one of Helen's trade,
With chasteness of Penelope[6]
100   the which did never fade.

A Lucrece for her constancy,
    and Thisby for her truth;

---

4. Son of Priam, king of Troy; he stole Helen, the wife of King Menelaus of Sparta, a theft that brought about the invasion of Troy by Menelaus and the Greeks.
5. Son of Priam, king of Troy; his fidelity to Cressida, who deserted him in favor of Diomedes, a Greek warrior, is recounted in a 4th century addition to the stories of the Trojan War.

6. Whitney alludes to women who exemplify fidelity: Penelope, who waited for the return of Odysseus from the Trojan War; Lucrece or Lucretia, who killed herself after confessing to her husband that she had been raped; and Thisby or Thisbe, who killed herself when she saw her dying lover, Pyramus.

If such thou have, then Peto[7] be,
　　not Paris, that were ruth.

105 Perchance, ye will think this thing rare
　　in one woman to find;
Save Helen's beauty, all the rest
　　the gods have me assigned.

These words I do not speak, thinking
110　from thy new love to turn thee.
Thou knowest by proof what I deserve;
　　I need not to inform thee.

But let that pass. Would God I had
　　Cassandra's gift[8] me lent;
115 Then either thy ill chance or mine
　　my foresight might prevent.

But all in vain for this I seek,
　　wishes may not attain it;
Therefore may hap° to me what shall,　　　　　happen
120　and I cannot refrain it.

Wherefore I pray God be my guide
　　and also thee defend;
No worser than I wish myself,
　　until thy life shall end.

125 Which life I pray God may again
　　King Nestor's[9] life renew,
And after that your soul may rest
　　amongst the heavenly crew.

Thereto I wish King Xerxes'[1] wealth,
130　or else King Croesus's gold,
With as much rest and quietness
　　as man may have on mold.°　　　　　in the world

And when you shall this letter have
　　let it be kept in store.
135 For she that sent the same hath sworn
　　as yet to send no more.

And now farewell, for why at large
　　my mind is here expressed?
The which you may perceive, if that
140　you do peruse the rest.

　　Finis.

　　　　　　　　　　　　　　c. 1567

---

7. The source of this name is unknown.
8. Daughter of Priam, king of Troy; she had prophetic powers, though her prophecies of the city's fall were not believed.
9. King of Pylos and wise counselor to all the Greeks during their siege of Troy.

1. Whitney names men of legendary wealth: Xerxes, king of the Persians, who, with enormous resources gathered from all Asia Minor, attacked Athens and was defeated there by Themistocles; and Croesus, king of Lydia, who was defeated by Cyrus, king of the Persians.

The Admonition by the Author

to All Young Gentlewomen, and to All Other Maids Being in Love

Ye virgins that from Cupid's tents
    do bear away the foil,[1]
Whose hearts as yet with raging love
    most painfully do boil.

5   To you I speak, for you be they
        that good advice do lack;
Oh, if I could good counsel give,
    my tongue should not be slack.

But such as I can give, I will.
10   here in few words express,
Which if you do observe, it will
    some of your care redress.

Beware of fair and painted talk,
    beware of flattering tongues;
15   The mermaids do pretend no good
    for all their pleasant songs.

Some use the tears of crocodiles
    contrary to their heart,
And if they cannot always weep,
20   they wet their cheeks by art.

Ovid, within his art of love,[2]
    doth teach them this same knack,
To wet their hand and touch their eyes,
    so oft as tears they lack.

25   Why have ye such deceit in store?
        have you such crafty wile?
Less craft than this, God knows, would soon
    us simple souls beguile.

And will ye not leave off? But still
30   delude us in this wise?
Since it is so, we trust we shall
    take heed to feigned lies.

Trust not a man at the first sight,
    but try him well before;
35   I wish all maids within their breasts
    to keep this thing in store:

For trial shall declare his truth,
    and show what he doth think,

---

1. The reference is obscure. Cupid's weapons were traditionally a bow and arrows; Whitney describes him rather as a fencer who wounds his victims with a foil or sword. By bearing his foil away, Whitney's virgins appear to have experienced but not acquiesced to love.

2. The *Ars Amatoria*, a facetious treatise in which the poet advises men how to court and make love to women. Here, Whitney implies that her readers either imitate or avoid the examples of legendary women whose stories she tells.

Whether he be a lover true,
    or do intend to shrink.

40

If Scylla[3] had not trust too much
    before that she did try,
She could not have been clean forsake°   *forsaken*
    when she for help did cry.

45

Or if she had had good advice,
    Nisus had lived long;
How durst she trust a stranger, and
    do her dear father wrong?

King Nisus had a hair by fate
50   which hair while he did keep
He never should be overcome
    neither on land nor deep.

The stranger that the daughter loved
    did war against the King,
55   And always sought how that he might
    them in subjection bring.

This Scylla stole away the hair
    for to obtain her will,
And gave it to the stranger that
60   did straight her father kill.

Then she, who thought herself most sure
    to have her whole desire,
Was clean reject,° and left behind   *rejected*
    when he did home retire.

65

Or if such falsehood had been once
    unto Oenone[4] known,
About the fields of Ida wood
    Paris had walked alone.

Or if Demophoon's deceit
70   to Phyllis[5] had been told,
She had not been transformed so,
    as poets tell of old.

Hero did try Leander's[6] truth
    before that she did trust,
75   Therefore she found him unto her
    both constant, true, and just.

---

3. Daughter of the mythical Nisus, king of Megara, Scylla trusted the love of Minos, king of Crete, who was beseiging her father's city. For love of Minos (whom Whitney refers to as "the stranger"), Scylla betrayed her father by stealing a lock of his hair, a guarantee that Megara would remain free. According to Virgil, Minos, having taken Megara, captured Scylla, tied her to his ship, and dragged her through the sea. She was eventually transformed into a ciris, or sea-bird.

4. A nymph of Mount Ida, who was abandoned by Paris, son of Priam, king of Troy.
5. A mythical princess of Thrace and loved by the Greek warrior Demophon (or Demophoon); believing that he would not return to her after the Trojan War, she hanged herself.
6. Hero's lover, Leander, drowned while swimming across the Hellespont to be with her, whereupon she, too, threw herself into the sea.

For always did he swim the sea
    when stars in sky did glide,
Till he was drowned by the way
80   near hand unto the side.

She scratched her face, she tore her hair
    (it grieveth me to tell)
When she did know the end of him,
    that she did love so well.

85   But like Leander there be few,
    therefore in time take heed;
And always try before ye trust,
    so shall you better speed.

The little fish that careless is
90   within the water clear,
How glad is he, when he doth see
    a bait for to appear.

He thinks his hap° right good to be,   *luck*
    that he the same could spy,
95   And so the simple fool doth trust
    too much before he try.

O little fish what hap hadst thou,
    to have such spiteful fate,
To come into one's cruel hands
100   out of so happy state?

Thou didst suspect no harm, when thou
    upon the bait didst look;
O that thou hadst had Linceus's[7] eyes
    for to have seen the hook.

105   Then hadst thou with thy pretty mates
    been playing in the streams,
Whereas Sir Phoebus° daily doth   *the sun god Apollo*
    show forth his golden beams.

But since thy fortune is so ill
110   to end thy life on shore,
Of this thy most unhappy end
    I mind to speak no more.

But of thy fellow's chance that late
    such pretty shift did make,
115   That he from fisher's hook did sprint
    before he could him take.

And now he pries on every bait,
    suspecting still that prick
    (For to lie hid in every thing)
120   wherewith the fishers strick.°   *strike*

7. A sharp-eyed mythical warrior of Greece.

And since the fish that reason lacks
    once warned doth beware,
Why should not we take heed to that
    that turneth us to care?

125   And I who was deceived late
    by one's unfaithful tears
Trust now for to beware, if that
    I live this hundred years.

Finis.

c. 1567

A Careful Complaint by the Unfortunate Author

Good Dido[1] stint thy tears,
    and sorrows all resign
To me that born was to augment
    misfortune's luckless line.
5   Or using still the same,
    good Dido do thy best,
In helping to bewail the hap
    that furthereth mine unrest.
For though thy Troyan mate,
10   that Lord Aeneas hight,
Requiting all thy steadfast love,
    from Carthage took his flight,
And foully broke his oath,
    and promise made before,
15   Whose falsehood finished thy delight,
    before thy hairs were hoar.
Yet greater cause of grief
    compels me to complain,
For Fortune fell° converted hath   *evil*
20   my health to heaps of pain.
And that she[2] swears my death,
    too plain it is (alas),
Whose end let malice still attempt
    to bring the same to pass.
25   O Dido, thou hadst lived
    a happy woman still,
If fickle fancy had not thralled°   *enslaved*
    thy wits to reckless will.
For as the man by whom
30   thy deadly dolors bred,
Without regard of plighted troth
    from Carthage city fled,
So might thy cares in time
    be banished out of thought,

1. Queen of Carthage, seduced and then abandoned by Aeneas on his way from Troy to Italy.

2. I.e., Fortune, whose end or purpose, Whitney's death, malice will bring to pass.

first

35   His absence might well salve the sore
      that erst° his presence wrought.
  For fire no longer burns
      than faggots° feed the flame,   *except when sticks*
  The want of things that breed annoy
40   may soon redress the same.[3]
  But I, unhappy most,
      and gripped with endless griefs,
  Despair (alas) amid my hope,
      and hope without relief.
45   And as the swelt'ring heat
      consumes the war away,
  So do the heaps of deadly harms
      still threaten my decay.
  O death delay not long
50   thy duty to declare.
  Ye Sisters three[4] dispatch my days
      and finish all my care.

The Manner of Her Will

The Author (though loath to leave the City) upon her friend's procurement is constrained to depart, wherefore she feigneth as she would die and maketh her will and testament, as followeth, with large legacies of such goods and riches which she most abundantly hath left behind her, and thereof maketh London sole executor to see her legacies performed.

A communication which the Author had to London, before she made her will.

  The time is come I must depart
      from thee, ah famous city.
  I never yet to rue my smart,
      did find that thou hadst pity.
5   Wherefore small cause there is that I
      should grieve from thee go.
  But many women foolishly,
      like me, and other mo'e,
  Do such a fixed fancy set,
10   on those which least deserve,
  That long it is ere° wit we get,   *before*
      away from them to swerve.°   *turn*
  But time with pity oft will tell
      to those that will her try,
15   Whether it best be more to mell,°   *associate with*
      or utterly defy.
  And now hath time me put in mind,
      of thy great cruelness,
  That never once a help would find,
20   to ease me in distress.
  Thou never yet wouldst credit give
      to board me for a year,
  Nor with apparel me relieve

---

3. I.e., "want," which breeds annoyance, will also end annoyance, as it will eventually result in death.

4. I.e., the three Fates, who determine the length of life and the time of death.

except thou paid were.
25   No, no, thou never didst me good,
        nor ever wilt, I know;
    Yet I am in no angry mood
        but will, or ere I go
    In perfect love and charity,
30   my testament here write,
    And leave to thee such treasury
        as I in it recite.
    Now stand aside and give me leave
        to write my latest will,
35   And see that none you do deceive
        of that I leave them till.[1]

The manner of her will, and what she left to London and to all those in it at her departing.

    I whole in body, and in mind,
        but very weak in purse,
    Do make, and write my testament
        for fear it will be worse.
5   And first I wholly do commend,
        my soul and body eke,°   *also*
    To God the Father and the Son,
        so long as I can speak.
    And after speech, my soul to him,
10   and body to the grave,
    Till time that all shall rise again,
        their judgment for to have.
    And then I hope they both shall meet,
        to dwell for aye° in joy   *ever*
15   Whereas I trust to see my friends
        released from all annoy.
    Thus have you heard touching my soul,
        and body what I mean,
    I trust you all will witness bear,
20   I have a steadfast brain.
    And now let me dispose such things,
        as I shall leave behind,
    That those which shall receive the same,
        may know my willing mind.
25   I first of all to London leave
        because I there was bred,
    Brave buildings rare, of churches store,
        and Paul's to the head.[2]
    Between the same, fair streets there be
30   and people goodly store;
    Because their keeping craveth° cost,   *requires*

---

1. I.e., you must not deceive my inheritors by taking what I leave them until I leave them.
2. St. Paul's Cathedral, in the heart of the City of Lon-
don; Whitney describes it as the foremost or "head" of London's public buildings.

I yet will leave him[3] more.
First for their food, I butchers leave,
    that every day shall kill;
35   By Thames you shall have brewers store,
    and bakers at your will.
And such as orders do observe,°   *clergymen*
    and eat fish thrice a week,
I leave two streets, full fraught therewith,
40   they need not far to seek.
Watling Street, and Canwick Street,
    I full of woolen leave,
And linen store in Friday Street,
    if they me not deceive.
45   And those which are of calling such,
    that costlier they require,
I mercers leave, with silk so rich,
    as any would desire.
In cheap of them, they store shall find,
50   and likewise in that street,[4]
I goldsmiths leave, with jewels such
    as are for ladies meet.
And plate to furnish cupboards with,
    full brave there shall you find,
55   With purl° of silver and of gold.   *cord*
    to satisfy your mind.
With hoods, bongraces,° hats or caps,   *sunshades*
    such store are in that street,
As if on one side you should miss,
60   the other serves you feat.
For nets of every kind of sort,
    I leave within the pawn,
French ruffs, high purls,° gorgets° and sleeves, *ruffs / collars*
    of any kind of lawn.°   *thin cloth*
65   For purse or knives, for comb or glass,
    or any needful knack,
I by the stocks have left a boy
    will ask you what you lack.
I hose do leave in Birchin Lane,
70   of any kind of size,
For women stitched, for men both trunks
    and those of Gascoigne guise,
Boots, shoes, or pantables° good store,   *slippers*
    Saint Martin's hath for you;
75   In Cornwall, there I leave you beds,
    and all that 'longs° thereto.   *belongs*
For women shall you tailors have,
    by Bow, the chiefest dwell,
In every lane you some shall find,
80   can do indifferent well.

---

3. St. Paul's, to whose district Whitney will leave "more" than the "goodly store" already there.

4. I.e., they shall also find much cheap cloth in that street.

And for the men, few streets or lanes,
  but bodymakers° be,   *suitmakers*
And such as make the sweeping cloaks,
  with guards° beneath the knee.   *ornamental borders*
85 Artillery at Temple Bar,
  and dagges° at Tower Hill,   *pistols*
Swords and bucklers of the best,
  are nigh the Fleet until.[5]
Now when thy folk are fed and clad
90 with such as I have named,
For dainty mouths, and stomachs weak
  some junkets° must be framed.   *milk puddings*
Wherefore I 'pothecaries° leave,   *apothecaries*
  with banquets in their shop,
95 Physicians also for the sick,
  diseases for to stop.
Some roisters° still, must bide in thee,   *thugs*
  and such as cut it out,
That with the guiltless quarrel will,
100 to let their blood about.[6]
For them I cunning surgeons leave,
  some plasters° to apply,   *bandages*
That ruffians may not still be hanged,
  nor quiet persons die.
105 For salt, oatmeal, candles, soap,
  or what you else do want,
In many places, shops are full,
  I left you nothing scant.
If they that keep what you I leave,
110 ask money, when they sell it,
At mint,° there is such store, it is   *the mint*
  unpossible to tell it.
At stillyard° store of wines there be,   *the distillery*
  your dulled minds to glad,
115 And handsome men, that must not wed
  except they leave their trade.[7]
They oft shall seek for proper girls,
  and some perhaps shall find,
That need compels, or lucre lures
120 to satisfy their mind.
And near the same, I houses leave
  for people to repair,
To bathe themselves, so to prevent
  infection of the air.
125 On Saturdays I wish that those,
  which all the week do drug,°   *drudge*
Shall thither trudge, to trim them up
  on Sundays to look smug.

5. I.e., near the Temple Bar up to Fleet Street.
6. I.e., those who assault men who have done them no
harm must remain in London.

7. I.e., because they deal in liquor, they are not fit husbands.

If any other thing be lacked
130   in thee, I wish them look,
For there it is, I little brought
    but nothing from thee took.
Now for the people in thee left,
    I have done as I may,
135   And that the poor, when I am gone,
    have cause for me to pray.
I will to prisons portions leave,
    what though but very small,
Yet that they may remember me,
140   occasion be it shall,
And first the counter they shall have,
    lest they should go to wrack,°   *ruin*
Some coggers,° and some honest men,   *crooks*
    that sergeants draw aback.[8]
145   And such as friends will not them bail,
    whose coin is very thin,
For them I leave a certain hole,
    and little ease within.
The Newgate once a month shall have
150   a sessions° for his share,   *court trials*
Lest being heaped, infection might
    procure a further care.[9]
And at those sessions some shall 'scape,
    with burning near the thumb,
155   And afterward to beg their fees,
    till they have got the sum.
And such whose deeds deserveth death,
    and twelve° have found the same,   *a jury*
They shall be drawn up Holborn Hill
160   to come to further shame.
Well, yet to such I leave a nag
    shall soon their sorrows cease,
For he shall either break their necks
    or gallop from the preace.°   *crowd*
165   The Fleet, not in their circuit is,[1]
    yet if I give him nought,
It might procure his curse, ere I
    unto the ground be brought.
Wherefore I leave some papist old
170   to underprop his roof,
And to the poor within the same,
    a box for their behoof.°   *benefit*
What makes you standers-by to smile,

8. Whitney seems to wish to endow prisons with a "counter," a device to keep track of accounts, lest the prisoners be ruined by tradesmen, both crooks and honest men, who sell goods to prisoners and who are also restrained in their commerce by sergeants.
9. I.e., Newgate prison shall hold trials once a month to avoid overcrowding and disease. Some prisoners, marked by a burn on the thumb, will be freed to beg for bail money.

1. In the 16th century the Fleet was a prison for people convicted of crimes by the Star Chamber, a court dealing with affairs of conscience, such as treason and differences of faith; hence it is where one would find a Catholic, a papist. It is not a prison for people convicted by the common law; hence it is not in the same "circuit" as Newgate.

and laugh so in your sleeve,
175 I think it is, because that I
to Ludgate° nothing give.   *a debtors' prison*
I am not now in case to lie,
here is no place of jest;
I did reserve that for myself,
180   if I my health possessed.
And ever came in credit so
a debtor for to be,
When days of payment did approach,
I thither meant to flee.
185 To shroud myself amongst the rest,
that choose to die in debt;
Rather than any creditor,
should money from them get.
Yet 'cause° I feel myself so weak   *because*
190   that none me credit° dare,   *give me credit*
I here revoke, and do it leave,
some bankrupts to his° share.   *their*
To all the bookbinders by Paul's°   *St. Paul's Cathedral*
because I like their art,
195 They every week shall money have,
when they from books depart.°   *sell their books*
Amongst them all, my printer must,
have somewhat to his share;
I will my friends these books to buy
200   of him, with other ware.
For maidens poor, I widowers rich
do leave, that oft shall dote,
And by that means shall marry them,
to set the girls afloat.
205 And wealthy widows will I leave,
to help young gentlemen,
Which when you° have, in any case   *i.e., gentlemen*
be courteous to them° then.   *i.e., widows*
And see their plate and jewels eke
210   may not be marred with rust,
Nor let their bags too long be full,
for fear that they do burst.
To every gate under the walls
that compass thee about,
215 I fruit wives leave to entertain
such as come in and out.
To Smithfield° I must something leave,   *the meat market*
my parents there did dwell;
So careless for to be of it,
220   none would account it well.
Wherefore it thrice a week shall have,
of horse and neat° good store,   *beef*
And in his spittle,² blind and lame,

2. In the hospital at Smithfield the blind and lame are always to dwell or find refuge.

to dwell for evermore.
225　And Bedlam[3] must not be forgot,
　　　for that was oft my walk,
　　I people there too many leave,
　　　that out of tune do talk.
　　At Bridewell[4] there shall beadles be,
230　　and matrons that shall still
　　See chalk well-chopped, and spinning plied,
　　　and turning of the mill.
　　For such as cannot quiet be,
　　　but strive for house or land,
235　At th'Inns of Court,[5] I lawyers leave
　　　to take their cause in hand.
　　And also leave I at each Inn,
　　　of Court or Chancery,
　　Of gentlemen, a youthful root,
240　　full of activity,
　　For whom I store of books have left,
　　　at each bookbinder's stall,
　　And part of all that London hath
　　　to furnish them withal.°　　　　　　　　　　　　*with*
245　And when they are with study cloyed,°　　　　　*tired*
　　　to recreate their mind,
　　Of tennis courts, of dancing schools,
　　　and fence they store shall find.
　　And every Sunday at the least,
250　　I leave to make them sport,
　　In divers places players that
　　　of wonder shall report.
　　Now London have I (for thy sake)
　　　within thee, and without,
255　As comes into my memory,
　　　dispersed round about
　　Such needful things, as they should have
　　　here left now unto thee,
　　When I am gone, with conscience
260　　let them dispersed be.
　　And though I nothing named have
　　　to bury me withal,
　　Consider that above the ground
　　　annoyance be I shall.°　　　　　　　　　　　　*I shall be*
265　And let me have a shrouding sheet
　　　to cover me from shame,
　　And in oblivion bury me
　　　and never more me name.
　　Ringings° nor other ceremonies　　　　　　　*of church bells*
270　　use you not for cost,
　　Nor at my burial, make no feast,

---

3. Asylum for the insane.
4. A prison for persons convicted for minor offenses; it also served as a workhouse for the unemployed.

5. The offices of those practicing common law; also the schools teaching common law.

your money were but lost.
Rejoice in God that I am gone,
  out of this vale so vile.
275 And that of each thing, left such store,
  as may your wants exile.
I make thee sole executor, because
  I loved thee best.
And thee I put in trust, to give
280 the goods unto the rest.
Because thou shalt a helper need,
  in this so great a charge,
I wish good Fortune be thy guide, lest
  thou shouldst run at large.
285 The happy days and quiet times,
  they both her servants be,
Which well will serve to fetch and bring,
  such things as need° to thee.   *are needed*
Wherefore (good London) not refuse,°   *do not refuse*
290 for helper her to take,
Thus being weak, and weary both
  an end here will I make.
To all that ask what end I made,
  and how I went away,
295 Thou answer mayest like those which here
  no longer tarry may.
And unto all that wish me well,
  or rue that I am gone,
Do me commend, and bid them cease
300 my absence for to moan.
And tell them further, if they would,
  my presence still have had,
They should have sought to mend my luck,
  which ever was too bad.
305 So fare thou well a thousand times,
  God shield thee from thy foe,
And still make thee victorious
  of those that seek thy woe.
And though I am persuade° that I   *persuaded*
310 shall never more thee see,
Yet to the last, I shall not cease
  to wish much good of thee.
This twenty of October, I,
  in Anno Domini,
315 A thousand five hundred seventy three,
  as almanacs descry,
Did write this will with mine own hand
  and it to London gave,
In witness of the standers-by,
320 whose names if you will have,
Paper, Pen, and Standish° were,   *inkstand*
  at that same present by,
With Time, who promised to reveal,

so fast as she could hie,
325   The same, lest of my nearer kin,
　　　for any thing should vary,
So finally I make an end
　　　no longer can I tarry.
Finis.

1573

Mary Herbert, Countess of Pembroke
1561–1621

Mary Herbert was like many women of her time in having two phases to her life: a period of service to men, followed by a phase of independent activity. Deeply attached to her brother, Sir Philip Sidney, she spent much of her young adulthood in his company. The estate she presided over as wife to Henry Herbert, Earl of Pembroke, was Sidney's place of refuge after Queen Elizabeth had exiled him from court. At Wilton House and in his sister's company he wrote *The Apology for Poetry* and the first version of his prose romance, *The Arcadia*. Mary Herbert was an interested party in yet another project, his translation of the psalms, and when he died in 1586, she resolved to finish the project. Picking up where he had left off, at Psalm 43, she completed the cycle. Her work was encouraged by the circle of friends that gathered frequently at Wilton House and included such writers and musicians as Francis Mere, Edmund Spenser, Samuel Daniel, Nicholas Breton, Fulke Greville, and Abraham Fraunce. The seventeenth-century biographer John Aubrey spoke of the group as a "college."

Translations of the psalms were popular among Protestant writers of the period; they fulfilled the obligation to know both the Word and the indwelling spirit of God. Poets of religious lyric in the next century, especially George Herbert, would seek and represent a similar knowledge. Mary Herbert dedicated her work to Queen Elizabeth in a poem entitled *Even Now That Care*, which was followed by an elegy for her brother Philip, *To Thee Pure Sprite*. Although riddled with ellipses or words that have been deliberately omitted, they convey the spiritual intensity that characterizes her translations. Some critics think that she did not write a second elegy (here attributed to her), *The Lay of Clorinda*; it is, however, what we might expect a woman of her station and training to have written about the death of a beloved friend. Milton would later give a profoundly political and religious dimension to the genre in his *Lycidas*, an elegy that is as much for an age and its temperament as it is for a person.

Even Now That Care[1]

Even now that care which on thy crown attends,
And with thy happy greatness daily grows,
Tells me, thrice sacred Queen, my Muse offends,
And of respect to thee the line outgoes.[2]
5   One instant will, or willing can she° lose   *Queen Elizabeth*
I say not reading, but receiving rhymes,

---

1. This poem prefaces Mary Herbert's translation of the psalms, dedicated to Queen Elizabeth.

2. I.e., my Muse oversteps the boundary of respect that your status demands.

On whom in chief dependeth to dispose
What Europe acts in these most active times?[3]

Yet dare I so, as humbleness may dare
Cherish some hope they shall acceptance find;
Not weighing less thy state, lighter thy care,
But knowing more thy grace, abler thy mind.
What heavenly powers thee highest throne assigned,
Assigned thee goodness suiting that degree,
And by thy strength thy burden so defined;
To others' toil, is exercise to thee.[4]

Cares though still great, cannot be greatest still;
Business must ebb, though leisure never flow.
Then these the posts of duty and goodwill
Shall press to offer what their senders owe,
Which once in two, now in one subject go,[5]
The poorer left, the richer reft away,
Who better might (O might! Ah, word of woe)
Have given for me what I for him defray.°   pay

How can I name whom sighing sighs extend,°   wordlessly amplify
And not unstop my tears' eternal spring?
But he did warp, I weaved this web to end.[6]
The stuff not ours, our work no curious thing,
Wherein yet well we thought the psalmist king,
Now English denizened though Hebrew born,
Would to thy music undispleased sing,
Oft having worse, without repining worn.[7]

And I the cloth in both our names present,
A livery robe to be bestowed by° thee,   on
Small parcel of that undischarged rent,
From which nor pains, nor payments can us free.
And yet enough to cause our neighbors see
We will our best, though scanted° in our will;   deficient
And those nigh fields where sown thy favors be
Unwealthy do, not else unworthy till.[8]

For in our work what bring we but thine own?
What English is, by many names is thine.
There humble laurels in thy shadows grown
To garland others' world, themselves repine.°   are sorrowful
Thy breast the cabinet, thy seat the shrine,
Where Muses hang their vowed memories,
Where wit, where art, where all that is divine
Conceived best, and best defended lies.

---

3. I.e., will she or can she lose an instant receiving rhymes—she, who is governing Europe?
4. I.e., thy burden, defined by thy strength, is to others toil, [but] to thee exercise.
5. I.e., Herbert and Sidney; the latter is the richer of the two subjects, the one who could better have offered the queen duty and good will.
6. I.e., he laid the warp of this web (placed its threads lengthwise); I wove it to completion (after his death).
7. I.e., you often had worse stuff than our web to wear (or our poems to listen to), which you did without complaining.
8. I.e., those near fields where thy favors are sown (as seed) we, not wealthy but not unworthy, cultivate. Herbert thanks the queen for her support.

Which if men did not (as they do) confess,
50 And wronging worlds would otherwise consent,[9]
  Yet here° who minds° so meet a patroness   *in England / finds*
  For author's state or writing's argument?
  A king° should only to a queen be sent.   *King David*
  God's loved choice unto his chosen love,
55 Devotion to devotion's president;°   *chief object*
  What all applaud, to her whom none reprove.

  And who sees aught,° but sees how justly square° *anything / suitable*
  His° haughty ditties to thy glorious days?   *King David's*
  How well beseeming thee his triumphs are?
60 His hope, his zeal, his prayer, plaint,° and praise, *complaint*
  Needless thy person to their height to raise,
  Less need to bend them down to thy degree;
  These holy garments each good soul assays,°   *tries on*
  Some sorting° all, all sort to none but thee.   *fitting*

65 For ev'n thy rule is painted° in his reign,   *illustrated*
  Both clear in right, both nigh° by wrong oppressed. *closely*
  And each at length (man crossing God in vain)
  Possessed of place,° and each in peace possessed. *office, rule*
  Proud Philistines did interrupt his rest,
70 The foes of heav'n no less have been thy foes;
  He with great conquest, thou with greater blessed;
  Thou sure to win, and he secure to lose.°   *secure against loss*

  Thus hand in hand with him thy glories walk,
  But who can trace them where alone they go?
75 Of thee two hemispheres on honor talk,
  And hands and seas thy trophies jointly show.
  The very winds did on thy party° blow,   *ally*
  And rocks in arms thy foemen eft defy;[1]
  But soft my muse, thy pitch is earthly low,
80 Forbear this heaven, where only eagles fly.

  Kings on a queen enforced their states to lay,
  Mainlands for empire waiting on an isle;
  Men drawn by worth a woman to obey,
  One moving all, herself unmoved the while.[2]
85 Truth's restitution, vanity's exile,
  Wealth sprung of want, war held without annoy;
  Let subject be of some inspired style,
  Till then the object of her subject's joy.[3]

  Thy utmost can but offer to her sight
90 Her handmaid's task, which most her will endears,

---

9. I.e., if men did not confess that your breast is the shrine of the Muses, even unfair worlds would otherwise agree that this was the case.
1. I.e., winds blew to help your allies; rocks defied your enemies who were up in arms. Herbert then protests that the level of her poetic skill is low; it must not aspire to a height that only "eagles," or poets of great power, attain.
2. I.e., kings are forced to place their "states" (authority

and power) on a queen; mainlands anticipating empire are forced to lay their "states" (conditions, resources) on an island, i.e., England.
3. Herbert defines the subjects of an inspired style of poetry: the restitution of truth, the exile of vanity, a "wealth" created by necessity (i.e., moral virtue), war without harm.

And pray unto thy pains life from that light
Which lively light some court and kingdom cheers.
What[4] wish she° may (far past her living peers   *the Queen*
And rival still to Judah's faithful king,
95   In more than he and more triumphant years),
Sing what God doth, and do what men may sing.

c. 1590

To Thee Pure Sprite[1]

To thee pure sprite,° to thee alone's addressed   *spirit*
    this coupled work, by double interest thine:
    first raised by thy blessed hand, and what is mine
Inspired by thee, thy secret power impressed.°   *informed by*
5   so dared my Muse with thine itself combine,
    as mortal stuff with that which is divine.
Thy lightening beams give lustre to the rest,

That heaven's king may deign his own transformed
    in substance no, but superficial tire°   *attire*
10   by thee° put on to praise,[2] not to aspire   *Sidney*
To those high tones so in themselves adorned,
    which angels sing in their celestial choir,
    and all of tongues with soul and voice admire.
These sacred hymns thy kingly prophet formed.

15   Oh, had that soul which honor brought to rest
    too soon not left, and reft the world of all
    what man could show, which we perfection call,
This half-maimed piece had sorted with° the best.   *matched*
    deep wounds enlarged, long festered in their gall,
20   fresh bleeding smart; not eye- but heart-tears fall.
Ah memory, what needs this new arrest?°   *delay*

Yet here behold, (oh, wert thou to behold!)
    this[3] finished now, thy matchless Muse begun,
    the rest but pieced, as left by thee undone.
25   Pardon (oh, blessed soul) presumption too too bold,
    if love and zeal such error ill-become,
    'tis zealous love, love which hath never done,
Nor can enough in world of words unfold.

And since it hath no further scope to go,
30   nor other purpose but to honor thee,
    thee in thy works, where all the Graces[4] be
As little streams with all their all do flow
    to their great sea, due tribute's grateful fee;[5]

4. I.e., court and kingdom.
1. Herbert's elegy is for her brother, Sir Philip Sidney. In
it she acknowledges his part in the translations.
2. I.e., your intelligence informs this verse not so that the
king of heaven will consider his own light transformed
substantially; rather it is that your own attire, clothing, is
put over that light to praise him. Herbert returns to the

idea, expressed earlier in her dedicatory poem to Elizabeth, that the psalms are a web or woven cloth.
3. I.e., the translation.
4. Personifications of the elements of courtesy and courteous expression; typically, they are attributes of poetic
and artistic work.
5. I.e., the streams are a tribute to the sea.

so press my thoughts, my burdened thoughts, in me,
35 To pay the debt of infinites I owe

To thy great worth. Exceeding nature's store,
  wonder of men, sole° born perfection's kind,   alone
  phoenix⁶ thou wert. So rare thy fairest mind,
Heav'nly adorned, Earth justly might adore,
40 where truthful praise in highest glory shined,
  for there alone was praise to truth confined;
And where but there, to live for ever more?

Oh! When to this account, this cast up sum,
  this reckoning made, this audit of my woe,
45 I call my thoughts, whence so strange passions flow,
How works my heart, my senses stricken dumb?
  that° would thee more than ever heart could show,   my thoughts
  and all too short,° who knew thee best doth know,   inadequate
There lives no wit that may thy praise become.°   express

50 Truth I invoke (who scorn elsewhere to move
  or here in aught my blood should partialize),⁷
  Truth, sacred Truth, thee sole to solemnize.
Those precious rights well known best mind's approve;
  and who but doth, hath wisdom's open eyes,
55 not owly° blind the fairest light still° flies,   owl-like/always
Confirm no less?⁸ At least 'tis sealed above.

Where thou art fixed among my fellow lights,
  my day put out, my life in darkness cast,
  thy angel's soul, with highest angels placed,
60 There blessed sings enjoying heaven, delights°   delights in
  thy maker's praise, as far from earthly taste
  as here thy works so worthily embraced
By all of worth, where never envy bites.

As goodly buildings to some glorious end
65 cut off by fate, before the Graces had
  each wond'rous part in all their beauties clad,
Yet so much done, as art would not amend;
  so thy rare works to which no wit can add,
  in all men's eyes, which are not blindly mad,
70 Beyond compare, above all praise extend.

Immortal monuments of thy fair fame,
  though not complete, nor in the reach of thought,
  how on that passing peacetime would have wrought
Had Heav'n so spared the life of life to frame
75 the rest?⁹ But ah, such loss! Hath this world aught
  can equal it? Or which like grievance brought?
Yet there will live thy ever-praised name.

---

6. A mythical bird, unique in the world, which is miraculously reborn from the ashes of its own funeral pyre.
7. I.e., I scorn that my blood (passion, temperament)
should favor anything in a partial or prejudicial way.

8. I.e., who that has wisdom's open eyes and is not
owlishly blind, fleeing strong light, does not confirm this?
9. I.e., had Heaven so spared your life so that you could
frame the life of the rest of mankind.

To which these dearest offerings of my heart,
   dissolved to ink, while pen's impressions move
80   the bleeding veins of never dying love,
I render here; these wounding lines of smart,
   sad characters indeed of simple love,
   not art nor skill which abler wits do prove,
Of my full soul receive the meanest part.

85 Receive these hymns, these obsequies receive,
   if any mark of thy sweet sprite appear,
   well are they born,[1] no title else shall bear.
I can no more. Dear soul, I take my leave;
   sorrow still strives, would mount thy highest sphere
90   presuming so just cause might meet thee there.[2]
Oh happy change! Could so I take my leave.

c. 1590

Psalm 71: In Te Domini Speravi

On thee my trust is grounded.
   Lord, let me never be
      With shame confounded,
        But set me free
5   And in thy justice rescue me;
     Thy gracious ear to meward° bend   *toward me*
       And me defend.

Be thou my rock, my tower,
   My ever safe resort,
10   Whose saving power
        Hath not been short°   *deficient*
To work my safety, for my fort
   On thee alone is built; in thee
     My strongholds be.

15 Me, O my God, deliver
   From wicked, wayward hand.
      God, my help-giver,
        On whom I stand
And stood since I could understand,
20   Nay, since by life I first became
     What now I am.

Since prisoned in my mother,
   By thee I prison brake,°   *broke from*
      I trust no other,
25   No other make
My stay, no other refuge take,
   Void of thy praise no time doth find
     My mouth and mind.

---

1. I.e, the hymns are of good parentage.
2. I.e., my sorrow would climb to your sphere in heaven,

presuming that so just a cause would allow my sorrow to be there.

Men for a monster took me,
30   Yet hope of help from thee
            Never forsook me.
                Make then by me
All men, with praise extolled, may see
        Thy glory,[1] thy magnificence,
35   Thy excellence.

When feeble years do leave me
    No stay of other sort,
        Do not bereave me
            Of thy support,
40 And fail not then to be my fort,
    When weakness, in me killing might,°   strength
            Usurps his right.[2]

For now against me banded,
    My foes have talked of me;
45   Now unwithstanded,°   not withstood
                Who° their spies be   whoever
Of me have made a firm decree:
    (Lo!) God to him hath bid adieu,
            Now then pursue.[3]

50 Pursue, say they, and take him;
        No succor can he win,
            No refuge make him.
                O God, begin
To bring with speed thy forces in.
55   Help me, my God, my God, I say
            Go not away.

But let them be confounded
    And perish by whose hate
        My soul is wounded;
60   And in one rate,°   as a class
Let them all share in shameful state
    Whose counsels, as their farthest end,°   goal
            My wrong intend.

For I will still persevere
65   My hopes on thee to raise,
            Augmenting ever
                Thy praise with praise.
My mouth shall utter forth always
    Thy truths, thy helps, whose sum surmounts
70   My best accounts.

1. I.e., cause all men to see, by my aid, thy glory magnified with praise.
2. I.e., when weakness, having overcome strength, takes

the place of strength in my soul.
3. I.e., my enemies' spies have decreed: God has said
goodbye to him, so now hunt him down.

Thy force keeps me from fearing,
　　Nor ever dread I aught;
　　　　Thy justice bearing
　　　　In mindful thought
75　　And glorious acts which thou hast taught
　　　　Me from my youth;[4] and I have shown
　　　　　　What I have known.

Now age doth overtake me
　　And paint my head with snow;
80　　　　Do not forsake me
　　　　Until I show
The ages which succeeding grow,
　　And every afterliving wight,°　　　　　　　*generation of men*
　　　　　　Thy power and might.

85　　How is thy justice raised
　　　　Above the height of thought;
　　　　　　How highly praised
　　　　　　What thou hast wrought.
Sought let be all that can be sought,
90　　　　None shall be found, nay none shall be,
　　　　　　O God, like thee.

What if thou down didst drive me
　　Into the gulf of woes;
　　　　Thou wilt revive me
95　　　　Again from those
And from the deep, which deepest goes;
　　Exalting me again will make
　　　　　　Me comfort take.

My greatness shall be greater
100　　By thee; by comfort thine
　　　　My good state better.
　　　　O lute of mine,
To praise his truth thy tunes incline;
　　My harp extol the Holy One
105　　　　In Judah known.

My voice to my harp join thee,[5]
　　My soul saved from decay,
　　　　My voice conjoin° thee,　　　　　　　*join with*
　　　　My tongue each day,
110　In all men's view his justice lay,°　　　　　*reveal*
　　Who° hath disgraced and shamed so,　　　*those who*
　　　　Who work my woe.

c. 1590

---

4. I.e., bearing thy justice and glorious acts in mindful thought.

5. I.e., let my voice, joined to my harp, join thee.

Miles Coverdale: Psalm 71[1]

In thee, O Lord, is my trust, let me never be put to confusion, but rid me and deliver me through thy righteousness. Incline thine ear unto me and help me. Be thou my stronghold (whereunto I may always fly), thou that hast promised to help me; for thou art my house of defense and my castle. Deliver me (O my God) out of the hand of the ungodly, out of the hand of the unrighteous and cruel man. For thou (O Lord God) art the thing that I long for, thou art my hope even from my youth. I have leaned upon thee ever since I was born, thou art he that took me out of my mother's womb, therefore is my praise always of thee. I am become a wonder unto the multitude, but my sure trust is in thee. Oh, let my mouth be filled with thy praise and honor all the day long. Cast me not away in mine old age, forsake me not when my strength faileth me. For mine enemies speak against me, and they that lay wait for my soul take their counsel together, saying, God hath forsaken him; persecute him, take him, for there is none to help him. Go not far from me, O God; my God haste thee to help me. Let them be confounded and perish that are against my soul; let them be covered with shame and dishonor that seek to do me evil. As for me, I will patiently abide always and will ever increase thy praise. My mouth shall speak of thy righteousness and saving health all the day long, for I know no end thereof. Let me go in (O Lord God) and I will make mention of thy power and righteousness only. Thou (O God) hast learned me from my youth up until now, therefore will I tell of thy wondrous works. Forsake me not (O God) in mine old age, when I am grey-headed; until I have showed thine arm unto children's children, and thy power to all them that are yet for to come. Thy righteousness (O God) is very high, thou that doest great things, O God, who is like unto thee? O what great troubles and adversity hast thou showed me, and yet didst thou turn and refresh me; yea, and broughtest me from the deep of the earth again. Thou hast brought me to great honor and comforted me on every side. Therefore will I praise thee and thy faithfulness (O God), playing upon the lute, unto thee will I sing upon the harp, O thou holy one of Israel. My lips would fain sing praises unto thee and so would my soul, whom thou hast delivered.

My tongue talketh of thy righteousness all the day long, for they are confounded and brought unto shame that sought to do me evil.

Psalm 121: Levavi Oculos

Unto the hills, I now will bend
    And list° with joy my hopeful sight;   *incline*
To him who me doth comfort send,
    My gracious God, the Lord of might.
5   Even he (who ever blessed be he named)
        Who Heaven and Earth and all therein hath framed.

By him thy foot, from slip shall stay,°   *prevent*
    Nor will he sleep who thee sustains;
Israel's great God by night or day
10   To sleep or slumber aye° disdains.   *always*

---

1. Miles Coverdale published his English translation of the Bible (using earlier translations into Latin and German as well as the English translation of William Tyndale) in 1535. Although the Authorized Version, commissioned by James I in 1604 and published in 1611, essentially reproduced Tyndale's translation of the New Testament and portions of the Hebrew Bible, the Prayer Book text of the psalms is considered to be Coverdale's work.

For he is still thy guard forever waking,
On thy right hand thy safety undertaking.

So undertakes that neither sun
    By day with heat shall thee molest,
15 Nor moon by night, when day is done,
    Offend thee, or disturb thy rest.
      Yea, from all evil thou still in his protection
      Shalt safely dwell from harm or ill infection.

This Lord (who never fails his flock)
20   Shall thee in all thy ways attend
At home, abroad, thy fort, thy rock
    From all annoy shall thee defend.
      Yea, from this time from age to age for ever
      Will be thy God, and thee forsaking never.

c. 1590

The Doleful Lay° of Clorinda   *ballad*

Ay me, to whom shall I my case complain
That may compassion° my impatient grief?   *sympathize with*
Or where shall I unfold my inward pain,
That my enriven° ear may find relief?   *dismayed*
5   Shall I unto the heavenly powers it show?
    Or unto earthly men that dwell below?

To heavens? Ah they, alas, the authors were
And workers of my unremedied woe;
For they foresee what to us happens here,
10 And they foresaw, yet suffered this be so.
    From them comes good, from them comes also ill;
    That which they made, who can them warn to spill.°   *destroy*

To men? Ah they, alas, like wretched be
And subject to the heavens' ordinance;
15 Bound to abide whatever they decree,
Their best redress is their best sufferance.[1]
    How then can they, like wretched, comfort me,
    The which no less, need comforted to be?[2]

Then to myself will I my sorrow mourn,
20 Since none alive like sorrowful remains;
And to myself my plaints shall back return,
To pay their usury with doubled pains.
    The woods, the hills, the rivers shall resound
    The mournful accent of my sorrow's ground.°   *cause*

25 Wood, hills, and rivers now are desolate,
Since he is gone the which them all did grace;
And all the fields do wail their widow state,

---

1. I.e., the best recourse for men subject to heaven is to tolerate its decrees.

2. I.e., how can they comfort me, wretched as I am, who themselves need to be comforted?

Since death their fairest flower did late deface.
   The fairest flower in field that ever grew,
30   Was Astrophel;[3] that was, we all may rue.

What cruel hand of cursed fate unknown,
Hath cropped the stalk which bore so fair a flower?
Untimely cropped, before it were well grown,
And clean defaced in untimely hour.
35   Great loss to all that ever him did see,
    Great loss to all, but greatest loss to me.

Break now your garlands, O ye shepherds' lasses,
Since the fair flower which them adorned is gone;
The flower which them adorned is gone to ashes,
40   Never again let lass put garland on.
    Instead of garland, wear sad cypress now,
    And bitter elder, broken from the bow.

Nor ever sing the love-lays which he made,
Who ever made such lays of love as he?
45   Nor ever read the riddles which he said
Unto yourselves to make you merry glee.
    Your merry glee is now laid all abed,
    Your merry maker now, alas, is dead.

Death, the devourer of all world's delight,
50   Hath robbed you and reft from me my joy;
Both you and me and all the world he quite
Hath robbed of joyance and left sad annoy.
    Joy of the world, and shepherds' pride was he,
    Shepherds' hope, never like again to see.

55   Oh death, that hast us of such riches reft,
Tell us at least, what hast thou with it done?
What is become of him whose flower here left
Is but the shadow of his likeness gone,
    Scarce like the shadow of that which he was,
60   Naught° like, but that he like a shade did pass?   *nothing*

But that immortal spirit, which was decked
With all the dowries of celestial grace,
By sovereign choice from the heavenly choirs select,
And lineally derived from angel's race,
65   O what is now of it become, aread—°   *tell*
    Ay me, can so divine a thing be dead?

Ah no, it is not dead, nor can it die,
But lives for aye° in blissful paradise,   *ever*
Where like a newborn babe it soft doth lie,
70   In bed of lilies wrapped in tender wise.°   *manner*

---

3. Astrophel or Astrophil: the principal speaker and the lover of "Stella," the figure representing the beloved woman, in Sir Philip Sidney's sonnet sequence *Astrophil and Stella*.

And compassed all about with roses sweet,
And dainty violets from head to feet.

There thousand birds all of celestial brood,
To him do sweetly carol day and night,
75   And with strange notes, or him well understood,
Lull him asleep in angel-like delight,
      While in sweet dream to him presented be
      Immortal beauties which no eye may see.

But he them sees and takes exceeding pleasure
80   Of their divine aspects, appearing plain,
And kindling love in him above all measure,
Sweet love still joyous, never feeling pain.
      For what so goodly form he there doth see,
      He may enjoy from jealous rancor free.

85   There liveth he in everlasting bliss,
Sweet spirit never fearing more to die,
Nor dreading harm from any foes of his,
Nor fearing salvage° beasts more cruelty.   *savage*
      While we here, wretches, wail his private lack,
90   And with vain vows do often call him back.

But live thou there still happy, happy spirit,
And give us leave thee here thus to lament.
Not thee that dost thy heaven's joy inherit,
But our own selves that here in dole are drent.°   *drenched*
95   Thus do we weep and wail and wear our eyes,
      Mourning others, our own miseries.

Elizabeth I

1533–1602

No British monarch has left posterity a more dazzling record of accomplishments than Elizabeth Tudor, second daughter of Henry VIII. In the course of her reign, England became a nation to rival France and Spain; England's cities became centers of commerce, her navy controlled the principal routes of trade, and her people pursued lucrative interests in Europe and the New World. Having ruled England for almost half a century, Elizabeth has lived on as a figure of compelling power in the history of her people. What Shakespeare said of his character Cleopatra—"Age cannot wither her, nor custom stale her infinite variety"—conveys something of the fascination the memory of this extraordinary woman has had for the English people as well as for others around the globe. Age did, of course, eventually touch her being; doubtless, too, the brilliant strategies by which she governed subjects who were ever jealous of her royal prerogative must finally have become predictable. But Elizabeth was brought up in the atmosphere of a volatile politics, given to shifts in the winds of chance, susceptible to the heat of violent controversy and even to the flames of rebellion. She did what she had to do to remain on the throne; her father's example, if nothing else, taught her how fragile was the rule

Robert Peake (attr.). *Queen Elizabeth Going in Procession to Blackfriars in 1600. This splendid painting is linked to no particular event. Its arrangement of figures suggests a Roman imperial triumph, and evokes the success of the queen's monarchy. She appears to be in a litter, but is actually in a chair on wheels pushed by attendants, and protected by a canopy held by courtiers. She is preceded by a knight, perhaps Gilbert Talbot, Earl of Shrewsbury, who carries the sword of state. Though Elizabeth was sixty-eight when this painting was made in 1601, she is shown as a much younger woman. Her wish to be recognized as always desirable and ever the object of courtly devotion is well illustrated by her pale, unlined face, her highly dressed hair and her stylized body, clothed in a bejeweled dress whose puffed sleeves and intricate lace ruff suggest an etherial and even divine creature. She is attended by six Knights of the Garter; the knight standing directly beside her (with a bald head and stiff grey beard) has been identified as her current favorite, Edward Somerset, Earl of Worcester; his two principal castles, Raglan and Chepstow, are probably those in the background of the painting.*

of a monarch who depended much more on the loyalty of subjects than on the authority of office or the power of the law.

Elizabeth's birth was itself a disappointment, at least to Henry VIII, who had hoped for a son. Her mother was the king's second wife, the charming Anne Boleyn, whom he married after divorcing Catherine of Aragon, the mother of his first daughter, Mary Tudor. The divorce precipitated the king's break with the Catholic Church, made Mary Tudor illegitimate, and effectively defined Anne's politics as unequivocally Protestant. But the new queen's influence was short-lived. Supporters of Catholicism, those who remained faithful to the memory of Catherine and respected the claims of Mary Tudor, may have been responsible for convincing the king that Anne had been unfaithful to him; in any case he ordered her execution. Ten days later, he married Jane Seymour, declared Elizabeth illegitimate, and again waited for the birth of a son. Elizabeth's half-brother, the future Edward VI, was born in 1537, when Elizabeth was four years old. Fortunately, at the age of ten, Elizabeth at last acquired a loving stepmother: Henry's sixth wife, Catherine

Parr, looked after her interests and education. An excellent student, fluent in Latin, French, and Italian and versed in history, Elizabeth was raised to be the subject of her brother, who became king after Henry's death in 1547. When he died in 1553, she became a pawn in a long and vicious struggle for the crown. Imprisoned in the Tower and then in Woodstock Castle in Oxfordshire by the Catholic supporters of her sister's claim to the throne, Elizabeth wrote lyrics that testify to both her fears and her faith during this dangerous time.

In 1558, Queen Mary died, and Elizabeth was crowned with much rejoicing; in the historian William Camden's words: "neither did the people ever embrace any other Prince with more willing and constant mind." Once on the throne, Elizabeth pursued a policy of exemplary discretion; she rewarded those who were loyal to her and punished those who showed signs of disobedience. In 1568, when her cousin Mary, Queen of Scots, abdicated the throne of Scotland in favor of her son, James VI, Elizabeth granted Mary refuge in England. Yet evidence later suggested that Mary, an ardent Catholic, had plotted to kill Elizabeth and restore Catholicism in England, and in 1587, Elizabeth ordered her execution with great regret. Reflecting on this action, also the subject of a speech to Parliament, the queen declared: "This death will wring my heart as long as I live."

A woman and reigning monarch, Elizabeth's position was anomalous. As a woman, she retained an important kind of social power only as long as she was an object of desire, to be courted and won; as a reigning monarch, she was expected not only to govern but also to secure the succession. In her speech to Parliament on the subject of marriage early in her reign, Elizabeth provided reasons why she would delay taking a husband. She probably never intended to take one. Continuing the fiction of courtship well past the age at which she could be expected to have a child, she saw to it that she remained at once attractive and unavailable. Most important, she succeeded in commanding the attention of her subjects by transforming her court into a center of literary and artistic activity. Late in life, she met her most serious suitor, the Duke of Alençon, brother to the French king, Henry III. A dwarf whose face was disfigured by smallpox, he was her "little frog," a man she is said to have loved dearly. The problem of succession required another kind of temporizing. She refused to name James VI of Scotland as the next king of England until shortly before she died—a silence that she maintained was necessary to preserve the peace.

Throughout her long reign she cultivated two personas. As a monarch, she could speak courageously (as she did to her soldiers at Tilbury on the Devon coast while they waited for the Spanish to invade); as a woman, she could convey understanding (as she did to her critics in her so-called Golden Speech curtailing her prerogative to create monopolies). Her government remained a conscientious one to its very end. She cultivated a habit of mind that must have helped to ensure its stability: as her translation of Boethius's *Consolation of Philosophy* (made when she was sixty years old) reminds us, she never allowed herself to forget the vicissitudes of fortune and her own mortality.

Written with a Diamond on Her Window at Woodstock[1]

> Much suspected by° me,   *to have been done by*
> Nothing proved can be,
>   Quoth Elizabeth prisoner.

---

1. Elizabeth was imprisoned at Woodstock Castle, near Oxford, from May 23, 1554, to sometime late in April 1555. The queen, Mary I, Elizabeth's half-sister, suspected her of treason. This and the following poem are thought to have been written at this time.

Written on a Wall at Woodstock

Oh fortune, thy wresting wavering state
Hath fraught with cares my troubled wit,
Whose witness this present prison late
Could bear, where once was joy's loan quit.[1]
5   Thou causedst the guilty to be loosed
From bands° where innocents were inclosed,   *bonds*
And caused the guiltless to be reserved,°   *bound*
And freed those that death had well deserved.
But all herein° can be nothing wrought,   *in prison*
10   So God send to my foes all they have thought.[2]

The Doubt of Future Foes

The doubt° of future foes exiles my present joy,   *fear*
And wit me warns to shun such snares as threaten mine annoy;[1]
For falsehood now doth flow, and subjects' faith doth ebb,
Which should not be if reason ruled or wisdom weaved the web.
5   But clouds of joys untried° do cloak aspiring minds,   *untested*
Which turn to rain of late repent by changed course of winds.[2]
The top of hope supposed the root upreared shall be,
And fruitless all their grafted guile, as shortly ye shall see.[3]
The dazzled eyes with pride, which great ambition blinds,
10   Shall be unsealed by worthy wights[4] whose foresight falsehood finds.
The daughter of debate that discord aye° doth sow   *ever*
Shall reap no gain where former rule[5] still peace hath taught to know.
No foreign banished wight[6] shall anchor in this port;
Our realm brooks not seditious sects, let them elsewhere resort.
15   My rusty sword through rest shall first his edge employ
To poll their tops[7] that seek such change or gape[8] for future joy.

On Monsieur's Departure[1]

I grieve and dare not show my discontent,
I love and yet am forced to seem to hate,
I do, yet dare not say I ever meant,
I seem stark mute but inwardly do prate.
5   I am and not,° I freeze and yet am burned,   *am not*
Since from myself another self I turned.

My care is like my shadow in the sun,
Follows me flying, flies when I pursue it,

---

1. I.e., this prison could bear witness recently to fortune's
wavering state, where once it did not have to borrow joy
[as it does now].
2. I.e., nothing can be done by one who is in prison, so
may God send to my foes what they have suspected me of
planning.
1. My harm.
2. I.e., because of a change of wind, my enemies' clouds of
joy can turn to the rain of repentance.
3. I.e., at their most hopeful, my enemies supposed that
the tree of my monarchy would be uprooted, but their
grafted limbs of guile will bear no fruit.

4. Men.
5. The rule of Elizabeth's father, Henry VIII, and brother,
Edward VI, both Protestants.
6. Any supporter of Philip II, king of Spain and consort of
Mary I.
7. Cut their heads off.
8. Smile.
1. The poem expresses Elizabeth's regret at the departure
of the Duke d'Alençon, who had sought her hand in marriage. After four years of visits and inconclusive negotiations, the courtship ended in 1583.

Stands and lies by me, doth what I have done.
10 His too familiar care doth make me rue° it.   *regret*
      No means I find to rid him from my breast,
      Till by the end of things° it be supprest.   *death*

Some gentler passion slide into my mind,
For I am soft and made of melting snow;
15 Or be more cruel, love, and so be kind.
Let me or° float or sink, be high or low.   *either*
      Or let me live with some more sweet content,
      Or die and so forget what love ere meant.

Psalm 13

Fools that true faith yet never had
Saith in their hearts, there is no God.
Filthy they are in their practice,
Of them not one is godly wise.
5   From heaven the Lord on man did look
To know what ways he undertook.
All they were vain and went astray,
Not one he found in the right way.
In heart and tongue have they deceit,
10 Their lips throw forth a poisoned bait.
Their minds are mad, their mouths° are wode,°   *speech/empty*
And swift they be in shedding blood.
So blind they are, no truth they know,
No fear of God in them will grow.
15 How can that cruel sort be good,
Of God's dear flock which suck the blood?
On him rightly shall they not call,
Despair will so their hearts appall.
At all times God is with the just,
20 Because they put in him their trust.
Who shall therefore from Sion[1] give
That health which hangeth in our belief?
When God shall take from his the smart,
Then will Jacob rejoice in heart.
25   Praise to God

from The Metres of Boethius's *Consolation of Philosophy*[1]
Book 1, No. 2

O in how headlong depth the drowned mind is dim!
      And losing light her own, to others' darkness drawn,
As oft as driven with earthly flaws the harmful care upward grows.[2]
      Once this man free in open field used the skies to view,

1. Zion, the heavenly city, source and object of salvation.
1. These poems are Elizabeth's translations, undertaken late in her life, of portions of the *De consolatione philosophiae* (*On the Consolation of Philosophy*) by the Christian martyr Anicius Manlius Severinus Boethius (475–525), written while Boethius was in prison, awaiting execution. The treatise's representation of a heavenly perspective from which earthly concerns appear trivial

made it a favorite work of moral philosophy through the Middle Ages and early modern period. Even at the height of her power, Elizabeth was attracted by Boethius's Stoic rejection of worldly ambition.
2. I.e., losing her own light, the mind is drawn to the darkness of others, just as care grows with the faults of others.

5   Of rosie sun the light beheld,
        Of frosty moon the planets saw,
    And what star else runs her wonted° course.   *accustomed*
        Bending by many circles this man had wone°   *used to*
    By number to know them all;[3]
10   Yea, causes each whence roaring winds the seas perturb.
    Acquainted with the spirit that rolls the steady world,
        And why the star that falls to the Hesperia's waters[4]
    From his reddy° root doth raise herself.[5]   *reddish*
        Who that gives the spring's mild hours their temper,
15   That with rosy flowers the earth bedeckt,
        Who made the fertile autumn at fullest of the year
    Abound with grape all swollen with ripest fruits.
        He, wonted to search and find sundry causes of hidden nature,
    Down lies of mind's light bereaved,[6]
20   With bruised neck by overheavy chains,
    A bowed low look by weight bearing,
        Driven, alas, the silly° earth behold.   *insignificant*

Book 1, No. 7

    Dim clouds,
    Sky close,
    Light none
    Can afford.
5   If roiling seas
    Boisterous soweth,°   *scatters*
    Mix his° foam,   *its*
    Greeny° once   *greenish*
    Like the clearest
10   Days, the water—
    Straight mud,
    Stirred up all foul—
    The sight gainsays.°   *prevents*
    Running stream
15   That pours
    From highest hills,
    Oft is stayed
    By slaked°   *cool*
    Stone of rock.
20   Thou, if thou wilt
    In clearest light
    The truth behold,
    By straight line
    Hit in the path.[1]
25   Chase joys,

---

3. I.e., this man was accustomed to know all the "circles" (cycles and epicycles of the stars and planets).
4. The sea to the west of the Hesperides, mythical islands located beyond the known horizon.
5. "His root" and "herself" both refer to the star that sinks in the west, perhaps the planet Mars, known for its red-

dish tinge.
6. I.e., happiness comes to the man who studies and knows nature; but when he contemplates the insignificance of the earth, he is weighed down with care.
1. I.e., keep to the path in a straight line.

Repulse fear,
Thrust out hope,
Woe not retain.
30   Cloudy is the mind
With snaffle° bound   *bridle-bit*
Where they reign.[2]

Book 2, No. 3

In pool when Phoebus with reddy wain[1]
   The light to spread begins,
The star,[2] dimmed with flames° uprising,   *of the sun*
   Pales her whitty° looks.   *whitish*
5   When wood° with Siphirus'[3] milding blast   *vegetation*
   Blusheth with the springing° roses,   *budding*
And cloudy soweth his blustering blasts,
   Away from stalk° the beauty goes.   *of the flower*
Some time with calmy fair° the sea   *a fair calm*
10   Void of waves doth run;
Oft boisterous tempests the north
   With foaming seas turns up.[4]
If rarely steady be the world's form,
   If turns so many it makes,
15   Believe slippar° mens' lucks,   *slippery*
   Trust that sliding° be their goods.   *impermanent*
Certain, and in eternal law is writ,
   Sure standeth naught° is made.   *nothing that*

SPEECHES

The speeches of Elizabeth I exemplify early modern public oratory at its most effective. But they are also marked by features uniquely derived from her sense of herself as a monarch who wished (and probably needed) to convince her subjects that their welfare was more important to her than her own. In the excerpts that follow, Elizabeth emphasizes that although nature made her a woman and therefore of the weaker sex, divine right has made her a "prince," a person endowed with a masculine persona whose function it is to command not obey. She further emphasizes that her principal care is for her subjects, who are her charges and in some sense her children. In her public dealings throughout her reign, she played the gender card for all it was worth; in so doing, she transformed the fact that she was a woman, potentially a liability, into an instrument of policy.

On Marriage[1]

I may say unto you that from my years of understanding, sith[2] I first had consideration of myself to be born a servitor of Almighty God, I happily chose this kind of life in which

---

2. Boethius extols the extreme indifference to fortune and the emotions that Stoic philosophers believed was necessary for the good life.
1. I.e., when Phoebus, or Apollo, god of the sun with his red chariot, spreads his light over the deep.
2. Venus, who as the morning star is known as Lucifer, or the light-bearer.
3. Zephyrus, god of the west wind.
4. This series of alterations in states of being—from darkness to light, from a breeze to a gale, and from a calm to a foaming sea—illustrate the "eternal law" of change.
1. In 1559, a year after she had acceded to the throne at

the age of twenty-five, Elizabeth addressed Parliament on the subject of marriage. Because the monarchy passed on by inheritance, it was expected that a monarch would marry and have children. In this speech, Elizabeth hints that she will never marry and also that she trusts God to provide for her successor, who, she guesses, may be more "beneficial" to the kingdom than any child of her own would be. She probably intended to convey to her subjects that she would never abandon the kingdom either to the rule of a foreign prince (as Mary I had) or to a succession crisis.
2. Since.

I yet live, which I assure you for mine own part hath hitherto best contented myself and I trust hath been most acceptable to God. From the which, if either ambition of high estate offered to me in marriage by the pleasure and appointment of my prince[3]—whereof I have some records in this presence, as you our Lord Treasurer[4] well know; or if the eschewing of the danger of mine enemies or the avoiding of the period of death, whose messenger or rather continual watchman, the prince's indignation, was not little time daily before mine eyes—by whose means, although I know or justly may suspect, yet I will not now utter; or if the whole cause were in my sister herself, I will not now burthen her therewith, because I will not charge the dead: if any of these I say, I had not now remained in this estate wherein you see me. But so constant have I always continued in this determination—although my youth and words may seem to some hardly to agree together—yet is it most true that at this day I stand free from any other meaning that either I have had in times past or have at this present. With which trade of life I am so thoroughly acquainted that I trust God, who hath hitherto therein preserved and led me by the hand, will not now of His goodness suffer me to go alone. * * *

Nevertheless—if any of you be in suspect—whensoever it may please God to incline my heart to another kind of life, ye may well assure yourselves my meaning is not to do or determine anything wherewith the realm may or shall have just cause to be discontented. And therefore put that clean out of your heads.[5] For I assure you—what credit my assurance may have with you I cannot tell, but what credit it shall deserve to have the sequence shall declare—I will never in that matter conclude anything that shall be prejudicial to the realm, for the weal, good, and safety whereof I will never shun to spend my life. And whomsoever my chance shall be to light upon, I trust he shall be as careful for the realm and you—I will not say as myself, because I cannot so certainly determine of any other; but at the least ways, by my good will and desire he shall be such as shall be as careful for the preservation of the realm and you as myself.

And albeit it might please Almightly God to continue me still in this mind to live out of the state of marriage, yet it is not to be feared but He will so work in my heart and in your wisdoms as good provision by His help may be made in convenient time, whereby the realm shall not remain destitute of an heir that may be a fit governor, and peradventure more beneficial to the realm than such offspring as may come of me. For, although I be never so careful of your well doings and mind ever so to be, yet may my issue grow out of kind and become perhaps ungracious. And in the end, this shall be for me sufficient, that a marble stone shall declare that a Queen, having reigned such a time, lived and died a virgin.

On Mary, Queen of Scots,[1]

The bottomless graces and immeasurable benefits bestowed upon me by the Almighty are and have been such, as I must not only acknowledge them but admire

---

3. The "prince" Elizabeth refers to is probably not Philip II, the consort of Mary I, but rather Mary herself, who in her official capacity as queen regnant might have offered her sister's hand in marriage to a suitable consort. Elizabeth can refer to Mary as her "sister" when she alludes to a "cause" that had no implications for the state but is rather personal, "in my sister herself."
4. The Marquis of Winchester.
5. Elizabeth emphasizes that her subjects and their representatives in Parliament have no authority to force her into marriage, however desirable they may think marriage is for the future of the kingdom.

1. The text is Elizabeth's answer to a petition from Parliament to execute Mary, Queen of Scots, who was reported to have conspired to depose her cousin Elizabeth and who had been a prisoner of the English queen for ten years. In August 1586, evidence of a new plot came to light, and the conspirators, led by Sir Thomas Babington, were executed. On the evidence in letters to Babington, Mary was then formally tried and convicted of treason by a special court of peers, counsellors, and judges. Elizabeth answered Parliament in October by asking for delay and divine enlightenment.

them, accounting them as well miracles as benefits; not so much in respect of His Divine Majesty—with whom nothing is more common than to do things rare and singular—as in regard of our weakness, who cannot sufficiently set forth His wonderful works and graces, which to me have been so many, so diversely folded and embroidered one upon another, as in no sort am I able to express them.

And although there liveth not any that may more justly acknowledge themselves infinitely bound unto God than I, whose life He hath miraculously preserved at sundry times (beyond my merit) from a multitude of perils and dangers, yet is not that the cause for which I count myself the deepliest bound to give Him my humblest thanks, or to yield Him greatest recognition; but this which I shall tell you hereafter, which will deserve the name of wonder, if rare things and seldom seen be worthy of account. Even this it is: that as I came to the crown with the willing hearts of subjects, so do I now, after twenty-eight years' reign, perceive in you no diminution of good wills, which, if haply I should want, well might I breathe but never think I lived.

And now, albeit I find my life hath been full dangerously sought, and death contrived by such as no desert procured it, yet am I thereof so clear from malice—which hath the property to make men glad at the falls and faults of their foes, and make them seem to do for other causes, when rancor is the ground—as I protest it is and hath been my grievous thought that one, not different in sex, of like estate, and my near kin, should be fallen into so great a crime. Yea, I had so little purpose to pursue her with any color of malice, that as it is not unknown to some of my Lords here—for now I will play the blab—I secretly wrote her a letter upon the discovery of sundry treasons, that if she would confess them, and privately acknowledge them by her letters unto myself, she never should need be called for them into so public question. Neither did I it of mind to circumvent her, for then I knew as much as she could confess; and so did I write.

And if, even yet, now the matter is made but too apparent, I thought she truly would repent—as perhaps she would easily appear in outward show to do—and that for her none other would take the matter upon them; or that we were but as two milk-maids, with pails upon our arms; or that there were no more dependency upon us, but mine own life were only in danger, and not the whole estate of your religion and well doings; I protest—wherein you may believe me, for although I may have many vices, I hope I have not accustomed my tongue to be an instrument of untruth—I would most willingly pardon and remit this offence. Or if by my death other nations and kingdoms might truly say that this realm had attained an ever prosperous and flourishing estate, I would (I assure you) not desire to live, but gladly give my life, to the end my death might procure you a better prince. And for your sakes it is that I desire to live: to keep you from a worse. For, as for me, I assure you I find no great cause I should be fond to live. I take no such pleasure in it that I should much wish it, nor conceive such terror in death that I should greatly fear it. And yet I say not but, if the stroke were coming, perchance flesh and blood would be moved with it, and seek to shun it.

I have had good experience and trial of this world. I know what it is to be a subject, what to be a sovereign, what to have good neighbors, and sometime meet evil-willers. I have found treason in trust, seen great benefits little regarded, and instead of gratefulness, courses[2] of purpose to cross. These former remembrances, present feeling, and future expectation of evils, (I say), have made me think an evil is much the better the less while it dureth,[3] and so them happiest that are soonest

2. Plans.   3. Lasts.

hence;[4] and taught me to bear with a better mind these treasons, than is common to my sex—yea, with a better heart perhaps than is in some men. Which I hope you will not merely impute to my simplicity or want of understanding, but rather that I thus conceived—that had their purposes taken effect, I should not have found the blow, before I had felt it; nor, though my peril should have been great, my pain should have been but small and short. Wherein, as I would be loath to die so bloody a death, so doubt I not but God would have given me grace to be prepared for such an event; which, when it shall chance, I refer to His good pleasure.

And now, as touching their treasons and conspiracies, together with the contriver of them. I will not so prejudicate myself and this my realm as to say or think that I might not, without the last statute, by the ancient laws of this land have proceeded against her; which[5] was not made particularly to prejudice her, though perhaps it might then be suspected in respect of the disposition of such as depend that way. It was so far from being intended to entrap her, that it was rather an admonition to warn the danger thereof. But sith it is made, and in the force of a law, I thought good, in that which might concern her, to proceed according thereunto rather than by course of common law. Wherein, if you the judges have not deceived me, or that the books you brought me were not false— which God forbid—I might as justly have tried her by the ancient laws of the land.

But you lawyers are so nice and so precise in sifting and scanning every word and letter, that many times you stand more upon form than matter, upon syllables than the sense of the law. For, in this strictness and exact following of common form, she must have been indicted in Staffordshire, been arraigned at the bar, holden up her hand, and then been tried by a jury: a proper course, forsooth, to deal in that manner with one of her estate! I thought it better, therefore, for avoiding of these and more absurdities, to commit the cause to the inquisition of a good number of the greatest and most noble personages of this realm, of the judges and others of good account, whose sentence I must approve.[6]

And all little enough: for we Princes, I tell you, are set on stages, in the sight and view of all the world duly observed. The eyes of many behold our actions; a spot is soon spied in our garments, a blemish quickly noted in our doings. It behoveth us, therefore, to be careful that our proceedings be just and honorable.

But I must tell you one thing more: that in this late Act of Parliament you have laid an hard hand on me—that I must give direction for her death, which cannot be but most grievous, and an irksome burden to me. And lest you might mistake mine absence from this Parliament—which I had almost forgotten: although there be no cause why I should willingly come amongst multitudes (for that amongst many, some may be evil), yet hath it not been the doubt of any such danger or occasion that kept me from thence, but only the great grief to hear this cause spoken of, especially that such one of state and kin should need so open a declaration, and that this nation should be so spotted with blots of disloyalty. Wherein, the less is my grief for that I hope the better part is mine; and those of the worse not much to be accounted of, for that in seeking my destruction they might have spoiled their own souls.

And even now could I tell you that which would make you sorry. It is a secret; and yet I will tell it you (although it be known I have the property to keep counsel but too well, often times to mine own peril). It is not long since mine eyes did see it

---

4. I.e., out of this world.
5. I.e., the Parliamentary statute of 1584–85, known as the Act for the Queen's Surety, which provided for the trial of Mary, Queen of Scots, should she be accused of treason.

6. Elizabeth claims that Mary could have been tried as a criminal in a common law court but that this would have been an improper way to proceed as Mary remained a Queen of Scotland and therefore was not liable under English law.

written that an oath was taken within few days either to kill me or to be hanged themselves; and that to be performed ere one month were ended. Hereby I see your danger in me, and neither can or will be so unthankful or careless of your consciences as to take no care for your safety.

I am not unmindful of your oath made in the Association,[7] manifesting your great good wills and affections, taken and entered into upon good conscience and true knowledge of the guilt, for safeguard of my person; done (I protest to God) before I ever heard it, or ever thought of such a matter, till a thousand hands, with many obligations, were showed me at Hampton Court, signed and subscribed with the names and seals of the greatest of this land. Which, as I do acknowledge as a perfect argument of your true hearts and great zeal to my safety, so shall my bond be stronger tied to greater care for all your good.

But, for that this matter is rare, weighty and of great consequence, and I think you do not look for any present resolution—the rather for that, as it is not my manner in matters of far less moment to give speedy answer without due consideration, so in this of such importance—I think it very requisite with earnest prayer to beseech His Divine Majesty so to illuminate mine understanding and inspire me with His grace, as I may do and determine that which shall serve to the establishment of His Church, preservation of your estates, and prosperity of this Commonwealth under my charge. Wherein, for that I know delay is dangerous, you shall have with all conveniency our resolution delivered by our message. And what ever any prince may merit of their subjects, for their approved testimony of their unfeigned sincerity, either by governing justly, void of all partiality, or sufferance of any injuries done (even to the poorest), that do I assuredly promise inviolably to perform, for requital of your so many deserts.

On Mary's Execution[1]

Full grievous is the way whose going on and end breeds cumber[2] for the hire of a laborious journey. I have strived more this day than ever in my life whether I should speak or use silence. If I speak and not complain, I shall dissemble; if I hold my peace, your labor taken were full vain.

For me to make my moan were strange and rare, for I suppose you shall find few that, for their own particular, will cumber you with such a care. Yet such, I protest, hath been my greedy desire and hungry will that of your consultation might have fallen out some other means to work my safety, joined with your assurance, than that for which you are become so earnest suitors, as I protest I must needs use complaint[3]— though not of you, but unto you, and of the cause; for that I do perceive, by your advices, prayers, and desires, there falleth out this accident, that only my injurer's bane must be my life's surety.

But if any there live so wicked of nature to suppose that I prolonged this time only pro forma, to the intent to make a show of clemency, thereby to set my praises to the wire-drawers[4] to lengthen them the more, they do me so great a wrong as they can hardly recompense. Or if any person there be that think or imagine that the least vain-

---

7. The Oath (or Bond) of Association was taken by the Queen's Council in October 1582. It provided for Mary's arrest and execution without a trial; in essence, it sanctioned a lynching.
1. Parliament had determined that Elizabeth's safety and the future of Protestantism in England could be secured only by Mary's execution; it sent a delegation to Eliza-

beth asking for her approval. Again Elizabeth demurred. It was only in February 1587, after a new conspiracy was discovered, that Elizabeth signed Mary's death warrant.
2. Distress.
3. Express regret.
4. One who draws metal into wire.

glorious thought hath drawn me further herein, they do me as open injury as ever was done to any living creature—as He that is the maker of all thoughts knoweth best to be true. Or if there be any that think that the Lords, appointed in commission, durst do no other, as fearing thereby to displease or to be suspected to be of a contrary opinion to my safety, they do but heap upon me injurious conceits. For, either those put in trust by me to supply my place have not performed their duty towards me, or else they have signified unto you all that my desire was that every one should do according to his conscience, and in the course of these proceedings should enjoy both freedom of voice and liberty of opinion, and what they would not openly, they might privately to myself declare. It was of a willing mind and great desire I had, that some other means might be found out, wherein I should have taken more comfort than in any other thing under the sun.

And since now it is resolved that my surety cannot be established without a princess's head, I have just cause to complain that I, who have in my time pardoned so many rebels, winked at so many treasons, and either not produced[5] them or altogether slipped them over with silence, should now be forced to this proceeding, against such a person. I have besides, during my reign, seen and heard many opprobrious books and pamphlets against me, my realm and state, accusing me to be a tyrant. I thank them for their alms. I believe therein their meaning was to tell me news: and news it is to me indeed. I would it were as strange to hear of their impiety. What will they not now say, when it shall be spread that for the safety of her life a maiden queen could be content to spill the blood even of her own kinswoman? I may therefore full well complain that any man should think me given to cruelty; whereof I am so guiltless and innocent as I should slander God if I should say He gave me so vile a mind. Yea, I protest, I am so far from it that for mine own life I would not touch her. Neither hath my care been so much bent how to prolong mine, as how to preserve both: which I am right sorry is made so hard, yea so impossible.

I am not so void of judgment as not to see mine own peril; nor yet so ignorant as not to know it were in nature a foolish course to cherish a sword to cut mine own throat; nor so careless as not to weigh that my life daily is in hazard. But this I do consider, that many a man would put his life in danger for the safeguard of a king. I do not say that so will I; but I pray you think that I have thought upon it.

But sith so many hath both written and spoken against me, I pray you give me leave to say somewhat for myself, and, before you return to your countries, let you know for what a one you have passed so careful thoughts. And, as I think myself infinitely beholding unto you all that seek to preserve my life by all the means you may, so I protest that there liveth no prince—nor ever shall be—more mindful to requite so good deserts. Wherein, as I perceive you have kept your old wont[6] in a general seeking the lengthening of my days, so am I sure that never shall I requite it, unless I had as many lives as you all; but for ever I will acknowledge it while there is any breath left me. Although I may not justify, but may justly condemn, my sundry faults and sins to God, yet for my care in this government let me acquaint you with my intents.

When first I took the sceptre, my title made me not forget the giver, and therefore [I] began as it became me, with such religion as both I was born in, bred in, and, I trust, shall die in; although I was not so simple as not to know what danger and peril so great an alteration might procure me—how many great princes of the contrary opinion would attempt all they might against me, and generally what enmity I should thereby breed unto myself. Which all I regarded not, knowing that He, for whose sake I did it,

---

5. Acted upon.   6. Desire.

might and would defend me. Rather marvel that I am, than muse that I should not be if it were not God's holy hand that continueth me beyond all other expectation.

I was not simply trained up, nor in my youth spent my time altogether idly; and yet, when I came to the crown, then entered I first into the school of experience, bethinking myself of those things that best fitted a king—justice, temper, magnanimity, judgment. As for the two latter, I will not boast. But for the two first, this may I truly say: among my subjects I never knew a difference of person, where right was one;[7] nor never to my knowledge preferred for favor what I thought not fit for worth; nor bent mine ears to credit a tale that first was told me; nor was so rash to corrupt my judgment with my censure, ere I heard the cause. I will not say but many reports might fortune[8] be brought me by such as must hear the matter, whose partiality might mar the right; for we princes cannot hear all causes ourselves. But this dare I boldly affirm: my verdict went with the truth of my knowledge.

But full well wished Alcibiades[9] his friend, that he should not give any answer till he had recited the letters of the alphabet. So have I not used over-sudden resolutions in matters that have touched me full near: you will say that with me, I think. And therefore, as touching your counsels and consultations, I conceive them to be wise, honest, and conscionable; so provident and careful for the safety of my life (which I wish no longer than may be for your good), that though I never can yield you of recompense your due, yet shall I endeavor myself to give you cause to think your good will not ill bestowed, and strive to make myself worthy for such subjects. And as for your petition: your judgment I condemn not, neither do I mistake your reasons, but pray you to accept my thankfulness, excuse my doubtfulness, and take in good part my answer-answerless. Wherein I attribute not so much to my own judgment, but that I think many particular persons may go before me, though by my degree I go before them. Therefore, if I should say, I would not do what you request, it might peradventure be more than I thought; and to say I would do it, might perhaps breed peril of that you labor to preserve, being more than in your own wisdoms and discretions would seem convenient,[1] circumstances of place and time being duly considered.

To the English Troops at Tilbury, Facing the Spanish Armada[1]

My loving people, we have been persuaded by some that are careful of our safety, to take heed how we commit ourselves to armed multitudes, for fear of treachery. But I assure you, I do not desire to live to distrust my faithful and loving people. Let tyrants fear. I have always so behaved myself that, under God, I have placed my chiefest strength and safeguard in the loyal hearts and good will of my subjects; and therefore I am come amongst you, as you see, at this time, not for my recreation and disport,[2] but being at this time resolved, in the midst and heat of the battle, to live or die amongst you all, to lay down for my God, and for my kingdom, and for my people, my honor and my blood, even in the dust. I know I have the body of a weak and feeble woman, but I have the heart and stomach of a king, and of a king of England too, and think

---

7. I.e., my justice was impartial; it did not regard rank, occupation, or property as factors in determining what was right.
8. By chance.
9. An Athenian statesman who took part in the Peloponnesian War; changed sides to support Athen's enemy, Sparta; and was finally assassinated by Persians with whom he sought an alliance. The source of Elizabeth's reference is unknown.

1. Elizabeth equivocates nicely. She refuses to disagree with Parliament, lest she not respect her own misgivings; she refuses to agree with Parliament, lest its policy not be in her own interest.
1. In 1588, with the Spanish fleet threatening the south coast of England, Elizabeth went to Tilbury, in Dorset, to speak to the troops who were guarding England against an invasion.
2. Amusement.

foul scorn[3] that Parma or Spain, or any prince of Europe should dare to invade the border of my realm; to which rather than any dishonor shall grow[4] by me, I myself will take up arms, I myself will be your general, judge, and rewarder of every one of your virtues in the field. I know, already for your forwardness[5] you have deserved rewards and crowns;[6] and we do assure you, in the word of a prince, they shall be duly paid you.

The Golden Speech[1]

Mr. Speaker, we have heard your declaration and perceive your care of our estate, by falling into a consideration of a grateful acknowledgment of such benefits as you have received; and that your coming is to present thanks to us, which I accept with no less joy than your loves can have desire to offer such a present.

I do assure you there is no prince that loves his subjects better, or whose love can countervail our love. There is no jewel, be it of never so rich a price, which I set before this jewel: I mean your love. For I do esteem it more than any treasure or riches; for that we know how to prize, but love and thanks I count unvaluable. And, though God hath raised me high, yet this I count the glory of my crown, that I have reigned with your loves. This makes me that I do not so much rejoice that God hath made me to be a queen, as to be a queen over so thankful a people. Therefore, I have cause to wish nothing more than to content the subject; and that is a duty which I owe. Neither do I desire to live longer days than I may see your prosperity; and that is my only desire. And as I am that person that still yet under God hath delivered you, so I trust, by the almighty power of God, that I shall be His instrument to preserve you from every peril, dishonor, shame, tyranny and oppression; partly by means of your intended helps which we take very acceptably, because it manifesteth the largeness of your good loves and loyalties unto your sovereign.

Of myself I must say this: I never was any greedy, scraping grasper, nor a strait, fast-holding prince, nor yet a waster. My heart was never set on any worldly goods, but only for my subjects' good. What you bestow on me, I will not hoard it up, but receive it to bestow on you again. Yea, mine own properties I account yours, to be expended for your good; and your eyes shall see the bestowing of all for your good. Therefore, render unto them, I beseech you, Mr. Speaker, such thanks as you imagine my heart yieldeth, but my tongue cannot express.

Since I was queen, yet did I never put my pen to any grant but that, upon pretext and semblance made unto me, it was both good and beneficial to the subject in general, though a private profit to some of my ancient servants who had deserved well at my hands. But the contrary being found by experience, I am exceedingly beholding to such subjects as would move the same at the first. And I am not so simple to suppose, but that there be some of the Lower House whom these grievances never touched: and for them, I think they spake out of zeal to their countries,[2] and not out of spleen or malevolent affection as being parties grieved; and I take it exceeding gratefully from them, because it gives us to know that no respects or interest had moved them, other than the minds they have to suffer no diminution of our

---

3. Shameful.
4. Be caused.
5. Courage.
6. Recompense.
1. The queen had the prerogative or absolute power to grant favored subjects a patent for an exclusive manufacture. But the monopolies so created were disliked by those who would otherwise have competed for business,

and a move to limit them was begun in Parliament. In response, in 1601, Elizabeth met with a committee of the House of Commons, led by the Speaker, thanked them for the subsidies recently granted the crown by the Commons, and promised to reform her practice.
2. I.e, those members who protested monopolies in behalf of their constituents, or "countries," and not on their own account.

honor and our subjects' love unto us. The zeal of which affection, tending to ease my people and knit their hearts unto me, I embrace with a princely care, for above all earthly treasure I esteem my people's love, more than which I desire not to merit.

That my grants should be grievous to my people and oppressions privileged under color of our patents, our kingly dignity shall not suffer[3] it. Yea, when I heard it, I could give no rest unto my thoughts until I had reformed it. Shall they, think you, escape unpunished that have thus oppressed you, and have been respectless of their duty, and regardless of our honor?[4] No, I assure you, Mr. Speaker, were it not more for conscience' sake than for any glory or increase of love that I desire, these errors, troubles, vexations and oppressions, done by these varlets and lewd persons, not worthy the name of subjects, should not escape without condign punishment. But I perceive they dealt with me like physicians who, ministering a drug, make it more acceptable by giving it a good aromatical savor, or when they give pills do gild them all over.[5]

I have ever used to set the Last-Judgment Day before mine eyes, and so to rule as I shall be judged to answer before a higher Judge, to whose judgment seat I do appeal, that never thought was cherished in my heart that tended not unto my people's good. And now, if my kingly bounties have been abused, and my grants turned to the hurt of my people, contrary to my will and meaning, and if any in authority under me have neglected or perverted what I have committed to them, I hope God will not lay their culps[6] and offences to my charge; who, though there were danger in repealing our grants, yet what danger would I not rather incur for your good, than I would suffer them still to continue?

I know the title of a king is a glorious title; but assure yourself that the shining glory of princely authority hath not so dazzled the eyes of our understanding, but that we well know and remember that we also are to yield an account of our actions before the great Judge. To be a king and wear a crown is a thing more glorious to them that see it, than it is pleasant to them that bear it. For myself, I was never so much enticed with the glorious name of a king or royal authority of a queen, as delighted that God hath made me His instrument to maintain His truth and glory, and to defend this kingdom (as I said) from peril, dishonor, tyranny and oppression.

There will never queen sit in my seat with more zeal to my country, care for my subjects, and that will sooner with willingness venture her life for your good and safety, than myself. For it is my desire to live nor reign no longer than my life and reign shall be for your good. And though you have had and may have many princes more mighty and wise sitting in this seat, yet you never had nor shall have any that will be more careful and loving.

Shall I ascribe anything to myself and my sexly weakness? I were not worthy to live then; and, of all, most unworthy of the mercies I have had from God, who hath given me a heart that yet never feared any foreign or home enemy. And I speak it to give God the praise, as a testimony before you, and not to attribute anything to myself. For I, oh Lord! what am I, whom practices and perils past should not fear? Or what can I do? That I should speak for any glory, God forbid.

This, Mr. Speaker, I pray you deliver unto the House, to whom heartily recommend me. And so I commit you all to your best fortunes and further counsels. And I pray you, Mr. Comptroller,[7] Mr. Secretary,[8] and you of my Council, that before these gentlemen go into their countries, you bring them all to kiss my hand.

3. Allow.
4. I.e., those who benefited from a monopoly without regard to the welfare of the general public.
5. Elizabeth compares unscrupulous patentees to physicians who coat bitter pills with sugar; in this case she is the patient who did not realize what was being given to her.
6. Sins.
7. Sir William Knollys.
8. Sir Robert Cecil.

---- ✦✦✦ ----

Aemilia Lanyer
1569–1645

Aemilia Lanyer was born Aemilia Bassano, the daughter of Queen Elizabeth's court musician, Baptista Bassano. Acquaintance with the nobility surrounding the Queen allowed her an education that was typically reserved for women of high station. At eighteen, shortly after her mother's death, she became the mistress of Henry Cary Hunsdon, the Lord Chancellor. Her position increased her presence at court until, at twenty-three, she became pregnant and was forced to marry a court musician. Their son, conspicuously named Henry, was born three months after the wedding. The first years of her married life were not auspicious. Alfonso Lanyer was a spendthrift, and the money Aemilia had acquired as Hunsdon's mistress was soon exhausted. Desperate for reassurance, she visited the astrologer Simon Forman to learn whether the stars indicated that Alfonso would gain a knighthood. The disreputable Forman appears to have had other ideas. His casebook records that on one occasion, he "went and supped with her and stayed all night, and she was familiar and friendly to him in all things. But only she would not halek [have intercourse] . . . he never obtained his purpose and she was a whore and dealt evil with him."

Lanyer's character is more accurately represented in the record of her long friendship with Margaret Clifford, Countess of Cumberland, and her daughter Anne. In 1610, partly in tribute to the loyal support of her patroness, Lanyer published a volume of poetry entitled *Salve Deus Rex Judaeorum*; this included a verse defense of women and a poem to Cookham, a country house leased by Margaret Clifford's brother, William Russell, and visited frequently by Lanyer until 1605. She particularly records two critical transformations in her sense of herself: a spiritual awakening, inspired by the piety of the Countess, and a confirmation of herself as a poet. Her impressions of Cookham express a unity among aesthetic elements that are usually opposed and antithetical: pagan culture and Christian vision, temporal experience and spiritual knowledge, and the erotic pleasure in the discipline of chastity.

The Description of Cookham

Farewell (sweet Cookham) where I first obtained
Grace from that Grace where perfit° grace remained;　　　　*perfect*
And where the Muses[1] gave their full consent,
I should have power the virtuous to content;
5　Where princely Palace willed me to indite,°　　　　*write*
The sacred story[2] of the soul's delight.
Farewell (sweet place) where virtue then did rest,
And all delights did harbor in her breast;
Never shall my said eyes again behold
10　Those pleasures which my thoughts did then unfold:
Yet you (great Lady),[3] Mistress of that place,
From whose desires did spring this work of grace;
Vouchsafe° to think upon those pleasures past,　　　　*agree*
As fleeting worldly joys that could not last,
15　Or, as dim shadows of celestial pleasures,
Which are desired above all earthly treasures.
Oh how (me thought) against you thither came,[4]

---

1. Divinities who presided over the arts and courtesy.
2. Possibly the story of the Passion, recounted in the poem *Salve Deus Rex Judaeorum*.

3. Margaret Clifford, the Countess of Cumberland.
4. In preparation for your arrival.

Each part did seem some new delight to frame!
The house received all ornaments to grace it,
20   And would endure no foulness to deface it.
The walks put on their summer liveries,°   *uniforms*
And all things else did hold like similies:°   *comparisons*
The trees with leaves, with fruits, with flowers clad,
Embraced each other, seeming to be glad,
25   Turning themselves to beauteous canopies,
To shade the bright sun from your brighter eyes.
The crystal streams with silver spangles graced,
While by the glorious sun they were embraced,
The little birds in chirping notes did sing,
30   To entertain both you and that sweet spring.
And Philomela⁵ with her sundry lays,°   *songs*
Both you and that delightful place did praise.
Oh, how me thought each plant, each flower, each tree
Set forth their beauties then to welcome thee:
35   The very hills right humbly did descend,
When you to tread upon them did intend.
And as you set your feet, they still did rise,
Glad that they could receive so rich a prize.
The gentle winds did take delight to be
40   Among those woods that were so graced by thee.
And in sad° murmur uttered pleasing sound,   *deep*
That pleasure in that place might more abound:
The swelling banks delivered all their pride,
When such a Phoenix⁶ once they had espied.
45   Each arbor, bank, each seat, each stately tree,
Thought themselves honored in supporting thee.
The pretty birds would oft come to attend thee,
Yet fly away for fear they should offend thee:
The little creatures in the burrow by°   *nearby*
50   Would come abroad to sport them in your eye;
Yet fearful of the bow in your fair hand,
Would run away when you did make a stand.
Now let me come unto that stately tree,
Wherein such goodly prospects you did see;
55   That oak that did in height his fellows pass,
As much as lofty trees, low growing grass
Much like a comely cedar straight and tall,
Whose beauteous stature far exceeded all.
How often did you visit this fair tree,
60   Which seeming joyful in receiving thee,
Would like a palm tree spread his arms abroad,
Desirous that you there should make abode:
Whose fair green leaves much like a comely veil,
Defended Phoebus when he would assail:⁷

5. In Greek mythology a woman who was transformed into a swallow; in Latin versions of her story she becomes a nightingale.
6. A mythical bird, always unique on earth, that regener-

ates itself in its own funeral pyre and therefore signifies eternity; here it figures the Countess.
7. The leaves of the palm tree protected the Countess from Phoebus, the god of the sun.

65 Whose pleasing boughs did yield a cool fresh air,
Joying his happiness when you were there.
Where being seated, you might plainly see,
Hills, vales, and woods, as if on bended knee
They had appeared, your honor to salute,

70 Or to prefer some strange unlooked for suit:
All interlaced with brooks and crystal springs,
A prospect fit to please the eyes of kings:
And thirteen shires appeared all in your sight,
Europe could not afford much more delight.

75 What was there then but gave you all content,
While you the time in meditation spent,
Of their Creator's power, which there you saw,
In all his creatures held a perfit law;
And in their beauties did you plain descry,°   discern

80 His beauty, wisdom, grace, love, majesty.
In these sweet woods how often did you walk,
With Christ and his apostles there to talk;
Placing his holy writ in some fair tree,
To meditate what you therein did see:

85 With Moses you did mount his holy hill,[8]
To know his pleasure, and perform his will.
With lovely David[9] you did often sing
His holy hymns to heaven's eternal king.
And in sweet music did your soul delight,

90 To sound his praises, morning, noon, and night.
With blessed Joseph you did often feed
Your pined° brethren, when they stood in need.[1]   poor
And that sweet lady sprung from Clifford's race,[2]
Of noble Bedford's blood, fair steam of grace,

95 To honorable Dorset now espoused,
In whose fair breast true virtue then was housed.
Oh, what delight did my weak spirits find
In those pure parts of her well framed mind,
And yet it grieves me that I cannot be

100 Near unto her, whose virtues did agree
With those fair ornaments of outward beauty,
Which did enforce from all both love and duty.
Unconstant Fortune, thou art most to blame,
Who casts us down into so low a frame,

105 Where our great friends we cannot daily see,
So great a diffrence is there in degree.
Many are placed in those orbs of state,
Parters° in honor, so ordained by Fate;   participants
Nearer in show, yet farther off in love,

8. Moses climbed Mount Sinai to receive the law of God (Exodus 24, 25).
9. King David the psalmist.
1. Sold by his jealous brothers into slavery, Joseph became Pharoah's right-hand man and granted these same brothers food and money during a famine many years later (Genesis 42.1–28).
2. The Lady is the Countess's daughter Anne, descended from Margaret Russell of Bedford and her father George Clifford, Duke of Cumberland. Anne married the Earl of Dorset in 1609 and is thus referred to as Dorset.

110 In which, the lowest always are above.³
    But whither am I carried in conceit?°   *imagination*
    My wit too weak to conster of° the great.   *understand*
    Why not? although we are but born of earth,
    We may behold the heavens, despising death;
115 And loving heaven that is so far above,
    May in the end vouchsafe us entire love.
    Therefore sweet memory do thou retain
    Those pleasures past, which will not turn again;
    Remember beauteous Dorset's former sports,
120 So far from being touched by ill reports;
    Wherein myself did always bear a part,
    While reverend Love presented my true heart.
    Those recreations let me bear in mind,
    Which her sweet youth and noble thoughts did find,
125 Whereof deprived, I evermore must grieve,
    Hating blind Fortune, careless to relieve.
    And you sweet Cookham, whom these ladies leave,
    I now must tell the grief you did conceive
    At their departure; when they went away,
130 How everything retained a sad dismay;
    Nay long before, when once an inkling came,
    Methought each thing did unto sorrow frame:
    The trees that were so glorious in our view,
    Forsook both flowers and fruit, when once they knew
135 Of your depart,° their very leaves did wither,   *departure*
    Changing their colors as they grew together.
    But when they saw this had no power to stay you,
    They often wept, though speechless, could not pray⁴ you;
    Letting their tears in your fair bosoms fall,
140 As if they said, "Why will ye leave us all?"
    This being vain, they cast their leaves away,
    Hoping that pity would have made you stay,
    Their frozen tops like age's hoary hairs,
    Shows their disasters, languishing in fears;
145 A swarthy riveled rine° all overspread,   *bark*
    Their dying bodies half alive, half dead.
    But your occasions called you so away,
    That nothing there had power to make you stay:
    Yet did I see a noble grateful mind,
150 Requiting each according to their kind,
    Forgetting not to turn and take your leave
    Of these sad creatures, powerless to receive
    Your favor when with grief you did depart,
    Placing their former pleasures in your heart;
155 Giving great charge to noble memory,
    There to preserve their love continually:
    But specially the love of that fair tree,

3. I.e., persons of low station or rank love more than   4. Beg.
those who are of the gentry or nobility.

That first and last you did vouchsafe to see:
In which it pleased you oft to take the air,
160   With noble Dorset, then a virgin fair:
Where many a learned book was read and scanned
To this fair tree, taking me by the hand,
You did repeat the pleasures which had passed,
Seeming to grieve they could no longer last.
165   And with a chaste, yet loving kiss took leave,
Of which sweet kiss I did it soon bereave:[5]
Scorning a senseless creature should possess
So rare a favor, so great happiness.
No other kiss it could receive from me,
170   For fear to give back what it took of thee:
So I ungrateful creature did deceive it,
Of that which you vouchsafed in love to leave it.
And though it oft° had given me much content,   *often*
Yet this great wrong I never could repent:
175   But of the happiest made it most forlorn,
To show that nothing's free from Fortune's scorn,
While all the rest with this most beauteous tree,
Made their sad consort° sorrow's harmony.   *music*
The flowers that on the banks and walks did grow,
180   Crept in the ground, the grass did weep for woe.
The winds and waters seemed to chide together,
Because you went away they know not whither:
And those sweet brooks that ran so fair and clear,
With grief and trouble wrinkled did appear.
185   Those pretty birds that wonted° were to sing,   *accustomed*
Now neither sing, nor chirp, nor use their wing;
But with their tender feet on some bare spray,
Warble forth sorrow, and their own dismay.
Fair Philomela leaves her mournful ditty,
190   Drowned in dead sleep, yet can procure no pity:
Each arbor, bank, each seat, each stately tree,
Looks bare and desolate now for want of thee;
Turning green tresses into frosty gray,
While in cold grief they wither all away.
195   The sun grew weak, his beams no comfort gave,
While all green things did make the earth their grave;
Each briar, each bramble, when you went away,
Caught fast your clothes, thinking to make you stay;
Delightful Echo[6] wonted° to reply   *used*
200   To our last words, did now for sorrow die:
The house cast off each garment that might grace it,
Putting on dust and cobwebs to deface it.
All desolation then there did appear,
When you were going whom they held so dear.
205   This last farewell to Cookham here I give,

5. I.e., I took their kiss from the tree on which they had
put it.

6. A nymph who can only repeat what she has heard; in
the absence of voices she dies.

When I am dead thy name in this may live,
Wherein I have performed her noble hest,°   *request*
Whose virtues lodge in my unworthy breast,
And ever shall, so long as life remains,
210   Tying my heart to her by those rich chains.

from Salve Deus Rex Judaeorum
To the Doubtful Reader

Gentle reader, if thou desire to be resolved, why I give this title, *Salve Deus Rex Judaeorum,* know for certain; that it was delivered unto me in sleep many years before I had any intent to write in this manner, and was quite out of my memory, until I had written the Passion of Christ, when immediately it came into my remembrance, what I had dreamed long before; and thinking it a significant token, that I was appointed to perform this work, I gave the very same words I received in sleep as the fittest title I could devise for this book.

To the Virtuous Reader[1]

Often have I heard, that it is the property of some women, not only to emulate the virtues and perfections of the rest, but also by all their powers of ill speaking, to eclipse the brightness of their deserved fame. Now contrary to this custom, which men I hope unjustly lay to their charge, I have written this small volume, or little book, for the general use of all virtuous ladies and gentlewomen of this kingdom; and in commendation of some particular persons of our own sex, such as for the most part are so well known to myself, and others, that I dare undertake fame dares not to call any better. And this have I done, to make known to the world that all women deserve not to be blamed, though some—forgetting they are women themselves and in danger to be condemned by the words of their own mouths—fall into so great an error as to speak unadvisedly against the rest of their sex; which if it be true, I am persuaded they can show their own imperfection in nothing more: and therefore could wish (for their own ease, modesties, and credit) they would refer[2] such points of folly to be practiced by evil disposed men, who forgetting they were born of women, nourished of women, and that if it were not by the means of women, they would be quite extinguished out of the world and a final end of them all, do like vipers deface the wombs wherein they were bred, only to give way and utterance to their want of discretion and goodness. Such as these, were they that dishonored Christ his apostles and prophets, putting them to shameful deaths. Therefore we are not to regard any imputations, that they undeservedly lay upon us, no[3] otherwise than to make use of them to our own benefits as spurs to virtue, making us fly all occasions that may color their unjust speeches to pass current,[4] especially considering that they have tempted even the patience of God himself, who gave power to wise and virtuous women, to bring down their pride and arrogance: As was cruel *Caesar* by the discreet counsel of noble

---

1. This preface is Lanyer's general introduction to her poem *Salve Deus Rex Judaeorum* (Hail, Lord God, King of the Jews). Three excerpts follow: the invocation, an argument against beauty without virtue, and Pilate's apology for Eve.

2. Assign.
3. Not.
4. To avoid occasions in which their unjust speeches might appear to have some truth.

Deborah,[5] judge and prophetess of Israel; and resolution of *Jael*, wife of *Heber* the Kenite; wicked *Haman*, by the divine prayers and prudent proceedings of beautiful *Hester*; blasphemous *Holofernes*, by the invincible courage, rare wisdom, and confident carriage of *Judith*; and the unjust judges, by the innocence of chaste *Susanna*; with infinite others, which for brevity's sake I will omit. As also in respect it pleased our Lord and Savior Jesus Christ, without the assistance of man, being free from original and all other sins from the time of his conception till the hour of his death, to be begotten of a woman, born of a woman, nourished of a woman, obedient to a woman; and that he healed woman,[6] pardoned women, comforted women; yea, even when he was in his greatest agony and bloody sweat, going to be crucified, and also in the last hour of his death, took care to dispose of a woman;[7] after his resurrection, appeared first to a woman, sent a woman to declare his most glorious resurrection to the rest of his disciples.[8] Many other examples I could allege of divers faithful and virtuous women, who have in all ages, not only been confessors, but also endured most cruel martyrdom for their faith in Jesus Christ. All which is sufficient to enforce all good Christians and honorable-minded men to speak reverently of our sex, and especially of all virtuous and good women. To the modest censures of both which, I refer these my imperfect endeavors, knowing that according to their own excellent dispositions, they will rather, cherish, nourish, and increase the least spark of virtue where they find it, by their favorable and best interpretations, than quench it by wrong constructions. To whom I wish all increase of virtue, and desire their best opinions.

[INVOCATION]

Sith *Cynthia*[9] is ascended to that rest
Of endless joy and true eternity,
That glorious place that cannot be expressed
By any wight° clad in mortality,   *person*
5   In her almighty love so highly blest,
And crowned with everlasting sovereignty;
  Where saints and angels do attend her throne,
  And she gives glory unto God alone.

To thee great Countess[1] now I will apply
10   My pen, to write thy never dying fame;
That when to heaven thy blessed soul shall fly,
These lines on earth record thy reverend name:
And to this task I mean my muse to tie,
  Though wanting skill I shall but purchase blame:

<hr/>

5. Lanyer lists virtuous women who benefited their people: Deborah, a wise judge and prophet of Israel, who urged the warrior Barak to attack their enemy, Sisera [Cesarus]; Jael, who killed Sisera with a blow to the head (both figures from Judges 4); Hester [Esther], the queen of the Israelites, who hanged Haman (Esther 5–7); the Jewish heroine Judith, who saved her town by killing King Nebuchadnezzar's general Holofernes (the Apocryphal Book of Judith 8–12); and Susanna, whose chastity was proved by the prophet Daniel (the Apocryphal History of Daniel and Susanna).
6. Womankind.

7. Jesus, from the cross, ordered a disciple (traditionally understood to be John) to care for his mother (John 19.25–27).
8. After his resurrection, Jesus appeared first to Mary Magdalene and "the other Mary," who then told the other disciples of this event (Matthew 28.8–10).
9. Goddess of the moon, also known as Diana; here she represents Queen Elizabeth I.
1. Lady Margaret Clifford, the Countess of Cumberland. Lanyer declares that the poem she is writing will be a memorial to her.

15   Pardon (dear Lady) want of woman's wit
   To pen thy praise, when few can equal it.

[AGAINST BEAUTY WITHOUT VIRTUE]

185   That outward beauty which the world commends
   Is not the subject I will write upon,
   Whose date expired, that tyrant Time soon ends;
   Those gaudy colors soon are spent and gone;
   But those fair virtues which on thee attends,
190   Are always fresh, they never are but one:
    They make thy beauty fairer to behold,
    Than was that queen's[2] for whom proud Troy was sold.

   As for those matchless colors red and white,
   Or perfit° features in a fading face,   *perfect*
195   Or due proportion pleasing to the sight;
   All these do draw but dangers and disgrace;
   A mind enriched with virtue, shines more bright,
   Adds everlasting beauty, gives true grace,
    Frames an immortal goddess on the earth,
200   Who though she dies, yet fame gives her new birth.

   That pride of nature which adorns the fair,
   Like blazing comets to allure all eyes,
   Is but the thread, that weaves their web of care,
   Who glories most, where most their danger lies;
205   For greatest perils do attend the fair,
   When men do seek, attempt, plot and devise,
    How they may overthrow the chastest dame,
    Whose beauty is the white[3] whereat they aim.

   'Twas beauty bred in Troy the ten years' strife,
210   And carried *Helen* from her lawful lord;
   'Twas beauty made chaste *Lucrece*[4] lose her life,
   For which proud *Tarquin's* fact° was so abhorr'd: *deed*
   Beauty the cause *Antonius*[5] wronged his wife,
   Which could not be decided but by sword:
215   Great *Cleopatra's* beauty and defects
    Did work *Octavia's* wrongs, and his neglects.

   What fruit did yield that fair forbidden tree,
   But blood, dishonor, infamy, and shame?
   Poor blinded queen,[6] could'st thou no better see,
220   But entertain disgrace, instead of fame?

---

2. Helen of Troy, wife of King Menelaus of Sparta. Renowned for her beauty, she was kidnapped by Paris, son of Priam, King of Troy. This brought about the Trojan War.
3. The "white" at which hunters aim is the breast of the deer (or dear), a common figure for the beloved lady.
4. Wife of the Roman nobleman Collatinus. She was raped by Sextus Tarquinius, son of Superbus, King of Rome. The crime aroused the people of Rome to over-throw the tyranny of the Tarquins and institute a republic.
5. Marc Antony, who married Octavia, sister to Octavius, who would become the Emperor Augustus; Antony later abandoned her in favor of Cleopatra, queen of Egypt.
6. Cleopatra, figuratively blinded by her passion for Marc Antony. The couple committed suicide after Marc Antony's defeat by Octavius at the battle of Actium.

Do these designs with majesty agree?
To stain thy blood, and blot thy royal name.
    That heart that gave consent unto this ill,
    Did give consent that thou thyself should'st kill.

[PILATE'S WIFE APOLOGIZES FOR EVE]

745   Now *Pontius Pilate*[7] is to judge the cause
    Of faultless *Jesus*, who before him stands;
    Who neither hath offended prince, nor laws,
    Although he now be brought in woeful bands:°   *bonds*
    "O noble governor, make thou you a pause,
750   Do not in innocent blood imbrue° thy hands;   *stain*
      But hear the words of thy most worthy wife,
      Who sends to thee, to beg her Saviour's life.

    Let barbarous cruelty far depart from thee,
    And in true justice take affliction's part;
755   Open thine eyes, that thou the truth mayest see;
    Do not the thing that goes against thy heart,
    Condemn not him that must thy Saviour be;
    But view his holy life, his good desert.
      Let not us women glory in men's fall,
760   Who had power given to overrule us all.

    Till now your indiscretion sets us free,
    And makes our former fault much less appear;[8]
    Our Mother *Eve*, who tasted of the tree,
    Giving to *Adam* what she held most dear,
765   Was simply good, and had no power to see,
    The after-coming harm did not appear:[9]
      The subtle serpent that our sex betrayed,
      Before our fall so sure a plot had laid.

    That undiscerning ignorance° perceived   *i.e., of Eve*
770   No guile, or craft that was by him intended;
    For had she known, of what we were bereaved,
    To his request she had not condescended.
    But she (poor soul) by cunning was deceived,
    No hurt therein her harmless heart intended:
775   For she alleged God's word, which he denies,
      That they should die, but even as gods, be wise.

    But surely *Adam* cannot be excused,
    Her fault though great, yet he was most to blame;
    What weakness offered, strength might have refused,

---

7. The Roman governor of Jerusalem, A.D. 26–36. He was
the judge at the trial of Jesus, who was accused of violating the laws of Rome. His wife warned him against condemning Jesus, saying, "Have thou nothing to do with
that just man: for I have suffered many things this day in
a dream because of him" (Matthew 27.19).
8. Lanyer recapitulates points raised by many writers who
denied that Eve should have all the blame for the loss of

Eden and paradise. Lanyer stresses Eve's innocence, and
emphasizes that Adam should have exercised authority
over Eve. This latter point is central to Milton's representation of Adam's sin in *Paradise Lost*, exonerating Eve
while also making her Adam's subordinate.
9. She could not foresee the harm that would follow her
disobedience.

780 Being Lord of all, greater was his shame:
Although the serpent's craft had her abused,
God's holy word ought all his actions frame,
　　For he was lord and king of all the earth,
　　Before poor *Eve* had either life or breath.

785 Who being framed by God's eternal hand,
The perfectest man that ever breathed on earth;
And from God's mouth received that strait° command,　　　　*stern*
The breach whereof he knew was present death:
Yea, having power to rule both sea and land,
790 Yet with one apple won to lose that breath
　　Which god had breathed in his beauteous face,
　　Bringing us all in danger and disgrace.

And then to lay the fault on Patience° back,　　　　*Patience's*
That we (poor women) must endure it all;
795 We know right well he did discretion lack,
Being not persuaded thereunto at all;
If *Eve* did err, it was for knowledge sake,
The fruit being fair, persuaded him to fall:
　　No subtle serpent's falsehood did betray him,
800 　　If he would eat it, who had power to stay him?

Not *Eve*, whose fault was only too much love,
Which made her give this present to her dear,
That what she tasted, he likewise might prove,
Whereby his knowledge might become more clear;
805 He never sought her weakness to reprove,
With those sharp words, which he of God did hear:
　　Yet men will boast of knowledge, which he took
　　From *Eve's* fair hand, as from a learned book.

If any evil did in her remain,
810 Being made of him, he was the ground of all;
If one of many worlds[1] could lay a stain
Upon our sex, and work so great a fall
To wretched man, by Satan's subtle train;
What will so foul a fault amongst you all?
815 　　Her weakness did the serpent's words obey;
　　But you in malice God's dear Son betray.

Whom, if unjustly you condemn to die,
Her sin was small, to what you do commit;
All mortal sins that do for vengeance cry,
820 Are not to be compared unto it:
If many worlds would altogether try,
By all their sins the wrath of God to get;
　　This sin of yours, surmounts them all as far
　　As doth the sun, another little star.

---

1. I.e., Adam who, as the father of all humankind, was of many people.

825   Then let us have our liberty again,
       And challenge° to your selves no sovereignty;[2]   *attribute*
       You came not in the world without our pain:
       Make that a bar against your cruelty;
       Your fault being greater, why should you disdain
830   Our being your equals, free from tyranny?
         If one weak woman simply did offend,
           This sin of yours, hath no excuse, nor end.

       To which (poor souls) we never gave consent,
       Witness thy wife (O *Pilate*) speaks for all,
835   Who did but dream, and yet a message sent,
       That thou should'st have nothing to do at all
       With that just man; which, if thy heart relent,
       Why wilt thou be a reprobate° with *Saul*?   *sinner*
         To seek the death of him that is so good,
840   For thy soul's health to shed his dearest blood.

⊶ ≖◆≖ ⊷

Sir Walter Raleigh
c. 1554–1618

Born in South Devon, a region in which ports and shipyards testified to the importance of
England's world trade and colonies abroad, Sir Walter Raleigh spent a considerable part of his
life outside his native land. As a boy, he fought with Huguenot armies in France; at twenty-
four he led an expedition to the West Indies with his half-brother, Sir Humphrey Gilbert; and
two years later, he commanded a contingent of English troops in Ireland. He is reported to
have been a great favorite of Elizabeth, at least until in 1592, when he secretly married one of
her ladies-in-waiting, Elizabeth Throckmorton; the queen, furious that she had had no say in
the match, imprisoned Raleigh in the Tower of London for a period that summer.

Raleigh was famous for his travels. His most challenging expedition was intended to
locate the legendary gold mines of El Dorado in South America. In 1595 he set out for the
Spanish colony of Guiana, penetrating the interior of that land by venturing up the Orinoco.
He described his trip in the brilliantly detailed *Discovery of the Large, Rich and Beautiful Empire
of Guiana*, and although he returned to England without the gold he had gone for, his leadership of an expedition to sack the harbor of Cadiz in 1596 was enough to restore him to royal
favor. But Raleigh was to encounter real trouble with the accession of James I. His enemies at
court convinced the king that Raleigh had committed treason, and in 1603 he was tried, convicted, and once again confined to the Tower of London, this time with his wife and family.
He remained there for thirteen years. His release was finally granted on the condition that he
lead another expedition to Guiana. He had informed the king that on his earlier trip he had
discovered an actual gold mine, and he now claimed that his new adventure would be successful. In fact, it was a disaster. Not only did he find no gold; the mine to whose existence he had
sworn was revealed to be a fabrication. On this occasion the grounds for proving treason were
stronger than they had been in 1603. Raleigh was executed in 1618.

---

2. Because men are afflicted with the weakness of Adam, they forfeit their original sovereignty over creation; their rule
over woman is therefore a tyranny.

During his long imprisonment, Raleigh began to write a complete history of the world, managing only to cover events in ancient history to 168 B.C. Entitled *The History of the World* and published in 1614, the work is primarily remembered for the stunning reflection on death that appears on its last page: "O eloquent, just and mighty Death! Whom none could advise, thou hast persuaded; what none hath dared, thou hast done; and whom all the world hath flattered, thou only hast cast out of the world and despised; thou hast drawn together all the far stretched greatness, all the pride, cruelty, and ambition of man, and covered it all over with those two narrow words, *Hic iacet*."

Much of Raleigh's poetry is occasional, written to address the circumstances and the moment in which he found himself. It possesses the quality Castiglione celebrated in his treatise on court life: a brilliance of self-expression that contemporary Italians termed *sprezzatura*, created by the supposedly artless use of artifice showing not the courtier's education, but rather his native wit and talent. Raleigh exploits images of common life but with an unusual intensity, adding sensuous detail to expressions of affection and reminders of mortality to celebrations of love. His longest and greatest poem, *The 21st and Last Book of the Ocean to Cynthia*, remained fragmentary at the time of his death. Occasioned when Queen Elizabeth imprisoned him for his marriage, the poem illustrates Raleigh's fury at the queen's inconsistent treatment of her "Ocean" or "Water," as Raleigh pronounced his first name. It ends in an equivocation: Raleigh professes his devotion to Elizabeth, instancing his good will that "knit up by faith shall ever last"; but he also concludes that despite this, they will not be reconciled: "Her love hath end; my woe must ever last."

Nature That Washed Her Hands in Milk

Nature that washed her hands in milk
    And had forgot to dry them,
Instead of earth took snow and silk,[1]
    At love's request to try them,
5   If she a mistress could compose
    To please love's fancy out of those.

Her eyes he would should be of light,
    A violet breath and lips of jelly,
Her hair not black nor over-bright,
10   And of the softest down her belly;
As for her inside he would have it
    Only of wantonness and wit.

At love's entreaty, such a one
    Nature made, but with her beauty
15 She hath framed a heart of stone,
    So as love by ill destiny
Must die for her whom nature gave him
    Because her darling would not save him.

But time, which nature doth despise,
20   And rudely gives her love the lie,
Makes hope a fool, and sorrow wise,
    His hands doth neither wash nor dry,

1. "And the Lord God formed man of the dust of the ground" (Genesis 2.7).

But being made of steel and rust,
Turns snow, and silk, and milk to dust.

25 The light, the belly, lips, and breath
     He dims, discolors, and destroys,
With those he feeds, but fills not death,
     Which sometimes were the food of joys;
Yea, time doth dull each lively wit
30 And dries all wantonness with it.

Oh cruel time which takes in trust
     Our youth, our joys, and all we have,
And pays us but with age and dust,
     Who in the dark and silent grave,
35 When we have wandered all our ways,
Shuts up the story of our days.[2]

c. 1592

To the Queen[1]

Our passions are most like to floods and streams,
The shallow murmur, but the deep are dumb.
So when affections yield discourse, it seems
The bottom is but shallow whence they come.
5   They that are rich in words must needs discover
      That they are poor in that which makes a lover.

Wrong not, dear empress of my heart,
     The merit of true passion,
With thinking that he feels no smart,
10   That sues for no compassion.
Since, if my plaints serve not to prove
     The conquest of your beauty,
It comes not from defect of love,
     But from excess of duty.

15 For knowing that I sue to serve
     A saint of such perfection,
As all desire, but none deserve,
     A place in her affection;
I rather choose to want relief
20   Than venture the revealing,
When glory recommends the grief,
     Despair distrusts the healing.

Thus those desires that aim too high
     For any mortal lover,

---

2. With one slight change and the addition of a final
couplet, the last stanza of this poem is also Raleigh's *Epitaph*.
1. This elaborate compliment is typical of the courtly

expressions of devotion Elizabeth I often inspired. Its
respectful complaint can be compared to the bitter regret
in Raleigh's later poem *The Shepherd of the Ocean to Cynthia*.

25   When reason cannot make them die,
          Discretion will them cover.
      Yet when discretion doth bereave
          The plaints that they should utter,
      Then your discretion may perceive
30   That silence is a suitor.

      Silence in love bewrays more woe
          Than words, though ne'er so witty,
      A beggar that is dumb, you know,
          Deserveth double pity.
35   Then misconceive not (dearest heart)
          My true, though secret passion,
      He smarteth most that hides his smart,
          And sues for no compassion.

c. 1590

On the Life of Man

What is our life? A play of passion,
Our mirth the music of division,
Our mothers' wombs the tiring houses be,
Where we are dressed for this short comedy,
Heaven the judicious sharp spectator is,
That sits and marks still who doth act amiss,
Our graves that hide us from the searching sun,
Are like drawn curtains when the play is done;
Thus march we playing to our latest rest,
Only we die in earnest, that's no jest.

1612

The Author's Epitaph, Made by Himself

Even such is time, which takes in trust
Our youth, our joys, and all we have,
And pays us but with age and dust,
Who in the dark and silent grave,
When we have wandered all our days,
Shuts up the story of our days;
And from which earth, and grave, and dust,
The Lord shall raise me up, I trust.

As You Came from the Holy Land

As you came from the holy land
    Of Walsingham[1]

___
1. A district in the county of Norfolk and site of Walsingham Abbey, one of the great shrines of medieval England.

          Met you not with my true love
            By the way as you came?[2]

5   How shall I know your true love
            That have met many one?
         As I went to the holy land
            That have come, that have gone.

         She is neither white nor brown
10   But as the heavens, fair.
         There is none hath a form so divine
            In the earth or the air.

         Such a one did I meet good sir,
            Such an angelic face,
15   Who like a queen, like a nymph did appear
            By her gait, by her grace.

         She hath left me here all alone,
            All alone as unknown,
         Who sometimes did me lead with herself,
20   And me loved as her own.

         What's the cause that she leaves you alone
            And a new way doth take,
         Who loved you once as her own,
            And her joy did you make?

25   I have loved her all my youth,
            But now old, as you see;
         Love likes not the falling fruit
            From the withered tree.

         Know that love is a careless child
30   And forgets promise past;
         He is blind, he is deaf, when he list,°   *wishes*
            And in faith never fast.

         His desire is a dureless content
            And a trustless joy;
35   He is won with a world of despair
            And is lost with a toy.

         Of womankind such indeed is the love
            Or the word love abused,
         Under which many childish desires
40   And conceits are excused.

         But love is a durable fire
            In the mind ever burning;
         Never sick, never old, never dead,
            From itself never turning.

---

2. This stanza is the first in the dialogue that constitutes the poem. Its first seven stanzas alternate statements between two speakers. Stanzas 7, 8, and 9 are spoken by the lover, the first speaker; the final two stanzas are spoken by the traveler.

from The 21st and Last Book of the Ocean to Cynthia[1]

Sufficeth to you, my joys interred,
In simple words that I my woes complain;
You that then died when first my fancy erred—[2]
Joys under dust that never live again.

5 If to the living were my muse addressed,
Or did my mind her own spirit still inhold,
Were not my living passion so repressed
As to the dead° the dead did these unfold,   *i.e., joys*

Some sweeter words, some more becoming verse
10 Should witness my mishap in higher kind;
But my love's wounds, my fancy in the hearse,
The idea but resting of a wasted mind,

The blossoms fallen, the sap gone from the tree,
The broken monuments of my great desires—
15 From these so lost what may the affections° be?   *passions*
What heat in cinders of extinguished fires?

Lost in the mud of those high-flowing streams,
Which through more fairer fields their courses bend,
Slain with self-thoughts, amazed in fearful dreams,
20 Woes without date, discomforts without end.

From fruitless trees I gather withered leaves,
And glean° the broken ears° with miser's hand,   *harvest / of grain*
Who sometime did enjoy the weighty sheaves;
I seek fair flowers amid the brinish° sand.   *salty*

25 All in the shade, even in the fair sun days,
Under those healthless trees I sit alone,
Where joyful birds sing neither lovely lays,
Nor Philomen° recounts her direful moan.   *the nightingale*

No feeding flocks, no shepherd's company,
30 That might renew my dolorous conceit,°   *imagination*
While happy then, while love and fantasy
Confined my thoughts on that fair flock to wait:

No pleasing streams fast to the ocean wending,
The messengers sometimes of my great woe;
35 But all on earth, as from the cold storms bending,
Shrink from my thoughts in high heavens or below.

1. This lyric complaint, a fragment of what was projected as a much longer work, is the most important of Raleigh's poems. It tells of his despair at losing the Queen's favor and reproaches her for indifference to his devoted service. Adopting the conventions of pastoral, Raleigh styles himself "The Shepherd of the Ocean," perhaps to draw attention to his first name, which he pronounced "Water." "Cynthia" is, of course, Elizabeth, figured here (as she was so often) as the moon, ever changeful, as well as Diana, the goddess of the moon and of chastity. Characterizing Cynthia as the moving force in his life,

Raleigh's verse illustrates how conventions of courtly love could acquire a political reference: both Elizabeth and her courtiers were accustomed to conveying their hopes and desires in the coded language of erotic compliment. Spenser's poem *Colin Clout's Come Home Again* (1591) notes that the subject of Raleigh's "Cynthia" is "the great unkindness" and "usage hard" of the "Lady of the Sea," who has "from her presence faultless him (i.e., the Shepherd) debarred."
2. The poet complains to his own "joys" that are now dead and buried.

Oh, hopeful love, my object and invention,
Oh, true desire, the spur of my conceit,
Oh, worthiest spirit, my mind's impulsion,°   *force*
40   Oh, eyes transpersant,° my affection's bait,   *that penetrate*

Oh princely form, my fancy's adamant,°   *magnet*
Divine conceit,° my pains' acceptance,   *image*
Oh, all in one! Oh, heaven on earth transparent!
The seat of joys and love's abundance!

45   Out of that mass of miracles, my muse
Gathered those flowers, to her pure senses pleasing;
Out of her eyes, the store of joys, did choose
Equal delights, my sorrow's counterpoising.

Her regal looks my vigorous sighs suppressed,
50   Small drops of joys sweetened great worlds of woes,
One gladsome day a thousand cares redressed—
Whom love defends, what fortune overthrows?

When she did well, what did there else amiss?
When she did ill, what empires would have pleased?
55   No other power affecting woe or bliss,
She gave, she took, she wounded, she appeased.

The honor of her love, love still devising,
Wounding my mind with contrary conceit,
Transferred itself sometime to her aspiring,
60   Sometime the trumpet of her thought's retreat.[3]

To seek new worlds for gold, for praise, for glory,
To try° desire, to try love severed far,   *test*
When I was gone, she sent her memory,
More strong than were ten thousand ships of war,

65   To call me back; to leave great honor's thought;
To leave my friends, my fortune, my attempt;
To leave the purpose[4] I so long had sought,
And hold both cares and comforts in contempt.

Such heat in ice, such fire in frost remained,
70   Such trust in doubt, such comfort in despair,
Which, like the gentle lamb, though lately weaned,
Plays with the dug, though finds no comfort there.

But as a body, violently slain,
Retaineth warmth although the spirit be gone,
75   And by a power in nature moves again
Till it be laid below the fatal stone;

3. The honor of being loved by her creating love (in me), wounding me with a contrary (twofold) conception, sometimes aspiring to (please) her, sometimes heralding the withdrawal of her attention. In other words, the poet is constantly aware that his love makes him have a conflicted conception of how to approach Cynthia: some-

times he pleases her, sometimes what he does causes her disdain.
4. Raleigh's "purpose" was to find gold for England in the wilderness of the New World; he continued to hope for success in this venture until 1617, when his last voyage to Guiana ended in nothing.

Or as the earth, even in cold winter days,
Left for a time by her life-giving sun,
Doth by the power remaining of his rays
80   Produce some green, though not as it hath done;

Or as a wheel, forced by the falling stream,
Although the course be turned some other way,
Doth for a time go round upon the beam,
Till, wanting strength to move, it stands at stay;

85   So my forsaken heart, my withered mind—
Widow of all the joys it once possessed,
My hopes clean out of sight with forced wind—
To kingdoms strange, to lands far off, addressed,

Alone, forsaken, friendless, on the shore
90   With many wounds, with death's cold pangs embraced,
Writes in the dust, as one that could no more,
Whom love, and time, and fortune, had defaced,

Of things so great, so long, so manifold,
With means so weak, the soul even then depicting
95   The weal, the woe, the passages of old,
And worlds of thoughts descried° by one last sighing.   *discerned*

As if, when after Phoebus° is descended,   *the sun*
And leaves a light much like the past day's dawning,
And every toil and labor wholly ended,
100   Each living creature draweth to his resting,

We should begin by such a parting light
To write the story of all ages past,
And end the same before approaching night.

Such is again the labor of my mind,
105   Whose shroud, by sorrow woven now to end,
Hath seen that ever shining sun declined,
So many years that so could not descend,

But that the eyes of my mind held her beams
In every part transferred by love's swift thought,
110   Far off or near, in waking or in dreams,
Imagination strong in lustre brought.

Such force her angelic appearance had
To master distance, time, or cruelty,
Such art to grieve, and after to make glad,
115   Such fear in love, such love in majesty.

My weary lines her memory embalmed;
My darkest ways her eyes make clear as day.
What storms so great but Cynthia's beams appeased?
What rage so fierce, that love could not allay?

120   Twelve years entire I wasted in this war,[5]
       Twelve years of my most happy younger days;
       But I in them, and they now wasted are,
       "Of all which past, the sorrow only stays."

                        . . .

       Yet as the air in deep caves underground
125   Is strongly drawn when violent heat hath vent
       Great clefts therein, till moisture do abound,
       And then the same, imprisioned and up-pent,°   *pent up*

       Breaks out in earthquakes, tearing all asunder,
       So in the center of my cloven heart—
130   My heart, to whom her beauties were such wonder—
       Lies the sharp, poisoned head of that love's dart

       Which, till all break and dissolve to dust,
       Thence drawn it cannot be, or therein known,
       There, mixed with my heart-blood, the fretting rust
135   The better part hath eaten and outgrown.

       But what of those or these? Or what of aught
       Of that which was, or that which is, to treat?
       What I possess is but the same I sought;
       My love was false, my labors were deceit.

140   Nor less than such they are esteemed to be,
       A fraud bought at the price of many woes,
       A guile, whereof the profits unto me—
       Could it be thought premediate° for those?   *plead*

       Witness those withered leaves left on the tree,
145   The sorrow-worn face, the pensive mind,
       The external shows, what may the internal be;
       Cold care hath bitten both the root and rind.

       But stay, my thoughts, make end, give fortune way;
       Harsh is the voice of woe and sorrow's sound;
150   Complaints cure not, and tears do but allay
       Griefs for a time, which after more abound.

       To seek for moisture in the Arabian sand
       Is but a loss of labor and of rest,
       The links which time did break of hearty bands

155   Words cannot knit, or wailings make anew,
       Seek not the sun in clouds when it is set. . . .
       On highest mountains, where those cedars[6] grew,
       Against whose banks the troubled ocean beat,

       And were the marks to find thy hoped port,
160   Into a soil far off themselves remove.
       On Sestos' shore, Leander's late resort,
       Hero hath left no lamp to guide her love.[7]

5. The 12 years of service to Elizabeth began with his command of troops in Ireland in 1580 and ended, in the terms the poem supplies, with his marriage and imprisonment in 1592. Raleigh was only 36 at the time.
6. The cedar was identified as a tree of royalty; so Raleigh can speak of the ocean beating against banks over which the cedar presides.
7. Leander and Hero were two lovers who lived on opposite shores of the Hellespont. When Leander swam at night from Abydos to visit Hero in Sestos, she hung out a lantern to guide him.

Thou lookest for light in vain, and storms arise,
She sleeps thy death, that erst thy danger sighed,
165   Strive then no more, bow down thy weary eyes—
Eyes which to all these woes thy heart have guided.

She is gone, she is lost, she is found, she is ever fair;
Sorrow draws weakly where love draws not too,
Woe's cries sound nothing, but only in love's ear.
170   Do then by dying what life cannot do.

Unfold thy flocks and leave them to the fields,
To feed on hills or dales, where likes them best,
Of what the summer or the springtime yields,
For love and time hath given thee leave to rest.

175   Thy heart which was their fold, now in decay
By often storms and winter's many blasts,
All torn and rent, becomes misfortune's prey,
False hope, my shepherd's staff, now age hath brast.°   broken

My pipe, which love's own hand gave my desire
180   To sing her praises and my woe upon—
Despair hath often threatened to the fire,
As vain to keep now all the rest are gone.

Thus home I draw, as death's long night draws on,
Yet every foot, old thoughts turn back mine eyes;
185   Constraint me guides, as old age draws a stone
Against a hill, which over-weighty lies

For feeble arms or wasted strength to move.
My steps are backward, gazing on my loss,
My mind's affection and my soul's sole love,
190   Not mixed with fancy's chaff or fortune's dross.

To God I leave it,° who first gave it me,   my soul
And I her gave, and she returned again,
As it was hers; so let His mercies be
Of my last comforts the essential mean.°   factor

195   But be it so or not, the effects are past;
Her love hath end, my woes must ever last.

from The Discovery of the Large, Rich and Beautiful Empire of Guiana[1]

from *Epistle Dedicatory*

To the Right Honorable my singular good lord and kinsman, Charles Howard,[2] Knight of the Garter, Baron, and Chancellor, and of the Admirals of England the most reknowned, and to the Right Honorable Sir Robert Cecil, Knight, Counselor in Her Highness's Privy Councils.[3]

---

1. A region in Venezuela. The full title of Raleigh's report is *The Discovery of the Large, Rich and Beautiful Empire of Guiana, with a relation of the Great and Golden City of Manoa (which the Spaniards call El Dorado) and the provinces of Emeria, Arromaia, Amapaia and other Countries, with their rivers, adjoining.* It was written and published in London in 1596, a year after Raleigh undertook his expedition.
2. Charles Howard (1536–1624) was Baron Howard of

Effingham and Earl of Nottingham, commander of the Queen's navy at the defeat of the Armada and the capture of Cadiz.
3. Sir Robert Cecil was the first Earl of Salisbury, son of a principal advisor to Elizabeth I. Robert Cecil became Elizabeth's secretary of state in 1589 and was a key figure in the administration of James I, in which he eventually held the office of Lord Treasurer.

For your Honors' many honorable and friendly parts, I have hitherto only returned promises, and now for answer of both your adventures, I have sent you a bundle of papers which I have divided between your Lordship and Sir Robert Cecil in these two respects chiefly. First, for it is reasonable that wasteful factors,[4] when they have consumed such stocks as they had in trust, do yield some color for the same in their account; secondly, for that I am assured that whatsoever shall be done or written by me shall need a double protection and defense. The trial that I had of both your loves, when I was left of all but of malice and revenge, makes me still presume that you will be pleased (knowing what little power I had to perform aught, and the great advantage of forewarned enemies) to answer that out of knowledge which others shall but object out of malice.[5] In my more happy times as I did especially honor you both, so I found that your loves sought me out in the darkest shadow of adversity, and the same affection which accompanied my better fortune, soared not away from me in my many miseries. All which, though I cannot requite, yet I shall ever acknowledge, and the great debt which I have no power to pay, I can do no more for a time but confess to be due. It is true that as my errors were great, so they have yielded very grievous effects, and if aught might have been deserved in former times to have counterpoised any part of offenses, the fruit thereof (as it seemeth) was long before fallen from the tree and the dead stock[6] only remained.[7] I did therefore even in the winter of my life undertake these travels, fitter for boys less blasted with misfortunes, for men of greater ability, and for minds of better encouragement, that thereby if it were possible I might recover but the moderation of excess and the least taste of the greatest plenty formerly possessed. If I had known other way to win, if I had imagined how greater adventures might have regained, if I could conceive what further means I might yet use but even to appease so powerful displeasure, I would not doubt but for one year more to hold fast my soul in my teeth til it were performed. Of that little remain I had, I have wasted in effect all therein,[8] I have undergone many constructions,[9] I have been accompanied with many sorrows, with labor, hunger, heat, sickness, and peril. It appeareth notwithstanding that I made no other bravado of going to sea than was meant, and that I was neither hidden in Cornwall or elsewhere, as was supposed.[1] They have grossly belied me, that forejudged that I would rather become a servant to the Spanish king than return; and the rest were much mistaken who would have persuaded that I was too easeful and sensual to undertake a journey of so great travel. But if what I have done receive the gracious construction[2] of a painful pilgrimage and purchase the least remission, I shall think all too little, and that there were wanting to the rest, many miseries.[3] But if both the times past, the present, and what may be in the future do all by one grain of gall continue in an eternal distaste, I do not then know whether I should bewail myself either for my too much travel and expense, or condemn myself for doing less than that which can

---

4. Raleigh refers to himself as a "factor," an agent who is commissioned to perform a certain function. Factors who exhausted the resources at their disposal had to account for their expenditures.
5. Raleigh presumes that Howard and Cecil will be able to answer his detractors (who speak from malice) with knowledge gained from this account of his travels to Guiana.
6. Trunk.
7. Raleigh admits that he has made errors and that the successes he had earlier in his career, which might have compensated for these errors, can no longer serve this purpose.

8. I.e., of what was left of my resources, I have effectually wasted everything.
9. Trials.
1. I.e., it is apparent that I made no other boast of going to sea than to state that I intended to do it and that I was not hidden in Cornwall or elsewhere. Here Raleigh addresses the rumor that he had never gone to Guiana but rather had waited for his men to return from there, then claimed that his expedition was a success.
2. Interpretation.
3. I.e., if I could get some credit for having taken this painful pilgrimage, I would wish that my miseries had been more severe.

deserve nothing.[4] From myself I have deserved no thanks, for I am returned a beggar, and withered, but that I might have bettered my poor estate it shall appear by the following discourse, if I had not only respected Her Majesty's future honor and riches. It became not the former fortune in which I once lived, to go journeys of picorie,[5] and it had sorted ill with the offices of honor which by Her Majesty's grace I hold this day in England to run from Cape to Cape and from place to place for the pillage of ordinary prizes. Many years since, I had knowledge by relation of that mighty, rich and beautiful Empire of Guiana and of that great and golden city which the Spaniards call El Dorado, and the naturals,[6] Manoa, which city was conquered, re-edified, and enlarged by a younger son of Guainacapa, Emperor of Peru, at such time as Francisco Pizarro[7] and others conquered the said empire from his two elder brethren, Guascar and Atabalipa, both then contending for the same, the one being favored by the Oreiones of Cuzco, the other by the people of Caximalca. I sent my servant Jacob Whiddon the year before to get knowledge of the passages, and I had some light from Captain Parker, sometime my servant and now attending on your Lordship, that such a place there was to the southward of the great bay of Charuas, or Guanipa, but I found that it was six hundred miles farther off than they supposed, and many other impediments to them unknown and unheard. After I had displanted[8] Don Antonio de Berreo, who was upon the same enterprise, leaving my ships at Trinidad, at the port called Curiapan, I wandered four hundred miles into the said country by land and river, the particulars I will leave to the following discourse.[9] The country hath more quantity of gold by manifold than the best parts of the Indies or Peru; all the most of the kings of the borders are already become Her Majesty's vassals and seem to desire nothing more than Her Majesty's protection and the return of the English nation.

To the Reader

Because there have been diverse opinions conceived of the gold ore brought from Guiana, and for that an alderman of London and an officer of Her Majesty's Mint hath given out that the same is of no price, I have thought good by the addition of these lines to give answer as well to the said malicious slander, as to other objections. It is true that while we abode at the Island of Trinidad, I was informed by an Indian that not far from the port where we were anchored there were found certain mineral stones which they esteemed to be gold and were thereunto persuaded the rather for that they had seen both English and French men gather and embark some quantities thereof. Upon this likelihood I sent forty men and gave order that each one should bring a stone of that mine to make trial of the goodness, which being performed, I assured them at their return that the same was marcasite[1] and of no riches or value.

---

4. I.e., if everything continues to go badly, I do not know whether I should regret my travel or condemn myself for doing less than what can deserve nothing (what is not enough to deserve anything).
5. Suitable for the *picaro*, or rogue in Spanish.
6. Indigenous people.
7. Pizarro (1475–1541) conquered Peru by capturing the Incan king Atahualpa, whom Raleigh refers to as Atabalipa. Atahualpa was the son of Guainacapa and the brother of Guascar, whom he killed to get the throne. This passage suggests that Guianacapa had three sons; Raleigh later states that he had only two sons. Pizarro captured Cuzco, the principal city of the Incas, in 1533.

The Oreiones were the native people of Cuzco; Caximalca or Casimarca was another large city in Peru.
8. Dislodged.
9. Here Raleigh claims that a Captain Parker told him that El Dorado was south of the bay of Guanipa (which opens onto the Gulf of Paria and has no connection with the Orinoco), but he discovered that it was 600 miles in the interior of the country and away from the shore. Don Antonio de Berreo was the Spanish Governor of Trinidad and Guiana; Trinidad is an island just off the Venezuelan coast. Presumably, Raleigh marched from that coast 400 miles inland.
1. Pyrite.

Notwithstanding, diverse,[2] trusting more to their own sense than to my opinion, kept of the said marcasite and have tried thereof, since my return, in diverse places. In Guiana itself I never saw marcasite, but all the rocks, mountains, all stones in the plains, in woods, and by the rivers' sides are in effect thereof shining, and appear marvelous rich, which being tried[3] to be no marcasite, are the true signs of rich minerals, but[4] are no other than *el madre del oro* (as the Spaniards term them), which is the mother of gold, or as it is said by others, the scum of gold. Of diverse sorts of these, many of my company brought also into England, every one taking the fairest for the best, which is not general.[5] For mine own part, I did not countermand any man's desire or opinion, and I could have afforded them little if I should have denied them the pleasing of their own fancies therein. But I was resolved that gold must be found either in grains separate from the stone (as it is in most of all the rivers in Guiana) or else in a kind of hard stone, which we call the white spar, of which I saw diverse hills and in sundry places but had neither time, nor men, nor instruments fit to labor. Near unto one of the rivers I found of the said white spar or flint a very great ledge or bank which I endeavored to break by all means I could, because there appeared on the outside some small grains of gold, but finding no means to work the same upon the upper part, seeking the sides and circuit of the said rock, I found a cleft in the same from whence with daggers and with the head of an ax we got out some small quantity thereof, of which kind of white stone (wherein gold is engendered) we saw diverse hills and rocks in every part of Guiana wherein we traveled. Of this there hath been made many trials, and in London it was first assayed by Master Westwood, a refiner dwelling in Wood Street, and it was held after the rate of 12,000 or 13,000 pounds a ton. Another sort was afterward tried by Master Bulmar and Master Dimoke, assay master, and it held after the rate of 23,000 pounds a ton. There was some of it again tried by Master Palmer, comptroller of the mint, and Master Dimoke in Goldsmith's Hall, and it held after 26,900 pounds a ton. There was also at the same time and by the same persons a trial made of the dust of the said mine, which held eight pounds, six ounces weight of gold in the hundred. There was likewise at the same time a trial made of an image of copper made in Guiana which held a third part gold, besides diverse trials made in the country and by others in London.[6] But because there came of ill with the good, and belike the said alderman was not presented with the best, it hath pleased him therefore to scandal[7] all the rest, and to deface[8] the enterprises as much as in him lieth. It hath also been concluded by diverse that if there had been any such ore in Guiana and the same discovered, that I would have brought home a greater quantity thereof. First, I was not bound to satisfy any man of the quantity, but such only as adventured, if any store had been returned thereof. But it is very true that had all their mountains been of massy gold, it was impossible for us to have made any longer stay to have wrought the same, and whosoever hath seen with what strength of stone the best gold is environed,[9] he will not think it easy to be had out in heaps and especially by us who had neither men, instruments, nor time (as it is said before) to perform the same. There were, on this discovery, no less than one hundred persons, who can all witness that when we passed any

---

2. Some men.
3. Discovered.
4. And.
5. I.e., the fairest mineral is judged to be best, provided that it is also rare or "not general."
6. Raleigh reports that the ore he brought back from Guiana was tested by several goldsmiths, who were

experts at refining the metal, and that it was found to be substantially gold. Throughout his address to the reader, Raleigh argues that he actually discovered gold and that this gold will allow England to rival Spain.
7. Disparage.
8. Criticize.
9. Embedded.

branch of the river to view the land within, and stayed from our boats but six hours, we were driven to wade to the eyes at our return, and if we attempted the same the day following, it was impossible either to ford it or to swim it,[1] both by reason of the swiftness and also for that the borders were so pestered[2] with fast[3] woods as neither boat nor man could find place either to land or to embark. For in June, July, August, and September, it is impossible to navigate any of those rivers, for such is the fury of the current and there are so many trees and woods overflowed as if any boat but touch upon any tree or stake, it is impossible to save any one person therein, and ere we departed the land, it ran with that swiftness as[4] we drove down most commonly against the wind little less than one hundred miles a day. Besides, our vessels were no other than wherries,[5] one little barge, a small cockboat,[6] and a bad galiota,[7] which we framed in haste for that purpose at Trinidad, and those little boats had nine or ten men apiece, with all their victuals and arms. It is further true that we were about four hundred miles from our ships and had been a month from them, which also we left weakly manned in an open road[8] and had promised our return in fifteen days. Others have devised that the same ore was had from Barbary,[9] and that we carried it with us into Guiana. Surely the singularity of that device I do not well comprehend; for my own part, I am not so much in love with these long voyages as to devise, thereby to cozen myself, to lie hard, to fare worse, to be subjected to perils, to diseases, to ill savors, to be parched and withered, and withal to sustain the care and labor of such an enterprise, except the same had more comfort than the fetching of marcasite in Guiana or buying of gold ore in Barbary.[1] But I hope the better sort will judge me by themselves, and that the way of deceit is not the way of honor or good opinion. I have herein consumed much time and many crowns, and I had no other respect or desire than to serve Her Majesty and my country thereby. If the Spanish nation had been of like belief to these detractors, we should little have feared or doubted their attempts wherewith we now are daily threatened.[2] But if we now consider of the actions both of Charles the Fifth,[3] who had the maidenhead of Peru and the abundant treasures of Atabalipa, together with the affairs of the Spanish king now living,[4] what territories he hath purchased, what he hath added to the acts of predecessors, how many kingdoms he hath endangered, how many armies, garrisons, and navies he hath and doth maintain, the great losses which he hath repaired, as in 1588, above one hundred sail of great ships with their artillery, and that no year is less unfortunate but that many vessels, treasures, and people are devoured, and yet notwithstanding he beginneth again like a storm to threaten shipwreck to us all, we shall find that these abilities rise not from the trades of sacks[5] and Seville oranges, nor from aught else that either Spain, Portugal, or any of his other provinces produce. It is his Indian gold that endangereth and disturbeth all the nations of Europe, it purchaseth intelligence, creepeth into councils, and setteth bound loyalty at liberty in the greatest monarchies of Europe. If the Spanish king can keep us from foreign enterprises and

1. The river Orinoco, which Raleigh describes as tidal.
2. Crowded.
3. Thick.
4. That.
5. Small barges.
6. Rowboat.
7. A small sailing ship, also equipped with oars.
8. An exposed anchorage, outside the protection of a harbor.
9. The regions along the coast of North Africa.
1. I.e., I would not have undergone such trials to bring marcasite from Guiana or to buy gold in Barbary.

2. Raleigh uses the Spaniards' interest in American gold as proof that his detractors are wrong.
3. Charles V (1500–1558) was the Holy Roman Emperor under whose rule the Spanish empire in the Americas was enormously enlarged.
4. Philip II (1527–1598). Raleigh alludes to the expenditures of that king—including the repair of his Armada, which was defeated by the English fleet in 1588—none of which stood in the way of his harrassing English interests and property. Spanish affluence and influence, Raleigh claims, are sustained by "Indian gold."
5. Wines.

from the empeachment of his trades, either by offer of invasions or by besieging us in Britain, Ireland, or elsewhere, he hath then brought the work of our peril in great forwardness.[6] Those princes which abound in treasure have great advantages over the rest, if they once constrain them[7] to a defensive war, where they are driven once a year or oftener to cast lots for their own garments, and from such shall all trades and intercourse be taken away, to the general loss and impoverishment of the kingdom and commonweal so reduced. Besides, when men are constrained to fight, it hath not the same hope as when they are pressed and encouraged by the desire of spoil and riches. Further, it is to be doubted how those that in time of victory seem to affect[8] their neighbor nations will remain after the first view of misfortunes or ill success. To trust also to the doubtfulness of a battle is but a fearful and uncertain adventure, seeing therein fortune is as likely to prevail as virtue. It shall not be necessary to allege all that might be said, and therefore I will thus conclude that whatsoever kingdom shall be enforced to defend itself may be compared to a body dangerously diseased, which for a season may be preserved with vulgar[9] medicines, but in a short time and by little and little, the same must needs fall to the ground and be dissolved. I have therefore labored all my life, both according to my small power and persuasion, to advance all those attempts that might either promise return of profit for ourselves or at least be a let[1] and empeachment to the quiet course and plentiful trades of the Spanish nation, who[2] in my weak judgment by such a war were as easily endangered and brought from his powerfulness as any prince in Europe, if it be considered from how many kingdoms and nations his revenues are gathered, and those so weak in their own beings and so far severed from mutual succour. But because such a preparation and resolution are not to be hoped for in haste, and that the time which our enemies embrace cannot be had again to advantage, I will hope that these provinces and that empire now by me discovered shall suffice to enable Her Majesty and the whole kingdom with no less quantities of treasure than the King of Spain hath in all the Indies, east and west, which he possesseth; which if the same be considered and followed ere the Spaniards enforce the same, and if Her Majesty will undertake it, I will be contented to lose Her Highness's favor and good opinion forever, and my life withal, if the same be not found rather to exceed than to equal whatsoever is in this discourse promised or declared. I will now refer the reader to the following discourse with the hope that the perilous and chargeable labors and endeavors of such as thereby seek the profit and honor of Her Majesty and the English nation shall by men of quality and virtue receive such construction and good acceptance as themselves would look to be rewarded withal in the like.

[THE AMAZONS]

I made inquiry amongst the most ancient and best traveled of the Orenoqueponi, and I had knowledge of all the rivers between Orenoque and [the river of the] Amazons, and was very desirous to understand the truth of those warlike women, because of some it is believed, of others not.[1] And though I digress from my purpose, yet I will set down what hath been delivered me for truth of those women, and I spake with a

---

6. I.e., he has advanced the work of our destruction.
7. I.e., the rest.
8. Support.
9. Ordinary.
1. Hindrance.
2. I.e., Philip II.

1. Raleigh takes his account of the Amazons from a native of Guiana. He associates this race of women, whose presence has never been verified, with a comparable people described in Greek mythology who are also warlike and consort with men only to conceive children.

Casique or Lord of people that told me he had been in the river, and beyond it also. The nations of these women are on the south side of the river in the provinces of Topago, and their chiefest strengths and retreats are in the Islands situated on the south side of the entrance, some 60 leagues within the mouth of the said river. The memories of the like women are very ancient as well in Africa as in Asia. In Africa those that had Medusa[2] for Queen: others in Scithia near the rivers of Tanais and Thermadon: we find also that Lampedo and Marthesia[3] were Queens of the Amazons: in many histories they are verified to have been, and in diverse ages and provinces. But they which are not far from Guiana do accompany with men but once a year, and for the time of one month, which I gather by their relation to be in April. At that time all the kings of the borders assemble, and the queens of the Amazons, and after the queens have chosen, the rest cast lots for their Valentines. This one month, they feast, dance, and drink of their wines in abundance, and the moon being done, they all depart to their own provinces. If they conceive, and be delivered of a son, they return him to the father, if of a daughter they nourish it, and retain it, and as many as have daughters send unto the begetters a present, all being desirous to increase their own sex and kind, but that they cut off the right dug of the breast I do not find to be true. It was further told me, that if in the wars they took any prisoners that they used to accompany with those also at what time soever, but in the end for certain they put them to death: for they are said to be very cruel and bloodthirsty, especially to such as offer to invade their territories.

[THE ORINOCO]

The great river of Orenoque or Baraquan hath nine branches which fall out on the north side of his own main mouth. On the south side it hath seven other fallings into the sea, so it disemboqueth[1] by sixteen arms in all, between islands and broken ground, but the islands are very great, many of them as big as the Isle of Wight[2] and bigger, and many less. From the first branch on the north to the last of the south it is at least one hundred leagues, so as the river's mouth is no less than three hundred miles wide at his entrance into the sea, which I take to be far bigger than that of [the] Amazons. All those that inhabit in the mouth of this river upon the several north branches are these Tiuitiuas,[3] of which there are two chief lords which have continual wars one with the other. The islands which lie on the right hand are called Pallamos, and the land on the left, Hororotomaka, and the river by which John Douglas returned within the land from Amana to Capuri, they call Macuri.

These Tiuitiuas are a very goodly people and very valiant, and have the most manly speech and most deliberate that ever I heard of, what nation so ever. In the summer they have houses on the ground as in other places, where they build very artificial towns and villages, as it is written in the Spanish story of the West Indies, that those people do in the low lands near the gulf of Uraba. For between May and September, the river of Orenoque riseth thirty foot upright, and then those islands overflow twenty foot high above the level of the ground, saving some few raised grounds in the middle of them, and for this cause they are enforced to live in this

2. A mythical monstrous woman, one of the Gorgons, who turned to stone whoever looked at her.
3. The legendary queen of the Amazons who fought in the Trojan war.
1. Discharges.

2. Island off the southern coast of England.
3. The Waraus, an indigenous people who live in the delta of the Orinoco and adjoining coasts. Spanish historians refer to them as the Guaraunos or Guaraunu.

manner. They never eat of anything that is set or sown, and as at home they use nei- ther planting nor other manurance, so when they come abroad they refuse to feed of aught but of that which nature without labor bringeth forth.[4] They use the tops of *palmitos* [palm trees] for bread and kill deer, fish, and porks for the rest of their suste- nance; they also have many sorts of fruits that grow in the woods and a great variety of birds and fowl.

And if to speak of them were not tedious and vulgar, surely we saw in those pas- sages of very rare colors and forms not elsewhere to be found, for as much as I have either seen or read. Of these poeple, those that dwell upon the branches of the Orenoque called Capuri and Macureo are for the most part carpenters of *canoas* [canoes], for they make the most and fairest houses and sell them into Guiana for gold, and into Trinidad for tobacco, in the excessive taking whereof they exceed all nations, and notwithstanding the moistness of the air in which they live, the hard- ness of their diet, and the great labors they suffer to hunt, fish, and fowl for their liv- ing, in all my life either in the Indies or in Europe did I never behold a more goodly or better-favored people, or a more manly. They were wont to make war upon all nations and especially on the Cannibals, so as none durst without a good strength trade by those rivers; but of late they are at peace with their neighbors, all holding the Spaniards for a common enemy.[5] When their commanders die, they use great lamentation, and when they think the flesh of their bodies is putrified and fallen from the bones, then they take up the carcass again and hang it in the Casique's house that died, and deck his skull with feathers of all colors and hang all his gold plates about the bones of his arms, thighs, and legs. Those nations which are called Arwacas,[6] which dwell on the south of Orenoque (of which place and nation our Indian pilot was), are dispersed in many other places and do use to beat the bones of their lords into powder, and their wives and friends drink it all in their several sorts of drinks.

[THE KING OF AROMAIA]

The next day we arrived at the port of Morequito,[1] and anchored there, sending away one of our pilots to seek the king of Aromaia, uncle to Morequito, slain by Berreo as aforesaid. The next day following, before noon he came to us on foot from his house, which was fourteen English miles (himself being 110 years old), and returned on foot the same day, and with him many of the borderers,[2] with many women and children that came to wonder at our nation and to bring us down victual, which they did in great plenty, as venison, pork, hens, chickens, fowl, fish, with diverse sorts of excel- lent fruits and roots, and great abundance of *pinas* [pineapples], the princess of fruits that grow under the sun, especially those of Guiana. They brought us also store of

4. As people that do not farm, the Tiuitiuas would have been categorized by many Europeans as having no con- ception of property and therefore incapable of being dis- possessed.
5. Here and throughout the narrative, Raleigh portrays the people of the region as desiring the protection of the English against the Spanish, whose mistreatment of the natives of the Americas was well publicized. Raleigh could claim that by making these natives vassals of the English monarch, England could acquire an empire to rival Spain's.
6. Known today as Arawaks, these people were neighbors of the Tiuitiuas.

1. A king whose territory bordered Guiana. He was cap- tured and executed by the Spanish Governor of Trinidad, Antonio de Berreo, for having killed a Spanish garrison. His uncle, here described as the king of Aromaia and lat- er named Topiawari, succeeded Morequito. His people are later identified as the Orenoqueponi, because they live on the shores of the Orinoco. The king's dignified report testifies to both his status as royalty and the culture of the Orenoqueponi, who are conscious of their history as one among many peoples of the territory which is now northern Venezuela.
2. People living on the borders of Aromaia.

bread, and of their wine, and a sort of *paraquitos* [parakeets], no bigger than wrens, and of all other sorts both small and great. One of them gave me a beast called by the Spaniards *armadilla* [armadillo] which they call *cassacam*, which seemeth to be all barred over with small plates somewhat like to a *renocero* [rhinoceros], with a white horn growing in his hinder parts as big as a great hunting horn, which they use to wind[3] instead of a trumpet. Monadarus writeth that a little of the powder of that horn put into the ear cureth deafness.

After this old king had rested a while in a little tent that I caused to be set up, I began by my interpretor to discourse with him of the death of Morequito his predecessor and afterward of the Spaniards, and ere I went any farther I made him know the cause of my coming thither, whose servant I was, and that the Queen's pleasure was I should undertake the voyage for their defense and to deliver them from the tyranny of the Spaniards, dilating[4] at large (as I had done before to those of Trinidad) Her Majesty's greatness, her justice, her charity to all oppressed nations, with as many of the rest of her beauties and virtues as either I could express or they conceive, all which being with great admiration attentively heard and marvellously admired, I began to sound the old man as touching Guiana and the state thereof, what sort of commonwealth it was, how governed, of what strength and policy, how far it extended, and what nations were friends or enemies adjoining, and finally of the distance and the way to enter the same; he told me that himself and his people, with all those down the river towards the sea, as far as Emeria, the province of Carapana, were of Guiana, but that they called themselves Orenoqueponi, because they bordered the great river of Orenoque, and that all the nations between the river and those mountains in sight called Wacarima were of the same cast and appellation, and that on the other side of the the mountains of Wacarima there was a large plain (which after I discovered in my return) called the valley of Amariocapana, in all that valley the people were also of the ancient Guianans. I asked what nations those were which inhabited on the further side of those mountains, beyond the valley of Amariocapana, he answered with a great sigh (as a man which had inward feeling of the loss of his country and liberty, especially for that his eldest son was slain in a battle on that side of the mountains, whom he most entirely loved) that he remembered in his father's lifetime, when he was very old and himself a young man, that there came down into that large valley of Guiana, a nation from so far off as the sun slept (for such were his own words) with so great a multitude as they could not be numbered or resisted, and that they wore large coats and hats of crimson color, which color he expressed by showing a piece of red wood wherewith my tent was supported, and that they were called Oreiones and Epuremei,[5] those that had slain and rooted out so many of the ancient people as there were leaves in the wood upon all the trees, and had now made themselves lords of all, even to that mountain foot called Curaa, saving only of two nations, the one called Iwarawaqueri, and the other Cassipagotos, and that in the last battle fought between the Epuremei and the Iwarawaqueri, his eldest son was chosen to carry to the aide of the Iwarawaqueri a great troop of the Orenoqueponi and was there slain with all his people and friends, and that he now had remaining but one son; and further told me that those Epuremei had built a great town called Macureguarai at the said mountain foot, at the beginning of the great plains of Guiana, which have no end, and that their houses have many rooms, one

3. Blow.
4. Describing.
5. The King of Aromaia describes a conquest of the

Orenoqueponi by the Oreiones, a "nation from so far off as the sun slept," i.e., Peru. His son, he reports, was killed in a battle with the Oreiones.

over the other, and that therein the great king of the Oreiones and Epuremei kept three thousand men to defend the borders against them and withal daily to invade and slay them; but that of late years, since the Christians offered to invade his territories and those frontiers, they were all at peace and traded one with another, saving only the Iwarawaqueri and those other nations upon the head of the river Caroli called Cassipagotos, which we afterwards discovered, each one holding the Spaniard for a common enemy.

After he had answered thus far, he desired leave to depart, saying that he had far to go, that he was old, and weak, and was every day called for by death, which was also his own phrase. I desired him to rest with us that night, but I could not entreat him. But he told me that at my return from the country above he would again come to us and in the mean time provide for us the best he could of all that his country yielded. The same night he returned to Orocotona, his own town, so as he went that day 28 miles, the weather being very hot, the country being situated between four and five degrees of the equator. This Topiawari is held for the proudest and wisest of all the Orenoqueponi, and so he behaved himself towards me in all his answers at my return, as I marvelled to find a man of that gravity and judgment and of so good discourse that had no help of learning or breed.

[THE NEW WORLD OF GUIANA]

To conclude, Guiana is a country that hath yet her maidenhead, never sacked, turned, nor wrought; the face of the earth hath not been torn, nor the virtue and salt of the soil spent by manurance, the graves have not been opened for gold, the mines not broken with sledges, nor their images pulled down out of their temples. It hath never been entered by any army of strength and never conquered or possessed by any Christian prince. It is besides so defensible that if two forts be builded in one of the provinces which I have seen, the flood setteth in so near the bank where the channel also lieth that no ship can pass but within a pike's length of the artillery, first of the one and afterwards of the other. Which two forts will be a sufficient guard both to the empire of *Inga* [Inca] and to an hundred other several kingdoms lying within the said river, even to the city of Quito in Peru.

There is therefore a great difference between the easiness of the conquest of Guiana and the defense of it being conquered, and the West or East Indies. Guiana hath but one entrance by the sea (if it have that) for any vessels of burden, so as whosoever shall first possess it, it shall be found inaccessible for any enemy except he come in wherries, barges, or *canoas,* or else in flat-bottomed boats; and if he do offer to enter it in that manner, the woods are so thick two hundred miles together upon the rivers of such entrance as a mouse cannot sit in a boat unhit from the bank. By land it is more impossible to approach, for it hath the strongest situation of any region under the sun, and is so environed with impassable mountains on every side as it is impossible to victual any company in the passage, which hath been well-proved by the Spanish nation, who, since the conquest of Peru have never left five years free from attempting this empire or discovering some way into it, and yet of twenty-three several gentlemen, knights, and noblemen, there was never any that knew which way to lead an army by land or to conduct ships by sea anything near the said country. Oreliano, of which the river of the Amazons taketh name, was the first, and Don Anthonio de Berreo (whom we displanted), the last; and I doubt much whether he himself or any of his yet know the best way into the said empire. It can therefore hardly be regained if any strength be formerly set down but in one or two places, and but two or three crumsters or galleys built and furnished upon the river within. The West Indies hath many ports, watering places, and landings, and nearer than three hundred miles to Guiana no man can harbor a ship, except he know one only place which is not learned in haste, and which I will undertake there is not any one of my companies that knoweth, whosoever hearkened after it.

Besides by keeping one good fort or building one town of strength, the whole empire is guarded, and whatsoever companies shall be afterwards planted within the land, although in twenty several provinces, those shall be able all to reunite themselves upon any occasion either by the way of one river or be able to march by land without either wood, bog, or mountain; whereas in the West Indies there are few towns or provinces that can succour or relieve one the other, either by land or sea. By land the countries are either desert, mountainous, or strong enemies. By sea, if any man invade to the eastward, those to the west cannot in many months turn against the breeze and east wind, besides the Spaniards are therein so dispersed as they are nowhere strong but in *Nueva Hispania* [New Spain] only. The sharp mountains, the thorns, the poisoned prickles, the sandy and deep ways in the valleys, the smothering heat and air, and want of water in other places are their only and best defense, which (because those nations that invade them are not victualled or provided to stay, neither have any place to friend adjoining) do serve them instead of good arms and great multitudes.

The West Indies were first offered Her Majesty's grandfather by Columbus,[1] a stranger in whom there might be doubt of deceit, and besides it was then thought incredible that there were such and so many lands and regions never written of before. This empire is made known to Her Majesty by her own vassal, and by him that oweth to her more duty than an ordinary subject, so that it shall ill sort with the many graces and benefits which I have received to abuse Her Highness either with fables or imaginations. The country is already discovered,[2] many nations won to Her Majesty's love and obedience, and those Spaniards which have latest and longest labored about the conquest, beaten out, discouraged and disgraced, which among these nations were thought invincible. Her Majesty may in this enterprise employ all those soldiers and gentlemen that are younger brethren, and all captains and chieftains that want employment, and the charge will be only the first setting out in victualling and arming them, for after the first or second year I doubt not but to see in London a contratation house of more receipt for Guiana than there is now in Seville for the West Indies.[3]

And I am resolved that if there were but a small army afoot in Guiana, marching towards Manoa, the chief city of *Inga,* he would yield Her Majesty by composition so many hundred thousand pounds yearly as should both defend all enemies abroad and defray all expenses at home and that he would besides pay a garrison of three or four thousand soldiers very royally to defend him against other nations. For he cannot but know how his predecessors, yea, how his own great uncles Guascar and Atibalipa,

1. The brother of Christopher Columbus, Bartholomew Columbus, who invited Henry VII, King of England and grandfather of Elizabeth I, to accept his brother's services in his effort to find a continent west of England. Henry is reported to have accepted this offer but not before Christopher Columbus had contracted his services to Queen Isabella of Spain. Therefore the West Indies were not ever offered to Henry VII; they were and remained Spanish through the 19th century.
2. The continent of which Guiana is a part.
3. Raleigh states that there will be a trading house or mercantile exchange for investors in Guiana that will exceed in its volume of business the comparable institution for the West Indian trade in Seville.

sons to Guanacapa, Emperor of Peru, were (while they contended for the empire) beaten out by the Spaniards and that both of late years and ever since the said conquest, the Spaniards have sought the passages and entry of his country; and of their cruelties used to the borderers he cannot be ignorant. In which respects no doubt but he will be brought to tribute with great gladness, if not, he hath neither shot nor iron weapon in all his empire and therefore may be easily conquered.

And I further remember that Berreo confessed to me and others (which I protest before the majesty of God to be true) that there was found among the prophecies of Peru (at such time as the empire was reduced to Spanish obedience) in their chiefest temples, among diverse others, which foreshadowed the loss of the said empire, that from *Inglatierra* [England] those *Ingas* should be again in time to come restored and delivered from the servitude of the said conquerors. And I hope, as we with these few hands have displanted the first garrison and driven them out of the said country, so Her Majesty will give order for the rest and either defend it and hold it as tributary, or conquer and keep it as Empress of the same. For whatsoever Prince shall possess it shall be greatest, and if the king of Spain enjoy it, he will become unresistable. Her Majesty hereby shall confirm and strengthen the opinions of all nations as touching her great and princely actions. And where the south border of Guiana reacheth to the dominion and empire of the Amazons, those women shall hereby hear the name of a virgin which is not only able to defend her own territories and her neighbors, but also to invade and conquer so great empires so far removed.[4]

To speak more at this time I fear would be but troublesome. I trust in God, this being true will suffice, and that he which is King of all Kings and Lord of all Lords will put it into her heart which is Lady of Ladies to possess it, if not, I will judge those men worthy to be kings thereof that by her grace and leave will undertake of it themselves.

THE DISCOVERY IN CONTEXT
Voyage Literature

During the second half of the sixteenth century in England, descriptions of the land and peoples of the New World increasingly found their way into print. Much of this material, including translations of treatises written in Spanish, French, and Portuguese, was gathered by Richard Hakluyt and published in volumes under the general title of *The Principal Navigations, Voyages, and Discoveries of the English Nation* (1598–1600). In some respects the observations and opinions of these adventurers to the Caribbean, Virginia, Newfoundland, and other points on the Atlantic coast can be appreciated as a kind of anthropology; the accounts Hakluyt collected by writers such as Arthur Barlow, Thomas Hariot, and René Landonnière convey their fascination with the cultures of the New World. In other respects their writing is obviously self-interested, motivated by a desire for wealth. Treatises encouraging trade with the natives of the New World were often punctuated with apologies for the use of violence, justifications for dispossession of native property, and professions of faith in a providence that allowed Europeans a chance to convert the heathen to Christianity and to civilize peoples that many judged to be "barbarians." In contrast, the great French essayist Michel de Montaigne, having declared that the term "barbarian" originally meant foreign rather than uncivilized, slyly drew on reports of cannibalism among the Indians in Brazil to condemn the European practice of torture as less humane than cannibalism.

---

4. This reference to the Amazons allows Raleigh to pay tribute to Elizabeth I, who represented herself as a powerful virgin queen.

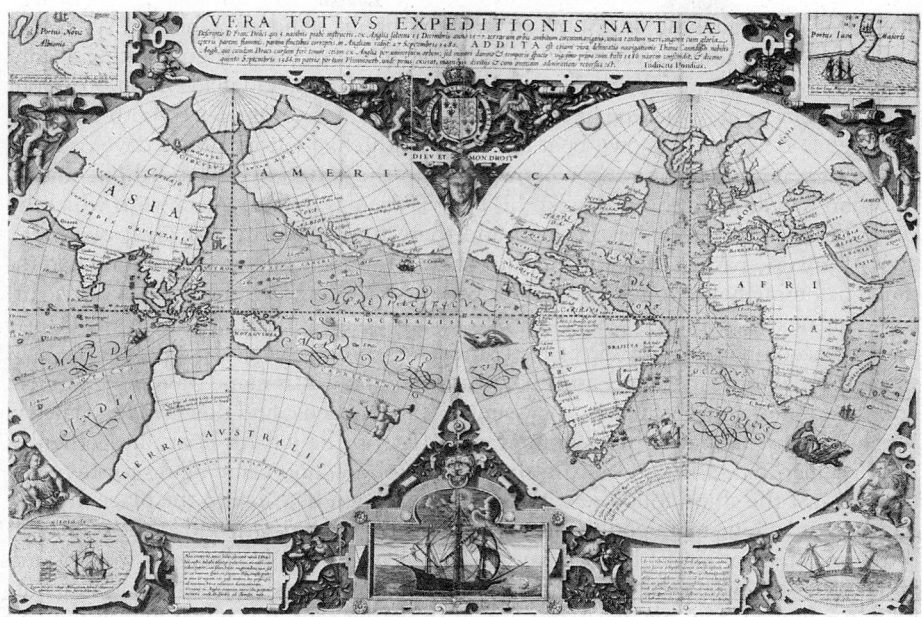

Hondius. *Sir Francis Drake's Map of the World*. ca. 1590.

Arthur Barlow
from *The First Voyage Made to the Coasts of America*[1]

This island had many goodly woods full of deer, coneys,[2] hares, and fowl, even in the midst of summer in incredible abundance. The woods are not such as you find in Bohemia, Muscovy, or Hercynia,[3] barren and fruitless, but the highest and reddest cedars of the world, far bettering the cedars of the Azores, of the Indies; or lybanus,[4] pines, cypress, sassafras, the lentisk, or the tree that beareth the mastic,[5] the tree that beareth the rind of black cinnamon, of which Master Winter brought from the straits of Magellan; and many other of excellent smell and quality. We remained by the side of this island two whole days before we saw any people of the country. The third day we espied one small boat rowing toward us, having in it three persons. This boat came to the island side, four harquebus[6]-shot from our ships, and there two of the people remaining, the third came along the shore side toward us, and, and we being then all within board, he walked up and down upon the point of the land next unto us. Then the master and the pilot of the Admiral,[7] Simon Ferdinando, and Captain Philip Amadas, myself, and others rowed to the land, whose coming this fellow

1. Published in 1600 in Hakluyt's third volume, Arthur Barlow's account describes events in a voyage he took to North America in the summer of 1584. His company landed on the coast of what is now Virginia on July 4 and, by a verbal declaration of "the right of the Queen's most excellent Majesty, as rightful Queen and Princess of the same," took possession of all the land that they could see on July 13. Barlow's account is notable for its picture of the Indians as hospitable people who were prepared to engage in trade with the English on the fairest of terms, although in general his judgments reflect his own Anglo-European experience. Describing the Indians' reliance on

prophecy, for example, Barlow compares it to the Romans' dependence on the oracle of Apollo.
2. Rabbits.
3. The woods of Virginia are described by what they are not like: those in Bohemia (now a region comprising portions of Hungary and the Czech Republic), Muscovy (the western portions of modern Russia), and Hercynia (now the Bavarian Alps in modern Germany).
4. Known for its incense.
5. Gum.
6. Gun.
7. The ship on which the admiral of the fleet sails.

attended, never making any show of fear and doubt. And after he had spoken of many things not understood by us, we brought him with his own good liking aboard the ship and gave him a shirt, a hat, and some other things, and made him taste of our wine and our meat, which he liked very well. And after having viewed both barks, he departed and went to his own boat again, which he had left in a little cove or creek adjoining. As soon as he was two bowshot into the water, he fell to fishing, and in less than half an hour, he had laden his boat as deep as it could swim, with which he came again to the point of the land and there he divided his fish into two parts, appointing one part to the ship and the other to the pinnace, which, after he had (as much as he might) requited the former benefits received, departed out of our sight.

The next day there came to us diverse boats, and in one of them the King's brother, accompanied with forty or fifty men, very handsome and goodly people, and in their behavior as mannerly and civil as any of Europe. His name was Granganimeo, and the king is called Wingina, the country Wingandacoa, and now by Her Majesty, Virginia. The manner of his coming was in this sort: he left his boats altogether, as the first man did, a little from the ships by the shore, and came along to the place over against the ships, followed with forty men. When he came to the place, his servants spread a long mat upon the ground, on which he sat down, and at the other end of the mat four others of his company did the like; the rest of his men stood round about him, somewhat afar off. When we came to the shore to him with our weapons, he never moved from his place, nor any of the other four, nor never mistrusted any harm to be offered from us, but sitting still, he beckoned us to come and sit by him, which we performed. And being set, he made all signs of joy and welcome, striking on his head with his breast and afterwards on ours, to show we were all one, smiling and making show the best he could of all love and familiarity. After he had made a long speech unto us, we presented him with diverse things, which he received very joyfully and thankfully. None of the company durst speak one word all the time, only the four which were at the other end spake one in the other's ear very softly.

The king is greatly obeyed, and his brothers and children reverenced. The king himself in person was, at our being there, sore wounded in a fight which he had with the king of the next country, called Wingina, and was shot in two places through the body, and once clean through the thigh, but yet he recovered. By reason whereof and for that he lay at the chief town of the country, being six days' journey off, we saw him not at all.

After we presented this his brother with such things as we thought he liked, we likewise gave somewhat to the other that sat with him on the mat. But presently he arose and took all from them and put it into his own basket, making signs and tokens that all things ought to be delivered unto him, and the rest were but his servants and followers. A day or two after this, we fell to trading with them, exchanging some things that we had for chamois, buff, and deerskins. When we showed him all our packet of merchandise, of all things that he saw, a bright tin dish most pleased him, which he presently took up and clapped it before his breast, and after made a hole in the brim thereof and hung it about his neck, making signs that it would defend him against his enemies' arrows; for those people maintain a deadly and terrible war, with the people and the king adjoining. We exchanged our tin dish for twenty skins, worth twenty crowns or twenty nobles, and a copper kettle for fifty skins worth fifty crowns. They offered us good exchange for our hatchets and axes, and for knives, and would have given anything for swords, but we would not depart with any. After two or three days the king's brother came aboard the ships and drank wine and eat of our meat and of our bread, and liked exceedingly thereof; and after a few days had overpassed, he brought his wife with him to the ships, his daughter, and two or three children. His wife was very well-favored, of mean stature and very bashful; she had on her back a long cloak of leather with the fur side next to her body and before her a piece of the same. About her forehead she had a band of white coral, and so had her husband many times. In her ears she had bracelets of pearls hanging to her middle (whereof we delivered your worship a little bracelet) and those were of the bigness of good peas. The rest of her women of the better sort had pendants of copper hanging in either ear, and some of the children of the king's brother and other noblemen have five or six in either ear. He himself had upon his head a broad plate of gold or copper, for being unpolished we knew not what metal it would be, neither would he by any means suffer us to take it off his head, but feeling it, it would bow very easily. His apparel was as his wife's, only the women wear their hair long on both sides and the men but on one. They are of color yellowish, and their hair black for the most part, and yet we saw children that had very fine auburn- and chestnut-colored hair.

After that these women had been there, there came down from all parts great store of people, bringing with them leather, coral, diverse kinds of dyes very excellent, and exchanged with us; but when Granganimeo the king's brother was present, none durst trade but himself, except such as wear red pieces of copper on their heads like himself, for that is the difference between the noblemen and the governors of countries, and the meaner sort. And we both noted there and you have understood since by these men which we have brought home, that no people in the world carry more respect to their king, nobility, and governors than these do. The king's brother's wife, when she came to us (as she did many times) was allowed with forty or fifty women always, and when she came into the ship, she left them all on land, saving her two daughters, her nurse, and one or two more. The king's brother always kept this order, as many boats as he would come withal to the ships, so many fires would he make on the shore afar off, to the end we might understand with what strength and company he approached. Their boats are made of one tree, either of pine or pitch trees, a wood not commonly known to our people, nor found growing in England. They have no edge tools to make them withal; if they have any, they are very few and those it seems they had twenty years since, which, as those two men declared, was out of a wreck which happened upon their coast of some Christian ship, being beaten that way by some storm and outrageous weather, whereof none of the people were saved, but only the ship, or some part of her being cast upon the sand out of whose sides they drew the nails and the spikes and with those they made their best instruments. The manner of making their boats is thus: They burn down some great tree, or take such as are wind-fallen, and putting gum and rosin upon one side thereof, they set fire into it, and when it hath burnt it hollow, they cut out the coal with their shells and everywhere they would burn it deeper or wider they lay on gums which burn away the timber and by this means they fashion very fine boats and such as will transport twenty men. Their oars are like scoops, and many times they set[8] with long poles as the depth serveth.

The king's brother had great liking of our armor, a sword, and diverse other things which we had, and offered to lay a great box of pearl in gage[9] for them; but we refused it for this time, because we would not make them know that we esteemed thereof until we had understood in what places of the country the pearl grew, which now your worship doth very well understand.

He was very just of his promise; for many times we delivered him merchandise upon his word, but ever he came within the day and performed his promise. He sent us everyday a brace or two of fat bucks, coneys, hares, fish, the best of the world. He

---

8. Punt.   9. Payment.

sent us diverse kinds of fruits, melons, walnuts, cucumbers, gourds, peas, and diverse roots, and fruits very excellent good, and of their country, corn,[1] which is very white, fair, and well-tasted, and growth three times in five months. In May they sow, in July they reap; in June they sow, in August they reap; in July they sow, in September they reap. Only they cast the corn into the ground, breaking a little of the soft turf with a wooden mattock or pickaxe. Ourselves proved the soil and put some of our peas in the ground, and in ten days they were of fourteen inches high. They have also beans very fair of diverse colors and wonderful plenty, some growing naturally and some in their gardens, and so have they wheat and oats.

The soil is the most plentiful, sweet, fruitful, and wholesome of all the world. There are above fourteen several sweet-smelling timber trees, and the most part of their underwoods are bays and such like. They have those oaks that we have, but far greater and better. After they had been diverse times aboard our ships, myself with seven more went twenty miles into the river that runneth toward the city of Skicoak, which river they call Occam; and the evening following, we came to an island which they call Raonoak,[2] distant from the harbor by which we entered seven leagues. And at the north end thereof was a village of nine houses, built of cedar and fortified round about with sharp trees to keep out their enemies, and the entrance into it made like a turnpike, very artificially. When we came toward it, standing near unto the water's side, the wife of Granganimeo, the king's brother, came running out to meet us very cheerfully and friendly; her husband was not then in the village. Some of her people she commanded to draw our boat on shore for the beating of the billow, others she appointed to carry us on their backs to the dry ground, and others to bring our oars into the house for fear of stealing. When we were come into the outer room, having five rooms in her house, she caused us to sit down by a great fire, and took off our clothes and washed them and dried them again. Some of the women plucked off our stockings and washed them, some washed our feet in warm water, and she herself took great pains to see all things ordered in the best manner she could, making great haste to dress some meat for us to eat.

After we had thus dried ourselves, she brought us into the inner room, where she set on the board standing along the house some wheat like fermenty,[3] sodden[4] venison and roasted; fish, sodden, boiled and roasted; melons raw and sodden; roots of diverse kinds, and diverse fruits. Their drink is commonly water, but while the grape lasteth, they drink wine, and for want of casks to keep it, all the year after they drink water, but it is sodden with ginger in it, and black cinnamon, and sometimes sassafras and diverse other wholesome and medicinable herbs and trees. We were entertained with all love and kindness, and with as much bounty (after their manner) as they could possibly devise. We found the people most gentle, loving and faithful, void of all guile and treason, and such as live after the manner of the golden age.[5] The people could only care how to defend themselves from the cold in their short winter, and to feed themselves with such meat as the soil affordeth. Their meat is very well sodden and they make broth very sweet and savory. Their vessels are earthen pots, very large,

---

1. Possibly buckwheat. The English used the term "maize" for the grain that in the United States is now known as corn.

2. Roanoke. A year later, this island in what is now North Carolina was to be the site of the first English colony in North America. Sir Walter Raleigh sent out settlers in 1585, who returned to England in 1586; another group, who tried to revive the colony in 1587, had vanished without a trace by 1591, when ships from England reached them with additional settlers and supplies.

3. Porridge.

4. Boiled.

5. The Indians of the Americas were sometimes compared with the people who were supposed to have lived during the mythical golden age, a period in which nature provided food without toil, property was common, and human society was free of conflict.

white, and sweet; their dishes are wooden platters of sweet timber. Within the place where they feed was their lodging, and within that, their idol which they worship, of whom they speak incredible things. While we were at meat, there came in at the gates two or three men with their bows and arrows from hunting, whom when we espied, we began to look one toward another and offered to reach our weapons; but as soon as she spied our mistrust, she was very much moved and caused some of her men to run out and take away their bows and arrows and break them and withal beat the poor fellows out of the gate again. When we departed in the evening and would not tarry all night, she was very sorry and gave us into our boat our supper half dressed, pots and all, and brought us to our boat's side, in which we lay all night, removing the same a pretty distance from the shore. She, perceiving our jealousy,[6] was much grieved, and sent diverse men and thirty women to sit all night on the bank side by us and sent us into our boats five mats to cover us from the rain, using many words to entreat us to rest in their houses. But because we were few men and if we had miscarried, the voyage had been in very great danger, we durst not adventure of anything, though there was no cause of doubt; for a more kind and loving people there cannot be found in the world, as far as we have hitherto had trial.

* * *

They wondered marvelously when we were amongst them at the whiteness of our skins, ever coveting[7] to touch our breast and to view the same. Besides they had our ships in marvelous admiration and all things else were so strange unto them as it appeared that none of them had ever seen the like. When we discharged any piece, were it but an harquebus, they would tremble thereat for very fear and for the strangeness of the same. For the weapons which themselves use are bows and arrows; the arrows are but of small canes, headed with a sharp shell or tooth of a fish sufficient enough to kill a naked man. Their swords be of wood hardened, likewise they use wooden breastplates for their defense. They have besides a kind of club, in the end whereof they fasten the sharp horns of a stag or other beast. When they go to wars they carry about with them their idol, of whom they ask counsel, as the Romans were wont of the Oracle of Apollo. They sing songs as they march toward the battle, instead of drums and trumpets. Their wars are very cruel and bloody by reason whereof, and of their civil dissensions which have happened of late years among them, the people are marvelously wasted,[8] and in some places the country left desolate.

Thomas Hariot
from *A Brief and True Report of the Newfound Land of Virginia*[1]

It resteth I speak a word or two of the natural inhabitants, their natures and manners, leaving large discourse thereof until time more convenient hereafter; now only so far forth as that you may know how they in respect of troubling our inhabiting and planting are not to be feared, but that they shall have cause both to fear and love us that shall inhabit with them.

---

6. Fear.
7. Wishing.
8. Reduced in numbers.
1. Thomas Hariot, an astronomer and mathematician, was a member of Sir Walter Raleigh's household. This account, published by Hakluyt in 1598, reports on his voyage to Virginia in 1586. He tells of an unanticipated yet terrible consequence of European colonization: the

death of numbers of Indians from diseases—brought by colonists—to which the Indians had no immunity. As a scientific matter, the phenomenon was not at all understood, and Hariot describes attempts by the English to explain what it meant in supposedly moral terms and also to take advantage of its practical effect—the reduction of the Indian population—as a way to colonize the region further.

They are a people clothed with loose mantles made of deerskins, and aprons of the same round about their middles, all else naked; of such a difference of statures only as we in England;[2] having no edge tools or weapons of iron or steel to offend us withal, neither know they how to make any. Those weapons that they have are only bows made of witch hazel and arrows of reeds, flat-edged truncheons also of wood about a yard long; neither have they anything to defend themselves but targets[3] made of barks and some armors made of sticks wickered together with thread. * * *

Their manner of war amongst themselves is either by sudden surprising one another, most commonly about the dawning of the day or moonlight, or else by ambushes or some subtle devices. Set battles are very rare, except it fall out where there are many trees, where either part may have some hope of defense after the delivery of every arrow, in leaping behind some or other.[4]

If there fall out any wars between us and them, what their fight is likely to be, we having advantages against them so many manner of ways, as by our discipline, our strong weapons and devices else, especially ordinance[5] great and small, it may easily be imagined. By the experience we have had in some places, the turning up of their heels against us in running away was their best defense.

In respect of us they are a people poor, and for want of skill and judgment in the knowledge and use of our things do esteem our trifles before things of greater value. Nothwithstanding, in their proper manner (considering the want of such means as we have), they seem very ingenious. For although they have no such tools, nor any such crafts, sciences, and arts as we, yet in those things they do, they show excellency of wit. And by how much they upon due consideration shall find our manner of knowledges and crafts to exceed theirs in perfection and speed for doing or execution, by so much the more is it probable that they should desire our friendship and love and have the greater respect for pleasing and obeying us. Whereby may be hoped, if means of good government be used, that they may in a short time be brought to civility and the embracing of true religion.

Some religion they have already, which although it be far from the truth, yet being as it is, there is hope that it may be the easier and sooner reformed.

They believe that there are many gods, which they call Mantoac, but of different sorts and degrees, one only chief and great God, which hath been from all eternity, who, as they affirm, when he purposed to make the world, made first other gods of a principal order to be as means and instruments to be used in the creation and government to follow, and after, the sun, moon, and stars as petty gods and the instruments of the other more principal. First (they say) were made waters, out of which by the gods was made all diversity of creatures that are visible or invisible.

For mankind, they say a woman was made first, which by the working of one of the gods, conceived and brought forth children; and in such sort they say they had their beginning. But how many years or ages have passed since, they say they can make no relation, having no letters or other such means as we to keep records of the particularities of times past, but only tradition from father to son.

---

2. I.e., the Indians are generally of the same stature as the English and have the same range of differences in height as the English.

3. Shields.

4. Europeans fought each other in "set battles." Typically, an army was led by its cavalry and supported by its infantry, who marched to a distance from which they could fire their guns and cannons at the enemy. Indians waged what is known in the modern period as guerilla warfare, attacking the enemy by surprise maneuvers and defending themselves in quick retreats.

5. Artillery.

* * *

Most things they saw with us, as mathematical instruments, sea compasses, the virtue of the loadstone[6] in drawing[7] iron, a perspective glass[8] whereby was showed many strange sights, burning glasses,[9] wild fireworks, guns, hooks, writing and reading, springclocks that seem to go of themselves, and many other things that we had were so strange unto them and so far exceeded their capacities to comprehend the reason and means how they should be made and done that they thought they were rather the works of gods than of men, or at the leastwise they had been given and taught us of the gods. Which made many of them to have such opinion of us as that if they knew not the truth of God and religion already, it was rather to be had from us whom God so specially loved than from a people that were so simple as they found themselves to be in comparison of us. Whereupon greater credit was given unto that we spoke of, concerning such matters. * * *

There could at no time happen any strange sickness, losses, hurts, or any other cross unto them but that they would impute to us the cause or means thereof, for offending or not pleasing us. One other rare and strange accident, leaving others, will I mention before I end, which moved the whole country that either knew or heard of us, to have us in wonderful admiration.

There was no town where we had any subtle devise[1] practiced against us, we leaving it unpunished or not revenged (because we sought by all means possible to win them by gentleness) but that within a few days after our departure from every such town, the people began to die very fast, and many in short space; in some towns about twenty, in some forty, and in one six score, which in truth was very many in respect of their numbers. This happened in no place that we could learn but where we had been where they used some practice against us, and after such time.[2] The disease also was so strange that they neither knew what it was, nor how to cure it, the like by report of the oldest men in the country never happened before, time out of mind. * * *

This marvelous accident in all the country wrought so strange opinions of us that some people could not tell whether to think us gods or men, and the rather because that all the space of their sickness, there was no man of ours known to die or that was especially sick; they noted also that we had no women among us, neither that we did care for any of theirs.

Some therefore were of opinion that we were not born of women, and therefore not mortal, but that we were men of an old generation many years past, then risen again to immortality.

Some would likewise seem to prophecy that there were more of our generation yet to come to kill theirs and take their places, as some thought the purpose was, by that which was already done. Those that were immediately to come after us they imagined to be in the air, yet invisible and without bodies, and that they by our entreaty and for the love of us did make the people to die in that sort as they did by shooting invisible bullets into them.

To confirm this opinion, their physicians (to excuse their ignorance in curing the disease) would not be ashamed to say but earnestly make the simple people believe that the strings of blood that they sucked out of the sick bodies were the

---

6. Magnet.
7. Attracting.
8. Telescope.
9. Magnifying glasses.
1. Trick.

2. Hariot moralizes the phenomenon of immunity by stating that Indian villages that came down with disease were those that had resisted or "used some practice against" the English.

strings wherewithal the invisible bullets were tied and cast. Some also thought that we shot them ourselves out of our pieces from the place where we dwelt and killed the people in any town that had offended us, as we listed, how far distant from us so ever it were. And other some said that it was the special work of God for our sakes as we ourselves have cause in some sort to think no less, whatsover some do or may imagine to the contrary, specially some astrologers, knowing of the eclipse of the sun which we saw the same year before in our voyage thitherward, which unto them appeared very terrible. And also of a comet which began to appear but a few days before the beginning of the said sickness.[3] But to exclude them[4] from being the special causes of so special an accident, there are further reasons than I think fit at this present to be alleged. These their[5] opinions I have set down the more at large that it may appear unto you that there is good hope that they may be brought through discreet dealing and government to the embracing of the truth and consequently to honor, obey, fear, and love us.

And although some of our company toward the end of the year showed themselves too fierce in slaying some of the people in some towns, upon causes that on our part might easily enough have been born withal; yet notwithstanding, because it was on their part justly deserved, the alteration of their opinions generally and for the most part concerning us is the less to be doubted.[6] And whatsoever else they may be, by carefulness[7] of ourselves need nothing at all to be feared.

René Landonnière
from *A Notable History Containing Four Voyages Made to Florida*[1]

My Lord Admiral of Chastillion, a nobleman more desirous of the public than of his private benefit, understanding the pleasure of the King his prince, which was to discover new and strange countries, caused vessels fit for this purpose to be made ready with all diligence and men to be levied meet for such an enterprise, among whom he chose Captain John Ribault, a man in truth expert in sea causes, which having received his charge, set himself to sea in the year 1562, the eighteenth of February, accompanied only with two of the king's ships, but so well furnished with gentlemen (of whose number I myself was one) and with old soldiers that he had means to achieve some notable thing and worthy of eternal memory. Having therefore sailed two months, never holding the usual course of the Spaniards, he arrived in Florida.

* * *

Having sailed twelve leagues at the least, we perceived a troop of Indians, which as soon as ever they espied the pinnaces[2] were so afraid that they fled into the woods leaving behind them a young lucerne[3] which they were turning upon a spit, for

---

3. The Indians attributed their disease to God's favor toward the English. Hariot observes that the English concurred in this opinion, despite the warnings of astrologers who saw a recent eclipse of the sun and the arrival of a comet as bad omens. He concludes that the Indians' sense of a divine power backing the English enterprise could be the basis for their further peaceful subjugation.
4. The eclipse and the comet.
5. I.e., the Indians'.
6. Hariot admits that the English were "too fierce" in killing Indians for insufficient reason; at the same time he states, without further explanation, that as these actions were "justly deserved," the English need fear no change in the Indians' attitude toward them.
7. Taking care.
1. Landonnière set sail with John (Jean) Ribault, a French captain under the command of the Admiral of Chastillon in 1562. This account of their adventures was translated from French into English and published in 1600 in Hakluyt's third volume.
2. Small sailing ships, often used to scout along rivers and bays.
3. Wildcat.

which cause the place was called Cape Lucerne. Proceeding forth on our way, we found another arm of the river, which ran toward the east, up which the Captain determined to sail and to leave the great current. A little while after, they began to espy diverse other Indians, both men and women, half hidden within the woods, who, knowing not that we were such as desired their friendship were dismayed at the first but soon after were emboldened, for the Captain caused store of merchandise to be showed them openly whereby they knew that we meant nothing but well unto them. And then they made a sign that we should come on land, which we would not refuse. At our coming on shore, diverse of them came to salute our general according to their barbarous fashion. Some of them gave him skins of chamois;[4] others, little baskets made of palm leaves. Some presented him with pearls, but no great number. Afterwards they went about to make an arbor to defend us in that place from the parching heat of the sun; but we would not stay as then. Wherefore the Captain thanked them much for their good will and gave presents to each of them, wherewith he pleased them so well before he went thence that his sudden departure was nothing pleasant unto them. For knowing him to be so liberal, they would have wished him to have stayed a little longer, seeking by all means to give him occasion to stay, showing him by signs that he should stay but that day only, and that they desired to advertise a great Indian lord which had pearls in great abundance and silver also, all which things should be given unto him at the king's[5] arrival, saying further that in the meantime while that this great lord came thither, they would lead him to their houses and show him there a thousand pleasures in shooting and seeing the stag killed, therefore they prayed him not to deny them their request. Notwithstanding, we returned to our ships. * * *

A few days afterward, John Ribault determined to return once again toward the Indians which inhabited that arm of the river which runneth toward the west, and to carry with him good store of soldiers. For his meaning was to take two Indians of this place to bring them into France, as the queen had commanded him. With this deliberation again we took our former course so far forth that at the last we came into the selfsame place where at the first we found the Indians, from thence we took two Indians by permission of the king, which thinking they were more favored than the rest thought themselves very happy to stay with us. But these two Indians, seeing we made no show at all that we would go on land but rather that we followed in the midst of the current, began to be somewhat offended and would by force have leapt into the water, for they are so good swimmers that immediately they would have gotten into the forests.[6] Nevertheless, being acquainted with their humor, we watched them narrowly and sought by all means to appease them, which we could not by any means do for that time, though we offered them things which they much esteemed, which things they disdained to take and gave back again whatever was given them, thinking that such gifts should have altogether bound them and that in restoring them they should be restored unto their liberty. In fine, perceiving that all that they did availed them nothing, they prayed us to give them those things which they had restored, which we did incontinent. Then they approached one toward the other and began to sing, agreeing so sweetly together that in hearing their song it seemed that they lamented the absence of their friends. They continued their songs all night

---

4. Deerskin.
5. I.e., of the Indians.

6. In effect, the Indians found that they were prisoners.

without ceasing, all which time we were constrained to lie at anchor by reason that the tide was against us; but we hoisted sail the next day very early in the morning and returned to our ships.[7] As soon as we were come to our ships, every one sought to gratify these two Indians and to show them the best countenance that was possible, to the intent that by such courtesies they might perceive the good desire and affection which we had to remain their friends in time to come. Then we offered them meat to eat, but they refused it and made us to understand that they were accustomed to wash their face and to stay until the sun were set before they did eat, which is a ceremony common to all the Indians of New France. Nevertheless in the end they were constrained to forget their superstitions and to apply themselves to our nature, which was somewhat strange to them at the first. They became therefore more jocund, every hour made us a thousand discourses, being marvelous sorry that we could not understand them. A few days after, they began to bear so goodwill toward me that, as I think, they would rather have taken perished with hunger and thirst than have taken their refection at any man's hand but mine. Seeing this their goodwill, I sought to learn some Indian words and began to ask them questions, showing them the thing whereof I desired to know the name and how they called it. They were very glad to tell it me and, knowing the desire that I had to learn their language, they encouraged me afterward to ask them everything. So that putting down in writing the words and phrases of the Indian speech, I was able to understand the greatest part of their discourses. Every day they did nothing but speak unto me of the desire that they had to use me well, if we returned unto their houses, and cause me to receive all the pleasures that they could devise, as well in hunting as in seeing their very strange and superstitious ceremonies at a certain feast which they call Toya, which feast they observe as straightly as we observe the Sunday. They gave me to understand that they would bring me to see the greatest lord of this country, which they call Chicola, who exceedeth them in height (as they told me) a good foot and a half. They said unto me that he dwelt within the land in a very large place and enclosed exceeding high, but I could not learn wherewith. And as far as I can judge, this place whereof they spoke unto me was a very fair city. For they said unto me that within the enclosure there was great store of houses which were built very high, wherein there was an infinite number of men like unto themselves which made none account of gold, of silver, nor of pearls, seeing they had thereof in abundance. * * * After they had stayed awhile in our ships, they began to be sorry and still demanded of me when they should return. I made them to understand that the Captain's will was to send them home again, but that first he would bestow apparel of them, which a few days after was delivered unto them. But seeing he would not give them license to depart, they resolved themselves to steal away by night and to get a little boat which we had, and by the help of the tide to sail home toward their dwellings and by this means to save themselves; which thing they failed not to do, and put their enterprise in execution, yet leaving behind them the apparel which the Captain had given them and carrying away nothing but that which was their own, showing well hereby that they were not void of reason. The Captain cared not greatly for their departure, considering they had not been used otherwise than well and that therefore they should not estrange themselves from the Frenchmen.

---

7. These "ships" were the larger sailing vessels, or galleons, having three masts, five or six sails, and three or four decks, on which most settlers crossed the ocean.

Michel de Montaigne
from *Of Cannibals*[1]

All [the Brazilians'] moral discipline containeth but these two articles; first, an undismayed resolution to war, then an inviolable affection to their wives. * * * They war against the nations that lie beyond their mountains, to which they go naked, having no other weapons than bows or wooden swords, sharp at one end, as our broaches are. It is an admirable thing to see the constant resolution of their combats, which never end but by effusion of blood and murder, for they know not what fear or routs are. Every victor brings home the head of the enemy he hath slain as a trophy of his victory, and fasteneth the same at the entrance of his dwelling place. After they have long time used and entreated their prisoners well and with all commodities they can devise, he that is the master of them, summoning a great assembly of his acquaintance, tieth a cord to one of his prisoner's arms, by the end whereof they hold him fast, with some distance from him for fear he might offend him, and giveth the other arm, bound in like manner, to the dearest friend he hath, and both in the presence of all the assembly kill him with swords. Which done, they roast and then eat him in common and send slices of him to such friends as are absent. It is not, as some imagine, to nourish themselves with it (as anciently the Scythians were wont to do), but to represent an extreme and inexpiable revenge. Which we prove thus: some of them perceiving the Portuguese, who had confederated themselves with their adversaries, to use another kind of death when they took them to be prisoners, which was to bury them up to the middle and against the upper part of the body to shoot arrows and then, being almost dead, to hang them up, they supposed that these people of the other world (as they who had sowed the knowledge of many vices amongst their neighbors and were much more cunning in all kinds of evils and michief than they) undertook not this manner of revenge without cause and that consequently it was more smartful and cruel than theirs, and thereupon began to leave their old fashion to follow this. I am not sorry we note the barbarous manner of such an action, but grieved that prying so narrowly into their faults we are so blinded in ours. I think there is more barbarism in eating men alive than to feed upon them, being dead; to mangle by tortures and torments a body full of lively sense, to roast him in pieces, to make dogs and swine to gnaw and tear him in mammocks[2] (as we have not only read but seen very lately, yea, and in our own memory, not amongst ancient enemies but our neighbors and fellow citizens and, which is worse, under the pretence of piety and religion) than to roast and eat him after he is dead. Chrysippus and Zeno,[3] arch-pillars of the Stoic sect, have supposed that it was no hurt at all, in time of need and to what end so ever, to make use of our carrion bodies and to feed upon them, as did our forefathers who, being beseiged by Caesar in the city of Alexia, resolved to sustain the famine of the seige with the bodies of old men, women, and other persons unserviceable and unfit to fight.

1. The great French humanist Michel de Montaigne virtually invented the modern essay, and actually coined the term *Essais* ("trials, attempts") for his collection, first published in 1580 and again in 1588 and 1595, each time with additions and revisions. The selection given here is from the first English translation (1603), by John Florio. This essay reflects on the account of French travelers to Brazil who reported on the manners and customs of the natives there. Montaigne comments especially on the Brazilians' practice of cannibalism, which consisted of a ritual eating of their dead prisoners of war, and compares it to the torture of prisoners in the religious wars that were being waged in France at that time. He concludes by declaring that the Brazilian practice is, in his view, less "barbarous," strange, and inhuman than the European.
2. Pieces.
3. Zeno was the founder of the Stoic school of philosophy in Athens, c. 315 B.C.; Stoics believed that happiness derived from a life in tune with nature and free from emotional attachments. Zeno was followed by Chrysippus (c. 204 B.C.).

Vascones (fama est) alimentis talibus usi
Produxere animas.
Gascoynes (as fame reports)
Lived with meats of such sorts.

And physicians fear not, in all kinds of compositions availful to our health, to make use of it, be it for outward or inward applications. But there was never any opinion found so unnatural and immodest that would excuse treason, treachery, disloyalty, tyranny, cruelty, and suchlike, which are our ordinary faults. We may then well call them barbarous, in regard of reason's rules, but not in respect of us that exceed them in all kind of barbarism. Their wars are noble and generous and have as much excuse and beauty as this human infirmity may admit. They aim at naught so much and have no other foundation amongst them but the mere jealousy of virtue. They contend not for the gaining of new lands, for to this day they yet enjoy that natural uberty[4] and fruitfulness which without laboring toil doth in such plenteous abundance furnish them with all necessary things that they need not enlarge their limits. They are yet in that happy estate as they desire no more than what their natural necessities direct them; whatsover is beyond it is to them superfluous.

Richard Barnfield

1577–1627

Richard Barnfield, a precocious yet only briefly productive poet, published four books of verse before his twenty-fifth birthday but then nothing else; we know merely that he lived to the age of fifty-two, comfortably settled on his Staffordshire estate, a husband and the father of a son, Robert. As a poet, he chose to follow the conventions of the amorous pastoral, fashionable for the ease with which they allowed the representation of lovers' intrigues. His frankly homoerotic verses express the love of a shepherd, Daphnis, for a boy called Ganimede or Ganymede, the mythological cup-bearer to Jupiter, the king of the gods. *The Tears of an Affectionate Shepherd* describes two phases to Daphnis's love; in *The Complaint* he offers Ganimede gifts from the pastoral world; in *The Lamentation*, claiming that what is fair is not necessarily good, he specifies steps to moral virtue. Complicating his narrative is the story of Ganimede's love for a woman, Queen Guendolen, whom Daphnis accuses of promiscuity. This rival threesome can be compared with the central figures of Shakespeare's (virtually contemporaneous) sonnet sequence: the poet, the young man, and the so-called dark lady. Finally, however, Barnfield creates his own poetic character, playing with occasional irony on the semantic and biblical association between shepherds and pastors. Barnfield's second collection of poems, published as *Cynthia*, continues to describe the competition for Ganimede's affection.

Slight as his total output was, Barnfield got the attention of readers. Francis Meres, his fellow student at Oxford and later critic of contemporary literature, placed him with Spenser, Sidney, and Abraham Fraunce as "best for pastoral." Barnfield's style is more vividly sensuous than theirs, however; his poems are best compared with the erotic pastoral verse of Theocritus, a Greek poet of the third century B.C., the first of its kind in Europe and a model for all subsequent examples of that genre.

---

4. Abundance.

The Affectionate Shepherd

To the Right Excellent and Most Beautiful Lady,
The Lady Penelope Rich[1]

Fair lovely Lady, whose angelic eyes
Are vestal candles of sweet beauty's treasure,
Whose speech is able to enchant the wise,
Converting joy to pain, and pain to pleasure;
5   Accept this simple toy of my soul's duty,
     Which I present unto thy matchless beauty,

And albeit the gift be all too mean,
Too mean an offering for thine ivory shrine;
Yet must thy beauty my just blame susteane,°   *sustain*
10 Since it is mortal, but thyself divine.
     Then (noble lady) take in gentle worth,
     This newborn babe which here my muse brings forth.

Your honors most affectionate
and perpetually devoted shepherd:
Daphnis.[2]

The Tears of an Affectionate Shepherd Sick for Love
or
The Complaint of Daphnis for the Love of Ganimede

Scarce had the morning star hid from the light
Heaven's crimson canopy with stars bespangled,
But I began to rue th'unhappy sight
Of that fair boy° that had my heart entangled;   *Ganimede*
5   Cursing the time, the place, the sense, the sin;
     I came, I saw, I viewed, I slipped in.

If it be sin to love a sweet-faced boy,
(Whose amber locks trussed up in golden trammels,°   *braids*
Dangle adown his lovely cheeks with joy,
10 When pearl and flowers his fair hair enamels)
     If it be sin to love a lovely lad;
     Oh then sin I, for whom my soul is sad.

His ivory-white and alabaster[3] skin
Is stained throughout with rare vermilion red,
15 Whose twinkling starry lights do never blin°   *cease*
To shine on lovely Venus (Beauty's bed):
     But as the lily and the blushing rose,
     So white and red on him in order grows.

1. Lady Penelope Rich (1562–1607) was the sister of Robert Devereux, Earl of Essex, the wife of Lord Rich, and the model for Sir Philip Sidney's "Stella."
2. A name conventionally assigned to a shepherd in pastoral poetry; Ganimede was frequently represented as his lover. Barnfield's Daphnis typifies the naive lover of pastoral who offers his beloved only the simple gifts of the countryside.
3. A white stone, prized for fine statuary.

Upon a time the nymphs bestirred themselves
20   To try who could his beauty soonest win:
But he accounted them but all as elves,
Except it were the fair Queen Guendolen,[4]
    Her he embraced, of her was beloved,
    With plaints he proved,° and with tears he moved.   *succeeded*

25   But her an old man had been suitor too,
That in his age began to dote again;
Her would he often pray, and often woo,
When through old age enfeebled was his brain:
    But she before had loved a lusty youth
30   That now was dead, the cause of all her ruth.

And thus it happened, Death and Cupid met
Upon a time at swilling Bacchus'° house,   *the god of wine*
Where dainty cates° upon the board were set,   *cakes*
And goblets full of wine to drink carouse:°   *riotously*
35   Where Love and Death did love the liquor so,
    That out they fall and to the fray° they go.   *to combat*

And having both their quivers at their back
Filled full of arrows; th'one of fatal steel,
The other all of gold; Death's shaft was black,
40   But Love's was yellow: Fortune turned her wheel;
    And from Death's quiver fell a fatal shaft,
    That under Cupid by the wind was waft.°   *blown*

And at the same time by ill hap° there fell   *misfortune*
Another arrow out of Cupid's quiver;
45   The which was carried by the wind at will,
And under Death the amorous shaft did shiver:
    They being parted, Love took up Death's dart,
    And Death took up Love's arrow (for his part.)

Thus as they wandered both about the world,
50   At last Death met with one of feeble age:
Wherewith he drew a shaft and at him hurled
The unknown arrow (with a furious rage),
    Thinking to strike him dead with Death's black dart,
    But he (alas) with Love did wound his heart.

55   This was the doting fool, this was the man
That loved fair Guendolena, Queen of Beauty;
She cannot shake him off, do what she can,
For he hath vowed to her his soul's last duty:
    Making him trim upon the holy-days;
60   And crowns his love with garlands made of bays.

Now doth he stroke his beard; and now (again)
He wipes the drivel from his filthy chin;
Now offers he a kiss; but high disdain

---

4. In Arthurian legend, Guendolen is a fay, or elf, who seduces King Arthur.

Will not permit her heart to pity him:
65   Her heart more hard than adamant° or steel,   *hard stone*
       Her heart more changeable than Fortune's wheel.

But leave we him in love (up to the ears),
And tell how Love behaved himself abroad;
Who seeing one that mourned still in tears
70   (A young man groaning under Love's great load),
       Thinking to ease his burden, rid his pains:
       For men have grief as long as life remains.

Alas (the while) that unawares he drew
The fatal shaft that death had dropped before;
75   By which deceit great harm did then ensue,
Staining his face with blood and filthy gore.
       His face, that was to Guendolen more dear
       Than love of lords, or any lordly peer.

This was that fair and beautiful young man,
80   Whom Guendolena so lamented for;
This is that love whom she doth curse and ban,
Because she doth that dismal chance abhor:
       And if it were not for his mother's[5] sake,
       Even Ganimede himself she would forsake.

85   Oh would she would forsake my Ganimede,
Whose surged love is full of sweet delight,
Upon whose forehead you may plainly read
Love's pleasure, graved in ivory tables bright:
       In whose fair eyeballs you may clearly see
90   Base Love still stained with foul indignity.

Oh, would to God he would but pity me,
That love him more than any mortal wight;
Then he and I with love would soon agree,
That now cannot abide his suitor's° sight.   *Guendolen's*
95   O would to God (so I might have my fee)°   *rightful reward*
       My lips were honey, and thy mouth a bee.

Then shouldst thou suck my sweet and my fair flower
That now is ripe, and full of honey-berries;
Then would I lead thee to my pleasant bower
100   Filled full of grapes, of mulberries, and cherries;
       Then shouldst thou be my wasp or else my bee,
       I would thy hive, and thou my honey be.

I would put amber bracelets on thy wrists,
Crownets° of pearl about thy naked arms;   *little crowns*
105   And when thou sitst at swilling° Bacchus's feasts   *drinking greedily*
My lips with charms should save thee from all harms:

---

5. Ganimede's mother is the mythological Callirrhoe, wife of Tros, King of Troy. Why this character is introduced at this point in the poem is unclear.

And when in sleep thou tookst thy chiefest pleasure,
Mine eyes should gaze upon thine eyelids' treasure.

And every morn by dawning of the day,
110   When Phoebus° riseth with a blushing face,   *the sun*
Silvanus'° chapel-clerks shall chant a lay,°   *a wood god / song*
And play thee hunts-up° in thy resting place: *a game*
    My cote° thy chamber, my bosom thy bed;   *shed*
    Shall be appointed for thy sleepy head.

115   And when it pleaseth thee to walk abroad,
(Abroad into the fields to take fresh air):
The meads with Flora's° treasure should be strowd,°   *goddess of spring / strewn*
(The mantled° meadows and the fields so fair).   *flower-covered*
    And by a silver well (with golden sands)
120   I'll sit me down, and wash thine ivory hands.

And in the sweltering heat of summertime,
I would make cabinets° for thee (my love:)   *shelters*
Sweet-smelling arbors made of eglantine
Should be thy shrine, and I would be thy dove.
125   Cool cabinets of fresh green laurel boughs
    Should shadow us, ore-set° with thick-set yews.   *overlaid*

Or if thou list to bathe thy naked limbs,
Within the crystal of a pearl-bright brook,
Paved with dainty pebbles to the brims;
130   Or clear, wherein thyself thyself mayst look;
    We'll go to Ladon,[6] whose still trickling noise,
    Will lull thee fast asleep amidst thy joys.

Or if thou'lt go unto the river side,
To angle for the sweet fresh-water fish;
135   Arm'd with thy implements that will abide
(Thy rod, hook, line) to take a dainty dish;
    Thy rods shall be of cane, thy lines of silk,
    Thy hooks of silver, and thy baits of milk.

Or if thou lovest to hear sweet melody,
140   Or pipe a round upon an oaten reed,
Or make thyself glad with some mirthful glee,
Or play them music whilst thy flock doth feed;
    To Pan's[7] own pipe I'll help my lovely lad,
    (Pan's golden pipe) which he of Syrinx had.

145   Or if thou darest to climb the highest trees
For apples, cherries, medlars, pears, or plums,
Nuts, walnuts, filberts, chestnuts, cervices,[8]
The hoary peach, when snowy winter comes;
    I have fine orchards full of mellowed fruit;
150   Which I will give thee to obtain my suit.

---

6. A river in Arcadia, the land of pastoral.
7. A woodland god, half man, half goat. He loved a
nymph, Syrinx, who, wishing to escape his attentions,

was changed into a reed by the gods. Pan named his pipe
of seven reeds after her.
8. The small edible fruit of a rose tree.

Not proud Alcynous[9] himself can vaunt,°   boast
Of goodlier orchards or of braver trees
Than I have planted; yet thou wilt not grant
My simple suit; but like the honeybees
155   Thou suckest the flower till all the sweet be gone;
    And lovest me for my coin till I have none.

Leave Guendolen (sweet heart), though she be fair
Yet is she light; not light in virtue shining:
But light in her behavior, to impair
160   Her honor in her chastity's declining;
    Trust not her tears, for they can wantonize,°   arouse you
    When tears in pearl are trickling from her eyes.

If thou wilt come and dwell with me at home;
My sheepcote shall be strowed° with new green rushes: strewn
165   We'll haunt the trembling prickets° as they roam   young buck
About the fields, along the hawthorn bushes;
    I have a piebald cur to hunt the hare:
    So we will live with dainty forest fare.

Nay more than this, I have a garden plot,
170   Wherein there wants nor herbs, nor roots, nor flowers;
(Flowers to smell, roots to eat, herbs for the pot),
And dainty shelters when the welkin° lowers: heaven
    Sweet-smelling beds of lilies and of roses,
    Which rosemary banks and lavender encloses.

175   There grows the gilliflower, the mint, the daisy
(Both red and white), the blew-veined-violet:
The purple hyacinth, the spike° to please thee,   lavender
The scarlet-dyed carnation bleeding yet;
    The sage, the savory, and sweet marjoram,
180   Hyssop, thyme, and eyebright,° good for the blind and dumb.   figwort

The pink, the primrose, cowslip, and daffadilly,
The harebell blue, the crimson columbine,
Sage, lettuce, parsley, and the milkwhite lily,
The rose, and speckled flower called sops-in-wine,
185   Fine pretty kingcups, and the yellow boots,°   buttercups
    That grows by rivers, and by shallow brooks.

And many thousand more (I cannot name)
Of herbs and flowers that in gardens grow,
I have for thee; and coneys° that be tame,   rabbits
190   Yong rabbits, white as swan, and black as crow,
    Some speckled here and there with dainty spots:
    And more I have two milch° and milkwhite goats.   milk

All these, and more, I'll give thee for thy love;
If these, and more, may 'tice° thy love away: entice

---

9. King of the Phaeacians, who gave Odysseus hospitality on his journey home from Troy to Ithaca. His gardens were reputed to be wonderful.

195   I have a pigeonhouse, in it a dove,
       Which I love more than mortal tongue can say:
          And last of all, I'll give thee a little lamb
          To play withal, new weaned from her dam.

    But if thou wilt not pity my complaint,
200   My tears, nor vows, nor oaths, made to thy beauty;
    What shall I do? But languish, die, or faint,
    Since thou dost scorn my tears, and my soul's duty:
        And tears contemned,° vows and oaths must fail;   *scorned*
        For where tears cannot, nothing can prevail.

205   Compare the love of fair Queen Guendolen
    With mine, and thou shalt see how she doth love thee:
    I love thee for thy qualities divine,
    But she doth love another swain above thee:
        I love thee for thy gifts, she for her pleasure;
210   I for thy virtue, she for beauty's treasure.

    And always (I am sure) it cannot last,
    But sometime nature will deny those dimples:
    Instead of beauty (when thy blossom's past)
    Thy face will be deformed, full of wrinkles:
215   Then she that loved thee for thy beauty's sake,
        When age draws on, thy love will soon forsake.

    But I that loved thee for thy gifts divine,
    In the December of thy beauty's waning,
    Will still admire (with joy) those lovely eyne,°   *eyes*
220   That now behold me with their beauty's baning:°   *poisoning*
        Though January will never come again,
        Yet April years[1] will come in showers of rain.

    When will my May come, that I may embrace thee?
    When will the hour be of my soul's joying?
225   Why dost thou seek in mirth still to disgrace me?
    Whose mirth's° my health, whose grief's my heart's annoying.   *mirth is*
        Thy bane my bale,° thy bliss my blessedness,   *misfortune*
        Thy ill my hell, thy weal my welfare is.

    Thus do I honor thee that love thee so,
230   And love thee so, that so do honor thee,
    Much more than any mortal man doth know,
    Or can discern by love or jealousy:
    But if that thou disdainest my loving ever;
    Oh happy I, if I had loved never.
                Finis.
        Plus fellus quam mellis Amor.[2]

---

1. The time of love when tears follow frustration, after the January of indifference and before the May of pleasure.

2. More bitter than sweet is Love.

The Second Day's Lamentation of the Affectionate Shepherd.[1]

Next morning when the golden sun was risen,
And new had bid good morrow to the mountains;
When night her silver light had locked in prison,
Which gave a glimmering on the crystal fountains:
5 Then ended sleep: and then my cares began,
  Even with the uprising of the silver Swan.[2]

O glorious sun, quoth I (viewing the sun),
That lightenest everything but me alone:
Why is my summer season almost done?
10 My springtime past, and age's autumn gone?
  My harvest's come, and yet I reaped no corn:
  My love is great, and yet I am forlorn.

Witness these wat'ry eyes my sad lament
(Receiving cisterns° of my ceaseless tears),   *tanks*
15 Witness my bleeding heart, my soul's intent,
Witness the weight distressed Daphnis bears:
  Sweet Love, come ease me of thy burthen's pain;[3]
  Or else I die, or else my heart is slain.

And thou love-scorning boy, cruel, unkind;
20 Oh let me once again entreat some pity:
May be thou wilt relent thy marble mind,
And lend thine ears unto my doleful ditty:
  Oh pity him, that pity craves so sweetly:
  Or else thou shalt be never named meekly.

25 If thou wilt love me, thou shalt be my boy,
My sweet delight, the comfort of my mind,
My love, my dove, my solace, and my joy:
But if I can no grace nor mercy find,
  I'll go to Caucasus to ease my smart,
30 And let a vulture gnaw upon my heart.[4]

Yet if thou wilt but show me one kind look,
(A small reward for my so great affection)
I'll grave thy name in beauty's golden book,
And shroud thee under Helicon's[5] protection;
35 Making the muses chant thy lovely praise:
  (For they delight in shepherds' lowly lays.)

And when th'art weary of thy keeping sheep
Upon a lovely down (to please thy mind),
I'll give thee fine ruff-footed doves to keep,

---

1. This poem is distinguished from its earlier counterpart by being a lamentation or expression of grief, rather than a complaint or protest that love has not been returned. It is presented on a "second day" in the sense that it is a reflection of a first day or an earlier time. In fact, the poet represents himself on the second day as an old man who has had ample time to consider matters of vice and virtue overlooked in his complaint.

2. Cygnus, a constellation.
3. I.e., ease me of the pain of loving you, a burden, because you do not love me.
4. An allusion to the fate of Prometheus, who, for having stolen fire from the gods to give to humans, was chained to the Caucasus Mountains to be eaten by a vulture.
5. A mountain in northern Greece, sacred to the muses.

40   And pretty pigeons of another kind:
           A robin-red-breast shall thy minstrel be,
           Chirping thee sweet, and pleasant melody.

      Or if thou wilt go shoot at little birds
      With bow and boult° (the thrustle-cock and sparrow)   *crossbow arrow*
45   Such as our country hedges can afford's;°   *afford us*
      I have a fine bow, and an ivory arrow:
           And if thou miss, yet meat thou shalt not lack,
           I'll hang a bag and a bottle at thy back.

      Wilt thou set springes° in a frosty night,   *traps*
50   To catch the long-billed woodcock and the snipe?
      (By the bright glimmering of the starry light),
      The partridge, pheasant, or the greedy gripe?°   *vulture*
           I'll lend thee lime-twigs, and fine sparrow calls,
           Wherewith the fowler silly birds enthrals.

55   Or in a misty morning if thou wilt
      Make pit-falls for the lark and pheldifare;
      Thy prop and sweak shall be both over-gilt:[6]
      With Cyparissus'[7] self thou shalt compare
           For gins° and wiles, the ouzels° to beguile;   *traps/blackbirds*
60   Whilst thou under a bush shalt sit and smile.

      Or with hare-pipes (set in a muset° hole)   *hedge*
      Wilt thou deceive the deep-earth-delving coney?°   *rabbit*
      Or wilt thou in a yellow boxen° bowl   *box tree*
      Taste with a wooden splint° the sweet lithe honey?   *a flat spoon*
65   Clusters of crimson grapes I'll pull thee down;
           And with vine-leaves make thee a lovely crown.

      Or wilt thou drink a cup of new-made wine
      Frothing at top, mixed with a dish of cream;
      And strawberries, or bilberries in their prime,
70   Bathed in a melting sugar-candy stream:
           Bunnell and Perry° I have for thee (alone)   *apple and pear liqueur*
           When vines are dead, and all the grapes are gone.

      I have a pleasant-noted nightingale,
      (That sings as sweetly as the silver swan),
75   Kept in a cage of bone; as white as whale,
      Which I with singing of Philemon[8] wan:
           Her shalt thou have, and all I have beside;
           If thou wilt be my boy, or else my bride.

      Then will I lay out all my lardary°   *dairy food*
80   (Of cheese, of cracknells,° curds and clotted-cream)   *biscuits*
      Before thy malcontent ill-pleasing eye:

6. Prop and sweak are parts of a trap to catch wild fowl;
Ganimede's trap will be gilded, in keeping with his
arrows, which are ivory.
7. A shepherd boy, beloved of Apollo, who killed him acci-
dently with a discus; he was changed into a cypress tree.

8. The legendary husband of Baucis. Together this old
couple were hospitable to Jupiter and Mercury; the
gods rewarded them by saving them from a universal
deluge.

But why do I of such great follies dream?
  Alas, he will not see my simple cote;
  For all my speckled lamb, nor milk-white goat.

85 Against° my birthday thou shalt be my guest: *for*
We'll have green cheeses and fine syllabubs;°   *puddings*
And thou shalt be the chief of all my feast.
And I will give thee two fine pretty cubs,°   *young foxes*
  With two young whelps,° to make thee sport withal,   *puppies*
90 A golden racket and a tennis ball

A gilded nutmeg and a race° of ginger,   *root*
A silken girdle and a drawn-work band,°   *woven bracelet*
Cuffs for thy wrists, a gold ring for thy finger,
And sweet rose-water for thy lily-white hand,
95 A purse of silk, bespanged with spots of gold,
  As brave a one as ere thou didst behold.

A pair of knives, a green hat and a feather,
New gloves to put upon thy milk-white hand
I'll give thee, for to keep thee from the weather;
100 With Phoenix[9] feathers shall thy face be fanned,
  Cooling those cheeks, that being cooled wax° red,   *grow*
  Like lilies in a bed of roses shed.

Why do thy coral lips disdain to kiss,
And suck that sweet, which many have desired?
105 That balm my bane, that means would mend my miss:[1]
Oh let me then with thy sweet lips b'inspired;
  When thy lips touch my lips, my lips will turn
  To coral too, and being cold ice will burn.

Why should thy sweet lovelock hang dangling down,
110 Kissing thy girdle-steed° with falling pride?   *waist*
Although thy skin be white, thy hair is brown:
Oh let not then thy hair thy beauty hide;
  Cut off thy lock, and sell it for gold wire:
  (The purest gold is tried in hottest fire).

Fair-long-hair-wearing Absolon[2] was killed,
Because he wore it in a bravery:°   *boastingly*
So that which graced his beauty, beauty spilled,
Making him subject to vile slavery,
  In being hanged: a death for him too good,
120 That sought his own shame, and his father's blood.

Again, we read of old King Priamus,[3]
(The hapless sire of valiant Hector slain)
That his hair was so long and odious

---

9. A legendary bird that regenerates itself.
1. I.e., that balm of your lips would cure my misfortune;
that means or way would repair my miss or lack.
2. Having led a failed revolt against his father King
David, Absalom fled but was caught when his long hair

tangled in a tree (2 Samuel 18).
3. King of Troy, father of the hero Hector. Barnfield
relates Priam's murder by the Greek hero Pyrrhus, also
known as Neoptolemus, the son of Achilles.

In youth, that in his age it bred his pain:
125   For if his hair had not been half so long,
      His life had been, and he had had no wrong.

For when his stately city was destroyed
(That monument of great antiquity)
When his poor heart (with grief and sorrow cloyed)
130 Fled to his wife (last hope in misery);
    Pyrrhus (more hard than adamantine rocks)
    Held him and hauled him by his aged locks.

These two examples by the way I show,
To prove th'indecency of men's long hair:
135 Though I could tell thee of a thousand moe,°   *more*
Let these suffice for thee (my lovely fair)
    Whose eye's my star; whose smiling is my sun;
    Whose love did end before my joys begun.

Fond love is blind, and so art thou (my dear),
140 For thou seest not my love, and great desart;°   *deserving*
Blind love is fond, and so thou dost appear;
For fond, and blind, thou grievest my grieving heart:
    Be thou fond-blind, blind-fond, or one, or all;
    Thou art my love, and I must be thy thrall.°   *slave*

145 Oh lend thine ivory forehead for love's book,
Thine eyes for candles to behold the same;
That when dim-sighted ones therein shall look
They may discern that proud disdainful dame;[4]
    Yet clasp that book, and shut that casement light;
150   Lest th'one obscured, the other shine too bright.

Sell thy sweet breath to'th'dainty musk-ball-makers;[5]
Yet sell it so as thou mayst soon redeem it:
Let others of thy beauty be partakers;
Else none but Daphnis will so well esteem it:
155   For what is beauty except it be well known?
    And how can it be known, except first shown?

Learn of the gentlewomen of this age,[6]
That set their beauties to the open view,
Making disdain their lord, true love their page;
160 A custom zeal doth hate, desert doth rue:
    Learn to look red, anon wax pale and wan,
    Making a mock of love, a scorn of man.

A candle light, and covered with a veil,
Doth no man good, because it gives no light;
165 So beauty of her beauty seems to fail,
    When being not seen it cannot shine so bright.

---

4. Barnfield personifies Ganimede's disdain for him by the figure of a proud lady.
5. Musk was a kind of perfume; a muskball was a receptacle to hold it.

6. This and the next stanza are ironic; Daphnis instructs Ganimede to show himself so that he will recognize his own pride.

Then show thyself and know thyself withal,
Lest climbing high thou catch too great a fall.

170 Oh, foul eclipser[7] of that fair sunshine,
Which is entitled beauty in the best;
Making that mortal, which is else divine,
That stains the fair which women 'steem not least:
    Get thee to Hell again (from whence thou art)
    And leave the center of a woman's heart.

175 Ah, be not stained (sweet boy) with this vile spot,°   *pride*
Indulgence daughter,° mother of mischance;   *daughter of indulgence*
A blemish that doth every beauty blot;
That makes them loathed, but never doth advance
    Her clients, fautors,° friends; or them that love her;   *patrons*
180   And hates them most of all, that most reprove her.

Remember age, and thou canst not be proud,
For age pulls down the pride of every man;
In youthful years by nature 'tis allowed
To have self-will, do nurture what she can;
185   Nature and nurture once together met,
    The soul and shape° in decent order set.   *body*

Pride looks aloft, still staring on the stars,
Humility looks lowly on the ground;
Th'one menaceth the gods with civil wars,
190 The other toils till he have virtue found:
    His thoughts are humble, not aspiring high;
    But pride looks haughtily with scornful eye.

Humility is clad in modest weeds,
But pride is brave and glorious to the show;
195 Humility his friends with kindness feeds,
But pride his friends (in need) will never know:
    Supplying not their wants, but them disdaining;
    Whilst they to pity never need complaining.

Humility in misery is relieved,
200 But pride in need of no man is regarded;
Pity and mercy weep to see him grieved
That in distress had them so well rewarded:
    But Pride is scorned, contemned, disdained, derided,
    Whilst humbleness of all things is provided.

205 Oh then be humble, gentle, meek, and mild;
So shalt thou be of every mouth commended;
Be not disdainful, cruel, proud, (sweet child)
So shalt thou be of no man much condemned;
    Care not for them that virtue do despise;
210   Virtue is loathed of fools; loved of the wise.

7. The pride of Queen Guendolen, whom the poet chastizes for seducing Ganimede.

O fair boy, trust not to thy beauty's wings,
They cannot carry thee above the sun:
Beauty and wealth are transitory things,
(For all must end that ever was begun)
215   But fame and virtue never shall decay;
     For fame is tombless, virtue lives for aye.

The snow is white, and yet the pepper's black,
The one is bought, the other is contemned:
Pebbles we have, but store of jeat° we lack;   *a black stone*
220 So white compared to black is much condemned:
     We do not praise the swan because she's white,
     But for she doth in music much delight.

And yet the silver-noted nightingale,
Though she be not so white is more esteemed;
225 Sturgeon is dun of hue, white is the whale,
Yet for the daintier dish the first is deemed;
     What thing is whiter than the milk-bred lily?
     Thou knows it not for naught, what man so silly?[8]

Yea what more noisomer° unto the smell   *vivid*
230 Than lilies are? What's sweeter than the sage?
Yet for pure white the lily bears the bell
Till it be faded through decaying age;
     Housedoves are white, and ouzels blackbirds be;
     Yet what a difference in the taste, we see.

235 Compare the cow and calf with ewe and lamb,
Rough hairy hides with softest downy fell;°   *wool*
Heifer and bull with wether and with ram,
And you shall see how far they do excel;
     White kine with black, black coney-skins with gray,
240   Kine, nesh° and strong; skin, dear° and cheap alway.   *weak/expensive*

The whitest silver is not always best,
Lead, tin, and pewter are of base esteem;
The yellow burnished gold, that comes from th'East,
And West (of late invented) may beseem
245   The world's rich treasury, or Midas'[9] eye;
     (The rich man's god, poor man's felicity).

Bugle° and jeat, with snow and alablaster   *black glass*
I will compare: white damascene° with black;   *inlaid metal*
Bullas and wheaton plums[1] (to a good taster),
250 The ripe red cherries have the sweetest smack;
     When they be green and young, th'are sour and naught;
     But being ripe, with eagerness th'are bought.

---

8. I.e., you do not know it because it is worthless; what man would be so silly as to give it value. Barnfield continues with his series of comparisons showing that unattractive objects are often valuable and vice versa. These comparisons introduce in turn a series of moral instructions that play on the concept of the shepherd as pastor, or clergyman.
9. Legendary King of Phrygia, who wished that all he touched were gold.
1. Bullas and wheaton plums are two varieties of plum.

Compare the wildcat to the brownish beaver,
Running for life, with hounds pursued sore;
255   When huntsmen of her precious stones bereave her
(Which with her teeth sh'had bitten off before):
    Restoratives, and costly curious felts
    Are made of them, and rich embroidered belts.

To what use serves a piece of crumbling chalk?
260   The agate stone is white, yet good for nothing;
Fie, fie, I am ashamed to hear thee talk;
Be not so much of thine on image doting:
    So fair Narcissus[2] lost his love and life.
    (Beauty is often with itself at strife).

265   Right diamonds are of a russet hue,
The brightsome carbuncles° are red to see too,   *garnets*
The sapphire stone is of a watchet° blue,   *deep*
(To this thou canst not choose but soon agree too):
    Pearls are not white but gray, rubies are red:
270   In praise of black, what can be better said?

For if we do consider of each thing
That flies in welkin,° or in water swims,   *heaven*
How everything increaseth with the spring,
And how the blacker still the brighter dims:
275   We cannot choose but needs we must confess,
    Sable excels milkwhite in more or less.

As for example, in the crystal clear
Of a sweet stream or pleasant running river,
Where thousand forms of fishes will appear,
280   (Whose names to thee I cannot now deliver):
    The blacker still the brighter have disgraced,
    For pleasant profit, and delicious taste.

Salmon and trout are of a ruddy color,
Whiting and dare is of a milkwhite hue:
285   Nature by them (perhaps) is made the fuller,
Little they nourish, be they old or new:
    Carp, loach, tench, eels (though black and bred in mud)
    Delight the tooth with taste, and breed good blood.

Innumerable be the kinds, if I could name them;
290   But I a shepherd, and no fisher am:
Little it skills whether I praise or blame them,
I only meddle with my ewe and lamb:
    Yet this I say, that black the better is,
    In birds, beasts, fruit, stones, flowers, herbs, metals, fish.

295   And last of all, in black there doth appear
Such qualities, as not in ivory;

2. The mythical youth, who, falling in love with his own image in a pool, died from grief that he could not possess it.

Black cannot blush for shame, look pale for fear,
Scorning to wear another livery.°   *servant's uniform*
   Black is the badge of sober modesty,
300   The wonted wear of ancient gravity.

The learned sisters suit themselves in black,
Learning abandons white and lighter hues:
Pleasure and pride light colors never lack;
But true religion doth such toys refuse:
305   Virtue and gravity are sisters grown,
   Since black by both and both by black are known.

White is the color of each paltry miller,
White is the ensign° of each common woman;   *sign*
White, is white virtue's for black vice's pillar;[3]
310 White makes proud fools inferior unto no man:
   White is the white of body, black of mind,
   (Virtue we seldom in white habit find).

Oh, then be not so proud because th'art fair,
Virtue is only the rich gift of God:
315 Let not self-pride thy virtue's name impair,
Beat not green youth with sharp repentance rod;
   (A fiend, a monster, a misshapen devil;
   Virtue's foe, vice's friend, the root of evil.)

Apply thy mind to be a virtuous man,
320 Avoid ill company (the spoil of youth);
To follow virtue's lore, do what thou can
(Whereby great profit unto thee ensueth):
   Read books, hate ignorance (the foe to art,
   The dam° of error, envy of the heart).   *mother*

325 Serve Jove (upon thy knees) both day and night,
Adore his name above all things on earth:
So shall thy vows be gracious in his sight,
So little babes are blessed in their birth;
   Think on no worldly woe, lament thy sin:
330   (For lesser cease, when greater griefs begin).

Swear no vain oaths; hear much but little say;
Speak ill of no man, tend thine own affairs,
Bridle thy wrath, thine angry mood delay;
(So shall thy mind be seldom cloyed with cares):
335   Be mild and gentle in thy speech to all,
   Refuse no honest gain when it doth fall.

Be not beguiled with words, prove not ungrateful,
Relieve thy neighbor in this greatest need,
Commit no action that to all is hateful,
340 Their want with wealth, the poor with plenty feed:
   Twit° no man in the teeth with what th'hast done;   *taunt*
   Remember flesh is frail and hatred shun.

---

3. White virtues support black vices by masking their true nature.

Leave wicked things, which men to mischief move,
(Least cross mishap° may thee in danger bring),   *evil chance*
345   Crave no preferment of thy heavenly Jove,
Nor any honor of thy earthly king:
    Boast not thyself before th'Almighty's sight,
    (Who knows thy heart and any wicked wight).

Be not offensive to the people's eye,
350   See that thy prayers heart's true zeal affords,
Scorn not a man that's fallen in misery,
Esteem no tattling tales, nor babbling words;
    That reason is exiled always think,
    When as a drunkard rails amidst his drink.

355   Use not thy lovely lips to loathsome lies,
By crafty means increase no worldly wealth;
Strive not with mighty men (whose fortune flies)
With temp'rate diet nourish wholesome health;
    Place well thy words, leave not thy friend for gold;
360   First try, then trust; in vent'ring° be not bold.   *adventuring*

In Pan[4] repose thy trust; extol his praise
(That never shall decay, but ever lives):
Honor thy parents (to prolong thy days),
Let not thy left hand know what right hand gives:
365   From needy men turn not thy face away,
    (Though charity be now yclad in clay).

Hear shepherds oft (thereby great wisdom grows),
With good advice a sober answer make:
Be not removed with every wind that blows,
370   (That course do only sinful sinners take).
    Thy talk will show thy fame or else thy shame;
    (A prattling tongue doth often purchase blame).

Obtain a faithful friend that will not fail thee,
Think on thy mother's pain in her childbearing,
375   Make no debate, lest quickly thou bewail thee,
Visit the sick with comfortable cheering;
    Pity the prisoner, help the fatherless,
    Revenge the widow's wrongs in her distress.

Think on thy grave, remember still thy end,
380   Let not thy winding sheet be stained with guilt,
Trust not a feigned reconciled friend,
More than an open foe (that blood hath spilt)
    (Who toucheth pitch, with pitch shall be defiled),
    Be not with wanton company beguiled.

385   Take not a flattering woman to thy wife,
A shameless creature, full of wanton words,
(Whose bad, thy good; whose lust will end thy life,

4. The god of flocks and shepherds; sometimes understood to refer to Christ.

Cutting thy heart with sharp two-edged swords):
 Cast not thy mind on her whose looks allure,
390 But she that shines in truth and virtue pure.

Praise not thyself, let other men commend thee:
Bear not a flattering tongue to glaver° any,   *wheedle*
Let parents' due correction not offend thee;
Rob not thy neighbor, seek the love of many;
395 Hate not to hear good counsel given thee,
  Lay not thy money unto usury.

Restrain thy steps from too much liberty,
Fulfill not th'envious man's malicious mind;
Embrace thy wife, live not in lechery;
400 Content thyself with what Fates have assigned:
  Be ruled by reason, warning dangers save;
  True age is reverend worship to thy grave.

Be patient in extreme adversity,
(Man's chiefest credit grows by doing well),
405 Be not highminded in prosperity;
Falsehood abhor, no lying fable tell.
  Give not thyself to sloth (the sink of shame,
  The moth of time, the enemy to fame).

This leare° I learned of a Beldame Trot,   *wisdom*
410 (When I was young and wild as now thou art):
But her good counsel I regarded not;
I marked it with my ears, not with my heart:
  But now I find it too-too true (my son),
  When my age-withered spring is almost done.

415 Behold my gray head, full of silver hairs,
My wrinkled skin, deep furrows in my face:
Cares bring old age, old age increaseth cares;
My time is come, and I have run my race;
  Winter hath snowed upon my hoary head,
420 And with my winter all my joys are dead.

And thou love-hating boy (whom once I loved),
Farewell, a thousand-thousand times farewell:
My tears the marble stones to ruth° have moved; *pity*
My sad complaints the babbling echoes tell:
425 And yet thou wouldst take no compassion on me,
  Scorning that cross which love hath laid upon me.

The hardest steel with fire doth mend his miss,
Marble is mollified° with drops of rain;   *softened*
But thou (more hard than steel or marble is)
430 Dost scorn my tears and my true love disdain,
  Which for thy sake shall everlasting be,
  Wrote in the annals of eternity.

By this, the night (with darkness overspread)
Had drawn the curtains of her coal-black bed;

435   And Cynthia° muffling her face with a cloud,   *the moon*
        (Lest all the world of her should be too proud)
           Had taken *conge*° of the sable night,   *leave*
           (That wanting her cannot be half so bright);

        When I poor forlorn man and outcast creature
440   (Despairing of my love, despised of° beauty)   *by*
        Grew malcontent, scorning his lovely feature
        That had disdained my ever zealous duty:
           I hied me homeward by the moonshine light;
           Forswearing love and all his fond delight.
                Finis.

                                       1594

Sonnets from *Cynthia*

1

    Sporting at fancy, setting light by love,
        There came a thief and stole away my heart,
        (And therefore robbed me of my chiefest part)
    Yet cannot reason him a felon prove.
5   For why his beauty (my heart's thief) affirmeth,
        Piercing no skin (the body's fensive° wall)   *defensive*
        And having leave, and free consent withal,
    Himself not guilty, from love guilty termeth,[1]
    Conscience the judge, twelve reasons are the jury,
10   They find mine eyes the beauty t'have let in,
        And on this verdict given, agreed they been,
    Wherefore, because his beauty did allure ye,[2]
        Your doom is this: in tears still to be drowned,
        When his fair forehead with disdain is frowned.

5

    It is reported of fair Thetis'[3] son,
        (Achilles, famous for his chivalry,
        His noble mind and magnanimity),
    That when the Trojan wars were new begun,
5   Whos'ever was deep-wounded with his spear,
        Could never be recurred° of his maim,°   *cured/wound*
        Nor ever after be made whole again;
    Except with that spear's rust he holpen were.°   *could be helped*
    Even so it fareth with my fortune now,
10   Who being wounded with his piercing eye,
        Must either thereby find a remedy,
    Or else to be relieved, I know not how,
        Then if thou hast a mind still to annoy me,
        Kill me with kisses, if thou wilt destroy me.

---

1. Himself not guilty, he puts a limit or term to guilty love.
2. You, i.e., the speaker addresses himself.

3. The mother of Achilles, the great Greek hero of the Trojan War.

9

Diana° (on a time) walking the wood,   *goddess of the hunt*
    To sport herself, of her fair train forlorn,
    Chancest for to prick her foot against a thorn,
And from thence issued out a stream of blood.
5 No sooner she was vanished out of sight,
    But love's fair Queen° came there by chance,   *Venus*
    And having of this hap a glimmering glance,
She put the blood into a crystal bright,
When being now come unto Mount Rhodope,
10   With her fair hands she forms a shape of snow,
    And blends it with this blood; from whence doth grow
A lovely creature, brighter than the day.
    And being christened in fair Paphos'⁴ shrine,
    She called him Ganimede: as all divine.

11

Sighing, and sadly sitting by my love,
    He asked the cause of my heart's sorrowing,
    Conjuring me by heaven's eternal king
To tell the cause which me so much did move.
5 Compelled (quoth I) to thee will I confess,
    Love is the cause; and only love it is
    That doth deprive me of my heavenly bliss.
Love is the pain that doth my heart oppress.
And what is she (quoth he) whom thou dost love?
10   Look in this glass (quoth I) there shalt thou see
    The perfect form of my felicity.
When, thinking that it would strange magic prove,
    He opened it; and taking off the cover,
    He straight perceived himself to be my lover.

13

Speak, Echo, tell; how may I call my love?   *Love⁵*
    But how his lamps that are so crystalline?   *Eyne°*   *eyes*
    Oh, happy stars that make your heavens divine:
And happy gems that admiration move.
5 How term'st his golden tresses waved with air?   *Hair*
    Oh, lovely hair of your more lovely master,
    Image of love, fair shape of alabaster,
Why dost thou drive thy lover to despair?
How dost thou call the bed where beauty grows?   *Rose*
10   Fair virgin rose, whose maiden blossoms cover
    The milk-white lily, thy embracing lover:
Whose kisses makes thee oft thy red to love.
    And blushing oft for shame, when he hath kissed thee,
    He vades° away, and thou rangest° where it list thee.   *fades/wander*

4. Cyprus, sacred to Venus.
5. This poem exploits a rhetorical figure called *paronoma-sia*, in which sounds are repeated; in this case the repetition is of the last syllable of a line, which produces the
effect of an echo.

Nicholas Hilliard. *The Young Man amongst Roses*. ca. 1597.

19

     Ah no; nor I myself: though my pure love
        (Sweet Ganimede) to thee hath still been pure,
        And even till my last gasp shall aye endure,
        Could ever thy obdurate beauty move:
5   Then cease, oh goddess' son (for sure thou are,
        A goddess' son that canst resist desire)
        Cease thy hard heart, and entertain love's fire,
     Within thy sacred breast: by nature's art.
     And as I love thee more than any creature,
10   (Love thee, because thy beauty is divine;
        Love thee because thyself, my soul, is thine:
     Wholly devoted to thy lovely feature)
        Even so of all the vowels, I and U,
        Are dearest unto me, as doth ensue.

Christopher Marlowe
1564–1593

When Christopher Marlowe began his career as a dramatist, the Elizabethan stage was at the height of its popularity and sophistication. Marlowe's plays were an immediate success, fascinating audiences with dazzling characters, exotic settings, and controversial subjects. Throughout his career—and even after his sudden death at the age of twenty-nine—Marlowe was Shakespeare's principal commercial and artistic rival.

A shoemaker's son, Marlowe went to Cambridge on a scholarship that was intended to prepare him for holy orders. His interests proved to be literary rather than religious, however, and he left Cambridge for London. As a student, he had composed a number of poems, notably the brilliant but unfinished *Hero and Leander*, a narrative of heterosexual and homosexual passion, but public recognition came with the production of his first play, *Tamburlaine the Great*, in 1587. This was followed by *The Second Part of Tamburlaine the Great*, *The Jew of Malta*, *Edward II*, *Dr. Faustus*, *Dido, Queen of Carthage*, and finally *The Massacre at Paris*, all composed within a period of six years. Marlowe's bold and inventive language captivated audiences; his blank verse, in which the sense of a sentence is not interrupted at the end of each line by the constraints of rhyme, brought the rhythms of natural speech to the language of theater. His characterizations of heroes were equally astonishing: driven by an incandescent desire that no conquest could satisfy, they revealed the torment and tragedy that were occasioned by pride.

Marlowe himself may have been employed in subversive activities. While still at Cambridge, he became a spy for Queen Elizabeth's secret service, dedicated to the infiltration and exposure of Catholic groups in England and abroad. How much activity he was responsible for remains guesswork. At the very least, the manner in which he died suggests his involvement in clandestine politics. In May 1593, the Queen's Privy Council issued a warrant for his arrest. The charge against him—blasphemy—seems to have come from Thomas Kyd, a fellow playwright with whom Marlowe shared lodgings. While in London waiting for a hearing, Marlowe, who was drinking in an alehouse, got into a fight with three men (all government spies), one of whom was Ingram Friser. Marlowe raised a dagger to stab Friser, but Friser, warding off the blow, managed to turn the dagger against Marlowe. It pierced his eye "in such sort that his brains coming out at the dagger point, he shortly after died." The affair did not end there; two days after Marlowe's death, Richard Baines (himself a former spy) accused him before the Privy Council of atheism, treason, and the opinion "that they that love not tobacco and boys were fools." Whether or not these accusations held any truth, they referred to views that were not unusual in the circles Marlowe traveled in; they indicate a skepticism in matters of religion and an indifference to social decorum that authorities responsible for political order would have considered dangerous. Some scholars think that Marlowe was murdered by government command. Although the mystery surrounding his death may never be solved, the mercurial brilliance of his work remains undisputed.

With the exception of the two parts of *Tamburlaine*, published in 1590, Marlowe's works were published after his death: *Edward II* and *Dido, Queen of Carthage* in 1594; *Hero and Leander* in 1598; *Dr. Faustus* in 1604; and *The Jew of Malta* in 1633. The celebrated lyric entitled *The Passionate Shepherd to His Love* first appeared in 1599 in an unauthorized collection of verse called *The Passionate Pilgrim* published by William Jaggard.

The Passionate Shepherd to His Love

Come live with me, and be my love,
And we will all the pleasures prove,
That valleys, groves, hills, and fields,
Woods, or steepy mountain yields.

5
And we will sit upon the rocks,
Seeing the shepherds feed their flocks,
By shallow rivers, to whose falls,
Melodious birds sing madrigals.

And I will make thee beds of roses,
10
And a thousand fragrant poesies,
A cap of flowers, and a kirtle,
Embroidered all with leaves of myrtle.

A gown made of the finest wool,
Which from our pretty lambs we pull,
15
Fair lined slippers for the cold,
With buckles of the purest gold.

A belt of straw, and ivy buds,
With coral clasps and amber studs,
And if these pleasures may thee move,
20
Come live with me, and be my love.

The shepherd swains shall dance and sing,
For thy delight each May morning,
If these delights thy mind may move,
Then live with me and be my love.

COMPANION READING

Sir Walter Raleigh: *The Nymph's Reply to the Shepherd*[1]

If all the world and love were young,
And truth in every shepherd's tongue,
These pretty pleasures might me move,
To live with thee, and be thy love.

5
Time drives the flocks from field to fold,
When rivers rage, and rocks grow cold,
And Philomel° becometh dumb,   *the nightingale*
The rest complain of cares to come.

The flowers do fade, and wanton fields,
10
To wayward winter reckoning yields,
A honey tongue, a heart of gall,
Is fancy's spring, but sorrow's fall.

Thy gowns, thy shoes, thy beds of roses,
Thy cap, thy kirtle, and thy poesies,
15
Soon break, soon wither, soon forgotten;
In folly ripe, in reason rotten.

Thy belt of straw and ivy buds,
Thy coral clasps and amber studs,
All these in me no means can move,
20
To come to thee, and be thy love.

---

1. Raleigh's *Reply* was published together with Marlowe's poem in Jaggard's collection.

But could youth last, and love still breed,
Had joys no date, nor age no need,
Then these delights my mind might move,
To live with thee, and be thy love.

Hero and Leander[1]

On Hellespont,[2] guilty of true love's blood,
In view and opposite, two cities stood,
Seaborders,° disjoined by Neptune's might.   seaports
The one Abydos, the other Sestos hight.
5   As Sestos, Hero dwelt, Hero the fair,
Whom young Apollo° courted for her hair,   god of the sun
And offered as a dower° his burning throne,   wedding gift
Where she should sit for men to gaze upon.
The outside of her garments were of lawn,°   fine cloth
10 The lining, purple silk, with gilt stars drawn,
Her wide sleeves green, and bordered with a grove,
Where Venus° in her naked glory strove,   goddess of love
To please the careless and disdainful eyes,
Of proud Adonis° that before her lies.   Venus's lover
15 Her kirtle° blue, whereon was many a stain,   gown
Made with the blood of wretched lovers slain.
Upon her head she wore a myrtle wreath,
From whence her veil reached to the ground beneath.
Her veil was artificial flowers and leaves,
20 Whose workmanship both man and beast deceives.
Many would praise the sweet smell as she passed,
When t'was the odor which her breath forth cast,
And there for honey, bees have fought in vain,
And beat from thence, have lighted there again.
25 About her neck hung chains of pebble stone,
Which, lightened by her neck, like diamonds shone.
She wore no gloves, for neither sun nor wind
Would burn or parch her hands, but to her mind,
Or warm or cool them, for they took delight
30 To play upon those hands, they were so white.
Buskins° of shells all silvered, used she,   boots
And branched° with blushing coral to the knee.   decorated
Where sparrows perched, of hollow pearl and gold,
Such as the world would wonder to behold.
35 Those with sweet water oft her handmaid fills,
Which as she went would chirrup through the° bills.[3]   their
Some say, for her the fairest Cupid pined,
And looking in her face, was strucken° blind.   struck
But this is true, so like was one the other,

---

1. In the early modern period the story of the lovers Hero
and Leander was attributed to the legendary poet
Musaeus; in fact, it appears to be the work of an anonymous Greek poet of the 4th or 5th century A.D.
2. The straits separating Asia Minor from Thracian

Greece, now the Dardanelles.
3. A fantastic costume: Hero's boots are decorated with
shells that are filled with water on which mechanical
sparrows made of pearl and gold perch and chirp.

40   As he imagined Hero was his mother.
      And oftentimes into her bosom flew,
      About her naked neck his bare arms threw.
      And laid his childish head upon her breast,
      And with still panting rocked, there took his rest.
45   So lovely fair was Hero, Venus' nun,
      As nature wept, thinking she was undone,
      Because she took more from her than she left,
      And of such wondrous beauty her bereft.
      Therefore in sign° her treasure suffered wrack,°   *to signify / loss*
50   Since Hero's time, hath half the world been black.

Amorous Leander, beautiful and young,
(Whose tragedy divine Musaeus sung)
Dwelt at Abidos, since him dwelt there none
For whom succeeding times make greater moan.
55   His dangling tresses that were never shorn,
      Had they been cut and unto Colchis[4] borne,
      Would have allured the vent'rous° youth of Greece,   *adventurous*
      To hazard more than for the golden fleece.
      Fair Cynthia° wished his arms might be her sphere,   *goddess of the moon*
60   Grief makes her pale, because she moves not there.
      His body was straight as Circe's[5] wand,
      Jove might have sipped out nectar from his hand.
      Even as delicious meat is to the taste,
      So was his neck in touching, and surpassed
65   The white of Pelops'[6] shoulder; I could tell ye
      How smooth his breast was, and how white his belly,
      And whose immortal fingers did imprint
      That heavenly path with many a curious dint
      That runs along his back, but my rude pen
70   Can hardly blazon° forth the loves of men,[7]   *list*
      Much less of powerful gods. Let it suffice,
      That my slack muse sings of Leander's eyes.
      Those orient° cheeks and lips, exceeding his   *shining*
      That leapt into the water for a kiss
75   Of his own shadow, and despising many,
      Died ere he could enjoy the love of any.
      Had wild Hippolytus[8] Leander seen,
      Enamored of his beauty had he been,
      His presence made the rudest peasant melt,
80   That in the vast uplandish° country dwelt;   *rustic*
      The barbarous Thracian[9] soldier, moved with nought,

---

4. A country at the east end of the Black Sea, to which the legendary golden fleece—a Greek treasure—had been taken. Colchis was raided by the Greek hero Jason and his men, the Argonauts, who carried the fleece back to their homeland.

5. The Greek divinity who with her magic wand turned the companions of Odysseus into swine (*Odyssey* 10).

6. A legendary figure whose father, Tantalus, had him cooked and served to the gods. Only his shoulder was eaten, however, and that was restored with a piece of ivory.

7. The homoerotic element in Marlowe's description of Leander becomes explicit here and continues to be prominent later in the poet's account of Neptune's love for Leander.

8. A legendary hero, vowed to hunting and chastity; at the command of Phaedra, his stepmother, he was consumed by a sea-monster for having refused to return her love for him.

9. Thrace was a mountainous region in northeastern Greece.

Was moved with him, and for his favor fought.
Some swore he was a maid in man's attire,
For in his looks were all that men desire,
85   A pleasant, smiling cheek, a speaking eye,
A brow for love to banquet royally,
And such as knew he was a man would say,
Leander, thou art made for amorous play;
Why art thou not in love, and loved of all?
90   Though thou be fair, yet be not thine own thrall.°   slave

The men of wealthy Sestos, every year
(For his sake whom their goddess° held so dear,   Venus
Rose-cheeked Adonis), kept a solemn feast;
Thither resorted many a wandering guest
95   To meet their loves; such as had none at all
Came lovers home from this great festival.
For every street like to a firmament°   sky
Glistered with breathing stars, who where they went,
Frighted the melancholy earth, which deemed,
100   Eternal heaven to burn, for so it seemed
As if another Phaeton[1] had got
The guidance of the sun's rich chariot.
But far above, the loveliest Hero shined,
And stole away th'enchanted gazer's mind,
105   For like sea-nymphs inveigling harmony,
So was her beauty to the standers-by.
Nor that night-wandering pale and watery star,[2]
(When yawning dragons draw her thirling° car,   spinning
From Latmos' mount up to the gloomy sky,
110   Where crowned with blazing light and majesty,
She proudly sits) more over-rules the flood,
Than she the hearts of those that near her stood.
Even as, when gaudy nymphs pursue the chase,
Wretched Ixion's shaggy-footed race,[3]
115   Incensed with savage heat, gallop amain,
From steep pine-bearing mountains to the plain,
So ran the people forth to gaze upon her,
And all that viewed her were enamored on her.
And as in fury of a dreadful fight,
120   Their fellows being slain or put to flight,
Poor soldiers stand with fear of death strucken,
So at her presence all surprised and tooken°   taken
Await the sentence of her scornful eyes;
He whom she favors lives, the other dies.
125   There might you see one sigh, another rage,
And some (their violent passions to assuage)
Compile sharp satires; but alas too late,
For faithful love will never turn to hate.

---

1. Apollo's son, who drove his father's chariot too near
the earth and was struck down by Jove's thunderbolt.
2. The moon, or Cynthia, whose seat is Mount Latmos.

3. Centaurs, creatures who were half-man, half-horse.
The sons of Ixion, they were punished for loving Juno,
the queen of the gods, by being bound on a wheel of fire.

And many, seeing great princes were denied,
130   Pined as they went and thinking on her, died.
On this feast day, O cursed day and hour,
Went Hero through Sestos, from her tower
To Venus' temple, where unhappily,
As after chanced, they did each other spy.
135   So fair a church as this had Venus none,
The walls were of discolored jasper stone,
Wherein was Proteus[4] carved, and o'erhead,
A lively vine of green sea agate spread,
Where by one hand, light-headed Bacchus° hung,   *god of wine*
140   And with the other, wine from grapes out-wrung.
Of crystal shining fair the pavement was,
The town of Sestos called it Venus' glass.
There might you see the gods in sundry shapes
Committing heady riots, incest, rapes.
145   For know that underneath this radiant flower
Was Danae's statue[5] in a brazen tower;
Jove, stealing from his sister's bed
To dally with Idalian Ganymede,
And for his love, Europa, bellowing loud,
150   And tumbling with the rainbow in a cloud;
Blood-quaffing Mars, heaving the iron net,
Which limping Vulcan and his Cyclops set;
Love kindling fire to burn such towns as Troy;
Sylvanus weeping for the lovely boy
155   That now is turned into a cypress tree,
Under whose shade the wood gods love to be.
And in the midst a silver altar stood,
There Hero, sacrificing turtle's° blood,   *dove's*
Veiled to the ground, veiling her eyelids close,
160   And modestly they opened as she rose;
Thence flew Love's arrow with the golden head,
And thus Leander was enamored.
Stone still he stood, and evermore he gazed,
Till with the fire that from his count'nance blazed,
165   Relenting Hero's gentle heart was struck,
Such force and virtue hath an amorous look.

It lies not in our power to love or hate,
For will in us is overruled by fate.
When two are stripped long ere the course begin,
170   We wish that one should lose, the other win.
And one especially do we affect,
Of two gold ingots like in each respect.
The reason no man knows, let it suffice,

---

4. A sea-god, who could change his shape at will.
5. The figure of the mythical woman Danae, whose father shut her up in a tower to keep her from suitors; Jupiter visited her there in a shower of gold. Marlowe continues his description of "Venus' glass" by allusions to popular mythological figures: Ganymede, Jove's cup-bearer and lover; Europa, carried off by Jove disguised as a bull; the lover of Venus, Mars, who was caught in the net of Vulcan, Venus' husband, assisted by his one-eyed helpers, the Cyclops; and Sylvanus, a wood god, who wept for his lover, Cyparissus, who had been turned into a tree.

What we behold is censured° by our eyes.   *judged*
175   Where both deliberate, the love is slight,
Who ever loved that loved not at first sight?

He kneeled, but unto her devoutly prayed.
Chaste Hero to herself thus softly said,
Were I the saint he worships, I would hear him,
180   And as she spoke those words, came somewhat near him.
He started up, she blushed as one ashamed,
Wherewith Leander much more was inflamed.
He touched her hand, in touching it she trembled,
Love deeply grounded, hardly is dissembled.
185   These lovers parled° by the touch of hands;   *spoke*
True love is mute, and oft amazed stands.
Thus while dumb signs their yielding hearts entangled,
The air with sparks of living fire was spangled,
And Night, deep-drenched in misty Acheron,°   *a river in hell*
190   Heaved up her head, and half the world upon
Breathed darkness forth (dark night is Cupid's day)
And now begins Leander to display
Love's holy fire with words, with sighs and tears,
Which like sweet music entered Hero's ears,
195   And yet at every word she turned aside,
And always cut him off as he replied.
At last, like to a bold, sharp sophister,°   *false reasoner*
With cheerful hope thus he accosted her.

Fair creature, let me speak without offence,
200   I would my rude words had the influence
To lead thy thoughts, as thy fair looks do mine,
Then shouldst thou be his prisoner who is thine.
Be not unkind and fair, misshapen stuff°   *ungainly persons*
Are of behavior boisterous and rough.
205   O shun me not, but hear me ere you go,
God knows I cannot force love, as you do.
My words shall be as spotless as my youth,
Full of simplicity and naked truth.
This sacrifice (whose sweet perfume descending
210   From Venus' altar to your footsteps bending)
Doth testify that you exceed her far,
To whom you offer, and whose nun you are.
Why should you worship her, her you surpass,
As much as sparkling diamonds flaring° glass.   *flashing*
215   A diamond set in lead his worth retains,
A heavenly nymph, beloved of human swains,°   *suitors*
Receives no blemish, but oft times more grace,
Which makes me hope, although I am but base,
Base in respect of thee, divine and pure,
220   Dutiful service may thy love procure,
And I in duty will excel all other,
As thou in beauty dost exceed Love's mother.
Nor heaven, nor thou, were made to gaze upon,

As heaven preserves all things, so save thou one.°   *Leander*
225   A stately builded ship, well-rigged and tall,
        The ocean maketh more majestical.
        Why vowest thou then to live in Sestos here,
        Who on Love's seas more glorious wouldst appear?
        Like untuned golden strings all women are,
230   Which, long time lie untouched, will harshly jar.
        Vessels of brass oft handled brightly shine,
        What difference betwixt the richest mine
        And basest mold, but use? For both not used
        Are of like worth. Then treasure is abused
235   When misers keep it; being put to loan,
        In time it will return us two for one.
        Rich robes, themselves and others do adorn,
        Neither themselves nor others, if not worn.
        Who builds a palace and rams up the gate,
240   Shall see it ruinous and desolate.
        Ah, simple Hero, learn thyself to cherish,
        Lone women, like to empty houses, perish.
        Less sins the poor rich man that starves himself,
        In heaping up a mass of drossy pelf,°   *worthless booty*
245   Than such as you; his golden earth remains,
        Which, after his decease, some other gains.
        But this fair gem, sweet in the loss alone,
        When you fleet hence, can be bequeathed to none.
        Or if it could, down from th'enamelled sky,
250   All heaven would come to claim this legacy,
        And with intestine broils° the world destroy,   *civil wars*
        And quite confound nature's sweet harmony.
        Well therefore by the gods decreed it is,
        We human creatures should enjoy that bliss.
255   One is no number, maids are nothing then,
        Without the sweet society of men.
        Wilt thou live single still? One shalt thou be,
        Though never-singling Hymen6 couple thee.
        Wild savages, that drink of running springs,
260   Think water far excels all earthly things.
        But they that daily taste neat° wine, despise it.   *unwatered*
        Virginity, albeit some highly prize it,
        Compared with marriage, had you tried them both,
        Differs as much as wine and water doth.
265   Base boullion° for the stamp's sake we allow,7   *metal*
        Even so for men's impression do we you.
        By which alone, our reverend fathers say,
        Women receive perfection every way.
        This idol which you term virginity,
270   Is neither essence subject to the eye,

6. Marlowe turns to paradox: Although Hero is coupled by Hymen, the god of marriage, she can also remain "one" or single.

7. Just as a coin has the value stamped on it, so a person is valued according to the impression she (or he) gives.

No, nor to any one exterior sense,
Nor hath it any place of residence,
Nor is't of earth or mold celestial,
Or capable of any form at all.
275 Of that which hath no being do not boast,
Things that are not at all are never lost.
Men foolishly do call it virtuous,
What virtue is it, that is born with us?
Much less can honor be ascribed thereto;
280 Honor is purchased by the deeds we do.
Believe me, Hero, honor is not won,
Until some honorable deed be done.
Seek you for chastity, immortal fame,
And know that some have wronged Diana's name?
285 Whose name is it, if she be false or not,
So she be fair, but some vile tongues will blot?
But you are fair (aye me), so wondrous fair,
So young, so gentle, and so debonair,°   *courteous*
As Greece will think if thus you live alone,
290 Some one or other keeps you as his own.
Then, Hero, hate me not, nor from me fly,
To follow swiftly blasting infamy.
Perhaps thy sacred priesthood makes thee loath,
Tell me, to whom mad'st thou that heedless oath?

295 To Venus, answered she, and as she spoke,
Forth from those two translucent cisterns broke
A stream of liquid pearl, which down her face
Made milk-white paths, whereon the gods might trace
To Jove's high court. He thus replied: the rites
300 In which love's beauteous empress most delights
Are banquets, Doric[8] music, midnight revel,
Plays, masques, and all that stern age counteth evil.
Thee as a holy Idiot doth she scorn,
For thou, in vowing chastity, hast sworn
305 To rob her name and honor, and thereby
Commit'st a sin far worse than perjury,
Even sacrilege against her deity,
Through regular and formal purity.
To expiate which sin, kiss and shake hands,
310 Such sacrifice as this Venus demands.

Thereat she smiled, and did deny him so,
As put thereby, yet might he hope for mo'e.
Which makes him quickly re-enforce his speech,
And her in humble manner thus beseech.

315 Though neither gods nor men may thee deserve,
Yet for her sake whom you have vowed to serve,
Abandon fruitless, cold virginity,

---

8. Pertaining to the Greek region of Doris, noted for the simplicity of its culture.

The gentle Queen of Love's sole enemy.
Then shall you most resemble Venus' nun,
320 When Venus' sweet rites are performed and done.
Flint-breasted Pallas⁹ joys in single life,
But Pallas and your mistress are at strife.
Love, Hero, then, and be not tyrannous,
But heal the heart that thou has wounded thus,
325 Nor stain thy youthful years with avarice,
Fair fools delight to be accounted nice.°   coy
The richest corn° dies if it be not reaped,   grain
Beauty alone is lost, too warily kept.
These arguments he used, and many more,
330 Wherewith she yielded, that was won before,
Hero's looks yielded, but her words made war;
Women are won when they begin to jar.°   quarrel
Thus having swallowed Cupid's golden hook,
The more she strived, the deeper was she struck.
335 Yet evilly feigning anger, strove she still,
And would be wrought to grant against her will.
So having paused a while, at last she said:
Who taught thee rhetoric to deceive a maid?
Aye me, such words as these should I abhor,
340 And yet I like them for the orator.

With that Leander stooped, to have embraced her,
But from his spreading arms away she cast her,
And thus bespake him: Gentle youth, forbear
To touch the sacred garments which I wear.

345 Upon a rock, and underneath a hill,
Far from the town (where all is whist° and still,   quiet
Save that sea playing on yellow sand
Sends forth a rattling murmur to the land,
Whose sound allures the golden Morpheus,°   god of sleep
350 In silence of the night to visit us)
My turret stands, and there God knows I play
With Venus' swans and sparrows all the day,
A dwarfish beldame° bears° me company,   old woman / keeps
That hops about the chamber where I lie,
355 And spends the night (that might be better spent)
In vain discourse and apish merriment.
Come thither; as she spake this, her tongue tripped,
For unawares (Come thither) from her slipped,
And suddenly her former color changed,
360 And here and there her eyes through anger ranged,
And like a planet, moving several ways,
At one self instant, she, poor soul, assays,
Loving, not to love at all, and every part,
Strove to resist the motions of her heart.
365 And hands so pure, so innocent, nay such,

9. Athena or Minerva, goddess of wisdom, justice, and war.

As might have made heaven stoop to have a touch,
Did she uphold to Venus, and again,
Vowed spotless chastity, but all in vain.
Cupid beat down her prayers with his wings,
370   Her vowes above the empty air he flings.
All deep enraged, his sinewy bow he bent,
And shot a shaft that burning from him went,
Wherewith she, stroocken,° looked so dolefully,   *struck*
As made Love sigh to see his tyranny.
375   And as she wept, her tears to pearl he turned,
And wound them on his arm, and for her mourned.
Then towards the palace of the Destinies,°   *the Fates*
Laden with languishment and grief, he flies.
And to those stern nymphs humbly made request,
380   Both might enjoy each other, and be blessed.
But with a ghastly dreadful countenance,
Threatening a thousand deaths at every glance,
They answered Love, nor would vouchsafe so much
As one poor word, their hate to him was such.
385   Harken a while, and I will tell you why:
Heaven's winged herald, Jove-born Mercury,[1]
The selfsame day that he asleep had laid
Enchanted Argus, spied a country maid,
Whose careless hair, instead of pearl t'adorn it,
390   Glistered with dew, as one that seemed to scorn it,
Her breath as fragrant as the morning rose,
Her mind pure and her tongue untaught to glose.°   *deceive*
Yet proud she was (for lofty pride that dwells
In towered courts, is oft in shepherd's cells),°   *cottages*
395   And too too well the fair vermillion knew,
And silver tincture of her cheeks, that drew
The love of every swain. On her, this god
Enamored was, and with his snakey rod,°   *Mercury's staff*
Did charm her nimble feet, and made her stay,
400   The while upon a hillock down he lay,
And sweetly on his pipe began to play,
And with his smooth speech, her fancy to assay,°   *attempt*
Till in his twining arms he locked her fast,
And then he wooed her with kisses and at last,
405   As shepherds do, her on the ground he laid,
And tumbling in the grass, he often strayed
Beyond the bounds of shame, in being bold
To eye those parts, which no eye should behold,
And like an insolent commanding lover,
410   Boasting his parentage, would needs discover
The way to new Elysium; but she,
Whose only dower° was her chastity,   *dowry, wealth*
Having striven in vain, was now about to cry,

---

1. The messenger god; he enchanted the many-eyed herdsman Argus (or Argos), whom Juno had ordered to guard the heifer Io, beloved of Jupiter.

And crave the help of the shepherds that were nigh.

415 Herewith he stayed his fury, and began
To give her leave to rise; away she ran,
After went Mercury, who used such cunning,
As she to hear his tale, left off running.
Maids are not wooed by brutish force and might,

420 But speeches full of pleasure and delight.
And knowing Hermes° courted her, was glad   *Mercury*
That she such loveliness and beauty had
As could provoke his liking, yet was mute,
And neither would deny, nor grant his suit.

425 Still vowed he love, she wanting no excuse
To feed him with delays, as women use,
Or thirsting after immortality,
All women are ambitious naturally,
Imposed upon her lover such a task,

430 As he ought not perform, nor yet she ask.
A draught of flowing nectar, she requested,
Wherewith the king of the gods and men is feasted.
He ready to accomplish what she willed,
Stole some from Hebe° (Hebe, Jove's cups filled)   *a goddess*

435 And gave it to his simple rustic love,
Which being known (as what is hid from Jove?)
He inly stormed, and waxed more furious
Than for the fire filched by Prometheus[2],
And thrusts him down from heaven; he wandering here,

440 In mournful terms, with sad and heavy cheer
Complained to Cupid. Cupid, for his° sake,   *Prometheus'*
To be revenged on Jove, did undertake,
And those on whom heaven, earth, and hell relies,
I mean the adamantine° Destinies,   *implacable*

445 He wounds with love, and forced them equally,
To dote upon deceitful Mercury.
They offered him the deadly, fatal knife,
That shears the slender threads of human life,
At his fair feathered feet, the engines laid,

450 Which th'earth from ugly Chaos'[3] den up-weighed:
These he regarded not, but did entreat
That Jove, usurper of his father's° seat,   *Saturn's*
Might presently be banished into hell,
And aged Saturn in Olympus dwell.

455 They granted what he craved, and once again,
Saturn and Ops° began their golden reign.   *Wealth (Saturn's wife)*
Murder, rape, war, lust, and treachery
Were, with Jove, closed in Stygian Emprie.°   *empire of hell*
But long this blessed time continued not,

460 As soon as he his wished purpose got;
He reckless of his promise, did despise

2. In Greek mythology the figure of "forethought"; he made mankind out of clay and, when Jupiter deprived them of fire, stole it from heaven.
3. The infinite space that precedes creation.

The love of the everlasting Destinies.
They seeing it, both Love and him abhorred,
And Jupiter unto his place restored.
465   And but that learning, in despite of Fate,
Will mount aloft and enter heaven's gate,
And to the seat of Jove itself advance,
Hermes[4] had slept in hell with ignorance.
Yet as a punishment they added this,
470   That he and Poverty should always kiss.
And to this day is every scholar poor,
Gross gold from them runs headlong to the boor.
Likewise the angry sisters° thus deluded,   *the Destinies*
To venge themselves on Hermes have concluded
475   That Midas' brood[5] shall sit in honor's chair,
To which the Muses' sons are only heir.
And fruitful wits that in aspiring° are,   *ambitious*
Shall, discontent, run into regions far,
And few great lords in virtuous deeds shall joy,
480   But be surprised with every garish toy.
And still enrich the lofty° servile clown,   *proud*
Who with encroaching guile keeps learning down.
Then muse not Cupid's suit no better sped,°   *succeeded*
Seeing in their loves the Fates were injured.

485   By this, sad Hero, with love unacquainted
Viewing Leander's face, fell down and fainted.
He kissed her and breathed life into her lips,
Wherewith as one displeased, away she trips.
Yet as she went full often looked behind,
490   And many poor excuses did she find
To linger by the way, and once she stayed,
And would have turned again, but was afraid,
In offering parley,° to be counted light.   *speech*
So on she goes, and in her idle flight,
495   Her painted fan of curled plumes let fall,
Thinking to train° Leander therewithal.   *tempt*
He, being a novice, knew not what she meant,
But stayed, and after her a letter sent.
Which joyful Hero answered in such sort,
500   As he had hope to scale the beauteous fort,
Wherein the liberal graces locked their wealth,
And therefore to her tower he got by stealth.
Wide open stood the door, he need not climb,
And she herself before the pointed° time,   *appointed*
505   Had spread the board, with roses strewed the room,
And oft looked out and mused he did not come.

4. Hermes (or Mercury), as Learning (or the messenger god), must rise to a god's status; he cannot therefore be imprisoned in ignorance for long. Marlowe's unprecedented mythology is complicated: he describes "deceitful Mercury" as instituting a new golden age, then as losing it because he neglects "the Destinies," and finally as regaining divine favor because of what he signifies.

5. Like their father, the children of Midas would have the golden touch, that is, money; ironically, the Destinies decree that money is also honor.

At last he came, O who can tell the greeting,
These greedy lovers had at their first meeting.
He asked, she gave, and nothing was denied,

510   Both to each other quickly were affied.°   *betrothed*
Look how their hands, so were their hearts united,
And what he did, she willingly requited.
(Sweet are the kisses, the embracements sweet,
When like desires and affections meet

515   For from the earth to heaven, is Cupid raised,
Where fancy is in equal balance paised),°   *poised*
Yet she this rashness suddenly repented,
And turned aside and to herself lamented.
As if her name and honor had been wronged,

520   By being possessed of him for whom she longed.
I, and she wished, albeit not from her heart,
That he would leave her turret and depart.
The mirthful god of amorous pleasure smiled,
To see how he this captive nymph beguiled.

525   For hitherto he did but fan the fire,
And kept it down that it might burn the higher.
Now waxed she jealous, lest his love abated,
Fearing her own thoughts made her to be hated.[6]
Therefore unto him hastily she goes,

530   And like light Salmacis,[7] her body throws
Upon his bosom, where with yielding eyes,
She offers up herself a sacrifice,
To slake his anger, if he were displeased,
O what god would not therewith be appeased?

535   Like Aesop's cock,[8] this jewel he enjoyed,
And as a brother with his sister toyed,
Supposing nothing else was to be done,
Now he her favor and good will had won.
But know you not that creatures wanting sense°   *inanimate*

540   By nature have a mutual appetence,°   *desire*
And wanting organs to advance a step,
Moved by Love's force, unto each other leap?
Much more in subjects having intellect,
Some hidden influence breeds like effect.

545   Albeit Leander, rude in love and raw,
Long dallying with Hero, nothing saw
That might delight him more, yet he suspected
Some amorous rites or other were neglected.
Therefore unto his body, hers he clung,°   *clasped*

550   She fearing on the rushes° to be flung,   *a floor covering*
Strived with redoubled strength; the more she strived,
The more a gentle pleasing heat revived,

6. I.e., fearing that she was hated, she imagined that she was hated.
7. A nymph who pursued the boy Hermaphroditus; when she embraced him they became one, half-girl, half-boy.
8. According to Aesop, a writer of animal fables supposed to have lived in Thrace in the 6th century B.C., his cock found a precious jewel in the barnyard but rejected it because it was not a barleycorn. In the context of Marlowe's story the comparison is ambiguous.

Which taught him all that elder lovers know,
And now the same 'gan° so to scorch and glow,   *began*
555 As in plain terms (yet cunningly) he craved it,
Love always makes those eloquent that have it.
She, with a kind of granting, put him by it,
And ever as he thought himself most nigh it,
Like to the tree of Tantalus[9] she fled,
560 And seeming lavish, saved her maidenhead.
Ne'er king more sought to keep his diadem
Than Hero this inestimable gem.
Above our life we love a steadfast friend,
Yet when a token of great wealth we send,
565 We often kiss it, often look thereon,
And stay the messenger that would be gone;
No marvel then, though Hero would not yield
So soon to part from that she dearly held.
Jewels being lost are found again; this, never.
570 T'is lost but once, and once lost, lost for ever.

Now had the morn° espied her lover's° steeds,   *Aurora/Apollo*
Whereat she starts, puts on her purple weeds,
And red for anger that he stayed so long,
All headlong throws herself the clouds among,
575 And now Leander, fearing to be missed,
Embraced her suddenly, took leave, and kissed,
Long was he taking leave, and loath to go,
And kissed again, as lovers use to do,
Sad Hero wrung him by the hand and wept,
580 Saying, let your vows and promises be kept.
Then standing at the door, she turned about,
As loath to see Leander going out.
And now the sun that through th'orizon peeps,
As pitying these lovers, downward creeps.
585 So that in silence of the cloudy night,
Though it was morning, did he take his flight.
But what the secret trusty night concealed,
Leander's amorous habit soon revealed,
With Cupid's myrtle was his bonnet crowned,
590 About his arms the purple ribbon wound,
Wherewith she wreathed her largely spreading hair.
Nor could the youth abstain, but he must wear
The sacred ring wherewith she was endowed
When first religious chastity she vowed,
595 Which made his love through Sestos to be known,
And thence to Abydos sooner blown
Than he could sail, for incorporeal Fame,°   *i.e., Rumor*
Whose weight consists of nothing but her name,
Is swifter than the wind, whose tardy plumes
600 Are reeking° water and dull earthly fumes.   *vaporizing*

---

9. Punished in hell for revealing the secrets of the gods, Tantalus was doomed to reach for fruit from a tree whose branches were always beyond his grasp.

Home when he came, he seemed not to be there,
But like exiled air thrust from his sphere,
Set in a foreign place, and straight from thence,
Alcides-like,° by mighty violence,   *like Heracles*
605 He would have chased away the swelling main,
That him from her unjustly did detain.
Like as the sun in a diameter[1]
Fires and enflames objects removed far,
And heateth kindly,° shining lat'rally,   *gently*
610 So beauty sweetly quickens when 'tis nigh.
But being separated and removed,
Burns where it cherished, murders where it loved.
Therefore even as an index to a book,
So to his mind was young Leander's look.°   *appearance*
615 O none but gods have power their love to hide,
Affection by the countenance is descried.
The light of hidden fire itself discovers,
And love that is concealed betrays poor lovers.
His secret flame apparently was seen,
620 Leander's father knew where he had been,
And for the same mildly rebuked his son,
Thinking to quench the fire new begun.
But love resisted once grows passionate,
And nothing more than counsel, lovers hate.
625 For as a hot, proud horse lightly disdains
To have his head controlled, but breaks the reins,
Spits forth the ringled bit° and with his hooves   *the bit with rings*
Checks the submissive ground, so he that loves,
The more he is restrained, the worse he fares,
630 What is it now but mad Leander dares?
O Hero, Hero, thus he cried full oft,
And then he got him to a rock aloft.
Where having spied her tower, long stared he on't,
And prayed the narrow toiling Hellespont
635 To part in twain, that he might come and go,
But still the rising billows answered no.
With that he stripped him to the ivory skin,
And crying, Love I come!, leapt lively° in.   *quickly*
Whereat the sapphire-visaged god[2] grew proud,
640 And made his capr'ing triton sound aloud,
Imagining that Ganymede, displeased,
Had left the heavens, therefore on him he seized.
Leander strived, the waves about him wound,
And pulled him to the bottom, where the ground
645 Was strewed with pearl and in low coral groves,
Sweet singing mermaids sported with their loves
On heaps of heavy gold, and took great pleasure
To spurn the careless sort, the shipwrack° treasure. *shipwrecked*

---

1. I.e., directly (as opposed to obliquely) above the earth.

2. Neptune, whose son, Triton, is both a shell and the creature who blows upon it.

For here the stately azure palace stood,
650   Where kingly Neptune and his train abode,
The lusty god embraced him, called him love,
And swore he never should return to Jove.
But when he knew it was not Ganymede,
For underwater he was almost dead,
655   He heaved him up, and looking on his face,
Beat down the gold waves with his triple mace,
Which mounted up, intending to have kissed him,
And fell in drops like tears because they missed him.
Leander, being up, began to swim,
660   And looking back, saw Neptune follow him.
Whereat aghast, the poor soul 'gan to cry,
O let me visit Hero ere I die!
The god put Helle's³ bracelet on his arm,
And swore the sea should never do him harm.
665   He clapped his plump cheeks, with his tresses played,
And smiling wantonly, his love bewrayed.°   *revealed*
He watched his arms, and as they opened wide,
At every stroke, betwixt them would he slide,
And steal a kiss, and then run out and dance,
670   And as he turned, cast many a lustful glance,
And threw him gaudy toys to please his eye,
And dive into the water, and there pry
Upon his breast, his thighs, and every limb,
And up again, and close beside him swim
675   And talk of love. Leander made reply,
You are deceived, I am no woman I.
Thereat smiled Neptune, and then told a tale,
How that a shepherd sitting in a vale,
Played with a boy so fair and kind,
680   As for his love both earth and heaven pined,
That of the cooling river durst not drink,
Lest water nymphs should pull him from the brink.
And when he sported in the fragrant lawns,
Goat-footed satyrs and up-staring fawns,⁴
685   Would steal him thence. Ere half this tale was done,
Aye me, Leander cried, th'enamored sun,
That now should shine on Thetis' glassy bower,⁵
Descends upon my radiant Hero's tower.
O that these tardy arms of mine were wings,
690   And as he spake, upon the waves he springs.
Neptune was angry that he gave no ear,
And in his heart, revenging malice bore.
He flung at him his mace, but as it went,
He called it in, for love made him repent.
695   The mace, returning back, his own hand hit,

3. The daughter of the mythical Athamas and Nephele, who had to escape from the wrath of her stepmother, Ino, on a flying ram; she fell off its back into the part of the sea called the Hellespont. Neptune is said to have res-cued her; the bracelet the god puts on Leander's arm sig-nifies divine protection.
4. Fauns, spirits who are guided by the heavens.
5. The bower of Thetis, a sea nymph, is the sea.

As meaning to be venged for darting it.
When this fresh-bleeding wound Leander viewed,
His color went and came, as if he rued
The grief which Neptune felt. In gentle breasts,
700 Relenting thoughts, remorse, and pity rests.
And who have hard hearts, and obdurate minds,
But vicious, harebrained, and illit'rate hinds?°   *rustics*
The god, seeing him with pity to be moved,
Thereon concluded that he was beloved.
705 (Love is too full of faith, too credulous,
With folly and false hope deluding us.)
Wherefore Leander's fancy to surprise,
To the rich ocean for gifts he flies.
'Tis wisdom to give much, a gift prevails,
710 When deep, persuading oratory fails.
By this, Leander, being near the land,
Cast down his weary feet and felt the sand.
Breathless albeit he were, he rested not,
Till to the solitary tower he got.
715 And knocked and called, at which celestial noise,
The longing heart of Hero much more joys
Than nymphs and shepherds when the timbrell° rings,   *tambourine*
Or crooked dolphin when the sailor sings.[6]
She stayed not her robes, but straight arose,
720 And drunk with gladness, to the door she goes,
Where seeing a naked man, she screeched for fear,
Such sighs as this to tender maids are rare.
And ran into the dark herself to hide;
Rich jewels in the dark are soonest spied.
725 Unto her he was led, or rather drawn,
By those white limbs which sparkled through the lawn.
The nearer he came, the more she fled,
And seeking refuge, slipped into her bed.
Whereon Leander sitting, thus begin,
730 Though numbing cold, all feeble, faint, and wan:

If not for love, yet love, for pity's sake,
Me in thy bed and maiden bosom take,
At least vouchsafe these arms some little room,°
735 Who hoping to embrace thee cheerily swome.°   *swam*
This head was beat with many a churlish billow,
And therefore let it rest upon thy pillow.
Herewith, afrighted, Hero shrunk away,
And in her lukewarm place Leander lay.
Whose lively head like fire from heaven fet,°   *fetched*
740 Would animate gross clay, and higher set
The drooping thoughts of base declining souls,
Than dreary° Mars, carousing nectar bowls.°   *bloody/bowls of nectar*
His hands he cast upon her like a snare,

6. The sailor is the musician Arion, who was saved by dolphins ("crooked" because of their curved backs) when they heard him sing.

She, overcome with shame and sallow fear,
745 Like chaste Diana when Actaeon spied her,
Being suddenly betrayed, dived down to hide her.
And as her silver body downward went,
With both her hands she made the bed a tent,
And in her own mind thought herself secure,
750 O'ercast with dim and darksome coverture.°   covering
And now she lets him whisper in her ear,
Flatter, entreat, promise, protest, and swear,
Yet ever as he greedily assayed
To touch those dainties, she the Harpy[7] played
755 And every limb did as a soldier stout,
Defend the fort, and keep the foe-man out.
For though the rising iv'ry mount he scaled,
Which is with azure circling lines empaled,
Much like a globe (a globe may I term this,
760 By which love sails to regions full of bliss),
Yet there with Sisyphus[8] he toiled in vain,
Till gentle parley° did the truce obtain.   speech
She trembling strove, this strife of hers (like that
Which made the world) another world begat,
765 Of unknown joy. Treason was in her thought,
And cunningly to yield herself she sought.
Seeming not won, yet won she was at length,
In such wars women use but half their strength.
Leander now like Thebian Hercules,[9]
770 Entered the orchard of Th'esperides.
Whose fruit none rightly can describe, but he
That pulls or shakes it from the golden tree.
Wherein Leander on her quivering breast,
Breathless spoke some thing and sighed out the rest,
775 Which so prevailed, as he with small ado,
Enclosed her in his arms and kissed her too.
And every kiss to her was as a charm,
And to Leander as a fresh alarm.
So that the truce was broke, and she alas,
780 (Poor silly maiden) at his mercy was.
Love is not full of pity (as men say)
But deaf and cruel, where he means to prey,
Even as a bird, which in our hands we wring,
Forth plungeth and oft flutters with her wing.
785 And now she wished this night were never done,
And sighed to think upon th'approaching sun,
For much it grieved her that the bright daylight
Should know the pleasure of this blessed night.
And then like Mars and Ericine° displayed,   Venus

7. One of the fierce birds who snatched food from the
Trojan companions of Aeneas on their way from Troy to
Italy (*Aeneid* 3.225ff.).
8. The legendary king of Corinth, who in the underworld
was eternally condemned to roll a large stone to the top

of a hill, only to have it roll down again.
9. The eleventh labor of Hercules was to steal the golden
apples of the Hesperides, daughters of the evening, who
watched over their orchard on an island in a distant western sea.

790   Both in each others' arms, chained as they laid,
      Again she knew not how to frame her look,
      Or speak to him who in a moment took
      That which so long, so charily she kept,
      And feign by stealth away she would have crept,
795   And to some corner secretly have gone,
      Leaving Leander in the bed alone.
      But as her naked feet were whipping out,
      He on the sudden clinged her so about,
      That mermaid-like unto the floor she slid,
800   One half appeared, the other half was hid.
      Thus near the bed she blushing stood upright,
      And from her countenance behold ye might,
      A kind of twilight break, which through the hair,
      As from an orient cloud, glimpse here and there.
805   And round about the chamber this false morn
      Brought forth the day before the day was born,
      So Hero's ruddy cheek, Hero betrayed,
      And her all naked to his sight displayed.
      Whence his admiring eyes more pleasure took
810   Than Dis on heaps of gold fixing his look.
      By this Apollo's golden harp began,
      To sound forth music to the ocean,
      Which watchful Hesperus[1] no sooner heard,
      But he the day bright-bearing car prepared
815   And ran before, as harbinger of light,
      And with his flaming beams mocked ugly Night,
      Till she, o'ercome with anguish, shame, and rage,
      Danged° down to Hell her loathsome carriage.   hurled
      Desunt nonnulla.[2]

The Tragical History of Dr. Faustus

Marlowe's play is the first dramatic rendition of the medieval legend of a man who sold his soul
to the devil. Sixteenth-century readers associated him with a necromancer named Dr. Faustus,
and Marlowe exploited this identification when he reworked the medieval plot for his play.
Rejecting the usual learning available to ambitious men—philosophy, medicine, law, and theology—Marlowe's Faustus signs a contract with the devil, represented in this case by his servant, Mephostophilis; in exchange for his soul, Faustus gains superhuman powers for twenty-
four years. He uses these powers to conjure the Pope in Rome into giving the Protestant
Emperor Charles V authority over the church through a surrogate Pope, Bruno; but his powers
are also deployed in the banal trickery of simple and even criminal characters. The play is
enigmatic on points of doctrine. Mephostophilis describes hell not as a locale but rather as the
state of mind of one who has rejected God—a description that Milton will later amplify—
telling Faustus: "this is hell, nor am I out of it." And Faustus, having worshipped the devil, is
nevertheless offered a chance to repent and find salvation even at the very end of his alloted
life. But he rejects God's love in favor of a night with Helen of Troy, praising her in lines that

---

1. Marlowe mistakes the evening star, Hesperus, for the
morning star, Venus.
2. "Some things are missing." Added in 1598 by Mar-

lowe's printer, Edward Blunt, who believed the poem was
unfinished.

are now famous: "Was this the face that launched a thousand ships, / And burnt the topless towers of Ilium?" The play concludes with a report of Faustus' mangled body, torn to bits by the demon to whom he had given his soul.

A short version of the play, in thirteen scenes, was published in 1604; known as the A text, it was probably used by touring companies. The longer B text, given here, was published in 1616, probably based on Marlowe's original manuscript but also incorporating revisions and additions by Marlowe or others, as (typically in this period) the play continued to evolve in performance.

The Tragical History of Dr. Faustus

Dramatis Personae

CHORUS	THE POPE
FAUSTUS	BRUNO
WAGNER, *Servant to Faustus*	RAYMOND, *King of Hungary*
GOOD ANGEL AND EVIL ANGEL	CHARLES, *the German Emperor*
VALDES ⎱ *Friends to Faustus*	MARTINO
CORNELIUS ⎰	FREDERICK
MEPHOSTOPHILIS	BENVOLIO
LUCIFER	SAXONY
BELZEBUB	DUKE OF VANHOLT
THE SEVEN DEADLY SINS	DUCHESS OF VANHOLT
CLOWN/ROBIN	SPIRITS IN THE SHAPES OF ALEXANDER
DICK	THE GREAT, DARIUS, PARAMOUR, AND
RAFE	HELEN
VINTNER	AN OLD MAN
CARTER	SCHOLARS, SOLDIERS, DEVILS, COURTIERS,
HOSTESS	CARDINALS, MONKS, CUPIDS

[*Enter Chorus.*]

CHORUS Not marching in the fields of Thrasimene,[1]
    Where Mars did mate the warlike Carthigens,
    Nor sporting in the dalliance of love
    In courts of kings where state is overturned,
5   Nor in the pomp of proud audacious deeds,
    Intends our muse to vaunt his heavenly verse.[2]
    Only this, gentles: we must now perform
    The form of Faustus' fortunes, good or bad.
    And now to patient judgments we appeal,
10   And speak for Faustus in his infancy.
    Now is he born, of parents base of stock,
    In Germany, within a town called Rhodes.
    At riper years to Wittenberg he went,
    Whereas his kinsmen chiefly brought him up.
15   So much he profits in divinity,
    The fruitful plot° of scholarism graced,   *field*

---

1. Trasimeno, a lake in Italy near Rome. The Carthaginian general Hannibal conquered Roman forces at Trasimeno in 217 B.C.; Marlowe's "Mars" is probably a reference to the Roman army, which "mated" or engaged the enemy opposition there.

2. These lines may refer to plays Marlowe had previously staged and whose subjects were war (*Tamburlaine*) and love (*Edward II, Dido, Queen of Carthage*).

That shortly he was graced with Doctor's name,
Excelling all; and sweetly can dispute
In th' heavenly matters of theology.
20   Till swol'n with cunning of a self-conceit,
His waxen wings did mount above his reach,
And melting, heavens conspired his overthrow.[3]
For falling to a devilish exercise,
And glutted now with learning's golden gifts,
25   He surfeits upon cursed necromancy.
Nothing so sweet as magic is to him,
Which he prefers before his chiefest bliss:
And this the man that in his study sits.

Act 1

Scene One

[*Faustus in his study.*]

FAUSTUS   Settle thy studies, Faustus, and begin
To sound the depth of that thou wilt profess.
Having commenced, be a divine in show,
Yet level at the end of every art
5   And live and die in Aristotle's works.
Sweet Analytics, 'tis thou hast ravished me.[4]
Bene disserere est finis logices.
Is "to dispute well logic's chiefest end"?
Affords this art no greater miracle?
10   Then read no more: thou hast attained that end.
A greater subject fitteth Faustus' wit.
Bid *on cai me on*° farewell. And Galen,[5] come.   *being and non-being*
Seeing, *ubi desinit philosophus, ibi incipit medicus.*
Be a physician, Faustus: heap up gold
15   And be eternized for some wondrous cure.
Summum bonum medicinae sanitas:
"The end of physic is our body's health."
Why, Faustus, hast thou not attained that end?
Is not thy common talk sound aphorisms?°   *wise sayings*
20   Are not thy bills hung up as monuments,
Whereby whole cities have escaped the plague,
And thousand desperate maladies been cured?
Yet art thou still but Faustus and a man.
Couldst thou make men to live eternally,
25   Or being dead, raise them to life again,
Then this profession were to be esteemed.

3. Faustus is compared to the legendary figure of Icarus, whose father, the master craftsman Daedalus, made him a pair of wings that were attached to his body with wax. Icarus flew too near the sun, the wax supporting his wings melted, and he fell to the sea. The legend is generally understood to signify the consequences of pride and presumption.

4. Aristotle (384–22 B.C.), the best known of the Greek philosophers, wrote on the natural and social sciences. His *Analytics* dealt with logic.
5. Greek physician (130–200) whose works on medicine were studied through the early modern period. Faustus welcomes his change of authorities with "where the philosopher ends, the physician begins."

Physic, farewell. Where is Justinian?[6]
Si una eademque res legatur duobus,
Alter rem, alter valorem rei etc.,
30   A petty case of paltry legacies!
Exhaereditare filium non potest pater, nisi—
Such is the subject of the institute
And universal body of the law.
This study fits a mercenary drudge,
35   Who aims at nothing but external trash,
Too servile and illiberal for me.
When all is done Divinity is best.
Jerome's Bible![7] Faustus, view it well.
Stipendium peccati mors est. Ha! Stipendium etc.,
40   "The reward of sin is death."[8] That's hard.
Si pecasse negamus, fallimur, et nulla est in nobis veritas.
"If we say that we have no sin
We deceive ourselves, and there is no truth in us."[9]
Why then, belike, we must sin,
45   And so consequently die.
Ay, we must die, an everlasting death.
What doctrine call you this? *Che sera, sera.*
"What will be, shall be." Divinity, adieu!
These necromantic books are heavenly,
50   Lines, circles, scenes, letters and characters:
Ay, these are those that Faustus most desires.
Oh, what a world of profit and delight,
Of power, of honor, of omnipotence,
Is promised to the studious artisan!
55   All things that move between the quiet poles
Shall be at my command. Emperors and kings
Are but obeyed in their several provinces.
Nor can they raise the wind or rend the clouds.
But his dominion that exceeds in this
60   Stretcheth as far as doth the mind of man:
A sound magician is a demi-god.
Here, tire° my brains to get° a deity.   use / engender
    [*Enter Wagner.*]
Wagner, commend me to my dearest friends,
The German Valdes and Cornelius.
65   Request them earnestly to visit me.
WAGNER I will, sir.   [*Exit.*]
FAUSTUS Their conference will be a greater help to me
    Than all my labors, plod I ne'er so fast.

---

6. Justinian, Emperor of Byzantium (483–565), codified all of Roman law; his *Institutes* provided the basis for civil law in England as well as on the continent. Faustus cites a principle of estate law: "if one and the same thing is bequeathed to two people, one of them should have the thing itself, and the other the value of it"; and "the father may not disinherit the son."
7. Jerome (347–420), a theologian who translated the Greek Bible and some of the Hebrew Bible into Latin, also wrote on Christian doctrine.
8. Romans 6.23.
9. 1 John 1.8.

[*Enter the Good and Evil Angels.*]

GOOD ANGEL Oh Faustus, lay that damned book aside,
70   And gaze not on it lest it tempt thy soul
        And heap God's heavy wrath upon thy head.
        Read, read the scriptures: that is blasphemy.
EVIL ANGEL Go forward, Faustus, in that famous art
        Wherein all nature's treasure is contained.
75   Be thou on earth as Jove[1] is in the sky,
        Lord and commander of these elements.   [*Exeunt Angels.*]
FAUSTUS How am I glutted with conceit° of this!   idea
        Shall I make spirits fetch me what I please,
        Resolve me of all ambiguities,
80   Perform what desperate enterprise I will?
        I'll have them fly to India for gold,
        Ransack the ocean for orient pearl,
        And search all corners of the new-found world
        For pleasant fruits and princely delicates.
85   I'll have them read me strange philosophy,
        And tell the secrets of all foreign kings.
        I'll have them wall all Germany with brass,
        And make swift Rhine circle fair Wittenberg.
        I'll have them fill the public schools° with silk,   college lecture halls
90   Wherewith the students shall be bravely clad.
        I'll levy soldiers with the coin they bring,
        And chase the Prince of Parma from our land,
        And reign sole king of all the provinces.
        Yea, stranger engines for the brunt of war
95   Than was the fiery keel[2] at Antwerp's bridge
        I'll make my servile spirits to invent.
        Come, German Valdes and Cornelius,
        And make me blest with your sage conference.
    [*Enter Valdes and Cornelius.*]
        Valdes, sweet Valdes and Cornelius!
100   Know that your words have won me at the last
        To practice magic and concealed arts.
        Yet not your words only but mine own fantasy
        That will receive no object° for my head,   idea
        But ruminates on necromantic skill.
105   Philosophy is odious and obscure.
        Both law and physic are for petty wits.
        Divinity is basest of the three,
        Unpleasant, harsh, contemptible and vile.
        'Tis magic, magic that hath ravished me.
110   Then, gentle friends, aid me in this attempt,
        And I, that have with subtle syllogisms
        Gravelled the pastors of the German Church

---

1. Roman god of the heavens and king of the gods.   2. In 1585 a fireship destroyed the Duke of Parma's bridge across the river Scheldt in the city of Antwerp.

And made the flowering pride of Wittenberg
Swarm to my problems as the infernal spirits
115   On sweet Musaeus[3] when he came to hell,
Will be as cunning as Agrippa was,
Whose shadow made all Europe honor him.

VALDES   Faustus, these books, thy wit and our experience
Shall make all nations to canonize us,
120   As Indian moors obey their Spanish lords.
So shall the spirits of every element
Be always serviceable to us three.
Like lions shall they guard us when we please;
Like Almain rutters° with their horsemen's staves;   *German knights*
125   Or Lapland giants trotting by our sides.
Sometimes like women or unwedded maids,
Shadowing more beauty in their airy brows
Than has the white breasts of the queen of love.
From Venice shall they drag huge argosies,°   *merchant ships*
130   And from America the golden fleece[4]
That yearly stuffs old Philip's treasury
If learned Faustus will be resolute.

FAUSTUS   Valdes, as resolute am I in this
As thou to live, therefore object° it not.   *reject*

CORNELIUS   The miracles that magic will perform
Will make thee vow to study nothing else.
He that is grounded in Astrology,
Enriched with tongues,° well seen° in minerals,   *languages/educated*
Hath all the principles magic doth require.
140   Then doubt not, Faustus, but to be renowned,
And more frequented° for this mystery   *sought after*
Than heretofore the Delphian oracle.[5]
The spirits tell me they can dry the sea,
And fetch the treasure of all foreign wracks,°   *wrecks*
145   Yea, all the wealth that our forefathers hid
Within the massy° entrails of the earth.   *massive*
Then tell me, Faustus, what shall we three want?

FAUSTUS   Nothing, Cornelius! Oh, this cheers my soul.
Come, show me some demonstrations magical,
150   That I may conjure in some bushy grove,
And have these joys in full possession.

VALDES   Then haste thee to some solitary grove,
And bear wise Bacon's and Albanus'[6] works,

3. Faustus wants to model himself on Musaeus, a legendary poet, said to have been a student of Orpheus, and Cornelius Agrippa of Nettesheim (1486–1535), a philosopher known for his works on scepticism and the occult.

4. The "golden fleece" refers to the treasure (the gold wool of a divine ram) sought and won by the legendary hero, Jason, and his companions, known as the Argonauts (from the name of their ship, the Argo). Faustus alludes to this treasure when he refers to the gold the King of Castile, Philip II, was taking from lands in the New World.

5. A shrine of Apollo, the god of the sun, music, and medicine, in his temple at Delphi, where his priestess, called the Pythia, spoke incoherent phrases that a priest later interpreted as prophecies.

6. Roger Bacon (1214–1294) was an English Franciscan monk and a lecturer at Oxford University who was interested in natural science, particularly alchemy. Albanus is perhaps Pietro D'Abano (1250–1360), who was supposed to be a sorcerer and was burned in effigy by the Inquisition after his death.

The Hebrew Psalter and New Testament;
155   And whatsoever else is requisite
         We will inform thee e're our conference cease.
CORNELIUS Valdes, first let him know the words of art,
         And then, all other ceremonies learned,
         Faustus may try his cunning by himself.
VALDES First I'll instruct thee in the rudiments,
         And then wilt thou be perfecter than I.
FAUSTUS Then come and dine with me, and after meat
         We'll canvass every quiddity° thereof,   *question*
         For ere I sleep, I'll try what I can do.
165   This night I'll conjure, though I die therefore.   [*Exeunt.*]

Scene Two

[*Enter two Scholars.*]
FIRST SCHOLAR I wonder what's become of Faustus, that was wont to make our
         schools ring with *sic probo*.[7]
         [*Enter Wagner.*]
SECOND SCHOLAR That shall we presently know. Here comes his boy.
FIRST SCHOLAR How now, sirrah, where's thy master?
WAGNER God in heaven knows.
SECOND SCHOLAR Why, dost not thou know then?
WAGNER Yes, I know, but that follows not.
FIRST SCHOLAR Go to, sirrah. Leave your jesting and tell us where he is.
WAGNER That follows not by force of argument, which you, being licentiates,[8]
10   should stand upon. Therefore, acknowledge your error and be attentive.
SECOND SCHOLAR Then you will not tell us?
WAGNER You are deceived, for I will tell you. Yet if you were not dunces, you would
         never ask me such a question. For is he not *Corpus naturale*?[9] And is not that
         mobile? Then wherefore should you ask me such a question? But that I am
15   by nature phlegmatic, slow to wrath and prone to lechery (to love, I would
         say), it were not for you to come within forty foot of the place of execution,
         although I do not doubt but to see you both hanged the next sessions. Thus,
         having triumphed over you, I will set my countenance like a precision,[1] and
         begin to speak thus: "Truly, my dear brethren, my master is within at dinner
20   with Valdes and Cornelius, as this wine, if it could speak, would inform your
         worships. And so the Lord bless you, preserve you and keep you, my dear
         brethren."   [*Exit.*]
FIRST SCHOLAR Oh Faustus, then I fear that which I have long suspected:
         That thou art fallen into that damned art
25   For which they two are infamous through the world.
SECOND SCHOLAR Were he a stranger, not allied to me,
         The danger of his soul would make me mourn.
         But come, let us go, and inform the Rector.
         It may be his grave counsel may reclaim him.
FIRST SCHOLAR I fear me nothing will reclaim him now.
SECOND SCHOLAR Yet let us see what we can do.   [*Exeunt.*]

---

7. "Thus I prove."   9. A natural body.
8. Postgraduates.   1. Puritan.

Scene Three

[Thunder. Enter Lucifer and Four Devils. Faustus to them with this speech.]

FAUSTUS Now that the gloomy shadow of the night,
      Longing to view Orion's drizzling look,
      Leaps from th'Antarctic world unto the sky,
      And dims the welkin° with her pitchy breath,   *heaven*
5   Faustus, begin thine incantations
      And try if devils will obey thy hest,°   *command*
      Seeing thou hast prayed and sacrificed to them.
      Within this circle is Jehovah's name
      Forward and backward anagrammatized:
10   The abbreviated names of holy saints,
      Figures of every adjunct to the heavens,
      And characters of signs and evening stars,
      By which the spirits are enforced to rise.
      Then fear not, Faustus, to be resolute
15   And try the utmost magic can perform.[2]
      [Thunder.]
      Sint mihi dei acherontis propitii, valeat numen triplex Jehovae, ignei areii, aquatani
      spiritus salvete: orientis princeps Belzebub, inferni ardentis monarcha et demigor-
      gon, propitiamus vos, ut appareat, et surgat Mephostophilis (Dragon)[3] quod tumer-
      aris: per Jehovam, gehennam, et consecratam aquam quam nunc spargo;
20   *signumque crucis quod nunc facio; et per vota nostra ipse nunc surgat nobis dicatus*
      Mephostophilis.
      [Enter a Devil.]
      I charge thee to return and change thy shape.
      Thou art too ugly to attend on me.
      Go, and return an old Franciscan friar:
25   That holy shape becomes a devil best.   *[Exit Devil.]*
      I see there's virtue in my heavenly words.
      Who would not be proficient in this art?
      How pliant is this Mephostophilis!
      Full of obedience and humility,
30   Such is the force of magic and my spells.
      Now, Faustus, thou art conjuror laureate:[4]
      Thou canst command great Mephostophilis.
      Quin redis Mephostophilis fratris imagine.
      [Enter Mephostophilis.]

MEPHOSTOPHILIS Now, Faustus, what wouldst thou have me do?

FAUSTUS I charge thee wait upon me whilst I live,
      To do whatever Faustus shall command,

---

2. Faustus styles himself an accomplished magician. He
now repeats, in Latin, his command to Mephostophilis to
appear in the guise of a friar: "May the gods of the underworld be kind to me; may the triple deity of Jehovah be
gone; to the spirits of fire, air, and water, greetings. Prince
of the east, Beelzebub, monarch of the fires below, and
Demogorgon, we appeal to you so that Mephostophilis
may appear and rise. Why do you delay? By Jehovah, hell
and the hallowed water which I now sprinkle, and the

sign of the cross, which I now make, and by our vows, let
Mephostophilis himself now arise to serve us."
3. This appears to be a stage direction that was inserted
into the playtext; it probably indicates that at this point
the figure of a dragon should come on stage.
4. Faustus, stating he is a "conjurer laureate" or honored
magician, asks again, in Latin: "Why do you not return,
Mephostophilis, in the guise of a friar?"

Be it to make the moon drop from her sphere,
Or the ocean to overwhelm the world.

MEPHOSTOPHILIS I am a servant to great Lucifer,
40   And may not follow thee without his leave.
            No more than he commands must we perform.

FAUSTUS Did not he charge thee to appear to me?

MEPHOSTOPHILIS No, I came now hither of mine own accord.

FAUSTUS Did not my conjuring speeches raise thee? Speak.

MEPHOSTOPHILIS That was the cause, but yet *per accidens;*°   *by accident*
            For when we hear one rack the name of God,
            Abjure the scriptures and his saviour Christ,
            We fly in hope to get his glorious soul.
            Nor will we come unless he use such means
50   Whereby he is in danger to be damned.
            Therefore the shortest cut for conjuring
            Is stoutly to abjure all godliness
            And pray devoutly to the price of hell.

FAUSTUS So Faustus hath already done, and holds this principle:
55   There is no chief but only Belzebub,
            To whom Faustus doth dedicate himself.
            This word "damnation" terrifies not me,
            For I confound hell in elysium.°   *heaven*
            My ghost be with the old philosophers.
60   But leaving these vain trifles of men's souls,
            Tell me, what is that Lucifer, thy lord?

MEPHOSTOPHILIS Arch-regent and commander of all spirits.

FAUSTUS Was not that Lucifer an angel once?

MEPHOSTOPHILIS Yes, Faustus, and most dearly loved of God.

FAUSTUS How comes it then that he is prince of devils?

MEPHOSTOPHILIS Oh, by aspiring pride and insolence,
            For which God threw him from the face of heaven.

FAUSTUS And what are you that live with Lucifer?

MEPHOSTOPHILIS Unhappy spirits that fell with Lucifer,
70   Conspired against our God with Lucifer,
            And are for ever damned with Lucifer.

FAUSTUS Where are you damned?

MEPHOSTOPHILIS In hell.

FAUSTUS How comes it then that thou art out of hell?

MEPHOSTOPHILIS Why, this is hell, nor am I out of it.
            Think'st thou that I that saw the face of God
            And tasted the eternal joys of heaven,
            Am not tormented with ten thousand hells
            In being deprived of everlasting bliss?
80   Oh, Faustus, leave these frivolous demands,
            Which strike a terror to my fainting soul.

FAUSTUS What, is great Mephostophilis so passionate
            For being deprived of the joys of heaven?
            Learn thou of Faustus manly fortitude,
85   And scorn those joys thou never shalt possess.

Go, bear these tidings to great Lucifer,
Seeing Faustus hath incurred eternal death
By desperate thoughts against Jove's deity.
Say he surrenders up to him his soul,
90   So he will spare him four and twenty years,
Letting him live in all voluptuousness,
Having thee ever to attend on me,
To give me whatsoever I shall ask,
To tell me whatsoever I demand,
95   To slay mine enemies and to aid my friends
And always be obedient to my will.
Go, and return to mighty Lucifer,
And meet me in my study at midnight,
And then resolve me of thy master's mind.

MEPHOSTOPHILIS I will, Faustus.   [Exit.]

FAUSTUS Had I as many souls as there be stars,
I'd give them all for Mephostophilis.
By him I'll be great emperor of the world,
And make a bridge through the air
105   To pass the ocean. With a band of men
I'll join the hills that bind the Affrick shore,
And make that country continent to Spain,
And both contributory to my crown.
The Emperor shall not live but by my leave,
110   Nor any potentate of Germany.
Now that I have obtained what I desired,
I'll live in speculation of this art
Till Mephostophilis return again.   [Exit.]

Scene Four

[*Enter Wagner and the Clown.*]

WAGNER Come hither, sirrah boy.

CLOWN Boy? Oh, disgrace to my person! Zounds! "Boy" in your face! You have seen
        many boys with beards, I am sure.

WAGNER Sirrah, hast thou no comings in?

CLOWN Yes, and goings out too, you may see, sir.

WAGNER Alas, poor slave. See how poverty jests in his nakedness. I know the vil-
        lain's out of service and so hungry that I know he would give his soul to the
        devil for a shoulder of mutton though it were blood-raw.

CLOWN Not so neither. I had need to have it well roasted, and good sauce to it, if I
10   pay so dear, I can tell you.

WAGNER Sirrah, wilt thou be my man and wait on me? And I will make thee go like
        Qui mihi discipulus.[5]

CLOWN What, in verse?

WAGNER No, slave, in beaten silk and stavesacre.[6]

CLOWN Stavesacre? That's good to kill vermin. Then belike, if I serve you I shall be
        lousy.

---

5. One who is my disciple.   6. A poison.

WAGNER Why, so thou shalt be whether thou dost it or no. For, sirrah, if thou dost not presently bind thyself to me for seven years, I'll turn all the lice about thee into familiars,[7] and make them tear thee in pieces.

CLOWN Nay, sir, you may save yourself a labor, for they are as familiar with me as if they paid for their meat and drink, I can tell you.

WAGNER Well, sirrah, leave your jesting and take these guilders.[8]

CLOWN Yes, marry, sir, and I thank you too.

WAGNER So, now thou art to be at an hour's warning, whensoever and wheresoever
25   the devil shall fetch thee.

CLOWN Here, take your guilders.

WAGNER Truly, I'll none of them.

CLOWN Truly but you shall.

WAGNER Bear witness I gave them him.

CLOWN Bear witness I give them you again.

WAGNER Not I. Thou art pressed. Prepare thyself, for I will presently raise up two devils, to carry thee away: Banio, Belcher!

CLOWN Belcher? And Belcher come here, I'll belch him! I am not afraid of a devil.
[Enter Two Devils and the Clown runs up and down crying.]

WAGNER How now, sir, will you serve me now?

CLOWN Ay, good Wagner. Take away the devil then.

WAGNER Baliol and Belcher, spirits, away!   [Exeunt Devils.]

CLOWN What, are they gone? A vengeance on them! They have vile long nails. There was a he-devil and a she-devil. I'll tell you how you shall know them: all he-devils has horns, and all she-devils has clifts[9] and cloven feet.

WAGNER Well, sirrah, follow me.

CLOWN But, do you hear, if I should serve you, would you teach me to raise up Banio's and Belcheo's?

WAGNER I will teach thee to turn thyself to anything, to a dog, or a cat, or a mouse, or a rat, or anything.

CLOWN How? A Christian fellow to a dog or a cat, a mouse or a rat? No, no, sir, if you turn me into anything, let it be in the likeness of a little pretty frisking flea, that I may be here and there and everywhere. Oh, I'll tickle the pretty wenches' plackets![1] I'll be amongst them, i'faith.

WAGNER Well, sirrah, come.

CLOWN But do you hear, Wagner?

WAGNER How? Baliol and Belcher!

CLOWN Oh Lord, I pray, sir, let Banio and Belcher go sleep.

WAGNER Villain, call me Master Wagner, and see that you walk attentively and let your right eye be always diametrically fixed upon my left heel, that thou
55   mayest Quasi vestigias nostras insistere.[2]   [Exit.]

CLOWN God forgive me, he speaks Dutch fustian![3] Well, I'll follow him. I'll serve him, that's flat.   [Exit.]

Scene Five

[Enter Faustus in his study.]

FAUSTUS Now, Faustus, must thou needs be damned?

---

7. Spirits.
8. Coins.
9. Clefts.
1. Petticoats.

2. Wagner mocks the Clown by telling him to walk "as if to tread in our footsteps," knowing that the clown's magic will never be as powerful as his own.
3. Nonsense.

And canst thou not be saved?
What boots it then to think on God or heaven?
Away with such vain fancies and despair,
5   Despair in God and trust in Belzebub.°   *the Devil*
Now go not backward. No, Faustus, be resolute.
Why waverest thou? Oh, something soundeth in mine ears
Abjure this magic, turn to God again.
Ay, and Faustus will turn to God again.
10   To God? He loves thee not.
The God thou servest is thine own appetite,
Wherein is fixed the love of Belzebub.
To him I'll build an altar and a church,
And offer lukewarm blood of new-born babes.
    [*Enter the Good and Evil Angels.*]
GOOD ANGEL   Sweet Faustus, leave that execrable art.
FAUSTUS   Contrition, prayer, repentance, what of these?
GOOD ANGEL   Oh, they are means to bring thee unto heaven.
EVIL ANGEL   Rather illusions, fruits of lunacy,
    That make men foolish that do trust them most.
GOOD ANGEL   Sweet Faustus, think of heaven and heavenly things.
EVIL ANGEL   No, Faustus, think of honor and of wealth.   [*Exeunt Angels.*]
FAUSTUS   Of wealth!
    Why, the signory of Emden⁴ shall be mine!
    When Mephostophilis shall stand by me,
25   What God can hurt thee, Faustus? Thou art safe.
    Cast no more doubts. Come, Mephostophilis,
    And bring glad tidings from great Lucifer.
    Is't not midnight? Come Mephostophilis!
    Veni, veni,° *Mephostophile!*   *come, come*
    [*Enter Mephostophilis.*]
30   Now tell me, what saith Lucifer, thy lord?
MEPHOSTOPHILIS   That I shall wait on Faustus whilst he lives,
    So he will buy my service with his soul.
FAUSTUS   Already Faustus hath hazarded that for thee.
MEPHOSTOPHILIS   But now thou must bequeath it solemnly,
35   And write a deed of gift with thine own blood,
    For that security craves great Lucifer.
    If thou deny it, I will back to hell.
FAUSTUS   Stay, Mephostophilis, and tell me
    What good will my soul do thy lord?
MEPHOSTOPHILIS   Enlarge his kingdom.
FAUSTUS   Is that the reason why he tempts us thus?
MEPHOSTOPHILIS   *Solamen miseris, socios habuisse doloris.*⁵
FAUSTUS   Why, have you any pain, that torture others?
MEPHOSTOPHILIS   As great as have the human souls of men.
45   But tell me, Faustus, shall I have thy soul?

---

4. At this point in his career, Faustus aspires to the governorship of Emden, an important trading town in Germany, a pathetic exchange for his immortal soul.

5. Mephostophilis states that misery loves company in
hell: "It is a comfort in wretchedness to have companions
in woe."

And I will be thy slave and wait on thee,
And give thee more than thou hast wit to ask.
FAUSTUS Ay, Mephostophilis, I'll give it thee.
MEPHOSTOPHILIS Then, Faustus, stab thy arm courageously,
50   And bind thy soul, that at some certain day
          Great Lucifer may claim it as his own,
          And then be thou as great as Lucifer.
FAUSTUS Lo, Mephostophilis, for love of thee
          I cut mine arm, and with my proper blood
55   Assure my soul to be great Lucifer's,
          Chief lord and regent of perpetual night.
          View here the blood that trickles from mine arm,
          And let it be propitious for my wish.
MEPHOSTOPHILIS But, Faustus, thou must write it in manner of a deed of gift.
FAUSTUS Ay, so I will. But, Mephostophilis,
          My blood congeals and I can write no more!
MEPHOSTOPHILIS I'll fetch thee fire to dissolve it straight.   [Exit.]
FAUSTUS What might the staying of my blood portend?
          Is it unwilling I should write this bill?
65   Why streams it not that I may write afresh?
          "Faustus gives to thee his soul": ah, there it stayed!
          Why shouldst thou not? Is not thy soul thine own?
          Then write again: "Faustus gives to thee his soul."
     [Enter Mephostophilis with a chafer of coals.]
MEPHOSTOPHILIS Here's fire. Come, Faustus, set it on.
FAUSTUS So, now my blood begins to clear again.
          Now will I make an end immediately.
MEPHOSTOPHILIS Oh what will not I do to obtain his soul!
FAUSTUS Consummatum est:[6] this bill is ended,
          And Faustus hath bequeathed his soul to Lucifer.
75   But what is this inscription on mine arm?
          Homo fuge!° Whither should I flee?   Flee, O man
          If unto heaven, he'll throw me down to hell.
          My senses are deceived: here's nothing writ!
          Oh, yes, I see it plain. Even here is writ
80   Homo fuge. Yet shall not Faustus fly.
MEPHOSTOPHILIS I'll fetch him somewhat to delight his mind.   [Exit.]
     [Enter Devils, giving crowns and rich apparel to Faustus; they dance and then depart.
     Enter Mephostophilis.]
FAUSTUS What means this show? Speak, Mephostophilis.
MEPHOSTOPHILIS Nothing, Faustus, but to delight thy mind,
          And let thee see what magic can perform.
FAUSTUS But may I raise such spirits when I please?
MEPHOSTOPHILIS Ay, Faustus, and do greater things than these.
FAUSTUS Then there's enough for a thousand souls.
          Here, Mephostophilis, receive this scroll,
          A deed of gift, of body and of soul:

---

6. Faustus speaks the last words of Jesus on the cross: "It is finished" (John 19.30), and then realizes he must try to avoid the consequences: "Flee, O man."

90   But yet conditionally, that thou perform
       All covenants and articles between us both.
MEPHOSTOPHILIS Faustus, I swear by hell and Lucifer
       To effect all promises between us both.
FAUSTUS Then hear me read it, Mephostophilis.
95   On these conditions following:
       First, that Faustus may be a spirit in form and substance.
       Secondly, that Mephostophilis shall be his servant, and be by him commanded.
       Thirdly, that Mephostophilis shall do for him, and bring him whatsoever.
       Fourthly, that he shall be in his chamber or house invisible.
100   Lastly, that he shall appear to the said John Faustus at all times, in what
          shape and form soever he please.
       I, John Faustus of Wittenberg Doctor, by these presents, do give both body
          and soul to Lucifer, Prince of the East, and his minister Mephostophilis,
          and furthermore grant unto them that four and twenty years being
105   expired, and these articles above written being inviolate, full power to
          fetch or carry the said John Faustus, body and soul, flesh, blood or goods,
          into their habitation wheresoever.
       By me, John Faustus.
MEPHOSTOPHILIS Speak, Faustus, do you deliver this as your deed?
FAUSTUS Ay, take it, and the devil give thee good of it.
MEPHOSTOPHILIS So now, Faustus, ask me what thou wilt.
FAUSTUS First I will question with thee about hell.
       Tell me, where is the place that men call hell?
MEPHOSTOPHILIS Under the heavens.
FAUSTUS Ay, so are all things else; but whereabouts?
MEPHOSTOPHILIS Within the bowels of these elements,
       Where we are tortured and remain for ever.
       Hell hath no limits, nor is circumscribed
       In one self place. But where we are is hell,
120   And where hell is there must we ever be.
       And to be short, when all the world dissolves
       And every creature shall be purified,
       All places shall be hell that is not heaven.
FAUSTUS Come, I think hell's a fable.
MEPHOSTOPHILIS Ay, think so still, till experience change thy mind.
FAUSTUS Why, dost thou think that Faustus shall be damned?
MEPHOSTOPHILIS Ay, of necessity, for here's the scroll
       In which thou hast given thy soul to Lucifer.
FAUSTUS Ay, and body too, but what of that?
130   Think'st thou that Faustus is so fond to imagine
       That after this life there is any pain?
       Tush, these are trifles and old wives' tales.
MEPHOSTOPHILIS But Faustus, I am an instance to prove the contrary,
       For I tell thee I am damned, and now in hell.
FAUSTUS How? Now in hell? Nay, and this be hell, I'll willingly be damned here.
       What! Sleeping, eating, walking and disputing? But leaving this, let me
       have a wife, the fairest maid in Germany, for I am wanton and lascivious,
       and can not live without a wife.
MEPHOSTOPHILIS How, a wife? I prithee, Faustus, talk not of a wife.

FAUSTUS Nay, sweet Mephostophilis, fetch me one, for I will have one.

MEPHOSTOPHILIS Well, thou wilt have one. Sit there till I come: I'll fetch thee a
    wife in the devil's name.

[*Enter a Devil dressed like a woman, with fireworks.*]

FAUSTUS What sight is this?

MEPHOSTOPHILIS Tell, Faustus, how dost thou like thy wife?

FAUSTUS A plague on her for a hot whore.

MEPHOSTOPHILIS Tut, Faustus, marriage is but a ceremonial toy.
    If thou lovest me, think no more of it.
    I'll cull thee out the fairest courtesans
    And bring them every morning to thy bed.

150   She whom thine eye shall like, thy heart shall have,
    Be she as chaste as was Penelope,[7]
    As wise as Saba, or as beautiful
    As was bright Lucifer before his fall.
    Here, take this book, and peruse it well.

155   The iterating° of these lines brings gold,   *repetition*
    The framing of this circle on the ground
    Brings thunder, whirlwinds, storm and lightning.
    Pronounce this thrice devoutly to thyself
    And men in harness shall appear to thee,

160   Ready to execute what thou commandest.

FAUSTUS Thanks, Mephostophilis. Yet fain would I have a book wherein I might
    behold all spells and incantations, that I might raise up spirits when I please.

MEPHOSTOPHILIS Here they are in this book.   [*There turn to them.*]

FAUSTUS Now would I have a book where I might see all characters and planets of

165   the heavens, that I might know their motions and dispositions.

MEPHOSTOPHILIS Here they are too.   [*Turn to them.*]

FAUSTUS Nay, let me have one book more, and then I have done, wherein I might
    see all plants, herbs and trees that grow upon the earth.

MEPHOSTOPHILIS Here they be.

FAUSTUS Oh thou art deceived.

MEPHOSTOPHILIS Tut, I warrant thee.   [*Turn to them.*]

Act 2

Scene One

[*Enter Faustus in his study, and Mephostophilis.*]

FAUSTUS When I behold the heavens then I repent,
    And curse thee, wicked Mephostophilis,
    Because thou hast deprived me of those joys.

MEPHOSTOPHILIS 'Twas thine own seeking, Faustus, thank thyself.

5   But thinkst thou heaven is such a glorious thing?
    I tell thee, Faustus, it is not half so fair
    As thou or any man that breathes on earth.

FAUSTUS How prov'st thou that?

MEPHOSTOPHILIS 'Twas made for man; then he's more excellent.

---

7. Mephostophilis compares the ideal woman to Penelope, the wife of Odysseus, who waited 20 years for him to return
from the Trojan wars, and to Saba, the wise Queen of Sheba, who taught King Solomon, known himself for his wisdom (1
Kings).

FAUSTUS If heaven was made for man, 'twas made for me.
　　　　I will renounce this magic and repent.
　　　　[*Enter the Good and Evil Angels.*]
GOOD ANGEL Faustus, repent. Yet God will pity thee.
EVIL ANGEL Thou art a spirit. God cannot pity thee.
FAUSTUS Who buzzeth in mine ears I am a spirit?
15　　　　Be I a devil, yet God may pity me.
　　　　Yea, God will pity me if I repent.
EVIL ANGEL Ay, but Faustus never shall repent.　　　　　　　[*Exeunt.*]
FAUSTUS My heart's so hardened I cannot repent.
　　　　Scarce can I name salvation, faith or heaven,
20　　　　But fearful echoes thunder in mine ears
　　　　"Faustus, thou art damned." Then swords and knives,
　　　　Poison, guns, halters and envenomed steel
　　　　Are laid before me to dispatch myself.
　　　　And long ere this I should have done the deed,
25　　　　Had not sweet pleasure conquered deep despair.
　　　　Have not I made blind Homer sing to me
　　　　Of Alexander's love and Oenon's death?[1]
　　　　And hath not he that built the walls of Thebes
　　　　With ravishing sound of his melodious harp
30　　　　Made music with my Mephostophilis?[2]
　　　　Why should I die then, or basely despair?
　　　　I am resolved, Faustus shall not repent.
　　　　Come, Mephostophilis, let us dispute again,
　　　　And reason of divine astrology.
35　　　　Speak, are there many spheres above the moon?
　　　　Are all celestial bodies but one globe,
　　　　As is the substance of this centric earth?[3]
MEPHOSTOPHILIS As are the elements, such are the heavens,
　　　　Even from the moon unto the empyrial orb,
40　　　　Mutually folded in each other's spheres,
　　　　And jointly move upon one axle-tree,
　　　　Whose termine° is termed the world's wide pole.　　　　　*end point*
　　　　Nor are the names of Saturn, Mars or Jupiter
　　　　Feigned, but are erring stars.
FAUSTUS But have they all one motion, both *situ et tempore*?[4]
MEPHOSTOPHILIS All move from east to west in four and twenty hours upon the
　　　　poles of the world, but differ in their motions upon the poles of the zodiac.
FAUSTUS Tush, these slender trifles Wagner can decide. Hath Mephostophilis no
　　　　greater skill? Who knows not the double motion of the planets? That the
50　　　　first is finished in a natural day? The second thus, as Saturn in thirty years,

---

1. Faustus claims he has made the poet Homer sing to
him of the love of Alexander the Great (356–323 B.C.),
who was married to Statira, daughter of the Emperor Darius of Persia; and of Oenone, a nymph of Mount Ida, who
died from grief when her lover, Paris of Troy, deserted her
for Helen, the wife of King Menalaus of Sparta.
2. Faustus further claims that the legendary Amphion,
whose music built the walls of Thebes, also made music

with Mephostophilis, now Faustus's servant.
3. Faustus alludes to the Ptolemaic universe in which the
earth, at the center, is surrounded by concentric spheres,
beginning with the moon. Beyond the spheres of the stars
that were thought to move (the constellations) were the
spheres of the fixed stars.
4. In place and in time.

Jupiter in twelve, Mars in four, the sun, Venus and Mercury in twenty-eight days. Tush, these are freshmen's suppositions. But tell me, hath every sphere a dominion or *intelligentia*?[5]

MEPHOSTOPHILIS Ay.

FAUSTUS How many heavens or spheres are there?

MEPHOSTOPHILIS Nine, the seven planets, the firmament, and the empyrial heaven.

FAUSTUS But is there not *coelum igneum et cristallinum?*

MEPHOSTOPHILIS No, Faustus, they be but fables.[6]

FAUSTUS Resolve me then in this one question. Why are not conjunctions, oppositions, aspects, eclipses, all at one time, but in some years we have more, in some less?

MEPHOSTOPHILIS *Per inaequalem motum, respectu totius.*[7]

FAUSTUS Well, I am answered. Now tell me, who made the world?

MEPHOSTOPHILIS I will not.

FAUSTUS Sweet Mephostophilis, tell me.

MEPHOSTOPHILIS Move me not, Faustus.

FAUSTUS Villain, have not I bound thee to tell me anything?

MEPHOSTOPHILIS Ay, that is not against our kingdom, but this is.
　　Think on hell, Faustus, for thou art damned.

FAUSTUS Think, Faustus, upon God, that made the world.

MEPHOSTOPHILIS Remember this—　　　　　　　　　　　　　　　　[*Exit.*]

FAUSTUS Ay, go, accursed spirit to ugly hell.
　　'Tis thou hast damned distressed Faustus' soul.
　　Is't not too late?

　　[*Enter the Good and Evil Angels.*]

EVIL ANGEL Too late.

GOOD ANGEL Never too late, if Faustus will repent.

EVIL ANGEL If thou repent devils will tear thee in pieces.

GOOD ANGEL Repent, and they shall never raze° thy skin.　　　　　*shave*
　　[*Exeunt Angels.*]

FAUSTUS Ah, Christ my savior,
80　　Seek to save distressed Faustus' soul.
　　[*Enter Lucifer, Belzebub and Mephostophilis.*]

LUCIFER Christ cannot save thy soul, for he is just.
　　There's none but I have interest in the same.

FAUSTUS Oh what art thou that look'st so terribly?

LUCIFER I am Lucifer, and this is my companion prince in hell.

FAUSTUS Oh Faustus, they are come to fetch away thy soul.

BELZEBUB We are come to tell thee thou dost injure us.

LUCIFER Thou call'st on Christ contrary to thy promise.

BELZEBUB Thou shouldst not think on God.

LUCIFER Think on the devil.

BELZEBUB And his dam too.

FAUSTUS Nor will I henceforth. Pardon me in this,
　　And Faustus vows never to look to heaven,

---

5. Guiding spirit.
6. Faustus asks whether there is a "fiery and crystalline heaven" beyond the "empyrial heaven" Mephostophilis has mentioned, and he is told it is a fiction.

7. Faustus asks why planetary and astral events do not occur uniformly, and Mephostophilis answers that they do "with respect to the whole" but each "by unequal motion."

Never to name God or to pray to him,
To burn his scriptures, slay his ministers,
95   And make my spirits pull his churches down.

LUCIFER Do so, and we will highly gratify thee.

BELZEBUB Faustus, we are come from hell in person to show thee some pastime. Sit down and thou shalt behold the seven deadly sins appear to thee in their own proper shapes and likeness.

FAUSTUS That sight will be as pleasant to me as Paradise was to Adam the first day of his creation.

LUCIFER Talk not of Paradise or Creation, but mark this show. Talk of the devil and nothing else. Go, Mephostophilis, fetch them in.

[Enter the Seven Deadly Sins.]

BELZEBUB Now, Faustus, question them of their names and dispositions.

FAUSTUS That shall I soon. What art thou, the first?

PRIDE I am Pride. I disdain to have any parents. I am like to Ovid's flea.[8] I can creep into every corner of a wench. Sometimes like a periwig I sit upon her brow. Next, like a necklace I hang about her neck. Then, like a fan of feathers, I kiss her. And then turning myself to a wrought smock do what I list. But fie,
110   what a smell is here! I'll not speak a word for a king's ransome, unless the ground be perfumed and covered with cloth of Arras.[9]

FAUSTUS Thou art a proud knave indeed. What art thou, the second?

COVETOUSNESS I am Covetousness. Begotten of an old churl in a leather bag. And might I now obtain my wish, this house, you and all, should turn to
115   gold, that I might lock you safe into my chest. Oh, my sweet gold!

FAUSTUS And what art thou, the third?

ENVY I am Envy, begotten of a chimney-sweeper and an oyster-wife. I cannot read and therefore wish all books were burnt. I am lean with seeing others eat. Oh, that there would come a famine over all the world, that all might die,
120   and I live alone, then thou should'st see how fat I'd be. But must thou sit and I stand? Come down, with a vengeance!

FAUSTUS Out, envious wretch. But what art thou, the fourth?

WRATH I am Wrath. I had neither father nor mother. I leapt out of a lion's mouth when I was scarce an hour old, and ever since have run up and down the world
125   with this case of rapiers, wounding myself when I could get none to fight withal. I was born in hell, and look to it, for some of you shall be my father.

FAUSTUS And what art thou, the fifth?

GLUTTONY I am Gluttony. My parents are all dead, and the devil a penny they have left me, but a small pension and that buys me thirty meals a day and
130   ten bevers:[1] a small trifle to suffice nature. I come of a royal pedigree; my father was a gammon of bacon and my mother was a hog's head of claret wine. My godfathers were these: Peter Pickle-herring and Martin Martlemas-beef. But my godmother, oh, she was an ancient gentlewoman, and well-beloved in every good town and city. Her name was Mistress Margery
135   March-beer. Now, Faustus, thou hast heard all my progeny, wilt thou bid me to supper?

---

8. One of the poems of the Roman poet Ovid (43 B.C.–A.D. 18) describes the journey of a flea around a woman's body.

9. Flemish cloth for tapestries.
1. Snacks.

FAUSTUS No, I'll see thee hanged. Thou wilt eat up all my victuals.

GLUTTONY Then the devil choke thee.

FAUSTUS Choke thyself, Glutton. What art thou, the sixth?

SLOTH Hey ho, I am Sloth. I was begotten on a sunny bank where I have lain ever since, and you have done me great injury to bring me from thence. Let me be carried thither again by Gluttony and Lechery. I'll not speak another word for a king's ransom.

FAUSTUS And what are you, Mistress Minx, the seventh and last?

LECHERY Who, I sir? I am one that loves an inch of raw mutton better than an ell of fried stockfish,[2] and the first letter of my name begins with Lechery.

FAUSTUS Away to hell! Away, on, piper!   [Exeunt the Seven Deadly Sins.]

LUCIFER Now, Faustus, how dost thou like this?

FAUSTUS Oh, this feeds my soul.

LUCIFER Tut, Faustus, in hell is all manner of delight.

FAUSTUS Oh, might I see hell and return again safe, how happy were I then!

LUCIFER Faustus, thou shalt. At midnight I will send for thee. Meanwhile, peruse this book and view it throughly, and thou shalt turn thyself into what shape thou wilt.

FAUSTUS Thanks, mighty Lucifer. This will I keep as chary as my life.

LUCIFER Now, Faustus, farewell, and think on the devil.

FAUSTUS Farewell, great Lucifer. Come, Mephostophilis.

[Exeunt omnes, several ways.]

Scene Two

[Enter the Clown.]

CLOWN What, Dick, look to the horses there till I come again. I have gotten one of Doctor Faustus' conjuring books, and now we'll have such knavery as't passes.
[Enter Dick.]

DICK What, Robin, you must come away and walk the horses.

ROBIN I walk the horses? I scorn't, faith. I have other matters in hand. Let the horses
5   walk themselves and they will. A per se a, t.h.e. the: o per se o deny orgon, gorgon.[3] Keep further from me, O thou illiterate and unlearned hostler.

DICK 'Snails![4] What hast thou got there? A book? Why, thou canst not tell ne'er a word on't.

ROBIN That thou shalt see presently. Keep out of the circle, I say, lest I send you
10   into the ostry[5] with a vengeance.

DICK That's like, faith. You had best leave your foolery, for, an my master come, he'll conjure you, faith!

ROBIN My master conjure me? I'll tell thee what, an my master come here, I'll clap as fair a pair of horns[6] on's head as e'er thou sawest in thy life.

DICK Thou need'st not do that, for my mistress hath done it.

ROBIN Ay, there be of us here, that have waded as deep into matters as other men, if they were disposed to talk.

---

2. Lechery implies that she would prefer a short but energetic penis to a yard-long but dry one.
3. Barely literate, Robin is trying to parse a Latin phrase, *atheo* Demigorgon ("godless Demigorgon").

4. Christ's nails.
5. Inn.
6. Sign of a cuckold.

DICK A plague take you! I thought you did not sneak up and down after her for noth-
    ing. But I prithee tell me, in good sadness, Robin, is that a conjuring book?
ROBIN Do but speak what thou't have me to do, and I'll do't. If thou't dance naked,
    put off thy clothes and I'll conjure thee about presently. Or if thou't go but
    to the tavern with me, I'll give thee white wine, red wine, claret wine, sack,
    muskadine, malmesey and whippincrust.[7] Hold, belly, hold; and we'll not
    pay one penny for it.
DICK Oh brave! Prithee, let's to it presently, for I am as dry as a dog.
ROBIN Come, then, let's away.   *[Exeunt.]*

A c t 3

Scene One

[*Enter the Chorus.*]
CHORUS Learned Faustus,
        To find the secrets of astronomy,
        Graven in the book of Jove's high firmament,
        Did mount him up to scale Olympus' top,
5   Where sitting in a chariot burning bright,
        Drawn by the strength of yoked dragons' necks,
        He views the clouds, the planets, and the stars,
        The tropic, zones, and quarters of the sky,
        From the bright circle of the horned moon,
10   Even to the height of *Primum Mobile*.[1]
        And whirling round with this circumference,
        Within the concave compass of the pole,
        From east to west his dragons swiftly glide,
        And in eight days did bring him home again.
15   Not long he stayed within his quiet house,
        To rest his bones after his weary toil,
        But new exploits do hale him out again,
        And mounted then upon a dragon's back,
        That with his wings did part the subtle air,
20   He now is gone to prove cosmography,
        That measures coasts and kingdoms of the earth;
        And as I guess will first arrive at Rome,
        To see the Pope and manner of his court,
        And take some part of holy Peter's feast,
25   The which this day is highly solemnized.   *[Exit.]*

Scene Two

[*Enter Faustus and Mephostophilis.*]
FAUSTUS Having now, my good Mephostophilis,
        Passed with delight the stately town of Trier,
        Environed round with airy mountain tops,

---

7. Robin lists various kinds of wine; "whippencrust" is
probably a corruption of "hippocras," a kind of sweet
wine.

1. The outermost of the heavenly spheres. Faustus is pictured as viewing the heavens from Mount Olympus to the
circle of the moon and beyond, to the *primum mobile*.

With walls of flint, and deep entrenched lakes,
5   Not to be won by any conquering prince,
From Paris next coasting the realm of France
We saw the river Main fall into Rhine,
Whose banks are set with groves of fruitful vines;
Then up to Naples, rich Campania,
10   Whose buildings fair and gorgeous to the eye,
The streets straight forth and paved with finest brick,
Quarters the town in four equivolence.°   parts
There saw we learned Maro's golden tomb,[2]
The way he cut an English mile in length,
15   Thorough a rock of stone in one night's space.
From thence to Venice, Padua and the rest,
In midst of which a sumptuous temple stands,
That threats the stars with her aspiring top,
Whose frame is paved with sundry colored stones,
20   And roofed aloft with curious work in gold.
Thus hitherto hath Faustus spent his time.
But tell me now, what resting place is this?
Hast thou, as erst I did command,
Conducted me within the walls of Rome?
MEPHOSTOPHILIS I have, my Faustus, and for proof thereof,
This is the goodly palace of the Pope;
And cause we are no common guests,
I choose his privy chamber for our use.
FAUSTUS I hope his Holiness will bid us welcome.
MEPHOSTOPHILIS All's one, for we'll be bold with his venison.
But now, my Faustus, that thou may'st perceive
What Rome contains for to delight thine eyes,
Know that this city stands upon seven hills
That underprop the groundwork of the same.
35   Just through the midst runs flowing Tiber's stream,
With winding banks that cut it in two parts,
Over the which four stately bridges lean,
That make safe passage to each part of Rome.
Upon the bridge called Ponto Angelo
40   Erected is a castle passing strong,
Where thou shalt see such store of ordinance
As that the double cannons forged of brass
Do match the number of the days contained
Within the compass of one complete year.
45   Beside the gates and high pyramides,
That Julius Caesar brought from Africa.[3]
FAUSTUS Now by the kingdoms of infernal rule,
Of Styx, or Acheron, and the fiery lake

---

2. Faustus' fiery chariot cut through rocks to go from Naples, where the Roman poet Publius Virgilius Maro, or Virgil, is buried, to Padua and Venice.

3. The Emperor Caligula brought an obelisk back from Heliopolis in Egypt, which stands before St. Peter's in Rome.

Of ever-burning Phlegethon,° I swear   *rivers in hell*
50   That I do long to see the monuments
        And situation of bright splendent Rome.
        Come, therefore, let's away.
MEPHOSTOPHILIS Now, stay, my Faustus. I know you'd see the Pope,
        And take some part of holy Peter's feast,
55   The which in state and high solemnity
        This day is held through Rome and Italy
        In honor of the Pope's triumphant victory.
FAUSTUS Sweet Mephostophilis, thou pleasest me.
        Whilst I am here on earth let me be cloyed
60   With all things that delight the heart of man.
        My four and twenty years of liberty
        I'll spend in pleasure and in dalliance,
        That Faustus' name, whilst this bright frame doth stand,
        May be admired through the furthest land.
MEPHOSTOPHILIS 'Tis well said, Faustus. Come then, stand by me,
        And thou shalt see them come immediately.
FAUSTUS Nay stay, my gentle Mephostophilis,
        And grant me my request, and then I go.
        Thou know'st within the compass of eight days
70   We viewed the face of heaven, of earth and hell.
        So high our dragons soared into the air,
        That looking down, the earth appeared to me
        No bigger than my hand in quantity.
        There did we view the kingdoms of the world,
75   And what might please mine eye, I there beheld.
        Then in this show let me an actor be,
        That this proud Pope may Faustus' cunning see.
MEPHOSTOPHILIS Let it be so, my Faustus, but first stay
        And view their triumphs° as they pass this way.   *procession*
80   And then devise what best contents thy mind
        By cunning in thine art to cross the Pope,
        Or dash the pride of this solemnity,
        To make his monks and abbots stand like apes,
        And point like antics° at his triple crown,   *clowns*
85   To beat the beads about the friars' pates,
        Or clap huge horns upon the cardinals' heads,
        Or any villainy thou canst devise,
        And I'll perform it, Faustus. Hark, they come!
        This day shall make thee be admired in Rome.
        [*Enter the Cardinals and Bishops, some bearing crosiers, some the pillars, Monks and
        Friars, singing their procession. Then the Pope and Raymond, King of Hungary with
        Bruno⁴ led in chains.*]
POPE   Cast down our footstool.
RAYMOND Saxon Bruno, stoop,

---

4. This character has no apparent historical counterpart or model.

Whilst on thy back his Holiness ascends
Saint Peter's chair and state pontifical.
BRUNO Proud Lucifer, that state belongs to me:
95   But thus I fall to Peter, not to thee.
POPE To me and Peter shalt thou grovelling lie,
And crouch before the papal dignity.
Sounds trumpets then, for thus Saint Peter's heir
From Bruno's back ascends Saint Peter's chair.
[*A flourish while he ascends.*]
100   Thus, as the gods creep on with feet of wool
Long ere with iron hands they punish men,
So shall our sleeping vengeance now arise,
And smite with death thy hated enterprise.
Lord cardinals of France and Padua,
105   Go forthwith to our holy consistory,
And read amongst the statutes decretal,
What by the holy council held at Trent[5]
The sacred synod hath decreed for them
That doth assume the papal government,
110   Without election and a true consent.
Away, and bring us word with speed!
FIRST CARDINAL We go, my lord.   [*Exeunt Cardinals.*]
POPE   Lord Raymond.
FAUSTUS Go, haste thee, gentle Mephostophilis,
115   Follow the cardinals to the consistory,
And as they turn their superstitious books,
Strike them with sloth and drowsy idleness,
And make them sleep so sound that in their shapes
Thyself and I may parly° with this Pope,   *speak*
120   This proud confronter of the Emperor,[6]
And in despite of all his holiness
Restore this Bruno to his liberty
And bear him to the states of Germany.
MEPHOSTOPHILIS Faustus, I go.
FAUSTUS Dispatch it soon,
The Pope shall curse that Faustus came to Rome.
[*Exeunt Faustus and Mephostophilis.*]
BRUNO Pope Adrian,[7] let me have some right of law:
I was elected by the Emperor.
POPE   We will depose the Emperor for that deed,
130   And curse the people that submit to him.
Both he and thou shalt stand excommunicate,
And interdict from Church's privilege

5. The council of Trent, called to meet the challenges posed by the Protestant Reformation, was held between 1545 and 1563.
6. The Holy Roman Emperor, Charles V, Emperor from 1519.
7. Possibly Marlowe means Hadrian VI (1522–23), although he was Pope before the Council of Trent, after which the action of the play is supposed to have taken place.

And all society of holy men.
He grows too proud in his authority,
135   Lifting his lofty head above the clouds
And like a steeple overpeers the Church.
But we'll pull down his haughty insolence,
And, as Pope Alexander, our progenitor,
Stood on the neck of German Frederick,[8]
140   Adding this golden sentence to our praise,
That Peter's heirs should tread on emperors
And walk upon the dreadful adder's back,
Treading the lion and the dragon down,
And fearless spurn the killing basilisk,[9]
145   So will we quell that haughty schismatic,
And by authority apostolical
Depose him from his regal government.
BRUNO   Pope Julius swore to princely Sigismond[1]
For him and the succeeding popes of Rome,
150   To hold the emperors their lawful lords.
POPE   Pope Julius did abuse the Church's rites,
And therefore none of his decrees can stand.
Is not all power on earth bestowed on us?
And therefore though we would we cannot err.
155   Behold this silver belt, whereto is fixed
Seven golden seals fast sealed with seven seals,
In token of our seven-fold power from heaven,
To bind or loose, lock fast, condemn or judge,
Resign or seal, or what so pleaseth us.
160   Then he and thou, and all the world, shall stoop,
Or be assured of our dreadful curse,
To light as heavy as the pains of hell.
[Enter Faustus and Mephostophilis, like the cardinals.]
MEPHOSTOPHILIS   Now tell me, Faustus, are we not fitted well?
FAUSTUS   Yes, Mephostophilis, and two such cardinals
165   Ne'er served a holy Pope as we shall do.
But whilst they sleep within the consistory,
Let us salute his reverend fatherhood.
RAYMOND   Behold, my lord, the cardinals are returned.
POPE   Welcome, grave fathers, answer presently
170   What have our holy council there decreed
Concerning Bruno and the Emperor,
In quittance of their late conspiracy
Against our state and papal dignity?
FAUSTUS   Most sacred patron of the Church of Rome,
175   By full consent of all the synod
Of priests and prelates, it is thus decreed:

---

8. Pope Alexander III (1159–81) forced Emperor Frederick Barbarossa to acknowledge his authority.
9. A mythical creature whose glance was lethal.

1. It is unclear to whom Marlowe refers; there was no
Pope Julius during the reign of the Emperor Sigismund
(1368–1436).

That Bruno and the German Emperor
Be held as lollards² and bold schismatics
And proud disturbers of the Church's peace.

180 And if that Bruno by his own assent,
Without enforcement of the German peers,
Did seek to wear the triple diadem
And by your death to climb Saint Peter's chair,
The statutes decretal have thus decreed:

185 He shall be straight condemned of heresy
And on a pile of faggots burnt to death.

POPE It is enough. Here, take him to your charge,
And bear him straight to Ponto Angelo,
And in the strongest tower enclose him fast.

190 Tomorrow, sitting in our consistory
With all our college of grave cardinals,
We will determine of his life or death.
Here, take his triple crown along with you,
And leave it in the Church's treasury.

195 Make haste again, my good lord cardinals,
And take our blessing apostolical.

MEPHOSTOPHILIS So, so, was never devil thus blessed before.

FAUSTUS Away, sweet Mephostophilis, be gone:
The cardinals will be plagued for this anon.

[Exeunt Faustus and Mephostophilis.]

POPE Go presently, and bring a banquet forth
That we may solemnize Saint Peter's feast,
And with Lord Raymond, King of Hungary,
Drink to our late and happy victory.   [Exeunt.]

Scene Three

[A sennet³ while the banquet is brought in, and then enter Faustus and Mephostophilis
in their own shapes.]

MEPHOSTOPHILIS Now, Faustus, come prepare thyself for mirth.
The sleepy cardinals are hard at hand
To censure Bruno that is posted° hence,   ridden
And on a proud paced steed as swift as thought

5 Flies o'er the Alps to fruitful Germany,
There to salute the woeful Emperor.

FAUSTUS The Pope will curse them for their sloth today,
That slept both Bruno and his crown away.
But now, that Faustus may delight his mind,

10 And by their folly make some merriment,
Sweet Mephostophilis, so charm me here,
That I may walk invisible to all,
And do what e'er I please unseen of any.

MEPHOSTOPHILIS Faustus, thou shalt. Then kneel down presently:

2. Heretics; in England, followers of John Wycliffe   3. A trumpet call.
(1328?–1384).

15   Whilst on thy head I lay my hand,
         And charm thee with this magic wand.
         First wear this girdle, then appear
         Invisible to all are here.
         The planets seven, the gloomy air,
20   Hell and the Furies'[4] forked hair,
         Pluto's[5] blue fire and Hecate's[6] tree,
         With magic spells so compass thee,
         That no eye may thy body see.
         So, Faustus, now for all their holiness,
25   Do what thou wilt, thou shalt not be discerned.
FAUSTUS Thanks, Mephostophilis. Now, friars, take heed
         Lest Faustus make your shaven crowns to bleed.
MEPHOSTOPHILIS Faustus, no more. See where the cardinals come.
      [*Enter the Pope and all the Lords. Enter the Cardinals with a book.*]
POPE   Welcome, lord cardinals. Come, sit down.
30   Lord Raymond, take your seat. Friars, attend
         And see that all things be in readiness
         As best beseems this solemn festival.
FIRST CARDINAL First, may it please your sacred Holiness,
         To view the sentence of the reverend synod
35   Concerning Bruno and the Emperor?
POPE   What needs this question? Did I not tell you
         Tomorrow we would sit i'the consistory
         And there determine of his punishment?
         You brought us word even now, it was decreed
40   That Bruno and the cursed Emperor
         Were by the holy Council both condemned
         For loathed lollards and base schismatics.
         Then wherefore would you have me view that book?
FIRST CARDINAL Your Grace mistakes. You gave us no such charge.
RAYMOND Deny it not. We all are witnesses
         That Bruno here was late delivered you,
         With his rich triple crown to be reserved
         And put into the Church's treasury.
BOTH CARDINALS By holy Paul, we saw them not.
POPE   By Peter, you shall die
         Unless you bring them forth immediately.
         Hale° them to prison, lade their limbs with gyves!°   *take/chains*
         False prelates, for this hateful treachery,
         Cursed be your souls to hellish misery.
FAUSTUS So, they are safe. Now Faustus, to the feast.
         The Pope had never such a frolic guest.
POPE   Lord Archbishop of Rheims, sit down with us.
BISHOP I thank your Holiness.
FAUSTUS Fall to, and the devil choke you an you spare.

4. Greek divinities instigating revenge.
5. The Roman god of the underworld.

6. Goddess representing death and the dark side of the moon.

POPE   Who's that spoke? Friars, look about.

FRIARS Here's nobody, if it like your Holiness.

POPE   Lord Raymond, pray fall to. I am beholding
            To the Bishop of Milan for this so rare a present.

FAUSTUS I thank you, sir. [*Snatches it.*]

POPE   How now? Who snatched the meat from me?
            Villains, why speak you not?
            My good Lord Archbishop, here's a most dainty dish
            Was sent me from a cardinal in France.

FAUSTUS I'll have that too. [*Snatches it.*]

POPE   What lollards do attend our Holiness
            That we receive such great indignity? Fetch me some wine.

FAUSTUS Ay, pray do, for Faustus is a-dry.

POPE   Lord Raymond, I drink unto your grace.

FAUSTUS I pledge your grace. [*Snatches the glass.*]

POPE   My wine gone too? Ye lubbers,° look about   *louts*
            And find the man that doth this villainy,
            Or by our sanctitude you all shall die.
            I pray, my lords, have patience at this
            Troublesome banquet.

BISHOP Please it your Holiness, I think it be some ghost crept out of Purgatory, and
            now is come unto your Holiness for his pardon.

POPE   It may be so.
            Go, then, command our priests to sing a dirge
            To lay the fury of this same troublesome ghost.
            [*The Pope crosseth himself.*]

FAUSTUS How now? Must every bit be spiced with a cross?
            Nay then, take that.
            [*Faustus hits him a box of the ear.*]

POPE   Oh, I am slain! Help me, my lords.
            Oh come, and help to bear my body hence.
            Damned be this soul for ever for this deed!
                                                      [*Exeunt the Pope and his train.*]

MEPHOSTOPHILIS Now, Faustus, what will you do now?
            For I can tell you, you'll be cursed with bell, book and candle.

FAUSTUS Bell, book and candle, candle, book and bell,
            Forward and backward, to curse Faustus to hell.
            [*Enter the Friars with bell, book and candle, for the dirge.*]

FIRST FRIAR Come, brethren, let's about our business with good devotion.

95   [*sing*] Cursed be he that stole his Holiness' meat from the table. *Maledicat
            dominus.*[7]
            Cursed be he that took his Holiness a blow on the face. *Maledicat dominus.*
            Cursed be he that struck Friar Sandelo a blow on the pate. *Maledicat dominus.*
100   Cursed be he that disturbeth our holy dirge. *Maledicat dominus.*
            Cursed be he that took away his Holiness' wine. *Maledicat dominus.*
            Et omnes sancti.[8] Amen.

---

7. May God curse you.   8. And all the saints.

[*Faustus and Mephostophilis beat the Friars, fling fireworks among them and exeunt. Enter Chorus.*]

CHORUS When Faustus had with pleasure ta'en the view
        Of rarest things and royal courts of kings,
105   He stayed his course and so returned home;
        Where such as bear his absence but with grief,
        I mean his friends and nearest companions,
        Did gratulate his safety with kind words,
        And in their conference of what befell,
110   Touching his journey through the world and air,
        They put forth questions of astrology,
        Which Faustus answered with such learned skill
        As they admired and wondered at his wit.
        Now is his fame spread forth in every land;
115   Amongst the rest, the Emperor is one,
        Carolus the Fifth, at whose palace now
        Faustus is feasted 'mongst his noblemen.
        What there he did in trial of his art,
        I leave untold: your eyes shall see performed.

Scene Four

[*Enter Robin the ostler[9] with a book in his hand.*]

ROBIN Oh this is admirable! Here I ha' stol'n one of Doctor Faustus' conjuring books, and, i'faith, I mean to search some circles for my own use. Now will I make all the maidens in our parish dance at my pleasure stark naked before me. And so by that means I shall see more than ere I felt or saw yet.

[*Enter Rafe calling Robin.*]

RAFE Robin, prithee come away! There's a gentleman tarries to have his horse, and he would have his things rubbed and made clean. He keeps such a chafing with my mistress about it, and she has sent me to look thee out. Prithee, come away!

ROBIN Keep out, keep out, or else you are blown up. You are dismembered, Rafe,
10   keep out, for I am about a roaring piece of work.

RAFE Come, what dost thou with that same book? Thou canst not read?

ROBIN Yes, my master and mistress shall find that I can read, he for his forehead, she for her private study. She's born to bear with me, or else my art fails.

RAFE Why, Robin, what book is that?

ROBIN What book? Why, the most intolerable book for conjuring that ere was invented by any brimstone devil.

RAFE Canst thou conjure with it?

ROBIN I can do all these things easily with it. First, I can make thee drunk with ippocras at any tavern in Europe, for nothing. That's one of my conjuring works!

RAFE Our master parson says that's nothing.

ROBIN True, Rafe. And more, Rafe, if thou hast any mind to Nan Spit, our kitchen maid, then turn her and wind her to thy own use as often as thou wilt, and at midnight.

---

9. Stableman.

RAFE   Oh brave Robin! Shall I have Nan Spit, and to mine own use? On that con-
25   dition, I'll feed thy devil with horsebread as long as he lives, of free cost.
ROBIN   No more, sweet Rafe. Let's go and make clean our boots which lie foul upon
             our hands, and then to our conjuring, in the devil's name.
        [*Exeunt. Re-enter Robin and Rafe with a silver goblet.*]
ROBIN   Come, Rafe, did I not tell thee we were for ever made by this Doctor Faus-
             tus' book? *Ecce signum,*[1] here's a simple purchase for horse-keepers. Our
30   horses shall eat no hay as long as this lasts.
        [*Enter the Vintner.*]
RAFE   But, Robin, here comes the vintner.
ROBIN   Hush, I'll gull[2] him supernaturally. Drawer, I hope all is paid. God be with
             you. Come, Rafe.
VINTNER Soft, sir, a word with you. I must yet have a goblet paid from you ere you go.
ROBIN   I, a goblet? Rafe, I a goblet? I scorn you, and you are but a etc. I, a goblet?
             Search me.
VINTNER I mean so, sir, with your favor.
ROBIN   How say you now?
VINTNER I must say somewhat to your fellow—you, sir.
RAFE   Me, sir? Me, sir? Search your fill. Now, sir, you may be ashamed to burden
             honest men with a matter of truth.
VINTNER Well, t'one of you hath this goblet about you.
ROBIN   You lie, drawer. 'Tis afore me! Sirrah, you! I'll teach ye to impeach honest
             men. Stand by, I'll scour you for a goblet. Stand aside, you were best. I
45   charge you in the name of Belzebub. Look to the goblet, Rafe.
VINTNER What mean you, sirrah?
ROBIN   I'll tell you what I mean. [*He reads*] *Sanctobolorum Periphrasticon.*[3] Nay, I'll
             tickle you, vintner—look to the goblet, Rafe. *Polypragmos Belseborams fra-
             manto pacostiphos tostu Mephostophilis, Etc.*
        [*Enter Mephostophilis, who sets squibs*[4] *at their backs. They run about.*]
VINTNER *O nomine Domine*[5] what mean'st thou, Robin? Thou hast no goblet.
RAFE   *Peccatum peccatorum*[6] here's thy goblet, good vintner.
ROBIN   *Misericordia pro nobis*[7] what shall I do? Good devil, forgive me now and I'll
             never rob thy library more.
        [*Enter to them Mephostophilis.*]
MEPHOSTOPHILIS Vainish villains! Th'one like an ape, another like a bear, the
55   third an ass, for doing this enterprise.
             Monarch of hell, under whose black survey
             Great potentates do kneel with awful fear,
             Upon whose altars thousand souls do lie,
             How am I vexed with these villains' charms?
60   From Constantinople am I hither come,
             Only for pleasure of these damned slaves.
ROBIN   How, from Constantinople? You have had a great journey. Will you take six
             pence in your purse to pay for your supper, and be gone?

---

1. "Behold, the sign"; i.e., of the truth.   5. In God's name.
2. Trick.   6. Sin of sins.
3. Gibberish.   7. Mercy on us.
4. Firecrackers.

MEPHOSTOPHILIS Well, villains, for your presumption I transform thee into an
65   ape and thee into a dog, and so be gone.   [*Exit.*]
ROBIN How, into an ape? That's brave! I'll have fine sport with the boys. I'll get
       nuts and apples enow.
RAFE And I must be a dog!
ROBIN I'faith thy head will never be out of the potage pot.   [*Exeunt.*]

Act 4

Scene One

[*The Emperor's Court. Enter Martino and Frederick at several doors.*]
MARTINO What ho, officers, gentlemen!
       Hie to the presence to attend the Emperor.
       Good Frederick, see the rooms be voided straight.
       His Majesty is coming to the hall;
5   Go back, and see the state in readiness.
FREDERICK But where is Bruno, our elected Pope,
       That on a fury's back came post from Rome?
       Will not his grace consort° the Emperor?   *greet*
MARTINO Oh yes, and with him comes the German conjuror,
10   The learned Faustus, fame of Wittenberg,
       The wonder of the world for magic art.
       And he intends to show great Carolus
       The race of all his stout progenitors,
       And bring in presence of his Majesty
15   The royal shapes and warlike semblances
       Of Alexander and his beauteous paramour.[1]
FREDERICK Where is Benvolio?
MARTINO Fast asleep, I warrant you.
       He took his rouse with stoups° of Rhenish wine   *large cups*
20   So kindly yesternight to Bruno's health,
       That all this day the sluggard keeps his bed.
FREDERICK See, see, his window's ope. We'll call to him.
MARTINO What ho, Benvolio?
       [*Enter Benvolio above at a window in his nightcap, buttoning.*]
BENVOLIO What a devil ail you two?
MARTINO Speak softly, sir, lest the devil hear you;
       For Faustus at the court is late arrived,
       And at his heels a thousand furies wait
       To accomplish whatsoever the Doctor please.
BENVOLIO What of this?
MARTINO Come, leave thy chamber first, and thou shalt see
       This conjuror perform such rare exploits
       Before the Pope and royal Emperor
       As never yet was seen in Germany.
BENVOLIO Has not the Pope enough of conjuring yet?
35   He was upon the devil's back late enough,

---

1. Alexander the Great and his wife, Roxana.

And if he be so far in love with him,
I would he would post with him to Rome again.

FREDERICK Speak, wilt thou come and see this sport?

BENVOLIO Not I.

MARTINO Wilt thou stand in thy window and see it, then?

BENVOLIO Ay, and I fall not asleep i' the meantime.

MARTINO The Emperor is at hand, who comes to see
What wonders by black spells may compassed be.

BENVOLIO Well, go you, attend the Emperor. I am content for this once to thrust
45   my head out at a window, for they say if a man be drunk over night the devil cannot hurt him in the morning. If that be true, I have a charm in my
head shall control him as well as the conjuror, I warrant you.

[Exeunt Martino and Frederick.]

Scene Two

[Sennet. Charles, the German Emperor, Bruno, Saxony, Faustus, Mephostophilis,
Frederick, Martino, and Attendants. Benvolio still at the window.]

EMPEROR Wonder of men, renowned magician,
Thrice-learned Faustus, welcome to our court.
This deed of thine, in setting Bruno free
From his and our professed enemy,
5   Shall add more excellence unto thine art,
Than if by powerful necromantic spells
Thou couldst command the world's obedience.
For ever be beloved of Carolus;
And if this Bruno thou hast late redeemed,
10   In peace possess the triple diadem
And sit in Peter's chair, despite of chance,
Thou shalt be famous through all Italy,
And honored of the German Emperor.

FAUSTUS These gracious words, most royal Carolus,
15   Shall make poor Faustus to his utmost power
Both love and serve the German Emperor,
And lay his life at holy Bruno's feet.
For proof whereof, if so your Grace be pleased,
The Doctor stands prepared, by power of art,
20   To cast his magic charms that shall pierce through
The ebon° gates of ever-burning hell,   *ebony*
And hale the stubborn furies from their caves,
To compass whatsoe'er your Grace commands.

BENVOLIO *[Aside]* Blood, he speaks terribly! But for all that, I do not greatly
25   believe him. He looks as like a conjuror as the Pope to a coster-monger.[2]

EMPEROR Then, Faustus, as thou late didst promise us,
We would behold that famous conqueror,
Great Alexander, and his paramour,
In their true shapes and state majestical,

2. Vegetable seller.

30   That we may wonder at their excellence.

FAUSTUS Your Majesty shall see them presently.
       Mephostophilis, away!
       And with a solemn noise of trumpets' sound,
       Present before this royal Emperor
35   Great Alexander and his beauteous paramour.

MEPHOSTOPHILIS Faustus, I will.

BENVOLIO Well, Master Doctor, an your devils come not away quickly, you shall
       have me asleep presently. Zounds, I could eat myself for anger, to think I
       have been such an ass all this while, to stand gaping after the devil's gover-
40   nor, and can see nothing.

FAUSTUS I'll make you feel something anon, if my art fail me not.
       My lord, I must forwarn your Majesty
       That when my spirits present the royal shapes
       Of Alexander and his paramour,
45   Your Grace demand no questions of the King,
       But in dumb silence let them come and go.

EMPEROR Be it as Faustus please, we are content.

BENVOLIO Ay, ay, and I am content too. And thou bring Alexander and his para-
       mour before the Emperor, I'll be Actaeon[3] and turn myself to a stag.

FAUSTUS And I'll play Diana, and send you the horns presently.
       [Sennet. Enter at one the Emperor Alexander, at the other Darius. They meet. Darius
       is thrown down; Alexander kills him, takes off his crown, and, offering to go out, his
       Paramour meets him. He embraceth her and sets Darius' crown upon her head, and
       coming back, both salute the Emperor, who, leaving his state, offers to embrace them,
       which Faustus seeing, suddenly stays him. Then trumpets cease and music sounds.]
       My gracious lord, you do forget yourself.
       These are but shadows, not substantial.

EMPEROR Oh pardon me, my thoughts are so ravished
       With sight of this renowned Emperor,
55   That in mine arms I would have compassed him.
       But, Faustus, since I may not speak to them,
       To satisfy my longing thoughts at full,
       Let me this tell thee: I have heard it said
       That this fair lady, whilst she lived on earth,
60   Had on her neck a little wart or mole.
       How may I prove that saying to be true?

FAUSTUS Your Majesty may boldly go and see.

EMPEROR Faustus, I see it plain,
       And in this sight thou better pleasest me
65   Than if I gained another monarchy.

FAUSTUS Away, be gone.   [Exit Show.]
       See, see, my gracious lord, what strange beast is yon, that
            thrusts his head out at window?

EMPEROR Oh, wondrous sight! See, Duke of Saxony,

---

3. Mythical hunter, changed by the goddess Diana into a stag because he had seen her naked as she bathed after a hunt;
he was then devoured by his own dogs.

70   Two spreading horns most strangely fastened
       Upon the head of young Benvolio!⁴

SAXONY What, is he asleep? Or dead?

FAUSTUS He sleeps, my lord: but dreams not of his horns.

EMPEROR This sport is excellent. We'll call and wake him.

75   What ho, Benvolio!

BENVOLIO A plague upon you! Let me sleep awhile.

EMPEROR I blame thee not to sleep much, having such a head of thine own.

SAXONY Look up, Benvolio, 'tis the Emperor calls.

BENVOLIO The Emperor? Where? Oh, zounds, my head!

EMPEROR Nay, and thy horns hold, 'tis no matter for thy head, for that's armed
       sufficiently.

FAUSTUS Why, how now, Sir Knight? What, hanged by the horns? This most
       horrible! Fie, fie! Pull in your head for shame; let not all the world wonder
       at you.

BENVOLIO Zounds, Doctor, is this your villainy?

FAUSTUS Oh, say not so, sir. The Doctor has no skill,
       No art, no cunning, to present these lords
       Or bring before this royal Emperor
       The mighty monarch, warlike Alexander.

90   If Faustus do it, you are straight resolved
       In bold Actaeon's shape to turn a stag.
       And therefore, my lord, so please your majesty,
       I'll raise a kennel of hounds shall hunt him so
       As all his footmanship shall scarce prevail

95   To keep his carcass from their bloody fangs.
       Ho, Belimote, Argiron, Asterote!

BENVOLIO Hold, hold! Zounds, he'll raise up a kennel of devils, I think anon.
       Good my lord, entreat for me. 'Sblood, I am never never able to endure
       these torments.

EMPEROR Then, good Master Doctor,
       Let me entreat you to remove his horns:
       He has done penance now sufficiently.

FAUSTUS My gracious lord, not so much for injury done to me, as to delight your
       majesty with some mirth, hath Faustus justly requited this injurious knight;

105   which being all I desire, I am content to remove his horns. Mephostophilis,
       transform him. And hereafter, sir, look you speak well of scholars.

BENVOLIO [Aside] Speak well of ye? 'Sblood, and scholars be such cuckold-makers
       to clap horns of honest men's heads o' this order, I'll ne'er trust smooth faces
       and small ruffs more. But an I be not revenged for this, would I might be

110   turned to a gaping oyster and drink nothing but salt water.

EMPEROR Come, Faustus, while the Emperor lives,
       In recompense of this thy high desert,°   merit
       Thou shalt command the state of Germany,
       And live beloved of mighty Carolus.   [Exeunt omnes.]

---

4. To be "horned" was to be cuckolded. Benvolio, who has insulted scholars, is given horns by Faustus, who takes a scholar's revenge. The insult is introduced as a reflection on the myth of Diana and Actaeon.

Scene Three

[*Enter Benvolio, Martino, Frederick and Soldiers.*]

MARTINO Nay, sweet Benvolio, let us sway thy thoughts
  From this attempt against the conjuror.
BENVOLIO Away, you love me not, to urge me thus.
  Shall I let slip° so great an injury,   *overlook*
5 When every servile groom jests at my wrongs,
  And in their rustic gambols proudly say
  Benvolio's head was graced with horns today?
  Oh, may these eyelids never close again
  Till with my sword I have that conjuror slain.
10 If you will aid me in this enterprise,
  Then draw your weapons and be resolute.
  If not, depart. Here will Benvolio die,
  But Faustus' death shall quit my infamy.
FREDERICK Nay, we will stay with thee, betide what may,
15 And kill that Doctor if he come this way.
BENVOLIO Then, gentle Frederick, hie° thee to the grove,   *take*
  And place our servants and our followers
  Close in an ambush there behind the trees.
  By this I know the conjuror is near:
20 I saw him kneel and kiss the Emperor's hand,
  And take his leave, laden with rich rewards.
  Then, soldiers, boldly fight. If Faustus die,
  Take you the wealth, leave us the victory.
FREDERICK Come, soldiers, follow me unto the grove.
25 Who kills him shall have gold and endless love.
             [*Exit Frederick with the Soldiers.*]
BENVOLIO My head is lighter than it was by th'horns,
  But yet my heart more ponderous than my head,
  And pants until I see that conjuror dead.
MARTINO Where shall we place ourselves, Benvolio?
BENVOLIO Here will we stay to bide the first assault.
  Oh, were that damned hell-hound but in place,
  Thou soon shouldst see me quit my foul disgrace.
  [*Enter Frederick.*]
FREDERICK Close, close! The conjuror is at hand,
  And all alone comes walking in his gown.
35 Be ready then, and strike the peasant down.
BENVOLIO Mine be that honor, then. Now sword, strike home.
  For horns he gave, I'll have his head anon.
  [*Enter Faustus with a false head.*]
MARTINO See, see, he comes.
BENVOLIO No words. This blow ends all.
40 Hell take his soul; his body thus must fall.   [*Attacks Faustus.*]
FAUSTUS Oh!
FREDERICK Groan you, Master Doctor?
BENVOLIO Break may his heart with groans! Dear Frederick, see,
  Thus will I end his griefs immediately.   [*Cuts off his head.*]

MARTINO Strike with a willing hand: his head is off.

BENVOLIO The devil's dead! The Furies now may laugh.

FREDERICK Was this that stern aspect, that awful frown,
    Made the grim monarch of infernal spirits
    Tremble and quake at his commanding charms?

MARTINO Was this that damned head, whose heart conspired
    Benvolio's shame before the Emperor?

BENVOLIO Ay, that's the head, and here the body lies,
    Justly rewarded for his villainies.

FREDERICK Come, let's devise how we may add more shame
55   To the black scandal of his hated name.

BENVOLIO First, on his head, in quittance° of my wrongs,   *payment*
    I'll nail huge forked horns, and let them hang
    Within the window where he yoked° me first,   *overcame*
    That all the world may see my just revenge.

MARTINO What use shall we put his beard to?

BENVOLIO We'll sell it to a chimney-sweeper: it will wear
    out ten birching° brooms, I warrant you.   *birch-twig*

FREDERICK What shall eyes do?

BENVOLIO We'll put out his eyes, and they shall serve for buttons to his lips, to
65   keep his tongue from catching cold.

MARTINO An excellent policy! And now, sirs, having divided him, what shall the
    body do?

    [*Faustus rises.*]

BENVOLIO Zounds, the devil's alive again!

FREDERICK Give him his head, for God's sake!

FAUSTUS Nay, keep it. Faustus will have heads and hands.
    I call your hearts to recompense this deed.
    Knew you not, traitors, I was limited
    For four and twenty years to breathe on earth?
    And had you cut my body with your swords,
75   Or hewed this flesh and bones as small as sand,
    Yet in a minute had my spirit returned,
    And I had breathed a man made free from harm.
    But wherefore do I dally° my revenge?   *delay*
    Asteroth, Belimoth, Mephostophilis!

    [*Enter Mephostophilis and other Devils.*]

80   Go, horse these traitors on your fiery backs,
    And mount aloft with them as high as heaven;
    Thence pitch them headlong to the lowest hell.
    Yet stay, the world shall see their misery,
    And hell shall after plague their treachery.
85   Go, Belimoth, and take this caitiff° hence,   *coward*
    And hurl him in some lake of mud and dirt.
    Take thou this other: drag him through the woods
    Amongst the pricking thorns and sharpest briars,
    Whilst with my gentle Mephostophilis,
90   This traitor flies unto some steepy rock,
    That rolling down may break the villain's bones,

As he intended to dismember me.
Fly hence, dispatch my charge immediately.
FREDERICK Pity us, gentle Faustus! Save our lives!
FAUSTUS Away!
FREDERICK He must needs go that the devil drives.
[*Exeunt Spirits with the Knights. Enter the Ambush Soldiers.*]
FIRST SOLDIER Come, sirs, prepare yourselves in readiness.
Make haste to help these noble gentlemen.
I heard them parley with the conjuror.
SECOND SOLDIER See, where he comes. Dispatch and kill the slave.
FAUSTUS What's here? An ambush to betray my life!
Then Faustus, try thy skill. Base peasants, stand!
For lo, these trees remove at my command,
And stand as bulwarks twixt yourselves and me,
105   To shield me from your hated treachery.
Yet, to encounter this your weak attempt,
Behold an army comes incontinent.°   *rapidly*
[*Faustus strikes the door, and enter a devil playing on a drum; after him another bearing an ensign;⁵ and divers with weapons; Mephostophilis with fireworks. They set upon the soldiers and drive them out.*]

Scene Four
[*Enter at several doors Benvolio, Frederick and Martino, their heads and faces bloody and besmeared with mud and dirt, all having horns on their heads.*]
MARTINO What ho, Benvolio!
BENVOLIO Here! What, Frederick, ho!
FREDERICK Oh help me, gentle friend. Where is Martino?
MARTINO Dear Frederick, here,
5   Half smothered in a lake of mud and dirt,
Through which the Furies dragged me by the heels.
FREDERICK Martino, see Benvolio's horns again!
MARTINO Oh misery! How now, Benvolio?
BENVOLIO Defend me, heaven! Shall I be haunted still?
MARTINO Nay, fear not, man; we have no power to kill.
BENVOLIO My friends transformed thus! Oh hellish spite!
Your heads are all set with horns!
FREDERICK You hit it right:
It is your own you mean. Feel on your head.
BENVOLIO Zounds, horns again!
MARTINO Nay, chafe not, man. We all are sped.°   *done for*
BENVOLIO What devil attends this damned magician,
That, spite of spite, our wrongs are doubled?
FREDERICK What may we do, that we may hide our shames?
BENVOLIO If we should follow him to work revenge,
He'd join long asses' ears to these huge horns,
And make us laughing stocks to all the world.

5. Flag.

MARTINO What shall we then do, dear Benvolio?
BENVOLIO I have a castle joining near these woods,
25   And thither we'll repair and live obscure,
     Till time shall alter these our brutish shapes.
     Sith° black disgrace hath thus eclipsed our fame,   *since*
     We'll rather die with grief, than live with shame.   [*Exeunt omnes.*]

                              Scene Five
          [*Enter Faustus and Mephostophilis.*]
FAUSTUS Now, Mephostophilis, the restless course
     That time doth run with calm and deadly foot,
     Shortening my days and thread of vital life,
     Calls for the payment of my latest years.
5   Therefore, sweet Mephostophilis, let us
     Make haste to Wittenberg.
MEPHOSTOPHILIS What, will you go on horseback, or on foot?
FAUSTUS Nay, till I am past this fair and pleasant green
     I'll walk on foot.
          [*Enter a Horse-Courser.*]⁶
HORSE-COURSER I have been all this day seeking one master Fustian.⁷ Mass, see
     where he is! God save you, Master Doctor.
FAUSTUS What, horse-courser! You are well met.
HORSE-COURSER Do you hear, sir? I have brought you forty dollars for your horse.
FAUSTUS I cannot sell him so. If thou likest him for fifty, take him.
HORSE-COURSER Alas, sir, I have no more. I pray you, speak for me.
MEPHOSTOPHILIS I pray you, let him have him. He is an honest fellow, and he
     has a great charge, neither wife nor child.
FAUSTUS Well, come, give me your money. My boy will deliver him to you. But I
     must tell you one thing before you have him: ride him not into the water at
20   any hand.
HORSE-COURSER Why, sir, will he not drink of all waters?
FAUSTUS Oh yes, he will drink of all waters; but ride him not into the water. Ride
     him over hedge or ditch or where thou wilt, but not into the water.
HORSE-COURSER Well, sir, now I am a made man for ever. I'll not leave my horse
25   for forty. If he had but the quality of hey ding ding, hey ding ding, I'd make
     a brave living on him. He has a buttock as slick as an eel. Well, God bye, sir.
     Your boy will deliver him me. But hark ye sir: if my horse be sick or ill at
     ease, if I bring his water to you, you'll tell me what is?
FAUSTUS Away, you villain! What, dost think I am a horse-doctor?
                                        [*Exit Horse-Courser.*]
30   What art thou, Faustus, but a man condemned to die?
     Thy fatal time doth draw to final end:
     Despair doth drive distrust into my thoughts.
     Confound these passions with a quiet sleep.
     Tush, Christ did call the thief upon the cross;

6. Horse trader.   7. Bombast.

35   Then rest thee, Faustus, quiet in conceit.
    [Sleeps in his chair. Enter Horse-Courser all wet, crying.]
HORSE-COURSER Alas, alas, Doctor Fustian quotha! Mass, Doctor Lopus[8] was
    never such a doctor. Has given me a purgation has purged me of forty dol-
    lars: I shall never see them more. But yet like an ass as I was, I would not be
    ruled by him, for he bade me I should ride him into no water. Now I, think-
40   ing my horse had had some rare quality that he would not have had me
    known of, I, like a venturous youth, rid him into the deep pond at the
    town's end. I was no sooner in the middle of the pond but my horse van-
    ished away, and I sat upon a bottle of hay, never so near drowning in my life.
    But I'll seek out my Doctor and have my forty dollars again, or I'll make it
45   the dearest horse. Oh, yonder is his snipper-snapper. Do you hear? You!
    Hey-pass, where's your master?
MEPHOSTOPHILIS Why, sir, what would you? You cannot speak with him.
HORSE-COURSER But I *will* speak with him.
MEPHOSTOPHILIS Why, he's fast asleep. Come some other time.
HORSE-COURSER I'll speak with him now, or I'll break his glass windows about his ears.
MEPHOSTOPHILIS I tell thee he has not slept this eight nights.
HORSE-COURSER And he have not slept this eight weeks I'll speak with him.
MEPHOSTOPHILIS See where he is fast asleep.
HORSE-COURSER Ay, this is he. God save ye, Master Doctor. Master Doctor!
55   Master Doctor Fustian! Forty dollars, forty dollars for a bottle of hay!
MEPHOSTOPHILIS Why, thou seest he hears thee not.
HORSE-COURSER So, ho, ho! So, ho, ho! *[Hollows in his ear.]*
    No, will you not wake? I'll make you wake e'er I go.
    [He pulls him by the leg, and pulls it away.]
    Alas, I am undone! What shall I do?
FAUSTUS Oh, my leg, my leg! Help, Mephostophilis. Call the officers. My leg, my leg!
MEPHOSTOPHILIS Come, villain, to the Constable.
HORSE-COURSER Oh lord, sir, let me go and I'll give you forty dollars more.
MEPHOSTOPHILIS Where be they?
HORSE-COURSER I have none about me. Come to my hostry and I'll give them you.
MEPHOSTOPHILIS Be gone, quickly!
    [Horse-Courser runs away.]
FAUSTUS What, is he gone? Farewell he. Faustus has his leg again, and the horse-
    courser, I take it, a bottle of hay for his labor. Well, this trick shall cost him
    forty dollars more.
    [Enter Wagner.]
FAUSTUS How now, Wagner, what news with thee?
WAGNER If it please you, the Duke of Vanholt[9] doth earnestly entreat your company,
    and hath sent some of his men to attend you with provision for your journey.
FAUSTUS The Duke of Vanholt's an honorable gentleman, and one to whom I
    must be no niggard[1] of my cunning. Come, away.   *[Exeunt.]*

8. Dr. Lopez, Queen Elizabeth's physician, who was executed in 1594 for alleged complicity in an attempt to
murder the Queen. Marlowe died in 1593, so the reference is not his but one of a later editor.
9. The Duchy of Anholt in Germany.
1. Miser.

Scene Six

[*Enter Clown, Dick, Horse-Courser and a Carter.*]

CARTER Come, my masters, I'll bring you to the best beer in Europe. What ho, hostess. Where be these whores?

[*Enter Hostess.*]

HOSTESS How now, what lack you? What, my old guests, welcome!

CLOWN Sirrah Dick, dost thou know why I stand so mute?

DICK No, Robin, why is't?

CLOWN I am eighteen pence on the score.[2] But say nothing. See if she have forgotten me.

HOSTESS Who's this, that stands so solemnly by himself? What, my old guest?

CLOWN Oh, hostess, how do you? I hope my score stands still.

HOSTESS Ay, there's no doubt of that, for methinks you make no haste to wipe it out.

DICK Why, hostess, I say, fetch us some beer.

HOSTESS You shall presently. Look up into the hall there, ho!   [*Exit.*]

DICK Come, sirs, what shall we do now till mine hostess comes?

CARTER Marry, sir, I'll tell you the bravest tale how a conjuror served me. You
15   know Doctor Faustus?

HORSE-COURSER Ay, a plague take him. Here's some on's have cause to know him. Did he conjure thee too?

CARTER I'll tell you how he served me. As I was going to Wittenberg t'other day, with a load of hay, he met me and asked me what he should give me for as
20   much hay as he could eat. Now, sir, I, thinking that a little would serve his turn, bade him take as much as he would for three-farthings. So he presently gave me my money and fell to eating. And, as I am a cursen man, he never left eating till he had eat up all my load of hay.

ALL Oh monstrous! Eat a whole load of hay?

CLOWN Yes, yes, that may be, for I have heard of one that has eat a load of logs.

HORSE-COURSER Now, sirs, you shall hear how villainously he served me. I went to him yesterday to buy a horse of him, and he would by no means sell him under forty dollars. So, sir, because I knew him to be such a horse as would run over hedge and ditch and never tire, I gave him his money. So when I
30   had my horse, Doctor Fauster bade me ride him night and day and spare him no time. But, quoth he, in any case ride him not into the water. Now, sir, I thinking the horse had some quality that he would not have me know of, what did I but ride him into a great river, and when I came just in the midst, my horse vanished away, and I sat straddling upon a bottle of hay.

ALL Oh brave Doctor!

HORSE-COURSER But you shall hear how bravely I served him for it: I went me home to his house, and there I found him asleep. I kept a-hallowing and whooping in his ears, but all could not wake him. I, seeing that, took him by the leg and never rested pulling, till I had pulled me his leg quite off, and
40   now 'tis at home in mine hostry.

CLOWN And has the Doctor but one leg, then? That's excellent, for one of his devils turned me into the likeness of an ape's face.

CARTER Some more drink, hostess.

2. Eighteen pence in debt.

CLOWN Hark you, we'll into another room and drink a while, and then we'll go seek
45   out the Doctor.   [*Exeunt omnes.*]

Scene Seven

[*Enter the Duke of Vanholt, his Duchess, Faustus and Mephostophilis.*]

DUKE Thanks, Master Doctor, for these pleasant sights. Nor know I how sufficiently to
      recompense your great deserts in erecting that enchanted castle in the air, the
      sight whereof so delighted me, as nothing in the world could please me more.

FAUSTUS I do think myself, my good lord, highly recompensed in that it pleaseth
5   your grace to think but well of that which Faustus hath performed. But, gra-
        cious lady, it may be that you have taken no pleasure in those sights. There-
        fore, I pray you tell me, what is the thing you most desire to have. Be it in
        the world, it shall be yours. I have heard that great-bellied women do long
        for things are rare and dainty.

LADY True, Master Doctor, and since I find you so kind, I will make known unto
      you what my heart desires to have; and were it now summer, as it is Janu-
      ary, a dead time of the winter, I would request no better meat than a dish
      of ripe grapes.

FAUSTUS This is but a small matter. Go, Mephostophilis, away.

                                                            [*Exit Mephostophilis.*]

15   Madame, I will do more than this for your content.
        [*Enter Mephostophilis again with the grapes.*]
        Here, now taste ye these. They should be good, for they come from a far coun-
        try, I can tell you.

DUKE This makes me wonder more than all the rest, that at this time of the year,
      when every tree is barren of his fruit, from whence you had these ripe grapes.

FAUSTUS Please it your grace, the year is divided into two circles over the whole
        world, so that when it is winter with us, in the contrary circle it is likewise
        summer with them, as in India, Saba and such countries that lie far East,
        where they have fruit twice a year. From whence, by means of a swift spirit
        that I have, I had these grapes brought as you see.

LADY And trust me, they are the sweetest grapes that e'er I tasted.
      [*The Clowns bounce at the gate within.*]

DUKE What rude disturbers have we at the gate?
      Go, pacify their fury. Set it ope,
      And then demand of them what they would have.
      [*They knock again and call out to talk with Faustus.*]

A SERVANT Why, how now, masters? What a coil[3] is there?
30   What is the reason you disturb the Duke?

DICK We have no reason for it, therefore a fig for him.

SERVANT Why, saucy varlets, dare you be so bold?

HORSE-COURSER I hope, sir, we have wit enough to be more bold than welcome.

SERVANT It appears so. Pray be bold elsewhere,
35   And trouble not the Duke.

DUKE   What would they have?

SERVANT They all cry out to speak with Doctor Faustus.

CARTER Ay, and we will speak with him.

---

3. Disturbance.

DUKE   Will you, sir? Commit the rascals.

DICK   Commit with us! He were as good commit with his father as commit with us.

FAUSTUS   I do beseech your grace let them come in.
They are good subject for a merriment.

DUKE   Do as thou wilt, Faustus; I give thee leave.

FAUSTUS   I thank your grace.

[Enter the Clown, Dick, Carter and Horse-Courser.]

45   Why, how now, my good friends?
Faith, you are too outrageous, but come near.
I have procured your pardons. Welcome all.

CLOWN   Nay, sir, we will be welcome for our money, and we will pay for what we
take. What ho! Give's half-a-dozen of beer here, and be hanged.

FAUSTUS   Nay, hark you. Can you tell me where you are?

CARTER   Ay, marry can I. We are under heaven.

SERVANT   Ay, but, sir sauce-box, know you in what place?

HORSE-COURSER   Ay, ay, the house is good enough to drink in. Zounds, fill us
some beer or we'll break all the barrels in the house and dash out all your
55   brains with your bottles.

FAUSTUS   Be not so furious. Come, you shall have beer.
My lord, beseech you give me leave awhile.
I'll gage my credit, 'twill content your Grace.

DUKE   With all my heart, kind Doctor; please thyself.
60   Our servants and our court's at thy command.

FAUSTUS   I humbly thank your Grace. Then fetch some beer.

HORSE-COURSER   Ay, marry. There spake a doctor indeed, and faith, I'll drink a
health to thy wooden leg for that word.

FAUSTUS   My wooden leg? What dost thou mean by that?

CARTER   Ha, ha, ha! Dost thou hear him, Dick? He has forgot his leg.

HORSE-COURSER   Ay, ay, he does not stand much upon that.

FAUSTUS   No, faith. Not much upon a wooden leg.

CARTER   Good lord! That flesh and blood should be so frail with your worship. Do
not you remember a horse-courser you sold a horse to?

FAUSTUS   Yes, I remember I sold one a horse.

CARTER   And do you remember you bid he should not ride into the water?

FAUSTUS   Yes, I do very well remember that.

CARTER   And do you remember nothing of your leg?

FAUSTUS   No, in good sooth.

CARTER   Then I pray remember your courtesy.[4]

FAUSTUS   I thank you, sir.

CARTER   'Tis not so much worth. I pray you, tell me one thing.

FAUSTUS   What's that?

CARTER   Be both your legs bedfellows every night together?

FAUSTUS   Wouldst thou make a colossus[5] of me, that thou askest me such questions?

CARTER   No, truly, sir. I would make nothing of you, but I would fain know that.

[Enter Hostess with drink.]

FAUSTUS   Then I assure thee certainly they are.

CARTER   I thank you, I am fully satisfied.

FAUSTUS   But wherefore dost thou ask?

CARTER For nothing, sir: but methinks you should have a wooden bedfellow of one of 'em.

HORSE-COURSER Why, do you hear, sir? Did not I pull off one of your legs when you were asleep?

FAUSTUS But I have it again now I am awake. Look you here, sir.

ALL   Oh horrible! Had the Doctor three legs?

CARTER Do you remember, sir, how you cozened[6] me and eat up my load of—

[Faustus charms him dumb.]

DICK   Do you remember how you made me wear an ape's—

HORSE-COURSER You whoreson conjuring scab, do you remember how you cozened me with a ho—

CLOWN Ha'you forgotten me? You think to carry it away with your hey-pass and repass. Do you remember the dog's fa—

[Faustus has charmed each dumb in turn; exeunt Clowns.]

HOSTESS Who pays for the ale? Hear you, Master Doctor, now you have sent away my guests, I pray who shall pay me for my a—?   [Exit Hostess.]

LADY   My lord,
100   We are much beholding to this learned man.

DUKE   So are we, madam, which we will recompense
       With all the love and kindness that we may.
       His artful sport drives all sad thoughts away.   [Exeunt.]

Act 5

Scene One

[Thunder and lightning. Enter Devils with covered dishes. Mephostophilis leads them into Faustus' study. Then enter Wagner.]

WAGNER I think my master means to die shortly.
       He hath made his will, and given me his wealth,
       His house, his goods, and store of golden plate,
       Besides two thousand ducats ready coined.
5   And yet methinks, if that death were near,
       He would not banquet and carouse and swill
       Amongst the students, as even now he doth,
       Who are at supper with such belly-cheer
       As Wagner ne'er beheld in all his life.
10   See where they come; belike the feast is ended.   [Exit.]

[Enter Faustus, Mephostophilis and two or three Scholars.]

FIRST SCHOLAR Master Doctor Faustus, since our conference about fair ladies, which was the beautifullest in all the world, we have determined with ourselves that Helen of Greece[1] was the admirablest lady that ever lived. Therefore Master Doctor, if you will do us so much favor, as to let us see that
15   peerless dame of Greece, whom all the world admires for majesty, we should think ourselves much beholding unto you.

FAUSTUS Gentlemen, for that I know your friendship is unfeigned,
       It is not Faustus' custom to deny
       The just request of those that wish him well.
20   You shall behold that peerless dame of Greece,

6. Tricked.
1. The mythical queen of Menelaus, King of Sparta, who

was abducted by Paris, son of King Priam of Troy. The action began the Trojan War.

No otherwise for pomp of majesty,
Than when Sir Paris crossed the seas with her,
And brought the spoils to rich Dardania.°   *Troy*
Be silent then, for danger is in words.
[*Music sounds. Mephostophilis brings in Helen; she passeth over the stage.*]

SECOND SCHOLAR Was this fair Helen, whose admired worth
    Made Greece with ten years wars afflict poor Troy?

THIRD SCHOLAR Too simple is my wit to tell her worth
    Whom all the world admires for majesty.

FIRST SCHOLAR Now we have seen the pride of nature's work,
30   We'll take our leaves, and for this blessed sight
    Happy and blest be Faustus evermore.
    [*Enter an Old Man.*]

FAUSTUS Gentlemen, farewell: the same wish I to you.

                                  [*Exeunt Scholars.*]

OLD MAN Oh gentle Faustus, leave this damned art,
    This magic, that will charm thy soul to hell,
35   And quite bereave thee of salvation.
    Though thou hast now offended like a man,
    Do not persever in it like a devil.
    Yet, yet, thou hast an amiable° soul,   *lovable*
    If sin by custom grow not into nature:
40   Then, Faustus, will repentance come too late,
    Then thou art banished from the sight of heaven;
    No mortal can express the pains of hell.
    It may be this my exhortation
    Seems harsh and all unpleasant; let it not,
45   For, gentle son, I speak it not in wrath,
    Or envy of thee, but in tender love,
    And pity of thy future misery.
    And so have hope, that this my kind rebuke,
    Checking thy body, may amend thy soul.

FAUSTUS Where art thou, Faustus? Wretch, what hast thou done?
    Damned art thou, Faustus, damned: despair and die.
    Hell claims his right, and with a roaring voice
    Says "Faustus, come, thine hour is almost come"
    [*Mephostophilis gives him a dagger.*]
    And Faustus now will come to do thee right.

OLD MAN Oh stay, good Faustus, stay thy desperate steps.
    I see an angel hover o'er thy head,
    And with a vial full of precious grace,
    Offers to pour the same into thy soul.
    Then call for mercy and avoid despair.

FAUSTUS Ah my sweet friend, I feel thy words
    To comfort my distressed soul.
    Leave me awhile to ponder on my sins.

OLD MAN I leave thee, but with grief of heart,
    Fearing the ruin of thy hopeless soul.   [*Exit.*]

FAUSTUS Accursed Faustus, wretch, what hast thou done?
    I do repent, and yet I do despair.

Hell strives with grace for conquest in my breast.
What shall I do to shun the snares of death?

MEPHOSTOPHILIS Thou traitor, Faustus, I arrest thy soul
70   For disobedience to my sovereign lord.
Revolt,[2] or I'll in piecemeal tear thy flesh.

FAUSTUS I do repent I e'er offended him.
Sweet Mephostophilis, entreat thy lord
To pardon my unjust presumption,
75   And with my blood again I will confirm
The former vow I made to Lucifer.

MEPHOSTOPHILIS Do it then, Faustus, with unfeigned heart,
Lest greater dangers do attend thy drift.

FAUSTUS Torment, sweet friend, that base and crooked age
80   That durst dissuade me from thy Lucifer,
With greatest torment that our hell affords.

MEPHOSTOPHILIS His faith is great: I cannot touch his soul.
But what I may afflict his body with
I will attempt, which is but little worth.

FAUSTUS One thing, good servant, let me crave of thee,
To glut the longing of my heart's desire,
That I may have unto my paramour
That heavenly Helen which I saw of late,
Whose sweet embraces may extinguish clear
90   Those thoughts that do dissuade me from my vow,
And keep my vow I made to Lucifer.

MEPHOSTOPHILIS This, or what else my Faustus shall desire,
Shall be performed in twinkling of an eye.

[Enter Helen again, passing over between two Cupids.]

FAUSTUS Was this the face that launched a thousand ships,
95   And burnt the topless towers of Ilium?
Sweet Helen, make me immortal with a kiss.
Her lips suck forth my soul: see where it flies.
Come, Helen, come, give me my soul again.
Here will I dwell, for heaven is in those lips,
100   And all is dross that is not Helena.

[Enter Old Man.]

I will be Paris,[3] and for love of thee
Instead of Troy shall Wittenberg be sacked,
And I will combat with weak Menelaus,
And wear thy colors on my plumed crest.
105   Yea, I will wound Achilles in the heel,
And then return to Helen for a kiss.
Oh, thou art fairer than the evening's air,
Clad in the beauty of a thousand stars.
Brighter art thou than flaming Jupiter,
110   When he appeared to hapless Semele:[4]

2. I.e., return to the terms of your bargain with the devil.
3. Faustus imagines he will be not only Paris, Helen's lover, but also the victor in combat with her husband,

King Menelaus, as well as with the greatest of the Greek warriors, Achilles.
4. The mortal woman to whom Jupiter appeared as lightening.

More lovely than the monarch of the sky,
In wanton Arethusa's[5] azure arms,
And none but thou shalt be my paramour.   [*Exeunt.*]

OLD MAN Accursed Faustus, miserable man,
115   That from thy soul exclud'st the grace of heaven,
And fliest the throne of his tribunal seat.

[*Enter the Devils.*]

Satan begins to sift° me with his pride,   scrutinize
As in this furnace God shall try my faith.
My faith, vile hell, shall triumph over thee.
120   Ambitious fiends, see how the heavens smiles
At your repulse, and laughs your state to scorn.
Hence, hell, for hence I fly unto my God.   [*Exeunt.*]

Scene Two

[*Thunder. Enter Lucifer, Belzebub and Mephostophilis.*]

LUCIFER Thus from infernal Dis° do we ascend   hell
To view the subjects of our monarchy,
Those souls which sin seals the black sons of hell,
'Mong which as chief, Faustus, we come to thee,
5   Bringing with us lasting damnation
To wait upon thy soul. The time is come
Which makes it forfeit.

MEPHOSTOPHILIS   And this gloomy night,
Here in this room will wretched Faustus be.

BELZEBUB And here we'll stay,
10   To mark him how he doth demean himself.

MEPHOSTOPHILIS How should he, but in desperate lunacy?
Fond worldling, now his heart blood dries with grief.
His conscience kills it, and his laboring brain
Begets a world of idle fantasies
15   To overreach the devil. But all in vain:
His store of pleasures must be sauced with pain.
He and his servant Wagner are at hand.
Both come from drawing Faustus' latest will.
See where they come.

[*Enter Faustus and Wagner.*]

FAUSTUS Say, Wagner, thou hast perused my will:
How dost thou like it?

WAGNER   Sir, so wondrous well
As in all humble duty I do yield
My life and lasting service for your love.

[*Enter the Scholars.*]

FAUSTUS Gramercies, Wagner. Welcome, gentlemen.

FIRST SCHOLAR Now, worthy Faustus, methinks your looks are changed.

FAUSTUS Oh gentlemen!

SECOND SCHOLAR What ails Faustus?

FAUSTUS Ah, my sweet chamber-fellow, had I lived with thee

---

5. A nymph beloved by the river-god Alpheus; no myth describes her as Jupiter's lover.

Then had I lived still, but now must die eternally.
30   Look, sirs, comes he not? Comes he not?
FIRST SCHOLAR Oh, my dear Faustus, what imports this fear?
SECOND SCHOLAR Is all our pleasure turned to melancholy?
THIRD SCHOLAR He is not well with being oversolitary.
SECOND SCHOLAR If it be so, we'll have physicians, and Faustus shall be cured.
THIRD SCHOLAR 'Tis but a surfeit, sir; fear nothing.
FAUSTUS A surfeit of deadly sin, that hath damned both body and soul.
SECOND SCHOLAR Yet Faustus, look up to heaven, and remember mercy is infinite.
FAUSTUS But Faustus' offence can ne'er be pardoned, The serpent that tempted
        Eve may be saved, but not Faustus. Oh gentlemen, hear with patience and
40   tremble not at my speeches. Though my heart pant and quiver to remember
        that I have been a student here these thirty years, oh would I had never seen
        Wittenberg, never read book. And what wonders I have done all Germany
        can witness, yea all the world, for which Faustus hath lost both Germany
        and the world, yea heaven itself, heaven, the seat of God, the throne of the
45   blessed, the kingdom of joy, and must remain in hell for ever. Hell, oh hell
        for ever. Sweet friends, what shall become of Faustus, being in hell for ever?
SECOND SCHOLAR Yet Faustus, call on God.
FAUSTUS On God, whom Faustus hath abjured? On God, whom Faustus hath blas-
        phemed? Oh my God, I would weep, but the devil draws in my tears. Gush
50   forth blood instead of tears, yea, life and soul. Oh, he stays my tongue. I
        would lift up my hands, but see, they hold them, they hold them.
ALL   Who, Faustus?
FAUSTUS Why, Lucifer and Mephostophilis: Oh gentlemen, I gave them my soul
        for my cunning.
ALL   Oh, God forbid.
FAUSTUS God forbade it indeed, but Faustus hath done it. For vain pleasure of four
        and twenty years hath Faustus lost eternal joy and felicity. I writ them a bill
        with mine own blood, the date is expired: this is the time, and he will fetch me.
FIRST SCHOLAR Why did not Faustus tell us of this before, that divines might
60   have prayed for thee?
FAUSTUS Oft have I thought to have done so, but the devil threatened to tear me
        in pieces if I named God; to fetch me body and soul if I once gave ear to
        divinity, and now 'tis too late. Gentlemen, away, lest you perish with me.
SECOND SCHOLAR Oh what may we do to save Faustus?
FAUSTUS Talk not of me, but save yourselves and depart.
THIRD SCHOLAR God will strengthen me. I will stay with Faustus.
FIRST SCHOLAR Tempt not God, sweet friend, but let us into the next room and
        pray for him.
FAUSTUS Ay, pray for me, pray for me. And what noise soever you hear, come not
70   unto me, for nothing can rescue me.
SECOND SCHOLAR Pray thou, and we will pray, that God may have mercy upon thee.
FAUSTUS Gentlemen, farewell. If I live till morning, I'll visit you. If not, Faustus is
        gone to hell.
ALL   Faustus, farewell.   [Exeunt Scholars.]
MEPHOSTOPHILIS Ay, Faustus, now thou hast no hope of heaven,
        Therefore despair, think only upon hell,
        For that must be thy mansion, there to dwell.
FAUSTUS Oh, thou bewitching fiend, 'twas thy temptation

Hath robbed me of eternal happiness.
MEPHOSTOPHILIS I do confess it, Faustus, and rejoice.
    'Twas I that, when thou were't i' the way to heaven,
    Dammed up thy passage; when thou took'st the book
    To view the scriptures, then I turned the leaves
    And led thine eye.
85   What, weep'st thou? 'Tis too late, despair. Farewell.
    Fools that will laugh on earth, must weep in hell.   *[Exit.]*
   [Enter the Good and the Evil Angel at several doors.]
GOOD ANGEL Oh Faustus, if thou hadst given ear to me,
    Innumerable joys had followed thee.
    But thou didst love the world.
EVIL ANGEL   Gave ear to me,
90   And now must taste hell's pains perpetually.
GOOD ANGEL Oh, what will all thy riches, pleasures, pomps,
    Avail thee now?
EVIL ANGEL   Nothing but vex thee more,
    To want in hell, that had on earth such store.
   [Music while the throne descends.]
GOOD ANGEL Oh, thou hast lost celestial happiness,
95   Pleasures unspeakable, bliss without end.
    Hadst thou affected sweet divinity,
    Hell, or the devil, had had no power on thee.
    Hadst thou kept on that way, Faustus, behold
    In what resplendent glory thou hadst sat
100   In yonder throne, like those bright shining saints,
    And triumphed over hell. That thou hast lost,
    And now, poor soul, must thy good angel leave thee:
    The jaws of hell are open to receive thee.   *[Exit.]*
   [Hell is discovered.]
EVIL ANGEL Now, Faustus, let thine eyes with horror stare
105   Into that vast perpetual torture-house.
    There are the furies tossing damned souls
    On burning forks. Their bodies broil in lead.
    There are live quarters broiling on the coals
    That ne'er can die. This ever-burning chair
110   Is for o'er-tortured souls to rest them in.
    These, that are fed with sops of flaming fire,
    Were gluttons, and loved only delicates,
    And laughed to see the poor starve at their gates.
    But yet all these are nothing. Thou shalt see
115   Ten thousand tortures that more horrid be.
FAUSTUS Oh, I have seen enough to torture me.
EVIL ANGEL Nay, thou must feel them, taste the smart of all:
    He that loves pleasure must for pleasure fall.
    And so I leave thee, Faustus, till anon.
120   Then wilt thou tumble in confusion.   *[Exit.]*
   [The clock strikes eleven.]
FAUSTUS Ah Faustus,
    Now hast thou but one bare hour to live,

And then thou must be damned perpetually.
Stand still, you ever-moving spheres of heaven,
125 That time may cease and midnight never come.
Fair nature's eye, rise, rise again, and make
Perpetual day. Or let this hour be but
A year, a month, a week, a natural day,
That Faustus may repent and save his soul.
130 O lente, lente, currite noctis equi.[6]
The stars move still, time runs, the clock will strike.
The devil will come, and Faustus must be damned.
Oh, I'll leap up to my God: who pulls me down?
See, see, where Christ's blood streams in the firmament.
135 One drop would save my soul, half a drop. Ah, my Christ!
Ah, rend not my heart for naming of my Christ!
Yet will I call on him. Oh, spare me, Lucifer!
Where is it now? 'Tis gone:
And see where God stretcheth out his arm,
140 And bends his ireful brows.
Mountains and hills, come, come, and fall on me,
And hide me from the heavy wrath of God.
No, no. Then will I headlong run into the earth.
Earth, gape! Oh no, it will not harbor me.
145 You stars that reigned at my nativity,
Whose influence hath allotted death and hell,
Now draw up Faustus like a foggy mist
Into the entrails of yon laboring cloud,
That when you vomit forth into the air
150 My limbs may issue from your smoky mouths,
So that my soul may but ascend to heaven.
   [The watch strikes.]
      Ah! half the hour is past,
      'Twill all be past anon.°   soon
      Oh God, if thou wilt not have mercy on my soul,
155 Yet, for Christ's sake whose blood hath ransomed me,
Impose some end to my incessant pain.
Let Faustus live in hell a thousand years,
A hundred thousand, and at last be saved.
Oh, no end is limited to damned souls.
160 Why wert thou not a creature wanting soul?
Or why is this immortal that thou hast?
Ah, Pythagoras' metempsychosis,[7] were that true
This soul should fly from me, and I be changed
Unto some brutish beast.
165 All beasts are happy, for when they die
Their souls are soon dissolved in elements,
But mine must live still to be plagued in hell.
Cursed be the parents that engendered me!

6. Faustus quotes from Ovid's Amores 1.13.40: "O slowly, slowly run, horses of the night."
7. The transmigration of souls. The Greek philosopher

Pythagoras speculated that souls were reborn in other bodies in an endless progression.

No, Faustus, curse thyself, curse Lucifer,
170   That hath deprived thee of the joys of heaven.
[The clock strikes twelve.]
    Oh, it strikes, it strikes! Now body turn to air,
    Or Lucifer will bear thee quick to hell.
[Thunder and lightning.]
    Oh soul, be changed into little water drops
    And fall into the ocean, ne'er be found.
[Thunder. Enter the Devils.]
175   My God, my God, look not so fierce on me.
    Adders and serpents, let me breathe awhile.
    Ugly hell, gape not, come not, Lucifer!
    I'll burn my books. Ah, Mephostophilis!   *[Exeunt with him.]*

Scene Three

[Enter the Scholars.]

FIRST SCHOLAR Come, gentlemen, let us go visit Faustus,
    For such a dreadful night was never seen
    Since first the world's creation did begin.
    Such fearful shrieks and cries were never heard.
5   Pray heaven the Doctor have escaped the danger.
SECOND SCHOLAR Oh help us, heaven! See, here are Faustus' limbs,
    All torn asunder by the hand of death.
THIRD SCHOLAR The devils whom Faustus served have torn him thus:
    For twixt the hours of twelve and one, methought
10   I heard him shriek and call aloud for help,
    At which self time the house seemed all on fire
    With dreadful horror of these damned fiends.
SECOND SCHOLAR Well, gentlemen, though Faustus' end be such.
    As every Christian heart laments to think on,
15   Yet, for he was a scholar once admired
    For wondrous knowledge in our German schools,
    We'll give his mangled limbs due burial,
    And all the students clothed in mourning black
    Shall wait upon his heavy funeral.   *[Exeunt.]*

Epilogue

[Enter the Chorus.]

CHORUS Cut is the branch that might have grown full straight,
    And burned is Apollo's laurel bough,
    That sometime grew within this learned man.
    Faustus is gone. Regard his hellish fall,
5   Whose fiendful fortune may exhort the wise
    Only to wonder at unlawful things,
    Whose deepness doth entice such forward wits,
    To practice more than heavenly power permits.

Terminat hora diem, Terminat Author opus.[8]
Finis.

---

8. The hour ends the day, the author ends the work.

William Shakespeare
1564–1616

English colonists venturing to the New World carried with them an English Bible; if they owned a single secular book, it was probably the works of Shakespeare. A humanist scripture of sorts, his works have never hardened into doctrine; rather, they have lent themselves to a myriad range of interpretations, each shaped by particular interests, tastes, and expectations. Ben Jonson's line—"He was not of an age, but for all time!"—describes the appeal Shakespeare has had for speakers of English and the many other languages into which his works have been translated.

Shakespeare was born in the provincial town of Stratford-on-Avon, a three-day journey from London by horse or carriage. His father, John Shakespeare, was a glover and local justice of the peace; his mother, Mary Arden, came from a family that owned considerable land in the county. He probably went to a local grammar school where he learned Latin and read histories of the ancient world. Jonson's disparaging comment, that Shakespeare knew "small Latin and less Greek," must not be taken too seriously. Shakespeare (unlike Jonson) was not classically inclined, but his mature works reveal a mind that was extraordinarily well informed and acutely aware of rhetorical techniques and logical argument. At eighteen, Shakespeare married Anne Hathaway, who was twenty-six; in the next three years they had a daughter, Susanna, and then twins, Hamnet and Judith. Six years later, perhaps after periods of teaching school in Stratford, he went to London, eventually (in 1594) to join one of the great theatrical companies of the day, the Chamberlain's Men. It was with this company that he began his career as actor, manager, and playwright. In 1599 the troupe began to put on plays at the Globe, an outdoor theater in Southwark, not far from the other principal theaters of the day—the Rose, the Bear Garden, and the Swan—and across the river from the city of London itself. Because these theaters were outside city limits, in a district known as "the liberties," they were free from the control of authorities responsible for civic order; in effect, the theater provided a place in which all kinds of ideas and ways of life, whether conventional or not, could be represented, examined, and criticized. When James I acceded to the throne in 1603, Shakespeare's company became the King's Men and played also at court and at Blackfriars, an indoor theater in London. Some critics think that the change in venue necessitated a degree of allusiveness and innuendo that was not evident in earlier productions.

During the years Shakespeare was writing for the theater, the populations of Europe were periodically devastated by the plague, and city authorities were obliged to close places of public gathering, including theaters. Shakespeare provided plays for seasons in which the theaters in London were open, composing them at lightning speed and helping to stage productions on very short notice. The plays that we now accept as Shakespeare's fall roughly into several general categories: first, the histories, largely based on the chronicles of the Tudor historian Raphael Holinshed, and the Roman plays, inspired by Plutarch's *Lives of the Ancient Romans*, written in Greek and translated by Sir Thomas North; second, the comedies, often set in the romantic world of the English countryside or an Italian town; third, the tragedies, some of which explore the dark legends of the past; and fourth, a group in the mixed genre of tragicomedy but also called, after critics in the nineteenth century, the romances. A fifth somewhat anomalous group—*All's Well That Ends Well*, *Measure for Measure*, and *Troilus and Cressida*—falls between comedy and satire; these plays are usually termed "problem comedies."

The early phase of Shakespeare's career, the decade beginning in the late 1580s, saw the first cycle of his English histories. In four plays (known as the first tetralogy) this cycle depicted events in the reigns of Henry VI and Richard III and concluded by dramatizing the accession of the first Tudor monarch, Henry VII. Fascinated by the fate of peoples governed by feeble or oppressive rulers, Shakespeare expressed his loathing of tyranny by showing how the misgovernment of a weak king can lead to despotic rule. The cycle ends with the death of the tyrant, Richard III, and the accession of the Duke of Richmond, later Henry VII (Elizabeth's grandfather)—an action that celebrates the founder of the Tudor dynasty and the providence that had selected this family to bring peace to England. A later play, *King John*, concerns an earlier monarch whose claim to the throne is suspect; here divine right, having validated the succession of the Tudor monarchy in the first tetralogy, is made doubtful by a monarch's own viciousness. The play implies a question that Shakespeare continues to ask of history for the rest of his career: in what sense may divine right to be understood as a principle of monarchic rule? History, as Shakespeare will go on to represent it, no longer clearly demonstrates the triumph of justice, but rather shows the interrelatedness of good and evil motives that end in morally ambiguous action. The first of the Roman plays, *The Tragedy of Titus Andronicus*, which tells of the Roman general's revenge for the rape of his daughter Lavinia, and the early comedies, *The Taming of the Shrew*, *The Comedy of Errors*, *Two Gentlemen of Verona*, and *Love's Labor's Lost*, which depicts the effects of mistaken identity and misunderstood speech, illustrate other themes that Shakespeare will continue to represent: the terrible consequences of the search for revenge and the unfortunate, as well as salutary, self-deceptions of love.

The second phase, culminating in productions around 1600, is marked by more and subtler comedy: *A Midsummer Night's Dream*, *The Merchant of Venice*, *The Merry Wives of Windsor*, *Much Ado About Nothing*, *As You Like It*, and *Twelfth Night*. These plays insert into plots that focus primarily on the courtship of young couples a dramatic commentary on darker kinds of human desire: a longing for possessions; a wish to control others, particularly children; and a self-love so intense that it leads to fantasy and delusion. A romantic tragedy of this period, *Romeo and Juliet*, shows how the gross unreason sustaining a family feud and a mysteriously malevolent fate combine to destroy the future of lovers. A second cycle of four English histories, beginning with the deposition of Richard II and ending in the triumphs of Henry V and the birth of Henry VI, reveals how Shakespeare complicates the genre. An ostensible motive for the second tetralogy was the celebration of an English monarchy that had been preserved through the ages by God's will. Yet the actions of even the least controversial of its kings are questionable: Henry V's conquest of France is driven by greed as much as by his claim to the French throne, which is represented as dubious even in the playtext. A second Roman play, *The Tragedy of Julius Caesar*, takes up the question of tyranny in relation to the liberty inherent in a republic; the play seems most tragic when its action suggests that the Roman people do not recognize the sacrifices that are necessary to preserve such freedom and even regard freedom itself as negligible. As a whole, these plays demonstrate the characteristics of Shakespeare's mature style. Certain recurring images unify the plays thematically and, more important, link them to contemporary habits of speech as well as to the intellectual discourse of the period. Visual images—the I and the eye of the lover—often clarify the language of love, and figures denoting the well-being of different kinds of "corporation," including the human body, the family, and the body politic, signal the comprehensive order that was supposed to govern relations among all the elements of creation.

Incorporating many of the themes in the "problem comedies," the tragedies of the same period preoccupied Shakespeare for the seven years following the accession of James I: *Hamlet*, *Othello*, *King Lear*, *Macbeth*, *Antony and Cleopatra*, and *Coriolanus*, together with *Timon of Athens*, a play that was apparently written in collaboration with Thomas Middleton. *All's Well That Ends Well* and *Measure for Measure* illustrate societies that contain rather than reject sordid or unregenerate characters, both noble and common, and thus provide opportunities for comic endings to situations that might otherwise have ended in tragedy. And making much of the need for order but exemplifying the deep disorder of the military societies of Greece and Troy, the characters in *Troilus and Cressida* reveal the extent to which Shakespeare could imagine language as ironic and the human spirit as utterly possessed by a cynical need to turn every occasion to its own advantage. These plays serve to introduce tragedies of unprecedented scope.

Featuring heroes who overreach the limits of their place in life and so fail to fulfill their obligations to themselves and their dependents, Shakespeare's later tragedies embrace a wider range of human experience than can be explained by traditional conceptions of sin and fate. Profoundly complex in their treatment of motivation and the operations of the will, the tragedies entertain the idea of a beneficent deity who both permits terrible suffering and infuses, to use Hamlet's words, a "special providence in the fall of a sparrow." They reveal the blinding egotism that causes fatal misperceptions of character, motive, and action; their heroes are at once terribly in error and also strangely sympathetic. The human capacity for evil is perhaps most fully realized in the characters of women: the bestial daughters of King Lear, Goneril and Regan; the diabolical Lady Macbeth; the shamelessly duplicitous Cleopatra. Yet even they are not entirely unsympathetic; in many ways their behavior responds to the challenges that other, essentially more authoritative characters represent. The romances—*Pericles, Cymbeline, The Winter's Tale*, and *The Tempest*—round out the final phase of Shakespeare's dramatic career, representing (like the comedies) the restoration of family harmony and (like the histories) the return of good government. The deeply troubling divisions within families and states that characterize the tragedies are the basis for the restorative unions in the romances. Their depiction of passages of time and space that allow providential recoveries of health and prosperity to both individual characters and whole bodies politic are largely owing to the intervention of women. Unlike the women of the tragedies, the daughters and wives of the romances are generative in the broadest sense. They heal their fathers and husbands by restoring to their futures the possibility of descendents and therefore of dynastic continuity. Their agency is, in turn, sustained by forces identified as divine and outside history. *Henry VIII*, a history, and *Two Noble Kinsmen*, a romance, both probably composed jointly with John Fletcher, conclude Shakespeare's career as a dramatist.

Shakespeare also wrote narrative and lyric poems of great power, notably *Venus and Adonis, The Rape of Lucrece*, and a cycle of 154 sonnets. In a bold departure from tradition the sonnets celebrate the poet's steadfast love for a young man (never identified), his competitive rivalry with another poet (sometimes identified as Christopher Marlowe), and his troubled relationship with a woman who has dark features. The cycle encourages an interpretation that accounts for its romantic elements, but it also thwarts any obvious construction of events. It is thought that most of the sonnets were composed in the mid-1590s, although they were not published until 1609, apparently without Shakespeare's oversight. Their order therefore cannot be assigned to Shakespeare, and for this reason alone their function as narrative must remain problematic. Still, the reader can trace their representation of successive relations between persons and themes: the young man, although himself derelict in the duties of friendship, will remain beloved by the poet and made immortal by his verse, while the dark lady, who is unscrupulous and afflicted with venereal disease, receives only expressions of desire and lust, shadowed by the poet's disdain and self-loathing.

In a sense, Shakespeare has always been up to date. True, his language is not what is heard today, and his characters are shaped by forces within his culture, not ours. Yet we continue to see his plays on stage and in film, sometimes as recreations of the productions that historians of theater think he knew and saw but more often as reconceived with the addition of modern costumes, settings, and music as well as some strategic cutting of the dramatic text. Earlier periods produced their own kinds of Shakespeare. The Restoration stage, with scenery that allowed audiences to imagine they were looking through a window to life itself, put on plays that were embellished and trimmed to satisfy the taste of the time. Some producers omitted characters who were considered superfluous (the porter in *Macbeth*); others added characters who were judged essential for balance (Miranda's sister, Dorinda, in *The Tempest*). *King Lear* acquired a happy ending when Edgar married Cordelia. No one production of any period has defined a play entirely; every director has had his or her vision of what Shakespeare meant an audience to see. These reinterpretations testify to the perennial vitality of a playwright who was indeed, as Jonson said, "for all time."

THE SONNETS

The entire sequence numbers 154 sonnets. The first fourteen encourage a young man to marry and have children and may have been commissioned by his family. Neither the young man nor his family has been identified, although some readers have thought Henry Wriosthesley, Earl of Southampton, a possible subject. In Sonnet 15, Shakespeare turns to a related topic: the young man will be made eternal not only by his descendants but by the poet's praise of him in verse. Sonnet 20 initiates a long sequence of sonnets addressed to a young man as the poet's lover; whether he is the man who featured in the earlier sonnets on procreation is unclear, but it has generally been assumed so. Beginning with Sonnet 78, the poet complains that a rival poet is stealing his subject—the young man's virtue and grace—to the detriment of his own poetry. Who Shakespeare's rival is (or whether he is in fact a single person) is not known, although some readers have considered Christopher Marlowe a possibility. A final set of twenty-eight sonnets introduces a new character to the sequence, a figure often referred to as "the dark lady," who is the lover of both the poet and the young man. The threesome make up a dramatic unity that is fraught with tension and anguish.

SONNETS

1

From fairest creatures we desire increase,		
That thereby beauty's rose might never die,		
But as the riper° should by time decease,		*the older person*
His tender heir might bear his memory;		
5 But thou, contracted° to thine own bright eyes,		*engaged, shrunk*
Feed'st thy light's flame with self-substantial fuel,		
Making a famine where abundance lies,		
Thyself thy foe, to thy sweet self too cruel.		
Thou that art now the world's fresh ornament		
10 And only herald to the gaudy spring,		
Within thine own bud buriest thy content,		
And, tender churl, mak'st waste in niggarding.°		*hoarding*
Pity the world, or else this glutton be:		
To eat the world's due, by the grave and thee.[1]		

12

When I do count the clock that tells the time,		
And see the brave day sunk in hideous night;		
When I behold the violet past prime,		
And sable° curls all silvered o'er with white;		*dark*
5 When lofty trees I see barren of leaves		
Which erst from heat did canopy the herd,		
And summer's green, all girded up in sheaves,		
Borne on the bier with white and bristly beard,[2]		
Then of thy beauty do I question make		
10 That thou among the wastes of time must go,		
Since sweets and beauties do themselves forsake[3]		

---

1. Have pity on the world and do not consume your own substance, refusing to engender the child you owe now to the world and finally to the grave.
2. The harvest of grain, once green, is gathered in bun-

dles; each stalk ends in clusters of kernels protected by husks that resemble a white and bristling beard, which, like a bier or coffin, suggests mortality.
3. Beauties fade, seeming to forsake themselves.

And die as fast as they see others grow;
   And nothing 'gainst Time's scythe can make defense
   Save breed, to brave° him when he takes thee hence.   *defy*

15

When I consider every thing that grows
Holds in perfection but a little moment,
That this huge stage presenteth naught but shows
Whereon the stars in secret influence comment;[4]
5 When I perceive that men as plants increase,
Cheerèd and checked even by the selfsame sky,
Vaunt° in their youthful sap, at height decrease,   *boast*
And wear their brave state out of memory;°   *until forgotten*
Then the conceit° of this inconstant stay   *idea*
10 Set you most rich in youth before my sight,
Where wasteful Time debateth with Decay
To change your day of youth to sullied° night,   *dark*
   And all in war with Time for love of you,
   As he takes from you, I ingraft you new.[5]

18

Shall I compare thee to a summer's day?
Thou art more lovely and more temperate.
Rough winds do shake the darling buds of May,
And summer's lease hath all too short a date.°   *duration*
5 Sometimes too hot the eye of heaven shines,
And often is his gold complexion dimmed;
And every fair from fair sometimes declines,
By chance or nature's changing course untrimmed.°   *stripped bare*
But thy eternal summer shall not fade
10 Nor lose possession of that fair thou ow'st;°   *own*
Nor shall Death brag thou wanderest in his shade,
When in eternal lines° to time thou grow'st.   *of verse*
   So long as men can breathe or eyes can see,
   So long lives this, and this gives life to thee.

20

A woman's face with Nature's own hand painted
Hast thou, the master-mistress of my passion;[6]
A woman's gentle heart, but not acquainted
With shifting change, as is false women's fashion;
5 An eye more bright than theirs, less false in rolling,°   *straying*
Gilding the object whereupon it gazeth;
A man in hue, all hues in his controlling,[7]
Which steals men's eyes and women's souls amazeth.

---

4. Human action is a kind of show, influenced by the stars or heavenly forces.
5. Renew by grafting, implanting new beauty in verse.
6. Feminine in appearance, the young man is both a master and a mistress of the poet's passion. This is the first of a series of sonnets in which Shakespeare addresses the young man in clearly erotic language.
7. A man in appearance, he determines the nature of what he sees, what is apparent to him.

	And for a woman wert thou first created,	
10	Till Nature, as she wrought thee, fell a-doting,°	*in love*
	And by addition me of thee defeated,[8]	
	By adding one thing to my purpose nothing.	
	But since she pricked thee out for women's pleasure,	
	Mine be thy love and thy love's use their treasure.	

29

	When, in disgrace with fortune and men's eyes,	
	I all alone beweep my outcast state,	
	And trouble deaf heaven with my bootless° cries,	*unavailing*
	And look upon myself and curse my fate,	
5	Wishing me like to one more rich in hope,	
	Featured like him, like him with friends possessed,	
	Desiring this man's art and that man's scope,°	*powers*
	With what I most enjoy contented least;	
	Yet in these thoughts myself almost despising,	
10	Haply° I think on thee, and then my state,	*perhaps*
	Like to the lark at break of day arising	
	From sullen earth, sings hymns at heaven's gate;	
	For thy sweet love remembered such wealth brings	
	That then I scorn to change° my state with kings.	*exchange*

31

	Thy bosom is endearèd with all hearts,	
	Which I by lacking have supposèd dead,	
	And there reigns love and all love's loving parts,	
	And all those friends which I thought burièd.[9]	
5	How many a holy and obsequious° tear	*mournful*
	Hath dear religious love stol'n from mine eye	
	As interest of the dead, which now appear	
	But things removed that hidden in thee lie!	
	Thou art the grave where buried love doth live,	
10	Hung with the trophies of my lovers gone,	
	Who all their parts° of me to thee did give;	*shares*
	That due of many now is thine alone.	
	Their images I loved I view in thee,[1]	
	And thou, all they, hast all the all of me.	

33

	Full many a glorious morning have I seen
	Flatter the mountaintops with sovereign eye,
	Kissing with golden face the meadows green,

---

8. The last four lines of the sonnet are full of double meanings: the thing loving nature adds to the young man is a penis; this points or "pricks" him out for women's pleasure or "use" (with the added suggestion that his body is capital, which through usury generates interest); but the poet reserves for himself the young man's love, which is beyond commerce and has no price.

9. I.e., my past loves seem to live again in your bosom; the affection they had is now made over to you.
1. Here Shakespeare plays with a convention of courtly love: the virtues of all previous loves are said to be summed up in a present love, who embodies a universal perfection.

Gilding pale streams with heavenly alchemy;
5   Anon° permit the basest clouds to ride   *soon*
With ugly rack° on his celestial face,   *driven clouds*
And from the forlorn world his visage hide,
Stealing unseen to west with this disgrace.
Even so my sun one early morn did shine
10 With all-triumphant splendor on my brow.
But out, alack! He was but one hour mine;
The region° cloud hath masked him from me now.   *of the upper air*
    Yet him for this my love no whit disdaineth;
    Suns of the world may stain when heaven's sun staineth.²

35

No more be grieved at that which thou hast done.
Roses have thorns, and silver fountains mud,
Clouds and eclipses stain both moon and sun,
And loathsome canker° lives in sweetest bud.   *worm*
5   All men make faults, and even I in this,
Authorizing thy trespass with compare,°   *comparisons*
Myself corrupting, salving thy amiss,
Excusing thy sins more than thy sins are.
For to thy sensual fault I bring in sense°—   *reason*
10 Thy adverse party° is thy advocate—   *accuser*
And 'gainst myself a lawful plea commence.
Such civil war is in my love and hate
    That I an accessary needs must be
    To that sweet thief which sourly robs from me.

55

Not marble nor the gilded monuments
Of princes shall outlive this powerful rhyme,
But you shall shine more bright in these contents
Than unswept stone besmeared with sluttish° time.   *dirty*
5   When wasteful war shall statues overturn,
And broils° root out the work of masonry,   *uprisings*
Nor° Mars his sword nor war's quick fire shall burn   *neither*
The living record of your memory.
'Gainst death and all-oblivious° enmity   *casting into oblivion*
10 Shall you pace forth; your praise shall still find room
Even in the eyes of all posterity
That wear this world out to the ending doom.°   *judgment day*
    So, till the judgment that yourself° arise,   *when you yourself*
    You live in this, and dwell in lovers' eyes.

60

Like as the waves make towards the pebbled shore,
So do our minutes hasten to their end;

---

2. If the sun may be covered by clouds, so too the suns (or sons) of the world may dim in their affections. This is the first of the poet's laments for his lover's insincerity.

Each changing place with that which goes before,
In sequent° toil all forwards do contend.°   *successive/strive*
5   Nativity, once in the main° of light,   *sea*
Crawls to maturity, wherewith being crowned,
Crookèd eclipses 'gainst his glory fight,
And Time that gave doth now his gift confound.°   *destroy*
Time doth transfix° the flourish set on youth   *puncture*
10 And delves° the parallels in beauty's brow,   *digs*
Feeds on the rarities of nature's truth,
And nothing stands but for his scythe to mow.
    And yet to times in hope my verse shall stand,
    Praising thy worth despite his cruel hand.

<h2 style="text-align:center">73</h2>

That time of year thou mayst in me behold
When yellow leaves, or none, or few, do hang
Upon those boughs which shake against the cold,
Bare ruined choirs[3] where late the sweet birds sang.
5   In me thou seest the twilight of such day
As after sunset fadeth in the west,
Which by and by black night doth take away,
Death's second self, that seals up all in rest.
In me thou seest the glowing of such fire
10 That on the ashes of his youth doth lie
As the deathbed whereon it must expire,
Consumed with that which it was nourished by.
    This thou perceiv'st, which makes thy love more strong,
    To love that well which thou must leave ere long.

<h2 style="text-align:center">80</h2>

O, how I faint when I of you do write,
Knowing a better spirit° doth use your name,   *the rival poet*
And in the praise thereof spends all his might
To make me tongue-tied, speaking of your fame!
5   But since your worth, wide as the ocean is,
The humble as° the proudest sail doth bear,   *as well as*
My saucy bark, inferior far to his,
On your broad main° doth willfully appear.   *sea*
Your shallowest° help will hold me up afloat,   *slightest*
10 Whilst he upon your soundless° deep doth ride;   *unfathomable*
Or, being wrecked, I am a worthless boat,
He of tall building° and of goodly pride.   *construction*
    Then if he thrive and I be cast away,
    The worst was this: my love was my decay.°   *ruin*

<h2 style="text-align:center">86</h2>

Was it the proud full sail of his great verse,
Bound for the prize° of all-too-precious you,   *captive booty*

---

3. The choir is the section of a church reserved for the singers in the choir. "Choir" puns on "quire," the gathering of pages in a book, and thus recalls the "leaves" in line 2.

That did my ripe thoughts in my brain inhearse,°   *entomb*
Making their tomb the womb wherein they grew?
5 Was it his spirit,° by spirits taught to write   *genius*
Above a mortal pitch, that struck me dead?[4]
No, neither he, nor his compeers by night
Giving him aid, my verse astonishèd.
He, nor that affable familiar ghost°   *spirit*
10 Which nightly gulls him with intelligence,
As victors of my silence cannot boast;
I was not sick of any fear from thence.
  But when your countenance filled up his line,[5]
  Then lacked I matter; that enfeebled mine.°   *my verse*

87

Farewell! Thou art too dear for my possessing,
And like enough thou know'st thy estimate.°   *value*
The charter of thy worth gives thee releasing;[6]
My bonds in thee are all determinate.°   *ended*
5 For how do I hold thee but by thy granting,
And for that riches where is my deserving?
The cause of this fair gift in me is wanting,
And so my patent[7] back again is swerving.
Thyself thou gav'st, thy own worth then not knowing,
10 Or me, to whom thou gav'st it, else mistaking;
So thy great gift, upon misprision° growing,   *error*
Comes home again, on better judgment making.
  Thus have I had thee as a dream doth flatter,
  In sleep a king, but waking no such matter.

93

So shall I live, supposing thou art true,
Like a deceivèd husband; so love's face
May still seem love to me, though altered new,
Thy looks with me, thy heart in other place.
5 For there can live no hatred in thine eye,
Therefore in that I cannot know thy change.°   *infidelity*
In many's looks the false heart's history
Is writ in moods and frowns and wrinkles strange,
But heaven in thy creation did decree
10 That in thy face sweet love should ever dwell;
Whate'er thy thoughts or thy heart's workings be,
Thy looks should nothing thence but sweetness tell.
  How like Eve's apple doth thy beauty grow,
  If thy sweet virtue answer not thy show![8]

---

4. Shakespeare ironically suggests that the rival poet writes with supernatural help, or at least what he claims is supernatural help. Shakespeare later implies that this help is actually no more than a gull's (trickster's) intelligence or gossip.
5. When you became his subject.

6. You are worth so much that you can pay off all obligations you owe me; in other words, I have no right to you.
7. Deed granting a monopoly.
8. Like Eve's deceptively attractive apple, the young man's beauty is a kind of temptation that leads to the death of him who succumbs to it.

104

To me, fair friend, you never can be old,
For, as you were when first your eye I eyed,
Such seems your beauty still. Three winters cold
Have from the forests shook three summers' pride,
5 Three beauteous springs to yellow autumn turned
In process of the seasons have I seen,
Three April perfumes in three hot Junes burned,
Since first I saw you fresh, which yet are green.
Ah, yet doth beauty, like a dial⁹ hand,
10 Steal from his figure and no pace perceived.
So your sweet hue, which methinks still doth stand,
Hath motion, and mine eye may be deceived,
    For fear of which, hear this, thou age unbred:°   *unborn*
    Ere you were born was beauty's summer dead.

106

When in the chronicle of wasted° time   *past*
I see descriptions of the fairest wights,°   *people*
And beauty making beautiful old rhyme
In praise of ladies dead and lovely knights,
5 Then, in the blazon° of sweet beauty's best,   *catalogue*
Of hand, of foot, of lip, of eye, of brow,
I see their antique pen would have expressed
Even such a beauty as you master° now.   *possess*
So all their praises are but prophecies
10 Of this our time, all you prefiguring;
And, for° they looked but with divining eyes,   *because*
They had not skill enough your worth to sing.
    For we, which now behold these present days,
    Have eyes to wonder, but lack tongues to praise.[1]

107

Not mine own fears nor the prophetic soul
Of the wide world dreaming on things to come[2]
Can yet the lease of my true love control,
Supposed as forfeit to a confined doom.°   *at a set time*
5 The mortal moon hath her eclipse endured,
And the sad augurs mock their own presage;
Incertainties now crown themselves assured,
And peace proclaims olives of endless age.[3]

9. Beauty is like the hand of a clock, a dial; it moves slowly but inexorably away from the height of the hour.
1. The poets of antiquity could not describe your perfection because they could only guess at it; we recognize
your perfection but lack but the skill to describe it.
2. Shakespeare may have had in mind the ancient concept of *anima mundi* (literally, a world soul), which was
imagined as breathing life into all creation.
3. A supposedly dangerous lunar eclipse has passed, and

those who predicted disaster now mock their own predictions. The moon may be Elizabeth I, who died in 1603;
the endless peace to follow may be the one that James I
negotiated with the Spanish in 1604. Or the moon's
eclipse may figure Elizabeth's sixty-third year, a numero-
logically suspect period; in this case the ensuing peace
describes a time in which anxiety over the future of the
kingdom diminished, or "uncertainties" were "assured,"
i.e., became certainties.

Now with the drops of this most balmy time[4]
10   My love looks fresh, and Death to me subscribes,°   *yields*
Since, spite of him, I'll live in this poor rhyme,
While he insults° o'er dull and speechless tribes;   *triumphs*
  And thou in this shalt find thy monument,
  When tyrants' crests and tombs of brass are spent.°   *worn away*

116

Let me not to the marriage of true minds
Admit impediments. Love is not love
Which alters when it alteration finds,°   *in the beloved*
Or bends with the remover to remove.
5   O, no, it is an ever-fixèd mark°   *landmark*
That looks on tempests and is never shaken;
It is the star to every wandering bark,
Whose worth's unknown, although his height be taken.[5]
Love's not Time's fool, though rosy lips and cheeks
10 Within his bending sickle's compass° come;   *range*
Love alters not with his brief hours and weeks,
But bears it out even to the edge of doom.°   *judgment day*
  If this be error and upon me proved,
  I never writ, nor no man ever loved.

123

No, Time, thou shalt not boast that I do change.
Thy pyramids[6] built up with newer might
To me are nothing novel, nothing strange;
They are but dressings of a former sight.
5   Our dates are brief, and therefore we admire
What thou dost foist upon us that is old,
And rather make them born to our desire
Than think that we before have heard them told.
Thy registers° and thee I both defy,   *records*
10 Not wondering at the present nor the past,
For thy records and° what we see doth lie,   *and also*
Made more or less by thy continual haste.
  This I do vow and this shall ever be:
  I will be true, despite thy scythe and thee.

124

If my dear love were but the child of state,
It might for Fortune's bastard be unfathered,
As subject to Time's love or to Time's hate,

---

4. A time that is restorative, as from the application of a medicinal ointment; a possible reference to the coronation of James I, celebrated by anointing the monarch with balm and other rituals.
5. The star by which ships navigate by measuring its altitude from the horizon (known values) is itself beyond valuation.
6. Any imposing structure; those built recently, "with newer might," are reconceptions, "dressings," of former structures.

Weeds among weeds, or flowers with flowers gathered.[7]
No, it was builded far from accident;
It suffers not in smiling pomp, nor falls
Under the blow of thrallèd° discontent,   *enslaved*
Whereto th' inviting time our fashion° calls.   *manner*
It fears not Policy,° that heretic,   *expediency*
Which works on leases of short-numbered hours,
But all alone stands hugely politic,[8]
That it nor grows with heat nor drowns with showers.
　　To this I witness call the fools of Time,
　　Which die for goodness, who have lived for crime.[9]

126

O thou, my lovely boy, who in thy power
Dost hold Time's fickle glass,° his sickle hour;   *hourglass*
Who hast by waning grown, and therein show'st
Thy lovers withering as thy sweet self grow'st;
If Nature, sovereign mistress over wrack,°   *destruction*
As thou goest onwards, still will pluck thee back,
She keeps thee to this purpose, that her skill
May Time disgrace and wretched minutes kill.[1]
Yet fear her, O thou minion° of her pleasure!   *slave*
She may detain, but not still keep, her treasure.
Her audit, though delayed, answered must be,
And her quietus° is to render thee.[2]   *settlement*

130[3]

My mistress' eyes are nothing like the sun;
Coral is far more red than her lips' red;
If snow be white, why then her breasts are dun;°   *brown*
If hairs be wires, black wires grow on her head.
I have seen roses damasked,° red and white,   *mingled*
But no such roses see I in her cheeks;
And in some perfumes is there more delight
Than in the breath that from my mistress reeks.
I love to hear her speak, yet well I know
That music hath a far more pleasing sound.
I grant I never saw a goddess go;
My mistress, when she walks, treads on the ground.

---

7. If my love for you were merely a product of circumstance, it would be no more than Fortune's bastard and not have a father; it would be subject to accidents, both good and bad.

8. His love is beyond the expedient maneuvers of mere "policy" because it is itself "politic" or a state.

9. This enigmatic couplet may mean that those who have lived as criminals and then die for goodness are Time's fools because deathbed repentance is folly; or that those who have lived as criminals and then die in a good cause are Time's fools in the sense that everyone who resists the temporizing ways of the world is a fool.

1. His lover's power can hold back time and prevent his sickle from mowing down his green youth; paradoxically, while others grow old, he grows young. Nature permits this expressly to defy Time.

2. Yet Nature owes you to Time and will pay her debt by handing you over at last. The sonnet ends short of the 14 lines the form demands, as if to emphasize the idea of brevity.

3. Sonnet 127 was the first to have a woman, not a man, as its principal subject; she is described as a woman of dark complexion.

And yet, by heaven, I think my love as rare
As any she belied with false compare.[4]

138

When my love swears that she is made of truth
I do believe her, though I know she lies,
That she might think me some untutored youth,
Unlearnèd in the world's false subtleties.
5 Thus vainly thinking that she thinks me young,
Although she knows my days are past the best,
Simply I credit her false-speaking tongue;
On both sides thus is simple truth suppressed.
But wherefore says she not she is unjust?
10 And wherefore say not I that I am old?
O, love's best habit is in seeming° trust,   *apparent*
And age in love loves not to have years told.
    Therefore I lie with her, and she with me,[5]
    And in our faults by lies we flattered be.

144

Two loves I have, of comfort and despair,
Which like two spirits do suggest° me still: *tempt*
The better angel is a man right fair,
The worser spirit a woman colored ill.
5 To win me soon to hell, my female evil
Tempteth my better angel from my side,
And would corrupt my saint to be a devil,
Wooing his purity with her foul pride.
And whether that my angel be turned fiend
10 Suspect I may, yet not directly tell;
But being both from me, both to each friend,
I guess one angel in another's hell.
    Yet this shall I ne'er know, but live in doubt
    Till my bad angel fire my good one out.[6]

152

In loving thee thou know'st I am forsworn,°   *faithless*
But thou art twice forsworn, to me love swearing:
In act thy bed-vow° broke, and new faith torn   *marriage vow*
In vowing new hate after new love bearing.[7]
5 But why of two oaths' breach do I accuse thee,
When I break twenty? I am perjured most,
For all my vows are oaths but to misuse° thee,   *deceive*

---

4. The couplet suggests ironic or hyperbolic compliment:
my mistress is exceptional in that she has set new standards for true beauty by a comparison that defies its standards.
5. We deceive each other; we have sex with each other.
6. The couplet suggests several interpretations. The
poet's lady or bad angel could fire or dismiss his "fair"

friend; she could infect him with a venereal disease, a
condition that would cause a fever; finally, she could be
the cause of his descent into hellfire, a consequence of
sin.
7. You have broken your marriage vow and your vow to
love me.

And all my honest faith in thee is lost.
For I have sworn deep oaths of thy deep kindness,
10   Oaths of thy love, thy truth, thy constancy,
And, to enlighten thee, gave eyes to blindness,[8]
Or made them swear against the thing they see;
For I have sworn thee fair. More perjured eye,
To swear against the truth so foul a lie!

Othello

Othello (1604) is a tragedy both of its time and ahead of its time. Basing Othello on a novella from Giraldi Cinthio's Hecatommithi (1565), Shakespeare takes an Italian Renaissance tale of greed, lust, and brutality and turns it into a timeless tragedy of ingenious evil spiraling toward destruction, and love haunted by demonic jealousy. A brief plot synopsis of the novella will make the point. Lusting after Desdemona and resenting Cassio for being given the position of lieutenant by Othello, Iago sets about convincing Othello that his wife has been unfaithful with Cassio. When Desdemona meets with Othello's suspicious jealousy, she concludes that she should never have married a Moor. Iago and Othello together plot to kill her. Bludgeoning her to death with sandbags, they pull down the plaster from the ceiling to make it look like an accident. The remorseful Othello betrays Iago, who then fingers Othello. Desdemona's family catches up with Othello and gets their revenge.

Although Shakespeare gives Iago the twin motives of sexual jealousy (he suspects his wife Emilia of having slept with Othello) and resentment, the intelligence and cunning of Iago make him resemble a politically calculating reader of Machiavelli's Prince rather than a brutal thug. To match this villain, Shakespeare creates a noble hero—not only a great general and war hero but a man enthralled by his wife, reluctant to believe her guilty, and manipulated into blaming her by the false evidence of the handkerchief. Faced with the protean shape-shifting ability of Iago to make not only himself but also the people around him appear to be what they are not, Othello is less a coconspirator than a victim. He is also a victim of his own status as outsider, an element that the tragedy plays up from the very first scene, where Iago shouts in the streets to Brabantio, Desdemona's father, "the black ram is tupping your white ewe." Othello loves Desdemona with a passionate intensity that is only equalled by the terrifying jealousy by which he undoes them both, "when I love thee not, / Chaos is come again." Shakespeare's Desdemona is also far more complex than her counterpart in the Italian novella. Portrayed from the outset of the play as a woman unafraid of incurring her father's wrath for marrying the man she loves, she loves Othello to the end—preferring to die rather than to live without his love.

Shakespeare makes his audience question preconceptions about sex, race, and identity in ways that are still urgent today. The play represents the sexual relation between Othello and Desdemona as one that is both passionate and yet somehow, at least from the point of view of Iago and Brabantio, obscene. The only time we see the couple in the bedroom together is in the final scene, where they both meet their deaths at Othello's hand. He likens himself to the "base Indian" ("Judean" in the Folio) who "sacrificed all his tribe for a pearl of great price." Othello sees himself as a cultural other, like the Turk he has been fighting throughout the play. There is no getting around the play's obsession with Othello's blackness; the language and imagery repeatedly impress upon us the issue of the hero's race.

Finally, identity itself is a central theme of Othello. The play abounds in incongruities of identity. Othello the Moor of Venice is a bit like Nanook of Las Vegas. And Venice, a city known for its decadent courtesans, is here the home of a woman of complete faithfulness. From the first act, where Iago declares "I am not what I am," to his declaration of love for Othello at

8. To make you seem fair, I saw what was not there or did not see what was there.

the moment where the audience knows he is enacting the greatest hatred, Shakespeare allows his audience to see the deceptively manipulative role-playing involved in the struggle for power. But rather than achieving power, Iago destroys not only Othello and Desdemona but also Emilia and himself. Whether Iago's evil is unfathomable or not, there is certainly something about it that is beyond the control of his own amazing powers of strategy and improvisation. It is an evil strong enough to overtake and inhabit even a man as noble as Othello.

Othello, the Moor of Venice

The Names of the Actors

OTHELLO, *the Moor*
BRABANTIO, *a senator, father to Desdemona*
CASSIO, *an honorable lieutenant to Othello*
IAGO, *Othello's ancient, a villain*
RODERIGO, *a gulled gentleman*
DUKE OF VENICE
SENATORS *of Venice*
MONTANO, *Governor of Cyprus*
GENTLEMEN *of Cyprus*
LODOVICO AND GRATIANO, *kinsmen*
  to Brabantio, two noble Venetians

SAILORS
CLOWN
DESDEMONA, *daughter to Brabantio*
  and wife to Othello
EMILIA, *wife to Iago*
BIANCA, *a courtesan and mistress to Cassio*
A MESSENGER
A HERALD
A MUSICIAN
SERVANTS, ATTENDANTS, OFFICERS,
  SENATORS, MUSICIANS, GENTLEMEN

Scene: *Venice; a seaport in Cyprus*

Act 1[1]

Scene 1

[Location: Venice. A street. Enter Roderigo and Iago.]

RODERIGO Tush, never tell me! I take it much unkindly
  That thou, Iago, who hast had my purse
  As if the strings were thine, shouldst know of this.[2]
IAGO 'Sblood,[3] but you'll not hear me.
5   If ever I did dream of such a matter,
  Abhor me.
RODERIGO Thou toldst me thou didst hold him in thy hate.
IAGO Despise me
  If I do not. Three great ones of the city,
10   In personal suit to make me his lieutenant,
  Off-capped to him;° and by the faith of man,   Othello
  I know my price, I am worth no worse a place.
  But he, as loving his own pride and purposes,
  Evades them with a bombast circumstance[4]
15   Horribly stuffed with epithets of war,
  And, in conclusion,
  Nonsuits° my mediators. For, "Certes,"° says he,   rejects/certainly
  "I have already chose my officer."
  And what was he?

---

1. Our text is taken, and the notes are adapted, from David Bevington, ed., *The Complete Works of Shakespeare*.
2. I.e., Desdemona's elopement.
3. By His (Christ's) blood.
4. Wordy evasion. *Bombast* is cotton padding.

20   Forsooth, a great arithmetician,[5]
        One Michael Cassio, a Florentine,
        A fellow almost damned in a fair wife,[6]
        That never set a squadron in the field
        Nor the division of a battle knows
25   More than a spinster[7]—unless the bookish theoric,°   *theory*
        Wherein the togaed consuls° can propose°   *senators/discuss*
        As masterly as he. Mere prattle without practice
        Is all his soldiership. But he, sir, had th'election;
        And I, of whom his° eyes had seen the proof   *Othello's*
30   At Rhodes, at Cyprus, and on other grounds
        Christened° and heathen, must be beleed and calmed[8]   *Christian*
        By debitor and creditor.[9] This countercaster,[1]
        He, in good time,° must his lieutenant be,   *opportunely*
        And I—God bless the mark![2]—his Moorship's ancient.°   *ensign*
RODERIGO By heaven, I rather would have been his hangman.
IAGO Why, there's no remedy. 'Tis the curse of service;
        Preferment° goes by letter and affection,[3]   *promotion*
        And not by old gradation,[4] where each second
        Stood heir to th' first. Now, sir, be judge yourself
40   Whether I in any just term° am affined°   *respect/bound*
        To love the Moor.
RODERIGO   I would not follow him then.
IAGO O sir, content you.[5]
        I follow him to serve my turn upon him.
        We cannot all be masters, nor all masters
45   Cannot be truly° followed. You shall mark   *faithfully*
        Many a duteous and knee-crooking knave
        That, doting on his own obsequious bondage,
        Wears out his time, much like his master's ass,
        For naught but provender, and when he's old, cashiered.°   *dismissed*
50   Whip me[6] such honest knaves. Others there are
        Who, trimmed in forms and visages of duty,[7]
        Keep yet their hearts attending on themselves,
        And, throwing but shows of service on their lords,
        Do well thrive by them, and when they have lined their coats,[8]
55   Do themselves homage.[9] These fellows have some soul,
        And such a one do I profess myself. For, sir,
        It is as sure as you are Roderigo,
        Were I the Moor I would not be Iago.[1]

---

5. A man whose military knowledge is merely theoretical, based on books of tactics.
6. Cassio does not seem to be married, but his counterpart in Shakespeare's source does have a woman in his house.
7. A housewife, one whose regular occupation is spinning.
8. Left to leeward without wind, becalmed (a sailing metaphor).
9. A name for a system of bookkeeping, here used as a contemptuous nickname for Cassio.
1. Bookkeeper, one who tallies with *counters*, or "metal disks." Said contemptuously.
2. Perhaps originally a formula to ward off evil; here an

expression of impatience.
3. Personal influence and favoritism.
4. Step-by-step seniority, the traditional way.
5. Don't you worry about that.
6. Whip, as far as I'm concerned.
7. Dressed up in the mere form and show of dutifulness.
8. Stuffed their purses.
9. Attend to self-interest solely.
1. If I were able to assume command, I certainly would not choose to remain a subordinate, or, I would keep a suspicious eye on a flattering subordinate.

In following him, I follow but myself—
60   Heaven is my judge, not I for love and duty,
But seeming so for my peculiar° end.   *particular*
For when my outward action doth demonstrate
The native° act and figure° of my heart   *innate/intent*
In compliment extern,[2] 'tis not long after
65   But I will wear my heart upon my sleeve
For daws[3] to peck at. I am not what I am.[4]
RODERIGO What a full° fortune does the thick-lips[5] owe°   *swelling/own*
If he can carry 't thus!°   *carry this off*
IAGO   Call up her father.
Rouse him, make after him, poison his delight,
70   Proclaim him in the streets; incense her kinsmen,
And, though he in a fertile climate dwell,
Plague him with flies.[6] Though that his joy be joy,[7]
Yet throw such changes of vexation° on 't   *vexing changes*
As it may lose some color.[8]
RODERIGO Here is her father's house. I'll call aloud.
IAGO Do, with like timorous° accent and dire yell   *frightening*
As when, by night and negligence, the fire
Is spied in populous cities.
RODERIGO What ho, Brabantio! Signor Brabantio, ho!
IAGO Awake! What ho, Brabantio! Thieves, thieves, thieves!
Look to your house, your daughter, and your bags!
Thieves, thieves!
[*Brabantio enters above at a window.*][9]
BRABANTIO What is the reason of this terrible summons?
What is the matter° there?   *your business*
RODERIGO Signor, is all your family within?
IAGO Are your doors locked?
BRABANTIO   Why, wherefore ask you this?
IAGO Zounds,[1] sir, you're robbed. For shame, put on your gown!
Your heart is burst; you have lost half your soul.
Even now, now, very now, an old black ram
90   Is tupping your white ewe.[2] Arise, arise!
Awake the snorting° citizens with the bell,   *snoring*
Or else the devil[3] will make a grandsire of you.
Arise, I say!
BRABANTIO   What, have you lost your wits?
RODERIGO Most reverend signor, do you know my voice?
BRABANTIO Not I. What are you?
RODERIGO My name is Roderigo.
BRABANTIO   The worser welcome.

---

2. Outward show (conforming in this case to the inner
workings and intention of the heart).
3. Small crowlike birds, proverbially stupid and avaricious.
4. I am not one who wears his heart on his sleeve.
5. Elizabethans often applied the term "Moor" to
Negroes.
6. Though he seems prosperous and happy now, vex him
with misery.

7. Although he seems fortunate and happy.
8. That may cause it to lose some of its fresh gloss.
9. This stage direction, from the Quarto, probably calls
for an appearance on the gallery above and rearstage.
1. By His (Christ's) wounds.
2. Covering, copulating with (said of sheep).
3. The devil was conventionally pictured as black.

I have charged thee not to haunt about my doors.
In honest plainness thou hast heard me say
My daughter is not for thee; and now, in madness,
100 Being full of supper and distempering° drafts,   *intoxicating*
Upon malicious bravery⁴ dost thou come
To start° my quiet.   *disrupt*
RODERIGO Sir, sir, sir—
BRABANTIO   But thou must needs be sure
My spirits and my place⁵ have in° their power   *have it in*
105 To make this bitter to thee.
RODERIGO   Patience, good sir.
BRABANTIO What tell'st thou me of robbing? This is Venice;
My house is not a grange.°   *country house*
RODERIGO   Most grave Brabantio,
In simple° and pure soul I come to you.   *sincere*
IAGO Zounds, sir, you are one of those that will not serve God if the devil bid you.
110   Because we come to do you service and you think we are ruffians, you'll have
your daughter covered with a Barbary⁶ horse; you'll have your nephews⁷ neigh
to you; you'll have coursers for cousins and jennets for germans.⁸
BRABANTIO What profane wretch art thou?
IAGO I am one, sir, that comes to tell you your daughter and the Moor are now mak-
115   ing the beast with two backs.
BRABANTIO Thou art a villain.
IAGO   You are—a senator.⁹
BRABANTIO This thou shalt answer.¹ I know thee, Roderigo.
RODERIGO Sir, I will answer anything. But I beseech you,
If 't be your pleasure and most wise° consent—   *well-informed*
120 As partly I find it is—that your fair daughter,
At this odd-even² and dull watch o' the night,
Transported with° no worse nor better guard   *by*
But with a knave of common hire,³ a gondolier,
To the gross clasps of a lascivious Moor—
125 If this be known to you and your allowance°   *permission*
We then have done you bold and saucy° wrongs.   *insolent*
But if you know not this, my manners tell me
We have your wrong rebuke. Do not believe
That, from° the sense of all civility,°   *contrary to/decency*
130 I thus would play and trifle with your reverence.⁴
Your daughter, if you have not given her leave,
I say again, hath made a gross revolt,
Tying her duty, beauty, wit,° and fortunes   *intelligence*
In an extravagant° and wheeling° stranger⁵   *expatriate/vagabond*
135 Of here and everywhere. Straight° satisfy yourself.   *straightway*

---

4. With hostile intent to defy me.
5. My temperament and my authority of office.
6. From northern Africa (and hence associated with Othello).
7. I.e., grandsons.
8. You'll have stallions for kinsmen and ponies for relatives.

9. Said with mock politeness, as though the word itself were an insult.
1. Be held accountable for.
2. Between one day and the next, i.e., about midnight.
3. Than by a low fellow, a servant.
4. The respect due to you.
5. Foreigner.

If she be in her chamber or your house,
Let loose on me the justice of the state
For thus deluding you.

BRABANTIO Strike on the tinder,[6] ho!
140   Give me a taper! Call up all my people!
This accident° is not unlike my dream.   event
Belief of it oppresses me already.
Light, I say, light!   [Exit above.]

IAGO   Farewell, for I must leave you.
It seems not meet° nor wholesome to my place°   fitting / position
145   To be producted[7]—as, if I stay, I shall—
Against the Moor. For I do know the state,
However this may gall° him with some check,°   oppress / rebuke
Cannot with safety cast° him, for he's embarked°   dismiss / engaged
With such loud reason[8] to the Cyprus wars,
150   Which even now stands in act,° that, for their souls,[9]   are going on
Another of his fathom[1] they have none
To lead their business; in which regard,[2]
Though I do hate him as I do hell pains,
Yet for necessity of present life°   livelihood
155   I must show out a flag and sign of love,
Which is indeed but sign. That you shall surely find him,
Lead to the Sagittary[3] the raisèd search,[4]
And there will I be with him. So farewell.   [Exit]

[Enter below, Brabantio in his nightgown[5] with servants and torches.]

BRABANTIO It is too true an evil. Gone she is;
160   And what's to come of my despisèd time[6]
Is naught but bitterness. Now, Roderigo,
Where didst thou see her?—O unhappy girl!—
With the Moor, sayst thou?—Who would be a father!—
How didst thou know 'twas she?—O, she deceives me
165   Past thought!—What said she to you?—Get more tapers.
Raise all my kindred.—Are they married, think you?

RODERIGO Truly, I think they are.

BRABANTIO O heaven! How got she out? O treason of the blood!
Fathers, from hence trust not your daughters' minds
170   By what you see them act. Is there not charms°   spells
By which the property° of youth and maidhood   nature
May be abused?° Have you not read, Roderigo,   deceived
Of some such thing?

RODERIGO   Yes, sir, I have indeed.

BRABANTIO Call up my brother.—O, would you had had her!—
175   Some one way, some another.—Do you know
Where we may apprehend her and the Moor?

---

6. Charred linen ignited by a spark from flint and steel, used to light torches or *tapers.*
7. Produced (as a witness).
8. Unanimous shout of confirmation (in the Senate).
9. To save themselves.
1. I.e., ability, depth of experience.
2. Out of regard for which.

3. An inn or house where Othello and Desdemona are staying, named for its sign of Sagittarius, or Centaur.
4. Search party roused out of sleep.
5. Dressing gown. (This costuming is specified in the Quarto text.)
6. I.e., remainder of life.

RODERIGO I think I can discover° him, if you please   *reveal*
    To get good guard and go along with me.
BRABANTIO Pray you, lead on. At every house I'll call;
180   I may command° at most.—Get weapons, ho!   *demand aid*
    And raise some special officers of night.—
    On, good Roderigo. I will deserve° your pains.   *reward*

                                   [Exeunt.]

Scene 2

[Location: Venice. Another street. Before Othello's lodgings. Enter Othello, Iago, attendants with torches.]

IAGO Though in the trade of war I have slain men,
    Yet do I hold it very stuff⁷ o' the conscience
    To do no contrived° murder. I lack iniquity   *premeditated*
    Sometimes to do me service. Nine or ten times
5   I had thought t' have yerked° him° here under the ribs.   *stabbed/Roderigo*
OTHELLO 'Tis better as it is.
IAGO   Nay, but he prated,
    And spoke such scurvy and provoking terms
    Against your honor
    That, with the little godliness I have,
10   I did full hard forbear him.⁸ But, I pray you, sir,
    Are you fast married? Be assured of this,
    That the magnifico⁹ is much beloved,
    And hath in his effect° a voice potential°   *command/powerful*
    As double as the Duke's. He will divorce you,
15   Or put upon you what restraint or grievance
    The law, with all his might to enforce it on,
    Will give him cable.°   *scope*
OTHELLO   Let him do his spite.
    My services which I have done the seigniory°   *government*
    Shall out-tongue his complaints. 'Tis yet to know°—   *not yet known*
20   Which, when I know that boasting is an honor,
    I shall promulgate—I fetch my life and being
    From men of royal siege,° and my demerits°   *rank/deserts*
    May speak unbonneted¹ to as proud a fortune
    As this that I have reached. For know, Iago,
25   But that I love the gentle Desdemona,
    I would not my unhousèd° free condition   *unconfined*
    Put into circumscription and confine°   *confinement*
    For the sea's worth.² But look, what lights come yond?
    [Enter Cassio and certain officers³ with torches.]
IAGO Those are the raisèd father and his friends.
30   You were best go in.
OTHELLO   Not I. I must be found.

---

7. Essence, basic material (continuing the metaphor of *trade* from line 1).
8. I restrained myself with great difficulty from assaulting him.
9. Venetian grandee, i.e., Brabantio.

1. Without removing the hat, i.e., on equal terms (or "with hat off," "in all due modesty").
2. All the riches at the bottom of the sea.
3. The Quarto text calls for "Cassio with lights, officers with torches."

My parts, my title, and my perfect soul[4]
Shall manifest me rightly. Is it they?

IAGO By Janus,[5] I think no.

OTHELLO The servants of the Duke? And my lieutenant?

35   The goodness of the night upon you, friends!
What is the news?

CASSIO   The Duke does greet you, General,
And he requires your haste-post-haste appearance
Even on the instant.

OTHELLO   What is the matter,° think you?   *business*

CASSIO Something from Cyprus, as I may divine.°   *guess*

40   It is a business of some heat.° The galleys   *urgency*
Have sent a dozen sequent° messengers   *successive*
This very night at one another's heels,
And many of the consuls,° raised and met,   *senators*
Are at the Duke's already. You have been hotly called for;

45   When, being not at your lodging to be found,
The Senate hath sent about[6] three several° quests   *separate*
To search you out.

OTHELLO   'Tis well I am found by you.
I will but spend a word here in the house
And go with you.   *[Exit.]*

CASSIO   Ancient, what makes° he here?   *does*

IAGO Faith, he tonight hath boarded[7] a land carrack.°   *merchant ship*
If it prove lawful prize,° he's made forever.   *booty*

CASSIO I do not understand.

IAGO   He's married.

CASSIO   To who?
    [Enter Othello.]

IAGO Marry,[8] to—Come, Captain, will you go?

OTHELLO Have with you.[9]

CASSIO Here comes another troop to seek for you.
    [Enter Brabantio, Roderigo, with officers and torches.][1]

IAGO It is Brabantio. General, be advised.[2]
He comes to bad intent.

OTHELLO   Holla! Stand there!

RODERIGO Signor, it is the Moor.

BRABANTIO   Down with him, thief!
    [They draw on both sides.]

IAGO You, Roderigo! Come, sir, I am for you.

OTHELLO Keep up° your bright swords, for the dew will rust them.   *sheathe*
Good signor, you shall more command with years
Than with your weapons.

---

4. My natural gifts, my position or reputation, and my unflawed conscience.
5. Roman two-faced god of beginnings.
6. All over the city.
7. Gone aboard and seized as an act of piracy (with sexual suggestion).

8. An oath, originally "by the Virgin Mary"; here used with wordplay on *married*.
9. Let's go.
1. The Quarto text calls for "others with lights and weapons."
2. Be on your guard.

BRABANTIO O thou foul thief, where hast thou stowed my daughter?
    Damned as thou art, thou hast enchanted her!
65   For I'll refer me to all things of sense,[3]
    If she in chains of magic were not bound
    Whether a maid so tender, fair, and happy,
    So opposite to marriage that she shunned
    The wealthy curlèd darlings of our nation,
70   Would ever have, t' incur a general mock,
    Run from her guardage[4] to the sooty bosom
    Of such a thing as thou—to fear, not to delight.
    Judge me the world if 'tis not gross in sense°   *obvious*
    That thou hast practiced on her with foul charms,
75   Abused her delicate youth with drugs or minerals°   *poisons*
    That weakens motion.[5] I'll have 't disputed on;[6]
    'Tis probable and palpable to thinking.
    I therefore apprehend and do attach° thee   *arrest*
    For an abuser of the world, a practicer
80   Of arts inhibited° and out of warrant.°—   *black magic / illegal*
    Lay hold upon him! If he do resist,
    Subdue him at his peril.
OTHELLO   Hold your hands,
    Both you of my inclining° and the rest.   *following*
    Were it my cue to fight, I should have known it
85   Without a prompter.—Whither will you that I go
    To answer this your charge?
BRABANTIO To prison, till fit time
    Of law and course of direct session[7]
    Call thee to answer.
OTHELLO   What if I do obey?
90   How may the Duke be therewith satisfied,
    Whose messengers are here about my side
    Upon some present business of the state
    To bring me to him?
OFFICER   'Tis true, most worthy signor.
    The Duke's in council, and your noble self,
95   I am sure, is sent for.
BRABANTIO   How? The Duke in council?
    In this time of the night? Bring him away.°   *right along*
    Mine's not an idle° cause. The Duke himself,   *trifling*
    Or any of my brothers of the state,
    Cannot but feel this wrong as 'twere their own;
100   For if such actions may have passage free,[8]
    Bondslaves and pagans shall our statesmen be.
    [*Exeunt.*]

---

3. Submit my case to creatures possessing common sense.
4. My guardianship of her.
5. Impair the vital faculties.
6. Argued in court by professional counsel, debated by experts.
7. Regular or specially convened legal proceedings.
8. Are allowed to go unchecked.

Scene 3

[*Location: Venice. A council chamber. Enter Duke and Senators and sit at a table,*
with lights, and Officers. The Duke and Senators are reading dispatches.][9]

DUKE There is no composition° in these news   consistency
    That gives them credit.

FIRST SENATOR Indeed, they are disproportioned.°   inconsistent
    My letters say a hundred and seven galleys.

DUKE And mine, a hundred forty.

SECOND SENATOR   And mine, two hundred.
    But though they jump° not on a just° account—   agree/exact
    As in these cases, where the aim° reports   conjecture
    'Tis oft with difference—yet do they all confirm
    A Turkish fleet, and bearing up to Cyprus.

DUKE Nay, it is possible enough to judgment.
    I do not so secure me in the error
    But the main article I do approve[1]
    In fearful sense.

SAILOR [*within*]   What ho, what ho, what ho!
    [*Enter Sailor.*]

OFFICER A messenger from the galleys.

DUKE Now, what's the business?

SAILOR The Turkish preparation[2] makes for Rhodes.
    So was I bid report here to the state
    By Signor Angelo.

DUKE How say you by° this change?   about

FIRST SENATOR   This cannot be
20   By no assay° of reason. 'Tis a pageant°   test/mere show
    To keep us in false gaze.[3] When we consider
    Th' importancy of Cyprus to the Turk,
    And let ourselves again but understand
    That, as it more concerns the Turk than Rhodes,
25   So may he with more facile question bear it,[4]
    For that° it stands not in such warlike brace,°   since/state
    But altogether lacks th' abilities°   means of defense
    That Rhodes is dressed in°—if we make thought of this,   equipped with
    We must not think the Turk is so unskillful°   careless
30   To leave that latest° which concerns him first,   last
    Neglecting an attempt of ease and gain
    To wake° and wage° a danger profitless.   stir up/risk

DUKE Nay, in all confidence, he's not for Rhodes.

OFFICER Here is more news.
    [*Enter a Messenger.*]

MESSENGER The Ottomites, reverend and gracious,
    Steering with due course toward the isle of Rhodes,

---

9. The Quarto text calls for the Duke and senators to "sit
at a table with lights and attendants."
1. I do not take such (false) comfort in the discrepancies
that I fail to perceive the main point, i.e., that the Turkish fleet is threatening.

2. Fleet prepared for battle.
3. Looking the wrong way.
4. So also he (the Turk) can more easily capture it
(Cyprus).

Have there injointed them[5] with an after° fleet.   *following*
FIRST SENATOR Ay, so I thought. How many, as you guess?
MESSENGER Of thirty sail; and now they do restem
40   Their backward course,[6] bearing with frank° appearance   *undisguised*
Their purposes toward Cyprus. Signor Montano,
Your trusty and most valiant servitor,°   *officer*
With his free duty[7] recommends[8] you thus,
And prays you to believe him.
DUKE 'Tis certain then for Cyprus.
Marcus Luccicos, is not he in town?
FIRST SENATOR He's now in Florence.
DUKE Write from us to him, post-post-haste. Dispatch.
FIRST SENATOR Here comes Brabantio and the valiant Moor.
[*Enter Brabantio, Othello, Cassio, Iago, Roderigo, and officers.*]
DUKE Valiant Othello, we must straight° employ you   *straightway*
Against the general enemy[9] Ottoman.
[*To Brabantio.*] I did not see you; welcome, gentle° signor.   *noble*
We lacked your counsel and your help tonight.
BRABANTIO So did I yours. Good Your Grace, pardon me;
55   Neither my place° nor aught I heard of business   *official position*
Hath raised me from my bed, nor doth the general care
Take hold on me, for my particular° grief   *personal*
Is of so floodgate[1] and o'erbearing nature
That it engluts° and swallows other sorrows   *engulfs*
60   And it is still itself.[2]
DUKE   Why, what's the matter?
BRABANTIO My daughter! O, my daughter!
DUKE AND SENATORS   Dead?
BRABANTIO
                                   Ay, to me.
She is abused,° stol'n from me, and corrupted   *deceived*
By spells and medicines bought of mountebanks;
For nature so preposterously to err,
65   Being not deficient,° blind, or lame of sense,   *defective*
Sans° witchcraft could not.   *without*
DUKE Whoe'er he be that in this foul proceeding
Hath thus beguiled your daughter of herself,
And you of her, the bloody book of law
You shall yourself read in the bitter letter
70   After your own sense[3]—yea, though our proper° son   *my own*
Stood in your action.[4]
BRABANTIO   Humbly I thank Your Grace.
Here is the man, this Moor, whom now it seems
Your special mandate for the state affairs
Hath hither brought.
ALL   We are very sorry for 't.

5. Joined themselves.   1. Overwhelming (as when floodgates are opened).
6. Retrace their original course.   2. Remains undiminished.
7. Freely given and loyal service.   3. According to your own interpretation.
8. Commends himself and reports to.   4. Were under your accusation.
9. Universal enemy to all Christendom.

DUKE [*to Othello*]

75   What, in your own part, can you say to this?

BRABANTIO Nothing, but this is so.

OTHELLO Most potent, grave, and reverend signors,
My very noble and approved° good masters: *esteemed*
That I have ta'en away this old man's daughter,
80   It is most true; true, I have married her.
The very head and front[5] of my offending
Hath this extent, no more. Rude° am I in my speech,   *unpolished*
And little blessed with the soft phrase of peace;
For since these arms of mine had seven years' pith,[6]
85   Till now some nine moons wasted,[7] they have used
Their dearest° action in the tented field;   *most valuable*
And little of this great world can I speak
More than pertains to feats of broils and battle,
And therefore little shall I grace my cause
90   In speaking for myself. Yet, by your gracious patience,
I will a round° unvarnished tale deliver   *plain*
Of my whole course of love—what drugs, what charms,
What conjuration, and what mighty magic,
For such proceeding I am charged withal,°   *with*
95   I won his daughter.

BRABANTIO   A maiden never bold;
Of spirit so still and quiet that her motion
Blushed at herself;[8] and she, in spite of nature,
Of years,[9] of country, credit,° everything,   *reputation*
To fall in love with what she feared to look on!
100   It is a judgment maimed and most imperfect
That will confess° perfection so could err   *concede (that)*
Against all rules of nature, and must be driven
To find out practices° of cunning hell   *plots*
Why this should be. I therefore vouch° again   *assert*
105   That with some mixtures powerful o'er the blood,°   *passions*
Or with some dram conjured to this effect,[1]
He wrought upon her.

DUKE To vouch this is no proof,
Without more wider° and more overt test°   *fuller / testimony*
Than these thin habits[2] and poor likelihoods°   *weak inferences*
110   Of modern seeming[3] do prefer° against him.   *bring forth*

FIRST SENATOR But Othello, speak.
Did you by indirect and forcèd courses[4]
Subdue and poison this young maid's affections?
Or came it by request and such fair question°   *conversation*
115   As soul to soul affordeth?

OTHELLO   I do beseech you,

---

5. Height and breadth, entire extent.
6. Since I was seven.
7. Until some nine months ago (since when Othello has evidently not been on active duty, but in Venice).
8. She blushed easily at herself. (*Motion* can suggest the impulse of the soul or of the emotions, or physical movement.)
9. I.e., difference in age.
1. Dose made by magical spells to have this effect.
2. Garments, i.e., appearances.
3. Commonplace assumption.
4. Means used against her will.

Send for the lady to the Sagittary
And let her speak of me before her father.
If you do find me foul in her report,
The trust, the office I do hold of you
120   Not only take away, but let your sentence
Even fall upon my life.

DUKE   Fetch Desdemona hither.

OTHELLO Ancient, conduct them. You best know the place.

                                    [Exeunt Iago and attendants.]

And, till she come, as truly as to heaven
I do confess the vices of my blood,°   *passions*
125   So justly° to your grave ears I'll present   *accurately*
How I did thrive in this fair lady's love,
And she in mine.

DUKE Say it, Othello.

OTHELLO Her father loved me, oft invited me,
130   Still° questioned me the story of my life   *continually*
From year to year—the battles, sieges, fortunes
That I have passed.
I ran it through, even from my boyish days
To th' very moment that he bade me tell it,
135   Wherein I spoke of most disastrous chances,
Of moving accidents° by flood and field,   *stirring happenings*
Of hairbreadth scapes i' th' imminent deadly breach,[5]
Of being taken by the insolent foe
And sold to slavery, of my redemption thence,
140   And portance° in my travels' history,   *conduct*
Wherein of antres° vast and deserts idle,°   *caverns/barren*
Rough quarries,° rocks, and hills whose heads touch heaven,   *rock formations*
It was my hint° to speak—such was my process— *opportunity*
And of the Cannibals that each other eat,
145   The Anthropophagi,[6] and men whose heads
Do grow beneath their shoulders. These things to hear
Would Desdemona seriously incline;
But still the house affairs would draw her thence,
Which ever as she could with haste dispatch
150   She'd come again, and with a greedy ear
Devour up my discourse. Which I, observing,
Took once a pliant° hour, and found good means *well-suiting*
To draw from her a prayer of earnest heart
That I would all my pilgrimage dilate,°   *relate in detail*
155   Whereof by parcels° she had something heard, *piecemeal*
But not intentively.° I did consent,   *continuously*
And often did beguile her of her tears,
When I did speak of some distressful stroke
That my youth suffered. My story being done,
160   She gave me for my pains a world of sighs.
She swore, in faith, 'twas strange, 'twas passing° strange, *exceedingly*

---

5. Death-threatening gaps made in a fortification.   6. Man-eaters (a term from Pliny's *Natural History*).

'Twas pitiful, 'twas wondrous pitiful.
She wished she had not heard it, yet she wished
That heaven had made her° such a man. She thanked me,   *created her to be*
165   And bade me, if I had a friend that loved her,
I should but teach him how to tell my story,
And that would woo her. Upon this hint° I spake.   *opportunity*
She loved me for the dangers I had passed,
And I loved her that she did pity them.
170   This only is the witchcraft I have used.
Here comes the lady. Let her witness it.
[*Enter Desdemona, Iago, and attendants.*]
DUKE   I think this tale would win my daughter too.
Good Brabantio,
175   Take up this mangled matter at the best.[7]
Men do their broken weapons rather use
Than their bare hands.
BRABANTIO   I pray you, hear her speak.
If she confess that she was half the wooer,
Destruction on my head if my bad blame
180   Light on the man!—Come hither, gentle mistress.
Do you perceive in all this noble company
Where most you owe obedience?
DESDEMONA   My noble Father,
I do perceive here a divided duty.
To you I am bound for life and education;°   *upbringing*
185   My life and education both do learn° me   *teach*
How to respect you. You are the lord of duty;[8]
I am hitherto your daughter. But here's my husband,
And so much duty as my mother showed
To you, preferring you before her father,
190   So much I challenge° that I may profess   *claim*
Due to the Moor my lord.
BRABANTIO   God be with you! I have done.
Please it Your Grace, on to the state affairs.
I had rather to adopt a child than get° it.   *beget*
195   Come hither, Moor. [*He joins the hands of Othello and Desdemona.*]
I here do give thee that with all my heart[9]
Which, but thou hast already, with all my heart°   *gladly*
I would keep from thee.—For your sake,° jewel,   *on your account*
I am glad at soul I have no other child,
200   For thy escape° would teach me tyranny,   *elopement*
To hang clogs[1] on them.—I have done, my lord.
DUKE   Let me speak like yourself,[2] and lay a sentence[3]
Which, as a grece° or step, may help these lovers   *step*
Into your favor.
205   When remedies° are past, the griefs are ended   *hopes of remedy*

7. Make the best of a bad bargain.
8. To whom duty is due.
9. Wherein my whole affection has been engaged.

1. Blocks of wood fastened to the legs of criminals or convicts to inhibit escape.
2. As you would, in your proper temper.
3. Apply a maxim.

By seeing the worst, which late on hopes depended.[4]
To mourn a mischief° that is past and gone   *misfortune*
Is the next° way to draw new mischief on.   *nearest*
What° cannot be preserved when fortune takes,   *whatever*
210   Patience her injury a mockery makes.[5]
     The robbed that smiles steals something from the thief;
     He robs himself that spends a bootless grief.[6]
BRABANTIO So let the Turk of Cyprus us beguile,
     We lose it not, so long as we can smile.
215   He bears the sentence well that nothing bears
     But the free comfort which from thence he hears,
     But he bears both the sentence and the sorrow
     That, to pay grief, must of poor patience borrow.[7]
     These sentences, to sugar or to gall,
220   Being strong on both sides, are equivocal.[8]
     But words are words. I never yet did hear
     That the bruisèd heart was piercèd through the ear.[9]
     I humbly beseech you, proceed to th' affairs of state.
DUKE The Turk with a most mighty preparation makes for Cyprus. Othello, the
225   fortitude[1] of the place is best known to you; and though we have there a sub-
     stitute[2] of most allowed[3] sufficiency, yet opinion, a sovereign mistress of
     effects, throws a more safer voice on you.[4] You must therefore be content to
     slubber[5] the gloss of your new fortunes with this more stubborn[6] and boister-
     ous expedition.
OTHELLO The tyrant custom, most grave senators,
     Hath made the flinty and steel couch of war
     My thrice-driven° bed of down. I do agnize[7]   *thrice sifted*
     A natural and prompt alacrity
     I find in hardness,° and do undertake   *hardship*
235   These present wars against the Ottomites.
     Most humbly therefore bending to your state,[8]
     I crave fit disposition for my wife,
     Due reference of place and exhibition,[9]
     With such accommodation° and besort°   *provision/attendance*
240   As levels° with her breeding.°   *suits/upbringing*
DUKE Why, at her father's.
BRABANTIO   I will not have it so.
OTHELLO Nor I.
DESDEMONA   Nor I. I would not there reside,
     To put my father in impatient thoughts

---

4. Which griefs were sustained until recently by hopeful anticipation.
5. Patience laughs at the injury inflicted by fortune (and thus eases the pain).
6. Indulges in unavailing grief.
7. A person well bears out your maxim who can enjoy its platitudinous comfort, free of all genuine sorrow, but anyone whose grief bankrupts his poor patience is left with your saying and his sorrow, too. (*Bears the sentence* also plays on the meaning, "receives judicial sentence.")
8. These fine maxims are equivocal, either sweet or bitter in their application.

9. I.e., surgically lanced and cured by mere words of advice.
1. Strength.
2. Deputy.
3. Acknowledged.
4. General opinion, an important determiner of affairs, chooses you as the best man.
5. Soil, sully.
6. Harsh, rough.
7. Know in myself, acknowledge.
8. Bowing to your authority.
9. Provision of appropriate place to live and allowance of money.

By being in his eye. Most gracious Duke,
245 To my unfolding° lend your prosperous° ear,   *proposal/propitious*
And let me find a charter° in your voice,   *authorization*
T' assist my simpleness.

DUKE What would you, Desdemona?

DESDEMONA That I did love the Moor to live with him,
250 My downright violence and storm of fortunes[1]
May trumpet to the world. My heart's subdued
Even to the very quality of my lord.[2]
I saw Othello's visage in his mind,
And to his honors and his valiant parts°   *qualities*
255 Did I my soul and fortunes consecrate.
So that, dear lords, if I be left behind
A moth[3] of peace, and he go to the war,
The rites[4] for why I love him are bereft me,
And I a heavy interim shall support
260 By his dear[5] absence. Let me go with him.

OTHELLO Let her have your voice.°   *consent*
Vouch with me, heaven, I therefor beg it not
To please the palate of my appetite,
Nor to comply with heat°—the young affects°   *sexual passion/desires*
265 In me defunct—and proper° satisfaction,   *personal*
But to be free° and bounteous to her mind.   *generous*
And heaven defend° your good souls that you think°   *forbid/should think*
I will your serious and great business scant
When she is with me. No, when light-winged toys
270 Of feathered Cupid seel[6] with wanton dullness
My speculative and officed instruments,[7]
That my disports corrupt and taint my business,[8]
Let huswives make a skillet of my helm,
And all indign° and base adversities   *unworthy, shameful*
275 Make head° against my estimation!°   *rise up/reputation*

DUKE Be it as you shall privately determine,
Either for her stay or going. Th' affair cries haste,
And speed must answer it.

A SENATOR   You must away tonight.

DESDEMONA Tonight, my lord?

DUKE   This night.

OTHELLO   With all my heart.

DUKE At nine i' the morning here we'll meet again.
Othello, leave some officer behind,
And he shall our commission bring to you,
With such things else of quality and respect[9]

---

1. My plain and total breach of social custom, taking my
future by storm and disrupting my whole life.
2. My heart is brought wholly into accord with Othello's
virtues; I love him for his virtues.
3. I.e., one who consumes merely.
4. Rites of love (with a suggestion, too, of "rights," sharing).

5. Heartfelt. Also, costly.
6. I.e., make blind (as in falconry, by sewing up the eyes
of the hawk during training).
7. Eyes and other faculties used in the performance of duty.
8. So that my sexual pastimes impair my work.
9. Of importance and relevance.

As doth import° you.   *concern*
OTHELLO   So please Your Grace, my ancient;
285 A man he is of honesty and trust.
To his conveyance I assign my wife,
With what else needful Your Good Grace shall think
To be sent after me.
DUKE   Let it be so.
Good night to everyone. [*To Brabantio.*] And, noble signor,
290 If virtue no delighted° beauty lack,   *delightful*
Your son-in-law is far more fair than black.
FIRST SENATOR Adieu, brave Moor. Use Desdemona well.
BRABANTIO Look to her, Moor, if thou hast eyes to see.
She has deceived her father, and may thee.
                    [*Exeunt Duke, Brabantio, Cassio, Senators, and officers.*]
OTHELLO My life upon her faith! Honest Iago,
My Desdemona must I leave to thee.
I prithee, let thy wife attend on her,
And bring them after in the best advantage.¹
Come, Desdemona. I have but an hour
300 Of love, of worldly matters and direction,°   *instructions*
To spend with thee. We must obey the time.²
                                                  [*Exit with Desdemona.*]
RODERIGO Iago—
IAGO What sayst thou, noble heart?
RODERIGO What will I do, think'st thou?
IAGO Why, go to bed and sleep.
RODERIGO I will incontinently° drown myself.   *immediately*
IAGO If thou dost, I shall never love thee after. Why, thou silly gentleman?
RODERIGO It is silliness to live when to live is torment; and then have we a pre-
scription³ to die when death is our physician.
IAGO O villainous!⁴ I have looked upon the world for four times seven years, and,
since I could distinguish betwixt a benefit and an injury, I never found man
that knew how to love himself. Ere I would say I would drown myself for the
love of a guinea hen,⁵ I would change my humanity with a baboon.
RODERIGO What should I do? I confess it is my shame to be so fond,⁶ but it is not in
315 my virtue⁷ to amend it.
IAGO Virtue? A fig!⁸ 'Tis in ourselves that we are thus or thus. Our bodies are our
gardens, to the which our wills are gardeners; so that if we will plant nettles or
sow lettuce, set hyssop⁹ and weed up thyme, supply it with one gender¹ of herbs
or distract it with² many, either to have it sterile with idleness³ or manured
320 with industry—why, the power and corrigible authority⁴ of this lies in our wills.

---

1. At the most favorable opportunity.
2. The urgency of the present crisis.
3. Right based on long-established custom. Also, doctor's
prescription
4. I.e., what perfect nonsense.
5. A slang term for a prostitute.
6. Infatuated.
7. Strength, nature.

8. To give a fig is to thrust the thumb between the first
and second fingers in a vulgar and insulting gesture.
9. An herb of the mint family.
1. Kind.
2. Divide it among.
3. Want of cultivation.
4. Power to correct.

If the beam[5] of our lives had not one scale of reason to poise[6] another of sensuality, the blood[7] and baseness of our natures would conduct us to most preposterous conclusions. But we have reason to cool our raging motions,[8] our carnal stings, our unbitted[9] lusts, whereof I take this that you call love to be a sect or
325   scion.[1]

RODERIGO   It cannot be.

IAGO   It is merely a lust of the blood and a permission of the will. Come, be a man. Drown thyself? Drown cats and blind puppies. I have professed me thy friend, and I confess me knit to thy deserving with cables of perdurable[2] toughness. I
330   could never better stead[3] thee than now. Put money in thy purse. Follow thou the wars; defeat thy favor[4] with an usurped[5] beard. I say, put money in thy purse. It cannot be long that Desdemona should continue her love to the Moor—put money in thy purse—nor he his to her. It was a violent commencement in her, and thou shalt see an answerable sequestration[6]—put but money
335   in thy purse. These Moors are changeable in their wills[7]—fill thy purse with money. The food that to him now is as luscious as locusts[8] shall be to him shortly as bitter as coloquintida.[9] She must change for youth; when she is sated with his body, she will find the error of her choice. She must have change, she must. Therefore put money in thy purse. If thou wilt needs damn thyself, do it a
340   more delicate way than drowning. Make[1] all the money thou canst. If sanctimony[2] and a frail vow betwixt an erring[3] barbarian and a supersubtle Venetian be not too hard for my wits and all the tribe of hell, thou shalt enjoy her. Therefore make money. A pox of drowning thyself! It is clean out of the way.[4] Seek thou rather to be hanged in compassing[5] thy joy than to be drowned and
345   go without her.

RODERIGO   Wilt thou be fast[6] to my hopes if I depend on the issue?[7]

IAGO   Thou art sure of me. Go, make money. I have told thee often, and I retell thee again and again, I hate the Moor. My cause is hearted;[8] thine hath no less reason. Let us be conjunctive[9] in our revenge against him. If thou canst cuckold
350   him, thou dost thyself a pleasure, me a sport. There are many events in the womb of time which will be delivered. Traverse,[1] go, provide thy money. We will have more of this tomorrow. Adieu.

RODERIGO   Where shall we meet i' the morning?

IAGO   At my lodging.

RODERIGO   I'll be with thee betimes.° [He starts to leave.]   early

IAGO   Go to, farewell.—Do you hear, Roderigo?

RODERIGO   What say you?

---

5. Balance.
6. Counterbalance.
7. Natural passions.
8. Appetites.
9. Unbridled, uncontrolled.
1. Cutting or offshoot.
2. Very durable.
3. Assist.
4. Disguise your face.
5. The suggestion is that Roderigo is not man enough to have a beard of his own.
6. A corresponding separation or estrangement.
7. Carnal appetites.

8. Fruit of the carob tree (see Matthew 3:4), or perhaps honeysuckle.
9. Colocynth or bitter apple, a purgative.
1. Raise, collect.
2. Sacred ceremony.
3. Wandering, vagabond, unsteady.
4. Entirely unsuitable as a course of action.
5. Encompassing, embracing.
6. True.
7. Successful outcome.
8. Fixed in the heart, heartfelt.
9. United.
1. A military marching term.

IAGO No more of drowning, do you hear?
RODERIGO I am changed.
IAGO Go to, farewell. Put money enough in your purse.
RODERIGO I'll sell all my land.   [Exit.]
IAGO Thus do I ever make my fool my purse;
 For I mine own gained knowledge should profane
 If I would time expend with such a snipe²
365 But for my sport and profit. I hate the Moor;
 And it is thought abroad° that twixt my sheets   rumored
 He's done my office.³ I know not if 't be true;
 But I, for mere suspicion in that kind,
 Will do as if for surety.⁴ He holds me well;⁵
370 The better shall my purpose work on him.
 Cassio's a proper° man. Let me see now: handsome
 To get his place and to plume⁶ up my will
 In double knavery—How, how?—Let's see:
 After some time, to abuse° Othello's ear   deceive
375 That he° is too familiar with his wife.   Cassio
 He hath a person and a smooth dispose°   disposition
 To be suspected, framed to make women false.
 The Moor is of a free° and open° nature,   frank / unsuspicious
 That thinks men honest that but seem to be so,
380 And will as tenderly° be led by the nose   readily
 As asses are.
 I have 't. It is engendered. Hell and night
 Must bring this monstrous birth to the world's light.
               [Exit.]

Act 2

Scene 1

[*A seaport in Cyprus. An open place near the quay. Enter Montano and two Gentlemen.*]
MONTANO What from the cape can you discern at sea?
FIRST GENTLEMAN Nothing at all. It is a high-wrought flood.° agitated sea
 I cannot, twixt the heaven and the main,°   ocean
 Descry a sail.
MONTANO Methinks the wind hath spoke aloud at land;
 A fuller blast ne'er shook our battlements.
 If it hath ruffianed° so upon the sea,   raged
 What ribs of oak, when mountains° melt on them, of water
 Can hold the mortise?⁷ What shall we hear of this?
SECOND GENTLEMAN A segregation° of the Turkish fleet. dispersal
 For do but stand upon the foaming shore,
 The chidden⁸ billow seems to pelt the clouds;
 The wind-shaked surge, with high and monstrous mane,⁹

---

2. Woodcock, i.e., fool.
3. My sexual function as husband.
4. Act as if on certain knowledge.
5. Regards me favorably.
6. Put a feather in the cap of, i.e., glorify, gratify.

7. Hold their joints together.
8. I.e., rebuked, repelled (by the shore), and thus shot into the air.
9. The surf is like the mane of a wild beast.

Seems to cast water on the burning Bear[1]
15 And quench the guards of th' ever-fixèd pole.
    I never did like molestation° view   *such a disturbance*
    On the enchafèd° flood.   *angry*
MONTANO   If that° the Turkish fleet   *if*
    Be not ensheltered and embayed,° they are drowned;   *in a harbor*
20 It is impossible to bear it out.°   *survive*
    Enter a [Third] Gentleman.
THIRD GENTLEMAN News, lads! Our wars are done.
    The desperate tempest hath so banged the Turks
    That their designment° halts.° A noble ship of Venice   *enterprise / is lame*
    Hath seen a grievous wreck° and sufferance°   *shipwreck / damage*
25 On most part of their fleet.
MONTANO How? Is this true?
THIRD GENTLEMAN   The ship is here put in,
    A Veronesa;[2] Michael Cassio,
    Lieutenant to the warlike Moor Othello,
    Is come on shore; the Moor himself at sea,
30 And is in full commission here for Cyprus.
MONTANO I am glad on 't. 'Tis a worthy governor.
THIRD GENTLEMAN But this same Cassio, though he speak of comfort
    Touching the Turkish loss, yet he looks sadly°   *gravely*
    And prays the Moor be safe, for they were parted
35 With foul and violent tempest.
MONTANO   Pray heaven he be,
    For I have served him, and the man commands
    Like a full° soldier. Let's to the seaside, ho!   *perfect*
    As well to see the vessel that's come in
    As to throw out our eyes for brave Othello,
40 Even till we make the main and th' aerial blue[3]
    An indistinct regard.[4]
THIRD GENTLEMAN   Come, let's do so,
    For every minute is expectancy°   *gives expectation*
    Of more arrivance.°   *arrival*
    [Enter Cassio.]
CASSIO Thanks, you the valiant of this warlike isle,
45 That so approve° the Moor! O, let the heavens   *honor*
    Give him defense against the elements,
    For I have lost him on a dangerous sea.
MONTANO Is he well shipped?
CASSIO His bark is stoutly timbered, and his pilot
50 Of very expert and approved allowance;°   *tested reputation*
    Therefore my hopes, not surfeited to death,[5]
    Stand in bold cure.[6]
                [A cry within:] "A sail, a sail, a sail!"

---

1. The constellation Ursa Minor or the Little Bear, which
includes the polestar (and hence regarded as the *guards of
th' ever-fixed pole* in the next line; sometimes the term
guards is applied to the two "pointers" of the Big Bear or
Dipper, which may be intended here.)
2. Fitted out in Verona for Venetian service, or possibly
Verennessa (the Folio spelling), i.e., *verrinessa*, a cutter

(from *verrinare*, "to cut through").
3. The sea and the sky.
4. Indistinguishable in our view.
5. Overextended, worn thin through repeated application
or delayed fulfillment.
6. In strong hopes of fulfillment.

CASSIO What noise?

A GENTLEMAN The town is empty. On the brow o' the sea[7]

55   Stand ranks of people, and they cry "A sail!"

CASSIO My hopes do shape him for[8] the governor.

    [A shot within.]

SECOND GENTLEMAN They do discharge their shot of courtesy;[9]

    Our friends at least.

CASSIO   I pray you, sir, go forth,

    And give us truth who 'tis that is arrived.

SECOND GENTLEMAN I shall. [Exit.]

MONTANO But, good Lieutenant, is your general wived?

CASSIO Most fortunately. He hath achieved a maid

    That paragons° description and wild fame,°   surpasses/rumor

    One that excels the quirks° of blazoning[1] pens,   witty conceits

65   And in th' essential vesture of creation

    Does tire the enginer.[2]

    [Enter Second Gentleman.][3]

                    How now? Who has put in?°   to harbor

SECOND GENTLEMAN 'Tis one Iago, ancient to the General.

CASSIO He's had most favorable and happy speed.

    Tempests themselves, high seas, and howling winds,

70   The guttered° rocks and congregated sands—   jagged

    Traitors ensteeped° to clog the guiltless keel—   lying under water

    As° having sense of beauty, do omit°   as if/suspend

    Their mortal° natures, letting go safely by   deadly

    The divine Desdemona.

MONTANO   What is she?

CASSIO She that I spake of, our great captain's captain,

    Left in the conduct of the bold Iago,

    Whose footing° here anticipates our thoughts   landing

    A sennight's° speed. Great Jove, Othello guard,   week's

    And swell his sail with thine own powerful breath,

80   That he may bless this bay with his tall° ship,   splendid

    Make love's quick pants in Desdemona's arms,

    Give renewed fire to our extincted spirits,

    And bring all Cyprus comfort!

    [Enter Desdemona, Iago, Roderigo, and Emilia.]

                    O, behold,

    The riches of the ship is come on shore!

85   You men of Cyprus, let her have your knees.

    [The gentlemen make curtsy to Desdemona.]

    Hail to thee, lady! And the grace of heaven

    Before, behind thee, and on every hand

    Enwheel thee round!

DESDEMONA   I thank you, valiant Cassio.

    What tidings can you tell me of my lord?

---

7. Cliff-edge.

8. I hope it is.

9. Fire a salute in token of respect and courtesy.

1. Setting forth as though in heraldic language.

2. In her real, God-given, beauty, (she) defeats any

attempt to praise her. The enginer [engineer] is the poet, one who devises.

3. So identified in the Quarto text here and in lines 57, 60, 67 and 95; the Folio calls him a gentleman.

CASSIO He is not yet arrived, nor know I aught
    But that he's well and will be shortly here.
DESDEMONA O, but I fear—How lost your company?
CASSIO The great contention of the sea and skies
    Parted our fellowship.
      [*Within: "A sail, a sail!" A shot.*]
                But hark. A sail!
SECOND GENTLEMAN They give their greeting to the citadel.
    This likewise is a friend.
CASSIO   See for the news.
    [*Exit Second Gentleman.*]
    Good Ancient, you are welcome. [*Kissing Emilia.*]
    Welcome, mistress.
    Let it not gall your patience, good Iago,
100   That I extend° my manners; 'tis my breeding[4]   *give scope to*
    That gives me this bold show of courtesy.
IAGO Sir, would she give you so much of her lips
    As of her tongue she oft bestows on me,
    You would have enough.
DESDEMONA Alas, she has no speech![5]
IAGO   In faith, too much.
    I find it still,° when I have list° to sleep.   *always/desire*
    Marry, before your ladyship, I grant,
    She puts her tongue a little in her heart
    And chides with thinking.[6]
EMILIA   You have little cause to say so.
IAGO Come on, come on. You are pictures out of doors,[7]
    Bells[8] in your parlors, wildcats in your kitchens,[9]
    Saints° in your injuries, devils being offended,   *martyrs*
    Players° in your huswifery,° and huswives[1] in your beds.   *idlers/housekeeping*
DESDEMONA O, fie upon thee, slanderer!
IAGO Nay, it is true, or else I am a Turk.[2]
    You rise to play, and go to bed to work.
EMILIA You shall not write my praise.
IAGO   No, let me not.
DESDEMONA What wouldst write of me, if thou shouldst praise me?
IAGO O gentle lady, do not put me to 't,
120   For I am nothing if not critical.°   *censorious*
DESDEMONA Come on, essay.°—There's one gone to the harbor?   *try*
IAGO Ay, madam.
DESDEMONA I am not merry, but I do beguile
    The thing I am[3] by seeming otherwise.
125   Come, how wouldst thou praise me?

---

4. Training in the niceties of etiquette.
5. She's not a chatterbox, as you allege.
6. In her thoughts only.
7. Silent and well-behaved in public.
8. Jangling, noisy, and brazen.

9. In domestic affairs. (Ladies would not do the cooking.)
1. Hussies (i.e., women are "busy" in bed, or unduly thrifty in dispensing sexual favors).
2. An infidel, not to be believed.
3. My anxious self.

IAGO I am about it, but indeed my invention
    Comes from my pate as birdlime[4] does from frieze—°   *coarse cloth*
    It plucks out brains and all. But my Muse labors,[5]
    And thus she is delivered:
130   If she be fair and wise, fairness and wit,
    The one's for use, the other useth it.[6]

DESDEMONA Well praised! How if she be black[7] and witty?

IAGO If she be black, and thereto have a wit,
    She'll find a white[8] that shall her blackness fit.[9]

DESDEMONA Worse and worse.

EMILIA How if fair and foolish?

IAGO She never yet was foolish that was fair,
    For even her folly[1] helped her to an heir.°   *to bear a child*

DESDEMONA These are old fond[2] paradoxes to make fools laugh i' th' alehouse.
140   What miserable praise hast thou for her that's foul[3] and foolish?

IAGO There's none so foul and foolish thereunto,°   *in addition*
    But does foul° pranks which fair and wise ones do.   *sluttish*

DESDEMONA O heavy ignorance! Thou praisest the worst best. But what praise
    couldst thou bestow on a deserving woman indeed, one that, in the authority
145   of her merit, did justly put on the vouch[4] of very malice itself?

IAGO She that was ever fair, and never proud,
    Had tongue at will, and yet was never loud,
    Never lacked gold and yet went never gay,°   *extravagantly clothed*
    Fled from her wish, and yet said, "Now I may,"[5]
150   She that being angered, her revenge being nigh,
    Bade her wrong stay[6] and her displeasure fly,
    She that in wisdom never was so frail
    To change the cod's head for the salmon's tail,[7]
    She that could think and ne'er disclose her mind,
155   See suitors following and not look behind,
    She was a wight, if ever such wight were—

DESDEMONA To do what?

IAGO To suckle fools and chronicle small beer.[8]

DESDEMONA O most lame and impotent conclusion! Do not learn of him, Emilia,
160   though he be thy husband. How say you, Cassio? Is he not a most profane and
    liberal[9] counselor?

CASSIO He speaks home,[1] madam. You may relish[2] him more in[3] the soldier than in
    the scholar.
    [*Cassio and Desdemona stand together, conversing intimately.*]

---

4. Sticky substance used to catch small birds.
5. Exerts herself. Also, prepares to deliver a child (with a following pun on "*delivered*" in line 130).
6. Her cleverness will make use of her beauty.
7. Dark-complexioned, brunette.
8. A fair person (with wordplay on "wight," a person).
9. With sexual suggestion of mating.
1. With added meaning of "lechery, wantonness."
2. Foolish.
3. Ugly.

4. Compel the approval.
5. Avoided temptation where the choice was hers.
6. Resolved to put up with her injury patiently.
7. To exchange a lackluster husband for a sexy lover(?) (*Cod's head* is slang for "penis.")
8. To nurse babies and keep petty household accounts.
9. Ribald and licentious.
1. Right to the target (a term from fencing).
2. Appreciate.
3. In the character of.

IAGO [*aside*] He takes her by the palm, Ay, well said,[4] whisper. With as little a web
165   as this will I ensnare as great a fly as Cassio. Aye, smile upon her, do; I will
gyve[5] thee in thine own courtship.[6] You say true;[7] 'tis so, indeed. If such tricks
as these strip you out of your lieutenantry, it had been better you had not kissed
your three fingers so oft, which now again you are most apt to play the sir[8] in.
Very good; well kissed! An excellent courtesy! 'Tis so, indeed. Yet again your
170   fingers to your lips? Would they were clyster pipes[9] for your sake! [*Trumpet
within.*] The Moor! I know his trumpet.

CASSIO 'Tis truly so.

DESDEMONA   Let's meet him and receive him.

CASSIO Lo, where he comes!

[*Enter Othello and attendants.*]

OTHELLO O my fair warrior!

DESDEMONA   My dear Othello!

OTHELLO It gives me wonder great as my content
To see you here before me. O my soul's joy,
If after every tempest come such calms,
May the winds blow till they have weakened death,
And let the laboring bark climb hills of seas
180   Olympus-high, and duck again as low
As hell's from heaven! If it were now to die,
'Twere now to be most happy, for I fear
My soul hath her content so absolute
That not another comfort like to this
185   Succeeds in unknown fate.[1]

DESDEMONA   The heavens forbid
But that our loves and comforts should increase
Even as our days do grow!

OTHELLO Amen to that, sweet powers!
I cannot speak enough of this content.
190   It stops me here; it is too much of joy.
And this, and this, the greatest discords be
[*They kiss.*][2]
That e'er our hearts shall make!

IAGO [*aside*] O, you are well tuned now!
But I'll set down[3] the pegs that make this music,
195   As honest as I am.[4]

OTHELLO Come, let us to the castle.
News, friends! Our wars are done, the Turks are drowned.
How does my old acquaintance of this isle?—
Honey, you shall be well desired° in Cyprus;   welcomed
200   I have found great love amongst them. O my sweet,
I prattle out of fashion,° and I dote   incoherently

---

4. Well done.
5. Fetter, shackle.
6. Courtesy, show of courtly manners.
7. That's right, go ahead.
8. The fine gentleman.

9. Tubes used for enemas and douches.
1. Can follow in the unknown future.
2. The direction is from the Quarto.
3. Loosen (and hence untune the instrument).
4. For all my supposed honesty.

In mine own comforts.—I prithee, good Iago,
Go to the bay and disembark my coffers.°   *chests*
Bring thou the master° to the citadel;   *ship's captain*
205   He is a good one, and his worthiness
Does challenge° much respect.—Come, Desdemona.—   *deserve*
Once more, well met at Cyprus!

               [Exeunt Othello and Desdemona and all but Iago and Roderigo.]

IAGO *[to an attendant]* Do thou meet me presently at the harbor. *[To Roderigo.]*
    Come hither. If thou be'st valiant—as, they say, base men[5] being in love have
210   then a nobility in their natures more than is native to them—list[6] me. The
    Lieutenant tonight watches on the court of guard.[7] First, I must tell thee this:
    Desdemona is directly in love with him.
RODERIGO With him? Why, 'tis not possible.
IAGO Lay thy finger thus,[8] and let thy soul be instructed. Mark me with what vio-
215   lence she first loved the Moor, but[9] for bragging and telling her fantastical lies.
    To love him still for prating? Let not thy discreet heart think it. Her eye must
    be fed; and what delight shall she have to look on the devil? When the blood is
    made dull with the act of sport,[1] there should be, again to inflame it and to give
    satiety a fresh appetite, loveliness in favor,[2] sympathy[3] in years, manners, and
220   beauties—all which the Moor is defective in. Now, for want of these required
    conveniences,[4] her delicate tenderness will find itself abused,[5] begin to heave
    the gorge,[6] disrelish and abhor the Moor. Very nature[7] will instruct her in it
    and compel her to some second choice. Now, sir, this granted—as it is a most
    pregnant[8] and unforced position—who stands so eminent in the degree[9] of this
225   fortune as Cassio does? A knave very voluble,[1] no further conscionable[2] than
    in putting on the mere form of civil and humane[3] seeming for the better com-
    passing of his salt[4] and most hidden loose affection.[5] Why, none, why, none. A
    slipper[6] and subtle knave, a finder out of occasions, that has an eye can stamp[7]
    and counterfeit advantages,[8] though true advantage never present itself; a dev-
230   ilish knave. Besides, the knave is handsome, young, and hath all those requi-
    sites in him that folly[9] and green[1] minds look after. A pestilent complete
    knave, and the woman hath found him[2] already.
RODERIGO I cannot believe that in her. She's full of most blessed condition.[3]
IAGO Blessed fig's end! The wine she drinks is made of grapes. If she had been
235   blessed, she would never have loved the Moor. Blessed pudding![4] Didst thou
    not see her paddle with the palm of his hand? Didst not mark that?

---

5. Even lowly born men.
6. Listen to.
7. Guardhouse. (Cassio is in charge of the watch.)
8. I.e., on your lips
9. Only.
1. Sex.
2. Appearance.
3. Correspondence, similarity.
4. Things conducive to sexual compatibility.
5. Cheated, revolted.
6. Experience nausea.
7. Her very instincts.
8. Evident, cogent.
9. As next in line for.

1. Facile, glib.
2. Conscientious, conscience-bound.
3. Polite, courteous.
4. Licentious.
5. Passion.
6. Slippery.
7. An eye that can coin, create.
8. Favorable opportunities.
9. Wantonness.
1. Immature.
2. Sized him up, perceived his intent.
3. Disposition.
4. Sausage.

RODERIGO Yes, that I did; but that was but courtesy.

IAGO Lechery, by this hand. An index[5] and obscure prologue to the history of lust and foul thoughts. They met so near with their lips that their breaths embraced
240 together. Villainous thoughts, Roderigo! When these mutualities[6] so marshal the way, hard at hand[7] comes the master and main exercise, th' incorporate[8] conclusion. Pish! But, sir, be you ruled by me. I have brought you from Venice. Watch you[9] tonight; for the command, I'll lay 't upon you.[1] Cassio knows you not. I'll not be far from you. Do you find some occasion to anger Cassio, either
245 by speaking too loud, or tainting[2] his discipline, or from what other course you please, which the time shall more favorably minister.[3]

RODERIGO Well.

IAGO Sir, he's rash and very sudden in choler,[4] and haply[5] may strike at you. Provoke him that he may, for even out of that will I cause these of Cyprus to
250 mutiny,[6] whose qualification[7] shall come into no true taste[8] again but by the displanting of Cassio. So shall you have a shorter journey to your desires by the means I shall then have to prefer[9] them, and the impediment most profitably removed, without the which there were no expectation of our prosperity.

RODERIGO I will do this, if you can bring it to any opportunity.

IAGO I warrant[1] thee. Meet me by and by[2] at the citadel. I must fetch his necessaries ashore. Farewell.

RODERIGO Adieu.   [Exit.]

IAGO That Cassio loves her, I do well believe 't;
     That she loves him, 'tis apt° and of great credit.°   *probable/credibility*
260 The Moor, howbeit that I endure him not,
     Is of a constant, loving, noble nature,
     And I dare think he'll prove to Desdemona
     A most dear husband. Now, I do love her too,
     Not out of absolute lust—though peradventure
265 I stand accountant° for as great a sin—   *accountable*
     But partly led to diet° my revenge   *feed*
     For that I do suspect the lusty Moor
     Hath leaped into my seat, the thought whereof
     Doth, like a poisonous mineral, gnaw my innards;
270 And nothing can or shall content my soul
     Till I am evened with him, wife for wife,
     Or failing so, yet that I put the Moor
     At least into a jealousy so strong
     That judgment cannot cure. Which thing to do,
275 If this poor trash of Venice, whom I trace[3]
     For[4] his quick hunting, stand[5] the putting on,

---

5. Table of contents.
6. Exchanges, intimacies.
7. Closely following.
8. Carnal.
9. Stand watch.
1. I'll arrange for you to be appointed, given orders.
2. Disparaging.
3. Provide.
4. Wrath.
5. Perhaps.
6. Riot.

7. Appeasement.
8. Acceptable state
9. Advance.
1. Assure.
2. Immediately.
3. Train, or follow (?), or perhaps *trash*, a hunting term, meaning to put weights on a hunting dog to slow him down.
4. To make more eager.
5. Respond properly when I incite him to quarrel.

I'll have our Michael Cassio on the hip,[6]
Abuse° him to the Moor in the rank garb°—   *slander/coarse manner*
For I fear Cassio with my nightcap[7] too—
280   Make the Moor thank me, love me, and reward me
For making him egregiously an ass
And practicing upon° his peace and quiet   *plotting against*
Even to madness. 'Tis here, but yet confused.
Knavery's plain face is never seen till used.   [*Exit.*]

Scene 2

[*Location: Cyprus. A street. Enter Othello's Herald with a proclamation.*]

HERALD It is Othello's pleasure, our noble and valiant general, that, upon certain
tidings now arrived, importing the mere perdition[8] of the Turkish fleet, every
man put himself into triumph:[9] some to dance, some to make bonfires, each
man to what sport and revels his addiction[1] leads him. For, besides these beneficial news, it is the celebration of his nuptial. So much was his pleasure should
be proclaimed. All offices[2] are open, and there is full liberty of feasting from
this present hour of five till the bell have told eleven. Heaven bless the isle of
Cyprus and our noble general Othello!

[*Exit.*]

Scene 3

[*Location: Cyprus. The citadel. Enter Othello, Desdemona, Cassio, and attendants.*]

OTHELLO Good Michael, look you to the guard tonight.
Let's teach ourselves that honorable stop°   *restraint*
Not to outsport° discretion.   *celebrate beyond*
CASSIO Iago hath direction what to do,
5   But notwithstanding, with my personal eye
Will I look to 't.
OTHELLO   Iago is most honest.
Michael, good night. Tomorrow with your earliest[3]
Let me have speech with you. [*To Desdemona.*] Come, my dear love,
The purchase made, the fruits are to ensue;
10   That profit's yet to come 'tween me and you.[4]—
Good night.

[*Exit Othello, with Desdemona and attendants.*]

[*Enter Iago.*]

CASSIO Welcome, Iago. We must to the watch.
IAGO Not this hour,[5] Lieutenant; 'tis not yet ten o' the clock. Our general cast[6] us
thus early for the love of his Desdemona; who[7] let us not therefore blame. He
15   hath not yet made wanton the night with her, and she is sport for Jove.
CASSIO She's a most exquisite lady.
IAGO And, I'll warrant her, full of game.

6. At my mercy, where I can throw him (a wrestling
term).
7. As a rival in my bed, as one who gives me cuckold's
horns.
8. Complete destruction.
9. Public celebration.
1. Inclination.

2. Rooms where food and drink are kept.
3. At your earliest convenience.
4. Though married, we haven't yet consummated our
love.
5. Not for an hour yet.
6. Dismissed.
7. Othello.

CASSIO Indeed, she's a most fresh and delicate creature.

IAGO What an eye she has! Methinks it sounds a parley[8] to provocation.

CASSIO An inviting eye, and yet methinks right modest.

IAGO And when she speaks, is it not an alarum[9] to love?

CASSIO She is indeed perfection.

IAGO Well, happiness to their sheets! Come, Lieutenant, I have a stoup[1] of wine, and here without[2] are a brace[3] of Cyprus gallants that would fain have a mea-
25   sure[4] to the health of black Othello.

CASSIO Not tonight, good Iago. I have very poor and unhappy brains for drinking. I could well wish courtesy would invent some other custom of entertainment.

IAGO O, they are our friends. But one cup! I'll drink for you.[5]

CASSIO I have drunk but one cup tonight, and that was craftily qualified[6] too, and
30   behold what innovation[7] it makes here.[8] I am unfortunate in the infirmity and dare not task my weakness with any more.

IAGO What, man? 'Tis a night of revels. The gallants desire it.

CASSIO Where are they?

IAGO Here at the door. I pray you, call them in.

CASSIO I'll do't, but it dislikes me.[9]   [Exit.]

IAGO If I can fasten but one cup upon him,
        With that which he hath drunk tonight already,
        He'll be as full of quarrel and offense[1]
        As my young mistress' dog. Now, my sick fool Roderigo,
40   Whom love hath turned almost the wrong side out,
        To Desdemona hath tonight caroused°   drunk off
        Potations pottle-deep;[2] and he's to watch.°   stand watch
        Three lads of Cyprus—noble swelling° spirits,   proud
        That hold their honors in a wary distance,[3]
45   The very elements° of this warlike isle—   typical sort
        Have I tonight flustered with flowing cups,
        And they watch° too. Now, 'mongst this flock of drunkards   are on guard
        Am I to put our Cassio in some action
        That may offend the isle.—But here they come.
        [Enter Cassio, Montano, and gentlemen; servants following with wine.]
50   If consequence do but approve my dream,[4]
        My boat sails freely both with wind and stream.°   current

CASSIO 'Fore God, they have given me a rouse° already.   large drink

MONTANA Good faith, a little one; not past a pint, as I am a soldier.

IAGO Some wine, ho!

55   [He sings.] "And let me the cannikin° clink, clink,   cup
        And let me the cannikin clink.

---

8. Calls for a conference, issues an invitation.
9. Signal calling men to arms (continuing the military metaphor of *parley*, line 21).
1. Measure of liquor, two quarts.
2. Outside.
3. Pair.
4. Gladly drink a toast.
5. In your place. (Iago will do the steady drinking to keep the gallants company while Cassio has only one cup.)

6. Diluted.
7. Disturbance, insurrection.
8. I.e., in my head.
9. I'm reluctant.
1. Readiness to take offense.
2. To the bottom of the tankard.
3. Are extremely sensitive of their honor.
4. If subsequent events will only substantiate my scheme.

A soldier's a man,
O, man's life's but a span;[5]
Why, then, let a soldier drink."

60   Some wine, boys!

CASSIO 'Fore God, an excellent song.

IAGO I learned it in England, where indeed they are most potent in potting.[6] Your Dane, your German, and your swag-bellied Hollander—drink, ho!—are nothing to your English.

CASSIO Is your Englishman so exquisite in his drinking?

IAGO Why, he drinks you,[7] with facility, your Dane dead drunk; he sweats not[8] to overthrow your Almain;[9] he gives your Hollander a vomit ere the next pottle can be filled.

CASSIO To the health of our general!

MONTANO I am for it, Lieutenant, and I'll do you justice.[1]

IAGO O sweet England! [*He sings.*]

"King Stephen was and-a worthy peer,
His breeches cost him but a crown;
He held them sixpence all too dear,
75   With that he called the tailor lown.°   *lout*

He was a wight of high renown,
And thou art but of low degree.
'Tis pride[2] that pulls the country down;
Then take thy auld° cloak about thee."   *old*

80   Some wine, ho!

CASSIO 'Fore God, this is a more exquisite song than the other.

IAGO Will you hear 't again?

CASSIO No, for I hold him to be unworthy of his place that does those things. Well, God's above all; and there be souls must be saved, and there be souls must not be saved.

IAGO It's true, good Lieutenant.

CASSIO For mine own part—no offense to the General, nor any man of quality[3]—I hope to be saved.

IAGO And so do I too, Lieutenant.

CASSIO Ay, but, by your leave, not before me; the lieutenant is to be saved before
90   the ancient. Let's have no more of this; let's to our affairs.—God forgive us our sins!—Gentlemen, let's look to our business. Do not think gentlemen, I am drunk. This is my ancient; this is my right hand, and this is my left. I am not drunk now. I can stand well enough, and speak well enough.

GENTLEMEN Excellent well.

CASSIO Why, very well then; you must not think then that I am drunk.   [*Exit.*]

MONTANO To th' platform, masters. Come, let's set the watch.[4]

---

5. Brief span of time. (Cf. Psalm 39.5 as rendered in the Book of Common Prayer: "Thou hast made my days as it were a span long.")
6. Drinking.
7. Drinks.
8. Need not exert himself.

9. German.
1. I'll drink as much as you.
2. Extravagance in dress.
3. Rank.
4. Mount the guard.

[*Exeunt Gentlemen.*]

IAGO You see this fellow that is gone before.
　　　He's a soldier fit to stand by Caesar
　　　And give direction; and do but see his vice.
100　'Tis to his virtue a just equinox,[5]
　　　The one as long as th' other. 'Tis pity of him.
　　　I fear the trust Othello puts him in,
　　　On some odd time of his infirmity,
　　　Will shake this island.
MONTANO　　　　　　　　But is he often thus?
IAGO 'Tis evermore the prologue to his sleep.
　　　He'll watch the horologe a double set,[6]
　　　If drink rock not his cradle.
MONTANO　　　　　　　　　　It were well
　　　The General were put in mind of it.
　　　Perhaps he sees it not, or his good nature
110　Prizes the virtue that appears in Cassio
　　　And looks not on his evils. Is not this true?
　　　[*Enter Roderigo.*]
IAGO [*aside to him*] How now, Roderigo?
　　　I pray you, after the Lieutenant; go.　　　　[*Exit Roderigo.*]
MONTANO And 'tis great pity that the noble Moor
115　Should hazard such a place as his own second
　　　With[7] one of an engraffed° infirmity.　　　　　　　*inveterate*
　　　It were an honest action to say so
　　　To the Moor.
IAGO　　　　　　Not I, for this fair island.
　　　I do love Cassio well and would do much
120　To cure him of this evil. [*Cry within:* "Help! Help!"]
　　　　　　　　　　　　But, hark! What noise?
　　　[*Enter Cassio, pursuing Roderigo.*][8]
CASSIO Zounds, you rogue! You rascal!
MONTANO What's the matter, Lieutenant?
CASSIO A knave teach me my duty? I'll beat the knave into a twiggen[9] bottle.
RODERIGO Beat me?
CASSIO Dost thou prate, rogue? [*He strikes Roderigo.*]
MONTANO Nay, good Lieutenant. [*Restraining him.*] I pray you, sir, hold your hand.
CASSIO Let me go, sir, or I'll knock you o'er the mazard.[1]
MONTANO Come, come, you're drunk.
CASSIO Drunk? [*They fight.*]
IAGO [*aside to Roderigo*]
130　Away, I say. Go out and cry a mutiny.[2]
　　　　　　　　　　　　　　　　　　[*Exit Roderigo.*]
　　　Nay, good Lieutenant—God's will, gentlemen—

---

5. Exact counterpart. (*Equinox* is an equal length of days and nights.)
6. Stay awake twice around the clock or *horologe*.
7. Risk giving such an important position as his second in command to.
8. The Quarto text reads, "driving in."

9. Wicker-covered. (Cassio vows to assail Roderigo until his skin resembles wickerwork or until he has driven Roderigo through the holes in a wickerwork.)
1. Head (literally, a drinking vessel).
2. Riot.

Help, ho!—Lieutenant—sir—Montano—sir—
Help, masters!°—Here's a goodly watch indeed!   *sirs*
[*A bell rings.*]³
Who's that which rings the bell?—Diablo,° ho!   *the devil*
135   The town will rise.° God's will, Lieutenant, hold!   *grow riotous*
You'll be ashamed forever.
[*Enter Othello and attendants with weapons*].
OTHELLO What is the matter here?
MONTANO   Zounds, I bleed still.
I am hurt to th' death. He dies! [*He thrusts at Cassio.*]
OTHELLO   Hold, for your lives!
IAGO Hold, ho! Lieutenant—sir—Montano—gentlemen—
140   Have you forgot all sense of place and duty?
Hold! The General speaks to you. Hold, for shame!
OTHELLO Why, how now, ho! From whence ariseth this?
Are we turned Turks, and to ourselves do that
Which heaven hath forbid the Ottomites?⁴
145   For Christian shame, put by this barbarous brawl!
He that stirs next to carve for⁵ his own rage
Holds his soul light;⁶ he dies upon his motion.⁷
Silence that dreadful bell. It frights the isle
From her propriety.° What is the matter, masters?   *proper state*
150   Honest Iago, that looks dead with grieving,
Speak. Who began this? On thy love, I charge thee.
IAGO I do not know. Friends all but now, even now,
In quarter⁸ and in terms° like bride and groom   *on good terms*
Devesting them° for bed; and then, but now—   *undressing*
155   As if some planet had unwitted men—
Swords out, and tilting one at others' breasts
In opposition bloody. I cannot speak°   *explain*
Any beginning to this peevish odds;°   *quarrel*
And would in action glorious I had lost
160   Those legs that brought me to a part of it!
OTHELLO How comes it, Michael, you are thus forgot?⁹
CASSIO I pray you, pardon me. I cannot speak.
OTHELLO Worthy Montano, you were wont° be civil;   *accustomed to be*
The gravity and stillness° of your youth   *sobriety*
165   The world hath noted, and your name is great
In mouths of wisest censure.° What's the matter   *judgment*
That you unlace¹ your reputation thus
And spend your rich opinion° for the name   *reputation*
Of a night-brawler? Give me answer to it.
MONTANO Worthy Othello, I am hurt to danger.
Your officer, Iago, can inform you—
While I spare speech, which something° now offends° me— *somewhat/pains*

---

3. This direction is from the Quarto, as are *Exit Roderigo*
at line 130, *They fight* at line 129, and *with weapons* at line
136.
4. Inflict on ourselves the harm that heaven has prevented the Turks from doing (by destroying their fleet).
5. Indulge, satisfy with his sword.

6. Places little value on his life.
7. If he moves.
8. In friendly conduct, within bounds.
9. Have forgotten yourself thus.
1. Undo, lay open (as one might loose the strings of a
purse containing reputation).

Of all that I do know; nor know I aught
By me that's said or done amiss this night,
175   Unless self-charity be sometimes a vice,
And to defend ourselves it be a sin
When violence assails us.

OTHELLO   Now, by heaven,
My blood[2] begins my safer guides[3] to rule,
And passion, having my best judgment collied,°   *darkened*
180   Essays° to lead the way. Zounds, if I stir,   *undertakes*
Or do but lift this arm, the best of you
Shall sink in my rebuke. Give me to know
How this foul rout° began, who set it on;   *riot*
And he that is approved in° this offense,   *found guilty of*
185   Though he had twinned with me, both at a birth,
Shall lose me. What? In a town of[4] war
Yet wild, the people's hearts brim full of fear,
To manage° private and domestic quarrel?   *undertake*
In night, and on the court and guard of safety?[5]
190   'Tis monstrous. Iago, who began 't?

MONTANO [*to Iago*] If partially affined,[6] or leagued in office,[7]
Thou dost deliver more or less than truth,
Thou art no soldier.

IAGO   Touch me not so near.
I had rather have this tongue cut from my mouth
195   Than it should do offense to Michael Cassio;
Yet, I persuade myself, to speak the truth
Shall nothing wrong him. Thus it is, General.
Montano and myself being in speech,
There comes a fellow crying out for help,
200   And Cassio following him with determined sword
To execute[8] upon him. Sir, this gentleman [*indicating Montano.*]
Steps in to Cassio and entreats his pause.°   *him to stop*
Myself the crying fellow did pursue,
Lest by his clamor—as it so fell out—
205   The town might fall in fright. He, swift of foot,
Outran my purpose, and I returned, the rather°   *sooner*
For that I heard the clink and fall of swords
And Cassio high in oath, which till tonight
I ne'er might say before. When I came back—
210   For this was brief—I found them close together
At blow and thrust, even as again they were
When you yourself did part them.
More of this matter cannot I report.
But men are men; the best sometimes forget.°   *forget themselves*
215   Though Cassio did some little wrong to him,
As men in rage strike those that wish them best,[9]
Yet surely Cassio, I believe, received
From him that fled some strange indignity,

---

2. Passion (of anger).
3. I.e., reason.
4. Town garrisoned for.
5. At the main guardhouse or headquarters and on watch.

6. Made partial by some personal relationship.
7. In league as fellow officers.
8. Give effect to (his anger).
9. Even those who are well disposed.

Which patience could not pass.°   *overlook*

OTHELLO   I know, Iago,

220   Thy honesty and love doth mince this matter,
      Making it light to Cassio. Cassio, I love thee,
      But nevermore be officer of mine.

      [*Enter Desdemona, attended.*]

      Look if my gentle love be not raised up.
      I'll make thee an example.

DESDEMONA What is the matter, dear?

OTHELLO   All's well now, sweeting;
      Come away to bed. [*To Montano.*] Sir, for your hurts,
      Myself will be your surgeon.[1]—Lead him off.

      [*Montano is led off.*]

      Iago, look with care about the town
      And silence those whom this vile brawl distracted.

230   Come, Desdemona. 'Tis the soldiers' life
      To have their balmy slumbers waked with strife.

                    [*Exit with all but Iago and Cassio.*]

IAGO What, are you hurt, Lieutenant?

CASSIO Ay, past all surgery.

IAGO Marry, God forbid!

CASSIO Reputation, reputation, reputation! O, I have lost my reputation! I have
      lost the immortal part of myself, and what remains is bestial. My reputation,
      Iago, my reputation!

IAGO As I am an honest man, I thought you had received some bodily wound; there
      is more sense in that than in reputation. Reputation is an idle and most false
240   imposition,[2] oft got without merit and lost without deserving. You have lost no
      reputation at all, unless you repute yourself such a loser. What, man, there are
      more ways to recover[3] the General again. You are but now cast in his mood[4]—
      a punishment more in policy[5] than in malice, even so as one would beat his
      offenseless dog to affright an imperious lion.[6] Sue[7] to him again and he's yours.

CASSIO I will rather sue to be despised than to deceive so good a commander with
      so slight,[8] so drunken, and so indiscreet an officer. Drunk? And speak parrot?[9]
      And squabble? Swagger? Swear? And discourse fustian with one's own shadow?
      O thou invisible spirit of wine, if thou hast no name to be known by, let us call
      thee devil!

IAGO What was he that you followed with your sword? What had he done to you?

CASSIO I know not.

IAGO Is 't possible?

CASSIO I remember a mass of things, but nothing distinctly; a quarrel, but nothing
      wherefore.[1] O God, that men should put an enemy in their mouths to steal
255   away their brains! That we should, with joy, pleasance, revel, and applause[2]
      transform ourselves into beasts!

IAGO Why, but you are now well enough. How came you thus recovered?

---

1. Make sure you receive medical attention.
2. Thing artificially imposed and of no real value.
3. Regain favor with.
4. Dismissed in a moment of anger.
5. Done for expediency's sake and as a public gesture.
6. Would make an example of a minor offender to deter more important and dangerous offenders.

7. Petition.
8. Worthless.
9. Talk nonsense, rant. (*Discourse fustian*, in the next line, has much the same meaning.)
1. Why.
2. Desire for applause.

CASSIO It hath pleased the devil drunkenness to give place to the devil wrath. One unperfectness shows me another, to make me frankly despise myself.

IAGO Come, you are too severe a moraler.[3] As the time, the place, and the condition of this country stands, I could heartily wish this had not befallen; but since it is as it is, mend it for your own good.

CASSIO I will ask him for my place again; he shall tell me I am a drunkard. Had I as many mouths as Hydra,[4] such an answer would stop them all. To be now a sen-
265   sible man, by and by a fool, and presently a beast! O, strange! Every inordinate cup is unblessed, and the ingredient is a devil.

IAGO Come, come, good wine is a good familiar creature, if it be well used. Exclaim no more against it. And, good Lieutenant, I think you think I love you.

CASSIO I have well approved[5] it, sir. I drunk!

IAGO You or any man living may be drunk at a time,[6] man. I'll tell you what you shall do. Our general's wife is now the general—I may say so in this respect, for that[7] he hath devoted and given up himself to the contemplation, mark, and denotement[8] of her parts[9] and graces. Confess yourself freely to her; importune her help to put you in your place again. She is of so free,[1] so kind, so apt, so
275   blessed a disposition, she holds it a vice in her goodness not to do more than she is requested. This broken joint between you and her husband entreat her to splinter;[2] and, my fortunes against any lay[3] worth naming, this crack of your love shall grow stronger than it was before.

CASSIO You advise me well.

IAGO I protest,[4] in the sincerity of love and honest kindness.

CASSIO I think it freely;[5] and betimes in the morning I will beseech the virtuous Desdemona to undertake for me. I am desperate of my fortunes if they check[6] me here.

IAGO You are in the right. Good night, Lieutenant. I must to the watch.

CASSIO Good night, honest Iago.   [Exit Cassio.]

IAGO And what's he then that says I play the villain,
When this advice is free[7] I give, and honest,
Probal° to thinking, and indeed the course   reasonable
To win the Moor again? For 'tis most easy
Th' inclining° Desdemona to subdue°   willing/persuade
290   In any honest suit; she's framed as fruitful[8]
As the free elements.[9] And then for her
To win the Moor—were 't to renounce his baptism,
All seals and symbols of redeemèd sin—
His soul is so enfettered to her love
295   That she may make, unmake, do what she list,
Even as her appetite[1] shall play the god
With his weak function.[2] How am I then a villain,

---

3. Moralizer.
4. The Lernaean Hydra, a monster with many heads and the ability to grow two heads when one was cut off, slain by Hercules as the second of his twelve labors.
5. Proved.
6. At one time or another.
7. In view of this fact, that.
8. Both words mean "observation."
9. Qualities.
1. Generous.
2. Bind with splints.

3. Stake, wager.
4. Insist, declare.
5. Unreservedly.
6. Repulse.
7. Free from guile. Also, freely given.
8. Created as generous.
9. I.e., earth, air, fire, and water, unrestrained and spontaneous.
1. Her desire, or, perhaps, his desire for her.
2. Exercise of faculties (weakened by his fondness for her).

To counsel Cassio to this parallel[3] course
Directly to his good? Divinity of hell![4]
300 When devils will the blackest sins put on,°   instigate
They do suggest° at first with heavenly shows,   tempt
As I do now. For whiles this honest fool
Plies Desdemona to repair his fortune,
And she for him pleads strongly to the Moor,
305 I'll pour this pestilence into his ear,
That she repeals him[5] for her body's lust;
And by how much she strives to do him good,
She shall undo her credit with the Moor.
So will I turn her virtue into pitch,[6]
310 And out of her own goodness make the net
That shall enmesh them all.
                    [*Enter Roderigo.*]
                    How now, Roderigo?

RODERIGO I do follow here in the chase, not like a hound that hunts, but one that
fills up the cry.[7] My money is almost spent; I have been tonight exceedingly
well cudgeled; and I think the issue will be I shall have so much[8] experience for
315 my pains, and so, with no money at all and a little more wit, return again to
Venice.

IAGO How poor are they that have not patience!
What wound did ever heal but by degrees?
Thou know'st we work by wit, and not by witchcraft,
320 And wit depends on dilatory time.
Does 't not go well? Cassio hath beaten thee,
And thou, by that small hurt, hast cashiered° Cassio.   dismissed
Though other things grow fair against the sun,
Yet fruits that blossom first will first be ripe.[9]
325 Content thyself awhile. By the Mass, 'tis morning!
Pleasure and action make the hours seem short.
Retire thee; go where thou art billeted.
Away, I say! Thou shalt know more hereafter.
Nay, get thee gone.   [*Exit Roderigo.*]
330 Two things are to be done.
My wife must move° for Cassio to her mistress;   plead
I'll set her on;
Myself the while to draw the Moor apart
And bring him jump° when he may Cassio find   precisely
335 Soliciting his wife. Ay, that's the way.
Dull not device° by coldness° and delay.   [*Exit.*]   plot/lack of zeal

Act 3

Scene 1

[*Location: Before the chamber of Othello and Desdemona. Enter Cassio and Musicians.*]

---

3. Corresponding to these facts and to his best interests.
4. Inverted theology of hell (which seduces the soul to its damnation).
5. Attempts to get him restored.
6. Foul blackness. Also a snaring substance.

7. Merely takes part as one of the pack.
8. Just so much and no more.
9. Plans that are well prepared and set expeditiously in motion will soonest ripen into success.

CASSIO Masters, play here—I will content your pains[1]—
    Something that's brief, and bid "Good morrow, General." [*They play.*]
    [*Enter Clown.*]
CLOWN Why, masters, have your instruments been in Naples, that they speak i' the
    nose[2] thus?
A MUSICIAN How, sir, how?
CLOWN Are these, I pray you, wind instruments?
A MUSICIAN Ay, marry, are they, sir.
CLOWN O, thereby hangs a tail.
A MUSICIAN Whereby hangs a tale, sir?
CLOWN Marry, sir, by many a wind instrument[3] that I know. But, masters, here's
    money for you. [*He gives money.*] And the General so likes your music that he
    desires you, for love's sake,[4] to make no more noise with it.
A MUSICIAN Well, sir, we will not.
CLOWN If you have any music that may not[5] be heard, to 't again; but, as they say,
15   to hear music the General does not greatly care.
A MUSICIAN We have none such, sir.
CLOWN Then put up your pipes in your bag, for I'll away.[6] Go, vanish into air, away!
                         [*Exeunt Musicians.*]
CASSIO Dost thou hear, mine honest friend?
CLOWN No, I hear not your honest friend; I hear you.
CASSIO Prithee, keep up[7] thy quillets.[8] There's a poor piece of gold for thee. [*He
    gives money.*] If the gentlewoman that attends the General's wife be stirring,
    tell her there's one Cassio entreats her a little favor of speech.[9] Wilt thou do
    this?
CLOWN She is stirring, sir. If she will stir[1] hither, I shall seem[2] to notify unto her.
CASSIO Do, good my friend.   [*Exit Clown.*]
    [*Enter Iago.*]
                  In happy time,[3] Iago.
IAGO You have not been abed, then?
CASSIO Why, no. The day had broke
    Before we parted. I have made bold, Iago,
    To send in to your wife. My suit to her
30   Is that she will to virtuous Desdemona
    Procure me some access.
IAGO I'll send her to you presently;
    And I'll devise a means to draw the Moor
    Out of the way, that your converse and business
35   May be more free.
CASSIO I humbly thank you for 't.   [*Exit Iago.*]
                  I never knew

---

1. Reward your efforts.
2. Sound nasal. Also sound like one whose nose has been attacked by syphilis. (Naples was popularly supposed to have a high incidence of venereal disease.)
3. With a joke on flatulence. The *tail* that hangs nearby the *wind instrument* suggests the penis.
4. Out of friendship and affection. Also, for the sake of lovemaking in Othello's marriage.

5. Cannot.
6. (Possibly a misprint, or a snatch of song?)
7. Do not bring out.
8. Quibbles, puns.
9. The favor of a brief talk.
1. Bestir herself (with a play on *stirring*, "rousing herself from rest").
2. Deem it good, think fit.
3. I.e., well met.

A Florentine[4] more kind and honest.
[*Enter Emilia.*]

EMILIA Good morrow, good Lieutenant. I am sorry
For your displeasure;° but all will sure be well.   *fall from favor*
40 The General and his wife are talking of it,
And she speaks for you stoutly.° The Moor replies   *spiritedly*
That he you hurt is of great fame° in Cyprus   *importance*
And great affinity,° and that in wholesome wisdom   *family connection*
He might not but refuse you; but he protests° he loves you   *insists*
45 And needs no other suitor but his likings
To take the safest occasion by the front[5]
To bring you in again.

CASSIO   Yet I beseech you,
If you think fit, or that it may be done,
Give me advantage of some brief discourse
50 With Desdemon alone.

EMILIA   Pray you, come in.
I will bestow you where you shall have time
To speak your bosom° freely.   *thoughts*

CASSIO I am much bound to you.   [*Exeunt.*]

Scene 2

[*Location: The citadel. Enter Othello, Iago, and Gentlemen.*]

OTHELLO [*giving letters*] These letters give, Iago, to the pilot,
And by him do my duties° to the Senate.   *give my respects*
That done, I will be walking on the works;°   *fortifications*
Repair° there to me.   *return*

IAGO   Well, my good lord, I'll do 't.

OTHELLO This fortification, gentlemen, shall we see 't?

GENTLEMEN We'll wait upon° your lordship.   [*Exeunt.*]   *attend*

Scene 3

[*Location: The garden of the citadel. Enter Desdemona, Cassio, and Emilia.*]

DESDEMONA Be thou assured, good Cassio, I will do
All my abilities in thy behalf.

EMILIA Good madam, do. I warrant it grieves my husband
As if the cause were his.

DESDEMONA O, that's an honest fellow. Do not doubt, Cassio,
But I will have my lord and you again
As friendly as you were.

CASSIO   Bounteous madam,
Whatever shall become of Michael Cassio,
He's never anything but your true servant.

DESDEMONA I know 't. I thank you. You do love my lord;
You have known him long, and be you well assured
He shall in strangeness° stand no farther off   *aloofness*

---

4. I.e., even a fellow Florentine. (Iago is a Venetian; Cassio is a Florentine.)

5. Opportunity by the forelock.

Than in a politic[6] distance.

CASSIO   Ay, but, lady,
    That policy may either last so long,
15   Or feed upon such nice and waterish diet,[7]
    Or breed itself so out of circumstance,[8]
    That, I being absent and my place supplied,[9]
    My general will forget my love and service.

DESDEMONA Do not doubt° that. Before Emilia here   *fear*
20   I give thee warrant° of thy place. Assure thee,   *guarantee*
    If I do vow a friendship I'll perform it
    To the last article. My lord shall never rest.
    I'll watch him tame[1] and talk him out of patience;[2]
    His bed shall seem a school, his board° a shrift;°   *table/confessional*
25   I'll intermingle everything he does
    With Cassio's suit. Therefore be merry, Cassio,
    For thy solicitor° shall rather die   *advocate*
    Than give thy cause away.°   *up*
    Enter Othello and Iago at a distance].

EMILIA Madam, here comes my lord.

CASSIO Madam, I'll take my leave.

DESDEMONA Why, stay, and hear me speak.

CASSIO Madam, not now. I am very ill at ease,
    Unfit for mine own purposes.

DESDEMONA Well, do your discretion.[3]   *[Exit Cassio.]*

IAGO Ha? I like not that.

OTHELLO   What dost thou say?

IAGO Nothing, my lord; or if—I know not what.

OTHELLO Was not that Cassio parted from my wife?

IAGO Cassio, my lord? No, sure, I cannot think it,
    That he would steal away so guiltylike,
40   Seeing you coming.

OTHELLO   I do believe 'twas he.

DESDEMONA How now, my lord?
    I have been talking with a suitor here,
    A man that languishes in your displeasure.

OTHELLO Who is 't you mean?

DESDEMONA Why, your lieutenant, Cassio. Good my lord,
    If I have any grace or power to move you,
    His present reconciliation take;[4]
    For if he be not one that truly loves you,
    That errs in ignorance and not in cunning,°   *wittingly*
50   I have no judgment in an honest face.
    I prithee, call him back.

OTHELLO   Went he hence now?

DESDEMONA Yes, faith, so humbled

---

6. Required by wise policy.
7. Or sustain itself at length upon such trivial and meager technicalities.
8. Continually renew itself so out of chance events, or yield so few chances for my being pardoned.
9. Filled by another person.

1. Tame him by keeping him from sleeping (a term from falconry).
2. Past his endurance.
3. Act according to your own discretion.
4. Let him be reconciled to you right away.

That he hath left part of his grief with me
To suffer with him. Good love, call him back.
OTHELLO Not now, sweet Desdemon. Some other time.
DESDEMONA But shall 't be shortly?
OTHELLO   The sooner, sweet, for you.
DESDEMONA Shall 't be tonight at supper?
OTHELLO   No, not tonight.
DESDEMONA Tomorrow dinner,° then?   *noontime*
OTHELLO   I shall not dine at home.
     I meet the captains at the citadel.
DESDEMONA Why, then, tomorrow night, or Tuesday morn,
     On Tuesday noon, or night, on Wednesday morn.
     I prithee, name the time, but let it not
     Exceed three days. In faith, he's penitent;
     And yet his trespass, in our common reason°—   *judgments*
65   Save that, they say, the wars must make example
     Out of her best⁵—is not almost° a fault   *scarcely*
     T' incur a private check.⁶ When shall he come?
     Tell me, Othello. I wonder in my soul
     What you would ask me that I should deny,
70   Or stand so mammering on.° What? Michael Cassio,   *wavering about*
     That came a-wooing with you, and so many a time,
     When I have spoke of you dispraisingly,
     Hath ta'en your part—to have so much to do
     To bring him in!° By 'r Lady, I could do much—   *restore him to favor*
OTHELLO Prithee, no more. Let him come when he will;
     I will deny thee nothing.
DESDEMONA   Why, this is not a boon.
     'Tis as I should entreat you wear your gloves,
     Or feed on nourishing dishes, or keep you warm,
     Or sue to you to do a peculiar° profit   *personal*
80   To your own person. Nay, when I have a suit
     Wherein I mean to touch° your love indeed,   *test*
     It shall be full of poise⁷ and difficult weight,
     And fearful to be granted.
OTHELLO   I will deny thee nothing.
     Whereon,° I do beseech thee, grant me this,   *in return*
85   To leave me but a little to myself.
DESDEMONA Shall I deny you? No. Farewell, my lord.
OTHELLO Farewell, my Desdemona. I'll come to thee straight.°   *straightway*
DESDEMONA Emilia, come.—Be as your fancies° teach you;   *inclinations*
     Whate'er you be, I am obedient.   [*Exit with Emilia.*]
OTHELLO Excellent wretch!⁸ Perdition catch my soul
     But I do love thee! And when I love thee not,
     Chaos is come again.⁹

---

5. Were it not that, as the saying goes, military discipline requires making an example of the very best men. (*Her* refers to *wars* as a singular concept.)
6. Even a private reprimand.
7. Weight, heaviness; or equipoise, delicate balance involving hard choice.

8. A term of affectionate endearment.
9. I.e., My love for you will last forever, until the end of time when chaos will return. (But with an unconscious, ironic suggestion that, if anything should induce Othello to cease loving Desdemona, the result would be chaos.)

IAGO My noble lord—
OTHELLO   What dost thou say, Iago?
IAGO Did Michael Cassio, when you wooed my lady,
95   Know of your love?
OTHELLO He did, from first to last. Why dost thou ask?
IAGO But for a satisfaction of my thought;
      No further harm.
OTHELLO   Why of thy thought, Iago?
IAGO I did not think he had been acquainted with her.
OTHELLO O, yes, and went between us very oft.
IAGO Indeed?
OTHELLO Indeed? Ay, indeed. Discern'st thou aught in that?
110   Is he not honest?
IAGO   Honest, my lord?
OTHELLO   Honest. Ay, honest.
IAGO My lord, for aught I know.
OTHELLO What dost thou think?
IAGO   Think, my lord?
OTHELLO "Think, my lord?" By heaven, thou echo'st me,
      As if there were some monster in thy thought
      Too hideous to be shown. Thou dost mean something.
      I heard thee say even now, thou lik'st not that,
110   When Cassio left my wife. What didst not like?
      And when I told thee he was of my counsel°   *in my confidence*
      In my whole course of wooing, thou criedst "Indeed?"
      And didst contract and purse° thy brow together   *knit*
      As if thou then hadst shut up in thy brain
115   Some horrible conceit.° If thou dost love me,   *fancy*
      Show me thy thought.
IAGO My lord, you know I love you.
OTHELLO   I think thou dost;
      And, for° I know thou'rt full of love and honesty,   *because*
      And weigh'st thy words before thou giv'st them breath,
120   Therefore these stops° of thine fright me the more; *pauses*
      For such things in a false disloyal knave
      Are tricks of custom,° but in a man that's just   *customary*
      They're close dilations,¹ working from the heart
      That passion cannot rule.²
IAGO   For° Michael Cassio,   *as for*
125   I dare be sworn I think that he is honest.
OTHELLO I think so too.
IAGO   Men should be what they seem;
      Or those that be not, would they might seem none!³
OTHELLO Certain, men should be what they seem.
IAGO Why, then, I think Cassio's an honest man.
OTHELLO Nay, yet there's more in this.
      I prithee, speak to me as to thy thinkings,

---

1. Secret or involuntary expressions or delays.
2. I.e., that are too passionately strong to be restrained
(referring to the workings), or that cannot rule its own
passions (referring to the heart).
3. I.e., not to be men, or not seem to be honest.

As thou dost ruminate, and give thy worst of thoughts
The worst of words.

IAGO   Good my lord, pardon me.
Though I am bound to every act of duty,
135   I am not bound to that° all slaves are free to.[4]   *that which*
Utter my thoughts? Why, say they are vile and false,
As where's that palace whereinto foul things
Sometimes intrude not? Who has that breast so pure
But some uncleanly apprehensions
140   Keep leets and law days,[5] and in sessions sit
With° meditations lawful?°   *along with/innocent*
OTHELLO Thou dost conspire against thy friend,[6] Iago,
If thou but think'st him wronged and mak'st his ear
A stranger to thy thoughts.
IAGO   I do beseech you,
145   Though I perchance am vicious° in my guess—   *wrong*
As I confess it is my nature's plague
To spy into abuses, and oft my jealousy°   *suspicious nature*
Shapes faults that are not—that your wisdom then,°   *on that account*
From one[7] that so imperfectly conceits,°   *conjectures*
150   Would take no notice, nor build yourself a trouble
Out of his scattering° and unsure observance.   *random*
It were not for your quiet nor your good,
Nor for my manhood, honesty, and wisdom,
To let you know my thoughts.
OTHELLO   What dost thou mean?
IAGO Good name in man and woman, dear my lord,
Is the immediate° jewel of their souls.   *essential*
Who steals my purse steals trash; 'tis something, nothing;
'Twas mine, 'tis his, and has been slave to thousands;
But he that filches from me my good name
160   Robs me of that which not enriches him
And makes me poor indeed.
OTHELLO By heaven, I'll know thy thoughts.
IAGO You cannot, if° my heart were in your hand,   *even if*
175   Nor shall not, whilst 'tis in my custody.
OTHELLO Ha?
IAGO   O, beware, my lord, of jealousy.
It is the green-eyed monster which doth mock
The meat it feeds on.[8] That cuckold lives in bliss
Who, certain of his fate, loves not his wronger;[9]
But O, what damnèd minutes tells° he o'er   *counts*
170   Who dotes, yet doubts, suspects, yet fondly loves!
OTHELLO O misery!
IAGO Poor and content is rich, and rich enough,[1]

---

4. Free with respect to.
5. I.e., hold court, set up their authority in one's heart.
Leets are a kind of manor court; *law days* are the days
courts sit in session, or those sessions.
6. I.e., Othello.
7. I.e., myself, Iago.

8. Mocks and torments the heart of its victim, the man
who suffers jealously.
9. I.e., his faithless wife. (The unsuspecting cuckold is
spared the misery of loving his wife only to discover she is
cheating on him.)
1. To be content with what little one has is the greatest
wealth of all (proverbial).

But riches fineless° is as poor as winter   *boundless*
To him that ever fears he shall be poor.
175   Good God, the souls of all my tribe defend
From jealousy!
OTHELLO   Why, why is this?
Think'st thou I'd make a life of jealousy,
To follow still the changes of the moon
With fresh suspicions?² No! To be once in doubt
180   Is once° to be resolved.³ Exchange me for a goat   *once and for all*
When I shall turn the business of my soul
To such exsufflicate and blown⁴ surmises
Matching thy inference.° 'Tis not to make me jealous   *allegation*
To say my wife is fair, feeds well, loves company,
185   Is free of speech, sings, plays, and dances well;
Where virtue is, these are more virtuous.
Nor from mine own weak merits will I draw
The smallest fear or doubt of her revolt,⁵
For she had eyes, and chose me. No, Iago,
190   I'll see before I doubt; when I doubt, prove;
And on the proof, there is no more but this—
Away at once with love or jealousy.
IAGO I am glad of this, for now I shall have reason
To show the love and duty that I bear you
195   With franker spirit. Therefore, as I am bound,
Receive it from me. I speak not yet of proof.
Look to your wife; observe her well with Cassio.
Wear your eyes thus, not° jealous nor secure.°   *neither / certain*
I would not have your free and noble nature,
200   Out of self-bounty,⁶ be abused.° Look to 't.   *deceived*
I know our country disposition well;
In Venice they do let God see the pranks
They dare not show their husbands; their best conscience
Is not to leave 't undone, but keep 't unknown.
OTHELLO Dost thou say so?
IAGO She did deceive her father, marrying you;
And when she seemed to shake and fear your looks,
She loved them most.
OTHELLO   And so she did.
IAGO   Why, go to,⁷ then!
She that, so young, could give out such a seeming,°   *false appearance*
210   To seel⁸ her father's eyes up close as oak,⁹
He thought 'twas witchcraft! But I am much to blame.
I humbly do beseech you of your pardon
For too much loving you.
OTHELLO   I am bound¹ to thee forever.

---

2. To be constantly imagining new causes for suspicion, changing incessantly like the moon.
3. Free of doubt, having settled the matter.
4. Inflated and blown up, rumored about, or, spat out and flyblown, hence loathsome, disgusting.
5. Fear of her unfaithfulness.

6. Inherent or natural goodness and generosity.
7. An expression of impatience.
8. Blind (a term from falconry).
9. A close-grained wood.
1. Indebted (but perhaps with the ironic sense of "tied").

IAGO I see this hath a little dashed your spirits.

OTHELLO Not a jot, not a jot.

IAGO   I' faith, I fear it has.
    I hope you will consider what is spoke
    Comes from my love. But I do see you're moved.
    I am to pray you not to strain my speech
    To grosser issues° nor to larger reach°   *significances/scope*
220   Than to suspicion.

OTHELLO I will not.

IAGO   Should you do so, my lord,
    My speech should fall into such vile success°   *effect*
    Which my thoughts aimed not. Cassio's my worthy friend.
    My lord, I see you're moved.

OTHELLO   No, not much moved.
225   I do not think but Desdemona's honest.°   *chaste*

IAGO Long live she so! And long live you to think so!

OTHELLO And yet, how nature erring from itself—

IAGO Ay, there's the point! As—to be bold with you—
    Not to affect° many proposèd matches   *prefer*
230   Of her own clime, complexion, and degree,[2]
    Whereto we see in all things nature tends—
    Foh! One may smell in such a will° most rank,   *sensuality*
    Foul disproportion,° thoughts unnatural.   *abnormality*
    But pardon me. I do not in position°   *argument*
235   Distinctly speak of her, though I may fear
    Her will, recoiling° to her better[3] judgment,   *reverting*
    May fall to match you with her country forms[4]
    And happily repent.[5]

OTHELLO   Farewell, farewell!
    If more thou dost perceive, let me know more.
240   Set on thy wife to observe. Leave me, Iago.

IAGO [*going*] My lord, I take my leave.

OTHELLO Why did I marry? This honest creature doubtless
    Sees and knows more, much more, than he unfolds.

IAGO [*returning*] My Lord, I would I might entreat your honor
245   To scan° this thing no farther. Leave it to time.   *scrutinize*
    Although 'tis fit that Cassio have his place—
    For, sure, he fills it up with great ability—
    Yet, if you please to hold him off awhile,
    You shall by that perceive him and his means.[6]
250   Note if your lady strain his entertainment[7]
    With any strong or vehement importunity;
    Much will be seen in that. In the meantime,
    Let me be thought too busy° in my fears—   *interfering*
    As worthy cause I have to fear I am—
255   And hold her free,[8] I do beseech your honor.

---

2. Country, color, and social position.
3. I.e., more natural and reconsidered.
4. Undertake to compare you with Venetian norms of handsomeness.

5. Perhaps repent her marriage.
6. The method he uses (to regain his post).
7. Urge his reinstatement.
8. Regard her as innocent.

OTHELLO Fear not my government.°   *conduct*
IAGO I once more take my leave.   *[Exit.]*
OTHELLO This fellow's of exceeding honesty,
    And knows all qualities,° with a learnèd spirit,   *natures*
260   Of human dealings. If I do prove her haggard,[9]
    Though that her jesses[1] were my dear heartstrings,
    I'd whistle her off and let her down the wind[2]
    To prey at fortune.[3] Haply, for[4] I am black
    And have not those soft parts of conversation[5]
265   That chamberers° have, or for I am declined   *gallants*
    Into the vale of years—yet that's not much—
    She's gone. I am abused,° and my relief   *deceived*
    Must be to loathe her. O curse of marriage,
    That we can call these delicate creatures ours
270   And not their appetites! I had rather be a toad
    And live upon the vapor of a dungeon
    Than keep a corner in the thing I love
    For others' uses. Yet, 'tis the plague of great ones;
    Prerogatived[6] are they less than the base.[7]
275   'Tis destiny unshunnable, like death.
    Even then this forkèd[8] plague is fated to us
    When we do quicken.[9] Look where she comes.
                [Enter Desdemona and Emilia.]
    If she be false, O, then heaven mocks itself!
    I'll not believe 't.
DESDEMONA   How now, my dear Othello?
280   Your dinner, and the generous° islanders   *noble*
    By you invited, do attend° your presence.   *await*
OTHELLO I am to blame.
DESDEMONA   Why do you speak so faintly?
    Are you not well?
OTHELLO I have a pain upon my forehead here.
DESDEMONA Faith, that's with watching.° 'Twill away again.   *too little sleep*
    [She offers her handkerchief.]
    Let me but bind it hard, within this hour
    It will be well.
OTHELLO   Your napkin° is too little.   *handkerchief*
    Let it alone.° Come, I'll go in with you.   *never mind*
    [He puts the handkerchief from him, and it drops.]
DESDEMONA I am very sorry that you are not well.
                          [Exit with Othello.]
EMILIA *[picking up the handkerchief]*
290   I am glad I have found this napkin.

---

9. Wild (like a wild female hawk).
1. Straps fastened around the legs of a trained hawk.
2. I'd let her go forever. (To release a hawk downwind
was to invite it not to return.)
3. Fend for herself in the wild.
4. Perhaps because.
5. Pleasing graces of social behavior.
6. Privileged (to have honest wives).

7. Ordinary citizens. (Socially prominent men are especially prone to the unavoidable destiny of being cuckolded and to the public shame that goes with it.)
8. An allusion to the horns of the cuckold.
9. Receive life. *Quicken* may also mean to swarm with maggots as the body festers, in which case these lines suggest that *even then*, in death, we are cuckolded by *forkèd* worms.

This was her first remembrance from the Moor.
My wayward° husband hath a hundred times   *capricious*
Wooed me to steal it, but she so loves the token—
For he conjured her she should ever keep it—
295   That she reserves it evermore about her
To kiss and talk to. I'll have the work ta'en out,[1]
And give 't Iago. What he will do with it
Heaven knows, not I;
I nothing but to please his fantasy.°   *whim*
[*Enter Iago.*]

IAGO How now? What do you here alone?

EMILIA Do not you chide. I have a thing for you.

IAGO You have a thing for me? It is a common thing[2]—

EMILIA Ha?

IAGO To have a foolish wife.

EMILIA O, is that all? What will you give me now
For that same handkerchief?

IAGO What handkerchief?

EMILIA What handkerchief?
Why, that the Moor first gave to Desdemona;
310   That which so often you did bid me steal.

IAGO Hast stolen it from her?

EMILIA No, faith. She let it drop by negligence,
And to th' advantage[3] I, being here, took 't up.
Look, here 'tis.

IAGO   A good wench! Give it me.

EMILIA What will you do with 't, that you have been so earnest
To have me filch it?

IAGO [*snatching it*]   Why, what is that to you?

EMILIA If it be not for some purpose of import,
Give 't me again. Poor lady, she'll run mad
When she shall lack° it.   *miss*

IAGO   Be not acknown on 't.[4]
320   I have use for it. Go, leave me.   [*Exit Emilia.*]
I will in Cassio's lodging lose[5] this napkin
And let him find it. Trifles light as air
Are to the jealous confirmations strong
As proofs of Holy Writ. This may do something.
325   The Moor already changes with my poison.
Dangerous conceits° are in their natures poisons,   *ideas*
Which at the first are scarce found to distaste,°   *be distasteful*
But with a little act° upon the blood   *action*
Burn like the mines of sulfur.
[*Enter Othello.*]
                          I did say so.
330   Look where he comes! Not poppy nor mandragora[6]

---

1. Design of the embroidery copied.
2. With bawdy suggestion; *common* suggests coarseness and availability to all comers, and *thing* is a slang term for the genitals.
3. Taking the opportunity.

4. Do not confess knowledge of it.
5. The Folio spelling, *loose*, is a normal spelling for "lose," but it may also contain the idea of "let go," "release."
6. An opiate made of the mandrake root.

Nor all the drowsy syrups of the world
Shall ever medicine thee to that sweet sleep
Which thou owedst° yesterday.   *you did own*

OTHELLO   Ha, ha, false to me?

IAGO Why, how now, General? No more of that.

OTHELLO Avaunt! Begone! Thou hast set me on the rack.
I swear 'tis better to be much abused
Than but to know 't a little.

IAGO   How now, my lord?

OTHELLO What sense had I of her stolen hours of lust?
I saw 't not, thought it not, it harmed not me.
340   I slept the next night well, fed well, was free° and merry;   *carefree*
I found not Cassio's kisses on her lips.
He that is robbed, not wanting° what is stolen,   *missing*
Let him not know 't and he's not robbed at all.

IAGO I am sorry to hear this.

OTHELLO I had been happy if the general camp,
Pioners⁷ and all, had tasted her sweet body,
So° I had nothing known. O, now, forever   *provided*
Farewell the tranquil mind! Farewell content!
Farewell the plumèd troops and the big° wars   *stately*
350   That makes ambition virtue! O, farewell!
Farewell the neighing steed and the shrill trump,
The spirit-stirring drum, th' ear-piercing fife,
The royal banner, and all quality,°   *character*
Pride,° pomp, and circumstance° of glorious war!   *display/pageantry*
And O, you mortal engines,⁸ whose rude throats
Th' immortal Jove's dread clamors° counterfeit,   *thunder*
Farewell! Othello's occupation's gone.

IAGO Is 't possible, my lord?

OTHELLO Villain, be sure thou prove my love a whore!
360   Be sure of it. Give me the ocular proof,
Or, by the worth of mine eternal soul,
Thou hadst been better have been born a dog
Than answer my waked wrath!

IAGO   Is 't come to this?

OTHELLO Make me to see 't, or at the least so prove it
365   That the probation° bear no hinge nor loop   *proof*
To hang a doubt on, or woe upon thy life!

IAGO My noble lord—

OTHELLO If thou dost slander her and torture me,
Never pray more; abandon all remorse;°   *pity*
370   On horror's head horrors accumulate;
Do deeds to make heaven weep, all earth amazed;
For nothing canst thou to damnation add
Greater than that.

IAGO   O grace! O heaven forgive me!
Are you a man? Have you a soul or sense?

7. Diggers of mines, the lowest grade of soldiers.   8. Cannon. (*Mortal* means "deadly.")

375 God b' wi' you; take mine office. O wretched fool,[9]
    That lov'st to make thine honesty a vice!°   *failing*
    O monstrous world! Take note, take note, O world,
    To be direct and honest is not safe.
    I thank you for this profit,° and from hence°   *instruction/henceforth*
380 I'll love no friend, sith° love breeds such offense.[1]   *since*
OTHELLO Nay, stay. Thou shouldst be honest.[2]
IAGO I should be wise, for honesty's a fool
    And loses that° it works for.   *what*
OTHELLO   By the world,
    I think my wife be honest and think she is not;
385 I think that thou art just and think thou art not.
    I'll have some proof. My name, that was as fresh
    As Dian's[3] visage, is now begrimed and black
    As mine own face. If there be cords, or knives,
    Poison, or fire, or suffocating streams,
390 I'll not endure it. Would I were satisfied!
IAGO I see, sir, you are eaten up with passion.
    I do repent me that I put it to you.
    You would be satisfied?
OTHELLO   Would? Nay, and I will.
IAGO And may; but how? How satisfied, my lord?
395 Would you, the supervisor,° grossly gape on?   *onlooker*
    Behold her topped?
OTHELLO   Death and damnation! O!
IAGO It were a tedious difficulty, I think,
    To bring them to that prospect. Damn them then,[4]
    If ever mortal eyes do see them bolster[5]
400 More° than their own.° What then? How then?   *other/own eyes*
    What shall I say? Where's satisfaction?
    It is impossible you should see this,
    Were they as prime° as goats, as hot as monkeys,   *wanton*
    As salt° as wolves in pride,° and fools as gross   *lustful/heat*
405 As ignorance made drunk. But yet I say,
    If imputation[6] and strong circumstances
    Which lead directly to the door of truth
    Will give you satisfaction, you might have 't.
OTHELLO Give me a living reason she's disloyal.
IAGO I do not like the office.
    But sith° I am entered in this cause so far,   *since*
    Pricked° to 't by foolish honesty and love,   *spurred*
    I will go on. I lay with Cassio lately,
    And being troubled with a raging tooth
415 I could not sleep. There are a kind of men
    So loose of soul that in their sleeps will mutter

9. Iago addresses himself as a fool for having carried honesty too far.
1. Harm to the one who offers help and friendship.
2. It appears that you are. (But Iago replies in the sense of
"ought to be.")

3. Diana, goddess of the moon and of chastity.
4. They would have to be really incorrigible.
5. Go to bed together, share a bolster.
6. Strong circumstantial evidence.

Their affairs. One of this kind is Cassio.
In sleep I heard him say, "Sweet Desdemona,
Let us be wary, let us hide our loves!"
420   And then, sir, would he grip and wring my hand,
Cry "O sweet creature!", then kiss me hard,
As if he plucked up kisses by the roots
That grew upon my lips; then laid his leg
Over my thigh, and sighed, and kissed, and then
425   Cried, "Cursèd fate that gave thee to the Moor!"
OTHELLO O monstrous! Monstrous!
IAGO   Nay, this was but his dream.
OTHELLO But this denoted a foregone conclusion.[7]
'Tis a shrewd doubt,[8] though it be but a dream.
IAGO And this may help to thicken other proofs
That do demonstrate thinly.
OTHELLO   I'll tear her all to pieces.
IAGO Nay, but be wise. Yet we see nothing done;
She may be honest yet. Tell me but this:
Have you not sometimes seen a handkerchief
Spotted° with strawberries in your wife's hand?   *embroidered*
OTHELLO I gave her such a one. 'Twas my first gift.
IAGO I know not that; but such a handkerchief—
I am sure it was your wife's—did I today
See Cassio wipe his beard with.
OTHELLO   If it be that—
IAGO If it be that, or any that was hers,
440   It speaks against her with the other proofs.
OTHELLO O, that the slave° had forty thousand lives!   *Cassio*
One is too poor, too weak for my revenge.
Now do I see 'tis true. Look here, Iago,
All my fond[9] love thus do I blow to heaven.
445   'Tis gone.
Arise, black vengeance, from the hollow hell!
Yield up, O love, thy crown and hearted° throne   *fixed in the heart*
To tyrannous hate! Swell, bosom, with thy freight,°   *burden*
For 'tis of aspics'° tongues!   *venomous serpents'*
IAGO   Yet be content.°   *calm*
OTHELLO O, blood, blood, blood!
IAGO Patience, I say. Your mind perhaps may change.
OTHELLO Never, Iago. Like to the Pontic Sea,[1]
Whose icy current and compulsive course
Ne'er feels retiring ebb, but keeps due on
455   To the Propontic[2] and the Hellespont,[3]
Even so my bloody thoughts with violent pace
Shall ne'er look back, ne'er ebb to humble love,

7. Concluded experience or action.
8. Suspicious circumstance.
9. Foolish (but also suggesting "affectionate").
1. Black Sea.

2. Sea of Marmora, between the Black Sea and the Aegean.
3. Dardanelles, straits where the Sea of Marmora joins with the Aegean.

Till that a capable° and wide revenge   *ample*
Swallow them up. Now, by yond marble[4] heaven,
460   [*Kneeling.*] In the due reverence of a sacred vow
I here engage my words.
IAGO   Do not rise yet.
[*He kneels.*][5] Witness, you ever-burning lights above,
You elements that clip° us round about,   *encompass*
Witness that here Iago doth give up
465   The execution° of his wit,° hands, heart,   *exercise / mind*
To wronged Othello's service. Let him command,
And to obey shall be in me remorse,[6]
What bloody business ever.° [*They rise.*]   *soever*
OTHELLO   I greet thy love,
Not with vain thanks, but with acceptance bounteous,
470   And will upon the instant put thee to 't.[7]
Within these three days let me hear thee say
That Cassio's not alive.
IAGO   My friend is dead;
'Tis done at your request. But let her live.
OTHELLO Damn her, lewd minx!° O, damn her, damn her!   *wanton*
475   Come, go with me apart. I will withdraw
To furnish me with some swift means of death
For the fair devil. Now art thou my lieutenant.
IAGO I am your own forever.
                                   [*Exeunt.*]

Scene 4

[*Location: Before the citadel. Enter Desdemona, Emilia, and Clown.*]
DESDEMONA Do you know, sirrah,[8] where Lieutenant Cassio lies?
CLOWN I dare not say he lies[9] anywhere.
DESDEMONA Why, man?
CLOWN He's a soldier, and for me to say a soldier lies, 'tis stabbing.
DESDEMONA Go to. Where lodges he?
CLOWN To tell you where he lodges is to tell you where I lie.
DESDEMONA Can anything be made of this?
CLOWN I know not where he lodges, and for me to devise a lodging and say he lies
    here, or he lies there, were to lie in mine own throat.[1]
DESDEMONA Can you inquire him out, and be edified by report?
CLOWN I will catechize the world for him; that is, make questions, and by them
    answer.
DESDEMONA Seek him, bid him come hither. Tell him I have moved[2] my lord on
    his behalf and hope all will be well.
CLOWN To do this is within the compass of man's wit, and therefore I will attempt
    the doing it.   [*Exit Clown.*]
DESDEMONA Where should I lose that handkerchief, Emilia?

---

4. I.e., gleaming like marble and unrelenting.
5. In the Quarto text, Iago kneels here after Othello has
knelt at line 460.
6. Pity (for Othello's wrongs).
7. To the proof.

8. A form of address to an inferior.
9. Lodges. (But the Clown makes the obvious pun.)
1. Lie egregiously and deliberately. Also, use the windpipe to speak a lie.
2. Petitioned.

EMILIA I know not, madam.

DESDEMONA Believe me, I had rather have lost my purse

20　　Full of crusadoes;° and but my noble Moor　　　　　*gold coins*

　　Is true of mind and made of no such baseness

　　As jealous creatures are, it were enough

　　To put him to ill thinking.

EMILIA　　　　　　　　　　　　Is he not jealous?

DESDEMONA Who, he? I think the sun where he was born

25　　Drew all such humors³ from him.

EMILIA　　　　　　　　　　　Look where he comes.

　　[*Enter Othello.*]

DESDEMONA I will not leave him now till Cassio

　　Be called to him.—How is 't with you, my lord?

OTHELLO Well, my good lady. [*Aside.*] O, hardness to dissemble!—

　　How do you, Desdemona?

DESDEMONA　　　　　　　　Well, my good lord.

OTHELLO Give me your hand. [*She gives her hand.*] This hand is moist, my lady.

DESDEMONA It yet hath felt no age nor known no sorrow.

OTHELLO This argues fruitfulness and liberal heart.⁴

　　Hot, hot, and moist. This hand of yours requires

　　A sequester° from liberty, fasting and prayer,　　　*separation*

35　　Much castigation,° exercise° devout;　　*discipline/prayer*

　　For here's a young and sweating devil here

　　That commonly rebels. 'Tis a good hand,

　　A frank⁵ one.

DESDEMONA　　　You may indeed say so,

　　For 'twas that hand that gave away my heart.

OTHELLO A liberal hand. The hearts of old gave hands,⁶

　　But our new heraldry is hands, not hearts.⁷

DESDEMONA I cannot speak of this. Come now, your promise.

OTHELLO What promise, chuck?⁸

DESDEMONA I have sent to bid Cassio come speak with you.

OTHELLO I have a salt and sorry rheum⁹ offends me;

　　Lend me thy handkerchief.

DESDEMONA　　　　　　　Here, my lord. [*She offers a handkerchief.*]

OTHELLO That which I gave you.

DESDEMONA　　　　　　　I have it not about me.

OTHELLO Not?

DESDEMONA No, faith, my lord.

OTHELLO　　　　　　　That's a fault. That handkerchief

50　　Did an Egyptian to my mother give.

　　She was a charmer,° and could almost read　　　*sorceress*

　　The thoughts of people. She told her, while she kept it

　　'Twould make her amiable° and subdue my father　　*desirable*

---

3. Refers to the four bodily fluids thought to determine temperament.
4. Gives evidence of amorousness, fecundity, and sexual freedom.
5. Generous, open (with sexual suggestion).
6. In former times, people would give their hearts when they gave their hands to something.
7. In our decadent times, the joining of hands is no longer a badge to signify the giving of hearts.
8. A term of endearment.
9. Distressful head cold or watering of the eyes.

55   Entirely to her love, but if she lost it
    Or made a gift of it, my father's eye
    Should hold her loathèd and his spirits should hunt
    After new fancies.° She, dying, gave it me,   *loves*
    And bid me, when my fate would have me wived,
    To give it her.[1] I did so; and take heed on 't;
60   Make it a darling like your precious eye.
    To lose 't or give 't away were such perdition°   *loss*
    As nothing else could match.

DESDEMONA   Is 't possible?

OTHELLO 'Tis true. There's magic in the web° of it.   *weaving*
    A sibyl, that had numbered in the world
65   The sun to course two hundred compasses,[2]
    In her prophetic fury[3] sewed the work;°   *embroidered pattern*
    The worms were hallowed that did breed the silk,
    And it was dyed in mummy[4] which the skillful
    Conserved of[5] maidens' hearts.

DESDEMONA   I' faith! Is 't true?

OTHELLO Most veritable. Therefore look to 't well.

DESDEMONA Then would to God that I had never seen 't!

OTHELLO Ha? Wherefore?

DESDEMONA Why do you speak so startingly and rash?[6]

OTHELLO Is 't lost? Is 't gone? Speak, is 't out o' the way?°   *misplaced*

DESDEMONA Heaven bless us!

OTHELLO Say you?

DESDEMONA It is not lost; but what an if° it were?   *if*

OTHELLO How?

DESDEMONA I say it is not lost.

OTHELLO   Fetch 't, let me see 't.

DESDEMONA Why, so I can, sir, but I will not now.
    This is a trick to put me from my suit.
    Pray you, let Cassio be received again.

OTHELLO Fetch me the handkerchief! My mind misgives.

DESDEMONA Come, come,
85   You'll never meet a more sufficient° man.   *able*

OTHELLO The handkerchief!

DESDEMONA   I pray, talk° me of Cassio.   *talk to*

OTHELLO The handkerchief!

DESDEMONA   A man that all his time[7]
    Hath founded his good fortunes on your love,
    Shared dangers with you—

OTHELLO The handkerchief!

DESDEMONA I' faith, you are to blame.

OTHELLO Zounds!   *[Exit Othello.]*

EMILIA Is not this man jealous?

DESDEMONA I ne'er saw this before.

---

1. I.e., to my wife.
2. Annual circlings. (The *sibyl*, or prophetess, was 200 years old.)
3. Frenzy of prophetic inspiration.

4. Medicinal or magical preparation drained from mummified bodies.
5. Prepared or preserved out of.
6. Disjointedly and impetuously, excitedly.
7. Throughout his career.

95   Sure, there's some wonder in this handkerchief.
      I am most unhappy in the loss of it.
EMILIA   'Tis not a year or two shows us a man.[8]
      They are all but° stomachs, and we all but food;   *nothing but*
      They eat us hungerly,° and when they are full   *hungrily*
100   They belch us.

            [Enter Iago and Cassio.]
            Look you, Cassio and my husband.

IAGO *[to Cassio]*
      There is no other way; 'tis she must do 't.
      And, lo, the happiness![9] Go and importune her.

DESDEMONA How now, good Cassio? What's the news with you?

CASSIO Madam, my former suit. I do beseech you
105   That by your virtuous° means I may again   *efficacious*
      Exist and be a member of his love
      Whom I, with all the office° of my heart,   *loyal service*
      Entirely honor. I would not be delayed.
      If my offense be of such mortal° kind   *fatal*
110   That nor° my service past, nor present sorrows,   *neither*
      Nor purposed merit in futurity
      Can ransom me into his love again,
      But to know so must be my benefit;[1]
      So shall I clothe me in a forced content,
115   And shut myself up in[2] some other course,
      To fortune's alms.[3]

DESDEMONA   Alas, thrice-gentle Cassio,
      My advocation° is not now in tune.   *advocacy*
      My lord is not my lord; nor should I know him,
      Were he in favor° as in humor° altered.   *appearance / mood*
120   So help me every spirit sanctified
      As I have spoken for you all my best
      And stood within the blank[4] of his displeasure
      For my free speech! You must awhile be patient.
      What I can do I will, and more I will
125   Than for myself I dare. Let that suffice you.

IAGO Is my lord angry?

EMILIA   He went hence but now,
      And certainly in strange unquietness.

IAGO Can he be angry? I have seen the cannon
130   When it hath blown his ranks into the air,
      And like the devil from his very arm
      Puffed his own brother—and is he angry?
      Something of moment[5] then. I will go meet him.
      There's matter in 't indeed, if he be angry.

DESDEMONA I prithee, do so. *[Exit Iago.]*

---

8. You can't really know a man even in a year or two of
experience (?), or, real men come along seldom (?).
9. In happy time, fortunately met.
1. Merely to know that my case is hopeless will have to
content me (and will be better than uncertainty).

2. Confine myself to.
3. Throwing myself on the mercy of fortune.
4. Within pointblank range. (The *blank* is the center of
the target.)
5. Of immediate importance, momentous.

Something, sure, of state,°   *state affairs*
Either from Venice, or some unhatched practice[6]
Made demonstrable here in Cyprus to him,
Hath puddled° his clear spirit; and in such cases   *muddied*
Men's natures wrangle with inferior things,
140   Though great ones are their object. 'Tis even so;
For let our finger ache, and it indues°   *induces*
Our other, healthful members even to a sense
Of pain. Nay, we must think men are not gods,
Nor of them look for such observancy°   *attentiveness*
145   As fits the bridal.[7] Beshrew me[8] much, Emilia,
I was, unhandsome° warrior as I am,   *unskillful*
Arraigning his unkindness with[9] my soul;
But now I find I had suborned the witness,[1]
And he's indicted falsely.

EMILIA   Pray heaven it be
150   State matters, as you think, and no conception
Nor no jealous toy° concerning you.   *fancy*

DESDEMONA Alas the day! I never gave him cause.

EMILIA But jealous souls will not be answered so;
They are not ever jealous for the cause,
155   But jealous for° they're jealous. It is a monster   *do because*
Begot upon itself,[2] born on itself.

DESDEMONA Heaven keep that monster from Othello's mind!

EMILIA Lady, amen.

DESDEMONA I will go seek him. Cassio, walk hereabout.
160   If I do find him fit, I'll move your suit
And seek to effect it to my uttermost.

CASSIO I humbly thank your ladyship.

                                    [Exit Desdemona with Emilia.]

  [Enter Bianca.]

BIANCA Save° you, friend Cassio!   *God save*

CASSIO   What make° you from home?   *do*
How is 't with you, my most fair Bianca?
165   I' faith, sweet love, I was coming to your house.

BIANCA And I was going to your lodging, Cassio.
What, keep a week away? Seven days and nights?
Eightscore-eight[3] hours? And lovers' absent hours
More tedious than the dial[4] eightscore times?
170   O weary reckoning!

CASSIO   Pardon me, Bianca.
I have this while with leaden thoughts been pressed;
But I shall, in a more continuate° time,   *uninterrupted*
Strike off this score[5] of absence. Sweet Bianca,

---

6. As yet unexecuted or undiscovered plot.
7. Wedding (when a bridegroom is newly attentive to his bride).
8. A mild oath.
9. Before the bar of.
1. Induced the witness to give false testimony.

2. Generated solely from itself.
3. One hundred sixty-eight, the number of hours in a week.
4. A complete revolution of the clock.
5. Settle this account.

[*Giving her Desdemona's handkerchief.*]
　　Take me this work out.[6]

BIANCA　　　　　　　　O Cassio, whence came this?

175　This is some token from a newer friend.°　　　　　　*mistress*
　　To the felt absence now I feel a cause.
　　Is 't come to this? Well, well.

CASSIO　　　　　　　　Go to, woman!
　　Throw your vile guesses in the devil's teeth,
　　From whence you have them. You are jealous now
180　That this is from some mistress, some remembrance.
　　No, by my faith, Bianca.

BIANCA　　　　　　　　Why, whose is it?

CASSIO　I know not, neither. I found it in my chamber.
　　I like the work well. Ere it be demanded°—　　　　　*inquired for*
　　As like° enough it will—I would have it copied.　　　*likely*
185　Take it and do 't, and leave me for this time.

BIANCA　Leave you? Wherefore?

CASSIO　I do attend here on the General,
　　And think it no addition,[7] nor my wish,
　　To have him see me womaned.

BIANCA　Why, I pray you?

CASSIO　Not that I love you not.

BIANCA　But that you do not love me.
　　I pray you, bring° me on the way a little,　　　　　*accompany*
　　And say if I shall see you soon at night.

CASSIO　'Tis but a little way that I can bring you,
　　For I attend here; but I'll see you soon.

BIANCA　'Tis very good. I must be circumstanced.[8]

　　　　　　　　　　　　　　　[*Exeunt omnes.*]

Act 4

Scene 1

[*Location: Before the citadel. Enter Othello and Iago.*]

IAGO　Will you think so?

OTHELLO　　　　　　　Think so, Iago?

IAGO　　　　　　　　　　　　What,
　　To kiss in private?

OTHELLO　　　　　　　An unauthorized kiss!

IAGO　Or to be naked with her friend in bed
　　An hour or more, not meaning any harm?

OTHELLO　Naked in bed, Iago, and not mean harm?
　　It is hypocrisy against the devil.
　　They that mean virtuously and yet do so,
　　The devil their virtue tempts, and they tempt heaven.

IAGO　If they do nothing, 'tis a venial° slip.　　　　　*pardonable*
10　But if I give my wife a handkerchief—

OTHELLO　What then?

---

6. Copy this embroidery for me.　　　　　8. Be governed by circumstance, yield to your conditions.
7. I.e., addition to my reputation.

IAGO Why then, 'tis hers, my lord, and being hers,
    She may, I think, bestow 't on any man.
OTHELLO She is protectress of her honor too.
15   May she give that?
IAGO Her honor is an essence that's not seen;
    They have it[9] very oft that have it not.
    But, for the handkerchief—
OTHELLO By heaven, I would most gladly have forgot it.
20   Thou saidst—O, it comes o'er my memory
    As doth the raven o'er the infectious house,[1]
    Boding to all—he had my handkerchief.
IAGO Ay, what of that?
OTHELLO   That's not so good now.
IAGO   What
    If I had said I had seen him do you wrong?
25   Or heard him say—as knaves be such abroad,°   *around about*
    Who having, by their own importunate suit,
    Or voluntary dotage[2] of some mistress,
    Convincèd or supplied[3] them, cannot choose
    But they must blab—
OTHELLO   Hath he said anything?
IAGO He hath, my lord; but, be you well assured,
    No more than he'll unswear.
OTHELLO   What hath he said?
IAGO Faith, that he did—I know not what he did.
OTHELLO What? What?
IAGO Lie—
OTHELLO With her?
IAGO   With her, on her; what you will.
OTHELLO Lie with her? Lie on her? We say "lie on her" when they belie[4] her. Lie with her? Zounds, that's fulsome.[5]—Handkerchief—confessions—handkerchief!—To confess and be hanged for his labor—first to be hanged and then to confess.[6]—I tremble at it. Nature would not invest herself in such shadowing
40   passion without some instruction.[7] It is not words[8] that shakes me thus. Pish!
    Noses, ears, and lips.—Is 't possible?—Confess—handkerchief!—O devil!
    [*Falls in a trance.*]
IAGO Work on, My medicine, work! Thus credulous fools are caught,
    And many worthy and chaste dames even thus,
    All guiltless, meet reproach.—What, ho! My lord!
45   My lord! I say! Othello!
    [*Enter Cassio.*]
                    How now, Cassio?
CASSIO What's the matter?

---

9. They enjoy a reputation for it.
1. Allusion to the belief that the raven hovered over a house of sickness or infection, such as one visited by the plague.
2. Willing infatuation.
3. Seduced or sexually gratified.
4. Slander.
5. Foul.

6. Othello reverses the proverbial *confess and be hanged;* Cassio is to be given no time to confess before he dies.
7. I.e., without some foundation in fact, nature would not have dressed herself in such an overwhelming passion that comes over me now and fills my mind with images, or in such a lifelike fantasy as Cassio had in his dream of lying with Desdemona.
8. Mere words.

IAGO My lord is fall'n into an epilepsy.
    This is his second fit. He had one yesterday.
CASSIO Rub him about the temples.
IAGO   No, forbear.
    The lethargy° must have his° quiet course.   *coma/its*
50   If not, he foams at mouth, and by and by
    Breaks out to savage madness. Look, he stirs.
    Do you withdraw yourself a little while.
    He will recover straight. When he is gone,
    I would on great occasion speak with you.

                                        [Exit Cassio.]

55   How is it, General? Have you not hurt your head?
OTHELLO Dost thou mock me?[1]
IAGO   I mock you not, by heaven.
    Would you would bear your fortune like a man!
OTHELLO A hornèd man's a monster and a beast.
IAGO There's many a beast then in a populous city,
60   And many a civil° monster.   *city-dwelling*
OTHELLO Did he confess it?
IAGO Good sir, be a man.
    Think every bearded fellow that's but yoked[2]
    May draw with you.[3] There's millions now alive
65   That nightly lie in those unproper° beds   *shared*
    Which they dare swear peculiar.° Your case is better.[4]   *their own*
    O, 'tis the spite of hell, the fiend's arch-mock,
    To lip° a wanton in a secure couch   *kiss*
    And to suppose her chaste! No, let me know,
70   And knowing what I am,[5] I know what she shall be.[6]
OTHELLO O, thou art wise. 'Tis certain.
IAGO   Stand you awhile apart;
    Confine yourself but in a patient list.[7]
    Whilst you were here o'erwhelmèd with your grief—
    A passion most unsuiting such a man—
75   Cassio came hither. I shifted him away,[8]
    And laid good 'scuse upon your ecstasy,°   *trance*
    Bade him anon return and here speak with me,
    The which he promised. Do but encave° yourself   *conceal*
    And mark the fleers,° the gibes, and notable° scorns *sneers/obvious*
80   That dwell in every region of his face;
    For I will make him tell the tale anew,
    Where, how, how oft, how long ago, and when
    He hath and is again to cope° your wife.   *have sex with*
    I say, but mark his gesture. Marry, patience!
85   Or I shall say you're all-in-all in spleen,[9]
    And nothing of a man.

---

1. Othello takes Iago's question about hurting his head to be a mocking reference to the cuckold's horns.
2. Married. Also, put into the yoke of infamy and cuckoldry.
3. Pull as you do, like oxen who are yoked, i.e., share your fate as cuckold.
4. I.e., because you know the truth.

5. I.e., a cuckold.
6. Will happen to her.
7. Within the bounds of patience.
8. Used a dodge to get rid of him.
9. Utterly governed by passionate impulses.

OTHELLO   Dost thou hear, Iago?
I will be found most cunning in my patience;
But—dost thou hear?—most bloody.
IAGO   That's not amiss;
But yet keep time[1] in all. Will you withdraw?
[Othello stands apart.]
90   Now will I question Cassio of Bianca,
A huswife° that by selling her desires   hussy
Buys herself bread and clothes. It is a creature
That dotes on Cassio—as 'tis the strumpet's plague
To beguile many and be beguiled by one.
95   He, when he hears of her, cannot restrain°   refrain
From the excess of laughter. Here he comes.
[Enter Cassio.]
As he shall smile, Othello shall go mad;
And his unbookish° jealousy must conster°   uninstructed / construe
Poor Cassio's smiles, gestures, and light behaviors
100   Quite in the wrong.—How do you now, Lieutenant?
CASSIO The worser that you give me the addition°   title
Whose want[2] even kills me.
IAGO Ply Desdemona well and you are sure on 't.
[Speaking lower.] Now, if this suit lay in Bianca's power,
105   How quickly should you speed!
CASSIO [laughing]   Alas, poor caitiff!°   wretch
OTHELLO [aside] Look how he laughs already!
IAGO I never knew a woman love man so.
CASSIO Alas, poor rogue! I think, i' faith, she loves me.
OTHELLO Now he denies it faintly, and laughs it out.
IAGO Do you hear, Cassio?
OTHELLO   Now he importunes him
To tell it o'er. Go to![3] Well said,° well said.   well done
IAGO She gives it out that you shall marry her.
Do you intend it?
CASSIO Ha, ha, ha!
OTHELLO Do you triumph, Roman?[4] Do you triumph?
CASSIO I marry her? What? A customer?[5] Prithee, bear some charity to my wit;[6] do
not think it so unwholesome. Ha, ha, ha!
OTHELLO So, so, so, so! They laugh that win.[7]
IAGO Faith, the cry goes that you shall marry her.
CASSIO Prithee, say true.
IAGO I am a very villain else.[8]
OTHELLO Have you scored me?[9] Well.
CASSIO This is the monkey's own giving out. She is persuaded I will marry her out
of her own love and flattery,[1] not out of my promise.

1. Keep yourself steady (as in music).
2. The lack of which.
3. An expression of remonstrance.
4. The Romans were noted for their *triumphs* or triumphal
processions.
5. Prostitute.

6. Be more charitable to my judgment.
7. I.e., they that laugh last laugh best.
8. Call me a complete rogue if I'm not telling the truth.
9. Scored off me, beaten me, made up my reckoning,
branded me.
1. Self-flattery, self-deception.

OTHELLO Iago beckons° me. Now he begins the story.   *signals*

CASSIO She was here even now; she haunts me in every place. I was the other day
    talking on the seabank[2] with certain Venetians, and thither comes the bauble,[3]
    and, by this hand,[4] she falls me thus about my neck—
    [*He embraces Iago.*]

OTHELLO Crying, "O dear Cassio!" as it were; his gesture imports it.

CASSIO So hangs and lolls and weeps upon me, so shakes and pulls me. Ha, ha, ha!

OTHELLO Now he tells how she plucked him to my chamber. O, I see that nose of
    yours, but not that dog I shall throw it to.[5]

CASSIO Well, I must leave her company.

IAGO Before me,[6] look where she comes.
    [*Enter Bianca with Othello's handkerchief.*]

CASSIO 'Tis such another fitchew![7] Marry, a perfumed one.—What do you mean by
    this haunting of me?

BIANCA Let the devil and his dam[8] haunt you! What did you mean by that same
    handkerchief you gave me even now? I was a fine fool to take it. I must take out
    the work? A likely piece of work,[9] that you should find it in your chamber and
140   know not who left it there! This is some minx's token, and I must take out the
    work? There; give it your hobbyhorse.[1] [*She gives him the handkerchief.*]
    Wheresoever you had it, I'll take out no work on 't.

CASSIO How now, my sweet Bianca? How now? How now?

OTHELLO By heaven, that should be[2] my handkerchief!

BIANCA If you'll come to supper tonight, you may; if you will not, come when you
    are next prepared for.[3]
                                                    [*Exit.*]

IAGO After her, after her.

CASSIO Faith, I must. She'll rail in the streets else.

IAGO Will you sup there?

CASSIO Faith, I intend so.

IAGO Well, I may chance to see you, for I would very fain speak with you.

CASSIO Prithee, come. Will you?

IAGO Go to. Say no more.   [*Exit Cassio.*]

OTHELLO [*advancing*] How shall I murder him, Iago?

IAGO Did you perceive how he laughed at his vice?

OTHELLO O, Iago!

IAGO And did you see the handkerchief?

OTHELLO Was that mine?

IAGO Yours, by this hand. And to see how he prizes the foolish woman your wife!
160   She gave it him, and he hath given it his whore.

OTHELLO I would have him nine years a-killing. A fine woman! A fair woman! A
    sweet woman!

---

2. Seashore.
3. Plaything.
4. I make my vow.
5. Othello imagines himself cutting off Cassio's nose and
throwing it to a dog.
6. On my soul.
7. What a polecat she is! Just like all the others. (Polecats

were often compared with prostitutes because of their
rank smell and presumed lechery.)
8. Mother.
9. A fine story.
1. Harlot.
2. Must be.
3. When I'm ready for you (i.e., never).

IAGO Nay, you must forget that.

OTHELLO Ay, let her rot and perish, and be damned tonight, for she shall not live.
165 No, my heart is turned to stone; I strike it, and it hurts my hand. O, the world hath not a sweeter creature! She might lie by an emperor's side and command him tasks.

IAGO Nay, that's not your way.[4]

OTHELLO Hang her! I do but say what she is. So delicate with her needle! An
170 admirable musician! O, she will sing the savageness out of a bear. Of so high and plenteous wit and invention![5]

IAGO She's the worse for all this.

OTHELLO O, a thousand, a thousand times! And then, of so gentle a condition![6]

IAGO Ay, too gentle.[7]

OTHELLO Nay, that's certain. But yet the pity of it, Iago! O, Iago, the pity of it, Iago!

IAGO If you are so fond[8] over her iniquity, give her patent[9] to offend, for if it touch not you it comes near nobody.

OTHELLO I will chop her into messes.[1] Cuckold me?

IAGO O, 'tis foul in her.

OTHELLO With mine officer?

IAGO That's fouler.

OTHELLO Get me some poison, Iago, this night. I'll not expostulate with her, lest her body and beauty unprovide[2] my mind again. This night, Iago.

IAGO Do it not with poison. Strangle her in her bed, even the bed she hath contami-
185 nated.

OTHELLO Good, good! The justice of it pleases. Very good.

IAGO And for Cassio, let me be his undertaker.[3] You shall hear more by midnight.

OTHELLO Excellent good. [A trumpet within.] What trumpet is that same?

IAGO I warrant, something from Venice.

[Enter Lodovico, Desdemona, and attendants.]
190 'Tis Lodovico. This comes from the Duke.
See, your wife's with him.

LODOVICO God save you, worthy General!

OTHELLO   With all my heart, sir.[4]

LODOVICO [giving him a letter] The Duke and the senators of Venice greet you.

OTHELLO I kiss the instrument of their pleasures.

[He opens the letter, and reads.]

DESDEMONA And what's the news, good cousin Lodovico?

IAGO I am very glad to see you, signor.
Welcome to Cyprus.

LODOVICO I thank you. How does Lieutenant Cassio?

IAGO Lives, sir.

DESDEMONA Cousin, there's fall'n between him and my lord
An unkind[5] breach; but you shall make all well.

---

4. I.e., the way you should think of her.
5. Imagination.
6. Wellborn and well-bred.
7. Generous, yielding (to other men).
8. Foolish.
9. License.

1. Portions of meat, i.e., bits.
2. Weaken, render unfit.
3. Undertake to dispatch him.
4. I thank you most heartily.
5. Unnatural, contrary to their natures; hurtful.

OTHELLO Are you sure of that?

DESDEMONA My lord?

OTHELLO [*reads*] "This fail you not to do, as you will—"

LODOVICO He did not call; he's busy in the paper.
    Is there division twixt my lord and Cassio?

DESDEMONA A most unhappy one. I would do much
    T' atone° them, for the love I bear to Cassio.   *reconcile*

OTHELLO Fire and brimstone!

DESDEMONA   My lord?

OTHELLO   Are you wise?

DESDEMONA What, is he angry?

LODOVICO   Maybe the letter moved him;
    For, as I think, they do command him home,
    Deputing Cassio in his government.°   *office*

DESDEMONA By my troth, I am glad on 't.°   *of it*

OTHELLO   Indeed?

DESDEMONA   My lord?

OTHELLO I am glad to see you mad.[6]

DESDEMONA   Why, sweet Othello—

OTHELLO [*striking her*] Devil!

DESDEMONA I have not deserved this.

LODOVICO My lord, this would not be believed in Venice,
    Though I should swear I saw 't. 'Tis very much.°   *outrageous*
    Make her amends; she weeps.

OTHELLO   O devil, devil!
    If that the earth could teem° with woman's tears,   *breed*
    Each drop she falls° would prove a crocodile.[7]   *lets fall*
    Out of my sight!

DESDEMONA   I will not stay to offend you. [*Going.*]

LODOVICO Truly, an obedient lady.
    I do beseech your lordship, call her back.

OTHELLO Mistress!

DESDEMONA [*returning*] My lord?

OTHELLO What would you with her, sir?

LODOVICO   Who, I, my lord?

OTHELLO Ay, you did wish that I would make her turn.[8]
    Sir, she can turn, and turn, and yet go on

230   And turn again; and she can weep, sir, weep;
    And she's obedient,[9] as you say, obedient,
    Very obedient.—Proceed you in your tears.—
    Concerning this, sir—O well-painted passion!—°   *grief*
    I am commanded home.—Get you away;

235   I'll send for you anon.—Sir, I obey the mandate
    And will return to Venice.—Hence, avaunt!

                              [*Exit Desdemona.*]

    Cassio shall have my place. And, sir, tonight

---

6. I.e., I am glad to see that you are insane enough to rejoice in Cassio's promotion. (Othello bitterly plays on Desdemona's *I am glad*.)

7. Crocodiles were supposed to weep hypocritical tears for their victims.

8. Othello implies that Desdemona is pliant and will do a *turn* for any man.

9. With much the same sexual connotation as *turn*.

I do entreat that we may sup together.
You are welcome, sir, to Cyprus.—Goats and monkeys!¹
LODOVICO Is this the noble Moor whom our full Senate
Call all in all sufficient? Is this the nature
Whom passion could not shake? Whose solid virtue
The shot of accident nor dart of chance
Could neither graze nor pierce?
IAGO   He is much changed.
LODOVICO Are his wits safe? Is he not light of brain?
IAGO He's that he is. I may not breathe my censure
What he might be. If what he might he is not,
I would to heaven he were!²
LODOVICO   What, strike his wife?
IAGO Faith, that was not so well; yet would I knew
250   That stroke would prove the worst!
LODOVICO   Is it his use?°   custom
Or did the letters work upon his blood°   passions
And new-create his fault?
IAGO   Alas, alas!
It is not honesty in me to speak
What I have seen and known. You shall observe him,
255   And his own courses will denote³ him so
That I may save my speech. Do but go after,
And mark how he continues.
LODOVICO I am sorry that I am deceived in him.   [*Exeunt.*]

Scene 2

[*Location: The Citadel. Enter Othello and Emilia.*]
OTHELLO You have seen nothing then?
EMILIA Nor ever heard, nor ever did suspect.
OTHELLO Yes, you have seen Cassio and she together.
EMILIA But then I saw no harm, and then I heard
5   Each syllable that breath made up between them.
OTHELLO What, did they never whisper?
EMILIA Never, my lord.
OTHELLO Nor send you out o' the way?
EMILIA Never.
OTHELLO To fetch her fan, her gloves, her mask, nor nothing?
EMILIA Never, my lord.
OTHELLO That's strange.
EMILIA I durst, my lord, to wager she is honest,
Lay down my soul at stake.° If you think other,   as the wager
15   Remove your thought; it doth abuse your bosom.°   deceive you
If any wretch have put this in your head,
Let heaven requite it with the serpent's curse!⁴

1. The most lustful animals.
2. I dare not venture an opinion as to whether he's of unsound mind, as you suggest, but, if he isn't, then it might be better to wish he were in fact insane, since only that could excuse his wild behavior.
3. Actions will reveal.
4. The curse pronounced by God on the serpent for deceiving Eve, just as some man has done to Othello and Desdemona. (See Genesis 3.14.)

For if she be not honest, chaste, and true,
There's no man happy; the purest of their wives
20   Is foul as slander.
OTHELLO   Bid her come hither. Go.

[Exit Emilia.]

She says enough; yet she's a simple bawd
That cannot say as much.⁵ This° is a subtle whore,   *Desdemona*
A closet lock and key of villainous secrets.
And yet she'll kneel and pray; I have seen her do 't.
[Enter Desdemona and Emilia.]
DESDEMONA My lord, what is your will?
OTHELLO Pray you, chuck, come hither.
DESDEMONA What is your pleasure?
OTHELLO   Let me see your eyes.
        Look in my face.
DESDEMONA   What horrible fancy's this?
OTHELLO [to Emilia] Some of your function,⁶ mistress.
30   Leave procreants° alone and shut the door;   *mating couples*
        Cough or cry "hem" if anybody come.
        Your mystery,° your mystery! Nay, dispatch.   *trade*

[Exit Emilia.]

DESDEMONA [kneeling] Upon my knees, what doth your speech import?
        I understand a fury in your words,
35   But not the words.
OTHELLO Why, what art thou?
DESDEMONA   Your wife, my lord, your true
        And loyal wife.
OTHELLO   Come, swear it, damn thyself,
        Lest, being like one of heaven,⁷ the devils themselves
        Should fear to seize thee. Therefore be double damned:
40   Swear thou art honest.
DESDEMONA   Heaven doth truly know it.
OTHELLO Heaven truly knows that thou art false as hell.
DESDEMONA To whom, my lord? With whom? How am I false?
OTHELLO [weeping] Ah, Desdemon! Away, away, away!
DESDEMONA Alas the heavy day! Why do you weep?
45   Am I the motive° of these tears, my lord?   *cause*
        If haply you my father do suspect
        An instrument of this your calling back,
        Lay not your blame on me. If you have lost him,
        I have lost him too.
OTHELLO   Had it pleased heaven
50   To try me with affliction, had they⁸ rained
        All kinds of sores and shames on my bare head,
        Steeped me in poverty to the very lips,
        Given to captivity me and my utmost hopes,
        I should have found in some place of my soul

---

5. Any procuress or go-between who couldn't make up as
plausible a story as Emilia's would have to be pretty stupid.
6. I.e., practice your chosen profession, that of bawd (by
guarding the door).
7. Looking like an angel.
8. I.e., heavenly powers.

55   A drop of patience. But, alas, to make me
     A fixèd figure for the time of scorn[9]
     To point his° slow and moving finger[1] at!   *its*
     Yet could I bear that too, well, very well.
     But there where I have garnered° up my heart,   *stored*
60   Where either I must live or bear no life,
     The fountain° from the which my current runs   *spring*
     Or else dries up—to be discarded thence!
     Or keep it as a cistern° for foul toads   *cesspool*
     To knot° and gender° in! Turn thy complexion there,[2]   *couple/engender*
65   Patience, thou young and rose-lipped cherubin—
     Ay, there look grim as hell![3]

DESDEMONA I hope my noble lord esteems me honest.°   *chaste*
OTHELLO O, ay, as summer flies are in the shambles,°   *slaughterhouse*
     That quicken° even with blowing.[4] O thou weed,   *come to life*
70   Who art so lovely fair and smell'st so sweet
     That the sense aches at thee, would thou hadst ne'er been born!
DESDEMONA Alas, what ignorant sin[5] have I committed?
OTHELLO Was this fair paper, this most goodly book,
     Made to write "whore" upon? What committed?
75   Committed? O thou public commoner!°   *prostitute*
     I should make very forges of my cheeks,
     That would to cinders burn up modesty,
     Did I but speak thy deeds. What committed?
     Heaven stops the nose at it and the moon winks;[6]
80   The bawdy[7] wind, that kisses all it meets,
     Is hushed within the hollow mine[8] of earth
     And will not hear 't. What committed?
     Impudent strumpet!
DESDEMONA   By heaven, you do me wrong.
OTHELLO Are not you a strumpet?
DESDEMONA No, as I am a Christian.
     If to preserve this vessel° for my lord   *body*
     From any other foul unlawful touch
     Be not to be a strumpet, I am none.
OTHELLO What, not a whore?
DESDEMONA No, as I shall be saved.
OTHELLO Is 't possible?
DESDEMONA O, heaven forgive us!
OTHELLO   I cry you mercy,° then.   *beg you pardon*
     I took you for that cunning whore of Venice
     That married with Othello. [*Calling out.*] You, mistress,
95   That have the office opposite to Saint Peter
     And keep the gate of hell!
     [*Enter Emilia.*]

---

9. Scornful world.
1. I.e., hour hand of the clock, moving so slowly it seems
hardly to move at all. (Othello envisages himself as being
eternally pointed at by the scornful world as the numbers
on a clock are pointed at by the hour hand.)
2. Change your color, grow pale, at such a sight.
3. Even Patience, that rose-lipped cherub, will look grim

and pale at this spectacle.
4. I.e., with the puffing up of something rotten in which
maggots are breeding.
5. Sin in ignorance.
6. Closes her eyes. (The moon symbolizes chastity.)
7. Kissing one and all.
8. Cave (where the winds were thought to dwell).

                                     You, you, ay, you!
    We have done our course.[9] There's money for your pains.   [*He gives money.*]
    I pray you, turn the key and keep our counsel.   [*Exit.*]
EMILIA Alas, what does this gentleman conceive?°   suppose
100   How do you, madam? How do you, my good lady?
DESDEMONA Faith, half asleep.[1]
EMILIA Good madam, what's the matter with my lord?
DESDEMONA With who?
EMILIA Why, with my lord, madam.
DESDEMONA Who is thy lord?
EMILIA   He that is yours, sweet lady.
DESDEMONA I have none. Do not talk to me, Emilia.
    I cannot weep, nor answers have I none
    But what should go by water.[2] Prithee, tonight
    Lay on my bed my wedding sheets, remember;
110   And call thy husband hither.
EMILIA Here's a change indeed! [*Exit.*]
DESDEMONA 'Tis meet° I should be used so, very meet.   fitting
    How have I been behaved, that he might stick°   attach
    The small'st opinion° on my least misuse?°   censure/misconduct
    [*Enter Iago and Emilia.*]
IAGO What is your pleasure, madam? How is 't with you?
DESDEMONA I cannot tell. Those that do teach young babes
    Do it with gentle means and easy tasks.
    He might have chid me so, for, in good faith,
    I am a child to chiding.
IAGO What is the matter, lady?
EMILIA Alas, Iago, my lord hath so bewhored her,
    Thrown such despite and heavy terms upon her,
    That true hearts cannot bear it.
DESDEMONA Am I that name, Iago?
IAGO What name, fair lady?
DESDEMONA Such as she said my lord did say I was.
EMILIA He called her whore. A beggar in his drink
    Could not have laid such terms upon his callet.°   whore
IAGO Why did he so?
DESDEMONA [*weeping*]
130   I do not know. I am sure I am none such.
IAGO Do not weep, do not weep. Alas the day!
EMILIA Hath she forsook so many noble matches,
    Her father and her country and her friends,
    To be called whore? Would it not make one weep?
DESDEMONA It is my wretched fortune.
IAGO   Beshrew° him for 't!   curse
    How comes this trick° upon him?   delusion
DESDEMONA   Nay, heaven doth know.
EMILIA I will be hanged if some eternal° villain,   inveterate

9. Business (with an indecent suggestion of "trick," turn   1. I.e., dazed.
at sex).   2. Be expressed by tears.

Some busy and insinuating° rogue,   *wheedling*
Some cogging,° cozening° slave, to get some office,   *cheating/defrauding*
140   Have not devised this slander. I will be hanged else.
IAGO   Fie, there is no such man. It is impossible.
DESDEMONA   If any such there be, heaven pardon him!
EMILIA   A halter° pardon him! And hell gnaw his bones!   *hangman's noose*
Why should he call her whore? Who keeps her company?
145   What place? What time? What form?° What likelihood?   *appearance*
The Moor's abused by some most villainous knave,
Some base notorious knave, some scurvy fellow.
O heaven, that such companions thou'dst unfold,[3]
And put in every honest hand a whip
150   To lash the rascals naked through the world
Even from the east to th' west!
IAGO   Speak within door.[4]
EMILIA   O, fie upon them! Some such squire° he was   *fellow*
That turned your wit the seamy side without°   *wrong side out*
And made you to suspect me with the Moor.
IAGO   You are a fool. Go to.[5]
DESDEMONA   Alas, Iago,
What shall I do to win my lord again?
Good friend, go to him; for, by this light of heaven,
I know not how I lost him. Here I kneel. [*She kneels.*]
If e'er my will did trespass 'gainst his love,
160   Either in discourse of thought or actual deed,
Or that° mine eyes, mine ears, or any sense   *if*
Delighted them° in any other form;   *took delight*
Or that I do not yet,° and ever did,   *still*
And ever will—though he do shake me off
165   To beggarly divorcement—love him dearly,
Comfort forswear[6] me! Unkindness may do much,
And his unkindness may defeat° my life,   *destroy*
But never taint my love. I cannot say "whore."
It does abhor[7] me now I speak the word;
170   To do the act that might the addition° earn   *title*
Not the world's mass of vanity° could make me.   *showy splendor*
[*She rises.*]
IAGO   I pray you, be content. 'Tis but his humor.°   *mood*
The business of the state does him offense,
And he does chide with you.
DESDEMONA   If 'twere no other—
IAGO   It is but so, I warrant. [*Trumpets within.*]
Hark, how these instruments summon you to supper!
The messengers of Venice stays the meat.°   *wait to dine*
Go in, and weep not. All things shall be well.
                              [*Exeunt Desdemona and Emilia.*]
[*Enter Roderigo.*]

---

3. If only you would expose such fellows.   6. May heavenly comfort forsake.
4. I.e., not so loud.   7. Fill me with abhorrence. Also, make me whorelike.
5. I.e., that's enough.

How now, Roderigo?

RODERIGO I do not find that thou deal'st justly with me.

IAGO What in the contrary?

RODERIGO Every day thou daff'st me[8] with some device,[9] Iago, and rather, as it seems to me now, keep'st from me all conveniency[1] than suppliest me with the least advantage[2] of hope. I will indeed no longer endure it, nor am I yet per-
185   suaded to put up[3] in peace what already I have foolishly suffered.

IAGO Will you hear me, Roderigo?

RODERIGO Faith, I have heard too much, for your words and performances are no kin together.

IAGO You charge me most unjustly.

RODERIGO With naught but truth. I have wasted myself out of my means. The jewels you have had from me to deliver[4] Desdemona would half have corrupted a votarist.[5] You have told me she hath received them and returned me expectations and comforts of sudden respect[6] and acquaintance, but I find none.

IAGO Well, go to, very well.

RODERIGO "Very well"! "Go to"! I cannot go to,[7] man, nor 'tis not very well. By this hand, I think it is scurvy, and begin to find myself fopped[8] in it.

IAGO Very well.

RODERIGO I tell you 'tis not very well.[9] I will make myself known to Desdemona. If she will return me my jewels, I will give over my suit and repent my unlawful
200   solicitation; if not, assure yourself I will seek satisfaction[1] of you.

IAGO You have said now?[2]

RODERIGO Ay, and said nothing but what I protest intendment[3] of doing.

IAGO Why, now I see there's mettle in thee, and even from this instant do build on thee a better opinion than ever before. Give me thy hand, Roderigo. Thou hast
205   taken against me a most just exception; but yet I protest I have dealt most directly in thy affair.

RODERIGO It hath not appeared.

IAGO I grant indeed it hath not appeared, and your suspicion is not without wit and judgment. But, Roderigo, if thou hast that in thee indeed which I have greater
210   reason to believe now than ever—I mean purpose, courage, and valor—this night show it. If thou the next night following enjoy not Desdemona, take me from this world with treachery and devise engines[4] for my life.

RODERIGO Well, what is it? Is it within reason and compass?

IAGO Sir, there is especial commission come from Venice to depute Cassio in
215   Othello's place.

RODERIGO Is that true? Why, then Othello and Desdemona return again to Venice.

IAGO O, no; he goes into Mauritania and takes away with him the fair Desdemona, unless his abode be lingered here by some accident; wherein none can be so determinate[5] as the removing of Cassio.

---

8. You put me off
9. Excuse, trick.
1. Advantage, opportunity.
2. Increase.
3. Submit to, tolerate.
4. Deliver to.
5. Nun.
6. Immediate consideration.
7. Roderigo changes Iago's *go to*, an expression urging patience, to *I cannot go to*, "I have no opportunity for suc-

cess in wooing."
8. Fooled, duped.
9. Roderigo changes Iago's *very well*, "all right, then," to *not very well*, "not at all good."
1. Repayment. (The term normally means settling of accounts in a duel.)
2. Have you finished?
3. Intention.
4. Plots against.
5. Conclusive.

RODERIGO How do you mean, removing of him?

IAGO Why, by making him uncapable of Othello's place—knocking out his brains.

RODERIGO And that you would have me to do?

IAGO Ay, if you dare do yourself a profit and a right. He sups tonight with a har-
lotry,⁶ and thither will I go to him. He knows not yet of his honorable fortune.
225   If you will watch his going thence, which I will fashion to fall out⁷ between
twelve and one, you may take him at your pleasure. I will be near to second
your attempt, and he shall fall between us. Come, stand not amazed at it, but
go along with me. I will show you such a necessity in his death that you shall
think yourself bound to put it on him. It is now high⁸ suppertime, and the
230   night grows to waste.⁹ About it.

RODERIGO I will hear further reason for this.

IAGO And you shall be satisfied.   [*Exeunt.*]

Scene 3

[*Location: The Citadel. Enter Othello, Lodovico, Desdemona, Emilia, and attendants.*]

LODOVICO I do beseech you, sir, trouble yourself no further.

OTHELLO O, pardon me; 'twill do me good to walk.

LODOVICO Madam, good night. I humbly thank your ladyship.

DESDEMONA Your honor is most welcome.

OTHELLO   Will you walk, sir?
5   O, Desdemona!

DESDEMONA My lord?

OTHELLO Get you to bed on th' instant. I will be returned forthwith. Dismiss your
attendant there. Look 't be done.

DESDEMONA I will, my lord.

[*Exit Othello, with Lodovico and attendants.*]

EMILIA How goes it now? He looks gentler than he did.

DESDEMONA He says he will return incontinent,°   *immediately*
And hath commanded me to go to bed,
And bid me to dismiss you.

EMILIA   Dismiss me?

DESDEMONA It was his bidding. Therefore, good Emilia,
15   Give me my nightly wearing, and adieu.
We must not now displease him.

EMILIA I would you had never seen him!

DESDEMONA So would not I. My love doth so approve him
That even his stubbornness,° his checks,° his frowns—   *roughness/rebukes*
20   Prithee, unpin me—have grace and favor in them.

[*Emilia prepares Desdemona for bed.*]

EMILIA I have laid those sheets you bade me on the bed.

DESDEMONA All's one.¹ Good faith, how foolish are our minds!
If I do die before thee, prithee shroud me
In one of these same sheets.

EMILIA   Come, come, you talk.°   *prattle*

6. Slut.
7. Occur.
8. Fully.

9. Wastes away.
1. All right. It doesn't really matter.

DESDEMONA My mother had a maid called Barbary.
She was in love, and he she loved proved mad°   *wild*
And did forsake her. She had a song of "Willow."
An old thing 'twas, but it expressed her fortune,
And she died singing it. That song tonight
30   Will not go from my mind; I have much to do
But to go hang² my head all at one side
And sing it like poor Barbary. Prithee, dispatch.
EMILIA Shall I go fetch your nightgown?°   *dressing gown*
DESDEMONA   No, unpin me here.
35   This Lodovico is a proper° man.   *handsome*
EMILIA A very handsome man.
DESDEMONA He speaks well.
EMILIA I know a lady in Venice would have walked barefoot to Palestine for a touch
of his nether lip.
DESDEMONA [*singing*] "The poor soul sat sighing by a sycamore tree,
40   Sing all a green willow;³
Her hand on her bosom, her head on her knee,
Sing willow, willow, willow.
The fresh streams ran by her and murmured her moans;
Sing willow, willow, willow;
45   Her salt tears fell from her, and softened the stones—"
Lay by these.
[*Singing*.] "Sing willow, willow, willow—"
Prithee, hie thee.° He'll come anon.°   *hurry/right away*
[*Singing*.] "Sing all a green willow must be my garland.
50   Let nobody blame him; his scorn I approve—"
Nay, that's not next.—Hark! Who is 't that knocks?
EMILIA It's the wind.
DESDEMONA [*singing*] "I called my love false love; but what said he then?
Sing willow, willow, willow;
55   If I court more women, you'll couch with more men."
So, get thee gone. Good night. Mine eyes do itch;
Doth that bode weeping?
EMILIA   'Tis neither here nor there.
DESDEMONA I have heard it said so. O, these men, these men!
60   Dost thou in conscience think—tell me, Emilia—
That there be women do abuse° their husbands   *deceive*
In such gross kind?
EMILIA   There be some such, no question.
DESDEMONA Wouldst thou do such a deed for all the world?
EMILIA Why, would not you?
DESDEMONA   No, by this heavenly light!
EMILIA Nor I neither by this heavenly light;
65   I might do 't as well i' the dark.
DESDEMONA Wouldst thou do such a deed for all the world?
EMILIA The world's a huge thing. It is a great price

For a small vice.

DESDEMONA Good troth, I think thou wouldst not.

EMILIA By my troth, I think I should, and undo 't when I had done. Marry, I would not do such a thing for a joint ring,[4] nor for measures of lawn,[5] nor for gowns, petticoats, nor caps, nor any petty exhibition.[6] But for all the whole world! Uds[7] pity, who would not make her husband a cuckold to make him a monarch? I should venture purgatory for 't.

DESDEMONA Beshrew me if I would do such a wrong
    For the whole world.

EMILIA Why, the wrong is but a wrong i' the world, and having the world for your labor, 'tis a wrong in your own world, and you might quickly make it right.

DESDEMONA I do not think there is any such woman.

EMILIA Yes, a dozen, and as many
    To th' vantage[8] as would store° the world they played[9] for.   *populate*
    But I do think it is their husbands' faults
    If wives do fall. Say that they slack their duties°   *marital duties*
    And pour our treasures into foreign laps,[1]
85   Or else break out in peevish jealousies,
    Throwing restraint upon us?[2] Or say they strike us,
    Or scant our former having in despite?[3]
    Why, we have galls,[4] and though we have some grace,
    Yet have we some revenge. Let husbands know
90   Their wives have sense° like them. They see, and smell,   *physical sense*
    And have their palates both for sweet and sour,
    As husbands have. What is it that they do
    When they change us for others? Is it sport?°   *sexual pastime*
    I think it is. And doth affection° breed it?   *passion*
95   I think it doth. Is 't frailty that thus errs?
    It is so, too. And have not we affections,
    Desires for sport, and frailty, as men have?
    Then let them use us well; else let them know,
    The ills we do, their ills instruct us so.

DESDEMONA Good night, good night. God me such uses° send   *practice*
    Not to pick bad from bad, but by bad mend![5]

                                    [Exeunt.]

Act 5

Scene 1

[Location: A street in Cyprus. Enter Iago and Roderigo.]

IAGO Here stand behind this bulk.[6] Straight will he come.
    Wear thy good rapier bare,° and put it home.   *unsheathed*
    Quick, quick! Fear nothing. I'll be at thy elbow.

---

4. A ring made in separate halves.
5. Fine linen.
6. Gift.
7. God's.
8. In addition, to boot.
9. Gambled. Also, sported sexually.
1. I.e., are unfaithful, give what is rightfully ours (semen) to other women.

2. I.e., jealously restricting our freedom to see other men.
3. Reduce our allowance to spite us.
4. Are capable of resenting injury and insult.
5. Not to learn bad conduct from others' badness (as Emilia has suggested women learn from men), but to mend my ways by perceiving what badness is, making spiritual benefit out of evil and adversity.
6. Framework projecting from the front of a shop.

It makes us or it mars us. Think on that,
5   And fix most firm thy resolution.
RODERIGO Be near at hand. I may miscarry in 't.
IAGO Here, at thy hand. Be bold, and take thy stand.
    [*Iago stands aside. Roderigo conceals himself.*]
RODERIGO I have no great devotion to the deed;
    And yet he hath given me satisfying reasons.
10   'Tis but a man gone. Forth, my sword! He dies.
    [*He draws.*]
IAGO I have rubbed this young quat° almost to the sense,°   *pimple/raw*
    And he grows angry. Now, whether he kill Cassio
    Or Cassio him, or each do kill the other,
    Every way makes my gain. Live Roderigo,[7]
15   He calls me to a restitution large
    Of gold and jewels that I bobbed° from him   *swindled*
    As gifts to Desdemona.
    It must not be. If Cassio do remain,
    He hath a daily beauty in his life
20   That makes me ugly; and besides, the Moor
    May unfold° me to him; there stand I in much peril.   *expose*
    No, he must die. Be 't so. I hear him coming.
    [*Enter Cassio.*]
RODERIGO [*coming forth*] I know his gait, 'tis he.—Villain, thou diest!
    [*He attacks Cassio.*]
CASSIO That thrust had been mine enemy indeed,
25   But that my coat[8] is better than thou know'st.
    I will make proof° of thine.   *a test*
    [*He draws, and wounds Roderigo.*]
RODERIGO   O, I am slain! [*He falls.*]
    [*Iago, from behind, wounds Cassio in the leg, and exit.*]
CASSIO I am maimed forever. Help, ho! Murder! Murder!
    [*Enter Othello.*]
OTHELLO The voice of Cassio! Iago keeps his word.
RODERIGO O, villain that I am!
OTHELLO   It is even so.
CASSIO O, help, ho! Light! A surgeon!
OTHELLO 'Tis he. O brave Iago, honest and just,
    That hast such noble sense of thy friend's wrong!
    Thou teachest me. Minion,[9] your dear lies dead,
    And your unblest fate hies.° Strumpet, I come.   *hastens on*
35   Forth of° my heart those charms, thine eyes, are blotted;   *from out*
    Thy bed, lust-stained, shall with lust's blood be spotted.   [*Exit Othello.*]
    [*Enter Lodovico and Gratiano.*]
CASSIO What ho! No watch? No passage?° Murder! Murder!   *passers-by*
GRATIANO 'Tis some mischance. The voice is very direful.
CASSIO O, help!
LODOVICO Hark!

7. If Roderigo lives.
8. Possibly a garment of mail under the outer clothing, or

simply a tougher coat than Roderigo expected.
9. Hussy (i.e., Desdemona).

RODERIGO O wretched villain!

LODOVICO Two or three groan. 'Tis heavy° night;   *thick, dark*
    These may be counterfeits. Let's think 't unsafe
    To come in° to the cry without more help.   *approach*
    [*They remain near the entrance.*]

RODERIGO Nobody come? Then shall I bleed to death.
    [*Enter Iago in his shirtsleeves, with a light.*]

LODOVICO Hark!

GRATIANO Here's one comes in his shirt, with light and weapons.

IAGO Who's there? Whose noise is this that cries on° murder?   *cries out*

LODOVICO We do not know.

IAGO   Did not you hear a cry?

CASSIO Here, here! For heaven's sake, help me!

IAGO   What's the matter?
    [*He moves toward Cassio.*]

GRATIANO [*to Lodovico*] This is Othello's ancient, as I take it.

LODOVICO [*to Gratiano*] The same indeed, a very valiant fellow.

IAGO [*to Cassio*] What° are you here that cry so grievously?   *who*

CASSIO Iago? O, I am spoiled,° undone by villains!   *ruined*
55   Give me some help.

IAGO O me, Lieutenant! What villains have done this?

CASSIO I think that one of them is hereabout,
    And cannot make° away.   *get*

IAGO   O treacherous villains!
    [*To Lodovico and Gratiano.*] What are you there? Come in, and
60   give some help. [*They advance.*]

RODERIGO O, help me there!

CASSIO That's one of them.

IAGO   O murderous slave! O villain!
    [*He stabs Roderigo.*]

RODERIGO O damned Iago! O inhuman dog!

IAGO Kill men i' the dark?—Where be these bloody thieves?—
    How silent is this town!—Ho! Murder, murder!—
    [*To Lodovico and Gratiano.*]
65   What may you be? Are you of good or evil?

LODOVICO As you shall prove us, praise° us.   *appraise*

IAGO Signor Lodovico?

LODOVICO He, sir.

IAGO I cry you mercy.[1] Here's Cassio hurt by villains.

GRATIANO Cassio?

IAGO How is 't, brother?

CASSIO My leg is cut in two.

IAGO Marry, heaven forbid!
    Light, gentlemen! I'll bind it with my shirt.
    [*He hands them the light and tends to Cassio's wound.*]
    [*Enter Bianca.*]

BIANCA What is the matter, ho? Who is 't that cried?

---

1. I beg your pardon.

IAGO Who is 't that cried?

BIANCA   O my dear Cassio!
    My sweet Cassio! O Cassio, Cassio, Cassio!

IAGO O notable strumpet! Cassio, may you suspect
    Who they should be that have thus mangled you?

CASSIO No.

GRATIANO I am sorry to find you thus. I have been to seek you.

IAGO Lend me a garter. [*He applies a tourniquet.*] So.—O, for a chair,°   *litter*
    To bear him easily hence!

BIANCA Alas, he faints! O Cassio, Cassio, Cassio!

IAGO Gentlemen all, I do suspect this trash
    To be a party in this injury.—
    Patience awhile, good Cassio.—Come, come;
    Lend me a light. [*He shines the light on Roderigo.*]
    Know we this face or no?

90   Alas, my friend and my dear countryman
    Roderigo! No.—Yes, sure.—O heaven! Roderigo!

GRATIANO What, of Venice?

IAGO Even he, sir. Did you know him?

GRATIANO Know him? Ay.

IAGO Signor Gratiano? I cry your gentle° pardon.   *noble*
    These bloody accidents° must excuse my manners   *sudden events*
    That so neglected you.

GRATIANO   I am glad to see you.

IAGO How do you, Cassio? O, a chair, a chair!

GRATIANO Roderigo!

IAGO He, he, 'tis he. [*A litter is brought in.*] O, that's well said;[2] the chair.
    Some good man bear him carefully from hence;
    I'll fetch the General's surgeon. [*To Bianca.*] For you, mistress,
    Save you your labor.[3] He that lies slain here, Cassio,
    Was my dear friend. What malice° was between you?   *enmity*

CASSIO None in the world, nor do I know the man.

IAGO [*to Bianca*] What, look you pale?—O, bear him out o' th' air.[4]
    [*Cassio and Roderigo are borne off.*]
    Stay you,[5] good gentlemen.—Look you pale, mistress?—
    Do you perceive the gastness° of her eye?—   *terror*
    Nay, if you stare,[6] shall hear more anon.—

110   Behold her well; I pray you, look upon her.
    Do you see, gentlemen? Nay, guiltiness
    Will speak, though tongues were out of use.
    [*Enter Emilia.*]

EMILIA 'Las, what's the matter? What's the matter, husband?

IAGO Cassio hath here been set on in the dark

115   By Roderigo and fellows that are scaped.
    He's almost slain, and Roderigo dead.

EMILIA Alas, good gentleman! Alas, good Cassio!

IAGO This is the fruits of whoring. Prithee, Emilia,

---

2. Well done.
3. Never you mind tending Cassio.
4. Fresh air was thought to be dangerous for a wound.

5. Lodovico and Gratiano are evidently about to leave.
6. Iago pretends to interpret Bianca's wild looks as an involuntary confession of guilt.

Go know° of Cassio where he supped tonight.   *learn*
120   [*To Bianca.*] What, do you shake at that?
BIANCA He supped at my house, but I therefore shake not.
IAGO O, did he so? I charge you go with me.
EMILIA O, fie upon thee, strumpet!
BIANCA I am no strumpet, but of life as honest°   *chaste*
125   As you that thus abuse me.
EMILIA As I? Faugh! Fie upon thee!
IAGO Kind gentlemen, let's go see poor Cassio dressed.[7]—
        Come, mistress, you must tell 's another tale.
        Emilia, run you to the citadel
130   And tell my lord and lady what hath happed.—
        Will you go on afore? [*Aside.*] This is the night
        That either makes me or fordoes° me quite.   [*Exeunt.*]   *ruins*

                                   Scene 2
[*Location: A bedchamber in the citadel.*
Enter Othello with a light, and Desdemona in her bed.][8]
OTHELLO It is the cause,[9] it is the cause, my soul.
        Let me not name it to you, you chaste stars!
        It is the cause. Yet I'll not shed her blood,
        Nor scar that whiter skin of hers than snow,
5   And smooth as monumental alabaster.[1]
        Yet she must die, else she'll betray more men.
        Put out the light, and then put out the light.[2]
        If I quench thee, thou flaming minister,[3]
        I can again thy former light restore,
10   Should I repent me;° but once put out thy light,   *change my mind*
        Thou cunning'st pattern[4] of excelling nature,
        I know not where is that Promethean heat[5]
        That can thy light relume.° When I have plucked thy rose,   *rekindle*
        I cannot give it vital growth again;
15   It needs must wither. I'll smell thee on the tree.
        [*He kisses her.*]
        O balmy breath, that dost almost persuade
        Justice to break her sword! One more, one more.
        Be thus when thou art dead, and I will kill thee,
        And love thee after. One more, and that's the last.
        [*He kisses her.*]
20   So sweet was ne'er so fatal. I must weep,
        But they are cruel° tears. This sorrow's heavenly;   *unrelenting*
        It strikes where it doth love.[6] She wakes.
DESDEMONA Who's there? Othello?
OTHELLO Ay, Desdemona.

---

7. Cassio's wounds dressed.
8. Either the curtains are drawn back to reveal the bed in a recessed area backstage or the bed is "thrust out" onstage as the scene begins.
9. Cause of justice, the offense itself, which Othello must correct as an agent of justice.
1. Used in making tombs and funeral monuments.

2. The torch or lamp . . . Desdemona's life.
3. Torch or lamp that serves me.
4. You skillfully wrought perfect example.
5. Divine fire (alluding to the theft of fire from heaven by Prometheus).
6. Compare Hebrews 12.6: "For whom the Lord loveth he chasteneth."

DESDEMONA Will you come to bed, my lord?

OTHELLO Have you prayed tonight, Desdemon?

DESDEMONA Ay, my lord.

OTHELLO If you bethink yourself of any crime°   *sin*
    Unreconciled as yet to heaven and grace,
30 Solicit° for it straight.°   *pray/immediately*

DESDEMONA Alack, my lord, what may you mean by that?

OTHELLO Well, do it, and be brief. I will walk by.
    I would not kill thy unpreparèd spirit.
    No, heaven forfend!° I would not kill thy soul.   *forbid*

DESDEMONA Talk you of killing?

OTHELLO   Ay, I do.

DESDEMONA   Then heaven
    Have mercy on me!

OTHELLO   Amen, with all my heart!

DESDEMONA If you say so, I hope you will not kill me.

OTHELLO Humh!

DESDEMONA And yet I fear you; for you're fatal then
40 When your eyes roll so. Why I should fear I know not,
    Since guiltiness I know not; but yet I feel I fear.

OTHELLO Think on thy sins.

DESDEMONA   They are loves I bear to you.[7]

OTHELLO Ay, and for that thou diest.

DESDEMONA That death's unnatural that kills for loving.
45 Alas, why gnaw you so your nether lip?
    Some bloody passion shakes your very frame.
    These are portents; but yet I hope, I hope,
    They do not point on[8] me.

OTHELLO Peace, and be still!

DESDEMONA I will so. What's the matter?

OTHELLO That handkerchief which I so loved and gave thee
    Thou gav'st to Cassio.

DESDEMONA   No, by my life and soul!
    Send for the man and ask him.

OTHELLO Sweet soul, take heed, take heed of perjury.
55 Thou art on thy deathbed.

DESDEMONA Ay, but not yet to die.

OTHELLO   Yes, presently.°   *immediately*
    Therefore confess thee freely of thy sin;
    For to deny each article with oath
    Cannot remove nor choke the strong conception[9]
60 That I do groan withal.[1] Thou art to die.

DESDEMONA Then Lord have mercy on me!

OTHELLO   I say, amen.

DESDEMONA And have you mercy too! I never did
    Offend° you in my life; never loved Cassio   *wrong*
    But with such general warranty° of heaven   *sanction*

---

7. If I sinned, it was in loving you more than my father or more than God.
8. Point at, predict what is to happen to.

9. Belief in your guilt. Also, plan in my mind.
1. Groan at in sorrow. Also, as in giving birth.

65   As I might love. I never gave him token.
OTHELLO By heaven, I saw my handkerchief in 's hand.
    O perjured woman! Thou dost stone° heart,   *harden*
    And makes me call what I intend to do
    A murder, which I thought a sacrifice.
    I saw the handkerchief.
DESDEMONA   He found it, then.
    I never gave it him. Send for him hither;
    Let him confess a truth.
OTHELLO   He hath confessed.
DESDEMONA What, my lord?
OTHELLO That he hath used thee.
DESDEMONA   How? Unlawfully?
OTHELLO   Ay.
DESDEMONA He will not say so.
OTHELLO   No, his mouth is stopped;
    Honest Iago hath ta'en order° for 't.   *taken measures*
DESDEMONA O, my fear interprets. What, is he dead?
OTHELLO Had all his hairs been lives, my great revenge
    Had stomach for them all.
DESDEMONA Alas, he is betrayed and I undone!   [*She weeps.*]
OTHELLO Out, strumpet! Weep'st thou for him to my face?
DESDEMONA O, banish me, my lord, but kill me not!
OTHELLO Down, strumpet!
DESDEMONA Kill me tomorrow; let me live tonight!
OTHELLO Nay, if you strive—
DESDEMONA But half an hour!
OTHELLO   Being done,² there is no pause.
DESDEMONA But while I say one prayer!
OTHELLO   It is too late. [*Smothers her.*]
EMILIA [*at the door*] My lord, my lord! What, ho! My lord, my lord!
OTHELLO What noise is this? Not dead? Not yet quite dead?
90   I that am cruel am yet merciful;
    I would not have thee linger in thy pain. [*He dispatches her.*]
    So, so.
EMILIA [*within*] What, ho! My lord, my lord!
OTHELLO   Who's there?
EMILIA [*within*] O, good my lord, I would speak a word with you!
OTHELLO Yes, 'tis Emilia.—By and by.—She's dead.
    'Tis like° she comes to speak of Cassio's death.—   *likely that*
    The noise was here.³ Ha! No more moving?
    Still as the grave. Shall she come in? Were 't good?—
    I think she stirs again. No. What's best to do?
100   If she come in, she'll sure speak to my wife.
    My wife! My wife! What wife? I have no wife.
    O, insupportable! O heavy hour!
    Methinks it should be now a huge eclipse
    Of sun and moon, and that th' affrighted globe

---

2. Since justice has begun its relentless course.

3. The Folio's *high* is possible, suggesting that the commotion of the attack on Cassio was loud.

Should yawn[4] at alteration.[5]

EMILIA [within]   I do beseech you
That I may speak with you, O, good my lord!

OTHELLO I had forgot thee. O, come in, Emilia.—
Soft,° by and by. Let me the curtains draw.—   *wait a minute*
[He closes the bed-curtains and opens the door.]
Where art thou?
[Enter Emilia.]
                    What's the matter with thee now?

EMILIA O, my good lord, yonder's foul murders done!

OTHELLO What, now?

EMILIA But now, my lord.

OTHELLO It is the very error° of the moon;   *aberration, irregularity*
She comes more nearer earth than she was wont,

115   And makes men mad.

EMILIA Cassio, my lord, hath killed a young Venetian
Called Roderigo.

OTHELLO   Roderigo killed?
And Cassio killed?

EMILIA   No, Cassio is not killed.

OTHELLO Not Cassio killed? Then murder's out of tune,

120   And sweet revenge grows harsh.

DESDEMONA O, falsely, falsely murdered!

EMILIA O Lord, what cry is that?

OTHELLO That? What?

EMILIA Out[6] and alas, that was my lady's voice.
[She opens the bed-curtains.]

125   Help, help, ho, help! O lady, speak again!
Sweet Desdemona! O sweet mistress, speak!

DESDEMONA A guiltless death I die.

EMILIA O, who hath done this deed?

DESDEMONA Nobody; I myself. Farewell.

130   Commend me to my kind lord. O, farewell! [She dies.]

OTHELLO Why, how should she be murdered?

EMILIA   Alas, who knows?

OTHELLO You heard her say herself it was not I.

EMILIA She said so. I must needs report the truth.

OTHELLO She's like a liar gone to burning hell!

135   'Twas I that killed her.

EMILIA   O, the more angel she,
And you the blacker devil!

OTHELLO She turned to folly,[7] and she was a whore.

EMILIA Thou dost belie° her, and thou art a devil.   *slander*

OTHELLO She was false as water.

---

4. Gape in amazement, i.e., move in an earthquake.
(According to Pliny, earthquakes often happen during
eclipses.)
5. At these cataclysmic events in nature, well suited to

express the horror of Desdemona's death.
6. A cry of dismay, intensifying *alas*.
7. I.e., wantonness, fleshly sin.

EMILIA   Thou art rash as fire to say
140   That she was false. O, she was heavenly true!
OTHELLO Cassio did top her. Ask thy husband else.[8]
        O, I were damned beneath all depth in hell
        But that I did proceed upon just grounds
        To this extremity. Thy husband knew it all.
EMILIA My husband?
OTHELLO   Thy husband.
EMILIA   That she was false to wedlock?
OTHELLO Ay, with Cassio. Nay, had she been true,
        If heaven would make me such another world
        Of one entire and perfect chrysolite,°   *precious topaz*
        I'd not have sold her for it.
EMILIA My husband?
OTHELLO Ay, 'twas he that told me on her first.
        An honest man he is, and hates the slime
        That sticks on filthy deeds.
EMILIA My husband?
OTHELLO What needs this iterance,° woman? I say thy husband.   *repetition*
EMILIA O mistress, villainy hath made mocks° with love!   *made sport*
        My husband say she was false?
OTHELLO   He, woman;
        I say thy husband. Dost understand the word?
        My friend, thy husband, honest, honest Iago.
EMILIA If he say so, may his pernicious soul
        Rot half a grain a day! He lies to th' heart.
        She was too fond of her most filthy bargain.
OTHELLO Ha? [*He draws.*]
EMILIA Do thy worst!
        This deed of thine is no more worthy heaven
        Than thou wast worthy her.
OTHELLO   Peace, you were best.[9]
EMILIA Thou hast not half that power to do me harm
        As I have to be hurt.° O gull!° O dolt!   *to endure hurt/dupe*
        As ignorant as dirt! Thou hast done a deed—
170   I care not for thy sword; I'll make thee known,
        Though I lost twenty lives.—Help! Help, ho, help!
        The Moor hath killed my mistress! Murder, murder!
        [*Enter Montano, Gratiano, and Iago.*]
MONTANO What is the matter? How now, General?
EMILIA O, are you come, Iago? You have done well,
175   That men must lay their murders on your neck.
GRATIANO What is the matter?
EMILIA [*to Iago*]
        Disprove this villain, if thou be'st a man.
        He says thou toldst him that his wife was false.
        I know thou didst not; thou'rt not such a villain.
180   Speak, for my heart is full.

---

8. I.e., if you don't believe me.   9. It would be best for you.

IAGO I told him what I thought, and told no more
    Than what he found himself was apt° and true.   *plausible*
EMILIA But did you ever tell him she was false?
IAGO I did.
EMILIA You told a lie, an odious, damnèd lie!
    Upon my soul, a lie, a wicked lie.
    She false with Cassio? Did you say with Cassio?
IAGO With Cassio, mistress. Go to, charm[1] your tongue.
EMILIA I will not charm my tongue; I am bound to speak.
190   My mistress here lies murdered in her bed—
ALL O heavens forfend!
EMILIA And your reports have set the murder on.
OTHELLO Nay, stare not, masters. It is true indeed.
GRATIANO 'Tis a strange truth.
MONTANO O monstrous act!
EMILIA   Villainy, villainy, villainy!
    I think upon 't—I think I smell 't! O villainy!
    I thought so then[2]—I'll kill myself for grief—
    O villainy, villainy!
IAGO What, are you mad? I charge you, get you home.
EMILIA Good gentlemen, let me have leave to speak.
    'Tis proper I obey him, but not now.
    Perchance, Iago, I will ne'er go home.
OTHELLO O! O! O! [*Othello falls on the bed.*][3]
EMILIA Nay, lay thee down and roar,
205   For thou hast killed the sweetest innocent
    That e'er did lift up eye.[4]
OTHELLO [*rising*]   O, she was foul!
    I scarce did know you, uncle. There lies your niece,
    Whose breath indeed these hands have newly stopped.
    I know this act shows° horrible and grim.   *looks*
GRATIANO Poor Desdemon! I am glad thy father's dead.
    Thy match was mortal to him, and pure grief
    Shore his old thread[5] in twain. Did he live now,
    This sight would make him do a desperate turn,°   *deed*
    Yea, curse his better angel from his side,
215   And fall to reprobance.[6]
OTHELLO 'Tis pitiful. But yet Iago knows
    That she with Cassio hath the act of shame
    A thousand times committed. Cassio confessed it;
    And she did gratify° his amorous works   *reward*
220   With that recognizance° and pledge of love   *token*
    Which I first gave her. I saw it in his hand;
    It was a handkerchief, an antique token
    My father gave my mother.
EMILIA O God! O heavenly God!
IAGO Zounds, hold your peace.

1. Keep silent (as though by a magic spell).
2. Perhaps in 3.3 and 4.2.
3. This direction is from the Quarto.
4. Lift her eyes to heaven.

5. Sheared the thread of his old age (as Atropos, one of the three Fates, was thought to do).
6. Damnation, i.e., suicide.

EMILIA   'Twill out, 'twill out! I peace?
No, I will speak as liberal as the north.[7]
Let heaven and men and devils, let them all,
All, all, cry shame against me, yet I'll speak.
IAGO Be wise, and get you home.
EMILIA   I will not.
   [*Iago threatens Emilia.*]
GRATIANO   Fie,
230   Your sword upon a woman?
EMILIA O thou dull Moor! That handkerchief thou speak'st of
   I found by fortune and did give my husband;
   For often, with a solemn earnestness,
   More than indeed belonged° to such a trifle,   *was appropriate*
235   He begged of me to steal 't.
IAGO   Villainous whore!
EMILIA She give it Cassio? No, alas! I found it,
   And I did give 't my husband.
IAGO   Filth, thou liest!
EMILIA By heaven, I do not, I do not, gentlemen.
   O murderous coxcomb![8] What should such a fool
240   Do with so good a wife?
OTHELLO   Are there no stones[9] in heaven
   But what serves for the thunder?—Precious° villain!   *utter*
   [*He runs at Iago; Montano disarms Othello. Iago, from behind, stabs Emilia.*][1]
GRATIANO The woman falls! Sure he hath killed his wife.
EMILIA Ay, ay. O, lay me by my mistress' side.
                                                               [*Exit Iago.*]
GRATIANO He's gone, but his wife's killed.
MONTANO 'Tis a notorious villain. Take you this weapon,
   Which I have here recovered from the Moor.
   Come, guard the door without. Let him not pass,
   But kill him rather. I'll after that same villain,
   For 'tis a damnèd slave.
   [*Exit with all but Othello and Emilia, who has been laid by Desdemona's side.*]
OTHELLO   I am not valiant neither,
250   But every puny whipster[2] gets my sword.
   But why should honor[3] outlive honesty?°   *integrity*
   Let it go all.
EMILIA   What did thy song bode, lady?
   Hark, canst thou hear me? I will play the swan,
   And die in music. [*She sings.*] "Willow, willow, willow."
255   Moor, she was chaste. She loved thee, cruel Moor.
   So come my soul to bliss as I speak true.
   So speaking as I think, alas, I die. [*She dies.*]
OTHELLO I have another weapon in this chamber;

7. Freely as the north wind (blows).
8. Fool (addressed to Othello).
9. Bolts, such as those used for thunderbolts.
1. The Quarto text reads, "The Moor runs at Iago. Iago kills his wife." The Quarto also specifies the exit of Iago below.

2. Contemptible fellow (one who is always ready to whip out his sword).
3. The bravery for which one enjoys a soldier's reputation.

It was a sword of Spain, the ice-brook's temper[4]—
260   O, here it is. [*He finds a sword.*] Uncle, I must come forth.
GRATIANO [*within*] If thou attempt it, it will cost thee dear.
 Thou hast no weapon, and perforce must suffer.
OTHELLO Look in upon me then and speak with me,
 Or, naked° as I am, I will assault thee.   *unarmed*
 [*Enter Gratiano.*]
GRATIANO What is the matter?
OTHELLO   Behold, I have a weapon;
 A better never did itself sustain
 Upon a soldier's thigh. I have seen the day
 That, with this little arm and this good sword,
 I have made my way through more impediments
270 Than twenty times your stop.[5] But O, vain boast!
 Who can control his fate? 'Tis not so now.
 Be not afraid, though you do see me weaponed;
 Here is my journey's end, here is my butt[6]
 And very seamark[7] of my utmost sail.
 [*Gratiano steps back.*]
275 Do you go back dismayed? 'Tis a lost° fear;   *wasted*
 Man but a rush[8] against Othello's breast
 And he retires. Where should Othello go?
 [*He turns to Desdemona.*]
 Now, how dost thou look now? O ill-starred wench!
 Pale as thy smock! When we shall meet at compt,° *Judgment Day*
280 This look of thine will hurl my soul from heaven,
 And fiends will snatch at it. Cold, cold, my girl?
 Even like thy chastity. O cursèd, cursèd slave![9]
 Whip me, ye devils,
 From the possession of this heavenly sight!
285 Blow me about in winds! Roast me in sulfur!
 Wash me in steep-down gulfs of liquid fire!
 O Desdemon! Dead, Desdemon! Dead! O! O!
 [*Enter Lodovico, Cassio (carried in a litter),[1] Montano, and Iago (prisoner), with
 officers.*]
LODOVICO Where is this rash and most unfortunate man?
OTHELLO That's he that was Othello. Here I am.
LODOVICO Where is that viper? Bring the villain forth.
 [*Iago is led forward.*]
OTHELLO I look down towards his feet;[2] but that's a fable.
 If that thou be'st a devil, I cannot kill thee.
 [*He wounds Iago.*]
LODOVICO Wrench his sword from him. [*Othello is disarmed.*]
IAGO   I bleed, sir, but not killed.
OTHELLO I am not sorry neither. I'd have thee live,
295 For in my sense[3] 'tis happiness to die.

4. Tempered in ice-cold water.   9. Othello himself.
5. Power (to stop).   1. The Quarto specifies that Cassio is "in a chair."
6. Goal, limit (an archery term).   2. I.e., to see if they are cloven, as the devil's are fabled to
7. Beacon (marking his destination or limit). be.
8. Wield no more than a reed.   3. To one who feels as I do.

LODOVICO O thou Othello, that was once so good,
    Fall'n in the practice[4] of a cursèd slave,°   *villain*
    What shall be said to thee?
OTHELLO   Why, anything.
    An honorable murderer, if you will,
300   For naught I did in hate, but all in honor.
LODOVICO This wretch hath part confessed his villainy.
    Did you and he consent° in Cassio's death?   *agree*
OTHELLO Ay.
CASSIO Dear General, I never gave you cause.
OTHELLO I do believe it, and I ask your pardon.
    Will you, I pray, demand that demi-devil
    Why he hath thus ensnared my soul and body?
IAGO Demand me nothing. What you know, you know.
    From this time forth I never will speak word.
LODOVICO What, not to pray?
GRATIANO Torments° will ope your lips.   *torture*
OTHELLO Well, thou dost best.
LODOVICO Sir, you shall understand what hath befall'n,
    Which, as I think, you know not. Here is a letter
315   Found in the pocket of the slain Roderigo;
    And here another. [*He produces letters.*] The one of them imports
    The death of Cassio, to be undertook
    By Roderigo.
OTHELLO O villain!
CASSIO   Most heathenish and most gross!°   *monstrous*
LODOVICO [*showing another paper*] Now here's another discontented paper
    Found in his pocket too. And this, it seems,
    Roderigo meant t' have sent this damnèd villain;
    But that belike° Iago in the interim   *most likely*
    Came in and satisfied him.[5]
OTHELLO O thou pernicious caitiff!—
    How came you, Cassio, by that handkerchief
    That was my wife's?
CASSIO   I found it in my chamber;
    And he himself confessed but even now
    That there he dropped it for a special purpose
330   Which wrought to his desire.[6]
OTHELLO   O fool, fool, fool!
CASSIO There is besides in Roderigo's letter
    How he upbraids Iago, that he made him
    Brave° me upon the watch, whereon it came[7]   *defy*
    That I was cast;° and even but now he spake,   *dismissed*
335   After long seeming dead, Iago hurt him,
    Iago set him on.
LODOVICO [*to Othello*] You must forsake this room and go with us.
    Your power and your command is taken off,°   *taken away*

---

4. Through the plotting, into the snare.
5. Interposed and gave him satisfactory explanation.

6. Worked out as he wished, fitted in with his plan.
7. Whereof it came about.

And Cassio rules in Cyprus. For this slave,
340   If there be any cunning cruelty
That can torment him much and hold him long,[8]
It shall be his. You shall close prisoner rest°   *remain*
Till that the nature of your fault be known
To the Venetian state.—Come, bring away.

OTHELLO Soft you;° a word or two before you go.   *one moment*
I have done the state some service, and they know't.
No more of that. I pray you, in your letters,
When you shall these unlucky° deeds relate,   *unfortunate*
Speak of me as I am; nothing extenuate,
350   Nor set down aught in malice. Then must you speak
Of one that loved not wisely but too well;
Of one not easily jealous but, being wrought,[9]
Perplexed° in the extreme; of one whose hand,   *distraught*
Like the base Indian,[1] threw a pearl away
355   Richer than all his tribe; of one whose subdued[2] eyes,
Albeit unusèd to the melting mood,
Drops tears as fast as the Arabian trees
Their medicinable gum.° Set you down this;   *myrrh*
And say besides that in Aleppo once,
360   Where a malignant and a turbaned Turk
Beat a Venetian and traduced the state,
I took by th' throat the circumcisèd dog
And smote him, thus. [*He stabs himself.*][3]

LODOVICO O bloody period!°   *end, conclusion*
GRATIANO   All that is spoke is marred.
OTHELLO I kissed thee ere I killed thee. No way but this,
Killing myself, to die upon a kiss.
[*He kisses Desdemona and dies.*]
CASSIO This did I fear, but thought he had no weapon;
For he was great of heart.
LODOVICO [*to Iago*]   O Spartan dog,[4]
More fell° than anguish, hunger, or the sea!   *cruel*
370   Look on the tragic loading of this bed.
This is thy work. The object poisons sight;
Let it be hid.[5] Gratiano, keep° the house,   *remain in*
[*The bed curtains are drawn*]
And seize upon the fortunes of the Moor,
For they succeed on you.[6] [*To Cassio.*] To you, Lord Governor,
375   Remains the censure° of this hellish villain,   *sentencing*
The time, the place, the torture. O, enforce it!
Myself will straight aboard, and to the state
This heavy act with heavy heart relate.   [*Exeunt.*]

---

8. Keep him alive a long time (during his torture).
9. Worked upon, worked into a frenzy.
1. This reading from the Quarto pictures an ignorant savage who cannot recognize the value of a precious jewel. The Folio reading, *Iudean* or *Judean*, i.e., infidel or disbeliever, may refer to Herod, who slew Mariam in a fit of jealousy, or to Judas Iscariot, the betrayer of Christ.

2. I.e., overcome by grief.
3. This direction is in the Quarto text.
4. Spartan dogs were noted for their savagery and silence.
5. I.e., draw the bed curtains. (No stage direction specifies that the dead are to be carried offstage at the end of the play.)
6. Take legal possession of Othello's property, which passes as though by inheritance to you.

OTHELLO IN CONTEXT

Ethnography in the Literature of Travel and Colonization

What would Shakespeare's audience have thought of the description of Othello as "the Moor"? Both the play itself and the literature on Africa that was available in English in the early modern period show that "Moor" was a synonym for "Negro." Two kinds of accounts of the Moors and North Africans were available to Shakespeare's audience: a kind of mythical travel literature inherited from such classical authors as Herodotus, Pliny, and Diodorus Siculus and more recent eyewitness accounts by seamen and traders who had traveled to Africa. While there were still many completely fantastical notions about non-European peoples such as Moors, Africans, and Turks, Leo Africanus's *History of Africa* enlightened sixteenth- and seventeenth-century European and English audiences about the peoples and customs of Africa.

This kind of writing, describing the physical features and social customs of a people, is called ethnography. The word comes from two Greek roots: *ethnos* ("nation") and *graphia* ("writing"). Rather than stressing the history of a people through time, ethnography reads as a timeless description of a people in space. Not surprisingly, ethnography was deployed mainly to describe cultural others, from the Scythians (the wild Northern Europeans of Book Four of Herodotus' *Histories*) to the Ethiopes of Philemon Holland's *Description of Africa*. Even within the British Isles, Spenser and other authors portrayed the Irish as barbarians because their language, customs, and religion were different from those of the English, who settled as colonists in Ireland.

Ethnography was also used to describe the people of the Caribbean. Columbus's description of the Caribes, or Canibes, gave rise to the word "cannibal." At the same time that Europeans traveled to and colonized the Americas, they also embarked on trade and took slaves in Africa. With the explorations of Portuguese navigators of the African coast came the exploitation of Africans as slaves in the plantations of the Caribbean. The British brought the first African slaves to Virginia in 1619. Leo Africanus himself was taken as a slave by Italian pirates. He was a learned man and was able to win his freedom through conversion. His accounts and those of eyewitnesses began to change the view of Africa as a place of such fantastical creatures as "men whose heads / Do grow beneath their shoulders" (*Othello* 1.3.145–46) to a place of prosperous kings and traders.

Peter Martyr

The Italian humanist Peter Martyr (Pietro Martire d'Anghiera, 1457?–1526) came to the court of Isabella and Ferdinand of Spain some time after 1480. Martyr became part of an intellectual movement that celebrated the consolidation of the monarchy's power over Spain and their conquests in the Americas. Although Martyr deplored the interventions of the French into Italy, he celebrated Spanish exploration and colonization around the world in *De Orbe Novo Decades* (1530). The style of this book has something in common with the tradition of travel writing and ethnography going back to Book 4 of Herodotus's *Histories* as well as Italian humanist letter writing as a method of disseminating information. Martyr himself never traveled beyond Europe, basing his accounts upon the reports of eyewitnesses.

Like Martyr, his English translator Richard Eden (1521?–1576) had a humanist education. Studying at Cambridge with Sir Thomas Smith prepared Eden for a life in government, in which he used his scholarship. He served as private secretary to Sir William Cecil in 1552 and gained a position in the English treasury of the Prince of Spain in 1554.

Eden added two eyewitness accounts of English voyages to Africa to his English translation of Martyr's work, *Decades of the New World* (1555). Although two papal bulls had given a monopoly over the West African coast to the Portuguese, two English seamen defied the ban: Thomas Windham voyaged to Guinea in 1553 and John Lok to Mina

Inigo Jones. *A Negro Nymph,* from the costume designs for Ben Jonson's *Masque of Blackness,* 1605. A designer of sets and costumes, Inigo Jones collaborated with Ben Jonson on many of his masques. In his notes on *The Masque of Blackness,* Jonson mentions Leo Africanus as a source. The ladies of the court painted their faces black to play the Negro Nymphs—among them Lady Mary Wroth, who would deploy metaphors of darkness and night to great effect in her poetry. Jones was also patronized by Lady Wroth's lover, William Herbert, the Earl of Pembroke, who financed the artist's journey to Italy where he studied Roman ruins and Palladio's buildings and writing on architecture. Jones became the first great English architect, designing such buildings as the earliest part of the Greenwich Hospital (1635) and the Church of Saint Paul, Covent Garden, with its square (1631–1638). In 1619 James I commissioned Jones to design the Banqueting House at Whitehall, the first English building to embody Palladian features such as rows of columns and symmetrical classical proportions. (See the engraving of the execution of Charles I before Jones's Banqueting House, page 1698.)

(Elmina) in 1554–1555. The account of Windham's voyage is the source for the first excerpt here, a description of the court of Benin, a kingdom in what is now Nigeria. Eden introduces these two accounts with his own "brief description of Africa" and interjects his comments throughout the eyewitness reports, as in the next excerpted passage taken from "Second Voyage." Eden mixes his informants' observations with fanciful fables about the mythical Christian king of Ethiopia, Preseter John, derived from medieval legend, and outlandish and bizarre ethnographic fictions, from Pliny's *Historia Naturalis.* Eden's accounts of Africa were later republished in Richard Haklyut's monumental *Principal Navigations* (1589).

from *Decades of the New World*

[THE COURT OF BENIN]

When they came they were brought with a great company to the presence of the king [of Benin], who being a black Moor[1] (although not so black as the rest) sat in a great huge hall, long and wide, the walls made of earth without windows, the roof of thin boards, open in sundry places, like unto louvers to let in the air.

And here to speak of the great reverence they give to their king being such that if we would give as much to our Savior Jesus Christ, we should remove from our heads many plagues which we daily deserve for our contempt and impiety.

* * *

And now to speak somewhat of the communication that was between the king and our men, you shall first understand that he himself could speak the Portugal tongue, which he had learned of a child. Therefore after that he had commanded our men to stand up and demanded of them the cause of their coming into that country, they answered by Pinteado[2] that they were merchants traveling into those parts for the commodities of his country for exchange of wares which they had brought from their countries, being such as should be no less commodious for him and his people.

[THE PEOPLE OF AFRICA]

Now therefore I will speak somewhat of the people and their manners and manner of living, with also another brief description of Africa. It is to understand that the people which now inhabit the regions of the coast of Guinea, and the mid parts of Africa, as Libya the inner, and Nubia,[3] with diverse other great and large regions about the same, were in old time called Ethiopes and Nigrite, which we now call Moors, Moorens, or Negros, a people of beastly living, without a god, law, religion, or commonwealth, and so scorched and vexed with the heat of the sun, that in many places they curse it when it riseth.[4] * * *

But to speak somewhat more of Ethiopia. Although there are many nations of people so named, yet is Ethiopia chiefly divided into two parts, whereof the one is called Ethiopia under Egypt, a great and rich region. To this pertaineth the Island of Meroe, embraced round about with the streams of the river Nilus.[5] In this island women reigned in old time. Josephus writeth, that it was sometime

1. Inhabitants of northwestern Africa (Morocco and Algeria), who were Islamic. From the Middle Ages to the 17th century, Europeans thought of the Moors primarily as blacks, and so the word became a synonym for Negro; hence the term "Blackamoor."

2. Captain Antonianes Pinteado was a Portuguese mariner and guide whom Windham used as translator. Once a member of the King of Portugal's household, Pinteado was "forced by poverty" into England. Eden portrays Pinteado as "a man worthy to serve any prince most vilely used." Both Windham and the crew derisively called him "a Jew," and after Windham's death, Pinteado was made a prisoner and died on board ship.

3. Nubia is in northeastern Africa. At its height the kingdom stretched from the first cataract of the Nile in Egypt to Khartoum in Sudan. During the time of the

Roman Emperor Diocletian, the Negro tribe the Nobatae settled in Nubia. The Nubian kingdom was converted to Christianity in the 6th century. After the Moslems moved into Nubia in 1366, Nubia was divided into smaller states.

4. Many Greek and Roman as well as early modern authors believed that Africans had black skin because of the intense heat of the sun. Sir Thomas Browne was one of the first to show this "common opinion" was an "error" in *Pseudodoxia Epidemica* (1646); see 6.10: "Of the Blackness of Negroes."

5. When the Nubians were expelled from Egypt in the 7th century B.C., they moved their capital to Meroe, which the Ethiopians conquered in A.D. 350. The site of ancient pyramids, Meroe, is on the Nile in Northern Sudan.

called Saba, and that the queen of Saba came from thence to Jerusalem to hear the wisdom of Solomon.[6] From hence toward the East reigneth the said Christian Emperor Prester John,[7] whom some call Papa Johannes, and others say that he is called Pean Juan (that is) great John, whose empire reacheth far beyond Nilus and is extended to the coasts of the Red Sea and Indian Sea. The middle of the region is almost in the 66 degrees of longitude, and 12 degrees of latitude. About this region inhabit the people called Clodii, Risophagi, Babilonii, Axiunite, Mosili, and Molibe. After these is the region called Trogloditica, whose inhabitants dwell in caves and dens, for these are their houses, and the flesh of serpents their meat, as writeth Pliny and Diodorus Siculus.[8] They have no speech, but rather a grinning and chattering. There are also people without heads, called Blemines, having their eyes and mouth in their breast. Likewise Strucophagi, and naked Ganphasantes; Satyrs also, which have nothing of men but only shape. Moreover Oripei, great hunters. Mennones also, and the region of Smyrnophara, which bringeth forth myrrh. After these is the region of Azania, in the which many elephants are found. A great part of the other regions of Africa that are beyond the equinoctial line, are now ascribed to the kingdom of Melinde,[9] whose inhabitants are accustomed to traffic with the nations of Arabie, and their kind is joined in friendship with the king of Portugal, and payeth tribute to Prester John.

The other Ethiope, called Ethiopia Interior (that is) the inner Ethiope, is not yet known for the greatness thereof, but only by the seacoasts. Yet is it described in this manner. First from the equinoctial toward the south is a great region of Ethiopians, which bringeth forth white elephants, tigers, and the beasts called Rhinocerontes. Also a region that bringeth forth plenty of cinnamon, lying between the branches of Nilus. Also the kingdom of Habech or Habassia,[1] a region of Christian men, lying both on this side and beyond Nilus. Here are also the Ethiopians, called Ichthiophagi (that is) such as live only by fish, and were sometimes subdued by the wars of great Alexander. Furthermore the Ethiopians calleth Rhapsii, and Anthropophagi, that are accustomed to man's flesh, inhabit the regions near unto the mountains called Montes Lunae (that is) the Mountains of the Moon.[2] Gazatia is under the Tropic of Capricorn.[3] After this followeth the front of Africa, the Cape of Buena Speranza, or Caput Bonae Spei (that is) the Cape of Good Hope,[4] by the which they pass that sail from Spain to Calicut. But by what names the capes and gulfs are called, for as much as the same are in every globe and card, it were here superfluous to rehearse them.

6. For the visit of the Queen of Sheba (Saba) to Solomon, see 1 Kings 10. See also *Antiquities of the Jews* by the Jewish historian Flavius Josephus (37–c. 95).

7. The medieval legend of Prester John placed this Christian king in either Asia or Africa. Marco Polo said that Prester John ruled over the Tartars, and some European writers thought of him as King of a Christian kingdom in either Ethiopia or India.

8. For Pliny, see *The History of the World* below. Diodorus Siculus (d. 21 B.C.) was a Sicilian author of a world history, including Ethiopia and North Africa, which is today considered unreliable.

9. Said to be in Arabia, 90 miles from Persia (Introduc-

tion to Martyr's *Decades*).

1. Possibly Abyssinia, another name for Ethiopia. In the 4th century the king of Northern Ethiopia was converted to Coptic Christianity, but later, in 451, the Alexandrian patriarch refused to recognize the Ethopian Christians as part of the Church. They believe that Christ has one nature in which his humanity is subsumed under his divinity.

2. This fantastical passage comes from Pliny.

3. The Southern Tropic.

4. The southern tip of Africa, around which the Portuguese sailed to India.

Pliny the Elder
from *The History of the World*[1]

All Ethiopia in general was in old time called Aetheria, afterwards Atlantia, and finally of Vulcan's son Aethops, it took the name Ethiopia. No wonder it is, that about the coasts thereof there be found both men and beasts of strange and monstrous shapes, considering the agility of the sun's fiery heat, so strong and powerful in those countries, which is able to frame bodies artificially of sundry proportions, and to imprint and grave[2] in them diverse forms. Certes, reported it is, that far within the country eastward there are a kind of people without any nose at all on their face, having their visage all plain and flat. Others again without any upper lip, and some tongueless. Moreover, there is a kind of them that want a mouth, framed apart from their nostrils, and at one and the same hole, and no more, taketh in breath, receiveth drink by drawing it in with an oaten straw; yea, and after the same manner feed themselves with the grains of oats, growing of their own accord without man's labor and tillage, for their only food. And others there be, who instead of speech and words, make signs, as well with nodding their heads, as moving their other members. There are also among them, that before the time of Ptolomaeus Lathyrus king of Egypt,[3] knew no use at all of fire.

Furthermore, writers there be, who have reported, that in the country near unto the mires and marshes from whence Nilus issueth, there inhabit those little dwarves called Pygmies * * * But then he [Dalion, the historian] telleth fabulous and incredible tales of those countries. Namely, that westward there are people called Nigroi, whose king hath but one eye, and that in the midst of his forehead. Also he talketh of the Agriophagi, who live most of panthers and lions flesh. Likewise of the Pomphagi, who eat all things whatsoever. Moreover, of the Anthopophagi, that feed on man's flesh. Furthermore, of the Cynamolgi,[4] who have heads like dogs. Over and besides, the Artabatites who wander and go up and down in the forests like four-footed savage beasts. Beyond whom, as he saith, be the Hesperioi and Perorsi, who, as we said before, were planted in the confines of Mauritania. In certain parts also of Ethiopia the people live off locusts only, which they powder with salt and hang up in smoke to harden, for their yearly provision, and these live not above 40 years at the most.

Leo Africanus

Born in Moorish Granada in the late 1480s and educated in Fez, to which his Moslem family fled in 1497, Al Hassan ibn Mohammed Al-Wezaz, Al-Fasi (Leo Africanus, 1488?–1552) was the first to write accurately about the interior of Africa. Captured by Italian pirates in the Mediterranean, he was at first enslaved and then presented to Pope Leo X, who freed him once he had converted to Christianity. In Rome, Leo Africanus learned Latin and taught Arabic. He wrote his history of Africa in 1526, but it was published in Venice only in 1550, when, according to one contemporary, Leo was living in Tunis, where he returned to his Moslem faith.

1. Pliny the Elder (Caius Plinius Secundus, A.D. 23–79) was a Roman naturalist from Cisalpine Gaul. His sole remaining work, the *Historia Naturalis*, is an encyclopedia of natural science, divided into 37 books, dealing with everything from the nature of the universe to geography, anthropology, and a history of the arts. Like the Greek historian Herodotus, Pliny knew more about Egypt than he did about the rest of Africa and had to rely on stories and legends for his accounts. The European view of Africa and Africans as wild, exotic, and unnatural derives

from such accounts as the following from Book 6 of *The History of the World* (1601), the English translation of Pliny by Philemon Holland. This passage was Shakespeare's source for Othello's description of the "Anthropophagi" (man-eaters) in Othello 1.3.144–46.
2. Engrave.
3. Ptolomeus Lathyrus (d. 81 B.C.), King of Ancient Egypt of the Macedonian dynasty.
4. Dog-milkers.

Encouraged by Richard Haklyut, who called Leo's work "the very best," John Pory first translated it into English as *A Geographical History of Africa* in 1600. Leo's history, which first appeared in Italian, was already known in England through Latin and French editions. Sir Thomas Smith owned a French translation, and Ben Jonson mentions Leo's work as a source for his *Masque of Blackness*. According to Lois Whitney and Eldred Jones, strong circumstantial evidence suggests that Shakespeare knew Leo's *Geographical History* and that it provided the background material for references to Africa in *Othello* and *Antony and Cleopatra*.

Pory prefaced his translation with Leo's biography, excerpted here, which makes for fascinating reading. There are some parallels between Leo's life and Othello's. A North African Moor, Leo had visited many parts of Africa but lived much of his life in Italy. Leo was not only a scholar and traveler but also a soldier; as Pory relates, Leo "did . . . personally serve king Mahumet of Fez in his wars." Like Leo who often recited poems and stories, Othello told his "travel's history." Both Leo and many of the African kingdoms that he describes emerge from his work as civilized, learned, and prosperous in contrast to the stereotyped ethnographies, which had portrayed Africans as barbarous, ignorant, and poor. While Leo's account of Africa was well known to Shakespeare's generation and even the generation that followed, subsequent scholarship chose either to misrepresent it, as in Peter Heylyn's highly selective choice of uncomplimentary passages, or to ignore it, as in Samuel Coleridge's false assertion that "at that time . . . negroes were not known except as slaves."

from *The History and Description of Africa*
from John Pory's Preface

Give me leave (gentle readers) if not to present unto your knowledge, because some perhaps may as well be informed as myself; yet, to call to your remembrance, some few particulars, concerning this geographical history and John Leo the author thereof.

Who albeit by birth a Moor, and by religion for many years a Mahumetan; yet if you consider his parentage, wit, education, learning, employments, travels, and his conversion to Christianity, you shall find him not altogether unfit to undertake such an enterprise, not unworthy to be regarded.

First therefore his parentage seemeth not to have been ignoble, seeing (as in his second book himself testifieth) an uncle of his was so honorable a person and so excellent an orator and poet, that he was sent as a principal ambassador, from the king of Fez to the king of Tombuto.[1]

And whether this our author were born at Granada in Spain (as it is most likely) or in some part of Africa,[2] certain it is, that in natural sharpness and vivacity of wit, he most lively resembled those great and classical authors, Pomponius Mela, Justinus Historicus, Columella, Seneca, Quintilian, Orosius, Prudentius, Martial, Juvenal, Avicen, etc., reputed all for Spanish writers, as likewise Terentius Afer, Tertullian, Saint Augustine, Victor, Optatus, etc. known to be writers of Africa.[3] But amongst great variety which are to be found in the process of this notable discourse, I will here

1. Timbuktu, near the Niger, with the Sahara to the north. Settled in 1087, Timbuktu was a center for trade and Moslem culture.

2. Pory's hesitation is due to a passage in the Latin translation (Antwerp 1556) that can be translated as "Africa, unto which country I stand indebted for my birth." But in the original Italian edition, this passage simply states that Africa was his "nurse," where he spent the early part of his life.

3. Pomponius Mela . . . Juvenal: Roman historians and rhetoricians; Avicen: the Arabic translator of Aristotle; Terentius Afer: a Roman writer of comedies, born in Carthage; Tertullian, Saint Augustine: the Church Fathers of late antiquity; Victorinus: a Neoplatonist convert to Christianity.

lay before your view our only pattern of his surpassing wit. In his second book therefore, if you peruse the description of Mount Teneves, you shall there find the learned and sweet Arabian verses of John Leo, not being then fully sixteen years of age, so highly esteemed by the prince of the same mountain that in recompense thereof, after bountiful entertainment, he dismissed him with gifts of great value.

Neither wanted he the best education that all Barbary could afford. For being even from his tender years trained up at the University of Fez, in grammar, poetry, rhetoric, philosophy, history, Cabala, astronomy, and other ingenuous sciences,[4] and having so great acquaintance and conversation in the king's court, how could he choose but prove in his kind a most accomplished and absolute man? So as I may justly say (if the comparison be tolerable) that as Moses was learned in all the wisdom of the Egyptians, so likewise was Leo, in that of the Arabians and Moors.

And that he was not meanly, but extraordinarily learned; let me keep silence, that the admirable fruits of his rare learning and this geographical history among the rest may bear record. Besides which, he wrote an Arabian grammar, highly commended by a great linguist of Italy who had the sight and examination thereof, as likewise a book of the lives of the Arabian philosophers and a discourse of the religion of Mahumet, with diverse excellent poems and other monuments of his industry, which are not come to light.

Now as concerning his employments, were they not such as might well beseem a man of good worth? For (to omit how many courts and camps of princes he had frequented) did not he, as himself in his third book witnesseth, personally serve king Mahumet of Fez in his wars against Arzilla?[5] And was he not at another time, as appeareth out of his second book, in service and honorable place under the same king of Fez, and sent ambassador by him to the king of Morocco? Yea, how often in regard of his singular knowledge and judgment in the laws of those countries, was he appointed and sometimes constrained at diverse strange cities and towns through which he traveled, to become a judge and arbiter in matters of greatest moment?

Moreover as touching his exceeding great travels, had he not at the first been a Moor and a Mahumetan in religion, and most skillful in the languages and customs of the Arabians and Africans, and for the most part traveled in caravans or under the authority, safe conduct, and commendation of great princes? I marvel much how ever he should have escaped so many thousands of imminent dangers. And (all the former notwithstanding) I marvel much more, how ever he escaped them. For how many desolate cold mountains and huge, dry, and barren deserts passed he? How often was he in hazard to have been captived or to have had his throat cut by the prowling Arabians and wild Moors? And how hardly many times escaped he the lion's greedy mouth and the devouring jaws of the crocodile? But if you will needs have a brief journal of his travels, you may see in the end of his eighth book, what he writeth for himself. Wherefore (saith he) if it shall please God to vouchsafe me longer life, I purpose to describe all the regions of Asia which I have traveled—to wit, Arabia Deserta, Arabia Petrea, Arabia Felix,[6] the Asian part of Egypt, Armenia, and some part of Tartaria—all which countries I saw and passed through in the time of my youth. Likewise I will describe my last voyages from Constantinople to Egypt and from

---

4. The University of Fez dated from the 13th-century Merinid dynasty. The Cabala, or Kabbala, was a system of occult wisdom and mystical interpretation of the Scriptures.

5. Leo served the Sultan Mohammed VI, who reigned in Fez (1508–1527), both in war and in diplomacy.
6. The ancients divided Arabia into three parts based on its principle place Petra, the desert, and the fertile area.

thence unto Italy, etc. Besides all which places he had also been at Tauris in Persia; and of his own country and other African regions adjoining and remote, he was so diligent a traveler that there was no kingdom, province, signory, or city, or scarcely any town, village, mountain, valley, river, or forest, etc. which he left unvisited. And so much the more credit and commendation deserveth this worthy history of his, in that it is (except the antiquities and certain other incidents) nothing else but a large itinerarium or journal of his African voyages, neither describeth he almost any one particular place, where himself had not sometime been an eyewitness.

But, not to forget his conversion to Christianity, amidst all these his busy and dangerous travels, it pleased the divine providence, for the discovery and manifestation of God's wonderful works and of his dreadful and just judgments performed in Africa (which before the time of John Leo, were either utterly concealed or unperfectly and fabulously reported both by ancient and late writers) to deliver this author of ours, and this present geographical history into the hands of certain Italian pirates about the isle of Gerbi, situated in the Gulf of Capes, between the cities of Tunis and Tripolis in Barbary. Being thus taken, the pirates presented him and his book unto Pope Leo the Tenth, who, esteeming of him as of a most rich and invaluable prize, greatly rejoiced at his arrival and gave him most kind entertainment and liberal maintenance, til such time as he had won him to be baptized in the name of Christ, and to be called John Leo, after the Pope's own name. And so during his abode in Italy, learning the Italian tongue, he translated this book thereinto, being before written in Arabic. Thus much of John Leo.

[On the Customs of the African People in Libya]

Those five kinds of people before rehearsed, to wit, the people of Zenega, of Gansiga, of Terga, of Leuta, and of Bardeoa, are called of the Latins Numidae;[7] and they live all after one manner, that is to say, without all law and civility. Their garment is a narrow and base piece of cloth, wherewith scarce half their body is covered. Some of them wrap their heads in a kind of black cloth, as it were with a scarf, such as the Turks use, which is commonly called a turbant.[8] Such as well be discerned from the common sort, for gentlemen wear a jacket made of blue cotton with wide sleeves. And cotton cloth is brought unto them by certain merchants from the land of negros. They have no beasts fit to ride upon except their camels, unto whom nature, between the bunch standing upon the hinder part of their backs and their necks, hath allotted a place, which may fitly serve to ride upon, instead of a saddle. Their manner of riding is most ridiculous. For sometimes they lay their legs across upon the camel's neck, and sometimes again (having no knowledge nor regard of stirrups) they rest their feet upon a rope, which is cast over his shoulders. Instead of spurs they use a truncheon of a cubit's length, having at the one end thereof a goad, wherewith they prick only the shoulders of their camels. Those camels which they use to ride upon have a hole bored through the gristles of their nose, in the which a ring of leather is fastened, whereby as with a bit, they are more easily curbed and mastered, after which manner I have seen buffles[9] used in Italy. For beds, they lie upon mats made of sedge and bul-

---

7. Numidia, an ancient kingdom in North Africa, north of the Sahara, was at one time a province of the Roman Empire. Leo here gives a description of the Tuareg, a pastoral people on the western and central Sahara, now located in Algeria, Mali, and Niger. The alphabet of the Tuareg is related to ancient Phoenician script.

8. Tuareg men traditionally wore dark blue robes and turbans.

9. Buffaloes.

rushes. Their tents are covered for the most part with coarse chamlet[1] or with a harsh kind of wool which commonly groweth upon the boughs of their date trees. As for their manner of living, it would seem to any man incredible what hunger and scarcity this nation will endure. Bread they have none at all, neither use they any seething or roasting; their food is camel's milk only, and they desire no other dainties. For their breakfast they drink off a great cup of camel's milk; for supper they have certain dried flesh steeped in butter and milk, whereof each man, taking his share, eateth it out of his fist. And that this their meat may not stay long undigested in their stomachs, they sup off the foresaid broth wherein their flesh was steeped; for which purpose they use the palms of their hands as a most fit instrument framed by nature to the same end. After that, each one drinks his cup of milk, & so their supper hath an end. These Numidians, while they have any store of milk, regard water nothing at all, which for the most part happeneth in the spring of the year, all which time you shall find some among them that will neither wash their hands nor their faces. Which seemeth not altogether to be unlikely; for (as we said before) while their milk lasteth, they frequent not those places where water is common; yea, and their camels, so long as they may feed upon grass, will drink no water at all. They spend their whole days in hunting and thieving; for all their endeavor and exercise is to drive away the camels of their enemies; neither will they remain above three days in one place, by reason that they have not pasture any longer for the sustenance of their camels. And albeit (as is aforesaid) they have no civility at all, nor any laws prescribed unto them, yet have they a certain governor or prince placed over them, unto whom they render obedience and due honor, as unto their king. They are not only ignorant of all good learning and liberal sciences, but are likewise altogether careless and destitute of virtue, insomuch that you shall find scarce one amongst them all which is a man of judgment or counsel. And if any injured party will go to the law with his adversary, he must ride continually five or six days before he can come to the speech of any judge. This nation hath all learning and good disciplines in such contempt that they will not once vouchsafe to go out of their deserts for the study and attaining thereof; neither, if any learned man shall chance to come among them, can they love his company and conversation, in regard of their most rude and detestable behavior. Howbeit, if they can find any judge, which can frame himself to live and continue among them, to him they give [a] most large yearly allowance. Some allow their judge a thousand ducats yearly, some more, and some less, according as themselves think good. They that will seem to be accounted of the better sort, cover their heads (as I said before) with a piece of black cloth, part whereof, like a vizard or mask, reacheth down over their faces, covering all their countenance except their eyes; and this is their daily kind of attire. And so often as they put meat into their mouths they remove the said mask, which being done, they forthwith cover their mouths again, alleging this fond reason: for (say they) as it is unseemly for a man, after he hath received meat into his stomach, to vomit it out of his mouth again and to cast it upon the earth; even so it is an undecent part to eat meat with a man's mouth uncovered.

The women of this nation be gross, corpulent, and of a swart[2] complexion. They are fattest upon their breast and paps, but slender about the girdle-stead.[3] Very civil they are, after their manner, both in speech and gestures. Sometimes they will accept

1. Chamlet, a fabric made from a mixture of silk and camel's hair.
2. Dark.
3. Waist.

of a kiss; but whoso tempteth them farther, putteth his own life in hazard. For by reason of jealousy you may see them daily one to be the death and destruction of another, and that in such savage and brutish manner that in this case they will show no compassion at all. And they seem to be more wise in this behalf than diverse of our people, for they will by no means match themselves unto a harlot.

The liberality of this people hath at all times been exceeding great. And when any travelers may pass through their dry and desert territories, they will never repair unto their tents, neither will they themselves travel upon the common highway. And if any caravan or multitude of merchants will pass those deserts, they are bound to pay certain custom unto the prince of the said people, namely, for every camel's load a piece of cloth worth a ducat. Upon a time I remember that traveling in the company of certain merchants over the desert called by them Araoan, it was our chance there to meet with the prince of Zanaga; who, after he had received his due custom, invited the said company of merchants, for their recreation, to go and abide with him in his tents four or five days. Howbeit, because his tents were too far out of our way, and for that we should have wandered farther than we thought good, esteeming it more convenient for us to hold on our direct course, we refused his gentle offer, and for his courtesy gave him great thanks. But not being satisfied therewith, he commanded that our camels should proceed on forward, but the merchants he carried along with him and gave them very sumptuous entertainment at his place of abode. Where we were no sooner arrived but this good prince caused camels of all kinds and ostriches, which he had hunted and taken by the way, to be killed for his household provision. Howbeit we requested him not to make such daily slaughters of his camels, affirming moreover that we never used to eat the flesh of a gelt[4] camel, but when all other victuals failed us. Whereunto he answered that he should deal uncivilly, if he welcomed so worthy and so seldom seen guests with the killing of small cattle only. Wherefore he wished us to fall to such provision as was set before us. Here might you have seen great plenty of roasted and sudden flesh. Their roasted ostriches were brought to the table in wicker platters, being seasoned with sundry kinds of herbs and spices. Their bread made of mill and panick[5] was of a most savory and pleasant taste; and always at the end of dinner or supper we had plenty of dates and great store of milk served in. Yea, this bountiful and noble prince, that he might sufficiently show how welcome we were unto him, would together with his nobility always bear us company; howbeit we ever dined and supped apart by ourselves. Moreover he caused certain religious and most learned men to come unto our banquet, who, all the time we remained with the said prince, used not to eat any bread at all, but fed only upon flesh and milk. Whereat we being somewhat amazed, the good prince gently told us that they all were born in such places whereas no kind of grain would grow, howbeit that himself, for the entertainment of strangers, had great plenty of corn laid up in store. Wherefore he bade us to be of good cheer, saying that he would eat only of such things as his own native soil afforded, affirming moreover, that bread was yet in use among them at their feast of passover, and at other feasts also, whereupon they used to offer sacrifice. And thus we remained with him for the space of two days, all which time, what wonderful and magnificent cheer we had made us, would seem incredible to report. But the third day, being desirous to take our leave, the prince accompanied us to that place where we overtook our camels and company sent before. And this I dare most deeply take mine oath on, that we spent the said prince

---

4. Gelded, castrated.   5. Varieties of millet, or grain.

ten times more than our custom which he received came to.[6] We thought it not amiss here to set down this history to declare in some sort the courtesy and liberality of the said nation. Neither could the prince aforesaid understand our language nor we his, but all our speech to and fro was made by an interpreter. And this which we have here recorded as touching this nation is likewise to be understood of the other four nations above mentioned, which are dispersed over the residue of the Numidian deserts.

Edmund Spenser

In addition to writing some of the greatest English poetry, Edmund Spenser wrote a colonialist tract promoting England's subjugation of Ireland. Spenser first came to Ireland as secretary to Lord Grey de Wilton, Lord Deputy of Ireland, in 1580. Through government service, Spenser acquired his land and house in Kilcoman, property confiscated from Sir John of Desmond, an "Old English" aristocrat who had rebelled against English rule. The Old English had been Anglo-Normans who settled in Ireland in the twelfth century. In *A View of the Present State of Ireland*, Spenser writes about the customs of the Irish, among whom he finds the Old English to be the most troublesome because they have gone native and become "more Irish than O'Hanlon's breech." Drawing heavily on the ethnographic stereotypes of the medieval *Topography of Ireland* by Gerald of Wales, Spenser wrote his text as a dialogue between Irenius, ("Peaceful") a veteran of English service in Ireland, and Eudoxus ("Of good opinion"), a younger man who questions why English policy in Ireland has not worked. In the 1590s, when Spenser was writing this text, another Irish rebellion had broken out under the command of Hugh O'Neill. Spenser and his family were driven out of Kilcoman. Creating a view of the Irish as a separate race, Spenser compares Irish customs with those of Africans and Moors. The description of the Irish as barbarous prepares for the conclusion of the text in which he recommends a military solution to the colonization of Ireland. Though not published until 1633, *A View of the Present State of Ireland* was entered in the Stationer's Register in 1598 and circulated widely in manuscript.

from *A View of the Present State of Ireland*

Eudoxus. Believe me, this observation of yours, Irenius,[1] is very good and delightful; far beyond the blind conceit of some, who (I remember) have upon the same word *Farragh*, made a very blunt conjecture, as namely Master Stanyhurst,[2] who though he be the same countryman born, that should search more nearly into the secret of these things, yet hath strayed from the truth all the heavens wide (as they say), for he thereupon groundeth a very gross imagination, that the Irish should descend from the Egyptians which came into that island, first under the leading of one Scota the daughter of Pharaoh, whereupon they use (saith he) in all their battles to call upon the name of Pharaoh, crying Ferragh, Ferragh.[3] Surely he shoots wide on the bow hand and very far from the mark. For I would first know of him what ancient ground of authority he hath for such a senseless fable, and if he have any of the rude Irish

6. Leo is saying that the prince gave them much more than they paid in tribute.
1. Irenius, who has greater experience of Ireland then Eudoxus, has just asserted that the Irish battle cry "Ferragh" is from the Scottish word "Fergus," which means that the Irish are Scots. The 17th-century Irish language historian Geoffrey Keating points out in his *History of Ireland* that the Irish etymology of "Ferragh" is "faire ó" or "ó faire" ("take care").

2. Richard Stanyhurst (1547–1618), a Dubliner and Catholic, wrote *Description of Ireland* in Holinshed's *Chronicles*, as well as *De rebus in Hibernia gestis*, in which he dismisses the Egyptian origin of the Irish war cry.
3. The notion that the Irish were descended from the Egyptian Scota dates back to the 8th–century life of St. Abban and is repeated in the medieval Irish *Book of Invasions* (*Leabhar gabhála*).

books, as it may be he hath, yet (me seems) that a man of his learning should not so lightly have been carried away with old wives' tales, from approvance of his own reason; for whether it be a smack of any learned judgment to say that Scota is like an Egyptian word, let the learned judge. But his Scota rather comes of the Greek *scotos*, that is, darkness, which hath not let him see the light of the truth.

Irenius. You know not, Eudoxus, how well Master Stanyhurst could see in the dark; perhaps he hath owls' or cats' eyes. But well I wot he seeth not well the very light in matters of more weight. * * * There be other sorts of cries also used among the Irish, which savor greatly of the Scythian barbarism,[4] as their lamentations at their burials, with despairful outcries, and immoderate wailings, the which Master Stanyhurst might also have used for an argument to prove them Egyptians. For so in scripture it is mentioned, that the Egyptians lamented for the death of Joseph.[5] Others think this custom to come from the Spaniards, for that they do immeasurably likewise bewail their dead. But the same is not proper Spanish, but altogether heathenish, brought in thither first either by the Scythians, or the Moors that were Africans and long possessed that country. For it is the manner of all pagans and infidels to be intemperate in their wailings of their dead, for that they had no faith nor hope of salvation. And this ill custom also is specially noted by Diodorus Siculus,[6] to have been in the Scythians, and is yet amongst the Northern Scots at this day, as you may read in their chronicles.

Eudoxus. This is sure an ill custom also, but yet doth not so much concern civil reformation, as abuse in religion.[7]

* * *

Eudoxus. It seemeth strange to me that the English should take more delight to speak that language than their own, whereas they should (me thinks) rather take scorn to acquaint their tongues thereto. For it hath ever been the use of the conqueror to despise the language of the conquered and to force him by all means to learn his. So did the Romans always use, insomuch that there is almost no nation in the world but is sprinkled with their language. It were good therefore (me seems) to search out the original cause of this evil; for, the same being discovered, a redress thereof will the more easily be provided. For I think it very strange that the English being so many, and the Irish so few, as they then were left, the fewer should draw the more unto their use.

Irenius. I suppose that the chief cause of bringing in the Irish language amongst them was especially their fostering[8] and marrying with the Irish, the which are two most dangerous infections; for first the child that sucketh the milk of the nurse must of necessity learn his first speech of her, the which being the first inured to his tongue, is ever after most pleasing unto him insomuch as though he afterwards be taught English, yet the smack of the first will always abide with him, and not only of speech but also of the manners and conditions. For besides that young children be like apes, which will affect and imitate what they see done before them, especially by their nurses whom they love so well, they moreover draw into themselves together with their suck even the nature and disposition of their nurses; for the mind fol-

---

4. Spenser claims both Irish and Scots are descended from the Scythians, described by Herodotus as a nomadic, barbarous people to the northwest of Greece.
5. Jacob, not Joseph (see Genesis 50.3).
6. Diodorus Siculus (d. 21 B.C.), a Sicilian author of a world history in Greek.
7. Irenius continues to discuss the Scythian, i.e., bar-

barous, character of Irish customs including going into battle naked, wearing glibs (masses of hair), and the women's riding facing right in the "old Spanish and as some say African" fashion, drinking blood and speaking the Irish language.
8. Gaelic custom of having children raised by clients, friends, or relatives to cement alliances.

loweth much the temperature of the body, and also the words are the image of the mind, so as they proceeding from the mind, the mind must needs be affected with the words. So that the speech being Irish, the heart must needs be Irish; for out of the abundance of the heart the tongue speaketh. The next is the marrying with the Irish, which how dangerous a thing it is in all commonwealths, appeareth to every simplest sense. And though some great ones have perhaps used such matches with their vassals and have of them nevertheless raised worthy issue, as Telamon did with Tocmissa, Alexander the Great with Roxanne, and Julius Caesar with Cleopatra,[9] yet the example is so perilous, as it is not to be adventured; for instead of those few good, I could count unto them infinite many evil. And indeed how can such matching but bring forth an evil race, seeing that commonly the child taketh most of his nature of the mother, besides speech, manners, and inclination, which are (for the most part) agreeable to the conditions of their mothers; for by them they are first framed and fashioned, so as what they receive once from them, they will hardly ever after forgo. Therefore are these evil customs of fostering and marrying with the Irish most carefully to be restrained; for of them two, the third evil, that is the custom of language (which I spake of), chiefly proceedeth.

Sir John Smith
from *The General History of Virginia, New England and the Summer Isles*[1]

Being thus satisfied with Europe and Asia, understanding of the wars in Barbary, he went from Gibraltar to Guta and Tanger, thence to Safee,[2] where growing into acquaintance with a French man-of-war,[3] the captain and some twelve more went to Morocco, to see the ancient monuments of that large renowned city. It was once the principal city in Barbary, situated in a goodly plain country, 14 miles from the great Mount Atlas and sixty miles from the Atlantic Sea, but now little remaining but the king's palace, which is like a city of itself, and the Christian church, on whose flat square steeple is a great brooch of iron, whereon is placed the three golden balls of Africa. The first is near three ells[4] in circumference, the next above it somewhat less, the uppermost the least over them, as it were, an half ball, and over all a pretty gilded pyramid. Against those golden balls hath been shot many a shot, their weight is recorded 700 weight of pure gold, hollow within, yet no shot did ever hit them, nor could ever any conspirator attain that honor as to get them down. They report the prince of Morocco betrothed himself to the king's daughter of Ethiopia, he dying before their marriage, she caused those three golden balls to be set up for his monument, and vowed virginity all her life. The Alfantica is also a place of note because it

9. All examples of interracial or cross-cultural marriages: the Phrygian Tecmessa with Greek Ajax, the Bactrian Roxana with the Macedonian Alexander, the Egyptian Cleopatra with the Roman Caesar.

1. Sir John Smith (1580–1631) spent his youth as a merchant's apprentice and then, at his father's death, set off to travel. He fought against the Turks in eastern Europe and was enslaved for a time in Turkey. On returning to England, he invested in the Virginia Company in 1606 and was appointed a member of the government council for the Jamestown settlement. He is probably best known for the much romanticized story of his being rescued from captivity by Pocahontas, the Indian princess and daughter of King Powhatan. After years of sea voyaging, war-

fare, and exploration, Smith returned to England. Among his many works of travel writing are *A Map of Virginia* (1612), *A Description of New England* (1616), and *The Generall Historie of Virginia New-England and the Summer Isles* (1624), from which the following passage describing the Barbary Coast (Tunisia and Morocco) is taken. Note Smith's mention of "that most excellent statesman, John de Leo,"—further evidence of how well known Leo Africanus' history of Africa was in early modern England.

2. From Gibraltar at the southern tip of Spain to Tangier in Morocco.

3. A large sailing ship equipped for warfare.

4. Twelve feet.

is environed with a great wall, wherein lie the goods of all the merchants securely guarded. The Juderea is also (as it were) a city of itself, where dwell the Jews. The rest for the most part is defaced, but by the many pinnacles and towers, with balls on their tops, hath much appearance of much sumptuousness and curiosity. There have been many famous universities, which are now but stables for fowls and beasts, and the houses in most parts lie tumbled one above another; the walls of earth are with the great fresh floods washed to the ground, nor is there any village in it, but tents for strangers, Larbes and Moors. Strange tales they will tell of a great garden, wherein were all sorts of birds, fishes, beasts, fruits and fountains, which for beauty, art and pleasure, exceeded any place known in the world, though now nothing but dunghills, pigeon houses, shrubs and bushes. There are yet many excellent fountains adorned with marble, and many arches, pillars, towers, ports and temples, but most only relics of lamentable ruins and sad desolation.

When Mully Hamet[5] reigned in Barbary he had three sons, Mully Sheck, Mully Sidan, and Mully Befferes—he, a most good and noble king that governed well with peace and plenty, til his empress, more cruel than any beast in Africa, poisoned him, her own daughter, Mully Sheck his eldest son born of a Portugal Lady, and his daughter, to bring Mully Sidan to the crown now reigning, which was the cause of all those brawls and wars that followed betwixt those brothers, their children, and a saint that start up, but he played the Devil.[6]

King Mully Hamet was not black, as many suppose, but Molata, or tawny, as are the most of his subjects, in every way noble, kind and friendly, very rich and pompous in state and majesty, though he sitteth not upon a throne nor chair of estate, but cross-legged upon a rich carpet, as doth the Turk, whose religion of Mahomet, with an incredible miserable curiosity they observe. His ordinary guard is at least 5,000 but in progress he goeth not with less than 20,000 horsemen, himself as rich in all his equipage as any prince in Christendom, and yet a contributor to the Turk. In all his kingdom were so few good artificers that he entertained from England, goldsmiths, plumbers, carvers and polishers of stone, and watchmakers, so much he delighted in the reformation of workmanship he allowed each of them ten shillings a day standing fee, linen, woolen, silks, and what they would for diet and apparel, and custom-free to transport or import what they would; for there were scare any of those qualities in his kingdoms, but those of which there are diverse of them living at this present in London. Amongst the rest, one Mr. Henry Archer, a watchmaker, walking in Morocco from the Alfantica to the Juderea, the way being very foul, met a great priest, or a Sante (as they call all great clergymen) who would have thrust him into the dirt for the way. But Archer, not knowing what he was, gave him a box on the ear; presently he was apprehended and condemned to have his tongue cut out and his hand cut off; but no sooner it was known at the king's court but 300 of his guard came and broke open the prison and delivered him, although the fact was next degree to treason. * * *

Fez also is a most large and plentiful country, the chief city is called Fez, divided into two parts, old Fez, containing about 80 thousand households, the other 4,000 pleasantly situated upon a river in the heart of Barbary, part upon hills, part upon plains, full of people and all sorts of merchandise. The great temple is called Carucer,

---

5. Sultan of Morocco.
6. A reference to the "battle of the three kings" (1578) in Alcazarquivir, in which the Moroccan sultan (whose army was victorious), his Portuguese-supported rival, and Sebastian of Portugal (a religiously fervent prince who led an army of mercenaries to disaster) all perished.

in breadth seventeen arches, in length 120 born up with 2,500 white marble pillars. Under the chief arch, where the tribunal is kept, hangeth a most huge lamp, compassed with 110 lesser; under the other also hang great lamps, and about some are burning fifteen hundred lights. They say they were all made of the bells the Arabians brought from Spain. It hath three gates of notable height, priests and officers so many that the circuit of the church, the yard, and other houses is little less than a mile and an half in compass. There are in this city 200 schools, 200 inns, 400 water mills, 600 water conduits, 700 temples and oratories, but fifty of them most stately and richly furnished. Their Alcazer[7] or Burse is walled about; it hath twelve gates and fifteen walks covered with tents to keep the sun from the merchants and them that come there. The king's palace, both for strength and beauty is excellent, and the citizens have many great privileges. Those two countries of Fez and Morocco are the best part of Barbary, abounding with people, cattle, and all good necessaries for man's use. For the rest, as the Larbes, or Mountainers, the kingdoms of Cocow, Algier, Tripoly, Tunis, and Egypt, there are so many large histories of them in diverse languages, especially that writ by that most excellent statesman, John de Leo [Africanus], who afterward turned Christian. The unknown countries of Ginny and Binne[8] this six and twenty years have been frequented with a few English ships only to trade, especially the river of Senega, by Captain Brimstead, Captain Brockit, Mr. Crump, and diverse others. Also the great river of Gambra, by Captain Jobson, who is returned in thither again in the year 1626 with Mr. William Grent and thirteen or fourteen others, to stay in the country, to discover some way to those rich mines of Gago or Tumbatu,[9] from whence is supposed the Moors of Barbary have their gold, and the certainty of those supposed descriptions and relations of those interior parts, which daily the more they are sought into, the more they are corrected. For surely, those interior parts of Africa are little known to either English, French, or Dutch, though they use much the coast; therefore we will make a little bold with the observations of the Portugals.

◆━━◆━━◆

Elizabeth Cary
1585?–1639

Elizabeth Cary was the first English woman to write and publish an original play, *The Tragedy of Mariam, The Fair Queen of Jewry*. She was also the first English woman to be the subject of a biography, her daughter's *The Lady Falkland: Her Life*. When we consider that the French poet Louise Labé was called a "common whore" by Calvin because she published her love poems and that Mary Wroth was forced to withdraw her work from publication, we can begin to get an idea of how unusual it was for Elizabeth Cary to publish her work. She showed similar independence by separating from her husband, by converting to Catholicism, and by translating controversial theological works. A prodigious scholar, a committed Catholic, and mother of eleven children, Elizabeth Cary was the extraordinary author of an extraordinary play.

---

6. A palace formed around a courtyard, here compared to a "Burse," or trading place.
7. Guinea and Benin, on the west coast of Africa.

8. Timbuktu, near the Niger with the Sahara to the north, a center of trade and Moslem culture.

Born Elizabeth Tanfield, the daughter of a wealthy lawyer, she had an independent mind and a passion for learning even as a child. Once, when the young Elizabeth observed her father hearing a case of witchcraft, the girl intervened, whispering in his ear the crucial question that exposed the evidence against the accused woman as a fraud. The precocious Elizabeth studied French, Spanish, and Italian, and she also studied the ancient languages of Latin and Hebrew, normally restricted to male students; she even translated some of Seneca's *Epistles* when she was only seven years old. She also translated Abraham Ortelius's *Le Miroir du Monde*, which described such places as China, India, and America. When Elizabeth was only twelve, the poet Michael Drayton praised her learning in his *Englands Heroicall Epistles*. She was such an avid reader that when her parents forbade her to read at night, she borrowed candles from the servants.

Her family arranged her marriage to Henry Cary in 1602. Master of the Queen's jewels and later made Viscount Falkland, Henry supplied the title and gentry status to the marriage, while Elizabeth supplied the money. Separated by Henry's military duty in the Protestant war against Spain in Holland during the early years of their marriage, they had their first child in 1609. Elizabeth's attempts to aid Henry's career by mortgaging her joint ownership of family property angered her father, who disinherited her.

In 1622 her husband became Lord Deputy of Ireland, and sharp disagreements arose between them. While he directed the colonial administration of Ireland, she studied the Irish language and set up a trade school for poor children in Dublin. While her husband attempted to enforce conformity to Protestantism in Catholic Ireland, Elizabeth's own desire to convert to Catholicism strengthened. From childhood she had found Calvinism inimical because of its emphasis on predestination, and she was also critical of Anglicanism. She returned to England at her husband's orders in 1625, and in 1626 she publicly converted to Catholicism. Nonconformity to the official church was dangerous for anyone in early modern England, but Elizabeth's open declaration of it was particularly dangerous for her husband, who was in government service. Henry was outraged and completely distanced himself from her. She complained to King Charles I that her husband did not support her financially; Henry excused himself by charging her with refusing to live "quietly." Their daughter claimed, nevertheless, that her parents were reconciled at Henry's deathbed in 1633.

Elizabeth moved to a small village outside London, where she continued to write until her death in 1639. She lived modestly, giving much of her income to charity. She arranged for her two youngest sons and four daughters, who had also converted, to live in Catholic France, where her daughters became Benedictine nuns. Her son Lucius, made famous by Ben Jonson's ode, remained behind in England. Not sharing his mother's religion, he was able to inherit his grandmother's money. He did, however, share his mother's love of languages and of theological dispute, which she continued to pursue. She translated the reply of a French theologian, Jacques Du Perron, to King James I's attack on Catholicism. A comment she made in the preface to her translation shows how thoroughly she rejected the conventional aristocratic and feminine stance of shunning publication: "I will not make use of the worn out form of saying I printed it against my will, moved by the importunity of friends; I was moved to it by my belief that it might make those English that understand not French . . . read Perron." She dedicated this work to the Catholic wife of Charles I, Queen Henrietta Maria. Published on the Continent, this work was immediately confiscated and burned when it was smuggled into England. At the time she died, Elizabeth was translating the Hebrew and Latin writings of the Flemish mystic Blosius.

During the early years of her marriage, Elizabeth Cary wrote a verse life of Tamberlain. Two texts about Edward II are now often attributed to her; one of these, *The History of the Life, Reign, and Death of Edward II*, contains the initials of Elizabeth Falkland on its title page. In addition to her numerous translations, she wrote occasional poetry which circulated in manuscript. Her former tutor Sir John Davies wrote verses praising two of her plays: a lost play set in Greece and *The Tragedy of Mariam*.

Though not published until 1613, *Mariam* was probably written sometime between 1604 and 1609. The play portrays Mariam's struggle between her own integrity and her loyalty to her husband Herod when confronted with his tyranny and tragically mistaken jealousy. The play also includes a subplot of political intrigue in which two minor characters, the sons of Baba, attempt to resist King Herod's tyranny. The story is taken from a pair of ancient sources, Josephus's *Jewish War* and *Antiquities of the Jews*, first translated into English in 1602. The dramatic influences may include Shakespeare's *Antony and Cleopatra* and *Othello*, although some would argue that Cary's *Mariam* could have influenced Shakespeare. Cary frequently attended the theater, and though her work was a closet drama—like Seneca's tragedies, meant to be read rather than performed—it is full of high emotion and dramatic action. In fact, *Othello* and *Mariam* have much in common. Both concern marriages that defy the expectations of the status quo, a husband's irrational jealousy, and the proper behavior of women. Cary surrounds the chaste yet outspoken Mariam with a range of vivid female characters: Salome, who promotes divorce for women; Graphina, who remains quiet and obedient; and Alexandra, who objects to her daughter's marriage.

Some of the conflicts in *The Tragedy of Mariam* can be related to those in Elizabeth Cary's own life. For example, the disparity between the royal Mariam and her upstart husband may reflect the social and financial disparity between Cary and her husband. The heroine's struggle between obedience to her husband and fidelity to herself may be related to the author's own crisis of conscience. Mariam's questioning of her "public voice" may be read as the text's questioning of the author's publication of her work. More generally, the play illustrates conflicts in the larger social context. The dissent of English Catholics, a long overlooked aspect of early modern English culture, surfaces in the figure of Herod. Catholics saw Herod as an allegorical figure for Henry VIII, because both kings killed their wives and imposed arbitrary dictates on their subjects. Cary's work can also be read as a comment on the norms of chastity, silence, and obedience for women of her time. Dramatic tension arises from the contrasts between the conventional pronouncements of the chorus on women's conduct and the perspectives of the female characters.

In her own time Elizabeth Cary was praised by her son's biographer, Edward Clarendon, as "a lady of a most masculine understanding," but she is now appreciated for representing a woman's subjectivity in the genre of tragedy. With its unique blend of popular Shakespearian and learned Senecan tragic style, *Mariam* gives us insight into the history of English drama. Along with the interracial couple of *Othello*, the mixed marriage of Cary's *Mariam* looks forward to a similar theme in Aphra Behn's *Oroonoko* (1688). For its questioning of power relationships, Elizabeth Cary's *Tragedy of Mariam* is a trenchant comment on perennial problems. In its emotional depth, *Mariam* can play a role in our understanding not only of the past but of ourselves.

The Tragedy of Mariam, The Fair Queen of Jewry[1]

To Diana's Earthly Deputess and My Worthy Sister, Mistress
Elizabeth Cary[2]

When cheerful Phoebus[3] his full course hath run,
His sister's fainter beams our hearts doth cheer;

---

1. The sole early modern edition, of 1613, contains some obvious misprints, and inconsistencies in spelling and punctuation, which this edition silently corrects. More problematic errors that have been corrected by modern editors are mentioned in the footnotes.

2. Two extant copies of the play contain this sonnet dedicated to the author's sister-in-law.

3. Apollo, the sun god, twin brother of Diana.

So your fair brother is to me the sun,
And you his sister as my moon appear.

5 You are my next beloved, my second friend,
For when my Phoebus' absence makes it night,
Whilst to the Antipodes[4] his beams do bend,
From you my Phoebe,[5] shines my second light.

He like to Sol,[6] clear-sighted, constant, free,
10 You Luna-like, unspotted, chaste, divine;
He shone on Sicily, you destined be,
To illumine the now obscurèd Palestine.
My first[7] was consecrated to Apollo,
My second to Diana now shall follow.

E.C.

The names of the speakers

Herod, *King of Judea*
Doris, *his first wife*
Mariam, *his second wife*
Salome, *Herod's sister*
Antipater, *his son by Doris*
Alexandra, *Mariam's mother*
Silleus, *Prince of Arabia*
Constabarus, *husband to Salome*
Pheroras, *Herod's brother*

Graphina, *his love*
Babas' first son
Babas' second son
Ananell, *the high Priest*
Sohemus, *a counselor to Herod*
Nuntio
Butler, *another messenger*
Chorus, *a company of Jews*

The Argument

Herod the son of Antipater (an Idumean[8]), having crept by the favor of the Romans into the Jewish monarchy, married Mariam the granddaughter of Hircanus, the rightful king and priest; and for her (besides her high blood, being of singular beauty) he repudiated Doris, his former wife, by whom he had children.

This Mariam had a brother called Aristobolus, and next him and Hircanus his grand-father, Herod in his wife's right had the best title. Therefore to remove them, he charged Hircanus with treason, and put him to death, and drowned Aristobolus under color of sport. Alexandra, daughter to the one and mother to the other, accused him for their deaths before Anthony.

So when he was forced to go answer this accusation at Rome, he left the custody of his wife to Josephus, his uncle that had married his sister Salome, and out of a violent affection (unwilling any should enjoy her after him) he gave strict and private commandment, that if he were slain, she should be put to death. But he returned with much honor, yet found his wife extremely discontented, to whom Josephus had (meaning it for the best, to prove Herod loved her) revealed his charge.

So by Salome's accusation he put Josephus to death, but was reconciled to Mariam, who still bare the death of her friends[9] exceeding hardly.

In the meantime Herod was again necessarily to revisit Rome, for Caesar, having over-thrown Anthony his great friend, was likely to make an alteration of Herod's fortune.

---

4. The opposite end of the earth.
5. Diana, or Luna, the moon.
6. The sun.
7. Cary's first play, which is now lost.

8. People of Edom, south of Judea, who had converted to Judaism but were not considered fully Jewish.
9. Family.

In his absence, news came to Jerusalem that Caesar had put him to death. Their will-
ingness it should be so, together with the likelihood, gave this rumor so good credit, as Sohe-
mus that had succeeded Josephus' charge,¹ succeeded him likewise in revealing it. So at
Herod's return, which was speedy and unexpected, he found Mariam so far from joy that
she showed apparent signs of sorrow. He, still desiring to win her to a better humor, she
being very unable to conceal her passion, fell to upbraiding him with her brother's death. As
they were thus debating, came in a fellow with a cup of wine, who, hired by Salome, said
first, it was a love potion, which Mariam desired to deliver to the king; but afterwards he
affirmed that it was a poison and that Sohemus had told her somewhat, which procured the
vehement hate in her.

The king, hearing this, more moved with jealousy of Sohemus than with this intent of
poison, sent her away; and presently after, by the instigation of Salome, Mariam was
beheaded. Which rashness was afterward punished in him, with an intolerable and almost
frantic passion for her death.

Act 1

Scene 1

[*Mariam alone.*]

MARIAM How oft have I with public voice run on?
    To censure Rome's last hero for deceit;
    Because he wept when Pompey's life was gone,
    Yet when he lived, he thought his name too great.
5   But now I do recant,° and, Roman lord,²   *renounce my error*
    Excuse too rash a judgment in a woman;
    My sex pleads pardon, pardon then afford,
    Mistaking is with us, but too too common.
    Now do I find by self-experience taught,
10   One object yields both grief and joy;
    You wept indeed, when on his worth you thought,
    But joyed that slaughter did your foe destroy.
    So at his death your eyes true drops did rain,
    Whom dead, you did not wish alive again.
15   When Herod lived, that now is done to death,
    Oft have I wished that I from him were free;
    Oft have I wished that he might lose his breath;
    Oft have I wished his carcass dead to see.
    Then rage and scorn had put my love to flight,
20   That love which once on him was firmly set;
    Hate hid his true affection from my sight,
    And kept my heart from paying him his debt.
    And blame me not, for Herod's jealousy
    Had power even constancy itself to change;
25   For he, by barring me from liberty,
    To shun° my ranging, taught me first to range.   *prevent*
    But yet too chaste a scholar was my heart,
    To learn to love another than my lord;

---

1. Who had taken on Josephus' duties.
2. Mariam addresses the absent Julius Caesar ("Rome's last hero"), who was said by Plutarch to have wept when

he saw the head of his slain rival Pompey. The characters frequently speak in apostrophe to an imagined or absent figure.

To leave his love, my lesson's former part,
30   I quickly learned, the other I abhorred.
But now his death to memory doth call,
The tender love, that he to Mariam bare;
And mine to him, this makes those rivers fall,
Which by another thought unmoistened are.
35   For Aristobolus the lowliest youth
That ever did in angel's shape appear,
The cruel Herod was not moved to ruth;°   *pity*
Then why grieves Mariam Herod's death to hear?
Why joy I not the tongue no more shall speak,
40   That yielded forth my brother's latest doom;
Both youth and beauty might thy° fury break,   *Herod's*
And both in him did ill befit a tomb.
And worthy grandsire ill did he requite,[3]
His high assent alone by thee procured,
45   Except he murdered thee to free the sprite°   *spirit*
Which still he thought on earth too long immured.°   *confined*
How happy was it that Sohemus' mind
Was moved to pity my distressed estate!
Might Herod's life a trusty servant find,[4]
50   My death to his had been unseparate.
These thoughts have power, his death to make me bear,
Nay more, to wish the news may firmly hold;
Yet cannot this repulse some falling tear,
That will against my will some grief unfold.
55   And more I owe him for his love to me,
The deepest love that ever yet was seen;
Yet had I rather much a milkmaid be,
Than be the monarch of Judea's queen.
It was for naught but love, he wished his end
60   Might to my death but the vaunt-courier° prove;   *forerunner*
But I had rather still be foe than friend,
To him that saves for hate, and kills for love.[5]
Hard-hearted Mariam, at thy discontent,
What floods of tears have drenched his manly face?
65   How canst thou then so faintly now lament,
Thy truest lover's death, a death's disgrace;[6]
Ay, now, mine eyes you do begin to right
The wrongs of your admirer and my lord.[7]
Long since you should have put your smiles to flight,
70   Ill doth a widowed eye with joy accord.
Why now methinks the love I bore him then,
When virgin freedom left me unrestrained,
Doth to my heart begin to creep again,
My passion now is far from being feigned.
75   But tears fly back, and hide you in your banks,[8]

3. Lines 43–46 are addressed to her dead grandfather Hircanus.
4. If Herod had been trustworthy while alive.
5. See *Othello*, 5.2.44, page 1252.

6. Her lack of grief dishonors his death.
7. Herod.
8. Her eyes.

You must not be to Alexandra seen;
For if my moan be spied, but little thanks
Shall Mariam have, from that incensèd queen.

Scene 2

[Mariam, Alexandra.]

ALEXANDRA What means these tears? My Mariam doth mistake,
    The news we heard did tell the tyrant's end;
    What° weepst thou for thy brother's murd'rer's sake,   *why*
    Will ever wight° a tear for Herod spend?   *a person*
5   My curse pursue his breathless trunk and spirit,
    Base Edomite the damnèd Esau's heir;
    Must he ere Jacob's child the crown inherit?[9]
    Must he, vile wretch, be set in David's chair°?   *throne*
    No David's soul within the bosom placed,
10   Of our forefather Abram was ashamed;
    To see his seat with such a toad disgraced,
    That seat that hath by Judah's race been famed.
    Thou fatal enemy to royal blood,[1]
    Did not the murder of my boy suffice,
15   To stop thy cruel mouth that gaping stood?
    But must thou dim the mild Hircanus' eyes?
    My gracious father, whose too ready hand
    Did lift this Idumean from the dust;[2]
    And he ungrateful caitiff° did withstand,°   *wretch / oppose*
20   The man that did in him most friendly trust.
    What kingdom's right could cruel Herod claim,
    Was he not Esau's issue, heir of hell?
    Then what succession can he have but shame?
    Did not his ancestor his birthright sell?
25   O yes, he doth from Edom's name derive
    His cruel nature which with blood is fed;[3]
    That made him me of sire and son deprive,
    He ever thirsts for blood, and blood is red.
    Weep'st thou because his love to thee was bent?
30   And read'st thou love in crimson characters?
    Slew he thy friends to work thy heart's content?
    No; hate may justly call that action hers.
    He gave the sacred priesthood for thy sake
    To Aristobolus, yet doomed him dead;
35   Before his back the ephod warm could make,
    And ere the miter settled on his head;[4]
    Oh, had he given my boy no less than right,
    The double oil should to his forehead bring
    A double honor, shining double bright;
40   His birth anointed him both priest and king.
    And say my father and my son he slew

9. The Edomites descended from Esau, who sold his birthright to his brother Jacob (Genesis 25.29–34).
1. Lines 13–16 are addressed to Herod.
2. Hircanus raised Herod's station by permitting his marriage to Miriam.
3. The root meaning of Edom is "red."
4. The ephod and the miter were Jewish priestly vestments.

To royalize by right your prince-born breath;[5]
Was love the cause, can Mariam deem it true,
That Mariam gave commandment for her death?
45   I know by fits he showed some signs of love,
And yet not love, but raging lunacy;
And this his hate to thee may justly prove,
That sure he hates Hircanus' family.
Who knows if he unconstant wavering lord,
50   His love to Doris[6] had renewed again?
And that he might his bed to her afford,
Perchance he wished that Mariam might be slain.

MARIAM Doris, alas her time of love was past,
Those coals were raked in embers long ago
55   Of Mariam's love, and she was now disgraced,[7]
Nor did I glory in her overthrow.
He not a whit his first-born son esteemed,
Because as well as his he was not mine;
My children only for his own he deemed,
60   These boys that did descend from royal line.
These did he style his heirs to David's throne,
My Alexander if he live, shall sit
In the majestic seat of Solomon,
To will it so, did Herod think it fit.

ALEXANDRA Why? Who can claim from Alexander's brood[8]
That gold-adornèd, lion-guarded chair?
Was Alexander not of David's blood?
And was not Mariam Alexander's heir?
What more than right could Herod then bestow,
70   And who will think except for more than right,
He did not raise them, for they were not low,[9]
But born to wear the crown in his despite.
Then send those tears away that are not sent
To thee by reason, but by passion's power;
75   Thine eyes to cheer, thy cheeks to smiles be bent,
And entertain with joy this happy hour.
Felicity, if when she comes, she finds
A mourning habit and a cheerless look,
Will think she is not welcome to thy mind,
80   And so perchance her lodging will not brook.°   *put up with*
Oh, keep her whilst thou hast her; if she go
She will not easily return again.
Full many a year have I endured in woe,
Yet still have sued her presence to obtain;
85   And did not I to her as presents send
A table,° that best art did beautify   *picture*

5. To make Mariam's son inherit royal power.
6. Herod's first wife.
7. "If" in the 1613 text is emended to "Of." "Mariam's love" (either Herod's love for Mariam or Mariam's for Herod) covers the coals of Doris's love with ashes.
8. Alexander was Mariam's father.

9. How could Herod grant Mariam's children anything more than what they were already entitled to? Whoever thinks Herod granted them "more than right" should know that "he did not raise them" since "they were not low" in the first place.

Of two, to whom heaven did best feature lend,
To woo her love by winning Anthony?
For when a prince's favor we do crave,
90   We first their minions'° loves do seek to win;   *favorites'*
So I, that sought felicity to have,
Did with her minion Anthony begin.
With double slight I sought to captivate
The warlike lover, but I did not right;
95   For if my gift had born but half the rate,
The Roman had been overtaken quite.
But now he farèd like a hungry guest,
That to some plenteous festival is gone;
Now this, now that, he deems to eat were best,
100   Such choice doth make him let them all alone.
The boy's large forehead first did fairest seem,
Then glanced his eye upon my Mariam's cheek;
And that without comparison did deem,
What was in either but he most did seek.
105   And, thus distracted, either's beauty's might
Within the other's excellence was drowned;
Too much delight did bare him from delight,
For either's love, the other's did confound.
Where if thy portraiture had only gone,
110   His life from Herod, Anthony had taken;
He would have lovèd thee, and thee alone,
And left the brown Egyptian clean forsaken.
And Cleopatra then to seek had been,[1]
So firm a lover of her wanèd° face;   *dark, gloomy*
115   Then great Antonius' fall we had not seen,
By her that fled to have him hold the chase.
Then Mariam in a Roman's chariot set,
In place of Cleopatra might have shown;
A mart of beauties in her visage met,
120   And part in this, that they were all her own.
MARIAM Not to be empress of aspiring Rome,
Would Mariam like to Cleopatra live;
With purest body will I press my tomb,
And wish no favors Anthony could give.[2]
ALEXANDRA Let us return us, that we may resolve
How now to deal in this reversèd state;
Great are the affairs that we must now revolve,
And great affairs must not be taken late.

Scene 3

[*Mariam, Alexandra, Salome.*]
SALOM More plotting yet? Why, now you have the thing
For which so oft you spent your suppliant° breath;   *humbly begging*

---

1. Cleopatra would have been left seeking.

2. Mariam disdains Cleopatra's quest for power through her affairs with Julius Caesar and Mark Antony.

And Mariam hopes to have another king.
Her eyes do sparkle joy for Herod's death.
ALEXANDRA If she desired another king to have,
    She might before she came in Herod's bed
    Have had her wish. More kings than one did crave,
    For leave to set a crown upon her head.
    I think with more than reason she laments,
10   That she is freed from such a sad annoy;
    Who is't will weep to part from discontent,
    And if she joy, she did not causeless joy.[3]
SALOME You durst not thus have given your tongue the rein,
    If noble Herod still remained in life;
15   Your daughter's betters far I dare maintain,
    Might have rejoiced to be my brother's wife.
MARIAM My betters far! Base woman, 'tis untrue,
    You scarce have ever my superiors seen;
    For Mariam's servants were as good as you,
20   Before she came to be Judea's queen.
SALOME Now stirs the tongue that is so quickly moved,
    But more then once your choler° have I borne;   *anger*
    Your fumish° words are sooner said than proved,   *hot-tempered*
    And Salome's reply is only scorn.
MARIAM Scorn those that are for thy companions held.
    Though I thy brother's face had never seen,
    My birth, thy baser birth so far excelled,
    I had to both of you the princess been.
    Thou parti-Jew, and parti-Edomite,[4]
30   Thou mongrel, issued from rejected race,
    Thy ancestors against the heavens did fight,[5]
    And thou like them wilt heavenly birth disgrace.
SALOME Still twit° you me with nothing but my birth,   *blame*
    What odds betwixt your ancestors and mine?
35   Both born of Adam, both were made of earth,
    And both did come from holy Abraham's line.
MARIAM I favor thee when nothing else I say,
    With thy black acts I'll not pollute my breath;
    Else to thy charge I might full justly lay
40   A shameful life, besides a husband's death.
SALOME 'Tis true indeed, I did the plots reveal,
    That passed betwixt your favorites and you;[6]
    I meant not, I, a traitor to conceal;
    Thus Salome your minion° Joseph slew.   *favorite*
MARIAM Heaven, dost thou mean this infamy to smother?
    Let slandered Mariam open thy closèd ear;
    Self-guilt hath ever been suspicion's mother,[7]
    And therefore I this speech with patience bear.

---

3. If she were delighted, it would be with good reason.
4. Part Jewish, part Edomite.
5. In resisting the power of Israel, the Edomites were portrayed as opposing God (Ezekiel 25.13,35).
6. Salome accused her first husband, Josephus, and Mari-

am of adultery. Herod judged Josephus's telling Mariam about the secret order that she be killed in the event of Herod's death as proof of Josephus's guilt, and so ordered his execution.
7. Your own guilt makes you suspicious of me.

50　No, had not Salome's unsteadfast heart,
　　In Josephus' stead her Constabarus placed[8]
　　To free herself, she had not used the art,
　　To slander hapless Mariam for unchaste.

ALEXANDRA Come Mariam, let us go: it is no boot°　　　　　use
　　To let the head contend against the foot.

Scene 4

[*Salome alone.*]

SALOME Lives Salome, to get so base a style°　　　　　name
　　As foot, to the proud Mariam? Herod's spirit
　　In happy time for her endured exile,[9]
　　For did he live she should not miss her merit;[1]
5　　But he is dead; and though he were my brother,
　　His death such store of cinders cannot cast
　　My coals of love to quench; for though they smother
　　The flames a while, yet will they out at last.
　　Oh blest Arabia, in best climate placed,
10　I by the fruit will censure of the tree;
　　'Tis not in vain, thy happy name thou hast,
　　If all Arabians like Silleus[2] be;
　　Had not my fate been too too contrary,
　　When I on Constabarus first did gaze,
15　Silleus had been object to mine eye,
　　Whose looks and personage must always amaze.
　　But now ill-fated Salome, thy tongue
　　To Constabarus by itself is tied;
　　And now except I do the Hebrew wrong
20　I cannot be the fair Arabian bride;
　　What childish lets° are these? Why stand I now　　　　　hindrances
　　On honorable points? 'Tis long ago
　　Since shame was written on my tainted brow;[3]
　　And certain 'tis, that shame is honor's foe.
25　Had I upon my reputation stood,
　　Had I affected an unspotted life,
　　Josephus' veins had still been stuffed with blood,
　　And I to him had lived a sober wife.
　　Then had I never cast an eye of love
30　On Constabarus' now detested face,
　　Then had I kept my thoughts without remove
　　And blushed at motion of the least disgrace;[4]
　　But shame is gone, and honor wiped away,
　　And Impudency on my forehead sits;
35　She bids me work my will without delay,
　　And for my will I will employ my wits.
　　He loves, I love; what then can be the cause
　　Keeps me from being the Arabian's wife?

---

8. Mariam claims that she was accused of adultery by
Salome because Salome wanted to get rid of her husband
so that she could marry Constabarus.
9. Separation of the soul from the body, i.e., death.

1. If he were alive, she would get what she deserves.
2. Salome's lover and minister to King Obodas of Arabia.
3. Since she showed any sign of shame.
4. Compare *Othello*, 1.3.96–97, page 1190.

It is the principles of Moses' laws;
40   For Constabarus still remains in life;
      If he to me did bear as earnest hate
      As I to him, for him there were an ease,
      A separating bill⁵ might free his fate
      From such a yoke that did so much displease.
45   Why should such privilege to man be given?
      Or given to them, why barred from women then?
      Are men than we in greater grace with Heaven?
      Or cannot women hate as well as men?⁶
      I'll be the custom-breaker, and begin
50   To show my sex the way to freedom's door,
      And with an offering will I purge my sin,
      The law was made for none but who are poor.
      If Herod had lived, I might to him accuse
      My present lord. But for the future's sake
55   Then would I tell the king he did refuse
      The sons of Baba in his power to take.⁷
      But now I must divorce him from my bed,
      That my Silleus may possess his room.
      Had I not begged his life he had been dead,⁸
60   I curse my tongue the hinderer of his doom;
      But then my wandering heart to him was fast,
      Nor did I dream of change. Silleus said,
      He would be here, and see he comes at last,
      Had I not named him longer had he stayed.

Scene 5

[Salome, Silleus.]

SILLEUS Well found fair Salome, Judea's pride!
         Hath thy innated° wisdom found the way   inborn
         To make Silleus deem him deified,
         By gaining thee a more than precious prey?
SALOME   I have devised the best I can devise:
         A more imperfect means was never found;
         But what cares Salome? It doth suffice
         If our endeavors with their end be crowned.
         In this our land we have an ancient use,
10   Permitted first by our law-giver's° head;   Moses'
         Who hates his wife, though for no just abuse,
         May with a bill divorce her from his bed.
         But in this custom women are not free,
         Yet I for once will wrest it; blame not thou
15   The ill I do, since what I do's for thee,
         Though others blame, Silleus should allow.

5. A bill of divorce, which only men could sue for.
6. Compare *Othello*, 4.3.88–99, page 1247.
7. Constabarus was supposed to have captured Herod's political enemies, the sons of Babas, but instead hid them on his own estate in hope that they might be useful to him in usurping power.
8. When Herod found out that Constabarus, as governor of Idumea, had tried to take over the kingdom, only Salome was able to convince Herod to spare his life.

SILLEUS Thinks Salome, Silleus hath a tongue
        To censure her fair actions? Let my blood
        Bedash my proper brow,[9] for such a wrong,
20   The being yours, can make even vices good;
        Arabia, joy, prepare thy earth with green,
        Thou never happy wert indeed 'til now;
        Now shall thy ground be trod by beauty's queen,
        Her foot is destined to depress thy brow.
25   Thou shalt fair Salome command as much
        As if the royal ornament were thine;
        The weakness of Arabia's king is such,
        The kingdom is not his so much as mine.
        My mouth is our Obodas' oracle,
30   Who thinks not aught but what Silleus will.
        And thou rare creature, Asia's miracle,
        Shalt be to me as it: Obodas' still.[1]
SALOME 'Tis not for glory I thy love accept,
        Judea yields me honor's worthy store;
35   Had not affection in my bosom crept,
        My native country should my life deplore.[2]
        Were not Silleus he with whom I go,
        I would not change my Palestine for Rome;
        Much less would I a glorious state to show,
40   Go far to purchase an Arabian tomb.
SILLEUS Far be it from Silleus so to think,
        I know it is thy gratitude requites
        The love that is in me, and shall not shrink
        'Til death do sever me from earth's delights.
SALOME But whist;° methinks the wolf is in our talk,[3]   *be silent*
        Be gone Silleus, who doth here arrive?
        'Tis Constabarus that doth hither walk,
        I'll find a quarrel, him from me to drive.
SILLEUS Farewell, but were it not for thy command,
50   In his despite Silleus here would stand.

Scene 6

[*Salome, Constabarus.*]
CONSTABARUS Oh Salome, how much you wrong your name,
        Your race, your country, and your husband most!
        A stranger's private conference is shame;[4]
        I blush for you, that have your blushing lost.
5   Oft have I found, and found you to my grief,
        Comforted with this base Arabian here;
        Heaven knows that you have been my comfort chief,
        Then do not now my greater plague appear.
        Now by the stately carved edifice

---

9. Splash against my own forehead.
1. Even though Obodas rules the Kingdom, he follows my judgment as I follow yours, Salome.
2. If it weren't for love of you, Silleus, I would regret leaving my country my whole life long.
3. In discussing our plot for power, we are in danger of being overheard.
4. Talking privately with a stranger is shameful.

10   That on Mount Sion makes so fair a show,[5]
        And by the altar fit for sacrifice,
        I love thee more than thou thyself dost know.
        Oft with a silent sorrow have I heard
        How ill Judea's mouth doth censure thee;
15   And did I not thine honor much regard,
        Thou shouldst not be exhorted thus for me.
        Didst thou but know the worth of honest fame,
        How much a virtuous woman is esteemed,
        Thou wouldst like hell eschew deservèd shame,
20   And seek to be both chaste and chastely deemed.
        Our wisest prince did say, and true he said,
        A virtuous woman crowns her husband's head.[6]
SALOME Did I for this uprear thy low estate?
        Did I for this requital beg thy life,
25   That thou hadst forfeited to hapless fate,
        To be to such a thankless wretch the wife?
        This hand of mine hath lifted up thy head,
        Which many a day ago had fall'n full low,
        Because the sons of Babas are not dead;
30   To me thou dost both life and fortune owe.
CONSTABARUS You have my patience often exercised,
        Use make my choler keep within the banks;[7]
        Yet boast no more, but be by me advised,
        A benefit upbraided, forfeits thanks.[8]
35   I prithee Salome, dismiss this mood,
        Thou dost not know how ill it fits thy place:
        My words were all intended for thy good,
        To raise thine honor and to stop disgrace.
SALOME To stop disgrace? Take thou no care for me,
40   Nay, do thy worst, thy worst I set not by;[9]
        No shame of mine is like to light on thee,
        Thy love and admonitions I defy.
        Thou shalt no hour longer call me wife,
        Thy jealousy procures my hate so deep;
45   That I from thee do mean to free my life,
        By a divorcing bill before I sleep.
CONSTABARUS Are Hebrew women now transformed to men?
        Why do you not as well our battles fight,
        And wear our armor? Suffer this, and then
50   Let all the world be topsy-turvèd° quite.   *upside down*
        Let fishes graze, beasts, swine, and birds descend,
        Let fire burn downwards whilst the earth aspires;
        Let winter's heat and summer's cold offend,
        Let thistles grow on vines, and grapes on briars,
55   Set us to spin or sow, or at the best

5. The temple of Jerusalem.
6. Proverbs 12.4; attributed to Solomon.
7. May habit control my anger.

8. If you blame someone for having granted him a benefit,
you lose his gratitude.
9. I couldn't care less about the worst you could do to me.

Make us wood-hewers, water-bearing wights;
For sacred service let us take no rest,
Use us as Joshua did the Gibonites.[1]

SALOME Hold on your talk, 'til it be time to end,
60   For me I am resolved it shall be so;
Though I be first that to this course do bend,
I shall not be the last full well I know.

CONSTABARUS Why then be witness heaven, the judge of sins,
Be witness spirits that eschew the dark;
65   Be witness angels, witness cherubins,
Whose semblance sits upon the holy Ark;
Be witness earth, be witness Palestine,
Be witness David's city, if my heart
Did ever merit such an act of thine;
70   Or if the fault be mine that makes us part,
Since mildest Moses, friend unto the Lord,
Did work his wonders in the land of Ham,[2]
And slew the first-born babes without a sword,
In sign whereof we eat the holy lamb;[3]
75   'Til now that fourteen hundred years are past,
Since first the Law[4] with us hath been in force;
You are the first, and will, I hope, be last,
That ever sought her husband to divorce.

SALOME I mean not to be led by precedent,
80   My will shall be to me instead of Law.

CONSTABARUS I fear me much you will too late repent,
That you have ever lived so void of awe;
This is Silleus' love that makes you thus
Reverse all order; you must next be his.
85   But if my thoughts aright the cause discuss,
In winning you, he gains no lasting bliss;
I was Silleus, and not long ago
Josephus then was Constabarus now;
When you became my friend° you proved his° foe,   *lover/Josephus's*
90   As now for him° you break to me your vow.   *Silleus*

SALOME If once I loved you, greater is your debt;
For certain 'tis that you deserve it not.
And undeserved love we soon forget,
And therefore that to me can be no blot.
95   But now fare ill my once belovèd lord,
Yet never more beloved than now abhorred.

CONSTABARUS Yet Constabarus biddeth thee farewell.
Farewell light creature. Heaven forgive thy sin;
My prophesying spirit doth foretell
100   Thy wavering thoughts do yet but new begin.
Yet I have better 'scaped than Joseph did;
But if our Herod's death had been delayed,
The valiant youths[5] that I so long have hid

---

1. Joshua enslaved the Gibonites (Joshua 9).
2. Egypt.
3. During the Passover celebration commemorating the

Israelites' deliverance from Egypt (Exodus 12).
4. The law of Moses.
5. Babas's sons.

Had been by her, and I for them betrayed.
105   Therefore in happy hour did Caesar give
The fatal blow to wanton Anthony;
For had he lived, our Herod then should live,
But great Anthonius' death made Herod die.
Had he enjoyed his breath, not I alone
110   Had been in danger of a deadly fall;
But Mariam had the way of peril gone,
Though by the tyrant most beloved of all.
The sweet-faced Mariam as free from guilt
As heaven from spots, yet had her lord come back
115   Her purest blood had been unjustly spilt.
And Salome it was would work her wrack.°   destruction
Though all Judea yield her innocent,
She often hath been near to punishment.   [Exit.]

CHORUS   Those minds that wholly dote upon delight,
120   Except° they only joy in inward good,   unless
Still hope at last to hop upon the right,[6]
And so from sand they leap in loathsome mud.
Fond wretches, seeking what they cannot find,
For no content attends a wavering mind.

125   If wealth they do desire, and wealth attain,
Then wondrous fain° would they to honor leap;   gladly
Of mean degree they do in honor gain,
They would but wish a little higher step.
Thus step to step, and wealth to wealth they add,
130   Yet cannot all their plenty make them glad.

Yet oft we see that some in humble state,
Are cheerful, pleasant, happy, and content;
When those indeed that are of higher state,
With vain additions do their thoughts torment.
135   Th' one would to his mind his fortune bind,
Th' other to his fortune frames his mind.

To wish variety is sign of grief,
For if you like your state as now it is,
Why should an alteration bring relief?
140   Nay change would then be feared as loss of bliss.
That man is only happy in his fate,
That is delighted in a settled state.

Still Mariam wished she from her lord were free,
For expectation of variety;
145   Yet now she sees her wishes prosperous be,
She grieves, because her lord so soon did die.
Who can those vast imaginations feed,
Where in a property contempt doth breed?[7]

6. To hop on to land on the right side meant to achieve a   7. Where what is possessed is despised.
good outcome.

150 Were Herod now perchance to love again,
    She would again as much be grieved at that;
    All that she may,⁸ she ever doth disdain,
    Her wishes guide her to she knows not what.
    And sad must be their looks, their honor sour,
    That care for nothing being in their power.

Act 2

Scene 1

*[Pheroras and Graphina.]*⁹

PHERORAS 'Tis true Graphina, now the time draws nigh
         Wherein the holy priest with hallowed right,
         The happy long-desired knot shall tie,
         Pheroras and Graphina to unite;
5   How oft have I with lifted hands implored
         This blessed hour, 'til now implored in vain,
         Which hath my wished liberty restored,
         And made my subject self my own again.
         Thy love, fair maid, upon mine eye doth sit,
10   Whose nature hot doth dry the moisture all,
         Which were in nature, and in reason fit
         For my monarchal brother's death to fall;
         Had Herod lived, he would have plucked my hand
         From fair Graphina's palm perforce; and tied
15   The same in hateful and despisèd band,
         For I had had a baby to my bride;¹
         Scarce can her infant tongue with easy voice
         Her name distinguish to another's ear;²
         Yet had he lived, his power, and not my choice
20   Had made me solemnly the contract swear.
         Have I not cause in such a change to joy?
         What? Though she be my niece, a princess born;
         Near-blood's without respect: high birth a toy,
         Since love can teach us blood and kindred's scorn.
25   What booted it³ that he did raise my head,
         To be his realm's copartner, kingdom's mate?
         Withall, he kept Graphina from my bed,
         More wished by me than thrice Judea's state.
         Oh, could not he be skilful judge in love,
30   That doted so upon his Mariam's face?
         He, for his passion, Doris did remove;
         I needed not a lawful wife displace.
         It could not be but he had power to judge,
         But he that never grudged a kingdom's share,
35   This well-known happiness to me did grudge,

---

8. All that she may have or do.
9. From the minor figure of a nameless slave girl in Jose-phus's *Jewish War*, Cary created Graphina, derived from *graphesis*, the Greek word for writing.
1. Herod would have ordered a marriage between his old-est daughter ("a baby") and Pheroras.
2. She is so young she can hardly say her own name clearly; "infant" from Latin *infans*, speechless.
3. What use was it?

And meant to be therein without compare.
Else had I been his equal in love's host,°   *army*
For though the diadem on Mariam's head
Corrupt the vulgar judgments, I will boast
40   Graphina's brow's as white, her cheeks as red.
Why speaks thou not fair creature? Move thy tongue,
For silence is a sign of discontent;
It were to both our loves too great a wrong
If now this hour do find thee sadly bent.

GRAPHINA Mistake me not my lord, too oft have I
Desired this time to come with wingèd feet,
To be enwrapped with grief when 'tis too nigh,
You know my wishes ever yours did meet;
If I be silent, 'tis no more but fear
50   That I should say too little when I speak;
But since you will my imperfections bear,
In spite of doubt I will my silence break;
Yet might amazement tie my moving tongue,
But that I know before Pheroras' mind.
55   I have admired° your affection long,   *marvelled at*
And cannot yet therein a reason find.
Your hand hath lifted me from lowest state,
To highest eminency's wondrous grace,
And me your handmaid have you made your mate,
60   Though all but you alone do count me base.
You have preserved me pure at my request,
Though you so weak a vassal[4] might constrain
To yield to your high will; then last not best
In my respect a princess you disdain;
65   Then need not all these favors study crave,
To be requited by a simple maid?[5]
And study still you know must silence have,
Then be my cause for silence justly weighed,
But study cannot boot nor I requite,
70   Except your lowly handmaid's steadfast love
And fast obedience may your mind delight,
I will not promise more then I can prove.

PHERORAS That study needs not let Graphina smile,
And I desire no greater recompense;
75   I cannot vaunt° me in a glorious style,   *boast, proclaim*
Nor show my love in far-fetched eloquence;
But this believe me, never Herod's heart
Hath held his prince-born beauty-famèd wife
In nearer place than thou, fair virgin, art,
80   To him that holds the glory of his life.
Should Herod's body leave the sepulcher,
And entertain the severed ghost again;[6]

---

4. The feudal relation between lord and subordinate with a pun on "vessel," as in woman as "the weaker vessel" (1 Peter 3.7).

5. All these favors will require effort for a simple maid to repay them.
6. The spirit separated from the body, an image of death.

He should not be my nuptial hinderer,
Except he hindered it with dying pain.
85   Come fair Graphina, let us go in state,
This wish-endearèd time to celebrate.

Scene 2

[*Constabarus and Babas' Sons.*]

FIRST SON Now valiant friend you have our lives redeemed,
Which lives as saved by you, to you are due;
Command and you shall see yourself esteemed,
Our lives and liberties belong to you.
5   This twice six years with hazard of your life,
You have concealed us from the tyrant's sword;
Though cruel Herod's sister were your wife,
You durst in scorn of fear this grace afford.
In recompense we know not what to say,
10   A poor reward were thanks for such a merit,[7]
Our truest friendship at your feet we lay,
The best requital to a noble spirit.
CONSTABARUS Oh how you wrong our friendship valiant youth,
With friends there is not such a word as debt,
15   Where amity is tied with bond of truth,
All benefits are therein common set.
Then is the golden age with them renewed,
All names of properties are banished quite;[8]
Division and distinction are eschewed;
20   Each hath to what belongs to other's right.[9]
And 'tis not sure so full a benefit,
Freely to give, as freely to require;
A bounteous act hath glory following it,
They cause the glory that the act desire.
25   All friendship should the pattern imitate,
Of Jesse's son and valiant Jonathan;[1]
For neither sovereign's nor father's hate,
A friendship fixed on virtue sever can.
Too much of this, 'tis written in the heart,
30   And need no amplifying with the tongue;
Now may you from your living tomb depart,
Where Herod's life hath kept you overlong.
Too great an injury to a noble mind,
To be quick buried;[2] you had purchased fame,
35   Some years ago, but that you were confined,
While thousand meaner did advance their name.
Your best of life the prime of all your years,
Your time of action is from you bereft,
Twelve winters have you overpassed in fears;

---

7. Thanks would be a poor reward for your saving our lives.
8. All individual ownership is forbidden.
9. Each one has a right to what belongs to the other.

1. See 1 Samuel 20 for how David (Jesse's son) was saved by Jonathan (Saul's son) from death at the hands of King Saul.
2. Buried alive.

40 Yet if you use it well, enough is left.
And who can doubt but you will use it well?
The sons of Babas have it by descent;
In all their thoughts each action to excel,
Boldly to act, and wisely to invent.

SECOND SON Had it not like the hateful cuckoo been,
Whose riper age his infant nurse doth kill;[3]
So long we had not kept ourselves unseen,
But Constabarus safely crossed our will;
For had the tyrant fixed his cruel eye,
50 On our concealèd faces wrath had swayed
His justice so, that he had forced us die.
And dearer price than life we should have paid;
For you our truest friend had fallen with us,
And we much like a house on pillars set,
55 Had clean depressed our prop, and therefore thus
Our ready will with our concealment met.
But now that you, fair lord, are dangerless,
The sons of Babas shall their rigor show;
And prove it was not baseness did oppress
60 Our hearts so long, but honor kept them low.

FIRST SON Yet do I fear this tale of Herod's death,
At last will prove a very tale indeed;
It gives me strongly in my mind, his breath
Will be preserved to make a number bleed;
65 I wish not therefore to be set at large,
Yet peril to myself I do not fear;
Let us for some days longer be your charge,°   care
'Til we of Herod's state the truth do hear.

CONSTABARUS What art thou turned a coward, noble youth,
70 That thou beginn'st to doubt undoubted truth?

FIRST SON Were it my brother's tongue that cast this doubt
I from his heart would have the question out
With this keen falchion,° but 'tis you my lord   curved sword
Against whose head I must not lift a sword:
I am so tied in gratitude.

CONSTABARUS   Believe
You have no cause to take it ill,
If any word of mine your heart did grieve
The word descended from the speakers's will;
I know it was not fear the doubt begun,
80 But rather valor and your care of me,
A coward could not be your father's son,
Yet know I doubts unnecessary be;
For who can think that in Anthonius' fall,
Herod his bosom friend should 'scape unbruised.[4]
85 Then, Caesar, we might thee an idiot call,

3. The cuckoo lays its eggs in other birds' nests, and when grown the chicks kill their foster parents.
4. The victory of Octavian over Anthony and Cleopatra in the battle of Actium made it seem unlikely that Herod would remain in power.

If thou by him should'st be so far abused.
SECOND SON Lord Constabarus, let me tell you this,
  Upon submission Caesar will forgive;
  And therefore though the tyrant did amiss,
90 It may fall out that he will let him live.
  Not many years agone it is since I
  Directed thither by my father's care,
  In famous Rome for twice twelve months did live,
  My life from Hebrew's cruelty to spare,
95 There though I were but yet of boyish age,
  I bent mine eye to mark, mine ears to hear.
  Where I did see Octavius then a page,
  When first he did to Julius' sight appear;[5]
  Methought I saw such mildness in his face,
100 And such a sweetness in his looks did grow,
  Withall, commixed with so majestic grace,
  His phis'nomy his fortune did foreshow;[6]
  For this I am indebted to mine eye,
  But then mine ear received more evidence,
105 How he with hottest choler° could dispense.   *anger*
CONSTABARUS But we have more than barely heard the news,
  It hath been twice confirmed. And though some tongue
  Might be so false, with false report t'abuse,
  A false report hath never lasted long.
110 But be it so that Herod have his life,
  Concealment would not then a whit avail;
  For certain 'tis, that she that was my wife,
  Would not to set her accusation fail.
  And therefore now as good the venture give,
115 And free ourselves from blot of cowardice,
  As show a pitiful desire to live,
  For, who can pity but they must despise?
FIRST SON I yield, but to necessity I yield;
  I dare upon this doubt engage mine arm:[7]
120 That Herod shall again this kingdom wield,
  And prove his death to be a false alarm.
SECOND SON I doubt° it too. God grant it be an error,   *fear*
  'Tis best without a cause to be in terror;
  And rather had I, though my soul be mine,
125 My soul should lie, than prove a true divine.[8]
CONSTABARUS Come, come, let fear go seek a dastard's nest,
  Undaunted courage lies in noble breast.

Scene 3

[*Doris and Antipater.*]
DORIS You royal buildings bow your lofty side,

---

5. Octavius (63 B.C.–A.D. 14), Julius Caesar's great-nephew and adopted heir, later became Augustus Caesar.
6. Octavius' courteous manners and graceful appearance (physiognomy) foretold his greatness.

7. I am willing to take up arms on the suspicion that Herod is still alive and will return to power.
8. I would rather that my suspicions be found false than that I be confirmed as a prophet.

And stoop to her that is by right your queen;
Let your humility upbraid the pride
Of those in whom no due respect is seen;
5   Nine times have we with trumpets' haughty sound,
And banishing sour leaven from our taste,
Observed the feast that takes the fruit from ground.[9]
Since I, fair city, did behold thee last,
So long it is since Mariam's purer cheek
10   Did rob from mine the glory.[1] And so long
Since I returned my native town to seek,
And with me nothing but the sense of wrong,
And thee my boy, whose birth though great it were,
Yet have thy after fortunes proved but poor;
15   When thou wert born how little did I fear
Thou shouldst be thrust from forth thy father's door.
Art thou not Herod's right begotten son?
Was not the hapless Doris, Herod's wife?
Yes: ere he had the Hebrew kingdom won,
20   I was companion to his private life.
Was I not fair enough to be a queen?
Why, ere thou wert to me false monarch tied,
My lake of beauty might as well be seen,
As after I had lived five years thy bride.
25   Yet then thine oath came powering like the rain,
Which all affirmed my face without compare,
And that if thou might'st Doris love obtain,
For all the world besides thou didst not care.
Then was I young, and rich, and nobly borne,
30   And therefore worthy to be Herod's mate;
Yet thou ungrateful cast me off with scorn,
When heaven's purpose raised your meaner fate.
Oft have I begged for vengeance for this fact,°   action
And with dejected° knees, aspiring hands   bent down
35   Have prayed the highest power to enact
The fall of her that on my trophy[2] stands.
Revenge I have according to my will,
Yet where I wished this vengeance did not light.
I wished it should high-hearted Mariam kill,
40   But it against my whilom° lord did fight.   former
With thee, sweet boy, I came, and came to try
If thou before his bastards might be placed
In Herod's royal seat and dignity.
But Mariam's infants here are only graced,
45   And now for us there doth no hope remain;
Yet we will not return 'til Herod's end
Be more confirmed, perchance he is not slain.
So glorious fortunes may my boy attend,
For if he° live, he'll think it doth suffice,   Herod

9. The feast of first fruits was observed on the day after   1. It had been nine years since Herod's divorce of Doris.
Passover (the feast of unleavened bread).   2. The spoils of my defeat.

50   That he to Doris shows such cruelty;
        For as he did my wretched life despise,
        So do I know I shall despisèd die.
        Let him but prove as natural to thee,
        As cruel to thy miserable mother;
55   His cruelty shall not upbraided be
        But in thy fortunes.³ I his faults will smother.

ANTIPATER Each mouth within the city loudly cries
        That Herod's death is certain. Therefore we
        Had best some subtle hidden plot devise,
60   That Mariam's children might subverted be,
        By poisons drink, or else by murderous knife,
        So we may be advanced, it skills not° how;   *makes no difference*
        They are but bastards, you were Herod's wife,
        And foul adultery blotteth Mariam's brow.

DORIS   They are too strong to be by us removed,
        Or else revenge's foulest spotted face;
        By our detested wrongs might be approved,
        But weakness must to greater power give place.
        But let us now retire to grieve alone,
70   For solitariness best fitteth moan. [*They exit.*]

                        Scene 4

[*Silleus and Constabarus.*]

SILLEUS Well met Judean lord, the only wight°   *person*
        Silleus wished to see. I am to call
        Thy tongue to strict account.

CONSTABARUS   For what despite
5   I ready am to hear, and answer all.
        But if directly at the cause I guess
        That breeds this challenge, you must pardon me;⁴
        And now some other ground of fight profess,
        For I have vowed, vows must unbroken be.

SILLEUS What may be your exception? Let me know.⁵

CONSTABARUS Why? Aught concerning Salome, my sword
        Shall not be wielded for a cause so low,
        A blow for her my arm will scorn t'afford.

SILLEUS It is for slandering her unspotted name,⁶
        And I will make thee in thy vows despite,
15   Suck up the breath that did my mistress blame,
        And swallow it again to do her right.

CONSTABARUS I prithee give some other quarrel ground
        To find beginning, rail against my name;
        Or strike me first, or let some scarlet wound
20   Inflame my courage, give me words of shame,
        Do thou our Moses' sacred laws disgrace,

---

3. I won't criticize his cruelty except in so far as it affects
your fortunes.
4. If I am right in guessing why you want to fight me, you'll
have to excuse me from responding to your challenge.

5. "Expectation" in the 1613 text has been emended
"exception," the reason why you will not fight.
6. I challenge you because you have slandered Salome.

Deprave our nation, do me some despite;
I'm apt enough to fight in any case,
But yet for Salome I will not fight.

SILLEUS Nor I for aught but Salome. My sword
  That owes his service to her sacred name
  Will not an edge for other cause afford;
  In other fight I am not sure of fame.

CONSTABARUS For her,[7] I pity thee enough already,
30 For her, I therefore will not mangle thee;
  A woman with a heart so most unsteady,
  Will of herself sufficient torture be.
  I cannot envy for so light a gain,
  Her mind with such inconstancy doth run;
35 As with a word thou didst her love obtain,
  So with a word she will from thee be won.
  So light as her possessions for most day
  Is her affections lost, to me 'tis known;[8]
  As good go hold the wind as make her stay,
40 She never loves, but 'til she call her own.[9]
  She merely is a painted sepulcher,[1]
  That is both fair, and vilely foul at once;
  Though on her outside graces garnish her,
  Her mind is filled with worse than rotten bones.
45 And ever ready lifted is her hand,
  To aim destruction at a husband's throat;
  For proofs, Josephus and myself do stand,
  Though once on both of us she seemed to dote.
  Her mouth though serpentlike it never hisses,
50 Yet like a serpent, poisons where it kisses.

SILLEUS Well Hebrew well, thou bark'st, but wilt not bite.

CONSTABARUS I tell thee still for her I will not fight.

SILLEUS Why then I call thee coward.

CONSTABARUS   From my heart
  I give thee thanks. A coward's hateful name,
55 Cannot to valiant minds a blot impart,
  And therefore I with joy receive the same.
  Thou know'st I am no coward. Thou wert by
  At the Arabian battle th'other day,
  And saw'st my sword with daring valiancy
60 Amongst the faint Arabians cut my way.
  The blood of foes no more could let it shine,
  And 'twas enamelèd with some of thine.
  But now have at thee;[2] not for Salome
  I fight, but to discharge a coward's style;°   name
65 Here 'gins the fight that shall not parted be,
  Before a soul or two endure exile. [*They fight.*]

---

7. Because of her.
8. You value her affection so little when you have it that
it is a light loss when you lose it.
9. She loves only up to the point when she gets what

she wants.
1. See Matthew 23.27: "Woe unto you, scribes and Pharisees, hypocrites! for ye are like unto whited sepulchres."
2. I'll fight you.

SILLEUS Thy sword hath made some windows for my blood,
　　　To show a horrid crimson phis'nomy;° *face*
　　　To breathe° for both of us methinks 'twere good, *catch breath*
70　　The day will give us time enough to die.
CONSTABARUS With all my heart take breath, thou shalt have time,
　　　And if thou list° a twelve month: let us end; *wish*
　　　Into thy cheeks there doth a paleness climb,
　　　Thou canst not from my sword thyself defend.
75　　What needest thou for Salome to fight?
　　　Thou hast her, and may'st keep her, none strives for her;
　　　I willingly to thee resign my right,
　　　For in my very soul I do abhor her.
　　　Thou seest that I am fresh, unwounded yet,
80　　Then not for fear I do this offer make;
　　　Thou art with loss of blood, to fight unfit.
　　　For here is one, and there another take.[3]
SILLEUS I will not leave, as long as breath remains
　　　Within my wounded body. Spare your words,
85　　My heart in blood's stead, courage entertains,
　　　Salome's love no place for fear affords.
CONSTABARUS Oh, could thy soul but prophesy like mine,
　　　I would not wonder thou should'st long to die;
　　　For Salome, if I aright divine,
90　　Will be than death a greater misery.
SILLEUS Then list, I'll breathe no longer.[4]
CONSTABARUS 　　　　　　　　　　Do thy will,
　　　I hateless fight, and charitably kill. [*They fight.*] Aye, aye,
　　　Pity thyself Silleus, let not death
　　　Intrude before his time into thy heart;
95　　Alas it is too late to fear, his breath
　　　Is from his body now about to part.
　　　How farest thou brave Arabian?
SILLEUS 　　　　　　　　　　　　Very well,
　　　My leg is hurt, I can no longer fight;
　　　It only grieves me, that so soon I fell,
100　Before fair Salom's wrongs[5] I came to right.
CONSTABARUS Thy wounds are less than mortal. Never fear,
　　　Thou shalt a safe and quick recovery find;
　　　Come, I will thee unto my lodging bear,
　　　I hate thy body, but I love thy mind.
SILLEUS Thanks, noble Jew, I see a courteous foe,
　　　Stern enmity to friendship can no art;[6]
　　　Had not my heart and tongue engaged me so,
　　　I would from thee no foe, but friend depart.
　　　My heart to Salome is tied too fast
110　To leave her love for friendship, yet my skill
　　　Shall be employed to make your favor last,

---

3. In this fight, each of us gives and takes.　　　　5. The wrong done to Salome.
4. Then listen, I won't pause or live any longer.　　6. Enmity doesn't know a way to friendship.

And I will honor Constabarus still.

CONSTABARUS I ope my bosom to thee, and will take
Thee in, as friend, and grieve for thy complaint;

115 But if we do not expedition make,
Thy loss of blood I fear will make thee faint.   [*They exit.*]

CHORUS To hear a tale with ears prejudicate,°   *prejudiced*
It spoils the judgment and corrupts the sense;
That human error given to every state,

120 Is greater enemy to innocence.[7]
It makes us foolish, heady, rash, unjust,
It makes us never try before we trust.[8]

It will confound the meaning, change the words,
For it our sense of hearing much deceives;

125 Besides no time to judgment it affords,
To weigh the circumstance our ear receives.
The ground of accidents[9] it never tries,
But makes us take for truth ten thousand lies.

Our ears and hearts are apt to hold for good,

130 That we ourselves do most desire to be;
And then we drown objections in the flood
Of partiality, 'tis that[1] we see
That makes false rumors long with credit passed,
Though they like rumors must conclude at last.

135 The greatest part of us prejudicate,°   *judge too soon*
With wishing Herod's death do hold it true;
The being once deluded doth not bate,°   *lessen*
The credit to a better likelihood due.[2]
Those few that wish it not, the multitude

140 Do carry headlong, so they doubts conclude.[3]

They° not object the weak uncertain ground,   *the few*
Whereon they built this tale of Herod's end;
Whereof the author scarcely can be found,
And all because their wishes that way bend.

145 They think not of the peril that ensu'th,°   *comes about*
If this should prove the contrary to truth.

On this same doubt, on this so light a breath,
They pawn their lives and fortunes. For they all
Behave them as the news of Herod's death,

150 They did of most undoubted credit call;
But if their actions now do rightly hit,°   *succeed*
Let them commend their fortune, not their wit.

---

7. The naive are more vulnerable to human error.
8. It makes us jump to conclusions before we test them.
9. Basis or cause of appearances.
1. I.e., partiality.
2. Having been once deceived before about Herod's

death doesn't lessen the belief that it might be true this
time.
3. Those who do not wish for Herod's death are swayed
by the majority and so stop doubting.

Act 3

Scene 1

[*Pheroras, Salome.*]

PHERORAS Urge me no more Graphina to forsake,
    Not twelve hours since I married her for love;
    And do you think a sister's power can make
    A resolute decree, so soon remove?
SALOME Poor minds they are that honor not affects.
PHERORAS Who hunts for honor, happiness neglects.
SALOME You might have been both of felicity,
    And honor too in equal measure seized.
PHERORAS It is not you can tell so well as I,
10   What 'tis can make me happy, or displeased.
SALOME To match for neither beauty nor respects
    One mean of birth, but yet of meaner mind,
    A woman full of natural defects,
    I wonder what your eye in her could find.
PHERORAS Mine eye found loveliness, mine ear found wit,
    To please the one, and to enchant the other;
    Grace on her eye, mirth on her tongue doth sit,
    In looks a child, in wisdom's house a mother.
SALOME But say you thought her fair, as none thinks else;
20   Knows not Pheroras, beauty is a blast;[4]
    Much like this flower which today excels,
    But longer than a day it will not last.
PHERORAS Her wit exceeds her beauty.
SALOME   Wit may show
    The way to ill as well as good you know.
PHERORAS But wisdom is the porter of her head,
    And bars all wicked words from issuing thence.
SALOME But of a porter, better were you sped,°   *provided*
    If she against their entrance made defense.[5]
PHERORAS But wherefore comes the sacred Ananell,[6]
30   That hitherward his hasty steps doth bend?
    Great sacrificer y'are arrived well,
    Ill news from holy mouth I not attend.°   *expect*

Scene 2

[*Pheroras, Salome, Ananell.*]

ANANELL My lips, my son, with peaceful tidings bless'd,
    Shall utter honey to your list'ning ear;
    A word of death comes not from priestly breast,
    I speak of life: in life there is no fear.
5   And for the news I did the Heavens salute,
    And filled the temple with my thankful voice;

---

4. A brief gust of wind.
5. See *Othello*, 3.3.136–41, page 1219.
6. Herod first had made Ananelus high priest, but then,
he gave the position to Mariam's brother Aristobolus.
After a year, jealous of Aristobolus' popularity, Herod
had him killed and made Ananelus high priest again.

For though that mourning may not me pollute,[7]
    At pleasing accidents I may rejoice.
PHERORAS Is Herod then revived from certain death?
SALOME What? Can your news restore my brother's breath?
ANANELL Both so, and so, the king is safe and sound,
    And did such grace in royal Caesar meet;
    That he with larger style than ever crowned,
    Within this hour Jerusalem will greet.
15   I did but come to tell you, and must back
    To make preparatives for sacrifice;
    I knew his death, your hearts like mine did rack,
    Though to conceal it, proved you wise. [*Exit.*]
SALOME How can my joy sufficiently appear?
PHERORAS A heavier tale did never pierce mine ear.
SALOME Now Salome of happiness may boast.
PHERORAS But now Pheroras is in danger most.
SALOME I shall enjoy the comfort of my life.
PHERORAS And I shall lose it, losing of my wife.
SALOME Joy heart, for Constabarus shall be slain.
PHERORAS Grieve soul, Graphina shall from me be ta'en.
SALOME Smile, cheeks, the fair Silleus shall be mine.
PHERORAS Weep, eyes, for I must with a child combine.
SALOME Well, brother, cease your moans, on one condition
30   I'll undertake to win the King's consent;
    Graphina still shall be in your tuition,°   *care*
    And her with you be ne'er the less content.
PHERORAS What's the condition? Let me quickly know,
    That I as quickly your command may act;
35   Were it to see what herbs in Ophir grow,
    Or that the lofty Tyrus might be sacked.[8]
SALOME 'Tis not so hard a task; it is no more,
    But tell the king that Constabarus hid
    The sons of Babas, done to death before;[9]
40   And 'tis no more than Constabarus did.
    And tell him more that he for Herod's sake,
    Not able to endure his brother's foe,
    Did with a bill our separation make,
    Though loath from Constabarus else to go.
PHERORAS Believe this tale for told, I'll go from hence,
    In Herod's ear the Hebrew to deface;
    And I that never studied eloquence,
    Do mean with eloquence this tale to grace. [*Exit.*]
SALOME This will be Constabarus' quick dispatch,
50   Which from my mouth would lesser credit find;
    Yet shall he not decease without a match,
    For Mariam shall not linger long behind.
    First, jealousy, if that avail not, fear

---

7. Priests had to avoid ritually defiling contact with corpses in mourning rites (Leviticus 21.1–2).
8. Ophir, on the west coast of Arabia or India, was a source of gold. Tyre, on the coast of Lebanon, was the greatest city of ancient Phoenicia.
9. Assumed to have been put to death.

Shall be my minister to work her end.
55   A common error moves not Herod's ear,
Which doth so firmly to his Mariam bend.
She shall be charged with so horrid crime,
As Herod's fear shall turn his love to hate;
I'll make some swear that she desires to climb,
60   And seeks to poison him for his estate.°   *royal position*
I scorn that she should love my birth t'upbraid,
To call me base and hungry Edomite;
With patient show her choler I betrayed,[1]
And watched the time to be revenged by slight.
65   Now tongue of mine with scandal load her name,
Turn hers to fountains, Herod's eyes to flame;
Yet first I will begin Pheroras' suit,
That he my earnest business may effect;
And I of Mariam will keep me mute,
70   'Till first some other doth her name detect.°   *accuse*
Who's there, Silleus' man? How fares your lord
That your aspects do bear the badge of sorrow?
SILLEUS' MAN He hath the marks of Constabarus' sword,
And for a while desires you sight to borrow.
SALOME My heavy curse the hateful sword pursue;
My heavier curse on the more hateful arm
That wounded my Silleus. But renew
Your tale again. Hath he no mortal harm?
SILLEUS' MAN No sign of danger doth in him appear,
80   Nor are his wounds in place of peril seen;
He bids you be assured you need not fear,
He hopes to make you yet Arabia's queen.
SALOME Commend my heart to be Silleus' charge.
Tell him my brother's sudden coming now
85   Will give my foot no room to walk at large,
But I will see him yet ere night I vow.

Scene 3

[*Mariam and Sohemus.*]
MARIAM Sohemus, tell me what the news may be
That makes your eyes so full, your cheeks so blue?
SOHEMUS I know not how to call them. Ill for me
'Tis sure they are; not so, I hope, for you.
Herod—
MARIAM   Oh what of Herod?
SOHEMUS   Herod lives.
MARIAM How! Lives? What, in some cave or forest hid?
SOHEMUS Nay, back returned with honor. Caesar gives
Him greater grace than ere Anthonius did.
MARIAM Foretell the ruin of my family,
Tell me that I shall see our city burned,

---

1. By pretending patience, I provoked her to anger.

10   Tell me I shall a death disgraceful die,
        But tell me not that Herod is returned.
SOHEMUS Be not impatient madam, be but mild,
        His love to you again will soon be bred.
MARIAM I will not to his love be reconciled,
15   With solemn vows I have forsworn his bed.
SOHEMUS But you must break those vows.
MARIAM   I'll rather break
        The heart of Mariam. Cursed is my fate.
        But speak no more to me, in vain ye speak°   tell me
        To live with him I so profoundly hate.
SOHEMUS Great Queen, you must to me your pardon give,
        Sohemus cannot now your will obey;
        If your command should me to silence drive,
        It were not to obey, but to betray.
        Reject and slight my speeches, mock my faith,
25   Scorn my observance, call my counsel nought
        Though you regard not what Sohemus saith,
        Yet will I ever freely speak my thought.
        I fear ere long I shall fair Mariam see
        In woeful state and by herself undone;
30   Yet for your issue's sake more temp'rate be,
        The heart by affability is won.
MARIAM And must I to my prison turn again?
        Oh, now I see I was an hypocrite;
        I did this morning for his death complain,
35   And yet do mourn, because he lives ere night.
        When I his death believed, compassion wrought,
        And was the stickler° 'twixt my heart and him;   mediator
        But now that curtain's drawn from off my thought,
        Hate doth appear again with visage grim,
40   And paints the face of Herod in my heart,
        In horrid colors with detested look.
        Then fear would come, but scorn doth play her part,
        And saith that scorn with fear can never brook.°   put up with
        I know I could enchain him with a smile,
45   And lead him captive with a gentle word;
        I scorn my look should ever man beguile,
        Or other speech, than meaning° to afford.   what I mean
        Else Salome in vain might spend her wind,
        In vain might Herod's mother whet her tongue,
50   In vain had they complotted and combined,
        For I could overthrow them all ere long.
        Oh what a shelter is mine innocence,
        To shield me from the pangs of inward grief,
        'Gainst all mishaps it is my fair defense,
55   And to my sorrows yields a large relief.
        To be commandress of the triple earth,
        And sit in safety from a fall secure:
        To have all nations celebrate my birth,
        I would not that my spirit were impure.

60   Let my distressed state unpitied be,
         Mine innocence is hope enough for me. [*Exit.*]
SOHEMUS Poor guiltless Queen. Oh that my wish might place
         A little temper° now about thy heart;   *moderation*
         Unbridled speech is Mariam's worst disgrace,
65   And will endanger her without desert.[2]
         I am in greater hazard. O'er my head,
         The fatal ax doth hang unsteadily;
         My disobedience once discovered
         Will shake it down: Sohemus so shall die.
70   For when the king shall find we thought his death
         Had been as certain as we see his life,
         And marks withall I slighted so his breath,°   *order*
         As to preserve alive his matchless wife.
         Nay more, to give to Alexander's hand[3]
75   The regal dignity. The sovereign power,
         How I had yielded up at her command
         The strength of all the city, David's Tower.
         What more than common death may I expect,
         Since I too well do know his cruelty?
80   'Twere death, a word of Herod's to neglect,
         What then to do directly contrary?
         Yet life I quit thee with a willing spirit,
         And think thou could'st not better be employed;
         I forfeit thee for her that more doth merit,
85   Ten such° were better dead than she destroyed.   *such as I*
         But fare thee well chaste Queen, well may I see
         The darkness palpable and rivers part,
         The sun stand still, nay more, retorted° be,   *turned backward*
         But never woman with so pure a heart.
90   Thine eyes' grave majesty keeps all in awe,
         And cuts the wings of every loose desire;
         Thy brow is table° to the modest law,   *tablet*
         Yet though we dare not love, we may admire.
         And if I die, it shall my soul content,
95   My breath in Mariam's service shall be spent.

CHORUS 'Tis not enough for one that is a wife
         To keep her spotless from an act of ill;
         But from suspicion she should free her life,[4]
         And bare herself of power as well as will.
100   'Tis not so glorious for her to be free,
         As by her proper° self restrained to be.   *own*

         When she hath spacious ground to walk upon,
         Why on the ridge should she desire to go?
         It is no glory to forebear alone°   *only*
105   Those things that may her honor overthrow.

---

2. Without her deserving it.
3. To Mariam's son.

4. Conduct books for women stressed that they should be pure not only in deed but also in reputation.

But 'tis thank-worthy, if she will not take
All lawful liberties for honor's sake.

That wife her hand against her fame doth rear,
That more than to her lord alone will give
110 A private word to any second ear,
And though she may with reputation live,
Yet though most chaste, she doth her glory blot,
And wounds her honor, though she kills it not.

When to their husbands they themselves do bind,
115 Do they not wholly give themselves away?
Or give they but their body not their mind,
Reserving that though best, for other's prey?
No sure, their thoughts no more can be their own,
And therefore should to none but one be known.

120 Then she usurps upon another's right,
That seeks to be by public language graced;
And though her thoughts reflect with purest light,
Her mind if not peculiar° is not chaste.   *kept private*
For in a wife it is no worse to find,
125 A common° body, than a common mind.   *shared, public*

And every mind though free from thought of ill,
That out of glory⁵ seeks a worth to show;
When any's ears but one therewith they fill,
Doth in a sort her pureness overthrow.
130 Now Mariam had (but that to this she bent)⁶
Been free from fear, as well as innocent.

Act 4

Scene 1

[Enter Herod and his attendants.]

HEROD Hail happy city, happy in thy store,°   *abundance*
And happy that thy buildings such we see;
More happy in the temple where w'adore,
But most of all that Mariam loves in thee. *[Enter Nuntio.]*
5   Art thou returned? How fares my Mariam? How?⁷
NUNTIO She's well my Lord, and will anon be here
As you commanded.
HEROD   Muffle up thy brow,
Thou day's dark taper.⁸ Mariam will appear.
And where she shines, we need not thy dim light.
10   Oh haste thy steps rare creature, speed thy pace,
And let thy presence make the day more bright,
And cheer the heart of Herod with thy face.

---

5. Out of a desire for glory.
6. Except that she wanted to speak about herself to more than one person.
7. Modern editors have added "How?" to correct the rhyme scheme.
8. Candle, "day's dark taper," as a metaphor for the sun.

It is an age since I from Mariam went,
Methinks our parting was in David's days;[9]
15   The hours are so increased by discontent,
Deep sorrow, Joshua-like the season stays;[1]
But when I am with Mariam, time runs on,
Her sight can make months minutes, days of weeks;
An hour is then no sooner come than gone,
20   When in her face mine eye for wonders seeks.
You world-commanding city, Europe's grace,
Twice hath my curious eye your streets surveyed,
And I have seen the statue-fillèd place,
That once if not for grief had been betrayed.
25   I all your Roman beauties have beheld,
And seen the shows your ediles° did prepare,   *Roman magistrates*
I saw the sum of what in you excelled,
Yet saw no miracle like Mariam rare.
The fair and famous Livia,[2] Caesar's love,
30   The world's commanding mistress did I see,
Whose beauties both the world and Rome approve,
Yet Mariam, Livia is not like to thee.
Be patient but a little, while mine eyes
Within your compassed limits be contained;
35   That object straight shall your desires suffice,
From which you were so long a while restrained.
How wisely Mariam doth the time delay,
Least sudden joy my sense should suffocate;
I am prepared, thou needst no longer stay.
40   Who's there, my Mariam, more than happy fate?
Oh no, it is Pheroras, welcome brother,
Now for a while, I must my passion smother.

Scene 2

[*Herod, Pheroras.*]

PHERORAS All health and safety wait upon my Lord,
And may you long in prosperous fortunes live
With Rome-commanding Caesar at accord,
And have all honors that the world can give.
HEROD Oh brother, now thou speakst not from thy heart;
No, thou hast struck a blow at Herod's love
That cannot quickly from my memory part,
Though Salome did me to pardon move.
Valiant Phasaelus,[3] now to thee farewell,
10   Thou wert my kind and honorable brother;
Oh hapless hour, when you self-stricken fell,
Thou father's image, glory of thy mother.
Had I desired a greater suit of thee

---

9. A thousand years before.
1. Joshua ordered the sun to keep shining so the Israelites could finish a battle (Joshua 10.12–14).
2. Wife of the Emperor Augustus.

3. Herod's brother Phasaelus killed himself to escape the disgrace of being executed by his enemies, who captured him in the war against Herod's rival, Antigonus.

Than to withhold thee from a harlot's bed,
15   Thou shouldst have granted it; but now I see
All are not like that in a womb are bred.
Thou wouldst not, hadst thou heard of Herod's death,
Have made his burial time, thy bridal hour;
Thou wouldst with clamors, not with joyful breath,
20   Have showed the news to be not sweet but sour.

PHERORAS Phasaelus' great worth I know did stain
Pheroras' petty valor; but they lie
(Excepting you yourself) that dare maintain
That he did honor Herod more than I.
25   For what I showed, love's power constrained me show,
And pardon loving faults[4] for Mariam's sake.

HEROD Mariam, where is she?

PHERORAS   Nay, I do not know,
But absent use of her fair name I make;
You have forgiven greater faults than this,
30   For Constabarus that against your will
Preserved the sons of Baba, lives in bliss,
Though you commanded him the youths to kill.

HEROD Go, take a present order for his death,
And let those traitors feel the worst of fears;
35   Now Salome will whine to beg his breath,
But I'll be deaf to prayers and blind to tears.

PHERORAS He is my lord from Salome divorced,
Though her affection did to leave him grieve;
Yet was she by her love to you enforced
40   To leave the man that would your foes relieve.

HEROD Then haste them to their death. I will requite
Thee gentle Mariam—Salome, I mean—
The thought of Mariam doth so steal my spirit,
My mouth from speech of her I cannot wean. [Exit.]

Scene 3

[Herod, Mariam.]

HEROD And here she comes indeed. Happily met
My best and dearest half. What ails my dear?
Thou doest the difference certainly forget
'Twixt dusky habits and a time so clear.[5]

MARIAM My lord, I suit my garment to my mind,
And there no cheerful colors can I find.

HEROD Is this my welcome? Have I longed so much
To see my dearest Mariam discontent?
What is't that is the cause thy heart to touch?
10   Oh speak, that I thy sorrow may prevent.
Art thou not Jewry's queen and Herod's too?
Be my commandress, be my sovereign guide;

4. Errors motivated by love.

5. You have forgotten how inappropriate dark clothes are for such a bright and joyful day.

To be by thee directed I will woo,
For in thy pleasure lies my highest pride.

15 Or if thou think Judea's narrow bound
Too strict a limit for thy great command,
Thou shalt be Empress of Arabia crowned,
For thou shalt rule, and I will win the land.
I'll rob the holy David's sepulcher

20 To give thee wealth, if thou for wealth do care;
Thou shalt have all they did with him inter,
And I for thee will make the temple bare.

MARIAM I neither have of power nor riches want,
I have enough, nor do I wish for more;

25 Your offers to my heart no ease can grant,
Except they could my brother's life restore.
No, had you wished the wretched Mariam glad,
Or had your love to her been truly tied,
Nay, had you not desired to make her sad,

30 My brother nor my grandsire had not died.

HEROD Wilt thou believe no oaths to clear thy lord?
How oft have I with execration° sworn   *curses*
Thou art by me beloved, by me adored;
Yet are my protestations heard with scorn.

35 Hircanus plotted to deprive my head
Of this long-settled honor that I wear.
And therefore I did justly doom him dead,
To rid the realm from peril, me from fear.
Yet I for Mariam's sake do so repent

40 The death of one whose blood she did inherit;
I wish I had a kingdom's treasure spent,
So I had ne'er expelled Hircanus' spirit.
As I affected that same noble youth,[6]
In lasting infamy my name enroll,

45 If I not mourned his death with hearty truth.
Did I not show to him my earnest love,
When I to him the priesthood did restore?
And did for him a living priest remove,
Which never had been done but once before.

MARIAM I know that moved by importunity,
You made him priest, and shortly after die.

HEROD I will not speak, unless to be believed,
This froward° humor will not do you good;   *perverse*
It hath too much already Herod grieved,

55 To think that you on terms of hate have stood.
Yet smile my dearest Mariam, do but smile,
And I will all unkind conceits° exile.   *thoughts*

MARIAM I cannot frame disguise, nor never taught
My face a look dissenting from my thought.

HEROD By heaven, you vex me, build not on my love.

---

6. Since I was fond of Aristobolus ("that same noble youth"), Mariam's young brother, whom Herod had murdered. There may be a missing line just before this one, since the rhyme scheme is interrupted here.

MARIAM I will not build on so unstable ground.
HEROD Nought is so fixed, but peevishness may move.
MARIAM 'Tis better slightest cause than none were found.
HEROD Be judge yourself, if ever Herod sought
65   Or would be moved a cause of change to find;
     Yet let your look declare a milder thought,
     My heart again you shall to Mariam bind.
     How oft did I for you my mother chide,
     Revile my sister, and my brother 'rate,°   *berate*
70   And tell them all my Mariam they belied,°   *told lies about*
     Distrust me still, if these be signs of hate.

Scene 4

[Enter Butler.]
HEROD What hast thou here?
BUTLER   A drink procuring love
     The queen desired me to deliver it.
MARIAM Did I? Some hateful practice° this will prove,   *intrigue*
     Yet can it be no worse than heaven's permit.
HEROD *[To the Butler.]* Confess the truth thou wicked instrument
     To her outrageous will, 'tis poison sure;[7]
     Tell true, and thou shalt 'scape the punishment,
     Which, if thou do conceal, thou shalt endure.
BUTLER I know not, but I doubt it be no less,
10   Long since the hate of you her heart did seize.
HEROD Know'st thou the cause thereof?
BUTLER   My Lord I guess
     Sohemus told the tale that did displease.
HEROD Oh heaven! Sohemus false! Go let him die,
     Stay not to suffer him to speak a word;
15   Oh damned villain, did he falsify
     The oath he swore ev'n of his own accord?
     Now did I know thy falsehood, painted devil,
     Thou white enchantress.[8] Oh thou art so foul
     That hyssop[9] cannot cleanse thee, worst of evil.
20   A beauteous body hides a loathsome soul,
     Your love Sohemus moved by his affection,
     Though he have ever heretofore been true
     Did blab forsooth, that I did give direction,
     If we were put to death to slaughter you.
25   And you in black revenge attended° now   *waited*
     To add a murther to your breach of vow.
MARIAM Is this a dream?
HEROD   Oh heaven, that 'twere no more
     I'll give my realm to who can prove it so;
     I would I were like any beggar poor,

---

7. The text reads "passion," but editors have emended this to "poison" to make sense of the plot and to follow Cary's source, Josephus's *Antiquities*.
8. "White," appearing to be good, with a possible allusion to the Renaissance notion of a "white devil," a hypocritical woman.
9. An herb used to treat lepers.

30 So I for false my Mariam did not know.
    Foul pith contained in the fairest rind,
    That ever graced a cedar. Oh thine eye
    Is pure as heaven, but impure thy mind,
    And for impurity shall Mariam die.
35 Why didst thou love Sohemus?
MARIAM   They can tell
    That say I loved him, Mariam says not so.
HEROD Oh cannot impudence the coals expel,
    That for thy love in Herod's bosom glow?
    It is as plain as water, and denial
40 Makes of thy falsehood but a greater trial.
    Hast thou beheld thyself, and couldst thou stain
    So rare perfection. Even for love of thee
    I do profoundly hate thee. Wert thou plain,
    Thou shouldst the wonder of Judea be.
45 But oh thou art not. Hell itself lies hid
    Beneath thy heavenly show. Yet never wert thou chaste;
    Thou might'st exalt, pull down, command, forbid,
    And be above the wheel of fortune placed.[1]
    Hadst thou complotted Herod's massacre,
50 That so thy son a monarch might be styled,
    Not half so grievous such an action were,
    As once to think, that Mariam is defiled.
    Bright workmanship of nature sullied o'er,
    With pitched darkness now thine end shall be.
55 Thou shalt not live fair fiend to cozen° more,   trick
    With heavy[2] semblance, as thou cozenest me.
    Yet must I love thee in despite of death,
    And thou shalt die in the despite of love;
    For neither shall my love prolong thy breath,
60 Nor shall thy loss of breath my love remove.
    I might have seen thy falsehood in thy face,
    Where couldst thou get thy stars that served for eyes?
    Except by theft, and theft is foul disgrace.
    This had appeared before were Herod wise,
65 But I'm a sot,° a very sot, no better;   fool
    My wisdom long ago a-wandering fell,
    Thy face encountering it, my wit did fetter,
    And made me for delight my freedom sell.
    Give me my heart, false creature, 'tis a wrong,
70 My guiltless heart should now with thine be slain;
    Thou hadst no right to lock it up so long,
    And with usurper's name I Mariam stain.
    [Enter Butler.]
HEROD Have you designed Sohemus to his end?
BUTLER I have my Lord.
HEROD   Then call our royal guard
75 To do as much for Mariam. [Exit Butler.] They offend

---

1. Free from reversals of fortune.   2. Perhaps an error for "heavenly."

Leave[3] ill unblamed, or good without reward. [*Enter soldiers.*]
Here, take her to her death. Come back, come back,
What meant I to deprive the world of light;
To muffle Jewry in the foulest black,
80   That ever was an opposite to white?
Why whither would you carry her?

SOLDIER   You bade
We should conduct her to her death my Lord.

HEROD Why, sure I did not, Herod was not mad.
Why should she feel the fury of the sword?
85   Oh now the grief returns into my heart,
And pulls me piecemeal. Love and hate do fight,
And now hath love acquired the greater part,
Yet now hath hate affection conquered quite.
And therefore bear her hence: and, Hebrew, why
90   Seize you with lion's paws the fairest lamb
Of all the flock? She must not, shall not, die.
Without her I most miserable am.
And with her more than most. Away, away,
But bear her but to prison not to death;
95   And is she gone indeed? Stay, villains, stay,
Her looks alone preserved your sovereign's breath.
Well, let her go, but yet she shall not die;
I cannot think she meant to poison me;
But certain 'tis she lived too wantonly,
100   And therefore shall she never more be free. [*They exit.*]

Scene 5

BUTLER Foul villain, can thy pitchy-colored soul
Permit thine ear to hear her causeless doom?°   fate
And not enforce thy tongue that tale control,[4]
That must unjustly bring her to her tomb?
5   Oh Salome thou hast thyself repaid
For all the benefits that thou hast done;
Thou art the cause I have the queen betrayed,
Thou hast my heart to darkest falsehood won.
I am condemned, Heav'n gave me not my tongue
10   To slander innocents, to lie, deceive,
To be that hateful instrument to wrong,
The earth of greatest glory to bereave.
My sin ascends and doth to Heav'n cry,
It is the blackest deed that ever was,
15   And there doth fit an angel notary,
That doth record it down in leaves of brass.
Oh how my heart doth quake. Achitophel,
Thou founds° a means thyself from shame to free;[5]   foundest

3. Who leave.
4. And not compel your tongue to hold back the tale.
5. When King David's son Absalom rebelled against his father, his counselor Achitophel urged a decisive quick

strike. Absalom rejected this advice; knowing their cause would be doomed by delay, Achitophel went home and hanged himself.

20 And sure my soul approves° thou didst not well,   *judges*
    All follow some, and I will follow thee. [*He exits.*]

Scene 6

[*Constabarus, Babas' sons, and their guard.*]

CONSTABARUS Now here we step our last, the way to death;
    We must not tread this way a second time;
    Yet let us resolutely yield our breath,
    Death is the only ladder, heaven to climb.

FIRST SON With willing mind I could myself resign,
    But yet it grieves me with a grief untold;
    Our death should be accompanied with thine,
    Our friendship we to thee have dearly sold.

CONSTABARUS Still wilt thou wrong the sacred name of friend?
10   Then shouldst thou never style it friendship more,
    But base mechanic traffic[6] that doth lend;
    Yet will be sure they shall the debt restore.
    I could with needless complement return,
    'Tis for thy ceremony I could say;
15   'Tis I that made the fire your house to burn,
    For but for me she would not you betray.
    Had not the damned woman sought mine end,
    You had not been the subject of her hate.
    You never did her hateful mind offend,
20   Nor could your deaths have freed her nuptial fate.
    Therefore fair friends, though you were still unborn,
    Some other subtlety devised should be,
    Whereby my life, though guiltless should be torn;
    Thus have I proved, 'tis you that die for me,
25   And therefore should I weakly now lament,
    You have but done your duties; friends should die
    Alone their friends' disaster to prevent,[7]
    Though not compelled by strong necessity.
    But now farewell, fair city, never more
30   Shall I behold your beauty shining bright;
    Farewell, of Jewish men the worthy store,
    But no farewell to any female wight.°   *creature*
    You wavering crew: my curse to you I leave,
    You had but one to give you any grace;
35   And you yourselves will Mariam's life bereave,
    Your commonwealth doth innocency chase.°   *drive out*
    You creatures made to be the human curse,
    You tigers, lionesses, hungry bears,
    Tear massacring hyenas:[8] nay far worse,
40   For they for prey do shed their feigned tears.
    But you will weep, (you creatures cross° to good)   *opposed*

---

6. Base business; "mechanics" are manual laborers, "traffic" is the exchange of goods or services.
7. Friends should be willing to die to save their friends' lives.

8. Hyenas were said to pretend to weep over their victims as they tore them to shreds. (See Pliny, *Natural History*, 8.44).

For your unquenchèd thirst of human blood;
You were the angels cast from Heav'n for pride,
And still do keep your angel's outward show,
45   But none of you are inly° beautified,   *inwardly*
For still your heaven-depriving pride doth grow.
Did not the sins of man[9] require a scourge,
Your place on earth had been by this withstood;[1]
But since a flood no more the world must purge,
50   You stayed in office of a second flood.[2]
You giddy creatures, sowers of debate,
You'll love today, and for no other cause,
But for you yesterday did deeply hate,
You are the wreck of order, breach of laws.
55   Your best are foolish, froward,° wanton, vain,   *perverse*
Your worst adulterous, murderous, cunning, proud;[3]
And Salome attends° the latter train,°   *follows/set*
Or rather she their leader is allowed.
I do the sottishness° of men bewail,   *foolishness*
60   That do with following you enhance your pride;
'Twere better that the human race should fail,
Than be by such a mischief multiplied.
Cham's servile curse to all your sex was given,
Because in Paradise you did offend;[4]
65   Then do we not resift the will of Heaven,
When on your wills like servants we attend?
You are to nothing constant but to ill,
You are with nought but wickedness indued,°   *endowed*
Your loves are set on nothing but your will,
70   And thus my censure I of you conclude.
You are the least of goods, the worst of evils,
Your best are worse than men; your worst than devils.
SECOND SON Come, let us to our death: are we not bless'd?
Our death will freedom from these creatures give;
75   Those trouble-quiet° sowers of unrest,   *peace-disturbing*
And this I vow that had I leave to live,
I would for ever lead a single life,
And never venture° on a devilish wife.   *take a risk*

Scene 7

[*Herod and Salome.*]
HEROD Nay, she shall die. Die quoth you? That she shall.
But for the means. The means! Methinks 'tis hard

---

9. The text reads "many," but as Weller and Ferguson point out, both the meter and the meaning of the line call for the emendation to "man."
1. By this time denied.
2. As God promised never to send another worldwide flood, women had to perform the function of "scourge" to mankind.
3. For the tradition of misogyny such as this, see the work of Joseph Swetnam in Perspectives: Tracts on Women and Gender, pages 1335–1338.
4. A combination of the pain of childbirth, the curse upon Eve after the fall (Genesis 3), with slavery, the curse upon Canaan (the son of Cham or Ham) after Ham brought his brothers to see their father Noah's nakedness. (Genesis 9).

To find a means to murther her withall,
Therefore I am resolved she shall be spared.

SALOME Why? Let her be beheaded.

HEROD   That were well,
Think you that swords are miracles like you?
Her skin will ev'ry curtlax° edge refell,°   *heavy sword/repel*
And then your enterprise you well may rue.
What if the fierce Arabian notice take
10   Of this your wretched weaponless estate;
They⁵ answer when we bid resistance make,
That Mariam's skin their falchions° did rebate.°   *broadswords/blunt*
Beware of this, you make a goodly hand,
If you of weapons do deprive our land.

SALOME Why, drown her then.

HEROD   Indeed, a sweet device,
Why? Would not ev'ry river turn her course
Rather than do her beauty prejudice?°   *harm*
And be reverted° to the proper source?   *driven back*
So not a drop of water should be found
20   In all Judea's quondam° fertile ground.   *once*

SALOME Then let the fire devour her.

HEROD   'Twill not be;
Flame is from her derived° into my heart;   *drawn off*
Thou nursest flame, flame will not murther thee,
My fairest Mariam, fullest of desert.

SALOME Then let her live for me.⁶

HEROD   Nay, she shall die.
But can you live without her?

SALOME   Doubt you that?

HEROD I'm sure I cannot; I beseech you try;
I have experience but I know not what.⁷

SALOME How should I try?

HEROD   Why, let my love be slain,
30   But if we cannot live without her sight
You'll find the means to make her breathe again,
Or else you will bereave my comfort quite.

SALOME Oh I, I warrant° you. [Exit.]   *assure*

HEROD   What is she gone?
35   And gone to bid the world be overthrown?
What? Is her heart's composure hardest stone?
To what a pass are cruel women grown? [Re-enter Salome.]
She is returned already: have you done?
Is't possible you can command so soon
40   A creature's heart to quench the flaming sun,
Or from the sky to wipe away the moon?

SALOME If Mariam be the sun and moon, it is;

---

5. The people of Jerusalem.
6. As far as I am concerned.

7. I know not either what to do in this instance or what
to do in the event of Mariam's death.

For I already have commanded this.

HEROD But have you seen her cheek?

SALOME   A thousand times.

HEROD But did you mark it too?

SALOME   Aye, very well.

HEROD What is't?

SALOME   A crimson bush, that ever limes[8]
                 The soul whose foresight doth not much excel.

HEROD Send word she shall not die. Her cheek a bush,
                 Nay, then I see indeed you marked it not.

SALOME 'Tis very fair, but yet will never blush,
                 Though foul dishonors do her forehead blot.

HEROD Then let her die, 'tis very true indeed,
                 And for this fault alone shall Mariam bleed.

SALOME What fault my Lord?

HEROD   What fault is't? You that ask,
55   If you be ignorant I know of none,
                 To call her back from death shall be your task,
                 I'm glad that she for innocent is known.
                 For on the brow of Mariam hangs a fleece,
                 Whose slenderest twine is strong enough to bind
60   The hearts of kings, the pride and shame of Greece,
                 Troy-flaming Helen's not so fairly shined.[9]

SALOME 'Tis true indeed, she lays them[1] out for nets,
                 To catch the hearts that do not shun a bait.
                 'Tis time to speak: for Herod sure forgets
65   That Mariam's very tresses hide deceit.

HEROD Oh do they so? Nay, then you do but well,
                 In sooth I thought it had been hair.
                 Nets call you then? Lord, how they do excel,
                 I never saw a net that showed so fair.
70   But have you heard her speak?

SALOME   You know I have.

HEROD And were you not amazed?

SALOME   No, not a whit.

HEROD Then 'twas not her you heard; her life I'll save,
                 For Mariam hath a world-amazing wit.

SALOME She speaks a beauteous language, but within
                 Her heart is false as powder, and her tongue
                 Doth but allure the auditors to sin,
                 And is the instrument to do you wrong.

HEROD It may be so: nay, 'tis so: she's unchaste,
80   Her mouth will ope° to ev'ry stranger's ear;   open
                 Then let the executioner make haste,
                 Lest she enchant him, if her words he hear.

---

8. Entraps.
9. Mariam's hair is compared to the golden fleece, sought
by Jason and the Argonauts, and the hair of Helen, the

great beauty whose abduction was the cause of the Trojan
War.
1. Strands of her hair.

Let him be deaf, lest she do him surprise
That shall to free her spirit be assigned.
85 Yet what boots° deafness if he have his eyes,   *good is*
Her murtherer must be both deaf and blind.
For if he see, he needs must see the stars
That shine on either side of Mariam's face,
Whose sweet aspect will terminate the wars,
90 Wherewith he should a soul so precious chase.
Her eyes can speak, and in their speaking move;
Oft did my heart with reverence receive
The world's mandates. Pretty tales of love
They utter, which can humane bondage weave.
95 But shall I let this Heaven's model die?
Which for a small self-portraiture she° drew?   *Heaven*
Her eyes like stars, her forehead like the sky,
She is like Heaven, and must be heavenly true.

SALOME Your thoughts do rave with doting on the queen,
100 Her eyes are ebon-hued,° and you'll confess,   *dark black*
A sable star hath been but seldom seen;
Then speak of reason more, of Mariam less.

HEROD Yourself are held a goodly creature here,
Yet so unlike my Mariam in your shape
105 That when to her you have approached near,
Myself hath often ta'en you for an ape.
And yet you prate of beauty: go your ways,
You are to her a sun-burnt blackamoor;[2]
Your paintings[3] cannot equal Mariam's praise,
110 Her nature is so rich, you are so poor.
Let her be stayed from death, for if she die,
We do we know not what to stop her breath.[4]
A world cannot another Mariam buy,
Why stay you lingering? countermand her death.

SALOME Then you'll no more remember what hath past,
Sohemus' love, and hers shall be forgot;
'Tis well in truth, that fault may be her last,
And she may mend, though yet she love you not.

HEROD Oh God, 'tis true. Sohemus! Earth and heaven,
120 Why did you both conspire to make me curs'd,
In coz'ning° me with shows and proofs unev'n?°   *tricking/unjust*
She showed the best, and yet did prove the worst.
Her show was such as had our singing king,
The holy David, Mariam's beauty seen,
125 The Hittite had then felt no deadly sting,
Nor Bathsheba had never been a queen.[5]

---

2. Female vice was often portrayed in terms of blackness. The Moors were thought of as black in the medieval and early modern periods.
3. Your face made up with cosmetics.
4. Compare with Luke 23.34, when Christ says of his exe-cutioners "they know not what they do."
5. When Bathsheba became pregnant by David, he ordered her husband Uriah the Hittite to go to war, where he would be killed in battle (2 Samuel 11).

Or had his son the wisest man of men,
Whose fond delight did most consist in change,[6]
Beheld her face, he had been stayed again;
130　No creature having her, can wish to range.
Had Asuerus seen my Mariam's brow,
The humble Jew, she might have walked alone,[7]
Her beauteous virtue should have stayed below,
Whiles Mariam mounted to the Persian throne.
135　But what avails it all? For in the weight°　　　　　　　　balance
She is deceitful, light as vanity.
Oh, she was made for nothing but a bait,
To train° some hapless man to misery.　　　　　　　　　mislead
I am the hapless man that have been trained
140　To endless bondage. I will see her yet;
Methinks I should discern her if she feigned;
Can human eyes be dazed by woman's wit?
Once more these eyes of mine with hers shall meet,
Before the headsman° do her life bereave.　　　　　　　executioner
145　Shall I forever part from thee, my sweet,
Without the taking of my latest leave?
SALOME You had as good resolve to save her now.
I'll stay her death, 'tis well determined;
For sure she nevermore will break her vow,
150　Sohemus and Josephus both are dead.
HEROD She shall not live, nor will I see her face;
A long-healed wound, a second time doth bleed;
With Joseph I remember her disgrace,
A shameful end ensues° a shameful deed.　　　　　　　　follows
155　Oh that I had not called to mind anew
The discontent of Mariam's wavering heart!
'Twas you, you foul-mouthed Até,[8] none but you,
That did the thought hereof to me impart.
Hence from my sight, my black tormenter hence,
160　For hadst not thou made Herod unsecure
I had not doubted Mariam's innocence,
But still had held her in my heart for pure.
SALOME I'll leave you to your passion; 'tis no time
To purge me now, though of a guiltless crime. [Exit.]
HEROD Destruction take thee; thou hast made my heart
As heavy as revenge, I am so dull,
Methinks I am not sensible of smart,
Though hideous horrors at my bosom pull.
My head weighs downwards; therefore will I go
170　To try if I can sleep away my woe. [Exit.]

Scene 8

[Mariam.]
MARIAM Am I the Mariam that presumed so much,

6. David's son Solomon was known for his wisdom and
his many concubines (1 Kings 4.11).
7. See Esther 2 for how Ahasuerus made Esther (the
humble Jew) queen.
8. "Até" in Greek means blindness or delusion and is goddess of discord.

And deemed my face must needs preserve my breath?
Ay, I it was that thought my beauty such,
As it alone could countermand my death.
5   Now death will teach me: he can pale as well
A cheek of roses as a cheek less bright,
And dim an eye whose shine doth most excel,
As soon as one that casts a meaner light.
Had not myself against myself conspired,
10   No plot, no adversary from without
Could Herod's love from Mariam have retired,
Or from his heart have thrust my semblance out.
The wanton queen that never loved for love,
False Cleopatra, wholly set on gain,
15   With all her flights did prove, yet vainly prove,°   *try*
For her the love of Herod to obtain.
Yet her allurements, all her courtly guile,
Her smiles, her favors, and her smooth deceit
Could not my face from Herod's mind exile,
20   But were with him of less than little weight.
That face and person that in Asia late
For beauty's goddess, Paphos' queen[9] was ta'en,
That face that did captive° great Julius'[1] fate,   *capture*
That very face that was Anthonius'[2] bane.°   *ruin*
25   That face that to be Egypt's pride was born,
That face that all the world esteemed so rare.
Did Herod hate, despise, neglect, and scorn
When with the same, he Mariam's did compare?
This made that I improvidently wrought,
30   And on the wager even my life did pawn,
Because I thought, and yet but truly thought,
That Herod's love could not from me be drawn.
But now, though out of time, I plainly see
It could be drawn, though never drawn from me;
35   Had I but with humility been graced
As well as fair, I might have proved me wise;
But I did think because I knew me chaste,
One virtue for a woman might suffice.
That mind for glory of our sex might stand,
40   Wherein humility and chastity
Doth march with equal paces, hand in hand.
But one if single seen, who setteth by?°   *values*
And I had singly one, but 'tis my joy,
That I was ever innocent, though sour.
45   And therefore can they but my life destroy;
My soul is free from adversary's power. [*Enter Doris.*]
You princes great in power and high in birth,
Be great and high, I envy not your hap;°   *fortune*
Your birth must be from dust, your power on earth,

9. Aphrodite or Venus.   2. Mark Antony.
1. Julius Caesar.

50   In heaven shall Mariam sit in Sarah's lap.[3]

DORIS In heaven! Your beauty cannot bring you thither,
       Your soul is black and spotted, full of sin;
       You in adult'ry lived nine year together,
       And Heav'n will never let adult'ry in.[4]

MARIAM What art thou that dost poor Mariam pursue?
        Some spirit sent to drive me to despair,
        Who sees for truth that Mariam is untrue?
        If fair she be, she is as chaste as fair.

DORIS I am that Doris that was once beloved,
60   Beloved by Herod, Herod's lawful wife.
       'Twas you that Doris from his side removed,
       And robbed from me the glory of my life.

MARIAM Was that adult'ry? Did not Moses say,
        That he that being matched did deadly hate
65   Might by permission put his wife away
        And take a more beloved to be his mate?

DORIS What did he hate me for: for simple truth?
       For bringing° beauteous babes for love to him,   *giving birth to*
       For riches, noble birth, or tender youth?
70   Or for no stain did Doris' honor dim?
       Oh tell me Mariam, tell me if you know,
       Which fault of these made Herod Doris' foe?
       These thrice three years have I with hands held up,
       And bowèd knees fast nailed to the ground,
75   Besought for thee the dregs of that same cup,
       That cup of wrath that is for sinners found.
       And now thou art to drink it: Doris' curse
       Upon thyself did all this while attend,
       But now it shall pursue thy children worse.

MARIAM Oh, Doris, now to thee my knees I bend,
        That heart that never bowed to thee doth bow;
        Curse not mine infants, let it thee suffice,
        That Heav'n doth punishment to me allow.
        Thy curse is cause that guiltless Mariam dies.

DORIS Had I ten thousand tongues, and ev'ry tongue
       Inflamed with poison's power and steeped in gall,
       My curses would not answer for my wrong,
       Though I in cursing thee employed them all.
       Hear thou that didst mount Gerizim[5] command,
90   To be a place whereon with cause to curse;
       Stretch thy revenging arm, thrust forth thy hand,
       And plague the mother much, the children worse.
       Throw flaming fire upon the base-born heads
       That were begotten in unlawful[6] beds.

---

3. With the wife of Abraham.
4. The charge of adultery against Mariam makes her analogous to Anne Boleyn, who was seen as an adulteress by
some who objected to Henry VIII's divorce.

5. Weller and Ferguson emend Gerarim to Gerizim,
named as the place of blessing in Deuteronomy 11, here
confused with the twin mountain Ebal, a place of cursing.
6. Outside of marriage.

95   But let them live 'til they have sense to know
        What 'tis to be in miserable state;
        Then be their nearest friends their overthrow,
        Attended be they by suspicious hate.
        And, Mariam, I do hope this boy of mine
100   Shall one day come to be the death of thine.[7] [*Exit.*]
MARIAM Oh! Heaven forbid. I hope the world shall see,
        This curse of thine shall be returned on thee.
        Now earth farewell, though I be yet but young;
        Yet I, methinks, have known thee too too long. [*Exit.*]

CHORUS The fairest action of our human life
        Is scorning to revenge an injury;
        For who forgives without a further strife,
        His adversary's heart to him doth tie.
        And 'tis a firmer conquest truly said,
110   To win the heart than overthrow the head.

        If we a worthy enemy do find,
        To yield to worth, it must be nobly done;[8]
        But if of baser metal be his mind,
        In base revenge there is no honor won.
115   Who would a worthy courage overthrow,
        And who would wrestle with a worthless foe?

        We say our hearts are great and cannot yield;
        Because they cannot yield it proves them poor;
        Great hearts are tasked beyond their power, but seld,°   seldom
120   The weakest lion will the loudest roar.
        Truths schooled for certain doth this same allow,
        High-heartedness doth sometimes teach to bow.

        A noble heart doth teach a virtuous scorn,
        To scorn to owe a duty over-long,[9]
125   To scorn to be for benefits foreborn,[1]
        To scorn to lie, to scorn to do a wrong.
        To scorn to bear an injury in mind,
        To scorn a free-born heart slave-like to bind.

        But if for wrongs we needs revenge must have,
130   Then be our vengeance of the noblest kind;[2]
        Do we his body from our fury save,
        And let our hate prevail against our mind?[3]

---

7. Doris foretells the future, in which her son Antipater turns Herod against Mariam's sons.

8. We act nobly when we concede victory to a worthy enemy.

9. To delay in fulfilling an obligation.

1. Not being required to fulfill an obligation because of previous good deeds.

2. Forgiveness.

3. Do we allow our enemy to escape injury from our anger but then turn that anger against ourselves by holding a grudge?

What can 'gainst him a greater vengeance be,
Then make his foe more worthy far than he?

135   Had Mariam scorned to leave a due unpaid,
She would to Herod then have paid her love,
And not have been by sullen passion swayed.
To fix her thoughts all injury above
Is virtuous pride. Had Mariam thus been proved,[4]
140   Long, famous life to her had been allowed.

Act 5

Scene 1

[*Nuntio.*]

NUNTIO   When, sweetest friend, did I so far offend
Your heavenly self, that you my fault to quit
Have made me now relator of your end,
The end of beauty, chastity and wit?[5]
5   Was none so hapless in the fatal place,
But I, most wretched, for the queen t' choose,
'Tis certain I have some ill-boding face
That made me culled° to tell this luckless news.   *picked*
And yet no news to Herod; were it new,
10   To him unhappy it had not been at all;[6]
Yet do I long to come within his view,
That he may know his wife did guiltless fall.
And here he comes. Your Mariam greets you well.

[*Enter Herod.*]

HEROD   What? Lives my Mariam? Joy, exceeding joy,
She shall not die.

NUNTIO   Heaven doth your will repel.

HEROD   Oh, do not with thy words my life destroy,
I prithee tell no dying-tale; thine eye
Without thy tongue doth tell but too too much;
Yet let thy tongue's addition make me die,
20   Death welcome, comes to him whose grief is such.

NUNTIO   I went amongst the curious gazing troop,
To see the last of her that was the best:
To see if death had heart to make her stoop,
To see the sun admiring phoenix'[7] nest.
25   When there I came, upon the way I saw
The stately Mariam not debased by fear;
Her look did seem to keep the world in awe,
Yet mildly did her face this fortune bear.

HEROD   Thou dost usurp my right, my tongue was framed

---

4. Had Mariam proved to be virtuously proud.
5. These lines are addressed to Mariam.
6. If Herod had been ignorant of (and not responsible for) Mariam's death, the news of it would not be tragic to him.

7. A mythical bird, which burnt itself every 500 years only to emerge from its ashes renewed. The phoenix symbolized Christ's resurrection. See the entry on the phoenix from Geoffrey Whitney's *Choice of Emblems* in Perspectives: Emblem, Style, and Metaphor, page 1599.

30   To be the instrument of Mariam's praise;
          Yet speak: she cannot be too often famed,
          All tongues suffice not her sweet name to raise.
NUNTIO But as she came she Alexandra met,
          Who did her death (sweet queen) no whit bewail,
35   But as if nature she did quite forget,
          She did upon her daughter loudly rail.°   *utter abuse*
HEROD Why stopped you not her mouth? Where had she words
          To darken that, that heaven made so bright?
          Our sacred tongue no epithet affords
40   To call her other than the world's delight.
NUNTIO She told her that her death was too too good,
          And that already she had lived too long;
          She said, she shamed to have a part in blood
          Of her that did the princely Herod wrong.
HEROD Base pick-thank° devil. Shame, 'twas all her glory   *flattering*
          That she to noble Mariam was the mother;
          But never shall it live in any story—
          Her name, except to infamy I'll smother.
          What answer did her princely daughter make?
NUNTIO She made no answer, but she looked the while,
          As if thereof she scarce did notice take,
          Yet smiled, a dutiful, though scornful smile.
HEROD Sweet creature, I that look to mind do call,
          Full oft hath Herod been amazed withall.
          Go on.
NUNTIO   She came unmoved with pleasant grace,
          As if to triumph her arrival were,
          In stately habit, and with cheerful face;
          Yet ev'ry eye was moist, but Mariam's there.
          When justly opposite to me she came,
60   She picked me out from all the crew;
          She beckoned to me, called me by my name,
          For she my name, my birth, and fortune knew.
HEROD What, did she name thee? Happy, happy man,
          Wilt thou not ever love that name the better?
65   But what sweet tune did this fair dying swan[8]
          Afford thine ear. Tell all, omit no letter.
NUNTIO Tell thou my Lord, said she.
HEROD   Me, meant she me?
          Is't true, the more my shame: I was her lord;
          Were I not mad, her lord I still should be;
70   But now her name must be by me adored.
          Oh say, what said she more? Each word she said
          Shall be the food whereon my heart is fed.
NUNTIO "Tell thou my Lord thou saw'st me loose[9] my breath."
HEROD Oh that I could that sentence now control![1]

---

8. The swan was said to sing at its death. See *Othello*,
5.2.253–57, page 1257.

9. Meaning "let go of" or "lose."

1. If only I could overturn her death sentence.

NUNTIO If guiltily eternal be my death,
HEROD I hold her chaste ev'n in my inmost soul.
NUNTIO By three days hence if wishes could revive,
    I know himself would make me oft alive.[2]
HEROD Three days, three hours, three minutes, not so much,
80   A minute in a thousand parts divided,
    My penitency for her death is such,
    As in the first[3] I wished she had not died.
    But forward in thy tale.
NUNTIO   Why on she went,
    And after she some silent prayer had said.
85   She did as if to die she were content,
    And thus to Heav'n her heavenly soul is fled.
HEROD But art thou sure there doth no life remain?
    Is't possible my Mariam should be dead?
    Is there no trick to make her breathe again?
NUNTIO Her body is divided from her head.
HEROD Why, yet methinks there might be found by art
    Strange ways of cure, 'tis sure rare things are done
    By an inventive head and willing heart.
NUNTIO Let not, my Lord, your fancies idly run.
95   It is as possible it should be seen
    That we should make the holy Abraham live,
    Though he entombed two thousand years had been,
    As breath again to slaughtered Mariam give.
    But now for more assaults prepare your ears.
HEROD There cannot be a further cause of moan;
    This accident shall shelter me from fears.
    What can I fear? Already Mariam's gone.
    Yet tell ev'n what you will.
NUNTIO   As I came by,
    From Mariam's death I saw upon a tree
105   A man that to his neck a cord did tie,
    Which cord he had designed his end to be.
    When me he once discerned, he downward bowed,
    And thus with fearful voice, he cried aloud:
    "Go tell the king he trusted ere he tried,
110   I am the cause that Mariam causeless died."
HEROD Damnation take him, for it was the slave
    That said she meant with poison's deadly force
    To end my life that she the crown might have,[4]
    Which tale did Mariam from herself divorce.
115   Oh pardon me thou pure unspotted ghost,
    My punishment must needs sufficient be,
    In missing that content I valued most,
    Which was thy admirable face to see.

---

2. The "three days" may allude to the time between Christ's death and resurrection.
3. The first thousandth of a minute.

4. The Butler's accusation that Mariam was attempting to take over the throne is not in Cary's source, Josephus's *Antiquities*.

I had but one inestimable jewel,[5]
120 Yet one I had no monarch had the like,
And therefore may I curse myself as cruel,
'Twas broken by a blow myself did strike.
I gazed thereon and never thought me bless'd,
But when on it my dazzled eye might rest,
125 A precious mirror made by wonderous art,
I prized it ten times dearer than my crown,
And laid it up fast-folded in my heart.
Yet I in sudden choler cast it down,
And pashed° it all to pieces. 'Twas no foe   *smashed*
130 That robbed me of it; no Arabian host,
Nor no Armenian guide hath used me so;
But Herod's wretched self hath Herod crossed.
She was my graceful moiety;° me accursed,   *half*
To slay my better half and save my worst.
135 But sure she is not dead, you did but jest,
To put me in perplexity a while;
'Twere well indeed if I could so be dressed:°   *treated*
I see she is alive, methinks you smile.
NUNTIO   If sainted Abel yet deceased be,[6]
140 'Tis certain Mariam is as dead as he.
HEROD   Why then go call her to me, bid her now
Put on fair habit, stately ornament,
And let no frown o'ershade her smoothest brow;
In her doth Herod place his whole content.
NUNTIO   She'll come in stately weeds° to please your sense,   *clothes*
If now she come attired in robe of Heav'n.
Remember you yourself did send her hence,
And now to you she can no more be given.
HEROD   She's dead, hell take her murderers, she was fair,
150 Oh what a hand she had, it was so white,
It did the whiteness of the snow impair.
I never more shall see so sweet a sight.
NUNTIO   'Tis true, her hand was rare.
HEROD   Her hand? Her hands.
She had not singly one of beauty rare,
155 But such a pair as here where Herod stands;
He dares the world to make to both compare.[7]
Accursed Salome, hadst thou been still,°   *silent*
My Mariam had been breathing by my side.
Oh never had I, had I had my will,
160 Sent forth command that Mariam should have died!
But Salome thou didst with envy vex,
To see thyself out-matchèd in thy sex;

---

5. See *Othello*, 5.2.353–55; "one whose hand / Like the base Indian, threw a pearl away / Richer than all his tribe", page 1260. The folio text reads "Judean" for "Indian" and thus may allude to Herod.

6. The death of innocent Abel in Genesis 4 was read as a prefiguration of Christ's death in the New Testament.
7. To find a pair of hands as beautiful as Mariam's.

Upon your sex's forehead Mariam sat,
To grace you all like an imperial crown;
165 But you, fond fool, have rudely pushed thereat,
And proudly pulled your proper glory down.
One smile of hers—nay—not so much—a look
Was worth a hundred thousand such as you;
Judea how canst thou the wretches brook,°   *put up with*
170 That robbed from thee the fairest of the crew?
You dwellers in the now deprived land,
Wherein the matchless Mariam was bred,
Why grasp not each of you a sword in hand,
To aim at me our cruel sovereign's head.
175 Oh, when you think of Herod as your king,
And owner of the pride of Palestine,
This act to your remembrance likewise bring,
'Tis I have overthrown your royal line.
Within her purer veins the blood did run,
180 That from her grandam Sarah she derived,
Whose beldam° age the love of kings hath won;   *old woman's*
Oh that her issue had as long been lived.
But can her eye be made by death obscure?°   *dull*
I cannot think but it must sparkle still;
185 Foul sacrilege to rob those lights so pure,
From out a temple made by heavenly skill.
I am the villain that have done the deed,
The cruel deed, though by another's hand;
My word though not my sword made Mariam bleed,
190 Hircanus' grandchild did at my command—
That Mariam that I once did love so dear,
The partner of my now detested bed,
Why shine you sun with an aspect so clear?
I tell you once again my Mariam's dead.
195 You could but shine, if some Egyptian blowse
Or Ethiopian dowdy lose her life;[8]
This was—then wherefore bend you not your brows?—
The King of Jewry's fair and spotless wife.
Deny thy beams, and moon refuse thy light,
200 Let all the stars be dark, let Jewry's eye
No more distinguish which is day and night;
Since her best birth did in her bosom die.
Those fond idolaters, the men of Greece,
Maintain these orbs are falsely governèd;[9]
205 That each within themselves have gods a piece
By whom their steadfast course is justly led.
But were it so, as so it cannot be,

---

8. A "blowse" was a beggar's prostitute; a "dowdy" was a
shabbily dressed woman. "Egyptian" here probably refers
to Cleopatra.
9. In Ptolemaic astronomy the orbs are the hollow

spheres that surround the earth and within which the
planets revolve around the earth. Each was thought to be
governed by one of the gods, each of whom embodied
human qualities.

They all would put their mourning garments on;
Not one of them would yield a light to me,
210   To me that is the cause that Mariam's gone.
For though they feign their Saturn melancholy,
Of sour behaviors and of angry mood,
They feign him likewise to be just and holy,
And justice needs must seek revenge for blood.
215   Their Jove, if Jove he were, would sure desire,
To punish him that slew so fair a lass;
For Leda's beauty set his heart on fire,[1]
Yet she not half so fair as Mariam was.
And Mars would deem his Venus had been slain,[2]
220   Sol[3] to recover her would never stick;°   *hesitate*
For if he want the power her life to gain,
Then physic's god is but an empiric.°   *quack*
The Queen of Love would storm for beauty's sake,
And Hermes too, since he bestowed her wit;
225   The night's pale light for angry grief would shake,
To see chaste Mariam die in age unfit.
But, oh, I am deceived, she pass'd° them all   *surpassed*
In every gift, in every property.°   *quality*
Her excellencies wrought her timeless fall,
230   And they rejoiced, not grieved to see her die.
The Paphian goddess did repent her waste[4]
When she to one such beauty did allow;
Mercurius thought her wit his wit surpassed,
And Cynthia envied Mariam's brighter brow.[5]
235   But these are fictions, they are void of sense;
The Greeks but dream, and dreaming falsehoods tell.
They neither can offend nor give defense,
And not by them it was my Mariam fell.
If she had been like an Egyptian black[6]
240   And not so fair, she had been longer lived;
Her overflow of beauty turned back,
And drowned the spring from whence it was derived.
Her heavenly beauty 'twas that made me think
That it with chastity could never dwell;
245   But now I see that heaven in her did link
A spirit and a person° to excel.   *appearance*
I'll muffle up myself in endless night,
And never let mine eyes behold the light.
Retire thyself vile monster, worse than he
250   That stained the virgin earth with brother's blood;[7]
Still in some vault or den enclosèd be,

1. Jove (or Jupiter) turned himself into a swan to rape Leda.
2. Mars, the god of war, was the lover of Venus, goddess of love and beauty.
3. Sol, or Apollo, was the god of the sun and of medicine.
4. The "Paphian goddess," Venus, would have regretted having given so much beauty to Mariam.
5. Cynthia, or Diana, goddess of chastity and of the moon.
6. Another allusion to Cleopatra.
7. Herod compares himself to Cain, who murdered Abel.

Where with thy tears thou mayst beget a flood,
Which flood in time may drown thee. Happy day
When thou at once shalt die and find a grave,
255   A stone upon the vault, someone shall lay,
Which monument shall an inscription have.
And these shall be the words it shall contain:
"Here Herod lies, that hath his Mariam slain." [*Exit.*]

CHORUS   Who ever hath beheld with steadfast eye
260   The strange events of this one only day?[8]
How many were deceived? How many die,
That once today did grounds of safety lay?
It will from them all certainty bereave,
Since twice six hours so many can deceive.

265   This morning Herod held for surely dead,
And all the Jews on Mariam did attend;
And Constabarus rise from Salom's bed,
And neither dreamed of a divorce or end.
Pheroras joyed that he might have his wife,
270   And Babas' sons for safety of their life.

Tonight our Herod doth alive remain,
The guiltless Mariam is deprived of breath;
Stout Constabarus both divorced and slain,
The valiant sons of Babas have their death.
275   Pheroras sure his love to be bereft,
If Salome her suit unmade had left.[9]

Herod this morning did expect with joy
To see his Mariam's much belovèd face;
And yet ere night he did her life destroy,
280   And surely thought she did her name disgrace.
Yet now again so short do humors last,
He both repents her death and knows her chaste.

Had he with wisdom now her death delayed,
He at his pleasure might command her death;
285   But now he hath his power so much betrayed,
As all his woes cannot restore her breath.
Now doth he strangely lunaticly rave,
Because his Mariam's life he cannot save.

This day's events were certainly ordained,
290   To be the warning to posterity;
So many changes are therein contained,
So admirably strange variety.
This day alone, our sagest Hebrews shall
In after-times the school of wisdom call.

8. The play follows the unity of time, "one day," as required by neoclassical critics.

9. Pheroras would have lost Graphina if Salome had not interceded on his behalf with Herod.

Tracts on Women and Gender

What is the nature of woman? Is she meant to be subordinate to man or an equal partner? What virtues is she capable of? Does she have intellectual ability, and if so, is it appropriate for her to write? How should she behave toward her husband? What are his responsibilities to her? What is the difference between a good woman and a bad one? What is the difference between manly behavior and womanly behavior? These are some of the questions that early modern English tracts on women and gender ask. Although we would not ask all of these questions in precisely the same way today, they are still of burning interest. The debate over these questions in early modern tracts on women sheds light on the representation of sex and gender in the poetry and drama of the period. By *sex* is meant the representation of biological difference; by *gender* is meant the representation of sex difference as it is socially constructed.

In the Middle Ages there were both attacks on women and defenses of them by both women and men, but intellectual and social changes modified the debate in the early modern period. One of the prominent medieval genres that continued to be imitated in the early mod-

Title page from *The English Gentlewoman*, by Richard Braithwait. 1631.

ern period was the praise of exemplary women, such as Boccaccio's *De Claris Mulieribus* ("concerning famous women"), Chaucer's *Legend of Good Women,* and Christine de Pisan's *Le Livre de la Cité des Dames* (translated into English in 1521 as *The Book of the City of Ladies*). Renaissance humanism brought a new intellectual rigor to the genre. The German humanist Heinrich Cornelius Agrippa (1486–1535) stands out in the early Tudor controversy of the 1540s. Agrippa's *De Nobilitate et Praecellentia Foemenei Sexus* (translated in 1542 as *A Treatise of the Nobilitie and Excellencye of Woman Kynde*) not only lists Biblical and classical heroines but also examines how the place of women in society is determined by culture rather than nature: "And thus by these lawes, the women being subdued as it were by force of arms, are constrained to give place to men, and to obey their subduers, not by no natural, no divine necessity or reason, but by custom, education, fortune, and a certain tyrannical occasion." However, even a humanist author such as Erasmus, who had enlightened views on other social issues, had very strict views about the absolute subordination of wife to husband. Indeed, this subordination seems to have increased in intensity in the early modern period as the nuclear family headed by the father superseded the extended family, in which power was more dispersed throughout the network of kinship.

Among the learned, the new classical humanist education was still largely reserved for young men. Such changes moved the historian Joan Kelly Gadol to ask, "Did women have a Renaissance?" At the same time, some early modern women were educated enough to represent themselves in the debate on the nature of women, and they brought new perspectives to it. Margaret Tyler was one of the first English women to speak in defense of women as writers. Rachel Speght, the first polemical or argumentative woman writer in English, wrote her defense of women in response to a controversy set in motion by the publication of Joseph Swetnam's *An Arraignment of Lewde, Idle, Froward, and Unconstant Women* (1615). Swetnam was a misogynist (woman hater), but his tract had the virtue of eliciting defenses of women. Among these responses were *A Muzzle for Melastomus,* written from the theological perspective of Rachel Speght, and *Esther Hath Hang'd Haman,* written from the more secular outlook of "Esther Sowernam" (a pen-name adopted to counter the "sweet" in the name Swetnam). Two other tracts of the 1620s, *Hic Mulier* ("the mannish woman") and *Haec Vir* ("the womanish man") humorously raised the problem of the blurring of genders and carried on a debate about the style of dress and behavior that men and women should adopt.

Whether these tracts take the form of an oration, a speech by one person, or a dialogue between two people (as in *Haec Vir*), they are all in lively conversation with each other, either directly or indirectly. They are also in a lively conversation with other texts in this period. Questions about marriage and a wife's relations with people other than her husband as well as a woman's speech and silence are dealt with directly in *Othello* and *The Tragedy of Mariam.* Representing only a fraction of the early modern literature on women and gender, these tracts attest to heightened interest in questions of gender, such as those posed by the speakers in Lady Mary Wroth's and Katherine Philips's poems and the cross-dressing, independent Moll Cutpurse of Thomas Dekker and Thomas Middleton's *The Roaring Girl.*

Desiderius Erasmus
1469?–1536

Erasmus was the author not only of the humorous *Encomium Morae* (*The Praise of Folly*), dedicated to his friend Thomas More, but also of numerous works on Christian morals. Although *The Praise of Folly* was translated into English only in 1551, Erasmus's *Coniugium* (c. 1523), a text on marriage, appeared in English as *A Mery Dialogue, Declaringe the Propertyes of Shrowde Shrewes, and Honest Wyves* as early as 1542. This text advocated wifely submissiveness but also domesticity for both men and women—concepts that influenced the English bourgeois notion of marriage. Richard Tavernour also translated Erasmus's writing on marriage as *A Ryght Frutefull Epystle Devised in Laude and Praise of Matrimony* (1534). The following passage from this text demonstrates a view of marriage as the closest possible bond between human beings—and, more than that, as a sacrament calling for the wife's sole loyalty to her husband and lasting even beyond death.

from In Laude and Praise of Matrimony

* * * if the most part of things (yea which be also bitter) are of a good man to be desired for none other purpose, but because they be honest, matrimony doubtless is chiefly to be desired whereof a man may doubt whether it hath more honesty than pleasure. For what thing is sweeter than with her to live, with whom ye may be most straightly coupled, not only in the benevolence of the mind, but also in the conjunction of the body? If a great delectation of mind be taken of the benevolence of our other kinsmen, since it is an especial sweetness to have one with whom ye may communicate the secret affections of your mind, with whom ye may speak even as it were with your own self, whom ye may safely trust, which supposeth your chances to be his, what felicity (think ye) have the conjunction of man and wife, than which no thing in the universal world may be found either greater or firmer. For with our other friends we be conjoined only with the benevolence of minds, with our wife we be coupled with most high love, with permixtion[1] of bodies, with the confederate band of the sacrament, and finally with the fellowship of all chances. Furthermore, in other friendships, how great simulation is there, how great falsity? Yea, they whom we judge our best friends, like as the swallows flee away when summer is gone, so they forsake us when fortune turneth her wheel. And sometime the fresher friend casts out the old. We hear of few whose fidelity endure till their lives' end. The wife's love is with no falsity corrupted, with no simulation obscured, with no chance of things minished,[2] finally with death only (nay not with death neither) withdrawn. She, the love of her parents, she, the love of her sisters, she, the love of her brethren, despiseth for the love of you, her only respect is to you, of you she hangeth,[3] with you she coveteth to die. * * *

* * * Do ye judge any pleasure to be compared with this so great a conjunction? If ye tarry at home there is at hand which shall drive away the tediousness of solitary being. If from home ye have one that shall kiss you when ye depart, long for you when ye be absent, receive you joyously when ye return. A sweet companion of youth, a kind solace of age. By nature yea any fellowship is delectable to man, as whom nature hath created to benevolence and friendship. This fellowship then how shall it not be most sweet, in which everything is common to them both? And contrarily, if we see the savage beasts also abhor[4] solitary living and delighted in fellowship, in my mind he is not once to be supposed a man, which abhoreth from[5] this fellowship most honest and pleasant of all. For what is more hateful than the man which (as though he were born only to himself) liveth for himself, seeketh for himself, spareth for himself, doth cost to himself, loveth no person, is loved of no person? Shall not such a monster be adjudged worthy to be cast out of all men's company into the mid sea with Timon the Athenian,[6] which because he fled all men's company, was called Misanthropus that is to say hate man * * *

---

1. A thorough mixture or mingling.
2. Diminished, lessened in power.
3. In the sense of clinging, holding fast, adhering.
4. Hate.

5. Shrink with horror from.
6. The story of how Timon shunned society after his friends abandoned him when he lost his wealth is told by Plutarch (the source for Shakespeare's *Timon of Athens*).

But I know well enough what among these, ye murmur against me. A blessed thing is wedlock, if all prove according to the desire, But what if a wayward wife chanceth?[7] What if an unchaste? What if unnatural children? There will run in your mind the examples of those whom wedlock have brought to utter destruction. Heap up as much as ye can, but yet these be the vices of men and not of wedlock. Believe me, an evil wife is not wont to chance, but to evil husbands. Put this unto it, that it lieth in you to choose out a good one. But what if after the marriage she be marred?[8] Of an evil husband (I will well) a good wife may be marred, but of a good, the evil is wont to be reformed and mended. We blame wives falsely. No man (if ye give any credence to men) had ever a shrew to his wife, but through his own default.[9]

— ⚜ —

Barnabe Riche
1542–1617

A veteran of wars in the Low Countries and Ireland and author of twenty-six books, Barnabe Riche led a life as fraught with contention as his writing. Best known as the author of *His Farewell to Military Profession* (1581), which contains the source for Shakespeare's *Twelfth Night,* Riche was both a keen observer of contemporary social life and a spy. Alongside his attacks on shameless city women in *My Lady's Looking Glass* (1616) and *A New Description of Ireland* (1610), he also portrays Dublin ladies as critics of his work in *A True and Kind Excuse* (1612)—an interesting episode documenting women's literacy in this period. His writing has the zealous spirit of reforming Protestantism and looks forward to the impassioned prose of radical dissenters in the Civil War. *My Lady's Looking Glass* was published by Thomas Adams, London, in 1616, and dedicated to Lady Saint Jones, wife of the Lord Deputy of Ireland. This text bears comparison with Riche's *Excellency of Good Women* (London, 1613), as well as numerous other Jacobean tracts on the conduct of women.

from My Lady's Looking Glass

But my promise was to give rules how to distinguish between a good woman and a bad, and promise is debt, but I must be well advised how I take the matter in hand; for we were better to charge a woman with a thousand defects in her soul, than with that one abuse of her body; and we must have two witnesses, besides our own eyes, to testify, or we shall not be believed: but I myself have thought of a couple that I hope will carry credit.

The first is the prophet Isaiah, that in his days challenged the daughters of Zion for their stretched-out necks, their wandering eyes, at their mincing and wanton demeanor as they passed through the streets: these signs and shows have ever been thought to be the special marks whereby to know a harlot.[1] But Solomon in a more particular manner better furnishes us with more assured notes, and to the end that we might the better distinguish the good woman from the bad, he delivereth their several qualities, and wherein they are opposite: and speaking of a good woman he saith, *She seeketh out wool and flax, and laboreth cheerfully with her hands: she overseeth the ways of her household, and eateth not the bread of idleness.*[2]

---

7. Comes about by chance.
8. Injured.
9. Fault.

1. See Isaiah 3.16.
2. See Proverbs 31.13, 27.

Solomon thinketh that a good woman should be a home *housewife*, he pointeth her out her housework. *She overseeth the ways of her household,* she must look to her children, her servants and family; but *the paths of a harlot* (he saith) *are movable, for now she is in the house, now in the streets, now she lies in wait in every corner,* she is still gadding from place to place, from person to person, from company to company; from custom to custom, she is evermore wandering: her feet are wandering, her eyes are wandering, her wits are wandering, *Her ways are like the ways of a serpent:* hard to be found out.[3]

A good woman (again) *opens her mouth with wisdom, the law of grace is in her tongue:* but *a harlot is full of words, she is loud and babbling,* saith Solomon.

She is bold, she is impudent, she is shameless, she cannot blush: and she that hath lost all these virtues hath lost her evidence of honesty: for the ornaments of a good woman are temperance in her mind, silence in her tongue, and bashfulness in her countenance.

It is not she that can lift up her heels highest in the dancing of a galliard,[4] she that is lavish of her lips or loose of her tongue.

Now if Solomon's testimony be good, the woman that is impudent, immodest, shameless, insolent, audacious, a night-walker, a company-keeper, a gadder from place to place, a reveller, a ramper, a roister, a rioter: she that has these properties, has the certain signs and marks of a harlot, as Solomon has avowed. Now what credit his words will carry in the Commissaries' court, I leave to those that be advocates, and proctors in women's causes.[5]

I have hitherto presented to your view the true resemblance of a harlot, as well what she is, as how she might be discerned: I would now give you the like notice of that notable *Strumpet, the whore of Babylon,*[6] that has made so many Kings and Emperors drunk with the cup of abominations, by whom the nations of the earth have so defiled themselves by their spiritual fornication, called in the Scripture by the name of *idolatry* (but now within the last five hundred years, amongst Christians) shadowed under the title of Popery. This harlot has her agents, Popes, Cardinals, Bishops, Abbots, Monks, Friars, Jesuits, Priests, with a number of other like, and all of them factors in her bands,[7] the professed enemies of the Gospel of Jesus Christ, that do superstitiously adore the crucifix, and are indeed enemies of the cross of Christ, and do tread his holy blood under their scornful feet: that build up devotion with ignorance, and do ring out their hot alarms in the ears of the unlearned, teaching that the light can be no light, that the Scriptures can be no Scriptures, nor the truth can be no truth, but by their allowance, and if they will say that high noon is midnight, we must believe them, and make no more ado but get us to bed.

⋆⋅ ⚎ ⋅⋆

Margaret Tyler
flourished 1578

Margaret Tyler is best known today for the preface to her translation of Diego Ortunez de Calahorra's Spanish prose romance *The Mirrour of Princely Deedes and Knighthood,* Book I (1578), in which she argues that women have the ability to write on any subject. She was a

---

3. See Proverbs 7.10–12.
4. A lively dance in triple time.
5. Commissaries' court: the court of a bishop's representative, which had jurisdiction over divorce and probate;

advocates: pleaders, legal counselors; proctors: attorneys.
6. An image from Revelation 17, taken by Protestants to symbolize the Roman Catholic Church.
7. Agents in her leagues, or covenants.

waiting woman in the Catholic household of the Duke of Norfolk in the 1560s, where she may have read her translation aloud to the Duchess and her circle. In the preface to her translation, Tyler refers both to the "friends" who wanted her to return to her "old reading" and defends herself against potential critics who might object to her translating "matter more manlike than becometh my sex." She argues that she is more interested in virtue than in war and that, in any case, war affects women as much as it does men. The sixteenth-century humanist Vives had viewed romances as unsuitable for women readers, while male authors of romances often dedicated their work to women. Arguing for women's right to an education, Tyler reasons that if men can dedicate their texts to women, then women can read them, and that if women can read texts on such subjects as war and government, then they can write them.

from Preface to The First Part of the Mirror of Princely Deeds

Thou hast here, gentle Reader, the history of Trebatio, an Emperor in Greece: whether a true history of him indeed, or a feigned fable, I wot[1] not, neither did I greatly seek after it in the translation, but by me it is done into English for thy profit and delight. The chief matter therein contained, is of exploits of wars, and the parties therein named are especially renowned for their magnanimity and courage. * * * Such delivery as I have made I hope thou wilt friendly accept, the rather for that it is a woman's work, though in a story profane, and a matter more manlike than becometh my sex. But as for any manliness of the matter, thou knowest that it is not necessary for every trumpeter or drumstare[2] in the war to be a good fighter. They take wages only to incite others, though themselves have privy maims,[3] and are thereby recure-less.[4] So, gentle reader, if my travail in Englishing this author may bring thee to a lik-ing of the virtues herein commended, and by example thereof in thy princes' and countries' quarrel to hazard thy person, and purchase good name, as for hope of well deserving myself that way, I neither bend my self thereto, nor yet fear the speech of people if I be found backward. I trust every man holds not the plough, which would that the ground were tilled, and it is no sin to talk of Robin Hood, though you never shot in his bow. Or be it that the attempt were bold to intermeddle in arms, as the ancient Amazons[5] did, and in this story Claridiana doth, and in other stories not a few, yet to report of arms is not so odious, but that it may be borne withall, not only in you men which yourselves are fighters, but in us women, to whom the benefit in equal part appertains of your victories, either the matter is so commendable that it carries no discredit from the homeliness of the speaker, or that it is so generally known, that it fits every man to speak thereof. * * * But my defense is by example of the best, amongst which, many have dedicated their labors, some stories, some of war, some physic, some law, some as concerning government, some divine matters, unto diverse ladies and gentlewomen. And if men may and do bestow such of their travails upon gentlewomen, then may we women read such of their works as they dedicate to us, and if we may read them, why not further wade in them to the search of truth. * * * But to return to whatever the truth is, whether that women may not at all discourse in learning, for men late in their claim to being sole possessioners of knowledge, or whether they may in some manner, that is by limitation or appoint-ment in some kind of learning, my persuasion hath been thus, that it is all one for a

---

1. Know.
2. Drummer.
3. Secret weaknesses.

4. Irrecoverable.
5. A tribe of female warriors described by Herodotus and other ancient Greek authors as living in Scythia.

woman to pen a story, as for a man to address his story to a woman. But amongst all my ill-willers, some I hope are not so straight that they would enforce me necessarily either not to write or to write of divinity. Whereas neither durst I trust mine own judgment sufficiently, if matter of controversy were handled, nor yet could I find any book in any tongue, which would not breed offense to some. But I perceive some may be rather angry to see their Spanish delight turned to all English pastime: they could well allow the story in Spanish, but they may not afford it so cheap, or they would have it proper to themselves. What natures such men be of, I list[6] not greatly to dispute, but my meaning hath been to make others partners of my liking, as I doubt not gentle reader, but if it shall please thee after serious matters to sport thyself with this Spaniard, that thou shalt find in him the just reward of malice and cowardice, with the good speed of honesty and courage, being able to furnish thee with sufficient store of foreign examples to both purposes. And as in such matters which have been rather devised to beguile time, than to breed matter of sad learning, he hath ever borne away any price which could season such delights with some profitable reading: so shalt thou have this stranger an honest man when need serveth, and at other times either a good companion to drive out a weary night, or a merry jest at thy board. And this much concerning this present story, that it is neither unseemly for a woman to deal in, neither greatly requiring a less staid age than mine is. But of these two points, gentle reader, I thought to give thee warning, lest perhaps understanding my name and years, there mightest be a wrong suspect[7] of my boldness and rashness, from which I would gladly free myself by this plain excuse, and if I may deserve thy good favor by like labor, when the choice is my own, I will have a special regard of thy liking. So I wish thee well.

Thine to use, M.T.[8]

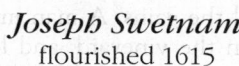

Joseph Swetnam
flourished 1615

Little is known about Joseph Swetnam other than that he stirred up an enormous controversy over the question of women when he wrote *An Arraignment of Lewde, Idle, Forward, and Unconstant Women* (1615). The work was published anonymously with an introductory letter signed by "Thomas Tel-troth." Trotting out all the negative stereotypes of women he could jumble together, Swetnam constructed his mock treatise as a piece of raucous comedy, aimed at the lowest common denominator. Reading Swetnam's work as a serious diatribe against women, Rachel Speght and the pseudonymous Esther Sowernam and Constantia Mundi produced critiques of misogyny. Speght unmasked Swetnam's authorship and identified him as a fencing master in Bristol. An anonymous comedy, *Swetnam the Woman-hater, Arraigned by Women* (1620), possibly by Thomas Heywood, dramatized the debate as a court trial with Swetnam prosecuting his case against women and the Amazon Atlanta (a soldier disguised as a woman) defending them. Swetnam is finally turned over to a court of women, who find him guilty and muzzle him (an obvious reference to Speght's *Muzzle for Melastomus*).

6. Wish.   8. Margaret Tyler.
7. Suspicion.

from **The Arraignment of Lewd, Idle, Forward, and Inconstant Women**

from *Chapter 2. The Second Chapter showeth the manner of such women as live upon evil report: it also showeth that the beauty of women has been the bane of many a man, for it hath overcome valiant and strong men, eloquent and subtle men. And in a word it hath overcome all men, as by examples following shall appear.*

First, that of Solomon unto whom God gave singular wit and wisdom, yet he loved so many women that he quite forgot his God which always did guide his steps, so long as he lived godly and ruled justly, but after he had glutted himself with women, then he could say, vanity of vanity all is but vanity. He also in many places of his book of Proverbs exclaims most bitterly against lewd women calling them all that naught is, and also displayeth their properties, and yet I cannot let men go blameless although women go shameless; but I will touch them both, for if there were not receivers then there would not be so many stealers: if there were not some knaves there would not be so many whores, for they both hold together to bolster each other's villainy, for always birds of a feather will flock together hand in hand to bolster each other's villainy.

Men, I say, may live without women, but women cannot live without men. For Venus, whose beauty was excellent fair, yet when she needeth man's help she took Vulcan, a clubfooted smith. And therefore if a woman's face glister,[1] and her gesture pierce the marble wall, or if her tongue be as smooth as oil or as soft as silk, and her words so sweet as honey, or if she were a very ape for wit, or a bag of gold for wealth, or if her personage have stolen away all that nature can afford, and if she be decked up in gorgeous apparel, then a thousand to one but she will love to walk where she may get acquaintance, and acquaintance bringeth familiarity, and familiarity setteth all follies abroach,[2] and twenty to one that if a woman love gadding but that she will pawn her honor to please her fantasy.

Man must be at all the cost and yet live by the loss. A man must take all the pains and women will spend all the gains. A man must watch and ward, fight and defend, till the ground, labor in the vineyard, and look what he getteth in seven years; a woman will spread it abroad with a fork in one year, and yet little enough to serve her turn but a great deal too little to get her good will. Nay, if thou give her ever so much and yet if thy person please not her humor, then will I not give a half-penny for her honesty at the year's end.

For then her breast will be the harborer of an envious heart, and her heart the storehouse of poisoned hatred; her head will devise villainy, and her hands are ready to practice that which their heart desireth. Then who can but say that women are sprung from the devil, whose heads, hands and hearts, minds and souls are evil, for women are called the hook of all evil, because men are taken by them as a fish is taken in with the hook.

For women have a thousand ways to entice thee, and ten thousand ways to deceive thee, and all such fools as are suitors unto them; some they keep in hand with promises, and some they feed with flattery, and some they delay with dalliances, and some they please with kisses. They lay out the folds of their hair to entangle men into their love; betwixt their breasts is the vale of destruction, and in their beds there is

---

1. Glitter, shine.   2. Flowing abroad.

hell, sorrow and repentance. Eagles do not eat men till they are dead, but women devour them alive, for a woman will pick thy pocket and empty thy purse, laugh in thy face and cut thy throat. They are ungrateful, perjured, full of fraud, flouting and deceit, unconstant, waspish,[3] toyish,[4] light, sullen, proud, discourteous and cruel, and yet they were by God created, and by nature formed, and therefore by policy and wisdom to be avoided, for good things abused are to be refused. Or else for a month's pleasure, she may make thee go stark naked. She will give thee roast meat, but she will beat thee with the spit. If thou hast crowns in thy purse, she will be thy heart's gold until she leave thee not a whit of white money. They are like summer birds, for they will abide no storm, but flock about thee in the pride of thy glory, and fly from thee in the storms of affliction; for they aim more at thy wealth than at thy person, and esteem more thy money than any man's virtuous qualities; for they esteem of a man without money as a horse does a fair stable without meat. They are like eagles which will always fly where the carrion is.

They will play the horse-leech to suck away thy wealth, but in the winter of thy misery, she will fly away from thee. Not unlike the swallow, which in the summer harboreth herself under the eaves of a house, and against winter flieth away, leaving nothing but dirt behind her.

Solomon saith, he that will suffer himself to be led away or to take delight in such women's company is like a fool which rejoiceth when he is led to the stocks. *Proverbs* 7.

Hosea, by marrying a lewd woman of light behavior was brought unto idolatry, *Hosea* 1. Saint Paul accounteth fornicators so odious, that we ought not to eat meat with them. He also showeth that fornicators shall not inherit the kingdom of Heaven, *1 Corinthians* the 9th and 11th verse.

And in the same chapter Saint Paul excommunicateth fornicators, but upon amendment he receiveth them again. Whoredom punished with death, *Deuteronomy* 22.21 and *Genesis* 38.24. Phineas a priest thrust two adulterers, both the man and the woman, through the belly with a spear, *Numbers* 25.

God detests the money or goods gotten by whoredom, *Deuteronomy* 23.17, 18. Whores called by diverse names, and the properties of whores, *Proverbs* 7.6 and 21. A whore envieth an honest woman, *Esdras* 16 and 24. Whoremongers God will judge, *Hebrews* 13 and 42. They shall have their portions with the wicked in the lake that burns with fire and brimstone, *Revelation* 21.8.

Only for the sin of whoredom God was sorry at heart, and repented that he ever made man, *Genesis* 6.67.

Saint Paul saith, to avoid fornication every man may take a wife, *1 Corinthians* 6.9.

Therefore he which hath a wife of his own and yet goeth to another woman is like a rich thief which will steal when he has no need.

There are three ways to know a whore: by her wanton looks, by her speech, and by her gait. *Ecclesiasticus* 26.[5] and in the same chapter he saith, that we must not give our strength unto harlots, for whores are the evil of all evils, and the vanity of all vanities, they weaken the strength of a man and deprive the body of his beauty, it furroweth his brows and maketh the eyes dim, and a whorish woman causeth the fever and the gout; and at a word, they are a great shortening to a man's life.

---

3. Spiteful
4. Frivolous, wanton.

5. Apocryphal book of the Old Testament.

For although they seem to be as dainty as sweet meat, yet in trial not so whole-some as sour sauce. They have wit, but it is all in craft; if they love it is vehement, but if they hate it is deadly.

Plato saith, that women are either angels or devils, and that they either love dearly or hate bitterly, for a woman hath no mean in her love, nor mercy in her hate, no pity in revenge, nor patience in her anger; therefore it is said, that there is noth-ing in the world which both pleases and displeases a man more than a woman, for a woman most delighteth a man and yet most deceiveth him, for as there is nothing more sweet to a man than a woman when she smiles, even so there is nothing more odious than the angry countenance of a woman.

Solomon in his 20th chapter of *Ecclesiastes*[6] saith, that an angry woman will foam at the mouth like a boar. If all this be true as most true it is, why shouldest thou spend one hour in the praise of women as some fools do, for some will brag of the beauty of such a maid, another will vaunt of the bravery of such a woman, that she goeth beyond all the women in the parish. Again, some study their fine wits how they may cunningly swooth[7] women, and with logic how to reason with them, and with eloquence to persuade them. They are always tempering their wits as fiddlers do their strings, who wrest them so high, that many times they stretch them beyond time, tune and reason.

Again, there are many that weary themselves with dallying, playing, and sport-ing with women, and yet they are never satisfied with the unsatiable desire of them; if with a song thou wouldest be brought asleep, or with a dance be led to delight, then a fair woman is fit for thy diet. If thy head be in her lap she will make thee believe that thou are hard by[8] God's seat, when indeed thou are just at hell gate.

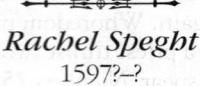

Rachel Speght
1597?–?

The daughter of the rector of two London churches and the wife of a minister, Rachel Speght was only about nineteen years old when she wrote *A Muzzle for Melastomus, the Cynical Baiter of, and Foul-Mouthed Barker Against Evah's Sex, or an Apologetical Answer to the Irreligious and Illiterate Pamphlet made by Io. Swe. and by him Intitled The Arraignment of Women.* Speght inter-preted Swetnam's *Arraignment* as a serious attack on women in order to show the faulty logic underpinning misogyny. Her title indicates the dual thrust of her analysis: the *irreligious* Swet-nam has misinterpreted Scripture, and the *illiterate* pamphlet is logically confused and rhetori-cally flawed. She argues for a view of marriage as a mutual partnership and the relation between the sexes as one of greater equality. Modern critics have debated the implications of Speght's work: Barbara Lewalski has called Rachel Speght "the first self-proclaimed and posi-tively identified female polemicist in England" while Ann Rosalind Jones has questioned whether Speght's work can be considered as feminist in the twentieth-century sense. All crit-ics of early modern gender studies agree, however, that Speght was a learned and committed author. She alone of the participants in the Jacobean controversy about women affixed her own name to the title page. And she reiterated her authorship with the publication of her poetic dream-vision *Moralities Memorandum* (1621), in which she defends women's education.

---

6. A faulty citation: in Ecclesiasticus 25, an angry woman is compared to a bear.

7. Sway, woo.
8. Close to.

from A Muzzle for Melastomus

Of Women's Excellency, with the causes of her creation, and of the sympathy which ought to be in man and wife each toward other

The work of creation being finished, this approbation thereof was given by God himself, that "All was very good."[1] If all, then woman, who—except man—is the most excellent creature under the canopy of heaven. But if it be objected by any:

First, that woman, though created good, yet by giving ear to Satan's temptations brought death and misery upon all her posterity.

Secondly, that "Adam was not deceived, but that the woman was deceived and was in the transgression."[2]

Thirdly, that St. Paul says "It were good for a man not to touch a woman."[3]

Fourthly and lastly, that of Solomon, who seems to speak against all of our sex: "I have found one man of a thousand, but a woman among them all I have not found,"[4] whereof in its due place.

To the first of these objections, I answer: that Satan first assailed the woman because where the hedge is lowest, most easy it is to get over, and she being the weaker vessel[5] was with more facility to be seduced—like as a crystal glass sooner receives a crack than a strong stone pot. Yet we shall find the offense of Adam and Eve almost to parallel; for as an ambitious desire to be made like God was the motive which caused her to eat, so likewise was it his, as may plainly appear by that *ironia*: "Behold, man is become as one of us"[6]—not that he was so indeed, but hereby his desire to attain a greater perfection than God had given him was reproved. Woman sinned, it is true, by her infidelity in not believing the word of God but giving credit to Satan's fair promises that "she should not die";[7] but so did the man, too. And if Adam had not approved of that deed which Eve had done, and been willing to tread the steps where she had gone, he—being her head—would have reproved her and have made the commandment a bit to restrain him from breaking his Maker's injunction. For if a man burn his hand in the fire, the bellows that blew the fire is not to be blamed, but himself rather for not being careful to avoid the danger. Yet if the bellows had not blown, the fire had not burned; no more is woman simply to be condemned for man's transgression. For by the free will which before his fall he enjoyed, he might have avoided and been free from being burned or singed with that fire which was kindled by Satan and blown by Eve. It therefore served not his turn a whit afterwards to say: "The woman which thou gavest me gave me of the tree, and I did eat."[8] For a penalty was inflicted upon him as well as on the woman, the punishment of her transgression being particular to her own sex and to none but the female kind, but for the sin of man the whole earth was cursed.[9] And he being better able than the woman to have resisted temptation, because the stronger vessel, was first called to account, to show that to whom much is given, of them much is required; and that he who was the sovereign of all creatures visible should have yielded greatest obedience to God.

---

1. Genesis 1.31. References to the Bible are indicated in the margins of Speght's text.
2. 1 Timothy 2.14.
3. 1 Corinthians 7.1.
4. Ecclesiastes 7.28.
5. "The weaker vessel," a phrase taken from 1 Peter 3.7, is frequently used in early modern English sermons to describe woman.

6. Genesis 3.22. "Ironia," or irony, is a figure of speech in which the meaning is the opposite of that of the words used and the tone of which is often mocking.
7. Genesis 3.4.
8. Genesis 3.12.
9. Genesis 3.17.

True it is (as is already confessed) that woman first sinned, yet find we no mention of spiritual nakedness till man had sinned. Then it is said "Their eyes were opened,"[1] the eyes of their mind and conscience; and then perceived they themselves naked, that is, not only bereft of that integrity which they originally had, but felt the rebellion and disobedience of their members in the disordered motions of their now corrupt nature, which made them for shame to cover their nakednesse. Then (and not afore) it is said that they saw it, as if sin were imperfect and unable to bring a deprivation of a blessing received, or death on all mankind, till man (in whom lay the active power of generation) had transgressed. The offense, therefore, of Adam and Eve is by St. Austin[2] thus distinguished: "the man sinned against God and himself, the woman against God, herself and her husband"; yet in her giving of the fruit to eat had she no malicious intent towards him, but did therein show a desire to make her husband partaker of that happiness, which she thought by their eating they should both have enjoyed. This her giving Adam of that sauce, wherewith Satan had served her, whose sourness, afore he had eaten, she did not perceive, was that which made her sin to exceed his. Wherefore, that she might not of him who ought to honor her be abhorred,[3] the first promise that was made in Paradise, God makes to woman, that by her seed should the serpent's head be broken.[4] Whereupon Adam calls her *Hevah*, Life, that as the woman had been an occasion of his sin so should woman bring forth the Savior from sin, which was in the fullness of time accomplished.[5] By which was manifested that he is a Savior of believing women no less than of men, that so the blame of sin may not be imputed to his creature, which is good, but to the will by which Eve sinned; and yet by Christ's assuming the shape of man was it declared that his mercy was equivalent to both sexes. So that by Hevah's blessed seed, as St. Paul affirms, it is brought to pass that "male and female are all one in Christ Jesus."[6]

To the second objection I answer: that the Apostle does not hereby exempt man from sin, but only giveth to understand that the woman was the primary transgressor, and not the man; but that man was not at all deceived was far from his meaning. For he afterwards expressly saith that "in Adam all die, so in Christ shall all be made alive."[7]

For the third objection, "It is good for a man not to touch a woman": the Apostle makes it not a positive prohibition but speaks it only because of the Corinth[ian]s' present necessity,[8] who were then persecuted by the enemies of the church. For which cause, and no other, he saith: "Art thou loosed from a wife? Seek not a wife"— meaning whilst the time of these perturbations should continue in their heat; "but if thou are bound, seek not to be loosed; if thou marriest, thou sinnest not," only increase thy care: "for the married careth for the things of this world. And I wish that you were without care that ye might cleave fast to the Lord without separation: for the time remaineth, that they which have wives be as though they had none, for the persecutors shall deprive you of them either by imprisonment, banishment or death." So that manifest it is, that the Apostle does not hereby forbid marriage, but only adviseth the Corinth[ian]s to forbear a while, till God in mercy should curb the fury of their adversaries. For (as Eusebius[9] writeth) Paul was afterward married himself,

---

1. Genesis 3.7.
2. Saint Augustine; this commonplace echoes parts of his sermon on Adam and Eve.
3. 1 Peter 3.7.
4. Genesis 3.15.
5. Galatians 4.4.

6. Galatians 3.28.
7. 1 Corinthians 15.22.
8. 1 Corinthians 7.
9. Eusebius (A.D. 260–340) was Bishop of Caesarea and a church historian. See *Ecclesiastical History* 3.30.

the which is very probable, being that interrogatively he saith: "Have we not power to lead about a wife being a sister, as well as the rest of the Apostles, and as the brethren of the Lord, and Cephas?"[1]

The fourth and last objection is that of Solomon: "I have found one man among a thousand, but a woman among them all have I not found.[2] For answer of which, if we look into the story of his life, we shall find therein a commentary upon this enigmatical[3] sentence included. For it is there said that Solomon had seven hundred wives and three hundred concubines, which number connected make one thousand. These women turning away his heart from being perfect with the Lord his God,[4] sufficient cause had he to say, that among the said thousand women found he not one upright. He saith not, that among a thousand women never any man found one worthy of commendation, but speaks in the first person singularly "I have not found," meaning in his own experience. For this assertion is to be held a part of the confession of his former follies, and no otherwise, his repentance being the intended drift of *Ecclesiastes*.

Thus having (by God's assistance) removed those stones whereat some have stumbled, others broken their shins, I will proceed toward the period of my intended task, which is to decipher the excellency of women. Of whose creation I will, for order's sake, observe: first, the efficient cause,[5] which was God; secondly, the material cause, or whereof she was made; thirdly, the formal cause, or fashion and proportion of her feature; fourthly and lastly, the final cause, the end or purpose for which she was made. To begin with the first.

The efficient cause of woman's creation was Jehovah the Eternal, the truth of which is manifest in Moses his narration of the six days' works, where he says, "God created them male and female."[6] And David, exhorting all "the earth to sing to the Lord" (meaning, by a metonymy,[7] "earth": all creatures that live on the earth, of whatever sex or nation) gives this reason: "For the Lord has made us."[8] That work then cannot choose but be good, yea very good, which is wrought by so excellent a workman as the Lord; for he, being a glorious Creator, must effect a worthy creature. Bitter water cannot proceed from a pleasant sweet fountain, nor bad work from that workman which is perfectly good—and, in propriety, none but he.[9]

Secondly, the material cause, or matter whereof woman was made, was of a refined mold, if I may so speak. For man was created of the dust of the earth,[1] but woman was made of a part of man after that he was a living soul. Yet she was not produced from Adam's foot, to be his too low inferior; nor from his head to be his superior; but from his side, near his heart, to be his equal: that where he is lord, she may be lady. And therefore saith God concerning man and woman jointly: "Let them rule over the fish of the sea, and over the fowls of the heaven, and over every beast that moves upon the earth."[2] By which words he makes their authority equal, and all creatures to be in subjection to them both. This, being rightly considered, doth teach men to make such account of their wives as Adam did of Eve: "This is bone of my bone, and flesh of my flesh."[3] As also, that they neither do or wish any more hurt

1. 1 Corinthians 9.5.
2. Ecclesiastes 7.30.
3. Mysterious.
4. 1 Kings 11.3.
5. The agent who makes something; see Aristotle's *Physics* 2.3.
6. Genesis 1.28 [27].

7. A figure of speech that substitutes one term for another to which it is closely related.
8. Psalms 100.3.
9. Psalms 100.5; Matthew 19.7.
1. Genesis 2.7.
2. Genesis 1.26.
3. Genesis 2.23.

unto them, than unto their own bodies. For men ought to love their wives as themselves, because he that loves his wife loves himself;[4] and never did man hate his own flesh (which the woman is) unless a monster in nature.

Thirdly, the formal cause, fashion and proportion, of woman was excellent. For she was neither like the beasts of the earth, fowls of the air, fishes of the sea, or any other inferior creature; but man was the only object which she did resemble. For as God gave man a lofty countenance that he might look up toward Heaven, so did he likewise give unto woman. And as the temperature of man's body is excellent, so is woman's. For whereas other creatures, by reason of their gross humors, have excrements for their habit—as fowls their feathers, beasts their hair, fishes their scales—man and woman only have their skin clear and smooth.[5] And (that more is) in the image of God were they both created; yea and to be brief, all the parts of their bodies, both external and internal, were correspondent and meet each for other.

Fourthly and lastly, the final cause or end for which woman was made was to glorify God, and to be a collateral companion for man to glory God, in using her body and all the parts, powers and faculties thereof as instruments for his honor. As with her voice to sound forth his praises, like Miriam, and the rest of her company;[6] with her tongue not to utter words of strife, but to give good counsel unto her husband, the which he must not despise. For Abraham was bidden to give ear to Sarah his wife.[7] Pilate was willed by his wife not to have any hand in the condemning of Christ;[8] and a sin it was in him that he listened not to her; Leah and Rachel counseled Jacob to do according to the word of the Lord;[9] and the Shunamite put her husband in mind of harboring the prophet Elisha.[1] Her hands should be open, according to her ability, in contributing towards God's service and distressed servants, like to that poor widow who cast two mites into the treasury;[2] and as Mary Magdalene, Susanna and Joanna, the wife of Herod's steward, with many others which of their substance ministered unto Christ.[3] Her heart should be a receptacle for God's word, like Mary that treasured the sayings of Christ in her heart.[4] Her feet should be swift in going to seek the Lord in his sanctuary, as Mary Magdalene made haste to seek Christ at his sepulcher.[5] Finally, no power external or internal ought woman to keep idle, but to employ it in some service of God, to the glory of her creator and comfort of her own soul.

The other end for which woman was made was to be a companion and helper for man; and if she must be a *helper*, and but a *helper*, then are those husbands to be blamed, which lay the whole burden of domestical affairs and maintenance on the shoulders of their wives. For, as yoke-fellows they are to sustain part of each other's cares, griefs and calamities. But as if two oxen be put into one yoke, the one being bigger than the other, the greater bears most weight; so the husband, being the stronger vessel, is to bear a greater burden than his wife. And therefore the Lord said to Adam: "In the sweat of your face shall you eat your bread, till you return to the dust."[6] And St. Paul says that "he that provideth not for his household is worse than

4. Ephesians 5.28.
5. Genesis 1.26.
6. Exodus 15.20.
7. Genesis 21.12.
8. Matthew 27.19.
9. Genesis 31.16.

1. 2 Kings 4.9.
2. Mark 12.43.
3. Luke 8.
4. Luke 1.45.
5. John 20.1.
6. Genesis 3.19.

an infidel."[7] Nature hath taught senseless creatures to help one another: as the male pigeon, when his hen is weary with sitting on her eggs and comes off from them, supplies her place, that in her absence they may receive no harm, until such time as she is fully refreshed. Of small birds, the cock always helps his hen to build her nest; and while she sits upon her eggs he flies abroad to get meat for her, who cannot then provide any for herself. The crowing cockerel helps his hen to defend her chickens from peril, and will endanger himself to save her and them from harm. Seeing then, that these unreasonable creatures by the instinct of nature bear such affection to each other, that without any grudge they willingly according to their kind help one another, I may reason, *a minore ad maius*,[8] that much more should man and woman, which are reasonable creatures, be helpers to each other in all things lawful, they having the law of God to guide them, his word to be a lantern to their feet and a light unto their paths, by which they are excited to a far more mutual participation of each other's burden than other creatures. So that neither the wife may say to her husband nor the husband to his wife: "I have no need of thee,"[9] no more than the members of the body may say to each other, between whom there is such a sympathy that if one member suffer, all suffer with it. Therefore though God bade Abraham forsake his country and kindred, yet he bade him not forsake his wife who, being "Flesh of his flesh, and bone of his bone," was to be copartner with him of whatsoever did betide him, whether joy or sorrow. Wherefore Solomon says "woe to him that is alone";[1] for when thoughts of discomfort, troubles of this world and fear of dangers do possess him, he wants a companion to lift him up from the pit of perplexity into which he is fallen.[2] For a good wife, saith Plautus, is the wealth of the mind and the welfare of the heart; and therefore a meet associate for her husband. And "woman," saith Paul, "is the glory of the man."[3]

Marriage is a merri-age, and this world's paradise, where there is mutual love. Our blessed Savior vouchsafed to honor a marriage with the first miracle that he wrought,[4] unto which miracle matrimonial estate may not unfitly be resembled. For as Christ turned water into wine, a far more excellent liquor (which, as the Psalmist saith, "Makes glad the hearts of man";[5] so the single man is changed by marriage from a bachelor to a husband, a far more excellent title: from a solitary life to a joyful union and conjunction with such a creature as God had made meet for man, for whom none was fit till she was made. The enjoying of this great blessing made Pericles more unwilling to part from his wife than to die for his country; and Antonius Pius to pour forth that pathetic exclamation against death for depriving him of his dearly beloved wife: "O cruel hard-hearted death in bereaving me of her whom I esteemed more than my own life!"[6] "A virtuous woman," saith Solomon, "is the crown of her husband";[7] by which metaphor he shows both the excellency of such a wife and what account her husband is to make of her. For a king does not trample his crown under his feet, but highly esteems it, gently handles it and carefully lays it up as the evidence of his kingdom; and therefore when David destroyed Rabbah[8] he

---

7. 1 Timothy 5.8.
8. From the lesser to the greater.
9. 1 Corinthians 12.21.
1. Ecclesiastes 4.10.
2. Ecclesiastes 4.10.
3. 1 Corinthians 11.7.
4. John 2.
5. Psalms 104.15.

6. Antonius Pius (A.D. 86–161) Roman emperor, founded a charity for orphaned girls in honor of his wife. Plutarch writes about how Pericles (495–429 B.C.), ruler of Athens, greatly loved Aspasia.
7. Proverbs 7.4.
8. 1 Chronicles 20.2. Joab destroyed Rabbah, while David took the king's crown.

took off the crown from their king's head. So husbands should not account their wives as their vassals but as those that are "heirs together of the grace of life,"[9] and with all lenity and mild persuasions set their feet in the right way if they happen to tread awry, bearing with their infirmities, as Elkanah did with his wife's barrenness.[1]

The kingdom of God is compared to the marriage of a king's son;[2] John calleth the conjunction of Christ and his chosen a marriage;[3] and not few but many times does our blessed Savior in the Canticles[4] set forth his unspeakable love towards his church under the title of a husband rejoicing with his wife, and often vouchsafeth to call her his sister a spouse—by which is showed that with God "is no respect of persons," nations, or sexes.[5] For whosoever, whether it be man or woman, that doth "believe in the lord Jesus, such shall be saved."[6] And if God's love, even from the beginning, had not been as great toward woman as to man, then he would not have preserved from the deluge of the old world as many women as men. Nor would Christ after his resurrection have appeared to a woman first of all other, had it not been to declare thereby, that the benefits of his death and resurrection are as available, by belief, for women as for men; for he indifferently died for the one sex as well as the other.

━━ ◄✦► ━━

"Esther Sowernam"

The pen name Esther Sowernam comes from the Old Testament heroine Esther, who defended her people against Haman, and the antithesis of Joseph Swetnam's last name (sweet/sour). The full title of her text also parodies Swetnam's: *Esther Hath Hanged Haman; or An Answer to a Lewd Pamphlet, Entitled The Arraignment of Women. With the arraignment of Lewd, Idle, Froward and Unconstant Men, and Husbands* (1617). On the whole the author of this pamphlet presents herself in a more secular light than Rachel Speght does. Sowernam's criticisms of misogyny are more psychological and social than moral and logical. Trained in classics as well as Scripture and a keen observer, Esther Sowernam finds that Swetnam has incorrectly stated that the Bible is the source of the statement that women are a necessary evil and finds that the true source is in Euripides' *Medea*. The occasion for Sowernam's writing is a dinner party at which Swetnam's book and Speght's response were discussed. Sowernam finds fault with both—Swetnam because he "damns all women" and Speght because she "undertaking to defend women doth rather charge and condemn them." Sowernam cites the double standard by which men are excused for what women are judged harshly for in order to assert women's superiority. She argues that women are judged more severely because they are thought to be more virtuous in the first place. The second half of her pamphlet may have helped to inspire the comedy that spoofed the entire controversy, *Swetnam the Woman-Hater Arraigned By Women* (1620).

from **Esther Hath Hanged Haman**

from Chapter 7. The answer to all objections which are material made against women

As for that crookedness and frowardness[1] with which you charge women, look from whence they have it. For of themselves and their own disposition it doth not proceed, which is proved directly by your own testimony. For in your 46th page, line

---

9. 1 Peter 3.7.
1. 1 Samuel 1.17.
2. Matthew 22.
3. Revelation 19.7.

4. The Song of Songs.
5. Romans 2.11.
6. John 3.18.
1. Perversity, unreasonableness.

15[16], you say: "A young woman of tender years is flexible, obedient, and subject to do anything, according to the will and pleasure of her husband." How cometh it then that this gentle and mild disposition is afterwards altered? Yourself doth give the true reason, for you give a great charge not to marry a widow. But why? Because, say you in the same page, "A widow is framed to the conditions[2] of another man." Why then, if a woman have froward conditions, they be none of her own, she was framed to them. Is not our adversary ashamed of himself to rail against women for those faults which do all come from men? Doth not he most grievously charge men to learn[3] their wives bad and corrupt behavior? For he saith plainly: "Thou must unlearn a widow, and make her forget and forego her former corrupt and disordered behavior." Thou must unlearn her; *ergo*, what fault she hath learned: her corruptness comes not from her own disposition but from her husband's destruction.

Is it not a wonder that your pamphlets are so dispersed? Are they not wise men to cast away time and money upon a book which cutteth their own throats? 'Tis pity but that men should reward you for your writing (if it be but as the Roman Sertorius[4] did the idle poet: he gave him a reward, but not for his writing—but because he should never write more). As for women, they laugh that men have no more able a champion. This author cometh to bait women or, as he foolishly saith, the "Bear-baiting of Women," and he bringeth but a mongrel cur who doth his kind[5] to brawl and bark, but cannot bite. The mild and flexible disposition of a woman is in philosophy proved in the composition of her body, for it is a maxim: *Mores animi sequntur temperaturam corporis* (the disposition of the mind is answerable to the temper of the body). A woman in the temperature of her body is tender, soft and beautiful, so doth her disposition in mind correspond accordingly: she is mild, yielding and virtuous. What disposition accidentally happeneth unto her is by the contagion of a froward husband, as Joseph Swetnam affirmeth.

And experience proveth. It is a shame for a man to complain of a froward woman— in many respects all concerning himself. It is a shame he hath no more government over the weaker vessel.[6] It is a shame he hath hardened her tender sides and gentle heart with his boisterous and Northern blasts. It is a shame for a man to publish and proclaim household secrets—which is a common practice amongst men, especially drunkards, lechers, and prodigal spendthrifts. These when they come home drunk, or are called in question for their riotous misdemeanors, they presently show themselves the right children of Adam. They will excuse themselves by their wives and say that their unquietness and frowardness at home is the cause that they run abroad: an excuse more fitter for a beast than a man. If thou wert a man thou wouldst take away the cause which urgeth a woman to grief and discontent, and not by thy frowardness increase her distemperature.[7] Forbear thy drinking, thy luxurious riot, thy gaming and spending, and thou shalt have thy wife give thee as little cause at home as thou givest her great cause of disquiet abroad. Men which are men, if they chance to be matched with froward wives—either of their own making or others' marring[8]—they would make a benefit of the discommodity:[9] either try his skill to make her mild or exercise his patience to endure her cursedness; for all crosses are inflicted either for punishment of sins or for exercise of virtues. But humorous[1] men will sooner mar a thousand women than out of a hundred make one good.

---

2. Circumstances, character traits.
3. Teach.
4. Quintus Sertorius, Roman general, appointed governor of Farther Spain in 83 B.C.
5. Nature.

6. From 1 Peter 3.7.
7. Disorder in mind and body.
8. Spoiling.
9. Inconvenience, disadvantageousness.
1. Moody.

And this shall appear in the imputation which our adversary chargeth upon our sex: to be lascivious, wanton and lustful. He saith: "Women tempt, allure and provoke men." How rare a thing is it for women to prostitute and offer themselves? How common a practice is it for men to seek and solicit women to lewdness? What charge do they spare? What travail do they bestow? What vows, oaths and protestations do they spend to make them dishonest? They hire panders, they write letters, they seal them with damnations and execrations to assure them of love when the end proves but lust. They know the flexible disposition of women, and the sooner to overreach them some will pretend they are so plunged in love that, except they obtain their desire, they will seem to drown, hang, stab, poison, or banish themselves from friends and country. What motives are these to tender dispositions? Some will pretend marriage, another offer continual maintenance; but when they have obtained their purpose, what shall a woman find?—just that which is her everlasting shame and grief: she hath made herself the unhappy subject to a lustful body and the shameful stall[2] of a lascivious tongue. Men may with foul shame charge woman with this sin which she had never committed, if she had not trusted; nor had ever trusted, if she had not been deceived with vows, oaths and protestations. To bring a woman to offend in one sin, how many damnable sins do they commit? I appeal to their own consciences. The lewd disposition of sundry men doth appear in this: if a woman or maid will yield to lewdness, what shall they want?[3]—but if they would live in honesty, what help shall they have? How much will they make of the lewd? How base an account of the honest? How many pounds will they spend in bawdy houses? But when will they bestow a penny upon an honest maid or woman, except it be to corrupt them?

Our adversary bringeth many examples of men which have been overthrown by women. It is answered before: the fault is their own. But I would have him, or anyone living, to show any woman that offended in this sin of lust, but that she was first solicited by a man.

Helen was the cause of Troy's burning: first, Paris did solicit her; next, how many knaves and fools of the male kind had Troy, which to maintain whoredom would bring their city to confusion?

When you bring in examples of lewd women and of men which have been stained by women, you show yourself both frantic and a profane irreligious fool to mention Judith,[4] for cutting off Holofernes' head, in that rank.

You challenge women for untamed and unbridled tongues; there was never woman was ever noted for so shameless, so brutish, so beastly a scold as you prove yourself in this base and odious pamphlet. Your blaspheme God, you rail at his creation, you abuse and slander his creatures; and what immodest or impudent scurrility is it which you do not express in this lewd and lying pamphlet?

Hitherto I have so answered all your objections against women that, as I have not defended the wickedness of any, so I have set down the true state of the question. As Eve did not offend without temptation of a serpent, so women do seldom offend but it is by provocation of men. Let not your impudency, nor your consorts' dishonesty, charge our sex hereafter with those sins of which you yourselves were the first procurers. I have, in my discourse, touched you, and all yours, to the quick. I have taxed you with bitter speeches; you will, perhaps, say I am a railing scold. In this

---

2. Target.
3. Lack, need.
4. A wealthy, attractive widow who saved her people from

Holofernes, an Assyrian general, by attracting and then killing him. (See The Book of Judith, part of the Catholic Bible, but viewed as apocryphal by Jews and Protestants.)

objection, Joseph Swetnam, I will teach you both wit and honesty. The difference between a railing scold and an honest accuser is this: the first rageth upon passionate fury without bringing cause or proof, the other bringeth direct proof for what she allegeth. You charge women with clamorous words, and bring no proof; I charge you with blasphemy, with impudency, scurrility, foolery and the like. I show just and direct proof for what I say. It is not my desire to speak so much; it is your dessert to provoke me upon just cause so far. It is not railing to call a crow black, or a wolf a ravenor,[5] or a drunkard a beast; the report of the truth is never to be blamed: the deserver of such a report deserves the shame.

Now, for this time, to draw to an end. Let me ask according to the question of Cassian, *cui bono?*[6]—what have you gotten by publishing your pamphlet? Good I know you can get none. You have, perhaps, pleased the humors of some giddy, idle, conceited persons. But you have dyed yourself in the colors of shame, lying, slandering, blasphemy, ignorance, and the like.

The shortness of time and the weight of business call me away, and urge me to leave off thus abruptly; but assure yourself, where I leave now I will by God's grace supply the next term, to your small content. You have exceeded in your fury against widows, whose defense you shall hear of at the time aforesaid. In the mean space, recollect your wits; write out of deliberation, not out of fury; write out of advice, not out of idleness: forbear to charge women with faults which come from the contagion of masculine serpents.

┄┄ ✦❖✦ ┄┄

Hic Mulier
and
Haec Vir

Hic Mulier and *Haec Vir* were published anonymously within a week of each other in February 1620. *Hic Mulier*, the first of the two pamphlets to appear, begins with the complaint that "since the days of Adam women were never so masculine." The title introduces this theme by a gender switch of its own: *Hic Mulier*, Latin for "This Woman," uses the masculine form *hic* instead of the feminine *haec*. The title page contains illustrations of two such mannish women—one wearing a man's hat, which she admires in a mirror, and another sitting in a barber's chair to get her hair cut. Structured as a "brief declamation," or oration, the text argues that such activities as hair bobbing and wearing men's clothes are immoral and unnatural for women. Furthermore, such gender crossing is also a threat to the entire political order: "most pernicious to the commonwealth for she hath power by example to do it a world of injury."

As its subtitle boasts, *Haec Vir* was "an answer to the late book intituled *Hic Mulier*" and was represented as "a brief dialogue between Haec Vir the Womanish Man, and Hic Mulier the Man-Woman." The effeminate man and the hermaphroditic woman first misrecognize each other's gender. Once that is cleared up, the foppish man launches into a diatribe against the woman, who defends herself by arguing that "custom is an idiot." The first half of the dialogue reads like a proclamation of the equality of the sexes, with the bare-breasted, dagger-swinging Hic Mulier exclaiming, "We are as free-born as men, have as free election, and as free spirits, we are compounded of like parts and may with like liberty make benefit of our creations." Despite this bold challenge, the text as a whole makes a rather conservative case for

---

5. An animal who seizes in order to devour.

6. "To whose beneift," a phrase attributed by Cicero to Lucius Cassius.

the need for gender distinctions, the overturning of which was seen as an assault on hierarchy. The dialogue ends with both participants agreeing to exchange clothes and Latin pronouns so that men will again be manly and women subservient to them.

These pamphlets display the early modern fascination with, and loathing of, transvestism. Not only did the fashionable young male favorites of King James I's court resemble the womanish man of *Haec Vir*, but there were more than a few documented cases of women wearing breeches on the streets. One of these women, the notorious Mary Frith, was immortalized in Dekker and Middleton's comedy, *The Roaring Girl*. A few women were actually brought before ecclesiastical courts for "shamefully" putting on "man's apparel."

While conforming to the comic pattern of disrupting and then reestablishing the status quo, these pamphlets show that questions about custom, nature, and sex and gender roles were being asked in the early seventeenth century.

from Hic Mulier; or, The Man-Woman

So I present these masculine women in their deformities as they are, that I may call them back to the modest comeliness in which they were.

The modest comeliness in which they were? Why, did ever these mermaids, or rather mere-monsters,[1] that wear the Car-man's block,[2] the Dutchman's feather *upse-van-muffe*, the poor man's pate pouled by a Treene dish, the French doublet trussed with points, to Mary Aubries' light nether skirts, the fool's baldric, and the devil's poniard. Did they ever know comeliness or modesty? Fie, no, they never walked in those paths, for these at the best are sure but rags of gentry, torn from better pieces for their foul stains, or else the adulterate branches of rich stocks,[3] that taking too much sap from the root, are cut away, and employed in base uses; or, if not so, they are the stinking vapors drawn from dunghills, which nourished in the higher regions of the air, become meteors and false fires blazing and flashing therein, and amazing men's minds with their strange proportions, till the substance of their pride being spent, they drop down again to the place from whence they came, and there rot and consume unpitied, and unremembered.

And questionless it is true, that such were the first beginners of these last deformities, for from any purer blood would have issued a purer birth; there would have been some spark of virtue: some excuse for imitation; but this deformity has no agreement with goodness, nor any difference against the weakest reason: it is all base, all barbarous. Base, in the respect it offends men in the example, and God in the most unnatural use: barbarous, in that it is exorbitant from nature, and an antithesis to kind,[4] going astray (with ill-favored affectation) both in attire, in speech, in manners, and (it is to be feared) in the whole courses and stories of their actions. What can be more true and curious consent of the most fairest colors and the wealthy gardens which fill the world with living plants? Do but you receive virtuous inmates (as what palaces are more rich to receive heavenly messengers?) and you shall draw men's souls to you with that severe, devout, and holy adoration, that you shall never want praise, never love, never reverence.

But now methinks I hear the witty-offending great ones reply in excuse of their deformities: What, is there no difference amongst women? no distinction of places, no respect of honors, nor no regard of blood, or alliance? Must but a bare pair of

---

1. Pure monsters.
2. A merchant's hat. Descriptions of ridiculous fashions follow: the *upse-van-muffe* is an elaborate feathered hat; the pate pouled by a Treene dish is hair cut short to the shape of a wooden dish; the French doublet is a man's

close-fitting upper body garment tied with laces; baldric: fancy belt; poniard: dagger.
3. Trunks or stems.
4. The opposite of what is natural to the gender.

shears pass between noble and ignoble, between the generous spirit and the base mechanic; shall we be all co-heirs of one honor, one estate, and one habit? O men, you are then too tyrannous, and not only injure nature, but also break the laws and customs of the wisest princes. Are not bishops known by their miters, princes by their crowns, judges by their robes, and knights by their spurs? But poor women have nothing (how great soever they be) to divide themselves from the enticing shows or moving images which do furnish most shops in the city. What is it that either the laws have allowed to the greatest ladies, custom found convenient, or their bloods or places challenged, which hath not been engrossed into the city with as great greediness, and pretense of true title; as if the surcease[5] from the imitation were the utter breach of their charter everlastingly.

For this cause, these apes of the city have enticed foreign nations to the cells, and there committing gross adultery with their gewgaws,[6] have brought out such unnatural conceptions, that the whole world is not able to make a *Democritus* big enough to laugh at their foolish ambitions.[7] Nay, the very art of painting (which to the last age shall ever be held in detestation) they have so cunningly stolen and hidden amongst their husbands' hoards of treasure, that the decayed stock of prostitution (having little other revenues) are hourly in bringing their action of *detinue*[8] against them. Hence (being thus troubled with these *Popeniars*,[9] and loath still to march in one rank with fools and *zanies*[1]) have proceeded these disguised deformities, not to offend the eyes of goodness, but to tire with ridiculous contempt the never to be satisfied appetites of these gross and unmannerly intruders. Nay, look if this very last edition of disguise, this which is so full of faults, corruptions, and false quotations, this bait which the devil had laid to catch the souls of wanton women, be not as frequent in the demi-palaces of burghers and citizens as it is either at masque, triumph, tilt-yard, or playhouse. Call but to account the tailors that are contained within the circumference of the walls of the city, and let but their heels and their hard reckonings be justly summed together, and it will be found they have raised more new foundations of this new disguise, and metamorphosed more modest old garments, to this new manner of short base and French doublet (only for the use of freemen's wives[2] and their children) in one month, than has been worn in court, suburbs, or country, since the unfortunate beginning of the first devilish invention.

Let therefore the powerful Statute of Apparel[3] but lift his battle-axe, and crush the offenders in pieces, so as every one may be known by the true badge of their blood, or fortune; and then these *Chimeras* of deformity will be sent back to hell, and there burn to cinders in the flames of their own malice.

Thus, methinks, I hear the best offenders argue, nor can I blame a high blood to swell when it is coupled and counter-checked with baseness and corruption; yet this shows an anger passing near akin to envy, and alludes much to the saying of an excellent poet:

> Women never
> Love beauty in their sex, but envy ever.

---

5. Cessation, stop.
6. Showy decorations.
7. Seneca recounts how Democritus laughed rather than cried at human life (*De tranquilitate animi* 15.2).
8. Legal action to recover personal property.
9. Popinjays, vain and empty people.
1. Parasites, those who play the fool for amusement.

2. Women married to men possessing the freedom of a city, borough, or corporation.
3. Laws governing dress that were intended to differentiate the aristocracy from the common people had been enacted from the Middle Ages through to the early modern period.

They have Caesar's ambition, and desire to be one and one alone, but yet to offend themselves, to grieve others, is a revenge dissonant to reason, and as *Euripides* says, a woman of that malicious nature is a fierce beast, and most pernicious to the commonwealth, for she has power by example to do it a world of injury. But far be such cruelty from the softness of their gentle dispositions: O let them remember what the poet saith:

> Women be
> Fram'd with the same parts of the mind as men
> Nay Nature triumph'd in their beauty's birth,
> And women made the glory of the earth,
> The life of beauty, in whose simple breast,
> (As in her fair lodging) Virtue rests:
> Whose towering thoughts attended with remorse,
> Do make their fairness be of greater force.

But when they thrust virtue out of doors, and give a shameless liberty to every loose passion, that either their weak thoughts engender, or the discourse of wicked tongues can charm into their yielding bosoms (much too apt to be opened with any pick-lock of flattering and deceitful insinuation) then they turn maskers, mummers, nay monsters in their disguises, and so they may catch the bridle in their teeth, and run away with their rulers, they care not into what dangers they plunge either their fortunes or reputations, the disgrace of the whole sex, or the blot and obloquy of their private families, according to the saying of the poets

> Such is the cruelty of women-kind,
> When they have shaken off the shamefac'd band
> With which wise nature did them strongly bind,
> T'obey the bests of man's well-ruling hand
> That then all rule and reason they withstand
> To purchase a licentious liberty;
> But virtuous women wisely understand,
> That they were born to mild humility,
> Unless the heavens them lift to lawful sovereignty.[4]

To you therefore that are fathers, husbands, of sustainers of these new hermaphrodites, belongs the cure of this imposture;[5] it is you that give fuel to the flames of their wild indiscretion. You add the oil which makes their stinking lamps defile the whole house with filthy smoke, and your purses purchase these deformities at rates both dear and unreasonable. Do you but hold close your liberal hands, or take a strict account of the employment of the treasure you give to their necessary maintenance, and these excesses will either cease, or else die smothered in prison in the tailors' trunks for want of redemption.

from Haec Vir; or, The Womanish Man

Hic-Mulier: Well, then to the purpose: first, you say, I am base in being a slave to novelty. What flattery can there be in freedom of election? Or what baseness to crown my delights with those pleasures which are most suitable to mine affections? Bondage or slavery is a restraint from those actions, which the mind (of its own

---

4. Description of the tyranny of the Amazonian ruler   5. Abcess.
Radigund in Spenser's *Faerie Queene* 5.5.25.

accord) doth most willingly desire: to perform the intents and purposes of another's disposition, and that not but by mansuetude[1] or sweetness of entreaty; but by the force of authority and strength of compulsion. Now for me to follow change, according to the limitation of my own will and pleasure, there cannot be a greater freedom. Nor do I in my delight of change otherwise than as the whole world doth, or as becometh a daughter of the world to do. For what is the world, but a very shop or warehouse of change? Sometimes winter, sometimes summer; day and night: they hold sometimes riches, sometimes poverty, sometimes health, sometimes sickness: now pleasure; presently anguish; now honor; then contempt: and to conclude, there is nothing but change, which doth surround and mix with all our fortunes. And will you have poor woman such a fixed star, that she shall not so much as move or twinkle in her own sphere? That would be true slavery indeed, and a baseness beyond the chains of the worst servitude. Nature to everything she hath created hath given a singular delight in change, as to herbs, plants, and trees a time to wither and shed their leaves, a time to bud and bring forth their leaves, and a time for their fruits and flowers; to worms and creeping things a time to hide themselves in the pores and hollows of the earth, and a time to come abroad and suck the dew; to beasts liberty to choose their food, liberty to delight in their food, and liberty to feed and grow fat with their food. The birds have the air to fly in, the waters to bathe in, and the earth to feed on. But to man, both these and all things else, to alter, frame, and fashion, according to his will and delight shall rule him. Again, who will rob the eye of the variety of objects, the ear of the delight of sounds, the nose of smells, the tongue of taste, and the hand of feeling? And shall only woman, excellent woman, so much better in that she is something purer, be only deprived of this benefit? Shall she be the bondslave of time, the handmaid of opinion, or the strict observer of every frosty or cold benumbed imagination? It would be a cruelty beyond the rack or strapado.[2]

But you will say it is not change, but novelty, from which you deter us: a thing that doth avert the good, and erect the evil; prefer the faithless, and confound desert; that with the change of opinions breeds the change of states, and with continual alterations thrusts headlong forward both ruin and subversion. Alas (soft Sir) what can you christen by that new imagined title, when the words of a wise man are: *that what was done, is but done again: all things do change, and under the cope of heaven there is no new thing.*[3] So that whatsoever we do or imitate, it is neither slavish, base, nor a breeder of novelty.

Next, you condemn me of unnaturalness, in forsaking my creation, and contemning[4] custom. How do I forsake my creation, that do all the right and offices due to my creation? I was created free, born free, and live free: what lets me then so to spin out my time, that I may die free?

To alter creation were to walk on my hands with my heels upward, to feed myself with my feet, or to forsake the sweet sound of sweet words, for the hissing noise of the serpent: but I walk with a face erected, with a body clothed, with a mind busied, and with a heart full of reasonable and devout cogitations; only offensive in attire, inasmuch as it is a stranger to the curiosity of the present times, and an enemy to custom. Are we then bound to be the flatterers of time, or the dependents on custom? O miserable servitude chained only to baseness and folly! For then custom, nothing is more absurd, nothing more foolish. * * *

---

1. Gentleless, meekness.
2. Rack: a frame with a roller at either end on which a person would be tortured; strapado: a form of torture in which the victim's hands would be hands tied behind his or her back and the victim would then be suspended by a pulley with a sharp jolt.
3. Ecclesiastes 1.9.
4. Disdaining, despising.

Cato Iunior held it for a custom, never to eat meat but sitting on the ground. The Venetians kiss one another ever at the first meeting; and even in this day it is a general received custom amongst our English, that when we meet or overtake any man in our travel or journeying, to examine him whither he rides, how far, to what purpose, and where he lodgeth? Nay, and with that unmannerly boldness of inquisition, that it is a certain ground of a most insufficient quarrel, not to receive a full satisfaction of those demands which go far astray from good manners, or comely civility; and will you have us to marry ourselves to these mimic and most fantastic customs? It is a fashion or custom with us to mourn in black, yet the Argian[5] and Roman ladies ever mourned in white; and (if we will tie the action upon the signification of colors) I see not but we may mourn in green, blue, red or any simple color used in heraldry. For us to salute strangers with a kiss is counted but civility, but with foreign nations immodesty; for you to cut the hair of your upper lips, familiar here in England, everywhere else almost thought unmanly. To ride on side-saddles at first was counted here abominable pride, and et cetera. I might instance in a thousand things that only custom and not reason hath approved. To conclude, Custom is an idiot, and whoever dependeth wholly upon him, without the discourse of reason, will take from him his pied[6] coat, and become a slave indeed to contempt and censure.

But you say we are barbarous and shameless and cast off all softness, to run wild through a wilderness of opinions. In this you express more cruelty than in all the rest, because I do not stand with my hands on my belly like a baby[7] at Bartholomew Fair,[8] that move not my whole body when I should but only stir my head like Jack of the clock house[9] which has no joints, that is not dumb when wantons court me, as if asslike I were ready for all burdens, or because I weep not when injury gripes me, like a worried deer in the fangs of many curs. Am I therefore barbarous or shameless? He is much injurious that so baptized us; we are as free-born as men, have as free election, and as free spirits, we are compounded of like parts, and may with like liberty make benefit of our creations; my countenance shall smile on the worthy, and frown on the ignoble, I will hear the wise, and be deaf to idiots, give counsel to my friend, but be dumb to flatterers, I have hands that shall be liberal to reward desert, feet that shall move swiftly to do good offices, and thoughts that shall ever accompany freedom and severity. If this be barbarous, let me leave the city and live with creatures of like simplicity.

* * *

Hic-Mulier: Therefore to take your proportion in a few lines, (my dear Feminine-Masculine) tell me what Charter, prescription or right of claim you have to those things you make our absolute inheritance? Why do you curl, frizzle and powder your hair, bestowing more hours and time in dividing lock from lock, and hair from hair, in giving every thread his posture, and every curl his true fence and circumference than ever Caesar did in marshalling his army, either at Pharsalia, in Spain, or Britain? Why do you rob us of our ruffs, our earrings, carkanets,[1] and mamillions,[2] of our fans and feathers, our busks and French bodies, nay, of our masks, hoods, shadows, and shapynas,[3] not so much as the very art of painting, but you have so greedily engrossed it, that were it not for that little fantastical sharp pointed dagger that

---

5. Of Argos.
6. Spotted, motley.
7. Doll.
8. A popular carnival fair held every year from 1133 to 1865 at West Smithfield on August 24, the feast day of Saint Bartholomew.

9. Figure that strikes the bell of a clock.
1. A jeweled or gold necklace.
2. Rounded protuberances (from French *mamelon*, nipple).
3. Disguises.

hangs at your chins, and the cross hilt which guards your upper lip, hardly would there be any difference between the fair mistress and the foolish servant. But is this theft the uttermost of our spoil? Fie, you have gone a world further, and even ravished from us our speech, our actions, sports, and recreations. Goodness leave me, if I have not heard a man court his mistress with the same words that Venus did Adonis, or as near as the book could instruct him;[4] where are the tilts and tourneys, and lofty galliards[5] that were danced in the days of old, when men capered in the air like wanton kids on the tops of mountains, and turned above ground as if they had been compact of fire or a purer element?[6] Tut, all's forsaken, all's vanished, those motions showed more strength than art, and more courage than courtship; it was much too robustious, and rather spent the body than prepared it, especially where any defect before reigned; hence you took from us poor women our traverses and tourneys, our modest stateliness and curious slidings, and left us nothing but the new French garb of puppet hopping and setting. Lastly, poor shuttlecock[7] that was only a female invention, how have you taken it out of our hands, and made yourselves such lords and rulers over it, that though it be a very emblem of us, and our lighter despised fortunes, yet it dare now hardly come near us; nay, you keep it so imprisoned within your bed-chambers and dining rooms, amongst your pages and panders, that a poor innocent maid to give but a kick with her battledore,[8] were more than halfway to the ruin of her reputation. For this you have demolished the noble schools of horsemanship (of which many were in this city) hung up your arms to rust, glued up those swords in their scabbards that would shake all Christendom with the brandish, and entertained into your mind such softness, dullness, and effeminate niceness that it would even make *Heraclitus*[9] himself laugh against his nature to see how pulingly[1] you languish in this weak entertained sin of womanish softness. To see one of your gender either show himself (in the midst of his pride or riches) at a playhouse or public assembly; how (before he dare enter) with the Jacob's-staff of his own eyes and his pages, he takes a full survey of himself, from the highest sprig in his feather, to the lowest spangle that shines in his shoestring: how he prunes and picks himself like a hawk set a-weathering, calls every several garment to auricular[2] confession, making them utter both their mortal great stains, and their venial and less blemishes, though the mote must be much less than an atom. Then to see him pluck and tug everything into the form of the newest received fashion; and by *Durer's* rules[3] make his leg answerable to his neck; his thigh proportionable with his middle, his foot with his hand, and a world of such idle disdained foppery. To see him thus patched up with symmetry, make himself complete, and even as a circle, and lastly, cast himself among the eyes of the people (as an object of wonder) with more niceness than a virgin goes to the sheets of her first lover would make patience herself mad with anger, and cry with the poet:

> O hominum mores, O gens, O tempora dura,
> Quantus in urbe dolor; quantus in orbe dolus![4]

---

4. Venus, goddess of love, fell in love with the beautiful youth Adonis.
5. A brisk dance in triple time.
6. Men were thought to be dominated by dry humors and women by humid ones.
7. A small piece of cork with feathers sticking out of it, batted back and forth in the game of battledoor and shuttlecock.
8. A small racket, used to hit a shuttlecock.

9. Heraclitus was said to weep whenever he went forth in public (See Seneca, *De tranquilitate animi* 15.2).
1. In a whining tone.
2. Told privately, to the ear.
3. Albrecht Dürer (1471–1528), German painter and engraver, wrote a work on human proportions that was published after his death.
4. O customs of men, O people, O hard times / what great sadness in the city; what great fraud in the world.

Now since according to your own inference, even by the laws of nature, by the rules of religion, and the customs of all civil nations, it is necessary there be a distinct and special difference between man and woman, both in their habit and behaviors, what could we poor weak women do less (being far too weak by force to fetch back those spoils you have unjustly taken from us) than to gather up those garments you have proudly cast away, and therewith to clothe both our bodies and our minds; since no other means was left us to continue our names, and to support a difference? For to have held the way in which our forefathers first set us, or to have still embraced the civil modesty, or gentle sweetness of our soft inclinations; why, you had so far encroached upon us, and so over-bribed the world, to be deaf to any grant of restitution, that as at our creation, our whole sex was contained in man our first parent, so we should have had no other being, but in you, and your most effeminate quality. Hence we have preserved (though to our own shames) those manly things which you have forsaken, which would you again accept, and restore to us the blushes we laid by, when first we put on your masculine garments; doubt not but chaste thoughts and bashfulness will again dwell in us, and our palaces being newly gilt, trimmed, and re-edified, draw to us all the Graces, all the Muses,[5] which that you may more willingly do, and (as we of yours) grow into detestation of that deformity you have purloined, to the utter loss of your honors and reputations. Mark how the brave Italian poet,[6] even in the infancy of your abuses, most lively describes you:

> About his neck a Carknet[7] rich he ware
> Of precious Stones, all set in gold well tried;
> His arms that erst all warlike weapons bare,
> In golden bracelets wantonly were tied:
> Into his ears two rings conveyed are
> Of golden wire, at which on either side,
> Two Indian pearls, in making like two pears,
> Of passing price were pendant at his ears.
>
> His locks bedewed with water of sweet savor,
> Stood curled round in order on his head;
> He had such wanton womanish behavior,
> At though in valor he had ne'er been bred:
> So chang'd in speech, in manners and in favor,
> So from himself beyond all reason led,
> By these enchantments of this amorous dame;
> He was himself in nothing, but in name.

Thus you see your injury to us is of an old and inveterate continuance, having taken such strong root in your bosoms, that it can hardly be pulled up, without some offense to the soil: ours young and tender, scarce freed from the swaddling clothes, and therefore may with as much ease be lost, as it was with little difficulty found. Cast then from you our ornaments, and put on your own armors. Be men in shape, men in show, men in words, men in actions, men in counsel, men in example: then will we love and serve you; then will we hear and obey you; then will we like rich jewels hang at your

---

5. The graces were the three sisters, Aglaia, Thalia, and Euphrosyne, viewed as bestowers of charm and beauty; the muses were the nine daughters of Zeus and Memory who inspire poetry and the arts.
6. Ludovico Ariosto (1474–1532), whose description of

Ruggiero's decadence when he is seduced by the sorceress Alcina in *Orlando Furioso* 7 is quoted here in the translation (1590) by Sir John Harington, Queen Elizabeth's godson.
7. Necklace.

ears to take our instructions, like true friends follow you through all dangers, and like careful leeches[8] pour oil into your wounds. Then shall you find delight in our words; pleasure in our faces; faith in our hearts; chastity in our thoughts, and sweetness both in our inward and outward inclinations. Comeliness shall be then our study; fear our armor, and modesty our practice: then shall we be all your most excellent thoughts can desire, and have nothing in us less than impudence and deformity.

Haec-Vir. Enough: you have both raised my eyelids, cleared my sight, and made my heart entertain both shame and delight at an instant; shame in my follies past; delight in our noble and worthy conversion. Away then from me these light vanities, the only ensigns[9] of a weak and soft nature: and come you grave and solid pieces, which arm a man with fortitude and resolution: you are too rough and stubborn for a woman's wearing, we will here change our attires, as we have changed our minds, and with our attires, our names. I will no more be *Haec-Vir,* but *Hic Vir,* nor you *Hic-Mulier,* but *Haec Mulier.* From henceforth deformity shall pack to Hell; and if at any time he hide himself upon the earth, yet it shall be with contempt and disgrace. He shall have no friend but Poverty; no favorer but Folly, nor no reward but Shame. Henceforth we will live nobly like ourselves, ever sober, ever discreet, ever worthy; true men, and true women. We will be henceforth like well-coupled doves, full of industry, full of love: I mean, not of sensual and carnal love, but heavenly and divine love, which proceeds from God, whose inexpressible nature none is able to deliver in words, since is like his dwelling, high and beyond the reach of human apprehension.

[END OF PERSPECTIVES: TRACTS ON WOMEN AND GENDER]

⤖

Thomas Dekker
1572?–1632

and

Thomas Middleton
1580?–1627

Thomas Dekker was one of the most talented and prolific of early modern dramatists, yet one of the most destitute. Though he wrote over seventy plays (many of them now lost) and more than a dozen tracts, Dekker was plagued by poverty throughout his life. In 1598, the same year that Francis Meres listed Dekker as one of the greatest English writers of tragedy, he was imprisoned for debt. The next year, he was arrested for owing money to the acting company of the Lord Chamberlain's Men. Later, he was sentenced to the King's Bench Prison from 1613 to 1619. His wife, Mary, died while he was in prison. While there, Dekker managed to publish the prose pamphlet *Villanies* (1616), the fourth edition of *Lantern and Candlelight,* to which he added descriptions of prison life.

Dekker's religious beliefs were as uncertain as his finances; he was twice indicted for recusancy—refusal to attend Church of England services. Yet he wrote many strongly Protestant works, among them *The Whore of Babylon,* a play castigating the evils of Catholic Spain and

---

8. Physicians.   9. Banners, signs.

celebrating the triumph of England over the Armada. He may have been avoiding church so as not to be apprehended for debt by officers of the law, who scouted Church of England services on Sundays.

Dekker began to write plays in 1593 for clients of Philip Henslowe, a theatrical entrepreneur, who paid close to six pounds per play (roughly $500 in today's purchasing power). Henslowe's *Diary* records that in one year alone, 1598, Dekker wrote fifteen plays. Jonson wrote of him in *Poetaster*, "He hath one of the most over-flowing rank wits in London."

Dekker frequently collaborated with other playwrights, including John Webster, and Shakespeare, with whom he wrote *The Play of Sir Thomas More* in 1595–1596. In 1604 Dekker worked on two plays with Thomas Middleton: *The Magnificent Entertainment*, which celebrated the accession of King James, and *The Honest Whore*, which combined a moralizing theme with a realistic depiction of London life. Then, in 1611, Dekker and Middleton cowrote *The Roaring Girl*, a romantic comedy built around the antics of the notorious London figure Moll Cutpurse. The same year, Dekker and Webster started a running debate with Jonson that began with their *Westward Ho!*, to which Jonson responded with his satire of the Puritan bourgeoisie called *Eastward Ho!*, which was in turn rebutted by Dekker and Webster's *Northward Ho!*

Dekker's work is notable for his colorful depiction of London life and his perspective—as one of their member—on the struggles of the working class and the poor. He wrote in a wide variety of dramatic genres: patriotic allegory, social satire, and romantic comedy, among others. All his work shows a reliance on the native English tradition. From the medieval mystery and morality play, Dekker took such features as the devil, allegory, moral teaching, and the simple folk as the bearers of truth. He combined these elements with the most contemporary topics, including the life of Wyatt, the defeat of the Armada, and the fortunes of Moll Cutpurse. From slang to fashion, from gender roles to class conflict, and from street crime to the venality of the middle class, Dekker's pamphlets and plays present the panorama of London with a vividness and humor that are unsurpassed in early modern English literature.

Like Dekker, Thomas Middleton was a Londoner, and although he came from a middle-class background, he was well acquainted with the London street life that they both wrote about. While Dekker made it only through grammar school, Middleton went to university and may even have studied at one of the Inns of Court. He started his writing career with verse satires, which, like Dekker's pamphlets, described the vices of London—including *Micro-Cynicon, or Six Snarling Satires* (1599). Middleton became a great but controversial success at the box office. One of his most popular plays, *A Game at Chess* (1624), was reported to the Privy Council for having "the boldness and presumption, in a rude and dishonorable fashion to represent on the stage the person of his majesty the King of Spain." Middleton was imprisoned for a brief time. Just a few years later, Middleton, like Dekker, died in poverty.

Middleton wrote for the public stage that featured the men's companies and for the more fashionable private theaters in which boy players acted. His first play, the now lost tragedy *Caesar's Fall* (1602), was commissioned by Philip Henslowe and written with John Webster. In comedy, Middleton's great collaboration was with Dekker, first on *The Honest Whore* (1604) and then on *The Roaring Girl* (1611), of which he may have been the chief author. From 1602 to 1608, Middleton wrote such witty satirical comedies as *Blurt, Master Constable*, for the Boys of Saint Paul's, and *The Family of Love*, for the Children of the Chapel Royal. Dekker may well have had a hand in both these plays. With the discontinuation of the children's companies after 1609, Middleton returned to the public stage, writing both comedies and tragedies such as *The Changeling* (1620–1621), in which a woman tries to win the man she loves but ends up as an accomplice to murder and the mistress of a murderer.

It has been said that with Middleton the great age of Elizabethan tragedy came to an end. Since T.S. Eliot drew modern attention back to Middleton as "a great recorder" of contemporary life, he has been admired mainly for his realism. But Middleton is also a great ironist and one of the finest writers of quick dialogue that turns on double meanings and innuendoes. *The

Roaring Girl is about an actual living person, known to the audience from the streets of London and from the stage of the Fortune Theater. This comedy portrays a woman who is not only quick and witty, like Shakespeare's cross-dressing heroines, but also fiercely independent and unattached to any man, a fact that has spurred a renewal of interest in how this unusual play represents sex and gender roles.

The Roaring Girl

The Roaring Girl (1611) is unique in early modern English drama for the presentation of a notorious figure of the London streets: Mary Frith. Other works attest to her popularity: an earlier play, now lost, *Long Meg* (1594), and the anonymous jest biography *Long Meg of Westminster* (1620). Like Long Meg, the dramatic heroine Moll dresses as a man to best her male opponent in a duel. City documents and letters record the public appearances of Moll Frith. *The Consistory of London Correction Book* for 27 January 1612 cites an appearance by the real Mary Frith on the stage of the Fortune Theater in spring of 1611. And a letter of John Chamberlain recounts her public penance at Paul's Cross. Although Mary Frith had connections with London criminal world, the Star Chamber suit of 1611 attests to her help in apprehending thieves. The fictional Moll is also a type of social bandit, who not only steals from the rich to give to the poor but even uncovers greed and hypocrisy.

Drawing on the popular pamphlet literature, Middleton and Dekker wove together such elements as the cross-dressing Robin Hood, the coney-catching plot (in which a trickster fools a gullible rube), the ruses of clever wives, and canting language (a kind of street slang). The subplot in which Laxton concocts a fake legal process in an attempt to extort money from the Gallipots plays off a commonplace from rogue literature. In *A Notable Discovery of Cosenage* a trickster plays husband off against wife through a pretended lawsuit. From another popular tradition, the comic debate on the battle between the sexes, *The Batchelar's Banquet* (1603) may have provided inspiration for such devices as passing off a lover as a relative and claiming pregnancy as an excuse for capriciousness.

All these elements are part of a larger design that interweaves three plot models: New Comedy, prodigal literature, and citizen comedy. To the stock New Comedy plot of the son who is barred from marrying the woman of his choice by his disapproving father, Middleton and Dekker added the novel element of the prodigal youth doting on a notorious woman. Young Sebastian Wengrave gains his father's approval by convincing him that marriage to anyone—even the less than wealthy Mary Fitzallard—would be better than marriage to Moll. In addition to the pretense of a young man sowing his wild oats, the play also presents a subplot that turns around the fidelity of two tradesmen's wives. The stock ending in citizen comedy confirmed the chastity of the good wives, but *The Roaring Girl* adds a new twist with the wives' condemnation of their seducers' deceptions.

Many critics have assigned credit for the plot to Middleton and credit for the rogue literature elements to Dekker, but most scenes appear to have been written by both writers. This play was the last joint project of these two playwrights, and with it they succeeded in fusing their respective talents. Middleton was known for his snappy dialogue liberally laced with *double entendres;* Dekker, more of a moralist than his partner, was known for his use of popular street slang, or canting. Though Act 5, scene 1, borrows heavily from Dekker's pamphlets *The Belman of London* and *Lantern and Candlelight,* even here evidence of Middleton's influence crops up in the language. It would appear that rather than dividing up scenes between them, each edited or rewrote the other's work. This collaboration resulted in a play and a character that were more memorable than any either writer had previously produced.

If the *Roaring Girl* was once overlooked in part because of the problems posed by joint authorship, it is now enjoying a resurgence of interest because of its fascinating representation of gender, sexuality, the marketplace, and class relations. Not only does Moll's cross-dressing pose questions about sex and gender roles, but Laxton's and Goshawk's seductions of Mistresses Gallipot and Openwork portray an unsentimental view of chastity. As Moll notes, "'tis impossible to know what woman is thoroughly honest because she's ne'er thoroughly tried" (2.1). The portrayal of sex is closely related to that of the marketplace; indeed, all relationships in the play are at times reduced to a question of power: "All that live in the world are but great fish and little fish, and feed upon one another" (3.3). Rising above all this is the disturbing and indomitable Moll. On stage in seven out of eleven scenes, Moll dominates the play with her charm and wit. She exercises moral judgment without being moralistic. Moll is her own woman and her own standard: "I please myself, and care not else who loves me" (5.2). Moll Cutpurse steals the show and makes *The Roaring Girl* one of the most innovative plays in English literature.

The Roaring Girl; or, Moll Cut-Purse

Dramatis Personae

SIR ALEXANDER WENGRAVE[1]
SEBASTIAN WENGRAVE, his son
SIR GUY FITZALLARD
SIR DAVY DAPPER
JACK DAPPER, his son
SIR ADAM APPLETON
SIR THOMAS LONG
SIR BEAUTEOUS GANYMEDE[2]
LORD NOLAND
GOSHAWK
LAXTON
GREENWIT
GALLIPOT, an apothecary
TILTYARD, a feather-seller
OPENWORK, a sempster°   *tailor*
NEATFOOT, Sir A. Wengrave's man
GULL,° page to Jack Dapper   *fool*
RALPH TRAPDOOR
TEARCAT[3]
CURTLEAX,° a sergeant   *broadsword*
HANGER,° his yeoman   *strap on a sword belt*
MOLL,[4] The Roaring Girl
MARY FITZALLARD, daughter to Sir Guy
MISTRESS GALLIPOT
MISTRESS TILTYARD
MISTRESS OPENWORK
Gentlemen, Cutpurses,° etc.   *pickpockets*
Coachman
Porter
Tailor

---

1. Many of the characters' names contain puns or humorous allusions: Wengrave/Went grave, Laxton/Lack-stone (lacks land or testicles), Jack Dapper/a dapper jack (a term of mockery).
2. Ganymede, the name of Zeus's cupbearer, came to

mean a young male homosexual lover.
3. "To tear a cat" means to act like a swaggering hero.
4. Moll was a common term for a prostitute as well as a nickname for Mary, a name symbolizing chastity.

Prologue

A play expected long makes the audience look
For wonders—that each scene should be a book
Composed to all perfection. Each one comes
And brings a play in's head with him; up he sums
What he would of a roaring girl have writ—
If that he finds not here, he mews at it.
Only we entreat you think our scene
Cannot speak high, the subject being but mean.
A roaring girl, whose notes till now never were,
Shall fill with laughter our vast theater:
That's all which I dare promise; tragic passion,
And such grave stuff, is this day out of fashion.
I see attention sets wide ope her gates
Of hearing, and with covetous listening waits
To know what girl this roaring girl should be—
For of that tribe are many. One is she
That roars at midnight in deep tavern bowls,
That beats the watch, and constables controls;
Another roars i'th' day-time, swears, stabs, gives braves,°   *acts tough*
Yet sells her soul to the lust of fools and slaves:
Both these are suburb-roarers. Then there's besides
A civil, city-roaring girl, whose pride,
Feasting, and riding, shakes her husband's state,
And leaves him roaring through an iron grate.
None of these roaring girls is ours: she flies
With wings more lofty. Thus her character lies—
Yet what need characters, when to give a guess
Is better than the person to express?
But would you know who 'tis? Would you hear her name?—
She is called Mad Moll; her life our acts proclaim!

Scene, LONDON.

Act 1

Scene 1

[*A room in Sir Alexander Wengrave's house. Enter Mary Fitzallard disguised like a sempster,*[5] *with a case for bands, and Neatfoot with her, a napkin on his shoulder, and a trencher*[6] *in his hand, as from table.*]

NEATFOOT The young gentleman, our young master, sir Alexander's son, is it into his ears, sweet damsel, emblem[7] of fragility, you desire to have a message transported, or to be transcendent?

MARY A private word or two, sir; nothing else.

NEATFOOT You shall fructify[8] in that which you come for; your pleasure shall be satisfied to your full contentation. I will, fairest tree of generation, watch when our young master is erected, that is to say, up, and deliver him to this your most white hand.

---

5. Tailor. Bands: collars.
6. A shallow wooden bowl.
7. Symbol.

8. Double meanings, such as those in "fructify" (flourish/become pregnant) and "erected" (gets up/gets it up), run throughout the play.

MARY Thanks, sir.

NEATFOOT And withal certify him, that I have culled out for him, now his belly is replenished, a daintier bit or modicum than any lay upon his trencher at dinner. Hath he notion of your name, I beseech your chastity?

MARY One, sir, of whom he bespake falling bands.[9]

NEATFOOT Falling bands? it shall so be given him. If you please to venture your modesty in the hall amongst a curl-pated company of rude serving-men, and take such as they can set before you, you shall be most seriously and ingeniously[1] welcome.

MARY I have dined indeed already, sir.

NEATFOOT Or will you vouchsafe to kiss the lip of a cup of rich Orleans in the buttery amongst our waiting-women?

MARY Not now, in truth, sir.

NEATFOOT Our young master shall then have a feeling of your being here; presently it shall so be given him.

MARY I humbly thank you, sir. But that my bosom

   [Exit Neatfoot.]

      Is full of bitter sorrows, I could smile
      To see this formal ape play antic tricks;
      But in my breast a poisoned arrow sticks,
      And smiles cannot become me. Love woven slightly,
      Such as thy false heart makes, wears out as lightly;
      But love being truly bred i' th' soul, like mine,
      Bleeds even to death at the least wound it takes,—
      The more we quench this [fire], the less it slakes:
      O me!

   [Enter Sebastian Wengrave with Neatfoot.]

SEBASTIAN A sempster speak with me, sayest thou?

NEATFOOT Yes, sir; she's there, *viva voce* to deliver her auricular confession.[2]

SEBASTIAN With me, sweetheart? what is't?

MARY I have brought home your bands, sir.

SEBASTIAN Bands?—Neatfoot.

NEATFOOT Sir?

SEBASTIAN Prithee, look in; for all the gentlemen are upon rising.

NEATFOOT Yes, sir; a most methodical attendance shall be given.

SEBASTIAN And dost hear? If my father call for me, say I am busy with a sempster.

NEATFOOT Yes, sir; he shall know it that you are busied with a needle-woman.[3]

SEBASTIAN In's ear, good Neatfoot.

NEATFOOT It shall be so given him. [Exit.]

SEBASTIAN Bands? You're mistaken, sweetheart, I bespake none:
      When, where, I prithee? What bands? Let me see them.

MARY Yes, sir; a bond fast sealed with solemn oaths,
      Subscribed unto, as I thought, with your soul;
      Delivered as your deed in sight of heaven
      Is this bond cancellèd? have you forgot me?

SEBASTIAN Ha! life of my life, sir Guy Fitzallard's daughter?
      What has transformed my love to this strange shape?

---

9. Flat collar, with a play on banns of marriage and bonds of marriage contract.
1. Honestly, without reserve.

2. Telling one's sins to a priest; here a sexual confession.
3. Needle: slang for penis.

Stay; make all sure. [*Shuts doors.*] So: now speak and be brief,
Because the wolf's at door that lies in wait
To prey upon us both. Albeit mine eyes
Are blest by thine, yet this so strange disguise
Holds me with fear and wonder.

MARY   Mine's a loathed sight;
Why from it are you banished else so long?

SEBASTIAN I must cut short my speech: in broken language
Thus much, sweet Moll; I must thy company shun;
I court another Moll my thoughts must run
As a horse runs that's blind round in a mill,
Out every step, yet keeping one path still.

MARY Umph! must you shun my company? in one knot
Have both our hands by th' hands of heaven been tied,
Now to be broke?[4] I thought me once your bride;
Our fathers did agree on the time when:
And must another bedfellow fill my room?

SEBASTIAN Sweet maid, let's lose no time; 'tis in heaven's book
Set down, that I must have thee; an oath we took
To keep our vows but when the knight your father
Was from mine parted, storms began to sit
Upon my covetous father's brows, which fell
From them on me. He reckoned up what gold
This marriage would draw from him; at which he swore,
To lose so much blood could not grieve him more:
He then dissuades me from thee, called thee not fair,
And asked what is she but a beggar's heir?
He scorned thy dowry of five thousand marks.[5]
If such a sum of money could be found,
And I would match with that, he'd not undo it,
Provided his bags might add nothing to it;
But vowed, if I took thee, nay, more, did swear it,
Save birth, from him I nothing should inherit.

MARY What follows then? my shipwreck?

SEBASTIAN   Dearest, no
Though wildly in a labyrinth I go,
My end is to meet thee: with a side-wind
Must I now sail, else I no haven can find,
But both must sink for ever. There's a wench
Called Moll, Mad Moll, or Merry Moll; a creature
So strange in quality, a whole city takes
Note of her name and person. All that affection
I owe to thee, on her in counterfeit passion
I spend, to mad° my father; he believes   *infuriate*
I doat upon this Roaring Girl, and grieves
As it becomes a father for a son
That could be so bewitched: yet I'll go on

4. Mary and Sebastian have pledged spousals *de futuro*, a
contract which was often secret and the equivalent of
marriage itself.

5. A small fortune. A mark equaled two-thirds of a
pound.

This crooked way, sigh still for her, feign° dreams   *pretend*
In which I'll talk only of her; these streams
Shall, I hope, force my father to consent
That here I anchor, rather than be rent
Upon a rock so dangerous. Art thou pleased,
Because thou seest we're waylaid, that I take
A path that's safe, though it be far about?

MARY My prayers with heaven guide thee!

SEBASTIAN   Then I will on
My father is at hand; kiss, and begone!
Hours shall be watched for meetings I must now,
As men for fear, to a strange idol bow.

MARY Farewell!

SEBASTIAN   I'll guide thee forth: when next we meet,
A story of Moll shall make our mirth more sweet.

                                                         [*Exeunt.*]

                              Scene 2

[*Enter Sir Alexander Wengrave, Sir Davy Dapper, Sir Adam Appleton, Goshawk,
Laxton, and Gentlemen.*]

ALL Thanks, good sir Alexander, for our bounteous cheer!

SIR ALEXANDER Fie, fie, in giving thanks you pay too dear.

SIR DAVY When bounty spreads the table, faith, 'twere sin,
At going off if thanks should not step in.

SIR ALEXANDER No more of thanks, no more. Ay, marry, sir.
Th' inner room was too close how do you like
This parlor, gentlemen?

ALL   O, passing° well!   *exceedingly*

SIR ADAM What a sweet breath the air casts here, so cool!

GOSHAWK I like the prospect best.

LAXTON   See how 'tis furnished!

SIR DAVY A very fair sweet room.

SIR ALEXANDER   Sir Davy Dapper,
The furniture that doth adorn this room[6]
Cost many a fair grey groat[7] ere it came here;
But good things are most cheap when they're most dear.
Nay, when you look into my galleries,[8]
How bravely they're trimmed up, you all shall swear
You're highly pleased to see what's set down there:
Stories of men and women, mixed together
Fair ones with foul, like sunshine in wet weather;
Within one square[9] a thousand heads are laid,
So close that all of heads the room seems made;
As many faces there, filled with blithe looks,
Show like the promising titles of new books
Writ merrily, the readers being their own eyes,

---

6. This speech describes what the Fortune Theater was like.
7. Four pence.
8. Rooms for artwork or theater balconies.
9. The Fortune was built on a square plan.

Which seem to move and to give plaudities;°   *applause*
And here and there, whilst with obsequious° ears   *servile*
Thronged heaps° do listen, a cut-purse thrusts and leers   *crowds*
With hawk's eyes for his prey; I need not show him;
By a hanging, villainous look yourselves may know him,
The face is drawn so rarely; then, sir, below
The very floor, as 'twere, waves to and fro,
And, like a floating island,[1] seems to move
Upon a sea bound in with shores above.
ALL These sights are excellent!
SIR ALEXANDER   I'll show you all:
    Since we are met, make our parting comical.
[*Reenter Sebastian Wengrave with Greenwit.*]
SEBASTIAN This gentleman, my friend, will take his leave, sir.
SIR ALEXANDER Ha! take his leave, Sebastian, who?
SEBASTIAN   This gentleman.
SIR ALEXANDER Your love, sir, has already given me some time,
    And if you please to trust my age with more,
    It shall pay double interest: good sir, stay.
GREENWIT I have been too bold.
SIR ALEXANDER   Not so, sir: a merry day
    'Mongst friends being spent, is better than gold saved.—
    Some wine, some wine! Where be these knaves I keep?
[*Reenter Neatfoot with several Servants.*]
NEATFOOT At your worshipful elbow, sir.
SIR ALEXANDER You're kissing my maids, drinking, or fast asleep.
NEATFOOT Your worship has given it us right.
SIR ALEXANDER You varlets,° stir!   *knaves*
    Chairs, stools, and cushions!—
[*Servants bring in wine, and place chairs, etc.*]
                          Prithee, sir Davy Dapper,
    Make that chair thine.
SIR DAVY   'Tis but an easy gift;
    And yet I thank you for it, sir: I'll take it.
SIR ALEXANDER A chair for old sir Adam Appleton!
NEATFOOT A back friend[2] to your worship.
SIR ADAM   Marry, good Neatfoot,
    I thank thee for't; back friends sometimes are good.
SIR ALEXANDER Pray, make that stool your perch, good master Goshawk.
GOSHAWL I stoop to your lure, sir.
SIR ALEXANDER   Son Sebastian,
    Take master Greenwit to you.
SEBASTIAN   Sit, dear friend.
SIR ALEXANDER Nay, master Laxton—furnish master Laxton
    With what he wants, a stone,—a stool, I would say,
    A stool.
LAXTON I had rather stand, sir.

---

1. The stage.   2. A backer. Also, a pretended friend.

SIR ALEXANDER I know you had, good master Laxton so, so.

[Exeunt Neatfoot and Servants.]

    Now here's a mess of friends; and, gentlemen,
    Because time's glass shall not be running long,
    I'll quicken it with a pretty tale.

SIR DAVY   Good tales do well
    In these bad days, where vice does so excel.

SIR ADAM Begin, Sir Alexander.

SIR ALEXANDER   Last day I met
    An aged man, upon whose head was scored
    A debt of just so many years as these
    Which I owe to my grave: the man you all know.

ALL His name, I pray you, sir?

SIR ALEXANDER   Nay, you shall pardon me:
    But when he saw me, with a sigh that brake,
    Or seemed to break, his heart-strings, thus he spake:
    O my good knight, says he (and then his eyes
    Were richer even by that which made them poor,
    They'd spent so many tears they had no more),
    O sir, says he, you know it! for you ha' seen
    Blessings to rain upon mine house and me:
    Fortune, who slaves men, was my slave; her wheel
    Hath spun me golden threads;[3] for, I thank heaven,
    I ne'er had but one cause to curse my stars.
    I ask'd him then what that one cause might be.

ALL So, sir.

SIR ALEXANDER He paused; and as we often see
    A sea so much becalmed, there can be found
    No wrinkle on his brow, his waves being drowned
    In their own rage; but when th' imperious winds
    Use strange invisible tyranny to shake
    Both heaven's and earth's foundation at their noise,
    The seas, swelling with wrath to part that fray,
    Rise up, and are more wild, more mad than they:
    Even so this good old man was by my question
    Stirred up to roughness; you might see his gall[4]
    Flow even in's eyes; then grew he fantastical.

SIR DAVY Fantastical? ha, ha!

SIR ALEXANDER   Yes; and talked oddly.

SIR ADAM Pray, sir, proceed:
    How did this old man end?

SIR ALEXANDER   Marry, sir, thus:
    He left his wild fit to read o'er his cards;
    Yet then, though age cast snow on all his hairs,
    He joyed, because, says he, the god of gold
    Has been to me no niggard; that disease,
    Of which all old men sicken, avarice,
    Never infected me—

---

3. A mixed image of Fortune's Wheel with the Fates'
spinning wheel.

4. Bile, resentment.

LAXTON [*Aside.*] He means not himself, I'm sure.
SIR ALEXANDER   For, like a lamp
    Fed with continual oil, I spend and throw
    My light to all that need it, yet have still
    Enough to serve myself: O but, quoth he,
    Though heaven's dew fall thus on this aged tree,
    I have a son that, like a wedge, doth cleave
    My very heart-root!
SIR DAVY   Had he such a son?
SEBASTIAN [*Aside.*] Now I do smell a fox strongly.[5]
SIR ALEXANDER Let's see; no, master Greenwit is not yet
    So mellow in years as he; but as like Sebastian,
    Just like my son Sebastian, such another.
SEBASTIAN [*Aside.*] How finely, like a fencer,
    My father fetches his by-blows to hit me!
    But if I beat you not at your own weapon
    Of subtilty—
SIR ALEXANDER This son, saith he, that should be
    The column and main arch unto my house,
    The crutch unto my age, becomes a whirlwind
    Shaking the firm foundation.
SIR ADAM   'Tis some prodigal.
SEBASTIAN [*Aside.*] Well shot, old Adam Bell!
SIR ALEXANDER No city-monster neither, no prodigal,
    But sparing, wary, civil, and, though wifeless,
    An excellent husband; and such a traveller,
    He has more tongues in his head than some have teeth.
SIR DAVY I have but two in mine.
GOSHAWK   So sparing and so wary?
    What, then, could vex his father so?
SIR ALEXANDER O, a woman!
SEBASTIAN A flesh-fly, that can vex any man.
SIR ALEXANDER A scurvy woman,
    On whom the passionate old man swore he doated;
    A creature, saith he, nature hath brought forth
    To mock the sex of woman. It is a thing
    One knows not how to name; her birth began
    Ere she was all made: 'tis woman more than man,
    Man more than woman; and, which to none can hap,
    The sun gives her two shadows to one shape;
    Nay, more, let this strange thing walk, stand, or sit,
    No blazing star draws more eyes after it.
SIR DAVY A monster! 'tis some monster!
SIR ALEXANDER   She's a varlet.
SEBASTIAN [*Aside.*] Now is my cue to bristle.
SIR ALEXANDER A naughty pack.[6]
SEBASTIAN   'Tis false!
SIR ALEXANDER   Ha, boy?

5. Smell a rat.   6. A bad person.

SEBASTIAN   'Tis false!
SIR ALEXANDER What's false? I say she's naught.
SEBASTIAN   I say, that tongue
    That dares speak so, but yours, sticks in the throat
    Of a rank villain set yourself aside—
SIR ALEXANDER So, sir, what then?
SEBASTIAN   Any here else had lied.—
    [*Aside.*] I think I shall fit you.
SIR ALEXANDER Lie?
SEBASTIAN   Yes.
SIR DAVY   Doth this concern him?
SIR ALEXANDER   Ah, sirrah-boy,
    Is your blood heated? boils it? are you stung?
    I'll pierce you deeper yet.—O my dear friends,
    I am that wretched father! this that son,
    That sees his ruin, yet headlong on doth run.
SIR ADAM Will you love such a poison?
SIR DAVY   Fie, fie.
SEBASTIAN   You're all mad.
SIR ALEXANDER Thou'rt sick at heart, yet feel'st it not of all these,
    What gentleman but thou, knowing his disease
    Mortal, would shun the cure!—O master Greenwit,
    Would you to such an idol bow?
GREENWIT   Not I, sir.
SIR ALEXANDER Here's master Laxton; has he mind to a woman
    As thou hast?
LAXTON   No, not I, sir.
SIR ALEXANDER   Sir, I know it.
LAXTON Their good parts are so rare, their bad so common,
    I will have nought to do with any woman.
SIR DAVY 'Tis well done, master Laxton.
SIR ALEXANDER   O thou cruel boy,
    Thou would'st with lust an old man's life destroy!
    Because thou see'st I'm half-way in my grave,
    Thou shovel'st dust upon me: would thou might'st have
    Thy wish, most wicked, most unnatural!
SIR DAVY Why, sir, 'tis thought sir Guy Fitzallard's daughter
    Shall wed your son Sebastian.
SIR ALEXANDER   Sir Davy Dapper,
    I have upon my knees wooed this fond boy
    To take that virtuous maiden.
SEBASTIAN   Hark you; a word, sir.
    You on your knees have cursed that virtuous maiden,
    And me for loving her; yet do you now
    Thus baffle[7] me to my face; wear not your knees
    In such entreats; give me Fitzallard's daughter.
SIR ALEXANDER I'll give thee rats-bane rather.
SEBASTIAN   Well, then, you know

---

7. Deceive, confound.

What dish I mean to feed upon.
SIR ALEXANDER   Hark, gentlemen! he swears
   To have this cut-purse drab,° to spite my gall.   *prostitute*
ALL Master Sebastian—
SEBASTIAN   I am deaf to you all.
   I'm so bewitched, so bound to my desires,
   Tears, prayers, threats, nothing can quench out those fires
   That burn within me. [*Exit.*]
SIR ALEXANDER [*Aside.*]   Her blood shall quench it, then.—
   Lose him not; O dissuade him, gentlemen!
SIR DAVY He shall be weaned, I warrant you.
SIR ALEXANDER   Before his eyes
   Lay down his shame, my grief, his miseries.
ALL No more, no more; away!
   [*Exeunt all but Sir Alexander Wengrave.*]
SIR ALEXANDER   I wash a negro,
   Losing both pains and cost:[8] but take thy flight,
   I'll be most near thee when I'm least in sight.
   Wild buck, I'll hunt thee breathless thou shalt run on,
   But I will turn thee when I'm not thought upon.—
   [*Enter Trapdoor with a letter.*]
Now, sirrah, what are you? leave your ape's tricks, and speak.
TRAPDOOR A letter from my captain to your worship.
SIR ALEXANDER O, O, now I remember; 'tis to prefer thee into my service.
TRAPDOOR To be a shifter under your worship's nose of a clean trencher, when
   there's a good bit upon't.
SIR ALEXANDER Troth, honest fellow—Hum—ha—let me see—
   [*Aside.*] This knave shall be the axe to hew that down
   At which I stumble; has a face that promiseth
   Much of a villain I will grind his wit,
   And, if the edge prove fine, make use of it.—
   Come hither, sirrah canst thou be secret, ha?
TRAPDOOR As two crafty attorneys plotting the undoing of their clients.
SIR ALEXANDER Did'st never, as thou'st walked about this town,
   Hear of a wench call'd Moll, mad, merry Moll?
TRAPDOOR Moll Cutpurse, sir?
SIR ALEXANDER   The same; dost thou know her, then?
TRAPDOOR As well as I know 'twill rain upon Simon and Jude's day next: I will sift
   all the taverns i' th' city, and drink half pots with all the water-men[9] a' th' Bank-
   side, but, if you will, sir, I'll find her out.
SIR ALEXANDER That task is easy; do't then: hold thy hand up.
   What's this? is't burnt?[1]
TRAPDOOR No, sir, no; a little singed with making fireworks.
SIR ALEXANDER There's money, spend it; that being spent, fetch more. [*Gives money.*]
TRAPDOOR O sir, that all the poor soldiers in England had such a leader! For fetch-
   ing, no water-spaniel is like me.
SIR ALEXANDER This wench we speak of strays so from her kind,

---

8. Proverbial. See Jeremiah 13.23: "Can the black Moor
change his skin? or the leopard his spots?"

9. Boatmen.
1. Branded, a common punishment for crime.

Nature repents she made her: 'tis a mermaid
Has toled° my son to shipwreck.   *lured*
TRAPDOOR I'll cut her comb° for you.   *put her down*
SIR ALEXANDER I'll tell out gold for thee, then. Hunt her forth,
   Cast out a line hung full of silver hooks
   To catch her to thy company; deep spendings
   May draw her that's most chaste to a man's bosom.
TRAPDOOR The gingling of golden bells, and a good fool with a hobbyhorse, will
   draw all the whores i' th' town to dance in a morris.
SIR ALEXANDER Or rather, for that's best (they say sometimes
   She goes in breeches), follow her as her man.
TRAPDOOR And when her breeches are off, she shall follow me.
SIR ALEXANDER Beat all thy brains to serve her.
TRAPDOOR Zounds, sir, as country wenches beat cream till butter comes.
SIR ALEXANDER Play thou the subtle spider; weave fine nets
   To ensnare her very life.
TRAPDOOR   Her life?
SIR ALEXANDER   Yes; suck
   Her heart-blood, if thou canst twist thou but cords
   To catch her, I'll find law to hang her up.
TRAPDOOR Spoke like a worshipful bencher!
SIR ALEXANDER Trace all her steps at this she-fox's den
   Watch what lambs enter; let me play the shepherd
   To save their throats from bleeding, and cut hers.
TRAPDOOR This is the goll° shall do't.   *hand*
SIR ALEXANDER   Be firm, and gain me
   Ever thine own this done, I entertain thee.
   How is thy name?
TRAPDOOR My name, sir, is Ralph Trapdoor, honest Ralph.
SIR ALEXANDER Trapdoor, be like thy name, a dangerous step
   For her to venture on; but unto me—
TRAPDOOR As fast as your sole to your boot or shoe, sir.
SIR ALEXANDER Hence, then; be little seen here as thou canst;
   I'll still be at thine elbow.
TRAPDOOR   The trapdoor's set.
   Moll, if you budge, you're gone: this me shall crown;
   A roaring boy the roaring girl puts down.
SIR ALEXANDER God-a-mercy, lose no time.   *[Exeunt.]*

Act 2

Scene 1

*[Three Shops open in a rank: the first an Apothecary's shop,[2] the next a Feather-shop, the
third a Sempster's shop; Mistress Gallipot in the first, Mistress Tiltyard in the next, Openwork and Mistress Openwork in the third. Enter Laxton, Goshawk, and Greenwit.]*
MISTRESS OPENWORK Gentlemen, what is't you lack? What is't you buy? See
   fine bands and ruffs, fine lawns, fine cambrics: What is't you lack, gentlemen?
   What is't you buy?

---

2. Apothecaries sold spices, medicines, and tobacco.

LAXTON Yonder's the shop.

GOSHAWK Is that she?

LAXTON Peace.

GREENWIT She that minces tobacco?

LAXTON Ay; she's a gentlewoman born, I can tell you, though it be her hard fortune now to shred Indian pot-herbs.

GOSHAWK O sir, 'tis many a good woman's fortune, when her husband turns bankrout,[3] to begin with pipes and set up again.

LAXTON And, indeed, the raising of the woman is the lifting up of the man's head at all times; if one flourish, t'other will bud as fast, I warrant ye.

GOSHAWK Come, thou'rt familiarly acquainted there, I grope[4] that.

LAXTON And you grope no better i' th' dark, you may chance lie i' th' ditch when you're drunk.

GOSHAWK Go, thou'rt a mystical lecher!

LAXTON I will not deny but my credit may take up an ounce of pure smoke.

GOSHAWK May take up an ell of pure smock! away, go! [Aside:] 'Tis the closest striker![5] Life, I think he commits venery forty foot deep; no man's aware on't. I, like a palpable smockster,[6] go to work so openly with the tricks of art, that I'm as apparently seen as a naked boy in a phial;[7] and were it not for a gift of treachery that I have in me, to betray my friend when he puts most trust in me—mass, yonder he is too!—and by his injury to make good my access to her, I should appear as defective in courting as a farmer's son the first day of his feather, that doth nothing at court but woo the hangings and glass windows for a month together, and some broken waiting-women for ever after. I find those imperfections in my venery, that were't not for flattery and falsehood, I should want discourse and impudence; and he that wants impudence among women is worthy to be kicked out at bed's feet. He shall not see me yet.

[At the tobacco shop.]

GREENWIT Troth, this is finely shred.

LAXTON O, women are the best mincers.

MISTRESS GALLIPOT 'T had been a good phrase for a cook's wife, sir.

LAXTON But 'twill serve generally, like the front of a new almanac, as thus:—calculated for the meridian of cooks' wives, but generally for all English women.

MISTRESS GALLIPOT Nay, you shall ha't, sir; I have filled it for you. [She puts it to the fire.]

LAXTON The pipe's in a good hand, and I wish mine always so.

GREENWIT But not to be used a' that fashion.

LAXTON O, pardon me, sir, I understand no French. I pray, be covered. Jack, a pipe of rich smoke!

GOSHAWK Rich smoke? that's sixpence a pipe, is't?

GREENWIT To me, sweet lady.

MISTRESS GALLIPOT Be not forgetful; respect my credit; seem strange: art and wit makes a fool of suspicion; pray, be wary.

LAXTON Push! I warrant you.—Come, how is't, gallants?

GREENWIT Pure and excellent.

---

3. Bankrupt.
4. Grasp.
5. Fornicator.

6. Go-between.
7. Abortions were considered monsters in Jacobean times and put on display in this way.

LAXTON I thought 'twas good, you were grown so silent: you are like those that love not to talk at victuals, though they make a worse noise i' th' nose than a common fiddler's 'prentice, and discourse a whole supper with snuffling.—I must speak a word with you anon.

MISTRESS GALLIPOT Make your way wisely, then.

GOSHAWK O, what else, sir? he's perfection itself; full of manners, but not an acre of ground belonging to 'em.

GREENWIT Ay, and full of form; has ne'er a good stool in's chamber.

GOSHAWK But above all, religious; he preyeth daily upon elder brothers.

GREENWIT And valiant above measure; has run three streets from a sergeant.

LAXTON Puh, puh. [*He blows tobacco in their faces.*]

GREENWIT O, puh!

GOSHAWK Ho, ho!

LAXTON So, so.

MISTRESS GALLIPOT What's the matter now, sir?

LAXTON I protest I'm in extreme want of money; if you can supply me now with any means, you do me the greatest pleasure, next to the bounty of your love, as ever poor gentleman tasted.

MISTRESS GALLIPOT What's the sum would pleasure ye, sir? though you deserve nothing less at my hands.

LAXTON Why, 'tis but for want of opportunity, thou knowest.—[*Aside:*] I put her off with opportunity still: by this light, I hate her, but for means to keep me in fashion with gallants; for what I take from her, I spend upon other wenches; bear her in hand[8] still: she has wit enough to rob her husband, and I ways enough to consume the money. —Why, how now? what, the chincough?[9]

GOSHAWK Thou hast the cowardliest trick to come before a man's face, and strangle him ere he be aware! I could find in my heart to make a quarrel in earnest.

LAXTON Pox, and thou dost—thou knowest I never use to fight with my friends—thou'lt but lose thy labor in't.—Jack Dapper!
    [*Enter Jack Dapper and Gull.*]

GREENWIT Monsieur Dapper, I dive down to your ankles.

JACK DAPPER Save ye, gentlemen, all three in a peculiar salute.

GOSHAWK He were ill to make a lawyer; he despatches three at once.

LAXTON So, well said.—But is this of the same tobacco, mistress Gallipot?[1]

MISTRESS GALLIPOT The same you had at first, sir.

LAXTON I wish it no better: this will serve to drink[2] at my chamber.

GOSHAWK Shall we taste a pipe on't?

LAXTON Not of this by my troth, gentlemen, I have sworn before you.

GOSHAWK What, not Jack Dapper?

LAXTON Pardon me, sweet Jack; I'm sorry I made such a rash oath, but foolish oaths must stand: where art going, Jack?

JACK DAPPER Faith to buy one feather.

LAXTON [*Aside.*] One feather? the fool's peculiar still.

JACK DAPPER Gull.

GULL Master?

---

8. Keep her in expectation.
9. Whooping cough.
1. When she slips him money, he pretends that she has

only given him tobacco.
2. Smoke.

JACK DAPPER Here's three halfpence for your ordinary,[3] boy; meet me an hour hence in Paul's.

GULL [*Aside.*] How? three single halfpence? life, this will scarce serve a man in sauce, a halp'orth of mustard, a halp'orth of oil, and a halp'orth of vinegar,— what's left then for the pickle herring?[4] This shows like small beer i' th' morning after a great surfeit of wine o'ernight: he could spend his three pound last night in a supper amongst girls and brave bawdyhouse[5] boys: I thought his pockets cackled not for nothing: these are the eggs of three pound, I'll go sup 'em up presently. [*Exit.*]

LAXTON Eight, nine, ten angels:[6] good wench, i'faith, and one that loves darkness well; she puts out a candle with the best tricks[7] of any drugster's wife in England: but that which mads her, I rail upon opportunity still, and take no notice on't. The other night she would needs lead me into a room with a candle in her hand to show me a naked picture, where no sooner entered, but the candle was sent of an errand: now, I not intending to understand her, but, like a puny[8] at the inns of venery, called for another light innocently; thus reward I all her cunning with simple mistaking. I know she cozens[9] her husband to keep me, and I'll keep her honest as long as I can, to make the poor man some part of amends. An honest mind of a whoremaster! how think you amongst you? What, a fresh pipe? draw in a third man?

GOSHAWK No, you're a hoarder, you engross by the ounces.
    [*At the feather-shop.*]

JACK DAPPER Pooh, I like it not.

MISTRESS TILTYARD   What feather is't you'd have, sir?
    These are most worn and most in fashion:
    Amongst the beaver gallants,[1] the stone riders,
    The private stage's audience, the twelvepenny-stool gentlemen,
    I can inform you 'tis the general feather.

JACK DAPPER And therefore I mislike it: tell me of general!
    Now, a continual Simon and Jude's rain
    Beat all your feathers as flat down as pancakes!
    Show me—a—spangled feather.

MISTRESS TILTYARD O, to go a-feasting with;
    You'd have it for a hench-boy,° you shall.   page
    [*At the sempster's shop.*]

OPENWORK Mass, I had quite forgot!
    His honor's footman was here last night, wife;
    Ha' you done with my lord's shirt?

MISTRESS OPENWORK   What's that to you, sir?
    I was this morning at his honor's lodging,
    Ere such a snake as you crept out of your shell.

OPENWORK O, 'twas well done, good wife!

MISTRESS OPENWORK I hold it better, sir,

---

3. An eating house that served fixed-price meals.
4. Three halfpence will buy the sauces but not the main dish.
5. Whorehouse.
6. He counts the money Mistress Gallipot give him.
7. I.e., like a prostitute.

8. A term for a first-year student at Oxford or the Inns-of-Court.
9. Deceives.
1. Men wearing expensive beaver hats; stone-riders: riders of stallions; to sit on a stool cost sixpence.

Than if you had done't yourself.

OPENWORK Nay, so say I:
 But is the countess's smock almost done, mouse?

MISTRESS OPENWORK Here lies the cambric, sir; but wants, I fear me.

OPENWORK I'll resolve you of that presently.

MISTRESS OPENWORK Heyday! O audacious groom!
 Dare you presume to noble women's linen?
 Keep you your yard[2] to measure shepherds' holland:
 I must confine you, I see that.
 [At the tobacco-shop.]

GOSHAWK What say you to this gear?

LAXTON I dare the arrant'st critic in tobacco
 To lay one fault upon't.
 [Enter Moll in a frieze jerkin[3] and a black saveguard.]

GOSHAWK Life, yonder's Moll!

LAXTON Moll! which Moll?

GOSHAWK Honest Moll.

LAXTON Prithee, let's call her.—Moll!

GOSHAWK Moll, Moll!

GREENWIT Pist, Moll!

MOLL How now? what's the matter?

GOSHAWK A pipe of good tobacco, Moll?

MOLL I cannot stay.

GOSHAWK Nay, Moll, pooh, prithee, hark; but one word, i'faith.

MOLL Well, what is't?

GREENWIT Prithee, come hither, sirrah.

LAXTON [Aside.] Heart, I would give but too much money to be nibbling with that wench! Life, sh'as the spirit of four great parishes, and a voice that will drown all the city! Methinks a brave captain might get all his soldiers upon her, and ne'er be beholding to a company of Mile End[4] milksops, if he could come on and come off quick enough: such a Moll were a marrow-bone[5] before an Italian;[6] he would cry *buona roba* till his ribs were nothing but bone.[7] I'll lay hard siege to her: money is that aquafortis[8] that eats into many a maidenhead; where the walls are flesh and blood, I'll ever pierce through with a golden augre.[9]

GOSHAWK Now, thy judgment, Moll? is't not good?

MOLL Yes, faith, 'tis very good tobacco.—How do you sell an ounce?—Farewell.— God b'i' you, mistress Gallipot.

GOSHAWK Why, Moll, Moll!

MOLL I cannot stay now, i'faith: I am going to buy a shag-ruff; the shop will be shut in presently.

GOSHAWK 'Tis the maddest fantasticalest girl! I never knew so much flesh and so much nimbleness put together.

---

2. Measuring stick; penis.
3. Man's short coat. "Saveguard": an outer petticoat to protect other clothes from the dirt.
4. Where London citizens were trained in military exercises.
5. A tasty morsel.

6. Italians were stereotyped as lustful.
7. See Florio's *A World of Words* (1598): "Buonarobba, as we say, good stuffe, a good wholesome plum-cheeked wench."
8. Nitric acid.
9. Tool for boring holes in wood.

LAXTON She slips from one company to another, like a fat eel between a Dutchman's fingers.—[*Aside.*] I'll watch my time for her.

MISTRESS GALLIPOT Some will not stick to say she is a man. And some, both man and woman.

LAXTON That were excellent: she might first cuckold the husband, and then make him do as much for the wife.

[*At the feather-shop.*]

MOLL Save you; how does mistress Tiltyard?

JACK DAPPER Moll!

MOLL Jack Dapper!

JACK DAPPER How dost, Moll?

MOLL I'll tell thee by and by; I go but to th' next shop.

JACK DAPPER Thou shalt find me here this hour about a feather.

MOLL Nay, and a feather hold you in play a whole hour, a goose will last you all the days of your life.—Let me see a good shag-ruff.

[*At the sempster's shop.*]

OPENWORK Mistress Mary, that shalt thou, i'faith, and the best in the shop.

MISTRESS OPENWORK How now? Greetings! Love-terms, with a pox, between you! Have I found out one of your haunts? I send you for hollands, and you're i' th' low countries with a mischief.[1] I'm served with good ware by th' shift; that makes it lie dead so long upon my hands: I were as good shut up shop, for when I open it I take nothing.

OPENWORK Nay, and you fall a-ringing once, the devil cannot stop you.—I'll out of the belfrey as fast as I can, Moll.

MISTRESS OPENWORK Get you from my shop!

MOLL I come to buy.

MISTRESS OPENWORK I'll sell ye nothing; I warn ye my house and shop.

MOLL You, goody[2] Openwork, you that prick out a poor living,
    And sews many a bawdy skin-coat together;
    Thou private pandress° between shirt and smock;   *go-between*
    I wish thee for a minute but a man,
    Thou shouldst ne'er use more shapes; but as thou art,
    I pity my revenge. Now my spleen's up,
    I would not mock it willingly.—

[*Enter a Fellow, with a long rapier by his side.*]

    Ha! be thankful;
    Now I forgive thee.

MISTRESS OPENWORK Marry, hang thee, I never asked forgiveness in my life.

MOLL You, goodman[3] swine's face!

FELLOW What, will you murder me?

MOLL You remember, slave, how you abused me t'other night in a tavern.

FELLOW Not I, by this light!

MOLL No, but by candle-light you did: you have tricks to save your oaths; reservations have you? and I have reserved somewhat for you. [*Strikes him.*] As you like that, call for more; you know the sign again.

---

1. "Low countries": the Netherlands, the low-life haunts of her husband, and the lower parts of the body; "shift": evasive device, underclothing; "good ware": good mer- chandise, bodily wares.
2. Housewife.
3. A man with status below a gentleman.

FELLOW [*Aside*.] Pox on't, had I brought any company along with me to have borne witness on't, 'twould ne'er have grieved me; but to be struck and nobody by, 'tis my ill fortune still. Why, tread upon a worm, they say 'twill turn tail; but indeed a gentleman should have more manners. [*Exit*.]

LAXTON Gallantly performed, i'faith, Moll, and manfully! I love thee for ever for't: base rogue, had he offered but the least counter-buff, by this hand, I was prepared for him!

MOLL You prepared for him? Why should you be prepared for him? Was he any more than a man?

LAXTON No, nor so much by a yard and a handful, London measure.

MOLL Why do you speak this then? do you think I cannot ride a stone-horse,[4] unless one lead him by th' snaffle?

LAXTON Yes, and sit him bravely; I know thou canst, Moll: 'twas but an honest mistake through love, and I'll make amends for't anyway. Prithee, sweet, plump Moll, when shall thou and I go out a' town together?

MOLL Whither? to Tyburn,[5] prithee?

LAXTON Mass, that's out a' town indeed: thou hangest so many jests upon thy friends still! I mean honestly to Brainford, Staines, or Ware.[6]

MOLL What to do there?

LAXTON Nothing but be merry and lie together: I'll hire a coach with four horses.

MOLL I thought 'twould be a beastly journey. You may leave out one well; three horses will serve, if I play the jade[7] myself.

LAXTON Nay, push, thou'rt such another kicking wench! Prithee, be kind, and let's meet.

MOLL 'Tis hard but we shall meet, sir.

LAXTON Nay, but appoint the place then; there's ten angels in fair gold, Moll: you see I do not trifle with you; do but say thou wilt meet me, and I'll have a coach ready for thee.

MOLL Why, here's my hand, I'll meet you, sir.

LAXTON [*Aside*.] O good gold!—The place, sweet Moll?

MOLL It shall be your appointment.

LAXTON Somewhat near Holborn,[8] Moll.

MOLL In Gray's-Inn-Fields then.

LAXTON A match.

MOLL I'll meet you there.

LAXTON The hour?

MOLL Three.

LAXTON That will be time enough to sup at Brainford.

OPENWORK I am of such a nature, sir, I cannot endure the house when she scolds: sh'as a tongue will be heard further in a still morning than Saint Antling's bell. She rails upon me for foreign wenching, that I being a freeman must needs keep a whore i' th' suburbs, and seek to impoverish the liberties.[9] When we fall out, I trouble you still to make all whole with my wife.

GOSHAWK No trouble at all; 'tis a pleasure to me to join things together.

OPENWORK [*Aside*.] Go thy ways, I do this but to try thy honesty, Goshawk.

[*At the feather-shop*.]

---

4. Stallion.
5. Place of public executions.
6. Towns north of London.
7. Worn-out horse; whore.

8. The area of the law schools, such as Gray's Inn.
9. Brothels flourished in the suburbs, over which the city had no control; the liberties just beyond the city were subject to its control.

JACK DAPPER How likest thou this, Moll?

MOLL O, singularly; you're fitted now for a bunch.—[*Aside.*] He looks for all the world, with those spangled feathers, like a nobleman's bed-post. The purity of your wench would I fain try; she seems like Kent unconquered, and, I believe, as many wiles are in her. O, the gallants of these times are shallow lechers! they put not their courtship home enough to a wench: 'tis impossible to know what woman is thoroughly honest, because she's ne'er thoroughly tried; I am of that certain belief, there are more queans[1] in this town of their own making than of any man's provoking: where lies the slackness then? Many a poor soul would down, and there's nobody will push 'em:

Women are courted, but ne'er soundly tried,
As many walk in spurs that never ride.

[*At the sempster's shop.*]

MISTRESS OPENWORK O, abominable!

GOSHAWK Nay, more, I tell you in private, he keeps a whore i' th' suburbs.

MISTRESS OPENWORK O spittle[2] dealing! I came to him a gentlewoman born: I'll show you mine arms when you please, sir.

GOSHAWK [*Aside.*] I had rather see your legs, and begin that way.

MISTRESS OPENWORK 'Tis well known he took me from a lady's service, where I was well beloved of the steward: I had my Latin tongue, and a spice of the French, before I came to him; and now doth he keep a suburbian whore under my nostrils?

GOSHAWK There's ways enough to cry quit with[3] him: hark in thine ear. [*Whispers to her.*]

MISTRESS OPENWORK There's a friend worth a million!

MOLL [*Aside.*] I'll try one spear against your chastity, mistress Tiltyard, though it prove too short by the burr.[4]

[*Enter Trapdoor.*]

TRAPDOOR [*Aside.*] Mass, here she is: I'm bound already to serve her, though it be but a sluttish trick.—Bless my hopeful young mistress with long life and great limbs; send her the upper hand of all bailiffs and their hungry adherents!

MOLL How now? what art thou?

TRAPDOOR A poor ebbing gentleman, that would gladly wait for the young flood of your service.

MOLL My service? what should move you to offer your service to me, sir?

TRAPDOOR The love I bear to your heroic spirit and masculine womanhood.

MOLL So, sir! put case we should retain you to us, what parts are there in you for a gentlewoman's service?

TRAPDOOR Of two kinds, right worshipful; moveable and immoveable—moveable to run of errands, and immoveable to stand when you have occasion to use me.

MOLL What strength have you?

TRAPDOOR Strength, mistress Moll? I have gone up into a steeple, and stayed the great bell as't has been ringing; stopped a windmill going—

MOLL And never struck down yourself?

TRAPDOOR Stood as upright as I do at this present.

[*Moll trips up his heels.*]

MOLL Come, I pardon you for this; it shall be no disgrace to you: I have struck up the heels of the high German's size ere now.[5] What, not stand?

TRAPDOOR I am of that nature, where I love, I'll be at my mistress' foot to do her service.

1. Harlots, strumpets.
2. Low-class.
3. Repay.

4. A broad iron ring on the handle of a lance.
5. A tall, strong German fencer in London at that time.

MOLL Why, well said; but say your mistress should receive injury, have you the spirit of fighting in you? durst you second her?

TRAPDOOR Life, I have kept a bridge myself, and drove seven at a time before me!

MOLL Ay?

TRAPDOOR [Aside.] But they were all Lincolnshire bullocks, by my troth.

MOLL Well, meet me in Gray's Inn Fields between three and four this afternoon, and, upon better consideration, we'll retain you.

TRAPDOOR I humbly thank your good mistresship.—

[Aside.] I'll crack your neck for this kindness. [Exit.]

LAXTON Remember three. [Moll meets Laxton.]

MOLL Nay, if I fail you, hang me.

LAXTON Good wench, i'faith!

MOLL Who's this? [Moll then meets Openwork.]

OPENWORK 'Tis I, Moll.

MOLL Prithee, tend thy shop and prevent bastards.

OPENWORK We'll have a pint of the same wine, i'faith, Moll.

[Exit with Moll. Bell rings.]

GOSHAWK Hark, the bell rings! come, gentlemen. Jack Dapper, where shall's all munch?

JACK DAPPER I am for Parker's ordinary.

LAXTON He's a good guest to'm, he deserves his board; he draws all the gentlemen in a term-time thither. We'll be your followers, Jack; lead the way.—Look you, by my faith, the fool has feathered his nest well.

[Exeunt Jack Dapper, Laxton, Goshawk, and Greenwit. Enter Gallipot, Tiltyard, and Servants, with water-spaniels and a duck.]

TILTYARD Come, shut up your shops. Where's master Openwork?

MISTRESS GALLIPOT Nay, ask not me, master Tiltyard.

TILTYARD Where's his water-dog? puh—pist—hur—hur—pist!

GALLIPOT Come, wenches, come; we're going all to Hogsdon.[6]

MISTRESS GALLIPOT To Hogsdon, husband?

GALLIPOT Ay, to Hogsdon, pigsnie.[7]

MISTRESS GALLIPOT I'm not ready, husband.

GALLIPOT Faith, that's well—hum—pist—pist.—

[Spits in the dog's mouth.]

Come, mistress Openwork, you are so long!

MISTRESS OPENWORK I have no joy of my life, master Gallipot.

GALLIPOT Push, let your boy lead his water-spaniel along, and we'll show you the bravest sport at Parlous Pond.—[8] Hey, Trug, hey, Trug, hey, Trug![9] here's the best duck in England, except my wife; hey, hey, hey! fetch, fetch, fetch!—

Come let's away:

Of all the year this is the sportful'st day. [Exeunt.]

Scene 2

[A Street. Enter Sebastian Wengrave.]

SEBASTIAN If a man have a free will, where should the use
     More perfect shine than in his will to love?
     All creatures have their liberty in that.

---

6. A holiday place for apprentices.
7. A term of endearment.
8. A swimming pond, called "parlous" (perilous) because

of those who drowned there.
9. Prostitute.

[*Enter behind Sir Alexander Wengrave listening.*]
    Though else kept under servile yoke and fear;
    The very bond-slave has his freedom there.
    Amongst a world of creatures voiced and silent,
    Must my desires wear fetters?—Yea, are you
    So near? then I must break with my heart's truth,
    Meet grief at a back way.—Well: why, suppose
    The two-leaved tongues[1] of slander or of truth
    Pronounce Moll loathsome; if before my love
    She appear fair, what injury have I?
    I have the thing I like: in all things else
    Mine own eye guides me, and I find 'em prosper.
    Life! what should ail it now? I know that man
    Ne'er truly loves,—if he gainsay't he lies,—
    That winks and marries with his father's eyes:
    I'll keep mine own wide open.
[*Enter Moll and a Porter with a viol on his back.*]
SIR ALEXANDER [*Aside.*]   Here's brave wilfulness!
    A made match! here she comes; they met a' purpose.
PORTER Must I carry this great fiddle to your chamber, mistress Mary?
MOLL Fiddle, goodman hog-rubber?[2] Some of these porters bear so much for others,
    they have no time to carry wit for themselves.
PORTER To your own chamber, mistress Mary?
MOLL Who'll hear an ass speak? Whither else, goodman pageant-bearer? They're
    people of the worst memories!

                                 [*Exit Porter.*]

SEBASTIAN Why, 'twere too great a burden, love, to have them
    Carry things in their minds and a' their backs together.
MOLL Pardon me, sir, I thought not you so near.
SIR ALEXANDER [*Aside.*] So, so, so!
SEBASTIAN I would be nearer to thee, and in that fashion
    That makes the best part of all creatures honest:
    No otherwise I wish it.
MOLL Sir, I am so poor to requite you, you must look for nothing but thanks of me: I
    have no humor to marry; I love to lie a' both sides a' th' bed myself: and again, a'
    th' other side, a wife, you know, ought to be obedient, but I fear me I am too head-
    strong to obey; therefore I'll ne'er go about it. I love you so well, sir, for your good
    will, I'd be loath you should repent your bargain after; and therefore we'll ne'er
    come together at first. I have the head now of myself, and am man enough for a
    woman: marriage is but a chopping and changing, where a maiden loses one head,
    and has a worse i' th' place.
SIR ALEXANDER [*Aside.*] The most comfortablest answer from a roaring girl
    That ever mine ears drunk in!
SEBASTIAN   This were enough
    Now to affright a fool for ever from thee,
    When 'tis the music that I love thee for.
SIR ALEXANDER [*Aside.*] There's a boy spoils all again!
MOLL   Believe it, sir,

---

1. Like forked tongues.   2. An abusive term for a swineherd.

I am not of that disdainful temper but I could love you faithfully.

SIR ALEXANDER [*Aside.*] A pox on you for that word! I like you not now. You're a cunning roarer, I see that already.

MOLL But sleep upon this once more, sir; you may chance shift a mind to-morrow: be not too hasty to wrong yourself; never while you live, sir, take a wife running; many have run out at heels that have done't. You see, sir, I speak against myself; and if every woman would deal with their suitor so honestly, poor younger brothers would not be so often gulled with old cozening widows,[3] that turn o'er all their wealth in trust to some kinsman, and make the poor gentleman work hard for a pension. Fare you well, sir.

SEBASTIAN Nay, prithee, one word more.

SIR ALEXANDER [*Aside.*] How do I wrong this girl! she puts him off still.

MOLL Think upon this in cold blood, sir: you make as much haste as if you were a-going upon a sturgeon voyage. Take deliberation, sir; never choose a wife as if you were going to Virginia.

SEBASTIAN And so we parted: my too-cursed fate!

SIR ALEXANDER [*Aside.*] She is but cunning, gives him longer time in't.
     [*Enter Tailor.*]

TAILOR Mistress Moll, mistress Moll! so ho, ho, so ho!

MOLL There, boy, there, boy! What, dost thou go a-hawking after me with a red clout on thy finger?

TAILOR I forgot to take measure on you for your new breeches.

SIR ALEXANDER [*Aside.*] Hoyda, breeches? What, will he marry a monster with two trinkets? What age is this! If the wife go in breeches, the man must wear long coats[4] like a fool.

MOLL What fiddling's here! Would not the old pattern have served your turn?

TAILOR You change the fashion: you say you'll have the great Dutch slop,[5] mistress Mary.

MOLL Why, sir, I say so still.

TAILOR Your breeches, then, will take up a yard more.

MOLL Well, pray, look it be put in then.

TAILOR It shall stand round and full, I warrant you.

MOLL Pray, make 'em easy enough.

TAILOR I know my fault now, t'other was somewhat stiff between the legs; I'll make these open enough, I warrant you.

SIR ALEXANDER [*Aside.*] Here's good gear[6] towards! I have brought up my son to marry a Dutch slop and a French doublet; a codpiece daughter!

TAILOR So, I have gone as far as I can go.

MOLL Why, then, farewell.

TAILOR If you go presently to your chamber, mistress Mary, pray, send me the measure of your thigh by some honest body.

MOLL Well, sir, I'll send it by a porter presently. [*Exit.*]

TAILOR So you had need, it is a lusty one; both of them would make any porter's back ache in England. [*Exit.*]

SEBASTIAN I have examined the best part of man,
          Reason and judgment; and in love, they tell me,
          They leave me uncontrolled; he that is swayed

---

3. Since by law a woman's property was given over to her husband when she married, widows put their wealth in the hands of relatives to avoid having to give it over to a second husband.

4. Petticoats worn by women, idiots, and court fools.
5. Wide loose breeches.
6. Business; genitals.

By an unfeeling blood, past heat of love,
His spring-time must needs err; his watch ne'er goes right
That sets his dial by a rusty clock.

SIR ALEXANDER [coming forward] So; and which is that rusty clock, sir, you?

SEBASTIAN The clock at Ludgate, sir; it ne'er goes true.

SIR ALEXANDER But thou go'st falser; not thy father's cares
Can keep thee right: when that insensible work
Obeys the workman's art, lets off the hour,
And stops again when time is satisfied:
But thou runn'st on; and judgment, thy main wheel,
Beats by all stops, as if the work would break,
Begun with long pains for a minute's ruin:
Much like a suffering man brought up with care,
At last bequeathed to shame and a short prayer.

SEBASTIAN I taste you bitterer than I can deserve, sir.

SIR ALEXANDER What has bewitched thee, son? what devil or drug
Hath wrought upon the weakness of thy blood,
And betrayed all her hopes to ruinous folly?
O, wake from drowsy and enchanted shame,
Wherein thy soul sits, with a golden dream
Flattered and poisoned! I am old, my son;
O, let me prevail quickly!
For I have weightier business of mine own
Than to chide thee: I must not to my grave
As a drunkard to his bed, whereon he lies
Only to sleep, and never cares to rise:
Let me despatch in time; come no more near her.

SEBASTIAN Not honestly? not in the way of marriage?

SIR ALEXANDER What sayst thou? marriage? in what place? the Sessions-house?
And who shall give the bride, prithee? an indictment?

SEBASTIAN Sir, now ye take part with the world to wrong her.

SIR ALEXANDER Why, wouldst thou fain marry to be pointed at?
Alas, the number's great! Do not o'erburden't.
Why, as good marry a beacon on a hill,
Which all the country fix their eyes upon,
As her thy folly doats on. If thou long'st
To have the story of thy infamous fortunes
Serve for discourse in ordinaries and taverns,
Thou'rt in the way; or to confound thy name,
Keep on, thou canst not miss it; or to strike
Thy wretched father to untimely coldness,
Keep the left hand still, it will bring thee to't.
Yet, if no tears wrung from thy father's eyes,
Nor sighs that fly in sparkles from his sorrows,
Had power to alter what is wilful in thee,
Methinks her very name should fright thee from her,
And never trouble me.

SEBASTIAN Why, is the name of Moll so fatal, sir?

SIR ALEXANDER Many one, sir, where suspect is entered;
For, seek all London from one end to t'other,
More whores of that name than of any ten other.

SEBASTIAN What's that to her? Let those blush for themselves:
    Can any guilt in others condemn her?
    I've vow'd to love her: let all storms oppose me
    That ever beat against the breast of man,
    Nothing but death's black tempest shall divide us.
SIR ALEXANDER O, folly that can doat on nought but shame!
SEBASTIAN Put case, a wanton itch runs through one name
    More than another; is that name the worse,
    Where honesty sits possest in't? It should rather
    Appear more excellent, and deserve more praise,
    When through foul mists a brightness it can raise.
    Why, there are of the devils honest gentlemen
    And well descended, keep an open house,
    And some a' th' good man's that are arrant knaves.
    He hates unworthily that by rote condemns,
    For the name neither saves nor yet condemns;
    And for her honesty, I've made such proof on't
    In several forms, so nearly watch'd her ways,
    I will maintain that strict against an army,
    Excepting you, my father. Here's her worst,
    Sh'as a bold spirit that mingles with mankind,
    But nothing else comes near it: and oftentimes
    Through her apparel somewhat shames her birth;
    But she is loose in nothing but in mirth:
    Would all Molls were no worse!
SIR ALEXANDER [Aside.] This way I toil in vain, and give but aim
    To infamy and ruin: he will fall;
    My blessing cannot stay him: all my joys
    Stand at the brink of a devouring flood,
    And will be wilfully swallowed, wilfully.
    But why so vain let all these tears be lost?
    I'll pursue her to shame, and so all's crost. [Exit.]
SEBASTIAN He's gone with some strange purpose, whose effect
    Will hurt me little if he shoot so wide,
    To think I love so blindly: I but feed
    His heart to this match, to draw on the other,
    Wherein my joy sits with a full wish crowned,
    Only his mood excepted, which must change
    By opposite policies, courses indirect;
    Plain dealing in this world takes no effect.
    This mad girl I'll acquaint with my intent,
    Get her assistance, make my fortunes known:
    'Twixt lovers' hearts she's a fit instrument,
    And has the art to help them to their own.
    By her advice, for in that craft she's wise,
    My love and I may meet, spite of all spies. [Exit.]

Act 3
Scene 1

[Gray's Inn Fields. Enter Laxton and Coachman.]
LAXTON Coachman.

COACHMAN Here, sir.

LAXTON There's a tester[7] more; prithee drive thy coach to the hither end of Mary-bone-park,[8] a fit place for Moll to get in.

COACHMAN Marybone-park, sir?

LAXTON Ay, it's in our way, thou knowest.

COACHMAN It shall be done, sir.

LAXTON Coachman.

COACHMAN Anon, sir.

LAXTON Are we fitted with good phrampel[9] jades?

COACHMAN The best in Smithfield,[1] I warrant you, sir.

LAXTON May we safely take the upper hand of any coached velvet cap, or tuftaffe-ty[2] jacket? for they keep a vild[3] swaggering in coaches now-a-days; the highways are stopt with them.

COACHMAN My life for yours, and baffle[4] 'em too, sir; why, they are the same jades, believe it, sir, that have drawn all your famous whores to Ware.

LAXTON Nay, then they know their business; they need no more instructions.

COACHMAN They're so used to such journeys, sir, I never use whip to 'em; for if they catch but the scent of a wench once, they run like devils.

[Exit Coachman with his whip.]

LAXTON Fine Cerberus![5] That rogue will have the start of a thousand ones; for whilst others trot a' foot, he'll ride prancing to hell upon a coach-horse. Stay, 'tis now about the hour of her appointment, but yet I see her not. [The clock strikes three.] Hark! What's this? One, two, three: three by the clock at Savoy;[6] this is the hour, and Gray's Inn Fields the place, she swore she'd meet me. Ha! yonder's two Inns-a'-court[7] men with one wench, but that's not she; they walk toward Islington out of my way. I see none yet drest like her; I must look for a shag-ruff, a frieze jerken, a short sword, and a safe-guard, or I get none. Why, Moll, prithee, make haste, or the coachman will curse us anon.

[Enter Moll, dressed as a man.]

MOLL [Aside.] O, here's my gentleman! If they would keep their days as well with their mercers[8] as their hours with their harlots, no bankrupt would give seven score pound for a sergeant's place; for would you know a catchpoll[9] rightly derived, the corruption of a citizen is the generation of a sergeant. How his eye hawks for venery![1] —Come, are you ready, sir?

LAXTON Ready? for what, sir?

MOLL Do you ask that now, sir?

Why was this meeting 'pointed?

LAXTON I thought you mistook me, sir; you seem to be some young barrister;[2]

I have no suit in law, all my land's sold;

I praise heaven for't, 't has rid me of much trouble,

MOLL Then I must wake you, sir; where stands the coach?

---

7. Sixpence.
8. Marybone Park was frequented by prostitutes.
9. Swift, restless.
1. The worst jades came from Smithfield.
2. Taffeta with velvet stripes, a rich fabric favored by the merchant class who enjoyed showing its wealth in dress when the sumptuary laws were repealed in 1603.
3. Vile.
4. Treat contemptuously.

5. The three-headed dog guarding the gates of Hades in classical myth.
6. Hospital built by Henry VIII.
7. Law schools.
8. Dealers in costly fabric, to whom gallants were often in debt.
9. Police who arrested debtors.
1. Hunting; sexual pleasure.
2. Lawyer.

LAXTON Who's this? Moll, honest Moll?

MOLL So young, and purblind?[3]

　　You're an old wanton in your eyes, I see that.

LAXTON Thou'rt admirably suited for the Three Pigeons[4] at Brainford. I'll swear I
　　knew thee not.

MOLL I'll swear you did not; but you shall know me now.

LAXTON No, not here; we shall be spied, i'faith; the coach is better: come.

MOLL Stay. [*Puts off her cloak.*]

LAXTON What, wilt thou untruss a point,[5] Moll?

MOLL Yes; here's the point [*Draws her sword.*]

　　　　That I untruss; 't has but one tag, 'twill serve though
　　　　To tie up a rogue's tongue.

LAXTON　　　　　　　　　　　　How!

MOLL　　　　　　　　　　　　　　　　　There's the gold
　　　　With which you hir'd your hackney,[6] here's her pace;
　　　　She racks hard, and perhaps your bones will feel it:
　　　　Ten angels of mine own I've put to thine;
　　　　Win 'em and wear 'em.

LAXTON　　　　　　　　　　　　　　Hold, Moll! mistress Mary—

MOLL Draw, or I'll serve an execution on thee,
　　　　Shall lay thee up till doomsday.

LAXTON Draw upon a woman! Why, what dost mean, Moll?

MOLL To teach thy base thoughts manners: thou'rt one of those
　　　　That thinks each woman thy fond flexible whore;
　　　　If she but cast a liberal eye upon thee,
　　　　Turn back her head, she's thine; or amongst company
　　　　By chance drink first to thee, then she's quite gone,
　　　　There is no means to help her; nay, for a need,
　　　　Wilt swear unto thy credulous fellow-lechers,
　　　　That thou art more in favor with a lady
　　　　At first sight than her monkey[7] all her lifetime.
　　　　How many of our sex, by such as thou,
　　　　Have their good thoughts paid with a blasted name
　　　　That never deserved loosely, or did trip
　　　　In path of whoredom beyond cup and lip!
　　　　But for the stain of conscience and of soul,
　　　　Better had women fall into the hands
　　　　Of an act silent than a bragging nothing;
　　　　There is no mercy in't. What durst move you, sir,
　　　　To think me whorish? a name which I'd tear out
　　　　From the high German's throat, if it lay leiger[8] there
　　　　To despatch privy slanders against me.
　　　　In thee I defy all men, their worst hates
　　　　And their best flatteries, all their golden witchcrafts,
　　　　With which they entangle the poor spirits of fools,
　　　　Distressed needle-women and trade-fallen wives;

3. Completely blind.
4. A famous inn.
5. Untie the laces of the breeches; points (laces) fastened
the hose to the doublet. "Untruss" also means unsheathe.

6. Horse; prostitute.
7. Pet.
8. Ambassador at a foreign court.

Fish that must needs bite, or themselves be bitten;
Such hungry things as these may soon be took
With a worm fastened on a golden hook:
Those are the lecher's food, his prey; he watches
For quarrelling wedlocks[9] and poor shifting sisters;
'Tis the best fish he takes. But why, good fisherman,
Am I thought meat for you, that never yet
Had angling rod cast towards me? 'cause, you'll say,
I'm given to sport, I'm often merry, jest:
Had mirth no kindred in the world but lust,
O shame take all her friends then! but howe'er
Thou and the baser world censure my life,
I'll send 'em word by thee, and write so much
Upon thy breast, 'cause thou shalt bear't in mind,
Tell them 'twere base to yield where I have conquered;
I scorn to prostitute myself to a man,
I that can prostitute a man to me;
And so I greet thee.

LAXTON   Hear me—
MOLL   Would the spirits
Of all my sland[er]ers were clasped in thine,
That I might vex an army at one time! [*They fight.*]
LOXTON I do repent me; hold!
MOLL You'll die the better Christian then.
LAXTON I do confess I have wronged thee, Moll.
MOLL Confession is but poor amends for wrong,
     Unless a rope would follow.
LAXTON   I ask thee pardon.
MOLL I'm your hired whore, sir!
LAXTON   I yield both purse and body.
MOLL Both are mine, and now at my disposing.
LAXTON Spare my life!
MOLL   I scorn to strike thee basely.
LAXTON Spoke like a noble girl, i'faith!—[*Aside.*] Heart, I think I fight with a
     familiar,[1] or the ghost of a fencer. Sh'as wounded me gallantly. Call you this a
     lecherous viage?[2] here's blood would have served me this seven year in broken
     heads and cut fingers; and it now runs all out together. Pox a' the Three
     Pigeons! I would the coach were here now to carry me to the chirurgeon's.
     [*Exit.*]
MOLL If I could meet my enemies one by one thus,
     I might make pretty shift with 'em in time,
     And make 'em know that she has wit and spirit,
     May scorn to live beholding to her body for meat;
     Or for apparel, like your common dame,
     That makes shame get her clothes to cover shame.
     Base is that mind that kneels unto her body,
     As if a husband stood in awe on's wife;

9. Wives.   2. Voyage.
1. Devil's spirit.

My spirit shall be mistress of this house
As long as I have time in't.—O,

[*Enter Trapdoor.*]

Here comes my man that would be: 'tis his hour.
Faith, a good well-set fellow, if his spirit
Be answerable to his umbles;° he walks stiff,   *insides*
But whether he'll stand to't stiffly, there's the point:
Has a good calf for't; and ye shall have many a woman
Choose him she means to make her head by his calf;
I do not know their tricks in't. Faith, he seems
A man without; I'll try what he's within.

TRAPDOOR She told me Gray's Inn Fields, 'twixt three and four;
I'll fit her mistress-ship with a piece of service:
I'm hired to rid the town of one mad girl.

[*Moll jostles him.*]

What a pox ails you, sir?

MOLL He begins like a gentleman.

TRAPDOOR Heart, is the field so narrow, or your eyesight—
Life, he comes back again!

MOLL Was this spoke to me, sir?

TRAPDOOR I cannot tell, sir.

MOLL   Go, you're a coxcomb!³

TRAPDOOR Coxcomb?

MOLL   You're a slave!

TRAPDOOR   I hope there's law for you, sir.

MOLL Yea, do you see, sir? [*Turns his hat.*]

TRAPDOOR Heart, this is no good dealing! pray, let me know what house you're of.

MOLL One of the Temple,⁴ sir. [*Fillips him.*]

TRAPDOOR   Mass, so methinks.

MOLL And yet sometime I lie about Chick Lane.

TRAPDOOR I like you the worse because you shift your lodging so often: I'll not meddle with you for that trick, sir.

MOLL A good shift; but it shall not serve your turn.

TRAPDOOR You'll give me leave to pass about my business, sir?

MOLL Your business? I'll make you wait on me
Before I ha' done, and glad to serve me too.

TRAPDOOR How, sir? serve you? not if there were no more men in England.

MOLL But if there were no more women in England,
I hope you'd wait upon your mistress then?

TRAPDOOR Mistress?

MOLL O, you're a tried spirit at a push, sir?

TRAPDOOR What would your worship have me do?

MOLL You a fighter!

TRAPDOOR No, I praise heaven, I had better grace and more manners.

MOLL As how, I pray, sir?

TRAPDOOR Life, 'thad been a beastly part of me to have drawn my weapons upon my mistress; all the world would a' cried shame of me for that.

MOLL Why, but you knew me not.

---

3. Fool.   4. A lawyer.

TRAPDOOR Do not say so, mistress; I knew you by your wide straddle, as well as if I
    had been in your belly.

MOLL Well, we shall try you further; i' th' mean time
    We give you entertainment.

TRAPDOOR   Thank your good mistress-ship.

MOLL How many suits have you?

TRAPDOOR No more suits than backs, mistress.

MOLL Well, if you deserve, I cast off this, next week,
    And you may creep into't.

TRAPDOOR   Thank your good worship.

MOLL Come, follow me to St. Thomas Apostle's:[5]
    I'll put a livery cloak upon your back
    The first thing I do.

TRAPDOOR   I follow, my dear mistress. [*Exeunt.*]

Scene 2

[*Gallipot's Shop. Enter Mistress Gallipot as from supper, Gallipot following her.*]

GALLIPOT What, Pru! nay, sweet Prudence!

MISTRESS GALLIPOT What a pruing keep you! I think the baby would have a
    teat, it kyes[6] so. Pray, be not so fond of me, leave your city humors;[7] I'm vexed at
    you, to see how like a calf you come bleating after me.

GALLIPOT Nay, honey Pru, how does your rising up before all the table show, and
    flinging from my friends so uncivilly! Fie, Pru, fie! Come.

MISTRESS GALLIPOT Then up and ride,[8] i'faith!

GALLIPOT Up and ride? nay, my pretty Pru, that's far from my thought, duck. Why,
    mouse, thy mind is nibbling at something; what is't? What lies upon thy stomach?

MISTRESS GALLIPOT Such an ass as you: Hoyda, you're best turn midwife, or
    physician! you're a 'pothecary already, but I'm none of your drugs.

GALLIPOT Thou art a sweet drug, sweetest Pru, and the more thou art pounded,[9]
    the more precious.

MISTRESS GALLIPOT Must you be prying into a woman's secrets, say ye?

GALLIPOT Woman's secrets?

MISTRESS GALLIPOT What! I cannot have a qualm come upon me, but your
    teeth waters till your nose hang over it!

GALLIPOT It is my love, dear wife.

MISTRESS GALLIPOT Your love? Your love is all words; give me deeds: I cannot
    abide a man that's too fond over me,—so cookish! Thou dost not know how to
    handle a woman in her kind.

GALLIPOT No, Pru? why, I hope I have handled—

MISTRESS GALLIPOT Handle a fool's head of your own,—fie, fie!

GALLIPOT Ha, ha, 'tis such a wasp! It does me good now to have her sting me, little
    rogue!

MISTRESS GALLIPOT Now, fie, how you vex me! I cannot abide these apron hus-
    bands;[1] such cotqueans![2] You overdo your things, they become you scurvily.[3]

---

5. Nearby the clothes shops.
6. Cries.
7. Moods.
8. Have an erection and sexual intercourse.

9. With a sexual double meaning.
1. Husbands who are tied to their wives' apron strings.
2. Men who interfere in women's business.
3. Badly.

GALLIPOT [*Aside.*] Upon my life she breeds: heaven knows how I have strained myself to please her night and day. I wonder why we citizens should get children so fretful and untoward in the breeding, their fathers being for the most part as gentle as milch kine.[4]—Shall I leave thee, my Pru?

MISTRESS GALLIPOT Fie, fie, fie!

GALLIPOT Thou shalt not be vexed no more, pretty, kind rogue; take no cold, sweet Pru? [*Exit.*]

MISTRESS GALLIPOT As your wit has done. Now, master Laxton, show your head; what news from you? Would any husband suspect that a woman crying, *Buy any scurvy-grass*, should bring love-letters amongst her herbs to his wife? Pretty trick! Fine conveyance! Had jealousy a thousand eyes, a silly woman with scurvy-grass blinds them all.

    Laxton, with bays
    Crown I thy wit for this, it deserves praise:
    This makes me affect thee more, this proves thee wise:
    'Lack, what poor shift is love forced to devise!—
To th' point. [*Reads letter.*] *O sweet creature*—a sweet beginning!—*pardon my long absence, for thou shalt shortly be possessed with my presence: though Demopho[o]n was false to Phyllis, I will be to thee as Pan-da-rus was to Cres-sida;*[5] *though Aeneas made an ass of Dido, I will die to thee ere I do so. O sweetest creature, make much of me! for no man beneath the silver moon shall make more of a woman than I do of thee: furnish me therefore with thirty pounds; you must do it of necessity for me; I languish till I see some comfort come from thee. Protesting not to die in thy debt, but rather to live, so as hitherto I have and will,*

                                          Thy true Laxton ever.

    Alas, poor gentleman! troth, I pity him.
    How shall I raise this money? thirty pound!
    'Tis thirty sure, a 3 before an O;
    I know his threes too well. My childbed linen,
    Shall I pawn that for him? Then if my mark
    Be known, I am undone; it may be thought
    My husband's bankrout.° Which way shall I turn?   *bankrupt*
    Laxton, what with my own fears and thy wants,
    I'm like a needle 'twixt two adamants.°   *magnates*
[*Reenter Gallipot hastily.*]

GALLIPOT Nay, nay, wife, the women are all up—[*Aside.*] Ha! how? reading a' letters? I smell a goose, a couple of capons, and a gammon of bacon, from her mother out of the country. I hold my life—steal, steal—

MISTRESS GALLIPOT O, beshrew your heart!

GALLIPOT   What letter's that? I'll see't.
[*Mistress Gallipot tears the letter.*]

MISTRESS GALLIPOT O, would thou had'st no eyes to see the downfall
    Of me and of thyself! I am for ever,
    For ever I'm undone!

GALLIPOT   What ails my Pru?

---

4. Milking cows.
5. Demophoon broke his promise to return to Phyllis, and Aeneas left Dido to found Rome. Both women committed suicide. Pandarus was a go-between for Troilus and Cressida.

What paper's that thou tear'st?

MISTRESS GALLIPOT   Would I could tear
My very heart in pieces! for my soul
Lies on the rack of shame, that tortures me
Beyond a woman's suffering.

GALLIPOT   What means this?

MISTRESS GALLIPOT Had you no other vengeance to throw down,
But even in height of all my joys—

GALLIPOT Dear woman—

MISTRESS GALLIPOT When the full sea of pleasure and content
Seemed to flow over me?

GALLIPOT   As thou desir'st
To keep me out of Bedlam,[6] tell what troubles thee!
Is not thy child at nurse fallen sick, or dead?

MISTRESS GALLIPOT O, no!

GALLIPOT   Heavens bless me! are my barns and houses
Yonder at Hockley-hole consumed with fire?
I can build more, sweet Pru.

MISTRESS GALLIPOT 'Tis worse, 'tis worse!

GALLIPOT My factor broke? or is the Jonas sunk?[7]

MISTRESS GALLIPOT Would all we had were swallowed in the waves,
Rather than both should be the scorn of slaves!

GALLIPOT I'm at my wit's end.

MISTRESS GALLIPOT   O my dear husband!
Where once I thought myself a fixed star,
Placed only in the heaven of thine arms,
I fear now I shall prove a wanderer.
O Laxton, Laxton! Is it then my fate
To be by thee o'erthrown?

GALLIPOT   Defend me, wisdom,
From falling into frenzy! On my knees,
Sweet Pru, speak; what's that Laxton, who so heavy
Lies on thy bosom?

MISTRESS GALLIPOT I shall sure run mad!

GALLIPOT I shall run mad for company then. Speak to me;
I'm Gallipot thy husband—Pru—why, Pru
Art sick in conscience for some villanous deed
Thou wert about to act? Didst mean to rob me?
Tush, I forgive thee: hast thou on my bed
Thrust my soft pillow under another's head?
I'll wink at all faults, Pru: 'las, that's no more
Than what some neighbors near thee have done before!
Sweet honey Pru, what's that Laxton?

MISTRESS GALLIPOT   O!

GALLIPOT Out with him!

MISTRESS GALLIPOT   O, he's born to be my undoer!

---

6. Insane asylum.

7. Factor: agent, commission merchant; Jonas: a trading ship.

This hand, which thou call'st thine, to him was given,
To him was I made sure[8] i' th' sight of heaven.
GALLIPOT I never heard this thunder.
GALLIPOT   Yes, yes, before
I was to thee contracted, to him I swore:
Since last I saw him, twelve months three times told
The moon hath drawn through her light silver bow;
For o'er the seas he went, and it was said,
But rumor lies, that he in France was dead;
But he's alive, O he's alive! He sent
That letter to me, which in rage I rent;
Swearing with oaths most damnably to have me,
Or tear me from this bosom: O heavens, save me!
GALLIPOT My heart will break; shamed and undone for ever!
MISTRESS GALLIPOT So black a day, poor wretch, went o'er thee never!
GALLIPOT If thou should'st wrestle with him at the law,
Thou'rt sure to fall. No odd slight? no prevention?
I'll tell him thou'rt with child.
MISTRESS GALLIPOT   Umh!
GALLIPOT   Or give out
One of my men was ta'en a-bed with thee.
MISTRESS GALLIPOT Umh, umh!
GALLIPOT   Before I lose thee, my dear Pru,
I'll drive it to that push.
MISTRESS GALLIPOT   Worse and worse still;
You embrace a mischief, to prevent an ill.
GALLIPOT I'll buy thee of him, stop his mouth with gold:
Think'st thou 'twill do?
MISTRESS GALLIPOT   O me! heavens grant it would!
Yet now my senses are set more in tune.
He writ, as I remember, in his letter,
That he in riding up and down had spent,
Ere he could find me, thirty pounds: send that;
Stand not on thirty with him.
GALLIPOT   Forty, Pru!
Say thou the word, 'tis done: we venture lives
For wealth, but must do more to keep our wives.
Thirty or forty, Pru?
MISTRESS GALLIPOT   Thirty, good sweet;
Of an ill bargain let's save what we can:
I'll pay it him with my tears; he was a man,
When first I knew him, of a meek spirit,
All goodness is not yet dried up, I hope.
GALLIPOT He shall have thirty pound, let that stop all:
Love's sweets taste best when we have drunk down gall.
[Enter Tiltyard, Mistress Tiltyard, Goshawk, and Mistress Openwork.]
God's-so, our friends! come, come, smooth your cheek:
After a storm the face of heaven looks sleek.
TILTYARD Did I not tell you these turtles were together?

8. Contracted.

MISTRESS TILTYARD How dost thou, sirrah? Why, sister Gallipot—
MISTRESS OPENWORK Lord, how she's chang'd!
GOSHAWK Is your wife ill, sir?
GALLIPOT Yes, indeed, la, sir, very ill, very ill, never worse.
MISTRESS TILTYARD How her head burns! Feel how her pulses work!
MISTRESS OPENWORK Sister, lie down a little; that always does me good.
MISTRESS TILTYARD In good sadness, I find best ease in that too. Has she laid
    some hot thing⁹ to her stomach?
MISTRESS GALLIPOT No, but I will lay something anon.
TILTYARD Come, come, fools, you trouble her.—Shall's go, master Goshawk?
GOSHAWK Yes, sweet master Tiltyard—Sirrah Rosamond, I hold my life Gallipot
    hath vext his wife.
MISTRESS OPENWORK She has a horrible high color indeed.
GOSHAWK We shall have your face painted with the same red soon at night, when
    your husband comes from his rubbers¹ in a false alley: thou wilt not believe me
    that his bowls run with a wrong bias.
MISTRESS OPENWORK It cannot sink into me that he feeds upon stale mutton²
    abroad, having better and fresher at home.
GOSHAWK What if I bring thee where thou shalt see him stand at rack and manger?
MISTRESS OPENWORK I'll saddle him in's kind, and spur him till he kick again.
GOSHAWK Shall thou and I ride our journey then?
MISTRESS OPENWORK Here's my hand.
GOSHAWK No more.—Come, master Tiltyard, shall we leap into the stirrups with
    our women, and amble home?
TILTYARD Yes, yes.—Come, wife.
MISTRESS TILTYARD In troth, sister, I hope you will do well for all this.
MISTRESS GALLIPOT I hope I shall. Farewell, good sister. Sweet master Goshawk.
GALLIPOT Welcome, brother; most kindly welcome, sir,
ALL Thanks, sir, for our good cheer.
    [Exeunt all but Gallipot and Mistress Gallipot.]
GALLIPOT It shall be so: because a crafty knave
    Shall not outreach me, nor walk by my door
    With my wife arm in arm, as 'twere his whore.
    I'll give him a golden coxcomb, thirty pound.
    Tush, Pru, what's thirty pound? Sweet duck, look cheerly.
MISTRESS GALLIPOT Thou'rt worthy of my heart, thou buy'st it dearly.
    [Enter Laxton muffled.³]
LAXTON [Aside.] Uds light, the tide's against me; a pox of your 'pothecaryship! O
    for some glister⁴ to set him going! 'Tis one of Hercules' labors to tread one of these
    city hens, because their cocks are still crowing over them. There's no turning tail
    here, I must on.
MISTRESS GALLIPOT O husband, see he comes!
GALLIPOT Let me deal with him.
LAXTON Bless you, sir.
GALLIPOT Be you blest too, sir, if you come in peace.

9. With a sexual double meaning.
1. Game of cards with three rounds, with a bawdy play on
"rub" and "alley." See Dekker, O Per Se O: "My bowls did
fit her alley."
2. Slang for a whore.
3. Hiding his face.
4. Suppository, enema.

LAXTON Have you any good pudding tobacco,[5] sir?

MISTRESS GALLIPOT O, pick no quarrels, gentle sir! my husband
    Is not a man of weapon, as you are;
    He knows all, I have open'd all before him,
    Concerning you.

LAXTON [Aside.]   Zounds, has she shown my letters?

MISTRESS GALLIPOT Suppose my case were yours, what would you do?
    At such a pinch, such batteries, such assaults
    Of father, mother, kindred, to dissolve
    The knot you tied, and to be bound to him;
    How could you shift this storm off?

LAXTON If I know, hang me!

MISTRESS GALLIPOT Besides a story of your death was read
    Each minute to me.

LAXTON [Aside.] What a pox means this riddling?

GALLIPOT Be wise, sir; let not you and I be tossed
    On lawyers' pens; they have sharp nibs, and draw
    Men's very heart-blood from them. What need you, sir,
    To beat the drum of my wife's infamy,
    And call your friends together, sir, to prove
    Your precontract, when sh'as confessed it?

LAXTON   Umh, sir,
    Has she confessed it?

GALLIPOT   Sh'as, 'faith, to me, sir,
    Upon your letter sending.

MISTRESS GALLIPOT I have, I have.

LAXTON [Aside.]   If I let this iron cool, call me slave.
    Do you hear, you dame Prudence? think'st thou, vile woman,
    I'll take these blows and wink?

MISTRESS GALLIPOT   Upon my knees. [Kneeling.]

LAXTON Out, impudence.

GALLIPOT   Good sir—

LAXTON   You goatish slaves![6]
    No wild fowl to cut up but mine?

GALLIPOT   Alas, sir,
    You make her flesh to tremble; fright her not:
    She shall do reason, and what's fit.

LAXTON   I'll have thee,
    Wert thou more common than an hospital,
    And more diseased.

GALLIPOT   But one word, good sir!

LAXTON   So, sir.

GALLIPOT I married her, have lien with her, and got
    Two children on her body: think but on that:
    Have you so beggarly an appetite,
    When I upon a dainty dish have fed
    To dine upon my scraps, my leavings? ha, sir?
    Do I come near you now, sir?

---

5. Pudding tobacco was compressed in rolls.   6. Slaves to lust.

LAXTON   Be-lady, you touch me!

GALLIPOT Would not you scorn to wear my clothes, sir?

LAXTON   Right, sir.

GALLIPOT Then, pray, sir, wear not her; for she's a garment
So fitting for my body, I am loath
Another should put it on: you'll undo both.
Your letter, as she said, complained you had spent,
In quest of her, some thirty pound; I'll pay it:
Shall that, sir, stop this gap up 'twixt you two?

LAXTON Well, if I swallow this wrong, let her thank you:
The money being paid, sir, I am gone:
Farewell. O women, happy's he trusts none!

MISTRESS GALLIPOT Despatch him hence, sweet husband.

GALLIPOT   Yes, dear wife:
Pray, sir, come in: ere master Laxton part,
Thou shalt in wine drink to him.

MISTRESS GALLIPOT   With all my heart.—[Exit Gallipot.]
How dost thou like my wit?

LAXTON   Rarely: that wile,
By which the serpent did the first woman beguile,
Did ever since all women's bosoms fill;
You're apple-eaters all, deceivers still. [Exeunt.]

Scene 3

[Holborn. Enter Sir Alexander Wengrave, Sir Davy Dapper, and Sir Adam Appleton
on one side, and Trapdoor on the other.]

SIR ALEXANDER Out with your tale, sir Davy, to sir Adam:
A knave is in mine eye deep in my debt.

SIR DAVY Nay, if he be a knave, sir, hold him fast.
[Sir Davy Dapper and Sir Adam Appleton talk apart.]

SIR ALEXANDER Speak softly; what egg is there hatching now?

TRAPDOOR A duck's egg, sir, a duck that has eaten a frog; I have cracked the shell,
and some villany or other will peep out presently: the duck that sits is the bounc-
ing ramp,[7] that roaring girl my mistress; the drake that must tread is your son
Sebastian.

SIR ALEXANDER Be quick.

TRAPDOOR As the tongue of an oyster-wench.

SIR ALEXANDER And see thy news be true.

TRAPDOOR As a barber's every Saturday night. Mad Moll—

SIR ALEXANDER Ah—

TRAPDOOR Must be let in, without knocking, at your back gate.

SIR ALEXANDER So.

TRAPDOOR Your chamber will be made bawdy.

SIR ALEXANDER Good.

TRAPDOOR She comes in a shirt of mail.

SIR ALEXANDER How? shirt of mail?

TRAPDOOR Yes, sir, or a male shirt; that's to say, in man's apparel.

---

7. An outspoken and outrageously bad woman or girl.

SIR ALEXANDER To my son?

TRAPDOOR Close to your son: your son and her moon will be in conjunction, if all almanacs lie not; her black saveguard is turned into a deep slop, the holes of her upper body to button-holes, her waistcoat to a doublet, her placket to the ancient seat of a codpiece, and you shall take 'em both with standing collars.[8]

SIR ALEXANDER Art sure of this?

TRAPDOOR As every throng is sure of a pick-pocket; as sure as a whore is of the clients all Michaelmas term,[9] and of the pox after the term.

SIR ALEXANDER The time of their tilting?

TRAPDOOR Three.

SIR ALEXANDER The day?

TRAPDOOR This.

SIR ALEXANDER Away; ply it, watch her.

TRAPDOOR As the devil doth for the death of a bawd; I'll watch her, do you catch her.

SIR ALEXANDER She's fast: here weave thou the nets. Hark.

TRAPDOOR They are made.

SIR ALEXANDER I told them thou didst owe me money: hold it up; maintain't.

TRAPDOOR Stiffly, as a Puritan does contention.—Pox, I owe thee not the value of a halfpenny halter.

SIR ALEXANDER Thou shalt be hanged in it ere thou 'scape so:
Varlet, I'll make thee look through a grate![1]

TRAPDOOR I'll do't presently, through a tavern grate: drawer! pish. [Exit.]

SIR ADAM Has the knave vexed you, sir?

SIR ALEXANDER   Asked him my money,
He swears my son received it. O, that boy
Will ne'er leave heaping sorrows on my heart,
Till he has broke it quite!

SIR ADAM   Is he still wild?

SIR ALEXANDER As is a Russian bear.

SIR ADAM   But he has left
His old haunt with that baggage?

SIR ALEXANDER   Worse still and worse;
He lays on me his shame, I on him my curse.

SIR DAVY My son, Jack Dapper, then shall run with him
All in one pasture.

SIR ADAM   Proves your son bad too, sir?

SIR DAVY As villany can make him: your Sebastian
Doats but on one drab, mine on a thousand;
A noise[2] of fiddlers, tobacco, wine, and a whore,
A mercer that will let him take up more,
Dice, and a water-spaniel with a duck,—O
Bring him a-bed with these: when his purse gingles,
Roaring[3] boys follow at's tail, fencers and ningles,[4]
Beasts Adam ne'er gave name to; these horse-leeches suck

---

8. Saveguard: outer petticoat; deep slop: wide breeches; placket: the front part of a woman's shift; codpiece: padded covering for the penis.
9. The fall term, here with reference to the Inns of Court.

1. Prison grating.
2. Company of musicians.
3. Riotous.
4. Favorites.

My son; he being drawn dry, they all live on smoke.

SIR ALEXANDER Tobacco?

SIR DAVY   Right: but I have in my brain
A windmill going that shall grind to dust
The follies of my son, and make him wise,
Or a stark fool. Pray lend me your advice.

SIR ALEXANDER ⎤
SIR ADAM   ⎦ That shall you, good sir Davy.

SIR DAVY Here's the springe
I ha' set to catch this woodcock in:[5] an action
In a false name, unknown to him, is entered
I' the Counter[6] to arrest Jack Dapper.

SIR ALEXANDER ⎤
SIR ADAM   ⎦ Ha, ha, he!

SIR DAVY Think you the Counter cannot break him?

SIR ADAM   Break him?
Yes, and break's heart too, if he lie there long.

SIR DAVY I'll make him sing a counter-tenor sure.

SIR ADAM No way to tame him like it; there he shall learn
What money is indeed, and how to spend it.

SIR DAVY He's bridled there.

SIR ALEXANDER   Ay, yet knows not how to mend it.
Bedlam cures not more madmen in a year
Than one of the Counters does; men pay more dear
There for their wit than anywhere: a Counter!
Why, 'tis an university, who not sees?
As scholars there, so here men take degrees,
And follow the same studies all alike.
Scholars learn first logic and rhetoric;
So does a prisoner: with fine honeyed speech
At's first coming in he doth persuade, beseech
He may be lodged with one that is not itchy,
To lie in a clean chamber, in sheets not lousy;
But when he has no money, then does he try,
By subtle logic and quaint sophistry,
To make the keepers trust him.

SIR ADAM   Say they do.

SIR ALEXANDER Then he's a graduate.

SIR DAVY   Say they trust him not.

SIR ALEXANDER Then is he held a freshman and a sot,
And never shall commence;[7] but being still barred,
Be expulsed from the Master's side to th' Twopenny ward,
Or else i' th' Hole beg place.

SIR ADAM   When then, I pray,
Proceeds a prisoner?

SIR ALEXANDER   When, money being the theme,
He can dispute with his hard creditors' hearts,

---

5. See *Hamlet* 1.4.115: "Springs to catch woodcocks,"
ways to trick the unsuspecting.

6. Debtors' prison.
7. Graduate.

And get out clear, he's then a master of arts.
Sir Davy, send your son to Wood Street college,
A gentleman can no where get more knowledge.

SIR DAVY There gallants study hard.

SIR ALEXANDER   True, to get money.

SIR DAVY 'Lies by th' heels, i'faith: thanks, thanks; I ha' sent
For a couple of bears shall paw him.

SIR ADAM   Who comes yonder?

SIR DAVY They look like puttocks;[8] these should be they.
[Enter Curtleax and Hanger.]

SIR ALEXANDER   I know 'em,
They are officers; sir, we'll leave you.

SIR DAVY   My good knights,
Leave me; you see I'm haunted now with sprites.[9]

SIR ALEXANDER } Fare you well, sir. [Exeunt.]
SIR ADAM

CURTLEAX This old muzzle-chops should be he by the fellow's description.—Save
you, sir.

SIR DAVY Come hither, you mad varlets; did not my man tell you I watched here for
you?

CURTLEAX One in a blue coat,[1] sir, told us that in this place an old gentleman
would watch for us; a thing contrary to our oath, for we are to watch for every
wicked member in a city.

SIR DAVY You'll watch then for ten thousand: what's thy name, honesty?

CURTLEAX Sergeant Curtleax I, sir.

SIR DAVY An excellent name for a sergeant, Curtleax:
Sergeants indeed are weapons of the law;
When prodigal ruffians far in debt are grown,
Should not you cut them, citizens were o'erthrown.
Thou dwell'st hereby in Holborn, Curtleax?

CURTLEAX That's my circuit, sir; I conjure most in that circle.

SIR DAVY And what young toward whelp is this?

HANGER Of the same litter; his yeoman, sir; my name's Hanger.

SIR DAVY Yeoman Hanger:
One pair of shears sure cut out both your coats;[2]
You have two names most dangerous to men's throats;
You two are villanous loads on gentlemen's backs;
Dear ware this Hanger and this Curtleax!

CURTLEAX We are as other men are, sir; I cannot see but he who makes a show of
honesty and religion, if his claws can fasten to his liking, he draws blood: all that
live in the world are but great fish and little fish, and feed upon one another; some
eat up whole men, a sergeant cares but for the shoulder of a man. They call us
knaves and curs; but many times he that sets us on worries more lambs one year
than we do in seven.

SIR DAVY Spoke like a noble Cerberus! is the action entered?

HANGER His name is entered in the book of unbelievers.

---

8. Birds of prey; sergeants.
9. Spirits.
1. Servant's dress.

2. "There was but a pair of shears between them," was a
proverbial expression.

SIR DAVY What book's that?

CURTLEAX The book where all prisoners' names stand; and not one amongst forty, when he comes in, believes to come out in haste.

SIR DAVY Be as dogged to him as your office allows you to be.

BOTH O sir!

SIR DAVY You know the unthrift, Jack Dapper?

CURTLEAX Ay, ay, sir, that gull, as well as I know my yeoman.

SIR DAVY And you know his father too, sir Davy Dapper?

CURTLEAX As damned a usurer as ever was among Jews: if he were sure his father's skin would yield him any money, he would, when he dies, flea it off, and sell it to cover drums for children at Bartholomew fair.

SIR DAVY What toads are these to spit poison on a man to his face! [Aside.]—Do you see, my honest rascals? yonder Greyhound is the dog he hunts with; out of that tavern Jack Dapper will sally: sa, sa; give the counter; on, set upon him!

BOTH We'll charge him upo' th' back, sir.

SIR DAVY Take no bail; put mace³ enough into his caudle; double your files, traverse your ground.

BOTH Brave, sir.

SIR DAVY Cry arm, arm, arm!

BOTH Thus, sir.

SIR DAVY There, boy, there, boy! away: look to your prey, my true English wolves; and so I vanish. [Exit.]

CURTLEAX Some warden of the sergeants begat this old fellow, upon my life: stand close.

HANGER Shall the ambuscado lie in one place?

CURTLEAX No; nook thou yonder. [They retire.]

[Enter Moll and Trapdoor.]

MOLL Ralph.

TRAPDOOR What says my brave captain male and female?

MOLL This Holborn is such a wrangling street!

TRAPDOOR That's because lawyers walks to and fro in't.

MOLL Here's such jostling, as if every one we met were drunk and reeled.

TRAPDOOR Stand, mistress! do you not smell carrion?

MOLL Carrion? No; yet I spy ravens.

TRAPDOOR Some poor, wind-shaken gallant will anon fall into sore labor, and these men-midwives must bring him to bed i' the Counter: there all those that are great with child with debts lie in.

MOLL Stand up.

TRAPDOOR Like your new Maypole.

HANGER Whist, whew!

CURTLEAX Hump, no.

MOLL Peeping? It shall go hard, huntsmen, but I'll spoil your game. They look for all the world like two infected malt-men coming muffled up in their cloaks in a frosty morning to London.

TRAPDOOR A course, captain; a bear comes to the stake.

[Enter Jack Dapper and Gull.]

MOLL It should be so, for the dogs struggle to be let loose.

HANGER Whew!

3. A spice; a sergeant's weapon.

CURTLEAX Hemp.

MOLL Hark, Trapdoor, follow your leader.

JACK DAPPER Gull

GULL Master?

JACK DAPPER Didst ever see such an ass as I am, boy?

GULL No, by my troth, sir; to lose all your money, yet have false dice of your own;
why, 'tis as I saw a great fellow used t'other day; he had a fair sword and buckler,
and yet a butcher dry beat him with a cudgel.

TRAPDOOR Honest servant, fly!

MOLL Fly, master Dapper! you'll be arrested else.

JACK DAPPER Run, Gull, and draw.

GULL Run, master; Gull follows you.

[Exeunt Dapper and Gull.]

CURTLEAX [Moll holding him.] I know you well enough; you're but a whore to hang
upon any man!

MOLL Whores, then, are like sergeants; so now hang you.—Draw, rogue, but strike
not: for a broken pate they'll keep their beds, and recover twenty marks damages.

CURTLEAX You shall pay for this rescue.—Run down Shoe Lane and meet him.

TRAPDOOR Shu! is this a rescue, gentlemen, or no?

MOLL Rescue? a pox on 'em! Trapdoor, let's away;

[Exeunt Curtleax and Hanger.]

    I'm glad I've done perfect one good work to day.
    If any gentleman be in scrivener's⁴ bands,
    Send but for Moll, she'll bail him by these hands.

                        [Exeunt.]

Act 4

Scene 1

[A room in Sir Alexander Wengrave's house. Enter Sir Alexander Wengrave.]

SIR ALEXANDER Unhappy in the follies of a son,
    Led against judgment, sense, obedience,
    And all the powers of nobleness and wit!

[Enter Trapdoor.]

    O wretched father!—Now, Trapdoor, will she come?

TRAPDOOR In man's apparel, sir; I'm in her heart now,
    And share in all her secrets.

SIR ALEXANDER   Peace, peace, peace!
    Here, take my German watch, hang't up in sight,
    That I may see her hang in English⁵ for't.

TRAPDOOR I warrant you for that now, next sessions rids her, sir. This watch will
bring her in better than a hundred constables. [Hangs up the watch.]

SIR ALEXANDER Good Trapdoor, sayst thou so? Thou cheer'st my heart
    After a storm of sorrow. My gold chain too;
    Here, take a hundred marks in yellow links.

TRAPDOOR That will do well to bring the watch to light, sir;
    And worth a thousand of your headborough's lanterns.⁶

---

4. Money-lender's.
5. Be hanged under English law.

6. Lanterns carried by the constable at night.

SIR ALEXANDER Place that a' the court-cupboard;[7] let it lie
     Full in the view of her thief-whorish eye.
TRAPDOOR She cannot miss it, sir; I see't so plain,
     That I could steal't myself. [*Places the chain.*]
SIR ALEXANDER   Perhaps thou shalt too,
     That or something as weighty: what she leaves
     Thou shalt come closely in and filch away,
     And all the weight upon her back I'll lay.
TRAPDOOR You cannot assure that, sir.
SIR ALEXANDER   No? what lets it?
TRAPDOOR Being a stout girl, perhaps she'll desire pressing;[8]
     Then all the weight must lie upon her belly.
SIR ALEXANDER Belly or back, I care not, so I've one.
TRAPDOOR You're of my mind for that, sir.
SIR ALEXANDER Hang up my ruff-band with the diamond at it;
     It may be she'll like that best.
TRAPDOOR [*Aside.*] It's well for her, that she must have her choice; he thinks noth-
     ing too good for her. —If you hold on this mind a little longer, it shall be the first
     work I do to turn thief myself; 'twould do a man good to be hanged when he is so
     well provided for. [*Hangs up the ruff-band.*]
SIR ALEXANDER So, well said; all hangs well: would she hung so too!
     The sight would please me more than all their glisterings.
     O that my mysteries[9] to such straits should run,
     That I must rob myself to bless my son! [*Exeunt.*]
[*Enter Sebastian Wengrave, Mary Fitzallard disguised as a page, and Moll in her male
dress.*]
SEBASTIAN Thou'st done me a kind office, without touch
     Either of sin or shame; our loves are honest.
MOLL I'd scorn to make such shift to bring you together else.
SEBASTIAN Now have I time and opportunity
     Without all fear to bid thee welcome, love!

                              [*Kisses Mary.*]

MARY Never with more desire and harder venture!
MOLL How strange this shows, one man to kiss another!
SEBASTIAN I'd kiss such men to choose, Moll;
     Methinks a woman's lip tastes well in a doublet.
MOLL Many an old madam[1] has the better fortune then,
     Whose breaths grew stale before the fashion came:
     If that will help 'em, as you think 'twill do,
     They'll learn in time to pluck on the hose too.
SEBASTIAN The older they wax, Moll, troth I speak seriously,
     As some have a conceit their drink tastes better
     In an outlandish cup than in our own,
     So methinks every kiss she gives me now
     In this strange form is worth a pair of two.
     Here we are safe, and furthest from the eye

7. Sideboard on which plate was displayed.
8. The loading of weights upon the accused to force a
confession; intercourse.
9. Devices.
1. Prostitute.

Of all suspicion: this is my father's chamber,
Upon which floor he never steps till night:
Here he mistrusts me not, nor I his coming;
At mine own chamber he still pries unto me,
My freedom is not there at mine own finding,
Still checked and curbed; here he shall miss his purpose.

MOLL And what's your business, now you have your mind, sir?
At your great suit I promised you to come:
I pitied her for name's sake, that a Moll
Should be so crost in love, when there's so many
That owes nine lays[2] a-piece, and not so little.
My tailor fitted her; how like you his work?

SEBASTIAN So well, no art can mend it, for this purpose:
But to thy wit and help we're chief in debt,
And must live still beholding.

MOLL   Any honest pity
I'm willing to bestow upon poor ringdoves.

SEBASTIAN I'll offer no worse play.

MOLL   Nay, and you should, sir,
I should draw first, and prove the quicker man.

SEBASTIAN Hold, there shall need no weapon at this meeting;
But 'cause thou shalt not loose thy fury idle,
Here take this viol, run upon the guts,
And end thy quarrel singing.

[Takes down and gives her a viol.]

MOLL   Like a swan above bridge;
For look you here's the bridge,[3] and here am I.

SEBASTIAN Hold on, sweet Moll!

MARY I've heard her much commended, sir, for one
That was ne'er taught.

MOLL   I'm much beholding to 'em.
Well, since you'll needs put us together, sir,
I'll play my part as well as I can: it shall ne'er
Be said I came into a gentleman's chamber,
And let his instrument hang by the walls.

SEBASTIAN Why, well said, Moll, i'faith; it had been a shame for that gentleman
then that would have let it hung still, and ne'er offered thee it.

MOLL There it should have been still then for Moll;
For though the world judge impudently of me,
I never came into that chamber yet
Where I took down the instrument myself.

SEBASTIAN Pish, let 'em prate abroad; thou'rt here where thou art known and
loved; there be a thousand close dames that will call the viol an unmannerly
instrument for a woman, and therefore talk broadly of thee, when you shall have
them sit wider to a worse quality.

MOLL Push,
I ever fall asleep and think not of 'em, sir;
And thus I dream.

---

2. Wagers.

3. I.e., of the viola da gamba.

SEBASTIAN   Prithee, let's hear thy dream, Moll.
MOLL [sings]

> I dream there is a mistress,
> And she lays out the money;
> She goes unto her sisters,
> She never comes at any.⁴

[Reenter Sir Alexander behind.]

> She says she went to th' Burse⁵ for patterns;
> You shall find her at Saint Kathern's,⁶
> And comes home with never a penny.

SEBASTIAN That's a free⁷ mistress, faith!
SIR ALEXANDER Ay, ay, ay,
            Like her that sings it; one of thine own choosing. [Aside.]
MOLL But shall I dream again? [Sings.]

> Here comes a wench will brave ye;
> Her courage was so great,
> She lay with one of the navy,
> Her husband lying i' the Fleet.°   prison
> Yet oft with him she cavilled;
> I wonder what she ails;
> Her husband's ship lay gravelled,°   aground
> When her's could hoise up sails:
> Yet she began, like all my foes,
> To call whore first; for so do those—
> A pox of all false tails!

SEBASTIAN Marry, amen, say I!
SIR ALEXANDER [Aside.] So say I too.
MOLL Hang up the viol now, sir: all this while I was in a dream; one shall lie rudely then;
            But being awake, I keep my legs together.
            A watch? what's a' clock here?
SIR ALEXANDER [Aside.] Now, now she's trapt!
MOLL Between one and two; nay, then I care not. A watch and a musician are
    cousin-germans⁸ in one thing, they must both keep time well, or there's no good-
    ness in 'em; the one else deserves to be dashed against a wall, and t'other to have
    his brains knocked out with a fiddle-case.
            What! a loose chain and a dangling diamond?
            Here were a brave booty for an evening thief now:
            There's many a younger brother would be glad
            To look twice in at a window for't,
            And wriggle in and out, like an eel in a sand-bag.
            O, if men's secret youthful faults should judge 'em,
            'Twould be the general'st execution
            That e'er was seen in England!

---

4. Money, sexual partners, sexual fulfillment.
5. Royal Exchange.
6. The dockside district in the east end of London, notorious for its taverns.
7. Generous, loose.
8. First cousins.

          There would be but few left to sing the ballads,
          There would be so much work: most of our brokers
          Would be chosen for hangmen; a good day for them;
          They might renew their wardrobes of free cost then.

SEBASTIAN This is the roaring wench must do us good.

MARY No poison, sir, but serves us for some use;
          Which is confirmed in her.

SEBASTIAN   Peace, peace—
          'Foot, I did hear him sure, where'er he be.

MOLL Who did you hear?

SEBASTIAN   My father;
          'Twas like a sigh of his: I must be wary.

SIR ALEXANDER [Aside.] No? wilt not be? am I alone so wretched
          That nothing takes? I'll put him to his plunge[9] for't.

SEBASTIAN Life! here he comes.—Sir, I beseech you take it;
          Your way of teaching does so much content me,
          I'll make it four pound; here's forty shillings, sir—
          I think I name it right—help me, good Moll—
          Forty in hand. [Offering money.]

MOLL   Sir, you shall pardon me:
          I've more of the meanest scholar I can teach;
          This pays me more than you have offered yet.

SEBASTIAN At the next quarter,
          When I receive the means my father 'lows me,
          You shall have t'other forty.

SIR ALEXANDER [Aside.]   This were well now,
          Were't to a man whose sorrows had blind eyes:
          But mine behold his follies and untruths
          With two clear glasses. [Coming forward.]
          How now?

SEBASTIAN   Sir?

SIR ALEXANDER   What's he there?

SEBASTIAN You're come in good time, sir; I've a suit to you; I'd crave your present
  kindness.

SIR ALEXANDER What's he there.

SEBASTIAN A gentleman, a musician, sir; one of excellent fingering.

SIR ALEXANDER Ay, I think so;—[Aside:] I wonder how they 'scaped her.

SEBASTIAN Has the most delicate stroke, sir.

SIR ALEXANDER A stroke indeed!—[Aside:] I feel it at my heart.

SEBASTIAN Puts down all your famous musicians.

SIR ALEXANDER [Aside.] Ay, a whore may put down a hundred of 'em.

SEBASTIAN Forty shillings is the agreement, sir, between us: Now, sir, my present
  means mounts but to half on't.

SIR ALEXANDER And he stands upon the whole?

SEBASTIAN Ay, indeed does he, sir.

SIR ALEXANDER And will do still; he'll ne'er be in other tale.

SEBASTIAN Therefore I'd stop his mouth, sir, and I could.

---

9. Plunge: difficulty, straits.

SIR ALEXANDER Hum, true; there is no other way indeed;—[*Aside:*] His folly
    hardens; shame must needs succeed.—
    Now, sir, I understand you profess music.
MOLL I'm a poor servant to that liberal science, sir.
SIR ALEXANDER Where is't you teach?
MOLL Right against Clifford's Inn.[1]
SIR ALEXANDER Hum, that's a fit place for't: you've many scholars?
MOLL And some of worth, whom I may call my masters.
SIR ALEXANDER [*Aside.*] Ay, true, a company of whoremasters.—
    You teach to sing, too?
MOLL Marry, do I, sir.
SIR ALEXANDER I think you'll find an apt scholar of my son,
    Especially for prick-song.
MOLL I've much hope of him.
SIR ALEXANDER [*Aside.*] I'm sorry for't, I have the less for that.—
    You can play any lesson?
MOLL At first sight, sir.
SIR ALEXANDER There's a thing call'd the Witch; can you play that?
MOLL I would be sorry any one should mend me in't.
SIR ALEXANDER [*Aside.*] Ay, I believe thee; thou'st so bewitched my son,
      No care will mend the work that thou hast done.
      I have bethought myself, since my art fails,
      I'll make her policy the art to trap her.
      Here are four angels marked with holes in them
      Fit for his cracked companions: gold he'll give her;
      These will I make induction to her ruin,
      And rid shame from my house, grief from my heart.—
      Here, son, in what you take content and pleasure,
      Want shall not curb you; pay the gentleman
      His latter half in gold. [*Gives money.*]
SEBASTIAN I thank you, sir.
SIR ALEXANDER [*Aside.*] O may the operation on't end three;
      In her life, shame in him, and grief in me! [*Exit.*]
SEBASTIAN Faith, thou shalt have 'em; 'tis my father's gift:
      Never was man beguiled with better shift.
MOLL He that can take me for a male musician,
      I can't choose but make him my instrument,
      And play upon him. [*Exeunt.*]

Scene 2

[*Before Gallipot's Shop. Enter Mistress Gallipot and Mistress Openwork.*]
MISTRESS GALLIPOT Is, then, that bird of yours, master Goshawk, so wild?
MISTRESS OPENWORK A Goshawk? a puttock;[2] all for prey: he angles for fish, but
    he loves flesh better.
MISTRESS GALLIPOT Is't possible his smooth face should have wrinkles in't, and
    we not see them?

---

1. One of the Inns of Chancery, a high court.   2. Kite, bird of prey.

MISTRESS OPENWORK Possible? Why, have not many handsome legs in silk stockings villanous splay feet, for all their great roses?[3]

MISTRESS GALLIPOT Troth, sirrah, thou sayst true.

MISTRESS OPENWORK Didst never see an archer, as thou'st walked by Bunhill,[4] look a-squint when he drew his bow?

MISTRESS GALLIPOT Yes, when his arrows have fline[5] toward Islington, his eyes have shot clean contrary towards Pimlico.[6]

MISTRESS OPENWORK For all the world so does master Goshawk double with me.

MISTRESS GALLIPOT O, fie upon him: if he double once, he's not for me.

MISTRESS OPENWORK Because Goshawk goes in a shag-ruff band, with a face sticking up in't which shows like an agate set in a cramp ring,[7] he thinks I'm in love with him.

MISTRESS GALLIPOT 'Las, I think he takes his mark amiss in thee!

MISTRESS OPENWORK He has, by often beating into me, made me believe that my husband kept a whore.

MISTRESS GALLIPOT Very good.

MISTRESS OPENWORK Swore to me that my husband this very morning went in a boat, with a tilt over it, to the Three Pigeons at Brainford, and his punk with him under his tilt.

MISTRESS GALLIPOT That were wholesome.

MISTRESS OPENWORK I believed it; fell a-swearing at him, cursing of harlots; made me ready to hoise up sail and be there as soon as he.

MISTRESS GALLIPOT So, so.

MISTRESS OPENWORK And for that voyage Goshawk comes hither incontinent-ly:[8] but, sirrah, this water-spaniel dives after no duck but me; his hope is having me at Brainford, to make me cry quack.

MISTRESS GALLIPOT Art sure of it?

MISTRESS OPENWORK Sure of it? My poor innocent Openwork came in as I was poking my ruff: presently hit I him i' the teeth with the Three Pigeons; he for-swore all; I up and opened all; and now stands he in a shop hard by, like a musket on a rest,[9] to hit Goshawk i' the eye, when he comes to fetch me to the boat.

MISTRESS GALLIPOT Such another lame gelding offered to carry me through thick and thin,—Laxton, sirrah,—but I am rid of him now.

MISTRESS OPENWORK Happy is the woman can be rid of 'em all! 'Las, what are your whisking gallants to our husbands, weigh 'em rightly, man for man?

MISTRESS GALLIPOT Troth, mere shallow things.

MISTRESS OPENWORK Idle, simple things, running heads; and yet let 'em run over us never so fast, we shopkeepers, when all's done, are sure to have 'em in our pursenets[1] at length; and when they are in, lord, what simple animals they are! Then they hang the head—

MISTRESS GALLIPOT Then they droop—

MISTRESS OPENWORK Then they write letters—

MISTRESS GALLIPOT Then they cog[2]—

---

3. Knots of ribbons worn on the shoes.
4. Where archery matches and artillery practice were held.
5. Flown.
6. Islington: a northern suburb; Pimlico: part of Hogsdon.
7. A ring consecrated on Good Friday that was supposed to preserve the wearer against cramp.

8. Immediately.
9. A support that consisted of a wooden pole with an iron spike at the end to fix it in the ground and a piece of iron at the top to put the musket in.
1. Nets whose ends are drawn together by a string.
2. "Cog" and "ingle" both mean "to wheedle."

MISTRESS OPENWORK Then deal they underhand with us, and we must ingle with our husbands a-bed; and we must swear they are our cousins, and able to do us a pleasure at court.

MISTRESS GALLIPOT And yet, when we have done our best, all's but put into a riven dish; we are but frumped at[3] and libelled upon.

MISTRESS OPENWORK O, if it were the good Lord's will there were a law made, no citizen should trust any of 'em all!

[Enter Goshawk.]

MISTRESS GALLIPOT Hush, sirrah! Goshawk flutters.

GOSHAWK How now? Are you ready?

MISTRESS OPENWORK Nay, are you ready? A little thing, you see, makes us ready.

GOSHAWK Us? Why, must she make one i' the voyage?

MISTRESS OPENWORK O, by any means! Do I know how my husband will handle me?

GOSHAWK [Aside.] 'Foot, how shall I find water to keep these two mills going? — Well, since you'll needs be clapped under hatches, if I sail not with you both till all split,[4] hang me up at the mainyard and duck me.—[Aside:] It's but liquoring them both soundly, and then you shall see their cork heels fly up high,[5] like two swans when their tails are above water, and their long necks under water diving to catch gudgeons.—Come, come, oars stand ready; the tide's with us; on with those false faces; blow winds and thou shalt take thy husband casting out his net to catch fresh salmon at Brainford.

MISTRESS GALLIPOT [Aside.] I believe you'll eat of a cod's head of your own dressing before you reach half way thither.

[She and Mistress Openwork mask themselves.]

GOSHAWK So, so, follow close; pin as you go.

[Enter Laxton muffled.]

LAXTON Do you hear?

MISTRESS GALLIPOT Yes, I thank my ears.

LAXTON I must have a bout with your 'pothecaryship.

MISTRESS GALLIPOT At what weapon?

LAXTON I must speak with you.

MISTRESS GALLIPOT No.

LAXTON No? You shall.

MISTRESS GALLIPOT Shall? Away, souced sturgeon! Half fish, half flesh.

LAXTON Faith, gib,[6] are you spitting? I'll cut your tail, puss-cat, for this.

MISTRESS GALLIPOT 'Las, poor Laxton, I think thy tail's cut already! your worst.

LAXTON If I do not—[Exit.]

GOSHAWK Come, ha' you done?

[Enter Openwork.]

'Sfoot, Rosamond, your husband!

OPENWORK How now? Sweet master Goshawk! None more welcome;
I've wanted your embracements: when friends meet,
The music of the spheres sounds not more sweet
Than does their conference. Who's this? Rosamond?
Wife? How now, sister?

GOSHAWK   Silence, if you love me!

---

3. Mocked.
4. Go to pieces.
5. The dramatists frequently refer to the cork heels worn

by women.
6. A scold.

OPENWORK Why masked?

MISTRESS OPENWORK Does a mask grieve you, sir?

OPENWORK   It does.

MISTRESS OPENWORK Then you're best get you a mumming.

GOSHAWK   'Sfoot, you'll spoil all!

MISTRESS GALLIPOT May not we cover our bare faces with masks,
    As well as you cover your bald heads with hats?

OPENWORK No masks; why, they're thieves to beauty, that rob eyes
    Of admiration in which true love lies.
    Why are masks worn? Why good? or why desired?
    Unless by their gay covers wits are fired
    To read the vildest[7] looks: many bad faces,
    Because rich gems are treasured up in cases,
    Pass by their privilege current; but as caves
    Damn misers' gold, so masks are beauties' graves.
    Men ne'er meet women with such muffled eyes,
    But they curse her that first did masks devise,
    And swear it was some beldam.[8] Come, off with't.

MISTRESS OPENWORK I will not.

OPENWORK Good faces masked are jewels kept by sprites;
    Hide none but bad ones, for they poison men's sights;
    Show, then, as shopkeepers do their broidered stuff,
    By owl-light; fine wares can't be open enough.
    Prithee, sweet Rose, come, strike this sail.

MISTRESS OPENWORK   Sail?

OPENWORK   Ha!
    Yes, wife, strike sail, for storms are in thine eyes.

MISTRESS OPENWORK They're here, sir, in my brows, if any rise.

OPENWORK Ha, brows?—What says she, friend? Pray, tell me why
    Your two flags were advanced;[9] the comedy,
    Come, what's the comedy?

MISTRESS GALLIPOT   Westward ho.[1]

OPENWORK   How?

MISTRESS OPENWORK 'Tis Westward ho, she says.

GOSHAWK   Are you both mad?

MISTRESS OPENWORK Is't market-day at Brainford, and your ware
    Not sent up yet?

OPENWORK   What market-day? what ware?

MISTRESS OPENWORK A pie with three pigeons in't: 'tis drawn,
    And stays your cutting up.

GOSHAWK As you regard my credit—

OPENWORK Art mad?

MISTRESS OPENWORK Yes, lecherous goat, baboon!

OPENWORK Baboon? then toss me in a blanket.

MISTRESS OPENWORK Do I it well?

MISTRESS GALLIPOT Rarely.

GOSHAWK Belike, sir, she's not well; best leave her.

7. Vilest.
8. Hag.
9. Flags were placed at the tops of theaters.

1. The boatmen's cry, and the title of a play by Webster
and Dekker printed in 1607.

OPENWORK   No;
    I'll stand the storm now, how fierce soe'er it blow.
MISTRESS OPENWORK Did I for this lose all my friends, refuse
    Rich hopes and golden fortunes, to be made
    A stale[2] to a common whore?
OPENWORK   This does amaze me.
MISTRESS OPENWORK O God, O God! Feed at reversion now?
    A strumpet's leaving?
OPENWORK   Rosamond!
GOSHAWK [Aside.] I sweat; would I lay in Cold Harbour![3]
MISTRESS OPENWORK Thou'st struck ten thousand daggers through my heart!
OPENWORK Not I, by heaven, sweet wife!
MISTRESS OPENWORK Go, devil, go; that which thou swear'st by damns thee!
GOSHAWK 'S heart, will you undo me?
MISTRESS OPENWORK Why stay you here? The star by which you sail
    Shines yonder above Chelsea; you lose your shore;
    If this moon light you, seek out your light whore.
OPENWORK Ha!
MISTRESS GALLIPOT Push, your western pug![4]
GOSHAWK   Zounds, now hell roars!
MISTRESS OPENWORK With whom you tilted in a pair of oars
    This very morning.
OPENWORK   Oars?
MISTRESS OPENWORK   At Brainford, sir.
OPENWORK Rack not my patience.—Master Goshawk,
    Some slave has buzzed this into her, has he not?
    I run a tilt in Brainford with a woman?
    'Tis a lie!
    What old bawd tells thee this? 's death, 'tis a lie!
MISTRESS OPENWORK 'Tis one who to thy face shall justify
    All that I speak.
OPENWORK   Ud'soul,[5] do but name that rascal!
MISTRESS OPENWORK No, sir, I will not.
GOSHAWK [Aside.]   Keep thee there, girl, then!
OPENWORK Sister, know you this varlet?
MISTRESS GALLIPOT   Yes.
OPENWORK   Swear true;
    Is there a rogue so low damned? a second Judas?—
    A common hangman, cutting a man's throat,
    Does it to his face,—bite me behind my back?
    A cur dog? swear if you know this hell-hound.
MISTRESS GALLIPOT In truth, I do.
OPENWORK   His name?
MISTRESS GALLIPOT   Not for the world;
    To have you to stab him.
GOSHAWK [Aside.]   O brave girls, worth gold![6]

---

2. A lover or mistress mocked by rivals; a decoy.
3. Poor neighborhood near London Bridge.
4. Barge man working on the Thames.

5. God bless my soul.
6. "A girl worth gold" was a proverbial expression and the subtitle of Heywood's Fair Maid of the West.

OPENWORK A word, honest master Goshawk. [*Drawing his sword.*]
GOSHAWK   What do you mean, sir?
OPENWORK Keep off, and if the devil can give a name
    To this new fury, holla it through my ear,
    Or wrap it up in some hid character.
    I'll ride to Oxford and watch out mine eyes,
    But I will hear the Brazen Head speak,[7] or else
    Show me but one hair of his head or beard,
    That I may sample it. If the fiend I meet
    In mine own house, I'll kill him; in the street,
    Or at the church-door,—there, 'cause he seeks t' untie
    The knot God fastens, he deserves most to die.
MISTRESS OPENWORK My husband titles him!
OPENWORK   Master Goshawk, pray, sir,
    Swear to me that you know him, or know him not,
    Who makes me at Brainford to take up a petticoat
    Besides my wife's.
GOSHAWK   By heaven, that man I know not!
MISTRESS OPENWORK Come, come, you lie!
GOSHAWK   Will you not have all out?
    By heaven, I know no man beneath the moon
    Should do you wrong, but if I had his name,
    I'd print it in text letters.
MISTRESS OPENWORK   Print thine own then:
    Didst not thou swear to me he kept his whore!
MISTRESS GALLIPOT And that in sinful Brainford they'd commit
    That which our lips did water at, sir,—ha?
MISTRESS OPENWORK Thou spider that Hast woven thy cunning web
    In mine own house t' ensnare me! hast not thou
    Sucked nourishment even underneath this roof,
    And turned it all to poison, spitting it
    On thy friend's face, my husband, (he as 'twere sleeping),
    Only to leave him ugly to mine eyes,
    That they might glance on thee?
MISTRESS GALLIPOT   Speak, are these lies?
GOSHAWK Mine own shame me confounds!
OPENWORK   No more; he's stung.
    Who'd think that in one body there could dwell
    Deformity and beauty, heaven and hell?
    Goodness I see is but outside; we all set
    In rings of gold stones that be counterfeit:
    I thought you none.
GOSHAWK   Pardon me!
OPENWORK   Truth I do:
    This blemish grows in nature, not in you;
    For man's creation stick even moles in scorn
    On fairest cheeks.—Wife, nothing's perfect born.
MISTRESS OPENWORK I thought you had been born perfect.
OPENWORK What's this whole world but a gilt rotten pill?

7. In the prose tract of the *Famous Historie of Fryer Bacon* (1589) it is related how "Friar Bacon made a Brazen Head to speak, by which he would have walled England about with brass."

For at the heart lies the old core still.
I'll tell you, master Goshawk, ay, in your eye
I have seen wanton fire; and then, to try
The soundness of my judgment, I told you
I kept a whore, made you believe 'twas true,
Only to feel how your pulse beat; but find
The world can hardly yield a perfect friend.
Come, come, a trick of youth, and 'tis forgiven;
This rub put by, our love shall run more even.

MISTRESS OPENWORK You'll deal upon men's wives no more?

GOSHAWK   No; you teach me
    A trick for that.

MISTRESS OPENWORK Troth, do not; they'll o'erreach thee.

OPENWORK Make my house yours, sir, still.

GOSHAWK   No.

OPENWORK   I say you shall:
    Seeing thus besieged it holds out, 'twill never fall.
    [*Enter Gallipot, followed by Greenwit disguised as a Sumner; and Laxton muffled
    aloof off.*[8]]

OPENWORK   }
GOSHAWK etc. } How now?

GALLIPOT With me, sir?

GREENWIT You, sir. I have gone snuffling up and down by your door this hour, to
    watch for you.

MISTRESS GALLIPOT What's the matter, husband?

GREENWIT I have caught a cold in my head, sir, by sitting up late in the Rose tav-
    ern; but I hope you understand my speech.

GALLIPOT So, sir.

GREENWIT I cite you by the name of Hippocrates Gallipot, and you by the name of
    Prudence Gallipot, to appear upon *Crastino,*—do you see?—*Crastino sancti Dun-
    stani,*[9] this Easter term, in Bow Church.

GALLIPOT Where, sir? what says he?

GREENWIT Bow, Bow Church, to answer to a libel of precontract on the part and
    behalf of the said Prudence and another: you're best, sir, take a copy of the cita-
    tion, 'tis but twelvepence.

OPENWORK   }
GALLIPOT etc.} A citation!

GOSHAWK You pocky-nosed rascal, what slave fees you to this!

LAXTON [*coming forward*] Slave? I ha' nothing to do with you; do you hear, sir?

GOSHAWK Laxton, is't not? What fagary[1] is this?

GALLIPOT Trust me, I thought, sir, this storm long ago
    Had been full laid, when, if you be remembered,
    I paid you the last fifteen pound, besides
    The thirty you had first; for then you swore—

LAXTON Tush, tush, sir, oaths,—
    Truth, yet I'm loath to vex you—tell you what,
    Make up the money I had an hundred pound,
    And take your bellyful of her.

---

8. Sumner: one employed to summon people to court;
aloof off: to hold aloof from.

9. May 20: the day after St. Dunstan's Day.
1. Vagary, trumped up expedition.

GALLIPOT   An hundred pound?

MISTRESS GALLIPOT What, a hundred pound? he gets none: what, a hundred pound?

GALLIPOT Sweet Pru, be calm; the gentleman offers thus:
    If I will make the moneys that are past
    A hundred pound, he will discharge all courts,
    And give his bond never to vex us more.

MISTRESS GALLIPOT A hundred pound? 'Las, take, sir, but threescore!
    Do you seek my undoing?

LAXTON   I'll not 'bate one sixpence.—
    I'll maul you, puss, for spitting.

MISTRESS GALLIPOT   Do thy worst.—
    Will fourscore stop thy mouth?

LAXTON   No.

MISTRESS GALLIPOT   You're a slave;
    Thou cheat, I'll now tear money from thy throat.—
    Husband, lay hold on yonder tawny coat.[2]

GREENWIT Nay, gentlemen, seeing your women are so hot, I must lose my hair[3] in
    their company, I see. [*Takes off his false hair.*]

MISTRESS OPENWORK His hair sheds off, and yet he speaks not so much in the
    nose as he did before.

GOSHAWK He has had the better chirurgeon.—Master Greenwit, is your wit so raw
    as to play no better a part than a summer's?

GALLIPOT I pray, who plays *A knack to know an honest man*,[4] in this company?

MISTRESS GALLIPOT Dear husband, pardon me, I did dissemble,
    Told thee I was his precontracted wife,
    When letters came from him for thirty pound:
    I had no shift but that.

GALLIPOT   A very clean shift,
    But able to make me lousy: on.

MISTRESS GALLIPOT   Husband, I plucked,
    When he had tempted me to think well of him,
    Gelt feathers[5] from thy wings, to make him fly
    More lofty.

GALLIPOT   A' the top of you, wife: on.

MISTRESS GALLIPOT He having wasted them, comes now for more,
    Using me as a ruffian doth his whore,
    Whose sin keeps him in breath. By heaven, I vow,
    Thy bed he ne'er wronged more than he does now!

GALLIPOT My bed? ha, ha! like enough; a shopboard will serve
    To have a cuckold's coat cut out upon:
    Of that we'll talk hereafter.—You're a villain.

LAXTON Here me but speak, sir, you shall find me none.

OPENWORK   ⎫
GOSHAWK etc.⎭ Pray, sir, be patient, and hear him.

GALLIPOT I'm muzzled for biting, sir; use me how you will.

---

2. Apparitors and bishop's retainers wore tawny coats.
3. "So hot . . . lose my hair": a joking allusion to venereal
disease.

4. Title of an anonymous comedy.
5. Golden feathers.

LAXTON The first hour that your wife was in my eye,
    Myself with other gentlemen sitting by
    In your shop tasting smoke, and speech being used,
    That men who've fairest wives are most abused,
    And hardly scape the horn, your wife maintained
    That only such spots in city dames were stained
    Justly but by men's slanders: for her own part,
    She vowed that you had so much of her heart,
    No man, by all his wit, by any wile
    Never so fine-spun, should yourself beguile
    Of what in her was yours.
GALLIPOT   Yet, Pru, 'tis well.—
    Play out your game at Irish,[6] sir: who wins?
MISTRESS OPENWORK The trial is when she comes to bearing.
LAXTON I scorned one woman thus should brave all men,
    And, which more vexed me, a she-citizen;
    Therefore I laid siege to her: out she held,
    Gave many a brave repulse, and me compelled
    With shame to sound retreat to my hot lust:
    Then, seeing all base desires raked up in dust,
    And that to tempt her modest ears, I swore
    Ne'er to presume again: she said, her eye
    Would ever give me welcome honestly;
    And, since I was a gentleman, if't run low,
    She would my state relieve, not to o'erthrow
    Your own and hers: did so; then seeing I wrought
    Upon her meekness, me she set at nought;
    And yet to try if I could turn that tide,
    You see what stream I strove with; but, sir, I swear
    By heaven, and by those hopes men lay up there,
    I neither have nor had a base intent
    To wrong your bed! What's done, is merriment:
    Your gold I pay back with this interest,
    When I'd most power to do't, I wronged you least.
GALLIPOT If this no gullery be, sir—
OPENWORK   ⎫
GOSHAWK etc. ⎬ No, no, on my life!
GALLIPOT Then, sir, I am beholden—not to you, wife,—
    But, master Laxton, to your want of doing
    Ill, which it seems you have not.—Gentlemen,
    Tarry and dine here all.
OPENWORK   Brother, we've a jest,
    As good as yours, to furnish out a feast.
GALLIPOT We'll crown our table with't.—Wife, brag no more
    Of holding out: who most brags is most whore.
    [Exeunt.]

6. A board game.

Act 5

Scene 1

[*A Street. Enter Jack Dapper, Moll, Sir Beauteous Ganymede, and Sir Thomas Long.*]

JACK DAPPER But, prithee, master captain Jack, be plain and perspicuous with me; was it your Meg of Westminster's[7] courage that rescued me from the Poultry puttocks[8] indeed?

MOLL The valor of my wit, I ensure you, sir, fetched you off bravely, when you were i' the forlorn hope among those desperates. Sir Beauteous Ganymede here, and sir Thomas Long, heard that cuckoo, my man Trapdoor, sing the note of your ransom from captivity.

SIR BEAUTEOUS Uds so, Moll, where's that Trapdoor?

MOLL Hanged, I think, by this time: a justice in this town, that speaks nothing but *make a mittimus, away with him to Newgate*,[9] used that rogue like a firework, to run upon a line betwixt him and me.

ALL How, how?

MOLL Marry, to lay trains of villany to blow up my life: I smelt the powder, spied what linstock gave fire to shoot against the poor captain of the galley-foist, and away slid I my man like a shovel-board shilling.[1] He struts up and down the suburbs, I think, and eats up whores, feeds upon a bawd's garbage.

SIR THOMAS Sirrah, Jack Dapper—

JACK DAPPER What sayst, Tom Long?

SIR THOMAS Thou hadst a sweet-faced boy, hail-fellow with thee, to your little Gull: how is he spent?

JACK DAPPER Troth, I whistled the poor little buzzard off a' my fist, because, when he waited upon me at the ordinaries, the gallants hit me i' the teeth still, and said I looked like a painted alderman's tomb, and the boy at my elbow like a death's head.—Sirrah Jack, Moll—

MOLL What says my little Dapper?

SIR BEAUTEOUS Come, come; walk and talk, walk and talk.

JACK DAPPER Moll and I'll be i' the midst.

MOLL These knights shall have squires' places belike then: well, Dapper, what say you?

JACK DAPPER Sirrah captain, mad Mary, the gull my own father, Dapper sir Davy, laid these London boot-halers,[2] the catchpolls, in ambush to set upon me.

ALL Your father? away, Jack!

JACK DAPPER By the tassels of this handkercher, 'tis true: and what was his warlike stratagem, think you? he thought, because a wicker cage tames a nightingale, a lousy prison could make an ass of me.

ALL A nasty plot!

JACK DAPPER Ay, as though a counter,[3] which is a park in which all the wild beasts of the city run head by head, could tame me!

MOLL Yonder comes my lord Noland.

[*Enter Lord Noland.*]

---

7. Meg of Westminster was celebrated in a popular tract entitled *The Life and Pranks of Long Meg of Westminster* (1582; reissued 1635). She was also the heroine of a lost play of 1594.
8. Officers, sergeants.
9. Mittimus: a warrant to commit to jail; "away with him to Newgate" was a proverbial expression for strict judges.

1. Linstock: the stick holding the gunner's match; galley foist: a long barge with oars; shovel-board shilling: a smooth coin that slipped easily used in the game of shovel-board.
2. Slang for robbers.
3. Prison.

ALL Save you, my lord.

LORD NOLAND Well met, gentlemen all.—Good sir Beauteous Ganymede, sir
   Thomas Long,—and how does master Dapper?

JACK DAPPER Thanks, my lord.

MOLL No tobacco, my lord?

LORD NOLAND No, faith, Jack.

JACK DAPPER My lord Noland, will you go to Pimlico[4] with us? We are making a
   boon voyage to that nappy[5] land of spice-cakes.

LORD NOLAND Here's such a merry ging,[6] I could find in my heart to sail to the
   world's end with such company: come, gentlemen, let's on.

JACK DAPPER Here's most amorous weather, my lord.

ALL Amorous weather! [They walk.]

JACK DAPPER Is not amorous a good word?

   [Enter Trapdoor disguised as a poor Soldier with a patch over one eye and Tearcat all
   in tatters.]

TRAPDOOR Shall we set upon the infantry, these troops of foot? Zounds, yonder comes
   Moll, my whorish master and mistress! would I had her kidneys between my teeth!

TEARCAT I had rather have a cow-heel.

TRAPDOOR Zounds, I am so patched up, she cannot discover me: we'll on.

TEARCAT Alla corago,[7] then!

TRAPDOOR Good your honors and worships, enlarge the ears of commiseration,
   and let the sound of a hoarse military organ-pipe penetrate your pitiful bowels, to
   extract out of them so many small drops of silver as may give a hard straw-bed
   lodging to a couple of maimed soldiers.

JACK DAPPER Where are you maimed?

TEARCAT In both our nether limbs.

MOLL Come, come, Dapper, let's give 'em something: 'las, poor men! What money
   have you? By my troth, I love a soldier with my soul.

SIR BEAUTEOUS Stay, stay; where have you served?

SIR THOMAS In any part of the Low Countries?

TRAPDOOR Not in the Low Countries, if it please your manhood, but in Hungary
   against the Turk at the siege of Belgrade.

LORD NOLAND Who served there with you, sirrah?

TRAPDOOR Many Hungarians, Moldavians, Vallachians, and Transylvanians, with
   some Sclavonians;[8] and retiring home, sir, the Venetian galleys took us prisoners,
   yet freed us, and suffered us to beg up and down the country.

JACK DAPPER You have ambled all over Italy, then?

TRAPDOOR O sir, from Venice to Roma, Vecchia, Bononia, Romagna, Bologna,
   Modena, Piacenza, and Tuscana, with all her cities, as Pistoia, Valteria, Mountep-
   ulchena, Arezzo; with the Siennois, and divers others.[9]

MOLL Mere rogues! put spurs to 'em once more.

JACK DAPPER Thou lookest like a strange creature, a fat butter-box, yet speakest
   English: what art thou?

---

4. The Pimlico Inn at Hogsden (Hoxton).
5. Heady, strong.
6. Gang, crowd.
7. A slang corruption of the Italian coraggio, courage.
8. Slavs; Transylvanians: people to the east of Austria;
Moldavia: a province along the Danube under the con-

trol of the Turks in the 16th century; Wallachia: south of
Moldavia, lay between the Hungarian and Turkish kingdoms.
9. All Italian cities. Bononia and Bologna are the same
place; Valteria is Volterra; Montepulchena is Montepul-
ciano; the Siennois are the people of Sienna.

TEARCAT *Ick, mine here? ick bin den ruffling Tearcat, den brave soldado; ick bin dorick all Dutchlant gereisen; der schellum das meer ine beasa ine woert gaeb, ick slaag um stroaques on tom cop; dastick den hundred touzun divel halle, frollick, mine here.*[1]

SIR BEAUTEOUS Here, here; let's be rid of their jobbering. [*About to give money.*]

MOLL Not a cross,[2] sir Beauteous—You base rogues, I have taken measure of you better than a tailor can; and I'll fit you, as you, monster with one eye, have fitted me.

TRAPDOOR Your worship will not abuse a soldier?

MOLL Soldier? Thou deservest to be hanged up by that tongue which dishonors so noble a profession: soldier? you skeldering[3] varlet! Hold, stand; there should be a trapdoor here abouts. [*Pulls off his patch.*]

TRAPDOOR The balls of these glasiers[4] of mine, mine eyes, shall be shot up and down in any hot piece of service for my invincible mistress.

JACK DAPPER I did not think there had been such knavery in black patches as now I see.[5]

MOLL O sir, he hath been brought up in the Isle of Dogs,[6] and can both fawn like a spaniel, and bite like a mastiff, as he finds occasion.

LORD NOLAND What are you, sirrah? a bird of this feather too?

TEARCAT A man beaten from the wars, sir.

SIR THOMAS I think so, for you never stood to fight.

JACK DAPPER What's thy name, fellow soldier?

TEARCAT I am called by those that have seen my valor, Tearcat.

ALL Tearcat?

MOLL A mere whip-jack,[7] and that is, in the commonwealth of rogues, a slave that can talk of sea-fight, name all your chief pirates, discover more countries to you than either the Dutch, Spanish, French, or English ever found out; yet indeed all his service is by land, and that is to rob a fair, or some such venturous exploit. Tearcat? 'foot, sirrah, I have your name, now I remember me, in my book of horners; horns for the thumb, you know how.[8]

TEARCAT No indeed, captain Moll, for I know you by sight, I am no such nipping Christian, but a maunderer upon the pad,[9] I confess; and meeting with honest Trapdoor here, whom you had cashiered from bearing arms, out at elbows, under your colors, I instructed him in the rudiments of roguery, and by my map made him sail over any country you can name, so that now he can maunder better than myself.

JACK DAPPER So, then, Trapdoor, thou art turned soldier now?

TRAPDOOR Alas, sir, now there's no wars, 'tis the safest course of life I could take!

MOLL I hope, then, you can cant, for by your cudgels, you, sirrah, are an upright man.[1]

1. Mainly in Low German: "I, my lord? I am the ruffling Tearcat, the brave soldier. I have traveled all over Deutschland. The scoundrel who gives a blow sooner than a word, I hit him with strokes on the head, to drive out a hundred thousand devils; enjoy it, my lord."
2. A piece of money marked with a cross.
3. Swindling.
4. Eyes.
5. Ornamental black patches were worn by ladies and fops.
6. A haunt of debtors and the title of a lost play by Ben Jonson.
7. There is a similar description of a "whipjacke" in Dekker's humorous pamphlet the *Belman of London* (1608).
8. "Horn-thumb": a cutpurse.
9. Cant for "beg on the high road."
1. All the cant terms used in this scene are described in the *Belman of London* and *Lantern and Candlelight*; see the excerpts on pages 1429–1432. An upright man was "a sturdy big-boned knave, that never walkes but (like a Commander) with a short truncheon in his hand, which he calls his Filchman."

TRAPDOOR As any walks the highway, I assure you.

MOLL And, Tearcat, what are you? a wild rogue, an angler, or a ruffler?[2]

TEARCAT Brother to this upright man, flesh and blood; ruffling Tearcat is my name, and a ruffler is my style, my title, my profession.

MOLL Sirrah, where's your doxy?[3] halt not with me.

ALL Doxy, Moll? what's that?

MOLL His wench.

TRAPDOOR My doxy? I have, by the salomon, a doxy that carries a kinchin mort in her slate at her back, besides my dell and my dainty wild dell, with all whom I'll tumble this next darkmans in the strommel, and drink ben bouse, and eat a fat gruntling cheat, a cackling cheat, and a quacking cheat.[4]

JACK DAPPER Here's old[5] cheating!

TRAPDOOR My doxy stays for me in a bousing ken,[6] brave captain.

MOLL He says his wench stays for him in an ale-house. You are no pure rogues!

TEARCAT Pure rogues? no, we scorn to be pure rogues; but if you come to our lib ken or our stalling ken, you shall find neither him nor me a queer cuffin.[7]

MOLL So, sir, no churl of you.

TEARCAT No, but a ben cove, a brave cove, a gentry cuffin.

LORD NOLAND Call you this canting?

JACK DAPPER Zounds, I'll give a schoolmaster half-a-crown a-week, and teach me this pedlar's French.[8]

TRAPDOOR Do but stroll, sir, half a harvest with us, sir, and you shall gabble your bellyful.

MOLL Come, you rogue, cant with me.

SIR THOMAS Well said, Moll—Cant with her, sirrah, and you shall have money, else not a penny.

TRAPDOOR I'll have a bout, if she please.

MOLL Come on, sirrah!

TRAPDOOR Ben mort, shall you and I heave a bough, mill a ken, or nip a bung, and then we'll couch a hogshead under the ruffmans, and there you shall wap with me, and I'll niggle with you.[9]

MOLL Out, you damned impudent rascal!

TRAPDOOR Cut benar whids, and hold your fambles and your stamps.[1]

LORD NOLAND Nay, nay, Moll, why art thou angry? what was his gibberish?

2. A wild rogue was "a spirit that cares not in what circle he rises, nor into the company of what Divels he falls." An angler was "a limb of an upright man, as being derived from him: their apparel in which they walk is commonly frieze jerkins and gall slops: in the daytime they beg from house to house, not so much for relief, as to spy what lies fit for their nets, which in the night following they fish for." And "the next in degree to him [the upright man] is called a ruffler: the ruffler and the upright man are so like in conditions, the you would swear them brothers: they walk with cudgels alike; they profess arms alike" (*Belman of London*).

3. Whore.

4. By the saloman: by the mass; kinchin "girls of a year or two old, which the Morts (their mothers) carry at their backs in the slates (which in the canting tongue are sheets)"; dell: "a young wench . . . but as yet not spoiled of her maidenhead. These dells are reserved for the upright men for none but they must have the first taste of them" (Dekker, *Lantern and Candlelight*). I'll tumble . . .

cheat: I'll tumble this next night in the straw, and drink good drink, and eat a fat pig, a capon, and a duck.

5. Fine, rare.

6. Alehouse.

7. "Lib ken, or our stalling ken," i.e., our house to lie in or our house to receive stolen goods. "The word cone or cofe, or cuffin, signifies a man, a fellow, etc. But differs something in his property according as it meets with other words; for a gentleman is called a gentry cove, or cofe. A good fellow is a bene cofe; a churle is called a queer cuffin; queer signifies naught" (*Lantern and Candlelight*).

8. "That pedlars French or that Canting language, which is to be found among none but beggars" (*Lantern and Candlelight*).

9. In the lines that follow, Moll interprets this passage of canting. "Heave a bough": rob a booth; "mill a ken": rob a house; "nip a bung": cut a purse; "niggling," companying with a woman." See *The Canter's Dictionary*, page 1431.

1. Cut . . . stamps: speak better words and hold your hands and legs.

MOLL Marry, this, my lord, says he: *Ben mort, good wench, shall you and I heave a bough, mill a ken, or nip a bung?* shall you and I rob a house or cut a purse?

ALL Very good.

MOLL *And then we'll couch a hogshead under the ruffmans;* and then we'll lie under a hedge.

TRAPDOOR That was my desire, captain, as 'tis fit a soldier should lie.

MOLL *And there you shall wap with me, and I'll niggle with you,*—and that's all.

SIR BEAUTEOUS Nay, nay, Moll, what's that wap?

JACK DAPPER Nay, teach me what niggling is; I'd fain be niggling.

MOLL Wapping and niggling is all one, the rogue my man can tell you.

TRAPDOOR 'Tis fadoodling,[2] if it please you.

SIR BEAUTEOUS This is excellent! One fit more, good Moll.

MOLL Come, you rogue, sing with me.

[*Song by Moll and Tearcat.*]

> *A gage of ben rom-bouse*
> *In a bousing ken of Rom-vile,*
> *Is benar than a caster,*
> *Peck, pennam, lap, or popler,*
> *Which we mill in deuse a vile.*
> *O I wud lib all the lightmans,*
> *O I wud lib all the darkmans*
> *By the salomon, under the ruffmans,*
> *By the salomon, in the hartmans,*
> *And scour the queer cramp ring,*
> *And couch till a palliard docked my dell,*
> *So my bousy nab might skew rom-bouse well.*
> *Avast to the pad, let us bing;*
> *Avast to the pad, let us bing.*[3]

ALL Fine knaves, i'faith!

JACK DAPPER The grating of ten new cart-wheels, and the gruntling of five hundred hogs coming from Rumford market, cannot make a worse noise than this canting language does in my ears. Pray, my lord Noland, let's give these soldiers their pay.

SIR BEAUTEOUS Agreed, and let them march.

LORD NOLAND Here, Moll. [*Gives money.*]

MOLL Now I see that you are stalled to the rogue, and are not ashamed of your professions: look you, my lord Noland here and these gentlemen bestows upon you two two boards and a half, that's two shillings sixpence.[4]

TRAPDOOR Thanks to your lordship.

TEARCAT Thanks, heroical captain.

MOLL Away!

TRAPDOOR We shall cut ben whids[5] of your masters and mistress-ship wheresoever we come.

---

2. Sexual intercourse.
3. "A quart pot of good wine in an alehouse of London is better than a cloak, meat, bread, butter-milk (or whey), or porridge, which we steal in the country. O I would lie all the day, O I would lie all the night, by the mass, under the woods (or bushes), by the mass, in the stocks, and wear bolts (or fetters), and lie till a palliard [lecher] lay

with my wench, so my drunken head might quaff wine well. Avast to the highway, let us hence, etc." (*Lantern and Candlelight*).
4. "Stalled to the rogue": initiated as a rogue; board: a shilling (*Lantern and Candlelight*).
5. Speak good words.

MOLL You'll maintain, sirrah, the old justice's plot to his face?

TRAPDOOR Else trine me on the cheats,[6]—hang me.

MOLL Be sure you meet me there.

TRAPDOOR Without any more maundering,[7] I'll do't.—Follow, brave Tearcat.

TEARCAT *I prae, sequor:*[8] let us go, mouse.

    [*Exeunt Trapdoor and Tearcat.*]

LORD NOLAND Moll, what was in that canting song?

MOLL Troth, my lord, only a praise of good drink, the only milk which these wild
    beasts love to suck, and thus it was:

> *A rich cup of wine,*
> *O it is juice divine!*
> *More wholesome for the head*
> *Than meat, drink, or bread:*
> *To fill my drunken pate*
> *With that, I'd sit up late;*
> *By the heels would I lie,*
> *Under a lowsy hedge die,*
> *Let a slave have a pull*
> *At my whore, so I be full*
> *Of that precious liquor:*

and a parcel of such stuff, my lord, not worth the opening.

    [*Enter a Cutpurse very gallant,*[9] *with four or five others, one having a wand.*]

LORD NOLAND What gallant comes yonder?

SIR THOMAS Mass, I think I know him; 'tis one of Cumberland.

FIRST CUTPURSE Shall we venture to shuffle in amongst yon heap of gallants, and
    strike?[1]

SECOND CUTPURSE 'Tis a question whether there be any silver shells[2] amongst
    them, for all their satin outsides.

THE REST Let's try.

MOLL Pox on him, a gallant? Shadow me, I know him; 'tis one that cumbers the land
    indeed: if he swim near to the shore of any of your pockets, look to your purses.

LORD NOLAND   }
SIR BEAUTEOUS etc. } Is't possible?

MOLL This brave[3] fellow is no better than a foist.

LORD NOLAND   }
SIR BEAUTEOUS etc. } Foist! what's that?

MOLL A diver with two fingers, a pickpocket; all his train study the figging-law,[4]
    that's to say, cutting of purses and foisting. One of them is a nip; I took him once
    i' the two-penny gallery at the Fortune: then there's a cloyer, or snap, that dogs
    any new brother in that trade, and snaps will have half in any booty. He with the
    wand is both a stale, whose office is to face a man i' the streets, whilst shells are
    drawn by another, and then with his black conjuring rod in his hand, he, by the

---

6. Hang me on the gallows.
7. Muttering.
8. You first, I'll follow.
9. Well dressed.
1. Pick a purse.
2. Money.
3. Finely dressed.
4. "Figging law" is described in the *Belman of London:* "He

that cuts the purse is called the *Nip.* He that is half with
him is the *Snap,* or the *Cloyer.* The knife is called a *Cut-tle-bung.* He that picks the pocket is called a *Foist.* He
that faceth the man is the *Stale.* The taking of the purse is
called *Drawing.* The spying of this villanie is called *Smok-ing* or *Boiling.* The purse is the *Bung.* The money the
Shels. The act doing is called *Striking."*

nimbleness of his eye and juggling stick, will, in cheaping a piece of plate at a goldsmith's stall, make four or five rings mount from the top of his *caduceus*,[5] and, as if it were at leap-frog, they skip into his hand presently.

SECOND CUTPURSE Zounds, we are smoked!

THE REST Ha!

SECOND CUTPURSE We are boiled,[6] pox on her! see, Moll, the roaring drab!

FIRST CUTPURSE All the diseases of sixteen hospitals boil her!—Away!

MOLL Bless you, sir.

FIRST CUTPURSE And you, good sir.

MOLL Dost not ken me, man?

FIRST CUTPURSE No, trust me, sir.

MOLL Heart, there's a knight, to whom I'm bound for many favors, lost his purse at the last new play i' the Swan,[7] seven angels in't: make it good, you're best; do you see? no more.

FIRST CUTPURSE A synagogue shall be called, mistress Mary; disgrace me not; *pacus palabros*,[8] I will conjure for you: farewell. [*Exit with his companions.*]

MOLL Did not I tell you, my lord?

LORD NOLAND I wonder how thou camest to the knowledge of these nasty villains.

SIR THOMAS And why do the foul mouths of the world call thee Moll Cutpurse? a name, methinks, damned and odious.

MOLL   Dare any step forth to my face and say,
     I've ta'en thee doing so, Moll? I must confess,
     In younger days, when I was apt to stray,
     I've sat amongst such adders; seen their stings,
     As any here might, and in full playhouses
     Watched their quick-diving hands, to bring to shame
     Such rogues, and in that stream met an ill name.
     When next, my lord, you spy any one of those,
     So he be in his art a scholar, question him;
     Tempt him with gold to open the large book
     Of his close villanies; and you yourself shall cant
     Better than poor Moll can, and know more laws
     Of cheaters, lifters, nips, foists, puggards, curbers,[9]
     With all the devil's black-guard,[1] than it's fit
     Should be discovered to a noble wit,
     I know they have their orders, offices,
     Circuits, and circles, unto which they're bound
     To raise their own damnation in.

JACK DAPPER How dost thou know it?

MOLL As you do; I show't you, they to me show it. Suppose, my lord, you were in Venice—

LORD NOLAND Well.

MOLL If some Italian pander there would tell

---

5. The wand of Mercury, god of thieves.
6. Spied, found out.
7. A playhouse on the Bankside.
8. A corruption of the Spanish *pocas palabras*, "few words."
9. "The Cheating Law, or the art of winning money by false dyce: Those that practice this study call themselves Cheators, the dyce Cheaters, and the money which they

purchase Cheates . . . the Curbing Law . . . teaches . . . how to hook goods out of a window . . . The Lifting Law . . . teacheth a kind of lifting of goods clean away" (*Belman of London*). "Puggards": thieves.
1. A group of attendants who were black in person, dress, or character; the kitchen-drudges who attended royal progresses.

All the close tricks of courtesans, would not you
Hearken to such a fellow?
LORD NOLAND   Yes.
MOLL   And here,
Being come from Venice, to a friend most dear
That were to travel thither, you'd proclaim
Your knowledge in those villanies, to save
Your friend from their quick danger: must you have
A black ill name, because ill things you know?
Good troth, my lord, I'm made Moll Cutpurse so.
How many are whores in small ruffs and still looks!
How many chaste whose names fill Slander's books!
Were all men cuckolds whom gallants in their scorns
Call so, we should not walk for goring horns.
Perhaps for my mad going some reprove me;
I please myself, and care not else who love me.
LORD NOLAND   ⎱ A brave mind, Moll, i'faith!
SIR BEAUTEOUS etc. ⎰
SIR THOMAS Come, my lord, shall's to the ordinary?
LORD NOLAND Ay, 'tis noon sure.
MOLL Good my lord, let not my name condemn me to you, or to the world: a fencer
    I hope may be called a coward; is he so for that? If all that have ill names in Lon-
    don were to be whipped, and to pay but twelvepence a-piece to the beadle, I
    would rather have his office than a constable's.
JACK DAPPER So would I, captain Moll: 'twere a sweet tickling office, i'faith.
    [Exeunt.]

Scene 2

[A Garden attached to Sir Alexander Wengrave's House. Enter Sir Alexander
Wengrave, Goshawk, Greenwit, and others.]
SIR ALEXANDER My son marry a thief, that impudent girl,
    Whom all the world stick their worst eyes upon!
GREENWIT How will your care prevent it?
GOSHAWK   'Tis impossible:
    They marry close, they're gone, but none knows whither.
SIR ALEXANDER O gentlemen, when has a father's heartstrings
    [Enter Servant.]
    Held out so long from breaking?—Now what news, sir?
SEBASTIAN They were met upo' th' water an hour since, sir,
    Putting in towards the Sluice.[2]
SIR ALEXANDER   The Sluice? Come, gentlemen,
    'Tis Lambeth works against us. [Exit Servant.]
GREENWIT   And that Lambeth
    Joins more mad matches than your six wet towns
    'Twixt that and Windsor Bridge,[3] where fares lie soaking.
SIR ALEXANDER Delay no time, sweet gentlemen: to Blackfriars![4]
    We'll take a pair of oars, and make after 'em.

2. A marshy riverside district, frequented by pickpockets
and prostitutes.
3. Bridge over the Thames connecting Windsor with

Eton.
4. A landing stage on the north side of the Thames.

[*Enter Trapdoor.*]

TRAPDOOR Your son and that bold masculine ramp⁵ my mistress
　　　Are landed now at Tower.

SIR ALEXANDER　　　　　　　　Hoyda, at Tower?

TRAPDOOR I heard it now reported.

SIR ALEXANDER　　　　　　　　Which way, gentlemen,
　　　Shall I bestow my care? I'm drawn in pieces
　　　Betwixt deceit and shame.

[*Enter Sir Guy Fitzallard.*]

SIR GUY　　　　　　　　Sir Alexander,
　　　You are well met, and most rightly served;
　　　My daughter was a scorn to you.

SIR ALEXANDER　　　　　　　　Say not so, sir.

SIR GUY A very abject she, poor gentlewoman!
　　　Your house had been dishonored. Give you joy, sir,
　　　Of your son's gascoyne bride!⁶ You'll be a grandfather shortly
　　　To a fine crew of roaring sons and daughters;
　　　'Twill help to stock the suburbs passing well, sir.

SIR ALEXANDER O, play not with the miseries of my heart!
　　　Wounds should be dressed and healed, not vexed, or left
　　　Wide open, to the anguish of the patient,
　　　And scornful air let in; rather let pity
　　　And advice charitably help to refresh 'em.

SIR GUY Who'd place his charity so unworthily?
　　　Like one that gives alms to a cursing beggar:
　　　Had I but found one spark of goodness in you
　　　Toward my deserving child, which then grew fond
　　　Of your son's virtues, I had eased you now;
　　　But I perceive both fire of youth and goodness
　　　Are raked up in the ashes of your age,
　　　Else no such shame should have come near your house,
　　　Nor such ignoble sorrow touch your heart.

SIR ALEXANDER If not for worth, for pity's sake assist me!

GREENWIT You urge a thing past sense; how can he help you?
　　　All his assistance is as frail as ours:
　　　Full as uncertain where's the place that holds 'em;
　　　One brings us water-news; then comes another
　　　With a full-charged mouth, like a culverin's° voice,　　　*gun's*
　　　And he reports the Tower: whose sounds are truest?

GOSHAWK In vain you flatter him.—Sir Alexander—

SIR GUY I flatter him? Gentlemen, you wrong me grossly.

GREENWIT He does it well, i'faith.

SIR GUY　　　　　　　　Both news are false,
　　　Of Tower or water; they took no such way yet.

SIR ALEXANDER O strange! Hear you this, gentlemen? Yet more plunges.⁷

SIR GUY They're nearer than you think for, yet more close
　　　Than if they were further off.

SIR ALEXANDER　　　　　　　　How am I lost

---

5. Wildwoman.　　　　　　　　　　　　7. Difficulties.
6. A bride who wears loose breeches.

                    In these distractions!
SIR GUY   For your speeches, gentlemen,
          In taxing me for rashness, 'fore you all
          I will engage my state to half his wealth,
          Nay, to his son's revenues, which are less,
          And yet nothing at all till they come from him,
          That I could, if my will stuck to my power,
          Prevent this marriage yet, nay, banish her
          For ever from his thoughts, much more his arms.
SIR ALEXANDER Slack not this goodness, though you heap upon me
          Mountains of malice and revenge hereafter!
          I'd willingly resign up half my state to him,
          So he would marry the meanest drudge I hire.
GREENWIT He talks impossibilities, and you believe 'em.
SIR GUY I talk no more than I know how to finish,
          My fortunes else are his that dares stake with me.
          The poor young gentleman I love and pity;
          And to keep shame from him (because the spring
          Of his affection was my daughter's first,
          Till his frown blasted all), do but estate him
          In those possessions which your love and care
          Once pointed out for him, that he may have room
          To entertain fortunes of noble birth,
          Where now his desperate wants casts him upon her;
          And if I do not, for his own sake chiefly,
          Rid him of this disease that now grows on him,
          I'll forfeit my whole state before these gentlemen.
GREENWIT Troth, but you shall not undertake such matches;
          We'll persuade so much with you.
SIR ALEXANDER   Here's my ring [Gives ring.]
          He will believe this token. 'Fore these gentlemen
          I will confirm it fully: all those lands
          My first love 'lotted him, he shall straight possess
          In that refusal.
SIR GUY   If I change it not,
          Change me into a beggar.
GREENWIT   Are you mad, sir?
SIR GUY 'Tis done.
GOSHAWK   Will you undo yourself by doing,
          And show a prodigal trick in your old days?
SIR ALEXANDER 'Tis a match, gentlemen.
SIR GUY   Ay, ay, sir, ay.
          I ask no favor, trust to you for none;
          My hope rests in the goodness of your son. [Exit.]
GREENWIT He holds it up well yet.
GOSHAWK   Of an old knight, i'faith.
SIR ALEXANDER Curst be the time I laid his first love barren,
          Wilfully barren, that before this hour
          Had sprung forth fruits of comfort and of honor!
          He loved a virtuous gentlewoman.
     [Enter Moll in her male dress.]

GOSHAWK   Life, here's Moll!

GREENWIT Jack?

GOSHAWK   How dost thou, Jack?

MOLL   How dost thou, gallant?

SIR ALEXANDER Impudence, where's my son?

MOLL   Weakness, go look him.

SIR ALEXANDER Is this your wedding gown?

MOLL   The man talks monthly:[8]
     Hot broth and a dark chamber for the knight!
     I see he'll be stark mad at our next meeting. [*Exit.*]

GOSHAWK Why, sir, take comfort now, there's no such matter,
     No priest will marry her, sir, for a woman
     Whiles that shape's on; and it was never known
     Two men were married and conjoined in one
     Your son hath made some shift to love another.

SIR ALEXANDER Whate'er she be, she has my blessing with her:
     May they be rich and fruitful, and receive
     Like comfort to their issue as I take
     In them! Has pleased me now; marrying not this,
     Through a whole world he could not choose amiss.

GREENWIT Glad you're so penitent for your former sin, sir.

GOSHAWK Say he should take a wench with her smock-dowry,
     No portion with her but her lips and arms?

SIR ALEXANDER Why, who thrive better, sir? They have most blessing,
     Though other have more wealth, and least repent:
     Many that want most know the most content.

GREENWIT Say he should marry a kind youthful sinner?

SIR ALEXANDER Age will quench that; any offence but theft
     And drunkenness, nothing but death can wipe away;
     Their sins are green even when their heads are grey.
     Nay, I despair not now; my heart's cheer'd, gentlemen;
     No face can come unfortunately to me.—
          [*Reenter Servant.*]
     Now, sir, your news?

SERVANT   Your son, with his fair bride,
     Is near at hand.

SIR ALEXANDER   Fair may their fortunes be!

GREENWIT Now you're resolved,[9] sir, it was never she.

SIR ALEXANDER I find it in the music of my heart.
     [*Enter Sebastian Wengrave leading in Moll in her female dress and masked and Sir
     Guy Fitzallard.*]
     See where they come.

GOSHAWK   A proper lusty presence, sir.

SIR ALEXANDER Now has he pleased me right: I always counselled him
     To choose a goodly, personable creature:
     Just of her pitch was my first wife his mother.

SEBASTIAN Before I dare discover my offence,

_____

8. Madly, at the full moon.   9. Convinced.

I kneel for pardon. [*Kneels.*]

SIR ALEXANDER My heart gave it thee
 Before thy tongue could ask it:
 Rise; thou hast raised my joy to greater height
 Than to that seat where grief dejected it.
 Both welcome to my love and care for ever!
 Hide not my happiness too long; all's pardoned;
 Here are our friends.—Salute her, gentlemen.

             [*They unmask her.*]

ALL Heart, who's this? Moll!

SIR ALEXANDER O my reviving shame! Is't I must live
 To be struck blind? Be it the work of sorrow,
 Before age take't in hand!

SIR GUY   Darkness and death!
 Have you deceived me thus? Did I engage
 My whole estate for this?

SIR ALEXANDER   You asked no favor,
 And you shall find as little; since my comforts
 Play false with me, I'll be as cruel to thee
 As grief to fathers' hearts.

MOLL   Why, what's the matter with you,
 'Less too much joy should make your age forgetful?
 Are you too well, too happy?

SIR ALEXANDER   With a vengeance!

MOLL Methinks you should be proud of such a daughter,
 As good a man as your son.

SIR ALEXANDER   O monstrous impudence!

MOLL You had no note before, an unmarked knight;
 Now all the town will take regard on you,
 And all your enemies fear you for my sake:
 You may pass where you list, through crowds most thick,
 And come off bravely with your purse unpicked.
 You do not know the benefits I bring with me;
 No cheat dares work upon you with thumb or knife,
 While you've a roaring girl to your son's wife.

SIR ALEXANDER A devil rampant!

SIR GUY   Have you so much charity
 Yet to release me of my last rash bargain,
 And I'll give in your pledge?

SIR ALEXANDER   No, sir, I stand to't;
 I'll work upon advantage, as all mischiefs
 Do upon me.

SIR GUY   Content. Bear witness all, then,
 His are the lands; and so contention ends:
 Here comes your son's bride 'twixt two noble friends.

[*Enter Lord Noland and Sir Beauteous Ganymede with Mary Fitzallard between
them; Gallipot, Tiltyard, Openwork, and their wives.*]

MOLL Now are you gulled as you would be; thank me for't,
 I'd a forefinger in't.

SEBASTIAN   Forgive me, father!

Though there before your eyes my sorrow feigned,
This still was she for whom true love complained.

SIR ALEXANDER Blessings eternal, and the joys of angels,
Begin your peace here to be signed in heaven!
How short my sleep of sorrow seems now to me,
To this eternity of boundless comforts,
That finds no want but utterance and expression!
My lord, your office here appears so honorably,
So full of ancient goodness, grace, and worthiness,
I never took more joy in sight of man
Than in your comfortable presence now.

LORD NOLAND Nor I more delight in doing grace to virtue
Than in this worthy gentlewoman your son's bride,
Noble Fitzallard's daughter, to whose honor
And modest fame I am a servant vowed;
So is this knight.

SIR ALEXANDER   Your loves make my joys proud.
Bring forth those deeds of land my care laid ready,
[Exit Servant, who presently returns with deeds.]
And which, old knight, thy nobleness may challenge,
Joined with thy daughter's virtues, whom I prize now
As dearly as that flesh I call mine own.
Forgive me, worthy gentlewoman; 'twas my blindness:
When I rejected thee, I saw thee not;
Sorrow and wilful rashness grew like films
Over the eyes of judgment; now so clear
I see the brightness of thy worth appear.

MARY Duty and love may I deserve in those!
And all my wishes have a perfect close.

SIR ALEXANDER That tongue can never err, the sound's so sweet.
Here, honest son, receive into thy hands
The keys of wealth, possession of those lands
Which my first care provided; they're thine own;
Heaven give thee a blessing with 'em! the best joys
That can in worldly shapes to man betide
Are fertile lands and a fair fruitful bride,
Of which I hope thou'rt sped.

SEBASTIAN   I hope so too, sir.

MOLL Father and son, I ha' done you simple service here.

SEBASTIAN For which thou shalt not part, Moll, unrequited.

SIR ALEXANDER Thou'rt a mad girl, and yet I cannot now
Condemn thee.

MOLL   Condemn me? troth, and you should, sir,
I'd make you seek out one to hang in my room:
I'd give you the slip at gallows, and cozen the people.
Heard you this jest, my lord?

LORD NOLAND   What is it, Jack?

MOLL He was in fear his son would marry me,
But never dream't that I would ne'er agree.

LORD NOLAND Why, thou had'st a suitor once, Jack: when wilt marry?

MOLL Who, I, my lord? I'll tell you when, i'faith;

When you shall hear
Gallants void from sergeants' fear,
Honesty and truth unslandered,
Woman manned, but never pandered,
Cheats booted, but not coached,
Vessels older ere they're broached;
If my mind be then not varied,
Next day following I'll be married.

LORD NOLAND This sounds like doomsday.

MOLL   Then were marriage best;
For if I should repent, I were soon at rest.

SIR ALEXANDER In troth thou'rt a good wench; I'm sorry now
The opinion was so hard I conceived of thee:
  [Enter Trapdoor.]
Some wrongs I've done thee.

TRAPDOOR [Aside.]   Is the wind there now?
'Tis time for me to kneel and confess first,
For fear it come too late, and my brains feel it.—
Upon my paws I ask you pardon, mistress!

MOLL Pardon! for what, sir? What has your rogueship done now?

TRAPDOOR I've been from time to time hired to confound you
By this old gentleman.

MOLL   How?

TRAPDOOR   Pray, forgive him:
But may I counsel you, you should never do't.
Many a snare t' entrap your worship's life
Have I laid privily; chains, watches, jewels;
And when he saw nothing could mount you up,
Four hollow-hearted angels he then gave you,
By which he meant to trap you, I to save you.

SIR ALEXANDER To all which shame and grief in me cry guilty.
Forgive me: now I cast the world's eyes from me,
And look upon thee freely with mine own,
I see the most of many wrongs before me,
Cast from the jaws of Envy and her people,
And nothing foul but that. I'll never more
Condemn by common voice, for that's the whore
That deceives man's opinion, mocks his trust,
Cozens his love, and makes his heart unjust.

MOLL Here be the angels, gentlemen; they were given me
As a musician: I pursue no pity;
Follow the law, and you can cuck me,[1] spare not;
Hang up my viol by me, and I care not.

SIR ALEXANDER So far I'm sorry, I'll thrice double 'em,
To make thy wrongs amends.
Come, worthy friends, my honorable lord,
Sir Beauteous Ganymede, and noble Fitzallard,

---

1. Set me in a cucking-stool, a punishment for scolds and shrews (women who were considered disorderly); the offender was fastened to a chair and exposed to the jeers of bystanders or ducked in water.

And you kind gentlewomen,[2] whose sparkling presence
Are glories set in marriage, beams of society,
For all your loves give lustre to my joys:
The happiness of this day shall be remembered
At the return of every smiling spring;
In my time now 'tis born; and may no sadness
Sit on the brows of men upon that day,
But as I am, so all go pleased away!   [*Exeunt omnes.*]

Epilogue

A painter having drawn with curious art
The picture of a woman, every part
Limned° to the life, hung out the piece to sell.   *portrayed*
People who passed along, viewing it well,
Gave several verdicts on it: some dispraised
The hair; some said the brows too high were raised;
Some hit her o'er the lips, misliked their color;
Some wished her nose were shorter; some, the eyes fuller;
Others said roses on her cheeks should grow,
Swearing they looked too pale; others cried no.
The workman still, as fault was found, did mend it,
In hope to please all: but this work being ended,
And hung open at stall, it was so vile,
So monstrous, and so ugly, all men did smile
At the poor painter's folly. Such, we doubt,
Is this our comedy: some perhaps do flout°   *mock*
The plot, saying, 'tis too thin, too weak, too mean;
Some for the person will revile the scene,
And wonder that a creature of her being
Should be the subject of a poet, seeing
In the world's eye none weighs so light: others look
For all those base tricks, published in a book
Foul as his brains they flowed from, of cutpurses,
Of nips° and foists,° nasty, obscene discourses,   *cutpurses/pickpockets*
As full of lies as empty of worth or wit,
For any honest ear or eye unfit.
And thus,
If we to every brain that's humorous°   *fanciful*
Should fashion scenes, we, with the painter, shall,
In striving to please all, please none at all.
Yet for such faults as either the writer's wit
Or negligence of the actors do commit,
Both crave your pardons: if what both have done
Cannot full pay your expectation,
The Roaring Girl herself, some few days hence,
Shall on this stage give larger recompence.
Which mirth that you may share in, herself does woo you,
And craves this sign, your hands to beckon her to you.

---

2. Addressed to Mistress Gallipot and the others.

THE ROARING GIRL IN CONTEXT
City Life

From 1400 to 1650, London grew from a small city to the second largest city in Europe, surpassed only by Paris. The population of London more than doubled from 70,000 in 1550 to 180,000 at the death of Elizabeth in 1603. Immigration from the countryside swelled the population as young single males came in search of work as laborers and apprentices. The larger workforce enabled a rise in manufacturing, especially of cloth. Increased production fed the growth of trade, created in part by the fall of Constantinople in 1453, which shifted activity from the Mediterranean to the Atlantic. England was at peace as religious wars raged in the Netherlands and France in the late sixteenth century, and London won a large share of continental trade. As its population and economy grew, London also experienced a burgeoning of culture and a rise in social problems.

Under the Tudor and Stuart reigns, London spread beyond the medieval walled city to encompass Westminster, the precinct of Court and Parliament, which expanded to become the West End of doctors, lawyers, and luxury dealers of all sorts, and the suburbs, a haven for theaters, bullbaiting and bearbaiting, pickpocketing, and prostitution. The part of London referred to as the City was the site of the guilds and the civic government and a stronghold of evangelical Protestantism. New building and development were carried on at a great rate. With the dissolution of the monasteries under Henry VIII's Reformation, many former church properties were turned into sumptuous private residences for courtiers. Indoor theater in London got its start in the 1540s, when a convent in Blackfriars was turned into a storehouse for props. One of a few religious institutions that Henry VIII had the city take over for the public welfare was the hospital of Saint Mary of Bethlehem, which became the notorious madhouse Bedlam.

A medieval city that had been dominated by the church was transformed into a center of trade. Woolen cloth was the chief export; imports ranged from silk, spices, and perfumes from the East to tobacco, sugar, and cotton from the Caribbean and North America. Joint stock companies such as the East India Company and the Virginia Company encouraged the high risks and profits of venture capitalism by financing privateering and plantation. A new architecture arose to house this commerce. Thomas Gresham, a merchant's son, built the Royal Exchange, opened by Queen Elizabeth as the commercial headquarters for London merchants. Under Charles I, the Earl of Bedford developed Covent ("convent") Garden to create arcaded housing, a Tuscan church, and a fruit and vegetable market in a piazza designed by the first great native English architect, Inigo Jones. In *Survey of London* (1598), John Stow, an environmentalist before his time, complained of the damage done to nature by the real estate boom. At the same time he celebrated the achievements of London, as did numerous mapmakers who portrayed the city's expansion over a landscape marked by the spire of Saint Paul's and by London Bridge, connecting the City's Guildhall and the Court's Whitehall with Southwark bearbaiting and theaters, all dominated by the Thames River, teeming with trading vessels.

The growth in manufacturing and trade produced an increasingly powerful city government. While the right to trade and participate as a citizen could still be inherited or bought, the chief route to citizenship was the seven-year apprenticeship in a guild. By the mid-sixteenth century, almost three-quarters of the city's adult males belonged to one of the guilds, six of which (the Mercers, Grocers, Drapers, Haberdashers, and Merchant Tailors) provided half of London's public officials. At the top of the power structure were the Lord Mayor and the Court of Alderman, who served as justices of the peace. Under these were the Court of Common Council, a legislative body with 200 representatives, elected each December by all freemen. The public pageants staged by the city government at the time of Elizabeth's corona-

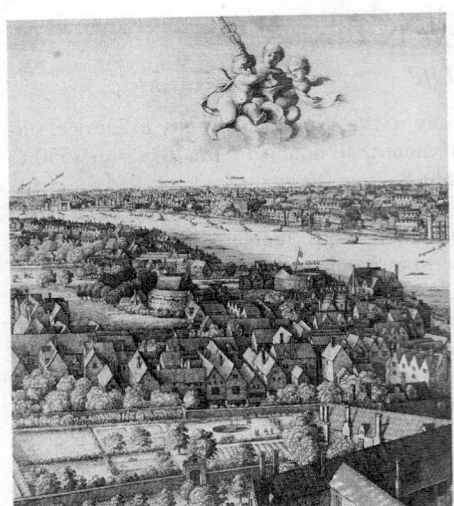

Wenceslaus Hollar. *Long View of London.* 1647.

tion influenced her strongly Protestant position. The Mayor and the Common Council initially supported Charles I, but in 1642, when the King attempted to arrest dissenters from Parliament who had fled for refuge into the City, the tradesmen and apprentices of London defended the cause of Cromwell. A ring of fortifications united the City and Westminster, and
London supported Cromwell's army with men and money.

A lively public culture accompanied this political and commercial activity. Theaters
flourished in the suburbs outside the control of city officials. The first playhouse, the Theater, was founded in Shoreditch in 1576 by the actor James Burbage, who later built the
Globe, in which Shakespeare had a tenth share. In competition with Burbage, William
Henslowe, the owner of the Rose and Curtain theaters as well as many brothels, built the
Fortune to the North in Aldersgate, where Middleton's and Dekker's *Roaring Girl* was performed. Not only were prostitution and plays associated with one another, but the theater
was viewed as a place where disease was spread. The playhouses were shut down with each
outbreak of the plague, generally during the summer months. From 1603 on, royal proclamations and statutes forbade Sunday performances, but Puritan complaints about violations of
these rules show that they were not very strictly enforced. Once in power, the Puritans shut
the theaters permanently in 1649; they were reopened only after the restoration of the
monarchy in 1660.

The city itself was a kind of theater in which one could observe everything from the
pomp of civic parades and the carnival atmosphere of the Saint Bartholomew's Day Fair to the
destitution of beggars who lived on the streets—if they were not arrested for vagrancy. A popular literature of broadsides, ballads, moral tracts, and tales of rogues was published by a thriving printing industry; London had twenty-four printers in 1585 and sixty by 1659. The audience for printed tracts and stories expanded with the rise in literacy. Half of the men who were
sentenced to death in early seventeenth-century Middlesex could read. Although female literacy was only at 10 percent in 1650, it rose to nearly five times that by 1690.

Rogue literature spoofed the naivete of those who were prey to the confidence scams of
city slickers and celebrated the escapades of such notorious city figures as Moll Cutpurse. Like
the comic drama, popular comic prose took place in shop, tavern, and marketplace in a constant interplay between civic and fictional life.

Barnabe Riche
from *My Lady's Looking Glass*[1]

It is said that Africa bringeth forth every year a new Monster,[2] the reason is, that in the deserts of that country, the wild and savage beasts that are both diverse in nature and contrary in kind will yet engender the one with the other: but England hatcheth up every month a new Monster, every week a new Sin, and every day a new Fashion: our Monsters are not bred in the Deserts, as those in Africa, but in every town and city: where they are so cheerily fostered and so daintily cherished that they multiply on heaps, by hundreds and by thousand. It were not possible for me now to set down how this monstrous generation thus hatched up by Sin hath been from time to time procreated and brought into the world, one sin still begetting another.[3]

Pride the eldest daughter of Sin was first spawned in Heaven. She was from thence expelled; but she drew after her a great dissolution of Angels. It was pride that begat Contempt in Paradise, where there was no Apple in the Garden so well pleasing to Eve as that which God had forbidden her.

It was Contempt that begot Malice. And Malice again begat Murder, when Cain killed his brother Abel.

1. Barnabe Riche (1542–1617) was a critic of the decadence of Jacobean Dublin and London. Riche ranted against the mores and politics of Catholics, the evils of "tobacco that draweth to drunkennesse," and the "gawdy attires" of women. He spent a good part of his adult life in Dublin, inveighing against what he saw as widespread corruption on every social level—from embezzlement by Protestant Archbishop Loftus (who tried to have Riche murdered) to the inflated prices of women alehouse keepers to the political dissent of Irish and English recusant Catholic gentry—that is, those who secretly defied the required conformity to the state church. Although Riche argued for such extreme measures as castration as a means to subdue the rebellious Irish, he was one of the few who

stressed the need of converting the people to Protestantism. One of the great qualities of his writing for the social critic is its uncensored quality. Seemingly disparate topics are all connected in Riche's writing, as in this passage from My Lady's Looking Glass (1616), in which he vividly portrays the loose morality of the overpopulated city as reminiscent of the monsters of Africa.
2. "Monster" has the sense of something unnatural, as in a misshapen birth or an abortion; something beastly, partly brute and partly human; and something huge or gigantic.
3. See Milton, *Paradise Lost* 2.705–844, where Sin is described as both the daughter and the incestuous consort of Satan.

As the sons of men increased in the world, so Sin began to multiply so fast that God repented him that he had made man.

To purge the world of her abominations, the Deluge came, and all were drowned, except eight persons. After the Flood, amongst the sons of Noah the generation of the accursed Cham[4] became to be great and mighty upon the earth; at which time Sin was grown up to that strength that she began on the sudden to play the Rebel, and with a tumultuous assembly gathered together in the plains of Shinar, she began to fortify herself against Heaven.

Amongst those Giants then reigning over the face of the earth, that greedy cur Covetousness, which the Apostle termeth to the root of all evils,[5] was (amongst a number of other monstrous sins) fostered up by Ambition.

Covetousness was the first parent of Oppression, Extortion, Bribery, Usury, Fraud, Deceit, Subtlety: and that common strumpet Idolatry was a bastard born of this brood.

Idolatry had issue, the Lady Lechery, who in process of time became conversant with the Pope and his Cardinals that they procreated amongst them that loathsome sin of Buggery.

It would be a matter of impossibility for me to set down the varieties of those sins that are hatched up in these days, when so many new fashioned iniquities doth swarm both in city, town, and country that were our bodies but half so diseased with sickness as our souls be with sins, it could not be avoided, but that some strange and unheard of mortality would ensue. The time hath been men would mask their vices with cloaked dissimulation from the eye of the world, but now iniquity is set forth bare faced without any mask of pretteries[6] to hide her ugly visage.

Robert Greene
from *A **Notable Discovery of Cosenage**[1]*

Ah gentlemen, merchants, yeomen and farmers, let this to you all, and to every degree else, be a caveat[2] to warn you from lust, that your inordinate desire be not a mean to impoverish your purses, discredit your good names, condemn your souls, but also that your wealth got with the sweat of your brows, or left by your parents as a patrimony, shall be a prey to those cozening cross-biters.[3] Some fond men are so far in with these detestable trugs[4] that they consume what they have upon them, and find nothing but a Neapolitan favor[5] for their labor. Read the seventh of Solomon's proverbs, and there at large view the description of a shameless and impudent courtesan:[6] yet is there another kind of cross-biting which is most pestilent, and that is this. There lives about this town certain householders, yet mere shifters and cozeners,

---

4. The offspring of Ham, who saw his father Noah naked, were cursed. See Genesis 9.22–26.

5. Chaucer's *Pardoner's Tale* turns on this theme from 1 Timothy 6.10.

6. Prettiness. The original reads "preteires."

1. Robert Greene (1560?–1592), born in Norwich, took his B.A. and M.A. from Cambridge, then toured the Continent. After marrying and then leaving his wife, a local Norwich woman who "tried to persuade him from his wilful wickedness," he settled in London. There, he became great friends with Thomas Nashe and a great enemy of Gabriel Harvey. Whereas Nashe delighted in Greene's florid and highly rhetorical style, popularized in Lyly's *Euphues*, Harvey called him "The Ass of Euphues." Harvey despised Greene so much that he actually published scurrilous stories about him after his death. Greene

died in isolation from the literary crowd and in poverty, leaving behind his mistress and his illegitimate son Fortunatus. In Greene's heyday, Nashe had praised him for the quickness of his pen: "he would have yanked a pamphlet in a night and a day as well as in a seven-year." Indeed, he was prolific, publishing twenty-eight romances and prose tracts. In one of the most popular of these, *A Notable Discovery of Cosenage*, Greene displays the tricks used by urban card sharps and pimps to hoodwink naive countrymen ("cozenage" means "cheating").

2. Caution.

3. Swindlers.

4. Prostitutes.

5. A form of syphilis.

6. See Proverbs 7.10–27, for the "woman with the attire of an harlot."

who, learning some insight in the civil law, walk abroad like paritors, summoners, and informers,[7] being none at all either in office or credit, and they go spying about where any merchant, or merchant's prentise,[8] citizen, wealthy farmer, or other of credit, either accompany with any woman familiarly, or else hath gotten some maid with child, as men's natures be prone to sin, straight they come over his fellows thus: they send for him to a tavern, and there open the matter unto him, which they have cunningly learned out, telling him he must be presented to the Arches,[9] and the citation shall be peremptorily served in his parish church. The party, afraid to have his credit cracked with the worshipful of the city and the rest of his neighbors, and grieving highly his wife should hear of it, straight takes composition with this cozener for some twenty marks, nay I heard of forty pound cross-bitten at one time, and then the cozening informer or cross-biter promiseth to wipe him out of the book and discharge him from the matter, when it was neither known nor presented: so go they to the woman and fetch her off if she be married, and though they have this gross sum yet oft times they cross-bite her for more: nay thus do they fear citizens, prentises, and farmers, that they find but any way suspicious of the like fault. The cross-biting bawds,[1] for no better can I term them, in that for lucre they conceal the sin, and smother up lust, do not only enrich themselves mightily thereby, but also discredit, hinder, and prejudice the court of the Arches, and the officers belonging to the same. There are some poor blind patches of that faculty, that have their tenements purchased and their plate on the board[2] very solemnly, who only get their gains by cross-biting, as is afore rehearsed.

Thomas Dekker
from *Lantern and Candlelight*[1]

from CHAPTER 1: OF CANTING: HOW LONG IT HATH BEEN A LANGUAGE;
HOW IT COMES TO BE A LANGUAGE; HOW IT IS DERIVED AND BY WHOM IT IS SPOKEN.[2]

Now because a language is nothing else than heaps of words orderly woven and composed together, and that, within so narrow a circle as I have drawn to myself, it is impossible to imprint a dictionary of all the canting phrases, I will at this time not make you surfeit on too much but, as if you were walking in a garden, you shall only pluck here a flower and there another, which, as I take it, will be more delightful than if you gathered them by handfuls.

---

7. Paritors were summoning officers of an ecclesiastical court; summoners were officers who warn people that they have to appear in court; informers gave information against lawbreakers.
8. Apprentice.
9. The Arches, or Court of Arches, the ecclesiastical court for the province of Canterbury.
1. Panderers.
2. Silver on the table.
1. Thomas Dekker (1572?–1632), in addition to being a playwright, was a witty and colorful author of prose pamphlets, describing London street life in a kind of early modern social criticism. Most pamphleteers were following the moralistic strain of Barnabe Riche rather than the satirical vein made popular by Nashe. Indeed, a bitter, satirical, and highly topical quarrel had brought on the banning of formal verse satire by the Archbishop of Canterbury in 1599. Dekker revived the satirical style in prose pamphlets that were humorous and fantastic. He took up this genre to make some money in the wake of

the closing of the theaters because of the plague of 1603. His first two pamphlets, the sardonically titled *Wonderful Year* and *Seven Deadly Sins*, were about the effects of the plague on London. Dekker's *Lantern and Candlelight* (1608), also about London street life, was so popular that it was reprinted in four different editions and, with some minor additions, under three other titles: *Villanies Discovered* (1616), *O per se—O* (1620), and *English Villanies* (1632).
2. This pamphlet tells the story of how the devil visits the earth only to find that peace and justice have fled to heaven. The only light of goodness that remains is the night watchman, or bellman, who wanders the streets of the city with his single candle. The devil finds a corrupt city in which he hears a Babel of canting, or street talk, spoken by vagabonds and beggars. Dekker's grim vision of the city is enlivened by sardonic humor and real sympathy for the poor. As he wrote in his *Work for Armourers* (1609), "God help the poor, the rich can shift."

But before I lead you into that walk, stay and hear a canter[3] in his own language making rhythms—albeit I think those charms of poesy which at the first made the barbarous tame and brought them to civility can upon these savage monsters work no such wonder. Yet this he sings, upon demand whether any of his own crew did come that way, to which he answers, "Yes," quoth he,

Canting Rhythms[4]

"Enough! With boozy cove maund nase,
Tower the patring cove in the darkman case,
Docked the dell for a copper make,
His watch shall feng a prounce's nab cheat,
Cyarum, by Salmon, and thou shalt peck my jeer
In thy gan, for my watch it is nase gear,
For the bene booze my watch hath a win, etc."

This short lesson I leave to be construed by him that is desirous to try his skill in the language, which he may do by help of the following dictionary, into which way that he may more readily come, I will translate into English this broken French that follows in prose. Two canters having wrangled a while about some idle quarrel, at length growing friends thus one of them speaks to the other, viz.

A Canter in Prose

Stow you, bene cofe, and cut benar whids, and bing we to Romeville to nip a bung. So shall we have lower for the boozing ken, and when we bing back to the Deuce-a-ville we will filch some duds off the ruffmans or mill the ken for a lag of duds.

Thus in English

Stow you, bene cofe, hold your peace, good fellow
and cut benar whids, and speak better words
and bing we to Romeville, and go we to London
to nip a bung, to cut a purse
So shall we have lower, so shall we have money
for the boozing ken, for the alehouse
and when we being back, and when we come back
to the Deuce-a-ville, into the country
we will filch some duds, we will filch some clothes
off the ruffmans, from the hedges
or mill the ken, or rob the house
for a lag of duds, for a buck[5] of clothes

Now turn to your dictionary; and because you shall not have one dish twice set before you, none of those canting words that are Englished before shall here be found, for our intent is to feast you with variety.

---

3. From Latin *cantus* (song, chant), canting was the street talk of thieves and beggars, who spoke in their own private language, sometimes intoned in a whining singsong.
4. These lines (untranslated by Dekker and perhaps intentionally nonsensical) come from Robert Copland's *The Highway to the Spital-House* (1536).
5. A "buck" was "a wash," the quantity of clothes washed at one time.

THE CANTER'S DICTIONARY

autem, a church
autem mort, a married woman
bung, a purse
bord, a shilling
half a bord, sixpence
booze, drink
boozing ken, an alehouse
bene, good
beneship, very good
bufe, a dog
bing awast, get you hence
caster, a cloak
a commission, a shirt
chates, the gallows
to cly the jerk, to be whipped
to cut, to speak
to cut bene, to speak gently
to cut bene whids, to speak good words
to cut queer whids, to give evil language
to cant, to speak
to couch a hogshead, to lie down asleep
drawers, hosen[6]
duds, clothes
darkmans, the night
Deuce-a-ville, the country
dup the jigger, open the door
fambles, hands
fambling cheat, a ring
flag, a groat[7]
glaziers, eyes
gan, a mouth
gage, a quart pot
grannam, corn
gybe, a writing
glimmer, fire
jigger, a door
gentry mort, a gentlewoman
gentry cofe's ken, a nobleman's house
harman beck, a constable
harmans, the stocks
heave a bough, rob a booth
jark, a seal
ken, a house
lag of duds, a buck of clothes

libbege, a bed
lower, money
lap, butter, milk or whey
libken, a house to lie in
lag, water
lightmans, the day
mint, gold
a make, a halfpenny
Margery prater, a hen
maunding, asking
to mill, to steal
mill a ken, rob a house
nosegent, a nun
niggling, companying a woman
prat, a buttock
peck, meat
poplars, pottage
prancer, a horse
prigging, riding
patrico, a priest
pad, a way
quaroms, a body
ruff peck, bacon
Roger or Tib of the buttery, a goose
Romeville, London
Rome booze, wine
Rome mort, a queen
ruffmans, the woods or bushes
Ruffian, the Devil
stamps, legs
stampers, shoes
slate, a sheet
skew, a cup
Solomon, the Mass
stuling ken, a house to receive stolen goods
skipper, a barn
strommel, straw
smelling cheat, an orchard or garden
to scour the cramp-ring, to wear bolts
stalling, making or ordaining
trining, hanging
to tower, to see
win, a penny
yarum, milk

And thus have I builded up a little mint where you may coin words for your pleasure. The payment of this was a debt, for the Bellman at his farewell in his first round which he walked promised so much. If he keep not touch by tendering the due sum, he

6. Leggings or stockings.   7. A coin valued at four pence.

desires forbearance and if any that is more rich in this canting commodity will lend him any more or any better he will pay his love double. In the meantime receive this and, to give it a little more weight, you shall have a canting song wherein you may learn how this cursed generation pray or, to speak truth, curse such officers as punish them.

A CANTING SONG

The Ruffian cly the nab of the harman beck!
If we maund pannam, lap or ruff peck
Or poplars of yarum, he cuts "Bing to the ruffmans!"
Or else he swears by the lightmans
5 To put our stamps in the harmans.
The Ruffian cly the ghost of the harman beck!
If we heave a booth we cly the jerk.

If we niggle or mill a boozing ken
Or nip a bung that has but a win,
10 Or dup the jigger of a gentry cofe's ken,
To the queer cuffin we bing
And then to the queer ken to scour the cramp-ring,
And then to be trined on the chates in the lightmans.
The bube and Ruffian cly the harman beck and harmans!

THUS ENGLISHED

The Devil take the Constable's head!
If we beg bacon, buttermilk or bread
Or pottage, "To the hedge!" he bids us hie
Or wears "by this light!" i' th' stocks we shall lie.
5 The Devil haunt the Constable's ghost!
If we rob but a booth we are whipped at a post.

If an alehouse we rob or be ta'en with a whore
Or cut a purse that has just a penny and no more
Or come but stealing in at a gentleman's door,
10 To the Justice straight we go
And then to the gaol to be shackled, and so
To be hanged on the gallows i' th' day-time. The pox
And the Devil take the Constable and his stocks!

We have canted, I fear, too much. Let us now give ear to the Bellman and hear what he speaks in English.

Thomas Deloney
from *Thomas of Reading*[1]

How Simon's wife of Southampton, being wholly bent to pride and pleasure, requested her husband to see London, which being granted, how she got good wife Sutton of Salis-

1. Thomas Nashe wrote of Thomas Deloney (1543?–1600?), "the ballading silk-weaver of Norwich hath rhyme enough for all miracles, and wit to make a 'Garland of Good Will' . . . his Muse from the first peeping forth hath stood at livery at an ale-house wisp, never exceeding a penny a quart a day nor night." Born in London, Thomas Deloney was a silk weaver but also became a popular writer of comical and historical ballads; he also wrote broadsides on contemporary events, such as *The Queen's Visiting the Camp at Tilsburie*. Most of his works have not survived. He is best known for three prose works: *The Gentle Craft* (1597), *Jack of Newbury, the Famous and Worthy Clothier of England* (8th edition, 1619), and *Thomas of Reading, or the Six Worthy Yeomen of the West* (c. 1600). In the following selection from this last work, Deloney creates broad comedy from the fascination of a countrywoman with the marvels of shopping in the metropolis. There were numerous editions of *Thomas of Reading*, but the earliest to survive is that of 1612.

bury to go with her, who took Crab to go along with them, and how he prophesied of many things.

The clothiers[2] being all come from London, Simon's wife of Southhampton, who was with her husband very merry and pleasant, brake[3] her mind unto him in this sort.

"Good Lord husband, will you never be so kind as let me go to London with you? Shall I be penned up in Southhampton, like a parrot in a cage, or a capon in a coop? I would request no more of you in lieu of all my pains, cark[4] and care, but to have one week's time to see that fair city: what is this life if it be not mixed with some delight? And what delight is more pleasing than to see the fashions and manners of unknown places? Therefore good husband, if thou lovest me, deny not this simple request. You know I am no common gadder,[5] nor have oft troubled you with travel. God knows, this may be the last thing that ever I shall request at your hands."

"Woman," quoth he, "I would willingly satisfy your desire, but you know it is not convenient for both of us to be abroad, our charge is great, and therefore our care ought not to be small. If you will go yourself, one of my men shall go with you, and money enough you shall have in your purse: but to go with you myself, you see my business will not permit me."

"Husband," said she, "I accept your gentle offer, and it may be I shall entreat my gossip[6] Sutton to go along with me."

"I shall be glad," quoth her husband, "prepare yourself when you will."

When she had obtained this license, she sent her man Weasell to Salisbury to know of good wife Sutton if she would keep her company to London. Sutton's wife being as willing to go, as she was to request, never rested till she had gotten leave of her husband; the which when she had obtained, casting in her mind their pleasure would be small, being but they twain; thereupon the wily woman sent letter by choleric[7] Crab her man, both to Graye's wife and Fitzallen's wife, that they would meet them at Reading; who liking well of the match, consented and did so provide that they met according to promise at Reading, and from thence with Cole's wife they went all together, with each of them a man to London, each one taking up a lodging with a several friend.

When the merchants of London understood they were in town, they invited them every day home to their own houses, where they had delicate good cheer: and when they went abroad to see the commodities of the city, the merchant's wives ever bore them company, being attired most dainty and fine: which when the clothier's wives did see, it grieved their hearts they had not the like.

Now when they were brought into Cheapside, there with great wonder they beheld the shops of the goldsmiths; and on the other side, the wealthy mercers,[8] whose shops shined of all sorts of colored silks; in Watling Street, they viewed the great number of drapers[9]; in Saint Martin's, shoemakers; at Saint Nicholas church, the flesh shambles[1]; at the end of the old change, the fishmongers; in Candlewick Street the weavers; then came into the Jew's Street, where all the Jews did inhabit; then went they to Blackwell Hall, where the country clothiers did use to meet.

Afterward they proceeded, and came to Saint Paul's church, whose steeple was so high that it seemed to pierce the clouds, on the top whereof was a great and mighty weathercock of clean silver, the which notwithstanding seemed as small as a

---

2. Makers and sellers of woolen cloth.
3. Opened.
4. Trouble, anxiety.
5. One who wanders from place to place.
6. Friend.

7. Irascible.
8. Dealers in silks, velvets, and other expensive fabrics.
9. Cloth merchants.
1. Slaughterhouse for meat, a place where meat was sold.

sparrow to men's eyes, it stood so exceeding high, the which goodly weathercock was afterwards stolen away by a cunning cripple, who found means one night to climb up to the top of the steeple, and took it down, with the which, and a great sum of money which he had got together by begging in his lifetime, he built a gate on the Northwest side of the city, which to this day is called Cripple Gate.

From thence they went to the Tower of London, which was built by Julius Caesar, who was emperor of Rome. And there they beheld salt and wine, which had lain there ever since the Romans invaded this land, which was many years before our Savior Christ was born, the wine was grown so thick that it might have been cut like a jelly. And in that place also they saw money that was made of leather, which in ancient time went current amongst the people.

When they had to their great contentation[2] beheld all this, they repaired to their lodgings, having also a sumptuous supper ordained for them, with all delight that might be. And you shall understand that when the country weavers, which came up with their dames, saw the weavers of Candlewick Street, they had great desire presently to have some conference with them, and thus one began to challenge the other for workmanship.

Quoth Weasell, "I'll work with any of you all for a crown, take it if you dare, and he that makes his yard of cloth soonest, shall have it."

"You shall be wrought withall," said the other, "and if it were for ten crowns; but we will make this bargain, that each of us shall wind their own quills."[3]

"Content," quoth Weasell.

And so to work they went, but Weasell lost. Whereupon another of them took the matter in hand, who lost likewise: so that the London weavers triumphed against the country, casting forth diverse frumps.[4]

"Alas, poor fellows," quoth they, "your hearts are good, but your hands are ill."

"Tush, the fault was in their legs," quoth another, "pray you friend, were you not born at home?"[5]

"Why do you ask?" quoth Weasell.

"Because," said he, "the biggest place of your leg is next to your shoe."

Crab hearing this, being choleric of nature, chafed like a man of law at the bar, and he wagers with them four crowns to twain,[6] the others agreed, to work they go: but Crab conquered them all. Whereupon the London weavers were nipped in the head like birds, and had not a word to say.

"Now," saith Crab, "as we have lost nothing, so you have won nothing, and because I know ye cannot be right weavers, except you be good fellows, therefore if you will go with us, we will bestow the ale upon you."

"That is spoken like a good fellow and like a weaver," quoth the other. So along they went as it were to the sign of the red cross.

When they were set down, and had drunk well, they began merrily to prattle and to extol Crab to the skies. Whereupon Crab protested that he would come and dwell among them.

"Nay, that must not be," said a London weaver. "The king hath given us privilege, that none shall live among us, but such as serve seven years in London."

With that Crab, according to his old manner of prophesying, said thus:

---

2. Contentment.

3. Bobbins or spools.

4. Jeers, derisive snorts.

5. A slighting reference to the lowly origins of the

provincial weavers, described as peasants with thick ankles.

6. A crown was a coin valued at five shillings; "twain": two.

"The day is very near at hand,
When as a king of this fair land
Shall privilege you more than so:
Then weavers shall in scarlet go.[7]

5   And to one brotherhood be brought,
The first that is in London wrought,
When other tradesmen by your fame,
Shall covet all to do the same.

Then shall you all live wondrous well,
10   But this one thing I shall you tell:
The day will come before the doom,
In Candlewick Street shall stand no loom.

Nor any weaver dwelling there,
But men that shall more credit bear:
15   For clothing shall be sore decayed,
And men undone that use that trade.

And yet the day some men shall see,
This trade again shall raised be,
When as bailiff of Sarum town,
20   Shall buy and purchase Bishop's down.

When there never man did sow,
Great store of goodly corn shall grow;
And woad,° that makes all colors sound   *blue dye*
Shall spring upon that barren ground.

25   At that same day I tell you plain,
Who so alive doth then remain,
A proper maiden there shall see,
Within the town of Salisbury.

Of favor sweet, of nature kind,
30   With goodly eyes, and yet stark blind,
This poor blind maiden I do say,
In age shall go in rich array.

And he that takes her to his wife
Shall lead a joyful happy life,
35   The wealthiest clothier shall he be,
That ever was in that country.

But clothing kept as it hath been
In London never shall be seen:
For weavers then the most shall win,
40   That work for clothing next the skin.

7. High rank was signified by an official scarlet robe.

Till pride the commonwealth doth peel,°   *exhaust*
And causeth housewives leave their wheel.°   *spinning wheel*
Then poverty upon each side
Unto those workmen shall betide.

45   At that time, from an eagle's nest,
That proudly built in the west,
A sort shall come with cunning hand.
To bring strange weaving in this land.

And by their gains that great will fall,
50   They shall maintain the weaver's hall:
But long they shall not flourish so,
But folly will them overthrow.

And men shall count it mickle° shame,   *much*
To bear that kind of weaver's name,
55   And this as sure will come to pass,
As here is ale within this glass."

When the silly souls that sat about him heard him speak in this sort, they admired and honored Crab for the same.

"Why my masters," said Weasell, "do you wonder at these words? He will tell you twenty of these tales, for which cause we call him our canvas prophet."

"His attire fits his title," said they, "and we never heard the like in our lives; and if this should be true, it would be strange."

"Doubt not but it will be true," quoth Weasell, "for I'll tell you what, he did but once see our Nick kiss Nel, and presently he powered out this rhyme.

That kiss, O Nel, God give thee joy,
Will nine months hence breed thee a boy.

"And I'll tell you what, you shall hear: we kept reckoning and it fell out as just as Jone's buttocks on a close stool, for which cause, our maids durst never kiss a man in his sight."

Upon this they broke company and went every one about his business, the London weavers to their frames and the country fellows to their dames, who after their great banqueting and merriment went every one home to their own houses, though with less money than they brought out, yet with more pride.

Especially Simon's wife of Southampton, who told the rest of her gossips that she saw no reason but that their husbands should maintain them as well as the merchants did their wives: "for I tell you what," quoth she, "we are as proper women (in my conceit) as the proudest of them all, as handsome of body, as fair of face, our legs as well made, and our feet as fine: then what reason is there (seeing our husbands are of as good wealth) but we should be as well maintained?"

"You say true, gossip," said Sutton's wife: "trust me, it made me blush, to see them brave it out so gallantly, and we to go so homely."

"But before God," said the other, "I will have my husband to buy me a London gown, or in faith he shall have little quiet."

"So shall mine," said another.

"And mine too," quoth the third.

And all of them sung the same note: so that when they came home, their husbands had no little to do.

Especially Simon, whose wife daily lay at him for London apparel, to whom he said, "Good woman, be content, let us go according to our place and ability: what will the bailiffs think, if I should prank thee up like a peacock, and thou in thy attire surpass their wives? They would either think I were mad, or else that I had more money than I could well use: consider I pray thee, good wife, that such as are in their youth wasters do prove in their age stark beggars.

"Beside that, it is enough to raise me up in the King's books:[8] for many times, men's coffers are judged by their garments. Why, we are country folks and must keep ourselves in good compass: gray russet and good homespun cloth doth best become us; I tell thee, wife, it were as undecent for us to go like Londoners as it is for Londoners to go like courtiers."

"What a coil keep you,"[9] quoth she. "Are not we God's creatures as well as Londoners? And the King's subjects, as well as they? Then finding our wealth to be as good as theirs, why should we not go as gay as Londoners? No, husband, no, here is the fault, we are kept without it, only because our husbands are not so kind as Londoners: why, man, a cobbler there keeps his wife better than the best clothier in this country: nay, I will affirm it, that the London oyster-wives, and the very kitchen-stuff criers,[1] do exceed us in their Sunday's attire: nay, more than that, I did see the water-bearer's wife which belongs to one of our merchants, come in with a tankard of water on her shoulder, and yet half a dozen gold rings on her fingers."

"You may think, wife," quoth he, "she got them not with idleness.

"But, wife, you must consider what London is, the chief and capital city of all the land, a place on the which all strangers cast their eyes. It is, wife, the King's chamber and his Majesty's royal seat: to that city repairs all nations under heaven. Therefore it is most meet and convenient that the citizens of such a city should not go in their apparel like peasants but, for the credit of our country, wear such seemly habits as do carry gravity and comeliness in the eyes of all beholders."

"But if we of the country went so," quoth she, "were it not as great credit for the land as the other?"

"Woman," quoth her husband, "it is altogether needless, and in diverse respects it may not be."

"Why then I pray you," quoth she, "let us go dwell at London."

"A word soon spoken," said her husband, "but not so easy to be performed: therefore, wife, I pray thee hold thy prating, for thy talk is foolish."

"Yea, yea, husband, your old churlish[2] conditions will never be left, you keep me here like a drudge and a droil,[3] and so you may keep your money in your purse. You care not for your credit, but before I will go so like a shepherdess, I will first go naked: and I tell you plain, I scorn it greatly that you should clap a gray gown on my back as if I had not brought you two pence. Before I was married, you swore I should have any thing that I requested, but now all is forgotten."

8. Taxation lists.
9. What a fuss you're making.
1. Hawkers, sellers of goods.

2. Grudging.
3. A servant.

And in saying this, she went in, and soon after she was so sick that needs she must go to bed: and when she was laid, she drave[4] out that night with many grievous groans, sighing and sobbing, and no rest she could take God wot.[5] And in the morning when she should rise, the good soul fell down in a swoon, which put her maidens in a great fright, who, running down to their master, cried out, "Alas, alas, our dame[6] is dead, our dame is dead."

The good man, hearing this, ran up in all haste, and there fell to rubbing and chafing of her temples, sending for *aqua vitae*, and saying, "Ah my sweet heart, speak to me, good wife, alack, alack, call in the neighbors, you queans,[7]" quoth he.

With that she lift up her head, fetching a great groan, and presently swooned again, and much ado iwis,[8] he had to keep life in her. But when she was come to herself, "How dost thou wife?" quoth he. "What wilt thou have? For God's sake, tell me if thou hast a mind to any thing, thou shalt have it."

"Away, dissembler," quoth she, "how can I believe thee? Thou hast said as much to me an hundred times, and deceived me, it is thy churlishness that hath killed my heart, never was woman matched to so unkind a man."

"Nay good wife, blame me not without cause; God knoweth how dearly I love thee."

"Love me! no, no, thou didst never carry my love but on the tip of thy tongue," quoth she, "I dare swear thou desirest nothing so much as my death, and for my part, I would to God thou hadst thy desire. But be content, I shall not trouble thee long," and with that fetching a sigh, she swooned and gave a great groan.

The man, seeing her in this case was wondrous woe. But so soon as they had recovered her he said, "O my dear wife, if any bad conceit hath engendered this sickness, let me know it; or if thou knowest any thing that may procure thy health, let me understand thereof, and I protest thou shalt have it, if it cost me all that ever I have."

"O husband," quoth she, "how may I credit your words, when for a paltry suit of apparel you denied me?"

"Well, wife, quoth he, "thou shalt have apparel or any thing else thou wilt request, if God send thee once health."

"O husband, if I may find you so kind, I shall think myself the happiest woman in the world; thy words have greatly comforted my heart, me thinketh if I had it, I could drink a good draught of Rhenish wine."

Well, wine was sent for.

"O Lord," said she, "that I had a piece of chicken, I feel my stomach desirous of some meat."

"Glad am I of that," said her husband, and so the woman within a few days after was very well.

But you shall understand that her husband was fain to dress her London-like ere he could get her quiet, neither would it please her, except the stuff were bought in Cheapside, for out of Cheapside nothing could content her, were it never so good: insomuch, that if she thought a tailor of Cheapside made not her gown, she would swear it was quite spoiled.

And having thus won her husband to her will, when the rest of the clothiers' wives heard thereof, they would be suited in the like sort too: so that ever since, the wives of Southampton, Salisbury, of Gloucester, Worcester, and Reading, went all as gallant and as brave as any Londoners' wives.

---

4. Drove.
5. Knows.
6. Lady.

7. Bold women, hussies.
8. Certainly.

Thomas Nashe
from *Pierce Penniless*[1]

That state or kingdom that is in league with all the world, and hath no foreign sword to vex it, is not half so strong or confirmed to endure, as that which lives every hour in fear of invasion. There is a certain waste of the people for whom there is no use, but war: and these men must have some employment still to cut them off. *Nam si foras hostem non habent, domi invenient.*[2] If they have no service abroad, they will make mutinies at home. Or if the affairs of the state be such, as cannot exhale all these corrupt excrements, it is very expedient they have some light toys to busy their heads withall, cast before them as bones to gnaw upon, which may keep them from having leisure to intermeddle with higher matters.

To this effect, the policy of plays is very necessary, howsoever some shallow-brained censurers (not the deepest searchers into the secrets of government) mightily oppugn[3] them. For whereas the afternoon being the idlest time of the day; wherein men that are their own masters (as gentlemen of the court, the inns of the court,[4] and the number of captains and soldiers about London) do wholly bestow themselves upon pleasure, and that pleasure they divide (how virtuously it skills not) either into gaming, following of harlots, drinking, or seeing a play: is it not then better (since of four extremes all the world cannot keep them but they will choose one) that they should betake them to the least, which is plays? Nay, what if I prove plays to be no extreme; but a rare exercise of virtue? First, for the subject of them (for the most part) it is borrowed out of our English chronicles, wherein our forefathers' valiant acts (that have lain long buried in rusty brass and worm-eaten books) are revived, and they themselves raised from the grave of oblivion and brought to plead their aged honors in open presence: than which, what can be a sharper reproof to these degenerate effeminate days of ours?

How would it have joyed brave Talbot (the terror of the French)[5] to think that after he had lain two hundred years in his tomb, he should triumph again on the stage, and have his bones new embalmed with the tears of ten thousand spectators at least (at several times), who, in the tragedian that represents his person, imagine they behold him fresh bleeding.

I will defend it against any collian[6] or clubfisted usurer of them all, there is no immortality can be given a man on earth like unto plays. What talk I to them of immortality, that are the only underminers of honor and do envy any man that is not sprung up by base brokery[7] like themselves? They care not if all the ancient houses

1. One of the most brilliant comic writers in the English language, Thomas Nashe (1567–1601) was a master satirist. After education at Cambridge, he came to London in 1588 to make a living as a writer. He first attracted attention for his invective against pseudo-poets and puritan reformers in *The Anatomie of Abuses* (1589). In his greatest satire *Pierce Penniless his Supplication to the Divell* (1592), Nashe exposed every kind of hypocrisy and deceit in contemporary society. This work proved a great popular success; it was reprinted six times within its first year. Among the objects of Nashe's satire was the pedantic and vindictive Gabriel Harvey, who quickly counterattacked by portraying Nashe as a boor and an academic failure. The Harvey-Nashe pamphlet war raged on until 1599, when the Archbishop of Canterbury ordered that "all Nashe's books and Harvey's books be taken wheresoever they may be, and that none of the same books be ever printed hereafter." Nashe also wrote an entertaining

parodic romance, *The Unfortunate Traveller*, whose realism has been compared to Defoe's novels. Nashe not only enjoyed the theater and befriended actors and playwrights but even cowrote the now lost play *The Isle of Dogs* with Ben Jonson. The following passage from *Pierce Penniless* shows Nashe's familiarity with the world of the theater and the realistic description that is the satirist's great skill.
2. Literally, "If they have no enemy abroad, they will find one at home."
3. Oppose.
4. The law schools of England.
5. For "fighting Talbot the terror of the French," see Shakespeare's *The First Part of King Henry VI* (1590), on Henry VI's war against France.
6. Cullion, from French *couillon*, testicle; a base person, a rascal.
7. Rascally dealing or trafficking.

were rooted out, so that, like the burgomasters of the Low-countries,[8] they might share the government amongst them as states, and be quartermasters[9] of our monarchy. All arts to them are vanity: and, if you tell them what a glorious thing it is to have Henry the Fifth represented on the stage, leading the French King prisoner, and forcing both him and the Dolphin to swear fealty, I, but (will they say) what do we get by it?[1] Respecting neither the right of fame that is due to true nobility deceased, nor what hopes of eternity are to be proposed to adventurous minds, to encourage them forward, but only their execrable lucre, and filthy unquenchable avarice.

They know when they are dead they shall not be brought upon the stage for any goodness, but in merriment of the usurer and the devil, or buying arms of the herald, who gives them the lion, without tongue, tail, or talents, because his master whom he must serve is a townsman, and a man of peace, and must not keep any quarreling beasts to annoy his honest neighbors.

In plays, all cozenages,[2] all cunning drifts overguiled with outward holiness, all strategems of war, all the cankerworms that breed on the rust of peace, are most lively anatomized: they show the ill success of treason, the fall of hasty climbers, the wretched end of usurpers, the misery of civil dissension, and how just God is evermore in punishing of murder. And to prove every one of these allegations, could I propound the circumstances of this play and that play, if I meant to handle this theme otherwise than *obiter*.[3] What should I say more? They are sour pills of reprehension, wrapt up in sweet words. Whereas some petitioners of the council against them object, they corrupt the youth of the city, and withdraw prentises from their work; they heartily wish they might be troubled with none of their youth nor their prentises; for some of them (I mean the ruder handicrafts servants) never come abroad, but they are in danger of undoing: and as for corrupting them when they come, that's false; for no play they have, encourageth any man to tumults or rebellion, but lays before such the halter and the gallows; or praiseth or approveth pride, lust, whoredom, prodigality, or drunkenness, but beats them down utterly. As for the hindrance of trades and traders of the city by them, that is an article foisted in by the vintners, alewives, and victuallers, who surmise, if there were no plays, they should have all the company that resort to them, lie boozing and beer-bathing in their houses every afternoon. Nor so, nor so, good brother bottle-ale, for there are other places besides where money can bestow itself: the sign of the smock will wipe your mouth clean: and yet I have heard ye have made her a tenant to your tap-houses. But what shall he do that hath spent himself? where shall he haunt? Faith, when dice, lust, and drunkenness, and all have dealt upon him, if there be never a play for him to go to for his penny, he sits melancholy in his chamber, devising upon felony or treason, and how he may best exalt himself by mischief.

In Augustus's time[4] (who was the patron of all witty sports) there happened a great fray in Rome about a player, insomuch as all the city was in an uproar: whereupon the emperor (after the broil was somewhat overblown) called the player before him, and asked what was the reason that a man of his quality durst presume to make such a brawl about nothing. He smilingly replied, "It is good for thee, O Caesar, that the people's heads are troubled with brawls and quarrels about us and our light matters: for otherwise they would look into thee and thy matters." Read Lipsius or any

---

8. Chief magistrates of Dutch towns.
9. Petty officers who steer the ship.
1. See Shakespeare's *Henry V*.
2. Tricks.

3. In passing.
4. Augustus (63 B.C.–16 A.D.) was the grandnephew of Julius Caesar and first Roman Emperor.

profane or Christian politician, and you shall find him of this opinion.[5] Our players are not as the players beyond sea, a sort of squirting bawdy comedians, that have whores and common courtesans to play women's parts, and forbear no immodest speech or unchaste action that may procure laughter;[6] but our scene is more stately furnished than ever it was in the time of Roscius,[7] our representations honorable, and full of gallant resolution, not consisting, like theirs of a pantaloon, a whore, and a zany,[8] but of emperors, kings, and princes; whose true tragedies (*Sophocleo cothurno*[9]) they do vaunt.

Not Roscius nor Aesop, those admired tragedians that have lived ever since before Christ was born, could ever perform more in action than famous Ned Allen.[1] I must accuse our poets of sloth and partiality, that they will not boast in large impressions what worthy men (above all nations) England affords. Other countries cannot have a fiddler break a string but they will put it in print, and the old Romans in the writings they published, thought scorn to use any but domestical examples of their own home-bred actors, scholars, and champions, and them they would extol to the third and fouth generation: cobblers, tinkers, fencers, none escaped them, but they mingled them all in one gallimaufry of glory.

Here I have used a like method, not of tying myself to mine own country, but by insisting in the experience of our time: and, if I ever write any thing in Latin (as I hope one day I shall), not a man of any desert here amongst us, but I will have up. Tarlton, Ned Allen, Knell, Bentley[2] shall be made known to France, Spain, and Italy: and not a part that they surmounted in, more than other, but I will there note and set down, with the manner of their habits and attire.

King James I
from *A Counterblast to Tobacco*[1]

That the manifold abuses of this vile custom of tobacco taking may the better be espied, it is fit that first you enter into consideration both of the first original thereof, and likewise of the reasons of the first entry thereof into this country. For certainly as such customs that have their first institution either from a godly, necessary, or honorable ground, and are first brought in by the means of some worthy, virtuous, and great personage, are ever, and most justly, holden in great and reverent estima-

5. Justus Lipsius (1547–1606) was a Flemish humanist who wrote on politics, edited Latin texts, and revived Stoicism.
6. Women played roles in the Renaissance Italian *commedia dell'arte*, but in Elizabethan and Jacobean times English players were all male.
7. Quintus Roscius (126–62 B.C.) was a famous Roman actor.
8. Stock *commedia dell'arte* characters: the pantaloon was a lean, foolish old man wearing pantaloons, and the zany was a servant who acted as a clown.
9. By the Sophoclean boot. Sophocles (496–c.406 B.C.), Greek tragic poet; "cothurnus," a high Greek boot worn by tragic actors.
1. A renowned English actor.
2. All English actors. Richard Tarlton (d. 1588) was well known for his jokes and jigs.
1. James I (1566–1625), the son of Mary Queen of Scots, became King of Scotland in 1567 and King of England in 1603. His tutor was the great Scots humanist George Buchanan, from whom the young prince learned a love of scholarship and literature. James wrote poetry and literary

theory in addition to political works like *The True Law of Free Monarchy* (1598), an argument in favor of the divine right of kings, and *Basilikon Doron* (1599), on the art of government. Though the loose mores of his own court allowed for his affair with Robert Carr and other favorites as well as the dalliances of Carr's wife Lady Frances Howard, who "played her pranks as the toy took her in the head," James asserted a strict control over his subjects, both economically and morally. This extract from *A Counterblast to Tobacco* (1616) asserts the corrupting effects of the new import from the Americas. In his *Commisso Pro Tobacco* (1604), James had actually imposed fines on merchants who brought tobacco into England. In this text, James argued that while "the better sort" used tobacco "only as physicke to preserve health" (in fact, as a cure for venereal disease), "a number of riotous and disordered persons of mean and base condition . . . do spend most of their time in that idle vanitie to the evil and corrupting of others, and also do consume the wages that many of them do get by their labor, wherewith their families should be relieved, not caring at what price they buy that drug."

tion and account, by all wise, virtuous, and temperate spirits: So should it by the contrary, justly bring a great disgrace into that sort of customs, which having their original from base corruption and barbarity, do in like sort, make their first entry into a country, by an inconsiderate and childish affectation of novelty, as is the true case of the first invention of tobacco taking, and of the first entry thereof among us. For tobacco being a common herb, which (though under diverse names) grows almost everywhere, was first found out by some of the barbarous Indians to be a preservative or antidote against the pox,[2] a filthy disease, whereunto these barbarous people are (as all men know) very much subject, what through the uncleanly and adult constitution of their bodies, and what through the intemperate heat of their climate: so that as from them was first brought into Christendom, that most detestable disease, so from them likewise was brought this use of tobacco, as a stinking and unsavory antidote, for so corrupted and execrable a malady, the stinking suffumigation[3] whereof they yet use against that disease, making so one canker or venom to eat out another.

And now good countrymen, let us (I pray you) consider, what honor or policy can move us to imitate the barbarous and beastly manners of the wild, godless, and slavish Indians, especially in so vile and stinking a custom? Shall we that disdain to imitate the manner of our neighbor France (having the style of the first Christian kingdom) and that cannot endure the spirit of the Spaniards (their king being now comparable in largeness of dominions to the great emperor of Turkey). Shall we, I say, that have been so long civil and wealthy in peace, famous and invincible in war, fortunate in both, we that have been ever able to aid any of our neighbors (but never deafed any of their ears with any of our supplications for assistance) shall we, I say, without blushing abase ourselves so far as to imitate these beastly Indians, slaves to the Spaniards, refuse to the world, and as yet aliens from the holy covenant of God? Why do we not as well imitate them in walking naked as they do? In preferring glasses, feathers, and such toys to gold and precious stones as they do? Yea why do we not deny God and adore the devil as they do?

Now to the corrupted baseness of the first use of this tobacco, doeth very well agree the foolish and groundless first entry thereof into this kingdom. It is not so long since the first entry of this abuse amongst us here, as this present age cannot yet very well remember both the first author and the form of the first introduction of it amongst us. It was neither brought in by king, great conqueror, nor learned doctor of physic.

With the report of a great discovery for a conquest, some two or three savage men were brought in, together with the savage custom. But the pity is, the poor wild barbarous men died, but that vile barbarous custom is yet alive, yea in fresh vigor: so as it seems a miracle to me, how a custom springing from so vile a ground, and brought in by a father so generally hated, should be welcomed upon so slender a warrant. For if they that first put it in practice here, had remembered for what respect it was used by them from whence it came, I am sure they would have been loath to have taken so far the imputation of that disease upon them as they did, by using the cure thereof: For *Sanis non est opus medico,*[4] and counterpoisons are never used, but where poison is thought to precede.

---

2. Syphilis.
3. In the medical sense, having fumes (vapors) penetrate

the body for a therapeutic effect.
4. It is not necessary to cure the healthy.

Ben Jonson
1572–1637

Ben Jonson's life was full of changes and contradictions. His earliest biographer, William Drummond, called him "passionately kind and angry, careless either to gain or keep, vindictive, but, if he be well answered, at himself." His father was Protestant, but Jonson turned Catholic, only to recant that conversion later; nevertheless, in his last years he called himself a "beadsman." The stepson of a bricklayer, he became Poet Laureate. He wrote poems of praise to win the patronage of king and court but also skewered their follies in satire. Though often assuming the role of moralist in his poetry and plays, Jonson admitted that as a younger man he was "given to venery" and pleaded guilty to the charge of murder. He was attached to admiring younger poets, "the tribe of Ben," yet he also enjoyed feuds, such as those with fellow dramatists Marston and Dekker. While espousing Horatian spareness and an acute sense of meter in both criticism and poetry, Jonson also had a keen ear for the colloquial language of London.

Indeed, London was one of the few constants in Jonson's turbulent career. Born in Harts-Born Lane near Charing Cross, he was buried in Poets' Corner at Westminster Abbey. Jonson portrayed the city as the world of those who lived by their wits. He dramatized literary infighting in *Every Man Out of His Humour* (1599), greedy schemes in *Volpone* (1606), intellectual confidence scams in *The Alchemist* (1610), and antitheatrical Puritan preaching in *Bartholomew Fair* (1614). The London audience at the Hope Theatre was reported to have exclaimed at a performance of *Bartholomew Fair*: "O rare Ben Jonson!"

Unlike other playwrights of his time (including Shakespeare), Jonson oversaw the publication of his plays, which appeared with his poems in the same deluxe folio volume, entitled *Works* (1616). The assertion of the dignity of popular drama surprised many of his readers, one of whom wrote, "Pray tell me Ben, where doth the mystery lurk, / What others call a play, you call a work?" That Jonson wanted his plays to be read as much as performed can be gathered from the comment printed on the title page of *Every Man Out of His Humour*: "as it was first composed by the author, Ben Jonson, containing more than hath been publicly spoken or acted."

Jonson viewed writing as his profession; he became the first poet in England to earn a living by his art. His achievement was recognized by James I, who made Jonson the first Poet Laureate of England and granted him a pension for life. Before becoming laureate, Jonson depended on a whole string of patrons. With the new Stuart king in power, Jonson was able to use his claim of Scots descent to advantage. He was supported by Esme Stuart Seigneur D'Aubigny (a cousin of King James), to whom he dedicated his first tragedy, *Sejanus* (1603). His patrons included Sir Walter Raleigh and Lady Mary Wroth, to whom he dedicated *The Alchemist*. Jonson's most important break came when he received a commission for a court masque. In 1605 he wrote *The Masque of Blackness* starring the Queen herself. To gain some idea of the extravagance of these masques, consider that in 1617, while 12,000 pounds were spent on the entire administration of Ireland, 4,000 pounds were spent on a single masque, *Pleasure Reconciled to Virtue*. The masques were lavish ventures that required costumes, music, and magnificent scenery, which was designed by Inigo Jones, who introduced the Italian invention of perspective.

If the pursuit of patronage was crucial to Jonson's advancement, his satire of politics and power repeatedly put his career and even his life at risk. In 1603 Jonson was called before the Privy Council for *Sejanus*; the charges included "popery and treason." Jonson's *Epicoene, or the Silent Woman*—which climaxes in the revelation that the silent woman is really a boy—was suppressed because it lampooned a love affair of the King's first cousin, Lady Arabella Stuart. One observer complained of the 1613 *Irish Masque at Court* that it was "no time . . . to exasperate that nation by making ridiculous." Jonson was imprisoned twice for the offense that his plays gave to the powerful—once for the now lost *The Isle of Dogs* (1597) and another time for *Eastward Ho!* (1605), in which he made fun of King James's Scots accent.

Jonson took reckless risks, whose consequences he barely managed to escape. While imprisoned for the murder of Gabriel Spencer in 1598, Jonson became a Catholic. Following his conversion, Jonson pleaded guilty to manslaughter (later calling it the result of a duel) but went free by claiming benefit of clergy. This medieval custom originally allowed clerics to be judged by the bishop's court but, by Jonson's time, permitted anyone who could translate the Latin Bible to go free. Jonson left prison with his belongings confiscated, his thumb branded for the felony, and his reputation marked by his profession of an outlaw religion. Like any other Catholic in Elizabethan England, Jonson could be fined or have his property confiscated for not attending Anglican services. Indeed, he and his wife were interrogated for their nonattendance in 1605; Jonson was also charged with being "a poet, and by fame a seducer of youth to the Popish religion." Threatened again with loss of property and another prison term, Jonson complied with the Court's order that he take instruction in Protestantism.

Not all Jonson's disputes were quite so dangerous. Like the characters in his plays, he enjoyed engaging in the game of vapors, a mock argument, drummed up for the display of wit. He not only engaged in combats of wit with Shakespeare (who acted in *Every Man Out of His Humour*), but also ridiculed Marston and Dekker in what critics call "the War of the Theaters." Jonson's *Every Man Out of His Humour* satirized Marston as a pseudo-intellectual. The same year, Jonson and Dekker collaborated on a play. Two years later, Dekker parodied Jonson as the bombastic Horace, constantly reading his work aloud and expecting praise in *Satiriomastix* (1601). The title of this play means "the whipping of the satirist," and it is full of barbs about Jonson's checkered past—both his imprisonment and his theatrical flops. Dekker called Jonson a "brown-bread mouth-stinker." Jonson responded with a "forced defense" against "base detractors and illiterate apes" in *Poetaster* (1601).

Jonson did have high regard for some of his contemporaries, as they did for him. Among these was John Donne, who wrote commendatory verses for *Volpone* and to whom Jonson wrote "Who shall doubt, Donne, whe'er I a poet be / When I dare send my epigrams to thee?" As an older man, Jonson held court at the Devil Tavern among his fellow poets as self-proclaimed *arbiter bibendi* (master of drinking), whose main object was "Not drinking much, but talking wittily." This vein of wit was carried on by Sir John Suckling's *A Session of Poets* and Herrick's *Prayer for Ben Jonson*. His servant Brome wrote an elegy for him, as did the many men of letters who contributed to *Jonsonius Virbius* ("Jonson Reborn"), the year after his death.

Jonson saw himself as a moral and poetic guide. His satire of moral depravity and intellectual delusion is hysterically funny. His plays include direct criticism of contemporary poetry and drama, contracts with the audience, and self-mockery—a foretaste of the break from realistic conventions in modernism. Jonson's comedies also persuade us that there is no reality without satire; we cannot know the world without laughing at its ridiculousness. The human foibles and obsessions portrayed in his comedies are captured in a language so vivid and oral that it has to be read aloud. Jonson's verse dazzles by concealing its art, allowing conversational words and rhythms to be perfectly wedded to poetic meters. The simplicity and restraint of his language, as in his elegy on the death of his son, are the vehicles for pure music and powerful emotion.

Volpone

Volpone was first performed in the spring of 1606 by the King's Men at the Globe Theatre on the Bankside. The King's Men, an acting troupe that included Shakespeare, produced most of Jonson's plays in the Globe, which they owned. The Globe seated some two thousand spectators of all stations—from aristocrats and prosperous merchants in the boxes to the "groundlings" who stood in the pit in front of the stage. Not only was *Volpone* a success in the public theater, but it was also performed for learned audiences at Oxford and Cambridge.

Volpone combines Jonson's unique blend of learned humanistic allusion and popular colloquial argot. The play conforms to the classical unities of place and time, taking place in Venice on a single day. Jonson drew on Erasmus's *The Praise of Folly* and translations of Lucian's dialogues, which both present mock praise, for Volpone's opening speech praising gold. Lucian had written of a childless rich old man who lived out his life playing with the various scoundrels who were trying to inherit his money. For the beastlike character of these moneygrubbing fools and his wily hero, Jonson drew on both the medieval beast fable and the Italian theatrical tradition of the improvisatory *commedia dell'arte,* with its stock figures of the old dotard and the cuckolded husband. Although the play ostensibly takes place in Italy, the commercial wealth that corrupts almost everyone in the play is as much a representation of London as of Venice. The play is not only about greed but also about manipulation and power, including the deceptive power of theater itself. As Volpone stage-manages his own supposed illness, Jonson satirizes the playwright who cons the audience into believing his illusions.

Volpone went to press in 1607 in quarto; it was published with a few changes in the 1616 folio, which is the basis of the present text. Stage directions and scene divisions have been added by the present editor to add greater clarity to the action.

Volpone; or, The Fox

Dramatis Personae[1]

Volpone, *a magnifico*

Mosca, *his parasite*

Voltore, *an advocate*

Corbaccio, *an old gentleman*

Corvino, *a merchant*

Bonario, *son to Corbaccio*

Sir Politic Would-be, *a knight*

Peregrine, *a gentleman traveler*

Nano, *a dwarf*

Castrone, *a eunuch*

Androgyno, *a hermaphrodite*

Grege (*mob*)

Commandadori (*officers of justice*)

Mercatori (*three merchants*)

Avocatori (*four magistrates*)

Notario (*the register*)

Lady Would-be, *Sir Politic's wife*

Celia, *Corvino's wife*

Servitori (*servants*), two Waiting-women, etc.

The Scene, Venice

The Argument

V *olpone, childless, rich, feigns sick, despairs,*

O *ffers his state to hopes of several heirs,*

L *ies languishing: his parasite receives*

P *resents of all, assures, deludes; then weaves*

O *ther cross plots, which ope themselves, are told.*

N *ew tricks for safety are sought; they thrive: when bold,*

E *ach tempts the other again, and all are sold.°*   enslaved

Prologue

Now, luck yet send us, and a little wit

  Will serve to make our play hit;

1. The characters' names all suggest their natures: in Italian, a *volpone* is an old fox, a sly deceiver; a *magnifico* is a nobleman; a *mosca* is a fly; a *voltore* is a vulture; a *corbaccio* is a large filthy raven; a *corvino* is a crow; *bonario* means good, honest; *politic* means scheming, as in a politic Machiavellian; *peregrine* is a falcon and a traveler; an *androgyno* is a man-woman (Greek); *commendatori* are officers of the court; *mercatori* are merchants; *avocatori* are lawyers; a *notario* is a recorder; *celia* (Latin *caelica*) means heavenly.

(According to the palates of the season)
   Here is rhyme, not empty of reason.
5 *This we were bid to credit from our poet,*
   Whose true scope, if you would know it,
In all his poems still hath been this measure,
   To mix profit with your pleasure;[2]
And not as some, whose throats their envy failing,
10 *Cry hoarsely, All he writes is railing:°*   sarcasm
And when his plays come forth, think they can flout them,
   With saying, he was a year about them.
To this there needs no lie but this his creature,
   Which was two months since no feature;[3]
15 *And though he dares give them five lives to mend it,*
   'Tis known, five weeks fully penned it,
From his own hand, without a co-adjutor,
   Novice, journeyman, or tutor.[4]
Yet thus much I can give you as a token
20 *Of his play's worth, no eggs are broken,*
Nor quaking custards with fierce teeth affrighted,
   Wherewith your rout° are so delighted;   crowd
Nor hales he in a gull° old ends reciting,   fool
   To stop gaps in his loose writing;[5]
25 *With such a deal of monstrous and forced action,*
   As might make Bethlem° a faction: Bedlam: the madhouse
Nor made he his play for jests stolen from each table,
   But makes jests to fit his fable;
And so presents quick comedy refined,
30 *As best critics have designed;*
The laws of time, place, persons he observeth,
   From no needful rule he swerveth.[6]
All gall and copperas° from his ink he draineth,   vitriol
   Only a little salt° remaineth,   wit
35 *Wherewith he'll rub your cheeks, till red, with laughter,*
   They shall look fresh a week after.

Act 1

Scene 1. A Room in Volpone's House

[*Enter Volpone and Mosca.*]

VOLPONE Good morning to the day; and next, my gold!—
    Open the shrine, that I may see my saint.
    [*Mosca withdraws the curtain, and discovers piles of gold, plate, jewels, etc.*]
    Hail the world's soul, and mine! more glad than is
    The teeming earth to see the longed-for sun

---

2. The goal of poetry according to Horace's *Ars Poetica*.
3. The proof that Jonson did not spend a year writing his plays is that *Volpone* ("his creature") did not exist two months ago.
4. A "co-adjutor" was a coauthor, while a "novice" was an apprentice; a "journeyman" was hired as the servant of a master, while a "tutor" revised another's work.

5. This play will not resort to slapstick (throwing eggs, or a custard pie in the face) or to the use of hackneyed proverbs, both popular in the Elizabethan theater.
6. The Aristotelian unities prescribed for drama by Renaissance critics included a period of 24 hours, and one location. Comic characters ("persons") were supposed to be lower- or middle-class.

5   Peep through the horns of the celestial Ram,[7]
       Am I, to view thy splendour darkening his;
       That lying here, amongst my other hoards,
       Shew'st like a flame by night, or like the day
       Struck out of chaos, when all darkness fled
10   Unto the center. O thou son of Sol,[8]
       But brighter than thy father, let me kiss,
       With adoration, thee, and every relic
       Of sacred treasure in this blessed room.
       Well did wise poets, by thy glorious name,
15   Title that age which they would have the best;[9]
       Thou being the best of things, and far transcending
       All style of joy, in children, parents, friends,
       Or any other waking dream on earth:
       Thy looks when they to Venus did ascribe,[1]
20   They should have given her twenty thousand Cupids;
       Such are thy beauties and our loves! Dear saint,
       Riches, the dumb god,[2] that giv'st all men tongues,
       Thou canst do nought, and yet mak'st men do all things;
       The price of souls;[3] even hell, with thee to boot,
25   Is made worth heaven. Thou art virtue, fame,
       Honor, and all things else. Who can get thee,
       He shall be noble valiant, honest, wise—
MOSCA And what he will, sir. Riches are in fortune
       A greater good than wisdom is in nature.
VOLPONE True, my beloved Mosca. Yet I glory
       More in the cunning purchase° of my wealth   *gaining*
       Than in the glad possession, since I gain
       No common way; I use no trade, no venture;
       I wound no earth with plough-shares, fat no beasts
35   To feed the shambles; have no mills for iron,
       Oil, corn, or men, to grind them into powder:
       I blow no subtle glass, expose no ships
       To threat'nings of the furrow-faced sea;
       I turn no monies° in the public bank,   *earn no interest*
40   Nor usure° private.   *make loans*
MOSCA   No, sir, nor devour
       Soft prodigals. You shall have some will swallow
       A melting heir as glibly as your Dutch
       Will pills of butter, and ne'er purge° for it;   *empty the bowels*
       Tear forth the fathers of poor families
45   Out of their beds, and coffin them alive
       In some kind clasping prison, where their bones
       May be forthcoming when the flesh is rotten:
       But your sweet nature doth abhor these courses;
       You loathe the widow's or the orphan's tears

---

7. The sun is in the Ram, or Aries, in mid-April.
8. Comparing gold to God's creation of the day out of
chaos (Genesis 1), when the darkness "retreated to the
underworld." Gold is the son of Sol (Latin "sun"), with a
pun on sol, short for Italian coins, *soldi.*
9. The Golden Age, see Ovid, *Metamorphoses* 1.89–122.

1. "Golden" is an epithet of Venus, goddess of love.
2. The god of riches, Mammon, was called dumb, because
"silence is golden."
3. Human souls were "bought with a price" (1 Corinthians 6.20) by Jesus Christ's sacrifice of his life.

50   Should wash your pavements, or their piteous cries
        Ring in your roofs, and beat the air for vengeance.
VOLPONE Right, Mosca; I do loathe it.
MOSCA   And besides, sir,
        You are not like the thresher that doth stand
        With a huge flail, watching a heap of corn,
55   And, hungry, dares not taste the smallest grain,
        But feeds on mallows and such bitter herbs;
        Nor like the merchant, who hath filled his vaults
        With Romagnia and rich Candian wines,
        Yet drinks the lees° of Lombard's vinegar:[4]   dregs
60   You will lie not in straw, whilst moths and worms
        Feed on your sumptuous hangings and soft beds;
        You know the use of riches, and dare give now
        From that bright heap, to me, your poor observer,
        Or to your dwarf, or your hermaphrodite,
65   Your eunuch, or what other household trifle
        Your pleasure allows maintenance—
VOLPONE   Hold thee, Mosca, [*Gives him money.*]
        Take of my hand; thou strik'st on truth in all,
        And they are envious term thee parasite.
        Call forth my dwarf, my eunuch, and my fool,
70   And let them make me sport. [*Exit Mosca.*] What should I do,
        But cocker up° my genius, and live free   indulge
        To all delights my fortune calls me to?
        I have no wife, no parent, child, ally,
        To give my substance to; but whom I make
75   Must be my heir: and this makes men observe me:
        This draws new clients daily to my house,
        Women and men of every sex and age,
        That bring me presents, send me plate, coin, jewels,
        With hope that when I die (which they expect
80   Each greedy minute) it shall then return
        Ten-fold upon them; whilst some, covetous
        Above the rest, seek to engross° me whole,   monopolize
        And counter-work the one unto the other,
        Contend in gifts, as they would seem in love:
85   All which I suffer, playing with their hopes,
        And am content to coin them into profit,
        And look upon their kindness, and take more,
        And look on that; still bearing them in hand,°   leading them on
        Letting the cherry knock against their lips,
90   And draw it by their mouths, and back again.[5]—
        How now!

                         Scene 2

    [*Reenter Mosca with Nano, Androgyno, and Castrone.*]
NANO *Now, room for fresh gamesters, who do will you to know,*

---

4. Romagnia was a sweet Greek wine; Candian was a Cre-   5. As in the game of bobbing for cherries.
tan wine. Italian wine was considered inferior.

They do bring you neither play nor university show;
And therefore do entreat you, that whatsoever they rehearse,
May not fare a whit the worse, for the false pace of the verse.[6]
5 If you wonder at this, you will wonder more ere we pass,
For know, here is enclosed the soul of Pythagoras,[7]
That juggler divine, as hereafter shall follow;
Which soul, fast and loose, sir, came first from Apollo,
And was breathed into Aethalides,[8] Mercurius his son,
10 Where it had the gift to remember all that ever was done.
From thence it fled forth, and made quick transmigration
To goldly-locked Euphorbus,[9] who was killed in good fashion,
At the siege of old Troy, by the cuckold of Sparta.[1]
Hermotimus was next (I find it in my charta)
15 To whom it did pass, where no sooner it was missing
But with one Pyrrhus of Delos it learned to go a fishing;
And thence did it enter the sophist of Greece.[2]
From Pythagore, she went into a beautiful piece,
Hight Aspasia, the meretrix;[3] and the next toss of her
20 Was again of a whore, she became a philosopher,
Crates the cynick, as it self doth relate it:
Since kings, knights, and beggars, knaves, lords, and fools gat it,
Besides ox and ass, camel, mule, goat, and brock,[4]
In all which it hath spoke, as in the cobler's cock.[5]
25 But I come not here to discourse of that matter,
Or his one, two, or three, or his great oath, By Quater![6]
His musics, his trigon, his golden thigh,
Or his telling how elements shift, but I
Would ask, how of late thou hast suffered translation,
30 And shifted thy coat in these days of reformation.
ANDROGYNO Like one of the reformed, a fool, as you see,
Counting all old doctrine heresie.
NANO But not on thine own forbid meats hast thou ventured?
ANDROGYNO On fish, when first a Carthusian I entered.[7]
NANO Why, then thy dogmatical silence hath left thee?
ANDROGYNO Of that an obstreperous lawyer bereft me.
NANO O wonderful change, when sir lawyer forsook thee!
For Pythagore's sake, what body then took thee?
ANDROGYNO A good dull mule.
NANO   And how! by that means
40 Thou wert brought to allow of the eating of beans?[8]
ANDROGYNO Yes.

---

6. The irregular meter recalls the four-stress line of the mortality plays.
7. Nano points at Androgyno. Nano's comic story of a divine lineage imitates Diogenes Laertius's life of Pythagoras, an ancient Greek philosopher who developed the theory of the transmigration of souls.
8. Herald of the Argonauts.
9. The Trojan hero who first wounded Patroclus.
1. Menelaus, whose wife went off with Paris.
2. Pythagoras, whose biography includes Hermotimus, a prophet whose soul frequently left his body, and Pyrrhus, a fisherman of Delos.

3. Prostitute; actually Aspasia was simply Pericles' lover.
4. Badger.
5. Lucian's *Gallus* (Cock) is a comic dialogue between a cobbler and a cock that also mocks Pythagoras.
6. "By four." A reference to the Pythagorean theory of the tetrad, by which the first four numbers when added yielded the number 10. Pythagoras, known for his theories of music and geometry, was also said to have a golden thigh.
7. As a Carthusian monk, he ate fish, forbidden to the vegetarian Pythagoreans.
8. Pythagoreans were not allowed to eat beans.

NANO   *But from the mule into whom didst thou pass?*
ANDROGYNO *Into a very strange beast, by some writers called an ass;*
                 By others, a precise, pure, illuminate brother,[9]
                 Of those devour flesh, and sometimes one another;
45   *And will drop you forth a libel, or a sanctified lie,*
                 Betwixt every spoonful of a nativity-pie.
NANO *Now quit thee, for heaven, of that profane nation,*
                 And gently report thy next transmigration.
ANDROGYNO *To the same that I am.*
NANO   *A creature of delight,*
50   *And, what is more than a fool, an hermaphrodite!*
                 Now, prithee, sweet soul, in all thy variation,
                 Which body would'st thou choose, to keep up thy station?
ANDROGYNO *Troth, this I am in: even here would I tarry.*
NANO *'Cause here the delight of each sex thou canst vary?*
ANDROGYNO *Alas, those pleasures be stale and forsaken;*
                 No, 'tis your fool wherewith I am so taken,
                 The only one creature that I can call blessed;
                 For all other forms I have proved most distressed.
NANO *Spoke true, as thou wert in Pythagoras still.*
60   *This learned opinion we celebrate will,*
                 Fellow eunuch, as behoves us, with all our wit and art,
                 To dignify that whereof ourselves are so great and special a part.
VOLPONE Now, very, very pretty! Mosca, this
                 Was thy invention?
MOSCA   If it please my patron,
65   Not else.
VOLPONE   It doth, good Mosca.
MOSCA   Then it was, sir.
         [*Nano and Castrone sing.*]

                 Fools, they are the only nation
                 Worth men's envy or admiration:
                 Free from care of sorrow-taking,
                 Selves and others merry making:
70   *All they speak or do is sterling.*
                 Your fool he is your great man's darling,
                 And your ladies' sport and pleasure;
                 Tongue and bauble are his treasure.
                 E'en his face begetteth laughter,
75   *And he speaks truth free from slaughter;*
                 He's the grace of every feast,
                 And sometimes the chiefest guest;
                 Hath his trencher° and his stool,   dish
                 When wit waits upon the fool.
80   *O, who would not be*
                 He, he, he?   [*Knocking without.*]

---

9. Describing the Puritans, who called each other "brother," as nit-picking and self-righteous, Johnson mocks their aversion to the word Christmas, for which they substituted "nativity."

VOLPONE Who's that? Away! [*Exeunt Nano and Castrone.*]
　　　　　　　　　　Look, Mosca. Fool, begone! [*Exit Androgyno.*]
MOSCA 'Tis signior Voltore, the advocate;
85　　　I know him by his knock.
VOLPONE　　　　　　　　　　Fetch me my gown,
　　　My furs and night-caps; say my couch is changing,
　　　And let him entertain himself awhile
　　　Without i' the gallery. [*Exit Mosca.*] Now, now, my clients
　　　Begin their visitation! Vulture, kite,
90　　　Raven, and gorcrow, all my birds of prey,
　　　That think me turning carcase, now they come;
　　　I am not for them yet—
　　　[*Reenter Mosca, with the gown, etc.*]
　　　　　　　　　　　How now! the news?
MOSCA A piece of plate,° sir.　　　　　　　　　　　　　　　　*silver plater*
VOLPONE　　　　　　　Of what bigness?
MOSCA　　　　　　　　　　　　　　Huge,
　　　Massy, and antique, with your name inscribed,
95　　　And arms engraven.
VOLPONE　　　　　　　Good! and not a fox
　　　Stretched on the earth, with fine delusive sleights,
　　　Mocking a gaping crow?[1] ha, Mosca!
MOSCA　　　　　　　　　　　　Sharp, sir.
VOLPONE Give me my furs. [*Puts on his sick dress.*]
　　　　　　　　　Why dost thou laugh so, man?
MOSCA I cannot choose, sir, when I apprehend
　　　What thoughts he has without now, as he walks:
　　　That this might be the last gift he should give;
　　　That this would fetch you; if you died to-day,
　　　And gave him all, what he should be to-morrow;
105　　　What large return would come of all his ventures;
　　　How he should worshipped be, and reverenced;
　　　Ride with his furs and foot-cloths; waited on
　　　By herds of fools and clients; have clear way
　　　Made for his mule, as lettered as himself;
110　　　Be called the great and learned advocate:
　　　And then concludes, there's nought impossible.
VOLPONE Yes, to be learned, Mosca.
MOSCA　　　　　　　　　　O, no: rich
　　　Implies it. Hood an ass with reverend purple,
　　　So you can hide his two ambitious ears,
115　　　And he shall pass for a cathedral doctor.°　　　　　　　　*of theology*
VOLPONE My caps, my caps, good Mosca. Fetch him in.
MOSCA Stay, sir; your ointment for your eyes.
VOLPONE　　　　　　　　　　　　That's true;
　　　Dispatch,° dispatch: I long to have possession　　　　　　*hurry*
　　　Of my new present.
MOSCA　　　　　　　That, and thousands more,

---

1. Volpone alludes to an animal fable about a fox who played dead to trick a crow.

120   I hope to see you lord of.
VOLPONE   Thanks, kind Mosca.
MOSCA And that, when I am lost in blended dust,
           And hundred such as I am, in succession—
VOLPONE Nay, that were too much, Mosca.
MOSCA   You shall live,
           Still, to delude these harpies.[2]
VOLPONE   Loving Mosca!
125   'Tis well: my pillow now, and let him enter. [*Exit Mosca.*]
           Now, my feigned cough, my phthisic,° and my gout,   asthma
           My apoplexy, palsy, and catarrhs,
           Help, with your forced functions, this my posture,
           Wherein, this three year, I have milked their hopes.
130   He comes; I hear him—Uh! [*Coughing.*] uh! uh! uh! O—

                              Scene 3
[*Reenter Mosca, introducing Voltore, with a piece of plate.*]
MOSCA You still are what you were, sir. Only you,
           Of all the rest, are he commands his love,
           And you do wisely to preserve it thus,
           With early visitation, and kind notes
5   Of your good meaning to him, which, I know,
           Cannot but come most grateful. Patron! sir!
           Here's signior Voltore is come—
VOLPONE [*faintly*]   What say you?
MOSCA Sir, signior Voltore is come this morning
           To visit you.
VOLPONE   I thank him.
MOSCA   And hath brought
10   A piece of antique plate, bought of St. Mark,°   in St. Mark's square
           With which he here presents you.
VOLPONE   He is welcome.
           Pray him to come more often.
MOSCA   Yes.
VOLTORE   What says he?
MOSCA He thanks you, and desires you see him often.
VOLPONE Mosca.
MOSCA   My patron!
VOLPONE   Bring him near, where is he?
15   I long to feel his hand.
MOSCA   The plate is here, sir.
VOLTORE How fare you, sir?
VOLPONE   I thank you, signior Voltore;
           Where is the plate? mine eyes are bad.
VOLTORE [*putting it into his hands*]   I'm sorry
           To see you still thus weak.
MOSCA [*aside*]   That he's not weaker.

2. Monstrous birds of vengeance; hence people who prey upon others.

VOLPONE You are too munificent.

VOLTORE   No, sir; would to heaven,

20   I could as well give health to you, as that plate!

VOLPONE You give, sir, what you can: I thank you. Your love
          Hath taste in this, and shall not be unanswered:
          I pray you see me often.

VOLTORE   Yes, I shall, sir.

VOLPONE Be not far from me.

MOSCA   Do you observe that, sir?

VOLPONE Hearken unto me still; it will concern you.

MOSCA You are a happy man, sir; know your good.

VOLPONE I cannot now last long—

MOSCA   You are his heir, sir.

VOLTORE Am I?

VOLPONE   I feel me going; Uh! uh! uh! uh!
          I'm sailing to my port, Uh! uh! uh! uh!

30   And I am glad I am so near my haven.

MOSCA Alas, kind gentleman! Well, we must all go—

VOLTORE But, Mosca—

MOSCA   Age will conquer.

VOLTORE   'Pray thee, hear me:
          Am I inscribed his heir for certain?

MOSCA   Are you!
          I do beseech you, sir, you will vouchsafe

35   To write me in your family. All my hopes
          Depend upon your worship: I am lost,
          Except the rising sun do shine on me.

VOLTORE It shall both shine and warm thee, Mosca.

MOSCA   Sir,
          I am a man, that hath not done your love

40   All the worst offices:° here I wear your keys,   *duties*
          See all your coffers and your caskets locked,
          Keep the poor inventory of your jewels,
          Your plate and monies; am your steward, sir,
          Husband° your goods here.   *protect*

VOLTORE   But am I sole heir?

MOSCA Without a partner, sir; confirmed this morning:
          The wax is warm yet, and the ink scarce dry
          Upon the parchment.

VOLTORE   Happy, happy me!
          By what good chance, sweet Mosca?

MOSCA   Your desert, sir;
          I know no second cause.

VOLTORE   Thy modesty

50   Is not to know it; well, we shall requite it.

MOSCA He ever liked your course, sir; that first took him.
          I oft have heard him say how he admired
          Men of your large profession, that could speak
          To every cause, and things mere contraries,

55   Till they were hoarse again, yet all be law;

That, with most quick agility, could turn,
And re-return; could make knots, and undo them;
Give forked° counsel; take provoking gold   *equivocal*
On either hand, and put it up:³ these men,
60   He knew, would thrive with their humility.
And for his part, he thought he should be blest
To have his heir of such a suffering spirit,
So wise, so grave, of so perplexed a tongue,
And loud withal, that would not wag, nor scarce
65   Lie still, without a fee; when every word
Your worship but lets fall, is a chequin!⁴—[*Knocking without.*]
Who's that? one knocks; I would not have you seen, sir.
And yet—pretend you came, and went in haste:
I'll fashion an excuse—and, gentle sir,
70   When you do come to swim in golden lard,
Up to the arms in honey, that your chin
Is borne up stiff with fatness of the flood,
Think on your vassal; but remember me:
I have not been your worst of clients.

VOLTORE Mosca!—
MOSCA   When will you have your inventory brought, sir?
Or see a copy of the will?—Anon!⁵—
I'll bring them to you, sir. Away, be gone,
Put business in your face.   [*Exit Voltore.*]
VOLPONE [*springing up*]   Excellent Mosca!
Come hither, let me kiss thee.
MOSCA   Keep you still, sir.
Here is Corbaccio.
VOLPONE   Set the plate away:
The vulture's gone, and the old raven's come!

Scene 4

MOSCA Betake you to your silence, and your sleep.
Stand there and multiply. [*Putting the plate to the rest.*]
                         Now, shall we see
A wretch who is indeed more impotent
Than this can feign to be; yet hopes to hop
5   Over his grave—
[*Enter Corbaccio.*]
                    Signior Corbaccio!
You're very welcome, sir.
CORBACCIO   How does your patron?
MOSCA Troth, as he did, sir; no amends.
CORBACCIO   What! mends he?
MOSCA No, sir: he's rather worse.
CORBACCIO   That's well. Where is he?
MOSCA Upon his couch, sir, newly fall'n asleep.

---

3. Accept money from opposing sides and keep it.   5. A response to the knocking at the door.
4. A gold coin.

CORBACCIO Does he sleep well?

MOSCA   No wink, sir, all this night.
    Nor yesterday; but slumbers.°   *catnaps*

CORBACCIO   Good! he should take
    Some counsel of physicians: I have brought him
    An opiate here, from mine own doctor.

MOSCA He will not hear of drugs.

CORBACCIO   Why? I myself
15   Stood by while it was made, saw all the ingredients:
    And know it cannot but most gently work:
    My life for his, 'tis but to make him sleep.

VOLPONE [*aside*] Ay, his last sleep, if he would take it.

MOSCA   Sir,
    He has no faith in physic.

CORBACCIO   Say you, say you?

MOSCA He has no faith in physic: he does think
    Most of your doctors are the greater danger,
    And worse disease, to escape. I often have
    Heard him protest that your physician
    Should never be his heir.

CORBACCIO   Not I his heir?

MOSCA Not your physician, sir.

CORBACCIO   O, no, no, no,
    I do not mean it.

MOSCA   No, sir, nor their fees
    He cannot brook: he says they flay a man,
    Before they kill him.

CORBACCIO   Right, I do conceive you.

MOSCA And then they do it by experiment;
30   For which the law not only doth absolve them,
    But gives them great reward: and he is loth
    To hire his death, so.

CORBACCIO   It is true, they kill
    With as much license as a judge.

MOSCA   Nay, more;
    For he but kills, sir, where the law condemns,
35   And these can kill him too.

CORBACCIO   Ay, or me;
    Or any man. How does his apoplex?
    Is that strong on him still?

MOSCA   Most violent.
    His speech is broken and his eyes are set,
    His face drawn longer than 'twas wont—

CORBACCIO   How! how!
40   Stronger than he was wont?

MOSCA   No, sir: his face
    Drawn longer than 'twas wont.

CORBACCIO   O, good!

MOSCA   His mouth
    Is ever gaping, and his eyelids hang.

CORBACCIO   Good.
MOSCA A freezing numbness stiffens all his joints,
       And makes the color of his flesh like lead.
CORBACCIO   'Tis good.
MOSCA His pulse beats slow and dull.
CORBACCIO   Good symptoms still.
MOSCA And from his brain—
CORBACCIO   I conceive you; good.
MOSCA Flows a cold sweat, with a continual rheum,
       Forth the resolved corners of his eyes.
CORBACCIO Is't possible? Yet I am better, ha!
50   How does he with the swimming of his head?
MOSCA O, sir, 'tis past the scotomy;° he now   *dizziness*
       Hath lost his feeling, and hath left to snort:
       You hardly can perceive him that he breathes.
CORBACCIO Excellent, excellent! sure I shall outlast him:
       This makes me young again, a score of years.
MOSCA I was a coming for you, sir.
CORBACCIO   Has he made his will?
       What has he given me?
MOSCA   No, sir.
CORBACCIO   Nothing! ha?
MOSCA He has not made his will, sir.
CORBACCIO   Oh, oh, oh!
       What then did Voltore, the lawyer, here?
MOSCA He smelt a carcase, sir, when he but heard
       My master was about his testament;
       As I did urge him to it for your good—
CORBACCIO He came unto him, did he? I thought so.
MOSCA Yes, and presented him this piece of plate.
CORBACCIO To be his heir?
MOSCA   I do not know, sir.
CORBACCIO   True:
       I know it too.
MOSCA [*aside*]   By your own scale, sir.
CORBACCIO   Well,
       I shall prevent him, yet. See, Mosca, look,
       Here, I have brought a bag of bright chequines,
       Will quite weigh down his plate.
MOSCA [*taking the bag*]   Yea, marry, sir.
70   This is true physic, this your sacred medicine;
       No talk of opiates to this great elixir![6]
CORBACCIO 'Tis aurum palpabile, if not potabile.[7]
MOSCA It shall be ministered to him in his bowl.
CORBACCIO Ay, do, do, do.
MOSCA   Most blessed cordial!
75   This will recover him.
CORBACCIO   Yes, do, do, do.

---

6. No sedative can compete with this great medicine.   7. Material gold, if not drinkable, as the elixir was.

MOSCA I think it were not best, sir.
CORBACCIO   What?
MOSCA   To recover him.
CORBACCIO O, no, no, no; by no means.
MOSCA   Why, sir, this
    Will work some strange effect, if he but feel it.
CORBACCIO 'Tis true, therefore forbear; I'll take my venture:
80   Give me it again.
MOSCA   At no hand; pardon me:
    You shall not do yourself that wrong, sir. I
    Will so advise you, you shall have it all.
CORBACCIO How?
MOSCA   All, sir; 'tis your right, your own: no man
    Can claim a part: 'tis yours, without a rival,
85   Decreed by destiny.
CORBACCIO   How, how, good Mosca?
MOSCA I'll tell you, sir. This fit he shall recover.
CORBACCIO I do conceive you.
MOSCA   And, on first advantage
    Of his gained sense, will I re-importune him
    Unto the making of his testament:
90   And shew him this. [*Pointing to the money.*]
CORBACCIO   Good, good.
MOSCA   'Tis better yet,
    If you will hear, sir.
CORBACCIO   Yes, with all my heart.
MOSCA Now would I counsel you, make home with speed;
    There, frame a will; whereto you shall inscribe
    My master your sole heir.
CORBACCIO   And disinherit
95   My son!
MOSCA   O, sir, the better: for that color
    Shall make it much more taking.[8]
CORBACCIO   O, but color?
MOSCA This will, sir, you shall send it unto me.
    Now when I come to inforce, as I will do,
    Your cares, your watchings, and your many prayers,
100   Your more than many gifts, your this day's present,
    And last, produce your will; where, without thought,
    Or least regard, unto your proper issue,
    A son so brave and highly meriting,
105   The stream of your diverted love hath thrown you
    Upon my master, and made him your heir:
    He cannot be so stupid or stone-dead,
    But out of conscience and mere gratitude—
CORBACCIO He must pronounce me his?
MOSCA   'Tis true.
CORBACCIO   This plot

---

8. If it seems that you are disinheriting your son, the trick will be more convincing.

110   Did I think on before.
MOSCA   I do believe it.
CORBACCIO Do you not believe it?
MOSCA   Yes, sir.
CORBACCIO   Mine own project.
MOSCA Which, when he hath done, sir—
CORBACCIO   Published me his heir?
MOSCA And you so certain to survive him—
CORBACCIO   Ay.
MOSCA Being so lusty a man—
CORBACCIO   'Tis true.
MOSCA   Yes, sir—
CORBACCIO I thought on that too. See, how he should be
        The very organ to express my thoughts!
MOSCA You have not only done yourself a good—
CORBACCIO But multiplied it on my son.
MOSCA   'Tis right, sir.
CORBACCIO Still, my invention.
MOSCA   'Las, sir! heaven knows,
120   It hath been all my study, all my care,
        (I e'en grow gray withal), how to work things—
CORBACCIO I do conceive, sweet Mosca.
MOSCA   You are he,
        For whom I labor here.
CORBACCIO   Ay, do, do, do:
        I'll straight about it. [Going.]
MOSCA   Rook go with you, raven!⁹
CORBACCIO I know thee honest.
MOSCA [aside]   You do lie, sir!
CORBACCIO And—
MOSCA Your knowledge is no better than your ears, sir.
CORBACCIO I do not doubt to be a father to thee.
MOSCA Nor I to gull my brother of his blessing.¹
CORBACCIO I may have my youth restored to me, why not?
MOSCA Your worship is a precious ass!
CORBACCIO   What say'st thou?
MOSCA I do desire your worship to make haste, sir.
CORBACCIO 'Tis done, 'tis done; I go. [Exit.]
VOLPONE [leaping from his couch]   O, I shall burst!
        Let out my sides, let out my sides²
MOSCA   Contain
        Your flux of laughter, sir: you know this hope
135   Is such a bait it covers any hook.
VOLPONE O, but thy working, and thy placing it!
        I cannot hold; good rascal, let me kiss thee:
        I never knew thee in so rare a humor.

9. Playing on the secondary meaning of rook, a crowlike
bird: cheat.
1. Mosca refers to Bonario, Corbaccio's son. Jacob robbed
his brother Esau of his blessing (Genesis 27).
2. Loosen my clothes.

MOSCA Alas, sir, I but do as I am taught;
140   Follow your grave instructions; give them words;
        Pour oil° into their ears, and send them hence.   *flattery*
VOLPONE 'Tis true, 'tis true. What a rare punishment
        Is avarice to itself!³
MOSCA   Ay, with our help, sir.
VOLPONE So many cares, so many maladies,
145   So many fears attending on old age,
        Yea, death so often called on, as no wish
        Can be more frequent with them, their limbs faint,
        Their senses dull, their seeing, hearing, going,
        All dead before them; yea, their very teeth,
150   Their instruments of eating, failing them:
        Yet this is reckoned life! nay, here was one
        Is now gone home, that wishes to live longer!
        Feels not his gout, nor palsy; feigns himself
        Younger by scores of years, flatters his age
155   With confident belying it, hopes he may,
        With charms, like Aeson,⁴ have his youth restored:
        And with these thoughts so battens as if fate
        Would be as easily cheated on as he,
        And all turns air! [*Knocking within.*] Who's that there, now? a third!
MOSCA Close, to your couch again; I hear his voice:
        It is Corvino, our spruce merchant.
VOLPONE [*lies down as before*]   Dead.
MOSCA Another bout, sir, with your eyes. [*Anointing them.*] —Who's there?

                              Scene 5

        [*Enter Corvino.*]
        Signior Corvino! come most wished for! O,
        How happy were you, if you knew it, now!
CORVINO Why? what? wherein?
MOSCA   The tardy hour is come, sir.
CORVINO He is not dead?
MOSCA   Not dead, sir, but as good;
        He knows no man.
CORVINO   How shall I do then?
MOSCA   Why, sir?
CORVINO I have brought him here a pearl.
MOSCA   Perhaps he has
        So much remembrance left as to know you, sir:
        He still calls on you; nothing but your name
        Is in his mouth. Is your pearl orient,⁵ sir?
CORVINO Venice was never owner of the like.
VOLPONE [*faintly*] Signior Corvino!
MOSCA   Hark.
VOLPONE   Signior Corvino!
MOSCA He calls you; step and give it him.—He's here, sir,

3. Seneca, *Epistle* 115.6.   5. From the east, where the pearls were most lustrous.
4. Jason's father, restored to life by Medea's magic.

And he has brought you a rich pearl.

CORVINO   How do you, sir?
    Tell him, it doubles the twelfth carat.

MOSCA   Sir,
15   He cannot understand, his hearing's gone;
    And yet it comforts him to see you—

CORVINO   Say,
    I have a diamond for him, too.

MOSCA   Best shew it, sir;
    Put it into his hand; 'tis only there
    He apprehends:[6] he has his feeling, yet.
20   See how he grasps it!

CORVINO   'Las, good gentleman!
    How pitiful the sight is!

MOSCA   Tut! forget, sir.
    The weeping of an heir should still be laughter
    Under a visor.

CORVINO   Why, am I his heir?

MOSCA Sir, I am sworn, I may not shew the will
25   Till he be dead; but here has been Corbaccio,
    Here has been Voltore, here were others too,
    I cannot number 'em, they were so many;
    All gaping here for legacies: but I,
    Taking the vantage of his naming you,
30   *Signior Corvino, Signior Corvino*, took
    Paper, and pen, and ink, and there I asked him,
    Whom he would have his heir? *Corvino*. Who
    Should be executor? *Corvino*. And,
    To any question he was silent to,
35   I still interpreted the nods he made,
    Through weakness, for consent: and sent home th' others,
    Nothing bequeathed them but to cry and curse.

CORVINO O, my dear Mosca! [*They embrace.*] Does he not perceive us?

MOSCA No more than a blind harper. He knows no man,
40   No face of friend, nor name of any servant,
    Who 'twas that fed him last, or gave him drink:
    Not those he hath begotten or brought up
    Can he remember.

CORVINO   Has he children?

MOSCA   Bastards,
    Some dozen or more, that he begot on beggars,
45   Gypsies, and Jews, and black-moors, when he was drunk.
    Knew you not that, sir? 'Tis the common fable.[7]
    The dwarf, the fool, the eunuch, are all his;
    He's the true father of his family,
    In all, save me:—but he has given them nothing.

CORVINO That's well, that's well! Art sure he does not hear us?

MOSCA Sure, sir! why, look you, credit your own sense. [*Shouts in Volpone's ear.*]
    The pox approach and add to your diseases,

---

6. Playing on the Latin *apprehendere*, "to take hold of."   7. It's widely believed.

If it would send you hence the sooner, sir,
For your incontinence, it hath deserved it
55   Thoroughly, and thoroughly, and the plague to boot!—
You may come near, sir.—Would you would once close
Those filthy eyes of yours, that flow with slime
Like two frog-pits; and those same hanging cheeks,
Covered with hide instead of skin—Nay, help, sir—
60   That look like frozen dish-clouts set on end!

CORVINO [aloud] Or like an old smoked wall on which the rain
    Ran down in streaks!

MOSCA   Excellent, sir! speak out:
    You may be louder yet; a culverin°   *cannon*
    Discharged in his ear would hardly bore it.

CORVINO His nose is like a common sewer, still running.

MOSCA 'Tis good! And what his mouth?

CORVINO   A very draught.°   *cesspool*

MOSCA O, stop it up—

CORVINO   By no means.

MOSCA   'Pray you, let me:
    Faith I could stifle him rarely with a pillow,
    As well as any woman that should keep him.

CORVINO Do as you will; but I'll begone.

MOSCA   Be so:
    It is your presence makes him last so long.

CORVINO I pray you, use no violence.

MOSCA   No, sir! why?
    Why should you be thus scrupulous, pray you, sir?

CORVINO Nay, at your discretion.

MOSCA   Well, good sir, begone.

CORVINO I will not trouble him now to take my pearl.

MOSCA Puh! nor your diamond. What a needless care
    Is this afflicts you? Is not all here yours?
    Am not I here, whom you have made your creature?
    That owe my being to you?

CORVINO   Grateful Mosca!
80   Thou art my friend, my fellow, my companion,
    My partner, and shalt share in all my fortunes.

MOSCA Excepting one.

CORVINO   What's that?

MOSCA   Your gallant wife, sir,—[Exit Corvino.]
    Now is he gone: we had no other means
    To shoot him hence, but this.

VOLPONE   My divine Mosca!
85   Thou hast today outgone thyself. [Knocking within.]—Who's there?
    I will be troubled with no more. Prepare
    Me music, dances, banquets, all delights;
    The Turk is not more sensual in his pleasures
    Than will Volpone. [Exit Mosca.] Let me see; a pearl!
90   A diamond! plate! chequines! Good morning's purchase.
    Why, this is better than rob churches, yet;
    Or fat, by eating, once a month, a man—

[*Reenter Mosca.*]
      Who is't?
MOSCA   The beauteous Lady Would-be, sir,
      Wife to the English knight Sir Politic Would-be
95   (This is the style, sir, is directed me),
      Hath sent to know how you have slept to-night,
      And if you would be visited?
VOLPONE   Not now:
      Some three hours hence—
MOSCA   I told the squire so much.
VOLPONE When I am high with mirth and wine; then, then:
100   'Fore heaven, I wonder at the desperate valor
      Of the bold English, that they dare let loose
      Their wives to all encounters!
MOSCA   Sir, this knight
      Had not his name for nothing, he is politic,°   *devious, subtle*
      And knows, howe'er his wife affect strange airs,
105   She hath not yet the face to be dishonest:
      But had she Signior Corvino's wife's face—
VOLPONE Has she so rare a face?
MOSCA   O, sir, the wonder,
      The blazing star of Italy! a wench
      Of the first year! a beauty ripe as harvest!
110   Whose skin is whiter than a swan all over
      Than silver, snow, or lilies! a soft lip
      Would tempt you to eternity of kissing!
      And flesh that melteth in the touch to blood!
      Bright as your gold, and lovely as your gold!
VOLPONE Why had not I known this before?
MOSCA   Alas, sir,
      Myself but yesterday discovered it.
VOLPONE How might I see her?
MOSCA   O, not possible;
      She's kept as warily as is your gold;
      Never does come abroad, never takes air,
120   But at a window. All her looks are sweet,
      As the first grapes or cherries, and are watched
      As near as they are.
VOLPONE   I must see her.
MOSCA   Sir,
      There is a guard of spies ten thick upon her,
      All his whole household; each of which is set
125   Upon his fellow, and have all their charge,
      When he goes out, when he comes in, examined.
VOLPONE I will go see her, though but at her window.
MOSCA In some disguise, then.
VOLPONE   That is true; I must
      Maintain mine own shape[8] still the same: we'll think. [*Exeunt.*]

8. Physical appearance, disguise, and theatrical role.

A c t 2

Scene 1. *St. Mark's Place; a retired corner before Corvino's house*

[*Enter Sir Politic Would-be and Peregrine.*]

SIR POLITIC Sir, to a wise man, all the world's his soil:
    It is not Italy, nor France, nor Europe
    That must bound me, if my fates call me forth.
    Yet, I protest, it is no salt desire
5   Of seeing countries, shifting a religion,
    Nor any disaffection to the state
    Where I was bred, and unto which I owe
    My dearest plots,° hath brought me out; much less   *ideas*
    That idle, antique, stale, gray-headed project
10   Of knowing men's minds and manners, with Ulysses!
    But a peculiar humor of my wife's,
    Laid for this height of Venice, to observe,
    To quote, to learn the language, and so forth—
    I hope you travel, sir, with license?°   *passport*
PEREGRINE   Yes.
SIR POLITIC I dare the safelier converse—How long, sir,
    Since you left England?
PEREGRINE   Seven weeks.
SIR POLITIC   So lately!
    You have not been with my lord ambassador?
PEREGRINE Not yet, sir.
SIR POLITIC   Pray you, what news, sir, vents our climate?[1]
    I heard last night a most strange thing reported
20   By some of my lord's followers, and I long
    To hear how 'twill be seconded.
PEREGRINE   What was't, sir?
SIR POLITIC Marry, sir, of a raven[2] that should build
    In a ship royal of the king's.
PEREGRINE [*aside*]   This fellow,
    Does he gull me, trow?[3] or is gull'd?—Your name, sir.
SIR POLITIC My name is Politic Would-be.
PEREGRINE [*aside*]   O, that speaks him.—
    A knight, sir?
SIR POLITIC   A poor knight, sir.
PEREGRINE   Your lady
    Lies here in Venice, for intelligence
    Of tires,° and fashions, and behavior   *attire*
    Among the courtesans?[4] the fine lady Would-be?
SIR POLITIC Yes, sir; the spider and the bee, ofttimes,
    Suck from one flower.
PEREGRINE   Good sir Politic,
    I cry you mercy; I have heard much of you:
    'Tis true, sir, of your raven.
SIR POLITIC   On your knowledge?

---

1. Comes from our country.
2. A bird that bodes ill.

3. Does he try to fool me; do you think?
4. Venetian prostitutes were famously stylish.

PEREGRINE Yes, and your lion's whelping in the Tower.[5]
SIR POLITIC Another whelp!
PEREGRINE   Another, sir.
SIR POLITIC   Now heaven!
    What prodigies be these? The fires at Berwick![6]
    And the new star![6] These things concurring, strange,
    And full of omen! Saw you those meteors?
PEREGRINE I did, sir.
SIR POLITIC   Fearful! Pray you, sir, confirm me,
40   Were there three porpoises seen above the bridge,
    As they give out?
PEREGRINE   Six, and a sturgeon, sir.
SIR POLITIC I am astonished.
PEREGRINE   Nay, sir, be not so;
    I'll tell you a greater prodigy than these.
SIR POLITIC What should these things portend?
PEREGRINE   The very day
45   (Let me be sure) that I put forth from London,
    There was a whale discovered in the river,
    As high as Woolwich, that had waited there,
    Few know how many months, for the subversion
    Of the Stode fleet.
SIR POLITIC   Is't possible? believe it,
50   'Twas either sent from Spain, or the Archduke's:
    Spinola's whale, upon my life, my credit![7]
    Will they not leave these projects? Worthy sir,
    Some other news.
PEREGRINE   Faith, Stone the fool is dead,
    And they do lack a tavern fool extremely.
SIR POLITIC Is Mass° Stone dead?   *master*
PEREGRINE   He's dead, sir; why, I hope
    You thought him not immortal?—[*Aside:*] O, this knight,
    Were he well known, would be a precious thing
    To fit our English stage; he that should write
    But such a fellow, should be thought to feign
60   Extremely, if not maliciously.
SIR POLITIC   Stone dead!
PEREGRINE Dead.—Lord! how deeply, sir, you apprehend it?
    He was no kinsman to you?
SIR POLITIC   That I know of.
    Well! that same fellow was an unknown fool.
PEREGRINE And yet you knew him, it seems?
SIR POLITIC   I did so. Sir,
65   I knew him one of the most dangerous heads
    Living within the state, and so I held him.
PEREGRINE Indeed, sir?

---

5. Lions were kept in the Tower of London.
6. Unusual northern lights had appeared over Berwick late in 1604, and a comet appeared that October.
7. Sir Politic believes the popular rumor that there was a whale sent to drown the people of London by the Spanish viceroy in the Netherlands, or by his general, Ambrosio Spinola.

SIR POLITIC   While he lived, in action.
    He has received weekly intelligence,
    Upon my knowledge, out of the Low Countries;
70   For all parts of the world, in cabbages;
    And those dispensed again to ambassadors,
    In oranges, musk-melons, apricocks,
    Lemons, pome-citrons, and such-like; sometimes
    In Colchester oysters, and your Selsey cockles.
PEREGRINE You make me wonder.
SIR POLITIC   Sir, upon my knowledge.
    Nay, I've observed him, at your public ordinary,°   *tavern*
    Take his advertisement° from a traveler,   *information*
    A concealed statesman, in a trencher of meat;
    And instantly, before the meal was done,
80   Convey an answer in a tooth-pick.
PEREGRINE   Strange!
    How could this be, sir?
SIR POLITIC   Why, the meat was cut
    So like his character, and so laid, as he
    Must easily read the cipher.
PEREGRINE   I have heard
    He could not read, sir.
SIR POLITIC   So 'twas given out,
85   In policy, by those that did employ him:
    But he could read, and had your languages,
    And to't,° as sound a noddle—   *what's more*
PEREGRINE   I have heard, sir,
    That your baboons were spies, and that they were
    A kind of subtle nation near to China.
SIR POLITIC Ay, ay, your Mamaluchi.[8] Faith, they had
    Their hand in a French plot or two; but they
    Were so extremely given to women, as
    They made discovery of all; yet I
    Had my advices here, on Wednesday last.
95   From one of their own coat they were returned,
    Made their relations, as the fashion is,
    And now stand fair for fresh employment.
PEREGRINE [*aside*]   'Heart!
    This sir Pol will be ignorant of nothing.
    It seems, sir, you know all.
SIR POLITIC   Not all, sir, but
100   I have some general notions. I do love
    To note and to observe; though I live out,
    Free from the active torrent, yet I'd mark
    The currents and the passages of things
    For mine own private use; and know the ebbs
105   And flows of state.
PEREGRINE   Believe it, sir, I hold
    Myself in no small tie unto my fortunes

8. A military body, ruling Egypt, originally coming from Asia Minor.

For casting me thus luckily upon you,
Whose knowledge, if your bounty equal it,
May do me great assistance, in instruction
110   For my behavior and my bearing, which
Is yet so rude and raw.
SIR POLITIC   Why, came you forth
Empty of rules for travel?
PEREGRINE   Faith, I had
Some common ones, from out that vulgar° grammar,   *vernacular*
Which he that cried Italian to me, taught me.
SIR POLITIC Why this it is that spoils all our brave bloods,
Trusting our hopeful gentry unto pedants,
Fellows of outside, and mere bark. You seem
To be a gentleman, of ingenuous race:°—   *honorable descent*
I not profess it, but my fate hath been
120   To be where I have been consulted with,
In this high kind, touching some great men's sons,
Persons of blood and honor.—

Scene 2

[*Enter Mosca and Nano disguised, followed by persons with materials for erecting a Stage.*]
PEREGRINE Who be these, sir?
MOSCA Under that window, there't must be. The same.
SIR POLITIC Fellows, to mount a bank. Did your instructor
In the dear tongues never discourse to you
5   Of the Italian mountebanks?⁹
PEREGRINE   Yes, sir.
SIR POLITIC   Why,
Here you shall see one.
PEREGRINE   They are quacksalvers;
Fellows that live by venting° oils and drugs.   *vending*
SIR POLITIC Was that the character he gave you of them?
PEREGRINE As I remember.
SIR POLITIC   Pity his ignorance.
10   They are the only knowing men of Europe!
Great general scholars, excellent physicians,
Most admired statesmen, profest favorites,
And cabinet counselors to the greatest princes;
The only languaged men of all the world!
PEREGRINE And I have heard they are most lewd° impostors;   *ignorant*
Made all of terms and shreds; no less beliers
Of great men's favors than their own vile medicines;
Which they will utter upon monstrous oaths:
Selling that drug for two-pence, ere they part,
20   Which they have valued at twelve crowns before.
SIR POLITIC Sir, calumnies are answered best with silence.
Yourself shall judge.—Who is it mounts, my friends?

9. Quacks who performed on a platform (a "bank") before selling fake medicines to their audience.

MOSCA Scoto of Mantua, sir.[1]

SIR POLITIC   Is't he? Nay, then
       I'll proudly promise, sir, you shall behold
25   Another man than has been fant'sied° to you.   described
       I wonder yet, that he should mount his bank
       Here in this nook, that has been wont t'appear
       In face of the Piazza!—Here he comes.
       [*Enter Volpone, disguised as a mountebank doctor, and followed by a crowd of people.*]

VOLPONE [*to Nano*] Mount, zany.°   fool, clown

MOB   Follow, follow, follow, follow!

SIR POLITIC See how the people follow him! he's a man
       May write ten thousand crowns in bank here. Note,
       [*Volpone mounts the Stage.*]
       Mark but his gesture:—I do use to observe
       The state he keeps in getting up.

PEREGRINE   'Tis worth it, sir.

VOLPONE *Most noble gentlemen, and my worthy patrons! It may seem strange that I, your Scoto Mantuano, who was ever wont to fix my bank in face of the public Piazza, near the shelter of the Portico to the Procuratia,[2] should now, after eight months' absence from this illustrious city of Venice, humbly retire myself into an obscure nook of the Piazza.*

SIR POLITIC Did not I now object the same?

PEREGRINE   Peace, sir.

VOLPONE *Let me tell you: I am not, as your Lombard proverb saith, cold on my feet; or content to part with my commodities at a cheaper rate than I accustomed: look not for it. Nor that the calumnious reports of that impudent detractor and shame to our profession (Alessandro Buttone, I mean), who gave out in public I was condemned a sforzato[3] to the galleys, for poisoning the cardinal Bembo's——cook,[4] hath at all attached, much less dejected me. No, no, worthy gentlemen; to tell you true, I cannot endure to see the rabble of these ground ciarlitani,[5] that spread their cloaks on the pavement as if they meant to do feats of activity, and then come in lamely with their moldy tales out of Boccaccio, like stale Tabarine,[6] the fabulist: some of them discoursing their travels and of their tedious captivity in the Turks' galleys, when, indeed, were the truth known, they were the Christians' galleys, where very temperately they eat bread and drunk water as a wholesome penance, enjoined them by their confessors for base pilferies.[7]*

SIR POLITIC Note but his bearing and contempt of these.

VOLPONE *These turdy-facy-nasty-paty-lousy-fartical rogues, with one poor groat's-worth of unprepared antimony,[8] finely wrapt up in several scartoccios,[9] are able, very well, to kill their twenty a week, and play; yet these meager, starved spirits, who have half stopped the organs of their minds with earthy oppilations,[1] want not their favorers among your shrivelled salad-eating artisans, who are overjoyed that they may have their ha'f-pe'rth[2] of physic; though it purge them into another world, it makes no matter.*

SIR POLITIC Excellent! have you heard better language, sir?

---

1. A juggler and magician who had performed before Queen Elizabeth.
2. The arcade along the north side of St. Mark's square.
3. Slave.
4. Comically suppressing some term like "mistress." This tale is absurd, though; Cardinal Bembo had died 50 years before the time of the play.
5. Charlatans.

6. An Italian comedian of the previous generation.
7. Condemned criminals rowed in the Venetian galley, where they were in fact treated miserably.
8. Antimony was used as an emetic.
9. Envelopes.
1. Obstructions.
2. Half-penny worth.

VOLPONE *Well, let them go. And gentlemen, honorable gentlemen, know, that for this time, our bank, being thus removed from the clamors of the canaglia,*[3] *shall be the scene of pleasure and delight; for I have nothing to sell, little or nothing to sell.*

SIR POLITIC I told you, sir, his end.

PEREGRINE   You did so, sir.

VOLPONE *I protest, I and my six servants are not able to make of this precious liquor, so fast as it is fetched away from my lodging by gentlemen of your city; strangers of the Terra-firma;*[4] *worshipful merchants; ay, and senators too: who, ever since my arrival, have detained me to their uses by their splendidous liberalities. And worthily; for what avails your rich man to have his magazines stuft with moscadelli,*[5] *or of the purest grape, when his physicians prescribe him, on pain of death, to drink nothing but water cocted with aniseeds? O, health! health! the blessing of the rich! the riches of the poor! who can buy thee at too dear a rate, since there is no enjoying this world without thee? Be not then so sparing of your purses, honorable gentlemen, as to abridge the natural course of life—*

PEREGRINE You see his end.

SIR POLITIC   Ay, is't not good?

VOLPONE *For when a humid flux or catarrh, by the mutability of air, falls from your head into an arm or shoulder, or any other part, take you a ducket, or your chequin of gold, and apply to the place affected: see what good effect it can work. No, no, 'tis this blessed unguento, this rare extraction, that hath only power to disperse all malignant humors that proceed either of hot, cold, moist, or windy causes—*

PEREGRINE I would he had put in dry too.

SIR POLITIC   'Pray you, observe.

VOLPONE *To fortify the most indigest and crude stomach, ay, were it of one that, through extreme weakness, vomited blood, applying only a warm napkin to the place after the unction and fricace;*[6]*—for the vertigine in the head, putting but a drop into your nostrils, likewise behind the ears; a most sovereign and approved remedy: the mal caduco, cramps, convulsions, paralyses, epilepsies, tremor-cordia, retired nerves, ill vapors of the spleen, stopping of the liver, the stone, the strangury, hernia ventosa, iliaca passio; stops a dysenteria immediately; easeth the torsion of the small guts; and cures melancholia hypondriaca, being taken and applied according to my printed receipt.* [Pointing to his bill and his vial.] *For this is the physician, this the medicine; this counsels, this cures; this gives the direction, this works the effect; and in sum, both together may be termed an abstract of the theoric and practic in the Aesculapian*[7] *art. 'Twill cost you eight crowns. And,—Zan Fritada,*[8] *prithee sing a verse extempore in honor of it.*

SIR POLITIC How do you like him, sir?

PEREGRINE   Most strangely, I!

SIR POLITIC Is not his language rare?

PEREGRINE   But alchemy,
    I never heard the like; or Broughton's books.[9]
                        [Nano sings.]

        Had old Hippocrates or Galen,[1]
        That to their books put med'cines all in,

---

3. The rabble.
4. The mainland.
5. A wine.
6. Anointing and rubbing in.
7. Medical.

8. Nano's stage name, Fried Fool.
9. Only alchemy and the tracts of the minor Puritan theologian Hugh Braughton are better.
1. Ancient Greek physicians.

But known this secret, they had never
(Of which they will be guilty ever)
Been murderers of so much paper,
Or wasted many a hurtless taper;
No Indian drug had e'er been famed,
Tobacco, sassafras not named;
Ne yet of guacum[2] one small stick, sir,
Nor Raymund Lully's great elixir.
Ne had been known the Danish Gonswart,
Or Paracelsus, with his long sword.[3]

PEREGRINE All this, yet, will not do; eight crowns is high.

VOLPONE No more.—Gentlemen, *if I had but time to discourse to you the miraculous effects of this oil, surnamed Oglio del Scoto; with the countless catalogue of those I have cured of the aforesaid and many more diseases; the patents and privileges of all the princes and commonwealths of Christendom; or but the depositions of those that appeared on my part, before the signiory of the Sanita[4] and most learned College of Physicians; where I was authorized, upon notice taken of the admirable virtues of my medicaments, and mine own excellency in matter of rare and unknown secrets, not only to disperse them publicly in this famous city, but in all the territories that happily joy under the government of the most pious and magnificent states of Italy. But may some other gallant fellow say, O, there be divers that make profession to have as good and as experimented receipts as yours. Indeed, very many have assayed, like apes, in imitation of that which is really and essentially in me, to make of this oil; bestowed great cost in furnices, stills, alembecks, continual fires, and preparation of the ingredients (as indeed there goes to it six hundred several simples,[5] besides some quality of human fat, for the conglutination, which we buy of the anatomists), but when these practitioners come to the last decoction, blow, blow, puff, puff, and all flies in fumo:[6] ha, ha, ha! Poor wretches! I rather pity their folly and indiscretion, than their loss of time and money; for these may be recovered by industry: but to be a fool born, is a disease incurable.*

For myself, I always from my youth have endeavored to get the rarest secrets, and book them, either in exchange, or for money. I spared not cost nor labor, where any thing was worthy to be learned. And, gentlemen, honorable gentlemen, I will undertake, by virtue of chemical art, out of the honorable hat that covers your head, to extract the four elements; that is to say, the fire, air, water, and earth, and return you your felt without burn or stain. For whilst others have been at the balloo,[7] I have been at my book; and am now past the craggy paths of study, and come to the flowery plains of honor and reputation.

SIR POLITIC I do assure you, sir, that is his aim.

VOLPONE But to our price—

PEREGRINE   And that withal, Sir Pol.

VOLPONE *You all know, honorable gentlemen, I never valued this ampulla, or vial, at less than eight crowns; but for this time, I am content to be deprived of it for six: six crowns is the price, and less in courtesy I know you cannot offer me; take it or leave it, howsoever,*

---

2. Like tobacco and sassafras, New World plant products thought to have medicinal properties.
3. Raymond Lull, a 13th-century Spanish mystic philosopher, was said to have discovered the elixir of life; Paracelsus, a 16th-century German doctor, was reputed

by legend to have kept medications in his sword handle.
4. Venetian medical board.
5. Separate herbs.
6. Up in smoke.
7. Balloon, a ball game.

both it and I am at your service. I ask you not as the value of the thing, for then I should demand of you a thousand crowns, so the cardinals Montalto, Farnese, the great Duke of Tuscany, my gossip, with divers other princes, have given me; but I despise money. Only to shew my affection to you honorable gentlemen and your illustrious State here, I have neglected the messages of these princes, mine own offices, framed my journey hither, only to present you with the fruits of my travels.—Tune your voices once more to the touch of your instruments, and give the honorable assembly some delightful recreation.

PEREGRINE What monstrous and most painful circumstance
    Is here, to get some three or four gazettes,[8]
    Some three-pence in the whole! for that 'twill come to.
        [*Nano sings.*]
    You that would last long, list to my song,
    Make no more coil,° but buy of this oil.   fuss
    Would you be ever fair and young?
    Stout of teeth, and strong of tongue?
    Tart of palate? quick of ear?
    Sharp of sight? of nostril clear?
    Moist of hand? and light of foot?
    Or, I will come nearer to't,
    Would you live free from all diseases?
    Do the act your mistress pleases,
    Yet fright all aches from your bones?
    Here's a medicine for the nones.°   purpose

VOLPONE *Well, I am in a humor at this time to make a present of the small quantity my coffer contains; to the rich in courtesy, and to the poor for God's sake. Wherefore now mark: I asked you six crowns; and six crowns, at other times, you have paid me; you shall not give me six crowns, nor five, nor four, nor three, nor two, nor one; nor half a ducat; no, nor a moccinigo.[9] Sixpence it will cost you, or six hundred pound—expect no lower price, for, by the banner of my front, I will not bate a bagatine[1]—that I will have, only, a pledge of your loves, to carry something from amongst you, to show I am not contemned by you. Therefore, now, toss your handkerchiefs, cheerfully, cheerfully; and be advertised that the first heroic spirit that designs to grace me with a handkerchief, I will give it a little remembrance of something, beside, shall please it better, than if I had presented it with a double pistolet.[2]*

PEREGRINE Will you be that heroic spark, sir Pol?
        [*Celia at a window above, throws down her handkerchief.*]
    O, see! the window has prevented you.

VOLPONE *Lady, I kiss your bounty; and for this timely grace you have done your poor Scoto of Mantua, I will return you, over and above my oil, a secret of that high and inestimable nature, shall make you for ever enamored on that minute wherein your eye first descended on so mean, yet not altogether to be despised, an object. Here is a powder concealed in this paper, of which, if I should speak to the worth, nine thousand volumes were but as one page, that page as a line, that line as a word; so short is this pilgrimage of man (which some call life) to the expressing of it. Would I reflect on the price? Why, the whole world is but as an empire, that empire as a province, the province as a bank, that bank as a private purse to the purchase of it. I will only tell you: it is the powder that*

8. Venetian coins worth less than a penny.   1. A fraction of a cent.
9. Dime.   2. A Spanish coin worth close to an English pound.

made Venus a goddess (given her by Apollo), that kept her perpetually young, cleared her wrinkles, firmed her gums, filled her skin, colored her hair; from her derived to Helen, and at the sack of Troy unfortunately lost: till now, in this our age, it was as happily recovered, by a studious antiquary, out of some ruins of Asia, who sent a moiety of it to the court of France (but much sophisticated), wherewith the ladies there now color their hair. The rest at this present remains with me; extracted to a quintessence: so that wherever it but touches, in youth it perpetually preserves, in age restores the complexion; seats your teeth, did they dance like virginal jacks,[3] firm as a wall; makes them while as ivory, that were black as—

Scene 3

[*Enter Corvino.*]

CORVINO Spite o' the devil, and my shame! come down here;
    Come down;—No house but mine to make your scene?
    Signior Flaminio,[4] will you down, sir? Down?
    What is my wife your Franciscina,[5] sir?
5   No windows on the whole Piazza here
    To make your properties, but mine? But mine?
[*Beats away Volpone, Nano, etc.*]
    Heart! Ere to-morrow I shall be new-christened,
    And called the Pantalone di Besogniosi[6]
    About the town.
PEREGRINE   What should this mean, Sir Pol?
SIR POLITIC Some trick of state, believe it; I will home.
PEREGRINE It may be some design on you.
SIR POLITIC   I know not,
    I'll stand upon my guard.
PEREGRINE   It is your best, sir.
SIR POLITIC This three weeks, all my advices, all my letters,
    They have been intercepted.
PEREGRINE   Indeed, sir!
15   Best have a care.
SIR POLITIC   Nay, so I will.
PEREGRINE   This knight,
    I may not lose him, for my mirth, till night. [*Exeunt.*]

Scene 4. A room in Volpone's house

[*Enter Volpone and Mosca.*]

VOLPONE O, I am wounded!
MOSCA   Where, sir?
VOLPONE   Not without;
    Those blows were nothing: I could bear them ever.
    But angry Cupid, bolting from her eyes,
    Hath shot himself into me like a flame;
5   Where now he flings about his burning heat,
    As in a furnace an ambitious fire

---

3. Quills that pluck the strings of a virginal, or harpsichord.
4. A Venetian actor of Jonson's time.

5. Name of the serving girl in the Italian popular comedies (*commedia dell'arte*).
6. In the *commedia dell'arte*, an old fool and cuckold.

Whose vent is stopped. The fight is all within me.
I cannot live except thou help me, Mosca;
My liver melts, and I, without the hope
10   Of some soft air, from her refreshing breath,
Am but a heap of cinders.

MOSCA   'Las, good sir,
Would you had never seen her!

VOLPONE   Nay, would thou
Had'st never told me of her!

MOSCA   Sir, 'tis true;
I do confess I was unfortunate,
15   And you unhappy: but I'm bound in conscience,
No less than duty, to effect my best
To your release of torment, and I will, sir.

VOLPONE Dear Mosca, shall I hope?

MOSCA   Sir, more than dear,
I will not bid you to despair of aught
20   With a human compass.

VOLPONE   O, there spoke
My better angel. Mosca, take my keys,
Gold, plate, and jewels, all's at thy devotion;
Employ them how thou wilt; nay, coin me too:
So thou in this but crown my longings, Mosca.

MOSCA Use but your patience.

VOLPONE   So I have.

MOSCA   I doubt not
To bring success to your desires.

VOLPONE   Nay, then,
I not repent me of my late disguise.

MOSCA If you can horn° him, sir, you need not.   cuckold

VOLPONE   True:
Besides, I never meant him for my heir.—
30   Is not the color of my beard and eyebrows
To make me known?

MOSCA   No jot.

VOLPONE   I did it well.

MOSCA So well, would I could follow you in mine
With half the happiness!—[Aside.] and yet I would
Escape your epilogue.

VOLPONE   But were they gulled
35   With a belief that I was Scoto?

MOSCA   Sir,
Scoto himself could hardly have distinguished!
I have not time to flatter you now; we'll part;
And as I prosper, so applaud my art.   [Exeunt.]

Scene 5. A room in Corvino's house

[Enter Corvino, with his sword in his hand, dragging in Celia.]

CORVINO Death of mine honor, with the city's fool!
A juggling, tooth-drawing, prating mountebank!

And at a public window! Where, whilst he,
With his strained action, and his dole° of faces,   *guile*
5   To his drug-lecture draws your itching ears,
A crew of old, unmarried, noted lechers
Stood leering up like satyrs; and you smile
Most graciously, and fan your favours forth
To give your hot spectators satisfaction!
10   What, was your mountebank their call? their whistle?
Or were you enamored on his copper rings,
His saffron jewel with the toad-stone in't,
Or his embroidered suit with the cope-stitch,
Made of a herse cloth?° or his old tilt-feather?   *coarse fabric*
15   Or his starched beard? Well, you shall have him, yes!
He shall come home, and minister unto you
The fricace for the mother.[7] Or, let me see,
I think you'd rather mount; would you not mount?[8]
Why, if you'll mount, you may; yes, truly, you may:
20   And so you may be seen down to the foot.
Get you a cittern,° lady Vanity,   *guitar*
And be a dealer with the virtuous man;
Make one: I'll but protest myself a cuckold,
And save your dowry.[9] I'm a Dutchman, I!
25   For, if you thought me an Italian,
You would be damned ere you did this, you whore![1]
Thou'dst tremble to imagine that the murder
Of father, mother, brother, all thy race,
Should follow as the subject of my justice.
CELIA   Good sir, have patience.
CORVINO   What couldst thou propose
Less to thyself, than in this heat of wrath
And stung with my dishonor, I should strike
This steel into thee, with as many stabs,
As thou wert gazed upon with goatish° eyes?   *lascivious*
CELIA   Alas, sir, be appeased! I could not think
My being at the window should more now
Move your impatience than at other times.
CORVINO   No! not to seek and entertain a parley
With a known knave, before a multitude!
40   You were an actor with your handkerchief,
Which he most sweetly kissed in the receipt,
And might, no doubt, return it with a letter,
And point the place where you might meet; your sister's,
Your mother's, or your aunt's might serve the turn.
CELIA   Why, dear sir, when do I make these excuses,
Or ever stir abroad, but to the church?
And that so seldom—

---

7. Massage for hysteria, the disease of the wandering womb.
8. Mount the stage—or the man.
9. A court that convicted a woman of adultery could grant her dowry to her husband.
1. The Dutch were stereotyped as unemotional, the Italians as intensely jealous.

CORVINO   Well, it shall be less;
            And thy restraint before was liberty
            To what I now decree; and therefore mark me.
50   First, I will have this bawdy light dammed up;
            And till't be done, some two or three yards off,
            I'll chalk a line: o'er which if thou but chance
            To set thy desperate foot, more hell, more horror,
            More wild remorseless rage shall seize on thee,
55   Than on a conjuror that had heedless left
            His circle's safety ere his devil was laid.[2]
            Then here's a lock which I will hang upon thee,
            And, now I think on't, I will keep thee backwards;
            Thy lodging shall be backwards; thy walks backwards;
60   Thy prospect, all be backwards; and no pleasure
            That thou shalt know but backwards. Nay, since you force
            My honest nature, know, it is your own,
            Being too open, makes me use you thus.
            Since you will not contain your subtle nostrils
65   In a sweet room, but they must snuff the air
            Of rank and sweaty passengers. [Knocking within.]—One knocks.
            Away, and be not seen, pain of thy life;
            Nor look toward the window: if thou dost—
            Nay, stay, hear this—let me not prosper, whore,
70   But I will make thee an anatomy,[3]
            Dissect thee mine own self, and read a lecture
            Upon thee to the city, and in public.
            Away!—[Exit Celia.]
      [Enter Servant.]
                                    Who's there?
SERVANT   'Tis Signior Mosca, sir.

                              Scene 6

CORVINO Let him come in. [Exit Servant.] His master's dead: there's yet
            Some good to help the bad. [Enter Mosca.]
                                    My Mosca, welcome!
            I guess your news.
MOSCA   I fear you cannot, sir.
CORVINO Is't not his death?
MOSCA   Rather the contrary.
CORVINO Not his recovery?
MOSCA   Yes, sir.
CORVINO   I am cursed,
            I am bewitched, my crosses meet to vex me.
            How? how? how? how?
MOSCA   Why, sir, with Scoto's oil;
            Corbaccio and Voltore brought of it,
            Whilst I was busy in an inner room—

---

2. The conjuror's magic circle was a protection against   3. A subject of moral examination and also of dissection.
the devils that he had called forth with spells.

CORVINO Death! that damned mountebank; but for the law
       Now, I could kill the rascal: it cannot be
       His oil should have that virtue. Have not I
       Known him a common rogue, come fiddling in
       To the osteria° with a tumbling whore,   *inn*
15   And, when he has done all his forced tricks, been glad
       Of a poor spoonful of dead wine, with flies in't?
       It cannot be. All his ingredients
       Are a sheep's gall, a roasted bitch's marrow,
       Some few sod earwigs, pounded caterpillars,
20   A little capon's grease, and fasting spittle:
       I know them to a dram.
MOSCA   I know not, sir;
       But some on't there they poured into his ears,
       Some in his nostrils, and recovered him;
       Applying but the fricace.
CORVINO   Pox o' that fricace!
MOSCA And since, to seem the more officious
       And flatt'ring of his health, there they have had,
       At extreme fees, the college of physicians
       Consulting on him, how they might restore him;
       Where one would have a cataplasm° of spices,   *poultice*
30   Another a flayed ape clapped to his breast,
       A third would have it a dog, a fourth an oil,
       With wild cats' skins: at last, they all resolved
       That to preserve him was no other means,
       But some young woman must be straight sought out,
35   Lusty, and full of juice, to sleep by him;
       And to this service, most unhappily,
       And most unwillingly, am I now employed,
       Which here I thought to preacquaint you with
       For your advice, since it concerns you most;
40   Because, I would not do that thing might cross
       Your ends, on whom I have my whole dependence, sir;
       Yet, if I do it not, they may delate
       My slackness to my patron, work me out
       Of his opinion; and there all your hopes,
45   Ventures, or whatsoever, are all frustrate!
       I do but tell you, sir. Besides, they are all
       Now striving who shall first present him; therefore—
       I could entreat you, briefly conclude somewhat;
       Prevent them if you can.
CORVINO   Death to my hopes,
50   This is my villainous fortune! Best to hire
       Some common courtesan.
MOSCA   Ay, I thought on that, sir;
       But they are all so subtle, full of art—
       And age again doting and flexible,
       So as—I cannot tell—we may, perchance,
55   Light on a quean° may cheat us all.   *harlot*
CORVINO   'Tis true.

MOSCA No, no: it must be one that has no tricks, sir,
    Some simple thing, a creature made unto it;
    Some wench you may command. Have you no kinswoman?
    God's so—Think, think, think, think, think, think, think, sir.
60   One o' the doctors offered there his daughter.
CORVINO   How!
MOSCA Yes, signior Lupo,° the physician.   *wolf*
CORVINO His daughter!
MOSCA   And a virgin, sir. Why, alas,
    He knows the state of's body, what it is;
    That nought can warm his blood, sir, but a fever;
65   Nor any incantation raise his spirit;
    A long forgetfulness hath seized that part.
    Besides sir, who shall know it? Some one or two—
CORVINO I pray thee give me leave. [*Walks aside.*] If any man
    But I had this luck—The thing in't self,
70   I know, is nothing—Wherefore should not I
    As well command my blood and my affections
    As this dull doctor? In the point of honor,
    The cases are all one of wife and daughter.
MOSCA [*Aside.*] I hear him coming.
CORVINO   She shall do't: 'tis done.
75   Slight! if this doctor, who is not engaged,
    Unless 't be for his counsel, which is nothing,
    Offer his daughter, what should I, that am
    So deeply in? I will prevent° him: Wretch!   *get ahead of*
    Covetous wretch!—Mosca, I have determined.
MOSCA How, sir?
CORVINO   We'll make all sure. The party you wot of
    Shall be mine own wife, Mosca.
MOSCA   Sir, the thing.
    But that I would not seem to counsel you,
    I should have motioned° to you at the first: *proposed*
    And make your count, you have cut all their throats.
85   Why, 'tis directly taking a possession!
    And in his next fit, we may let him go.
    'Tis but to pull the pillow from his head,
    And he is throttled: it had been done before,
    But for your scrupulous doubts.
CORVINO   Ay, a plague on't,
90   My conscience fools my wit! Well, I'll be brief,
    And so be thou, lest they should be before us:
    Go home, prepare him, tell him with what zeal
    And willingness I do it; swear it was
    On the first hearing, as thou may'st do, truly,
95   Mine own free motion.
MOSCA   Sir, I warrant you,
    I'll so possess him with it that the rest
    Of his starved clients shall be banished all;
    And only you received. But come not, sir,
    Until I send, for I have something else

100   To ripen for your good, you must not know't.
CORVINO But do not you forget to send now.
MOSCA   Fear not. [*Exit.*]

Scene 7

CORVINO Where are you, wife? my Celia! wife!
  [*Reenter Celia, weeping.*]
                                        —What, blubbering?
      Come, dry those tears. I think thou thought'st me in earnest;
      Ha! by this light I talked so but to try thee:
      Methinks the lightness of the occasion
5   Should have confirmed thee. Come, I am not jealous.
CELIA No?
CORVINO Faith I am not, I, nor never was;
      It is a poor unprofitable humor.
      Do not I know, if women have a will,
      They'll do 'gainst all the watches of the world,[4]
10   And that the fiercest spies are tamed with gold?
      Tut, I am confident in thee, thou shalt see't;
      And see I'll give thee cause too to believe it.
      Come kiss me. Go, and make thee ready, straight,
      In all thy best attire, thy choicest jewels,
15   Put them all on, and with them thy best looks:
      We are invited to a solemn feast
      At old Volpone's, where it shall appear
      How far I am free from jealousy or fear. [*Exeunt.*]

Act 3

Scene 1. *A street*

  [*Enter Mosca.*]
MOSCA I fear, I shall begin to grow in love
      With my dear self and my most prosperous parts,
      They do so spring and burgeon; I can feel
      A whimsy in my blood: I know not how,
5   Success hath made me wanton. I could skip
      Out of my skin, now, like a subtle snake,
      I am so limber. O! your parasite
      Is a most precious thing, dropt from above,
      Not bred 'mongst clods and clodpoles,° here on earth.   *thick heads*
10   I muse, the mystery° was not made a science,   *secret art*
      It is so liberally professed! almost
      All the wise world is little else, in nature,
      But parasites or sub-parasites.—And yet,
      I mean not those that have your bare town-art,
15   To know who's fit to feed them; have no house,
      No family, no care, and therefore mold
      Tales for men's ears, to bait that sense; or get
      Kitchen-invention, and some stale receipts

4. Have sex no matter how well they are guarded.

To please the belly, and the groin; nor those,
20   With their court dog-tricks, that can fawn and fleer,°   *grin falsely*
Make their revenue out of legs and faces,[1]
Echo my lord, and lick away a moth:
But your fine elegant rascal, that can rise,
And stoop, almost together, like an arrow;
25   Shoot through the air as nimbly as a star;
Turn short as doth a swallow; and be here,
And there, and here, and yonder, all at once;
Present to any humor, all occasion;
And change a visor,° swifter than a thought!   *facial disguise*
30   This is the creature had the art born with him;
Toils not to learn it, but doth practise it
Out of most excellent nature: and such sparks
Are the true parasites, others but their zanies.°   *clown's side-kicks*

Scene 2

[*Enter Bonario.*]
            Who's this? Bonario, old Corbaccio's son?
            The person I was bound to seek.—Fair sir,
            You are happily met.
BONARIO   That cannot be by thee.
MOSCA Why, sir?
BONARIO   Nay, pray thee, know thy way, and leave me:
5   I would be loth to interchange discourse
       With such a mate as thou art.
MOSCA   Courteous sir,
            Scorn not my poverty.
BONARIO   Not I, by heaven;
            But thou shalt give me leave to hate thy baseness.
MOSCA Baseness!
BONARIO   Ay; answer me, is not thy sloth
10   Sufficient argument? Thy flattery?
       Thy means of feeding?
MOSCA   Heaven be good to me!
       These imputations are too common, sir,
       And easily stuck on virtue when she's poor.
       You are unequal to me, and however
15   Your sentence may be righteous, yet you are not
       That, ere you know me, thus proceed in censure;
       St. Mark bear witness 'gainst you, 'tis inhuman. [*Weeps.*]
BONARIO [*aside*] What! does he weep? the sign is soft and good:
            I do repent me that I was so harsh.
MOSCA 'Tis true, that, swayed by strong necessity,
       I am enforced to eat my careful bread
       With too much obsequy;° 'tis true, beside,   *servility*
       That I am fain to spin mine own poor raiment°   *clothing*
       Out of my mere observance,° being not born   *service*

1. Bows and smiles.

25 To a free fortune: but that I have done
   Base offices, in rending friends asunder,
   Dividing families, betraying counsels,
   Whispering false lies, or mining men with praises,
   Trained their credulity with perjuries,
30 Corrupted chastity, or am in love
   With mine own tender ease, but would not rather
   Prove the most rugged, and laborious course,
   That might redeem my present estimation,
   Let me here perish, in all hope of goodness.
BONARIO [*aside*] This cannot be a personated° passion.—   *pretended*
   I was to blame, so to mistake thy nature;
   Prithee, forgive me: and speak out thy business.
MOSCA Sir, it concerns you; and though I may seem,
   At first to make a main offence in manners,
40 And in my gratitude unto my master,
   Yet, for the pure love, which I bear all right,
   And hatred of the wrong, I must reveal it.
   This very hour your father is in purpose
   To disinherit you—
BONARIO   How!
MOSCA   And thrust you forth,
45 As a mere stranger to his blood; 'tis true, sir,
   The work no way engageth me, but, as
   I claim an interest in the general state
   Of goodness and true virtue, which I hear
   To abound in you: and, for which mere respect,
50 Without a second aim, sir, I have done it.
BONARIO This tale hath lost thee much of the late trust
   Thou hadst with me; it is impossible:
   I know not how to lend it any thought,
   My father should be so unnatural.
MOSCA It is a confidence that well becomes,
   Your piety; and formed, no doubt, it is
   From your own simple innocence, which makes
   Your wrong more monstrous and abhorred. But, sir,
   I now will tell you more. This very minute,
60 It is, or will be doing; and, if you
   Shall be but pleased to go with me, I'll bring you,
   I dare not say where you shall see, but where
   Your ear shall be a witness of the deed;
   Hear yourself written bastard, and profest
65 The common issue of the earth.
BONARIO   I am amazed!
MOSCA Sir, if I do it not, draw your just sword,
   And score your vengeance on my front and face:
   Mark me your villain: you have too much wrong,
   And I do suffer for you, sir. My heart
70 Weeps blood in anguish—
BONARIO   Lead; I follow thee. [*Exeunt.*]

Scene 3. *A room in Volpone's house*

[*Enter Volpone.*]

VOLPONE Mosca stays long, methinks.—Bring forth your sports,
　　And help to make the wretched time more sweet.

[*Enter Nano, Androgyno, and Castrone.*]

NANO *Dwarf, fool, and eunuch, well met here we be.*
　　A question it were now, whether of us three,
5　　*Being all the known delicates° of a rich man,*　　　　　objects of pleasure
　　In pleasing him, claim the precedency can?

CASTRONE *I claim for myself.*

ANDROGYNO　　　　　　　　*And so doth the fool.*

NANO *'Tis foolish indeed: let me set you both to school.*
　　First for your dwarf, he's little and witty,
10　　*And every thing, as it is little, is pretty;*
　　Else why do men say to a creature of my shape,
　　So soon as they see him, "It's a pretty little ape?"
　　And why a pretty ape, but for pleasing imitation
　　Of greater men's actions, in a ridiculous fashion?
15　　*Beside, this feat° body of mine doth not crave*　　　　　fit
　　Half the meat, drink, and cloth, one of your bulks will have.
　　Admit your fool's face be the mother of laughter,
　　Yet, for his brain, it must always come after:
　　And though that do feed him, it's a pitiful case,
20　　*His body is beholding to such a bad face.* [*Knocking within.*]

VOLPONE Who's there? my couch; away! look! Nano, see:

[*Exeunt Androgyno and Castrone.*]

　　Give me my caps, first—go, enquire. [*Exit Nano.*]—Now, Cupid
　　Send it be Mosca, and with fair return!

NANO [*within*] It is the beauteous madam—

VOLPONE　　　　　　　　　　　　　　Would-be—is it?

NANO The same.

VOLPONE　　　　　　Now torment on me! Squire her in;
　　For she will enter, or dwell here forever.
　　Nay, quickly. [*Retires to his couch.*]—That my fit were past! I fear
　　A second hell too, that my loathing this
　　Will quite expel my appetite to the other:[2]
30　　Would she were taking now her tedious leave.
　　Lord, how it threats me what I am to suffer!

Scene 4

[*Re-enter Nano, with Lady Politic Would-be.*]

LADY POLITIC I thank you, good sir. 'Pray you signify
　　Unto your patron, I am here.—This band
　　Shows not my neck enough.—I trouble you, sir;
　　Let me request you, bid one of my women
5　　Come hither to me.—In good faith, I am dressed
　　Most favorably to-day! It is no matter;

2. "This" is Lady Politic; "the other" is Celia.

'Tis well enough.—
                    [Enter First Waiting-woman.]
              Look, see, these petulant things,
      How they have done this!

VOLPONE *[aside]*   I do feel the fever
      Entering in at mine ears; O, for a charm
10   To fright it hence!

LADY POLITIC   Come nearer: is this curl
      In his right place, or this? Why is this higher
      Than all the rest? You have not washed your eyes, yet!
      Or do they not stand even in your head?
      Where is your fellow? Call her. *[Exit First Woman.]*

NANO   Now, St. Mark
15   Deliver us! Anon, she'll beat her women,
      Because her nose is red.
                   [Re-enter First with Second Woman.]

LADY POLITIC   I pray you, view
      This tire,° forsooth: are all things apt, or no?   *headdress*

FIRST WOMAN One hair a little, here, sticks out, forsooth.

LADY POLITIC Does't so, forsooth? and where was your dear sight,
20   When it did so, forsooth? What now! Bird-eyed?
      And you, too? 'Pray you, both approach and mend it.
      Now, by that light, I muse you are not ashamed!
      I, that have preached these things so oft unto you,
      Read you the principles, argued all the grounds,
25   Disputed every fitness, every grace,
      Called you to counsel of so frequent dressings—

NANO *[aside]* More carefully than of your fame or honor.

LADY POLITIC Made you acquainted, what an ample dowry
      The knowledge of these things would be unto you,
30   Able, alone, to get you noble husbands
      At your return; and you thus to neglect it!
      Besides you seeing what a curious° nation   *particular*
      The Italians are, what will they say of me?
      The English lady cannot dress herself.
35   Here's a fine imputation to our country!
      Well, go your ways, and stay in the next room.
      This fucus° was too coarse too; it's no matter.—   *cosmetic*
      Good sir, you'll give them entertainment?
   [Exeunt Nano and Waiting-women.]

VOLPONE The storm comes toward me.

LADY POLITIC *[goes to the couch]*   How does my Volpone?

VOLPONE Troubled with noise, I cannot sleep; I dreamt
      That a strange fury entered, now, my house,
      And, with the dreadful tempest of her breath,
      Did cleave my roof asunder.

LADY POLITIC   Believe me, and I
      Had the most fearful dream, could I remember't—

VOLPONE *[aside]* Out on my fate! I have given her the occasion
      How to torment me: she will tell me her's.

LADY POLITIC Me thought, the golden mediocrity,°   *mean*
    Polite and delicate—
VOLPONE   O, if you do love me,
    No more: I sweat, and suffer, at the mention
50   Of any dream; feel how I tremble yet.
LADY POLITIC Alas, good soul! the passion of the heart.
    Seed-pearl were good now, boiled with syrup of apples,
    Tincture of gold, and coral, citron-pills,
    Your elicampane root, myrobalanes—[3]
VOLPONE [*aside*] Ah me, I have ta'en a grass-hopper by the wing!
LADY POLITIC Burnt silk, and amber;[4] you have muscadel
    Good in the house—
VOLPONE   You will not drink, and part?
LADY POLITIC No, fear not that. I doubt, we shall not get
    Some English saffron, half a dram would serve;
60   Your sixteen cloves, a little musk, dried mints,
    Bugloss, and barley-meal—
VOLPONE [*aside*]   She's in again!
    Before I feigned diseases, now I have one.
LADY POLITIC And these applied with a right scarlet cloth.
VOLPONE [*aside*]
65   Another flood of words! a very torrent!
LADY POLITIC Shall I, sir, make you a poultice?
VOLPONE   No, no, no,
    I'm very well, you need prescribe no more.
LADY POLITIC I have a little studied physic; but now,
    I'm all for music, save, in the forenoons,
    An hour or two for painting. I would have
70   A lady, indeed, to have all, letters and arts,
    Be able to discourse, to write, to paint—
    But principal, as Plato holds, your music,[5]
    And so does wise Pythagoras, I take it—
    Is your true rapture, when there is concent°   *harmony*
75   In face, in voice, and clothes, and is, indeed,
    Our sex's chiefest ornament.
VOLPONE   The poet
    As old in time as Plato, and as knowing,
    Says, that your highest female grace is silence.[6]
LADY POLITIC Which of your poets? Petrarch, or Tasso, or Dante?
80   Guarini? Ariosto? Aretine?
    Cieco di Hadria?[7] I have read them all.
VOLPONE [*aside*] Is every thing a cause to my destruction?
LADY POLITIC I think I have two or three of them about me.
VOLPONE [*aside*] The sun, the sea, will sooner both stand still
85   Than her eternal tongue! nothing can 'scape it.

---

3. Elicampane is a stimulant; myrobalanes is medicine for
diarrhea.
4. Remedies for smallpox.
5. According to Plato's *Republic*, education in music was

for men, not women.
6. Sophocles, *Ajax*, line 293.
7. Famous Italian Renaissance poets.

LADY POLITIC Here's Pastor Fido—[8]
VOLPONE [*aside*]   Profess obstinate silence;
    That's now my safest.
LADY POLITIC   All our English writers,
    I mean such as are happy in the Italian,
    Will deign to steal out of this author, mainly:
90   Almost as much as from Montagnié.[9]
    He has so modern and facile a vein,
    Fitting the time, and catching the court-ear!
    Your Petrarch is more passionate, yet he,
    In days of sonnetting, trusted them with much.
95   Dante is hard, and few can understand him.
    But, for a desperate wit, there's Aretine;
    Only, his pictures are a little obscene—[1]
    You mark me not.
VOLPONE   Alas, my mind's perturbed.
LADY POLITIC Why, in such cases, we must cure ourselves,
100   Make use of our philosophy—
VOLPONE   Oh me!
LADY POLITIC And as we find our passions do rebel,
    Encounter them with reason, or divert them,
    By giving scope unto some other humor
    Of lesser danger: as, in politic bodies,°   *governments*
105   There's nothing more doth overwhelm the judgment,
    And cloud the understanding, than too much
    Settling and fixing, and, as 'twere, subsiding
    Upon one object. For the incorporating
    Of these same outward things, into that part,
110   Which we call mental, leaves some certain faeces°   *dregs*
    That stop the organs, and as Plato says,
    Assassinate our knowledge.
VOLPONE [*aside*]   Now, the spirit
    Of patience help me!
LADY POLITIC   Come, in faith, I must
    Visit you more a days; and make you well.
115   Laugh and be lusty.
VOLPONE [*aside*]   My good angel save me!
LADY POLITIC There was but one sole man in all the world,
    With whom I e'er could sympathize; and he
    Would lie you, often, three, four hours together
    To hear me speak; and be sometimes so rapt,
120   As he would answer me quite from the purpose,
    Like you, and you are like him, just. I'll discourse,
    An't be but only, sir, to bring you asleep,
    How we did spend our time and loves together,
    For some six years.

---

8. A pastoral by Guarini (1590).
9. Author of the *Essays*, which Jonson's friend John Florio had recently translated into English.

1. Aretino's "Sonnets of Lust" (*Sonnetti Lussuriosi*, 1532) were accompanied by engravings based on pornographic drawings by Giulio Romano.

VOLPONE   Oh, oh, oh, oh, oh, oh!
LADY POLITIC For we were coaetanei,° and brought up—   *the same age*
VOLPONE Some power, some fate, some fortune rescue me!

Scene 5

[*Enter Mosca.*]

MOSCA God save you, madam!
LADY POLITIC   Good sir.
VOLPONE   Mosca! welcome,
    Welcome to my redemption.
MOSCA   Why, sir?
VOLPONE   Oh,
    Rid me of this my torture, quickly, there;
    My madam, with the everlasting voice:
5   The bells, in time of pestilence, ne'er made
    Like noise, or were in that perpetual motion!
    The cock-pit comes not near it. All my house,
    But now, steamed like a bath with her thick breath,
    A lawyer could not have been heard; nor scarce
10   Another woman, such a hail of words
    She has let fall. For hell's sake, rid her hence.
MOSCA Has she presented?
VOLPONE   O, I do not care;
    I'll take her absence, upon any price,
    With any loss.
MOSCA   Madam—
LADY POLITIC   I have brought your patron
15   A toy, a cap here, of mine own work.
MOSCA   'Tis well.
    I had forgot to tell you, I saw your knight.
    Where you would little think it.—
LADY POLITIC   Where?
MOSCA   Marry,
    Where yet, if you make haste, you may apprehend
    Rowing upon the water in a gondola
20   With the most cunning courtesan of Venice.
LADY POLITIC Is't true?
MOSCA   Pursue them, and believe your eyes:
    Leave me, to make your gift. [*Exit Lady Politic, hastily.*]
                —I knew 'twould take:
    For, lightly, they that use themselves most license,
    Are still most jealous.
VOLPONE   Mosca, hearty thanks,
25   For thy quick fiction, and delivery of me.
    Now to my hopes, what say'st thou?
          [*Re-enter Lady Politic Would-be.*]
LADY POLITIC   But do you hear, sir?—
VOLPONE Again! I fear a paroxysm.
LADY POLITIC   Which way
    Rowed they together?

MOSCA   Toward the Rialto.

LADY POLITIC I pray you lend me your dwarf.

MOSCA   I pray you take him.—[*Exit Lady Politic.*]

30   Your hopes, sir, are like happy blossoms, fair,
       And promise timely fruit, if you will stay
       But the maturing; keep you at your couch,
       Corbaccio will arrive straight, with the will;
       When he is gone, I'll tell you more. [*Exit.*]

VOLPONE   My blood,

35   My spirits are returned; I am alive:
       And, like your wanton gamester at primero,[2]
       Whose thought had whispered to him, not go less,
       Methinks I lie, and draw—for an encounter.
       [*The scene closes upon Volpone.*]

Scene 6. *The passage leading to Volpone's chamber*

[*Enter Mosca and Bonario.*]

MOSCA Sir, here concealed, [*shews him a closet*] you may hear all—But, pray you,
       Have patience, sir; [*knocking within.*]—the same's your father knocks:
       I am compelled to leave you. [*Exit.*]

BONARIO   Do so.—Yet
       Cannot my thought imagine this a truth. [*Goes into the closet.*]

Scene 7. *Another part of the same*

[*Enter Mosca and Corvino, Celia following.*]

MOSCA Death on me! you are come too soon, what meant you?
       Did not I say, I would send?

CORVINO   Yes, but I feared
       You might forget it, and then they prevent us.

MOSCA [*aside*] Prevent! did e'er man haste so, for his horns?
5   A courtier would not ply it so, for a place.
       Well, now there is no helping it, stay here;
       I'll presently return. [*Crosses stage to Bonario.*]

CORVINO   Where are you, Celia?
       You know not wherefore I have brought you hither?

CELIA Not well, except you told me.

CORVINO   Now, I will:
       Hark hither. [*He leads her to one side and whispers to her.*]

MOSCA [*to Bonario*] Sir, your father hath sent word,
       It will be half an hour ere he come;
       And therefore, if you please to walk the while
       Into that gallery—at the upper end,
       There are some books to entertain the time:
15   And I'll take care no man shall come unto you, sir.

BONARIO Yes, I will stay there.—[*aside*] I do doubt this fellow. [*Exit Bonario.*]

MOSCA [*looking after him*] There; he is far enough; he can hear nothing:
       And, for his father, I can keep him off.

---

2. A Spanish card game; "go less" means "make a smaller bet"; "lie" means "place a bet"; "draw—for an encounter" means "pick a winning card," with a sexual double meaning.

[*Mosca goes to Volpone's couch, and, sitting by him, whispers.*]

CORVINO [*to Celia*] Nay, now, there is no starting back, and therefore,

20   Resolve upon it; I have so decreed.
    It must be done. Nor would I move't afore,
    Because I would avoid all shifts and tricks
        That might deny me.

CELIA   Sir, let me beseech you,
    Affect not these strange trials; if you doubt

25   My chastity, why, lock me up forever;
    Make me the heir of darkness. Let me live,
    Where I may please your fears, if not your trust.

CORVINO Believe it, I have no such humor, I.
    All that I speak I mean; yet I'm not mad;

30   Nor horn-mad,[3] see you? Go to, show yourself
    Obedient, and a wife.

CELIA   O heaven!

CORVINO   I say it,
    Do so.

CELIA   Was this the train?°   *scheme*

CORVINO   I've told you reasons;
    What the physicians have set down: how much
    It may concern me; what my engagements are;

35   My means; and the necessity of those means,
    For my recovery: wherefore, if you be
    Loyal, and mine, be won, respect my venture.[4]

CELIA Before your honor?

CORVINO   Honor! tut, a breath:
    There's no such thing in nature: a mere term

40   Invented to awe fools. What is my gold
    The worse for touching, clothes for being looked on?
    Why, this is no more. An old decrepit wretch,
    That has no sense, no sinew; takes his meat
    With others' fingers; only knows to gape,

45   When you do scald his gums; a voice, a shadow;
    And, what can this man hurt you?

CELIA [*aside*]   Lord! what spirit
    Is this hath entered him?

CORVINO   And for your fame,
    That's such a jig;° as if I would go tell it,   *joke*
    Cry it on the Piazza! who shall know it,

50   But he that cannot speak it, and this fellow,
    Whose lips are in my pocket? save yourself,
    (If you'll proclaim't, you may,) I know no other
    Should come to know it.

CELIA   Are heaven and saints then nothing?
    Will they be blind or stupid?

CORVINO   How!

CELIA   Good sir,

---

3. Driven mad by having been cuckolded.

4. Business transaction—i.e., his prostitution of Celia to Volpone.

55   Be jealous still, emulate them; and think
        What hate they burn with toward every sin.
CORVINO I grant you; if I thought it were a sin,
        I would not urge you. Should I offer this
        To some young Frenchman, or hot Tuscan blood
60   That had read Aretine, conned all his prints,[5]
        Knew every quirk within lust's labyrinth,
        And were professed critic in lechery;
        And I would look upon him, and applaud him,
        This were a sin: but here, 'tis contrary,
65   A pious work, mere° charity for physic,°   *pure / health*
        And honest polity, to assure mine own.
CELIA O heaven! canst thou suffer such a change?
VOLPONE Thou art mine honor, Mosca, and my pride,
        My joy, my tickling, my delight! Go bring them.
MOSCA [*advancing*] Please you draw near, sir.
CORVINO   Come on, what—
        You will not be rebellious? By that light—
MOSCA Sir, Signior Corvino, here, is come to see you.
VOLPONE Oh!
MOSCA   And hearing of the consultation had,
        So lately, for your health, is come to offer,
75   Or rather, sir, to prostitute—
CORVINO   Thanks, sweet Mosca.
MOSCA Freely, unasked, or unintreated—
CORVINO   Well.
MOSCA As the true fervent instance of his love,
        His own most fair and proper wife; the beauty,
        Only of price in Venice—
CORVINO   'Tis well urged.
MOSCA To be your comfortress, and to preserve you.
VOLPONE Alas, I am past, already! Pray you, thank him
        For his good care and promptness; but for that,
        'Tis a vain labor e'en to fight 'gainst heaven;
        Applying fire to stone—uh, uh, uh, uh! [*Coughing.*]
85   Making a dead leaf grow again. I take
        His wishes gently, though; and you may tell him,
        What I have done for him: marry, my state is hopeless.
        Will him to pray for me; and to use his fortune
        With reverence, when he comes to't.
MOSCA   Do you hear, sir?
90   Go to him with your wife.
CORVINO   Heart of my father!
        Wilt thou persist thus? come, I pray thee, come.
        Thou seest 'tis nothing, Celia. By this hand,
        I shall grow violent. Come, do't, I say.
CELIA Sir, kill me, rather: I will take down poison,
95   Eat burning coals,[6] do anything.—

---

5. Knew all the sexually explicit illustrations to Aretino's
poems.

6. Portia, the virtuous wife of Brutus, killed herself by eating burning coals.

CORVINO   Be damned!
           Heart, I will drag thee hence, home, by the hair;
           Cry thee a strumpet through the streets; rip up
           Thy mouth unto thine ears; and slit thy nose,[7]
           Like a raw rochet!°—Do not tempt me; come,   *large-headed fish*
100   Yield, I am loth—Death! I will buy some slave
           Whom I will kill, and bind thee to him, alive;[8]
           And at my window hang you forth, devising
           Some monstrous crime, which I, in capital letters,
           Will eat into thy flesh with aquafortis,°   *acid*
105   And burning corsives,° on this stubborn breast.   *corrosives*
           Now, by the blood thou hast incensed, I'll do it!
CELIA   Sir, what you please, you may, I am your martyr.
CORVINO   Be not thus obstinate, I have not deserved it:
           Think who it is intreats you. 'Prithee, sweet;—
110   Good faith, thou shalt have jewels, gowns, attires,
           What thou wilt think, and ask. Do but go kiss him.
           Or touch him, but. For my sake.—At my suit.—
           This once.—No! not! I shall remember this.
           Will you disgrace me thus? Do you thirst my undoing?
MOSCA   Nay, gentle lady, be advised.
CORVINO   No, no.
           She has watched her time. God's precious, this is scurvy,°   *evil*
           'Tis very scurvy; and you are—
MOSCA   Nay, good sir.
CORVINO   An arrant locust,[9] by heaven, a locust!
           Whore, crocodile, that hast thy tears prepared,[1]
120   Expecting how thou'lt bid them flow—
MOSCA   Nay, 'pray you, sir!
           She will consider.
CELIA   Would my life would serve
           To satisfy—
CORVINO   S'death! if she would but speak to him,
           And save my reputation, it were somewhat;
           But spightfully to affect my utter ruin!
MOSCA   Ay, now you have put your fortune in her hands.
           Why i'faith, it is her modesty, I must quit° her.   *exonerate*
           If you were absent, she would be more coming;
           I know it: and dare undertake for her.
           What woman can before her husband? 'pray you,
130   Let us depart, and leave her here.
CORVINO   Sweet Celia,
           Thou may'st redeem all, yet; I'll say no more:
           If not, esteem yourself as lost. Nay, stay there.
           [*Shuts the door and exits with Mosca.*]
CELIA   O God, and his good angels! whither, whither,
           Is shame fled human breasts? That with such ease,

---

7. There were cases of prostitutes being publicly mutilated in early modern Venice, although this was illegal.
8. The rapist Tarquin made similar threats to the chaste

Roman heroine Lucretia.
9. A notorious devouring creature.
1. The crocodile trapped its prey with fake tears.

135   Men dare put off your honors, and their own?
Is that, which ever was a cause of life,
Now placed beneath the basest circumstance,
And modesty an exile made, for money?

VOLPONE *[leaping from his couch]* Ay, in Corvino, and such earth-fed minds,
140   That never tasted the true heaven of love.
Assure thee, Celia, he that would sell thee,
Only for hope of gain, and that uncertain,
He would have sold his part of Paradise
For ready money, had he met a cope-man.°   *dealer*
145   Why art thou mazed to see me thus revived?
Rather applaud thy beauty's miracle;
'Tis thy great work that hath, not now alone,
But sundry times raised me, in several shapes,
And, but this morning, like a mountebank,
150   To see thee at thy window. Ay, before
I would have left my practice, for thy love,
In varying figures, I would have contended
With the blue Proteus, or the horned flood.[2]
Now art thou welcome.

CELIA   Sir!

VOLPONE   Nay, fly me not.
155   Nor let thy false imagination
That I was bed-rid, make thee think I am so:
Thou shalt not find it. I am, now, as fresh,
As hot, as high, and in as jovial plight,
As when, in that so celebrated scene,
160   At recitation of our comedy,
For entertainment of the great Valois,[3]
I acted young Antinous;[4] and attracted
The eyes and ears of all the ladies present,
To admire each graceful gesture, note, and footing. *[Sings.]*[5]

165   *Come, my Celia, let us prove,*
While we can, the sports of love,
Time will not be ours for ever,
He, at length, our good will sever;
Spend not then his gifts in vain;
170   *Suns, that set, may rise again;*
But if once we lose this light,
'Tis with us perpetual night.
Why should we defer our joys?
Fame and rumor are but toys.
175   *Cannot we delude the eyes*
Of a few poor household spies?
Or his easier ears beguile,
Thus removed by our wile?—

2. Both Proteus, the sea god, and Achelous, the horned river god, transformed themselves into many different shapes.
3. The future Henry III of France visited Venice in 1574.

4. The young male lover of Emperor Hadrian, or one of Penelope's suitors in the *Odyssey*.
5. The song is based on the Latin poet Catullus's "Let us live, my Lesbia, and love."

'Tis no sin love's fruits to steal:
180   *But the sweet thefts to reveal;*
To be taken, to be seen,
These have crimes accounted been.

CELIA   Some serene° blast me, or dire lightning strike   *noxious mist*
This my offending face!

VOLPONE   Why droops my Celia?
185   Thou hast, in place of a base husband, found
A worthy lover: use thy fortune well,
With secrecy and pleasure. See, behold,
What thou art queen of; not in expectation,
As I feed others: but possessed and crowned.
190   See, here, a rope of pearl; and each more orient
Than that the brave Aegyptian queen⁶ caroused:
Dissolve and drink them. See, a carbuncle,°   *ruby*
May put out both the eyes of our St. Mark;
A diamond, would have bought Lollia Paulina,⁷
195   When she came in like star-light, hid with jewels,
That were the spoils of provinces; take these,
And wear, and lose them: yet remains an ear-ring
To purchase them again, and this whole state.
A gem but worth a private patrimony,
200   Is nothing: we will eat such at a meal.
The heads of parrots, tongues of nightingales,
The brains of peacocks, and of ostriches,
Shall be our food: and, could we get the phoenix,
Though nature lost her kind, she were our dish.

CELIA   Good sir, these things might move a mind affected
With such delights; but I, whose innocence
Is all I can think wealthy, or worth th' enjoying,
And which, once lost, I have nought to lose beyond it,
Cannot be taken with these sensual baits:
If you have conscience—

VOLPONE   'Tis the beggar's virtue;
If thou hast wisdom, hear me, Celia.
Thy baths shall be the juice of July-flowers,
Spirit of roses, and of violets,
The milk of unicorns, and panthers' breath
215   Gathered in bags, and mixt with Cretan wines.
Our drink shall be prepared gold and amber;
Which we will take, until my roof whirl round
With the vertigo: and my dwarf shall dance,
My eunuch sing, my fool make up the antic,
220   Whilst we, in changed shapes, act Ovid's tales,⁸
Thou, like Europa now, and I like Jove,
Then I like Mars, and thou like Erycine:

---

6. Cleopatra.
7. The Emperor Caligula's wife.
8. Ovid's *Metamorphoses* contains stories of shape changing and the pursuit of desire. The god Jupiter in the form

of a bull raped Europa (*Metamorphoses* 2.858). Ericyna,
from Mount Eryx in Sicily, was a name for Venus, who
had an affair with Mars, god of War (*Metamorphoses*
4.171).

So, of the rest, till we have quite run through,
And wearied all the fables of the gods.
225   Then will I have thee in more modern forms,
Attired like some sprightly dame of France,
Brave Tuscan lady, or proud Spanish beauty;
Sometimes, unto the Persian sophy's wife;
Or the grand signior's mistress;[9] and, for change,
230   To one of our most artful courtesans,
Or some quick Negro, or cold Russian;
And I will meet thee in as many shapes:
Where we may so transfuse our wandering souls
Out at our lips, and score up sums of pleasures, [*Sings.*]

235   *That the curious shall not know*
        How to tell them as they flow;
        And the envious, when they find
        What their number is, be pined.°   *tormented*

CELIA   If you have ears that will be pierced—or eyes
240   That can be opened—a heart that may be touched—
Or any part that yet sounds man about you—
If you have touch of holy saints—or heaven—
Do me the grace to let me 'scape—if not,
Be bountiful and kill me. You do know,
245   I am a creature, hither ill betrayed,
By one, whose shame I would forget it were:
If you will deign me neither of these graces,
Yet feed your wrath, sir, rather than your lust,
(It is a vice comes nearer manliness,)
250   And punish that unhappy crime of nature,
Which you miscall my beauty: flay my face,
Or poison it with ointments, for seducing
Your blood to this rebellion. Rub these hands,
With what may cause an eating leprosy,
255   E'en to my bones and marrow: any thing,
That may disfavor me, save in my honor—
And I will kneel to you, pray for you, pay down
A thousand hourly vows, sir, for your health;
Report, and think you virtuous—

VOLPONE   Think me cold,
260   Frozen and impotent, and so report me?
That I had Nestor's hernia,[1] thou wouldst think.
I do degenerate, and abuse my nation,
To play with opportunity thus long;
I should have done the act, and then have parleyed.
265   Yield, or I'll force thee. [*Seizes her.*]
CELIA   O! just God!
VOLPONE   In vain—
BONARIO [*rushing in*] Forbear, foul ravisher, libidinous swine!

---

9. The Sultan of Turkey's mistress. The "Sophy" was the Shah of Persia.

1. Juvenal described the old impotent Greek warrior as having a hernia (*Satires* 6.326).

Free the forced lady, or thou diest, impostor.
But that I'm loth to snatch thy punishment
Out of the hand of justice, thou shouldst, yet,
270   Be made the timely sacrifice of vengeance,
Before this altar, and this dross, thy idol.—
Lady, let's quit the place, it is the den
Of villainy; fear nought, you have a guard:
And he, ere long, shall meet his just reward.

    [*Exeunt Bonario and Celia.*]

VOLPONE Fall on me, roof, and bury me in ruin!
Become my grave, that wert my shelter! O!
I am unmasked, unspirited, undone,
Betrayed to beggary, to infamy—

Scene 8

    [*Enter Mosca, wounded and bleeding.*]

MOSCA Where shall I run, most wretched shame of men,
    To beat out my unlucky brains?

VOLPONE   Here, here.
    What! dost thou bleed?

MOSCA   O that his well-driven sword
    Had been so courteous to have cleft me down
5   Unto the navel, ere I lived to see
    My life, my hopes, my spirits, my patron, all
    Thus desperately engaged, by my error!

VOLPONE Woe on thy fortune!

MOSCA   And my follies, sir.

VOLPONE Thou hast made me miserable.

MOSCA   And myself, sir.
10   Who would have thought he would have hearkened so?

VOLPONE What shall we do?

MOSCA   I know not; if my heart
    Could expiate the mischance, I'd pluck it out.
    Will you be pleased to hang me, or cut my throat?
    And I'll requite you, sir. Let's die like Romans,
15   Since we have lived like Grecians.[2] [*Knocking within.*]

VOLPONE   Hark! who's there?
    I hear some footing; officers, the saffi,°   *police*
    Come to apprehend us! I do feel the brand
    Hissing already at my forehead; now,
    Mine ears are boring.

MOSCA   To your couch, sir, you,
20   Make that place good, however. [*Volpone lies down, as before.*]—Guilty men
    Suspect what they deserve still.

    [*Enter Corbaccio.*]

                           Signior Corbaccio!

CORBACCIO Why, how now, Mosca?

MOSCA   O, undone, amazed, sir.

---

2. To "die like Romans" means to commit suicide; to live "like Grecians" means to enjoy luxury.

Your son, I know not by what accident,
Acquainted with your purpose to my patron,
25   Touching your will, and making him your heir,
Entered our house with violence, his sword drawn
Sought for you, called you wretch, unnatural,
Vowed he would kill you.

CORBACCIO   Me!

MOSCA   Yes, and my patron.

CORBACCIO This act shall disinherit him indeed;
Here is the will.

MOSCA   'Tis well, sir.

CORBACCIO   Right and well:
Be you as careful now for me.

                    [*Enter Voltore, behind.*]

MOSCA   My life, sir,
Is not more tendered; I am only yours.

CORBACCIO How does he? will he die shortly, think'st thou?

MOSCA   I fear
He'll outlast May.

CORBACCIO   Today?

MOSCA   No, last out May, sir.

CORBACCIO Could'st thou not give him a dram?

MOSCA   O, by no means, sir.

CORBACCIO Nay, I'll not bid you.

VOLTORE [*coming forward*]   This is a knave, I see.

MOSCA [*seeing Voltore*] How! signior Voltore! [*Aside.*] Did he hear me?

VOLTORE   Parasite!

MOSCA Who's that?—O, sir, most timely welcome—

VOLTORE   Scarce,
To the discovery of your tricks, I fear.
40   You are his, *only?* and mine also, are you not?

MOSCA Who? I, sir?

VOLTORE   You, sir. What device is this
About a will?

MOSCA   A plot for you, sir.

VOLTORE   Come,
Put not your foists° upon me; I shall scent them.   *tricks, stinks*

MOSCA Did you not hear it?

VOLTORE   Yes, I hear Corbaccio
Hath made your patron there his heir.

MOSCA   'Tis true,
By my device, drawn to it by my plot,
With hope—

VOLTORE   Your patron should reciprocate?
And you have promised?

MOSCA   For your good, I did, sir.
Nay, more, I told his son, brought, hid him here,
50   Where he might hear his father pass the deed:
Being persuaded to it by this thought, sir,
That the unnaturalness, first, of the act,

And then his father's oft disclaiming in him,
(Which I did mean t'help on,) would sure enrage him
55   To do some violence upon his parent,
On which the law should take sufficient hold,
And you be stated in a double hope:
Truth be my comfort, and my conscience,
My only aim was to dig you a fortune
60   Out of these two old rotten sepulchres—
VOLTORE I cry thee mercy, Mosca.
MOSCA   Worth your patience,
And your great merit, sir. And see the change!
VOLTORE Why, what success?
MOSCA   Most hapless! You must help, sir.
Whilst we expected the old raven, in comes
65   Corvino's wife, sent hither by her husband—
VOLTORE What, with a present?
MOSCA   No, sir, on visitation;
(I'll tell you how anon;) and staying long,
The youth he grows impatient, rushes forth,
Seizeth the lady, wounds me, makes her swear
70   (Or he would murder her, that was his vow)
To affirm my patron to have done her rape:
Which how unlike it is, you see! and hence,
With that pretext he's gone, to accuse his father,
Defame my patron, defeat you—
VOLTORE   Where's her husband?
Let him be sent for straight.
MOSCA   Sir, I'll go fetch him.
VOLTORE Bring him to the Scrutineo.[3]
MOSCA   Sir, I will.
VOLTORE This must be stopped.
MOSCA   O you do nobly, sir.
Alas, 'twas labored all, sir, for your good;
Nor was there want of counsel in the plot:
80   But fortune can, at any time, o'erthrow
The projects of a hundred learnèd clerks, sir.
CORBACCIO [listening] What's that?
VOLTORE   Will't please you, sir, to go along?
    [Exit Corbaccio, followed by Voltore.]
MOSCA Patron, go in, and pray for our success.
VOLPONE [rising from his couch] Need makes devotion: heaven your labor bless!
    [Exeunt.]

Act 4

Scene 1. A street

[Enter Sir Politic Would-be and Peregrine.]
SIR POLITIC I told you, sir, it was a plot; you see
What observation is! You mentioned me

3. Law court in the Senate-house.

For some instructions: I will tell you, sir,
(Since we are met here in this height[1] of Venice,)
5   Some few particulars I have set down,
Only for this meridian, fit to be known
Of your crude traveler; and they are these.
I will not touch, sir, at your phrase, or clothes,
For they are old.
PEREGRINE   Sir, I have better.
SIR POLITIC   Pardon,
I meant, as they are themes.
PEREGRINE   O, sir, proceed:
I'll slander you no more of wit, good sir.
SIR POLITIC First, for your garb,° it must be grave and serious,   *behavior*
Very reserved and locked; not tell a secret
On any terms, not to your father; scarce
15   A fable, but with caution: make sure choice
Both of your company, and discourse; beware
You never speak a truth—
PEREGRINE   How!
SIR POLITIC   Not to strangers,
For those be they you must converse with most;
Others I would not know, sir, but at distance,
20   So as I still might be a saver[2] in them:
You shall have tricks else past upon you hourly.
And then, for your religion, profess none,
But wonder at the diversity, of all:
And, for your part, protest, were there no other
25   But simply the laws o' the land, you could content you,
Nic. Machiavel, and Monsieur Bodin, both
Were of this mind.[3] Then must you learn the use
And handling of your silver fork at meals,[4]
The metal of your glass; (these are main matters
30   With your Italian) and to know the hour
When you must eat your melons, and your figs.
PEREGRINE Is that a point of state too?
SIR POLITIC   Here it is:
For your Venetian, if he see a man
Preposterous in the least, he has him straight;
35   He has; he strips him. I'll acquaint you, sir,
I now have lived here, 'tis some fourteen months
Within the first week of my landing here,
All took me for a citizen of Venice,
I knew the forms so well—
PEREGRINE [*aside*]   And nothing else.
SIR POLITIC I had read Contarene,[5] took me a house,

---

1. Climate, constitution.
2. A gambling term meaning to avoid either winning or losing.
3. Niccolo Machiavelli (1469–1526) analyzed the political expediency of religion, while Jean Bodin (1530–1596) saw religious toleration as way to avoid civil war.
4. The fork, a Renaissance invention, was not yet used in early 17th century England.
5. Gasparo Contarini wrote a book on the Venetian constitution, translated as *The Commonwealth and Government of Venice* (1599).

Dealt with my Jews[6] to furnish it with moveables—
Well, if I could but find one man, one man
To mine own heart, whom I durst trust, I would—

PEREGRINE What, what, sir?

SIR POLITIC   Make him rich; make him a fortune:
45   He should not think again. I would command it.

PEREGRINE As how?

SIR POLITIC   With certain projects that I have;
Which I may not discover.°   reveal

PEREGRINE [aside]   If I had
But one to wager with, I would lay odds now,
He tells me instantly.

SIR POLITIC   One is, and that
50   I care not greatly who knows, to serve the state
Of Venice with red herrings for three years,
And at a certain rate, from Rotterdam,
Where I have correspondence. There's a letter,
Sent me from one o' the States,[7] and to that purpose:
55   He cannot write his name, but that's his mark.

PEREGRINE He is a chandler?°   candle maker

SIR POLITIC   No, a cheesemonger.
There are some others too with whom I treat
About the same negotiation;
And I will undertake it; for, 'tis thus.
60   I'll do't with ease, I have cast it all; Your hoy°   small fishing boat
Carries but three men in her, and a boy;
And she shall make me three returns a year:
So, if there come but one of three, I save;
If two, I can defalk:°—but this is now,   cut back the amount
If my main project fail.

PEREGRINE   Then you have others?

SIR POLITIC I should be loath to draw the subtle air
Of such a place, without my thousand aims.
I'll not dissemble, sir: where'er I come,
I love to be considerative; and 'tis true,
70   I have at my free hours thought upon
Some certain goods unto the state of Venice,
Which I do call my Cautions; and, sir, which
I mean, in hope of pension, to propound
To the Great Council, then unto the Forty,
75   So to the Ten.[8] My means are made already—

PEREGRINE By whom?

SIR POLITIC   Sir, one that, though his place be obscure,
Yet he can sway, and they will hear him. He's
A commandatore.

PEREGRINE   What! a common sergeant?

SIR POLITIC Sir, such as they are, put it in their mouths,

---

6. Borrowed money from Jews who lived in the Venetian
ghetto.
7. A citizen of the United Provinces of the Netherlands;

a member of the Dutch assembly, the States-General.
8. Representative assemblies of Venetian government.

80   What they should say, sometimes; as well as greater:
        I think I have my notes to show you—[*Searching his pockets.*]
PEREGRINE   Good sir.
SIR POLITIC But you shall swear unto me, on your gentry,
        Not to anticipate—
PEREGRINE   I, sir!
SIR POLITIC   Nor reveal
        A circumstance—My paper is not with me.
PEREGRINE O, but you can remember, sir.
SIR POLITIC   My first is
        Concerning tinder-boxes.° You must know,   *match boxes*
        No family is here without its box.
        Now, sir, it being so portable a thing,
        Put case, that you or I were ill affected
90   Unto the state, sir; with it in our pockets,
        Might not I go into the Arsenal,[9]
        Or you, come out again, and none the wiser?
PEREGRINE Except yourself, sir.
SIR POLITIC   Go to, then. I therefore
        Advertise to the state, how fit it were,
95   That none but such as were known patriots,
        Sound lovers of their country, should be suffered
        To enjoy them in their houses; and even those
        Sealed at some office, and at such a bigness
        As might not lurk in pockets.
PEREGRINE   Admirable!
SIR POLITIC My next is, how to enquire, and be resolved,
        By present demonstration, whether a ship,
        Newly arrived from Syria, or from
        Any suspected part of all the Levant,°   *the Middle East*
        Be guilty of the plague: and where they use
105   To lie out forty, fifty days, sometimes,
        About the Lazaretto,[1] for their trial;
        I'll save that charge and loss unto the merchant,
        And in an hour clear the doubt.
PEREGRINE   Indeed, sir!
SIR POLITIC Or—I will lose my labor.
PEREGRINE   'My faith, that's much.
SIR POLITIC Nay, sir, conceive me. It will cost me in onions,
        Some thirty livres[2]—
PEREGRINE   Which is one pound sterling.
SIR POLITIC Beside my waterworks: for this I do, sir
        First, I bring in your ship 'twixt two brick walls;
        But those the state shall venture: On the one
115   I strain me a fair tarpauling,° and in that   *waterproofed canvas*
        I stick my onions, cut in halves: the other
        Is full of loop-holes, out at which I thrust

---

9. Venetian shipyard.
1. Plague hospital on an island outside Venice, where the passengers of foreign ships were held until deemed

free of disease.
2. Peeled onions were used to protect the air from the plague; the livre was a French coin.

The noses of my bellows; and those bellows
I keep, with water-works, in perpetual motion,
120   Which is the easiest matter of a hundred.
Now, sir, your onion, which doth naturally
Attract the infection, and your bellows blowing
The air upon him, will show, instantly,
By his changed color, if there be contagion;
125   Or else remain as fair as at the first.
    —Now it is known, 'tis nothing.

PEREGRINE   You are right, sir.
SIR POLITIC I would I had my note.
PEREGRINE   'Faith, so would I:
    But you have done well for once, sir.
SIR POLITIC   Were I false,
    Or would be made so, I could show you reasons
130   How I could sell this state now to the Turk,
    Spite of their gallies, or their—[*Examining his papers.*]
PEREGRINE   Pray you, Sir Pol.
SIR POLITIC I have them not about me.
PEREGRINE   That I feared:
    The're there, sir.
SIR POLITIC   No, this is my diary,
    Wherein I note my actions of the day.
PEREGRINE Pray you, let's see, sir. What is here? [*Reads.*] *Notandum,*[3]
    A rat had gnawn my spur-leathers; notwithstanding,
    I put on new, and did go forth: but first
    I threw three beans over the threshold. Item,
    I went and bought two tooth-picks, whereof one
140   *I burst immediately, in a discourse*
    With a Dutch merchant, 'bout ragion del stato.[4]
    From him I went and paid a moccinigo°   *a dime*
    For piecing my silk stockings; by the way
    I cheapened sprats;[5] and at St. Mark's I urined.
145   'Faith these are politic notes!
SIR POLITIC   Sir, I do slip
    No action of my life, but thus I quote it.
PEREGRINE Believe me, it is wise!
SIR POLITIC   Nay, sir, read forth.

Scene 2

[*Enter, at a distance, Lady Politic Would-be, Nano, and two Waiting-women.*]
LADY POLITIC Where should this loose knight be, trow? Sure he's housed.[6]
NANO Why, then he's fast.
LADY POLITIC   Ay, he plays both[7] with me.
    I pray you stay. This heat will do more harm

---

3. It must be noted.
4. Reasons of state, the notion that political ends justify immoral means.

5. Haggled over the price of fish.
6. Secure; involved with a courtesan.
7. Fast and loose.

To my complexion, than his heart is worth.

5   (I do not care to hinder, but to take him.)
     How it[8] comes off! [*Rubbing her cheeks.*]

1 WOMAN   My master's yonder.

LADY POLITIC   Where?

2 WOMAN With a young gentleman.

LADY POLITIC   That same's the party;
     In man's apparel! 'Pray you, sir, jog my knight:
     I will be tender to his reputation,
     However he demerit.

SIR POLITIC [*seeing her*]   My lady!

PEREGRINE   Where?

SIR POLITIC 'Tis she indeed, sir; you shall know her. She is,
     Were she not mine, a lady of that merit,
     For fashion and behavior; and for beauty
     I durst compare—

PEREGRINE   It seems you are not jealous,
     That dare commend her.

SIR POLITIC   Nay, and for discourse—

PEREGRINE Being your wife, she cannot miss that.

SIR POLITIC [*introducing Peregrine*]   Madam,
     Here is a gentleman, pray you, use him fairly;
     He seems a youth, but he is—

LADY POLITIC   None?

SIR POLITIC   Yes, one
     Has put his face as soon into the world—

LADY POLITIC You mean, as early? But to-day?

SIR POLITIC   How's this?

LADY POLITIC Why, in this habit, sir; you apprehend me:—
     Well, master Would-be, this doth not become you;
     I had thought the odor, sir, of your good name
     Had been more precious to you; that you would not

25   Have done this dire massacre on your honor;
     One of your gravity and rank besides!
     But knights, I see, care little for the oath
     They make to ladies; chiefly, their own ladies.

SIR POLITIC Now, by my spurs, the symbol of my knighthood,[9]—

PEREGRINE [*Aside.*] Lord, how his brain is humbled for an oath!

SIR POLITIC I reach you not.

LADY POLITIC   Right, sir, your policy
     May bear it through thus.—Sir, a word with you. [*To Peregrine.*]
     I would be loth to contest publicly
     With any gentlewoman, or to seem

35   Froward, or violent, as the courtier says;[1]
     It comes too near rusticity in a lady,
     Which I would shun by all means: and however

---

8. Her make-up.
9. A swipe at James I's bestowal of an excessively large number of knighthoods.

1. Castiglione's *Il Cortegiano* (1528), a conduct book, translated in 1561 by Hoby as *The Courtier*.

I may deserve from master Would-be, yet
T'have one fair gentlewoman thus be made
40   The unkind instrument to wrong another,
And one she knows not, ay, and to persèver;
In my poor judgment, is not warranted
From being a solecism² in our sex,
If not in manners.
PEREGRINE   How is this?
SIR POLITIC   Sweet madam,
45   Come nearer to your aim.
LADY POLITIC   Marry, and will, sir.
Since you provoke me with your impudence,
And laughter of your light land-siren here,
Your Sporus,³ your hermaphrodite—
PEREGRINE   What's here?
Poetic fury, and historic storms!
SIR POLITIC The gentleman, believe it, is of worth,
And of our nation.
LADY POLITIC   Ay, your White-friars nation.⁴
Come, I blush for you, master Would-be, I;
And am ashamed you should have no more forehead,°   modesty
Than thus to be the patron, or St. George,
55   To a lewd harlot, a base fricatrice,°   prostitute
A female devil, in a male outside.
SIR POLITIC   Nay,
An you be such a one, I must bid adieu
To your delights. The case appears too liquid. [Exit.]
LADY POLITIC Ay, you may carry't clear, with your state-face!—
60   But for your carnival⁵ concupiscence,
Who here is fled for liberty of conscience,
From furious persecution of the marshal,
Her will I dis'ple.⁶
PEREGRINE   This is fine, i'faith!
And do you use this often? Is this part
65   Of your wit's exercise, 'gainst you have occasion?
Madam—
LADY POLITIC   Go to, sir.
PEREGRINE   Do you hear me, lady?
Why, if your knight have set you to beg shirts,
Or to invite me home, you might have done it
A nearer way, by far.⁷
LADY POLITIC   This cannot work you
65   Out of my snare.
PEREGRINE   Why, am I in it, then?
Indeed your husband told me you were fair.

---

2. An error in language use rather than in behavior, so this is itself a solecism.
3. The Roman Emperor Nero's transvestite eunuch.
4. White-friars, a section of London frequented by prostitutes.

5. Festival characterized by sexual license and transvestism.
6. Discipline, a reference to the English marshall's public punishment of prostitutes by whipping.
7. Peregrine suggests that Sir Politic has been pimping his wife.

And so you are; only your nose inclines,
That side that's next the sun, to the queen-apple.[8]
LADY POLITIC This cannot be endured by any patience.

Scene 3

[Enter Mosca.]
MOSCA What is the matter, madam?
LADY POLITIC   If the senate
    Right not my quest in this, I will protest them
    To all the world, no aristocracy.
MOSCA What is the injury, lady?
LADY POLITIC   Why, the callet°   *whore*
5   You told me of, here I have ta'en disguised.
MOSCA Who? This! What means your ladyship? The creature
    I mentioned to you is apprehended now,
    Before the senate; you shall see her—
LADY POLITIC   Where?
MOSCA I'll bring you to her. This young gentleman,
10   I saw him land this morning at the port.
LADY POLITIC Is't possible! How has my judgment wandered?
    Sir, I must, blushing, say to you, I have erred;
    And plead your pardon.
PEREGRINE   What, more changes yet!
LADY POLITIC I hope you have not the malice to remember
15   A gentlewoman's passion. If you stay
    In Venice here, please you to use me, sir—
MOSCA Will you go, madam?
LADY POLITIC   'Pray you, sir, use me; in faith,
    The more you see me, the more I shall conceive
    You have forgot our quarrel.
    [Exeunt Lady Would-be, Mosca, Nano, and waiting-women.]
PEREGRINE   This is rare!
20   Sir Politic Would-be? No; sir Politic Bawd,°   *pimp*
    To bring me thus acquainted with his wife!
    Well, wise Sir Pol, since you have practised thus
    Upon my freshman-ship,° I'll try your salt-head,[9]   *innocence*
    What proof it is against a counter-plot. [Exit.]

Scene 4. The Scrutineo, or Senate-House

[Enter Voltore, Corbaccio, Corvino, and Mosca.]
VOLTORE Well, now you know the carriage of the business,
    Your constancy is all that is required
    Unto the safety of it.
MOSCA   Is the lie
    Safely conveyed amongst us? Is that sure?
    Knows every man his burden?
CORVINO   Yes.
MOSCA   Then shrink not.

---

8. Her nose is red as an apple.   9. Lecherousness.

CORVINO But knows the advocate the truth?

MOSCA   O, sir,
By no means; I devised a formal tale,
That salv'd your reputation. But be valiant, sir.

CORVINO I fear no one but him, that this his pleading
Should make him stand for a co-heir—

MOSCA   Co-halter!
Hang him; we will but use his tongue, his noise,
As we do Croaker's[1] here.

CORVINO   Ay, what shall he do?

MOSCA When we have done, you mean?

CORVINO   Yes.

MOSCA   Why, we'll think:
Sell him for mummia;[2] he's half dust already.

15   [To Voltore.] Do you not smile, to see this buffalo,
How he doth sport it with his head?[3]—[aside] I should,
If all were well and past.—[To Corbaccio.] Sir, only you
Are he that shall enjoy the crop of all,
And these not know for whom they toil.

CORBACCIO   Ay, peace.

MOSCA [Turning to Corvino.]
20   But you shall eat it. [Aside:] Much!
        [To Voltore.]   —Worshipful sir,
Mercury sit upon your thundering tongue,
Or the French Hercules,[4] and make your language
As conquering as his club, to beat along,
As with a tempest, flat, our adversaries;
25   But much more yours, sir.

VOLTORE   Here they come, have done.

MOSCA I have another witness, if you need, sir,
I can produce.

VOLTORE   Who is it?

MOSCA   Sir, I have her.

Scene 5

[Enter Avocatori and take their seats, Bonario, Celia, Notario, Commendatori, Saffi,
and other Officers of justice.]

1 AVOCATORE The like of this the senate never heard of.

2 AVOCATORE 'Twill come most strange to them when we report it.

4 AVOCATORE The gentlewoman[5] has been ever held
Of unreproved name.

3 AVOCATORE   So has the youth.[6]

4 AVOCATORE The more unnatural part that of his father.[7]

2 AVOCATORE More of the husband.[8]

1 AVOCATORE   I not know to give

---

1. Corbaccio's, referring to the way he speaks.
2. Medicine made from mummies.
3. Enjoy the cuckold's horns on his head.
4. Mercury was the god of skill in speech; Lucian described the French Hercules as eloquent.
5. Celia.
6. Bonario.
7. Corbaccio.
8. Corvino.

His act a name, it is so monstrous!

4 AVOCATORE But the impostor,° he's a thing created   *Volpone*
To exceed example!

1 AVOCATORE   And all after-times!

2 AVOCATORE I never heard a true voluptuary[9]
Described, but him.

3 AVOCATORE   Appear yet those were cited?

NOTARIO All but the old magnifico, Volpone.

1 AVOCATORE Why is not he here?

MOSCA   Please your fatherhoods,
Here is his advocate: himself's so weak,
So feeble—

4 AVOCATORE   What are you?

BONARIO   His parasite,
His knave, his pandar:° I beseech the court,   *procurer*
He may be forced to come, that your grave eyes
May bear strong witness of his strange impostures.

VOLTORE Upon my faith and credit with your virtues,
20   He is not able to endure the air.

2 AVOCATORE Bring him, however.

3 AVOCATORE   We will see him.

4 AVOCATORE   Fetch him.

VOLTORE Your fatherhoods' fit pleasures be obeyd;
  [*Exeunt Officers.*]
      But sure, the sight will rather move your pities,
      Than indignation. May it please the court,
25   In the mean time, he may be heard in me;
      I know this place most void of prejudice,
      And therefore crave it, since we have no reason
      To fear our truth should hurt our cause.

3 AVOCATORE   Speak free.

VOLTORE Then know, most honored fathers, I must now
30   Discover to your strangely abused ears,
      The most prodigious and most frontless° piece   *shameless*
      Of solid impudence, and treachery,
      That ever vicious nature yet brought forth
      To shame the state of Venice. This lewd woman,
35   That wants no artificial looks or tears
      To help the visor° she has now put on,   *mask*
      Hath long been known a close° adulteress   *secret*
      To that lascivious youth there; not suspected,
      I say, but known, and taken in the act
40   With him; and by this man, the easy husband,
      Pardoned; whose timeless bounty makes him now
      Stand here, the most unhappy, innocent person,
      That ever man's own goodness made accused.
      For these not knowing how to owe a gift
45   Of that dear grace, but with their shame; being placed

---

9. Person addicted to pleasure.

So above all powers of their gratitude,
Began to hate the benefit; and, in place
Of thanks, devise to extirp° the memory   *root out*
Of such an act: wherein I pray your fatherhoods
50   To observe the malice, yea, the rage of creatures
Discovered in their evils; and what heart
Such take, even from their crimes:—but that anon
Will more appear.—This gentleman, the father,
Hearing of this foul fact, with many others,
55   Which daily struck at his too tender ears,
And grieved in nothing more than that he could not
Preserve himself a parent, (his son's ills
Growing to that strange flood,) at last decreed
To disinherit him.

1 AVOCATORE   These be strange turns!
2 AVOCATORE The young man's fame was ever fair and honest.
VOLTORE So much more full of danger is his vice,
That can beguile so under shade of virtue.
But, as I said, my honored sires, his father
Having this settled purpose, by what means
65   To him betrayed, we know not, and this day
Appointed for the deed; that parricide,
I cannot style him better, by confederacy°   *conspiracy*
Preparing this his paramour to be there,
Entered Volpone's house, (who was the man,
70   Your fatherhoods must understand, designed
For the inheritance,) there sought his father:—
But with what purpose sought he him, my lords?
I tremble to pronounce it, that a son
Unto a father, and to such a father,
75   Should have so foul, felonious intent!
It was to murder him: when being prevented
By his more happy absence, what then did he?
Not check his wicked thoughts; no, now new deeds,
(Mischief doth never end where it begins)
80   An act of horror, fathers! He dragged forth
The aged gentleman that had there lain bed-rid
Three years and more, out of his innocent couch,
Naked upon the floor, there left him; wounded
His servant in the face: and, with this strumpet
85   The stale° to his forged practice, who was glad   *decoy*
To be so active—(I shall here desire
Your fatherhoods to note but my collections,°   *conclusions*
As most remarkable)— thought at once to stop
His father's ends, discredit his free choice
90   In the old gentleman, redeem themselves,
By laying infamy upon this man,°   *Corvino*
To whom, with blushing, they should owe their lives.

1 AVOCATORE What proofs have you of this?
BONARIO   Most honored fathers,

I humbly crave there be no credit given
To this man's mercenary tongue.

2 AVOCATORE   Forbear.

BONARIO His soul moves in his fee.

3 AVOCATORE   O, sir.

BONARIO   This fellow,
For six sols° more, would plead against his Maker   *coins*

1 AVOCATORE You do forget yourself.

VOLTORE   Nay, nay, grave fathers,
Let him have scope: can any man imagine
100   That he will spare his accuser, that would not
Have spared his parent?

1 AVOCATORE   Well, produce your proofs.

CELIA I would I could forget I were a creature.

VOLTORE Signior Corbaccio! [*Corbaccio comes forward.*]

4 AVOCATORE   What is he?

VOLTORE   The father.

2 AVOCATORE Has he had an oath?

NOTARIO   Yes.

CORBACCIO   What must I do now?

NOTARIO Your testimony's craved.

CORBACCIO   Speak to the knave?
I'll have my mouth first stopped with earth; my heart
Abhors his knowledge: I disclaim in him.

1 AVOCATORE But for what cause?

CORBACCIO   The mere portent of nature!
He is an utter stranger to my loins.

BONARIO Have they made you to this?

CORBACCIO   I will not hear thee,
Monster of men, swine, goat, wolf, parricide!
Speak not, thou viper.

BONARIO   Sir, I will sit down,
And rather wish my innocence should suffer,
Than I resist the authority of a father.

VOLTORE Signior Corvino! [*Corvino comes forward.*]

AVOCATORE   This is strange.

1 AVOCATORE   Who's this?

NOTARIO The husband.

4 AVOCATORE   Is he sworn?

NOTARIO   He is.

3 AVOCATORE   Speak, then.

CORVINO This woman, please your fatherhoods, is a whore,
Of most hot exercise, more than a partrich,[1]
Upon record—

1 AVOCATORE   No more.

CORVINO   Neighs like a jennet.°   *small horse*

NOTARIO Preserve the honor of the court.

---

1. The most lustful of birds.

CORVINO   I shall,
    And modesty of your most reverend ears.
    And yet I hope that I may say, these eyes
    Have seen her glued unto that piece of cedar,
    That fine well-timbered gallant; and that here
125   The letters may be read, thorough the horn,
    That make the story perfect.
MOSCA   Excellent! sir.
CORVINO [aside to Mosca] There is no shame in this now, is there?
MOSCA   None.
CORVINO Or if I said, I hoped that she were onward
    To her damnation, if there be a hell
130   Greater than whore and woman; a good Catholic[2]
    May make the doubt.
3 AVOCATORE   His grief hath made him frantic.
1 AVOCATORE Remove him hence.
2 AVOCATORE   Look to the woman. [Celia swoons.]
CORVINO   Rare!
    Prettily feigned, again!
4 AVOCATORE   Stand from about her.
1 AVOCATORE Give her the air.
3 AVOCATORE [to Mosca]   What can you say?
MOSCA   My wound,
135   May it please your wisdoms, speaks for me, received
    In aid of my good patron, when he mist
    His sought-for father,[3] when that well-taught dame
    Had her cue given her, to cry out, A rape!
BONARIO O most laid impudence! Fathers—
3 AVOCATORE   Sir, be silent;
140   You had your hearing free, so must they theirs.
2 AVOCATORE I do begin to doubt the imposture here.
4 AVOCATORE This woman has too many moods.
VOLTORE   Grave fathers,
    She is a creature of a most profest
    And prostituted lewdness.
CORVINO   Most impetuous,
145   Unsatisfied, grave fathers!
VOLTORE   May her feignings
    Not take your wisdoms: but this day she baited
    A stranger, a grave knight, with her loose eyes,
    And more lascivious kisses. This man saw them
    Together on the water, in a gondola.
MOSCA Here is the lady herself, that saw them too;
    Without; who then had in the open streets
    Pursued them, but for saving her knight's honor.
1 AVOCATORE Produce that lady.
2 AVOCATORE   Let her come. [Exit Mosca.]
4 AVOCATORE   These things,

2. The 1607 Quarto, printed when Jonson was still a   "Catholic."
Catholic, reads "Christian," whereas the 1616 Folio reads   3. Corbaccio.

They strike with wonder.

3 AVOCATORE   I am turned a stone.

Scene 6

[*Reenter Mosca with Lady Would-be.*]

MOSCA Be resolute, madam.

LADY POLITIC [*pointing to Celia*] Ay, this same is she.
    Out, thou chameleon[4] harlot! now thine eyes
    Vie tears with the hyaena.[5] Dar'st thou look
    Upon my wronged face?—I cry your pardons,
5   I fear I have forgettingly transgressed
    Against the dignity of the court—

2 AVOCATORE   No, madam.

LADY POLITIC And been exorbitant°—   *excessive*

2 AVOCATORE   You have not, lady.

4 AVOCATORE These proofs are strong.

LADY POLITIC   Surely, I had no purpose
    To scandalize your honors, or my sex's.

3 AVOCATORE We do believe it.

LADY POLITIC   Surely, you may believe it.

2 AVOCATORE Madam, we do.

LADY POLITIC   Indeed you may; my breeding
    Is not so coarse—

4 AVOCATORE   We know it.

LADY POLITIC   To offend
    With pertinacy—

3 AVOCATORE   Lady—

LADY POLITIC   Such a presence!
    No surely.

1 AVOCATORE We well think it.

LADY POLITIC   You may think it.

1 AVOCATORE Let her o'ercome. What witnesses have you
    To make good your report?

BONARIO   Our consciences.

CELIA And heaven, that never fails the innocent.

4 AVOCATORE These are no testimonies.

BONARIO   Not in your courts,
    Where multitude, and clamor overcomes.

1 AVOCATORE Nay, then you do wax insolent.

    [*Reenter Officers, bearing Volpone on a couch.*]

VOLTORE   Here, here,
    The testimony comes, that will convince,
    And put to utter dumbness their bold tongues:
    See here, grave fathers, here's the ravisher,
    The rider on men's wives, the great impostor,
25   The grand voluptuary! Do you not think
    These limbs should affect venery?° or these eyes   *lust*

---

4. An animal that changes colors, a symbol of fraud.

5. The hyena was known for luring its victims and then devouring them.

Covet a concubine? Pray you mark these hands;
Are they not fit to stroke a lady's breasts?—
Perhaps he doth dissemble!

BONARIO   So he does.

VOLTORE Would you have him tortured?

BONARIO   I would have him proved.

VOLTORE Best try him then with goads, or burning irons;
Put him to the strappado:⁶ I have heard
The rack hath cured the gout; 'faith, give it him,
And help him of a malady; be courteous.

35   I'll undertake, before these honored fathers,
He shall have yet as many left diseases,
As she has known adulterers, or thou strumpets.—
O, my most equal hearers, if these deeds,
Acts of this bold and most exorbitant strain,

40   May pass with sufferance, what one citizen
But owes the forfeit of his life, yea, fame,
To him that dares traduce him? Which of you
Are safe, my honored fathers? I would ask,
With leave of your grave fatherhoods, if their plot

45   Have any face or color like to truth?
Or if, unto the dullest nostril here,
It smell not rank, and most abhorred slander?
I crave your care of this good gentleman,
Whose life is much endangered by their fable;

50   And as for them, I will conclude with this,
That vicious persons, when they're hot and fleshed
In impious acts, their constancy abounds:
Damned deeds are done with greatest confidence.

1 AVOCATORE Take them to custody, and sever them.

2 AVOCATORE 'Tis pity two such prodigies should live.

1 AVOCATORE Let the old gentleman be returned with care.

    [Exeunt Officers with Volpone.]
    I'm sorry our credulity hath wronged him.

4 AVOCATORE These are two creatures!

3 AVOCATORE   I've an earthquake in me.

2 AVOCATORE Their shame, even in their cradles, fled their faces.

4 AVOCATORE [to Voltore]

60   You have done a worthy service to the state, sir,
In their discovery.

1 AVOCATORE   You shall hear, ere night,
What punishment the court decrees upon them.

    [Exeunt Avocatori, Notario, and Officers with Bonario and Celia.]

VOLTORE We thank your fatherhoods.—How like you it?

MOSCA   Rare.
I'd have your tongue, sir, tipped with gold for this;

65   I'd have you be the heir to the whole city;
The earth I'd have want men, ere you want living:°   lack a livelihood

---

6. A form of torture to extort confession in which the victim's hands were tied across his back; he was then hoisted from the ground by a pulley and let down with a jerk.

They're bound to erect your statue in St. Mark's.
Signior Corvino, I would have you go
And show yourself, that you have conquered.

CORVINO   Yes.

MOSCA It was much better that you should profess
     Yourself a cuckold thus, than that the other
     Should have been proved.

CORVINO   Nay, I considered that:
     Now it is her fault.

MOSCA   Then it had been yours.

CORVINO True; I do doubt this advocate still.

MOSCA   I'faith
75   You need not, I dare ease you of that care.

CORVINO I trust thee, Mosca.

MOSCA   As your own soul, sir. [Exit Corvino.]

CORBACCIO   Mosca!

MOSCA Now for your business, sir.

CORBACCIO   How! Have you business?

MOSCA Yes, yours, sir.

CORBACCIO   O, none else?

MOSCA   None else, not I.

CORBACCIO Be careful, then.

MOSCA   Rest you with both your eyes, sir.

CORBACCIO Dispatch it.

MOSCA   Instantly.

CORBACCIO   And look that all,
     Whatever, be put in, jewels, plate, moneys,
     Household stuff, bedding, curtains.

MOSCA   Curtain-rings, sir:
     Only the advocate's fee must be deducted.

CORBACCIO I'll pay him now; you'll be too prodigal.

MOSCA Sir, I must tender it.

CORBACCIO   Two chequines is well.

MOSCA No, six, sir.

CORBACCIO   'Tis too much.

MOSCA   He talked a great while;
     You must consider that, sir.

CORBACCIO   Well, there's three—

MOSCA I'll give it him.

CORBACCIO   Do so, and there's for thee. [Exit.]

MOSCA [aside] Bountiful bones! What horrid strange offence
90   Did he commit 'gainst nature, in his youth,
     Worthy this age? [To Voltore.]—You see, sir, how I work
     Unto your ends: take you no notice.

VOLTORE   No,
     I'll leave you. [Exit.]

MOSCA   All is yours, the devil and all:
     Good advocate!—Madam, I'll bring you home.

LADY POLITIC No, I'll go see your patron.

MOSCA   That you shall not:

I'll tell you why. My purpose is to urge
My patron to reform his will; and for
The zeal you have shown to-day, whereas before
You were but third or fourth, you shall be now
100　　　　Put in the first: which would appear as begged,
If you were present. Therefore—

LADY POLITIC　　　　　　　　　　You shall sway me. [*Exeunt.*]

Act 5

Scene 1. *A room in Volpone's house*

[*Enter Volpone.*]

VOLPONE Well, I am here, and all this brunt° is past.　　　　　　　*crisis*
　　　　I ne'er was in dislike with my disguise
　　　　Till this fled moment: here 'twas good, in private;
　　　　But in your public,—*cave*° whilst I breathe.　　　　*watch out (Latin)*
5　　　'Fore God, my left leg 'gan to have the cramp,
　　　　And I apprehended straight some power had struck me
　　　　With a dead palsy: Well! I must be merry,
　　　　And shake it off. A many of these fears
　　　　Would put me into some villainous disease,
10　　　Should they come thick upon me: I'll prevent 'em.
　　　　Give me a bowl of lusty wine, to fright
　　　　This humor from my heart. [*Drinks.*]—Hum, hum, hum!
　　　　'Tis almost gone already; I shall conquer.
　　　　Any device, now, of rare ingenious knavery,
15　　　That would possess me with a violent laughter,
　　　　Would make me up° again. [*Drinks again.*]—So, so, so, so!　　*restore me*
　　　　This heat is life; 'tis blood by this time:[1]—Mosca!

Scene 2

[*Enter Mosca.*]

MOSCA How now, sir? Does the day look clear again?
　　　　Are we recovered, and wrought out of error,
　　　　Into our way, to see our path before us?
　　　　Is our trade free once more?

VOLPONE　　　　　　　　　　Exquisite Mosca!

MOSCA Was it not carried learnedly?

VOLPONE　　　　　　　　　　　And stoutly:
　　　　Good wits are greatest in extremities.

MOSCA It were a folly beyond thought, to trust
　　　　Any grand act unto a cowardly spirit:
　　　　You are not taken with it enough, methinks.

VOLPONE O, more than if I had enjoyed the wench:
　　　　The pleasure of all womankind's not like it.

MOSCA Why now you speak, sir. We must here be fixed;
　　　　Here we must rest; this is our masterpiece;
　　　　We cannot think to go beyond this.

VOLPONE　　　　　　　　　　　　True,

----

1. Early modern medicine held that wine metabolized into blood quickly.

15   Thou hast played thy prize, my precious Mosca.

MOSCA   Nay, sir,
To gull the court—

VOLPONE   And quite divert the torrent
Upon the innocent.

MOSCA   Yes, and to make
So rare a music out of discords—

VOLPONE   Right.
That yet to me's the strangest, how thou hast borne it!

20   That these, being so divided 'mongst themselves,
Should not scent somewhat, or in me or thee,
Or doubt their own side.

MOSCA   True, they will not see't.
Too much light blinds them, I think. Each of them
Is so possessed and stuffed with his own hopes,

25   That any thing unto the contrary,
Never so true, or never so apparent,
Never so palpable, they will resist it—

VOLPONE Like a temptation of the devil.

MOSCA   Right, sir.
Merchants may talk of trade, and your great signiors

30   Of land that yields well; but if Italy
Have any glebe° more fruitful than these fellows,   *land*
I am deceived. Did not your advocate rare?[2]

VOLPONE O—*My most honored fathers, my grave fathers,*
Under correction of your fatherhoods,

35   *What face of truth is here? If these strange deeds*
*May pass, most honored fathers—*I had much ado
To forbear laughing.

MOSCA   It seemed to me, you sweat, sir.

VOLPONE In troth, I did a little.

MOSCA   But confess, sir,
Were you not daunted?

VOLPONE   In good faith, I was

40   A little in a mist, but not dejected;
Never, but still my self.

MOSCA   I think it, sir.
Now, so truth help me, I must needs say this, sir,
And out of conscience for your advocate,
He has taken pains, in faith, sir, and deserved,

45   In my poor judgment, I speak it under favor,
Not to contrary you, sir, very richly—
Well—to be cozened.

VOLPONE   Troth, and I think so too,
By that I heard him, in the latter end.

MOSCA O, but before, sir: had you heard him first

50   Draw it to certain heads, then aggravate,
Then use his vehement figures[3] —I looked still

---

2. Didn't Voltore do a great job as a lawyer?   3. Strong rhetoric.

change

When he would shift° a shirt: and, doing this
Out of pure love, no hope of gain—

VOLPONE   'Tis right.
I cannot answer him, Mosca, as I would,

55   Not yet; but for thy sake, at thy entreaty,
I will begin, even now—to vex them all,
This very instant.

MOSCA   Good sir.

VOLPONE   Call the dwarf
And eunuch forth.

MOSCA   Castrone, Nano!
[*Enter Castrone and Nano.*]

NANO   Here.

VOLPONE Shall we have a jig now?

MOSCA   What you please, sir.

VOLPONE   Go,

60   Straight give out about the streets, you two,
That I am dead; do it with constancy,
Sadly, do you hear? Impute it to the grief
Of this late slander. [*Exeunt Castrone and Nano.*]

MOSCA   What do you mean, sir?

VOLPONE   O,
I shall have instantly my vulture, crow,

65   Raven, come flying hither, on the news,
To peck for carrion, my she-wolf, and all,
Greedy, and full of expectation—

MOSCA And then to have it ravished from their mouths!

VOLPONE 'Tis true. I will have thee put on a gown,

70   And take upon thee, as thou wert mine heir:
Show them a will. Open that chest, and reach
Forth one of those that has the blanks; I'll straight
Put in thy name.

MOSCA   It will be rare, sir. [*Gives him a paper.*]

VOLPONE   Ay,
When they ev'n gape, and find themselves deluded—

MOSCA Yes.

VOLPONE   And thou use them scurvily! Dispatch,
Get on thy gown.

MOSCA [*putting on a gown*] But what, sir, if they ask
After the body?

VOLPONE   Say, it was corrupted.

MOSCA I'll say, it stunk, sir; and was fain to have it
Coffined up instantly, and sent away.

VOLPONE Any thing; what thou wilt. Hold, here's my will.
Get thee a cap, a count-book, pen and ink,
Papers afore thee; sit as thou wert taking
An inventory of parcels: I'll get up
Behind the curtain, on a stool, and hearken;

85   Sometime peep over, see how they do look,
With what degrees their blood doth leave their faces,

O, 'twill afford me a rare meal of laughter!

MOSCA [*putting on a cap, and setting out the table, etc.*]
　　　　Your advocate will turn stark dull upon it.

VOLPONE It will take off his oratory's edge.

MOSCA But your clarissimo,[4] old round-back, he
　　　　Will crump you like a hog-louse, with the touch.

VOLPONE And what Corvino?

MOSCA　　　　　　　　　O, sir, look for him,
　　　　To-morrow morning, with a rope and dagger,
　　　　To visit all the streets; he must run mad.
95　　　My lady too, that came into the court,
　　　　To bear false witness for your worship—

VOLPONE　　　　　　　　　　　　　Yes,
　　　　And kissed me 'fore the fathers, when my face
　　　　Flowed all with oils.

MOSCA　　　　　　　And sweat, sir. Why, your gold
　　　　Is such another medicine, it dries up
100　　All those offensive savors: it transforms
　　　　The most deformed, and restores them lovely,
　　　　As 'twere the strange poetical girdle.[5] Jove
　　　　Could not invent t' himself a shroud more subtle
　　　　To pass Acrisius' guards.[6] It is the thing
105　　Makes all the world her grace, her youth, her beauty.

VOLPONE I think she loves me.

MOSCA　　　　　　　Who? the lady, sir?
　　　　She's jealous° of you.　　　　　　　　　　　　　　　　　　*devoted to*

VOLPONE　　　　　　Dost thou say so? [*Knocking within.*]

MOSCA　　　　　　　　　　　Hark,
　　　　There's some already.

VOLPONE　　　　　　Look.

MOSCA　　　　　　　　　　It is the Vulture;
　　　　He has the quickest scent.

VOLPONE　　　　　　　　　I'll to my place,
　　　　Thou to thy posture. [*Goes behind the curtain.*]

MOSCA　　　　I am set.

VOLPONE　　　　　　　　But, Mosca,
　　　　Play the artificer° now, torture them rarely.　　　*craftsman, trickster*

Scene 3

[*Enter Voltore.*]

VOLTORE How now, my Mosca?

MOSCA [*writing*]　　　　　Turkey carpets, nine—

VOLTORE Taking an inventory! That is well.

MOSCA *Two suits of bedding, tissue[7]*—

VOLTORE　　　　　　　　Where's the will?
　　　　Let me read that the while.

---

4. A Venetian grandee, here referring to Corbaccio.
5. Venus's belt made its wearers beautiful and seductive.
6. Acrisius kept his daughter Danae in a tower protected

by guards, but Zeus escaped them by coming to her in golden shower.
7. Fine fabric woven with gold and silver.

[*Enter Servants, with Corbaccio in a chair.*]
CORBACCIO   So, set me down,
      And get you home. [*Exeunt Servants.*]
VOLTORE   Is he come now, to trouble us!
MOSCA *Of cloth of gold, two more—*
CORBACCIO   Is it done, Mosca?
MOSCA *Of several velvets eight—*
VOLTORE   I like his care.
CORBACCIO Dost thou not hear?
      [*Enter Corvino.*]
CORVINO   Ha! is the hour come, Mosca?
VOLPONE [*peeping over the curtain*] Ay, now they muster.
CORVINO   What does the advocate here,
      Or this Corbaccio?
CORBACCIO   What do these here?
      [*Enter Lady Politic Would-be.*]
LADY POLITIC   Mosca!
      Is his thread spun?[8]
MOSCA   *Eight chests of linen—*
VOLPONE   O,
      My fine dame Would-be, too!
CORVINO   Mosca, the will,
      That I may shew it these, and rid them hence.
MOSCA *Six chests of diaper, four of damask.[9]—There.*
      [*Gives them the will carelessly, over his shoulder.*]
CORBACCIO Is that the will?
MOSCA   *Down-beds and bolsters—*
VOLPONE   Rare!
      Be busy still. Now they begin to flutter:
      They never think of me. Look, see, see, see!
      How their swift eyes run over the long deed,
      Unto the name, and to the legacies,
      What is bequeathed them there—
MOSCA   *Ten suits of hangings°—*   tapestries
VOLPONE Ay, in their garters, Mosca. Now their hopes
      Are at the gasp.
VOLTORE   Mosca the heir!
CORBACCIO   What's that?
VOLPONE My advocate is dumb; look to my merchant,
      He has heard of some strange storm, a ship is lost,
25   He faints; my lady will swoon. Old glazen eyes,[1]
      He hath not reached his despair yet.
CORBACCIO   All these
      Are out of hope; I am, sure, the man. [*Takes the will.*]
CORVINO   But, Mosca—
MOSCA *Two cabinets.*
CORVINO   Is this in earnest?

---

8. The thread of life, spun and cut by the Fates.
9. Diaper is a linen fabric woven with patterns; damask is

a rich silk fabric woven with designs.
1. Corbaccio wears glasses.

MOSCA   *One*
          Of ebony—
CORVINO   Or do you but delude me?
MOSCA *The other, mother of pearl*—I am very busy.
          Good faith, it is a fortune thrown upon me—
          Item, one salt° *of agate*—not my seeking.   *saltcellar*
LADY POLITIC. Do you hear, sir?
MOSCA   *A perfumed box*—'Pray you forbear,
          You see I'm troubled—*made of an onyx*—
LADY POLITIC   How!
MOSCA Tomorrow or next day, I shall be at leisure
          To talk with you all.
CORVINO   Is this my large hope's issue?
LADY POLITIC Sir, I must have a fairer answer.
MOSCA   Madam!
          Marry, and shall: 'pray you, fairly quit my house.
          Nay, raise no tempest with your looks; but hark you,
40   Remember what your ladyship offered me
          To put you in an heir; go to, think on it:
          And what you said e'en your best madams did
          For maintenance; and why not you? Enough.
          Go home, and use the poor Sir Pol, your knight, well,
45   For fear I tell some riddles; go, be melancholy.
          [*Exit Lady Would-be.*]
VOLPONE O, my fine devil!
CORVINO   Mosca, 'pray you a word.
MOSCA Lord! will you not take your dispatch hence yet?
          Methinks, of all, you should have been the example.
          Why should you stay here? With what thought, what promise?
50   Hear you; do you not know, I know you an ass,
          And that you would most fain have been a wittol,[2]
          If fortune would have let you? That you are
          A declared cuckold, on good terms? This pearl,
          You'll say, was yours? Right: this diamond?
55   I'll not deny't, but thank you. Much here else?
          It may be so. Why, think that these good works
          May help to hide your bad. I'll not betray you;
          Although you be but extraordinary,
          And have it only in title,[3] it sufficeth:
60   Go home, be melancholy too, or mad. [*Exit Corvino.*]
VOLPONE Rare Mosca! How his villainy becomes him!
VOLTORE Certain he doth delude all these for me.
CORBACCIO Mosca the heir!
VOLPONE   O, his four eyes have found it.
CORBACCIO I am cozened, cheated, by a parasite slave;
          Harlot, thou hast gulled me.
MOSCA   Yes, sir. Stop your mouth,
          Or I shall draw the only tooth is left.

---

2. A man who encourages the infidelity of his own wife.   3. Not a real cuckold but a seeming one.

Are not you he, that filthy covetous wretch,
With the three legs,[4] that here, in hope of prey,
Have, any time this three years, snuffed about,
70   With your most groveling nose, and would have hired
Me to the poisoning of my patron, sir?
Are not you he that have today in court
Professed the disinheriting of your son?
Perjured yourself? Go home, and die, and stink.
75   If you but croak a syllable, all comes out:
Away, and call your porters! [*Exit Corbaccio.*] Go, go, stink.

VOLPONE Excellent varlet!

VOLTORE   Now, my faithful Mosca,
I find thy constancy.

MOSCA   Sir!

VOLTORE   Sincere.

MOSCA [*writing*]   *A table*
Of porphyry—I mar'l° you'll be thus troublesome.   marvel

VOLTORE Nay, leave off now, they are gone.

MOSCA   Why, who are you?
What! Who did send for you? O, cry you mercy,
Reverend sir! Good faith, I am grieved for you,
That any chance of mine should thus defeat
Your (I must needs say) most deserving travails:
85   But I protest, sir, it was cast upon me,
And I could almost wish to be without it,
But that the will o' the dead must be observed.
Marry, my joy is that you need it not;
You have a gift, sir, (thank your education,)
90   Will never let you want, while there are men,
And malice, to breed causes. Would I had
But half the like, for all my fortune, sir!
If I have any suits, as I do hope,
Things being so easy and direct, I shall not,
95   I will make bold with your obstreperous aid,
Conceive me,—for your fee, sir. In mean time,
You that have so much law, I know have the conscience
Not to be covetous of what is mine.
Good sir, I thank you for my plate; 'twill help
100   To set up a young man. Good faith, you look
As you were costive;[5] best go home and purge, sir. [*Exit Voltore.*]

VOLPONE [*comes from behind the curtain*]
Bid him eat lettuce well. My witty mischief,
Let me embrace thee. O that I could now
Transform thee to a Venus!—Mosca, go,
105   Straight take my habit of clarissimo,[6]
And walk the streets; be seen, torment them more:
We must pursue, as well as plot. Who would
Have lost this feast?

---

4. Two legs and a cane.
5. Constipated.

6. By publicly wearing the clothes of a clarissimo, Mosca flouts the laws against dressing above one's rank.

MOSCA   I doubt it will lose them.

VOLPONE O, my recovery shall recover all.

110   That I could now but think on some disguise
         To meet them in, and ask them questions:
         How I would vex them still at every turn!

MOSCA Sir, I can fit you.

VOLPONE   Canst thou?

MOSCA   Yes, I know
         One o' the commandatori, sir, so like you;

115   Him will I straight make drunk, and bring you his habit.[7]

VOLPONE A rare disguise, and answering thy brain!
         O, I will be a sharp disease unto them.

MOSCA Sir, you must look for curses—

VOLPONE   Till they burst;
         The Fox fares over best when he is cursed. [Exeunt.]

Scene 4. A hall in Sir Politic's house

[Enter Peregrine disguised, and three Merchants.]

PEREGRINE Am I enough disguised?

1 MERCHANT   I warrant you.

PEREGRINE All my ambition is to fright him only.

2 MERCHANT If you could ship him away, 'twere excellent.

3 MERCHANT To Zant, or to Aleppo?[8]

PEREGRINE   Yes, and have his

5   Adventures put i' the Book of Voyages,
         And his gulled story[9] registered for truth.
         Well, gentlemen, when I am in a while,
         And that you think us warm in our discourse,
         Know your approaches.

1 MERCHANT   Trust it to our care. [Exeunt Merchants.]

         [Enter Waiting-woman.]

PEREGRINE Save you, fair lady! Is Sir Pol within?

WOMAN I do not know, sir.

PEREGRINE   Pray you say unto him,
         Here is a merchant, upon earnest business,
         Desires to speak with him.

WOMAN   I will see, sir. [Exit.]

PEREGRINE Pray you.—

15   I see the family is all female here.[1]

         [Reenter Waiting-woman.]

WOMAN He says, sir, he has weighty affairs of state,
         That now require him whole; some other time
         You may possess him.

PEREGRINE   Pray you say again,
         If those require him whole, these will exact him,

20   Whereof I bring him tidings. [Exit Woman.]—What might be

---

7. Volpone puts on a sergeant's uniform.
8. Zant or Zakynthos, an Ionian island, was then under Venetian rule; Aleppo is a town in Syria.

9. Story of his being tricked.
1. The family, as in Latin familia, refers to the household of servants.

20   His grave affair of state now! How to make
            Bolognian sausages here in Venice, sparing
            One o' the ingredients?
            [*Reenter Waiting-woman.*]
WOMAN   Sir, he says, he knows
            By your word *tidings*, that you are no statesman,[2]
            And therefore wills you stay.
PEREGRINE   Sweet, pray you return him;
25   I have not read so many proclamations,
            And studied them for words, as he has done—
            But—here he deigns to come. [*Exit Woman.*]
            [*Enter Sir Politic.*]
SIR POLITIC   Sir, I must crave
            Your courteous pardon. There hath chanced today,
            Unkind disaster 'twixt my lady and me;
30   And I was penning my apology,
            To give her satisfaction, as you came now.
PEREGRINE Sir, I am grieved I bring you worse disaster:
            The gentleman you met at the port today,
            That told you, he was newly arrived—
SIR POLITIC   Ay, was
            A fugitive punk?°   *prostitute*
PEREGRINE   No, sir, a spy set on you;
            And he has made relation to the senate,
            That you professed to him to have a plot
            To sell the State of Venice to the Turk.
SIR POLITIC O me!
PEREGRINE   For which, warrants are signed by this time,
40   To apprehend you, and to search your study
            For papers—
SIR POLITIC   Alas, sir, I have none, but notes
            Drawn out of play-books—
PEREGRINE   All the better, sir.
SIR POLITIC And some essays. What shall I do?
PEREGRINE   Sir, best
            Convey yourself into a sugar-chest;
45   Or, if you could lie round, a frail° were rare,   *rush basket*
            And I could send you aboard.
SIR POLITIC   Sir, I but talked so,
            For discourse sake merely. [*Knocking within.*]
PEREGRINE   Hark! they are there.
SIR POLITIC I am a wretch, a wretch!
PEREGRINE   What will you do, sir?
            Have you ne'er a currant-butt° to leap into?   *cask for currants*
50   They'll put you to the rack; you must be sudden.
SIR POLITIC Sir, I have an engine—
3 MERCHANT [*within*]   Sir Politic Would-be!
2 MERCHANT [*within*] Where is he?

2. A statesman would receive intelligence rather than tidings.

SIR POLITIC   That I have thought upon before time.
PEREGRINE What is it?
SIR POLITIC   I shall ne'er endure the torture.
      Marry, it is, sir, of a tortoise-shell,
55   Fitted for these extremities; pray you, sir, help me.
      Here I've a place, sir, to put back my legs,
      Please you to lay it on, sir, [*lies down while Peregrine places the shell upon
          him*]—with this cap,
      And my black gloves. I'll lie, sir, like a tortoise,
      'Till they are gone.
PEREGRINE   And call you this an engine?
SIR POLITIC Mine own device[3]———Good sir, bid my wife's women
      To burn my papers. [*Exit Peregrine.*]
      [*The three Merchants rush in.*]
1 MERCHANT   Where is he hid?
3 MERCHANT   We must,
      And will sure find him.
2 MERCHANT   Which is his study?
      [*Reenter Peregrine.*]
1 MERCHANT   What
      Are you, sir?
PEREGRINE   I am a merchant, that came here
      To look upon this tortoise.
3 MERCHANT   How!
1 MERCHANT   St. Mark!
      What beast is this!
PEREGRINE   It is a fish.
2 MERCHANT   Come out here!
PEREGRINE Nay, you may strike him, sir, and tread upon him;
      He'll bear a cart.
1 MERCHANT   What, to run over him?
PEREGRINE   Yes, sir.
3 MERCHANT Let's jump upon him.
2 MERCHANT   Can he not go?
PEREGRINE   He creeps, sir.
1 MERCHANT Let's see him creep.
PEREGRINE   No, good sir, you will hurt him.
2 MERCHANT Heart, I will see him creep, or prick his guts.
3 MERCHANT Come out here!
PEREGRINE [*aside to Sir Politic*] Pray you, sir!—Creep a little.
1 MERCHANT   Forth.
2 MERCHANT Yet farther.
PEREGRINE   Good sir!—Creep.
2 MERCHANT   We'll see his legs.
      [*They pull off the shell and discover him.*]
3 MERCHANT God's so, he has garters!
1 MERCHANT   Ay, and gloves!

---

3. Contrivance, but also an emblem, or symbol; the tortoise was an emblem of prudence.

2 MERCHANT   Is this
    Your fearful tortoise?
PEREGRINE [*discovering himself*] Now, Sir Pol, we are even;
75   For your next project I shall be prepared:
    I am sorry for the funeral of your notes, sir.
1 MERCHANT 'Twere a rare motion to be seen in Fleet-street.⁴
2 MERCHANT Ay, in the Term.
1 MERCHANT   Or Smithfield, in the fair.⁵
3 MERCHANT Methinks 'tis but a melancholy sight.
PEREGRINE Farewell, most politic tortoise!
    [*Exeunt Peregrine and Merchants. Reenter Waiting-woman.*]
SIR POLITIC   Where's my lady?
    Knows she of this?
WOMAN   I know ·not, sir.
SIR POLITIC   Enquire.—
    O, I shall be the fable of all feasts,
    The freight of the gazetti,⁶ ship-boy's tale;
    And, which is worst, even talk for ordinaries.
WOMAN My lady's come most melancholy home,
    And says, sir, she will straight to sea, for physic.
SIR POLITIC And I to shun this place and clime for ever,
    Creeping with house on back, and think it well
    To shrink my poor head in my politic shell. [*Exeunt.*]

Scene 5. A room in Volpone's house

    [*Enter Mosca in the habit of a Clarissimo and Volpone in that of a Commendatore.*]
VOLPONE Am I then like him?
MOSCA   O, sir, you are he;
    No man can sever° you.   distinguish
VOLPONE   Good.
MOSCA   But what am I?
VOLPONE 'Fore heaven, a brave clarissimo; thou becom'st it!
    Pity thou wert not born one.
MOSCA   If I hold
    My made one, 'twill be well. [*Aside.*]
VOLPONE   I'll go and see
    What news first at the court. [*Exit.*]
MOSCA   Do so. My Fox
    Is out of his hole, and ere he shall reenter,
    I'll make him languish in his borrowed case,°   false costume
    Except he come to composition° with me.—   financial agreement
    Androgyno, Castrone, Nano!
    [*Enter Androgyno, Castrone, and Nano.*]
ALL   Here.
MOSCA Go, recreate yourselves abroad; go sport.— [*Exeunt.*]

---

4. A rare motion was a puppet show; Fleet Street in central London was frequented by lawyers during the terms of
the Inns of Court where plays were frequently performed.

5. The site of the Bartholomew Fair.
6. Gossip of the news-sheets.

So, now I have the keys, and am possessed.
Since he will needs be dead afore his time,
I'll bury him, or gain by him: I am his heir,
15   And so will keep me, till he share at least.
To cozen him of all, were but a cheat
Well placed; no man would construe it a sin:
Let his sport pay for't. This is called the Fox-trap.

Scene 6. A *street*

[*Enter Corbaccio and Corvino.*]

CORBACCIO They say, the court is set.
CORVINO   We must maintain
   Our first tale good, for both our reputations.
CORBACCIO Why, mine's no tale: my son would there have killed me.
CORVINO That's true, I had forgot: [*aside:*]—mine is, I'm sure.
   But for your will, sir.
CORBACCIO   Ay, I'll come upon him
   For that hereafter, now his patron's dead.
   [*Enter Volpone in disguise.*]
VOLPONE Signior Corvino! and Corbaccio! sir,
   Much joy unto you.
CORVINO   Of what?
VOLPONE   The sudden good
   Dropped down upon you—
CORBACCIO   Where?
VOLPONE   And none knows how,
10   From old Volpone, sir.
CORBACCIO   Out, arrant knave!
VOLPONE Let not your too much wealth, sir, make you furious.
CORBACCIO Away, thou varlet!
VOLPONE   Why, sir?
CORBACCIO   Dost thou mock me?
VOLPONE You mock the world, sir; did you not change wills?
CORBACCIO Out, harlot!
VOLPONE   O! belike you are the man.
15   Signior Corvino? 'faith, you carry it well;
   You grow not mad withal; I love your spirit:
   You are not overleavened with your fortune.
   You should have some would swell now, like a wine-fat,
   With such an autumn—Did he give you all, sir?
CORVINO Avoid, you rascal!
VOLPONE   Troth, your wife has shown
   Herself a very woman; but you are well,
   You need not care, you have a good estate,
   To bear it out, sir, better by this chance:
   Except Corbaccio have a share.
CORBACCIO   Hence, varlet.
VOLPONE You will not be aknown, sir; why, 'tis wise.
   Thus do all gamesters, at all games, dissemble:

No man will seem to win. [*Exeunt Corvino and Corbaccio.*]—
                 Here comes my vulture,
Heaving his beak up in the air, and snuffing.

Scene 7

[*Enter Voltore.*]

VOLTORE Outstripped thus, by a parasite! a slave,
    Would run on errands, and make legs° for crumbs!   *bows*
    Well, what I'll do—
VOLPONE   The court stays for your worship.
    I e'en rejoice, sir, at your worship's happiness,
5   And that it fell into so learned hands,
    That understand the fingering—
VOLTORE   What do you mean?
VOLPONE I mean to be a suitor to your worship,
    For the small tenement, out of reparations,°   *repair*
    That, to the end of your long row of houses,
10   By the Piscaria:° it was, in Volpone's time,   *fish market*
    Your predecessor, ere he grew diseased,
    A handsome, pretty, customed° bawdy-house   *used by customers*
    As any was in Venice, none dispraised;
    But fell with him: his body and that house
    Decayed together.
VOLTORE   Come, sir, leave your prating.
VOLPONE Why, if your worship give me but your hand,
    That I may have the refusal, I have done.
    'Tis a mere toy to you, sir; candle-rents;[7]
    As your learned worship knows—
VOLTORE What do I know?
VOLPONE   Marry, no end of your wealth, sir; God decrease it!
VOLTORE Mistaking knave! what, mock'st thou my misfortune? [*Exit.*]
VOLPONE His blessing on your heart, sir; would 'twere more!—
    Now to my first again, at the next corner. [*Exit.*]

Scene 8. *Another part of the street*

[*Enter Corbaccio and Corvino;—Mosca passes over the stage, before them.*]

CORBACCIO See, in our habit![8] see the impudent varlet!
CORVINO That I could shoot mine eyes at him like gun-stones!
    [*Enter Volpone.*]
VOLPONE But is this true, sir, of the parasite?
CORBACCIO Again, to afflict us! monster!
VOLPONE   In good faith, sir,
5   I'm heartily grieved, a beard of your grave length
    Should be so overreached. I never brooked°   *could stand*
    That parasite's hair; methought his nose should cozen:°   *cheat*
    There still was somewhat in his look, did promise
    The bane of a clarissimo.

---

7. Rents from poor properties that were only enough to
buy candles with.   8. The dress reserved for members of our class.

CORBACCIO   Knave—
VOLPONE   Methinks
10   Yet you, that are so traded in the world,
          A witty merchant, the fine bird, Corvino,
          That have such moral emblems on your name,
          Should not have sung your shame, and dropt your cheese,
          To let the Fox laugh at your emptiness.
CORVINO Sirrah, you think the privilege of the place,
          And your red saucy cap, that seems to me
          Nailed to your jolt-head° with those two chequines,[9]   *blockhead*
          Can warrant your abuses; come you hither:
          You shall perceive, sir, I dare beat you; approach.
VOLPONE No haste, sir, I do know your valor well,
          Since you durst publish what you are, sir.
CORVINO   Tarry,
          I'd speak with you.
VOLPONE   Sir, sir, another time—
CORVINO Nay, now.
VOLPONE   O lord, sir! I were a wise man,
          Would stand the fury of a distracted cuckold.
          [*As he is running off, reenter Mosca.*]
CORBACCIO What, come again!
VOLPONE   Upon 'em, Mosca; save me.
CORBACCIO The air's infected where he breathes.
CORVINO   Let's fly him.
          [*Exeunt Corvino and Corbaccio.*]
VOLPONE Excellent basilisk![1] turn upon the vulture.

                              Scene 9
          [*Enter Voltore.*]
VOLTORE Well, flesh-fly,[2] it is summer with you now;
          Your winter will come on.
MOSCA   Good advocate,
          Prithee not rail, nor threaten out of place thus;
          Thou'lt make a solecism,[3] as madam says.
5   Get you a biggin[4] more, your brain breaks loose. [*Exit.*]
VOLTORE Well, sir.
VOLPONE   Would you have me beat the insolent slave,
          Throw dirt upon his first good clothes?
VOLTORE   This same
          Is doubtless some familiar.[5]
VOLPONE   Sir, the court,
10   In troth, stays for you. I am mad, a mule
          That never read Justinian,[6] should get up,

---

9. Coinlike buttons that were part of the commendatore's
uniform.
1. Mythical reptile whose look could kill.
2. The blowfly, which lays its eggs in carrion; the meaning of Mosca's name.

3. A mistake in speech.
4. Lawyer's skullcap.
5. Household member; attending demon.
6. The Emperor Justinian drew up the Roman legal code.

And ride an advocate. Had you no quirk
To avoid gullage,° sir, by such a creature?   *trickery*
I hope you do but jest; he has not done it,
'Tis but confederacy, to blind the rest.
You are the heir?
VOLTORE   A strange, officious,
Troublesome knave! thou dost torment me.
VOLPONE   I know—
It cannot be, sir, that you should be cozened;
'Tis not within the wit of man to do it;
You are so wise, so prudent; and 'tis fit
20   That wealth and wisdom still should go together. [*Exeunt.*]

Scene 10. *The Scrutineo or Senate-House*

[*Enter Avocatori, Notario, Bonario, Celia, Corbaccio, Corvino, Commendatori, Saf-*
fi, etc.]

1 AVOCATORE Are all the parties here?
NOTARIO   All but the advocate.
2 AVOCATORE And here he comes.
    [*Enter Voltore and Volpone.*]
1 AVOCATORE   Then bring them forth to sentence.
VOLTORE O, my most honored fathers, let your mercy
    Once win upon your justice, to forgive—
    I am distracted—
VOLPONE [*aside*]   What will he do now?
VOLTORE   O,
    I know not which to address myself to first;
    Whether your fatherhoods, or these innocents—
CORVINO [*aside*] Will he betray himself?
VOLTORE   Whom equally
    I have abused, out of most covetous ends—
CORVINO The man is mad!
CORBACCIO   What's that?
CORVINO   He is possessed.°   *by the devil*
VOLTORE For which, now struck in conscience, here, I prostrate
    Myself at your offended feet, for pardon.
1, 2 AVOCATORE Arise.
CELIA   O heaven, how just thou art!
VOLPONE [*aside*]   I am caught
    In mine own noose—
CORVINO [*to Corbaccio*] Be constant, sir: nought now
    Can help, but impudence.
1 AVOCATORE   Speak forward.
COMMENDATORE   Silence!
VOLTORE It is not passion in me, reverend fathers,
    But only conscience, conscience, my good sires,
    That makes me now tell truth. That parasite,
    That knave, hath been the instrument of all.

1 AVOCATORE Where is that knave? fetch him.

VOLPONE   I go. [*Exit.*]

CORVINO   Grave fathers,
    This man's distracted; he confessed it now:
    For, hoping to be old Volpone's heir,
    Who now is dead—

3 AVOCATORE   How!

2 AVOCATORE   Is Volpone dead?

CORVINO Dead since, grave fathers.

BONARIO   O sure vengeance!

1 AVOCATORE   Stay,
    Then he was no deceiver?

VOLTORE   O no, none:
    The parasite, grave fathers.

CORVINO   He does speak
    Out of mere envy, 'cause the servant's made
    The thing he gaped for; please your fatherhoods,
    This is the truth, though I'll not justify

30   The other,° but he may be some-deal faulty.   *Mosca*

VOLTORE Ay, to your hopes, as well as mine, Corvino:
    But I'll use modesty. Pleaseth your wisdoms,
    To view these certain notes, and but confer them;
    As I hope favor, they shall speak clear truth.

CORVINO The devil has entered him!

BONARIO   Or bides in you.

4 AVOCATORE We have done ill, by a public officer
    To send for him, if he be heir.

2 AVOCATORE   For whom?

4 AVOCATORE Him that they call the parasite.

3 AVOCATORE   'Tis true,
    He is a man of great estate, now left.

4 AVOCATORE Go you, and learn his name, and say, the court
    Entreats his presence here, but to the clearing
    Of some few doubts. [*Exit Notary.*]

2 AVOCATORE   This same's a labyrinth!

1 AVOCATORE Stand you unto your first report?

CORVINO   My state,
    My life, my fame—

BONARIO   Where is it?

CORVINO   Are at the stake.

1 AVOCATORE Is yours so too?

CORBACCIO   The advocate's a knave,
    And has a forked tongue—

2 AVOCATORE   Speak to the point.

CORBACCIO So is the parasite too.

1 AVOCATORE   This is confusion.

VOLTORE I do beseech your fatherhoods, read but those—[*Giving them papers.*]

CORVINO And credit nothing the false spirit hath writ:

50   It cannot be, but he's possessed, grave fathers. [*The scene closes.*]

Scene 11. *A street*

[*Enter Volpone.*]

VOLPONE To make a snare for mine own neck! and run
  My head into it, wilfully! with laughter!
  When I had newly 'scaped, was free, and clear,
  Out of mere wantonness! O, the dull devil
5 Was in this brain of mine, when I devised it,
  And Mosca gave it second; he must now
  Help to sear up° this vein, or we bleed dead.—   *cauterize*

[*Enter Nano, Androgyno, and Castrone.*]

  How now! who let you loose? whither go you now?
  What, to buy gingerbread, or to drown kitlings?

NANO Sir, master Mosca called us out of doors,
  And bid us all go play, and took the keys.

ANDROGYNO   Yes.

VOLPONE Did master Mosca take the keys? why so!
  I'm farther in. These are my fine conceits!
  I must be merry, with a mischief to me!
15 What a vile wretch was I, that could not bear
  My fortune soberly? I must have my crotchets,
  And my conundrums! Well, go you, and seek him:
  His meaning may be truer than my fear.
  Bid him, he straight come to me to the court;
20 Thither will I, and, if't be possible,
  Unscrew my advocate, upon new hopes:
  When I provoked him, then I lost myself. [*Exeunt.*]

Scene 12. *The Scrutineo, or Senate-House*

[*Avocatori, Bonario, Celia, Corbaccio, Corvino, Commendatori, Saffi, etc., as before.*]

1 AVOCATORE These things can ne'er be reconciled. He, here, [*Showing the papers.*]
  Professeth, that the gentleman was wronged,
  And that the gentlewoman was brought thither,
  Forced by her husband, and there left.

VOLTORE   Most true.

CELIA How ready is heaven to those that pray!

1 AVOCATORE   But that
  Volpone would have ravished her, he holds
  Utterly false, knowing his impotence.

CORVINO Grave fathers, he's possessed; again, I say,
  Possessed: nay, if there be possession, and
  Obsession, he has both.[7]

3 AVOCATORE   Here comes our officer.

[*Enter Volpone, still in disguise.*]

VOLPONE The parasite will straight be here, grave fathers.

4 AVOCATORE You might invent some other name, sir varlet.

3 AVOCATORE Did not the notary meet him?

---

7. In possession the devil controls the body from within, in obsession from without.

VOLPONE   Not that I know.

4 AVOCATORE His coming will clear all.

2 AVOCATORE   Yet, it is misty.

VOLTORE May't please your fatherhoods—

VOLPONE [*whispers to Voltore*]

15   Sir, the parasite
    Willed me to tell you, that his master lives;
    That you are still the man; your hopes the same;
    And this was only a jest—

VOLTORE   How?

VOLPONE   Sir, to try
    If you were firm, and how you stood affected.

VOLTORE Art sure he lives?

VOLPONE   Do I live, sir?

VOLTORE   O me!
    I was too violent.

VOLPONE   Sir, you may redeem it.
    They said, you were possessed; fall down, and seem so:
    I'll help to make it good. [*Voltore falls.*]—God bless the man!—
    Stop your wind hard, and swell—See, see, see, see!

25   He vomits crooked pins! His eyes are set,
    Like a dead hare's hung in a poulter's° shop!   *poultry dealer*
    His mouth's running away![8] Do you see, signior?
    Now it is in his belly.

CORVINO   Ay, the devil!

VOLPONE Now in his throat.

CORVINO   Ay, I perceive it plain.

VOLPONE 'Twill out, 'twill out! Stand clear. See where it flies,
    In shape of a blue toad, with a bat's wings!
    Do you not see it, sir?

CORBACCIO   What? I think I do.

CORVINO 'Tis too manifest.

VOLPONE   Look! he comes to himself!

VOLTORE Where am I?

VOLPONE   Take good heart, the worst is past, sir.
    You are dispossessed.

1 AVOCATORE   What accident is this!

2 AVOCATORE Sudden, and full of wonder!

3 AVOCATORE   If he were
    Possessed, as it appears, all this is nothing.

CORVINO He has been often subject to these fits.

1 AVOCATORE Show him that writing:—Do you know it, sir?

VOLPONE [*whispers to Voltore*] Deny it, sir, forswear it; know it not.

VOLTORE Yes, I do know it well, it is my hand;
    But all that it contains is false.

BONARIO   O practice!°   *deceit*

2 AVOCATORE What maze is this!

---

8. Early modern English accounts of fraudulent exorcisms of demonic possession describe similar symptoms.

1 AVOCATORE   Is he not guilty then,
     Whom you there name the parasite?
VOLTORE   Grave fathers,
45   No more than his good patron, old Volpone.
4 AVOCATORE Why, he is dead.
VOLTORE   O no, my honored fathers,
     He lives—
1 AVOCATORE   How! lives?
VOLTORE   Lives.
2 AVOCATORE   This is subtler yet!
3 AVOCATORE You said he was dead.
VOLTORE   Never.
3 AVOCATORE   You said so.
CORVINO   I heard so.
4 AVOCATORE Here comes the gentleman; make him way.
     [Enter Mosca as a clarissimo.]
3 AVOCATORE   A stool.
4 AVOCATORE [aside]
50   A proper man; and, were Volpone dead,
     A fit match for my daughter.
3 AVOCATORE   Give him way.
VOLPONE [aside to Mosca] Mosca, I was almost lost; the advocate
     Had betrayed all; but now it is recovered;
     All's on the hinge° again—Say, I am living.   running well
MOSCA What busy knave is this!—Most reverend fathers,
     I sooner had attended your grave pleasures,
     But that my order for the funeral
     Of my dear patron, did require me—
VOLPONE [aside]   Mosca!
MOSCA Whom I intend to bury like a gentleman.
VOLPONE [aside] Ay, quick,° and cozen me of all   alive
2 AVOCATORE   Still stranger!
     More intricate!
1 AVOCATORE   And come about again!
4 AVOCATORE [aside] It is a match, my daughter is bestowed.
MOSCA [aside to Volpone] Will you give me half?
VOLPONE   First, I'll be hanged.
MOSCA   I know
     Your voice is good, cry not so loud.
1 AVOCATORE   Demand
65   The advocate.—Sir, did you not affirm
     Volpone was alive?
VOLPONE   Yes, and he is;
     This gentleman told me so.—[Aside to Mosca:] Thou shalt have half.
MOSCA Whose drunkard is this same? Speak, some that know him:
     I never saw his face.—[Aside to Volpone:] I cannot now
     Afford it you so cheap.
VOLPONE   No!
1 AVOCATORE   What say you?

VOLTORE The officer told me.
VOLPONE   I did, grave fathers,
      And will maintain he lives, with mine own life,
      And that this creature [*points to Mosca*] told me.—[*Aside.*] I was born
      With all good stars my enemies.
MOSCA   Most grave fathers,
75   If such an insolence as this must pass
      Upon me, I am silent: 'twas not this
      For which you sent, I hope.
2 AVOCATORE Take him away.
VOLPONE   Mosca!
3 AVOCATORE Let him be whipped.
VOLPONE   Wilt thou betray me?
      Cozen me?
3 AVOCATORE   And taught to bear himself
      Toward a person of his rank.
4 AVOCATORE   Away. [*The Officers seize Volpone.*]
MOSCA I humbly thank your fatherhoods.
VOLPONE [*aside*]   Soft, soft. Whipped!
      And lose all that I have! If I confess,
      It cannot be much more.
4 AVOCATORE [*to Mosca*]   Sir, are you married?
VOLPONE They'll be allied anon; I must be resolute:
      The Fox shall here uncase. [*Throws off his disguise.*]
MOSCA   Patron!
VOLPONE   Nay, now
      My ruins shall not come alone: your match
      I'll hinder sure: my substance shall not glue you,
      Nor screw you into a family.
MOSCA   Why, patron!
VOLPONE I am Volpone, and this is my knave; [*pointing to Mosca*]
      This, [*to Voltore*] his own knave; this, [*to Corbaccio*] avarice's fool;
      This, [*to Corvino*] a chimera⁹ of wittol, fool, and knave:
      And, reverend fathers, since we all can hope
      Nought but a sentence, let's not now despair it.
      You hear me brief.
CORVINO   May it please your fatherhoods—
COMMENDATORE   Silence.
1 AVOCATORE The knot is now undone by miracle.
2 AVOCATORE Nothing can be more clear.
3 AVOCATORE   Or can more prove
      These innocent.
1 AVOCATORE   Give them their liberty.
BONARIO Heaven could not long let such gross crimes be hid.
2 AVOCATORE If this be held the highway to get riches,
      May I be poor!
3 AVOCATORE   This is not the gain, but torment.

---

9. A fantastical creature made up of a lion's head, a goat's body, and a serpent's tail.

1 AVOCATORE These possess wealth, as sick men possess fevers,
    Which trulier may be said to possess them.[1]
2 AVOCATORE Disrobe that parasite.
CORVINO AND MOSCA   Most honored fathers!—
1 AVOCATORE Can you plead aught to stay the course of justice?
    If you can, speak.
CORVINO AND VOLTORE We beg favor.
CELIA   And mercy.
1 AVOCATORE You hurt your innocence, suing for the guilty.
    Stand forth; and first the parasite. You appear
    T'have been the chiefest minister, if not plotter,
110   In all these lewd impostures; and now, lastly,
    Have with your impudence abused the court,
    And habit of a gentleman of Venice,
    Being a fellow of no birth or blood,[2]
    For which our sentence is, first, thou be whipped;
115   Then live perpetual prisoner in our gallies.
VOLPONE I thank you for him.
MOSCA   Bane° to thy wolvish nature!   *poison*
1 AVOCATORE Deliver him to the saffi. [*Mosca is carried out.*]—
                Thou, Volpone,
    By blood and rank a gentleman, canst not fall
    Under like censure; but our judgment on thee
120   Is, that thy substance all be straight confiscate
    To the hospital of the Incurabili:[3]
    And, since the most was gotten by imposture,
    By feigning lame, gout, palsy, and such diseases,
    Thou art to lie in prison, cramped with irons,
125   Till thou be'st sick and lame indeed.—Remove him.
                      [*He is taken from the Bar.*]
VOLPONE This is called mortifying of a Fox.
1 AVOCATORE Thou, Voltore, to take away the scandal
    Thou hast given all worthy men of thy profession,
    Art banished from their fellowship, and our state.
130   Corbaccio!—bring him near—We here possess
    Thy son of all thy state, and confine thee
    To the monastery of San Spirito;
    Where, since thou knewest not how to live well here,
    Thou shalt be learned° to die well.   *taught*
CORBACCIO   Ah! what said he?
    Commendatore. You shall know anon, sir.
1 AVOCATORE   Thou, Corvino, shalt
    Be straight embarked from thine own house, and rowed
    Round about Venice, through the grand canale,
    Wearing a cap, with fair long ass's ears,
    Instead of horns; and so to mount, a paper
    Pinned on thy breast, to the Berlina[4]—

---

1. Seneca, *Epistle* 119.2.
2. Mosca's sentence is the harshest because of his class status.
3. The Venetian Hospital of Incurables, founded in 1522 for orphans, beggars, and prostitutes.
4. Pillory.

CORVINO   Yes,
    And have mine eyes beat out with stinking fish,
    Bruised fruit, and rotten eggs—'Tis well. I am glad
    I shall not see my shame yet.
1 AVOCATORE   And to expiate
    Thy wrongs done to thy wife, thou art to send her
145   Home to her father, with her dowry trebled.
    And these are all your judgments.
ALL   Honored fathers.—
1 AVOCATORE Which may not be revoked. Now you begin,
    When crimes are done, and past, and to be punished,
    To think what your crimes are: away with them.
150   Let all that see these vices thus rewarded,
    Take heart and love to study 'em! Mischiefs feed
    Like beasts, till they be fat, and then they bleed. [*Exeunt.*]
[*Volpone comes forward.*]
    The seasoning of a play, is the applause.
    Now, though the Fox be punished by the laws,
155   *He yet doth hope, there is no suffering due,*
    For any fact which he hath done 'gainst you;
    If there be, censure him; here he doubtful stands:
    If not, fare jovially, and clap your hands. [*Exit.*]

On Something, That Walks Somewhere[1]

    At court I met it, in clothes brave° enough,   *showy*
      To be a courtier; and looks grave enough,
    To seem a statesman: as I near it came,
      It made me a great face, I asked the name.
    "A lord," it cried, "buried in flesh, and blood,
      And such from whom let no man hope least good,
    For I will do none; and as little ill,
      For I will dare none." Good lord, walk dead still.

On My First Daughter[1]

    Here lies to each her parents' ruth,°   *grief*
    Mary, the daughter of their youth;
    Yet, all heaven's gifts, being heaven's due,
    It makes the father, less, to rue.
5   At six months' end, she parted hence
    With safety of her innocence;
    Whose soul heaven's Queen (whose name she bears),
    In comfort of her mother's tears,
    Hath placed amongst her virgin-train;
10   Where, while that severed doth remain,
    This grave partakes the fleshly birth;[2]
    Which cover lightly, gentle earth.

---

1. This and the following four poems were all first printed in the collected *Works* of 1616 under the heading "Epigrams." An epigram is a short witty poem of invective or satire. Jonson's "Epigrams" include epitaphs, poems of praise, and a verse letter.
1. Probably written in the late 1590s.
2. While the soul is in heaven, the grave holds the body.

To John Donne

Donne, the delight of Phoebus,[1] and each Muse,
    Who, to thy one, all other brains refuse;[2]
Whose every work, of thy most early wit
    Came forth example, and remains so, yet;
Longer a-knowing than most wits do live;
    And which no affection praise enough can give!
To it,[3] thy language, letters, arts, best life,
    Which might with half mankind maintain a strife.
All which I meant to praise, and, yet, I would,
    But leave, because I cannot as I should.

On My First Son[1]

Farewell, thou child of my right hand,[2] and joy;
    My sin was too much hope of thee, loved boy.
Seven years thou wert lent to me, and I thee pay,
    Exacted by thy fate, on the just day.
O, could I lose all father, now![3] For why
    Will man lament the state he should envy?
To have so soon 'scaped world's and flesh's rage,
    And, if no other misery, yet age?
Rest in soft peace, and, asked, say, "Here doth lie
    Ben Jonson his best piece of poetry."
For whose sake, henceforth, all his vows be such,
    As what he loves may never like too much.[4]

Inviting a Friend to Supper[1]

Tonight, grave sir, both my poor house and I
    Do equally desire your company:
Not that we think us worthy such a guest,
    But that your worth will dignify our feast
5   With those that come; whose grace may make that seem
    Something, which else could hope for no esteem.
It is the fair acceptance, Sir, creates
    The entertainment perfect, not the cates.°   *food*
Yet shall you have, to rectify your palate,
10   An olive, capers, or some better salad
Ushering the mutton; with a short-legged hen
    If we can get her, full of eggs, and then
Lemons, and wine for sauce: to these, a coney°   *rabbit*
    Is not to be despaired of, for our money;
15   And though fowl now be scarce, yet there are clerks,°   *scholars*
    The sky not falling, think we may have larks.

---

1. God of poetry.
2. The Muses give the inspiration to your brain that they
deny to others.
3. In addition to your wit.
1. Benjamin, who died of the plague on his birthday in 1603.
2. In Hebrew, Benjamin means "son of the right hand;
dexterous, fortunate."

3. Let go of fatherly feeling.
4. "If you wish . . . to beware of sorrows that gnaw the
heart, to no man make yourself too much a comrade"
(Martial 12.34, lines 8–11).
1. Based on three poems of invitation by the Roman poet
Martial, 11.52, 5.78, and 10.48.

I'll tell you of more, and lie, so you will come:
    Of partridge, pheasant, woodcock, of which some
May yet be there; and godwit, if we can;
20   Knat, rail, and ruff,° too. Howsoe'er, my man   *gamebirds*
Shall read a piece of Virgil, Tacitus,
    Livy, or of some better book to us,
Of which we'll speak our minds, amidst our meat;
    And I'll profess no verses to repeat;
25 To this, if aught appear, which I not know of,
    That will the pastry, not my paper, show of.[2]
Digestive cheese and fruit there sure will be;
    But that, which most doth take my muse and me,
Is a pure cup of rich Canary wine,
30   Which is the Mermaid's,[3] now, but shall be mine:
Of which had Horace, or Anacreon tasted,
    Their lives, as do their lines, till now had lasted.[4]
Tobacco, nectar, or the Thespian spring
    Are all but Luther's beer to this I sing.[5]
35 Of this we will sup free, but moderately,
    And we will have no Poley, or Parrot by;[6]
Nor shall our cups make any guilty men,
    But, at our parting, we will be, as when
We innocently met. No simple word
40   That shall be uttered at our mirthful board
Shall make us sad next morning, or affright
    The liberty, that we'll enjoy tonight.

To Penshurst[1]

Thou art not, Penshurst, built to envious show,
    Of touch,° or marble; nor canst boast a row   *black marble*
Of polished pillars, or a roof of gold;
    Thou hast no lantern,° whereof tales are told,   *turret*
5 Or stair, or courts; but stand'st an ancient pile,[2]
    And these grudged at, art reverenced the while.
Thou joy'st in better marks, of soil, of air,
    Of wood, of water; therein thou art fair.
Thou hast thy walks for health, as well as sport:
10   Thy mount to which the dryads° do resort,   *wood nymphs*
Where Pan, and Bacchus their high feasts have made,[3]
    Beneath the broad beech and the chestnut shade;
That taller tree, which of a nut was set,
    At his great birth, where all the Muses met.

2. Add to this that if there is any paper, it will only be that used to keep the pastry from sticking to the pan.
3. A famous tavern in Cheapside, London.
4. Horace praised wine in Latin verse, as did Anacreon in Greek.
5. The Thespian spring, inspiration of poetry, and all these things are but Luther's beer in comparison with Canary.
6. Government spies; talkative birds.
1. First published in the 1616 *Works* in "The Forest," a title inspired by the Latin *silva* (timber), suggesting raw materials to be worked, used by classical authors for an improvised collection of poems. Penshurst was the Sidney family's house in Kent since 1552, the "great lord" (line 91) of which was Robert Sidney, Baron Sidney of Penshurst and Viscount of Lille, younger brother of Sir Philip Sidney.
2. The castle was built in 1340.
3. Pan was the god of forest, field, and pasture; Bacchus was the god of wine.

15   There, in the writhèd bark, are cut the names
      Of many a sylvan,° taken with his flames;   *wood sprite*
    And thence, the ruddy satyrs oft provoke
      The lighter fauns, to reach thy Lady's oak.[4]
    Thy copse,° too, named of Gamage, thou hast there,   *a small wood*
20   That never fails to serve thee seasoned deer
    When thou wouldst feast, or exercise thy friends.
      The lower land, that to the river bends,
    Thy sheep, thy bullocks, kine° and calves do feed;   *cows*
      The middle grounds thy mares and horses breed.
25   Each bank doth yield thee conies,° and the tops   *rabbits*
      Fertile of wood, Ashour and Sydney's copse,
    To crown thy open table, doth provide
      The purpled pheasant with the speckled side;
    The painted partridge lies in every field,
30   And, for thy mess, is willing to be killed.
    And if the high-swoll'n Medway[5] fail thy dish,
      Thou hast thy ponds, that pay thee tribute fish:
    Fat, agèd carps, that run into thy net.
      And pikes, now weary their own kind to eat,
35   As loath, the second draught, or cast to stay,
      Officiously, at first, themselves betray;
    Bright eels, that emulate them, and leap on land,
      Before the fisher, or into his hand.
    Then hath thy orchard fruit, thy garden flowers,
40   Fresh as the air, and new as are the hours.
    The early cherry, with the later plum,
      Fig, grape, and quince, each in his time doth come;
    The blushing apricot and woolly peach
      Hang on thy walls, that every child may reach.
45   And though thy walls be of the country stone,
      They're reared with no man's ruin, no man's groan;
    There's none, that dwell about them, wish them down;
      But all come in, the farmer, and the clown,°   *peasant*
    And no one empty-handed, to salute
50   Thy lord, and lady, though they have no suit.
    Some bring a capon, some a rural cake,
      Some nuts, some apples; some that think they make
    The better cheeses, bring 'em; or else send
      By their ripe daughters, whom they would commend
55   This way to husbands; and whose baskets bear
      An emblem of themselves in plum, or pear.
    But what can this (more than express their love)
      Add to thy free provisions, far above
    The need of such? whose liberal board doth flow
60   With all that hospitality doth know!
    Where comes no guest, but is allowed to eat

---

4. In Greek mythology the satyr with a man's body and a goat's legs was devoted to lechery. Robert Sidney's wife Bar-

bara Gamage was said to have given birth under this oak.
5. The local river.

Without his fear, and of thy lord's own meat;
Where the same beer, and bread, and self-same wine
That is his lordship's shall be also mine,
65   And I not fain to sit (as some this day
At great men's tables) and yet dine away.
Here no man tells my cups; nor, standing by,
A waiter, doth my gluttony envy,
But gives me what I call, and lets me eat;
70   He knows below he shall find plenty of meat,
Thy tables hoard not up for the next day.
Nor, when I take my lodging, need I pray
For fire, or lights, or livery:° all is there,   *provisions, food*
As if thou then wert mine, or I reigned here;
75   There's nothing I can wish, for which I stay.
That found King James, when, hunting late this way
With his brave son, the Prince, they saw thy fires
Shine bright on every hearth as the desires
Of thy Penates[6] had been set on flame
80   To entertain them; or the country came,
With all their zeal, to warm their welcome here.
What (great, I will not say, but) sudden cheer
Didst thou, then, make 'em! and what praise was heaped
On thy good lady, then, who therein reaped
85   The just reward of her high housewifery;
To have her linen, plate, and all things nigh,
When she was far, and not a room, but dressed
As if it had expected such a guest!
These, Penshurst, are thy praise, and yet not all.
90   Thy lady's noble, fruitful, chaste withall.
His children thy great lord may call his own,
A fortune, in this age, but rarely known.
They are, and have been, taught religion; thence
Their gentler spirits have sucked innocence.
95   Each morn and even, they are taught to pray,
With the whole household, and may every day
Read in their virtuous parents' noble parts
The mysteries of manners, arms, and arts.
Now, Penshurst, they that will proportion° thee   *compare*
100 With other edifices, when they see
Those proud, ambitious heaps, and nothing else,
May say, their lords have built, but thy lord dwells.

Song to Celia

Drink to me only with thine eyes,
And I will pledge with mine;
Or leave a kiss but in the cup,
And I'll not look for wine.
5   The thirst that from the soul doth rise

6. Household gods.

Doth ask a drink divine;
But might I of Jove's nectar sup,
   I would not change for thine.
I sent thee late a rosy wreath,
10   Not so much honoring thee
As giving it a hope that there
   It could not withered be.
But thou thereon didst only breathe,
   And sent'st it back on me;
15 Since when it grows, and smells, I swear,
   Not of itself, but thee.

Queen and Huntress[1]

Queen and huntress, chaste and fair,
Now the sun is laid to sleep,
Seated in thy silver chair,
State in wonted manner keep;
5   Hesperus° entreats thy light,   *the evening star*
   Goddess excellently bright.

Earth, let not thy envious shade
Dare itself to interpose;
Cynthia's shining orb was made
10 Heaven to clear, when day did close.
   Bless us then with wishèd sight,
   Goddess excellently bright.

Lay thy bow of pearl apart,
And thy crystal-shining quiver;
15 Give unto the flying hart
Space to breathe, how short soever.
   Thou that mak'st a day of night,
   Goddess excellently bright.

To the Memory of My Beloved, the Author, Mr. William Shakespeare, and What He Hath Left Us[1]

To draw no envy, Shakespeare, on thy name,
   Am I thus ample[2] to thy book, and fame,
While I confess thy writings to be such,
   As neither man, nor muse, can praise too much.
5 'Tis true, and all men's suffrage. But these ways
   Were not the paths I meant unto thy praise;
For silliest ignorance on these may light,
   Which, when it sounds at best, but echoes right;
Or blind affection, which doth ne'er advance
10   The truth, but gropes, and urgeth all by chance;
Or crafty malice, might pretend this praise,
   And think to ruin, where it seemed to raise.

---

1. From *Cynthia's Revels*, 5.6.1–18. Cynthia, another name for Diana, goddess of the moon and the hunt, and of chastity, an image associated with Queen Elizabeth.

1. Prefixed to the first folio of Shakespeare's plays (1623).
2. From Latin *amplus*: copious; an *amplus orator* was one who spoke richly and with dignity.

These are as some infamous bawd or whore
Should praise a matron. What could hurt her more?
15 But thou art proof against them, and indeed
Above the ill fortune of them, or the need.
I, therefore will begin. Soul of the age!
The applause! delight! the wonder of our stage!
My Shakespeare, rise; I will not lodge thee by
20 Chaucer, or Spenser, or bid Beaumont lie
A little further, to make thee a room;[3]
Thou art a monument without a tomb,
And art alive still while thy book doth live,
And we have wits to read, and praise to give.
25 That I not mix thee so, my brain excuses,
I mean with great, but disproportioned, Muses;
For, if I thought my judgment were of years,
I should commit thee surely with thy peers,
And tell how far thou didst our Lyly outshine,
30 Or sporting Kid, or Marlowe's mighty line.[4]
And though thou hadst small Latin, and less Greek,
From thence to honor thee, I would not seek
For names, but call forth thundering Aeschylus,
Euripides, and Sophocles to us,
35 Pacuvius, Accius, him of Cordova dead,
To life again, to hear thy buskin[5] tread
And shake a stage; or, when thy socks[6] were on,
Leave thee alone for the comparison
Of all that insolent Greece or haughty Rome
40 Sent forth, or since did from their ashes come.
Triumph, my Britain; thou hast one to show
To whom all scenes of Europe homage owe.
He was not of an age, but for all time!
And all the muses still were in their prime
45 When like Apollo he came forth to warm
Our ears, or like a Mercury to charm![7]
Nature herself was proud of his designs,
And joyed to wear the dressing of his lines,
Which were so richly spun, and woven so fit
50 As, since, she will vouchsafe no other wit.
The merry Greek, tart Aristophanes,
Neat Terence, witty Plautus,[8] now not please,
But antiquated, and deserted lie,
As they were not of Nature's family.
55 Yet must I not give Nature all; thy Art,
My gentle Shakespeare, must enjoy a part.
For though the poet's matter, Nature be,
His art doth give the fashion. And, that he,

3. Chaucer, Spenser, and Francis Beaumont were buried in Westminster Abbey; Shakespeare was buried in Stratford.
4. Lyly was an author of English prose comedies; Kyd and Marlowe were authors of English verse tragedies.
5. Boot worn by tragic actors. Jonson compares Shakespeare to tragedians of Ancient Greece (Aeschylus, Sophocles, Euripides) and Rome (Pacuvius, Accius, and "him of Cordova," Seneca).
6. Symbols of comedy.
7. Apollo and Mercury were the gods of poetry and eloquence.
8. Aristophanes was an ancient Greek comic playwright; Terence and Plautus were authors of Roman comedy.

60 Who casts to write a living line must sweat
        (Such as thine are) and strike the second heat
    Upon the Muses' anvil: turn the same,
        And himself with it, that he thinks to frame;[9]
    Or for the laurel, he may gain a scorn;
        For a good poet's made as well as born.
65 And such wert thou! Look how the father's face
        Lives in his issue; even so, the race
    Of Shakespeare's mind, and manners brightly shines
        In his well-turnèd, and true-filèd lines:
    In each of which, he seems to shake a lance,[1]
70   As brandished at the eyes of ignorance.
    Sweet Swan of Avon, what a sight it were
        To see thee in our waters yet appear,
    And make those flights upon the banks of Thames,
        That so did take Eliza, and our James![2]
75 But stay, I see thee in the hemisphere
        Advanced, and made a constellation there!
    Shine forth, thou star of poets, and with rage
        Or influence chide or cheer the drooping stage,[3]
    Which, since thy flight from hence, hath mourned like night,
80   And despairs day, but for thy volume's light.

To the Immortal Memory, and Friendship of that Noble Pair, Sir Lucius Cary and Sir H. Morison[1]

The Turne[2]

    Brave infant of Saguntum, clear
    Thy coming forth in that great year,
    When the prodigious Hannibal did crown
    His rage with razing your immortal town.[3]
5   Thou, looking then about,
    Ere thou wert half got out,
    Wise child, didst hastily return,
    And mad'st thy mother's womb thine urn.
    How summed° a circle[4] didst thou leave mankind   *complete*
10   Of deepest lore, could we the center find!

The Counter-Turn

    Did wiser Nature draw thee back
    From out the horror of that sack,

9. See Horace, *Ars Poetica* 441: "return the ill-tuned verses to the anvil."
1. Pun on "Shake-speare."
2. Queen Elizabeth and King James.
3. Like an ancient hero, Shakespeare is given a place
among the stars; as the "rage" and "influence" of the
planets affect life on earth, Shakespeare affects the world
of the stage.
1. Sir Lucius Cary (1610?–1643), second Viscount Falkland, son of Elizabeth Cary (author of *The Tragedy of
Mariam*). He befriended Jonson and wrote an elegy on his
death. Sir Henry Morison, son of Sir Richard Morison
and nephew of the travel writer Fynes Morison, died on
or near his twenty-first birthday.

2. "Turn," "counter-turn," and "stand" represent the
Greek "strophe," "antistrophe," and "epode." Jonson's
poem is the first Great Ode in English. Often in the form
of an address, the ode is a dignified lyric poem, in commemoration of a person, occasion, or theme. The Greek
poet Pindar wrote odes praising winners of the Olympics.
His odes were sung by a chorus in a three-part scheme,
which Jonson imitates here.
3. Pliny, *History* 7.3.40–42: "an infant of Saguntum . . . at
once went back into the womb in the year in which the
city was destroyed by Hannibal" (the great Carthaginian
general in the Second Punic War).
4. Emblem of perfection.

Where shame, faith, honor, and regard of right
Lay trampled on?—the deeds of death, and night,
15   Urged, hurried forth, and hurled
Upon th'affrighted world?
Sword, fire, and famine, with fell fury met;
And all on utmost ruin set;
As, could they but life's miseries foresee,
20   No doubt all infants would return like thee.

The Stand

For, what is life, if measured by the space,
Not by the act?
Or maskèd man, if valued by his face,
Above his fact?°   *deeds*
25   Here's one outlived his peers
And told forth fourscore years;
He vexèd time, and busied the whole state;
Troubled both foes, and friends,
But ever to no ends:
30   What did this stirrer, but die late?
How well at twenty had he fallen, or stood!
For three of his fourscore, he did no good.

The Turn

He entered well by virtuous parts,
Got up and thrived with honest arts:
35   He purchased friends, and fame, and honors then,
And had his noble name advanced with men:
But weary of that flight,
He stooped in all men's sight!
To sordid flatteries, acts of strife,
40   And sunk in that dead sea of life
So deep, as he did then death's waters sup;
But that the cork of title buoyed him up.

The Counter-Turn

Alas, but Morison fell young!
He never fell: thou fall'st,[5] my tongue.
45   He stood, a soldier to the last right end,
A perfect patriot, and a noble friend,
But most, a virtuous son.
All offices were done
By him, so ample, full, and round,
50   In weight, in measure, number, sound,
As, though his age imperfect might appear,
His life was of humanity the sphere.

The Stand

Go now, and tell out days summed up with fears;
And make them years;
55   Produce thy mass of miseries on the stage,
To swell thine age;

---

5. Slip, with a pun on the Latin *fallere*, to deceive, to be mistaken.

Repeat of things a throng,
To show thou hast been long,
Not lived; for life doth her great actions spell
60   By what was done and wrought
In season, and so brought
To light: her measures are, how well
Each syllabe° answered, and was formed, how fair;   *syllable*
These make the lines of life, and that's her air.

The Turn

65   It is not growing like a tree
In bulk, doth make man better be;
Or standing long an oak, three hundred year,
To fall a log at last, dry, bald, and sere:
A lily of a day
70   Is fairer far, in May,
Although it fall and die that night;
It was the plant and flower of light.
In small proportions, we just beauty see,
And in short measures life may perfect be.

The Counter-Turn

75   Call, noble Lucius, then for wine,
And let thy looks with gladness shine;
Accept this garland,[6] plant it on thy head;
And think, nay know, thy Morison's not dead.
He leaped the present age,
80   Possessed with holy rage,
To see that bright eternal day,
Of which we priests, and poets say
Such truths, as we expect for happy men,
And there he lives with memory, and Ben

The Stand

85   Jonson, who sung this of him, ere he went
Himself to rest,
Or taste a part of that full joy he meant
To have expressed
In this bright asterism;°   *constellation*
90   Where it were friendship's schism
(Were not his Lucius long with us to tarry)
To separate these twi-
Lights, the Dioscuri;[7]
And keep the one half from his Harry.
95   But fate doth so alternate the design,
Whilst that in heaven, this light on earth must shine.

The Turn

And shine as you exalted are;
Two names of friendship, but one star:

6. The poem itself.
7. "Twin lights": the mythical Greek brothers, Castor and

Pollux. After Castor's death the twin brothers exchanged places on earth and in the underworld at regular intervals.

Of hearts the union. And those not by chance
100 Made, or indentured,° or leased out t' advance   *contracted for*
The profits for a time.
No pleasures vain did chime,
Of rhymes, or riots, at your feasts,
Orgies of drink, or feigned protests;
105 But simple love of greatness, and of good;
That knits brave minds, and manners, more than blood.

The Counter-Turn

This made you first to know the why
You liked; then after, to apply
That liking; and approach so one the t'other,
110 Till either grew a portion of the other:
Each stylèd, by his end,
The copy of his friend.
You lived to be the great surnames
And titles by which all made claims
115 Unto the virtue. Nothing perfect done,
But as a Cary, or a Morison.

The Stand

And such a force the fair example had,
As they that saw
The good, and durst not practise it, were glad
120 That such a law
Was left yet to mankind;
Where they might read, and find
Friendship in deed was written, not in words.
And with the heart, not pen,
125 Of two so early° men,   *youthful*
Whose lines her rolls were, and records.
Who, ere the first down bloomèd on the chin,
Had sowed these fruits, and got the harvest in.

Pleasure Reconciled to Virtue

A Masque as It Was Presented at Court Before King James. 1618.[1]

The Scene was the Mountain Atlas, who had his top ending in the figure of an old man, his head and beard all hoary and frost, as if his shoulders were covered with snow; the rest wood and rock. A grove of ivy at his feet, out of which, to a wild music of cymbals, flutes, and tabors, is brought forth Comus,[2] the god of cheer or the belly, riding in triumph, his head crowned with roses and other flowers, his hair curled; they that wait upon him, crowned with ivy, their javelins done about with it; one of them going with Hercules' bowl[3] bare before him, while the rest presented him, with this

1. A masque was an entertainment performed by members of the court that included elaborate sets, dance, music, and poetry. Designed to compliment the monarch, the masque portrayed him as an ideal ruler in a moral allegory. The myth on which this masque is based is the story of Hercules' choice between pleasure and virtue, in

which King James is represented as harmonizing voluptuous enjoyment and right action.
2. Allied with Dionysus, the god of wine, Comus is the god of sensual excess.
3. Hercules used the bowl that the Sun gave him as a sailing ship.

Hymn

Room, room, make room for the boucing belly,
First father of sauce and deviser of jelly,
Prime master of arts, and the giver of wit,
That found out the excellent engine, the spit,
5   The plough and the flail, the mill, and the hopper,
The hutch, and the bolter, the furnace and copper.
The oven, the bavin, the mawkin, and peel,
The hearth and the range, the dog and the wheel.[4]
He, he first invented both hogshead° and tun,°   cask / barrel
10 The gimlet and vice, too, taught them to run.[5]
And since, with the funnel, an Hippocras bag
He's made of himself, that now he cries swag.[6]
Which shows, though the pleasure be but of four inches,
Yet he is a weezle,° the gullet that pinches,   throat
15 Of any delight, and not spares from the back
Whatever, to make of the belly a sack.
Hail, hail, plump paunch! O the founder of taste
For fresh meats, or powdered, or pickle, or paste;
Devourer of broiled, baked, roasted, or sod,°   boiled
20 And emptier of cups, be they even, or odd;
All which have now made thee, so wide i' the waist
As scarce with no pudding thou art to be laced;
But eating and drinking, until thou dost nod,
Thou break'st all thy girdles, and break'st forth[7] a god.

To this, the
Bowl-bearer

Do you hear, my friends, to whom do you sing all this now? Pardon me only that I ask you, for I do not look for an answer; I'll answer myself. I know it is now such a time as the Saturnals[8] for all the world, that every man stands under the eaves of his own hat and sings what pleases him; that's the right and the liberty of it. Now you sing of god Comus here, the Belly-god. I say it is well, and I say it is not well. It is well, as it is a ballad, and the belly worthy of it I must needs say, and 'twere forty yards of ballad, more—as much ballad as tripe.[9] But when the belly is not edified by it, it is not well; for where did you ever read, or hear, that the belly had any ears? Come, never pump for an answer, for you are defeated. Our fellow Hunger there, that was as ancient a retainer to the belly as any of us, was turned away, for being unseasonable—not unreasonable, but unseasonable—and now is he (poor thin-gut) fain to get his living with teaching of starlings, magpies, parrots, and jackdaws, those things he would have taught the belly. Beware of dealing with the Belly; the Belly will not be talked to, especially when he is full. Then there is no venturing upon Venter,[1] then he will blow you all up; he will thunder, indeed la; some in derision call him the father of farts. But I say, he was the

4. Flail: tool for threshing corn; mill: apparatus for grinding grain; hopper: a cone through which grain is conveyed to the mill; hutch: a box for sifting grain; bolter: a sieve; bavin: bundle of light wood used in bakers' ovens; mawkin: mop for cleaning a baker's oven; peel: a baker's shovel. A dog connected to a wheel turned the roasting spit.
5. The gimlet and vice were used to tap the cask.
6. A Hippocras bag was a strainer for wine. To cry swag

was to let out a hanging belly.
7. With a double meaning of fart.
8. The Roman Saturnalia was a wild festival at the end of the year, similar to Twelfth Night, part of the English Christmas season, at the celebration of which this masque was performed.
9. Edible animal intestines, and also the human stomach.
1. Belly (Latin).

first inventor of great ordinance,[2] and taught us to discharge them on festival days. Would we had a fit feast for him i'faith, to show his activity. I would have something now fetched in now to please his five senses, the throat; or the two senses, the eyes. Pardon me, for my two senses; for I that carry Hercules' bowl[3] in the service may see double by my place, for I have drunk like a frog today. I would have a tun[4] now, brought in to dance, and so many bottles about him. Ha? You look as if you would make a problem of this. Do you see? a problem: why bottles? and why a tun? and why a tun? and why bottles to dance? I say that men that drink hard and serve the belly in any place of quality (as *The Jovial Tinkers*, or *The Lusty Kindred*)[5] are living measures of drink, and can transform themselves, and do every day, to bottles or tuns when they please; and when they have done all they can, they are, as I say again (for I think I said somewhat like it afore), but moving measures of drink. And there is a piece-in-the-cellar can hold more than all they. This will I make good, if it please our new god but to give a nod; for the belly does all by signs, and I am all for the belly, the truest clock in the world to go by.

> *Here the first Anti-masque[6] [danced by men*
> *in the shape of bottles, tuns, etc.] after which,*

HERCULES What rites are these? Breeds earth more monsters yet?
       Antaeus[7] scarce is cold; what can beget
       This store? and stay such contraries upon her?
       Is earth so fruitful of her own dishonor?
5   Or 'cause his vice was inhumanity,
       Hopes she, by vicious hospitality
       To work an expiation first?[8] and then
       (Help, Virtue) these are sponges, and not men.
       Bottles? mere vessels? half a tun of paunch?
10   How? and the other half thrust forth in haunch?[9]
       Whose feast? the belly's! Comus'! and my cup
       Brought in to fill the drunken orgies up
       And here abused! That was the crowned reward
       Of thirsty heroes after labor hard!
15   Burdens and shames of nature, perish, die;
       For yet you never lived, but in the sty
       Of vice have wallowed, and in that swine's strife
       Been buried under the offense of life.
       Go, reel, and fall, under the load you make,
20   Till your swoll'n bowels burst with what you take.
       Can this be pleasure, to extinguish man?
       Or so quite change him in his figure? Can
       The belly love his pain, and be content
       With no delight, but what's a punishment?
25   These monsters plague themselves, and fitly too,
       For they do suffer what and all they do.
       But here must be no shelter, nor no shroud
       For such: sink grove, or vanish into cloud.

---

2. Artillery.
3. "To carry Hercules 'bowl" means to drink heavily.
4. Keg.
5. Taverns.
6. A grotesque, comic interlude.
7. Antaeus was a Libyan giant slain by Hercules.

8. Hercules assumes that Comus is another monster, like Antaeus, produced by the Earth and that Earth hopes to expiate her guilt by giving birth to one monster after another.
9. The area between the ribs and thighs.

After this, the whole grove vanished, and the whole music was discovered,
sitting at the foot of the mountain, with Pleasure and Virtue seated above them.
The Choir invited Hercules to rest with this

Song

> Great friend and servant of the good,
> Let cool a while thy heated blood,
> And from thy mighty labor cease.
> Lie down, lie down,
5 > And give thy troubled spirits peace,
> Whilst Virtue, for whose sake
> Thou dost this godlike travail take,
> May of the choicest herbage° make,   *plants*
> Here on this mountain bred,
10 > A crown, a crown
> For thy immortal head.

Here Hercules being laid down at their feet,
the second anti-masque, which was of pygmies,[1] appeared.

1ST PYGMY Antaeus dead? And Hercules yet live!
Where is this Hercules? What would I give
To meet him, now? Meet him? Nay, three such other,
If they had hand in murder of our brother![2]
5 With three? with four? with ten? nay, with as many
As the name yields![3] Pray anger there by any
Whereon to feed my just revenge and soon!
How shall I kill him? Hurl him 'gainst the moon,
And break him in small portions! Give to Greece
10 His brain, and every tract of earth a piece!
2ND PYGMY He is yonder.
1ST   Where?
3RD   At the hill foot, asleep.
1ST Let one go steal his club.
15 2ND   My charge; I'll creep.
4TH He's ours.
1ST   Yes, peace.
3RD   Triumph, we have him, boy.
4TH Sure, sure, he's sure.
20 1ST   Come, let us dance for joy.

At the end of their dance they thought to surprise him, when suddenly,
being awaked by the music, he roused himself, and they all ran into holes.

Song

CHOIR Wake, Hercules, awake, but heave up thy black eye,
'Tis only asked from thee to look and these will die,
Or fly.

---

1. In ancient Greek history, the pygmies were supposed to
have been a tribe of very short people in Africa or India;
the term was also used of dwarves.
2. Antaeus.

3. The Pygmies' assumption that there is more than one
Hercules is a joke alluding to the many different stories
about Hercules put forward by the mythographers.

Already they are fled,

Whom scorn had else left dead.

At which Mercury[4] descendeth from the hill, with a garland of poplar to crown him.

MERCURY Rest still, thou active friend of Virtue: these
       Should not disturb the peace of Hercules.
       Earth's worms and honor's dwarfs, at too great odds,
       Prove or provoke the issue of the gods.
5   See here, a crown, the agèd hill hath sent thee,
       My grandsire Atlas, he that did present thee
       With the best sheep that in his fold were found,
       Or golden fruit, on the Hesperian ground,
       For rescuing his fair daughters, then the prey
10   Of a rude pirate, as thou cam'st this way;
       And taught thee all the learning of the sphere,
       And how, like him, thou mightst the heaven up-bear,
       As that thy labors virtuous recompense.[5]
       He, though a mountain now, hath yet the sense
15   Of thanking thee for more, thou being still
       Constant to goodness, guardian of the hill;
       Antaeus, by thee suffocated here,
       And the voluptuous Comus, god of cheer,
       Beat from his grove, and that defaced. But now
20   The time's arrived, that Atlas told thee of: how
       By unaltered law, and working of the stars,
       There should be a cessation of all jars°   *fights*
       'Twixt Virtue and her noted opposite,
       Pleasure, that both should meet here, in the sight
25   Of Hesperus, the glory of the west,[6]
       The brightest star, that from his burning crest
       Lights all on this side the Atlantic seas
       As far as to thy pillars Hercules.[7]
       See where he shines, Justice and Wisdom placed
30   About his throne and those with Honor graced,
       Beauty and Love. It is not with his brother
       Bearing the world, but ruling such another
       Is his renown.[8] Pleasure, for his delight,
       Is reconciled to Virtue; and this night
35   Virtue brings forth twelve princes have been bred
       In this rough mountain and near Atlas' head,
       The hill of Knowledge; one, and chief of whom
       Of the bright race of Hesperus is come,
       Who shall in time the same that he is, be,
40   And now is only a less light than he.[9]
       These now she trusts with Pleasure, and to these
       She gives an entrance to the Hesperides,
       Fair Beauty's garden; neither can she fear
       They should grow soft or wax effeminate here,

---

4. The messenger god.
5. Atlas was an astronomer. His labor of holding up the heavens was taken over by Hercules so that Atlas could capture the golden apples of the Hesperides.
6. Hesperus, the brother of Atlas, was the evening star

and the protector of the western isles.
7. The Pillars of Hercules are the Straits of Gibraltar.
8. Hesperus is similar to King James, who also rules "another" world: England.
9. King James's 18-year-old son Prince Charles.

45   Since in her sight and by her charge all's done,
        Pleasure the servant, Virtue looking on.

Here the whole choir of music called the masquers forth from
the lap of the mountain, which now opens with this

Song

        Ope, agèd Atlas, open then thy lap,
        And from thy beamy bosom, strike a light,
        That men may read in thy mysterious map
                    All lines
5   And signs
        Of royal education, and the right,
                See how they come, and show,
                That are but born to know.
                            Descend,
10   Descend,
        Though pleasure lead,
                    Fear not to follow:
        They who are bred
                    Within the hill
15   Of skill,
                May safely tread
                What path they will:
        No ground of good is hollow.

In their descent from the hill Daedalus[1] came down
before them of whom Hercules questioned Mercury.

HERCULES But Hermes, stay a little, let me pause:
    Who's this that leads?
MERCURY   A guide that gives them laws
    To all their motions. Daedalus the wise.
HERCULES And doth in sacred harmony comprise
    His precepts?
MERCURY   Yes.
HERCULES   They may securely prove°   experience
    Then, any labyrinth, though it be of love.

Here, while they put themselves in form, Daedalus hath his first

Song

        Come on, come on, and where you go,
            So interweave the curious knot,
        As even th'observer scarce may know
            Which lines are Pleasures, and which not.

5   First, figure out the doubtful way
            At which, a while all youth should stay
        Where she and Virtue did contend
            Which should have Hercules to friend.[2]

---

1. Daedalus here acts as choreographer for the dance. As architect of the labyrinth, or maze, Daedalus may symbolize Inigo Jones, the set designer of the masque.
2. The story of how Hercules had to choose the arduous path of Virtue over the easy road offered to him by Vice is related by the ancient Greek author Xenophon (*Memorabilia* 2.1.21–34).

Then, as all actions of mankind.
10   Are but a labyrinth or maze,
So let your dances be entwined,
    Yet not perplex men unto gaze;

But measured, and so numerous° too,   *rhythmical*
    As men may read each act you do,
15 And when they see the graces meet,
    Admire the wisdom of your feet.

For dancing is an exercise
    Not only shows the mover's wit,
But maketh the beholder wise,
20   As he hath power to rise to it.

The first dance.
After which Daedalus again.

Song 2

O more, and more! this was so well
    As praise wants half his voice to tell;
        Again yourselves compose;
    And now put all the aptness on
5   Of figure, that proportion
        Or color can disclose.

That if those silent arts were lost,
Design and picture, they might boast
        From you a newer ground;
10   Instructed to that height'ning sense
        Of dignity and reverence
        In your true motions found:

Begin, begin; for look, the fair
Do longing listen to what air
15   You form your second touch;
That they may vent their murmuring hymns
Just to the tune you move your limbs,
        And wish their own were such.

Make haste, make haste, for this
20   The labyrinth of Beauty is.

The second dance.
That ended, Daedalus:

Song 3

It follows now, you are to prove
    The subtlest maze of all, that's love,
        And if you stay too long,
        The fair will think you do 'em wrong,
5 Go choose among—but with a mind
    As gentle as the stroking wind
        Runs o'er the gentler flowers.

And so let all your actions smile,
    As if they meant not to beguile
10   The ladies, but the hours.

Grace, laughter and discourse may meet,
　　And yet the beauty not go less:
For what is noble should be sweet,
　　But not dissolved in wantonness.

15　Will you, that I give the law
　　　To all your sport and sum it?
　　It should be such should envy draw,
　　　But ever overcome it.

Here they danced with the ladies, and the whole revels³ followed; which ended, Mercury
called to Daedalus in this following speech, which was after repeated in song, by two trebles,
two tenors, a bass, and the whole chorus.

Song 4

An eye of looking back were well,
　Or any murmur that would tell
　　Your thoughts, how you were sent
　　　And went,
5　To walk with Pleasure, not to dwell.

These, these are hours by Virtue spared
Herself, she being her own reward,
　　But she will have you know
　　　That though
10　Her sports be soft, her life is hard.

　　You must return unto the hill,
　　　And there advance
With labor and inhabit still
　　　That height and crown
15　From whence you ever may look down
　　　Upon triumphed Chance.

She, she it is, in darkness shines.
’Tis she that still herself refines
　　By her own light, to every eye,
20　More seen, more known, when Vice stands by.

And though a stranger here on earth,
In heaven she hath her right of birth.
　　There, there is Virtue’s seat,
Strive to keep her your own;
25　　’Tis only she can make you great,
Though place, here, make you known.

After which they danced their last dance, and returned into the scene,
which closed, and is a mountain again, as before.

The End.

This pleased the king so well, as he would see it again; when it was presented with
these additions.⁴

---

3. The audience, including members of the court.　　　4. The additions were another masque, *For the Honor of*
Wales.

John Donne
1572–1631

John Donne wrote some of the most passionate love poems and most moving religious verse in the English language. Even his contemporaries wondered how one mind could express itself in such different modes. Eliciting a portrait of the artist as a split personality, Donne's letters mention the melancholic lover "Jack Donne," succeeded by the Anglican priest "Doctor Donne." Izaak Walton's *Life of Donne* (1640) portrays an earnest aspiring clergyman who wrote love poetry to his wife. Yet Donne actually wrote most of his poetry—both the love lyrics and the *Holy Sonnets*—before he entered the ministry at forty-three. An ambitious, talented, and handsome young man, Donne struggled to attain secular patronage; later he resigned himself to life in the church and, after his wife's death, came to terms with his own mortality.

Donne was born into a Catholic family. His mother was the great-niece of Sir Thomas More; she went into exile in Antwerp for a time to seek religious toleration. One of Donne's uncles was imprisoned in the Tower of London because he was a Jesuit priest. Donne wrote of his family that none "hath endured and suffered more in their persons and fortunes, for obeying the Teachers of Roman Doctrine, then it hath done." Donne and his brother Henry entered Hart Hall, Oxford, when they were just eleven and ten, young enough to be spared the required oath recognizing the Queen as head of the church. The Donne brothers later studied law at Lincoln's Inn, where Henry was arrested for harboring a priest in 1593. The priest was drawn and quartered; Henry died in Newgate prison of the plague.

Though shadowed by his brother's death, Donne's student years in London had their pleasures. Donne was distracted from studying law by "the worst voluptuousness . . . an Hydroptique immoderate desire of humane learning and languages." The young Donne was described by his friend Sir Richard Baker as "a great visitor of ladies, a great frequenter of Playes, a great writer of conceited Verses." Among these were Donne's erotic *Elegies*, including *To His Mistress Going to Bed* and *Love's Progress*, both of which were refused a license for publication in the 1633 edition of his collected verse.

Shortly after gaining a position as secretary to Sir Thomas Egerton, Lord Keeper of the Great Seal, in 1597, Donne met and fell in love with Ann More. His noble employer's niece, she was so far above Donne's station that they married secretly. When Ann's father heard the news, he asked Egerton to have Donne fired and saw to it that he was incarcerated. At this time, Donne is said to have written to Ann: *"John Donne, Ann Donne, un-done."* As a result of Donne's petition, the Court of Audience for Canterbury declared the marriage lawful; nevertheless, Ann was disinherited.

John and Ann made a love match, but their life was not easy. She bore twelve children in fifteen years, not counting miscarriages. Donne lamented the "poorness of [his] fortune and the greatness of [his] charge." After thirteen years of marriage, however, he could also still say: "we had not one another at so cheap a rate, as that we should ever be weary of one another." A few of the love poems in *Songs and Sonnets* express a mixture of bliss and hardship linked with their marriage.

Relations with friends and patrons also influenced Donne's poetry. He is said to have addressed several poems to Magdalen Herbert, mother of the poet George. Living in Mitcham near London, Donne cemented his friendship with Ben Jonson, who wrote two epigrams in praise of Donne in thanks for his Latin verses on *Volpone* (1607). Donne was also introduced to Lucy, Countess of Bedford, who asked Jonson to get her a copy of Donne's *Satires*. Donne not only addressed several verse letters to her but also enjoyed her poems. An even more generous patron was Sir Robert Drury, for the death of whose young daughter Elizabeth the poet composed *A Funeral Elegie*, the inspiration for his two *Anniversaries* (1612) on the nature of the cosmos and death.

Donne's writing from 1607 to 1611 dealt with theological and moral controversies. His *Pseudo-Martyr* (1610) argued that Catholics should take the Oath of Allegiance to the King and that resistance to him should not be glorified as a form of martyrdom. This work won him James I's advice to enter the ministry, but, still skeptical, Donne held off. He protested against sectarianism: "You know I never fettered nor imprisoned the word Religion . . . immuring it in a Rome, or a Wittenberg, or a Geneva." Donne also examined the morality of suicide in *Biathanatos* (written 1607, published 1646). His *Holy Sonnets* (some of which may have been written as early as 1608–1610) reveal an obsession with his own death and fear of damnation: "I dare not move my dim eyes any way, / Despair behind, and death before doth cast / Such terror."

Donne was plagued by professional bad luck until he became an Anglican priest. With the exception of Sir Robert Drury, Donne never found a dependable patron. His applications for secretaryships in Ireland and Virginia were unsuccessful. In search of the Earl of Somerset's patronage, Donne wrote an epithalamion for his marriage to Frances Howard and even volunteered to justify her earlier controversial divorce. Fortunately for Donne, his attempts to win a position through Somerset failed, since a year later the Earl fell from power. Giving up his long quest for secular preferment, Donne took holy orders in 1615. Once an Anglican priest, he was made a royal chaplain and received an honorary Doctorate of Divinity from Cambridge. Two years later, he became reader in divinity at his old law school Lincoln's Inn.

Prosperity was followed by tragic loss. Ann Donne died giving birth in 1617. The death of his wife turned Donne more completely toward God. His later prose viewed death from a different perspective from his earlier personal torment. Suffering from a recurring fever, he wrote *Devotions upon Emergent Occasions* (1624). In the midst of a major epidemic, at the height of his fever, distraught and sleepless, he realizes our common mortality: "never send to know for whom the bell tolls; it tolls for thee." He became a prolific and stirring preacher of sermons. Some of these, such as that urging the Company of the Virginia Plantation to spread the gospel (1622), were printed in his lifetime. One written just before his death shows confidence in God's forgiveness: "I cannot plead innocency of life, especially of my youth: But I am to be judged by a merciful God."

If Donne's life can be split into the secular and religious, his poetic sensibility cannot. His verse fuses flesh and spirit through metaphysical conceits that create fascinating connections between apparently unrelated topics. In Donne's erotic lyrics, sex excites spiritual ecstasy along with hot lust and seductive wit. Similarly, Donne's religious poems express his relation with God not as an intellectual construct but as an emotional need, articulated in intimate and even erotic language. Later ages did not always appreciate either Donne's sensuality or his intellectual extravagance; remarkably, none of his poems were included in the most important nineteenth-century anthology of poetry, Palgraves's *Golden Treasury*. Donne's fame was revived early in the twentieth century, when modernist poets, especially T. S. Eliot, took inspiration from Donne's complex mixture of immediacy and artifice, passion and subtle thought.

The Good Morrow[1]

I wonder by my troth, what thou, and I
Did, till we loved? Were we not weaned till then?
But sucked on country pleasures, childishly?
Or snorted we in the seven sleepers' den?[2]

---

1. Donne's love poems, written over a period of 20 years, cannot be dated with any certainty. They were first printed in 1633, scattered throughout the entire collection of poems. Then in the 1635 edition the love poems were printed as a group under the title *Songs and Sonnets*.

There is no certainty that the titles were chosen by Donne.
2. Legendary cave where seven Ephesian youths were put to sleep by God to escape the persecution of Christians by the Emperor Decius (249).

5   'Twas so; but this, all pleasures fancies be.
    If ever any beauty I did see,
    Which I desired, and got, 'twas but a dream of thee.

    And now good morrow to our waking souls,
    Which watch not one another out of fear;
10   For love, all love of other sights controls,
    And makes one little room, an everywhere.
    Let sea-discoverers to new worlds have gone,
    Let maps to others, worlds on worlds have shown,
    Let us possess one world, each hath one, and is one.

15   My face in thine eye, thine in mine appears,
    And true plain hearts do in the faces rest,
    Where can we find two better hemispheres
    Without sharp north, without declining west?
    What ever dies, was not mixed equally;[3]
20   If our two loves be one, or, thou and I
    Love so alike, that none do slacken, none can die.

Song

    Go, and catch a falling star,
        Get with child a mandrake root,[1]
    Tell me, where all past years are,
        Or who cleft the Devil's foot,
5   Teach me to hear mermaids singing,
    Or to keep off envy's stinging,
           And find
           What wind
    Serves to advance an honest mind.

10   If thou be borne to strange sights,
        Things invisible to see,
    Ride ten thousand days and nights,[2]
        Till age snow white hairs on thee,
    Thou, when thou return'st, will tell me
15   All strange wonders that befell thee,
           And swear
           No where
    Lives a woman true, and fair.

    If thou findest one, let me know,
20   Such a pilgrimage were sweet;
    Yet do not, I would not go,
        Though at next door we might meet,
    Though she were true, when you met her,
    And last, till you write your letter,
25   Yet she

3. According to ancient medicine, death was caused by an imbalance of elements in the body.

1. A fork-rooted plant, resembling the human body in its form.

2. See *Faerie Queene* 3.7.56–61, where Spenser's Squire of Dames searches the country for a chaste woman.

Will be
False, ere I come, to two, or three.

The Undertaking

I have done one braver thing
    Than all the Worthies did,[1]
And yet a braver thence doth spring,
    Which is, to keep that hid.

5   It were but madness now to impart
    The skill of specular stone,[2]
When he which can have learned the art
    To cut it, can find none.

So, if I now should utter this,
10   Others (because no more
Such stuff to work upon, there is,)
    Would love but as before.

But he who loveliness within
    Hath found, all outward loathes,
15   For he who color loves, and skin,
    Loves but their oldest clothes.

If, as I have, you also do
    Virtue attired in woman see,
And dare love that, and say so too,
20   And forget the He and She;

And if this love, though placèd so,
    From profane men you hide,
Which will no faith on this bestow,
    Or, if they do, deride:

25   Then you have done a braver thing
    Than all the Worthies did;
And a braver thence will spring,
    Which is, to keep that hid.

The Sun Rising[1]

Busy old fool, unruly Sun,
    Why dost thou thus
Through windows, and through curtains call on us?
Must to thy motions lovers' seasons run?
5   Saucy pedantic wretch, go chide
    Late schoolboys, and sour prentices,°   *apprentices*
Go tell court-huntsmen, that the king will ride,
Call country ants to harvest offices;

---

1. The nine great military heroes of ancient and medieval legend and history.
2. Transparent stone of ancient times, but now lost, that required great skill to cut in strips.

1. In the tradition of the alba, a love song addressing the dawn, as in Ovid's *Amores* 1.13 and Petrarch's *Canzoniere* 188.

Love, all alike, no season knows, nor clime,
10   Nor hours, days, months, which are the rags of time.

Thy beams, so reverend, and strong
Why shouldst thou think?
I could eclipse and cloud them with a wink,
But that I would not lose her sight so long:
15   If her eyes have not blinded thine,
Look, and tomorrow late, tell me,
Whether both th'Indias of spice and mine²
Be where thou left'st them, or lie here with me.
Ask for those kings whom thou saw'st yesterday,
20   And thou shalt hear, all here in one bed lay.

She is all states, and all princes, I,
Nothing else is.
Princes do but play us; compared to this,
All honor's mimic; all wealth alchemy.°   *fake science*
25   Thou sun art half as happy as we,
In that the world's contracted thus;
Thine age asks ease, and since thy duties be
To warm the world, that's done in warming us.
Shine here to us, and thou art everywhere;
30   This bed thy center is, these walls, thy sphere.

The Indifferent

I can love both fair and brown,
Her whom abundance melts, and her whom want betrays,
Her who loves loneness best, and her who masks and plays,
Her whom the country formed, and whom the town,
5   Her who believes, and her who tries,°   *questions*
Her who still weeps with spongy eyes,
And her who is dry cork, and never cries;
I can love her, and her, and you and you,
I can love any, so she be not true.

10   Will no other vice content you?
Will it not serve your turn to do, as did your mothers?
Or have you old vices spent, and now would find out others?
Or doth a fear, that men are true, torment you?
Oh we are not, be not you so,
15   Let me, and do you, twenty know.
Rob me, but bind me not, and let me go.
Must I, who came to travail,¹ thorough you
Grow your fixed subject, because you are true?

Venus heard me sigh this song,
20   And by love's sweetest part, variety, she swore,
She heard not this till now; and that it should be so no more.

---

2. The East Indies was the source of spice; the West Indies was the source of gold.

1. In three senses: to make love, to undergo hardship, to travel or move on to another woman.

She went, examined, and returned ere long,
And said, "Alas, some two or three
Poor heretics in love there be,
25 Which think to establish dangerous constancy.
But I have told them, 'Since you will be true,
You shall be true to them, who are false to you.'"

The Canonization[1]

For God's sake hold your tongue, and let me love,
    Or° chide my palsy, or my gout,   *either*
My five gray hairs, or ruined fortune flout,
    With wealth your state, your mind with arts improve,
5   Take you a course, get you a place,
        Observe his Honor, or his Grace,
Or the King's real, or his stampèd face[2]
    Contemplate, what you will, approve,
    So you will let me love.

10 Alas, alas, who's injured by my love?
        What merchant's ships have my sighs drowned?
Who says my tears have overflowed his ground?
        When did my colds a forward spring remove?
            When did the heats which my veins fill
15   Add one more to the plaguy bill?[3]
Soldiers find wars, and lawyers find out still
        Litigious men, which quarrels move
        Though she and I do love.

Call us what you will, we are made such by love;
20   Call her one, me another fly,
We are tapers° too, and at our own cost die,[4]   *candles*
    And we in us find the eagle and the dove.
        The phoenix riddle hath more wit[5]
        By us; we two being one, are it.
25 So to one neutral thing both sexes fit,
        We die and rise the same, and prove
        Mysterious by this love.

We can die by it, if not live by love,
    And if unfit for tombs and hearse
30 Our legend be, it will be fit for verse;
    And if no piece of chronicle we prove,
        We'll build in sonnets pretty rooms;[6]
        As well a well wrought urn becomes
The greatest ashes, as half-acre tombs,
35   And by these hymns, all shall approve
        Us canonized for love:

---

1. The making of saints.
2. The King's actual face or his image stamped on coins.
3. Daily list of those who have died issued during outbreaks of the plague.

4. To die is to experience orgasm.
5. The mythical bird that was burned and reborn out of its own ashes, a symbol of perfection.
6. A play on *stanza*, Italian for "room."

And thus invoke us: You whom reverend love
    Made one another's hermitage;°   *refuge, retreat*
You, to whom love was peace, that now is rage;
40   Who did the whole world's soul contract, and drove
    Into the glasses° of your eyes[7]   *lenses*
    (So made such mirrors, and such spies,
That they did all to you epitomize)
    Countries, towns, courts: beg from above
45   A pattern of your love!

Air and Angels

Twice or thrice had I loved thee,
Before I knew thy face or name;
So in a voice, so in a shapeless flame,
Angels affect us oft, and worshipped be;
5   Still when, to where thou wert, I came,
Some lovely glorious nothing I did see.[1]
    But since my soul, whose child love is,
Takes limbs of flesh, and else could nothing do,
    More subtle than the parent is
10   Love must not be, but take a body too,
    And therefore what thou wert, and who,
      I bid love ask, and now
That it assume thy body, I allow,
And fix itself in thy lip, eye, and brow.

15   Whilst thus to ballast love, I thought,
And so more steadily to have gone,
With wares which would sink admiration,
I saw, I had love's pinnace° overfraught,   *light sailing ship*
    Every thy hair for love to work upon
20   Is much too much, some fitter must be sought;
    For, nor in nothing, nor in things
Extreme, and scattering bright, can love inhere;
    Then as an angel, face and wings
Of air, not pure as it, yet pure doth wear,
25   So thy love may be my love's sphere;[2]
      Just such disparity
As is twixt air and angel's purity,[3]
'Twixt women's love, and men's will ever be.

Break of Day[1]

'Tis true, 'tis day; what though it be?
Oh wilt thou therefore rise from me?

7. The lovers gazing into each other's eyes saw there a compact version or microcosm of the larger world or macrocosm.
1. A divine light shining through the body that Neoplatonists thought was the true object of desire rather than the body, which only reflected that beauty.
2. The analogy is between his love as the intelligence

controlling a heavenly body and her love as the heavenly sphere, or material body.
3. Metaphysical doctrine separates being into celestial, aerial, and material. If the material lady returns his aerial love, then they will be united in a celestial union.
1. First printed, with music, in W. Corkine's *Second Book of Airs* (1612).

Why should we rise, because 'tis light?
Did we lie down, because 'twas night?
5   Love, which in spite of darkness brought us hither,
Should in despite of light keep us together.

Light hath no tongue, but is all eye;
If it could speak as well as spy,
This were the worst, that it could say,
10   That being well, I fain would stay,
And that I loved my heart and honor so,
That I would not from him, that had them, go.

Must business thee from hence remove?
Oh, that's the worst disease of love,
15   The poor, the foul, the false, love can
Admit, but not the busied man.
He which hath business, and makes love, does do
Such wrong, as when a married man doth woo.

A Valediction:° of Weeping   *farewell*

Let me pour forth
My tears before thy face, whilst I stay here,
For thy face coins them, and thy stamp° they bear,   *image*
And by this mintage they are something worth,
5   For thus they be
        Pregnant of thee;
Fruits of much grief they are, emblems° of more,   *symbols*
When a tear falls, that thou falls which it bore,
So thou and I are nothing then, when on a diverse shore.

10   On a round ball
A workman that hath copies by, can lay
A Europe, Africa, and an Asia,
And quickly make that, which was nothing, all,[1]
        So doth each tear,
15   Which thee doth wear,
A globe, yea world by that impression grow,
Till thy tears mixed with mine do overflow
This world, by waters sent from thee, my heaven dissolvèd so.

        Oh more than moon,
20   Draw not up seas to drown me in thy sphere,[2]
Weep me not dead, in thine arms, but forbear
To teach the sea, what it may do too soon;
        Let not the wind
        Example find,
25   To do me more harm, than it purposeth;
Since thou and I sigh one another's breath,
Whoe'er sighs most, is cruelest, and halts the other's death.

1. The blank ball looks like a zero ("nothing") until the
continents are painted on it to represent the entire world
("all").

2. An astral sphere with a power of attraction greater
than the moon might draw the seas up to itself.

Love's Alchemy

Some that have deeper digged love's mine than I,
Say, where his centric° happiness doth lie: *central*
   I have loved, and got, and told,
But should I love, get, tell, till I were old,
5   I should not find that hidden mystery;
      Oh, 'tis imposture all:
And as no chemic° yet the elixir got,[1]   *alchemist*
    But glorifies his pregnant pot,
    If by the way to him befall
10 Some odoriferous thing, or medicinal,
     So, lovers dream a rich and long delight,
     But get a winter-seeming summer's night.

Our ease, our thrift, our honor, and our day,
Shall we, for this vain bubble's shadow pay?
15   Ends love in this, that my man,°   *servant*
Can be as happy as I can; if he can
Endure the short scorn of a bridegroom's play?
    That loving wretch that swears,
'Tis not the bodies marry, but the minds,
20   Which he in her angelic finds,
     Would swear as justly, that he hears,
In that day's rude hoarse minstrelsy, the spheres.[2]
    Hope not for mind in women; at their best
    Sweetness and wit, they're but mummy,[3] possessed.

The Flea[1]

Mark but this flea, and mark in this,
How little that which thou deniest me is;
It sucked me first,[2] and now sucks thee,
And in this flea, our two bloods mingled be;
5   Thou know'st that this cannot be said
A sin, nor shame, nor loss of maidenhead,
    Yet this enjoys before it woo,
    And pampered swells with one blood made of two,
    And this, alas, is more than we would do.

10 Oh stay, three lives in one flea spare,
Where we almost, nay more than married are.
This flea is you and I, and this
Our marriage bed, and marriage temple is;
Though parents grudge, and you, we are met,
15 And cloistered in these living walls of jet.°   *black*
    Though use make you apt to kill me,
    Let not to that, self murder added be,
    And sacrilege, three sins in killing three.

---

1. A goal of alchemy was to produce a pure essence with the power to heal and prolong life.
2. The concentric globes that created sublime music as they revolved around the earth.

3. Medicine made from mummies; dead bodies.
1. Based on a poem attributed to Ovid, the poem plays on the belief that intercourse involved the mixing of bloods.
2. "Me it sucked first" in the 1635 edition.

Cruel and sudden, hast thou since
20   Purpled thy nail, in blood of innocence?
Wherein could this flea guilty be,
Except in that drop which it sucked from thee?
Yet thou triumph'st, and say'st that thou
Find'st not thy self, nor me the weaker now;
25   'Tis true, then learn how false, fears be;
Just so much honor, when thou yield'st to me,
Will waste, as this flea's death took life from thee.

The Bait[1]

Come live with me, and be my love,
And we will some new pleasures prove
Of golden sands, and crystal brooks,
With silken lines, and silver hooks.

5   There will the river whispering run
Warmed by thy eyes, more than the sun.
And there the enamored fish will stay,
Begging themselves they may betray.

When thou wilt swim in that live bath,
10   Each fish, which every channel hath,
Will amorously to thee swim,
Gladder to catch thee, then thou him.

If thou, to be so seen, be'st loath,
By sun, or moon, thou darkenest both,
15   And if myself have leave to see,
I need not their light, having thee.

Let others freeze with angling reeds,
And cut their legs, with shells and weeds,
Or treacherously poor fish beset,
20   With strangling snare, or windowy net:

Let coarse bold hands, from slimy nest
The bedded fish in banks out-wrest,
Or curious traitors, sleave-silk flies[2]
Bewitch poor fishes' wandering eyes.

25   For thee, thou need'st no such deceit,
For thou thyself are thine own bait;
That fish, that is not catched thereby,
Alas, is wiser far than I.

The Apparition

When by thy scorn, O murderess, I am dead,
And that thou thinkst thee free

---

1. Parodies Marlowe's *The Passionate Shepherd to His Love*
and Raleigh's *The Nymph's Reply*; see pages 1098–1100.

2. Artificial flies made from silk threads.

From all solicitation from me,
Then shall my ghost come to thy bed,
5 And thee, feigned vestal,° in worse arms shall see;   *virgin priestess*
Then thy sick taper will begin to wink,
And he, whose thou art then, being tired before,
Will, if thou stir, or pinch to wake him, think
      Thou call'st for more,
10 And in false sleep will from thee shrink,
And then poor aspen[1] wretch, neglected thou
Bathed in a cold quicksilver[2] sweat will lie
      A verier° ghost than I;   *truer*
What I will say, I will not tell thee now,
15 Lest that preserve thee; and since my love is spent,
I had rather thou shouldst painfully repent,
Than by my threatenings rest still innocent.

A Valediction: Forbidding Mourning[1]

As virtuous men pass mildly away,
    And whisper to their souls, to go,
Whilst some of their sad friends do say,
    The breath goes now, and some say, no:

5 So let us melt, and make no noise,
    No tear-floods, nor sigh-tempests move,
'Twere profanation° of our joys   *desecration*
    To tell the laity[2] of our love.

Moving of th'earth brings harms and fears,
10   Men reckon what it did and meant,
But trepidation of the spheres,[3]
    Though greater far, is innocent.

Dull sublunary[4] lovers' love
    (Whose soul is sense) cannot admit
15 Absence, because it doth remove
    Those things which elemented° it.   *composed*

But we by a love, so much refined,
    That our selves know not what it is,
Inter-assurèd of the mind,
20   Care less, eyes, lips, and hands to miss.

Our two souls therefore, which are one,
    Though I must go, endure not yet
A breach, but an expansion,
    Like gold to airy thinness beat.[5]

---

1. Trembling like an aspen leaf in the wind.
2. Liquid mercury, used to treat venereal disease.
1. In his *Life of Dr. John Donne* (1640), Walton describes the occasion as Donne's farewell to his wife before his journey to France in 1611.
2. The uninitiated.

3. Though the movement of the spheres is greater than an earthquake, we feel its effects less.
4. Under the sphere of the moon, hence sensual.
5. Gold was beaten to produce gold leaf. "Airy" suggests their love will become so fine that it will be spiritual.

25   If they be two, they are two so
            As stiff twin compasses[6] are two,
        Thy soul the fixed foot, makes no show
            To move, but doth, if th' other do.

        And though it in the center sit,
30   Yet when the other far doth roam,
        It leans, and hearkens after it,
            And grows erect, as that comes home.

        Such wilt thou be to me, who must
            Like th' other foot, obliquely run;
35   Thy firmness makes my circle just,°   *complete*
            And makes me end, where I begun.

The Ecstasy[1]

        Where, like a pillow on a bed,
            A pregnant bank swelled up, to rest
        The violet's reclining head,[2]
            Sat we two, one another's best.

5   Our hands were firmly cemented
            With a fast balm, which thence did spring,
        Our eye-beams twisted, and did thread
            Our eyes, upon one double string;[3]

        So to intergraft our hands, as yet
10   Was all the means to make us one,
        And pictures in our eyes to get
            Was all our propagation.[4]

        As 'twixt two equal armies, Fate
            Suspends uncertain victory,
15   Our souls (which to advance their state
            Were gone out) hung 'twixt her and me.

        And whilst our souls negotiate there,
            We like sepulchral statues lay;
        All day, the same our postures were,
20   And we said nothing, all the day.

        If any, so by love refined,
            That he soul's language understood,
        And by good love were grown all mind,
            Within convenient distance stood,

25   He (though he knew not which soul spake
            Because both meant, both spake the same)

6. A common emblem of constancy amidst change.
1. From *ekstasis* (Greek) meaning passion and the withdrawal of the soul from the body. A beautiful and secluded pastoral spot was a frequent setting for love poetry.
2. The violet was an emblem of faithfulness.

3. The lovers are totally enthralled by gazing into each other's eyes.
4. The act of reflecting each other's image was called "making babies."

Might thence a new concoction[5] take,
   And part far purer than he came.

This ecstasy doth unperplex,
30   We said, and tell us what we love,
We see by this, it was not sex,
   We see, we saw not what did move:

But as all several souls contain
   Mixture of things, they know not what,
35 Love, these mixed souls, doth mix again,
   And makes both one, each this and that.

A single violet transplant,
   The strength, the color, and the size,
(All which before was poor and scant)
40   Redoubles still, and multiplies.

When love with one another so
   Interinanimates two souls,
That abler soul, which thence doth flow,
   Defects of loneliness controls.

45 We then, who are this new soul, know,
   Of what we are composed and made,
For, th' atomies° of which we grow,   *components, parts*
   Are souls, whom no change can invade.

But O alas, so long, so far
50   Our bodies why do we forbear?
They are ours, though they are not we, we are
   The intelligences, they the sphere.[6]

We owe them thanks, because they thus,
   Did us to us at first convey,
55 Yielded their forces, sense, to us,
   Nor are dross° to us, but allay.°   *refuse / a mixture*

On man heaven's influence works not so,
   But that it first imprints the air,[7]
So soul into the soul may flow,
60   Though it to body first repair.

As our blood labors to beget
   Spirits, as like souls as it can,
Because such fingers need to knit
   That subtle knot, which makes us man:[8]

65 So much pure lovers' souls descend
   T'affections,° and to faculties,°[9]   *feelings / powers*

---

5. Refining of metals by heat.
6. In Aristotelian cosmology, each planet moved in a sphere (the form of its motion around the earth) and was guided by an inner spiritual force, or intelligence.
7. An angel has to put on clothes of air to be seen by men; in hermetic medicine the air mediates the influence of the stars. Just as spirits need a material medium, so souls need the union of bodies.
8. In scholastic philosophy a human being is composed of body and soul, and vapors called spirits produced by the blood link the body with the soul.
9. As the blood mediates between body and soul, so the lovers' feelings mediate between flesh and spirit.

Which sense may reach and apprehend,
    Else a great prince in prison lies.

70   To our bodies turn we then, that so
       Weak men on love revealed may look;
Love's mysteries in souls do grow,
    But yet the body is his book.

And if some lover, such as we,
    Have heard this dialogue of one,
75   Let him still mark us, he shall see
    Small change, when we are to bodies gone.

The Funeral

Whoever comes to shroud me, do not harm
       Nor question much
That subtle wreath of hair, which crowns my arm;
The mystery, the sign you must not touch,
5   For 'tis my outward soul,
Viceroy to that, which then to heaven being gone,
       Will leave this to control,
And keep these limbs her provinces, from dissolution.

For if the sinewy thread my brain lets fall
10   Through every part,
Can tie those parts, and make me one of all;[1]
These hairs which upward grew, and strength and art
       Have from a better brain,
Can better do it;[2] except she meant that I
15   By this should know my pain,
As prisoners then are manacled when they're condemned to die.

Whate'er she meant by it, bury it with me,
       For since I am
Love's martyr, it might breed idolatry,
20   If into others' hands these relics[3] came;
       As 'twas humility
To afford to it all a soul can do,
       So, 'tis some bravery,
That since you would save[4] none of me, I bury some of you.

The Relic

When my grave is broke up again
    Some second guest to entertain,
    (For graves have learned that woman-head[1]
    To be to more than one a bed)

---

1. There was a theory that nerves emanating from the brain held the entire body together.
2. Her hairs coming from a better brain could better preserve his body.
3. Objects, often body parts, that served as memorials of a saint.

4. Editions from 1633 to 1669 read "have," as do some manuscripts.
1. A feminine trait, with a play on maidenhead. The reference is to the custom of burying more than one corpse in the same grave.

5   And he that digs it, spies
  A bracelet of bright hair about the bone,
    Will he not let us alone,
  And think that there a loving couple lies,
  Who thought that this device might be some way
10 To make their souls, at the last busy day,
  Meet at this grave, and make a little stay?

    If this fall in a time, or land,
    Where misdevotion[2] doth command,
    Then, he that digs us up, will bring
15   Us, to the Bishop, and the King,
     To make us relics; then
  Thou shalt be a Mary Magdalen, and I
    A something else thereby;[3]
  All women shall adore us, and some men;
20 And since at such time, miracles are sought,
  I would have that age by this paper taught
  What miracles we harmless lovers wrought.

    First, we loved well and faithfully,
    Yet knew not what we loved, nor why,
25   Difference of sex no more we knew,
    Than our guardian angels do;
     Coming and going, we
  Perchance might kiss, but not between those meals;
    Our hands ne'er touched the seals,
30 Which nature, injured by late law, sets free:[4]
  These miracles we did; but now alas,
  All measure, and all language, I should pass,
  Should I tell what a miracle she was.

Elegy 19: To His Mistress Going to Bed[1]

Come, Madam, come, all rest my powers defy,
Until I labor, I in labor° lie.   *suffering*
The foe oft-times having the foe in sight,
Is tired with standing though he never fight.
5 Off with that girdle,° like heaven's zone° glistering, *belt/zodiac*
But a far fairer world encompassing.
Unpin that spangled breastplate[2] which you wear,
That th'eyes of busy fools may be stopped there.
Unlace your self, for that harmonious chime,
10 Tells me from you, that now it is bed time.
Off with that happy busk,° which I envy,   *bodice*
That still can be, and still can stand so nigh.

2. Idolatry, as in *The Second Anniversary*, where Donne calls prayers to saints "misdevotion."
3. Possibly Jesus Christ or one of Mary's lovers.
4. Nature permits a free love forbidden by human law.
1. In Latin poetry an elegy was a poem in "elegiacs" (alternating lines of dactylic hexameters and pentame-

ters). Most of these, like Ovid's *Amores*, were about love and sex; Donne imitates Ovid's wit and eroticism. This poem was refused a license to be printed in 1633; it was first printed in *The Harmony of the Muses* (1654).
2. The stomacher, a covering for the chest worn under the bodice and covered with jewels.

Your gown going off, such beauteous state reveals,
As when from flowery meads th' hill's shadow steals.
15 Off with that wiry coronet and show
The hairy diadem which on you doth grow:
Now off with those shoes, and then safely tread
In this love's hallowed temple, this soft bed.
In such white robes, heaven's angels used to be
20 Received by men; thou angel bring'st with thee
A heaven like Mahomet's paradise;³ and though
Ill spirits walk in white, we easily know,
By this these angels from an evil sprite,
Those set our hairs, but these our flesh upright.
25   License my roving hands, and let them go,
Before, behind, between, above, below.
Oh my America! my new-found-land,
My kingdom, safliest when with one man manned,
My mine of precious stones, my empery,°   empire
30 How blest I am in this discovering thee!
To enter in these bonds, is to be free;
Then where my hand is set, my seal shall be.⁴
        Full nakedness! All joys are due to thee.
As souls unbodied, bodies unclothed must be,
35 To taste whole joys. Gems which you women use
Are like Atlanta's balls, cast in men's views,⁵
That when a fool's eye lighteth on a gem,
His earthly soul may covet theirs, not them.
Like pictures, or like books' gay coverings made
40 For laymen, are all women thus arrayed;
Themselves are mystic books, which only we
(Whom their imputed grace will dignify)
Must see revealed.⁶ Then since that I may know,
As liberally, as to a midwife, show
45 Thyself: cast all, yea, this white linen hence,
Here is no penance much less innocence.⁷
To teach thee, I am naked first; why then
What need'st thou have more covering than a man?

Holy Sonnets¹
Divine Meditations

1

As due by many titles° I resign   legal rights
Myself to thee, Oh God, first I was made
By thee, and for thee, and when I was decayed
Thy blood bought that, the which before was thine,

---

3. A heaven of sensual pleasure.
4. He has signed an agreement which he will now stamp with his seal. Also, he has put his hand where he will consummate his desire.
5. Donne changes the story of how Atalanta was distracted from racing her suitor Hippomenes when he threw three golden apples before her, which she paused to pick up.

6. The analogy is between the grace that man cannot merit from God in Calvinist doctrine and the undeserved favors women grant their lovers.
7. The 1669 edition and some manuscripts read: "There is no penance due to innocence."
1. The first twelve of the sonnets are printed in the sequence of the 1633 edition, which, according to Helen Gardner, represents Donne's order.

5 I am thy son, made with thyself to shine,
 Thy servant, whose pains thou has still repaid,
 Thy sheep, thine image, and, till I betrayed
 Myself, a temple of thy Spirit divine;
 Why doth the devil then usurp in me?
10 Why doth he steal, nay ravish that's thy right?
 Except thou rise and for thine own work fight,
 Oh I shall soon despair, when I do see
 That thou lov'st mankind well, yet wilt not choose me,
 And Satan hates me, yet is loth to lose me.

2

 Oh my black soul! Now thou art summoned
 By sickness, death's herald, and champion;
 Thou art like a pilgrim, which abroad hath done
 Treason, and durst not turn to whence he is fled,
5 Or like a thief, which till death's doom be read,
 Wisheth himself delivered from prison;
 But damned and haled° to execution,   *dragged*
 Wisheth that still he might be imprisoned;
 Yet grace, if thou repent, thou canst not lack;
10 But who shall give thee that grace to begin?
 Oh make thyself with holy mourning black,
 And red with blushing, as thou art with sin;
 Or wash thee in Christ's blood, which has this might
 That being red, it dyes red souls to white.

3

 This is my play's last scene, here heavens appoint
 My pilgrimage's last mile; and my race
 Idly, yet quickly run, hath this last pace,
 My span's last inch, my minute's latest point,
5 And gluttonous death, will instantly unjoint
 My body, and soul, and I shall sleep a space,
 But my ever-waking part shall see that face,
 Whose fear already shakes my every joint:
 Then, as my soul, to heaven her first seat, takes flight,
10 And earth-borne body, in the earth shall dwell,
 So, fall my sins, that all may have their right,
 To where they're bred, and would press me, to hell.
 Impute me righteous, thus purged of evil,[2]
 For thus I leave the world, the flesh, and devil.

4

 At the round earth's imagined corners, blow[3]
 Your trumpets, angels, and arise, arise
 From death, you numberless infinities
 Of souls, and to your scattered bodies go,
5 All whom the flood did, and fire shall o'erthrow,[4]
 All whom war, dearth, age, agues, tyrannies,

---

2. Protestant theology held that even when a man repented of his sins, he was still marked by the sin of Adam and needed to be made righteous by Christ's grace.

3. "I saw four angels standing on the four corners of the earth, holding the four winds of the earth" (Revelation 7.1).

4. The flood that Noah survived (Genesis 7) and the fire that will destroy the world at the last judgment (Revelation 6.11)

Despair, law, chance, hath slain, and you whose eyes,
Shall behold God, and never taste death's woe.[5]
But let them sleep, Lord, and me mourn a space,
10   For, if above all these, my sins abound,
'Tis late to ask abundance of thy grace,
When we are there; here on this lowly ground,
Teach me how to repent; for that's as good
As if thou'hadst sealed my pardon with thy blood.

5

If poisonous minerals, and if that tree,
Whose fruit threw death on else immortal us,
If lecherous goats, if serpents envious
Cannot be damned; alas, why should I be?
5   Why should intent or reason, born in me,
Make sins, else equal, in me more heinous?
And mercy being easy, and glorious
To God, in his stern wrath, why threatens he?
But who am I, that dare dispute with thee?
10   O God, Oh! of thine only worthy blood,
And my tears, make a heavenly Lethean[6] flood,
And drown in it my sins' black memory.
That thou remember them, some claim as debt,
I think it mercy, if thou wilt forget.

6

Death be not proud, though some have called thee
Mighty and dreadful, for thou are not so.
For, those, whom thou think'st thou dost overthrow,
Die not, poor death, nor yet canst thou kill me;
5   From rest and sleep, which but thy pictures be,
Much pleasure, then from thee, much more must flow,
And soonest our best men with thee do go,
Rest of their bones, and soul's delivery.
Thou art slave to fate, chance, kings, and desperate men,
10   And dost with poison, war, and sickness dwell,
And poppy,° or charms can make us sleep as well,   *a narcotic*
And better than thy stroke; why swell'st° thou then?   *grow in pride*
One short sleep past, we wake eternally,
And death shall be no more, Death thou shalt die.[7]

7

Spit in my face ye Jews, and pierce my side,
Buffet, and scoff, scourge, and crucify me,
For I have sinned, and sinned, and only he,
Who could do no iniquity, hath died:
5   But by my death cannot be satisfied°   *atoned for*
My sins, which pass the Jews' impiety:
They killed once an inglorious[8] man, but I
Crucify him daily, being now glorified.[9]

---

5. The resurrection of the body (see 1 Corinthians 15.51–52).
6. Of Lethe, the river of forgetfulness in the underworld of ancient mythology.
7. "The last enemy that shall be destroyed is death" (1

Corinthians 15.26).
8. Unknown; not yet ascended into glory.
9. Every sin knowingly committed is another torture of Christ. (See Hebrews 6.6: "They crucify to themselves the Son of God afresh.")

Oh let me then, his strange love still admire:
Kings pardon, but he bore our punishment.
And Jacob came clothed in vile harsh attire
But to supplant, and with gainful intent:[1]
God clothed himself in vile man's flesh, that so
He might be weak enough to suffer woe.

8

Why are we by all creatures waited on?
Why do the prodigal elements supply
Life and food to me, being more pure than I,
Simple, and further from corruption?[2]
Why brook'st thou, ignorant horse, subjection?
Why dost thou bull, and boar so sillily
Dissemble weakness, and by one man's stroke die,[3]
Whose whole kind, you might swallow and feed upon?
Weaker I am, woe is me, and worse than you,
You have not sinned, nor need be timorous.
But wonder at a greater wonder, for to us
Created nature doth these things subdue,
But their Creator, whom sin, nor nature tied,
For us, his creatures, and his foes, hath died.

9

What if this present were the world's last night?
Mark in my heart, O soul, where thou dost dwell,
The picture of Christ crucified, and tell
Whether that countenance can thee affright,
Tears in his eyes quench the amazing light,
Blood fills his frowns, which from his pierced head fell,
And can that tongue adjudge thee unto hell,
Which prayed forgiveness for his foes' fierce spite?
No, no; but as in my idolatry[4]
I said to all my profane mistresses,
Beauty, of pity, foulness only is
A sign of rigor:[5] so I say to thee,
To wicked spirits are horrid shapes assigned,
This beauteous form assures a piteous mind.

10

Batter my heart, three-personed God;[6] for, you
As yet but knock, breathe, shine, and seek to mend;
That I may rise, and stand, o'erthrow me, and bend
Your force, to break, blow, burn and make me new.
I, like an usurped town, to another due,
Labor to admit you, but oh, to no end,
Reason your viceroy° in me, me should defend,   *ruler*
But is captived, and proves weak or untrue,
Yet dearly I love you, and would be loved fain,°   *willingly*

---

1. Jacob tricked his father Isaac into giving him his blessing by disguising himself in goatskin as his hairy brother Esau (see Genesis 27.1–36).
2. The elements are physically and morally pure, while humans are a complex mixture of all four elements, prone to decay, and moral agents, capable of sin.
3. The slaughterman's blow, and Adam's sin, causing death to all creation.
4. Erotic devotion to women.
5. Beautiful women show compassion; only ugly ones refuse their lovers.
6. The Trinity: God the Father, Son, and Holy Spirit.

10   But am betrothed unto your enemy,
    Divorce me, untie, or break that knot again,
    Take me to you, imprison me, for I
    Except you enthrall me, never shall be free,
    Nor ever chaste, except you ravish me.

11

    Wilt thou love God, as he thee? Then digest,°   *consider*
    My soul, this wholesome meditation,
    How God the Spirit, by angels waited on
    In heaven, doth make his temple in thy breast.
5   The Father having begot a Son most blest,
    And still begetting, (for he ne'er begun)[6]
    Hath deigned to choose thee by adoption,
    Coheir to his glory, and Sabbath's endless rest;
    And as a robbed man, which by search doth find
10   His stol'n stuff sold, must lose or buy it again:
    The Son of glory came down, and was slain,
    Us whom he had made, and Satan stol'n, to unbind.
    'Twas much, that man was made like God before,
    But, that God should be made like man, much more.

12

    Father, part of his double interest
    Unto thy kingdom, thy Son gives to me,
    His jointure° in the knotty Trinity,   *joint tenancy*
    He keeps, and gives me his death's conquest.
5   This Lamb, whose death, with life the world hath blest,
    Was from the world's beginning slain, and he[7]
    Hath made two wills, which with the legacy[8]
    Of his and thy kingdom, do thy sons invest.
    Yet such are those laws, that men argue yet
10   Whether a man those statutes can fulfill;
    None doth, but all-healing grace and Spirit,
    Revive again what law and letter kill.
    Thy law's abridgement, and thy last command
    Is all but love; oh let that last will stand![9]

from Devotions Upon Emergent Occasions[1]

["FOR WHOM THE BELL TOLLS"]

Nunc lento sonitu dicunt, morieris.
Now this bell tolling softly for another, says to me, Thou must die.

Perchance he for whom this bell[2] tolls may be so ill as that he knows not it tolls for him; and perchance I may think myself so much better than I am, as that they who are about me, and see my state may have caused it to toll for me, and I know not that. The Church is catholic, universal, so are all her actions; all that she does, belongs to all. When she baptises a child, that action concerns me; for that child is thereby connected to that

---

6. God's existence and begetting of his Son are both eternal.
7. Christ, "the Lamb slain from the foundation of the world" (Revelation 13.8).
8. Old and New Testaments.
9. "A new commandment I give unto you, that ye love

one another" (John 13.34).
1. Donne wrote the *Devotions* (1624) following an illness he suffered in winter 1623. Each meditation concerns a phase of his disease.
2. The passing-bell rung slowly when a person was dying.

Head which is my Head too, and engrafted into that body,[3] whereof I am a member. And when she buries a man, that action concerns me: all mankind is of one Author, and is of one volume; when one man dies, one chapter is not torn out of the book, but translated[4] into a better language; and every chapter must be so translated. God employs several translators; some pieces are translated by age, some by sickness, some by war, some by justice; but God's hand is in every translation, and his hand shall bind up all our scattered leaves again, for that library where every book shall lie open to one another. As therefore the bell that rings to a sermon calls not upon the preacher only, but upon the congregation to come, so this bell calls us all; but how much more me, whom am brought so near the door by this sickness. There was a contention as far as a suit, (in which both piety and dignity, religion, and estimation, were mingled) which of the religious orders should ring to prayers first in the morning; and it was determined that they should ring first that rose earliest. If we understand aright the dignity of this bell that tolls for our evening prayer, we would be glad to make it ours by rising early, in that application, that it might be ours, as well as his whose indeed it is. The bell doth toll for him that thinks it doth; and though it intermit again, yet from that minute that occasion wrought upon him, he is united to God. Who casts not up his eye to the sun when it rises? but who takes off his eye from a comet when that breaks out? Who bends not his ear to any bell which upon any occasion rings? but who can remove it from that bell which is passing a piece of himself out of this world? No man is an island, entire of itself; every man is a piece of the Continent, a part of the main. If a clod be washed away by the sea, Europe is the less, as well as if a promontory were, as well as if a manor of thy friends or of thine own were Any man's death diminishes me, because I am involved in mankind; and therefore never send to know for whom the bell tolls; it tolls for thee. Neither can we call this a begging of misery or a borrowing of misery, as though we were not miserable enough of ourselves but must fetch in more from the next house in taking upon us the misery of our neighbors. Truly it were an excusable covetousness if we did; for affliction is a treasure, and scarce any man hath enough of it. No man hath affliction enough that is not matured and ripened by it, and made fit for God by that affliction. If a man carry treasure in bullion, or in a wedge of gold, and have none coined into current moneys, his treasure will not defray him as he travels. Tribulation is treasure in the nature of it, but it is not current money in the use of it, except we get nearer and nearer our home, heaven, by it. Another man may be sick too, and sick to death, and this affliction may lie in his bowels as gold in a mine and be of no use to him: but this bell that tells me of his affliction digs out and applies that gold to me, if by this consideration of another's danger I take mine own into contemplation and so secure myself by making my recourse to my God who is our only security.

from A Sermon Preached to the Honorable Company of the Virginia Plantation[1]

Beloved in him, whose kingdom, and Gospel you seek to advance, in this plantation, our Lord and Savior Christ Jesus, if you seek to establish a temporal kingdom[2]

---

3. United with the church.
4. From Latin *translatus*, "having been carried across."
1. This sermon was preached on November 13, 1622. It was printed three times before Donne died. The Virginia Company was founded in 1606 for the purpose of colonizing North America. In 1609 the Company split into the Virginia Company of London and the Plymouth Company. Dissension within the company arose over whether

there should be martial law or a liberal form of government. By May 1624, when King James disbanded this corporation of private stockholders, 14,000 emigrants had been sent to Virginia.
2. The sermon interprets Acts 1.8: "But ye shall receive power, after that the Holy Ghost is come upon you, and ye shall be witnesses unto me both in Jerusalem, and in all Judea, and in Samaria, and unto the uttermost part of the earth."

there, you are not rectified, if you seek to be kings in either acceptation of the word; to be a king signifies liberty and independency, and supremacy, to be under no man, and to be a king signifies abundance, and omnisufficiency, to need no man. If those that govern there, would establish such a government, as should not depend upon this, or if those that thither, propose to themselves an exemption from laws, to live at their liberty; this is to be kings, to divest allegiance, to be under no man: and if those that adventure thither, propose to themselves present benefit, and profit, a sudden way to be rich, and an abundance of all desirable commodities from thence, this is to be sufficient of themselves, and to need no man: and to be under no man, and to need no man, are the two acceptations of being kings. Whom liberty draws to go, or present profit draws to adventure, are not yet in the right way. O, if you could once bring a catechism to be as good ware amongst them as a bugle, as a knife, as a hatchet! O, if you would be as ready to harken at the return of a ship, how many Indians were converted to Christ Jesus, as what trees, or drugs, or dyes that ship had brought, then you were in your right way, and not till then; liberty and abundance, are characters of kingdoms, and a kingdom is excluded in the Text; the Apostles were not to look for it, in their employment, nor you in this your plantation. * * *

God says to you, "No kingdom, not ease, not abundance; nay nothing at all yet; the plantation shall not discharge the charges, not defray itself yet; but yet already, now at first, it shall conduce to great uses; it shall redeem many a wretch from the jaws of death,[3] from the hands of the executioner, upon whom, perchance a small fault, or perchance a first fault, or perchance a fault heartily and sincerely repented, perchance no fault, but malice, had otherwise cast a present, and ignominious death. It shall sweep your streets, and wash your doors, from idle persons, and the children of idle persons, and employ them: and truly, if the whole country were but such a Bridewell,[4] to force idle persons to work, it has a good use. But it is already, not only a spleen, to drain the ill humors of the body, but a liver, to breed good blood; already the employment breeds mariners; already the place gives assays,[5] nay freights of marketable commodities; already it is a mark for the envy, and for the ambition of our enemies. I speak but of our doctrinal, not national enemies; as they are papists, they are sorry we have this country; and surely, twenty lectures in matter of controversy, does not so much vex them as one ship that goes, and strengthens that plantation. Neither can I recommend it to you, by any better rhetoric than their malice. They would gladly have it, and therefore let us be glad to hold it. * * *

Those amongst you, that are old now, shall pass out of this world with this great comfort, that you contributed to the beginning of that Commonwealth, and of that Church, though they live not to see the growth thereof to perfection. Apollos[6] watered, but Paul planted; he that began the work, was the greater man. And you that are young now, may live to see the enemy as much empeached by that place, and your friends, yea, children, as well accommodated in that place, as any other. You shall have made this island, which is but as the suburbs of the Old World, a bridge, a gallery to the New, to join all to that world that shall never grow old, the kingdom of heaven; you shall add persons to this kingdom, and to the kingdom of heaven, and add names to the books of our chronicles, and to the Book of Life.

To end all, as the orators which declaimed in the presence of the Roman emperors, in their panegyrics, took that way to make those emperors see, what they were

---

3. Many of those who were brought from England to Virginia were freed from imprisonment and execution in England by becoming indentured servants.

4. A London prison.
5. Returns of profit.
6. Paul's successor at Corinth. See 1 Corinthians 3.6.

bound to do, to say in those public orations, that those emperors had done so, (for that increased the love of the subject to the prince, to be so told, that he had done those great things, and then it conveyed a counsel into the prince to do them after). As their way was to procure things to be done, by saying they were done, so beloved I have taken a contrary way: for when I, by way of exhortation, all this while have seemed to tell you what should be done by you, I have, indeed, but told the congregation what has been done already; neither do I speak to move a wheel that stood still, but to keep the wheel in due motion; nor persuade you to begin, but to continue a good work, nor propose foreign, but your own examples, to do still, as you have done hitherto. For, for that, that which is especially in my contemplation, the conversion of the people, as I have received, so I can give this testimony, that of those persons, who have sent in moneys, and concealed their names, the greatest part, almost all, have limited their devotion, and contribution upon that point, the propagation of religion, and the conversion of the people; for the building and beautifying of the house of God, and for the instruction and education of their young children. Christ Jesus himself "is yesterday, and today, and the same forever."[7] In the advancing of his glory, be you so too, yesterday, and today, and the same forever, here; and hereafter, when time shall be no more, no more yesterday, no more today, yet forever and ever, you shall enjoy that joy, and that glory, which no ill accident can attain to diminish, or eclipse it.

Lady Mary Wroth
1586–1640

Lady Mary Wroth was born the same year that her uncle Sir Philip Sidney died in battle. Like her uncle, she wrote brilliant sonnets and an entertaining and complex prose romance, but whereas his death and writing became the stuff of myth, she died in obscurity. Appreciated by the finest poets of her time, her writing was neglected for the next 300 years; she has only recently been rediscovered as one of the most compelling women writers of her age. Her *Pamphilia to Amphilanthus*, the first Petrarchan sonnet sequence in English by a woman, was first printed in 1621 but was not reprinted until 1977. Wroth's work has finally become available outside rare book libraries, thanks to Josephine Robert's editions of Wroth's complete poems (1983) and her prose romance *The Countess of Montgomeries Urania* (1995), along with Michael Brennan's edition of her pastoral tragicomedy *Love's Victory* (1988). Recent criticism has stressed the formal complexity and variety of her poetry and prose, their creation of female subjectivity, and their relationship to her life and social context, shedding new light on one of the most emotionally powerful and stylistically innovative authors of the Jacobean period.

Mary Wroth was born into the cultivated and distinguished Sidney family. Mary and her mother, two brothers, and seven sisters lived at the family estate Penshurst in Kent. She sometimes visited her father in the Low Countries, where he commanded the English troops fighting for the Protestant cause against the Spanish. Ben Jonson sang the praises of Lady Mary's family and their way of life in *To Penshurst* (see pages 1533–1535), a place where the children not only enjoyed natural beauty—"broad beech" and "chest-nut shade"—but also learned the "mysteries of manners, arms and arts." Mary also spent a great deal of time in London with her

7. Hebrews 13.8.

aunt for whom she was named, Mary (Sidney) Herbert, Countess of Pembroke, hostess to and patron of a circle of poets that included George Chapman and Ben Jonson.

Mary found a mentor in her aunt, who herself wrote poems as well as translations of the Psalms and of Petrarch. Mary Herbert's translation of Petrarch's *Trionfo della Morte* ("Triumph of Death") portrays the poet's beloved Laura not as a passive object but as a lively and eloquent speaker. Mary Wroth's own sonnets similarly portray the woman as the suffering and desiring subject of love rather than the mute object that was common in earlier English Petrarchan poetry. Mary Wroth took the title of her *Urania* from a character in Philip Sidney's *The Countess of Pembrokes Arcadia*, whose publication had been overseen by his sister, Mary Sidney Herbert. Mary Wroth even created the character of the Queen of Naples as a fictional version of her aunt and perhaps saw *Urania* as a continuation of *Arcadia*.

When Mary married Sir Robert Wroth, Lord of Durance and Laughton House and juror for the Gunpowder Plot, she continued her close family ties with her aunt and father (yet another poet), but she also moved into the larger world of the Jacobean court. She served as Queen Anne's companion, and she became at once an observer and a center of attention in the aristocratic circle at court. In 1605, shortly after the first recorded performance of *Othello* at Whitehall, Lady Mary Wroth played in Ben Jonson's *Masque of Blackness*, in which she was presented to the court with Lady Frances Walsingham as the embodiment of gravity and dignity. Later, Wroth would deploy metaphors of darkness and night to great effect in her lyric poems.

It was in this court context that she attracted the attention of Ben Jonson, who not only wrote a poem complimenting her husband but also dedicated a sonnet and two epigrams to her. Jonson paid tribute to her as a subject and inspiration for poetry and as a powerfully moving poet in her own right. He claimed that since writing out her sonnets, he had "become / A better lover and much better poet." Dedicating his great play *The Alchemist* to her, he portrayed her as inheriting her uncle's mantle as poet: "To that Lady Most Deserving her Name and Blood, Lady Mary Wroth,"—a pun on her name, as Wroth was pronounced "worth." While she, too, punned on her married name in her poetry, Mary clung to her identity as a Sidney, using the Sidney device in her letters.

Her marriage was not particularly happy and pales in comparison with her literary friendship and love affair with her cousin William Herbert, by whom she had two illegitimate children, after she was widowed in 1614. During the years of her early widowhood she wrote the first part of her prose romance *Urania*, which was printed with *Pamphilia to Amphilanthus* in 1621. The *Urania* not only presents a fictional account of her relationship with her cousin and her parents' own happy marriage but also was read at the time as a criticism of the mores of the court. King James's courtiers, taking offense at the satire of their private lives, attacked her, prompting her to ask for the book to be removed from publication a few months after it first appeared. The early modern prejudice against women writing surfaces in Lord Denny's punning condescension to Wroth: "leave idle books alone / For wiser and worthier women have writ none."

Fortunately for us, she didn't take his advice and continued to write the second book of the *Urania*, which survives in manuscript. Indeed, no record of a warrant to recall the book survives. Her final years remain a mystery; she lived in retirement after her cousin's death. She left behind a body of poetry challenging the status quo of the court, proclaiming the suffering she had endured for love, and singing the beauty of spiritual love in a woman's voice. Imitating not only her uncle Philip's *Arcadia* but also the *Heptameron* of the French writer Marguerite de Navarre, Mary Wroth made the prose romance a complex combination of novelistic fantasy, roman à clef, and social satire. The greatest English woman writer of her age, Mary Wroth fashioned a new voice and new perspectives within literary tradition that convey the fullness and complexity of her life as woman, lover, and writer.

from **Pamphilia to Amphilanthus**[1]

1

When night's black mantle could most darkness prove,
    And sleep death's image did my senses hire
From knowledge of myself, then thoughts did move
    Swifter than those most swiftness need require:
5   In sleep, a chariot drawn by winged desire
    I saw, where sat bright Venus, Queen of love,
And at her feet her son,[2] still adding fire
    To burning hearts which she did hold above,
But one heart flaming more than all the rest
10   The goddess held, and put it to my breast.
"Dear son, now shut?"[3] said she, "thus must we win."
He her obeyed, and martyred my poor heart,
    I, waking, hoped as dreams it would depart;[4]
    Yet since, O me, a lover I have been.

16

Am I thus conquered? Have I lost the powers
    That to withstand, which joys to ruin me?
Must I be still while it my strength devours
    And captive leads me prisoner, bound, unfree?
5   Love first shall leave men's fant'sies to them free,[5]
    Desire shall quench love's flames, spring hate sweet showers,
Love shall loose all his darts, have sight, and see
    His shame, and wishings hinder happy hours.[6]
Why should we not Love's purblind° charms resist?   *totally blind*
10   Must we be servile, doing what he list?°   *wants*
No, seek some host to harbor thee: I fly
Thy babish° tricks, and freedom do profess;   *childish*
    But O my hurt, makes my lost heart confess
    I love, and must. So farewell liberty.

17

Truly poor Night thou welcome art to me;
    I love thee better in this sad attire
Than that which raiseth some men's fant'sies higher
    Like painted outsides which foul inward be.[7]
5   I love thy grave, and saddest looks to see,
    Which seems my soul, and dying heart entire,

---

1. The title means "From the All-loving one to the Dual Lover." First published in 1621, the sonnet sequence is here printed according to the numbering in Josephine Robert's 1983 edition.
2. Cupid. Compare the image of the chariot here with that in Petrarch's *Triumph of Love*. Also see Giordano Bruno on the symbolic meanings of Venus in Perspectives: Emblem, Metaphor, and Style, page 1605.
3. Enclose that flaming heart within Pamphilia.

4. Pamphilia's experience of love is represented as a dream vision, a symbolic narrative in which the dreamer discovers hidden truth.
5. Before I surrender to Love, Love will allow men to realize their fantasies freely.
6. Cupid blindfolded was a popular figure in Renaissance iconography.
7. Like the whitewashed sepulchers (tombs) in Matthew 23.27.

Like to the ashes of some happy fire
That flamed in joy, but quenched in misery.
I love thy count'nance,° and thy sober pace   *face, expression*
10   Which evenly goes, and as of loving grace
To us, and me me among the rest oppressed
Gives quiet, peace to my poor self alone,
And freely grants day leave when thou art gone
To give clear light to see all ill redressed.

26

When everyone to pleasing pastime hies°   *goes in haste*
Some hunt, some hawk,[8] some play, while some delight
In sweet discourse, and music shows joy's might
Yet I my thoughts do far above these prize.
5   The joy which I take is that free from eyes
I sit, and wonder at this day-like night
So to dispose themselves, as void of right,
And leave true pleasure for poor vanities;
When others hunt, my thoughts I have in chase;
10   If hawk, my mind at wishèd end doth fly,
Discourse, I with my spirit talk, and cry
While others music choose as greatest grace.
O God, say I, can these fond pleasures move?
Or music be but in sweet thoughts of love?

28. Song

Sweetest love, return again,
Make not too long stay;
Killing mirth and forcing pain,
Sorrow leading way,
5   Let us not thus parted be,
Love and absence ne'er agree;

But since you must needs depart,
And me hapless° leave,   *unlucky*
In your journey take my heart
10   Which will not deceive,
Yours it is, to you it flies
Joying in those lovèd eyes,

So in part, we shall not part
Though we absent be;
15   Time, nor place, nor greatest smart
Shall my bands make free.
Tied I am, yet think it gain,
In such knots I feel no pain.

But can I live having lost
20   Chiefest part of me?

8. To hunt game with hawks.

Heart is fled, and sight is crossed,
    These my fortunes be;
Yet dear heart go, soon return,
As good there as here to burn.

39

Take heed mine eyes, how you your looks do cast,
    Lest they betray my heart's most secret thought;
    Be true unto yourselves for nothing's bought
    More dear than doubt which brings a lover's fast.
5 Catch you all watching eyes, ere they be past,
    Or take yours fixed where your best love hath sought
    The pride of your desires; let them be taught
    Their faults for shame, they could no truer last;
Then look, and look with joy for conquest won,
10   Of those that searched your hurt in double kind;
    So you kept safe, let them themselves look blind;
Watch, gaze, and mark 'til they to madness run,
While you, mine eyes, enjoy full sight of love
Contented that such happinesses move.

40

False hope which feeds but to destroy, and spill°   *kill*
    What it first breeds; unnatural to the birth
    Of thine own womb; conceiving but to kill,[9]
    And plenty gives to make the greater dearth,
5 So tyrants do who falsely ruling earth
    Outwardly grace them, and with profits fill,
    Advance those who appointed are to death
    To make their greater fall to please their will.
Thus shadow they their wicked vile intent,
10 Coloring evil with a show of good
    While in fair shows their malice so is spent;
    Hope kills the heart, and tyrants shed the blood.
For hope deluding brings us to the pride[1]
Of our desires the farther down to slide.

48

If ever Love had force in human breast?
    If ever he could move in pensive heart?
    Or if that he such power could but impart
    To breed those flames whose heat brings joy's unrest,
5 Then look on me: I am to these addressed.
    I am the soul that feels the greatest smart,
    I am that heartless trunk of heart's depart,
    And I, that one, by love and grief oppressed;
None ever felt the truth of Love's great miss°   *need, want*
10 Of eyes, 'til I deprived was of bliss;
    For had he seen, he must have pity showed;

---

9. The image is of a miscarriage or infanticide.   1. Arrogance, but also elation and pleasure.

I should not have been made this stage of woe
   Where sad disasters have their open show;
   O no, more pity he had sure bestowed.

68

My pain, still smothered in my grièved breast
   Seeks for some ease, yet cannot passage find
   To be discharged of this unwelcome guest;
   When most I strive, more fast his burdens bind,
5 Like to a ship, on Goodwins[2] cast by wind
   The more she strives, more deep in sand is pressed
   Till she be lost; so am I, in this kind°   *way*
   Sunk and devoured, and swallowed by unrest,
Lost, shipwracked, spoiled, debarred of smallest hope
10 Nothing of pleasure left; save thoughts have scope,
   Which wander may. Go then, my thoughts, and cry
Hope's perished, Love tempest-beaten, Joy lost:
   Killing Despair hath all these blessings crossed.
   Yet Faith still cries, Love will not falsify.

74. Song

Love a child is ever crying,
   Please him, and he straight is flying;
   Give him, he the more is craving,
   Never satisfied with having.

5 His desires have no measure,
   Endless folly is his treasure;
   What he promiseth he breaketh;
   Trust not one word that he speaketh.

He vows nothing but false matter,
10 And to cozen° you he'll flatter.   *trick*
   Let him gain the hand[3] he'll leave you,
   And still glory to deceive you.

He will triumph in your wailing,
   And yet cause be of your failing.
15 These his virtues are, and slighter
   Are his gifts, his favors lighter.

Feathers are as firm in staying,
   Wolves no fiercer in their preying;
   As a child then leave him crying,
20 Nor seek him so given to flying.

from *A Crown of Sonnets Dedicated to Love*[1]

77

In this strange labyrinth how shall I turn?
   Ways° are on all sides while the way I miss: *paths*

---

2. A dangerous shoal off the south eastern coast of England.
3. Let him take control.
1. The crown (Italian *corona*) is a form in which the last

line of each poem is repeated as the first line of the next.
The last poem of the sequence ends with the first line of
the first poem.

If to the right hand, there, in love I burn;
    Let me go forward, therein danger is;
5 If to the left, suspicion hinders bliss,
    Let me turn back, shame cries I ought return,
    Nor faint° though crosses with my fortunes kiss;[2]   *lose heart*
    Stand still is harder, although sure to mourn.[3]
Thus let me take the right, or left-hand way,
10   Go forward, or stand still, or back retire;
    I must these doubts endure without allay°   *relief*
    Or help, but travail[4] find for my best hire.
Yet that which most my troubled sense doth move
Is to leave all, and take the thread of love.[5]

83

How blessed be they then, who his favors prove,
    A life whereof the birth is just desire,
    Breeding sweet flame which hearts invite to move
    In these loved eyes which kindle Cupid's fire,
5 And nurse his longings with his thoughts entire,
    Fixed on the heat of wishes formed by love;
    Yet whereas fire destroys this doth aspire,
    Increase, and foster all delights above;
Love will a painter make you, such as you
10   Shall able be to draw your only dear
    More lovely, perfect, lasting, and more true
Than rarest workman, and to you more near.
These be the least, then all must needs confess
He that shuns love doth love himself the less.

103

My muse now happy, lay thyself to rest,
    Sleep in the quiet of a faithful love,
    Write you no more, but let these fant'sies move
    Some other hearts, wake not to new unrest;
5 But if you study, be those thoughts addressed
    To truth, which shall eternal goodness prove,
    Enjoying of true joy, the most, and best,
    The endless gain which never will remove.
Leave the discourse to Venus, and her son
10   To young beginners, and their brains inspire
    With stories of great love, and from that fire
    Get heat to write the fortunes they have won,
And thus leave off; what's past shows you can love,
Now let your constancy your honor prove.

                      Pamphilia.[6]

---

2. Though troubles embrace my luck, or fate.
3. It is more difficult to do nothing, although this is sure to make me mourn.
4. Hard work, with word play on "Travel," which occurs in the 1621 text.
5. An allusion to the myth of Ariadne, beloved of Theseus, to whom she gave a thread to unwind behind him on his path through the labyrinth so that, after slaying the Minotaur, he could retrace his steps on his way out.
6. According to the 1621 *Urania*, when Pamphilia accepts the keys to the Throne of Love, the virtue Constancy disappears and is transformed into Pamphilia's breast.

Robert Herrick
1591–1674

The urbane and at times pagan poet Robert Herrick might seem an unlikely candidate for rural vicar, but such were his connections that he was promoted from deacon to priest in a day. He spent most of his life as vicar of the Devonshire parish of Dean, where he wrote poetry about country customs and church liturgy. A hundred and fifty years after his death, a writer in the *Quarterly Review* was able to find people in the village who could recite from memory Herrick's *Farewell to Dean Bourn:* "I never look to see / Dean, or thy warty incivility," lines that "they said he uttered as he crossed the brook, upon being ejected from the vicarage by Cromwell." Referring to Herrick's return to the vicarage after the Restoration, these locals "added with an air of innocent triumph, 'He did see it again.'" The villagers also recalled stories of how the bachelor vicar threw his sermon at the congregation one day for their inattention and how he taught his pet pig to drink from a tankard. Many of his best poems, such as *Corinna's Going A-Maying* and *The Hock-Cart, or Harvest Home,* celebrate the landscape and the life of the country in the idealized tradition of pastoral poetry.

The son of a goldsmith in Cheapside, Herrick was apprenticed to the trade at age fourteen. After taking his B.A. from Cambridge in 1617, he returned to London, where he spent his poetic apprenticeship until he was appointed chaplain to the Duke of Buckingham in his failed expedition to aid the French Protestants of Rhé in 1627. Only a year later, Herrick moved to the vicarage at Dean, but many of his poems recount his London days, recalling the feasts frequented by Ben Jonson, whose verse "out-did the meat, out-did the frolic wine." The influence of Jonson's classical concision, wit, and urbanity can be felt in such poems as *Delight in Disorder* and his *Prayer* to the poet. While in London, Herrick also became friends with William Lawes, the court composer who wrote the music for Milton's masque *Comus.* When Lawes set Herrick's *To the Virgins to Make Much of Time* to music, this poem became one of the most popular drinking songs of the seventeenth century—often sung as a "catch," which meant that its words could be played with to produce ribald double meanings. His poems circulated in manuscript until his volume of verse was printed in 1648, with his secular poetry entitled *Hesperides* and his religious poetry entitled *Noble Numbers.* He first achieved a wide readership in the early nineteenth century with the romantic revival of interest in rural life and poetry.

The Argument of His Book[1]

I sing of brooks, of blossoms, birds, and bowers,
Of April, May, of June, and July flowers.
I sing of Maypoles, hock carts, wassails, wakes,[2]
Of bridegrooms, brides, and of their bridal cakes.
5   I write of youth, of love, and have access
By these, to sing of cleanly wantonness.°   *carefree abandon*
I sing of dews, of rains, and piece by piece,
Of balm, of oil, of spice, and ambergris.[3]

---

1. All of Herrick's poems were published in 1648. The "Argument" introduces the book's themes.
2. Hock carts: harvest wagons; wassails: drinking toasts; wakes: celebrations in honor of the dedication of a parish church.
3. Secretion from the intestines of sperm whales, used to make perfume.

10

I sing of times trans-shifting;[4] and I write
How roses first came red, and lilies white.
I write of groves, of twilights, and I sing
The court of Mab,[5] and of the fairy king.
I write of hell; I sing (and ever shall)
Of Heaven, and hope to have it after all.

Delight in Disorder

5

10

A sweet disorder in the dress
Kindles in clothes a wantonness:
A lawn° about the shoulders thrown   *scarf*
Into a fine distraction;
An erring° lace, which here and there   *wandering*
Enthralls the crimson stomacher:[1]
A cuff neglectful, and thereby
Ribbons to flow confusedly:
A winning wave, deserving note,
In the tempestuous petticoat;
A carelesse shoestring, in whose tie
I see a wild civility:
Do more bewitch me, than when art
Is too precise[2] in every part.

Corinna's Going A-Maying

5

10

15

Get up, get up for shame! the blooming morn
Upon her wings presents the god unshorn.[1]
        See how Aurora[2] throws her fair
        Fresh-quilted colors through the air:
        Get up, sweet slug-a-bed, and see
        The dew-bespangling herb and tree.
Each flower has wept, and bowed toward the east,
Above an hour since; yet you not dressed,
        Nay! not so much as out of bed?
        When all the birds have matins° said,   *morning prayer*
        And sung their thankfull hymns: 'tis sin,
        Nay, profanation° to keep in,   *impiety*
Whenas a thousand virgins on this day
Spring, sooner than the lark, to fetch in May.[3]

Rise, and put on your foliage, and be seen
To come forth, like the springtime, fresh and green,
        And sweet as Flora.[4] Take no care

4. Times changing and passing; the cycle of the seasons.
5. Queen of the fairies.
1. Ornamental covering for the chest worn under the lacing of the bodice.
2. "Precise" was often used to describe the strictness of the Puritans.

1. Apollo, the sun god, whose beams are seen as his flowing locks.
2. Goddess of the dawn in Roman mythology.
3. The custom on May Day morning was to gather blossoms.
4. Ancient Italian goddess of fertility and flowers.

For jewels for your gown, or hair:
Fear not; the leaves will strew
20   Gems in abundance upon you;
Besides, the childhood of the day has kept,
Against you come, some orient° pearls unwept;   *oriental, shining*
    Come, and receive them while the light
    Hangs on the dew-locks of the night,
25   And Titan[5] on the eastern hill
    Retires himself, or else stands still
Till you come forth. Wash, dress, be brief in praying:
Few beads are best,[6] when once we go a-Maying.

Come, my Corinna, come; and coming, mark
30 How each field turns a street; each street a park
    Made green, and trimmed with trees; see how
    Devotion gives each house a bough,
    Or branch: each porch, each door, ere this,
    An ark, a tabernacle is,[7]
35 Made up of whitethorn neatly interwove;
As if here were those cooler shades of love.
    Can such delights be in the street
    And open fields, and we not see't?
    Come, we'll abroad; and let's obey
40   The proclamation made for May,
And sin no more, as we have done, by staying;
But my Corinna, come, let's go a-Maying.

There's not a budding boy, or girl, this day,
But is got up, and gone to bring in May.
45   A deal of youth, ere this, is come
    Back, and with whitethorn laden home.
    Some have dispatched their cakes and cream,
    Before that we have left to dream:
And some have wept, and wooed, and plighted troth,
50 And chose their priest, ere we can cast off sloth.
    Many a green-gown has been given,
    Many a kiss, both odd and even:[8]
    Many a glance, too, has been sent
    From out the eye, love's firmament:
55 Many a jest told of the keys betraying
This night, and locks picked; yet we're not a-Maying.

Come, let us go, while we are in our prime,
And take the harmless folly of the time.
    We shall grow old apace, and die
60   Before we know our liberty.
    Our life is short; and our days run
    As fast away as does the sun;

---

5. The sun god.
6. An allusion to Catholic rosary beads.
7. The Hebrew ark of the Covenant contained the tablets of the laws; a tabernacle is an ornamental niche to hold the consecrated host.
8. Green gown . . . given: by lying in the grass. Kisses are odd and even in kissing games.

And as a vapor, or a drop of rain
Once lost, can ne'er be found again,
65   So when or you or I are made
      A fable, song, or fleeting shade,°   *soul*
All love, all liking, all delight
Lies drowned with us in endless night.
Then while time serves, and we are but decaying,
70 Come, my Corinna, come, let's go a-Maying.

To the Virgins, to Make Much of Time

Gather ye rosebuds while ye may,
    Old time is still a-flying;[1]
And this same flower that smiles today,
    Tomorrow will be dying.[2]

5 The glorious lamp of heaven, the sun,
    The higher he's a-getting;
The sooner will his race be run,[3]
    And nearer he's to setting.

That age is best, which is the first,
10   When youth and blood are warmer;
But being spent, the worse, and worst
    Times still succeed the former.

Then be not coy, but use your time,
    And while ye may, go marry;
15 For having lost but once your prime,
    You may for ever tarry.

The Hock-Cart,[1] or Harvest Home

To the Right Honorable, Mildmay, Earl of Westmoreland[2]

Come, sons of summer, by whose toil,
We are the lords of wine and oil;
By whose tough labors, and rough hands,
We rip up first, then reap our lands.
5 Crowned with the ears of corn, now come,
And, to the pipe, sing harvest home.
Come forth, my Lord, and see the cart
Dressed up with all the country art.
See, here a maukin°, there a sheet,   *scarecrow*
10 As spotless pure, as it is sweet,
The horses, mares, and frisking fillies,
(Clad, all, in linen, white as lilies.)
The harvest swains,° and wenches bound   *young men*
For joy, to see the hock-cart crowned.

---

1. The Latin tag *tempus fugit* ("time flies").
2. "Dying" was also a euphemism for orgasm.
3. In Greek mythology the sun was seen as the chariot of Phoebus Apollo drawn across the sky each day as in a race.

1. Wagon carrying the last load of harvest crops.
2. The landlord, Mildmay Fane (Earl of Westmoreland), was one of Herrick's patrons.

15   About the cart, hear how the rout
         Of rural younglings raise the shout,
         Pressing before, some coming after,
         Those with a shout and these with laughter.
         Some blesse the cart, some kiss the sheaves;
20   Some prank° them up with oaken leaves: *decorate*
         Some cross the fill-horse, some with great
         Devotion stroke the home-borne wheat:[3]
         While other rustics, less attent
         To prayers, than to merriment,
25   Run after with their breeches rent.
            Well, on, brave boys, to your Lord's hearth,
         Glittering with fire; where, for your mirth,
         Ye shall see first the large and chief
         Foundation of your feast, fat beef:
30   With upper stories, mutton, veal,
         And bacon, (which makes full the meal)
         With several dishes standing by,
         As here a custard, there a pie,
         And here all tempting frumenty.°   *pudding*
35   And for to make the merry cheer,
         If smirking° wine be wanting here,   *sparkling*
         There's that, which drowns all care, stout beer:
         Which freely drink to your Lord's health,
         Then to the plough, (the common-wealth),
40   Next to your flails, your fanes, your vats;[4]
         Then to the maids with wheaten hats:
         To the rough sickle, and crook'd sythe,
         Drink, frolic boys, till all be blithe.
            Feed, and grow fat; and as ye eat,
45   Be mindfull, that the laboring neat[5]
         As you, may have their fill of meat.
         And know, besides, ye must revoke°   *call back*
         The patient ox unto the yoke,
         And all go back unto the plow
50   And harrow, though they're hanged up now.
         And, you must know, your Lord's word's true,
         Feed him ye must, whose food fills you,
         And that this pleasure is like rain,
         Not sent ye for to drown your pain,
55   But for to make it spring again.

His Prayer to Ben Jonson[1]

     When I a verse shall make,
     Know I have prayed thee,

---

3. The fill-horse is harnessed between the shafts of the cart. Crossing the horse and kissing the sheaves of wheat were old English Catholic customs.
4. Flails: instruments for threshing; fans: used to separate wheat from chaff.

5. Cattle, whose "meat" is grain or hay.
1. The humorous conceit in this poem is of Ben Jonson as a saint in the "religion" of poetry, aiding Herrick as a saint would intercede for a sinner. Herrick pays homage to Jonson's style both in his humor and verse form.

For old religion's sake,[2]
Saint Ben to aid me.

5   Make the way smooth for me,
When I, thy Herrick,
Honoring thee, on my knee
Offer my lyric.

Candles I'll give to thee
10   And a new altar;
And thou Saint Ben shall be
Writ in my psalter.°   *hymn book*

Upon Julia's Clothes

When as in silks my Julia goes,
Then, then, me thinks, how sweetly flows
That liquefaction of her clothes.
Next, when I cast mine eyes and see
That brave° vibration each way free;   *splendid*
O how that glittering taketh me!

Upon His Spaniel Tracie

Now thou art dead, no eye shall ever see,
For shape and service, spaniel like to thee.
This shall my love do, give thy sad death one
Tear, that deserves of me a million.

George Herbert
1593–1633

George Herbert spent the last three years of his life as a country parson. In an age in which such a church living was often a mere sinecure, Herbert had a genuine vocation, which he chose over other paths open to him through his talent and the connections of his distinguished Welsh family. His education and vocation were most influenced by his mother Magdalene Herbert, a woman with a great appreciation for poetry and strong devotion to the Church of England. When she died in 1627, John Donne gave the funeral sermon, extolling not only her grace, wit, and charm but especially her extraordinary charity to those who suffered from the plague of 1625, among whom was Donne himself. Herbert's mother had been widowed when he was just three years old. She brought up ten children, first in Oxford and then in London, where she saw to it that they were well read in the Bible and the classics.

    Herbert studied at Cambridge University, where he became Reader in Rhetoric in 1616; in 1620 he was elected Public Orator, a post that he held for eight years. He wrote poetry and delivered public addresses in Latin and worked on the Latin version of Francis Bacon's *The Advancement of Learning*. Herbert also stood for Parliament and served there in 1624, when the Virginia Company, in which many of his friends and family were stockholders, was beset by financial difficulties and ultimately dissolved by James I.

2. A reference to Jonson's Catholicism.

Though his book *The Temple*, which included all his English poems, was not published until just after his death in 1633, Herbert was already writing verse as an undergraduate in 1610, when he dedicated two sonnets to his mother that advocated religious rather than secular love as the subject for poetry. His first published poems were written in Latin, commemorating the death of Prince Henry (1612). Herbert also wrote three different collections of Latin poems during his Cambridge years: *Musae Responsoriae*, polemical poems that defended the rites of the Church of England from Puritan criticism; *Passio discerpta*, religious verse that focused on Christ's passion and death in a style reminiscent of Crashaw; and *Lucas*, a collection of brief epigrams, such as this one on pride: "Each man is earth, and the field's child. Tell me, / Will you be a sterile mountain or a fertile valley?" The sardonic and mocking tone of these epigrams may surprise a reader of his English poems, but the wit and the rhetorical finish of his Latin poetry recur in his later verse.

Herbert's poetry is some of the most complex and innovative of all English verse. In a very pared-down style, enlivened by gentle irony, Herbert produces complexity of meaning through allegory and emblem, directly or more often indirectly alluding to biblical images, events, and insights, which take on their own moral and poetic meaning in the life of the speaker and the reader. Each of his poems is a kind of spiritual event, enacting in its form, both visual and aural, the very theological experiences and beliefs—or conflict of beliefs— expressed. Herbert allows us to make the spiritual journey with him through suffering and redemption, through doubt and hope. The meaning of one of his poems unravels like a discovery, each line and stanza raising alternative possibilities and altering the meaning of the one before. His spirituality is not a matter of easy acceptance but one of struggle, portrayed with wit, logic, and passion that recall the best of Donne's verse. The humility, subtle hesitancy, and whimsical irony are Herbert's alone, as when he addresses a love poem, *The Pearl*, to God:

> I know the ways of pleasure, the sweet strains,
> The lullings and the relishes of it . . .
> My stuff is flesh, not brass; my senses live,
> And grumble oft, that they have more in me
> Then he that curbs them, being but one to five:
>   Yet I love thee.

The Altar[1]

> A broken ALTAR, Lord, thy servant rears,
> Made of a heart, and cemented with tears:
>   Whole parts are as thy hand did frame;
>   No workman's tool has touched the same.[2]
5   A HEART alone
>   Is such a stone,
>   As nothing but
>   Thy power doth cut.
>   Wherefore each part
10   Of my hard heart
>   Meets in this frame,
>   To praise thy Name.
>   That, if I chance to hold my peace,
>   These stones to praise thee may not cease.[3]
15   Oh let thy blessed SACRIFICE be mine,
>   and sanctify this ALTAR to be thine.

1. All of Herbert's poems were published in *The Temple* (1633).
2. See Exodus 20.5, where God tells Moses: "And if thou wilt make me an altar of stone, thou shalt not build it of hewn stone: for if thou lift up thy tool upon it thou has polluted it."
3. See Luke 19.40: "I tell you that, if these should hold their peace, the stones would immediately cry out."

Redemption[1]

Having been tenant long to a rich lord,
    Not thriving, I resolvèd to be bold,
    And make a suit unto him, to afford
A new small-rented° lease, and cancel the old.   *cheaper*

5   In heaven at his manor I him sought:
    They told me there, that he was lately gone
    About some land, which he had dearly bought
Long since on earth, to take possession.

I straight returned, and knowing his great birth,
10   Sought him accordingly in great resorts—
    In cities, theaters, gardens, parks, and courts:
At length I heard a ragged noise and mirth

    Of thieves and murderers: there I him espied,
    Who straight, "Your suit is granted," said, and died.

Easter

Rise heart, thy Lord is risen. Sing his praise
          Without delays,
Who takes thee by the hand, that thou likewise
          With him may'st rise:
5   That, as his death calcinèd° thee to dust,   *reduced by fire*
His life may make thee gold, and much more just.

Awake, my lute, and struggle for thy part
          With all thy art.
The cross taught all wood to resound his name
10   Who bore the same.
His stretchèd sinews taught all strings, what key
Is best to celebrate this most high day.

Consort° both heart and lute, and twist a song   *harmonize*
          Pleasant and long:
15   Or, since all music is but three parts vied
          And multiplied,[1]
Oh let thy blessed spirit bear a part,
And make up our defects with his sweet art.

I got me flowers to strew thy way;
20   I got me boughs off many a tree:
But thou wast up by break of day,
And brought'st thy sweets along with thee.

---

1. "Redemption," means deliverance from sin and comes from the Latin *redimere,* to buy back, to ransom.

1. Since music is increased by three-part harmony.

The sun arising in the east,
Though he give light, and th' east perfume,
25   If they should offer to contest
With thy arising, they presume.

Can there be any day but this,
Though many suns to shine endeavor?
We count three hundred, but we miss:[2]
30   There is but one, and that one ever.

Easter Wings[1]

Lord, who createdst man in wealth and store,[2]
Though foolishly he lost the same,
Decaying more and more,
Till he became
Most poor:
With thee
Oh let me rise
As larks, harmoniously,
And sing this day thy victories:
Then shall the fall[3] further the flight in me.

My tender age in sorrow did begin
And still with sickness and shame
Thou didst so punish sin,
That I became
Most thin.
With thee
Let me combine,
And feel this day thy victory:
For, if I imp[4] my wing on thine,
Affliction shall advance the flight in me.

Affliction (1)[1]

When first thou didst entice to thee my heart,
    I thought the service brave:
So many joys I wrote down for my part,
    Besides what I might have
5   Out of my stock of natural delights,
Augmented with thy gracious benefits.

2. We are mistaken in reckoning that there are 300-plus days in the year, since they are all but as one day when compared to the light of the Son (Christ) rising.
1. As in the first editions of Herbert, this poem is printed sideways to represent the shape of wings.
2. Plenty.

3. The human frailty of sin, as well as the speaker's own descent into sin and suffering, which Christ redeems through his rising from the dead on Easter.
4. In falconry, to insert feathers in a bird's wing.
1. Editors assign numbers to poems that Herbert gave the same title to in order to distinguish them from one another.

I lookèd on thy furniture so fine,
          And made it fine to me:
Thy glorious household stuff did me entwine,
          And 'tice me unto thee.
10   Such stars I counted mine: both heaven and earth
Paid me my wages in a world of mirth.

What pleasures could I want, whose king I served,
          Where joys my fellows were?
15   Thus argued into hopes, my thoughts reserved
          No place for grief or fear;
Therefore my sudden soul caught at the place,
And made her youth and fierceness seek thy face.

At first thou gav'st me milk and sweetness;
20   I had my wish and way:
My days were strawed° with flowers and happiness;   *strewed*
          There was no month but May.
But with my years sorrow did twist and grow,
And made a party unawares for woe.

25   My flesh began unto my soul in pain,[2]
          Sicknesses cleave° my bones;   *penetrate*
Consuming agues dwell in every vein,
          And tune my breath to groans,
Sorrow was all my soul, I scarce believed,
30   Till grief did tell me roundly, that I lived.

When I got health, thou took'st away my life,
          And more; for my friends die:
My mirth and edge was lost; a blunted knife
          Was of more use than I.
35   Thus thin and lean without a fence or friend,
I was blown through with every storm and wind.

Whereas my birth and spirit rather took
          The way that takes the town,
Thou didst betray me to a lingering book,
40   And wrap me in a gown.
I was entangled in the world of strife,
Before I had the power to change my life.

Yet, for I threatened often the siege to raise,
          Not simpering all mine age,
45   Thou often did with academic praise
          Melt and dissolve my rage.
I took thy sweetened pill, till I came near;
I could not go away, nor persevere.

2. The body speaks to the soul from this point on.

Yet, lest perchance I should too happy be
                In my unhappiness,
50   Turning my purge³ to food, thou throwest me
                Into more sickness.
Thus does thy power cross-bias⁴ me, not making
Thine own gift good, yet me from my ways taking.

55   Now I am here, what thou wilt do with me
                None of my books will show:
I read, and sigh, and wish I were a tree,
                For sure then I should grow
To fruit or shade; at least some bird would trust
60   Her household to me, and I should be just.

Yet, though thou troublest me, I must be meek;
                In weakness must be stout.
Well, I will change the service, and go seek
                Some other master out.
65   Ah my dear God! though I am clean forgot,
Let me not love thee, if I love thee not.

Prayer (1)

Prayer the church's banquet; angels' age,
    God's breath in man returning to his birth;
    The soul in paraphrase, heart in pilgrimage;
The Christian plummet¹ sounding heaven and earth;

5   Engine against th'Almighty, sinner's tower,²
    Reversèd thunder, Christ-side-piercing spear,
    The six-days world transposing in an hour;
A kind of tune, which all things hear and fear;

Softness, and peace, and joy, and love, and bliss;
10   Exalted manna,³ gladness of the best;
    Heaven in ordinary,⁴ man well dressed,
The milky way, the bird of paradise,⁵

    Church bells beyond the stars heard, the soul's blood,
    The land of spices; something understood.

Jordan (1)¹

Who says that fictions only and false hair
Become a verse? Is there in truth no beauty?
Is all good structure in a winding stair?

---

3. Medicine inducing evacuation of the bowels.
4. To give an inclination running counter to another.
1. A metal weight used to measure, or sound, the depth of water; figuratively, the criterion of truth.
2. A stronghold or fortress, used for purposes of defense.
3. The food that God supplied to the Jews during their

wandering in the wilderness.
4. What is usual; or, a meal in a tavern.
5. A bird, found in New Guinea, known for its beautiful feathers.
1. To cross the River Jordan symbolizes entering the Promised Land.

May no lines pass, except they do their duty
5   Not to a true, but painted chair?

Is it no verse, except enchanted groves
And sudden arbors shadow coarse-spun lines?
Must purling° streams refresh a lover's loves?   *rippling*
Must all be veiled, while he that reads, divines,[2]
10   Catching the sense at two removes?

Shepherds are honest people; let them sing:
Riddle who list,[3] for me, and pull for prime:[4]
I envy no man's nightingale or spring;
Nor let them punish me with loss of rhyme,
15   Who plainly say, My *God*, My *King*.

Church Monuments

While that my soul repairs to her devotion,
Here I entomb my flesh, that it betimes
May take acquaintance of this heap of dust;
To which the blast of death's incessant motion,
5   Fed with the exhalation of our crimes,
Drives all at last. Therefore I gladly trust

My body to this school, that it may learn
To spell his elements and find his birth
Written in dusty heraldry and lines
10   Which dissolution sure does best discern,
Comparing dust with dust, and earth with earth.[1]
These[2] laugh at jet and marble, put for signs

To sever the good fellowship of dust
And spoil the meeting. What shall point out them[3]
15   When they shall bow, and kneel, and fall down flat
To kiss those heaps, which now they have in trust?
Dear flesh, while I do pray, learn here thy stem
And true descent; that when thou shalt grow fat,

And wanton in thy cravings, thou may'st know,
20   That flesh is but the glass, which holds the dust
That measures all our time, which also shall
Be crumbled into dust. Mark here below
How tame these ashes are, how free from lust,
That thou may'st set thyself against thy fall.

The Windows

Lord, how can man preach thy eternal word?
      He is a brittle, crazy° glass,   *cracked*

2. To interpret what is obscure through magical insight or
intuitive conjecture.
3. Whoever wants to may interpret.
4. Draw a lucky card, or hit upon a lucky guess.
1. An allusion to Genesis 3.19: "for dust thou art and to

dust shalt thou return."
2. Dust and earth.
3. The souls that cling to "those heaps," the dust of their
bodies and of the earth.

Yet in thy temple thou do him afford
    This glorious and transcendent place,
5   To be a window, through thy grace.

But when thou dost anneal[1] in glass thy story,
    Making thy life to shine within
The holy preachers, then the light and glory
    More reverent grows, and does win
10   Which else shows watr'ish, bleak, and thin

Doctrine and life, colors and light, in one
    When they combine and mingle, bring
A strong regard and awe; but speech alone
    Doth vanish like a flaring thing,
15   And in the ear, not conscience ring.

Denial

When my devotions could not pierce
        Thy silent ears;
Then was my heart broken, as was my verse:
    My breast was full of tears
5   And disorder:

My bent thoughts, like a brittle bow,
        Did fly asunder:
Each took his way; some would to pleasures go,
    Some to the wars and thunder
10   Of alarms.

As good go anywhere, they say,
        As to benumb
Both knees and heart in crying night and day,
    Come, come, my God, Oh come!
15   But no hearing.

O that thou shouldst give dust a tongue
        To cry to thee,
And then not hear it crying! All day long
    My heart was in my knee,
20   But no hearing.

Therefore my soul lay out of sight,
        Untuned, unstrung;
My feeble spirit, unable to look right,
    Like a nipped bloom, hung
25   Discontented.

Oh cheer and tune my heartless breath,
        Defer no time,
That so thy favors granting my request,
    They and my mind may chime,°   *ring together, agree*
30   And mend my rhyme.

1. To burn in colors on glass.

Virtue

Sweet day, so cool, so calm, so bright,
The bridal° of the earth and sky: *wedding*
The dew shall weep thy fall tonight,
      For thou must die.

5   Sweet rose, whose hue, angry and brave
Bids the rash gazer wipe his eye:
Thy root is ever in its grave,
      And thou must die.

Sweet spring, full of sweet days and roses,
10   A box where sweets° compacted lie;   *pleasant fragrances*
My music shows ye have your closes,[1]
      And all must die.

Only a sweet and virtuous soul,
Like seasoned timber, never gives;
15   But though the whole world turn to coal,[2]
      Then chiefly lives.

Man

My God, I heard this day
That none doth build a stately habitation,
    But he that means to dwell therein.
What house more stately hath there been,
5   Or can be, than is man? to[1] whose creation
    All things are in decay.

    For man is everything,
And more; he is a tree, yet bears more[2] fruit;
    A beast, yet is, or should be more:
10   Reason and speech we only bring.
Parrots may thank us, if they are not mute:
    They go upon the score.[3]

    Man is all symmetry,
Full of proportions, one limb to another,
15   And all to all the world besides:
    Each part may call the farthest, brother;
For head with foot has private amity,
    And both with moons and tides.

    Nothing hath got so far
20   But man hath caught and kept it as his prey.
    His eyes dismount the highest star:
    He is in little all the sphere.[4]

1. Cadences, indicating that Herbert wanted this poem to
be sung.
2. Reduced to ashes as at the Last Judgment.
1. In comparison to.

2. An alternative reading is "no."
3. They are indebted to us.
4. See Robert Fludd's engraving of the human body as
microcosm of the universe, page 1598.

Herbs gladly cure our flesh; because that they
　　　　Find their acquaintance there.

25　　　　For us the winds do blow,
The earth doth rest, heav'n move, and fountains flow;
　　　Nothing we see, but means our good,
　　　　As our delight, or as our treasure.
The whole is, either our cupboard of food,
30　　　　Or cabinet of pleasure.

　　　　The stars have us to bed;
Night draws the curtain, which the sun withdraws,
　　　Music and light attend our head.
　　　All things unto our flesh are kind
35　In their descent and being; to our mind
　　　　In their ascent and cause.

　　　　Each thing is full of duty.
Waters united are our navigation,
　　　　Distinguished, our habitation;
40　　　Below, our drink; above, our meat;
Both are our cleanliness. Hath one such beauty?
　　　　Then how are all things neat?

　　　　More servants wait on man
Than he'll take notice of: in ev'ry path,
45　　　He treads down that which doth befriend him,
　　　When sickness makes him pale and wan.
Oh mighty love! Man is one world, and hath
　　　　Another to attend him.

　　　　Since then, my God, thou hast
50　So brave a palace built, O dwell in it,
　　　That it may dwell with thee at last!
　　　Till then, afford us so much wit,
That, as the world serves us, we may serve thee,
　　　　And both thy servants be.

Jordan (2)

When first my lines of heav'nly joys made mention,
Such was their luster, they did so excel,
That I sought out quaint° words, and trim invention;　　　*clever*
My thoughts began to burnish,° sprout, and swell,　　　*spread out*
5　Curling with metaphors a plain intention,
Decking the sense, as if it were to sell.[1]

Thousands of notions in my brain did run,
Off'ring their service, if I were not sped:[2]
I often blotted what I had begun;
10　This was not quick° enough, and that was dead.　　　*lively*

---

1. Decorating the meaning as if it were for sale.　　　2. Dealt with so that I was satisfied.

Nothing could seem too rich to clothe the sun,
Much less those joys which trample on his head.[3]

As flames do work and wind, when they ascend,
So did I weave my self into the sense.
15 But while I bustled, I might hear a friend
Whisper, "How wide° is all this long pretence!   *beside the point*
There is in love a sweetness ready penn'd:
Copy out only that, and save expense."

Time

Meeting with time, "Slack thing," said I,
"Thy scythe is dull; whet it for shame."
"No marvel sir," he did reply,
"If it at length deserve some blame:
5   But where one man would have me grind it,
        Twenty for one too sharp do find it."

"Perhaps some such of old did pass,[1]
Who above all things lov'd this life;
To whom thy scythe a hatchet was,
10 Which now is but a pruning knife.
        Christ's coming hath made man thy debtor,
        Since by thy cutting he grows better.

"And in this blessing thou art blest:
For where thou only wert before
15 An executioner at best,
Thou art a gard'ner now, and more,
        An usher to convey our souls
        Beyond the utmost stars and poles.

"And this is that makes life so long,
20 While it detains us from our God.
Ev'n pleasures here increase the wrong,
And length of days lengthen the rod.
        Who wants° the place, where God doth dwell,   *lacks*
        Partakes already half of hell.

"Of what strange length must that needs be,
Which ev'n eternity excludes!"
Thus far Time heard me patiently:
Then chafing° said, "This man deludes: *getting angry*
        What do I here before his door?
30   He doth not crave less time, but more."

The Collar

I struck the board,° and cried, "No more.   *table*
                I will abroad!

3. The sun is a symbol for Christ; the sun's head is the
Son's head.

1. Herbert is the speaker in stanzas 2, 3, and 4, and the
first two lines of stanza 5.

What? Shall I ever sigh and pine?
My lines and life are free; free as the road,
5   Loose as the wind, as large as store.°   *abundance*
            Shall I be still in suit?[1]
Have I no harvest but a thorn
To let me blood, and not restore
What I have lost with cordial[2] fruit?
10   Sure there was wine
Before my sighs did dry it; there was corn
    Before my tears did drown it.
Is the year only lost to me?
    Have I no bays[3] to crown it?
15 No flowers, no garlands gay? all blasted?
                All wasted?
Not so, my heart; but there is fruit,
            And thou hast hands.
Recover all thy sigh-blown age
20 On double pleasures: leave thy cold dispute
Of what is fit and not forsake thy cage,
            Thy rope of sands,
Which petty thoughts have made, and made to thee
    Good cable, to enforce and draw,
25   And be thy law,
While thou didst wink[4] and wouldst not see.
            Away! take heed:
            I will abroad.
Call in thy death's head[5] there: tie up thy fears.
30   He that forbears
    To suit and serve his need,
        Deserves his load."
But as I raved and grew more fierce and wild
            At every word,
35   Me thoughts I heard one calling, *Child!*
        And I replied, *My Lord.*

The Pulley

When God at first made man,
Having a glass of blessings standing by,
"Let us," said he "pour on him all we can:
Let the world's riches, which dispersèd lie,
5   Contract into a span."

So strength first made a way;
Then beauty flowed, then wisdom, honor, pleasure:
When almost all was out, God made a stay,

1. Engaged in a lawsuit.
2. Invigorating to the heart.
3. The poet's laurel wreath.

4. Shut your eyes to.
5. The skull as an emblem of human mortality.

Perceiving that alone of all his treasure
10   Rest in the bottom lay.[1]

"For if I should," said he,
"Bestow this jewel also on my creature,
He would adore my gifts instead of me,
And rest in Nature, not the God of Nature.
15   So both should losers be.

"Yet let him keep the rest,
But keep them with repining° restlessness: *complaining*
Let him be rich and weary, that at least,
If goodness lead him not, yet weariness
20   May toss him to my breast."

The Forerunners

The harbingers[1] are come: see, see their mark;
White is their color, and behold my head.
But must they have my brain? Must they dispark°   *turn out*
Those sparkling notions, which therein were bred?
5   Must dullness turn me to a clod?
Yet have they left me, "Thou art still my God."

Good men ye be, to leave me my best room,
Ev'n all my heart, and what is lodged there:
I pass not, I, what of the rest become,
10 So "Thou art still my God," be out of fear.[2]
        He will be pleasèd with that ditty;
And if I please him, I write fine and witty.

Farewell, sweet phrases, lovely metaphors:
But will ye leave me thus? when ye before
15 Of stews[3] and brothels only knew the doors,
Then did I wash you with my tears, and more,
        Brought you to Church well-dressed and clad:
My God must have my best, ev'n all I had.

Lovely enchanting language, sugarcane,
20 Honey of roses, whither wilt thou fly?
Hath some fond lover 'ticed thee to thy bane?
And wilt thou leave the Church, and love a sty?
        Fie, thou wilt soil thy 'broidered coat,
And hurt thy self, and him that sings the note.

25 Let foolish lovers, if they will love dung,
With canvas, not with arras° clothe their shame: *rich tapestry*
Let Folly speak in her own native tongue.
True Beauty dwells on high; ours is a flame

---

1. "Rest" in the sense of repose, or freedom from distress, and in the sense of remainder, or surplus.
1. Men sent out before a royal train to requisition lodgings by marking the doors with chalk.

2. I don't care about anything except being left with the thought that "Thou art still my God."
3. Public hot bathhouses, brothels.

> But borrowed thence to light us thither:
30   Beauty and beauteous words should go together.

> Yet if you go, I pass not; take your way.
> For, "Thou art still my God" is all that ye
> Perhaps with more embellishment can say,
> Go, birds of spring; let winter have his fee;
35   Let a bleak paleness chalk the door.
> So all within be livelier than before.

Love (3)

> Love bade me welcome: yet my soul drew back,
>   Guilty of dust and sin.
> But quick-eyed Love, observing me grow slack°   *slow, weak*
>   From my first entrance in,
5 Drew nearer to me, sweetly questioning,
>   If I lacked anything.

> "A guest," I answered, "worthy to be here":
>   Love said, "You shall be he."
> "I the unkind, ungrateful? Ah my dear,
10   I cannot look on thee."
> Love took my hand, and smiling did reply,
>   "Who made the eyes but I?"

> "Truth Lord, but I marred them; let my shame
>   Go where it doth deserve."
15 "And know you not," says Love, "who bore the blame?"
>   "My dear, then I will serve."
> "You must sit down," says Love, "and taste my meat."
>   So I did sit and eat.[1]

PERSPECTIVES

Emblem, Style, and Metaphor

The early modern period in England began at a cultural moment that was still medieval and ended at one on the verge of the modern. At the outset of the period, in the reign of Henry VIII, science was magic, symbols were biblical, and poetry was the work of makers who imitated nature; at the close of the era, with the end of the Interregnum and the Restoration, science had become more empirical, symbols had become more idiosyncratic, and poetry was the work of individual geniuses, who more than imitating nature transformed it with the unusual correspondences that they created. The in-between or liminal aspect of early modern culture helps to explain the way in which early modern art had much in common with medieval forms of representation but also began to move beyond these forms.

---

1. The speaker takes Communion, which symbolizes union with God.

The early modern emblem is a good example of this transitional aspect of the period's culture. Emblems were visual symbols that appeared in medieval coats of arms, illuminated manuscripts of the Bible, and church decoration. With early modern printing, books of emblems were produced that included not only the visual symbol, but also a poem and a Latin motto, either a proverb or a classical quotation. Whereas medieval iconography, or visual symbolism, was dominated largely by reference to the Bible, Renaissance iconography showed a stronger influence of classical mythology, though still often harmonized with a Christian framework. For example, the popular emblem of the phoenix, the mythological Egyptian bird that was reborn every thousand years out of its own ashes, was also a symbol of Christ. Geoffrey Whitney's use of this symbol to describe the rebirth of the town of Nantwich after a fire exemplifies the local and particular character of the early modern emblem, in contrast to the medieval symbol, which usually could be read as part of the book of the world that reflected the book of the Word, or the Bible.

More classically and (increasingly) scientifically inflected, the system of resemblances would still have made sense to a medieval audience. Early modern writers often thought in terms of a "Great Chain of Being," as the historian Arthur Lovejoy called it in 1936. This mode of thinking is well illustrated by a set of linkages made by the Italian playwright and scientist Giambattista della Porta in a treatise called *Natural Magic* (1558):

> the plant stands convenient to the brute beast, so through feeling does the brutish animal to man, who is conformable to the rest of the stars by his intelligence; these links proceed so strictly that they appear as a rope stretched from the first cause as far as the lowest and the smallest of things.

The concept of *aemulatio*, or emulation, accounts for the way in which images mirror various aspects of the world. The concept of Venus, for example, as described by Giordano Bruno, comprehends various human and cosmic qualities, including charm, beauty, natural harmony, the relationship between love and death, and "every form of pleasure." Venus's son Cupid "sets [us] on fire with his heat and enthralls with his chains," while at the same time her triumphal chariot represents wisdom and prudence. The concept of *analogia*, or analogy, expresses the relationship between the macrocosm and the microcosm in Renaissance art. Not only are human beings midway between angels and beasts, but the proportions of the human body correspond to those of the universe—a notion that is well illustrated by Robert Fludd's engraving of a human figure outstretched over the concentric circles of the Ptolemaic universe.

These conventional symbols inherited from classical and medieval culture often existed side by side with ingenious new metaphors. The symbols that allowed the world to be read as united in reference to God's word in the Bible were supplemented and even challenged by new images created by poets. For example the rood of medieval English poetry was at once a tree and the cross on which Christ died. But an early modern poet such as John Donne could shock his audience with his ingenuity by likening the sexual union of lovers to the canonization of saints. Emmanuele Tesauro's description of metaphor shows that it was the qualities of ingenuity and marvelousness that were prized in the seventeenth-century conceit, or metaphor. Whereas medieval symbols had relied on culturally accepted associations, early modern metaphors created new and unexpected associations through a transference of meaning. The term "metaphor" comes from the Greek verb *metaphorein*, which means "to transfer" or "to carry across," and this is precisely what the metaphysical conceit did: it transferred meaning from one thing to another.

Like the freshness of the poetic conceit, the simplicity and clarity of what Ben Jonson called the concise style with its brevity, pointedness, and wit characterized the new style of

Title page to volume 2 of *Utriusque cosmi, maioris scilicet et minoris, metaphysica atque technica historia,* ("Metaphysical and Technical History of both the Greater and Lesser Universe"), by Robert Fludd, 1619. After taking his degree at Oxford, Robert Fludd studied chemistry and medicine on the Continent, where he came into contact with the occult philosophy of the Rosicrucians, whose goals ranged from alchemy to moral reformation. Returning to London, he practiced medicine and published numerous works expressing his belief that science was a form of divine revelation and that all creation reflected a divinely ordered design. This engraving shows the image of a male body spread out over the cosmos as a circle, portraying the human body's perfect proportions, and their analogy to the proportions of the universe: man is a little world, the microcosm to the universe's macrocosm. The engraving also depicts the earth-centered Ptolemaic universe, the constellations and astrological signs. The innermost circles are the four bodily humors (choleric, melancholic, phlegmatic, and sanguine), and the outermost circles are the supernatural faculties of reason, intellect, and mind.

writing. Calling for a concentration on meaning rather than an abundance of ornamentation, this new style strongly influenced the development of modern English prose. The great champion of the concise or Senecan style of prose, Francis Bacon, ushered in a whole new rhythm in the English sentence and a new form known as the essay. At the very time that poets such as Donne and Marvell were using images taken from science in their poetry, Bacon was creating a new form of English prose that would help to make English the language of science that it is today.

Geoffrey Whitney
1548?–1601

Geoffrey Whitney composed one of the most important English emblem books, A *Choice of Emblems* (1586). Each emblem contains a woodcut, prefixed by a Latin motto and accompanied by verses in six-line stanzas. The book was dedicated to the Earl of Leicester and was published in Leyden, where Whitney was studying at the university. Although only twenty-three of the emblems are original and another 235 loosely or exactly copy Continental models by Alciati, Paradin, Sambucus, and Junius, Whitney gives many of the emblems a specifically English interpretation. Sometimes an emblem is used to support the politics of the Leicester court faction, who urged an active role in defending Protestants in the Low Countries. At other times, Whitney's Englishness surfaces in references to local events. For example, he applies the emblem of the phoenix to the fire of Nantwich, not far from his birthplace in Chesire, where he would retire after the death of his patron Leicester. Possibly because of the decline of the Leicester faction, Whitney's book was not republished in his lifetime. Nevertheless, his influence is seen in later Jacobean emblem books, such as Peacham's *Minerva Britanna* (London 1612), and in decorations in domestic architecture and furnishings. Whitney's work helped to make the Continental emblem tradition known to such English poets as Shakespeare, Spenser, Donne, and Philips, whose poetry is enriched by emblematic metaphor, conjuring up both a visual image and its complex symbolic associations.

The Phoenix
Unica semper avis.[1]

To my countrymen of the Nampwiche in Cheshire.

1. "The bird that is ever unique." The picture shows a phoenix with wings outstretched rising from the flames of a fire. See Ovid, *Metamorphoses* 15, 393–407.

The Phoenix rare, with feathers fresh of hue,
Arabia's right, and sacred to the sun:
Whom, other birds with wonder seem to view,
Doth live until a thousand years be run:

5   Then makes a pile: which, when with sun it burns,
She flies therein, and so to ashes turns.

Whereof, behold, another Phoenix rare,
With speed doth rise most beautiful and fair:
And though for truth, this many do declare,

10   Yet thereunto, I mean not for to swear:
Although I know that author's witness true,
What here I write, both of the old, and new.

Which when I weighed, the new, and eke the old,
I thought upon your town destroyed with fire:

15   And did in mind, the new Nampwiche behold,
A spectacle for any man's desire:
Whose buildings brave, where cinders were but late,
Did represent (me thought) the Phoenix fate.

And as the old, was many hundred years,

20   A town of fame, before it felt that cross:
Even so, (I hope) this Wiche,[2] that now appears,
A Phoenix age shall last, and know no loss:
Which God vouchsafe, who make you thankful, all:
That see this rise, and saw the other fall.

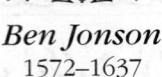

Ben Jonson
1572–1637

Jonson's observations on style are contained in papers first found after his death by his literary executor Sir Kenelm Digby. First published in 1640, *Timber, or Discoveries*, contains not only Jonson's observations but also those of authors whose work on rhetoric and poetics he greatly admired, such as Quintilian and Horace. The following passages, based on Quintilian's *De institutione oratoria* and on Vives' *On the Proper Method of Speaking* (1532), give us insight into Jonson's approach to the process of writing, his taste in literature, and his firm conviction that an essential step in perfecting the craft of writing is to read the best authors.

For more on Jonson, see his principal listing, page 1443.

from Timber: or Discoveries

For a man to write well, there are required three necessaries: to read the best authors, observe the best speakers, and much exercise of his own style. In style to consider, what ought to be written, and after what manner; he must first think and excogitate[1] his matter, then choose his words, and examine the weight of either. Then take care in placing and ranking both matter and words, that the composition be comely; and to do this with diligence, and often. No matter how slow the style be at first, so it be

---

2. Originally meaning the group of buildings connected with a salt pit, "wich" was the name given to such salt-making towns as Nantwich and Northwich in Chesire.

1. Devise.

labored,[2] and accurate; seek the best, and be not glad of the froward conceits,[3] or first words, that offer themselves to us; but judge of what we invent, and order what we approve. Repeat often, what we have formerly written; which beside that it helps the consequence, and makes the juncture better, it quickens the heat of imagination, that often cools in the time of setting down, and gives it new strength, as if it grew lustier, by the going back. As we see in the contention of leaping, they jump farthest, that fetch their race largest: or, as in throwing a dart, or javelin, we force back our arms, to make our loose[4] the stronger. Yet if we have a fair gale of wind, I forbid not the steering out of our sail, so the favor of the gale deceive us not. For all that we invent doth please us in the conception, or birth, else we would never set it down. But the safest is to return to our judgment, and handle over again those things, the easiness of which might make them justly suspected. So did the best writers in their beginnings; they imposed upon themselves care, and industry; they did nothing rashly. They obtained first to write well, and then custom made it easy and a habit. By little and little their matter showed itself to them more plentifully; their words answered, their composition followed; and all, as in a well-ordered family, presented itself in the place. So that the sum of all is: Ready writing makes not good writing; but good writing brings on ready writing.

Yet, when we think we have got the faculty, it is even then good to resist it, as to give a horse a check sometimes with [a] bit, which doth not so much stop his course, as stir his mettle. Again, whither a man's genius is best able to reach, thither it should more and more contend, lift and dilate itself; as men of low stature raise themselves on their toes, and so ofttimes get even, if not eminent. Besides, as it is fit for grown and able writers to stand of themselves, and work with their own strength, to trust and endeavor by their own faculties: so it is fit for the beginner and learner to study others, and the best. For the mind, and memory are more sharply exercised in comprehending another man's things, than our own; and such as accustom themselves and are familiar with the best authors shall ever and anon find somewhat of them in themselves, and in the expression of their minds, even when they feel it not, be able to utter something like theirs, which hath an authority above their own. Nay, sometimes it is the reward of a man's study, the praise of quoting another man fitly. And though a man be more prone, and able for one kind of writing, than another, yet he must exercise all. For as in an instrument, so in style, there must be a harmony, and consent of parts.

I take this labor in teaching others, that they should not be always to be taught; and I would bring my precepts into practice. For rules are ever of less force, and value, than experiments. Yet with this purpose, rather to show the right way to those that come after, than to detect any that have slipped before by error, and I hope it will be more profitable. For men do more willingly listen, and with more favor to precept, than reprehension.[5] Among diverse opinions of an art, and most of them contrary in themselves, it is hard to make election; and therefore, though a man cannot invent new things after so many, he may do a welcome work yet to help posterity to judge rightly of the old. But arts and precepts avail nothing, except nature be beneficial, and aiding. And therefore these things are no more written to a dull disposition, than rules of husbandry to a barren soil. No precepts will profit a fool; no more than beauty will the blind, or music the deaf. As we should take care, that our style in writing, be neither dry,

---

2. Painstakingly worked on.
3. The initial concepts.

4. Throw.
5. Censure.

nor empty, we should look again it be not winding, or wanton with far-fetched descriptions; either is a vice. But that is worse which proceeds out of want, than that which riots out of plenty. The remedy of fruitfulness is easy, but no labor will help the contrary; I will like, and praise some things, in a young writer, which yet if he continue in, I cannot, but justly hate him for the same. There is a time to be given all things for maturity; and that even your country-husbandman can teach, who to a young plant will not put the pruning knife, because it seems to fear the iron, as not able to admit the scar. No more would I tell a green writer all his faults, lest I should make him grieve and faint, and at last despair. For nothing doth more hurt, than to make him so afraid of all things, as he can endeavor nothing. Therefore youth ought to be instructed betimes, and in the best things; for we hold those longest, we take soonest. As the first scent of a vessel lasts; and that tinct[6] the wool first receives. Therefore a master should temper his own powers, and descend to the other's infirmity. If you pour a glut of water upon a bottle, it receives little of it; but with a funnel, and by degrees, you shall fill many of them and spill little of your own; to their capacity they will all receive, and be full. And as it is fit to read the best authors to youth first, so let them be of the openest, and clearest. As Livy before Sallust,[7] Sidney before Donne; and beware of letting them taste Gower or Chaucer at first, lest falling too much in love with antiquity and, and not apprehending the weight, they grow rough and barren in language only. When their judgments are firm, and out of danger, let them read both, the old and the new: but no less take heed, that their new flowers, and sweetness do not as much corrupt, as the others dryness and squalor, if they choose not carefully. Spenser, in affecting the ancients, wrote no language.[8] Yet I would have him read for his manner; but as Virgil read Ennius.[9] The reading of Homer and Virgil is counseled by Quintilian, as the best way of informing youth, and confirming man. For besides that, the mind is raised with the height, and sublimity of such a verse, it takes spirit from the greatness of the matter, and is tincted with the best things. Tragic and lyric poetry is good too: and comic with the best, if the manners of the reader be once in safety. In the Greek poets, as also in Plautus,[1] we shall see the economy, and disposition of poems better observed than in Terence, and the latter, who thought the sole grace, and virtue of their fable, the sticking in of sentences, as ours do the forcing of jests. * * *

Custom is the most certain mistress of language, as the public stamp makes the current money.[2] But we must not be too frequent with the mint, every day coining; nor fetch words from the extreme and utmost ages, since the chief virtue of a style is perspicuity, and nothing so vicious in it as to need an interpreter. Words borrowed of antiquity do lend a kind of majesty to style, and are not without their delight sometimes. For they have the authority of years, and out of their intermission do win to themselves a kind of gracelike newness. But the eldest of the present and newest of the past language is the best. For what was the ancient language, which some men so dote upon, but the ancient custom? Yet when I name custom, I

6. Dye, color.
7. Sallust (86–c. 34 B.C.) and Livy (59 B.C.–A.D. 17), Roman historians.
8. A reference to Spenser's self-consciously archaic diction, spelling, and syntax.
9. The great epic poet Virgil (70–19 B.C.) studied but also

went beyond his poetic predecessor Ennius (239–169? B.C.).
1. Plautus (254–184 B.C.) and Terence (c. 185–159 B.C.) were Roman comic playwrights.
2. The beginning of this passage is based on Quintillian, and the rest on Vives, *On the Proper Method of Speaking* (1532).

understand not the vulgar custom, for that were a precept no less dangerous to language than life, if we should speak or live after the manner of the vulgar. But that I call custom of speech which is the consent of the learned, as custom of life which is the consent of the good. Virgil was most loving of antiquity; yet how rarely doth he insert *aquai* and *pictai!*[3] Lucretius[4] is scabrous and rough in these; he seeks them, as some do Chaucerisms with us, which were better expunged and banished. Some words are to be culled out for ornament and color, as we gather flowers to strew houses or make garlands; but they are better when they grow to our style as in a meadow, where, though the mere grass and greenness delights, yet the variety of flowers doth heighten and beautify. Marry, we must not play or riot too much with them, as in paronomasias;[5] nor use too swelling or ill-sounding words, *quae per salebras altaque saxa cadunt.*[6] It is true, there is not sound but shall find some lovers, as the bitterest confections are grateful to some palates. Our composition must be more accurate in the beginning and end than in the midst, and in the end more than in the beginning; for through the midst the stream bears us. And this is attained by custom more than care or diligence. We must express readily and fully, not profusely. There is difference between a liberal and a prodigal hand. As it is a great point of art, when our matter requires it, to enlarge and veer out all sail, so to take it in and contract it is of no less praise when the argument doth ask it. Either of them hath their fitness in the place. A good man always profits by his endeavor, by his help; yea, when he is absent; nay, when he is dead, by his example and memory. So good authors in their style.

A strict and succinct style is that where you can take away nothing without loss, and that loss to be manifest. The brief style is that which expresseth much in little. The concise style, which expresseth not enough, but leaves somewhat to be understood. The abrupt style, which hath many breaches, and doth not seem to end but fall. The congruent style and harmonious fitting of parts in a sentence hath almost the fastening and force of knitting and connection, as in stones well squared, which will rise strong a great way without mortar. Periods[7] are beautiful when they are not too long, for so they have their strength too, as in a pike or javelin. As we must take the care that our words and sense be clear, so if the obscurity happen through the hearer's or the reader's want of understanding, I am not to answer for them, no more than for their not listening or marking.[8] I must neither find them ears nor mind. But a man cannot put a word so in sense but something about it will illustrate it, if the writer understand himself. For order helps much to perspicuity, as confusion hurts. *Rectitudo lucem adfert; obliquitas et circumductio offuscat.*[9] We should therefore speak what we can the nearest way, so as we keep our gait, not leap; for too short may as well not be let into the memory as too long not kept in. Whatsoever loseth the grace and clearness converts into a riddle; the obscurity is marked, but not the value. That perisheth, and is passed by, like the pearl in the fable.[1] Our style should be like a skein of silk, to be carried and found by the right thread, not ravelled and perplexed; then all is a knot, a heap.

---

3. Archaic forms of *aquae* (waters) and *pictae* (embroidered), that occur once each in the *Aeneid.*
4. Roman poet (c. 99–55 B.C.) who wrote *De rerum natura.*
5. Puns.
6. Martial: "Which fall on rough ground and boulders."
7. Subordinated sentences.

8. Taking to heart.
9. Vives: "Directness enlightens, shiftiness and indirection obscure matters."
1. In Plato's *Phaedrus* 3.12, a cock finds a pearl on a dunghill but simply leaves it there.

Giordano Bruno
1548–1600

Best known for having been burned at the stake as a heretic in Rome, and still suspected of having been a spy in England, the Italian philosopher Giordano Bruno was one of the great theorists of the esoteric symbolic correspondences generated by hermeticism. Sixteenth-century intellectuals believed that a work called *The Hermetic Corpus* was written by the ancient Egyptian magus Hermes Trismegistus and that its complex system of analogies linking pagan gods, planets, and their attributes with the human personality was a key to secret knowledge in astronomy, medicine, mnemonics or memory theory, and magic. Although Isaac Causabon proved in 1614 that *The Hermetic Corpus* was not an ancient Egyptian but a second-century Greek work, the philosophy that it inspired in Bruno influenced other thinkers such as the English astrologer John Dee and the German astronomer Johannes Kepler. Later, such writers as Coleridge and Joyce also had a strong interest in Bruno's work.

During his stay in England from 1583 to 1586, Bruno lectured on Copernican theory and Platonism at Cambridge and made friendships among English writers. He is said to have sung Ariosto's *Orlando Furioso* to Sir Philip Sidney while riding horseback from Oxford to London. Bruno published no fewer than six works in England. Among these, *Spaccio della bestia trionfante (The Expulsion of the Triumphant Beast)* presents ideas developed in his last work, *De imaginum compositione (On the Composition of Images, Signs, and Ideas)*, published in Frankfurt in 1591. Bruno's final book views the imagination as the means through which God communicates with humanity. Bruno sought to discover the images that could unite the multiplicity of the universe. His writing about the connections between images and words, and between painting and poetry, offers insight into how Renaissance poets conceived of the world as composed of a complex chain of analogies. His chapter on Venus shows the association of a mythological figure with many different images expressing a variety of qualities. For Bruno, as for many Renaissance poets, mythology provided not only a rich repertoire of visual symbols but also a way of creating layers of mysterious meaning in poetry.

from On the Composition of Images, Signs, and Ideas[1]

The idea, imagination, shape, designation, notation, all are the universe of God, both the work of nature and of reason. The idea is controlled by analogy with nature and reason, so that nature admirably reflects divine action, and our innate human ability to reason rivals nature. Who cannot see how nature makes so many diverse things with so few elements? Nature orders the same four elements, and under various signs, in accord with the thing formed, she drives them out of the abyss of possibility into the apex of actuality. By God, what can be easier than counting? First, since there is one, two, three and then four; second because one is not two, two is not three, three is not four. And finally because one and two make three, and one and three make four. To do this is to do everything: imagining, signifying and retaining render all things as objects that can be apprehended, and understood once apprehended, and remembered once understood.

* * *

I spoke of a certain marvelous kinship that exists among true poets, who are referred to as musicians, and that also connects true painters and true philosophers.[2] For true philosophy, music, or poetry is also painting, and true painting is also music and philosophy; and true poetry or music is a kind of divine wisdom and painting.

---

1. From the Dedicatory Letter. Translated by Clare Carroll.   2. From Book 1, Part 2, Chapter 20.

In other places, I have discussed how any painter naturally establishes infinite images, and how his capacity to form images creates out of sense impressions—sights and sounds—and combines them in a multiplicity of ways.

* * *

Let us relate the pleasure derived from the seven courts by viewing the image of the goddess.[3] The first image of Venus is a girl rising from the sea's foam, who, as she approaches dry land, wipes off the wetness of the sea with her dainty hands.

In her second image she appears as a naked girl whom the Hours[4] cloak in robes, and whose head they crown with a garland of flowers.

In her third image, she is a girl advancing, who produces lilies and violets in her footprints. Her accessory is a cestus,[5] in which are contained all the charms of face, word, and gesture. A prophetess carrying a willow rod follows her.[6]

The fourth image of Venus is connected with a shining chariot of amber, which is pulled by gentle swans, amorous doves, and erotic pigeons. There is a lively inner force that moves the chariot along.

In her fifth image, Venus is a queen leading a triumphal procession.[7] She holds a scepter in her right hand, and at the top of this is the image of the Sun, while in her left hand she holds a globe in the shape of the universe, decorated with stars. In the middle of this sphere Tellus appears. All applaud her divinity, which is delightful to all. In her chariot she carries a trophy, which she bears as a testament to her victory over the Parcae.[8]

In her sixth image, Venus appears as a lovely woman, with the sky above her head. She holds a poppy in her right hand and a pomegranate in her left.

In her seventh image, Venus is related to three heroic women who stand beside a shepherd with a golden apple in his hand.[9]

In the eighth image, she is with a young man slain by a boar, whom she buries.[1]

In her ninth image, she is linked with a naked boy who is marked by his bow and arrow. Shining rays stream out of his body and an atmosphere of amiability. He appears to each person variously, according to each person's own temperment. So he hits each person with his arrows in conformity to his likeness; he sets on fire with his heat and enthralls with his chains.

The last image is of a man crowned and seated on a camel, dressed in a colorful robe, carrying beside him a naked girl; a chorus of girls dance in a circle; with the blessing of Zephyrus[2] comes the court of Venus with every form of pleasure.

Conte Emmanuele Tesauro
1591–1677

The son of a poet, Emmanuele Tesauro was one of the major theorists of the *concetto*, or conceit, a defining characteristic of the metaphysical style in the poetry of Donne, Crashaw, Herbert, and Marvell. Tesauro's patron was the Duke of Savoy who sent him on many diplomatic missions and

---

3. From Book 2, Chapter 13.
4. The four seasons.
5. Venus's belt.
6. Either Cybele, mother of the gods, or Manto, the seer and daughter of Tiresias.
7. Venus in this aspect represents wisdom and prudence.

8. The Fates.
9. When Paris was asked to decide whether Venus, Minerva, or Juno was the most desirable goddess, he chose Venus and was granted the love of the beautiful Helen.
1. Adonis, with whom Venus fell in love.
2. The west wind.

even knighted him. In addition to his histories of Turin, Piemonte, and Italy, he also wrote poetry, tragedy, and moral philosophy. He developed the theory of metaphor in *Il Cannochiale Aristotelico* (literally "the Aristotelian telescope," translated here as *Through the Lens of Aristotle*). Written in the late 1620s and published in Turin in 1654, *Il Cannochiale* treats, as its subtitle indicates, "ideas of heroic wittiness popularly called "imprese" [heraldic devices and mottos] and of the whole symbolic aphoristic art." Heraldic devices were a daily feature of early modern life. Not only did aristocratic coats of arms feature *imprese*, but so did university insignia, guild banners, and even tavern signs. Tesauro based his concept of metaphor on Aristotle's *Rhetoric* and stressed that metaphor was a way of comprehending the correspondences, or connections, between widely disparate things. In the following excerpt from *Il Cannochiale*, Tesauro stresses the two qualities that distinguish metaphor as the greatest of all figures of speech. Metaphor is *ingegnoso*, witty or ingenious— sparking a new idea, creating a new relationship between disparate things—and *mirabile*, awesome or marvelous—inspiring a sensual impression and a feeling of wonder in the beholder.

from Through the Lens of Aristotle

And indeed at last we have arrived step by step to the highest peak of the ingenious figures, in comparison to which all the other figures described up to this point lose their value, metaphor being the most ingenious and acute, the most outlandish and wonderful, the most enjoyable and helpful, the most eloquent and fecund part of the human intellect. Most ingenious truly, because, if ingenuity consists (as we say) in tying together remote and separate notions of proposed objects, this is precisely the function of metaphor, and not of any other figure: hence, drawing the mind, no less than the word, from one genus to another, metaphor expresses one concept [*concetto*] through the means of another much different from it, finding similarity in dissimilarities. So that our author Aristotle concludes that constructing metaphors is a labor of a perspicacious and agile wit [*ingegno*]. Consequently metaphor is among the figures the most acute; since the others are formed almost grammatically and finished in the surfaces of vocabulary, but metaphor reflexively penetrates and investigates the most abstruse notions by combining them; and where those other figures clothe the concepts of words, metaphor clothes the words themselves in the concepts.

Therefore metaphor is of all others the most outlandish by the newness of ingenious accompaniment: without this novelty, ingenuity loses its glory, and the metaphor its force. So that our author advises that metaphor wants to be born only out of us, and not from anywhere else, almost like a birth, sought on loan. And out of this is born wonder, while the soul of the listener, from the overwhelming novelty, considers the acuteness of the ingenuity representing and the unexpected image of the object represented.

And if this is so full of wonder, it is also just so entertaining and delightful because from marvel delight is born, just like what you experience from unexpected combinations of scenes and from having seen many spectacles. If delight proceeds from rhetorical figures (as our author[1] teaches) from the desire of the human mind to learn new things without hard work and many things in a little space, certainly more delightful than all the other figures is metaphor: which, carrying in flight our mind from one genus to another, causes one to see one thing through another in a single word more than an object. Therefore if you say: "meadows are pleasant," you do not represent anything other than the greening of the meadows; but if you were to say: "Meadows laugh," you make me see (as you speak) the earth as an animated man, the meadow being the face, the pleasantness the happy smile. So that in a little word all these notions are transposed from different categories: earth, meadow,

---

1. Aristotle.

pleasantness, man, soul, smile, happiness. And reciprocally with a swift passage I observe in the human face the notions of meadows and all the relationships that pass between these and those, not observed by me at another time. And this is that swift and easy instruction from which is born delight, appearing to the mind of him who hates to see in a single word a full theater of marvels.

Richard Crashaw
1613?–1649

Richard Crashaw was one of the chief poets to introduce the Italian poetic style of *concettismo* into English. Marked by an intense concentration of visual imagery that strove to create a striking newness and intellectual ingenuity, the conceited style provided the vehicle for Crashaw's passionate spirituality. A poet whose work is distinguished by the vividness, subtlety, and intricacy of its conceits, or metaphors, Richard Crashaw was also an artist, and twelve engravings based on his designs accompanied the third edition of his verse, published posthumously in Paris in 1652. In this same edition, two poems addressed to the Countess of Denbigh appeared for the first time. The one printed here, urging her conversion to Catholicism, had been written in 1644 in Paris, where Crashaw went to live in exile after being expelled from Peterhouse, Cambridge, whose chapel was sacked by the Puritan army. Crashaw had himself converted to Catholicism in Paris. His conversion was inspired by the Spanish mystic Saint Theresa of Avila and by his friend Nicholas Ferrar, whose religious community at Little Gidding the poet often visited. Crashaw's passionate and protean visual imagination influenced both Milton and Coleridge, and the experience of Crashaw and others at Little Gidding is alluded to in the last section of T. S. Eliot's *Four Quartets*.

Non VI.[1]

'Tis not the work of force but skill
To find the way into man's will.
'Tis love alone can hearts unlock.
Who knows the WORD, he needs not knock.

---

1. "Not by force," the motto of the emblem that introduces this poem: a heart with a hinge to the right, demonstrating that it can be opened, and a lock on the left with a scroll inscribed with letters standing for the Word of God's Law, the key to opening the heart.

To the Noblest and best of Ladies, the Countess of Denbigh

Persuading her to Resolution in Religion &
to render herself without further delay into the Communion of the
Catholic Church.[2]

What heaven-entreated heart is this?
Stands trembling at the gate of bliss,
Holds fast the door, yet dares not venture
Fairly to open it, and enter?
5   Whose definition is a doubt
Twixt life and death, twixt in and out.
Say, ling'ring fair! why comes the birth
Of your brave soul so slowly forth?
Plead your pretenses (oh you strong
10   In weakness!) why you choose so long
In labor of your self to lie?
Nor daring quite to live nor die.
Ah, linger not, loved soul! a slow
And late consent was a long no,
15   Who grants at last, long time tried
And did his best to have denied.
What magic bolts, what mystic bars,
Maintain the will in these strange wars!
What fatal yet fantastic bands
20   Keep the free heart from its own hands!
So when the year takes cold, we see
Poor waters their own prisoners be;
Fettered and locked up fast they lie
In a sad self-captivity.
25   The astonished nymphs their flood's strange fate deplore,
To see themselves their own severer shore.
    Thou that alone canst thaw this cold,
And fetch the heart from its stronghold,
Almighty Love! end this long war,
30   And of a meteor make a star.
Oh fix this fair Indefinite.
And 'mongst thy shafts of sovereign light
Choose out that sure decisive dart
Which has the key of this close heart,
35   Knows all the corners of't, and can control
The self-shut cabinet of an unsearched soul.
Oh let it be at last, love's hour!
Raise this tall trophy of thy power;
Come once the conquering way, not to confute
40   But kill this rebel-word, *irresolute*,
That so, in spite of all this peevish strength
Of weakness, she may write *resolved at length*,
    Unfold at length, unfold, fair flower

---

2. When she lost her husband, who died fighting for the King in the Civil War, Susan, Countess of Denbigh, went to live with the Queen in Paris, where she began to think about converting to Catholicism.

And use the season of love's shower.
45 Meet his well-meaning wounds, wise heart,
And haste to drink the wholesome dart,
That healing shaft, which heaven till now
Hath in love's quiver hid for you.
Oh dart of love! arrow of light!
50 Oh happy you, if it hit right,
It must not fall in vain, it must
Not mark the dry, regardless dust.
Fair one, it is your fate, and brings
Eternal worlds upon its wings.
55 Meet it with widespread arms; and see
Its seat your soul's just center be.
Disband dull fears; give faith the day.
To save your life, kill your delay,
It is love's siege, and sure to be
60 Your triumph, though his victory.
'Tis cowardice that keeps this field,
And want of courage not to yield.
Yield then, O yield, that love may win
The fort at last and let life in.
65 Yield quickly, lest perhaps you prove
Death's prey, before the prize of love.
This fort of your fair self, if't be not won,
He is repulsed indeed; but you are undone.

[END OF PERSPECTIVES: EMBLEM, STYLE, AND METAPHOR]

++ ⊞◊⊞ ++

Richard Lovelace
1618–1657

In *To His Noble Friend*, Andrew Marvell portrays Richard Lovelace as an amorous and chivalrous courtier from a world destroyed by "Our Civil Wars." Marvell depicts the consternation that arose

> When the beauteous ladies came to know
> That their dear Lovelace was endangered so:
> Lovelace that thawed the most congealèd breast
> He who loved best and them defended best.

The dashing and handsome Lovelace was the last exemplar of courtly *sprezzatura* in the history of English poetry, recalling the eroticism and finesse of Wyatt and the chivalry of Sidney and Raleigh. The voluptuousness and elegance that characterized his poetry no less than the Carolinian court was destroyed by the Puritan Revolution.

Lovelace's brief life was indeed endangered more than once—all because of his allegiance to the Royalist cause. After only two years at Cambridge University, he left school to fight in the army of King Charles I, serving as senior ensign in the First Scottish expedition of 1639 and captain in the second of 1640. Both expeditions were disasters for the King's forces. Lovelace was imprisoned twice, first in 1642 for presenting an anti-Parliamentary petition from his home county Kent and again in 1648, when Marvell's patron Lord Fairfax brought the Roundhead (Puritan) army right to the doors of Lovelace's country estate. During his first stint in prison, Lovelace wrote one of his most memorable poems, *To Althea, from Prison*. Released on bail, he lived a precarious life, aiding the King's cause by selling his property and giving money to supply arms. In 1649, when he was released from prison the second time, Lovelace was reduced to selling all of his property, even his family portraits.

Lovelace is a representative of the cultural milieu of the court of Charles I, which included many poets and painters of great distinction. The regime was graced by such poets as Sir John Suckling, Thomas Carew, Abraham Cowley, and Edmund Waller, sometimes referred to as the Cavalier poets, among whom Lovelace is considered the greatest. Lovelace admired not only the works of his fellow poets but also the paintings of Rubens, Van Dyck, and Lely, which adorned the court. Lovelace was great friends with, and wrote poems praising, Lely, who designed plates for Lovelace's two books of poems, published in 1649 and 1659. Lovelace enjoyed painting and music as a gentleman amateur, the characteristic persona of a Cavalier poet. His poems express a tone of extravagant passion tempered with courtly poise achieved through lush images conveying a sensuous *joie de vivre* and a perspective of brave insouciance mixed with self-deprecating irony. His deft rhythms create songlike poems with a spontaneous grace and ease, stylistic ideals of the Cavaliers.

We know nothing about Lovelace after 1649. His brother Philip had been colonel in the King's army but survived the Interregnum to become governor of New York in 1688. Of his brother William's death on the field of battle in the Civil War, Richard had written these Stoic lines to Philip:

> Iron decrees of Destiny
> Are ne'er wiped out with a wet eye.
> But this way you may gain the field,
> Oppose but sorrow, and 'twill yield;
> One gallant thorough made resolve
> Doth starry influence dissolve.

To Lucasta, Going to the Wars

> Tell me not, sweet, I am unkind,
>   That from the nunnery
> Of thy chaste breast and quiet mind
>   To war and arms I fly.
>
> 5   True, a new mistress now I chase,
>   The first foe in the field;
> And with a stronger faith embrace
>   A sword, a horse, a shield.
>
> Yet this inconstancy is such
> 10   As you too shall adore;
> I could not love thee, dear, so much,
>   Loved I not honor more.

1649

The Grasshopper[1]
To My Noble Friend, Mr. Charles Cotton[2]

> O thou that swing'st upon the waving hair
>   Of some well-fillèd oaten beard,

---

1. The grasshopper was associated with a carefree life.
2. Charles Cotton was a learned and literary man. This poem describes the atmosphere of Puritan rule during the Interregnum.

Drunk ev'ry night with a delicious tear
   Dropped thee from heav'n, where now th' art reared,

5 The joys of earth and air are thine entire,
   That with thy feet and wings dost hop and fly;
And when thy poppy[3] works thou dost retire
   To thy carved acorn-bed to lie.

Up with the day, the sun thou welcom'st then,
10   Sport'st in the gilt-plats° of his beams,   *golden fields*
And all these merry days mak'st merry men,
   Thyself, and melancholy streams.

But ah the sickle! golden ears are cropped,
   Ceres and Bacchus[4] bid good night;
15 Sharp frosty fingers all your flowers have topped,
   And what scythes spared, winds shave off quite.

Poor verdant fool! and now green ice! thy joys,
   Large and as lasting as thy perch of grass,
Bid us lay in 'gainst winter, rain, and poise°   *counterbalance*
20   Their floods, with an o'erflowing glass.

Thou best of men and friends! We will create
   A genuine summer in each other's breast;
And spite of this cold time and frozen fate[5]
   Thaw us a warm seat to our rest.

25 Our sacred hearths shall burn eternally
   As vestal flames;[6] the North Wind, he
Shall strike his frost-stretched wings, dissolve and fly
   This Etna[7] in epitome.

Dropping December shall come weeping in,
30   Bewail th' usurping of his reign;
But when in showers of old Greek[8] we begin,
   Shall cry, he hath his crown[9] again!

Night as clear Hesper shall our tapers whip
   From the light casements where we play,
35 And the dark hag from her black mantle strip,
   And stick there everlasting day.[1]

Thus richer than untempted kings are we,
   That asking nothing, nothing need:
Though Lord of all what seas embrace; yet he
40   That wants himself is poor indeed.

1649

---

3. A plant with narcotic powers.
4. The goddess of agriculture and the god of wine.
5. A reference to the persecution of Royalists during the rule of the Puritans.
6. The Roman Vestal Virgins attended to the eternal flame.

7. A volcano, here symbolizing the force and warmth of friendship.
8. The wine that was most prized in ancient Rome.
9. Wreath worn at a drinking party.
1. Hesperus, the morning star; casements: frames forming windows; the dark hag: Hecate, daughter of Night.

To Althea, from Prison

When love with unconfined wings
   Hovers within my gates,
And my divine Althea brings
   To whisper at the grates:
5   When I lie tangled in her hair
     And fettered to her eye,
The gods[1] that wanton° in the air,   *play*
   Know no such liberty.

When flowing cups run swiftly round,
10   With no allaying Thames,[2]
Our careless heads with roses bound,
   Our hearts with loyal flames;
When thirsty grief in wine we steep,
   When healths and draughts go free,
15   Fishes that tipple in the deep
   Know no such liberty.

When, like committed° linnets,° I   *confined/songbirds*
   With shriller throat shall sing
The sweetness, mercy, majesty,
20   And glories of my king;
When I shall voice aloud, how good
   He is, how great should be,
Enlargèd winds that curl the flood,
   Know no such liberty.

25   Stone walls do not a prison make,
    Nor iron bars a cage;
Minds innocent and quiet take
   That for an hermitage;°   *hermit's dwelling*
If I have freedom in my love,
30   And in my soul am free,
Angels alone that soar above,
   Enjoy such liberty.

                        1649

Love Made in the First Age: To Chloris[1]

In the nativity of time,
Chloris, it was not thought a crime
   In direct Hebrew for to woo.[2]
Now we make love, as all on fire,
5   Ring retrograde[3] our loud desire,
   And court in English backward too.

---

1. Some editions read "birds" rather than "gods."
2. River running through London; the meaning of this line is "with no water to dilute the wine."
1. "The First Age" refers to the golden age of Greek and Roman mythology, a time of idyllic plenty in which there was no need for laws or work.
2. Hebrew, which reads from right to left, was believed to have been the original language.
3. In backward or reverse direction; an imitation of notes in contrary motion.

Thrice happy was that golden age,
When compliment was construed rage,[4]
   And fine words in the center hid;
10   When cursed *No* stained no maid's bliss,
And all discourse was summed in *Yes,*
   And nought forbade, but to forbid.

Love then unstinted, love did sip,
And cherries plucked fresh from the lip,
15   On cheeks and roses free he fed;
Lasses like autumn plums did drop,
And lads, indifferently did crop
   A flower, and a maidenhead.

Then unconfinèd each did tipple
20   Wine from the bunch, milk from the nipple;
   Paps tractable as udders were;
Then equally the wholesome jellies
Were squeezed from olive-trees, and bellies,
   Nor suits of trespass did they fear.

25   A fragrant bank of strawberries,
Diapered° with violet's eyes,   *decorated*
   Was table, tablecloth, and fare;
No palace to the clouds did swell
Each humble princess then did dwell
30   In the piazza[5] of her hair.

Both broken faith, and the cause of it,
All-damning gold was damned to the pit;
   Their troth sealed with a clasp and kiss,
Lasted until that extreme day,
35   In which they smiled their souls away,
   And, in each other breathed new bliss.

Because no fault, there was no tear;
No groan did grate the granting ear;
   No false foul breath their delicate smell:
40   No serpent kiss poisoned the taste,
Each touch was naturally chaste,
   And their mere sense a miracle.

Naked as their own innocence,
And unembroidered[6] from offense
45   They went, above poor riches, gay;
On softer than the cygnet's° down,   *young swan's*
In beds they tumbled of their own;
   For each within the other lay.

Thus did they live: thus did they love,
50   Repeating only joys above;

---

4. When compliments were interpreted as passionate proposals.

5. A colonnade surrounding a square.
6. Not ornamented with the trappings of authority.

       And angels were, but with clothes on,
       Which they would put off cheerfully,
       To bathe them in the galaxy,[7]
       Then gird them with the heavenly zone.[8]

55   Now, Chloris, miserably crave
       The offered bliss you would not have;
         Which evermore I must deny,
       Whilst ravished with these noble dreams
       And crownèd with mine own soft beams,
60   Enjoying of myself I lie.

                                    1659

Henry Vaughan
1622–1695

Henry Vaughan grew up speaking Welsh among the woods and streams of Newton in the parish of Llansantffraed. He responded to the sound of his first language and to the beauty of this countryside in the music and imagery of his poetry. For example, the slope of mount Allt, on which he lived, provided a striking image: "those faint beams in which this hill is dressed,/ After the Sun's remove" The Welsh influence can be heard in his poetry's alliteration and assonance; his piling up of comparisons, as in *The Night*, is called *dyfalu* ("to liken") in Welsh poetic technique. On the title page to his second book of verse, *Olor Iscanus* ("The Swan of Usk" [a local river]), he is called a "Silurist," a member of an ancient Welsh tribe. Though his verse is written in English, Vaughan's poetry and identity were always bound up with his native land.

    Henry Vaughan's Welsh childhood was followed by education at Oxford, where he studied with his twin brother Thomas, and then at the Inns of Court in London, where he began his poetic apprenticeship. An admirer of Ben Jonson's verse, Vaughan praised and imitated Jonson in his first book of poetry, *Poems with the Tenth Satyre of Juvenal Englished* (1646). The mysticism and Neoplatonism of Vaughan's best known collection of poems, *Silex Scintillans* ("The Fiery Flint") (1650), link him to the metaphysical tradition of Donne, Herbert, and Crashaw, yet his verse continued to show fondness for the wit and spareness of Jonson.

    At the outbreak of the Civil War, Vaughan returned to Wales in August 1642. He worked as secretary to the Circuit Chief Justice of the Great Sessions until 1645, when he joined the company of soldiers who fought for King Charles's cause with Sir Herbert Price at Chester. The poems in *Silex Scintillans* express his anger and disappointment at the outcome of the Civil War. In *Prayer in Time of Persecution*, Vaughan rails against the Puritans for confiscating the woods of his family's estate. The 1650 Act for the Propagation of the Gospel in Wales gave a committee of Puritan commissioners the power to purge the Welsh royalist clergy. Among these was Henry's brother Thomas, who was stripped of his position and livelihood. In *The World*, Vaughan describes a "darksome statesman" reminiscent of Cromwell; and in several poems, Vaughan complains of the Puritan "zeal" that brought about regicide and persecution of the Church of England. In *Christ's Nativity*, Vaughan lamented the Puritans's prohibition of the observance of Christmas and Good Friday:

---

7. The Milky Way.   8. The zodiac of stars.

Shall he that came down from thence,
    And here for us was slain,
Shall he be now cast off? no sense
    Of all his woes remain?
Can neither Love, nor sufferings bind?
    Are we all stone, and Earth?
Neither his bloody passions mind,
    Nor one day bless his birth?
Alas, my God! Thy birth now here
Must not be numbered in the year.

There is even evidence in one poem, *The Proffer*, that Vaughan disdained offers of power from Cromwell's government: "I'll not stuff my story / With your Commonwealth and glory." Some time after 1650, Vaughan decided to study and practice medicine.

    The 1650s were troubled years for Vaughan. During this time he grieved for the deaths of his brother Thomas and his first wife Catherine. In the preface to the second edition of *Silex Scintillans* in 1655, Vaughan refers to an illness he had suffered, which seems to have been spiritual and may even have resulted in a kind of conversion experience. In this same preface, Vaughan also praises George Herbert: "his holy life and verse gained many pious Converts of whom I am the least." Along with the Bible, Herbert's verse is the main influence on Vaughan's. The titles of twenty-six lyrics in *Silex Scintillans* are taken from Herbert's *The Temple*. Both poets describe a spiritual paradise, but while Herbert's is ineffable, Vaughan's has the physical beauty of an actual landscape. Vaughan's temple stretches beyond the pristine church architecture of Herbert's imagery to touch flowers and trees and to contemplate the stars. Vaughan's feeling for nature is unsurpassed in English verse until Wordsworth. Vaughan's intense sense of the transitoriness of natural beauty and the immanence of mortality make his verse worth contemplating and savoring.

Regeneration

A ward, and still in bonds, one day
    I stole abroad;
It was high spring, and all the way
    Primrosed, and hung with shade;
5   Yet, was it frost within,
        And surly winds
Blasted my infant buds, and sin
    Like clouds eclipsed my mind.

Stormed thus, I straight perceived my spring
10   Mere stage and show,
My walk a monstrous, mountained thing,
    Roughcast with rocks, and snow;
        And as a pilgrim's eye
        Far from relief,
15 Measures the melancholy sky,
    Then drops, and rains for grief,

So sighed I upwards still, at last
       'Twixt steps, and falls
I reached the pinnacle, where placed
20   I found a pair of scales,
    I took them up and laid

In th'one late pains,
The other smoke, and pleasures weighed,
But proved the heavier grains.

25 With that, some cried, "Away!" Straight I
Obeyed, and led
Full east, a fair, fresh field could spy;
Some called it, Jacob's bed,[1]
A virgin soil, which no
30 Rude feet ere trod,
Where, since he stepped there, only go
Prophets, and friends of God.

Here, I reposed; but scarce well set,
A grove descried
35 Of stately height, whose branches met
And mixed on every side;
I entered, and once in,
Amazed to see't,
Found all was changed, and a new spring
40 Did all my senses greet;

The unthrift° sun shot vital gold   *spendthrift*
A thousand pieces,
And heaven its azure did unfold,
Checkered with snowy fleeces,
45 The air was all in spice,
And every bush
A garland wore; thus fed my eyes,
But all the ear lay hush.

Only a little fountain lent
50 Some use for ears,
And on the dumb shades language spent
The music of her tears;
I drew her near, and found
The cistern full
55 Of divers stones, some bright, and round
Others ill-shaped, and dull.

The first, pray mark, as quick as light
Danced through the flood,
But, th'last more heavy than the night
60 Nailed to the center stood;
I wondered much, but tired
At last with thought,
My restless eye that still desired
As strange an object brought;

65 It was a bank of flowers, where I descried,
Though 'twas mid-day,
Some fast asleep, others broad-eyed

---

1. See Genesis 28.11–19. Sleeping outdoors, Jacob had a vision of a ladder in the sky leading up to God.

And taking in the ray,
Here musing long, I heard
70   A rushing wind
Which still increased, but whence it stirred
Nowhere I could not find.

I turned me round, and to each shade
Dispatched an eye,
75   To see, if any leaf had made
Least motion, or reply;
But while I listening sought
My mind to ease
By knowing, where 'twas, or where not,
80   It whispered, "Where I please."[2]

"Lord," then said I, "on me one breath,
And let me die before my death!"

1650

The Retreat

Happy those early days! when I
Shined in my angel infancy.
Before I understood this place
Appointed for my second race,[1]
5   Or taught my soul to fancy ought
But a white, celestial thought;
When yet I had not walked above
A mile or two from my first love,
And looking back, at that short space,
10   Could see a glimpse of his bright face;
When on some gilded cloud, or flower
My gazing soul would dwell an hour,
And in those weaker glories spy
Some shadows of eternity;
15   Before I taught my tongue to wound
My conscience with a sinful sound,
Or had the black art to dispense
A several° sin to every sense,   *separate*
But felt through all this fleshly dress
20   Bright shoots of everlastingness.
    O, how I long to travel back,
And tread again that ancient track!
That I might once more reach that plain
Where first I left my glorious train,
25   From whence th' enlightened spirit sees
That shady city of palm trees.[2]

---

2. John 3.8: "The wind bloweth where it listeth, and thou hearest the sound thereof, but canst not tell whence it cometh, and whither it goeth: so is every one that is born of the Spirit." See also Genesis 2.7 for the breath of life that God breathed into humanity.

1. "Second race" implies a Platonic belief in the reincarnation of the soul and in the preexistence of the soul in the world of perfect forms.
2. The New Jerusalem, the Paradise of Heaven.

But, ah! my soul with too much stay°   *hesitation*
      Is drunk, and staggers in the way.
      Some men a forward motion love;
30   But I by backward steps would move,
      And when this dust falls to the urn
      In that state I came, return.

                                                        1650

Silence, and Stealth of Days[1]

      Silence, and stealth of days! 'tis now
            Since thou art gone,
      Twelve hundred hours, and not a brow[2]
            But clouds hang on.
5   As he that in some cave's thick damp
            Locked from the light,
      Fixeth a solitary lamp,
            To brave the night
      And walking from his sun, when past
10   That glim'ring ray,
      Cuts through the heavy mists in haste
            Back to his day,[3]
      So o'er fled minutes I retreat
            Unto that hour
15   Which showed thee last, but did defeat
            Thy light, and pow'r,
      I search, and rack my soul to see
            Those beams again,
      But nothing but the snuff[4] to me
20   Appeareth plain;
      That dark, and dead sleeps in its known
            And common urn,
      But those fled to their Maker's throne,
            There shine, and burn;
25   O could I track them! but souls must
            Track one the other,
      And now the spirit, not the dust,
            Must be thy brother.
      Yet I have one Pearl[5] by whose light
30   All things I see,
      And in the heart of earth and night,
            Find Heaven and thee.

                                                        1650

The World

      I saw eternity the other night,
      Like a great ring of pure and endless light,

1. The poem is about the death of Vaughan's younger
brother William, who died in July 1648.
2. Facial expression, but also a gallery in a coal mine,
since the following lines depict the image of a miner
making his way through dark mist.

3. When the miner walks a little beyond the area lit by
his lamp into the dark, he then rushes back to the light.
4. The part of a candle wick burnt in order to give light;
an image of his brother's body turned to dust.
5. The Bible.

All calm as it was bright;
And round beneath it, Time, in hours, days, years,
5   Driven by the spheres,[1]
Like a vast shadow moved, in which the world
          And all her train were hurled.
The doting lover in his quaintest strain[2]
          Did there complain;
10 Near him, his lute, his fancy, and his flights,
          Wit's sour delights,
With gloves and knots,[3] the silly snares of pleasure,
          Yet his dear treasure,
All scattered lay, while he his eyes did pour
15   Upon a flower.

The darksome statesman[4] hung with weights and woe
Like a thick midnight fog moved there so slow
          He did not stay nor go;
Condemning thoughts, like sad eclipses, scowl
20   Upon his soul,
And clouds of crying witnesses without
          Pursued him with one shout.
Yet digged the mole, and lest his ways be found,
          Worked underground,
25 Where he did clutch his prey. But one did see
          That policy:
Churches and altars fed him; perjuries
          Were gnats and flies;
It rained about him blood and tears; but he
30   Drank them as free.

The fearful miser on a heap of rust
Sat pining all his life there, did scarce trust
          His own hands with the dust;
Yet would not place° one piece above, but lives   *invest*
35   In fear of thieves.
Thousands there were as frantic as himself,
          And hugged each one his pelf:°   *money*
The downright epicure placed heaven in sense,[5]
          And scorned pretense;
40 While others, slipped into a wide excess,
          Said little less;
The weaker sort slight, trivial wares enslave,
          Who think them brave,°   *showy*
And poor, despisèd Truth sat counting by,°   *reckoning*
45   Their victory.

Yet some, who all this while did weep and sing,
And sing and weep, soared up into the ring;
          But most would use no wing,
"O fools!" said I, "thus to prefer dark night

---

1. The spheres of the heavenly bodies circling the earth.
2. Most intricate melody.
3. Ties or bows worn as love tokens.

4. Possibly a reference to Cromwell.
5. An "epicure" is a person who finds the greatest good in sensual pleasure.

50
              Before true light!
To live in grots° and caves, and hate the day   *caverns*
           Because it shows the way;
The way which from the dead and dark abode
           Leads up to God,

55
A way where you might tread the sun and be
           More bright than he!"
But as I did their madness so discuss,
           One whispered thus:
"This ring the bridegroom did for none provide,

60
           But for his bride."[6]

1650

They Are All Gone into the World of Light!

They are all gone into the world of light!
    And I alone sit lingering here;
Their very memory is fair and bright,
    And my sad thoughts doth clear.

5
It glows and glitters in my cloudy breast
    Like stars upon some gloomy grove,
Or those faint beams in which this hill is dressed,
    After the sun's remove.

I see them walking in an air of glory,
10
    Whose light doth trample on my days:
My days, which are at best but dull and hoary,
    Mere glimmering and decays.

O holy hope! and high humility,
    High as the heavens above!
15
These are your walks, and you have showed them me
    To kindle my cold love,

Dear, beauteous death! the jewel of the just,
    Shining no where, but in the dark;
What mysteries do lie beyond thy dust,
20
    Could man outlook that mark!

He that hath found some fledged birds nest, may know
    At first sight, if the bird be flown;
But what fair well, or grove he sings in now,
    That is to him unknown.

25
And yet, as angels in some brighter dreams
    Call to the soul, when man doth sleep,
So some strange thoughts transcend our wonted themes,
    And into glory peep.

If a star were confined into a tomb
30
    Her captive flames must needs burn there;
But when the hand that locked her up, gives room,
    She'll shine through all the sphere.

6. For the union of Christ and his Church as that between husband and wife, see Ephesians 5.23.

O Father of eternal life, and all
    Created glories under thee!
35   Resume thy spirit from this world of thrall°   *slavery*
       Into true liberty.

Either disperse these mists, which blot and fill
    My perspective[1] still as they pass,
Or else remove me hence unto that hill,[2]
40   Where I shall need no glass.

1655

The Night

John 3.2[1]

Through that pure virgin-shrine,
That sacred veil drawn o'er thy glorious noon
That men might look and live as glowworms shine,
      And face the moon:
5   Wise Nicodemus saw such light
    As made him know his God by night.

      Most blest believer he!
Who in that land of darkness and blind eyes
Thy long expected healing wings could see,
10   When thou didst rise,
    And what can never more be done,
    Did at midnight speak with the Sun!

      O who will tell me, where
He found thee at that dead and silent hour?
15   What hallowed solitary ground did bear
      So rare a flower,
    Within whose sacred leaves did lie
    The fullness of the Deity?

      No mercy-seat of gold,[2]
20   No dead and dusty cherub, nor carved stone,
But his own living works did my Lord hold
      And lodge alone;
    Where trees and herbs did watch and peep
    And wonder, while the Jews did sleep.

25   Dear night! this world's defeat;[3]
The stop to busy fools; cares check and curb;
    The day of spirits; my soul's calm retreat
      Which none disturb!
    Christ's progress, and his prayer time;
30   The hours to which high heaven doth chime;

---

1. Telescope; vision.
2. Sion Hill, a symbol for union with God.
1. In John 3.2, the Pharisee Nicodemus tells Jesus: "Rabbi, we know that thou art a teacher come from God: for no man can do these miracles that thou doest except God be with him."

2. God told the Israelites to build "a mercy seat of pure gold" with a cherub on either end to place above the ark (see Exodus 25.17–21).
3. This and the next stanza echo George Herbert's *Prayer (1)*; see page 1588.

God's silent, searching flight,
When my Lord's head is filled with dew, and all
His locks are wet with the clear drops of night;
    His still, soft call;
35   His knocking time; the souls dumb watch,
When spirits their fair kindred catch.

    Were all my loud, evil days
Calm and unhaunted as is thy dark tent,
Whose peace but by some angel's wing or voice
40   Is seldom rent;
Then I in heaven all the long year
Would keep, and never wander here.

    But living where the sun
Doth all things wake, and where all mix and tire
45 Themselves and others, I consent and run
    To ev'ry mire,°   bog
And by this world's ill-guiding light,
Ere more then I can do by night.

    There is in God (some say)
50 A deep, but dazzling darkness; as men here
Say it is late and dusky, because they
    See not all clear;
O for that night! where I in him
Might live invisible and dim.

                                      1655

Andrew Marvell
1621–1678

Praised by his nephew for "joining the most peculiar graces of wit and learning" and berated by his antagonist Samuel Parker for speaking the language of "boat-swains and cabin boys," Andrew Marvell left little evidence for his biographers. Most of what remains of his verse has been bequeathed to posterity by virtue of a shady banking scheme on his part and an implausible claim by his housekeeper to be "Mrs. Marvell." Though she couldn't remember the date of his death, Mary Palmer tried to prove that she was the poet's wife to get at money that her master had squirrelled away in an account for some bankrupt acquaintances. To further her claim, she saw to it that Marvell's *Miscellaneous Poems* were published in 1681. In his own name, Marvell published only a few occasional poems and a satire attacking religious intolerance and political authoritarianism.

If it is thanks to Mrs. Palmer's rummaging through the poet's papers that such exquisite poems as *To His Coy Mistress* and *The Definition of Love* saw the light of day, it is largely thanks to T. S. Eliot that modern critical attention was turned to Marvell's poetry. The Augustans and Romantics neglected him, and it was not until Eliot that such features of Marvell's verse as Latinate gravity, metaphysical wit, and muscular syntax came to be fully appreciated. For ingenious ambiguity and sheer seductive sensuousness, Marvell is one of the greatest poets of all time.

As tantalizing as the verse is, it leaves little solid evidence of what was a very private life. Marvell grew up in a house surrounded by gardens in the Yorkshire town of Hull on the Humber, where his father was the Anglican rector. There is a story that Marvell once left university for London to flirt with Catholicism, but his father made sure he returned to Cambridge and Protestantism. After his father's death, Marvell traveled in Holland, France, Italy, and Spain (1642–1647). He later tutored Mary Fairfax, daughter of Lord Fairfax of Nun-Appleton House (1650–1652), and taught William Dutton, Cromwell's ward (1653–1656). Initially recommended by Milton to serve as Assistant Latin Secretary in 1653, Marvell was first appointed Latin Secretary to the Council of State in 1657. He was elected Member of Parliament for Hull in 1659, a position he held until 1678. When Charles I returned to power, Marvell interceded on Milton's behalf and made sure his old friend and fellow poet was released from prison. Later in life, Marvell wrote satires criticizing the corruption of the Restoration regime, all but one published anonymously.

Marvell chose to keep his cards close to his chest in the ideologically volatile atmosphere of the Civil War and Restoration. A contemporary biographer remarked that Marvell "was wont to say that, he would not play the good-fellow in any man's company in whose hands he would not trust his life." He did not fight in the Civil War, since he was in Europe at the time, and as he later ambiguously maintained, "the Cause was too good to have been fought for." His strategy in dealing with change involved publicly siding with the faction in power while maintaining politically incorrect friendships and finding himself "inclinable to favor the weaker party"—whether it was a Royalist who had given his life for the King, such as Lord Hastings, or a Republican who went to prison for his convictions, such as Milton. Marvell wrote poems praising both royalists and revolutionaries. He was nothing if not tolerant.

He was also something of a chameleon, an assumer of numerous poetic personae and disguises. In *Tom May's Death*, Marvell satirized the Royalist turned Republican, here portrayed arriving in heaven drunk. Marvell equivocally praised Cromwell in *An Horatian Ode*, ironically maintaining that it was the Irish whom Cromwell had so brutally massacred who could "best affirm his praises." When he became tutor to Cromwell's ward William Dutton, Marvell wrote poems praising Cromwell in such slavishly glowing terms that the poet was made Latin Secretary to the Council of State.

The last word should go to Marvell, whose choice to translate the following chorus from Seneca's *Thyestes* shows his outlook on the vicissitudes of power:

> Climb at court for me that will
> Giddy favor's slippery hill;
> All I seek is to lie still,
> Settled in some secret nest.
> In calm leisure let me rest,
> And far off the public stage
> Pass away my silent age.
> Thus, when without noise, unknown,
> I have lived out all my span,
> I shall die without a groan,
> An old honest countryman,
> Who exposed to others' eyes,
> Into his own heart ne'er pries.
> Death to him's a strange surprise.

The Coronet[1]

When for the thorns with which I long, too long,
　　With many a piercing wound,
　　My Savior's head have crowned,
I seek with garlands to redress that wrong:
5　　Through every garden, every mead,
I gather flow'rs (my fruits are only flow'rs)
　　Dismantling all the fragrant towers°　　　　*tall headdresses*
That once adorned my shepherdess's head.
And now when I have summed up all my store,
10　　Thinking (so I myself deceive)
　　So rich a chaplet° thence to weave　　　　*wreath*
As never yet the King of Glory wore:
　　Alas, I find the serpent old
　　That, twining in his speckled breast,[2]
15　　About the flowers disguised does fold,°　　　　*wind*
　　With wreaths° of fame and interest.　　　　*coils*
Ah, foolish man, that wouldst debase with them,
And mortal glory, Heaven's diadem!
But Thou who only couldst the serpent tame,
20　　Either his slippery knots at once untie,
　　And disentangle all his winding snare:
Or shatter too with him my curious frame:[3]
And let these wither, so that he may die,
Though set with skill and chosen out with care:
25　　That they, while Thou on both their spoils[4] dost tread,
May crown thy feet, that could not crown thy head.[5]

Bermudas[1]

Where the remote Bermudas ride
In th' ocean's bosom unespied,
From a small boat, that rowed along,
The list'ning winds received this song.
5　　"What should we do but sing his praise
That led us through the watry maze,
Unto an isle so long unknown,[2]
And yet far kinder than our own?
Where he the huge sea-monsters wracks,°　　　　*shipwrecks*
10　　That lift the deep upon their backs.
He lands us on a grassy stage,
Safe from the storms, and prelate's[3] rage.
He gave us this eternal spring,

1. Marvell's poems were first published in 1681.
2. See Spenser, *Faerie Queene* 1.11.15.
3. Ingenious structure (the chaplet).
4. Sloughing of the snake's skin; plundering.
5. See Genesis 3.15, for the prophecy that the seed of Eve
will bruise the serpent's head.
1. Probably composed sometime after 1653, when Marvell was living in the house of John Oxenbridge, who had

made two trips to the Bermudas. Marvell could also have
known Captain John Smith's 1624 work *The General History of Virginia, New England and the Summer Isles* (as the
Bermudas were called).
2. Unknown to Europeans; Juan Bermudez first came
there in 1515.
3. Clergyman's, bishop's.

15   Which here enamels everything;
      And sends the fowl to us in care,
      On daily visits through the air.
      He hangs in shades the orange bright,
      Like golden lamps in a green night,
      And does in the pom'granates close,
20   Jewels more rich than Ormus⁴ shows.
      He makes the figs our mouths to meet,
      And throws the melons at our feet,
      But apples° plants of such a price,   *pineapples*
      No tree could ever bear them twice.
25   With cedars, chosen by his hand,
      From Lebanon, he stores the land,
      And makes the hollow seas, that roar,
      Proclaim the ambergris⁵ on shore.
      He cast (of which we rather boast)
30   The gospel's pearl upon our coast,
      And in these rocks for us did frame
      A temple, where to sound his name.
      Oh let our voice his praise exalt,
      Till it arrive at heaven's vault:
35   Which thence (perhaps) rebounding, may
      Echo beyond the Mexique Bay.⁶
      Thus sung they, in the English boat,
      An holy and a cheerful note,
      And all the way, to guide their chime,
40   With falling oars they kept the time.

The Nymph Complaining for the Death of Her Fawn¹

      The wanton troopers² riding by
      Have shot my fawn, and it will die.
      Ungentle men! They cannot thrive
      To kill thee. Thou ne'er didst alive
5   Them any harm: alas, nor could
      Thy death yet do them any good.
      I'm sure I never wished them ill;
      Nor do I for all this; nor will:
      But, if my simple prayers may yet
10   Prevail with Heaven to forget
      Thy murder, I will join my tears
      Rather then fail. But, O my fears!
      It cannot die so. Heaven's King
      Keeps register of everything:
15   And nothing may we use in vain.
      E'en beasts must be with justice slain,

4. Hormuz on the Persian Gulf.
5. Musky secretion of the sperm whale that is used in perfumes.
6. Gulf of Mexico.
1. Ancient Roman poets such as Catullus and Ovid had

written poems on the death of pets, as did the early 16th-century English poet John Skelton in *Philip Sparrow*.
2. A term used for the Presbyterian Scots Covenanting Army that attacked England in 1640.

Else men are made their deodands.[3]
Though they should wash their guilty hands
In this warm life-blood, which doth part
20   From thine, and wound me to the heart,
Yet could they not be clean: their stain
Is dyed in such a purple grain.
There is not such another in
The world, to offer for their sin.
25   Unconstant Sylvio, when yet
I had not found him counterfeit,
One morning (I remember well)
Tied in this silver chain and bell,
Gave it to me: nay, and I know
30   What he said then; I'm sure I do.
Said he, "Look how your huntsman here
Hath taught a fawn to hunt his dear."
But Sylvio soon had me beguiled.
This waxèd tame, while he grew wild,
35   And quite regardless of my smart,
Left me his fawn, but took his heart.
        Thenceforth I set myself to play
My solitary time away
With this: and very well content,
40   Could so mine idle life have spent.
For it was full of sport; and light
Of foot, and heart; and did invite
Me to its game: it seemed to bless
Itself in me. How could I less
45   Than love it? O I cannot be
Unkind, t' a beast that loveth me.
        Had it lived long, I do not know
Whether it too might have done so
As Sylvio did: his gifts might be
50   Perhaps as false or more than he.
But I am sure, for ought that I
Could in so short a time espie,
Thy Love was far more better then
The love of false and cruel men.
55   With sweetest milk, and sugar, first
I it at mine own fingers nursed.
And as it grew, so every day
It waxed more white and sweet than they,
It had so sweet a breath! And oft
60   I blushed to see its foot more soft,
And white, (shall I say than my hand?)
Nay any lady's of the land.
        It is a wondrous thing, how fleet
'Twas on those little silver feet.

3. Otherwise; men would become forfeited objects. In early modern English law, any personal property that caused a
human death had to be given up as part of the reparation for the crime.

65   With what a pretty skipping grace,
      It oft would challenge me the race:
      And when 't had left me far away,
      'Twould stay, and run again, and stay.
      For it was nimbler much than hinds;
70   And trod, as on the four winds.
          I have a garden of my own,
      But so with roses overgrown,
      And lilies, that you would it guess
      To be a little wilderness.
75   And all the springtime of the year
      It only lovèd to be there.
      Among the beds of lilies, I
      Have sought it oft, where it should lie;
      Yet could not, till itself would rise,
80   Find it, although before mine eyes.
      For, in the flaxen lilies' shade,
      It like a bank of lilies laid.
      Upon the roses it would feed,
      Until its lips e'en seemed to bleed:
85   And then to me 'twould boldly trip,
      And print those roses on my lip.
      But all its chief delight was still
      On roses thus itself to fill:
      And its pure virgin limbs to fold
90   In whitest sheets of lilies cold.
      Had it lived long, it would have been
      Lilies without, roses within.
      O help! O help! I see it faint:
      And die as calmly as a saint.
95   See how it weeps. The tears do come
      Sad, slowly dropping like a gum.
      So weeps the wounded balsam: so
      The holy frankincense doth flow.
      The brotherless Heliades
100   Melt in such amber tears as these.[4]
          I in a golden vial will
      Keep these two crystal tears; and fill
      It till it do o'reflow with mine;
      Then place it in Diana's[5] shrine.
105   Now my sweet fawn is vanished to
      Whither the swans and turtles° go: doves
      In fair Elysium to endure,
      With milk-white lambs, and ermines pure.
      O do not run too fast: for I
110   Will but bespeak thy grave, and die.
          First my unhappy statue shall
      Be cut in marble; and withal,

4. Grieving the death of their brother Phaethon, the   tears of amber.
Heliades were transformed into poplar trees which wept   5. Goddess of chastity and of the hunt.

Let it be weeping too:[6] but there
Th' engraver sure his art may spare;
115 For I so truly thee bemoan,
That I shall weep though I be stone:
Until my tears, still dropping, wear
My breast, themselves engraving there.
There at my feet shalt thou be laid,
120 Of purest alabaster made:
For I would have thine image be
White as I can, though not as thee.

To His Coy Mistress[1]

Had we but world enough, and time,
This coyness, Lady, were no crime.
We would sit down, and think which way
To walk, and pass our long love's day.
5 Thou by the Indian Ganges' side
Shouldst rubies find: I by the tide
Of Humber would complain.[2] I would
Love you ten years before the flood:
And you should if you please refuse
10 Till the conversion of the Jews.[3]
My vegetable love should grow
Vaster then empires, and more slow.[4]
An hundred years should go to praise
Thine eyes, and on thy forehead gaze.
15 Two hundred to adore each breast:
But thirty thousand to the rest.
An age at least to every part,
And the last age should show your heart.
For Lady you deserve this State;
20 Nor would I love at lower rate.
But at my back I always hear
Times wingèd chariot hurrying near:
And yonder all before us lie
Deserts of vast eternity.
25 Thy beauty shall no more be found;
Nor, in thy marble vault, shall sound
My echoing song: then worms shall try
That long preserved virginity:
And your quaint honor turn to dust;[5]
30 And into ashes all my lust.
The grave's a fine and private place,

6. Niobe was turned into a weeping stone for her pride in her children.
1. A poem on the theme of *carpe diem* ("seize the day") that includes a blazon, or description of the lady from head to toe, and a logical argument: "If . . . But . . . Therefore."
2. Marvell grew up in Hull on the Humber River.
3. The ends of time: the Flood occurred in the distant past, and Christians prophesied that Jews would convert to Christianity at the end of the world.
4. The "vegetable" was characterized only by growth, in contrast to the sensitive, which felt, and the rational, which could reason.
5. "Quaint honor," proud chastity. Note the pun on *queynte* (Middle English), woman's genitals.

But none, I think, do there embrace.
    Now, therefore, while the youthful hue
Sits on thy skin like morning dew,[6]
35   And while thy willing soul transpires
At every pore with instant fires,
Now let us sport us while we may;
And now, like amorous birds of prey,
Rather at once our time devour,
40   Than languish in his slow-chapped° power.   *slowly biting*
Let us roll all our strength, and all
Our sweetness, up into one ball:
And tear our pleasures with rough strife,
Thorough the iron gates of life.[7]
45   Thus, though we cannot make our sun
Stand still, yet we will make him run.[8]

The Definition of Love

My Love is of a birth as rare
As 'tis for object strange and high:
It was begotten by Despair
Upon Impossibility.

5   Magnanimous Despair alone
Could show me so divine a thing,
Where feeble Hope could ne'er have flown
But vainly flapped its tinsel wing.

And yet I quickly might arrive
10   Where my extended soul is fixed,
But Fate does iron wedges drive,
And always crowds itself betwixt.

For Fate with jealous eye does see
Two perfect loves, nor lets them close:°   *unite*
15   Their union would her ruin be,
And her tyrannic power depose.

And therefore her decrees of steel
Us as the distant poles have placed,
(Though Love's whole world on us doth wheel)
20   Not by themselves to be embraced.

Unless the giddy heaven fall,
And earth some new convulsion tear;
And, us to join, the world should all
Be cramped into a planisphere.[1]

25   As lines (so loves) oblique[2] may well
Themselves in every angle greet:

---

6. In the 1681 Folio, "dew" reads "glue," and in two manuscripts the rhymes in lines 33 and 34 are "glue" and "dew."
7. One manuscript reads "grates" for "gates."
8. Joshua made the sun stand still in the war against

Gibeon (see Joshua 10.12).
1. A two-dimensional map of the globe.
2. Slanting at an angle other than a right angle, and also veering away from right morals.

But ours so truly parallel,
Though infinite, can never meet.

Therefore the love which us doth bind.
30   But Fate so enviously debars,
Is the conjunction of the mind,
And opposition of the stars.³

The Mower Against Gardens

Luxurious man, to bring his vice in use,¹
    Did after him the world seduce,
And from the fields the flowers and plants allure,
    Where Nature was most plain and pure.
5   He first enclosed within the garden's square
    A dead and standing pool of air,
And a more luscious earth for them did knead,
    Which stupefied them while it fed.
The pink grew then as double as his mind;²
10   The nutriment did change the kind.
With strange perfumes he did the roses taint,
    And flowers themselves were taught to paint.
The tulip, white, did for complexion seek,
    And learned to interline its cheek:
15   Its onion root they then so high did hold,
    That one was for a meadow sold.³
Another world was searched, through oceans new,
    To find the Marvel of Peru.⁴
And yet these rarities might be allowed
20   To man, that sovereign thing and proud,
Had he not dealt between the bark and tree,⁵
    Forbidden mixtures there to see.
No plant now knew the stock from which it came;
    He grafts upon the wild the tame:
25   That the uncertain and adult'rate fruit
    Might put the palate in dispute.
His green seraglio⁶ has its eunuchs too;
    Lest any tyrant him outdo.
And in the cherry he does nature vex,
30   To procreate without a sex.⁷
'Tis all enforced; the fountain and the grot,°   *grotto*
    While the sweet fields do lie forgot:
Where willing Nature does to all dispense
    A wild and fragrant innocence:
35   And fauns and fairies do the meadows till,

---

3. Conjunction: coming together in the same sign of the zodiac; union. Stars in opposition are diametrically opposed to one another.
1. To make current.
2. Double, both in the sense of having two blooms and being the result of sophisticated (duplicitous) thought.
3. Marvell alludes to the 17th-century lucrative trade in Dutch tulips.
4. *Mirabilis jalapa*, also known as the four-o'clock, a multicolored flower native to tropical America.
5. An expression used to describe interfering in another's affairs, especially those of a married couple.
6. Secluded place; Turkish palace; harem.
7. To grow by grafting one strain of cherry onto another.

More by their presence than their skill.
Their statues polished by some ancient hand,
    May to adorn the gardens stand:
But howsoe'er the figures do excel,
40   The gods themselves with us do dwell.

The Mower's Song

My mind was once the true survey
Of all these meadows fresh and gay;
And in the greenness of the grass
Did see its hopes as in a glass;°   *mirror*
5   When Juliana came, and she,
What I do to the grass, does to my thoughts and me.[1]

But these, while I with sorrow pine,
Grew more luxuriant still and fine,
That not one blade of grass you spied,
10 But had a flower on either side;
When Juliana came, and she,
What I do to the grass, does to my thoughts and me.

Unthankful meadows, could you so
A fellowship so true forgo,
15 And in your gaudy May-games meet,[2]
While I lay trodden under feet?
When Juliana came, and she,
What I do to the grass, does to my thoughts and me.

But what you in compassion ought,
20 Shall now by my revenge be wrought:
And flowers, and grass, and I and all,
Will in one common ruin fall.
For Juliana comes, and she,
What I do to the grass, does to my thoughts and me.

25 And thus, ye meadows, which have been
Companions of my thoughts more green,
Shall now the heraldry become
With which I shall adorn my tomb;
For Juliana comes, and she,
30 What I do to the grass, does to my thoughts and me.

The Garden

How vainly men themselves amaze
To win the palm, the oak, or bays,[1]
And their uncessant labors see
Crowned from some single herb or tree,
5   Whose short and narrow-vergèd shade

1. This 12-syllable line (an alexandrine) is the only
instance of a refrain in all of Marvell's poetry.
2. Festivals celebrated on May 1.

1. Vainly: arrogantly, in vain. Amaze: bewilder, go mad.
The palm, the oak, or bays: prizes symbolic of military,
political, and poetic excellence.

Does prudently their toils upbraid,
While all flowers and all trees do close°   unite
To weave the garlands of repose.

10 Fair quiet, have I found thee here,
    And innocence thy sister dear!
    Mistaken long, I sought you then
    In busy companies of men.
    Your sacred plants, if here below,
    Only among the plants will grow.
15 Society is all but rude,
    To this delicious solitude.[2]

    No white nor red[3] was ever seen
    So am'rous as this lovely green.
    Fond lovers, cruel as their flame,
20 Cut in these trees their mistress' name.
    Little, alas, they know, or heed,
    How far these beauties hers exceed!
    Fair trees! whereso'er your barks I wound,
    No name shall but your own be found.

25 When we have run our passion's heat,
    Love hither makes his best retreat.
    The gods, that mortal beauty chase,
    Still in a tree did end their race.
    Apollo hunted Daphne so,
30 Only that she might laurel grow,
    And Pan did after Syrinx speed,
    Not as a nymph, but for a reed.[4]

    What wondrous life in this I lead!
    Ripe apples drop about my head;
35 The luscious clusters of the vine
    Upon my mouth do crush their wine;
    The nectarine, and curious peach,
    Into my hands themselves do reach;
    Stumbling on melons, as I pass,
40 Insnared with flowers, I fall on grass.

    Meanwhile the mind, from pleasure less,
    Withdraws into its happiness:
    The mind, that ocean where each kind
    Does straight its own resemblance find,[5]
45 Yet it creates, transcending these,
    Far other worlds, and other seas,

2. Compare to Katherine Philips's *A Country-life:* "Then welcome dearest solitude, / My great felicity; / Though some are pleased to call thee rude."
3. Colors used to describe the beloved's beauty.
4. As god of poetry, Apollo seeks the laurel (the bays), while Pan seeks the syrinx (pipe) of pastoral poetry. Apollo chased Daphne, who prayed to be saved from him

and was transformed into a laurel tree, just as Syrinx escaped Pan's lust when she was turned into a reed.
5. It was popularly believed that animals and plants on land had counterparts in the sea. This line describes the mind as innately possessing ideas, a concept of Platonic philosophy.

Annihilating all that's made
To a green thought in a green shade.

Here at the fountain's sliding foot,
50   Or at some fruit-tree's mossy root,
Casting the body's vest aside,
My soul into the boughs does glide:
There like a bird it sits and sings,
Then whets and combs its silver wings;
55   And, till prepared for longer flight,
Waves in its plumes the various light.

Such was that happy garden-state,
While man there walked without a mate:
After a place so pure and sweet,
60   What other help could yet be meet!
But 'twas beyond a mortal's share
To wander solitary there:
Two paradises 'twere in one
To live in paradise alone.

65   How well the skillful gardener drew
Of flowers and herbs this dial new;[6]
Where from above the milder sun
Does through a fragrant zodiac run;
And, as it works, th' industrious bee
70   Computes its time as well as we.[7]
How could such sweet and wholesome hours
Be reckoned but with herbs and flowers!

from **Upon Appleton House:**
To my Lord Fairfax[1]

1

Within this sober frame expect
Work of no foreign architect,
That unto caves the quarries drew,
And forests did to pastures hew,
5   Who of his great design in pain
Did for a model vault° his brain,   *arch*
Whose columns should so high be raised
To arch the brows that on them gazed.

2

Why should of all things man unruled
10   Such unproportioned dwellings build?
The beasts are by their dens expressed:
And birds contrive an equal nest;[2]

---

6. The garden is arranged as a floral sundial.
7. Computes its time: a pun on thyme.
1. Nun Appleton in Yorkshire was the home of Lord Fairfax, whose daughter Mary was tutored by Marvell. With
the dissolution of the monasteries, the estate, which had
once been a Cistercian priory, was taken over by the Fairfax family.
2. A nest in proportion to their own size.

The low-roofed tortoises do dwell
In cases fit of tortoise shell:

15   No creature loves an empty space;
Their bodies measure out their place.

3

But he, superfluously spread,
Demands more room alive than dead.
And in his hollow palace goes

20   Where winds as he themselves may lose;
What need of all this marble crust
T'impark the wanton mote of dust,
That thinks by breadth the world t'unite
Though the first builders failed in height?[3]

4

25   But all things are composèd here
Like Nature, orderly and near:
In which we the dimensions find
Of that more sober age and mind,
When larger-sizèd men did stoop

30   To enter at a narrow loop;
As practising, in doors so strait,
To strain themselves through heaven's gate.

5

And surely when the after age
Shall hither come in pilgrimage,

35   These sacred places to adore,
By Vere[4] and Fairfax trod before,
Men will dispute how their extent
Within such dwarfish confines went:
And some will smile at this, as well

40   As Romulus his bee-like cell.[5]

6

Humility alone designs
Those short but admirable lines,
By which, ungirt and unconstrained,
Things greater are in less contained.

45   Let others vainly strive t'immure°   *enclose*
The circle in the quadrature!
These holy mathematics can
In ev'ry figure equal man.[6]

7

Yet thus the laden house does sweat,

50   And scarce endures the Master great:
But where he comes the swelling hall

---

3. The builders of the Tower of Babel failed in their attempt to make it reach heaven.
4. Lady Fairfax.
5. Romulus, founder of Rome, was said to have lived in a small hut.
6. The circle symbolized perfection, and the square symbolized virtue and justice.

Stirs, and the square grows spherical;
More by his magnitude distressed,
Then he is by its straitness pressed:
55   And too officiously it slights
That in itself which him delights.

8

So honor better lowness bears,
Than that unwonted greatness wears:
Height with a certain grace does bend,
60   But low things clownishly ascend.
And yet what needs there here excuse,
Where everything does answer use?
Where neatness nothing can condemn,
Nor pride invent what to contemn?

9

65   A stately frontispiece of poor
Adorns without the open door:[7]
Nor less the rooms within commends
Daily new furniture of friends.
The house was built upon the place
70   Only as for a mark of grace;
And for an inn to entertain
Its lord a while, but not remain.

* * *

37

When in the east the morning ray
290   Hangs out the colors of the day,
The bee through these known alleys hums,
Beating the *dian*° with its drums.   *morning call*
Then flowers their drowsy eyelids raise,
Their silken ensigns° each displays,   *banners*
295   And dries its pan[8] yet dank with dew,
And fills its flask[9] with odors new.

38

These, as their governor goes by,
In fragrant volleys they let fly;
And to salute their governess
300   Again as great a charge they press:
None for the virgin nymph;[1] for she
Seems with the flowers a flower to be.
And think so still! though not compare
With breath so sweet, or cheek so fair.

39

305   Well shot ye firemen! Oh how sweet,
And round your equal fires do meet,

---

7. The poor waiting to receive alms.
8. Part of the musket lock.
9. Powder flask.

1. Mary Fairfax, Lord Fairfax's daughter, whom Marvell
was tutoring. She was between 12 and 14 at the time of
the poem.

Whose shrill report no ear can tell,
But echoes to the eye and smell.
See how the flowers, as at parade,
310   Under their colors stand displayed:
Each regiment in order grows,
That of the tulip, pink, and rose.

40

But when the vigilant patrol
Of stars walks round about the Pole,
315   Their leaves, that to the stalks are curled,
Seem to their staves the ensigns furled.
Then in some flower's belovèd hut
Each bee as sentinel is shut;
And sleeps so too: but, if once stirred,
320   She runs you through, or asks the word.

41

Oh thou, that dear and happy isle
The garden of the world ere while,
Thou paradise of four seas,
Which heaven planted us to please,
325   But, to exclude the world, did guard
With watery if not flaming sword;
What luckless apple did we taste,
To make us mortal, and thee waste?

42

Unhappy! shall we never more
330   That sweet militia restore,
When gardens only had their towers,
And all the garrisons were flowers,
When roses only arms might bear,
And men did rosy garlands wear?
335   Tulips, in several colors barred,
Were then the Switzers of our Guard.[2]

43

The gardener had the soldier's place,
And his more gentle forts did trace.
The nursery of all things green
340   Was then the only magazine.°   *storehouse*
The winter quarters were the stoves,
Where he the tender plants removes.
But war all this doth overgrow;
We ordnance° plant and powder sow.   *artillery*

44

345   And yet their walks one on the sod
Who, had it pleasèd him and God,
Might once have made our gardens spring

2. A reference to the black, yellow, and red stripes of the papal Swiss guards.

Fresh as his own and flourishing.
But he preferred to the Cinque Ports[3]
350 These five imaginary forts:
And, in those half-dry trenches, spanned°   *held in*
Power which the ocean might command.

45

For he did, with his utmost skill,
Ambition weed, but conscience till.
355 Conscience, that heaven-nursèd plant,
Which most our earthly gardens want.
A prickling leaf it bears, and such
As that which shrinks at every touch;
But flowers eternal, and divine,
360 That in the crowns of saints do shine.

46

The sight does from these bastions ply,
Th' invisible artillery;
And at proud Cawood Castle[4] seems
To point the battery of its beams.
365 As if it quarreled° in the seat   *criticized*
Th' ambition of its prelate great.
But o'er the meads below it plays,
Or innocently seems to gaze.

47

And now to the abyss I pass
370 Of that unfathomable grass,
Where men like grasshoppers appear,
But grasshoppers are giants there:
They, in their squeaking laugh, contemn°   *scorn*
Us as we walk more low than them:
375 And, from the precipices tall
Of the green spires, to us do call.

48

To see men through this meadow dive,
We wonder how they rise alive.
As, under water, none does know
380 Whether he fall through it or go.
But, as the mariners that sound,
And show upon their lead the ground,
They bring up flowers so to be seen,
And prove they've at the bottom been.

49

385 No scene that turns with engines strange
Does oft'ner then these meadows change.
For when the sun the grass hath vexed,
The tawny mowers enter next;

3. Five ports on the southeast coast of England.   4. Estate of the Archbishop of York.

Who seem like Israelites to be,
390   Walking on foot through a green sea.[5]
To them the grassy deeps divide,
And crowd a lane to either side.[6]

* * *

71

Thus I, easy philosopher,
Among the birds and trees confer:
And little now to make me wants
Or of the fowls, or of the plants.
565   Give me but wings as they, and I
Straight floating on the air shall fly:
Or turn me but, and you shall see
I was but an inverted tree.

72

Already I begin to call
570   In their most learned original:
And where I language want, my signs
The bird upon the bough divines;
And more attentive there doth sit
Than if she were with lime-twigs knit.
575   No leaf does tremble in the wind
Which I, returning, cannot find.

73

Out of these scattered sibyl's leaves[7]
Strange prophecies my fancy weaves:
And in one history consumes,
580   Like Mexique paintings, all the plumes.[8]
What Rome, Greece, Palestine, ere said
I in this light mosaic read.
Thrice happy he who, not mistook,
Hath read in Nature's mystic book.

74

585   And see how chance's better wit
Could with a mask my studies hit!
The oak leaves me embroider all,
Between which caterpillars crawl:
And ivy, with familiar trails,
590   Me licks, and clasps, and curls, and hales.
Under this antic° cope I move   *fantastic*
Like some great prelate° of the grove.   *bishop*

75

Then, languishing with ease, I toss
On pallets swoll'n of velvet moss;
595   While the wind, cooling through the boughs,

---

5. An allusion to the parting of the Red Sea in Exodus
14.21–31.
6. Create a crowd on either side to form a lane.
7. The Cumaean Sibyl was a prophetess who recorded her
predictions on leaves.
8. Feathers used to form "Mexique paintings."

Flatters with air my panting brows.
Thanks for my rest, ye mossy banks,
And unto you cool zephyrs,° thanks,   *mild west winds*
Who, as my hair, my thoughts too shed,
600   And winnow from the chaff my head.

76

How safe, methinks, and strong, behind
These trees have I encamped my mind;
Where beauty, aiming at the heart,
Bends in some tree its useless dart;
605   And where the world no certain shot
Can make, or me it toucheth not.
But I on it securely play,
And gall its horsemen all the day.

77

Bind me, ye woodbines, in your twines,
610   Curl me about, ye gadding vines,
And, oh, so close your circles lace,
That I may never leave this place:
But, lest your fetters prove too weak,
Ere I your silken bondage break,
615   Do you, O brambles, chain me too,
And courteous briars, nail me through.

78

Here in the morning tie my chain,
Where the two woods have made a lane;
While, like a guard on either side,
620   The trees before their Lord divide;
This, like a long and equal thread,
Betwixt two labyrinths does lead.
But, where the floods did lately drown,
There at the evening stake me down.

79

625   For now the waves are fallen and dried,
And now the meadows fresher dyed;
Whose grass, with moister color dashed,
Seems as green silks but newly washed.
No serpent new nor crocodile
630   Remains behind our little Nile;
Unless itself you will mistake,
Among these meads the only snake.

80

See in what wanton harmless folds
It everywhere the meadow holds;
635   And its yet muddy back doth lick,
Till as a crystal mirror slick;
Where all things gaze themselves, and doubt
If they be in it or without.

And for his shade which therein shines,
640   Narcissus-like, the sun too pines.[9]

81

Oh what a pleasure 'tis to hedge
My temples here with heavy sedge;
Abandoning my lazy side,
Stretched as a bank unto the tide;
645   Or to suspend my sliding foot
On the osier's° undermined root,   *willow's*
And in its branches tough to hang,
While at my lines the fishes twang!

82

But now away my hooks, my quills,
650   And angles, idle utensils.
The young Maria[1] walks tonight:
Hide trifling youth thy pleasures slight.
'Twere shame that such judicious eyes
Should with such toys a man surprise;
655   She that already is the law
Of all her sex, her age's awe.

83

See how loose Nature, in respect
To her, itself doth recollect;
And every thing so whisht° and fine,   *silent*
660   Starts forth with to its *bonne mine*.[2]
The sun himself, of her aware,
Seems to descend with greater care;
And lest she see him go to bed,
In blushing clouds conceals his head.

84

665   So when the shadows laid asleep
From underneath these banks do creep,
And on the river as it flows
With eben shuts° begin to close;   *black shutters*
The modest halcyon° comes in sight,   *kingfisher*
670   Flying betwixt the day and night;
And such an horror calm and dumb,
Admiring Nature does benumb.

85

The viscous air, wheres'e'er she fly,
Follows and sucks her azure dye;
675   The jellying stream compacts below,
If it might fix her shadow so;
The stupid fishes hang, as plain
As flies in crystal overta'en;
And men the silent scene assist,
680   Charmed with the sapphire-wingèd mist.

9. Narcissus fell in love with his own reflection in the
water and, in pining for it, was turned into a flower.

1. Mary Fairfax.
2. Good appearance.

86

Maria such, and so doth hush
The world, and through the evening rush.
No new-born comet such a train
Draws through the sky, nor star new-slain.[3]

685   For straight those giddy rockets fail,
Which from the putrid earth exhale,
But by her flames, in heaven tried,
Nature is wholly vitrified.°   *converted into glass*

87

'Tis she that to these gardens gave
690   That wondrous beauty which they have;
She straightness on the woods bestows;
To her the meadow sweetness owes;
Nothing could make the river be
So crystal pure but only she;
695   She yet more pure, sweet, straight, and fair,
Than gardens, woods, meads, rivers are.

88

Therefore what first she on them spent,
They gratefully again present:
The meadow, carpets where to tread;
700   The garden, flowers to crown her head;
And for a glass the limpid brook,
Where she may all her beauties look;
But, since she would not have them seen,
The wood about her draws a screen.

89

705   For she, to higher beauties raised,
Disdains to be for lesser praised.
She counts her beauty to converse
In all the languages as hers;
Nor yet in those herself employs
710   But for the wisdom, not the noise;
Nor yet that wisdom would affect,
But as 'tis heaven's dialect.

90

Blessed nymph! that couldst so soon prevent
Those trains by youth against thee meant;
715   Tears (watery shot that pierce the mind;)
And sighs (Love's cannon charg'd with wind;)
True praise (that breaks through all defense;)
And feigned complying innocence;
But knowing where this ambush lay,
720   She 'scaped the safe, but roughest way.

91

This 'tis to have been from the first
In a domestic heaven nursed,
Under the discipline severe

---

3. A shooting star.

Of Fairfax, and the starry Vere;
725 Where not one object can come nigh
But pure, and spotless as the eye;
And goodness doth itself entail
On females, if there want a male.

92

Go now fond sex that on your face
730 Do all your useless study place,
Nor once at vice your brows dare knit
Lest the smooth forehead wrinkled sit:
Yet your own face shall at you grin,
Thorough the black-bag of your skin;
735 When knowledge only could have filled
And virtue all those furrows tilled.

93

Hence she with graces more divine
Supplies beyond her sex the line;
And, like a sprig of mistletoe,
740 On the Fairfacian oak does grow;
Whence, for some universal good,
The priest shall cut the sacred bud;
While her glad parents most rejoice,
And make their destiny their choice.

94

745 Meantime, ye fields, springs, bushes, flowers,
Where yet she leads her studious hours,
(Till fate her worthily translates,
And find a Fairfax for our Thwaites)[4]
Employ the means you have by her,
750 And in your kind yourselves prefer;
That, as all virgins she precedes,
So you all woods, streams, gardens, meads.

95

For you Thessalian Tempe's Seat[5]
Shall now be scorned as obsolete;
755 Aranjuez, as less, disdain'd;
The Bel-Retiro as constrain'd;[6]
But name not the Idalian grove,[7]
For 'twas the seat of wanton love;
Much less the dead's Elysian Fields,
760 Yet nor to them your beauty yields.

96

'Tis not, what once it was, the world;
But a rude heap together hurled;
All negligently overthrown,
Gulfs, deserts, precipices, stone.
765 Your lesser world contains the same.
But in more decent order tame;

---

4. Piece of forest or waste land that has been cleared; also
a surname.
5. A vale in Thessaly that was celebrated as a place of
pleasure and love.
6. Spanish palaces known for their gardens.
7. Cyprus, a haunt of Venus.

You heaven's center, Nature's lap.
And paradise's only map.

97

But now the salmon-fishers moist
770   Their leathern boats begin to hoist;
    And, like Antipodes in shoes,[8]
    Have shod their heads in their canoes.
    How tortoise-like, but not so slow,
    These rational amphibii[9] go?
775   Let's in: for the dark hemisphere
    Does now like one of them appear.

An Horatian Ode Upon Cromwell's Return from Ireland[1]

The forward youth that would appear
Must now forsake his muses dear,
    Nor in the shadows sing
    His numbers[2] languishing.
5   'Tis time to leave the books in dust,
And oil th' unusèd armor's rust:
    Removing from the wall
    The corslet[3] of the hall.
So restless Cromwell could not cease
10   In the inglorious arts of peace,
    But through adventurous war
    Urgèd his active star.
And, like the three-forked lightning, first
Breaking the clouds where it was nursed,
15   Did thorough his own side
    His fiery way divide:[4]
For 'tis all one to courage high
The emulous or enemy;
    And with such to enclose
20   Is more than to oppose.
Then burning through the air he went,
And palaces and temples rent:
    And Caesar's head at last
    Did through his laurels blast.[5]
25   'Tis madness to resist or blame
The force of angry heaven's flame:
    And, if we would speak true,
    Much to the man is due,
Who, from his private gardens, where
30   He lived reservèd and austere,

8. Like those who dwell on the opposite side of the earth.
9. The salmon fishers are amphibii because they move on both land and water.
1. Cromwell returned from his military campaign in Ireland in May 1650. After General Fairfax resigned as commander of the parliamentary army because he refused to invade Scotland, Cromwell assumed his position and attacked the Scots. This poem was printed in the 1681 edition but then was canceled from printed copies until 1776. The influence of Horace's Odes (especially I. 35,

37; IV. 4, 5, 14, 15) surfaces in the poised dignity of the verse and its subtly ambiguous attitude toward power.
2. Conformity to a rhythmical pattern in verse or music.
3. Defensive armor covering the upper body.
4. Cromwell's overtaking his rivals in Parliament is described as an elemental force similar to the "three-forked lightning" of Zeus.
5. Although lightning was thought not to strike the laurel (symbolizing the royal crown), Cromwell had struck down Charles I (Caesar).

As if his highest plot
To plant the bergamot,[6]
Could by industrious valor climb
To ruin the great work of Time,
35   And cast the kingdom old
Into another mold;
Though justice against fate complain,
And plead the ancient rights in vain:
But those do hold or break,
40   As men are strong or weak.
Nature, that hateth emptiness,
Allows of penetration less:[7]
And therefore must make room
Where greater spirits come.
45   What field of all the Civil Wars,
Where his were not the deepest scars?
And Hampton[8] shows what part
He had of wiser art,
Where, twining subtle fears with hope,
50   He wove a net of such a scope,
That Charles himself might chase
To Carisbrooke's narrow case:
That thence the royal actor borne,
The tragic scaffold might adorn;
55   While round the armèd bands
Did clap their bloody hands.
He nothing common did or mean
Upon that memorable scene:
But with his keener eye
60   The axe's[9] edge did try;
Nor called the gods with vulgar spite
To vindicate his helpless right,
But bowed his comely head,
Down, as upon a bed.
65   This was that memorable hour
Which first assured the forcèd power.
So when they did design
The Capitol's first line,
A bleeding head where they begun,
70   Did fright the architects to run;
And yet in that the State
Foresaw it's happy fate.[1]
And now the Irish are ashamed
To see themselves in one year tamed:[2]

6. A pear known as the "prince's pear."
7. Nature abhors not only a vacuum but even more so the penetration of one body's space by another body.
8. Hampton Court where Charles I was held captive before his execution in 1649. He had fled to Carisbrooke Castle on the Isle of Wight, where he was betrayed to the Governor in 1647.
9. Marvell plays on the Latin "*acies*," the sharp edge of a sword, a keen glance, and the vanguard of battle.

1. In digging the foundations of the temple of Jupiter Capitolinum, the excavators found a human's head (*caput*), which was interpreted as prophesying that Rome should be the capitol of the Empire (see Livy, *Annals* I.55.6).
2. From August 1649 to his return to England in May 1650, Cromwell went on a savage military campaign that included the slaughter of Irish civilians.

75   So much one man can do,
          That does both act and know.
        They can affirm his praises best,
        And have, though overcome, confessed
          How good he is, how just,
80   And fit for highest trust.[3]
        Nor yet grown stiffer with command,
        But still in the Republic's hand:
          How fit he is to sway
          That can so well obey.[4]
85   He to the commons' feet presents
        A kingdom, for his first year's rents:
          And, what he may, forbears
          His fame to make it theirs:
        And has his sword and spoils ungirt,
90   To lay them at the public's skirt.
          So when the falcon high
          Falls heavy from the sky,
        She, having killed, no more does search,
        But on the next green bough to perch;
95   Where, when he first does lure,
          The falconer has her sure.
        What may not then our isle presume
        While victory his crest does plume!
          What may not others fear
100   If thus he crown each year!
        A Caesar he ere long to Gaul,
        To Italy an Hannibal,[5]
          And to all states not free
          Shall climactéric° be.   *period of change*
105   The Pict no shelter now shall find
        Within his particolored mind;
          But from this valor sad°   *severe*
          Shrink underneath the plaid;[6]
        Happy if in the tufted brake
110   The English hunter him mistake;
          Nor lay his hounds in near
          The Caledonian° deer.   *Scottish*
        But thou the wars' and fortune's son
        March indefatigably on;
115   And for the last effect
          Still keep thy sword erect:
        Besides the force it has to fright
        The spirits of the shady night,[7]
          The same arts that did gain
120   A power must it maintain.

3. An example of one of the many equivocal statements in this poem; of course, the Irish did not affirm Cromwell's greatness.
4. A saying attributed to the Athenian Solon the lawgiver.
5. Neither Caesar nor Hannibal gave freedom to peoples whose countries they invaded and conquered.

6. Marvell uses "Picts" the ancient name for the Scots, creating a play on *picti* (Latin: painted) and particolored.
7. There was an ancient tradition of dead spirits being frightened by raised swords (Homer, *Odyssey* 11; Virgil, *Aeneid* 6). The dead spirits referred to here include the dead in the wars in Ireland and England, including the king.

—·— ⚜ —·—

Katherine Philips
1631–1664

Idolized as the "Matchless Orinda" in her own day, Katherine Philips is now taking her place in the history of English verse after two centuries of neglect. During her lifetime, her work circulated in manuscript among a close network of friends. The first edition of her poems appeared posthumously in 1664. The second edition of 1667 was evidently a commercial success, since it was reprinted in 1669, 1678, and 1710. The next complete edition of her poems did not appear until 1994.

John Keats esteemed Philips's *To Mrs. Mary Awbrey at Parting* as an example of "real feminine Modesty"; today, by contrast, critics praise her poems to women friends as reminiscent of the ancient Greek Sappho's erotic lyrics. By imitating Donne's love lyrics in her poems to women, Philips poetically conceives of these friendships as no less world-changing, no less ennobling and enthralling, than Donne's romantic liaisons. Some of the best poets of her own day were able to appreciate her as a fellow poet rather than as Keats's romanticized ideal woman. Marvell paid tribute to her by subtly alluding to lines of her poetry in one of his greatest poems, *The Garden*. And Henry Vaughan insisted that "No laurel grows, but for [her] brow."

Katherine Philips's work was particularly important for other women writers. Philips's lyric poetry influenced such other early modern women poets as Aphra Behn and Anne Killigrew. Yet it is impossible to pigeonhole Philips as stereotypically feminine. She wrote on public and political themes as well as personal subjects, endowing traditional genres such as the parting poem, the elegy, and the epitaph, with a particular directness and clarity all her own.

Katherine Philips was born in London to a well-to-do Presbyterian family. Her father was a prosperous merchant, and her mother was the daughter of a Fellow of the Royal College of Physicians. Philips's father was wealthy enough to invest two hundred pounds for a thousand acres in Ulster, a scheme that was begun in 1642 by the Puritan Parliament but, ironically, not realized until the Restoration, when we find Katherine in Ireland pursuing lawsuits to obtain this land. As a girl, Katherine attended Mrs. Salmon's Presbyterian School, where she learned to love poetry and began to write verses. In 1646 her widowed mother married Sir Richard Philips, and the family moved to his castle in Wales. Philips herself married Sir Richard's kinsman James Philips, and they lived together for twelve years in the small Welsh town of Cardigan when not in London, where her husband served as Member of Parliament during the Interregnum.

However Presbyterian and Cromwellian were the associations of her family and marriage, she emerged after the Restoration as a complete Anglican. Not only did she write poetry against the regicide, such as *Upon the Double Murder of King Charles*, but she became a favorite author at court. She was encouraged to write poetry by her friend "Poliarchus," Sir Charles Cotterell, Master of Ceremonies in the Court of Charles II, who showed her poems to the royal family. An Anglo-Irish nobleman, the Earl of Orrery, encouraged her to complete a translation of Corneille's *Pompey* and actually produced and had the play printed in Dublin in 1663.

Katherine Philips developed friendships that became the theme of what most critics regard as her best poems. Perhaps the most intense of these friendships was that with Mrs. Anne Owen, the Lucasia of Philips's most passionate poems, several of which echo love poems by Donne. Her friend Sir Edward Dering, whom she called "the Noble Silvander," lamented Katherine Philips's death in recounting the extraordinary accomplishment of both her poetry and her life, which had attempted

> the most generous design . . . to unite all those of her acquaintance which she found worthy or desired to make so (among which later number she was pleased to give me a place)

into one society, and by the bands of friendship to make an alliance more firm than what nature, our country or equal education can produce.

Friendship in Emblem,
or the Seal,[1]

TO MY DEAREST LUCASIA[2]

The hearts thus intermixèd speak
A love that no bold shock can break;
For joined and growing, both in one,
Neither can be disturbed alone.

5 That means a mutual knowledge too;
For what is't either heart can do,
Which by its panting sentinel°   *guard*
It does not to the other tell?

That friendship hearts so much refines,
10 It nothing but itself designs:
The hearts are free from lower ends,
For each point to the other tends.

They flame, 'tis true, and several ways,
But still those flames do so much raise,
15 That while to either they incline
They yet are noble and divine.

From smoke or hurt those flames are free,
From grossness or mortality:
The hearts (like Moses bush presumed)[3]
20 Warmed and enlightened, not consumed.

The compasses that stand above
Express this great immortal Love;[4]
For friends, like them, can prove this true,
They are, and yet they are not, two.

25 And in their posture is expressed
Friendship's exalted interest:
Each follows where the other leans,
And what each does, the other means.

And as when one foot does stand fast,
30 And t'other circles seeks to cast,
The steady part does regulate
And make the wanderer's motion straight:

---

1. A symbolic picture, which appeared with a motto and a poem in such books as Whitney's *Choice of Emblems* (see Perspectives: Emblem, Style, and Metaphor). The central emblematic image of this poem is "the compasses" (line 21); another emblem is "those flames" (line 14). 2. Anne Owen, to whom many of Philips's poems are dedicated, was a neighbor of hers in Wales and a close

friend from 1651 until Philips's death. 3. See Exodus 3.2–5 for the burning bush through which the angel of the Lord appeared to and from which God called Moses. 4. Compare the image of the compasses here to the "twin compasses" in Donne's *A Valediction: Forbidding Mourning*, pages 1559–1560.

So friends are only two in this,
T'reclaim each other when they miss:
35   For whose'er will grossly fall,
Can never be a friend at all.

And as that useful instrument
For even lines was ever meant;
So friendship from good angels[5] springs,
40   To teach the world heroic things.

As these are found out in design
To rule and measure every line;
So friendship governs actions best,
Prescribing law to all the rest.

45   And as in nature nothing's set
So just as lines and numbers met;
So compasses for these being made,
Do friendship's harmony persuade.

And like to them, so friends may own
50   Extension, not division:
Their points, like bodies, separate;
But head, like souls, knows no such fate.

And as each part so well is knit,
That their embraces ever fit:
55   So friends are such by destiny,
And no third can the place supply.

There needs no motto to the seal:
But that we may the mine[6] reveal
To the dull eye, it was thought fit
60   That friendship only should be writ.

But as there is degrees of bliss,
So there's no friendship meant by this,
But such as will transmit to fame
Lucasia's and Orinda's name.

Upon the Double Murder of King Charles

in Answer to a Libelous Rhyme Made by V. P.[1]

I think not on the state, nor am concerned
Which way soever that great helm is turned,
But as that son whose father's danger nigh
Did force his native dumbness, and untie
5   The fettered organs: so here is a cause

---

5. Guardian spirits, with puns on angels, and *angeli*
(Latin), messengers.
6. A mass of gold, a store of plenty, as well as a pun on the
possessive pronoun meaning "my own" and perhaps also
on "mind."

1. Vavasor Powell, a Fifth Monarchist who believed that
Christ's second coming was imminent, and an ardent
Republican, whose verses on the murder of the king are
lost. According to Philips's poem, Powell argued that
Charles I had usurped God's power.

That will excuse the breach of nature's laws.[2]
Silence were now a sin: nay passion now
Wise men themselves for merit would allow.
What noble eye could see, (and careless pass)
10 The dying lion kicked by every ass?
Hath Charles so broke God's laws, he must not have
A quiet crown, nor yet a quiet grave?
Tombs have been sanctuaries; thieves lie here
Secure from all their penalty and fear.
15 Great Charles his double misery was this,
Unfaithful friends, ignoble enemies;
Had any heathen been this prince's foe,
He would have wept to see him injured so.
His title was his crime, they'd reason good
20 To quarrel at the right they had withstood.
He broke God's laws, and therefore he must die,
And what shall then become of thee and I?
Slander must follow treason; but yet stay,
Take not our reason with our king away.
25 Though you have seized upon all our defense,
Yet do not sequester° our common sense.   *excommunicate, confiscate*
But I admire not at this new supply:
No bounds will hold those who at scepters fly.
Christ will be King, but I ne'er understood,
30 His subjects built his kingdom up with blood,
(Except their own) or that he would dispense
With his commands, though for his own defense.
Oh! to what height of horror are they come,
Who dare pull down a crown, tear up a tomb![3]

On the Third of September, 1651[1]

As when the glorious magazine of light[2]
Approaches to his canopy of night,
He with new splendor clothes his dying rays,
And double brightness to his beams conveys;
5 As if to brave and check his ending fate,
Puts on his highest looks in 's lowest state;
Dressed in such terror as to make us all
Be anti-Persians,[3] and adore his fall;
Then quits the world, depriving it of day,
10 While every herb and plant does droop away:
So when our gasping English royalty
Perceived her period now was drawing nigh,
She summons her whole strength to give one blow,

---

2. Breaking the prohibition against women speaking on public affairs. See Margaret Tyler, Perspectives: Tracts on Women and Gender, page 1334, for a defense of woman's ability to write about war, traditionally considered only appropriate to male authors.
3. Possibly a reference to the unearthing of the regicides' bodies.

1. Cromwell defeated Charles II at the Battle of Worcester on this date.
2. The sun; a magazine is a storehouse for gunpowder.
3. Anti-sun, since the Persians were thought to worship the sun, and anti-monarchist, possibly with reference to Darius I, the Persian king who put down many revolts during his lifetime.

To raise her self, or pull down others too.
15 Big with revenge and hope, she now spake more
Of terror than in many months before;
And musters her attendants, or to save
Her from, or wait upon her to the grave:
Yet but enjoyed the miserable fate
20 Of setting majesty, to die in state.
    Unhappy Kings! who cannot keep a throne,
Nor be so fortunate to fall alone!
Their weight sinks others: Pompey could not fly,
But half the world must bear him company;[4]
25 Thus captive Sampson could not life conclude,
Unless attended with a multitude.[5]
Who'd trust to greatness now, whose food is air,
Whose ruin sudden, and whose end despair?
Who would presume upon his glorious birth,
30 Or quarrel for a spacious share of earth,
That sees such diadems° become thus cheap,   crowns
And heroes tumble in the common heap?
    O! give me virtue then, which sums up all,
And firmly stands when crowns and scepters fall.

To the Truly Noble, and Obliging Mrs. Anne Owen
(on My First Approaches)[1]

Madam,
As in a triumph conquerors admit
Their meanest captives to attend on it,[2]
Who, though unworthy, have the power confessed,
And justified the yielding of the rest:
5 So when the busy world (in hope t'excuse
Their own surprise) your conquests do peruse,
And find my name, they will be apt to say
Your charms were blinded, or else thrown away.
There is no honor got in gaining me,
10 Who am a prize not worth your victory.
But this will clear you, that 'tis general
The worst applaud what is admired by all.
But I have plots in't: for the way to be
Secure of fame to all posterity,
15 Is to obtain the honor I pursue,
To tell the world I was subdued by you.
And since in you all wonders common are,
Your votaries° may in your virtues share,   devoted admirers
While you by noble magic worth impart:

4. Caesar defeated Pompey at the battle of Pharsalus, where 15,000 of Pompey's men were killed. Afterward, Pompey fled to Egypt, where he was assassinated.
5. The blind Israelite hero Sampson tore down the temple at Gaza, thus killing both himself and his enemies (Judges 16).

1. Mrs. Anne Owen of Orielton, Wales, was Philips's close friend and the Lucasia of her poems; she was married to John Owen and was the heiress to the ancient seat of Presaddfed in Anglesey.
2. Here, "triumph" means military victory and the triumphal procession that announced it.

20   She that can conquer, can reclaim a heart.
Of this creation I shall not despair,
Since for your own sake it concerns your care:
For 'tis more honor that the world should know
You made a noble soul, than found it so.

To Mrs. Mary Awbrey at Parting[1]

I have examined, and do find,
    Of all that favor me,
There's none I grieve to leave behind
    But only, only thee.
5   To part with thee I needs must die,
Could parting separate thee and I.

But neither chance nor compliment
    Did element our love;
'Twas sacred sympathy was lent
10   Us from the choir above.
That friendship fortune did create,
Which fears a wound from time or fate.

Our changed and mingled souls are grown
    To such acquaintance now,
15 That if each would assume their own,
    Alas! we know not how.
We have each other so engrossed,
That each is in the union lost.

And thus we can no absence know,
20   Nor shall we be confined;
Our active souls will daily go
    To learn each other's mind.
Nay, should we never meet to sense,
Our souls would hold intelligence.[2]

25 Inspired with a flame divine,
    I scorn to court a stay;
For from the noble soul of thine
    I can ne'er be away.
But I shall weep when thou dost grieve;
30 Nor can I die whilst thou dost live.

By my own temper I shall guess
    At thy felicity,
And only like my happiness
    Because it pleaseth thee.
35 Our hearts at any time will tell
If thou, or I, be sick, or well.

---

1. Mrs. Mary Awbrey, one of Philips's classmates at Mrs. Salmon's school. Quoting the entire poem, John Keats praises it as an example of "real feminine Modesty" in a letter to J. H. Reynolds of 21 September 1817.

2. A Neoplatonic idea, that the souls would know each other not by physical contact but by spiritual communion. Compare Donne's A Valediction: Forbidding Mourning, pages 1559–1560.

All honor sure I must pretend,
 All that is good or great;
She that would be Rosania's[3] friend,
40 Must be at least complete.
If I have any bravery,
 'Tis cause I am so much of thee.

Thy leiger° soul in me shall lie,   *lighter*
 And all thy thoughts reveal;
45 Then back again with mine shall fly,
 And thence to me shall steal.
Thus still to one another tend;
Such is the sacred name of friend.

Thus our twin souls in one shall grow,
50 And teach the world new love;
Redeem the age and sex, and show
 A flame fate dares not move:
And courting death to be our friend,
Our lives together too shall end.

55 A dew shall dwell upon our tomb
 Of such a quality,
That fighting armies, thither come,
 Shall reconciled be.
We'll ask no epitaph, but say
60 Orinda and Rosania.

To My Excellent Lucasia, on Our Friendship.
17th. July 1651[1]

I did not live until this time
 Crowned my felicity,
When I could say without a crime,
 I am not thine, but thee.
5 This carcass breathed, and walked, and slept,
  So that the world believed
There was a soul the motions kept;
 But they were all deceived.
For as a watch by art is wound
10 To motion, such was mine:
But never had Orinda found
 A soul till she found thine;
Which now inspires, cures and supplies,
 And guides my darkened breast:
15 For thou art all that I can prize,
 My joy, my life, my rest.
Nor bridegroom's nor crowned conqueror's mirth
  To mine compared can be:

---

3. Rosania was the poetic name that Philips gave to her
friend Mary Awbrey.

1. Philips met her friend Anne Owen (called Lucasia) in
1651.

20   They have but pieces of this earth,
    I've all the world in thee.
   Then let our flame still light and shine,
    (And no bold fear control)
   As innocent as our design,
    Immortal as our soul.

The World

We falsely think it due unto our friends,
That we should grieve for their too early ends:
He that surveys the world with serious eyes,
And strips her from her gross and weak disguise,[1]
5 Shall find 'tis injury to mourn their fate;
He only dies untimely who dies late.
For if 'twere told to children in the womb,
To what a stage of mischief they must come;
Could they foresee with how much toil and sweat
10 Men court that gilded nothing, being great;
What pains they take not to be what they seem,
Rating their bliss by others' false esteem,
And sacrificing their content, to be
Guilty of grave and serious vanity;
15 How each condition hath its proper thorns,
And what one man admires, another scorns;
How frequently their happiness they miss,
And so far from agreeing what it is,
That the same person we can hardly find,
20 Who is an hour together in a mind;
Sure they would beg a period of their breath,
And what we call their birth would count their death.
Mankind is mad; for none can live alone,
Because their joys stand by comparison:
25 And yet they quarrel at society,
And strive to kill they know not whom, nor why.
We all live by mistake, delight in dreams,
Lost to ourselves, and dwelling in extremes;
Rejecting what we have, though ne'er so good,
30 And prizing what we never understood.
Compared to our boisterous inconstancy
Tempests are calm, and discords harmony.
Hence we reverse the world, and yet do find
The God that made can hardly please our mind.
35 We live by chance, and slip into events;
Have all of beasts except their innocence.
The soul, which no man's power can reach, a thing
That makes each woman man, each man a king,
Doth so much loose, and from its height so fall,
40 That some contend to have no soul at all.

---

1. The Platonic notion that the body is a covering for the soul.

'Tis either not observed, or at the best
By passion fought withall, by sin depressed.
Freedom of will (God's image) is forgot;
And if we know it, we improve it not.
45   Our thoughts, though nothing can be more our own,
Are still unguided, very seldom known.
Time 'scapes our hands as water in a sieve,
We come to die ere we begin to live.
Truth, the most suitable and noble prize,
50   Food of our spirits, yet neglected lies.
Errors and shadows are our choice, and we
Owe our perdition to our own decree.
If we search truth, we make it more obscure;
And when it shines, we can't the light endure.
55   For most men who plod on, and eat, and drink,
Have nothing less their business than to think;
And those few that enquire, how small a share
Of truth they find! how dark their notions are!
That serious evenness that calms the breast,
60   And in a tempest can bestow a rest,
We either not attempt, or else decline,
By every trifle snatched from our design.
(Others he must in his deceits involve,
Who is not true unto his own resolve.)
65   We govern not ourselves, but loose the reins,
Courting our bondage to a thousand chains;
And with as many slaveries content,
As there are tyrants ready to torment,
We live upon a rack, extended still
70   To one extreme, or both, but always ill.
For since our fortune is not understood,
We suffer less from bad than from the good.
The sting is better dressed and longer lasts,
As surfeits are more dangerous than fasts.
75   And to complete the misery to us,
We see extremes are still contiguous.
And as we run so fast from what we hate,
Like squibs on ropes,[2] to know no middle state;
So (outward storms strengthened by us) we find
80   Our fortune as disordered as our mind.
But that's excused by this, it doth its part;
A treacherous world befits a treacherous heart.
All ill's our own; the outward storms we loathe
Receive from us their birth, or sting, or both;
85   And that our vanity be past a doubt,
'Tis one new vanity to find it out.
Happy are they to whom God gives a grave,
And from themselves as from his wrath doth save.
'Tis good not to be born; but if we must,
90   The next good is, soon to return to dust:

---

2. A display of fireworks on a line.

When th'uncaged[3] soul, fled to eternity,
Shall rest, and live, and sing, and love, and see.
Here we but crawl and grope, and play and cry;[4]
Are first our own, then other's enemy:
95   But there shall be defaced both stain and score,
For time, and death, and sin shall be no more.[5]

The Development of English Prose

In the seventeenth century, English prose developed as a major language for both popular and learned texts. Such English prose texts as the *Geneva Bible* and Foxe's *Book of Martyrs* had been the most widely read texts of the sixteenth century. The King James Bible of 1611 brought a balanced rhythm and memorable phrasing to the language of the Church of England that would influence the poetry of the age as well. Pamphlets, both humorous and political, were popular, and the prose romance produced an early version of the entertainment that would later become the novel. Although Latin continued to be the language of academic discourse, such great philosophers as Francis Bacon and Thomas Hobbes began to use English for intellectual inquiry into science, education, and political theory. Though many of his prose works were in Latin, Milton made English an impassioned and incisive language for public debate in such prose masterpieces as *Areopagitica,* on freedom of speech, and *Reason of Church Government,* in defense of the principles of the Puritan Revolution. Even enormously learned authors such as Robert Burton could become popular authors by writing in English. Burton's *Anatomy of Melancholy*, with its meandering sentences that seem strangely fanciful to today's reader, was read as a mixture of medicine, entertainment, politics, and therapy.

Burton uses the Ciceronian, or Asian, style, which competed with the Senecan, or Attic, style in the early modern period. The Ciceronian style was characterized by *copia* (abundance), pleonasm (elegant restatement), and hypotaxis (complex sentence structure full of subordinated clauses). In contrast, the Senecan style was marked by brevity, broken rhythms, and parataxis (clauses of equal importance, which resulted in either short or loosely organized sentences). Not all authors neatly followed one or the other style. Sir Thomas Browne, for example, fuses the two in his skeptical writing, which contrasts strongly with the utopianism of Bacon. In his *Essays*, Francis Bacon was one of the first to reject the strictly Ciceronian model. The three editions of this work show Bacon refining his style for greater clarity and precision, as he strove to make English a language that could describe the material world empirically and would emphasize thought rather than style. Indeed, Bacon created the concise style that would dominate English prose even into this century, as adopted by such writing handbooks as Strunk and White's *The Elements of Style.*

❖❖❖

Francis Bacon
1561–1626

Commenting on his one and only lyric poem, an eleventh-hour political maneuver to help reconcile the rebellious Earl of Essex and the outraged Queen Elizabeth, Francis Bacon once wrote that he had to confess himself "not to be a poet." He was, however, a great essayist. In addition to being one of the most politically powerful men of his time, Bacon was one of the

---

3. Free from the body.
4. See 1 Corinthians 13.11–12.

5. See Revelation 21.4.

most powerful influences on the development of English prose style. He was a master of the terse and succinct Senecan style, if still an eclectic practitioner at times of the more elaborate Ciceronianism. Bacon was also a pioneer in scientific theory. When we think of such concepts as social progress through science or the scientific method for gathering exact empirical data, we are thinking of concepts that were promoted through the writing of Francis Bacon.

If Bacon was one of the most influential men in early modern England, he was also one of the most disgraced. Little did Bacon know at the time of his former patron Essex's trial for treason in 1601 that twenty years later, he would suffer his own political fall from grace. At age sixty, he had been in every Parliament since he entered the House of Commons at age twenty-three; he had held every important legal position in the kingdom—Solicitor General, Attorney General, and finally Lord Chancellor. Charged with bribery, Bacon was fined 40,000 pounds, disqualified from holding office, and sentenced to the Tower. Although he was released from these punishments, he spent the last five years of his life largely retired from the world of power and devoted to his writing.

Bacon was the first to use the word "essay" in English, a term from the French *essayer* (to try or attempt), coined by Michel de Montaigne in 1580 to describe his skeptical and introspective prose compositions. Bacon writes about topics that admit of more than one point of view, but his end is practical rather than speculative. Indeed, in the *Essays*, Bacon faults both Montaigne and the French in general for their lack of political effectiveness. The purpose of Bacon's *Essays* is more like that of Castiglione's *Courtier* or Machiavelli's *The Prince*. In a sense, all of these are how-to books, designed to instruct the reader in the political virtue of practical wisdom.

Bacon's *Essays* appeared in three different editions: 1597, 1612, and 1625. The first edition contained only ten essays and their style was extremely terse. He added forty-eight more essays in the later editions and revised the style of his earlier essays. Thinking that his Latin works would outlast those in English, Bacon translated the *Essays* into Latin. Bacon also wrote his major philosophical work in Latin; the *Novum Organum* (1620) was the basis for his new approach to the search for knowledge. At the same time, Bacon helped to make English a language capable of philosophical and scientific expression that would ultimately overtake Latin and help to promote the democratization of knowledge that he argued for in his *Advancement of Learning* (1605). Through his works, Bacon helped to define both the prose style and the ideology of modernity.

Of Truth[1]

"What is truth?" said jesting Pilate; and would not stay for an answer.[2] Certainly there be that delight in giddiness,[3] and count it a bondage to fix a belief; affecting free-will in thinking, as well as in acting. And though the sects of philosophers of that kind[4] be gone, yet there remain certain discoursing wits[5] which are of the same veins, though there be not so much blood in them as was in those of the ancients. But it is not only the difficulty and labor which men take in finding out of truth; nor again that when it is found it imposeth upon men's thoughts; that doth bring lies in favor; but a natural though corrupt love of the lie itself. One of the later school of the Grecians examineth the matter, and is at a stand[6] to think what should be in it, that men should love lies, where neither they make for pleasure, as with poets, nor for advantage, as with the merchant; but for the lie's sake. But I cannot tell: this same truth is a naked and open daylight, that doth not show the masks and mummeries and triumphs of the world half so stately and daintily as candle-lights. Truth may perhaps come to the price of a pearl, that showeth best by day; but it will not rise to the price of a diamond or carbuncle,[7] that showeth best in varied lights. A mixture of a

---

1. The first essay in the 1625 edition, from which all essays here, except the 1597 *Of Studies*, are taken.
2. According to John 18.38, Pilot dismissively asks Jesus this question during his trial.
3. Unsteadiness.

4. The ancient Greek Skeptics argued that there is no certain basis from which to know the truth.
5. Rationally arguing minds.
6. Is puzzled.
7. Ruby.

lie doth ever add pleasure. Doth any man doubt, that if there were taken out of men's minds vain opinions, flattering hopes, false valuations, imaginations as one would, and the like, but it would leave the minds of a number of men poor shrunken things, full of melancholy and indisposition, and unpleasing to themselves? One of the Fathers,[8] in great severity, called poesy *vinum daemonum*[9], because it filleth the imagination; and yet it is but with the shadow of a lie. But it is not the lie that passeth through the mind, but the lie that sinketh in and settleth in it, that doth the hurt, such as we spake of before. But howsoever these things are thus in men's depraved judgments and affections, yet truth, which only doth judge itself, teacheth that the inquiry of truth, which is the love-making or wooing of it, the knowledge of truth, which is the presence of it, and the belief of truth, which is the enjoying of it, is the sovereign good of human nature. The first creature of God, in the works of the days, was the light of the sense;[1] the last was the light of reason; and his sabbath work ever since, is the illumination of his Spirit. First he breathed light upon the face of the matter or chaos; then he breathed light into the face of man; and still he breatheth and inspireth light into the face of his chosen. The poet that beautified the sect that was otherwise inferior to the rest,[2] saith yet excellently well: "It is a pleasure to stand upon the shore, and to see ships tossed upon the sea; a pleasure to stand in the window of a castle, and to see a battle and the adventures thereof below; but no pleasure is comparable to the standing upon the vantage ground of truth" (a hill not to be commanded,[3] and where the air is always clear and serene), "and to see the errors, and wanderings, and mists, and tempests, in the vale below": so always that this prospect be with pity, and not with swelling or pride. Certainly, it is heaven upon earth, to have a man's mind move in charity, rest in providence, and turn upon the poles of truth.

To pass from theological and philosophical truth, to the truth of civil business, it will be acknowledged even by those that practise it not, that clear and round dealing is the honor of man's nature, and that mixture of falsehood is like allay in coin of gold and silver, which may make the metal work the better, but it embaseth it.[4] For these winding and crooked courses are the goings of the serpent;[5] which goeth basely upon the belly, and not upon the feet. There is no vice that doth so cover a man with shame as to be found false and perfidious. And therefore Montaigne saith prettily, when he inquired the reason, why the word of the lie should be such a disgrace and such an odious charge? Saith he, "If it be well weighed, to say that a man lieth, is as much to say as that he is brave towards God and a coward towards men."[6] For a lie faces God, and shrinks from man. Surely the wickedness of falsehood and breach of faith cannot possibly be so highly expressed, as in that it shall be the last peal to call the judgments of God upon the generations of men, it being foretold, that when Christ cometh, he shall not "find faith upon the earth."[7]

Of Marriage and Single Life

He that hath wife and children hath given hostages to fortune; for they are impediments to great enterprises, either of virtue or mischief. Certainly the best works, and of greatest merit for the public, have proceeded from the unmarried or childless men,

---

8. Early Christian theologians.
9. Devil's wine.
1. "And God said, Let there be light" (Genesis 1.3).
2. Bacon thought that the Epicurean belief that pleasure is the greatest good was inferior. See Lucretius, *On the Nature of Things* 2.1–13.

3. Captured.
4. Debases it.
5. The devil.
6. *Essays* 2.18.
7. Luke 18.8.

which both in affection and means have married and endowed the public. Yet it were great reason that those that have children should have greatest care of future times, unto which they know they must transmit their dearest pledges. Some there are, who though they lead a single life, yet their thoughts do end with themselves, and account future times impertinences.[1] Nay, there are some other that account wife and children but as bills of charges. Nay more, there are some foolish rich covetous men that take a pride in having no children, because they may be thought so much the richer. For perhaps they have heard some talk, "Such an one is a great rich man," and another except to it, "Yea, but he hath a great charge of children"; as if it were an abatement to his riches. But the most ordinary cause of a single life is liberty, especially in certain self-pleasing and humorous[2] minds, which are so sensible of every restraint, as they will go near to think their girdles and garters to be bonds and shackles. Unmarried men are best friends, best masters, best servants, but not always best subjects, for they are light to run away, and almost all fugitives are of that condition. A single life doth well with churchmen, for charity will hardly water the ground where it must first fill a pool. It is indifferent for judges and magistrates; for if they be facile[3] and corrupt, you shall have a servant five times worse than a wife. For soldiers, I find the generals commonly in their hortatives[4] put men in mind of their wives and children; and I think the despising of marriage amongst the Turks maketh the vulgar soldier more base. Certainly wife and children are a kind of discipline of humanity; and single men, though they may be many times more charitable, because their means are less exhaust,[5] yet, on the other side, they are more cruel and hardhearted (good to make severe inquisitors), because their tenderness is not so oft called upon. Grave natures, led by custom, and therefore constant, are commonly loving husbands, as was said of Ulysses, *vetulam suam praetulit immortalitati*:[6] Chaste women are often proud and froward,[7] as presuming upon the merit of their chastity. It is one of the best bonds both of chastity and obedience in the wife, if she think her husband wise, which she will never do if she find him jealous. Wives are young men's mistresses, companions for middle age, and old men's nurses. So as a man may have a quarrel[8] to marry when he will. But yet he was reputed one of the wise men, that made answer to the question, when a man should marry: "A young man not yet, an elder man not at all."[9] It is often seen that bad husbands have very good wives; whether it be that it raiseth the price of their husband's kindness when it comes, or that the wives take a pride in their patience. But this never fails, if the bad husbands were of their own choosing, against their friend's consent; for then they will be sure to make good their own folly.

Of Superstition

It were better to have no opinion of God at all, than such an opinion as is unworthy of him. For the one is unbelief, the other is contumely:[1] and certainly superstition is the reproach of the deity. Plutarch saith well to that purpose: "Surely" (saith he) "I had rather a great deal men should say there was no such man at all as Plutarch, than that they should say that there was one Plutarch that would eat his children as soon

1. Irrelevant matters.
2. Flighty.
3. Easily led.
4. Speeches to troops before battle.
5. Used up.
6. He preferred his old wife to immortality. See *Odyssey* 5 for the story of how Odysseus chose to return home to his

wife and son and accept death rather than live forever with the nymph Calypso.
7. Perverse.
8. Excuse.
9. Quoting Thales, one of the sages—unmarried—of ancient Greece.
1. Contempt.

as they were born," as the poets speak of Saturn.[2] And as the contumely is greater towards God, so the danger is greater towards men. Atheism leaves a man to sense, to philosophy, to natural piety, to laws, to reputation, all which may be guides to an outward moral virtue, though religion were not; but superstition dismounts all these, and erecteth an absolute monarchy in the minds of men. Therefore atheism did never perturb states; for it makes men wary of themselves, as looking no further: and we see the times inclined to atheism (as the time of Augustus Caesar) were civil times.[3] But superstition hath been the confusion of many states, and bringeth in a new *primum mobile*, that ravisheth all the spheres of government.[4] The master of superstition is the people; and in all superstition wise men follow fools; and arguments are fitted to practice, in a reversed order. It was gravely said by some of the prelates in the council of Trent, where the doctrine of the schoolmen bare great sway, "that the schoolmen[5] were like astronomers, which did feign eccentrics and epicycles, and such engines of orbs, to save the phaenomena; though they knew there were no such things;"[6] and in like manner, that the schoolmen had framed a number of subtle and intricate axioms and theorems, to save the practice of the church. The causes of superstition are, pleasing and sensual rites and ceremonies; excess of outward and pharisaical holiness;[7] over-great reverence of traditions, which cannot but load the church; the stratagems of prelates for their own ambition and lucre; the favoring too much of good intentions, which openeth the gate to conceits[8] and novelties; the taking an aim at divine matters by human, which cannot but breed mixture of imaginations: and, lastly, barbarous times, especially joined with calamities and disasters. Superstition, without a veil, is a deformed thing; for as it addeth deformity to an ape to be so like a man, so the similitude of superstition to religion makes it the more deformed. And as wholesome meat corrupteth to little worms, so good forms and orders corrupt into a number of petty observances. There is a superstition in avoiding superstition, when men think to do best if they go furthest from the superstition formerly received; therefore care would be had that (as it fareth in ill purgings) the good be not taken away with the bad, which commonly is done when the people is the reformer.[9]

Of Plantations[1]

Plantations are amongst ancient, primitive, and heroical works. When the world was young it begat more children; but now it is old it begets fewer: for I may justly account new plantations to be the children of former kingdoms. I like a plantation in a pure soil; that is, where people are not displanted to the end to plant in others. For else it is rather an extirpation than a plantation.[2] Planting of countries is like planting of woods; for you must make account to leese[3] almost twenty years profit, and

2. Saturn, the Roman god of time, who ate his children. Bacon refers to Plutarch's *Of Superstition*.
3. The Roman emperor Augustus's rule was peaceful. Atheism, in the early modern period could describe any belief that was not Christian or that did not agree with one's own.
4. The *primum mobile* (prime mover) controlled the motions of the other spheres.
5. Medieval scholastic philosophers.
6. "To save the phenomena" means to account for appearances. Ptolemaic astronomy, based on the mistaken geocentric theory, had many inconsistencies to explain.
7. Like the Pharisees, an ancient Jewish sect, who stressed adherence to the letter of the law and believed that this proved their spiritual superiority.
8. Fanciful notions.
9. Bacon refers to the radically antiritualistic Puritans.
1. Settlements of farmers in colonized territory. Classical and Renaissance authors discussed the pros and cons of different methods of colonization, including both armed garrisons and plantations.
2. In the 17th century, plantations of Scotts Presbyterians in the North of Ireland and of the English in North America were established on land confiscated from native inhabitants.
3. Lose.

expect your recompense in the end. For the principal thing that hath been the destruction of most plantations hath been the base and hasty drawing of profit in the first years. It is true, speedy profit is not to be neglected, as far as may stand[4] with the good of the plantation, but no further. It is a shameful and unblessed thing to take the scum of people, and wicked condemned men, to be the people with whom you plant;[5] and not only so, but it spoileth the plantation, for they will ever live like rogues, and not fall to work, but be lazy, and do mischief, and spend victuals, and be quickly weary, and then certify over[6] to their country to the discredit of the plantation. The people wherewith you plant ought to be gardeners, ploughmen, laborers, smiths, carpenters, joiners,[7] fishermen, fowlers, with some few apothecaries, surgeons, cooks, and bakers. In a country of plantation, first look about what kind of victual the country yields of itself to hand, as chestnuts, walnuts, pineapples, olives, dates, plums, cherries, wild honey, and the like, and make use of them. Then consider what victual or esculent[8] things there are, which grow speedily, and within the year; as parsnips, carrots, turnips, onions, radish, artichokes of Jerusalem, maize, and the like. For wheat, barley, and oats, they ask too much labor; but with peas and beans you may begin, both because they ask less labor, and because they serve for meat[9] as well as for bread. And of rice likewise cometh a great increase, and it is a kind of meat. Above all, there ought to be brought store of biscuit, oatmeal, flour, meal, and the like, in the beginning, till bread may be had. For beasts, or birds, take chiefly such as are least subject to diseases, and multiply fastest; as swine, goats, cocks, hens, turkeys, geese, house-doves, and the like. The victual in plantations ought to be expended almost as in a besieged town; that is, with certain allowance. And let the main part of the ground employed to gardens or corn be to a common stock; and to be laid in, and stored up, and then delivered out in proportion; besides some spots of ground that any particular person will manure[1] for his own private. Consider likewise what commodities the soil where the plantation is doth naturally yield, that they may some way help to defray the charge of the plantation, (so it be not, as was said, to the untimely prejudice of the main business,) as it hath fared with tobacco in Virginia. Wood commonly aboundeth but too much; and therefore timber is fit to be one. If there be iron ore, and streams whereupon to set the mills, iron is a brave[2] commodity, where wood aboundeth. Making of bay-salt,[3] if the climate be proper for it, would be put in experience. Growing silk likewise, if any be, is a likely commodity. Pitch and tar, where store of firs and pines are, will not fail. So drugs and sweet woods, where they are, cannot but yield great profit. Soap-ashes[4] likewise, and other things that may be thought of. But moil[5] not too much under ground; for the hope of mines is very uncertain, and useth to make the planters lazy in other things.

For government, let it be in the hands of one, assisted with some counsel; and let them have commission to exercise martial laws, with some limitation. And above all, let men make that profit of being in the wilderness, as they have God always, and his service, before their eyes. Let not the government of the plantation depend upon too many counselors and undertakers[6] in the country that planteth,

---

4. Accord.
5. Convicted criminals were brought to the English colonies as indentured servants.
6. Send reports home.
7. Finish carpenters.
8. Edible.
9. For a main course.
1. Enrich, cultivate.

2. Splendid.
3. Bay salt was made from evaporating seawater.
4. Ashes used in making soap.
5. Work hard.
6. The term "undertakers" was first used to describe those who held crown lands and attempted to meet the requirements for plantation in Ireland; more generally, farm managers.

but upon a temperate number; and let those be rather noblemen and gentlemen, than merchants; for they look ever to the present gain. Let there be freedom from custom,[7] till the plantation be of strength; and not only freedom from custom, but freedom to carry their commodities where they may make their best of them, except there be some special cause of caution. Cram not in people, by sending too fast company after company; but rather harken how they waste,[8] and send supplies proportionably; but so as the number may live well in the plantation, and not by surcharge[9] be in penury.

It hath been a great endangering to the health of some plantations, that they have built along the sea and rivers, in marish[1] and unwholesome grounds. Therefore, though you begin there, to avoid carriage and other like discommodities, yet build still rather upwards from the streams, than along. It concerneth likewise the health of the plantation that they have good store of salt with them, that they may use it in their victuals when it shall be necessary. If you plant where savages are, do not only entertain them with trifles and jingles, but use them justly and graciously, with sufficient guard nevertheless; and do not win their favor by helping them to invade their enemies, but for their defense it is not amiss; and send oft of them over to the country that plants, that they may see a better condition than their own, and commend it when they return. When the plantation grows to strength, then it is time to plant with women as well as with men, that the plantation may spread into generations, and not be ever pieced[2] from without. It is the sinfullest thing in the world to forsake or destitute a plantation once in forwardness; for besides the dishonor, it is the guiltiness of blood of many commiserable[3] persons.

Of Studies
[VERSION OF 1597]

Studies serve for pastimes, for ornaments and for abilities. Their chief use for pastime is in privateness and retiring; for ornament is in discourse, and for abilities is in judgment. For expert[1] men can execute, but learned men are fittest to judge or censure.

¶ To spend too much time in them is sloth, to use them too much for ornament is affectation: to make judgment wholly by their rules is the humor[2] of a scholar. ¶ They perfect nature, and are perfected by experience. ¶ Crafty men contemn[3] them, simple men admire them, wise men use them: For they teach not their own use, but that is a wisdom without them:[4] and above them won by observation. ¶ Read not to contradict, nor to believe, but to weigh and consider. ¶ Some books are to be tasted, others to be swallowed, and some few to be chewed and digested: That is, some books are to be read only in parts; others to be read, but cursorily;[5] and some few to be read wholly and with diligence and attention. ¶ Reading maketh a full man, conference[6] a ready man, and writing an exact man. And therefore if a man write little, he had need have a great memory, if he confer little, he had need have a present wit, and if he read little, he had need have much cunning, to seem to know

---

7. Import taxes.
8. Decline in number.
9. Overburden in population.
1. Swampy.
2. Penetrated.
3. Pitiable.
1. Experienced.

2. Fixed habit.
3. The original reads "continue," corrected by pen in the British Museum copy to "contemn."
4. Knowledge must be used outside of the books that convey it.
5. Quickly without care.
6. Discussion.

that he doth not. ¶ Histories make men wise, Poets witty:[7] the Mathematics subtle, natural Philosophy deep: Moral grave, Logic and Rhetoric able to contend.

Of Studies
[VERSION OF 1625]

Studies serve for delight, for ornament, and for ability. Their chief use for delight is in privateness and retiring; for ornament, is in discourse; and for ability, is in the judgment and disposition of business. For expert[1] men can execute, and perhaps judge of particulars, one by one; but the general counsels, and the plots and marshalling of affairs, come best from those that are learned. To spend too much time in studies is sloth; to use them too much for ornament is affectation; to make judgment wholly by their rules is the humor[2] of a scholar. They perfect nature, and are perfected by experience; for natural abilities are like natural plants, that need pruning by study; and studies themselves do give forth directions too much at large, except they be bounded in by experience. Crafty men contemn studies, simple men admire them, and wise men use them; for they teach not their own use; but that is a wisdom without them,[3] and above them, won by observation. Read not to contradict and confute; nor to believe and take for granted; nor to find talk and discourse; but to weigh and consider. Some books are to be tasted, others to be swallowed, and some few to be chewed and digested; that is, some books are to be read only in parts; others to be read, but not curiously;[4] and some few to be read wholly, and with diligence and attention. Some books also may be read by deputy, and extracts made of them by others; but that would be only in the less important arguments, and the meaner sort of books; else distilled books are like common distilled waters,[5] flashy things. Reading maketh a full man; conference[6] a ready man; and writing an exact man. And therefore, if a man write little, he had need have a great memory; if he confer little, he had need have a present wit: and if he read little, he had need have much cunning, to seem to know that he doth not. Histories make men wise; poets witty;[7] the mathematics subtle; natural philosophy deep; moral grave; logic and rhetoric able to contend. *Abeunt studia in mores*.[8] Nay, there is no stond[9] or impediment in the wit, but may be wrought out by fit studies, like as diseases of the body may have appropriate exercises. Bowling is good for the stone and reins;[1] shooting for the lungs and breast; gentle walking for the stomach; riding for the head; and the like. So if a man's wit be wandering, let him study the mathematics; for in demonstrations, if his wit be called away never so little, he must begin again. If his wit be not apt to distinguish or find differences, let him study the schoolmen; for they are *cumini sectores*.[2] If he be not apt to beat over matters and to call up one thing to prove and illustrate another, let him study the lawyers' cases. So every defect of the mind may have a special receipt.[3]

---

7. Ingenious.
1. Experienced.
2. Fixed habit.
3. Knowledge must be used outside of the books that convey it.
4. With interest.
5. Ineffective herbal remedies.
6. Discussion.
7. Imaginative, ingenious.

8. Studies lead to ways of life (Ovid, *Heroides* 15.13).
9. Obstacle.
1. The gall bladder and kidneys.
2. "Dividers of cuminseed," or hair-splitters. The schoolmen are the medieval scholastic philosophers who Bacon thought were more concerned with the abstract logic of an argument than with its practical ramifications.
3. Remedy.

The King James Bible

Many earlier English translations of the Bible prepared the way for the King James Bible of 1611. As early as the late fourteenth century, the popular religious reformer John Wycliff had rendered the Latin of the Vulgate into Middle English, and in the following century the Lollards used his translation. With the Reformation, translation became both more crucial and more dangerous—crucial because one of the chief principles of the Reformation was the need for the individual to read Scripture directly; dangerous because individual readings could conflict with church authority and the authority of the state.

In the case of William Tyndale, translation of the Bible into English led to death. The first Englishman to translate the Bible directly from Hebrew and Greek in accord with humanist principles, Tyndale had to go the Continent to work on and publish his New Testament (1525–1526). When copies of it entered England, the bishops suppressed them. He then angered Henry VIII by condemning his divorce in *The Practice of Prelates* (1530). Tyndale was ultimately seized in Antwerp and burned at the stake for heresy.

Soon after Tyndale's Bible came a translation by Miles Coverdale. Then Tyndale's and Coverdale's translations were fused in the Great Bible (1540), issued as the official version in English after Henry VIII's break from Roman Catholicism. Later, the Bishop's Bible (1568), which also reworked Tyndale's translation, was meant to stand for the Elizabethan religious compromise—neither too Catholic nor too Puritan—and against the strict Calvinism of the Geneva Bible (1560). The translation of the Protestant exiles, who left England in the reign of Catholic Queen Mary in search of religious freedom, the Geneva Bible was particularly controversial because of its marginal commentary that interprets biblical history as prophetic of the judgment of God on churches, kings, and nations.

The King James Bible, or Authorized Version, of 1611 was compiled by a learned committee of forty-seven different humanist scholars and theologians, headed by Lancelot Andrews. Much of the phraseology of the Authorized Version comes from Tyndale's translation. The language of the King James Bible is distinguished by its elegant variation, its direct and memorable phrasing, and its grave and sonorous cadences. Echoes of this language can be heard throughout seventeenth-century prose and poetry, especially in Milton's *Paradise Lost*. Particularly important for Milton's great epic are the stories of the creation and fall in the second and third chapters of Genesis, here printed in their entirety.

from The King James Bible

from *Genesis*

CHAPTER 2

Thus the heavens and the earth were finished, and all the host of them.

2 And on the seventh day God ended his work which he had made; and he rested on the seventh day from all his work which he had made.

3 And God blessed the seventh day, and sanctified it: because that in it he had rested from all his work which God created and made.

4 ¶These *are*[1] the generations of the heavens and of the earth when they were created, in the day that the LORD God made the earth and the heavens,

5 And every plant of the field before it was in the earth, and every herb of the field before it grew: for the LORD God had not caused it to rain upon the earth, and *there was* not a man to till the ground.

---

1. Concerned to reflect the Hebrew original as accurately as possible, the translators italicize words that are needed in English but not present in Hebrew.

6 But there went up a mist from the earth, and watered the whole face of the ground.

7 And the LORD God formed man *of* the dust of the ground, and breathed into his nostrils the breath of life; and man became a living soul.

8 ¶And the LORD God planted a garden eastward in Ē'dĕn;[2] and there he put the man whom he had formed.

9 And out of the ground made the LORD God to grow every tree that is pleasant to the sight, and good for food; the tree of life also in the midst of the garden, and the tree of knowledge of good and evil.

10 And a river went out of Ē'dĕn to water the garden; and from thence it was parted, and became into four heads.

11 The name of the first *is* Pī'sŏn: that *is* it which compasseth the whole land of Hăv'ĭläh, where *there is* gold;

12 And the gold of that land *is* good: there *is* bdellium[3] and the onyx stone.

13 And the name of the second river *is* Gī'hŏn: the same *is* it that compasseth the whole land of Ēthĭō'pĭa.

14 And the name of the third river *is* Hĭd'ĕkĕl: that *is* it which goeth toward the east of Ăssўrĭă. And the fourth river *is* Eūphrā'tēs.

15 And the LORD God took the man, and put him into the garden of Ē'dĕn to dress it and to keep it.

16 And the LORD God commanded the man, saying, Of every tree of the garden thou mayest freely eat:

17 But of the tree of the knowledge of good and evil, thou shalt not eat of it: for in the day that thou eatest thereof thou shalt surely die.

18 ¶And the LORD God said, *It is* not good that the man should be alone; I will make him an help meet for him.

19 And out of the ground the LORD God formed every beast of the field, and every fowl of the air; and brought *them* unto Ăd'ăm to see what he would call them: and whatsoever Ăd'ăm called every living creature, that *was* the name thereof.

20 And Ăd'ăm gave names to all cattle, and to the fowl of the air, and to every beast of the field; but for Ăd'ăm there was not found an help meet for him.

21 And the LORD God caused a deep sleep to fall upon Ăd'ăm, and he slept: and he took one of his ribs, and closed up the flesh instead thereof;

22 And the rib, which the LORD God had taken from man, made he a woman, and brought her unto the man.

23 And Ăd'ăm said, This *is* now bone of my bones, and flesh of my flesh: she shall be called Woman, because she was taken out of Man.

24 Therefore shall a man leave his father and his mother, and shall cleave unto his wife: and they shall be one flesh.

25 And they were both naked, the man and his wife, and were not ashamed.

CHAPTER 3

Now the serpent was more subtil than any beast of the field which the LORD God had made. And he said unto the woman, Yea, hath God said, Ye shall not eat of every tree of the garden?

2 And the woman said unto the serpent, We may eat of the fruit of the trees of the garden:

---

2. To facilitate reading by individuals and families, the translators indicate how to pronounce all names.

3. A Latin word taken from the Greek to translate the Hebrew *b'dolakh,* a precious stone, pearl.

3 But of the fruit of the tree which *is* in the midst of the garden, God hath said, Ye shall not eat of it, neither shall ye touch it, lest ye die.

4 And the serpent said unto the woman, Ye shall not surely die:

5 For God doth know that in the day ye eat thereof, then your eyes shall be opened, and ye shall be as gods, knowing good and evil.

6 And when the woman saw that the tree *was* good for food, and that it *was* pleasant to the eyes, and a tree to be desired to make *one* wise, she took of the fruit thereof, and did eat, and gave also unto her husband with her; and he did eat.

7 And the eyes of them both were opened, and they knew that they *were* naked; and they sewed fig leaves together, and made themselves aprons.

8 And they heard the voice of the Lord God walking in the garden in the cool of the day: and Ăd'ăm and his wife hid themselves from the presence of the Lord God amongst the trees of the garden.

9 And the Lord God called unto Ăd'ăm and said unto him, Where *art* thou?

10 And he said, I heard thy voice in the garden, and I was afraid, because I *was* naked; and I hid myself.

11 And he said, Who told thee that thou *wast* naked? Hast thou eaten of the tree, whereof I commanded thee that thou shouldest not eat?

12 And the man said, The woman whom thou gavest *to be* with me, she gave me of the tree, and I did eat.

13 And the Lord God said unto the woman, What *is* this *that* thou hast done? And the woman said, The serpent beguiled me, and I did eat.

14 And the Lord God said unto the serpent, Because thou hast done this, thou *art* cursed above all cattle, and above every beast of the field; upon thy belly shalt thou go, and dust shalt thou eat all the days of thy life:

15 And I will put enmity between thee and the woman, and between thy seed and her seed; it shall bruise thy head, and thou shalt bruise his heel.

16 Unto the woman he said, I will greatly multiply thy sorrow and thy conception; in sorrow thou shalt bring forth children; and thy desire *shall be* to thy husband, and he shall rule over thee.

17 And unto Ăd'ăm he said, Because thou hast hearkened unto the voice of thy wife, and hast eaten of the tree, of which I commanded thee, saying, Thou shalt not eat of it: cursed *is* the ground for thy sake; in sorrow shalt thou eat *of* it all the days of thy life;

18 Thorns also and thistles shall it bring forth to thee; and thou shalt eat the herb of the field;

19 In the sweat of thy face shalt thou eat bread, till thou return unto the ground; for out of it wast thou taken: for dust thou *art*, and unto dust shalt thou return.

20 And Ăd'ăm called his wife's name Ēve; because she was the mother of all living.

21 Unto Ăd'ăm also and to his wife did the Lord God make coats of skins, and clothed them.

22 ¶And the Lord God said, Behold, the man is become as one of us, to know good and evil: and now, lest he put forth his hand, and take also of the tree of life, and eat, and live for ever:

23 Therefore the Lord God sent him forth from the garden of Eden, to till the ground from whence he was taken.

24 So he drove out the man; and he placed at the east of the garden of Ē'dĕn Chĕr'ūbĭms, and a flaming sword which turned every way, to keep the way of the tree of life.

—◆— ⚓ —◆—

Lady Mary Wroth
1586–1640

Lady Mary Wroth's *Urania* is the first work of original prose fiction by an Englishwoman. The book was first published in 1621 at a time when the controversy over women was raging and when one of the first great Continental novels, Cervantes's *Don Quixote*, had recently been translated into English by Thomas Shelton (part 1, 1612; part 2, 1620). Some of the women characters in *Urania* are not only central protagonists but also unconventional heroines who go beyond the confines of conventional gender roles. Similarly, Wroth's treatment of the romance genre in some ways exceeds the limits of the conventional romance, propelled by stereotypically feminine desire. In Book Four, for instance, English ladies simply walk away from the Prince of Florence's praises rather than swoon over them. Another bit of satire involves Pelarina, "a distressed creature in the habits of a pilgrim," who like Quixote is obsessed with an ideal of perfect love that is completely disjointed from any real love object. The first episode of the *Urania*, included here, recalls the beginning of her uncle Sir Philip Sidney's *Arcadia*, in which the shepherds mourn for Urania, yet Wroth's Urania is not a passive object but actively helps others and embarks on her own quest to discover her identity.

The text is in two parts; one part corresponds to the published version of 1621, the other to a unique manuscript in the author's hand at the Newberry Library in Chicago. The publishers entered *Urania* in the Stationer's Register in 1621; it is not clear whether or not they had the author's permission. Once in print, the book provoked attacks from powerful courtiers, who did not like to see their foibles fictionalized. In her defense, Wroth claimed that she never intended to have her work published. This may have been simply an aristocratic disclaimer against the taint of publication, but the remark may also carry a concern with the prohibition against women's publishing. Although Wroth asked for a King's warrant to recall the book, no record of such a warrant exists.

For more on Wroth, see her principal listing, page 1571.

from The Countess of Montgomery's Urania
from *Book 1*

When the spring began to appear like the welcome messenger of summer, one sweet (and in that more sweet) morning, after Aurora[1] had called all careful eyes to attend the day, forth came the fair shepherdess Urania,[2] (fair indeed; yet that far too mean a title for her, who for beauty deserved the highest style could be given by best knowing judgments). Into the mead[3] she came, where usually she drove her flocks to feed, whose leaping and wantonness showed they were proud of such a guide: But she, whose sad thoughts led her to another manner of spending her time, made her soon leave them, and follow her late begun custom; which was (while they delighted themselves) to sit under some shade, bewailing her misfortune; while they fed, to feed upon her own sorrow and tears, which at this time she began again to summon, sitting down under the shade of a well-spread beech; the ground (then blest) and the tree with full and fine leaved branches growing proud to bear and shadow such perfections. But she regarding nothing, in comparison of her woe, thus proceeded in her grief:

---

1. Goddess of the dawn.
2. Urania represents Susan Herbert, countess of Montgomery (1587–1629), the author's close friend. In

Spenser's *Colin Clouts Come Home Again*, Urania stands for Wroth's aunt, Mary Sidney, Countess of Pembroke.
3. Meadow.

"Alas Urania," said she (the true servant to misfortune); "of any misery that can befall woman, is not this the most and greatest which thou art fallen into? Can there be any near the unhappiness of being ignorant, and that in the highest kind, not being certain of mine own estate or birth? Why was I not still continued in the belief I was, as I appear, a shepherdess, and daughter to a shepherd? My ambition then went no higher than this estate, now flies it to a knowledge; then was I contented, now perplexed. O ignorance, can thy dullness yet procure so sharp a pain? and that such a thought as makes me now aspire unto knowledge? How did I joy in this poor life being quiet? blest in the love of those I took for parents, but now by them I know the contrary, and by that knowledge, not to know myself. Miserable Urania, worse art thou now than these thy lambs; for they know their dams, while thou dost live unknown of any."

By this were others come into that mead with their flocks: but she esteeming her sorrowing thoughts her best, and choicest company, left that place, taking a little path which brought her to the further side of the plain, to the foot of the rocks, speaking as she went these lines, her eyes fixed upon the ground, her very soul turned into mourning.

> Unseen, unknown, I here alone complain
>   To rocks, to hills, to meadows and to springs,
> Which can no help return to ease my pain,
>   But back my sorrows the sad echo brings.
> Thus still increasing are my woes to me,
>   Doubly resounded by that moanful voice,
> Which seems to second me in misery,
>   And answer gives like friend of mine own choice.
> Thus only she doth my companion prove,
>   The others silently do offer ease:
> But those that grieve, a grieving note do love;
>   Pleasures to dying eyes bring but disease:
> And such am I, who daily ending live,
> Wailing a state which can no comfort give.

In this passion she went on, till she came to the foot of a great rock, she thinking of nothing less than ease, sought how she might ascend it; hoping there to pass away her time more peaceably with loneliness, though not to find least respite from her sorrow, which so dearly she did value, as by no means she would impart it to any. The way was hard, though by some windings making the ascent pleasing. Having attained the top, she saw under some hollow trees the entry into the rock: she fearing nothing but the continuance of her ignorance, went in; where she found a pretty room, as if that stony place had yet in pity, given leave for such perfections to come into the heart as chiefest, and most beloved place, because most loving. The place was not unlike the ancient (or the descriptions of ancient) hermitages,[4] instead of hangings, covered and lined with ivy, disdaining aught else should come there, that being in such perfection. This richness in nature's plenty made her stay to behold it, and almost grudge the pleasant fullness of content that place might have, if sensible, while she must know to taste of torments. As she was thus in passion mixed with pain, throwing her eyes as wildly as timorous lovers do for fear of discovery, she perceived a little light, and such a one, as a chink doth oft discover to our sights. She

4. Hermits' cells.

curious to see what this was, with her delicate hands put the natural ornament aside, discerning a little door, which she putting from her, passed through it into another room, like the first in all proportion; but in the midst there was a square stone, like to a pretty table, and on it a wax-candle burning; and by that a paper, which had suffered itself patiently to receive the discovering of so much of it, as presented this sonnet (as it seemed newly written) to her sight.

> Here all alone in silence might I mourn:
>   But how can silence be where sorrows flow?
>   Sighs with complaints have poorer pains out-worn;
>   But broken hearts can only true grief show.
>
> Drops of my dearest blood shall let love know
>   Such tears for her I shed, yet still do burn,
>   As no spring can quench least part of my woe,
>   Till this live earth, again to earth do turn.
>
> Hateful all thought of comfort is to me,
>   Despised day, let me still night possess;
>   Let me all torments feel in their excess,
>   And but this light[5] allow my state to see.
>
> Which still doth waste, and wasting as this light,
>   Are my sad days unto eternal night.

"Alas Urania!" sighed she. "How well do these words, this place, and all agree with thy fortune? Sure poor soul thou wert here appointed to spend thy days, and these rooms ordained to keep thy tortures in; none being assuredly so matchlessly unfortunate."

Turning from the table, she discerned in the room a bed of boughs, and on it a man lying, deprived of outward sense, as she thought, and of life, as she at first did fear, which struck her into a great amazement: yet having a brave spirit, though shadowed under a mean habit, she stepped unto him, whom she found not dead, but laid upon his back, his head a little to her wards,[6] his arms folded on his breast, hair long, and beard disordered, manifesting all care; but care itself had left him: curiousness thus far afforded him, as to be perfectly discerned the most exact piece of misery; apparel he had suitable to the habitation, which was a long gray robe. This grievefull spectacle did much amaze the sweet and tender-hearted shepherdess; especially, when she perceived (as she might by the help of the candle) the tears which distilled from his eyes; who seeming the image of death, yet had this sign of worldly sorrow, the drops falling in that abundance, as if there were a kind strife among them, to rid their master first of that burdenous carriage; or else meaning to make a flood, and so drown their woeful patient in his own sorrow, who yet lay still, but then fetching a deep groan from the profoundest part of his soul, he said:

"Miserable Perissus,[7] canst thou thus live, knowing she that gave thee life is gone? Gone, O me! and with her all my joy departed. Wilt thou (unblessed creature) lie here complaining for her death, and know she died for thee? Let truth and shame make thee do something worthy of such a love, ending thy days like thyself, and one fit to be her servant. But that I must not do: then thus remain and softer storms, still

---

5. A candle. The story of Cleophila finding a poem atop a table in a dark cave (Philip Sidney, Old Arcadia) is the source for the story of Urania's finding the sonnet.

6. Toward her.
7. Lost one.

to torment thy wretched soul withall, since all are little, and too too little for such a loss. O dear Limena,[8] loving Limena, worthy Limena, and more rare, constant Limena: perfections delicately feigned to be in women were verified in thee, was such worthiness framed only to be wondered at by the best, but given as a prey to base and unworthy jealousy? When were all worthy parts joined in one, but in thee (my best Limena)? Yet all these grown subject to a creature ignorant of all but ill; like unto a fool, who in a dark cave, that hath but one way to get out, having a candle, but not the understanding what good it doth him, puts it out:[9] this ignorant wretch not being able to comprehend thy virtues, did so by thee in thy murder, putting out the world's light, and men's admiration: Limena, Limena, O my Limena."

With that he fell from complaining into such a passion, as weeping and crying were never in so woeful a perfection, as now in him; which brought as deserved a compassion from the excellent shepherdess, who already had her heart so tempered with grief, as that it was apt to take any impression that it would come to feel withall. Yet taking a brave courage to her, she stepped unto him, kneeling down by his side, and gently pulling him by the arm, she thus spake.

"Sir," said she, "having heard some part of your sorrows, they have not only made me truly pity you, but wonder at you; since if you have lost so great a treasure, you should not lie thus leaving her and your love unrevenged, suffering her murderers to live, while you lie here complaining; and if such perfections be dead in her, why make you not the phoenix[1] of your deeds live again, as to new life raised out of revenge you should take on them? Then were her end satisfied, and you deservedly accounted worthy of her favor, if she were so worthy as you say."

"If she were? O God," cried out Perissus, "what devilish spirit art thou, that thus dost come to torture me? But now I see you are a woman; and therefore not much to be marked, and less resisted: but if you know charity, I pray now practice it, and leave me who am afflicted sufficiently without your company; or if you will stay, discourse not to me."

"Neither of these will I do," said she.

"If you be then," said he, "some fury of purpose sent to vex me, use your force to the uttermost in martyring me; for never was there a fitter subject, than the heart of poor Perissus is."

"I am no fury," replied the divine Urania, "not hither come to trouble you, but by accident lighted on this place; my cruel hap[2] being such, as only the like can give me content, while the solitariness of this like cave might give me quiet, though not ease, seeking for such a one, I happened hither; and this is the true cause of my being here, though now I would use it to a better end if I might. Wherefore favor me with the knowledge of your grief; which heard, it may be I shall give you some counsel, and comfort in your sorrow."

"Cursed may I be," cried he, "if ever I take comfort, having such case of mourning: but because you are, or seem to be afflicted, I will not refuse to satisfy your demand, but tell you the saddest story that ever was rehearsed by dying man to living woman; and such a one, as I fear will fasten too much sadness in you; yet should I deny it, I were to blame, being so well known to these senseless places; as were they sensible of sorrow, they would condole, or else amazed at such cruelty, stand dumb as they do, to find that man should be so inhuman."

---

8. Woman of the home or threshold.
9. An allusion to the Myth of the Cave in Plato's *Republic*.

1. The mythical bird that burned and was then reborn from its ashes.
2. Fate, chance.

⊶ ⊷

Thomas Hobbes
1588–1679

In an autobiographical poem that Hobbes wrote toward the end of his life, he described himself as having been born with a twin brother: fear. Born the year of the Spanish Armada, Hobbes felt that the fear of war had influenced his life. According to his friend and biographer Aubrey, Hobbes was an *enfant terrible*, having translated Euripides' *Medea* out of Greek into Latin iambics before the age of fourteen when he went to study at Magdalen Hall, Oxford. He was an incredibly well-read man and one of the great translators of his day; he produced the first (probably the greatest in English) translation of Thucydides' *The History of the Grecian War* (1628). An atmosphere that he described as "boiling hot with questions about dominion and the obedience due from subjects" affected his writing of *De Cive* (On the Citizen, 1647) in the years leading up to the Civil War. He also wrote on geometry and physics as well as on rhetoric and logic, and he tutored Margaret and William Cavendish's son, who later became Earl of Devonshire and host to his old bachelor tutor in retirement.

Best known today as the author of *Leviathan, or the Matter, Form, and Power of a Commonwealth Ecclesiastical and Civil* (1651), Hobbes was a controversial figure in his own century. Thought by many to be an atheist, he was even denounced by the University of Oxford in 1683. One of the great works of political philosophy, Hobbes's *Leviathan* imagines a social contract to explain political relations. The forceful and memorable style of this work, with its directness, clarity, and logical rigor, make it one of the masterpieces of English prose.

from **Leviathan**[1]

Chapter 13. Of the Natural Condition of Mankind as Concerning their Felicity, and Misery.

Nature hath made men so equal, in the faculties of the body, and mind; as that though there be found one man sometimes manifestly stronger in body, or of quicker mind than another; yet when all is reckoned together, the difference between man, and man, is not so considerable, as that one man can thereupon claim to himself any benefit, to which another may not pretend, as well as he. For as to the strength of body, the weakest has strength enough to kill the strongest, either by secret machination, or by confederacy[2] with others, that are in the same danger with himself.

And as to the faculties of the mind, setting aside the arts grounded upon words, and especially that skill of proceeding upon general, and infallible rules, called science; which very few have, and but in few things; as being not a native faculty, born with us; nor attained, as prudence, while we look after somewhat else, I find yet a greater equality amongst men, than that of strength. For prudence, is but experience; which equal time, equally bestows on all men, in those things they equally apply

---

1. The frontispiece to Hobbes's *Leviathan* pictures the body of a giant made up of little men, over which appears the Latin quotation: "Non est potestas super terram qui comparetur ei" (There is no power on earth to be compared with him). This line, from Job 41.33, refers to the primordial sea creature Leviathan, whom God cites as evidence of his all-creating power. The ensuing verse concludes by describing Leviathan as "king over all the sons of pride." Hobbes conceives of the secular state as both humanly constructed and the result of natural conflict.

2. Alliance.

themselves unto. That which may perhaps make such equality incredible, is but a vain conceit of one's own wisdom, which almost all men think they have in a greater degree, than the vulgar; that is, than all men but themselves, and a few others, whom by fame, or for concurring with themselves, they approve. For such is the nature of men, that howsoever they may acknowledge many others to be more witty, or more eloquent, or more learned; yet they will hardly believe there be many so wise as themselves; for they see their own wit at hand, and other men's at a distance. But this proveth rather that men are in that point equal, than unequal. For there is not ordinarily a greater sign of the equal distribution of any thing, than that every man is contented with his share.

From this equality of ability, ariseth equality of hope in the attaining of our ends. And therefore if any two men desire the same thing, which nevertheless they cannot both enjoy, they become enemies; and in the way to their end, which is principally their own conservation, and sometimes their delectation[3] only, endeavor to destroy, or subdue one another. And from hence it comes to pass, that where an invader hath no more to fear, than another man's single power; if one plant, sow, build, or possess a convenient seat, others may probably be expected to come prepared with forces united, to dispossess, and deprive him, not only of the fruit of his labor, but also of his life, or liberty. And the invader again is in the like danger of another.

And from this diffidence[4] of one another, there is no way for any man to secure himself, so reasonable, as anticipation; that is, by force, or wiles, to master the persons of all men he can, so long, till he see no other power great enough to endanger him: and this is no more than his own conservation requireth, and is generally allowed. Also because there be some, that taking pleasure in contemplating their own power in the acts of conquest, which they pursue farther than their security requires; if others, that otherwise would be glad to be at ease within modest bounds, should not by invasion increase their power, they would not be able, long time, by standing only on their defence, to subsist. And by consequence, such augmentation of dominion over men being necessary to a man's conservation, it ought to be allowed him.

Again, men have no pleasure, but on the contrary a great deal of grief, in keeping company, where there is no power able to overawe them all. For every man looketh that his companion should value him, at the same rate he sets upon himself: and upon all signs of contempt, or undervaluing, naturally endeavors, as far as he dares, (which amongst them that have no common power to keep them in quiet, is far enough to make them destroy each other), to extort a greater value from his contemners,[5] by damage; and from others, by the example.

So that in the nature of man, we find three principal causes of quarrel. First, competition; secondly, diffidence; thirdly, glory. The first, maketh men invade for gain; the second, for safety; and the third, for reputation. The first use violence, to make themselves masters of other men's persons, wives, children, and cattle; the second, to defend them; the third, for trifles, as a word, a smile, a different opinion, and any other sign of undervalue, either direct in their persons, or by reflection in their kindred, their friends, their nation, their profession, or their name.

---

3. Enjoyment.
4. Suspicion.

5. Scorners.

Hereby it is manifest, that during the time men live without a common power to keep them all in awe, they are in that condition which is called war; and such a war, as is of every man, against every man. For WAR, consisteth not in battle only, or the act of fighting; but in a tract of time, wherein the will to contend by battle is sufficiently known: and therefore the notion of *time*, is to be considered in the nature of war; as it is in the nature of weather. For as the nature of foul weather, lieth not in a shower or two of rain; but in an inclination thereto of many days together: so the nature of war, consisteth not in actual fighting; but in the known disposition thereto, during all the time there is no assurance to the contrary. All other time is PEACE.

Whatsoever therefore is consequent to a time of war, where every man is enemy to every man; the same is consequent to the time, wherein men live without other security, than what their own strength, and their own invention shall furnish them withal. In such condition, there is no place for industry; because the fruit thereof is uncertain: and consequently no culture of the earth; no navigation, nor use of the commodities that may be imported by sea; no commodious building; no instruments of moving, and removing, such things as require much force; no knowledge of the face of the earth; no account of time; no arts; no letters; no society; and which is worst of all, continual fear, and danger of violent death; and the life of man, solitary, poor, nasty, brutish, and short.

It may seem strange to some man, that has not well weighed these things; that nature should thus dissociate, and render men apt to invade, and destroy one another: and he may therefore, not trusting to this inference, made from the passions, desire perhaps to have the same confirmed by experience. Let him therefore consider with himself, when taking a journey, he arms himself, and seeks to go well accompanied; when going to sleep, he locks his doors; when even in his house he locks his chests; and this when he knows there be laws, and public officers, armed, to revenge all injuries shall be done him; what opinion he has of his fellow-subjects, when he rides armed; of his fellow citizens, when he locks his doors; and of his children, and servants, when he locks his chests. Does he not there as much accuse mankind by his actions, as I do by my words? But neither of us accuse man's nature in it. The desires, and other passions of man, are in themselves no sin. No more are the actions, that proceed from those passions, till they know a law that forbids them: which till laws be made they cannot know: nor can any law be made, till they have agreed upon the person that shall make it.

It may peradventure be thought, there was never such a time, nor condition of war as this; and I believe it was never generally so, over all the world: but there are many places, where they live so now. For the savage people in many places of America, except the government of small families, the concord whereof dependeth on natural lust, have no government at all; and live at this day in that brutish manner, as I said before. Howsoever, it may be perceived what manner of life there would be, where there were no common power to fear, by the manner of life, which men that have formerly lived under a peaceful government, use to degenerate into, in a civil war.

But though there had never been any time, wherein particular men were in a condition of war one against another; yet in all times, kings, and persons of sovereign authority, because of their independency, are in continual jealousies, and in the state and posture of gladiators; having their weapons pointing, and their eyes fixed on one another; that is, their forts, garrisons, and guns upon the frontiers of their kingdoms; and continual spies upon their neighbors; which is a posture of war. But because they uphold thereby, the industry of their subjects; there does not follow from it, that misery, which accompanies the liberty of particular men.

To this war of every man, against every man, this also is consequent; that nothing can be unjust. The notions of right and wrong, justice and injustice have there no place. Where there is no common power, there is no law: where no law, no injustice. Force, and fraud, are in war the two cardinal virtues. Justice, and injustice are none of the faculties neither of the body, nor mind. If they were, they might be in a man that were alone in the world, as well as his senses, and passions. They are qualities, that relate to men in society, not in solitude. It is consequent also to the same condition, that there be no propriety,[6] no dominion, no *mine* and *thine* distinct; but only that to be every man's, that he can get; and for so long, as he can keep it. And thus much for the ill condition, which man by mere nature is actually placed in; though with a possibility to come out of it, consisting partly in the passions, partly in his reason.

The passions that incline men to peace, are fear of death; desire of such things as are necessary to commodious living; and a hope by their industry to obtain them. And reason suggesteth convenient articles of peace, upon which men may be drawn to agreement. These articles, are they, which otherwise are called the Laws of Nature: whereof I shall speak more particularly, in the two following chapters.

⊷⊷⊱◆⊰⊷

Sir Thomas Browne
1605–1682

Coleridge described Sir Thomas Browne as "the Humorist constantly mingling with & flashing across the Philosopher." There is both a whimsical wit and a metaphysical depth to Browne's writing that make him the favorite author of Lord Peter Wimsey (the dandified detective of Dorothy Sayers's mysteries). Like Dorothy Sayers, Browne was a great lover of Dante, and like her character Wimsey, Browne was imperturbably "in England under any meridian." So modest that he was known to blush on being complimented, Browne had a gentle humor and peaceful nature that make him stand out in an age that was rife with vituperative polemics. The tact and understatement of his writing style express the equipoise between faith and reason that is the hallmark of this doctor's creed.

Browne became a public figure in 1642 with the surreptitious publication of *Religio Medici* ("A Doctor's Religion"). Having studied medicine at Oxford and Padua, Browne settled down to a medical practice and then married life in Norwich sometime after 1637. The manuscript of *Religio Medici* had at first circulated among friends; Browne wrote in the preface to the first authorized edition of 1643 that he had written the work "some seven years past . . . for my private exercise and satisfaction." Both Protestants and Catholics objected to *Religio Medici* and accused Browne of atheism. An attempt to publish the Latin translation by John Merryweather in Leyden met with rejection from the Protestant intellectual Salmasius, who asserted that it would meet with "but frowning entertainment among the ministers." The text's Paris publisher was convinced that though Browne declared himself a Protestant, he was really Roman Catholic. The papacy put the treatise on the Index Expurgatorius. The militantly Protestant Alexander Ross, who also criticized Bacon, Harvey, and Hobbes, wrote *Arcana Microcosmi* "with a refutation of Dr. Browne's Vulgar Errors" in 1652. After reading the book, one of

6. Personal property.

Browne's friends tried to convert him to Quakerism. Browne's independent-minded yet religious sensibility is best summed up in his own words: "I borrow not the rules of my religion from Rome or Geneva but the dictates of my own reason."

What Browne meant by reason, however, was not the disembodied individual rationality of the Enlightenment, but rather the cosmic reason of Platonism, one of the chief schools of philosophy at Cambridge in the mid-seventeenth century. Like Giordano Bruno, Browne had an interest in the hermetic tradition, which reconciled the occult writing of Hermes Trismegistus with Zoroastrianism, Platonism, and Christianity. Browne believed not only in the Ptolemaic universe but also in alchemy, astrology, and witchcraft. Indeed, he was even consulted to give his opinion on a case of witchcraft in 1644, at which he is recorded to have commented that "the fits were natural, but heightened by the devil's cooperating with the malice of the witches." By the same token, Browne, like Bacon, refuted the superstition of received ideas, as can be seen in his next important work, *Pseudodoxia Epidemica*, subtitled "Enquiries into Many Received Tenets and Commonly Presumed Truths, Which Examined Proved but Vulgar and Common Errors" (1646). He was also a kind of anthropologist in his *Hydriotaphia, Urn Burial* (1658), which uses the burial customs of various cultures as the basis for a profound meditation on mortality.

His family life appears to have been an unusually happy one. He and his intelligent and beautiful wife Dorothy Mileham had ten children, and if Browne's letters are any evidence, he was very devoted to them. Browne also had a great correspondence with people who wrote to him for information. One, a Lutheran minister who lived in Iceland, visited Browne in England for medical treatment. Browne seems to have been one of those who knew how to follow Voltaire's dictum that we must "cultivate our gardens." Browne's last work, *The Garden of Cyrus* (1658), exemplifies his dual interests in the natural and the metaphysical. This study treats the history of horticulture from Eden to the gardens of the Persian King Cyrus, supposedly the first person to plant the quincunx, which expressed the mystical properties of the number five.

Politically, Browne had royalist sympathies; he was eventually knighted by Charles II in 1671. As the story goes, that honor was conferred on Browne only by default, since the mayor of Norwich declined and the King wanted to knight someone. Browne's greatest honor is in the number of writers who admired his work. Coleridge, Lamb, and De Quincy wrote of the imaginative fantasy in Browne's writing. Among American authors, Melville particularly prized Browne's writing for its combination of the scientific and the transcendental. The effect of Browne's prose style is one of flowing harmony. Animated by biblical parallelism and a profound reverence for the power of the word, Browne's prose flows harmoniously while giving the illusion of spontaneous organization.

from **Religio Medici**

from *Part 1*

1. For my religion, though there be several circumstances that might persuade the world I have none at all, as the general scandal of my profession,[1] the natural course of my studies, the indifferency[2] of my behavior and discourse in matters of religion (neither violently defending one, nor with that common ardor and contention opposing another), yet, in despite hereof, I dare without usurpation assume the honorable style of a Christian. Not that I merely owe this title to the font,[3] my education, or the clime wherein I was born, as being bred up either to confirm those principles my parents instilled into my unwary understanding, or by a general consent proceed

---

1. The "scandal of his profession" was the notion that doctors were often atheists. Natural: scientific.

2. Lack of bias.
3. The baptismal font.

in the religion of my country; but that having, in my riper years and confirmed judgment, seen and examined all, I find myself obliged, by the principles of grace, and the law of mine own reason, to embrace no other name but this: neither doth herein my zeal so far make me forget the general charity I owe unto humanity, as rather to hate than pity Turks, Infidels, and (what is worse) Jews;[4] rather contenting myself to enjoy that happy style, than maligning those who refuse so glorious a title.

2. But, because the name of a Christian is become too general to express our faith, there being a geography of religion as well as lands, and every clime not only distinguished by its laws and limits, but circumscribed by its doctrines and rules of faith, to be particular, I am of that reformed new-cast religion, wherein I dislike nothing but the name;[5] of the same belief our Savior taught, the Apostles disseminated, the Fathers authorized,[6] and the Martyrs confirmed; but, by the sinister ends of princes, the ambition and avarice of prelates, and the fatal corruption of times, so decayed, impaired, and fallen from its native beauty, that it required the careful and charitable hands of these times to restore it to its primitive integrity. Now, the accidental occasion whereupon, the slender means whereby, the low and abject condition of the person by whom, so good a work was set on foot,[7] which in our adversaries beget contempt and scorn, fill me with wonder, and are the very same objections the insolent pagans first cast at Christ and his disciples.[8]

3. Yet I have not so shaken hands with those desperate resolutions[9] who had rather venture at large their decayed bottom, than bring her in to be new trimmed in the dock, who had rather promiscuously retain all, than abridge any, and obstinately be what they are, than what they have been, as to stand in diameter and sword's point with them. We have reformed from them, not against them: for, omitting those improperations[1] and terms of scurrility betwixt us, which only difference[2] our affections, and not our cause, there is between us one common name and appellation, one faith and necessary body of principles common to us both; and therefore I am not scrupulous to converse and live with them, to enter their churches in defect of ours, and either pray with them or for them. I could never perceive any rational consequence from those many texts which prohibit the children of Israel to pollute themselves with the temples of the heathens; we being all Christians, and not divided by such detested impieties as might profane our prayers, or the place wherein we make them; or that a resolved conscience may not adore her Creator anywhere, especially in places devoted to his service; where, if their devotions offend him, mine may please him; if theirs profane it, mine may hallow it. Holy water and crucifix (dangerous to the common people) deceive not my judgment, nor abuse my devotion at all. I am, I confess, naturally inclined to that which misguided zeal terms superstition: my common conversation I do acknowledge austere, my behavior full of rigor, sometimes not without morosity; yet, at my devotion I love to use the civility of my knee, my hat, and hand, with all those outward and sensible motions which may express or promote my invisible devotion. I should violate my own arm rather than a church, nor willingly deface the memory[3] of saint or martyr. At the sight of a cross, or crucifix, I can dispense with my hat, but scarce with the thought or memory of my Savior.

---

4. Brown thinks that it would be against charity to hate rather than pity Turks and infidels, and even worse in the case of the Jews.
5. Protestant.
6. The Church Fathers of the first few centuries of the church, in particular St. Augustine, were a major influence on the Protestant Reformation.
7. Martin Luther was the son of a miner.

8. See Mark 6.2–3: "From whence hath this man these things. . . . Is not this the carpenter, the son of Mary?"
9. Roman Catholics, whose church is described as a leaky boat.
1. Taunts.
2. Make different.
3. Memorial.

I cannot laugh at, but rather pity, the fruitless journeys of pilgrims, or contemn the miserable condition of friars; for, though misplaced in circumstances, there is something in it of devotion. I could never hear the Ave Maria bell without an elevation,[4] or think it a sufficient warrant, because they erred in one circumstance, for me to err in all,—that is, in silence and dumb contempt. Whilst, therefore, they directed their devotions to her, I offered mine to God; and rectified the errors of their prayers by rightly ordering mine own. At a solemn procession I have wept abundantly, while my consorts, blind with opposition and prejudice, have fallen into an excess of scorn and laughter. There are, questionless, both in Greek, Roman, and African churches, solemnities and ceremonies, whereof the wiser zeals do make a Christian use; and which stand condemned by us, not as evil in themselves, but as allurements and baits of superstition to those vulgar heads that look asquint on the face of truth, and those unstable judgments that cannot consist in the narrow point and center of virtue without a reel or stagger to the circumference.

4. As there were many reformers, so likewise many reformations; every country proceeding in a particular way and method, according as their national interest, together with their constitution and clime, inclined them: some angrily and with extremity; others calmly and with mediocrity, not rending, but easily dividing, the community, and leaving an honest possibility of a reconciliation; which, though peaceable spirits do desire, and may conceive that revolution of time and the mercies of God may effect, yet that judgment that shall consider the present antipathies between the two extremes, their contrarieties in condition, affection, and opinion, may, with the same hopes, expect a union in the poles of heaven.

5. But, to difference myself nearer, and draw into a lesser circle; there is no church whose every part so squares unto my conscience, whose articles, constitutions, and customs, seem so consonant unto reason, and, as it were, framed to my particular devotion, as this whereof I hold my belief—the church of England; to whose faith I am a sworn subject, and therefore, in a double obligation, subscribe unto her articles, and endeavor to observe her constitutions: whatsoever is beyond, as points indifferent, I observe according to the rules of my private reason, or the humor and fashion of my devotion; neither believing this because Luther affirmed it, nor disapproving that because Calvin hath disavouched it. I condemn not all things in the council of Trent, nor approve all in the synod of Dort.[5] In brief, where the Scripture is silent, the church is my text; where that speaks, 't is but my comment; where there is a joint silence of both, I borrow not the rules of my religion from Rome or Geneva, but from the dictates of my own reason. It is an unjust scandal of our adversaries, and a gross error in ourselves, to compute the nativity of our religion from Henry the Eighth; who, though he rejected the Pope, refused not the faith of Rome, and effected no more than what his own predecessors desired and essayed in ages past, and it was conceived the state of Venice would have attempted in our days. It is as uncharitable a point in us to fall upon those popular scurrilities and opprobrious scoffs of the bishop of Rome, to whom, as a temporal prince, we owe the duty of good language. I confess there is a cause of passion between us: by his sentence I stand excommunicated; heretic is the best language he affords me: yet can no ear witness I ever returned to him the name of antichrist, man of sin, or whore of Babylon.[6] It is the method of

---

4. Browne's marginalia: "A Church Bell that tolls every day at 6 and 12 of the clock, at the hearing whereof every one in what ever place soever either of house or street betakes him to his prayers, which is commonly directed to the Virgin."

5. Theological councils: for Catholicism in Trento, Italy (1545–1563) and for Calvinism in Dordrecht, Holland (1618–1619).
6. Images taken from Revelation used in Protestant polemics against Catholics.

charity to suffer without reaction: those usual satires and invectives of the pulpit may perchance produce a good effect on the vulgar, whose ears are opener to rhetoric than logic; yet do they, in no wise, confirm the faith of wiser believers, who know that a good cause needs not be patroned by passion, but can sustain itself upon a temperate dispute.

6. I could never divide myself from any man upon the difference of an opinion, or be angry with his judgment for not agreeing with me in that from which, perhaps, within a few days, I should dissent myself. I have no genius to disputes in religion; and have often thought it wisdom to decline them, especially upon a disadvantage, or when the cause of truth might suffer in the weakness of my patronage. Where we desire to be informed, 'tis good to contest with men above ourselves; but, to confirm and establish our opinions, 'tis best to argue with judgments below our own, that the frequent spoils and victories over their reasons may settle in ourselves an esteem and confirmed opinion of our own. Every man is not a proper champion for truth, nor fit to take up the gauntlet in the cause of verity: many, from the ignorance of these maxims, and an inconsiderate zeal unto truth, have too rashly charged the troops of error, and remain as trophies unto the enemies of truth. A man may be in as just possession of truth as of a city, and yet be forced to surrender; 'tis therefore far better to enjoy her with peace than to hazard her on a battle. If, therefore, there rise any doubts in my way, I do forget them, or at least defer them, till my better settled judgment and more manly reason be able to resolve them; for I perceive every man's own reason is his best Oedipus,[7] and will, upon a reasonable truce, find a way to loose those bonds wherewith the subtleties of error have enchained our more flexible and tender judgments. In philosophy, where truth seems doublefaced, there is no man more paradoxical than myself: but in divinity I love to keep the road; and, though not in an implicit, yet an humble faith, follow the great wheel of the church, by which I move; not reserving any proper poles, or motion from the epicycle[8] of my own brain. By this means I leave no gap for heresy, schisms, or errors, of which at present, I hope I shall not injure truth to say, I have no taint or tincture. I must confess my greener studies have been polluted with two or three; not any begotten in the latter centuries, but old and obsolete, such as could never have been revived but by such extravagant and irregular heads as mine. For, indeed, heresies perish not with their authors; but, like the river Arethusa,[9] though they lose their currents in one place, they rise up again in another. One general council is not able to extirpate one single heresy; it may be canceled for the present; but revolution of time, and the like aspects from heaven, will restore it, when it will flourish till it be condemned again. For, as though there were a metempsychosis,[1] and the soul of one man passed into another, opinions do find, after certain revolutions, men and minds like those that first begat them. To see ourselves again, we need not look for Plato's year;[2] every man is not only himself; there have been many Diogeneses, and as many Timons,[3] though but few of that name; men are lived over again; the world is now as it was in ages past; there was none then, but there hath been some one since, that parallels him, and is, as it were, his revived self.

7. Searcher after truth.

8. The revolving of a planet within a smaller circle within its larger orbit around the earth, a concept used by Ptolemaic astronomy to account for inconsistencies in its system, which were resolved by the simpler model of the solar system.

9. A Greek nymph who fled the sexual advances of the river god Alphaeus. She was turned into a stream but Alphaeus still pursued her. Diana rescued Arethusa by pushing the stream underground until it emerged in Sicily.

1. Transmigration of the soul.

2. Browne's marginalia: "A revolution of certain thousand years when all things should return unto their former estate and he be teaching again in his school as when he delivered this opinion."

3. Cynics and misanthropes.

from **Pseudodoxia Epidemica**

from *Book 1*

CHAPTER 1

Of the first Cause of Common Errors; the common infirmity of Human Nature

The first and father cause of common error is the common infirmity of human nature; of whose deceptible[1] condition, although, perhaps, there should not need any other eviction[2] than the frequent errors we shall ourselves commit, even in the express declarement hereof, yet shall we illustrate the same from more infallible constitutions, and persons presumed as far from us in condition as time, that is, our first and ingenerated[3] forefathers. From whom, as we derive our being, and the several wounds of constitution, so may we in some manner excuse our infirmities in the depravity of those parts, whose traductions[4] were pure in them, and their originals but once removed from God. Who, notwithstanding, (if posterity may take leave to judge of the fact, as they are assured to suffer in the punishment,) were grossly deceived in their perfection, and so weakly deluded in the clarity of their understanding, that it hath left no small obscurity in ours, how error should gain upon them.

For first, they were deceived by Satan; and that not in an invisible insinuation, but an open and discoverable apparition, that is, in the form of a serpent;[5] whereby, although there were many occasions of suspicion, and such as could not easily escape a weaker circumspection, yet did the unwary apprehension of Eve take no advantage thereof. It hath therefore seemed strange unto some, she should be deluded by a serpent, or subject her reason to a beast, which God had subjected unto hers. It hath empuzzled the enquiries of others to apprehend, and enforced them unto strange conceptions, to make out, how without fear or doubt she could discourse with such a creature, or hear a serpent speak, without suspicion of imposture. The wits of others have been so bold as to accuse her simplicity, in receiving his temptation so coldly; and, when such specious effects of the fruit were promised as to make them like gods, not to desire, at least not to wonder, he pursued not that benefit himself. And had it been their own case, would perhaps have replied, if the taste of this fruit maketh the eaters like Gods why remainest thou a beast? If it maketh us but *like* gods, we are so already. If thereby our eyes shall be opened hereafter, they are at present quick enough to discover thy deceit; and we desire them no opener to behold our own shame. If to know good and evil be our advantage, although we have free will unto both, we desire to perform but one. We know 'tis good to obey the commandment of God, but evil if we transgress it.

They were deceived by one another, and in the greatest disadvantage of delusion, that is, the stronger by the weaker: for Eve presented the fruit, and Adam received it from her. Thus the serpent was cunning enough to begin the deceit in the weaker; and the weaker of strength sufficient to consummate the fraud in the stronger. Art and fallacy was used unto her; a naked offer proved sufficient to him; so his superstruction was his ruin, and the fertility of his sleep[6] an issue of death unto him. And although the condition of sex, and posteriority of creation,[7] might somewhat extenuate the error of the woman, yet was it very strange and inexcusable in

---

1. Deceivable.
2. Proof.
3. Not humanly generated, Adam and Eve were created by God.

4. Transmissions of the soul from the parents to the child.
5. See Genesis 2–3, and Milton's *Paradise Lost*.
6. Eve.
7. Eve's being created after Adam.

the man: especially, if, as some affirm, he was the wisest of all men since; or if, as others have conceived, he was not ignorant of the fall of the angels, and had thereby example and punishment to deter him.

They were deceived from themselves, and their own apprehensions; for Eve either mistook, or traduced the commandment of God. "Of every tree of the garden thou mayest freely eat, but of the tree of knowledge of good and evil thou shalt not eat: for in the day thou eatest thereof, thou shalt surely die."[8] Now Eve upon the question of the serpent, returned the precept in different terms: "You shall not eat of it, neither shall you touch it, lest perhaps you die." In which delivery there were no less than two mistakes, or rather additional mendacities: for the commandment forbad not the touch of the fruit; and positively said, ye shall surely die, but she extenuating replied, *ne forte moriamini*, lest perhaps ye die. For so in the vulgar translation it runneth, and so it is expressed in the Thargum or paraphrase of Jonathan.[9] And therefore although it be said, and that very truly, that the Devil was a liar from the beginning, yet was the woman herein the first express beginner, and falsified twice, before the reply of Satan. And therefore also, to speak strictly, the sin of the fruit was not the first offence. They first transgressed the rule of their own reason, and after, the commandment of God.

They were deceived through the conduct of their senses, and by temptations from the object itself; whereby although their intellectuals[1] had not failed in the theory of truth, yet did the inservient and brutal[2] faculties control the suggestion of reason: pleasure and profit already overswaying the instructions of honesty, and sensuality perturbing the reasonable commands of virtue. For so it is delivered in the text; that when the woman saw "that the tree was good for food," and "that it was pleasant unto the eye," and "a tree to be desired to make one wise, she took of the fruit thereof and did eat."[3] Now hereby it appeareth, that Eve, before the fall, was by the same and beaten way of allurements inveigled, whereby her posterity hath been deluded ever since; that is, those three delivered by St. John, "the lust of the flesh, the lust of the eye, and the pride of life:"[4] where indeed they seemed as weakly to fail, as their debilitated posterity, ever after. Whereof, notwithstanding, some in their imperfection have resisted more powerful temptations, and in many moralities condemned the facility of their seductions.

Again, they might, for aught we know, be still deceived in the unbelief of their mortality, even after they had eat of the fruit. For, Eve observing no immediate execution of the curse, she delivered the fruit unto Adam; who after the taste thereof, perceiving himself still to live, might yet remain in doubt, whether he had incurred death; which perhaps he did not indubitably believe, until he was after convicted in the visible example of Abel. For he that would not believe the menace of God at first, it may be doubted whether, before an ocular example, he believed the curse at last. And therefore they are not without all reason, who have disputed the fact of Cain; that is, although he purposed to do mischief, whether he intended to kill his brother; or designed that, whereof he had not beheld an example in his own kind. There might be somewhat in it, that he would not have done, or desired undone, when he brake forth as desperately, as before he had done uncivilly, my iniquity is greater than can be forgiven me.[5]

---

8. Genesis 2.16–17.
9. The vulgar translation: the Vulgate, the Latin translation of the Bible by St. Jerome; Thargum: Aramaic translations of the Old Testament.
1. Reasoning.
2. Servile and animalistic.
3. Genesis 3.6.
4. John 2.16.
5. Genesis 4.13–14.

Some niceties I confess there are which extenuate, but many more that aggravate this delusion; which exceeding the bounds of this discourse, and perhaps our satisfaction, we shall at present pass over. And therefore whether the sin of our first parents were the greatest of any since; whether the transgression of Eve seducing did not exceed that of Adam seduced; or whether the resistibility of his reason, did not equivalence the facility of her seduction, we shall refer it to the schoolman.[6] Whether there was not in Eve as great injustice in deceiving her husband, as imprudence in being deceived herself, especially, if foretasting the fruit, her eyes were opened before his, and she knew the effect of it, before he tasted of it, we leave it unto the moralist. Whether the whole relation be not allegorical, that is, whether the temptation of the man by the woman be not the seduction of the rational and higher parts by the inferior and feminine faculties; or whether the tree in the midst of the garden, were not that part in the center of the body, in which was afterward the appointment of circumcision in males, we leave it unto the talmudist. Whether there were any policy in the devil to tempt them before the conjunction, or whether the issue, before tentation,[7] might in justice have suffered with those after, we leave it unto the lawyer. Whether Adam foreknew the advent of Christ, or the reparation of his error by his Savior; how the execution of the curse should have been ordered, if, after Eve had eaten, Adam had yet refused; whether, if they had tasted the tree of life, before that of good and evil, they had yet suffered the curse of mortality; or whether the efficacy of the one had not overpowered the penalty of the other, we leave it unto God. For he alone can truly determine these, and all things else; who, as he hath proposed the world unto our disputation, so hath he reserved many things unto his own resolution; whose determination we cannot hope from flesh, but must with reverence suspend unto that great day, whose justice shall either condemn our curiosities, or resolve our disquisitions.

Lastly, man was not only deceivable in his integrity, but the angels of light in all their clarity. He that said, he would be like the highest,[8] did err, if in some way he conceived not himself so already: but in attempting so high an effect from himself, he misunderstood the nature of God, and held a false apprehension of his own; whereby vainly attempting not only insolencies, but impossibilities, he deceived himself as low as hell. In brief, there is nothing infallible but God, who cannot possibly err. For things are really true, as they correspond unto His conception; and have so much verity, as they hold of conformity unto that intellect, in whose idea they had their first determinations.[9] And, therefore, being the rule, he cannot be irregular; nor, being truth itself, conceivably admit the impossible society of error.

from Hydriotaphia, Urn Burial
or a Discourse of the Sepulchral Urns lately found in Norfolk

FROM CHAPTER 1

In the deep discovery of the subterranean world, a shallow part would satisfy some enquirers; who, if two or three yards were open about the surface, would not care to rake the bowels of Potosi,[1] and regions towards the center. Nature hath furnished one part of the earth, and man another. The treasures of time lie high, in

---

6. Medieval scholastic philosopher.
7. Temptation.
8. Lucifer.
9. According to Renaissance Platonism, the idea of each

thing first existed in the mind of God.
1. Browne's marginalia: "the rich mountain of Peru," a major source of silver.

urns, coins, and monuments, scarce below the roots of some vegetables. Time hath endless rarities, and shows of all varieties; which reveals old things in heaven, makes new discoveries in earth, and even earth itself a discovery. That great antiquity America lay buried for thousands of years, and a large part of the earth is still in the urn unto us.

Though if Adam were made out of an extract of the earth,[2] all parts might challenge a restitution, yet few have returned their bones far lower than they might receive them; not affecting the graves of giants, under hilly and heavy coverings, but content with less than their own depth, have wished their bones might lie soft, and the earth be light upon them. Even such as hope to rise again, would not be content with central interment, or so desperately to place their relics as to lie beyond discovery; and in no way to be seen again; which happy contrivance hath made communication with our forefathers, and left unto our view some parts, which they never beheld themselves.

Though earth hath engrossed the name, yet water[3] hath proved the smartest grave; which in forty days swallowed almost mankind, and the living creation; fishes not wholly escaping, except the salt ocean were handsomely contempered[4] by a mixture of the fresh element.

Many have taken voluminous pains to determine the state of the soul upon disunion; but men have been most fantastical in the singular contrivances of their corporal dissolution: whilst the soberest nations have rested in two ways, of simple inhumation and burning.

That carnal interment or burying was of the elder date, the old examples of Abraham and the patriarchs are sufficient to illustrate;[5] and were without competition, if it could be made out, that Adam was buried near Damascus, or Mount Calvary, according to some tradition. God himself, that buried but one, was pleased to make choice of this way, collectible from Scripture expression, and the hot contest between Satan and the archangel, about discovering the body of Moses.[6] But the practice of burning was also of great antiquity, and of no slender extent. For (not to derive the same from Hercules) noble descriptions there are hereof in the Grecian funerals of Homer, in the formal obsequies of Patroclus, and Achilles;[7] and somewhat elder in the Theban war, and solemn combustion of Meneccus, and Archemorus, contemporary unto Jair the eighth judge of Israel.[8] Confirmable also among the Trojans, from the funeral pyre of Hector, burnt before the gates of Troy: and the burning of Penthesilea the Amazonian queen:[9] and long continuance of that practice, in the inward countries of Asia; while as low as the reign of Julian,[1] we find that the king of Chionia burnt the body of his son, and interred the ashes in a silver urn.[2]

The same practice extended also far west; and, besides Herulians, Getes, and Thracians,[3] was in use with most of the Celtae, Sarmatians, Germans, Gauls, Danes, Swedes, Norwegians; not to omit some use thereof among Carthaginians and Americans. Of greater antiquity among the Romans than most opinion, or Pliny[4] seems to allow: for (beside the old table laws of burning or burying within the city,[5] of

2. There was a traditional belief that Adam was formed of dust from the four quarters of the earth.
3. The Flood; see Genesis 7.17ff.
4. Moderated.
5. Genesis 25.9.
6. Deuteronomy 34.6; Jude 9.
7. Hercules cremated Argeus; for Homer's funerals, see *Iliad* 23.161ff. and *Odyssey* 24.65ff.
8. For Meneceus and Archemorus, see Statius, *Thebaid*

12.60ff. and 6.1ff.; for Jair, see Judges 10.3–5.
9. *Iliad* 24.782ff.
1. Roman emperor (361–363).
2. Browne's marginalia: "Gumbrates King of Chionia a Country near Persia. Ammianus Marcellinus [Roman historian, c. 390]."
3. Eastern European tribe.
4. Pliny (A.D. 23–79) author of *Historia naturalis*.
5. In the Roman code of the Twelve Tables.

making the funeral fire with planed wood, or quenching the fire with wine,) Manlius the consul burnt the body of his son: Numa,[6] by special clause of his will, was not burnt but buried; and Remus was solemnly burned, according to the description of Ovid.[7]

Cornelius Sylla was not the first whose body was burned in Rome, but the first of the Cornelian family; which, being indifferently, not frequently used before; from that time spread, and became the prevalent practice. Not totally pursued in the highest run of cremation; for when even crows were funereally burnt, Poppaea the wife of Nero found a peculiar grave interment.[8] Now as all customs were founded upon some bottom of reason, so there wanted not grounds for this; according to several apprehensions of the most rational dissolution. Some being of the opinion of Thales,[9] that water was the original of all things, thought it most equal to submit unto the principle of putrefaction, and conclude in a moist relentment.[1] Others conceived it most natural to end in fire, as due unto the master principle in the composition, according to the doctrine of Heraclitus;[2] and therefore heaped up large piles, more actively to waft them toward that element, whereby they also declined a visible degeneration into worms, and left a lasting parcel of their composition.

Some apprehended a purifying virtue in fire, refining the grosser commixture, and firing out the ethereal particles so deeply immersed in it. And such as by tradition or rational conjecture held any hint of the final pyre of all things; or that this element at last must be too hard for all the rest; might conceive most naturally of the fiery dissolution. Others pretending no natural grounds, politicly declined the malice of enemies upon their buried bodies. Which consideration led Sylla unto this practice; who having thus served the body of Marius, could not but fear a retaliation upon his own; entertained after in the civil wars, and revengeful contentions of Rome.[3]

But as many nations embraced, and many left it indifferent, so others too much affected, or strictly declined this practice. The Indian Brachmans[4] seemed too great friends unto fire, who burnt themselves alive, and thought it the noblest way to end their days in fire; according to the expression of the Indian, burning himself at Athens, in his last words upon the pyre unto the amazed spectators, thus I make myself immortal.[5]

But the Chaldeans[6] the great idolaters of fire, abhorred the burning of their carcasses, as a pollution of that deity. The Persian magi declined it upon the like scruple, and being only solicitous about their bones, exposed their flesh to the prey of birds and dogs. And the Persees now in India, which expose their bodies unto vultures, and endure not so much as *feretra* or biers of wood, the proper fuel of fire, are led on with such niceties. But whether the ancient Germans, who burned their dead, held any such fear to pollute their deity of Herthus, or the earth, we have no authentic conjecture.

6. Numa, legendary King of Rome and founder of Roman religion.
7. Browne's marginalia quotes Ovid, *Fasti* 4.856 (in Latin): "At last the flame lit the funeral pyre."
8. Tacitus, *Annals* 16.6.
9. Thales (c. 636–c. 546 B.C.), Greek Milesian philosopher.
1. Putrefaction: decay; relentment: dissolution.
2. The pre-Socratic philosopher Heraclitus (c. 535–c. 475 B.C.) believed that because fire was the underlying substance of the universe, everything in the world would ultimately be consumed by fire.

3. The rivalry between the Roman generals Marius and Sulla (Sylla) over the command of the army resulted in civil war. When Sulla won, Marius fled from Rome, but he later returned to seek revenge by killing his opponents (88 B.C.).
4. The highest Hindu caste.
5. Browne's marginalia: "And therefore the Inscription of his Tomb was made accordingly." Browne's source is Nicholas of Damascus as reported by the scholar Perucci (*Pompe funebri*, 1639).
6. Inhabitants of the Tigris and Euphrates valley.

The Egyptians were afraid of fire, not as a deity, but a devouring element, mercilessly consuming their bodies, and leaving too little of them; and therefore by precious embalments, depositure in dry earths, or handsome inclosure in glasses, contrived the notablest ways of integral conservation. And from such Egyptian scruples, imbibed by Pythagoras,[7] it may be conjectured that Numa and the Pythagorical sect first waved the fiery solution.

The Scythians,[8] who swore by wind and sword, that is, by life and death, were so far from burning their bodies, that they declined all interment, and made their graves in the air: and the Ichthyophagi, or fish-eating nations about Egypt, affected the sea for their grave; thereby declining visible corruption, and restoring the debt of their bodies. Whereas the old heroes, in Homer, dreaded nothing more than water or drowning; probably upon the old opinion of the fiery substance of the soul, only extinguishable by that element; and therefore the poet emphatically implieth the total destruction in this kind of death, which happened to Ajax Oileus.[9]

The old Balearians[1] had a peculiar mode, for they used great urns and much wood, but no fire in their burials, while they bruised the flesh and bones of the dead, crowded them into urns, and laid heaps of wood upon them.[2] And the Chinese without cremation or urnal interment of their bodies, make use of trees and much burning, while they plant a pine tree by their grave, and burn great numbers of printed draughts of slaves and horses over it, civilly content with their companies in *effigy*, which barbarous nations exact unto reality.[3]

Christians abhorred this way of obsequies,[4] and though they sticked not to give their bodies to be burnt in their lives, detested that mode after death; affecting rather a depositure than absumption,[5] and properly submitting unto the sentence of God, to return not unto ashes but unto dust again, conformable unto the practice of the patriarchs, the interment of our Savior, of Peter, Paul, and the ancient martyrs. And so far at last declining promiscuous interment with Pagans, that some have suffered ecclesiastical censures, for making no scruple thereof.[6]

The Musselman believers will never admit this fiery resolution. For they hold a present trial from their black and white angels in the grave; which they must have made so hollow, that they may rise upon their knees.

The Jewish nation, though they entertained the old way of inhumation, yet sometimes admitted this practice. For the men of Jabesh burnt the body of Saul;[7] and by no prohibited practice, to avoid contagion or pollution, in time of pestilence, burnt the bodies of their friends.[8] And when they burnt not their dead bodies, yet sometimes used great burnings near and about them, deducible from the expressions concerning Jehoram, Zedechias, and the sumptuous pyre of Asa.[9] And were so little averse from Pagan burning, that the Jews lamenting the death of Caesar their friend, and revenger on Pompey,[1] frequented the place where his body was burnt for many

7. Ancient Greek philosopher who believed in the transmigration of souls.
8. People who lived on the north shore of the Black Sea who were viewed as barbarians by the Greeks.
9. Ajax, hero of Trojan War, was struck dead by lightning.
1. Natives of the Mediterranean islands Minorca and Majorca.
2. Browne's marginalia: "Diodorus Siculus [Greek historian] 5.18."
3. Browne's marginalia: "See Ramusius" (a 16th-century

Venetian collector of travel literature).
4. Funeral rites.
5. Preferring to be buried rather than cremated.
6. Browne's marginalia: "Bishop Martialis, as reported by Cyprian" (Bishop of Carthage, d. 258).
7. 1 Samuel 31.12.
8. Amos 6.10.
9. Jeremiah 34.5; 2 Chronicles 16.14, 21.19.
1. Julius Caesar defeated Pompey's forces in the Roman Civil War (48 B.C.)

nights together.[2] And as they raised noble monuments and mausoleums for their own nation,[3] so they were not scrupulous in erecting some for others, according to the practice of Daniel, who left that lasting sepulchral pile in Ecbatana, for the Median and Persian kings.[4]

But even in times of subjection and hottest use,[5] they conformed not unto the Roman practice of burning; whereby the prophecy was secured concerning the body of Christ, that it should not see corruption, or a bone should not be broken;[6] which we believe was also providentially prevented, from the soldier's spear and nails that passed by the little bones both in his hands and feet; not of ordinary contrivance, that it should not corrupt on the cross, according to the laws of Roman crucifixion, or an hair of his head perish, though observable in Jewish customs, to cut the hairs of malefactors.

Nor in their long cohabitation with Egyptians, crept into a custom of their exact embalming, wherein deeply slashing the muscles, and taking out the brains and entrails, they had broken the subject[7] of so entire a resurrection, nor fully answered the types of Enoch, Elijah, or Jonah,[8] which yet to prevent or restore, was of equal facility unto that rising power, able to break the fasciations[9] and bands of death, to get clear out of the cerecloth, and an hundred pounds of ointment, and out of the sepulchre before the stone was rolled from it.

But though they embraced not this practice of burning, yet entertained they many ceremonies agreeable unto Greek and Roman obsequies. And he that observeth their funeral feasts, their lamentations at the grave, their music, and weeping mourners; how they closed the eyes of their friends, how they washed, anointed, and kissed the dead; may easily conclude these were not mere pagan civilities. But whether that mournful burthen, and treble calling out after Absalom, had any reference unto the last conclamation,[1] and triple valediction, used by other nations, we hold but a wavering conjecture.

Civilians[2] make sepulture[3] but of the law of nations, others do naturally found it and discover it also in animals. They that are so thick-skinned[4] as still to credit the story of the Phoenix, may say something for animal burning. More serious conjectures find some examples of sepulture in elephants, cranes, the sepulchral cells of pismires, and practice of bees, which civil society carrieth out their dead, and hath exequies,[5] if not interments.

CHAPTER 5

Now since these dead bones have already outlasted the living ones of Methuselah,[6] and in a yard under ground, and thin walls of clay, outworn all the strong and specious buildings above it; and quietly rested under the drums and tramplings of three conquests:[7] what prince can promise such diuturnity[8] unto his relics, or might not gladly say,

2. Browne's marginalia: "So Suetonius [Roman historian], *Julius* 84.5."
3. Browne's marginalia: "As that magnificent monument erected by Simon." See 1 Macabees 1.13.
4. Browne's marginalia: "'A wonderfully made work' [quoted in Greek from Josephus, *Jewish Antiquities* 10.11.7] whereof the Jewish Priest had always the custody unto Josephus his days."
5. Most violent treatment.
6. Psalms 16.10; Acts 2.31; John 19.36.
7. Substance.
8. Enoch and Elijah are prefigurations of the Resurrection in that they were assumed into heaven; Jonah was saved from the whale.

9. Bandages.
1. Shout of many together. Browne marginalia: "O Absolom, Absolom, Absolom. 1 Samuel 18.33."
2. "Experts in those things that appertain to the administration of a commonwealth." Sir Thomas Elyot, *Dictionary* (1538).
3. Burial.
4. Stupid. Browne is thinking about Alexander Ross, who defended the existence of the phoenix and the unicorn in *Arcana Microcosmi* (1651).
5. Funeral rites.
6. Said to have lived for 969 years (Genesis 5.21).
7. I.e., Anglo-Saxon, Danish, and Norman.
8. Long duration.

Sic ego componi versus in ossa velim.[9]

Time, which antiquates antiquities, and hath an art to make dust of all things, hath yet spared these minor monuments. In vain we hope to be known by open and visible conservatories,[1] when to be unknown was the means of their continuation, and obscurity their protection. If they died by violent hands, and were thrust into their urns, these bones become considerable, and some old philosophers would honor them, whose souls they conceived most pure, which were thus snatched from their bodies, and to retain a stronger propension[2] unto them; whereas they weariedly left a languishing corpse, and with faint desires of reunion. If they fell by long and aged decay, yet wrapped up in the bundle of time, they fall into indistinction,[3] and make but one blot with infants. If we begin to die when we live, and long life be but a prolongation of death, our life is a sad composition; we live with death, and die not in a moment. How many pulses made up the life of Methuselah, were work for Archimedes: common counters sum up the life of Moses his man.[4] Our days become considerable, like petty sums, by minute accumulations; where numerous fractions make up but small round numbers; and our days of a span long, make not one little finger.[5]

If the nearness of our last necessity brought a nearer conformity unto it, there were a happiness in hoary hairs, and no calamity in half senses. But the long habit of living indisposeth us for dying; when avarice makes us the sport of death, when even David grew politicly cruel, and Solomon could hardly be said to be the wisest of men.[6] But many are too early old, and before the date of age. Adversity stretcheth our days, misery makes Alcmena's nights,[7] and time hath no wings unto it. But the most tedious being is that which can unwish itself, content to be nothing, or never to have been, which was beyond the malcontent of Job, who cursed not the day of his life, but his nativity; content to have so far been, as to have a title to future being, although he had lived here but in an hidden state of life, and as it were an abortion.[8]

What song the Sirens sang, or what name Achilles assumed when he hid himself among women, though puzzling questions, are not beyond all conjecture.[9] What time the persons of these ossuaries entered the famous nations of the dead,[1] and slept with princes and counselors,[2] might admit a wide solution. But who were the proprietaries of these bones, or what bodies these ashes made up, were a question above antiquarism; not to be resolved by man, nor easily perhaps by spirits, except we consult the provincial guardians, or tutelary observators.[3] Had they made as good provision for their names, as they have done for their relics, they had not so grossly erred in the art of perpetuation. But to subsist in bones, and be but pyramidally extant, is a fallacy in duration. Vain ashes which in the oblivion of names, persons, times, and sexes, have found unto themselves a fruitless continua-

---

9. Thus, when naught is left of me but bones, would I be laid to rest. (Quoting the Roman elegiac poet Tibullus 3.2.26.)
1. Places to preserve things.
2. Propensity.
3. Undistinguishableness.
4. Browne's marginalia: "In the Psalm of Moses." See Psalm 90.10. The Greek mathematician Archimedes gave directions in *The Sand Reckoner* for counting the grains of sand in the universe.
5. Browne's marginalia: "According to the ancient arithmetic of the hand wherein the little finger of the right hand contracted, signified an hundred. Pierius in *Hieroglyph [1556]*."

6. Samuel 8.2 and 1 Kings 11.1.
7. Browne's marginalia: "One night as long as three," so that Zeus could have more pleasure with Alcmena, his lover and mother of Hercules.
8. Job 3.1ff.
9. The Roman emperor Tiberius tested his grammarians by asking them such questions; see the Roman historian Suetonius, *Tiberius* 70.
1. *Odyssey* 10.526; ossuaries are urns for bones.
2. Job 3.13–15.
3. See *Religio Medici* 33: "Not only whole countries, but particular persons have their tutelary and guardian angels."

tion, and only arise unto late posterity, as emblems of mortal vanities, antidotes against pride, vainglory, and madding vices. Pagan vainglories which thought the world might last for ever, had encouragement for ambition; and, finding no *Atropos*[4] unto the immortality of their names, were never damped with the necessity of oblivion. Even old ambitions had the advantage of ours, in the attempts of their vainglories, who acting early, and before the probable meridian of time,[5] have by this time found great accomplishment of their designs, whereby the ancient heroes have already outlasted their monuments, and mechanical preservations. But in this latter scene of time, we cannot expect such mummies unto our memories, when ambition may fear the prophecy of Elias,[6] and Charles the Fifth can never hope to live within two Methuselahs of Hector.[7]

And therefore, restless inquietude for the diuturnity[8] of our memories unto present considerations seems a vanity almost out of date, and superannuated piece of folly. We cannot hope to live so long in our names, as some have done in their persons. One face of Janus[9] holds no proportion unto the other. 'Tis too late to be ambitious. The great mutations of the world are acted, or time may be too short for our designs. To extend our memories by monuments, whose death we daily pray for, and whose duration we cannot hope, without injury to our expectations in the advent of the last day, were a contradiction to our beliefs. We whose generations are ordained in this setting part of time, are providentially taken off from such imaginations; and, being necessitated to eye the remaining particle of futurity, are naturally constituted unto thoughts of the next world, and cannot excusably decline the consideration of that duration, which maketh pyramids pillars of snow, and all that's past a moment.

Circles and right lines limit and close all bodies, and the mortal right lined circle[1] must conclude and shut up all. There is no antidote against the opium of time, which temporally considereth all things: our fathers find their graves in our short memories, and sadly tell us how we may be buried in our survivors. Gravestones tell truth scarce forty years.[2] Generations pass while some trees stand, and old families last not three oaks. To be read by bare inscriptions like many in Gruter,[3] to hope for eternity by enigmatical epithets or first letters of our names, to be studied by antiquaries, who we were, and have new names given us like many of the mummies,[4] are cold consolations unto the students of perpetuity, even by everlasting languages.

To be content that times to come should only know there was such a man, not caring whether they knew more of him, was a frigid ambition in Cardan;[5] disparaging his horoscopal inclination and judgment of himself. Who cares to subsist like

4. The name of the Fate who cut short human life.
5. About 1000 B.C., the supposed midpoint of the world's history.
6. Browne's marginalia: "That the world may last but six thousand years" (i.e., from 4000 B.C. to A.D. 2000).
7. "Hector's fame lasting above two lives of Methuselah" (2 × 969, or 1,938 years). The fame of Charles V (born 1500) can last for only 500 years before the end of the world.
8. Long duration.
9. Roman god of doorways whose temple was shut in peace and open in war.

1. Browne's marginalia: "θ The character of death." The Greek letter theta (θ) is the initial letter in *thanatos* (death).
2. Browne's marginalia: "Old one's being taken up, and other bodies laid under them."
3. Janus Gruterus, the Dutch scholar, died c. 1607.
4. Browne's note: "Which men show in several countries, giving them what names they please; and unto some the names of the old Egyptian kings out of Herodotus."
5. Girolamo Cardano (1501–1576), Italian physician and mathematician.

Hippocrates's patients, or Achilles's horses in Homer,[6] under naked nominations, without deserts and noble acts, which are the balsam of our memories, the *entelechia*[7] and soul of our subsistences? To be nameless in worthy deeds, exceeds an infamous history. The Canaanitish woman lives more happily without a name, than Herodias with one.[8] And who had not rather have been the good thief, than Pilate?

But the iniquity of oblivion blindly scattereth her poppy, and deals with the memory of men without distinction to merit of perpetuity. Who can but pity the founder of the pyramids? Herostratus lives that burnt the temple of Diana, he is almost lost that built it.[9] Time hath spared the epitaph of Adrian's horse, confounded that of himself. In vain we compute our felicities by the advantage of our good names, since bad have equal durations, and Thersites[1] is like to live as long as Agamemnon. Who knows whether the best of men be known, or whether there be not more remarkable persons forgot, than any that stand remembered in the known account of time? Without the favor of the everlasting register, the first man had been as unknown as the last, and Methuselah's long life had been his only chronicle.

Oblivion is not to be hired. The greater part must be content to be as though they had not been, to be found in the register of God, not in the record of man. Twenty seven names make up the first story before the flood, and the recorded names ever since contain not one living century. The number of the dead long exceedeth all that shall live. The night of time far surpasseth the day, and who knows when was the equinox? Every hour adds unto that current arithmetic, which scarce stands one moment. And since death must be the *Lucina*[2] of life, and even pagans could doubt, whether thus to live were to die; since our longest sun sets at right descensions, and makes but winter arches,[3] and therefore it cannot be long before we lie down in darkness, and have our light in ashes;[4] since the brother of death[5] daily haunts us with dying mementos, and time that grows old in itself, bids us hope no long duration;—diuturnity is a dream and folly of expectation.

Darkness and light divide the course of time, and oblivion shares with memory a great part even of our living beings; we slightly remember our felicities, and the smartest strokes of affliction leave but short smart upon us. Sense endureth no extremities, and sorrows destroy us or themselves. To weep into stones are fables. Afflictions induce callosities;[6] miseries are slippery, or fall like snow upon us, which notwithstanding is no unhappy stupidity. To be ignorant of evils to come, and forgetful of evils past, is a merciful provision in nature, whereby we digest the mixture of our few and evil days, and, our delivered senses not relapsing into cutting remembrances, our sorrows are not kept raw by the edge of repetitions. A great part of antiquity contented their hopes of subsistency with a

---

6. For Achilles's horses, see *Iliad* 16.149–52.

7. The essence of actual being according to Aristotle, *On the Soul* 312a.

8. Herodias demanded the head of John the Baptist; the Canaanite woman offered water to Christ (Matthew 14.6, 15.22).

9. For Chersiphon, who built the temple of Diana, see Pliny 36.21.

1. Obnoxious soldier who criticized Agamemnon (*Iliad* 2).

2. Roman goddess of childbirth.

3. Our longest life is but the length of a winter's day.

4. Browne's note: "According to the custom of the Jews, who place a lighted wax candle in a pot of ashes by the corps."

5. Sleep.

6. Callousness.

transmigration of their souls,—a good way to continue their memories, while, having the advantage of plural successions, they could not but act something remarkable in such variety of beings, and enjoying the fame of their passed selves, make accumulation of glory unto their last durations. Others, rather than be lost in the uncomfortable night of nothing, were content to recede into the common being, and make one particle of the public soul of all things, which was no more than to return into their unknown and divine original again. Egyptian ingenuity was more unsatisfied, contriving their bodies in sweet consistencies, to attend the return of their souls. But all was vanity, feeding the wind,[7] and folly. The Egyptian mummies, which Cambyses[8] or time hath spared, avarice now consumeth. Mummy[9] is become merchandise, Mizraim cures wounds, and Pharaoh is sold for balsams.

In vain do individuals hope for immortality, or any patent from oblivion, in preservations below the moon: men have been deceived even in their flatteries, above the sun, and studied conceits to perpetuate their names in heaven. The various cosmography of that part hath already varied the names of contrived constellations; Nimrod is lost in Orion, and Osiris in the dog-star. While we look for incorruption in the heavens, we find they are but like the earth;—durable in their main bodies, alterable in their parts; whereof, beside comets and new stars, perspectives begin to tell tales,[1] and the spots that wander about the sun, with Phaeton's favor, would make clear conviction.

There is nothing strictly immortal, but immortality. Whatever hath no beginning, may be confident of no end;—which is the peculiar of that necessary essence that cannot destroy itself;—and the highest strain of omnipotency, to be so powerfully constituted as not to suffer even from the power of itself: all others have a dependent being and within the reach of destruction. But the sufficiency of Christian immortality frustrates all earthly glory, and the quality of either state after death, makes a folly of posthumous memory. God who can only destroy our souls, and hath assured our resurrection, either of our bodies or names hath directly promised no duration. Wherein there is so much of chance, that the boldest expectants have found unhappy frustration; and to hold long subsistence, seems but a scape in oblivion. But man is a noble animal, splendid in ashes, and pompous in the grave, solemnizing nativities and deaths with equal lustre, nor omitting ceremonies of bravery in the infamy of his nature.

Life is a pure flame, and we live by an invisible sun within us. A small fire sufficeth for life, great flames seemed too little after death, while men vainly affected precious pyres, and to burn like Sardanapalus;[2] but the wisdom of funeral laws found the folly of prodigal blazes, and reduced undoing fires unto the rule of sober obsequies, wherein few could be so mean as not to provide wood, pitch, a mourner, and an urn.[3]

Five languages secured not the epitaph of Gordianus.[3] The man of God lives longer without a tomb than any by one, invisibly interred by angels, and adjudged to obscurity, though not without some marks directing human discovery. Enoch

---

7. Ecclesiastes 1.14.
8. Ancient Persian king who attacked Egypt.
9. Ground up, as a drug.
1. "Perspectives" (telescopes) showed that comets penetrated the region above the moon, an area that Aristotle claimed was "incorruptible."
2. Assyrian king who had his whole court buried with him.
3. Browne's note: "In Greek, Latin, Hebrew, Egyptian, Arabic, defaced by Licinus the Emperor."

and Elias,[4] without either tomb or burial, in an anomalous state of being, are the great examples of perpetuity, in their long and living memory, in strict account being still on this side death, and having a late part yet to act upon this stage of earth. If in the decretory term of the world[5] we shall not all die but be changed, according to received translation, the last day will make but few graves; at least quick resurrections will anticipate lasting sepultures. Some graves will be opened before they be quite closed, and Lazarus[6] be no wonder. When many that feared to die, shall groan that they can die but once, the dismal state is the second and living death,[7] when life puts despair on the damned; when men shall wish the coverings of mountains, not of monuments, and annihilation shall be courted.

While some have studied monuments, others have studiously declined them, and some have been so vainly boisterous, that they durst not acknowledge their graves; wherein Alaricus seems most subtle, who had a river turned to hide his bones at the bottom.[8] Even Sylla, that thought himself safe in his urn, could not prevent revenging tongues, and stones thrown at his monument. Happy are they whom privacy makes innocent, who deal so with men in this world, that they are not afraid to meet them in the next; who, when they die, make no commotion among the dead, and are not touched with that poetical taunt of Isaiah.[9]

Pyramids, arches, obelisks, were but the irregularities of vainglory, and wild enormities of ancient magnanimity. But the most magnanimous resolution rests in the Christian religion, which trampleth upon pride, and sits on the neck of ambition, humbly pursuing that infallible perpetuity, unto which all others must diminish their diameters, and be poorly seen in angles of contingency.[1]

Pious spirits who passed their days in raptures of futurity, made little more of this world, than the world that was before it, while they lay obscure in the chaos of preordination, and night of their forebeings. And if any have been so happy as truly to understand Christian annihilation, ecstasies, exolution, liquefaction, transformation, the kiss of the Spouse, gustation of God, and ingression into the divine shadow,[2] they have already had an handsome anticipation of heaven; the glory of the world is surely over, and the earth in ashes unto them.

To subsist in lasting monuments, to live in their productions, to exist in their names and predicament of chimaeras,[3] was large satisfaction unto old expectations, and made one part of their Elysiums. But all this is nothing in the metaphysics of true belief. To live indeed, is to be again ourselves, which being not only an hope, but an evidence in noble believers, 't is all one to lie in St. Innocent's churchyard,[4] as in the sands of Egypt. Ready to be any thing, in the ecstasy of being ever, and as content with six foot as the *moles* of Adrianus.[5]

> —*tabésne cadavera solvat,*
> *An rogus, haud refert.*—Lucan.[6]

4. Believed to be the "two witnesses" of Revelation 11.3ff., who would appear at the end of time.
5. I.e., the Last Judgment.
6. Raised from death by Christ (John 11).
7. Revelation 20.14, 21.8.
8. Browne's marginalia: "According to Jordandes [6th-century historian of the Goths]."
9. Browne's marginalia: "Isaiah 14.4–17."
1. Browne's marginalia: "*Angulus contingentiae,* the least of Angles."
2. Exolution: the soul's release; the Spouse: the Church; ingression into the divine shadow: echoes the Platonic philosopher Ficino, who expressed the paradox that light is the shadow of God.
3. Predicament is a term in logic, meaning that which is asserted. Chimaeras were creatures with a lion's head, a goat's body, and a serpent's tale; hence a fanciful notion or unfounded conception.
4. Browne's marginalia: "In Paris where bodies soon consume."
5. Roman mausoleum.
6. It does not matter whether the corpses are placed on the pyre or decompose (Lucan, *Civil War* 7.809–10).

Robert Burton

(1577–1640)

One of the most learned authors of his generation, Robert Burton was also one of the most popular and influential. While he spent most of his life at Oxford, where he was elected a student of Christ Church and took his Bachelor of Divinity in 1614, Burton wrote *The Anatomy of Melancholy* (1621) which went through many different editions (eight alone in the seventeenth century) and made a bundle of money for its publisher Henry Cripps. The topic was based on the ancient theory of the humors, which still dominated both medicine and personality theory in the early modern period. The sanguine humor was hot and moist and characterized a happy disposition; the choleric humor was hot and dry and characterized an angry one; the phlegmatic humor was cold and moist and characterized an impassive one; and the melancholic humor was cold and dry and signified the pensive and imaginative soul of Hamlet and so many other lovelorn sonneteers, scholars, and mystics.

An anatomy, exhaustively dissecting the topic into its parts, the book treats the full body of knowledge on the disease of melancholy with an encyclopedic thoroughness, covering the inherited wisdom of a whole gamut of ancient authors. The book is huge, a veritable brick even in paperback. It is divided into three parts: the causes and symptoms of melancholy, cures for melancholy, and love melancholy and religious melancholy. One of the liveliest parts of the book is its preface, *Democritus to the Reader*, in which Burton writes of his "silent, sedentary, solitary, private life" and of "the diseases in a commonwealth."

As this brief quotation suggests, Burton was a master of the elegant pleonasm, prolific in the elegantly varied synonym. His syntax is almost the opposite of Bacon's. Where Bacon's sentences are terse and pointed, Burton's are long and meandering. Part of the pleasure in reading this unfamiliar prose style comes from its unexpected digressions. Much loved in the author's own lifetime, Burton's *Anatomy* influenced Milton's *L'Allegro* and *Il Penseroso*. Later, Dr. Johnson wrote that *The Anatomy* was the only book that could get him out of bed two hours earlier than he was used to. Closest to Sir Thomas Browne's style in its humor, Robert Burton's *Anatomy* is a delightful read, a cure for boredom in any age.

from The Anatomy of Melancholy

[THE UTOPIA OF DEMOCRITUS][1]

Kingdoms, provinces, and politic bodies are likewise sensible and subject to this disease, as Boterus in his Politics hath proved at large.[2] "As in human bodies," saith he, "there be divers alterations proceeding from humors, so there be many diseases in a commonwealth, which do as diversely happen from several distempers," as you may easily perceive by their particular symptoms. For where you shall see the people civil, obedient to God and Princes, judicious, peaceable and quiet, rich, fortunate, and flourish, to live in peace, in unity and concord, a country well tilled, many fair built and populous cities, as old Cato said,[3] the people are neat, polite and terse, where they live well and happily, which our politicians make the chief end of a commonwealth; and which Aristotle calls a general blessing, Polybius a desirable and favor-

---

1. Democritus was an ancient Greek philosopher who held that all things were composed of atoms. Though melancholy by nature, he laughed at the world. Burton's purpose in his *Anatomy* is to find the cause of melancholy as Democritus searched for the cause of melancholy when he cut up beasts and looked at their insides.

2. Giovanni Botero, *De politia illustrium,* translated into English as *Of the Greatness and Magnificance of Cities* (1606).
3. Cato the Elder (234–149 B.C.) in his *De re rustica* (On Farming).

able condition, that country is free from melancholy;[4] as it was in Italy in the time of Augustus, now in China, now in many other flourishing kingdoms of Europe. But whereas you shall see many discontents, common grievances, complaints, poverty, barbarism, beggary, plagues, wars, rebellions, seditions, mutinies, contentions, idleness, riot, epicurism,[5] the land lie untilled, waste, full of bogs, fens, deserts, &c., cities decayed, base and poor towns, villages depopulated, the people squalid, ugly, uncivil; that kingdom, that country, must needs be discontent, melancholy, hath a sick body, and had need to be reformed.

Now that cannot well be effected, till the causes of these maladies be first removed, which commonly proceed from their own default, or some accidental inconvenience: as to be sited in a bad clime, too far North, sterile, in a barren place, as the desert of Libya, deserts of Arabia, places void of waters, as those of Lop and Belgian in Asia, or in a bad air, as at Alexandretta, Bantam, Pisa, Durazzo, S. John de Ullua, &c., or in danger of the sea's continual inundations, as in many places of the Low Countries, and elsewhere, or near some bad neighbors, as Hungarians to Turks, Podolians to Tartars,[6] or almost any bordering countries, they live in fear still, and by reason of hostile incursions are oftentimes left desolate. So are cities by reason of wars, fires, plagues, inundations, wild beasts, decay of trades, barred havens, the sea's violence, as Antwerp may witness of late, Syracuse of old, Brundusium in Italy, Rye & Dover with us, and many that at this day suspect the sea's fury and rage, and labor against it, as the Venetians, to their inestimable charge. But the most frequent maladies are such as proceed from themselves, as first when religion & God's service is neglected, innovated or altered, where they do not fear God, obey their Prince, where Atheism, Epicurism, Sacrilege, Simony,[7] &c., and all such impieties are freely committed, that country cannot prosper. When Abraham came to Gerar, and saw a bad land, he said, sure the fear of God was not in that place.[8] Cyprian Echovius, a Spanish Chorographer,[9] above all other Cities of Spain commends Barcino,[1] "in which there was no beggar, no man poor, &c., but all rich and in good estate, and he gives the reason, because they were more religious than their neighbors." Why was Israel so often spoiled by their enemies, led into captivity, &c., but for their idolatry, neglect of God's word, for sacrilege, even for one Achan's fault?[2] And what shall we expect that have such multitudes of Achans, Church-robbers, Simoniacal Patrons, &c.? How can they hope to flourish, that neglect divine duties, that live most part like Epicures?[3]

Other common grievances are generally noxious to a body politic; alteration of laws and customs, breaking privileges, general oppressions, seditions, &c., observed by Aristotle,[4] Bodine, Boterus, Junius, Arniseus, &c. I will only point at some of the chiefest. Confusion, ill government, which proceeds from unskillful, slothful, griping, covetous, unjust, rash, or tyrannizing magistrates, when they are fools, idiots, children, proud, wilful, partial, indiscreet, oppressors, giddy heads, tyrants, not able or unfit to manage such offices.[5] Many noble cities and flourishing kingdoms by that

---

4. The commonweal of Aristotle, *Politics* 3.4; see also Polybius 6 and Plato, *Laws* 5.
5. The philosophy of Epicurus, devotion to a life of ease, in which pleasure is the greatest good.
6. Podolians: inhabitants of West central Ukraine; Tartars: inhabitants of Central Asia.
7. The selling of church offices, benefices, or preferments.
8. Genesis 10.19, 20.1.
9. Cyprian Echovius, a writer of geographical description,

Deliciis Hispaniae (1604).
1. Barcelona.
2. Achan, a Judahite who was stoned for keeping some of the spoil from Jericho. Joshua 7.1; Chronicles 2.7.
3. Those who think pleasure is the greatest good.
4. Aristotle, *Politics* 5.3.
5. A reference to *Polycraticus*, a treatise on government, by John of Salisbury, 12th-century English scholastic philosopher.

means are desolate, the whole body groans under such heads, and all the members must needs be misaffected, as at this day those goodly provinces in Asia Minor, &c., groan under the burden of a Turkish government; and those vast kingdoms of Muscovia, Russia,[6] under a tyrannizing Duke. Who ever heard of more civil and rich populous countries than those of Greece, Asia Minor, "abounding with all wealth, multitude of inhabitants, force, power, splendor, and magnificence?" and that miracle of countries, the Holy Land, that in so small a compass of ground could maintain so many towns, cities, produce so many fighting men? Egypt, another Paradise, now barbarous and desert, and almost waste, by the despotical government of an imperious Turk, sent into an intolerable slavery (one saith); not only fire and water, goods or lands, but such is their slavery, their lives and souls depend upon his insolent will and command: a tyrant that spoils all wheresoever he comes, insomuch that an historian complains, "If an old inhabitant should now see them, he would not know them, if a traveler, or stranger, it would grieve his heart to behold them." Where, as Aristotle notes, new burdens and exactions daily come upon them, like those of which Zosimus [speaks],[7] so grievous, as that men prostituted their wives, fathers their sons, for the profit of overseers, &c., they must needs be discontent, as Tully holds,[8] hence come those complaints and tears of cities, poor, miserable, rebellious, and desperate subjects, as Hippolytus[9] adds: and as a judicious countryman of ours observed not long since in a survey of that great Duchy of Tuscany, the people lived much grieved and discontent, as appeared by their manifold and manifest complainings in that kind; "that the State was like a sick body which had lately taken physic, whose humors were not yet well settled, and weakened so much by purging, that nothing was left but melancholy."

Whereas the Princes and Potentates are immoderate in lust, hypocrites, epicures, of no religion, but in show: what so brittle and unsure? what sooner subverts their estates than wandering & raging lusts on their subjects' wives, daughters, to say no worse? They that should lead the way to all virtuous actions, are the ringleaders oftentimes of all mischief and dissolute courses, and by that means their countries are plagued, "and they themselves often ruined, banished or murdered by conspiracy of their subjects,"[1] as Sardanapulus was, Dionysius Junior, Heliogabalus, Periander, Pisistratus, Tarquinius, Timocrates, Childericus, Appius Claudius, Andronicus, Galeazzo Sforza, Alexander de Medici, &c.

Whereas the Princes or great men are malicious, envious, factious, ambitious, emulators, they tear a commonwealth asunder, as so many Guelfs and Ghibellines,[2] disturb the quietness of it, and with mutual murders let it bleed to death. Our histories are too full of such barbarous inhumanities, and the miseries that issue from them.

Whereas they be like so many horse-leeches, hungry, griping, corrupt, covetous, greedy for property, ravenous as wolves (for as Tully writes, "Whoso rules is a benefit, and he who rules cattle should study their interests"), or such prefer their private before the public good (for as he said long since, "private interests always interfere with public benefits"), or whereas they be illiterate, ignorant, empirics[3] in policy, lacking in capacity, courage, & knowledge, wise only by inheritance, and in authority

---

6. See Dr. Giles Fletcher's *Of the Russe Common Wealth* (1591).
7. Zosimus, a strongly anti-Christian, Greek author (fl. 450), who wrote a history of the Roman empire.
8. Marcus Tullius Cicero, *Epistulae ad Atticum* 2.18.
9. Hippolytus Collibus, early modern Swiss author of *The*

Growth of Cities.
1. Boterus *De Politia illustrium* 9.4.
2. The warring parties of the Pope and of the Emperor in late medieval Florence.
3. Those who draw their practice only from experience.

by birthright, favor, or for their wealth and titles; there must needs be a fault, a great defect: because, as an old philosopher affirms, such men are not always fit: "Of an infinite number few alone are Senators, and of those few fewer good, and of that small number of honest good and noble men, few that are learned, wise, discreet and sufficient, able to discharge such places;" it must needs turn to the confusion of a State.

For as the Princes are, so are the people;[4] and which Antigonus right well said of old, he that teacheth the King of Macedon, teacheth all his subjects, is a true saying still.

> For Princes are the glass, the school, the book,
> Where subjects' eyes do learn, do read, do look.
>
> *Shakespeare*[5]

> ———*Swiftly, in a trice,*
> *We are corrupted by domestic vice;*
> *When precedents of sin our great ones give,*
> *Few are the youths that free from vice can live.*
>
> *Juvenal*[6]

Their examples are soonest followed, vices entertained; if they be profane, irreligious, lascivious, riotous, epicures, factious, covetous, ambitious, illiterate, so will the commons most part be idle, unthrifts, prone to lust, drunkards, and therefore poor and needy (for poverty begets sedition and villainy), upon all occasions ready to mutiny and rebel, discontent still, complaining, murmuring, grudging, apt to all outrages, thefts, treasons, murders, innovations, in debt, shifters, cozeners, outlaws, men of evil life and reputation. It was an old Politician's Aphorism, "They that are poor and bad envy rich, hate good men, abhor the present government, wish for a new, and would have all turned topsy-turvy."[7] When Catiline rebelled in Rome, he got a company of such debauched rogues together, they were his familiars and coadjutors; and such have been your rebels most part in all ages, Jack Cade, Tom Straw, Kett, and his companions.[8]

Where they be generally riotous and contentious, where there be many discords, many laws, many lawsuits, many lawyers, and many physicians, it is a manifest sign of a distempered, melancholy state, as Plato long since maintained: for where such kind of men swarm, they will make more work for themselves, and that body politic diseased, which was otherwise sound. A general mischief in these our times, an insensible plague, and never so many of them: "which are now multiplied" (saith Mat. Geraldus, a Lawyer himself,) "as so many locusts, not the parents, but the plagues of the country, & for the most part a supercilious, bad, covetous, litigious generation of men;" a purse-milking nation, a clamorous company, gowned vultures, "who live by violence and bloodshed, thieves and seminaries of discord; worse than any pollers[9] by the highway side, gold-hawks, gold-borers, money-fishers, temple thieves, market-jinglers, horrible wretches, slave-traders, &c.," that take upon them to make peace, but are indeed the very disturbers of our peace, a company of irreligious Harpies, scraping, griping catchpoles (I mean our common hungry pettifoggers; I love and honor in the mean time all good laws, and worthy lawyers, that are so many oracles

---

4. Cicero, *De legibus* 3.
5. Shakespeare, *The Rape of Lucrece*, 615–16.
6. Juvenal 14.31–33.
7. Sallust, *Cataline* 37.3.

8. Jack Cade led the 1450 rebellion in Kent. Robert Kett (d. 1549) led an agrarian revolt in Norfolk against the enclosure of common land for sheep grazing.
9. Robbers.

and pilots of a well-governed commonwealth), without art, without judgment, that do more harm, as Livy said, than sickness, wars, hunger, diseases; "and cause a most incredible destruction of a Commonwealth," saith Sesellius, a famous Civilian some-time in Paris. As ivy doth by an oak, embrace it so long, until it hath got the heart out of it, so do they by such places they inhabit, no counsel at all, no justice, no speech to be had, he must be fee'd still, or else he is as mute as a fish, better open an oyster without a knife. "I speak out of experience," saith Sarisburiensis,[1] "I have been a thousand times amongst them, & Charon[2] himself is more gentle than they; he is contented with his single pay, but they multiply still, they are never satisfied:" besides, they have pernicious tongues, as he terms it, they must be fee'd to say noth-ing, and get more to hold their peace than we can to say our best. They will speak their clients fair, and invite them to their tables, but, as he follows it, "of all injustice there is none so pernicious as that of theirs, which, when they deceive most, will seem to be honest men." They take upon them to be peacemakers, and to espouse the cause of the humble, to help them to their right, they play patron to the afflicted, but all is for their own good, that they may drain the moneybags of the rich, they plead for poor men free, but they are but as a stale to catch others. If there be no jar, they can make a jar, out of the law itself find still some quirk or other, to set them at odds, and continue causes so long, I know not how many years before the cause is heard, and when 'tis judged and determined, by reason of some tricks and errors it is as fresh to begin, after twice seven years sometimes, as it was at first; and so they prolong time, delay suits, till they have enriched themselves, and beggared their clients. And as Cato inveighed against Isocrates' scholars,[3] we may justly tax our wrangling lawyers, they do grow old in lawsuits, are so litigious & busy here on earth, that I think they will plead their clients' causes hereafter, some of them in hell. Simlerus complains, amongst the Switzers, of the Advocates in his time, that when they should make an end, they begin controversies, and "protract their causes many years, persuading them their title is good, till their patrimonies be consumed, and that they have spent more in seeking than the thing is worth, or they shall get by the recov-ery."[4] So he that goes to law, as the proverb is, holds a wolf by the ears, or, as a sheep in a storm runs for shelter to a briar, if he prosecute his cause he is consumed, if he surcease his suit he loseth all; what difference? They had wont, heretofore, saith Austin,[5] to end matters by common arbitrators, and so in Switzerland, (we are informed by Simlerus,) "they had some common arbitrators, or daysmen in every town, that made a friendly composition betwixt man and man; and he much wonders at their honest simplicity, that could keep peace so well, and end such great causes by that means." At Fez, in Africa, they have neither lawyers nor advocates; but if there be any controversies amongst them, both parties, plaintiff and defendant, come to their Alfakins or chief Judges, "& at once, without any further appeals or pitiful delays, the cause is heard and ended. Our forefathers, as a worthy Chorographer[6] of ours observes, had wont with a few golden crosses, and lines in verse, [to] make all conveyances, assurances. And such was the candor & integrity of succeeding ages, that a deed (as I have oft seen), to convey a whole manor, was succinctly contained

1. John of Salisbury, *Polycraticus*, 1. Prologue.
2. Mythological figure who conveyed the souls of the dead across the River Styx.
3. Plutarch, *Life of Cato* 23.
4. Simlerus, 16th century Swiss theologian and author of

a history of the Helvetian Republic.
5. Saint Augustine (354–430).
6. Describer of particular regions referring to William Camden, author of *Brittania* (1586).

in some twenty lines or thereabouts; like that Schede or Scytala Laconica,[7] so much renowned of old in all contracts, which Tully so earnestly commends to Atticus,[8] Plutarch in his Lysander, Aristotle, Thucydides, Diodorus, and Suidas, approve and magnify for that Laconic brevity in this kind; and well they might, for, according to Tertullian,[9] there is much more certainty in fewer words. And so was it of old throughout: but now many skins of parchment will scarce serve turn; he that buys and sells a house, must have a house full of writings, there be so many circumstances, so many words, such tautological repetitions of all particulars (to avoid cavillation, they say), but we find, by our woeful experience, that to subtle wits it is a cause of much more contention and variance, and scarce any conveyance so accurately penned by one, which another will not find a crack in, or cavil at; if any one word be misplaced, any little error, all is disannulled. That which is law today is none tomorrow, that which is sound in one man's opinion, is most faulty to another; that, in conclusion, here is nothing amongst us but contention and confusion, we band one against another. And that which long since Plutarch complained of them in Asia, may be verified in our times. "These men here assembled, come not to sacrifice to their gods, to offer Jupiter their first fruits, or merriments to Bacchus; but a yearly disease exasperating Asia hath brought them hither, to make an end of their controversies and law suits." 'Tis a destructive rout that seek one another's ruin. Such most part are our ordinary suitors, termers, clients; new stirs every day, mistakes, errors, cavils, and at this present, as I have heard, in some one Court, I know not how many thousand causes: no person free, no title almost good, with such bitterness in following, so many slights, procrastinations, delays, forgery, such cost (for infinite sums are inconsiderately spent), violence and malice, I know not by whose fault, lawyers, clients, laws, both or all: but as Paul reprehended the Corinthians long since,[1] I may more appositely infer now: "There is a fault amongst you, & I speak it to your shame; is there not a wise man amongst you, to judge between his brethren; but that a brother goes to law with a brother?" And Christ's counsel concerning lawsuits was never so fit to be inculcated, as in this age: "Agree with thine adversary quickly," &c.[2] I could repeat many such particular grievances, which must disturb a body politic. To shut up all in brief, where good government is, prudent and wise Princes, there all things thrive and prosper, peace and happiness is in that land: where it is otherwise, all things are ugly to behold, incult,[3] barbarous, uncivil, a Paradise is turned to a wilderness. This Island amongst the rest, our next neighbors the French and Germans, may be a sufficient witness, that in a short time, by that prudent policy of the Romans, was brought from barbarism; see but what Caesar reports of us, and Tacitus of those old Germans; they were once as uncivil as they in Virginia, yet by planting of colonies and good laws, they became, from barbarous outlaws, to be full of rich and populous cities, as now they are, and most flourishing kingdoms. Even so might Virginia, and those wild Irish, have been civilized long since, if that order had been heretofore taken, which now begins, of planting colonies, &c. I have read a discourse, printed in the year 1612, "discovering the true causes why Ireland was never entirely subdued, or brought under obedience to the Crown of England, until the beginning of his Majesty's happy reign."[4] Yet if his reasons were thoroughly scanned

---

7. Spartan ordinance.
8. Cicero, *Epistulae ad Atticum* 10.3.
9. Roman theologian (c. A.D. 150–230).
1. 1 Corinthians 6.5–6.

2. Matthew 5.25.
3. Uncultivated, rough.
4. The author is Sir John Davies (1529–1626), Attorney General for Ireland.

by a judicious politician, I am afraid he would not altogether be approved, but that it would turn to the dishonor of our nation, to suffer it to lie so long waste. Yea, and if some travelers should see (to come nearer home) those rich United Provinces of Holland, Zealand, &c., over against us; those neat cities and populous towns, full of most industrious artificers, so much land recovered from the sea, and so painfully preserved by those artificial inventions, so wonderfully approved, as that of Bemster in Holland, so that you would find nothing equal to it or like it in the whole world, saith Bertius the Geographer, all the world cannot match it, so many navigable channels from place to place, made by men's hands, &c., and on the other side so many thousand acres of our fens lie drowned, our cities thin, and those vile, poor, and ugly to behold in respect of theirs, our trades decayed, our still running rivers stopped, and that beneficial use of transportation wholly neglected, so many havens void of ships and towns, so many parks and forests for pleasure, barren heaths, so many villages depopulated, &c., I think sure he would find some fault.

I may not deny but that this nation of ours doth bear a good name amongst foreigners, is a most noble, a most flourishing kingdom, by common consent of all Geographers, Historians, Politicians, 'tis an unique stronghold, and which Quintius in Livy said of the inhabitants of Peloponnesus, may be well applied to us, we are like so many tortoises in our shells, safely defended by an angry sea, as a wall on all sides. Our Island hath many such honorable elogiums;[5] and as a learned countryman of ours right well hath it, "Ever since the Normans' first coming into England, this country both for military matters, and all other of civility, hath been paralleled with the most flourishing kingdoms of Europe & our Christian world,"[6] a blessed, a rich country, and one of the fortunate Isles: and for some things preferred before other countries, for expert seamen, our laborious discoveries, art of navigation, true merchants, they carry the bell away from all other nations, even the Portugals and Hollanders themselves; "without all fear," saith Boterus,[7] "furrowing the ocean winter and summer, and two of their captains, with no less valor than fortune, have sailed round about the world." We have besides many particular blessings, which our neighbors want, the Gospel truly preached, Church discipline established, long peace and quietness, free from exactions, foreign fears, invasions, domestical seditions, well manured, fortified by art and nature, and now most happy in that fortunate union of England and Scotland,[8] which our forefathers have labored to effect, and desired to see. But in which we excel all others, a wise, learned, religious King, another Numa, a second Augustus, a true Josiah,[9] most worthy senators, a learned clergy, an obedient commonalty, &c. Yet amongst many roses some thistles grow, some bad weeds and enormities, which much disturb the peace of this body politic, eclipse the honor and glory of it, fit to be rooted out, and with all speed to be reformed.

Division of the Body, Humors, Spirits[1]

Of the parts of the Body, there be many divisions: the most approved is that of Laurentius,[2] out of Hippocrates: which is, into parts contained, or containing. Contained are either humors or spirits.

5. Eulogies.
6. Camden, *Brittania* (1586).
7. Giovanni Botero, an Italian political theorist.
8. Effected by James VI of Scotland's becoming James I of England.

9. Numa, founder of Roman religion; Augustus, first Roman emperor; Josiah, reformer of Jewish law.
1. Part I, Section I, Member ii, Subsection II.
2. Andreas Laurentius, 16th-century writer on anatomy; Hippocrates, Greek founder of medicine.

A humor is a liquid or fluent part of the body, comprehended in it, for the preservation of it; and is either innate or born with us, or adventitious and acquisite. The radical or innate is daily supplied by nourishment, which some call cambium, and make those secondary humors of ros and gluten to maintain it; or acquisite, to maintain these four first primary humors, coming and proceeding from the first concoction in the liver, by which means chyle[3] is excluded. Some divide them into profitable and excrementitious. But Crato[4] out of Hippocrates will have all four to be juice, and not excrements, without which no living creature can be sustained: which four, though they be comprehended in the mass of blood, yet they have their several affections, by which they are distinguished from one another, and from those adventitious, peccant, or diseased humors, as Melancthon[5] calls them.

Blood is a hot, sweet, temperate, red humor, prepared in the meseraic[6] veins, and made of the most temperate parts of the chylus in the liver, whose office is to nourish the whole body, to give it strength and color, being dispersed by the veins through every part of it. And from it spirits are first begotten in the heart, which afterwards by the arteries are communicated to the other parts.

Pituita, or phlegm, is a cold and moist humor, begotten of the colder parts of the chylus (or white juice coming out of the meat digested in the stomach) in the liver; his office is to nourish and moisten the members of the body, which, as the tongue, are moved, that they be not over dry.

Choler is hot and dry, bitter, begotten of the hotter parts of the chylus, and gathered to the gall: it helps the natural heat and senses, and serves to the expelling of excrements.

Melancholy, cold and dry, thick, black, and sour, begotten of the more feculent[7] part of nourishment, and purged from the spleen, is a bridle to the other two hot humors, blood and choler, preserving them in the blood, and nourishing the bones. These four humors have some analogy with the four elements, and to the four ages in man.

To these humors you may add serum, which is the matter of urine, & those excrementitious humors of the third concoction, sweat & tears.

Spirit is a most subtle vapor, which is expressed from the blood, and the instrument of the soul, to perform all his actions; a common tie or medium betwixt the body and the soul, as some will have it; or, as Paracelsus,[8] a fourth soul of itself. Melancthon holds the fountain of these spirits to be the heart; begotten there, and afterwards conveyed to the brain, they take another nature to them: Of these spirits there be three kinds, according to the three principal parts, brain, heart, liver; natural, vital, animal. The natural are begotten in the liver, and thence dispersed through the veins, to perform those natural actions. The vital spirits are made in the heart of the natural, which by the arteries are transported to all the other parts: if these spirits cease, then life ceaseth, as in a syncope or swooning. The animal spirits formed of the vital, brought up to the brain, and diffused by the nerves, to the subordinate members, give sense and motion to them all.

---

3. The white milky fluid formed by the action of the pancreatic juice and the bile on the chyme, or pulpy acid matter into which food is converted in the stomach.
4. Johann Craton, 16th-century German author of medical treatises.
5. Philip Melanchthon (1497–1560), a humanist and one

of the leading figures of the Lutheran Reformation.
6. A vein of the middle belly.
7. Of the nature of feces.
8. Swiss physician, alchemist, and chemist (1493?–1541). His work was first translated into English as *One Hundred and Fourteen Experiments and Cures* (1590).

The Execution of Charles I. Seventeenth-century German print.

PERSPECTIVES

The Civil War, or the Wars of Three Kingdoms

The English Civil War arose out of citizens' revolutionary demands for their rights and those of their legislature, and out of England's attempt to dominate Ireland and Scotland. The armed conflicts that arose from the demand for political self-determination in every part of the British Isles would have consequences for centuries to come. During the period from 1639 to 1651, war raged not only in England but also in Ireland, Scotland, and Wales; hence, historians now prefer to call this period of conflict the Wars of Three Kingdoms. The origins of the conflict in England were between Parliament and a King who had an absolutist style of governing. Charles I reigned without Parliament from 1629 to 1640, a period referred to as the "Eleven Years' Tyranny." He also imposed unpopular heavy taxes in the form of ship money levies to build up the fleet. Even more controversial was his imposition of Anglican worship and episcopal authority on Puritans and Presbyterians, who felt that such ritual was tantamount to Roman Catholicism. The King placed two Anglican bishops on the court of Star Chamber, who used the arbitrary power of this body to enforce unpopular religious practices.

When the King decided to impose an Anglican liturgy on the Scottish Kirk in 1639, riots broke out in Edinburgh, and Scottish Lowlanders united in a National Covenant against English interference. In 1639 and 1640, Scottish military uprisings necessitated Charles I's recalling Parliament to ask for financial aid. The Parliament was already angered by the eleven-year shutdown by the King, his imposition of taxes without its consent, and his support for Archbishop Laud, whom Parliament viewed as too dictatorial and too high church, shutting out both Puritans (who elected their ministers and disdained Catholic sacraments) and Presbyterians (who favored central church government but not Anglo-Catholic authority or ritual). When Parliament refused after three weeks to grant the King's request for money, the King decided to dissolve the "Short Parliament." In the wake of the dissolution of Parliament, soldiers went on rampages against churches, smashing stained glass windows and altar rails that smacked to them of Roman Catholicism. In some places, soldiers mutinied against their aristocratic commanders.

When the Scots defeated the King's army in the fall of 1640, he had to recall Parliament to petition for more funds. Led by John Pym, the "Long Parliament" seized the opportunity to criticize the King. It passed a Bill of Attainder, condemning to death as a traitor the general of the King's army, Viscount Strafford, who had been accused of instigating the war against Scotland and of suggesting that an Irish Catholic army could be used against England. No proof of guilt was necessary, only assent from the House of Lords and the King. Despite the King's reluctance, the combined opposition of the House of Commons and armed mobs in London in the spring of 1641 pressured him into signing Strafford's death warrant.

That fall two rebellions broke out in Ireland—one organized by Catholic Irish gentry, another arising more spontaneously among the native Gaelic Irish in Ulster against Scots and English settlers who had dispossessed them of their land. Pym blamed the unrest on the King and his Catholic court. Although there was terrible violence, especially in the popular uprisings, the English press wildly exaggerated the extent of the bloodshed, claiming a figure for Protestant deaths in the North of Ireland that was greater than the number of Protestants then living in the whole country. Pym, the leader of the House of Commons, moved that Parliament should offer no help in repressing Irish rebellion unless Charles agreed to dismiss his guilty counselors. The next day, Oliver Cromwell moved that the Parliament empower the Puritan Earl of Essex to head the English militia. Attacks on the King became stronger: his irresponsibility and violation of the security and rights of the people mandated Parliament's wresting power from him. On May 12, Archbishop Laud was executed. Although the King made some concessions, by January 1642 he decided to impeach Pym, four other members of Commons, and one from the House of Lords for treason. However, the accused were safely hidden in the City, and the King left London, not to return until he was put on trial and beheaded six years later. Just on the eve of the outbreak of the war, the "Gentlewomen and Tradesmen's Wives of London" presented their petition to Parliament, complaining against Archbishop Laud's Anglicanism and the threat of violence from Ireland. The first part of the English Civil War (1642–1646), arising from the disputes between Parliament and the King, culminated in the victory of Parliament's New Model Army, headed by Sir Thomas Fairfax.

With the King defeated by the combined forces of the New Model Army and the Scots Covenanters in 1646, new conflicts arose between the army and the Parliament. Closely tied to the army, the Levellers, led by John Lilburne, agitated for a fundamental revision of the constitution: a single representative body, universal suffrage for men, and the abolition of monarchy and noble privilege. Colonel Ludlow, a leader of the republicans, opposed any negotiations with the King and petitioned Parliament to reform the constitution and to put the King on trial. When the House of Commons refused to listen to the army and continued to negotiate with the King, Colonels Ludlow, Ireton, and Pride purged Parliament, placing forty-five members under arrest and prohibiting another 186 from entering the House. This Rump Parliament set up a high court to try the King. On 27 January 1649, Charles I was condemned to death as a tyrant and traitor who had shed the blood of his people. John Bradshaw, President of the Court, proclaimed that the King was subject to the law and the law proceeded from Parliament. Arising out of these events came both the King's own memoir, *Eikon Basilike* ("the

Peter Paul Rubens. *Peace and War*. 1630. One of the greatest painters of the Flemish school, Rubens grew up in Antwerp, where he married and set up his studio. After the death of his wife in 1626, he entered the diplomatic service, traveling to Spain to negotiate a treaty between Philip IV and England in 1628. Idolized and knighted in London, Rubens painted *Peace and War* for Charles I to commemorate the English-Spanish peace treaty of 1629–30. Charles later walked to his death through the Banqueting Hall under a ceiling Rubens painted. *Peace and War* optimistically represents both the court of Charles I at its zenith and the hope for European peace that would be dashed ten years later. The painting is charged with movement. A satyr grasps the fruits of peace, while to the right, Minerva, goddess of wisdom, drives out Mars, god of war, and Fury Allecto. At the center, Peace extends her full breast to the baby Plutus, god of riches.

Royal Image"), ghostwritten and published after his execution by John Gauden, and Milton's militantly republican response *Eikonoklastes* ("Image-Breaker").

In the last stage of the civil war, the dead king's son, Charles II, attempted to regain power through Irish and Scottish aid. In Ireland the Marquis of Ormonde led a coalition of royalists that secured the support of Irish troops for the King in exchange for the free exercise of Catholicism. Before Charles II could land in Dublin, the English sent troops there to put down the uprising. Cromwell slaughtered many at the siege of Drogheda; his campaign throughout Munster killed many civilians. In the aftermath of Cromwell's conquest, what remained of an Irish intelligentsia was either exiled or killed off, and large numbers of native inhabitants were either thrown off their land onto poorer farming land in western Ireland or sent into indentured servitude in the Caribbean. Following policies begun by Elizabeth and James, Cromwell granted Irish land to English settlers. The late events of the war in Ireland are represented here by one of Cromwell's letters from his campaign in Ireland, and by *John O'Dwyer of the Glenn*, a translation of one of the many Irish-language laments for the devastation of the Cromwellian conquest.

In Scotland, Charles II found allies among Presbyterian Covenanters, infuriated with the English Parliament for executing a Scottish monarch, and in the Marquis of Montrose, who recruited the Highland clans. When the Covenanters met with Charles II for the Treaty of Breda in Holland, they imposed on him a promise to reestablish Presbyterianism as the religion of both England and Scotland, to reinstate the Scottish Parliament, and to repudiate his pledges to Ormonde and Montrose. When Charles landed in Scotland, he learned that Montrose, most loyal of all royalists, had been hanged and quartered as a traitor. The political intrigue of Argyle against Montrose can be seen in the Earl of Clarendon's account of Montrose's death. The Covenanters, fighting for Scotland rather than for the King, were defeated by Cromwell at Dunbar. The Scots' losses were so huge that Scottish royalism was revived for one last battle between the King's Cavaliers and Cromwell's Roundheads. Facing Cromwell's army at Worcester in 1651, the forces of Scots and English royalists were vastly outnumbered and easily defeated. Charles II escaped to France, where he remained until the Restoration. Two years later, Cromwell became Lord Protector of the Commonwealth.

━━ ❧❧❧ ━━

John Gauden
1605–1662

John Gauden wrote the most influential account of the royalist cause, *Eikon Basilike* ("Royal Portrait"), advance copies of which were sold on the day of Charles I's execution in 1649. Although Gauden at first sided with Parliament and the Presbyterians, he did not agree to the abolition of the bishops. In 1647 supporters of Charles I, then confined at Hampton Court by Parliament, sought Gauden's help to revise the King's meditations for publication. When the manuscript was complete, Gauden showed it to the King, who hesitated about having it published under his name. Meanwhile, the King was preoccupied first by his attempts to escape and then by his confinement, trial, and execution. When Royston first printed the book in January 1649, he believed that King Charles was the author. Just months later, William Duggard published another edition based on a manuscript that had been revised by the King; Gauden's authorship remained publically unknown until 1690.

Throughout the interregnum, Gauden managed to keep his deanery at Brockton by conforming to Presbyterianism. With the Restoration in 1660, he was made Bishop of Exeter. In letters to Sir Edward Hyde, Gauden admitted his authorship and complained that his reward had not been sufficient. He was then promoted to the bishopric of Worcester, just a year before his death.

Eikon Basilike was written to influence public opinion and to guide the Prince of Wales, who waited in exile to regain his father's throne. A collection of meditations written in a lofty style, *Eikon Basilike* justified the King's views and evoked sympathy for his plight. The emblematic frontispiece shows the King in a saintly light—kneeling in prayer. Admirers of the work called it "most charitable, most heavenly" and "most pious, most ravishing." By the end of 1649, thirty-five editions had been printed in England. The most important of these, that of March 1649, added the King's prayers, the Prince of Wales's letter to his father, and an epitaph on the King's death. An English-language edition was published in Ireland in 1649, and twenty foreign language editions were published on the Continent for the English community in exile as well as their European supporters.

The text aroused both support and criticism. Parliament had the printer Duggard arrested but released him when he produced a license to publish the book. Parliament prohibited the further sale of the book in May 1649, but by the end of 1649, five clandestine editions and two responses had appeared. *The Princely Pellican* explained how Charles had come to write the book, and *Eikon Alethine* attacked it as a fraud. Milton wrote his own rebuttal in *Eikonoklastes,* a savagely satirical prosecution of the King. *Eikonoklastes* merely went through two editions, showing that it could not compete in popularity with *Eikon Basilike.*

from **Eikon Basilike**

from *Chapter 4. Upon the Insolency of the Tumults*

I never thought anything, except our sins, more ominously presaging all these mischiefs which have followed, than those tumults in London and Westminster soon after the convening of this Parliament which were not like a storm at sea, (which yet wants not its terror,) but like an earthquake, shaking the very foundation of all; than which nothing in the world hath more of horror.

As it is one of the most convincing arguments that there is a God, while His power sets bounds to the raging of the sea, so it is no less that He restrains the madness of the people. Nor does anything portend more God's displeasure against a nation than when He suffers the confluence and clamors of the vulgar to pass all boundaries of laws and reverence to authority.

Which those tumults did to so high degrees of insolence, that they spared not to invade the honor and freedom of the two Houses, menacing, reproaching, shaking, yea, and assaulting some members of both Houses as they fancied or disliked them; nor did they forbear most rude and unseemly deportments, both in contemptuous words and actions, to myself and my court.

Nor was this a short fit or two of shaking, as an ague, but a quotidian fever, always increasing to higher inflammations, impatient of any mitigation, restraint, or remission.

First, they must be a guard against those fears which some men scared themselves and others withal; when, indeed, nothing was more to be feared, and less to be used by wise men, than those tumultuary confluxes of mean and rude people who are taught first to petition, then to protect, then to dictate, at last to command and overawe the Parliament.

All obstructions of Parliament, that is, all freedom of differing in votes, and debating matters with reason and candor, must be taken away with these tumults. By these must the Houses be purged, and all rotten members (as they pleased to count them) cast out; by these the obstinacy of men, resolved to discharge their consciences, must be subdued; by these all factious, seditious, and schismatical proposals against government, ecclesiastical or civil, must be backed and abetted till they prevailed.

Generally, whoever had most mind to bring forth confusion and ruin upon Church and State used the midwifery of those tumults, whose riot and impatience was such as they would not stay the ripening and season of counsels, or fair production of acts, in the order, gravity, and deliberateness befitting a Parliament, but ripped up with barbarous cruelty, and forcibly cut out abortive notes, such as their inviters and encouragers most fancied.

Yea, so enormous and detestable were their outrages, that no sober man could be without infinite shame and sorrow to see them so tolerated and connived at by some, countenanced, encouraged, and applauded by others.

What good man had not rather want anything he most desired for the public good, than obtain it by such unlawful and irreligious means? But men's passions and God's directions seldom agree; violent designs and motions must have suitable engines; such as too much attend their own ends, seldom confine themselves to God's means. Force must crowd in what reason will not lead.

Who were the chief demagogues and patrons of tumults, to send for them, to flatter and embolden them, to direct and tune their clamorous importunities, some men yet living are too conscious to pretend ignorance. God in His due time will let these see that those were no fit means to be used for attaining His ends.

But as it is no strange thing for the sea to rage when strong winds blow upon it, so neither for multitudes to become insolent when they have men of some reputation for parts and piety to set them on.

That which made their rudeness most formidable was, that many complaints being made, and messages sent by myself and some of both Houses yet no order for redress could be obtained with any vigor and efficacy proportionable to the malignity of that now far-spread disease and predominant mischief.

Such was some men's stupidity, that they feared no inconvenience; others' petulancy, that they joyed to see their betters shamefully outraged and abused, while they knew their only security consisted in vulgar flattery, so insensible were they of mine or the two Houses common safety and honors.

Nor could ever any order be obtained impartially to examine, censure, and punish the known boutefeus[1] and impudent incendiaries, who boasted of the influence they had, and used to convoke those tumults as their advantages served.

Yea some, who should have been wiser statesmen, owned them as friends, commending their courage, zeal, and industry, which to sober men could seem no better than that of the devil, who goes about seeking whom he may deceive and devour.

I confess, when I found such a deafness, that no declaration from the bishops, who were first foully insolenced and assaulted, nor yet from other lords and gentlemen of honor, nor yet from myself, could take place for the due repression of these tumults, and securing not only our freedom in Parliament, but our very persons in the streets; I thought myself not bound by my presence to provoke them to higher boldness and contempts; I hoped by my withdrawing[2] to give time both for the ebbing of their tumultuous fury, and others regaining some degrees of modesty and sober sense.

Some may interpret it as an effect of pusillanimity[3] in any man, for popular terrors, to desert his public station; but I think it is hardiness beyond true valor for a wise man to set himself against the breaking in of a sea, which to resist at present threatens imminent danger, but to withdraw gives it space to spend its fury, and gains a fitter time to repair the breach. Certainly a gallant man had rather fight to great disadvantages for number and place in the field in an orderly way, than scuffle with an undisciplined rabble.

Some suspected and affirmed that I meditated a war, when I went from Whitehall only to redeem my person and conscience from violence: God knows I did not then think of a war. Nor will any prudent man conceive that I would, by so many former and some after acts, have so much weakened myself if I had purposed to engage in a war, which to decline by all means I denied myself in so many particulars. It is evident I had then no army to fly unto for protection and vindication.

Who can blame me, or any other, for withdrawing ourselves from the daily baitings of the tumults, not knowing whether their fury and discontent might not fly so high as to worry and tear those in pieces whom as yet they but played with in their paws? God, who is my sole judge, is my witness in heaven that I never had any thoughts of my going from my house at Whitehall if I could have had but any reasonable fair quarter. I was resolved to bear much, and did so; but I did not think myself bound to prostitute the majesty of my place and person, the safety of my wife and

---

1. Firebrands.
2. Charles decided to flee from London on the night of 10 January 1642, in response to rioting that erupted as a result of his failed attempts to arrest the five opposition leaders in the House of Commons. Charles returned to Whitehall only as a prisoner just before his execution.
3. Cowardice.

children, to those who are prone to insult most when they have objects and opportunity most capable of their rudeness and petulancy.

But this business of the tumults, whereof some have given already an account to God, others yet living know themselves desperately guilty, time and the guilt of many has so smothered up and buried, that I think it best to leave it as it is; only I believe the just avenger of all disorders will in time make those men and that city see their sin in the glass of their punishment. It is more than an even lay, that they may one day see themselves punished by that way they offended.

Had this Parliament, as it was in its first election and constitution, sat full and free, the members of both Houses, being left to their freedom of voting, as in all reason, honor, and religion they should have been, I doubt not but things would have been so carried as would have given no less good content to all good men than they wished or expected.

For I was resolved to hear reason in all things, and to consent to it as far as I could comprehend it; but as swine are to gardens and orderly plantations, so are tumults to Parliaments, and plebeian concourses to public counsels, turning all into disorders and sordid confusions.

I am prone sometimes to think that had I called this Parliament to any other place in England, as I might opportunely enough have done, the sad consequences in all likelihood, with God's blessing, might have been prevented. A Parliament would have been welcome in any place; no place afforded such confluence of various and vicious humors as that where it was unhappily convened. But we must leave all to God, who orders our disorders, and magnifies His wisdom most when our follies and miseries are most discovered.

⊷ ⊰✠⊱ ⊷

John Milton
1608–1674

With the popularity of the royalist tract *Eikon Basilike* after the execution of Charles I, the new Puritan government needed to find someone to defend its cause against the growing support for the King. The Puritans found their man in the newly appointed Secretary for Foreign Tongues to the Council of State, John Milton. In *Eikonoklastes* ("Image Breaker"), Milton focused his attack on the arguments of *Eikon Basilike* more than on its authorship. He doubted whether the King wrote his own defense, but he chose to concentrate on a chapter-by-chapter refutation of the book's account of history—in terms of both events and the perspective on them. Milton also revealed that one the prayers attributed to the King was really Pamela's prayer from Sir Philip Sidney's prose romance *Arcadia*. For the Puritan Milton this was a shocking piece of paganism and plagiarism by one who presented himself as pious. Milton's language in *Eikonoklastes* is iconoclastic—mocking and sarcastic, marked by invective and sharply stinging *ad hominem* argument. One royalist called *Eikonoklastes* a "blackguardly book" in which Milton "blows his viper's breath upon those immortal devotions." Some royalists even viewed Milton's blindness as God's punishment for his having attacked the King. Shortly after the Restoration of Charles II in 1660 the House of Commons ordered the burning of *Eikonoklastes* and had Milton arrested. He was imprisoned for several months before being released through the aid of his friend Andrew Marvell. *Eikonklastes* was first published in October 1649; the second and final edition in Milton's lifetime appeared in 1650.

For more about Milton, see his principal listing, page 1729.

from **Eikonoklastes**

from *Chapter 1. Upon the King's Calling This Last Parliament*

"The odium and offenses which some men's rigor, or remissness in church and state had contracted upon his government, he resolved to have expiated with better laws and regulations." And yet the worst of misdemeanors committed by the worst of all his favorites, in the height of their dominion, whether acts of rigor or remissness, he hath from time to time continued, owned, and taken upon himself by public declarations, as often as the clergy, or any other of his instruments felt themselves overburdened with the people's hatred. And who knows not the superstitious rigor of his Sunday's chapel, and the licentious remissness of his Sunday's theater;[1] accompanied with that reverend statute for dominical jigs and maypoles,[2] published in his own name, and derived from the example of his father James? Which testifies all that rigor in superstition, all that remissness in religion to have issued out originally from his own house, and from his own authority.

Much rather then may those general miscarriages in State, his proper sphere, be imputed to no other person chiefly than to himself. And which of all those oppressive acts, or impositions did he ever disclaim or disavow, till the fatal awe of this Parliament hung ominously over him. Yet here he smoothly seeks to wipe off all the envy of his evil government upon his substitutes, and under-officers: and promises, though much too late, what wonders he purposed to have done in the reforming of religion—a work wherein all his undertakings heretofore declare him to have had little or no judgment. Neither could his breeding, or his course of life acquaint him with a thing so spiritual. Which may well assure us what kind of reformation we could expect from him; either some politic form of an imposed religion, or else perpetual vexation, and persecution to all those that complied not with such a form.

The like amendment he promises in State; not a step further "than his reason and conscience told him was fit to be desired"; wishing "he had kept within those bounds, and not suffered his own judgment to have been overborne in some things," of which things one was the Earl of Strafford's execution.[3] And what signifies all this, but that still his resolution was the same, to set up an arbitrary government of his own; and that all Britain was to be tied and chained to the conscience, judgment, and reason of one man; as if those gifts had been only his peculiar and prerogative, entailed upon him with his fortune to be a king? When as doubtless no man so obstinate, or so much a tyrant, but professes to be guided by that which he calls his reason, and his judgment, though never so corrupted; and pretends also his conscience. In the meanwhile, for any Parliament or the whole nation to have either reason, judgment, or conscience, by this rule was altogether in vain, if it thwarted the king's will; which was easy for him to call by any other more plausible name. He himself hath

---

1. While observers such as the Spanish ambassador noted Charles's sincere piety, Milton considered traditional ritual "superstitious" ironically linking it to irreligious theater life. Like the Puritans, Milton abhorred Sunday theater performances, and in *Of Reformation* he attacked the bishops for promoting "gaming, jigging, wassailing, and mixed dancing" on Sundays.
2. The *Book of Sports* (1633) forbade bearbaiting and bullbaiting on Sundays, but also rebuked the Puritans for condemning other forms of recreation such as dancing and archery.

3. Thomas Wentworth, Earl of Strafford, was executed in May 1641. Charles had recalled Strafford from the Lord Deputyship in Ireland to help with the war against the Scots Covenanters. Parliament accused Wentworth of planning to use the Irish army to suppress the King's opponents in Scotland and England. Even though Strafford was successfully defended against the charges, Charles signed his death warrant, fearing retaliation against himself and the Queen for their part in a plot to rescue Strafford.

many times acknowledged to have no right over us but by law; and by the same law to govern us: but law in a free nation hath been ever public reason, the enacted reason of a Parliament; which he denying to enact, denies to govern us by that which ought to be our law; interposing his own private reason, which to us is no law. And thus we find these fair and specious promises, made upon the experience of many hard sufferings, and his most mortified retirements, being thoroughly sifted, to contain nothing in them much different from his former practices, so cross, and so averse to all his Parliaments, and both the nations of this island. What fruits they could in likelihood have produced in his restorement, is obvious to any prudent foresight.

And this is the substance of his first section, till we come to the devout of it, modeled into the form of a private psalter. Which they who so much admire, either for the matter or the manner, may as well admire the archbishop's late breviary,[4] and many other as good *Manuals*, and *Handmaids of Devotion*, the lip-work of every prelatical liturgist, clapped together, and quilted out of Scripture phrase, with as much ease, and as little need of Christian diligence, or judgment, as belongs to the compiling of any ordinary and salable piece of English divinity, that the shops value. But he who from such a kind of psalmistry, or any other verbal devotion, without the pledge and earnest of suitable deeds, can be persuaded of a zeal, and true righteousness in the person, hath much yet to learn; and knows not that the deepest policy of a tyrant hath been ever to counterfeit religious. And Aristotle in his *Politics*, hath mentioned that special craft among twelve other tyrannical sophisms.[5] Neither want we examples. Andronicus Comnenus the Byzantine Emperor, though a most cruel tyrant, is reported by Nicetas[6] to have been a constant reader of Saint Paul's Epistles; and by continual study had so incorporated the phrase and style of that transcendent apostle into all his familiar letters, that the imitation seemed to vie with the original. Yet this availed not to deceive the people of that empire; who notwithstanding his saint's vizard, tore him to pieces for his tyranny.

From stories of this nature both ancient and modern which abound, the poets also, and some English, have been in this point so mindful of decorum, as to put never more pious words in the mouth of any person, than of a tyrant. I shall not instance an abstruse author, wherein the King might be less conversant, but one whom we well know was the closet companion of these his solitudes, William Shakespeare, who introduces the person of Richard the Third, speaking in as high a strain of piety, and mortification, as is uttered in any passage of this book, and sometimes to the same sense and purpose with some words in this place, "I intended," saith he, "not only to oblige my friends but mine enemies." The like saith Richard, Act 2. Scene 1,

> I do not know that Englishman alive
> With whom my soul is any jot at odds,
> More than the infant that is born tonight;
> I thank my God for my humility.

Other stuff of this sort may be read throughout the whole tragedy, wherein the poet used not much license in departing from the truth of history, which delivers him a deep dissembler, not of his affections only, but of religion.

---

4. Milton's name for Archbishop Laud's *Prayer Book*, which the Puritans hated because of its similarity to Roman Catholic ritual.
5. See Aristotle, *Politics* 5.9.15, for the notion that care in religious ritual is a device of tyrants.
6. A 12th-century historian who recorded the cruelty of Comnenus's reign (1183–1185).

from *Chapter 4. Upon the Insolency of the Tumults*

And that the King was so emphatical and elaborate on this theme against tumults, and expressed with such a vehemence his hatred of them, will redound less perhaps, than he was aware, to the commendation of his government. For besides that in good governments they happen seldomest, and rise not without cause, if they prove extreme and pernicious, they were never counted so to monarchy, but to monarchical tyranny; and extremes one with another are at most antipathy. If then the King so extremely stood in fear of tumults, the inference will endanger him to be the other extreme. Thus far the occasion of this discourse against tumults; now to the discourse itself, voluble enough, and full of sentence,[1] but that, for the most part, either specious rather than solid, or to his cause nothing pertinent.

"He never thought any thing more to presage the mischiefs that ensued, than those tumults." Then was his foresight but short, and much mistaken. Those tumults were but the mild effects of an evil and injurious reign; not signs of mischiefs to come, but seeking relief for mischiefs past; those signs were to be read more apparent in his rage and purposed revenge of those free expostulations, and clamors of the people against his lawless government. "Not any thing," saith he, "portends more God's displeasure against a nation than when he suffers the clamors of the vulgar to pass all bounds of law & reverence to authority." It portends rather his displeasure against a tyrannous King, whose proud throne he intends to overturn by that contemptible vulgar; the sad cries and oppressions of whom his royalty regarded not. As for that supplicating people they did no hurt either to law or authority, but stood for it rather in the Parliament against whom they feared would violate it.

That "they invaded the honor and freedom of the two Houses," is his own officious accusation, not seconded by the Parliament, who had they seen cause, were themselves best able to complain. And if they "shook & menaced" any, they were such as had more relation to the Court, than to the Commonwealth; enemies, not patrons of the people. But if their petitioning unarmed were an invasion of both Houses, what was his entrance into the House of Commons, besetting it with armed men, in what condition then was the honor, and freedom of that House?

"They forbore not rude deportments, contemptuous words and actions to himself and his Court."

It was more wonder, having heard what treacherous hostility he had designed against the city, and his whole kingdom, that they forbore to handle him as people in their rage have handled tyrants heretofore for less offenses.

"They were not a short ague, but a fierce quotidian fever:" He indeed may best say it, who most felt it; for the shaking was within him; and it shook him by his own description "worse than a storm, worse then an earthquake, Belshazzar's Palsy."[2] Had not worse fears, terrors, and envies made within him that commotion, how could a multitude of his subjects, armed with no other weapon then petitions, have shaken all his joints with such a terrible ague. Yet that the Parliament should entertain the least fear of bad intentions from him or his party, he endures not; but would persuade

1. Significance, meaning.
2. In *Of Reformation*, Milton compares the feasting of Anglican bishops to that of Belshazzar in his palace in Babylon on the eve of the fall of the city to the Medes and Persians. When King Belshazzar saw the mysterious writing on the wall that foretold his doom, "the joints of his loins were loosed, and his knees smote one against another" (Daniel 5.6).

us that "men scare themselves and others without cause;" for he thought fear would be to them a kind of armor, and his design was, if it were possible, to disarm all, especially of a wise fear and suspicion; for that he knew would find weapons.

He goes on therefore with vehemence to repeat the mischiefs done by these tumults. "They first petitioned, then protected, dictate next, and lastly overawe the Parliament. They removed obstructions, they purged the Houses, cast out rotten members." If there were a man of iron, such as Talus, by our poet Spenser, is feigned to be the page of Justice, who with his iron flail could do all this, and expeditiously, without those deceitful forms and circumstances of law, worse than ceremonies in religion; I say God send it down, whether by one Talus, or by a thousand.[3]

"But they subdued the men of conscience in Parliament, backed and abetted all seditious and schismatical proposals against government ecclesiastical and civil."

Now we may perceive the root of his hatred whence it springs. It was not the King's grace or princely goodness, but this iron flail the people, that drove the bishops out of their baronies, out of their cathedrals, out of the Lord's house, out of their copes and surplices, and all those papistical innovations,[4] threw down the High Commission and Star Chamber, gave us a triennial Parliament, and what we most desired;[5] in revenge whereof he now so bitterly inveighs against them; these are those seditious and scismatical proposals, then by him condescended to, as acts of grace, now of another name; which declares him, touching matters of Church and State, to have been no other man in the deepest of his solitude, than he was before at the highest of his sovereignty.

But this was not the worst of these tumults, they played the hasty "midwives," and "would not stay the ripening, but went straight to ripping up, and forcibly cut out abortive votes."

They would not stay perhaps the Spanish demurring, and putting off such wholesome acts and counsels, as the politic cabin at Whitehall had no mind to. But all this is complained here as done to the Parliament, and yet we heard not the Parliament at that time complain of any violence from the people, but from him. Wherefore intrudes he to plead the cause of Parliament against the people, while the Parliament was pleading their own cause against him; and against him were forced to seek refuge of the people? 'Tis plain then that those confluxes and resorts interrupted not the Parliament, nor by them were thought tumultuous, but by him only and his court faction.

"But what good Man had not rather want any thing he most desired for the public good, then attain it by such unlawful and irreligious means;" as much as to say, had not rather sit still and let his country be tyrannized, then that the people, finding no other remedy, should stand up like men and demand their rights and liberties. This is the artificialest piece of fineness to persuade men into slavery that the wit of court could have invented. But hear how much better the moral of this lesson would befit the teacher. What good man had not rather want a boundless and arbitrary power, and those fine flowers of the crown, called prerogatives, then for them to use force and perpetual vexation to his faithful subjects, nay to wade for them through blood and civil war? So that

3. Talus is the iron flail who ruthlessly cuts down all who oppose Artegal, the Knight of Justice, in Spenser's *Faerie Queene* 5, much of which is about the subjugation of Ireland by England.
4. Milton refers to the London petition calling for the abolition of the bishops' power, introduced into Parliament in December 1640, that resulted in their exclusion from the House of Lords.

5. The High Commission, the highest ecclesiastical court, investigated such matters as heresy, recusancy, and any writing against the Book of Common Prayer; Parliament abolished it on July 5, 1641. The Star Chamber was also abolished because it was viewed as a special tool of government favoring the special right of the sovereign above all other persons and the common law. A triennial Parliament is a parliament convened every three years.

this and the whole bundle of those following sentences may be applied better to the convincement of his own violent courses, then of those pretended tumults.

"Who were the chief demagogues to send for those tumults, some alive are not ignorant." Setting aside the affrightment of this goblin word; for the King by his leave cannot coin English as he could money, to be current (and tis believed this wording was above his known style and orthography, and accuses the whole composure to be conscious of some other author)[6] yet if the people "were sent for, emboldened and directed" by those "demagogues," who, saving his Greek, were good patriots, and by his own confession "Men of some repute for parts and piety," it helps well to assure us there was both urgent cause, and the less danger of their coming.

"Complaints were made, yet no redress could be obtained." The Parliament also complained of what danger they sat in from another party, and demanded of him a guard, but it was not granted. What marvel then if it cheered them to see some store of their friends, and in the Roman not the pettifogging sense, their clients so near about them; a defense due by nature both from whom it was offered, and to whom; as due as to their parents; though the Court stormed, and fretted to see such honor given to them, who were then best fathers of the Commonwealth. And both the Parliament and people complained, and demanded justice for those assaults, if not murders done at his own doors, by that crew of rufflers, but he, instead of doing justice on them, justified and abetted them in what they did, as in his public "Answer to a Petition from the City" may be read. Neither is it slightly to be passed over, that in the very place where blood was first drawn in this cause, as the beginning of all that followed, there was his own blood shed by the executioner. According to that sentence of divine justice, "In the place where dogs licked the blood of Naboth, shall dogs lick thy blood, even thine."

From hence he takes occasion to excuse that improvident and fatal error of his absenting from the Parliament. "When he found that no declaration of the bishops could take place against those tumults." Was that worth his considering, that foolish and self-undoing declaration of twelve cypher bishops, who were immediately appeached of treason for that audacious declaring?[7] The bishops peradventure were now and then pulled by the rochets,[8] and deserved another kind of pulling; but what amounted this to "the fear of his own person in the streets"? Did he not the very next day after his irruption into the House of Commons, than which nothing had more exasperated the people, go in his coach unguarded into the city? did he receive the least affront, much less violence in any of the streets, but rather humble demeanors, and supplications? Hence may be gathered, that however in his own guiltiness he might have justly feared, yet that he knew the people so full of awe and reverence to his person, as to dare commit himself single among the thickest of them, at a time when he had most provoked them. Besides in Scotland they had handled the Bishops in a more robustious manner; Edinburgh had been full of tumults,[9] two armies from thence had entered England against him;[1] yet after all this, he was not fearful, but very forward to take so long a journey to Edinburgh;[2] which argues first, as did also his rendition afterward to the Scotch Army,[3] that to England he continued still, as he was indeed, a stranger, and full of diffidence; to the Scots

---

6. Milton believed that Charles I could not have written *Eikon Basilike* because such passages as this one showed a word choice and style different from Charles's.
7. The Bishops' Exclusion Bill was Parliament's reaction to the assertion by 12 bishops that any legislation passed by the House of Lords when the bishops were absent was void.
8. Vestments.
9. When Charles attempted to force the Book of Common Prayer on the Scottish churches, the people rioted.
1. The first Scottish war ended with the Treaty of Berwick in June 1639, the second with the Treaty of Ripon in October 1640.
2. Charles went to Edinburgh in 1641, hoping to pit the Covenanters against their opponents.
3. Charles surrendered himself to the Scottish army commanders in May 1646.

only a native King,[4] in his confidence, though not in his dealing towards them. It shows us next beyond doubting, that all this his fear of tumults was but a mere color and occasion taken of his resolved absence from the Parliament, for some other end not difficult to be guessed. And those instances wherein valor is not to be questioned for not "scuffling with the sea, or an undisciplined rabble," are but subservient to carry on the solemn jest of his fearing tumults: if they discover not withall, the true reason why he departed; only to turn his slashing at the court gate, to slaughtering "in the field"; his disorderly bickering, to an orderly invading: which was nothing else but a more orderly disorder.

"Some suspected and affirmed, that he meditated a War when he went first from Whitehall." And they were not the worst heads that did so, nor did "any of his former acts weaken him" to that, as he alleges for himself, or if they had, they clear him only for the time of passing them, not for what ever thoughts might come after into his mind. Former actions of improvidence or fear, not with him unusual, cannot absolve him of all after meditations.

He goes on protesting his "no intention to have left Whitehall," had these horrid tumults given him but "fair quarter," as if he himself, his wife and children had been in peril. But to this enough hath been answered.

"Had this Parliament as it was in its first election," namely, with the Lord and Baron Bishops, "sat full and free," he doubts not but all had gone well. What warrant this of his to us? Whose not doubting was all good men's greatest doubt.

"He was resolved to hear reason, and to consent so far as he could comprehend." A hopeful resolution; what if his reason were found by oft experience to comprehend nothing beyond his own advantages, was this a reason fit to be intrusted with the common good of three nations?

"But," saith he, "as swine are to gardens, so are tumults to Parliaments." This the Parliament, had they found it so, could best have told us. In the meanwhile, who knows not that one great hog may do as much mischief in a garden, as many little swine.[5]

"He was sometimes prone to think that had he called this last Parliament to any other place in England, the sad consequences might have been prevented." But change of air changes not the mind. Was not his first Parliament at Oxford dissolved after two subsidies given him, and no justice received? Was not his last in the same place, where they sat with as much freedom, as much quiet from tumults, as they could desire, a Parliament both in his account, and their own, consisting of all his friends, that fled after him, and suffered for him, and yet by him nicknamed, and cashiered for a "mongrel Parliament that vexed his Queen with their base and mutinous motions," as his cabinet letter tells us?[6] Whereby the world may see plainly, that no shifting of place, no sifting of members to his own mind, no number, no paucity, no freedom from tumults, could ever bring his arbitrary wilfulness, and tyrannical designs to brook the least shape or similitude, the least counterfeit of a Parliament.

Finally instead of praying for his people as a good King should do, he prays to be delivered from them, as "from wild beasts, inundations, and raging seas, that had overborne all loyalty, modesty, laws, justice, and religion." God save the people from such intercessors.

---

4. Charles was born in Scotland, and he made special appeals to the Scots to be their king in both 1641 and 1646.
5. Milton may echo the identification of the hog with Henry VIII for his failure to carry out a thorough and consistent reformation in Anthony Gilby's *An Admonition to England and Scotland to Call Them to Repentance* (Geneva, 1558).

6. Charles called an opposition Parliament that met in Oxford in January 22, 1644, and that he ordered closed after disagreement with them. This Parliament first attempted a peaceful settlement with the Westminster Parliament and then declared it guilty of treason. The King called it his "mongrel Parliament."

━━◆━━

The Petition of Gentlewomen and Tradesmen's Wives

A month after the King tried to have the five chief members of Parliament arrested, two petitions were presented to the Commons by "Gentlewomen and Tradesmen's Wives" of London. In the first of these, dated 1 February 1642, the women complained about the lack of trade, which caused great want and blamed the "opposition of some bishops or lords" for the neglect of the women's earlier petitions. In the second petition, reprinted here, the women complain about threats to the security of the state posed by the bishops and Catholic lords in the House of Lords, the still not yet executed Archbishop Laud, and the Catholic Mass. From the London women's vantage point, the 1641 rebellion of the Catholics in Ireland demonstrated the risk to Puritans of attacks from Catholics (indistinguishable from Anglicans) within England. The violence unleashed by the more spontaneous and popular revolts in Ireland had been luridly portrayed and grossly exaggerated in the English press. Nevertheless, the Catholic revolt did bring much bloodshed, which increased with the Protestant retaliation. Interestingly, some of the Irish uprisings were led by women, a fact that would not have made any difference to the London women, even if they had known it.

The chief terms of the petition, like the chief terms of the Wars of the Three Kingdoms, were religious. Archbishop Laud is attacked here, but the King is not. Even the women's justification of their right to approach Parliament with a petition is articulated in religious terms. They argue that women are the same as men in Christ's eyes and that women have suffered as much religious persecution as men. If these women argue that women are equal to men, it is mainly insofar as they are believers in the Puritan practice of religion. Delegated by his fellow members to make a reply, Pym publicly reassured the women that their petition had been read and that they would receive "satisfaction . . . to [their] just and lawful desires." The next day, the House of Lords passed a bill excluding the Bishops, and so Parliament met at least one of the women petitioners' demands.

A True Copy of the Petition of the Gentlewomen and Tradesmen's Wives, In and About the City of London[1]

Delivered to the Honorable, the Knights, Citizens, and Burgesses of the House of Commons in Parliament, the 4th of February, 1642

Together with their several reasons why their sex ought thus to petition, as well as the men; and the manner how both their petition and reasons was delivered.

Likewise the answer which the Honorable Assembly sent to them by Mr. Pym,[2] as they stood at the house door.

To the Honorable Knights, Citizens and Burgesses,[3] of the House of Commons assembled in Parliament. The most humble Petition of the Gentlewomen, Tradesmen's Wives, and many others of the female sex, all inhabitants of the city of London, and the suburbs thereto.

With lowest submission showing,

1. Printed in the *Parliamentary History* ii.1074.
2. John Pym (1583?–1643) was a strong Puritan opponent of episcopacy and a leader of the House of Commons, one of the five members whom Charles I unsuc-

cessfully attempted to have arrested in 1642.
3. Members of Parliament representing boroughs or corporate towns.

That we also with all thankful humility acknowledging the unwearied pains, care and great charge, besides hazard of health and life, which you the noble worthies of this honorable and renowned assembly have undergone, for the safety both of church and commonwealth, for a long time already past; for which not only we your humble petitioners, and all well affected in this kingdom, but also all other good Christians are bound now and at all times acknowledge; yet notwithstanding that many worthy deeds have been done by you, great danger and fear do still attend us, and will, as long as Popish Lords and superstitious bishops are suffered to have their voice in the House of Peers, and that accursed and abominable idol of the Mass suffered in the kingdom, and that archenemy[4] of our prosperity and reformation lieth in the Tower, yet not receiving his deserved punishment.

All these under correction, gives us great cause to suspect that God is angry with us, and to be the chief causes why your pious endeavors for a further reformation proceedeth not with that success as you desire, and is most earnestly prayed for of all that wish well to true religion, and the flourishing estate both of king and kingdom; the insolencies of the papists and their abettors, raiseth a just fear and suspicion of sowing sedition, and breaking out into bloody persecution in this kingdom, as they have done in Ireland, the thoughts of which sad and barbarous events maketh our tender hearts to melt within us, forcing us humbly to petition to this honorable assembly, to make safe provision for yourselves and us, before it be too late.

And whereas we, whose hearts have joined cheerfully with all those petitions which have been exhibited unto you in the behalf of the purity of religion, and the liberty of our husbands' persons and estates, recounting ourselves to have an interest in the common privileges with them, do with the same confidence assure ourselves to find the same gracious acceptance with you, for easing of those grievances, which in regard of our frail condition, do more nearly concern us, and do deeply terrify our souls: our domestical dangers with which this kingdom is so much distressed, especially growing on us from those treacherous and wicked attempts already are such as we find ourselves to have as deep a share as any other.

We cannot but tremble at the very thoughts of the horrid and hideous facts which modesty forbids us now to name, occasioned by the bloody wars in Germany,[5] his Majesty's late Northern Army, how often did it affright our hearts, whilst their violence began to break out so furiously upon the persons of those whose husbands or parents were not able to rescue: we wish we had no cause to speak of those insolencies, and savage usage and unheard-of rapes, exercised upon our sex in Ireland, and have we not just cause to fear they will prove the forerunners of our ruin, except Almighty God by the wisdom and care of this Parliament be pleased to succor us, our husbands and children, which are as dear and tender unto us as the lives and blood of our hearts, to see them murdered and mangled and cut in pieces before our eyes, to see our children dashed against the stones, and the mothers' milk mingled with the infants' blood, running down the streets, to see our houses on flaming fire over our heads: oh how dreadful would this be?[6] We thought it misery enough (though nothing to that we have just cause to fear) but few years since for some of our sex, by

---

4. Archbishop Laud (1573–1645), who enforced forms of worship that were Anglican High Church, or similar to Roman Catholicism, and promoted church government by Anglican bishops. His policies and support for Charles I won Laud impeachment in 1642; in 1643 he was condemned to death by the Commons.
5. The Thirty Years War (1618–1648) was a European-

wide war fought mainly in Germany between Protestant opponents to Hapsburg rule and Catholic supporters of the Holy Roman Empire.
6. While there was violence on both sides, woodcuts of the Irish rebellions in the English press sensationalized the violence of Catholics against Protestant settlers by depicting the murder of infants and attacks upon women.

unjust divisions from their bosom comforts, to be rendered in a manner widows, and the children fatherless, husbands were imprisoned from the society of their wives, even against the laws of God and nature, and little infants suffered in their fathers' banishments: thousands of our dearest friends have been compelled to fly from Episcopal persecutions into desert places amongst wild beasts, there finding more favor than in their native soil, and in the midst of all their sorrows such hath the pity of the Prelates[7] been, that our cries could never enter into their ears or hearts, not yet through multitudes of obstructions could never have access or come nigh to those royal mercies of our most gracious sovereign, which we confidently hope would have relieved us: but after all these pressures ended, we humbly signify that our present fears are, that unless the bloodthirsty faction of the Papists and Prelates be hindered in their designs, ourselves here in England as well as they in Ireland, shall be exposed to the misery which is more intolerable than that which is already past, as namely to the rage not of men alone, but of devils incarnate (as we may so say), besides the thralldom of our souls and consciences in matters concerning God, which of all things are most dear unto us.

Now the remembrance of all these fearful accidents aforementioned do strongly move us from the example of the woman of Tekoa (II Samuel 14.2–20)[8] to fall submissively at the feet of his Majesty, our dread sovereign, and cry Help, oh King, help oh ye the noble Worthies now sitting in Parliament: And we humbly beseech you, that you will be a means to his Majesty and the House of Peers, that they will be pleased to take our heartbreaking grievances into timely consideration, and to add strength and encouragement to your noble endeavors, and further that you would move his Majesty with our humble requests, that he would be graciously pleased according to the example of the good King Asa,[9] to purge both the court and kingdom of that great idolatrous service of the Mass, which is tolerated in the Queen's court, this sin (as we conceive) is able to draw down a greater curse upon the whole kingdom than all your noble and pious endeavors can prevent, which was the cause that the good and pious King Asa would not suffer idolatry in his own mother, whose example if it shall please his Majesty's gracious goodness to follow, in putting down Popery and idolatry both in great and small, in court and in the kingdom throughout, to subdue the Papists and their abettors, and by taking away the power of the Prelates, whose government by long and woeful experience we have found to be against the liberty of our conscience and the freedom of the Gospel, and the sincere profession and practice thereof, then shall our fears be removed, and we may expect that God will pour down his blessings in abundance both upon his Majesty, and upon this Honorable Assembly, and upon the whole land.

For which your new petitioners shall pray affectionately.

The reasons follow.

It may be thought strange and unbeseeming our sex to show ourselves by way of petition to this Honorable Assembly: but the matter being rightly considered, of the right and interest we have in the common and public cause of the church, it will, as we conceive (under correction) be found a duty commanded and required.

7. Churchmen, bishops.
8. The wise woman of Tekoa went before King David and urged him to act mercifully toward his son Absalom. King David had been failing to act decisively against rape and

murder within his own household.
9. Charles I is asked to banish Catholics and the Mass just as King Asa banished sodomites and idolatry in 1 Kings 15.8–12.

First, because Christ hath purchased us at as dear a rate as he hath done men, and therefore requireth the like obedience for the same mercy as of men.

Secondly, because in the free enjoying of Christ in his own laws, and a flourishing estate of the church and commonwealth, consisteth the happiness of women as well as men.

Thirdly, because women are sharers in the common calamities that accompany both church and commonwealth, when oppression is exercised over the church or kingdom wherein they live; and an unlimited power have been given to Prelates to exercise authority over the consciences of women, as well as men, witness Newgate, Smithfield,[1] and other places of persecution, wherein women as well as men have felt the smart of their fury.

Neither are we left without example in scripture, for when the state of the church, in the time of King Ahasuerus, was by the bloody enemies thereof sought to be utterly destroyed, we find that Esther the Queen and her maids fasted and prayed, and that Esther petitioned to the King in the behalf of the church:[2] and though she enterprised this duty with the hazard of her own life, being contrary to the law to appear before the King before she were sent for, yet her love to the church carried her through all difficulties, to the performance of that duty.

On which grounds we are emboldened to present our humble petition unto this Honorable Assembly, not weighing the reproaches which may and are by many cast upon us, who (not well weighing the premises) scoff and deride our good intent. We do it not out of any self-conceit, or pride of heart, as seeking to equal ourselves with men, either in authority or wisdom: But according to our places to discharge that duty we owe to God, and the cause of the church, as far as lieth in us, following herein the example of the men which have gone in this duty before us.

A relation of the manner how it was delivered, with their answer, sent by Mr. Pym.

This petition, with their reasons, was delivered the 4th of Feb. 1641/2, by Mrs. Anne Stagg, a gentlewoman and brewer's wife, and many others with her of like rank and quality, which when they had delivered it, after some time spent in reading of it, the Honorable Assembly sent them an answer by Mr. Pym, which was performed in this manner.

Mr. Pym came to the Commons door, and called for the women, and spake unto them in these words: Good women, your petition and the reasons have been read in the house; and is very thankfully accepted of, and is come in a seasonable time: You shall (God willing) receive from us all the satisfaction which we can possibly give to your just and lawful desires. We entreat you to repair to your houses, and turn your petition which you have delivered here into prayers at home for us; for we have been, are and shall be (to our utmost power) ready to relieve you, your husbands, and children, and to perform the trust committed unto us towards God, our King and country, as becometh faithful Christians and loyal subjects.

---

1. Persecutions at Smithfield and Newgate.
2. The Jewish Esther became the Queen of Ahasuerus and saved the Jews from Haman, who planned to mas-

sacre the Jews; see the Book of Esther and also *Esther Hath Hang'd Haman* in Perspectives: Tracts on Women and Gender, page 1344.

＊＋ 〓◆〓 ＋＊

John Lilburne
1614?–1657

John Lilburne was one of the most tireless political reformers of the Civil War in England. His pamphlets against the Anglican Church in 1638 got him arrested and brought before the Star Chamber (the secret royal tribunal that judged and punished without a jury). Lilburne seized the opportunity to question the court's procedures by refusing to incriminate himself. With Cromwell's help in the House of Commons, Lilburne was released from prison and became a lieutenant in the Parliamentary army (1642–45), from which he resigned in objection to Presbyterianism as the state religion. Examined several times by the House of Commons for his criticisms of its policies and members, Lilburne became the chief exponent of the Levellers, derisively called such because of their egalitarianism. The Levellers wanted fundamental changes in the government, including universal suffrage, freedom of speech and religion, freedom from exorbitant taxation, care of the poor and aged, and trial by jury. Though a convinced antimonarchist, Lilburne even protested against the condemnation of Charles I without a proper trial.

The House of Commons rejected Leveller reforms in January 1648. This defeat, combined with Lilburne's fear that the Levellers would be brought to trial for their dissent, provoked his speech to Commons in February. This speech was published as *England's New Chains Discovered*. The first part (a selection from which is reprinted here) reviews the Leveller's concerns, and the second part criticizes the members of Parliament, who condemned Lilburne's speech as seditious. Lilburne went on to publish tracts criticizing Cromwell, monopolies, and enclosures but was ordered into exile by Parliament in 1652 only for attacking his uncle's business enemy, Sir Arthur Hesilrige, as a man "fit to be spewed out of all human society." In 1653, Lilburne returned to England in defiance of Cromwell and was arrested on arrival. His plight aroused popular petitions in his favor, and he was finally acquitted. Nevertheless, the government would not let him go free. Having converted to Quakerism, he died in confinement just a year before the death of Cromwell.

from England's New Chains Discovered

or, *The serious apprehensions of a part of the People, in behalf of the Commonwealth; (being Presenters, Promoters, and Approvers of the Large Petition of September 11. 1648.)*

Presented to the Supreme Authority of England, the Representers of the people in Parliament assembled.

By Lieut. Col. John Lilburn, and divers other Citizens of London, and Borough of Southwark; February 26. 1648. Whereunto his speech delivered at the Bar is annexed.

Since you have done the nation so much right, and yourselves so much honor as to declare that the people (under God) are the original of all just powers; and given us thereby fair grounds to hope, that you really intend their freedom and prosperity; yet the way thereunto being frequently mistaken, and through haste or error of judgment, those who mean the best, are many times misled so far to the prejudice of those that trust them, as to leave them in a condition nearest to bondage, when they have thought they had brought them into a way of freedom. And since woeful experience hath manifested this to be a truth, there seemeth no small reason that you should seriously lay to heart what at present we have to offer, for discovery and prevention of so great a danger.

And because we have been the first movers in and concerning an Agreement of the People,[1] as the most proper and just means for the settling the long and tedious distractions of this nation, occasioned by nothing more, than the uncertainty of our government; and since there hath been an Agreement prepared and presented by some officers of the army to this honorable House,[2] as what they thought requisite to be agreed unto by the people (you approving thereof) we shall in the first place deliver our apprehensions thereupon.

That an Agreement between those that trust, and those who are trusted, hath appeared a thing acceptable to this honorable House, his Excellency, and the officers of the army, is as much to our rejoicing, as we conceive it just in itself, and profitable for the Commonwealth,[3] and cannot doubt but that you will protect those of the people, who have no ways forfeited their birthright, in their proper liberty of taking this, or any other, as God and their own considerations[4] shall direct them.

Which we the rather mention, for that many particulars in the Agreement before you, are upon serious examination thereof, dissatisfactory to most of those who are very earnestly desirous of an Agreement, and many very material things seem to be wanting therein, which may be supplied in another: As

1. They are now much troubled there should be any intervals between the ending of this Representative, and the beginning of the next as being desirous that this present Parliament that hath lately done so great things in so short a time, tending to their liberties, should sit; until with certainty and safety they can see them delivered into the hands of another Representative, rather than to leave them (though never so small a time) under the dominion of a Council of State; a Constitution of a new and unexperienced nature, and which they fear, as the case now stands, may design to perpetuate their power, and to keep off Parliaments for ever.

2. They now conceive no less danger, in that it is provided that Parliaments for the future are to continue but 6 months, and a Council of State 18. In which time, if they should prove corrupt, having command of all forces by sea and land, they will have great opportunities to make themselves absolute and unaccountable: And because this is a danger, than which there cannot well be a greater; they generally incline to Annual Parliaments, bounded and limited as reason shall devise, not dissolvable, but to be continued or adjourned as shall seem good in their discretion, during that year, but no longer; and then to dissolve of course, and give way to those who shall be chosen immediately to succeed them, and in the intervals of their adjournments, to entrust an ordinary Committee of their own members, as in other cases limited and bounded with express instructions, and accountable to the next session, which will avoid all those dangers feared from a Council of State, as at present this is constituted.

3. They are not satisfied with the clause, wherein it is said, that the power of the Representatives shall extend to the erecting and abolishing of Courts of Justice; since the alteration of the usual way of trials by twelve sworn men of the neighborhood, may be included therein: a constitution so equal and just in itself, as that they conceive it ought to remain unalterable. Neither is it clear what is meant by these

---

1. The Levellers published their proposals for "An Agreement of the People" in *Foundations of Freedom* (15 December 1648). The beginning of this speech complains about how the government has betrayed the principles set forth in the Leveller "Agreement."
2. *An Agreement Prepared for the People of England* was

submitted to Parliament on January 20, 1649.
3. Commonwealth, meaning both public good and body politic, and specifically the republican government established in England between the execution of Charles I in 1649 and the Restoration in 1660.
4. Attentive thoughts.

words, (viz.) That the Representatives have the highest final judgment. They conceiving that their authority in these cases, is only to make laws, rules, and directions for other courts and persons assigned by law for the execution thereof; unto which every member of the Commonwealth, as well those of the Representative, as others, should be alike subject; it being likewise unreasonable in itself, and an occasion of much partiality, injustice, and vexation to the people, that the law-makers should be law-executors.[5]

4. Although it doth provide that in the laws hereafter to be made, no person by virtue of any tenure, grant, charter, patent, degree, or birth, shall be privileged from subjection thereunto, or from being bound thereby, as well as others. Yet doth it not null and make void those present protections by law, or otherwise; nor leave all persons, as well Lords as others, alike liable in person and estate, as in reason and conscience they ought to be.[6]

5. They are very much unsatisfied with what is expressed as a reserve from the Representative, in matters of religion, as being very obscure, and full of perplexity, that ought to be most plain and clear; there having occurred no greater trouble to the nation about any thing than by the intermeddling of Parliaments in matters of religion.[7]

6. They seem to conceive it absolutely necessary, that there be in their agreement, a reserve from ever having any kingly government, and a bar against restoring the House of Lords, both which are wanting in the agreement which is before you.

7. They seem to be resolved to take away all known and burdensome grievances, as tithes,[8] that great oppression of the country's industry and hindrance of tillage: excise, and customs, those secret thieves, and robbers, drainers of the poor and middle sort of people, and the greatest obstructers of trade, surmounting all the prejudices of ship money, patents, and projects,[9] before this Parliament: also to take away all monopolizing companies of merchants, the hinderers and decayers of clothing and cloth-working, dying, and the like useful professions; by which thousands of poor people might be set at work, that are now ready to starve, were merchandising restored to its due and proper freedom: they conceive likewise that the three grievances before mentioned, (viz.) monopolizing companies, excise, and customs, do exceedingly prejudice shipping and navigation, and consequently discourage seamen, and mariners, and which have had no small influence upon the late unhappy revolts which have so much endangered the nation, and so much advantaged your enemies. They also incline to direct a more equal and less burdensome way for levying monies for the future, those other forementioned being so chargeable in the receipt, as that the very stipends and allowance to the officers attending thereupon would defray a very great part of the charge of the army; whereas now they engender and support a corrupt interest. They also have in mind to take away all imprisonment of disabled men, for debt; and to provide some effectual course to enforce all that are able to a

---

5. Lilburne is calling for a clear distinction between the power of the House of Commons to legislate and the power of the Courts to interpret the law.
6. The Commonwealth did not thoroughly abolish the privileges of the landed classes and so did not provide a government in which all classes would be treated equally under the law.
7. Lilburne criticizes the Commons for not completely separating Church and State, which he sees as a major danger, since the King's imposition of the rituals of the

Anglican Church was one of the reasons the English Civil War was fought.
8. The tenth part of the annual produce of agriculture, due as payment for the Church.
9. "Ship money" was an ancient tax levied in time of war on maritime cities, which was revived by Charles I and applied to inland counties as well; patents were the sole right or license to sell or deal in a commodity; and projects were plans or schemes, here especially those by the government to get money.

speedy payment, and not suffer them to be sheltered in prisons, where they live in plenty, whilst their creditors are undone. They have also in mind to provide work, and comfortable maintenance for all sorts of poor, aged, and impotent people, and to establish some more speedy, less troublesome and chargeable way for deciding of controversies in law, whole families having been ruined by seeking right in the ways yet in being. All which, though of greatest and most immediate concernment to the people, are yet omitted in their Agreement before you.

These and the like are their intentions in what they purpose for an Agreement of the people, as being resolved (so far as they are able) to lay an impossibility upon all whom they shall hereafter trust, of ever wronging the Commonwealth in any considerable measure, without certainty of ruining themselves, and as conceiving it to be an improper tedious, and unprofitable thing for the people, to be ever running after their Representatives with petitions for redress of such grievances as may at once be removed by themselves, or to depend for these things so essential to their happiness and freedom, upon the uncertain judgments of several Representatives, the one being apt to renew what the other hath taken away.

+--=◆=--+

Oliver Cromwell
1599–1658

Cromwell's brutal conquest of Ireland (1649–1650) was the culmination of a long military, political, and religiously zealous career and the turning point in his rise to the position of Lord Protector. He had risen steadily in the Parliamentary Army, serving in the early days of the Civil War as captain of a troop of horses and finally becoming the chief of the New Model Army. Not only did he have a genius for military strategy but he was one of those who "never stirred from their troops . . . but fought to the last minute." He and his men were both called "Ironsides" in tribute to their indomitability. As a member of Parliament, he argued vigorously for the Puritan cause, and when Parliament was purged of Presbyterians in 1649, Cromwell's power and that of his fellow Congregationalists or Independents increased. At the trial of Charles I in January 1649, Cromwell adamantly demanded execution. Afterward, when the new Commonwealth was set up, one of Parliament's first charges was to send Cromwell to subdue Ireland, where Irish Royalists and Rebels, once pitted against each other, had formed a coalition and were gaining ground.

Cromwell's treatment of the Irish tested the limits of the principles of the Puritan Revolution and left a legacy of devastation. If Cromwell was a strong member of the English Parliament, he helped to bring about the abolition of both Irish and Scottish Parliaments with his military defeats of both kingdoms. In September 1644, Cromwell urged the Presbyterian Parliament to guarantee liberty of conscience to the Independents among his troops, but when the Catholics of New Ross, Ireland, called for similar toleration in October 1649, Cromwell refused them: "if by liberty of conscience, you mean a liberty to exercise the Mass, I judge it best to use plain dealing, and to let you know, where the Parliament of England have power, that will not be allowed of." Indeed during Cromwell's rule in England, only Jews and non-Anglican Protestants were tolerated. Furthermore, Cromwell escalated the policy (begun under Elizabeth and James) of giving lands confiscated from native Irish inhabitants to English colonists. The massacre of Drogheda—including civilians as well as troops—made the Irish remember Cromwell as cruel. In the following letter of September 17, 1649, Cromwell presents his troops' massacre of the people of Drogheda as "the righteous judgment of God." The same religious conviction that had made him and his New Model Army such valiant defenders of English liberty was used to justify Irish slaughter.

Cromwell also used his letters to keep Parliament informed of his progress, to ask for further supplies, and to promote his political power. He was to go on to defeat the Scots in 1650. Ultimately, his power grew to such an extent that in 1657 he became Lord Protector, assuming the pomp and trappings of royalty. When his son Richard succeeded him at his death in September 1658, it seemed as if Oliver Cromwell's rule had led to a new monarchy. His son proved a weak successor, and the Commonwealth was restored in May 1659, only to collapse with the Restoration of 1660. If Cromwell's participation in parliamentary politics and the New Model Army contributed to the cause of republican liberty, his conquest of Ireland marked one of the bleakest chapters in the English colonization of Ireland.

from Letters from Ireland

Relating the Several Great Success It Hath Pleased God to Give Unto the Parliament's Forces There, in the Taking of Drogheda, Trym, Dundalk, Carlingford, and the Nury . . . .

For the Honorable *William Lenthal* Esq;
Speaker of the Parliament of *England*

Sir,
Your army[1] being safely arrived at Dublin, and the enemy endeavoring to draw all his forces together about Trym and Tecroghan[2] (as my intelligence gave me); from whence endeavors were used by the Marquis of Ormonde, to draw Owen Roe O'Neal with his forces to his assistance, but with what success I cannot yet learn.[3] I resolved after some refreshment taken for our weather beaten men and horses, and accommodations for a march, to take the field; and accordingly upon Friday the thirtieth of August last, rendezvoused with eight regiments of foot, and six of horse, and some troops of dragoons, three miles on the north side of Dublin; the design was, to endeavor the regaining of Drogheda,[4] or tempting the enemy, upon his hazard of the loss of that place, to fight. Your army came before the town upon Monday following, where having pitched, as speedy course as could be was taken to frame our batteries,[5] which took up the more time, because divers of the battering guns were on shipboard. Upon Monday the ninth of this instant, the batteries began to play; whereupon I sent Sir Arthur Ashton the then Governor a summons, to deliver the town to the use of the Parliament of England; to the which I received no satisfactory answer, but proceeded that day to beat down the steeple of the church on the south side of the town, and to beat down a tower not far from the same place, which you will discern by the card[6] enclosed. Our guns not being able to do much that day, it was resolved to endeavor to do our utmost the next day to make breaches[7] assaultable, and by the help of God to storm them. The places pitched upon, were that part of the town wall next a church, called St. Marie's, which was the rather chosen, because we did hope that if we did enter and possess that church, we should be the better able to keep it against their horse and foot, until we could make way for the entrance of our horse,

---

1. The letter is addressed to Parliament from the commander of the parliamentary army, hence "your army."
2. A town and townland in County Meath, northwest of Dublin.
3. James Butler, Earl of Ormonde, represented Charles I in Ireland throughout the 1640s. At first opposed to the Catholic Confederation led by Owen Roe O'Neill (c. 1590–1649), Ormonde joined forces with O'Neill against

the incursion of Cromwell's army.
4. Drogheda (Droichead átha, "Bridge of the ford"), a city in County Louth, was under royalist command when Cromwell arrived there on 2 September 1649.
5. Platforms on which artillery was mounted.
6. Chart, map.
7. Gaps in fortifications.

which we did not conceive that any part of the town would afford the like advantage for that purpose with this. The batteries planted were two, one was for that part of the wall against the east end of the said church, the other against the wall on the south side; being somewhat long in battering, the enemy made six retrenchments, three of them from the said church to Duleek Gate, and three from the east end of the church to the town wall, and so backward. The guns after some two or three hundred shot, beat down the corner tower, and opened two reasonable good breaches in the east and south wall. Upon Tuesday the tenth of this instant, about five of the clock in the evening, we began the storm, and after some hot dispute, we entered about seven or eight hundred men, the enemy disputing it very stiffly with us; and indeed through the advantages of the place, and the courage God was pleased to give the defenders, our men were forced to retreat quite out of the breach, not without some considerable loss; Colonel Cassel being there shot in the head, whereof he presently died, and divers soldiers and officers doing their duty, killed and wounded. There was a tenalia[8] to flanker the south wall of the town, between Duleek Gate, and the corner tower before mentioned, which our men entered, wherein they found some forty or fifty of the enemy, which they put to the sword, and this they held; but it being without[9] the wall, and the sallyport[1] through the wall into that tenalia being choked up with some of the enemy which were killed in it, it proved of no use for our entrance into the town that way.

Although our men that stormed the breaches were forced to recoil, as before is expressed, yet being encouraged to recover their loss, they made a second attempt, wherein God was pleased to animate them, that they got ground of the enemy, and by the goodness of God, forced him to quit his entrenchments; and after a very hot dispute, the enemy having both horse and foot, and we only foot within the wall, the enemy gave ground, and our men became masters; but of their retrenchments and the church, which indeed although they made our entrance the more difficult, yet they proved of excellent use to us, so that the enemy could not annoy us with their horse, but thereby we had advantage to make good the ground, that so we might let in our own horse, which accordingly was done, though with much difficulty; the enemy retreated divers of them into the Mill-Mount, a place very strong and of difficult access, being exceeding high, having a good graft[2] and strongly pallisadoed;[3] the Governor Sir Arthur Ashton and divers considerable officers being there, our men getting up to them, were ordered by me to put them all to the sword; and indeed being in the heat of action, I forbade them to spare any that were in arms in the town, and I think that night they put to the sword about two thousand men, divers of the officers and soldiers being fled over the bridge into the other part of the town, where about one hundred of them possessed St. Peter's church steeple, some the west gate, and others, a round strong tower next the gate, called St. Sunday's. These being summoned to yield to mercy, refused; whereupon I ordered the steeple of St. Peter's church to be fired, where one of them was heard to say in the midst of the flames, "God damn me, God confound me, I burn, I burn." The next day the other two towers were summoned,[4] in one of which was about six or seven score, but they refused to yield themselves; and we knowing that hunger must compel them, set only good guards to secure them from running away, until their stomachs were come down.

---

8. A low fortification to protect the wall from the side.
9. Outside.
1. An opening for troops to pass through.

2. Ditch, moat.
3. Defended with a strong fence of pointed stakes.
4. Called to surrender.

From one of the said towers, notwithstanding their condition, they killed and wounded some of our men; when they submitted, their officers were knocked on the head, and every tenth man of the soldiers killed, and the rest shipped for the Barbados;[5] the soldiers in the other tower were all spared, as to their lives only, and shipped likewise for the Barbados. I am persuaded that this is a righteous judgment of God upon these barbarous wretches, who have imbrued their hands in so much innocent blood, and that it will tend to prevent the effusion of blood for the future, which are the satisfactory grounds to such actions, which otherwise cannot but work remorse and regret.

The officers and soldiers of this garrison were the flower of all their army; and their great expectation was that our attempting this place would put fair to ruin us; they being confident of the resolution of their men, and the advantage of the place; if we had divided our force into two quarters, to have besieged the north town and the south town, we could not have had such a correspondency between the two parts of our army, but that they might have chosen to have brought their army, and have fought with which part they pleased, and at the same time have made a sally with two thousand men upon us, and have left their walls manned, they having in the town the numbers specified in this inclosed, by some say near four thousand. Since this great mercy vouchsafed to us, I sent a party of horse and dragoons to Dundalk, which the enemy quitted, and we are possessed of; as also another castle they deserted between Trym and Drogheda, upon the Boynes.[6] I sent a party of horse and dragoons to a house within five miles of Trym, there being then in Trym some Scots companies which the Lord of Ards[7] brought to assist the Lord of Ormonde; but upon the news of Drogheda they ran away, leaving their great guns behind them, which we also have possessed. And now give me leave to say how it comes to pass that this work is wrought. It was set upon some of our hearts, that a great thing should be done, not by power, or might, but by the Spirit of God; and is it not so clear? That which caused your men to storm so courageously, it was the Spirit of God, who gave your men courage, and took it away again, and gave the enemy courage, and took it away again, and gave your men courage again, and therewith this happy success; and therefore it is good that God alone have all the glory.

It is remarkable, that these people at the first set up the Mass in some places of the town that had been monasteries; but afterwards grew so insolent, that the last Lord's day before the Storm,[8] the Protestants were thrust out of the great church, called St. Peter's, and they had public Mass there; and in this very place near one thousand of them were put to the sword, flying thither for safety: I believe all their friars were knocked on the head promiscuously, but two, the one of which was Father Peter Taaff (Brother to the Lord Taaff)[9] whom the Soldiers took the next day, and made an end of; the other was taken in the round tower, under the repute of lieutenant, and when he understood the officers in that tower had no quarter, he confessed he was a friar, but that did not save him. A great deal of loss in this business, fell upon Col. Hewson, Col. Cassel, and Colonel Ewers' regiments; Colonel Ewers having two field-officers in his regiment shot, Colonel Cassel and a captain of his

---

5. In the Cromwellian period in Ireland, not only men captured in battle but also women and children were sent into indentured servitude to English colonies in the Caribbean.
6. The Boyne River.
7. Hugh Montgomery (c. 1623–1663), 3rd Viscount of Ards.
8. I.e., Cromwell's attack on the town.
9. Theobald, 2nd Viscount Taaff (d. 1677). An uncle of Lord Taaff, Lucas was forced to surrender New Ross to Cromwell in October 1649.

regiment slain, Colonel Hewson's captain-lieutenant slain; I do not think we lost one hundred men upon the place, though many be wounded. I most humbly pray, the Parliament will be pleased this army may be maintained, and that a consideration may be had of them, and of the carrying on of the affairs here, as may give a speedy issue to this work, to which there seems to be a marvelous fair opportunity offered by God. And although it may seem very chargeable to the State of England to maintain so great a force, yet surely to stretch a little for the present, in following God's Providence, in hope the charge will not be long, I trust it will not be thought by any (that have no irreconcilable or malicious principles) unfit for me to move for a constant supply, which in humane probability, as to outward means, is most likely to hasten and perfect this work; and indeed, if God please to finish it here, as he hath done in England, the war is like to pay itself. We keep the field much, our tents sheltering us from the wet and cold, but yet the country sickness overtakes many, and therefore we desire recruits, and some fresh regiments of foot may be sent us; for it is easily conceived by what the garrisons already drink up, what our field army will come to, if God shall give more garrisons into our hands. Craving pardon for this great trouble, I rest,

Dublin, Sept. 17. 1649

Your most humble Servant,
O. CROMWELL

✦ ⊰⊱ ✦

John O'Dwyer of the Glenn
c. 1651

John O'Dwyer of the Glenn (Seán O'Duibhir an Ghleanna) is one of the most beautiful popular Irish-language songs commemorating the war against the Cromwellian conquest of Ireland and its aftermath. According to James Hardiman, who collected this song in his *Irish Minstrelsy, or Bardic Remains of Ireland* (1831), John O'Dwyer was "a distinguished officer who commanded in the Counties of Waterford and Tipperary in 1651." The poem is listed under the heading "Jacobite Relics," which places it in a long tradition of support for the Stuart kings, which began with the celebration of the accession of James I in elite bardic poetry and continued into the eighteenth century with support for Bonnie Prince Charlie in popular ballads.

The imagery of the natural world in *John O'Dwyer of the Glenn* symbolizes the state of Ireland. The lyric begins with a pastoral idyll, as the speaker describes awakening in the morning to the sound of birds singing. The intrusion of a fox signals the advent of war, and a sad old woman who stands by the side of the road reckoning her geese evokes Ireland weeping for those she has lost. Some of the geese (*geidh*), here referred to as "that prowler's spoil," died in battle; others, like the "wild geese" (*geidh fiádháin*) who left Ireland after the defeat of the Gaelic chiefs in 1603, fled to the Continent. John O'Dwyer and his men were said by Hardiman to have embarked for Spain.

The translation here is that of Thomas Furlong as printed in Hardiman's *Irish Minstrelsy*. The song originated in County Tipperary in the mid-seventeenth century, and there are more verses in Irish. It is still sung in both English and Irish. The best edition of the Irish text is that edited by Padraig de Brún and Breandán O Buachalla in *Nua-Dhuanaire* (1971), which also contains poems by such mid-seventeenth-century Irish poets as Piaras Feiritéar and Dáibhí O Bruadair.

John O'Dwyer of the Glenn

Blithe the bright dawn found me,
Rest with strength had crown'd me,

Sweet the birds sung round me,
　　Sport was all their toil.
5　The horn its clang was keeping,
　　Forth the fox was creeping,
　　Round each dame stood weeping,
　　　　O'er that prowler's spoil.
　　Hark, the foe is calling,
10　Fast the woods are falling,
　　Scenes and sights appalling
　　　　Mark the wasted soil.[1]

　　War and confiscation
　　Curse the fallen nation;
15　Gloom and desolation
　　　　Shade the lost land o'er.
　　Chill the winds are blowing,
　　Death aloft is going;
　　Peace or hope seems growing
20　　　For our race no more.
　　Hark the foe is calling,
　　Fast the woods are falling,
　　Scenes and sights appalling
　　　　Throng our blood-stained shore.

25　Where's my goat to cheer me,[2]
　　Now it plays not near me;
　　Friends no more can hear me;
　　　　Strangers round me stand.
　　Nobles once high-hearted,
30　From their homes have parted,
　　Scatter'd, scar'd and started
　　　　By a base-born band.
　　Hark the foe is calling,
　　Fast the woods are falling;
35　Scenes and sights appalling
　　　　Thicken round the land.

　　Oh! that death had found me
　　And in darkness bound me,
　　Ere each object round me
40　　　Grew so sweet, so dear.
　　Spots that once were cheering,
　　Girls beloved endearing,
　　Friends from whom I'm steering,
　　　　Take this parting tear.
45　Hark, the foe is calling,
　　Fast the woods are falling;
　　Scenes and sights appalling
　　　　Plague and haunt me here.

---

1. The falling woods are the old Irish families who have
been thrown off their land, and the "wasted soil" is the
country after war.

2. The goat stands for both Charles II in exile and the
defeated Irish lords.

⊶ ⩢⬦⩢ ⊷

The Story of Alexander Agnew

Alexander Agnew is seen by contemporary Scots writers such as Booker Prize–winning novelist James Kelman as something of a hero. An unrepentant freethinker, Agnew was the first man in Scots history publicly to deny the existence of God. Offending the Presbyterian laws of Scotland, Agnew was found guilty of blasphemy and hanged. The following journalistic account of his trial gives the sense of a man being driven to greater and greater levels of vitriolic sarcasm by the nitpicking detail of his Presbyterian examiners. Since the story begins with his refusing to go to church, saying, "Hang God, God was hanged long since," the ninth count against him—that he refused to say grace—seems oddly anticlimactic.

The story was printed in *Mercurius Politicus,* a pamphlet founded by Marchamont Needham in June 1650. In 1649, Parliament had had Needham arrested for the royalist *Mercurius Pragmaticus,* a pamphlet he had been editing since 1647, and ordered John Milton to examine Needham on his political views. Less than a year after his brush with the law, Needham reemerged as the editor of *Mercurius Politicus, the Common-Wealth of England Stated . . . With a Discourse of Excellencie of a Free-State, above a Kingly-Government.* Needham's editorial style has been described as slangy, even reminiscent of Dekker's canting. For example, in Needham's first sentence in *Mercurius Politicus* 15, he refers to the Scots Prebyterians as "our gown'd Granado's." Needham clearly had it in for the Scots, whose independence he and his pamphlet's republican English audience saw as one of the greatest obstacles to the Commonwealth.

The Story of Alexander Agnew; or Jock of Broad Scotland[1]

Alexander Agnew, commonly called Jock of broad Scotland, being accused; forasmuch as by the Divine Law of Almighty God, and Acts of Parliament of this nation, the committers of the horrid crime of blasphemy are punished by death; nevertheless, in plain contempt of the said Laws and Acts of Parliament, the said Alexander Agnew uttered heinous and grievous blasphemies against the Omnipotent and Almighty God; and second and third persons of the Trinity, as the same is set down in diverse articles in manner following; to wit,

First, the said Alexander being desired to go to church answered, "Hang God, God was hanged long since." What had he to do with God? He had nothing to do with God. Secondly, he answered, he was nothing in God's common,[2] God gave him nothing, and he was no more obliged to God than to the Devil, and God was very greedy. Thirdly, when he was desired to seek anything in God's name, he said he would never seek anything for God's sake, and that it was neither God nor the Devil that gave the fruits of the ground, the wives of the country gave him his meat. Fourthly, being asked, wherein he believed, answered, he believed in white meal, water, and salt. Fifthly, being asked how many persons were in the Godhead, answered there was only one person in the Godhead who made all, but for Christ he was not God, because he was made, and came into the world after it was made, and died as other men, being nothing but a mere man.

Sixthly, he declared that he knew not whether God or the Devil had the greater power, but he thought the Devil had the greatest, "And when I die," said he, "let God and the Devil strive for my soul, and let him that is strongest take it." Seventhly, he denied there was a holy Ghost, or knew there was a Spirit, and denied he was a

---

1. From *Mercurius Politicus,* 3 July 1656.   2. Community.

sinner or needed mercy. Eighthly, he denied he was a sinner and that he scorned to seek God's mercy. Ninthly, he ordinarily mocked all exercise of God's worship, and invocation on his name, in derision saying, "Pray you to your God and I will pray to mine when I think time." And when he was desired by some to give thanks for his meat, he said, "Take a sackful of prayers to the mill and shell them, and grind them and take your breakfast of them." To others he said, "I will give you a twopence, and pray until a bowl of meal and one stone[3] of butter fall down from heaven through the house rigging to you." To others he said when bread and cheese was given him, and was laid on the ground by him, he said, "If I leave this, I will long cry to God before he give it me again." To others he said, "Take a bannock[4] and break it in two, and lay down the one half thereof, and ye will long pray to God before he put the other half to it again."

Tenthly, being posed whether or not he knew God or Christ, he answered, he had never had any profession, nor never would; he never had any religion, nor never would: also that there was no God nor Christ, and that he never received anything from God but from nature, which he said ever reigned, and ever would, and that to speak of God and their persons was an idle thing, and that he would never name such names, for he had shaken his cap of these things long since, and he denied that a man has a soul, or that there is a heaven or a hell, or that the Scriptures are the word of God. Concerning Christ he said, that he heard of such a man, but for the second person of the Trinity, he had been the second person of the Trinity, if the ministers had not put him in prison, and that he was no more obliged to God nor the Devil. And these aforesaid blasphemies are not rarely or seldom uttered by him, but frequently and ordinarily in several places where he resorted, to the entangling, deluding, and seducing of the common people: through the committing of which blasphemies he hath contravened the tenor of the said Laws and Acts of Parliament and incurred the pain of death mentioned therein, which ought to be inflicted upon him with all rigor, in manner specified in the indictment.

Which indictment being put to the knowledge of an assize,[5] the said Alexander Agnew called Jock of broad Scotland, was by the said assize, all in one voice, by the mouth of William Carlile, late baily[6] of Dumfrize their chancellor[7] found guilty of the crime of blasphemy mentioned in his indictment. For which the commissioners ordained him upon Wednesday, 21 May 1656, betwixt 2 and 4 hours in the afternoon to be taken to the ordinary place of execution for the burgh of Dumfrize, and there to be hanged on a gibbet while he be dead, and all his movable goods to be escheat.[8]

Edward Hyde, Earl of Clarendon
1609–1674

Bound up in the politics of his day, Edward Hyde was also often at odds with the powerful. From a long line of lawyers, he was neither noble nor wealthy by birth but rose to power through the law. Hyde played the observer in his roles as scholar, legislator, and diplomat. At law school at the Middle Temple in 1627 he complained that the whole country was a "sea of wine, and women, and quarrels, and gaming." A member of a humanist circle surrounding Sir Lucius Cary, Secretary

---

3. Fourteen pounds.
4. In Scotland and the North of England, a large round loaf of bread.
5. In Scotland, a trial by jury.

6. In Scotland, the chief magistrate of a county who functions as a sheriff.
7. In Scotland, the foreman of a jury.
8. Forfeited to the state.

of State under Charles I, Clarendon found them too naive about the realities of power. Entering Parliament in 1640, Hyde initially supported Parliament's curbs on royal absolutism, such as the impeachment of the King's man in Ireland, the Earl of Strafford. Later, however, fearing that parliamentary radicalism was a threat to the English constitution, Clarendon sided with the King. Serving Charles I closely throughout the 1640s by urging compromise with Parliament rather than war, Clarendon was no more comfortable among the King's followers than among the Parliamentarians. After the execution of Charles I, Clarendon was hired by Charles II in exile only when all other policies had been tried and failed. After the Restoration he held the position of Lord Chancellor until he was removed from power by Charles II's rakish courtiers, who resented his political ethos of moderation and tradition. Exiled in disgrace, he wrote the final version of *The History of the Rebellion and Civil Wars in England,* published a quarter century after his death (1702–1704).

Ironic detachment in tension with partisanship characterizes the history as it does his life. Strangely enough, neither his autobiography nor his history contains an account of how he abandoned the Parliamentarians for Charles I. Yet his scathing criticism of those who crossed the royalists—Presbyterians, Scots, Irish, Independents—reveals a private audience of like-minded royalists among family and friends. At times, Clarendon's irony escalates to sarcasm, as in his comments on the Scottish nobleman Argyle in the following account of the death of the great Scots military hero Montrose. Montrose's support of Charles I had thwarted Argyle's rise to power in Scotland. When Montrose returned to Scotland in 1649 as Charles II's Lieutenant General, Argyle succeeded in having him arrested on charges of heresy. A vacillating Charles II did not intervene, and Montrose was executed with theatrical brutality. As Martine Brownley has commented, there are "no unalloyed heroes or villains" in Clarendon's history, and so Montrose is portrayed in understated terms, and the narrative does not shrink from revealing Charles II's betrayal of his old ally. Clarendon's style eschews high rhetoric and opts for a middle style in a syntax uniting periods in a loose linear fashion. The poised detachment and sober gravity of his style produce the kind of authority that caused the German historian Ranke to say of Clarendon's *History of the Rebellion:* "the view of the event in England itself and in the educated world generally . . . has been determined by the book."

from True Historical Narrative of the Rebellion
[THE DEATH OF MONTROSE]

Permission was then given to him[1] to speak; and without the least trouble in his countenance, or disorder, upon all the indignities he had suffered, he told them, since the King had owned them so far as to treat with them, he had appeared before them with reverence, and bareheaded, which otherwise he would not have done: that he had done nothing of which he was ashamed, or had cause to repent; that the first Covenant he had taken,[2] and complied with it, and with them who took it, as long as the ends for which it was ordained were observed; but when he discovered, which was now evident to all the world, that private and particular men designed to satisfy their own ambition and interest, instead of considering the public benefit, and that under the pretence of reforming some errors in religion they resolved to abridge and take away the King's just power and lawful authority, he had withdrawn himself from that engagement: that for the League and Covenant,[3] he had never taken it, and therefore could not break it; and it was now too apparent to the whole Christian world what monstrous mischiefs it had produced: that when, under color of it, an army from Scotland had invaded England in assistance of the rebellion that was then against their lawful King, he had, by his

1. Montrose.
2. Montrose had sworn to the National Covenant of 1638, a pact drawn up by the Scots Presbyterians to drive out Anglicanism and the innovations of Archbishop Laud, particularly the English Book of Common Prayer.

3. The Solemn League and Covenant (1643) was an Anglo-Scottish alliance to establish a state Presbyterian Church in Scotland and Ireland and to pledge military aid against the King, both funding for the Scots Presbyterian forces in Ulster and the entrance of these forces into England.

majesty's command, received a commission from him to raise forces in Scotland, that he might thereby divert them from the other odious prosecution: that he had executed that commission with the obedience and duty that he owed to the King, and in all the circumstances of it had proceeded like a gentleman, and had never suffered any blood to be shed but in the heat of the battle; and that he saw many persons there whose lives he had saved: when the King commanded him, he laid down his arms, and withdrew out of the kingdom, which they could not have compelled him to have done. He said he was now again entered into the kingdom by his majesty's command and with his authority; and what success soever it might have pleased God to have given him, he would always have obeyed any command he should have received from him. He advised them to consider well of the consequence before they proceeded against him, and that all his actions might be examined and judged by the laws of the land, or those of nations.

As soon as he had ended his discourse he was ordered to withdraw, and after a short space was again brought in, and told by the Chancellor that he was on the morrow, being the one and twentieth of May 1650, to be carried to Edinborough cross, and there to be hanged upon a gallows thirty foot high, for the space of three hours, and then to be taken down, and his head to be cut off upon a scaffold, and hanged on Edinborough tollbooth, and his legs and arms to be hanged up in other public towns of the kingdom, and his body to be buried at the place where he was to be executed, except the Kirk should take off his excommunication, and then his body might be buried in the common place of burial. He desired that he might say somewhat to them, but was not suffered, and so was carried back to the prison.

That he might not enjoy any ease or quiet during the short remainder of his life, their ministers came presently to insult over him with all the reproaches imaginable, pronounced his damnation, and assured him that the judgment he was the next day to undergo was but an easy prologue to that which he was to undergo afterward. And after many such barbarities, they offered to intercede for him to the Kirk upon his repentance, and to pray with him; but he too well understood the form of their common prayers in those cases to be only the most virulent and insolent imprecations against the persons of those they prayed against ("Lord, vouchsafe yet to touch the obdurate heart of this proud incorrigible sinner, this wicked, perjured, traitorous, and profane person, who refuses to hearken to the voice of thy Kirk," and the like charitable expressions), and therefore he desired them to spare their pains, and to leave him to his own devotions. He told them that they were a miserable, deluded, and deluding people; and would shortly bring that poor nation under the most insupportable servitude ever people had submitted to. He told them he was prouder to have his head set upon the place it was appointed to be, than he could have been to have had his picture hung in the King's bedchamber: that he was so far from being troubled that his four limbs were to be hanged in four cities of the kingdom, that he heartily wished that he had flesh enough to be sent to every city in Christendom, as a testimony of the cause for which he suffered.

The next day they executed every part and circumstance of that barbarous sentence with all the inhumanity imaginable; and he bore it with all the courage and magnanimity, and the greatest piety, that a good Christian could manifest. He magnified the virtue, courage, and religion of the last King, exceedingly commended the justice and goodness and understanding of the present King, and prayed that they might not betray him as they had done his father. When he had ended all he meant to say, and was expecting to expire, they had yet one scene more to act of their tyranny. The hangman brought the book that had been published of his truly heroic actions whilst he had commanded in that kingdom, which book was tied in a small cord that was put about his neck. The marquis smiled at this new instance of their malice, and thanked them for it; and said he was pleased that it should be there, and was prouder of wearing it than ever he had been of the Garter;[4] and so renewing some devout ejaculations, he patiently endured the last act of the executioner.

Soon after, the officers who had been taken with him, Sir William Hurry, Sir Francis Hay, and many others of as good families as any in the kingdom, were executed, to the number of thirty or forty, in several quarters of the kingdom; many of them being suffered to be beheaded. There was one whom they thought fit to save, one Colonel Whitford; who, when he was brought to die, said, he knew the reason why he was put to death, which was only because he had killed Dorislaus at the Hague, who was one of those who had murdered the last King. One of the magistrates, who were present to see the execution, caused it to be suspended, till he presently informed the council what the man had said; and they thought fit to avoid the reproach, and so preserved the gentleman, who was not before known to have had a hand in that action.

Thus died the gallant Marquis of Montrose, after he had given as great a testimony of loyalty and courage as a subject can do, and performed as wonderful actions in several battles, upon as great inequality of numbers and as great disadvantages in respect of arms and other preparations for war, as hath been performed in this age. He was a gentleman of a very ancient extraction, many of whose ancestors had exercised the highest charges under the King in that kingdom, and had been allied to the Crown itself. He was of very good parts, which were improved by a good education: he had always a great emulation, or rather a great contempt, of the Marquis of Argyle (as he was too apt to contemn those he did not love), who wanted nothing but honesty and courage to be a very extraordinary man, having all other good talents in a great degree. He was in his nature fearless of danger, and never declined any enterprise for the difficulty of going through with it, but exceedingly affected those which seemed desperate to other men and did believe somewhat to be in him[self] which other men were not acquainted with, which made him live more easily towards those who were, or were willing to be, inferior to him, and towards whom he exercised wonderful civility and generosity, than with his superiors or equals. He was naturally jealous, and suspected those who did not concur with him in the way not to mean so well as he. He was not without vanity, but his virtues were much superior, and he well deserved to have his memory preserved and celebrated amongst the most illustrious persons of the age in which he lived.

The King received an account and information of all these particulars before he embarked from Holland, without any other apology for the affront and indignity to himself than that they assured him that the proceeding against the late Marquis of Montrose had been for his service. They who were most displeased with Argyle and his faction were not sorry for this inhuman and monstrous prosecution; which at the same time must render him the more odious, and had rid them of an enemy that they thought would have been more dangerous to them; and they persuaded the King, who was enough afflicted with the news and all the circumstances of it, that he might sooner take revenge upon that people by a temporary complying with them and going to them, than by staying away and absenting himself, which would invest them in an absolute dominion in that kingdom, and give them power to corrupt or destroy all those who yet remained faithful to him, and were ready to spend their lives in his service: and so he pursued his former resolution and embarked for Scotland.

[END OF PERSPECTIVES: THE CIVIL WAR, OR THE WARS OF THREE KINGDOMS]

4. The Order of the Garter is the oldest and most important order of knighthood in England, instituted by Edward III (c. 1346).

John Milton
1608–1674

While writing *Paradise Lost*, Milton would rise early to begin composing poetry; when his secretary arrived late, the old blind man would complain, "I want to be milked." Prodigious in his memory and ingenuity, austere in his frugality and discipline, Milton devoted his life to learning, politics, and art. He put his eloquence at the service of the Puritan Revolution, which brought on the beheading of a king and the institution of a republican commonwealth. Milton entered controversies on divorce and freedom of the press. He showed courage in defending the Puritan republic when he could have lost his life for doing so. Radical, scholar, sage—Milton is above all the great epic poet of England.

Milton's life was marked by a passionate devotion to his religious, political, and artistic ideals, a devotion that ran in his family. Milton's father was said to have been disinherited for his Protestantism by his own father, who was Roman Catholic. When the Civil War broke out, Milton sided with Cromwell while his brother fought for the King. The oldest of three children in a prosperous middle-class family, young John read Virgil, Ovid, and Livy; he especially loved "our sage and serious Spenser," whom he called "a better teacher than Aquinas." Milton later wrote that from the age of twelve he "hardly ever gave up reading for bed till midnight." After his first year at Christ's College, Cambridge, the poet was expelled. While in exile, Milton excoriated academia: "How wretchedly suited that place is to the worshippers of Phoebus! It is disgusting to be constantly subjected to the threats of a rough tutor and to other indignities my spirit cannot endure." Returning to Cambridge, he took his B.A. in 1629 and his M.A. in 1632. On vacations during these years he wrote two of his most musical lyrics, the erotic *L'Allegro* and the Platonic *Il Penseroso*. After leaving university, Milton lived with his parents in Berkshire, where he wrote *Lycidas*, a haunting elegy for the early death of his Cambridge friend Edward King, and *Comus*, a masque for the prominent noble Egerton family at Ludlow Castle.

After his mother's death in 1638, Milton traveled to Europe. He stayed longest in Italy, where his poems were greatly admired by the Florentine literati, who welcomed him into their academies. He later reflected that it was in Italy that he first sensed his vocation as an epic poet, hoping to "perhaps leave something so written, as they should not willingly let it die." Visiting Rome, Naples, and Venice, Milton collected Monteverdi's music, which he would later sing and play. He also met the famed astronomer Galileo, the censorship of whose works Milton would later protest. Concerned about political turmoil in England, he returned home at the outbreak of the Civil War.

From 1640 to 1660, Milton devoted himself to "the cause of real and substantial liberty," by which he meant religious, domestic, and civil liberties. Defending religious liberty, he decried Anglican hierarchy and ritualism—"the new vomited paganism of sensual idolatry"—in a series of tracts, including *Of Reformation* (1641) and *The Reason of Church Government* (1642).

That same year, Milton married seventeen-year-old Mary Powell, who came from a royalist Oxfordshire family. After only a month, she left Milton alone to his "philosophical" life for a more sociable one at home. Troubled by the unhappiness of his marriage, Milton wrote four treatises on divorce, for which he was publicly condemned. He argued that incompatibility should be grounds for divorce, that both husband and wife should be allowed to remarry, and that to maintain otherwise was contrary to reason and scripture. According to his nephew, whom Milton tutored during this time, he was interested in marrying another woman but by 1645 was reunited with Mary. They had a daughter soon afterward. They were joined for several years by Mary's family, who had lost their estate in the Civil War.

Along with "the true conception of marriage," Milton's concept of domestic liberty included "the sound education of children, and freedom of thought and speech." In *Of Education* (1644), opposing strictly vocational instruction, Milton called for the study of languages, rhetoric, poetry, philosophy, and science, the goal of which was "to perform justly, skillfully and magnanimously all of the offices both private and public of peace and war." In *Areopagitica* (1644), Milton fought against censorship before publication but counseled control of printed texts posing political or religious danger. In the 1640s, Milton steered a course midway between the religious conformity demanded by the once dissenting Presbyterians and the complete separation of church and state advocated by such radicals as Roger Williams, who ultimately went to America in search of greater toleration.

After Oliver Cromwell defeated the Royalists and the King was tried and executed by order of the "Rump" parliament purged of dissenters, Milton wrote *The Tenure of Kings and Magistrates* (1649) to argue that subjects could justly overthrow a tyrant. This tract won him the job of Latin Secretary to the Council of State, handling all correspondence to foreign governments. After the beheading of Charles I in 1649, *Eikon Basilike*, "the Royal Image" appeared, pieced together from the King's papers by his chaplain John Gauden. To counteract sympathy for the King's cause that this work might elicit, Milton wrote a chapter-by-chapter refutation of it entitled *Eikonoklastes, or Image-Breaker* (1649). Milton also defended Cromwell's government in three Latin works that were in some measure self-defenses: *First* and *Second Defense of the English People* (1651, 1654) and *Defense of Himself* (1656).

His eyes weakened by the strain of so much writing, Milton went blind. His wife Mary died, leaving three daughters and one son. The boy died soon after, in May 1652. That same month, Milton wrote a sonnet exhorting the Lord General Cromwell to "Help us to save free conscience from the paw of hireling wolves," a reference to ministers who wanted to exclude dissenters from a unified established church. Sounding the cry for liberty again in *Avenge, O Lord these Slaughtered Saints* (1655), Milton lamented the massacre of Italian Protestants. One of Milton's most beautiful and best-known sonnets, *Me thought I saw my late espoused saint*, is said to be about his second wife, Katherine Woodcock, who, after just two years of marriage, died following the birth of her child in 1558.

Cromwell died the same year, and his son Richard's succession to power began a period of political confusion. Milton continued to write political tracts, now even more radical in arguing for universal education and freedom from allegiance to *any* established church and against the abuse of church positions for money. In *De Doctrina Christiana* (written 1655–1660, published 1823), Milton set forth his individualistic theology; he was convinced that no one should be required to attend church and that everyone should interpret scripture in his own way. Committed to the cause of the republic even after the Restoration of Charles II, Milton published *The Ready and Easy Way to Establish a Free Commonwealth* in 1660. Shortly after its appearance, Milton went into hiding. The House of Commons ordered the burning of *Eikonoklastes* and had Milton arrested. He was held in prison for several months. For a time threatened with heavy fines and even death by hanging, Milton was finally released through the aid of his friend Andrew Marvell.

In the aftermath of the Restoration, Milton lived in obscurity and desolation. On the anniversary of Charles I's execution, Cromwell's body was dug up and hanged. More than a few of Milton's friends were either executed or forced into exile. The republic to which he had devoted his life's work had been defeated. Amid this experience of defeat, he worked on *Paradise Lost*, with its themes of fall, damnation, war in heaven, and future redemption for an erring humanity.

While writing his epic, he was much helped by the companionship and housekeeping of his young and amiable third wife Elizabeth Minshull, whom he married in 1663. Young pupils, secretaries, and his daughters read to him in many languages (some of which they didn't understand). The Miltons lived frugally on the money that he had saved from his salary as Latin Secretary (1649–1659). Milton had begun writing *Paradise Lost* by 1658–1659, but he only completed the first edition for publication in 1667. First conceiving of this work as a drama, he had written a soliloquy for the rebellious Lucifer in 1642, which later appeared near the opening of the epic's fourth book. Milton explained that he had put off writing *Paradise Lost* because it was "a work to be raised . . . by devout prayer to that eternal Spirit who can enrich with all utterance and knowledge."

In the last ten years of his life, Milton also wrote *Paradise Regained* (1671), a short epic about the temptation of Christ, based on the model of the Book of Job. Published in the same year was *Samson Agonistes*, a verse tragedy about the Biblical hero, who, betrayed by his lover Delilah, brought down destruction on himself as well as his enemies. In 1673 he published an expanded edition of his *Poems* (1645), to which he added his translations of the Psalms. Finally, in 1674, all twelve books of *Paradise Lost* as we know it were published. That same year, Milton died in a fit of gout and was buried in Saint Giles Cripplegate alongside his father.

Milton combined the traditional erudition of a Renaissance poet with the committed politics of a Puritan radical, both of which contributed to his crowning achievement, *Paradise Lost*. Milton draws on the Bible, Homer, Virgil, and Dante to create his own original sound and story. The vivid sensual imagery of *L'Allegro*, echoing Shakespeare and Spenser, suggests the pastoral idyll of Adam and Eve in Paradise. The intellectual rebelliousness of his prose works inflects the epic's dramatic embodiment of such problems as the origin of evil, sin, and death. Like *Samson Agonistes*, *Paradise Lost* reaches humanity's psychological depths: arrogance, despair, revenge, self-destruction, desire, and self-knowledge. Most of all, *Paradise Lost* dramatizes human wayfaring in the face of the Fall, not unlike Milton's own heroic perseverance in writing his epic after the loss of the world he had helped to create.

L'Allegro[1]

Hence loathèd Melancholy
   Of Cerberus,[2] and blackest midnight born,
In Stygian cave forlorn.
   'Mongst horrid shapes, and shreiks, and sights unholy,
5   Find out some uncouth° cell,   *unknown*
   Where brooding darkness spreads his jealous wings,
And the night-raven[3] sings;
   There under ebon shades, and low-brow'd rocks,
   As ragged as thy Locks,
10   In dark Cimmerian[4] desert ever dwell.
But come thou goddess fair and free,
   In Heaven yclept° Euphrosyne,   *called*
And by men, heart-easing Mirth,
   Whom lovely Venus at a birth
15   With two sister Graces more
   To ivy-crownèd Bacchus bore;[5]
Or whether (as some sager sing)
   The frolic wind that breathes the spring,
Zephyr with Aurora playing,
20   As he met her once a-Maying,[6]

---

1. The happy person. This and the companion poem *Il Penseroso* (the pensive one) were composed around 1631; they were first published in 1645.
2. For the underworld cave of the three-headed dog Cerberus, see Virgil, *Aeneid* 6.418. Milton makes Cerberus and Night the parents of Melancholy, which is the subject of *Il Penseroso*.
3. Ominous bird.

4. The Cimmerians lived at the extreme limit of the known world (see *Odyssey* 11.13–22).
5. The Graces: Euphrosyne (Mirth), Aglaia (Brightness), and Thalia (Bloom). Servius's commentary to the *Aeneid* makes Venus and Bacchus their parents.
6. Milton invented this parentage of the Graces by Aurora, the dawn, and Zephyr, the west wind.

There on beds of violets blue,
And fresh-blown roses washed in dew,
Filled her with thee a daughter fair,
So buxom,° blithe, and debonair.   *yielding*
25 Haste thee nymph, and bring with thee
Jest and youthful Jollity,
Quips and cranks,° and wanton wiles,   *jests*
Nods, and becks, and wreathèd smiles,
Such as hang on Hebe's[7] cheek,
30 And love to live in dimple sleek;
Sport that wrinkled Care derides,
And Laughter holding both his sides.
Come, and trip it as you go
On the light fantastic toe,
35 And in thy right hand lead with thee,
The mountain nymph, sweet Liberty;
And if I give thee honor due,
Mirth, admit me of thy crew
To live with her, and live with thee,
40 In unreprovèd pleasures free;
To hear the lark begin his flight,
And singing startle the dull night,
From his watch-tower in the skies,
Till the dappled dawn doth rise;
45 Then to come in spite of sorrow,
And at my window bid good morrow,
Through the sweetbriar, or the vine,
Or the twisted eglantine.°   *honey-suckle*
While the cock with lively din,
50 Scatters the rear of darkness thin,
And to the stack, or the barn door,
Stoutly struts his dames before,
Oft listening how the hounds and horn
Cheerly rouse the slumbring morn,
55 From the side of some hoar° hill,   *grey with mist*
Through the high wood echoing shrill.
Sometime walking not unseen
By hedge-row elms, on hillocks green,
Right against the eastern gate,
60 Where the great sun begins his state,°   *progress*
Robed in flames, and amber light,
The clouds in thousand liveries dight,°   *dressed*
While the plowman near at hand,
Whistles ore the furrowed land,
65 And the milkmaid singeth blithe,
And the mower whets his scythe,
And every shepherd tells his tale
Under the hawthorn in the dale.
Straight mine eye hath caught new pleasures

7. Goddess of youth and daughter of Zeus and Hera.

70   Whilst the landscape round it measures,
    Russet lawns, and fallows° gray,   *plowed lands*
    Where the nibling flocks do stray,
    Mountains on whose barren breast
    The laboring clouds do often rest;
75   Meadows trim with daisies pied,°   *variegated*
    Shallow brooks, and rivers wide.
    Towers and battlements it sees
    Bosomed high in tufted trees,
    Where perhaps some beauty lies,
80   The cynosure[8] of neighboring eyes.
    Hard by, a cottage chimney smokes
    From betwixt two agèd oaks,
    Where Corydon and Thyrsis met,
    Are at their savory dinner set
85   Of herbs, and other country messes,
    Which the neat-handed Phyllis dresses;
    And then in haste her bower she leaves,
    With Thestylis[9] to bind the sheaves;
    Or if the earlier season lead
90   To the tanned haycock° in the mead,   *heaps of hay*
    Sometimes with secure delight
    The upland hamlets will invite,
    When the merry bells ring round,
    And the jocond rebecks° sound   *fiddles*
95   To many a youth, and many a maid,
    Dancing in the checkered shade;
    And young and old come forth to play
    On a sunshine holiday,
    Till the livelong daylight fail,
100   Then to the spicy nut-brown ale,
    With stories told of many a feat,
    How fairy Mab[1] the junkets° eat,   *cream cheeses*
    She was pinched, and pulled she said,
    And by the friar's lantern led
105   Tells how the drudging goblin sweat,
    To earn his cream-bowl duly set,
    When in one night, ere glimpse of morn,
    His shadowy flail hath threshed the corn
    That ten day-laborers could not end;
110   Then lies him down the lubber fiend.[2]
    And stretched out all the chimney's length,
    Basks at the fire his hairy strength;
    And crop-full out of doors he flings,
    Ere the first cock his matin rings.
115   Thus done the tales, to bed they creep,
    By whispering winds soon lulled asleep.

---

8. The North Star, here meaning, the center of attention.
9. The shepherds' names are common in Renaissance pastoral.
1. Queen of the fairies, and the topic of Mercutio's

famous speech (*Romeo and Juliet* 1.4.54–95).
2. Slaving demon, like Robin Goodfellow called "lob of spirits" in *Midsummer Night's Dream* 2.1.16.

Towered cities please us then,
And the busy hum of men,
Where throngs of knights and barons bold,
120   In weeds° of peace high triumphs° hold,   *clothes/tournaments*
With store of ladies, whose bright eyes
Rain influence,[3] and judge the prize,
Of wit, or arms, while both contend
To win her grace, whom all commend.
125   There let Hymen[4] oft appear
In saffron robe, with taper clear,
And pomp, and feast, and revelry,
With mask, and antique pageantry;
Such sights as youthful poets dream
130   On summer eves by haunted stream.
Then to the well-trod stage anon,
If Jonson's learned sock[5] be on,
Or sweetest Shakespeare fancy's child,
Warble his native wood-notes wild,
135   And ever against eating cares
Lap me in soft Lydian airs,[6]
Married to immortal verse
Such as the meeting soul may pierce
In notes, with many a winding bout
140   Of linkèd sweetness long drawn out,
With wanton heed and giddy cunning,
The melting voice through mazes running,
Untwisting all the chains that tie
The hidden soul of harmony.
145   That Orpheus' self may heave his head
From golden slumber on a bed
Of heaped Elysian flowers, and hear
Such strains as would have won the ear
Of Pluto, to have quite set free
150   His half regained Eurydice.[7]
These delights, if thou canst give,
Mirth with thee, I mean to live.[8]

Il Penseroso[1]

Hence vain deluding joys,
    The brood of Folly without father bred,
How little you bestead,°   *help*
    Or fill the fixèd mind with all your toys;
5   Dwell in some idle brain,

---

3. In astrology, the process by which an etherial fluid emanating from the stars ruled human fate.
4. Roman wedding god.
5. Low-heeled slipper of the comic actor in ancient Greece and Rome.
6. Plato considered the Lydian mode to be morally corrupting and loose; others found it a source of relaxed enjoyment.

7. When Orpheus attempted to rescue his wife Eurydice from Hades, he lost her by violating the command that he not look back to see if she were behind him.
8. The concluding lines recall the final couplet of Marlowe's lyric *The Passionate Shepherd to His Love*: "If these delights thy mind may move, / Then live with me, and be my love."
1. The pensive one.

And fancies fond with gaudy shapes possess,
　　As thick and numberless
　　As the gay motes that people the sunbeams,
　　Or likest hovering dreams,

10　　The fickle pensioners° of Morpheus'[2] train.　　　　　　*guards*
But hail thou Goddess, sage and holy,
Hail divinest Melancholy,
Whose saintly visage is too bright
To hit° the sense of human sight,　　　　　　　　　　　　　*fit*

15 And therefore to our weaker view,
O'er laid with black staid Wisdom's hue;[3]
Black, but such as in esteem,
Prince Memnon's sister[4] might beseem,
Or that starred Ethiope Queen[5] that strove

20 To set her beauties praise above
The sea nymphs, and their powers offended.
Yet thou art higher far descended,
Thee bright-haired Vesta[6] long of yore,
To solitary Saturn bore;

25 His daughter she (in Saturn's reign
Such mixture was not held a stain)[7]
Oft in glimmering bowers, and glades
He met her, and in secret shades
Of woody Ida's inmost grove,

30 While yet there was no fear of Jove.
Come pensive nun, devout and pure,
Sober, steadfast, and demure,
All in a robe of darkest grain,
Flowing with majestic train,

35 And sable° stole of cypress lawn,°　　　　　　　　　*dark / fine linen*
Over thy decent shoulders drawn.
Come, but keep thy wonted state,
With even step, and musing gait,
And looks commercing with the skies,

40 Thy rapt soul sitting in thine eyes:
There held in holy passion still,
Forget thyself to marble,[8] till
With a sad leaden downward cast,
Thou fix them on the earth as fast.

45 And join with thee calm Peace, and Quiet,
Spare Fast, that oft with gods doth diet,
And hears the Muses in a ring,
Ay round about Jove's altar sing.
And add to these retired leisure;

---

2. God of dreams and son of Sleep.
3. Melancholy was governed by the black bile in the body and manifested itself in a black face.
4. The Ethiopian Prince Memnon (*Odyssey* 11.521) had a sister named Himera (Greek, "light of day").
5. Cassiopea was turned into a constellation because she boasted that she was more beautiful than the Nereids.

6. Milton makes Vesta a mother; by tradition, she was a virgin, daughter of Saturn, and goddess of the hearth.
7. The Golden Age was a time of plenty and sexual freedom.
8. Turning to stone through grief comes from the story of Niobe.

50	That in trim gardens takes his pleasure;
	But first, and chiefest, with thee bring
	Him that yon soars on golden wing,
	Guiding the fiery-wheelèd throne,[9]
	The cherub Contemplation;[1]
55	And the mute Silence hist° along,
	'Less Philomel[2] will deign a song,
	In her sweetest, saddest plight,
	Smoothing the rugged brow of night,
	While Cynthia[3] checks her dragon yoke,
60	Gently o'er th'accustomed oak;
	Sweet bird that shunn'st the noise of folly,
	Most musical, most melancholy!
	Thee chantress oft the woods among,
	I woo to hear thy evensong;
65	And missing thee, I walk unseen
	On the dry smooth-shaven green,
	To behold the wandring moon,
	Riding near her highest noon,
	Like one that had been led astray
70	Through the heaven's wide pathless way;
	And oft, as if her head she bowed,
	Stooping through a fleecy cloud.
	Oft on a plat° of rising ground,
	I hear the far-off curfew sound,
75	Over some wide-watered shore,
	Swinging slow with sullen roar;
	Or if the air will not permit,
	Some still removèd place will fit,
	Where glowing embers through the room
80	Teach light to counterfeit a gloom,
	Far from all resort of mirth,
	Save the cricket on the hearth,
	Or the bellman's drowsy charm,[4]
	To bless the doors from nightly harm;
85	Or let my lamp at midnight hour,
	Be seen in some high lonely tower,
	Where I may oft out-watch the Bear,[5]
	With thrice great Hermes,[6] or unsphere[7]
	The spirit of Plato to unfold
90	What worlds, or what vast regions hold
	The immortal mind that hath forsook
	Her mansion in this fleshly nook;
	And of those demons that are found

a call (gloss for line 55)

plot (gloss for line 73)

9. See Ezekiel 1.4–6.
1. The angel Cherubim contemplate God.
2. The nightingale (Greek).
3. The moon goddess, another name for Hecate; for her dragons, see Ovid, *Metamorphoses* 7.218–19.
4. The night-watchman, or bellman, cries out the hours in a chant, or charm (from *carmen*, Latin for song).
5. The constellation of the Great Bear, which never sets, symbolizes perfection.
6. Hermes Trismegistus was believed to be the author of the Hermetica, texts of esoteric neoplatonism and magic. See Giordano Bruno in Perspectives: Emblem, Style, and Metaphor, page 1604.
7. To remove from the eternal sphere and make reappear on earth.

In fire, air, flood, or under ground,
95   Whose power hath a true consent
With planet, or with element.
Sometime let gorgeous Tragedy
In scepter'd pall° come sweeping by,   *robe*
Presenting Thebes, or Pelops line,
100   Or the tale of Troy divine.[8]
Or what (though rare) of later age
Ennobled hath the buskined stage.[9]
But, O sad virgin, that thy power
Might raise Musaeus[1] from his bower,
105   Or bid the soul of Orpheus[2] sing
Such notes as warbled to the string,
Drew iron tears down Pluto's cheek,
And made Hell grant what Love did seek.
Or call up him[3] that left half told
110   The story of Cambuscan bold,
Of Camball, and of Algarsife,
And who had Canace to wife,
That owned the virtuous° ring and glass,   *magical*
And of the wondrous horse of brass,
115   On which the Tartar king did ride;
And if aught else, great bards beside,[4]
In sage and solemn tunes have sung,
Of tourneys and of trophies hung;
Of forests, and enchantments drear,
120   Where more is meant then meets the ear.
Thus, Night, oft see me in thy pale career,
Till civil-suited Morn appear,
Not tricked and frounced[5] as she was wont,
With the Attic boy[6] to hunt,
125   But kerchiefed in a comely cloud,
While rocking winds are piping loud,
Or ushered with a shower still,°   *quiet*
When the gust hath blown his fill,
Ending on the rustling leaves,
130   With minute drops from off the eaves.
And when the sun begins to fling
His flaring beams, me, Goddess, bring
To archèd walks of twilight groves,
And shadows brown that Sylvan[7] loves
135   Of pine, or monumental oak,
Where the rude ax with heavèd stroke.

8. Thebes was the birthplace of Oedipus, tragic hero of
Sophocles' *Oedipus Rex*. Pelops's descendants Agamemnon and Orestes are the subject of Aeschylus' tragedy
Oresteia. Troy was the city destroyed by the Trojan War,
the tragic consequences of which are the subject of
Euripides' *The Trojan Women*.
9. The high boots of tragic actors. Compare *L'Allegro* line
132.
1. Prophet and poet, who studied with the mythic bard

Orpheus.
2. See *L'Allegro* 145–50.
3. Chaucer; the "story" is the unfinished *Squire's Tale*.
4. Lines 116–20 refer to Spenser's allegorical *Faerie
Queene*.
5. Richly attired and wearing ringlets.
6. Cephalus, beloved of Aurora, who met him while he
was hunting. (See Ovid, *Metamorphoses* 7.700–13.)
7. Roman god of the forest.

Was never heard the nymphs to daunt,
Or fright them from their hallowed haunt.
There in close covert by some brook,
140 Where no prophaner eye may look,
Hide me from day's garish eye,
While the bee with honeyed thigh,
That at her flowery work doth sing,
And the waters murmuring
145 With such consort° as they keep,   *musical harmony*
Entice the dewy-feathered sleep;
And let some strange mysterious dream
Wave at his wings in airy stream
Of lively portraiture displayed,
150 Softly on my eye-lids laid.
And as I wake, sweet music breathe
Above, about, or underneath,
Sent by some spirit to mortals good,
Or th'unseen genius° of the wood.   *presiding local god*
155 But let my due feet never fail
To walk the studious cloisters° pale,   *enclosure*
And love the high embowèd° roof,   *arched*
With antic pillars massy proof,°   *impenetrability*
And storied[8] windows richly dight,°   *decorated*
160 Casting a dim religious light.
There let the pealing organ blow
To the full voiced choir below,
In service high, and anthems clear,
As may with sweetness, through mine ear,
165 Dissolve me into ecstasies,
And bring all heaven before mine eyes.
And may at last my weary age
Find out the peaceful hermitage,
The hairy gown and mossy cell,
170 Where I may sit and rightly spell°   *find out about*
Of every star that heaven doth shew,
And every herb that sips the dew,
Till old experience do attain
To something like prophetic strain.
175 These pleasures Melancholy give,
And I with thee will choose to live.[9]

Lycidas

In this Monody[1] the Author bewails a learned Friend,[2] unfortunately drowned in his passage from Chester on the Irish Seas, 1637. And by occasion foretells the ruin of our corrupted Clergy then in their height.

---

8. With stories from the Bible.
9. See *L'Allegro* 151–52.
1. A mournful song sung by one voice. *Lycidas* is a pastoral elegy, a lament for the dead through language evoking nature and the rural life of shepherds. The first *Idyll* of Theocritus and Virgil's fifth *Eclogue* are classical prece-

dents for *Lycidas*. Shelley's *Adonais* and Arnold's *Thyrsis* are later examples of this form.
2. Edward King, who attended Cambridge when Milton did, and drowned 10 August 1637. He had planned to enter the clergy and had written some Latin poems.

Yet once more, O ye laurels, and once more
Ye myrtles brown, with ivy[3] never sear,°   *withered*
I come to pluck your berries harsh and crude,°   *unripe*
And with forced fingers rude,
5 Shatter your leaves before the mellowing year.
Bitter constraint, and sad occasion dear,
Compels me to disturb your season due:
For Lycidas is dead, dead ere his prime,[4]
Young Lycidas, and hath not left his peer:
10 Who would not sing for Lycidas? he knew
Himself to sing, and build the lofty rhyme.
He must not float upon his watery bier
Unwept, and welter° to the parching wind,   *writhe*
Without the meed° of some melodious tear.°   *recompense/elegy*
15   Begin then, sisters of the sacred well,[5]
That from beneath the seat of Jove doth spring,
Begin, and somewhat loudly sweep the string.
Hence with denial vain, and coy excuse,
So may some gentle Muse
20 With lucky words favor my destined urn,
And as he passes turn,
And bid fair peace be to my sable° shroud.   *black*
For we were nursed upon the self-same hill,
Fed the same flock; by fountain, shade, and rill.
25   Together both, ere the high lawns appeared
Under the opening eyelids of the morn,
We drove a field, and both together heard
What time the grayfly[6] winds her sultry horn,
Battening° our flocks with the fresh dews of night,   *fattening*
30 Oft till the star that rose, at evening, bright,
Toward heaven's descent had sloped his westering wheel.
Meanwhile the rural ditties were not mute,
Tempered to th' oaten flute,
Rough satyrs danced, and fauns with cloven heel,
35 From the glad sound would not be absent long,
And old Damaetas[7] lov'd to hear our song.
But O the heavy change, now thou art gone,
Now thou art gone, and never must return!
Thee shepherd, thee the woods, and desert caves,
40 With wild thyme and the gadding° vine o'ergrown,   *wandering*
And all their echoes mourn.
The willows, and the hazle copses green,
Shall now no more be seen,
Fanning their joyous leaves to thy soft lays.
45 As killing as the canker° to the rose,   *cankerworm*
Or taint-worm[8] to the weanling herds that graze,

---

3. Laurels . . . myrtles . . . ivy: the leaves used to crown respectively poets, lovers, and scholars.
4. King ("Lycidas") was 25 when he died.
5. Sisters: the nine muses; well: Aganippe, on Mount Helicon, where there was an altar to Jove.

6. Name used to designate various kinds of insect.
7. "Damaetas" is etymologically derived from the Greek verb meaning "to tame"; thus a tutor is meant.
8. An intestinal worm that can kill newly weaned calves.

Or frost to flowers, that their gay wardrop wear,
When first the white thorn blows;
Such, Lycidas, thy loss to shepherd's ear.

50   Where were ye nymphs when the remorseless deep
Closed o'er the head of your loved Lycidas?
For neither were ye playing on the steep
Where your old Bards, the famous Druids,° lie,   pagan Celtic priests
Nor on the shaggy top of Mona[9] high,
55   Nor yet where Deva spreads her wizard stream:
Ay me, I fondly dream!
Had ye been there—for what could that have done?
What could the Muse[1] herself that Orpheus bore,
The Muse her self for her inchanting son
60   Whom universal nature did lament,
When by the rout that made the hideous roar
His gory visage down the stream was sent,
Down the swift Hebrus to the Lesbian shore.[2]
Alas! What boots° it with incessant care   avails
65   To tend the homely slighted shepherd's trade,
And strictly meditate the thankless Muse,
Were it not better done as others use,
To sport with Amaryllis in the shade,
Or with the tangles of Neaera's hair?[3]
70   Fame is the spur that the clear spirit doth raise
(That last infirmity of noble mind)
To scorn delights, and live laborious days;
But the fair guerdon° when we hope to find,   reward
And think to burst out into sudden blaze,
75   Comes the blind Fury[4] with th'abhorred shears,
And slits the thin spun life. "But not the praise,"
Phoebus replied, and touched my trembling ears;[5]
"Fame is no plant that grows on mortal soil,
Nor in the glistering foil[6]
80   Set off to the world, nor in broad rumor lies,
But lives and spreds aloft by those pure eyes,
And perfet witness of all-judging Jove;
As he pronounces lastly on each deed,
Of so much fame in heaven expect thy meed."
85   O Fountain Arethuse, and thou honored flood,
Smooth-sliding Mincius, crowned with vocal reeds,
That strain I heard was of a higher mood.[7]
But now my oat proceeds,

---

9. The island of Anglesey; Deva: the river Dee, viewed as magical and prophetic by the inhabitants.
1. Calliope, Orpheus' mother.
2. Ovid, *Metamorphoses*, 11.1–55, relates how Orpheus was torn to pieces by the Thracian women and how his severed head floated down the Hebrus and was carried across to the island of Lesbos.
3. Amaryllis symbolizes erotic poetry (Virgil, *Eclogues* 2.14–5; Neaera: see *Eclogues* 3.3.
4. Atropos, one of the Fates, who cut the thread of life

spun by her sisters.
5. Echoing Virgil, *Eclogues* 6.3–4: "the Cynthian plucked my ear and warned me."
6. A reflecting leaf of gold or silver placed under a precious stone.
7. The "higher mood" is the lofty tone of Phoebus' speech. The invocation to the river Arethuse (in Sicily) and the Mincius (Virgil's native river) marks a return to pastoral.

90 And listens to the herald of the sea
   That came in Neptune's plea.[8]
   He asked the waves, and asked the felon° winds,   *savage*
   "What hard mishap hath doomed this gentle swain?"
   And questioned every gust of rugged wings
95 That blows from off each beakèd promontory;
   They knew not of his story,
   And sage Hippotades[9] their answer brings,
   That not a blast was from his dungeon strayed,
   The air was calm, and on the level brine,
   Sleek Panope[1] with all her sisters played.
100 It was that fatal and perfidious bark,
   Built in th' eclipse,° and rigged with curses dark,   *period of evil omen*
   That sunk so low that sacred head of thine.
       Next Camus,[2] reverend sire, went footing slow,
   His mantle hairy, and his bonnet sedge,[3]
105 Inwrought with figures dim, and on the edge
   Like to that sanguine flower inscribed with woe.[4]
   "Ah! who hath reft (quoth he) my dearest pledge?"°   *child*
   Last came, and last did go,
   The Pilot of the Galilean lake,[5]
110 Two massy keys he bore of metals twain,
   (The golden opes, the iron shuts amain°)   *vehemently*
   He shook his mitered[6] locks, and stern bespake,
   "How well could I have spared for thee, young swain,
   Enow° of such as for their bellies' sake,   *enough*
115 Creep and intrude, and climb into the fold?[7]
   Of other care they little reckoning make,
   Than how to scramble at the shearer's feast,
   And shove away the worthy bidden guest.
   Blind mouths![8] that scarce themselves know how to hold
120 A sheep-hook, or have learned aught else the least
   That to the faithfull herdman's art belongs!
   What recks it them?[9] What need they? They are sped;°   *satisfied*
   And when they list,° their lean and flashy° songs   *please/insipid*
   Grate on their scrannel° pipes of wretched straw,   *feeble*
125 The hungry sheep look up, and are not fed,
   But swoln with wind, and the rank mist they draw,
   Rot inwardly, and foul contagion spread.
   Besides what the grim woolf[1] with privy° paw   *secret, hidden*
   Daily devours apace, and nothing said,
130 But that two-handed engine at the door,

---

8. The herald Triton came to defend Neptune from blame for King's death.
9. God of winds, son of Hippotes.
1. One of the 50 Nereids (sea nymphs), mentioned by Virgil, *Aeneid* 5.240.
2. The River Cam, representing Cambridge University.
3. "Hairy" refers to the fur of the academic gown; "sedge" is a rushlike plant growing near water.
4. The hyacinth; see Ovid, *Metamorphoses* 10.214–6: "the flower bore the marks AI AI, letters of lamentation."

5. St. Peter bearing the keys of heaven given to him by Christ (Matthew 16.19).
6. Wearing a bishop's headdress.
7. See John 10.1: "He that entereth not by the door into the sheepfold, but climbeth up some other way, the same is a thief and a robber."
8. Milton's charge against the greed of the clergy.
9. What business is it of theirs?
1. The Roman Catholic Church.

Stands ready to smite once, and smite no more."[2]
   Return Alpheus,[3] the dread voice is past,
That shrunk thy streams; return Sicilian muse,
And call the vales, and bid them hither cast
135   Their bells, and flowerets of a thousand hues.
Ye valleys low where the mild whispers use,°   *often go*
Of shades and wanton winds, and gushing brooks,
On whose fresh lap the swart star[4] sparely looks,
Throw hither all your quaint enameled eyes,
140   That on the green turf suck the honeyed showers,
And purple all the ground with vernal flowers.
Bring the rathe° primrose that forsaken dies.   *early*
The tufted crow-toe,° and pale jessamine,°   *hyacinth/jasmine*
The white pink, and the pansie freaked° with jet,   *adorned*
145   The glowing violet.
The musk-rose, and the well attired woodbine,
With cowslips wan° that hang the pensive head,   *pale*
And every flower that sad embroidery wears:
Bid amaranthus[5] all his beauty shed,
150   And daffadillies fill their cups with tears,
To strew the laureate hearse where Lycid lies.
For so to interpose a little ease,
Let our frail thoughts dally with false surmise.[6]
Ay me! whilst thee the shores, and sounding seas
155   Wash far away, where'er thy bones are hurled,
Whether beyond the stormy Hebrides[7]
Where thou perhaps under the whelming tide
Visit'st the bottom of the monstrous world;
Or whether thou to our moist° vows denied,   *tearful*
160   Sleep'st by the fable of Bellerus[8] old,
Where the great vision of the guarded mount
Looks toward Namancos and Bayona's hold;[9]
Look homeward angel° now, and melt with ruth.°   *Michael/pity*
And, O ye dolphins, waft the haples youth.[1]
165   Weep no more, woeful shepherds weep no more,
For Lycidas your sorrow is not dead,
Sunk though he be beneath the wat'ry floor,
So sinks the day-star° in the ocean bed,   *the sun*
And yet anon repairs his drooping head,
170   And tricks° his beams, and with new spangled ore,°   *arrays/gold*
Flames in the forehead of the morning sky:
So Lycidas sunk low, but mounted high,
Through the dear might of him[2] that walked the waves

2. Indicates that the corrupted clergy will be punished;
see 1 Samuel 26.8.
3. The Arcadian hunter, who pursued Arethusa, the
nymph he loved, under the sea to Sicily.
4. The Dog-star, Sirius. Its rising brings on the dog-days
of heat.
5. The eternal flower (see *Paradise Lost*, 3.353–7).
6. The surmise is false since King's body drowned and will
have no hearse.
7. Islands off the northwest coast of Scotland.

8. A giant of Bellerium, the Latin name for Land's End.
9. Namancos: an ancient name for a district in northwestern Spain; Bayona: a fortress town about 50 miles
south of Cape Finisterre. The two names represent the
threat of Spanish Catholicism, against which St. Michael
guards England.
1. The dolphin is a symbol of Christ; waft: convey by
water.
2. Christ, who walks on the sea in Matthew 14.25–6.

Where other groves, and other streams along,
175 With nectar pure his oozy lock's he laves,[3]
And hears the unexpressive nuptial[4] song,
In the blest kingdoms meek of joy and love.
There entertain him all the saints above,
In solemn troops, and sweet societies
180 That sing, and singing in their glory move,
And wipe the tears for ever from his eyes.[5]
Now Lycidas the shepherds weep no more;
Henceforth thou art the genius° of the shore,   *local deity*
In thy large recompense, and shalt be good
185 To all that wander in that perilous flood.
     Thus sang the uncouth° swain to th' oaks and rills,   *unknown*
While the still morn went out with sandals gray,
He touched the tender stops of various quills,[6]
With eager thought warbling his Doric° lay: *pastoral*
190 And now the sun had stretched out all the hills,[7]
And now was dropped into the western bay;
At last he rose, and twitch'd his mantle blue:[8]
Tomorrow to fresh woods, and pastures new.

1638

How Soon Hath Time

How soon hath time the subtle thief of youth,
    Stol'n on his wing my three and twentieth year![1]
    My hasting days fly on with full career,°   *speed*
    But my late spring no bud or blossom shew'th.
5 Perhaps my semblance° might deceive the truth,   *appearance*
    That I to manhood am arrived so near,
    And inward ripeness doth much less appear,
    That some more timely-happy spirits[2] endu'th.°   *gives, endows*
    Yet be it less or more, or soon or slow,
10 It shall be still° in strictest measure even,°   *always/level with*
    To that same lot, however mean or high,
    Toward which Time leads me, and the will of Heaven;
    All is, if I have grace to use it so,
    As ever in my great task Master's° eye.   *God's*

On the New Forcers of Conscience Under the Long Parliament[1]

Because you have thrown off your prelate Lord,[2]
    And with stiff vows renounced his liturgy[3]

---

3. The brooks in Eden run with nectar, *Paradise Lost* 4.240; oozy: slimy from contact with the sea.
4. Relating to the marriage of the Lamb, or Christ, to the Church (Revelation 19.7).
5. See Revelation 7.17: "God shall wipe away all tears from their eyes"; see also Revelation 21.4.
6. Stops are the finger-holes in the pipes; quills are the hollow reeds of the shepherd's pipe.
7. The setting sun had shone over the hills and length-ened their shadows.

8. Blue is the traditional symbol of hope.
1. Written when Milton was 23, this sonnet was pub-lished in 1645.
2. Those individuals of Milton's age who have already achieved success.
1. Written c. 1646, but printed in 1673.
2. Refers to the abolishment of episcopacy in England in September 1646.
3. The House of Commons forbade the use of the *Book of Common Prayer* in August 1645.

To seize the widowed whore Plurality[4]
     From them whose sin ye envied, not abhored,
5 Dare ye for this adjure° the civil sword   *entreat*
     To force our consciences that Christ set free,[5]
     And ride us with a classic hierarchy[6]
Taught ye by meer A. S. and Rutherford?[7]
Men whose life, learning, faith and pure intent
10   Would have been held in high esteem with Paul
     Must now be named and printed heretics
By shallow Edwards[8] and Scotch what d'ye call:
     But we do hope to find out all your tricks,
     Your plots and packing worse then those of Trent[9]
15   That so the Parliament
May with their wholsome and preventive shears
Clip your phylacteries,[1] though balk° your ears,[2]   *stop short of*
          And succor our just fears
When they shall read this clearly in your charge
20 *New presbyter* is but *old priest* writ large.[3]

To the Lord General Cromwell

Cromwell, our chief of men, who through a cloud[1]
     Not of war only, but detractions rude,
     Guided by faith and matchless fortitude
     To peace and truth thy glorious way hast ploughed,
5 And on the neck of crownèd Fortune[2] proud
     Hast reard° God's trophies and his work pursued,   *raised, erected*
     While Darwen stream[3] with blood of Scotts imbrued,°   *stained*
     And Dunbarr field[4] resounds thy praises loud,
     And Worester's laureate wreath;[5] yet much remains
10   To conquer still; peace hath her victories
     No less renownd than war, new foes arise

---

4. The practice of holding more than one living identified with episcopacy but subsequently supported by the Presbyterian system.
5. Milton complains of the Westminster Assembly's attempt to impose Presbyterianism by force.
6. Parliament resolved that the English congregations were to be grouped in Presbyteries or "Classes," which could impose rules after the Scottish pattern.
7. A. S.: Dr. Adam Stewart, Scottish Presbyterian controversialist; Rutherford: Samuel Rutherford, author of pamphlets in defense of Presbyterianism.
8. Thomas Edwards, author of *Antapologia*, advocating strict Presbyterianism, and *Gangraena* (1646), which included a denunciation of Milton's views on divorce.
9. Comparing the overwhelming Presbyterian predominance in the Assembly to the anti-protestant Roman Catholic Council of Trent (1545–1563).
1. Small leather boxes containing scriptural texts worn by Jews as a mark of obedience. Christ in Matthew 23.5 uses the phrase "make broad their phylacteries" in the sense

"vaunt their own righteousness."
2. William Prynne, who had attacked one of the Bishops in print, actually did have both of his ears cut off. Milton's manuscript of this poem contains the line: "Crop ye as close as marginal P—'s ears."
3. "Priest" is etymologically a contracted form of Latin "presbyter" (an elder). The Presbyterians now appeared as dictatorial as the bishops had been.
1. In Virgil, Aeneas prevails through the "war-cloud" of battle as he conquers Italy (*Aeneid* 10.809).
2. Refers to Charles I and to his successor, whose army Cromwell defeated at Worcester after he had been crowned king in Scotland on 1 January 1651. This poem was written in 1652 but not published until 1694.
3. Near Preston, where, on 17–19 August 1648, Cromwell routed the invading Scottish army.
4. At Dunbar, on 3 September 1650, after being virtually surrounded, Cromwell routed the Scottish army.
5. At Worcester, on 3 September 1651, Cromwell virtually annihilated Charles II's Royalist Scottish army.

Threatening to bind our souls with secular chains:
   Help us to save free conscience from the paw
   Of hireling wolves whose gospel is their maw.

On the Late Massacre in Piedmont[1]

Avenge O Lord thy slaughtered saints, whose bones
   Lie scattered on the Alpine mountains cold,[2]
   Even them who kept thy truth so pure of old
   When all our Fathers worshiped stocks and stones,[3]
5 Forget not: in thy book[4] record their groans
   Who were thy sheep and in their ancient fold
   Slain by the bloody Piemontese that rolled
   Mother with infant down the rocks. Their moans
The vales redoubled to the hills, and they
10   To Heaven. Their martyred blood and ashes sow
   O'er all th' Italian fields where still doth sway
The triple tyrant:[5] that from these may grow
   A hundred-fold,[6] who having learnt thy way
   Early may fly the Babylonian[7] woe.

When I Consider How My Light Is Spent[1]

When I consider how my light is spent,
   Ere half my days, in this dark world and wide,
   And that one talent which is death to hide,[2]
   Lodged with me useless, though my soul more bent
5 To serve therewith my Maker, and present
   My true account, lest he returning chide,
   Doth God exact day-labor, light denied,
   I fondly° ask; but Patience to prevent   *foolishly*
That murmur, soon replies, "God doth not need
10   Either man's work or his own gifts,[3] who best
   Bear his mild yoke,[4] they serve him best, his state
   Is kingly. Thousands at his bidding speed
   And post o'er land and ocean without rest:
   They also serve who only stand and wait."

---

1. The poem protests the persecution of Protestants in northern Italy in 1655.
2. See Luke 18.7: "shall not God avenge his own elect," and Psalms 141.7: "Our bones are scattered at the grave's mouth."
3. Gods of wood and stone.
4. See Revelation 5.1: "I saw in the right hand of him that sat on the throne a book."
5. The Pope with his three-tiered crown.
6. Lines 10–13 combine the parable of the sower (Matthew 13.3–23) with the legend of Cadmus, in which an army of warriors sprouts from the sowing of a dragon's teeth.

7. The Puritans used the corrupt Babylon of Revelation as a symbol for the Roman Catholic Church.
1. Probably written around 1652, as Milton's blindness became complete.
2. In the parable of the talents, Jesus tells of a servant who is given a talent (a large sum of money) to keep for his master. He buries the money; his master condemns him for not having invested it wisely. Matthew 25.14–30.
3. See Job 22.2.
4. See Matthew 11.30: "My yoke is easy."

Methought I Saw My Late Espoused Saint[1]

Methought I saw my late espousèd saint°   *soul in heaven*
    Brought to me like Alcestis[2] from the grave,
    Whom Jove's great son to her glad husband gave,
    Rescued from death by force though pale and faint.
5 Mine as whom washed from spot of child-bed taint,
    Purification in the old Law[3] did save,
    And such, as yet once more I trust to have
    Full sight of her in Heaven without restraint,
Came vested all in white, pure as her mind:
10   Her face was veiled, yet to my fancied sight,
    Love, sweetness, goodness, in her person shined
So clear, as in no face with more delight,
    But O, as to embrace me she enclined,
    I waked, she fled, and day brought back my night.[4]

Areopagitica

The title *Areopagitica* refers to the Areopagus, the ancient Athenian Council of State. Milton wrote *Areopagitica* to criticize the Parliamentary Ordinance of June 14, 1643 "to prevent and suppress the licence of printing." Although *Areopagitica* was unlicensed, Milton made the bold move of affixing his name to the title page, which made no mention of the printer. Also on the title page are these lines from Euripides' *Suppliant Women* (436–441):

There is true Liberty when free born men
Having to advise the public may speak free,
Which he who can and will, deserv'd high praise,
Who neither can nor will, may hold his peace;
What can be juster in a state than this?

from Areopagitica[1]
A Speech of Mr. John Milton
for the Liberty of Unlicensed Printing,
to the Parliament of England

* * * Good and evil we know in the field of this world grow up together almost inseparably; and the knowledge of good is so involved and interwoven with the knowledge of evil, and in so many cunning resemblances hardly to be discerned, that those confused seeds which were imposed on Psyche as an incessant labor to cull out and sort

1. The date of composition is placed at 1658; the poem appears as the last sonnet in the 1673 edition.
2. In Euripides' *Alcestis* she gives her life for her husband Admetus, but Hercules ("Jove's great son") wrestles with death and brings her back from the grave.
3. According to Leviticus 12.4–8, after bearing a female child, a woman shall be unclean "two weeks, as in her separation: and she shall continue in the blood of her purifying threescore and six days" (i.e., during this period "she shall touch no hallowed thing, nor come into the sanctuary"). Some critics construe this line as evidence

that the sonnet is about the death of Milton's second wife Katherine Woodcock, who died three months after childbirth in 1658.
4. In Virgil, Aeneas sees the ghost of his wife Creusa amid the ruins of Troy; when he tries to embrace her, "she withdrew into thin air . . . most like a winged dream" (*Aeneid* 2.791–794).
1. The Areopagus was the seat of the Council of State, organized as a judicial tribunal by Solon in the sixth century B.C. The Athenian orator Isocrates argues for its renewal in his *Areopagiticus*.

asunder, were not more intermixed.[2] It was from out the rind of one apple tasted, that the knowledge of good and evil, as two twins cleaving together, leaped forth into the world. And perhaps this is that doom which Adam fell into of knowing good and evil, that is to say, of knowing good by evil.[3]

As therefore the state of man now is, what wisdom can there be to choose, what continence to forbear without the knowledge of evil? He that can apprehend and consider vice with all her baits and seeming pleasures, and yet abstain, and yet distinguish, and yet prefer that which is truly better, he is the true wayfaring[4] Christian. I cannot praise a fugitive and cloistered virtue, unexercised and unbreathed, that never sallies out and sees her adversary, but slinks out of the race where that immortal garland is to be run for, not without dust and heat. Assuredly we bring not innocence into the world, we bring impurity much rather: that which purifies us is trial, and trial is by what is contrary. That virtue therefore which is but a youngling in the contemplation of evil, and knows not the utmost that vice promises to her followers, and rejects it, is but a blank virtue, not a pure; her whiteness is but an excremental[5] whiteness; which was the reason why our sage and serious poet Spenser, whom I dare be known to think a better teacher than Scotus or Aquinas, describing true temperance under the person of Guyon, brings him in with his palmer through the cave of Mammon and the bower of earthly bliss, that he might see and know, and yet abstain.[6]

Since therefore, the knowledge and survey of vice is in this world so necessary to the constituting of human virtue, and the scanning of error to the confirmation of truth, how can we more safely and with less danger scout into the regions of sin and falsity than by reading all manner of tractates and hearing all manner of reason? And this is the benefit which may be had of books promiscuously read.

But of the harm that may result hence, three kinds are usually reckoned. First is feared the infection that may spread; but then all human learning and controversy in religious points must remove out of the world, yea the Bible itself; for that ofttimes relates blasphemy not nicely,[7] it describes the carnal sense of wicked men not unelegantly, it brings in holiest men passionately murmuring against providence through all the arguments of Epicurus;[8] in other great disputes it answers dubiously and darkly to the common reader; and ask a Talmudist what ails the modesty of his marginal Keri, that Moses and all the prophets cannot persuade him to pronounce the textual Chetiv.[9] For these causes we all know the Bible itself put by the papist into the first rank of prohibited books. The ancientest fathers must be next removed, as Clement of Alexandria, and that Eusebian book of Evangelic preparation transmitting our ears through a hoard of heathenish obscenities to receive the Gospel. Who finds not that Irenaeus, Epiphanius, Jerome,[1] and others discover more heresies than they well confute, and that oft for heresy which is the truer opinion?[2]

---

2. Furious over her son Cupid's love for Psyche, Venus ordered Psyche to sort out a huge mass of seeds, but the ants, sympathizing with her plight, sorted them for her. See Apuleius, *Golden Ass* 4–6.

3. See *Paradise Lost* 4.222: "Knowledge of Good bought dear by knowing ill."

4. The original reads "warfaring," but in several copies this is corrected by hand to "wayfaring."

5. Superficial.

6. Duns Scotus and Thomas Aquinas here represent types of the scholastic theologian. For the cave of Mammon, see *The Faerie Queene* 2.7 (the Palmer is not with Guyon in Mammon's Cave); the "Bower of Bliss," 2.12.

7. Delicately.

8. The Greek philosopher who propounded a morality based on pleasure.

9. Talmudist: a student of the Talmud, the Jewish commentaries on the Bible; Keri: marginal emendations of rabbinical scholars on the Chetiv, the text of the Bible.

1. Early apologists of Christianity: St. Clement of Alexandria (2nd century) and Eusebius, who describes pagan depravity to promote faith in Christianity, as do St. Irenaeus (2nd century), Epiphanius (4th century), and St. Jerome (early 5th century).

2. Milton goes on to argue that the effect of books depends upon the teacher, who, if really good, needs no books. Milton stresses the role of the reader: A wise person can find something instructive in even the worst books.

* * *

Impunity and remissness, for certain, are the bane of a commonwealth; but here the great art lies, to discern in what the law is to bid restraint and punishment, and in what things persuasion only is to work. If every action which is good or evil in man at ripe years, were to be under pittance and prescription and compulsion, what were virtue but a name, what praise could be then due to well-doing, what gramercy[3] to be sober, just, or continent?

Many there be that complain of divine providence for suffering Adam to transgress. Foolish tongues! when God gave him reason, he gave him freedom to choose, for reason is but choosing; he had been else a mere artificial Adam, such an Adam as he is in the motions.[4] We ourselves esteem not of that obedience, or love, or gift, which is of force. God therefore left him free, set before him a provoking object, ever almost in his eyes; herein consisted his merit, herein the right of his reward, the praise of his abstinence. Wherefore did he create passions within us, pleasures round about us, but that these rightly tempered are the very ingredients of virtue? They are not skilful considerers of human things who imagine to remove sin by removing the matter of sin. For, besides that it is a huge heap increasing under the very act of diminishing, though some part of it may for a time be withdrawn from some persons, it cannot from all, in such a universal thing as books are; and when this is done, yet the sin remains entire. Though ye take from a covetous man all his treasure, he has yet one jewel left—ye cannot bereave him of his covetousness. Banish all objects of lust, shut up all youth into the severest discipline that can be exercised in any hermitage, ye cannot make them chaste that came not thither so: such great care and wisdom is required to the right managing of this point.

Suppose we could expel sin by this means; look how much we thus expel of sin, so much we expel of virtue: for the matter of them both is the same; remove that, and ye remove them both alike. This justifies the high providence of God, who, though he command us temperance, justice, continence, yet pours out before us, even to a profuseness, all desirable things, and gives us minds that can wander beyond all limit and satiety. Why should we then affect a rigor contrary to the manner of God and of nature, by abridging or scanting those means which books freely permitted are, both to the trial of virtue and the exercise of truth?[5]

* * *

And lest some should persuade ye, Lords and Commons, that these arguments of learned men's discouragement at this your Order are mere flourishes, and not real, I could recount what I have seen and heard in other countries where this kind of inquisition tyrannizes; when I have sat among their learned men, for that honor I had, and been counted happy to be born in such a place of philosophic freedom as they supposed England was, while themselves did nothing but bemoan the servile condition into which learning amongst them was brought; that this was it which had damped the glory of Italian wits; that nothing had been there written now these many years but flattery and fustian. There it was that I found and visited the famous Galileo, grown old, a prisoner to the Inquisition[6] for thinking in astronomy otherwise

---

3. Thanks.
4. Puppet shows. For this statement about Adam, see *Paradise Lost* 3.103–28, page 1802.
5. Milton argues that no intelligent person will be willing to take on the job of censorship and that an unintelligent person would be prone to commit serious errors. In addition to giving power to stupid people, censorship would

actually encourage people to read banned books and to adhere to the perverse opinions expressed in such books.
6. In 1633 the great Italian astronomer Galileo was tried by the Inquisition at Rome and forced to abjure his earlier assertion that his findings confirmed the Copernican heliocentric theory of the universe. He was under house arrest in Florence when Milton visited there in 1638–39.

than the Franciscan and Dominican licensers thought. And though I knew that England then was groaning loudest under the prelatical yoke, nevertheless I took it as a pledge of future happiness that other nations were so persuaded of her liberty.

Yet was it beyond my hope that those worthies were then breathing in her air, who should be her leaders to such a deliverance as shall never be forgotten by any revolution of time that this world hath to finish. When that was once begun, it was as little in my fear, that what words of complaint I heard among learned men of other parts uttered against the Inquisition, the same I should hear by as learned men at home uttered in time of Parliament against an order of licensing; and that so generally, that when I had disclosed myself a companion of their discontent, I might say, if without envy, that he whom an honest quaestorship had endeared to the Sicilians, was not more by them importuned against Verres,[7] than the favorable opinion which I had among many who honor ye, and are known and respected by ye, loaded me with entreaties and persuasions that I would not despair to lay together that which just reason should bring into my mind toward the removal of an undeserved thraldom upon learning.

That this is not, therefore, the disburdening of a particular fancy, but the common grievance of all those who had prepared their minds and studies above the vulgar pitch to advance truth in others, and from others to entertain it, thus much may satisfy. And in their name I shall for neither friend nor foe conceal what the general murmur is; that if it come to inquisitioning again and licensing, and that we are so timorous of ourselves and so suspicious of all men as to fear each book and the shaking of every leaf, before we know what the contents are; if some who but of late were little better than silenced from preaching, shall come now to silence us from reading, except what they please, it cannot be guessed what is intended by some but a second tyranny over learning; and will soon put it out of controversy that bishops and presbyters are the same to us both name and thing.

* * *

But I am certain that a state governed by the rules of justice and fortitude, or a church built and founded upon the rock of faith and true knowledge, cannot be so pusillanimous.[8] While things are yet not constituted in religion, that freedom of writing should be restrained by a discipline imitated from the prelates, and learnt by them from the Inquisition, to shut us up all again into the breast of a licenser, must needs give cause of doubt and discouragement to all learned and religious men. Who cannot but discern the fineness of this politic drift, and who are the contrivers: that while bishops were to be baited down, then all presses might be open; it was the people's birthright and privilege in time of parliament, it was the breaking forth of light.

But now, the bishops abrogated and voided out of the church, as if our reformation sought no more but to make room for others into their seats under another name, the episcopal arts begin to bud again; the cruse[9] of truth must run no more oil; liberty of printing must be enthralled again under a prelatical commission of twenty, the privilege of the people nullified; and, which is worse, the freedom of learning must groan again, and to her old fetters: all this the parliament yet sitting. Although their own late arguments and defenses against the prelates might remember them that this obstructing violence meets for the most part with an event utterly opposite to the end which it drives at; instead of suppressing sects and

---

7. Cicero exposed the corruption of Verres' government in 75 B.C.

8. Mean-spirited, cowardly.
9. Small vessel; see 1 Kings 17.12–16.

schisms, it raises them and invests them with a reputation: "The punishing of wits enhances their authority," saith the Viscount St. Albans,[1] "and a forbidden writing is thought to be a certain spark of truth that flies up in the faces of them who seek to tread it out."

This Order, therefore, may prove a nursing mother to sects, but I shall easily show how it will be a stepdame to Truth; and first by disenabling us to the maintenance of what is known already.

Well knows he who uses to consider, that our faith and knowledge thrives by exercise, as well as our limbs and complexion. Truth is compared in scripture to a streaming fountain;[2] if her waters flow not in a perpetual progression, they sicken into a muddy pool of conformity and tradition. A man may be a heretic in the truth; and if he believe things only because his pastor says so, or the Assembly so determines, without knowing other reason, though his belief be true, yet the very truth he holds becomes his heresy. There is not any burden that some would gladlier post off to another than the charge and care of their religion. There be, who knows not that there be, of protestants and professors who live and die in as arrant an implicit faith, as any lay papist of Loreto.[3]

A wealthy man addicted to his pleasure and to his profits, finds religion to be a traffic so entangled, and of so many piddling accounts, that of all mysteries[4] he cannot skill to keep a stock going upon that trade. What should he do? Fain he would have the name to be religious, fain he would bear up with his neighbors in that. What does he, therefore, but resolves to give over toiling, and to find himself out some factor to whose care and credit he may commit the whole managing of his religious affairs; some Divine of note and estimation that must be. To him he adheres, resigns the whole warehouse of his religion with all the locks and keys into his custody; and indeed makes the very person of that man his religion; esteems his associating with him a sufficient evidence and commendatory of his own piety. So that a man may say his religion is now no more within himself, but is become a dividual movable,[5] and goes and comes near him, according as that good man frequents the house. He entertains him, gives him gifts, feasts him, lodges him. His religion comes home at night, prays, is liberally supped, and sumptuously laid to sleep, rises, is saluted, and after the malmsey, or some well spiced brewage, and better breakfasted than he[6] whose morning appetite would have gladly fed on green figs between Bethany and Jerusalem, his religion walks abroad at eight, and leaves his kind entertainer in the shop trading all day without his religion.

Another sort there be, who, when they hear that all things shall be ordered, all things regulated and settled, nothing written but what passes through the customhouse of certain publicans[7] that have the tonnaging and the poundaging of all freespoken truth, will straight give themselves up into your hands, make 'em and cut 'em out what religion ye please. There be delights, there be recreations and jolly pastimes that will fetch the day about from sun to sun, and rock the tedious year as in a delightful dream. What need they torture their heads with that which others have taken so strictly and so unalterably into their own purveying? These are the fruits which a dull ease and cessation of our knowledge will bring forth among the people.

1. Sir Francis Bacon, *An Advertisement Touching the Controversies of the Church of England.*
2. See Psalms 85.11.
3. Professors: those who profess religion; Loreto: a Catholic shrine supposed to have been transported to Italy from the Holy Land.
4. Trades, crafts.
5. A separate piece of property.
6. For this description of Christ, see Mark 11.12–14.
7. Tax collectors.

How goodly, and how to be wished, were such an obedient unanimity as this, what a fine conformity would it starch us all into! Doubtless a staunch and solid piece of framework, as any January could freeze together.[8]

* * *

Truth indeed came once into the world with her divine Master, and was a perfect shape most glorious to look on. But when he ascended, and his apostles after him were laid asleep, then straight arose a wicked race of deceivers, who, as that story goes of the Egyptian Typhon with his conspirators, how they dealt with the good Osiris, took the virgin Truth, hewed her lovely form into a thousand pieces, and scattered them to the four winds.[9] From that time ever since, the sad friends of Truth, such as durst appear, imitating the careful search that Isis made for the mangled body of Osiris, went up and down gathering up limb by limb still as they could find them. We have not yet found them all, Lords and Commons, nor ever shall do, till her Master's second coming. He shall bring together every joint and member, and shall mold them into an immortal feature of loveliness and perfection. Suffer not these licensing prohibitions to stand at every place of opportunity, forbidding and disturbing them that continue seeking, that continue to do our obsequies to the torn body of our martyred saint.

We boast our light; but if we look not wisely on the sun itself, it smites us into darkness. Who can discern those planets that are oft combust, and those stars of brightest magnitude that rise and set with the sun, until the opposite motion of their orbs bring them to such a place in the firmament, where they may be seen evening or morning. The light which we have gained, was given us, not to be ever staring on, but by it to discover onward things more remote from our knowledge. It is not the unfrocking of a priest, the unmitering of a bishop, and the removing him from off the Presbyterian shoulders that will make us a happy nation; no, if other things as great in the church, and in the rule of life both economical and political, be not looked into and reformed, we have looked so long upon the blaze that Zwinglius[1] and Calvin hath beaconed up to us, that we are stark blind.

There be who perpetually complain of schisms and sects, and make it such a calamity that any man dissents from their maxims. It is their own pride and ignorance which causes the disturbing, who neither will hear with meekness, nor can convince, yet all must be suppressed which is not found in their syntagma.[2] They are the troublers, they are the dividers of unity, who neglect and permit not others to unite those dissevered pieces which are yet wanting to the body of Truth. To be still searching what we know not by what we know, still closing up truth to truth as we find it (for all her body is homogeneal[3] and proportional), this is the golden rule in theology as well as in arithmetic, and makes up the best harmony in a church; not the forced and outward union of cold and neutral and inwardly divided minds.

Lords and Commons of England, consider what nation it is whereof ye are, and whereof ye are the governors; a nation not slow and dull, but of a quick, ingenious, and piercing spirit, acute to invent, subtle and sinewy to discourse, not beneath the reach of any point the highest that human capacity can soar to. Therefore the studies of learning in her deepest sciences have been so ancient and so eminent among us that writers of good antiquity and ablest judgment have been persuaded that even the

---

8. Milton goes on to argue that censorship will make the clergy lazy and will hinder the Reformation's goal of seeking truth.
9. Typhon tore apart and scattered Osiris's body, and his wife Isis and son Horus collected it. The interpretation

here is based on Plutarch's allegory in *Isis and Osiris*.
1. Ulrich Zwingli (1484–1531), the Protestant reformer of Zurich.
2. Systematic doctrinal treatise.
3. Homogeneous.

school of Pythagoras and the Persian wisdom took beginning from the old philosophy of this island.[4] And that wise and civil Roman, Julius Agricola, who governed once here for Caesar, preferred the natural wits of Britain before the labored studies of the French.[5] Nor is it for nothing that the grave and frugal Transylvanian[6] sends out yearly from as far as the mountainous borders of Russia and beyond the Hercynian wilderness,[7] not their youth, but their staid men to learn our language and our theologic arts.

Yet that which is above all this, the favor and the love of Heaven, we have great argument to think in a peculiar manner propitious and propending towards us. Why else was this nation chosen before any other, that out of her as out of Sion should be proclaimed and sounded forth the first tidings and trumpet of reformation to all Europe? And had it not been the obstinate perverseness of our prelates against the divine and admirable spirit of Wycliffe[8] to suppress him as a schismatic and innovator, perhaps neither the Bohemian Huss and Jerome,[9] no, nor the name of Luther, or of Calvin, had been ever known; the glory of reforming all our neighbors had been completely ours. But now, as our obdurate clergy have with violence demeaned the matter, we are become hitherto the latest and the backwardest scholars of whom God offered to have made us the teachers.

Now once again by all concurrence of signs, and by the general instinct of holy and devout men, as they daily and solemnly express their thoughts, God is decreeing to begin some new and great period in his Church, even to the reforming of reformation itself. What does he then but reveal himself to his servants, and, as his manner is, first to his Englishmen? I say as his manner is, first to us, though we mark not the method of his counsels and are unworthy. Behold now this vast city, a city of refuge, the mansion house of liberty, encompassed and surrounded with his protection. The shop of war hath not there more anvils and hammers waking, to fashion out the plates and instruments of armed justice in defense of beleaguered Truth, than there be pens and heads there, sitting by their studious lamps, musing, searching, revolving new notions and ideas wherewith to present, as with their homage and their fealty, the approaching reformation; others as fast reading, trying all things, assenting to the force of reason and convincement.

What could a man require more from a nation so pliant and so prone to seek after knowledge? What wants there to such a towardly[1] and pregnant soul but wise and faithful laborers to make a knowing people, a nation of prophets, of sages, and of worthies? We reckon more than five months yet to harvest; there need not be five weeks, had we but eyes to lift up; the fields are white already. Where there is much desire to learn, there of necessity will be much arguing, much writing, many opinions; for opinion in good men is but knowledge in the making. Under these fantastic terrors of sect and schism, we wrong the earnest and zealous thirst after knowledge and understanding which God hath stirred up in this city.

What some lament of, we rather should rejoice at, should rather praise this pious forwardness among men, to reassume the ill-deputed care of their religion into their own hands again. A little generous prudence, a little forbearance of one another, and

---

4. For the connection between the Druids and Zoroastrian and Pythagorean philosophy, see Pliny, *Natural History* 30.2.
5. See Tacitus, *Agricola* 21.
6. Seventeenth-century Transylvania was Protestant and independent.

7. South central Germany.
8. English Protestants viewed John Wycliff (1320?–84) as the initiator of the Reformation in England.
9. Jerome of Prague (c. 1365–1416), a disciple of Wycliff, and John Huss of Bohemia (1373–1415).
1. Promising.

some grain of charity might win all these diligences to join and unite into one general and brotherly search after truth; could we but forego this prelatical tradition of crowding free consciences and Christian liberties into canons and precepts of men. I doubt not, if some great and worthy stranger should come among us, wise to discern the mold and temper of a people, and how to govern it, observing the high hopes and aims, the diligent alacrity of our extended thoughts and reasonings in the pursuance of truth and freedom, but that he would cry out as Pyrrhus did, admiring the Roman docility and courage, "If such were my Epirots, I would not despair the greatest design that could be attempted to make a church or kingdom happy."[2]

Yet these are the men cried out against for schismatics and sectaries;[3] as if, while the temple of the Lord was building, some cutting, some squaring the marble, others hewing the cedars, there should be a sort of irrational men who could not consider there must be many schisms and many dissections made in the quarry and in the timber, ere the house of God can be built. And when every stone is laid artfully together, it cannot be united into a continuity, it can but be contiguous in this world; neither can every piece of the building be of one form; nay rather the perfection consists in this, that out of many moderate varieties and brotherly dissimilitudes that are not vastly disproportional, arises the goodly and the graceful symmetry that commends the whole pile and structure.

Let us, therefore, be more considerate builders, more wise in spiritual architecture, when great reformation is expected. For now the time seems come, wherein Moses, the great prophet, may sit in heaven rejoicing to see that memorable and glorious wish of his fulfilled, when not only our seventy elders, but all the Lord's people, are become prophets.

* * *

Methinks I see in my mind a noble and puissant nation rousing herself like a strong man after sleep, and shaking her invincible locks. Methinks I see her as an eagle muing[4] her mighty youth, and kindling her undazzled eyes at the full midday beam; purging and unscaling her long-abused sight at the fountain itself of heavenly radiance; while the whole noise of timorous and flocking birds, with those also that love the twilight, flutter about, amazed at what she means, and in their envious gabble would prognosticate a year of sects and schisms.

What should ye do then, should ye suppress all this flowery crop of knowledge and new light sprung up and yet springing daily in this city? Should ye set an oligarchy of twenty engrossers[5] over it, to bring a famine upon our minds again, when we shall know nothing but what is measured to us by their bushel? Believe it, Lords and Commons, they who counsel ye to such a suppressing, do as good as bid ye suppress yourselves; and I will soon show how.

* * *

And now the time in special is, by privilege, to write and speak what may help to the further discussing of matters in agitation. The temple of Janus with his two controversal faces might now not unsignificantly be set open.[6] And though all the winds of doctrine were let loose to play upon the earth, so Truth be in the field, we do injuriously by licensing and prohibiting to misdoubt her strength. Let her and Falsehood grapple; who ever knew Truth put to the worse, in a free and open encounter. Her

---

2. King Pyrrhus of Epirus defeated the Romans at Hereclea in 280 B.C.
3. Dividers of the church.
4. Renewing.

5. Monopolists.
6. The Roman god Janus's head had two faces looking in opposite directions. During times of war the gates of Janus were open.

confuting is the best and surest suppressing. He who hears what praying there is for light and clearer knowledge to be sent down among us, would think of other matters to be constituted beyond the discipline of Geneva, framed and fabriced already to our hands.[7]

Yet when the new light which we beg for shines in upon us, there be who envy and oppose, if it come not first in at their casements. What a collusion[8] is this, whenas we are exhorted by the wise man to use diligence, to seek for wisdom as for hidden treasures[9] early and late, that another order shall enjoin us to know nothing but by statute. When a man hath been laboring the hardest labor in the deep mines of knowledge, hath furnished out his findings in all their equipage, drawn forth his reasons as it were a battle ranged, scattered and defeated all objections in his way, calls out his adversary into the plain, offers him the advantage of wind and sun, if he please, only that he may try the matter by dint of argument; for his opponents then to skulk, to lay ambushments, to keep a narrow bridge of licensing where the challenger should pass, though it be valor enough in soldiership, is but weakness and cowardice in the wars of Truth.

For who knows not that Truth is strong, next to the Almighty. She needs no policies, nor stratagems, nor licensings to make her victorious—those are the shifts and the defenses that error uses against her power. Give her but room, and do not bind her when she sleeps, for then she speaks not true, as the old Proteus did, who spake oracles only when he was caught and bound,[1] but then rather she turns herself into all shapes except her own, and perhaps tunes her voice according to the time, as Micaiah did before Ahab,[2] until she be adjured into her own likeness.

Yet is it not impossible that she may have more shapes than one. What else is all that rank of things indifferent, wherein Truth may be on this side, or on the other, without being unlike herself? What but a vain shadow else is the abolition of those ordinances, that handwriting nailed to the cross;[3] what great purchase is this Christian liberty which Paul so often boasts of? His doctrine is, that he who eats, or eats not, regards a day, or regards it not, may do either to the Lord.[4] How many other things might be tolerated in peace and left to conscience, had we but charity, and were it not the chief stronghold of our hypocrisy to be ever judging one another. I fear yet this iron yoke of outward conformity hath left a slavish print upon our necks; the ghost of a linen decency[5] yet haunts us. We stumble and are impatient at the least dividing of one visible congregation from another, though it be not in fundamentals; and through our forwardness to suppress, and our backwardness to recover any enthralled piece of truth out of the gripe of custom, we care not to keep truth separated from truth, which is the fiercest rent and disunion of all. We do not see that while we still affect by all means a rigid external formality, we may as soon fall again into a gross conforming stupidity, a stark and dead congealment of "wood, and hay, and stubble"[6] forced and frozen together, which is more to the sudden degenerating of a church than many subdichotomies[7] of petty schisms.

Not that I can think well of every light separation, or that all in a church is to be expected "gold and silver and precious stones."[8] It is not possible for man to sever the wheat from the tares, the good fish from the other fry; that must be the angels' min-

---

7. Discipline of Geneva: Calvinism; fabriced: fabricated.
8. Secret agreement for purposes of trickery; ambiguity in words or reasoning.
9. The wise man is Solomon; see Proverbs 8.11 and Matthew 13.44.
1. The story of Proteus is in *Odyssey* 384–93.
2. 1 Kings 22.

3. Colossians 2.14.
4. Romans 14.1–13.
5. A reference to the controversy over ecclesiastical vestments.
6. See 1 Corinthians 3.12.
7. Inconsequential divisions.
8. 1 Corinthians 3.12.

istry at the end of mortal things.[9] Yet if all cannot be of one mind,—as who looks they should be?—this doubtless is more wholesome, more prudent, and more Christian, that many be tolerated, rather than all compelled. I mean not tolerated popery and open superstition, which, as it extirpates all religions and civil supremacies, so itself should be extirpate, provided first that all charitable and compassionate means be used to win and regain the weak and the misled; that also which is impious or evil absolutely, either against faith or manners, no law can possibly permit, that intends not to unlaw itself; but those neighboring differences, or rather indifferences, are what I speak of, whether in some point of doctrine or of discipline, which though they may be many, yet need not interrupt "the unity of spirit," if we could but find among us the "bond of peace."[1]

In the meanwhile, if any one would write and bring his helpful hand to the slow-moving reformation which we labor under, if truth have spoken to him before others, or but seemed at least to speak, who hath so bejesuited us that we should trouble that man with asking license to do so worthy a deed? And not consider this, that if it come to prohibiting, there is not aught more likely to be prohibited than truth itself; whose first appearance to our eyes bleared and dimmed with prejudice and custom, is more unsightly and unplausible than many errors, even as the person is of many a great man slight and contemptible to see to. And what do they tell us vainly of new opinions, when this very opinion of theirs, that none must be heard but whom they like, is the worst and newest opinion of all others; and is the chief cause why sects and schisms do so much abound, and true knowledge is kept at distance from us; besides yet a greater danger which is in it. For when God shakes a kingdom with strong and healthful commotions to a general reforming, it is not untrue that many sectaries and false teachers are then busiest in seducing; but yet more true it is that God then raises to his own work men of rare abilities and more than common industry, not only to look back and revise what hath been taught heretofore, but to gain further and go on some new enlightened steps in the discovery of truth.

PARADISE LOST

Paradise Lost is about devastating loss attended by redemption. The reader's knowledge of the Fall creates a sense of tragic inevitability. And Satan, no less than Adam and Eve, appears in all the psychological complexity and verbal grandeur of a tragic hero. Indeed, there is even a manuscript in which Milton outlined the story as a tragedy. In that version, "Lucifer's contriving Adam's ruin" is Act 3. Following epic tradition, Milton places this part of the action at the forefront of his poem, beginning *in medias res*.

So powerful is Milton's opening portrayal of Satan that the Romantic poets thought Satan was the hero of the poem. Focusing on the first two books, the romantic reading sees him as a dynamic rebel. From a Renaissance point of view, Satan is more like an Elizabethan hero-villain, with his many soliloquies and his tortured psychology of brilliance twisted toward evil. Only in Book 9, however, does Milton say, "I now must change these notes to tragic," thereby signaling that he is about to narrate the fall of Adam and Eve. From this point on the poem follows Adam and Eve's tragic movement from sin to despair to the recognition of sin and the need for repentance. Adam and Eve's learning through suffering and the prophecy of the Son's redemption of sin make this a story of gain as well as loss, on the order of Aeschylean tragedy.

Like all epics, *Paradise Lost* is encyclopedic, combining many different genres. To read this poem is to have an education in everything from literary history to astronomy. Milton draws on a vast wealth of reading, with the Bible as his main source—not only Genesis, but

---

9. Matthew 13.24.   1. Ephesians 4.3.

also Exodus, the Prophets, Revelation, Saint Paul, and especially the Psalms, which he had translated. Milton also makes great use of biblical commentary from rabbinical, patristic, and contemporary sources. Early on, Milton had envisaged a poem about the Arthurian legend, and his choice of the nonmartial, seemingly unheroic biblical story of Adam and Eve marks a bold departure from epic tradition. While Spenser's *Faerie Queene* is Milton's most important vernacular model, among epic poets his closest affinity is with Virgil and Dante, both of whom had written of the underworld; Dante especially devoted himself to humanity's free choice of sin. Like Dante, Milton creates his poem as a microcosm of the natural universe. His ideal vision of the world before the Fall is one where day and night are equal and the sun is always in the same sign of the zodiac, an image that embodies in poetic astronomy the world of simplicity and perfection that humans have lost through sin. Milton does not choose between the earth-centered Ptolemaic and the heliocentric Copernican systems but presents both as alternative explanations for the order of the universe.

Although we know nothing about the order in which the parts of the poem were composed, we do know that Milton typically composed at night or in the early morning. Sometimes he lay awake unable to write a line; at others he was seized "with a certain impetus and *oestro*" [frenzy]. He would dictate forty lines from memory and then reduce them to half that number. According to his nephew, the poem was written from 1658 to 1663.

The one extant manuscript of the poem, which contains the first book, reveals that Milton revised for punctuation and spelling. There were two editions in Milton's lifetime, both printed by Samuel Simmons. The first edition, *Paradise Lost: A poem in ten books,* was printed in six different issues in 1667, 1668, and 1669. From the fourth issue of the poem on, such paratexts as "The Printer to Reader," "The Argument" (which stood altogether), and Milton's note on the verse appear. With the second octave edition of 1674, Milton divided Books 7 and 10 into two books each to create twelve books in all. Prefaced by dedicatory Latin verses, one of which was by his old friend Andrew Marvell, this 1674 edition, which appeared in the year of Milton's death, is the basis for the present text.

FROM **PARADISE LOST**[1]

Book 1

The Argument

This first Book proposes, first in brief, the whole Subject, *Man's disobedience, and the loss thereupon of Paradise wherein he was plac't:* Then touches *the prime cause of his fall, the Serpent, or rather* Satan *in the Serpent; who revolting from God, and drawing to his side many Legions of Angels, was by the command of God driven out of Heaven with all his Crew into the great Deep.* Which action past over, the Poem hastes into the midst of things,[2] presenting *Satan with his Angels now fallen into Hell,* describ'd here, *not in the Centre* (for Heaven and Earth may be suppos'd as yet not made, certainly not yet accurst) *but in a place of utter darkness, fitliest call'd* Chaos: *Here* Satan *with his Angels lying on the burning Lake, thunder-struck and astonisht, after a certain space recovers, as from confusion, calls up him who next in Order and Dignity lay by him; they confer of thir miserable fall.* Satan *awakens all his Legions, who lay till then in the same manner confounded; They rise, thir Numbers, array of Battle, thir chief Leaders nam'd, according to the Idols known afterwards in* Canaan *and the Countries adjoining. To these* Satan *directs his Speech, comforts them with hope yet of regaining Heaven, but tells them lastly of a new World and new kind of Creature to be created, according to an ancient Prophecy or report*

---

1. Our text is taken, and the notes are adapted, from John Carey and Alastair Fowler, eds., *The Poems of John Milton.*

2. Following Horace's rule that the epic should plunge "*in medias res.*"

in Heaven; for that Angels were long before this visible Creation, was the opinion of many ancient Fathers. To find out the truth of this Prophecy, and what to determine thereon he refers to a full Council. What his Associates thence attempt. Pandemonium *the Palace of* Satan *rises, suddenly built out of the Deep: The infernal Peers there sit in Council.*

Of Man's First Disobedience, and the Fruit
Of that Forbidden Tree, whose mortal[3] taste
Brought Death into the World, and all our woe,[4]
With loss of *Eden,* till one greater Man[5]
5   Restore us, and regain the blissful Seat,
Sing Heav'nly Muse,[6] that on the secret top
Of *Oreb,* or of *Sinai,* didst inspire
That Shepherd, who first taught the chosen Seed,[7]
In the Beginning how the Heav'ns and Earth
10   Rose out of *Chaos:* Or if *Sion* Hill[8]
Delight thee more, and *Siloa's* Brook[9] that flow'd
Fast° by the Oracle of God; I thence   *close*
Invoke thy aid to my advent'rous Song,
That with no middle flight intends to soar
15   Above th' *Aonian* Mount,[1] while it pursues
Things unattempted yet in Prose or Rhyme.[2]
And chiefly Thou O Spirit, that dost prefer
Before all Temples th' upright heart and pure,[3]
Instruct me, for Thou know'st; Thou from the first
20   Wast present, and with mighty wings outspread
Dove-like satst brooding on the vast Abyss
And mad'st it pregnant:[4] What in me is dark
Illumine, what is low raise and support;
That to the highth of this great Argument°   *theme*
25   I may assert Eternal Providence,
And justify[5] the ways of God to men.
    Say first, for Heav'n hides nothing from thy view
Nor the deep Tract of Hell, say first what cause
Mov'd our Grand[6] Parents in that happy State,

---

3. "Death-bringing" (Latin *mortalis*) but also "to mortals."
4. This definition of the first sin follows Calvin's Catechism.
5. Christ, in Pauline theology the second Adam (see Romans 5.19). The people and events referred to in these lines have a typological connection, i.e., the Christian interpretation of the Old Testament as a prefiguration of the New.
6. Rhetorically, lines 1–49 are the *invocatio,* consisting of an address to the Muse, and the *principium* that states the whole scope of the poem's action. The "Heavenly Muse," later addressed as the muse of astronomy Urania (7.1), is here identified with the Holy Spirit of the Bible, which inspires Moses.
7. The "Shepherd" is Moses, who was granted the vision of the burning bush on Mount Oreb (Exodus 3) and received the Law, either on Mount Oreb (Deuteronomy 4.10) or on its lower part, Mount Sinai (Exodus 19.20). Moses, the first Jewish writer, taught "the chosen seed," the children of Israel, about the beginning of the world in

Genesis.
8. The sanctuary, a place of ceremonial song but also (Isaiah 2.3) of oracular pronouncements.
9. A spring immediately west of Mount Zion and beside Calvary, often used as a symbol of the operation of the Holy Ghost.
1. Helicon, sacred to the Muses.
2. Ironically translating Ariosto's boast in the invocation to *Orlando Furioso.*
3. The Spirit is the voice of God, which inspired the Hebrew prophets.
4. Identifying the Spirit present at the creation (Genesis 1.2) with the Spirit in the form of a dove that descended on Jesus at the beginning of his ministry (John 1.32). Vast: large; deserted (Latin *vastus*).
5. Does not mean merely "demonstrate logically" but has its biblical meaning and implies spiritual rather than rational understanding.
6. Implies not only greatness, but also inclusiveness of generality or parentage.

30 Favor'd of Heav'n so highly, to fall off
    From thir Creator, and transgress his Will
    For° one restraint, Lords of the World besides?°   *because of/otherwise*
    Who first seduc'd them to that foul revolt?
    Th' infernal Serpent;[7] hee it was, whose guile
35 Stirr'd up with Envy and Revenge, deceiv'd
    The Mother of Mankind; what time his Pride
    Had cast him out from Heav'n, with all his Host
    Of Rebel Angels, by whose aid aspiring
    To set himself in Glory above his Peers,
40 He trusted to have equall'd the most High,[8]
    If he oppos'd; and with ambitious aim
    Against the Throne and Monarchy of God
    Rais'd impious War in Heav'n and Battle proud
    With vain attempt. Him the Almighty Power
45 Hurl'd headlong flaming from th' Ethereal Sky[9]
    With hideous ruin and combustion down
    To bottomless perdition, there to dwell
    In Adamantine Chains[1] and penal Fire,
    Who durst defy th' Omnipotent to Arms.
50 Nine times the Space that measures Day and Night[2]
    To mortal men, hee with his horrid crew
    Lay vanquisht, rolling in the fiery Gulf
    Confounded though immortal: But his doom
    Reserv'd him to more wrath; for now the thought
55 Both of lost happiness and lasting pain
    Torments him; round he throws his baleful° eyes   *evil, suffering*
    That witness'd huge affliction and dismay
    Mixt with obdúrate° pride and steadfast hate: *unyielding*
    At once as far as Angels' ken° he views   *power of vision*
60 The dismal° Situation waste and wild,   *dreadful, sinister*
    A Dungeon horrible, on all sides round
    As one great Furnace flam'd, yet from those flames
    No light, but rather darkness visible
    Serv'd only to discover sights of woe,[3]
65 Regions of sorrow, doleful shades, where peace
    And rest can never dwell, hope never comes
    That comes to all;[4] but torture without end
    Still urges,° and a fiery Deluge, fed   *presses*
    With ever-burning Sulphur unconsum'd:

---

7. "That old serpent, called the Devil, and Satan" (Revelation 12.9) both because Satan entered the body of a serpent to tempt Eve and because his nature is guileful and dangerous to humans.

8. Satan's crime was not his aspiring "above his peers" but aspiring "To set himself in [divine] Glory." Numerous verbal echoes relate lines 40–48 to the biblical accounts of the fall and binding of Lucifer, in 2 Peter 2.4, Revelation 20.1–2, and Isaiah 14.12–15: "Thou hast said . . . I will exalt my throne above the stars of God . . . I will be like the most High. Yet thou shalt be brought down to hell."

9. Mingling an allusion to Luke 10.18, "I beheld Satan as lightning fall from heaven," with one to Homer, *Iliad* 1.591, Hephaistos "hurled from the ethereal threshold."
1. 2 Peter 2.4; "God spared not the angels that sinned, but . . . delivered them into chains of darkness."
2. The devils fall for the same number of days that the Titans fall from heaven when overthrown by the Olympian gods (see Hesiod, *Theogony* 664–735).
3. See the account of the land of the dead in Job 10.22: "the light is as darkness."
4. The phrase echoes Dante's *Inferno:* "All hope abandon, ye who enter here."

70   Such place Eternal Justice had prepar'd
For those rebellious, here thir Prison ordained
In utter° darkness, and thir portion set   *complete, outer*
As far remov'd from God and light of Heav'n
As from the Center thrice to th' utmost Pole.[5]

75   O how unlike the place from whence they fell!
There the companions of his fall, o'erwhelm'd
With Floods and Whirlwinds of tempestuous fire,
He soon discerns, and welt'ring by his side
One next himself in power, and next in crime,

80   Long after known in *Palestine*, and nam'd
Beëlzebub.[6] To whom th' Arch-Enemy,
And thence in Heav'n call'd Satan,[7] with bold words
Breaking the horrid silence thus began.[8]
        If thou beest hee; But O how fall'n! how chang'd

85   From him, who in the happy Realms of Light
Cloth'd with transcendent brightness didst outshine
Myriads though bright:[9] If he whom mutual league,
United thoughts and counsels, equal hope,
And hazard in the Glorious Enterprise,

90   Join'd with me once, now misery hath join'd
In equal ruin: into what Pit thou seest
From what highth fall'n, so much the stronger prov'd
He with his Thunder: and till then who knew
The force of those dire Arms? yet not for those,

95   Nor what the Potent Victor in his rage
Can else inflict, do I repent or change,
Though chang'd in outward luster; that fixt mind
And high disdain, from sense of injur'd merit,
That with the mightiest rais'd me to contend,

100   And to the fierce contention brought along
Innumerable force of Spirits arm'd
That durst dislike his reign, and mee preferring,
His utmost power with adverse power oppos'd
In dubious Battle on the Plains of Heav'n,

105   And shook his throne.[1] What though the field be lost?
All is not lost; the unconquerable Will,
And study° of revenge, immortal hate,   *pursuit*
And courage never to submit or yield:
And what is else not to be overcome?

---

5. Milton refers to the Ptolemaic universe in which the earth is at the center of ten concentric spheres. Milton draws attention to the numerical proportion, heaven-earth:earth-hell—i.e., earth divides the interval between heaven and hell in the proportion that Neoplatonists believed should be maintained between reason and concupiscence.

6. Hebrew, "Lord of the flies"; Matthew 12.24, "the prince of the devils."

7. Hebrew, "enemy." After his rebellion, Satan's "former name" (Lucifer) was no longer used (5.658).

8. Rhetorically, the opening of the action proper. The 41-line speech beginning here, the first speech in the book, exactly balances the last, which also is spoken by Satan and also consists of 41 lines (12.622–662).

9. The break in grammatical concord (between "him" and "didst") reflects Satan's doubt whether Beelzebub is present and so whether second-person forms are appropriate.

1. The Son's chariot, not Satan's armies, shakes heaven to its foundations, as we learn in Book 6. Throughout the present passage, Satan sees himself as the hero of a pagan epic.

110   That Glory² never shall his wrath or might
      Extort from me. To bow and sue for grace
      With suppliant knee, and deify his power
      Who from the terror of this Arm so late
      Doubted° his Empire, that were low indeed,   *feared for*
115   That were an ignominy and shame beneath
      This downfall; since by Fate the strength of Gods
      And this Empyreal substance cannot fail,³
      Since through experience of this great event
      In Arms not worse, in foresight much advanc't,
120   We may with more successful hope resolve
      To wage by force or guile eternal War
      Irreconcilable to our grand Foe,
      Who now triúmphs, and in th' excess of joy
      Sole reigning holds the Tyranny of Heav'n.⁴
125   So spake th' Apostate Angel, though in pain,
      Vaunting aloud, but rackt with deep despair:
      And him thus answer'd soon his bold Compeer.°   *comrade*
          O Prince, O Chief of many Throned Powers,
      That led th' imbattl'd Seraphim⁵ to War
130   Under thy conduct, and in dreadful deeds
      Fearless, endanger'd Heav'n's perpetual King;
      And put to proof his high Supremacy,
      Whether upheld by strength, or Chance, or Fate;⁶
      Too well I see and rue the dire event,
135   That with sad overthrow and foul defeat
      Hath lost us Heav'n, and all this mighty Host
      In horrible destruction laid thus low,
      As far as Gods and Heav'nly Essences
      Can perish: for the mind and spirit remains
140   Invincible, and vigor soon returns,
      Though all our Glory extinct, and happy state
      Here swallow'd up in endless misery.
      But what if he our Conqueror (whom I now
      Of force° believe Almighty, since no less   *necessarily*
145   Than such could have o'erpow'rd such force as ours)
      Have left us this our spirit and strength entire
      Strongly to suffer and support our pains,
      That we may so suffice° his vengeful ire,   *satisfy*
      Or do him mightier service as his thralls
150   By right of War, whate'er his business be
      Here in the heart of Hell to work in Fire,
      Or do his Errands in the gloomy Deep;
      What can it then avail though yet we feel
      Strength undiminisht, or eternal being

2. Either "the glory of overcoming me" or "my glory of
will."
3. Implying not only that as angels they are immortal, but
also that the continuance of their strength is assured by
fate.
4. An obvious instance of the devil's bias.
5. The traditional nine orders of angels are seraphim,

cherubim, thrones, dominions, virtues, powers, principalities, archangels, and angels, but Milton does not use
these terms systematically.
6. The main powers recognized in the devils' ideology.
God's power rests on a quality that does not occur to
Beelzebub: goodness.

155   To undergo eternal punishment?[7]
        Whereto with speedy words th' Arch-fiend repli'd.
            Fall'n Cherub, to be weak is miserable
        Doing or Suffering: but of this be sure,
        To do aught good never will be our task,
160   But ever to do ill our sole delight,
        As being the contrary to his high will
        Whom we resist.[8] If then his Providence
        Out of our evil seek to bring forth good,
        Our labor must be to pervert that end,
165   And out of good still to find means of evil;
        Which oft-times may succeed, so as perhaps
        Shall grieve him, if I fail not, and disturb
        His inmost counsels from thir destin'd aim.
        But see the angry Victor hath recall'd
170   His Ministers of vengeance and pursuit
        Back to the Gates of Heav'n: the Sulphurous Hail
        Shot after us in storm, o'erblown hath laid°   subdued
        The fiery Surge, that from the Precipice
        Of Heav'n receiv'd us falling, and the Thunder,
175   Wing'd with red Lightning and impetuous rage,
        Perhaps hath spent his shafts, and ceases now
        To bellow through the vast and boundless Deep.
        Let us not slip° th' occasion, whether scorn,   lose
        Or satiate fury yield it from our Foe.
180   Seest thou yon dreary Plain, forlorn and wild,
        The seat of desolation, void of light,
        Save what the glimmering of these livid flames
        Casts pale and dreadful? Thither let us tend
        From off the tossing of these fiery waves,
185   There rest, if any rest can harbor there,
        And reassembling our afflicted° Powers,   downcast
        Consult how we may henceforth most offend°   harm
        Our Enemy, our own loss how repair,
        How overcome this dire Calamity,
190   What reinforcement we may gain from Hope,
        If not what resolution from despair.
            Thus Satan talking to his nearest Mate
        With Head up-lift above the wave, and Eyes
        That sparkling blaz'd, his other Parts besides
195   Prone on the Flood, extended long and large
        Lay floating many a rood,° in bulk as huge   six to eight yards
        As whom the Fables name of monstrous size,
        Titanian, or Earth-born, that warr'd on Jove,
        Briareos or Typhon,[9] whom the Den

---

7. Being that is eternal, merely so that our punishment may also be eternal.

8. This fundamental disobedience and disorientation make Satan's heroic virtue into the corresponding excess of vice. Lines 163–165 look forward to 12.470–78 and Adam's wonder at the astonishing reversal whereby God will turn the Fall into an occasion for good.

9. The serpent-legged Briareos was a Titan, the serpent-headed Typhon (Typhoeus) a Giant. Each was a son of Earth; each fought against Jupiter; and each was eventually confined beneath Aetna (see lines 232–37). Typhon was so powerful that when he first made war on the Olympians, they had to resort to metamorphoses to escape (Ovid, Metamorphoses 5.325–31 and 346–58).

200   By ancient *Tarsus*[1] held, or that Sea-beast
     Leviathan,[2] which God of all his works
     Created hugest that swim th' Ocean stream:
     Him haply slumb'ring on the *Norway* foam
     The Pilot of some small night-founder'd° Skiff,   *sunk in night*
205   Deeming some Island, oft, as Seamen tell,
     With fixed Anchor in his scaly rind
     Moors by his side under the Lee, while Night
     Invests° the Sea, and wished Morn delays: *wraps*
     So stretcht out huge in length the Arch-fiend lay
210   Chain'd on the burning Lake, nor ever thence
     Had ris'n or heav'd his head, but that the will
     And high permission of all-ruling Heaven
     Left him at large to his own dark designs,
     That with reiterated crimes he might
215   Heap on himself damnation, while he sought
     Evil to others, and enrag'd might see
     How all his malice serv'd but to bring forth
     Infinite goodness, grace and mercy shown
     On Man by him seduc't, but on himself
220   Treble confusion, wrath and vengeance pour'd.
     Forthwith upright he rears from off the Pool
     His mighty Stature; on each hand the flames
     Driv'n backward slope thir pointing spires, and roll'd
     In billows, leave i' th' midst a horrid° Vale.   *bristling*
225   Then with expanded wings he steers his flight
     Aloft, incumbent[3] on the dusky Air
     That felt unusual weight, till on dry Land
     He lights, if it were Land that ever burn'd
     With solid, as the Lake with liquid fire
230   And such appear'd in hue;[4] as when the force
     Of subterranean wind transports a Hill
     Torn from *Pelorus*,[5] or the shatter'd side
     Of thund'ring *AEtna*, whose combustible
     And fuell'd entrails thence conceiving Fire,
235   Sublim'd[6] with Mineral fury,[7] aid the Winds,
     And leave a singed bottom all involv'd°   *wreathed*
     With stench and smoke: Such resting found the sole
     Of unblest feet. Him follow'd his next Mate,
     Both glorying to have scap't the *Stygian*[8] flood
240   As Gods, and by thir own recover'd strength,
     Not by the sufferance of supernal Power.
       Is this the Region, this the Soil, the Clime,
     Said then the lost Arch-Angel, this the seat
     That we must change° for Heav'n, this mournful gloom   *exchange*

---

1. The biblical Tarsus was the capital of Cilicia, and both Pindar and Aeschylus describe Typhon's habitat as a Cilician cave or "den."
2. The monster of Job 41, identified in Isaiah's prophecy of judgement as "the crooked serpent" (Isaiah 27.1) but also sometimes thought of as a whale.
3. Pressing with his weight.

4. In the 17th century, "hue" referred to surface appearance and texture as well as color.
5. Pelorus and Aetna are volcanic mountains in Sicily.
6. Converted directly from solid to vapor by volcanic heat in such a way as to resolidify on cooling.
7. Disorder of minerals, or subterranean disorder.
8. Of the River Styx—i.e., hellish.

245   For that celestial light? Be it so, since he
       Who now is Sovran can dispose and bid
       What shall be right: fardest° from him is best   *farthest*
       Whom reason hath equall'd, force hath made supreme
       Above his equals. Farewell happy Fields
250   Where Joy for ever dwells: Hail horrors, hail
       Infernal world, and thou profoundest Hell
       Receive thy new Possessor: One who brings
       A mind not to be chang'd by Place or Time.
       The mind is its own place, and in itself
255   Can make a Heav'n of Hell, a Hell of Heav'n.⁹
       What matter where, if I be still the same,
       And what I should be, all but less than hee
       Whom Thunder hath made greater? Here at least
       We shall be free; th' Almighty hath not built
260   Here for his envy, will not drive us hence:
       Here we may reign secure, and in my choice
       To reign is worth ambition¹ though in Hell:
       Better to reign in Hell, than serve in Heav'n.
       But wherefore let we then our faithful friends,
265   Th' associates and copartners of our loss
       Lie thus astonisht on th' oblivious Pool,²
       And call them not to share with us their part
       In this unhappy Mansion: or once more
       With rallied Arms to try what may be yet
270   Regain'd in Heav'n, or what more lost in Hell?
           So *Satan* spake, and him *Beëlzebub*
       Thus answer'd. Leader of those Armies bright,
       Which but th' Omnipotent none could have foiled,
       If once they hear that voice, thir liveliest pledge
275   Of hope in fears and dangers, heard so oft
       In worst extremes, and on the perilous edge°   *front line*
       Of battle when it rag'd, in all assaults
       Thir surest signal, they will soon resume
       New courage and revive, though now they lie
280   Groveling and prostrate on yon Lake of Fire,
       As we erewhile, astounded and amaz'd;
       No wonder, fall'n such a pernicious highth.
           He scarce had ceas't when the superior Fiend
       Was moving toward the shore; his ponderous shield
285   Ethereal temper,³ massy, large and round,
       Behind him cast; the broad circumference
       Hung on his shoulders like the Moon, whose Orb
       Through Optic Glass the *Tuscan* Artist⁴ views
       At Ev'ning from the top of *Fesole*,

---

9. The view that heaven and hell are states of mind was held by Amaury de Bene, a medieval heretic often cited in 17th-century accounts of atheism.
1. Worth striving for (Latin *ambitio*). Satan refers not merely to a mental state but also to an active effort that is the price of power.
2. The pool attended by forgetfulness.

3. Tempered in celestial fire.
4. Galileo, who looked through a telescope ("optic glass"), had been placed under house arrest by the Inquisition near Florence, which is in the "Valdarno" or the Valley of the Arno, overlooked by the hills of "Fesole" or Fiesole.

290 Or in *Valdarno*, to descry new Lands,
  Rivers or Mountains in her spotty Globe.
  His Spear, to equal which the tallest Pine
  Hewn on *Norwegian* hills, to be the Mast
  Of some great Ammiral,° were but a wand,   *flagship*
295 He walkt with to support uneasy steps
  Over the burning Marl,° not like those steps   *ground*
  On Heaven's Azure, and the torrid Clime
  Smote on him sore besides, vaulted with Fire;
  Nathless° he so endur'd, till on the Beach   *nevertheless*
300 Of that inflamed Sea, he stood and call'd
  His Legions, Angel Forms, who lay intrans't
  Thick as Autumnal Leaves that strow the Brooks
  In *Vallombrosa*, where th' *Etrurian* shades
  High overarch't imbow'r;[5] or scatter'd sedge
305 Afloat, when with fierce Winds *Orion* arm'd
  Hath vext the Red-Sea Coast,[6] whose waves o'erthrew
  Busiris and his *Memphian* Chivalry,
  While with perfidious hatred they pursu'd
  The Sojourners of *Goshen*, who beheld
310 From the safe shore thir floating Carcasses
  And broken Chariot Wheels;[7] so thick bestrown
  Abject and lost lay these, covering the Flood,
  Under amazement of thir hideous change.
  He call'd so loud, that all the hollow Deep
315 Of Hell resounded. Princes, Potentates,
  Warriors, the Flow'r of Heav'n, once yours, now lost,
  If such astonishment as this can seize
  Eternal spirits; or have ye chos'n this place
  After the toil of Battle to repose
320 Your wearied virtue,° for the ease you find   *strength*
  To slumber here, as in the Vales of Heav'n?
  Or in this abject posture have ye sworn
  To adore the Conqueror? who now beholds
  Cherub and Seraph rolling in the Flood
325 With scatter'd Arms and Ensigns,° till anon *battle flags*
  His swift pursuers from Heav'n Gates discern
  Th' advantage, and descending tread us down
  Thus drooping, or with linked Thunderbolts
  Transfix us to the bottom of this Gulf.
330 Awake, arise, or be for ever fall'n.
   They heard, and were abasht, and up they sprung
  Upon the wing; as when men wont to watch

---

5. See Isaiah 34.4: "and all their host shall fall down, as the leaf falleth off from the vine, and as a falling fig from the fig tree." Fallen leaves were an enduring simile for the numberless dead; see Homer, *Iliad* 6.146; Virgil, *Aeneid* 6.309; Dante, *Inferno* 3.112. Milton adds an actual locality, Vallombrosa, again near Florence.
6. Commentators on Job 9.9 and Amos 5.8 interpreted the creation of Orion as a symbol of God's power to raise tempests and floods to execute his judgments. Thus Mil-

ton's transition to the Egyptians overwhelmed by God's judgment in lines 306–11 is a natural one. The Hebrew name for the Red Sea was "Sea of Sedge."
7. Contrary to his promise, the Pharaoh with his Memphian (i.e., Egyptian) charioteers pursued the Israelites—who had been in captivity in Goshen—across the Red Sea. The Israelites passed over safely; but the Egyptians' chariot wheels were broken (Exodus 14.25), and the rising sea engulfed them and cast their corpses on the shore.

On duty, sleeping found by whom they dread,
Rouse and bestir themselves ere well awake.
335   Nor did they not perceive the evil plight
In which they were, or the fierce pains not feel;
Yet to thir General's Voice they soon obey'd
Innumerable. As when the potent Rod
Of *Amram's* Son[8] in *Egypt's* evil day
340   Wav'd round the Coast, up call'd a pitchy cloud
Of *Locusts,* warping° on the Eastern Wind,   *floating*
That o'er the Realm of impious *Pharaoh* hung
Like Night, and darken'd all the Land of *Nile:*
So numberless were those bad Angels seen
345   Hovering on wing under the Cope° of Hell   *canopy*
'Twixt upper, nether, and surrounding Fires;
Till, as a signal giv'n, th' uplifted Spear
Of thir great Sultan waving to direct
Thir course, in even balance down they light
350   On the firm brimstone, and fill all the Plain;
A multitude, like which the populous North
Pour'd never from her frozen loins, to pass
Rhene or the *Danaw,* when her barbarous Sons
Came like a Deluge on the South, and spread
355   Beneath *Gibraltar* to the *Lybian* sands.[9]
Forthwith from every Squadron and each Band
The Heads and Leaders thither haste where stood
Thir great Commander; Godlike shapes and forms
Excelling human, Princely Dignities,
360   And Powers that erst in Heaven sat on Thrones;
Though of thir Names in heav'nly Records now
Be no memorial, blotted out and ras'd
By thir Rebellion, from the Books of Life.[1]
Nor had they yet among the Sons of *Eve*
365   Got them new Names, till wand'ring o'er the Earth,
Through God's high sufferance for the trial of man,
By falsities and lies the greatest part
Of Mankind they corrupted to forsake
God thir Creator, and th' invisible
370   Glory of him that made them, to transform
Oft to the Image of a Brute, adorn'd
With gay Religions° full of Pomp and Gold,   *ceremonies*
And Devils to adore for Deities:[2]
Then were they known to men by various Names,
375   And various Idols through the Heathen World.
Say, Muse, thir Names then known, who first, who last,
Rous'd from the slumber on that fiery Couch,
At thir great Emperor's call, as next in worth

---

8. Moses, who used his rod to bring down on the Egyptians a plague of locusts (Exodus 10.12–15).
9. The barbarian invasions of Rome began with crossings of the Rhine ("Rhene") and Danube ("Danaw") Rivers and spread to North Africa.

1. See Revelation 3.5 ("He that overcometh . . . I will not blot out his name out of the book of life") and Exodus 32.32–3.
2. The catalogue of gods here is an epic convention.

Came singly where he stood on the bare strand,
380   While the promiscuous crowd stood yet aloof?
The chief were those who from the Pit of Hell
Roaming to seek thir prey on earth, durst fix
Thir Seats long after next the Seat of God,
Thir Altars by his Altar, Gods ador'd
385   Among the Nations round, and durst abide
Jehovah thund'ring out of *Sion*, thron'd
Between the Cherubim; yea, often plac'd
Within his Sanctuary itself thir Shrines,
Abominations; and with cursed things
390   His holy Rites, and solemn Feasts profan'd,
And with thir darkness durst affront his light.
First *Moloch*,[3] horrid King besmear'd with blood
Of human sacrifice, and parents' tears,
Though for the noise of Drums and Timbrels° loud   *tambourines*
395   Thir children's cries unheard, that pass'd through fire
To his grim Idol. Him the *Ammonite*
Worshipt in *Rabba* and her wat'ry Plain,
In *Argob* and in *Basan*, to the stream
Of utmost *Arnon*.[4] Nor content with such
400   Audacious neighborhood, the wisest heart
Of *Solomon*[5] he led by fraud to build
His Temple right against the Temple of God
On that opprobrious Hill,[6] and made his Grove
The pleasant Valley of *Hinnom*, *Tophet* thence
405   And black *Gehenna* call'd, the Type of Hell.[7]
Next *Chemos*,[8] th' obscene dread of *Moab's* Sons,
From *Aroar* to *Nebo*, and the wild
Of Southmost *Abarim*; in *Hesebon*
And *Horonaim*, *Seon's* Realm, beyond
410   The flow'ry Dale of *Sibma* clad with Vines,
And *Eleale* to th' *Asphaltic* Pool.[9]
Peor[1] his other Name, when he entic'd
Israel in *Sittim* on thir march from *Nile*

3. Satan gathers twelve disciples: Moloch, Chemos, Baalim, Ashtaroth, Astoreth, Thammuz, Dagon, Rimmon, Osiris, Isis, Horus, and Belial. The literal meaning of *Moloch* is "king."

4. Though ostensibly magnifying Moloch's empire, these lines look forward to his eventual defeat; for Rabba, the Ammonite royal city, is best known for its capture by David after his repentance (2 Samuel 12), while the Israelite conquest of the regions of Argob and Basan, as far as the boundary river Arnon, is recalled by Moses as particularly crushing (Deuteronomy 3.1–13).

5. Solomon's wives drew him into idolatry (1 Kings 11.5–7); but the "high places that were before Jerusalem . . . on the right hand of the mount of corruption which Solomon . . . had builded for Ashtoreth the abomination of the Zidonians, and for Chemosh the abomination of the Moabites, and Milcom the abomination of the children of Ammon" were later destroyed by Josiah (2 Kings 23.13–14).

6. The Mount of Olives, because of Solomon's idolatry

called "mount of corruption." Throughout the poem, Solomon functions as a type both of Adam and of Christ.

7. To abolish sacrifice to Moloch, Josiah "defiled Topheth, which is in the valley of the children of Hinnom" (2 Kings 23.10). Gehenna, for "Valley of Hinnom," is used in Matthew 10.28 as a name for hell.

8. "The abomination of Moab," associated with the neighboring god Moloch in 1 Kings 11.7.

9. Most of these places are named in Numbers 32 as the formerly Moabite inheritance assigned by Moses to the tribes of Reuben and Gad. Numbers 21.25–30 rejoices at the Israelite capture of Hesebon (Heshbon), a Moabite city which had been taken by the Amorite King Seon, or Sihon. Heshbon, Horonaim, "the vine of Sibmah," and Elealeh all figure in Isaiah's sad prophecy of the destruction of Moab (Isaiah 15.5, 16.8f). The Asphaltic Pool is the Dead Sea.

1. For the story of Peor, see Numbers 25.1–3 and Hosea 9.10.

To do him wanton rites, which cost them woe.[2]
415 Yet thence his lustful Orgies he enlarg'd
Even to that Hill of scandal, by the Grove
Of *Moloch* homicide, lust hard by hate;
Till good *Josiah*[3] drove them thence to Hell.
With these came they, who from the bord'ring flood
420 Of old *Euphrates*[4] to the Brook that parts
Egypt from *Syrian* ground, had general Names
Of *Baalim* and *Ashtaroth*,[5] those male,
These Feminine. For Spirits when they please
Can either Sex assume, or both; so soft
425 And uncompounded is thir Essence pure,
Not ti'd or manacl'd with joint or limb,
Nor founded on the brittle strength of bones,
Like cumbrous flesh; but in what shape they choose
Dilated° or condens't, bright or obscure,   *expanded*
430 Can execute thir aery purposes,
And works of love or enmity fulfil.
For those the Race of *Israel* oft forsook
Thir living strength,[6] and unfrequented left
His righteous Altar, bowing lowly down
435 To bestial Gods; for which thir heads as low
Bow'd down in Battle, sunk before the Spear
Of despicable foes. With these in troop
Came *Astoreth*, whom the *Phoenicians* call'd
Astarte, Queen of Heav'n, with crescent Horns;[7]
440 To whose bright Image nightly by the Moon
Sidonian Virgins paid thir Vows and Songs,
In *Sion* also not unsung, where stood
Her Temple on th' offensive Mountain, built
By that uxorious King, whose heart though large,
445 Beguil'd by fair Idolatresses, fell
To Idols foul. *Thammuz*[8] came next behind,
Whose annual wound in *Lebanon* allur'd
The *Syrian* Damsels to lament his fate
In amorous ditties all a Summer's day,
450 While smooth *Adonis* from his native Rock
Ran purple to the Sea, suppos'd with blood
Of *Thammuz* yearly wounded: the Love-tale
Infected *Sion's* daughters with like heat,

---

2. A plague that killed 24,000 (Numbers 25.9).
3. Always a favorite with the Reformers because of his destruction of idolatrous images.
4. An area stretching from the northeast limit of Syria to the southwest limit of Canaan, the river Besor.
5. Baal is the general name for most idols; the Phoenician and Canaanite sun gods were collectively called Baalim (plural form). Astartes (Ishtars) were manifestations of the moon goddess.
6. See 1 Samuel 15.29: "Strength of Israel," a formulaic periphrasis for Jehovah.
7. The image of Astoreth or Astarte, the Sidonian (Phoenician) moon goddess and Venus, was the statue of a woman with the head of a bull above her head with horns resembling the crescent moon. "Queen of heaven": from Jeremiah 44.17–19.
8. The lover of Astarte. His identification with Adonis was based on St. Jerome's commentary on the passage in Ezekiel 8.14, drawn on by Milton in lines 454–456. The Syrian festival of Tammuz was celebrated after the summer solstice; the slaying of the young god by a boar was mourned as a symbol of the southward withdrawal of the sun and the death of vegetation. Each year when the River Adonis became discolored with red mud, it was regarded as a renewed sign of the god's wound.

455 Whose wanton passions in the sacred Porch
    Ezekiel saw, when by the Vision led
    His eye survey'd the dark Idolatries
    Of alienated *Judah*. Next came one
    Who mourn'd in earnest, when the Captive Ark
460 Maim'd his brute Image, head and hands lopt off
    In his own Temple, on the grunsel° edge,   *threshold*
    Where he fell flat, and sham'd his Worshippers:
    Dagon his Name, Sea Monster, upward Man
    And downward Fish:⁹ yet had his Temple high
    Rear'd in *Azotus*, dreaded through the Coast
465 Of *Palestine*, in *Gath* and *Ascalon*,
    And *Accaron* and *Gaza's* frontier bounds.¹
    Him follow'd *Rimmon*, whose delightful Seat
    Was fair *Damascus*, on the fertile Banks
    Of *Abbana* and *Pharphar*, lucid streams.²
470 He also against the house of God was bold:
    A Leper once he lost and gain'd a King,
    Ahaz his sottish Conqueror, whom he drew
    God's Altar to disparage and displace
    For one of *Syrian* mode, whereon to burn
475 His odious off'rings, and adore the Gods
    Whom he had vanquisht.³ After these appear'd
    A crew who under Names of old Renown,
    Osiris, Isis, Orus and thir Train
    With monstrous shapes and sorceries abus'd°   *deceived*
480 Fanatic *Egypt* and her Priests, to seek
    Thir wand'ring Gods disguis'd in brutish forms
    Rather than human.⁴ Nor did *Israel* scape
    Th' infection when thir borrow'd Gold compos'd
    The Calf in *Oreb*:⁵ and the Rebel King⁶
485 Doubl'd that sin in *Bethel* and in *Dan*,
    Lik'ning his Maker to the Grazed Ox,⁷
    Jehovah, who in one Night when he pass'd
    From *Egypt* marching, equall'd with one stroke
    Both her first born and all her bleating Gods.⁸

9. When the Philistines put the ark of the Lord, which they had captured, into the temple of Dagon, "on the morrow morning, behold, Dagon was fallen upon his face to the ground . . . and the head of Dagon and both the palms of his hands were cut off upon the threshold" (1 Samuel 5.4).

1. Divine vengeance on these Philistine cities is prophesied in Zephaniah 2.4.

2. When Elisha told Naaman that his leprosy would be cured if he washed in the Jordan, the Syrian was at first angry (2 Kings 5.12: "Are not Abana and Pharpar, rivers of Damascus, better than all the waters of Israel?") but then humbled himself and was cured.

3. After engineering the overthrow of Damascus by the Assyrians, the sottish (foolish) King Ahaz became interested in the cult of Rimmon and had an altar of the Syrian type put in the temple of the Lord (2 Kings 16.9–17).

4. Milton alludes to the myth of the Olympian gods fleeing from the Giant Typhoeus into Egypt and hiding in bestial forms (Ovid, *Metamorphoses* 5.319–31) afterward worshipped by the Egyptians.

5. Perhaps the most familiar of all Israelite apostasies was their worship of "a calf in Horeb" (Psalms 106.19) made by Aaron while Moses was away receiving the tables of the Law (Exodus 32).

6. Jeroboam, who led the revolt of the ten tribes of Israel against Rehoboam, Solomon's successor; he "doubled" Aaron's sin, since he made "two calves of gold," placing one in Bethel and the other in Dan (1 Kings 12.28–9).

7. "Thus they changed their glory into the similitude of an ox that eateth grass" (Psalms 106.20).

8. At the passover, Jehovah smote all the Egyptian first-born, "both man and beast" (Exodus 12.12); presumably, this stroke would extend to their sacred animals.

490	Belial came last,[9] than whom a Spirit more lewd	
	Fell not from Heaven, or more gross to love	
	Vice for itself: To him no Temple stood	
	Or Altar smok'd; yet who more oft than hee	
	In Temples and at Altars, when the Priest	
495	Turns Atheist, as did Ely's Sons, who fill'd	
	With lust and violence the house of God.[1]	
	In Courts and Palaces he also Reigns	
	And in luxurious Cities, where the noise	
	Of riot ascends above thir loftiest Tow'rs,	
500	And injury and outrage: And when Night	
	Darkens the Streets, then wander forth the Sons	
	Of Belial, flown° with insolence and wine.[2]	swollen
	Witness the Streets of Sodom, and that night	
	In Gibeah, when the hospitable door	
505	Expos'd a Matron to avoid worse rape.[3]	
	These were the prime in order and in might;	
	The rest were long to tell, though far renown'd,	
	Th' Ionian Gods,[4] of Javan's Issue held	
	Gods, yet confest later than Heav'n and Earth	
510	Thir boasted Parents; Titan Heav'n's first born	
	With his enormous° brood, and birthright seiz'd	monstrous
	By younger Saturn, he from mightier Jove	
	His own and Rhea's Son like measure found;	
	So Jove usurping reign'd: these first in Crete	
515	And Ida known,[5] thence on the Snowy top	
	Of cold Olympus rul'd the middle Air	
	Thir highest Heav'n; or on the Delphian Cliff,[6]	
	Or in Dodona, and through all the bounds	
	Of Doric Land;° or who with Saturn old	Greece
520	Fled over Adria to th' Hesperian Fields,	
	And o'er the Celtic roam'd the utmost Isles.[7]	
	All these and more came flocking; but with looks	
	Downcast and damp,° yet such wherein appear'd	depressed
	Obscure some glimpse of joy, to have found thir chief	
525	Not in despair, to have found themselves not lost	
	In loss itself; which on his count'nance cast	
	Like doubtful hue: but he his wonted pride	
	Soon recollecting,° with high words, that bore	recovering
	Semblance of worth, not substance, gently rais'd	
530	Thir fainting courage, and dispell'd thir fears.	

9. Belial comes last, both because he had no local cult and because in the poem he is "timorous and slothful" (2.117). Properly, "Belial" is an abstract noun meaning "iniquity."

1. The impiety and fornication of Ely's sons are described in 1 Samuel 2.12–24.

2. The Puritans referred to their enemies as the Sons of Belial.

3. See Genesis 19 and Judges 19.

4. The Ionian Greeks were held by some to be the issue of

Javan the son of Japhet the son of Noah, on the basis of the Septuagint version of Genesis 10.

5. Jove was born and secretly reared on Mount Ida, in Crete.

6. Delphi was famed as the site of the Pythian oracle of Apollo, but cults of Ge, Poseidon, and Artemis were also celebrated there.

7. After Saturn's downfall he fled across the Adriatic Sea (Adria) to Italy (Hesperian Fields), France (the Celtic), and the British Isles (Utmost Isles).

Then straight commands that at the warlike sound
Of Trumpets loud and Clarions° be uprear'd   *shrill trumpets*
His mighty Standard; that proud honor claim'd
Azazel as his right, a Cherub tall:[8]
535   Who forthwith from the glittering Staff unfurl'd
Th' Imperial Ensign, which full high advanc't
Shone like a Meteor streaming to the Wind
With Gems and Golden lustre rich imblaz'd,[9]
Seraphic arms and Trophies: all the while
540   Sonorous metal blowing Martial sounds:
At which the universal Host upsent
A shout that tore Hell's Concave,° and beyond   *vault*
Frighted the Reign of *Chaos* and old Night.[1]
All in a moment through the gloom were seen
545   Ten thousand Banners rise into the Air
With Orient° Colors waving: with them rose   *brilliant*
A Forest huge of Spears: and thronging Helms
Appear'd, and serried° Shields in thick array   *locked together*
Of depth immeasurable: Anon they move
550   In perfect *Phalanx*[2] to the *Dorian*° mood   *solemn*
Of Flutes and soft Recorders; such as rais'd
To highth of noblest temper Heroes old
Arming to Battle, and instead of rage
Deliberate valor breath'd, firm and unmov'd
555   With dread of death to flight or foul retreat,
Nor wanting power to mitigate and swage°   *assuage*
With solemn touches, troubl'd thoughts, and chase
Anguish and doubt and fear and sorrow and pain
From mortal or immortal minds. Thus they
560   Breathing united force with fixed thought
Mov'd on in silence to soft Pipes that charm'd
Thir painful steps o'er the burnt soil; and now
Advanc't in view they stand, a horrid° Front   *bristling*
Of dreadful length and dazzling Arms, in guise
565   Of Warriors old with order'd Spear and Shield,
Awaiting what command thir mighty Chief
Had to impose: He through the armed Files
Darts his experienc't eye, and soon traverse°   *across*
The whole Battalion views, thir order due,
570   Thir visages and stature as of Gods;
Thir number last he sums. And now his heart
Distends with pride, and hard'ning in his strength
Glories: For never since created man,[3]
Met such imbodied° force, as nam'd with these   *united*
575   Could merit more than that small infantry

---

8. Azazel was one of the chief fallen angels who are the object of God's wrath in the apocryphal apocalypse The Book of Enoch. For the healing of the earth he is bound and cast into the same wilderness where the scapegoat was led (Enoch 10.4–8).

9. Adorned with heraldic devices.
1. Chaos and Night, rulers of the region of unformed matter between Heaven and Hell.
2. A square battle formation.
3. Since humanity was created.

Warr'd on by Cranes:[4] though all the Giant brood
Of *Phlegra* with th' Heroic Race were join'd
That fought at *Thebes* and *Ilium*, on each side
Mixt with auxiliar Gods;[5] and what resounds
580 In Fable or *Romance of Uther's* Son°   *King Arthur*
Begirt with *British* and *Armoric*[6] Knights;
And all who since, Baptiz'd or Infidel
Jousted in *Aspramont* or *Montalban*,
Damasco, or *Marocco*, or *Trebisond*,
585 Or whom *Biserta* sent from *Afric* shore
When *Charlemain* with all his Peerage fell
By *Fontarabbia*.[7] Thus far these beyond
Compare of mortal prowess, yet observ'd°   *obeyed*
Thir dread commander: he above the rest
590 In shape and gesture proudly eminent
Stood like a Tow'r; his form had yet not lost
All her Original brightness, nor appear'd
Less than Arch-Angel ruin'd, and th' excess
Of Glory obscur'd: As when the Sun new ris'n
595 Looks through the Horizontal misty Air
Shorn of his Beams, or from behind the Moon
In dim Eclipse disastrous twilight sheds
On half the Nations, and with fear of change
Perplexes Monarchs.[8] Dark'n'd so, yet shone
600 Above them all th' Arch-Angel: but his face
Deep scars of Thunder had intrencht, and care
Sat on his faded cheek, but under Brows
Of dauntless courage, and considerate° Pride   *deliberate*
Waiting revenge: cruel his eye, but cast
605 Signs of remorse and passion to behold
The fellows of his crime, the followers rather
(Far other once beheld in bliss) condemn'd
For ever now to have thir lot in pain,
Millions of Spirits for his fault amerc't°   *deprived*
610 Of Heav'n, and from Eternal Splendors flung
For his revolt, yet faithful how they stood,
Thir Glory wither'd. As when Heaven's Fire
Hath scath'd the Forest Oaks, or Mountain Pines,
With singed top thir stately growth though bare
615 Stands on the blasted Heath. He now prepar'd
To speak; whereat thir doubl'd Ranks they bend

4. When compared with the Devil's, any army would seem no bigger than pygmies ("that small infantry"), who were portrayed by Pliny as tiny men who fought with canes.
5. To amplify the heroic stature of the angels, Milton mentions a series of armies that had been thought worthy of epic treatment only to dismiss them. The Giants, who fought with the Olympians at Phlegra, join with the heroes of Thebes and Troy (Ilium).
6. From Brittany.
7. Aspramont was a castle near Nice, and Montalban was

the castle of Rinaldo; these castles figure in Ariosto's *Orlando Furioso* and the romances concerned with chivalric wars between Christians and Saracens. Milton would know late versions of the Charlemagne legend. Charlemagne's whole rearguard, led by Roland, one of the 12 peers or paladins, was massacred at Roncesvalles, about 40 miles from Fontarabbia (Fuenterrabia).
8. The comparison is ironically double-edged, for the ominous solar eclipse presages not only disaster for creation but also the doom of the godlike ruler for whom the sun was a traditional symbol.

From wing to wing, and half enclose him round
With all his Peers: attention held them mute.
Thrice he assay'd, and thrice in spite of scorn,
620 Tears such as Angels weep, burst forth: at last
Words interwove with sighs found out thir way.
  O Myriads of immortal Spirits, O Powers
Matchless, but with th' Almighty, and that strife
Was not inglorious, though th' event° was dire,   *result*
625 As this place testifies, and this dire change
Hateful to utter: but what power of mind
Foreseeing or presaging, from the Depth
Of knowledge past or present, could have fear'd
How such united force of Gods, how such
630 As stood like these, could ever know repulse?
For who can yet believe, though after loss,
That all these puissant° Legions, whose exíle   *powerful*
Hath emptied Heav'n, shall fail to re-ascend
Self-rais'd, and repossess thir native seat?
635 For mee be witness all the Host of Heav'n,
If counsels different, or danger shunn'd
By me, have lost our hopes. But he who reigns
Monarch in Heav'n, till then as one secure
Sat on his Throne, upheld by old repute,
640 Consent or custom, and his Regal State
Put forth at full, but still his strength conceal'd,
Which tempted our attempt, and wrought our fall.
Henceforth his might we know, and know our own
So as not either to provoke, or dread
645 New War, provok't; our better part remains
To work in close° design, by fraud or guile   *secret*
What force effected not: that he no less
At length from us may find, who overcomes
By force, hath overcome but half his foe.
650 Space may produce new Worlds; whereof so rife°   *common*
There went a fame° in Heav'n that he ere long   *rumor*
Intended to create, and therein plant
A generation, whom his choice regard
Should favor equal to the Sons of Heaven:
655 Thither, if but to pry, shall be perhaps
Our first eruption, thither or elsewhere:
For this Infernal Pit shall never hold
Celestial Spirits in Bondage, nor th' Abyss
Long under darkness cover. But these thoughts
660 Full Counsel must mature: Peace is despair'd,
For who can think Submission? War then, War
Open or understood, must be resolv'd.
  He spake: and to confirm his words, out-flew
Millions of flaming swords, drawn from the thighs
665 Of mighty Cherubim; the sudden blaze
Far round illumin'd hell: highly they rag'd

Against the Highest, and fierce with grasped Arms
Clash'd on thir sounding shields the din of war,
Hurling defiance toward the Vault of Heav'n.
670   There stood a Hill not far whose grisly top
Belch'd fire and rolling smoke; the rest entire
Shone with a glossy scurf, undoubted sign
That in his womb was hid metallic Ore,
The work of Sulphur.[9] Thither wing'd with speed
675   A numerous Brígad° hasten'd. As when bands   *brigade*
Of Píoners° with Spade and Pickax arm'd   *engineers*
Forerun the Royal Camp, to trench a Field,
Or cast a Rampart. *Mammon*[1] led them on,
Mammon, the least erected° Spirit that fell   *elevated*
680   From Heav'n, for ev'n in Heav'n his looks and thoughts
Were always downward bent, admiring more
The riches of Heav'n's pavement, trodd'n Gold,
Than aught divine or holy else enjoy'd
In vision beatific: by him first
685   Men also, and by his suggestion taught,
Ransack'd the Center, and with impious hands
Rifl'd the bowels of thir mother Earth
For Treasures better hid. Soon had his crew
Op'n'd into the Hill a spacious wound
690   And digg'd out ribs of Gold. Let none admire°   *wonder*
That riches grow in Hell; that soil may best
Deserve the precious bane. And here let those
Who boast in mortal things, and wond'ring tell
Of *Babel,* and the works of *Memphian* Kings,[2]
695   Learn how thir greatest Monuments of Fame,
And Strength and Art are easily outdone
By Spirits reprobate, and in an hour
What in an age they with incessant toil
And hands innumerable scarce perform.
700   Nigh on the Plain in many cells prepar'd,
That underneath had veins of liquid fire
Sluic'd° from the Lake, a second multitude   *led by channels*
With wondrous Art founded the massy Ore,
Severing each kind, and scumm'd the Bullion dross:
705   A third as soon had form'd within the ground
A various mould, and from the boiling cells
By strange conveyance fill'd each hollow nook:
As in an Organ from one blast of wind
To many a row of Pipes the sound-board breathes.
710   Anon out of the earth a Fabric huge

9. The traditional physiognomy of the fiend is in Milton's
hell displaced onto the landscape. It is a dead or corrupt
body imaged as scurf (i.e., scales, crust), belching, ransacked womb, bowels, entrails, and ribs.
1. In Matthew 6.24 and Luke 16.13, "Mammon" is an
abstract noun meaning wealth, but later it was used as the

name of "the prince of this world" (John 12.31).
Medieval and Renaissance tradition often associated
Mammon with Plutus, the Greek god of riches.
2. The Tower of Babel was built by the ambitious Nimrod. The works of Memphian kings, the Pyramids, were
regarded as memorials of vanity.

Rose like an Exhalation,[3] with the sound
Of Dulcet Symphonies and voices sweet,
Built like a Temple, where *Pilasters*° round   *columns*
Were set, and Doric pillars overlaid
715   With Golden Architrave; nor did there want
Cornice or Frieze, with bossy° Sculptures grav'n;   *embossed*
The Roof was fretted° Gold. Not *Babylon*,[4]   *patterned*
Nor great *Alcairo* such magnificence
Equall'd in all thir glories,[5] to inshrine
720   *Belus*[6] or *Serapis*[7] thir Gods, or seat
Thir Kings, when *Egypt* with *Assyria* strove
In wealth and luxury. Th' ascending pile
Stood fixt her stately highth, and straight the doors
Op'ning thir brazen folds discover wide
725   Within, her ample spaces, o'er the smooth
And level pavement: from the arched roof
Pendant by subtle Magic many a row
Of Starry Lamps and blazing Cressets[8] fed
With *Naphtha* and *Asphaltus*[9] yielded light
730   As from a sky. The hasty multitude
Admiring enter'd, and the work some praise
And some the Architect: his hand was known
In Heav'n by many a Tow'red structure high,
Where Scepter'd Angels held thir residence,
735   And sat as Princes, whom the supreme King
Exalted to such power, and gave to rule,
Each in his Hierarchy, the Orders bright.
Nor was his name unheard or unador'd
In ancient *Greece*; and in *Ausonian* land
740   Men call'd him *Mulciber*;[1] and how he fell
From Heav'n, they fabl'd, thrown by angry *Jove*
Sheer o'er the Crystal Battlements: from Morn
To Noon he fell, from Noon to dewy Eve,
A Summer's day; and with the setting Sun
745   Dropt from the Zenith like a falling Star,
On *Lemnos* th' *Aegean* Isle:[2] thus they relate,
Erring; for he with this rebellious rout

3. Pandaemonium rises to music, since in the Renaissance it was believed that musical proportions governed the forms of architecture.

4. An ironic allusion to Ovid's description of the Palace of the Sun built by Mulciber (*Metamorphoses* 2. 1–4). Pandaemonium has a classical design, complete in every respect, like that of the ancient (but still surviving) gilt-roofed Pantheon, the most admired building of Milton's time. Doric is the oldest and simplest order of Greek architecture.

5. In traditional biblical exegesis, Babylon, a place of proud iniquity, was often a figure of Antichrist or of hell. Memphis (modern Cairo) was the most splendid city of heathen Egypt.

6. Bel, the Babylonian Baal; see lines 421–423n and Jeremiah 51.44: "I will punish Bel in Babylon."

7. An Egyptian deity.

8. Basketlike lamps.

9. *Naphtha* is an oily constituent of asphalt (asphaltus).

1. The Greek god Hephaistos, in Latin *Mulciber* or Vulcan, presided over all arts, such as metal-working, that required the use of fire. He built all the palaces of the gods. "Ausonian land" is the old Greek name for Italy. Milton emulates Homer's description of the daylong fall of Hephaistos (*Iliad* 1.591–95) and then deflates it in the casual but commanding dismissal of 2.746–48.

2. In Homer (*Iliad* 2.87–90) the Achaians going to a council are compared to bees, as are the Carthaginians; in Virgil (*Aeneid* 1.430–436). Milton also glances at Virgil's mock-epic account of the ideal social organization of the hive (*Georgics* 4.149–227).

Fell long before; nor aught avail'd him now
To have built in Heav'n high Tow'rs; nor did he scape
750   By all his Engines, but was headlong sent
With his industrious crew to build in hell.
Meanwhile the winged Heralds by command
Of Sovran power, with awful Ceremony
And Trumpets' sound throughout the Host proclaim
755   A solemn Council forthwith to be held
At *Pandaemonium*, the high Capitol
Of Satan and his Peers: thir summons call'd
From every Band and squared Regiment
By place or choice the worthiest; they anon
760   With hunderds and with thousands trooping came
Attended: all access was throng'd, the Gates
And Porches wide, but chief the spacious Hall
(Though like a cover'd field, where Champions bold
Wont ride in arm'd, and at the Soldan's° chair   *Sultan's*
765   Defi'd the best of *Paynim*° chivalry   *pagan*
To mortal combat or career with Lance)
Thick swarm'd, both on the ground and in the air,
Brusht with the hiss of rustling wings. As Bees
In spring time, when the Sun with *Taurus*[3] rides,
770   Pour forth thir populous youth about the Hive
In clusters; they among fresh dews and flowers
Fly to and fro, or on the smoothed Plank,
The suburb of thir Straw-built Citadel,
New rubb'd with Balm, expatiate° and confer   *debate*
775   Thir State affairs. So thick the aery crowd
Swarm'd and were strait'n'd; till the Signal giv'n,
Behold a wonder! they but now who seem'd
In bigness to surpass Earth's Giant Sons
Now less than smallest Dwarfs, in narrow room
780   Throng numberless, like that Pigmean Race
Beyond the *Indian* Mount, or Faery Elves,
Whose midnight Revels, by a Forest side
Or Fountain some belated Peasant sees,
Or dreams he sees, while over-head the Moon
785   Sits Arbitress, and nearer to the Earth
Wheels her pale course;[4] they on thir mirth and dance
Intent, with jocund Music charm his ear;
At once with joy and fear his heart rebounds.
Thus incorporeal Spirits to smallest forms
790   Reduc'd thir shapes immense, and were at large,
Though without number still amidst the Hall
Of that infernal Court. But far within
And in thir own dimensions like themselves

---

3. In Milton's time the sun entered the second sign of the zodiac in mid-April, according to the Julian calendar.
4. Echoing *A Midsummer Night's Dream* 2.1.28f and 141.

"The moon / Sits arbitress" because the moon-goddess was queen of faery.

795   The great Seraphic Lords and Cherubim

    In close° recess and secret conclave⁵ sat   *secret*

    A thousand Demi-Gods on golden seats,

    Frequent° and full. After short silence then   *crowded*

    And summons read, the great consult began.

          The End of the First Book.

Book 2
The Argument

The Consultation begun, Satan debates whether another Battle be to be hazarded for the recovery of Heaven: some advise it, others dissuade: A third proposal is preferr'd, mention'd before by Satan, to search the truth of that Prophecy or Tradition in Heaven concerning another world, and another kind of creature equal or not much inferior to themselves, about this time to be created: Thir doubt who shall be sent on this difficult search: Satan thir chief undertakes alone the voyage, is honor'd and applauded. The Council thus ended, the rest betake them several ways and to several employments, as thir inclinations lead them, to entertain the time till Satan return. He passes on his Journey to Hell Gates, finds them shut, and who sat there to guard them, by whom at length they are op'n'd, and discover¹ to him the great Gulf between Hell and Heaven; with what difficulty he passes through, directed by Chaos, the Power of that place, to the sight of this new World which he sought.

    High on a Throne of Royal State,² which far

    Outshone the wealth of *Ormus* and of *Ind*,³

    Or where the gorgeous East with richest hand

    Show'rs on her Kings *Barbaric* Pearl and Gold,

5   Satan exalted sat, by merit rais'd

    To that bad eminence; and from despair

    Thus high uplifted beyond hope, aspires

    Beyond thus high, insatiate to pursue

    Vain War with Heav'n, and by success° untaught   *result*

10   His proud imaginations thus display'd.

        Powers and Dominions,⁴ Deities of Heav'n,

    For since no deep within her gulf can hold

    Immortal vigor, though opprest and fall'n,

    I give not Heav'n for lost. From this descent

15   Celestial Virtues rising, will appear

    More glorious and more dread than from no fall

    And trust themselves to fear no second fate:

    Mee though just right and the fixt Laws of Heav'n

    Did first create your Leader, next, free choice,

20   With what besides, in Counsel or in Fight,

    Hath been achiev'd of merit, yet this loss

---

5. "Conclave" could refer to any assembly in secret session but already had the specifically ecclesiastical meaning on which Milton's satire here depends.
1. Disclose.
2. Compare Spenser's description of the bright throne of the Phaethonlike Lucifera, embodiment of pride in *The*

Faerie Queene 1.4.8, page 778.
3. India. Ormus, an island town in the Persian Gulf, was famous as a jewel market.
4. Two angelic orders mentioned by St. Paul in Colossians 1.16.

Thus far at least recover'd, hath much more
Establisht in a safe unenvied Throne
Yielded with full consent. The happier state
25 In Heav'n, which follows dignity, might draw
Envy from each inferior; but who here
Will envy whom the highest place exposes
Foremost to stand against the Thunderer's aim[5]
Your bulwark, and condemns to greatest share
30 Of endless pain? where there is then no good
For which to strive, no strife can grow up there
From Faction; for none sure will claim in Hell
Precedence, none, whose portion is so small
Of present pain, that with ambitious mind
35 Will covet more. With this advantage then
To union, and firm Faith, and firm accord,
More than can be in Heav'n, we now return
To claim our just inheritance of old,
Surer to prosper than prosperity
40 Could have assur'd us; and by what best way,
Whether of open War or covert guile,
We now debate; who can advise, may speak.
        He ceas'd, and next him *Moloch*, Scepter'd King
Stood up, the strongest and the fiercest Spirit
45 That fought in Heav'n; now fiercer by despair:
His trust was with th' Eternal to be deem'd
Equal in strength, and rather than be less
Car'd not to be at all; with that care lost
Went all his fear: of God, or Hell, or worse
50 He reck'd° not, and these words thereafter spake.   cared
        My sentence° is for open War: Of Wiles,   opinion
More unexpert,° I boast not: them let those   inexperienced
Contrive who need, or when they need, not now.
For while they sit contriving, shall the rest,
55 Millions that stand in Arms, and longing wait
The Signal to ascend, sit ling'ring here
Heav'n's fugitives, and for thir dwelling place
Accept this dark opprobrious Den of shame,
The Prison of his Tyranny who Reigns
60 By our delay? no, let us rather choose
Arm'd with Hell flames and fury[6] all at once
O'er Heav'n's high Tow'rs to force resistless way,
Turning our Tortures into horrid Arms
Against the Torturer; when to meet the noise
65 Of his Almighty Engine[7] he shall hear
Infernal Thunder, and for Lightning see
Black fire and horror shot with equal rage
Among his Angels; and his Throne itself

---

5. By identifying him with thunder, the attribute of Jupiter, Satan reduces God to a mere Olympian tyrant.
6. The violent yoking of concrete and abstract words is one of the most characteristic figures of Milton's style.
7. Machine of war, probably here referring to the Messiah's chariot or perhaps to his thunder.

Mixt with *Tartarean* Sulphur, and strange fire,[8]
70 His own invented Torments. But perhaps
The way seems difficult and steep to scale
With upright wing against a higher foe.
Let such bethink them, if the sleepy drench[9]
Of that forgetful Lake benumb not still,
75 That in our proper motion we ascend
Up to our native seat: descent and fall
To us is adverse. Who but felt of late
When the fierce Foe hung on our brok'n Rear
Insulting,° and pursu'd us through the Deep,   assaulting, exulting
80 With what compulsion and laborious flight
We sunk thus low? Th' ascent is easy then;
Th' event° is fear'd; should we again provoke   outcome
Our stronger, some worse way his wrath may find
To our destruction: if there be in Hell
85 Fear to be worse destroy'd: what can be worse
Than to dwell here, driv'n out from bliss, condemn'd
In this abhorred deep to utter woe;
Where pain of unextinguishable fire
Must exercise° us without hope of end   afflict
90 The Vassals[1] of his anger, when the Scourge
Inexorably, and the torturing hour
Calls us to Penance? More destroy'd than thus
We should be quite abolisht and expire.
What fear we then? what doubt we to incense
95 His utmost ire? which to the highth enrag'd,
Will either quite consume us, and reduce
To nothing this essential,° happier far   essence
Than miserable to have eternal being:
Or if our substance be indeed Divine,
100 And cannot cease to be, we are at worst
On this side nothing;[2] and by proof we feel
Our power sufficient to disturb his Heav'n,
And with perpetual inroads to Alarm,
Though inaccessible, his fatal Throne:
105 Which if not Victory is yet Revenge.
    He ended frowning, and his look denounc'd
Desperate revenge, and Battle dangerous
To less than Gods. On th' other side up rose
Belial, in act more graceful and humane;
110 A fairer person lost not Heav'n; he seem'd
For dignity compos'd and high exploit:
But all was false and hollow; though his Tongue
Dropt Manna, and could make the worse appear

8. In the classical underworld, Tartarus was the place of the guilty. For "strange fire" see Leviticus 10.1–2: "Nadab and Abihu, the sons of Aaron . . . offered strange fire before the Lord, which he commanded them not. And there went out fire from the Lord, and devoured them." 9. A draught of medicine for an animal.

1. Servants, slaves. Also an allusion to Romans 9.22: "What if God, willing to show his wrath, and to make his power known, endured with much longsuffering the vessels of wrath fitted to destruction . . . ?" 2. Already we are in the worst condition possible, short of being nothing, being annihilated.

The better reason,[3] to perplex and dash
Maturest Counsels: for his thoughts were low;
To vice industrious, but to Nobler deeds
Timorous and slothful: yet he pleas'd the ear,
And with persuasive accent thus began.
    I should be much for open War, O Peers,
As not behind in hate; if what was urg'd
Main reason to persuade immediate War,
Did not dissuade me most, and seem to cast
Ominous conjecture on the whole success:
When he who most excels in fact° of Arms,   *feat*
In what he counsels and in what excels
Mistrustful, grounds his courage on despair
And utter dissolution, as the scope
Of all his aim, after some dire revenge.
First, what Revenge? the Tow'rs of Heav'n are fill'd
With Armed watch, that render all access
Impregnable; oft on the bordering Deep
Encamp thir Legions, or with obscure[4] wing
Scout far and wide into the Realm of night,
Scorning surprise. Or could we break our way
By force, and at our heels all Hell should rise
With blackest Insurrection, to confound
Heav'n's purest Light, yet our great Enemy
All incorruptible would on his Throne
Sit unpolluted, and th' Ethereal mould
Incapable of stain would soon expel
Her mischief, and purge off the baser fire
Victorious.[5] Thus repuls'd, our final hope
Is flat° despair: we must exasperate   *absolute*
Th' Almighty Victor to spend all his rage,
And that must end us, that must be our cure,
To be no more; sad cure; for who would lose,
Though full of pain, this intellectual being,
Those thoughts that wander through Eternity,
To perish rather, swallow'd up and lost
In the wide womb of uncreated night,
Devoid of sense and motion? and who knows,
Let this be good,[6] whether our angry Foe
Can give it, or will ever? how he can
Is doubtful; that he never will is sure.
Will he, so wise, let loose at once his ire,
Belike° through impotence, or unaware,   *no doubt*
To give his Enemies thir wish, and end
Them in his anger, whom his anger saves
To punish endless? wherefore cease we then?

115
120
125
130
135
140
145
150
155

3. This was the claim of the Greek Sophists, who taught their students how to use rhetoric to win an argument.
4. "Obscure" is stressed on the first syllable here.
5. Criticizing Moloch's proposal to mix God's throne with sulphur (lines 68–9) and shoot "black fire" among

his angels. This "baser fire" Belial contrasts with the "ethereal" (derived from ether, the fifth and purest element) fire of the throne.
6. Suppose it is good to be destroyed.

160   Say they who counsel War, we are decreed,
Reserv'd and destin'd to Eternal woe;
Whatever doing, what can we suffer more,
What can we suffer worse? is this then worst,
Thus sitting, thus consulting, thus in Arms?

165   What when we fled amain,° pursu'd and strook°   *headlong/struck*
With Heav'n's afflicting Thunder, and besought
The Deep to shelter us? this Hell then seem'd
A refuge from those wounds: or when we lay
Chain'd on the burning Lake? that sure was worse.

170   What if the breath that kindl'd those grim fires
Awak'd should blow them into sevenfold rage
And plunge us in the flames? or from above
Should intermitted vengeance arm again
His red right hand to plague us? what if all

175   Her° stores were op'n'd, and this Firmament   *Hell's*
Of Hell should spout her Cataracts of Fire,
Impendent° horrors, threat'ning hideous fall   *threatening*
One day upon our heads; while we perhaps
Designing or exhorting glorious war,

180   Caught in a fiery Tempest shall be hurl'd
Each on his rock transfixt, the sport and prey
Of racking whirlwinds, or for ever sunk
Under yon boiling Ocean, wrapt in Chains;
There to converse with everlasting groans,

185   Unrespited, unpitied, unrepriev'd,
Ages of hopeless end; this would be worse.
War therefore, open or conceal'd, alike
My voice dissuades; for what can force or guile
With him, or who deceive his mind, whose eye

190   Views all things at one view? he from Heav'n's highth
All these our motions° vain, sees and derides;   *schemes*
Not more Almighty to resist our might
Than wise to frustrate all our plots and wiles.
Shall we then live thus vile, the race of Heav'n

195   Thus trampl'd, thus expell'd to suffer here
Chains and these Torments? better these than worse
By my advice; since fate inevitable
Subdues us, and Omnipotent Decree,
The Victor's will. To suffer, as to do,

200   Our strength is equal, nor the Law unjust
That so ordains: this was at first resolv'd,
If we were wise, against so great a foe
Contending, and so doubtful what might fall.
I laugh, when those who at the Spear are bold

205   And vent'rous, if that fail them, shrink and fear
What yet they know must follow, to endure
Exile, or ignominy, or bonds, or pain,
The sentence of thir Conqueror: This is now
Our doom; which if we can sustain and bear,

210   Our Supreme Foe in time may much remit

His anger, and perhaps thus far remov'd
Not mind us not offending, satisfi'd
With what is punisht; whence these raging fires
Will slack'n, if his breath stir not thir flames.

215 Our purer essence then will overcome
Thir noxious vapor, or enur'd° not feel,   *accustomed*
Or chang'd at length, and to the place conform'd
In temper[7] and in nature, will receive
Familiar the fierce heat, and void of pain;

220 This horror will grow mild, this darkness light,[8]
Besides what hope the never-ending flight
Of future days may bring, what chance, what change
Worth waiting, since our present lot appears
For happy though but ill, for ill not worst,[9]

225 If we procure not to ourselves more woe.
      Thus *Belial* with words cloth'd in reason's garb
Counsell'd ignoble ease, and peaceful sloth,
Not peace: and after him thus *Mammon* spake.
      Either to disinthrone the King of Heav'n

230 We war, if war be best, or to regain
Our own right lost: him to unthrone we then
May hope, when everlasting Fate shall yield
To fickle Chance, and *Chaos* judge the strife:
The former vain to hope argues as vain

235 The latter: for what place can be for us
Within Heav'n's bound, unless Heav'n's Lord supreme
We overpower? Suppose he should relent
And publish Grace to all, on promise made
Of new Subjection; with what eyes could we

240 Stand in his presence humble, and receive
Strict Laws impos'd, to celebrate his Throne
With warbl'd Hymns, and to his Godhead sing
Forc't Halleluiahs;[1] while he Lordly sits
Our envied Sovran, and his Altar breathes

245 Ambrosial[2] Odors and Ambrosial Flowers,
Our servile offerings. This must be our task
In Heav'n, this our delight; how wearisome
Eternity so spent in worship paid
To whom we hate. Let us not then pursue

250 By force impossible, by leave obtain'd
Unácceptable, though in Heav'n, our state
Of splendid vassalage, but rather seek
Our own good from ourselves, and from our own
Live to ourselves, though in this vast recess,

255 Free, and to none accountable, preferring

---

7. Temperament, the mixture or adjustment of humors. Thus the phrase means "adjusted psychologically and physically to the new environment."
8. Easy to bear, and illumination.
9. Though as far as happiness is concerned, the devils are but ill off, as far as evil is concerned, they could be worse.

1. The word "hallelujah" (Hebrew, "praise Jehovah") occurred in so many psalms that it came to mean a song of praise to God.
2. Fragrant and perfumed, immortal. Ambrosia was the fabled food or drink of the gods.

Hard liberty before the easy yoke
Of servile Pomp.[3] Our greatness will appear
Then most conspicuous, when great things of small,
Useful of hurtful, prosperous of adverse
260 We can create, and in what place soe'er
Thrive under evil, and work ease out of pain
Through labor and endurance. This deep world
Of darkness do we dread? How oft amidst
Thick clouds and dark doth Heav'n's all-ruling Sire
265 Choose to reside, his Glory unobscur'd,
And with the Majesty of darkness round
Covers his Throne; from whence deep thunders roar
Must'ring thir rage, and Heav'n resembles Hell?
As he our darkness, cannot we his Light
270 Imitate when we please? This Desert soil
Wants not her hidden lustre, Gems and Gold;
Nor want we skill or art, from whence to raise
Magnificence; and what can Heav'n show more?
Our torments also may in length of time
275 Become our Elements, these piercing Fires
As soft as now severe, our temper chang'd
Into their temper;[4] which must needs remove
The sensible of pain.[5] All things invite
To peaceful Counsels, and the settl'd State
280 Of order, how in safety best we may
Compose° our present evils, with regard   *order*
Of what we are and where, dismissing quite
All thoughts of War; ye have what I advise.
      He scarce had finisht, when such murmur fill'd
285 Th' Assembly, as when hollow Rocks retain
The sound of blust'ring winds, which all night long
Had rous'd the Sea, now with hoarse cadence lull
Sea-faring men o'erwatcht, whose Bark by chance
Or Pinnace anchors in a craggy Bay
290 After the Tempest: Such applause was heard
As *Mammon* ended, and his Sentence° pleas'd,   *opinion*
Advising peace: for such another Field
They dreaded worse than Hell: so much the fear
Of Thunder and the Sword of *Michaël*[6]
295 Wrought still within them; and no less desire
To found this nether Empire, which might rise
By policy,[7] and long process of time,
In emulation opposite to Heav'n.

3. In *Samson Agonistes* 271, Samson condemns those who are fonder of "bondage with ease than strenuous liberty." The antithesis is from the Roman historian, Sallust, who assigns it to an opponent of the dictator Sulla. See also Jesus' words in Matthew 11.28–30: "Come unto me. . . . For my yoke is easy."
4. Milton alludes to an idea of St. Augustine's, that the devils are bound to tormenting fires as if to bodies (*City of*

God, 21.10).
5. The part of pain apprehended through the senses.
6. In the war in Heaven, Michael's two-handed sword felled "squadrons at once" and wounded even Satan. "Michael" here has three syllables.
7. Statesmanship, often in a bad sense, implying Machiavellian strategems. "Process" is stressed on the second syllable.

Which when *Beëlzebub*[8] perceiv'd, than whom,
300 *Satan* except, none higher sat, with grave
Aspect he rose, and in his rising seem'd
A Pillar of State; deep on his Front° engraven   *forehead*
Deliberation sat and public care;
And Princely counsel in his face yet shone,
305 Majestic though in ruin: sage he stood
With *Atlantean*[9] shoulders fit to bear
The weight of mightiest Monarchies; his look
Drew audience and attention still as Night
Or Summer's Noon-tide air, while thus he spake.
310   Thrones and Imperial Powers, off-spring of Heav'n,
Ethereal Virtues; or these Titles now
Must we renounce, and changing style be call'd
Princes of Hell? for so the popular vote
Inclines, here to continue, and build up here
315 A growing Empire; doubtless; while we dream,
And know not that the King of Heav'n hath doom'd
This place our dungeon, not our safe retreat
Beyond his Potent arm, to live exempt
From Heav'n's high jurisdiction, in new League
320 Banded against his Throne, but to remain
In strictest bondage, though thus far remov'd,
Under th' inevitable curb, reserv'd
His captive multitude: For he, be sure,
In highth or depth, still first and last will Reign
325 Sole King, and of his Kingdom lose no part
By our revolt, but over Hell extend
His Empire, and with Iron Sceptre rule
Us here, as with his Golden those in Heav'n.
What° sit we then projecting peace and war?   *why*
330 War hath determin'd[1] us, and foil'd with loss
Irreparable; terms of peace yet none
Voutsaf't[2] or sought; for what peace will be giv'n
To us enslav'd, but custody severe,
And stripes, and arbitrary punishment
335 Inflicted? and what peace can we return,
But to our power[3] hostility and hate,
Untam'd reluctance,° and revenge though slow,   *resistance*
Yet ever plotting how the Conqueror least
May reap his conquest, and may least rejoice
340 In doing what we most in suffering feel?[4]
Nor will occasion want, nor shall we need
With dangerous expedition to invade

8. Satan's closest associate.
9. Worthy of Atlas, who was forced by Jupiter to carry the heavens on his shoulders as a punishment for his part in the rebellion of the Titans.
1. Finished, but the context also activates a subsidiary meaning, "war has given us a settled aim."

2. "Vouchsafed": granted; Milton's spelling, "Voutsaf't," indicates the 17th-century pronunciation he preferred.
3. To the limit of our power.
4. How God may get the least happiness from our pain. Beelzebub portrays God as similar in his motives to the devils.

Heav'n, whose high walls fear no assault or Siege,
Or ambush from the Deep. What if we find
345   Some easier enterprise? There is a place
(If ancient and prophetic fame in Heav'n
Err not) another World, the happy seat
Of some new Race call'd *Man*, about this time
To be created like to us, though less
350   In power and excellence, but favor'd more
Of him who rules above;[5] so was his will
Pronounc'd among the Gods, and by an Oath,
That shook Heav'n's whole circumference, confirm'd.[6]
Thither let us bend all our thoughts, to learn
355   What creatures there inhabit, of what mould,
Or substance, how endu'd,° and what thir Power,   *gifted*
And where thir weakness, how attempted° best,   *attacked*
By force or subtlety: Though Heav'n be shut,
And Heav'n's high Arbitrator sit secure
360   In his own strength, this place may lie expos'd
The utmost border of his Kingdom, left
To their defense who hold it: here perhaps
Some advantageous act may be achiev'd
By sudden onset, either with Hell fire
365   To waste his whole Creation, or possess
All as our own, and drive as we were driven,
The puny° habitants, or if not drive,   *weak*
Seduce them to our Party, that thir God
May prove thir foe, and with repenting hand
370   Abolish his own works. This would surpass
Common revenge, and interrupt his joy
In our Confusion, and our Joy upraise
In his disturbance; when his darling Sons
Hurl'd headlong to partake with us,[7] shall curse
375   Thir frail Original,° and faded bliss,   *author*
Faded so soon. Advise if this be worth
Attempting, or to sit in darkness here
Hatching vain Empires. Thus *Beëlzebub*
Pleaded his devilish Counsel, first devis'd
380   By *Satan*, and in part propos'd: for whence,
But from the Author of all ill could Spring
So deep a malice, to confound the race
Of mankind in one root,[8] and Earth with Hell
To mingle and involve, done all to spite
385   The great Creator? But thir spite still serves
His glory to augment. The bold design
Pleas'd highly those infernal States,[9] and joy

5. The creation of humanity was the subject of a public oath by God, but the time of the creation was the subject of a rumor only ("it is not for you to know the times or season," Acts 1.7).
6. See Isaiah 13.12–3: "I will make a man more precious than fine gold. . . . Therefore I will shake the Heavens."
7. Share in our condition; also, take sides with us.
8. Adam, the root of the genealogical tree of man.
9. Estates of the realm, people of rank and authority.

Sparkl'd in all thir eyes; with full assent
They vote: whereat his speech he thus renews.
390   Well have ye judg'd, well ended long debate,
Synod[1] of Gods, and like to what ye are,
Great things resolv'd, which from the lowest deep
Will once more lift us up, in spite of Fate,
Nearer our ancient Seat; perhaps in view
395 Of those bright confines, whence with neighboring Arms
And opportune excursion we may chance
Re-enter Heav'n; or else in some mild Zone
Dwell not unvisited of Heav'n's fair Light
Secure, and at the bright'ning Orient beam
400 Purge off this gloom; the soft delicious Air,
To heal the scar of these corrosive Fires
Shall breathe her balm. But first whom shall we send
In search of this new world, whom shall we find
Sufficient? who shall tempt° with wand'ring feet   *venture upon*
405 The dark unbottom'd infinite Abyss
And through the palpable obscure[2] find out
His uncouth° way, or spread his aery flight   *unknown*
Upborne with indefatigable wings
Over the vast abrupt,[3] ere he arrive
410 The happy Isle; what strength, what art can then
Suffice, or what evasion bear him safe
Through the strict Senteries° and Stations thick   *sentries*
Of Angels watching round? Here he had need
All circumspection, and wee now no less
415 Choice in our suffrage;[4] for on whom we send,
The weight of all and our last hope relies.
    This said, he sat; and expectation held
His look suspense, awaiting who appear'd
To second, or oppose, or undertake
420 The perilous attempt; but all sat mute,
Pondering the danger with deep thoughts; and each
In other's count'nance read his own dismay
Astonisht: none among the choice and prime
Of those Heav'n-warring Champions could be found
425 So hardy as to proffer° or accept   *offer*
Alone the dreadful voyage; till at last
Satan, whom now transcendent glory rais'd
Above his fellows, with Monarchal pride
Conscious of highest worth, unmov'd thus spake.
430   O Progeny of Heav'n, Empyreal Thrones,
With reason hath deep silence and demur°   *delay*
Seiz'd us, though undismay'd: long is the way
And hard, that out of Hell leads up to light;

1. A meeting of councillors.
2. See Exodus 10.21: "The Lord said unto Moses, Stretch out thine hand toward heaven, that there may be darkness over the land of Egypt, even darkness which may be felt."
3. The adjective (precipitous, broken off) is here used as a noun and refers to the abyss between hell and heaven.
4. Care in our vote (to elect him).

Our prison strong, this huge convex° of Fire,   *vault*
435   Outrageous to devour, immures us round
Ninefold, and gates of burning Adamant
Barr'd over us prohibit all egress.
These past, if any pass, the void profound
Of unessential° Night receives him next   *empty*
440   Wide gaping, and with utter loss of being
Threatens him, plung'd in that abortive gulf.
If thence he scape into whatever world,
Or unknown Region, what remains him less
Than⁵ unknown dangers and as hard escape.
445   But I should ill become this Throne, O Peers,
And this Imperial Sov'ranty, adorn'd
With splendor, arm'd with power, if aught propos'd
And judg'd of public moment, in the shape
Of difficulty or danger could deter
450   Mee from attempting. Wherefore do I assume
These Royalties, and not refuse to Reign,
Refusing⁶ to accept as great a share
Of hazard as of honor, due alike
To him who Reigns, and so much to him due
455   Of hazard more, as he above the rest
High honor'd sits? Go therefore mighty Powers.
Terror of Heav'n, though fall'n; intend° at home,   *consider*
While here shall be our home, what best may ease
The present misery, and render Hell
460   More tolerable; if there be cure or charm
To respite° or deceive, or slack the pain   *rest*
Of this ill Mansion: intermit no watch
Against a wakeful Foe, while I abroad
Through all the Coasts of dark destruction seek
465   Deliverance for us all: this enterprise
None shall partake with me. Thus saying rose
The Monarch, and prevented all reply,
Prudent, lest from his resolution rais'd°   *encouraged*
Others among the chief might offer now
470   (Certain to be refus'd) what erst they fear'd;
And so refus'd might in opinion stand
His Rivals, winning cheap the high repute
Which he through hazard huge must earn. But they
Dreaded not more th' adventure than his voice
475   Forbidding; and at once with him they rose;
Thir rising all at once was as the sound
Of Thunder heard remote. Towards him they bend
With awful° reverence prone; and as a God   *respectful*
Extol him equal to the highest in Heav'n:
480   Nor fail'd they to express how much they prais'd,
That for the general safety he despis'd
His own: for neither do the Spirits damn'd

5. What awaits him except.   6. If I refuse.

Lose all thir virtue; lest bad men should boast[7]
Thir specious° deeds on earth, which glory excites,   *pretending*
485   Or close° ambition varnisht o'er with zeal.   *secret*
Thus they thir doubtful consultations dark
Ended rejoicing in their matchless Chief:
As when from mountain tops the dusky clouds
Ascending, while the North wind sleeps, o'erspread
490   Heav'n's cheerful face, the low'ring Element
Scowls o'er the dark'n'd lantskip° Snow, or show'r;   *landscape*
If chance the radiant Sun with farewell sweet
Extend his ev'ning beam, the fields revive,
The birds thir notes renew, and bleating herds
495   Attest thir joy, that hill and valley rings.
O shame to men! Devil with Devil damn'd
Firm concord holds, men only disagree
Of Creatures rational, though under hope
Of heavenly Grace; and God proclaiming peace,
500   Yet live in hatred, enmity, and strife
Among themselves, and levy cruel wars,
Wasting the Earth, each other to destroy:
As if (which might induce us to accord)
Man had not hellish foes anow° besides,   *enough*
505   That day and night for his destruction wait.
    The *Stygian* Council thus dissolv'd; and forth
In order came the grand infernal Peers:
Midst came thir mighty Paramount,° and seem'd   *ruler*
Alone th' Antagonist of Heav'n, nor less
510   Than Hell's dread Emperor with pomp Supreme,[8]
And God-like imitated State; him round
A Globe° of fiery Seraphim inclos'd   *band*
With bright imblazonry,° and horrent° Arms.   *heraldry/bristling*
Then of thir Session ended they bid cry
515   With Trumpet's regal sound the great result:
Toward the four winds four speedy Cherubim
Put to thir mouths the sounding Alchymy[9]
By Herald's voice explain'd: the hollow Abyss
Heard far and wide, and all the host of Hell
520   With deaf'ning shout, return'd them loud acclaim.
Thence more at ease thir minds and somewhat rais'd°   *encouraged*
By false presumptuous hope, the ranged powers[1]
Disband, and wand'ring, each his several way
Pursues, as inclination or sad choice
525   Leads him perplext, where he may likeliest find
Truce to his restless thoughts, and entertain
The irksome hours, till this great Chief return.
Part on the Plain, or in the Air sublime°   *uplifted*
Upon the wing, or in swift Race contend,

---

7. So that men ought not to boast.
8. Lines 510–520 may portray the English mob's easy gulli-
bility and their passion (which Milton detested) for the
regalia of monarchy.

9. Trumpets made of the alloy brass, associated with
alchemy.
1. Armies drawn up in ranks.

530 As at th' *Olympian* Games or *Pythian* fields;[2]
  Part curb thir fiery Steeds, or shun the Goal
  With rapid wheels, or fronted Brígads form.
  As when to warn proud Cities war appears
  Wag'd in the troubl'd Sky, and Armies rush
535 To Battle in the Clouds, before each Van
  Prick forth the Aery Knights, and couch thir spears
  Till thickest Legions close; with feats of Arms
  From either end of Heav'n the welkin° burns.   *sky*
  Others with vast *Typhoean*[3] rage more fell
540 Rend up both Rocks and Hills, and ride the Air
  In whirlwind; Hell scarce holds the wild uproar.
  As when *Alcides* from *Oechalia* Crown'd
  With conquest, felt th' envenom'd robe, and tore
  Through pain up by the roots *Thessalian* Pines,
545 And *Lichas* from the top of *Oeta* threw
  Into th' *Euboic* Sea.[4] Others more mild,
  Retreated in a silent valley, sing
  With notes Angelical to many a Harp
  Thir own Heroic deeds and hapless fall
550 By doom of Battle; and complain that Fate
  Free Virtue should enthrall to Force or Chance.
  Thir Song was partial,° but the harmony   *prejudiced*
  (What could it less when Spirits immortal sing?)
  Suspended° Hell, and took with ravishment   *enthralled*
555 The thronging audience. In discourse more sweet
  (For Eloquence the Soul, Song charms the Sense,)
  Others apart sat on a Hill retir'd,
  In thoughts more elevate, and reason'd high
  Of Providence, Foreknowledge, Will, and Fate,
560 Fixt Fate, Free will, Foreknowledge absolute,
  And found no end, in wand'ring mazes lost.
  Of good and evil much they argu'd then,
  Of happiness and final misery,
  Passion and Apathy, and glory and shame,
565 Vain wisdom all, and false Philosophie:[5]
  Yet with a pleasing sorcery could charm
  Pain for a while or anguish, and excite
  Fallacious hope, or arm th' obdured° breast   *hardened*
  With stubborn patience as with triple steel.
570 Another part in Squadrons and gross° Bands, *dense*
  On bold adventure to discover wide
  That dismal World, if any Clime perhaps

---

2. Epic models for lines 528–569 include the sports of the Myrmidons during Achilles' absence from the war (Homer, *Iliad* 2.774ff.), the Greek funeral games of *Iliad* 23 and the Trojan of *Aeneid* 5, and the amusements of the blessed dead in Virgil's Elysium (*Aeneid* 6.642–59). To "shun the goal" (line 531) is to drive a chariot as close as possible around a post without touching it.
3. Like that of Typhon, the hundred-headed Titan. A pun, for "typhon" was also an English word meaning "whirlwind."

4. "Alcides" (Hercules) returning as victor from "Oechalia" (Ovid, *Metamorphoses* 9.136) put on a ritual robe that had inadvertently been soaked by his wife in corrosive poison. Mad with pain, he blamed his friend Lichas, who had brought the robe, and hurled him far into the "Euboic" (Euboean) Sea.
5. Directed against Stoicism, the most formidable ethical challenge to Christianity; "apathy," or complete freedom from passion, was a Stoic ideal.

Might yield them easier habitation, bend
Four ways thir flying March, along the Banks
575 Of four infernal Rivers that disgorge
Into the burning Lake thir baleful° streams;[6]   *evil*
Abhorred *Styx* the flood of deadly hate,
Sad *Acheron* of sorrow, black and deep;
Cocytus, nam'd of lamentation loud
580 Heard on the rueful stream; fierce *Phlegeton*
Whose waves of torrent fire inflame with rage.
Far off from these a slow and silent stream,
Lethe the River of Oblivion rolls
Her wat'ry Labyrinth, whereof who drinks,
585 Forthwith his former state and being forgets,
Forgets both joy and grief, pleasure and pain.
Beyond this flood a frozen Continent
Lies dark and wild, beat with perpetual storms
Of Whirlwind and dire Hail, which on firm land
590 Thaws not, but gathers heap, and ruin seems
Of ancient pile; all else deep snow and ice,
A gulf profound as that *Serbonian* Bog[7]
Betwixt *Damiata* and Mount *Casius* old,
Where Armies whole have sunk: the parching° Air   *withering*
595 Burns frore,° and cold performs th' effect of Fire.   *frozen*
Thither by harpy-footed Furies hal'd,[8]
At certain revolutions all the damn'd
Are brought: and feel by turns the bitter change
Of fierce extremes, extremes by change more fierce,
600 From Beds of raging Fire to starve° in Ice   *stifle*
Thir soft Ethereal warmth, and there to pine
Immovable, infixt, and frozen round,
Periods of time, thence hurried back to fire.
They ferry over this *Lethean* Sound
605 Both to and fro, thir sorrow to augment,
And wish and struggle, as they pass, to reach
The tempting stream, with one small drop to lose
In sweet forgetfulness all pain and woe,
All in one moment, and so near the brink;
610 But Fate withstands, and to oppose th' attempt
Medusa[9] with *Gorgonian* terror guards
The Ford, and of itself the water flies
All taste of living wight, as once it fled
The lip of *Tantalus*.[1] Thus roving on
615 In confus'd march forlorn, th' advent'rous Bands

---

6. This description of the four rivers of hell takes its broad outline from Virgil's (*Aeneid* 6), Dante's *Inferno* 14, and Spenser's *Faerie Queene* 2.7.56ff. Milton adds the detail of confluence in the "burning lake." The epithet or description attached to each river translates its Greek name (e.g., "Styx" means hateful).
7. Serbonis, a lake bordered by quicksands on the Egyptian coast.

8. Milton combines the hooked clawed Harpies of Dante and Virgil with the ancient Greek Furies, daughters of Acheron and Night and agencies of divine vengeance.
9. One of the Gorgons, mythical sisters with snakes for hair, whose look turned the beholder into stone.
1. In Homer's hell, Tantalus is tormented by thirst, standing in a pool that recedes whenever he tries to drink (*Odyssey* 11.582–92).

With shudd'ring horror pale, and eyes aghast
View'd first thir lamentable lot, and found
No rest: through many a dark and dreary Vale
They pass'd, and many a Region dolorous,
620   O'er many a Frozen, many a Fiery Alp,
Rocks, Caves, Lakes, Fens, Bogs, Dens, and shades of death,
A Universe of death, which God by curse
Created evil, for evil only good,
Where all life dies, death lives, and Nature breeds,
625   Perverse, all monstrous, all prodigious things,
Abominable, inutterable, and worse
Than Fables yet have feign'd, or fear conceiv'd,
Gorgons and Hydras, and Chimeras dire.[2]
        Meanwhile the Adversary of God and Man,
630   Satan with thoughts inflam'd of highest design,
Puts on swift wings, and towards the Gates of Hell
Explores his solitary flight; sometimes
He scours the right hand coast, sometimes the left,
Now shaves with level wing the Deep, then soars
635   Up to the fiery concave tow'ring high.
As when far off at Sea a Fleet descri'd
Hangs in the Clouds, by Equinoctial Winds
Close sailing from Bengala, or the Isles
Of Ternate and Tidore, whence Merchants bring
640   Thir spicy Drugs:[3] they on the Trading Flood
Through the wide Ethiopian to the Cape
Ply stemming nightly toward the Pole. So seem'd
Far off the flying Fiend: at last appear
Hell bounds high reaching to the horrid Roof,
645   And thrice threefold the Gates; three folds were Brass,
Three Iron, three of Adamantine Rock,
Impenetrable, impal'd° with circling fire,   *enclosed*
Yet unconsum'd. Before the Gates there sat
On either side a formidable shape;
650   The one seem'd Woman to the waist, and fair,[4]
But ended foul in many a scaly fold
Voluminous and vast, a Serpent arm'd
With mortal° sting: about her middle round   *death-dealing*
A cry of Hell Hounds never ceasing bark'd
655   With wide Cerberean mouths full loud, and rung
A hideous Peal:[5] yet, when they list, would creep,
If aught disturb'd thir noise, into her womb,
And kennel there, yet there still bark'd and howl'd
Within unseen. Far less abhorr'd than these

2. The Hydra was many-headed, and the Chimeras breathed flame.
3. In Milton's time there was increased trade with "Bengala" (Bengal) and "Ternate" and "Tidore" (two of the "spice islands," or Moluccas). The spice ships would cross the "Ethiopian" Sea (the Indian Ocean) before rounding the Cape of Good Hope.
4. The nearest analogue to Milton's Sin is probably

Spenser's Errour, who is half serpent and half woman, has a "mortal sting," and swallows her young (*The Faerie Queene* 1.1.14–16, pages 748–749). The serpent of sin that tempted Adam and Eve was traditionally portrayed as having a woman's head or bust.
5. There is a whole "cry" (pack) of hounds, because one sin engenders many consequences, sometimes hidden. Cerberus was the many-headed dog who guarded Hades.

660   Vex'd *Scylla* bathing in the Sea that parts
        Calabria from the hoarse *Trinacrian* shore:[6]
        Nor uglier follow the Night-Hag,[7] when call'd
        In secret, riding through the Air she comes
        Lur'd with the smell of infant blood, to dance
665   With *Lapland* Witches, while the laboring Moon
        Eclipses at thir charms. The other shape,
        If shape it might be call'd that shape had none
        Distinguishable in member, joint, or limb,
        Or substance might be call'd that shadow seem'd,
670   For each seem'd either; black it stood as Night,
        Fierce as ten Furies, terrible as Hell,
        And shook a dreadful Dart;[8] what seem'd his head
        The likeness of a Kingly Crown had on.
        Satan was now at hand, and from his seat
675   The Monster moving onward came as fast,
        With horrid strides; Hell trembled as he strode.
        Th' undaunted Fiend what this might be admir'd,°   *wondered*
        Admir'd, not fear'd; God and his Son except,
        Created thing naught valu'd he nor shunn'd;
680   And with disdainful look thus first began.
            Whence and what are thou, execrable shape,
        That dar'st, though grim and terrible, advance
        Thy miscreated Front athwart my way
        To yonder Gates? through them I mean to pass,
685   That be assured, without leave askt of thee:
        Retire, or taste thy folly, and learn by proof,°   *experience*
        Hell-born, not to contend with Spirits of Heav'n.
            To whom the Goblin full of wrath repli'd:
        Art thou that Traitor Angel, art thou hee,
690   Who first broke peace in Heav'n and Faith, till then
        Unbrok'n, and in proud rebellious Arms
        Drew after him the third part of Heav'n's Sons
        Conjur'd[9] against the Highest, for which both Thou
        And they outcast from God, are here condemn'd
695   To waste Eternal days in woe and pain?
        And reck'n'st thou thyself with Spirits of Heav'n,
        Hell-doom'd, and breath'st defiance here and scorn,
        Where I reign King, and to enrage thee more,
        Thy King and Lord? Back to thy punishment,
700   False fugitive, and to thy speed add wings,
        Lest with a whip of Scorpions I pursue
        Thy ling'ring, or with one stroke of this Dart
        Strange horror seize thee, and pangs unfelt before.

6. Circe, jealous of the nymph Scylla, changed her lower parts into a knot of "gaping dogs' heads, such as a Cerberus might have" (Ovid, *Metamorphoses* 14.50–74). Later Scylla was again transformed, into a dangerous rock between "Trinacria" (Sicily) and Calabria. In the medieval moralized Ovid, she became a symbol of lust or of sin.
7. Hecate, whose charms were used by Circe in her spell

against Scylla. Milton may allude here to the hellish yeth hounds, which, according to popular superstition, followed the queen of darkness across the sky in pursuit of the souls of the damned.
8. The "dreadful dart" was a traditional attribute of Death, signifying his sharpness and suddenness.
9. Sworn together in conspiracy; bewitched.

So spake the grisly terror, and in shape,
705 So speaking and so threat'ning, grew tenfold
More dreadful and deform: on th' other side
Incens't with indignation *Satan* stood
Unterrifi'd, and like a Comet burn'd,
That fires the length of *Ophiucus*[1] huge
710 In th' Artic Sky, and from his horrid hair
Shakes Pestilence and War. Each at the Head
Levell'd his deadly aim; thir fatal hands
No second stroke intend, and such a frown
Each cast at th' other, as when two black Clouds
715 With Heav'n's Artillery fraught, come rattling on
Over the *Caspian*, then stand front to front
Hov'ring a space, till Winds the signal blow
To join thir dark Encounter in mid air:
So frown'd the mighty Combatants, that Hell
720 Grew darker at thir frown, so matcht they stood;
For never but once more was either like
To meet so great a foe:[2] and now great deeds
Had been achiev'd, whereof all Hell had rung,
Had not the Snaky Sorceress that sat
725 Fast by Hell Gate, and kept the fatal Key,
Ris'n, and with hideous outcry rush'd between.
  O Father, what intends thy hand, she cri'd,
Against thy only Son?[3] What fury O Son,
Possesses thee to bend that mortal Dart
730 Against thy Father's head? and know'st for whom;
For him who sits above and laughs the while
At thee ordain'd his drudge, to execute
Whate'er his wrath, which he calls Justice, bids,
His wrath which one day will destroy ye both.
735   She spake, and at her words the hellish Pest
Forbore, then these to her *Satan* return'd:
  So strange thy outcry, and thy words so strange
Thou interposest, that my sudden hand
Prevented spares to tell thee yet by deeds
740 What it intends; till first I know of thee,
What thing thou art, thus double-form'd, and why
In this infernal Vale first met thou call'st
Me Father, and that Phantasm call'st my Son?
I know thee not, nor ever saw till now
745 Sight more detestable than him and thee.
  T' whom thus the Portress of Hell Gate repli'd:[4]
Hast thou forgot me then, and do I seem

---

1. The comet referred to here may be a magnificent one that appeared in 1618 in the constellation *Ophiuchus*. In his diary, John Evelyn held it responsible for the Thirty Years' War. Ophiuchus (Serpent Bearer) is also chosen to allude to Satan's later transformation into a serpent.
2. When Christ destroys "him that had the power of death, that is, the devil" (Hebrews 2.14), as well as "the last enemy . . . death" (1 Corinthians 15.26).
3. The allegory whereby Sin is daughter of Satan and mother of Death is from St. Basil's *Hexameron*.
4. Sin's office is an allegorical statement of the idea that access to hell is by sinning.

Now in thine eye so foul, once deem'd so fair
In Heav'n, when at th' Assembly, and in sight
750 Of all the Seraphim with thee combin'd
In bold conspiracy against Heav'n's King,
All on a sudden miserable pain
Surpris'd thee, dim thine eyes, and dizzy swum
In darkness, while thy head flames thick and fast
755 Threw forth, till on the left side op'ning wide,
Likest to thee in shape and count'nance bright,
Then shining heav'nly fair, a Goddess arm'd
Out of thy head I sprung:[5] amazement seiz'd
All th' Host of Heav'n; back they recoil'd afraid
760 At first, and call'd me *Sin*, and for a Sign
Portentous held me; but familiar grown,
I pleas'd, and with attractive graces won
The most averse, thee chiefly, who full oft
Thyself in me thy perfect image viewing
765 Becam'st enamor'd, and such joy thou took'st
With me in secret, that my womb conceiv'd
A growing burden. Meanwhile War arose,
And fields were fought in Heav'n: wherein remain'd
(For what could else) to our Almighty Foe
770 Clear Victory, to our part loss and rout
Through all the Empyrean: down they fell
Driv'n headlong from the Pitch° of Heaven, down   summit
Into this Deep, and in the general fall
I also; at which time this powerful Key
775 Into my hand was giv'n, with charge to keep
These Gates for ever shut, which none can pass
Without my op'ning. Pensive here I sat
Alone, but long I sat not, till my womb
Pregnant by thee, and now excessive grown
780 Prodigious motion felt and rueful throes.
At last this odious offspring whom thou seest
Thine own begotten, breaking violent way
Tore through my entrails, that with fear and pain
Distorted, all my nether shape thus grew
785 Transform'd: but he my inbred enemy
Forth issu'd, brandishing his fatal Dart
Made to destroy: I fled, and cri'd out *Death*;
Hell trembl'd at the hideous Name, and sigh'd
From all her Caves, and back resounded *Death*.
790 I fled, but he pursu'd (though more, it seems,
Inflam'd with lust than rage) and swifter far,
Mee overtook his mother all dismay'd,
And in embraces forcible and foul
Ingend'ring with me, of that rape begot

5. The circumstances of Sin's birth recall the ancient myth about Athena springing fully formed from the head of Zeus. It is thus presented as a parody of God's generation of the Son, since Minerva's birth had traditionally been allegorized by theologians in that sense.

795 These yelling Monsters that with ceasless cry
    Surround me, as thou saw'st, hourly conceiv'd
    And hourly born, with sorrow infinite
    To me, for when they list, into the womb
    That bred them they return, and howl and gnaw
800 My Bowels, thir repast; then bursting forth
    Afresh with conscious terrors vex° me round,   *harass*
    That rest or intermission none I find.⁶
    Before mine eyes in opposition sits
    Grim *Death* my Son and foe, who sets them on,
805 And me his Parent would full soon devour
    For want of other prey, but that he knows
    His end with mine involv'd; and knows that I
    Should prove a bitter Morsel, and his bane,
    Whenever that shall be; so Fate pronounc'd.
810 But thou O Father, I forewarn thee, shun
    His deadly arrow; neither vainly hope
    To be invulnerable in those bright Arms,
    Though temper'd heav'nly, for that mortal dint,
    Save he who reigns above, none can resist.⁷
815   She finish'd, and the subtle Fiend his lore
    Soon learn'd, now milder, and thus answer'd smooth.
    Dear Daughter, since thou claim'st me for thy Sire,
    And my fair Son here shows't me, the dear pledge
    Of dalliance had with thee in Heav'n, and joys
820 Then sweet, now sad to mention, through dire change
    Befall'n us unforeseen, unthought of, know
    I come no enemy, but to set free
    From out this dark and dismal house of pain,
    Both him and thee, and all the heav'nly Host
825 Of Spirits that in our just pretenses arm'd
    Fell with us from on high: from them I go
    This uncouth° errand sole, and one for all   *strange*
    Myself expose, with lonely steps to tread
    Th' unfounded° deep, and through the void immense   *bottomless*
830 To search with wand'ring quest a place foretold
    Should be, and, by concurring signs, ere now
    Created vast and round, a place of bliss
    In the Purlieus° of Heav'n, and therein plac't   *outskirts*
    A race of upstart Creatures, to supply
835 Perhaps our vacant room, though more remov'd,
    Lest Heav'n surcharg'd° with potent multitude   *too full*
    Might hap to move new broils: Be this or aught
    Than this more secret now design'd, I haste
    To know, and this once known, shall soon return,
840 And bring ye to the place where Thou and Death
    Shall dwell at ease, and up and down unseen

6. Here Sin's offspring appear to symbolize the pangs of   7. "Dint," stroke given with a weapon. Only God is
guilt or fear. "Conscious terrors" are terrors of guilty   immune to death.
knowledge.

Wing silently the buxom° Air, imbalm'd[8]　　　　　　　　*unresisting*
With odors; there ye shall be fed and fill'd
Immeasurably, all things shall be your prey.
845　　He ceas'd, for both seem'd highly pleas'd, and Death
Grinn'd horrible a ghastly smile, to hear
His famine° should be fill'd, and blest his maw　　　　*hunger*
Destin'd to that good hour: no less rejoic'd
His mother bad, and thus bespake her Sire.
850　　The key of this infernal Pit by due,
And by command of Heav'n's all-powerful King
I keep, by him forbidden to unlock
These Adamantine Gates; against all force
Death ready stands to interpose his dart,
855　　Fearless to be o'ermatcht by living might.
But what owe I to his commands above
Who hates me, and hath hither thrust me down
Into this gloom of *Tartarus* profound,
To sit in hateful Office here confin'd,
860　　Inhabitant of Heav'n, and heav'nly-born,
Here in perpetual agony and pain,
With terrors and with clamors compasst round
Of mine own brood, that on my bowels feed:
Thou art my Father, thou my Author, thou
865　　My being gav'st me; whom should I obey
But thee, whom follow? thou wilt bring me soon
To that new world of light and bliss, among
The Gods who live at ease, where I shall Reign
At thy right hand voluptuous, as beseems
870　　Thy daughter and thy darling, without end.[9]
　　Thus saying, from her side the fatal Key,
Sad instrument of all our woe, she took;[1]
And towards the Gate rolling her bestial train,
Forthwith the huge Portcullis high up drew,
875　　Which but herself not all the *Stygian* powers
Could once have mov'd; then in the key-hole turns
Th' intricate wards,[2] and every Bolt and Bar
Of massy Iron or solid Rock with ease
Unfast'ns: on a sudden op'n fly
880　　With impetuous recoil and jarring sound
Th' infernal doors, and on thir hinges grate
Harsh Thunder, that the lowest bottom shook
Of *Erebus*.[3] She op'n'd, but to shut
Excell'd her power; the Gates wide op'n stood,
885　　That with extended wings a Banner'd Host
Under spread Ensigns marching might pass through
With Horse and Chariots rankt in loose array;

8. Balmy, rendered resistent to decay.
9. Parodying the Nicene creed ("on the right hand of the Father . . . [Christ] whose kingdom shall have no end"). In Sin's fantasy she enjoys glory like Christ's. Satan, Sin, and Death form a complete anti-Trinity.

1. "Sad instrument" may stand in apposition to "she" as well as to "key"; it could mean "a person made use of by another, for the accomplishment of a purpose."
2. The incisions in a key's bit.
3. Classical name for Hell.

So wide they stood, and like a Furnace mouth
Cast forth redounding° smoke and ruddy flame.   *surging*
890   Before thir eyes in sudden view appear
The secrets of the hoary deep, a dark
Illimitable Ocean without bound,
Without dimension, where length, breadth, and highth,
And time and place are lost; where eldest *Night*
895   And *Chaos*, Ancestors of Nature, hold
Eternal Anarchy, amidst the noise
Of endless wars, and by confusion stand.
For hot, cold, moist, and dry, four Champions fierce
Strive here for Maistry, and to Battle bring
900   Thir embryon Atoms;[4] they around the flag
Of each his Faction, in thir several Clans,
Light-arm'd or heavy, sharp, smooth, swift or slow,
Swarm populous, unnumber'd as the Sands
Of *Barca* or *Cyrene's* torrid soil,[5]
905   Levied° to side with warring Winds, and poise   *enlisted*
Thir lighter wings. To whom these most adhere,
Hee rules a moment; *Chaos* Umpire sits,
And by decision more imbroils the fray
By which he Reigns: next him high Arbiter
910   *Chance* governs all. Into this wild Abyss,
The Womb of nature and perhaps her Grave,
Of neither Sea, nor Shore, nor Air, nor Fire,
But all these in thir pregnant causes mixt
Confus'dly, and which thus must ever fight,
915   Unless th' Almighty Maker them ordain
His dark materials to create more Worlds,
Into this wild Abyss the wary fiend
Stood on the brink of Hell and look'd a while,
Pondering his Voyage: for no narrow frith°   *channel*
920   He had to cross. Nor was his ear less peal'd°   *dinned*
With noises loud and ruinous (to compare
Great things with small) than when *Bellona*[6] storms,
With all her battering Engines bent to rase
Some Capital City; or less than if this frame
925   Of Heav'n were falling, and these Elements
In mutiny had from her Axle torn
The steadfast Earth. At last his Sail-broad Vans°   *wings*
He spreads for flight, and in the surging smoke
Uplifted spurns the ground, thence many a League
930   As in a cloudy Chair ascending rides
Audacious, but that seat soon failing, meets
A vast vacuity: all unawares

---

4. In works such as Hesiod's *Theogony* and Boccaccio's
De genealogis, Chaos and Night were made "ancestors"
of nature. Milton's description of the strife between
contrary qualities that preceded the emergence of the
cosmos is close to Ovid's account of the primeval chaos
in which "cold things strove with hot, moist with dry,

soft with hard, weightless with heavy" (*Metamorphoses*
1.19ff.).
5. "Barca," an ancient city of Cyrenaica, of which
"Cyrene" was the capital.
6. Goddess of war, here a metonymy for war itself.

	Flutt'ring his pennons° vain plumb down he drops	*wings*
	Ten thousand fadom° deep, and to this hour	*fathoms*
935	Down had been falling, had not by ill chance	
	The strong rebuff of some tumultuous cloud	
	Instinct° with Fire and Nitre hurried him	*inflamed*
	As many miles aloft: that fury stay'd,	
	Quencht in a Boggy *Syrtis*, neither Sea,[7]	
940	Nor good dry Land, nigh founder'd on he fares,	
	Treading the crude consistence, half on foot,	
	Half flying;[8] behoves him now both Oar and Sail.	
	As when a Gryfon through the Wilderness	
	With winged course o'er Hill or moory Dale,	
945	Pursues the *Arimaspian*, who by stealth	
	Had from his wakeful custody purloin'd	
	The guarded Gold: So eagerly the fiend	
	O'er bog or steep, through strait, rough, dense, or rare,	
	With head, hands, wings, or feet pursues his way,	
950	And swims or sinks, or wades, or creeps, or flies:	
	At length a universal hubbub wild	
	Of stunning sounds and voices all confus'd	
	Borne through the hollow dark assaults his ear	
	With loudest vehemence: thither he plies,	
955	Undaunted to meet there whatever power	
	Or Spirit of the nethermost Abyss	
	Might in that noise reside, of whom to ask	
	Which way the nearest coast of darkness lies	
	Bordering on light; when straight behold the Throne	
960	Of *Chaos*, and his dark Pavilion spread	
	Wide on the wasteful Deep; with him Enthron'd	
	Sat Sable-vested *Night*, eldest of things,	
	The Consort of his Reign; and by them stood	
	Orcus and *Ades*, and the dreaded name	
965	Of *Demogorgon*;[9] *Rumor* next and *Chance*,	
	And *Tumult* and *Confusion* all imbroil'd,	
	And *Discord* with a thousand various mouths.	
	T' whom *Satan* turning boldly, thus. Ye Powers	
	And Spirits of this nethermost Abyss,	
970	*Chaos* and *ancient Night*, I come no Spy,	
	With purpose to explore or to disturb	
	The secrets of your Realm, but by constraint	
	Wand'ring this darksome Desert, as my way	
	Lies through your spacious Empire up to light,	

7. The Syrtes were two huge and proverbially dangerous shifting sandbanks off the North African shore.
8. Spenser's dragon of evil is similarly described as "halfe flying, and halfe footing in his hast" (*The Faerie Queene* 1.11.8). The legend of "gold-guarding griffins" in Scythia, from whom the one-eyed Arimaspi steal, was often retold out of Herodotus (3.116) and Pliny (*Natural History* 7.10). The griffin (a composite monster: half eagle, half lion) is appropriate here partly because it was subdued by the sun god Apollo, as Satan will be by Christ.

9. In general, this court of personifications resembles Virgil's halls of Pluto (*Aeneid* 6.268–81), though the only member common to both is Discord. Milton's Demogorgon is from Boccaccio's *De genealogiis deorum*, in which he comes first of all the dark gods. Among his brood are Night, Tartarus, Erebus, the serpent Python, Litigium (cf. Milton's Tumult and Discord), and Fama (Milton's Rumor). Orcus and Ades are Latin and Greek names of Pluto, god of hell.

975 Alone, and without guide, half lost, I seek
 What readiest path leads where your gloomy bounds
 Confine with° Heav'n; or if some other place   *border on*
 From your Dominion won, th' Ethereal King
 Possesses lately, thither to arrive
980 I travel this profound,° direct my course;   *deep pit*
 Directed, no mean recompence it brings
 To your behoof, if I that Region lost,
 All usurpation thence expell'd, reduce
 To her original darkness and your sway
985 (Which is my present journey) and once more
 Erect the Standard there of *ancient Night;*
 Yours be th' advantage all, mine the revenge.
  Thus *Satan;* and him thus the Anarch[1] old
 With falt'ring speech and visage incompos'd°   *disordered*
990 Answer'd. I know thee, stranger, who thou art,
 That mighty leading Angel, who of late
 Made head against Heav'n's King, though overthrown.
 I saw and heard, for such a numerous Host
 Fled not in silence through the frighted deep
995 With ruin upon ruin, rout on rout,
 Confusion worse confounded; and Heav'n Gates
 Pour'd out by millions her victorious Bands
 Pursuing. I upon my Frontiers here
 Keep residence; if all I can will serve,
1000 That little which is left so to defend,
 Encroacht on still through our intestine broils
 Weak'ning the Sceptre of old *Night:* first Hell
 Your dungeon stretching far and wide beneath;
 Now lately Heaven and Earth, another World
1005 Hung o'er my Realm, link'd in a golden Chain
 To that side Heav'n from whence your Legions fell:
 If that way be your walk, you have not far;
 So much the nearer danger; go and speed;
 Havoc and spoil and ruin are my gain.
1010 He ceas'd; and *Satan* stay'd not to reply,
 But glad that now his Sea should find a shore,
 With fresh alacrity and force renew'd
 Springs upward like a Pyramid of fire
 Into the wild expanse, and through the shock
1015 Of fighting Elements, on all sides round
 Environ'd wins his way; harder beset
 And more endanger'd, than when *Argo* pass'd
 Through *Bosporus* betwixt the justling° Rocks:[2]   *jostling*
 Or when *Ulysses* on the Larboard shunn'd
1020 *Charybdis,* and by th' other whirlpool steer'd.[3]

1. Chaos, ruler or antiruler of the "eternal anarchy" (line 896).
2. When Jason and the Argonauts sailed through the Bosporus (Straits of Constantinople) en route to Colchis, their boat, the *Argo,* narrowly escaped destruction between the Symplegades, the clashing or "jostling"

rocks. See Apollonius Rhodius, *Argonautica* 2.317, 552–611.
3. Homer tells how Odysseus followed Circe's advice in avoiding Charybdis and sailing close by Scylla ("the other whirlpool") in his passage through the Straits of Messina between Sicily and Italy (*Odyssey* 12).

So he with difficulty and labor hard
Mov'd on, with difficulty and labor hee;
But hee once past, soon after when man fell,
Strange alteration! Sin and Death amain°   *without delay*
1025 Following his track, such was the will of Heav'n,
Pav'd after him a broad and beat'n way
Over the dark Abyss, whose boiling Gulf
Tamely endur'd a Bridge of wondrous length
From Hell continu'd reaching th' utmost Orb
1030 Of this frail World; by which the Spirits perverse
With easy intercourse pass to and fro
To tempt or punish mortals, except whom
God and good Angels guard by special grace.
But now at last the sacred influence
1035 Of light appears, and from the walls of Heav'n
Shoots far into the bosom of dim Night
A glimmering dawn; here Nature first begins
Her fardest° verge, and *Chaos* to retire   *farthest*
As from her outmost works a brok'n foe
1040 With tumult less and with less hostile din,
That *Satan* with less toil, and now with ease
Wafts on the calmer wave by dubious light
And like a weather-beaten Vessel holds°   *remains in*
Gladly the Port, though Shrouds and Tackle torn;
1045 Or in the emptier waste, resembling Air,
Weighs his spread wings, at leisure to behold
Far off th' Empyreal Heav'n, extended wide
In circuit, undetermin'd square or round,[4]
With Opal Tow'rs and Battlements adorn'd
1050 Of living° Sapphire, once his native Seat;   *unshaped*
And fast by hanging in a golden Chain[5]
This pendant world, in bigness as a Star
Of smallest Magnitude close by the Moon.
Thither full fraught with mischievous revenge,
1055 Accurst, and in a cursed hour he hies.
                    The End of the Second Book.

from **Book 3**
The Argument

God *sitting on his Throne sees* Satan *flying towards this world, then newly created;
shows him to the Son who sat at his right hand; foretells the success of* Satan *in pervert-
ing mankind; clears his own Justice and Wisdom from all imputation, having created
Man free and able enough to have withstood his Tempter; yet declares his purpose of
grace towards him, in regard he fell not of his own malice, as did* Satan, *but by him
seduc't. The Son of God renders praises to his Father for the manifestation of his gra-*

---

4. So wide that it was impossible to tell whether the boundary was rectilinear or curved.
5. Homer's Zeus asserts his transcendence by claiming that if a golden chain were lowered from Heaven, he could draw up by it all the other gods, together with the earth and the sea, and hang them from a pinnacle of Olympus (*Iliad* 8.18–27). Milton interprets this chain as "the universal concord and sweet union of all things which Pythagoras poetically figures as harmony" (*Prolusion* 2), thus accepting a philosophical and literary tradition that runs from Plato through Boethius, Chaucer, and Spenser.

cious purpose towards Man; but God again declares, that Grace cannot be extended towards Man without the satisfaction of divine Justice; Man hath offended the majesty of God by aspiring to Godhead, and therefore with all his Progeny devoted to death must die, unless some one can be found sufficient to answer for his offense, and undergo his Punishment. The Son of God freely offers himself a Ransom for Man: the Father accepts him, ordains his incarnation, pronounces his exaltation above all Names in Heaven and Earth; commands all the Angels to adore him; they obey, and hymning to thir Harps in full Choir, celebrate the Father and the Son. Meanwhile Satan alights upon the bare convex of this World's outermost Orb; where wand'ring he first finds a place since call'd The Limbo of Vanity; what persons and things fly up thither; thence comes to the Gate of Heaven, describ'd ascending by stairs, and the waters above the Firmament that flow about it: His passage thence to the Orb of the Sun; he finds there Uriel the Regent of that Orb, but first changes himself into the shape of a meaner Angel; and pretending a zealous desire to behold the new Creation and Man whom God had plac't there, inquires of him the place of his habitation, and is directed; alights first on Mount Niphates.

	Hail holy Light, offspring of Heav'n first-born,	
	Or of th' Eternal Coeternal beam	
	May I express thee unblam'd?[1] since God is Light,	
	And never but in unapproached Light	
5	Dwelt from Eternity, dwelt then in thee,	
	Bright effluence° of bright essence increate.[2]	*radiance*
	Or hear'st thou rather[3] pure Ethereal stream,	
	Whose Fountain who shall tell? before the Sun,	
	Before the Heavens thou wert, and at the voice	
10	Of God, as with a Mantle didst invest°	*cover*
	The rising world of waters dark and deep,	
	Won from the void° and formless infinite.[4]	*chaos*
	Thee I revisit now with bolder wing,	
	Escap't the *Stygian* Pool, though long detain'd	
15	In that obscure sojourn, while in my flight	
	Through utter and through middle darkness borne[5]	
	With other notes than to th' *Orphean* Lyre	
	I sung of *Chaos* and *Eternal Night*,	
	Taught by the heav'nly Muse° to venture down	*Urania*
20	The dark descent, and up to reascend,	
	Though hard and rare:[6] thee I revisit safe,	
	And feel thy sovran vital Lamp; but thou	

1. The light of the invocation has been interpreted as the Son of God, as physical light, and as the principal image of God and the divine emanation itself, according to the Platonic system. Milton proposes three images or forms of address, "offspring," "beam," and "stream," each of which associates the divine Light or Wisdom with a different aspect of deity. The blame could attach only to using the second name, "co-eternal beam"; it is this name that is justified by the implicit appeal to scriptural authority. 2. "God is Light," from 1 John 1.5. God "only hath immortality, dwelling in the light which no man can approach unto" (1 Timothy 6.16). "Essence increate," the uncreated divine essence. In the physics and metaphysics of Milton's time, light was regarded as an "acci-

dent" (quality), not a body or substance.
3. Do you prefer to be called.
4. See Genesis 1.1–5.
5. The "Stygian pool" and the "utter" (outer) darkness are hell; the "middle darkness" is chaos.
6. Alluding to the "fable of Orpheus, whom they faigne to have recovered his Euridice from Hell with his Musick, that is, Truth and Equity from darkenesse of Barbarisme and Ignorance with his profound and excellent Doctrines; but, that in the way to the upper-earth, she was lost againe" (Henry Reynolds, *Mythomystes*). "Other notes," because Milton, unlike Orpheus, claims not to have lost his Eurydice.

Revisit'st not these eyes, that roll in vain
To find thy piercing ray, and find no dawn;
25 So thick a drop serene[7] hath quencht thir Orbs,
Or dim suffusion° veil'd. Yet not the more   *cataract*
Cease I to wander where the Muses haunt
Clear Spring, or shady Grove, or Sunny Hill,
Smit with the love of sacred Song;[8] but chief
30 Thee *Sion*[9] and the flow'ry Brooks beneath
That wash thy hallow'd feet, and warbling flow,
Nightly I visit: nor sometimes forget
Those other two equall'd with me in Fate,
So were I equall'd with them in renown,
35 Blind *Thamyris* and blind *Maeonides*,
And *Tiresias* and *Phineus* Prophets old.[1]
Then feed on thoughts, that voluntary move
Harmonious numbers;° as the wakeful Bird[2]   *rhythmic measure*
Sings darkling,° and in shadiest Covert hid   *in the dark*
40 Tunes her nocturnal Note. Thus with the Year
Seasons return, but not to me returns
Day, or the sweet approach of Ev'n or Morn,
Or sight of vernal bloom, or Summer's Rose,
Or flocks, or herds, or human face divine;
45 But cloud instead, and ever-during dark
Surrounds me, from the cheerful ways of men
Cut off, and for the Book of knowledge[3] fair
Presented with a Universal blanc°   *blank*
Of Nature's works to me expung'd and ras'd,°   *erased*
50 And wisdom at one entrance quite shut out.
So much the rather thou Celestial Light
Shine inward, and the mind through all her powers
Irradiate, there plant eyes, all mist from thence
Purge and disperse, that I may see and tell
55 Of things invisible to mortal sight.
　　Now had th' Almighty Father from above,
From the pure Empyrean where he sits
High Thron'd above all highth, bent down his eye,
His own works and their works at once to view:
60 About him all the Sanctities of Heaven
Stood thick as Stars, and from his sight receiv'd
Beatitude past utterance; on his right
The radiant image of his Glory sat,
His only Son; On Earth he first beheld

7. Literally translating *gutta serena*, the medical term for the form of blindness from which Milton suffered.
8. An allusion to Virgil's prayer that "smitten with a great love" of the Muses, he may be shown by them the secrets of nature (*Georgics* 2.475–489).
9. The mountain of scriptural inspiration.
1. Thamyris was a Thracian poet who fell in love with the Muses and challenged them to a contest in which the loser was to give the winner whatever he wanted. The Muses, having won, took Thamyris's eyes and his lyre.

Maeonides was Homer's surname; the contrast between his outward blindness and inner vision was a commonplace. In *De Idea Platonica*, Milton writes of Tiresias that his "very blindness gave him boundless light." The Thracian king Phineus lost his sight because he had become too good a prophet.
2. The nightingale. The soul of Thamyris passed into a nightingale.
3. The Book of Nature.

65   Our two first Parents, yet the only two
      Of mankind, in the happy Garden plac't,
      Reaping immortal fruits of joy and love,
      Uninterrupted joy, unrivall'd love
      In blissful solitude; he then survey'd
70   Hell and the Gulf between, and *Satan* there
      Coasting the wall of Heav'n on this side Night
      In the dun° Air sublime,° and ready now   *dusky/aloft*
      To stoop with wearied wings, and willing feet
      On the bare outside of this World, that seem'd
75   Firm land imbosom'd without Firmament,[4]
      Uncertain which, in Ocean or in Air.
      Him God beholding from his prospect high,
      Wherein past, present, future he beholds,
      Thus to his only Son foreseeing spake.
80   Only begotten Son, seest thou what rage
      Transports our adversary, whom no bounds
      Prescrib'd, no bars of Hell, nor all the chains
      Heapt on him there, nor yet the main Abyss
      Wide interrupt° can hold; so bent he seems   *divided*
85   On desperate revenge, that shall redound
      Upon his own rebellious head. And now
      Through all restraint broke loose he wings his way
      Not far off Heav'n, in the Precincts of light,
      Directly towards the new created World,
90   And Man there plac't, with purpose to assay°   *test*
      If him by force he can destroy, or worse,
      By some false guile pervert; and shall pervert;
      For Man will heark'n to his glozing° lies,   *flattering*
      And easily transgress the sole Command,[5]
95   Sole pledge of his obedience: So will fall
      Hee and his faithless Progeny: whose fault?
      Whose but his own? ingrate, he had of mee
      All he could have; I made him just and right,
      Sufficient to have stood, though free to fall.
100   Such I created all th' Ethereal Powers
      And Spirits, both them who stood and them who fail'd;
      Freely they stood who stood, and fell who fell.
      Not free, what proof could they have giv'n sincere
      Of true allegiance, constant Faith or Love,
105   Where only what they needs must do, appear'd,
      Not what they would? what praise could they receive?
      What pleasure I from such obedience paid,
      When Will and Reason (Reason also is choice)
      Useless and vain, of freedom both despoil'd,
110   Made passive both, had serv'd necessity,
      Not mee. They therefore as to right belong'd,
      So were created, nor can justly accuse

---

4. The firmament or atmosphere, being inside the shell of   5. I.e., not to taste the fruit of the forbidden tree.
the universe that Satan stands on, is invisible to him.

Thir maker, or thir making, or thir Fate;
As if Predestination over-rul'd

115 Thir will, dispos'd by absolute Decree
Or high foreknowledge; they themselves decreed
Thir own revolt, not I: if I foreknew,
Foreknowledge had no influence on their fault,
Which had no less prov'd certain unforeknown.

120 So without least impulse or shadow of Fate,
Or aught by me immutably foreseen,
They trespass, Authors to themselves in all
Both what they judge and what they choose; for so
I form'd them free, and free they must remain,

125 Till they enthrall themselves: I else must change
Thir nature, and revoke the high Decree
Unchangeable, Eternal, which ordain'd
Thir freedom: they themselves ordain'd thir fall.
The first sort[6] by thir own suggestion° fell,   *temptation*

130 Self-tempted, self-deprav'd: Man falls deceiv'd
By th' other first: Man therefore shall find grace,
The other none: in Mercy and Justice both,
Through Heav'n and Earth, so shall my glory excel,
But Mercy first and last shall brightest shine.

135   Thus while God spake, ambrosial fragrance fill'd
All Heav'n, and in the blessed Spirits elect[7]
Sense of new joy ineffable diffus'd:
Beyond compare the Son of God was seen
Most glorious, in him all his Father shone

140 Substantially express'd, and in his face
Divine compassion visibly appear'd,
Love without end, and without measure Grace,
Which uttering thus he to his Father spake.
    O Father, gracious was that word which clos'd

145 Thy sovran° sentence, that Man should find grace;   *sovereign*
For which both Heav'n and Earth shall high extol
Thy praises, with th' innumerable sound
Of Hymns and sacred Songs, wherewith thy Throne
Encompass'd shall resound thee ever blest.

150 For should Man finally be lost, should Man
Thy creature late so lov'd, thy youngest Son
Fall circumvented thus by fraud, though join'd
With his own folly? that be from thee far,
That far be from thee, Father, who art Judge

155 Of all things made, and judgest only right.
Or shall the Adversary[8] thus obtain
His end, and frustrate thine, shall he fulfil
His malice, and thy goodness bring to naught,
Or proud return though to his heavier doom,

6. Satan and the rebel angels.
7. The "elect angels" of 1 Timothy 5.21, explained in Milton's *De doctrina* 1.9 as angels "who have not revolted."
8. The literal meaning of "Satan."

160   Yet with revenge accomplish't and to Hell
        Draw after him the whole Race of mankind,
        By him corrupted? or wilt thou thyself
        Abolish thy Creation, and unmake,
        For him, what for thy glory thou hast made?
165   So should thy goodness and thy greatness both
        Be question'd and blasphem'd without defense.
            To whom the great Creator thus repli'd.
        O Son, in whom my Soul hath chief delight,[9]
        Son of my bosom, Son who art alone
170   My word, my wisdom, and effectual might,
        All hast thou spok'n as my thoughts are, all
        As my Eternal purpose hath decreed:
        Man shall not quite be lost, but sav'd who will,
        Yet not of will in him, but grace in me
175   Freely voutsaf't;° once more I will renew   *vouchsafed*
        His lapsed° powers, though forfeit and enthrall'd   *decayed*
        By sin to foul exorbitant desires;
        Upheld by me, yet once more he shall stand
        On even ground against his mortal foe,
180   By me upheld, that he may know how frail
        His fall'n condition is, and to me owe
        All his deliv'rance, and to none but me.
        Some I have chosen of peculiar grace
        Elect above the rest; so is my will:[1]
185   The rest shall hear me call, and oft be warn'd
        Thir sinful state, and to appease betimes
        Th' incensed Deity while offer'd grace
        Invites; for I will clear thir senses dark,
        What may suffice, and soft'n stony hearts
190   To pray, repent, and bring obedience due.
        To Prayer, repentance, and obedience due,
        Though but endeavor'd with sincere intent,
        Mine ear shall not be slow, mine eye not shut.
        And I will place within them as a guide
195   My Umpire *Conscience*, whom if they will hear,
        Light after light well us'd they shall attain,
        And to the end persisting, safe arrive.
        This my long sufferance and my day of grace
        They who neglect and scorn, shall never taste;
200   But hard be hard'n'd, blind be blinded more,
        That they may stumble on, and deeper fall;
        And none but such from mercy I exclude.
        But yet all is not done; Man disobeying,

9. Echoing Mark 1.11, the words out of the heavens at Jesus' baptism: "Thou art my beloved Son, in whom I am well pleased."
1. In *De doctrina* 1.4, Milton sets out an Arminian position, explicitly opposed to the Calvinist, on such doctrines as predestination, election, and reprobation, and he could be regarded as doing something similar here (lines 173–202); e.g., his God seems to make salvation depend on humans' will to avail themselves of grace, or on "prayer, repentance, and obedience" (line 191), whereas Calvinists regarded humans as incapable of contributing in any way to their own salvation. By the term "elect," Milton usually means no more than "whoever believes and continues in the faith."

Disloyal breaks his fealty, and sins
205 Against the high Supremacy of Heav'n,
Affecting° God-head, and so losing all,   *seeking*
To expiate his Treason hath naught left,
But to destruction sacred and devote,°   *dedicated*
He with his whole posterity must die,
210 Die hee or Justice must; unless for him
Some other able, and as willing, pay
The rigid satisfaction, death for death.[2]
Say Heav'nly Powers, where shall we find such love,
Which of ye will be mortal[3] to redeem
215 Man's mortal crime, and just th' unjust to save,
Dwells in all Heaven charity° so dear?   *compassionate love*
      He ask'd, but all the Heav'nly Choir stood mute,
And silence was in Heav'n: on man's behalf
Patron or Intercessor none appear'd,
220 Much less that durst upon his own head draw
The deadly forfeiture, and ransom set.[4]
And now without redemption all mankind
Must have been lost, adjudg'd to Death and Hell
By doom° severe, had not the Son of God,   *judgment*
225 In whom the fulness dwells of love divine,
His dearest mediation thus renew'd.
      Father, thy word is past,[5] man shall find grace;
And shall grace not find means, that finds her way,
The speediest of thy winged messengers,
230 To visit all thy creatures, and to all
Comes unprevented,° unimplor'd, unsought?   *unanticipated*
Happy for man, so coming; he her aid
Can never seek, once dead in sins and lost;
Atonement for himself or offering meet,
235 Indebted and undone, hath none to bring:
Behold mee then, mee for him, life for life
I offer, on mee let thine anger fall;
Account mee man; I for his sake will leave
Thy bosom, and this glory next to thee
240 Freely put off, and for him lastly die
Well pleas'd, on me let Death wreck all his rage;
Under his gloomy power I shall not long
Lie vanquisht; thou hast giv'n me to possess
Life in myself for ever, by thee I live,[6]
245 Though now to Death I yield, and am his due
All that of me can die, yet that debt paid,
Thou wilt not leave me in the loathsome grave
His prey, nor suffer my unspotted Soul

2. Note that human death is here regarded by God not
as a punishment, but as a "satisfaction" for the treason.
See *De doctrina* 1.16: "The satisfaction of Christ is the
complete reparation made by him . . . by the fulfilment
of the Law, and payment of the required price for all
mankind."

3. Is willing to be subject to death.
4. Put down the ransom price (by giving his own life).
5. Your word of honor is pledged.
6. See John 5.26: "As the Father hath life in himself: so
hath he given to the Son to have life in himself."

For ever with corruption there to dwell;
250 But I shall rise Victorious, and subdue
My vanquisher, spoil'd of his vaunted spoil;
Death his death's wound shall then receive, and stoop
Inglorious, of his mortal sting disarm'd.[7]
I through the ample Air in Triumph high
255 Shall lead Hell Captive maugre° Hell, and show   despite
The powers of darkness bound. Thou at the sight
Pleas'd, out of Heaven shalt look down and smile,
While by thee rais'd I ruin all my Foes,
Death last, and with his Carcass glut the Grave:[8]
260 Then with the multitude of my redeem'd
Shall enter Heav'n long absent, and return,
Father, to see thy face, wherein no cloud
Of anger shall remain, but peace assur'd,
And reconcilement; wrath shall be no more
265 Thenceforth, but in thy presence Joy entire.
     His words here ended, but his meek aspéct
Silent yet spake, and breath'd immortal love
To mortal men, above which only shone
Filial obedience: as a sacrifice
270 Glad to be offer'd, he attends° the will   awaits
Of his great Father. Admiration seiz'd
All Heav'n, what this might mean, and whither tend
Wond'ring; but soon th' Almighty thus repli'd:
     O thou in Heav'n and Earth the only peace
275 Found out for mankind under wrath, O thou
My sole complacence! well thou know'st how dear
To me are all my works, nor Man the least
Though last created, that for him I spare
Thee from my bosom and right hand, to save,
280 By losing thee a while, the whole Race lost.
Thou therefore whom thou only canst redeem,
Thir Nature also to thy Nature join;
And be thyself Man among men on Earth,
Made flesh, when time shall be, of Virgin seed,
285 By wondrous birth: Be thou in *Adam's* room°   place
The Head of all mankind, though *Adam's* Son.
As in him perish all men, so in thee
As from a second root shall be restor'd,
As many as are restor'd, without thee none.[9]
290 His crime makes guilty all his Sons, thy merit
Imputed shall absolve them who renounce
Thir own both righteous and unrighteous deeds,[1]

---

7. See 1 Corinthians 15.55–6: "O death, where is thy sting? O grave, where is thy victory? The sting of death is sin; and the strength of sin is the law."
8. Alludes to 1 Corinthians 15.26: "The last enemy that shall be destroyed is death."
9. See 1 Corinthians 15.22: "As in Adam all die, even so in Christ shall all be made alive."

1. See *De doctrina* 1.22: "As therefore our sins are imputed to Christ, so the merits or righteousness of Christ are imputed to us through faith." If one simply renounced dependence on "righteous" deeds, one would be justified by faith alone; but for the "living faith"—faith issuing in works—that Milton believes necessary, one has to renounce (in a different sense) "unrighteous" deeds.

And live in thee transplanted, and from thee
Receive new life. So Man, as is most just,
295   Shall satisfy for Man, be judg'd and die,
And dying rise, and rising with him raise
His Brethren, ransom'd with his own dear life.
So Heav'nly love shall outdo Hellish hate,
Giving to death, and dying to redeem,
300   So dearly to redeem what Hellish hate
So easily destroy'd, and still destroys
In those who, when they may, accept not grace.
Nor shalt thou by descending to assume
Man's Nature, lessen or degrade thine own.
305   Because thou hast, though Thron'd in highest bliss
Equal to God, and equally enjoying
God-like fruition, quitted[2] all to save
A world from utter loss, and hast been found
By Merit more than Birthright Son of God,
310   Found worthiest to be so by being Good,
Far more than Great or High; because in thee
Love hath abounded more than Glory abounds,
Therefore thy Humiliation shall exalt
With thee thy Manhood also to this Throne;
315   Here shalt thou sit incarnate, here shalt Reign
Both God and Man, Son both of God and Man,
Anointed[3] universal King; all Power
I give thee, reign for ever, and assume
Thy Merits; under thee as Head Supreme
320   Thrones, Princedoms, Powers, Dominions I reduce:
All knees to thee shall bow, of them that bide
In Heaven, or Earth, or under Earth in Hell;
When thou attended gloriously from Heav'n
Shalt in the Sky appear, and from thee send
325   The summoning Arch-Angels to proclaim
Thy dread Tribunal: forthwith from all Winds
The living, and forthwith the cited° dead   *summoned*
Of all past Ages to the general Doom°   *judgment*
Shall hast'n, such a peal shall rouse thir sleep.
330   Then all thy Saints° assembl'd, thou shalt judge   *elect*
Bad men and Angels, they arraign'd shall sink
Beneath thy Sentence; Hell, her numbers full,
Thenceforth shall be for ever shut. Meanwhile
The World shall burn, and from her ashes spring
335   New Heav'n and Earth, wherein the just shall dwell
And after all thir tribulations long
See golden days, fruitful of golden deeds,
With Joy and Love triumphing, and fair Truth.[4]
Then thou thy regal Sceptre shalt lay by,
340   For regal Sceptre then no more shall need,

2. A pun, since "quitted" meant "redeemed, remitted" as well as "left."

3. The "Anointed" in Hebrew is the Messiah.
4. The burning of Earth is based on 2 Peter 3.12ff.

God shall be All in All. But all ye Gods,°   *angels*
Adore him, who to compass all this dies,
Adore the Son, and honor him as mee.
        No sooner had th' Almighty ceas't, but all
345 The multitude of Angels with a shout
Loud as from numbers without number, sweet
As from blest voices, uttering joy, Heav'n rung
With Jubilee, and loud Hosannas fill'd
Th' eternal Regions: lowly reverent
350 Towards either Throne they bow, and to the ground
With solemn adoration down they cast
Thir Crowns inwove with Amarant and Gold,
Immortal Amarant,[5] a Flow'r which once
In Paradise, fast by the Tree of Life
355 Began to bloom, but soon for man's offense
To Heav'n remov'd where first it grew, there grows,
And flow'rs aloft shading the Fount of Life,
And where the river of Bliss through midst of Heav'n
Rolls o'er *Elysian* Flow'rs her Amber stream;[6]
360 With these that never fade the Spirits elect
Bind thir resplendent locks inwreath'd with beams,
Now in loose Garlands thick thrown off, the bright
Pavement that like a Sea of Jasper shone
Impurpl'd with Celestial Roses smil'd.
365 Then Crown'd again thir gold'n Harps they took,
Harps ever tun'd, that glittering by thir side
Like Quivers hung, and with Preamble sweet
Of charming symphony they introduce
Thir sacred Song, and waken raptures high;
370 No voice exempt,° no voice but well could join   *debarred*
Melodious part, such concord is in Heav'n.
        Thee Father first they sung Omnipotent,
Immutable, Immortal, Infinite,[7]
Eternal King; thee Author of all being,
375 Fountain of Light, thyself invisible
Amidst the glorious brightness where thou sit'st
Thron'd inaccessible, but° when thou shad'st   *except*
The full blaze of thy beams, and through a cloud
Drawn round about thee like a radiant Shrine,
380 Dark with excessive bright thy skirts appear,
Yet dazzle Heav'n, that brightest Seraphim
Approach not, but with both wings veil thir eyes.
Thee next they sang of all Creation first,
Begotten Son, Divine Similitude,
385 In whose conspicuous count'nance, without cloud
Made visible, th' Almighty Father shines,

---

5. "Amaranth" in Greek means "unwithering"; a purple
flower that was a "symbol of immortality"; the amaran-
tine crown was an ancient pagan symbol of untroubled
tranquillity and health.
6. Allusion to Virgil, *Aeneid* 6.656–59, the description of

spirits chanting in chorus beside the Eridanus, in the
Elysian fields; "amber" was a standard of purity or clarity.
7. Line 373 is transplanted in its entirety from Sylvester's
translation of Du Bartas's poem on creation.

Whom else no Creature can behold;[8] on thee
Impresst th' effulgence of his Glory abides,
Transfus'd on thee his ample Spirit rests.
390 Hee Heav'n of Heavens and all the Powers therein
By thee created, and by thee threw down
Th' aspiring Dominations:° thou that day   *rebel angels*
Thy Father's dreadful Thunder didst not spare,
Nor stop thy flaming Chariot wheels, that shook
395 Heav'n's everlasting Frame, while o'er the necks
Thou drov'st of warring Angels disarray'd.
Back from pursuit thy Powers with loud acclaim
Thee only extoll'd, Son of thy Father's might,
To execute fierce vengeance on his foes:
400 Not so on Man; him through their malice fall'n,
Father of Mercy and Grace, thou didst not doom°   *judge*
So strictly, but much more to pity incline:
No sooner did thy dear and only Son
Perceive thee purpos'd not to doom frail Man
405 So strictly, but much more to pity inclin'd,[9]
Hee to appease thy wrath, and end the strife
Of Mercy and Justice in thy face discern'd,
Regardless of the Bliss wherein hee sat
Second to thee, offer'd himself to die
410 For man's offense. O unexampl'd love,
Love nowhere to be found less than Divine!
Hail Son of God, Savior of Men, thy Name
Shall be the copious matter of my Song
Henceforth, and never shall my Harp thy praise
415 Forget, nor from thy Father's praise disjoin.
   Thus they in Heav'n, above the starry Sphere,
Thir happy hours in joy and hymning spent.
Meanwhile upon the firm opacous Globe
Of this round World, whose first convex divides
420 The luminous inferior Orbs, enclos'd
From *Chaos* and th' inroad of Darkness old,[1]
Satan alighted walks: a Globe far off
It seem'd, now seems a boundless Continent
Dark, waste, and wild, under the frown of Night
425 Starless expos'd, and ever-threat'ning storms
Of *Chaos* blust'ring round, inclement sky;
Save on that side which from the wall of Heav'n,
Though distant far, some small reflection gains
Of glimmering air less vext° with tempest loud: *tossed about*
430 Here walk'd the Fiend at large in spacious field.
As when a Vultur on *Imaus* bred,
Whose snowy ridge the roving *Tartar* bounds,

8. See John 1.18 and 14.9.
9. Most editors say that "but" or "than" has to be supplied
before "He" (line 406). However, if "much more to pity
inclined" refers to the Son, the "but" immediately preceding is available for the main clause.

1. The "starry Sphere," is either the sphere of the fixed
stars or, more loosely, the stars and planets together. The
stars are enclosed within the *primum mobile* or "first convex" (sphere). Both heaven and chaos lie outside that
opaque ("opacous") shell.

Dislodging from a Region scarce of prey
To gorge the flesh of Lambs or yeanling Kids
435   On Hills where Flocks are fed, flies toward the Springs
Of *Ganges* or *Hydaspes*, *Indian* streams;
But in his way lights on the barren Plains
Of *Sericana*, where *Chineses* drive
With Sails and Wind thir cany Waggons light:
440   So on this windy Sea of Land, the Fiend
Walk'd up and down alone bent on his prey,[2]
Alone, for other Creature in this place
Living or lifeless to be found was none,
None yet, but store hereafter from the earth
445   Up hither like Aereal vapors flew
Of all things transitory and vain, when Sin
With vanity had fill'd the works of men:[3]
Both all things vain, and all who in vain things
Built thir fond hopes of Glory or lasting fame,
450   Or happiness in this or th' other life;
All who have thir reward on Earth, the fruits
Of painful Superstition and blind Zeal,
Naught seeking but the praise of men, here find
Fit retribution, empty as thir deeds;
455   All th' unaccomplisht works of Nature's hand,
Abortive, monstrous, or unkindly mixt,
Dissolv'd on Earth, fleet hither, and in vain,
Till final dissolution, wander here,
Not in the neighboring Moon, as some have dream'd;
460   Those argent Fields more likely habitants,
Translated Saints,[4] or middle Spirits hold
Betwixt th' Angelical and Human kind:
Hither of ill-join'd Sons and Daughters born
First from the ancient World those Giants came
465   With many a vain exploit, though then renown'd:[5]
The builders next of *Babel* on the Plain
Of *Sennaar*, and still with vain design
New *Babels*, had they wherewithal, would build:[6]
Others came single; he who to be deem'd
470   A God, leap'd fondly into *AEtna* flames,
Empedocles, and hee who to enjoy
Plato's Elysium, leap'd into the Sea,

---

2. The simile compares the vulture's journey to Satan's. One journey is from Imaus, (a mountain range said to run through Afghanistan), to the rivers of India; the other is from the "frozen continent" (2.587) of Tartarus, which did not keep Satan from roving, to Eden with its rivers. The "barren plains of Sericana" correspond to the *primum mobile* because both are stopping places and in both the elements are confused. (The Chinese use sails, the means of propulsion for ships, on their land vehicles; and the *primum mobile* is a "sea of land.")
3. In *Orlando Furioso* 34.73ff., a passage from which Milton quotes in *Of Reformation*, Ariosto tells how Astolfo searches for his lost wits in a Limbo of Vanity on the moon.
4. Probably such as Enoch (Genesis 5.24) and Elijah (2 Kings 2).
5. The first group of fools are the Giants, "mighty men . . . of renown," born of the misunion of "sons of God" with "daughters of men" (Genesis 6.4).
6. At 12.45–47 the builders of Babel are said to have formed their "vain design" out of a desire for fame. "New Babels" suggests the New Babylon of anti-Papist propaganda.

Cleombrotus,[7] and many more too long,
Embryos, and Idiots, Eremites and Friars
475　White, Black and Grey, with all thir trumpery.[8]
Here Pilgrims roam, that stray'd so far to seek
In Golgotha[9] him dead, who lives in Heav'n;
And they who to be sure of Paradise
Dying put on the weeds of Dominic,
480　Or in Franciscan think to pass disguis'd;[1]
They pass the Planets seven, and pass the fixt,
And that Crystalline Sphere whose balance weighs
The Trepidation talkt, and that first mov'd;[2]
And now Saint Peter at Heav'n's Wicket seems
485　To wait them with his Keys, and now at foot
Of Heav'n's ascent they lift thir Feet, when lo
A violent cross wind from either Coast
Blows them transverse ten thousand Leagues awry
Into the devious Air; then might ye see
490　Cowls, Hoods and Habits with thir weares tost
And flutter'd into Rags, then Reliques, Beads,
Indulgences, Dispenses,[3] Pardons, Bulls,
The sport of Winds: all these upwhirl'd aloft
Fly o'er the backside of the World far off
495　Into a Limbo° large and broad, since call'd   *empty region*
The Paradise of Fools, to few unknown
Long after, now unpeopl'd and untrod;
All this dark Globe the Fiend found as he pass'd,
And long he wander'd, till at last a gleam
500　Of dawning light turn'd thither-ward in haste
His travell'd steps; far distant he descries
Ascending by degrees magnificent
Up to the wall of Heaven a Structure high,
At top whereof, but far more rich appear'd
505　The work as of a Kingly Palace Gate
With Frontispiece[4] of Diamond and Gold
Imbellisht; thick with sparkling orient° Gems   *brilliant*
The Portal shone, inimitable on Earth
By Model, or by shading Pencil drawn.
510　The Stairs were such as whereon Jacob saw
Angels ascending and descending, bands

7. Empedocles and Cleombrotus were not associated by classical writers but occur together in Lactantius' chapter on "Pythagoreans and Stoics who, Believing in the Immortality of the Soul, Foolishly Persuade a Voluntary Death" (*Divinae Institutiones* 3.18). Cleombrotus drowned himself after an unwise reading of Plato's *Phaedo;* Empedocles' motive was to conceal his own mortality.
8. Milton here satirizes a Catholic tradition that consigned cretins and unbaptized infants to a much debated *limbo infantum.* The friars were specified by robe color; "white" meant Carmelite, "black" Dominican, and "grey" Franciscan. The contemptuous juxtaposition of all three colors ridicules the importance assigned to external trappings. "Eremites" were Order of Friars Hermits.

9. The hill where Christ was crucified and buried.
1. Compare *Inferno* 27.67–84, in which Dante tells how Guido da Montefeltro hoped to get into heaven by virtue of Franciscan robes but found to his cost that absolution without repentance is vain.
2. In order of proximity to earth, the spheres passed are the seven planetary spheres; the eighth sphere, containing the "fixed" stars; the ninth, "crystalline sphere"; and the tenth sphere, the "first moved" or *primum mobile.*
3. A "dispense" or dispensation was an exemption from a solemn obligation by licence of an ecclesiastical dignitary, especially the Pope.
4. A decorated entrance or a pediment over the gate.

Of Guardians bright, when he from *Esau* fled
To *Padan-Aram* in the field of *Luz,*
Dreaming by night under the open Sky,
515   And waking cri'd, *This is the Gate of Heav'n.*[5]
Each Stair mysteriously° was meant,[6] nor stood   *symbolically*
There always, but drawn up to Heav'n sometimes
Viewless, and underneath a bright Sea flow'd
Of Jasper, or of liquid Pearl, whereon
520   Who after came from Earth, sailing arriv'd,
Wafted by Angels, or flew o'er the Lake
Rapt in a Chariot drawn by fiery Steeds.
The Stairs were then let down, whether to dare
The Fiend by easy ascent, or aggravate
525   His sad exclusion from the doors of Bliss.
Direct against which op'n'd from beneath,
Just o'er the blissful seat of Paradise,
A passage down to th' Earth, a passage wide,
Wider by far than that of after-times
530   Over Mount *Sion,* and, though that were large,
Over the *Promis'd Land* to God so dear,
By which, to visit oft those happy Tribes,
On high behests his Angels to and fro
Pass'd frequent, and his eye with choice° regard   *careful*
535   From *Paneas* the fount of *Jordan's* flood
To *Beërsaba,*[7] where the *Holy Land*
Borders on *Egypt* and th' *Arabian* shore;
So wide the op'ning seem'd, where bounds were set
To darkness, such as bound the Ocean wave.
540   *Satan* from hence now on the lower stair
That scal'd by steps of Gold to Heaven Gate
Looks down with wonder at the sudden view
Of all this World at once. As when a Scout
Through dark and desert ways with peril gone
545   All night; at last by break of cheerful dawn
Obtains° the brow of some high-climbing Hill,   *reaches*
Which to his eye discovers unaware
The goodly prospect of some foreign land
First seen, or some renown'd Metropolis
550   With glistering Spires and Pinnacles adorn'd,
Which now the Rising Sun gilds with his beams.
Such wonder seiz'd, though after Heaven seen,
The Spirit malign, but much more envy seiz'd
At sight of all this World beheld so fair.[8]* * *

5. The unregenerate Jacob was terrified by the vision of a ladder reaching to heaven just after he had cheated Esau out of his father's blessing (Genesis 27–8). The experience awed him into belief and a vow to the Lord.
6. Jacob's ladder had been identified with Homer's golden chain linking the universe to Jupiter. Each "stair," or step, could be interpreted as a spiritual stage extending "from the supreme God even to the bottomest dregs of the universe."

7. "Paneas," is a later Greek name for Dan—not the city of Dan but the spring of the same name, "the easternmost fountain of Jordan." Beersaba was the southern limit of Canaan, as Dan was the northern.
8. Seeing the archangel Uriel, Satan now disguises himself as a cherub and asks the way to Eden. Uriel directs him, not realizing who he is—"For neither Man nor Angel can discern / Hypocrisy, the only evil that walks / Invisible, except to God alone" (lines 682–5).

from **Book 4**

The Argument

Satan *now in prospect of* Eden, *and nigh the place where he must now attempt the bold enterprise which he undertook alone against God and Man, falls into many doubts with himself, and many passions, fear, envy, and despair; but at length confirms himself in evil, journeys on to Paradise, whose outward prospect and situation is described, over-leaps the bounds, sits in the shape of a Cormorant on the Tree of Life, as highest in the Garden to look about him. The Garden describ'd; Satan's first sight of Adam and Eve; his wonder at thir excellent form and happy state, but with resolution to work thir fall; overhears thir discourse, thence gathers that the Tree of Knowledge was forbidden them to eat of, under penalty of death; and thereon intends to found his Temptation, by seducing them to transgress: then leaves them a while, to know further of thir state by some other means. Meanwhile* Uriel *descending on a Sun-beam warns* Gabriel, *who had in charge the Gate of Paradise, that some evil spirit had escap'd the Deep, and past at Noon by his Sphere in the shape of a good Angel down to Paradise, discovered after by his furious gestures in the Mount.* Gabriel *promises to find him ere morning. Night com-ing on,* Adam *and* Eve *discourse of going to thir rest: thir Bower describ'd; thir Evening worship.* Gabriel *drawing forth his Bands of Night-watch to walk the round of Paradise, appoints two strong Angels to* Adam's *Bower, lest the evil spirit should be there doing some harm to* Adam *or* Eve *sleeping; there they find him at the ear of* Eve, *tempting her in a dream, and bring him, though unwilling, to* Gabriel; *by whom question'd, he scorn-fully answers, prepares resistance, but hinder'd by a Sign from Heaven, flies out of Par-adise.*

      O for that warning voice, which he who saw
    Th' *Apocalypse*, heard cry in Heav'n aloud,
    Then when the Dragon, put to second rout,
    Came furious down to be reveng'd on men,
5   *Woe to the inhabitants on Earth!*[1] that now,
    While time was, our first Parents had been warn'd
    The coming of thir secret foe, and scap'd
    Haply so scap'd his mortal snare; for now
    Satan, now first inflam'd with rage, came down,
10 The Tempter ere th' Accuser of man-kind,
    To wreck° on innocent frail man his loss   *avenge*
    Of that first Battle, and his flight to Hell:
    Yet not rejoicing in his speed, though bold,
    Far off and fearless, nor with cause to boast,
15 Begins his dire attempt, which nigh the birth
    Now rolling, boils in his tumultuous breast,
    And like a devilish Engine back recoils
    Upon himself; horror and doubt distract
    His troubl'd thoughts, and from the bottom stir
20 The Hell within him, for within him Hell
    He brings, and round about him, nor from Hell
    One step no more than from himself can fly
    By change of place: Now conscience wakes despair

---

1. The *Apocalypse* of St. John relates a vision of a second battle in heaven between Michael and "the Dragon," Satan.

That slumber'd, wakes the bitter memory
25   Of what he was, what is, and what must be
Worse; of worse deeds worse sufferings must ensue.
Sometimes towards *Eden* which now in his view
Lay pleasant,[2] his griev'd look he fixes sad,
Sometimes towards Heav'n and the full-blazing Sun,
30   Which now sat high in his Meridian Tow'r:
Then much revolving, thus in sighs began.
        O thou that with surpassing Glory crown'd,
Look'st from thy sole Dominion like the God
Of this new World; at whose sight all the Stars
35   Hide thir diminisht heads; to thee I call,
But with no friendly voice, and add thy name
O Sun, to tell thee how I hate thy beams
That bring to my remembrance from what state
I fell, how glorious once above thy Sphere;
40   Till Pride and worse Ambition threw me down
Warring in Heav'n against Heav'n's matchless King:[3]
Ah wherefore! he deserv'd no such return
From me, whom he created what I was
In that bright eminence, and with his good
45   Upbraided none;[4] nor was his service hard.
What could be less than to afford him praise,
The easiest recompense, and pay him thanks,
How due! yet all his good prov'd ill in me,
And wrought but malice; lifted up so high
50   I sdein'd° subjection, and thought one step higher   *disdained*
Would set me highest, and in a moment quit°   *pay off*
The debt immense of endless gratitude,
So burdensome, still paying, still to owe;
Forgetful what from him I still receiv'd,
55   And understood not that a grateful mind
By owing owes not, but still pays, at once
Indebted and discharg'd; what burden then?[5]
O had his powerful Destiny ordain'd
Me some inferior Angel, I had stood
60   Then happy; no unbounded hope had rais'd
Ambition. Yet why not? some other Power
As great might have aspir'd, and me though mean
Drawn to his part; but other Powers as great
Fell not, but stand unshak'n, from within
65   Or from without, to all temptations arm'd.
Hadst thou the same free Will and Power to stand?
Thou hadst: whom hast thou then or what to accuse,
But Heav'n's free Love dealt equally to all?

2. The etymological meaning of "Eden" is "pleasure, delight."
3. According to Edward Phillips, lines 32–41 were shown to him and some others "before the Poem was begun,"
when Milton intended to write a tragedy on the Fall.
4. Demanded no return for his benefits; see James 1.5.
5. Simply by owning an obligation gratefully, one ceases to owe it.

Be then his Love accurst, since love or hate,
70   To me alike, it deals eternal woe.
Nay curs'd be thou; since against his thy will
Chose freely what it now so justly rues.
Me miserable! which way shall I fly
Infinite wrath, and infinite despair?
75   Which way I fly is Hell; myself am Hell;
And in the lowest deep a lower deep
Still threat'ning to devour me opens wide,
To which the Hell I suffer seems a Heav'n.
O then at last relent: is there no place
80   Left for Repentance, none for Pardon left?
None left but by submission; and that word
Disdain forbids me, and my dread of shame
Among the Spirits beneath, whom I seduc'd
With other promises and other vaunts
85   Than to submit, boasting I could subdue
Th' Omnipotent. Ay me, they little know
How dearly I abide that boast so vain,
Under what torments inwardly I groan:
While they adore me on the Throne of Hell,
90   With Diadem and Sceptre high advanc'd
The lower still I fall, only Supreme
In misery; such joy Ambition finds.
But say I could repent and could obtain
By Act of Grace[6] my former state; how soon
95   Would highth recall high thoughts, how soon unsay
What feign'd submission swore: ease would recant
Vows made in pain, as violent and void.
For never can true reconcilement grow
Where wounds of deadly hate have pierc'd so deep:
100   Which would but lead me to a worse relapse,
And heavier fall: so should I purchase dear
Short intermission bought with double smart.
This knows my punisher; therefore as far
From granting hee, as I from begging peace:
105   All hope excluded thus, behold instead
Of us out-cast, exil'd, his new delight,
Mankind created, and for him this World.
So farewell Hope, and with Hope farewell Fear,
Farewell Remorse: all Good to me is lost;
110   Evil be thou my Good; by thee at least
Divided Empire with Heav'n's King I hold
By thee, and more than half perhaps will reign;
As Man ere long, and this new World shall know.
        Thus while he spake, each passion dimm'd his face,
115   Thrice chang'd with pale, ire, envy and despair,

---

6. By concession of favor, not of right; often used for a formal pardon by Parliament.

Which marr'd his borrow'd visage, and betray'd
Him counterfeit, if any eye beheld.
For heav'nly minds from such distempers foul
Are ever clear. Whereof hee soon aware,

120   Each perturbation smooth'd with outward calm,
Artificer° of fraud; and was the first   *inventor*
That practis'd falsehood under saintly show,
Deep malice to conceal, couch't° with revenge: *hidden*
Yet not anough had practis'd to deceive

125   *Uriel* once warn'd; whose eye pursu'd him down
The way he went, and on th' *Assyrian* mount°   *Niphates*
Saw him disfigur'd, more than could befall
Spirit of happy sort: his gestures fierce
He mark'd and mad demeanor, then alone,

130   As he suppos'd, all unobserv'd, unseen.
So on he fares, and to the border comes
Of *Eden*, where delicious Paradise,
Now nearer, Crowns with her enclosure green,
As with a rural mound the champaign° head   *unenclosed, level*

135   Of a steep wilderness, whose hairy sides
With thicket overgrown, grotesque and wild,
Access deni'd; and over head up grew
Insuperable highth of loftiest shade,
Cedar, and Pine, and Fir, and branching Palm,

140   A Silvan Scene, and as the ranks ascend
Shade above shade, a woody Theatre
Of stateliest view. Yet higher than thir tops
The verdurous wall of Paradise up sprung:
Which to our general Sire° gave prospect large   *Adam*

145   Into his nether Empire neighboring round.
And higher than that Wall a circling row
Of goodliest Trees loaden with fairest Fruit,
Blossoms and Fruits at once of golden hue
Appear'd, with gay enamell'd° colors mixt: *lustrous*

150   On which the Sun more glad impress'd his beams
Than in fair Evening Cloud, or humid Bow,°   *rainbow*
When God hath show'r'd the earth; so lovely seem'd
That Lantskip:° And of pure now purer air   *landscape*
Meets his approach, and to the heart inspires

155   Vernal delight and joy, able to drive
All sadness but despair: now gentle gales
Fanning thir odoriferous wings dispense
Native perfúmes, and whisper whence they stole
Those balmy spoils. As when to them who sail

160   Beyond the *Cape* of *Hope,* and now are past
Mozambic,[7] off at Sea North-East winds blow
Sabean[8] Odors from the spicy shore

---

7. Mozambique, a Portuguese colony on the east coast of Africa; the trade route lay between Mozambique and Madagascar.

8. Of Saba or Sheba (now Yemen). Milton draws on the description of "Araby the blest"—"Arabia felix"— in Diodorus Siculus 3.46.

Of *Araby* the blest, with such delay
Well pleas'd they slack thir course, and many a League
165   Cheer'd with the grateful smell old Ocean smiles.
So entertain'd those odorous sweets the Fiend
Who came thir bane, though with them better pleas'd
Than *Asmodeus* with the fishy fume,
That drove him, though enamor'd, from the Spouse
170   Of *Tobit's* Son, and with a vengeance sent
From *Media* post to *Egypt*, there fast bound.[9]
          Now to th' ascent of that steep savage° Hill   wild
Satan had journey'd on, pensive and slow;
But further way found none, so thick entwin'd,
175   As one continu'd brake, the undergrowth
Of shrubs and tangling bushes had perplext
All path of Man or Beast that pass'd that way:
One Gate there only was, and that look'd East
On th' other side: which when th' arch-felon saw
180   Due entrance he disdain'd, and in contempt,
At one slight bound high overleap'd all bound
Of Hill or highest Wall, and sheer within
Lights on his feet. As when a prowling Wolf,
Whom hunger drives to seek new haunt for prey,
185   Watching where Shepherds pen thir Flocks at eve
In hurdl'd Cotes° amid the field secure,   shelters
Leaps o'er the fence with ease into the Fold:
Or as a Thief bent to unhoard the cash
Of some rich Burgher, whose substantial doors,
190   Cross-barr'd and bolted fast, fear no assault,
In at the window climbs, or o'er the tiles:
So clomb° this first grand Thief into God's Fold: climbed
So since into his Church lewd Hirelings[1] climb.
Thence up he flew, and on the Tree of Life,
195   The middle Tree and highest there that grew,
Sat like a Cormorant;[2] yet not true Life
Thereby regain'd, but sat devising Death
To them who liv'd; nor on the virtue thought
Of that life-giving Plant, but only us'd
200   For prospect,° what well us'd had been the pledge   lookout
Of immortality. So little knows
Any, but God alone, to value right
The good before him, but perverts best things
To worst abuse, or to thir meanest use.
205   Beneath him with new wonder now he views
To all delight of human sense expos'd
In narrow room Nature's whole wealth, yea more,

9. The apocryphal book Tobit relates the story of Tobit's son Tobias, who was sent into Media on an errand and there married Sara. Sara had previously been given to seven men, but all were killed by the jealous spirit Asmodeus before their marriages could be consummated.

By the advice of Raphael, however, Tobias succeeded by creating a fishy smoke to drive away the devil Asmodeus.
1. Wicked men motivated only by material gain.
2. A voracious sea bird, often used to describe greedy clergy.

A Heaven on Earth: for blissful Paradise
Of God the Garden was, by him in the East
210   Of *Eden* planted; *Eden* stretch'd her Line
From *Auran* Eastward to the Royal Tow'rs
Of Great *Seleucia*, built by *Grecian* Kings,
Or where the Sons of *Eden* long before
Dwelt in *Telassar*:³ in this pleasant soil
215   His far more pleasant Garden God ordain'd;
Out of the fertile ground he caus'd to grow
All Trees of noblest kind for sight, smell, taste;
And all amid them stood the Tree of Life,
High eminent, blooming Ambrosial Fruit
220   Of vegetable Gold; and next to Life
Our Death the Tree of Knowledge grew fast by,
Knowledge of Good bought dear by knowing ill.⁴
Southward through *Eden* went a River large,
Nor chang'd his course, but through the shaggy hill
225   Pass'd underneath ingulft, for God had thrown
That Mountain as his Garden mould high rais'd
Upon the rapid current, which through veins
Of porous Earth with kindly° thirst up-drawn,   *natural*
Rose a fresh Fountain, and with many a rill
230   Water'd the Garden;⁵ thence united fell
Down the steep glade, and met the nether Flood,
Which from his darksome passage now appears,
And now divided into four main Streams,
Runs diverse, wand'ring many a famous Realm
235   And Country whereof here needs no account,
But rather to tell how, if Art could tell,
How from that Sapphire Fount the crisped° Brooks,   *wavy*
Rolling on Orient Pearl and sands of Gold,
With mazy error° under pendant shades   *wandering*
240   Ran Nectar, visiting each plant, and fed
Flow'rs worthy of Paradise which not nice° Art   *careful*
In Beds and curious Knots, but Nature boon°   *bounteous*
Pour'd forth profuse on Hill and Dale and Plain,
Both where the morning Sun first warmly smote
245   The open field, and where the unpierc't shade
Imbrown'd° the noontide Bow'rs: Thus was this place,   *darkened*
A happy rural seat of various view:
Groves whose rich Trees wept odorous Gums and Balm,
Others whose fruit burnisht with Golden Rind
250   Hung amiable,° *Hesperian* Fables true,⁶   *lovely*
If true, here only, and of delicious taste:

3. Auran was an eastern boundary of the land of Israel. Great Seleucia was built by Alexander's general Seleucus Nicator as a seat of government for his Syrian empire. The mention of Telassar prophesies war in Eden; see 2 Kings 14.11ff., where Telassar is an instance of lands destroyed utterly.
4. See Genesis 2.9.
5. See Genesis 2.10.
6. Golden fruit like the legendary apples of the western islands, the Hesperides.

Betwixt them Lawns, or level Downs, and Flocks
Grazing the tender herb, were interpos'd,
Or palmy hillock, or the flow'ry lap
255 Of some irriguous° Valley spread her store,   *well-watered*
Flow'rs of all hue, and without Thorn the Rose:⁷
Another side, umbrageous° Grots and Caves   *shady*
Of cool recess, o'er which the mantling Vine
Lays forth her purple Grape, and gently creeps
260 Luxuriant; meanwhile murmuring waters fall
Down the slope hills, disperst, or in a Lake,
That to the fringed Bank with Myrtle crown'd,
Her crystal mirror holds, unite thir streams.
The Birds thir choir apply;° airs, vernal airs,⁸   *practice*
265 Breathing the smell of field and grove, attune
The trembling leaves, while Universal *Pan*⁹
Knit with the *Graces* and the *Hours* in dance
Led on th' Eternal Spring.¹ Not that fair field
Of *Enna*, where *Proserpin* gath'ring flow'rs
270 Herself a fairer Flow'r by gloomy *Dis*
Was gather'd, which cost *Ceres* all that pain
To seek her through the world;² nor that sweet Grove
Of *Daphne* by *Orontes*, and th' inspir'd
Castalian Spring³ might with this Paradise
275 Of *Eden* strive; nor that *Nyseian* Isle
Girt with the River *Triton*, where old *Cham*,
Whom Gentiles *Ammon* call and *Lybian Jove*,
Hid *Amalthea* and her Florid° Son,   *ruddy-complexioned*
Young *Bacchus*, from his Stepdame *Rhea's* eye;⁴
280 Nor where *Abassin* Kings thir issue Guard,
Mount *Amara*, though this by some suppos'd
True Paradise under the *Ethiop* Line
By *Nilus* head, enclos'd with shining Rock,
A whole day's journey high,⁵ but wide remote
285 From this *Assyrian* Garden, where the Fiend
Saw undelighted all delight, all kind
Of living Creatures new to sight and strange:
Two of far nobler shape erect and tall,
Godlike erect, with native Honor clad
290 In naked Majesty seem'd Lords of all,

---

7. The thornless rose was used to symbolize the sinless state of humanity before the Fall; or the state of grace.
8. Breezes and melodies.
9. Pan (Greek for "all") was a symbol of universal nature.
1. Neoplatonists thought the triadic pattern of their dance expressed the movement underlying all natural generation.
2. The rape of Proserpina by Dis, the king of hell, was located in Enna by Ovid (*Fasti* 4.420ff.). The search for her made the world barren, and even when she was found, she was restored to Ceres—and fruitfulness to the world—only for half the year.

3. The grove called "Daphne" beside the River Orontes, near Antioch, had an Apolline oracle and a stream named after the famous Castalian spring of Parnassus.
4. Ammon, King of Libya, had an illicit affair with a maiden Amaltheia, who gave birth to a marvelous son Dionysus (Bacchus). To protect mother and child from the jealousy of his wife Rhea, Ammon hid them on Nysa, an island near modern Tunis. The identifications of Ammon with the Libyan Jupiter and with Noah's son Ham were widely accepted.
5. Milton takes his description of Mount Amara from Peter Heylyn's *Cosmographie* 4.64.

And worthy seem'd, for in thir looks Divine
The image of thir glorious Maker shone,[6]
Truth, Wisdom, Sanctitude severe and pure,
Severe, but in true filial freedom plac't;
295 Whence true autority in men; though both
Not equal, as thir sex not equal seem'd;
For contemplation hee and valor form'd,
For softness shee and sweet attractive Grace,
Hee for God only, shee for God in him:[7]
300 His fair large Front° and Eye sublime° declar'd   *forehead/uplifted*
Absolute rule; and Hyacinthine Locks
Round from his parted forelock manly hung
Clust'ring, but not beneath his shoulders broad:
Shee as a veil down to the slender waist
305 Her unadorned golden tresses wore
Dishevell'd, but in wanton ringlets wav'd
As the Vine curls her tendrils, which impli'd
Subjection, but requir'd with gentle sway,
And by her yielded, by him best receiv'd,
310 Yielded with coy° submission, modest pride,   *modest*
And sweet reluctant amorous delay.
Nor those mysterious parts were then conceal'd,
Then was not guilty shame: dishonest shame
Of Nature's works, honor dishonorable,
315 Sin-bred, how have ye troubl'd all mankind
With shows instead, mere shows of seeming pure,
And banisht from man's life his happiest life,
Simplicity and spotless innocence.
So pass'd they naked on, nor shunn'd the sight
320 Of God or Angel, for they thought no ill:
So hand in hand they pass'd, the loveliest pair
That ever since in love's imbraces met,
Adam the goodliest man of men since born
His Sons, the fairest of her Daughters *Eve*.
325 Under a tuft of shade that on a green
Stood whispering soft, by a fresh Fountain side
They sat them down, and after no more toil
Of thir sweet Gard'ning labor than suffic'd
To recommend cool *Zephyr*,[8] and made ease
330 More easy, wholesome thirst and appetite
More grateful, to thir Supper Fruits they fell,
Nectarine Fruits which the compliant boughs
Yielded them, side-long as they sat recline°   *lying down*
On the soft downy Bank damaskt with flow'rs:
335 The savory pulp they chew, and in the rind
Still as they thirsted scoop the brimming stream;

6. See Genesis 1.27: "God created man in his own image."
7. See 1 Corinthians 11.3: "The head of every man is Christ; and the head of the woman is the man; and the head of Christ is God."
8. The west wind.

Nor gentle purpose,° nor endearing smiles   *conversation*
Wanted,° nor youthful dalliance as beseems   *lacked*
Fair couple, linkt in happy nuptial League,
340 Alone as they. About them frisking play'd
All Beasts of th' Earth, since wild, and of all chase
In Wood or Wilderness, Forest or Den;
Sporting the Lion ramp'd,° and in his paw   *reared up*
Dandl'd the Kid; Bears, Tigers, Ounces,° Pards°   *lynxes/leopards*
345 Gamboll'd before them, th' unwieldy Elephant
To make them mirth us'd all his might, and wreath'd
His Lithe Proboscis; close the Serpent sly
Insinuating,⁹ wove with Gordian twine¹
His braided train, and of his fatal guile
350 Gave proof unheeded; others on the grass
Coucht, and now fill'd with pasture gazing sat,
Or Bedward ruminating;² for the Sun
Declin'd was hasting now with prone career
To th' Ocean Isles,³ and in th' ascending Scale
355 Of Heav'n the Stars that usher Evening rose:
When *Satan* still in gaze, as first he stood,
Scarce thus at length fail'd speech recover'd sad.
     O Hell! what do mine eyes with grief behold,
Into our room of bliss thus high advanc't
360 Creatures of other mould, earth-born perhaps,
Not Spirits, yet to heav'nly Spirits bright
Little inferior; whom my thoughts pursue
With wonder, and could love, so lively shines
In them Divine resemblance, and such grace
365 The hand that form'd them on thir shape hath pour'd.
Ah gentle pair, yee little think how nigh
Your change approaches, when all these delights
Will vanish and deliver ye to woe,
More woe, the more your taste is now of joy;
370 Happy, but for so happy ill secur'd
Long to continue, and this high seat your Heav'n
Ill fenc't for Heav'n to keep out such a foe
As now is enter'd; yet no purpos'd foe
To you whom I could pity thus forlorn
375 Though I unpitied: League with you I seek,
And mutual amity so strait,° so close,   *intimate*
That I with you must dwell, or you with me
Henceforth; my dwelling haply may not please
Like this fair Paradise, your sense, yet such
380 Accept your Maker's work; he gave it me,
Which I as freely give; Hell shall unfold,⁴

---

9. Penetrating by sinuous ways.
1. Coil, convolution, as difficult to undo as the Gordian
knot, which it took the hero Alexander to cut.
2. Chewing the cud before going to rest.

3. The Azores.
4. A blasphemous echo of Matthew 10.8 ("freely ye have
received, freely give").

To entertain you two, her widest Gates,
And send forth all her Kings; there will be room,
Not like these narrow limits, to receive
385   Your numerous offspring; if no better place,
Thank him who puts me loath to this revenge
On you who wrong me not for him who wrong'd.
And should I at your harmless innocence
Melt, as I do, yet public reason[5] just,
390   Honor and Empire with revenge enlarg'd,
By conquering this new World, compels me now
To do what else though damn'd I should abhor.
     So spake the Fiend, and with necessity,
The Tyrant's plea, excus'd his devilish deeds.
395   Then from his lofty stand on that high Tree
Down he alights among the sportful Herd
Of those fourfooted kinds, himself now one,
Now other, as thir shape serv'd best his end
Nearer to view his prey, and unespi'd
400   To mark what of thir state he more might learn
By word or action markt: about them round
A Lion now he stalks with fiery glare,
Then as a Tiger, who by chance hath spi'd
In some Purlieu° two gentle Fawns at play,   *edge of a forest*
405   Straight couches close, then rising changes oft
His couchant watch, as one who chose his ground
Whence rushing he might surest seize them both
Gript in each paw: when *Adam* first of men
To first of women *Eve* thus moving speech,
410   Turn'd him° all ear to hear new utterance flow.   *Satan*
     Sole partner and sole part of all these joys,[6]
Dearer thyself than all; needs must the Power
That made us, and for us this ample World
Be infinitely good, and of his good
415   As liberal and free as infinite,
That rais'd us from the dust and plac't us here
In all this happiness, who at his hand
Have nothing merited, nor can perform
Aught whereof hee hath need, hee who requires
420   From us no other service than to keep
This one, this easy charge, of all the Trees
In Paradise that bear delicious fruit
So various, not to taste that only Tree
Of Knowledge, planted by the Tree of Life,[7]
425   So near grows Death to Life, whate'er Death is,
Some dreadful thing no doubt; for well thou know'st
God hath pronounc't it death to taste that Tree,

---

5. Reason of state, a perversion of the Ciceronian principle (*Laws* 3.3.8) that the good of the people is the
supreme law.

6. The first "sole" means "only"; the second, "unrivalled."
7. See Genesis 2.16ff.

The only sign of our obedience left
Among so many signs of power and rule
430 Conferr'd upon us, and Dominion giv'n
Over all other Creatures that possess
Earth, Air, and Sea.[8] Then let us not think hard
One easy prohibition, who enjoy
Free leave so large to all things else, and choice
435 Unlimited of manifold delights:
But let us ever praise him, and extol
His bounty, following our delightful task
To prune these growing Plants, and tend these Flow'rs,
Which were it toilsome, yet with thee were sweet.
440 To whom thus Eve repli'd. O thou for whom
And from whom I was form'd flesh of thy flesh,[9]
And without whom am to no end, my Guide
And Head, what thou hast said is just and right.[1]
For wee to him indeed all praises owe,
445 And daily thanks, I chiefly who enjoy
So far the happier Lot, enjoying thee
Preëminent by so much odds,° while thou   *advantage*
Like consort to thyself canst nowhere find.
That day I oft remember, when from sleep
450 I first awak't, and found myself repos'd
Under a shade on flow'rs, much wond'ring where
And what I was, whence thither brought, and how.
Not distant far from thence a murmuring sound
Of waters issu'd from a Cave and spread
455 Into a liquid Plain, then stood unmov'd
Pure as th' expanse of Heav'n; I thither went
With unexperienc't thought, and laid me down
On the green bank, to look into the clear
Smooth Lake, that to me seem'd another Sky.
460 As I bent down to look, just opposite,
A Shape within the wat'ry gleam appear'd
Bending to look on me, I started back,
It started back, but pleas'd I soon return'd,
Pleas'd it return'd as soon with answering looks
465 Of sympathy and love; there I had fixt
Mine eyes till now, and pin'd with vain desire,[2]
Had not a voice thus warn'd me, What thou seest,
What there thou seest fair Creature is thyself,
With thee it came and goes: but follow me,
470 And I will bring thee where no shadow stays°   *awaits*

8. See Genesis 1.28: "God said unto them . . . have
dominion over the fish of the sea, and over the fowl of
the air, and over every living thing that moveth upon the
earth."
9. See 1 Corinthians 11.9: "Neither was the man created
for the woman; but the woman for the man." See Genesis
2.23.

1. See 1 Corinthians 11.3: "The head of every man is
Christ; and the head of the woman is the man; and the
head of Christ is God."
2. Alluding to Ovid's story of the proud youth Narcissus,
who was punished for his scornfulness by being made to
fall in love with his own reflection in a pool.

Thy coming, and thy soft imbraces, hee
Whose image thou art, him thou shalt enjoy
Inseparably thine, to him shalt bear
Multitudes like thyself, and thence be call'd
475   Mother of human Race: what could I do,
But follow straight, invisibly thus led?
Till I espi'd thee, fair indeed and tall,
Under a Platan, yet methought less fair,
Less winning soft, less amiably mild,
480   Than that smooth wat'ry image; back I turn'd,
Thou following cri'd'st aloud, Return fair *Eve*,
Whom fli'st thou? whom thou fli'st, of him thou art,
His flesh, his bone; to give thee being I lent
Out of my side to thee, nearest my heart
485   Substantial Life, to have thee by my side
Henceforth an individual° solace dear;   *inseparable*
Part of my Soul I seek thee, and thee claim
My other half: with that thy gentle hand
Seiz'd mine, I yielded, and from that time see
490   How beauty is excell'd by manly grace
And wisdom, which alone is truly fair.
        So spake our general Mother, and with eyes
Of conjugal attraction unreprov'd,°   *innocent*
And meek surrender, half imbracing lean'd
495   On our first Father, half her swelling Breast
Naked met his under the flowing Gold
Of her loose tresses hid: hee in delight
Both of her Beauty and submissive Charms
Smil'd with superior Love, as *Jupiter*
500   On *Juno* smiles, when he impregns° the Clouds   *impregnates*
That shed *May* Flowers; and press'd her Matron lip
With kisses pure: aside the Devil turn'd
For envy, yet with jealous leer malign
Ey'd them askance, and to himself thus plain'd.°   *complained*
505   Sight hateful, sight tormenting! thus these two
Imparadis't in one another's arms
The happier *Eden*, shall enjoy thir fill
Of bliss on bliss, while I to Hell am thrust,
Where neither joy nor love, but fierce desire,
510   Among our other torments not the least,
Still unfulfill'd with pain of longing pines;°   *troubles*
Yet let me not forget what I have gain'd
From thir own mouths; all is not theirs it seems:
One fatal Tree there stands of Knowledge call'd,
515   Forbidden them to taste: Knowledge forbidd'n?
Suspicious, reasonless. Why should thir Lord
Envy them that? can it be sin to know,
Can it be death? and do they only stand
By Ignorance, is that thir happy state,
520   The proof of thir obedience and thir faith?

O fair foundation laid whereon to build
Thir ruin! Hence I will excite thir minds
With more desire to know, and to reject
Envious commands, invented with design
525 To keep them low whom Knowledge might exalt
Equal with Gods; aspiring to be such,
They taste and die: what likelier can ensue?
But first with narrow search I must walk round
This Garden, and no corner leave unspi'd;
530 A chance but chance³ may lead where I may met
Some wand'ring Spirit of Heav'n, by Fountain side,
Or in thick shade retir'd, from him to draw
What further would be learnt. Live while ye may,
Yet happy pair; enjoy, till I return,
535 Short pleasures, for long woes are to succeed.
      So saying, his proud step he scornful turn'd,
But with sly circumspection, and began
Through wood, through waste, o'er hill, o'er dale his roam.
Meanwhile in utmost Longitude,⁴ where Heav'n
540 With Earth and Ocean meets, the setting Sun
Slowly descended, and with right aspect
Against the eastern Gate of Paradise
Levell'd his ev'ning Rays: it was a Rock
Of Alablaster,° pil'd up to the Clouds,   *alabaster*
545 Conspicuous far, winding with one ascent
Accessible from Earth, one entrance high;
The rest was craggy cliff, that overhung
Still as it rose, impossible to climb.⁵
Betwixt these rocky Pillars *Gabriel*⁶ sat
550 Chief of th' Angelic Guards, awaiting night;
About him exercis'd Heroic Games
Th' unarmed Youth of Heav'n, but nigh at hand
Celestial Armory, Shields, Helms, and Spears
Hung high with Diamond flaming, and with Gold.
555 Thither came *Uriel*, gliding through the Even
On a Sun-beam, swift as a shooting Star
In *Autumn* thwarts° the night, when vapors fir'd   *crosses*
Impress the Air, and shows the Mariner
From what point of his Compass to beware
560 Impetuous winds:⁷ he thus began in haste.
      Gabriel, to thee thy course by Lot hath giv'n
Charge and strict watch that to this happy place
No evil thing approach or enter in;
This day at highth of Noon came to my Sphere
565 A Spirit, zealous, as he seem'd, to know

---

3. An accident and an opportunity.
4. The farthest west.
5. A possible source is the paradise of Mount Amara in Heylyn's *Cosmographie*.

6. "Strength of God," one of the four archangels ruling the corners of the world.
7. Shooting stars were thought to be a sign of storm because in falling they were thrust down by winds.

More of th' Almighty's works, and chiefly Man
God's latest Image: I describ'd° his way   *observed*
Bent all on speed, and markt his Aery Gait;
But in the Mount that lies from *Eden* North,
570   Where he first lighted, soon discern'd his looks
Alien from Heav'n, with passions foul obscur'd:
Mine eye pursu'd him still, but under shade
Lost sight of him; one of the banisht crew
I fear, hath ventur'd from the Deep, to raise
575   New troubles; him thy care must be to find.
　　　To whom the winged Warrior thus return'd:
Uriel,[8] no wonder if thy perfect sight,
Amid the Sun's bright circle where thou sitst,
See far and wide: in at this Gate none pass
580   The vigilance here plac't, but such as come
Well known from Heav'n; and since Meridian hour
No Creature thence: if Spirit of other sort,
So minded, have o'erleapt these earthy bounds
On purpose, hard thou know'st it to exclude
585   Spiritual substance with corporeal bar.
But if within the circuit of these walks
In whatsoever shape he lurk, of whom
Thou tell'st, by morrow dawning I shall know.
　　　So promis'd hee, and *Uriel* to his charge
590   Return'd on that bright beam, whose point now rais'd
Bore him slope downward to the Sun now fall'n
Beneath th' *Azores*; whither the prime Orb,
Incredible how swift, had thither roll'd
Diurnal,° or this less volúbil[9] Earth   *in one day*
595   By shorter flight to th' East, had left him there
Arraying with reflected Purple and Gold
The Clouds that on his Western Throne attend:[1]
Now came still Ev'ning on, and Twilight gray
Had in her sober Livery all things clad;
600   Silence accompanied, for Beast and Bird,
They to thir grassy Couch, these to thir Nests
Were slunk, all but the wakeful Nightingale;
She all night long her amorous descant sung;
Silence was pleas'd: now glow'd the Firmament
605   With living Sapphires: *Hesperus*[2] that led
The starry Host, rode brightest, till the Moon
Rising in clouded Majesty, at length
Apparent Queen unveil'd her peerless light,
And o'er the dark her Silver Mantle threw.
610   　　　When *Adam* thus to *Eve*: Fair Consort, th' hour
Of night, and all things now retir'd to rest
Mind us of like repose, since God hath set

---

8. "Light of God."
9. Capable of ready rotation on its axis.
1. The appearance of sunset can be regarded as caused

either by orbital motion of the sun about the earth or by
the earth's rotation (a lesser movement).
2. The evening star.

Labor and rest, as day and night to men
Successive, and the timely dew of sleep
615 Now falling with soft slumbrous weight inclines
Our eye-lids; other Creatures all day long
Rove idle unimploy'd, and less need rest;
Man hath his daily work of body or mind
Appointed, which declares his Dignity,
620 And the regard of Heav'n on all his ways;
While other Animals unactive range,
And of thir doings God takes no account.
Tomorrow ere fresh Morning streak the East
With first approach of light, we must be ris'n,
625 And at our pleasant labor, to reform
Yon flow'ry Arbors, yonder Alleys green,
Our walk at noon, with branches overgrown,
That mock our scant manuring,° and require   *cultivating*
More hands than ours to lop thir wanton growth:
630 Those Blossoms also, and those dropping Gums,
That lie bestrown unsightly and unsmooth,
Ask riddance, if we mean to tread with ease;
Meanwhile, as Nature wills, Night bids us rest.
     To whom thus *Eve* with perfect beauty adorn'd.
635 My Author° and Disposer, what thou bidd'st   *origin*
Unargu'd I obey; so God ordains,
God is thy Law, thou mine: to know no more
Is woman's happiest knowledge and her praise.
With thee conversing I forget all time,
640 All seasons and thir change, all please alike.[3]
Sweet is the breath of morn, her rising sweet,
With charm° of earliest Birds; pleasant the Sun   *song*
When first on this delightful Land he spreads
His orient Beams, on herb, tree, fruit, and flow'r,
645 Glist'ring with dew; fragrant the fertile earth
After soft showers; and sweet the coming on
Of grateful Ev'ning mild, then silent Night
With this her solemn Bird and this fair Moon,
And these the Gems of Heav'n, her starry train:
650 But neither breath of Morn when she ascends
With charm of earliest Birds, nor rising Sun
On this delightful land, nor herb, fruit, flow'r,
Glist'ring with dew, nor fragrance after showers,
Nor grateful Ev'ning mild, nor silent Night
655 With this her solemn Bird, nor walk by Moon,
Or glittering Star-light without thee is sweet.
But wherefore all night long shine these, for whom
This glorious sight, when sleep hath shut all eyes?
     To whom our general Ancestor repli'd.
660 Daughter of God and Man, accomplisht *Eve*,

_____

3. Time of day; not "seasons of the year," since it is still eternal spring.

Those have thir course to finish, round the Earth,
By morrow Ev'ning, and from Land to Land
In order, though to Nations yet unborn,
Minist'ring light prepar'd, they set and rise;
665   Lest total darkness should by Night regain
Her old possession, and extinguish life
In Nature and all things, which these soft fires
Not only enlighten, but with kindly heat
Of various influence foment and warm,
670   Temper or nourish, or in part shed down
Thir stellar virtue on all kinds that grow
On Earth, made hereby apter to receive
Perfection from the Sun's more potent Ray.[4]
These then, though unbeheld in deep of night,
675   Shine not in vain, nor think, though men were none,
That Heav'n would want spectators, God want praise;
Millions of spiritual Creatures walk the Earth
Unseen, both when we wake, and when we sleep:
All these with ceaseless praise his works behold
680   Both day and night: how often from the steep
Of echoing Hill or Thicket have we heard
Celestial voices to the midnight air,
Sole, or responsive each to other's note
Singing thir great Creator: oft in bands
685   While they keep watch, or nightly rounding walk,
With Heav'nly touch of instrumental sounds
In full harmonic number join'd, thir songs
Divide the night, and lift our thoughts to Heaven.
      Thus talking hand in hand alone they pass'd
690   On to thir blissful Bower; it was a place
Chos'n by the sovran Planter, when he fram'd
All things to man's delightful use; the roof
Of thickest covert was inwoven shade
Laurel and Myrtle, and what higher grew
695   Of firm and fragrant leaf; on either side
Acanthus, and each odorous bushy shrub
Fenc'd up the verdant wall; each beauteous flow'r,
Iris all hues, Roses, and Jessamin°   jasmine
Rear'd high thir flourisht heads between, and wrought
700   Mosaic; underfoot the Violet,
Crocus, and Hyacinth with rich inlay
Broider'd the ground, more color'd than with stone
Of costliest Emblem:[5] other Creature here

---

4. In Neoplatonic astrology, Sol was said to accomplish the generation of new life by acting through each of the other planets in turn; their function was only to modulate his influence or to select from his complete spectrum of virtues. After the Fall, the influence of the stars becomes less "kindly" (benign; natural).

5. Any ornament of inlaid work; the other sense of "emblem" (pictorial symbol) also operates here, to draw attention to the emblematic properties of the flowers (the humility of the violet, prudence of the hyacinth, amiability of the jasmine, etc.). The bower as a whole is an emblem of true married love.

705 Beast, Bird, Insect, or Worm durst enter none;
Such was thir awe of Man. In shadier Bower
More sacred and sequester'd, though but feign'd,
Pan or *Silvanus* never slept, nor Nymph,
Nor *Faunus* haunted.[6] Here in close recess
With Flowers, Garlands, and sweet-smelling Herbs

710 Espoused *Eve* deckt first her Nuptial Bed,
And heav'nly Choirs the Hymenaean° sung,   *wedding hymn*
What day the genial° Angel to our Sire   *nuptial, generative*
Brought her in naked beauty more adorn'd,
More lovely than *Pandora,* whom the Gods

715 Endow'd with all thir gifts, and O too like
In sad event, when to the unwiser Son
Of *Japhet* brought by *Hermes,* she ensnar'd
Mankind with her fair looks, to be aveng'd
On him who had stole *Jove's* authentic fire.[7]

720 Thus at thir shady Lodge arriv'd, both stood,
Both turn'd, and under op'n Sky ador'd
The God that made both Sky, Air, Earth and Heav'n
Which they beheld, the Moon's resplendent Globe
And starry Pole:° Thou also mad'st the Night,   *sky*

725 Maker Omnipotent, and thou the Day,
Which we in our appointed work imploy'd
Have finisht happy in our mutual help
And mutual love, the Crown of all our bliss
Ordain'd by thee, and this delicious place

730 For us too large, where thy abundance wants
Partakers, and uncropt falls to the ground.
But thou hast promis'd from us two a Race
To fill the Earth, who shall with us extol
Thy goodness infinite, both when we wake,

735 And when we seek, as now, thy gift of sleep.
This said unanimous, and other Rites
Observing none, but adoration pure
Which God likes best, into thir inmost bower
Handed they went; and eas'd the putting off

740 These troublesome disguises which wee wear,
Straight side by side were laid, nor turn'd I ween
Adam from his fair Spouse, nor *Eve* the Rites
Mysterious of connubial Love refus'd:

6. Pan, Silvanus, and Faunus were confused, for all were represented as half man, half goat. Pan was a symbol of fecundity; Silvanus, god of woods, symbolized gardens and limits; Faunus, the Roman Pan, a wood god, and the father of satyrs, was an emblem of concupiscence.
7. Milton has followed Charles Estienne's version of the myth: "Pandora ... is feigned by Hesiod the first woman—made by Vulcan at Jupiter's command— ... she was called Pandora, either because she was 'endowed with all [the gods'] gifts,' or because she was endowed

with gifts by all." She was "sent with a closed casket to Epimetheus, since Jupiter wanted revenge on the human race for the boldness of Prometheus, who had stolen fire from heaven and taken it ... down to earth; and that Epimetheus received her and opened the casket, which contained every kind of evil, so that it filled the world with diseases and calamaties." Prometheus and Epimetheus were sons of Iapetus, the Titan son of Coelus and Terra. Milton identifies Iapetus with Iaphet (Noah's son).

Whatever Hypocrites austerely talk
745   Of purity and place and innocence,
Defaming as impure what God declares
Pure, and commands to some, leaves free to all.
Our Maker bids increase,[8] who bids abstain
But our Destroyer, foe to God and Man?
750   Hail wedded Love, mysterious Law, true source
Of human offspring, sole propriety
In Paradise of all things common else.
By thee adulterous lust was driv'n from men
Among the bestial herds to range, by thee
755   Founded in Reason, Loyal, Just, and Pure,
Relations dear, and all the Charities°   *affections*
Of Father, Son, and Brother first were known.
Far be it, that I should write thee sin or blame,
Or think thee unbefitting holiest place,
760   Perpetual Fountain of Domestic sweets,
Whose bed is undefil'd and chaste pronounc't,[9]
Present, or past, as Saints and Patriarchs us'd.
Here Love his golden shafts imploys,[1] here lights
His constant Lamp, and waves his purple wings,
765   Reigns here and revels; not in the bought smile
Of Harlots, loveless, joyless, unindear'd,
Casual fruition, nor in Court Amours,
Mixt Dance, or wanton Mask, or Midnight Ball,
Or Serenate, which the starv'd Lover sings
770   To his proud fair, best quitted with disdain.
These lull'd by Nightingales imbracing slept,
And on thir naked limbs the flow'ry roof
Show'r'd Roses, which the Morn repair'd.° Sleep on,   *made up for*
Blest pair; and O yet happiest if ye seek
775   No happier state, and know to know no more.[2]
      Now had night measur'd with her shadowy Cone
Half way up Hill this vast Sublunar Vault,[3]
And from thir Ivory Port the Cherubim
Forth issuing at th' accustom'd hour stood arm'd
780   To thir night watches in warlike Parade,
When *Gabriel* to his next in power thus spake.
      Uzziel,[4] half these draw off, and coast the South
With strictest watch; these other wheel the North;
Our circuit meets full West. As flame they part
785   Half wheeling to the Shield, half to the Spear.[5]

8. See Genesis 1.28.
9. See Hebrews 13.4: "Marriage is honourable in all, and the bed undefiled."
1. Cupid's "golden shafts" were sharp and gleaming and kindled love, while those of lead were blunt and put love to flight (Ovid, *Metamorphoses* 1.468–471).
2. Either "know that it is best not to seek new knowledge (by eating the forbidden fruit)" or "know how to limit your experience to the state of innocence."
3. The earth's shadow is a cone that appears to circle around it in diametrical opposition to the sun. When the axis of the cone reaches the meridian, it is midnight; but here it is only "Half way up," so the time is nine o'clock.
4. "Uzziel" (Strength of God) occurs in the Bible as an ordinary human name (e.g., Exodus 6.18), and so does "Zephon" (Searcher of Secrets: Numbers 26.15). "Ithuriel" (Discovery of God) is not from the Bible.
5. "Shield" for "left" and "spear" for "right" were ancient military terms.

From these, two strong and subtle Spirits he call'd
That near him stood, and gave them thus in charge.
   Ithuriel and *Zephon*, with wing'd speed
Search through this Garden, leave unsearcht no nook,
790   But chiefly where those two fair Creatures Lodge,
Now laid perhaps asleep secure° of harm.   *careless*
This Ev'ning from the Sun's decline arriv'd
Who tells of some infernal Spirit seen
Hitherward bent (who could have thought?) escap'd
795   The bars of Hell, on errand bad no doubt:
Such where ye find, seize fast, and hither bring.
   So saying, on he led his radiant Files,
Dazzling the Moon; these to the Bower direct
In search of whom they sought: him there they found
800   Squat like a Toad, close at the ear of *Eve;*
Assaying by his Devilish art to reach
The Organs of her Fancy, and with them forge
Illusions as he list, Phantasms° and Dreams,   *illusions*
Or if, inspiring venom, he might taint
805   Th' animal spirits[6] that from pure blood arise
Like gentle breaths from Rivers pure, thence raise
At least distemper'd,° discontented thoughts,   *vexed*
Vain hopes, vain aims, inordinate desires
Blown up with high conceits ingend'ring pride.
810   Him thus intent *Ithuriel* with his Spear
Touch'd lightly; for no falsehood can endure
Touch of Celestial temper, but returns
Of force to its own likeness: up he starts
Discover'd and surpris'd. As when a spark
815   Lights on a heap of nitrous[7] Powder, laid
Fit for the Tun[8] some Magazin to store
Against° a rumor'd War, the Smutty grain   *preparing for*
With sudden blaze diffus'd, inflames the Air:
So started up in his own shape the Fiend.
820   Back stepp'd those two fair Angels half amaz'd
So sudden to behold the grisly King;
Yet thus, unmov'd with fear, accost him soon.
   Which of those rebel Spirits adjudg'd to Hell
Com'st thou, escap'd thy prison, and transform'd,
825   Why satst thou like an enemy in wait
Here watching at the head of these that sleep?
   Know ye not then said *Satan*, fill'd with scorn,
Know ye not mee?[9] * * *

---

6. Spirits in this sense were fine vapors, regarded by some as a medium between body and soul, by others as a separate soul. Animal spirits (Latin *anima*, soul) ascended to the brain and issued through the nerves to impart motion to the body. Local movement of the animal spirits could also produce imaginative apparitions, by which angels were thought to affect the human mind.
7. Mixed with niter (potassium nitrate or saltpeter, an ingredient in gunpowder) to form an explosive.
8. In proper condition for casking, ready for use.
9. Ithuriel and Zephon take Satan to Gabriel, who orders him to return to Hell. Satan rises up to fight the assembled angels—"His Stature reacht the Sky, and on his Crest / Sat horror Plum'd"—but then God displays scales in heaven, showing victory tilting to Gabriel, and Satan flees.

from **Book 5**

The Argument

Morning approacht, Eve *relates to Adam her troublesome dream; he likes it not, yet comforts her: They come forth to thir day labors: Thir Morning Hymn at the Door of thir Bower. God to render Man inexcusable sends Raphael to admonish him of his obedience, of his free estate, of his enemy near at hand; who he is, and why his enemy, and whatever else may avail Adam to know. Raphael comes down to Paradise, his appearance describ'd, his coming discern'd by Adam afar off sitting at the door of his Bower; he goes out to meet him, brings him to his lodge, entertains him with the choicest fruits of Paradise got together by Eve; thir discourse at Table: Raphael performs his message, minds Adam of his state and of his enemy; relates at Adam's request who that enemy is, and how he came to be so, beginning from his first revolt in Heaven, and the occasion thereof; how he drew his Legions after him to the parts of the North, and there incited them to rebel with him, persuading all but only Abdiel a Seraph, who in Argument dissuades and opposes him, then forsakes him.*

     Now Morn her rosy steps in th' Eastern Clime
     Advancing, sow'd the Earth with Orient Pearl,
     When *Adam* wak't, so custom'd, for his sleep
     Was Aery light, from pure digestion bred,
5   And temperate vapors bland, which th' only sound
     Of leaves and fuming rills, *Aurora's* fan,
     Lightly dispers'd, and the shrill Matin° Song   *morning*
     Of Birds on every bough;[1] so much the more
     His wonder was to find unwak'n'd *Eve*
10   With Tresses discompos'd, and glowing Cheek,
     As through unquiet rest: hee on his side
     Leaning half-rais'd, with looks of cordial Love
     Hung over her enamor'd, and beheld
     Beauty, which whether waking or asleep,
15   Shot forth peculiar° graces; then with voice   *distinctive*
     Mild, as when *Zephyrus*[2] on *Flora* breathes,
     Her hand soft touching, whisper'd thus. Awake
     My fairest, my espous'd, my latest found,
     Heav'n's last best gift, my ever new delight,
20   Awake, the morning shines, and the fresh field
     Calls us; we lose the prime,[3] to mark how spring
     Our tended Plants, how blows° the Citron Grove,   *blossoms*
     What drops the Myrrh, and what the balmy Reed,
     How Nature paints her colors, how the Bee
25   Sits on the Bloom extracting liquid sweet.[4]
     Such whispering wak'd her, but with startl'd eye
     On *Adam*, whom imbracing, thus she spake.
     O Sole in whom my thoughts find all repose,
     My Glory, my Perfection, glad I see

---

1. The "only" (mere) sound of leaves, water, and birds was enough to rouse Adam. The fan of Aurora, the goddess of morning, is the leaves.
2. The west wind. Zephyrus's sweet breath was supposed to produce flowers, as was that of his wife, the flower-goddess Flora.
3. The first hour of the day.
4. For lines 18–25, see Song of Solomon 2.10–13 and 7.12.

30 Thy face, and Morn return'd, for I this Night,
Such night till this I never pass'd, have dream'd,
If dream'd, not as I oft am wont, of thee,
Works of day past, or morrow's next design,
But of offense and trouble, which my mind
35 Knew never till this irksome night; methought
Close at mine ear one call'd me forth to walk
With gentle voice, I thought it thine; it said,
Why sleep'st thou Eve? now is the pleasant time,
The cool, the silent, save where silence yields
40 To the night-warbling Bird, that now awake
Tunes sweetest his love-labor'd song; now reigns
Full Orb'd the Moon, and with more pleasing light
Shadowy sets off the face of things; in vain,
If none regard; Heav'n wakes with all his eyes,
45 Whom to behold but thee, Nature's desire,
In whose sight all things joy, with ravishment
Attracted by thy beauty still to gaze.
I rose as at thy call, but found thee not;
To find thee I directed then my walk;
50 And on, methought, alone I pass'd through ways
That brought me on a sudden to the Tree
Of interdicted Knowledge: fair it seem'd,
Much fairer to my Fancy than by day:
And as I wond'ring lookt, beside it stood
55 One shap'd and wing'd like one of those from Heav'n
By us oft seen; his dewy locks distill'd
Ambrosia;[5] on that Tree he also gaz'd;
And O fair Plant, said he, with fruit surcharg'd,
Deigns none to ease thy load and taste thy sweet,
60 Nor God, nor Man; is Knowledge so despis'd?
Or envy, or what reserve[6] forbids to taste?
Forbid who will, none shall from me withhold
Longer thy offer'd good, why else set here?
This said he paus'd not, but with vent'rous Arm
65 He pluckt, he tasted; mee damp horror chill'd
At such bold words voucht with a deed so bold:
But he thus overjoy'd, O Fruit Divine,
Sweet of thyself, but much more sweet thus cropt,
Forbidd'n here, it seems, as only fit
70 For Gods, yet able to make Gods of Men:
And why not Gods of Men, since good, the more
Communicated, more abundant grows,
The Author not impair'd, but honor'd more?
Here, happy Creature, fair Angelic Eve,
75 Partake thou also; happy though thou art,
Happier thou may'st be, worthier canst not be:
Taste this, and be henceforth among the Gods

5. The fabled anointing oil of the gods.
6. Limitation, restriction, or knowledge kept secret on

the part of God; but perhaps also inhibition, self-restraint
on the part of humans.

Thyself a Goddess, not to Earth confin'd,
But sometimes in the Air, as wee, sometimes
80   Ascend to Heav'n, by merit thine, and see
What life the Gods live there, and such live thou.
So saying, he drew nigh, and to me held,
Even to my mouth of that same fruit held part
Which he had pluckt; the pleasant savory smell[7]
85   So quick'n'd appetite, that I, methought,
Could not but taste. Forthwith up to the Clouds
With him I flew, and underneath beheld
The Earth outstretcht immense, a prospect wide
And various: wond'ring at my flight and change
90   To this high exaltation; suddenly
My Guide was gone, and I, methought, sunk down,
And fell asleep; but O how glad I wak'd
To find this but a dream! Thus *Eve* her Night
Related, and thus *Adam* answer'd sad.°   *gravely*
95   Best Image of myself and dearer half,
The trouble of thy thoughts this night in sleep
Affects me equally; nor can I like
This uncouth° dream, of evil sprung I fear;   *strange*
Yet evil whence? in thee can harbor none,
100   Created pure. But know that in the Soul
Are many lesser Faculties that serve
Reason as chief; among these Fancy next
Her office holds; of all external things,
Which the five watchful Senses represent,
105   She forms Imaginations, Aery shapes,
Which Reason joining or disjoining, frames
All what we affirm or what deny, and call
Our knowledge or opinion; then retires
Into her private Cell when Nature rests.[8]
110   Oft in her absence mimic Fancy wakes
To imitate her; but misjoining shapes,
Wild work produces oft, and most in dreams,
Ill matching words and deeds long past or late.
Some such resemblances methinks I find
115   Of our last Ev'ning's talk,[9] in this thy dream,
But with addition strange; yet be not sad.
Evil into the mind of God[1] or Man
May come and go, so unapprov'd, and leave
No spot or blame behind: Which gives me hope
120   That what in sleep thou didst abhor to dream,
Waking thou never wilt consent to do.

---

7. The fruit has an appetizing, fragrant scent, but "savory" could also mean "spiritually edifying."
8. For the psychology involved here, see Burton, *Anatomy of Melancholy* 1.1.2.7: "Phantasy, or imagination . . . is an inner sense which doth more fully examine the species perceived by common sense, of things present or absent. . . . In time of sleep this faculty is free, and many times

conceives strange, stupend, absurd shapes . . . it is subject and governed by reason, or at least should be."
9. Their discussion of the prohibition of the Tree of Knowledge (4.421ff.).
1. Probably "angel." But Milton (if not Adam) may also intend a reference to the doctrine that God's omniscience extends to evil.

Be not disheart'n'd then, nor cloud those looks
That wont to be more cheerful and serene
Than when fair Morning first smiles on the World,
125 And let us to our fresh imployments rise
Among the Groves, the Fountains, and the Flow'rs
That open now thir choicest bosom'd° smells   *hidden*
Reserv'd from night, and kept for thee in store.
    So cheer'd he his fair Spouse, and she was cheer'd,
130 But silently a gentle tear let fall
From either eye, and wip'd them with her hair;
Two other precious drops that ready stood,
Each in thir crystal sluice, hee ere they fell
Kiss'd as the gracious signs of sweet remorse
135 And pious awe, that fear'd to have offended.
    So all was clear'd, and to the Field they haste.
But first from under shady arborous roof,
Soon as they forth were come to open sight
Of day-spring,° and the Sun, who scarce up risen   *daybreak*
140 With wheels yet hov'ring o'er the Ocean brim,
Shot parallel to the earth his dewy ray,
Discovering in wide Lantskip° all the East   *landscape*
Of Paradise and *Eden's* happy Plains,
Lowly they bow'd adoring, and began
145 Thir Orisons,° each Morning duly paid   *prayers*
In various style, for neither various style
Nor holy rapture wanted they to praise
Thir Maker, in fit strains pronounct or sung
Unmeditated, such prompt eloquence
150 Flow'd from thir lips, in Prose or numerous Verse,
More tuneable° than needed Lute or Harp   *tuneful*
To add more sweetness, and they thus began.[2]
    These are thy glorious works, Parent of good,
Almighty, thine this universal Frame,[3]
155 Thus wondrous fair; thyself how wondrous then!
Unspeakable, who sit'st above these Heavens
To us invisible or dimly seen
In these thy lowest works, yet these declare
Thy goodness beyond thought, and Power Divine:
160 Speak yee who best can tell, ye Sons of Light,
Angels, for yee behold him, and with songs
And choral symphonies, Day without Night,
Circle his Throne rejoicing, yee in Heav'n;
On Earth join all ye Creatures to extol
165 Him first, him last, him midst, and without end.
Fairest of Stars,[4] last in the train of Night,
If better thou belong not to the dawn,

---

2. The hymn (lines 153–208) is based on Psalms 148 and on the Canticle *Benedicite, omnia opera* (in the 1549 *Book of Common Prayer*).
3. Used of heaven, earth, or the universe regarded as structures fabricated by God.
4. The planet Venus rises in the east just before sunrise and is known as the morning star.

Sure pledge of day, that crown'st the smiling Morn
With thy bright Circlet, praise him in thy Sphere
170   While day arises, that sweet hour of Prime.
Thou Sun, of this great World both Eye and Soul,[5]
Acknowledge him thy Greater, sound his praise
In thy eternal course, both when thou climb'st,
And when high Noon hast gain'd, and when thou fall'st.
175   Moon, that now meet'st the orient Sun, now fli'st
With the fixt Stars, fixt in thir Orb that flies,
And yee five other wand'ring Fires that move
In mystic Dance not without Song,[6] resound
His praise, who out of Darkness call'd up Light.
180   Air, and ye Elements the eldest birth
Of Nature's Womb, that in quaternion run
Perpetual Circle, multiform, and mix
And nourish all things, let your ceaseless change
Vary to our great Maker still new praise.
185   Ye Mists and Exhalations that now rise
From Hill or steaming Lake, dusky or grey,
Till the Sun paint your fleecy skirts with Gold,
In honor to the World's great Author rise,
Whether to deck with Clouds th' uncolor'd sky,
190   Or wet the thirsty Earth with falling showers,
Rising or falling still advance his praise.
His praise ye Winds, that from four Quarters blow,
Breathe soft or loud; and wave your tops, ye Pines,
With every Plant, in sign of Worship wave.
195   Fountains and yee, that warble, as ye flow,
Melodious murmurs, warbling tune his praise.
Join voices all ye living Souls; ye Birds,
That singing up to Heaven Gate ascend,
Bear on your wings and in your notes his praise;
200   Yee that in Waters glide, and yee that walk
The Earth, and stately tread, or lowly creep;
Witness if I be silent, Morn or Even,
To Hill, or Valley, Fountain, or fresh shade
Made vocal by my Song, and taught his praise.
205   Hail universal Lord, be bounteous still
To give us only good; and if the night
Have gather'd aught of evil or conceal'd,
Disperse it, as now light dispels the dark.
      So pray'd they innocent, and to thir thoughts
210   Firm peace recover'd soon and wonted calm.
On to thir morning's rural work they haste
Among sweet dews and flow'rs; where any row

---

5. The metaphor of the sun as an eye implied a connection between seeing and understanding and hence an identification of the sun with the creative word. The sun is "soul" of the world in the sense that it gives life.
6. The music of the spheres, inaudible now to fallen humans' gross hearing. The elements are a form of the quaternion, or tetrad, a group of four regarded as one: air, earth, fire, and water. For the transformation of the elements into one another, see Cicero, *De natura deorum* 2.33.

Of Fruit-trees overwoody reach'd too far
Thir pamper'd boughs, and needed hands to check
215 Fruitless imbraces: or they led the Vine
To wed her Elm; she spous'd about him twines
Her marriageable arms, and with her brings
Her dow'r th' adopted Clusters, to adorn
His barren leaves. Them thus imploy'd beheld
220 With pity Heav'n's high King, and to him call'd
    Raphael, the sociable Spirit, that deign'd
To travel with *Tobias,* and secur'd
His marriage with the seven-times-wedded Maid.
Raphael, said hee, thou hear'st what stir on Earth
225 *Satan* from Hell scap't through the darksome Gulf
Hath rais'd in Paradise, and how disturb'd
This night the human pair, how he designs
In them at once to ruin all mankind.
Go therefore, half this day as friend with friend
230 Converse with *Adam,* in what Bow'r or shade
Thou find'st him from the heat of Noon retir'd,
To respite his day-labor with repast,
Or with repose; and such discourse bring on,
As may advise him of his happy state,
235 Happiness in his power left free to will,
Left to his own free Will, his Will though free,
Yet mutable; whence warn him to beware
He swerve not too secure:⁷ tell him withal
His danger, and from whom, what enemy
240 Late fall'n himself from Heaven, is plotting now
The fall of others from like state of bliss;
By violence, no, for that shall be withstood,
But by deceit and lies; this let him know,
Lest wilfully transgressing he pretend
245 Surprisal, unadmonisht, unforewarn'd.⁸
                  * * *
350 Meanwhile our Primitive great Sire, to meet
His god-like Guest, walks forth, without more train
Accompanied than with his own complete
Perfections; in himself was all his state,°   *dignity*
More solemn than the tedious pomp that waits
355 On Princes, when thir rich Retinue long
Of Horses led, and Grooms besmear'd with Gold
Dazzles the crowd, and sets them all agape.
Nearer his presence *Adam* though not aw'd,
Yet with submiss° approach and reverence meek,   *submissive*
360 As to a superior Nature, bowing low,
    Thus said. Native of Heav'n, for other place
None can than Heav'n such glorious shape contain;
Since by descending from the Thrones above,

7. To be careful not to err through overconfidence.   8. Raphael now flies to Eden to see Adam.

Those happy places thou hast deign'd a while
365   To want,° and honor these, voutsafe with us   *miss*
Two only, who yet by sovran gift possess
This spacious ground, in yonder shady Bow'r
To rest, and what the Garden choicest bears
To sit and taste, till this meridian heat
370   Be over, and the Sun more cool decline.
    Whom thus the Angelic Virtue answer'd mild.
Adam, I therefore came, nor art thou such
Created, or such place hast here to dwell,
As may not oft invite, though Spirits of Heav'n
375   To visit thee; lead on then where thy Bow'r
O'ershades; for these mid-hours, till Ev'ning rise
I have at will. So to the Silvan Lodge
They came, that like *Pomona's* Arbor smil'd
With flow'rets deck't and fragrant smells; but *Eve*
380   Undeckt, save with herself more lovely fair
Than Wood-Nymph,[9] or the fairest Goddess feign'd
Of three that in Mount *Ida* naked strove,[1]
Stood to entertain her guest from Heav'n; no veil
Shee needed, Virtue-proof, no thought infirm
385   Alter'd her cheek. On whom the Angel *Hail*
Bestow'd, the holy salutation us'd
Long after to blest *Mary,* second *Eve.*
    Hail Mother of Mankind, whose fruitful Womb
Shall fill the World more numerous with thy Sons
390   Than with these various fruits the Trees of God
Have heap'd this Table. Rais'd of grassy turf
Thir Table was, and mossy seats had round,
And on her ample Square from side to side
All *Autumn* pil'd, though *Spring* and *Autumn* here
395   Danc'd hand in hand. A while discourse they hold;
No fear lest Dinner cool; when thus began
Our Author.° Heav'nly stranger, please to taste   *ancestor*
These bounties which our Nourisher, from whom
All perfet good unmeasur'd out, descends,
400   To us for food and for delight hath caus'd
The Earth to yield; unsavory food perhaps
To spiritual Natures; only this I know,
That one Celestial Father gives to all.
    To whom the Angel. Therefore what he gives
405   (Whose praise be ever sung) to man in part
Spiritual, may of purest Spirits be found
No ingrateful food:[2] and food alike those pure
Intelligential substances[3] require

---

9. The Roman wood-nymph Pomona presided over gardens and especially fruit trees.
1. The three goddesses Juno, Minerva, and Venus all claimed the apple of Strife, inscribed TO THE FAIREST, and the mortal Paris, famed for his wisdom, was appointed arbiter. The judgment of Paris was delivered on Mount

Ida, where the goddesses appeared before him naked and without ornament.
2. Food acceptable to the angels ("purest spirits") because acceptable to humans ("in part spiritual").
3. Intellectual beings.

410 As doth your Rational; and both contain
Within them every lower faculty
Of sense, whereby they hear, see, smell, touch, taste,
Tasting concoct, digest, assimilate,
And corporeal to incorporeal turn.[4]
415 For know, whatever was created, needs
To be sustain'd and fed; of Elements
The grosser feeds the purer, Earth the Sea,
Earth and the Sea feed Air, the Air those Fires
Ethereal, and as lowest first the Moon;
Whence in her visage round those spots, unpurg'd
420 Vapors not yet into her substance turn'd.
Nor doth the Moon no nourishment exhale[5]
From her moist Continent to higher Orbs.
The Sun that light imparts to all, receives
From all his alimental° recompense   *nutritive*
425 In humid exhalations, and at Even
Sups with the Ocean:[6] though in Heav'n the Trees
Of life ambrosial fruitage bear, and vines
Yield Nectar, though from off the boughs each Morn
We brush mellifluous° Dews, and find the ground   *sweetly flowing*
430 Cover'd with pearly grain:[7] yet God hath here
Varied his bounty so with new delights,
As may compare with Heaven; and to taste
Think not I shall be nice.° So down they sat,   *overrefined*
And to thir viands fell, nor seemingly[8]
435 The Angel, nor in mist, the common gloss
Of Theologians, but with keen dispatch
Of real hunger, and concoctive heat
To transubstantiate;[9] what redounds,° transpires   *remains in excess*
Through Spirits with ease; nor wonder; if by fire
440 Of sooty coal the Empiric Alchemist
Can turn, or holds it possible to turn
Metals of drossiest Ore to perfet Gold
As from the Mine. Meanwhile at Table *Eve*
Minister'd naked, and thir flowing cups
445 With pleasant liquors crown'd: O innocence
Deserving Paradise! if ever, then,
Then had the Sons of God° excuse to have been   *angels*
Enamour'd at that sight; but in those hearts
Love unlibidinous reign'd, nor jealousy

4. Physiological theory distinguished three stages of digestion: the "first concoction," or digestion in the stomach ("concoct"); the "second concoction," or conversion to blood ("digest"); and the "thirst concoction," or secretion ("assimilate").

5. The ancient theory was that vapors drawn up to the moon from the earth caused lunar spots. Galileo explained them as landscape features, a theory used above at lines 287–291.

6. This version of the Great Chain of Being was held by Stoics and Epicureans and was also popular in Milton's own time with mystical and alchemic Platonists such as Robert Fludd.

7. Manna, the "corn of heaven."

8. Refers to the Docetist theories about angelic appearances, devised to explain away the awkwardly materialistic accounts of angels in the Bible (e.g., at Genesis 18.8, "they did eat"). The Reformers on the whole rejected such evasions.

9. Transubstantiation is the Roman Catholic doctrine that the bread and wine of the Eucharist become the body and blood of Christ so "transubstantiate" contrasts sharply with the direct concrete simplicity of "keen . . . hunger."

450   Was understood, the injur'd Lover's Hell.
               Thus when with meats and drinks they had suffic't,
           Not burd'n'd Nature, sudden mind arose
           In *Adam*, not to let th' occasion pass
           Given him by this great Conference to know
455   Of things above his World, and of thir being
           Who dwell in Heav'n, whose excellence he saw
           Transcend his own so far, whose radiant forms
           Divine effulgence, whose high Power so far
           Exceeded human, and his wary speech
460   Thus to th' Empyreal° Minister he fram'd.   *heavenly*
               Inhabitant with God, now know I well
           Thy favor, in this honor done to Man,
           Under whose lowly roof thou hast voutsaf't
           To enter, and these earthly fruits to taste,
465   Food not of Angels, yet accepted so,
           As that more willingly thou couldst not seem
           At Heav'n's high feasts to have fed: yet what compare?
               To whom the winged Hierarch repli'd.
           O *Adam*, one Almighty is, from whom
470   All things proceed, and up to him return,
           If not deprav'd from good, created all
           Such to perfection, one first matter all,
           Indu'd with various forms, various degrees
           Of substance, and in things that live, of life;[1]
475   But more refin'd, more spiritous, and pure,
           As nearer to him plac't or nearer tending
           Each in thir several active Spheres assign'd,
           Till body up to spirit work, in bounds
           Proportion'd to each kind. So from the root
480   Springs lighter the green stalk, from thence the leaves
           More aery, last the bright consummate° flow'r   *perfected*
           Spirits odorous breathes: flow'rs and thir fruit
           Man's nourishment, by gradual scale sublim'd°   *raised*
           To vital spirits aspire, to animal,
485   To intellectual, give both life and sense,[2]
           Fancy° and understanding, whence the Soul   *imagination*
           Reason receives, and reason is her being,
           Discursive, or Intuitive; discourse
           Is oftest yours, the latter most is ours,
490   Differing but in degree, of kind the same.[3]
           Wonder not then, what God for you saw good
           If I refuse not, but convert, as you,
           To proper substance; time may come when men

1. Raphael's world picture is characterized by a cyclic movement of emanation and return that marks it as Platonic, just as does the notion of successive degrees of spirituousness. The plant simile explains the notion of a scale of being from vegetable to animal, human, and angelic natures.
2. "Vital spirits" were fine pure fluids, given off by the blood of the heart and sustaining life; "animal spirits" had

their seat in the brain and controlled sensation and voluntary motion.
3. The distinction between the "intuitive," simple undifferentiated operation of the contemplating intellect and the "discursive" or ratiocinative, piecemeal operation of the intellect working in conjuction with the reason goes back ultimately to Plato.

With Angels may participate, and find
495 No inconvenient Diet, nor too light Fare:
And from these corporal nutriments perhaps
Your bodies may at last turn all to spirit,
Improv'd by tract of time, and wing'd ascend
Ethereal, as wee, or may at choice
500 Here or in Heav'nly Paradises dwell;
If ye be found obedient, and retain
Unalterably firm his love entire
Whose progeny you are. Meanwhile enjoy
Your fill what happiness this happy state
505 Can comprehend, incapable of more.
     To whom the Patriarch of mankind repli'd:
O favorable Spirit, propitious guest,
Well hast thou taught the way that might direct
Our knowledge, and the scale of Nature set
510 From centre to circumference, whereon
In contemplation of created things
By steps we may ascend to God.[4] But say,
What meant that caution join'd, *if ye be found
Obedient?* can we want obedience then
515 To him, or possibly his love desert
Who form'd us from the dust, and plac'd us here
Full to the utmost measure of what bliss
Human desires can seek or apprehend?
     To whom the Angel. Son of Heav'n and Earth,
520 Attend: That thou art happy, owe to God;
That thou continu'st such, owe to thyself,
That is, to thy obedience; therein stand.
This was that caution giv'n thee; be advis'd.
God made thee perfet, not immutable;
525 And good he made thee, but to persevere
He left it in thy power, ordain'd thy will
By nature free, not over-rul'd by Fate
Inextricable, or strict necessity;
Our voluntary service he requires,
530 Not our necessitated, such with him
Finds no acceptance, nor can find, for how
Can hearts, not free, be tri'd whether they serve
Willing or no, who will but what they must
By Destiny, and can no other choose?
535 Myself and all th' Angelic Host that stand
In sight of God enthron'd, our happy state
Hold, as you yours, while our obedience holds;
On other surety none; freely we serve,
Because we freely love, as in our will
540 To love or not; in this we stand or fall:
And some are fall'n, to disobedience fall'n,

---

4. In the scale or ladder of nature, Adam refers to the Platonic ascent from image to universal, up the hierarchic grades of existence.

And so from Heav'n to deepest Hell; O fall
From what high state of bliss into what woe!
        To whom our great Progenitor. Thy words
545   Attentive, and with more delighted ear
Divine instructor, I have heard, than when
Cherubic Songs by night from neighboring Hills
Aereal Music send: nor knew I not
To be both will and deed created free;
550   Yet that we never shall forget to love
Our maker, and obey him whose command
Single, is yet so just, my constant thoughts
Assur'd me and still assure: though what thou tell'st
Hath past in Heav'n, some doubt within me move,
555   But more desire to hear, if thou consent,
The full relation, which must needs be strange,
Worthy of Sacred silence to be heard;
And we have yet large day, for scarce the Sun
Hath finisht half his journey, and scarce begins
560   His other half in the great Zone of Heav'n.
        Thus *Adam* made request, and *Raphaël*
After short pause assenting, thus began.[5] * * *

Book 6
The Argument

Raphael *continues to relate how* Michael *and* Gabriel *were sent forth to Battle against* Satan *and his Angels. The first fight describ'd:* Satan *and his Powers retire under Night: He calls a Council, invents devilish Engines, which in the second day's Fight put* Michael *and his Angels to some disorder; but they at length pulling up Mountains overwhelm'd both the force and Machines of* Satan: *Yet the Tumult not so ending, God on the third day sends* Messiah *his Son for whom he had reserv'd the glory of the Victory: Hee in the Power of his Father coming to the place, and causing all his Legions to stand still on either side, with his Chariot and Thunder driving into the midst of his Enemies, pursues them unable to resist towards the wall of Heaven; which opening they leap down with horror and confusion in the place of punishment prepar'd for them in the Deep:* Messiah *returns with triumph to his Father.*

from Book 7
The Argument

Raphael *at the request of Adam relates how and wherefore this world was first created; that God, after the expelling of Satan and his Angels out of Heaven, declar'd his pleasure to create another World and other Creatures to dwell therein; sends his Son with Glory and attendance of Angels to perform the work of Creation in six days: the Angels celebrate with Hymns the performance thereof, and his reascension into Heaven.*

---

5. Raphael's account of the war in heaven continues to the end of Book 6. It is one of the two long "episodes," or inset narrations, that conclude the two halves of the poem (the other is at the end of Book 11).

[THE INVOCATION]

Descend from Heav'n *Urania*,[1] by that name
If rightly thou art call'd, whose Voice divine
Following, above th' *Olympian* Hill I soar,
Above the flight of *Pegasean* wing.[2]
5   The meaning, not the Name I call: for thou
Nor of the Muses nine, nor on the top
Of old *Olympus* dwell'st, but Heav'nly born,
Before the Hills appear'd, or Fountain flow'd,
Thou with Eternal Wisdom didst converse,
10   Wisdom thy Sister, and with her didst play
In presence of th' Almighty Father, pleas'd
With thy Celestial Song. Up led by thee
Into the Heav'n of Heav'ns I have presum'd,
An Earthly Guest, and drawn Empyreal Air,
15   Thy temp'ring;[3] with like safety guided down
Return me to my Native Element:
Lest from this flying Steed unrein'd, (as once
Bellerophon, though from a lower Clime)
Dismounted, on th' *Aleian* Field I fall
20   Erroneous° there to wander and forlorn.[4]   *wandering, erring*
Half yet remains unsung, but narrower bound
Within the visible Diurnal Sphere;
Standing on Earth, not rapt° above the Pole,[5]   *entranced*
More safe I Sing with mortal voice, unchang'd
25   To hoarse or mute, though fall'n on evil days,
On evil days though fall'n, and evil tongues;
In darkness, and with dangers compast round,
And solitude;[6] yet not alone, while thou
Visit'st my slumbers Nightly, or when Morn
30   Purples the East: still govern thou my Song,
Urania, and fit audience find, though few.
But drive far off the barbarous dissonance
Of *Bacchus* and his Revellers, the Race
Of that wild Rout that tore the *Thracian* Bard
35   In *Rhodope,* where Woods and Rocks had Ears
To rapture, till the savage clamor drown'd
Both Harp and Voice;[7] nor could the Muse defend
Her Son. So fail not thou, who thee implores:
For thou art Heavn'ly, shee an empty dream. * * *

1. Only in this invocation is the Muse ever named. *Urania* was the Muse of Astronomy. Milton's denial that his Urania is one "of the Muses nine" directs attention to a more recent, single Muse. Since Du Bartas's *Uranie,* the name had been used for the Christian Muse of the divine poetry movement.
2. The winged horse Pegasus was an emblem for the inspired poet.
3. The air of the "first region" (3.562–64) was fatal to mortals.
4. When Bellerephon tried to fly to heaven on Pegasus, Jupiter sent an insect to sting the horse and throw the rider. Bellerephon fell on the Aleian plain and wandered

blind and lonely until his death.
5. Either the celestial pole or a synecdoche for the sky.
6. The obfuscated syntax conceals an allusion to Milton's dangerous situation during the persecutions that immediately followed the Restoration.
7. Orpheus as a type of the inspired poet. The myth of his dismemberment by Thracian women during orgies of Bacchus seems to have focused some of Milton's deepest fears. Rhodope was a mountain range in Thrace. In Ovid, *Metamorphoses* 11.1–60, the "woods and rocks" mourned Orpheus's loss, though they were the instruments of his murder.

from **Book 8**

The Argument

Adam *inquires concerning celestial Motions, is doubtfully answer'd, and exhorted to search rather things more worthy of knowledge:* Adam *assents, and still desirous to detain* Raphael, *relates to him what he remember'd since his own Creation, his placing in Paradise, his talk with* God *concerning solitude and fit society, his first meeting and Nuptials with* Eve, *his discourse with the Angel thereupon; who after admonitions repeated departs.*

	To whom thus Adam clear'd of doubt, repli'd.	
180	How fully hast thou satisfi'd me, pure	
	Intelligence° of Heav'n, Angel serene,	*spirit*
	And freed from intricacies, taught to live	
	The easiest way, nor with perplexing thoughts	
	To interrupt the sweet of Life, from which	
185	God hath bid dwell far off all anxious cares,	
	And not molest us, unless we ourselves	
	Seek them with wand'ring thoughts, and notions vain.	
	But apt the Mind or Fancy is to rove	
	Uncheckt, and of her roving is no end;	
190	Till warn'd, or by experience taught, she learn	
	That not to know at large of things remote	
	From use, obscure and subtle, but to know	
	That which before us lies in daily life,	
	Is the prime Wisdom; what is more, is fume,°	*smoke*
195	Or emptiness, or fond impertinence,°	*foolish irrelevance*
	And renders us in things that most concern	
	Unpractic'd, unprepar'd, and still to seek.	
	Therefore from this high pitch let us descend	
	A lower flight, and speak of things at hand	
200	Useful, whence haply mention may arise	
	Of something not unseasonable to ask	
	By sufferance,° and thy wonted favor deign'd.	*permission*
	Thee I have heard relating what was done	
	Ere my remembrance: now hear mee relate	
205	My Story, which perhaps thou hast not heard;	
	And Day is yet not spent; till then thou seest	
	How subtly to detain thee I devise,	
	Inviting thee to hear while I relate,	
	Fond, were it not in hope of thy reply:	
210	For while I sit with thee, I seem in Heav'n,	
	And sweeter thy discourse is to my ear	
	Than Fruits of Palm-tree pleasantest to thirst	
	And hunger both, from labor, at the hour	
	Of sweet repast; they satiate, and soon fill,	
215	Though pleasant, but thy words with Grace Divine	
	Imbu'd, bring to thir sweetness no satiety.	
	To whom thus *Raphael* answer'd heav'nly meek.	
	Nor are thy lips ungraceful, Sire of men,	
	Nor tongue ineloquent; for God on thee	
220	Abundantly his gifts hath also pour'd	

Inward and outward both, his image fair:
Speaking or mute all comeliness and grace
Attends thee, and each word, each motion forms.
Nor less think wee in Heav'n of thee on Earth
225 Than of our fellow servant, and inquire
Gladly into the ways of God with Man:
For God we see hath honor'd thee, and set
On Man his Equal Love: say therefore on;
For I that Day was absent, as befell,
230 Bound on a voyage uncouth° and obscure,   *unfamiliar*
Far on excursion toward the Gates of Hell;
Squar'd in full Legion (such command we had)
To see that none thence issu'd forth a spy,
Or enemy, while God was in his work,
235 Lest hee incenst at such eruption bold,
Destruction with Creation might have mixt.
Not that they durst without his leave attempt,
But us he sends upon his high behests
For state,° as Sovran King, and to enure   *ceremony*
240 Our prompt obedience. Fast we found, fast shut
The dismal Gates, and barricado'd strong;
But long ere our approaching heard within
Noise, other than the sound of Dance or Song,
Torment, and loud lament, and furious rage.
245 Glad we return'd up to the coasts of Light
Ere Sabbath Ev'ning: so we had in charge.
But thy relation now; for I attend,
Pleas'd with thy words no less than thou with mine.
    So spake the Godlike Power, and thus our Sire.
250 For man to tell how human Life began
Is hard; for who himself beginning knew?
Desire with thee still longer to converse
Induc'd me. As new wak't from soundest sleep
Soft on the flow'ry herb I found me laid
255 In Balmy Sweat, which with his Beams the Sun
Soon dri'd, and on the reeking moisture fed.
Straight toward Heav'n my wond'ring Eyes I turn'd,
And gaz'd a while the ample Sky, till rais'd
By quick instinctive motion up I sprung,
260 As thitherward endeavoring, and upright
Stood on my feet; about me round I saw
Hill, Dale, and shady Woods, and sunny Plains,
And liquid Lapse of murmuring Streams; by these,
    Creatures that liv'd, and mov'd, and walk'd, or flew,
265 Birds on the branches warbling; all things smil'd,
With fragrance and with joy my heart o'erflow'd.
Myself I then perus'd, and Limb by Limb
Survey'd, and sometimes went,° and sometimes ran   *walked*
With supple joints, as lively vigor led:
270 But who I was, or where, or from what cause,
Knew not; to speak I tri'd, and forthwith spake,

My Tongue obey'd and readily could name
Whate'er I saw. Thou Sun, said I, fair Light,
And thou enlight'n'd Earth, so fresh and gay,
275 Ye Hills and Dales, ye Rivers, Woods, and Plains
And ye that live and move, fair Creatures, tell,
Tell, if ye saw, how came I thus, how here?
Not of myself; by some great Maker then,
In goodness and in power preëminent;
280 Tell me, how may I know him, how adore,
From whom I have that thus I move and live,[1]
And feel that I am happier than I know.
While thus I call'd, and stray'd I knew not whither,
From where I first drew Air, and first beheld
285 This happy Light, when answer none return'd,
On a green shady Bank profuse of Flow'rs
Pensive I sat me down; there gentle sleep
First found me, and with soft oppression seiz'd
My drowsed sense, untroubl'd, though I thought
290 I then was passing to my former state
Insensible, and forthwith to dissolve:
When suddenly stood at my Head a dream,
Whose inward apparition gently mov'd
My fancy to believe I yet had being,
295 And liv'd: One came, methought, of shape Divine,
And said, thy Mansion° wants thee, *Adam*, rise,   home
First Man, of Men innumerable ordain'd
First Father, call'd by thee I come thy Guide
To the Garden of bliss, thy seat prepar'd.[2]
300 So saying, by the hand he took me rais'd,
And over Fields and Waters, as in Air
Smooth sliding without step, last led me up
A woody Mountain; whose high top was plain,
A Circuit wide, enclos'd, with goodliest Trees
305 Planted, with Walks, and Bowers, that what I saw
Of Earth before scarce pleasant seem'd. Each Tree
Load'n with fairest Fruit, that hung to the Eye
Tempting, stirr'd in me sudden appetite
To pluck and eat; whereat I wak'd, and found
310 Before mine Eyes all real, as the dream
Had lively shadow'd: Here had new begun
My wand'ring, had not hee who was my Guide
Up hither, from among the Trees appear'd,
Presence Divine. Rejoicing, but with awe,
315 In adoration at his feet I fell
Submiss:° he rear'd me, and Whom thou sought'st I am,[3]   submissive
Said mildly, Author of all this thou seest

---

1. See St. Paul's Mars' hill sermon on the Unknown God,
Acts 17.28: "For in him we live, and move, and have our
being."
2. See Genesis 2.8 and 2.15.

3. See Exodus 3.14: "I AM THAT I AM. . . . Thus
shalt thou say unto the children of Israel, I AM hath
sent me unto you."

Above, or round about thee or beneath.
This Paradise I give thee, count it thine
320 To Till and keep, and of the Fruit to eat:
Of every Tree that in the Garden grows
Eat freely with glad heart; fear here no dearth:[4]
But of the Tree whose operation brings
Knowledge of good and ill, which I have set
325 The Pledge of thy Obedience and thy Faith,
Amid the Garden by the Tree of Life,
Remember what I warn thee, shun to taste,
And shun the bitter consequence: for know,
The day thou eat'st thereof, my sole command
330 Transgrest, inevitably thou shalt die;
From that day mortal, and this happy State
Shalt lose, expell'd from hence into a World
Of woe and sorrow. Sternly he pronounc'd
The rigid interdiction,° which resounds   *prohibition*
335 Yet dreadful in mine ear, though in my choice
Not to incur; but soon his clear aspect
Return'd and gracious purpose° thus renew'd.   *discourse*
Not only these fair bounds, but all the Earth
To thee and to thy Race I give; as Lords
340 Possess it, and all things that therein live,
Or live in Sea, or Air, Beast, Fish, and Fowl.[5]
In sign whereof each Bird and Beast behold
After thir kinds; I bring them to receive
From thee thir Names, and pay thee fealty
345 With low subjection; understand the same
Of Fish within thir wat'ry residence,
Not hither summon'd, since they cannot change
Thir Element to draw the thinner Air,
As thus he spake, each Bird and Beast behold
350 Approaching two and two, These cow'ring low
With blandishment, each Bird stoop'd on his wing.
I nam'd them, as they pass'd, and understood
Thir Nature, with such knowledge God endu'd
My sudden apprehension: but in these
355 I found not what methought I wanted still;
And to the Heav'nly vision thus presum'd.
    O by what Name, for thou above all these,
Above mankind, or aught than mankind higher,
Surpassest far my naming, how may I
360 Adore thee, Author of this Universe,
And all this good to man, for whose well being
So amply, and with hands so liberal
Thou hast provided all things: but with mee
I see not who partakes. In solitude
365 What happiness, who can enjoy alone,
Or all enjoying, what contentment find?

---

4. See Genesis 2.15ff.   5. See Genesis 1.28.

Thus I presumptuous; and the vision bright,
As with a smile more bright'n'd, thus repli'd.
   What call'st thou solitude? is not the Earth
370   With various living creatures, and the Air
Replenisht, and all these at thy command
To come and play before thee; know'st thou not
Thir language and thir ways? They also know,[6]
And reason not contemptibly; with these
375   Find pastime, and bear rule; thy Realm is large.
So spake the Universal Lord, and seem'd
So ordering. I with leave of speech implor'd,
And humble deprecation thus repli'd.
   Let not my words offend thee, Heav'nly Power,
380   My Maker, be propitious while I speak.
Hast thou not made me here thy substitute,
And these inferior far beneath me set?
Among unequals what society
Can sort,° what harmony or true delight?   agree
385   Which must be mutual, in proportion due
Giv'n and receiv'd; but in disparity
The one intense, the other still remiss
Cannot well suit with either, but soon prove
Tedious alike:[7] Of fellowship I speak
390   Such as I seek, fit to participate
All rational delight, wherein the brute
Cannot be human consort; they rejoice
Each with thir kind, Lion with Lioness;
So fitly them in pairs thou hast combin'd;
395   Much less can Bird with Beast, or Fish with Fowl
So well converse, nor with the Ox the Ape;
Worse then can Man with Beast, and least of all.
   Whereto th' Almighty answer'd, not displeas'd.
A nice and subtle happiness I see
400   Thou to thyself proposest, in the choice
Of thy Associates, *Adam*, and wilt taste
No pleasure, though in pleasure, solitary.
What think'st thou then of mee, and this my State,
Seem I to thee sufficiently possest
405   Of happiness, or not? who am alone
From all Eternity, for none I know
Second to mee or like, equal much less.
How have I then with whom to hold converse
Save with the Creatures which I made, and those
410   To me inferior, infinite descents
Beneath what other Creatures are to thee?
   He ceas'd, I lowly answer'd. To attain
The highth and depth of thy Eternal ways
All human thoughts come short, Supreme of things;

---

6. It was a widespread Jewish belief that before the Fall, Adam understood the language of the beasts. The original language was usually supposed to have been Hebrew, but sometimes Syriac, Greek, or Aramaic.

7. In a stringed instrument the strings should bear a due ratio of length and frequency. But the human string is too strained ("intense") and therefore high in pitch, while the animal string is too "remiss," i.e., low in pitch.

415   Thou in thyself art perfet, and in thee
       Is no deficience found; not so is Man,
       But in degree, the cause of his desire
       By conversation with his like to help,
       Or solace his defects. No need that thou
420   Shouldst propagate, already infinite;
       And through all numbers absolute, though One;[8]
       But Man by number is to manifest
       His single imperfection, and beget
       Like of his like, his Image multipli'd,
425   In unity defective, which requires
       Collateral love, and dearest amity.
       Thou in thy secrecy although alone,
       Best with thyself accompanied, seek'st not
       Social communication, yet so pleas'd,
430   Canst raise thy Creature to what highth thou wilt
       Of Union or Communion, deifi'd;
       I by conversing cannot these erect
       From prone, nor in thir ways complacence° find.   *source of pleasure*
       Thus I embold'n'd spake, and freedom us'd
435   Permissive, and acceptance found, which gain'd
       This answer from the gracious voice Divine.
           Thus far to try thee, *Adam*, I was pleas'd,
       And find thee knowing not of Beasts alone,
       Which thou hast rightly nam'd, but of thyself,
440   Expressing well the spirit within thee free,
       My Image, not imparted to the Brute,
       Whose fellowship therefore unmeet for thee
       Good reason was thou freely shouldst dislike,
       And be so minded still; I, ere thou spak'st,
445   Knew it not good for Man to be alone,
       And no such company as then thou saw'st
       Intended thee, for trial only brought,
       To see how thou couldst judge of fit and meet:
       What next I bring shall please thee, be assur'd,
450   Thy likeness, thy fit help, thy other self,
       Thy wish, exactly to thy heart's desire.
           Hee ended, or I heard no more, for now
       My earthly° by his Heav'nly overpower'd,   *earthly nature*
       Which it had long stood under, strain'd to the highth
455   In that celestial Colloquy sublime,
       As with an object that excels the sense,
       Dazzl'd and spent, sunk down, and sought repair
       Of sleep, which instantly fell on me, call'd
       By Nature as in aid, and clos'd mine eyes.[9]
460   Mine eyes he clos'd, but op'n left the Cell
       Of Fancy my internal sight, by which
       Abstract° as in a trance methought I saw,   *withdrawn*
       Though sleeping, where I lay, and saw the shape

8. The divine monad contains all other numbers and is therefore complete and perfect through them all. The monad is like God because it is the fountain and origin of all numbers, as God is the origin of created being.
9. For lines 452–486, see Genesis 2.21ff.

Still glorious before whom awake I stood;
465 Who stooping op'n'd my left side, and took
From thence a Rib, with cordial spirits warm,
And Life-blood streaming fresh; wide was the wound,
But suddenly with flesh fill'd up and heal'd:
The Rib he form'd and fashion'd with his hands;
470 Under his forming hands a Creature grew,
Manlike, but different sex, so lovely fair,
That what seem'd fair in all the World, seem'd now
Mean, or in her summ'd up, in her contain'd
And in her looks, which from that time infus'd,
475 Sweetness into my heart, unfelt before,
And into all things from her Air inspir'd
The spirit of love and amorous delight.
Shee disappear'd, and left me dark, I wak'd
To find her, or for ever to deplore
480 Her loss, and other pleasures all abjure:
When out of hope, behold her, not far off,
Such as I saw her in my dream, adorn'd
With what all Earth or Heaven could bestow
To make her amiable: On she came,
485 Led by her Heav'nly Maker, though unseen,
And guided by his voice, nor uninform'd
Of nuptial Sanctity and marriage Rites:
Grace was in all her steps, Heav'n in her Eye,
In every gesture dignity and love.
490 I overjoy'd could not forbear aloud.°   *saying aloud*
     This turn hath made amends; thou hast fulfill'd
Thy words, Creator bounteous and benign,
Giver of all things fair, but fairest this
Of all thy gifts, nor enviest. I now see
495 Bone of my Bone, Flesh of my Flesh, my Self
Before me; Woman is her Name, of Man
Extracted; for this cause he shall forgo
Father and Mother, and to his Wife adhere;
And they shall be one Flesh, one Heart, one Soul.[1]
500   She heard me thus, and though divinely brought,
Yet Innocence and Virgin Modesty,
Her virtue and the conscience° of her worth,   *consciousness*
That would be woo'd, and not unsought be won,
Not obvious, not obtrusive, but retir'd,
505 The more desirable, or to say all,
Nature herself, though pure of sinful thought,
Wrought in her so, that seeing me, she turn'd;
I follow'd her, she what was Honor knew,
And with obsequious° Majesty approv'd   *compliant*
510 My pleaded reason. To the Nuptial Bow'r
I led her blushing like the Morn: all Heav'n,
And happy Constellations on that hour
Shed thir selectest influence; the Earth

---

1. See *Genesis* 3.23ff. The biblical expression "one flesh" is replaced by the familiar Platonic tripartite division into parts.

	Gave sign of gratulation,° and each Hill;	*joy*
515	Joyous the Birds; fresh Gales and gentle Airs	
	Whisper'd it to the Woods, and from thir wings	
	Flung Rose, flung Odors from the spicy Shrub,	
	Disporting, till the amorous Bird of Night[2]	
	Sung Spousal, and bid haste the Ev'ning Star	
520	On his Hill top, to light the bridal Lamp.	
	Thus I have told thee all my State, and brought	
	My Story to the sum of earthly bliss	
	Which I enjoy, and must confess to find	
	In all things else delight indeed, but such	
525	As us'd or not, works in the mind no change,	
	Nor vehement desire, these delicacies	
	I mean of Taste, Sight, Smell, Herbs, Fruits, and Flow'rs,	
	Walks, and the melody of Birds; but here	
	Far otherwise, transported I behold,	
530	Transported touch; here passion first I felt,	
	Commotion strange, in all enjoyments else	
	Superior and unmov'd, here only weak	
	Against the charm of Beauty's powerful glance.	
	Or° Nature fail'd in mee, and left some part	*either*
535	Not proof enough such Object to sustain,	
	Or from my side subducting,° took perhaps	*subtracting*
	More than enough; at least on her bestow'd	
	Too much of Ornament, in outward show	
	Elaborate, of inward less exact.°	*perfect*
540	For well I understand in the prime end	
	Of Nature her th' inferior, in the mind	
	And inward Faculties, which most excel,	
	In outward also her resembling less	
	His Image who made both, and less expressing	
545	The character of that Dominion giv'n	
	O'er other Creatures; yet when I approach	
	Her loveliness, so absolute she seems	
	And in herself complete, so well to know	
	Her own, that what she wills to do or say,	
550	Seems wisest, virtuousest, discreetest, best;	
	All higher knowledge in her presence falls	
	Degraded, Wisdom in discourse with her	
	Loses discount'nanc't, and like folly shows;	
	Authority and Reason on her wait,	
555	As one intended first, not after made	
	Occasionally;° and to consummate all,	*accidentally*
	Greatness of mind and nobleness thir seat	
	Build in her loveliest, and create an awe	
	About her, as a guard Angelic plac't.	
560	To whom the Angel with contracted brow.	
	Accuse not Nature, she hath done her part;	
	Do thou but thine, and be not diffident°	*mistrustful*
	Of Wisdom, she deserts thee not, if thou	

---

2. The nightingale; see 5.40–41, page 1833.

Dismiss not her, when most thou need'st her nigh,
565   By attribúting overmuch to things
Less excellent, as thou thyself perceiv'st.
For what admir'st thou, what transports thee so,
An outside? fair no doubt, and worthy well
Thy cherishing, thy honoring, and thy love,
570   Not thy subjection: weigh with her thyself;
Then value: Oft-times nothing profits more
Than self-esteem, grounded on just and right
Well manag'd; of that skill the more thou know'st,
The more she will acknowledge thee her Head,[3]
575   And to realities yield all her shows;
Made so adorn for thy delight the more,
So awful, that with honor thou may'st love
Thy mate, who sees when thou art seen least wise.
But if the sense of touch whereby mankind
580   Is propagated seem such dear delight
Beyond all other, think the same voutsaf't
To Cattle and each Beast; which would not be
To them made common and divulg'd, if aught
Therein enjoy'd were worthy to subdue
585   The Soul of Man, or passion in him move.
What higher in her society thou find'st
Attractive, human, rational, love still;
In loving thou dost well, in passion not,
Wherein true Love consists not; Love refines
590   The thoughts, and heart enlarges, hath his seat
In Reason, and is judicious, is the scale[4]
By which to heav'nly Love thou may'st ascend,
Not sunk in carnal pleasure, for which cause
Among the Beasts no Mate for thee was found.[5]
595   To whom thus half abash't *Adam* repli'd.[6]
Neither her out-side form'd so fair, nor aught
In procreation common to all kinds
(Though higher of the genial° Bed by far,   *nuptial*
And with mysterious reverence I deem)
600   So much delights me, as those graceful acts,
Those thousand decencies that daily flow
From all her words and actions, mixt with Love
And sweet compliance, which declare unfeign'd
Union of Mind, or in us both one Soul;
605   Harmony to behold in wedded pair
More grateful than harmonious sound to the ear.

---

3. Alludes to 1 Corinthians 11.3: "The head of every man is Christ; and the head of the woman is the man; and the head of Christ is God."
4. The Neoplatonic ladder of love.
5. Raphael here expounds the very familiar Neoplatonic distinction between divine or celestial love, human or terrestrial love, and bestial love. The first (Milton's "heavenly love") is the love of the contemplative, belonging to mind alone. The second ("true love") is the

force that drives humans to propagate the earthly image of divine beauty but may also, in its ideal form, lead them to the first. The third ("sunk . . . pleasure") is experienced by humans who stoop to debauchery.
6. The conversation of Raphael and Adam does in some respects resemble a debate between Heavenly Love and Human Love in which the angel/human distinction is intensified into an antithesis.

Yet these subject not; I to thee disclose
What inward thence I feel, not therefore foil'd,°   *overcome*
Who meet with various objects, from the sense
610   Variously representing; yet still free
Approve the best, and follow what I approve.
To Love thou blam'st me not, for Love thou say'st
Leads up to Heav'n, is both the way and guide;
Bear with me then, if lawful what I ask;
615   Love not the heav'nly Spirits, and how thir Love
Express they, by looks only, or do they mix
Irradiance, virtual or immediate touch?
        To whom the Angel with a smile that glow'd
Celestial rosy red, Love's proper hue,
620   Answer'd. Let it suffice thee that thou know'st
Us happy, and without Love no happiness.
Whatever pure thou in the body enjoy'st
(And pure thou wert created) we enjoy
In eminence, and obstacle find none
625   Of membrance, joint, or limb, exclusive bars:
Easier than Air with Air, if Spirits embrace,
Total they mix, Union of Pure with Pure
Desiring; nor restrain'd conveyance need
As Flesh to mix with Flesh, or Soul with Soul.
630   But I can now no more; the parting Sun
Beyond the Earth's green Cape and verdant Isles
Hesperian sets, my Signal to depart.[7]
Be strong, live happy, and love, but first of all
Him whom to love is to obey, and keep
635   His great command; take heed lest Passion sway
Thy Judgment to do aught, which else free Will
Would not admit; thine and of all thy Sons
The weal or woe in thee is plac't; beware.
I in thy persevering shall rejoice,
640   And all the Blest: stand fast; to stand or fall
Free in thine own Arbitrement it lies.
Perfet within, no outward aid require;
And all temptation to transgress repel.
        So saying, he arose; whom *Adam* thus
645   Follow'd with benediction. Since to part,
Go heavenly Guest, Ethereal Messenger,
Sent from whose sovran goodness I adore.
Gentle to me and affable hath been
Thy condescension, and shall be honor'd ever
650   With grateful Memory: thou to mankind
Be good and friendly still, and oft return.
        So parted they, the Angel up to Heav'n
From the thick shade, and *Adam* to his Bow'r.
                The End of the Eighth Book.

---

7. Where the sun sets "beneath the Azores." Here the "green Cape" is Cape Verde, and the "verdant Isles" are the Cape Verde Islands.

Book 9

The Argument

Satan *having compast the Earth, with meditated guile returns as a mist by Night into Paradise, enters into the Serpent sleeping.* Adam *and* Eve *in the Morning go forth to thir labors, which* Eve *proposes to divide in several places, each laboring apart:* Adam *consents not, alleging the danger, lest that Enemy, of whom they were forewarn'd, should attempt her found alone:* Eve *loath to be thought not circumspect or firm enough, urges her going apart, the rather desirous to make trial of her strength;* Adam *at last yields: The Serpent finds her alone; his subtle approach, first gazing, then speaking, with much flattery extolling* Eve *above all other Creatures.* Eve *wond'ring to hear the Serpent speak, asks how he attain'd to human speech and such understanding not till now; the Serpent answers, that by tasting of a certain Tree in the Garden he attain'd both to Speech and Reason, till then void of both:* Eve *requires him to bring her to that Tree, and finds it to be the Tree of Knowledge forbidden: The Serpent now grown bolder, with many wiles and arguments induces her at length to eat; she pleas'd with the taste deliberates awhile whether to impart thereof to* Adam *or not, at last brings him of the Fruit, relates what persuaded her to eat thereof:* Adam *at first amaz'd, but perceiving her lost, resolves through vehemence[1] of love to perish with her; and extenuating[2] the trespass, eats also of the Fruit: The effects thereof in them both; they seek to cover thir nakedness; then fall to variance and accusation of one another.*

	No more of talk where God or Angel Guest	
	With Man, as with his Friend, familiar us'd	
	To sit indulgent, and with him partake	
	Rural repast, permitting him the while	
5	Venial° discourse unblam'd: I now must change	*permissible*
	Those Notes to Tragic; foul distrust, and breach	
	Disloyal on the part of Man, revolt,	
	And disobedience: On the part of Heav'n	
	Now alienated, distance and distaste,	
10	Anger and just rebuke, and judgment giv'n,	
	That brought into this World a world of woe,	
	Sin and her shadow Death, and Misery	
	Death's Harbinger: Sad task, yet argument	
	Not less but more Heroic than the wrath	
15	Of stern *Achilles* on his Foe pursu'd	
	Thrice Fugitive about *Troy* Wall; or rage	
	Of *Turnus* for *Lavinia* disespous'd,	
	Or *Neptune's* ire or *Juno's,* that so long	
	Perplex'd the *Greek* and *Cytherea's* Son;[3]	
20	If answerable° style I can obtain	*equal, accountable*
	Of my Celestial Patroness,[4] who deigns	
	Her nightly visitation unimplor'd,	

1. The root meaning of Latin "vehementia" is mindlessness.
2. Carrying further, drawing out.
3. *Achilles* is "stern" in his "wrath" because he refused any covenant with Hector, and Turnus dies fighting Aeneas for the hand of Lavinia, whereas Messiah, more heroically, is not implacable in his anger. He issued his sole commandment "sternly" (8.333); but when it is disobeyed, he works for reconciliation. Similarly, God's anger is distinguished from "Neptune's ire" and "Juno's" (which merely "perplexed" Odysseus and Aeneas) in that it is expressed in justice rather than in victimization.
4. The heavenly Muse, Urania. Both ancient and modern epics had always had war, or at least fighting, as a principal ingredient. (So has *Paradise Lost,* in the first half of the poem; but in the second half this subject is transcended.) Milton now glances unfavorably at the typical matter of the romantic epic.

And dictates to me slumb'ring, or inspires
Easy my unpremeditated Verse:
25   Since first this Subject for Heroic Song
Pleas'd me long choosing, and beginning late;
Not sedulous by Nature to indite
Wars, hitherto the only Argument
Heroic deem'd, chief maistry to dissect
30   With long and tedious havoc fabl'd Knights
In Battles feign'd; the better fortitude
Of Patience and Heroic Martyrdom
Unsung; or to describe Races and Games,
Or tilting Furniture, emblazon'd Shields,
35   Impreses[5] quaint, Caparisons[6] and Steeds;
Bases and tinsel Trappings, gorgeous Knights
At Joust and Tournament; then marshall'd Feast
Serv'd up in Hall with Sewers,° and Seneschals;°   *waiters/stewards*
The skill of Artifice or Office mean,
40   Not that which justly gives Heroic name
To Person or to Poem.[7] Mee of these
Nor skill'd nor studious, higher Argument
Remains, sufficient of itself to raise
That name,[8] unless an age too late, or cold
45   Climate, or Years damp my intended wing
Deprest; and much they may, if all be mine,
    Not Hers who brings it nightly to my Ear.
The Sun was sunk, and after him the Star
Of *Hesperus*,° whose Office is to bring   *the planet Venus*
50   Twilight upon the Earth, short Arbiter
Twixt Day and Night, and now from end to end
Night's Hemisphere had veil'd the Horizon round:
When *Satan* who late fled before the threats
Of *Gabriel* out of *Eden*,[9] now improv'd°   *intensified*
55   In meditated fraud and malice, bent
On Man's destruction, maugre what might hap
Of heavier on himself,[1] fearless return'd.
By Night he fled, and at Midnight return'd
From compassing the Earth, cautious of day,
60   Since *Uriel* Regent of the Sun descri'd
His entrance, and forewarn'd the Cherubim
That kept thir watch; thence full of anguish driv'n,
The space of seven continu'd Nights he rode
With darkness, thrice the Equinoctial Line
65   He circl'd, four times cross'd the Car of Night
From Pole to Pole, traversing each Colure;[2]
On th'eighth return'd, and on the Coast averse
From entrance or Cherubic Watch, by stealth

---

5. Heraldic devices, often with accompanying mottos.
6. Ornamented coverings spread over the saddle of a horse.
7. Artifice implies mechanic or applied art. It is beneath the dignity of epic to teach etiquette and social ceremony and heraldry.
8. The name of epic.
9. I.e., at the end of Book 4, a week earlier.

1. Despite the danger of heavier punishment.
2. By keeping to earth's shadow, Satan contrives to experience a whole week of darkness. The two colures were great circles, intersecting at right angels at the poles and dividing the equinoctial circle (the equator) into four equal parts.

Found unsuspected way. There was a place,
70 Now not, though Sin, not Time, first wrought the change,
Where *Tigris* at the foot of Paradise
Into a Gulf shot under ground, till part
Rose up a Fountain by the Tree of Life;
In with the River sunk, and with it rose
75 *Satan* involv'd in rising Mist, then sought
Where to lie hid; Sea he had searcht and Land
From *Eden* over *Pontus*, and the Pool
Maeotis, up beyond the River *Ob*;[3]
Downward as far Antarctic; and in length
80 West from *Orontes* to the Ocean barr'd
At *Darien*, thence to the Land where flows
Ganges and *Indus*:[4] thus the Orb he roam'd
With narrow search; and with inspection deep
Consider'd every Creature, which of all
85 Most opportune might serve his Wiles, and found
The Serpent subtlest Beast of all the Field.[5]
Him after long debate, irresolute°   *undecided*
Of thoughts revolv'd, his final sentence° chose   *judgment*
Fit Vessel, fittest Imp° of fraud, in whom   *offshoot*
90 To enter, and his dark suggestions hide
From sharpest sight: for in the wily Snake,
Whatever sleights none would suspicious mark,
As from his wit and native subtlety
Proceeding, which in other Beasts observ'd
95 Doubt° might beget of Diabolic pow'r   *suspicion*
Active within beyond the sense of brute.
Thus he resolv'd, but first from inward grief
His bursting passion into plaints thus pour'd:
    O Earth, how like to Heav'n, if not preferr'd
100 More justly, Seat worthier of Gods, as built
With second thoughts, reforming what was old!
For what God after better worse would build?
Terrestrial Heav'n, danc't round by other Heav'ns
That shine, yet bear thir bright officious Lamps,
105 Light above Light, for thee alone, as seems,
In thee concentring all thir precious beams
Of sacred influence:[6] As God in Heav'n
Is Centre, yet extends to all, so thou
Centring receiv'st from all those Orbs; in thee,
110 Not in themselves, all thir known virtue appears
Productive in Herb, Plant, and nobler birth
Of Creatures animate with gradual life
Of Growth, Sense, Reason, all summ'd up in Man.[7]

---

3. In his north-south circles, Satan passed Pontus (the Black Sea), the "pool / Maeotis" (the Sea of Azov), and the Siberian River Ob, which flows north into the Gulf of Ob and from there into the Arctic Ocean.
4. In his westward circling of the equinoctial line, he crossed the Syrian River Orontes, then the Pacific ("peaceful") "Ocean barred" by the Isthmus of Darien

(Panama) and India.
5. See Genesis 3.1.
6. The case for an earth-centered universe, put at 8.86–114 by Raphael, is now put by Satan.
7. "Growth, sense, reason" are the activities of the vegetable, animal, and rational souls, respectively, in humans.

With what delight could I have walkt thee round,
115 If I could joy in aught, sweet interchange
Of Hill and Valley, Rivers, Woods and Plains,
Now Land, now Sea, and Shores with Forest crown'd,
Rocks, Dens, and Caves; but I in none of these
Find place or refuge; and the more I see
120 Pleasures about me, so much more I feel
Torment within me, as from the hateful siege°   *conflict*
Of contraries; all good to me becomes
Bane,° and in Heav'n much worse would be my state.   *poison*
But neither here seek I, no nor in Heav'n
125 To dwell, unless by maistring Heav'n's Supreme;
Nor hope to be myself less miserable
By what I seek, but others to make such
As I, though thereby worse to me redound:
For only in destroying I find ease
130 To my relentless thoughts; and him destroy'd,
Or won to what may work his utter loss,
For whom all this was made, all this will soon
Follow, as to him linkt in weal or woe,
In woe then: that destruction wide may range:[8]
135 To mee shall be the glory sole among
Th'infernal Powers, in one day to have marr'd
What he *Almight* styl'd, six Nights and Days
Continu'd making, and who knows how long
Before had been contriving, though perhaps
140 Not longer than since I in one Night freed
From servitude inglorious well nigh half
Th' Angelic Name, and thinner left the throng
Of his adorers: hee to be aveng'd,
And to repair his numbers thus impair'd,
145 Whether such virtue° spent of old now fail'd   *power*
More Angels to Create, if they at least
Are his Created, or to spite us more,
Determin'd to advance into our room
A Creature form'd of Earth, and him endow,
150 Exalted from so base original,
With Heav'nly spoils, our spoils; What he decreed
He effected; Man he made, and for him built
Magnificent this World, and Earth his seat,
Him Lord pronounc'd, and, O indignity!
155 Subjected to his service Angel wings,
And flaming Ministers to watch and tend
Thir earthy Charge: Of these the vigilance
I dread, and to elude, thus wrapt in mist
Of midnight vapor glide obscure, and pry
160 In every Bush and Brake, where hap may find
The Serpent sleeping, in whose mazy folds
To hide me, and the dark intent I bring.
O foul descent! that I who erst contended

8. The created cosmos will follow humans to destruction.

With Gods to sit the highest, am now constrain'd
165 Into a Beast, and mixt with bestial slime,
This essence to incarnate and imbrute,
That to the highth of Deity aspir'd;
But what will not Ambition and Revenge
Descend to? who aspires must down as low
170 As high he soar'd, obnoxious° first or last   *exposed*
To basest things. Revenge, at first though sweet,
Bitter ere long back on itself recoils;
Let it, I reck not, so it light well aim'd,
Since higher I fall short, on him who next
175 Provokes my envy, this new Favorite
Of Heav'n, this Man of Clay, Son of despite,
Whom us the more to spite his Maker rais'd
From dust: spite then with spite is best repaid.
        So saying, through each Thicket Dank or Dry,
180 Like a black mist low creeping, he held on
His midnight search, where soonest he might find
The Serpent: him fast sleeping soon he found
In Labyrinth of many a round self-roll'd,
His head the midst, well stor'd with subtle wiles:
185 Not yet in horrid Shade or dismal Den,
Nor nocent° yet, but on the grassy Herb   *harmful, guilty*
Fearless unfear'd he slept: in at his Mouth
The Devil enter'd, and his brutal sense,
In heart or head, possessing soon inspir'd
190 With act intelligential; but his sleep
Disturb'd not, waiting close° th' approach of Morn.   *concealed*
Now whenas sacred Light began to dawn
In *Eden* on the humid Flow'rs, that breath'd
Thir morning incense, when all things that breathe,
195 From th' Earth's great Altar send up silent praise
To the Creator, and his Nostrils fill
With grateful Smell, forth came the human pair
And join'd thir vocal Worship to the Choir
Of Creatures wanting voice; that done, partake
200 The season, prime for sweetest Scents and Airs:
Then cómmune how that day they best may ply
Thir growing work: for much thir work outgrew
The hands' dispatch of two Gard'ning so wide.
And *Eve* first to her Husband thus began.
205   *Adam*, well may we labor still to dress
This Garden, still to tend Plant, Herb and Flow'r,
Our pleasant task enjoin'd, but till more hands
Aid us, the work under our labor grows,
Luxurious by restraint; what we by day
210 Lop overgrown, or prune, or prop, or bind,
One night or two with wanton growth derides
Tending to wild. Thou therefore now advise
Or hear what to my mind first thoughts present,
Let us divide our labors, thou where choice
215 Leads thee, or where most needs, whether to wind

The Woodbine round this Arbor, or direct
The clasping Ivy where to climb, while I
In yonder Spring of Roses intermixt
With Myrtle, find what to redress till Noon:
220   For while so near each other thus all day
Our task we choose, what wonder if so near
Looks intervene and smiles, or object new
Casual discourse draw on, which intermits
Our day's work brought to little, though begun
225   Early, and th' hour of Supper comes unearn'd.
     To whom mild answer *Adam* thus return'd.
Sole *Eve*, Associate sole, to me beyond
Compare above all living Creatures dear,
Well hast thou motion'd,° well thy thoughts imploy'd   *proposed*
230   How we might best fulfil the work which here
God hath assign'd us, nor of me shalt pass
Unprais'd: for nothing lovelier can be found
In Woman, than to study household good,
And good works in her Husband to promote.
235   Yet not so strictly hath our Lord impos'd
Labor, as to debar us when we need
Refreshment, whether food, or talk between,
Food of the mind, or this sweet intercourse
Of looks and smiles, for smiles from Reason flow,
240   To brute deni'd, and are of Love the food,
Love not the lowest end of human life.
For not to irksome toil, but to delight
He made us, and delight to Reason join'd.
These paths and Bowers doubt not but our joint hands
245   Will keep from Wilderness with ease, as wide
As we need walk, till younger hands ere long
Assist us: But if much converse perhaps
Thee satiate, to short absence I could yield.
For solitude sometimes is best society,
250   And short retirement urges sweet return.
But other doubt possesses me, lest harm
Befall thee sever'd from me; for thou know'st
What hath been warn'd us, what malicious Foe
Envying our happiness, and of his own
255   Despairing, seeks to work us woe and shame
By sly assault; and somewhere nigh at hand
Watches, no doubt, with greedy hope to find
His wish and best advantage, us asunder,
Hopeless to circumvent us join'd, where each
260   To other speedy aid might lend at need;
Whether his first design be to withdraw
Our fealty from God, or to disturb
Conjugal Love, than which perhaps no bliss
Enjoy'd by us excites his envy more;
265   Or this, or worse,[9] leave not the faithful side

---

9. Whether this or worse (be his first design).

That gave thee being, still shades thee and protects.
The Wife, where danger or dishonor lurks,
Safest and seemliest by her Husband stays,
Who guards her, or with her the worst endures.

270   To whom the Virgin° Majesty of *Eve*,   *chaste, innocent*
As one who loves, and some unkindness meets,
With sweet austere composure thus repli'd.
Offspring of Heav'n and Earth, and all Earth's Lord,
That such an Enemy we have, who seeks

275   Our ruin, both by thee inform'd I learn,
And from the parting Angel over-heard
As in a shady nook I stood behind,
Just then return'd at shut of Ev'ning Flow'rs.
But that thou shouldst my firmness therefore doubt

280   To God or thee, because we have a foe
May tempt it, I expected not to hear.
His violence thou fear'st not, being such,
As wee, not capable of death or pain,
Can either not receive, or can repel.

285   His fraud is then thy fear, which plain infers
Thy equal fear that my firm Faith and Love
Can by his fraud be shak'n or seduc't;
Thoughts, which how found they harbor in thy breast,
Adam, misthought of her to thee so dear?

290   To whom with healing words *Adam* repli'd.
Daughter of God and Man, immortal *Eve*,
For such thou art, from sin and blame entire:°   *free*
Not diffident° of thee do I dissuade   *mistrustful*
Thy absence from my sight, but to avoid

295   Th' attempt itself, intended by our Foe.
For hee who tempts, though in vain, at least asperses°   *falsely charges*
The tempted with dishonor foul, suppos'd
Not incorruptible of Faith, not proof
Against temptation: thou thyself with scorn

300   And anger wouldst resent the offer'd wrong,
Though ineffectual found: misdeem not then,
If such affront I labor to avert
From thee alone, which on us both at once
The Enemy, though bold, will hardly dare,

305   Or daring, first on mee th' assault shall light.
Nor thou his malice and false guile contemn;
Subtle he needs must be, who could seduce
Angels, nor think superfluous others' aid.
I from the influence of thy looks receive

310   Access° in every Virtue, in thy sight   *increase*
More wise, more watchful, stronger, if need were
Of outward strength; while shame, thou looking on,
Shame to be overcome or over-reacht
Would utmost vigor raise, and rais'd unite.

315   Why shouldst not thou like sense within thee feel
When I am present, and thy trial choose
With me, best witness of thy Virtue tri'd.

So spake domestic *Adam* in his care
And Matrimonial Love; but *Eve,* who thought
320 Less° attribúted to her Faith sincere,   *too little*
Thus her reply with accent sweet renew'd.
　　If this be our condition, thus to dwell
In narrow circuit strait'n'd by a Foe,
Subtle or violent, we not endu'd
325 Single with like defense, wherever met,
How are we happy, still in fear of harm?
But harm precedes not sin: only our Foe
Tempting affronts us with his foul esteem
Of our integrity: his foul esteem
330 Sticks no dishonor on our Front,° but turns   *face*
Foul on himself; then wherefore shunn'd or fear'd
By us? who rather double honor gain
From his surmise prov'd false, find peace within,
Favor from Heav'n, our witness from th' event.
335 And what is Faith, Love, Virtue unassay'd
Alone, without exterior help sustain'd?
Let us not then suspect our happy State
Left so imperfet by the Maker wise,
As not secure to single or combin'd.
340 Frail is our happiness, if this be so,
And *Eden* were no Eden[1] thus expos'd.
　　To whom thus Adam fervently repli'd.
O Woman, best are all things as the will
Of God ordain'd them, his creating hand
345 Nothing imperfet or deficient left
Of all that he Created, much less Man,
Or aught that might his happy State secure,
Secure from outward force; within himself
The danger lies, yet lies within his power:
350 Against his will he can receive no harm.
But God left free the Will, for what obeys
Reason, is free, and Reason he made right,
But bid her well beware, and still erect,[2]
Lest by some fair appearing good surpris'd
355 She dictate false, and misinform the Will
To do what God expressly hath forbid.
Not then mistrust, but tender love enjoins,
That I should mind thee oft, and mind thou me.
Firm we subsist, yet possible to swerve,
360 Since Reason not impossibly may meet
Some specious object by the Foe suborn'd,
And fall into deception unaware,
Not keeping strictest watch, as she was warn'd.
Seek not temptation then, which to avoid
365 Were better, and most likely if from mee
Thou sever not: Trial will come unsought.
Wouldst thou approve° thy constancy, approve   *demonstrate*

---

1. I.e., no pleasure, the literal Hebrew meaning of "Eden."　　2. Always attentive, but also with a glance at upright.

First thy obedience; th' other who can know,
Not seeing thee attempted, who attest?
370 But if thou think, trial unsought may find
Us both securer° than thus warn'd thou seem'st,   *more careless*
Go; for thy stay, not free, absents thee more;
Go in thy native innocence, rely
On what thou hast of virtue, summon all,
375 For God towards thee hath done his part, do thine.
        So spake the Patriarch of Mankind, but *Eve*
Persisted, yet submiss, though last, repli'd.
        With thy permission then, and thus forewarn'd
Chiefly by what thy own last reasoning words
380 Touch'd only, that our trial, when least sought,
May find us both perhaps far less prepar'd,
The willinger I go, nor much expect
A Foe so proud will first the weaker seek;
So bent, the more shall shame him his repulse.
385 Thus saying, from her Husband's hand her hand
Soft she withdrew, and like a Wood-Nymph light,
Oread or *Dryad*, or of *Delia's* Train,[3]
Betook her to the Groves, but *Delia's* self
In gait surpass'd and Goddess-like deport,
390 Though not as shee with Bow and Quiver arm'd,
But with such Gard'ning Tools as Art yet rude,
Guiltless° of fire had form'd, or Angels brought.[4]   *innocent, ignorant*
To Pales, or Pomona, thus adorn'd,
Likest she seem'd, Pomona when she fled
395 *Vertumnus*, or to *Ceres* in her Prime,
Yet Virgin of *Proserpina* from *Jove*.[5]
Her long and ardent look his Eye pursu'd
Delighted, but desiring more her stay.
Oft he to her his charge of quick return
400 Repeated, shee to him as oft engag'd
To be return'd by Noon amid the Bow'r,
And all things in best order to invite
Noontide repast, or Afternoon's repose.
O much deceiv'd, much failing, hapless *Eve*,
405 Of thy presum'd return! event perverse!
Thou never from that hour in Paradise
Found'st either sweet repast, or sound repose;
Such ambush hid among sweet Flow'rs and Shades
Waited with hellish rancor imminent
410 To intercept thy way, or send thee back
Despoil'd of Innocence, of Faith, of Bliss.
For now, and since first break of dawn the Fiend,
Mere° Serpent in appearance, forth was come,   *plain*
And on his Quest, where likeliest he might find

---

3. Oreads, were mountain nymphs, such as attended on
Diana; dryads were wood nymphs. Neither class of
nymphs were immortal.
4. Only as a result of the Fall did it become necessary for
humans to have some means of warming themselves.
There may also be an allusion to the fire stolen from

heaven by Prometheus.
5. Pales was the Roman goddess of pastures; Pomona was
the nymph or goddess of fruit trees, seduced by the disguised Vertumnus; Ceres was the goddess of corn and
agriculture who bore Proserpina to Jove.

415	The only two of Mankind, but in them	
	The whole included Race, his purpos'd prey.	
	In Bow'r and Field he sought, where any tuft	
	Of Grove or Garden-Plot more pleasant lay,	
	Thir tendance° or Plantation for delight,	*object of care*
420	By Fountain or by shady Rivulet,	
	He sought them both, but wish'd his hap° might find	*chance*
	Eve separate, he wish'd, but not with hope	
	Of what so seldom chanc'd, when to his wish,	
	Beyond his hope, *Eve* separate he spies,	
425	Veil'd in a Cloud of Fragrance, where she stood,	
	Half spi'd, so thick the Roses bushing round	
	About her glow'd, oft stooping to support	
	Each Flow'r of slender stalk, whose head though gay	
	Carnation, Purple, Azure, or speckt with Gold,	
430	Hung drooping unsustain'd, them she upstays	
	Gently with Myrtle band, mindless the while,	
	Herself, though fairest unsupported Flow'r,	
	From her best prop so far, and storm so nigh.[6]	
	Nearer he drew, and many a walk travers'd	
435	Of stateliest Covert, Cedar, Pine, or Palm,	
	Then voluble and bold, now hid, now seen	
	Among thick-wov'n Arborets and Flow'rs	
	Imborder'd on each Bank, the hand° of *Eve:*	*handiwork*
	Spot more delicious than those Gardens feign'd	
440	Or of reviv'd *Adonis,* or renown'd	
	Alcinoüs, host of old *Laertes'* Son,	
	Or that, not Mystic, where the Sapient King	
	Held dalliance with his fair *Egyptian* Spouse.[7]	
	Much hee the Place admir'd, the Person more.	
445	As one who long in populous City pent,	
	Where Houses thick and Sewers annoy the Air,	
	Forth issuing on a Summer's Morn to breathe	
	Among the pleasant Villages and Farms	
	Adjoin'd, from each thing met conceives delight,	
450	The smell of Grain, or tedded° Grass, or Kine,°	*mown/cows*
	Or Dairy, each rural sight, each rural sound;	
	If chance with Nymphlike step fair Virgin pass,	
	What pleasing seem'd, for her now pleases more,	
	She most, and in her look sums all Delight.	
455	Such Pleasure took the Serpent to behold	
	This Flow'ry Plat,° the sweet recess of *Eve*	*piece of ground*
	Thus early, thus alone; her Heav'nly form	
	Angelic, but more soft, and Feminine,	
	Her graceful Innocence, her every Air	
460	Of gesture or least action overaw'd	
	His Malice, and with rapine sweet bereav'd	

6. See 4.270, page 1819, where Proserpina (and by implication Eve) was "Herself a fairer flower" when she was carried off by the king of hell.
7. "The sapient king" was Solomon (*Song of Solomon* 6.2). Milton alludes to Spenser's addition to the myth of Ado-

nis, that Venus keeps Adonis hidden in a secret garden (*The Faerie Queene* 3.6). "Laertes' son" was Odysseus; much-traveled as he was, he marveled when he saw the Garden of Alcinoüs (Homer, *Odyssey* 7).

His fierceness of the fierce intent it brought:
That space the Evil one abstracted stood
From his own evil, and for the time remain'd
465　　Stupidly good, of enmity disarm'd,
Of guile, of hate, of envy, of revenge;
But the hot Hell that always in him burns,
Though in mid Heav'n, soon ended his delight,
And tortures him now more, the more he sees
470　　Of pleasure not for him ordain'd: then soon
Fierce hate he recollects, and all his thoughts
Of mischief, gratulating,° thus excites.　　　　　　　*rejoicing*
　　Thoughts, whither have ye led me, with what sweet
Compulsion thus transported to forget
475　　What hither brought us, hate, not love, nor hope
Of Paradise for Hell, hope here to taste
Of pleasure, but all pleasure to destroy,
Save what is in destroying, other joy
To me is lost. Then let me not let pass
480　　Occasion which now smiles, behold alone
The Woman, opportune° to all attempts,　　　　　　　*exposed*
Her Husband, for I view far round, not nigh,
Whose higher intellectual more I shun,
And strength, of courage haughty, and of limb
485　　Heroic built, though of terrestrial mould,°　　　　*formed of earth*
Foe not informidable, exempt from wound,
I not; so much hath Hell debas'd, and pain
Infeebl'd me, to what I was in Heav'n.
Shee fair, divinely fair, fit Love for Gods,
490　　Not terrible, though terror be in Love
And beauty, not approacht by stronger hate,
Hate stronger, under show of Love well feign'd,
The way which to her ruin now I tend.
　　So spake the Enemy of Mankind, enclos'd
495　　In Serpent, Inmate bad, and toward *Eve*
Address'd his way, not with indented wave,
Prone on the ground, as since, but on his rear,
Circular base of rising folds, that tow'r'd
Fold above fold a surging Maze, his Head
500　　Crested aloft, and Carbuncle his Eyes;[8]
With burnisht Neck of verdant Gold, erect
Amidst his circling Spires,° that on the grass　　　　*coils*
Floated redundant:° pleasing was his shape,　　　　*abundant to excess*
And lovely, never since of Serpent kind
505　　Lovelier, not those that in *Illyria* chang'd
Hermione and *Cadmus*, or the God
In *Epidaurus*;[9] nor to which transform'd
Ammonian Jove, or *Capitoline* was seen,
Hee with *Olympias*, this with her who bore

---

8. "Carbuncle" or reddish eyes denoted rage.
9. Cadmus was turned into a serpent first; only after he had
embraced his wife Hermione (Harmonia) in his new form
did she too change (Ovid, *Metamorphoses* 4.572–603).

Aesculapius, the god of healing, once changed into a serpent to help the Romans in that form (Ovid, *Metamorphoses* 15.626–744).

510   *Scipio* the highth of Rome.[1] With tract oblique
      At first, as one who sought access, but fear'd
      To interrupt, side-long he works his way.
      As when a Ship by skilful Steersman wrought
      Nigh River's mouth or Foreland, where the Wind
515   Veers oft, as oft so steers, and shifts her Sail;
      So varied hee, and of his tortuous Train
      Curl'd many a wanton wreath in sight of *Eve*,
      To lure her Eye; shee busied heard the sound
      Of rustling Leaves, but minded not, as us'd
520   To such disport before her through the Field,
      From every Beast, more duteous at her call,
      Than at *Circean* call the Herd disguis'd.[2]
      Hee bolder now, uncall'd before her stood;
      But as in gaze admiring: Oft he bow'd
525   His turret Crest, and sleek enamell'd Neck,
      Fawning, and lick'd the ground whereon she trod.
      His gentle dumb expression turn'd at length
      The Eye of *Eve* to mark his play; he glad
      Of her attention gain'd, with Serpent Tongue
530   Organic, or impulse of vocal Air,
      His fraudulent temptation thus began.
          Wonder not, sovran Mistress, if perhaps
      Thou canst, who are sole Wonder, much less arm
      Thy looks, the Heav'n of mildness, with disdain,
535   Displeas'd that I approach thee thus, and gaze
      Insatiate, I thus single, nor have fear'd
      Thy awful brow, more awful thus retir'd.
      Fairest resemblance of thy Maker fair,
      Thee all things living gaze on, all things thine
540   By gift, and thy Celestial Beauty adore
      With ravishment beheld, there best beheld
      Where universally admir'd: but here
      In this enclosure wild, these Beasts among,
      Beholders rude, and shallow to discern
545   Half what in thee is fair, one man except,
      Who sees thee? (and what is one?) who shouldst be seen
      A Goddess among Gods, ador'd and serv'd
      By Angels numberless, thy daily Train.
          So gloz'd° the Tempter, and his Proem° tun'd;   *flattered/prelude*
550   Into the Heart of *Eve* his words made way,
      Though at the voice much marvelling; at length
      Not unamaz'd she thus in answer spake.
          What may this mean? Language of Man pronounc't
      By Tongue of Brute, and human sense exprest?[3]
555   The first at least of these I thought deni'd
      To Beasts, whom God on thir Creation-Day

1. Jupiter Ammon, the "Lybian Jove," as a serpent mated with Olympias to father Alexander the Great, just as the Roman Jupiter, Capitolinus, took the form of a snake to father the great general Scipio.
2. Homer's Circe changed men into beasts who surprised Odysseus's company by fawning on them like dogs (*Odyssey*

10.212–219).
3. Milton is unusually favorable to Eve in making her ask the serpent how it came by its voice. The Eve of Scriptural exegesis, by contrast, is carried away by the words and makes no inquiry into their source.

Created mute to all articulate sound;
The latter I demur,° for in thir looks   *hesitate about*
Much reason, and in thir actions oft appears.
560   Thee, Serpent, subtlest beast of all the field
I knew, but not with human voice endu'd;
Redouble then this miracle, and say,
How cam'st thou speakable of mute,⁴ and how
To me so friendly grown above the rest
565   Of brutal kind, that daily are in sight?
Say, for such wonder claims attention due.
        To whom the guileful Tempter thus repli'd.
Empress of this fair World, resplendent *Eve*,
Easy to mee it is to tell thee all
570   What thou command'st and right thou should'st be obey'd:
I was at first as other Beasts that graze
The trodden Herb, of abject° thoughts and low,   *mean-spirited*
As was my food, nor aught but food discern'd
Or Sex, and apprehended nothing high:
575   Till on a day roving the field, I chanc'd
A goodly Tree far distant to behold
Loaden with fruit of fairest colors mixt,
Ruddy and Gold: I nearer drew to gaze;
When from the boughs a savory odor blown,
580   Grateful to appetite, more pleas'd my sense
Than smell of sweetest Fennel, or the Teats
Of Ewe or Goat dropping with Milk at Ev'n,
Unsuckt of Lamb or Kid, that tend thir play.
To satisfy the sharp desire I had
585   Of tasting those fair Apples, I resolv'd
Not to defer; hunger and thirst at once,
Powerful persuaders, quick'n'd at the scent
Of that alluring fruit, urg'd me so keen.
About the mossy Trunk I wound me soon,
590   For high from ground the branches would require
Thy utmost reach or *Adam's*: Round the Tree
All other Beasts that saw, with like desire
Longing and envying stood, but could not reach.
Amid the Tree now got, where plenty hung
595   Tempting so nigh, to pluck and eat my fill
I spar'd not, for such pleasure till that hour
At Feed or Fountain never had I found.
Sated at length, ere long I might perceive
Strange alteration in me, to degree
600   Of Reason in my inward Powers, and Speech
Wanted not long, though to this shape retain'd.
Thenceforth to Speculations high or deep
I turn'd my thoughts, and with capacious mind
Consider'd all things visible in Heav'n,
605   Or Earth, or Middle, all things fair and good;
But all that fair and good in thy Divine

4. How did you become capable of speech from being dumb?

Semblance, and in thy Beauty's heav'nly Ray
United I beheld; no Fair° to thine   *beauty*
Equivalent or second, which compell'd
610   Mee thus, though importune perhaps, to come
And gaze, and worship thee of right declar'd
Sovran of Creatures, universal Dame.
      So talk'd the spirited[5] sly Snake; and *Eve*,
Yet more amaz'd unwary thus repli'd.
615   Serpent, thy overpraising leaves in doubt
The virtue° of that Fruit, in thee first prov'd: *power*
But say, where grows the Tree, from hence how far?
For many are the Trees of God that grow
In Paradise, and various, yet unknown
620   To us, in such abundance lies our choice,
As leaves a greater store of Fruit untoucht,
Still hanging incorruptible, till men
Grow up to thir provision, and more hands
Help to disburden Nature of her Birth.
625   To whom the wily Adder, blithe and glad.
Empress, the way is ready, and not long,
Beyond a row of Myrtles, on a Flat,
Fast by a Fountain, one small Thicket past
Of blowing° Myrrh and Balm; if thou accept   *blooming*
630   My conduct,° I can bring thee thither soon.   *guidance*
      Lead then, said Eve. Hee leading swiftly roll'd
In tangles, and made intricate seem straight,
To mischief swift. Hope elevates, and joy
      Bright'ns his Crest, as when a wand'ring Fire,
635   Compact° of unctuous vapor, which the Night   *made up*
Condenses, and the cold invirons round,
Kindl'd through agitation to a Flame,
Which oft, they say, some evil Spirit attends,
Hovering and blazing with delusive Light,
640   Misleads th' amaz'd Night-wanderer from his way
To Bogs and Mires, and oft through Pond or Pool,
There swallow'd up and lost, from succor far.
So glister'd the dire Snake, and into fraud
Led *Eve* our credulous Mother, to the Tree
645   Of prohibition, root of all our woe;
Which when she saw, thus to her guide she spake.
      Serpent, we might have spar'd our coming hither,
Fruitless to mee, though Fruit be here to excess,
The credit of whose virtue rest with thee,
650   Wondrous indeed, if cause of such effects.
But of this Tree we may not taste nor touch;
God so commanded, and left that Command
Sole Daughter of his voice;[6] the rest, we live
Law to ourselves, our Reason is our Law.
655   To whom the Tempter guilefully repli'd.
Indeed? hath God then said that of the Fruit

---

5. Endowed with an animating spirit, stirred up; also   6. A Hebraism for "voice sent from heaven."
energetic, enterprising, possessed by a spirit.

Of all these Garden Trees ye shall not eat,
Yet Lords declar'd of all in Earth or Air?[7]
To whom thus *Eve* yet sinless. Of the Fruit
660 Of each Tree in the Garden we may eat,
But of the Fruit of this fair Tree amidst
The Garden, God hath said, Ye shall not eat
Thereof, nor shall ye touch it, lest ye die.
She scarce had said, though brief, when now more bold
665 The Tempter, but with show of Zeal and Love
To Man, and indignation at his wrong,
New part puts on, and as to passion mov'd,
Fluctuates disturb'd, yet comely, and in act
Rais'd, as of some great matter to begin.
670 As when of old some Orator renown'd
In *Athens* or free *Rome*, where Eloquence
Flourish'd, since mute, to some great cause addrest,
Stood in himself collected, while each part,
Motion, each act won audience ere the tongue,
675 Sometimes in highth began, as no delay
Of Preface brooking through his Zeal of Right.[8]
So standing, moving, or to highth upgrown
The Tempter all impassion'd thus began.
O Sacred, Wise, and Wisdom-giving Plant,
680 Mother of Science,° Now I feel thy Power   *knowledge*
Within me clear, not only to discern
Things in thir Causes, but to trace the ways
Of highest Agents, deem'd however wise.
Queen of this Universe, do not believe
685 Those rigid threats of Death; ye shall not Die:
How should ye? by the Fruit? it gives you Life
To° Knowledge: By the Threat'ner? look on mee,   *in addition to*
Mee who have touch'd and tasted, yet both live,
And life more perfet have attain'd than Fate
690 Meant mee, by vent'ring higher than my Lot.
Shall that be shut to Man, which to the Beast
Is open? or will God incense his ire
For such a petty Trespass, and not praise
Rather your dauntless virtue, whom the pain
695 Of Death denounc't, whatever thing Death be,
Deterr'd not from achieving what might lead
To happier life, knowledge of Good and Evil;
Of good, how just? of evil, if what is evil
Be real, why not known, since easier shunn'd?[9]
700 God therefore cannot hurt ye, and be just;
Not just, not God; not fear'd then, nor obey'd:
Your fear itself of Death removes the fear.
Why then was this forbid? Why but to awe,

---

7. Lines 655–58 closely follow Genesis. 3.1.
8. This simile blends oratorical, theatrical, and theological meanings. Thus "part" means "part of the body," "dramatic role," and "moral act"; "motion" means "gesture," "mime" (or "puppet-show"), and "instigation, persuasive force, inclination"; "act" means "action," "performance of

a play," and "the accomplished deed itself."
9. If the knowledge is good, how is it just to prohibit it? Here occurs the most egregious logical fallacy in speech. (For evil to be "shunned," it is not at all necessary that it should be "known" in the sense of being experienced.)

705
710
715
720
725
730
735
740
745

Why but to keep ye low and ignorant,
His worshippers; he knows that in the day
Ye Eat thereof, your Eyes that seem so clear,
Yet are but dim, shall perfetly be then
Op'n'd and clear'd, and ye shall be as Gods,
Knowing both Good and Evil as they know.[1]
That ye should be as Gods, since I as Man,
Internal Man,[2] is but proportion meet,
I of brute human, thee of human Gods.
So ye shall die perhaps, by putting off
Human, to put on Gods, death to be wisht,
Though threat'n'd, which no worse than this can bring.[3]
And what are Gods that Man may not become
As they, participating° God-like food?   *sharing*
The Gods are first, and that advantage use
On our belief, that all from them proceeds;
I question it, for this fair Earth I see,
Warm'd by the Sun, producing every kind,
Them nothing: If they° all things, who enclos'd   *if they produce*
Knowledge of Good and Evil in this Tree,
That who so eats thereof, forthwith attains
Wisdom without their leave? and wherein lies
Th' offense, that Man should thus attain to know?
What can your knowledge hurt him, or this Tree
Impart against his will if all be his?
Or is it envy, and can envy dwell
In heav'nly breasts?[4] these, these and many more
Causes import° your need of this fair Fruit.   *suggest*
Goddess humane, reach then, and freely taste.
     He ended, and his words replete with guile
Into her heart too easy entrance won:
Fixt on the Fruit she gaz'd, which to behold
Might tempt alone, and in her ears the sound
Yet rung of his persuasive words, impregn'd°   *impregnated*
With Reason, to her seeming, and with Truth;
Meanwhile the hour of Noon drew on, and wak'd
An eager appetite, rais'd by the smell
So savory of that Fruit, which with desire,
Inclinable now grown to touch or taste,
Solicited her longing eye;[5] yet first
Pausing a while, thus to herself she mus'd.
     Great are thy Virtues, doubtless, best of Fruits,
Though kept from Man, and worthy to be admir'd,
Whose taste, too long forborne, at first assay
Gave elocution to the mute, and taught
The Tongue not made for Speech to speak thy praise:[6]

---

1. See Genesis 3.5.
2. The serpent's pretence is that his "inward powers" are human.
3. Satan offers a travesty of Christian mortification and death to sin; see *Colossians* 3.1–15: "ye have put off the old man with his deeds; And have put on the new man, which is renewed in knowledge after the image of him

that created him."
4. See Virgil, *Aeneid* 1.11; Satan is inviting Eve to participate in a pagan epic, complete with machinery of jealous gods.
5. For lines 735–43, see Genesis 3.6.
6. Eve has trusted Satan's account of the fruit and consequently argues from false premises, such as its magical power.

750 Thy praise hee also who forbids thy use,
    Conceals not from us, naming thee the Tree
    Of Knowledge, knowledge both of good and evil;
    Forbids us then to taste, but his forbidding
    Commends thee more, while it infers the good
755 By thee communicated, and our want:
    For good unknown, sure is not had, or had
    And yet unknown, is as not had at all.
    In plain° then, what forbids he but to know,   *plainly*
    Forbids us good, forbids us to be wise?
760 Such prohibitions bind not. But if Death
    Bind us with after-bands, what profits then
    Our inward freedom? In the day we eat
    Of this fair Fruit, our doom is, we shall die.
    How dies the Serpent? hee hath eat'n and lives,
765 And knows, and speaks, and reasons, and discerns,
    Irrational till then. For us alone
    Was death invented? or to us deni'd
    This intellectual food, for beasts reserv'd?
    For Beasts it seems: yet that one Beast which first
770 Hath tasted, envies not, but bring with joy
    The good befall'n him, Author unsuspect,[7]
    Friendly to man, far from deceit or guile.
    What fear I then, rather what know to fear[8]
    Under this ignorance of Good and Evil,
775 Of God or Death, of Law or Penalty?
    Here grows the Cure of all, this Fruit Divine,
    Fair to the Eye, inviting to the Taste,
    Of virtue° to make wise: what hinders then   *power*
    To reach, and feed at once both Body and Mind?
780   So saying, her rash hand in evil hour
    Forth reaching to the Fruit, she pluck'd, she eat:°   *ate*
    Earth felt the wound, and Nature from her seat
    Sighing through all her Works gave signs of woe,
    That all was lost. Back to the Thicket slunk
785 The guilty Serpent, and well might, for *Eve*,
    Intent now wholly on her taste, naught else
    Regarded, such delight till then, as seem'd,
    In Fruit she never tasted, whether true
    Or fancied so, through expectation high
790 Of knowledge, nor was God-head from her thought.[9]
    Greedily she ingorg'd without restraint,
    And knew not eating Death:[1] Satiate at length,
    And hight'n'd as with Wine, jocund and boon,°   *jolly*
    Thus to herself she pleasingly began.
795   O Sovran, virtuous, precious of all Trees
    In Paradise, of operation blest
    To Sapience,[2] hitherto obscur'd, infam'd,°   *defamed*

7. Eve means "informant not subject to suspicion."
8. What fear I, then—or rather (since I'm not allowed to
know anything) what do I know that is to be feared?
9. She expected to achieve godhead.
1. She knew not that she was eating death; "she was

unaware, while she ate death" or even "she 'knew'; not
eating (immediate) death."
2. "Sapience" is derived from Latin *sapientia* (discernment, taste) and ultimately from *sapere* (to taste).

And thy fair Fruit let hang, as to no end
Created; but henceforth my early care,
800 Not without Song, each Morning, and due praise
Shall tend thee, and the fertile burden ease
Of thy full branches offer'd free to all;
Till dieted by thee I grow mature
In knowledge, as the Gods who all things know;
805 Though others[3] envy what they cannot give;
For had the gift been theirs, it had not here
Thus grown. Experience, next to thee I owe,
Best guide; not following thee, I had remain'd
In ignorance, thou op'n'st Wisdom's way,
810 And giv'st access, though secret she retire.
And I perhaps am secret; Heav'n is high,
High and remote to see from thence distinct
Each thing on Earth; and other care perhaps
May have diverted from continual watch
815 Our great Forbidder, safe with all his Spies
About him. But to *Adam* in what sort
Shall I appear? shall I to him make known
As yet my change, and give him to partake
Full happiness with mee, or rather not.
820 But keep the odds of Knowledge in my power
Without Copartner? so to add what wants
In Female Sex, the more to draw his Love,
And render me more equal, and perhaps,
A thing not undesirable, sometime
825 Superior: for inferior who is free?
This may be well: but what if God have seen,
And Death ensue? then I shall be no more,
And *Adam* wedded to another *Eve*,
Shall live with her enjoying, I extinct;
830 A death to think. Confirm'd then I resolve,
Adam shall share with me in bliss or woe:
So dear I love him, that with him all deaths
I could endure, without him live no life.
    So saying, from the Tree her step she turn'd,
835 But first low Reverence done, as to the power
That dwelt within, whose presence had infus'd
Into the plant sciential[4] sap, deriv'd
From Nectar, drink of Gods. *Adam* the while
Waiting desirous her return, had wove
840 Of choicest Flow'rs a Garland to adorn
Her Tresses, and her rural labors crown,
As Reapers oft are wont thir Harvest Queen.
Great joy he promis'd to his thoughts, and new
Solace in her return, so long delay'd;
845 Yet oft his heart, divine° of something ill,   *prophet*
Misgave him; hee the falt'ring measure[5] felt;
And forth to meet her went, the way she took

---

3. I.e., God. Eve's language is now full of lapses in logic   4. Endowed with knowledge.
and evasions in theology.   5. The rhythm of his own heart.

That Morn when first they parted; by the Tree
Of Knowledge he must pass; there he her met,
850   Scarce from the Tree returning; in her hand
A bough of fairest fruit that downy smil'd,
New gather'd, and ambrosial smell diffus'd.
To him she hasted, in her face excuse
Came Prologue, and Apology to prompt,[6]
855   Which with bland words at will she thus addrest.
     Hast thou not wonder'd, *Adam*, at my stay?
Thee I have misst, and thought it long, depriv'd
Thy presence, agony of love till now
Not felt, nor shall be twice, for never more
860   Mean I to try, what rash untri'd I sought,
The pain of absence from thy sight. But strange
Hath been the cause, and wonderful to hear:
This Tree is not as we are told, a Tree
Of danger tasted,° nor to evil unknown   *if tasted*
865   Op'ning the way, but of Divine effect
To open Eyes, and make them Gods who taste;
And hath been tasted such: the Serpent wise,
Or not restrain'd as wee, or not obeying,
Hath eat'n of the fruit, and is become,
870   Not dead, as we are threat'n'd, but thenceforth
Endu'd with human voice and human sense,
Reasoning to admiration, and with mee
Persuasively hath so prevail'd, that I
Have also tasted, and have also found
875   Th' effects to correspond, opener mine Eyes,
Dim erst, dilated Spirits, ampler Heart,
And growing up to Godhead; which for thee
Chiefly I sought, without thee can despise.
For bliss, as thou hast part, to me is bliss,
880   Tedious, unshar'd with thee, and odious soon.
Thou therefore also taste, that equal Lot
May join us, equal Joy, as equal Love;
Lest thou not tasting, different degree[7]
Disjoin us, and I then too late renounce
885   Deity for thee, when Fate will not permit.
     Thus *Eve* with Count'nance blithe her story told;
But in her Cheek distemper[8] flushing glow'd.
On th' other side, *Adam*, soon as he heard
The fatal Trespass done by *Eve*, amaz'd,
890   Astonied° stood and Blank, while horror chill   *stunned*
Ran through his veins, and all his joints relax'd;
From his slack hand the Garland wreath'd for *Eve*,
Down dropp'd, and all the faded Roses shed:
Speechless he stood and pale, till thus at length
895   First to himself he inward silence broke.

6. The expression on Eve's face is visible in advance as she approaches and so is like the prologue-speaker of a play. But it also remains on her face as she speaks, to help out her words, and so is like the prompter of the play. The actor prompted is apology, i.e., justification or defense personified.
7. Differing position in the scale of creatures.
8. A disordered condition due to disturbance of the temperament of the bodily humors.

O fairest of Creation, last and best
Of all God's Works, Creature in whom excell'd
Whatever can to sight or thought be form'd,
Holy, divine, good, amiable, or sweet!
900   How art thou lost, how on a sudden lost,
Defac't, deflow'r'd, and now to death devote?°   *given over*
Rather how hast thou yielded to transgress
The strict forbiddance, how to violate
The sacred Fruit forbidd'n! some cursed fraud
905   Of Enemy hath beguil'd thee, yet unknown,
And mee with thee hath ruin'd, for with thee
Certain my resolution is to Die;
How can I live without thee, how forgo
Thy sweet Converse and Love so dearly join'd,
910   To live again in these wild Woods forlorn?
Should God create another *Eve*, and I
Another Rib afford, yet loss of thee
Would never from my heart; no no, I feel
The Link of Nature draw me: Flesh of Flesh,
915   Bone of my Bone thou art, and from thy State
Mine never shall be parted, bliss or woe.
      So having said, as one from sad dismay
Recomforted, and after thoughts disturb'd
Submitting to what seem'd remediless,
920   Thus in calm mood his Words to *Eve* he turn'd.
      Bold deed thou hast presum'd, advent'rous *Eve*,
And peril great provok't, who thus hath dar'd
Had it been only coveting to Eye
That sacred Fruit, sacred° to abstinence,   *devoted*
925   Much more to taste it under ban to touch.
But past who can recall, or done undo?
Not God Omnipotent, nor Fate; yet so
Perhaps thou shalt not Die, perhaps the Fact°   *crime, deed*
Is not so heinous now, foretasted Fruit,
930   Profan'd first by the Serpent, by him first
Made common and unhallow'd ere our taste;
Nor yet on him found deadly, he yet lives,
Lives, as thou said'st, and gains to live as Man
Higher degree of Life, inducement strong
935   To us, as likely tasting to attain
Proportional ascent, which cannot be
But to be Gods, or Angels Demi-gods.
Nor can I think that God, Creator wise,
Though threat'ning, will in earnest so destroy
940   Us his prime Creatures, dignifi'd so high,
Set over all his Works, which in our Fall,
For us created, needs with us must fail,
Dependent made; so God shall uncreate,
Be frustrate, do, undo, and labor lose,
945   Not well conceiv'd of God, who though his Power
Creation could repeat, yet would be loath
Us to abolish, lest the Adversary

Triumph and say; Fickle their State whom God
Most Favors, who can please him long? Mee first
950   He ruin'd, now Mankind; whom will he next?
Matter of scorn, not to be given the Foe.
However I with thee have fixt my Lot,
Certain to undergo like doom;[9] if Death
Consort with thee, Death is to mee as Life;
955   So forcible within my heart I feel
The Bond of Nature draw me to my own,
My own in thee, for what thou art is mine;
Our State cannot be sever'd, we are one,
One Flesh; to lose thee were to lose myself.
960   So *Adam*, and thus *Eve* to him repli'd.
O glorious trial of exceeding Love,
Illustrious evidence, example high!
Ingaging me to emulate, but short
    Of thy perfection, how shall I attain,
965   *Adam*, from whose dear side I boast me sprung,
And gladly of our Union hear thee speak,
One Heart, one Soul in both; whereof good proof
This day affords, declaring thee resolv'd,
Rather than Death or aught than Death more dread
970   Shall separate us, linkt in Love so dear,
To undergo with mee one Guilt, one Crime,
If any be, of tasting this fair Fruit,
Whose virtue, for of good still good proceeds,
Direct, or by occasion[1] hath presented
975   This happy trial of thy Love, which else
So eminently never had been known.
Were it I thought Death menac't would ensue
This my attempt, I would sustain alone
The worst, and not persuade thee, rather die
980   Deserted, than oblige° thee with a fact   °make liable
Pernicious to thy Peace, chiefly assur'd
Remarkably so late of thy so true,
So faithful Love unequall'd; but I feel
Far otherwise th' event,° nor Death, but Life   °result
985   Augmented, op'n'd Eyes, new Hopes, new Joys,
Taste so Divine, that what of sweet before
Hath toucht my sense, flat seems to this, and harsh.
On my experience, *Adam*, freely taste,
And fear of Death deliver to the Winds.
990   So saying, she embrac'd him, and for joy
Tenderly wept, much won that he his Love
Had so ennobl'd, as of choice to incur
Divine displeasure for her sake, or Death.
In recompense (for such compliance bad
995   Such recompense best merits) from the bough
She gave him of that fair enticing Fruit
With liberal hand: he scrupl'd not to eat

9. Three separate meanings are possible: judgment, irrev-   1. I.e., directly or indirectly.
ocable destiny, and death.

Against his better knowledge, not deceiv'd,
But fondly overcome with Female charm.[2]
1000   Earth trembl'd from her entrails, as again
In pangs, and Nature gave a second groan,
Sky low'r'd, and muttering Thunder, some sad drops
Wept at completing of the mortal Sin
Original;[3] while *Adam* took no thought,
1005   Eating his fill, nor *Eve* to iterate
Her former trespass fear'd, the more to soothe
Him with her lov'd society, that now
As with new Wine intoxicated both
They swim in mirth, and fancy that they feel
1010   Divinity within them breeding wings
Wherewith to scorn the Earth: but that false Fruit
Far other operation first display'd,
Carnal desire inflaming, hee on *Eve*
Began to cast lascivious Eyes, she him
1015   As wantonly repaid; in Lust they burn:
Till *Adam* thus 'gan *Eve* to dalliance move.
          Eve, now I see thou are exact of taste,
And elegant, of Sapience[4] no small part,
Since to each meaning savor[5] we apply,
1020   And Palate call judicious; I the praise
Yield thee, so well this day thou hast purvey'd.°   *provided*
Much pleasure we have lost, while we abstain'd
From this delightful Fruit, nor known till now
True relish, tasting; if such pleasure be
1025   In things to us forbidden, it might be wish'd,
For this one Tree had been forbidden ten.
But come, so well refresh't, now let us play,
As meet is, after such delicious Fare;
For never did thy Beauty since the day
1030   I saw thee first and wedded thee, adorn'd
With all perfections, so inflame my sense
With ardor to enjoy thee, fairer now
Than ever, bounty of this virtuous Tree.[6]
          So said he, and forbore not glance or toy°   *caress*
1035   Of amorous intent, well understood
Of° *Eve*, whose Eye darted contagious Fire.   *by*
Her hand he seiz'd, and to a shady bank,
Thick overhead with verdant roof imbowr'd
He led her nothing loath; Flow'rs were the Couch,
1040   Pansies, and Violets, and Asphodel,
And Hyacinth, Earth's freshest softest lap.
There they thir fill of Love and Love's disport
Took largely, of thir mutual guilt the Seal,

---

2. See 1 Timothy 2.14: "And Adam was not deceived, but the woman being deceived was in the transgression."
3. The only occurrence in *Paradise Lost* of the term "Original Sin." In his *De doctrina* (1.11) where Milton defines Original Sin as "the sin which is common to all men, that which our first parents, and in them all their posterity committed, when, casting off their obedience

to God, they tasted the fruit of the forbidden tree."
4. Wisdom, from Latin *sapere*, to taste.
5. Tastiness, understanding.
6. See Homer, *Iliad*. 14, where Hera, bent on deceiving Zeus, comes to him wearing Aphrodite's belt and seems more charming to him than ever before.

The solace of thir sin, till dewy sleep
1045   Oppress'd them, wearied with thir amorous play.
Soon as the force of that fallacious Fruit,
That with exhilarating vapor bland°   *pleasing*
About thir spirits had play'd, and inmost powers
Made err, was now exhal'd, and grosser sleep
1050   Bred of unkindly fumes,[7] with conscious dreams
Encumber'd, now had left them, up they rose
As from unrest, and each the other viewing,
Soon found thir Eyes how op'n'd, and thir minds
How dark'n'd;[8] innocence, that as a veil
1055   Had shadow'd them from knowing ill, was gone,
Just confidence, and native righteousness,
And honor from about them, naked left
To guilty shame: hee cover'd, but his Robe
Uncover'd more. So rose the *Danite* strong
1060   *Herculean Samson* from the Harlot-lap
Of *Philistean Dalilah*, and wak'd
Shorn of his strength, They destitute and bare
Of all thir virtue:[9] silent, and in face
Confounded long they sat, as struck'n mute,
1065   Till *Adam*, though not less than *Eve* abasht,
At length gave utterance to these words constrain'd.
      O *Eve,* in evil hour thou didst give ear
To that false Worm, of whomsoever taught
To counterfeit Man's voice, true in our Fall,
1070   False in our promis'd Rising; since our Eyes
Op'n'd we find indeed, and find we know
Both Good and Evil, Good lost, and Evil got,
Bad Fruit of Knowledge, if this be to know,
Which leaves us naked thus, of Honor void,
1075   Of Innocence, of Faith, of Purity,
Our wonted Ornaments now soil'd and stain'd,
And in our Faces evident the signs
Of foul concupiscence; whence evil store;
Even shame, the last of evils; of the first
1080   Be sure then. How shall I behold the face
Henceforth of God or Angel, erst with joy
And rapture so oft beheld? those heav'nly shapes
Will dazzle now this earthly, with thir blaze
Insufferably bright. O might I here
1085   In solitude live savage, in some glade
Obscur'd, where highest Woods impenetrable
To Star or Sun-light, spread thir umbrage broad,
And brown as Evening: Cover me ye Pines,
Ye Cedars, with innumerable boughs
1090   Hide me, where I may never see them more.
But let us now, as in bad plight, devise
What best may for the present serve to hide

7. Unnatural vapors or exhalations rising from the stomach to the brain.
8. See Genesis 3.7: "The eyes of them both were opened,
and they knew that they were naked."
9. See Judges 16 for the story of Samson's betrayal by Delilah.

The Parts of each from other, that seem most
To shame obnoxious,° and unseemliest seen,   *exposed*
1095 Some Tree whose broad smooth Leaves together sew'd,
And girded on our loins, may cover round
Those middle parts, that this new comer, Shame,
There sit not, and reproach us as unclean.[1]
    So counsell'd hee, and both together went
1100 Into the thickest Wood, there soon they chose
The Figtree,[2] not that kind for Fruit renown'd,
But such as at this day to *Indians* known
In *Malabar* or *Decan* spreads her Arms
Branching so broad and long, that in the ground
1105 The bended Twigs take root, and Daughters grow
About the Mother Tree, a Pillar'd shade
High overarch't, and echoing Walks between;
There oft the *Indian* Herdsman shunning heat
Shelters in cool, and tends his pasturing Herds
1110 At Loopholes cut through thickest shade: Those Leaves
They gather'd, broad as Amazonian Targe,°   *shield*
And with what skill they had, together sew'd,
To gird thir waist, vain Covering if to hide
Thir guilt and dreaded shame; O how unlike
1115 To that first naked Glory. Such of late
Columbus found th' *American* so girt
With feather'd Cincture,° naked else and wild   *belt*
Among the Trees on Isles and woody Shores.
Thus fenc't, and as they thought, thir shame in part
1120 Cover'd, but not at rest or ease of Mind,
They sat them down to weep, nor only Tears
Rain'd at thir Eyes, but high Winds worse within
Began to rise, high Passions, Anger, Hate,
Mistrust, Suspicion, Discord, and shook sore
1125 Thir inward State of Mind, calm Region once
And full of Peace, now toss't and turbulent:
For Understanding rul'd not, and the Will
Heard not her lore, both in subjection now
To sensual Appetite, who from beneath
1130 Usurping over sovran Reason claim'd
Superior sway: From thus distemper'd breast,
Adam, estrang'd in look and alter'd style,
Speech intermitted thus to *Eve* renew'd.
    Would thou hadst heark'n'd to my words, and stay'd
1135 With me, as I besought thee, when that strange
Desire of wand'ring this unhappy Morn,
I know not whence possess'd thee; we had then
Remain'd still happy, not as now, despoil'd
Of all our good, sham'd, naked, miserable.
1140 Let none henceforth seek needless cause to approve°   *give proof of*
The Faith they owe;[3] when earnestly they seek
Such proof, conclude, they then begin to fail.

---

1. See Genesis 3.7.
2. Milton's description of the banyan or Indian fig comes

from Gerard's *Herball* (1597).
3. Be under obligation to render or possess.

To whom soon mov'd with touch of blame thus *Eve*.
What words have past thy Lips,[4] *Adam* severe,
1145   Imput'st thou that to my default, or will
Of wand'ring, as thou call'st it, which who knows
But might as ill have happ'n'd thou being by,
Or to thyself perhaps: hadst thou been there,
Or here th' attempt, thou couldst not have discern'd
1150   Fraud in the Serpent, speaking as he spake;
No ground of enmity between us known,
Why hee should mean me ill, or seek to harm.
Was I to have never parted from thy side?
As good have grown there still a lifeless Rib.
1155   Being as I am, why didst not thou the Head[5]
Command me absolutely not to go,
Going into such danger as thou said'st?
Too facile° then thou didst not much gainsay,   *permissive*
Nay, didst permit, approve, and fair dismiss.
1160   Hadst thou been firm and fixt in thy dissent,
Neither had I transgress'd, nor thou with mee.
    To whom then first incenst Adam repli'd.
Is this the Love, is this the recompense
Of mine to thee, ingrateful *Eve*, express't
1165   Immutable° when thou wert lost, not I,   *unchangeable*
Who might have liv'd and joy'd immortal bliss,
Yet willingly chose rather Death with thee:
And am I now upbraided, as the cause
Of thy transgressing? not enough severe,
1170   It seems, in thy restraint: what could I more?
I warn'd thee, I admonish'd thee, foretold
The danger, and the lurking Enemy
That lay in wait; beyond this had been force,
And force upon free Will hath here no place.
1175   But confidence then bore thee on, secure
Either to meet no danger, or to find
Matter of glorious trial; and perhaps
I also err'd in overmuch admiring
What seem'd in thee so perfet, that I thought
1180   No evil durst attempt thee, but I rue
That error now, which is become my crime,
And thou th' accuser. Thus it shall befall
Him who to worth in Woman overtrusting
Lets her Will rule; restraint she will not brook,
1185   And left to herself, if evil thence ensue,
Shee first his weak indulgence will accuse.
    Thus they in mutual accusation spent
The fruitless hours, but neither self-condemning,
And of thir vain contést appear'd no end.
      The End of the Ninth Book.

4. Echoes Odysseus's disapproval of a speech of Agamemnon's (*Iliad* 14.83).
5. Alludes to 1 Corinthians 11.3: "The head of every man is Christ; and the head of the woman is the man; and the head of Christ is God."

Book 10
The Argument

Man's transgression known, the Guardian Angels forsake Paradise, and return up to Heaven to approve thir vigilance, and are approv'd, God declaring that the entrance of Satan could not be by them prevented. He sends his Son to judge the Transgressors, who descends and gives Sentence accordingly; then in pity clothes them both, and reascends. Sin and Death sitting till then at the Gates of Hell, by wondrous sympathy feeling the success of Satan in this new World, and the sin by Man there committed, resolve to sit no longer confin'd in Hell, but to follow Satan thir Sire up to the place of Man: To make the way easier from Hell to this World to and fro, they pave a broad Highway or Bridge over Chaos, according to the Track that Satan first made; then preparing for Earth, they meet him proud of his success returning to Hell; thir mutual gratulation. Satan arrives at Pandemonium, in full assembly relates with boasting his success against Man; instead of applause is entertained with a general hiss by all his audience, transform'd with himself also suddenly into Serpents, according to his doom giv'n in Paradise; then deluded with a show of the forbidden Tree springing up before them, they greedily reaching to take of the Fruit, chew dust and bitter ashes. The proceedings of Sin and Death; God foretells the final Victory of his Son over them, and the renewing of all things; but for the present commands his Angels to make several alterations in the Heavens and Elements. Adam more and more perceiving his fall'n condition heavily bewails, rejects the condolement of Eve; she persists and at length appeases him: then to evade the Curse likely to fall on thir Offspring, proposes to Adam violent ways, which he approves not, but conceiving better hope, puts her in mind of the late Promise made them, that her Seed should be reveng'd on the Serpent, and exhorts her with him to seek Peace of the offended Deity, by repentance and supplication.

>   Meanwhile the heinous and despiteful act
> Of *Satan* done in Paradise, and how
> Hee in the Serpent had perverted *Eve,*
> Her Husband shee, to taste the fatal fruit,
> 5 Was known in Heav'n;[1] for what can scape the Eye
> Of *God* All-seeing, or deceive his Heart
> Omniscient, who in all things wise and just,
> Hinder'd not *Satan* to attempt the mind
> Of Man, with strength entire, and free will arm'd,
> 10 Complete to have discover'd and repulst
> Whatever wiles of Foe or seeming Friend.
> For still they knew, and ought to have still remember'd
> The high Injunction not to taste that Fruit,
> Whoever tempted; which they not obeying,
> 15 Incurr'd, what could they less, the penalty,
> And manifold[2] in sin, deserv'd to fall.
>   Up into Heav'n from Paradise in haste
> Th' Angelic Guards ascended, mute and sad

---

1. Rhetorically, lines 1–16 function both as *principium,* stating the subject of the book, and as *initium,* introducing the first scene. They also sum up the theological content of Book 3, which will receive specific application in the present book, in the exchanges between the Father and the Son (lines 34–84) and between the Son and

Adam (lines 124ff.). Note the structural symmetry whereby the divine decrees of the third book are balanced by those of the third last.
2. Multiplied; alluding to Psalms 38.19: "they that hate me wrongfully are multiplied."

For Man, for of his state by this they knew,
20   Much wond'ring how the subtle Fiend had stol'n
Entrance unseen. Soon as th' unwelcome news
From Earth arriv'd at Heaven Gate, displeas'd
All were who heard, dim sadness did not spare
That time Celestial visages, yet mixt
25   With pity, violated not thir bliss.
About the new-arriv'd, in multitudes
Th' ethereal People ran, to hear and know
How all befell: they towards the Throne Supreme
Accountable made haste to make appear
30   With righteous plea, thir utmost vigilance,
And easily approv'd; when the most High
Eternal Father from his secret Cloud,
Amidst in Thunder utter'd thus his voice.
        Assembl'd Angels, and ye Powers return'd
35   From unsuccessful charge, be not dismay'd,
Nor troubl'd at these tidings from the Earth,
Which your sincerest care could not prevent,
Foretold so lately what would come to pass,
When first this Tempter cross'd the Gulf from Hell.
40   I told ye then he should prevail and speed°   succeed
On his bad Errand, Man should be seduc't
And flatter'd out of all, believing lies
Against his Maker; no Decree of mine
Concurring to necessitate his Fall,
45   Or touch with lightest moment of impulse
His free Will, to her own inclining left
In even scale.³ But fall'n he is, and now
What rests, but that the mortal Sentence pass
On his transgression. Death denounc't that day,
50   Which he presumes already vain and void,
Because not yet inflicted, as he fear'd,
By some immediate stroke; but soon shall find
Forbearance no acquittance ere day end.
Justice shall not return as bounty scorn'd.
55   But whom send I to judge them? whom but thee
Vicegerent Son, to thee I have transferr'd
All Judgment, whether in Heav'n, or Earth, or Hell.
Easy it may be seen that I intend
Mercy colleague with Justice, sending thee
60   Man's Friend, his Mediator, his design'd
Both Ransom and Redeemer voluntary,
And destin'd Man himself to judge Man fall'n.⁴
        So spake the Father, and unfolding bright
Toward the right hand his Glory, on the Son

3. "Moment" is a term applied to the smallest increment that could affect the equilibrium of a balance. If man had been protected from the tempter, then there would have been real interference with the free action of the scales of justice.

4. The double syntax—line 62 can be read as either "himself a man, destined to judge man" (primary) or "destined to judge man himself, man fallen"—mimes the close identification of Christ with humanity.

65	Blaz'd forth unclouded Deity; he full
	Resplendent all his Father manifest
	Express'd, and thus divinely answer'd mild.
	Father Eternal, thine is to decree,
	Mine both in Heav'n and Earth to do thy will
70	Supreme, that thou in mee thy Son belov'd
	May'st ever rest well pleas'd.[5] I go to judge
	On Earth these thy transgressors, but thou know'st,
	Whoever judg'd, the worst on mee must light,
	When time shall be, for so I undertook
75	Before thee; and not repenting, this obtain
	Of right, that I may mitigate thir doom
	On me deriv'd, yet I shall temper so
	Justice with Mercy, as may illustrate most
	Them fully satisfied, and thee appease.
80	Attendance none shall need, nor Train, where none
	Are to behold the Judgment, but the judg'd,
	Those two; the third[6] best absent is condemn'd,
	Convict° by flight, and Rebel to all Law:
	Conviction to the Serpent none belongs.[7]
85	Thus saying, from his radiant Seat he rose
	Of high collateral° glory: him Thrones and Powers,
	Princedoms, and Dominations ministrant
	Accompanied to Heaven Gate, from whence
	Eden and all the Coast in prospect lay.
90	Down he descended straight; the speed of Gods
	Time counts not, though with swiftest minutes wing'd.
	Now was the Sun in Western cadence° low[8]
	From Noon, and gentle Airs due at thir hour
	To fan the Earth now wak'd, and usher in
95	The Ev'ning cool, when he from wrath more cool
	Came the mild Judge and Intercessor both
	To sentence Man: the voice of God they heard
	Now walking in the Garden, by soft winds
	Brought to thir Ears, while day declin'd, they heard,
100	And from his presence hid themselves among
	The thickest Trees, both Man and Wife, till God
	Approaching, thus to Adam call'd aloud.
	Where art thou *Adam*, wont with joy to meet
	My coming seen far off? I miss thee here,
105	Not pleas'd, thus entertain'd with solitude,
	Where obvious duty erewhile appear'd unsought:
	Or come I less conspicuous, or what change
	Absents thee, or what chance detains? Come forth.
	He came, and with him *Eve*, more loath, though first
110	To offend, discount'nanc't both, and discompos'd;
	Love was not in thir looks, either to God

Marginal glosses:
- *convicted* (line 83)
- *side by side* (line 86)
- *falling* (line 92)

5. Echoing Matthew 3.17.
6. Satan.
7. "Conviction" has both the legal sense (proof of guilt) and the theological (the condition of being convinced of sin).
8. Lines 92–123 follow Genesis 3.8–11.

Or to each other, but apparent guilt,
And shame, and perturbation, and despair,
Anger, and obstinacy, and hate, and guile.

115   Whence *Adam* falt'ring long, thus answer'd brief.
    I heard thee in the Garden, and of thy voice
Afraid, being naked, hid myself. To whom
The gracious Judge without revile repli'd.
    My voice thou oft hast heard, and hast not fear'd,

120   But still rejoic't, how is it now become
So dreadful to thee? that thou art naked, who
Hath told thee? hast thou eaten of the Tree
Whereof I gave thee charge thou shouldst not eat?
    To whom thus *Adam* sore beset repli'd.

125   O Heav'n! in evil strait this day I stand
Before my Judge, either to undergo
Myself the total Crime, or to accuse
My other self, the partner of my life;
Whose failing, while her Faith to me remains,

130   I should conceal, and not expose to blame
By my complaint; but strict necessity
Subdues me, and calamitous constraint,
Lest on my head both sin and punishment,
However insupportable, be all

135   Devolv'd;[9] though should I hold my peace, yet thou
Wouldst easily detect what I conceal.
This Woman whom thou mad'st to be my help,
And gav'st me as thy perfet gift, so good,
So fit, so acceptable, so Divine,

140   That from her hand I could suspect no ill,
And what she did, whatever in itself,
Her doing seem'd to justify the deed;
Shee gave me of the Tree, and I did eat.[1]
    To whom the sovran Presence thus repli'd.

145   Was shee thy God, that her thou didst obey
Before his voice, or was shee made thy guide,
Superior, or but equal, that to her
Thou didst resign thy Manhood, and the Place
Wherein God set thee above her made of thee,

150   And for thee, whose perfection far excell'd
Hers in all real° dignity:[2] Adorn'd   *regal*
She was indeed, and lovely to attract
Thy Love, not thy Subjection, and her Gifts
Were such as under Government well seem'd,

155   Unseemly to bear rule, which was thy part°   *role*
And person,° hadst thou known thyself aright.   *character*
    So having said, he thus to Eve in few:
Say Woman, what is this which thou hast done?

---

9. Caused to fall upon.
1. See Genesis 3.12.
2. See 1 Corinthians 11.8ff.: "For the man is not of the woman; but the woman of the man. Neither was the man created for the woman; but the woman for the man."

To whom sad *Eve* with shame nigh overwhelm'd,
160   Confessing soon, yet not before her Judge
Bold or loquacious, thus abasht repli'd.
    The Serpent me beguil'd and I did eat.[3]
    Which when the Lord God heard, without delay
To Judgment he proceeded on th' accus'd
165   Serpent though brute, unable to transfer
The Guilt on him who made him instrument
Of mischief, and polluted from the end
Of his Creation; justly then accurst,
As vitiated in Nature: more to know
170   Concern'd not Man (since he no further knew)
Nor alter'd his offense; yet God at last
To Satan first in sin his doom appli'd,
Though in mysterious° terms, judg'd as then best: *mystical*
And on the Serpent thus his curse let fall.
175   Because thou hast done this, thou art accurst
Above all Cattle, each Beast of the Field;
Upon thy Belly groveling thou shalt go,
And dust shalt eat all the days of thy Life.
Between Thee and the Woman I will put
180   Enmity, and between thine and her Seed;
Her Seed shall bruise thy head, thou bruise his heel.[4]
    So spake this Oracle, then verifi'd
When *Jesus* son of *Mary* second *Eve*,
Saw Satan fall like Lightning down from Heav'n,[5]
185   Prince of the Air; then rising from his Grave
Spoil'd Principalities and Powers, triumpht
In open show, and with ascension bright
Captivity led captive through the Air,[6]
The Realm itself of Satan long usurpt,
190   Whom he shall tread at last under our feet;[7]
Ev'n hee who now foretold his fatal bruise,
And to the Woman thus his Sentence turn'd.
    Thy sorrow I will greatly multiply
By thy Conception; Children thou shalt bring
195   In sorrow forth, and to thy Husband's will
Thine shall submit, hee over thee shall rule.
    On *Adam* last thus judgment he pronounc'd.
Because thou hast heark'n'd to the voice of thy Wife,
And eaten of the Tree concerning which
200   I charg'd thee, saying: Thou shalt not eat thereof,
Curs'd is the ground for thy sake, thou in sorrow
Shalt eat thereof all the days of thy Life;[8]
Thorns also and Thistles it shall bring thee forth
Unbid, and thou shalt eat th' Herb of the Field,

3. Repeating Genesis 3.13.
4. See Genesis 3.14ff.
5. "I beheld Satan as lightning fall from heaven" (Luke 10.18).
6. Psalms 68.18: "Thou hast ascended on high, thou hast

led captivity captive": applied to Christ in Ephesians 4.8.
7. See Romans 16.20: "And the God of peace shall bruise Satan under your feet shortly."
8. See Genesis 3.17.

205   In the sweat of thy Face shalt thou eat Bread,
       Till thou return unto the ground, for thou
       Out of the ground wast taken, know thy Birth,
       For dust thou art, and shalt to dust return.[9]
           So judg'd he Man, both Judge and Savior sent,
210   And th' instant stroke of Death denounc't that day
       Remov'd far off;[1] then pitying how they stood
       Before him naked to the air, that now
       Must suffer change, disdain'd not to begin
       Thenceforth the form of servant to assume,[2]
215   As when he wash'd his servants' feet, so now
       As Father of his Family he clad
       Thir nakedness with Skins of Beasts, or slain,
       Or as the Snake with youthful Coat repaid;
       And thought not much to clothe his Enemies:
220   Nor hee thir outward only with the Skins
       Of Beasts, but inward nakedness, much more
       Opprobrious, with his Robe of righteousness,
       Arraying cover'd from his Father's sight.
       To him with swift ascent he up return'd,
225   Into his blissful bosom reassum'd
       In glory as of old, to him appeas'd
       All, though all-knowing, what had past with Man
       Recounted, mixing intercession sweet.[3]
                          * * *
                    Th' other way *Satan* went down
415   The Causey° to Hell Gate; on either side   *causeway*
       Disparted *Chaos* over-built exclaim'd,
       And with rebounding surge the bars assail'd,
       That scorn'd his indignation: through the Gate,
       Wide open and unguarded, *Satan* pass'd,
420   And all about found desolate; for those
       Appointed to sit there,[4] had left thir charge,
       Flown to the upper World; the rest were all
       Far to th'inland retir'd, about the walls
       Of *Pandaemonium*, City and proud seat
425   Of *Lucifer*, so by allusion call'd,
       Of that bright Star to *Satan* paragon'd.°   *compared*
       There kept thir Watch the Legions, while the Grand
       In Council sat, solicitous° what chance   *anxious*
       Might intercept thir Emperor sent, so hee
430   Departing gave command, and they observ'd.
       As when the Tartar from his *Russian* Foe
       By *Astracan*[5] over the Snowy Plains
       Retires, or *Bactrian* Sophi[6] from the horns

---

9. See Genesis 3.18–9.
1. Christ removes the fear that physical death will follow the eating of the fruit on the same day.
2. See Phillipians. 2.7: "made himself of no reputation, and took upon him the form of a servant, and was made in the likeness of men."
3. Sin and Death now pave a highway across Chaos from

Hell to earth. Satan meets them and sends them on to dwell on earth; he heads home to Hell.
4. Sin and Death.
5. Astracan, or Astrakhan, was a Tartar kingdom and capital city near the outh of the Volga.
6. Persian king.

Of *Turkish* Crescent,[7] leaves all waste beyond
435 The Realm of *Aladule*,[8] in his retreat
To *Tauris* or *Casbeen:*[9] So these the late
Heav'n-banisht Host, left desert utmost Hell
Many a dark League, reduc't in careful Watch
Round thir Metropolis, and now expecting
440 Each hour their great adventurer from the search
Of Foreign Worlds: he through the midst unmark't,
In show Plebeian Angel militant
Of lowest order, pass't; and from the door
Of that *Plutonian*[1] Hall, invisible
445 Ascended his high Throne, which under state°   canopy
Of richest texture spread, at th' upper end
Was plac't in regal lustre. Down a while
He sat, and round about him saw unseen:
At last as from a Cloud his fulgent head
450 And shape Star-bright appear'd, or brighter, clad
With what permissive glory since his fall
Was left him, or false glitter: All amaz'd
At that so sudden blaze the Stygian throng
Bent thir aspect, and whom they wish'd beheld,
455 Thir mighty Chief return'd: loud was th' acclaim:
Forth rush'd in haste the great consulting Peers,
Rais'd from thir dark *Divan*,[2] and with like joy
Congratulant approach'd him, who with hand
Silence, and with these words attention won.
460   Thrones, Dominations, Princedoms, Virtues, Powers,
For in possession such, not only of right,
I call ye and declare ye now, return'd
Successful beyond hope, to lead ye forth
Triumphant out of this infernal Pit
465 Abominable, accurst, the house of woe,
And Dungeon of our Tyrant: Now possess,
As Lords, a spacious World, to our native Heaven
Little inferior, by my adventure hard
With peril great achiev'd. Long were to tell
470 What I have done, what suffer'd, with what pain
Voyag'd th' unreal, vast, unbounded deep
Of horrible confusion, over which
By Sin and Death a broad way now is pav'd
To expedite your glorious march; but I
475 Toil'd out my úncouth° passage, forc't to ride   strange
Th' untractable Abyss, plung'd in the womb
Of unoriginal° *Night* and *Chaos* wild,   uncreated
That jealous of thir secrets fiercely oppos'd
My journey strange, with clamorous uproar

7. Refers not only to the Turkish ensign, but also to their battle formations.
8. Greater Armenia.
9. Tauris (modern Tabriz) is in the extreme northwest of Persia; Casbeen, or Kazvin, is north of Teheran.
1. Pertaining to Pluto, ruler of the classical underworld.
2. Turkish council of state.

480 Protesting Fate supreme; thence how I found
     The new created World, which fame in Heav'n
     Long had foretold, a Fabric wonderful
     Of absolute perfection, therein Man
     Plac't in a Paradise, by our exile
485 Made happy: Him by fraud I have seduc'd
     From his Creator, and the more to increase
     Your wonder, with an Apple; he thereat
     Offended, worth your laughter, hath giv'n up
     Both his beloved Man and all his World,
490 To Sin and Death a prey, and so to us,
     Without our hazard, labor, or alarm,
     To range in, and to dwell, and over Man
     To rule, as over all he should have rul'd.
     True is, mee also he hath judg'd, or rather
495 Mee not, but the brute Serpent in whose shape
     Man I deceiv'd: that which to mee belongs,
     Is enmity, which he will put between
     Mee and Mankind; I am to bruise his heel;
     His Seed, when is not set, shall bruise my head:
500 A World who would not purchase with a bruise,
     Or much more grievous pain? Ye have th' account
     Of my performance: What remains, ye Gods,
     But up and enter now into full bliss.
          So having said, a while he stood, expecting
505 Thir universal shout and high applause
     To fill his ear, when contrary he hears
     On all sides, from innumerable tongues
     A dismal universal hiss, the sound
     Of public scorn; he wonder'd, but not long
510 Had leisure, wond'ring at himself now more;
     His Visage drawn he felt to sharp and spare,
     His Arms clung to his Ribs, his Legs entwining
     Each other, till supplanted° down he fell   tripped
     A monstrous Serpent on his Belly prone,[3]
515 Reluctant,° but in vain: a greater power   resisting
     Now rul'd him, punisht in the shape he sinn'd,
     According to his doom: he would have spoke,
     But hiss for hiss return'd with forked tongue
     To forked tongue, for now were all transform'd
520 Alike, to Serpents all as accessories
     To his bold Riot: dreadful was the din
     Of hissing through the Hall, thick swarming now
     With complicated° monsters, head and tail,   compound
     Scorpion and Asp, and *Amphisbaena* dire,
525 *Cerastes* horn'd, *Hydrus,* and *Ellops* drear,
     And *Dipsas*[4] (not so thick swarm'd once the Soil

3. See the metamorphosis of Cadmus in Ovid, *Metamorphoses* 4.572–603, and the mutual interchange of serpentine forms in Dante's canto of the thieves, *Inferno* 25. 4. The amphisbaena is a serpent with a head at either end. The cerastes has four horns on its head. The hydrus is a water snake. The ellops, though sometimes identified as the swordfish, is mentioned as a serpent in Pliny, *Natural History* 32.5. The dipsas causes raging thirst by its bite.

Bedropt with blood of *Gorgon*, or the Isle
Ophiusa) but still greatest hee the midst,[5]
Now Dragon grown, larger than whom the Sun
530　Ingender'd in the *Pythian* Vale on slime,
Huge *Python*, and his Power no less he seem'd
Above the rest still to retain;[6] they all
Him follow'd issuing forth to th' open Field,
Where all yet left of that revolted Rout
535　Heav'n-fall'n, in station stood or just array,
Sublime° with expectation when to see　　　　　　　*uplifted*
In Triumph issuing forth thir glorious Chief;
They saw, but other sight instead, a crowd
Of ugly Serpents; horror on them fell,
540　And horrid sympathy; for what they saw,
They felt themselves now changing; down thir arms,
Down fell both Spear and Shield, down they as fast,
And the dire hiss renew'd, and the dire form
Catcht by Contagion, like in punishment,
545　As in thir crime. Thus was th' applause they meant,
Turn'd to exploding hiss, triumph to shame
Cast on themselves from thir own mouths. There stood
A Grove hard by, sprung up with this thir change,
His will who reigns above, to aggravate
550　Thir penance, laden with fair Fruit, like that
Which grew in Paradise, the bait of *Eve*
Us'd by the Tempter: on that prospect strange
Thir earnest eyes they fix'd, imagining
For one forbidden Tree a multitude
555　Now ris'n, to work them furder° woe or shame;　　　*further*
Yet parcht with scalding thirst and hunger fierce,
Though to delude them sent, could not abstain,
But on they roll'd in heaps, and up the Trees
Climbing, sat thicker than the snaky locks
560　That curl'd *Megaera*:[7] greedily they pluck'd
The Fruitage fair to sight, like that which grew
Near that bituminous Lake where *Sodom* flam'd;[8]
This more delusive, not the touch, but taste
Deceiv'd; they fondly thinking to allay
565　Thir appetite with gust,° instead of Fruit　　　　*taste*
Chew'd bitter Ashes, which th' offended taste
With spattering noise rejected: oft they assay'd,
Hunger and thirst constraining, drugg'd° as oft,　　*nauseated*
With hatefullest disrelish writh'd thir jaws
570　With soot and cinders fill'd; so oft they fell
Into the same illusion, not as Man

---

5. When Perseus was bringing back the severed head of
Medusa, drops of blood fell to earth and became serpents.
"Ophiusa" means literally "full of serpents"; a name
anciently given to several islands, including Rhodes and
one of the Balearic group.
6. For the birth of Python from the slime remaining after
the flood, see Ovid, *Metamorphoses* 1.438–440. Python
was slain by Apollo. Satan's dragon shape is that of the

"old dragon" of Christian apocalypse; see Revelation
12.9: "the great dragon was cast out, that old serpent,
called the Devil, and Satan."
7. One of the Furies, often described as snaky-haired.
8. The allusion is to Josephus, *Wars* 4.8.4, where it is said
that traces still remain of the divine fire that burnt
Sodom, such as tasty-looking fruits that turned to ashes
when plucked.

Whom they triumph'd, once lapst. Thus were they plagu'd
And worn with Famine long, and ceaseless hiss,
Till thir lost shape, permitted, they resum'd,
575   Yearly enjoin'd, some say, to undergo
This annual humbling certain number'd days,
To dash thir pride, and joy for Man seduc't.
However some tradition they dispers'd
Among the Heathen of thir purchase got,
580   And Fabl'd how the Serpent, whom they call'd
Ophion with *Eurynome*, the wide-
Encroaching *Eve* perhaps, had first the rule
Of high *Olympus*, thence by Saturn driv'n
And Ops, ere yet *Dictaean Jove* was born.[9]
585   Meanwhile in Paradise the hellish pair
Too soon arriv'd, *Sin* there in power before,
Once actual, now in body, and to dwell
Habitual habitant; behind her *Death*
Close following pace for pace, not mounted yet
590   On his pale Horse:[1] to whom *Sin* thus began.
        Second of *Satan* sprung, all conquering *Death*,
What think'st thou of our Empire now, though earn'd
With travail difficult, not better far
Than still at Hell's dark threshold to have sat watch,
595   Unnam'd, undreaded, and thyself half starv'd?
        Whom thus the Sin-born Monster answer'd soon.
To mee, who with eternal Famine pine,
Alike is Hell, or Paradise, or Heaven,
There best, where most with ravin I may meet;
600   Which here, though plenteous, all too little seems
To stuff this Maw, this vast unhide-bound Corpse.
        To whom th' incestuous Mother thus repli'd.
Thou therefore on these Herbs, and Fruits, and Flow'rs
Feed first, on each Beast next, and Fish, and Fowl,
605   No homely morsels, and whatever thing
The Scythe of Time mows down, devour unspar'd,
Till I in Man residing through the Race,
His thoughts, his looks, words, actions all infect,
And season him thy last and sweetest prey.
610   This said, they both betook them several ways,
Both to destroy, or unimmortal make
All kinds, and for destruction to mature
Sooner or later; which th' Almighty seeing
From his transcendent Seat the Saints among,
615   To those bright Orders utter'd thus his voice.
        See with what heat these Dogs of Hell advance
To waste and havoc° yonder World, which I   devastate
So fair and good created, and had still
Kept in that state, had not the folly of Man

---

9. Ophion and Eurynome ruled Olympus until the one
yielded to Cronos (Saturn) and the other to Rhea (Ops).
Their two successors then ruled the Titans, while Zeus
lived in the Dictaean cave. See Apollonius Rhodius, *Arg-*
onautica 1.503–9.
1. See Revelation 6.8: "I looked, and behold a pale horse:
and his name that sat on him was Death, and Hell followed with him."

620   Let in these wasteful Furies, who impute
        Folly to mee, so doth the Prince of Hell
        And his Adherents, that with so much ease
        I suffer them to enter and possess
        A place so heav'nly, and conniving seem
625   To gratify my scornful Enemies,
        That laugh, as if transported with some fit
        Of Passion, I to them had quitted° all,   *yielded*
        At random yielded up to their misrule;
        And know not that I call'd and drew them thither
630   My Hell-hounds, to lick up the draff° and filth   *refuse*
        Which man's polluting Sin with taint hath shed
        On what was pure, till cramm'd and gorg'd, nigh burst
        With suckt and glutted offal, at one sling
        Of thy victorious Arm, well-pleasing Son,
635   Both *Sin*, and *Death,* and yawning *Grave* at last
        Through *Chaos* hurl'd, obstruct the mouth of Hell
        For ever, and seal up his ravenous Jaws.
        Then Heav'n and Earth renew'd shall be made pure
        To sanctity that shall receive no stain:
640   Till then the Curse pronounc't on both precedes.[2]
                          * * *
                                        Thus began
        Outrage from lifeless things; but Discord first
        Daughter of Sin, among th' irrational,
        Death introduc'd through fierce antipathy:
710   Beast now with Beast gan war, and Fowl with Fowl,
        And Fish with Fish; to graze the Herb all leaving,
        Devour'd each other; nor stood much in awe
        Of Man, but fled him, or with count'nance grim
        Glar'd on him passing: these were from without
715   The growing miseries, which *Adam* saw
        Already in part, though hid in gloomiest shade,
        To sorrow abandon'd, but worse felt within,
        And in a troubl'd Sea of passion tost,
        Thus to disburd'n sought with sad complaint.
720   O miserable of happy! is this the end
        Of this new glorious World, and mee so late
        The Glory of that Glory, who now become
        Accurst of blessed, hide me from the face
        Of God, whom to behold was then my highth
725   Of happiness: yet well, if here would end
        The misery, I deserv'd it, and would
        My own deservings; but this will not serve;
        All that I eat or drink, or shall beget,
        Is propagated curse.[3] O voice once heard
730   Delightfully, *Increase and multiply,*[4]

2. See Genesis 3.17: "Cursed is the ground for thy sake."
God next commands the angels to make the earth turn
on its axis and so cause the change of seasons, and to disrupt the order of the planets, making their effect on the
world negative as well as positive.
3. Handed down from one generation to another. Food

prolongs life and thus extends the curse, while begetting
children hands it on. Note also that eating and sex are
jointly the concerns of the concupiscible faculty, which
was often regarded as the special field of operation of concupiscence or the "body of sin."
4. See Genesis 1.28.

Now death to hear! for what can I increase
Or multiply, but curses on my head?
Who of all Ages to succeed, but feeling
The evil on him brought by me, will curse
735   My Head; Ill fare our Ancestor impure,
For this we may thank *Adam*; but his thanks
Shall be the execration; so besides
Mine own that bide upon me, all from mee
Shall with a fierce reflux on mee redound,°   *overflow, come back*
740   On mee as on thir natural centre light
Heavy, though in thir place. O fleeting joys
Of Paradise, dear bought with lasting woes!
Did I request thee, Maker, from my Clay
To mould me Man, did I solicit thee
745   From darkness to promote me, or here place
In this delicious Garden? as my Will
Concurr'd not to my being, it were but right
And equal° to reduce me to my dust,   *just*
Desirous to resign, and render back
750   All I receiv'd, unable to perform
Thy terms too hard, by which I was to hold
The good I sought not. To the loss of that,
Sufficient penalty, why hast thou added
The sense of endless woes? inexplicable
755   Thy Justice seems; yet to say truth, too late
I thus contest; then should have been refus'd
Those terms whatever, when they were propos'd:
Thou didst accept them; wilt thou enjoy the good,
Then cavil the conditions? and though God
760   Made thee without thy leave, what if thy Son
Prove disobedient, and reprov'd, retort,
Wherefore didst thou beget me? I sought it not:
Wouldst thou admit for his contempt of thee
That proud excuse? yet him not thy election,°   *choice*
765   But Natural necessity begot.
God made thee of choice his own, and of his own
To serve him, thy reward was of his grace,
Thy punishment then justly is at his Will.
Be it so, for I submit, his doom° is fair,   *judgment*
770   That dust I am, and shall to dust return:[5]
O welcome hour whenever! why delays
His hand to execute what his Decree
Fix'd on this day? why do I overlive,
Why am I mockt with death, and length'n'd out
775   To deathless pain? How gladly would I meet
Mortality my sentence, and be Earth
Insensible, how glad would lay me down
As in my Mother's lap![6] There I should rest
And sleep secure; his dreadful voice no more
780   Would Thunder in my ears, no fear of worse

5. Alluding to Genesis 3.19.   6. Adam's lament echoes Job 3.

To mee and to my offspring would torment me
With cruel expectation. Yet one doubt
Pursues me still, lest all I cannot die,
Lest that pure breath of Life, the Spirit of Man
785 Which God inspir'd, cannot together perish
With this corporeal Clod; then in the Grave,
Or in some other dismal place, who knows
But I shall die a living Death? O thought
Horrid, if true! yet why? it was but breath
790 Of Life that sinn'd; what dies but what had life
And sin? the Body properly hath neither.
All of me then shall die:[7] let this appease
The doubt, since human reach no further knows.
For though the Lord of all be infinite,
795 Is his wrath also? be it, Man is not so,
But mortal doom'd. How can he exercise
Wrath without end on Man whom Death must end?
Can he make deathless Death? that were to make
Strange contradiction, which to God himself
800 Impossible is held, as Argument
Of weakness, not of Power. Will he draw out,
For anger's sake, finite to infinite
In punisht Man, to satisfy his rigor
Satisfi'd never; that were to extend
805 His Sentence beyond dust and Nature's Law,
By which all Causes else according still
To the reception of thir matter act,
Not to th' extent of thir own Sphere.[8] But say
That Death be not one stroke, as I suppos'd,
810 Bereaving sense, but endless misery
From this day onward, which I feel begun
Both in me, and without me, and so last
To perpetuity; Ay me, that fear
Comes thund'ring back with dreadful revolution
815 On my defenseless head; both Death and I
Am found Eternal, and incorporate° both,   *united, embodied*
Nor I on my part single, in mee all
Posterity stands curst:[9] Fair Patrimony
That I must leave ye, Sons; O were I able
820 To waste it all myself, and leave ye none!
So disinherited how would ye bless
Me now your Curse! Ah, why should all mankind
For one man's fault thus guiltless be condemn'd,
If guiltless? But from me what can proceed,
825 But all corrupt, both Mind and Will deprav'd,

---

7. Adam's question is like Milton's in *De doctrina* 1.13: "What could be more absurd than that the mind, which is the part principally offending, should escape the threatened death; and that the body alone, to which immortality was equally allotted, before death came into the world by sin, should pay the penalty of sin by undergoing death, though not implicated in the transgression?" Milton's belief in the joint extinction and joint resurrection of man's body and mind was not an eccentric heresy but good biblical theology.

8. Adam tries to comfort himself with an argument drawn from medieval philosophy. Here Adam means that God would be going beyond a natural law, that any agent acts according to the powers of what receives its action, not according to its own powers.

9. Not only are Death and I double, two in one, but so also am I, since I am both myself and my descendants.

Not to do only, but to will the same
With me? how can they then acquitted stand
In sight of God? Him after all Disputes
Forc't I absolve: all my evasions vain
830 And reasonings, though through Mazes, lead me still
But to my own conviction:[1] first and last
On mee, mee only, as the source and spring
Of all corruption, all the blame lights due;
So might the wrath. Fond wish! couldst thou support
835 That burden heavier than the Earth to bear,
Than all the World much heavier, though divided
With that bad Woman? Thus what thou desir'st,
And what thou fear'st, alike destroys all hope
Of refuge, and concludes thee miserable
840 Beyond all past example and futúre,
To *Satan* only like both crime and doom.
O Conscience, into what Abyss of fears
And horrors hast thou driv'n me; out of which
I find no way, from deep to deeper plung'd!
845   Thus *Adam* to himself lamented loud
Through the still Night, not now, as ere man fell,
Wholesome and cool and mild, but with black Air
Accompanied, with damps and dreadful gloom,
Which to his evil Conscience represented
850 All things with double terror: On the ground
Outstretcht he lay, on the cold ground, and oft
Curs'd his Creation, Death as oft accus'd
Of tardy execution, since denounc't
The day of his offense. Why comes not Death,
855 Said he, with one thrice àcceptable stroke
To end me? Shall Truth fail to keep her word,
Justice Divine not hast'n to be just?
But Death comes not at call, Justice Divine
Mends not her slowest pace for prayers or cries.
860 O Woods, O Fountains, Hillocks, Dales and Bow'rs,
With other echo late I taught your Shades
To answer, and resound far other Song.
Whom thus afflicted when sad Eve beheld,
Desolate where she sat, approaching nigh,
865 Soft words to his fierce passion she assay'd:
But her with stern regard he thus repell'd.
     Out of my sight, thou Serpent, that name best
Befits thee with him leagu'd, thyself as false
And hateful; nothing wants, but that thy shape,
870 Like his, and color Serpentine may show
Thy inward fraud, to warn all Creatures from thee
Henceforth; lest that too heav'nly form, pretended[2]
To hellish falsehood, snare them. But for thee
I had persisted happy, had not thy pride

---

1. Adam at last reaches full conviction of his sin; but being unable yet to pass to contrition, the next stage of repentance, he falls instead into despair. The present pas-sage should be compared with Satan's similar fall into conscience-stricken despair at 4.86–113.

2. Stretched in front as a covering serving as a mask.

875 And wand'ring vanity, when least was safe,
    Rejected my forewarning, and disdain'd
    Not to be trusted, longing to be seen
    Though by the Devil himself, him overweening
    To over-reach, but with the Serpent meeting
880 Fool'd and beguil'd, by him thou, I by thee,
    To trust thee from my side, imagin'd wise,
    Constant, mature, proof against all assaults,
    And understood not all was but a show
    Rather than solid virtue, all but a Rib
885 Crooked by nature, bent, as now appears,
    More to the part siníster³ from me drawn,
    Well if thrown out, as supernumerary
    To my just number found. O why did God,
    Creator wise, that peopl'd highest Heav'n
890 With Spirits Masculine, create at last
    This novelty on Earth, this fair defect
    Of Nature, and not fill the World at once
    With Men as Angels without Feminine,
    Or find some other way to generate
895 Mankind?⁴ this mischief had not then befall'n,
    And more that shall befall, innumerable
    Disturbances on Earth through Female snares,
    And strait conjunction with this Sex: for either
    He never shall find out fit Mate, but such
900 As some misfortune brings him, or mistake,
    Or whom he wishes most shall seldom gain
    Through her perverseness, but shall see her gain'd
    By a far worse, or if she love, withheld
    By Parents, or his happiest choice too late
905 Shall meet, already linkt and Wedlock-bound
    To a fell° Adversary, his hate or shame: *bitter*
    Which infinite calamity shall cause
    To Human life, and household peace confound.
        He added not, and from her turn'd, but *Eve*
910 Not so repulst, with Tears that ceas'd not flowing,
    And tresses all disorder'd, at his feet
    Fell humble, and imbracing them, besought
    His peace, and thus proceeded in her plaint.
        Forsake me not thus, *Adam*, witness Heav'n
915 What love sincere, and reverence in my heart
    I bear thee, and unweeting° have offended,   *unintentionally*
    Unhappily deceiv'd; thy suppliant
    I beg, and clasp thy knees; bereave me not,
    Whereon I live, thy gentle looks, thy aid,
920 Thy counsel in this uttermost distress,
    My only strength and stay: forlorn of thee,
    Whither shall I betake me, where subsist?

---

3. Left; also corrupt, evil, base. The notion that woman is formed from a bent rib, and therefore crooked, had appeared in tracts like Swetnam's *The Araignment of Lewd, Idle, Forward, and Inconstant Women* (page 1335).

4. Another ancient piece of antifeminism; see Euripides, *Hippolytus* 616ff. Aristotle had said in the *De generatione* that the female is a defective male.

While yet we live, scarce one short hour perhaps,
Between us two let there be peace, both joining,
925 As join'd in injuries, one enmity
Against a Foe by doom express assign'd us,
That cruel Serpent: On me exercise not
Thy hatred for this misery befall'n,
On me already lost, mee than thyself
930 More miserable; both have sinn'd, but thou
Against God only, I against God and thee,
And to the place of judgment will return,
There with my cries importune Heaven, that all
The sentence from thy head remov'd may light
935 On me, sole cause to thee of all this woe,
Mee mee only just object of his ire.
    She ended weeping, and her lowly plight,
Immovable till peace obtain'd from fault
Acknowledg'd and deplor'd,[5] in *Adam* wrought
940 Commiseration; soon his heart relented
Towards her, his life so late and sole delight,
Now at his feet submissive in distress,
Creature so fair his reconcilement seeking,
His counsel whom she had displeas'd, his aid;
945 As one disarm'd, his anger all he lost,
And thus with peaceful words uprais'd her soon.
    Unwary, and too desirous, as before,
So now of what thou know'st not, who desir'st
The punishment all on thyself; alas,
950 Bear thine own first, ill able to sustain
His full wrath whose thou feel'st as yet least part,
And my displeasure bear'st so ill. If Prayers
Could alter high Decrees, I to that place
Would speed before thee, and be louder heard,
955 That on my head all might be visited,
Thy frailty and infirmer Sex forgiv'n,
To me committed and by me expos'd.
But rise, let us no more contend, nor blame
Each other, blam'd enough elsewhere,[6] but strive
960 In offices of Love, how we may light'n
Each other's burden in our share of woe;
Since this day's Death denounc't, if aught I see,
Will prove no sudden, but a slow-pac't evil,
A long day's dying to augment our pain,
965 And to our Seed (O hapless Seed!) deriv'd.
    To whom thus *Eve*, recovering heart, repli'd.
Adam, by sad experiment I know
How little weight my words with thee can find,
Found so erroneous, thence by just event°   consequence
970 Found so unfortunate; nevertheless,

5. Eve cannot be moved from Adam's feet until he for-   6. Either "heaven" or the "place of judgment" of line 932.
gives her.

Restor'd by thee, vile as I am, to place
Of new acceptance, hopeful to regain
Thy Love, the sole contentment of my heart
Living or dying, from thee I will not hide
975   What thoughts in my unquiet breast are ris'n,
Tending to some relief of our extremes,
Or end, though sharp and sad, yet tolerable,
As in our evils, and of easier choice.
If care of our descent° perplex° us most,   descendants/torment
980   Which must be born to certain woe, devour'd
By Death at last, and miserable it is
To be to other cause of misery,
Our own begott'n, and of our Loins to bring
Into this cursed World a woeful Race,
985   That after wretched Life must be at last
Food for so foul a Monster, in thy power
It lies, yet ere Conception to prevent
The Race unblest, to being yet unbegot.
Childless thou art, Childless remain: So Death
990   Shall be deceiv'd his glut, and with us two
Be forc'd to satisfy his Rav'nous Maw.
But if thou judge it hard and difficult,
Conversing, looking, loving, to abstain
From Love's due Rites, Nuptial embraces sweet,
995   And with desire to languish without hope,[7]
Before the present object° languishing   Eve
With like desire, which would be misery
And torment less than none of what we dread,
Then both ourselves and Seed at once to free
1000   From what we fear for both, let us make short,
Let us seek Death, or he not found, supply
With our own hands his Office on ourselves;
Why stand we longer shivering under fears,
That show no end but Death, and have the power,
1005   Of many ways to die the shortest choosing,
Destruction with destruction to destroy.
     She ended here, or vehement despair
Broke off the rest; so much of Death her thoughts
Had entertain'd, as dy'd her Cheeks with pale.
1010   But *Adam* with such counsel nothing sway'd,
To better hopes his more attentive mind
Laboring had rais'd, and thus to *Eve* replied.
     Eve, thy contempt of life and pleasure seems
To argue in thee something more sublime
1015   And excellent than what thy mind contemns;
But self-destruction therefore sought, refutes
That excellence thought in thee, and implies,
Not thy contempt, but anguish and regret
For loss of life and pleasure overlov'd.

7. See Dante, *Inferno* 4.42, "without hope we live in desire."

1020   Or if thou covet death, as utmost end
            Of misery, so thinking to evade
            The penalty pronounc't, doubt not but God
            Hath wiselier arm'd his vengeful ire than so
            To be forestall'd; much more I fear lest Death
1025   So snatcht will not exempt us from the pain
            We are by doom to pay; rather such acts
            Of contumacy° will provoke the Highest   *contempt*
            To make death in us live: Then let us seek
            Some safer resolution, which methinks
1030   I have in view, calling to mind with heed
            Part of our Sentence, that thy Seed shall bruise
            The Serpent's head; piteous amends, unless
            Be meant, whom I conjecture, our grand Foe
            Satan, who in the Serpent hath contriv'd
1035   Against us this deceit: to crush his head
            Would be revenge indeed; which will be lost
            By death brought on ourselves, or childless days
            Resolv'd, as thou proposest; so our Foe
            Shall 'scape his punishment ordain'd, and wee
1040   Instead shall double ours upon our heads.
            No more be mention'd then of violence
            Against ourselves, and wilful barrenness,
            That cuts us off from hope, and savors only
            Rancor and pride, impatience and despite,
1045   Reluctance° against God and his just yoke   *resistance*
            Laid on our Necks. Remember with what mild
            And gracious temper he both heard and judg'd
            Without wrath or reviling; wee expected
            Immediate dissolution, which we thought
1050   Was meant by Death that day, when lo, to thee
            Pains only in Child-bearing were foretold,
            And bringing forth, soon recompens't with joy,
            Fruit of thy Womb: On mee the Curse aslope
            Glanc'd on the ground, with labor I must earn
1055   My bread;[8] what harm? Idleness had been worse;
            My labor will sustain me; and lest Cold
            Or Heat should injure us, his timely care
            Hath unbesought provided, and his hands
            Cloth'd us unworthy, pitying while he judg'd;
1060   How much more, if we pray him, will his ear
            Be open, and his heart to pity incline,[9]
            And teach us further by what means to shun
            Th' inclement Seasons, Rain, Ice, Hail and Snow,
            Which now the Sky with various Face begins
1065   To show us in this Mountain, while the Winds
            Blow moist and keen, shattering the graceful locks
            Of these fair spreading Trees; which bids us seek

---

8. Referring to Christ's words at lines 201–5.   9. Biblical diction; see Psalms 24.4, 119.36, 112; and 1
                                                              Peter 3.12.

	Some better shroud,° some better warmth to cherish	*shelter*
	Our Limbs benumb'd, ere this diurnal Star[1]	
1070	Leave cold the Night, how we his gather'd beams	
	Reflected, may with matter sere foment,[2]	
	Or by collision of two bodies grind	
	The Air attrite° to Fire, as late the Clouds	*ground down*
	Justling° or pusht with Winds rude in thir shock	*jostling*
1075	Tine° the slant Lightning, whose thwart flame driv'n down	*ignite*
	Kindles the gummy bark of Fir or Pine,	
	And sends a comfortable heat from far,	
	Which might supply° the Sun: such Fire to use,	*take the place of*
	And what may else be remedy or cure	
1080	To evils which our own misdeeds have wrought,	
	Hee will instruct us praying, and of Grace	
	Beseeching him, so as we need not fear	
	To pass commodiously this life, sustain'd	
	By him with many comforts, till we end	
1085	In dust, our final rest and native home.	
	What better can we do, than to the place	
	Repairing where he judg'd us, prostrate fall	
	Before him reverent, and there confess	
	Humbly our faults, and pardon beg, with tears	
1090	Watering the ground, and with our sighs the Air	
	Frequenting,° sent from hearts contrite, in sign	*filling*
	Of sorrow unfeign'd, and humiliation meek.[3]	
	Undoubtedly he will relent and turn	
	From his displeasure; in whose look serene,	
1095	When angry most he seem'd and most severe,	
	What else but favor, grace, and mercy shone?	
	So spake our Father penitent, nor Eve	
	Felt less remorse: they forthwith to the place	
	Repairing where he judg'd them prostrate fell	
1100	Before him reverent, and both confess'd	
	Humbly thir faults, and pardon begg'd, with tears	
	Watering the ground, and with thir sighs the Air	
	Frequenting, sent from hearts contrite, in sign	
	Of sorrow unfeign'd, and humiliation meek.[4]	

    The End of the Tenth Book.

Book 11

The Argument

The Son of God present to his Father the Prayers of our first Parents now repenting, and intercedes for them: God accepts them, but declares that they must no longer abide in Paradise; sends Michael with a Band of Cherubim to dispossess them; but first to reveal to

1. The sun.
2. Cherish; but alluding also to Latin *fomes* (tinder). Adam envisages making fire: focusing the sun's rays onto dry combustibles ("matter sere") with a parabolic mirror.
3. Having passed on from conviction of sin Adam, now "contrite" (line 1103), is ready for confession, the third

stage of repentance. An allusion to the Penitential Psalm: "The sacrifices of God are a broken spirit: a broken and a contrite heart, O God, thou wilt not despise" (Psalms 51.17).
4. Repeating lines 1086–92, modulated into narrative discourse (only the last two verses remain identical).

Adam *future things; Michael's coming down. Adam shows to Eve certain ominous signs; he discerns Michael's approach, goes out to meet him: the Angel denounces thir departure. Eve's Lamentation. Adam pleads, but submits: The Angel leads him up to a high Hill, sets before him in vision what shall happ'n till the Flood.*

Book 12
The Argument

The Angel Michael continues from the Flood to relate what shall succeed; then, in the mention of Abraham, comes by degrees to explain, who that Seed of the Woman shall be, which was promised Adam and Eve in the Fall; his Incarnation, Death, Resurrection, and Ascension; the state of the Church till his second Coming. Adam greatly satisfied and recomforted by these Relations and Promises descends the Hill with Michael; wakens Eve, who all this while had slept, but with gentle dreams compos'd to quietness of mind and submission. Michael in either hand leads them out of Paradise, the fiery Sword waving behind them, and the Cherubim taking thir Stations to guard the Place.

	As one who in his journey bates° at Noon,	*pauses*
	Though bent on speed, so here the Arch-Angel paus'd	
	Betwixt the world destroy'd and world restor'd,	
	If *Adam* aught perhaps might interpose;	
5	Then with transition sweet new Speech resumes.	
	Thus thou hast seen one World begin and end;	
	And Man as from a second stock proceed.[1]	
	Much thou hast yet to see, but I perceive	
	Thy mortal sight to fail; objects divine	
10	Must needs impair and weary human sense:	
	Henceforth what is to come I will relate,	
	Thou therefore give due audience, and attend.	
	This second source of Men, while yet but few,	
	And while the dread of judgment past remains	
15	Fresh in thir minds, fearing the Deity,	
	With some regard to what is just and right	
	Shall lead thir lives, and multiply apace,	
	Laboring° the soil, and reaping plenteous crop,	*tilling*
	Corn, wine and oil; and from the herd or flock,	
20	Oft sacrificing Bullock, Lamb, or Kid,	
	With large Wine-offerings pour'd, and sacred Feast,	
	Shall spend thir days in joy unblam'd, and dwell	
	Long time in peace by Families and Tribes	
	Under paternal rule; till one shall rise[2]	
25	Of proud ambitious heart, who not content	
	With fair equality, fraternal state,	
	Will arrogate Dominion undeserv'd	

1. "Stock," an ambiguity, refers not only to the literal replacement of one source of the human line of descent (Adam) by another (Noah), but also to the grafting of mankind onto the stem of Christ, according to the Pauline allegory of regeneration (Romans 11). The covenant with Noah was a type of the New Covenant.
2. Nimrod is not connected with the builders of the Tower in Genesis 10.8. The connection is made, however, in Josephus, *Antiquities* 1.4.2ff., where we also learn that Nimrod "changed the government into tyranny."

Over his brethren, and quite dispossess
Concord and law of Nature from the Earth;[3]
30   Hunting (and Men not Beasts shall be his game)
With War and hostile snare such as refuse
Subjection to his Empire tyrannous:[4]
A mighty Hunter thence he shall be styl'd
Before the Lord, as in despite of Heav'n,
35   Or from Heav'n claiming second Sovranty;[5]
And from Rebellion shall derive his name,
Though of Rebellion others he accuse.
Hee with a crew, whom like Ambition joins
With him or under him to tyrannize,
40   Marching from *Eden* towards the West, shall find
The Plain, wherein a black bituminous gurge°   *whirlpool*
Boils out from under ground, the mouth of Hell;
Of Brick, and of that stuff they cast to build
A City and Tow'r, whose top may reach to Heav'n;[6]
45   And get themselves a name, lest far disperst
In foreign Lands thir memory be lost,
Regardless whether good or evil fame.[7]
But God who oft descends to visit men
Unseen, and through thir habitations walks
50   To mark thir doings, them beholding soon,
Comes down to see thir City, ere the Tower
Obstruct Heav'n Tow'rs, and in derision sets
Upon thir Tongues a various Spirit to rase
Quite out thir Native Language, and instead
55   To sow a jangling noise of words unknown:
Forthwith a hideous gabble rises loud
Among the Builders; each to other calls
Not understood, till hoarse, and all in rage,
As mockt they storm;[8] great laughter was in Heav'n
60   And looking down, to see the hubbub strange
And hear the din; thus was the building left
Ridiculous, and the work Confusion nam'd.[9]
          Whereto thus *Adam* fatherly displeas'd.
O execrable Son so to aspire
65   Above his Brethren, to himself assuming
Authority usurpt, from God not giv'n:
He gave us only over Beast, Fish, Fowl
Dominion absolute; that right we hold

---

3. In *The Tenure of Kings and Magistrates*, Milton denies
the natural right of kings and insists that their power is
committed to them in trust by the people.
4. See *Eikonoklastes:* "The Bishops could have told him,
that 'Nimrod,' the first that hunted after Faction is reputed, by ancient Tradition, the first that founded monarchy; whence it appears that to hunt after Faction is more
properly the Kings Game."
5. "Before the Lord," Genesis 10.9; Milton takes it in a
constitutional sense; see *The Tenure:* "To say Kings are

accountable to none but God, is the overturning of all
Law."
6. The materials of the Tower—brick with bitumen as
mortar—are specified in Genesis 11.3.
7. See Genesis 11.4.
8. In the 17th century it was generally believed that the
separation of language into distinct individual languages
had its beginning at the confusion of tongues at Babel.
9. See Genesis 11.9, "Therefore is the name of it called
Babel"; marginal gloss: "that is, Confusion."

By his donation; but Man over men

70   He made not Lord; such title to himself
Reserving, human left from human free.
But this Usurper his encroachment proud
Stays not on Man; to God his Tower intends
Siege and defiance: Wretched man! what food

75   Will he convey up thither to sustain
Himself and his rash Army, where thin Air
Above the Clouds will pine his entrails gross,
And famish him of breath, if not of Bread?
       To whom thus *Michael*. Justly thou abhorr'st

80   That Son, who on the quiet state of men
Such trouble brought, affecting to subdue
Rational Liberty;[1] yet know withal,
Since thy original lapse, true Liberty
Is lost, which always with right Reason dwells

85   Twinn'd, and from her hath no dividual° being: *separate*
Reason in man obscur'd, or not obey'd,
Immediately inordinate desires
And upstart Passions catch the Government
From Reason, and to servitude reduce

90   Man till then free. Therefore since hee permits
Within himself unworthy Powers to reign
Over free Reason, God in Judgment just
Subjects him from without to violent Lords;
Who oft as undeservedly enthral

95   His outward freedom: Tyranny must be,
Though to the Tyrant thereby no excuse.
Yet sometimes Nations will decline so low
From virtue, which is reason, that no wrong,
But Justice, and some fatal curse annext

100   Deprives them of thir outward liberty,
Thir inward lost:[2] * * *
       So spake th' Arch-Angel *Michaël*, then paus'd,
As at the World's great period;[3] and our Sire
Replete with joy and wonder thus repli'd.
       O goodness infinite, goodness immense![4]

470   That all this good of evil shall produce,
And evil turn to good; more wonderful
Than that which by creation first brought forth
Light out of darkness! full of doubt I stand,
Whether I should repent me now of sin

1. Lines 80–101 recall the regicide tracts and follow St. Augustine's *City of God* 19.15, where we read that the derivation of servitude, whose mother is sin, is the "first cause of man's subjection to man: which notwithstanding comes not to pass but by the direction of the highest, in whom is no injustice." For the connection between psychological and political enslavement, see 9.1127–31.
2. Michael goes on to describe the history of Israel, from Abraham to King David, then tells of the birth of the

Messiah, who will crush Satan and defeat Sin and Death.
3. This is Michael's second pause; the first was at 12.2. The three divisions of Adam's instruction are meant to correspond to "three drops" of the well of life placed in his eyes (11.416). Here the pause is compared with the world's period the dawning of the present age, from the first to the second coming of Christ.
4. The Final Cause or end of the Fall: a greater "glory" for God and an opportunity for him to show his surpassing love through the sacrifice of Christ.

475   By mee done and occasion'd, or rejoice
      Much more, that much more good thereof shall spring,
      To God more glory, more good will to Men
      From God, and over wrath grace shall abound.[5]
      But say, if our deliverer up to Heav'n
480   Must reascend, what will betide the few
      His faithful, left among th' unfaithful herd,
      The enemies of truth; who then shall guide
      His people, who defend? will they not deal
      Worse with his followers than with him they dealt?
485   Be sure they will, said th' Angel; but from Heav'n
      Hee to his own a Comforter will send,[6]
      The promise of the Father, who shall dwell
      His Spirit within them, and the Law of Faith
      Working through love, upon thir hearts shall write,[7]
490   To guide them in all truth, and also arm
      With spiritual Armor, able to resist
      Satan's assaults, and quench his fiery darts,[8]
      What Man can do against them, not afraid,
      Though to the death, against such cruelties
495   With inward consolations recompens't,
      And oft supported so as shall amaze
      Thir proudest persecutors: for the Spirit
      Pour'd first on his Apostles, whom he sends
      To evangelize the Nations, then on all
500   Baptiz'd, shall them with wondrous gifts endue°   *endow*
      To speak all Tongues, and do all Miracles,
      As did thir Lord before them. Thus they win
      Great numbers of each Nation to receive
      With joy the tidings brought from Heav'n: at length
505   Thir Ministry perform'd, and race well run,
      Thir doctrine and thir story written left,
      They die; but in thir room, as they forewarn,
      Wolves shall succeed for teachers, grievous Wolves,[9]
      Who all the sacred mysteries of Heav'n
510   To thir own vile advantages shall turn
      Of lucre and ambition, and the truth
      With superstitions and traditions taint,
      Left only in those written Records pure,
      Though not but by the Spirit understood.[1]
515   Then shall they seek to avail themselves of names,
      Places and titles, and with these to join
      Secular power, though feigning still to act
      By spiritual, to themselves appropriating

---

5. See Romans 5.20 ("where sin abounded, grace did much more abound") and 2 Corinthians 4.15.
6. The Holy Spirit. See John 14.18 and 15.26.
7. See Galations 5.6: "faith which worketh by love."
8. Alluding to the allegory in Ephesians 6.16: "Above all, taking the shield of faith, wherewith ye shall be able to quench all the fiery darts of the wicked."

9. "For I know this, that after my departing shall grievous wolves enter in among you, not sparing the flock" (Acts 20.29). See the simile comparing Satan to a wolf in the fold, at 4.183–87; see also *Lycidas* 113ff, page 1741.
1. It was an important article of Protestant belief that in doctrinal matters the ultimate arbiter is individual conscience rather than mere authority.

worldly

520   The Spirit of God, promis'd alike and giv'n
     To all Believers;[2] and from that pretense,
     Spiritual Laws by carnal° power shall force
     On every conscience; Laws which none shall find
     Left them inroll'd, or what the Spirit within
     Shall on the heart engrave.[3] What will they then
525   But force the Spirit of Grace itself, and bind
     His consort Liberty; what, but unbuild
     His living Temples, built by Faith to stand,[4]
     Thir own Faith not another's: for on Earth
     Who against Faith and Conscience can be heard
530   Infallible?[5] yet many will presume:
     Whence heavy persecution shall arise
     On all who in the worship persevere
     Of Spirit and Truth; the rest, far greater part,
     Will deem in outward Rites and specious forms
535   Religion satisfi'd; Truth shall retire
     Bestuck with sland'rous darts, and works of Faith
     Rarely be found: so shall the World go on,
     To good malignant, to bad men benign,
     Under her own weight groaning, till the day
540   Appear of respiration[6] to the just,
     And vengeance to the wicked, at return
     Of him so lately promis'd to thy aid,
     The Woman's seed, obscurely then foretold,
     Now amplier known thy Saviour and thy Lord,
545   Last in the Clouds from Heav'n to be reveal'd
     In glory of the Father, to dissolve
     Satan with his perverted World, then raise

burning

     From the conflagrant° mass, purg'd and refin'd,
     New Heav'ns, new Earth, Ages of endless date
550   Founded in righteousness and peace and love,
     To bring forth fruits Joy and eternal Bliss.
         He ended; and thus *Adam* last repli'd.
     How soon hath thy prediction, Seer blest,
     Measur'd this transient World, the Race of time,
555   Till time stand fixt: beyond is all abyss,
     Eternity, whose end no eye can reach.
     Greatly instructed I shall hence depart,
     Greatly in peace of thought, and have my fill
     Of knowledge, what this Vessel can contain;
560   Beyond which was my folly to aspire.
     Henceforth I learn, that to obey is best,

---

2. The corruption of the Church through its pursuit of "secular power" is a subject Milton had dealt with in *Of Reformation*. In *De doctrina* 1.30 he condemns the enforcement of obedience to human opinions or authority.

3. The wolves will enforce laws written neither in Scripture nor in the individual conscience.

4. See 1 Corinthians 3.17: "The temple of God is holy, which temple ye are."

5. Even though the doctrine of papal infallibility was not formally adapted until 1870, there can be no doubt that Rome is Milton's main target here. In *A Treatise of Civil Power* he writes that the "Pope assumes infallibility over conscience and scripture."

6. Opportunity for breathing again; rest.

And love with fear the only God, to walk
As in his presence, ever to observe
His providence, and on him sole depend,
565   Merciful over all his works, with good
Still overcoming evil, and by small
Accomplishing great things, by things deem'd weak
Subverting worldly strong, and worldly wise
By simply meek; that suffering for Truth's sake
570   Is fortitude to highest victory,
And to the faithful Death the Gate of Life;
Taught this by his example whom I now
Acknowledge my Redeemer ever blest.
      To whom thus also th' Angel last repli'd:
575   This having learnt, thou hast attain'd the sum
Of wisdom; hope no higher, though all the Stars
Thou knew'st by name, and all th' ethereal Powers,
All secrets of the deep, all Nature's works,
Or works of God in Heav'n, Air, Earth, or Sea,
580   And all the riches of this World enjoy'dst,
And all the rule, one Empire; only add
Deeds to thy knowledge answerable, add Faith,
Add Virtue, Patience, Temperance, add Love,
By name to come call'd Charity, the soul
585   Of all the rest:[7] then wilt thou not be loath
To leave this Paradise, but shalt possess
A paradise within thee, happier far.
Let us descend now therefore from this top
Of Speculation;[8] for the hour precise
590   Exacts our parting hence; and see the Guards,
By mee encampt on yonder Hill, expect
Thir motion,[9] at whose Front a flaming Sword,
In signal of remove, waves fiercely round;
We may no longer stay: go, waken *Eve*;
595   Her also I with gentle Dreams have calm'd
Portending good, and all her spirits compos'd
To meek submission: thou at season fit
Let her with thee partake what thou hast heard,
Chiefly what may concern her Faith to know,
600   The great deliverance by her Seed to come
(For by the Woman's Seed)[1] on all Mankind,
That ye may live, which will be many days,[2]
Both in one Faith unanimous though sad,
With cause for evils past, yet much more cheer'd
605   With meditation on the happy end.

---

7. Compare 2 Peter 1.5–7: "Add to your faith virtue; and to virtue knowledge; and to knowledge temperance; and to temperance patience; and to patience godliness; and to godliness brotherly kindness; and to brotherly kindness charity."

8. Vantage point but also height of theological speculation.
9. Await deployment, marching orders.
1. Alluding to the birth of Jesus.
2. Adam lived to be 930 years of age (Genesis 5.5).

He ended, and they both descend the Hill;
Descended, *Adam* to the Bow'r where *Eve*
Lay sleeping ran before, but found her wak't;
And thus with words not sad she him receiv'd.

610   Whence thou return'st, and whither went'st, I know;
For God is also in sleep, and Dreams advise,
Which he hath sent propitious, some great good
Presaging, since with sorrow and heart's distress
Wearied I fell asleep: but now lead on;

615 In mee is no delay; with thee to go,
Is to stay here; without thee here to stay,
Is to go hence unwilling; thou to mee
Art all things under Heav'n, all places thou,
Who for my wilful crime art banisht hence.[3]

620 This further consolation yet secure
I carry hence; though all by mee is lost,
Such favor I unworthy am voutsaf't,
By mee the Promis'd Seed shall all restore.

     So spake our Mother *Eve*, and *Adam* heard

625 Well pleas'd, but answer'd not; for now too nigh
Th' Arch-Angel stood, and from the other Hill
To thir fixt Station, all in bright array
The Cherubim descended; on the ground
Gliding meteorous,° as Ev'ning Mist   *meteoric*

630 Ris'n from a River o'er the marish° glides,   *marsh*
And gathers ground fast at the Laborer's heel
Homeward returning. High in Front advanc't,
The brandisht Sword of God before them blaz'd
Fierce as a Comet; which with torrid heat,

635 And vapor as the *Libyan* Air adust,°   *scorched*
Began to parch that temperate Clime; whereat
In either hand the hast'ning Angel caught
Our ling'ring Parents, and to th' Eastern Gate
Led them direct, and down the Cliff as fast

640 To the subjected° Plain; then disappear'd.   *underlying*
They looking back, all th' Eastern side beheld
Of Paradise, so late thir happy seat,
Wav'd over by that flaming Brand,[4] the Gate
With dreadful Faces throng'd and fiery Arms:

645 Some natural tears they dropp'd, but wip'd them soon;
The World was all before them, where to choose
Thir place of rest, and Providence thir guide:[5]
They hand in hand with wand'ring steps and slow,
Through *Eden* took thir solitary way.

The End

3. Eve has assimilated Michael's exhortation at 11.292: "where [Adam] abides, think there thy native soil." There is also a resonance with Eve's song at 4.635–56 (every time of day is pleasing with Adam, none is pleasing without him).

4. See Genesis. 3.24: "a flaming sword which turned every way."

5. Note that "Providence" can be the object of "choose": decisions of faith lie ahead.

Samson Agonistes

Milton's readers knew Samson as the hero in Judges 13–16, whose strength Delila destroys by cutting his hair. Samson's Philistine enemies then blind him and set him to turn a millstone. When they bring him out to mock him during a feast in honor of their god Dagon, Samson prays to God for strength, and pulls down the pillars upholding the palace roof; he and several thousand Philistines are killed. The epithet "Agonistes" in Milton's title expresses Milton's reshaping of the biblical myth as tragedy, since "Agonistes" (from *agon*, Greek for combat) means "in struggle, under trial." Milton's Samson not only struggles with his external enemies—the Philistines, Delila, and a giant named Harapha—but with himself.

Though a "closet" drama rather than one intended to be staged, Milton's *Samson* is a work of profound psychological complexity, and Milton's reworking of his biblical material highlights the poem's tragic mystery. In the Bible, Samson's father Manoa does not plan to ransom his son as he does in Milton's work. Manoa's belief that he can save his son's life, along with the prophetic realization that Samson has regained his strength so that God might "use him further yet in some great service," strike notes of tragic irony. Milton also deepens the sense of Samson's part in his own downfall as a tragic hero. In speaking to his father, Milton's Samson accepts his suffering as a just punishment for breaking his vow as a Nazarite never to drink wine or cut his hair.

Milton's portrayal of Dalila is similarly complex. Milton makes her Samson's wife rather than his mistress, as she is in the Bible. The poet intensifies both her treachery and Samson's love for her. When she begs Samson's forgiveness for having betrayed him to save her country, she pleads jealousy as the cause. In contrast to the Chorus's view that she is "a manifest serpent by her sting" and "wanton, whose distrustful eye / Was fixed upon reward," Samson takes the full responsibility for his downfall upon himself: "she was not the prime cause / But I myself."

Like Greek tragedy, Milton's play works simultaneously on psychological, political, and spiritual levels. Many critics have seen the tragedy as related to Milton's own personal and public struggles—his blindness as well as his imprisonment following the Restoration. The poem may also allude to political conflicts, as in Harapha's arrogant challenge of Samson, which has been construed as reminiscent of the dueling challenges of the Cavaliers, who fought for the King and disdained the Puritans. Through defeating Harapha, Samson regains a faith in himself that leads to his final victory in suicide. Though suicide was seen as a sin by Christianity, Milton makes Samson's self-destruction at once an act of fate and of spiritual redemption. As in Greek tragedy, the *daimon* or spirit from within Samson ineluctably overtakes him—"self killed / Not willingly, but tangled in the fold / Of dire necessity." As in Christian resurrection, Samson is spiritually reborn like the phoenix: "His fiery virtue roused / From under ashes into sudden flame." The phoenix image defies any one explanation. "Like that self-begotten bird," Samson paradoxically arises triumphant in his own destruction.

Though some critics have argued that Milton may have begun *Samson Agonistes* as early as the 1640s, the text was first published along with *Paradise Regained* in 1671. Our text and notes are adapted from John Grey and Alastair Fowler, eds., *The Poems of John Milton*.

Samson Agonistes
a Dramatic Poem

OF THAT SORT OF DRAMATIC POEM WHICH IS CALLED TRAGEDY

Tragedy, as it was anciently composed, hath been ever held the gravest, moralest, and most profitable of all other Poems: therefore said by Aristotle to be of power by raising pity and fear, or terror, to purge the mind of those and such like passions, that is to temper and reduce them to just measure with a kind of delight, stirred up by reading or seeing those passions well imitated. Nor is Nature wanting in her own effects to make good his assertion: for so in Physic things of melancholic hue and quality are used against melancholy, sour against sour, salt to remove salt humours. Hence Philosophers and other gravest Writers, as Cicero, Plutarch and others, frequently cite out of Tragic Poets, both to adorn and illustrate their discourse. The Apostle Paul himself thought it not unworthy to insert a verse of Euripides into the Text of Holy Scripture, I Cor. 15.33, and Paraeus,[1] commenting on the Revelation, divides the whole Book as a Tragedy, into Acts distinguisht each by a Chorus of Heavenly Harpings and Song between. Heretofore Men in highest dignity have laboured not a little to be thought able to compose a Tragedy. Of that honour Dionysius[2] the elder was no less ambitious, than before of his attaining to the Tyranny. Augustus Caesar also had begun his *Ajax*, but unable to please his own judgment with what he had begun, left it unfinisht. Seneca[3] the Philosopher is by some thought the Author of those Tragedies (at lest the best of them) that go under that name. Gregory Nazianzen,[4] a Father of the Church, thought it not unbeseeming the sanctity of his person to write a Tragedy, which he entitled *Christ suffering*. This is mentioned to vindicate Tragedy from the small esteem, or rather infamy, which in the account of many it undergoes at this day with other common Interludes; hap'ning through the Poet's error of intermixing Comic stuff with Tragic sadness and gravity; or introducing trivial and vulgar persons, which by all judicious hath been counted absurd; and brought in without discretion, corruptly to gratify the people. And though ancient Tragedy use no Prologue,[5] yet using sometimes, in case of self-defence, or explanation, that which Martial[6] calls an Epistle; in behalf of this Tragedy coming forth after the ancient manner, much different from what among us passes for best, thus much beforehand may be Epistled; that *Chorus* is here introduced after the Greek manner, not ancient only but modern, and still in use among the Italians. In the modelling therefore of this Poem, with good reason, the Ancients and Italians[7] are rather followed, as of much more authority and fame. The measure of Verse used in the Chorus is of all sorts, called by the Greeks Monostrophic, or rather Apolelymenon, without regard had to Strophe, Antistrophe or Epode,[8] which were a kind of Stanzas framed only for the Music then used with the Chorus that sung; not essential to the Poem, and therefore not material; or being divided into Stanzas or Pauses, they may be called Allaeostropha. Division into Act and Scene referring chiefly to the Stage (to which this work never was intended) is here omitted.

It suffices if the whole Drama be found not produc't beyond the fifth Act. Of the style and uniformity, and that commonly called the Plot, whether intricate or explicit, which is nothing indeed but such economy[9] or disposition of the fable as may

---

1. David Paraeus, a German Calvinist whose *Commentary on Romans* (1609) was publicly burned by the universities of Oxford and Cambridge. Milton here refers to his work *On the Divine Apocalypse* (1618).

2. Tyrant of Syracuse (431–367 B.C.).

3. Lucius Annaeus Seneca (3 B.C.–A.D. 65). The doubt as to his authorship of his ten tragedies is due to a mistake of Sidonius Apollinaris, *Carmen* 9.230–38, who distinguishes between Seneca the philosopher and Seneca the tragedian.

4. Bishop of Constantinople (A.D. 325?–390?).

5. Milton uses the term "prologue" in its modern sense (a preliminary address to the audience), not in Aristotle's sense (the part of a tragedy that precedes the entrance of the chorus).

6. Martial notes that tragedies and comedies may need epistles since "they cannot speak for themselves" (*Epigrams* 2).

7. Tasso's *Aminta* and Guarini's *Pastor Fido*, for example, both have a chorus, as did 16th-century Italian tragic drama frequently.

8. Apolelymenon: Greek "freed" (i.e., from the restraint of any firm stanza pattern). In Greek drama the strophe was a stanza sung by the chorus as it moved from right to left, and the antistrophe corresponded exactly to the strophe in structure, as it moved in the opposite direction. The concluding epode was sung standing still. Milton says that if his choruses do seem at times to divide into stanzas, then they should be called "allaeostropha" (Greek: "of irregular strophes").

9. "Intricate . . . explicit": Aristotle, *Poetics* 6, divides plots into two classes, simple and complex; "which is nothing indeed," i.e., the plot is merely the management ("economy") of the events: the "putting together of the incidents," as Aristotle calls it.

stand best with verisimilitude and decorum; they only will best judge who are not unacquainted with Aeschulus,[1] Sophocles, and Euripides, the three Tragic Poets unequalled yet by any, and the best rule to all who endeavor to write Tragedy. The circumscription of time wherein the whole Drama begins and ends, is according to ancient rule,[2] and best example, within the space of 24 hours.

THE ARGUMENT

SAMSON made captive, blind, and now in the prison at Gaza, there to labor as in a common workhouse, on a Festival day, in the general cessation from labor, comes forth into the open air, to a place nigh, somewhat retired there to sit a while and bemoan his condition. Where he happens at length to be visited by certain friends and equals of his tribe, which make the Chorus, who seek to comfort him what they can; then by his old father, Manoa, who endeavours the like, and withal tells him his purpose to procure his liberty by ransom; lastly, that this feast was proclaimed by the Philistines as a day of thanksgiving for their deliverance from the hands of Samson, which yet more troubles him. Manoa then departs to prosecute his endeavor with the Philistian Lords for Samson's redemption; who in the mean while is visited by other persons; and lastly by a public Officer to require his coming to the feast before the Lords and People, to play or show his strength in their presence; he at first refuses, dismissing the public Officer with absolute denial to come; at length persuaded inwardly that this was from God, he yields to go along with him, who came now the second time with great threatenings to fetch him; the Chorus yet remaining on the place, Manoa returns full of joyful hope, to procure ere long his Son's deliverance: in the midst of which discourse an Hebrew comes in haste confusedly at first; and afterward more distinctly relating the catastrophe, what Samson had done to the Philistines, and by accident to himself; wherewith the tragedy ends.

The Persons

SAMSON	PUBLIC OFFICER
MANOA, *the father of Samson*	MESSENGER
DALILA, *his wife*	CHORUS OF DANITES
HARAPHA OF GATH	

THE SCENE BEFORE THE PRISON IN GAZA

SAMSON A little onward lend thy guiding hand
        To these dark steps, a little further on;[3]
        For yonder bank hath choice of sun or shade,
        There I am wont to sit, when any chance
5   Relieves me from my task of servile toil,
        Daily in the common prison else enjoined me,
        Where I a prisoner chained, scarce freely draw
        The air imprisoned also, close and damp,
        Unwholsome draught: but here I feel amends,
10   The breath of Heaven fresh-blowing, pure and sweet,
        With day-spring[4] born; here leave me to respire.
        This day a solemn feast the people hold

1. Milton is unusual among 17th-century scholars in ranking Aeschylus with Sophocles and Euripides.
2. "The unity of time," Aristotle, *Poetics* 5.
3. See Sophocles, *Oedipus at Colonus*, where Oedipus is led forward by Antigone, and Euripides, *Phoenician Maidens* 834–35, where Tiresias asks his daughter to lead him on and says she is as eyes to his "blind feet." In Sidney's *Arcadia* 2.10.3, the blinded King of Paphlagonia complains that there is no one to "lend [him] a hande to guide [his] dark steps."
4. Daybreak; see Luke 1.78: "The day-spring from on high hath visited us."

To Dagon[5] their sea-idol, and forbid
Laborious works, unwillingly this rest
15   Their superstition yields me; hence with leave
Retiring from the popular noise, I seek
This unfrequented place to find some ease,
Ease to the body some, none to the mind
From restless thoughts, that like a deadly swarm
20   Of hornets armed, no sooner found alone,
But rush upon me thronging, and present
Times past, what once I was, and what am now.
O wherefore was my birth from heaven foretold
Twice[6] by an angel, who at last in sight
25   Of both my parents all in flames ascended
From off the altar, where an offering burned,
As in a fiery column charioting
His godlike presence, and from some great act
Or benefit revealed to Abraham's race?
30   Why was my breeding ordered and prescribed
As of a person separate to God,[7]
Designed for great exploits; if I must die
Betrayed, captived, and both my eyes put out,
Made of my enemies the scorn and gaze;
35   To grind in brazen fetters under task
With this heaven-gifted strength? O glorious strength
Put to the labor of a beast, debas't
Lower then bondslave! Promise was that I
Should Israel from Philistian yoke deliver;[8]
40   Ask for this great deliverer now, and find him
Eyeless in gaza at the mill with slaves,
Himself in bonds under Philistian yoke;
Yet stay, let me not rashly call in doubt
Divine prediction; what if all foretold
45   Had been fulfilled but through mine own default,
Whom have I to complain of but myself?
Who this high gift of strength committed to me,
In what part lodged, how easily bereft me,
Under the seal of silence could not keep,
50   But weakly to a woman must reveal it,
O'ercome with importunity and tears.
O impotence of mind, in body strong![9]
But what is strength without a double share
Of wisdom, vast, unwieldy, burdensom,[1]
55   Proudly secure, yet liable to fall
By weakest suttleties, not made to rule,
But to subserve where wisdom bears command.

---

5. National deity of the Philistines, presented in *Paradise
Lost* 1.462–3 as half-man, half-fish (the name is possibly
derived from Hebrew *dag*, "fish").
6. First to his mother alone (Judges 13.3–5) and later to
both parents (Judges 13.10–20).
7. "Nazarite" is derived from Hebrew *nazar*, "to separate
oneself." The angel says to Samson's mother "The child

shall be a Nazarite unto God" (Judges 13.7).
8. See Judges 13.5: "He shall begin to deliver Israel out of
the hand of the Philistines."
9. Samson's weak-mindedness is unique to Milton.
1. See Horace, *Odes* 3.4.65: "Brute force bereft of wisdom
falls to ruin by its own weight."

God, when he gave me strength, to show withal
How slight the gift was, hung it in my hair.
60 But peace, I must not quarrel with the will
Of highest dispensation, which herein
Happ'ly had ends above my reach to know:
Suffices that to me strength is my bane,
And proves the sourse of all my miseries;
65 So many, and so huge, that each apart
Would ask a life to wail, but chief of all,
O loss of sight, of thee I most complain!
Blind among enemies, O worse then chains,
Dungeon, or beggery, or decrepit age!
70 Light the prime work of God to me is extinct,
And all her various objects of delight
Annulled, which might in part my grief have eased,
Inferior to the vilest now become
Of man or worm; the vilest here excel me,
75 They creep, yet see, I dark in light exposed
To daily fraud, contempt, abuse and wrong,
Within doors, or without, still° as a fool,   *always*
In power of others, never in my own;
Scarce half I seem to live, dead more then half.
80 O dark, dark, dark, amid the blaze of noon,
Irrecoverably dark, total eclipse
Without all hope of day!
O first created beam, and thou great Word,
Let there be light, and light was over all;[2]
85 Why am I thus bereaved thy prime decree?
The sun to me is dark
And silent as the moon,[3]
When she deserts the night
Hid in her vacant interlunar cave.
90 Since light so necessary is to life,
And almost life itself, if it be true
That light is in the soul,
She all in every part;[4] why was the sight
To such a tender ball as th' eye confined?
95 So obvious° and so easie to be quench't,   *exposed*
And not as feeling through all parts diffused,
That she might look at will through every pore?
Then had I not been thus exiled from light;
As in the land of darkness yet in light,
100 To live a life half dead, a living death,
And buried; but O yet more miserable!
My self my sepulcher, a moving grave,
Buried, yet not exempt
By privilege of death and burial
105 From worst of other evils, pains and wrongs,

---

2. See Genesis 1.3.
3. Silent: not shining; vacant: Milton thinks of the moon
at leisure (Latin *vacare*) resting in a cave.

4. The theory that the soul is diffused throughout the
body; see Augustine, *De Trinitate* 6.6: "The soul . . . in
any body, is both all in the whole, and all in every part."

But made hereby obnoxious° more   *liable to*
To all the miseries of life,
Life in captivity
Among inhuman foes.
110   But who are these? for with joint pace I hear
The tread of many feet stearing this way;
Perhaps my enemies who come to stare
At my affliction, and perhaps to insult,
Their daily practice to afflict me more.

CHORUS   This, this is he; softly a while,
Let us not break in upon him;
O change beyond report, thought, or belief!
See how he lies at random, carelessly diffused,
With languish't head unpropt,
120   As one past hope, abandoned,
And by himself given over;
In slavish habit, ill-fitted weeds
O'er worn and soiled;
Or do my eyes misrepresent? Can this be he,
125   That heroic, that renowned,
Irresistible Samson? whom unarmed
No strength of man, or fiercest wild beast could withstand;
Who tore the lion, as the lion tears the kid,[5]
Ran on embattled armies clad in iron,
130   And weaponless himself,
Made arms ridiculous, useless the forgery°   *forging*
Of brazen shield and spear, the hammered cuirass,
Chalybean[6] tempered steel, and frock of mail
Adamantean proof;[7]
135   But safest he who stood aloof,
When insupportably° his foot advanc't,   *irresistibly*
In scorn of their proud arms and warlike tools,
Spurned them to death by troops. The bold Ascalonite[8]
Fled from his lion° ramp,° old warriors turned   *lionlike / rearing up*
140   Their plated° backs under his heel;   *armored*
Or groveling soiled their crested helmets in the dust.
Then with what trivial weapon came to hand,
The jaw of a dead ass, his sword of bone,[9]
A thousand foreskins[1] fell, the flower of Palestine,
145   In Ramath-lechi[2] famous to this day:
Then by main force pulled up, and on his shoulders bore
The gates of Azza, post, and massie bar
Up to the hill by Hebron, seat of giants old,[3]

---

5. See Judges 14.6: "And he rent him [the young lion] as he would have rent a kid."
6. See Virgil, *Georgics* 1.58: "the naked Chalybes give us iron." They were famous metal workers.
7. "Adamant" (Latin *adamas*) was the name applied to the hardest known substance—at first steel, later diamond; "proof armor" was considered to be impenetrable.
8. Ascalon was one of the five main cities of the Philistines. In Judges 14.19, Samson goes down to Ascalon and kills 30 men there.

9. In Judges 15.15–6, Samson finds the jawbone of an ass and kills 1,000 men with it.
1. Uncircumcised Philistines.
2. The name of the city means "the lifting up" or "casting away of the jawbone."
3. This exploit is narrated in Judges 16.3. "Azza" is a variant form of Gaza; "Hebron" was the city of Arba (Joshua 14.15), father of Anak, 15.13–4, whose children, the Anakim, were giants (Numbers 13.33).

No journey of a Sabbath day, and loaded so;
150 Like whom° the Gentiles feign to bear up heav'n.   *Atlas*
Which shall I first bewail,
Thy bondage or lost sight,
Prison within Prison
Inseparably dark?
155 Thou art become (O worst imprisonment!)
The dungeon of thyself; thy soul
(Which men enjoying sight oft without cause complain)[4]
Imprisoned now indeed,
In real darkness of the body dwells,
160 Shut up from outward light
To incorporate with gloomy night;
For inward light alas
Puts forth no visual beam.°   *beam of eyesight*
O mirror of our fickle state,
165 Since man on earth unparalleled!
The rarer thy example stands,
By how much from the top of wondrous glory,
Strongest of mortal men,
To lowest pitch of abject fortune thou art fallen.
170 For him I reckon not in high estate
Whom long descent of birth
Or the sphere of fortune raises;
But thee whose strength, while virtue was her mate,
Might have subdued the earth,
175 Universally crowned with highest praises.
SAMSON I hear the sound of words, their sense the air
Dissolves unjointed e'er it reach my ear.
CHORUS He speaks, let us draw nigh. Matchless in might,
The glory late of Israel, now the grief;
180 We come thy friends and neighbours not unknown
From Eshtaol and Zora's fruitful vale[5]
To visit or bewail thee, or if better,
Counsel or consolation we may bring,
Salve to thy sores, apt words have power to suage
185 The tumors of a troubled mind,
And are as balm to festered wounds.
SAMSON Your coming, friends, revives me, for I learn
Now of my own experience, not by talk,
How counterfeit a coin they are who friends
190 Bear in their superscription° (of the most   *the stamp on a coin*
I would be understood) in prosperous days
They swarm, but in adverse withdraw their head
Not to be found, though sought. Yee see, O friends,
How many evils have enclosed me round;
195 Yet that which was the worst now least afflicts me,
Blindness, for had I sight, confused with shame,

4. I.e., men often complain that the soul is imprisoned in the body.
5. Samson was born at Zora (Judges 13.2) and buried between Zora and Eshtaol (Judges 16.31). These towns lay "in the valley" and are ascribed to both Judah and Dan (Joshua 15.33 and 19.41).

How could I once look up, or heave the head,
Who like a foolish pilot have shipwrack't,
My vessel trusted to me from above,
200   Gloriously rigged; and for a word, a tear,
Fool, have divulged the secret gift of God
To a deceitful woman: tell me, friends,
Am I not sung and proverbed[6] for a fool
In every street, do they not say, "How well
205   Are come upon him his deserts?" Yet why?
Immeasurable strength they might behold
In me, of wisdom nothing more then mean;°   *average*
This with the other should, at least, have paired,
These two proportioned ill drove me transverse.°   *sideways*

CHORUS   Tax not divine disposal, wisest men
Have erred, and by bad women been deceived;
And shall again, pretend they ne'er so wise.
Deject not then so overmuch thyself,
Who hast of sorrow thy full load besides;
215   Yet truth to say, I oft have heard men wonder
Why thou shouldst wed Philistian women rather
Then of thine own tribe fairer, or as fair,
At least of thy own nation, and as noble.

SAMSON   The first I saw at Timna, and she pleased
220   Me, not my Parents, that I sought to wed,
The daughter of an infidel: they knew not
That what I motioned was of God; I knew
From intimate impulse, and therefore urged
The marriage on; that by occasion hence
225   I might begin Israel's deliverance,
The work to which I was divinely called;[7]
She proving false,[8] the next I took to wife
(O that I never had! fond wish too late!)
Was in the vale of Sorec,[9] Dalila,
230   That specious° monster, my accomplished snare.   *falsely attractive*
I thought it lawful from my former act,
And the same end; still watching to oppress
Israel's oppressours: of what now I suffer
She was not the prime cause, but I myself,
235   Who vanquished with a peal[1] of words (O weakness!)
Gave up my fort of silence to a woman.

CHORUS   In seeking just occasion to provoke
The Philistine, thy country's enemy,

---

6. See Psalms 69.11: "I became a proverb to them," and
Job 30.9: "and now am I their song, yea, I am their
byword."
7. In lines 219–26, Milton follows the account in Judges
14.1–4 exactly, except in the detail of Samson's "intimate
impulse," which is not found in Judges; the reason Samson gives there for the match is "that she pleaseth me
well."
8. In Judges 14.5–20 she extracts from Samson the
answer to the riddle he has set the young men of Timna

and tells it to them. Her father then gives her to Samson's "companion, whom he had used as his friend,"
meaning groomsman; the Samson of Judges was not married to Dalila.
9. See Judges 16.4: "He loved a woman in the valley of
Sorek."
1. An artillery term. A peal of guns was used as a salute or
sign of rejoicing; the guns were not weapons of attack
when pealing.

Thou never wast remiss, I bear thee witness:
240   Yet Israel still serves with all his sons.
SAMSON That fault I take not on me, but transfer
On Israel's governours, and heads of tribes,
Who seeing those great acts which God had done
Singly by me against their conquerors
245   Acknowledged not, or not at all considered
Deliverance offered: I on th' other side
Used no ambition[2] to commend my deeds,
The deeds themselves, though mute, spoke loud the doer;
But they persisted deaf, and would not seem
250   To count them things worth notice, till at length
Their lords the Philistines with gathered powers
Entered Judea seeking me, who then
Safe to the rock of Etham was retired,
Not flying, but fore-casting in what place
255   To set upon them, what advantaged best;[3]
Meanwhile the men of Judah to prevent
The harrass of their land, beset me round;[4]
I willingly on some conditions came[5]
Into their hands, and they as gladly yield me
260   To the uncircumcised a welcome prey,
Bound with two cords; but cords to me were threads
Touched with the flame: on their whole host I flew
Unarmed, and with a trivial weapon felled
Their choicest youth; they only lived who fled.[6]
265   Had Judah that day joined, or one whole tribe,
They had by this° possessed the towers of Gath,[7]   *by this time*
And lorded over them whom now they serve;
But what more oft in nations grown corrupt,
And by their vices brought to servitude,
270   Then to love bondage more than liberty,[8]
Bondage with ease than strenuous liberty;
And to despise, or envy, or suspect
Whom God hath of his special favor raised
As their deliverer; if he aught begin,
275   How frequent° to desert him, and at last   *accustomed*
To heap ingratitude on worthiest deeds?
CHORUS Thy words to my remembrance bring
How Succoth and the Fort of Penuel
Their great deliverer contemned,
280   The matchless Gideon[9] in pursuit

2. In the sense of Latin *ambitio,* which means "walking about to solicit votes or applause."
3. In Judges 15, Samson burns the Philistines' standing corn. They, in revenge, burn his wife and her father (Judges 15.5–6); he smites them "hip and thigh with a great slaughter" and goes to dwell "in the top of the rock Etam" (Judges 15.8). "Then the Philistines went up, and pitched in Judah" (Judges 15.9).
4. See Judges 15.11–12.
5. Judges 15.12: "Swear unto me, that ye will not fall

upon me yourselves."
6. See Judges 15.13–16.
7. A city of Philistia.
8. See Matthew 11.28–30, where Jesus says, "Come unto me. . . . For my yoke is easy."
9. See Judges 8.5–9, where Gideon, pursuing Zebah and Zalmunna, kings of Midian, asks for bread for his 300 followers from Succoth and Penuel but is refused; "Madian" is the Vulgate form of Midian.

Of Madian and her vanquished kings:
And how ingrateful Ephraim
Had dealt with Jephtha,[1] who by argument,
Not worse then by his shield and spear
285   Defended Israel from the Ammonite,
Had not his prowess quelled their pride
In that sore battle when so many died
Without reprieve adjudged to death,
For want of well pronouncing Shibboleth.[2]
SAMSON Of such examples add me to the roll,[3]
Me easily indeed mine° may neglect,   *my people*
But God's proposed deliverance not so.
CHORUS Just are the ways of God,
And justifiable to men;
295   Unless there be who think not God at all,
If any be, they walk obscure;
For of such doctrine never was there school,
But the heart of the fool,[4]
And no man therein doctor but himself.
300   Yet more there be who doubt his ways not just,
As to his own edicts, found contradicting,
Then give the reins to wandering thought,
Regardless of his glory diminution;
Till by their own perplexities involved
305   They ravel° more, still less resolved,   *become entangled*
But never find self-satisfying solution.
      As if they would confine th' interminable,
And tie him to his own prescript,
Who made our laws to bind us, not himself,
310   And hath full right to exempt
Whom so it pleases him by choice
From national obstriction,[5] without taint
Of sin, or legal debt;°   *duty to Mosaic law*
For with his own laws he can best dispense.
315   He would not else who never wanted means,
Nor in respect of the enemy just cause
To set his people free,
Have prompted this heroic Nazarite,
Against his vow of strictest purity,[6]
320   To seek in marriage that fallacious bride,
Unclean, unchaste.

---

1. See Judges 11.12–33 and 12.1–4, where the Ephraimites refuse to help Jephtha against the Ammonites, whom he first refutes in argument and then defeats in battle.

2. Judges 12.5–6; Ephraimites had a distinctive dialect. When they deny their identity in order to escape punishment, Jephtha asks them to say the word "shibboleth" (ear of corn), which they can only pronounce as "sibboleth," thereby giving themselves away.

3. Gideon and Jephtha were considered saints like Sam-

son and for the same reason. See Hebrews 11.32.

4. See Psalms 14.1: "The fool hath said in his heart, There is no God."

5. Obstruction; the obligation referred to is recorded in Deuteronomy 7.1–3, which, however, does not prohibit marriage specifically with Philistines.

6. Celibacy was not included in the Nazarite vow (Numbers 6.1–21), and marriage with Gentiles was not impurity until after the reformation of Ezra.

Down Reason then, at least vain reasonings down,
Though Reason here aver
That moral verdict quits° her of unclean: *acquits*
325   Unchaste was subsequent,[7] her stain not his.
But see here comes thy reverend sire
With careful step, locks white as down,
Old Manoah: advise
Forthwith how thou ought'st to receive him.
SAMSON Ay me, another inward grief awaked,
With mention of that name renews th' assault.
MANOA Brethren and men of Dan, for such ye seem,
Though in this uncouth° place; if old respect,   *unknown*
As I suppose, towards your once gloried friend,
335   My son now captive, hither hath informed
Your younger feet, while mine cast back with age
Came lagging after; say if he be here.
CHORUS As signal° now in low dejected state,   *remarkable*
As erst in highest, behold him where he lies.
MANOA O miserable change! Is this the man,
That invincible Samson, far renowned,
The dread of Israel's foes, who with a strength
Equivalent to angels walked their streets,
None offering fight; who single combatant
345   Duelled their armies ranked in proud array,
Himself an army, now unequal match
To save himself against a coward armed
At one spear's length. O ever failing trust
In mortal strength! And oh, what not in man
350   Deceivable and vain! Nay, what thing good
Prayed for, but often proves our woe, our bane?
I prayed for children, and thought barrenness
In wedlock a reproach; I gained a son,
And such a son as all men hailed me happy;
355   Who would be now a father in my stead?
O wherefore did God grant me my request,
And as a blessing with such pomp adorned?
Why are his gifts desirable, to tempt
Our earnest prayers, then given with solemn hand
360   As graces, draw a scorpion's tail behind?
For this did the angel twice descend? for this
Ordained thy nurture holy, as of a plant;
Select, and sacred, glorious for a while,
The miracle of men: then in an hour
365   Ensnared, assaulted, overcome, led bound,
Thy foes' derision, captive, poor, and blind
Into a dungeon thrust, to work with slaves?
Alas, methinks whom God hath chosen once
To worthiest deeds, if he through frailty err,

---

7. The woman of Timna was unclean only in a legal sense, as a Gentile, and her unchastity took place afterward ("was subsequent"); see Judges 14.20: "Samson's wife was given to his companion."

370 He should not so o'erwhelm, and as a thrall
     Subject him to so foul indignities,
     Be it but for honor's sake of former deeds.
SAMSON Appoint not heavenly disposition, father,
     Nothing of all these evils hath befallen me
375 But justly; I myself have brought them on,
     Sole author I, sole cause: if aught seem vile,
     As vile hath been my folly, who have profaned[8]
     The mystery of God given me under pledge
     Of vow, and have betrayed it to a woman,
380 A Canaanite,[9] my faithless enemy.
     This well I knew, nor was at all surprised,
     But warned by oft experience: did not she
     Of Timna first betray me,[1] and reveal
     The secret wrested from me in her highth
385 Of nuptial love profest, carrying it straight
     To them who had corrupted her, my spies
     And rivals? In this other was there found
     More faith? who also in her prime of love,
     Spousal embraces, vitiated° with gold,[2]   *corrupted*
390 Though offered only, by the scent conceived
     Her spurious first-born; treason against me?
     Thrice[3] she assayed with flattering prayers and sighs,
     And amorous reproaches[4] to win from me
     My capital[5] secret, in what part my strength
395 Lay stored, in what part summed, that she might know:
     Thrice I deluded her, and turned to sport
     Her importunity, each time perceiving
     How openly, and with what impudence
     She purposed to betray me, and (which was worse
400 Than undissembled hate) with what contempt
     She sought to make me traitor to myself;
     Yet the fourth time, when mustering all her wiles,
     With blandished parlies,° feminine assaults,   *flattering words*
     Tongue-batteries, she surceased not day nor night
405 To storm me over-watched,° and wearied out.   *kept awake*
     At times when men seek most repose and rest,
     I yielded, and unlocked her all my heart,
     Who with a grain of manhood well resolved
     Might easily have shook off all her snares:
410 But foul effeminacy held me yoked
     Her bond-slave; O indignity, O blot
     To honor and religion! Servile mind
     Rewarded well with servile punishment!
     The base degree to which I now am fallen,

8. Published (Latin *profanus*, "outside the temple," hence "public").
9. The Philistines were immigrants into Canaan from Caphtor. See Amos 9.7.
1. See line 227.
2. See Judges 16.5: "And we will give thee every one of us

eleven hundred pieces of silver."
3. See Judges 16.6–14.
4. See Judges 16.15: "How canst thou say, I love thee, when thine heart is not with me?"
5. A pun: "most important," and also "pertaining to the head" (Latin *caput*).

415 These rags, this grinding, is not yet so base
    As was my former servitude, ignoble,
    Unmanly, ignominious, infamous,
    True slavery, and that blindness worse then this,
    That saw not how degenerately I served.

MANOA I cannot praise thy marriage choices, son,
    Rather approved them not; but thou didst plead
    Divine impulsion prompting how thou might'st
    Find some occasion to infest° our foes.   *harass*
    I state[6] not that; this I am sure; our foes
425 Found soon occasion thereby to make thee
    Their captive, and their triumph; thou the sooner
    Temptation found'st, or over-potent charms
    To violate the sacred trust of silence
    Deposited within thee; which to have kept
430 Tacit, was in thy power; true; and thou bear'st
    Enough and more the burden of that fault:
    Bitterly hast thou paid, and still art paying
    That rigid score.° A worse thing yet remains: *account of a debt*
    This day the Philistines a popular feast
435 Here celebrate in Gaza; and proclaim
    Great pomp, and sacrifice, and praises loud
    To Dagon, as their God who hath delivered
    Thee, Samson, bound and blind into their hands,
    Them[7] out of thine, who slew'st them many a slain.
440 So Dagon shall be magnified, and God,
    Besides whom is not God, compared with idols,
    Disglorified, blasphemed, and had in scorn
    By th' Idolatrous rout amidst their wine;
    Which to have come to pass by means of thee,
    Samson, of all thy sufferings think the heaviest,
    Of all reproach the most with shame that ever
    Could have befallen thee and thy father's house.

SAMSON Father, I do acknowledge and confess
    That I this honor, I this pomp have brought
450 To Dagon, and advanced his praises high
    Among the heathen round; to God have brought
    Dishonor, obloquy, and oped the mouths
    Of idolists° and atheists; have brought scandal   *idolaters*
    To Israel, diffidence of God, and doubt
455 In feeble hearts, propense° enough before   *inclined*
    To waver, or fall off and join with idols;
    Which is my chief affliction, shame and sorrow,
    The anguish of my soul, that suffers not
    Mine eye to harbor sleep, or thoughts to rest.
460 This only hope relieves me, that the strife
    With me hath end; all the contést is now
    'Twixt God and Dagon; Dagon hath presumed,
    Me overthrown, to enter lists° with God,   *competition*

---

6. "Assign a value to, have an opinion upon."   7. An imitation of a Latin dative: "to them."

	His deity comparing and preferring	
465	Before the God of Abraham. He, be sure,	
	Will not connive,° or linger, thus provoked,	*stay dormant*
	But will arise and his great name assert:	
	Dagon must stoop, and shall ere long receive	
	Such a discomfit,° as shall quite despoil him	*defeat*
470	Of all these boasted trophies won on me,	
	And with confusion blank° his worshippers.	*nonplus*

MANOA With cause this hope relieves thee, and these words
　　　I as a prophecy receive: for God,
　　　Nothing more certain, will not long defer
475　　To vindicate the glory of his name
　　　Against all competition, nor will long
　　　Endure it, doubtful whether God be Lord,
　　　Or Dagon. But for thee what shall be done?
　　　Thou must not in the meanwhile here forgot
480　　Lie in this miserable loathsome plight
　　　Neglected. I already have made way
　　　To some Philistian lords, with whom to treat
　　　About thy ransom:[8] well they may by this
　　　Have satisfied their utmost of revenge
485　　By pains and slaveries, worse than death inflicted
　　　On thee, who now no more canst do them harm.

SAMSON Spare that proposal, father, spare the trouble
　　　Of that solicitation; let me here,
　　　As I deserve, pay on my punishment;
490　　And expiate, if possible, my crime,
　　　Shameful garrulity. To have revealed
　　　Secrets of men, the secrets of a friend,
　　　How heinous had the fact been, how deserving
　　　Contempt and scorn of all, to be excluded
495　　All friendship, and avoided as a blab,
　　　The mark of fool set on his front? But I
　　　God's counsel have not kept, his holy secret
　　　Presumptuously have published, impiously,
　　　Weakly at least, and shamefully: A sin
500　　That Gentiles in their parables condemn[9]
　　　To their abyss and horrid pains confined.

MANOA Be penitent and for thy fault contrite,
　　　But act not in thy own affliction, son,
　　　Repent the sin, but if the punishment
505　　Thou canst avoid, self-preservation bids;
　　　Or th' execution leave to high disposal,
　　　And let another hand, not thine, exact
　　　Thy penal forfeit from thyself;[1] perhaps
　　　God will relent, and quit thee all his debt;[2]

---

8. Having Manoa sue with the Philistines for the release of his son is a Miltonic innovation to the story.
9. Alluding to the myth of Tantalus, who was placed in Hades for revealing the secrets of the gods.
1. See Augustine, *De Doctrina* 2.8: "The love of man

towards himself consists in loving himself next to God . . . Opposed to this is, first, a perverse hatred of self . . . In this class are to be reckoned those who lay violent hands on themselves."
2. Remit all your debt to him ("thee" is a dative).

510 Who evermore approves and more accepts
(Best pleased with humble and filial submission)
Him who imploring mercy sues for life,
Then who self-rigorous chooses death as due;
Which argues over-just,[3] and self-displeased
515 For self-offence, more than for God offended.
Reject not then what offered means, who knows
But God hath set before us, to return thee
Home to thy country and his sacred house,
Where thou mayst bring thy offerings, to avert
520 His further ire, with prayers and vows renewed.
SAMSON His pardon I implore; but as for life,
To what end should I seek it? When in strength
All mortals I excelled, and great in hopes
With youthful courage and magnanimous thoughts
525 Of birth from heaven foretold and high exploits,
Full of divine instinct, after some proof
Of acts indeed heroic, far beyond
The sons of Anak,[4] famous now and blazed,°   *published*
Fearless of danger, like a petty God
530 I walked about admired of all and dreaded
On hostile ground, none daring my affront.
Then swollen with pride into the snare I fell
Of fair fallacious looks, venereal trains,°   *sexual snares*
Softned with pleasure and voluptuous life;
535 At length to lay my head and hallowed pledge
Of all my strength in the lascivious lap[5]
Of a deceitful concubine who shore[6] me
Like a tame wether,° all my precious fleece,   *castrated sheep*
Then turned me out ridiculous, despoiled,
540 Shaven, and disarmed among my enemies.
CHORUS Desire of wine and all delicious drinks,[7]
Which many a famous warrior overturns,
Thou couldst repress, nor did the dancing ruby
Sparkling, outpoured, the flavor or the smell,
545 Or taste that cheers the heart of Gods and men,[8]
Allure thee from the cool Crystálline stream.
SAMSON Wherever fountain or fresh current flowed
Against[9] the eastern ray, translucent, pure,
With touch etheral of heavens fiery rod
550 I drank, from the clear milky[1] juice allaying
Thirst, and refreshed; nor envied them the grape
Whose heads that turbulent liquor fills with fumes.
CHORUS O madness, to think use of strongest wines

---

3. Proves a man just to excess.
4. Giants; see line 148.
5. See Judges 16.19: "She made him sleep upon her knees."
6. Shaved. In Judges 16.19, Dalila calls for a man to shave Samson's head; here, she apparently does it herself.
7. As a Nazarite, Samson vowed to abstain from strong drink, Numbers 6.3.

8. See Judges 9.13: "wine, which cheereth God and man."
9. In the direction of. In Ezekiel 47.8–9 the waters that flow eastward are said to have life-giving powers.
1. The concept is of earth as mother; possibly Milton recalls Song of Solomon 5.12: "doves by the rivers of water, washed with milk," where the last phrase can be translated as "splashed by the milky water."

And strongest drinks our chief support of health,
555   When God with these forbidden made choice to rear
His mighty champion, strong above compare,
Whose drink was only from the liquid° brook.   *transparent*
SAMSON But what availed this temperance, not complete
Against another object more enticing?
560   What boots it° at one gate to make defence,   *what use is it*
And at another to let in the foe
Effeminately vanquished? by which means,
Now blind, disheartened, shamed, dishonored, quelled,
To what can I be useful, wherein serve
565   My nation, and the work from heaven imposed,
But to sit idle on the houshold hearth,
A burdenous drone; to visitants a gaze°   *object gazed at*
Or pitied object, these redundant° locks   *abounding*
Robustious° to no purpose clustering down,   *robust*
570   Vain monument of strength; till length of years
And sedentary numbness craze° my limbs   *weaken*
To a contemptible old age obscure.
Here rather let me drudge and earn my bread,
Till vermin or the draff° of servile food   *pig-swill*
575   Consume me, and oft-invocated death
Hasten the welcome end of all my pains.
MANOA Wilt thou then serve the Philistines with that gift
Which was expressly given thee to annoy° them?   *molest*
Better at home lie bed-rid, not only idle,
580   Inglorious, unemployed, with age out-worn.
But God who caused a fountain at thy prayer
From the dry ground to spring, thy thirst to allay
After the brunt of battle,[2] can as easy
Cause light again within thy eyes to spring,
585   Wherewith to serve him better then thou hast;
And I persuade me so; why else this strength
Miraculous yet remaining in those locks?
His might continues in thee not for naught,
Nor shall his wondrous gifts be frustrate thus.
SAMSON All otherwise to me my thoughts portend,
That these dark orbs no more shall treat with light,
Nor th' other light of life continue long,
But yield to double darkness nigh at hand:
So much I feel my genial[3] spirits droop,
595   My hopes all flat,° nature within me seems   *overthrown*
In all her functions weary of herself;
My race of glory run, and race of shame,
And I shall shortly be with them that rest.[4]
MANOA Believe not these suggestions which proceed

---

2. See Judges 15.19: "But God clave an hollow place that was in the jaw [or "in Lehi"], and there came water thereout."

3. Pertaining to genius or natural disposition.

4. In lines 581–98, Milton seems to have remembered the exchange between Jason and Phineus in Apollonius Rhodius, *Argonautica* 2.438–48.

600 From anguish of the mind and humors black,[5]
    That mingle with thy fancy.° I however   *imagination*
    Must not omit a Father's timely care
    To prosecute° the means of thy deliverance   *persist in*
    By ransom or how else: meanwhile be calm,
605 And healing words from these thy friends admit.
SAMSON O that torment should not be confined
    To the body's wounds and sores
    With maladies innumerable
    In heart, head, breast, and reins;°   *kidneys*
610 But must secret passage find
    To th' inmost mind,
    There exercise all his fierce accidents,°   *symptoms*
    And on her purest spirits prey,
    As on entrails, joints, and limbs,
615 With answerable° pains, but more intense,   *corresponding*
    Though void of corporal sense.
       My griefs not only pain me
    As a lingring disease,
    But finding no redress, ferment and rage,
620 Nor less than wounds immedicable
    Rankle, and fester, and gangrene,
    To black mortification.°   *decay*
    Thoughts, my tormenters, armed with deadly stings
    Mangle my apprehensive° tenderest parts,   *sensitive*
625 Exasperate,° exulcerate,° and raise   *worsen/infect*
    Dire inflammation which no cooling herb
    Or medicinal liquor can assuage,
    Nor breath of vernal air from snowy alp.
    Sleep hath forsook and given me o'er
630 To death's benumbing opium as my only cure.
    Thence faintings, swoonings of despair,
    And sense of heaven's desertion.
       I was his nursling once and choice delight,
    His destined from the womb,
635 Promised by heavenly message twice descending.
    Under his special eye
    Abstemious I grew up and thrived amain;
    He led me on to mightiest deeds
    Above the nerve° of mortal arm   *muscle*
640 Against the uncircumcised, our enemies.
    But now hath cast me off as never known,
    And to those cruel enemies,
    Whom I by his appointment° had provok't,   *command*
    Left me all helpless with th' irreparable loss
645 Of sight, reserved alive to be repeated°   *spoken of as*
    The subject of their cruelty or scorn.
    Nor am I in the list of them that hope;

5. The black humor was melancholy (black bile).

Hopeless are all my evils, all remediless;
This one prayer yet remains, might I be heard,
650   No long petition: speedy death,
The close of all my miseries, and the balm.

CHORUS Many are the sayings of the wise
In antient and in modern books enrolled;
Extolling patience as the truest fortitude;
655   And to the bearing well of all calamities,
All chances incident to man's frail life[6]
Consolatories° writ   *writings of comfort*
With studied argument, and much persuasion sought[7]
Lenient of grief and anxious thought,[8]
660   But with th' afflicted in his pangs their sound
Little prevails, or rather seems a tune,
Harsh, and of dissonant mood from his complaint,
Unless he feel within
Some source of consolation from above;
665   Secret refreshings, that repair his strength,
And fainting spirits uphold.
            God of our Fathers, what is man![9]
That thou towards him with hand so various,
Or might I say contrarious,°   *opposed*
670   Temper'st thy providence through his short course,
Not evenly, as thou rulest
The angelic orders and inferiour creatures mute,
Irrational and brute.
Nor do I name of men the common rout,
675   That wandring loose about
Grow up and perish, as the summer fly,
Heads without name no more rememberd,
But such as thou hast solemnly elected,
With gifts and graces eminently adorned
680   To some great work, thy glory,
And people's safety, which in part they effect:
Yet toward these thus dignified, thou oft
Amidst their height of noon,
Changest thy countenance, and thy hand with no regard
685   Of highest favors past
From thee on them, or them to thee of service.
            Nor only dost degrade them, or remit
To life obscured, which were a fair dismission,° *dismissal*
But throw'st them lower than thou didst exalt them high,
690   Unseemly falls in human eye,
Too grievous for the trespass or omission,
Oft leav'st them to the hostile sword
Of heathen and profane, their carcasses

---

6. Echoing Shakespeare's *Timon of Athens* 5.1.203–5:
"With other incident throes / That nature's fragile vessel
doth sustain / In life's uncertain voyage."
7. Persuasion painstakingly constructed.
8. Tending to soothe; see Horace, *Epistles* 1.1.34: "There

are words and sayings with which you may soothe the
pain."
9. See Psalms 8.4: "What is man, that thou art mindful of
him?"

To dogs and fowls a prey, or else captíved:[1]
695　Or to the unjust tribunals, under change of times,
And condemnation of the ingrateful multitude.
If these they scape, perhaps in poverty
With sickness and disease thou bow'st them down,
Painful diseases and deformed,
700　In crude° old age;　　　　　　　　　　　　　　　　*premature*
Though not disordinate,° yet causless suffering　　　*immoderate*
The punishment of dissolute days, in fine,
Just or unjust, alike seem miserable,
For oft alike, both come to evil end.
705　　So deal not with this once thy glorious champion,
The image of thy strength, and mighty minister.
What do I beg? how hast thou dealt already?
Behold him in this state calamitous, and turn
His labors, for thou canst, to peaceful end.
710　　But who is this, what thing of sea or land?
Femal of sex it seems,
That so bedeckt, ornate, and gay,
Comes this way sailing
Like a stately ship
715　Of Tarsus,[2] bound for th' Isles
Of Javan or Gadier[3]
With all her bravery on, and tackle trim,
Sails filled, and streamers waving,
Courted by all the winds that hold them play,°　　　*move them*
720　An amber scent of odorous perfume
Her harbinger, a damsel train behind;
Some rich Philistian matron she may seem,
And now at nearer view, no other certain
Than Dalila thy wife.
SAMSON My wife, my traitress, let her not come near me.
CHORUS Yet on she moves, now stands and eyes thee fixed,
About t' have spoke, but now, with head declined
Like a fair flower surcharged with dew, she weeps
And words addressed seem into tears dissolved,
730　Wetting the borders of her silken veil:
But now again she makes address° to speak.　　　　*prepares*
DALILA With doubtful feet and wavering resolution
I came, still dreading thy displeasure, Samson,
Which to have merited, without excuse
735　I cannot but acknowledge; yet if tears
May expiate° (though the fact° more evil drew　　　*make amends for/deed*
In the perverse event° than I foresaw)　　　　　　*outcome*
My penance hath not slackened, though my pardon
No way assured. But conjugal affection
740　Prevailing over fear, and timerous doubt

---

1. Echoing Homer, *Iliad* 1.4–5: the dead in the Trojan war are "made a spoil for dogs and all manner of birds."
2. The biblical phrase "ships of Tarshish" (i.e., probably Tartessus in southern Spain) is found in Isaiah 23.1, 14 and Psalm 48.7.
3. Ionian isles. Javan, son of Japhet (Genesis 10.2) and grandson of Noah, was the supposed ancestor of the Ionians. "Gadire" is Cadiz, on the southern coast of Spain.

Hath led me on desirous to behold
Once more thy face, and know of thy estate.
If aught in my ability may serve
To lighten what thou suffer'st, and appease
745   Thy mind with what amends is in my power,
Though late, yet in some part to recompense
My rash but more unfortunate misdeed.

SAMSON Out, out Hyaena;[4] these are thy wonted arts,
And arts of every woman false like thee,
750   To break all faith, all vows, deceive, betray,
Then as repentant to submit, beseech,
And reconcilement move with feigned remorse,
Confess, and promise wonders in her change,
Not truly penitent, but chief to try
755   Her husband, how far urged his patience bears,
His virtue or weakness which way to assail:
Then with more cautious and instructed skill
Again transgresses, and again submits;
That wisest and best men full oft beguiled
760   With goodness principled not to reject
The penitent, but ever to forgive,
Are drawn to wear out miserable days,
Entangled with a poisonous bosom snake,
If not by quick destruction soon cut off
765   As I by thee, to ages an example.

DALILA Yet hear me, Samson; not that I endeavor
To lessen or extenuate my offence,
But that on th' other side if it be weighed
By itself, with aggravations° not surcharged,   *exaggerations*
770   Or else with just allowance counterpoised,
I may, if possible, thy pardon find
The easier towards me, or thy hatred less.
First granting, as I do, it was a weakness
In me, but incident to all our sex,
775   Curiosity, inquisitive, importune
Of secrets,[5] then with like infirmity
To publish them, both common female faults:
Was it not weakness also to make known
For importunity, that is for naught,
780   Wherein consisted all thy strength and safety?
To what I did thou show'dst me first the way.
But I to enemies revealed, and should not.
Nor shouldst thou have trusted that to womans frailty
E'er I to thee, thou to thyself wast cruel.[6]
785   Let weakness then with weakness come to parle°   *talk*

4. According to Pliny 8.44, the hyena is believed to contain within itself both sexes, to imitate the human voice and thus lure men out to devour them, and to be the only animal that digs up graves to get at the bodies of the dead. Magicians, he says (28.27), believe that it has magical powers and can deprive human beings of their senses.

All these attributes help to give point to Samson's abuse. See also Jonson, *Volpone* 4.6.3: "now, thine eyes / Vie tears with the hyaena."
5. Irksomely persistent in discovering secrets.
6. See Shakespeare, Sonnet 1: "to thy sweet self too cruel" (page 1169).

So near related, or the same of kind,
Thine forgive mine; that men may censure thine
The gentler, if severely thou exact not
More strength from me than in thyself was found.
790 And what if Love, which thou interpret'st hate,
The jealousy of love, powerful of sway
In human hearts, nor less in mine towards thee,
Caused what I did? I saw thee mutable
Of fancy, feared lest one day thou wouldst leave me
795 As her at Timna, sought by all means therefore
How to endear and hold thee to me firmest:
No better way I saw than by importuning
To learn thy secrets, get into my power
Thy key of strength and safety: thou wilt say,
800 Why then revealed? I was assured by those
Who tempted me, that nothing was designed
Against thee but safe custody, and hold:[7]
That made for me,° I knew that liberty   *was to my advantage*
Would draw thee forth to perilous enterprises,
805 While I at home sat full of cares and fears
Wailing thy absence in my widowed bed;
Here I should still enjoy thee day and night
Mine and love's prisoner, not the Philistines',
Whole to myself, unhazarded abroad,
810 Fearless at home of partners in my love.
These reasons in Love's law have passed for good,
Though fond and reasonless to some perhaps;
And love hath oft, well meaning, wrought much woe,
Yet always pity or pardon hath obtained.
815 Be not unlike all others, not austere
As thou art strong, inflexible as steel.
If thou in strength all mortals dost exceed,
In uncompassionate anger do not so.
SAMSON How cunningly the sorceress displays
820 Her own transgressions, to upbraid me mine!
That malice not repentance brought thee hither,
By this appears: I gave, thou say'st, th' example,
I led the way; bitter reproach, but true,
I to myself was false ere thou to me,
825 Such pardon therefore as I give my folly,
Take to thy wicked deed: which when thou seest
Impartial, self-severe, inexorable,
Thou wilt renounce thy seeking, and much rather
Confess it feigned; weakness is thy excuse,
830 And I believe it, weakness to resist
Philistian gold: if weakness may excuse,
What murderer, what traitor, parricide,
Incestuous, sacrilegious, but may plead it?
All wickedness is weakness: that plea therefore

7. In Judges 16.5 the Lords of the Philistines say to Dalila: "Entice him . . . that we may bind him to afflict him."

835   With God or man will gain thee no remission.
        But love constrained thee; call it furious rage
        To satisfy thy lust: love seeks to have love;
        My love how couldst thou hope, who tookst the way
        To raise in me inexpiable hate,
840   Knowing, as needs I must, by thee betrayed?
        In vain thou striv'st to cover shame with shame,
        Or by evasions thy crime uncover'st more.
DALILA Since thou determin'st weakness for no plea
        In man or woman, though to thy own condemning,
845   Hear what assaults I had, what snares besides,
        What sieges girt me round, ere I consented;
        Which might have awed the best resolved of men,
        The constantest to have yielded without blame.
        It was not gold, as to my charge thou lay'st,
850   That wrought with me: thou know'st the magistrates
        And princes of my country came in person,
        Solicited, commanded, threatened, urged,
        Adjured by all the bonds of civil duty
        And of religion, pressed how just it was,
855   How honorable, how glorious to entrap
        A common enemy, who had destroyed
        Such numbers of our nation: and the priest[8]
        Was not behind, but ever at my ear,
        Preaching how meritorious with the gods
860   It would be to ensnare an irreligious
        Dishonorer of Dagon: what had I
        To oppose against such powerful arguments?
        Only my love of thee held long debate;
        And combated in silence all these reasons
865   With hard contest: at length that grounded maxim
        So rife and celebrated in the mouths
        Of wisest men; that to the public good
        Private respects must yield; with grave authority
        Took full possession of me and prevailed;
870   Virtue, as I thought, truth, duty so enjoining.
SAMSON I thought where all thy circling wiles would end;
        In feigned religion, smooth hypocrisy.
        But had thy love, still odiously pretended,
        Been, as it ought, sincere, it would have taught thee
875   Far other reasonings, brought forth other deeds.
        I before all the daughters of my tribe
        And of my nation chose thee from among
        My enemies, loved thee, as too well thou knew'st,
        Too well, unbosomed all my secrets to thee,
880   Not out of levity, but over-powered
        By thy request, who could deny thee nothing;[9]
        Yet now am judged an enemy. Why then

8. No priest is mentioned in the biblical account.
9. Echoes *Othello* 3.3.76: "I will deny thee nothing," and 5.2.351, where Othello says he "lov'd not wisely, but too well" (pages 1217 and 1260).

Didst thou at first receive me for thy husband?
Then, as since then, thy country's foe professed:
885   Being once a wife, for me thou wast to leave
Parents and country; nor was I their subject,
Nor under their protection but my own,
Thou mine, not theirs: if aught against my life
Thy country sought of thee, it sought unjustly,
890   Against the law of nature, law of nations,[1]
No more thy country, but an impious crew
Of men conspiring to uphold their state
By worse then hostile deeds, violating the ends
For which our country is a name so dear;
895   Not therefore to be obeyed. But zeal moved thee;
To please thy gods thou didst it; gods unable
To acquit themselves and prosecute their foes
But by ungodly deeds, the contradiction
Of their own deity, Gods cannot be:
900   Less therefore to be pleased, obeyed, or feared,
These false pretexts and varnished colors° failing,   *specious excuses*
Bare in thy guilt how foul must thou appear?
DALILA In argument with men a woman ever
Goes by the worse, whatever be her cause.
SAMSON For want of words no doubt, or lack of breath,
Witness when I was worried with thy peals.[2]
DALILA I was a fool, too rash, and quite mistaken
In what I thought would have succeeded best.
Let me obtain forgiveness of thee, Samson,
910   Afford me place to show what recompense
Towards thee I intend for what I have misdone,
Misguided; only what remains past cure
Bear not too sensibly,° nor still insist   *feel not too acutely*
To afflict thyself in vain: though sight be lost,
915   Life yet hath many solaces, enjoyed
Where other senses want not their delights
At home in leisure and domestic ease,
Exempt from many a care and chance to which
Eye-sight exposes daily men abroad.
920   I to the lords will intercede, not doubting
Their favorable ear, that I may fetch thee
From forth this loathsome prison-house, to abide
With me, where my redoubled love and care
With nursing diligence, to me glad office,
925   May ever tend about thee to old age
With all things grateful cheered, and so supplied,
That what by me thou hast lost thou least shalt miss.
SAMSON No, no, of my condition take no care;
It fits not; thou and I long since are twain;
930   Nor think me so unwary or accurst

---

1. Echoes *Troilus and Cressida* 2.2.184–5: "these moral   2. See line 235.
laws / Of nature and of nations."

To bring my feet again into the snare
Where once I have been caught; I know thy trains°   *snares*
Though dearly to my cost, thy gins° and toils;°   *traps / harassment*
Thy fair enchanted cup and warbling charms[3]
935   No more on me have power, their force is nulled,
So much of adder's wisdom I have learned
To fence my ear against thy sorceries.[4]
If in my flower of youth and strength, when all men
Loved, honoured, feared me, thou alone could hate me
940   Thy husband, slight me, sell me, and forgo me;
How wouldst thou use me now, blind, and thereby
Deceiveable, in most things as a child
Helpless, thence easily contemned, and scorned,
And last neglected? How wouldst thou insult
945   When I must live uxorious to thy will
In perfet thraldom, how again betray me,
Bearing my words and doings to the lords
To gloss upon, and censuring, frown or smile?
This gaol° I count the house of liberty   *jail*
950   To thine whose doors my feet shall never enter.
DALILA Let me approach at least, and touch thy hand.
SAMSON Not for thy life, lest fierce remembrance wake
My sudden rage to tear thee joint by joint.
At distance I forgive thee, go with that;
955   Bewail thy falsehood, and the pious works
It hath brought forth to make thee memorable
Among illustrious women, faithful wives:
Cherish thy hastened widowhood with the gold
Of matrimonial treason: so farewell.
DALILA I see thou art implacable, more deaf
To prayers, than winds and seas, yet winds to seas
Are reconciled at length, and sea to shore:
Thy anger, unappeasable, still rages,
Eternal tempest never to be calmed.
965   Why do I humble thus myself, and suing
For peace, reap nothing but repulse and hate?
Bid go with evil omen and the brand
Of infamy upon my name denounced?
To mix with thy concernments I desist
970   Henceforth, nor too much disapprove my own.
Fame if not double-faced is double-mouthed,[5]
And with contrary blast proclaims most deeds,
On both his wings, one black, th' other white,
Bears greatest names in his wild airy flight.
975   My name perhaps among the circumcised

---

3. Alludes to the Circe story (*Odyssey* 10).
4. The proverb "As deaf as an adder" originated in Psalm 58.4: "They are like the deaf adder that stoppeth her ears."
5. No source has been found for Milton's representation

of Fame as male, double-mouthed, and with one wing black and one wing white. In Chaucer's *House of Fame* (1571–1582, 1637), Fame employs Aeolus, god of winds, as trumpeter, and he has two trumpets, one golden, "Clear Laud," and the other black, "Slander."

In Dan,[6] in Judah, and the bordering tribes,
To all posterity may stand defamed,
With malediction mentioned, and the blot
Of falsehood most unconjugal traduced.
980 But in my country where I most desire,
In Ekron, Gaza, Asdod, and in Gath[7]
I shall be named among the famousest
Of women, sung at solemn festivals,
Living and dead recorded, who to save
985 Her country from a fierce destroyer, chose
Above the faith of wedlock-bands, my tomb
With odors° visited and annual flowers.   *from burnt spices*
Not less renowned than in Mount Ephraim,
Jael, who with inhospitable guile
990 Smote Sisera sleeping through the temples nailed.[8]
Nor shall I count it heinous to enjoy
The public marks of honor and reward
Conferred upon me, for the piety
Which to my country I was judged to have shown.
995 At this who ever envies or repines
I leave him to his lot, and like my own.[9]

CHORUS She's gone, a manifest serpent by her sting
Discovered in the end, till now concealed.

SAMSON So let her go; God sent her to debase me,
1000 And aggravate my folly who committed
To such a viper his most sacred trust
Of secrecy, my safety, and my life.

CHORUS Yet beauty, though injurious, hath strange power,
After offense returning, to regain
1005 Love once possessed, nor can be easily
Repulsed, without much inward passion felt
And secret sting of amorous remorse.

SAMSON Love-quarrels oft in pleasing concord end,
Not wedlock-treachery endangering life.

CHORUS It is not virtue, wisdom, valor, wit,
Strength, comeliness of shape, or amplest merit
That woman's love can win or long inherit;°   *hold*
But what it is, hard is to say,
Harder to hit,
1015 (Which way soever men refer it)
Much like thy riddle,[1] Samson, in one day
Or seven, though one should musing sit;
If any of these or all, the Timnian bride

---

6. Samson's tribe.
7. Four of the five chief Philistine cities.
8. In Judges 4.21, Jael, Heber's wife, kills Sisera, the Canaanite general, by driving a nail into his temples as he sleeps after taking refuge in her tent from Barak and the Israelites. Jael's praises are sung (Judges 5.24) by Barak and by the prophetess Deborah, who lived (Judges 4.5) in Mount Ephraim.

9. See Sophocles, *Ajax* 1038–39: "If there be any in whose mind this wins no favor, let him hold to his own thoughts, as I hold to mine."
1. See Judges 14.8–14: Samson, finding that bees have made honey in the carcass of the lion he killed, sets the 30 companions a riddle, "Out of the eater came forth meat, and out of the strong came forth sweetness," and gives them seven days to solve it.

	Had not so soon preferred
1020	Thy paranymph,[2] worthless to thee compared,
	Successor in thy bed,
	Nor both° so loosely disallied

Nor both° so loosely disallied   *both wives*
Their nuptials, nor this last so treacherously
Had shorn the fatal harvest of thy head.
1025 Is it for that such outward ornament
Was lavished on their sex, that inward gifts
Were left for haste unfinished, judgment scant,
Capacity not raised to apprehend
Or value what is best
1030 In choice, but oftest to affect the wrong?
Or was too much of self-love mixed,
Of constancy no root infixed,
That either they love nothing, or not long?
Whate'er it be, to wisest men and best
1035 Seeming at first all heavenly under virgin veil,
Soft, modest, meek, demure,
Once joined, the contrary she proves,[3] a thorn[4]
Intestine°, far within defensive arms   *domestic*
A cleaving[5] mischief, in his way to virtue
1040 Adverse and turbulent, or by her charms
Draws him awry enslaved
With dotage, and his sense depraved
To folly and shameful deeds which ruin ends.
What pilot so expert but needs must wreck
1045 Embarked with such a steers-mate at the helm?
Favored of Heaven who finds
One virtuous rarely found,
That in domestic good combines:
Happy that house! his way to peace is smooth:[6]
1050 But virtue which breaks through all opposition,
And all temptation can remove,
Most shines and most is acceptable above.
Therefore God's universal law
Gave to the man despotic power
1055 Over his female in due awe,
Nor from that right to part an hour,
Smile she or lour:
So shall he least confusion draw
On his whole life, not swayed
1060 By female usurpation, nor dismayed.
But had we best retire, I see a storm?
SAMSON Fair days have oft contracted wind and rain.

---

2. Groomsman. In Judges 14.20, Samson's wife is given to his groomsman; see line 227.

3. In the *Doctrine and Discipline of Divorce*, Milton says that "The sobrest and best govern'd men are least practiz'd in these affairs; and who knows not that the bashful mutenes of a virgin may oft-times hide all the unlivelines and naturall sloth which is really unfit for conversation."

4. See 2 Corinthians 12.7: "a thorn in the flesh."

5. Perhaps a reference to the poisoned shirt sent to Hercules by Deianira in hope of regaining his love (Sophocles, *Trachiniae*); see Euripides, *Orestes* 605–606: "Women were born to mar the lives of men / Ever, unto their surer overthrow."

6. See Proverbs 31.10–28.

CHORUS But this another kind of tempest brings.

SAMSON Be less abstruse, my riddling days[7] are past.

CHORUS Look now for no enchanting voice, nor fear
    The bait of honeyed words; a rougher tongue
    Draws hitherward, I know him by his stride,
    The giant Harapha[8] of Gath, his look
    Haughty as is his pile° high-built and proud.   *frame*
1070   Comes he in peace? What wind hath blown him hither
    I less conjecture than when first I saw
    The sumptuous Dalila floating this way:
    His habit carries peace, his brow defiance.

SAMSON Or peace or not, alike to me he comes.

CHORUS His fraught° we soon shall know, he now arrives.   *cargo*

HARAPHA I come not, Samson, to condole thy chance,
    As these perhaps, yet wish it had not been,
    Though for no friendly intent. I am of Gath;
    Men call me Harapha, of stock renowned
1080   As Og or Anak and the Emims old
    That Kiriathaim held,[9] thou knowst me now
    If thou at all art known.° Much I have heard   *knowledgeable*
    Of thy prodigious might and feats performed
    Incredible to me, in this displeased,
1085   That I was never present on the place
    Of those encounters where we might have tried
    Each other's force in camp or listed° field: *open or enclosed*
    And now am come to see of whom such noise
    Hath walked about, and each limb to survey,
1090   If thy appearance answer loud report.

SAMSON The way to know were not to see but taste.°   *try*

HARAPHA Dost thou already single° me; I thought   *challenge*
    Gyves° and the mill had tamed thee; O that fortune   *chains*
    Had brought me to the field where thou art famed
1095   To have wrought such wonders with an Ass's jaw;
    I should have forced thee soon with other arms,
    Or left thy carcass where the ass lay thrown:
    So had the glory of prowess been recovered
    To Palestine, won by a Philistine
1100   From the unforeskinned race, of whom thou bear'st
    The highest name for valiant acts, that honor
    Certain to have won by mortal duel from thee,
    I lose, prevented by thy eyes put out.

SAMSON Boast not of what thou wouldst have done, but do
1105   What then thou would'st; thou seest it in thy hand.

HARAPHA To combat with a blind man I disdain,

---

7. See lines 1016–17.

8. Milton has invented this giant, a Philistine whose sons were slain by David and his servants (an allusion to 2 Samuel 21.20). The name "Harapha" translates as "the giant."

9. "Og," see Deuteronomy 3.2: "Only Og king of Bashan remained of the remnant of the giants"; "Anak," see Numbers 13.33: "And there we saw the giants, the sons of Anak . . . and we were in our own sight as grasshoppers"; "Emims . . . Kiriathaim," see Deuteronomy 2.10–11: "The Emims dwelt therein . . . Which also were accounted giants," and Genesis 14.5: "the Emims in Shaveh ['the plain of'] Kiriathaim."

And thou hast need much washing to be touched.

SAMSON Such usage as your honorable lords
    Afford me assassinated° and betrayed,   *wounded by treachery*
1110   Who durst not with their whole united powers
    In fight withstand me single and unarmed,
    Nor in the house with chamber ambushes
    Close-banded durst attack me, no not sleeping,
    Till they had hired a woman with their gold
1115   Breaking her marriage faith to circumvent me.
    Therefore without feigned shifts let be assigned
    Some narrow place enclosed, where sight may give thee,
    Or rather flight, no great advantage on me;
    Then put on all thy gorgeous arms, thy helmet
1120   And brigandine of brass, thy broad habergeon,
    Vant-brass and greaves, and gauntlet, add thy spear
    A weaver's beam, and seven-times-folded shield,[1]
    I only with an oaken staff will meet thee,
    And raise such outcries on thy clattered iron,
1125   Which long shall not withhold me from thy head,
    That in a little time while breath remains thee,
    Thou oft shalt wish thy self at Gath to boast
    Again in safety what thou wouldst have done
    To Samson, but shalt never see Gath more.

HARAPHA Thou durst not thus disparage glorious arms
    Which greatest heroes have in battle worn,
    Their ornament and safety, had not spells
    And black enchantments, some magician's art
    Armed thee or charmed thee strong, which thou from heaven
1135   Feignd'st at thy birth was given thee in thy hair,
    Where strength can least abide, though all thy hairs
    Were bristles ranged like those that ridge the back
    Of chaf't° wild boars, or ruffled porcupines.   *angered*

SAMSON I know no spells, use no forbidden arts;
1140   My trust is in the living God who gave me
    At my nativity this strength, diffused
    No less through all my sinews, joints and bones,
    Then thine, while I preserved these locks unshorn,
    The pledge of my unviolated vow.
1145   For proof hereof, if Dagon be thy god,
    Go to his temple, invocate his aid
    With solemnest devotion, spread before him
    How highly it concerns his glory now
    To frustrate and dissolve these magic spells,
1150   Which I to be the power of Israel's God
    Avow, and challenge Dagon to the test,
    Offering to combat thee, his champion bold,
    With th' utmost of his godhead seconded:

---

1. Brigandine: body armor of metal rings or plates sewn on canvas or leather; habergeon: sleeveless coat of mail; vantbrace: armor for the fore-arm; weaver's beam: the wooden roller in a loom on which the warp is wound before weaving, and the similar roller on which the cloth is wound as it is woven—(see 1 Samuel 17.7, of Goliath: "the staff of his spear was like a weaver's beam"); shield: see the shield of Ajax (*Iliad* 7.220), made of seven layers of bull's hide.

Then thou shalt see, or rather to thy sorrow
1155   Soon feel, whose God is strongest, thine or mine.

HARAPHA Presume not on thy God, whate'er he be,
Thee he regards not, owns not, hath cut off
Quite from his people, and delivered up
Into thy enemies' hand, permitted them
1160   To put out both thine eyes, and fettered send thee
Into the common prison, there to grind
Among the slaves and asses, thy comrades,
As good for nothing else, no better service
With those thy boist'rous locks, no worthy match
1165   For valor to assail, nor by the sword
Of noble warrior, so to stain his honor,
But by the barber's razor best subdued.

SAMSON All these indignities, for such they are
From thine,° these evils I deserve and more,   *thy people*
1170   Acknowledge them from God inflicted on me
Justly, yet despair not of his final pardon
Whose ear is ever open; and his eye
Gracious to re-admit the suppliant;
In confidence whereof I once again
1175   Defy thee to the trial of mortal fight,
By combat to decide whose god is God,
Thine or whom I with Israel's sons adore.

HARAPHA Fair honor that thou dost thy God, in trusting
He will accept thee to defend his cause,
1180   A murderer, a revolter, and a robber.

SAMSON Tongue-doughty giant, how dost thou prove me these?

HARAPHA Is not thy nation subject to our lords?
Their magistrates confest it, when they took thee
As a league-breaker and delivered bound
1185   Into our hands:[2] for hadst thou not committed
Notorious murder on those thirty men
At Askalon, who never did thee harm,
Then like a robber stripd'st them of their robes?[3]
The Philistines, when thou hadst broke the league,
1190   Went up with armed powers thee only seeking,
To others did no violence nor spoil.

SAMSON Among the daughters of the Philistines
I chose a wife, which argued me no foe;
And in your city held my nuptial feast:
1195   But your ill-meaning politician lords,
Under pretense of bridal friends and guests,
Appointed to await me thirty spies,[4]
Who threatening cruel death constrained the bride

2. See lines 259–64.
3. See Judges 14.19. Samson had wagered "thirty change
of garments" that his "companions" would not be able to
solve his riddle. They extracted the answer from his wife,
so he killed 30 men at Ascalon and took their clothes to
be able to pay the wager.
4. There is nothing in Judges to support this claim that

the 30 "companions" were spies. However, Josephus,
Antiquities 5.8, says, "now the people of Timnath, out of
dread of the young man's strength, gave him during the
time of the wedding feast . . . thirty of the most stout of
their youth, in pretence to be his companions, but in
reality to be a guard upon him, that he might not attempt
to give them any disturbance."

To wring from me and tell to them my secret,
1200   That solved the riddle which I had proposed.
When I perceived all set on enmity,
As on my enemies, wherever chanced,
I used hostility, and took their spoil
To pay my underminers in their coin.[5]
1205   My nation was subjected to your lords.
It was the force of conquest; force with force
Is well ejected when the conquered can.
But I a private person, whom my country
As a league-breaker gave up bound, presumed
1210   Single rebellion and did hostile acts.
I was no private but a person raised
With strength sufficient and command from heaven
To free my Country; if their servile minds
Me their deliverer sent would not receive,
1215   But to their masters gave me up for nought,
Th' unworthier they; whence to this day they serve.
I was to do my part from heaven assigned,
And had performed it if my known offense
Had not disabled me, not all your force:
1220   These shifts refuted, answer thy appellant°   *challenger*
Though by his blindness maimed for high attempts,
Who now defies thee thrice[6] to single fight,
As a petty enterprise of small enforce.°   *effort*
HARAPHA   With thee a man condemned, a slave enrolled,
1225   Due by the law to capital punishment?
To fight with thee no man of arms will deign.
SAMSON   Camest thou for this, vain boaster, to survey me,
To descant on my strength, and give thy verdict?
Come nearer, part not hence so slight informed;
1230   But take good heed my hand survey not thee.
HARAPHA   O Baal-zebub![7] can my ears unused
Hear these dishonors, and not render death?
SAMSON   No man withholds thee, nothing from thy hand
Fear I incurable; bring up thy van,°   *vanguard*
1235   My heels are fettered, but my fist is free.
HARAPHA   This insolence other kind of answer fits.
SAMSON   Go, baffled° coward, lest I run upon thee,   *disgraced*
Though in these chains, bulk without spirit vast,
And with one buffet lay thy structure low,
1240   Or swing thee in the air, then dash thee down
To the hazard of thy brains and shattered sides.
HARAPHA   By Astaroth[8] ere long thou shalt lament
These braveries in irons loaden on thee.
CHORUS   His Giantship is gone somewhat crestfallen,

---

5. They threatened to kill to win a wager; he killed to pay
it; underminers: secret assailants.
6. Previously at lines 1151 and 1175.
7. Baal-zebub: God of the flies; a Philistine idol, with
temple at Ekron, 2 Kings 1.2. Unused: not used to hear-

ing "dishonors."
8. The plural form of Astareth, supreme goddess of the
Phoenicians representing fertility and passion; identical
with the Syrian Astarte.

1245   Stalking with less unconscionable° strides,   *excessive*
       And lower looks, but in a sultry chafe.
SAMSON I dread him not, nor all his giant-brood,
       Though fame divulge him father of five sons
       All of gigantic size, Goliah chief.⁹
CHORUS He will directly to the lords, I fear,
       And with malicious counsel stir them up
       Some way or other yet further to afflict thee.
SAMSON He must allege some cause, and offered fight
       Will not dare mention, lest a question rise
1255   Whether he durst accept the offer or not,
       And that he durst not plain enough appeared.
       Much more affliction then already felt
       They cannot well impose, nor I sustain;
       If they intend advantage of my labors
1260   The work of many hands, which earns my keeping
       With no small profit daily to my owners.
       But come what will, my deadliest foe will prove
       My speediest friend, by death to rid me hence,
       The worst that he can give, to me the best.
1265   Yet so it may fall out, because their end
       Is hate, not help to me, it may with mine
       Draw their own ruin who attempt the deed.
CHORUS Oh how comely it is¹ and how reviving
       To the Spirits of just men long opprest!
1270   When God into the hands of their deliverer
       Puts invincible might
       To quell the mighty of the earth, th' oppressor,
       The brute and boist'rous force of violent men
       Hardy and industrious to support
1275   Tyrannic power, but raging to pursue
       The righteous and all such as honor truth;
       He all their ammunition°   *military supplies*
       And feats of war defeats
       With plain heroic magnitude of mind
1280   And celestial vigor armed,
       Their armories and magazines contemns,
       Renders them useless, while
       With winged expedition
       Swift as the lightning glance he executes
1285   His errand on the wicked, who surprised
       Lose their defence distracted and amazed.
          But patience is more oft the exercise
       Of saints, the trial of their fortitude,
       Making them each his own deliverer,
1290   And victor over all
       That tryranny or fortune can inflict,
       Either of these is in thy lot,

9. See 2 Samuel 21.16–22.   1. See Ecclesiasticus 25.4–5: "O how comely a thing is
                                   judgment . . . O how comely is the wisdom of old men!"

Samson, with might endued
Above the sons of men; but sight bereaved
1295 May chance to number thee with those
Whom patience finally must crown.
This idol's day hath bin to thee no day of rest,
Laboring thy mind
More than the working day thy hands,
1300 And yet perhaps more trouble is behind.
For I descry this way
Some other tending, in his hand
A scepter or quaint° staff he bears,   *elaborate*
Comes on amain, speed in his look.
1305 By his habit I discern him now
A public officer, and now at hand.
His message will be short and voluble.°   *straightforward*
OFFICER Hebrews, the prisoner Samson here I seek.
CHORUS His manacles remark° him, there he sits.   *distinguish*
OFFICER Samson, to thee our lords thus bid me say;
This day to Dagon is a solemn feast,
With sacrifices, triumph, pomp, and games;
Thy strength they know surpassing human rate,
And now some public proof thereof require
1315 To honor this great feast and great assembly;
Rise therefore with all speed and come along,
Where I will see thee heartened and fresh clad
To appear as fits before th' illustrious lords.
SAMSON Thou knowst I am an Hebrew, therefore tell them,
1320 Our law forbids² at their religious rites
My presence; for that cause I cannot come.
OFFICER This answer, be assured, will not content them.
SAMSON Have they not sword-players, and every sort
Of gymnic° artists, wrestlers, riders, runners,   *gymnastic*
1325 Juglers and dancers, antics,° mummers,° mimics,   *clowns / mimes*
But they must pick me out with shackles tired,
And over-labored at their public mill,
To make them sport with blind activity?
Do they not seek occasion of new quarrels
1330 On my refusal to distress me more,
Or make a game of my calamities?
Return the way thou camest, I will not come.
OFFICER Regard thyself, this will offend them highly.
SAMSON My self? My conscience and internal peace.
1335 Can they think me so broken, so debased
With corporal servitude, that my mind ever
Will condescend to such absurd commands?
Although their drudge, to be their fool or jester,
And in my midst of sorrow and heart-grief
1340 To show them feats and play before their god,
The worst of all indignities, yet on me

2. See Exodus 20.4–5, 23.24.

Joined° with extreme contempt? I will not come.   *charged*
OFFICER My message was imposed on me with speed,
        Brooks no delay: is this thy resolution?
SAMSON So take it with what speed thy message needs.
OFFICER I am sorry what this stoutness° will produce.   *pride*
SAMSON Perhaps thou shalt have cause to sorrow indeed.
CHORUS Consider, Samson; matters now are strained
        Up to the height, whether to hold or break;
1350   He's gone, and who knows how he may report
        Thy words by adding fuel to the flame?
        Expect another message more imperious,
        More lordly thundering than thou well wilt bear.
SAMSON Shall I abuse this consecrated gift
1355   Of strength, again returning with my hair
        After my great transgression, so requite
        Favor renewed, and add a greater sin
        By prostituting holy things to idols;
        A Nazarite in place abominable
1360   Vaunting my strength in honor to their Dagon?
        Besides, how vile, contemptible, ridiculous,
        What act more execrably unclean, profane?
CHORUS Yet with this strength thou serv'st the Philistines,
        Idolatrous, uncircumcised, unclean.
SAMSON Not in their idol-worship, but by labor
        Honest and lawful to deserve my food
        Of those who have me in their civil power.
CHORUS Where the heart joins not, outward acts defile not.[3]
SAMSON Where outward force constrains, the sentence° holds   *maxim*
1370   But who constrains me to the temple of Dagon,
        Not dragging? the Philistian lords command.
        Commands are no constraints. If I obey them,
        I do it freely; venturing to displease
        God for the fear of man, and man prefer,
1375   Set God behind: which in his jealousy[4]
        Shall never, unrepented, find forgiveness.
        Yet that he may dispense with° me or thee   *grant pardon to*
        Present in temples at idolatrous rites
        For some important cause, thou needst not doubt.
CHORUS How thou wilt here come off° surmounts my reach.   *escape*
SAMSON Be of good courage, I begin to feel
        Some rousing motions in me which dispose
        To something extraordinary my thoughts.
        I with this messenger will go along,
1385   Nothing to do, be sure, that may dishonor
        Our law, or stain my vow of Nazarite.
        If there be aught of presage in the mind,
        This day will be remarkable in my life

3. See Aristotle, *Ethics* 3.1.1: "It is only voluntary actions for which praise and blame are given; those that are involuntary are condoned, and sometimes even pitied."

4. See Exodus 20.5: "I the Lord thy God am a jealous God."

By some great act, or of my days the last.[5]

CHORUS In time thou hast resolved, the man returns.

OFFICER Samson, this second message from our lords
        To thee I am bid say. Art thou our slave,
        Our captive, at the public mill our drudge,
        And dar'st thou at our sending and command
1395   Dispute thy coming? Come without delay;
        Or we shall find such engines to assail
        And hamper thee, as thou shalt come of force,
        Though thou wert firmlier fastened than a rock.

SAMSON I could be well content to try their art,
1400   Which to no few of them would prove pernicious.
        Yet knowing their advantages too many,
        Because they shall not trail me through their streets
        Like a wild beast, I am content to go.
        Masters' commands come with a power resistless
1405   To such as owe them absolute subjection;
        And for a life who will not change his purpose?
        (So mutable are all the ways of men.)
        Yet this be sure, in nothing to comply
        Scandalous or forbidden in our law.

OFFICER I praise thy resolution, doff these links:
        By this compliance thou wilt win the lords
        To favor, and perhaps to set thee free.

SAMSON Brethren farewell, your company along
        I will not wish, lest it perhaps offend them
1415   To see me girt with friends; and how the sight
        Of me as of a common enemy,
        So dreaded once, may now exasperate them
        I know not. Lords are lordliest in their wine;
        And the well-feasted priest then soonest fired
1420   With zeal, if aught religion seem concerned:
        No less the people on their holy-days
        Impetuous, insolent, unquenchable;[6]
        Happen what may, of me expect to hear
        Nothing dishonorable, impure, unworthy
1425   Our God, our law, my nation, or myself,
        The last of me or no I cannot warrant.

CHORUS Go, and the Holy One
        Of Israel be thy guide
        To what may serve his glory best, and spread his name
1430   Great among the heathen round:
        Send thee the angel of thy birth, to stand
        Fast by thy side, who from thy father's field
        Rode up in flames after his message told
        Of thy conception,[7] and be now a shield

---

5. Milton is perhaps indebted to Sophocles, *Trachiniae* 1169–73, where Heracles realizes that the oracle that foretold release from his labors meant death to him, not final prosperity.

6. See Horace, *Ars Poetica* 224: "The spectator, after the rites had been observed, was drunk and in a lawless mood."

7. See line 24ff.

1435   Of fire; that spirit that first rusht on thee
        In the camp of Dan[8]
        Be efficacious in thee now at need.
        For never was from heaven imparted
        Measure of strength so great to mortal seed,
1440   As in thy wond'rous actions hath been seen.
        But wherefore comes old Manoa in such haste
        With youthful steps? much livelier then erewhile
        He seems: supposing here to find his son,
        Or of him bringing to us some glad news?
MANOA Peace with you brethren; my inducement hither
        Was not at present here to find my son,
        By order of the lords new parted hence
        To come and play before them at their feast.
        I heard all as I came, the city rings
1450   And numbers thither flock, I had no will,
        Lest I should see him forced to things unseemly.
        But that which moved my coming now, was chiefly
        To give ye part with me what hope I have
        With good success° to work his liberty.   *outcome*
CHORUS That hope would much rejoice us to partake
        With thee; say, reverend sire, we thirst to hear.
MANOA I have attempted° one by one the lords   *sought to influence*
        Either at home, or through the high street passing,
        With supplication prone° and father's tears   *prostrated*
1460   To accept of ransom for my son their prisoner,
        Some much averse I found and wondrous harsh,
        Contemptuous, proud, set on revenge and spite;
        That part most reverenced Dagon and his priests,
        Others more moderate seeming, but their aim
1465   Private reward, for which both god and state
        They easily would set to sale, a third
        More generous far and civil, who confessed
        They had enough revenged, having reduced
        Their foe to misery beneath their fears,
1470   The rest was magnanimity to remit,
        If some convenient ransom were proposed.
        What noise or shout was that? it tore the sky.
CHORUS Doubtless the people shouting to behold
        Their once great dread, captive, and blind before them,
1475   Or at some proof of strength before them shown.
MANOA His ransom, if my whole inheritance
        May compass it, shall willingly be paid
        And numbered down: much rather I shall choose
        To live the poorest in my tribe, than richest,
1480   And he in that calamitous prison left.
        No, I am fixed not to part hence without him.
        For his redemption all my patrimony,
        If need be, I am ready to forgo

8. See Judges 13.25, also 14.6: "the Spirit of the Lord came mightily upon him."

And quit: not wanting him, I shall want nothing.
CHORUS Fathers are wont to lay up for their sons,
   Thou for thy son art bent to lay out all;
   Sons wont to nurse their parents in old age,
   Thou in old age carest how to nurse thy son
   Made older then thy age through eyesight lost.
MANOA It shall be my delight to tend his eyes,
   And view him sitting in the house, enobled
   With all those high exploits by him achieved,
   And on his shoulders waving down those locks,
   That of a nation armed the strength contained:
1495 And I persuade me God had not permitted
   His strength again to grow up with his hair
   Garrisoned round about him like a camp
   Of faithful soldiery, were not his purpose
   To use him further yet in some great service,
1500 Not to sit idle with so great a gift
   Useless, and thence ridiculous about him.
   And since his strength with eyesight was not lost,
   God will restore him eyesight to his strength.
CHORUS Thy hopes are not ill founded, nor seem vain
1505 Of his delivery, and thy joy thereon
   Conceived, agreeable to a father's love,
   In both which we, as next° participate.   *of kin*
MANOA I know your friendly minds and—O what noise!
   Mercy of heaven, what hideous noise was that!
1510 Horribly loud unlike the former shout.
CHORUS Noise call you it or universal groan
   As if the whole inhabitation perished,
   Blood, death, and deathful deeds are in that noise,
   Ruin, destruction at the utmost point.
MANOA Of ruin indeed methought I heard the noise,
   Oh it continues, they have slain my son.
CHORUS Thy Son is rather slaying them, that outcry
   From slaughter of one foe could not ascend.
MANOA Some dismal accident it needs must be;
1520 What shall we do, stay here or run and see?
CHORUS Best keep together here, lest running thither
   We unawares run into danger's mouth.[9]
   This evil on the Philistines is fallen,
   From whom could else a general cry be heard?
1525 The sufferers then will scarce molest us here,
   From other hands we need not much to fear.
   What if his eyesight (for to Israel's God
   Nothing is hard) by miracle restored,
   He now be dealing dole[1] among his foes,
1530 And over heaps of slaughtered walk his way?
MANOA That were a joy presumptuous to be thought.
CHORUS Yet God hath wrought things as incredible

---

9. There is a similarly hesitant chorus in Euripides, *Hippolytus* 782–85.

1. A pun; "dole" means "that which is dealt" and also "grief, pain."

For his people of old; what hinders now?
MANOA He can, I know, but doubt to think he will;
1535   Yet Hope would fain subscribe, and tempts belief.
    A little stay will bring some notice hither.
CHORUS Of good or bad so great, of bad the sooner;
    For evil news rides post, while good news baits.°   *travels slowly*
    And to our wish I see one hither speeding,
1540   An Hebrew, as I guess, and of our tribe.
MESSENGER O whither shall I run, or which way fly
    The sight of this so horrid spectacle
    Which erst my eyes beheld and yet behold;
    For dire imagination still persues me.
1545   But providence or instinct of nature seems,
    Or reason though disturbed, and scarse consulted
    To have guided me aright, I know not how,
    To thee first reverend Manoa, and to these
    My Countrymen, whom here I knew remaining,
1550   As at some distance from the place of horror,
    So in the sad event too much concerned.
MANOA The accident was loud, and here before thee
    With rueful cry, yet what it was we hear not,
    No preface needs, thou seest we long to know.
MESSENGER It would burst forth, but I recover breath
    And sense distract, to know well what I utter.
MANOA Tell us the sum, the circumstance defer.
MESSENGER Gaza yet stands, but all her sons are fallen,
    All in a moment overwhelmed and fallen.
MANOA Sad, but thou knowst to Israelites not saddest
    The desolation of a hostile city.
MESSENGER Feed on that first, there may in grief be surfeit.[2]
MANOA Relate by whom.
MESSENGER   By Samson.
MANOA   That still lessens
    The sorrow, and converts it nigh to joy.
MESSENGER Ah, Manoa, I refrain, too suddenly
    To utter what will come at last too soon;
    Lest evil tidings with too rude irruption°   *bursting in*
    Hitting thy aged ear should pierce too deep.
MANOA Suspense in news is torture, speak them out.
MESSENGER Then take the worst in brief: Samson is dead.[3]
MANOA The worst indeed, O all my hope's defeated
    To free him hence! but death who sets all free
    Hath paid his ransom now and full discharge.
    What windy° joy this day had I conceived   *vain*
1575   Hopeful of his delivery, which now proves
    Abortive as the first-born bloom of spring
    Nipped with the lagging rear of winter's frost.[4]

---

2. Echoes Shakespeare's *Two Gentlemen of Verona* 3.1.220–1: "O, I have fed upon this woe already, / And now excess of it will make me surfeit."
3. See the announcement of Orestes' death in Sophocles,

Electra 673: "In short, Orestes is dead."
4. Echoing *Love's Labour's Lost* 1.1.100–101: "An envious-sneaping frost, / That bites the first born infants of the spring."

Yet ere I give the rains to grief, say first,
How died he? death to life is crown or shame.
1580 All by him fell, thou say'st, by whom fell he,
What glorious hand gave Samson his death's wound?
MESSENGER Unwounded of his enemies he fell.
MANOA Wearied with slaughter then, or how? Explain.
MESSENGER By his own hands.
MANOA   Self-violence? What cause
1585   Brought him so soon at variance with himself
Among his foes?
MESSENGER   Inevitable cause
At once both to destroy and be destroyed;
The edifice where all were met to see him
Upon their heads and on his own he pulled.
MANOA O lastly over-strong against thy self!
A dreadful way thou took'st to thy revenge.
More than enough we know; but while things yet
Are in confusion, give us if thou canst,
Eye-witness of what first or last was done,
1595   Relation more particular and distinct.
MESSENGER Occasions° drew me early to this city,   *business*
And as the gates I entered with sun-rise,
The morning trumpets festival proclaimed
Through each high street: little° I had dispatched   *little business*
1600   When all abroad was rumored that this day
Samson should be brought forth to show the people
Proof of his mighty strength in feats and games;
I sorrowed at his captive state, but minded
Not to be absent at that spectacle.
1605   The building was a spacious theatre
Half round on two main pillars vaulted high,
With seats where all the lords and each degree
Of sort, might sit in order to behold,
The other side was open, where the throng
1610   On banks° and scaffolds under sky might stand;[5]   *benches*
I among these aloof obscurely stood.
The feast and noon grew high, and sacrifice
Had filled their hearts with mirth, high cheer, and wine,
When to their sports they turned. Immediately
1615   Was Samson as a public servant brought,
In their state livery clad; before him pipes
And timbrels, on each side went armed guards,
Both horse and foot before him and behind
Archers, and slingers, cataphracts° and spears.°   *soldiers / spearsmen*
1620   At sight of him the people with a shout
Rifted the air clamoring their god with praise,
Who had made their dreadful enemy their thrall.
He patient but undaunted where they led him,
Came to the place, and what was set before him
1625   Which without help of eye, might be assayed,

5. See Judges 16.27, where the building is called a "house" and has 3,000 men and women on the roof.

To heave, pull, draw, or break, he still performed
All with incredible, stupendious force,
None daring to appear antagonist.
At length for intermission sake they led him
1630   Between the pillars; he his guide requested
(For so from such as nearer stood we heard)
As overtired to let him lean a while
With both his arms on those two massy pillars
That to the arched roof gave main support.[6]
1635   He unsuspicious led him; which when Samson
Felt in his arms, with head a while inclined,
And eyes fast fixed he stood, as one who prayed,[7]
Or some great matter in his mind revolved.
At last with head erect thus cried aloud,
1640   "Hitherto, Lords, what your commands imposed
I have performed, as reason was, obeying,
Not without wonder or delight beheld.
Now of my own accord such other trial
I mean to show you of my strength, yet greater;
1645   As with amaze° shall strike all who behold."   *confusion*
This uttered, straining all his nerves he bowed,
As with the force of winds and waters pent,
When mountains tremble, those two massy pillars
With horrible convulsion to and fro
1650   He tugged, he shook, till down they came and drew
The whole roof after them, with burst of thunder
Upon the heads of all who sat beneath,
Lords, ladies, captains, councellors, or priests,
Their choice nobility and flower, not only
1655   Of this but each Philistian city round
Met from all parts to solemnize this feast.
Samson with these immixed, inevitably
Pulled down the same destruction on himself;
The vulgar° only scaped who stood without.[8]   *commoners*
CHORUS O dearly-bought revenge, yet glorious!
Living or dying thou hast fulfilled
The work for which thou wast foretold
To Israel, and now liest victorious
Among thy slain self-killed
1665   Not willingly, but tangled in the fold
Of dire necessity, whose law in death conjoined
Thee with thy slaughtered foes in number more
Then all thy life had slain before.[9]
SEMICHORUS While their hearts were jocund and sublime,°   *exalted*
1670   Drunk with idolatry, drunk with wine,
And fat regorged° of bulls and goats,   *reswallowed*

6. See Judges 16.26: "And Samson said unto the lad that held him by the hand, Suffer me that I may feel the pillars whereupon the house standeth, that I may lean upon them."
7. In Judges 16.30, Samson prays: "Let me [Hebrew: "my soul"] die with the Philistines." The speech, with its suicidal implications, was one of the major obstacles to those who wished to regard Samson as a saint. In the Scholastic period his suicide was excused as the prompting of the Holy Ghost.
8. Not found in the scriptural account (Judges 16.30).
9. See Judges 16.30: "The dead which he slew at his death were more than they which he slew in his life."

Chaunting their idol, and preferring
Before our living Dread who dwells
In Silo[1] his bright sanctuary:
1675 Among them he a spirit of frenzy sent,
Who hurt their minds,
And urged them on with mad desire
To call in haste for their destroyer;
They only set on sport and play
1680 Unweetingly importuned
Their own destruction to come speedy upon them.
So fond° are mortal men   foolish
Fallen into wrath divine,
As their own ruin on themselves to invite,
1685 Insensate left, or to sense reprobate,[2]
And with blindness internal struck.
SEMICHORUS But he though blind of sight,
Despised and thought extinguished quite,
With inward eyes illuminated
1690 His fiery virtue roused
From under ashes into sudden flame,
And as an evening dragon° came,   huge python
Assailant on the perched roosts,
And nests in order ranged
1695 Of tame villatic° fowl; but as an eagle   farmyard
His cloudless thunder bolted on their heads.
So virtue given for lost,
Depressed, and overthrown, as seemed,
Like that self-begotten bird[3]
1700 In the Arabian woods embossed,°   sheltered
That no second knows nor third,[4]
And lay erewhile a holocaust,[5]
From out her ashy womb now teemed,°   delivered
Revives, reflourishes, then vigorous most
1705 When most unactive deemed,
And though her body die, her fame survives,
A secular° bird, ages of lives.   centuries-long
MANOA Come, come, no time for lamentation now,
Nor much more cause; Samson hath quit himself
1710 Like Samson, and heroicly hath finished
A life heroic, on his enemies
Fully revenged, hath left them years of mourning,
And lamentation to the sons of Caphtor[6]
Through all Philistian bounds. To Israel
1715 Honour hath left, and freedom, let but them
Find courage to lay hold on this occasion,

1. Where the ark remained from the time of Joshua until "the people sent to Shiloh, that they might bring from thence the ark of the covenant" (1 Samuel 4.4).
2. Either left senseless, or left to a reprobate sense; see Romans 1.28: "God gave them over to a reprobate mind."
3. The Phoenix, a symbol of resurrection. See Geoffrey

Whitney, The Phoenix, in Perspectives: Emblem, Style and Metaphor, page 1599.
4. Only one phoenix lives at a time.
5. A thing wholly consumed by fire.
6. The Philistines; see line 380.

To himself and father's house eternal fame;
And which is best and happiest yet, all this
With God not parted from him, as was feared,
1720   But favoring and assisting to the end.
Nothing is here for tears, nothing to wail
Or knock the breast, no weakness, no contempt,
Dispraise, or blame, nothing but well and fair,
And what may quiet us in a death so noble.
1725   Let us go find the body where it lies
Soaked in his enemies' blood, and from the stream
With lavers° pure and cleansing herbs wash off   *washbasins*
The clotted gore. I with what speed° the while   *what speed I can*
(Gaza is not in plight to say us nay)
1730   Will send for all my kindred, all my friends
To fetch him hence and solemnly attend
With silent obsequy° and funeral train   *burial rite*
Home to his father's house:[7] there will I build him
A monument, and plant it round with shade
1735   Of laurel ever green, and branching palm,
With all his trophies hung, and acts enrolled
In copious legend, or sweet lyric song.
Thither shall all the valiant youth resort,
And from his memory inflame their breasts
1740   To matchless valor, and adventures high:
The virgins also shall on feastful days
Visit his tomb with flowers, only bewailing
His lot unfortunate in nuptial choice,
From whence captivity and loss of eyes.
CHORUS All is best, though we oft doubt,
What th' unsearchable dispose
Of highest wisdom brings about,
And ever best found in the close.[8]
Oft he seems to hide his face,[9]
1750   But unexpectedly returns
And to his faithful champion hath in place°   *at hand*
Bore witness gloriously; whence Gaza mourns
And all that band them to resist
His uncontrollable intent,
1755   His servants he with new acquist°   *acquisition*
Of true experience from this great event
With peace and consolation hath dismissed,
And calm of mind all passion spent.[1]

The End.

7. See Judges 16.31: "Then his brethren and all the house of his father came down, and took him, and brought him up, and buried him."
8. See the closing chorus of Euripides, *Alcestis* 1160–64: "Manifold things unhoped-for the gods to accomplishment bring . . . So fell this marvelous thing." The same chorus is used at the end of *Andromache, Bacchae, Helen,* and in *Medea* (with a different first line: "All dooms be of Zeus in Olympus: 'tis his to reveal them").

9. See Psalm 104.29: "Thou hidest thy face, they are troubled" (also Psalm 30.7 and 27.9).
1. The poem ends in the rhyme scheme of a sonnet, which is noteworthy considering Milton's argument on "The Verse" prefacing *Paradise Lost:* "Rime being no necessary Adjunct or true Ornament of Poem or good Verse . . . , but the Invention of a barbarous Age, to set off wretched matter and lame meter."

PERSPECTIVES

Spiritual Self-Reckonings

As the title of this section suggests, autobiographical writing in early modern England was tied to religious experience, the individual, and the act of reckoning. Just as the Civil War was fought largely over religious differences, so allegiance to a particular interpretation of Christianity, usually tied to a specific institution and set of beliefs and practices, was one of the chief shapers of identity in the seventeenth century. All the accounts in this section relate a life as lived from the perspective of belief—from Elizabeth Cary's conversion to Catholicism to John Bunyan's Puritan salvation by grace, from Anna Trapnel's ecstatic visions to the preacher Ralph Josselin's sober reflections on his daily blessings. The fictional Robinson Crusoe experiences a dramatic conversion on being saved from death by drowning, just as Alice Thornton renews her trust in salvation every time she recovers from the sickness brought on by the death of a child or a near-fatal labor.

The status of the self is necessarily qualified by religion; it is impossible to speak of self-knowledge in isolation from knowledge of God in this period. The selves that are described in these accounts are shaped by the literary forms their narratives take. In the case of Elizabeth Cary, Lady Falkland, her daughter chose to tell her story as a kind of spiritual biography, in which all the events, even including her quarrels with Calvinist theology in youth, tend to converge on the moment of her conversion. In some sense the mother's story may also be a way for the daughter, a Benedictine nun as well as a convert to Catholicism, to witness her own religious experience. For Anna Trapnel the life story takes the form of a testimonial that relates her trial for witchcraft, a drama of persecution from which she emerges triumphant in her reliance on God. Diarists such as Alice Thornton and Ralph Josselin also rely on God as they struggle with their daily trials. Among these is often the struggle for life itself, as in the pregnancies and labors of Alice Thornton and of Ralph Josselin's wife. With Bunyan and Defoe, autobiography is fictionalized as both travel novel and salvational allegory. Both heroes are on journeys; both journeys, according to the authors, have allegorical significance.

The other major influence on these life stories is the rise of a certain way of accounting for material experience—that of time and of money. Reckoning entails counting, calculating, and recording. The journals of Alice Thornton and Ralph Josselin record dates. In his journal, Robinson Crusoe keeps a strict record of the number of days since his shipwreck. If Ralph Josselin reckons his capital in gains and debits, he also reckons his blessings to shore himself up against his losses. Similarly, Robinson Crusoe takes stock of himself by writing a ledger of his spiritual goods and evils. The language of credit gains importance toward the close of the century. As England becomes not just the battleground of saints, as it was in the Civil War, but the seat of empire, as it develops as a world trader and a colonial power, the "self" expresses itself in relation to Lady Credit as well as the Lord.

----- ⟨◆⟩ -----

The Lady Falkland: Her Life

The Lady Falkland: Her Life is the first known biography of an Englishwoman by a woman. The text survives in a manuscript located in the Archives of the Départment du Nord in Lille, France, a collection that contains documents from the Benedictine monastery of Our Blessed Lady of Consolation in Cambray, where four of Elizabeth Cary's six daughters became Benedictine nuns. Donald Foster has connected the italic hand of the manuscript with Anne Cary, who was born in 1615 and entered the convent in 1639. However, Margaret Ferguson and Barry Weller argue that Lucy Cary cannot be ruled out as possible author, since her obituary makes reference to the "Life of Lady Falkland," written by "one who knew her well."

The passage reprinted here, from the first half of the biography, highlights Elizabeth Cary's intellectual precociousness, theological questioning, obedience to her husband, devotion to her children, and, above all, her strong spiritual life despite her many trials. One of the most palpable expressions of Cary's spirituality was her philanthropy in Ireland. When her husband was Lord Deputy there (1622–29), Elizabeth set up a trade school to help poor children. In a characteristically seventeenth-century God-centered view of life, Cary, according to her daughter, viewed the failure of the enterprise as God's punishment for the forced conversion of the children from Catholicism to Protestantism. Although the selection here stops short of Cary's own conversion from Protestantism to Catholicism, her daughter writes from the perspective of that change as the defining event of her mother's spiritual life.

from The Lady Falkland Her Life, by one of Her Daughters

Her mother's name was Elizabeth Symondes. She was their only child. She was christened Elizabeth. She learnt to read very soon and loved it much. When she was but four or five year old they put her to learn French, which she did about five weeks and, not profiting at all, gave it over. After, of herself, without a teacher, whilst she was a child, she learnt French, Spanish, Italian, which she always understood very perfectly. She learnt Latin in the same manner (without being taught) and understood it perfectly when she was young, and translated the Epistles of Seneca out of it into English; after having long discontinued it, she was much more imperfect in it, so as a little afore her death, translating some (intending to have done it all had she lived) of Blosius[1] out of Latin, she was fain to help herself somewhat with the Spanish translation. Hebrew she likewise, about the same time, learnt with very little teaching; but for many year neglecting it, she lost it much; yet not long before her death, she again beginning to use it, could in the Bible understand well, in which she was most perfectly well read. She then learnt also, of a Transylvanian, his language, but never finding any use of it, forgot it entirely. She was skilful and curious in working,[2] ⟨but⟩ never having been helped by anybody; those that knew her would never have believed she knew how to hold a needle unless they had seen it.

Being once present when she was ⟨about⟩ ten year old, when a poor old woman was brought before her father for a witch, and, being accused for having bewitched two or 3 to death, the witness not being found convincing, her father asked the woman what she said for herself? She falling down before him trembling and weeping confessed all to be true, desiring him to be good to her and she would mend. Then he asking her particularly, did you bewitch such a one to death? she answered yes. He asked her how she did it? One of her accusers, preventing her, said, "Did not you send your familiar in the shape of a black dog, a hare or a ⟨toad?⟩ cat, and he finding him asleep, licked his hand, or breathed on him, or stepped over him, and he presently came home sick and languished away?" She, quaking, begging pardon, acknowledged all, and the same of each particular accusation, with a several manner of doing it. Then the standers-by said, what would they have more than her own confession? But the child, seeing the poor woman in so terrible a fear, and in so simple a manner confess all, thought fear had made her idle,[3] so she whispered her father and desired him to ask her whether she had bewitched to death Mr John Symondes of such a place

1. Louis de Blois (1506–66), Benedictine mystic and author of devotional works such as *Institutio Spiritualis* ("Spiritual Instruction") and *Consolatio Pusillanimium* ("Comfort for the Fainthearted").

2. Needleworking. In the next phrase and onward, angle brackets indicate likely readings of illegible words in the manuscript.

3. Delirious.

(her uncle that was one of the standers-by). He did so, to which she said yes, just as she had done to the rest, promising to do so no more if they would have pity on her. He asked how she did it? She told one of her former stories; then (all the company laughing) he asked her what she ailed to say so? told her the man was alive, and stood there. She cried, "Alas, sir, I knew him not, I said so because you asked me." Then he, "Are you no witch then?" ⟨⟨says he⟩⟩ "No, God knows," says she, "I know no more what belongs to it than the child newborn." "Nor did you never see the devil?" She answered, "No, God bless me, never in all my life." Then he examined her what she meant to confess all this, if it were false? She answered they had threatened her if she would not confess, and said, if she would, she should have mercy showed her— which she said with such simplicity that (the witness brought against her being of lit-tle force, and her own confession appearing now to be of less) she was easily believed innocent, and [ac]quitted.

She having neither brother nor sister, nor other companion of her age, spent her whole time in reading; to which she gave herself so much that she frequently read all night; so as her mother was fain to forbid her servants to let her have candles, which command they turned to their own profit, and let themselves be hired by her to let her have them, selling them to her at half a crown apiece, so was she bent to reading; and she not having money so free, was to owe it them, and in this fashion was she in debt a hundred pound afore she was twelve year old, which with two hundred more ⟨afore⟩ for the like bargains and promises she paid on her wedding day; this will not seem strange to those that knew her well. When she was twelve year old, her father (who loved much to have her read, and she as much to please him) gave her Calvin's *Institutions*[4] and bid her read it, against which she made so many objections, and found in him so many contradictions, and with all of them she still went to her father, that he said, "This girl hath a spirit averse from Calvin."

At fifteen year old, her father married her to one Sir Harry Cary (son to Sir Edward Cary of Barkhamsteed in Harfordshire), then Master of the Jewel House to Queen Elizabeth. He married her only for being an heir, for he had no acquaintance with her (she scarce ever having spoke to him) and she was nothing handsome, though then very fair. The first year or more she lived at her own father's; her hus-band about that time went into Holland, leaving her ⟨there⟩ still with her own friends.[5] He, in the time they had been married, had been for the most part at the court or his father's house, from her, and ⟨so⟩ had heard her speak little, and those letters he had received from her had been indited by others, by her mother's appoint-ment, so he knew her then very little.

Soon after his being gone, his mother must needs have her to her, and, her friends not being able to satisfy the mother-in-law with any excuse, were fain to send her; though her husband had left her with them till his return, knowing his own mother well, and desiring (though he did not care for his wife) to have her be where she should be best content. Her mother-in-law having her, and being one that loved much to be humored, and finding her not to apply herself to it, used her very hardly, so far, as at last, to confine her to her chamber; which seeing she little cared for, but entertained herself with reading, the mother-in-law took away all her books, with command to have no more brought her; then she set herself to make verses. There was only two in the whole house (besides her own servants) that ever came to see

---

4. *Institutes of the Christian Religion* (1536) defines the central doctrines of Calvinist theology, including moral election and predestination for redemption.
5. Relatives.

her, which they did by stealth: one of her husband's sisters and a gentlewoman that waited on her mother-in-law. (To the first of them, she always, all her life after, showed herself a very true friend in all occasions wheresoever she was able ⟨to⟩; of the other (being gone from her mother-in-law's service) she never gave over to take care till she died, she [the gentlewoman] having continual recourse to her when she had need, who ever provided her places with her children or friends, and helped her in the meantime.) But her husband returning (who had been taken prisoner in the Low Countries by the Spaniards, and carried prisoner into Spain, where he was kept a year whilst his father was raising his ransom),[6] all this was soon at an end, he being much displeased to see her so used.

In his absence he had received some letters from her, since she came from her mother, which seemed to him to be in a very different style from the former, which he had thought to have been her own. These he liked much, but believed some other did them, till, having examined her about it and found the contrary, he grew better acquainted with her and esteemed her more. From this time she writ many things for her private recreation, on several subjects, and occasions, all in verse (out of which she scarce ever writ anything that was not translations). One of them was after stolen out of that sister-in-law's (her friend's) chamber and printed, but by her own procurement was called in. Of all she then writ, that which was said to be the best was the life of Tamberlaine in verse.[7]

She continued to read much, and when she was about twenty year old, through reading, she grew into much doubt of her religion. The first occasion of it was reading a Protestant book much esteemed, called Hooker's *Ecclesiastical Polity*.[8] It seemed to her, he left her hanging in the air, for having brought her so far (which she thought he did very reasonably), she saw not how, nor at what, she could stop, till she returned to the church from whence they were come. This was more confirmed in her by a brother of her husband's returning out of Italy, with a good opinion of Catholic religion. His wit, judgment and ⟨company⟩ conversation she was much pleased withal. He was a great reader of the Fathers, especially St Augustine, whom he affirmed to be of the religion of the Church of Rome. He persuaded her to read the Fathers also (what she had read till then having been for the most part poetry and history, except Seneca, and some other such, whose Epistles it is probable she translated afore she left her father's house, because the only copy of it was found by her son in her father's study)—which she did upon his persuasion, all that she could meet with in French, Spanish or Italian. It may be she might then read some in Latin, but for many year only in the others.

Her distrust of her religion increased by reading them, so far as that at two several times she refused to go to church for a long while together. The first time she satisfied herself she might continue as she was, having a great mind to do so. The second time, going much to the house of a Protestant bishop,[9] which was frequented by many of the learnedest of their divines (out of the number of whose chaplains, those of the King's were frequently chosen, and some of their greatest bishops), she there grew acquaint[ed] with many of them, making great account of them, and using them with much respect (being ever more inclined to do so to any for their learning and

---

6. Spanish troops captured Henry Cary in October 1605, when he was fighting with a joint English-Dutch force.
7. Tamerlane (1336–1405), the Mongol military leader whose conquests are the subject of Christopher Marlowe's *Tamberlaine the Great*, Parts I and II (1587–1588).

8. Richard Hooker wrote *Of the Laws of Ecclesiastical Polity* (Books 1–4, 1593; Book 5, 1597) to defend the bishops of the Church of England.
9. Richard Neile, dean of Westminster (1605) and archbishop of York (1631).

worth, than for their greatness of quality, and she had learnt in the Fathers, and histories of former Christian times to bear a high reverence to the dignity they pretended to). By them she was persuaded she might lawfully remain as she was, she never making question for all that but that to be in the Roman Church were infinitely better and securer. Thus (from the first) she remained about two and twenty year, flattering herself with good intentions. She was in the house of the same bishop divers times present at the examination of such beginners, or receivers, of new opinions, as were by them esteemed heretics, where some (strangers to her), wondering to see her, asked the bishop how he durst trust that young lady to be there? who answered, he would warrant she would never be in danger to be an heretic, so much honor and adherence did she ever render to authority, where she ⟨conceived⟩ imagined it to be, much more where she knew it to be.

She was married seven year without any child; after, had eleven born alive.[1] When she had some children, she and her husband went to keep house by themselves, where she, taking the care of her family, which at first was but little, did seem to show herself capable of what she would apply herself to. She was very careful and diligent in the disposition of the affairs of her house of all sorts; and she herself would work hard, together with her women and her maids, curious pieces of work, teaching them and directing all herself; nor was her care of her children less, to whom she was so much a mother that she nursed them all herself, but only her eldest son[2] (whom her father took from her to live with him from his birth), and she taught 3 or 4 of the eldest. After, having other occasions to divert her, she left that to others, of whose care long experience might make her confident, for she never changed her servants about them, and whilst she was with them she was careful nothing in that kind might be wanting.

Her first care was (whether by herself or others) to have them soon inclined to the knowledge, love, and esteem of all moral virtue; and to have them according to their capacities instructed in the principles of Christianity, not in manner of a catechism (which would have instructed them in the particular Protestant doctrines, of the truth of which she was little satisfied), but in a manner more apt to make an impression in them (than things learnt by rote and not understood), as letting them know, when they loved anything, that they were to love God more than it; that he made it, and them, and all things; they must love him, and honor him, more than their father; he gave them their father, he sent them every good thing, and made it for them; the King was his servant, he made all kings, and gave them their kingdom[s?].

* * *

Being once like to die, whilst she had but two or 3 children, and those very little, that her care of them might not die with her, she writ (directed to her two eldest, a daughter and a son) a letter of some sheets of paper (to be given them when they were come to a more capable age), full of such moral precepts as she judged most proper for them, and such effect had this care of hers in the mind of her eldest daughter (for the forming of whose spirit and her instruction (though she were of a good nature) she had taken extraordinary pains, and ever found her again the most dutiful and best loving of all her children), that being married afore she was thirteen year old, and going then to live in the house of her mother-in-law (in which she yielded a great obedience to her father's will) where she lived till her death (which was

---

1. She had five sons and six daughters.
2. Lucius Cary (1610–1643), second Viscount Falkland,

about whom Ben Jonson wrote in the *Cary-Morison Ode* (page 1538).

between sixteen and seventeen year old, in childbed of her first child), she being exceedingly beloved by her mother-in-law and all her family, her own mother asked her what she had done to gain all their affections in so great a degree? She said, indeed, she knew not anything that she did, unless that she had been careful to observe, as exactly as she could, the rule she had given her, when she took her leave of her at her first going from her: that wheresoever conscience and reason would permit her, she should prefer the will of another before her own.

Neither did she neglect to have those that were of a bigness capable of it (whilst she was with them) learn all those things that might be fit for them. She always thought it a most misbecoming thing in a mother to make herself more her business than her children and, whilst she had care of herself, to neglect them. Her doing was most contrary to this, being excessive in all that concerned their clothes or recreation, and she that never (not in her youth) could take care or delight in her own fineness, could apply herself to have too much care and take pleasure in theirs.

To her husband she bore so much respect that she taught her children, as a duty, to love him better than herself; and, though she saw it was a lesson they could learn without teaching, and that all but her eldest son did it in a very high degree, it never lessened her love or kindness to any of them. He was very absolute, and though she had a strong will, she had learnt to make it obey his. The desire to please him ⟨would⟩ had power to make her do that, that others would have scarce believed possible for her: as taking care of her house in all things (to which she could have no inclination but what his will gave her); the applying herself to use and love work;[3] and, being most fearful of a horse, both before and after, she did (he loving hunting and desiring to have her a good horsewoman) for many year ride so much, and so desperately, as if she had no fear but much delight in it; and so she had, to see him pleased, and did really make herself love it as long as that lasted. But after (as before) she neither had the courage, nor the skill, to sit upon a horse; ⟨and he left to desire it, after her having had a fall from her horse (leaping a hedge and ditch being with child of her fourth child, when she was taken up for dead though both she and her child did well), she being continually after as long as she lived with him either with child or giving suck⟩.

Dressing was all her life a torture to her, yet because he would have it so, she willingly supported it, all the while she lived with him, in her younger days, even to tediousness; but all that ever she could do towards it, was to have those about her that could do it well, and to take order that it should be done, and then endure the trouble; for though she was very careful it should be so, she was not able to attend to it all, nor ever was her mind the least engaged in it, but her women were fain to walk round the room after her (which was her custom) while she was seriously thinking on some other business, and pin on her things and braid her hair; and while she writ or read, curl her hair and dress her head; and it did sufficiently appear how alone for his will she did undergo the trouble by the extraordinary great carelessness she had of herself after he was angry with her, from which time she never went out of plain black, frieze or coarse stuff, or cloth.

Where his interest was concerned, she seemed not able to have any consideration of her own; which amongst other things, she showed in this: a considerable part of her jointure[4] (which upon her marriage had been made sufficiently good) having been reassumed to the crown, to which it had formerly belonged, a greater part of it (being all that remained, but some very small thing) she did on his occasions consent

---

3. Needlework.   4. The holding of property by a wife to be granted her in widowhood.

to have mortgaged; which act of hers did so displease her own father that he disinherited her upon it, putting before her, her two eldest (and then only) sons, tying his estate on the eldest and, in case he failed,[5] on the second. She showed herself always no less ready to avoid whatsoever might displease him. Of this all her life she gave many proofs; and after she was a Catholic, when he would neither speak to her nor see her, she forbore things most ordinarily done by all, and which she did much delight in, for hearing from some other that he seemed to dislike it; and where she did but apprehend it would not please him, she would not do the least thing, though on good occasion; so as she seemed to prefer nothing but religion and her duty to God before his will. The rules which she did, in some things she writ (and in her opinions), seem to think fit to be held in this, did displease many as overstrict. She did always much disapprove ⟨a⟩ the practice ⟨with⟩ of satisfying oneself with their conscience being free from fault, not forbearing all that might have the least show, ⟨of unfit⟩ or suspicion, of uncomeliness, or unfitness; what she thought to be required in this she expressed in this motto (which she caused [to be inscribed] in her daughter's wedding ring): be and seem.

In this time she had some occasions of trouble, which afflicted her so much as twice to put her into so deep melancholy ⟨(while she was with child of her 2$^{\rm d}$ and 4$^{\rm th}$ child) that she lost the perfect use of her reason, and was in much danger of her life. She had ground for the beginning of her apprehensions, but she giving full way to them (which were always apt to go as far as she would let them), they arrived so far as to be plain distractedness. It is like she at first gave the more way to it at those times, thinking her husband would then be most sensible of her trouble, knowing he was extraordinary careful of her when she was with child or gave suck, as being a most tenderly loving father.⟩ One of these times for fourteen days together she eat nor drunk nothing in the world, but only a little beer with a toast, yet without touching the toast, so as being great with child and quick, the child left to stir, and she became as flat as if she had not been with child at all. Yet after, coming out of her melancholy, the child and she did well.

From this time she seemed so far to have overcome all sadness that she was scarce ever subject to it on any occasion (but only once), but always looked on the best side of everything, and what good every accident brought with it. Her greatest sign of sadness (after) was sleeping, which she was used to say she could do when she would, and then had most will to when she had occasion to have sad thoughts waking; which she much sought to avoid, and it seemed could (for the most part) do it, when she gave herself to it; and she could well divert others in occasions of trouble, having sometimes with her conversation much lightened the grief of some, suddenly, in that which touched them nearliest. This occasion of her own trouble being past, she did so far pardon the causers of it as to some of them she showed herself a most faithful and constant friend, to others so careful a provider and reliever in their necessities that she was by some (that knew her but afar off, and were not witness of what she had suffered) thought almost guilty of their faults.

She continued the care of her house till, her husband being made Controller of the King's Household, she came to live frequently at his lodgings at court; and her father-in-law dying, their family being increased, she put it into the hands of others. She continued her opinion of religion, and bore a great and high reverence to our Blessed Lady, to whom, being with child of her last daughter[6] (and still a Protestant) she offered up that child, promising if it were a girl it should (in devotion to her) bear

---

5. Died without a male heir.   6. Mary Cary, born c. 1621.

her name, and that as much as was in her power, she would endeavor to have it be a nun. Whilst she yet gave suck to the same child, she went into Ireland,[7] with her lord and all her children, except her eldest daughter (who, just before her going, was married into Scotland). Being there, she had much affection to that nation, and was very desirous to have made use of ⟨her⟩ what power she had on any occasion in their behalf, as also in that of any Catholics. She there learnt to read Irish in an Irish Bible; but it being very hard (so as she could scarce find one that could teach it) and few books in it, she quickly lost what she had learnt.

Here chiefly the desire of the benefit and commodity of that nation set her upon a great design. It was to bring up the use of all trades in that country, which is fain to be beholding to others for the smallest commodities. To this end she procured some of each kind to come from those other places where those trades are exercised (as several sorts of linen and woolen weavers, dyers, all sorts of spinners, and knitters, hatters, lace makers, and many other trades) at the very beginning; and for this purpose she took of beggar children (with which that country swarms) more than 8 score prentices, refusing none above seven year old, and taking some less. These were disposed to their several masters and mistresses to learn those trades they were thought most fit for, the least amongst them being set to something, as making points, tags, buttons, or lace, or some other thing. They were parted in their several rooms and houses, where they exercised their trades, many rooms being filled with little boys or girls, sitting all round at work; besides those that were bigger, for trades needing more understanding and strength. She brought it to that pass that they there made broadcloth so fine and good (of Irish wool, and spun and weaved and dyed and dressed there) that her Lord, being Deputy, wore it.

Yet it came to nothing; which she imputed to a judgment of God on her, because the overseers made all those poor children go to church; and she had great losses by fire and water (which she judged extraordinary, others but casual).[8] Her workhouse, with all that was in it, much cloth and much materials, was burnt; her fulling mills carried away; and much of her things spoiled with water—all which when she was a Catholic she took to be the punishment of God for the children's going to church, and that therefore her business did not succeed. But others thought it rather that she was better at contriving than executing, and that too many things were undertaken at the very first, and that she was fain (having little choice) to employ either those that had little skill in the matters they dealt in, or less honesty, and so she was extremely cozened,[9] which she was most easily, though she were not a little suspicious in her nature; but chiefly the ill order she took for paying money in this (as in all other occasions). Having the worst memory, in such things, in the world, and wholly trusting to it (or them she dealt with), and never keeping any account of what she did, she was most subject to pay the same thing often (as she hath had it confessed to her, by some, that they have (in a small matter) made her pay them the same thing five times in five days). Neither would she suffer herself to be undeceived by them that stood by and saw her do it frequently; rather suspecting they said it out of dislike of her designs, and to divert her from them; and the same unwillingness she had to see she was cozened, in all things on which she was set with such violence (as she was on all the things she undertook, which were many), which violence in all

---

7. Henry Cary's tenure as Lord Deputy of Ireland (1622–1629) was characterized by such policies as the suppression of the Roman Catholic clergy and continued colonization.

8. She thought these events were due to God's anger while others saw them as accidents.
9. Tricked or deceived.

occasions made her ever subject to necessities (even when she had most), and made her continually pawn and sell anything she had (though it were a thing she should need (almost) within an hour after) to procure what she had a mind to at the present: the same violence made her subject to make great promises to those that assisted her in those things which, being many, could not always be performed. It made her, too, to acknowledge small things, done at the instants she desired them, so great (and without regarding to whom it was) that, if it chanced to be to such as would claim a requital according to the acknowledgment (and not the worth of the thing), at a greater distance, looking on it with truer eyes, what she had said could not always be stood to.

About these works, after the beginning of them, her lord seemed often displeased with her; yet rather with the manner of ordering it than the thing itself, which she knew not how to mend. It would have been in his power easily to have made her give over; but she conceived what he showed in it was rather not to engage his own credit in the success of it, than that he desired to have her leave it; and in this she after saw herself not deceived; for, some letters of his, to others, came after to her hands, where she saw he highly praised that for which he had often chidden her, and that he affirmed it would have been to the exceeding great benefit of that kingdom, could it have been well prosecuted.

+→ ≍◆≍ ←+

Anna Trapnel
fl. 1654–1658

During the English Civil War, some 300 women publicly testified to their visions. Among them one of the most outspoken was Anna Trapnel, whose prophecies (either written by her or transcribed from her testimony) were published in *The Cry of a Stone* (1654), *Strange and Wonderful Newes from White-Hall* (1654), *Anna Trapnel's Report and Plea* (1654), *A Legacy for Saints* (1654), and *A Voice for the King of Saints* (1658). Anna first discovered her power of prophecy while listening to a sermon the day after her mother's death. Inspired by visions and by Scripture, Anna was a Fifth Monarchist, belonging to a radical Puritan group who believed that Jesus was about to return to reign on earth. Supporters of the overthrow of Charles I, they turned against Cromwell when he set himself up as Lord Protector in Charles's place. Trapnel's excited spontaneous performances—a mixture of prophecy, trances, visions, and songs—drew large audiences and brought on the wrath of the government. She was charged with witchcraft and sentenced to prison for almost six months. When she was brought to trial, the authorities tried to silence her, but she spoke out, calling on the crowds outside to witness that it was God who spoke through her. In her remarks "To the Reader," she indicates that the civil and religious authorities viewed her behavior as madness and witchcraft. Such charges against her, including that she was "a monster or some ill-shaped creature" rather than "a woman like others that were modest and civil," necessitated her going into print. Her *Report and Plea* (1654), from which the following excerpt is taken, is an autobiography that contains several different forms—the narrative of events, political argument, and even the drama of her interrogation in court. At the close of her text she triumphantly reports that she had effectively convinced her audience that "this woman is no witch."

from Anna Trapnel's Report and Plea

Then the Lord made his rivers flow, which soon broke down the banks of an ordinary capacity, and extraordinarily mounted my spirits into a praying and singing frame, and so they remained till morning light, as I was told, for I was not capable of that.

But when I had done, and was a while silent, I came to speak weakly to those about me, saying, "I must go to bed, for I am very weak"; and the men and women went away, and my friend that tended me, and some other maids, helped me to bed, where I lay till the afternoon, they said, silent. And that time I had a vision of the minister's wife stirring against me; and she was presented to me as one enviously bent against me, calling that falsity which she understood not. And I saw the clergyman and the jurors contriving an indictment against me, and I saw myself stand before them; in a vision I saw this. And I sang with much courage, and told them I feared not them nor their doings, for that I had not deserved such usage.

But while I was singing praises to the Lord for his love to me, the justices sent their constable to fetch me, who came and said he must have me with him. And he pulled, and called me, they said that were by, but I was not capable thereof. They said he was greatly troubled how to have me to his master; they told him he had better obey God than man. And his hand shook, they said, while he was pulling me. Then some went to the justices to tell them I could not come. But they would not be pacified. Some offered to be bound for my appearance next day, if I were in a capacity, but this was refused. They would have me out of my bed, unless some would take their oaths that it would endanger my life to be taken out of my bed, which none could do, without they had loved to take false oaths, like some others in those parts. Then a friend persuaded them to see whether they could put me out of that condition, and told them I was never known to be put out of it; so they came. Justice Launce, now a Parliament-man, was one of them, I was told. These justices that came to fetch me out of my bed, they made a great tumult, them and their followers, in the house, and some came upstairs crying "A witch! A witch!", making a great stir on the stairs. And a poor honest man rebuking such that said so, he was tumbled downstairs and beaten too, by one of the justices' followers. And the justices made a great noise in putting out of my chamber where I lay many of my friends; and they said if my friends would not take me up, they would have some should take me up. One of my friends told them that they must fetch their silk gowns to do it then, for the poor would not do it. And they threatened much, but the Lord overruled them. They caused my eyelids to be pulled up, for they said I held them fast, because I would deceive the people; they spake to this purpose. One of the justices pinched me by the nose, and caused my pillow to be pulled from under my head, and kept pulling me, and calling me; but I heard none of all this stir and bustle. Neither did I hear Mr. Welstead, which I was told called to the rulers, saying, "a whip will fetch her up"; and he stood at the chamber door talking against me, and said, "She speaks nonsense." The women said, "Hearken, for you cannot hear, there is such a noise"; then he listened, and said, "Now she hears me speak, she speaks sense." And this clergyman durst not come till the rulers came, for then, they say, the witches can have no power over them: so that one depends upon another, rulers upon clergy, and clergy upon rulers.

And again, after they had made all the fury appear that the Lord permitted them to vent against me, they then went away, saying, "She will fall in a trance when we shall at any time call for her." The Lord kept me this day from their cruelty, which they had a good mind further to have let out against me. And that witch-trier woman of that town, some would fain have had come with her great pin which she used to thrust into witches to try them, but the Lord my God in whom I trust delivered me from their malice, making good that word to me in the Psalms,[1] "The rage of man

1. Psalm 76.10.

shall turn to thy praise, and the remnant of rages thou wilt restrain." Then further, to tell you how the Lord carried me in singing and prayer after they were gone two hours, as I was told, and then I came to myself; and being all alone, I blessed God for that quiet still day that I had. And the gentlewoman of the house coming into the chamber, I said, "Have I lain alone all this day? I have had a sweet day." She replied, and said, did not I hear the justices there, and the uproar that was in my chamber? I said, "No." Then she told me how they dealt by her house, bringing in their follow-ers, and what a noise they made. Then another friend asked me whether I did not hear that stir. I said, "No." They wondered, and so did I when I heard the relation, which is much more than I will write, for I don't take delight to stir in such puddles, it's no pleasant work to me. But that truth engageth me to let the world know what men have acted against the pourings-out of the spirit in a dispensation beyond their understanding; they hearkened not to scripture advice, which would not have any judge that they know not.

After that day's tumult, at night many came to catch at my words. And it was very probable that the rulers sent some to watch for what could be had further against me. And there were two women, that they had got their names, who had promised them to swear against me, and of this I shall further speak when I come to it. But now I am telling of what passed that night mentioned: many people spake much to me, asking me questions, the which the Lord helped me to answer. And my friends kept most part of that night in prayer on my behalf. And many watched what they said in prayer, for there were listeners under the window, which fain would have had some-thing to have informed against them. There was great endeavoring to have found a bill of indictment against Captain Langdon, but they could not; they could not vent their spleen, though they to the utmost desired it, the Lord would not let them have their evil desires herein. For though they in this would have brought him into con-tempt, yet they endeavored this that so I might want a surety, and then they had what they desired, which was to have cast me into the jail. But to leave that, and to tell you that I had the presence of the Lord with me that night abundantly, and my sleep was sweeter than at other times. My sister Langdon lay with me that night, and in the morning she told me that she could not sleep all night for thinking of my going to the sessions that day. She told me she wondered I could sleep so soundly all night. I told her I never had a sweeter night in my life, and as for my going before the rulers, I was no whit afraid or thoughtful, for I had cast my care upon the Lord, which I was persuaded would speak for me. Therefore I was not troubled nor afraid, for the Lord said to me, "Fear not, be not dismayed, I am thy God, and will stand by thee."[2]

Then I rose up, and prepared to go before them at sessions-house; and walking out in the garden before I went, I was thinking what I should say before the justices. But I was taken off from my own thoughts quickly, through the word, "Take no heed what thou shalt say; being brought before them for the Lord Christ's sake, he will give thee words. Dost thou know what they will ask thee? Therefore look to the Lord, who will give thee answers suitable to what shall be required of thee." So I was resolved to cast myself upon the Lord and his teaching. And though I had heard how the form of bills run, and of that word "Not guilty," according to the form of the bill, yet I said, "I shall not remember to say thus, if the Lord don't bid me say so; and if he bids me, I will say it." And this I thought, I would be nothing, the Lord should have all the praise, it being his due. So I went, the officer coming for me; and as I went

2. Isaiah 41.10.

along the street, I had followed me abundance of all manner of people, men and women, boys and girls, which crowded after me. And some pulled me by the arms, and stared me in the face, making wry faces at me, and saying, "How do you now? How is it with you now?" And thus they mocked and derided at me as I went to the sessions. But I was never in such a blessed self-denying lamb-like frame of spirit in my life as then; I had such lovely apprehensions of Christ's sufferings, and of that scripture which saith, "He went as a sheep, dumb before the shearers, he opened not his mouth; and when reviled, he reviled not again."[3] The Lord kept me also, so that I went silent to the sessions-house, which was much thronged with people: some said the sessions-house was never so filled since it was a sessions-house. So that I was a gazing-stock for all sorts of people, but I praise the Lord, this did not daunt me, nor a great deal more that I suffered that day, for the eternal grace of Jehovah surrounded me, and kept me from harm. So way was made for me to draw near to the table, which stood lower than the justices; and round the table sat the lawyers and others that attended them, and I with my friends that went with me stood by the lawyers, and the justices leaned over a rail, which railed them in together. Only I espied a clergyman at their elbow, who helped to make up their indictment, so that he could not be absent, though his pulpit wanted him, it being a fast-day, set apart by authority, which he broke without any scruple that so he might keep close to the work of accusation. But though he and the witch-trying woman looked steadfastly in my face, it did no way dismay me, nor the grim fierce looks of the justices did not daunt me, for as soon as I beheld them I remembered a dear friend to Christ, who smiled in the face of a great man that looked fiercely on him, and sat as a judge to condemn him for the testimony of Jesus; but this servant of the Lord looked cheerfully all the time of his accusations charged upon him. So I thinking upon that posture of his before those that acted against him, I begged the same cheerfulness, and I had the same courage to look my accusers in the face, which was no carnal boldness, though they called it so.

And when I came before them, Lobb, being the mouth of the court, as he was foreman of the jury he represented the whole court, and he first demanded my name, and I told him. And he said, "Anna Trapnel, here is a bill of indictment to be read, for you to give your answer concerning." Then Justice Lobb said, "Read the bill," so it was read to me; and Lobb said, "Are you guilty, or not?" I had no word to say at the present, but the Lord said to me, "Say 'not guilty,' according to the form of the bill." So I spoke it as from the Lord, who knew I was not guilty of such an indictment. Then said Lobb, "Traverse the bill to the next assizes";[4] so that was done. Then Lobb said I must enter into bond for my appearance at the next assizes, unto which I agreed. Then they demanded sureties, so I desired Captain Langdon and Major Bawden to be my sureties, unto which they were willing. So there were two recognizances drawn, one for my appearance, and the other bound me to the good behavior; and I was entered into both the recognizances £300, and my sureties as much, to both the recognizances. And this being done, they whispered a while, and I thought they had done with me at that time. So they had, if they had gone according to true law, which was not to have brought their interrogatories then; but the report was that I would discover myself to be a witch when I came before the justices, by having never a word to answer for myself, for it used to be so among the witches, they could not

---

3. Isaiah 53.7; 1 Peter 2.23.
4. Carry the case over to the next court session; Trapnel is next ordered to pledge a large sum (guaranteed by two

wealthy friends) to ensure that she will reappear for the trial.

speak before the magistrates, and so they said it would be with me. But the Lord quickly defeated them herein, and caused many to be of another mind. Then Lobb said, "Tender her the book which was written from something said at Whitehall," so the book was reached out to me, and Justice Lobb said, "What say you to that book? Will you own it? Is it yours?"

A. T. "I am not careful to answer you in that matter."

Then they said, "She denies her book." Then they whispered with those behind them. Then spake Justice Lobb again, and said, "Read a vision of the horns out of the book," so that was read. Then Justice Lobb said, "What say you to this? Is this yours?"

A. T. "I am not careful to answer you in that matter, touching the whole book. As I told you before, so I say again. For what was spoken was at Whitehall, at a place of concourse of people, and near a council I suppose wise enough to call me into question if I offended, and unto them I appeal." But though it was said I appealed unto Caesar and unto Caesar should I go, yet I have not been brought before him which is called Caesar; so much by the by. Again, I said I supposed they had not power to question me for that which was spoke in another county; they said yea, that they had. Then the book was put by, and they again whispered.

Then Justice Lobb asked me about my coming into that country, how it came to pass that I came into that country.

I answered I came as others did that were minded to go into the country.

Lobb. "But why did you come into this country?"

A. T. "Why might not I come here, as well as into another country?"

Lobb. "But you have no lands, nor livings, nor acquaintance to come to in this country."

A. T. "What though I had not? I am a single person, and why may I not be with my friends anywhere?"

Lobb. "I understand you are not married."

A. T. "Then having no hindrance, why may not I go where I please, if the Lord so will?"

Then spoke Justice Launce, "But did not some desire you to come down?" And this Lobb asked me too, but I told them I would accuse none, I was there to answer as to what they should charge my own particular with.

Launce said, "Pray, Mistress, tell us what moved you to come such a journey?"

A. T. "The Lord gave me leave to come, asking of him leave, whitherever I went. I used still to pray for his direction in all I do, and so I suppose ought you," I said.

Justice Launce. "But pray tell us, what moved you to come such a journey?"

A. T. "The Lord moved me, and gave me leave."

Launce. "But had you not some extraordinary impulses of spirit that brought you down? Pray tell us what those were."

A. T. "When you are capable of extraordinary impulses of spirit, I will tell you; but I suppose you are not in a capacity now," for I saw how deridingly he spoke. And for answering him thus, he said I was one of a bold spirit, but he soon took me down: so himself said. But some said it took them down, for the Lord carried me so to speak, that they were in a hurry and confusion and sometimes would speak all together, that I was going to say, "What, are you like women, all speakers and no hearers?" But I said thus, "What, do you speak all at a time? I cannot answer all, when speaking at once. I appeal to the civilest of you," and I directed my speech to Justice Lobb, who spake very moderately, and gave me a civil answer, saying, "You are not acquainted with the manner of the court, which is to give in their sayings."

A. T. "But I cannot answer all at once. Indeed I do not know the manner of the court, for I never was before any till now."

Justice Lobb. "You prophesy against Truro."

A. T. "Indeed I pray against the sins of the people of Truro, and for their souls' welfare. Are you angry for that?"

Lobb. "But you must not judge authority, but pray for them, and not speak so suspiciously of them," and more to this purpose he spoke to me.

A. T. "I will take up your word, in which you said I was not to judge. You said well, for so saith the scripture, 'Who art thou that judgest another man's servant? To his own master he standeth or falleth; yea, he shall be holden up, for God is able to make him stand.'[5] But you have judged me, and never heard me speak: you have not dealt so well by me as Agrippa dealt by Paul. Though Agrippa was an heathen, he would have Paul speak before he gave in his judgment concerning him."[6]

Justice Tregagle. "Oh, you are a dreamer!"

A. T. "So they called Joseph, therefore I wonder not that you call me so."[7]

Justice Selye said, "You knew we were with you yesterday."

A. T. "I did not."

Justice Selye. "He which is the major said you will not say so."

A. T. "I will speak it, being it's truth."

He said, "Call the women that will witness they heard you say you knew we were with you." And he pulled out a writing, and named their names, calling to some to fetch them.

A. T. "You may suborn false witnesses against me, for they did so against Christ." And I said, "Produce your witnesses."

Justice Selye. "We shall have them for you at next assizes."

They put it off long enough, because one was fallen in a swoon before she got out of the house where she dwelt; and the other was come into the sessions-house. And Mrs Grose, a gentlewoman of the town, standing by her that was their false witness, said, "Wilt thou take an oath thus? Take heed what thou dost, it's a dangerous thing to take a false oath." And she ran out of the sessions-house; this was credibly reported. And here ended their witnesses that they had procured against me as to that. There was a soldier that smiled to hear how the Lord carried me along in my speech, and Justice Selye called to the jailer to take him away, saying he laughed at the court. He thought him to be one of my friends, and for his cheerful looking the jailer had like to have had him. Then I said, "Scripture speaks of such who 'make a man an offender for a word,'[8] but you make a man an offender for a look." They greatly bustled, as if they would have taken him away; but this was quickly squashed, their heat as to this lasted not long. In the meantime, the other, Selye, was talking to Major Bawden, wondering such a man as he, who had been so well reputed for a judicious, sober, understanding man, should hearken to me; many words were used to him to that purpose. I said, "Why may not he and others try all things, and hold fast that which is best?" But they still cast grim looks on me. And they had a saying to Major Bawden, and to Captain Langdon then, whom they derided in a letter sent from Truro by some of their learned court, which wrote that Captain Langdon and Major Bawden stood up and made a learned defence. They had indeed such learning from the spirit of wisdom and of a sound mind, which the jurors and their companions

5. Romans 14.4.
6. Acts 25–26.

7. Genesis 37.5–11.
8. Isaiah 29.21.

were not able to contend against, their speech and whole deportment was so humble and self-denying, and so seasoned with the salt of grace,[9] which their flashy unsavory spirits could not endure. Those that are raised from the dunghill and set on thrones cannot sit there without vaunting and showing their fool's coat of many colors, as envy, and pride, and vainglory; these and other colors they show, which delights not King Jesus nor his followers. Justice Lobb told me I made a disturbance in the town. I asked wherein. He said by drawing so many people after me. I said, "How did I draw them?" He said I set open my chamber doors and my windows for people to hear.

A. T. "That's a very unlikely thing, that I should do so, for I prayed the maid to lock my chamber door when I went to bed, and I did not rise in the night sure to open it." I said, "Why may not I pray with many people in the room, as well as your professing woman that prays before men and women, she knowing them to be there; but I know not that there is anybody in the room when I pray. And if you indict one for praying, why not another? Why are you so partial in your doings?"

Justice Lobb. "But you don't pray so, as others."

A. T. "I pray in my chamber."

Justice Trevill. "Your chamber!"

A. T. "Yea, that it's my chamber while I am there, through the pleasure of my friends."

They used more words to me, sometimes slighting and mockingly they spoke, and sometimes seeming to advise me to take heed how I spoke and prayed so again. Many such kind of words Justice Trevill used, and Justice Lobb. And one thing I omitted in telling you when I told you how I answered Justice Launce: I should have told you how I said to him, if he would know what the ordinary impulse of spirit was that I had to bring me into that country, I would tell him. So I related the scriptures, as that in the Psalms, and in the prophet Isaiah, how the presence and spirit of the Lord should be with me, and he would uphold me and strengthen me with the right hand of his righteousness.[1] He answered such impulse was common, they hoped they had that, they were not ignorant of such impulse of spirit; much to this effect was spoken. I seeing they were very willing to be gone, I said, "Have you done with me?" Answer was I might now go away. But I said, "Pray, what is it to break the good behavior you have bound me over to? I know not what you may make a breaking of it: is it a breaking the good behavior to pray and sing?" Justice Trevill said no, so I did it at the habitation where I abode. "It's well," said I, "you will give me leave it shall be anywhere." I said, "I will leave one word with you, and that is this: a time will come when you and I shall appear before the great judge of the tribunal seat of the most high, and then I think you will hardly be able to give an account for this day's work before the Lord, at that day of true judgment." Said Tregagle, "Take you no care for us." So they were willing to have no more discourse with me.

And as I went in the crowd, many strangers were very loving and careful to help me out of the crowd; and the rude multitude said, "Sure this woman is not witch, for she speaks many good words, which the witches could not." And thus the Lord made the rude rabble to justify his appearance. For in all that was said by me, I was nothing, the Lord put all in my mouth, and told me what I should say, and that from the written word, he put it in my memory and mouth; so that I will have nothing ascribed to me, but all honor and praise given to him whose right it is, even to Jehovah, who is the king that lives for ever. I have left out some things that I thought were not so

9. Colossians 4.6.   1. Psalm 139.7–10; Isaiah 29.21.

material to be written; and what I have written of this, it's to declare as much as is convenient to take off those falsities and contrary reports that are abroad concerning my sufferings, some making it worse than it was, and some saying it was little or nothing. Now to inform all people's judgments, I have thought it meet to offer this relation to the world's view, and with as much covering as I can of saints' weaknesses herein, praying the Lord to forgive them; and as for the Lord's enemies, that he would confound them; but as for my enemies, I still pray.

⊱─⊰

Alice Thornton
fl. 1645–1662

Alice Thornton wrote three volumes of an autobiography, spanning the years 1629 to 1660. From a royalist family, she tells in the early part of her story how her mother protected herself and her daughter from Scots soldiers who wanted to be quartered in their home. When one Captain Innis demanded that he have Alice in marriage, her mother hid her and paid another family to house him. The threat of rape in wartime was a real one, and when Alice learned that Captain Innis planned to kidnap her, she never ventured out of the house. The two passages printed here are from the decade after the Civil War, during her married life, in which the dangers she suffered were mainly due to the perils of reproduction. Her perspective is at once religious and biological. Images and allusions from the Bible as well as a belief in salvation color her narrative. At the same time, Mrs. Thornton depicts her physical suffering in the most graphic and realistic detail. Most married women of the early modern period were pregnant during most of their adult lives, and they often died in childbirth, as did their infants. Even if the mother survived labor, her risk of sickness was great. Alice Thornton relates her ordeal following her first two labors and expresses thanks to God for helping her through the sicknesses that followed.

from Book of Remembrances

Meditations upon my deliverance of my first child;
and of the great sickness followed for three quarters of a year;
August 6, 1652, lasted till May 2, 1653

About seven weeks after I married it pleased God to give me the blessing of conception. The first quarter I was exceeding sickly in breeding, till I was with quick child; after which I was very strong and healthy, I bless God, only much hotter than formerly, as is usual in such cases from a natural cause, insomuch that my nose bled much when I was about half gone, by reason of the increase of heat. Being helped more forward in the distemper by the extreme heat of the weather at that time, when the extreme great eclipse of the sun was in its height, and a great and total eclipse fell out this year 1652. At which time I was big with child, and the sight of it much affrighted me, it being so dark in the morning that [one] could not see to eat his breakfast without a candle. But this did amaze me much, and I could not refrain going out into the garden and look on the eclipse in water, discovering the power of God so great to a miracle, who did withdraw His light from our sun so totally that the sky was dark, and stars appeared, and a cold storm for a time did possess the earth. Which dreadful change did put me into most serious and deep consideration of the day of judgment which would come as sudden and as certainly upon all the earth as this eclipse fell out, which caused me to desire and beg of His Majesty that He would prepare me for this great day in repentance, faith, and a holy life, for the judgments of God was just and certain upon all sins and sinners. O prepare me, O God, for all Thy dispensations and trials in this world, and make me ready and prepared with oil in my lamp, as the wise virgins, against the coming of the sweet Bridegroom of my soul.

About a month after, Mr. Thornton desired and his relations that I should go to see them both at Crathorne, Buttercrambe, York, and at Hull and Beverley, at Burn Park where his mother lived then . . . and by God's mercy did I go to all those places where his friends lived, and [was] most kindly received and entertained. I bless God who gave me favor in the eyes of my husband's friends. When I came to Hull, Dr. Witty would have had me advised to be let blood. . . . In my return home by Newton when I saw the old house the remains of it, as I was in the great chamber, the door into a little room was so low as I got a great knock on my forehead which struck me down, and I fell with the force of the blow, at which my husband was troubled. But I recovering my astonishment (because he should not be too much concerned), smiled, said I hoped I was not much worse, but said I had taken possession, which made him smile, and said it was to my hurt, and indeed so it was many ways. For in my going homeward he carried me to that place of the great rocks and cliffs which is called Whitson Cliff. . . . But this my husband would not have had me go down this way, but by Ampleford, about, and plain way, but for Mr. Bradley, who told him it would not do me no hurt, because his wife went down that way and was no worse. However, the effect to me was contrary, for I being to go to my cousin Ascough's, she did admire that I came that way, and wished I might get safe home. It was indeed the good pleasure of my God to bring me safe home to my dear mother's house, Hipswell.

But my dangerous journey the effects of it did soon appear on me, and Dr. Witty's words came true. For as soon as I got home I fell into the most dreadful sickness that ever any creature could possibly be saved out of, and by a strong and putrid fever, which was on me eleven days before Dr. Witty came from Hull, had so putrefied my whole blood that both myself and poor infant was like to go. . . . The more particular description of this great and long-lasting sickness I have related in my first book of my Life, and with the miraculous deliverance was towards me in all that time. Mr. Thornton had a desire that I should visit his friends, in which I freely joined, his mother living about fifty miles from Hipswell, and all at Newton and Buttercrambe. In my passage thither I sweat exceedingly, and was much inclining to be feverish wanting not eight weeks of my time, so that Dr. Witty said that I should go near to fall into a fever, or some desperate sickness, if I did not cool my blood, by taking some away, and if I had stayed but two days longer, I had followed his advice. In his return home from Newton, his own estate, I was carried over Hambleton towards Sir William Ascough's house, where I passed down on foot a very high wall betwixt Hud-hill and Whitson Cliff, which is above a mile steep down, and indeed so bad that I could not scarce tread the narrow steps, which was exceeding bad for me in that condition, and sore to endure, the way so straight and none to lead me but my maid [Susan Gosling], which could scarce make shift to get down herself, all our company being gone down before. Each step did very much strain me, being so big with child, nor could I have got down if I had not then been in my full strength and nimble on foot. But, I bless God, I got down safe at last, though much tired, and hot and weary, finding myself not well, but troubled with pains after my walk. Mr. Thornton would not have brought me that way if he had known it so dangerous, and I was a stranger in that place; but he was advised by some to go that way before we came down the hill.

This was the first occasion which brought me a great deal of misery, and killed my sweet infant in my womb. For I continued ill in pain by fits upon this journey, and within a fortnight fell into a desperate fever at Hipswell. Upon which my old doctor, Mr. Mahum, was called, but could do little towards the cure, because of being with child. I was willing to be ordered by him, but said I found it absolutely necessary to be let blood if they would save my life, but I was freely willing to resign my will to God's, if He saw fit for me, to spare my life, yet to live with my husband; but still with subserviency to my Heavenly Father. Nor was I wanting to supplicate my God for direction what to do, either for life or death. I had very often and frequent impressions to desire the latter before the former, finding no true joy in this life, but I confess also that which moved me to use all means for my recovery, in regard of the great sorrow of my dear and aged mother and my dear husband took for me, far exceeding my deserts, made me more willing to save my life for them, and that I might render praises to my God in the land of the living. But truly, I found my heart still did cleave to my Maker that I never found myself more desirous of a change to be delivered from this wicked world and body of sin and death, desiring to be dissolved and to be with Christ. Therefore endured I all the rigors and extremity of my sickness with such a share of patience as my God gave me.

As for my friends, they were so much concerned for me that, upon the importunity of my husband, although I was brought indeed very weak and desperately ill about eleventh day of my sickness, I did let him send for Dr. Witty, if it were not too late. The doctor came post the next day, when he found me very weak, and durst not let me blood that night, but gave me cordials, etc., till the next day, and if I got but one hour's rest that night, he would do it the morning following. That night the two doctors had a dispute about the letting me blood. Mr. Mahum was against it, and Dr. Witty for it; but I soon decided that dispute, and told them, if they would save my life, I must bleed. So the next day I had six or seven ounces taken which was turned very bad by my sickness, but I found a change immediately in my sight, which was exceeding dim before, and then I see as well as ever clearly, and my strength began a little to return; these things I relate that I may set forth the mercy of my ever-gracious God, who had blessed the means in such manner. Who can sufficiently extol his Majesty for his boundless mercies to me his weak creature, for from that time I was better, and he had hopes of my life.

The doctor stayed with me seven days during my sickness; my poor infant within me was greatly forced with violent motions perpetually, till it grew so weak that it had left stirring, and about the 27th of August I found myself in great pains as it were the colic, after which I began to be in travail, and about the next day at night I was delivered of a goodly daughter, who lived not so long as that we could get a minister to baptize it, though we presently sent for one. This my sweet babe and first child departed this life half an hour after its birth, being received, I hope, into the arms of Him that gave it. She was buried that night, being Friday, the 27th of August, 1652, at Easby Church.

The effects of this fever remained by several distempers successively, first, after the miscarriage I fell into a most terrible shaking ague, lasting one quarter of a year, by fits each day twice, in much violency, so that the sweat was great with faintings, being thereby weakened till I could not stand or go. The hair on my head came off, my nails of my fingers and toes came off, my teeth did shake, and ready to come out and grew black. After the ague left me, upon a medicine of London treacle, I fell into the jaundice, which vexed me very hardly one full quarter and a half more. I finding Dr. Witty's judgment true, that it would prove a chronical[1] distemper; but blessed be the Lord, upon great and many means used and all remedies, I was at length cured of all distempers and weaknesses, which, from its beginning, had lasted three quarters of a year full out. Thus had I a sad entertainment and beginning of my change of life, the comforts thereof being turned into much discomforts and weaknesses, but still I was upheld by an Almighty Power, therefore will I praise the Lord my God. Amen.

Upon the birth of my second child and daughter,
born at Hipswell on the 3rd of January in the year 1654.

Alice Thornton, my second child, was born at Hipswell near Richmond in Yorkshire the 3rd day of January, 1654, baptized the 5th of the same. Witnesses, my mother the Lady Wandesforde, my uncle Mr. Major Norton, and my cousin York his daughter, at Hipswell, by Mr. Michell Siddall, minister then of Caterick.

It was the pleasure of God to give me but a weak time after my daughter Alice her birth, and she had many preservations from death in the first year, being one night delivered from being overlaid by her nurse, who laid in my dear mother's chamber a good while. One night my mother was writing pretty late, and she heard my dear child make a groaning troublesomely, and stepping immediately to nurse's bedside she saw the nurse fallen asleep, with her breast in the child's mouth, and lying over the child; at which she, being affrighted, pulled the nurse suddenly off from her, and so preserved my dear child from being smothered . * * *

After I was delivered [of her third child, Elizabeth], and in my weary bed and very weak, it fell out that my little daughter Alice, being then newly weaned, and about a year old, being asleep in one cradle and the young infant [Elizabeth] in another, she fell into a most desperate fit, of the convulsions as supposed to be, her breath stopped, grew black in her face, which sore frighted her maid Jane Flouer. She took her up immediately, and with the help of the midwife, Jane Rimer, to open her teeth and to bring her to life again.

But still, afterwards, no sooner that she was out of one fit but fell into another fit, and the remedies could be by my dear mother and aunt Norton could scarce keep her alive, she having at least twenty fits; all friends expecting when she should have died. But I lying the next chamber to her and did hear her, when she came out of them, to give great shrieks and suddenly, that it frighted me extremely, and all the time of this poor child's illness I myself was at death's door by the extreme excess of those, upon the fright and terror came upon me, so great floods that I was spent, and my breath lost, my strength departed from me, and I could not speak for faintings, and dispirited so that my dear mother and aunt and friends did not expect my life, but overcome with sorrow for me. Nor durst they tell me in what a condition my dear Naly [Alice's nickname] was in her fits, lest grief for her, added to my own extremity, with loss of blood, might have extinguished my miserable life: but removing her in her cradle into the Blue Parlor, a great way off me, lest I hearing her sad shrieks should renew my sorrows. These extremities did so lessen my milk, that though I began to recruit strength, yet I must be subject to the changes of my condition. After my dear Naly was in most miraculous mercy restored to me the next day, and recruited my strength; within a fortnight I recovered my milk, and was overjoyed to give my sweet Betty suck, which I did, and

---

1. Chronic, lasting a long time.

began to recover to a miracle, blessed be my great and gracious Lord God, who remembered mercy towards me.

·—+ ⇥◆⇤ +—·

Ralph Josselin
1616–1683

Vicar of an Essex parish, Ralph Josselin kept a diary for forty-two years; it became one of the most substantial diaries of the century. It included an extensive annual accounting of his finances, recorded each March at the start of the church year, followed by three or four entries each week describing events—"God's dealings." Financial language pervades Josselin's reckonings of his financial dealings and his spiritual debts alike, as he strives to improve both his material and his spiritual well-being.

from Diary

Nov: 18: God good to me, and mine in manifold outward mercies, but I find such a vanity in my spirit that boweth down my soul, yet this trouble is my hope for surely there is the spirit stirring against the flesh, but when shall Christ so strengthen me that I shall in his grace be more than a conqueror.

19: We killed a good hog, which proved neat and clean, a mercy to be observed, at night a violent wind and snow which covered the earth die 20.[1] so that we gave our cattle meat twice in the day, having begun to give once a day ever since octob. 29.

21. Received in a little wood from Sprigs marsh, its a mercy when God is our own to have any thing to call our own.

Nov: 25. The season somewhat more winterly then formerly. I observe how apt we are to account a harsh time the hardest we ever felt and a mild the best, letting slip out of our mind what was formerly, and very commonly not eying God that giveth both, God good to me in many mercies, a zeal in me in preaching the word, Lord warm their souls in the love, and embracement of the truth as it is in Jesus.

* * *

March. 24: A sad season for wet, yet some sow their oats. God good to me and mine in mercies, Bettie more quiet in nights then formerly. Mr. H. very ill which is a great trouble to me. Lord bear up my heart to thee, that nothing may overset my soul; God good to me in the word, awakening my heart unto him, the Lord stablish me in his fear, prayed earnestly for fair weather, this evening was the most hopeful and clear I have seen of many for which mercy I praise the Lord, but the next morning wet as formerly Lord be not angry with the prayers of thy people.

27. Rid[2] to choose Knights of the shire, we lost it, and my heart quiet, the Lord liveth and reigneth and if he put his own servants and things on suffering his will be done. Went on to London. returned safe.

30. with a vain heart, Lord be my help, and stir up my soul to endeavor it.

March. 31. My dear friend Mr R. H. under a visible distraction, the Lord in infinite mercy raise him up again. When I come to view my expenses I find I have laid out 233li. 9s. 6d. ob.[3] I have received in all receipts whatsoever only. 146. 16. 0. but my stock which I valued last year at. 25li. is worth now about. 55li. so though I have

---

1. On the twentieth day.
2. Rode.

3. 233 pounds, 9 shillings, 6 pence, "ob," short for Latin *obolus*, a halfpenny.

laid out. 87. 6. 5. ob more then received yet on the whole matter I am not abated in my stock above. 50li. and in lieu of that I am sure I have laid out. above 80li. on the house on the green.

My roll of debts as in the blew book are 80li. about. owing unto me. ———— 167. 10. 0

I have in cash towards my building about 50li. and my uncle Shepheard being dead, I have a meadow befalls my wife worth about. 50li. more, which when it cometh into my hand I shall value.

Yet God even in outward things is good to me, Lord make me upright before thee in all my ways, I humbly entreat thee and continue thy kindness to me, and all that fear thy name.

April. 1. 2. 3. I sew oats on lay, and other land. Lord command a blessing for my hope is in thee. went towards London on Mr H. account, a sad providence, oh Lord melt my bowels, accept my praises for my family's health, reason, return to them in favor: die. 6. I came home, God with me in the journey.

Ap: 7. The season very good, springing. God merciful to me in many outward mercies, but sensible I am my heart is out of frame, the Lord sanctify my thoughts, help me to watch over them, the Lord command mercy for me and mine in Christ Jesus, I had but little time for my sermons this day, Lord help me to trust thee but not for any thing to neglect any opportunities

God gave an answer to prayer in the season from March 27. yet, so that men are at work on all hands for their employment.

⚜

Daniel Defoe
1660–1731

Son of a butcher, Daniel Defoe was one of the most prolific and influential English journalists and novelists, publishing 566 separate works. His rise to fame was fraught with financial and political crises. A merchant and trader, Defoe speculated in land and overseas ventures, risking such enormous sums of capital that by 1692 he owed his creditors seventeen thousand pounds. After a short stint running a brick and tile factory, Defoe turned to political writing and journalism to pay his debts. His many works included propaganda for William III, and two important essays on the capitalist economy, *An Essay Upon Public Credit* and—a subject he knew all too well—*An Essay upon Loans* (1710).

His literary career began at the age of fifty-nine with *The Life and Strange Surprizing Adventures of Robinson Crusoe, Mariner of York* (1719). This became Part One of a trilogy, followed by *The Farther Adventures of Robinson Crusoe* (1719) and in 1720 by *The Serious Reflections of . . . Robinson Crusoe*. The story is about a young man who rebels against his father by sailing the high seas rather than following the "middle life" at home. After a series of adventures, Crusoe becomes a planter in Brazil and finally, en route to Africa to buy slaves, he is shipwrecked on an island off the northeast coast of South America, where he lives alone for twenty-eight years. A fascinating mixture of fiction and fact, Defoe's novel had its immediate source in the popular story of Alexander Selkirk, a Scottish sailor marooned from 1704 to 1709 on an island 300 miles west of Chile, as related in Captain Woodes Rogers's *Cruising Voyage Round the World* (1712).

Defoe plays with the factual status of his fiction by maintaining in the preface that the story was "a just history of fact," yet later, accused of being a liar, he explained in his *Serious Reflections* (1720) that the novel was an allegory of his own life. One can find plenty of parallels between Defoe's life and Crusoe's and between the form of the novel and autobiography. In the first-person narrative, Crusoe portrays himself as a self-destructive risk taker—"the wilful agent of my own miseries" thanks to a "rash and immoderate desire of rising faster." Commenting on his reckless love of danger is the voice of a sober inward-looking Presbyterian, who attempts to control all this chaos in whatever way he can. Once shipwrecked, Crusoe begins the process of taking stock of himself by reckoning his spiritual credits and debits, by keeping track of time and writing a journal of his experiences. While money is no longer valuable to him—"O drug . . . what art thou good for?" he says to the thirty-six pounds he finds in the shipwreck—his assets are expressed in terms of capital, as if they could be reckoned as pluses and minuses in a financial accounting.

For more on Defoe, see his principal listing, page 2289.

from The Life and Strange and Surprizing Adventures of Robinson Crusoe, of York, Mariner

I now began to consider seriously my condition, and the circumstance I was reduced to, and I drew up the state of my affairs in writing, not so much to leave them to any that were to come after me, for I was like to have but few heirs, as to deliver my thoughts from daily poring upon them, and afflicting my mind; and as my reason began now to master my despondency, I began to comfort my self as well as I could, and to set the good against the evil, that I might have something to distinguish my case from worse, and I stated it very impartially, like debtor and creditor, the comforts I enjoyed, against the miseries I suffered, thus,

Evil.	Good.
I am cast upon a horrible desolate island, void of all hope of recovery.	But I am alive, and not drowned as all my ship's company was.
I am singled out and separated, as it were, from all the World to be miserable.	But I am singled out too from all the ship's crew to be spared from death; and he that miraculously saved me from death, can deliver me from this condition.
I am divided from mankind, a solitaire, one banished from humane society.	But I am not starved and perishing on a barren place, affording no sustenance.
I have not clothes to cover me.	But I am in a hot climate, where if I had clothes I could hardly wear them.
I am without any defence or means to resist any violence of man or beast.	But I am cast on an island, where I see no wild beasts to hurt me, as I saw on the coast of Africa: And what if I had been shipwrecked there?
I have no soul to speak to, or relieve me.	But God wonderfully sent the ship in near enough to the shore, that I have gotten out so many necessary things as will either supply my wants, or enable me to supply my self even as long as I live.

Upon the whole, here was an undoubted testimony, that there was scarce any condition in the world so miserable, but there was something *negative* or something *positive* to be thankful for in it; and let this stand as a direction from the experience of the most miserable of all conditions in this world, that we may always find in it something to comfort our selves from, and to set in the description of good and evil, on the credit side of the accompt.

⊷ ⊰⊱ ⊷

John Bunyan
1628–1688

Born at Elstow near Bedford in 1628, John Bunyan was descended from a family of small farmers, or yeomen, who had fallen on hard times. His father was forced to become a traveling tinker, a mender of pots and household utensils. As a child, Bunyan learned to read and write at a grammar school. At the age of sixteen he joined the local militia to fight on the parliamentary side in the Civil War. Some time around 1648, Bunyan underwent a crisis of faith. He was plagued with doubts about his faith and fear of damnation. This ordeal ultimately led to his conversion. Bunyan became a Noncomformist preacher and set out to spread the good news of the Bible to others. With the Restoration of Charles II and the Church of England, Bunyan was arrested for preaching. Refusing to conform to the Church of England and to stop his Nonconformist preaching, he spent first twelve years in prison and then another six months. While in prison for this second short stay, Bunyan wrote *The Pilgrim's Progress* (1678), the great classic of Puritan literature. A dream vision, the allegorical journey of the protagonist Christian begins with his falling asleep in a "den," which is designated in the margin of the text as "the gaol" (jail). Christian is both a kind of everyman and a representative of Bunyan himself. Christian's experiences symbolically relate the crises of Bunyan's life—his falling into despair, figured as the Slough of Despond, and his temptation by the things of this world, portrayed as Vanity Fair. The most popular book of its time and for long afterward a favorite text of English Protestant missionaries around the world, *Pilgrim's Progress* presents the myth of life as a war between the forces of good and evil, light and darkness, God and the devil, in a powerful and symbolically complex narrative of spiritual despair, struggle with temptation, longing for salvation, and redemption through dependence on God's grace.

from The Pilgrim's Progress from This World to That Which Is to Come.
The Author's Apology for His Book

> When at the first I took my pen in hand
> Thus for to write, I did not understand
> That I at all should make a little book
> In such a mode; nay, I had undertook
> 5   To make another, which when almost done,
> Before I was aware, I this begun.
>   And thus it was: I writing of the way
> And race of saints, in this our Gospel-day,
> Fell suddenly into an allegory
> 10 About their journey, and the way to glory,
> In more than twenty things which I set down;
> This done, I twenty more had in my crown,
> And they again began to multiply,
> Like sparks that from the coals of fire do fly.
> 15 Nay then, thought I, if that you breed so fast,
> I'll put you by yourselves, lest you at last

Should prove *ad infinitum*, and eat out
The book that I already am about.
 Well, so I did; but yet I did not think
20 To show to all the world my pen and ink
In such a mode; I only thought to make
I knew not what: nor did I undertake
Thereby to please my neighbor; no, not I,
I did it mine own self to gratify.
25 Neither did I but vacant seasons spend
In this my scribble: nor did I intend
But to divert myself in doing this,
From worser thoughts which make me do amiss.
 Thus I set pen to paper with delight,
30 And quickly had my thoughts in black and white.
For, having now my method by the end,
Still as I pulled, it came; and so I penned
It down, until it came at last to be
For length and breadth the bigness which you see.
35 Well, when I had thus put mine ends together,
I showed them others, that I might see whether
They would condemn them, or them justify:
And some said, "Let them live"; some, "Let them die."
Some said, "John, print it"; others said, "Not so."
40 Some said, "It might do good" others said, "No."
 Now was I in a strait, and did not see
Which was the best thing to be done by me:
At last I thought, since you are thus divided,
I print it will, and so the case decided.
45 For, thought I, some I see would have it done,
Though others in that channel do not run.
To prove then who advised for the best,
Thus I thought fit to put it to the test.
 I further thought, if now I did deny
50 Those that would have it thus, to gratify,
I did not know, but hinder them I might,
Of that which would to them be great delight.
 For those which were not for its coming forth,
I said to them, Offend you I am loth;°   *unwilling*
55 Yet since your brethren pleased with it be,
Forbear to judge, till you do further see.
 If that thou wilt not read, let it alone;
Some love the meat, some love to pick the bone:
Yea, that I might them better palliate,
60 I did too with them thus expostulate.
 May I not write in such a style as this?
In such a method too, and yet not miss
Mine end, thy good? why may it not be done?
Dark clouds bring waters, when the bright bring none;
65 Yea, dark or bright, if they their silver drops
Cause to descend, the earth, by yielding crops
Gives praise to both, and carpeth not at either,

But treasures up the fruit they yield together;
Yea, so commixes both, that in her fruit
70   None can distinguish this from that, they suit
Her well, when hungry, but if she be full
She spews out both, and makes their blessings null.
        You see the ways the fisherman doth take
To catch the fish, what engines doth he make?
75   Behold! how he engageth all his wits
Also his snares, lines, angles, hooks, and nets.
Yet fish there be, that neither hook, nor line,
Nor snare, nor net, nor engine can make thine;
They must be groped for, and be tickled too,
80   Or they will not be catched, whate'er you do.
        How doth the fowler seek to catch his game
By divers means, all which one cannot name?
His gun, his nets, his lime-twigs, light, and bell:
He creeps, he goes, he stands; yea who can tell
85   Of all his postures? Yet there's none of these
Will make him master of what fowls he please.
Yea, he must pipe, and whistle to catch *this*,
Yet if he does so, *that* bird he will miss.
        If that a pearl may in a toad's head dwell,
90   And may be found too in an oyster-shell;
If things that promise nothing do contain
What better is than gold, who will disdain,
That have an inkling of it, there to look,
That they may find it? Now my little book
95   (Though void of all those paintings that may make
It with this or the other man to take)
Is not without those things that do excel,
What do in brave but empty notions dwell.
        Well, yet I am not fully satisfied,
100   That this your book will stand, when soundly tried.
        Why, what's the matter? "It is dark." What tho'?
"But it is feigned."° What of that I trow?   *invented/suppose*
Some men, by feigning words as dark as mine,
Make truth to spangle, and its rays to shine.
105   "But they want solidness." Speak man thy mind.
"They drowned the weak; metaphors make us blind."
        Solidity, indeed becomes the pen
Of him that writeth things divine to men;
But must I needs want solidness, because
110   By metaphors I speak? Were not God's laws,
His Gospel-laws, in olden time held forth
By types, shadows, and metaphors? Yet loth
Will any sober man be to find fault
With them, lest he be found for to assault
115   The highest wisdom. No, he rather stoops,
And seeks to find out what by pins and loops,
By calves, and sheep, by heifers, and by rams,
By birds, and herbs, and by the blood of lambs,

God speaketh to him: and happy is he
120   That finds the light and grace that in them be.
      Be not too forward therefore to conclude
That I want solidness, that I am rude:
All things solid in show not solid be;
All things in parables despise not we
125   Lest things most hurtful lightly we receive;
And things that good are, of our souls bereave.
      My dark and cloudy words they do but hold
The truth, as cabinets enclose the gold.
      The prophets used much by metaphors
130   To set forth truth; yea, who so considers
Christ, his Apostles too, shall plainly see,
That truths to this day in such mantles° be.   *cloaks, coverings*
      Am I afraid to say that Holy Writ,
Which for its style and phrase puts down all wit,
135   Is everywhere so full of all these things,
(Dark figures, allegories), yet there springs
From that same book that lustre, and those rays
Of light, that turns our darkest nights to days.
      Come, let my carper to his life now look,
140   And find there darker lines than in my book
He findeth any, Yea, and let him know
That in his best things there are worse lines too.
      May we but stand before impartial men,
To his poor one, I dare adventure ten,
145   That they will take my meaning in these lines
Far better than his lies in silver shrines.
Come, truth, although in swaddling-clouts, I find
Informs the judgment, rectifies the mind,
Pleases the understanding, makes the will
150   Submit; the memory too it doth fill
With what doth our imagination please,
Likewise, it tends our troubles to appease.
      Sound words I know Timothy is to use,
And old wives' fables he is to refuse,
155   But yet grave Paul him nowhere doth forbid
The use of parables; in which lay hid
That gold, those pearls, and precious stones that were
Worth digging for, and that with greatest care.
      Let me add one word more. O man of God!
160   Art thou offended? Dost thou wish I had
Put forth my matter in another dress,
Or that I had in things been more express?
Three things let me propound, then I submit
To those that are my betters, (as is fit).
165   1. I find not that I am denied the use
Of this my method, so I no abuse
Put on the words, things, readers, or be rude
In handling figure, or similitude,
In application; but, all that I may,

170   Seek the advance of Truth this or that way.
        Denied, did I say? Nay, I have leave
        (Example too, and that from them that have
        God better pleased, by their words or ways
        Than any man that breatheth nowadays),
175   Thus to express my mind, thus to declare
        Things unto thee, that excellentest are.
            2. I find that men (as high as trees) will write
        Dialogue-wise; yet no man doth them slight
        For writing so: Indeed if they abuse
180   Truth, cursed be they, and the craft they use
        To that intent; but yet let truth be free
        To make her sallies upon thee and me,
        Which way it pleases God. For who knows how,
        Better than he that taught us first to plow,
185   To guide our Mind and Pens for his design?
        And he makes base things usher in divine.
            3. I find that Holy Writ in many places
        Hath semblance with this method, where the cases
        Do call for one thing, to set forth another;
190   Use it I may then, and yet nothing smother
        Truth's golden beams: nay, by this method may
        Make it cast forth its rays as light as day.
            And now, before I do put up my pen,
        I'll show the profit of my book, and then
195   Commit both thee and it unto that hand
        That pulls the strong down, and makes weak ones stand.
            This book it chalketh out before thine eyes
        The man that seeks the everlasting prize;
        It shows you whence he comes, whither he goes,
200   What he leaves undone, also what he does:
        It also shows you how he runs and runs,
        Till he unto the Gate of Glory comes.
            It shows too who set out for life amain,
        As if the lasting Crown they would obtain:
205   Here also you may see the reason why
        They lose their labor, and like fools do die.
            This book will make a traveler of thee,
        If by its counsel thou wilt ruled be;
        It will direct thee to the Holy Land,
210   If thou wilt its directions understand:
        Yea, it will make the slothful active be;
        The blind also delightful things to see.
            Art thou for something rare and profitable?
        Wouldst thou see a truth within a fable?
215   Art thou forgetful? Wouldest thou remember
        From New-year's-day to the last of December?
        Then read my fancies, they will stick like burrs,
        And may be to the helpless, comforters.
            This Book is writ in such a dialect
220   As may the minds of listless men affect:
        It seems a novelty, and yet contains

Nothing but sound and honest Gospel strains.
   Wouldst thou divert thyself from melancholy?
Wouldst thou be pleasant, yet be far from folly?
225   Wouldst thou read riddles, and their explanation?
Or else be drowned in thy contemplation?
Dost thou love picking meat? Or wouldst thou see
A man i' th' clouds, and hear him speak to thee?
Wouldst thou be in a dream, and yet not sleep?
230   Or wouldst thou in a moment laugh and weep?
Wouldest thou lose thyself, and catch no harm,
And find thyself again without a charm?
Wouldst read thyself, and read thou know'st not what,
And yet know whether thou art blest or not,
235   By reading the same lines? O then come hither,
And lay my book, thy head and heart together.
         JOHN BUNYAN.

[The Slough of Despond[1] and Mr. Worldly Wisdom]

Now I saw in my dream, that just as they had ended this talk, they drew near to a very miry Slough, that was in the midst of the plain; and they being heedless did both fall suddenly into the bog. The name of the slough was Despond. Here, therefore, they wallowed for a time, being grievously bedaubed with the dirt; and Christian, because of the burden that was on his back, began to sink in the mire.

Pli. Then said Pliable, Ah, neighbor Christian, where are you now?

Chr. Truly, said Christian, I do not know.

Pli. At that Pliable began to be offended, and angrily said to his fellow, Is this the happiness you have told me all this while of? If we have such ill speed at our first setting out, what may we expect 'twixt this and our journey's end? May I get out again with my life, you shall possess the brave country alone for me. And with that he gave a desperate struggle or two, and got out of the mire on that side of the slough which was next to his own house: so away he went, and Christian saw him no more.

Wherefore Christian was left to tumble in the Slough of Despond alone: but still he endeavored to struggle to that side of the slough that was still further from his own house, and next to the wicket-gate; the which he did, but could not get out, because of the burden that was upon his back: but I beheld in my dream, that a man came to him, whose name was Help, and asked him what he did there?

Chr. Sir, said Christian, I was bid go this way by a man called *Evangelist;* who directed me also to yonder gate, that I might escape the wrath to come; and as I was going thither, I fell in here.

Help. But why did you not look for the steps?

Chr. Fear followed me so hard, that I fled the next way, and fell in.

Help. Then said he, Give me thy hand. So he gave him his hand, and he drew him out, and set him upon sound ground, and bid him go on his way.

Then I stepped to him that pluckt him out, and said, Sir, wherefore (since over this place is the way from the City of Destruction to yonder gate), is it that this plat[2] is not mended, that poor travelers might go thither with more security? And he said unto me, This miry Slough is such a place as cannot be mended; it is the descent

1. "Slough" rhymes with "cow." "Despond" means dejec-   2. Piece of ground.
tion, loss of hope.

whither the scum and filth that attends conviction for sin doth continually run, and therefore it is called the Slough of Despond; for still as the sinner is awakened about his lost condition, there ariseth in his soul many fears and doubts, and discouraging apprehensions, which all of them get together, and settle in this place: And this is the reason of the badness of this ground.

It is not the pleasure of the King that this place should remain so bad. His laborers also have, by the direction of His Majesty's surveyors, been for above these sixteen hundred years employed about this patch of ground, if perhaps it might have been mended. Yea, and to my knowledge, saith he, here hath been swallowed up at least twenty thousand cart-loads, yea, millions of wholesome instructions, that have at all seasons been brought from all places of the King's dominions, and they that can tell say they are the best materials to make good ground of the place. If so be it might have been mended, but it is the Slough of Despond still, and so will be when they have done what they can.

True, there are by the direction of the lawgiver, certain good and substantial steps,[3] placed even through the very midst of this Slough; but at such time as this place doth much spew out its filth, as it doth against change of weather, these steps are hardly seen; or if they be, men through the dizziness of their heads, step besides; and then they are bemired to purpose, notwithstanding the steps be there; but the ground is good when they are once got in at the gate.

[VANITY FAIR][4]

Then I saw in my dream, that when they were got out of the wilderness, they presently saw a town before them, and the name of that town is Vanity; and at the town there is a Fair kept, called Vanity Fair: it is kept all the year long; it beareth the name of Vanity Fair, because the town where 'tis kept is lighter than Vanity; and also because all that is there sold, or that cometh thither, is vanity. As is the saying of the wise, "All that cometh is vanity."[5]

This fair is no new erected business, but a thing of ancient standing; I will show you the original of it.

Almost five thousand years agone, there were pilgrims walking to the Caelestial City, as these two honest persons are; and Beelzebub, Apollyon, and Legion,[6] with their Companions, perceiving by the path that the Pilgrims made, that their way to the City lay through this Town of Vanity, they contrived here to set up a Fair; a Fair wherein should be sold of all sorts of Vanity, and that it should last all the year long: therefore at this Fair are all such merchandise sold, as houses, lands, trades, places, honors, preferments, titles, countries, kingdoms, lusts, pleasures, and delights of all sorts, as whores, bawds, wives, husbands, children, masters, servants, lives, blood, bodies, souls, silver, gold, pearls, precious stones, and what not.

And moreover, at this Fair there is at all times to be seen jugglings, cheats, games, plays, fools, apes, knaves, and rogues, and that of all sorts.

Here are to be seen too, and that for nothing, thefts, murders, adulteries, false-swearers, and that of a blood-red color.

And as in other fairs of less moment, there are the several rows and streets under their proper names, where such and such wares are vended; so here likewise you have the proper places, rows, streets (*viz.* countries and kingdoms) where the wares of this

3. The steps are promises of forgiveness and acceptance through a life by faith in Christ.
4. From the image of a local fair, Bunyan creates a symbol of the emptiness and material worldliness that tempt the Christian.

5. Ecclesiastes 1.2, 1.14; 2.11, 2.17; Isaiah 40.17.
6. Beelzebub, the prince of demons (Matthew 12.24); Apollyon, "the angel of the bottomless pit" (Revelation 9.11); Legion, the "unclean spirit" (Mark 5.9).

Fair are soonest to be found: Here is the Britain Row, the French Row, the Italian Row, the Spanish Row, the German Row, where several sorts of vanities are to be sold. But as in other fairs, some one commodity is as the chief of all the fair, so the ware of Rome and her Merchandise is greatly promoted in this Fair; only our English nation, with some others, have taken a dislike thereat.

Now, as I said, the way to the Caelestial City lies just through this Town where this lusty Fair is kept; and he that will go to the City, and yet not go through this town, must needs go out of the World. The Prince of Princes himself, when here, went through this Town to his own Country, and that upon a Fair-day too; yea, and as I think, it was Beelzebub, the chief lord of this Fair, that invited him to buy of his vanities: yea, would have made him Lord of the Fair, would he but have done him reverence as he went through the town. Yea, because he was such a person of honor, Beelzebub had him from street to street, and showed him all the kingdoms of the world in a little time, that he might (if possible) allure that Blessed One to cheapen and buy some of his vanities. But he had no mind to the merchandise, and therefore left the town, without laying out so much as one farthing upon these vanities. This Fair therefore is an ancient thing, of long standing, and a very great Fair.

Now these pilgrims, as I said, must needs go through this Fair: well, so they did: but behold, even as they entered into the Fair, all the people in the Fair were moved, and the town itself as it were in a hubbub about them; and that for several reasons: for,

First, the pilgrims were clothed with such kind of raiment as was diverse from the raiment of any that traded in that Fair. The people therefore of the Fair made a great gazing upon them: Some said they were fools, some they were bedlams,[7] and some they are outlandish-men.

Secondly, and as they wondered at their Apparel, so they did likewise at their speech; for few could understand what they said: they naturally spoke the language of Canaan,[8] but they that kept the Fair were the men of this world; so that, from one end of the Fair to the other, they seemed barbarians each to the other.

Thirdly, but that which did not a little amuse the merchandisers was, that these pilgrims set very light by all their wares, they cared not so much as to look upon them; and if they called upon them to buy, they would put their fingers in their ears, and cry, "Turn away mine eyes from beholding vanity," and look upwards, signifying that their trade and traffic was in Heaven.[9]

One chanced mockingly, beholding the carriages of the men, to say unto them, What will ye buy? But they, looking gravely upon him, answered, "We buy the Truth."[1] At that there was an occasion taken to despise the men the more; some mocking, some taunting, some speaking reproachfully, and some calling upon others to smite them. At last things came to an hubbub and great stir in the Fair, insomuch that all order was confounded. Now was word presently brought to the great one of the Fair, who quickly came down and deputed some of his most trusty friends to take these men into examination, about whom the Fair was almost overturned. So the men were brought to examination; and they that sat upon them,[2] asked them whence they came, whither they went, and what they did there in such an unusual garb? The men told them that they were pilgrims and strangers in the world, and that they were going to their own country, which was the heavenly Jerusalem;[3] and that they had given none occasion to

---

7. Mad people from Bedlam, the Hospital of St. Mary of Bethlehem, which was made an insane asylum in 1647. In 1 Corinthians 2.7 St. Paul says that Christian wisdom looks like folly to worldly observers.
8. The Promised Land in the Bible.

9. Psalm 119.37; Philippians 3.19, 3.20.
1. Proverbs 23.23.
2. Questioned them.
3. Hebrews 11.13–16.

the men of the town, nor yet to the merchandisers, thus to abuse them, and to let[4] them in their journey, except it was for that, when one asked them what they would buy, they said they would buy the truth. But they that were appointed to examine them did not believe them to be any other than bedlams and mad, or else such as came to put all things into a confusion in the Fair. Therefore they took them and beat them, and besmeared them with dirt, and then put them into the cage, that they might be made a spectacle to all the men of the Fair. There therefore they lay for some time, and were made the objects of any man's sport, or malice, or revenge, the great one of the Fair laughing still at all that befell them. But the men being patient, and not rendering railing for railing, but contrariwise blessing, and giving good words for bad, and kindness for injuries done, some men in the Fair that were more observing, and less prejudiced than the rest, began to check and blame the baser sort for their continual abuses done by them to the men; they therefore in angry manner let fly at them again, counting them as bad as the men in the cage, and telling them that they seemed confederates, and should be made partakers of their misfortunes. The other replied, that for aught they could see, the men were quiet, and sober, and intended nobody any harm; and that there were many that traded in their Fair that were more worthy to be put into the cage, yea, and pillory[5] too, than were the men that they had abused. Thus, after divers words had passed on both sides, (the men behaving themselves all the while very wisely and soberly before them) they fell to some blows among themselves, and did harm one to another. Then were these two poor men brought before their examiners again, and there charged as being guilty of the late hubbub that had been in the Fair. So they beat them pitifully and hanged irons upon them, and led them in chains up and down the Fair, for an example and a terror to others, lest any should further speak in their behalf, or join themselves unto them. But Christian and Faithful behaved themselves yet more wisely, and received the ignominy and shame that was cast upon them, with so much meekness and patience, that it won to their side (though but few in comparison of the rest) several of the men in the Fair. This put the other party yet into a greater rage, insomuch that they concluded the death of these two men. Wherefore they threatened, that the cage nor irons should serve their turn, but that they should die, for the abuse they had done, and for deluding the men of the Fair.

> Behold Vanity Fair; the Pilgrims there
> Are chained and stoned beside;
> Even so it was, our Lord passed here,
> And on Mount Calvary died.

Then were they remanded to the cage again, until further order should be taken with them. So they put them in, and made their feet fast in the stocks.

Here also they called again to mind what they had heard from their faithful friend Evangelist, and were the more confirmed in their way and sufferings, by what he told them would happen to them. They also now comforted each other, that whose lot it was to suffer, even he should have the best on't; therefore each man secretly wished that he might have that preferment: but committing themselves to the allwise dispose of Him that ruleth all things, with much content they abode in the condition in which they were, until they should be otherwise disposed of.

[END OF PERSPECTIVES: SPIRITUAL SELF-RECKONINGS]

4. Hinder.
5. A wooden framework with holes through which the head and the hands of the offender were placed, in which state he or she was subjected to the public hurling verbal abuse and such objects as rotten vegetables.

Thomas Bowles. *The Bubblers' Medley, or a Sketch of the Times.* 1720

The Restoration and
the Eighteenth Century

◆❖◆

On 25 May 1660, Charles II set foot on the shore of Dover and brought his eleven-year exile to an end. The arrival was recorded by the great diarist Samuel Pepys, and his words preserve for us a form of the event:

> I went, and Mr. Mansell, and one of the King's footmen, with a dog that the King loved (which beshat the boat, which made us laugh, and methink that a king and all that belong to him are but just as others are), in a boat by ourselves, and so got on shore when the King did, who was received . . . with all imaginable love and respect at his entrance upon the land of Dover. Infinite the crowd of people and the horsemen, citizens, and noblemen of all sorts. The Mayor of the town came and gave him his white staff, the badge of his place, which the King did give him again. The Mayor also presented him from the town a very rich Bible, which he took and said it was the thing that he loved above all things in the world. . . . The shouting and joy expressed by all is past imagination.

Pepys captures and creates a brilliant mix of materials and experiences: his words compound jubilation and skepticism, images of authority and obeisance, tropes of spirituality and irony, and they remind us of the elements and passions by which all men live. Every gesture and exchange in this scene forecast the world to come, but what most signals the future is the paradox of remembering and forgetting that the diarist performs even as he records this scene. And all who witnessed the king's descent at Dover committed similar acts of memory and oblivion. Many of those (Pepys included) who were drunk with pleasure at the return of Charles Stuart had endorsed the destruction of his father eleven years before. The entire Restoration and the events that would follow over the ensuing years would prove a complex unfolding of memory and forgetfulness.

The jubilant crowds at Dover thought to make flux stop here: forever to banish the turbulence of civil war and political innovation, to restore all the old familiar forms, utterly to erase what had come between the death of the father and the restoration of the son. Charles II would soon institute an Act of Oblivion to those ends, forgiving proponents of rebellion by officially forgetting their misdeeds. But civil war and revolution would not be erased, nor could monarchy, the Anglican Church, aristocratic privilege, political patronage, and the old social hierarchies be revived as though nothing had intervened. Much of the old was brought back with the return of the Stuart monarchy, but the consequence of layering the present over a willfully suppressed past was an instability of feelings and forms that ensured the ever-changing triumph of different memories and different oblivions during the ensuing decades. No one celebrating the return of ancient ways in 1660 could have foreseen the ruptures and innovations that lay ahead in the next half of the century when crises of conspiracy and the birth of party politics would produce further shifts in monarchy, through a sequence of three ruling houses from three different countries. But even in 1660 the innocent acclaim on the shores of Dover was accompanied by hidden guilts and ironies, by vindictive desires, even for some by millenarian hopes. And while such stresses and tensions were unacknowledged in May 1660, they soon enough surfaced; and they unsettled not only the pleasures of this king's rule but the politics of an entire age.

MONARCHS, MINISTERS, EMPIRE

The coronation of Charles II in May 1661 marked the beginning of both the first and the eleventh year of his rule. The king's laws were named as if he had taken possession of the crown at the moment of his father's execution in 1649. And fictions, legal and not so legal, were to prove a hallmark of Stuart rule. The king openly proclaimed his love of parliaments, his devotion to the immemorial constitution of balance and moderation, his Protestant fervor, and his pious hopes for a national church. Yet he often postponed his parliaments; he claimed a tender conscience for Protestant dissenters, but he maneuvered for the toleration of Roman Catholics; he conducted an aggressive, nationalist program against European powers, but he signed a secret and deeply compromising treaty with Louis XIV; he took communion in the Anglican Church, but on his deathbed he sealed his own conversion to Catholicism; he was tenderly affectionate to his barren queen, yet he publicly flaunted his whoring tastes; he repeatedly exiled his unpopular brother James, Duke of York, while promoting and indulging his own bastard sons, yet he staunchly resisted any effort to displace his brother from the line of succession. The dominance of masquerade surely derived from Charles's temper, but fiction and falsehood were also the structural principles and aesthetic features of an entire world.

In December 1678, a series of events started to unfold that proved the very emblem of the masking, the fears, and the psychology of Charles II's rule. It began with legal depositions: one Titus Oates, a baker's son and self-annointed savior of a Protestant people, claimed to have knowledge of a secret plot to kill the king, crown his Catholic brother, and begin the wholesale conversion of English souls—and, just as frightening, English properties—to Rome. Oates offered to a public hungry for scandal and change a Popish plot and a familiar mix of images and idioms: priests and idols, the Roman Antichrist, conspiracy, murder, and mayhem. His depositions and fabrications played brilliantly on memories of the past and on fears of a future under a Catholic king. Nor did it help that the Duke of York's private secretary, Edward Coleman, was caught with treasonous correspondence in his chamber. The plot seemed compounded of sufficient truths to challenge the stability of the Crown. From the midst of the plot, and under the hand of the Earl of Shaftesbury, a political party emerged that took advantage of Popish facts and fears by proposing the Bill of Exclusion in Parliament that would bar the Duke of York and any future Catholic monarchs from the English throne. In the event, the bill failed, Charles died of natural causes, and the duke succeeded his brother in February 1685.

During James's brief reign, no plots, conspiracies, or political parties proved so costly to his rule as did the new king himself. He succeeded his brother in a mood of surprising public affirmation. At his accession, James returned the embrace of Anglican England by promising to honor the national church and that most beloved of Protestant properties, a tender conscience. There would be no forcing of religious uniformity in this reign. But soon enough James began to move against Anglican interests: he staffed his army with Catholic officers, he imposed Catholic officials on Oxford University, and he insisted that his Declarations of Toleration be read aloud from the pulpits of Anglican churches. Such a program challenged interest, property, and propriety, and it spelled the quick demise of Catholic rule.

As Duke of York, James had been famed for martial valor. But now, when confronted in November 1688 by the army of his Dutch son-in-law, William of Orange, he fled under cover of night to France. What had in part provoked James's flight were memories of the past—of civil war and of the execution of his father, Charles I. What had provoked the invasion by William of Orange was not merely the specter of Louis XIV hovering behind James's rule or the open presence of Jesuits at James's court. It was the birth of James Francis Edward Stuart, son of James II and Mary of Modena. Protestants would suffer not only the inconvenience of one Catholic monarch but the possibility of an endless Catholic succession. The prospect was too much to bear. Secret negotiations were begun between powerful English artistocrats—Whigs and Tories alike—and William, the governor (stadholder) of Holland, resulting in what many called the Glorious Revolution. But the deceits and pretenses—the gaps and silences—of this palace coup did not strike all contemporaries as glorious. The stadholder who chased a Catholic king from England was not only an invading hero (though some did call him William the Conqueror), he was also the son-in-law of James II. Those who clung to the binding ties of loyalty and gratitude accused William and Mary of deep impiety, indeed, of parricide.

But the astonishing invitation to William of Orange produced no bloodshed. What it did produce was a Protestant monarchy under the rule of King William III and Queen Mary. Members of Parliament, meeting to invent the laws that would sanctify this revolutionary change, decided that it would be best to say they had discovered the throne of England mysteriously vacant and that this William was no conqueror but a rightful claimant on a vacant throne. Of course, not everyone was pleased by such a revolution—sacred oaths had been broken, binding ties were cast aside, vows were juggled as mere words. Those who would not accept a convenient revolution were called Jacobites; that is, supporters of King James (*Jacobus* in Latin); they remained a force that would trouble British political life by threatening a Stuart restoration in the fervent but failed Jacobite rebellions of 1715 and 1745.

Most of William's subjects, though, were content with the evasions of this Glorious Revolution. Many were not content, though, with the program of European war in which the English were now plunged by their new king, intent on thwarting the ambitions of Louis XIV, his lifelong nemesis. The ruinous expense of war demanded taxes and fiscal innovation; it produced a stream of grumbling satire, complaint against Dutch favorites, and more than one conspiracy and attempted assassination. No such disaffection or turbulence disturbed the reign (1701–1714) of William's successor, Queen Anne. Her years were the twilight of Stuart monarchy, a time of political nostalgia and commercial confidence whose mood the young Alexander Pope captured in the lines of *Windsor-Forest* (1713), where softened memories and strategic elisions of the years of Stuart rule are mingled with images of triumph—of imperial expansion and a swelling commerce of domestic and foreign trade.

But luxury was not England's only import. At the death of Queen Anne an entire court and new ruling house were shipped to England from the German state of Hanover. George I was the grandson of James I; beyond lineage, George's communion in a Protestant Church was the virtue that most recommended his succession. He spoke no English, knew nothing of his new subjects, and could not be bothered to learn. Nor was he much implicated in the management of a state whose rule would successively become less the prerogative of kings than the business of ministers and the function of parties, interest, and corruption. This displacement of monarch by minister was cemented during the period caustically nicknamed "Robin's Reign": two decades (1721–1742), transversing the reigns of George I and George II, when politics were dominated by Robert Walpole, who bought loyalties, managed kings, and ran the state with such ruthless efficency as to earn him the new label "prime minister" (the phrase was meant as an insult, aimed at the perceived excess of his power in a government where ministers were only supposed to advise their colleagues and their king). The South Sea Bubble, a state-endorsed investment scheme which ruined many, was the making of Robert Walpole. As the only cabinet minister untainted by the scandal (he had initially argued against the scheme, then lost money in it), he was put in charge of the subsequent governmental housecleaning. Once empowered, he cheerfully shed his scruples, devising a political machine fueled by patronage that made his cronies rich, his opposition apoplectic. By the firmness of his rule and the prudence of his policies, Walpole consolidated a long period of Whig supremacy that supplanted the party contest of the preceding decades, when Whigs and Tories had see-sawed more swiftly in and out of power.

The parties had begun to crystallize during the Exclusion crisis of the early 1680s, when Whigs fought to bar the king's Catholic brother from the throne, and Tories upheld the established continuity of the Stuart line. Like "prime minister," the two party names began as insult, "Tory" denoting an Irish-Catholic bandit, "Whigs" identifying a group of Scotch rebels during the civil wars. Late in the eighteenth century, Samuel Johnson summed up their polarities: "The prejudice of the Tory is for establishment; the prejudice of the Whig is for innovation." "Establishment" meant preserving monarchic prerogatives, upholding the Anglican church, lamenting the advent of the Hanoverians, and—for some Tories, not all—actively yearning for the restoration of the Stuart line, and abetting the attempts to achieve this in the Jacobite rebellions of 1715 and 1745. Whig "innovation" entailed enthusiastic support for both the Glorious Revolution and the House of Hanover, for policies of religious tolerance, and for all measures that advanced the interests of the newly prosperous and powerful merchant class. In the late seventeenth century, party politics had begun for the first time to supplant long-running religious conflicts as the main articulation of interest and power. For all its noise and rage, the new structure produced a paradoxical calm, not by the suppression of difference but by its recognition. The division into parties amounted to a sanctioned fragmentation of the whole. Even during the reign of Anne, when party conflict was at its most feverish, what the machinery of the party seemed to ensure was the containment of partisan interest within the dynamic, even organic, coherence of the state.

During Walpole's "reign," portions of the two parties coalesced in an uneasy alliance. The arrogance, obstinacy, and efficacy of Walpole's methods galvanized an opposition consisting of both Tories and alienated Whigs; their endeavors acquired luster from the contributions of a remarkable array of writers (the Tories Jonathan Swift, Alexander Pope, John Gay, and Henry Fielding, and the Whig James Thomson) who opposed the prime minister on grounds of personality, principle, and of course self-interest. Walpole, recognizing that the best writers worked for the opposition, strove to suppress them by all the strategies of censorship he could devise. But by his greatness as a character and his force as an opponent, Walpole loomed for a long while as both literature's nemesis and its muse.

In fact, Walpole enforced the policies endorsed by only a fraction of his party—those moderate Whigs deeply interested in cultivating the country's wealth by commerce, deeply resistant to waging war. "My *politics*," he once wrote emphatically, "*are to keep free from all engagements, as long as we possibly can*"; by "engagements," he meant military commitments abroad. By the late 1730s, he discovered that he could keep free from them no longer. Britons feared that powers on the Continent—Spain, Austria, and above all France—were encroaching on their rights, and the popular clamor to wage European war prevailed. "When trade is at stake," the oppositionist William Pitt warned the British, "it is your last retrenchment; you must defend it or perish." Under the pressure of such sentiments Walpole eventually resigned, having led the state through two decades of comparative peace, growing national prosperity, and a new stability in government, but leaving behind him an army and a navy debilitated by disuse. Nonetheless, with trade at stake and the navy rebuilt, Britain embarked on a series of wars that ran almost unbroken for the rest of the century. Pitt presided brilliantly over many of them, wars waged directly or indirectly against France for trading privileges and territories abroad. By 1763, Britain had secured possession of Bengal in India, many islands and coastal territories in the Caribbean, and virtually all of North America (including Canada) east of the Mississippi, as well as half of all the international trade transpiring on the planet. So great was the impetus towards empire that even Britain's humiliating defeat in the American War of Independence (1775–1783) could not really halt the momentum; territories in India were still expanding, and settlement of Australia lay in the offing.

By now, the throne was occupied by the first Hanoverian monarch born in Britain—George III. His long reign (1760–1820) teemed with troubles: the popular scorn for his chosen ministers; the loss of the American war; the aftershocks of the French Revolution; the defiance of his heirs; the torments of his own slow-encroaching madness. But almost from beginning to end he ruled over the richest nation and the widest empire in the world. In 1740, a new song could be heard with a catchy refrain: "Rule, Britannia, rule the waves / Britons never will be slaves." The words were the work of the Scots-born poet James Thomson, now a proud adherent of "Britannia" by virtue of the Act of Union (1707) which had fused Scotland with England and Wales into a new nation, newly named: Great Britain. Over the ensuing years the song took hold because of the seductively prophetic ways in which it forecast Britain's greatness, and partly because of the proud but peculiar resonances of the refrain's last line. There, Thomson contrasts British liberties with the slave-like constraints supposedly suffered by subjects of absolute monarchy elsewhere. Less directly, "slaves" also points to those peoples upon whose subjugation British privilege and British prosperity were increasingly to depend. Throughout the century, Britons profited spectacularly from the capture, transport, sale, and labor of African slaves in current and former colonies; "no nation," William Pitt the Younger proclaimed in 1792, had "plunged so deeply into this guilt as Great Britain."

There were also whole populations whose condition often evoked the analogy of slavery in the minds of the few who paid reformist attention to their plight: the oppressed indigenous peoples of the colonies, and women and the poor at home. Conversation about such issues became louder and more purposeful near the end of the eighteenth century, as particular champions began to turn social questions into moral causes: John Wilkes on the widening of liberties and voting rights; Mary Wollstonecraft on the rights of women; William Blake (and later, William Cobbett) on the economic inequities of the whole social structure. The problems themselves did not even begin to find redress until the following century, but the emergence of such advocacies, quickened by the audacities of the French Revolution, marked a turning point toward the Romanticism that seized poetic and political imaginations in the 1790s. For most Britons of the eighteenth century, however, the new prosperity produced no special promptings of conscience. As their Restoration forebears had actively encouraged oblivion in an effort to anesthetize themselves to their past, men and women now sustained a moral and social oblivion that eased their use of others, and their pleasure in new wealth. Out of such adroitly managed oscillations, Britons fabricated a new sense of themselves as a nation and an empire.

This new construct was in large measure the work of a prominent breed of economic architects: the capital-wielding middle classes. For centuries, wealth had derived primarily from land: tenant farmers performed the labor; the landed gentry collected the often enormous profits. The new wealth was amassed, even created, by people situated between these two extremes, constituting what was often referred to as "the middling rank," "the middling station," or "the middling orders." What set the middling orders apart was the comparatively new way in which they made their money: not by landed inheritance, not by tenancy or wagework, but by the adroit deployment of money itself. Having acquired a sum by inheritance, wage, or loan, they used it as capital, investing it, along with their own efforts, in potentially lucrative enterprises: in shops, in factories, and in the enormous new financial structures (banks, stocks) that underwrote the nation's economic expansiveness. They hired helpers, reinvested profits, and when their schemes succeeded, they made their money grow. With wealth, of course, grew clout. The interests of the "City"—that is, of the eastern half of London where bustling merchants made their deals—increasingly shaped the affairs of state, the appetites for empire. Empire also shaped the progress of the arts: members of the middle class became the chief consumers and energetic producers of the period's most conspicuous new forms of literature: newspapers and novels. But nowhere were the new powers of the burgeoning bourgeoisie more striking than in the theater, that cultural site they often visited and ultimately revised.

MONEY, MANNERS, AND THEATRICS

No event more exactly and more economically signals the return of an aristocratic court to the center of English culture than the reopening of the London theaters in 1662. The intimacy, indeed the complicity, of court with theater throughout the early modern period was such that when in the 1640s Parliament took aim at monarchy, aristocracy, and privilege, it not only struck off the heads of the Duke of Buckingham and Archbishop Laud, it also banished play acting and shut tight the doors of the London stage. But Puritans could not banish the theater from the English imagination, and no sooner were the playhouses closed than publishers issued new editions of old plays, and the theater made a secret return in domestic spaces and before private audiences. Print and memory would be the preservative of an entire culture. In 1660, monarchy and theater were restored in tandem. But this artistic restoration, like the political one that made it possible, irresistibly mingled the old with the new. Pepys captured all the excitement and splendor of this restoration; as usual he proves adroit at reckoning innovation:

> [T]he stage is now . . . a thousand times better and more glorious than heretofore. Now, wax-candles, and many of them; then, not above three pounds of tallow. Now, all things civil, no rudeness anywhere; then, as in a bear garden. Then, two or three fiddlers; now, nine or ten of the best. Then, nothing but rushes upon the ground and everything mean; and now all otherwise. Then the Queen seldom and the King never would come; now not the King only for state but all civil people do think they may come as well as any.

One reason that "all civil people" thought so was a matter of simple geography. Whereas the theaters of Shakespeare's day had been located in seedy districts on the outskirts of the city, this new and sumptuous theatrical world was ensconced in new neighborhoods strategically located for maximum social confluence, on the border between Westminster—home of the court—and the City of London, dwelling place of a "mighty band of citizens and prentices" whose sudden convergence with royalty seemed a dramatic innovation. They had all gathered to witness the most astonishing new spectacle of all: women on stage in a public theater.

Before the Restoration, aristocratic women had tantalized the court in private and privileged masquing; now the pleasures of display and consumption were democratized in several ways. For women, theatricality was no longer a pastime reserved for the very few but a plausible—though precarious—profession. For audiences at the new theaters, actresses represented the possibility of erotic spectacle for the price of a ticket—a chance to gaze on women who everyone knew were managing the pleasures, and often the policies, of kings and courtiers. Inevitably new strategies of theatricality suffused this audience, where women might model seductive conduct on the teasing combinations of concealment and display enacted before them. Pepys eavesdropped on the libertine Sir Charles Sedley in urgent banter with two women: "And one of the women would and did sit with her mask on, all the play. He would fain know who she was, but she would not tell; yet did give him many pleasant hints of her knowledge of him, by that means setting his brains at work to find out who she was, and did give him leave to use all means but pulling off her mask." Display and disguise not only animated the stage, they quickened social exchange in the intimate spaces of stalls and boxes. The traffic between revelation and concealment defined this theater. It drove the plots of plays and galvanzied audiences, modeling and scripting their fashions, their language, their lives.

In such a world the theater provided a national mask, a fantasy of empire and heroism, and yet at the same time sustained a critique of masquerade, a brutal exposure of deceptions rampant in the culture. On the one hand, the heroic drama displayed, indeed reveled in, outsized acts of conquest in exotic lands, valor, and virtue: on stage, princes slaughtered infidels by the thousands; virgins sustained honor through impossible ordeals of abduction and assault. Yet in 1667, at the same moment such dramas were thriving in the king's and the duke's playhouses, the royal fleet was being burned and sunk by a Dutch navy that breached all defenses, invading the very precincts and privacy of London's docks and shipyards. And while the fleet burned, the king busied himself with other depradations, sustaining a series of intrigues, some with the very actresses who wore such incomparable honor and virtue on the stage. (The mix of myth and mischief was popular in pictures too—for example, in the portrait of Barbara Villiers, Countess of Castlemaine, perhaps the most notorious of all the king's mistresses, gotten up in the guise of Minerva, Roman goddess of wisdom.) The heroic drama celebrated military conquest and colonial glory, and displayed them at a moment in national history that produced nothing so much as shame and humiliation: defeat at the hands of Dutch ships and Dutch commerce.

At the same time, but in a far different dramatic mode, the stage sustained a brilliant critique of a whole culture of incongruity, masquerade, and self-delusion. Restoration comedy took as its subject appetite and opportunism, social hypocrisy and sexual power play. The London audience watched scenes of seduction and connivance set in the very vicinities they had traversed to reach the playhouse: St. James's Park, Covent Garden. Such aristocratic libertines as Sir Charles Sedley and Lord Rochester, intent on their own intrigues, might admire themselves in a theatrical mirror, where the rake-hero conducted endless parry-and-thrust with his equals,

Sir Peter Lely (1616–1680). *Barbara Villiers, Countess of Castlemaine.* ca. 1665. Theatricality disseminated: Charles II's favorite painter portrays Charles II's favorite mistress, in costume as Minerva, Roman goddess of wisdom, against a stormy background. Castlemaine's countenance was reproduced in less costly ways as well, in engravings from Lely's portraits that made the visage of the king's mistress possessible by ordinary mortals. The diarist Samuel Pepys records a visit to Lely's sumptuous studio, where he "saw the so-much-by-me-desired picture of my Lady Castlemaine, which is a most blessed picture and that I must have a copy of."

brutalized his inferiors, and laid hands and claim on any moveable object of desire: fruits and foodstuffs, silks and sonnets, housemaids and women of high estate. But the rakes in the playhouse might see themselves mocked as well. The best comic writers—Wycherley, Etherege, Behn, Congreve—showed the libertines equalled and often bested in cunning by the women they pursued, baffled where they would be most powerful, enslaved where they would be most free. In brilliant volleys of dialogue, these lovers mixed passion and poison in volatile measures, chasing one another through a maze of plots, counterplots, and subplots so convoluted as to suggest a world of calculation run mad. Over the thirty years of its triumphs, Restoration comedy, in an astounding fugue of excesses and depravities, laid bare the turbulence and toxins of this culture.

That the heroic drama, with all its exaggerations and flatteries, found a market, is hardly surprising; what is more puzzling is the commercial triumph of Restoration comedy, a theatrical mode that entertained by punishing and humiliating its audience—though it is hardly surprising that this theater should itself have fallen victim in the 1690s to prudery and what would come to be called "taste." In the wake of the Protestant revolution of 1688 that typed Stuart rule as the very emblem of self-indulgence, agents of moral improvement and social propriety made their assault on Restoration comedy the stalking horse for a broad program of Christian reform. Restoration comedy, which had erupted as a repudiation of Puritan prohibitions, now seemed to prompt a new wave of moral rectitude.

Under such pressures, the playhouse redirected its mirror, away from the aristocracy towards the upper strata of the "middling sort": London merchants, colonial
profiteers. During the Restoration, the newly prosperous mercantile classes who converged with courtiers at the theater had watched themselves either derided or
ignored on stage, their social pretensions and ineptitudes put down in the comedies,
their commercial concerns absent from the heroic drama. In the early eighteenth
century, they saw themselves glorified instead, in "domestic tragedy," which displayed the tribulations of commercial households, and in sentimental comedy, which
sought by a mix of tears and modest laughter to inculcate family values and to portray
the merchant class as the nation's moral core. Richard Steele's *The Conscious Lovers*
(1722) sounded the fanfare for a newly theatric social self-conception. "We merchants," a businessman informs an aristocrat, "are a species of gentry that have grown
into the world this last century, and are as honorable and almost as useful as you
landed folk, that have always thought yourself so much above us."

Nor was the stage the only venue to promulgate this new cultural self-awareness.
By its very title *The Spectator* (1711–1713), one of the most widely read periodicals of
the century, assured its largely middle-class audience that they moved under the constant, thoughtful scrutiny of a virtual playgoer, the paper's fictive author, "Mr. Spectator," who made all London a kind of theater, in which he (and his eagerly imitative
readers) might perpetually enjoy the privileges of making observations and forming
judgments. The very energies that had been drained away from the stage now found a
new home in the theatricalized world of commerce, fashion, manners, taste.

The cast members in this new theater were numerous, varied, and eager for
direction, mostly because, as a "new species of gentry," they aspired to roles for which
they had formerly been deemed unfit. Terms like "esquire" and "gentleman" had
operated in previous centuries as proof of literal "entitlement." They were secured by
registration with the College of Heralds, and they calibrated not merely monetary
wealth but lineage, landholdings, education, and social standing. In the eighteenth
century, men and women with sufficient money and nerve assumed these titles for
themselves, confident enough that they might learn to play the part. "In our days,"
noted a 1730 dictionary, "all are accounted gentlemen that have money." But since
"the money" was now so variously attainable—by shopkeeping, by manufacture, by
international trade—the "middle station" was itself subdivided into many striations,
and since the very point of capital was accumulation and improvement, ascent by
emulation became a master plot in the new social theater. "Everyone," observed one
commentator, "is flying from his inferiors in pursuit of his superiors, who fly from him
with equal alacrity."

Amid the flux, fashion and commodity—what one wore, what one owned—
mattered enormously. Wigs, fans, scarves, silks, petticoats, and jewels; china, silver,
family portraits—these were the costumes, these the props of the new commercial
theater, by which members of the middle orders pleased themselves and imitated the
gentry. The commercial classes who had begun by catering to the aristocracy gradually became, in their waxing prosperity, their own best customers, selling garb and
goods to one another. Shrewd marketers saw that novelty itself possessed an intrinsic
and urgent appeal for people constantly in social flight, tirelessly engaged in remaking themselves. Advertising came into its own, filling the pages and underwriting the
costs of the daily, weekly, and monthly periodicals. The listing of consumables
became a prevalent mode of print, in everything from auction catalogues (the still-
dominant houses of Christie's and Sotheby's got their start near the middle of the

century) to poems and novels, where long lists of products and possessions became a means of recording the culture's appetites and at times of satirizing them. In the hands of Swift and Pope, the catalogue itself became a form of art. The taste in literary miscellany reflected a more general taste for omnivorous consumption: variety indexed abundance, and proved power. Tea from China, coffee from the Caribbean, tobacco from Virginia—all were relatively new, comparatively inexpensive, and enormously popular. In daily rituals of drink and smoke, the middling orders imbibed and inhaled a pleasing sense of their global reach, their comfortable centrality on a planet newly commercialized.

Commodities formed part of a larger discourse, involving speech and gesture as well as prop and costume. A cluster of precepts, gathered under the umbrella-term "politeness," supplied the stage directions, even at times the script, for the new social theater in which everyone was actor, and everyone was audience. Eager to shine in their recently acquired roles, the merchant classes pursued the polish implicit in the word "polite." They hired "dancing masters" to teach them graceful motions and proper manners; "bear leaders" (tutors) to guide their sons on the Grand Tour of France and Italy in the footsteps of the nobility; elocution coaches to help them purge inappropriate accents; teachers of painting and music to supply their daughters with marriageable competence. For the newly prosperous, politeness was the epitome of distinction: it went beyond gesture and accomplishment to suggest a state of mind, a refinement of perception, a mix of knowledge, responsiveness, and judgment often summarized as "taste." "The man of polite imagination," said the *Spectator*, "is let into a great many pleasures that the vulgar are not capable of receiving." Eager to gain access, middle-class readers avidly sought instruction.

Politeness (which Samuel Johnson once defined as "fictitious benevolence") required considerable self-control; the passions (rage, greed, lust) were to be contained and channeled into the appearance of abundant and abiding goodwill. The middle classes embraced such constraints partly to allay widespread suspicion of their commercial aggressions, their social ambitions. Their preoccupation with politeness has helped to foster a recurrent misimpression of the period: that, setting aside the occasional rake or wench, it was all manners and morals, dignity and decorum, fuss and formality, reason and enlightenment. Not so. Even among the merchant classes, politeness afforded only provisional concealment for roiling energies; amid the impoverished and the gentry, it held less purchase still. In no succeeding epoch until our own was language so openly and energetically obscene, drunkenness so rampant, sexual conduct so various and unapologetic. Even among the "officially" polite, the very failure of containment could produce a special thrill. In one of the century's most often-used phrases, a speaker announces that "I cannot forebear"—that is, cannot restrain myself—from saying or doing what the verb itself suggests were better left unsaid or undone. The formula declares helpless and pleasurable surrender to an unmastered impulse, and the condition was apparently endemic. James Boswell records the memorable self-summary of an elderly lawyer: "I have tried . . . in my time to be a philosopher, but—I don't know how—cheerfulness was always breaking in." Such "breakings-in" (and breakings-out) of feeling were common, even cherished. The scholar Donald Greene has argued well that the eighteenth century was less an "age of reason" (as has often been said) than an age of exuberance. Certainly much of what the middle classes read and wrote is a literature of outburst: of hilarity, of lament, of rage, of exaltation. The copious diaries that the century brought forth deal in all such exclamations; they are the prose of people who have chosen to write rather than repress the thoughts and actions that strict politeness might proscribe. Even the *Spectator*, that manual of polished taste, presents itself as the daily outpouring of a writer who, after maintaining an eccentric lifelong silence, has found that he can no longer keep his "discoveries"—moral, social, experiential—to himself.

Such self-publicizing was more complex for women than for men. When women represented their own lives—in manuscript (letters, journals) and increasingly in print—they sometimes chafed at the paradoxical mix of tantalizing possibilities and painful limitations that their privilege produced. Post-Restoration prosperity and politeneness supplied women with many new venues for self-display and sociability, in playhouses and pleasure gardens, ballrooms, spas, and shops. Society exalted and paraded women as superior consumers: wearing the furs, fragrances, and fabrics of distant climes, they furnished evidence of empire, proud proof of their fathers' and husbands' economic attainments. They consumed print, too; near the start of the eighteenth century, male editors invented the women's periodical, and found the new genre immensely profitable. Increasingly, women not only purchased print but produced it, deploying their words and wit as a kind of cultural capital, which when properly expended might reap both cash and fame. During the eighteenth century, for the first time, books by women—of poems, of precepts, and above all of fiction—became not exotic but comparatively commonplace.

Still, books by women remained controversial, as did all manifestations of female autonomy and innovation. The very excitement aroused by women's new conspicuousness in the culture provoked counter-efforts at containment. Preachers and moralists argued endlessly that female virtue resided in domesticity. Marriage itself offered an age-old instrument of social control, newly retooled to meet the needs of ambitious merchants, for whom daughters were the very currency of social mobility. If parents could arrange the right marriage, the whole family's status promptly rose. The dowry that the bride brought with her was an investment in future possibilities: in the rank and connections that the union secured, in the inheritance that would descend to its heirs, in the annual income ("jointure") that the wife herself would receive following the death of the husband. Financially, a widow (or for that matter, a well-born woman who never married) was often far more independent than a wife, whose wedding led to a kind of sanctioned erasure. She possessed little or no control over marital property (including the wealth she had brought to the union); "in marriage," wrote the codifier of English law William Blackstone, "husband and wife are one person, and that person is the husband." The sums that the husband undertook to hand over to his wife were dubbed "pin money" (a suggestive trivialization): funds for managing the household, that sphere wherein, as the moral literature insisted, a woman might best deploy her innate talents and find her sanctioned satisfactions. These consisted first and foremost in producing children and in shaping their manners and morals. In a time of improvisatory birth control, precarious obstetrics, and high infant mortality, the bearing of children was a relentless, dangerous, and emotionally exhausting process. The upbringing of children provided more pleasure, and possessed a new cachet: the conduct literature endorsed busy, attentive child-rearing as the highest calling possible for women whose prosperity freed them from the need to work for wages. (Guidebooks for parents and pleasure books for children both had their origins in the eighteenth century.) Apart from the duties of motherhood and household management—the supervision of servants, meals, shopping, and social occasions—the woman of means was encouraged to pursue those pleasures for which her often deliberately constricted education had prepared her: music, embroidery, letter writing, and talk at the tea table—the domestic counterpart of the clubs and coffeehouses, where women were not permitted to appear.

In the late seventeenth century, the possibilities for women had seemed at moments more various and more audacious. In the plays of Aphra Behn, female characters pursued their pleasures with an almost piratical energy and ingenuity; in *A Serious Proposal to the Ladies* (1694), the feminist Mary Astell imagined academies where women could withdraw to pursue the pleasures of learning and escape the drudgeries of marriage. In the eighteenth century, though, despite women's increasing authorial presence, these early audacities tended to go underground. Protests by women against their secondary status are most overt in manuscript—in the acerbic poems and letters that Mary Wortley Montagu circulated among her friends, in the journal entries wherein the brewer's wife Hester Thrale vented her frustrations. In print, women's desire for autonomy became a tension in the text, rather than its explicit point or outcome. Novelists explored women's psyches with subtlety; their plots, however, nearly always culminated in marriage, and more rarely in catastrophe, as though those were the only alternatives. Even the Bluestocking Circle, an eminent late-century group of intellectual women, preached tenets of essential sexual difference and subordination; they argued (for example) in favor of improving girls' educations, but as a way of preparing them for better and happier work within the home rather than for adventures abroad. During the eighteenth century, the middle classes did much to spell out the gendered divison of labor—father as the family's champion in the marketplace, mother as cheerfully efficient angel in the house—that remained a cultural commonplace, among families who could afford it, for the next two hundred years.

Among the poor, such divisions were not tenable; most manual labor paid so little that everyone in the family had to work if all were to survive. Wives not only managed their frugal households; they also worked for wages, in fields, in shops, or in cottage manufacture of fabrics, gloves, basketry. Children often began wage work at age four or five, treading laundry, scaring crows, sweeping chimneys; boys began the more promising role of apprenticeships around the age of ten. For many of the poor, domestic service offered employment comparatively secure and endlessly demanding. Darker prospects included prostitution, and crime; shoplifting was punishable by death. In the case of the helplessly indigent, local government was responsible for providing relief; but the Poor Law provided large loopholes by which the parish could drive out any unwanted supplicant—an unwed mother, for example—who could not meet the intricate and restrictive criteria for legal residence. The poor had no vote, no voice in government; as the century progressed, their predicament attracted increasing attention and advocacy. Philanthropists instituted charity schools designed, in the words of their proponent Hannah More, "to train up the lower classes in habits of industry and piety." Two convictions informed even the most ambitious philanthropy: that poverty was part of a divine plan and that it was the fault of the indolent poor themselves; they thus found themselves caught between the rock of providence and the hard place of reproach. Yet charity schools did increase literacy, and with it perhaps the sense of possibilities. Other late-century developments, too, were mixed. Improvements in sanitation, medicine, and hygiene contributed to a surge in population, which in turn produced among the rural poor a labor surplus: too many people, too little work. At the same time, wealthy landholders increased the practice of "enclosure," acquiring and sequestering acreage formerly used by the poor for common pasturage and family farming. As a result, many rural families left the land on which they had worked for centuries, and traveled to alien terrain: the textile mills that capitalists had newly built, and the industrial cities developing rapidly around them.

As the poor became poorer, the very rich—landowning lords and gentry—became very much richer, both by the means they now shared with the middle class (capital investment in banks and stocks), and through their own long-held resources. Land increased in value, partly because there were now so many merchant families passion-ately eager to buy into the landscape and the life of their aristocratic betters, among whom the spectacle of emulation provoked amusement and revulsion. The landed gen-try preserved their distance by many means: social practices (they often flaunted their adulteries, for example, as contrast to middle-class proprieties); artistic allegiance (with the advent of the bourgeois drama, aristocratic audiences defected from the theater to the opera house, where elaborate productions and myth-based plots sustained the aris-tocratic values of the heroic drama); and by the sheer ostentation of their leisure and the magnitude of their consumption. But the pivotal difference remained political: by the award of offices, by the control of elections, landowners maintained their strangle-hold on local and national power, despite all the waxing wealth of trade.

At the same time, their very absorption in pleasure and power demanded a continual traffic with their inferiors. Merchants and shopkeepers catered to them; professionals managed their transactions; household servants contrived their com-forts; aspiring artists sought to cultivate their taste and profit by their patronage. Transactions among the aristocracy and the middle classes took other forms as well. A lord low on money often found it lucrative to marry the daughter of a thriving merchant. And middle-class modes of life could exert a subtler magnet-ism, too—particularly for George III, who prized mercantile decorum over aristo-cratic swagger. In the portrait of his queen and her two eldest sons on the next page, the artist Johann Zoffany (himself an expensive German import) celebrates not their royal state but their domestic felicity: the heroic trappings (helmet, spear, turban) so conspicuous in Lely's portrait of the scandalous Lady Castle-maine (see page 1986) are here reduced to the props of child's play in the domes-tic theater of family relations.

King George had commissioned Johann Zoffany in pursuit of precisely this effect. By his eager emulation of the middling orders, George III broke with monar-chic traditions, but he inaugurated a new one that would be sustained and expanded in various ways by Queen Victoria in the nineteenth century and her successors in the twentieth. During George's reign, too, the middle classes began to pursue more practical convergence with the aristocracy: a wider distribution of voting rights, a firmer political power base. For the first time, the phrase "middle classes" itself came into use, as a way of registering this cohort's recognition of its own coherence and interests, its unique, often combative relations with the classes above and below; the plural ("classes") registered the abiding diversity—of income, of lifestyle—within the cohesion. In the years since the Restoration, the middle classes had moved them-selves energetically, in the theater of social and economic relations, from a place in the audience towards center stage, exerting enormous power over the working lives of the poor, posing challenges to the elite. Increasingly, their money, manners, appetites, and taste came to be perceived as the essence of national life, as the part that might stand for the whole. "Trade," Henry Fielding remarked in 1751, "has indeed given a new face to the nation."

Johann Zoffany. *Queen Charlotte with her Two Eldest Sons*. 1764. Theatricality domesticated: a century after Lely painted the king's mistress in the garb of the goddess of wisdom, such mythological trappings are reduced to dress-up for George III's two young sons at play. Amid sumptuous furnishings, Zofanny's conversation piece emphasizes not the grandeur of the royal family but its intimacy and affection; a new era of majesty as "good example" has commenced.

It gave the nation new momentum, too, literal as well as figurative. The engineering marvels of the eighteenth century—the harnessing of steam power, the innovations in factory design, the acceleration of production—were instruments of capital. So were improvements in the rate of transport. Over the course of the century, the government collaborated with private investors to construct a proliferating network of smooth turnpikes and inland waterways: canal boats delivered coal and other cargo with new celerity; stagecoaches sped between cities on precise schedules with crowded timetables. Timekeeping itself became a source of national wealth and pride. During the 1660s, British clockmakers established themselves as the best in Europe. A century later, the clockmaker John Harrison invented the "marine chronometer," a large watch so sturdy and so precise that it could keep time to the minute throughout a voyage around the world, amid all vicissitudes of wind and weather. Harrison's invention made it possible accurately to calculate a ship's longitude, thus solving a problem that had bedeviled navigation for centuries (and sometimes sunk whole fleets). The innovation further paved the way for trade and empire-building, and did much to establish

Greenwich, a town just east of London, as the reference point for world time-keeping. Trade was giving a new face—a new distribution of power and priority—not only to the nation but also to the globe, placing Britain (so Britons liked to think) at its center.

FAITH AND KNOWLEDGE, THOUGHT AND FEELING

Clockwork functioned another way too: as a new, theologically unsettling metaphor for the relations between God and his creation. In his *Principia Mathematica* (1687), Isaac Newton set forth the mathematical principles—the laws of motion, the workings of gravity—by which, it turned out, the universe could be seen to operate more consistently and efficiently than even the finest clockwork. What need had this flawless mechanism for any further adjustments by its divine clockmaker? Some of Newton's admirers—though never the pious scientist himself—found in his discoveries the cue for a nearly omnivorous skepticism. The boldest deists and "freethinkers" dismissed Christianity as irrational fiction, to be supplanted by the stripped-down doctrine of "natural religion." In the intricate design of nature they found the proof of a creator whose existence and infinite wisdom, they argued, are all we know on earth and all we need to know. The fashion for such thought—at least in its purest form—proved fleeting. To most minds, the "argument from design" simply furnished further proof of God's benevolence. Amid such comfortable conviction, the blasphemies of a virtuoso skeptic like David Hume appeared an aberration, even an entertainment, rather than a trend. "There is a great cry about infidelity," Samuel Johnson remarked in 1775, "but there are, in reality, very few infidels." From deep belief and ingrained habit, Christianity retained its hold over the entire culture; though a few pietists voiced alarm, science tended to enhance faith, not destroy it.

Still, the relation of religion to public life had changed. In the mid-seventeenth century, politics was inevitably suffused with spirituality. Charles I had gone to the scaffold as an Anglican martyr; he had ruled according to the dictum "No bishop, no king." For many English men and women the war of Parliament against the king was a holy war; Puritans had typed Charles I as that "man of blood," Cromwell's army had gone to battle singing David's psalms. By the eighteenth century, ardors had cooled; no one went to war for creed alone. But that is not to say that these were lives bereft of the spiritual; deep religious feeling remained, even as violence of expression abated. The Restoration had reinstated Anglicanism as the national faith; its adherents were admitted to the full privileges of education and office. Over the ensuing century, the Church of England pursued a strategic but controversial mix of old exclusions and new accommodations. For dissenters (offspring of the Puritans), new laws proffered certain permissions (to teach, to congregate for public worship) in exchange for certain oaths. Catholics, by contrast, were kept beyond the pale; they received no such concessions until late in the eighteenth century, when even a limited act provoked angry Protestant riots. Early in the century, the Anglican faithful were divided between the "high flyers," who perennially claimed that the church was in danger of dilution, and the Latitudinarians, who argued that all kinds of dissent might finally be accommodated within the structure of the church. Latitudinarians prevailed, but as the Church of England broadened, it began to lose the force of its exclusiveness; attendance at services shrank markedly as the century advanced, but alternative forms of communal worship flourished. In the eighteenth century, evangelical religions came to occupy the crucial space of fervent spirituality that the church of Donne and Herbert had once claimed as its own. By mid-century, in the new movement called Methodism, John Wesley expressed a vehement response against the skeptical rationalism of the freethinkers and the monied complacency of the established church. Wesley preached the truth of scriptural revelation. He urged his followers to purge their sins methodically—by a constant self-monitoring, partly modeled on earlier Puritan practices—and enthusiastically, by attending revival meetings, hearing electrifying sermons. Wesley delivered some 40,000 sermons over the course of a phenomenally energetic life, and his no less relentless brother Charles composed some 6,000 hymns to quicken evangelical spirits. Methodism found its most ardent following among the poor, who discovered in the doctrine a sympathy for their condition and a recognition of their worth, epitomized in one of Charles Wesley's verses: "Our Savior by the rich unknown / Is worshipped by the poor alone." Their worship was loud and fervent; intensity of feeling attested authenticity of faith.

The middle class and gentry located their own fervor in the more polished idioms of sentiment and sensibility. The terms named a code of conduct and of feeling current in the mid-eighteenth century, when men and women increasingly came to pride themselves on an emotional responsiveness highly cultivated and conspicuously displayed: tears of pity at the spectacle of suffering, admiration for the achievements of art or the magnificence of nature. For many in the middle class, the cult of sentiment held out the appealing prospect of a democratization of manners; the elaborate protocols of the aristocracy might remain elusive, but pure *feeling* was surely more accessible, to anyone with the leisure and the training. For many women the cult afforded the added attraction of honoring that very susceptibility to feeling and that renunciation of reason that had long and pejoratively been gendered female. The sufferings of the poor, of children, of animals, became a testing ground for empathy; majestic mountains became favorite proving grounds for heightened response. The fashion for benevolence helped focus attention on the plight of the poor and the oppressed, prompting new charities and social movements. For many of the conventionally religious, sentimentality became an adjunct article of faith. They found their scriptures in treatises that posited proper feeling as a chief measure of human worth—Adam Smith's *Theory of Moral Sentiments* (1759); in sentimental dramas that modeled the cultivation (and the performance) of elaborate emotion; in novels that paid minute attention to the protagonist's every emotional nuance—Samuel Richardson's *Pamela* (1740–1741) and *Clarissa* (1747–1749); Laurence Sterne's *Life and Opinions of Tristram Shandy* (1759–1767) and *A Sentimental Journey* (1768); Henry Mackenzies's *The Man of Feeling* (1771); in travel books that transported readers geographically and emotionally by charged descriptions of mighty vistas. For both deists and pietists earlier in the century, nature had testified the existence of a God; for connoisseurs of the sublime near century's end, nature itself was beginning to serve as surrogate for the divine.

In the articulation of eighteenth-century faith and science, thought and feeling, the most conspicuous and continuous voice was that of the first person. The "I" was omnipresent, observing world and self alike: in the experiment-reports of the scientists and the thought-experiments of the philosophers; in the Methodists' self-monitoring, the sentimentalist's self-approbation, the sublimity-seekers' recorded raptures; in the copious autobiographical writings—diaries, letters, memoirs—of characters in novels and people in the real world. Always and everywhere, it seems, someone was setting down the nuances of his or her experience. The self-reckoning promulgated in the past by dissenters was now a broad cultural preoccupation. Its dominion may help to explain why the literature of this era famed for the dominance and delight of its conversation returns us, again and again, to a sense of fundamental solitude.

WRITERS, READERS, CONVERSATIONS

The century and a half from the English Civil Wars to the brink of the French Revolution brought startling change to the structures of politics, social relations, scientific knowledge, and the economy; and no change was more intimate to all these revolutions than the transformations in the relations between writers and readers. From our present perspective, perhaps no scene seems more familiar, even eternal, than that of reader with book in hand. We imagine Virgil's readers and Dante's, Austen's and Wilde's, Pound's and Pynchon's similarly situated, alone with a book, communing silently with an oracular author. But these configurations have changed radically from age to age—sometimes driven by shifts in technology, at other times by social changes. In the eighteenth century, the sea change in relations between writers and readers derived from new social transactions and a new marketplace of letters. And this change did much to shape the modern reckoning of the mix of the solitary and the social, the commerical and the therapeutic within the act of reading. In its refiguring of the social contract between writers and readers, the eighteenth century was nearly as eruptive as our own time with its marketplace of e-mail and Internet, where everyone can potentially operate as both consumer and purveyor—and no one knows for sure the shape of literary things to come.

In 1661, the Earl of Argyle wrote to his son with advice on books, their acquisition, and their proper use:

> Think no cost too much in purchasing rare books; next to that of acquiring good friends I look upon this purchase; but buy them not to lay by or to grace your library, with the name of such a manuscript, or by such a singular piece, but read, revolve him, and lay him up in your memory where he will be far the better ornament. Read seriously whatever is before you, and reduce and digest it to practice and observation, otherwise it will be Sisyphus's labor to be always revolving sheets and books at every new occurence which will require the oracle of your reading. Trust not to your memory, but put all remarkable, notable things you shall meet with in your books *sub slava custodia* [under the sound care] of pen and ink, but so alter the property by your own scholia and annotations on it, that your memory may speedily recur to the place it was committed to.

The earl's account displays all the elements of the traditional reading program of Renaissance humanism: book or manuscript as surrogate friend; as "ornament" of the gentleman's mind and library; as "oracle" of enduring truths; as "property" to be possessed, marked, transcribed, and committed to memory. In the decades that followed all these constructions remained in play, yet every one of the earl's crucial terms broadened in application to include print genres and transactions that Argyle would not have imagined: the periodical review, the monthly miscellany; epistolary fiction; the three-volume novel; as well as the coffeehouses and penny-lending libraries that broadly circulated these new forms of print. With these new genres and modes of distribution, the text's status as friend, ornament, oracle, and property changed markedly.

Nothing had demonstrated (some even thought created) the material force and oracular authority of print so much as the English Civil Wars. Sermons and prophecies bearing the names of "oracles" and "revelations" forecast the demise of the Beast, the triumph of Parliament, indeed the imminence of the thousand-year rule of Christ on earth. Nor had the Restoration of the Stuart monarchy wholly denatured print as prophecy—royalists and radicals continued to publish apocalyptic claims. And yet, over the ensuing decades the repeated threat of contest and rebellion began to exhaust both the authority of print as prophecy and the appetite of readers for a textual diet of frenzy and apocalypse. Not that party warfare in print forms declined, but rather that partisanship yoked political contest to forms of confrontation that cooled apocalyptic tempers and supplanted military combat with paper controversy. The uneven course of government censorship, the issuing and lapsing of the licensing laws that governed press freedom, meant that paper wars with their full armory of ephemera—pamphlets, broadsides, pasquinades—raged at moments of crisis and parliamentary inattention when printers might cash in on the market for opposition and confrontation.

But not all the action of print contest was situated in the gutter of journalism. Satire, that most venerable mode of attack and advocacy, flourished in England as it had in Augustan Rome. Horace and Juvenal were indeed the models for Dryden, Pope, and Swift, who not only translated the forms of Roman satire into native idioms but were themselves possessed by all the Roman delight in outrage and invective, in civic engagement and political contest. But the genius of satire is never solely political. Satirists always score their most important points by wit, by cool savagery, by the thrust and parry of language, by the most brilliant and damaging metaphors and rhymes. Their peers, their rivals, even their enemies ruefully conceded that Dryden, Pope, and Swift had brought the verse couplet and the prose sentence to an unprecedented suppleness and precision. Satire in the years of civil war and Stuart agitations had begun in politics; pamphlet wars, swelled by periodicals, continued to rage through the Georgian age. But the classic verse satire had moved to a more exalted ground where the aesthetic often overwhelmed the political, and satire itself became an object of admiration, even of theorizing, and of the most vivid and polite conversation.

"Conversation" had once meant the entire conduct of life itself; now, "conversation" had narrowed to signify social exchange; yet social exchange in its turn had expanded to govern the conduct of life itself. Many of the most striking literary developments in the period—its poetic modes and tastes, the popularity and prominence of letter and journal writing, the advent of the newspaper and the novel—can perhaps best be understood as new ways devised by writers for performing conversation on the page—conversation with readers, with other writers, and within the texts themselves. The cultural critic Mikhail Bakhtin has pinpointed as one key feature of the novel its "heteroglossia": its capacity to speak, almost concurrently, many different languages, in the various voices and viewpoints of its characters and narrators, the range of its concerns (across social ranks and geograpical spaces), even the variabilities of its style (each with its own cultural connotations) from page to page, paragraph to paragraph. But in this respect as in so many, the novel, usually reckoned the greatest literary invention of the period, is the product of a time when virtually all modes of writing were involved with diversity and dialogue.

One of the most popular ways of buying and reading poetry, for example, was in the form of "miscellanies"—anthologies of work by many hands ancient and modern in many modes, brought together in intriguing juxtapositions. Such juxtapositions could also take place within a single poem. For poets, a crucial procedure was the "imitation"—a poem in English that closely echoes the tone, structure, and sequence of a classical model, while applying the predecessor's form and thought to contemporary topics. Where the Roman poet Juvenal, for example, begins his tenth Satire by declaring that wise men are hard to find even if you search every country from Spain to India (roughly the extent of the known Roman world), Samuel Johnson begins his imitation of Juvenal's poem (*The Vanity of Human Wishes*) this way:

> Let Observation, with extensive view,
> Survey mankind from China to Peru . . .

The known world, Johnson tacitly reminds his knowing reader, is much larger than it was when Juvenal wrote (and hence the rarity of discerning mortals will be all the more striking). The opening couplet prepares us for the poem's close, where it will turn out that moral possibilities are larger too: there, Johnson will supplant Juvenal's characteristically Roman resignation to "Fortune" with an expressly Christian reliance on the cardinal virtues (faith, hope, charity) as a means of protection from the delusions of desire. The writer of a poetic imitation always conducts at least a double dialogue: between poet and predecessor, and between the present writer and the ideal reader who knows enough of the "original" to savor the poetic exchange, the cultural cross talk, in all its echoes, divergences, and diversions.

Johnson here practices a more general kind of imitation as well, by casting his poem in heroic couplets: iambic pentameter lines paired in a sequence of successive rhymes. The rhymed pairs are often "closed," so that the moment of the rhyme coincides with and clinches the completion of a sentence and a thought. The verse form was called "heroic" because of its frequent use in the heroic drama and other high-aspiring poetry of the Restoration; the rhymed, closed pentameter was also thought to imitate, as closely as English allowed, the grandeur and the sonority of the lines in which ancient poets composed their epics. Throughout the century following Restoration, the heroic couplet prevailed as the most commonly used poetic structure, adaptable to all genres and occasions, deployed by every sort of poet from hacks to John Dryden and Alexander Pope, the supreme masters of the mode. It was in this form that Dryden translated Virgil's *Aeneid* (1697), and Pope translated Homer's *Iliad* (1715–1720) and *Odyssey* (1725–1726); it was in this form that they wrote original poems of high seriousness and savage satire; and it was in this form that they aspired (like many of their contemporaries) to write new epics of their own. Neither ever did; both complained intermittently that they lived in an unheroic age. But the mesh of mighty ancient models with trivial modern subjects produced a new mode of satire, the mock-heroic, and disclosed astonishing suppleness in the heroic couplet itself.

In the hands of Dryden, Pope, and many others, the mock mode—high style, low subject matter—performed brilliant accommodations and solved large problems. It allowed poets to turn what they perceived as the crassness of modern culture to satiric advantage. If the triviality of modern life prevented them from recapturing epic grandeur whole, they could at least strive to match the epic's inclusiveness, its capacity to encompass all the things and actions of the world: the accessories of a young woman's dressing table (Pope's *Rape of the Lock*); the clutter in a gutter after rain (Swift's *Description of a City Shower*); the glut of print itself and the folly of those who produce so much bad writing (Pope's *Dunciad*). After Pope's death, though, this vein of mockery seemed exhausted. The heroic couplet persisted in poetry to the end of the century; but other verse forms became prominent too, partly in the service of an even wider inclusiveness, of paying new kinds of attention to modes of life and literature that lay outside the heroic and the mock: the predicament of the poor, the pleasures of domesticity, the discoveries of science, the tones and textures of medieval English balladry, the modalities of melancholy, the improvisatory motions of human thought and feeling. Blank verse—iambic pentameter without rhyme—offered one manifestation of the impulse to open-endedness. James Thomson's *The Seasons* (1730) and William Cowper's *The Task* (1785), huge works in blank verse, are epic in their own kind: they mingle genres, and move from topic to topic, with the improvisatory energy of a barely stoppable train of thought. They perform the world's miscellany, the mind's conversation with itself and others, in a new poetic language—one that Wordsworth had absorbed by century's end, when he cast his *Prelude* in a capacious blank verse, and praised in the preface to *Lyrical Ballads* that kind of poetry which deploys "the real language" of "a man speaking to men."

In the new prose forms of the eighteenth century—both nonfiction and fiction—the dominion of miscellany, the centrality of conversation, is if anything more palpable than in poetry. The first daily newspaper and the first magazines both appeared early in the century, providing a regularly recurrent compendium of disparate items, intended to appeal to a variety of tastes and interests. These periodicals formed part of a larger and highly visible print mix: coffeehouses attracted a burgeoning clientele of urbanites by laying out copies of the current gazettes, mercuries, newsletters, playbooks and satiric verses. Customers took pleasure in the literary montage, the ever-shifting anthology on the tabletops (of which the pictorial medley on page 1978 conveys a vivid visual idea). Coffeehouse customers gathered to consume new drink and new print in a commerce of pleasure, intellect, and gossip. Some read silently, others aloud to listeners who eagerly seized on texts and topics. Habits of social reading that would have been familiar to Chaucer and his audience (even to Virgil performing his epic at the court of Augustus Caesar) contributed to sociable debate on the persons and personalities of public life, foreign potentates, military campaigns, theatrical rivalries, monsters, and prodigies. In the eighteenth century, the papers and the consequent conversations broadened to encompass questions of personal conduct, relations between the sexes, manner and fashion. Writers of papers still claimed oracular authority: "Isaac Bickerstaff" of the *Tatler* dubbed himself the Censor of Great Britain, Mr. Spectator claimed to watch everyone who read his paper, and the *Athenian Gazette* dispensed advice as though with the authority of a supremely learned society. But writers made such claims at least partly with tongue in cheek; they knew that their oracular "truths" would trickle down into the commerce of conversation.

The press not only stimulated but also simulated conversation. Newspapers had always depended on "correspondents"—not (as now) professional reporters, but local letter writers who sent in the news of their parish and county in exchange for free copies of the paper. To read a newspaper was to read in part the work of fellow readers. Other periodicals—the scientific monthly as well as the journal of advice and the review of arts—adopted the practice of printing letters as a reliable source of copy and as an act and model of sociability. Printed correspondence ran longer, more ambitiously, and more lucratively. For the first time, the collected letters of the eminent became an attractive commercial genre (Pope was a pioneer), and travel books in the form of copious letters home sold by the thousands.

The printed letter would prove crucial too to the development of the newest form of all, the "novel." Aphra Behn had pioneered epistolary fiction in the Restoration, and Samuel Richardson recast the mode on an epic scale in *Pamela* and *Clarissa*, among the most important and talked-about fictions of the eighteenth century. In discussing the fate of his characters, Richardson's readers joined a conversation already in progress; Richardson's characters, in their lively exchange of letters, performed and modeled what their creator called "the converse of the pen."

Yet letters were only one among the many kinds of conversation that novelists contrived to carry on. "The rise of the novel"—the emergence over the course of the eighteenth century of so curious, capacious, and durable a genre—has long excited interest and controversy among scholars, who explain the phenomenon in various ways: by the emergence of a large middle-class readership with the money to obtain, the leisure to read, and the eagerness to absorb long narratives that mirrored their circumstances, their aspirations, and their appetites; by a tension between the aristocratic virtues central to older forms of fiction, and the constructs of human merit prized by a proud commercial culture; by the passion for journalistic and experiential fact (in newspapers, criminal autobiographies, scientific experiments, etc.), shading over imperceptibly into new practices of fiction.

All of these explanations are true, and each is revelatory when applied to particular clusters of novels. Still, definition and explanation remain elusive, as they clearly were for the genre's early readers and practitioners. The very word "novel"—identifying the genre by no other marks than newness itself—performs a kind of surrender in the face of a form whose central claim to novelty was its barely definable breadth. Mimicry, motion, and metamorphosis are the genre's stock in trade. Novels absorbed all the modes of literature around them: letters, diaries, memoirs, news items, government documents, drawings, verses, even sheet music all crop up within the pages of the early novels, one representational mode supplanting another with often striking speed. Novelists moved with equal alacrity through space: through England (Henry Fielding's *Tom Jones*), Britain more broadly (Tobias Smollett's *Humphry Clinker*), Europe (Smollett's *Roderick Random*), the entire globe as it is ordinarily mapped (Behn's *Oroonoko*, Defoe's *Robinson Crusoe*) or as it could be extraordinarily imagined (Swift's *Gulliver's Travels*). Traversing geographies, the genre crossed cultures too, mostly by means of mimicry, and parroted a range of accents, for purposes either of mockery—the malapropisms of a semiliterate housemaid, the fulminations of a Scots soldier, the outrage of an Irish cuckold—or of pathos: the lamentations of the African slave Oroonoko, the delirium of the violated Clarissa. Many novels, too, made a point of spanning the social spectrum, often compassing destitution and prosperity, labor and luxury within the career of a single ambitious character. Social mobility was perhaps the one plot element that novel readers savored most.

But the novel's supplest means of self-conveyance, its subtlest modes of conversation, were grounded in its attention to the workings of the mind. In his *Essay Concerning Human Understanding* (1690), the philosopher John Locke had explained the mind as a capacious, absorptive instrument engaged in constant motion, linking mixed memories, impressions, and ideas in a ceaseless chain of "associations." In the eighteenth century, novelists took Locke's cue; their works both mimicked the mind's capacity, heterogeneity, and associativeness, and explored them too, tracking over many pages the subtlest modulations in the characters' thoughts and feelings. Richardson famously boasted that his epistolary mode, featuring "familiar letters written as it were to the moment" by characters in their times of crisis, enabled him to track the course of their "hopes and fears" with unprecedented precision—and he trusted that the value of such a process would surely excuse the "bulk" of the huge novels themselves. In the nine volumes of Laurence Sterne's *Life and Opinions of Tristram Shandy*, the title narrator is so committed to following his digressive trains of thought wherever they may lead, that the pronouncement of his opinions leaves him preposterously little time to narrate his life. Moving widely over space, freely through society, minutely through time, and deeply into mind, the novelists devised new strategies for achieving that epic inclusiveness that writers sought, in various ways, throughout the century.

The new tactics of miscellany, the new conversations conducted by means of pen and printing press, poetry and prose, refigured the practices of reading that the Earl of Argyle had wished to transmit to his son. In the aristocratic world of Renaissance letters, the book as friend had intimated a sphere of male pedagogy and sociability. The grammar school classroom, the college lecture hall, the estate library, the world of the tutor and his high-born protégé, all these figured reading principally as the privilege and the pleasure of a limited few, mostly males in positions of some leisure, comfort, and power. The links between reading and power were sustained through patterns of production and consumption in which authors received benefits from aristocratic patrons, and manuscripts passed from hand to hand. Donne refused to imagine his verse circulating in any other fashion. After the Restoration, Dryden, Behn, and Pope all pursued the compensations of print, but they nonetheless remained eager to participate in patronage and coterie circulation. Even when printed, their satires purveyed the pleasurable sense of shared knowledge that had constituted the *frisson* of coterie reading. Printers and poets understood that concealing a public name behind initials and dashes provided safety from censors and litigants while at the same time garnering a market share among readers who pleased themselves by decoding "dangerous matter."

By the middle of the eighteenth century, the patronage model of literary production and the coterie mode of distribution had been complicated (some thought ruined) by the commerce of print. For print had become the principal mode of literary distribution. Samuel Johnson, a bookseller's son, thought of literature as print and rarely circulated a manuscript as a gesture of literary sociability. ("None but a blockhead," he famously intoned, "ever wrote except for money.") As a consequence of the dominance of print and its broad distribution, the audiences for texts proliferated into new mixtures. Readers from many strata could afford a penny paper; apprentices and merchants' daughters might read the same novel. Assumptions of commonality that had underwritten the intimate sociability of Renaissance reading had been exploded by civil conflict in the mid-seventeenth century, by the profusion of print and the proliferation of genres that drove and were driven by the appetite of contest and conversation. During the eighteenth century, the print marketplace generated audiences on a scale vaster than ever before, circulating widely across the boundaries of class and gender. Print may have cancelled some of the intimacies of the coterie, but it generated new convergences, even new consciousness—a public sphere in which aesthetics, politics, conduct, and taste were all objects of perpetual, often pleasurable debate. To an unprecedented extent, print furnished its readers with the substance for sustained conversation and continual contact.

It also kept them apart. Nothing was more evident to eighteenth-century men and women than the burgeoning of their domestic economy, the vastness of their colonial empire, and the growth in wealth and population which both entailed. The proliferation of consumables was evident in the village market, the Royal Exchange, and the bookstalls of country towns and capitol. The sheer bulk and variety of these consumables were strikingly evident in the length and scope of that capacious new genre, the novel. But even in the midst of abundance and sociability, eighteenth-century consumers were instructed in their paradoxical solitude. Defoe inscribes the condition of the novel as isolation—Robinson Crusoe, a man alone on an island, opines that human life "is, or ought to be, one universal act of solitude." And in novel after novel the very transactions of commerce produce isolation, as ambition and acquisition drive each character into the solitary, often melancholy corner of his or her own self-interest. The novel itself as a reading experience produced comparable sensations. Readers might now empathize with an entire world of fictional characters; but in order to savor such imaginative pleasures, they spent long hours in the privacy of their own quarters, in silent acts of reading.

A sense of solitude underwrote all this century's celebrated gregariousness. This held true even for sociable transactions that might take place between a reader and a text. In the Renaissance, it had long been a practice to annotate texts with comments echoing and endorsing the author's oracular wisdom. Under the pressure of civil war, the dialogue between author and reader often became more heated as the manuscript marginalia expressed anger and outrage at the partisan zeal of the printed text. But one form of textual reverence persisted. Throughout the seventeenth century readers took pleasure in writing marginalia that epitomized the text, making its wisdom portable. They filled blank books with pithy sentences, "commonplaces" drawn from their favorite works and organized in ways that would allow them to recirculate these sayings in their own writing and conversation.

By the eighteenth century, print had managed to appropriate all these modes of study and sociability. Through print, the manuscript collation of wit and wisdom turned into popular commodities—the printed commonplace book, the miscellany, the anthology. Even annotation itself migrated from manuscript markings into print, as Swift and Pope (among others) found ways of exploding scholarly pretension and of rendering the breath of gossip and scandal in the elaborate apparatus of the printed page. By century's end, all of manuscript's august authority and its most cherished genres—letters and memoirs—had been commandeered by print. In the mid-1730s, Pope alarmed and outraged his contemporaries by publishing his letters as if they deserved to partake of eternity with Cicero's. By the early nineteenth century, even that most secretive mode of self-communion, the private journal, had made its way into the marketplace. In 1825, Pepys's *Diary* appeared in two large printed folios, laying bare the elaborate machinery of public life, the secrets and scandals of the Restoration court, and the diarist's own experiences, transgressions, and sequestered musings, which he had written in shorthand code and shown to no one. The communal and commodified medium of print had found yet another way to market signal acts of solitude.

CODA

Mrs. Abington as Miss Prue (1771), by the pre-eminent portraitist Sir Joshua Reynolds, shows a solitary figure engaged in intricate conversation with the viewer. Some of the intricacy inheres in the life history of the sitter, whose career many of the painting's first viewers would have known well. The daughter of a cobbler, Frances Abington had worked in childhood as a flower seller, in her early teens as a prostitute, and (beginning around age fifteen) as an actress, quickly establishing herself as "by far the most eminent performer in comedy of her day" (these words, and others to follow, are the testimony of contemporaries). When an unknown, she had married her music teacher; as fame increased, she carried on several well-publicized affairs with members of parliament and the aristocracy. By her sexual frankness, she scandalized—and of course fascinated—the multitudes. By her grace

Joshua Reynolds. *Mrs. Abington as "Miss Prue."* 1771. Restoration theatricality transposed and transformed.

and taste, she became "a favorite of the public" and "the high priestess of fashion"; her costumes on stage instantly set new trends among her audience. Reynolds, who greatly admired her, here captures the complexity of her character and reputation. Her dress is supremely stylish, her pose deliberately provocative. For a woman to lean casually over the back of a chair this way violated all propriety; in earlier portraits, only men had struck such a pose. The thumb at her lips suggests vulgarity verging on the lascivious. The portrait's title purports to explain such seeming aberrations: the actress here appears in her celebrated role as Miss Prue, the "silly, awkward country girl" in William Congreve's Restoration comedy *Love for Love* (1695), who comes to London with the intention, frankly lustful and loudly declared, of getting herself a husband. In Reynolds's painting, of course, Mrs. Abington plays a role more layered: a hybrid of Miss Prue, of the matchlessly fashionable figure into which the actress had transformed herself, and of the whole range of experiences, the prodigious lifelong motion from poverty to polish, which formed part of her self-creation and her fame. Impersonating Miss Prue some seventy-five years after the comedy's first production, Mrs. Abington here infuses Restoration wantonness with Georgian elegance, transgression with high taste, theatricality with self-assertive authenticity. Like the century she inhabits, she is miscellany incarnate.

Stuart Sherman and
Steven N. Zwicker

Samuel Pepys

1633–1703

Twice in his life, Samuel Pepys embarked on long projects that allowed him to use the methods of the bureaucrat with an inventiveness that amounted to genius. The longer project, which occupied him from his mid-twenties through his mid-fifties, was a fundamental restructuring of the Royal Navy. The shorter project began just a few months earlier. Starting on January 1, 1660, and continuing for the next nine years, Pepys devised the diary form as we know it today: a detailed, private, day-by-day account of daily doings.

Halfway through the diary, Pepys delights to describe himself as "a very rising man," and he wrote the diary in part to track his ascent. The rise began slowly. Born in London to a tailor and a butcher's sister, Pepys studied at Puritan schools; he then attended Magdalene College, Cambridge, as a scholarship student. His B.A. left him well educated but short on cash. A year later he married the fifteen-year-old Elizabeth St. Michel, a French Protestant whose poverty surpassed his own. By his mid-twenties (when the diary commences), neither his accomplishments nor his prospects were particularly striking: he was working as factotum for two powerful men, one of them his high-born cousin Edward Mountagu, First Earl of Sandwich, an important naval officer once devoted to Cromwell but recently turned Royalist.

The diary begins at a calendrical turning point (the first day of a new week, a new year, and a new decade) and on a kind of double bet: that the coming time would bring changes worth writing up, both in the life of the diarist and in the history of the state. The two surmises quickly proved true. As a schoolboy taught by Puritans, Pepys had attended and applauded the execution of Charles I, but the Restoration of Charles II was the making of him, and he recalibrated his loyalties readily enough. His cousin secured for him the Clerkship of the Acts in the Navy Office, a secretarial post that Pepys transformed into something more. By mastering the numberless details of shipbuilding and supplying—from the quality of timber to the composition of tar and hemp—he contrived to control costs and produce results to an extent unmatched by any predecessor.

He managed all these matters so carefully that he soon became the ruler of the Royal Navy, in effect if not in name. When the Test Act of 1673 forced Charles's Catholic brother James to resign as Lord High Admiral, Pepys took his place (in the newly created post of Admiralty Secretary) and ran the operation. He immediately launched a systematic reform of the institution, which he had come to see as dangerously slipshod. By devising (in the words of one biographer) "a rule for all things, great or small," and by enforcing the new disciplines through a method of tireless surveillance and correspondence with ports extending from the Thames to Tangier, Pepys made the navy immeasurably more efficient than ever before. His efforts were interrupted by the political tribulations of his patron James: Pepys spent two brief terms in prison on trumped-up charges of Catholic sympathies, and in 1688 the Glorious Revolution drove him from office into a prosperous retirement. At the height of his power, though, as his biographer Richard Ollard observes, Pepys was the "master builder" of the permanent, professional navy that made possible the expansion of trade and the conquest of colonies over the ensuing century. Energetic in his king's service and in his own (the taking of bribes was one of the perquisites of office that Pepys mastered most adroitly), the tailor's son functioned formidably as an early architect of empire.

Pepys's schooling and profession had immersed him in the two practices most central to earlier English diaries, Puritanism and financial bookkeeping. But where account books and religious diaries emphasize certain kinds of moment—exchanges of money and goods, instances of moral redemption and relapse—Pepys tries for something more comprehensive. He implicitly commits himself to tracking the whole day's experience: the motions of the body as it makes its way through the city in boats, in coaches, and on foot, and the motions of the mind as it shuttles between business and pleasure. He sustained his narrative over a virtually unbroken series of daily entries before stopping out of fear that his work on the diary had helped to damage his eyesight to the brink of blindness. "None of Pepys's contemporaries," writes his editor Robert Latham, "attempted a diary in the all-inclusive Pepysian sense and on the Pepysian scale." To the efficiency of the bookkeeper and the discipline of the Puritan, Pepys added the ardor of the virtuoso, eager (as he observes at one point) "to see any strange thing" and capable of finding wonder in ordinary things: music, plays, books, food, clothes, conversation. The phrase "with great pleasure" recurs in the diary as a kind of leitmotiv, and superlatives play leapfrog through the pages: many, many experiences qualify in turn as the "best" thing that the diarist ever ate, read, thought, saw, heard. To achieve the diary's seeming immediacy, Pepys put his entries through as many as five stages of revision, sometimes days or even months after the events recorded. Even at the final stage, in the bound, elegantly formatted volumes of the diary manuscript, he often crammed new detail or comment into margins and between the lines. Comparable pressures operated in connection with the diary's complex privacy. Pepys took pains to secure secrecy for his text. He hid it from view in drawers or in cabinets. He wrote most of it in a secretarial shorthand, and where he most wanted secrecy, as in the accounts of his many flirtations and infidelities, he obscured things further by an improvised language made up of Spanish, French, Latin, and other tongues. (Elizabeth Pepys figures throughout the diary as a kind of muse and countermuse, the narrative's most recurrent and obsessive subject, and the person most urgently to be prevented from reading it.) At the same time, the manuscript makes notable gestures toward self-display. Pepys frequently shifts to a readily readable longhand, especially for names, places, titles of books, plays, and persons; at times even his secret sexual language opens out into longhand.

This ambivalent secrecy persisted past the diarist's death. Pepys bequeathed the manuscript to Magdalene College without calling any special attention to it. It was included among his many collections: of naval books and papers, of broadsheet ballads, and of instruction manuals on shorthand methods—including the one Pepys used to write the diary. The manuscript kept its secrets long. In the early nineteenth century, the diary was discovered and painstakingly decoded (by a transcriber who, missing the connection between the manuscript and the shorthand manuals on adjacent shelves, treated the text as a million-word cryptogram); it was finally published, in a severely shortened and expurgated version, in 1825. Readers and reviewers soon called for more, recognizing that Pepys possessed (in the words of one reviewer) "the most indiscriminating, insatiable, and miscellaneous curiosity, that ever . . . supplied the pen, of a daily chronicler." Expanded (but still bowdlerized) editions appeared throughout the century, and only in the 1970s did the semisecret manuscript make its way wholly into print.

from The Diary

[FIRST ENTRIES][1]

$$16\frac{59}{60}.$$

Blessed be God, at the end of the last year I was in very good health, without any sense of my old pain[2] but upon taking of cold.

---

1. England still adhered to the Old Style calendar, in which the new year officially began on March 25. Pepys wrote this "prelude" in early January 1659 according to the English reckoning, but 1660 (New Style) in the rest of Europe.

2. Pepys had suffered from stones in the bladder from babyhood until 1658, when he underwent a risky but successful operation.

I lived in Axe Yard,[3] having my wife and servant Jane, and no more in family than us three.

My wife, after the absence of her terms[4] for seven weeks, gave me hopes of her being with child, but on the last day of the year she hath them again. The condition of the state was thus. *Viz.* the Rump, after being disturbed by my Lord Lambert, was lately returned to sit again.[5] The officers of the army all forced to yield. Lawson lies still in the river and Monck is with his army in Scotland.[6] Only my Lord Lambert is not yet come in to the Parliament; nor is it expected that he will, without being forced to it.

The new Common Council of the City doth speak very high; and hath sent to Monck their sword-bearer, to acquaint him with their desires for a free and full Parliament, which is at present the desires and the hopes and expectation of all—22 of the old secluded members having been at the House door the last week to demand entrance; but it was denied them, and it is believed that they nor the people will not be satisfied till the House be filled.[7]

My own private condition very handsome; and esteemed rich, but indeed very poor, besides my goods of my house and my office, which at present is somewhat uncertain. Mr Downing master of my office.[8]

1 January 1659/60. Lord's Day. This morning (we lying lately in the garret) I rose, put on my suit with great skirts,[9] having not lately worn any other clothes but them.

Went to Mr. Gunning's church at Exeter House, where he made a very good sermon upon these words: that in the fullness of time God sent his Son, made of a woman, etc., showing that by "made under the law" is meant his circumcision, which is solemnized this day.[1]

Dined at home in the garret, where my wife dressed the remains of a turkey, and in the doing of it she burned her hand.

I stayed at home all the afternoon, looking over my accounts.

Then went with my wife to my father's; and in going, observed the great posts which the City hath set up[2] at the Conduit in Fleet Street.

Supped at my father's, where in came Mrs. Theophila Turner and Madam Morris[3] and supped with us. After that, my wife and I went home with them, and so to our own home.

---

3. In Westminster.
4. Menstrual periods.
5. John Lambert, a skilled general under Oliver Cromwell, now opposed the convening of the Rump Parliament, which had governed England since the fall of Cromwell's son Richard in 1659.
6. At this point, the political intentions and allegiance of General George Monck were the object of much speculation; he led his army back from Scotland into England on January 1 and became one of the principal engineers of the Restoration. Vice-Admiral John Lawson supported the Rump.
7. A Parliament that would include the "old secluded members"—the representatives expelled in 1648—was understood to be a first step toward restoration of the monarchy.

8. Pepys was at this point a clerk in the office of the Exchequer.
9. I.e., with a long coat.
1. Peter Gunning had held illegal Anglican services during the Commonwealth. His sermon text is Galatians 4.4: "But, when the fullness of the time was come, God sent forth his Son, made of a woman, made under the law."
2. As defensive barriers during its opposition to the Rump Parliament.
3. A relative and a friend, respectively. "Mistress" ("Mrs.") was applied to unmarried as well as to married women; Theophila was eight years old.

[THE CORONATION OF CHARLES II][4]

[23 April 1661] I lay with Mr. Shiply,[5] and about 4 in the morning I rose.

Coronation Day.

And got to the Abbey,[6] where I followed Sir J. Denham the surveyor with some company that he was leading in. And with much ado, by the favor of Mr Cooper his man, did get up into a great scaffold across the north end of the Abbey—where with a great deal of patience I sat from past 4 till 11 before the King came in. And a pleasure it was to see the Abbey raised in the middle, all covered with red and a throne (that is a chair) and footstool on the top of it. And all the officers of all kinds, so much as the very fiddlers, in red vests.

At last comes in the Dean and prebends of Westminster with the Bishops (many of them in cloth-of-gold copes); and after them the nobility all in their Parliament robes, which was a most magnificent sight. Then the Duke[7] and the King with a scepter (carried by my Lord of Sandwich) and sword and mond before him, and the crown too.

The King in his robes, bare-headed, which was very fine. And after all had placed themselves, there was a sermon and the service. And then in the choir at the high altar he passed all the ceremonies of the coronation—which, to my very great grief, I and most in the Abbey could not see. The crown being put upon his head, a great shout begun. And he came forth to the throne and there passed more ceremonies: as, taking the oath and having things read to him by the Bishop, and his lords (who put on their caps as soon as the King put on his crown) and bishops came and kneeled before him.

And three times the King-at-Arms went to the three open places on the scaffold and proclaimed that if any one could show any reason why Charles Stuart should not be King of England, that now he should come and speak.

And a general pardon also was read by the Lord Chancellor;[8] and medals flung up and down by my Lord Cornwallis—of silver; but I could not come by any.

But so great a noise, that I could make but little of the music; and indeed, it was lost to everybody. But I had so great a list[9] to piss, that I went out a little while before the King had done all his ceremonies and went round the Abbey to Westminster Hall, all the way within rails, and 10,000 people, with the ground covered with blue cloth—and scaffolds all the way. Into the hall I got—where it was very fine with hangings and scaffolds, one upon another, full of brave[1] ladies. And my wife in one little one on the right hand.

Here I stayed walking up and down; and at last, upon one of the side-stalls, I stood and saw the King come in with all the persons (but the soldiers) that were yesterday in the cavalcade;[2] and a most pleasant sight it was to see them in their several robes. And the King came in with his crown on and his scepter in his hand—under a canopy borne up by six silver staves, carried by Barons of the Cinqueports—and little bells at every end.

---

4. Charles II had returned to England in May 1660; he scheduled his coronation for St. George's Day, honoring England's patron saint.
5. Edward Shipley was steward to Pepys's cousin Edward Mountagu.
6. Westminster Abbey, site of English coronations.
7. Charles's brother James, Duke of York, later James II.

8. Charles II's Act of Oblivion forgave the crimes of all those on the parliamentary side, with the principal exception of those who had participated in the trial, sentencing, and execution of his father.
9. Desire.
1. Splendid.
2. The previous day's procession.

And after a long time he got up to the farther end, and all set themselves down at their several tables—and that was also a rare sight. And the King's first course carried up by the Knights of the Bath. And many fine ceremonies there was of the heralds leading up people before him and bowing; and my Lord of Albemarle's[3] going to the kitchen and eat[4] a bit of the first dish that was to go to the King's table.

But above all was these three Lords, Northumberland and Suffolk and the Duke of Ormond, coming before the courses on horseback and staying so all dinner-time; and at last, to bring up Dymock the King's champion, all in armor on horseback, with his spear and target carried before him. And a herald proclaim that if any dare deny Charles Stuart to be lawful King of England, here was a champion that would fight with him; and with those words the champion flings down his gauntlet; and all this he doth three times in his going up toward the King's table. At last, when he is come, the King drinks to him and then sends him the cup, which is of gold; and he drinks it off and then rides back again with the cup in his hand.

I went from table to table to see the bishops and all others at their dinner, and was infinite pleased with it. And at the lords' table I met with Will Howe and he spoke to my Lord for me and he did give him four rabbits and a pullet; and so I got it, and Mr. Creed and I got Mr. Mitchell to give us some bread and so we at a stall eat it, as everybody else did what they could get.[5]

I took a great deal of pleasure to go up and down and look upon the ladies—and to hear the music of all sorts; but above all, the 24 violins.

About 6 at night they had dined; and I went up to my wife and there met with a pretty lady (Mrs. Franklin, a doctor's wife, a friend of Mr. Bowyer's) and kissed them both—and by and by took them down to Mr. Bowyer's. And strange it is, to think that these two days have held up fair till now that all is done and the King gone out of the Hall; and then it fell a-raining and thundering and lightening as I have not seen it do some years—which people did take great notice of God's blessing of the work of these two days—which is a foolery, to take too much notice of such things.

I observed little disorder in all this; but only the King's footmen had got hold of the canopy and would keep it from the Barons of the Cinqueports; which they endeavored to force from them again but could not do it till my Lord Duke of Albemarle caused it to be put into Sir R. Pye's hand till tomorrow to be decided.

At Mr. Bowyer's, a great deal of company; some I knew, others I did not. Here we stayed upon the leads[6] and below till it was late, expecting to see the fireworks; but they were not performed tonight. Only, the City had a light like a glory round about it, with bonfires.

At last I went to King Street; and there sent Crockford to my father's and my house to tell them I could not come home tonight, because of the dirt and a coach could not be had.

And so after drinking a pot of ale alone at Mrs. Harper's, I returned to Mr. Bowyer's; and after a little stay more, I took my wife and Mrs. Franklin (who I proferred the civility of lying with my wife at Mrs. Hunt's tonight) to Axe Yard. In which, at the further end, there was three great bonfires and a great many great gallants, men and women; and they laid hold of us and would have us drink the King's

3. In 1660 Charles II had made George Monck Duke of Albemarle as a reward for his role in the Restoration.
4. Ate (pronounced "ett"), to test for poison.
5. Will Howe and John Creed served as clerks to Sand-

wich, whom the diarist invariably refers to as "my Lord." Miles Mitchell was a local bookseller.
6. Rooftop.

health upon our knee, kneeling upon a fagot; which we all did, they drinking to us one after another—which we thought a strange frolic. But these gallants continued thus a great while, and I wondered to see how the ladies did tipple.

At last I sent my wife and her bedfellow to bed, and Mr. Hunt and I went in with Mr. Thornbury (who did give the company all their wines, he being yeoman of the wine-cellar to the King) to his house; and there, with his wife and two of his sisters and some gallant sparks that were there, we drank the King's health and nothing else, till one of the gentlemen fell down stark drunk and there lay spewing. And I went to my Lord's pretty well. But no sooner a-bed with Mr. Shiply but my head begun to turn and I to vomit, and if ever I was foxed[7] it was now—which I cannot say yet, because I fell asleep and sleep till morning—only, when I waked I found myself wet with my spewing. Thus did the day end, with joy everywhere; and blessed be God, I have not heard of any mischance to anybody through it all, but only to Sergeant Glynne, whose horse fell upon him yesterday and is like to kill him; which people do please themselves with, to see how just God is to punish that rogue at such a time as this—he being now one of the King's sergeants and rode in the cavalcade with Maynard, to whom people wished the same fortune.[8]

There was also this night, in King Street, a woman had her eye put out by a boy's flinging of a firebrand into the coach.

Now after all this, I can say that besides the pleasure of the sight of these glorious things, I may now shut my eyes against any other objects, or for the future trouble myself to see things of state and show, as being sure never to see the like again in this world.

[24 April 1661] Waked in the morning with my head in a sad taking through the last night's drink, which I am very sorry for. So rise and went out with Mr. Creed to drink our morning draught, which he did give me in chocolate to settle my stomach. And after that to my wife, who lay with Mrs. Franklin at the next door to Mrs. Hunt's.

And they were ready, and so I took them up in a coach and carried the lady to Paul's[9] and there set her down; and so my wife and I home—and I to the office.

That being done, my wife and I went to dinner to Sir W. Batten;[1] and all our talk about the happy conclusion of these last solemnities.

After dinner home and advised with my wife about ordering things in my house; and then she went away to my father's to lie, and I stayed with my workmen, who do please me very well with their work.

At night set myself to write down these three days' diary; and while I am about it, I hear the noise of the chambers and other things of the fireworks, which are now playing upon the Thames before the King. And I wish myself with them, being sorry not to see them.

So to bed.

[THE PLAGUE YEAR]

[7 June 1665] This morning my wife and mother rose about 2 a-clock, and with Mercer, Mary, the boy, and W. Hewer,[2] as they had designed, took boat and down to refresh themselves on the water to Gravesend. I lay till 7 a-clock; then up, and to the

---

7. Drunk.
8. Sir John Glynne and Sir John Maynard were lawyers who had served under Cromwell.
9. St. Paul's Cathedral.

1. Surveyor of the Navy.
2. Mary Mercer was Elizabeth Pepys's paid companion; Will Hewer was Pepys's office clerk and lifelong friend; Mary and "the boy" are household servants.

office upon Sir G. Carteret's accounts again—where very busy.[3] Thence abroad and to the Change, no news of certainty being yet come from the fleet.[4] Thence to the Dolphin Tavern, where Sir J. Mennes, Lord Brouncker, Sir Thomas Harvey and myself dined upon Sir G. Carteret's charge—and very merry we were, Sir Thomas Harvey being a very droll.[5] Thence to the office; and meeting Creed, away with him to my Lord Treasurer's, there thinking to have met the goldsmiths, or at Whitehall; but did not, and so appointed another time for my lord to speak to them to advance us some money. Thence, it being the hottest day that ever I felt in my life, and it is confessed so by all other people the hottest they ever knew in England in the beginning of June—we to the New Exchange and there drunk whey; with much entreaty, getting it for our money, and would not be entreated to let us have one glass more. So took water, and to Foxhall[6] to the Spring Garden and there walked an hour or two with great pleasure, saving our minds ill at ease concerning the fleet and my Lord Sandwich, that we have no news of them, and ill reports run up and down of his being killed, but without ground. Here stayed, pleasantly walking and spending but 6d, till 9 at night; and then by water to Whitehall, and there I stopped to hear news of the fleet, but none come, which is strange; and so by water home—where, weary with walking and with the mighty heat of the weather, and for my wife's not coming home—I staying walking in the garden till 12 at night, when it begun to lighten exceedingly through the greatness of the heat. Then, despairing of her coming home, I to bed.

This day, much against my will, I did in Drury Lane see two or three houses marked with a red cross upon the doors, and "Lord have mercy upon us" writ there[7]—which was a sad sight to me, being the first of that kind that to my remembrance I ever saw. It put me into an ill conception of myself and my smell, so that I was forced to buy some roll-tobacco to smell to and chaw—which took away the apprehension.[8]

[30 July 1665] Lord's Day. Up, and in my nightgown, cap, and neck-cloth, undressed all day long; lost not a minute, but in my chamber setting my Tangier accounts to rights, which I did by night, to my very heart's content; not only that it is done, but I find everything right and even beyond what, after so long neglecting them, I did hope for. The Lord of Heaven be praised for it.

Will was with me today and is very well again. It was a sad noise to hear our bell to toll and ring so often today, either for deaths or burials; I think five or six times.

At night, weary with the day's work but full of joy at my having done it—I to bed, being to rise betimes tomorrow to go to the wedding at Dagnams.

So to bed—fearing I have got some cold sitting in my loose garment all this day.

[31 July 1665[9]] Up, and very betimes, by 6 a-clock, at Deptford; and there find Sir G. Carteret and my lady ready to go—I being in my new colored-silk suit and coat, trimmed with gold buttons and gold broad lace round my hands, very rich and fine. By water to the ferry, where, when we came, no coach there—and tide of ebb so far spent as the horse-boat could not get off on the other side the river to bring away the coach. So we were fain to stay there in the unlucky Isle of Dogs—in a chill place, the

---

3. George Carteret was Navy Treasurer.
4. The Royal Exchange was the City's central location for luxury shopping, business dealings, and newsgathering. Pepys wanted news of the ongoing Second Dutch War; his patron Sandwich was in command of the fleet.
5. All these men were colleagues on the Navy Board. *Droll*: jester.
6. Vauxhall, a cluster of riverside gardens, immensely

popular for its avenues, covered walks, and wine stalls.
7. The red cross marked houses infected by plague.
8. Tobacco was thought to prevent infection.
9. The wedding day of Lady Jemimah Mountagu, Sandwich's eldest daughter, and Philip Carteret, eldest son of Pepys's colleague Sir George. Pepys had helped to arrange the match.

morning cool and wind fresh, above two if not three hours, to our great discontent. Yet being upon a pleasant errand, and seeing that could not be helped, we did bear it very patiently; and it was worth my observing, I thought as ever anything, to see how upon these two scores, Sir G. Carteret, the most passionate man in the world and that was in greatest haste to be gone, did bear with it, and very pleasant all the while, at least not troubled much so as to fret and storm at it.

Anon the coach comes—in the meantime there coming a citizen thither with his horse to go over, that told us he did come from Islington this morning, and that Proctor the vintner of the Mitre in Wood Street, and his son, is dead this morning there—of the plague. He having laid out abundance of money there—and was the greatest vintner for some time in London for great entertainments.

We, fearing the canonical hour would be past before we got thither,[1] did with a great deal of unwillingness send away the license and wedding ring. So that when we came, though we drove hard with six horses, yet we found them gone from home; and going toward the church, met them coming from church—which troubled us. But however, that trouble was soon over—hearing it was well done—they being both in their old clothes. My Lord Crew giving her—there being three coach-fulls of them. The young lady mighty sad, which troubled me; but yet I think it was only her gravity, in a little greater degree than usual. All saluted her,[2] but I did not till my Lady Sandwich did ask me whether I had not saluted her or no. So to dinner, and very merry we were; but yet in such a sober way as never almost any wedding was in so great families—but it was much better. After dinner, company divided, some to cards—others to talk. My Lady Sandwich and I up to settle accounts and pay her some money—and mighty kind she is to me, and would fain have had me gone down for company with her to Hinchingbrooke—but for my life I cannot.

At night to supper, and so to talk and, which methought was the most extraordinary thing, all of us to prayers as usual, and the young bride and bridegroom too. And so after prayers, soberly to bed; only, I got into the bridegroom's chamber while he undressed himself, and there was very merry—till he was called to the bride's chamber and into bed they went. I kissed the bride in bed, and so the curtains drawn with the greatest gravity that could be, and so good-night.

But the modesty and gravity of this business was so decent, that it was to me, indeed, ten times more delightful than if it had been twenty times more merry and jovial.

Whereas I feared I must have sat up all night, we did here all get good beds—and I lay in the same I did before, with Mr. Brisband, who is a good scholar and sober man; and we lay in bed, getting him to give me an account of Rome, which is the most delightful talk a man can have of any traveler. And so to sleep—my eyes much troubled already with the change of my drink.

Thus I ended this month with the greatest joy that ever I did any in my life, because I have spent the greatest part of it with abundance of joy and honor, and pleasant journeys and brave entertainments, and without cost of money. And at last live to see that business ended[3] with great content on all sides.

This evening with Mr. Brisband speaking of enchantments and spells, I telling him some of my charms,[4] he told me this of his own knowledge at Bourdeaux in France. The words these—

---

1. Church law stipulated that marriages could be performed only during certain hours of the day.
2. Greeted her with a kiss.
3. The marriage concluded.

4. At the end of the previous year, Pepys had written into his diary a set of incantations ("charms") for healing cuts, burns, etc.

Voicy un corps mort
Royde comme un baston
Froid comme marbre
Leger comme un esprit,
Levons te au nom de Jesus Christ.[5]

He saw four little girls, very young ones, all kneeling, each of them upon one knee; and one begin the first line, whispering in the ear of the next, and the second to the third, and the third to the fourth, and she to the first. Then the first begun the second line, and so round quite through. And putting each one finger only to a boy that lay flat upon his back on the ground, as if he was dead. At the end of the words they did with their four fingers raise this boy as high as they could reach. And he being there and wondering at it (as also being afeared to see it—for they would have had him to have bore a part in saying the words in the room of one of the little girls, that was so young that they could hardly make her learn to repeat the words), did, for fear there might be some sleight used in it by the boy, or that the boy might be light, called the cook of the house, a very lusty fellow, as Sir G. Carteret's cook, who is very big, and they did raise him just in the same manner.

This is one of the strangest things I ever heard, but he tells it me of his own knowledge and I do heartily believe it to be true. I inquired of him whether they were Protestant or Catholic girls, and he told me they were Protestant—which made it the more strange to me.

Thus we end this month, as I said, after the greatest glut of content that ever I had; only, under some difficulty because of the plague, which grows mightily upon us, the last week being about 1,700 or 1,800 [dead] of the plague.

My Lord Sandwich, at sea with a fleet of about 100 sail to the Norward, expect De Ruyter or the Dutch East-India fleet.

My Lord Hinchingbrooke[6] coming over from France, and will meet his sister at Scott's Hall.

Myself having obliged both these families in this business very much, as both my lady and Sir G. Carteret and his lady do confess exceedingly; and the latter two also now call me cousin, which I am glad of.

So God preserve us all friends long, and continue health among us.

[15 August 1665] Up by 4 a-clock and walked to Greenwich, where called at Captain Cocke's[7] and to his chamber, he being in bed—where something put my last night's dream into my head, which I think is the best that ever was dreamed—which was, that I had my Lady Castlemaine[8] in my arms and was admitted to use all the dalliance I desired with her, and then dreamed that this could not be awake but that it was only a dream. But that since it was a dream and that I took so much real pleasure in it, what a happy thing it would be, if when we are in our graves (as Shakespeare resembles it),[9] we could dream, and dream but such dreams as this—that then we should not need to be so fearful of death as we are this plague-time.

* * *

5. Here is a dead body / Stiff as a rod / Cold as marble / Light as a spirit, / We raise thee in the name of Jesus Christ.
6. Sandwich's son.
7. George Cocke, supplier to the navy and Pepys's colleague on the board.
8. Barbara Palmer, Countess of Castlemaine, was a cele-

brated beauty and at this point the foremost among the King's mistresses.
9. Shakespeare compares ("resembles") death to sleep in Hamlet's famous soliloquy, though Hamlet fears what he might dream when dead: "To die, to sleep— / To sleep— perchance to dream: ay, there's the rub, / For in that sleep of death what dreams may come" (*Hamlet* 3.1.60–62).

It was dark before I could get home; and so land at church-yard-stairs, where to my great trouble I met a dead corpse, of the plague, in the narrow ally, just bringing down[1] a little pair of stairs—but I thank God I was not much disturbed at it. However, I shall beware of being late abroad again.

[10 September 1665] *Lord's day*. Walked home, being forced thereto by one of my watermen falling sick yesterday; and it was God's great mercy I did not go by water with them yesterday, for he fell sick on Saturday night and it is to be feared of the plague. So I sent him away to London with his fellow.

But another boat came to me this morning, whom I sent to Blackwell for Mr. Andrews; I walked to Woolwich,[2] and there find Mr. Hill, and he and I all the morning at music and a song he hath set, of three parts; methinks very good. Anon comes Mr. Andrews, though it be a very ill day. And so after dinner we to music and sang till about 4 or 5 a-clock, it blowing very hard, and now and then raining—and, wind and tide being against us, Andrews and I took leave and walked to Greenwich—my wife before I came out telling me the ill news that she hears, that her father is very ill; and then I told her I feared of the plague, for that the house is shut up.[3] And so, she much troubled, she did desire me to send them something, and I said I would, and will do so.

But before I came out, there happened news to come to me by an express from Mr. Coventry, telling me the most happy news of my Lord Sandwich's meeting with part of the Dutch; his taking two of their East India ships and six or seven others, and very good prize—and that he is in search of the rest of the fleet, which he hopes to find upon the Well Bank—with the loss only of the *Hector*, poor Captain Cuttle. This news doth so overjoy me, that I know not what to say enough to express it; but the better to do it, I did walk to Greenwich;[4] and there sending away Mr. Andrews, I to Captain Cocke's, where I find my Lord Brouncker and his mistress and Sir J. Mennes—where we supped (there was also Sir W. Doyly and Mr. Evelyn);[5] but the receipt of this news did put us all into such an ecstasy of joy, that it inspired into Sir J. Mennes and Mr. Evelyn such a spirit of mirth, that in all my life I never met with so merry a two hours as our company this night was. Among other humors, Mr. Evelyn's repeating of some verses made up of nothing but the various acceptations of May and Can, and doing it so aptly, upon occasion of something of that nature, and so fast, did make us all die almost with laughing, and did so stop the mouth of Sir J. Mennes in the middle of all his mirth (and in a thing agreeing with his own manner of genius) that I never saw any man so outdone in all my life; and Sir J. Mennes's mirth too, to see himself outdone, was the crown of all our mirth.

In this humor we sat till about 10 at night; and so my Lord and his mistress home, and we to bed—it being one of the times of my life wherein I was the fullest of true sense of joy.

[14 September 1665] Up, and walked to Greenwich and there fitted myself in several businesses to go to London, where I have not been now a pretty while. But before I went from the office, news is brought by word of mouth that letters are now just now

---

1. Being carried down.
2. A navy yard on the Thames, east of London, where Pepys, his wife, and their servants had taken lodgings in an effort to avoid the plague.
3. Quarantined.
4. A town on the Thames, east of London, where the

Navy Office had temporarily relocated during plague time.
5. John Evelyn (1620–1706), author, virtuoso, and fellow diarist. During the Second Dutch War, both Evelyn and William Doyly served the Navy as Commissioners for the Sick and Wounded.

brought from the Fleet of our taking a great many more of the Dutch fleet—in which I did never more plainly see my command of my temper, in my not admitting myself to receive any kind of joy from it till I had heard the certainty of it. And therefore went by water directly to the Duke of Albemarle, where I find a letter of the 12th from Solebay, from my Lord Sandwich, of the fleet's meeting with about 18 more of the Dutch fleet and his taking of most of them; and the messenger says they had taken three after the letter was wrote and sealed; which being 21, and the 14 took the other day, is 45 sail—some of which are good, and others rich ships—which is so great a cause of joy in us all, that my Lord and every body is highly joyed thereat. And having taken a copy of my Lord's letter, I away back again to the Bear at the bridge-foot, being full of wind and out of order, and there called for a biscuit and a piece of cheese and gill of sack[6]—being forced to walk over the bridge toward the Change, and the plague being all thereabouts. Here my news was highly welcome, and I did wonder to see the Change so full, I believe 200 people; but not a man or merchant of any fashion, but plain men all. And Lord, to see how I did endeavor all I could to talk with as few as I could, there being now no observation of shutting up of houses infected, that to be sure we do converse and meet with people that have the plague upon them. I to Sir Robert Viners, where my main business was about settling the business of Debusty's 5000*l* tallies—which I did for the present to enable me to have some money. And so home, buying some things for my wife in the way. So home and put up several things to carry to Woolwich—and upon serious thoughts, I am advised by W. Griffin to let my money and plate[7] rest there, as being as safe as any place, nobody imagining that people would leave money in their houses now, when all their families are gone. So for the present, that being my opinion, I did leave them there still. But Lord, to see the trouble that it puts a man to to keep safe what with pain a man hath been getting together; and there is good reason for it. Down to the office, and there wrote letters to and again about this good news of our victory, and so by water home late—

Where when I came home, I spent some thoughts upon the occurrences of this day, giving matter for as much content on one hand and melancholy on another as any day in all my life—for the first, the finding of my money and plate and all safe at London and speeding in my business of money this day—the hearing of this good news, to such excess after so great a despair of my Lord's doing anything this year—adding to that, the decrease of 500 and more, which is the first decrease we have yet had in the sickness since it begun—and great hopes that the next week it will be greater. Then on the other side—my finding that though the Bill[8] in general is abated, yet the City within the walls[9] is increased and likely to continue so and is close to our house there—my meeting dead corpses of the plague, carried to be buried close to me at noonday through the City in Fanchurch Street—to see a person sick of the sores carried close by me by Grace Church in a hackney-coach—my finding the Angel Tavern at the lower end of Tower Hill shut up; and more than that, the alehouse at the Tower stairs; and more than that, that the person was then dying of the plague when I was last there, a little while ago at night, to write a short letter there, and I overheard the mistress of the house sadly saying to her husband somebody was very ill, but did not think it was of the plague—to hear that poor Payne my waterman

---

6. Quarter pint of white wine.
7. Silver.
8. The Bill of Mortality, a weekly, parish-by-parish

account of the deaths in London.
9. London had spread beyond its original walls, but the area within those walls was still known as "the City."

hath buried a child and is dying himself—to hear that a laborer I sent but the other day to Dagnams to know how they did there is dead of the plague; and that one of my own watermen, that carried me daily, fell sick as soon as he had landed me on Friday morning last, when I had been all night upon the water (and I believed he did get his infection that day at Brainford) is now dead of the plague—to hear that Captain Lambert and Cuttle are killed in the taking these ships and that Mr. Sidney Mountagu is sick of a desperate fever at my Lady Carteret's at Scott's Hall—to hear that Mr. Lewes hath another daughter sick—and lastly, that both my servants, W. Hewer and Tom Edwards, have lost their fathers, both in St. Sepulcher's parish, of the plague this week—doth put me into great apprehensions of melancholy, and with good reason. But I put off the thoughts of sadness as much as I can; and the rather to keep my wife in good heart, and family also. After supper (having eat nothing all this day) upon a fine tench[1] of Mr. Sheldon's taking, we to bed.

[THE FIRE OF LONDON]

[2 September 1666] Lord's Day. Some of our maids sitting up late last night to get things ready against our feast today, Jane called us up, about 3 in the morning, to tell us of a great fire they saw in the City. So I rose, and slipped on my nightgown and went to her window, and thought it to be on the back side of Mark Lane at the furthest; but being unused to such fires as followed, I thought it far enough off, and so went to bed again and to sleep. About 7 rose again to dress myself, and there looked out at the window and saw the fire not so much as it was, and further off. So to my closet[2] to set things to rights after yesterday's cleaning. By and by Jane comes and tells me that she hears that above 300 houses have been burned down tonight by the fire we saw, and that it was now burning down all Fish Street by London Bridge. So I made myself ready presently, and walked to the Tower and there got up upon one of the high places, Sir J. Robinson's little son going up with me; and there I did see the houses at that end of the bridge all on fire, and an infinite great fire on this and the other side the end of the bridge—which, among other people, did trouble me for poor little Mitchell and our Sarah on the bridge.[3] So down, with my heart full of trouble, to the Lieutenant of the Tower, who tells me that it begun this morning in the King's baker's house in Pudding Lane, and that it hath burned down St. Magnus's Church and most part of Fish Street already. So I down to the water-side and there got a boat and through bridge,[4] and there saw a lamentable fire. Poor Mitchell's house, as far as the Old Swan, already burned that way and the fire running further, that in a very little time it got as far as the Steelyard while I was there. Everybody endeavoring to remove their goods, and flinging into the river or bringing them into lighters[5] that lay off. Poor people staying in their houses as long as till the very fire touched them, and then running into boats or clambering from one pair of stair by the water-side to another. And among other things, the poor pigeons I perceive were loath to leave their houses, but hovered about the windows and balconies till they were some of them burned, their wings, and fell down.

    Having stayed, and in an hour's time seen the fire rage every way, and nobody to my sight endeavoring to quench it, but to remove their goods and leave all to the fire;

---

1. A kind of fish.
2. Private room, study.
3. London Bridge was lined with shops and houses, including the liquor shop of Pepys's friend Michael

Mitchell and the residence of his former servant Sarah.
4. Under the bridge.
5. Barges.

and having seen it get as far as the Steelyard, and the wind mighty high and driving it into the City, and everything, after so long a drought, proving combustible, even the very stones of churches, and among other things, the poor steeple by which pretty Mrs. Horsley lives, and whereof my old school-fellow Elborough is parson, taken fire in the very top and there burned till it fall down—I to Whitehall with a gentleman with me who desired to go off from the Tower to see the fire in my boat—to Whitehall, and there up to the King's closet in the chapel, where people came about me and I did give them an account dismayed them all; and word was carried in to the King, so I was called for and did tell the King and Duke of York what I saw, and that unless his Majesty did command houses to be pulled down, nothing could stop the fire. They seemed much troubled, and the King commanded me to go to my Lord Mayor from him and command him to spare no houses but to pull down before the fire every way. The Duke of York bid me tell him that if he would have any more soldiers, he shall; and so did my Lord Arlington afterward, as a great secret. Here meeting with Captain Cocke, I in his coach, which he lent me, and Creed with me, to Paul's; and there walked along Watling Street as well as I could, every creature coming away loaden with goods to save—and here and there sick people carried away in beds. Extraordinary good goods carried in carts and on backs. At last met my Lord Mayor in Canning Street, like a man spent, with a hankercher about his neck. To the King's message, he cried like a fainting woman, "Lord, what can I do? I am spent! People will not obey me. I have been pulling down houses. But the fire overtakes us faster than we can do it." That he needed no more soldiers; and that for himself, he must go and refresh himself, having been up all night. So he left me, and I him, and walked home—seeing people all almost distracted and no manner of means used to quench the fire. The houses too, so very thick thereabouts, and full of matter for burning, as pitch and tar, in Thames Street—and warehouses of oil and wines and brandy and other things. Here I saw Mr. Isaac Houblon, that handsome man—prettily dressed and dirty at his door at Dowgate, receiving some of his brothers' things whose houses were on fire; and as he says, have been removed twice already, and he doubts (as it soon proved) that they must be in a little time removed from his house also—which was a sad consideration. And to see the churches all filling with goods, by people who themselves should have been quietly there at this time.

By this time it was about 12 a-clock, and so home and there find my guests, which was Mr. Wood and his wife, Barbary Shelden, and also Mr. Moone—she mighty fine, and her husband, for aught I see, a likely man. But Mr. Moone's design and mine, which was to look over my closet and please him with the sight thereof, which he hath long desired, was wholly disappointed, for we were in great trouble and disturbance at this fire, not knowing what to think of it. However, we had an extraordinary good dinner, and as merry as at this time we could be.

While at dinner, Mrs. Batelier came to inquire after Mr. Woolfe and Stanes (who it seems are related to them), whose houses in Fish Street are all burned, and they in a sad condition. She would not stay in the fright.

As soon as dined, I and Moone away and walked through the City, the streets full of nothing but people and horses and carts loaden with goods, ready to run over one another, and removing goods from one burned house to another—they now removing out of Canning Street (which received goods in the morning) into Lombard Street and further; and among others, I now saw my little goldsmith Stokes receiving some friend's goods, whose house itself was burned the day after. We parted at Paul's, he home and I to Paul's Wharf, where I had appointed a boat to attend me;

and took in Mr. Carkesse and his brother, whom I met in the street, and carried them below and above bridge, to and again, to see the fire, which was now got further, both below and above, and no likelihood of stopping it. Met with the King and Duke of York in their barge, and with them to Queenhithe and there called Sir Richard Browne to them. Their order was only to pull down houses apace, and so below bridge at the water-side; but little was or could be done, the fire coming upon them so fast. Good hopes there was of stopping it at the Three Cranes above, and at Buttolph's Wharf below bridge, if care be used; but the wind carries it into the City, so as we know not by the water-side what it doth there. River full of lighters and boats taking in goods, and good goods swimming in the water; and only, I observed that hardly one lighter or boat in three that had the goods of a house in, but there was a pair of virginals[6] in it. Having seen as much as I could now, I away to Whitehall by appointment, and there walked to St. James's Park, and there met my wife and Creed and Wood and his wife and walked to my boat, and there upon the water again, and to the fire up and down, it still increasing and the wind great. So near the fire as we could for smoke; and all over the Thames, with one's face in the wind you were almost burned with a shower of firedrops—this is very true—so as houses were burned by these drops and flakes of fire, three or four, nay five or six houses, one from another. When we could endure no more upon the water, we to a little alehouse on the Bankside over against the Three Cranes, and there stayed till it was dark almost and saw the fire grow; and as it grow darker, appeared more and more, and in corners and upon steeples and between churches and houses, as far as we could see up the hill of the City, in a most horrid malicious bloody flame, not like the fine flame of an ordinary fire. Barbary and her husband away before us. We stayed till, it being darkish, we saw the fire as only one entire arch of fire from this to the other side the bridge, and in a bow up the hill, for an arch of above a mile long. It made me weep to see it. The churches, houses, and all on fire and flaming at once, and a horrid noise the flames made, and the cracking of houses at their ruin. So home with a sad heart, and there find everybody discoursing and lamenting the fire; and poor Tom Hayter[7] came with some few of his goods saved out of his house, which is burned upon Fish Street Hill. I invited him to lie at my house, and did receive his goods: but was deceived in his lying there, the noise coming every moment of the growth of the fire, so as we were forced to begin to pack up our own goods and prepare for their removal. And did by moonshine (it being brave,[8] dry, and moonshine and warm weather) carry much of my goods into the garden, and Mr. Hayter and I did remove my money and iron-chests into my cellar—as thinking that the safest place. And got my bags of gold into my office ready to carry away, and my chief papers of accounts also there, and my tallies into a box by themselves. So great was our fear, as Sir W. Batten had carts come out of the country to fetch away his goods this night. We did put Mr. Hayter, poor man, to bed a little; but he got but very little rest, so much noise being in my house, taking down of goods.

[3 September 1666] About 4 a-clock in the morning, my Lady Batten sent me a cart to carry away all my money and plate and best things to Sir W. Rider's at Bethnell Green; which I did, riding myself in my nightgown in the cart; and Lord, to see how the streets and the highways are crowded with people, running and riding and getting of carts at any rate to fetch away things. I find Sir W. Rider tired with being called up[9] all night

---

6. A small harpsichord.
7. One of Pepys's clerks in the Navy Office.

8. Pleasant.

and receiving things from several friends. His house full of goods—and much of Sir W. Batten and Sir W. Penn's.[1] I am eased at my heart to have my treasure so well secured. Then home with much ado to find a way. Nor any sleep all this night to me nor my poor wife. But then, and all this day, she and I and all my people laboring to get away the rest of our things, and did get Mr. Tooker to get me a lighter to take them in, and we did carry them (myself some) over Tower Hill, which was by this time full of people's goods, bringing their goods thither. And down to the lighter, which lay at the next quay above the Tower Dock. And here was my neighbor's wife, Mrs. Buckworth, with her pretty child and some few of her things, which I did willingly give way to be saved with mine. But there was no passing with anything through the postern,[2] the crowd was so great.

The Duke of York came this day by the office and spoke to us, and did ride with his guard up and down the City to keep all quiet (he being now general, and having the care of all).

This day, Mercer being not at home, but against her mistress's order gone to her mother's, and my wife going thither to speak with W. Hewer, met her there and was angry; and her mother saying that she was not a prentice girl, to ask leave every time she goes abroad, my wife with good reason was angry, and when she came home, bid her be gone again. And so she went away, which troubled me; but yet less than it would, because of the condition we are in fear of coming into in a little time, of being less able to keep one in her quality. At night, lay down a little upon a quilt of W. Hewer in the office (all my own things being packed up or gone); and after me, my poor wife did the like—we having fed upon the remains of yesterday's dinner, having no fire nor dishes, nor any opportunity of dressing anything.

[4 September 1666] Up by break of day to get away the remainder of my things, which I did by a lighter at the Iron Gate; and my hands so few, that it was the afternoon before we could get them all away.

Sir W. Penn and I to Tower Street, and there met the fire burning three or four doors beyond Mr. Howell's; whose goods, poor man (his trays and dishes, shovels, etc., were flung all along Tower Street in the kennels, and people working therewith from one end to the other), the fire coming on in that narrow street, on both sides, with infinite fury. Sir W. Batten, not knowing how to remove his wine, did dig a pit in the garden and laid it in there; and I took the opportunity of laying all the papers of my office that I could not otherwise dispose of. And in the evening Sir W. Penn and I did dig another and put our wine in it, and I my parmesan cheese as well as my wine and some other things.

The Duke of York was at the office this day at Sir W. Penn's, but I happened not to be within. This afternoon, sitting melancholy with Sir W. Penn in our garden and thinking of the certain burning of this office without extraordinary means, I did propose for the sending up of all our workmen from Woolwich and Deptford yards (none whereof yet appeared), and to write to Sir W. Coventry to have the Duke of York's permission to pull down houses rather then lose this office, which would much hinder the King's business. So Sir W. Penn he went down this night, in order to the sending them up tomorrow morning; and I wrote to Sir W. Coventry about the business, but received no answer.

This night Mrs. Turner (who, poor woman, was removing her goods all this day—good goods, into the garden, and knew not how to dispose of them)—and her husband supped with my wife and I at night in the office, upon a shoulder of mutton

9. Called on, woken.
1. William Penn, Pepys's colleague on the Navy Board

(and father of the founder of Pennsylvania).
2. Back or side gate.

from the cook's, without any napkin or anything, in a sad manner but were merry. Only, now and then walking into the garden and saw how horridly the sky looks, all on a fire in the night, was enough to put us out of our wits; and indeed it was extremely dreadful—for it looks just as if it was at us, and the whole heaven on fire. I after supper walked in the dark down to Tower Street, and there saw it all on fire at the Trinity House on that side and the Dolphin Tavern on this side, which was very near us—and the fire with extraordinary vehemence. Now begins the practice of blowing up of houses in Tower Street, those next the Tower, which at first did frighten people more than anything; but it stopped the fire where it was done—it bringing down the houses to the ground in the same places they stood, and then it was easy to quench what little fire was in it, though it kindled nothing almost. W. Hewer this day went to see how his mother did, and comes late home, but telling us how he hath been forced to remove her to Islington, her house in Pye Corner being burned. So that it is got so far that way and all the Old Bailey, and was running down to Fleet Street. And Paul's is burned, and all Cheapside. I wrote to my father this night; but the post-house being burned, the letter could not go.

COMPANION READING

John Evelyn: from Kalendarium[1]

[2 September 1666] This fatal night about ten, began that deplorable fire, near Fish Street in London. 2: I had public prayers at home: after dinner the fire continuing, with my wife and son took coach and went to the Bankside in Southwark,[2] where we beheld that dismal spectacle, the whole City in dreadful flames near the water-side, and had now consumed all the houses from the bridge all Thames Street and upwards towards Cheapside, down to the Three Cranes, and so returned exceedingly astonished, what would become of the rest. 3: The fire having continued all this night (if I may call that night, which was as light as day for 10 miles round about after a dreadful manner) when conspiring with a fierce eastern wind, in a very dry season, I went on foot to the same place, when I saw the whole south part of the City burning from Cheapside to the Thames, and all along Cornhill (for it likewise kindled back against the wind, as well as forward) Tower Street, Fenchurch Street, Gracious Street and so along to Baynard Castle, and was now taking hold of St. Paul's Church, to which the scaffolds contributed exceedingly. The conflagration was so universal, and the people so astonished, that from the beginning (I know not by what desponding or fate), they hardly stirred to quench it, so as there was nothing heard or seen but crying out and lamentation, and running about like distracted creatures, without at all attempting to

1. John Evelyn (1620–1706), versatile author (on air pollution, architecture, gardening, forestry, and other subjects), wrote up his life on a plan very different from that of his friend Pepys. His *Kalendarium*, commenced when he was 40 years old, narrates selected dates (and omits many), starting with his birth and ending shortly before his death; the thousand-page manuscript encompasses (in legible longhand) his extensive travels in Europe during the Civil Wars and his busy social, court, and civic life after the Restoration. Evelyn's vantage on the Fire of London (as on much else) contrasts with Pepys's. A land-owning gentleman, Evelyn dwelt at a remove from the City on a country estate across the river. A devout Anglican, he saw the catastrophe as an

apocalypse steeped in biblical precedent and prophecy. A tireless projector of plans and improvements, he reckoned the City's losses and began to imagine its renewal. Nine days after the fire's outbreak, Evelyn presented the king and queen "with a survey of the ruins and a plot for a new city. . . . [They seemed] extremely pleased with what I had so early thought on"—though in the event, no unified plan for rebuilding was followed. For another account of the fire, see the selection from the *London Gazette* in Perspectives: Reading Papers, pages 2313–2314.

2. The southern bank of the Thames, across the river from the fire.

save even their goods; such a strange consternation there was upon them, so as it burned both in breadth and length, the churches, public halls, Exchange, hospitals, monuments, and ornaments, leaping after a prodigious manner from house to house and street to street, at great distance one from the other, for the heat (with a long set of fair and warm weather) had even ignited the air, and prepared the materials to conceive the fire, which devoured after an incredible manner, houses, furniture, and everything. Here we saw the Thames covered with goods floating, all the barges and boats laden with what some had time and courage to save, as on the other, the carts etc. carrying out to the fields, which for many miles were strewed with moveables of all sorts, and tents erecting to shelter both people and what goods they could get away: O the miserable and calamitous spectacle, such as haply the whole world had not seen the like since the foundation of it, nor to be outdone, till the universal conflagration of it. All the sky were of a fiery aspect, like the top of a burning oven, and the light seen above 40 miles round about for many nights. God grant mine eyes may never behold the like, who now saw above ten thousand houses all in one flame, the noise and crackling and thunder of the impetuous flames, the shrieking of women and children, the hurry of people, the fall of towers, houses and churches was like an hideous storm, and the air all about so hot and inflamed that at the last one was not able to approach it, so as they were forced to stand still, and let the flames consume on which they did for near two whole miles in length and one in breadth. The clouds also of smoke were dismal, and reached upon computation near 50 miles in length. Thus I left it this afternoon burning, a resemblance of Sodom, or the last day.[3] It called to mind that of 4 *Heb: non enim hic habemus stabilem Civitatem:*[4] the ruins resembling the picture of *Troy: London* was,[5] but is no more. Thus I returned.

[4 September 1666] The burning still rages; I went now on horseback, and it was now gotten as far as the Inner Temple; all Fleet Street, Old Bailey, Ludgate Hill, Warwick Lane, Newgate, Paul's Chain, Watling Street now flaming and most of it reduced to ashes, the stones of Paul's flew like granados,[6] the lead melting down the streets in a stream, and the very pavements of them glowing with fiery redness, so as nor horse nor man was able to tread on them, and the demolitions had stopped all the passages, so as no help could be applied; the eastern wind still more impetuously driving the flames forwards. Nothing but the almighty power of God was able to stop them, for vain was the help of man. On the fourth it crossed towards Whitehall, but O the confusion was then at that court. It pleased his Majesty to command me among the rest to look after the quenching of Fetter Lane end, to preserve (if possible) that part of Holborn, whilst the rest of the gentlemen took their several posts, some at one part, some at another, for now they began to bestir themselves, and not till now, who till now had stood as men interdict, with their hands a cross,[7] and began to consider that nothing was like to put a stop, but the blowing up of so many houses, as might make a wider gap, than any had yet been made by the ordinary method of pulling them down with engines.[8] This some stout seamen proposed early enough to have saved the whole City; but some tenacious and avaricious men, aldermen etc., would not

3. In Genesis, the Lord destroys the sinful city of Sodom by raining "fire and brimstone . . . out of heaven" (19.24). "The last day" is the Day of Judgment, when the city of Babylon (emblem of the corrupt world) "shall be utterly burned with fire" (Revelation 18.8).
4. For here we have no lasting city (Hebrews 13.14; the sentence continues: "but we seek one to come").

5. Echoing the *Aeneid*'s account of the fall of Troy: on the night the Greeks burn the city, a Trojan priest declares *fuit Ilium* ("Troy was"; 2.325).
6. Grenades.
7. Immobilized, with their arms crossed (a conventional posture of passivity).
8. Machines.

permit, because their houses must have been of the first. It was therefore now commanded to be practiced, and my concern being particularly for the Hospital of St. Bartholomew's near Smithfield, where I had many wounded and sick men, made me the more diligent to promote it;[9] nor was my care for the Savoy less. So as it pleased Almighty God by abating of the wind, and the industry of people, now when all was lost, infusing a new spirit into them (and such as had if exerted in time undoubtedly preserved the whole) that the fury of it began sensibly to abate, about noon, so as it came no farther than the Temple westward, nor than the entrance of Smithfield north; but continued all this day and night so impetuous toward Cripplegate, and the Tower, as made us even all despair. It also brake out again in the Temple: but the courage of the multitude persisting, and innumerable houses blown up with gunpowder, such gaps and desolations were soon made, as also by the former three days' consumption, as the back fire did not so vehemently urge upon the rest, as formerly. There was yet no standing near the burning and glowing ruins near a furlong's space. The coal and wood wharves and magazines of oil, rosin, chandler, etc.[1] did infinite mischief; so as the invective I but a little before dedicated to his Majesty and published, giving warning what might probably be the issue of suffering those shops to be in the City, was looked on as prophetic.[2] But there I left this smoking and sultry heap, which mounted up in dismal clouds night and day, the poor inhabitants dispersed all about St. George's, Moorfields, as far as Highgate, and several miles in circle, some under tents, others under miserable huts and hovels, without a rag, or any necessary utensils, bed or board, who from delicateness, riches and easy accommodations in stately and well-furnished houses, were now reduced to extremest misery and poverty. In this calamitous condition I returned with a sad heart to my house, blessing and adoring the distinguishing mercy of God, to me and mine, who in the midst of all this ruin, was like Lot, in my little Zoar, safe and sound.[3]

[THE ROYAL SOCIETY][1]

[14 November 1666] Up, and by water to Whitehall; and thence to Westminister, where I bought several things—as, a hone—ribband—gloves—books. And then took coach and to Knepp's[2] lodging, whom I find not ready to go home with me, so I away to do a little business; among others, to call upon Mr. Osborne for my Tangier warrant for the last quarter, and so to the New Exchange for some things for my wife, and then to Knepp again and there stayed, reading of Waller's[3] verses while she finished her dressing—her husband being by, I had no other pastime. Her lodging very mean, and the condition she lives in; yet makes a show without doors, God bless us. I carried him along with us into the City, and set him down in Bishopsgate Street and then home with her. She tells me how Smith of the Duke's house hath killed a man upon a quarrel in play—which makes everybody sorry, he being a good actor, and they say a good

9. Evelyn served on the Navy Board as a commissioner, charged with the care of sick and wounded seamen.

1. Different sorts of fuel, stored and sold in shops along the Thames.

2. In 1661 Evelyn had warned of these dangers in a pamphlet entitled *Fumifugium: or the Inconveniency of the Air and Smoke of London Dissipated. Together with Some Remedies Humbly Proposed by J. E., Esq; to His Sacred Majesty, and to the Parliament Now Assembled.*

3. Lot, a prosperous inhabitant of Sodom, is warned by angels of the city's impending destruction. He escapes to Zoar, a small city nearby (Genesis 19.20–22).

1. This next selection from Pepys was written two months after the fire, when life had begun to return to normal.

2. Elizabeth Knepp, actress, singer, and friend of Pepys.

3. Sir Edmund Waller (1606–1687), widely read poet and pioneer of the heroic couplet; he wrote much love poetry in praise of "Sacharissa," a woman he wooed without success.

man, however this happens. The ladies of the court do much bemoan him, she says. Here she and we alone at dinner, to some good victuals that we could not put off,[4] that was intended for the great dinner of my Lord Hinchingbrooke, if he had come. After dinner, I to teach her my new recitative of *It is decreed*[5]—of which she learnt a good part; and I do well like it, and believe shall be well pleased when she hath it all, and that it will be found an agreeable thing. Then carried her home, and my wife and I intended to have seen my Lady Jemima at Whitehall; but the Exchange street was so full of coaches, everybody as they say going thither to make themselves fine against tomorrow night,[6] that after half an hour's stay we could not do any; but only, my wife to see her brother, and I to go speak one word with Sir G. Carteret about office business. And talk of the general complexion of matters; which he looks upon, as I do, with horror, and gives us all for an undone people—that there is no such thing as a peace in hand, nor a possibility of any without our begging it, they[7] being as high, or higher, in their terms than ever. And tells me that just now my Lord Hollis had been with him, and wept to think in what a condition we are fallen. He showed me my Lord Sandwich's letter to him, complaining of the lack of money; which Sir G. Carteret is at a loss how in the world to get the King to supply him[8] with—and wishes him for that reason here, for that he fears he will be brought to disgrace there, for want of supplies. He says the House is yet in a bad humor; and desiring to know whence it is that the King stirs not, he says he minds it not, nor will be brought to it—and that his servants of the House do, instead of making the Parliament better, rather play the rogue one with another, and will put all in fire.[9] So that upon the whole, we are in a wretched condition, and I went from him in full apprehensions of it. So took up my wife, her brother being yet very bad, and doubtful whether he will recover or no; and so to St. Ellen's and there sent my wife home, and myself to the Pope's Head, where all the Houblons were, and Dr. Croone;[1] and by and by to an exceeding pretty supper—excellent discourse of all sorts; and indeed, are a set of the finest gentlemen that ever I met withal in my life. Here Dr. Croone told me that at the meeting[2] at Gresham College tonight (which it seems they now have every Wednesday again) there was a pretty experiment, of the blood of one dog let out (till he died) into the body of another on one side, while all his own run out on the other side. The first died upon the place, and the other very well, and likely to do well. This did give occasion to many pretty wishes, as of the blood of a Quaker to be let into an archbishop, and such like. But, as Dr. Croone says, may if it takes be of mighty use to man's health, for the amending of bad blood by borrowing from a better body.

After supper James Houblon and another brother took me aside, and to talk of some businesses of their own, where I am to serve them, and will. And then to talk of public matters; and I do find that they, and all merchants else, do give over trade and the nation for lost—nothing being done with care or foresight—no convoys[3] granted, nor anything done to satisfaction. But do think that the Dutch and French will master us the next year, do what we can; and so do I, unless God Almighty makes the king to mind his business; which might yet save all.

4. Delay (because the food would spoil).
5. Pepys enjoyed composing music (here setting words from Ben Jonson's play *Catiline*).
6. When a court ball was to be held for the queen's birthday.
7. The Dutch.
8. Sandwich, now ambassador to Spain.
9. Into ruin.

1. The Houblons were a merchant family—a father and five sons—whom Pepys and others admired for their affection and generosity. Dr. William Croone, a specialist in anatomy, was an original Fellow and First Secretary of the Royal Society for the Improving of Natural Knowledge.
2. Of the Royal Society.
3. Protective escort for merchant ships.

Here we sat talking till past one in the morning, and then home—where my people sat up for me, my wife and all; and so to bed.

[30 May 1667] Up, and to the office, where all the morning. At noon dined at home; being, without any words, friends with my wife, though last night I was very angry, and do think I did give her as much cause to be angry with me. After dinner I walked to Arundel House, the way very dusty (the day of meeting of the Society being changed from Wednesday to Thursday; which I knew not before because the Wednesday is a Council day and several of the Council are of the Society, and would come but for their attending the King at Council); where I find much company, indeed very much company, in expectation of the Duchess of Newcastle,[4] who had desired to be invited to the Society, and was, after much debate pro and con, it seems many being against it, and we do believe the town will be full of ballets[5] of it. Anon comes the Duchess, with her women attending her; among others, that Ferrabosco[6] of whom so much talk is, that her lady would bid her show her face and kill the gallants. She is indeed black[7] and hath good black little eyes, but otherwise but a very ordinary woman I do think; but they say sings well. The Duchess hath been a good comely woman; but her dress so antic and her deportment so unordinary, that I do not like her at all, nor did I hear her say anything that was worth hearing, but that she was full of admiration, all admiration.[8] Several fine experiments were shown her of colors, loadstones, microscope, and of liquors: among others, of one that did while she was there turn a piece of roasted mutton into pure blood—which was very rare. Here was Mr. Moore of Cambridge, whom I had not seen before, and I was glad to see him—as also a very pretty black boy that run up and down the room, somebody's child in Arundel House. After they had shown her many experiments, and she cried still she was "full of admiration," she departed, being led out and in by several lords that were there; among others, Lord George Berkeley and the Earl of Carlisle and a very pretty young man, the Duke of Somerset.

She gone, I by coach home and there busy at my letters till night; and then with my wife in the evening, singing with her in the garden with great pleasure. And so home to supper and to bed.

[21 November 1667] Up, and to the office, where all the morning; and at noon home, where my wife not very well, but is to go to Mr. Mill's child's christening, where she is godmother, Sir. J. Mennes and Sir R. Brookes her companions. I left her after dinner (my clerks dining with me) to go with Sir J. Mennes, and I to the office, where did much business till after candlelight; and then, my eyes beginning to fail me, I out and took coach and to Arundel House, where the meeting of Gresham College was broke up; but there meeting Creed, I with him to the tavern in St. Clement's churchyard, where was Dean Wilkins, Dr. Whistler[9] * * * and others. * * * Among the rest, they discourse of a man that is a little frantic (that hath been a kind of minister, Dr. Wilkins saying that he hath read for him in his church) that is a poor and debauched man, that the college have hired for 20s[1] to have some of the blood of

---

4. Margaret Cavendish, Duchess of Newcastle, had published poems, plays, and treatises on natural philosophy highly critical of the Society's methods (see pages 2058–2073).
5. Ballads (Evelyn wrote one on Cavendish's visit).
6. An Italian family of this name was eminent in England for its musical talents.

7. I.e., of dark complexion and hair.
8. Wonder, amazement.
9. The mathematician John Wilkins was one of the founders of the Royal Society; the physician Daniel Whistler was a Fellow.
1. s: Shillings.

a sheep let into his body; and it is to be done on Saturday next. They purpose to let in about twelve ounces, which they compute is what will be let in in a minute's time by a watch. They differ in the opinion they have of the effects of it; some think that it may have a good effect upon him as a frantic man, by cooling his blood; others, that it will not have any effect at all. But the man is a very healthy man, and by this means will be able to give an account what alteration, if any, he doth find in himself, and so may be useful. On this occasion Dr. Whistler told a pretty story related by Muffett, a good author, of Dr. Caius that built Key's College: that being very old and lived only at that time upon woman's milk, while he fed upon the milk of an angry fretful woman, was so himself; and then being advised to take of a good-natured patient woman, he did become so, beyond the common temper of his age. Thus much nutriment, they observed, might do. Their discourse was very fine; and if I should be put out of my office,[2] I do take great content in the liberty I shall be at of frequenting these gentlemen's companies. Broke up thence and home, and there to my wife in her chamber, who is not well (of those[3]); and there she tells me great stories of the gossiping women of the parish, what this and what that woman was; and among the rest, how Mrs. Hollworthy is the veriest confident bragging gossip of them all, which I should not have believed—but that Sir R. Brookes, her partner,[4] was mighty civil to her and taken with her and what not. My eyes being bad, I spent the evening with her in her chamber, talking and inventing a cipher to put on a piece of plate[5] which I must give, better than ordinary, to the parson's child; and so to bed, and through my wife's illness had a bad night of it, and she a worse, poor wretch.

[30 November 1667] Then to Cary House, a house now of entertainment, * * * next my Lord Ashly's; and there, where I have heretofore heard Common Prayer in the time of Dr. Mossum,[6] we after two hours' stay, sitting at the table with our napkins open, had our dinners brought; but badly done. But here was good company, I choosing to sit next Dr. Wilkins, Sir George Ent, and others whom I value. And there talked of several things; among others, Dr. Wilkins, talking of the universal speech, of which he hath a book coming out,[7] did first inform me how man was certainly made for society, he being of all creatures the least armed for defense; and of all creatures in the world, the young ones are not able to do anything to help themselves, nor can find the dug without being put to it, but would die if the mother did not help it. And he says were it not for speech, man would be a very mean creature. Much of this good discourse we had. But here above all, I was pleased to see the person who had his blood taken out. He speaks well, and did this day give the Society a relation thereof in Latin, saying that he finds himself much better since, and as a new man. But he is cracked a little in his head, though he speaks very reasonably and very well. He had but 20s for his suffering it, and is to have the same again tried upon him—the first sound man that ever had it tried on him in England, and but one that we hear of in France, which was a porter hired by the virtuosi.

2. Pepys's position was in jeopardy because of a parliamentary investigation into Navy Office mismanagement during the Second Dutch War.
3. Her menstrual period.
4. As godfather at the christening.
5. I.e., a coded message to be engraved on a silver dish (so that the gift includes a kind of game).
6. Robert Mossum had conducted illegal Anglican services (using the forbidden Book of Common Prayer) during the Interregnum.
7. In his *Essay toward a Real Character, and a Philosophical Language* (1668), Wilkins argued for (and attempted) the creation of a newly precise and logical language based not on an arbitrary alphabet but on written symbols representing ideas and things.

[THEATER AND MUSIC]

[5 October 1667] Up, and to the office and there all the morning, none but my Lord Anglesey and myself. But much surprised with the news of the death of Sir W. Batten, who died this morning, having been but two days sick. Sir W. Penn and I did dispatch a letter this morning to Sir W. Coventry[8] to recommend Colonel Middleton, who we think a most honest and understanding man, and fit for that place. Sir G. Carteret did also come this morning, and walked with me in the garden and concluded not to concern or have any advice made to Sir W. Coventry in behalf of my Lord Sandwich's business; so I do rest satisfied, though I do think they are all mad,[9] that they will judge Sir W. Coventry an enemy, when he is indeed no such man to anybody, but is severe and just, as he ought to be, where he sees things ill done. At noon home, and by coach to Temple Bar to a India shop[1] and there bought a gown and sash, which cost me 26s. And so she and Willett[2] away to the Change, and I to my Lord Crew and there met my Lord Hinchingbrooke and Lady Jemima, and there dined with them and my Lord—where pretty merry. And after dinner, my Lord Crew and Hinchingbrooke and myself went aside to discourse about my Lord Sandwich's business, which is in a very ill state for want of money; and so parted, and I to my tailor's and there took up my wife and Willet, who stayed there for me, and to the Duke of York's playhouse;[3] but the House so full, it being a new play The Coffee-House, that we could not get in, and so to the King's House; and there going in, met with Knepp and she took us up into the tiring-rooms and to the women's shift,[4] where Nell[5] was dressing herself and was all unready; and is very pretty, prettier then I thought; and so walked all up and down the house above, and then below into the scene-room, and there sat down and she gave us fruit; and here I read the Qu's[6] to Knepp while she answered me, through all her part of Flora's Figarys, which was acted today. But Lord, to see how they were both painted would make a man mad—and did make me loathe them—and what base company of men comes among them, and how lewdly they talk—and how poor the men are in clothes, and yet what a show they make on the stage by candlelight, is very observable. But to see how Nell cursed for having so few people in the pit was pretty, the other house carrying away all the people at the new play, and is said nowadays to have generally most company, as being better players. By and by into the pit and there saw the play; which is pretty good, but my belly was full of what I had seen in the house; and so after the play done, away home and there to the writing my letters; and so home to supper and to bed.

[27 February 1668] All the morning at the office, and at noon home to dinner; and thence with my wife and Deb[7] to the King's House to see Virgin Martyr,[8] the first time it hath been acted a great while, and it is mighty pleasant; not that the play is worth much, but it is finely acted by Becke Marshall; but that which did please me

---

8. A commissioner on the Navy Board.
9. "They" are the Parliament investigators looking into the Board's (and Sandwich's) conduct during the Second Dutch War.
1. Dealing in goods imported from India.
2. Deborah Willett, recently hired as Elizabeth Pepys's companion.
3. There were only two licensed theater companies in Restoration London, one officially sponsored by the

duke, the other by the king.
4. Attiring rooms; women's dressing room.
5. Nell Gwyn, a popular comic actress; she would later become the king's mistress.
6. Cues.
7. Deborah Willett.
8. A tragedy by Thomas Dekker and Philip Massinger, first performed c. 1620.

beyond anything in the whole world was the wind-music when the angel comes down, which is so sweet that it ravished me; and indeed, in a word, did wrap up my soul so that it made me really sick, just as I have formerly been when in love with my wife; that neither then, nor all the evening going home and at home, I was able to think of anything, but remained all night transported, so as I could not believe that ever any music hath that real command over the soul of a man as this did upon me; and makes me resolve to practice wind-music and to make my wife do the like.

[ELIZABETH PEPYS AND DEBORAH WILLETT]

[25 October 1668] *Lord's Day.* Up, and discoursing with my wife about our house and many new things we are doing of; and so to church I, and there find Jack Fen come, and his wife, a pretty black woman; I never saw her before, nor took notice of her now. So home and to dinner; and after dinner, all the afternoon got my wife and boy to read to me. And at night W. Batelier comes and sups with us; and after supper, to have my head combed by Deb, which occasioned the greatest sorrow to me that ever I knew in this world; for my wife, coming up suddenly, did find me embracing the girl con my hand sub su coats; and indeed, I was with my main in her cunny.[9] I was at a wonderful loss upon it, and the girl also; and I endeavored to put it off, but my wife was struck mute and grew angry, and as her voice came to her, grew quite out of order; and I do say little, but to bed; and my wife said little also, but could not sleep all night; but about 2 in the morning waked me and cried, and fell to tell me as a great secret that she was a Roman Catholic and had received the Holy Sacrament; which troubled me but I took no notice of it, but she went on from one thing to another, till at last it appeared plainly her trouble was at what she saw; but yet I did not know how much she saw and therefore said nothing to her. But after her much crying and reproaching me with inconstancy and preferring a sorry girl before her, I did give her no provocations but did promise all fair usage to her, and love, and foreswore any hurt that I did with her—till at last she seemed to be at ease again; and so toward morning, a little sleep; [26][1] and so I, with some little repose and rest, rose, and up and by water to Whitehall, but with my mind mightily troubled for the poor girl, whom I fear I have undone by this, my wife telling me that she would turn her out of door. However, I was obliged to attend the Duke of York, thinking to have had a meeting of Tangier today, but had not; but he did take me and Mr. Wren into his closet, and there did press me to prepare what I had to say upon the answers of my fellow-officers to his great letter; which I promised to do against his coming to town again the next week; and so to other discourse, finding plainly that he is in trouble and apprehensions of the reformers, and would be found to do what he can towards reforming himself.[2] And so thence to my Lord Sandwich; where after long stay, he being in talk with others privately, I to him; and there he taking physic and keeping his chamber, I had an hour's talk with him about the ill posture of things at this time, while the King gives countenance to Sir Charles Sedley and Lord Buckhurst,[3] telling

9. I.e., with his hand under her petticoats and his hand in her vagina. Here as often, Pepys reports his illicit sexual activities in a "secret" language compounded of Latin, French, Spanish, and English.
1. Pepys wedges the new date into the margin, beside the run-on narrative.

2. The duke was Lord High Admiral of the navy; on his behalf Pepys had composed a letter to the Navy Board proposing reforms in response to parliamentary investigations of the disastrous Second Dutch War.
3. Notorious libertines (Buckhurst was Nell Gwyn's current lover).

him their late story of running up and down the streets a little while since all night, and their being beaten and clapped up all night by the constable, who is since chid and imprisoned for his pains.

He tells me that he thinks his matters do stand well with the King—and hopes to have dispatch to his mind; but I doubt it, and do see that he doth fear it too. He told me my Lady Carteret's trouble about my writing of that letter[4] of the Duke of York's lately to the office; which I did not own, but declared to be of no injury to G. Carteret, and that I would write a letter to him to satisfy him therein. But this I am in pain how to do without doing myself wrong, and the end I had, of preparing a justification to myself hereafter, when the faults of the Navy come to be found out. However, I will do it in the best manner I can.

Thence by coach home and to dinner, finding my wife mightily discontented and the girl sad, and no words from my wife to her. So after dinner, they out with me about two or three things; and so home again, I all the evening busy and my wife full of trouble in her looks; and anon to bed—where about midnight, she wakes me and there falls foul on me again, affirming that she saw me hug and kiss the girl; the latter I denied, and truly; the other I confessed and no more. And upon her pressing me, did offer to give her under my hand that I would never see Mrs. Pearse[5] more, nor Knepp, but did promise her particular demonstrations of my true love to her, owning some indiscretion in what I did, but that there was no harm in it. She at last on these promises was quiet, and very kind we were, and so to sleep; [27] and in the morning up, but with my mind troubled for the poor girl, with whom I could not get opportunity to speak; but to the office, my mind mighty full of sorrow for her, where all the morning, and to dinner with my people and to the office all the afternoon; and so at night home and there busy to get some things ready against tomorrow's meeting of Tangier; and that being done and my clerks gone, my wife did towards bedtime begin to be in a mighty rage from some new matter that she had got in her head, and did most part of the night in bed rant at me in most high terms, of threats of publishing my shame; and when I offered to rise, would have rose too, and caused a candle to be lit, to burn by her all night in the chimney while she ranted; while I, that knew myself to have given some grounds for it, did make it my business to appease her all I could possibly, and by good words and fair promises did make her very quiet; and so rested all night and rose with perfect good peace, being heartily afflicted for this folly of mine that did occasion it; but was forced to be silent about the girl, which I have no mind to part with, but much less that the poor girl should be undone by my folly. [28] So up, with mighty kindness from my wife and a thorough peace; and being up, did by a note advise the girl what I had done and owned, which note I was in pain for till she told me that she had burned it. This evening, Mr. Spong came and sat late with me, and first told me of the instrument called parrallogram, which I must have one of, showing me his practice thereon by a map of England.[6]

So by coach with Mr. Gibson[7] to Chancery Lane, and there made oath before a master of chancery to my Tangier account of fees; and so to Whitehall, where by and by a committee met; my Lord Sandwich there, but his report was not received, it

---

4. The "great letter" on naval reform.
5. Elizabeth Pearse, wife of a naval surgeon.
6. The parallelogram was a device for making copies of

diagrams and maps on the same or on a different scale.
7. A favorite assistant of Pepys's.

being late; but only a little business done, about the supplying the place with victuals; but I did get, to my great content, my account allowed of fees, with great
applause by my Lord Ashley and Sir W. Penn. Thence home, calling at one or two
places, and there about our workmen, who are at work upon my wife's closet and other parts of my house, that we are all in dirt. So after dinner, with Mr. Gibson all the
afternoon in my closet; and at night to supper and to bed, my wife and I at good
peace, but yet with some little grudgings of trouble in her, and more in me, about the
poor girl.

[14 November 1668] Up, and had a mighty mind to have seen or given a note to Deb
or to have given her a little money; to which purpose I wrapped up 40s in a paper,
thinking to give her; but my wife rose presently, and would not let me be out of her
sight; and went down before me into the kitchen, and came up and told me that she
was in the kitchen, and therefore would have me go round the other way; which she
repeating, and I vexed at it, answered her a little angrily; upon which she instantly
flew out into a rage, calling me dog and rogue, and that I had a rotten heart; all
which, knowing that I deserved it, I bore with; and word being brought presently up
that she was gone away by coach with her things, my wife was friends; and so all quiet, and I to the office with my heart sad, and find that I cannot forget the girl, and
vexed I know not where to look for her—and more troubled to see how my wife is by
this means likely for ever to have her hand over me, that I shall for ever be a slave to
her; that is to say, only in matters of pleasure, but in other things she will make her
business, I know, to please me and to keep me right to her—which I will labor to be
indeed, for she deserves it of me, though it will be I fear a little time before I shall be
able to wear Deb out of my mind. At the office all the morning, and merry at noon at
dinner; and after dinner to the office, where all the afternoon and doing much business late; my mind being free of all troubles, I thank God, but only for my thoughts of
this girl, which hang after her. And so at night home to supper, and there did sleep
with great content with my wife. I must here remember that I have lain with my
moher[8] as a husband more times since this falling-out then in I believe twelve
months before—and with more pleasure to her than I think in all the time of our
marriage before.

[20 November 1668] This morning up, with mighty kind words between my poor
wife and I; and so to Whitehall by water, W. Hewer with me, who is to go with me
everywhere until my wife be in condition to go out along with me herself; for she
doth plainly declare that she dares not trust me out alone, and therefore made it a
piece of our league that I should alway take somebody with me, or her herself;
which I am mighty willing to, being, by the grace of God resolved never to do her
wrong more.[9]
    We landed at the Temple, and there I did bid him call at my cousin Roger
Pepys's lodgings, and I stayed in the street for him; and so took water again at the
Strand stairs and so to Whitehall, in my way I telling him plainly and truly my resolutions, if I can get over this evil, never to give new occasion for it. He is, I

---

8. Spanish *mujer*: wife. For the first time, Pepys applies
his secret language to Elizabeth.
9. Two nights earlier, Pepys had traced Deborah Willett
to her new lodgings, and caressed her in his coach. The

next day, Elizabeth told him that she knew about the
assignation, and he signed a pledge "never to see or speak
with Deb while I live."

think, so honest and true a servant to us both, and one that loves us, that I was not much troubled at his being privy to all this, but rejoiced in my heart that I had him to assist in the making us friends; which he did do truly and heartily, and with good success—for I did get him to go to Deb to tell her that I had told my wife all of my being with her the other night, that so, if my wife should send, she might not make the business worse by denying it. While I was at Whitehall with the Duke of York doing our ordinary business with him, here being also the first time the new treasurers, W. Hewer did go to her and come back again; and so I took him into St. James's Park, and there he did tell me he had been with her and found what I said about my manner of being with her true, and had given her advice as I desired. I did there enter into more talk about my wife and myself, and he did give me great assurance of several particular cases to which my wife had from time to time made him privy of her loyalty and truth to me after many and great temptations, and I believe them truly. I did also discourse the unfitness of my leaving of my employment now in many respects, to go into the country as my wife desires—but that I would labor to fit myself for it; which he thoroughly understands, and doth agree with me in it; and so, hoping to get over this trouble, we about our business to Westminster Hall to meet Roger Pepys; which I did, and did there discourse of the business of lending him 500*l* to answer some occasions of his, which I believe to be safe enough; and so took leave of him and away by coach home, calling on my coach-maker by the way, where I like my little coach mightily. But when I came home, hoping for a further degree of peace and quiet, I find my wife upon her bed in a horrible rage afresh, calling me all the bitter names; and rising, did fall to revile me in the bitterest manner in the world, and could not refrain to strike me and pull my hair; which I resolved to bear with, and had good reason to bear it. So I by silence and weeping did prevail with her a little to be quiet, and she would not eat her dinner without me; but yet by and by into a raging fit she fell again worse than before, that she would slit the girl's nose; and at last W. Hewer came in and came up, who did allay her fury, I flinging myself in a sad desperate condition upon the bed in the blue room, and there lay while they spoke together; and at last it came to this, that if I would call Deb "whore" under my hand,[1] and write to her that I hated her and would never see her more, she would believe me and trust in me—which I did agree to; only, as to the name of "whore" I would have excused, and therefore wrote to her sparing that word; which my wife thereupon tore it, and would not be satisfied till, W. Hewer winking upon me, I did write so, with the name of a whore, as that I did fear she might too probably have been prevailed upon to have been[2] a whore by her carriage to me, and therefore, as such, I did resolve never to see her more. This pleased my wife, and she gives it W. Hewer to carry to her, with a sharp message from her. So from that minute my wife begun to be kind to me, and we to kiss and be friends, and so continued all the evening and fell to talk of other matters with great comfort, and after supper to bed.

This evening comes Mr. Billup to me to read over Mr. Wren's alterations of my draft of a letter for the Duke of York to sign, to the board; which I like mighty well, they being not considerable, only in mollifying some hard terms which I had thought fit to put in. From this to other discourse; I do find that the Duke of

---

1. In writing.   2. Become.

York and his servant Mr. Wren do look upon this service of mine as a very seasonable service to the Duke of York, as that which he will have to show to his enemies in his own justification of his care of the King's business. And I am sure I am heartily glad of it—both for the King's sake and the Duke of York's, and my own also—for if I continue, my work, by this means, will be the less, and my share in the blame[3] also.

He being gone, I to my wife again and so spent the evening with very great joy, and the night also, with good sleep and rest, my wife only troubled in her rest, but less than usual—for which the God of Heaven be praised. I did this night promise to my wife never to go to bed without calling upon God upon my knees by prayer; and I begun this night, and hope I shall never forget to do the like all my life—for I do find that it is much the best for my soul and body to live pleasing to God and my poor wife—and will ease me of much care, as well as much expense.

[31 May 1669] Up very betimes, and so continued all the morning, with W. Hewer, upon examining and stating my accounts, in order to the fitting myself to go abroad beyond sea,[4] which the ill condition of my eyes, and my neglect for a year or two, hath kept me behindhand in, and so as to render it very difficult now, and troublesome to my mind to do it; but I this day made a satisfactory entrance therein.[5] Dined at home, and in the afternoon by water to Whitehall, calling by the way at Mitchell's,[6] where I have not been many a day till just the other day; and now I met her mother there and knew her husband to be out of town. And here yo did besar ella, but have not opportunity para hazer mas[7] with her as I would have offered if yo had had it. And thence had another meeting with the Duke of York at Whitehall with the Duke of York on yesterday's work, and made a good advance; and so being called by my wife, we to the park, Mary Batelier, a Dutch gentleman, a friend of hers, being with us. Thence to the World's End, a drinking-house by the park, and there merry; and so home late.

And thus ends all that I doubt I shall ever be able to do with my own eyes in the keeping of my journal, I being not able to do it any longer, having done now so long as to undo my eyes almost every time that I take a pen in my hand; and therefore, whatever comes of it, I must forbear; and therefore resolve from this time forward to have it kept by my people in longhand, and must therefore be contented to set down no more than is fit for them and all the world to know; or if there be anything (which cannot be much, now my amours to Deb are past, and my eyes hindering me in almost all other pleasures), I must endeavor to keep a margin in my book open, to add here and there a note in shorthand with my own hand.[8] And so I betake myself to that course which is almost as much as to see myself go into my grave—for which, and all the discomforts that will accompany my being blind, the good God prepare me.

May. 31. 1669.   S.P.

---

3. For Navy Board misconduct.
4. Pepys and his wife planned a tour of Holland, Flanders, and France. Near journey's end, Elizabeth Pepys caught a fever; she died in London on 10 November 1669.
5. Pepys suffered from a painful combination of farsightedness and astigmatism which doctors did not know how to diagnose or to treat; he feared (mistakenly) that he was going blind.
6. Michael Mitchell sold liquor in a shop on London Bridge; his wife Betty is the "her" of the ensuing clauses.
7. I did kiss her but had no chance to do more.
8. Pepys never produced the continuation of his journal that he envisions here.

Mary Carleton
1642?–1673

Even during her highly publicized life, little was known for certain about the woman called Mary Carleton, and that uncertainty generated fascination. She claimed that she was Maria de Wolway, a German-born, convent-educated noblewoman who had traveled to England, where she had been wooed and wedded by an eighteen-year-old lawyer named John Carleton. He, his family, and others claimed instead that she was a con-woman named Mary Moders, a musician's daughter from Canterbury who had tricked Carleton into false nuptials when she was already married to a shoemaker from her hometown.

The dispute came to a head in 1663, with her arrest and trial on charges of bigamy. While in prison awaiting trial, Carleton became a popular attraction, with Londoners paying fees for the privilege of seeing her, assessing her conduct, and surmising her actual identity. At her trial many in the crowd applauded her lively self-defense and quick acquittal (her accusers almost certainly had the truer case but couldn't muster the necessary evidence). In his diary, Samuel Pepys hinted at some components of Carleton's complex popularity: "My Lady Batten inveighed mightily against the German princess, and I [was] as high in the defense of her wit and spirit, and glad that she is cleared at the sessions." The Lady rages and the tailor's son rejoices at the freedom of a woman who had shown how readily high rank might be counterfeited.

Nine months later, strapped for cash, Carleton appeared in a play *The German Princess*, a comedy based on her story. She played, of course, herself—ineptly by all accounts. ("Never," Pepys observed, "was anything so well done in earnest worst performed in jest upon the stage.") Deception proved precarious in life as well. Following several more arrests, Carleton was hanged for theft in 1673.

Both at her initial trial and her eventual execution, the Carleton enigma fed the presses. Pamphlets appeared in abundance, purportedly written by her accusers, by supporters, by disinterested observers who mocked or moralized, and by the woman herself. *The Case of Madam Mary Carleton*, which appeared shortly after the trial, presents the fullest first-person account; like all the other texts in the controversy, it raises basic questions of authenticity and authorship. Is it truthful autobiography or an outright fiction? Probably a mix: the account of her German childhood is almost certainly false; that of her London escapades is partly corroborated by other sources, though wittily elaborated here. Is the text hers or a ghostwriter's? Again, perhaps a hybrid—and a sturdy one. In an audacious, even defiant, voice, the writer recounts dubious activities and improvisatory impersonations in a purported autobiography whose credibility remains stubbornly open to question. This is one of the early templates for the novel. Daniel Defoe, who sixty years later wrote several long fictions on just such a model, knew of Carleton's case and drew on it ("I might as well have been the German Princess," remarks Roxana, one of his most accomplished self-inventors). The Carleton papers bespeak a culture suffused with the suspicion that identity might be a mere construct, an impersonation.

from The Case of Madam Mary Carleton
TO THE NOBLE LADIES AND GENTLEWOMEN OF ENGLAND

Madames,

Be pleased to lay aside that severity of your judgment, by which you examine and castigate the licitness and convenience of every of your actions or passages of moment, and therefore seldom run into the misgovernment of Fortune, and cast a favorable eye upon these novels[1] of my life, not much unlike those of Boccace[2] but that they are more serious and tragical.

The breach that is made in my credit and reputation, I do feel and understand to be very wide, and past my repairing, whatever materials of defense, excuse, and purgation I can bring to the scrutiny of men; who are not sensible to what sudden changes our natures are subjected, and that from airy thoughts and motions, things of great influence, sometimes good, sometimes bad, have been exhibited to the world, equal to the most sober and firm resolutions of the valiant and the wise.

It hath been my mishap for one among many others to miscarry in an affair to which there are more intrigues and perplexities of kin and alliance, and necessary dependence, than to any other thing in the world, i.e. marriage (Hymen[3] is as blind as Fortune and gives her favors by guess): the mistaken advantages whereof have turned to my real damage: so that when I might have been happy in myself, I must needs transplant my content into a sterile ungrateful soul, and be miserable by another. Yet have I done nothing dishonorable to your better beloved sex, there is nothing of lewdness, baseness, or meanness in the whole carriage of this noised story, nor which I will not, cannot justify, as the actions of a gentlewoman; with the account of which, from the beginning of my life, I here present you.

My fortune not being competent to my mind, though proportionable to my gentele degree,[4] hath forwardly shrunk into nothing, but I doubt not to buoy both my honor and estate up together, when these envious clouds are dispelled that obscure my brightness; the shadows are at the longest, and my fame shall speedily rise in its due luster. Till then, and ever, I am,

Ladies, your devoted hand-maid,

MARY CARLETON

The Case of Madam Mary Carleton
The Wife of Mr. John Carleton, formerly styled a German Princess

* * *

The time of my deliberated departure being come,[5] and other intervening accidents having confirmed me to the pursuance of that journey (some piecemeal rumors whereof have been scattered up and down, not far distant from the truth, namely constraint and awe of an unliked and unsuitable match, which the freedom of my soul most highly abominated and resented), I privately by night withdrew from my governess, and by the way of Utrecht, where I stayed a while incognito, thence passed to Amsterdam, and so to Rotterdam, I came to the Brill,[6] and there took shipping for England, the Elysium[7] of my wishes and expectations being in hope to find it a land of angels,[8] but I perceive it now to be, as to me, a place of torments.

1. The word (meaning "new things") refers here to both fictions and factual "news."
2. The Renaissance writer Giovanni Boccaccio (1313?–1375), whose *Decameron* collects 100 short tales.
3. God of marriage.
4. I.e., my high birth.
5. By this point in the text, Carleton has recounted her youth in the German city of Cologne, as the orphaned daughter of wealthy parents. Educated in a nunnery, she rejected the religious life, returned to her family seat,

"addicted [her]self to the reading of history," and mastered several languages. Wooed pressingly by two unappetizing bachelors, she resolved to leave Germany for England.
6. Brielle, a Dutch port.
7. A place or condition of ideal happiness; paradise.
8. By an old pun, "England" was deemed to mean "Angelland," because the light-haired inhabitants resembled angels.

I am not single,[9] or the first woman, that hath put herself upon such hazards or pilgrimages; the stories of all times abound with such examples, enough to make up a volume. I might as well have given luster to a romance[1] as any of those supposed heroines: and since it is the method of those pieces, and the art of that way of writing, to perplex and intricate[2] the commencement and progress of such adventures with unexpected and various difficulties and troubles, and at last bring them to the long desired fruition of their dear-bought content, I am not altogether out of heart, but that Providence may have some tender and more courteous consideration of me; for I protest I know not what crime, offense, or demerit of mine hath rendered her so averse and intractable as she hath proved to my designs.

Nor do the modern and very late times want examples of the like adventures. I could mention a princess and great personage out of the north,[3] who not long since came into my country, and hath passed two or three times between Italy and France, and keeps her design yet undiscovered, and is the only lady errant in the world. I could mention another of a far worse consequence in this country, a she-general,[4] who followed the camp to the other world in America, etc., and was the occasion of the loss of the design. Mine compared with those are mere puny stories and inconsiderable. I neither concerned my travail in negotiating peace or carrying war, but was merely my own free agent.

Nor can I be blamed for this course, for besides the necessity and enforcements of forsaking my country, without running into a more insupportable condition of marriage than this I am now in (for my patience and suffering and continence I have, I trust in my own power, and shall endeavor to keep them undisturbed and uncorrupted, whatever temptations or occasions, by reason of this unjust separation, now are, or shall be put upon me hereafter; but my life is not in my disposal or preservation, which I had certainly endangered at home, if I had been bedded to him whom my heart abhorred); and besides other reasons, which I cannot in prudence yet render to the world, the very civility and purity of my design, without any lustful or vicious appertenant,[5] would fairly excuse me.

What harm have I done in pretending to great titles? Ambition and affection of greatness to good and just purposes was always esteemed and accounted laudable and praiseworthy, and the sign and character of a virtuous mind, nor do I think it an unjust purpose in me to contrive my own advancement by such illustrious pretenses as they say I made use of, to grant the question that I am not so honorably descended as I insinuated to the catchdolt[6] my father-in-law (which yet by their favor they shall first better and more evidently disprove than as yet they have done, before I relinquish my just claim to my honor), I think I do rather deserve commendation than reproach; if the best *things are to be imitated;* I had a good precept and warrant for my assumption of such a personage as they were willing to believe me to be. If indeed by any misbecoming act unhandsome and unbefitting such a person, I had profaned that quality and bewrayed and discovered any inconsistent meanness therewith (as it was very difficult to personate greatness for so long a time without slips or mistakes), I had deserved to be severely punished and abominated by all gentlemen; whereas after all these loads

---

9. The only.
1. "A tale of wild adventure in war and love" (Johnson's *Dictionary*); a genre immensely popular in the 17th century.
2. Complicate.
3. Christina (1626–1689), queen of Sweden (1632–1654), who abdicated in 1654, and thereafter wandered through

Europe, often dressed as a man. In A *Relation of the Life of Christina Queen of Sweden* (1656), she is described as a lady errant (the female counterpart to a knight errant).
4. This "she-general" has not been identified.
5. Element.
6. Swindler.

of imputations which my enemies have heaped upon me, I do (with my acknowl-edgments to them for it) enjoy, and am happy in many of their loves and good estimation.

And I will yet continue the same respects, and make the world to know that there is no possibility of such perfections, without a more intent care and elegancy of learning, to which I have by great labor and industry attained.

I need not therefore engage further in this preliminary part of my defense, only as an irrefragable[7] confutation of the poorness of my birth, and in this kingdom I would have my adversaries know, as some of them do, though they don't well under-stand, that the several languages I have ready and at my command, as the Greek, Latin, French, Italian, Spanish, English, and something of the Oriental tongues, all which I pronounce with a Dutch dialect and idiom, are not common and ordinary endowments of an English spinster, no not of the best rank of the city. And since I must praise myself, in short, I came not here to learn anything for use or ornament of a woman, but only the ways to a better fortune.

I come now to the matter of fact. The first place I touched at was Gravesend, where I arrived towards the end of March, and without any stay took a tideboat,[8] came to London in company with a parson or minister, who officiously, but I suppose out of design, gave me the trouble of his service and attendance to the Exchange Tavern right against the stock,[9] betwixt the Poultry and Cornhill, the house of one Mr. King, not having any knowledge of the master or his acquaintance, and free, God knows, from any design, for I would have entered any other house if I had found the doors open or could have raised the folks nearer to my landing, for I was distempered with the night's passage; but it was so early in the morning, five a-clock, that there was nobody stirring elsewhere, only here by mishap Mr. King himself was up and standing at the bar, telling of brass farthings, whom the parson desired to fill a pint of wine, which he readily performed, and brought to a room behind the bar. While the wine was a-drinking (which was Rhenish wine, the compliment being put upon me by the parson as the fruit of my own happy country), Sir John very rudely began to accost me and to offer some incivilities to me, which I found no other way to avoid than by pretending want of rest to the master of the house, and acquainting him with my charge of jewels, and that I was as I do justify myself to be a person of quality. Hereupon a room was provided for me to repose myself in, and the clergyman took his leave with a troublesome promise of waiting upon me another day to give me a visit, which I was forced to admit and to tell him I would leave word wherever I went; but he considering as I suppose of the unfeasibleness of his desires and the pub-licness of the place, neglected his promise and troubled me no more.

He being gone, Mr. King began to question me, what country-woman I was, and of what religion. I frankly told him, and acquainted him with all what charge I had about me, which to secure from the danger of the town, that was full of cozenage and villainy, he advised me to stay with him till I could better provide for myself.

I rested myself here till eleven a-clock at noon; when I arose, and was very civil-ly treated by Mr. King, who well knowing I was a stranger and well furnished with money, omitted no manner of respect to me, nor did I spend parsimoniously and at an ordinary rate, but answerable to the quality and account, at their fetching and itching questions, I gave of myself.

---

7. Unquestionable.
8. A vessel that traveled up the Thames with the tide.

9. Next to the public pillory; the tavern is at the center of the City's commercial district.

This invited him earnestly with all submissive address to request my staying with them till I had dispatched and had provided all things for my public appearance, for the better furnishing and equipping whereof, I acquainted him I would send by post to my steward, for the return of some moneys to defray the expenses thereof, which letters he viewed, and conceived such imaginations in his head thereupon that it never left working till it had wrought the effect of his finely begun and hopefully continued enterprise.

These letters he himself delivered at my desire to have them carefully put into the mail, to the posthouse;[1] and thereafter observed me with most manifest respects.[2] In the interim of[3] the return of these moneys, I was slightly, and as it were by the by, upon discourse of my country (wherein they took occasion to be liberally copious[4]), engaged into some discovery of myself, my estate and quality, and the nature of both, the causes of my coming hither, etc., but I did it so unconcernedly and negligently, as a matter of no moment or disturbance to me, though I had hinted at the discontent of my match,[5] that this did assure them that all was real, and therefore it was time to secure my estate to them by a speedy and secret marriage.

Let the world now judge whether being prompted by such plain and public signs of a design upon me, to counterplot them I have done any more than what the rule, and a received principle of justice directs: *to deceive the deceiver is no deceit.*

I knew not nevertheless which way their artifices tended, till Master King brought into my acquaintance old Mr. Carleton his father-in-law, and soon after Mr. John Carleton his son: it seems it had been consulted to have preferred George, the elder brother: he, troubled with a simple modesty, and a mind no way competent to so much greatness, was laid aside, and the younger flushed and encouraged to set upon me. By this time they had obtained my name from me, viz. Maria de Wolway, which passage also hath suffered by another lewder imposture, and allusory sound of De Vulva:[6] in the language of which I am better versed than to pick out no civiller and eleganter impress.[7]

To the addresses of Mr. John Carleton, I carried myself with so much indifference, not superciliously refusing his visits or readily admitting his suit, not disheartening him with a severe retiredness or challenges of his imparity,[8] nor encouraging him with a freedom or openness of heart or arrogance of my own condition, that he and his friends were upon the spur to consummate the match, which yet I delayed and dissembled with convenient pretenses, but herein I will be more particular in the ensuing pages.

In the meanwhile, to prevent all notice of me, and the disturbance of their proceedings that might be occasioned thereby, they kept me close in the nature of a prisoner, which though I perceived, yet I made no semblance thereof[9] at all, but colluded with them in their own arts, and pretended some averseness to all company but only my innamorato,[1] Mr. Carleton: nor was anybody else suffered to come near me or to speak with me; insomuch, as I have been informed, that they promised to one Sackvil (whom for his advice they had too forwardly, as they thought, imparted the

1. The post office (King hand-delivers them to prevent tampering).
2. Obvious attention.
3. While awaiting.
4. I.e., King and others at the house often brought up the subject.
5. Projected marriage (in Cologne).
6. This sexual pun had been popularized by writers of several pamphlets deriding Carleton's claims.
7. Carleton may mean that she knows all three languages (German, Latin, English) better than to have chosen a name so susceptible to punning. (Her point is that it is her given name; she never chose it.)
8. Inequality to me in rank.
9. Didn't reveal that I saw what they were up to.
1. Beloved.

business) the sum of £200 to be silent, lest that it should be heard at Court, and so the estate and honor which they had already swallowed[2] would be lost from their son and seized by some courtier, who should next come to hear of this great lady.

After many visits passed betwixt Mr. Carleton and myself, old Mr. Carleton and Mr. King came to me and very earnestly pressed the dispatch of the marriage, and that I would be pleased to give my assent, setting forth with all the qualities and great sufficiencies of that noble person, as they pleased to style him. I knew what made them so urgent, for they had now seen the answers I had received by the post, by which I was certified of the receipt of mine, and that accordingly some thousands of crowns should be remitted instantly to London, and coach and horses sent by the next shipping, with other things I had sent for, and to reinforce this their *commendamus*[3] the more effectually, they acquainted me that if I did not presently grant the suit and their request, Mr. Carleton was so far in love with me, that he would make away with himself, or presently travail beyond sea and see England no more.

I cannot deny but that I could hardly forbear smiling, to see how serious these elders and brokers were in this love-killing story, but keeping to my business, after some demurs and demands, I seemed not to consent, and then they began passionately, urging me with other stories.

* * *

And now my lord spoke nothing but rodomantades[4] of the greatness of his family, of the delights and stateliness of his lands and houses, the game of his parks, the largeness of his stables, and convenience of fish and foul, for furnishing his liberal and open housekeeping, that I should see *England afforded more pleasure than any place in the world,* but they were (without the host) reckoned and charged beforehand to my account,[5] and to be purchased with my estate, which was his, by a figure of anticipation, when we two should be all one, and therefore he lied not but only equivocated a little.

But he did not in the least mention any such thing to me, nor made any offer of inquiry what I was, no not the least semblance or shadow of it; he seemed to take no notice of my fortunes, it was my person he only courted, which having so happily and accidentally seen, he could not live if I cherished not his affections. Nor did I think it then convenient or civil to question the credit of his words and the report given me of him. His demeanor I confess was light, but I imputed that to his youth, and the vanity of a gallant, as necessary a quality and as much admired as wit in a woman.

The last day of my virgin state, Easter eve, the tailor brought me my gown to my lodging. I being dressed and adorned with my jewels, he again renewed his suit to me, with all importunity imaginable. His courteous mother was also now most forward, pressing me to consent by telling me that *she should lose her son* and *he his wits,* he being already impatient with denials and delays, adding withal, that he was a person hopeful, and might deserve my condescension. I withstood all their solicitation, although they continued it until twelve of the clock that night. The young lord, at his taking his leave of me, told me he would attend me betimes the next morning and carry me to St. Paul's Church,[6] to hear the organs, saying, that there would be very excellent anthems performed by rare voices, the morrow being Sunday the 19th of

---

2. Captured.
3. Their self-recommendation (their argument in favor of the marriage).
4. Boasts.
5. To "reckon without the host" is to calculate one's debt

without consulting the person to whom one owes it (in this case, the author).
6. The City of London's cathedral, and central place of worship.

April last. In the morning betimes,[7] the young lord cometh to my chamber door, desiring admittance, which I refused, in regard I was not ready; yet so soon as my head was dressed, I let him have access. He hastened me, and told me his coach was ready at the door, in which he carried me to his mother's in the Greyfriars, London,[8] where I was assaulted by the young lord's tears, and others to give my consent to marry him, telling me that they had a parson and a license ready, which was a mere falsehood and temporary fallacy to secure the match.

So on Easter morning, with three coaches, in which with the bride and bridegroom were all the kindred that were privy to the business, and pretended a license,[9] they carried me to Cloth Fair by Smithfield, and in the church of great St. Bartholomew's, married me by one Mr. Smith, who was well paid for his pains. And now they thought themselves possessed of their hopes, but because they would prevent the noise and fame of their good fortune from public discourse, that no sinister accident might intervene before Mr. Carleton had bedded me, offense being likely to be taken at Court (as they whispered to themselves) that a private subject had married a foreign princess, they had before determined to go to Barnet,[1] and thither immediately after the celebration of the marriage we were driven in the coaches, where we had a handsome treatment, and there we stayed Sunday and Monday, both which nights Mr. Carleton lay with me, and on Tuesday morning we were married again, a license being then obtained to make the match more fast and sure, at their instance with me to consent to it.

This being done, and their fears over, they resolved to put me in a garb befitting the estate and dignity they fancied I had; and they were so far possessed with a belief of it, that they gave out I was worth no less than £80,000 per annum, and my husband, as I must now style him, published[2] so much in a coffeehouse; adding withal, to the extolling of his good hap, that there was a further estate but that it was my modesty or design to conceal it, and that he could not attribute his great fortune to anything but the Fates, for he had not anything to balance with the least of my estate and merits. So do conceited[3] heights of sudden prosperity and greatness dazzle the eyes and judgment of the most, nor could this young man be much blamed for his vainglorious mistake.

My clothes being made at the charge of my father-in-law, and other fineries of the mode and fashion sent me by some of his kindred and friends (who prided themselves in this happy affinity, and who had an eye upon some advantages also, and therefore gave me this early bribe, as testimonies of their early respect), and as for jewels I had of mine own of all sorts, for necklaces, pendants and bracelets, of admirable splendor and brightness. I was in a prince-like attire, and a splendid equipage and retinue, accoutered for public view among all the great ladies of the Court and the town on May Day[4] ensuing. At which time in my Lady Bludworth's[5] coach, which the same friends procured for my greater accommodation, and accompanied with the same lady with footmen and pages, I rode to Hyde Park[6] in open view of that celebrious[7] cavalcade and assembly, much gazed upon by them all, the eximiousness[8] of my fortune drawing their eyes upon me; particularly that that noble lady gave me precedence and the right hand, and a neat treatment after our divertisement of turning up and down the park.

---

7. Early.
8. Once the site of a monastery, this was now an area of prosperous residences.
9. Either they pretended to have a license or they had a fake license and pretended it was real.
1. A village north of London.
2. Announced.
3. Imagined.

4. May 1, exuberantly celebrated as a spring festival.
5. "Blood-worth": a name concocted by Carleton that indicates high rank and birth.
6. A fashionable gathering place.
7. Fine and crowded.
8. Excellence; Carleton is pointedly showing off her vocabulary and her learning.

I was altogether ignorant of what estate my husband was, and therefore made no nicety to take those places his friends gave me, and if I be taxed for incivility herein, it was his fault that he instructed me no better in my quality, for I conceited still that he was some landed, honorable, and wealthy man.

Things yet went fairly on, the same observances and distances continued, and lodgings befitting a person of quality taken for me in Durham Yard,[9] at one Mr. Green's, where my husband and I enjoyed one another with mutual complacency, till the return of the moneys out of Germany failing the day and their rich hopes, old Mr. Carleton began to suspect he was deceived in his expectation, and that all was not gold that glistered. But to remove such a prejudice from himself, as if he were the author of those scandals that were now prepared against my innocence, a letter is produced and sent from some then unknown hand, which reflected much upon my honor and reputation;[1] and thereupon on the fifth or sixth of May ensuing, I was by a warrant dragged forth of my new lodgings, with all the disgrace and contumely that could be cast upon the vilest offender in the world, at the instigation of old Mr. Carleton, who was the prosecutor, and by him and his agents divested and stripped of all my clothes, and plundered of all my jewels and my money, my very bodice and a pair of silk stockings being also pulled from me, and in a strange array carried before a justice.

* * *

See the fickleness and vanity of human things, today embellished, and adorned with all the female arts of bravery and gallantry, and courted and attended on by the best rank of my sex, who are jealous observers what honor and respect they give among themselves, to a very punctilio;[2] and now disrobed and disfigured in misshapen garments and almost left naked, and haled[3] and pulled by beadles,[4] and such like rude and boisterous fellows, before a tribunal, like a lewd criminal.

The justice's name was Mr. Godfrey,[5] by whose *mittimus*,[6] upon an accusation managed by old Mr. Carleton, that I had married two husbands, both of them in being, I was committed to the Gatehouse. Being interrogated by the justice, whether or no I had not two husbands as was alleged, I answered, if I had, he was one of them, which I believe incensed him something the more against me, but I did not know the authority and dignity of his place, so much am I a stranger to this kingdom.

There were other things and crimes of a high nature objected against me besides: That I cheated a vintner[7] of sixty pounds, and was for that committed to Newgate; but that lie quickly vanished, for it was made appear that I was never a prisoner there, nor was my name ever recorded in their books; and that I picked a Kentish lord's pocket, and cheated a French merchant of rings, jewels, and other commodities, that I made an escape, when sold and shipped for the Barbados,[8] but these were urged only as surmises; and old Carleton bound over to prosecute only for bigamy, for my having two husbands.

Thus the world may see how industrious mischief is to ruin a poor helpless and destitute woman, who had neither money, friends, nor acquaintance left me; yet I

---

9. A fashionable London neighborhood.
1. The letter (which Carleton quotes in a section omitted here) came from Canterbury, and described her as an "absolute cheat" who had already "married several men in our county."
2. A small detail.
3. Harried; molested.
4. Minor parish officers.

5. Sir Edmund Berry Godfrey (1622–1678), justice of the peace. He became one of the century's most famous corpses; his murder, and the accusations surrounding it, initiated the anti-Catholic furor called the Popish Plot.
6. Latin, meaning "we send"; a warrant stipulating that the accused be imprisoned.
7. Wine dealer.
8. I.e., as punishment for a previous crime.

cannot deny that my husband lovingly came to me at the Gatehouse the same day I was committed, and did very passionately complain of his father's usage of me, merely upon the disappointment, as he said, of their expectations, and that he could be contented to love me as well as ever, to live with me and own me as a wife, and used several other expressions of tenderness to me.

Nor have I less affection and kind sentiments for him, whom I own and will own till death dissolve the union, and did acquaint him with so much there and protested my innocence to him, nor do I doubt, could he have prevailed with his father, but that these things had never happened. If now after my vindication he prove faithless and renege[9] me, his fault will be doubly greater in that he neither assisted my innocence when endangered, or cherished it when vindicated by the law.

In this prison of the Gatehouse I continued six weeks, in a far better condition than I promised myself, but the greater civilities I owe to the keeper: as I am infinitely beholding to several persons of quality, who came at first I suppose out of curiosity to see me, and did thereafter nobly compassionate my calamitous, and injurious restraint. * * * I may in some measure thank my stars that out of this misfortune extracted so much bliss as the honor of their acquaintance, which otherwise at large I had been in no capacity to attain.[1]

* * *

And now let all the world judge of the cheat I have put upon this worshipful family of the Carletons. I have of theirs not a thread nor piece of anything, to be a token or remembrance of my beloved lord, which I might preserve and lay up as a sacred relic of a person dear to me (I think indeed the dearest that ever woman had).

I am advised howsoever to prosecute my adversaries[2] in the same manner, and at the same bar where they arraigned me for a suspicion, of a real suit of felony, for that riot against the public peace committed upon my person: which I am resolved to do, in case I receive not better satisfaction from them before the Sessions:[3] nor shall my husband's dilating entreaties and persuasions befool me any longer.[4]

> Either love me, or leave me,
> And do not deceive me.

The fashions and customs here are much different from those of our country, where the wife shares an equal portion with her husband in all things of weal and woe, and can *liber intentare*,[5] begin and commence, and finish a suit in her own name; they buy and sell, and keep accounts, manage the affairs of household and the trade, and do all things relating to their several stations and degrees. I have heard and did believe the proverb *that England was a Heaven for women*. But I never saw that Heaven described in its proper terms. For as to as much as I see of it, 'tis a very long prospect, and almost disappears to view; it is to be enjoyed but at second hand, and all by the husband's title; quite contrary to the custom of the Russians, where it

---

9. Denounce.
1. Carleton proceeds to recount her trial and her acquittal.
2. I.e., the Carleton family.

3. The period appointed for new trials.
4. Since her arrest, her husband had made intermittent overtures of reconciliation.
5. Be free to bring an action.

is a piece of their divinity that because it's said that the bishop must be the husband of one wife, they put out of orders[6] and from all ecclesiastical function such clergymen who by the canon being bound to be married, are by death deprived of their wives; so that their tenure to their livings and preferments clearly depends upon the welfare and long life of their yoke-fellows, in whose choice, as of such moment to their well-being, they are very curious, as they are afterwards in their care and preservation of them.

I could instance in many other customs of nearer nations, in respect to female right and propriety in their own dowers, as well as in their husbands' estates: but, *cum fueris Romae, Romano vivite more.*[7] I will not quarrel with the English laws, which I question not are calculated and well accommodated to the genius and temper of the people.

While I mention these customs, I cannot forbear to complain of a very great rudeness and incivility to which the mass and generality of the English vulgar are most pronely inclined, that is, to hoot and hallow and pursue strangers with their multitudes through the streets, pressing upon them even to the danger of their lives; and when once a cry or some scandalous humor is bruited[8] among them, they become brutes indeed. A barbarity I thought could not possibly be in this nation, whom I heard famed for so much civility and urbanity. This I experimented the other day in Fenchurch Street, as I was passing through it upon some occasion, which being noised and scattered among the 'prentices, I was forced to bethink of some shift and stratagem to avoid them, which was by putting my maid into a coach that by a good hap was at hand, and stepping into an adjoining tavern; which the herd mistaking my maid for me, and following the coach as supposing there for the convenience thereof, gave me the opportunity of escaping from them. A regulation of this kind of uproar by some severe penalties would much conduce not only to the honor of the government of the city, but the whole nation in general; having heard the French very much complain of the like injuries and affronts: but those to me I may justly place to my husband's account, who hath exposed me to the undeserved wonder, and to be a May-game[9] to the town. * * *

1663   1663

PERSPECTIVES

The Royal Society and the New Science

In the late 1600s, the antiquarian John Aubrey looked back to the middle of his century as a turning point in intellectual history: "Till about the year 1649, when experimental philosophy was first cultivated by a club at Oxford, 'twas held a strange presumption for a man to attempt an innovation in learnings; and not to be good manners, to be more knowing than his neighbors and forefathers." The "club" consisted of a group of inquirers for whom the university at Oxford offered a place of retreat in time of civil war. As Aubrey implies,

---

6. Dismiss from office.
7. "When in Rome do as the Romans do." St. Ambrose's advice to St. Augustine had become proverbial.

8. Rumored.
9. A source of entertainment, like the games on May Day.

their "innovation" consisted in a kind of bad manners. They refused to take the word of their intellectual "forefathers" (notably Aristotle) for how the natural world worked, and instead pursued knowledge of it through direct experiment, preferring new data to old theory, the testimony of the senses over the constructs of the intellect; the works of Francis Bacon, who had articulated such a method half a century earlier, served for these investigators as something akin to scripture. The members continued to meet during the Interregnum. In 1662, Charles II granted the group (which had relocated to London) a charter, a seal, and with his patronage, a new prominence. The informal club had become the "Royal Society for the Improving of Natural Knowledge."

That "Improving" was to take place on many fronts. The Society's charter stipulated that its experiments should be aimed at "promoting the knowledge of natural things and useful arts": science and technology. In its first decades its members made enormous advances in both realms, producing (among innumerable innovations) new explanations of heat, cold, and light; an air pump capable of creating a vacuum; a newly efficient pocket watch; and a newly coherent and durable account of the universe. A Fellow of the Society might work simultaneously at many endeavors that have since become specialties, investigating biology, physics, and astronomy, inventing scientific instruments and domestic appliances, advancing inquiries into theology, astrology, even demonology.

The group liked to portray itself as inclusive demographically too. Its Fellows represented many religious views, political persuasions, and social strata, from dukes to merchants to "mechanicks." Still, the early records evince an initial emphasis on high rank: aristocrats, courtiers, politicians, and "gentlemen" made up more than half the original membership (women were excluded altogether). Many of these men were mere names on the rolls, enlisted to bolster the respectability of the new enterprise; others were occasional spectators, intermittently attending the meetings to observe (amused, amazed, often baffled) the experiments performed there. But the Society also fostered a new category of inquirer: the "Christian virtuoso," a man of birth, means, merit, brains, and leisure, whose dissociation from any one profession was taken to guarantee the objectivity of his investigations, and whose rank and goodness underwrote the integrity of his findings. The Honorable Robert Boyle, who coined the phrase, was also its epitome. Well-born, devout, and dazzlingly gifted at science, he was the Society's prime mover and first star. But the type also found a less rarified, more popular incarnation in a new kind of amateur: the prosperous person who read, contemplated, talked the new philosophy, and kept a "cabinet of curiosities"—a closet or small room in which were arranged, and proudly displayed, antiquarian objects, scientific specimens, anything whose strangeness might arouse interest. The Society was amassing comparable collections on a much larger scale; the history of museums begins within the cabinets of the virtuosi.

The Society's emphasis on gentlemanly virtuosity was partly a form of self-defense against attacks from many quarters, where the "experimental philosophy" was regarded as ludicrous or dangerous or both. The influential wits of the day scoffed at the earnestness of the investigators and the seeming preposterousness of their findings (even Charles II laughed out loud when he learned that the members were busy weighing air); some clergymen and politicians saw in the new enterprise a threat to religion and to social hierarchy, a challenge against past, present, and divine authority, mounted by persons so presumptuous as to suppose that the truths of the world could be determined by human investigation rather than by Christian revelation.

The Society answered (again in the language of its charter) that it was intent upon serving "the glory of God and the good of mankind." The "good of mankind" was to be enhanced by technological improvements which would make work more productive, life easier, and commerce more abundant, in contrast to the dark old days when (as Aubrey reminisces) "even to attempt an improvement in husbandry [agriculture], though it succeeded with profit, was looked upon with an ill eye." The "glory of God" would be served by a new form of attention to the world God made. A long tradition ascribed to the Deity two sacred texts: the Book of Scripture, and the Book of Nature. The faithful had long pondered the first; the Society now undertook to read the second anew and aright. "Each page in the great volume of nature," observed Boyle, "is full of real hieroglyphs, where (by an inverted way of expression) things stand for words"—objects and actions incarnate truths. To disclose the divine intricacy in the Book of Nature (so the Society's advocates argued) could only enlarge wonder and increase worship.

The new reading of that old text reshaped other texts as well. In the 1660s and after, manuscripts, periodicals, and printed books all explored new forms, as writers attempted to render in language what Michel Foucault has called "the prose of the world," to grapple with new relations between words and things, and to make the written or the printed page (like the closet and the cabinet) a copious repository of newfound curiosities.

Thomas Sprat
1635–1713

Given the date of its first appearance, the *History of the Royal Society* seems puzzlingly titled. The Oxford-educated clergyman Thomas Sprat wrote much of it in 1663, just a year after the Society received its charter, and published it (after delays caused by fire, plague, and other distractions) in 1667. Both title and timing reflect the pressures that produced the book in the first place. As he acknowledges at the outset, Sprat has produced not so much a "plain history" of the Society as an "apology," in the Greek-based sense of the word current in the seventeenth century: an energetic defense of the new institution's policies and methods.

From its inception, the Society's directors felt the need for such a defense, and they brought Sprat in specifically to provide it, appointing him a Founding Fellow and anxiously inquiring after his progress on the book. They had chosen him not for his knowledge of science (negligible) but for his status as a divine and for his skill as a rhetorician. In response to its detractors, Sprat insists that the Society will enhance piety (by detailing the wonders of Creation); will uphold hierarchy (as evidenced by the predominance of gentlemen and aristocrats among the Fellowship); and will cultivate community (in order to appease fears that the Fellows will revive "disputation" when the new Restoration needs it least, Sprat downplays the importance of argument in the new science, and stresses instead the accumulation of raw data). Above all, Sprat focuses on the Society's capacity to improve ordinary life by producing "new inventions and shorter ways of labor" that will make possible an easier and more prosperous existence for the English, whose national "Genius" is uniquely suited to such advances.

As Michael Hunter notes, Sprat's "generalized attempt to appeal to everybody and antagonize nobody" fell short. It appealed mainly to adherents, and provided critics with a new target for their attacks. In the selection printed here Sprat navigates a particularly delicate portion of his argument. He sets forth the Fellows' attempts to simplify the prose style in which they wrote up their inquiries and discoveries. The degree to which the Society actually sought and managed to implement a new "mathematical plainness" has long remained a matter of dispute. In contemporary writing, clarity and "ornament" were often seen as mutually supportive; even when Sprat is arguing for a "naked" prose, he intermittently resorts to the very "amplifications, digressions, and swellings of style" that he is ruling out. As its sponsors intended, Sprat's *History* applies a polished rhetoric to a pointed claim: that the Royal Society was creating a "common-stock" of knowledge on which all might draw, and from which all might profit.

from The History of the Royal Society of London, for the Improving of Natural Knowledge

Thus they have directed, judged, conjectured upon, and improved experiments. But lastly, in these and all other businesses that have come under their care, there is one thing more about which the Society has been most solicitous, and that is the manner of their discourse, which unless they have been watchful to keep in due temper, the whole spirit and vigor of their design had been soon eaten out by the luxury and redundance of speech. The ill effects of this superfluity of talking have already overwhelmed most other arts and professions, insomuch that when I consider the means of happy living and the causes of their corruption, I can hardly forbear recanting what I said before, and concluding that eloquence ought to be banished out of all civil societies as a thing fatal to peace and good manners. To this opinion I should wholly incline, if I did not find that it is a weapon which may be as easily procured by bad men as good, and that, if these should only cast it away and those retain it, the naked innocence of virtue would be upon all occasions exposed to the armed malice of the wicked. This is the chief reason that should now keep up the ornaments of speaking in any request, since they are so much degenerated from their original usefulness. They were at first, no doubt, an admirable instrument in the hands of wise men, when they were only employed to describe goodness, honesty, obedience, in larger, fairer, and more moving images; to represent truth, clothed with bodies; and to bring knowledge back again to our very senses, from whence it was at first derived to our understandings. But now they are generally changed to worse uses. They make the fancy disgust[1] the best things, if they come sound and unadorned. They are in open defiance against reason, professing not to hold much correspondence with that, but with its slaves, the passions. They give the mind a motion too changeable and bewitching to consist with right practice. Who can behold, without indignation, how many mists and uncertainties these specious tropes and figures[2] have brought on our knowledge? How many rewards, which are due to more profitable and difficult arts, have been still snatched away by the easy vanity of fine speaking? For now I am warmed with this just anger, I cannot withhold myself from betraying the shallowness of all these seeming mysteries upon which we writers and speakers look so big. And, in few words, I dare say that of all the studies of men, nothing may be sooner obtained than this vicious abundance of phrase, this trick of metaphors, this volubility of tongue, which makes so great a noise in the world. But I spend words in vain; for the evil is now so inveterate that it is hard to know whom to blame or where to begin to reform. We all value one another so much upon this beautiful deceit and labor so long after it in the years of our education that we cannot but ever after think kinder of it than it deserves. And indeed, in most other parts of learning, I look on it to be a thing almost utterly desperate in its cure. And I think it may be placed amongst those general mischiefs such as the dissension of Christian princes,[3] the want[4] of practice in religion and the like, which have been so long spoken against, that men are become insensible about them, every one shifting off the fault from himself to others, and so they are only made bare commonplaces of complaint. It will suffice my present purpose to point out what has been done by the Royal Society towards the correcting of its[5] excesses in natural philosophy, to which it is, of all others, a most professed enemy.

1. They make the imagination reject.
2. Figures of speech.
3. Disputes between Christian monarchs.

4. Lack.
5. I.e., eloquence's.

They have therefore been most rigorous in putting in execution the only remedy that can be found for this extravagance. And that has been a constant resolution to reject all the amplifications, digressions, and swellings of style; to return back to the primitive purity and shortness, when men delivered so many *things*, almost in an equal number of *words*. They have exacted from all their members a close, naked, natural way of speaking; positive expressions; clear senses; a native easiness; bringing all things as near the mathematical plainness as they can and preferring the language of artisans, countrymen, and merchants before that of wits or scholars.[6]

And here there is one thing not to be passed by, which will render this established custom of the Society well nigh everlasting; and that is, the general constitution of the minds of the English. I have already often insisted on some of the prerogatives of England, whereby it may justly lay claim to be the head of a philosophical league, above all other countries in Europe. I have urged its situation,[7] its present genius, and the disposition of its merchants, and many more such arguments to encourage us still remain to be used. But of all others, this, which I am now alleging, is of the most weighty and important consideration. If there can be a true character given of the universal temper of any nation under heaven, then certainly this must be ascribed to our countrymen: that they have commonly an unaffected sincerity; that they love to deliver their minds with a sound simplicity; that they have the middle qualities between the reserved, subtle southern and the rough, unhewn northern people; that they are not extremely prone to speak; that they are more concerned what others will think of the strength, than of the fineness of what they say; and that an universal modesty possesses them. These qualities are so conspicuous and proper to our soil that we often hear them objected to us by some of our neighbor satirists in more disgraceful expressions. For they are wont to revile the English with a want of familiarity; with a melancholy dumpishness,[8] with slowness, silence, and with the unrefined sullenness of their behavior. But these are only the reproaches of partiality or ignorance. For they ought rather to be commended for an honorable integrity; for a neglect of circumstances and flourishes; for regarding things of greater moment,[9] more than less; for a scorn to deceive as well as to be deceived, which are all the best endowments that can enter into a philosophical mind. So that even the position of our climate, the air, the influence of the heaven, the composition of the English blood, as well as the embraces of the ocean, seem to join with the labors of the Royal Society to render our country a land of experimental knowledge. And it is a good sign that nature will reveal more of its secrets to the English than to others because it has already furnished them with a genius so well proportioned for the receiving and retaining its mysteries.

And now to come to a close of the second part of the narration. The Society has reduced its principal observations into one common-stock[1] and laid them up in public registers to be nakedly transmitted to the next generation of men, and so from them to their successors. And as their purpose was to heap up a mixed mass of experiments, without digesting them into any perfect model, so to this end, they confined themselves to no order of subjects; and whatever they have recorded, they have done it, not as complete schemes of opinions, but as bare, unfinished histories.

6. For a parody of this position, see Swift's depiction of the Academy in *Gulliver's Travels* (pages 2392–2397).
7. I.e., its location. Sprat has earlier emphasized that England's status as an island, and as "mistress of the Ocean," gives it a privileged position from which to supervise international scientific experiments and correspondence.
8. Tendency to depression.
9. Importance.
1. Property and resource for the use of all.

━━ ✠ ━━

Philosophical Transactions

Philosophical Transactions first appeared in 1665 and continues to the present day; it is the longest running periodical in English, and the oldest scientific journal in the world. It was created by Henry Oldenburg (1618–1677), a German-born diplomat who came to England in 1653 as an emissary to Oliver Cromwell and found himself powerfully drawn to the ideas and the company of the practitioners of the new science at Oxford. His gift for copious, accurate reporting on scientific matters prompted the Royal Society to enlist him as Fellow and Secretary, charged with attending the meetings, keeping the minutes, and managing the new institution's huge correspondence with scientific inquirers in England and abroad. Oldenburg produced the monthly *Transactions* as a private venture, but he drew its material from the documents in which his Society work immersed him, particularly from the correspondence that provided so plentiful an account (in the words of the journal's subtitle) "of the present undertakings, studies, and labors of the ingenious in many considerable parts of the world." The *Transactions'* content ranged wide conceptually as well as geographically, readily shifting from systematic searches for natural laws, to reports on technological innovations, to eager surmises about random oddities: monstrous births, human and otherwise, were a recurrent favorite. The new journal combined in text the attractions of the scientific treatise and the cabinet of curiosities; the insatiable curiosity of the journal's most assiduous contributor, Oldenburg's patron Robert Boyle, helped to ensure this variety and texture.

More than any other instrument, the *Transactions* established the Royal Society as central to the new philosophy, and fostered the conviction that the advancement of learning was a communal pursuit of truth to which (as Francis Bacon had predicted) everyone from a mariner to a virtuoso could contribute indispensable information. The *Transactions* influenced nonscientific journalism as well: with its topical headlines, variegated matter, and detailed tables of contents, it resembled no periodical of its time, but many that came after.

from Philosophical Transactions
[THE INTRODUCTION][1]

Whereas there is nothing more necessary for promoting the improvement of philosophical matters than the communicating, to such as apply their studies and endeavors that way, such things as are discovered or put in practice by others, it is therefore thought fit to employ the press as the most proper way to gratify those whose engagement in such studies and delight in the advancement of learning and profitable discoveries doth entitle them to the knowledge of what this kingdom or other parts of the world do from time to time afford, as well of the progress of the studies, labors, and attempts of the curious and learned in things of this kind, as of their complete discoveries and performances. To the end that such productions being clearly and truly communicated, desires after solid and useful knowledge may be further entertained, ingenious endeavors and undertakings cherished, and those addicted to and conversant in such matters may be invited and encouraged to search, try, and find out new things, impart their knowledge to one another, and contribute what they can to the grand design of improving natural knowledge and perfecting all philosophical arts and sciences. All for the glory of God, the honor and advantage of these kingdoms, and the universal good of mankind.

* * *

1. This and the following two selections appeared in Vol. 1, No. 1, 6 March 1665.

An Account of a Very Odd Monstrous Calf

By the same noble person[2] was lately communicated to the Royal Society an account of a very odd, monstrous birth produced at Limmington in Hampshire, where a butcher, having caused a cow (which calved her first calf the year before) to be covered that she might the sooner be fatted, killed her when fat, and opening the womb, which he found heavy to admiration, saw in it a calf, which had begun to have hair, whose hinderlegs had no joints and whose tongue was, Cerebus-like,[3] triple—to each side of his mouth one, and one in the midst. Between the forelegs and the hinderlegs was a great stone, on which the calf rid.[4] The *sternum*, or that part of the breast where the ribs lie, was also perfect stone. And the stone on which it rid weighed twenty pounds and a half. The outside of the stone was of greenish color, but some small parts being broken off, it appeared a perfect free-stone. The stone, according to the letter of Mr. David Thomas, who sent this account to Mr. Boyle, is with Dr. Haughten of Salisbury, to whom he also refers for further information.

* * *

An observation imparted to the noble Mr. Boyle by Mr. David Thomas touching some particulars further considerable in the monster mentioned in the first papers of these *Philosophical Transactions*.[5]

Upon the strictest inquiry, I find by one that saw the monstrous calf and stone, within four hours after it was cut out of the cow's belly, that the breast of the calf was not stony (as I wrote) but that the skin of the breast and between the legs and of the neck (which parts lay on the smaller end of the stone) was very much thicker than on any other part, and that the feet of the calf were so parted as to be like the claws of a dog. The stone I have since seen. It is bigger at one end than the other, of no plain *superficies*,[6] but full of little cavities. The stone, when broken, is full of small pebble stones of an oval figure. Its color is gray—like freestone, but intermixed with veins of yellow and black. A part of it I have begged of Dr. Haughten for you, which I have sent to Oxford, whither a more exact account will be conveyed by the same person.

* * *

A letter of the Honorable Robert Boyle of Sept. 13, 1673, to the publisher concerning Amber Greece and its being a vegetable production[7]

Sir,

Some occasions calling me this afternoon up to London, I was met there with a very intelligent gentleman, who was ready to go out of it. But before he did so, he willingly spared me some time to discourse with him about some of the affairs of our East Indian Company,[8] of which he was very lately Deputy Governor, and, his year being expired, is still one of the chief of the Court of Committees, which a foreigner would call Directors that manage all the affairs of that considerable society. And among other things, talking with him about some contents of a journal lately taken

2. Rober Boyle.
3. Resembling the mythical three-headed dog that guarded the entrance to Hades, the underworld of the dead.
4. Rode (i.e., straddled).
5. A "follow-up" from Vol. 1, No. 2.
6. Smooth surface.
7. Ambergris (Latin, "gray amber") is a gray waxy substance formed in the intestines of sperm whales; it was valued as a component in perfumes and medicines. Because ambergris, once emitted by the whale, often floats along the sea coast, traders and scientists were uncertain about its origins. (Boyle's letter appeared in Vol. 8, No. 97.)
8. A company chartered by Elizabeth I in 1600 to develop trade with India and the Far East.

in a Dutch East Indian prize,[9] I learned from him that he, who understands that language very well, is now perusing that manuscript; and among many things recorded there that concern the economical and political affairs of the said Dutch company, he met with one physical observation which he thought so rare that, remembering the curiosity I had expressed for such things, he put it into English and transcribed it for me; and immediately drawing it out of his pocket, he presented me the short paper, whereof I now show you the copy. Upon perusal of which, you will very easily believe, that not only his civility obliged me, but the information it brought me surprised me too. For the several trials and observations of my own about amber greece have long kept me from acquiescing either in the vulgar opinions[1] or those of some learned men concerning it. Yet I confess, my experiments did much less discover what it is than this paper has done, in case we may safely and entirely give credit to its information, and that it reach to all kinds of amber greece. And probably you will be invited to look on this account, though not as complete, yet as very sincere, and on that score credible if you consider that this was not written by a philosopher to broach[2] a paradox or serve a hypothesis, but by a merchant or factor[3] for his superiors to give them an account of a matter of fact. And that this passage is extant in an authentic journal, wherein the affairs of the company were by public order from time to time registered at their chief colony Batavia.[4] And it appears by the paper itself that the relation was not looked upon as a doubtful thing, but as a thing from which a practical way may be deduced to make this discovery easily lucriferous[5] to the Dutch Company. And I could heartily wish that in those countries that are addicted to long navigations, more notice than is usual were taken and given of the natural rarities that occur to merchants and seamen. On which occasion I remember when I had in compliance with my curiosity put myself into our East Indian Company and had by their civility to me been chosen of their Committee as long as my health allowed me to continue so, I had the opportunity in some register books of merchants English and Dutch to observe some things which would easily justify this wish of mine, if my haste and their interest would permit me to acquaint others with them. But to return to our account of amber greece I think you will easily believe that if I had received it not by a paper but immediately from the writer,[6] I should by proposing diverse questions, have been enabled to give you a much more satisfactory account than this short one contains. But the obliging person that gave it me, being just going out of town, I could not civilly stay him to receive my queries about it, which though (God permitting) I may propose ere long, if I can light on him again, yet I fear he has given me in these few lines all that he found about this matter. However, this relation, as short as it is, being about the nature of a drug so precious and so little known will not, I hope, be unwelcome to the curious. To whom none is so like to convey it so soon and so well as Mr. O,[7] whose forwardness to oblige others by his various communications challenges returns of the like nature from others and particularly from his affectionate humble servant.

Follows the extract itself out of a Dutch journal belonging to the Dutch East Indian Company:

---

9. I.e., the ship's log of a Dutch trading vessel recently captured by the English.
1. Received ideas of ordinary people.
2. Penetrate, untangle.
3. Company agent. Boyle reaffirms the Royal Society's interest in raw data over cooked theory, in the testimony of experienced "mechanics" over that of abstract "philosophers."
4. A seaport on the island of Java.
5. Profitable.
6. I.e., in conversation.
7. Henry Oldenburg, editor of the *Transactions*.

Amber greece is not the scum or excrement of the whale, etc., but issues out of the root of a tree, which tree how far soever it stands on the land, always shoots forth its roots towards the sea, seeking the warmth of it, thereby to deliver the fattest gum that comes out of it, which tree otherwise by its copious fatness might be burnt and destroyed. Wherever that fat gum is shot into the sea, it is so tough that it is not easily broken from the root, unless its own weight and the working of the warm sea doth it,[8] and so it floats on the sea.

There was found by a soldier 7/8 of a pound and by the chief two pieces weighing five pounds. If you plant the trees where the stream sets to the shore, then the stream will cast it up to great advantage. March 1, 1672, in Batavia.

⊷•⊷ ⊯✦⊒ ⊷•⊷

Robert Hooke
1635–1703

In a long life, Robert Hooke got little sleep. From the age of twenty-eight until his death, he lived in rooms at Gresham College, the Royal Society headquarters, in order to make himself maximally available to meet the ceaseless demands of his many concurrent employ-ments, as the Society's first Curator of Experiments, as the College's lecturer in geometry, as Surveyor and rebuilder of London after the Great Fire, and as restless, relentless inventor and improver of scientific instruments. Hooke's friend John Aubrey described him as "the greatest mechanick this day in the world"; the jostle between the high superlative and the equivocal noun captures Hooke's uncertain status in the Society to which he devoted his prodigiously productive working life. The mechanical arts were in many ways the lifeblood of the Society's enterprise, but "mechanicks" were not gentry. In an institution founded and headed by aristocrats and gentlemen, this gifted son of a provincial clergyman was often treated (in Stephen Shapin's words) "as a tradesman, as a servant." Hooke's contract as Curator required that he prepare and perform "three or four substantial experiments" at each of the Society's weekly meetings, as well as any other experiments the Fellows might (in the recurrent wording of the meeting minutes) "order" or "direct" him to undertake. The empirical life of the Society during its first four decades would have been unimaginable without Hooke, but the Fellows registered his indispensability by irritation at the outside interests through which he pursued autonomy and income. "I could wish," wrote Sir Robert Moray, "he had finished the task laid upon him rather than to learn a dozen trades." Hooke's variegated pursuits, though, produced dozens of inventions and discoveries: newly efficient lenses, lamps, telescopes, watches; new theories of optics, chemistry, and gravity that in some cases anticipated Issac Newton's. Constitutionally irascible, Hooke spent much energy asserting, angrily but often accurately, the priority and/or superiority of his many innovations.

Hooke produced *Micrographia* at the Society's behest. The book doubled as a work of sci-ence and a piece of institutional propaganda, designed to promote the Society's methods. It fulfilled both purposes. In Hooke's sixty word-and-picture "Observations" of magnified objects, readers could see for the first time how far the useful artifice of the microscope had extended the "knowledge of natural things" into realms unreachable by the eye and mind alone. At the same time, the book touched a cultural pulse point. At its Greek root, Hooke's title suggests "the writing down of small things," and this is what many of his fellow Fellows—Pepys, Olden-burg, Evelyn, Aubrey—were in their different ways newly up to. (Pepys thought *Micrographia* "the most ingenious book that I ever read in my life.") Small things, it had been discovered, could produce large amazements when written up.

---

8. I.e., breaks it off.

from **Micrographia**

Or Some Physiological Description of Minute Bodies Made by Magnifying Glasses with Observations and Inquiries thereupon

To the King

Sir,

I do here most humbly lay this small present at your Majesty's royal feet. And though it comes accompanied with two disadvantages, the meanness of the author and of the subject; yet in both I am encouraged by the greatness of your mercy and your knowledge. By the one I am taught, that you can forgive the most presumptuous offenders. And by the other, that you will not esteem the least work of nature or art unworthy of your observation. Amidst the many felicities that have accompanied your Majesty's happy restoration and government, it is none of the least considerable that philosophy and experimental learning have prospered under your royal patronage.[1] And as the calm prosperity of your reign has given us the leisure to follow these studies of quiet and retirement, so it is just that the fruits of them should, by way of acknowledgment, be returned to your Majesty. There are, Sir, several other of your subjects, of your Royal Society, now busy about nobler matters: the improvement of manufactures and agriculture, the increase of commerce, the advantage of navigation—in all which they are assisted by your Majesty's encouragement and example. Amidst all those greater designs, I here presume to bring in that which is more proportional to the smallness of my abilities and to offer some of the least of all visible things to that mighty king that has established an empire over the best of all invisible things of this world, the minds of men. Your Majesty's most humble and most obedient subject and servant,

Robert Hooke

To the Royal Society

After my address to our great founder and patron, I could not but think myself obliged, in consideration of those many engagements you have laid upon me, to offer these my poor labors to this most illustrious assembly. You have been pleased formerly to accept of these rude drafts.[2] I have since added to them some descriptions and some conjectures of my own. And therefore, together with your acceptance, I must also beg your pardon. The rules you have prescribed yourselves in your philosophical progress do seem the best that have ever yet been practiced. And particularly that of avoiding dogmatizing and the espousal of any hypothesis not sufficiently grounded and confirmed by experiments. This way seems the most excellent and may preserve both philosophy and natural history from its former corruptions. In saying which, I may seem to condemn my own course in this treatise, in which there may perhaps be some expressions, which may seem more positive than your prescriptions will permit. And though I desire to have them understood only as conjectures and queries (which your method does not altogether disallow) yet if even in those I have exceeded, 'tis fit that I should declare that it was not done by your directions. For it is most unreasonable that you should undergo the imputation of the faults of my conjectures, seeing you can receive so small advantage of reputation by the slight observations of Your most humble and most faithful servant,

Robert Hooke.

---

1. Charles II had granted the Society a royal charter in 1662.
2. Hooke had originally drawn many of the book's illustrations for use in the public presentation of experiments, which, as the Society's Curator of Experiments, he was obliged to perform regularly.

from *The Preface*

[A]ll the uncertainty and mistakes of human actions proceed either from the narrowness and wandering of our senses, from the slipperiness or delusion of our memory, from the confinement or rashness of our understanding, so that 'tis no wonder that our power over natural causes and effects is so slowly improved, seeing we are not only to contend with the obscurity and difficulty of the things whereon we work and think, but even the forces of our own minds conspire to betray us.

These being the dangers in the process of human reason, the remedies of them all can only proceed from the real, the mechanical, the experimental philosophy, which has this advantage over the philosophy of discourse and disputation, that whereas that chiefly aims at the subtlety of its deductions and conclusions, without much regard to the first groundwork, which ought to be well laid on the sense and memory, so this intends the right ordering of them all and the making them serviceable to each other.

The first thing to be undertaken in this weighty work is a watchfulness over the failings and an enlargement of the dominion of the senses.

To which end it is requisite, first, that there should be a scrupulous choice and a strict examination of the reality, constancy, and certainty of the particulars that we admit.[3] This is the first rise[4] whereon truth is to begin, and here the most severe and most impartial diligence must be employed. The storing up of all, without any regard to evidence or use, will only tend to darkness and confusion. We must not therefore esteem the riches of our philosophical treasure by the number only, but chiefly by the weight. The most vulgar instances[5] are not to be neglected, but above all, the most instructive are to be entertained.[6] The footsteps of Nature are to be traced, not only in her ordinary course, but when she seems to be put to her shifts,[7] to make many doublings and turnings, and to use some kind of art in endeavoring to avoid our discovery.

The next care to be taken, in respect of the senses, is a supplying of their infirmities with instruments, and as it were, the adding of artificial organs to the natural; this in one of them has been of late years accomplished with prodigious benefit to all sorts of useful knowledge by the invention of optical glasses. By the means of telescopes, there is nothing so far distant but may be represented to our view; and by the help of microscopes, there is nothing so small as to escape our inquiry; hence there is a new visible world discovered to the understanding. By this means the heavens are opened, and a vast number of new stars and new motions and new productions appear in them to which all the ancient astronomers were utterly strangers. By this the earth itself, which lies so near us under our feet, shows quite a new thing to us; and in every little particle of its matter, we now behold almost as great a variety of creatures as we were able before to reckon up in the whole universe itself. * * *

I here present to the world my imperfect endeavors, which though they shall prove no other way considerable, yet I hope they may be in some measure useful to the main design of a reformation in philosophy, if it be only by showing that there is

---

3. I.e., as experimental data.
4. Elevation (with "truth" imagined as a progressive ascent).

5. Familiar particulars.
6. Considered.
7. Up to her tricks.

not so much required towards it any strength of imagination or exactness of method or depth of contemplation (though the addition of these, where they can be had, must needs produce a much more perfect composure) as[6] a sincere hand and a faithful eye to examine and to record the things themselves as they appear.

And I beg my reader to let me take the boldness to assure him that in this present condition of knowledge, a man so qualified as I have endeavored to be, only with resolution and integrity and plain intentions of employing his senses aright, may venture to compare the reality and the usefulness of his services towards the true philosophy with those of other men that are of much stronger and more acute speculations that shall not make uses of the same method by the senses. * * *

from *Observation 1. Of the point of a sharp small needle*

As in geometry, the most natural way of beginning is from a mathematical point, so is the same method in observations and natural history the most genuine, simple, and instructive. We must first endeavor to make letters, and draw single strokes true, before we venture to write whole sentences, or to draw large pictures. And in physical inquiries, we must endeavor to follow Nature in the more plain and easy ways she treads in the most simple and uncompounded bodies, to trace her steps, and be acquainted with her manner of walking there, before we venture ourselves into the multitude of meanders she has in bodies of a more complicated nature; lest, being unable to distinguish and judge of our way, we quickly lose both Nature our guide, and ourselves too, and are left to wander in the labyrinth of groundless opinions; wanting both judgment, that light, and experience, that clue, which should direct our proceedings.

We will begin these our inquiries therefore with the observations of bodies of the most simple nature first, and so gradually proceed to those of a more compounded one. In prosecution of which method, we shall begin with a physical point; of which kind the point of a needle is commonly reckoned for one, and is indeed, for the most part, made so sharp, that the naked eye cannot distinguish any parts of it. It very easily pierces and makes its way through all kinds of bodies softer than itself. But if viewed with a very good microscope, we may find that the top of a needle (though as to the sense very sharp) appears a broad, blunt, and very irregular end; not resembling a cone, as is imagined, but only a piece of a tapering body, with a great part of the top removed, or deficient. The points of pins are yet more blunt, and the points of the most curious mathematical instruments so very seldom arrive at so great a sharpness. How much therefore can be built upon demonstrations made only by the productions of the ruler and compasses, he will be better able to consider that shall but view those points and lines with a microscope.

* * *

The image we have here exhibited in the first figure, was the top of a small and very sharp needle, whose point *aa* nevertheless appeared through the microscope above a quarter of an inch broad, not round nor flat, but irregular and uneven; so that it seemed to have been big enough to have afforded a hundred armed mites room enough to be ranged by each other without endangering the breaking one another's necks, by being thrust off on either side. The surface of which, though appearing to the naked eye very smooth, could not nevertheless hide a multitude of holes and scratches and ruggednesses from being discovered by the microscope to invest it, several of which inequalities (as A, B, C, seemed holes made by some small specks of

6. But only.

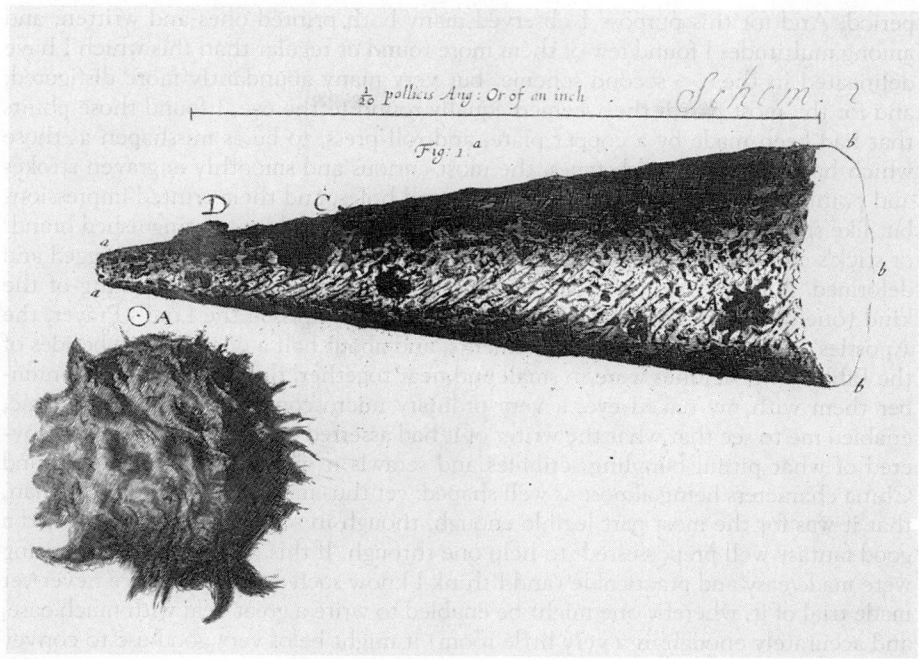

Robert Hooke. *Schema ii: Needle point and period,* from *Micrographia.* 1665.

rust; and D some adventitious[1] body, that stuck very close to it) were casual.[2] All the rest that roughen the surface, were only so many marks of the rudeness and bungling of art.[3] So unaccurate is it, in all its productions, even in those which seem most neat, that if examined with an organ more acute than that by which they were made, the more we see of their shape, the less appearance will there be of their beauty; whereas in the works in nature, the deepest discoveries show us the greatest excellencies. An evident argument, that He that was the author of all these things, was no other than omnipotent; being able to include as great a variety of parts and contrivances in the yet smallest discernible point, as in those vaster bodies (which comparatively are called also points) such as the earth, sun, or planets. Nor need it seem strange that the earth itself may be by an analogy called a physical point: for as its body, though now so near us as to fill our eyes and fancies with a sense of the vastness of it, may by a little distance, and some convenient diminishing glasses, be made vanish into a scarce visible speck, or point (as I have often tried on the moon, and—when not too bright—on the sun itself), so, could a mechanical contrivance successfully answer our theory, we might see the least spot as big as the earth itself; and discover, as Descartes also conjectures,[4] as great a variety of bodies in the moon, or planets, as in the earth.

But leaving these discoveries to future industries, we shall proceed to add one observation more of a point commonly so called, that is, the mark of a full stop, or

1. Chance-encountered.
2. Accidental.
3. Artifice; human (as opposed to natural) creation.

4. René Descartes (1596–1650); French mathematician and philosopher.

period. And for this purpose I observed many both printed ones and written; and among multitudes I found few of them more round or regular than this which I have delineated in the * * * second scheme, but very many abundantly more disfigured; and for the most part if they seemed equally round to the eye, I found those points that had been made by a copper plate, and roll-press, to be as misshapen as those which had been made with types, the most curious and smoothly engraven strokes and points looking but as so many furrows and holes, and their printed impressions but like smutty daubings on a mat or uneven floor with a blunt extinguished brand[5] or stick's end. And as for points made with a pen they were much more rugged and deformed. Nay, having viewed certain pieces of exceeding curious writing of the kind (one of which in the breadth of a two-pence comprised the Lord's Prayer, the Apostles' Creed, the Ten Commandments, and about half a dozen verses besides of the Bible[6]), whose lines were so small and near together, that I was unable to number them with my naked eye, a very ordinary microscope, I had then about me, enabled me to see that what the writer of it had asserted was true, but withal discovered of what pitiful bungling scribbles and scrawls it was composed, Arabian and China characters being almost as well shaped; yet thus much I must say for the man, that it was for the most part legible enough, though in some places there wanted a good fantasy well prepossessed[7] to help one through. If this manner of small writing were made easy and practicable (and I think I know such a one,[8] but have never yet made trial of it, whereby one might be enabled to write a great deal with much ease, and accurately enough in a very little room) it might be of very good use to convey secret intelligence without any danger of discovery or mistrusting. But to come again to the point. The irregularies of it are caused by three or four coadjutors,[9] one of which is the uneven surface of the paper, which at best appears no smoother than a very coarse piece of shagged cloth; next the irregularity of the type of engraving; and a third is the rough daubing of the printing ink that lies upon the instrument that makes the impression; to all which, add the variation made by the different lights and shadows, and you may have sufficient reason to guess that a point may appear much more ugly than this, which I have here presented, which though it appeared through the microscope grey, like a great splatch of London dirt, about three inches over; yet to the naked eye it was black, and no bigger than that in the midst of the Circle A. And could I have found room in this plate to have inserted an O you should have seen that the letters were not more distinct than the points of distinction, nor a drawn circle more exactly so, than we have now shown a point to be a point.

from *Observation 53. Of a Flea*

The strength and beauty of this small creature, had it no other relation at all to man, would deserve a description.

For its strength, the microscope is able to make no greater discoveries of it than the naked eye, but only the curious contrivance of its legs and joints, for the exerting that strength, is very plainly manifested, such as no other creature I have yet observed has anything like it; for the joints of it are so adapted, that he can, as

---

5. Torch.
6. In the mid-17th century, this minuscule writing was practiced as a craft; specimens (often of the scriptural texts Hooke lists here) were prized by collectors.

7. Imagination kindly disposed.
8. I.e., an instrument.
9. Factors.

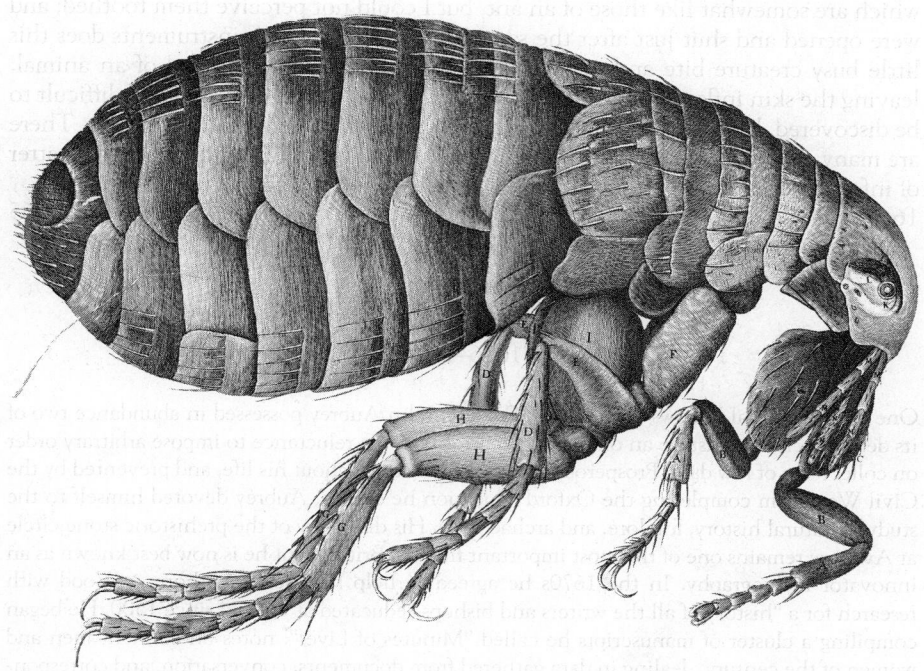

Robert Hooke. *Schema xxxiv: A Flea,* from *Micrographia.* 1665

'twere, fold them short one within another, and suddenly stretch, or spring them out to their whole length, that is, of the forelegs. The part A * * * lies within B, and B within C, parallel to, or side by side each other; but the parts of the two next lie quite contrary, that is, D without E, and E without F, but parallel also; but the parts of the hinder legs G, H, and I, bend one within another, like the parts of a double jointed ruler, or like the foot, leg, and thigh of a man; these six legs he clitches[1] up altogether, and when he leaps, springs them all out, and thereby exerts his whole strength at once.

But, as for the beauty of it, the microscope manifests it to be all over adorned with a curiously polished suit of sable armor, neatly jointed, and beset with multitudes of sharp pins, shaped almost like porcupine's quills, or bright conical steel bodkins[2]; the head is either side beautified with a quick and round black eye K, behind each of which also appears a small cavity, L, in which he seems to move to and fro a certain thin film beset with many small transparent hairs, which probably may be his ears. In the forepart of his head, between the two forelegs, he has two small long jointed feelers, or rather smellers, M M, which have four joints, and are hairy, like those of several other creatures. Between these, it has a small proboscis, or probe, N N O, that seems to consist of a tube N N, and a tongue or sucker O, which I have perceived him to flip in and out. Besides these, it has also two chaps or biters P P,

---

1. Clutches.

2. "An instrument with a small blade and sharp point, used to bore holes" (Johnson's *Dictionary*).

which are somewhat like those of an ant, but I could not perceive them toothed; and were opened and shut just after the same manner. With these instruments does this little busy creature bite and pierce the skin, and suck out the blood of an animal, leaving the skin inflamed with a small round red spot. These parts are very difficult to be discovered, because for the most part, they lie covered between the forelegs. There are many other particulars, which, being more obvious, and affording no great matter of information, I shall pass by, and refer the reader to the figure.
1663–1665   1665

John Aubrey
1626–1697

One of the original Fellows of the Royal Society, John Aubrey possessed in abundance two of its defining characteristics: an omnivorous curiosity and a reluctance to impose arbitrary order on collections of raw data. Prosperous by birth, sickly throughout his life, and prevented by the Civil Wars from completing the Oxford education he craved, Aubrey devoted himself to the study of natural history, folklore, and archaeology. His discovery of the prehistoric stone circle at Avebury remains one of the most important finds in Britain, but he is now best known as an innovator in biography. In the 1670s he agreed to help his friend Anthony à Wood with research for a "history of all the writers and bishops" educated at Oxford since 1500. He began compiling a cluster of manuscripts he called "Minutes of Lives": notes on eminent men and women of the century, dealing in data gathered from documents, conversation, and correspondence with the subjects and their survivors, and from Aubrey's own prodigious (if at times unreliable) memory.

The life stories thus produced display an obsessive particularity, an abiding preference for the telling detail over the big picture (which in the conventional biographies of Aubrey's time took the form of hagiography: pious summations of pious lives). Aubrey's *Lives,* notes his editor Oliver Lawson Dick, "were the first biographies that did not point a moral."

Throughout his "Minutes," Aubrey performs a kind of textual archaeology. He dwells on the physical objects, natural and man-made, which marked the early seventeenth-century world inhabited by most of his subjects, and by his younger self. The Civil Wars, destroying buildings, communities, and bodies, had rendered that world as remote in some respects as the ancient tribes elusively commemorated at Avebury. Aubrey writes the *Lives* out of a passion for recovery and an awareness of the precariousness of his whole enterprise. "'Tis pity," he observed to Wood, "that such minutes had not been taken 100 years since or more: for want whereof many worthy men's names and notions are swallowed up in oblivion." This urgency infuses the *Lives'* odd form. Aubrey cares more to get the facts down than to set them in order: he repeatedly describes himself as writing his notes "tumultuarily," that is, "as they occurred to my thoughts or as occasionally I had information" or (more succinctly) as if "tumbled out of a sack." Such an unmethodical method sorted well with the Royal Society's program as Sprat had elaborated it: "to heap up a mixed mass of experiments, without digesting them into any perfect model"; to record findings not "as complete schemes of opinions, but as bare unfinished histories."

Aubrey's notes have outlasted their original purpose as preparatory adjuncts to Wood's more "finished" history. Rediscovered and published over the course of the nineteenth century, they have exerted considerable influence over the twentieth, primarily through their talky, energetic language and their unabashed attention to bodily functions and ignoble motives as defining elements in the course of a human life. Lytton Strachey and James

Joyce both display distinctly Aubreyan characteristics, as do more recent practitioners of the tell-all biography and the contemporary novel. In the "bare unfinished histories" of Aubrey's "Minutes," the techniques and protocols of the new science begin to infuse the craft of biography.

from Brief Lives

[FRANCIS BACON][1]

* * * He came often to Sir John Danvers[2] at Chelsea. Sir John told me that when his lordship had wrote the *History of Henry 7*, he sent the manuscript copy to him to desire his opinion of it before 'twas printed. Qd.[3] Sir John, "Your lordship knows that I am no scholar." "'Tis no matter," said my lord, "I know what a scholar can say; I would know what *you* can say." Sir John read it, and gave his opinion what he misliked which Tacitus[4] did not omit (which I am sorry I have forgot) which my lord acknowledged to be true, and mended it: "Why," said he, "a scholar would never have told me this."

Mr. Thomas Hobbes (Malmesburiensis[5]) was beloved by his lordship, who was wont to have him walk with him in his delicate groves where he did meditate: and when a notion darted into his mind, Mr. Hobbes was presently to write it down, and his lordship was wont to say that he did it better than anyone else about him; for that many times, when he read their[6] notes he scarce understood what they writ, because they understood it not clearly themselves.

In short, all that were *great* and *good* loved and honored him. * * *

His lordship would many times have music in the next room where he meditated.

The aviary at York House[7] was built by his lordship; it did cost £300.

At every meal, according to the season of the year, he had his table strewn with sweet herbs and flowers, which he said did refresh his spirits and memory.

When his lordship was at his country house at Gorhambery,[8] St. Albans seemed as if the Court were there, so nobly did he live. His servants had liveries with his crest (a boar . . .[9]); his watermen[1] were more employed by gentlemen than any other, even the King's.

King James sent a buck to him, and he gave the keeper fifty pounds.

He was wont to say to his servant Hunt (who was a notable thrifty man, and loved this world, and the only servant he had that he could never get to become bound for[2] him), "The world was made for man, Hunt; and not man for the world." Hunt left an estate of £1000 per annum in Somerset.

None of his servants durst appear before him without Spanish leather boots:[3] for he would smell the neat's leather which offended him. * * *

---

1. Statesman, scholar, philosopher, and writer (1561–1626); in his *Advancement of Learning* (1605) and *Novum Organum* (1620) he articulated the experimental methods that would later be championed by the Royal Society.
2. Danvers was a relative of Aubrey's and "a great acquaintance and favorite" of Bacon's.
3. *Quod:* "said" (Latin).
4. Publius Tacitus (c. A.D. 56–c. 117), Roman historian; the sense here seems to be that Bacon has left out some element in history that Tacitus would have included.
5. Of Malmesbury (Hobbes's birthplace). Hobbes was a

close friend of Aubrey's, and his is the longest and the fullest of the *Brief Lives*.
6. Anyone else's.
7. In London; Bacon's birthplace and residence.
8. Gornhambry, Bacon's estate on the river Ver, near the city of St. Albans.
9. Aubrey inserts this ellipsis, presumably for filling in later.
1. Ferrymen, busy bringing guests to and from the house.
2. I.e., legally committed to serve.
3. Cordovan leather from Spain was more highly processed than ordinary English "neat's (cattle) leather."

He was a παιδεραστής.[4] His Ganimeds[5] and favorites took bribes; but his lordship always gave judgment *secundum aequum et bonum*.[6] His decrees in Chancery[7] stand firm, i.e., there are fewer of his decrees reversed than any other Chancellor.

His dowager[8] married her gentleman-usher,[9] Sir (Thomas, I think) Underhill, whom she made deaf and blind with too much of Venus.[1] She was living since the beheading of the late King.—Quaere[2] where and when she died.

He had a delicate, lively hazel eye; Dr. Harvey told me it was like the eye of a viper.

I have now forgot what Mr. Bushnell said, whether his lordship enjoyed his Muse[3] best at night, or in the morning.

Apothegmata[4]

His lordship being in York House garden looking on fishers as they were throwing their net, asked them what they would take for their draught;[5] they answered *so much:* his lordship would offer them no more but *so much.* They drew up their net, and in it were only 2 or 3 little fishes: his lordship then told them it had been better for them to have taken his offer. They replied, they hoped to have had a better draught. "But," said his lordship, "hope is a good breakfast, but an ill supper." * * *

The Bishop of London did cut down a noble cloud of trees at Fulham. The Lord Chancellor told him that he was *a good expounder of dark places.*[6]

Upon his being in disfavor his servants suddenly went away; he compared them to the flying of the vermin when the house was falling.

One told his lordship it was now time to look about him. He replied, "I do not look *about* me, I look *above* me." * * *

His lordship would often drink a good draught of strong beer (March beer) tobedwards, to lay his working fancy[7] asleep: which otherwise would keep him from sleeping great part of the night. * * *

Mr. Hobbes told me that the cause of his lordship's death was trying an experiment: viz., as he was taking the air in a coach with Dr. Witherborne (a Scotchman, physician to the king) towards Highgate, snow lay on the ground, and it came into my lord's thought, why flesh might not be preserved in snow, as in salt. They were resolved they would try the experiment presently. They alighted out of the coach, and went into a poor woman's house at the bottom of Highgate Hill, and bought a hen, and made the woman exenterate[8] it, and then stuffed the body with snow, and my lord did help to do it himself. The snow so chilled him, that he immediately fell so extremely ill, that he could not return to his lodgings (I suppose then at Gray's Inn), but went to the Earl of Arundel's house at Highgate, where they put him into a good bed warmed with a pan, but it was a damp bed that had not been lain in in about a year before, which gave him such a cold that in 2 or 3 days, as I remember he told me, he died of suffocation.

---

4. Greek: pederast, a homosexual lover of boys.
5. Beloved boys (so called after the Trojan youth Ganymede, Zeus's cupbearer).
6. "Fairly and well." Bacon had served as attorney-general and Lord Chancellor until he was impeached for taking bribes.
7. The law court presided over by the Lord Chancellor.
8. Widow.
9. A gentleman acting as attendant to a person of superior rank.

1. Sex.
2. "Find out" (Aubrey's most frequent instruction to himself in his notes).
3. I.e., wrote and thought.
4. Witty sayings.
5. Catch.
6. Bacon puns on the Bishop's duty to shed light on obscure passages in scripture.
7. Busy mind.
8. Clean it; remove its innards.

[WILLIAM HARVEY][1]

He was always very contemplative, and the first that I hear of that was curious in anatomy in England. He had made dissections of frogs, toads, and a number of other animals, and had curious observations on them, which papers, together with his goods, in his lodgings at Whitehall, were plundered at the beginning of the Rebellion, he being for the King, and with him at Oxon;[2] but he often said, that of all the losses he sustained, no grief was so crucifying to him as the loss of these papers, which for love or money he could never retrieve or obtain. When Charles I by reason of the tumults left London, he attended him, and was at the fight of Edgehill with him; and during the fight, the Prince and Duke of York were committed to his care. He told me that he withdrew with them under a hedge, and took out of his pocket a book and read; but he had not read very long before a bullet of a great gun grazed on the ground near him, which made him remove his station. He told me that Sir Adrian Scrope was dangerously wounded there, and left for dead amongst the dead men, stripped; which happened to be the saving of his life. It was cold, clear weather, and a frost that night; which staunched his bleeding, and about midnight, or some hours after his hurt, he awaked, and was fain to draw a dead body upon him for warmth-sake. * * *

He did delight to be in the dark, and told me he could then best contemplate. He had a house heretofore at Combe, in Surrey, a good air and prospect, where he had caves made in the earth, in which in summer time he delighted to meditate.—He was pretty well versed in the mathematics, and had made himself master of Mr. Oughtred's *Clavis Math*.[3] in his old age; and I have seen him perusing it, and working problems, not long before he died, and that book was always in his meditating apartment. * * *

At Oxford, he grew acquainted with Dr. Charles Scarborough,[4] then a young physician (since by King Charles II knighted), in whose conversation he much delighted; and whereas before he marched up and down with the army, he took him to him and made him lie in his chamber, and said to him, "Prithee leave off thy gunning, and stay here; I will bring thee into practice."[5]

I remember he kept a pretty young wench to wait on him, which I guess he made use of for warmth-sake as King David did,[6] and took care of her in his will, as also of his man servant. * * *

He was, as all the rest of the brothers, very choleric;[7] and in his young days wore a dagger (as the fashion then was, nay I remember my old schoolmaster, old Mr. Latimer, at 70, wore a dudgeon, with a knife, and bodkin, as also my old grandfather Lyte, and alderman Whitson of Bristowe, which I suppose was the common fashion in their young days), but this Dr. would be too apt to draw out his dagger upon every slight occasion.

He was not tall; but of the lowest stature, round faced, olivaster[8] complexion; little eye, round, very black, full of spirit; his hair was black as a raven, but quite white 20 years before he died. * * *

He was much and often troubled with the gout,[9] and his way of cure was thus: he would then sit with his legs bare, if it were frost, on the leads[1] of Cockaine house, put

1. Physician and anatomist (1578–1657); he discovered the circulation of the blood, and set forth his findings in *De Motu Cordis* ("on the heart's motion"), 1628.
2. Oxford, to which Charles I removed himself and his Court in 1643.
3. William Oughtred (1575–1660), mathematician; his *Clavis Mathematicae* ("the key of mathematics") was a widely used textbook on algebra and arithmetic (it introduced the symbol "x" for multiplication).

4. Charles Scarburgh (1616–1694) assisted Harvey with his work on the generation of animals.
5. I.e., medical practice.
6. In his old age David was warmed in bed at night by a young woman (1 Kings 1.1–4).
7. Prone to anger.
8. Olive-colored.
9. Inflammation of the joints in the hands and feet.
1. Rooftop (lined with lead).

them into a pail of water, till he was almost dead with cold, and betake himself to the stove, and so 'twas gone.

He was hot-headed, and his thoughts working would many times keep him from sleeping; he told me that then his way was to rise out of his bed and walk about his chamber in his shirt till he was pretty cool, i.e., till he began to have a horror,[2] and then return to bed, and sleep very comfortably.

I remember he was wont to drink coffee; which he and his brother Eliab did, before coffeehouses were in fashion in London.[3] * * *

It is now fit, and but just, that I should endeavor to undeceive the world in a scandal that I find strongly runs of him, which I have met amongst some learned young men: viz. that he made himself away[4] to put himself out of his pain, by opium; not but that, had he labored under great pains, he had been ready enough to have done it; I do not deny that it was not according to his principles upon certain occasions to . . . .[5] But the manner of his dying was really, and *bona fide*, thus, viz.: The morning of his death about 10 a clock, he went to speak, and found he had the dead palsy[6] in his tongue; then he saw what was to become of him, he knew there was then no hopes of his recovery, so presently sends for his young nephews to come up to him, to whom he gives one his watch ('twas a minute watch with which he made his experiments);[7] to another, another remembrance, etc.; made sign to . . . [8] Sambroke, his apothecary (in Blackfriars), to let him blood in[9] the tongue, which did little or no good; and so he ended his days. His practice was not very great towards his later end; he declined it, unless to a special friend—e.g. my Lady Howland, who had a cancer in her breast, which he did cut off and seared, but at last she died of it.

* * *

I was at his funeral, and helped to carry him into the vault.

1680s   1813

[END OF PERSPECTIVES: THE ROYAL SOCIETY AND THE NEW SCIENCE]

Margaret Cavendish, Duchess of Newcastle
1623–1674

The youngest child in a wealthy family whose social arrogance and Royalist sympathies brought it near ruin during the Civil Wars, Margaret Lucas combined a near immobilizing shyness with a passion for fame. She spent the years of war and Interregnum on the continent, first as maid of honor to Charles's exiled queen, then as wife to the Royalist general William Cavendish, Marquis of Newcastle; he was made Duke by Charles II after the couple returned to England at the Restoration. Neglected by the Court, they lived far from London on their northern estates, where they cultivated their passions: his, riding and fencing; hers, reading and writing. Words poured from her pen, into a variety of genres: verse (*Poems and Fancies*, 1653), fiction (*Nature's Pictures*, 1656), plays (*Love's Adventure*, *The Matrimonial Trouble*, *The Female Academy*, and some fifteen others: all printed, none performed); essays (*The World's*

---

2. Shiver.
3. The drink was rare in England before mid-century, hugely popular thereafter; London's first coffeehouse opened in 1652.
4. Killed himself.
5. Aubrey leaves the blank, perhaps intending a phrase

like "commit suicide."
6. Paralysis caused by stroke.
7. At this time, most clocks and watches told only the hour, not the minutes.
8. Aubrey's blank.
9. Draw blood from.

Olio, 1655); scientific speculations (*Philosophical and Physical Opinions*, 1663; *Observations upon Experimental Philosophy*, 1665); biography (of her husband); and autobiography (*A True Relation*, 1656; *Sociable Letters*, 1664). Cavendish and her husband published much of her work (and some of his) in sumptuous editions at their own expense.

It was rare for a woman to write and publish, rarer still for an aristocrat to write so revealingly and emphatically about her own fears, desires, opinions, and aspirations. The combination of her gender, rank, and work brought the Duchess an equivocal celebrity, a mix of amazement and derision which her occasional trips to London did much to animate. After one such visit, Mary Evelyn (wife of the diarist John) tried to capture Cavendish's impact in a letter to a friend: "I was surprised to find so much extravagancy and vanity in any person not confined within four walls" (of a madhouse). Her clothing, Evelyn reported, was "fantastical"; her behavior outstripped "the imagination of poets, or the descriptions of a romance heroine's greatness; her gracious bows, seasonable nods, courteous stretching out of hands, twinkling of her eyes, and various gestures of approbation, show what may be expected from her discourse, which is as airy, empty, whimsical, and rambling as her books, aiming at science, difficulties, high notions . . ." Evelyn voices a satiric hostility shared by many London onlookers, but she also pinpoints some of Cavendish's range and intensity: her idiosyncratic engagement with the new science of her day, and her variable, highly conscious self-presentation.

At letter's end, Evelyn despairs of description. The Duchess "is not of mortal race, and therefore cannot be defined." Cavendish, though, knew herself mortal. She repeatedly made clear that the threat of oblivion impelled her pen, and she worked constantly and inventively to define herself, sometimes in familiar genres, sometimes in modes of her own making—most notably that mix of fantasy, science fiction, argument, and autobiography she called *The Blazing World* (1665). The Duchess's extraordinary energies and kaleidoscopic output have transmuted seventeenth-century ridicule into late twentieth-century fascination with a woman's voice in relentless pursuit of (a favorite Cavendish term) "singularity."

from POEMS AND FANCIES[1]
The Poetress's Hasty Resolution

> Reading my verses, I liked them so well,
> Self-love did make my judgment to rebel;
> And thinking them so good, thought more to make,
> Considering not how others would them take.
> 5   I writ so fast, thought, lived I many a year,
> A pyramid of fame thereon to rear.[2]
> Reason, observing which way I was bent,
> Did stay my hand, and asked me what I meant.
> "Will you," said he, "thus waste your time in vain,
> 10   On that which in the world small praise shall gain?
> For shame leave off, and do the printer spare:
> He'll lose by your ill poetry, I fear.
> Besides, the world already hath great store
> Of useless books, wherefore do write no more,
> 15   But pity take, do the world a good turn,
> And all you write cast in the fire and burn."
> Angry I was, and Reason struck away,

---

1. This was Cavendish's first publication; the first three pieces presented here functioned as verse preface to the collection. The texts are taken from the second edition

(1664), "much altered and corrected."

2. I.e., I thought that if I were to live a long time I would be able to create a poetic monument to myself.

When I did hear what he to me did say.
Then all in haste I to the press it sent,
20   Fearing persuasion might my book prevent.
But now 'tis done, repent with grief do I,
Hang down my head with shame, blush, sigh, and cry.
Take pity, and my drooping spirits raise,
Wipe off my tears with handkerchiefs of praise.

The Poetress's Petition

Like to a fever's pulse my heart doth beat,
For fear my book some great repulse should meet.
If it be naught, let it in silence lie;
Disturb it not; let it in quiet die;
5   Let not the bells of your dispraise ring loud,
But wrap it up in silence as a shroud;
Cause black oblivion on its hearse to lie,
Instead of tapers, let dark night stand by;
Instead of flowers, on its grave to strew,
10   Before its hearse, sleepy, dull poppy throw;
Instead of scutcheons,[3] let my tears be hung,
Which grief and sorrow from my eyes out wrung.
Let those that bear its corpse no jesters be,
But sober, sad, and grave mortality.
15   No satyr° poets by its grave appear,   *satirical*
No altars raised, to write inscriptions there.
Let dust of all forgetfulness be cast
Upon its corpse, there let it lie and waste.
Nor let it rise again, unless some know,
20   At Judgments some good merits it can show;
Then shall it live in Heavens of high praise,
And for its glory, garlands have of bays.[4]

An Apology for Writing So Much upon This Book

Condemn me not, I make so much ado
About this book; it is my child, you know;
Just like a bird, when her young are in nest,
Goes in, and out, and hops, and takes no rest;
5   But when their young are fledged,[5] their heads out peep,
Lord! what a chirping does the old one keep.
So I, for fear my strengthless child should fall
Against a door, or stool, aloud I call,
Bid have a care of such a dangerous place.
10   Thus write I much, to hinder all disgrace.

The Hunting of the Hare

Betwixt two ridges of plowed land sat Wat,[6]
Whose body, pressed to the earth, lay close and squat;

3. Escutcheons: funeral ornaments, shield-shaped, exhibiting the deceased's coat of arms.
4. Wreaths of laurel leaves, awarded for military victory

or literary excellence.
5. Feathered; ready to fly.
6. Conventional nickname for a hare.

His nose upon his two forefeet did lie,
With his gray eyes he glared obliquely;
5   His head he always set against the wind,
His tail when turned, his hair blew up behind,
And made him to get cold; but he being wise,
Doth keep his coat still down, so warm he lies.
Thus rests he all the day, til th' sun doth set,
10   Then up he riseth his relief to get,
And walks about, until the sun doth rise,
Then coming back in's° former posture lies.   *in his*
At last poor Wat was found, as he there lay,
By huntsmen, which came with their dogs that way,
15   Whom seeing, he got up, and fast did run,
Hoping some ways the cruel dogs to shun;
But they by nature had so quick a scent,
That by their nose they traced what way he went,
And with their deep wide mouths set forth a cry,
20   Which answered was by echo in the sky;
Then Wat was struck with terror and with fear,
Seeing each shadow thought the dogs were there,
And running out some distance from their cry,
To hide himself, his thoughts he did employ;
25   Under a clod of earth in sand pit wide
Poor Wat sat close, hoping himself to hide,
There long he had not been, but straight in's ears
The winding° horns and crying dogs he hears;   *blowing*
Then starting up with fear, he leaped, and such
30   Swift speed he made, the ground he scarce did touch;
Into a great thick wood straight ways he got,
And underneath a broken bough he sat,
Where every leaf that with the wind did shake
Brought him such terror, that his heart did ache;
35   That place he left, to champaign° plains he went,   *open*
Winding about, for to deceive their scent,
And while they snuffling were to find his track,
Poor Wat being weary, his swift pace did slack;
On his two hinder legs for ease he sat;
40   His forefeet rubbed his face from dust and sweat;
Licking his feet, he wiped his ears so clean
That none could tell that Wat had hunted been;
But casting round about his fair gray eyes,
The hounds in full career he near him 'spies.
45   To Wat it was so terrible a sight,
Fear gave him wings and made his body light;
Though he was tired before by running long,
Yet now his breath he never felt more strong—
Like those that dying are, think health returns,
50   When 'tis but a faint blast which life out-burns;
For spirits seek to guard the heart about,
Striving with death, but death doth quench them out.
The hounds so fast came on, and with such cry,
That he no hopes had left, nor help could 'spy;

55   With that the winds did pity poor Wat's case,
        And with their breath the scent blew from that place;
        Then every nose was busily employed,
        And every nostril was set open wide,
        And every head did seek a several way,
60   To find the grass or track where the scent lay;
        For witty industry° is never slack,   *cunning diligence*
        'Tis like to witchcraft, and brings lost things back;
        But though the wind had tied the scent up close,
        A busy dog thrust in his snuffling nose
65   And drew it out, with that did foremost run,
        Then horns blew loud, the rest to follow on;
        The great slow hounds their throats did set a base,
        The fleet, swift hounds, as tenors next in place,
        The little beagles did a treble sing,
70   And through the air their voices round did ring,
        Which made such consort as they ran along,
        That, had they spoken words, 't had been a song;
        The horns kept time, the men did shout for joy,
        And seemed most valiant, poor Wat to destroy;
75   Spurring their horses to a full career,
        Swum rivers deep, leaped ditches without fear,
        Endangered life and limbs, so fast they'd ride,
        Only to see how patiently Wat died;
        At last the dogs so near his heels did get,
80   That their sharp teeth they in his breech did set;
        Then tumbling down he fell, with weeping eyes
        Gave up his ghost; and thus poor Wat he dies.
        Men whooping loud, such acclamations made,
        As if the Devil they imprisoned had,
85   When they but did a shiftless creature kill;
        To hunt, there needs no valiant soldier's skill;
        But men do think that exercise and toil,
        To keep their health, is best, which makes most spoil,
        Thinking that food and nourishment so good,
90   Which doth proceed from others' flesh and blood.
        When they do lions, wolves, bears, tigers see
        Kill silly sheep, they say, they cruel be,
        But for themselves all creatures think too few,
        For luxury, wish God would make more new;
95   As if God did make creatures for man's meat,
        And gave them life and sense for man to eat,
        Or else for sport or recreation's sake
        For to destroy those lives that God did make,
        Making their stomachs graves, which full they fill
100   With murdered bodies, which in sport they kill;
        Yet man doth think himself so gentle and mild,
        When of all creatures he's most cruel, wild,
        Nay, so proud, that he only[7] thinks to live,

---

7. Alone, with no other creature.

That God a God-like nature him did give,
105   And that all creatures for his sake alone
Were made, for him to tyrannize upon.

1653, 1664

---

from A True Relation of My Birth, Breeding, and Life[1]

My father was a gentleman,[2] which title is grounded and given by merit, not by princes; and 'tis the act of time, not favor. And though my father was not a peer of the realm, yet there were few peers who had much greater estates, or lived more noble therewith. * * *

As for my breeding, it was according to my birth and the nature of my sex, for my birth was not lost in my breeding; for as my sisters was or had been bred, so was I in plenty, or rather with superfluity. Likewise we were bred virtuously, modestly, civilly, honorably, and on honest principles. As for plenty, we had not only for necessity, conveniency, and decency, but for delight and pleasure to a superfluity. 'Tis true, we did not riot, but we lived orderly; for riot, even in kings' courts and princes' palaces, brings ruin without content or pleasure, when order in less fortune shall live more plentifully and deliciously than princes that lives in a hurly-burly, as I may term it, in which they are seldom well served, for disorder obstructs. Besides, it doth disgust life,[3] distract the appetites, and yield no true relish to the senses; for pleasure, delight, peace, and felicity live in method and temperance.

As for our garments, my mother[4] did not only delight to see us neat and cleanly, fine and gay, but rich and costly, maintaining us to the height of her estate, but not beyond it. For we were so far from being in debt, before the Wars,[5] as we were rather beforehand with the world, buying all with ready money, not on the score.[6] For although after my father's death the estate was divided between my mother and her sons, paying such a sum of money for portions to her daughters either at the day of their marriage or when they should come to age, yet by reason she and her children agreed with a mutual consent, all their affairs were managed so well as she lived not in a much lower condition than when my father lived. 'Tis true my mother might have increased her daughters' portions by a thrifty sparing, yet she chose to bestow it on our breeding, honest pleasures, and harmless delights, out of an opinion that if she bred us with needy necessity it might chance to create in us sharking[7] qualities, mean[8] thoughts, and base actions, which she knew my father as well as herself did abhor. Likewise we were bred tenderly, for my mother naturally did strive to please and delight her children, not to cross or torment them, terrifying them with threats or lashing them with slavish whips. But instead of threats, reason was used to persuade us, and instead of lashes, the deformities of vices was discovered, and the graces and virtues were presented unto us. Also we were bred with respectful attendance,

1. Cavendish published her autobiography as the closing piece in a collection of her fiction called *Nature's Pictures* (1656), which she wrote while living in exile at Antwerp during the years of Cromwell's commonwealth. This work (like many of her others) was privately printed, at the author's expense, in a lavish folio, whose title page suggests the autobiography's particular place in the scheme: "In this volume there are several feigned stories . . . comical, tragical, and tragicomical, poetical, romantical, philosophical, and historical. . . . And a true story at the latter end, wherein there is no feignings." In a later edition (1671), published after she and her husband had returned to England, Cavendish omitted the autobiography.

2. Thomas Lucas (c.1573–1625), whose forebears had risen to the gentry in the 16th century. He died when Margaret was two years old.

3. I.e., makes life unpleasant.

4. Elizabeth Lucas, née Leighton (?–1647).

5. The English Civil Wars, begun in 1642.

6. On credit.

7. Greedy.

8. Ignoble.

every one being severally waited upon. And all her servants in general used the same respect to her children (even those that were very young) as they did to herself, for she suffered not her servants either to be rude before us or to domineer over us, which all vulgar servants are apt and ofttimes have leave to do. Likewise she never suffered the vulgar servingmen to be in the nursery amongst the nursemaids, lest their rude lovemaking[9] might do unseemly actions, or speak unhandsome words in the presence of her children, knowing that youth is apt to take infection by ill examples, having not the reason of distinguishing good from bad. Neither were we suffered to have any familiarity with the vulgar servants, or conversation; yet caused us to demean ourselves[1] with an humble civility towards them, as they with a dutiful respect to us. Not because they were servants were we so reserved, for many noble persons are forced to serve through necessity, but by reason the vulgar sort of servants are as ill bred as meanly born, giving children ill examples, and worse counsel. * * *

But some time after this war began, I knew not how they[2] lived. For though most of them were in Oxford, where the King was, yet after the Queen went from Oxford, and so out of England, I was parted from them.[3] For when the Queen was in Oxford, I had a great desire to be one of her Maids of Honor, hearing the Queen had not the same number she was used to have. Whereupon I wooed and won my mother to let me go, for my mother being fond of all her children was desirous to please them, which made her consent to my request. But my brothers and sisters seemed not very well pleased, by reason I had never been from home, nor seldom out of their sight; for though they knew I would not behave myself to their or my own dishonor, yet they thought I might to my disadvantage, being inexperienced in the world. Which indeed I did, for I was so bashful when I was out of my mother's, brothers', and sisters' sight, whose presence used to give me confidence, thinking I could not do amiss while any one of them were by, for I knew they would gently reform me if I did. Besides, I was ambitious they should approve of my actions and behavior, that when I was gone from them I was like one that had no foundation to stand, or guide to direct me, which made me afraid lest I should wander with ignorance out of the ways of honor so that I knew not how to behave myself. Besides, I had heard the world was apt to lay aspersions even on the innocent, for which I dared neither look up with my eyes, nor speak, nor be any way sociable, insomuch as I was thought a natural fool.[4] Indeed I had not much wit, yet I was not an idiot; my wit was according to my years. And though I might have learned more wit, and advanced my understanding by living in a court, yet being dull, fearful, and bashful, I neither heeded what was said or practiced, but just what belonged to my loyal duty and my own honest reputation. And indeed I was so afraid to dishonor my friends and family by my indiscreet actions that I rather chose to be accounted a fool than to be thought rude or wanton. In truth my bashfulness and fears made me repent my going from home to see the world abroad, and much I did desire to return to my mother again, or to my sister Pye,[5] with whom I often lived when she was in London, and loved with a supernatural affection. But my mother advised me there to stay, although I put her to more charges than if she had kept me at home, and the more, by reason she and my brothers were

---

9. Flirtation.
1. To behave.
2. Her mother and siblings.
3. In 1643, Charles I had moved his family, court, and military base to Oxford as the Civil Wars rendered Lon-

don unsafe. In 1644 his queen, Henrietta Maria, escaped to her native Paris in hopes of raising money and support for the Royalist cause.
4. I.e., born mentally defective.
5. Catherine, wife of Edmond Pye.

sequestered from their estates and plundered of all their goods.[6] Yet she maintained me so, that I was in a condition rather to lend than to borrow, which courtiers usually are not, being always necessitated by reason of great expenses courts put them to. But my mother said it would be a disgrace for me to return out of the court so soon after I was placed.

So I continued almost two years, until such time as I was married from thence. For my Lord the Marquis of Newcastle[7] did approve of those bashful fears which many condemned, and would choose such a wife as he might bring to his own humors,[8] and not such an one as was wedded to self-conceit, or one that had been tempered to the humors of another, for which he wooed me for his wife. And though I did dread marriage, and shunned men's companies as much as I could, yet I could not nor had not the power to refuse him, by reason my affections were fixed on him, and he was the only person I ever was in love with. Neither was I ashamed to own it, but gloried therein, for it was not amorous love. I never was infected therewith—it is a disease, or a passion, or both, I know by relation, not by experience. Neither could title, wealth, power, or person entice me to love. But my love was honest and honorable, being placed upon merit; which affection joyed at the fame of his worth, pleased with delight in his wit, proud of the respects he used to me, and triumphing in the affections he professed for me; which affections he hath confirmed to me by a deed[9] of time, sealed by constancy, and assigned by an unalterable decree of his promise, which makes me happy in despite of Fortune's frowns. For though misfortunes may and do oft dissolve base, wild, loose, and ungrounded affections, yet she hath no power of those that are united either by merit, justice, gratitude, duty, fidelity, or the like. And though my Lord hath lost his estate, and banished out of his country for his loyalty to his King and country, yet neither despised poverty nor pinching necessity could make him break the bonds of friendship, or weaken his loyal duty to his King or country.

But not only the family I am linked to is ruined, but the family from which I sprung, by these unhappy Wars—which ruin my mother lived to see, and then died, having lived a widow many years, for she never forgot my father so as to marry again. Indeed he remained so lively in her memory, and her grief was so lasting, as she never mentioned his name, though she spoke often of him, but love and grief caused tears to flow, and tender sighs to rise, mourning in sad complaints. She made her house her cloister, enclosing herself as it were therein, for she seldom went abroad, unless to church, but these unhappy Wars forced her out by reason she and her children were loyal to the King, for which they plundered her and my brothers of all their goods, plate, jewels, money, corn, cattle, and the like, cut down their woods, pulled down their houses, and sequestered them from their lands and livings. But in such misfortunes my mother was of an heroic spirit, in suffering patiently where there is no remedy, or to be industrious where she thought she could help. She was of a grave behavior, and had such a majestic grandeur, as it were continually hung about her, that it would strike a kind of an awe to the beholders, and command respect from the rudest. I mean the rudest of civilized people; I mean not such barbarous people as plundered her and used her cruelly, for they would have pulled God out of Heaven,

6. The Lucas family took the king's side in the Civil Wars; its property was raided during anti-Royalist riots in 1642.
7. William Cavendish (1593–1676), a general in the king's army. In 1644, after suffering defeat in a pivotal

battle, he departed for the Continent. He married Margaret (his second wife) at Paris in 1645.
8. Inclinations, ways of thinking.
9. A legal document (here used metaphorically).

had they had power, as they did royalty out of his throne. Also her beauty was beyond the ruin of time, for she had a well-favored loveliness in her face, a pleasing sweetness in her countenance, and a well-tempered complexion, as neither too red nor too pale, even to her dying hour, although in years. And by her dying, one might think death was enamored with her, for he embraced her in a sleep, and so gently, as if he were afraid to hurt her. Also she was an affectionate mother, breeding her children with a most industrious care and tender love. * * * Likewise my mother was a good mistress to her servants, taking care of her servants in their sickness, not sparing any cost she was able to bestow for their recovery. Neither did she exact more from them in their health than what they with ease or rather like pastime could do. She would freely pardon a fault, and forget an injury. Yet sometimes she would be angry, but never with her children; the sight of them would pacify her. Neither would she be angry with others but when she had cause, as with negligent or knavish servants that would lavishly or unnecessarily waste, or subtly and thievishly steal. And though she would often complain that her family was too great for her weak management, and often pressed my brother to take it upon him, yet I observe she took a pleasure and some little pride in the governing thereof. * * *

But howsoever our fortunes are, we are both content, spending our time harmlessly, for my Lord pleaseth himself with the management of some few horses, and exercises himself with the use of the sword. Which two arts he hath brought by his studious thoughts to an absolute perfection. And though he hath taken as much pains in those arts, both by study and practice, as chemists[1] for the philosopher's stone, yet he hath this advantage of them, that he hath found the right and the truth thereof and therein, which chemists never found in their art and I believe never will. Also he recreates himself with his pen, writing what his wit dictates to him. But I pass my time rather with scribbling than writing, with words than wit. Not that I speak much, because I am addicted to contemplation, unless I am with my Lord; yet then I rather attentively listen to what he says, than impertinently speak. Yet when I am writing any sad feigned stories or serious humors or melancholy passions, I am forced many times to express them with the tongue before I can write them with the pen, by reason those thoughts that are sad, serious, and melancholy are apt to contract and to draw too much back, which oppression doth as it were overpower or smother the conception in the brain. But when some of those thoughts are sent out in words, they give the rest more liberty to place themselves in a more methodical order, marching more regularly with my pen on the ground of white paper. But my letters seem rather as a ragged rout, than a well-armed body, for the brain being quicker in creating than the hand in writing, or the memory in retaining, many fancies are lost by reason they ofttimes outrun the pen. Where I, to keep speed in the race, write so fast as I stay not so long as to write my letters plain, insomuch as some have taken my handwriting for some strange character.[2] And being accustomed so to do, I cannot now write very plain. When I strive to write my best, indeed my ordinary handwriting is so bad as few can read it so as to write it fair for the press. But however that[3] little wit I have, it delights me to scribble it out and disperse it about. For I being addicted from my childhood to contemplation rather than conversation, to solitariness rather than society, to melancholy rather than mirth, to write with the

---

1. Alchemists, who devoted themselves to the search for the "philosopher's stone"—the substance that would turn base metals into gold.

2. Code, cryptography.
3. Whatever.

pen than to work with a needle, passing my time with harmless fancies, their company being pleasing, their conversation innocent, in which I take such pleasure as I neglect my health. For it is as great a grief to leave their society, as a joy to be in their company. My only trouble is lest my brain should grow barren, or that the root of my fancies should become insipid, withering into a dull stupidity, for want of maturing subjects to write on. * * *

But since I have writ in general thus far of my life, I think it fit I should speak something of my humor, particular practice, and disposition. As for my humor, I was from my childhood given to contemplation, being more taken or delighted with thoughts than in conversation with a society. * * * Also I did dislike any should follow my fashions, for I always took delight in a singularity, even in accoutrements of habits. But whatsoever I was addicted to, either in fashions of clothes, contemplation of thoughts, actions of life, they were lawful, honest, honorable, and modest, of which I can avouch to the world with a great confidence, because it is a pure truth. * * * Likewise I am neither spiteful, envious, nor malicious. I repine not at[4] the gifts that Nature or Fortune bestows upon others, yet I am a great emulator. For though I wish none worse than they are, nor fear any should be better than they are, yet it is lawful for me to wish myself the best, and to do my honest endeavor thereunto. For I think it no crime to wish myself the exactest[5] of Nature's works, my thread of life the longest, my chain of destiny the strongest, my mind the peaceablest, my life the pleasantest, my death the easiest, and the greatest saint in Heaven. * * * As I am not covetous, so I am not prodigal.[6] But of the two I am inclining to be prodigal, yet I cannot say to a vain prodigality, because I imagine it is to a profitable end; for perceiving the world is given or apt to honor the outside more than the inside, worshipping show more than substance; and I am so vain, if it be a vanity, as to endeavor to be worshipped rather than not to be regarded. Yet I shall never be so prodigal as to impoverish my friends,[7] or go beyond the limits or facility of our estate. And though I desire to appear at the best advantage whilst I live in the view of the public world, yet I could most willingly exclude myself, so as never to see the face of any creature but my Lord as long as I live, enclosed myself like an anchorite,[8] wearing a frieze gown[9] tied with a cord about my waist. But I hope my readers will not think me vain for writing my life, since there have been many that have done the like, as Caesar, Ovid,[1] and many more, both men and women, and I know no reason I may not do it as well as they. But I verily believe some censuring readers will scornfully say, "Why hath this lady writ her own life, since none cares to know whose daughter she was or whose wife she is, or how she was bred, or what fortunes she had, or how she lived, or what humor or disposition she was of?" I answer that it is true, that 'tis to no purpose, to the readers, but it is to the authoress, because I write it for my own sake, not theirs. Neither did I intend this piece for to delight, but to divulge, not to please the fancy, but to tell the truth, lest after-ages should mistake, in not knowing I was daughter to one Master Lucas of St. Johns near Colchester in Essex, second wife to the Lord Marquis of Newcastle; for my Lord having had two wives, I might easily have been mistaken, especially if I should die, and my Lord marry again.

1656

---

4. Do not fret about.
5. Most perfected.
6. Spendthrift, lavish.
7. Family members.
8. Religious recluse.

9. Coarse woolen robe.
1. Julius Caesar (c.100–44 B.C.), Roman general and statesman, wrote memoirs of his military campaigns; the Roman poet Ovid (43 B.C.–A.D. 17) wrote many autobiographical poems.

from Observations upon Experimental Philosophy. To which is added, The Description of a New Blazing World[1]
Of Micrography, and of Magnifying and Multiplying Glasses[2]

Although I am not able to give a solid judgment of the art of micrography and the several dioptrical[3] instruments belonging thereto, by reason I have neither studied nor practiced that art, yet of this I am confident: that this same art, with all its instruments, is not able to discover the interior natural motions of any part or creature of nature. Nay, the question is whether it can represent yet the exterior shapes and motions so exactly as naturally they are, for art[4] doth more easily alter than inform. As, for example, art makes cylinders, concave and convex glasses, and the like, which represent the figure of an object in no part exactly and truly, but very deformed and misshaped. Also a glass that is flawed, cracked, or broke, or cut into the figure of lozenges, triangles, squares, or the like, will present numerous pictures of one object. Besides, there are so many alterations made by several lights, their shadows, refractions, reflections, as also several lines, points, mediums, interposing and intermixing parts, forms, and positions, as the truth of an object will hardly be known.[5] For the perception of sight, and so of the rest of the senses, goes no further than the exterior parts of the object presented, and though the perception may be true when the object is truly presented, yet when the presentation is false, the information must be false also. And it is to be observed that art for the most part makes hermaphroditical,[6] that is, mixed figures, as partly artificial and partly natural. For art may make some metal as pewter, which is between tin and lead, as also brass, and numerous other things of mixed natures; in the like manner may artificial glasses present objects partly natural and partly artificial. Nay, put the case they can present the natural figure of an object; yet that natural figure may be presented in as monstrous a shape as it may appear misshapen rather than natural. For example, a louse by the help of a magnifying glass appears like a lobster,[7] where the microscope enlarging and magnifying each part of it makes them bigger and rounder than naturally they are. The truth is, the more the figure by art is magnified, the more it appears misshapen from the natural, inasmuch as each joint will appear as a diseased, swelled and tumid body, ready and ripe for incision. But mistake me not; I do not say that no glass presents the true picture of an object, but only that magnifying, multiplying, and the like optic glasses may and do oftentimes present falsely the picture of an exterior object. I say the picture because it is not the real body of the object which the glass presents, but the glass only figures or patterns out the picture presented in and by the glass, and there may easily mistakes be committed in taking copies from copies. Nay, artists[8] do confess themselves that flies and the like will appear of several figures or shapes, according to the several reflections, refractions, mediums, and positions of several lights. Which if so, how can they tell or judge which is the truest light, position, or

---

1. The *Observations* is a critique of science, the *Blazing World* a work of fantasy; Cavendish published them together in a single volume as complementary texts. The "experimental philosophy" was that method and outlook pursued and exalted by the Royal Society; the group itself makes a sustained parodic appearance in the *Blazing World*. The Society held that copious experiment was the necessary basis for reliable study of the natural world. Cavendish challenges any such investigation grounded in human perceptions and the machines (microscopes, telescopes) contrived to enhance them; in the excerpt here she specifically takes on the work of Robert Hooke (see

page 2047), whose *Micrographia* (1665) may well have prompted her to write the *Observations*, which includes the first selection given here.
2. Lenses.
3. Vision-enhancing (by means of refraction).
4. Artifice, like that of the lens-makers.
5. Early microscopes in England used simple lenses that blurred the image.
6. Composed of two opposite qualities.
7. As in Hooke's *Micrographia* illustration.
8. Technicians.

medium, that doth present the object naturally as it is? And if not, then an edge may very well seem flat, and a point of a needle a globe;[9] but if the edge of a knife, or point of a needle were naturally and really so as the microscope presents them, they would never be so useful as they are, for a flat or broad plain-edged knife would not cut, nor a blunt globe pierce so suddenly another body. Neither would or could they pierce without tearing and rending, if their bodies were so uneven. And if the picture of a young beautiful lady should be drawn according to the representation of the microscope, or according to the various refraction and reflection of light through such like glasses, it would be so far from being like her, as it would not be like a human face, but rather a monster than a picture of nature.

Wherefore those that invented microscopes and suchlike dioptrical glasses at first did, in my opinion, the world more injury than benefit. For this art has intoxicated so many men's brains, and wholly employed their thoughts and bodily actions about phenomena, or the exterior figures of objects, as[1] all better arts and studies are laid aside. Nay, those that are not as earnest and active in such employments as they, are by many of them accounted unprofitable subjects to the commonwealth of learning. But though there be numerous books written of the wonders of these glasses, yet I cannot perceive any such; at best, they are but superficial wonders, as I may call them.

But could experimental philosophers find out more beneficial arts than our forefathers have done, either for the better increase of vegetables and brute animals to nourish our bodies, or better and commodious contrivances in the art of architecture to build us houses, or for the advancing of trade and traffic to provide necessaries for us to live, or for the decrease of nice[2] distinctions and sophistical[3] disputes in churches, schools, and courts of judicature, to make men live in unity, peace, and neighborly friendship, it would not only be worth their labor, but of as much praise as could be given to them. But as boys that play with watery bubbles, or sling dust into each other's eyes, or make a hobbyhorse of snow, are worthy of reproof rather than praise, for wasting their time with useless sports, so those that addict themselves to unprofitable arts spend more time than they reap benefit thereby. Nay, could they benefit men either in husbandry, architecture, or the like necessary and profitable employments, yet before the vulgar sort[4] would learn to understand them, the world would want bread to eat, and houses to dwell in, as also clothes to keep them from the inconveniences of the inconstant weather. But truly, although spinsters[5] were most experienced in this art, yet they will never be able to spin silk, thread, or wool, etc., from loose atoms; neither will weavers weave a web of light from the sun's rays, nor an architect build a house of the bubbles of water and air, unless they be poetical spinsters, weavers, and architects. And if a painter should draw a louse as big as a crab, and of that shape as the microscope presents, can anybody imagine that a beggar would believe it to be true?[6] But if he did, what advantage would it be to the beggar? For it doth neither instruct him how to avoid breeding them, or how to catch them, or to hinder them from biting. Again, if a painter should paint birds according to those colors the microscope presents, what advantage would it be for fowlers to take them? Truly, no fowler will be able to distinguish several birds through a microscope,

---

9. Cavendish evidently refers to Hooke's micrographic depiction of a needle's point, a printed period (her "globe"), and (in the original illustration) a razor's edge; see page 2051.
1. That.
2. Minute, subtle, trivial.

3. Complicatedly and falsely argued.
4. Common people.
5. People who spin yarn or thread (possibly, here, with the additional sense of "unmarried woman").
6. Beggars were assumed to be most familiar (because most often afflicted) with lice.

neither by their shapes nor colors; they will be better discerned by those that eat their flesh than by micrographers that look upon their colors and exterior figures through a magnifying glass.

In short, magnifying glasses are like a high heel to a short leg, which if it be made too high, it is apt to make the wearer fall, and at the best can do no more than represent exterior figures in a bigger, and so in a more deformed shape and posture than naturally they are. But as for the interior form and motions of a creature, as I said before, they can no more represent them, than telescopes can the interior essence and nature of the sun, and what matter it consists of. For if one that never had seen milk before should look upon it through a microscope, he would never be able to discover the interior parts of milk by that instrument, were it the best that is in the world—neither the whey, nor the butter, nor the curds. Wherefore the best optic[7] is a perfect natural eye, and a regular sensitive perception, and the best judge is reason, and the best study is rational contemplation joined with the observations of regular sense, but not deluding arts. For art is not only gross[8] in comparison to nature, but for the most part deformed and defective, and at best produces mixed or hermaphroditical figures—that is, a third figure between nature and art. Which proves that natural reason is above artificial sense, as I may call it. Wherefore those arts are the best and surest informers that alter nature least, and they the greatest deluders that alter nature most—I mean, the particular nature of each particular creature. (For art is so far from altering infinite Nature that it is no more in comparison to it than a little fly to an elephant;[9] no, not so much, for there is no comparison between finite and infinite.) But wise Nature, taking delight in variety, her parts, which are her creatures, must of necessity do so too.

from The Description of a New Blazing World

FROM TO THE READER

If you wonder that I join a work of fancy[1] to my serious philosophical contemplations, think not that it is out of a disparagement to philosophy, or out of an opinion as if this noble study were but a fiction of the mind * * * The end of reason is truth, the end of fancy is fiction. But mistake me not when I distinguish fancy from reason; I mean not as if fancy were not made by the rational parts of matter, but by "reason" I understand a rational search and inquiry into the causes of natural effects, and by "fancy" a voluntary creation or production of the mind, both being effects, or rather actions, of the rational part of matter, of which, as that[2] is a more profitable and useful study than this, so it is also more laborious and difficult, and requires sometimes the help of fancy to recreate the mind and withdraw it from its more serious contemplations.

And this is the reason, why I added this piece of fancy to my philosophical observations, and joined them as two worlds at the ends of their poles; both for my own sake, to divert my studious thoughts, which I employed in the contemplation thereof, and to delight the reader with variety, which is always pleasing. But lest my fancy should stray too much, I chose such a fiction as would be agreeable to

7. Lens.
8. Rough, approximate.
9. Cavendish probably refers to Hooke's illustration of a

flea (see page 2053).
1. Imagination.
2. Philosophy.

the subject treated of in the former parts; it is a description of a new world, not such as Lucian's, or the Frenchman's world in the moon;[3] but a world of my own creating, which I call the Blazing World: the first part whereof is romancical, the second philosophical, and the third is merely fancy, or (as I may call it) fantastical, which if it add any satisfaction to you, I shall account myself a happy creatoress.[4] If not, I must be content to live a melancholy life in my own world; I cannot call it a poor world, if poverty be only want of gold, silver, and jewels; for there is more gold in it than all the chemists ever did, and (as I verily believe) will ever be able to make.[5] As for the rocks of diamonds, I wish with all my soul they might be shared amongst my noble female friends, and upon that condition, I would willingly quit my part;[6] and of the gold I should only desire so much as might suffice to repair my noble Lord and husband's losses:[7] for I am not covetous, but as ambitious as ever any of my sex was, is, or can be; which makes, that though I cannot be Henry the Fifth, or Charles the Second,[8] yet I endeavor to be Margaret the First; and although I have neither power, time, nor occasion to conquer the world as Alexander and Caesar did; yet rather than not to be mistress of one, since Fortune and the Fates would give me none, I have made a world of my own: for which nobody, I hope, will blame me, since it is in everyone's power to do the like.

[CREATING WORLDS]

At last, when the Duchess[9] saw that no patterns would do her any good in the framing of her world, she resolved to make a world of her own invention, * * * which world after it was made, appeared so curious and full of variety, so well ordered and wisely governed, that it cannot possibly be expressed by words, nor the delight and pleasure which the Duchess took in making this world of her own.

In the meantime the Empress was also making and dissolving several worlds in her own mind, and was so puzzled, that she could not settle in any of them; wherefore she sent for the Duchess, who being ready to wait on the Empress, carried her beloved world along with her, and invited the Empress's soul to observe the frame, order, and government of it. Her Majesty was so ravished with the perception of it, that her soul desired to live in the Duchess's world; but the Duchess advised her to make such another world in her own mind; for, said she, your Majesty's mind is full of rational corporeal motions, and the rational motions of my mind shall assist you by the help of sensitive expressions, with the best instructions they are able to give you.

3. The *True History*, by the Greek satirist Lucian (2nd century A.D.), initiated a long literary tradition of imaginary voyages, to which the French writer Savinien Cyrano de Bergerac's account of a trip to the moon (*Histoire comique contenant les états et empires de la lune* [1657]) was a recent, celebrated contribution.
4. In the first part of *The Blazing World*, a "virtuous lady" survives her abduction at sea and is transported into a "Blazing World" that touches Earth at the North Pole; quickly wooed and wedded by the Emperor of this utopia, she becomes its Empress. In the second, "philosophical" section, she hears the testimony of various scholars, scientists, theologians, and philosophers; in the third, "fantastical" section, the Empress summons the soul of Margaret Cavendish to travel from England to the Blazing World, in order to serve as her companion and secretary.

The excerpts below are from the third part of the narrative.
5. Alchemists sought to turn base metals into gold.
6. Give up my share.
7. During the civil wars, William Cavendish had lost much wealth and property, of which he had recovered only part since the Restoration.
8. Henry V of England (1387–1422) was celebrated for his conquest of France; Charles II for his restoration of the monarchy after the Interregnum.
9. Cavendish herself, whose soul has been transported to the Blazing World at the Empress's request. At this point in the story she and the Empress have been experimenting with creating worlds in accordance with the theories established by various experts, ancient and modern (Pythagoras, Plato, Aristotle, Descartes, Hobbes).

The Empress being thus persuaded by the Duchess to make an imaginary world of her own, followed her advice; and after she had quite finished it, and framed all kinds of creatures proper and useful for it, strengthened it with good laws, and beautified it with arts and sciences; having nothing else to do, unless she did dissolve her imaginary world, or made some alterations in the Blazing World she lived in, which yet she could hardly do, by reason it was so well ordered that it could not be mended.[1]

[EMPRESS, DUCHESS, DUKE]

At last, they entered into the Duke's house,[2] an habitation not so magnificent, as useful; and when the Empress saw it, "Has the Duke," said she, "no other house but this?" "Yes," answered the Duchess, "some five miles from this place, he has a very fine castle, called Bolsover."[3] "That place then," said the Empress, "I desire to see." "Alas!" replied the Duchess, "it is but a naked house, and unclothed of all furniture." "However," said the Empress, "I may see the manner of its structure and building." "That you may," replied the Duchess. And as they were thus discoursing, the Duke came out of the house into the court, to see his horses of manage;[4] whom when the Duchess's soul perceived, she was so overjoyed, that her aerial vehicle[5] became so splendorous, as if it had been enlightened by the sun; by which we may perceive, that the passions of souls or spirits can alter their bodily vehicles. Then these two ladies' spirits went close to him, but he could not perceive them; and after the Empress had observed the art of manage, she was much pleased with it, and commended it as a noble pastime, and an exercise fit and proper for noble and heroic persons; but when the Duke was gone into the house again, those two souls followed him; where the Empress observing, that he went to the exercise of the sword, and was such an excellent and unparalleled master thereof, she was as much pleased with that exercise, as she was with the former. But the Duchess's soul being troubled, that her dear lord and husband used such a violent exercise before meat, for fear of overheating himself, without any consideration of the Empress's soul, left her aerial vehicle, and entered into her lord. The Empress's soul perceiving this, did the like: and then the Duke had three souls in one body; and had there been but some such souls more, the Duke would have been like the Grand Signior in his seraglio,[6] only it would have been a Platonic seraglio.[7] But the Duke's soul being wise, honest, witty, complaisant, and noble, afforded such delight and pleasure to the Empress's soul by her conversation, that these two souls became enamored of each other; which the Duchess's soul perceiving, grew jealous at first, but then considering that no adultery could be committed amongst Platonic lovers, and that Platonism was divine, as being derived from divine Plato, cast forth of her mind that idea of jealousy. Then the conversation of these three souls was so pleasant, that it cannot be expressed; for the Duke's soul entertained the Empress's soul with scenes,

---

1. Instead, the Empress resolves "to see the world the Duchess came from," and so "those two female souls" travel together "as lightly as two thoughts," into England.
2. Welbeck Abbey, north-country birthplace and family seat of Cavendish's husband the Duke of Newcastle.
3. The Duke's favorite residence.
4. Well-disciplined in the actions and paces of *ménage*, or systematic horse training. The Duke, an expert equestri-

an, had published two books on the subject; when Charles II was a boy, Newcastle had taught him how to ride.
5. Form made out of air.
6. Harem.
7. One where the pleasures of the flesh would be repudiated in favor of the contemplation of pure, disembodied Ideas.

songs, music, witty discourses, pleasant recreations, and all kinds of harmless sports; so that the time passed away faster than they expected. At last, a spirit came and told the Empress, that although neither the Emperor, nor any of his subjects knew that her soul was absent; yet the Empress's soul was so sad and melancholy, for want of his own beloved soul, that all the imperial court took notice of it. Wherefore he advised the Empress's soul to return into the Blazing World, into her own body she left there; which both the Duke's and Duchess's soul was very sorry for, and wished, that if it had been possible, the Empress's soul might have stayed a longer time with them; but seeing it could not be otherwise, they pacified themselves. * * *

Epilogue

TO THE READER

By this poetical description, you may perceive, that my ambition is not only to be Empress, but Authoress of a whole world; and that the worlds I have made, both the Blazing and the other Philosophical World, mentioned in the first part of this description, are framed and composed of the most pure, that is, the rational parts of matter, which are the parts of my mind; which creation was more easily and suddenly effected, than the conquests of the two famous monarchs of the world, Alexander and Caesar. Neither have I made such disturbances, and caused so many dissolutions of particulars,[8] otherwise named deaths, as they did; for I have destroyed but some few men in a little boat,[9] which died through the extremity of cold, and that by the hand of Justice, which was necessitated to punish their crime of stealing away a young and beauteous lady. And in the formation of those worlds, I take more delight and glory, than ever Alexander or Caesar did in conquering this terrestrial world; and though I have made my Blazing World a peaceable world, allowing it but one religion, one language, and one government; yet could I make another world, as full of factions, divisions, and wars, as this is of peace and tranquility; and the rational figures of my mind might express as much courage to fight, as Hector and Achilles had; and be as wise as Nestor, as eloquent as Ulysses, and as beautiful as Helen.[1] But I esteeming peace before war, wit before policy, honesty before beauty; instead of the figures of Alexander, Caesar, Hector, Achilles, Nestor, Ulysses, Helen, etc. chose rather the figure of honest Margaret Newcastle, which now I would not change for all this terrestrial world; and if any should like the world I have made, and be willing to be my subjects, they may imagine themselves such, and they are such, I mean, in their minds, fancies, or imaginations; but if they cannot endure to be subjects, they may create worlds of their own, and govern themselves as they please: but yet let them have a care, not to prove unjust usurpers, and to rob me of mine; for concerning the Philosophical World, I am Empress of it myself; and as for the Blazing World, it having an Empress already, who rules it with great wisdom and conduct, which Empress is my dear Platonic friend; I shall never prove so unjust, treacherous, and unworthy to her, as to disturb her government, much less to depose her from her imperial throne, for the sake of any other; but rather choose to create another world for another friend.

1666

8. Individuals.
9. The sailor-abductors of the "virtuous lady," who die during the boat's passage through the North Pole to the

Blazing World.
1. Characters in the *Iliad*, Homer's epic poem about the Trojan War.

John Dryden
1631–1700

In his last years, Dryden often felt the need to defend his morals, his religion, his politics, even his writing. For nearly a quarter of a century, he had held high literary office and mingled with the great; he had curried royal favor and aristocratic patronage, bolstering officialdom, aiming to injure the Crown's enemies and to caress its friends. He wrote about politics and religion, about trade and empire; he wrote for the theater and for public occasions; he composed songs, fables, odes, and panegyrics, brilliant satire and savage polemic; he translated from many languages and formulated an idiomatic, familiar, and fluent prose style. Dryden virtually invented the idea of a commercial literary career; and through all the turns of a difficult public life, he fashioned from his own unlikely personality—from his privacy, self-doubts, and hesitations—a public figure of literary distinction. But he attained this celebrity at the cost of gossip and scandal, and in the last decade of his life (after the Glorious Revolution and his deposition from the Poet Laureateship) he faced suspicion and scorn.

The poet's beginnings give no hint of literary greatness or the likelihood of fame. He was born in 1631 in a country town and to comfortable circumstance; he was educated at Westminster School and graduated from Trinity College, Cambridge. He held minor public office in the 1650s but had written almost nothing before he was twenty-seven. Dryden then began his long career as public poet. He mourned the Lord Protector in 1659 (*Heroic Stanzas*) and then, in what looks like a convenient turn of allegiance, he celebrated the return of monarchy in 1660, writing poems to Charles II, to the Lord Chancellor, and to the Duchess of York; he praised the Royal Society (*To Doctor Charleton*) and defended the Royal Navy and its aristocratic high command (*Annus Mirabilis,* 1667).

The first years seem a series of calculated moves; and the combination of talent, application, and opportunity was crowned when Dryden was named Poet Laureate in 1667. But in addition to fashioning a career in the 1660s, Dryden also forged a new drama—an epic theater whose themes and language echoed the idioms of heroic verse—and a body of literary criticism that itself would have made his lasting reputation. Indeed, the great text of the first decade was the *Essay of Dramatic Poesy* (1668), Dryden's formulation of a pointedly English poetics and theater. Along with Sir Philip Sidney's *Defence of Poesy*, and Samuel Johnson's *Lives of the Poets*, Dryden's *Essay* is central to the long-standing canon of English literary criticism. Some of Dryden's early plays have been forgotten, but he worked steadily at a craft that would enable him to turn Milton's *Paradise Lost* into theater (*The State of Innocence,* 1677), create a superb adaptation of Shakespeare's *Antony and Cleopatra* in *All for Love* (1678), the finest of Restoration tragedies in *Don Sebastian* (1690), and the texts of one of England's first operas, *King Arthur* (1691), and last masques, *The Pilgrim* (1700).

By the late 1670s Dryden was famed as publicist for the Crown, and his theatrical work had come to dominate the stage; but he had hardly begun the career as satirist by which he is now best known. Its opening move was *Mac Flecknoe* (1676), and in the next few years Dryden fashioned masterpieces of literary mockery and political invective, poems that virtually created literary genres and dominated satire for decades to come. *Mac Flecknoe* allowed Dryden to ridicule and crush his rivals, all the while conjuring the suave tones and elegant manners of literary supremacy. In the abuse of rivals, only Pope surpasses Dryden as a master of scorn. But *Mac Flecknoe* was only the first act in a theater of invective. In the fall of 1681 Dryden wrote *Absalom and Achitophel*, a biblical allegory occasioned by the crisis of succession. The king had failed to beget a legitimate heir, and the king's Catholic brother waited ominously in the wings. It was Dryden's job to defend the Crown, to extenuate royal indulgence, and, especially, to defuse anxieties. With *Absalom and Achitophel*, Dryden wove together the Bible and contemporary politics with such deftness that mere diversionary tactics were spun into an incomparable allegory of envy, ambition, and misdeed. The satire was read, marked, circulated, and treasured as a masterpiece and a menace.

The masterpiece secured Dryden's fame; the menace exacted a cost. The poet had attacked powerful men: aristocrats, politicans, and their partisan hacks who intrigued against the Crown. They failed in the early 1680s to foment rebellion, but by 1688 they were able to effect a revolution that deposed Catholic monarchy and the Poet Laureate himself. Dryden was reputed a brilliant and damaging advocate of Stuart rule; he had collaborated with court publicity and polemic; he had even converted to Roman Catholicism after James ascended the throne. Indeed, Dryden wrote his longest and most elaborate original poem—*The Hind and the Panther* (1687)—in defense of that king's rule and religion, and of his own conversion to Roman Catholicism. Once James II had been chased into exile, the poet felt he had nowhere to turn. In 1688 Dryden was fifty-seven, an old man by contemporary standards. He was forced from office, his pension was cancelled, and he was driven back to the venues of commercial writing: the theater, translation, publication by subscription, even editing and anthologizing. He often expressed a keen sense of loss and abandonment in the 1690s, yet the decade would prove to be a remarkable phase of his career. Between his loss of the laureateship in 1689 and his death in 1700, Dryden wrote a series of superb translations that included selections from the satires of Juvenal and Persius, Ovid's *Metamorphoses* and *Amores,* Boccaccio's and Chaucer's tales. In these same years he wrote odes and epitaphs, and collaborated with his publisher Jacob Tonson in the new fashion for literary anthologies. Most remarkably, he produced *The Works of Virgil,* which set the standard for the translation of Latin poetry. He had come to his project late, and more than once he wrote of his inadequacy for this daunting task: "What Virgil wrote in the vigor of his age, in plenty and at ease, I have undertaken to translate in my declining years, struggling with wants, oppressed with sickness, curbed in my genius, liable to be misconstrued in all I write; and my judges . . . already prejudiced against me, by the lying character which has been given them of my morals." But Dryden's *Virgil* was a resounding, rehabilitating commercial and artistic success.

Nor were the twelve thousand lines of translated Virgil the close of this career. What followed was *Fables Ancient and Modern,* an anthology of original verse and new translations that included Ovid, Boccaccio, and Chaucer as well as a trial for what Dryden hoped would be his English Homer. He saw commercial opportunity in this new collection; but he must also have understood it as a crowning achievement in this life of theatricality and ventriloquism. He had begun by seeking a voice in the idioms and gestures of other poets; he now belonged wholly to himself as he casually turned their verse into his own. It is something of a paradox that a life of literary self-assertion, of aggressive, even calculating, careerism, should have closed with Dryden rummaging among other poets' verse, pausing over favorite lines, translating Ovid's Latin and Boccaccio's Italian into what was unmistakably his own voice. And the paradox of self-assertion ending in translation helps us to identify what is so particularly and so brilliantly Dryden's art. In the early modern world, writing meant belonging to others—to the authority of antiquity, to the opinions and fickle pleasure of patrons, to favor, to obligation, to taste, even to the emerging appetites of a reading public. Many of Dryden's contemporaries—Donne, Milton, Rochester—appeal to us by their seeming defiance of such self-denying ordinances. We read Dryden today not just for the skill with which he picked his way through political dangers or negotiated social minefields, not even for the savage cartooning of enemies or baroque praise of friends, but for the achievement of belonging to others as he became more exactly and more generously himself.

Absalom and Achitophel

Dryden wrote *Absalom and Achitophel* as a piece of propaganda; he was, after all, Poet Laureate. He may even have written it at the personal request of Charles II, and he surely intended to please the king, to entertain his friends, to embarrass their enemies. He performed these offices amidst tangled circumstances and under extraordinary partisan and civic pressures.

Charles had sired many children by many mistresses, but no heir by his wife. These habits and accidents of royal procreation had created a succession crisis: in the absence of a legitimate heir, the crown would pass to Charles's brother James, an openly professed Roman Catholic. This prospect excited every fear of absolute rule—of Popery, slavery, subjugation to France and to Rome. The crisis, in turn, helped crystallize an opposition of Protestants, rebels, republicans, and opportunists who mustered support for an audacious proposal: exclude the duke from succession and appoint as substitute the dim but charming, Protestant but (alas) bastard off-spring of the king, James, Duke of Monmouth.

To bolster its program, the opposition made ingenious use of a conspiracy theory, widely entertained though largely false. In 1678 the mysterious murder of an eminent judge, a cloud of perjured witnesses, and a blizzard of broadsides, rumors, and innuendos persuaded many that the Queen, the Duke of York, and a band of Jesuits had conspired in a "Popish Plot" to kill the king and inaugurate Catholic rule. At the height of the mania, thirty-five Catholics were executed for their supposed complicity in this "plot." After the bloodletting, and in the face of much evidence to suggest that the plot itself was fiction, the rage subsided. The Whig opposition, now emerging from thuggery and faction into England's first organized political party, tested its powers by parliamentary maneuver. In 1680 its leader, the Earl of Shaftesbury, tried twice to pass a bill excluding Charles's brother James from the succession. In 1681 Shaftesbury publicly urged Charles to legitimate Monmouth. The king had had enough: he dismissed Parliament in March, and on July 2 had Shaftesbury imprisoned on charges of high treason. Four months later, a packed jury produced the verdict *ignoramus* ("we don't know").

Dryden's poem, appearing the week before the trial, told these busy stories in terms both daring and familiar. He cast the crisis as biblical drama: Charles became King David, Monmouth was David's wayward son Absalom, Shaftesbury the wily counselor Achitophel. Of course, factions of all sorts had long deployed parallels between England and Israel for instruction, for prophecy and exhortation, for mockery and even scandal. But no one had set all the possibilities of irony and celebration simultaneously in motion. Against the king's enemies Dryden turned their own rhetoric of scriptural sanctimony; in support of the king's friends he wrote hymns of praise; but on behalf of that complex client the king himself, Dryden discovered a way of portraying monarchy in a spirit at once appreciative, ironic, and delicately abrasive. In the poem's mischievous opening lines we hear these possibilities fully orchestrated. Charles's sexual energies, mapped as Davidic fecundity, are simultaneously grand and titillating, munificent and comic. Such mixtures of tone suffuse all the actions and arguments of Dryden's poem—its images of authority, its satiric portraits, its theories of governance, its monologues and declamations—all its traffic with the dangerous world of politics, plots, and promiscuity.

Absalom and Achitophel: A Poem.

—Si propiùs stes
Te capiet magis—[1]

TO THE READER

'Tis not my intention to make an apology for my poem: some will think it needs no excuse, and others will receive none. The design, I am sure, is honest, but he who

---

1. "If you stand closer, it will capture you more readily" (Horace, *Ars Poetica*, 361–362); Horace is here developing his argument that a poem works like a picture (*ut pictura poesis*).

draws his pen for one party must expect to make enemies of the other. For wit and fool are consequents of Whig and Tory, and every man is a knave or an ass to the contrary side. There's a treasury of merits in the fanatic church, as well as in the Papist, and a pennyworth to be had of saintship, honesty, and poetry, for the lewd, the factious, and the blockheads.[2] But the longest chapter in Deuteronomy has not curses enough for an anti-Bromingham.[3] My comfort is, their manifest prejudice to my cause will render their judgment of less authority against me. Yet if a poem have a genius, it will force its own reception in the world. For there's a sweetness in good verse, which tickles even while it hurts, and no man can be heartily angry with him who pleases him against his will. The commendation of adversaries is the greatest triumph of a writer, because it never comes unless extorted. But I can be satisfied on more easy terms: if I happen to please the more moderate sort, I shall be sure of an honest party and, in all probability, of the best judges, for the least concerned are commonly the least corrupt. And, I confess, I have laid in for those, by rebating[4] the satire (where justice would allow it) from carrying too sharp an edge. They who can criticize so weakly as to imagine I have done my worst may be convinced, at their own cost, that I can write severely with more ease than I can gently. I have but laughed at some men's follies, when I could have declaimed against their vices; and other men's virtues I have commended as freely as I have taxed[5] their crimes. And now, if you are a malicious reader, I expect you should return upon me that I affect to be thought more impartial than I am. But if men are not to be judged by their professions,[6] God forgive you commonwealthsmen[7] for professing so plausibly for the government. You cannot be so unconscionable as to charge me for not subscribing of my name, for that would reflect too grossly upon your own party, who never dare, though they have the advantage of a jury to secure them.[8] If you like not my poem, the fault may, possibly, be in my writing (though 'tis hard for an author to judge against himself); but, more probably, 'tis in your morals, which cannot bear the truth of it. The violent on both sides will condemn the character of Absalom as either too favorably or too hardly drawn. But they are not the violent whom I desire to please. The fault, on the right hand, is to extenuate, palliate, and indulge; and, to confess freely, I have endeavored to commit it. Besides the respect which I owe his birth, I have a greater for his heroic virtues; and David himself could not be more tender of the young man's life than I would be of his reputation. But since the most excellent natures are always the most easy,[9] and, as being such, are the soonest perverted by ill counsels, especially when baited with fame and glory, 'tis no more a wonder that he withstood not the temptations of Achitophel than it was for Adam not to have resisted the two devils, the serpent and the woman. The conclusion of the story I purposely forbore to prosecute, because I could not obtain from myself to show Absalom unfortunate.[1] The frame of it was cut out but for a picture to the waist; and if the draught be so far true, 'tis as much as I designed.

---

2. Roman Catholic doctrine posited the existence in heaven of a fund of surplus "merits," accumulated through the goodness of Christ and the saints, on which ordinary mortals might draw for absolution. Dryden suggests that the dissenting Protestant sects ("the fanatic church"), like the Catholic ("Papist") church, confer forgiveness (even "saintship") too freely and too cheaply.
3. Tory (Royalist). Deuteromony 28 includes a long list of curses against those who "shall not enter into the congregation of the Lord" because they have disobeyed his law.
4. Abating, softening.
5. Denounced.
6. What they say (profess).

7. Here and throughout the poem, Dryden conflates the supporters of Monmouth with the supporters of Cromwell, as enemies of the monarchy.
8. Dryden published his politically volatile poem anonymously. He accuses Whig writers of similar caution, and hence of greater cowardice, because the London juries that adjudicated cases of seditious libel were handpicked by Whig sheriffs for their bias in the party's favor.
9. Easily persuaded.
1. I.e., Dryden decided to leave off the end of the biblical story (in which Absalom is killed), because he could not bring himself to show Absalom's misfortune.

Were I the inventor, who am only the historian, I should certainly conclude the piece with the reconcilement of Absalom to David. And who knows but this may come to pass? Things were not brought to an extremity where I left the story. There seems yet to be room left for a composure;[2] hereafter, there may only be for pity. I have not so much as an uncharitable wish against Achitophel, but am content to be accused of a good-natured error and to hope with Origen[3] that the Devil himself may, at last, be saved. For which reason, in this poem he is neither brought to set his house in order nor to dispose of his person afterwards as he in wisdom shall think fit.[4] God is infinitely merciful, and his vicegerent[5] is only not so because he is not infinite.

The true end of satire is the amendment of vices by correction. And he who writes honestly is no more an enemy to the offender than the physician to the patient, when he prescribes harsh remedies to an inveterate disease; for those are only in order to prevent the surgeon's work of an *ense rescindendum*,[6] which I wish not to my very enemies. To conclude all, if the body politic have any analogy to the natural, in my weak judgment, an Act of Oblivion were as necessary in a hot, distempered state as an opiate would be in a raging fever.

Absalom and Achitophel: A Poem

In pious times, ere priestcraft did begin,
Before polygamy was made a sin;[7]
When man on many multiplied his kind,
Ere one to one was cursedly confined;
5   When Nature prompted, and no law denied
Promiscuous use of concubine and bride;
Then Israel's monarch, after Heaven's own heart,
His vigorous warmth did variously impart
To wives and slaves; and, wide as his command,
10   Scattered his Maker's image through the land.
Michal,[8] of royal blood, the crown did wear,
A soil ungrateful to the tiller's care:
Not so the rest, for several mothers bore
To godlike David several sons before.
15   But since like slaves his bed they did ascend,
No true succession could their seed attend.[9]
Of all this numerous progeny was none
So beautiful, so brave as Absolon:
Whether, inspired by some diviner lust,
20   His father got° him with a greater gust,°   *begot/pleasure*
Or that his conscious destiny made way
By manly beauty to imperial sway.

---

2. Reconciliation.
3. An early Christian theologian.
4. Dryden insinuatingly echoes the biblical account of Achitophel's disappointment and suicide (2 Samuel 23).
5. The king.
6. "Something to be cut out" in order to prevent infection of the whole organism. Dryden next suggests that an "Act of Oblivion" forgiving the rebels, like the one Charles II enacted at his Restoration, might constitute a gentler remedy.

7. "Priestcraft" is "religious fraud" (Johnson's *Dictionary*); Dryden mimics the anti-Catholicism of the Whigs, while insinuating that monogamy is an unnatural restriction imposed by power-hungry priests.
8. Daughter of David's predecessor King Saul; here she represents Charles's childless wife, Catherine of Braganza.
9. Their offspring could not succeed to the throne because of their illegitimacy.

Early in foreign fields he won renown,
With kings and states allied to Israel's crown:
25   In peace the thoughts of war he could remove,
And seemed as he were only born for love.
Whate'er he did was done with so much ease,
In him alone 'twas natural to please.
His motions all accompanied with grace;
30   And paradise was opened in his face.
With secret joy indulgent David viewed
His youthful image in his son renewed:
To all his wishes nothing he denied,
And made the charming Annabel[1] his bride.
35   What faults he had (for who from faults is free?)
His father could not, or he would not see.
Some warm excesses, which the law forbore,
Were construed youth that purged by boiling o'er:
And Amnon's murder,[2] by a specious name,
40   Was called a just revenge for injured fame.
Thus praised and loved the noble youth remained,
While David, undisturbed, in Sion[3] reigned.
But life can never be sincerely blest:
Heaven punishes the bad, and proves° the best.   *tests*
45   The Jews,[4] a headstrong, moody, murmuring race,
As ever tried th' extent and stretch of grace;
God's pampered people whom, debauched with ease,
No king could govern, nor no God could please
(Gods they had tried of every shape and size
50   That god-smiths could produce, or priests devise);
These Adam-wits, too fortunately free,
Began to dream they wanted° liberty;   *lacked, desired*
And when no rule, no precedent was found
Of men by laws less circumscribed and bound,
55   They led their wild desires to woods and caves,
And thought that all but savages were slaves.
They who when Saul was dead, without a blow,
Made foolish Ishbosheth[5] the crown forgo;
Who banished David did from Hebron bring,[6]
60   And with a general shout proclaimed him King:
Those very Jews, who, at their very best,
Their humor more than loyalty expressed,
Now wondered why so long they had obeyed
An idol monarch which their hands had made;
65   Thought they might ruin him they could create,
Or melt him to that golden calf, a state.
But these were random bolts; no formed design,

---

1. Anne, Countess of Buccleuch.
2. In 2 Samuel 8, Amnon rapes Absalom's half sister, and Absalom orders his murder; the correspondence with events in Monmouth's life is uncertain.
3. Jerusalem (hence, London).
4. The English.

5. Ishbosheth briefly succeeded his father Saul; correspondingly, Richard Cromwell was Protector for a few months after the death of his father, Oliver.
6. David ruled in Hebron seven years before becoming king of Israel. Charles had been crowned in Scotland in 1651.

Nor interest made the factious crowd to join:
The sober part of Israel, free from stain,
70 Well knew the value of a peaceful reign:
And, looking backward with a wise afright,
Saw seams of wounds, dishonest to the sight;
In contemplation of whose ugly scars
They cursed the memory of Civil Wars.
75 The moderate sort of men, thus qualified,
Inclined the balance to the better side:
And David's mildness managed it so well,
The bad found no occasion to rebel.
But when to sin our biased nature leans,
80 The careful Devil is still° at hand with means;   *always*
And providently pimps for ill desires:
The Good Old Cause⁷ revived, a Plot requires.
Plots, true or false, are necessary things,
To raise up commonwealths and ruin kings.
85   Th' inhabitants of old Jerusalem
Were Jebusites:⁸ the town so called from them;
And theirs the native right—
But when the chosen people grew more strong,
The rightful cause at length became the wrong:
90 And every loss the men of Jebus bore,
They still were thought God's enemies the more.
Thus, worn and weakened, well or ill content,
Submit they must to David's government:
Impoverished, and deprived of all command,
95 Their taxes doubled as they lost their land,
And, what was harder yet to flesh and blood,
Their gods disgraced, and burnt like common wood.⁹
This set the heathen priesthood in a flame;
For priests of all religions are the same:
100 Of whatsoe'er descent their godhead be,
Stock, stone, or other homely pedigree,
In his defense his servants are as bold
As if he had been born of beaten gold.
The Jewish rabbins,¹ though their enemies,
105 In this conclude them honest men and wise:
For 'twas their duty, all the learned think,
T' espouse his cause by whom they eat and drink.
From hence began that Plot,² the nation's curse,
Bad in itself, but represented worse:
110 Raised in extremes, and in extremes decried;
With oaths affirmed, with dying vows denied:
Not weighed or winnowed by the multitude,
But swallowed in the mass, unchewed and crude.
Some truth there was, but dashed and brewed with lies,

---

7. Popular name for the Cromwellian opposition to the
monarchy.
8. Jebusites inhabited Jerusalem before the Israelites;
here, they represent the Catholics.

9. Dryden alludes to a variety of anti-Catholic penal laws.
1. Anglican clergy.
2. The Popish Plot.

115 To please the fools, and puzzle all the wise.
Succeeding times did equal folly call
Believing nothing, or believing all.
Th' Egyptian rites the Jebusites embraced,
Where gods were recommended by their taste.[3]
120 Such savory deities must needs be good,
As served at once for worship and for food.
By force they could not introduce these gods,
For ten to one[4] in former days was odds.
So fraud was used (the sacrificer's trade):
125 Fools are more hard to conquer than persuade.
Their busy teachers mingled with the Jews,
And raked, for converts, even the court and stews:°   *brothels*
Which Hebrew priests the more unkindly took,
Because the fleece[5] accompanies the flock.
130 Some thought they God's anointed[6] meant to slay
By guns, invented since full many a day:[7]
Our author swears it not; but who can know
How far the Devil and Jebusites may go?
This Plot, which failed for want of common sense,
135 Had yet a deep and dangerous consequence:
For, as when raging fevers boil the blood,
The standing lake soon floats into a flood,
And every hostile humor,[8] which before
Slept quiet in its channels, bubbles o'er:
140 So several factions from this first ferment
Work up to foam, and threat the government.
Some by their friends, more by themselves thought wise,
Opposed the power to which they could not rise.
Some had in courts been great, and thrown from thence,
145 Like fiends were hardened in impenitence.
Some, by their monarch's fatal mercy, grown,
From pardoned rebels, kinsmen to the throne,
Were raised in power and public office high:
Strong bands, if bands ungrateful men could tie.
150   Of these the false Achitophel[9] was first:
A name to all succeeding ages cursed:
For close° designs and crooked counsels fit;   *secret*
Sagacious, bold, and turbulent of wit:
Restless, unfixed in principles and place;
155 In power unpleased, impatient of disgrace:
A fiery soul, which working out its way, ⎫
Fretted the pygmy body to decay: ⎬
And o'er-informed the tenement of clay.[1] ⎭
A daring pilot in extremity;

---

3. Here, and in the lines following, Dryden mocks the Catholic belief in transubstantiation.
4. Protestants to Catholics.
5. Tithe, paid by the "flock" (the parishioners).
6. The king.
7. Long since; Dryden playfully acknowledges this anachronism.

8. Bodily fluid, thought to determine temperament.
9. David's counselor, who encourages Absalom to rebel against his father; here representing Anthony Ashley Cooper, first Earl of Shaftesbury, counselor to both Cromwell and Charles II.
1. The body; Dryden contrasts Shaftesbury's large ambition with his small and sickly body.

160 Pleased with the danger, when the waves went high
     He sought the storms; but for a calm unfit,
     Would steer too nigh the sands, to boast his wit.
     Great wits are sure to madness near allied;
     And thin partitions do their bounds divide:
165 Else why should he, with wealth and honor blessed,
     Refuse his age² the needful hours of rest?
     Punish a body which he could not please;
     Bankrupt of life, yet prodigal of ease?
     And all to leave what with his toil he won,
170 To that unfeathered, two-legged thing, a son:
     Got while his soul did huddled notions try;
     And born a shapeless lump, like anarchy.
     In friendship false, implacable in hate:
     Resolved to ruin or to rule the state.
175 To compass this the triple bond³ he broke,
     The pillars of the public safety shook,   }
     And fitted Israel for a foreign yoke.
     Then, seized with fear, yet still affecting° fame,   *desiring*
     Usurped a patriot's all-atoning name.⁴
180 So easy still it proves in factious times,
     With public zeal to cancel private crimes:
     How safe is treason, and how sacred ill,
     Where none can sin against the people's will:
     Where crowds can wink,⁵ and no offense be known,
185 Since in another's guilt they find their own.
     Yet fame deserved no enemy can grudge;
     The statesman we abhor, but praise the judge.
     In Israel's courts ne'er sat an Abbethdin⁶
     With more discerning eyes, or hands more clean:
190 Unbribed, unsought, the wretched to redress,
     Swift of dispatch, and easy of access.
     Oh, had he been content to serve the crown,
     With virtues only proper to the gown;
     Or had the rankness of the soil been freed
195 From cockle,° that oppressed the noble seed: *weeds*
     David for him his tuneful harp had strung,
     And heaven had wanted one immortal song.⁷
     But wild ambition loves to slide, not stand,
     And fortune's ice prefers to virtue's land:
200 Achitophel, grown weary to possess°   *of possessing*
     A lawful fame and lazy happiness,
     Disdained the golden fruit to gather free,
     And lent the crowd his arm to shake the tree.
     Now, manifest° of crimes contrived long since,   *clearly guilty*
205 He stood at bold defiance with his prince:
     Held up the buckler° of the people's cause   *shield*

2. Shaftesbury was 60 in 1681.
3. England's 1668 alliance with Sweden and Holland
(against France).
4. Name that excuses anything.

5. Turn a blind eye.
6. Chief justice of the Jewish supreme court.
7. David would have composed one psalm fewer because
he would be employed in writing praise of Achitophel.

Against the crown; and skulked behind the laws.
The wished occasion of the Plot he takes,
Some circumstances finds, but more he makes;
210   By buzzing emissaries fills the ears
Of list'ning crowds with jealousies and fears
Of arbitrary counsels brought to light,
And proves the King himself a Jebusite:
Weak arguments! which yet he knew full well
215   Were strong with people easy to rebel.
For, governed by the moon, the giddy Jews
Tread the same track when she the prime renews;[8]
And once in twenty years, their scribes record,
By natural instinct they change their lord.
220   Achitophel still wants a chief, and none
Was found so fit as warlike Absolon:
Not that he wished his greatness to create
(For politicians neither love nor hate),
But for he knew his title not allowed,
225   Would keep him still depending on the crowd,
That kingly power, thus ebbing out, might be
Drawn to the dregs of a democracy.[9]
Him he attempts with studied arts to please,
And sheds his venom in such words as these.
230   "Auspicious Prince! at whose nativity
Some royal planet ruled the southern sky;
Thy longing country's darling and desire;
Their cloudy pillar, and their guardian fire:
Their second Moses, whose extended wand
235   Divides the seas and shows the promised land:[1]
Whose dawning day, in every distant age,
Has exercised the sacred prophet's rage:
The people's prayer, the glad diviners' theme,
The young men's vision, and the old men's dream!
240   Thee, savior, thee, the nation's vows confess,
And, never satisfied with seeing, bless:
Swift, unbespoken pomps° thy steps proclaim,   *unsought honors*
And stammering babes are taught to lisp thy name.
How long wilt thou the general joy detain,
245   Starve and defraud the people of thy reign?
Content ingloriously to pass thy days
Like one of virtue's fools that feeds on praise;
Till thy fresh glories, which now shine so bright,
Grow stale and tarnish with our daily sight.
250   Believe me, royal youth, thy fruit must be
Or° gathered ripe, or rot upon the tree.   *either*
Heav'n has to all allotted, soon or late,
Some lucky revolution of their fate:

---

8. A lunar cycle lasts about 20 years; Dryden alludes to the constitutional crises of 1640, 1660, and 1680.
9. Like "commonwealth" and "state," a pejorative term used to suggest a government of mob rule.

1. On the way to Canaan, God's "promised land," Moses led the Israelites across the Red Sea and through the desert; they followed a pillar of cloud by day and a pillar of fire by night.

Whose motions, if we watch and guide with skill
255 (For human good depends on human will),
Our Fortune rolls as from a smooth descent,
And from the first impression takes the bent:
But, if unseized, she glides away like wind,
And leaves repenting folly far behind.[2]
260 Now, now she meets you with a glorious prize,
And spreads her locks before her as she flies.
Had thus old David, from whose loins you spring,
Not dared, when Fortune called him, to be King,
At Gath[3] an exile he might still remain,
265 And heaven's anointing oil had been in vain.
Let his successful youth your hopes engage,
But shun the example of declining age:
Behold him setting in his western skies,
The shadows length'ning as the vapors rise.
270 He is not now as when on Jordan's sand
The joyful people thronged to see him land,
Cov'ring the beach, and black'ning all the strand:[4]
But, like the Prince of Angels[5] from his height,
Comes tumbling downward with diminished light;
275 Betrayed by one poor plot to public scorn
(Our only blessing since his curst return),
Those heaps of people which one sheaf did bind,
Blown off and scattered by a puff of wind.
What strength can he to your designs oppose,
280 Naked of friends, and round beset with foes?
If Pharaoh's doubtful succor he should use,[6]
A foreign aid would more incense the Jews:
Proud Egypt would dissembled friendship bring,
Foment the war, but not support the King:
285 Nor would the royal party e'er unite
With Pharaoh's arms t' assist the Jebusite;
Or if they should, their interest soon would break,
And with such odious aid make David weak.
All sorts of men by my successful arts,
290 Abhorring kings, estrange their altered hearts
From David's rule; and 'tis the general cry,
'Religion, Commonwealth, and Liberty.'[7]
If you, as champion of the public good,
Add to their arms a chief of royal blood,
295 What may not Israel hope, and what applause
Might such a general gain by such a cause?
Not barren praise alone, that gaudy flower,
Fair only to the sight, but solid power:
And nobler is a limited command,

---

2. Fortune, represented as a woman with streaming hair, needs to be grasped at the first opportunity.
3. Brussels, where Charles spent the last phase of his exile.
4. Dryden refers to Charles's triumphant landing at Dover in May of 1660.

5. Lucifer (light-bearer) rebelled against God and was cast out from heaven.
6. I.e., if Charles should turn for assistance to Louis XIV, Catholic king of France.
7. A slogan of the Good Old Cause.

300	Giv'n by the love of all your native land,
	Than a successive° title, long and dark,	*inherited*
	Drawn from the moldy rolls of Noah's ark."
	What cannot praise effect in mighty minds,
	When flattery soothes, and when ambition blinds!
305	Desire of power, on earth a vicious weed,
	Yet, sprung from high, is of celestial seed:
	In God 'tis glory, and when men aspire,
	'Tis but a spark too much of heavenly fire.
	Th' ambitious youth, too covetous of fame,
310	Too full of angel's metal[8] in his frame,
	Unwarily was led from virtue's ways,
	Made drunk with honor, and debauched with praise.
	Half loath, and half consenting to the ill
	(For royal blood within him struggled still),
315	He thus replied: "And what pretense have I
	To take up arms for public liberty?
	My father governs with unquestioned right;
	The faith's defender, and mankind's delight:
	Good, gracious, just, observant of the laws;
320	And heav'n by wonders has espoused his cause.
	Whom has he wronged in all his peaceful reign?
	Who sues for justice to his throne in vain?
	What millions has he pardoned[9] of his foes,
	Whom just revenge did to his wrath expose!
325	Mild, easy, humble, studious of our good,
	Inclined to mercy, and averse from blood.
	If mildness ill with stubborn Israel suit,
	His crime is God's beloved attribute.
	What could he gain, his people to betray,
330	Or change his right for arbitrary sway?
	Let haughty Pharaoh curse, with such a reign,
	His fruitful Nile, and yoke a servile train.
	If David's rule Jerusalem displease,
	The dog star[1] heats their brains to this disease.
335	Why then should I, encouraging the bad,
	Turn rebel and run popularly mad?
	Were he a tyrant who, by lawless might,
	Oppressed the Jews and raised the Jebusite,
	Well might I mourn; but nature's holy bands
340	Would curb my spirits and restrain my hands:
	The people might assert their liberty,
	But what was right in them were crime in me.
	His favor leaves me nothing to require,
	Prevents my wishes, and outruns desire.
345	What more can I expect while David lives?
	All but his kingly diadem he gives;
	And that—" But there he paused; then sighing said,

8. Dryden puns on "angel" (a coin as well as a supernatural being) and on "metal/mettle" ("spriteliness," "courage"— Johnson's *Dictionary*).

9. By the Act of Oblivion of 1660.
1. Sirius, which presides over the madness-inducing "dog days" of summer.

"Is justly destined for a worthier head.
For when my father from his toils shall rest,
350   And late augment the number of the blest,
His lawful issue shall the throne ascend,
Or the collateral line² where that shall end.
His brother, though oppressed with vulgar spite,³
Yet dauntless and secure of native right,
355   Of every royal virtue stands possessed;
Still dear to all the bravest and the best.
His courage foes, his friends his truth proclaim;
His loyalty the King, the world his fame.
His mercy ev'n th' offending crowd will find,
360   For sure he comes of a forgiving kind.°   family
Why should I then repine at Heaven's decree,
Which gives me no pretense to royalty?
Yet O that Fate, propitiously inclined,
Had raised my birth, or had debased my mind;
365   To my large soul not all her treasure lent,
And then betrayed it to a mean descent.
I find, I find my mounting spirits bold,
And David's part disdains my mother's mold.
Why am I scanted by a niggard⁴ birth?
370   My soul disclaims the kindred of her earth:
And, made for empire, whispers me within,
'Desire of greatness is a godlike sin.'"
        Him staggering so when Hell's dire agent found,⁵
While fainting Virtue scarce maintained her ground,
375   He pours fresh forces in, and thus replies:
        "Th' eternal God, supremely good and wise,
Imparts not these prodigious gifts in vain;
What wonders are reserved to bless your reign?
Against your will, your arguments have shown
380   Such virtue's only given to guide a throne.
Not that your father's mildness I condemn;
But manly force becomes the diadem.
'Tis true, he grants the people all they crave,
And more perhaps than subjects ought to have:
385   For lavish grants suppose° a monarch tame,   suggest
And more his goodness than his wit proclaim.
But when should people strive their bonds to break,
If not when kings are negligent or weak?
Let him give on till he can give no more,
390   The thrifty Sanhedrin⁶ shall keep him poor:
And every shekel° which he can receive,   coin
Shall cost a limb of his prerogative.⁷

2. That which passed through Charles's brother, James.
3. The hostility of the common people.
4. Stingy; i.e., Monmouth's illegitimacy prevents him
from acquiring all he desires.
5. The Miltonic inversion of syntax helps to link Achi-

tophel's speech to the temptation of Eve by Satan in
Book 9 of *Paradise Lost*.
6. The Jewish council; here the English Parliament.
7. Royal privileges (which Parliament sought to limit).

To ply him with new plots shall be my care,
Or plunge him deep in some expensive war;
395   Which when his treasure can no more supply,
He must with the remains of kingship buy.
His faithful friends our jealousies and fears
Call Jebusites, and Pharaoh's pensioners:
Whom, when our fury from his aid has torn,
400   He shall be naked left to public scorn.
The next successor,[8] whom I fear and hate,
My arts have made obnoxious to the state;
Turned all his virtues to his overthrow,
And gained our elders[9] to pronounce a foe.
405   His right, for sums of necessary gold,
Shall first be pawned, and afterwards be sold:
Till time shall ever-wanting David draw,
To pass your doubtful title into law:
If not, the people have a right supreme
410   To make their kings, for kings are made for them.
All empire is no more than power in trust,
Which, when resumed, can be no longer just.
Succession, for the general good designed,
In its own wrong a nation cannot bind:
415   If altering that the people can relieve,
Better one suffer than a nation grieve.
The Jews well know their power: ere Saul they chose,
God was their King, and God they durst depose.[1]
Urge now your piety, your filial name,
420   A father's right, and fear of future fame;
The public good, that universal call
To which even Heav'n submitted, answers all.
Nor let his love enchant your generous mind;
'Tis Nature's trick to propagate her kind.
425   Our fond begetters, who would never die,
Love but themselves in their posterity.
Or let his kindness by th' effects be tried,
Or let him lay his vain pretense aside.
God said he loved your father; could he bring
430   A better proof than to anoint him King?
It surely showed he loved the shepherd well,
Who gave so fair a flock as Israel.
Would David have you thought his darling son?
What means he then to alienate° the crown?   give away
435   The name of godly he may blush to bear:
'Tis after God's own heart to cheat his heir.
He to his brother gives supreme command;
To you a legacy of barren land,[2]

8. James, Duke of York.
9. Shaftesbury's supporters, who included members of
both the gentry and the aristocracy.
1. The prophet Samuel warned the Israelites that in

choosing a king they would displace their true king, God
(1 Samuel 8).
2. In 1678 Charles had promoted James and in the following year banished Monmouth.

Perhaps th' old harp on which he thrums his lays,[3]
440   Or some dull Hebrew ballad in your praise.
Then the next heir, a prince severe and wise,
Already looks on you with jealous eyes;
Sees through the thin disguises of your arts,
And marks your progress in the people's hearts.
445   Though now his mighty soul its grief contains,
He meditates revenge who least complains;
And like a lion, slumbering in the way,
Or sleep dissembling, while he waits his prey,
His fearless foes within his distance draws,
450   Constrains his roaring, and contracts his paws;
Till at the last, his time for fury found,
He shoots with sudden vengeance from the ground:
The prostrate vulgar passes o'er and spares,
But with a lordly rage his hunters tears.
455   Your case no tame expedients will afford;
Resolve on death, or conquest by the sword,
Which for no less a stake than life you draw;
And self-defense is nature's eldest law.
Leave the warm people no considering time,
460   For then rebellion may be thought a crime.
Prevail° yourself of what occasion gives,   *avail*
But try your title while your father lives:
And that your arms may have a fair pretense,
Proclaim you take them in the King's defense,
465   Whose sacred life each minute would expose
To plots from seeming friends and secret foes.
And who can sound the depth of David's soul?
Perhaps his fear his kindness may control.
He fears his brother, though he loves his son,
470   For plighted vows too late to be undone.
If so, by force he wishes to be gained,
Like women's lechery, to seem constrained:
Doubt not, but when he most affects the frown,
Commit a pleasing rape upon the crown.
475   Secure his person to secure your cause;
They who possess the prince, possess the laws."
      He said, and this advice above the rest,
With Absalom's mild nature suited best;
Unblamed of° life (ambition set aside),   *blameless in*
480   Not stained with cruelty, nor puffed with pride;
How happy had he been, if destiny
Had higher placed his birth, or not so high!
His kingly virtues might have claimed a throne,
And blessed all other countries but his own:
485   But charming greatness, since so few refuse,
'Tis juster to lament him than accuse.
Strong were his hopes a rival to remove,

---

3. David was said to have composed the Psalms.

With blandishments to gain the public love;
To head the faction while their zeal was hot,
490   And popularly prosecute the Plot.
To farther this, Achitophel unites
The malcontents of all the Israelites;
Whose differing parties he could wisely join,
For several ends, to serve the same design:
495   The best, and of the princes some were such,
Who thought the power of monarchy too much:
Mistaken men, and patriots in their hearts;
Not wicked, but seduced by impious arts.
By these the springs of property were bent,
500   And wound so high they cracked the government.
The next for interest sought t' embroil the state,
To sell their duty at a dearer rate;
And make their Jewish markets of the throne,
Pretending public good, to serve their own.
505   Others thought kings an useless heavy load,
Who cost too much, and did too little good.
These were for laying honest David by,
On principles of pure good husbandry.°   *economy*
With them joined all th' haranguers of the throng,
510   That thought to get preferment by the tongue.
Who follow next a double danger bring,
Not only hating David, but the King;
The Solymaean rout,[4] well versed of old
In godly faction, and in treason bold;
515   Cowering and quaking at a conqueror's sword,
But lofty° to a lawful prince restored;   *arrogant*
Saw with disdain an ethnic[5] plot begun,
And scorned by Jebusites to be outdone.
Hot Levites[6] headed these; who, pulled before
520   From th' ark, which in the judges' days they bore,[7]
Resumed their cant, and with a zealous cry
Pursued their old beloved theocracy:[8]
Where Sanhedrin and priest enslaved the nation,
And justified their spoils by inspiration;[9]
525   For who so fit for reign as Aaron's race,[1]
If once dominion they could found in grace?
These led the pack; though not of surest scent,
Yet deepest-mouthed against the government.
A numerous host of dreaming saints succeed;
530   Of the true old enthusiastic[2] breed:
'Gainst form and order they their power employ,

---

4. Solymas was another name for Jerusalem, hence, "the London mob."
5. Here, Catholic.
6. Dissenting clergymen.
7. The 1662 Act of Uniformity deprived Presbyterian clergy of their livings which they had acquired during the commonwealth (the judges' days, when they bore the ark).

8. I.e., sought to restore the commonwealth.
9. Members of dissenting sects sometimes claimed to be inspired directly by God.
1. Priests (who, in Jewish law, had to be descendants of Moses's brother Aaron).
2. A pejorative term, applied to those who claimed special inspiration.

Nothing to build and all things to destroy.
But far more numerous was the herd of such
Who think too little, and who talk too much.
535 These out of mere instinct, they knew not why,
Adored their fathers' God and property:
And, by the same blind benefit of fate,
The Devil and the Jebusite did hate:
Born to be saved, even in their own despite,°   *despite themselves*
540 Because they could not help believing right.
Such were the tools, but a whole Hydra[3] more
Remains, of sprouting heads too long to score.
Some of their chiefs were princes of the land:
In the first rank of these did Zimri[4] stand:
545 A man so various, that he seemed to be
Not one, but all mankind's epitome.
Stiff in opinions, always in the wrong;
Was everything by starts, and nothing long:
But, in the course of one revolving moon,
550 Was chemist, fiddler, statesman, and buffoon:
Then all for women, painting, rhyming, drinking;
Besides ten thousand freaks° that died in thinking.   *whims*
Blest madman, who could every hour employ,
With something new to wish, or to enjoy!
555 Railing° and praising were his usual themes;   *criticizing*
And both (to show his judgment) in extremes:
So over-violent, or over-civil,
That every man, with him, was god or devil.
In squand'ring wealth was his peculiar art:
560 Nothing went unrewarded but desert.°   *true worth*
Beggared by fools, whom still he found° too late: *found out*
He had his jest, and they had his estate.
He laughed himself from court, then sought relief
By forming parties, but could ne'er be chief:
565 For, spite of him, the weight of business fell
On Absalom and wise Achitophel:
Thus, wicked but in will, of means bereft,
He left not faction, but of that was left.
    Titles and names 'twere tedious to rehearse
570 Of lords below the dignity of verse.
Wits, warriors, commonwealthsmen, were the best:
Kind husbands and mere nobles all the rest.
And therefore, in the name of dullness, be
The well-hung Balaam[5] and cold Caleb free.

---

3. Many-headed monster, who would sprout new heads
every time one was cut off.
4. An Old Testament conspirator and regicide (1 Kings
16. 9–20); here, George Villiers, Second Duke of Buckingham, a prominent Whig. He had satirized the playwright Dryden in *The Rehearsal* (1671).
5. Balaam was a prophet who first resisted and then
accepted God's will (Numbers 22–24); here, he probably
represents Theophilus Hastings, Earl of Huntingdon, who

initially supported Shaftesbury but was subsequently forgiven by Charles. *Well-hung:* Eloquent, or sexually
impressive ("Lord Huntingdon," wrote one of the poem's
early readers in a marginal inscription, "is said to have a
swinging p——"). Caleb (a spy in Numbers 13) has been
identified as either Lord Grey, whose wife was reputedly
Monmouth's mistress, or Arthur Capel, an efficient
administrator and ally of Shaftesbury.

575 And canting Nadab[6] let oblivion damn,
Who made new porridge for the paschal lamb.[7]
Let friendship's holy band some names assure:
Some their own worth, and some let scorn secure.
Nor shall the rascal rabble here have place,
580 Whom kings no titles gave, and God no grace:
Not bull-faced Jonas,[8] who could statutes draw
To mean rebellion, and make treason law.
But he, though bad, is followed by a worse,
The wretch who heaven's anointed dared to curse:
585 Shimei,[9] whose youth did early promise bring
Of zeal to God, and hatred to his King;
Did wisely from expensive sins refrain,
And never broke the Sabbath, but for gain:
Nor ever was he known an oath to vent,
590 Or curse, unless against the government.
Thus heaping wealth by the most ready way
Among the Jews, which was to cheat and pray;
The city, to reward his pious hate
Against his master, chose him magistrate:
595 His hand a vare° of justice did uphold;   *staff*
His neck was loaded with a chain of gold.
During his office, treason was no crime;
The sons of Belial[1] had a glorious time:
For Shimei, though not prodigal of pelf,[2]
600 Yet loved his wicked neighbor as himself:
When two or three were gathered to declaim[3] ⎤
Against the monarch of Jerusalem,   ⎬
Shimei was always in the midst of them: ⎦
And, if they cursed the King when he was by,
605 Would rather curse than break good company.
If any durst his factious friends accuse,
He packed a jury of dissenting Jews,
Whose fellow-feeling in the godly cause
Would free the suff'ring saint from human laws.
610 For laws are only made to punish those
Who serve the King, and to protect his foes.
If any leisure time he had from power
(Because 'tis sin to misemploy an hour),
His business was, by writing, to persuade
615 That kings were useless, and a clog to trade:
And that his noble style he might refine,

6. The priest Nadab tries to institute improper rites of worship, and is slain by God (Leviticus 10); probably William, Lord Howard of Escrick, a dissenting preacher.
7. Howard was said to have celebrated communion (the commemoration of Christ's sacrifice as "paschal lamb") not with bread and wine but with ale and roasted apples—a concoction known as "lamb's wool." Dissenters such as Howard referred disparagingly to the Anglican Book of Common Prayer as "porridge."
8. Sir William Jones, attorney general and fierce prosecu-

tor of alleged Popish plotters.
9. Shimei cursed David as he fled Absalom's rebellion. Here, he is Slingsby Bethel, one of London's sheriffs.
1. Rebellious, debauched men.
2. Free with money.
3. The description of Shimei echoes two of Christ's pronouncements: "Thou shalt love thy neighbor as thyself" (Matthew 22.39); "When two or three are gathered together in my name, there am I in the midst of them" (Matthew 18.20).

No Rechabite[4] more shunned the fumes of wine.
Chaste were his cellars, and his shrieval board[5]
The grossness of a city feast abhorred:
620　His cooks, with long disuse, their trade forgot;
Cool was his kitchen, though his brains were hot.
Such frugal virtue malice may accuse,
But sure 'twas necessary to the Jews:
For towns once burnt[6] such magistrates require
625　As dare not tempt God's providence by fire.
With spiritual food he fed his servants well,
But free from flesh that made the Jews rebel:
And Moses's laws he held in more account,
For forty days of fasting in the mount.[7]
630　To speak the rest, who better are forgot,
Would tire a well-breathed witness of the Plot:
Yet, Corah,[8] thou shalt from oblivion pass;
Erect thyself, thou monumental brass,°　　　　　*shamelessness*
High as the serpent of thy metal made,[9]
635　While nations stand secure beneath thy shade.
What though his birth were base, yet comets rise
From earthy vapors ere they shine in skies.
Prodigious actions may as well be done
By weaver's issue,[1] as by prince's son.
640　This arch-attestor for the public good
By that one deed ennobles all his blood.
Who ever asked the witnesses' high race,
Whose oath with martyrdom did Stephen[2] grace?
Ours was a Levite, and as times went then,
645　His tribe were God Almighty's gentlemen.
Sunk were his eyes, his voice was harsh and loud,
Sure signs he neither choleric° was, nor proud:　　*hot-tempered*
His long chin proved his wit; his saintlike grace
A church vermilion, and a Moses's face;[3]
650　His memory, miraculously great,
Could plots, exceeding man's belief, repeat;
Which therefore cannot be accounted lies,
For human wit could never such devise.
Some future truths are mingled in his book;
655　But where the witness failed, the prophet spoke:
Some things like visionary flights appear;
The spirit caught him up, the Lord knows where,
And gave him his rabbinical degree

---

4. Rechabites drank no wine.
5. Sheriff's hospitality.
6. A reference to the Fire of London (1666).
7. Shimei attempts to justify his frugality by citing the precedent of Moses, who fasted on Mount Sinai before receiving the Ten Commandments.
8. A rebellious Levite; here, Titus Oates, the ambitious informer who did more than anyone to arouse suspicions of a "Popish Plot."

9. Moses set up a brass serpent that saved the Jews from dying of snakebite (Numbers 21).
1. Oates's father was a weaver.
2. The first Christian martyr, sworn against and stoned by false witness (Acts 6–7).
3. After Moses received the tables of the law on Mount Sinai, his face shone with divine illumination; Oates's face, by contrast, is flushed with debauchery.

Unknown to foreign university.[4]
660 His judgment yet his memory did excel;
Which pieced his wondrous evidence so well,
And suited to the temper of the times,
Then groaning under Jebusitic crimes.
Let Israel's foes suspect his heav'nly call,
665 And rashly judge his writ apocryphal;[5]
Our laws for such affronts have forfeits made:
He takes his life, who takes away his trade.
Were I myself in witness Corah's place,
The wretch who did me such a dire disgrace
670 Should whet my memory, though once forgot,
To make him an appendix of my plot.
His zeal to heav'n made him his prince despise,
And load his person with indignities:
But zeal peculiar privilege affords,
675 Indulging latitude to deeds and words;
And Corah might for Agag's murder[6] call,
In terms as coarse as Samuel used to Saul.
What others in his evidence did join
(The best that could be had for love or coin)
680 In Corah's own predicament will fall:
For *witness* is a common name to all.
    Surrounded thus with friends of every sort,
Deluded Absalom forsakes the court:
Impatient of high hopes, urged with renown,
685 And fired with near possession of a crown:
Th' admiring crowd are dazzled with surprise,
And on his goodly person feed their eyes:
His joy concealed, he sets himself to show,
On each side bowing popularly low:
690 His looks, his gestures, and his words he frames,
And with familiar ease repeats their names.
Thus, formed by nature, furnished out with arts,
He glides unfelt into their secret hearts:
Then with a kind compassionating look,
695 And sighs bespeaking pity ere he spoke,
Few words he said, but easy those and fit:
More slow than Hybla° drops, and far more sweet.   *honey*
    "I mourn, my countrymen, your lost estate,
Though far unable to prevent your fate:
700 Behold a banished man, for your dear cause
Exposed a prey to arbitrary laws!
Yet O! that I alone could be undone,
Cut off from empire, and no more a son!

---

4. Oates pretended to hold a doctorate of divinity from the University of Salamanca.
5. Not part of the canon of biblical texts.

6. Oates denounced Lord Stafford, who was then executed, as Samuel denounced Agag, who was murdered by Saul (1 Samuel 15).

Now all your liberties a spoil are made,
705 Egypt and Tyrus° intercept your trade,   *France and Holland*
And Jebusites your sacred rites invade.
My father, whom with reverence yet I name,
Charmed into ease, is careless of his fame:
And bribed with petty sums of foreign gold,
710 Is grown in Bathsheba's[7] embraces old:
Exalts his enemies, his friends destroys,
And all his pow'r against himself employs.
He gives, and let him give, my right away:
But why should he his own, and yours betray?
715 He only, he can make the nation bleed,
And he alone from my revenge is freed.
Take then my tears" (with that he wiped his eyes)
" 'Tis all the aid my present power supplies:
No court informer can these arms accuse,
720 These arms may sons against their fathers use,
And 'tis my wish, the next successor's reign
May make no other Israelite complain."
        Youth, beauty, graceful action seldom fail:
But common interest always will prevail:
725 And pity never ceases to be shown
To him, who makes the people's wrongs his own.
The crowd (that still believe their kings oppress)
With lifted hands their young Messiah bless:
Who now begins his progress to ordain,[8]
730 With chariots, horsemen, and a numerous train:
From east to west his glories he displays:
And, like the sun, the promised land surveys.
Fame runs before him, as the morning star,
And shouts of joy salute him from afar:
735 Each house receives him as a guardian god,
And consecrates the place of his abode:
But hospitable treats did most commend
Wise Issachar,[9] his wealthy western friend.
This moving court, that caught the people's eyes,
740 And seemed but pomp, did other ends disguise:
Achitophel had formed it, with intent
To sound the depths, and fathom, where it went,
The people's hearts; distinguish friends from foes,
And try their strength before they came to blows:
745 Yet all was colored with a smooth pretense
Of specious love, and duty to their prince.
Religion, and redress of grievances,
Two names that always cheat and always please,
Are often urged, and good King David's life
750 Endangered by a brother and a wife.[1]

---

7. Louise de Kéroualle, Duchess of Portsmouth, Charles's French, Catholic mistress.
8. Monmouth traveled through the west of England in 1680, rallying popular support.

9. Thomas Thynne, a wealthy Whig.
1. Both James and Catherine were Catholic and were thought by some to be implicated in Popish plotting.

Thus, in a pageant show, a plot is made,
And peace itself is war in masquerade.
O foolish Israel! never warned by ill,
Still the same bait, and circumvented still!
755 Did ever men forsake their present ease,
In midst of health imagine a disease;
Take pains contingent mischiefs to foresee,
Make heirs for monarchs, and for God decree?
What shall we think! can people give away,
760 Both for themselves and sons, their native sway?
Then they are left defenseless to the sword
Of each unbounded, arbitrary lord:
And laws are vain, by which we right enjoy,
If kings unquestioned can those laws destroy.
765 Yet, if the crowd be judge of fit and just,
And kings are only officers in trust,
Then this resuming cov'nant was declared
When kings were made, or is forever barred:
If those who gave the scepter could not tie
770 By their own deed their own posterity,
How then could Adam bind his future race?
How could his forfeit on mankind take place?
Or how could heavenly justice damn us all,
Who ne'er consented to our father's fall?
775 Then kings are slaves to those whom they command,
And tenants to their people's pleasure stand.
Add, that the pow'r for property² allowed
Is mischievously seated in the crowd:
For who can be secure of private right,
780 If sovereign sway may be dissolved by might?
Nor is the people's judgment always true:
The most may err as grossly as the few,
And faultless kings run down by common cry
For vice, oppression, and for tyranny.
785 What standard is there in a fickle rout,
Which, flowing to the mark,° runs faster out?   high-water mark
Nor only crowds, but Sanhedrins may be
Infected with this public lunacy,
And share the madness of rebellious times,
790 To murder monarchs for imagined crimes.
If they may give and take whene'er they please,
Not kings alone (the Godhead's images),
But government itself at length must fall
To nature's state, where all have right to all.
795 Yet, grant our lords the people kings can make,
What prudent men a settled throne would shake?
For whatsoe'er their sufferings were before,
That change they covet makes them suffer more.

---

2. Political influence derived from ownership of land.

All other errors but disturb a state,
800 But innovation is the blow of fate.
If ancient fabrics nod, and threat to fall,
To patch the flaws, and buttress up the wall,
Thus far 'tis duty; but here fix the mark:
For all beyond it is to touch our ark.[3]
805 To change foundations, cast the frame anew,
Is work for rebels who base ends pursue,
At once divine and human laws control,
And mend the parts by ruin of the whole.
The tampering world is subject to this curse,
810 To physic their disease into a worse.
       Now what relief can righteous David bring?
How fatal 'tis to be too good a king!
Friends he has few, so high the madness grows;
Who dare be such, must be the people's foes:
815 Yet some there were, ev'n in the worst of days;
Some let me name, and naming is to praise.
       In this short file Barzillai[4] first appears;
Barzillai crowned with honor and with years:
Long since, the rising rebels he withstood
820 In regions waste, beyond the Jordan's flood:[5]
Unfortunately brave to buoy the state,
But sinking underneath his master's fate:
In exile with his godlike prince he mourned;
For him he suffered, and with him returned.
825 The court he practised, not the courtier's art:
Large was his wealth, but larger was his heart:
Which well the noblest objects knew to choose,
The fighting warrior, and recording Muse.[6]
His bed could once a fruitful issue boast:
830 Now more than half a father's name is lost:
His eldest hope,[7] with every grace adorned,
By me (so Heaven will have it) always mourned,
And always honored, snatched in manhood's prime
By unequal Fates, and Providence's crime:
835 Yet not before the goal of honor won,
All parts fulfilled of subject and of son;
Swift was the race, but short the time to run.
Oh narrow circle, but of pow'r divine,
Scanted in space, but perfect in thy line!
840 By sea, by land, thy matchless worth was known;
Arms thy delight, and war was all thy own:
Thy force, infused, the fainting Tyrians[8] propped:
And haughty Pharaoh found his fortune stopped.
O ancient honor, O unconquered hand,

3. To touch the ark was to commit sacrilege.
4. James Butler, Duke of Ormonde, loyal to Charles I and II.
5. I.e., in Ireland.
6. I.e., he gave money to support the Stuart cause and was
also a patron to authors.
7. Ormonde's eldest son, who died in 1680.
8. The Dutch, whom Ormonde's son had aided against the French.

845 Whom foes unpunished never could withstand!
But Israel was unworthy of thy name;
Short is the date of all immoderate fame.
It looks as Heaven our ruin had designed,
And durst not trust thy fortune and thy mind.

850 Now, free from earth, thy disencumbered soul
Mounts up, and leaves behind the clouds and starry pole:
From thence thy kindred legions mayst thou bring,
To aid the guardian angel of thy King.
Here stop, my Muse, here cease thy painful flight;

855 No pinions° can pursue immortal height: *wings*
Tell good Barzillai thou canst sing no more,
And tell thy soul she should have fled before;
Or fled she with his life, and left this verse
To hang on her departed patron's hearse?

860 Now take thy steepy flight from heaven, and see
If thou canst find on earth another *he*;
Another *he* would be too hard to find,
See then whom thou canst see not far behind:
Zadock⁹ the priest, whom, shunning power and place,

865 His lowly mind advanced to David's grace:
With him the Sagan¹ of Jerusalem,
Of hospitable soul and noble stem;
Him of the western dome,² whose weighty sense
Flows in fit words and heavenly eloquence.

870 The prophets' sons³ by such example led,
To learning and to loyalty were bred:
For colleges on bounteous kings depend,
And never rebel was to arts a friend.
To these succeed the pillars of the laws,

875 Who best could plead and best can judge a cause.
Next them a train of loyal peers ascend:
Sharp-judging Adriel,⁴ the Muses' friend,
Himself a Muse—in Sanhedrin's debate
True to his prince, but not a slave of state:

880 Whom David's love with honors did adorn,
That from his disobedient son were torn.⁵
Jotham⁶ of piercing wit and pregnant thought,
Indued° by nature, and by learning taught   *endowed*
To move assemblies, who but only tried

885 The worse awhile, then chose the better side;
Nor chose alone, but turned the balance too;
So much the weight of one brave man can do.
Hushai,⁷ the friend of David in distress,

9. William Sancroft, Archbishop of Canterbury.
1. Henry Compton, Bishop of London.
2. John Dolben, Dean of Westminster ("the western dome").
3. Students of the Westminster School.
4. John Sheffield, Earl of Mulgrave, poet and a patron of Dryden.
5. In 1679 Mulgrave received two offices that had previ-

ously belonged to Monmouth.
6. George Savile, Marquis of Halifax, formerly a critic but now a supporter of Charles's policies, was instrumental in defeating the exclusion bill.
7. Laurence Hyde, Earl of Rochester, negotiated several European treaties and became the first Lord of the Treasury.

In public storms of manly steadfastness;
890   By foreign treaties he informed his youth,
And joined experience to his native truth.
His frugal care supplied the wanting throne,
Frugal for that, but bounteous of his own:
'Tis easy conduct when exchequers[8] flow,
895   But hard the task to manage well the low:
For sovereign power is too depressed or high,
When kings are forced to sell, or crowds to buy.
Indulge one labor more, my weary Muse,
For Amiel,[9] who can Amiel's praise refuse?
900   Of ancient race by birth, but nobler yet
In his own worth, and without title great:
The Sanhedrin long time as chief he ruled,
Their reason guided and their passion cooled;
So dexterous was he in the crown's defense,
905   So formed to speak a loyal nation's sense,
That, as their band was Israel's tribes in small,
So fit was he to represent them all.
Now rasher charioteers the seat ascend,
Whose loose careers his steady skill commend:
910   They like th' unequal ruler of the day,[1]
Misguide the seasons and mistake the way;
While he, withdrawn, at their mad labor smiles,
And safe enjoys the sabbath of his toils.
      These were the chief, a small but faithful band ⎤
915   Of worthies, in the breach who dared to stand, ⎬
And tempt th' united fury of the land. ⎦
With grief they viewed such powerful engines bent,
To batter down the lawful government:
A numerous faction with pretended frights,
920   In Sanhedrins to plume° the regal rights: *pluck away*
The true successor from the court removed:[2]
The Plot by hireling witnesses improved.
These ills they saw, and as their duty bound,
They showed the King the danger of the wound:
925   That no concessions from the throne would please,
But lenitives fomented[3] the disease:
That Absalom, ambitious of the crown,
Was made the lure to draw the people down:
That false Achitophel's pernicious hate
930   Had turned the Plot to ruin Church and State:
The council violent, the rabble worse:
That Shimei taught Jerusalem to curse.
      With all these loads of injuries oppressed,

---

8. Treasurers/treasuries.
9. Edward Seymour, speaker of the Commons (1673–1678) and treasurer of the Navy (1673–1681); opponent of exclusion.
1. Phaëton, who drove (with disastrous results) the chariot of the sun that belonged to his father, Apollo.

2. In 1679, at the height of the furor over the Popish Plot, Charles II had ordered his brother to withdraw to the Continent, where James remained for six months.
3. I.e., soothing measures/medicines only encouraged the disease.

And long revolving, in his careful breast,
935 Th' event of things, at last, his patience tired,
Thus from his royal throne by Heav'n inspired,
The godlike David spoke: with awful fear
His train their Maker in their master hear.
　　"Thus long have I, by native mercy swayed,
940 My wrongs dissembled, my revenge delayed:
So willing to forgive th' offending age,
So much the father did the king assuage.
But now so far my clemency they slight,
Th' offenders question my forgiving right.
945 That one was made for many, they contend:
But 'tis to rule, for that's a monarch's end.
They call my tenderness of blood my fear:
Though manly tempers can the longest bear.
Yet, since they will divert my native course,
950 'Tis time to show I am not good by force.
Those heaped affronts that haughty subjects bring,
Are burdens for a camel, not a king:
Kings are the public pillars of the state,
Born to sustain and prop the nation's weight:
955 If my young Samson[4] will pretend a call
To shake the column, let him share the fall:
But O that yet he would repent and live!
How easy 'tis for parents to forgive!
With how few tears a pardon might be won
960 From Nature, pleading for a darling son!
Poor pitied youth, by my paternal care
Raised up to all the height his frame could bear:
Had God ordained his fate for empire born,
He would have given his soul another turn:
965 Gulled with a patriot's name, whose modern sense
Is one that would by law supplant his prince:
The people's brave,° the politicians' tool;　　　　　*bully*
Never was patriot yet, but was a fool.
Whence comes it that religion and the laws
970 Should more be Absalom's than David's cause?
His old instructor,[5] ere he lost his place,
Was never thought indued with so much grace.
Good heavens, how faction can a patriot paint!
My rebel ever proves my people's saint:
975 Would they impose an heir upon the throne?
Let Sanhedrins be taught to give their own.
A king's at least a part of government,
And mine as requisite as their consent:
Without my leave a future king to choose,
980 Infers a right the present to depose:
True, they petition me t' approve their choice,

4. Monmouth, who threatens, Samson-like, to bring　　5. Achitophel/Shaftesbury.
down the nation.

But Esau's hands suit ill with Jacob's voice.[6]
My pious subjects for my safety pray,
Which to secure they take my power away.
985 From plots and treasons Heaven preserve my years,
But save me most from my petitioners.
Unsatiate as the barren womb or grave;
God cannot grant so much as they can crave.
What then is left but with a jealous eye
990 To guard the small remains of royalty?
The law shall still direct my peaceful sway,
And the same law teach rebels to obey:
Votes shall no more established pow'r control,
Such votes as make a part exceed the whole:
995 No groundless clamors shall my friends remove,
Nor crowds have power to punish ere they prove:
For gods, and godlike kings, their care express,
Still to defend their servants in distress.
O that my power to saving were confined:
1000 Why am I forced, like Heaven, against my mind, }
To make examples of another kind?
Must I at length the sword of justice draw?
O cursed effects of necessary law!
How ill my fear they by my mercy scan;[7]
1005 Beware the fury of a patient man.
Law they require, let law then show her face;
They could not be content to look on Grace,
Her hinder parts, but with a daring eye
To tempt the terror of her front, and die.
1010 By their own arts, 'tis righteously decreed,
Those dire artificers of death shall bleed.
Against themselves their witnesses will swear,
Till viper-like their mother Plot they tear:
And suck for nutriment that bloody gore
1015 Which was their principle of life before.
Their Belial with their Belzebub[8] will fight;
Thus on my foes, my foes shall do me right:
Nor doubt th' event: for factious crowds engage,
In their first onset, all their brutal rage;
1020 Then let 'em take an unresisted course,
Retire and traverse, and delude their force:
But when they stand all breathless, urge the fight,
And rise upon 'em with redoubled might:
For lawful pow'r is still superior found,
1025 When long driven back, at length it stands the ground."
He said. Th' Almighty, nodding, gave consent;

6. In Genesis 27, Esau is a hunter and a "hairy man"; his younger brother Jacob steals his birthright by impersonating him before their blind father Isaac, covering his own smooth hands with rough goatskin. David/Charles here accuses his opposition of Esau-like violence and Jacob-like deception.
7. How wrong ("ill") they are to see ("scan") fear in my mercy.
8. Both devils.

And peals of thunder shook the firmament.
Henceforth a series of new time began,
The mighty years in long procession ran:

1030   Once more the godlike David was restored,
And willing nations knew their lawful lord.

1681   1681

COMPANION READING

Charles II: His Majesty's Declaration to all His Loving Subjects,
Touching the Causes and Reasons that Moved Him
to Dissolve the Two Last Parliaments[1]

It was with exceeding great trouble that We were brought to the dissolving of the two last Parliaments, without more benefit to Our people by the calling of them. But having done Our part in giving so many opportunities of providing for their good, it cannot be justly imputed to Us that the success hath not answered Our expectation.

We cannot at this time but take notice of the particular causes of Our dissatisfaction, which at the beginning of the last Parliament we did recommend to their care to avoid, and expected We should have no new cause to remember them.

We opened the last Parliament, which was held at Westminster, with as gracious expressions of Our readiness to satisfy the desires of Our good subjects and to secure them against all their just fears, as the weighty consideration, either of preserving the established religion, and the liberty and property of Our subjects at home, or of supporting Our neighbors and allies abroad, could fill Our heart with, or possibly require from Us.

And We do solemnly declare that We did intend, as far as would have consisted with the very being of the government, to have complied with anything that could have been proposed to Us to accomplish those ends.

We asked of them the supporting the alliances We had made for the preservation of the general peace in Christendom;[2] We recommended to them the further examination of the Plot;[3] We desired their advice and assistance concerning the preservation of Tangier;[4] We offered to concur in any remedies that could be proposed for the security of the Protestant religion, that might consist with preserving the succession

---

1. In the wake of the "Popish Plot," the Whigs tried repeatedly to pass an exclusion bill barring the Catholic Duke of York from succeeding to the throne. In response, the increasingly exasperated Charles dissolved the Parliament twice in quick succession: On 18 January 1681, he dismissed the Commons at Westminster and called for a new Parliament at Oxford; on 28 March he abruptly dissolved this second Parliament after only seven days of bitterly contentious sessions. By his peremptory actions, the king had laid himself open to charges of arbitrary and despotic rule. In *His Majesty's Declaration*, Charles tried to lay these charges to rest. Recent votes in the House of Commons, he argued, had so encroached upon the king's prerogatives and the country's laws as to endanger the stability of the Restoration and revive the possibility of

civil war; throughout the pamphlet, Charles plays adroitly on his audience's memories of midcentury strife. Read aloud from pulpits throughout the land, this unusually direct statement by the monarch to his subjects made a considerable impression—though not so conclusive an impact as Dryden was willing to imagine in the closing lines of *Absalom and Achitophel*, where the king of Israel's arguments occasionally echo Charles's *Declaration*.
2. Charles had begun to cultivate—and to boast about—a defensive alliance with Spain against France.
3. At the first of the two Parliaments, Charles had consented to the execution of the one of the accused Popish "conspirators."
4. This seaport on the Straits of Gibraltar, claimed by the English, was now under attack by the Moors.

of the Crown in its due and legal course of descent; to all which We met with most unsuitable returns from the House of Commons: addresses, in the nature of remonstrances, rather than of answers; arbitrary orders for taking Our subjects into custody, for matters that had no relation to privileges of Parliament; strange illegal votes, declaring diverse eminent persons to be enemies to the King and Kingdom, without any order or process of law, any hearing of their defense, or any proof so much as offered against them.[5] * * *

[The Parliamentary] Votes, instead of giving Us assistance to support our allies, or enable Us to preserve Tangier, tended rather to disable Us from contributing towards either, by Our own revenue or credit; not only exposing Us to all dangers that might happen either at home, or abroad, but endeavoring to deprive Us of the possibility of supporting the government itself, and to reduce Us to a more helpless condition than the meanest of Our subjects. * * *

These were some of the unwarrantable proceedings of the House of Commons, which were the occasion of Our parting with that Parliament.

Which We had no sooner dissolved, but We caused another to be forthwith assembled at Oxford; at the opening of which, We thought it necessary to give them warning of the errors of the former, in hopes to have prevented the like miscarriages; and We required of them to make the laws of the land their rule, as We did, and do, resolve they shall be Ours. We further added, that what We had formerly and so often declared concerning the succession, We could not depart from. But, to remove all reasonable fears that might arise from the possibility of a Popish successor's coming to the Crown, if means could be found that in such a case the administration of the government might remain in Protestant hands, We were ready to hearken to any expedient by which the religion established might be preserved, and the Monarchy not destroyed.

But contrary to Our offers and expectation, We saw that no expedient would be entertained but that of a total Exclusion, which, We had so often declared, was a point that, in Our own royal judgment, so nearly concerned Us both in honor, justice, and conscience, that We could never consent to it. In short, We cannot, after the sad experience We have had of the late Civil Wars, that murdered Our father of blessed memory and ruined the Monarchy, consent to a law that shall establish another most unnatural war, or at least make it necessary to maintain a standing force for the preserving the government and the peace of the Kingdom.

And We have reason to believe, by what passed in the last Parliament at Westminster, that if We could have been brought to give Our consent to a Bill of Exclusion, the intent was not to rest there, but to pass further, and to attempt some other great and important changes even in present. * * *

But, notwithstanding all this, let not the restless malice of ill men who are laboring to poison Our people, some out of fondness of their old beloved Commonwealth principles, and some out of anger at their being disappointed in the particular designs they had for the accomplishment of their own ambition and greatness, persuade any of Our good subjects that We intend to lay aside the use of Parliaments. For We do still declare that no irregularities in Parliaments shall ever make Us out of love with Parliaments, which We look upon as the best method for healing the distempers of the Kingdom, and the only means to preserve the Monarchy in that due credit and respect which it ought to have both at home and abroad.

---

5. At the first of the two Parliaments, the Whigs had demanded the expulsion of several "eminent persons" who had worked successfully to defeat an exclusion bill.

And for this cause We are resolved, by the blessing of God, to have frequent Parliaments, and, both in and out of Parliament, to use Our utmost endeavors to extirpate Popery, and to redress all the grievances of Our good subjects, and in all things to govern according to the laws of the Kingdom.

And We hope that a little time will so far open the eyes of all Our good subjects, that Our next meeting in Parliament shall perfect all that settlement and peace which shall be found wanting either in Church or State.

To which, as We shall contribute Our utmost endeavors, so We assure Ourself that We shall be assisted therein by the loyalty and good affections of all those who consider the rise and progress of the late troubles and confusions, and desire to preserve their country from a relapse.

And who cannot but remember that Religion, Liberty, and Property were all lost and gone when the Monarchy was shaken off, and could never be revived till that was restored.

Given at Our Court at Whitehall, the eighth day of April 1681.

Mac Flecknoe

In *Mac Flecknoe*, Dryden put on display a literary culture dangerously debased. The poem's title ("Son of Flecknoe") announces a royal succession in the kingdom of bad writing. A literary "father," the priest and minor poet Richard Flecknoe (c.1605–c.1677), anoints as his true heir Thomas Shadwell (1640–1692), a playwright whom Dryden loathed as a tiresome controversialist and an ardent (worse, successful) rival for public favor and aristocratic patronage. Dryden wages his attack in an idiom at once elevated and scandalous, in language whose allegiance alternates (even within a single line) between epic poetry and the privy. Like much libelous and bawdy verse, Dryden's demolitionary masterpiece circulated in manuscript for several years; it was eventually printed in a pirated edition (1682) by a publisher seeking to capitalize on the recent success of *Absalom and Achitophel*. Like that poem, *Mac Flecknoe* plays upon the question of monarchic succession, but stages it in such a way as to implicate bad politics in bad taste. Dryden maps a City of London where foul writing chokes the streets, and dim-witted citizens get—and applaud—the poet-monarchs they deserve.

Mac Flecknoe

All human things are subject to decay,
And, when Fate summons, monarchs must obey.
This Flecknoe found, who, like Augustus, young
Was called to empire,[1] and had governed long:
In prose and verse was owned, without dispute,
Through all the realms of Nonsense, absolute.
This aged prince, now flourishing in peace,
And blest with issue of a large increase,
Worn out with business, did at length debate
To settle the succession of the state:
And, pondering which of all his sons was fit
To reign, and wage immortal war with wit,
Cried, " 'Tis resolved; for Nature pleads that he

5

10

---

1. Augustus became the first Roman emperor at the age of 32.

15 Should only rule, who most resembles me:
Sh—— alone my perfect image bears,
Mature in dullness from his tender years.
Sh—— alone, of all my sons, is he
Who stands confirmed in full stupidity.
The rest to some faint meaning make pretense,
20 But Sh—— never deviates into sense.
Some beams of wit on other souls may fall,
Strike through and make a lucid interval,
But Sh——'s genuine night admits no ray,
His rising fogs prevail upon the day.
25 Besides, his goodly fabric° fills the eye,   large body
And seems designed for thoughtless majesty:
Thoughtless as monarch oaks that shade the plain,
And, spread in solemn state, supinely reign.
Heywood and Shirley were but types of thee,[2]
30 Thou last great prophet of tautology:
Even I, a dunce of more renown than they,
Was sent before but to prepare thy way;
And coarsely clad in Norwich drugget[3] came
To teach the nations in thy greater name.[4]
35 My warbling lute, the lute I whilom° strung   once
When to King John of Portugal I sung,[5]
Was but the prelude to that glorious day
When thou on silver Thames didst cut thy way,
With well-timed oars before the royal barge,
40 Swelled with the pride of thy celestial charge;
And big with hymn, commander of an host,
The like was ne'er in Epsom blankets tossed.[6]
Methinks I see the new Arion[7] sail,
The lute still trembling underneath thy nail.
45 At thy well-sharpened thumb from shore to shore
The treble squeaks for fear, the basses roar:
Echoes from Pissing Alley[8] "Sh——" call,
And "Sh——" they resound from A—— Hall.[9]
About thy boat the little fishes throng,
50 As at the morning toast° that floats along.   sewage
Sometimes as prince of thy harmonious band
Thou wield'st thy papers in thy threshing hand.
St. André's feet[1] ne'er kept more equal time,
Not ev'n the feet of thy own *Psyche*'s rhyme,
55 Though they in number as in sense excel;

2. Thomas Heywood and James Shirley, popular and prolific playwrights from the first half of the 17th century. As "types," they foreshadow or prepare for Shadwell, just as Old Testament figures such as Moses or Isaac were interpreted in Christian theology as forerunners of Jesus.
3. Woolen cloth; Shadwell came from Norwich.
4. Here, Flecknoe is John the Baptist ("coarsely clad" in camel's hair) to Shadwell's Jesus.
5. Flecknoe claimed that, during his travels in Europe, he had been summoned to perform before the king of Portugal.

6. A glance at two of Shadwell's plays: *Epsom Wells* and *The Virtuoso*, in which Sir Samuel Hearty is tossed in a blanket; tossing in a blanket was also a means of inducing childbirth.
7. Greek musician-poet rescued from drowning by music-loving dolphins.
8. West of Temple Bar, it led from the Strand down to the Thames.
9. Unidentified.
1. St. André, a French dancer who choreographed the opera *Psyche* (1675), for which Shadwell wrote the libretto.

So just, so like tautology they fell,
That, pale with envy, Singleton foreswore ⎤
The lute and sword which he in triumph bore, ⎬
And vowed he ne'er would act Villerius[2] more. ⎦
60 Here stopped the good old sire, and wept for joy
In silent raptures of the hopeful boy.
All arguments, but most his plays, persuade,
That for anointed dullness he was made.
     Close to the walls which fair Augusta bind[3]
65 (The fair Augusta much to fears inclined[4]),
An ancient fabric,[5] raised t' inform the sight,
There stood of yore, and Barbican it hight:[6]
A watchtower once, but now, so Fate ordains,
Of all the pile an empty name remains.
70 From its old ruins brothel-houses rise,
Scenes of lewd loves and of polluted joys;
Where their vast courts the mother-strumpets keep
And, undisturbed by watch,° in silence sleep.[7]   police
Near these a nursery[8] erects its head,
75 Where queens[9] are formed and future heroes bred;
Where unfledged actors learn to laugh and cry,
Where infant punks° their tender voices try,   prostitutes
And little Maximins[1] the gods defy.
Great Fletcher never treads in buskins here,
80 Nor greater Jonson dares in socks appear.[2]
But gentle Simkin[3] just reception finds
Amidst this monument of vanished minds:
Pure clinches° the suburbian Muse[4] affords,   puns
And Panton[5] waging harmless war with words.
85 Here Flecknoe, as a place to fame well known,
Ambitiously designed his Sh——'s throne.
For ancient Dekker[6] prophesied long since, ⎤
That in this pile should reign a mighty prince, ⎬
Born for a scourge of wit, and flail of sense: ⎦
90 To whom true dullness should some *Psyches* owe,
But Worlds of *Misers* from his pen should flow;
Humorists and *Hypocrites*[7] it should produce,
Whole Raymond families, and tribes of Bruce.

2. John Singleton, one of the king's musicians; Villerius, a character in William Davenant's opera, *The Siege of Rhodes*.
3. The old wall of the City of London (Augusta).
4. Fears aroused by the Popish Plot.
5. Structure.
6. Was named; the Barbican, a medieval gatehouse, gave its name to a disreputable district of gaming and prostitution; adjoining it was Grub Street, the center of hack journalism.
7. Parodying Abraham Cowley, *Davideis* (1656), "Where their vast court the mother-waters keep, / And undisturbed by moons in silence sleep."
8. A training theater for the two main playhouses.
9. Dryden puns on queen (stage-monarch)/quean (prostitute). During the Restoration, actresses were often thought to moonlight as sexual companions.

1. Maximin is the fulminating protagonist of Dryden's *Tyrannic Love*.
2. John Fletcher and Ben Jonson, major playwrights of the previous generations. The buskin is the symbol of tragedy (Fletcher's forte) and the sock of comedy (Jonson's). Shadwell promoted himself as Jonson's successor in the tradition of "humors" comedy.
3. A clownish character in a series of popular farces.
4. I.e., the muse presiding over the disreputable area outside the City walls.
5. Another farce character.
6. Thomas Dekker (1570?–1632), prolific dramatist whose plays focused on London life.
7. Shadwell was the author of *The Miser* (1672), *The Humorists* (1671), and *The Hypocrite* (1669). Raymond and Bruce appear in *The Humorists* and *The Virtuoso*, respectively.

Now Empress Fame had published the renown
95   Of Sh——'s coronation through the town.
Roused by report of Fame, the nations meet,
From near Bunhill, and distant Watling Street.[8]
No Persian carpets spread th' imperial way,
But scattered limbs of mangled poets lay:
100 From dusty shops neglected authors come,
Martyrs of pies, and relics of the bum.[9]
Much Heywood, Shirley, Ogilby[1] there lay,
But loads of Sh—— almost choked the way.
Bilked stationers for yeomen stood prepared,
105 And H——[2] was captain of the guard.
The hoary prince in majesty appeared,
High on a throne of his own labors reared.
At his right hand our young Ascanius[3] sate,
Rome's other hope, and pillar of the state.
110 His brows thick fogs, instead of glories, grace,
And lambent° dullness played around his face.   *glowing*
As Hannibal did to the altars come,
Sworn by his sire a mortal foe to Rome,[4]
So Sh—— swore, nor should his vow be vain,
115 That he till death true dullness would maintain;
And in his father's right, and realm's defense,
Ne'er to have peace with wit, nor truce with sense.
The king himself the sacred unction[5] made,
As king by office, and as priest by trade:
120 In his sinister° hand, instead of ball,   *left*
He placed a mighty mug of potent ale;
Love's Kingdom[6] to his right he did convey,
At once his scepter and his rule of sway,[7]
Whose righteous lore the prince had practiced young,
125 And from whose loins[8] recorded Psyche sprung.
His temples last with poppies[9] were o'erspread,
That nodding seemed to consecrate his head:
Just at that point of time, if Fame not lie,
On his left hand twelve reverend owls[1] did fly.
130 So Romulus,[2] 'tis sung, by Tiber's brook,
Presage of sway from twice six vultures took.
Th' admiring throng loud acclamations make,
And omens of his future empire take.

---

8. Fame draws her crowd both from cemeteries (like Bunhill Fields) and from mercantile districts (like Watling Street); thus, these devotees of Shadwell include both the dead and the living.

9. Unsold books might be recycled as pie wrappers or as toilet paper; the bones of martyrs were often venerated as relics.

1. John Ogilby, printer, cartographer, and translator (like Dryden) of Virgil.

2. Henry Herringman, a prominent bookseller-publisher; he had published both Shadwell and Dryden.

3. The son of Aeneas, marked for greatness by a heaven-sent flame about his head.

4. According to Livy, Hannibal's father made the young boy swear himself Rome's enemy.

5. The oil with which the king was anointed during the coronation ceremony.

6. A play by Flecknoe.

7. Dryden parodies the rituals and props of the coronation ceremony.

8. Prounounced "lines" (a fact that permits Dryden a significant pun).

9. Symbolizing sleep.

1. Symbols of ignorance and darkness (because nocturnal).

2. Co-founder of Rome (through which the Tiber runs).

The sire then shook the honors[3] of his head,
135   And from his brows damps of oblivion shed
Full on the filial dullness: long he stood,
Repelling from his breast the raging God; }
At length burst out in this prophetic mood: }
      "Heavens bless my son, from Ireland let him reign
140   To far Barbados on the western main;[4]
Of his dominion may no end be known,
And greater than his father's be his throne.
Beyond *Love's Kingdom* let him stretch his pen!"
He paused, and all the people cried, "Amen."
145   "Then thus," continued he, "my son, advance
Still in new impudence, new ignorance.
Success let others teach, learn thou from me
Pangs without birth, and fruitless industry.
Let *Virtuosos* in five years be writ,
150   Yet not one thought accuse thy toil of wit.
Let gentle George[5] in triumph tread the stage,
Make Dorimant betray, and Loveit rage;
Let Cully, Cockwood, Fopling charm the pit,
And in their folly show the writer's wit.
155   Yet still thy fools shall stand in thy defense,
And justify° their author's want of sense.   prove
Let 'em be all by thy own model made
Of dullness, and desire no foreign aid:
That they to future ages may be known,
160   Not copies drawn, but issue[6] of thy own.
Nay let thy men of wit too be the same,
All full of thee, and differing but in name;
But let no alien S—dl—y[7] interpose
To lard with wit thy hungry *Epsom* prose.
165   And when false flowers of rhetoric thou would'st cull,
Trust nature, do not labor to be dull;
But write thy best, and top; and in each line,
Sir Formal's[8] oratory will be thine.
Sir Formal, though unsought, attends thy quill,
170   And does thy northern dedications[9] fill.
Nor let false friends seduce thy mind to fame,
By arrogating Jonson's hostile name.
Let father Flecknoe fire thy mind with praise,
And uncle Ogilby thy envy raise.
175   Thou art my blood, where Jonson has no part;
What share have we in nature or in art?
Where did his wit on learning fix a brand,

---

3. Ornaments, and by extension, hair—a Virgilian expression.
4. His kingdom will be the Atlantic Ocean.
5. Sir George Etherege, comic playwright; characters from his plays follow.
6. A pun: both progeny and printing.
7. Sir Charles Sedley, courtier, poet, and intimate of Dry-

den's circle; he wrote a prologue for *Epsom Wells*.
8. Sir Formal Trifle, a character in Shadwell's *The Virtuoso*, described by Shadwell as "the Orator, a florid coxcomb."
9. Both Flecknoe and Shadwell dedicated several of their works to the Duke and Duchess of Newcastle, (a town in the north of England).

And rail at arts he did not understand?
Where made he love in Prince Nicander's[1] vein,
180   Or swept the dust in *Psyche*'s humble strain?
Where sold he bargains,[2] "whip-stitch, kiss my arse,"
Promised a play and dwindled to a farce?
When did his Muse from Fletcher scenes purloin,
As thou whole Eth'rege dost transfuse to thine?
185   But so transfused as oil on waters flow,
His always floats above, thine sinks below.
This is thy province, this thy wondrous way,
New humors to invent for each new play:[3]
This is that boasted bias of thy mind,
190   By which one way, to dullness, 'tis inclined;
Which makes thy writings lean on one side still,
And in all changes that way bends thy will.
Nor let thy mountain belly make pretense
Of likeness; thine's a tympany[4] of sense.
195   A tun of man in thy large bulk is writ,
But sure thou'rt but a kilderkin[5] of wit.
Like mine thy gentle numbers feebly creep;
Thy tragic Muse gives smiles, thy comic sleep.
With whate'er gall thou sett'st thyself to write,
200   Thy inoffensive satires never bite.
In thy felonious heart, though venom lies,
It does but touch thy Irish[6] pen, and dies.
Thy genius calls thee not to purchase fame
In keen iambics,[7] but mild anagram:
205   Leave writing plays, and choose for thy command
Some peaceful province in acrostic land.
There thou may'st wings display and altars[8] raise,
And torture one poor word ten thousand ways.
Or if thou would'st thy diff'rent talents suit,
210   Set thy own songs, and sing them to thy lute."
He said, but his last words were scarcely heard, ⎤
For Bruce and Longvil had a trap prepared,[9] ⎬
And down they sent the yet declaiming bard. ⎦
Sinking he left his drugget robe behind,
215   Borne upwards by a subterranean wind.
The mantle fell to the young prophet's part,[1]
With double portion of his father's art.

c. 1676   1682

1. A character in *Psyche*.
2. "To sell bargains" is to respond to an innocent question with a coarse phrase, as in this line. Dryden sharpens the insult by quoting the slangy nonsense phrase "whip-stitch" from Shadwell's own play, *The Virtuoso*.
3. I.e., by these contemptible means, you purport to out-do Ben Jonson.
4. A swelling of the abdomen, caused by air or gas.
5. A tun was a large cask of wine; a kilderkin a quarter of a tun.
6. Neither Flecknoe nor Shadwell was actually Irish; Ireland was regarded in England as an abode of savages.

7. Sharp satire (written in iambic meter by classical satirists).
8. Dryden here mocks the practice of writing emblematic verse, poems in the shape of their subjects (e.g., George Herbert's *Easter Wings* and *The Altar*). He lumps this practice together with other forms of empty ingenuity.
9. In Shadwell's *The Virtuoso*, Bruce and Longvil open a trap door beneath the long-winded Sir Formal Trifle.
1. A burlesque of 2 Kings 2.8–14, in which the prophet Elijah is borne up to heaven, while his mantle falls to his successor, Elisha.

To the Memory of Mr. Oldham[1]

Farewell, too little and too lately known,
Whom I began to think and call my own;
For sure our souls were near allied; and thine
Cast in the same poetic mold with mine.[2]
5   One common note on either lyre did strike,
And knaves and fools[3] we both abhorred alike:
To the same goal did both our studies drive,
The last set out the soonest did arrive.
Thus Nisus[4] fell upon the slippery place,
10   While his young friend performed and won the race.
O early ripe! to thy abundant store
What could advancing age have added more?
It might (what Nature never gives the young)
Have taught the numbers[5] of thy native tongue.
15   But satire needs not those, and wit will shine
Through the harsh cadence of a rugged line:
A noble error, and but seldom made,
When poets are by too much force betrayed.
Thy generous fruits, though gathered ere their prime, ⎫
20   Still showed a quickness;[6] and maturing time   ⎬
But mellows what we write to the dull sweets of rhyme. ⎭
Once more, hail and farewell;[7] farewell thou young,
But ah too short, Marcellus of our tongue;
Thy brows with ivy, and with laurels bound;
25   But fate and gloomy night encompass thee around.[8]

1684

Ode to Mrs. Anne Killigrew

By her birth and through her accomplishments, Anne Killigrew (1660–1685) moved in an elevated sphere where politics, theater, poetry, and painting were intimately linked. Her uncles, the playwrights Thomas and Sir William Killigrew, were Dryden's associates; her father was chaplain to the Duke of York, and she was Maid of Honor to the Duke's wife. In this aristocratic circle, she wrote and painted. When she died of smallpox at age 25, Dryden made her early death the occasion for an elegy mapping her several worlds. By her varied talents she conquers adjacent provinces in the "spacious empire" of the Muses; by virtue of her family connections she participates in the more material empire of English commerce and conquest; by her saintly chastity she mediates between earth and heaven. To represent such scope, Dryden

1. John Oldham (1653–1683) achieved fame at age 28 with his *Satires upon the Jesuits* (1681). Three years later, an aging Dryden mourned him in a tribute that prefaced the *Remains of Mr. John Oldham in Verse and Prose.* Within his poem's brief compass, Dryden echoes many poets—Virgil, Catullus, Milton, and Oldham himself—and invokes several modes: satire, celebration, elegy.
2. An echo of Oldham's poem *David's Lamentation:* "Oh, dearer than my soul! if I can call it mine, / For sure we had the same, 'twas very thine."
3. Satire's traditional targets.
4. In Book 5 of Virgil's *Aeneid,* Nisus slips near the finish line during a footrace, falling in a manner that permits "his young friend" Euryalus to win.

5. Metrical patterns and harmonies.
6. Liveliness; also, sharpness of taste.
7. Dryden echoes a phrase in Catullus's elegy for his brother: "Ave atque vale" (101.10).
8. In Book 6 of Virgil's *Aeneid,* the hero visits the underworld, where his dead father shows him a vision of Rome's future. This vision concludes with a sight of Augustus Caesar's adopted son and heir Marcellus, who after a glorious military career died at the age of 20. The last line of Dryden's elegy reworks Virgil's conclusion: "But hov'ring mists around his brows are spread, / And night, with sable shades, involves his head." (*Aeneid* 6.866; Dryden's translation).

chose the capacious structure of the Pindaric ode; its formal complexities and varied meters had long provoked admiration and imitation among English poets. A century later, Samuel Johnson deemed Dryden's performance a triumph, "undoubtedly the noblest ode that our language has produced."

To the Pious Memory of the Accomplished Young Lady Mrs. Anne Killigrew[1]

Excellent in the two Sister Arts of Poesy and Painting.
An Ode

1

Thou youngest virgin-daughter of the skies,
Made in the last promotion of the blest;
Whose palms,[2] new plucked from paradise,
In spreading branches more sublimely rise,
5   Rich with immortal green above the rest:
Whether, adopted to some neighboring star,
Thou roll'st above us in thy wandering race,
    Or in procession fixed and regular,
    Moved with the heavens' majestic pace,[3]
10   Or called to more superior bliss,
Thou tread'st with seraphims the vast abyss:
Whatever happy region is thy place,
Cease thy celestial song a little space
(Thou wilt have time enough for hymns divine,
15   Since heav'n's eternal year is thine).
Hear then a mortal Muse thy praise rehearse,
        In no ignoble verse;
But such as thy own voice did practice here,
When thy first fruits of poesy were given,
20   To make thyself a welcome inmate there,
        While yet a young probationer,
            And candidate of heaven.

2

If by traduction[4] came thy mind,
    Our wonder is the less to find
25   A soul so charming from a stock so good;
Thy father was transfused into thy blood:
So wert thou born into the tuneful strain
(An early, rich, and inexhausted vein).
        But if thy pre-existing soul
30   Was formed at first with myriads more,[5]
    It did through all the mighty poets roll
        Who Greek or Latin laurels wore,

---

1. The term Mistress (Mrs.) applied to married and single women alike (Anne Killigrew died unmarried).
2. Symbols of victory (and also of martyrdom).
3. Dryden makes imaginative use of the geocentric cosmos of Ptolemy, which surrounds the earth with nine transparent spheres. Beyond the seven spheres of the

luminous bodies that roll "above us" is the sphere of the stars "fix'd and regular"; beyond this is the Prime Mover.
4. By descent, derivation from ancestry.
5. Dryden offers an alternative explanation for Killigrew's poetic gifts by mentioning the doctrine of metempsychosis, or transmigration of souls.

And was that Sappho[6] last which one it was before.
 If so, then cease thy flight, O heaven-born mind!
35 Thou hast no dross to purge from thy rich ore:
 Nor can thy soul a fairer mansion find,
 Than was the beauteous frame she left behind:
Return, to fill or mend the choir of thy celestial kind.

3

 May we presume to say, that at thy birth
40 New joy was sprung in heav'n, as well as here on earth.
 For sure the milder planets did combine
 On thy auspicious horoscope to shine,
 And ev'n the most malicious were in trine.[7]
  Thy brother-angels at thy birth
45 Strung each his lyre and tuned it high,
  That all the people of the sky
 Might know a poetess was born on earth.
  And then, if ever, mortal ears
  Had heard the music of the spheres![8]
50 And if no clustering swarm of bees
 On thy sweet mouth distilled their golden dew,[9]
  'Twas that such vulgar miracles
  Heav'n had not leisure to renew:
 For all the blest fraternity of love
55 Solemnized there thy birth, and kept thy holiday above.

4

  O gracious God! How far have we
Profaned thy heavenly gift of poesy?
Made prostitute and profligate the Muse,
Debased to each obscene and impious use,
60 Whose harmony was first ordained above
For tongues of angels and for hymns of love?
O wretched we! Why were we hurried down
  This lubric[1] and adult'rate age
  (Nay added fat pollutions of our own)
65 T' increase the steaming ordures of the stage?
What can we say t' excuse our second fall?
Let this thy vestal,[2] Heaven, atone for all!
 Her Arethusian[3] stream remains unsoiled,
 Unmixed with foreign filth, and undefiled;
70 Her wit was more than man, her innocence a child!

5

  Art she had none, yet wanted[4] none:
  For nature did that want supply,
  So rich in treasures of her own,

---

6. Ancient Greek female poet.
7. Favorably aligned.
8. The celestial music generated by the motion of the planets, inaudible to humans.
9. This "vulgar miracle" was said to have accompanied the birth of the ancient Greek poet Pindar, celebrated for

his odes.
1. Lewd.
2. Virgin tender of a shrine.
3. Arethusa was changed into a spring to save her from the lustful river god Alpheus.
4. Lacked.

She might our boasted stores defy:
75   Such noble vigor did her verse adorn,
That it seemed borrowed, where 'twas only born.
Her morals too were in her bosom bred
        By great examples daily fed,
What in the best of books, her father's life, she read.
80   And to be read herself she need not fear;
Each test and every light her Muse will bear,
Though Epictetus[5] with his lamp were there.
Even love (for love sometimes her Muse expressed)
Was but a lambent[6] flame which played about her breast:
85   Light as the vapors of a morning dream,
So cold herself, whilst she such warmth expressed,
'Twas Cupid bathing in Diana's stream.

6

Born to the spacious empire of the Nine,[7]
One would have thought she should have been content
90   To manage well that mighty government:
But what can young ambitious souls confine?
        To the next realm she stretched her sway, ⎫
        For painture near adjoining lay,   ⎬
        A plenteous province, and alluring prey.   ⎭
95   A chamber of dependences[8] was framed
        (As conquerors will never want pretense,
        When armed, to justify the offense),
And the whole fief in right of Poetry she claimed.
The country open lay without defense:
100   For poets frequent inroads there had made,
        And perfectly could represent
The shape, the face, with every lineament;
And all the large domains which the dumb Sister[9] swayed,
        All bowed beneath her government,
105   Received in triumph wheresoe'er she went.
Her pencil drew whate'er her soul designed,
And oft the happy draught surpassed the image in her mind:
        The sylvan scenes of herds and flocks,
        And fruitful plains and barren rocks;
110   Of shallow brooks that flowed so clear,
        The bottom did the top appear;
        Of deeper too and ampler floods,
        Which, as in mirrors, showed the woods;
        Of lofty trees with sacred shades,
115   And perspectives of pleasant glades,
        Where nymphs of brightest form appear, ⎫
        And shaggy satyrs standing near,   ⎬
        Which them at once admire and fear;   ⎭
        The ruins too of some majestic piece,

---

5. Stoic philosopher noted for his rigorous system of
ethics.
6. Glowing.
7. The nine Muses.

8. This refers to a legislative device used by Louis XIV to
annex lands adjoining France.
9. The silent Muse (painting).

120   Boasting the pow'r of ancient Rome or Greece,
                 Whose statues, friezes, columns broken lie,
                 And though defaced, the wonder of the eye;
                 What nature, art, bold fiction e'er durst frame,
                 Her forming hand gave feature to the name.
125   So strange a concourse ne'er was seen before,
        But when the peopled ark the whole creation bore.

7

         The scene then changed; with bold erected look
         Our martial King[1] the sight with reverence strook:
         For not content t' express his outward part,
130   Her hand called out the image of his heart;
                 His warlike mind, his soul devoid of fear,
                 His high-designing thoughts, were figured there, }
                 As when, by magic, ghosts are made appear.
         Our phoenix Queen[2] was portrayed too, so bright,
135   Beauty alone could beauty take so right:
                 Her dress, her shape, her matchless grace,
                 Were all observed, as well as heav'nly face.
                 With such a peerless majesty she stands,
                 As in that day she took the crown from sacred hands:[3]
140   Before a train of heroines was seen,
                 In beauty foremost, as in rank, the queen!
             Thus nothing to her[4] genius was denied,
            But like a ball of fire, the further thrown,
             Still with a greater blaze she shone,
145   And her bright soul broke out on ev'ry side.
                 What next she had designed, Heaven only knows; }
                 To such immod'rate growth her conquest rose,
                 That fate alone its progress could oppose.

8

         Now all those charms, that blooming grace,
150   The well-proportioned shape, and beauteous face,
         Shall never more be seen by mortal eyes;
         In earth the much-lamented virgin lies!
             Not wit, nor piety, could fate prevent;
             Nor was the cruel destiny content
155   To finish all the murder at a blow,
         To sweep at once her life and beauty too;
         But, like a hardened felon, took a pride
              To work more mischievously slow,
              And plundered first, and then destroyed.
160   O double sacrilege on things divine,
         To rob the relic, and deface the shrine!
            But thus Orinda[5] died:
         Heaven, by the same disease, did both translate,
         As equal were their souls, so equal was their fate.

---

1. James II, who fought in the Dutch wars, and whose portrait Killigrew had painted.
2. Queen of matchless beauty (James's wife Mary, whom Killigrew also painted).
3. The Archbishop of Canterbury officiated at James's coronation.
4. Killigrew's.
5. The pen name of the poet Katherine Philips, who had died, also of smallpox, in 1664.

9

165   Meantime her warlike brother[6] on the seas
His waving streamers to the winds displays,
And vows for his return with vain devotion pays.
        Ah, generous youth, that wish forbear;
        The winds too soon will waft thee here!
        Slack all thy sails, and fear to come;
170   Alas, thou know'st not, thou art wrecked at home!
No more shalt thou behold thy sister's face;
Thou hast already had her last embrace.
But look aloft, and if thou ken'st° from far,   *you see*
175   Among the Pleiads[7] a new-kindled star,
If any sparkles than the rest more bright,
'Tis she that shines in that propitious light.

10

When in mid-air the golden trump shall sound,
        To raise the nations under ground;
180   When in the valley of Jehosaphat,
The judging God shall close the book of fate,[8]
        And there the last assizes[9] keep,
        For those who wake, and those who sleep;
        When rattling bones together fly,
185   From the four corners of the sky;
When sinews o'er the skeletons are spread,
Those clothed with flesh, and life inspires the dead;
The sacred poets first shall hear the sound, ⎫
        And foremost from the tomb shall bound: ⎬
190   For they are covered with the lightest ground, ⎭
And straight, with inborn vigor, on the wing,
Like mounting larks, to the new morning sing.
There thou, sweet saint, before the choir shalt go, ⎫
As harbinger of heaven, the way to show, ⎬
195   The way which thou so well hast learned below. ⎭
1685   1685

Alexander's Feast

or, The Power of Music
An Ode in Honor of St. Cecilia's Day[1]

1

'Twas at the royal feast, for Persia won
        By Philip's warlike son:[2]

---

6. Henry Killigrew, a naval officer.
7. A cluster of seven stars in the constellation Taurus, associated with a group of 16th-century French poets (who called themselves la *Pléiade*).
8. "Let the heathen be wakened, and come up to the valley of Jehoshaphat: for there will I sit to judge all the heathen round about" (Joel 3:12).
9. Trial session.
1. The early martyr Cecilia is the patron saint of music and musicians. Her feast day (22 November) was annually celebrated in London by a concert featuring a new piece with words by an eminent poet and music by a dis-

tinguished composer. The musical society in charge of the occasion commissioned two odes from Dryden, ten years apart: *A Song for St. Cecilia's Day* (1687) and *Alexander's Feast*. Dryden undertook the commission with some reluctance, but after the piece's successful premiere, he noted with pleasure that *Alexander's Feast* "is esteemed the best of all my poetry, by all the town. I thought so myself when I writ it, but being old, I mistrusted my own judgment."
2. Alexander the Great, son of Philip of Macedon; Dryden depicts the feast that Alexander held after defeating the Persians and their emperor Darius in B.C. 331.

Aloft in awful state
The godlike hero sate
5   On his imperial throne:
His valiant peers were placed around;
Their brows with roses and with myrtles bound
  (So should desert in arms be crowned).
The lovely Thais[3] by his side
10 Sat like a blooming Eastern bride
In flow'r of youth and beauty's pride.
   Happy, happy, happy pair!
   None but the brave
   None but the brave
15   None but the brave deserves the fair.

Chorus

Happy, happy, happy pair!
None but the brave
None but the brave
None but the brave deserves the fair.

2

20 Timotheus,[4] placed on high
  Amid the tuneful choir,
   With flying fingers touched the lyre:
The trembling notes ascend the sky,
     And heav'nly joys inspire.
25 The song began from Jove,
Who left his blissful seats above
(Such is the power of mighty love).
A dragon's fiery form belied[5] the god:
Sublime on radiant spires° he rode,   coils
30   When he to fair Olympia pressed:
   And while he sought her snowy breast:
Then, round her slender waist he curled,
And stamped an image of himself, a sov'reign of the world.
The listening crowd admire the lofty sound:
35 "A present deity," they shout around:
"A present deity," the vaulted roofs rebound.
     With ravished ears
     The monarch hears,
     Assumes the god,[6]
40   Affects to nod,
And seems to shake the spheres.

Chorus

With ravished ears
The monarch hears,
Assumes the god,

---

3. Alexander's Greek concubine.
4. Celebrated poet and musician.
5. Timotheus tells the alternative story of Alexander's parentage, that he was begotten by Jove—disguised

("belied") as a serpent—upon Philip's wife Olympias.
6. Behaves like Jove, whose nod is said by Virgil to cause earthquakes.

45   *Affects to nod,*
         And seems to shake the spheres.

3

     The praise of Bacchus then the sweet musician sung,
        Of Bacchus ever fair and ever young:
           The jolly god in triumph comes;
50   Sound the trumpets; beat the drums:
             Flushed with a purple grace
             He shows his honest face,
Now give the hautboys° breath; he comes, he comes.   *oboes*
         Bacchus, ever fair and young,
55   Drinking joys did first ordain:
         Bacchus' blessings are a treasure;
         Drinking is the soldier's pleasure;
             Rich the treasure,
             Sweet the pleasure;
60   Sweet is pleasure after pain.

Chorus

        Bacchus' blessings are a treasure;
        Drinking is the soldier's pleasure;
           Rich the treasure,
           Sweet the pleasure;
65   *Sweet is pleasure after pain.*

4

    Soothed with the sound, the king grew vain;
     Fought all his battles o'er again;
And thrice he routed all his foes, and thrice he slew the slain.
        The master saw the madness rise,
70   His glowing cheeks, his ardent eyes;
        And, while he heav'n and earth defied,
        Changed his hand, and checked his pride.[7]
           He chose a mournful Muse
           Soft pity to infuse:
75   He sung Darius great and good,
            By too severe a fate
      Fallen, fallen, fallen, fallen,
         Fallen from his high estate
            And welt'ring in his blood:
80   Deserted at his utmost need,
     By those his former bounty fed:
     On the bare earth exposed he lies,
     With not a friend to close his eyes.

    With downcast looks the joyless victor sat,
85   Revolving° in his altered soul   *pondering*
       The various turns of chance below;
     And, now and then, a sigh he stole,
       And tears began to flow.

7. Timotheus ("the master") changes the music in order to restrain Alexander's swelling pride.

Chorus

Revolving in his altered soul
90   *The various turns of chance below;*
        And, now and then, a sigh he stole;
        And tears began to flow.

5

        The mighty master smiled to see
        That love was in the next degree:
95   'Twas but a kindred sound to move;[8]
        For pity melts the mind to love.
                Softly sweet, in Lydian measures,[9]
                Soon he soothed his soul to pleasures.
                "War," he sung, "is toil and trouble,
100   Honor but an empty bubble.
                        Never ending, still° beginning,   *always*
                Fighting still, and still destroying,
                        If the world be worth thy winning,
                Think, O think, it worth enjoying.
105   Lovely Thais sits beside thee,
                        Take the good the gods provide thee."

        The many[1] rend the skies with loud applause;
        So love was crowned, but music won the cause.
                The prince, unable to conceal his pain,
110   Gazed on the fair
                        Who caused his care,
                And sighed and looked, sighed and looked,
        Sighed and looked, and sighed again:
        At length, with love and wine at once oppressed,
115   The vanquished victor sunk upon her breast.

Chorus

        The prince, unable to conceal his pain,
                Gazed on the fair
                Who caused his care,
                And sighed and looked, sighed and looked,
120   *Sighed and looked, and sighed again:*
        At length, with love and wine at once oppressed,
        The vanquished victor sunk upon her breast.

6

        Now strike the golden lyre again:
        A louder yet, and yet a louder strain.
125   Break his bands of sleep asunder,
        And rouse him, like a rattling peal of thunder.
                        Hark, hark, the horrid sound
                        Has raised up his head,
                        As awaked from the dead,

8. All it took to "move" Alexander to the "next degree"
of feeling was to shift ("move") musical registers.
9. In ancient Greek music, the mode associated with

pathos.
1. The retinue or company.

130   And, amazed, he stares around.
    "Revenge, revenge," Timotheus cries,
        "See the Furies[2] arise!
        See the snakes that they rear,
        How they hiss in their hair,
135   And the sparkles that flash from their eyes!
        Behold a ghastly band,
        Each a torch in his hand!
  Those are Grecian ghosts, that in battle were slain,
                And unburied remain
140   Inglorious on the plain.
        Give the vengeance due
        To the valiant crew.
  Behold how they toss their torches on high,
        How they point to the Persian abodes,
145 And glitt'ring temples of their hostile gods!"
  The princes applaud, with a furious joy;
  And the king seized a flambeau,[3] with zeal to destroy;
        Thais led the way,
        To light him to his prey,
150 And, like another Helen, fired another Troy.[4]

         Chorus

And the king seized a flambeau, with zeal to destroy;
        Thais led the way,
        To light him to his prey,
And, like another Helen, fired another Troy.

           7
155   Thus, long ago,
    Ere heaving bellows learned to blow,
      While organs yet were mute,
    Timotheus, to his breathing flute,
        And sounding lyre,
160 Could swell the soul to rage, or kindle soft desire.
    At last divine Cecilia came,
    Inventress of the vocal frame;[5]
  The sweet enthusiast,[6] from her sacred store,
      Enlarged the former narrow bounds,
165   And added length to solemn sounds,
  With nature's mother wit, and arts unknown before.
    Let old Timotheus yield the prize,
      Or both divide the crown;
    He raised a mortal to the skies;
170   She drew an angel down.[7]

---

2. Spirits of punishment.
3. Torch.
4. Stolen away to Troy by Paris, Helen was blamed for setting in motion the chain of events that led to the burning of the city by the Greeks.
5. Cecilia was believed to have invented the organ.

6. One possessed by spirits or by a god.
7. Dryden alludes to his earlier ode to music, *A Song for St. Cecilia's Day* (1687): as Cecilia plays the organ, "An angel heard and straight appear'd, / Mistaking earth for heaven."

Grand Chorus

> *At last divine Cecilia came,*
> *Inventress of the vocal frame;*
> *The sweet enthusiast, from her sacred store,*
> *Enlarged the former narrow bounds,*
175   *And added length to solemn sounds,*
> *With nature's mother wit, and arts unknown before.*
> *Let old Timotheus yield the prize,*
> *Or both divide the crown;*
> *He raised a mortal to the skies;*
> *She drew an angel down.*

1697   1697

from Fables Ancient and Modern[1]

from *the Preface*

'Tis with a poet as with a man who designs to build, and is very exact, as he supposes, in casting up the cost beforehand. But generally speaking, he is mistaken in his account, and reckons short of the expense he first intended. He alters his mind as the work proceeds, and will have this or that convenience more, of which he had not thought when he began. So has it happened to me; I have built a house where I intended but a lodge, yet with better success than a certain nobleman,[2] who beginning with a dog kennel, never lived to finish the palace he had contrived.

From translating the first of Homer's *Iliads* (which I intended as an essay to[3] the whole work) I proceeded to the translation of the twelfth book of Ovid's *Metamorphoses*,[4] because it contains, among other things, the causes, the beginning, and ending, of the Trojan War. Here I ought in reason to have stopped; but the speeches of Ajax and Ulysses lying next in my way, I could not balk 'em. When I had compassed them, I was so taken with the former part of the fifteenth book[5] (which is the masterpiece of the whole *Metamorphoses*) that I enjoined myself the pleasing task of rendering it into English. And now I found, by the number of my verses, that they began to swell into a little volume; which gave me an occasion of looking backward on some beauties of my author, in his former books: there occurred to me the hunting of the boar, Cinyras and Myrrha, the good-natured story of Baucis and Philemon, with the rest, which I hope I have translated closely enough, and given them the same turn of

---

1. Following the triumph of his *Virgil* (1697), Dryden turned again to translation. He had frequently collaborated with others in the assembly of anthologies; now he undertook to make one of his own, containing poets both "Ancient"—Ovid and Homer—and "Modern"—Boccaccio, Chaucer, and Dryden himself. In the *Fables*, Dryden's pleasure and assurance in his own technical mastery are everywhere on display: in the expansiveness of his translations; in the bravado with which he plunders his own works as a treasury of echo and allusion; in the arrangement of his materials, so that fable talks to fable in an almost calculated sequence; and in his preface, where he lays out the history of his book's development with a conspicuous delight in the improvisatory logic of his creative process, and then proudly argues for the

greatness of Chaucer, whose career and craft he celebrates in such a way as to suggest parallels with his own.
2. Probably the Duke of Buckingham (whom Dryden had ridiculed as Zimri in *Absalom and Achitophel* line 544), and Buckingham's house at Cliveden.
3. First attempt at, and "taste of" (Johnson's *Dictionary*).
4. Ovid (43 B.C.–A.D. 17), Roman poet who spent the last decade of his life in exile. His *Metamorphoses* is a collection of ancient legends; in many, the characters undergo bodily transformations, from one form of life into another.
5. In which Ovid puts into verse the philosophy of the Greek mystic Pythagoras, who propounded a doctrine of reincarnation, arguing that "all things are but altered, nothing dies."

verse, which they had in the original; and this, I may say without vanity, is not the talent of every poet. He who has arrived the nearest to it, is the ingenious and learned Sandys,[6] the best versifier of the former age, if I may properly call it by that name, which was the former part of this concluding century. For Spenser and Fairfax[7] both flourished in the reign of Queen Elizabeth: great masters in our language, and who saw much farther into the beauties of our numbers than those who immediately followed them. Milton was the poetical son of Spenser, and Mr. Waller[8] of Fairfax; for we have our lineal descents and clans, as well as other families. Spenser more than once insinuates that the soul of Chaucer was transfused into his body, and that he was begotten by him two hundred years after his decease. Milton has acknowledged to me that Spenser was his original, and many besides myself have heard our famous Waller own that he derived the harmony of his numbers from the *Godfrey of Bulloign*, which was turned into English by Mr. Fairfax.

But to return: having done with Ovid for this time, it came into my mind that our old English poet Chaucer in many things resembled him, and that with no disadvantage on the side of the modern author, as I shall endeavor to prove when I compare them. And as I am and always have been studious to promote the honor of my native country, so I soon resolved to put their merits to the trial, by turning some of the *Canterbury Tales* into our language, as it is now refined, for by this means, both the poets being set in the same light, and dressed in the same English habit, story to be compared with story, a certain judgment may be made betwixt them by the reader, without obtruding my opinion on him: or if I seem partial to my countryman, and predecessor in the laurel, the friends of antiquity are not few. And besides many of the learned, Ovid has almost all the beaux,[9] and the whole fair sex, his declared patrons. Perhaps I have assumed somewhat more to myself than they allow me, because I have adventured to sum up the evidence. But the readers are the jury; and their privilege remains entire to decide according to the merits of the cause or, if they please, to bring it to another hearing before some other court. In the meantime, to follow the thread of my discourse (as thoughts, according to Mr. Hobbes,[1] have always some connection) so from Chaucer I was led to think on Boccace,[2] who was not only his contemporary, but also pursued the same studies; wrote novels in prose, and many works in verse; particularly is said to have invented the octave rhyme, or stanza of eight lines, which ever since has been maintained by the practice of all Italian writers who are, or at least assume the title of, heroic poets. He and Chaucer, among other things, had this in common, that they refined their mother tongues; but with this difference, that Dante had begun to file their language,[3] at least in verse, before the time of Boccace, who likewise received no little help from his master Petrarch.[4] But the reformation of their prose was wholly owing to Boccace himself, who is yet the standard of purity in the Italian tongue, though many of his phrases are become obsolete, as in process of time it must needs happen. Chaucer (as you have formerly been told by our learned Mr. Rymer) first adorned and amplified our barren

6. George Sandys (1578–1644), poet and translator, whose *Ovid's Metamorphosis Englished* was issued in 1626 and often republished.
7. Edward Fairfax (c. 1580–1635), poet and translator.
8. Edmund Waller (1606–1687), poet, early practitioner of the heroic couplet; Dryden praised him as "the father" of English versification.
9. Fashionable gentlemen.
1. In his *Leviathan* (1651), Thomas Hobbes includes a chap-

ter on "The Consequence or Train of Imaginations" (1.3).
2. Giovanni Boccaccio (1313–1375), Italian writer, authored *The Decameron* (a collection of 100 tales) and was one of Chaucer's chief influences.
3. Dante Alighieri (1265–1321), author of the *Divine Comedy*, was the first great vernacular poet in Italy; *to file*: to smooth (into graceful verse).
4. Italian poet (1304–1374), whose cycle of love sonnets exerted enormous influence over English writers.

tongue from the Provençal, which was then the most polished of all the modern languages.[5] But this subject has been copiously treated by that great critic, who deserves no little commendation from us his countrymen. For these reasons of time, and resemblance of genius, in Chaucer and Boccace, I resolved to join them in my present work, to which I have added some original papers of my own, which whether they are equal or inferior to my other poems, an author is the most improper judge; and therefore I leave them wholly to the mercy of the reader. I will hope the best, that they will not be condemned; but if they should, I have the excuse of an old gentleman, who mounting on horseback before some ladies, when I was present, got up somewhat heavily, but desired of the fair spectators that they would count fourscore and eight before they judged him. By the mercy of God, I am already come within twenty years of his number, a cripple in my limbs, but what decays are in my mind, the reader must determine. I think myself as vigorous as ever in the faculties of my soul, excepting only my memory, which is not impaired to any great degree; and if I lose not more of it, I have no great reason to complain. What judgment I had increases rather than diminishes; and thoughts, such as they are, come crowding in so fast upon me that my only difficulty is to choose or to reject; to run them into verse, or to give them the other harmony of prose. I have so long studied and practiced both that they are grown into a habit, and become familiar to me. In short, though I may lawfully plead some part of the old gentleman's excuse, yet I will reserve it till I think I have greater need, and ask no grains of allowance for the faults of this my present work but those which are given of course to human frailty. I will not trouble my reader with the shortness of time in which I writ it, or the several intervals of sickness. They who think too well of their own performances are apt to boast in their prefaces how little time their works have cost them, and what other business of more importance interfered. But the reader will be as apt to ask the question, why they allowed not a longer time to make their works more perfect? and why they had so despicable an opinion of their judges, as to thrust their indigested stuff upon them, as if they deserved no better?

With this account of my present undertaking, I conclude the first part of this discourse. In the second part, as at a second sitting, though I alter not the draught, I must touch the same features over again, and change the dead-coloring[6] of the whole.

* * *

It remains that I say somewhat of Chaucer in particular.

In the first place, as he is the father of English poetry, so I hold him in the same degree of veneration as the Grecians held Homer, or the Romans Virgil. He is a perpetual fountain of good sense; learned in all sciences; and therefore speaks properly on all subjects. As he knew what to say, so he knows also when to leave off, a continence which is practiced by few writers, and scarcely by any of the Ancients, excepting Virgil and Horace. One of our late great poets[7] is sunk in his reputation, because he could never forgive any conceit which came in his way, but swept like a dragnet, great and small. There was plenty enough, but the dishes were ill sorted; whole pyramids of sweet-meats for boys and women, but little of solid meat for men. All this proceeded not from any want of knowledge, but of judgment; neither did he want that in discerning the beauties

---

5. In his *Short View of Tragedy* (1693), Thomas Rymer writes that Chaucer seized "all Provençal [Old French], French, or Latin that came in his way, gives them a new garb . . . and mingles them amongst our English."

6. The prepatory layer of paint applied to a canvas.
7. Abraham Cowley (1618–1667), whom Dryden admired and imitated.

and faults of other poets, but only indulged himself in the luxury of writing; and perhaps knew it was a fault, but hoped the reader would not find it. For this reason, though he must always be thought a great poet, he is no longer esteemed a good writer; and for ten impressions,[8] which his works have had in so many successive years, yet at present a hundred books are scarcely purchased once a twelvemonth. For, as my last Lord Rochester said, though somewhat profanely, "Not being of God, he could not stand."

Chaucer followed Nature everywhere, but was never so bold to go beyond her. And there is a great difference of being *poeta* and *nimis poeta*,[9] if we may believe Catullus, as much as betwixt a modest behavior and affectation. The verse of Chaucer, I confess, is not harmonious to us; but 'tis like the eloquence of one whom Tacitus commends: it was *auribus istius temporis accommodata*.[1] They who lived with him, and some time after him, thought it musical, and it continues so even in our judgment, if compared with the numbers of Lydgate and Gower, his contemporaries. There is the rude sweetness of a Scotch tune in it, which is natural and pleasing, though not perfect. 'Tis true, I cannot go so far as he who published the last edition of him,[2] for he would make us believe the fault is in our ears, and that there were really ten syllables in a verse where we find but nine. But this opinion is not worth confuting; 'tis so gross and obvious an error that common sense (which is a rule in everything but matters of faith and revelation) must convince the reader that equality of numbers, in every verse which we call heroic,[3] was either not known or not always practiced in Chaucer's age. It were an easy matter to produce some thousands of his verses which are lame for want of half a foot, and sometimes a whole one, and which no pronunciation can make otherwise. We can only say that he lived in the infancy of our poetry, and that nothing is brought to perfection at the first. We must be children before we grow men. There was an Ennius, and in process of time a Lucilius and a Lucretius, before Virgil and Horace; even after Chaucer there was a Spenser, a Harrington, a Fairfax, before Waller and Denham were in being.[4] And our numbers were in their nonage[5] till these last appeared. I need say little of his parentage, life, and fortunes. They are to be found at large in all the editions of his works. He was employed abroad, and favored by Edward the Third, Richard the Second, and Henry the Fourth, and was poet, as I suppose, to all three of them. In Richard's time, I doubt, he was a little dipped in the rebellion of the Commons, and being brother-in-law to John of Gaunt, it was no wonder if he followed the fortunes of that family, and was well with Henry the Fourth when he had deposed his predecessor.[6] Neither is it to be admired[7] that Henry, who was a wise as well as a valiant prince, who claimed by succession, and was sensible that his title was not sound, but was rightfully in Mortimer, who had married the heir of York—it was not to be admired, I say, if that great politician should be pleased to have the greatest wit of those times in his interests, and to be the trumpet of his praises. Augustus had given him the example, by the advice of Maecenas,[8] who recommended Virgil and Horace to him; whose praises helped to make him popular while he was alive, and after his death have made him precious to

---

8. Printings.
9. "A poet" and "too much a poet"; the Latin poet Martial, and not his predecessor Catullus, made this observation.
1. "Suited to the ears of those times": Cornelius Tacitus, Roman historian.
2. Thomas Speght, who argued (correctly) that Chaucer's versification was skillful and smooth but misrepresented by transcribers and misunderstood by readers.
3. I.e., consistent iambic pentameter.

4. Dryden traces a "descent and lineage" of influence first in Latin and then in English poetry.
5. Early youth.
6. Henry Bolingbroke (son to John of Gaunt) deposed his cousin Richard II in 1499; Chaucer survived political upheaval, and received patronage from both kings.
7. Wondered at.
8. Roman patron of the poets Virgil, Horace, and Propertius.

posterity. As for the religion of our poet, he seems to have some little bias towards the opinions of Wyclif,[9] after John of Gaunt his patron; somewhat of which appears in the *Tale of Piers Plowman*.[1] Yet I cannot blame him for inveighing so sharply against the vices of the clergy in his age. Their pride, their ambition, their pomp, their avarice, their worldly interest deserved the lashes which he gave them, both in that, and in most of his *Canterbury Tales*. Neither has his contemporary Boccace spared them. Yet both those poets lived in much esteem, with good and holy men in orders, for the scandal which is given by particular priests reflects not on the sacred function. Chaucer's Monk, his Canon, and his Friar took not[2] from the character of his Good Parson. A satirical poet is the check of the laymen on bad priests. We are only to take care that we involve not the innocent with the guilty in the same condemnation. The good cannot be too much honored, nor the bad too coarsely used, for the corruption of the best becomes the worst. When a clergyman is whipped, his gown is first taken off, by which the dignity of his order is secured. If he be wrongfully accused, he has his action of slander, and 'tis at the poet's peril if he transgress the law. But they will tell us that all kind of satire, though never so well deserved by particular priests, yet brings the whole order into contempt. Is then the peerage of England any thing dishonored, when a peer suffers for his treason? If he be libeled, or any way defamed, he has his *scandalum magnatum* [legal recourse] to punish the offender. They who use this kind of argument seem to be conscious to themselves of somewhat which has deserved the poet's lash, and are less concerned for their public capacity than for their private. At least, there is pride at the bottom of their reasoning. If the faults of men in orders are only to be judged among themselves, they are all in some sort parties. For, since they say the honor of their order is concerned in every member of it, how can we be sure that they will be impartial judges? How far I may be allowed to speak my opinion in this case I know not, but I am sure a dispute of this nature caused mischief in abundance betwixt a King of England and an Archbishop of Canterbury; one standing up for the laws of his land, and the other for the honor (as he called it) of God's Church; which ended in the murder of the prelate, and in the whipping of his Majesty from post to pillar for his penance.[3] The learned and ingenious Dr. Drake[4] has saved me the labor of inquiring into the esteem and reverence which the priests have had of old; and I would rather extend than diminish any part of it. Yet I must needs say that when a priest provokes me without any occasion given him, I have no reason, unless it be the charity of a Christian, to forgive him. *Prior laesit*[5] is justification sufficient in the civil law. If I answer him in his own language, self-defense, I am sure, must be allowed me, and if I carry it farther, even to a sharp recrimination, somewhat may be indulged to human frailty. Yet my resentment has not wrought so far, but that I have followed Chaucer in his character of a holy man, and have enlarged on that subject with some pleasure, reserving to myself the right, if I shall think fit hereafter, to describe another sort of priests, such as are more easily to be found than the Good Parson; such as have given the last blow to Christianity in this age, by a practice so contrary to their doctrine. But this will keep cold till another time.

9. John Wyclif (c. 1330–1384), theologian and religious reformer.
1. This tale had been mistakenly attributed to Chaucer; there is no evidence that he was a follower of Wyclif.
2. I.e., did not detract.
3. Thomas Becket, Archbishop of Canterbury, was murdered in 1170 on the orders of his king, Henry II, after a long dispute over the powers and rights of the church. (The pilgrims in *The Canterbury Tales* are traveling to Becket's shrine.)
4. James Drake (1667–1707), physician, dramatist, and ally of Dryden in literary controversies.
5. He injured first (i.e., "he started it").

In the meanwhile, I take up Chaucer where I left him. He must have been a man of a most wonderful comprehensive nature, because, as it has been truly observed of him, he has taken into the compass of his *Canterbury Tales* the various manners and humors (as we now call them) of the whole English nation in his age. Not a single character has escaped him. All his pilgrims are severally distinguished from each other; and not only in their inclinations, but in their very physiognomies and persons. Baptista Porta[6] could not have described their natures better than by the marks which the poet gives them. The matter and manner of their tales, and of their telling, are so suited to their different educations, humors, and callings, that each of them would be improper in any other mouth. Even the grave and serious characters are distinguished by their several sorts of gravity: their discourses are such as belong to their age, their calling, and their breeding; such as are becoming of them, and of them only. Some of his persons are vicious, and some virtuous; some are unlearned, or (as Chaucer calls them) *lewd*, and some are learned. Even the ribaldry of the low characters is different: the Reeve, the Miller, and the Cook, are several men, and distinguished from each other, as much as the mincing Lady Prioress and the broad-speaking gap-toothed Wife of Bath. But enough of this: there is such a variety of game springing up before me that I am distracted in my choice, and know not which to follow. 'Tis sufficient to say according to the proverb, that here is God's plenty. We have our forefathers and great grand-dames all before us, as they were in Chaucer's days; their general characters are still remaining in mankind, and even in England, though they are called by other names than those of monks, and friars, and canons, and lady abbesses, and nuns. For mankind is ever the same, and nothing lost out of nature, though everything is altered. May I have leave to do myself the justice (since my enemies will do me none, and are so far from granting me to be a good poet that they will not allow me so much as to be a Christian, or a moral man) may I have leave, I say, to inform my reader, that I have confined my choice to such tales of Chaucer as savor nothing of immodesty.[7] If I had desired more to please than to instruct, the Reeve, the Miller, the Shipman, the Merchant, the Summoner, and above all, the Wife of Bath, in the Prologue to her Tale, would have procured me as many friends and readers as there are beaux and ladies of pleasure in the town. But I will no more offend against good manners. I am sensible as I ought to be of the scandal I have given by my loose writings;[8] and make what reparation I am able, by this public acknowledgment. If anything of this nature, or of profaneness, be crept into these poems, I am so far from defending it, that I disown it. *Totum hoc indictum volo.*[9] Chaucer makes another manner of apology for his broad speaking, and Boccace makes the like; but I will follow neither of them. Our countryman, in the end of his characters, before the *Canterbury Tales,* thus excuses the ribaldry, which is very gross, in many of his novels.

> But first, I pray you, of your courtesy,
> That ye ne arrete it nought my villany,
> Though that I plainly speak in this mattere
> To tellen you her words, and eke her chere:

---

6. Giambattista della Porta (c. 1538–1615), a physician whose book *De humana physiognomia* catalogued the effects of the emotional life on the look of the face.
7. The *Fables* includes Dryden's translations of *The Knight's Tale, The Nun's Priest's Tale (The Cock and the Fox), The Wife of Bath's Tale,* and the portrait of the Parson from the *General Prologue (The Character of a Good Parson; Imitated from Chaucer and Inlarg'd).*
8. Throughout his career, Dryden had found it necessary to defend his plays against charges of immorality.
9. I wish all this unsaid.

Ne though I speak her words properly,
For this ye knowen as well as I,
Who shall tellen a tale after a man
He mote rehearse as nye as ever he can:
Everich word of it been in his charge,
All speke he never so rudely, ne large.
Or else he mote tellen his tale untrue,
Or feine things, or find words new:
He may not spare, altho he were his brother,
He mote as well say o word as another.
Christ spake himself full broad in holy writ,
And well I wote no villany is it.
Eke Plato saith, who so can him rede,
The words mote been cousin to the dede.[1]

Yet if a man should have inquired of Boccace or of Chaucer, what need they had of introducing such characters, where obscene words were proper in their mouths, but very undecent to be heard, I know not what answer they could have made. For that reason, such tales shall be left untold by me. You have here a specimen of Chaucer's language, which is so obsolete that his sense is scarce to be understood; and you have likewise more than one example of his unequal numbers, which were mentioned before. Yet many of his verses consist of ten syllables, and the words not much behind our present English, as for example, these two lines, in the description of the carpenter's young wife:

Wincing she was, as is a jolly colt,
Long as a mast, and upright as a bolt.[2]

I have almost done with Chaucer, when I have answered some objections relating to my present work. I find some people are offended that I have turned these tales into modern English, because they think them unworthy of my pains, and look on Chaucer as a dry, old-fashioned wit, not worth receiving. I have often heard the late Earl of Leicester[3] say that Mr. Cowley himself was of that opinion, who having read him over at my Lord's request, declared he had no taste of him. I dare not advance my opinion against the judgment of so great an author. But I think it fair, however, to leave the decision to the public. Mr. Cowley was too modest to set up for a dictator, and being shocked perhaps with his old style, never examined into the depth of his good sense. Chaucer, I confess, is a rough diamond, and must first be polished ere he shines. I deny not likewise, that living in our early days of poetry, he writes not always of a piece; but sometimes mingles trivial things with those of greater moment. Sometimes also, though not often, he runs riot, like Ovid, and knows not when he has said enough. But there are more great wits, beside Chaucer, whose fault is their excess of conceits, and those ill sorted. An author is not to write all he can, but only all he ought. Having observed this redundancy in Chaucer (as it is an easy matter for a man of ordinary parts to find a fault in one of greater) I have not tied myself to a literal translation, but have often omitted what I judged unnecessary, or not of dignity enough to appear in the company of better thoughts. I have presumed farther in some places, and added somewhat of my own where I thought my author was deficient, and

1. *The General Prologue*, lines 727–744 (see pages 310–311).
2. *The Miller's Tale*, lines 155–156 (see page 317).

3. Philip Sidney (1619–1698), patron of Dryden, to whom the poet had dedicated his tragedy *Don Sebastian* (1690).

had not given his thoughts their true luster, for want of words in the beginning of our language. And to this I was the more emboldened, because (if I may be permitted to say it of myself) I found I had a soul congenial to his, and that I had been conversant in the same studies. Another poet, in another age, may take the same liberty with my writings, if at least they live long enough to deserve correction. It was also necessary sometimes to restore the sense of Chaucer, which was lost or mangled in the errors of the press. Let this example suffice at present; in the story of Palamon and Arcite,[4] where the Temple of Diana is described, you find these verses in all the editions of our author:

> There saw I Danè turned unto a tree,
> I mean not the goddess Diane,
> But Venus daughter, which that hight Danè.

Which after a little consideration I knew was to be reformed into this sense, that Daphne the daughter of Peneus was turned into a tree. I durst not make thus bold with Ovid, lest some future Milbourn[5] should arise, and say I varied from my author because I understood him not.

But there are other judges who think I ought not to have translated Chaucer into English, out of a quite contrary notion. They suppose there is a certain veneration due to his old language, and that it is little less than profanation and sacrilege to alter it. They are farther of opinion that somewhat of his good sense will suffer in this transfusion, and much of the beauty of his thoughts will infallibly be lost, which appear with more grace in their old habit. Of this opinion was that excellent person whom I mentioned, the late Earl of Leicester, who valued Chaucer as much as Mr. Cowley despised him. My Lord dissuaded me from this attempt (for I was thinking of it some years before his death) and his authority prevailed so far with me as to defer my undertaking while he lived, in deference to him. Yet my reason was not convinced with what he urged against it. If the first end of a writer be to be understood, then as his language grows obsolete, his thoughts must grow obscure: *multa renascentur quae nunc cecidere; cadentque quae nunc sunt in honore vocabula, si volet usus, quem penes arbitrium est & jus & norma loquendi.*[6] When an ancient word for its sound and significancy deserves to be revived, I have that reasonable veneration for antiquity to restore it. All beyond this is superstition. Words are not like landmarks, so sacred as never to be removed. Customs are changed, and even statutes are silently repealed when the reason ceases for which they were enacted. As for the other part of the argument, that his thoughts will lose of their original beauty by the innovation of words: in the first place, not only their beauty, but their being is lost, where they are no longer understood, which is the present case. I grant that something must be lost in all transfusion, that is, in all translations; but the sense will remain, which would otherwise be lost, or at least be maimed, when it is scarce intelligible, and that but to a few. How few are there who can read Chaucer so as to understand him perfectly? And if imperfectly, then with less profit, and no pleasure. 'Tis not for the use of some old Saxon friends[7] that I have taken these pains with him. Let them neglect my version, because they have no need of it. I made it for their sakes who understand sense and poetry as well as they, when that poetry and sense is put into words which they understand. I will go farther, and dare to add, that what beauties I lose in some

---

4. *The Knight's Tale.*
5. Luke Milbourne (1649–1720), a clergyman and translator who had attacked Dryden's *Virgil.*
6. Many terms that have fallen out of use shall be born

again, and those shall fall which that are now in use, if usage so will it, in whose hands lies the judgment, the right, and the rule of speech (Horace, *Ars Poetica* 70–72).
7. Friends who were scholars of Anglo-Saxon literature.

places, I give to others which had them not originally. But in this I may be partial to myself; let the reader judge, and I submit to his decision. Yet I think I have just occasion to complain of them who, because they understand Chaucer, would deprive the greater part of their countrymen of the same advantage, and hoard him up, as misers do their grandam gold,[8] only to look on it themselves, and hinder others from making use of it. In sum, I seriously protest that no man ever had, or can have, a greater veneration for Chaucer than myself. I have translated some part of his works, only that I might perpetuate his memory, or at least refresh it, amongst my countrymen. If I have altered him anywhere for the better, I must at the same time acknowledge that I could have done nothing without him. *Facile est inventis addere*[9] is no great commendation, and I am not so vain to think I have deserved a greater. I will conclude what I have to say of him singly, with this one remark: a lady of my acquaintance, who keeps a kind of correspondence with some authors of the fair sex in France, has been informed by them, that Mademoiselle de Scudery,[1] who is as old as Sibyl,[2] and inspired like her by the same god of poetry, is at this time translating Chaucer into modern French. From which I gather, that he has been formerly translated into the old Provençal (for how she should come to understand old English, I know not). But the matter of fact being true, it makes me think that there is something in it like fatality; that after certain periods of time, the fame and memory of great wits should be renewed, as Chaucer is both in France and England. If this be wholly chance, 'tis extraordinary; and I dare not call it more, for fear of being taxed with superstition. * * *

from *The Cock and the Fox*[1]

    A yard she had with pales enclosed about,
Some high, some low, and a dry ditch without.
Within this homestead lived, without a peer
For crowing loud, the noble Chanticleer.
5   So hight° her cock, whose singing did surpass   *was named*
The merry notes of organs at the mass.
More certain was the crowing of a cock
To number hours, than is an abbey clock;
And sooner than the matin-bell was rung,
10   He clapped his wings upon his roost, and sung.
For when degrees fifteen ascended right,
By sure instinct he knew 'twas one at night.
High was his comb, and coral-red withal,
In dents embattled like a castle wall.
15   His bill was raven-black, and shone like jet,
Blue were his legs, and orient° were his feet.   *pearl-white*
White were his nails, like silver to behold,
His body glitt'ring like the burnished gold.
    This gentle cock for solace of his life,
20   Six misses had beside his lawful wife;
Scandal that spares no king, though ne'er so good,
Says, they were all of his own flesh and blood:
His sisters both by sire and mother's side,

8. Long-stored-up wealth.
9. It is easy to add to what has already been discovered.
1. Madeleine de Scudéry (1607–1701), author of chivalric romances.

2. The Sybil of Cumae was a prophetess who served Apollo, god of poetry; he granted her wish to live a thousand years.
1. *The Nun's Priest's Tale*, lines 81–115 and 670–680 (see pages 374–375 and 386–387).

And sure their likeness showed them near allied.
25   But make the worst, the monarch did no more
Than all the Ptolemies² had done before:
When incest is for int'rest of a nation,
'Tis made no sin by holy dispensation.
Some lines have been maintained by this alone,
30   Which by their common ugliness are known.
     But passing this as from our tale apart,
Dame Partlet was the sovereign of his heart:
Ardent in love, outrageous in his play,
He feathered her a hundred times a day:
35   And she that was not only passing fair,
But was withal discreet and debonair,
Resolved the passive doctrine to fulfil
Though loath: and let him work his wicked will.
At board and bed was affable and kind,
40   According as their marriage-vow did bind, }
And as the church's precept had enjoined. }
Ev'n since she was a sennight° old, they say, }   *week*
Was chaste and humble to her dying day, }
Nor chick nor hen was known to disobey. }
45   By this her husband's heart she did obtain.
What cannot beauty joined with virtue, gain!
She was his only joy, and he her pride;
She, when he walked, went pecking by his side;
If, spurning up the ground, he sprung a corn,
50   The tribute in his bill to her was born.
But O! what joy it was to hear him sing
In summer, when the day began to spring,
Stretching his neck, and warbling in his throat,
Solus cum Sola then was all his note.
55   For in the days of yore, the birds of parts
Were bred to speak, and sing, and learn the lib'ral arts.

THE MORAL

     In this plain fable you th' effect may see
Of negligence, and fond credulity;
And learn besides of flatt'rers to beware,
60   Then most pernicious when they speak too fair.
The Cock and Fox, the Fool and Knave imply;
The truth is moral, though the tale a lie.
Who spoke in parables, I dare not say;³
But sure, he knew it was a pleasing way,
65   Sound sense, by plain example, to convey.
And in a heathen author we may find,
That pleasure with instruction should be joined:⁴
So take the corn, and leave the chaff behind.

1700

2. Kings of Egypt, some of whom married their sisters.
3. In the Gospels, Jesus often speaks in parables.
4. The Roman poet Horace wrote that the most success-

ful writers are those who have combined the "useful"
(*utile*) with the "sweet" (*dulce*; *Ars Poetica* 343–344).

Aphra Behn
164?–1689

Aphra Behn's career was unprecedented, her output prodigious, her fame extensive, and her voice distinctive. Her origins, though, remain elusive. We know nothing certain about her birth, family, education, or marriage. She may have been born at the start or at the end of the 1640s, to parents of low or "gentle" station, named Johnson, Amies, or Cooper. Her Catholicism and her firm command of French suggest the possibility of a prosperous upbringing in a convent at home or abroad; the running argument against marriage for money that she sustains through much of her work suggests that her own marriage, to the otherwise unidentifiable "Mr. Behn," may have been obligatory and unhappy. In any case it was brief—and just possibly fictitious, since a widow could pursue a profession more freely than a spinster.

Behn's first appearances in the historical record suggest a propensity for self-invention. In 1663–1664, during a short stay with her family in the South American sugar colony of Surinam, a government agent there reported that she was conducting a flirtation with William Scott, an antimonarchist on the run from the Restoration. The agent referred to Scott as "Celadon" and Aphra as "Astraea," names the lovers may well have chosen for themselves from a popular French romance; Behn kept hers, as *nom de plume,* for the whole of her writing life. Within two years, her loyalties had shifted and her self-invention had grown more intricate. In 1666 Behn herself became the king's spy, sent from London to Antwerp to persuade her old flame Scott to turn informer against his fellow Republicans and to apprise King Charles of rebellious plots. She did useful but costly work, garnering good information that her handlers ignored and spending much money that they were slow to reimburse. Returning to England later that year, and threatened with imprisonment for debt, she wrote her supervisor, "I have cried myself dead and could find in my heart to break through all and get to the King and never rise till he were pleased to pay this, but I am sick and weak and unfit for it or a prison . . . Sir, if I have not the money tonight you must send me something to keep [sustain] me in prison, for I will not starve." The king paid up, and Behn forestalled any further threat of starvation by writing plays for money—the first woman in England to earn a living by her pen. She had been "forced to write for bread," she later declared, and she was "not ashamed to own it."

Throughout her career Behn transmuted such "shamelessness" into a positive point of pride and a source of literary substance. Many of her plays, poems, and fictions focus on the difficulty with which intelligent, enterprising women pursue their desires against the current of social convention. In the prologues, prefaces, postscripts, and letters by which she provided a running commentary on her work, Behn sometimes aligned herself with the large fraternity of male authors who "like good tradesmen" sell whatever is "in fashion," but she often stood apart to muse acerbically on her unique position as a *female* purveyor of literary product. Once, surveying the panoply of contemporary male playwrights, she declared that "except for our most unimitable Laureate [Dryden], I dare say I know of none that write at such a formidable rate, but that a woman may well hope to reach their greatest heights." "Formidable rate" suggests both speed and skill; Behn made good on both boasts, producing twenty plays in twenty years, along with much poetry (including fervent pro-Stuart propaganda), copious translations, one of the earliest epistolary novels in English, and a cluster of innovative shorter fiction. In her range and her dexterity, she approached the stature of the "unimitable Laureate" himself, who knew her and praised her repeatedly. With her greatest successes—the comedy *The Rover* (1677), the novella *Oroonoko* (1688)—she secured both an audience and a reputation that continued without pause well into the following century.

Other pieces worked less well. Changes in literary fashion often obliged Behn to try new modes; she switched to fiction, for example, in the 1680s, when plays became less lucrative.

Out of her vicissitudes—professional and personal, amorous, financial, literary—she fashioned a formidable celebrity, becoming the object of endless speculation in talk and in ink. "I value fame," she once wrote, and she cultivated it by what seemed an unprecedented frankness. ("All women together," wrote Virginia Woolf, "ought to let flowers fall upon the grave of Aphra Behn . . . for it was she who earned them the right to speak their minds.") In an age of libertines, when men like Rochester paraded their varied couplings in verse couplets, Behn undertook to proclaim and to analyze women's sexual desire, as manifested in her characters and in herself. Her disclosures, though, were intricately orchestrated. Living and writing at the center of a glamorous literary circle, Behn may have fostered, as the critic Janet Todd suggests, the "fantasy of a golden age of sexual and social openness," but she performed it for her readers rather than falling for it herself. Throughout her work Behn adroitly conceals the "self" that she purports to show and sell. She sometimes likens herself to those other female denizens of the theater, the mask-wearing prostitutes who roamed the audience in search of customers. The critic Catherine Gallagher has argued that Behn's literary persona—defiant, vulnerable, hypnotic—functions like the prostitute's vizard, promising the woman's "availability" as commodity while at the same time implying "the impenetrability of the controlling mind" behind the mask.

In Gallagher's reckoning, as in Woolf's, Behn's total career is more important than any particular work it produced. This is fitting tribute to a writer who, in an era of spectacular self-performers (Charles II, Dryden, Rochester), brought off, by virtue of her gender and her art, one of the most intricate performances of all. That performance now looks set for a long second run. After a hiatus in the nineteenth century, when both the writer and the work were dismissed as indecent, Behn's fame has undergone extraordinary revival. She dominates cultural-studies discourse as both a topic and a set of texts. The texts in particular are worth attending to: many are as astonishing as the career that engendered them.

The Disappointment[1]

> One day the amorous Lysander,
> By an impatient passion swayed,
> Surprised fair Cloris, that loved maid,
> Who could defend herself no longer.
5 > All things did with his love conspire;
> The gilded planet of the day,
> In his gay chariot drawn by fire,
> Was now descending to the sea,
> And left no light to guide the world,
10 > But what from Cloris' brighter eyes was hurled.
>
> In a lone thicket made for love,
> Silent as yielding maid's consent,
> She with a charming languishment
> Permits his force, yet gently strove;
15 > Her hands his bosom softly meet,
> But not to put him back designed,
> Rather to draw 'em[2] on inclined;
> Whilst he lay trembling at her feet,

1. Behn based this poem partly on a French source, *Sur une impuissance* (1661), itself derived in part from Ovid's poem on impotence in *Amores*, which also provided the model for Rochester's *Imperfect Enjoyment* (see page 2196). Behn's poem and Rochester's first appeared in the

same volume, *Poems on Several Occasions* (1680); she later included hers, with alterations, in her own collection, *Poems on Several Occasions* (1684).

2. Behn's earlier version reads "him."

Resistance 'tis in vain to show;
20   She wants° the power to say, "Ah! What d'ye do?"   lacks

Her bright eyes sweet, and yet severe,
Where love and shame confusedly strive,
Fresh vigor to Lysander give;
And breathing faintly in his ear,
25   She cried, "Cease, cease your vain desire,
Or I'll call out—what would you do?
My dearer honor even to you
I cannot, must not give—retire,
Or take this life, whose chiefest part
30   I gave you with the conquest of my heart."

But he as much unused to fear,
As he was capable of love,
The blessed minutes to improve,
Kisses her mouth, her neck, her hair;
35   Each touch her new desire alarms,
His burning trembling hand he pressed
Upon her swelling snowy breast,
While she lay panting in his arms.
All her unguarded beauties lie
40   The spoils and trophies of the enemy.

And now without respect or fear,
He seeks the object of his vows,
(His love no modesty allows)
By swift degrees advancing—where
45   His daring hand that altar seized,
Where gods of love do sacrifice:
That awful° throne, that paradise   awe-inspiring
Where rage is calmed, and anger pleased;
That fountain where delight still flows,
50   And gives the universal world repose.

Her balmy lips encountering his,
Their bodies, as their souls, are joined;
Where both in transports unconfined
Extend themselves upon the moss.
55   Cloris half dead and breathless lay;
Her soft eyes cast a humid light,
Such as divides the day and night;
Or falling stars, whose fires decay:
And now no signs of life she shows,
60   But what in short-breathed sighs returns and goes.

He saw how at her length she lay;
He saw her rising bosom bare;
Her loose thin robes, through which appear
A shape designed for love and play;
65   Abandoned by her pride and shame,
She does her softest joys dispense,

Offering her virgin innocence
A victim to love's sacred flame;
While the o'er-ravished shepherd lies
70   Unable to perform the sacrifice.

Ready to taste a thousand joys,
The too transported hapless swain[3]
Found the vast pleasure turned to pain;
Pleasure which too much love destroys.
75   The willing garments by he laid,
And Heaven all opened to his view,
Mad to possess, himself he threw
On the defenseless lovely maid.
But oh what envying god conspires
80   To snatch his power, yet leave him the desire!

Nature's support[4] (without whose aid
She can no human being give)
Itself now wants the art to live.
Faintness its slackened nerves invade.
85   In vain the enraged youth essayed
To call its fleeting vigor back,
No motion 'twill from motion take.
Excess of love his love betrayed.
In vain he toils, in vain commands;
90   The insensible[5] fell weeping in his hand.

In this so amorous cruel strife,
Where love and fate were too severe,
The poor Lysander in despair
Renounced his reason with his life.
95   Now all the brisk and active fire
That should the nobler part inflame,
Served to increase his rage and shame,
And left no spark for new desire.
Not all her naked charms could move
100   Or calm that rage that had debauched° his love.   *corrupted*

Cloris returning from the trance
Which love and soft desire had bred,
Her timorous hand she gently laid
(Or° guided by design or chance)   *either*
105   Upon that fabulous Priapus,[6]
That potent god, as poets feign;
But never did young shepherdess,
Gathering of fern upon the plain,
More nimbly draw her fingers back,
110   Finding beneath the verdant leaves a snake,

---

3. In English pastoral poetry, this is the conventional
term for the shepherd/lover.
4. I.e., the erect penis.

5. The unfeeling object.
6. Greek god of male fertility, often depicted as possessing
a permanent erection.

Than Cloris her fair hand withdrew,
Finding that god of her desires
Disarmed of all his awful fires,
And cold as flowers bathed in the morning dew.
115   Who can the nymph's confusion guess?
The blood forsook the hinder place,
And strewed with blushes all her face,
Which both disdain and shame expressed.
And from Lysander's arms she fled,
120   Leaving him fainting on the gloomy bed.

Like lightning through the grove she hies,
Or Daphne from the Delphic god,[7]
No print upon the grassy road
She leaves, to instruct pursuing eyes.
125   The wind that wantoned in her hair,
And with her ruffled garments played,
Discovered in the flying maid
All that the gods e'er made, if fair.
So Venus, when her love was slain,
130   With fear and haste flew o'er the fatal plain.[8]

The nymph's resentments none but I
Can well imagine or condole.
But none can guess Lysander's soul,
But those who swayed his destiny.
135   His silent griefs swell up to storms,
And not one god his fury spares;
He cursed his birth, his fate, his stars;
But more the shepherdess's charms,
Whose soft bewitching influence
140   Had damned him to the hell of impotence.

1680

To Lysander,[1] on Some Verses He Writ, and Asking More for His Heart than 'Twas Worth

Take back that heart you with such caution give,
   Take the fond[2] valued trifle back;
I hate love-merchants that a trade would drive;
   And meanly cunning bargains make.

5   I care not how the busy market goes,
   And scorn to chaffer° for a price: *bargain*
Love does one staple° rate on all impose,   *fixed*
   Nor leaves it to the trader's choice.

A heart requires a heart unfeigned and true,
10   Though subtly you advance the price,

---

7. Apollo, who pursued the nymph Daphne until she was turned into a laurel tree in order to escape his advances.
8. When her beloved Adonis was wounded by a boar, the goddess of love rushed to help him, but in vain.
1. "Lysander," the addressee of several of Behn's poems

(and, in name at least, the male lover in *The Disappointment*), has not been identified; the poem suggests that he was a married man.
2. The word meant both "foolish" and "affectionate."

And ask a rate that simple love ne'er knew:
    And the free trade monopolize.

An humble slave the buyer must become,
    She must not bate[3] a look or glance,
15   You will have all, or you'll have none;
    See how love's market° you enhance.°   *price / increase*

Is't not enough, I gave you heart for heart,
    But I must add my lips and eyes?
I must no friendly smile or kiss impart;
20   But you must dun[4] me with advice?

And every hour still more unjust you grow.
    Those freedoms you my life deny,
You to Adraste[5] are obliged to show,
    And give her all my rifled° joy.   *stolen*

25   Without control she gazes on that face,
    And all the happy envied night,
In the pleased circle of your fond embrace:
    She takes away the lover's right.

From me she ravishes those silent hours,
30   That are by sacred love my due;
Whilst I in vain accuse the angry powers,
    That make me hopeless love pursue.

Adraste's ears with that dear voice are blest,
    That charms my soul at every sound,
35   And with those love-enchanting touches pressed:
    Which I ne'er felt without a wound.

She has thee all: whilst I with silent grief,
    The fragments of thy softness feel,
Yet dare not blame the happy licensed[6] thief:
40   That does my dear-bought pleasures steal.

Whilst like a glimmering taper still I burn,
    And waste myself in my own flame,
Adraste takes the welcome rich return:
    And leaves me all the hopeless pain.

45   Be just, my lovely swain, and do not take
    Freedoms you'll not to me allow;
Or give Amynta[7] so much freedom back:
    That she may rove as well as you.

---

3. Withhold (by way of reducing love's "price").
4. Badger, demand payment from.
5. Apparently his wife.

6. Permitted (by the marriage license).
7. I.e. the poem's speaker.

Let us then love upon the honest square,[8]
50   Since interest neither have designed.[9]
     For the sly gamester,[1] who ne'er plays me fair,
         Must trick for trick expect to find.

1684

To Lysander at the Music-Meeting

     It was too much, ye gods, to see and hear,
     Receiving wounds both from the eye and ear.
     One charm might have secured a victory;
     Both, raised the pleasure even to ecstasy.
5   So ravished lovers in each other's arms,
     Faint with excess of joy, excess of charms.
     Had I but gazed and fed my greedy eyes,
     Perhaps you'd pleased no farther than surprise.
     That heav'nly form might admiration move,
10   But, not without the music, charmed° with love: *have charmed*
     At least so quick the conquest had not been;
     You stormed without, and harmony within.
     Nor could I listen to the sound alone,
     But I alas must look—and was undone:
15   I saw the softness that composed your face,
     While your attention heightened every grace:
     Your mouth all full of sweetness and content,
     And your fine killing eyes of languishment:
     Your bosom now and then a sigh would move,
20   (For music has the same effects with love).
     Your body easy and all tempting lay,
     Inspiring wishes which the eyes betray,
     In all that have the fate to glance that way.
     A careless and a lovely negligence,
25   Did a new charm to every limb dispense.
     So look young angels, listening to the sound,
     When the tuned spheres glad[1] all the heav'ns around:
     So raptured lie amidst the wondering crowd,
     So charmingly extended on a cloud.
30   When from so many ways love's arrows storm,
     Who can the heedless heart defend from harm?
     Beauty and music must the soul disarm;
     Since harmony, like fire to wax, does fit
     The softened heart impressions to admit:
35   As the brisk sounds of war the courage move,
     Music prepares and warms the soul to love.
     But when the kindling sparks such fuel meet,
     No wonder if the flame inspired be great.

1684

8. I.e., by rules that apply to both sides equally.
9. Neither of us has intended to make a profit (on our investment in each other).
1. Trickster or gambler.

1. Gladden. In the Ptolemaic view of the universe that Behn invokes here, the heavens were composed of concentric crystalline spheres, whose motion produced a sublime music. Angels could hear it, humans could not.

A Letter to Mr. Creech at Oxford[1]

Written in the Last Great Frost[2]

Daphnis, because I am your debtor,
(And other causes which are better)
I send you here by debt of letter.
You should have had a scrap of nonsense,
5 You may remember left at Tonson's.[3]
(Though by the way that's scurvy rhyme Sir,
But yet 'twill serve to tag° a line Sir.)   *round off*
A *billet-doux*° I had designed then,   *sweet note*
But you may think I was in wine then;
10 Because it being cold, you know
We warmed it with a glass—or so.
I grant you that shy° wine's the devil,   *cheap*
To make one's memory uncivil;
But when, 'twixt every sparkling cup,
15 I so much brisker wit took up;
Wit, able to inspire a thinking;
And make one solemn even in drinking;
Wit that would charm and stock a poet,
Even instruct ————[4] who has no wit;
20 Wit that was hearty, true, and loyal,
Of wit, like Bays'[5] Sir, that's my trial;
I say 'twas most impossible,
That after that one should be dull.
Therefore because you may not blame me,
25 Take the whole truth as —— shall sa'me.[6]
        From Whitehall[7] Sir, as I was coming,
His sacred Majesty from dunning—
Who oft in debt is, truth to tell,
For Tory farce, or doggerel—[8]
30 When every street as dangerous was,
As ever the Alpian hills° to pass,   *the Alps*
When melted snow and ice confound one,
Whether to break one's neck or drown one,
And *billet-doux* in pocket lay,
35 To drop as° coach should jolt that way,   *whenever*
Near to that place of fame called Temple,[9]
(Which I shall note by sad example)
Where college dunce is cured of simple,[1]

1. Thomas Creech (1659–1700), classicist and translator. Behn had praised his work in a previous poem, in which (as here) she addresses him by the pastoral name "Daphnis." Here she produces a less solemn piece, explaining why a love letter from her has failed to reach him, and conveying (in the postscript) a compliment from an unnamed well-wisher.
2. The winter of 1683–1684 was so severe that the surface of the river Thames froze solid.
3. The eminent bookseller Jacob Tonson (1656–1737) had published several of Behn's plays and her *Poems on Several Occasions* (1684). The route through London that Behn traces in this poem would have taken her past Tonson's shop.
4. An in-joke, probably referring to some mutually

despised Whig poet.
5. John Dryden, poet laureate (so nicknamed because in ancient Rome the laureate wore a wreath of bay leaves); Behn here implies that Dryden sets the standard ("trial") for true wit.
6. As Christ shall save me.
7. The royal palace in London; Behn has apparently been trying to collect payment from the king for a poem she wrote in his support.
8. I.e., Charles II frequently owes money to the partisan poets who write for him.
9. A cluster of buildings on Fleet Street containing residences, offices, and lecture halls for lawyers and students.
1. Simplicity, foolishness.

Against that sign of whore called scarlet,[2]
40   My coachman fairly laid pilgarlic.[3]
        Though scribbling fist was out of joint,
And every limb made great complaint;
Yet missing the dear assignation,[4]
Gave me most cause of tribulation.
45   To honest H——le[5] I should have shown ye,
A wit that would be proud t'have known ye;
A wit uncommon, a facetious,
A great admirer of Lucretius.[6]
But transitory hopes do vary,
50   And high designments oft miscarry.
Ambition never climbed so lofty,
But may descend too fair and softly.
But would you'd seen how sneakingly
I looked with this catastrophe.
55   So saucy Whig, when plot broke out,
Dejected hung his sniveling snout;[7]
So Oxford member looked, when Rowley
Kicked out the rebel crew so foully;[8]
So Perkin, once that god of Wapping,
60   Whom slippery turn of state took napping,
From hopes of James the Second fell
Into the native scoundrel.[9]
So lover looked of joy defeated,
When too much fire his vigor cheated.[1]
65   Even so looked I, when bliss-depriving
Was caused by over-hasty driving.
Who saw me could not choose but think,
I looked like brawn in sousing drink,[2]
Or Lazarello[3] who was showed
70   For a strange fish, to the gaping crowd.
        Thus you by fate (to me, sinister)
At shop of book my *billet* missed Sir.
And home I went as discontent,   ⎤
As a new routed° Parliament,   ⎬   *dismissed*
75   Not seeing Daphnis ere he went. ⎦

2. The Pope's Head tavern, so nicknamed because anti-
Catholic literature identified the Roman church with the
"whore . . . in scarlet" of Revelation 17.
3. The word originally denoted baldness (with "a head
like peeled garlic"), but had become slang for any unfortunate person.
4. I.e., with Creech.
5. John Hoyle, a rakish lawyer with whom Aphra Behn
had carried on a much-talked-about amorous relationship
and to whom she had addressed many poems.
6. Roman author of *De rerum natura* (*On the Nature of
Things*), which Creech had translated (1683). Lucretius's
insistence on worldly pleasure had established him as the
patron philosopher of Restoration libertines.
7. Behn imagines a partisan disappointed by the exposure
(and hence the failure) of the Rye House plot, an alleged
Whig scheme to assassinate the king and his brother in
1683.

8. In March 1681, Charles II (often dubbed "Rowley" in
casual talk and satiric ballads) dismissed the Parliament
at Oxford to frustrate the ambitions of the Whig faction.
9. "Perkin" is Charles II's illegitimate son James, Duke of
Monmouth, who (like the medieval pretender Perkin
Warbeck) claimed that he was the legitimate heir to the
crown; his cause was at one point popular in the rough
neighborhood of Wapping. Had he made good on his
claim, he (rather than his like-named uncle the Duke of
York) would have become James II. Disappointed of that
prospect, Behn suggests, he has now "fallen back" into
what he truly is: a born rascal.
1. I.e., because of premature ejaculation.
2. Like pickled pig's flesh, bruised and discolored.
3. Hero of Juan de Luna's picaresque narrative *Lazarillo de
Tormes*, who is rescued in fishermen's nets after a shipwreck and displayed as a sea monster.

And sure his grief beyond expressing,
Of joy proposed to want the blessing.[4]
Therefore to pardon pray incline,
Since disappointment all was mine.
80   Of Hell we have no other notion,
Than all the joys of Heaven's privation;
So Sir with recommendations fervent,
I rest your very humble servant.

Postscript

On Twelfth Night Sir, by that good token,
85   When lamentable cake was broken,[5]
You had a friend, a man of wit,
A man whom I shall ne'er forget,
For every word he did impart,
'Twas worth the keeping in a heart.
90   True Tory all! and when he spoke,
A god of wit, though man in look.
"To this your friend Daphnis, address
The humblest of my services.
Tell him how much—yet do not, too.
95   My vast esteem no words can show.
Tell him—that he is worthy—you."

1685

To the Fair Clarinda, Who Made Love to Me, Imagined More than Woman

Fair lovely maid, or if that title be
Too weak, too feminine for nobler thee,
Permit a name that more approaches truth,
And let me call thee, lovely charming youth.
5   This last will justify my soft complaint,
While that may serve to lessen my constraint;
And without blushes I the youth pursue,
When so much beauteous woman is in view.
Against thy charms we struggle but in vain,
10   With thy deluding form thou giv'st us pain,
While the bright nymph betrays us to the swain.[1]
In pity to our sex sure thou wert sent,
That we might love, and yet be innocent:
For sure no crime with thee we can commit;
15   Or if we should—thy form excuses it.
For who that gathers fairest flowers believes
A snake lies hid beneath the fragrant leaves.

4. Certainly he, having missed out on a promised pleasure, suffers inexpressible grief.
5. On the Twelfth Night of Christmas (6 January, "lamentable," perhaps, because it marked the holiday's conclusion), the traditional festivities included the cutting of
a cake in which a pea and bean had been concealed. The

recipients of the "prize" pieces presided over the celebration as king and queen (cf. the poem's final line, where
Behn and Creech are linked in praise).
1. The conventional pastoral term for a male lover or a
country lad.

Thou beauteous wonder of a different kind,
Soft Cloris with the dear Alexis[2] joined;
20   Whene'er the manly part of thee would plead
Thou tempts us with the image of the maid,
While we the noblest passions do extend
The love to Hermes, Aphrodite the friend.[3]

1688

APHRA BEHN IN CONTEXT
Coterie Writing

To Lysander, To the Fair Clarinda, A Letter to Mr. Creech: Some of Behn's poetry, like much other verse in the seventeenth century, proffered its readers the voyeuristic sense that they were being let in on the poet's correspondence. Sometimes this was so. In literary families and in friendships, verse often served as a medium of communication. A poem might make its way first from the writer to a designated recipient, then to a larger circle of acquaintances, and finally (with or without the author's consent) to the printing press. The practice of circulating manuscripts has come to be called "coterie writing," and its antecedents were ancient. Theocritus, the Greek poet credited with inventing pastoral verse, cast many of his poems as expressions of love and friendship (sung rather than written) among shepherds and nymphs living in a Golden Age. The Greek names of these ardent Arcadians—all those swooning "Lysanders" and "Clarindas"—came down to the English poets through the *Eclogues* of Virgil, Theocritus's immeasurably influential Roman imitator. Another Roman, Horace, had pioneered the durable paradigm of the verse epistle, a wittily self-conscious poetic performance addressed to a real-life, explicitly identified contemporary. In the seventeenth century, the resurgence of coterie writing began with the work of Katherine Philips, who celebrated her friendships with women in poems published to great acclaim shortly after her early death. (Behn admired Philips enormously, but reworked the tradition by addressing many of her poems to men—lovers and literary colleagues—in a boldly specific, often sexual language that contrasted sharply with Philips's celebrated chastity.) Both men and women produced poems of friendship in great numbers, but for women writers the practice appears to have held a particular attraction. In addressing other women, they could enact a solidarity, cultivate a self-discovery, define and develop a resistance otherwise muted in a male-dominated world; they often depict themselves as building from female friendship what the critic Janet Todd calls "the last buttress against the irrationality always implied in the female condition." The equivocal "privacy" of the coterie poem made it a particularly supple medium, capable of combining fact and fiction, disguise and revelation, intimacy and declamation. The three practitioners sampled here worked many variations in this pliable, powerful mode of writing.

Mary, Lady Chudleigh[1]
To the Ladies

Wife and servant are the same,
But only differ in the name:

---

2. "Cloris" is female, "Alexis" male.
3. Named after the offspring of these two gods, a hermaphrodite combines the characteristics of both sexes.
1. Born Mary Lee, and wed at age 17 into a family as aristocratic as her own, Lady Chudleigh (1656–1710) lived and wrote in the west coast county of Devon. After years of dispatching manuscript verses among a widening circle of writing friends (including the laureate John Dryden and the pioneering feminist Mary Astell), Chudleigh made her first foray into print with *The Ladies Defense*

(1701), a satiric retort to a parson who had exhorted all women (in her mocking paraphrase) to "give up their reason, and their wills resign" to the dictates of their husbands. In her *Defense*, and in the two collections of shorter poems that followed (1703, 1710), Chudleigh sought to expand her coterie into a larger collective readership consisting of "all ingenious ladies": women willing, in defiance of male presumption and social convention, "to read and think, and think and read again," and thereby to "make it our whole business to be wise."

For when that fatal knot is tied,
Which nothing, nothing can divide:
5   When she the word *obey* has said,
And man by law supreme has made,
Then all that's kind is laid aside,
And nothing left but state° and pride: *dignity*
Fierce as an Eastern Prince he grows,
10   And all his innate rigor shows:
Then but to look, to laugh, or speak,
Will the nuptial contract break.
Like mutes she signs alone must make,
And never any freedom take:
15   But still be governed by a nod,
And fear her husband as her God:
Him still must serve, him still obey,
And nothing act, and nothing say,
But what her haughty lord thinks fit,
20   Who with the power, has all the wit.°   *intelligence*
Then shun, oh! shun that wretched state,
And all the fawning flatterers hate:
Value your selves, and men despise,
You must be proud, if you'll be wise.

1703

To Almystrea[1]

1

Permit Marissa[2] in an artless lay
To speak her wonder, and her thanks repay:
Her creeping Muse can ne'er like yours ascend;
She has not strength for such a towering flight.
5   Your wit, her humble fancy does transcend;
She can but gaze at your exalted height:
Yet she believed it better to expose
    Her failures, than ungrateful prove;
    And rather chose
10   To show a want of sense, than want of love:
But taught by you, she may at length improve,
And imitate those virtues she admires.
Your bright example leaves a tract divine,
She sees a beamy brightness in each line,
15   And with ambitious warmth aspires,
Attracted by the glory of your name,
To follow you in all the lofty roads of fame.

2

Merit like yours can no resistance find,
But like a deluge overwhelms the mind;
20   Gives full possession of each part,
Subdues the soul, and captivates the heart.

---

1. The name is an anagram for Mary Astell, feminist   2. Chudleigh's pen name.
author of *Some Reflections upon Marriage* (see page 2280).

Let those whom wealth, or interest[3] unite,
    Whom avarice, or kindred sway,[4]
    Who in the dregs of life delight,
25   And every dictate of their sense° obey,   *appetites*
Learn here to love at a sublimer rate,
To wish for nothing but exchange of thoughts,
    For intellectual joys,
    And pleasures more refined
30   Than earth can give, or fancy can create.
Let our vain sex be fond of glittering toys,
Of pompous titles, and affected noise,
Let envious men by barb'rous custom led
    Descant° on faults,   *expound*
35   And in detraction° find   *criticisms*
Delights unknown to a brave generous mind,
While we resolve a nobler path to tread,
    And from tyrannic custom free,
View the dark mansions of the mighty dead,
40   And all their close recesses see;
    Then from those awful shades retire,
        And take a tour above,
    And there, the shining scenes admire,
    The opera of eternal love;
45   View the machines,[5] on the bright actors gaze,
Then in a holy transport, blest amaze,
To the great Author our devotion raise,
And let our wonder terminate in praise.

1703

Anne Finch, Countess of Winchilsea[1]
The Introduction

Did I my lines intend for public view,
How many censures would their faults pursue!
Some would, because such words they do affect,
Cry they're insipid, empty, uncorrect.
5   And many have attained, dull and untaught
The name of wit, only by finding fault.
True judges might condemn their want of wit,
And all might say they're by a woman writ.

---

3. Self-interest, desire for power and material prosperity.
4. I.e., who are motivated by greed or desire for family status.
5. The stage mechanisms used to move scenery and produce striking effects (including the appearances of gods and angels).
1. In the early 1680s, while serving as Maid of Honor to Mary of Modena (wife of the future James II), Anne Kingsmill (1661–1720) met and married Colonel Heneage Finch, and savored the splendors of the Stuart court. When that world vanished in the Revolution of 1688, she and her husband withdrew to his country estate, where she suffered recurrent depression, cultivated friendships, wrote poetry, and saw her work published in several miscellanies. In 1713, despite her wariness of the censures heaped on women writers, she published anonymously a collection of her own, *Miscellany Poems on Several Occasions*. (*The Introduction*, in which she most memorably confronts the censurers, remained like much of her verse unpublished until the 20th century.) The book brought her some fame in her own time and much more a century later, when William Wordsworth proclaimed his admiration for her work. Her poetry moves adroitly among polarities: city and country, satire and affection, solitude and friendship.

Alas! A woman that attempts the pen,
10   Such an intruder on the rights of men,
Such a presumptuous creature is esteemed,
The fault can by no virtue be redeemed.
They tell us we mistake our sex and way;
Good breeding, fashion, dancing, dressing, play
15   Are the accomplishments we should desire;
To write, or read, or think, or to inquire
Would cloud our beauty, and exhaust our time,
And interrupt the conquests of our prime;
Whilst the dull manage of a servile house
20   Is held by some our utmost art, and use.
    Sure 'twas not ever thus, nor are we told
Fables,° of women that excelled of old;   *false stories*
To whom, by the diffusive° hand of heaven   *scattering*
Some share of wit and poetry was given.
25   On that glad day, on which the Ark returned,[2]
The holy pledge for which the land had mourned,
The joyful tribes attend it on the way,
The Levites do the sacred charge convey,
Whilst various instruments before it play;
30   Here, holy virgins in the concert join,
The louder notes to soften, and refine,
And with alternate verse,[3] complete the hymn divine.
Lo! The young poet,[4] after God's own heart,
By Him inspired, and taught the Muse's art,
35   Returned from conquest, a bright chorus meets,
That sing his slain ten thousand in the streets.
In such loud numbers° they his acts declare,   *verses*
Proclaim the wonders of his early war,
That Saul upon the vast applause does frown,
40   And feels its mighty thunder shake the crown.[5]
What can the threatened judgment now prolong?[6]
Half of the kingdom is already gone:
The fairest half, whose influence guides the rest,
Have David's empire o'er their hearts confessed.
45   A woman[7] here leads fainting Israel on,
She fights, she wins, she triumphs with a song,
Devout, majestic, for the subject fit,
And far above her arms, exalts her wit,
Then to the peaceful, shady palm withdraws,
50   And rules the rescued nation with her laws.

---

2. The Ark of the Covenant was a chest containing the stone tablets of the Ten Commandments. Recovered by King David, it was carried into Jerusalem by members of the Levite tribe (1 Chronicles 15).

3. Responsive singing: the male and the female choruses sing by turns, answering line with line.

4. David, who in his youth was skilled both as a fighter, conquering the Philistines, and as a harper, credited with composing the Psalms.

5. Saul, first king of Israel, had made David his general but tried to kill him after hearing the women of Israel singing, "Saul has slain his thousands, and David his ten thousands" (1 Samuel 18.7).

6. Postpone; the prophet Samuel had foretold an untimely end to Saul's reign.

7. Deborah, judge and prophet who led the Israelites to victory over the Canaanites (Judges 4–5).

How are we fal'n, fal'n by mistaken rules?
And education's, more than nature's fools,
Debarred from all improvements of the mind,
And to be dull, expected and designed°;   *intended*
55   And if someone would soar above the rest,
With warmer fancy[8] and ambition pressed,
So strong the opposing faction still appears,
The hopes to thrive can ne'er outweigh the fears.
Be cautioned then my Muse, and still retired;
60   Nor be despised, aiming to be admired;
Conscious of wants, still with contracted wing,
To some few friends and to thy sorrows sing;
For groves of laurel[9] thou wert never meant;
Be dark enough thy shades, and be thou there content.

1903

Friendship Between Ephelia and Ardelia[1]

Eph. What friendship is, Ardelia, show.
Ard. 'Tis to love, as I love you.
Eph. This account, so short (though kind)
Suits not my inquiring mind.
5   Therefore farther now repeat:
What is friendship when complete?
Ard. 'Tis to share all joy and grief;
'Tis to lend all due relief
From the tongue, the heart, the hand;
10   'Tis to mortgage house and land;
For a friend be sold a slave;
'Tis to die upon a grave,
If a friend therein do lie.
Eph. This indeed, though carried high,
15   This, though more than e'er was done
Underneath the rolling sun,
This has all been said before.
Can Ardelia say no more?
Ard. Words indeed no more can show:
20   But 'tis to love, as I love you.

1713

A Ballad to Mrs. Catherine Fleming in London
from Malshanger Farm in Hampshire

From me, who whilom° sung the town,   *formerly*
   This second ballad comes;
To let you know we are got down
   From hurry, smoke, and drums:

8. Livelier imagination.   1. "Ardelia" is Finch's pastoral pen name.
9. Tree whose leaves were used to crown celebrated poets.

5   And every visitor that rolls
          In restless coach from Mall to Paul's,[1]
             With a fa-la-la-la-la-la.

       And now were I to paint the seat[2]
          (As well-bred poets use°)   do
10   I should embellish our retreat,
             By favor of the Muse:
       Though to no villa we pretend,
       But a plain farm at the best end,
             With a fa-la etc.

15   Where innocence and quiet reigns,
             And no distrust is known;
       His nightly safety none maintains,
             By ways they do in town,
       Who rising loosen bolt and bar;
20   We draw the latch and out we are,
             With a fa-la etc.

       For jarring sounds in London streets,
             Which still are passing by;
       Where "Cowcumbers"[3] with "Sand ho" meets,
25   And for loud mastery vie:
       The driver whistling to his team
       Here wakes us from some rural dream,
             With a fa-la etc.

       From rising hills through distant views,
30   We see the sun decline;
       Whilst everywhere the eye pursues
             The grazing flocks and kine:
       Which home at night the farmer brings,
       And not the post's but sheep's bell rings,
35   With a fa-la etc.

       We silver trouts and crayfish eat,
             Just taken from the stream;
       And never think our meal complete,
             Without fresh curds and cream:
40   And as we pass by the barn floor,
       We choose our supper from the door,
             With a fa-la etc.

       Beneath our feet the partridge springs,
             As to the woods we go;
45   Where birds scarce stretch their painted wings,
             So little fear they show:
       But when our outspread hoops° they spy,   hoop skirts
       They look when we like them should fly,
             With a fa-la etc.

50   Through verdant circles as we stray,
             To which no end we know;

---

1. From Pall Mall, a fashionable promenade in London,   2. The "country seat": the farm.
to St. Paul's Cathedral.   3. Cucumbers; these are the cries of street peddlers.

As we o'erhanging boughs survey,
    And tufted grass below:
Delight into the fancy falls,
55 And happy days and verse recalls,
    With a fa-la etc.

Oh! Why did I these shades forsake,
    And shelter of the grove;
The flowering shrub, the rustling brake,°   *thicket*
60   The solitude I love:
Where emperors have fixed their lot,
And greatly chose to be forgot,
    With a fa-la etc.

Then how can I from hence depart,
65   Unless my pleasing friend
Should now her sweet harmonious art
    Unto these shades extend:
And, like old Orpheus' powerful song,[4]
Draw me and all my woods along,
70   With a fa-la etc.

So charmed like Birnam's they would rise,
    And march in goodly row,[5]
But since it might the town surprise
    To see me travel so,
75 I must from soothing joys like these,
Too soon return in open chaise°   *carriage*
    With a fa-la etc.

Meanwhile accept what I have writ,
    To show this rural scene;
80 Nor look for sharp satiric wit
    From off the balmy plain:
The country breeds no thorny bays,
    But mirth and love and honest praise,
    With a fa-la etc.

c. 1719   1929

Mary Leapor[1]
The Headache. To Aurelia

Aurelia, when your zeal makes known
Each woman's failing but your own,

---

4. The mythological poet's music charmed trees and stones into motion.
5. In Shakespeare's *Macbeth*, the forest of Birnam "comes" to Dunsinane (fulfilling the witches' prophecy) when soldiers carry boughs as camouflage.
1. The daughter of a gardener, Mary Leapor (1722–1746) worked as a kitchen maid, read voraciously, wrote plentifully, and sustained the tradition of the social poem (complete with pastoral pseudonyms) into a new era and a new register. Her manuscripts, circulating among neighbors, brought her the attention, friendship, and support of Bridget Freemantle, who undertook to arrange their publication. Leapor died of measles at age 24 before

she could see her work in print. Her *Poems upon Several Occasions* appeared in 1748; its success prompted an additional volume three years later. Though the books were marketed as (in the words of one contemporary) the work of "a most extraordinary, uncultivated genius," the poems themselves prove otherwise. They display influences absorbed from Greek and Roman classics, Restoration drama, and Augustan literature—particularly Swift and Pope. Leapor transports these elements across boundary lines of class and gender to produce a new, arresting voice speaking from an old position: that of the woman who must labor in order to live.

How charming Silvia's teeth decay,
And Celia's hair is turning grey;
5   Yet Celia gay has sparkling eyes,
But (to your comfort) is not wise:
Methinks you take a world of pains
To tell us Celia has no brains.

Now you wise folk, who make such a pother°   *fuss*
10   About the wit of one another,
With pleasure would your brains resign,
Did all your noddles° ache like mine.   *heads*

Not cuckolds half my anguish know,
When budding horns[2] begin to grow;
15   Nor battered skull of wrestling Dick,
Who late was drubbed at singlestick;[3]
Nor wretches that in fevers fry,
Not Sappho[4] when her cap's awry,
E'er felt such torturing pangs as I;
20   Not forehead of Sir Jeffrey Strife,
When smiling Cynthio kissed his wife.

Not lovesick Marcia's languid eyes,
Who for her simpering Corin dies,
So sleepy look or dimly shine,
25   As these dejected eyes of mine:
Not Claudia's brow such wrinkles made
At sight of Cynthia's new brocade.

Just so, Aurelia, you complain
Of vapors, rheums, and gouty pain;
30   Yet I am patient, so should you,
For cramps and headaches are our due:
We suffer justly for our crimes,
For scandal you, and I for rhymes;
Yet we (as hardened wretches do)
35   Still the enchanting vice pursue;
Our reformation ne'er begin
But fondly hug the darling sin.

Yet there's a might difference too
Between the fate of me and you;
40   Though you with tottering age shall bow,
And wrinkles scar your lovely brow,
Your busy tongue may still proclaim
The faults of every sinful dame:
You still may prattle nor give o'er,
45   When wretched I must sin no more.
The sprightly Nine° must leave me then,   *Muses*
This trembling hand resign its pen:

---

2. Folklore held that the husband of an unfaithful wife
would sprout horns from his forehead.
3. Beaten in a fencing match using short, heavy sticks.

4. Apparently a mutual friend; the ensuing names, too,
refer to either real or imaginary people, otherwise
unidentified.

No matron ever sweetly sung,
Apollo° only courts the young.   *god of poetry*
50   Then who would not (Aurelia, pray)
Enjoy his favors while they may?
Nor cramps nor headaches shall prevail:
I'll still write on, and you shall rail.

                                                                    1748

Advice to Sophronia

When youth and charms have ta'en their wanton flight,
And transient beauty bids the fair good-night;
When once her sparkling eyes shall dimly roll,
Then let the matron dress her lofty soul;
5   Quit affectation, partner of her youth,
For goodness, prudence, purity, and truth.
These virtues will her lasting peace prepare,
And give a sanction to her silver hair.
These precepts let the fond Sophronia prove,
10   Nor vainly dress her blinking eyes with love.
Can roses flourish on a leafless thorn,
Or dewy woodbines grace a wintry morn?
The weeping Cupids languish in your eye;
On your brown cheek the sickly beauties die.
15   Time's rugged hand has stroked your visage o'er;
The gay vermilion stains your lip no more.
None can with justice now your shape admire;
The drooping lilies on your breast expire.
Then, dear Sophronia, leave thy foolish whims:
20   Discard your lover with your favorite sins.
Consult your glass; then prune your wanton mind,
Nor furnish laughter for succeeding time.
'Tis not your own; 'tis gold's all-conquering charms
Invite Myrtillo to your shrivelled arms:
25   And shall Sophronia, whose once-lovely eyes
Beheld those triumphs which her heart despised,
Who looked on merit with a haughty frown,
At five-and-fifty take a beardless clown?
Ye pitying Fates, this withered damsel save,
30   And bear her safely to her virgin grave.

                                                                    1751

An Essay on Woman

Woman, a pleasing but a short-lived flower,
Too soft for business and too weak for power:
A wife in bondage, or neglected maid;
Despised, if ugly; if she's fair, betrayed.
5   'Tis wealth alone inspires every grace,
And calls the raptures to her plenteous face.

What numbers for those charming features pine,
If blooming acres round her temples twine![1]
Her lip the strawberry, and her eyes more bright
10   Than sparkling Venus in a frosty night;
Pale lilies fade and, when the fair appears,
Snow turns a negro[2] and dissolves in tears,
And, where the charmer treads her magic toe,
On English ground Arabian odors grow;
15   Till mighty Hymen° lifts his sceptred rod,   *god of marriage*
And sinks her glories with a fatal nod,
Dissolves her triumphs, sweeps her charms away,
And turns the goddess to her native clay.

But, Artemisia,[3] let your servant sing
20   What small advantage wealth and beauties bring.
Who would be wise, that knew Pamphilia's[4] fate?
Or who be fair, and joined to Sylvia's mate?
Sylvia, whose cheeks are fresh as early day,
As evening mild, and sweet as spicy May:
25   And yet that face her partial husband tires,
And those bright eyes, that all the world admires.
Pamphilia's wit who does not strive to shun,
Like death's infection or a dog-day's sun?
The damsels view her with malignant eyes,
30   The men are vexed to find a nymph so wise:
And wisdom only serves to make her know
The keen sensation of superior woe.
The secret whisper and the listening ear,
The scornful eyebrow and the hated sneer,
35   The giddy censures of her babbling kind,
With thousand ills that grate a gentle mind,
By her are tasted in the first degree,
Though overlooked by Simplicus and me.
Does thirst of gold a virgin's heart inspire,
40   Instilled by Nature or a careful sire?
Then let her quit extravagance and play,
The brisk companion and expensive tea,
To feast with Cordia in her filthy sty
On stewed potatoes or on mouldy pie;
45   Whose eager eyes stare ghastly at the poor,
And fright the beggars from her hated door;
In greasy clouts° she wraps her smokey chin,   *rags*
And holds that pride's a never-pardoned sin.

If this be wealth, no matter where it falls;
50   But save, ye Muses, save your Mira's[5] walls:

---

1. I.e., if her dowry includes valuable land.
2. I.e., seems black by comparison.
3. The name of an ancient ruler celebrated as a patron of literature; Leapor applies it to her friend and sponsor Bridget Freemantle.

4. The lines about "Pamphilia" suggest that she may serve here as Leapor's alter ego; the other pastoral names (Sylvia, Simplicus, etc.) conjure up acquaintances real or imaginary.
5. Leapor's pen name (derived from "Mary").

Still give me pleasing indolence and ease,
A fire to warm me and a friend to please.

    Since, whether sunk in avarice or pride,
    A wanton virgin or a starving bride,
55   Or° wondering crowds attend her charming tongue,   *whether*
    Or, deemed an idiot, ever speaks the wrong;
    Though Nature armed us for the growing ill
    With fraudful cunning and a headstrong will;
    Yet, with ten thousand follies to her charge,
60   Unhappy woman's but a slave at large.

                                   1751

The Epistle of Deborah Dough

Dearly beloved Cousin, these
Are sent to thank you for your cheese;
The price of oats is greatly fell:
I hope your children all are well
5   (Likewise the calf you take delight in),
As I am at this present writing.
But I've no news to send you now;
Only I've lost my brindled° cow,   *spotted*
And that has greatly sunk my dairy.
10   But I forgot our neighbor Mary;
Our neighbor Mary—who, they say,
Sits scribble-scribble all the day,
And making—what—I can't remember;
But sure 'tis something like December;
15   A frosty morning—let me see—
O! Now I have it to a T:
She throws away her precious time
In scrawling nothing else but rhyme;[1]
Of which, they say, she's mighty proud,
20   And lifts her nose above the crowd;
Though my young daughter Cicely
Is taller by a foot than she,
And better learned (as people say);
Can knit a stocking in a day;
25   Can make a pudding, plump and rare;
And boil her bacon to an hair;
Will coddle° apples nice and green,   *cook*
And fry her pancakes—like a queen.

    But there's a man, that keeps a dairy,
30   Will clip the wings of neighbor Mary:
Things wonderful they talk of him,
But I've a notion 'tis a whim.

---

1. A pun on "rime" (frost), which is why her work is "like December."

Howe'er, 'tis certain he can make
Your rhymes as thick as plums in cake;
35   Nay more, they say that from the pot
He'll take his porridge, scalding hot,
And drink 'em down;—and yet they tell ye
Those porridge shall not burn his belly;
A cheesecake o'er his head he'll throw,
40   And when 'tis on the stones below,
It shan't be found so much as quaking,
Provided 'tis of his wife's making.
From this some people would infer
That this good man's a conjuror:
45   But I believe it is a lie;
I never thought him so, not I,
Though Win'fred Hobble who, you know,
Is plagued with corns on every toe,
Sticks on his verse with fastening spittle,
50   And says it helps her feet a little.
Old Frances too his paper tears,
And tucks it close behind her ears;
And (as she told me t'other day)
It charmed her toothache quite away.

55   Now as thou'rt better learned than me,
Dear Cos', I leave it all to thee
To judge about this puzzling man,
And ponder wisely—for you can.

Now Cousin, I must let you know
60   That, while my name is Deborah Dough,
I shall be always glad to see ye,
And what I have, I'll freely gi' ye.

'Tis one o'clock, as I'm a sinner;
The boys are all come home to dinner,
65   And I must bid you now farewell.
I pray remember me to Nell;
And for your friend I'd have you know
Your loving Cousin,
                              DEBORAH DOUGH

1751

Oroonoko

"I am very ill and have been dying this twelve month," Behn wrote an acquaintance late in 1687; she suffered from degenerative arthritis, and had some eighteen months' dying still to do. Now, near the end of her writing career, she set down a narrative of events that had pre-dated its beginnings, a story that she claimed to recall from the months she spent in 1663–1664 as a young woman in Surinam, an English colony on the northeastern coast of South America. A friend records that during the intervening decades Behn had often told the story of an African prince enslaved on the plantation where she dwelt; prompted by his love for a slave from his own country, he mounted a rebellion against his English masters. In *Oroonoko*, Behn displayed Surinam as a world where the appetites of trade and empire had brought several cultures—indigenous "Indians," colonizing Europeans, abducted Africans—into violent and precarious fusion.

Writing the narrative, Behn undertook volatile fusions of her own. On the title page, the single name "Oroonoko" sits above two subtitles in which both hero and text are implicitly split in two. The hero is both "royal" and a "slave"; the text's "true history" is so suffused with fictional conventions that for a long while historians suspected that Behn had never been to Surinam and had made the whole thing up (the truth of many of the story's details has been neither established nor refuted). Oroonoko and his beloved Imoinda play out the love-and-loss plot of a heroic romance—a genre favored by Restoration aristocracy—within the far more realistic context of a world driven by bourgeois imperatives and political aspirations. Behn's boldest fusion involves not only cultures, identities, and modes but also times. Oroonoko, "the chief actor in this history," comes to embody the history of Stuart sovereignty, playing the roles of all three kings to whom Behn had devoted her own obsessive loyalties: Charles I, whose 1649 execution haunts the narrative, particularly in its last few pages; Charles II, whose 1660 Restoration Behn pointedly invokes at the celebratory moment of the African prince's arrival at Surinam; and James II, the beleaguered Catholic king whose three-year reign was hurtling toward its close at the very moment of *Oroonoko*'s publication, and whose predicament as the embattled champion of an oppressed minority finds many echoes in the royal slave's rebellion and his fate.

Mapping all these convergences—of culture with culture, of monarch with slave, of man with woman—Behn places herself as narrator problematically near their center. The story is driven by her empathy for the slave couple, for whom she acts as mentor, friend, and advocate. Yet her empathy is complicated, perhaps even compromised. She shows less pity for less "royal" slaves, she acknowledges the possibility of her own complicity (however inadvertent) in her hero's pain, and she is oddly absent at the height of his suffering. She also participates in the profitable systems that enmesh him. Even before she tells his story, she presents herself as a kind of trader, who has brought back from Surinam butterflies for the Royal Society and exotic feathers for the dress of the "Indian Queen" in the popular heroic tragedy of that name. As Laura Brown points out, Behn's "treatment of slavery . . . is neither coherent nor fully critical." The narrative is by turns empathetic with the oppressed and complicit with the powerful; the crossing vectors of Behn's allegiance produce no conclusive sum.

In *Oroonoko*, cultural compounds prove unstable. Again and again in the story, human bodies are torn apart, and these sunderings foretell other dissolutions. Behn repeatedly reminds her readers that shortly after the events she narrates, the entire colony at Surinam disappeared: the English traded it away to the Dutch (they got New York in return). As colonist she laments this loss; as Tory, she anticipates another: the loss of James II in the parliamentary overthrow that would soon supplant the English Catholic with the Dutch Protestant William of Orange. Stuart rule, which had "ended" once with regicide, would end again (like the world of her youth in Surinam) with revolution.

Behn died shortly after publishing her narrative; she was buried in Westminster Abbey, where William would be crowned just five days later. After Behn's death, *Oroonoko* did more than any of her other works to sustain her fame. As a prose narrative and in an oft-revived dramatic adaptation, it became one of the touchstone texts for the antislavery movement that grew in England and America over the next century and a half. Only with the appearance of *Uncle Tom's Cabin* in the 1850s did the advocates of abolition find a more contemporary narrative that could take its place. Behn's intricately fictionalized "true history" had survived its initial moment and helped shape history thereafter.

Oroonoko

or

The Royal Slave
A True History

I do not pretend, in giving you the history of this royal slave, to entertain my reader with the adventures of a feigned hero, whose life and fortunes fancy may manage at the poet's pleasure; nor in relating the truth, design to adorn it with any accidents, but such as arrived in earnest to him. And it shall come simply into the world, recommended by its own proper merits, and natural intrigues; there being enough of reality to support it, and to render it diverting, without the addition of invention.

I was myself an eyewitness to a great part of what you will find here set down; and what I could not be witness of, I received from the mouth of the chief actor in this history, the hero himself, who gave us the whole transactions of his youth; and though I shall omit, for brevity's sake, a thousand little accidents of his life, which, however pleasant to us, where history was scarce, and adventures very rare, yet might prove tedious and heavy to my reader, in a world where he finds diversions for every minute, new and strange. But we who were perfectly charmed with the character of this great man were curious to gather every circumstance of his life.

The scene of the last part of his adventures lies in a colony in America called Surinam, in the West Indies.

But before I give you the story of this gallant slave, 'tis fit I tell you the manner of bringing them to these new colonies; for those they make use of there, are not natives of the place; for those we live with in perfect amity, without daring to command them; but on the contrary, caress them with all the brotherly and friendly affection in the world, trading with them for their fish, venison, buffaloes, skins, and little rarities; as marmosets, a sort of monkey as big as a rat or weasel, but of a marvelous and delicate shape, and has face and hands like an human creature; and cousheries,[1] a little beast in the form and fashion of a lion, as big as a kitten; but so exactly made in all parts like that noble beast, that it is it in miniature. Then for little parakeets, great parrots, macaws, and a thousand other birds and beasts of wonderful and surprising forms, shapes, and colors. For skins of prodigious snakes, of which there are some threescore yards in length; as is the skin of one that may be seen at His Majesty's Antiquaries,[2] where are also some rare flies,[3] of amazing forms and colors, presented to them by myself, some as big as my fist, some less; and all of various excellencies, such as art cannot imitate. Then we trade for feathers, which they order into all shapes, make themselves little short habits of them, and glorious wreaths for their heads, necks, arms, and legs, whose tinctures are inconceivable. I had a set of these presented to me, and I gave them to the King's Theater, and it was the dress of the *Indian Queen*,[4] infinitely admired by persons of quality, and were inimitable. Besides these, a thousand little knacks and rarities in nature, and some of art; as their baskets, weapons, aprons, etc. We dealt with them with beads of all colors, knives, axes, pins, and needles, which they used only as tools to drill holes with in their ears, noses, and lips, where they hang a great many little things; as long beads, bits of tin,

1. Other writers mention this animal, but its identity remains uncertain.
2. Probably the "Repository" (museum) of the Royal Society.

3. Butterflies.
4. A heroic drama (1664) by Robert Howard and John Dryden, celebrated for its sumptuous costumes and design.

brass, or silver, beat thin, and any shining trinket. The beads they weave into aprons about a quarter of an ell[5] long, and of the same breadth, working them very prettily in flowers of several colors of beads; which apron they wear just before them, as Adam and Eve did the fig leaves; the men wearing a long strip of linen, which they deal with us for. They thread these beads also on long cotton threads, and make girdles to tie their aprons to, which come twenty times or more about the waist and then cross, like a shoulder-belt, both ways, and round their necks, arms, and legs. This adornment, with their long black hair, and the face painted in little specks or flowers here and there, makes them a wonderful figure to behold. Some of the beauties which indeed are finely shaped, as almost all are, and who have pretty features, are very charming and novel; for they have all that is called beauty except the color, which is a reddish yellow; or after a new oiling, which they often use to themselves, they are of the color of a new brick, but smooth, soft, and sleek. They are extreme modest and bashful, very shy, and nice[6] of being touched. And though they are all thus naked, if one lives forever among them, there is not to be seen an indecent action or glance; and being continually used to see one another so unadorned, so like our first parents before the Fall, it seems as if they had no wishes; there being nothing to heighten curiosity, but all you can see, you see at once, and every moment see; and where there is no novelty, there can be no curiosity. Not but I have seen a handsome young Indian, dying for love of a very beautiful young Indian maid; but all his courtship was, to fold his arms, pursue her with his eyes, and sighs were all his language; while she, as if no such lover were present, or rather, as if she desired none such, carefully guarded her eyes from beholding him; and never approached him, but she looked down with all the blushing modesty I have seen in the most severe and cautious of our world. And these people represented to me an absolute idea of the first state of innocence, before man knew how to sin; and 'tis most evident and plain, that simple Nature is the most harmless, inoffensive, and virtuous mistress. 'Tis she alone, if she were permitted, that better instructs the world than all the inventions of man; religion would here but destroy that tranquillity they possess by ignorance, and laws would but teach them to know offense, of which now they have no notion. They once made mourning and fasting for the death of the English governor, who had given his hand to come on such a day to them, and neither came, nor sent; believing, when once a man's word was past, nothing but death could or should prevent his keeping it. And when they saw he was not dead, they asked him, what name they had for a man who promised a thing he did not do? The governor told them, such a man was a liar, which was a word of infamy to a gentleman. Then one of them replied, "Governor, you are a liar, and guilty of that infamy." They have a native justice which knows no fraud, and they understand no vice, or cunning, but when they are taught by the white men. They have plurality of wives which, when they grow old, they serve those that succeed them, who are young; but with a servitude easy and respected; and unless they take slaves in war, they have no other attendants.

Those on that continent where I was had no king; but the oldest war captain was obeyed with great resignation.

A war captain is a man who has led them on to battle with conduct[7] and success, of whom I shall have occasion to speak more hereafter, and of some other of their customs and manners, as they fall in my way.

---

5. Forty-five inches.
6. Shy.

7. Skillful management.

With these people, as I said, we live in perfect tranquillity and good understand-ing, as it behooves us to do; they knowing all the places where to seek the best food of the country, and the means of getting it; and for very small and invaluable trifles, supply us with what 'tis impossible for us to get; for they do not only in the wood, and over the savannahs, in hunting, supply the parts of hounds, by swiftly scouring through those almost impassable places, and by the mere activity of their feet, run down the nimblest deer, and other eatable beasts; but in the water, one would think they were gods of the rivers, or fellow citizens of the deep, so rare an art they have in swimming, diving, and almost living in water, by which they command the less swift inhabitants of the floods. And then for shooting, what they cannot take, or reach with their hands, they do with arrows, and have so admirable an aim, that they will split almost a hair; and at any distance that an arrow can reach, they will shoot down oranges and other fruit, and only touch the stalk with the darts' points, that they may not hurt the fruit. So that they being, on all occasions, very useful to us, we find it absolutely necessary to caress them as friends, and not to treat them as slaves; nor dare we do other, their numbers so far surpassing ours in that continent.

Those then whom we make use of to work in our plantations of sugar are Negroes, black slaves altogether, which are transported thither in this manner.

Those who want slaves make a bargain with a master, or captain of a ship, and contract to pay him so much apiece, a matter of twenty pound a head for as many as he agrees for, and to pay for them when they shall be delivered on such a plantation. So that when there arrives a ship laden with slaves, they who have so contracted go aboard, and receive their number by lot; and perhaps in one lot that may be for ten, there may happen to be three or four men; the rest, women and children; or be there more or less of either sex, you are obliged to be contented with your lot.

Coramantien,[8] a country of blacks so called, was one of those places in which they found the most advantageous trading for these slaves, and thither most of our great traders in that merchandise trafficked; for that nation is very warlike and brave, and having a continual campaign, being always in hostility with one neighboring prince or other, they had the fortune to take a great many captives; for all they took in battle were sold as slaves, at least, those common men who could not ransom themselves. Of these slaves so taken, the general only has all the profit; and of these generals, our captains and masters of ships buy all their freights.

The King of Coramantien was himself a man of a hundred and odd years old, and had no son, though he had many beautiful black wives; for most certainly, there are beauties that can charm of that color. In his younger years he had had many gallant men to his sons, thirteen of which died in battle, conquering when they fell; and he had only left him for his successor one grandchild, son to one of these dead victors; who, as soon as he could bear a bow in his hand, and a quiver at his back, was sent into the field, to be trained up by one of the oldest generals to war; where, from his natural inclination to arms, and the occasions given him, with the good conduct of the old general, he became, at the age of seventeen, one of the most expert captains, and bravest soldiers, that ever saw the field of Mars; so that he was adored as the wonder of all that world, and the darling of the soldiers. Besides, he was adorned with a native beauty so transcending all those of his gloomy race, that he struck an awe and reverence, even in those that knew not his quality; as he did in me, who beheld him with surprise and wonder, when afterwards he arrived in our world.

---

8. Koromantyn, a fort and trading post on the western coast of Africa (in modern Ghana).

He had scarce arrived at his seventeenth year when, fighting by his side, the general was killed with an arrow in his eye, which the Prince Oroonoko (for so was this gallant Moor[9] called) very narrowly avoided; nor had he, if the general, who saw the arrow shot, and perceiving it aimed at the Prince, had not bowed his head between, on purpose to receive it in his own body rather than it should touch that of the Prince, and so saved him.

'Twas then, afflicted as Oroonoko was, that he was proclaimed general in the old man's place; and then it was, at the finishing of that war, which had continued for two years, that the Prince came to court, where he had hardly been a month together, from the time of his fifth year to that of seventeen; and 'twas amazing to imagine where it was he learned so much humanity or, to give his accomplishments a juster name, where 'twas he got that real greatness of soul, those refined notions of true honor, that absolute generosity, and that softness that was capable of the highest passions of love and gallantry, whose objects were almost continually fighting men, or those mangled or dead; who heard no sounds but those of war and groans. Some part of it we may attribute to the care of a Frenchman of wit and learning, who finding it turn to very good account to be a sort of royal tutor to this young black, and perceiving him very ready, apt, and quick of apprehension, took a great pleasure to teach him morals, language, and science, and was for it extremely beloved and valued by him. Another reason was, he loved, when he came from war, to see all the English gentlemen that traded thither, and did not only learn their language but that of the Spaniards also, with whom he traded afterwards for slaves.

I have often seen and conversed with this great man, and been a witness to many of his mighty actions, and do assure my reader, the most illustrious courts could not have produced a braver man, both for greatness of courage and mind, a judgment more solid, a wit more quick, and a conversation more sweet and diverting. He knew almost as much as if he had read much: he had heard of, and admired the Romans; he had heard of the late Civil Wars in England, and the deplorable death of our great monarch,[1] and would discourse of it with all the sense, and abhorrence of the injustice imaginable. He had an extreme good and graceful mien, and all the civility of a well-bred great man. He had nothing of barbarity in his nature, but in all points addressed himself as if his education had been in some European court.

This great and just character of Oroonoko gave me an extreme curiosity to see him, especially when I knew he spoke French and English, and that I could talk with him. But though I had heard so much of him, I was as greatly surprised when I saw him as if I had heard nothing of him, so beyond all report I found him. He came into the room, and addressed himself to me, and some other women, with the best grace in the world. He was pretty tall, but of a shape the most exact that can be fancied; the most famous statuary[2] could not form the figure of a man more admirably turned from head to foot. His face was not of that brown, rusty black which most of that nation are, but a perfect ebony, or polished jet. His eyes were the most awful that could be seen, and very piercing, the white of them being like snow, as were his teeth. His nose was rising and Roman, instead of African and flat; his mouth, the finest shaped that could be seen, far from those great turned lips which are so natural to the rest of the Negroes. The whole proportion and air of his face was so noble and

---

9. The word originally meant "Moroccan," but was often used more generally for any person of African descent. Oroonoko's name may echo the river Orinoco in Venezuela, or the African god Oro.

1. Charles I, whose beheading in 1649 by sentence of the House of Commons marked the culmination of the wars between Royalists and Parliament.
2. Sculptor.

exactly formed that, bating[3] his color, there could be nothing in nature more beautiful, agreeable, and handsome. There was no one grace wanting that bears the standard of true beauty. His hair came down to his shoulders by the aids of art, which was, by pulling it out with a quill and keeping it combed, of which he took particular care. Nor did the perfections of his mind come short of those of his person, for his discourse was admirable upon almost any subject; and whoever had heard him speak, would have been convinced of their errors, that all fine wit is confined to the white men, especially to those of Christendom; and would have confessed that Oroonoko was as capable even of reigning well, and of governing as wisely, had as great a soul, as politic maxims,[4] and was as sensible of power as any prince civilized in the most refined schools of humanity and learning, or the most illustrious courts.

This prince, such as I have described him, whose soul and body were so admirably adorned, was (while yet he was in the court of his grandfather) as I said, as capable of love as 'twas possible for a brave and gallant man to be; and in saying that, I have named the highest degree of love; for sure, great souls are most capable of that passion.

I have already said the old general was killed by the shot of an arrow, by the side of this prince, in battle; and that Oroonoko was made general. This old dead hero had one only daughter left of his race; a beauty that, to describe her truly, one need say only, she was female to the noble male; the beautiful black Venus to our young Mars; as charming in her person as he, and of delicate virtues. I have seen an hundred white men sighing after her, and making a thousand vows at her feet, all vain and unsuccessful; and she was, indeed, too great for any but a prince of her own nation to adore.

Oroonoko coming from the wars (which were now ended) after he had made his court to his grandfather, he thought in honor he ought to make a visit to Imoinda, the daughter of his foster-father, the dead general; and to make some excuses to her, because his preservation was the occasion of her father's death; and to present her with those slaves that had been taken in this last battle, as the trophies of her father's victories. When he came, attended by all the young soldiers of any merit, he was infinitely surprised at the beauty of this fair Queen of Night, whose face and person was so exceeding all he had ever beheld; that lovely modesty with which she received him, that softness in her look and sighs, upon the melancholy occasion of this honor that was done by so great a man as Oroonoko, and a prince of whom she had heard such admirable things; the awfulness[5] wherewith she received him, and the sweetness of her words and behavior while he stayed, gained a perfect conquest over his fierce heart, and made him feel the victor could be subdued. So that having made his first compliments, and presented her a hundred and fifty slaves in fetters, he told her with his eyes that he was not insensible of her charms; while Imoinda, who wished for nothing more than so glorious a conquest, was pleased to believe she understood that silent language of new-born love; and from that moment, put on all her additions to beauty.

The Prince returned to court with quite another humor[6] than before; and though he did not speak much of the fair Imoinda, he had the pleasure to hear all his followers speak of nothing but the charms of that maid; insomuch that, even in the presence of the old king, they were extolling her, and heightening, if possible, the beauties they had found in her; so that nothing else was talked of, no other sound was heard in every corner where there were whisperers, but "Imoinda! Imoinda!"

'Twill be imagined Oroonoko stayed not long before he made his second visit; nor, considering his quality, not much longer before he told her he adored her. I have often heard him say that he admired by what strange inspiration he came to talk things so soft and so passionate, who never knew love, nor was used to the conversation of women; but (to use his own words) he said, most happily, some new, and till then unknown power instructed his heart and tongue in the language of love, and at the same time, in favor of him, inspired Imoinda with a sense of his passion. She was touched with what he said, and returned it all in such answers as went to his very heart, with a pleasure unknown before. Nor did he use those obligations ill that love had done him; but turned all his happy moments to the best advantage; and as he knew no vice, his flame aimed at nothing but honor, if such a distinction may be made in love; and especially in that country, where men take to themselves as many as they can maintain, and where the only crime and sin with woman is to turn her off, to abandon her to want, shame, and misery. Such ill morals are only practiced in Christian countries, where they prefer the bare name of religion; and, without virtue or morality, think that's sufficient. But Oroonoko was none of those professors; but as he had right notions of honor, so he made her such propositions as were not only and barely such; but, contrary to the custom of his country, he made her vows she should be the only woman he would possess while he lived; that no age or wrinkles should incline him to change, for her soul would be always fine, and always young; and he should have an eternal idea in his mind of the charms she now bore, and should look into his heart for that idea, when he could find it no longer in her face.

After a thousand assurances of his lasting flame, and her eternal empire over him, she condescended to receive him for her husband; or rather, received him, as the greatest honor the gods could do her.

There is a certain ceremony in these cases to be observed, which I forgot to ask him how performed; but 'twas concluded on both sides that, in obedience to him, the grandfather was to be first made acquainted with the design; for they pay a most absolute resignation to the monarch, especially when he is a parent also.

On the other side, the old king, who had many wives, and many concubines, wanted not court flatterers to insinuate in his heart a thousand tender thoughts for this young beauty; and who represented her to his fancy as the most charming he had ever possessed in all the long race of his numerous years. At this character his old heart, like an extinguished brand, most apt to take fire, felt new sparks of love and began to kindle; and now grown to his second childhood, longed with impatience to behold this gay thing, with whom, alas, he could but innocently play. But how he should be confirmed she was this wonder, before he used his power to call her to court (where maidens never came, unless for the King's private use) he was next to consider; and while he was so doing, he had intelligence brought him, that Imoinda was most certainly mistress to the Prince Oroonoko. This gave him some chagrin; however, it gave him also an opportunity, one day, when the Prince was a-hunting, to wait on a man of quality, as his slave and attendant, who should go and make a present to Imoinda, as from the Prince; he should then, unknown, see this fair maid, and have an opportunity to hear what message she would return the Prince for his present; and from thence gather the state of her heart, and degree of her inclination. This was put in execution, and the old monarch saw, and burned; he found her all he had heard, and would not delay his happiness, but found he should have some obstacle to overcome her heart; for she expressed her sense of the present the Prince had sent her, in terms so sweet, so soft and pretty, with an air of love and joy that could not be dissembled, insomuch that 'twas past doubt whether she loved Oroonoko entirely. This gave the old king some affliction, but he salved it with this, that the obedience the people pay their king was not at all inferior to what they paid their gods, and what love would not oblige Imoinda to do, duty would compel her to.

He was therefore no sooner got to his apartment, but he sent the royal veil to Imoinda, that is, the ceremony of invitation; he sends the lady, he has a mind to honor with his bed, a veil, with which she is covered and secured for the King's use; and 'tis death to disobey; besides, held a most impious disobedience.

'Tis not to be imagined the surprise and grief that seized this lovely maid at this news and sight. However, as delays in these cases are dangerous, and pleading worse than treason, trembling and almost fainting, she was obliged to suffer herself to be covered and led away.

They brought her thus to court; and the King, who had caused a very rich bath to be prepared, was led into it, where he sat under a canopy in state, to receive this longed for virgin; whom he having commanded should be brought to him, they (after disrobing her) led her to the bath and, making fast the doors, left her to descend. The King, without more courtship, bade her throw off her mantle and come to his arms. But Imoinda, all in tears, threw herself on the marble on the brink of the bath, and besought him to hear her. She told him, as she was a maid, how proud of the divine glory she should have been of having it in her power to oblige her king; but as by the laws he could not, and from his royal goodness would not take from any man his wedded wife, so she believed she should be the occasion of making him commit a great sin, if she did not reveal her state and condition, and tell him she was another's, and could not be so happy to be his.

The King, enraged at this delay, hastily demanded the name of the bold man that had married a woman of her degree without his consent. Imoinda, seeing his eyes fierce and his hands tremble, whether with age or anger I know not, but she fancied the last, almost repented she had said so much, for now she feared the storm would fall on the prince; she therefore said a thousand things to appease the raging of his flame, and to prepare him to hear who it was with calmness; but before she spoke, he imagined who she meant, but would not seem to do so, but commanded her to lay aside her mantle and suffer herself to receive his caresses; or by his gods, he swore, that happy man whom she was going to name should die, though it were even Oroonoko himself. "Therefore," said he, "deny this marriage, and swear thyself a maid." "That," replied Imoinda, "by all our powers I do, for I am not yet known to my husband." " 'Tis enough," said the king, " 'tis enough to satisfy both my conscience and my heart." And rising from his seat, he went and led her into the bath, it being in vain for her to resist.

In this time the Prince, who was returned from hunting, went to visit his Imoinda, but found her gone; and not only so, but heard she had received the royal veil. This raised him to a storm, and in his madness they had much ado to save him from laying violent hands on himself. Force first prevailed, and then reason. They urged all to him that might oppose his rage; but nothing weighed so greatly with him as the King's old age, incapable of injuring him with Imoinda. He would give way to that hope, because it pleased him most, and flattered best his heart. Yet this served not altogether to make him cease his different passions, which sometimes raged within him, and sometimes softened into showers. 'Twas not enough to appease him, to tell him his grandfather was old, and could not that way injure him, while he retained that awful[7] duty which the young men are used there to pay to their grave relations. He could not be convinced he had no cause to sigh and mourn for the loss of a mistress he could not with all his strength and courage retrieve. And he would often cry, "O my friends! Were she in walled cities, or confined from me in fortifications of the greatest strength; did enchantments or monsters detain her from me, I would venture through any hazard to free her. But here, in the arms of a feeble old man, my youth, my violent love, my trade in arms, and all my vast desire of glory avail me nothing. Imoinda is as irrecoverably lost to me as if she were snatched by the cold arms of death. Oh! she is never to be retrieved. If I would wait tedious years, till fate should bow the old king to his grave, even that would not leave me Imoinda free; but still that custom that makes it so vile a crime for a son to marry his father's wives or mistress would hinder my happiness; unless I would either ignobly set an ill precedent to my successors, or abandon my country and fly with her to some unknown world, who never heard our story."

But it was objected to him that his case was not the same; for Imoinda being his lawful wife, by solemn contract, 'twas he was the injured man, and might, if he so pleased, take Imoinda back, the breach of the law being on his grandfather's side; and that if he could circumvent him, and redeem her from the otan, which is the palace of the King's women, a sort of seraglio, it was both just and lawful for him so to do.

This reasoning had some force upon him, and he should have been entirely comforted, but for the thought that she was possessed by his grandfather. However, he loved so well that he was resolved to believe what most favored his hope, and to endeavor to learn from Imoinda's own mouth what only she could satisfy him in: whether she was robbed of that blessing, which was only due to his faith and love. But as it was very hard to get a sight of the women, for no men ever entered into the otan but when the King went to entertain himself with some one of his wives or mistresses, and 'twas death at any other time for any other to go in, so he knew not how to contrive to get a sight of her.

While Oroonoko felt all the agonies of love, and suffered under a torment the most painful in the world, the old king was not exempted from his share of affliction. He was troubled for having been forced by an irresistible passion to rob his son of a treasure he knew could not but be extremely dear to him, since she was the most beautiful that ever had been seen; and had besides all the sweetness and innocence of youth and modesty, with a charm of wit surpassing all. He found that however she was forced to expose her lovely person to his withered arms, she could only sigh and weep there, and think of Oroonoko; and oftentimes could not forbear speaking of him, though her life were, by custom, forfeited by owning her passion. But she spoke not of a lover only, but of a prince dear to him to whom she spoke; and of the praises of a man, who, till now, filled the old man's soul with joy at every recital of his bravery, or even his name. And 'twas this dotage on our young hero that gave Imoinda a thousand privileges to speak of him without offending, and this condescension in the old king that made her take the satisfaction of speaking of him so very often.

Besides, he many times inquired how the Prince bore himself; and those of whom he asked, being entirely slaves to the merits and virtues of the Prince, still answered what they thought conduced best to his service; which was, to make the old

7. Reverential.

king fancy that the Prince had no more interest in Imoinda, and had resigned her willingly to the pleasure of the King; that he diverted himself with his mathematicians, his fortifications, his officers, and his hunting.

This pleased the old lover, who failed not to report these things again to Imoinda, that she might, by the example of her young lover, withdraw her heart and rest better contented in his arms. But however she was forced to receive this unwelcome news, in all appearance, with unconcern and content, her heart was bursting within, and she was only happy when she could get alone, to vent her griefs and moans with sighs and tears.

What reports of the Prince's conduct were made to the King, he thought good to justify as far as possibly he could by his actions; and when he appeared in the presence of the King, he showed a face not at all betraying his heart; so that in a little time the old man, being entirely convinced that he was no longer a lover of Imoinda, he carried him with him, in his train to the otan, often to banquet with his mistress. But as soon as he entered one day into the apartment of Imoinda with the King, at the first glance from her eyes, notwithstanding all his determined resolution, he was ready to sink in the place where he stood; and had certainly done so, but for the support of Aboan, a young man who was next to him; which, with his change of countenance, had betrayed him, had the King chanced to look that way. And I have observed, 'tis a very great error in those who laugh when one says a Negro can change color; for I have seen them as frequently blush, and look pale, and that as visibly as ever I saw in the most beautiful white. And 'tis certain that both these changes were evident, this day, in both these lovers. And Imoinda, who saw with some joy the change in the Prince's face, and found it in her own, strove to divert the King from beholding either, by a forced caress, with which she met him, which was a new wound in the heart of the poor dying Prince. But as soon as the King was busied in looking on some fine thing of Imoinda's making, she had time to tell the Prince with her angry but love-darting eyes, that she resented his coldness, and bemoaned her own miserable captivity. Nor were his eyes silent, but answered hers again, as much as eyes could do, instructed by the most tender and most passionate heart that ever loved. And they spoke so well, and so effectually, as Imoinda no longer doubted but she was the only delight, and the darling of that soul she found pleading in them its right of love, which none was more willing to resign than she. And 'twas this powerful language alone that in an instant conveyed all the thoughts of their souls to each other, that they both found there wanted but opportunity to make them both entirely happy. But when he saw another door opened by Onahal, a former old wife of the King's who now had charge of Imoinda, and saw the prospect of a bed of state made ready with sweets and flowers for the dalliance of the King, who immediately led the trembling victim from his sight into that prepared repose, what rage, what wild frenzies seized his heart! Which forcing to keep within bounds, and to suffer without noise, it became the more insupportable and rent his soul with ten thousand pains. He was forced to retire to vent his groans, where he fell down on a carpet, and lay struggling a long time, and only breathing now and then, "O Imoinda!" When Onahal had finished her necessary affair within, shutting the door, she came forth to wait till the king called; and hearing some one sighing in the other room, she passed on, and found the Prince in that deplorable condition which she thought needed her aid. She gave him cordials but all in vain, till finding the nature of his disease by his sighs, and naming Imoinda. She told him he had not so much cause as he imagined to afflict himself; for if he knew the King so well as she did, he would not lose a moment in jealousy, and that she was confident that Imoinda bore, at this minute, part in his affliction. Aboan was of the same opinion; and both together persuaded him to reassume his courage; and all sitting down on the carpet, the Prince said so many obliging things to Onahal, that he half persuaded her to be of his party. And she promised him she would thus far comply with his just desires, that she would let Imoinda know how faithful he was, what he suffered, and what he said.

This discourse lasted till the King called, which gave Oroonoko a certain satisfaction; and with the hope Onahal had made him conceive, he assumed a look as gay as 'twas possible a man in his circumstances could do; and presently after, he was called in with the rest who waited without. The King commanded music to be brought, and several of his young wives and mistresses came all together by his command, to dance before him, where Imoinda performed her part with an air and grace so passing all the rest as her beauty was above them, and received the present ordained as a prize. The Prince was every moment more charmed with the new beauties and graces he beheld in this fair one; and while he gazed and she danced, Onahal was retired to a window with Aboan.

This Onahal, as I said, was one of the past mistresses of the old king; and 'twas these (now past their beauty) that were made guardians, or governants to the new and the young ones; and whose business it was, to teach them all those wanton arts of love with which they prevailed and charmed heretofore in their turn; and who now treated the triumphing happy ones with all the severity, as to liberty and freedom, that was possible, in revenge of those honors they rob them of; envying them those satisfactions, those gallantries and presents, that were once made to themselves, while youth and beauty lasted, and which they now saw pass regardless by, and paid only to the bloomings. And certainly, nothing is more afflicting to a decayed beauty than to behold in itself declining charms that were once adored, and to find those caresses paid to new beauties to which once she laid a claim; to hear them whisper as she passes by, "That once was a delicate woman." These abandoned ladies therefore endeavor to revenge all the despites and decays of time on these flourishing happy ones. And 'twas this severity that gave Oroonoko a thousand fears he should never prevail with Onahal to see Imoinda. But, as I said, she was now retired to a window with Aboan.

This young man was not only one of the best quality, but a man extremely well made and beautiful; and coming often to attend the King to the otan, he had subdued the heart of the antiquated Onahal, which had not forgot how pleasant it was to be in love. And though she had some decays in her face, she had none in her sense and wit; she was there agreeable still, even to Aboan's youth, so that he took pleasure in entertaining her with discourses of love. He knew also, that to make his court to these she-favorites was the way to be great; these being the persons that do all affairs and business at court. He had also observed that she had given him glances more tender and inviting than she had done to others of his quality. And now, when he saw that her favor could so absolutely oblige the Prince, he failed not to sigh in her ear, and to look with eyes all soft upon her, and give her hope that she had made some impressions on his heart. He found her pleased at this, and making a thousand advances to him; but the ceremony ending, and the King departing, broke up the company for that day, and his conversation.

Aboan failed not that night to tell the Prince of his success, and how advantageous the service of Onahal might be to his amour with Imoinda. The Prince was overjoyed with this good news, and besought him, if it were possible, to caress her, so as to engage her entirely; which he could not fail to do, if he complied with her desires. "For then," said the Prince, "her life lying at your mercy, she must grant you the request you make in my behalf." Aboan understood him, and assured him he would make love so effectually, that he would defy the most expert mistress of the art to find out whether he dissembled it or had it really. And 'twas with impatience they waited the next opportunity of going to the otan.

The wars came on, the time of taking the field approached, and 'twas impossible for the Prince to delay his going at the head of his army to encounter the enemy; so that every day seemed a tedious year, till he saw his Imoinda, for he believed he could not live if he were forced away without being so happy. 'Twas with impatience therefore that he expected the next visit the King would make; and, according to his wish, it was not long.

The parley of the eyes of these two lovers had not passed so secretly, but an old jealous lover could spy it; or rather, he wanted not flatterers who told him they observed it. So that the prince was hastened to the camp, and this was the last visit he found he should make to the otan; he therefore urged Aboan to make the best of this last effort, and to explain himself so to Onahal, that she, deferring her enjoyment of her young lover no longer, might make way for the Prince to speak to Imoinda.

The whole affair being agreed on between the Prince and Aboan, they attended the King, as the custom was, to the otan; where, while the whole company was taken up in beholding the dancing and antic[8] postures the women royal made to divert the King, Onahal singled out Aboan, whom she found most pliable to her wish. When she had him where she believed she could not be heard, she sighed to him, and softly cried, "Ah, Aboan! When will you be sensible of my passion? I confess it with my mouth, because I would not give my eyes the lie; and you have but too much already perceived they have confessed my flame. Nor would I have you believe that because I am the abandoned mistress of a king I esteem myself altogether divested of charms. No, Aboan; I have still a rest of beauty enough engaging, and have learned to please too well, not to be desirable. I can have lovers still, but will have none but Aboan." "Madam," replied the half-feigning youth, "you have already, by my eyes, found you can still conquer; and I believe 'tis in pity of me, you condescend to this kind confession. But, Madam, words are used to be so small a part of our country courtship, that 'tis rare one can get so happy an opportunity as to tell one's heart; and those few minutes we have are forced to be snatched for more certain proofs of love than speaking and sighing; and such I languish for."

He spoke this with such a tone that she hoped it true, and could not forbear believing it; and being wholly transported with joy, for having subdued the finest of all the King's subjects to her desires, she took from her ears two large pearls and commanded him to wear them in his. He would have refused them, crying, "Madam, these are not the proofs of your love that I expect; 'tis opportunity, 'tis a lone hour only, that can make me happy." But forcing the pearls into his hand, she whispered softly to him, "Oh! Do not fear a woman's invention when love sets her a-thinking." And pressing his hand she cried, "This night you shall be happy. Come to the gate of the orange groves, behind the otan, and I will be ready, about midnight, to receive you." 'Twas thus agreed, and she left him, that no notice might be taken of their speaking together.

---

8. Fantastic or grotesque.

The ladies were still dancing, and the King, laid on a carpet, with a great deal of pleasure was beholding them, especially Imoinda, who that day appeared more lovely than ever, being enlivened with the good tidings Onahal had brought her of the constant passion the Prince had for her. The Prince was laid on another carpet at the other end of the room, with his eyes fixed on the object of his soul; and as she turned or moved so did they; and she alone gave his eyes and soul their motions. Nor did Imoinda employ her eyes to any other use than in beholding with infinite pleasure the joy she produced in those of the Prince. But while she was more regarding him than the steps she took, she chanced to fall, and so near him as that leaping with extreme force from the carpet, he caught her in his arms as she fell; and 'twas visible to the whole presence, the joy wherewith he received her. He clasped her close to his bosom, and quite forgot that reverence that was due to the mistress of a king, and that punishment that is the reward of a boldness of this nature; and had not the presence of mind of Imoinda (fonder of his safety than her own) befriended him in making her spring from his arms and fall into her dance again, he had at that instant met his death; for the old king, jealous to the last degree, rose up in rage, broke all the diversion, and led Imoinda to her apartment, and sent out word to the Prince to go immediately to the camp; and that if he were found another night in court, he should suffer the death ordained for disobedient offenders.

You may imagine how welcome this news was to Oroonoko, whose unseasonable transport and caress of Imoinda was blamed by all men that loved him; and now he perceived his fault, yet cried that for such another moment, he would be content to die.

All the otan was in disorder about this accident; and Onahal was particularly concerned, because on the Prince's stay depended her happiness, for she could no longer expect that of Aboan. So that e'er they departed, they contrived it so that the Prince and he should come both that night to the grove of the otan, which was all of oranges and citrons, and that there they should wait her orders.

They parted thus, with grief enough, till night, leaving the King in possession of the lovely maid. But nothing could appease the jealousy of the old lover. He would not be imposed on, but would have it that Imoinda made a false step on purpose to fall into Oroonoko's bosom, and that all things looked like a design on both sides, and 'twas in vain she protested her innocence. He was old and obstinate, and left her more than half assured that his fear was true.

The King going to his apartment, sent to know where the Prince was, and if he intended to obey his command. The messenger returned and told him he found the Prince pensive, and altogether unpreparing for the campaign; that he lay negligently on the ground, and answered very little. This confirmed the jealousy of the King, and he commanded that they should very narrowly and privately watch his motions; and that he should not stir from his apartment, but one spy or other should be employed to watch him. So that the hour approaching, wherein he was to go to the citron grove, and taking only Aboan along with him, he leaves his apartment, and was watched to the very gate of the otan, where he was seen to enter, and where they left him, to carry back the tidings to the King.

Oroonoko and Aboan were no sooner entered but Onahal led the Prince to the apartment of Imoinda, who, not knowing anything of her happiness, was laid in bed. But Onahal only left him in her chamber to make the best of his opportunity, and took her dear Aboan to her own, where he showed the height of complaisance[9] for his prince, when, to give him an opportunity, he suffered himself to be caressed in bed by Onahal.

The Prince softly wakened Imoinda, who was not a little surprised with joy to find him there, and yet she trembled with a thousand fears. I believe he omitted saying nothing to this young maid that might persuade her to suffer him to seize his own and take the rights of love; and I believe she was not long resisting those arms where she so longed to be; and having opportunity, night and silence, youth, love and desire, he soon prevailed, and ravished in a moment what his old grandfather had been endeavoring for so many months.

'Tis not to be imagined the satisfaction of these two young lovers; nor the vows she made him, that she remained a spotless maid till that night; and that what she did with his grandfather had robbed him of no part of her virgin honor, the gods in mercy and justice having reserved that for her plighted lord, to whom of right it belonged. And 'tis impossible to express the transports he suffered while he listened to a discourse so charming from her loved lips, and clasped that body in his arms for whom he had so long languished; and nothing now afflicted him but his sudden departure from her; for he told her the necessity and his commands; but should depart satisfied in this, that since the old king had hitherto not been able to deprive him of those enjoyments which only belonged to him, he believed for the future he would be less able to injure him. So that abating the scandal of the veil, which was no otherwise so than that she was wife to another, he believed her safe even in the arms of the king, and innocent; yet would he have ventured at the conquest of the world, and have given it all, to have had her avoided that honor of receiving the royal veil. 'Twas thus, between a thousand caresses, that both bemoaned the hard fate of youth and beauty, so liable to that cruel promotion; 'twas a glory that could well have been spared here, though desired and aimed at by all the young females of that kingdom.

But while they were thus fondly employed, forgetting how time ran on and that the dawn must conduct him far away from his only happiness, they heard a great noise in the otan, and unusual voices of men; at which the Prince, starting from the arms of the frighted Imoinda, ran to a little battle-ax he used to wear by his side; and having not so much leisure as to put on his habit, he opposed himself against some who were already opening the door; which they did with so much violence that Oroonoko was not able to defend it, but was forced to cry out with a commanding voice, "Whoever ye are that have the boldness to attempt to approach this apartment thus rudely, know that I, the Prince Oroonoko, will revenge it with the certain death of him that first enters. Therefore stand back, and know this place is sacred to love and me this night; tomorrow 'tis the King's."

This he spoke with a voice so resolved and assured that they soon retired from the door, but cried, "'Tis by the King's command we are come; and being satisfied by thy voice, O Prince, as much as if we had entered, we can report to the King the truth of all his fears, and leave thee to provide for thy own safety, as thou art advised by thy friends."

At these words they departed, and left the Prince to take a short and sad leave of his Imoinda; who trusting in the strength of her charms, believed she should appease the fury of a jealous king by saying she was surprised, and that it was by force of arms

9. Desire to please.

he got into her apartment. All her concern now was for his life, and therefore she hastened him to the camp, and with much ado prevailed on him to go. Nor was it she alone that prevailed; Aboan and Onahal both pleaded, and both assured him of a lie that should be well enough contrived to secure Imoinda. So that at last, with a heart sad as death, dying eyes, and sighing soul, Oroonoko departed, and took his way to the camp.

It was not long after the King in person came to the otan, where beholding Imoinda with rage in his eyes, he upbraided her wickedness and perfidy, and threatening her royal lover, she fell on her face at his feet, bedewing the floor with her tears and imploring his pardon for a fault which she had not with her will committed, as Onahal, who was also prostrate with her, could testify that, unknown to her, he had broke into her apartment, and ravished her. She spoke this much against her conscience; but to save her own life, 'twas absolutely necessary she should feign this falsity. She knew it could not injure the Prince, he being fled to an army that would stand by him against any injuries that should assault him. However, this last thought of Imoinda's being ravished changed the measures of his revenge, and whereas before he designed to be himself her executioner, he now resolved she should not die. But as it is the greatest crime in nature amongst them to touch a woman after having been possessed by a son, a father, or a brother, so now he looked on Imoinda as a polluted thing, wholly unfit for his embrace; nor would he resign her to his grandson, because she had received the royal veil. He therefore removes her from the otan, with Onahal, whom he put into safe hands, with order they should be both sold off as slaves to another country, either Christian or heathen; 'twas no matter where.

This cruel sentence, worse than death, they implored might be reversed; but their prayers were vain, and it was put in execution accordingly, and that with so much secrecy that none, either without or within the otan, knew anything of their absence or their destiny.

The old king, nevertheless, executed this with a great deal of reluctance; but he believed he had made a very great conquest over himself when he had once resolved, and had performed what he resolved. He believed now that his love had been unjust, and that he could not expect the gods, or Captain of the Clouds (as they call the unknown power) should suffer a better consequence from so ill a cause. He now begins to hold Oroonoko excused and to say he had reason for what he did; and now everybody could assure the King, how passionately Imoinda was beloved by the Prince; even those confessed it now who said the contrary before his flame was abated. So that the King being old and not able to defend himself in war, and having no sons of all his race remaining alive but only this to maintain him on the throne; and looking on this as a man disobliged, first by the rape of his mistress, or rather, wife, and now by depriving him wholly of her, he feared, might make him desperate, and do some cruel thing, either to himself, or his old grandfather the offender; he began to repent him extremely of the contempt he had, in his rage, put on Imoinda. Besides, he considered he ought in honor to have killed her for this offense, if it had been one. He ought to have had so much value and consideration for a maid of her quality, as to have nobly put her to death, and not to have sold her like a common slave, the greatest revenge, and the most disgraceful of any, and to which they a thousand times prefer death, and implore it as Imoinda did, but could not obtain that honor. Seeing therefore it was certain that Oroonoko would highly resent this affront, he thought good to make some excuse for his rashness to him, and to that end he sent a messenger to the camp with orders to treat with him about the matter, to gain his pardon, and to endeavor to mitigate his grief; but that by no means he should tell him she was sold, but secretly put to death; for he knew he should never obtain his pardon for the other.

When the messenger came, he found the Prince upon the point of engaging with the enemy, but as soon as he heard of the arrival of the messenger he commanded him to his tent, where he embraced him and received him with joy; which was soon abated, by the downcast looks of the messenger, who was instantly demanded the cause by Oroonoko, who, impatient of delay, asked a thousand questions in a breath, and all concerning Imoinda. But there needed little return, for he could almost answer himself of all he demanded from his sighs and eyes. At last, the messenger casting himself at the Prince's feet and kissing them with all the submission of a man that had something to implore which he dreaded to utter, he besought him to hear with calmness what he had to deliver to him, and to call up all his noble and heroic courage to encounter with his words, and defend himself against the ungrateful things he must relate. Oroonoko replied, with a deep sigh and a languishing voice, "I am armed against their worst efforts—for I know they will tell me, Imoinda is no more—and after that, you may spare the rest." Then, commanding him to rise, he laid himself on a carpet under a rich pavilion, and remained a good while silent, and was hardly heard to sigh. When he was come a little to himself, the messenger asked him leave to deliver that part of his embassy which the Prince had not yet divined, and the Prince cried, "I permit thee." Then he told him the affliction the old king was in for the rashness he had committed in his cruelty to Imoinda, and how he deigned to ask pardon for his offense, and to implore the Prince would not suffer that loss to touch his heart too sensibly which now all the gods could not restore him, but might recompense him in glory which he begged he would pursue; and that death, that common revenger of all injuries, would soon even the account between him and a feeble old man.

Oroonoko bade him return his duty to his lord and master, and to assure him there was no account of revenge to be adjusted between them; if there were, 'twas he was the aggressor, and that death would be just, and, maugre[1] his age, would see him righted; and he was contented to leave his share of glory to youths more fortunate, and worthy of that favor from the gods. That henceforth he would never lift a weapon, or draw a bow, but abandon the small remains of his life to sighs and tears, and the continual thoughts of what his lord and grandfather had thought good to send out of the world, with all that youth, that innocence, and beauty.

After having spoken this, whatever his greatest officers and men of the best rank could do, they could not raise him from the carpet, or persuade him to action and resolutions of life, but commanding all to retire, he shut himself into his pavilion all that day, while the enemy was ready to engage; and wondering at the delay, the whole body of the chief of the army then addressed themselves to him, and to whom they had much ado to get admittance. They fell on their faces at the foot of his carpet, where they lay, and besought him with earnest prayers and tears to lead them forth to battle, and not let the enemy take advantages of them; and implored him to have regard to his glory, and to the world that depended on his courage and conduct. But he made no other reply to all their

---

1. In spite of; i.e., despite Oroonoko's youth, death will avenge the king by taking Oroonoko first.

supplications but this, that he had now no more business for glory; and for the world, it was a trifle not worth his care. "Go," continued he, sighing, "and divide it amongst you; and reap with joy what you so vainly prize, and leave me to my more welcome destiny."

They then demanded what they should do, and whom he would constitute in his room, that the confusion of ambitious youth and power might not ruin their order, and make them a prey to the enemy. He replied, he would not give himself the trouble; but wished them to choose the bravest man amongst them, let his quality or birth be what it would. "For, O my friends!" said he, "it is not titles make men brave, or good; or birth that bestows courage and generosity, or makes the owner happy. Believe this, when you behold Oroonoko, the most wretched, and abandoned by fortune of all the creation of the gods." So turning himself about, he would make no more reply to all they could urge or implore.

The army beholding their officers return unsuccessful, with sad faces and ominous looks that presaged no good luck, suffered a thousand fears to take possession of their hearts, and the enemy to come even upon them, before they would provide for their safety by any defense; and though they were assured by some, who had a mind to animate them, that they should be immediately headed by the Prince, and that in the meantime Aboan had orders to command as general, yet they were so dismayed for want of that great example of bravery that they could make but a very feeble resistance, and at last downright fled before the enemy, who pursued them to the very tents, killing them. Nor could all Aboan's courage, which that day gained him immortal glory, shame them into a manly defense of themselves. The guards that were left behind about the Prince's tent, seeing the soldiers flee before the enemy and scatter themselves all over the plain in great disorder, made such outcries as roused the prince from his amorous slumber, in which he had remained buried for two days without permitting any sustenance to approach him. But in spite of all his resolutions, he had not the constancy of grief to that degree as to make him insensible of the danger of his army; and in that instant he leapt from his couch and cried, "Come, if we must die, let us meet death the noblest way; and 'twill be more like Oroonoko to encounter him at an army's head, opposing the torrent of a conquering foe, than lazily, on a couch, to wait his lingering pleasure, and die every moment by a thousand wrecking thoughts; or be tamely taken by an enemy and led a whining, love-sick slave, to adorn the triumphs of Jamoan, that young victor, who already is entered beyond the limits I had prescribed him."

While he was speaking, he suffered his people to dress him for the field; and sallying out of his pavilion, with more life and vigor in his countenance than ever he showed, he appeared like some divine power descended to save his country from destruction; and his people had purposely put him on all things that might make him shine with most splendor, to strike a reverend awe into the beholders. He flew into the thickest of those that were pursuing his men, and being animated with despair, he fought as if he came on purpose to die, and did such things as will not be believed that human strength could perform, and such as soon inspired all the rest with new courage and new order. And now it was that they began to fight indeed, and so, as if they would not be outdone even by their adored hero, who turning the tide of the victory, changing absolutely the fate of the day, gained an entire conquest; and Oroonoko having the good fortune to single out Jamoan, he took him prisoner with his own hand, having wounded him almost to death.

This Jamoan afterwards became very dear to him, being a man very gallant and of excellent graces and fine parts, so that he never put him amongst the rank of captives, as they used to do, without distinction, for the common sale or market, but kept him in his own court, where he retained nothing of the prisoner but the name, and returned no more into his own country, so great an affection he took for Oroonoko; and by a thousand tales and adventures of love and gallantry, flattered his disease of melancholy and languishment, which I have often heard him say had certainly killed him, but for the conversation of this prince and Aboan, [and] the French governor he had from his childhood, of whom I have spoken before, and who was a man of admirable wit, great ingenuity and learning, all which he had infused into his young pupil. This Frenchman was banished out of his own country for some heretical notions he held; and though he was a man of very little religion, he had admirable morals, and a brave soul.

After the total defeat of Jamoan's army, which all fled, or were left dead upon the place, they spent some time in the camp, Oroonoko choosing rather to remain a while there in his tents, than enter into a palace, or live in a court where he had so lately suffered so great a loss. The officers therefore, who saw and knew his cause of discontent, invented all sorts of diversions and sports to entertain their prince: so that what with those amusements abroad and others at home, that is, within their tents, with the persuasions, arguments, and care of his friends and servants that he more peculiarly prized, he wore off in time a great part of that chagrin and torture of despair which the first effects of Imoinda's death had given him; insomuch as having received a thousand kind embassies from the King, and invitations to return to court, he obeyed, though with no little reluctance; and when he did so, there was a visible change in him, and for a long time he was much more melancholy than before. But time lessens all extremes, and reduces them to mediums and unconcern; but no motives or beauties, though all endeavored it, could engage him in any sort of amour, though he had all the invitations to it, both from his own youth and others' ambitions and designs.

Oroonoko was no sooner returned from this last conquest, and received at court with all the joy and magnificence that could be expressed to a young victor, who was not only returned triumphant but beloved like a deity, when there arrived in the port an English ship.

This person had often before been in these countries, and was very well known to Oroonoko, with whom he had trafficked for slaves, and had used to do the same with his predecessors.

This commander was a man of a finer sort of address and conversation, better bred and more engaging than most of that sort of men are; so that he seemed rather never to have been bred out of a court than almost all his life at sea. This captain therefore was always better received at court than most of the traders to those countries were; and especially by Oroonoko, who was more civilized, according to the European mode, than any other had been, and took more delight in the white nations, and, above all, men of parts and wit. To this captain he sold abundance of his slaves, and for the favor and esteem he had for him made him many presents, and obliged him to stay at court as long as possibly he could. Which the captain seemed to take as a very great honor done him, entertaining the Prince every day with globes and maps, and mathematical discourses and instruments; eating, drinking, hunting, and living with him with so much familiarity that it was not to be doubted but he had gained very greatly upon the heart of this gallant young man. And the captain, in return of all these mighty favors, besought the Prince to honor his vessel with his presence, some day or other, to dinner, before he should set sail; which he condescended to accept, and appointed his day. The captain, on his part, failed not to have all things in a readiness, in the most magnificent order he could possibly. And the day being come, the captain, in his boat richly adorned with carpets and velvet cushions, rowed to the shore to receive the Prince; with another longboat, where was placed all his music and trumpets, with which Oroonoko was extremely delighted, who met him on the shore, attended by his French governor, Jamoan, Aboan, and about an hundred of the noblest of the youths of the court. And after they had first carried the Prince on board, the boats fetched the rest off; where they found a very splendid treat, with all sorts of fine wines, and were as well entertained as 'twas possible in such a place to be.

The Prince having drunk hard of punch, and several sorts of wine, as did all the rest (for great care was taken they should want nothing of that part of the entertainment) was very merry, and in great admiration of the ship, for he had never been in one before; so that he was curious of beholding every place where he decently might descend. The rest, no less curious, who were not quite overcome with drinking, rambled at their pleasure fore and aft, as their fancies guided them: so that the captain, who had well laid his design before, gave the word and seized on all his guests; they clapping great irons suddenly on the Prince when he was leaped down in the hold to view that part of the vessel, and locking him fast down, secured him. The same treachery was used to all the rest; and all in one instant, in several places of the ship, were lashed fast in irons and betrayed to slavery. That great design over, they set all hands to work to hoist sail; and with as treacherous and fair a wind they made from the shore with this innocent and glorious prize, who thought of nothing less than such an entertainment.

Some have commended this act, as brave in the captain; but I will spare my sense of it, and leave it to my reader to judge as he pleases.

It may be easily guessed in what manner the Prince resented this indignity, who may be best resembled to a lion taken in a toil; so he raged, so he struggled for liberty, but all in vain; and they had so wisely managed his fetters that he could not use a hand in his defense, to quit himself of a life that would by no means endure slavery; nor could he move from the place where he was tied to any solid part of the ship against which he might have beat his head, and have finished his disgrace that way; so that being deprived of all other means, he resolved to perish for want of food. And pleased at last with that thought, and toiled and tired by rage and indignation, he laid himself down, and sullenly resolved upon dying, and refused all things that were brought him.

This did not a little vex the captain, and the more so because he found almost all of them of the same humor; so that the loss of so many brave slaves, so tall and goodly to behold, would have been very considerable. He therefore ordered one to go from him (for he would not be seen himself) to Oroonoko, and to assure him he was afflicted for having rashly done so inhospitable a deed, and which could not be now remedied, since they were far from shore; but since he resented it in so high a nature, he assured him he would revoke his resolution, and set both him and his friends ashore on the next land they should touch at; and of this the messenger gave him his oath, provided he would resolve to live. And Oroonoko, whose honor was such as he never had violated a word in his life himself, much less a solemn asseveration, believed in an instant what this man said, but replied he expected for a confirmation of this to have his shameful fetters dismissed. This demand was carried to the captain, who returned him answer that the offense had been so great which he had put upon the Prince, that he durst not trust him with liberty while he remained in the ship, for fear lest by a valor natural to him, and a revenge that would animate that valor, he might commit some outrage fatal to himself and the King his master, to whom his vessel did belong. To this Oroonoko replied, he would engage his honor to behave himself in all friendly order and manner, and obey the command of the captain, as he was lord of the King's vessel, and general of those men under his command.

This was delivered to the still doubting captain, who could not resolve to trust a heathen he said, upon his parole,[2] a man that had no sense or notion of the God that he worshipped. Oroonoko then replied he was very sorry to hear that the captain pretended to the knowledge and worship of any gods who had taught him no better principles, than not to credit as he would be credited; but they told him the difference of their faith occasioned that distrust: for the captain had protested to him upon the word of a Christian, and sworn in the name of a great God, which if he should violate, he would expect eternal torment in the world to come. "Is that all the obligation he has to be just to his oath?" replied Oroonoko. "Let him know I swear by my honor, which to violate, would not only render me contemptible and despised by all brave and honest men, and so give myself perpetual pain, but it would be eternally offending and diseasing all mankind, harming, betraying, circumventing, and outraging all men; but punishments hereafter are suffered by oneself; and the world takes no cognizances whether this god have revenged them, or not, 'tis done so secretly, and deferred so long; while the man of no honor suffers every moment the scorn and contempt of the honester world, and dies every day ignominiously in his fame, which is more valuable than life. I speak not this to move belief, but to show you how you mistake, when you imagine that he who will violate his honor will keep his word with his gods." So turning from him with a disdainful smile, he refused to answer him when he urged him to know what answer he should carry back to his captain; so that he departed without saying any more.

The captain pondering and consulting what to do, it was concluded that nothing but Oroonoko's liberty would encourage any of the rest to eat, except the Frenchman, whom the captain could not pretend to keep prisoner, but only told him he was secured because he might act something in favor of the Prince, but that he should be freed as soon as they came to land. So that they concluded it wholly necessary to free the Prince from his irons that he might show himself to the rest, that they might have an eye upon him, and that they could not fear a single man.

This being resolved, to make the obligation the greater, the captain himself went to Oroonoko; where, after many compliments, and assurances of what he had already promised, he receiving from the Prince his parole, and his hand, for his good behavior, dismissed his irons, and brought him to his own cabin; where, after having treated and reposed him a while, for he had neither eaten nor slept in four days before, he besought him to visit those obstinate people in chains, who refused all manner of sustenance; and entreated him to oblige them to eat, and assure them of their liberty the first opportunity.

Oroonoko, who was too generous not to give credit to his words, showed himself to his people, who were transported with excess of joy at the sight of their darling prince, falling at his feet, and kissing and embracing them, believing, as some divine

2. Word of honor.

oracle, all he assured them. But he besought them to bear their chains with that bravery that became those whom he had seen act so nobly in arms; and that they could not give him greater proofs of their love and friendship, since 'twas all the security the captain (his friend) could have against the revenge, he said, they might possibly justly take, for the injuries sustained by him. And they all, with one accord, assured him they could not suffer enough when it was for his repose and safety.

After this they no longer refused to eat, but took what was brought them and were pleased with their captivity, since by it they hoped to redeem the Prince, who, all the rest of the voyage, was treated with all the respect due to his birth, though nothing could divert his melancholy; and he would often sigh for Imoinda, and think this a punishment due to his misfortune, in having left that noble maid behind him that fatal night in the otan, when he fled to the camp.

Possessed with a thousand thoughts of past joys with this fair young person, and a thousand griefs for her eternal loss, he endured a tedious voyage, and at last arrived at the mouth of the river of Surinam, a colony belonging to the King of England, and where they were to deliver some part of their slaves. There the merchants and gentlemen of the country going on board to demand those lots of slaves they had already agreed on, and amongst those the overseers of those plantations where I then chanced to be, the captain, who had given the word, ordered his men to bring up those noble slaves in fetters, whom I have spoken of; and having put them, some in one, and some in other lots, with women and children (which they call pickaninnies), they sold them off as slaves to several merchants and gentlemen; not putting any two in one lot, because they would separate them far from each other; not daring to trust them together, lest rage and courage should put them upon contriving some great action, to the ruin of the colony.

Oroonoko was first seized on and sold to our overseer, who had the first lot, with seventeen more of all sorts and sizes, but not one of quality with him. When he saw this, he found what they meant; for, as I said, he understood English pretty well; and being wholly unarmed and defenseless, so as it was in vain to make any resistance, he only beheld the captain with a look all fierce and disdainful; upbraiding him with eyes that forced blushes on his guilty cheeks, he only cried in passing over the side of the ship, "Farewell, Sir! 'Tis worth my suffering to gain so true a knowledge both of you and of your gods by whom you swear." And desiring those that held him to forbear their pains, and telling them he would make no resistance, he cried, "Come, my fellow slaves, let us descend, and see if we can meet with more honor and honesty in the next world we shall touch upon." So he nimbly leapt into the boat, and showing no more concern, suffered himself to be rowed up the river with his seventeen companions.

The gentleman that bought him was a young Cornish gentleman, whose name was Trefry, a man of great wit and fine learning, and was carried into those parts by the Lord——, Governor, to manage all his affairs.[3] He reflecting on the last words of Oroonoko to the captain, and beholding the richness of his vest,[4] no sooner came into the boat, but he fixed his eyes on him; and finding something so extraordinary in his face, his shape and mien, a greatness of look, and haughtiness in his air, and finding he spoke English, had a great mind to be inquiring into his quality and fortune;

---

3. John Treffry (?–1674) supervised the plantation at Parham for Francis, Lord Willoughby (1613?–1686), a nobleman long involved with colonization, who received from Charles II both the governorship and a grant of land in Surinam; his appointment of Behn's father to the post of lieutenant-governor appears to account for her sojourn in the colony (though her father died en route).
4. Robe.

which, though Oroonoko endeavored to hide by only confessing he was above the rank of common slaves, Trefry soon found he was yet something greater than he confessed; and from that moment began to conceive so vast an esteem for him, that he ever after loved him as his dearest brother, and showed him all the civilities due to so great a man.

Trefry was a very good mathematician and a linguist, could speak French and Spanish, and in the three days they remained in the boat (for so long were they going from the ship to the plantation) he entertained Oroonoko so agreeably with his art and discourse, that he was no less pleased with Trefry, than he was with the Prince; and he thought himself, at least, fortunate in this, that since he was a slave, as long as he would suffer himself to remain so, he had a man of so excellent wit and parts for a master. So that before they had finished their voyage up the river, he made no scruple of declaring to Trefry all his fortunes and most part of what I have here related, and put himself wholly into the hands of his new friend, whom he found resenting all the injuries were done him, and was charmed with all the greatnesses of his actions, which were recited with that modesty and delicate sense, as wholly vanquished him, and subdued him to his interest. And he promised him on his word and honor, he would find the means to reconduct him to his own country again; assuring him, he had a perfect abhorrence of so dishonorable an action; and that he would sooner have died, than have been the author of such a perfidy. He found the Prince was very much concerned to know what became of his friends, and how they took their slavery; and Trefry promised to take care about the inquiring after their condition, and that he should have an account of them.

Though, as Oroonoko afterwards said, he had little reason to credit the words of a backearary,[5] yet he knew not why, but he saw a kind of sincerity and awful truth in the face of Trefry; he saw an honesty in his eyes, and he found him wise and witty enough to understand honor; for it was one of his maxims, "A man of wit could not be a knave or villain."

In their passage up the river they put in at several houses for refreshment, and ever when they landed numbers of people would flock to behold this man; not but their eyes were daily entertained with the sight of slaves, but the fame of Oroonoko was gone before him, and all people were in admiration of his beauty. Besides, he had a rich habit on, in which he was taken, so different from the rest, and which the captain could not strip him of because he was forced to surprise his person in the minute he sold him. When he found his habit made him liable, as he thought, to be gazed at the more, he begged Trefry to give him something more befitting a slave; which he did, and took off his robes. Nevertheless, he shone through all and his osenbrigs (a sort of brown holland suit he had on)[6] could not conceal the graces of his looks and mien; and he had no less admirers than when he had his dazzling habit on. The royal youth appeared in spite of the slave, and people could not help treating him after a different manner without designing it; as soon as they approached him they venerated and esteemed him; his eyes insensibly commanded respect, and his behavior insinuated it into every soul. So that there was nothing talked of but this young and gallant slave, even by those who yet knew not that he was a prince.

---

5. An African-derived term for "white master."

6. Osnaburg and holland were thick cotton or linen fabrics.

I ought to tell you, that the Christians never buy any slaves but they give them some name of their own, their native ones being likely very barbarous, and hard to pronounce; so that Mr. Trefry gave Oroonoko that of Caesar, which name will live in that country as long as that (scarce more) glorious one of the great Roman, for 'tis most evident, he wanted no part of the personal courage of that Caesar, and acted things as memorable, had they been done in some part of the world replenished with people and historians that might have given him his due. But his misfortune was to fall in an obscure world, that afforded only a female pen to celebrate his fame, though I doubt not but it had lived from others' endeavors, if the Dutch, who immediately after his time took that country,[7] had not killed, banished, and dispersed all those that were capable of giving the world this great man's life, much better than I have done. And Mr. Trefry, who designed it, died before he began it, and bemoaned himself for not having undertook it in time.

For the future therefore, I must call Oroonoko Caesar, since by that name only he was known in our western world, and by that name he was received on shore at Parham House, where he was destined a slave. But if the King himself (God bless him) had come ashore, there could not have been greater expectations by all the whole plantation, and those neighboring ones, than was on ours at that time; and he was received more like a governor than a slave. Notwithstanding, as the custom was, they assigned him his portion of land, his house, and his business, up in the plantation. But as it was more for form than any design to put him to his task, he endured no more of the slave but the name, and remained some days in the house, receiving all visits that were made him, without stirring towards that part of the plantation where the Negroes were.

At last, he would needs go view his land, his house, and the business assigned him. But he no sooner came to the houses of the slaves, which are like a little town by itself, the Negroes all having left work, but they all came forth to behold him, and found he was that prince who had, at several times, sold most of them to these parts; and, from a veneration they pay to great men, especially if they know them, and from the surprise and awe they had at the sight of him, they all cast themselves at his feet, crying out, in their language, "Live, O King! Long live, O King!" And kissing his feet, paid him even divine homage.

Several English gentlemen were with him; and what Mr. Trefry had told them was here confirmed, of which he himself before had no other witness than Caesar himself. But he was infinitely glad to find his grandeur confirmed by the adoration of all the slaves.

Caesar, troubled with their over-joy, and over-ceremony, besought them to rise, and to receive him as their fellow slave, assuring them, he was no better. At which they set up with one accord a most terrible and hideous mourning and condoling, which he and the English had much ado to appease. But at last they prevailed with them, and they prepared all their barbarous music, and everyone killed and dressed something of his own stock (for every family has their land apart, on which, at their leisure times, they breed all eatable things) and clubbing it together, made a most magnificent supper, inviting their grandee captain, their prince, to honor it with his presence, which he did, and several English with him, where they all waited on him,

***

7. In 1667 Surinam twice changed hands. The Dutch briefly captured the colony and the English won it back, but immediately ceded it to the Dutch (in exchange for New York) at the Treaty of Breda.

some playing, others dancing before him all the time, according to the manners of their several nations, and with unwearied industry endeavoring to please and delight him.

While they sat at meat Mr. Trefry told Caesar that most of these young slaves were undone in love, with a fine she-slave, whom they had had about six months on their land. The Prince, who never heard the name of love without a sigh, nor any mention of it without the curiosity of examining further into that tale which of all discourses was most agreeable to him, asked, how they came to be so unhappy, as to be all undone for one fair slave? Trefry, who was naturally amorous, and loved to talk of love as well as anybody, proceeded to tell him, they had the most charming black that ever was beheld on their plantation, about fifteen or sixteen years old, as he guessed; that, for his part, he had done nothing but sigh for her ever since she came; and that all the white beauties he had seen never charmed him so absolutely as this fine creature had done; and that no man of any nation ever beheld her, that did not fall in love with her; and that she had all the slaves perpetually at her feet; and the whole country resounded with the fame of Clemene, "for so," said he, "we have christened her. But she denies us all with such a noble disdain, that 'tis a miracle to see that she, who can give such eternal desires, should herself be all ice, and all unconcern. She is adorned with the most graceful modesty that ever beautified youth; the softest sigher—that, if she were capable of love, one would swear she languished for some absent happy man; and so retired, as if she feared a rape even from the God of Day,[8] or that the breezes would steal kisses from her delicate mouth. Her task of work some sighing lover every day makes it his petition to perform for her, which she accepts blushing, and with reluctance, for fear he will ask her a look for a recompense, which he dares not presume to hope, so great an awe she strikes into the hearts of her admirers." "I do not wonder," replied the Prince, "that Clemene should refuse slaves, being as you say so beautiful, but wonder how she escapes those who can entertain her as you can do. Or why, being your slave, you do not oblige her to yield." "I confess," said Trefry, "when I have, against her will, entertained her with love so long as to be transported with my passion even above decency, I have been ready to make use of those advantages of strength and force nature has given me. But oh! she disarms me, with that modesty and weeping so tender and so moving, that I retire, and thank my stars she overcame me." The company laughed at his civility to a slave, and Caesar only applauded the nobleness of his passion and nature, since that slave might be noble, or, what was better, have true notions of honor and virtue in her. Thus passed they this night, after having received from the slaves all imaginable respect and obedience.

The next day Trefry asked Caesar to walk, when the heat was allayed, and designedly carried him by the cottage of the fair slave, and told him, she whom he spoke of last night lived there retired. "But," says he, "I would not wish you to approach, for I am sure you will be in love as soon as you behold her." Caesar assured him he was proof against all the charms of that sex, and that if he imagined his heart could be so perfidious to love again after Imoinda, he believed he should tear it from his bosom. They had no sooner spoke, but a little shock dog,[9] that Clemene had presented her, which she took great delight in, ran out, and she, not knowing anybody

---

8. The sun.   9. A thick-haired dog.

was there, ran to get it in again, and bolted out on those who were just speaking of her. When seeing them she would have run in again, but Trefry caught her by the hand and cried, "Clemene, however you fly a lover, you ought to pay some respect to this stranger" (pointing to Caesar). But she, as if she had resolved never to raise her eyes to the face of a man again, bent them the more to the earth when he spoke, and gave the Prince the leisure to look the more at her. There needed no long gazing or consideration to examine who this fair creature was. He soon saw Imoinda all over her; in a minute he saw her face, her shape, her air, her modesty, and all that called forth his soul with joy at his eyes, and left his body destitute of almost life. It stood without motion, and, for a minute, knew not that it had a being. And I believe he had never come to himself, so oppressed he was with overjoy, if he had not met with this allay,[1] that he perceived Imoinda fall dead in the hands of Trefry. This awakened him, and he ran to her aid, and caught her in his arms, where, by degrees, she came to herself; and 'tis needless to tell with what transports, what ecstasies of joy, they both a while beheld each other, without speaking, then snatched each other to their arms, then gaze again, as if they still doubted whether they possessed the blessing they grasped. But when they recovered their speech, 'tis not to be imagined what tender things they expressed to each other, wondering what strange fate had brought them again together. They soon informed each other of their fortunes, and equally bewailed their fate; but at the same time, they mutually protested that even fetters and slavery were soft and easy, and would be supported with joy and pleasure, while they could be so happy to possess each other, and to be able to make good their vows. Caesar swore he disdained the empire of the world while he could behold his Imoinda, and she despised grandeur and pomp, those vanities of her sex, when she could gaze on Oroonoko. He adored the very cottage where she resided, and said, that little inch of the world would give him more happiness than all the universe could do, and she vowed, it was a palace, while adorned with the presence of Oroonoko.

Trefry was infinitely pleased with this novel,[2] and found this Clemene was the fair mistress of whom Caesar had before spoke; and was not a little satisfied, that Heaven was so kind to the Prince as to sweeten his misfortunes by so lucky an accident, and leaving the lovers to themselves, was impatient to come down to Parham House (which was on the same plantation) to give me an account of what had happened. I was as impatient to make these lovers a visit, having already made a friendship with Caesar, and from his own mouth learned what I have related, which was confirmed by his Frenchman, who was set on shore to seek his fortunes, and of whom they could not make a slave because a Christian, and he came daily to Parham Hill to see and pay his respects to his pupil prince. So that concerning and interesting myself in all that related to Caesar, whom I had assured of liberty as soon as the governor arrived, I hasted presently to the place where the lovers were, and was infinitely glad to find this beautiful young slave (who had already gained all our esteems, for her modesty and her extraordinary prettiness) to be the same I had heard Caesar speak so much of. One may imagine then, we paid her a treble respect; and though from her being carved in fine flowers and birds all over her body, we took her to be of quality before, yet, when we knew Clemene was Imoinda, we could not enough admire her.

---

1. Reduction; release.   2. New development.

I had forgot to tell you, that those who are nobly born of that country are so delicately cut and raced[3] all over the fore part of the trunk of their bodies, that it looks as if it were japanned;[4] the works being raised like high point[5] round the edges of the flowers. Some are only carved with a little flower or bird at the sides of the temples, as was Caesar; and those who are so carved over the body resemble our ancient Picts,[6] that are figured in the chronicles, but these carvings are more delicate.

From that happy day Caesar took Clemene for his wife, to the general joy of all people, and there was as much magnificence as the country would afford at the celebration of this wedding. And in a very short time after she conceived with child; which made Caesar even adore her, knowing he was the last of his great race. This new accident made him more impatient of liberty, and he was every day treating with Trefry for his and Clemene's liberty; and offered either gold, or a vast quantity of slaves, which should be paid before they let him go, provided he could have any security that he should go when his ransom was paid. They fed him from day to day with promises, and delayed him, till the Lord Governor should come, so that he began to suspect them of falsehood, and that they would delay him till the time of his wife's delivery, and make a slave of that too, for all the breed is theirs to whom the parents belong. This thought made him very uneasy, and his sullenness gave them some jealousies[7] of him, so that I was obliged, by some persons who feared a mutiny (which is very fatal sometimes in those colonies that abound so with slaves that they exceed the whites in vast numbers), to discourse with Caesar, and to give him all the satisfaction I possibly could. They knew he and Clemene were scarce an hour in a day from my lodgings, that they ate with me, and that I obliged them in all things I was capable of: I entertained him with the lives of the Romans, and great men, which charmed him to my company, and her, with teaching her all the pretty works that I was mistress of, and telling her stories of nuns, and endeavoring to bring her to the knowledge of the true God. But of all discourses Caesar liked that the worst, and would never be reconciled to our notions of the Trinity, of which he ever made a jest; it was a riddle, he said, would turn his brain to conceive, and one could not make him understand what faith was. However, these conversations failed not altogether so well to divert him, that he liked the company of us women much above the men, for he could not drink, and he is but an ill companion in that country that cannot. So that obliging him to love us very well, we had all the liberty of speech with him, especially myself, whom he called his Great Mistress; and indeed my word would go a great way with him. For these reasons, I had opportunity to take notice to him, that he was not well pleased of late, as he used to be, was more retired and thoughtful, and told him, I took it ill he should suspect we would break our words with him, and not permit both him and Clemene to return to his own kingdom, which was not so long away, but when he was once on his voyage he would quickly arrive there. He made me some answers that showed a doubt in him, which made me ask him, what advantage it would be to doubt? It would but give us a fear of him, and possibly compel us to treat him so as I should be very loath to behold: that is, it might occasion his confinement. Perhaps this was not so luckily spoke of me, for I perceived he resented that word, which I strove to soften again in vain. However, he assured me, that whatsoever resolutions he should take, he would act nothing upon the white people. And

3. Carved.
4. Varnished with a glossy black lacquer.
5. Intricate lace.
6. Ancient inhabitants of northern Britain, possibly so

named by the Romans because of the "pictures" (tattoos and other ornaments) they bore on their skin.
7. Suspicions.

as for myself, and those upon that plantation where he was, he would sooner forfeit his eternal liberty, and life itself, than lift his hand against his greatest enemy on that place. He besought me to suffer no fears upon his account, for he could do nothing that honor should not dictate, but he accused himself for having suffered slavery so long; yet he charged that weakness on love alone, who was capable of making him neglect even glory itself, and for which now he reproaches himself every moment of the day. Much more to this effect he spoke, with an air impatient enough to make me know he would not be long in bondage, and though he suffered only the name of a slave, and had nothing of the toil and labor of one, yet that was sufficient to render him uneasy, and he had been too long idle, who used to be always in action, and in arms. He had a spirit all rough and fierce, and that could not be tamed to lazy rest, and though all endeavors were used to exercise himself in such actions and sports as this world afforded, as running, wrestling, pitching the bar,[8] hunting and fishing, chasing and killing tigers of a monstrous size, which this continent affords in abundance; and wonderful snakes, such as Alexander[9] is reported to have encountered at the river of Amazons, and which Caesar took great delight to overcome; yet these were not actions great enough for his large soul, which was still panting after more renowned action.

Before I parted that day with him, I got, with much ado, a promise from him to rest yet a little longer with patience, and wait the coming of the Lord Governor, who was every day expected on our shore. He assured me he would, and this promise he desired me to know was given perfectly in complaisance to me, in whom he had an entire confidence.

After this, I neither thought it convenient to trust him much out of our view, nor did the country who feared him; but with one accord it was advised to treat him fairly, and oblige him to remain within such a compass, and that he should be permitted as seldom as could be to go up to the plantations of the Negroes; or if he did, to be accompanied by some that should be rather in appearance attendants than spies. This care was for some time taken, and Caesar looked upon it as a mark of extraordinary respect, and was glad his discontent had obliged them to be more observant to him. He received new assurance from the overseer, which was confirmed to him by the opinion of all the gentlemen of the country, who made their court to him. During this time that we had his company more frequently than hitherto we had had, it may not be unpleasant to relate to you the diversions we entertained him with, or rather he us.

My stay was to be short in that country, because my father died at sea, and never arrived to possess the honor was designed him (which was lieutenant-general of six and thirty islands, besides the continent[1] of Surinam), nor the advantages he hoped to reap by them, so that though we were obliged to continue on our voyage, we did not intend to stay upon the place. Though, in a word, I must say thus much of it, that certainly had his late Majesty,[2] of sacred memory, but seen and known what a vast and charming world he had been master of in that continent, he would never have parted so easily with it to the Dutch. 'Tis a continent whose vast extent was never yet known, and may contain more noble earth than all the universe besides; for they say it reaches from east to west, one way as far as China, and another to Peru. It

---

8. Hurling a heavy rod for purposes of exercise or sport.
9. Legends surrounding Alexander the Great included his encounter with the mythical woman warriors called Amazons, and with the formidable snakes inhabiting

their territories.
1. Mainland.
2. Charles II.

affords all things both for beauty and use; 'tis there eternal spring, always the very months of April, May, and June. The shades are perpetual, the trees, bearing at once all degrees of leaves and fruit from blooming buds to ripe autumn, groves of oranges, lemons, citrons, figs, nutmegs, and noble aromatics, continually bearing their fragrancies. The trees appearing all like nosegays adorned with flowers of different kind; some are all white, some purple, some scarlet, some blue, some yellow; bearing, at the same time, ripe fruit and blooming young, or producing every day new. The very wood of all these trees have an intrinsic value above common timber, for they are, when cut, of different colors, glorious to behold, and bear a price considerable, to inlay withal. Besides this, they yield rich balm and gums, so that we make our candles of such an aromatic substance as does not only give a sufficient light but, as they burn, they cast their perfumes all about. Cedar is the common firing, and all the houses are built with it. The very meat we eat, when set on the table, if it be native, I mean of the country, perfumes the whole room, especially a little beast called an armadillo, a thing which I can liken to nothing so well as a rhinoceros. 'Tis all in white armor so jointed that it moves as well in it as if it had nothing on. This beast is about the bigness of a pig of six weeks old. But it were endless to give an account of all the diverse wonderful and strange things that country affords, and which we took a very great delight to go in search of, though those adventures are oftentimes fatal and at least dangerous. But while we had Caesar in our company on these designs we feared no harm, nor suffered any.

As soon as I came into the country, the best house in it was presented me, called St. John's Hill. It stood on a vast rock of white marble, at the foot of which the river ran a vast depth down, and not to be descended on that side. The little waves still dashing and washing the foot of this rock made the softest murmurs and purlings in the world, and the opposite bank was adorned with such vast quantities of different flowers eternally blowing,[3] and every day and hour new, fenced behind them with lofty trees of a thousand rare forms and colors, that the prospect was the most ravishing that sands can create. On the edge of this white rock, towards the river, was a walk or grove of orange and lemon trees, about half the length of the Mall[4] here, whose flowery and fruity branches meet at the top, and hindered the sun, whose rays are very fierce there, from entering a beam into the grove, and the cool air that came from the river made it not only fit to entertain people in at all the hottest hours of the day, but refreshed the sweet blossoms, and made it always sweet and charming, and sure the whole globe of the world cannot show so delightful a place as this grove was. Not all the gardens of boasted Italy can produce a shade to out-vie this, which Nature had joined with Art to render so exceeding fine. And 'tis a marvel to see how such vast trees, as big as English oaks, could take footing on so solid a rock, and in so little earth, as covered that rock, but all things by nature there are rare, delightful, and wonderful. But to our sports.

Sometimes we would go surprising,[5] and in search of young tigers in their dens, watching when the old ones went forth to forage for prey, and oftentimes we have been in great danger, and have fled apace for our lives, when surprised by the dams. But once, above all other times, we went on this design, and Caesar was with us, who had no sooner stolen a young tiger from her nest, but going off, we encountered the

---

3. Blossoming.
4. A walk extending alongside London's St. James's Park.

5. I.e., surprise-attacking.

dam, bearing a buttock of a cow, which he[6] had torn off with his mighty paw, and going with it towards his den. We had only four women, Caesar, and an English gentleman, brother to Harry Martin, the great Oliverian.[7] We found there was no escaping this enraged and ravenous beast. However, we women fled as fast as we could from it, but our heels had not saved our lives if Caesar had not laid down his cub, when he found the tiger quit her prey to make the more speed towards him, and taking Mr. Martin's sword desired him to stand aside, or follow the ladies. He obeyed him, and Caesar met this monstrous beast of might, size, and vast limbs, who came with open jaws upon him, and fixing his awful stern eyes full upon those of the beast, and putting himself into a very steady and good aiming posture of defense, ran his sword quite through his breast down to his very heart, home to the hilt of the sword. The dying beast stretched forth her paw, and going to grasp his thigh, surprised with death in that very moment, did him no other harm than fixing her long nails in his flesh very deep, feebly wounded him, but could not grasp the flesh to tear off any. When he had done this, he hollowed to us to return, which, after some assurance of his victory, we did, and found him lugging out the sword from the bosom of the tiger, who was laid in her blood on the ground. He took up the cub, and with an unconcern, that had nothing of the joy or gladness of a victory, he came and laid the whelp at my feet. We all extremely wondered at his daring, and at the bigness of the beast, which was about the height of an heifer, but of mighty, great, and strong limbs.

Another time, being in the woods, he killed a tiger, which had long infested that part, and borne away abundance of sheep and oxen and other things, that were for the support of those to whom they belonged. Abundance of people assailed this beast, some affirming they had shot her with several bullets quite through the body, at several times, and some swearing they shot her through the very heart, and they believed she was a devil rather than a mortal thing. Caesar had often said he had a mind to encounter this monster, and spoke with several gentlemen who had attempted her, one crying, I shot her with so many poisoned arrows, another with his gun in this part of her, and another in that. So that he remarking all these places where she was shot, fancied still he should overcome her, by giving her another sort of a wound than any had yet done, and one day said (at the table), "What trophies and garlands, ladies, will you make me, if I bring you home the heart of this ravenous beast that eats up all your lambs and pigs?" We all promised he should be rewarded at all our hands. So taking a bow, which he chose out of a great many, he went up in the wood, with two gentlemen, where he imagined this devourer to be. They had not passed very far in it, but they heard her voice, growling and grumbling, as if she were pleased with something she was doing. When they came in view, they found her muzzling in the belly of a new ravished sheep which she had torn open, and seeing herself approached, she took fast hold of her prey with her forepaws, and set a very fierce raging look on Caesar, without offering to approach him, for fear, at the same time, of losing what she had in possession. So that Caesar remained a good while, only taking aim, and getting an opportunity to shoot her where he designed. 'Twas some time before he could accomplish it, and to wound her and not kill her would but have enraged her more, and endangered him. He had a quiver of arrows at his side, so that if one failed he could be supplied. At last, retiring a little, he gave her opportunity to

---

6. The "dam" is the cub's mother, but Behn has surprisingly shifted the gender of the pronoun from "she" to "he"; she will do so again in reference to another tiger in the next paragraph.

7. Supporter of Oliver Cromwell.

eat, for he found she was ravenous, and fell to as soon as she saw him retire, being more eager of her prey than of doing new mischiefs. When he going softly to one side of her, and hiding his person behind certain herbage that grew high and thick, he took so good aim that, as he intended, he shot her just into the eye, and the arrow was sent with so good a will, and so sure a hand, that it stuck in her brain, and made her caper and become mad for a moment or two, but being seconded by another arrow, he fell dead upon the prey. Caesar cut him open with a knife, to see where those wounds were that had been reported to him, and why he did not die of them. But I shall now relate a thing that possibly will find no credit among men, because 'tis a notion commonly received with us that nothing can receive a wound in the heart and live; but when the heart of this courageous animal was taken out, there were seven bullets of lead in it, and the wounds seamed up with great scars, and she lived with the bullets a great while, for it was long since they were shot. This heart the conqueror brought up to us, and 'twas a very great curiosity, which all the country came to see; and which gave Caesar occasion of many fine discourses, of accidents in war and strange escapes.

At other times he would go a-fishing, and discoursing on that diversion, he found we had in that country a very strange fish, called a numb eel[8] (an eel of which I have eaten), that while it is alive, it has a quality so cold that those who are angling, though with a line of never so great a length, with a rod at the end of it, it shall, in the same minute the bait is touched by this eel, seize him or her that holds the rod with benumbedness, that shall deprive them of sense for a while. And some have fallen into the water, and others dropped as dead on the banks of the rivers where they stood, as soon as this fish touches the bait. Caesar used to laugh at this, and believed it impossible a man could lose his force at the touch of a fish; and could not understand that philosophy, that a cold quality should be of that nature. However, he had a great curiosity to try whether it would have the same effect on him it had on others, and often tried, but in vain. At last, the sought-for fish came to the bait as he stood angling on the bank; and instead of throwing away the rod, or giving it a sudden twitch out of the water, whereby he might have caught both the eel and have dismissed the rod before it could have too much power over him for experiment sake, he grasped it but the harder, and fainting fell into the river. And being still possessed of the rod, the tide carried him senseless as he was a great way, till an Indian boat took him up, and perceived, when they touched him, a numbness seize them, and by that knew the rod was in his hand, which with a paddle (that is, a short oar) they struck away, and snatched it into the boat, eel and all. If Caesar were almost dead with the effect of this fish, he was more so with that of the water, where he had remained the space of going a league, and they found they had much ado to bring him back to life. But at last they did, and brought him home, where he was in a few hours well recovered and refreshed, and not a little ashamed to find he should be overcome by an eel, and that all the people who heard his defiance would laugh at him. But we cheered him up and he, being convinced, we had the eel at supper, which was a quarter of an ell about, and most delicate meat, and was of the more value, since it cost so dear as almost the life of so gallant a man.

About this time we were in many mortal fears about some disputes the English had with the Indians, so that we could scarce trust ourselves, without great numbers, to go to any Indian towns or place where they abode, for fear they should fall upon us,

8. An electric eel.

as they did immediately after my coming away, and that it was in the possession of the Dutch, who used them not so civilly as the English, so that they cut in pieces all they could take, getting into houses, and hanging up the mother, and all her children about her, and cut a footman, I left behind me, all in joints, and nailed him to trees.

This feud began while I was there, so that I lost half the satisfaction I proposed, in not seeing and visiting the Indian towns. But one day, bemoaning of our misfortunes upon this account, Caesar told us we need not fear, for if we had a mind to go he would undertake to be our guard. Some would, but most would not venture. About eighteen of us resolved, and took barge, and after eight days arrived near an Indian town. But approaching it, the hearts of some of our company failed, and they would not venture on shore, so we polled who would, and who would not. For my part, I said, if Caesar would, I would go. He resolved, so did my brother and my woman, a maid of good courage. Now none of us speaking the language of the people, and imagining we should have a half diversion in gazing only and not knowing what they said, we took a fisherman that lived at the mouth of the river, who had been a long inhabitant there, and obliged him to go with us. But because he was known to the Indians, as trading among them, and being, by long living there, become a perfect Indian in color, we, who resolved to surprise them, by making them see something they never had seen (that is, white people) resolved only myself, my brother, and woman should go. So Caesar, the fisherman, and the rest, hiding behind some thick reeds and flowers, that grew on the banks, let us pass on towards the town, which was on the bank of the river all along. A little distant from the houses, or huts, we saw some dancing, others busied in fetching and carrying of water from the river. They had no sooner spied us but they set up a loud cry, that frighted us at first. We thought it had been for those that should kill us, but it seems it was of wonder and amazement. They were all naked, and we were dressed, so as is most commode for the hot countries, very glittering and rich, so that we appeared extremely fine. My own hair was cut short, and I had a taffeta cap, with black feathers, on my head. My brother was in a stuff[9] suit, with silver loops and buttons, and abundance of green ribbon. This was all infinitely surprising to them, and because we saw them stand still, till we approached them, we took heart and advanced, came up to them, and offered them our hands, which they took, and looked on us round about, calling still for more company; who came swarming out, all wondering, and crying out *tepeeme*, taking their hair up in their hands, and spreading it wide to those they called out to, as if they would say (as indeed it signified) "numberless wonders," or not to be recounted, no more than to number the hair of their heads. By degrees they grew more bold, and from gazing upon us round, they touched us, laying their hands upon all the features of our faces, feeling our breasts and arms, taking up one petticoat, then wondering to see another, admiring our shoes and stockings, but more our garters, which we gave them, and they tied about their legs, being laced with silver lace at the ends, for they much esteem any shining things. In fine, we suffered them to survey us as they pleased, and we thought they would never have done admiring us. When Caesar and the rest saw we were received with such wonder, they came up to us, and finding the Indian trader whom they knew (for 'tis by these fishermen, called Indian traders, we hold a commerce with them; for they love not to go far from home, and we never go to them), when they saw him therefore they set up a new joy, and cried, in their language, "Oh! here's our *tiguamy*, and we shall now know whether those things can

9. Woolen.

speak." So advancing to him, some of them gave him their hands, and cried, "*Amora tiguamy*," which is as much as, "How do you," or "Welcome friend," and all, with one din, began to gabble to him, and asked, If we had sense, and wit? If we could talk of affairs of life, and war, as they could do? If we could hunt, swim, and do a thousand things they use? He answered them, we could. Then they invited us into their houses, and dressed venison and buffalo for us; and, going out, gathered a leaf of a tree, called a sarumbo leaf, of six yards long, and spread it on the ground for a tablecloth, and cutting another in pieces instead of plates, setting us on little bow Indian stools, which they cut out of one entire piece of wood, and paint in a sort of japan work. They serve everyone their mess on these pieces of leaves, and it was very good, but too high seasoned with pepper. When we had eaten, my brother and I took out our flutes and played to them, which gave them new wonder, and I soon perceived, by an admiration that is natural to these people, and by the extreme ignorance and simplicity of them, it were not difficult to establish any unknown or extravagant religion among them, and to impose any notions or fictions upon them. For seeing a kinsman of mine set some paper afire with a burning-glass, a trick they had never before seen, they were like to have adored him for a god, and begged he would give them the characters or figures of his name, that they might oppose it against winds and storms, which he did, and they held it up in those seasons, and fancied it had a charm to conquer them, and kept it like a holy relic. They are very superstitious, and called him the great *peeie*, that is, prophet. They showed us their Indian *peeie*, a youth of about sixteen years old, as handsome as Nature could make a man. They consecrate a beautiful youth from his infancy, and all arts are used to complete him in the finest manner, both in beauty and shape. He is bred to all the little arts and cunning they are capable of, to all the legerdemain tricks and sleight of hand whereby he imposes upon the rabble, and is both a doctor in physic and divinity. And by these tricks makes the sick believe he sometimes eases their pains, by drawing from the afflicted part little serpents, or odd flies, or worms, or any strange thing; and though they have besides undoubted good remedies for almost all their diseases, they cure the patient more by fancy than by medicines, and make themselves feared, loved, and reverenced. This young *peeie* had a very young wife, who seeing my brother kiss her, came running and kissed me; after this, they kissed one another, and made it a very great jest, it being so novel, and new admiration and laughing went round the multitude, that they never will forget that ceremony, never before used or known. Caesar had a mind to see and talk with their war captains, and we were conducted to one of their houses, where we beheld several of the great captains, who had been at council. But so frightful a vision it was to see them no fancy can create; no such dreams can represent so dreadful a spectacle. For my part I took them for hobgoblins, or fiends, rather than men. But however their shapes appeared, their souls were very humane and noble, but some wanted their noses, some their lips, some both noses and lips, some their ears, and others cut through each cheek, with long slashes, through which their teeth appeared; they had several other formidable wounds and scars, or rather dismemberings. They had *comitias*, or little aprons before them, and girdles of cotton, with their knives naked, stuck in it, a bow at their backs, and a quiver of arrows on their thighs, and most had feathers on their heads of diverse colors. They cried "*Amora tiguamy*" to us at our entrance, and were pleased we said as much to them. They feted us, and gave us drink of the best sort, and wondered, as much as the others had done before, to see us. Caesar was marveling as much at their faces, wondering how they should all be so wounded in war; he was impatient to know how they all came by those frightful marks of rage or malice, rather than wounds got in noble battle. They told us, by our interpreter, that when any war was waging, two men chosen out by some old captain, whose fighting was past, and who could only teach the theory of war, these two men were to stand in competition for the generalship, or Great War Captain, and being brought before the old judges, now past labor, they are asked, what they dare do to show they are worthy to lead an army? When he who is first asked, making no reply, cuts off his nose, and throws it contemptibly[1] on the ground, and the other does something to himself that he thinks surpasses him, and perhaps deprives himself of lips and an eye. So they slash on till one gives out, and many have died in this debate. And 'tis by a passive valor they show and prove their activity, a sort of courage too brutal to be applauded by our black hero; nevertheless he expressed his esteem of them.

In this voyage Caesar begot so good an understanding between the Indians and the English, that there were no more fears or heartburnings during our stay, but we had a perfect, open, and free trade with them. Many things remarkable, and worthy reciting, we met with in this short voyage, because Caesar made it his business to search out and provide for our entertainment, especially to please his dearly adored Imoinda, who was a sharer in all our adventures; we being resolved to make her chains as easy as we could, and to compliment the Prince in that manner that most obliged him.

As we were coming up again, we met with some Indians of strange aspects, that is, of a larger size, and other sort of features, than those of our country. Our Indian slaves, that rowed us, asked them some questions, but they could not understand us, but showed us a long cotton string with several knots on it, and told us, they had been coming from the mountains so many moons as there were knots. They were habited in skins of a strange beast, and brought along with them bags of gold dust, which, as well as they could give us to understand, came streaming in little small channels down the high mountains, when the rains fell, and offered to be the convoy to anybody, or persons, that would go to the mountains. We carried these men up to Parham, where they were kept till the Lord Governor came. And because all the country was mad to be going on this golden adventure, the governor, by his letters, commanded (for they sent some of the gold to him) that a guard should be set at the mouth of the river of Amazons (a river so called, almost as broad as the river of Thames), and prohibited all people from going up that river, it conducting to those mountains of gold. But we going off for England before the project was further prosecuted, and the Governor being drowned in a hurricane, either the design died, or the Dutch have the advantage of it. And 'tis to be bemoaned what His Majesty lost by losing that part of America.

Though this digression is a little from my story, however since it contains some proofs of the curiosity and daring of this great man, I was content to omit nothing of his character.

It was thus, for some time we diverted him. But now Imoinda began to show she was with child, and did nothing but sigh and weep for the captivity of her lord, herself, and the infant yet unborn, and believed, if it were so hard to gain the liberty of two, 'twould be more difficult to get that for three. Her griefs were so many darts in the great heart of Caesar, and taking his opportunity one Sunday, when all the whites were overtaken in drink, as there were abundance of several trades, and slaves

1. Contemptuously.

for four years,[2] that inhabited among the Negro houses, and Sunday was their day of debauch (otherwise they were a sort of spies upon Caesar), he went pretending out of goodness to them, to feast amongst them, and sent all his music, and ordered a great treat for the whole gang, about three hundred Negroes. And about a hundred and fifty were able to bear arms, such as they had, which were sufficient to do execution with spirits accordingly. For the English had none but rusty swords, that no strength could draw from a scabbard, except the people of particular quality, who took care to oil them and keep them in good order. The guns also, unless here and there one, or those newly carried from England, would do no good or harm, for 'tis the nature of that country to rust and eat up iron, or any metals but gold and silver. And they are very inexpert at the bow, which the Negroes and Indians are perfect masters of.

Caesar, having singled out these men from the women and children, made a harangue to them of the miseries and ignominies of slavery; counting up all their toils and sufferings, under such loads, burdens, and drudgeries as were fitter for beasts than men, senseless brutes than human souls. He told them it was not for days, months, or years, but for eternity; there was no end to be of their misfortunes. They suffered not like men who might find a glory and fortitude in oppression, but like dogs that loved the whip and bell,[3] and fawned the more they were beaten. That they had lost the divine quality of men, and were become insensible asses, fit only to bear. Nay worse, an ass, or dog, or horse having done his duty, could lie down in retreat, and rise to work again, and while he did his duty endured no stripes; but men, villainous, senseless men such as they, toiled on all the tedious week till black Friday, and then, whether they worked or not, whether they were faulty or meriting, they promiscuously, the innocent with the guilty, suffered the infamous whip, the sordid stripes, from their fellow slaves till their blood trickled from all parts of their body, blood whose every drop ought to be revenged with a life of some of those tyrants that impose it. "And why," said he, "my dear friends and fellow sufferers, should we be slaves to an unknown people? Have they vanquished us nobly in fight? Have they won us in honorable battle? And are we, by the chance of war, become their slaves? This would not anger a noble heart, this would not animate a soldier's soul. No, but we are bought and sold like apes, or monkeys, to be the sport of women, fools, and cowards, and the support of rogues, runagades, that have abandoned their own countries, for raping, murders, thefts, and villainies. Do you not hear every day how they upbraid each other with infamy of life below the wildest salvages, and shall we render obedience to such a degenerate race, who have no one human virtue left to distinguish them from the vilest creatures? Will you, I say, suffer the lash from such hands?" They all replied, with one accord, "No, no, no; Caesar has spoke like a great captain, like a great king."

After this he would have proceeded, but was interrupted by a tall Negro of some more quality than the rest. His name was Tuscan, who bowing at the feet of Caesar, cried, "My lord, we have listened with joy and attention to what you have said, and, were we only men, would follow so great a leader through the world. But oh! consider, we are husbands and parents too, and have things more dear to us than life: our wives and children unfit for travel, in these impassable woods, mountains, and bogs. We have not only difficult lands to overcome, but rivers to wade, and monsters to encounter, ravenous beasts of prey—" To this, Caesar replied, that honor was the

---

2. I.e., whites who, as punishment for crime or debt, had been forced into service for fixed periods of time.

3. Because rigorous training has taught them to cherish their punishment.

first principle in nature that was to be obeyed; but as no man would pretend to that, without all the acts of virtue, compassion, charity, love, justice, and reason, he found it not inconsistent with that, to take an equal care of their wives and children, as they would of themselves, and that he did not design, when he led them to freedom and glorious liberty, that they should leave that better part of themselves to perish by the hand of the tyrant's whip. But if there were a woman among them so degenerate from love and virtue to choose slavery before the pursuit of her husband, and with the hazard of her life to share with him in his fortunes, that such an one ought to be abandoned, and left as a prey to the common enemy.

To which they all agreed—and bowed. After this, he spoke of the impassable woods and rivers, and convinced them, the more danger, the more glory. He told them that he had heard of one Hannibal, a great captain, had cut his way through mountains of solid rocks,[4] and should a few shrubs oppose them, which they could fire before them? No, 'twas a trifling excuse to men resolved to die, or overcome. As for bogs, they are with a little labor filled and hardened, and the rivers could be no obstacle, since they swam by nature, at least by custom, from their first hour of their birth. That when the children were weary they must carry them by turns, and the woods and their own industry would afford them food. To this they all assented with joy.

Tuscan then demanded, what he would do? He said, they would travel towards the sea; plant a new colony, and defend it by their valor; and when they could find a ship, either driven by stress of weather, or guided by Providence that way, they would seize it, and make it a prize, till it had transported them to their own countries. At least, they should be made free in his kingdom, and be esteemed as his fellow sufferers, and men that had the courage and the bravery to attempt, at least, for liberty. And if they died in the attempt it would be more brave than to live in perpetual slavery.

They bowed and kissed his feet at this resolution, and with one accord vowed to follow him to death. And that night was appointed to begin their march; they made it known to their wives, and directed them to tie their hamaca[5] about their shoulder, and under their arm like a scarf; and to lead their children that could go, and carry those that could not. The wives who pay an entire obedience to their husbands obeyed, and stayed for them where they were appointed. The men stayed but to furnish themselves with what defensive arms they could get, and all met at the rendezvous, where Caesar made a new encouraging speech to them, and led them out.

But, as they could not march far that night, on Monday early, when the overseers went to call them all together to go to work, they were extremely surprised to find not one upon the place, but all fled with what baggage they had. You may imagine this news was not only suddenly spread all over the plantation, but soon reached the neighboring ones, and we had by noon about six hundred men, they call the militia of the county, that came to assist us in the pursuit of the fugitives. But never did one see so comical an army march forth to war. The men of any fashion would not concern themselves, though it were almost the common cause, for such revoltings are very ill examples, and have very fatal consequences oftentimes in many colonies. But they had a respect for Caesar, and all hands were against the Parhamites, as they called those of Parham Plantation, because they did not, in the first place, love the Lord Governor, and secondly, they would have it that Caesar was ill used, and baffled with.[6] And 'tis not impossible but some of the best in the country was of his counsel

---

4. The Carthaginian general (B.C. 247–182) had accomplished this while crossing the Alps to invade Rome.

5. Hammock.
6. Cheated.

in this flight, and depriving us of all the slaves, so that they of the better sort would not meddle in the matter. The deputy governor,[7] of whom I have had no great occasion to speak, and who was the most fawning fair-tongued fellow in the world, and one that pretended the most friendship to Caesar, was now the only violent man against him, and though he had nothing, and so need fear nothing, yet talked and looked bigger than any man. He was a fellow whose character is not fit to be mentioned with the worst of the slaves. This fellow would lead his army forth to meet Caesar, or rather to pursue him. Most of their arms were of those sort of cruel whips they call cat-with-nine-tails; some had rusty useless guns for show; others old basket-hilts, whose blades had never seen the light in this age, and others had long staffs, and clubs. Mr. Trefry went along rather to be a mediator than a conqueror in such a battle, for he foresaw and knew, if by fighting they put the Negroes into despair, they were a sort of sullen fellows that would drown or kill themselves before they would yield, and he advised that fair means was best. But Byam was one that abounded in his own wit, and would take his own measures.

It was not hard to find these fugitives, for as they fled they were forced to fire and cut the woods before them, so that night or day they pursued them by the light they made, and by the path they had cleared. But as soon as Caesar found he was pursued, he put himself in a posture of defense, placing all the women and children in the rear, and himself, with Tuscan by his side, or next to him, all promising to die or conquer. Encouraged thus, they never stood to parley, but fell on pell-mell upon the English, and killed some, and wounded a good many, they having recourse to their whips, as the best of their weapons. And as they observed no order, they perplexed the enemy so sorely, with lashing them in the eyes. And the women and children, seeing their husbands so treated, being of fearful cowardly dispositions, and hearing the English cry out, "Yield and live, yield and be pardoned," they all ran in amongst their husbands and fathers, and hung about them, crying out, "Yield, yield, and leave Caesar to their revenge," that by degrees the slaves abandoned Caesar, and left him only Tuscan and his heroic Imoinda, who, grown big as she was, did nevertheless press near her lord, having a bow, and a quiver full of poisoned arrows, which she managed with such dexterity that she wounded several, and shot the governor into the shoulder, of which wound he had like to have died but that an Indian woman, his mistress, sucked the wound, and cleansed it from the venom. But however, he stirred not from the place till he had parleyed with Caesar, who he found was resolved to die fighting, and would not be taken; no more would Tuscan, or Imoinda. But he, more thirsting after revenge of another sort, than that of depriving him of life, now made use of all his art of talking and dissembling, and besought Caesar to yield himself upon terms which he himself should propose, and should be sacredly assented to and kept by him. He told him, it was not that he any longer feared him, or could believe the force of two men, and a young heroine, could overcome all them, with all the slaves now on their side also, but it was the vast esteem he had for his person, the desire he had to serve so gallant a man, and to hinder himself from the reproach hereafter of having been the occasion of the death of a prince, whose valor and magnanimity deserved the empire of the world. He protested to him, he looked upon this action as gallant and brave, however tending to the prejudice of his lord and master, who would by it have lost so considerable a number of slaves, that this flight of his should be looked on as a heat of youth, and rashness of a too forward courage, and an unconsidered impatience of liberty, and no more; and that he labored in vain to accomplish

---

7. William Byam, who during a decade as administrator in Surinam had acquired a reputation for arrogance and severity.

that which they would effectually perform, as soon as any ship arrived that would touch on his coast. "So that if you will be pleased," continued he, "to surrender yourself, all imaginable respect shall be paid you; and yourself, your wife, and child, if it be here born, shall depart free out of our land." But Caesar would hear of no composition, though Byam urged, if he pursued and went on in his design, he would inevitably perish, either by great snakes, wild beasts, or hunger, and he ought to have regard to his wife, whose condition required ease, and not the fatigues of tedious travel, where she could not be secured from being devoured. But Caesar told him, there was no faith in the white men, or the gods they adored, who instructed them in principles so false that honest men could not live amongst them; though no people professed so much, none performed so little; that he knew what he had to do, when he dealt with men of honor, but with them a man ought to be eternally on his guard, and never to eat and drink with Christians without his weapon of defense in his hand, and, for his own security, never to credit one word they spoke. As for the rashness and inconsiderateness of his action he would confess the governor is in the right, and that he was ashamed of what he had done, in endeavoring to make those free, who were by nature slaves, poor wretched rogues, fit to be used as Christians' tools; dogs, treacherous and cowardly, fit for such masters, and they wanted only but to be whipped into the knowledge of the Christian gods to be the vilest of all creeping things, to learn to worship such deities as had not power to make them just, brave, or honest. In fine, after a thousand things of this nature, not fit here to be recited, he told Byam, he had rather die than live upon the same earth with such dogs. But Trefry and Byam pleaded and protested together so much, that Trefry believing the governor to mean what he said, and speaking very cordially himself, generously put himself into Caesar's hands, and took him aside, and persuaded him, even with tears, to live, by surrendering himself, and to name his conditions. Caesar was overcome by his wit and reasons, and in consideration of Imoinda, and demanding what he desired, and that it should be ratified by their hands in writing, because he had perceived that was the common way of contract between man and man amongst the whites. All this was performed, and Tuscan's pardon was put in, and they surrender to the governor, who walked peaceably down into the plantation with them, after giving order to bury their dead. Caesar was very much toiled with the bustle of the day, for he had fought like a Fury, and what mischief was done he and Tuscan performed alone, and gave their enemies a fatal proof that they durst do anything, and feared no mortal force.

But they were no sooner arrived at the place where all the slaves receive their punishments of whipping, but they laid hands on Caesar and Tuscan, faint with heat and toil; and surprising them, bound them to two several stakes, and whipped them in a most deplorable and inhumane manner, rending the very flesh from their bones; especially Caesar, who was not perceived to make any moan, or to alter his face, only to roll his eyes on the faithless governor, and those he believed guilty, with fierceness and indignation. And, to complete his rage, he saw every one of those slaves, who, but a few days before, adored him as something more than mortal, now had a whip to give him some lashes, while he strove not to break his fetters, though if he had, it were impossible. But he pronounced a woe and revenge from his eyes, that darted fire, that 'twas at once both awful and terrible to behold.

When they thought they were sufficiently revenged on him, they untied him, almost fainting with loss of blood from a thousand wounds all over his body, from which they had rent his clothes, and led him bleeding and naked as he was, and loaded him all over with irons, and then rubbed his wounds, to complete their cruelty, with Indian pepper, which had like to have made him raving mad, and in this condition made him so fast to the ground that he could not stir, if his pains and wounds would have given him leave. They spared Imoinda, and did not let her see this barbarity committed towards her lord, but carried her down to Parham, and shut her up, which was not in kindness to her, but for fear she should die with the sight, or miscarry, and then they should lose a young slave, and perhaps the mother.

You must know, that when the news was brought on Monday morning, that Caesar had betaken himself to the woods, and carried with him all the Negroes, we were possessed with extreme fear, which no persuasions could dissipate, that he would secure himself till night, and then, that he would come down and cut all our throats. This apprehension made all the females of us fly down the river, to be secured, and while we were away, they acted this cruelty. For I suppose I had authority and interest enough there, had I suspected any such thing, to have prevented it, but we had not gone many leagues, but the news overtook us that Caesar was taken, and whipped like a common slave. We met on the river with Colonel Martin, a man of great gallantry, wit, and goodness, and, whom I have celebrated in a character of my new comedy,[8] by his own name, in memory of so brave a man. He was wise and eloquent, and, from the fineness of his parts, bore a great sway over the hearts of all the colony. He was a friend to Caesar, and resented this false dealing with him very much. We carried him back to Parham, thinking to have made an accommodation; when we came, the first news we heard was that the governor was dead of a wound Imoinda had given him, but it was not so well. But it seems he would have the pleasure of beholding the revenge he took on Caesar, and before the cruel ceremony was finished, he dropped down, and then they perceived the wound he had on his shoulder was by a venomed arrow, which, as I said, his Indian mistress healed, by sucking the wound.

We were no sooner arrived, but we went up to the plantation to see Caesar, whom we found in a very miserable and inexpressible condition, and I have a thousand times admired how he lived, in so much tormenting pain. We said all things to him that trouble, pity, and good nature could suggest, protesting our innocence of the fact, and our abhorrence of such cruelties; making a thousand professions of services to him, and begging as many pardons for the offenders, till we said so much, that he believed we had no hand in his ill treatment, but told us, he could never pardon Byam. As for Trefry, he confessed he saw his grief and sorrow for his suffering, which he could not hinder, but was like to have been beaten down by the very slaves, for speaking in his defense. But for Byam, who was their leader, their head—and should, by his justice, and honor, have been an example to them—for him, he wished to live, to take a dire revenge of him, and said, "It had been well for him if he had sacrificed me, instead of giving me the contemptible whip." He refused to talk much, but begging us to give him our hands, he took them, and protested never to lift up his, to do us any harm. He had a great respect for Colonel Martin, and always took his counsel, like that of a parent, and assured him, he would obey him in anything but his revenge on Byam. "Therefore," said he, "for his own safety, let him speedily dispatch me, for if I could dispatch myself, I would not, till that justice were done to my injured person, and the contempt of a soldier. No, I would not kill myself, even after a whipping, but will be content to live with that infamy, and be pointed at by

---

8. *The Younger Brother: or the Amorous Jilt*, produced posthumously in 1696.

every grinning slave, till I have completed my revenge; and then you shall see that Oroonoko scorns to live with the indignity that was put on Caesar." All we could do could get no more words from him, and we took care to have him put immediately into a healing bath, to rid him of his pepper, and ordered a chirurgeon[9] to anoint him with healing balm, which he suffered, and in some time he began to be able to walk and eat. We failed not to visit him every day, and, to that end, had him brought to an apartment at Parham.

The governor was no sooner recovered, and had heard of the menaces of Caesar, but he called his council, who (not to disgrace them, or burlesque the government there) consisted of such notorious villains as Newgate[1] never transported, and possibly originally were such, who understood neither the laws of God or man, and had no sort of principles to make them worthy the name of men, but at the very council table would contradict and fight with one another, and swear so bloodily that 'twas terrible to hear and see them. (Some of them were afterwards hanged, when the Dutch took possession of the place; others sent off in chains.) But calling these special rulers of the nation together, and requiring their counsel in this weighty affair, they all concluded that (damn them) it might be their own cases, and that Caesar ought to be made an example to all the Negroes, to fright them from daring to threaten their betters, their lords and masters, and, at this rate, no man was safe from his own slaves, and concluded, *nemine contradicente*,[2] that Caesar should be hanged.

Trefry then thought it time to use his authority, and told Byam his command did not extend to his lord's plantation, and that Parham was as much exempt from the law as Whitehall; and that they ought no more to touch the servants of the Lord——— (who there represented the King's person) than they could those about the King himself; and that Parham was a sanctuary, and though his lord were absent in person, his power was still in being there, which he had entrusted with him, as far as the dominions of his particular plantations reached, and all that belonged to it; the rest of the country, as Byam was lieutenant to his lord, he might exercise his tyranny upon. Trefry had others as powerful, or more, that interested themselves in Caesar's life, and absolutely said he should be defended. So turning the governor, and his wise council, out of doors (for they sat at Parham House) we set a guard upon our landing place, and would admit none but those we called friends to us and Caesar.

The governor having remained wounded at Parham till his recovery was completed, Caesar did not know but he was still there, and indeed, for the most part, his time was spent there, for he was one that loved to live at other people's expense, and if he were a day absent, he was ten present there, and used to play, and walk, and hunt, and fish, with Caesar. So that Caesar did not at all doubt, if he once recovered strength, but he should find an opportunity of being revenged on him. Though, after such a revenge, he could not hope to live, for if he escaped the fury of the English mobile,[3] who perhaps would have been glad of the occasion to have killed him, he was resolved not to survive his whipping, yet he had, some tender hours, a repenting softness, which he called his fits of coward, wherein he struggled with love for the victory of his heart, which took part with his charming Imoinda there, but, for the most part, his time was passed in melancholy thought, and black designs. He considered, if he should do this deed, and die either in the attempt, or after it, he left his

9. Surgeon.
1. London prison from which convicts were sent to work in the colonies.
2. No one disagreeing.
3. Mob.

lovely Imoinda a prey, or at best a slave, to the enraged multitude; his great heart could not endure that thought. "Perhaps," said he, "she may be first ravished by every brute, exposed first to their nasty lusts, and then a shameful death." No, he could not live a moment under that apprehension, too insupportable to be borne. These were his thoughts, and his silent arguments with his heart, as he told us afterwards, so that now resolving not only to kill Byam, but all those he thought had enraged him, pleasing his great heart with the fancied slaughter he should make over the whole face of the plantation. He first resolved on a deed that (however horrid it at first appeared to us all), when we had heard his reasons, we thought it brave and just. Being able to walk and, as he believed, fit for the execution of his great design, he begged Trefry to trust him into the air, believing a walk would do him good, which was granted him, and taking Imoinda with him, as he used to do in his more happy and calmer days, he led her up into a wood where, after (with a thousand sighs, and long gazing silently on her face, while tears gushed, in spite of him, from his eyes), he told her his design first of killing her, and then his enemies, and next himself, and the impossibility of escaping, and therefore he told her the necessity of dying. He found the heroic wife faster pleading for death than he was to propose it, when she found his fixed resolution, and on her knees besought him not to leave her a prey to his enemies. He (grieved to death) yet pleased at her noble resolution, took her up, and embracing her with all the passion and languishment of a dying lover, drew his knife to kill this treasure of his soul, this pleasure of his eyes. While tears trickled down his cheeks, hers were smiling with joy she should die by so noble a hand, and be sent in her own country (for that's their notion of the next world) by him she so tenderly loved, and so truly adored in this, for wives have a respect for their husbands equal to what any other people pay a deity, and when a man finds any occasion to quit his wife, if he love·her, she dies by his hand, if not, he sells her, or suffers some other to kill her. It being thus, you may believe the deed was soon resolved on, and 'tis not to be doubted, but the parting, the eternal leave-taking of two such lovers, so greatly born, so sensible,[4] so beautiful, so young, and so fond, must be very moving, as the relation of it was to me afterwards.

All that love could say in such cases being ended, and all the intermitting irresolutions being adjusted, the lovely, young, and adored victim lays herself down before the sacrificer, while he, with a hand resolved, and a heart breaking within, gave the fatal stroke, first cutting her throat, and then severing her yet smiling face from that delicate body, pregnant as it was with fruits of tenderest love. As soon as he had done, he laid the body decently on leaves and flowers, of which he made a bed, and concealed it under the same coverlid of nature, only her face he left yet bare to look on. But when he found she was dead, and past all retrieve, never more to bless him with her eyes and soft language, his grief swelled up to rage; he tore, he raved, he roared, like some monster of the wood, calling on the loved name of Imoinda. A thousand times he turned the fatal knife that did the deed toward his own heart, with a resolution to go immediately after her, but dire revenge, which now was a thousand times more fierce in his soul than before, prevents him, and he would cry out, "No, since I have sacrificed Imoinda to my revenge, shall I lose that glory which I have purchased so dear, as at the price of the fairest, dearest, softest creature that ever Nature made? No, no!" Then, at her name, grief would get the ascendant of rage, and he would lie down by her side, and water her face with showers of tears, which never

4. Sensitive.

were wont to fall from those eyes. And however bent he was on his intended slaughter, he had not power to stir from the sight of this dear object, now more beloved and more adored than ever.

He remained in this deploring condition for two days, and never rose from the ground where he had made his sad sacrifice. At last, rousing from her side, and accusing himself with living too long now Imoinda was dead, and that the deaths of those barbarous enemies were deferred too long, he resolved now to finish the great work; but offering to rise, he found his strength so decayed, that he reeled to and fro, like boughs assailed by contrary winds, so that he was forced to lie down again, and try to summon all his courage to his aid. He found his brains turn round, and his eyes were dizzy, and objects appeared not the same to him as they were wont to do; his breath was short, and all his limbs surprised with a faintness he had never felt before. He had not eaten in two days, which was one occasion of this feebleness, but excess of grief was the greatest; yet still he hoped he should recover vigor to act his design, and lay expecting it yet six days longer, still mourning over the dead idol of his heart, and striving every day to rise, but could not.

In all this time you may believe we were in no little affliction for Caesar and his wife. Some were of opinion he was escaped never to return; others thought some accident had happened to him. But however, we failed not to send out a hundred people several ways to search for him. A party of about forty went that way he took, among whom was Tuscan, who was perfectly reconciled to Byam. They had not gone very far into the wood, but they smelt an unusual smell, as of a dead body, for stinks must be very noisome that can be distinguished among such a quantity of natural sweets, as every inch of that land produces. So that they concluded they should find him dead, or somebody that was so. They passed on towards it, as loathsome as it was, and made such a rustling among the leaves that lie thick on the ground, by continual falling, that Caesar heard he was approached, and though he had, during the space of these eight days, endeavored to rise, but found he wanted strength, yet looking up, and seeing his pursuers, he rose, and reeled to a neighboring tree, against which he fixed his back. And being within a dozen yards of those that advanced and saw him, he called out to them, and bid them approach no nearer, if they would be safe; so that they stood still, and hardly believing their eyes, that would persuade them that it was Caesar that spoke to them, so much was he altered, they asked him what he had done with his wife, for they smelt a stink that almost struck them dead. He, pointing to the dead body, sighing, cried, "Behold her there." They put off the flowers that covered her with their sticks, and found she was killed, and cried out, "Oh monster! that hast murdered thy wife." Then asking him, why he did so cruel a deed, he replied, he had no leisure to answer impertinent questions. "You may go back," continued he, "and tell the faithless governor he may thank Fortune that I am breathing my last, and that my arm is too feeble to obey my heart in what it had designed him." But his tongue faltering, and trembling, he could scarce end what he was saying. The English taking advantage by his weakness, cried, "Let us take him alive by all means." He heard them; and, as if he had revived from a fainting, or a dream, he cried out, "No, gentlemen, you are deceived, you will find no more Caesars to be whipped, no more find a faith in me. Feeble as you think me, I have strength yet left to secure me from a second indignity." They swore all anew, and he only shook his head, and beheld them with scorn. Then they cried out, "Who will venture on this single man? Will nobody?" They stood all silent while Caesar replied, "Fatal will be the attempt to the first adventurer, let him assure himself," and, at that word, held up his knife in a menacing posture. "Look ye, ye faithless crew," said he, "'tis not life I seek, nor am I afraid of dying," and, at that word, cut a piece of flesh from his own throat, and threw it at them, "yet still I would live if I could, till I had perfected my revenge. But oh! it cannot be. I feel life gliding from my eyes and heart, and, if I make not haste, I shall yet fall a victim to the shameful whip." At that, he ripped up his own belly, and took his bowels and pulled them out, with what strength he could, while some, on their knees imploring, besought him to hold his hand. But when they saw him tottering, they cried out, "Will none venture on him?" A bold English cried, "Yes, if he were the Devil" (taking courage when he saw him almost dead) and swearing a horrid oath for his farewell to the world he rushed on. Caesar with his armed hand met him so fairly, as stuck him to the heart, and he fell dead at his feet. Tuscan seeing that, cried out, "I love thee, oh Caesar, and therefore will not let thee die, if possible." And, running to him, took him in his arms, but at the same time, warding a blow that Caesar made at his bosom, he received it quite through his arm, and Caesar having not the strength to pluck the knife forth, though he attempted it, Tuscan neither pulled it out himself, nor suffered it to be pulled out, but came down with it sticking in his arm, and the reason he gave for it was because the air should not get into the wound. They put their hands across, and carried Caesar between six of them, fainted as he was, and they thought dead, or just dying, and they brought him to Parham, and laid him on a couch, and had the chirurgeon immediately to him, who dressed his wounds, and sewed up his belly, and used means to bring him to life, which they effected. We ran all to see him; and, if before we thought him so beautiful a sight, he was now so altered that his face was like a death's head blacked over, nothing but teeth and eye-holes. For some days we suffered nobody to speak to him, but caused cordials to be poured down his throat, which sustained his life, and in six or seven days he recovered his senses. For you must know, that wounds are almost to a miracle cured in the Indies, unless wounds in the legs, which rarely ever cure.

When he was well enough to speak, we talked to him, and asked him some questions about his wife, and the reasons why he killed her. And he then told us what I have related of that resolution, and of his parting, and he besought us we would let him die, and was extremely afflicted to think it was possible he might live. He assured us, if we did not dispatch him, he would prove very fatal to a great many. We said all we could to make him live, and gave him new assurances, but he begged we would not think so poorly of him, or of his love to Imoinda, to imagine we could flatter him to life again; but the chirurgeon assured him he could not live, and therefore he need not fear. We were all (but Caesar) afflicted at this news; and the sight was gashly.[5] His discourse was sad; and the earthly smell about him so strong, that I was persuaded to leave the place for some time (being myself but sickly, and very apt to fall into fits of dangerous illness upon any extraordinary melancholy). The servants, and Trefry, and the chirurgeons, promised all to take what possible care they could of the life of Caesar, and I, taking boat, went with other company to Colonel Martin's, about three days' journey down the river; but I was no sooner gone, but the governor taking Trefry about some pretended earnest business a day's journey up the river, having communicated his design to one Banister, a wild Irishman, and one of the council, a fellow of absolute barbarity, and fit to execute any villainy, but was rich, he came up to Parham, and forcibly took Caesar, and had him carried to the same post where he was whipped, and causing him to be tied to it, and a great fire made before him, he

5. Ghastly.

told him he should die like a dog, as he was. Caesar replied, this was the first piece of bravery that ever Banister did, and he never spoke sense till he pronounced that word, and, if he would keep it, he would declare, in the other world, that he was the only man, of all the whites, that ever he heard speak truth. And turning to the men that bound him, he said, "My friends, am I to die, or to be whipped?" And they cried, "Whipped! no; you shall not escape so well." And then he replied, smiling, "A blessing on thee," and assured them, they need not tie him, for he would stand fixed, like a rock, and endure death so as should encourage them to die. "But if you whip me," said he, "be sure you tie me fast."

He had learned to take tobacco, and when he was assured he should die, he desired they would give him a pipe in his mouth, ready lighted, which they did, and the executioner came, and first cut off his members,[6] and threw them into the fire. After that, with an ill-favored knife, they cut his ears and his nose, and burned them; he still smoked on, as if nothing had touched him. Then they hacked off one of his arms, and still he bore up, and held his pipe. But at the cutting off the other arm, his head sunk, and his pipe dropped, and he gave up the ghost, without a groan, or a reproach. My mother and sister were by him all the while, but not suffered to save him, so rude and wild were the rabble, and so inhuman were the justices, who stood by to see the execution, who after paid dearly enough for their insolence. They cut Caesar in quarters, and sent them to several of the chief plantations. One quarter was sent to Colonel Martin, who refused it, and swore he had rather see the quarters of Banister and the governor himself than those of Caesar on his plantations, and that he could govern his Negroes without terrifying and grieving them with frightful spectacles of a mangled king.

Thus died this great man, worthy of a better fate, and a more sublime wit than mine to write his praise. Yet, I hope, the reputation of my pen is considerable enough to make his glorious name to survive to all ages, with that of the brave, the beautiful, and the constant Imoinda.

1688

John Wilmot, Earl of Rochester
1647–1680

In one of his many notorious escapades, John Wilmot, Earl of Rochester, drunkenly smashed to pieces one of the king's costliest timekeepers. He always lived at odds with ordinary time, mostly ahead of it: he became Earl at age ten, when his father died; received his M.A. from Oxford at fourteen; conducted a Grand Tour of Europe during the next three years; tried to abduct his future wife Elizabeth Malet (a much-sought woman of wealth, wit, and beauty) when he was eighteen, and was briefly imprisoned for the attempt; married her at twenty; and died, after long libertinage and precipitate piety, at thirty-three. Rochester's wit and beauty, the stupendous energies of his mind (erudite, inventive), of his language (adroit, obscene), of his body (alcoholic, bisexual), and of his convictions (hedonistic, atheistic) made him the fascination of the Restoration court, whose proclivities for theatrics, for combat, and for amorous entanglement he pushed to matchless extremes. Theatrics: Rochester wrote plays of his own and produced plays by others; he tutored the stage novice Elizabeth Barry, soon to become the

---

6. Genitals.

greatest actress of the age (they carried on a volatile affair, and had a daughter); at times he could don a disguise himself and play a role so successfully (in order to go underground, to escape punishment, to bring off a seduction) that close friends could not recognize him. Combat: Rochester distinguished himself for courage by plunging into the thick of the fighting during several sea battles; he once disgraced himself for cowardice in running away during a nocturnal street brawl, "frighted" (he later wrote) "at my own mischiefs" and leaving one of his own defenders dead. In the lesser combats of the court, those endless verbal cutting contests of improvised insult and impromptu verse, Rochester was virtually unbeatable (though the king, when cut, could cut back: the earl's status shifted often and quickly between favorite and outcast). Amorous entanglement: Rochester's letters to his wife bespeak a marriage of extraordinary tenderness; his poems boast a career of fornication scarcely credible in its range and ferocity. In 1680, ill and exahusted, Rochester left London for his ancestral country estate where, frighted by his own mischiefs on a grander scale, he pursued a highly publicized course of penitence under the tutelage of the clergyman Gilbert Burnet, who later published a detailed account of their conversations. The authenticity of this deathbed conversion was questioned then, and has been questioned since, but its results were real enough: Rochester asked his mother to burn his papers, and she did. Fewer than a hundred poems survive. Rochester had never troubled to publish any of them himself; a pirated collection appeared a few months after his death. Yet these pieces, and the conflicting accounts of the life that produced them, have been enough to make him last. Soon after his death, the poet Aphra Behn claimed in verse to have received a visit from his "lovely phantom." "The great, the god-like Rochester" comes before her in order both to praise and to correct her poetry. Since then he has haunted many—pietists, poets, and others—as object of veneration, or reproach, or both together: as admonitory example, verbal virtuoso, extraordinary mortal.

Against Constancy

Tell me no more of constancy,
    The frivolous pretense
Of cold age, narrow jealousy,
    Disease, and want of sense.

5   Let duller fools, on whom kind chance
    Some easy heart has thrown,
Despairing higher to advance,
    Be kind to one alone.

Old men and weak, whose idle flame
10   Their own defects discovers,
Since changing can but spread their shame,
    Ought to be constant lovers.

But we, whose hearts do justly swell
    With no vainglorious pride,
15   Who know how we in love excel,
    Long to be often tried.

Then bring my bath, and strew my bed,
    As each kind night returns;
I'll change a mistress till I'm dead—
20   And fate change me to worms.

The Disabled Debauchee

As some brave admiral, in former war
    Deprived of force, but pressed with courage still,
Two rival fleets appearing from afar,
    Crawls to the top of an adjacent hill;

5   From whence, with thoughts full of concern, he views
    The wise and daring conduct of the fight,
Whilst each bold action to his mind renews
    His present glory and his past delight;

From his fierce eyes flashes of fire he throws,
10   As from black clouds when lightning breaks away;
Transported, thinks himself amidst the foes,
    And absent, yet enjoys the bloody day;

So, when my days of impotence approach,
    And I'm by pox and wine's unlucky chance
15   Forced from the pleasing billows of debauch
    On the dull shore of lazy temperance,

My pains at least some respite shall afford
    While I behold the battles you maintain
When fleets of glasses sail about the board,[1]
20   From whose broadsides volleys of wit shall rain.

Nor let the sight of honorable scars,
    Which my too forward valor did procure,
Frighten new-listed soldiers from the wars:
    Past joys have more than paid what I endure.

25   Should any youth (worth being drunk) prove nice,
    And from his fair inviter meanly shrink,
'Twill please the ghost of my departed Vice[2]
    If, at my counsel, he repent and drink.

Or should some cold-complexioned sot forbid,
30   With his dull morals, our bold night-alarms,
I'll fire his blood by telling what I did
    When I was strong and able to bear arms.

I'll tell of whores attacked, their lords at home;
    Bawds' quarters beaten up, and fortress won;
35   Windows demolished, watches overcome;
    And handsome ills by my contrivance done.

Nor shall our love-fits, Chloris,[3] be forgot,
    When each the well-looked linkboy[4] strove t' enjoy,
And the best kiss was the deciding lot
40   Whether the boy fucked you, or I the boy.

---

1. I.e., wine glasses passed around the table.
2. A character bearing this name had been a staple figure in medieval morality plays, as the comic, scoffing incarnation of depravity.
3. A woman's name, common in pastoral verse (and in Rochester's).
4. A boy employed to accompany walkers on the city streets at night, lighting their way by means of a torch ("link").

With tales like these I will such thoughts inspire
    As to important mischief shall incline:
I'll make him long some ancient church to fire,
    And fear no lewdness he's called to by wine.

45   Thus, statesmanlike, I'll saucily impose,
    And safe from action, valiantly advise;
Sheltered in impotence, urge you to blows,
    And being good for nothing else, be wise.

1675?   1680

Song

Love a woman? You're an ass!
    'Tis a most insipid passion
To choose out for your happiness
    The silliest part of God's creation.

5   Let the porter and the groom,
    Things designed for dirty slaves,
Drudge in fair Aurelia's womb
    To get supplies for age and graves.

Farewell, woman! I intend
10   Henceforth every night to sit
With my lewd, well-natured friend,
    Drinking to engender wit.

Then give me health, wealth, mirth, and wine,
    And, if busy love entrenches,
15   There's a sweet, soft page of mine
    Does the trick worth forty wenches.

                                        1680

The Imperfect Enjoyment

Naked she lay, clasped in my longing arms,
I filled with love, and she all over charms;
Both equally inspired with eager fire,
Melting through kindness, flaming in desire.
5   With arms, legs, lips close clinging to embrace,
She clips me to her breast, and sucks me to her face.
Her nimble tongue, Love's lesser lightning, played
Within my mouth, and to my thoughts conveyed
Swift orders that I should prepare to throw
10   The all-dissolving thunderbolt below.
My fluttering soul, sprung with the pointed kiss,
Hangs hovering o'er her balmy brinks of bliss.
But whilst her busy hand would guide that part
Which should convey my soul up to her heart,
15   In liquid raptures I dissolve all o'er,
Melt into sperm, and spend at every pore.
A touch from any part of her had done 't:
Her hand, her foot, her very look's a cunt.

Smiling, she chides in a kind murmuring noise,
20 And from her body wipes the clammy joys,
When, with a thousand kisses wandering o'er
My panting bosom, "Is there then no more?"
She cries. "All this to love and rapture's due;
Must we not pay a debt to pleasure too?"
25 But I, the most forlorn, lost man alive,
To show my wished obedience vainly strive:
I sigh, alas! and kiss, but cannot swive.°   *screw*
Eager desires confound my first intent,
Succeeding shame does more success prevent,
30 And rage at last confirms me impotent.
Ev'n her fair hand, which might bid heat return
To frozen age, and make cold hermits burn,
Applied to my dead cinder, warms no more
Than fire to ashes could past flames restore.
35 Trembling, confused, despairing, limber, dry,
A wishing, weak, unmoving lump I lie.
This dart of love, whose piercing point, oft tried,
With virgin blood ten thousand maids have dyed,
Which nature still directed with such art
40 That it through every cunt reached every heart—
Stiffly resolved, 'twould carelessly invade
Woman or man, nor ought° its fury stayed:°   *anything/stopped*
Where'er it pierced, a cunt it found or made—
Now languid lies in this unhappy hour,
45 Shrunk up and sapless like a withered flower.
Thou treacherous, base deserter of my flame,
False to my passion, fatal to my fame,
Through what mistaken magic dost thou prove
So true to lewdness, so untrue to love?
50 What oyster-cinder-beggar-common whore
Didst thou e'er fail in all thy life before?
When vice, disease, and scandal lead the way,
With what officious haste doest thou obey!
Like a rude, roaring hector° in the streets   *bully*
55 Who scuffles, cuffs, and justles all he meets,
But if his king or country claim his aid,
The rakehell villain shrinks and hides his head;
Ev'n so thy brutal valor is displayed,
Breaks every stew,° does each small whore invade,   *brothel*
60 But when great Love the onset does command,
Base recreant to thy prince, thou dar'st not stand.
Worst part of me, and henceforth hated most,
Through all the town a common fucking post,
On whom each whore relieves her tingling cunt
65 As hogs on gates do rub themselves and grunt,
Mayst thou to ravenous chancres° be a prey,   *syphilis sores*
Or in consuming weepings waste away;
May strangury and stone[1] thy days attend;

---

1. Painful diseases of the bladder and urinary tract that block the flow of urine.

70   May'st thou never piss, who didst refuse to spend
      When all my joys did on false thee depend.
          And may ten thousand abler pricks agree
          To do the wronged Corinna right for thee.

                                                    1680

Upon Nothing

Nothing! thou elder brother even to Shade:
Thou hadst a being ere the world was made,
And well fixed, art alone of ending not afraid.

5   Ere Time and Place were, Time and Place were not,
     When primitive Nothing Something straight begot;
     Then all proceeded from the great united What.

Something, the general attribute of all,
Severed from thee, its sole original,
Into thy boundless self must undistinguished fall;

10   Yet Something did thy mighty power command,
     And from thy fruitful Emptiness's hand
     Snatched men, beasts, birds, fire, water, air, and land.

Matter, the wicked'st offspring of thy race,
By Form assisted, flew from thy embrace,
15   And rebel Light obscured thy reverend dusky face.

With Form and Matter, Time and Place did join;
Body, thy foe, with these did leagues combine
To spoil thy peaceful realm, and ruin all thy line;

But turncoat Time assists the foe in vain,
20   And bribed by thee, destroys their short-lived reign,
     And to thy hungry womb drives back thy slaves again.

Though mysteries are barred from laic° eyes,   uninitiated
And the divine alone with warrant pries
Into thy bosom, where the truth in private lies,

25   Yet this of thee the wise may truly say:
     Thou from the virtuous nothing dost delay,
     And to be part of thee the wicked wisely pray.

Great Negative, how vainly would the wise
Inquire, define, distinguish, teach, devise,
30   Didst thou not stand to point their blind philosophies!

Is or Is Not, the two great ends of Fate,
And True or False, the subject of debate,
That perfect or destroy the vast designs of state—

When they have racked the politician's breast,
35   Within thy bosom most securely rest,
     And when reduced to thee, are least unsafe and best.

But Nothing, why does Something still permit
That sacred monarchs should in council sit
With persons highly thought at best for nothing fit,

40 While weighty Something modestly abstains
From princes' coffers, and from statesmen's brains,
And Nothing there like stately Nothing reigns?

Nothing! who dwellst with fools in grave disguise,
For whom they reverend shapes and forms devise,
45 Lawn[1] sleeves and furs and gowns, when they like thee look wise:

French truth, Dutch prowess, British policy,
Hibernian learning, Scotch civility,
Spaniards' dispatch, Danes' wit are mainly seen in thee;

The great man's gratitude to his best friend,
50 Kings' promises, whores' vows—towards thee they bend,
Flow swiftly into thee, and in thee ever end.

1678   1679

A Satyr[1] Against Reason and Mankind

Were I (who to my cost already am
One of those strange, prodigious creatures, man)
A spirit free to choose, for my own share,
What case of flesh and blood I pleased to wear,
5 I'd be a dog, a monkey, or a bear,
Or anything but that vain animal
Who is so proud of being rational.
    The senses are too gross, and he'll contrive
A sixth, to contradict the other five,
10 And before certain instinct, will prefer
Reason, which fifty times for one does err;
Reason, an *ignis fatuus*[2] in the mind,
Which, leaving light of nature, sense, behind,
Pathless and dangerous wandering ways it takes
15 Through error's fenny bogs and thorny brakes;
Whilst the misguided follower climbs with pain
Mountains of whimseys, heaped in his own brain;
Stumbling from thought to thought, falls headlong down
Into doubt's boundless sea, where, like to drown,
20 Books bear him up awhile, and make him try
To swim with bladders of philosophy;
In hopes still to o'ertake th' escaping light,
The vapor dances in his dazzling sight
Till, spent, it leaves him to eternal night.
25 Then old age and experience, hand in hand,
Lead him to death, and make him understand,
After a search so painful and so long,
That all his life he has been in the wrong.
Huddled in dirt the reasoning engine lies,
30 Who was so proud, so witty, and so wise.

---

1. Linen; worn (like the furs and gowns) as a mark of rank
by eminent professionals: lawyers, scholars, statesmen
etc.
1. Possibly a pun, identifying both the genre (satire) and

the speaker (a satyr: half-man, half-animal).
2. Literally "foolish fire": a marshland phosphorescence
that, appearing now here and now there, was thought to
be created by sprites to mislead night travelers.

Pride drew him in, as cheats their bubbles° catch,   *victims*
And made him venture to be made a wretch.
His wisdom did his happiness destroy,
Aiming to know that world he should enjoy.
35   And wit was his vain, frivolous pretense
Of pleasing others at his own expense,
For wits are treated just like common whores:
First they're enjoyed, and then kicked out of doors.
The pleasure past, a threatening doubt remains
40   That frights th' enjoyer with succeeding pains.
Women and men of wit are dangerous tools,
And ever fatal to admiring fools:
Pleasure allures, and when the fops escape,
'Tis not that they're belov'd, but fortunate,
45   And therefore what they fear at heart, they hate.
But now, methinks, some formal band and beard³
Takes me to task. Come on, sir; I'm prepared.
"Then, by your favor, anything that's writ
Against this gibing, jingling knack called wit
50   Likes° me abundantly; but you take care   *pleases*
Upon this point, not to be too severe.
Perhaps my muse were fitter for this part,
For I profess I can be very smart
On wit, which I abhor with all my heart.
55   I long to lash it in some sharp essay,
But your grand indiscretion bids me stay
And turns my tide of ink another way.
"What rage ferments in your degenerate mind
To make you rail at reason and mankind?
60   Blest, glorious man! to whom alone kind heaven
An everlasting soul has freely given,
Whom his great Maker took such care to make
That from himself he did the image take
And this fair frame in shining reason dressed
65   To dignify his nature above beast;
Reason, by whose aspiring influence
We take a flight beyond material sense,
Dive into mysteries, then soaring pierce
The flaming limits of the universe,
70   Search heaven and hell, find out what's acted there,
And give the world true grounds of hope and fear."
Hold, mighty man, I cry, all this we know
From the pathetic pen of Ingelo,
From Patrick's *Pilgrim*, Stillingfleet's replies,⁴
75   And 'tis this very reason I despise:
This supernatural gift, that makes a mite
Think he's the image of the infinite,

3. I.e., a clergyman, wearing these marks of office. In 1675 one clergyman in particular, the king's chaplain Edward Stillingfleet, had denounced in a sermon an earlier version of Rochester's *Satyr*, prompting the poet to alter and add some portions of the dialogue that follows.

4. Rochester names three pious inspirational writers: Nathaniel Ingelo (?1621–1683); Simon Patrick, whose *Parable of the Pilgrim* appeared in 1664; and Stillingfleet, Rochester's clerical critic.

Comparing his short life, void of all rest,
To the eternal and the ever blest;
80   This busy, puzzling stirrer-up of doubt
That frames deep mysteries, then finds 'em out,
Filling with frantic crowds of thinking fools
Those reverend bedlams,° colleges and schools;   *madhouses*
Borne on whose wings, each heavy sot can pierce
85   The limits of the boundless universe;
So charming ointments make an old witch fly
And bear a crippled carcass through the sky.
'Tis this exalted power, whose business lies
In nonsense and impossibilities,
90   This made a whimsical philosopher
Before the spacious world, his tub prefer,⁵
And we have modern cloistered coxcombs who
Retire to think, 'cause they have nought to do.
      But thoughts are given for action's government;
95   Where action ceases, thought's impertinent.
Our sphere of action is life's happiness,
And he who thinks beyond, thinks like an ass.
Thus, whilst against false reasoning I inveigh,
I own⁶ right reason, which I would obey:
100   That reason which distinguishes by sense
And gives us rules of good and ill from thence,
That bounds desires with a reforming will
To keep 'em more in vigor, not to kill.
Your reason hinders, mine helps to enjoy,
105   Renewing appetites yours would destroy.
My reason is my friend, yours is a cheat;
Hunger calls out, my reason bids me eat;
Perversely, yours your appetite does mock:
This asks for food, that answers, "What's o'clock?"
110   This plain distinction, sir, your doubt secures:
'Tis not true reason I despise, but yours.
      Thus I think reason righted, but for man,
I'll ne'er recant; defend him if you can.
For all his pride and his philosophy,
115   'Tis evident beasts are, in their degree,
As wise at least, and better far than he.
Those creatures are the wisest who attain,
By surest means, the ends at which they aim.
If therefore Jowler⁷ finds and kills his hares
120   Better than Meres⁸ supplies committee chairs,
Though one's a statesman, th' other but a hound,
Jowler, in justice, would be wiser found.
      You see how far man's wisdom here extends;

---

5. Diogenes (c. 400–325 B.C.), Greek philosopher who supposedly lived in an earthenware tub, as an emblem of his scorn for the shallowness of more opulent modes of life.
6. Acknowledge. "Right reason" refers to natural instinct or common sense, as opposed to the more elaborate modes of thought Rochester is attacking.
7. A dog's name, emphasizing the animal's appetites.
8. Sir Thomas Meres (1634–1715), politician noted for his energy, efficacy, and self-serving flexibility in questions of party allegiance.

Look next if human nature makes amends:

125 Whose principles most generous are, and just,
And to whose morals you would sooner trust.
Be judge yourself, I'll bring it to the test:
Which is the basest creature, man or beast?
Birds feed on birds, beasts on each other prey,

130 But savage man alone does man betray.
Pressed by necessity, they kill for food;
Man undoes man to do himself no good.
With teeth and claws by nature armed, they hunt
Nature's allowance, to supply their want.

135 But man, with smiles, embraces, friendship, praise,
Inhumanly his fellow's life betrays;
With voluntary pains works his distress,
Not through necessity, but wantonness.
     For hunger or for love they fight and tear,

140 Whilst wretched man is still in arms for fear.
For fear he arms, and is of arms afraid,
By fear to fear successively betrayed;
Base fear, the source whence his best passions came:
His boasted honor, and his dear-bought fame;

145 That lust of power, to which he's such a slave,
And for the which alone he dares be brave;
To which his various projects are designed;
Which makes him generous, affable, and kind;
For which he takes such pains to be thought wise,

150 And screws his actions in a forced disguise,
Leading a tedious life in misery
Under laborious, mean hypocrisy.
Look to the bottom of his vast design,
Wherein man's wisdom, power, and glory join:

155 The good he acts, the ill he does endure,
'Tis all from fear, to make himself secure.
Merely for safety, after fame we thirst,
For all men would be cowards if they durst.
     And honesty's against all common sense:

160 Men must be knaves, 'tis in their own defence.
Mankind's dishonest; if you think it fair
Amongst known cheats to play upon the square,
You'll be undone.
Nor can weak truth your reputation save:

165 The knaves will all agree to call you knave.
Wronged shall he live, insulted o'er, oppressed,
Who dares be less a villain than the rest.
     Thus, sir, you see what human nature craves:
Most men are cowards, all men should be knaves.

170 The difference lies, as far as I can see,
Not in the thing itself, but the degree,
And all the subject matter of debate
Is only: Who's a knave of the first rate?

All this with indignation have I hurled
175   At the pretending part of the proud world,
Who, swollen with selfish vanity, devise
False freedoms, holy cheats, and formal lies
Over their fellow slaves to tyrannize.
    But if in court so just a man there be
180   (In court a just man, yet unknown to me)
Who does his needful flattery direct,
Not to oppress and ruin, but protect
(Since flattery, which way soever laid,
Is still a tax on that unhappy trade);
185   If so upright a statesman you can find,
Whose passions bend to his unbiased mind,
Who does his arts and policies apply
To raise his country, not his family,
Nor, whilst his pride owned avarice withstands,
190   Receives close bribes through friends' corrupted hands—
    Is there a churchman who on God relies;
Whose life, his faith and doctrine justifies?
Not one blown up with vain prelatic pride,
Who, for reproof of sins, does man deride;
195   Whose envious heart makes preaching a pretense,
With his obstreperous, saucy eloquence,
To chide at kings, and rail at men of sense;
None of that sensual tribe whose talents lie
In avarice, pride, sloth, and gluttony;
200   Who hunt good livings, but abhor good lives;
Whose lust exalted to that height arrives
They act adultery with their own wives,
And ere a score of years completed be,
Can from the lofty pulpit proudly see
205   Half a large parish their own progeny;
Nor doting bishop who would be adored
For domineering at the council board,
A greater fop in business at fourscore,
Fonder of serious toys, affected more,
210   Than the gay, glittering fool at twenty proves
With all his noise, his tawdry clothes, and loves;
    But a meek, humble man of honest sense,
Who, preaching peace, does practice continence;
Whose pious life's a proof he does believe
215   Mysterious truths, which no man can conceive.
If upon earth there dwell such God-like men,
I'll here recant my paradox to them,
Adore those shrines of virtue, homage pay,
And, with the rabble world, their laws obey.
220   If such there be, yet grant me this at least:
Man differs more from man, than man from beast.

1674–1676   1679

George Etherege
c. 1636–1692

In *The Man of Mode*, the last of his three comedies, George Etherege drew a world that he knew well. Nicknamed "Easy Etherege" for the dexterity of his talk and the looseness of his morals, the playwright was a member of the reigning "critics of the circle," a group of influential courtiers and wits that his protagonist Dorimant mentions reverentially in the play. Others in the circle—Sir Charles Sedley, the Earl of Rochester, the Earl of Dorset, and the Duke of Buckingham—were born to the aristocracy and fell naturally into the group which refereed fashion and taste. Etherege, by contrast, acquired that position through his brilliance and perseverance. He was a judge self-made, not born.

Etherege's father had been one of Queen Henrietta Maria's purveyors, responsible for purchasing food for the royal household; he accompanied the Queen into exile in 1644. His son returned to London, was apprenticed to a lawyer at age eighteen, and went on to study at Clement's Inn, working toward the equivalent of a law degree. The seventeenth century posited an unbridgeable gap between a lawyer and a fashionable courtier. As Sir Fopling Flutter declares in *The Man of Mode*, no one could possibly mistake an "Inns of Court man" for his own exquisite self, any more than Fopling's elegant French carriage could be thought a farmer's cart. But Etherege shook off the dust of Clement's Inn; by 1663, he was exchanging bawdy verse letters with Lord Buckhurst, the future Earl of Dorset to whom he dedicated his first (hugely successful) play, *The Comical Revenge*, the following year. The Inns of Court man had transformed himself into a full-fledged wit and courtier.

He played the new role to the hilt. He gambled; he wrote poetry, songs, and three plays; he drank and seduced and engaged in tavern brawls. He was knighted in 1679, and married a rich widow; in 1685 James II appointed him the English diplomat in Ratisbon, Germany. Etherege's most bitter complaint about Germany was the "reservedness in the ladies." "I can assure your Grace," he wrote to the Duke of Buckingham, "that an amour is not to be managed here." But two weeks later his discontented secretary wrote home describing Etherege as having had "two sisters in his chamber that night, where they all danced stark naked," and of having "tormented the whole town with coaching, fiddling, piping, and dancing till two, three, or four o'clock in the morning." A disgruntled contemporary insisted that Etherege "was exactly his own Sir Fopling Flutter."

Etherege himself would heartily have disagreed. He crafts the entire comedy in order to draw a sharp distinction between the clownish Fopling and the more formidable Dorimant. Dorimant is a wit; Fopling is merely (as his name implies) a fop—a "man of mode," narcissistically absorbed in his dress and manners. It was the business of the true wit to distinguish himself from such fashion-conscious fools, primarily by his way with words. If fops are besotted by clothes, wits are "rhetorically drunk," in Dorimant's magnificent phrase. Medley and Dorimant are intoxicated by words, by the power of language to flout, mock, and jeer.

In Dorimant, the only passion that compares with language is love: in the course of a single day his heart is stirred by Bellinda, by Mrs. Loveit, and by Harriet. Yet "baring" his experienced heart is a game played for amorous gain, a calculated and highly controlled risk, as only the discerning Harriet fully understands. The knowledge gives her power. She becomes a brilliant impiety, a blasphemous intruder into Dorimant's man-run world. As Dorimant notes, she is witty, wild, and beautiful; her serious fault is that she is also virtuous. If Dorimant is akin to "Easy Etherege," Harriet is *not* easy, and she sharply tells him so.

What might happen to an accomplished libertine if, roaming from petticoat to petticoat, he were to meet a woman with a wit so captivating as to match his own, combined with a virtue so clear-headed that she demanded "church security" or marriage? Dorimant is justly wary: "I love her and dare not let her know it. I fear she has an ascendant o'er me . . ." In 1686 Etherege wrote from Germany that the heir to the throne of Bavaria was in love with the wife of the Count von Kaunitz. He had pursued her, Etherege reported, unsuccessfully but unceasingly, "she having an ascendant over [his] spirit, and being like to keep it by her subtlety and wit." The battle for sexual "ascendancy" was waged by a tussle between wit and virtue, in which the reputation and self-regard of both parties were at stake.

The Man of Mode, or Sir Fopling Flutter opened in 1676 before an audience of dukes, courtiers, wits, and the king himself. That audience immediately noticed that Medley's name rhymed with that of Sir Charles Sedley, and that the actor playing Dorimant was dressed like the Earl of Rochester, mimicked his mannerisms, and quoted his favorite poet, Edmund Waller. They watched with delight, as Etherege confronted them with an intriguingly distortive but highly polished mirror.

The Man of Mode
or
Sir Fopling Flutter
A Comedy

TO HER ROYAL HIGHNESS
THE DUCHESS[1]

MADAM,

Poets, however they may be modest otherwise, have always too good an opinion of what they write. The world, when it sees this play dedicated to your Royal Highness, will conclude I have more than my share of that vanity. But I hope the honor I have of belonging to you[2] will excuse my presumption. 'Tis the first thing I have produced in your service, and my duty obliges me to what my choice durst not else have aspired.

I am very sensible,[3] madam, how much it is beholding to your indulgence for the success it had in the acting, and your protection will be no less fortunate to it in the printing; for all are so ambitious of making their court to you that none can be severe to what you are pleased to favor.

This universal submission and respect is due to the greatness of your rank and birth; but you have other illustrious qualities which are much more engaging. Those would but dazzle, did not these really charm the eyes and understandings of all who have the happiness to approach you.

Authors on these occasions are never wanting to publish a particular[4] of their patron's virtues and perfections; but your Royal Highness's are so eminently known that, did I follow their examples, I should but paint those wonders here of which everyone already has the idea in his mind. Besides, I do not think it proper to aim at

---

1. Mary of Modena (1658–1718), Duchess of York. She became queen when her husband ascended the throne as James II in 1685.
2. It is not clear in what capacity Etherege served the

duchess; her husband gave him a pension in 1682 and appointed him envoy to Ratisbon in 1685.
3. Aware.
4. Never stop themselves from publishing a list.

that in prose which is so glorious a subject for verse, in which hereafter if I show more zeal than skill, it will not grieve me much, since I less passionately desire to be esteemed a poet than to be thought,

Madam,
Your Royal Highness's
most humble, most obedient,
and most faithful servant,

GEORGE ETHEREGE

Prologue
BY SIR CAR SCROOPE, BARONET[5]

	Like dancers on the ropes poor poets fare:	
	Most perish young, the rest in danger are.	
	This, one would think, should make our authors wary,	
	But, gamester-like, the giddy fools miscarry;[6]	
5	A lucky hand or two so tempts 'em on,	
	They cannot leave off play till they're undone.	
	With modest fears a muse does first begin,	
	Like a young wench newly enticed to sin;	
	But tickled once with praise, by her good will,	
10	The wanton fool would never more lie still.	
	'Tis an old mistress[7] you'll meet here tonight,	
	Whose charms you once have looked on with delight.	
	But now, of late, such dirty drabs° have known ye,[8]	prostitutes
	A muse o' th' better sort's ashamed to own° ye.	acknowledge
15	Nature well-drawn and wit must now give place	
	To gaudy nonsense and to dull grimace;	
	Nor is it strange that you should like so much	
	That kind of wit, for most of yours is such.	
	But I'm afraid that while to France we go,	
20	To bring you home fine dresses, dance, and show,	
	The stage, like you, will but more foppish[9] grow.	
	Of foreign wares why should we fetch the scum,	
	When we can be so richly served at home?	
	For, heav'n be thanked, 'tis not so wise an age	
25	But your own follies may supply the stage.	
	Though often plowed, there's no great fear the soil	
	Should barren grow by the too-frequent toil,	
	While at your doors are to be daily found	
	Such loads of dunghill to manure the ground.	
30	'Tis by your follies that we players thrive,	
	As the physicians by diseases live;	
	And as each year some new distemper reigns,	
	Whose friendly poison helps to increase their gains,	
	So, among you, there starts up every day	
35	Some new, unheard-of fool for us to play.	

---

5. A courtier and poet; one of Etherege's friends in the circle of Court wits.
6. Lose (like gamblers).
7. I.e., Etherege's muse. The playwright was famous for his earlier success, *The Comical Revenge* (1664).
8. Scroope's sexual innuendo ("know") jeers at the audience for loving "gaudy nonsense."
9. Foolishly obsessed with fashionable dress and manners.

Then, for your own sakes, be not too severe,
Nor what you all admire at home, damn here.
Since each is fond of his own ugly face,
Why should you, when we hold it, break the glass?°   mirror

Dramatis Personae

MR. DORIMANT
MR. MEDLEY *his friend*
OLD BELLAIR
YOUNG BELLAIR *his son (in love with Emilia)*   Gentlemen
SIR FOPLING FLUTTER

LADY TOWNLEY *Old Bellair's sister*
EMILIA
MRS. LOVEIT (in love with Dorimant)   Gentlewomen
BELLINDA (in love with Dorimant)
LADY WOODVILL
HARRIET *Lady Woodvill's daughter*

PERT, *Mrs. Loveit's waiting woman*
BUSY, *Harriet's waiting woman*
A SHOEMAKER
AN ORANGE-WOMAN
THREE SLOVENLY BULLIES
TWO CHAIRMEN
MR. SMIRK, *a parson*
HANDY, *Dorimant's personal attendant*
PAGES, FOOTMEN *etc.*

A c t I

A dressing room. A table covered with a toilet;[1] *clothes laid ready. Enter Dorimant in his gown and slippers, with a note in his hand made up,*[2] *repeating verses.*

DORIMANT

> "Now, for some ages, had the pride of Spain
> Made the sun shine on half the world in vain."[3]

[*Then looking on the note.*]

"For Mrs. Loveit." What a dull, insipid thing is a *billet-doux*[4] written in cold blood, after the heat of the business is over! It is a tax upon good nature which I have here been laboring to pay, and have done it, but with as much regret as ever fanatic paid the Royal Aid or church duties.[5] 'Twill have the same fate, I know, that all my notes to her have had of late; 'twill not be thought kind enough. Faith, women are i' the right when they jealously examine our letters, for in them we always first discover our decay of passion.—Hey! Who waits?

[*Enter Handy.*]

HANDY Sir—
DORIMANT Call a footman.

---

1. Cloth or lace cover for a dressing table.
2. Ready to be sent.
3. The opening couplet of a poem by Edmund Waller (1606–1687), *Of a War with Spain, and a Fight at Sea*. Dorimant's habit of quoting Waller has been taken as

evidence that the character is modeled on the Earl of Rochester, who often did the same.
4. Love letter.
5. Religious dissenters ("fanatics") resisted paying taxes levied by the Crown and by the established church.

HANDY None of 'em are come yet.

DORIMANT Dogs! Will they ever lie snoring abed till noon?

HANDY 'Tis all one, sir: if they're up, you indulge 'em so, they're ever poaching[6] after whores all the morning.

DORIMANT Take notice henceforward who's wanting in his duty; the next clap[7] he gets, he shall rot for an example. What vermin are those chattering without?

HANDY Foggy Nan, the orange-woman, and swearing Tom, the shoemaker.

DORIMANT Go, call in that overgrown jade[8] with the flasket[9] of guts before her. Fruit is refreshing in a morning.

[Exit Handy.]

"It is not that I love you less,
Than when before your feet I lay—"[1]

[Enter Orange-Woman and Handy].

How now, double-tripe,[2] what news do you bring?

ORANGE-WOMAN News! Here's the best fruit has come to town t' year. Gad,[3] I was up before four o'clock this morning and bought all the choice i' the market.

DORIMANT The nasty refuse of your shop.

ORANGE-WOMAN You need not make mouths at it. I assure you, 'tis all culled ware.[4]

DORIMANT The citizens buy better on a holiday in their walk to Totnam.[5]

ORANGE-WOMAN Good or bad, 'tis all one; I never knew you commend anything. Lord, would the ladies had heard you talk of 'em as I have done.

[Sets down the fruit.]

Here, bid your man give me an angel.[6]

DORIMANT [to Handy] Give the bawd her fruit again.

ORANGE-WOMAN Well, on my conscience, there never was the like of you.— God's my life, I had almost forgot to tell you, there is a young gentlewoman, lately come to town with her mother, that is so taken with you.

DORIMANT Is she handsome?

ORANGE-WOMAN Nay, gad, there are few finer women, I tell you but so, and a hugeous fortune, they say. Here, eat this peach, it comes from the stone;[7] 'tis better than any Newington[8] y' have tasted.

DORIMANT [taking the peach] This fine woman, I'll lay my life, is some awkward, ill-fashioned country toad, who, not having above four dozen of black hairs on her head, has adorned her baldness with a large white fruz,[9] that she may look sparkishly[1] in the forefront of the King's box[2] at an old play.

ORANGE-WOMAN Gad, you'd change your note quickly if you did but see her!

DORIMANT How came she to know me?

ORANGE-WOMAN She saw you yesterday at the Change.[3] She told me you came and fooled with the woman at the next shop.

DORIMANT I remember, there was a mask[4] observed me, indeed. Fooled, did she say?

---

6. Hunting illicitly.

7. Attack of venereal disease.

8. Ill-tempered horse.

9. Tub.

1. Waller, from *The Self-Banished*.

2. Guts.

3. God.

4. Choice merchandise.

5. Tottenham, a northern suburb favored by London tradespeople as a day-trip destination.

6. Gold coin.

7. It's so ripe that it falls away from the pit.

8. Variety of peach.

9. Wig of frizzled hair.

1. Chic.

2. The box seats would be vacant because the king did not attend "old plays."

3. The New Exchange, a fashionable shopping complex.

4. I.e., a woman wearing a mask (as was fashionable among ladies).

ORANGE-WOMAN Ay; I vow she told me twenty things you said too, and acted with her head and with her body so like you—

[Enter Medley.]

MEDLEY Dorimant, my life, my joy, my darling sin! How dost thou?

[Embraces him.]

ORANGE-WOMAN Lord, what a filthy trick these men have got of kissing one another!

[She spits.]

MEDLEY Why do you suffer this cartload of scandal to come near you and make your neighbors think you so improvident to need a bawd?[5]

ORANGE-WOMAN [to Dorimant] Good, now we shall have it! You did but want him to help you. Come, pay me for my fruit.

MEDLEY Make us thankful for it, huswife,[6] bawds are as much out of fashion as gentlemen-ushers:[7] none but old formal ladies use the one, and none but foppish old stagers[8] employ the other. Go, you are an insignificant brandy bottle.

DORIMANT Nay, there you wrong her. Three quarts of canary[9] is her business.

ORANGE-WOMAN What you please, gentlemen.

DORIMANT To him! Give him as good as he brings.

ORANGE-WOMAN Hang him, there is not such another heathen in the town again, except it be the shoemaker without.

MEDLEY I shall see you hold up your hand at the bar next sessions[1] for murder, huswife. That shoemaker can take his oath you are in fee with the doctors to sell green fruit to the gentry, that the crudities[2] may breed diseases.

ORANGE-WOMAN Pray give me my money.

DORIMANT Not a penny! When you bring the gentlewoman hither you spoke of, you shall be paid.

ORANGE-WOMAN The gentlewoman! The gentlewoman may be as honest[3] as your sisters, for aught as I know. Pray pay me, Mr. Dorimant, and do not abuse me so. I have an honester way of living; you know it.

MEDLEY Was there ever such a resty[4] bawd?

DORIMANT Some jade's tricks she has, but she makes amends when she's in good humor.—Come, tell me the lady's name, and Handy shall pay you.

ORANGE-WOMAN I must not; she forbid me.

DORIMANT That's a sure sign she would have you.

MEDLEY Where does she live?

ORANGE-WOMAN They lodge at my house.

MEDLEY Nay, then she's in a hopeful way.

ORANGE-WOMAN Good Mr. Medley, say your pleasure of me, but take heed how you affront[5] my house. God's my life, in a hopeful way!

DORIMANT Prithee, peace. What kind of woman's the mother?

ORANGE-WOMAN A goodly, grave gentlewoman. Lord, how she talks against the wild young men o' the town! As for your part, she thinks you an arrant devil: should she see you, on my conscience she would look if you had not a cloven foot.

DORIMANT Does she know me?

---

5. So unresourceful as to depend upon a procuress.
6. Hussy, slut.
7. Male servants, notoriously bribable.
8. Old-timers.
9. A sweet wine from the Canary Islands, often served in whorehouses. "Canary" was also slang for "whore."

1. In the law court when the judge next sits.
2. The indigestibility of her oranges.
3. Chaste.
4. Stubborn, irritable.
5. Insult.

ORANGE-WOMAN Only by hearsay. A thousand horrid stories have been told her of you, and she believes 'em all.

MEDLEY By the character, this should be the famous Lady Woodvill and her daughter Harriet.

ORANGE-WOMAN [aside] The devil's in him for guessing, I think.

DORIMANT Do you know 'em?

MEDLEY Both very well. The mother's a great admirer of the forms and civility of the last age.[6]

DORIMANT An antiquated beauty may be allowed to be out of humor at the freedoms of the present. This is a good account of the mother. Pray, what is the daughter?

MEDLEY Why, first, she's an heiress, vastly rich.

DORIMANT And handsome?

MEDLEY What alteration a twelvemonth may have bred in her, I know not, but a year ago she was the beautifulest creature I ever saw: a fine, easy, clean shape; light brown hair in abundance; her features regular; her complexion clear and lively; large, wanton eyes; but above all, a mouth that has made me kiss it a thousand times in imagination—teeth white and even, and pretty, pouting lips, with a little moisture ever hanging on them, that look like the Provins rose[7] fresh on the bush, ere the morning sun has quite drawn up the dew.

DORIMANT Rapture, mere rapture!

ORANGE-WOMAN Nay, gad, he tells you true. She's a delicate creature.

DORIMANT Has she wit?

MEDLEY More than is usual in her sex, and as much malice. Then, she's as wild as you would wish her, and has a demureness in her looks that makes it so surprising.

DORIMANT Flesh and blood cannot hear this and not long to know her.

MEDLEY I wonder what makes her mother bring her up to town? An old, doting keeper[8] cannot be more jealous of his mistress.

ORANGE-WOMAN She made me laugh yesterday. There was a judge came to visit 'em, and the old man (she told me) did so stare upon her and, when he saluted her, smacked[9] so heartily—who would think it of 'em?

MEDLEY God-a-mercy, Judge!

DORIMANT Do 'em right, the gentlemen of the long robe[1] have not been wanting[2] by their good examples to countenance the crying sin o' the nation.[3]

MEDLEY Come, on with your trappings; 'tis later than you imagine.

DORIMANT Call in the shoemaker, Handy!

ORANGE-WOMAN Good Mr. Dorimant, pay me. Gad, I had rather give you my fruit than stay to be abused by that foul-mouthed rogue. What you gentlemen say, it matters not much; but such a dirty fellow does one more disgrace.

DORIMANT [to Handy] Give her ten shillings. [To Orange-Woman.] And be sure you tell the young gentlewoman I must be acquainted with her.

ORANGE-WOMAN Now do you long to be tempting this pretty creature. Well, heavens mend you!

MEDLEY Farewell, bog! [Exeunt Orange-Woman and Handy.]
Dorimant, when did you see your pis aller,[4] as you call her, Mrs. Loveit?

---

6. I.e., of the court of Charles I, who reigned 1625–1649.   1. Judges.
7. A double red rose.   2. Lacking.
8. A man who maintains a woman as his paid lover.   3. I.e., fornication.
9. Kissed.   4. Last resource.

DORIMANT Not these two days.

MEDLEY And how stand affairs between you?

DORIMANT There has been great patching of late, much ado; we make a shift[5] to hang together.

MEDLEY I wonder how her mighty spirit bears it?

DORIMANT Ill enough, on all conscience. I never knew so violent a creature.

MEDLEY She's the most passionate in her love and the most extravagant in her jealousy of any woman I ever heard of. What note is that?

DORIMANT An excuse I am going to send her for the neglect I am guilty of.

MEDLEY Prithee, read it.

DORIMANT No, but if you will take the pains, you may.

MEDLEY [reads] "I never was a lover of business, but now I have a just reason to hate it, since it has kept me these two days from seeing you. I intend to wait upon you in the afternoon, and in the pleasure of your conversation forget all I have suffered during this tedious absence."—This business of yours, Dorimant, has been with a vizard[6] at the playhouse; I have had an eye on you. If some malicious body should betray you, this kind note would hardly make your peace with her.

DORIMANT I desire no better.

MEDLEY Why, would her knowledge of it oblige[7] you?

DORIMANT Most infinitely; next to the coming to a good understanding with a new mistress, I love a quarrel with an old one. But the devil's in't, there has been such a calm in my affairs of late, I have not had the pleasure of making a woman so much as break her fan, to be sullen, or forswear herself, these three days.

MEDLEY A very great misfortune! Let me see, I love mischief well enough to forward this business myself. I'll about it presently, and though I know the truth of what y'ave done will set her a-raving, I'll heighten it a little with invention, leave her in a fit o' the mother,[8] and be here again before y'are ready.

DORIMANT Pray, stay; you may spare yourself the labor. The business is undertaken already by one who will manage it with as much address[9] and, I think, with a little more malice than you can.

MEDLEY Who i' the devil's name can this be?

DORIMANT Why, the vizard, that very vizard you saw me with.

MEDLEY Does she love mischief so well as to betray herself to spite another?

DORIMANT Not so neither, Medley; I will make you comprehend the mystery. This mask, for a farther confirmation of what I have been these two days swearing to her, made me yesterday at the playhouse make her a promise, before her face, utterly to break off with Loveit; and because she tenders[1] my reputation and would not have me do a barbarous thing, has contrived a way to give me a handsome occasion.

MEDLEY Very good.

DORIMANT She intends, about an hour before me this afternoon, to make Loveit a visit; and (having the privilege by reason of a professed friendship between 'em to talk of her concerns)—

MEDLEY Is she a friend?

DORIMANT Oh, an intimate friend!

---

5. Are trying.
6. I.e., a woman wearing a mask: the customary covering for prostitutes who frequented the theaters.
7. Please.

8. Hysteria.
9. Skill.
1. Is solicitous of.

MEDLEY Better and better! Pray proceed.

DORIMANT She means insensibly to insinuate[2] a discourse of me and artificially raise her jealousy to such a height that, transported with the first motions of her passion, she shall fly upon me with all the fury imaginable as soon as ever I enter. The quarrel being thus happily begun, I am to play my part: confess and justify all my roguery, swear her impertinence and ill humor makes her intolerable, tax[3] her with the next fop that comes into my head, and in a huff march away, slight her, and leave her to be taken by whosoever thinks it worth his time to lie down before her.

MEDLEY This vizard is a spark,[4] and has a genius that makes her worthy of yourself, Dorimant.

[Enter Handy, Shoemaker, and Footman.]

DORIMANT [to Footman] You rogue there, who sneak like a dog that has flung down a dish! If you do not mend your waiting, I'll uncase you[5] and turn you loose to the wheel of fortune.—Handy, seal this and let him run with it presently. [Exit Footman.]

MEDLEY Since y'are resolved on a quarrel, why do you send her this kind note?

DORIMANT To keep her at home in order to the business. [To the Shoemaker.] How now, you drunken sot?

SHOEMAKER 'Zbud,[6] you have no reason to talk. I have not had a bottle of sack[7] of yours in my belly this fortnight.

MEDLEY The orange-woman says your neighbors take notice what a heathen you are, and design to inform the bishop and have you burned for an atheist.

SHOEMAKER Damn her, dunghill! If her husband does not remove her, she stinks so, the parish intend to indict him for a nuisance.

MEDLEY I advise you like a friend, reform your life. You have brought the envy of the world upon you by living above yourself. Whoring and swearing are vices too genteel for a shoemaker.

SHOEMAKER 'Zbud, I think you men of quality will grow as unreasonable as the women: you would engross[8] the sins o' the nation. Poor folks can no sooner be wicked but th'are railed at[9] by their betters.

DORIMANT Sirrah,[1] I'll have you stand i' the pillory[2] for this libel.

SHOEMAKER Some of you deserve it, I'm sure. There are so many of 'em that our journeymen[3] nowadays, instead of harmless ballads, sing nothing but your damned lampoons.[4]

DORIMANT Our lampoons, you rogue?

SHOEMAKER Nay, good master, why should not you write your own commentaries as well as Caesar?[5]

MEDLEY The rascal's read, I perceive.

SHOEMAKER You know the old proverb, ale and history.[6]

DORIMANT Draw on my shoes, sirrah.

SHOEMAKER Here's a shoe—

DORIMANT Sits with more wrinkles than there are in an angry bully's forehead.

SHOEMAKER 'Zbud, as smooth as your mistress's skin does upon her. So, strike your foot in home. 'Zbud, if e'er a monsieur of 'em all make more fashionable ware, I'll be content to have my ears whipped off with my own paring knife.

MEDLEY And served up in a ragout,[7] instead of coxcombs[8], to a company of French shoemakers for a collation.[9]

SHOEMAKER Hold, hold! Damn 'em caterpillars,[1] let 'em feed upon cabbage!— Come master, your health this morning next my heart now.[2]

DORIMANT Go, get you home, and govern your family better! Do not let your wife follow you to the alehouse, beat your whore, and lead you home in triumph.

SHOEMAKER 'Zbud, there's never a man i' the town lives more like a gentleman with his wife than I do. I never mind her motions;[3] she never inquires into mine. We speak to one another civilly, hate one another heartily, and because 'tis vulgar to lie and soak[4] together, we have each of us our several settle-bed.[5]

DORIMANT [to Handy] Give him half a crown.

MEDLEY Not without he will promise to be bloody drunk.

SHOEMAKER Tope's[6] the word, i' the eye of the world. [To Handy.[7]] For my master's honor, Robin!

DORIMANT Do not debauch[8] my servants, sirrah.

SHOEMAKER I only tip him the wink;[9] he knows an alehouse from a hovel.

[Exit Shoemaker.]

DORIMANT [to Handy] My clothes, quickly!

MEDLEY Where shall we dine today?

[Enter Young Bellair.]

DORIMANT Where you will. Here comes a good third man.

YOUNG BELLAIR Your servant, gentlemen.

MEDLEY Gentle sir, how will you answer[1] this visit to your honorable mistress? 'Tis not her interest you should keep company with men of sense, who will be talking reason.

YOUNG BELLAIR I do not fear her pardon, do you but grant me yours for my neglect of late.

MEDLEY Though y'ave made us miserable by the want of your good company, to show you I am free from all resentment, may the beautiful cause of our misfortune give you all the joys happy lovers have shared ever since the world began.

YOUNG BELLAIR You wish me in heaven, but you believe me on my journey to hell.

MEDLEY You have a good strong faith, and that may contribute much towards your salvation. I confess I am but of an untoward[2] constitution, apt to have doubts and scruples; and in love they are no less distracting than in religion. Were I so near marriage, I should cry out by fits as I ride in my coach, "Cuckold, cuckold!" with no less fury than the mad fanatic does "Glory!" in Bethlem.[3]

7. Stew.
8. Cocks' combs (used by the French in stews).
9. Light snack.
1. People who prey on society; here, particularly referring to the French.
2. The shoemaker asks for money to drink Dorimant's health (which he will do with hand on heart).
3. Activities.
4. Sweat.
5. They sleep apart, on long wooden benches.

6. A more fashionable term for "drunk."
7. Inviting him to drink, too.
8. Corrupt.
9. Give him the signal.
1. Explain.
2. Rebellious, perverse.
3. A reference to Oliver Cromwell's porter, Daniel, who ended up in Bethlehem Hospital, the insane asylum also known as Bedlam.

YOUNG BELLAIR Because religion makes some run mad, must I live an atheist?

MEDLEY Is it not great indiscretion for a man of credit, who may have money enough on his word, to go and deal with Jews, who for little sums make men enter into bonds and give judgments?[4]

YOUNG BELLAIR Preach no more on this text; I am determined, and there is no hope of my conversion.

DORIMANT [to Handy, who is fiddling about him] Leave your unnecessary fiddling. A wasp that's buzzing about a man's nose at dinner is not more troublesome than thou art.

HANDY You love to have your clothes hang just, sir.

DORIMANT I love to be well-dressed, sir, and think it no scandal to my understanding.

HANDY Will you use the essence,[5] or orange-flower water?

DORIMANT I will smell as I do today, no offense to the ladies' noses.

HANDY Your pleasure, sir.   [Exit Handy.]

DORIMANT That a man's excellency should lie in neatly tying of a ribbon or a cravat?[6] How careful's nature in furnishing the world with necessary coxcombs![7]

YOUNG BELLAIR That's a mighty pretty suit of yours, Dorimant.

DORIMANT I am glad 't has your approbation.

YOUNG BELLAIR No man in town has a better fancy in his clothes than you have.

DORIMANT You will make me have an opinion of my genius.

MEDLEY There is a great critic, I hear, in these matters lately arrived piping hot from Paris.

YOUNG BELLAIR Sir Fopling Flutter, you mean.

MEDLEY The same.

YOUNG BELLAIR He thinks himself the pattern of modern gallantry.

DORIMANT He is indeed the pattern of modern foppery.

MEDLEY He was yesterday at the play, with a pair of gloves up to his elbows and a periwig[8] more exactly curled than a lady's head newly dressed for a ball.

YOUNG BELLAIR What a pretty lisp he has!

DORIMANT Ho, that he affects in imitation of the people of quality of France.

MEDLEY His head stands for the most part on one side, and his looks are more languishing than a lady's when she lolls at stretch[9] in her coach or leans her head carelessly against the side of a box i' the playhouse.

DORIMANT He is a person indeed of great acquired follies.

MEDLEY He is like many others, beholding to his education for making him so eminent a coxcomb. Many a fool had been lost to the world, had their indulgent parents wisely bestowed neither learning nor good breeding on 'em.

YOUNG BELLAIR He has been, as the sparkish word is, brisk upon the ladies already. He was yesterday at my Aunt Townley's and gave Mrs. Loveit a catalogue of his good qualities, under the character[1] of a complete gentleman, who (according to Sir Fopling) ought to dress well, dance well, fence well, have a genius for love letters, an agreeable voice for a chamber,[2] be very amorous, something discreet, but not overconstant.

MEDLEY Pretty ingredients to make an accomplished person!

DORIMANT I am glad he pitched upon Loveit.

4. Take out loans and pledge possessions as security.
5. Perfume.
6. Fine scarf tied in a bow with flowing ends.
7. Men who are naturally conceited and showy.

8. A man's long-haired wig.
9. Lies back.
1. I.e., as an example of.
2. Bedchamber.

YOUNG BELLAIR How so?

DORIMANT I wanted a fop to lay to her charge;[3] and this is as pat as may be.

YOUNG BELLAIR I am confident she loves no man but you.

DORIMANT The good fortune were enough to make me vain, but that I am in my nature modest.

YOUNG BELLAIR Hark you, Dorimant.—With your leave, Mr. Medley. 'Tis only a secret concerning a fair lady.

MEDLEY Your good breeding, sir, gives you too much trouble. You might have whispered without all this ceremony.

YOUNG BELLAIR [to Dorimant] How stand your affairs with Bellinda of late?

DORIMANT She's a little jilting baggage.

YOUNG BELLAIR Nay, I believe her false enough, but she's ne'er the worse for your purpose. She was with you yesterday in a disguise at the play.

DORIMANT There we fell out and resolved never to speak to one another more.

YOUNG BELLAIR The occasion?

DORIMANT Want of courage to meet me at the place appointed. These young women apprehend[4] loving as much as the young men do fighting at first; but once entered, like them too, they all turn bullies straight.

[Enter Handy.]

HANDY [to Young Bellair] Sir, your man without desires to speak with you.

YOUNG BELLAIR Gentlemen, I'll return immediately.   [Exit Young Bellair.]

MEDLEY A very pretty fellow, this.

DORIMANT He's handsome, well-bred, and by much the most tolerable of all the young men that do not abound in wit.

MEDLEY Ever well-dressed, always complaisant,[5] and seldom impertinent; you and he are grown very intimate, I see.

DORIMANT It is our mutual interest to be so. It makes the women think the better of his understanding and judge more favorably of my reputation; it makes him pass upon some for[6] a man of very good sense, and I upon others for a very civil person.

MEDLEY What was that whisper?

DORIMANT A thing which he would fain have known, but I did not think it fit to tell him. It might have frighted him from his honorable intentions of marrying.

MEDLEY Emilia, give her her due, has the best reputation of any young woman about the town who has beauty enough to provoke detraction. Her carriage[7] is unaffected, her discourse modest—not at all censorious nor pretending, like the counterfeits of the age.

DORIMANT She's a discreet maid, and I believe nothing can corrupt her but a husband.

MEDLEY A husband?

DORIMANT Yes, a husband. I have known many women make a difficulty of losing a maidenhead, who have afterwards made none of making a cuckold.

MEDLEY This prudent consideration, I am apt to think, has made you confirm poor Bellair in the desperate resolution he has taken.

DORIMANT Indeed, the little hope I found there was of her, in the state she was in, has made me by my advice contribute something towards the changing of her condition.[8]

[Enter Young Bellair.]

3. Blame her for.
4. Fear.
5. Amiable, well-mannered.

6. Be accepted by people as.
7. Bearing.
8. Her unmarried state.

Dear Bellair, by heavens I thought we had lost thee! Men in love are never to be reckoned on when we would form a company.

YOUNG BELLAIR Dorimant, I am undone. My man has brought the most surprising news i' the world.

DORIMANT Some strange misfortune is befall'n your love?

YOUNG BELLAIR My father came to town last night and lodges i' the very house where Emilia lies.

MEDLEY Does he know it is with her you are in love?

YOUNG BELLAIR He knows I love, but knows not whom, without[9] some officious sot has betrayed me.

DORIMANT Your Aunt Townley is your confidante and favors the business.

YOUNG BELLAIR I do not apprehend any ill office from her. I have received a letter, in which I am commanded by my father to meet him at my aunt's this afternoon. He tells me farther he has made a match for me, and bids me resolve to be obedient to his will or expect to be disinherited.

MEDLEY Now's your time, Bellair. Never had lover such an opportunity of giving a generous proof of his passion.

YOUNG BELLAIR As how, I pray?

MEDLEY Why, hang an estate, marry Emilia out of hand, and provoke your father to do what he threatens. 'Tis but despising a coach, humbling yourself to a pair of galoshes,[1] being out of countenance[2] when you meet your friends, pointed at and pitied wherever you go by all the amorous fops that know you, and your fame will be immortal.

YOUNG BELLAIR I could find in my heart to resolve not to marry at all.

DORIMANT Fie, fie! That would spoil a good jest and disappoint the well-natured town of an occasion of laughing at you.

YOUNG BELLAIR The storm I have so long expected hangs o'er my head and begins to pour down upon me. I am on the rack and can have no rest till I'm satisfied in what I fear. Where do you dine?

DORIMANT At Long's or Locket's.[3]

MEDLEY At Long's let it be.

YOUNG BELLAIR I'll run and see Emilia and inform myself how matters stand. If my misfortunes are not so great as to make me unfit for company, I'll be with you.

[Exit Young Bellair. Enter a Footman, with a letter.]

FOOTMAN [to Dorimant] Here's a letter, sir.

DORIMANT The superscription's right: "For Mr. Dorimant."

MEDLEY Let's see. [Looks at the letter.] The very scrawl and spelling of a true-bred whore.

DORIMANT I know the hand. The style is admirable, I assure you.

MEDLEY Prithee, read it.

DORIMANT [reads] "I told a you you dud not love me, if you dud, you would have seen me again ere now. I have no money and am very malicolly. Pray send me a guynie to see the operies. Your servant to command, Molly."

MEDLEY Pray let the whore have a favorable answer, that she may spark it in a box and do honor to her profession.

DORIMANT She shall, and perk up i' the face of quality. [To Handy.] Is the coach at door?

---

9. Unless.
1. Wooden-soled shoes, worn by the lower classes.

2. Disconcerted.
3. Fashionable taverns.

HANDY You did not bid me send for it.

DORIMANT Eternal blockhead! [*Handy offers to go out.*] Hey, sot!

HANDY Did you call me, sir?

DORIMANT I hope you have no just exception[4] to the name, sir?

HANDY I have sense,[5] sir.

DORIMANT Not so much as a fly in winter.—How did you come, Medley?

MEDLEY In a chair.[6]

FOOTMAN You may have a hackney coach[7] if you please, sir.

DORIMANT I may ride the elephant[8] if I please, sir. Call another chair and let my coach follow to Long's.

[*Exeunt Footman and Handy.*]

"Be calm, ye great parents, etc."[9]

[*Exeunt, singing.*]

Act II

Scene 1

[*Lady Townley's house. Enter my Lady Townley and Emilia.*]

LADY TOWNLEY I was afraid, Emilia, all had been discovered.

EMILIA I tremble with the apprehension still.

LADY TOWNLEY That my brother should take lodgings i' the very house where you lie!

EMILIA 'Twas lucky we had timely notice to warn the people to be secret. He seems to be a mighty good-humored old man.

LADY TOWNLEY He ever had a notable smirking way with him.

EMILIA He calls me rogue, tells me he can't abide me, and does so bepat[1] me.

LADY TOWNLEY On my word, you are much in his favor then.

EMILIA He has been very inquisitive, I am told, about my family, my reputation, and my fortune.

LADY TOWNLEY I am confident he does not i' the least suspect you are the woman his son's in love with.

EMILIA What should make him then inform himself so particularly of me?

LADY TOWNLEY He was always of a very loving temper himself. It may be he has a doting fit upon him, who knows?

EMILIA It cannot be.

[*Enter Young Bellair.*]

LADY TOWNLEY Here comes my nephew.—Where did you leave your father?

YOUNG BELLAIR Writing a note within.—Emilia, this early visit looks as if some kind jealousy would not let you rest at home.

EMILIA The knowledge I have of my rival gives me a little cause to fear your constancy.

YOUNG BELLAIR My constancy! I vow—

EMILIA Do not vow. Our love is frail as is our life, and full as little in our power; and are you sure you shall outlive this day?

---

4. Objection.

5. Feelings.

6. A vehicle seating one person, carried by two "chairmen."

7. A coach for hire.

8. An elephant had recently been exhibited as an extraordinary curiosity at Bartholomew Fair.

9. Line from Thomas Shadwell's operatic version of Shakespeare's *Tempest* (1674).

1. Pat.

YOUNG BELLAIR I am not, but when we are in perfect health, 'twere an idle thing to fright ourselves with the thoughts of sudden death.

LADY TOWNLEY Pray, what has passed between you and your father i' the garden?

YOUNG BELLAIR He's firm in his resolution, tells me I must marry Mrs. Harriet, or swears he'll marry himself and disinherit me. When I saw I could not prevail with him to be more indulgent, I dissembled an obedience to his will, which has composed[2] his passion and will give us time—and I hope opportunity—to deceive him.

[Enter Old Bellair, with a note in his hand.]

LADY TOWNLEY Peace, here he comes.

OLD BELLAIR Harry, take this and let your man carry it for me to Mr. Fourbe's[3] chamber—my lawyer, i' the Temple.[4]

[Exit Young Bellair.]

[To Emilia.] Neighbor, adod[5] I am glad to see thee here.—Make much of her, sister. She's one of the best of your acquaintance. I like her countenance and behavior well; she has a modesty that is not common i' this age, adod she has.

LADY TOWNLEY I know her value, brother, and esteem her accordingly.

OLD BELLAIR Advise her to wear a little more mirth in her face. Adod, she's too serious.

LADY TOWNLEY The fault is very excusable in a young woman.

OLD BELLAIR Nay, adod, I like her ne'er the worse; a melancholy beauty has her charms. I love a pretty sadness in a face which varies now and then, like changeable colors,[6] into a smile.

LADY TOWNLEY Methinks you speak very feelingly, brother.

OLD BELLAIR I am but five-and-fifty, sister, you know—an age not altogether insensible.[7] [To Emilia.] Cheer up, sweetheart, I have a secret to tell thee may chance to make thee merry. We three will make collation together anon.[8] I' the meantime, mum! [Aloud.] I can't abide you; go, I can't abide you.

[Enter Young Bellair.]

Harry! Come, you must along with me to my Lady Woodvill's.—I am going to slip[9] the boy at a mistress.

YOUNG BELLAIR At a wife, sir, you would say.

OLD BELLAIR You need not look so glum, sir. A wife is no curse when she brings the blessing of a good estate with her. But an idle town flirt, with a painted face, a rotten reputation, and a crazy[1] fortune, adod, is the devil and all; and such a one I hear you are in league with.

YOUNG BELLAIR I cannot help detraction, sir.

OLD BELLAIR Out, a pize[2] o' their breeches, there are keeping fools enough for such flaunting baggages, and they are e'en too good for 'em. [To Emilia.] Remember night. [Aloud.] Go, y'are a rogue, y'are a rogue. Fare you well, fare you well. [To Young Bellair.] Come, come, come along, sir.

[Exeunt Old and Young Bellair.]

LADY TOWNLEY On my word, the old man comes on apace. I'll lay my life he's smitten.

---

2. Calmed.

3. From the French *fourbe*, meaning deceitful, untrustworthy.

4. The district of London where lawyers lived and worked.

5. By God.

6. Fabrics (like silk) whose hue alters with their motion.

7. Passionless.

8. Soon.

9. Let loose (like a hunting dog pursuing prey).

1. Unsound.

2. Old Bellair's characteristic curse, of uncertain meaning.

EMILIA This is nothing but the pleasantness of his humor.

LADY TOWNLEY I know him better than you. Let it work; it may prove lucky.

[*Enter a Page.*]

PAGE Madam, Mr. Medley has sent to know whether a visit will not be troublesome this afternoon?

LADY TOWNLEY Send him word his visits never are so.   [*Exit Page.*]

EMILIA He's a very pleasant man.

LADY TOWNLEY He's a very necessary man among us women. He's not scandalous i' the least, perpetually contriving to bring good company together, and always ready to stop up a gap at ombre.³ Then, he knows all the little news o' the town.

EMILIA I love to hear him talk o' the intrigues. Let 'em be never so dull in themselves, he'll make 'em pleasant i' the relation.

LADY TOWNLEY But he improves things so much one can take no measure of the truth from him. Mr. Dorimant swears a flea or a maggot is not made more monstrous by a magnifying glass than a story is by his telling it.

[*Enter Medley.*]

EMILIA Hold, here he comes.

LADY TOWNLEY Mr. Medley.

MEDLEY Your servant, madam.

LADY TOWNLEY You have made yourself a stranger of late.

EMILIA I believe you took a surfeit of ombre last time you were here.

MEDLEY Indeed I had my bellyful of that termagant Lady Dealer. There never was so insatiable a carder;⁴ an old gleeker⁵ never loved to sit to 't like her. I have played with her now at least a dozen times, till she 'as worn out all her fine complexion and her tour⁶ would keep in curl no longer.

LADY TOWNLEY Blame her not, poor woman. She loves nothing so well as a black ace.

MEDLEY The pleasure I have seen her in when she has had hope in drawing for a matadore!⁷

EMILIA 'Tis as pretty sport to her as persuading masks off is to you, to make discoveries.

LADY TOWNLEY Pray, where's your friend Mr. Dorimant?

MEDLEY Soliciting his affairs. He's a man of great employment—has more mistresses now depending⁸ than the most eminent lawyer in England has causes.⁹

EMILIA Here has been Mrs. Loveit so uneasy and out of humor these two days.

LADY TOWNLEY How strangely love and jealousy rage in that poor woman!

MEDLEY She could not have picked out a devil upon earth so proper¹ to torment her. H'as made her break a dozen or two of fans already, tear half a score points² in pieces, and destroy hoods and knots³ without number.

LADY TOWNLEY We heard of a pleasant serenade he gave her t'other night.

MEDLEY A Danish serenade,⁴ with kettledrums and trumpets.

EMILIA Oh, barbarous!

MEDLEY What, you are of the number of the ladies whose ears are grown so delicate since our operas, you can be charmed with nothing but *flûtes douces* and French hautboys?⁵

---

3. A card game for three players.
4. Cardplayer.
5. "Gleek" was a card game for three players.
6. Crescent of false hair.
7. Slang for the best cards (such as black aces).
8. I.e., pending, on the horizon.

9. Cases.
1. Suited.
2. Ten lace handkerchieves.
3. Clusters or bows of ribbon ornamenting a dress.
4. Denmark was noted for raucous drinking practices.
5. Recorders and oboes.

EMILIA Leave your raillery and tell us, is there any new wit come forth—songs, or novels?

MEDLEY A very pretty piece of gallantry, by an eminent author, called *The Diversions of Brussels*[6]—very necessary to be read by all old ladies who are desirous to improve themselves at questions and commands,[7] blindman's buff, and the like fashionable recreations.

EMILIA Oh, ridiculous!

MEDLEY Then there is *The Art of Affectation*,[8] written by a late beauty of quality, teaching you how to draw up your breasts, stretch up your neck, to thrust out your breech,[9] to play with your head, to toss up your nose, to bite your lips, to turn up your eyes, to speak in a silly soft tone of a voice, and use all the foolish French words that will infallibly make your person and conversation charming; with a short apology at the latter end, in the behalf of young ladies who notoriously wash and paint,[1] though they have naturally good complexions.

EMILIA What a deal of stuff[2] you tell us!

MEDLEY Such as the town affords, madam. The Russians, hearing the great respect we have for foreign dancing, have lately sent over some of their best balladines,[3] who are now practicing a famous ballet which will be suddenly[4] danced at the Bear Garden.[5]

LADY TOWNLEY Pray forbear your idle stories, and give us an account of the state of love as it now stands.

MEDLEY Truly there has been some revolutions in those affairs: great chopping and changing[6] among the old, and some new lovers, whom malice, indiscretion, and misfortune have luckily brought into play.

LADY TOWNLEY What think you of walking into the next room and sitting down, before you engage in this business?

MEDLEY I wait upon you; and I hope (though women are commonly unreasonable) by the plenty of scandal I shall discover,[7] to give you very good content, ladies.

[*Exeunt.*]

Scene 2

[*Mrs. Loveit's. Enter Mrs. Loveit and Pert; Mrs. Loveit putting up[8] a letter, then pulling out her pocket glass and looking in it.*]

MRS. LOVEIT Pert.

PERT Madam?

MRS. LOVEIT I hate myself, I look so ill today.

PERT Hate the wicked cause on't, that base man Mr. Dorimant, who makes you torment and vex yourself continually.

MRS. LOVEIT He is to blame, indeed.

PERT To blame to be two days without sending, writing, or coming near you, contrary to his oath and covenant! 'Twas to much purpose to make him swear! I'll lay my life there's not an article but he has broken: talked to the vizards i' the pit,[9]

6. A reference to Richard Flecknoe's *A Treatise of the Sports of Wit* (1675).
7. Old-fashioned game in which one player (the "King") makes ludicrous inquiries and demands of the others.
8. A reference to Hannah Woolley's *The Gentlewoman's Companion* (1675).
9. Buttocks.
1. Use cosmetics.
2. Lot of nonsense.

3. Theatrical dancers, but also buffoons.
4. Soon.
5. A riverside arena largely devoted to animal combat: cockfighting, bear baiting (which pitted many dogs against a single bear), etc.
6. Playing fast and loose, vacillating.
7. Reveal.
8. Away.
9. The main-floor section of the theater.

waited upon the ladies from the boxes to their coaches, gone behind the scenes and fawned upon those little insignificant creatures, the players. 'Tis impossible for a man of his inconstant temper to forbear, I'm sure.

MRS. LOVEIT I know he is a devil, but he has something of the angel yet undefaced in him, which makes him so charming and agreeable that I must love him, be he never so wicked.

PERT I little thought, madam, to see your spirit tamed to this degree, who banished poor Mr. Lackwit but for taking up another lady's fan in your presence.

MRS. LOVEIT My knowing of such odious fools contributes to the making of me love Dorimant the better.

PERT Your knowing of Mr. Dorimant, in my mind, should rather make you hate all mankind.

MRS. LOVEIT So it does, besides himself.

PERT Pray, what excuse does he make in his letter?

MRS. LOVEIT He has had business.

PERT Business in general terms would not have been a current[1] excuse for another. A modish man is always very busy when he is in pursuit of a new mistress.

MRS. LOVEIT Some fop has bribed you to rail at him. He had business; I will believe it and will forgive him.

PERT You may forgive him anything, but I shall never forgive him his turning me into ridicule, as I hear he does.

MRS. LOVEIT I perceive you are of the number of those fools his wit has made his enemies.

PERT I am of the number of those he's pleased to rally,[2] madam; and if we may believe Mr. Wagfan and Mr. Caperwell, he sometimes makes merry with yourself, too, among his laughing companions.

MRS. LOVEIT Blockheads are as malicious to witty men as ugly women are to the handsome; 'tis their interest, and they make it their business to defame 'em.

PERT I wish Mr. Dorimant would not make it his business to defame you.

MRS. LOVEIT Should he, I had rather be made infamous by him than owe my reputation to the dull discretion of those fops you talk of.

[Enter Bellinda.]

Bellinda!

[Running to her.]

BELLINDA My dear!

MRS. LOVEIT You have been unkind of late.

BELLINDA Do not say unkind, say unhappy.

MRS. LOVEIT I could chide you. Where have you been these two days?

BELLINDA Pity me rather, my dear, where I have been so tired with two or three country gentlewomen, whose conversation has been more insufferable than a country fiddle.

MRS. LOVEIT Are they relations?

BELLINDA No, Welsh acquaintance I made when I was last year at St. Winifred's.[3] They have asked me a thousand questions of the modes and intrigues of the town, and I have told 'em almost as many things for news that hardly were so when their gowns were in fashion.

MRS. LOVEIT Provoking creatures, how could you endure 'em?

1. Acceptable.
2. Ridicule.
3. The Welsh town of Holywell.

BELLINDA [*aside*] Now to carry on my plot; nothing but love could make me capable of so much falsehood. 'Tis time to begin, lest Dorimant should come before her jealousy has stung her.

[*Laughs and then speaks on.*]

I was yesterday at a play with 'em, where I was fain to show 'em the living, as the man at Westminster[4] does the dead. That is Mrs. Such-a-one, admired for her beauty; this is Mr. Such-a-one, cried up for a wit; that is sparkish Mr. Such-a-one, who keeps reverend[5] Mrs. Such-a-one; and there sits fine Mrs. Such-a-one, who was lately cast off by my Lord Such-a-one.

MRS. LOVEIT Did you see Dorimant there?

BELLINDA I did; and imagine you were there with him and have no mind to own it.

MRS. LOVEIT What should make you think so?

BELLINDA A lady masked, in a pretty *déshabillé*,[6] whom Dorimant entertained with more respect than the gallants do a common vizard.

MRS. LOVEIT [*aside*] Dorimant at the play entertaining a mask! Oh, heavens!

BELLINDA [*aside*] Good!

MRS. LOVEIT Did he stay all the while?

BELLINDA Till the play was done, and then led her out; which confirms me it was you.

MRS. LOVEIT Traitor!

PERT Now you may believe he had business, and you may forgive him too.

MRS. LOVEIT Ungrateful, perjured man!

BELLINDA You seem so much concerned, my dear, I fear I have told you unawares what I had better have concealed for your quiet.

MRS. LOVEIT What manner of shape had she?

BELLINDA Tall and slender. Her motions were very genteel. Certainly she must be some person of condition.[7]

MRS. LOVEIT Shame and confusion be ever in her face when she shows it!

BELLINDA I should blame your discretion for loving that wild man, my dear; but they say he has a way so bewitching that few can defend their hearts who know him.

MRS. LOVEIT I will tear him from mine, or die i' the attempt!

BELLINDA Be more moderate.

MRS. LOVEIT Would I had daggers, darts, or poisoned arrows in my breast, so I could but remove the thoughts of him from thence!

BELLINDA Fie, fie, your transports are too violent, my dear. This may be but an accidental gallantry, and 'tis likely ended at her coach.

PERT Should it proceed farther, let your comfort be, the conduct Mr. Dorimant affects[8] will quickly make you know your rival, ten to one let you see her ruined, her reputation exposed to the town—a happiness none will envy her but yourself, madam.

MRS. LOVEIT Whoe'er she be, all the harm I wish her is, may she love him as well as I do, and may he give her as much cause to hate him!

PERT Never doubt the latter end of your curse, madam.

MRS. LOVEIT May all the passions that are raised by neglected love—jealousy, indignation, spite, and thirst of revenge—eternally rage in her soul, as they do now in mine!

[*Walks up and down with a distracted air.*]

---

4. The guide to the Abbey tombs.
5. Respected.
6. Casual and seductive dress.

7. Rank.
8. Has a taste for.

[*Enter a Page.*]

PAGE Madam, Mr. Dorimant—

MRS. LOVEIT I will not see him.

PAGE I told him you were within, madam.

MRS. LOVEIT Say you lied, say I'm busy—shut the door—say anything!

PAGE He's here, madam.

[*Enter Dorimant. Exit Page.*]

DORIMANT

> "They taste of death who do at heaven arrive;
> But we this paradise approach alive."[9]

[*To Mrs. Loveit.*] What, dancing the galloping nag[1] without a fiddle?

   [*Offers to catch her by the hand; she flings away and walks on.*]

I fear this restlessness of the body, madam, [*pursuing her*] proceeds from an unquietness of the mind. What unlucky accident puts you out of humor—a point ill-washed, knots spoiled i' the making up, hair shaded awry,[2] or some other little mistake in setting you in order?

PERT A trifle, in my opinion, sir, more inconsiderable than any you mention.

DORIMANT Oh, Mrs. Pert! I never knew you sullen enough to be silent. Come, let me know the business.

PERT The business, sir, is the business that has taken you up these two days. How have I seen you laugh at men of business, and now to become a man of business yourself!

DORIMANT We are not masters of our own affections; our inclinations daily alter. Now we love pleasure, and anon we shall dote on business. Human frailty will have it so, and who can help it?

MRS. LOVEIT Faithless, inhuman, barbarous man—

DORIMANT [*aside*] Good. Now the alarm strikes.

MRS. LOVEIT —Without sense of love, of honor, or of gratitude! Tell me, for I will know, what devil masked she was, you were with at the play yesterday.

DORIMANT Faith, I resolved as much as you, but the devil was obstinate and would not tell me.

MRS. LOVEIT False in this as in your vows to me! You do know!

DORIMANT The truth is, I did all I could to know.

MRS. LOVEIT And dare you own it to my face? Hell and furies!

[*Tears her fan in pieces.*]

DORIMANT Spare your fan, madam. You are growing hot and will want it to cool you.

MRS. LOVEIT Horror and distraction seize you! Sorrow and remorse gnaw your soul and punish all your perjuries to me! [*Weeps.*]

DORIMANT [*turning to Bellinda*]

> "So thunder breaks the cloud in twain.
> And makes a passage for the rain."[3]

[*To Bellinda.*] Bellinda, you are the devil that have raised this storm. You were at the play yesterday and have been making discoveries to your dear.

BELLINDA Y'are the most mistaken man i' the world.

---

9. Lines from Waller's *Of Her Chamber*.
1. A country dance.
2. Parted incorrectly.

3. Lines from *An Elegie* by Matthew Roydon (1580–1622).

DORIMANT It must be so, and here I vow revenge—resolve to pursue and persecute you more impertinently than ever any loving fop did his mistress, hunt you i' the Park, trace you i' the Mail,[4] dog you in every visit you make, haunt you at the plays and i' the drawing room,[5] hang my nose in your neck and talk to you whether you will or no, and ever look upon you with such dying eyes till your friends grow jealous of me, send you out of town, and the world suspect your reputation. [*In a lower voice.*] At my Lady Townley's when we go from hence.

[*He looks kindly on Bellinda.*]

BELLINDA I'll meet you there.

DORIMANT Enough.

MRS. LOVEIT [*pushing Dorimant away*] Stand off! You shall not stare upon her so.

DORIMANT Good, there's one made jealous already.

MRS. LOVEIT Is this the constancy you vowed?

DORIMANT Constancy at my years? 'Tis not a virtue in season; you might as well expect the fruit the autumn ripens i' the spring.

MRS. LOVEIT Monstrous principle!

DORIMANT Youth has a long journey to go, madam. Should I have set up my rest[6] at the first inn I lodged at, I should never have arrived at the happiness I now enjoy.

MRS. LOVEIT Dissembler, damned dissembler!

DORIMANT I am so, I confess. Good nature and good manners corrupt me. I am honest in my inclinations and would not, wer't not to avoid offense, make a lady a little in years believe I think her young, wilfully mistake art for nature, and seem as fond of a thing I am weary of as when I doted on't in earnest.

MRS. LOVEIT False man!

DORIMANT True woman.

MRS. LOVEIT Now you begin to show yourself.

DORIMANT Love gilds us over and makes us show fine things to one another for a time; but soon the gold wears off, and then again the native brass appears.

MRS. LOVEIT Think on your oaths, your vows, and protestations, perjured man!

DORIMANT I made 'em when I was in love.

MRS. LOVEIT And therefore ought they not to bind? Oh, impious!

DORIMANT What we swear at such a time may be a certain proof of a present passion; but to say truth, in love there is no security to be given for the future.

MRS. LOVEIT Horrid and ungrateful, begone! And never see me more!

DORIMANT I am not one of those troublesome coxcombs who, because they were once well-received, take the privilege to plague a woman with their love ever after. I shall obey you, madam, though I do myself some violence.

[*He offers to go, and Mrs. Loveit pulls him back.*]

MRS. LOVEIT Come back, you sha' not go! Could you have the ill nature to offer it?

DORIMANT When love grows diseased, the best thing we can do is to put it to a violent death. I cannot endure the torture of a lingering and consumptive passion.

MRS. LOVEIT Can you think mine sickly?

DORIMANT Oh, 'tis desperately ill! What worse symptoms are there than your being always uneasy when I visit you, your picking quarrels with me on slight occasions, and in my absence kindly list'ning to the impertinences of every fashionable fool that talks to you?

---

4. The Mall, a fashionable walk bordering St. James's Park.

5. A room used for formal receptions.

6. Settled down permanently.

MRS. LOVEIT What fashionable fool can you lay to my charge?

DORIMANT Why, the very cock-fool of all those fools, Sir Fopling Flutter.

MRS. LOVEIT I never saw him in my life but once.

DORIMANT The worse woman you, at first sight to put on all your charms, to entertain him with that softness in your voice and all that wanton kindness in your eyes you so notoriously affect when you design a conquest.

MRS. LOVEIT So damned a lie did never malice yet invent. Who told you this?

DORIMANT No matter. That ever I should love a woman that can dote on a senseless caper,[7] a tawdry French ribbon, and a formal cravat!

MRS. LOVEIT You make me mad!

DORIMANT A guilty conscience may do much. Go on, be the game-mistress[8] of the town and enter[9] all our young fops, as fast as they come from travel.

MRS. LOVEIT Base and scurrilous!

DORIMANT A fine mortifying reputation 'twill be for a woman of your pride, wit, and quality!

MRS. LOVEIT This jealousy's a mere pretense, a cursed trick of your own devising. I know you.

DORIMANT Believe it and all the ill of me you can. I would not have a woman have the least good thought of me that can think well of Fopling. Farewell. Fall to,[1] and much good may do you with your coxcomb.

MRS. LOVEIT Stay! Oh stay, and I will tell you all.

DORIMANT I have been told too much already.

[Exit Dorimant.]

MRS. LOVEIT Call him again!

PERT E'en let him go. A fair riddance!

MRS. LOVEIT Run, I say, call him again. I will have him called!

PERT The devil should carry him away first, were it my concern.

[Exit Pert.]

BELLINDA H'as frighted me from the very thoughts of loving men. For heav'n sake, my dear, do not discover what I told you. I dread his tongue as much as you ought to have done his friendship.

[Enter Pert.]

PERT He's gone, madam.

MRS. LOVEIT Lightning blast him!

PERT When I told him you desired him to come back, he smiled, made a mouth[2] at me, flung into his coach, and said—

MRS. LOVEIT What did he say?

PERT "Drive away"; and then repeated verses.

MRS. LOVEIT Would I had made a contract to be a witch when first I entertained this greater devil. Monster, barbarian! I could tear myself in pieces. Revenge, nothing but revenge can ease me. Plague, war, famine, fire, all that can bring universal ruin and misery on mankind—with joy I'd perish to have you in my power but this moment!   *[Exit Mrs. Loveit.]*

PERT Follow, madam. Leave her not in this outrageous passion.

[Pert gathers up the things.]

---

7. Springy leap in a dance.
8. Leader of amorous games.
9. Initiate, break in (as with horses).

1. Go ahead.
2. Smirked.

BELLINDA H'as given me the proof which I desired of his love; but 'tis a proof of his ill nature too. I wish I had not seen him use her so.

I sigh to think that Dorimant may be
One day as faithless and unkind to me.   [*Exeunt.*]

Act III

Scene 1

[*Lady Woodvill's lodgings. Enter Harriet and Busy, her woman.*]

BUSY Dear madam, let me set that curl in order.

HARRIET Let me alone, I will shake 'em all out of order!

BUSY Will you never leave this wildness?

HARRIET Torment me not.

BUSY Look, there's a knot falling off.

HARRIET Let it drop.

BUSY But one pin, dear madam.

HARRIET How do I daily suffer under thy officious fingers!

BUSY Ah, the difference that is between you and my Lady Dapper! How uneasy she is if the least thing be amiss about her!

HARRIET She is indeed most exact. Nothing is ever wanting to make her ugliness remarkable.

BUSY Jeering people say so.

HARRIET Her powdering, painting, and her patching[1] never fail in public to draw the tongues and eyes of all the men upon her.

BUSY She is indeed a little too pretending.

HARRIET That women should set up for[2] beauty as much in spite of nature as some men have done for wit!

BUSY I hope without offense one may endeavor to make one's self agreeable.

HARRIET Not when 'tis impossible. Women then ought to be no more fond of dressing than fools should be of talking. Hoods and modesty, masks and silence, things that shadow and conceal—they should think of nothing else.

BUSY Jesu, madam! What will your mother think is become of you? For heav'n's sake, go in again.

HARRIET I won't.

BUSY This is the extravagant'st thing that ever you did in your life, to leave her and a gentleman who is to be your husband.

HARRIET My husband! Hast thou so little wit to think I spoke what I meant when I overjoyed her in the country with a low curtsy and "What you please, madam; I shall ever be obedient"?

BUSY Nay, I know not, you have so many fetches.[3]

HARRIET And this was one, to get her up to London. Nothing else, I assure thee.

BUSY Well! The man, in my mind, is a fine man.

HARRIET The man indeed wears his clothes fashionably and has a pretty, negligent way with him, very courtly and much affected. He bows, and talks, and smiles so agreeably as he thinks.

BUSY I never saw anything so genteel.

---

1. Setting a small disk of black silk on one's cheek as an ornament.   2. Aim at.
3. Tricks.

HARRIET Varnished over with good breeding, many a blockhead makes a tolerable show.

BUSY I wonder you do not like him.

HARRIET I think I might be brought to endure him, and that is all a reasonable woman should expect in a husband; but there is duty i' the case,[4] and like the haughty Merab, I

> "Find much aversion in my stubborn mind,"

which

> "Is bred by being promised and designed."[5]

BUSY I wish you do not design your own ruin. I partly guess your inclinations, madam. That Mr. Dorimant—

HARRIET Leave your prating[6] and sing some foolish song or other.

BUSY I will—the song you love so well ever since you saw Mr. Dorimant.

Song

> When first Amintas charmed my heart,
>   My heedless sheep began to stray;
> The wolves soon stole the greatest part,
>   And all will now be made a prey.
>
> Ah, let not love your thoughts possess,
>   'Tis fatal to a shepherdess;
> The dang'rous passion you must shun,
>   Or else like me be quite undone.

HARRIET Shall I be paid down[7] by a covetous parent for a purchase? I need no land. No, I'll lay myself out[8] all in love. It is decreed.

[Enter Young Bellair.]

YOUNG BELLAIR What generous resolution are you making, madam?

HARRIET Only to be disobedient, sir.

YOUNG BELLAIR Let me join hands with you in that.

HARRIET With all my heart. I never thought I should have given you mine so willingly. Here.

[They join hands.]

I, Harriet—

YOUNG BELLAIR And I, Harry—

HARRIET Do solemnly protest—

YOUNG BELLAIR And vow—

HARRIET That I with you—

YOUNG BELLAIR And I with you—

HARRIET. YOUNG BELLAIR. Will never marry.

HARRIET A match!

YOUNG BELLAIR And no match! How do you like this indifference now?

HARRIET You expect I should take it ill, I see.

YOUNG BELLAIR 'Tis not unnatural for you women to be a little angry, you miss a conquest—though you would slight the poor man were he in your power.

---

4. Involved.
5. King Saul's eldest daughter, Merab, was promised to David but married Adriel (1 Samuel 18.19). The lines are from Abraham Cowley's description of Merab in *Davideis*

(1656).
6. Chattering.
7. Given as a down payment.
8. Spend myself.

HARRIET There are some, it may be, have an eye like Bart'lomew,[9] big enough for the whole fair; but I am not of the number, and you may keep your gingerbread. 'Twill be more acceptable to the lady whose dear image it wears.

YOUNG BELLAIR I must confess, madam, you came a day after the fair.

HARRIET You own then you are in love?

YOUNG BELLAIR I do.

HARRIET The confidence is generous, and in return I could almost find in my heart to let you know my inclinations.

YOUNG BELLAIR Are you in love?

HARRIET Yes—with this dear town, to that degree I can scarce endure the country in landscapes and in hangings.[1]

YOUNG BELLAIR What a dreadful thing 'twould be to be hurried back to Hampshire!

HARRIET Ah, name it not.

YOUNG BELLAIR As for us, I find we shall agree well enough. Would we could do something to deceive the grave people!

HARRIET Could we delay their quick proceeding, 'twere well. A reprieve is a good step towards the getting of a pardon.

YOUNG BELLAIR If we give over the game, we are undone. What think you of playing it on booty?[2]

HARRIET What do you mean?

YOUNG BELLAIR Pretend to be in love with one another. 'Twill make some dilatory[3] excuses we may feign pass the better.

HARRIET Let us do 't, if it be but for the dear pleasure of dissembling.

YOUNG BELLAIR Can you play your part?

HARRIET I know not what it is to love, but I have made pretty remarks[4] by being now and then where lovers meet. Where did you leave their gravities?

YOUNG BELLAIR I' th' next room. Your mother was censuring our modern gallant.

[Enter Old Bellair and Lady Woodvill.]

HARRIET Peace, here they come. I will lean against this wall and look bashfully down upon my fan while you, like an amorous spark, modishly entertain me.

LADY WOODVILL [to Old Bellair] Never go about to excuse 'em. Come, come, it was not so when I was a young woman.

OLD BELLAIR Adod, they're something disrespectful—

LADY WOODVILL Quality was then considered and not rallied by every fleering[5] fellow.

OLD BELLAIR Youth will have its jest, adod it will.

LADY WOODVILL 'Tis good breeding now to be civil to none but players and Exchange women.[6] They are treated by 'em as much above their condition as others are below theirs.

OLD BELLAIR Out, a pize on 'em! Talk no more; the rogues ha' got an ill habit of preferring beauty, no matter where they find it.

LADY WOODVILL See your son and my daughter. They have improved their acquaintance since they were within.

OLD BELLAIR Adod, methinks they have! Let's keep back and observe.

---

9. A character in Ben Jonson's *Bartholomew Fair* (1614) who is robbed of everything, including his gingerbread (sold in the shape of a person) and the heiress he was to marry.
1. Tapestries.

2. Joining together to fool the other players.
3. Dawdling.
4. Learned a bit.
5. Jeering.
6. Women working in the shops of the New Exchange.

YOUNG BELLAIR [to Harriet] Now for a look and gestures that may persuade 'em I am saying all the passionate things imaginable.

HARRIET Your head a little more on one side. Ease yourself on your left leg and play with your right hand.

YOUNG BELLAIR Thus, is it not?

HARRIET Now set your right leg firm on the ground, adjust your belt, then look about you.

YOUNG BELLAIR A little exercising will make me perfect.

HARRIET Smile, and turn to me again very sparkish.

YOUNG BELLAIR Will you take your turn and be instructed?

HARRIET With all my heart.

YOUNG BELLAIR At one motion play your fan, roll your eyes, and then settle a kind look upon me.

HARRIET So.

YOUNG BELLAIR Now spread your fan, look down upon it, and tell the sticks[7] with a finger.

HARRIET Very modish.

YOUNG BELLAIR Clap your hand up to your bosom, hold down your gown. Shrug a little, draw up your breasts and let 'em fall again, gently, with a sigh or two, *etc.*

HARRIET By the good instructions you give, I suspect you for one of those malicious observers who watch people's eyes, and from innocent looks make scandalous conclusions.

YOUNG BELLAIR I know some, indeed, who out of mere love to mischief are as vigilant as jealousy itself, and will give you an account of every glance that passes at a play and i' th' Circle.[8]

HARRIET 'Twill not be amiss now to seem a little pleasant.

YOUNG BELLAIR Clap your fan then in both your hands, snatch it to your mouth, smile, and with a lively motion fling your body a little forwards. So! Now spread it, fall back on the sudden, cover your face with it, and break out into a loud laughter.—Take up![9] Look grave and fall a-fanning of yourself. Admirably well acted!

HARRIET I think I am pretty apt at these matters.

OLD BELLAIR [to Lady Woodvill] Adod, I like this well.

LADY WOODVILL This promises something.

OLD BELLAIR [coming forward] Come, there is love i' th' case, adod there is, or will be. —What say you, young lady?

HARRIET All in good time, sir. You expect we should fall to and love as gamecocks fight, as soon as we are set together. Adod, y'are unreasonable!

OLD BELLAIR Adod, sirrah, I like thy wit well.

[Enter a Servant.]

SERVANT The coach is at the door, madam.

OLD BELLAIR Go, get you and take the air together.

LADY WOODVILL Will not you go with us?

OLD BELLAIR Out a pize! Adod, I ha' business and cannot. We shall meet at night at my sister Townley's.

YOUNG BELLAIR [aside] He's going to Emilia. I overheard him talk of a collation.

[Exeunt.]

7. Caress each, as if counting them.   9. Now stop!
8. The fashionable walk in Hyde Park, also called the Ring.

Scene 2

[*Lady Townley's. Enter Lady Townley, Emilia, and Medley.*]

LADY TOWNLEY I pity the young lovers we last talked of, though to say truth, their conduct has been so indiscreet they deserve to be unfortunate.

MEDLEY Y' have an exact account, from the great lady i' th' box down to the little orange-wench.

EMILIA Y'are a living libel, a breathing lampoon. I wonder you are not torn in pieces.

MEDLEY What think you of setting up an office of intelligence for these matters? The project may get money.

LADY TOWNLEY You would have great dealings with country ladies.

MEDLEY More than Muddiman[1] has with their husbands!

[*Enter Bellinda.*]

LADY TOWNLEY Bellinda, what has been become of you? We have not seen you here of late with your friend Mrs. Loveit.

BELLINDA Dear creature, I left her but now so sadly afflicted.

LADY TOWNLEY With her old distemper,[2] jealousy?

MEDLEY Dorimant has played her some new prank.

BELLINDA Well, that Dorimant is certainly the worst man breathing.

EMILIA I once thought so.

BELLINDA And do you not think so still?

EMILIA No, indeed.

BELLINDA Oh, Jesu!

EMILIA The town does him a great deal of injury, and I will never believe what it says of a man I do not know, again, for his sake.

BELLINDA You make me wonder.

LADY TOWNLEY He's a very well-bred man.

BELLINDA But strangely ill-natured.

EMILIA Then he's a very witty man.

BELLINDA But a man of no principles.

MEDLEY Your man of principles is a very fine thing, indeed!

BELLINDA To be preferred to men of parts[3] by women who have regard to their reputation and quiet. Well, were I minded to play the fool, he should be the last man I'd think of.

MEDLEY He has been the first in many ladies' favors, though you are so severe, madam.

LADY TOWNLEY What he may be for a lover, I know not; but he's a very pleasant acquaintance, I am sure.

BELLINDA Had you seen him use Mrs. Loveit as I have done, you would never endure him more.

EMILIA What, he has quarreled with her again?

BELLINDA Upon the slightest occasion. He's jealous of Sir Fopling.

LADY TOWNLEY She never saw him in her life but yesterday; and that was here.

EMILIA On my conscience, he's the only man in town that's her aversion. How horribly out of humor she was all the while he talked to her!

BELLINDA And somebody has wickedly told him—

---

1. Henry Muddiman (1629–1692) wrote a newsletter popular with country gentry.

2. Ailment.

3. Abilities.

[*Enter Dorimant.*]

EMILIA Here he comes.

MEDLEY Dorimant, you are luckily come to justify yourself. Here's a lady—

BELLINDA —Has a word or two to say to you from a disconsolate person.

DORIMANT You tender your reputation too much, I know, madam, to whisper with me before this good company.

BELLINDA To serve Mrs. Loveit, I'll make a bold venture.

DORIMANT Here's Medley, the very spirit of scandal.

BELLINDA No matter.

EMILIA 'Tis something you are unwilling to hear, Mr. Dorimant.

LADY TOWNLEY Tell him, Bellinda, whether he will or no.

BELLINDA [*aloud*] Mrs. Loveit—

DORIMANT Softly, these are laughers; you do not know 'em.

BELLINDA [*to Dorimant, apart*] In a word, y'ave made me hate you, which I thought you never could have done.

DORIMANT In obeying your commands?

BELLINDA 'Twas a cruel part you played. How could you act it?

DORIMANT Nothing is cruel to a man who could kill himself to please you. Remember, five o'clock tomorrow morning.

BELLINDA I tremble when you name it.

DORIMANT Be sure you come.

BELLINDA I shall not.

DORIMANT Swear you will.

BELLINDA I dare not.

DORIMANT Swear, I say!

BELLINDA By my life, by all the happiness I hope for—

DORIMANT You will.

BELLINDA I will.

DORIMANT Kind.

BELLINDA I am glad I've sworn. I vow I think I should have failed you else.

DORIMANT Surprisingly kind! In what temper did you leave Loveit?

BELLINDA Her raving was prettily[4] over, and she began to be in a brave way of defying you and all your works. Where have you been since you went from thence?

DORIMANT I looked in at the play.

BELLINDA I have promised and must return to her again.

DORIMANT Persuade her to walk in the Mail this evening.

BELLINDA She hates the place and will not come.

DORIMANT Do all you can to prevail with her.

BELLINDA For what purpose?

DORIMANT Sir Fopling will be here anon. I'll prepare him to set upon her there before me.

BELLINDA You persecute her too much. But I'll do all you'll ha' me.

DORIMANT [*aloud*] Tell her plainly, 'tis grown so dull a business I can drudge on no longer.

EMILIA There are afflictions in love, Mr. Dorimant.

DORIMANT You women make 'em, who are commonly as unreasonable in that as you are at play:[5] without the advantage be on your side, a man can never quietly give over when he's weary.

---

4. Nearly.   5. Cards, gambling.

MEDLEY If you would play without being obliged to complaisance, Dorimant, you should play in public places.[6]

DORIMANT Ordinaries[7] were a very good thing for that, but gentlemen do not of late frequent 'em. The deep play is now in private houses.

[*Bellinda offering to steal away.*]

LADY TOWNLEY Bellinda, are you leaving us so soon?

BELLINDA I am to go to the Park with Mrs. Loveit, madam.

[*Exit Bellinda.*]

LADY TOWNLEY This confidence will go nigh to spoil this young creature.

MEDLEY 'Twill do her good, madam. Young men who are brought up under practicing lawyers prove the abler counsel when they come to be called to the bar themselves.

DORIMANT The town has been very favorable to you this afternoon, my Lady Townley. You use to have an *embarras*[8] of chairs and coaches at your door, an uproar of footmen in your hall, and a noise of fools above here.

LADY TOWNLEY Indeed, my house is the general rendezvous and, next to the playhouse, is the common refuge of all the young idle people.

EMILIA Company is a very good thing, madam, but I wonder you do not love it a little more chosen.

LADY TOWNLEY 'Tis good to have an universal taste. We should love wit, but for variety be able to divert ourselves with the extravagancies of those who want[9] it.

MEDLEY Fools will make you laugh.

EMILIA For once or twice; but the repetition of their folly after a visit or two grows tedious and insufferable.

LADY TOWNLEY You are a little too delicate, Emilia.

[*Enter a Page.*]

PAGE Sir Fopling Flutter, madam, desires to know if you are to be seen.

LADY TOWNLEY Here's the freshest fool in town, and one who has not cloyed you yet.—Page!

PAGE Madam?

LADY TOWNLEY Desire him to walk up.   [*Exit Page.*]

DORIMANT Do not you fall on him, Medley, and snub him. Soothe him up[1] in his extravagance. He will show the better.

MEDLEY You know I have a natural indulgence for fools and need not this caution, sir.

[*Enter Sir Fopling, with his Page after him.*]

SIR FOPLING Page, wait without.   [*Exit Page.*]

[*To Lady Townley.*] Madam, I kiss your hands. I see yesterday was nothing of chance; the *belles assemblées* form themselves[2] here every day. [*To Emilia.*] Lady, your servant.—Dorimant, let me embrace thee. Without lying, I have not met with any of my acquaintance who retain so much of Paris as thou dost—the very air thou hadst when the marquise mistook thee i' th' Tuileries[3] and cried "Hé, chevalier!" and then begged thy pardon.

DORIMANT I would fain wear in fashion as long as I can, sir. 'Tis a thing to be valued in men as well as baubles.[4]

---

6. I.e., if he doesn't want to be courteous (as required in private houses), he should play only in public.
7. Restaurants where gambling took place.
8. A crush (French).
9. Lack.

1. Humor him.
2. Beautiful women assemble.
3. Garden of the Palace of Tuileries in Paris.
4. Trinkets, but also a jester's emblem (a sarcastic reference to Fopling's folly).

SIR FOPLING Thou art a man of wit and understands the town. Prithee let thee and I be intimate. There is no living without making some good man the confidant of our pleasures.

DORIMANT 'Tis true; but there is no man so improper for such a business as I am.

SIR FOPLING Prithee, why hast thou so modest an opinion of thyself?

DORIMANT Why, first, I could never keep a secret in my life; and then, there is no charm so infallibly makes me fall in love with a woman as my knowing a friend loves her. I deal honestly with you.

SIR FOPLING Thy humor's very gallant, or let me perish. I knew a French count so like thee.

LADY TOWNLEY Wit, I perceive, has more power over you than beauty, Sir Fopling, else you would not have let this lady stand so long neglected.

SIR FOPLING [to Emilia] A thousand pardons, madam. Some civility's due of course upon the meeting a long absent friend. The éclat[5] of so much beauty, I confess, ought to have charmed me sooner.

EMILIA The brillant[6] of so much good language, sir, has much more power than the little beauty I can boast.

SIR FOPLING I never saw anything prettier than this high work on your point d'Espaigne.[7]

EMILIA 'Tis not so rich as point de Venise.[8]

SIR FOPLING Not altogether, but looks cooler, and is more proper for the season.— Dorimant, is not that Medley?

DORIMANT The same, sir.

SIR FOPLING [to Medley] Forgive me, sir; in this embarras of civilities I could not come to have you in my arms sooner. You understand an equipage[9] the best of any man in town, I hear.

MEDLEY By my own you would not guess it.

SIR FOPLING There are critics who do not write, sir.

MEDLEY Our peevish poets will scarce allow it.

SIR FOPLING Damn 'em, they'll allow no man wit who does not play the fool like themselves and show it! Have you taken notice of the gallesh[1] I brought over?

MEDLEY Oh, yes! 'T has quite another air than th' English makes.

SIR FOPLING 'Tis as easily known from an English tumbril[2] as an Inns of Court man[3] is from one of us.

DORIMANT Truly there is a bel air[4] in galleshes as well as men.

MEDLEY But there are few so delicate[5] to observe it.

SIR FOPLING The world is generally very grossier[6] here, indeed.

LADY TOWNLEY [to Emilia] He's very fine.

EMILIA Extreme proper!

SIR FOPLING A slight suit I made to appear in at my first arrival—not worthy your consideration, ladies.

DORIMANT The pantaloon is very well mounted.[7]

SIR FOPLING The tassels are new and pretty.

MEDLEY I never saw a coat better cut.

---

5. Brilliant display (French).
6. Dazzle.
7. Raised needlework on Spanish lace.
8. Venetian lace.
9. Elegant carriage.
1. Light French carriage.

2. Rough cart, often used for hauling dung.
3. Lawyer.
4. Elegant look.
5. Discerning (but also effeminate).
6. Coarse.
7. Puffed out from the leg.

SIR FOPLING It makes me show long-waisted, and I think slender.

DORIMANT That's the shape our ladies dote on.

MEDLEY Your breech,[8] though, is a handful too high, in my eye, Sir Fopling.

SIR FOPLING Peace, Medley, I have wished it lower a thousand times; but a pox on't, 'twill not be!

LADY TOWNLEY His gloves are well fringed, large and graceful.

SIR FOPLING I was always eminent for being *bien ganté*.[9]

EMILIA He wears nothing but what are originals of the most famous hands in Paris.

SIR FOPLING You are in the right, madam.

LADY TOWNLEY The suit?

SIR FOPLING Barroy.[1]

EMILIA The garniture?[2]

SIR FOPLING Le Gras.

MEDLEY The shoes?

SIR FOPLING Piccar.

DORIMANT The periwig?

SIR FOPLING Chedreux.

LADY TOWNLEY. EMILIA The gloves?

SIR FOPLING Orangerie.[3] You know the smell, ladies.—Dorimant, I could find in my heart for an amusement to have a gallantry with some of our English ladies.

DORIMANT 'Tis a thing no less necessary to confirm the reputation of your wit than a duel will be to satisfy the town of your courage.

SIR FOPLING Here was a woman yesterday—

DORIMANT Mrs. Loveit.

SIR FOPLING You have named her!

DORIMANT You cannot pitch on a better for your purpose.

SIR FOPLING Prithee, what is she?

DORIMANT A person of quality, and one who has a rest[4] of reputation enough to make the conquest considerable. Besides, I hear she likes you too.

SIR FOPLING Methoughts she seemed, though, very reserved and uneasy all the time I entertained her.

DORIMANT Grimace and affectation! You will see her i' th' Mail tonight.

SIR FOPLING Prithee, let thee and I take the air together.

DORIMANT I am engaged to Medley, but I'll meet you at Saint James's[5] and give you some information upon the which you may regulate your proceedings.

SIR FOPLING All the world will be in the Park tonight.—Ladies, 'twere pity to keep so much beauty longer within doors and rob the Ring[6] of all those charms that should adorn it.—Hey, page!

[*Enter Page.*]

See that all my people be ready.   [*Page goes out again.*]

Dorimant, *au revoir*.   [*Exit Sir Fopling.*]

MEDLEY A fine-mettled[7] coxcomb.

DORIMANT Brisk and insipid.

---

8. Medley is punning: "breech" can mean pantaloon or buttocks.
9. Well-gloved.
1. Fopling answers this and the ensuing questions with the names of fashionable Parisian merchants.
2. Trimmings.
3. Scented with perfume extracted from the orange flower.
4. Sufficiency.
5. The park bordered by the Mall.
6. The fashionable walk in Hyde Park, also called the Circle.
7. Spirited.

MEDLEY Pert and dull.

EMILIA However you despise him, gentlemen, I'll lay my life he passes for a wit with many.

DORIMANT That may very well be. Nature has her cheats, stums[8] a brain, and puts[9] sophisticate[1] dullness often on the tasteless multitude for true wit and good humor.—Medley, come.

MEDLEY I must go a little way; I will meet you i' the Mail.

DORIMANT I'll walk through the garden thither. [To the women.] We shall meet anon and bow.

LADY TOWNLEY Not tonight. We are engaged about a business, the knowledge of which may make you laugh hereafter.

MEDLEY Your servant, ladies.

DORIMANT Au revoir, as Sir Fopling says.   [Exeunt Medley and Dorimant.]

LADY TOWNLEY The old man will be here immediately.

EMILIA Let's expect him i' th' garden.

LADY TOWNLEY Go, you are a rogue!

EMILIA I can't abide you!   [Exeunt.]

Scene 3

[The Mail. Enter Harriet and Young Bellair, she pulling him.]

HARRIET Come along!

YOUNG BELLAIR And leave your mother?

HARRIET Busy will be sent with a hue and cry after us; but that's no matter.

YOUNG BELLAIR 'Twill look strangely in me.

HARRIET She'll believe it a freak[2] of mine and never blame your manners.

YOUNG BELLAIR [pointing] What reverend acquaintance is that she has met?

HARRIET A fellow beauty of the last king's time,[3] though by the ruins you would hardly guess it.   [Exeunt.]

[Enter Dorimant and crosses the stage. Enter Young Bellair and Harriet.]

YOUNG BELLAIR By this time your mother is in a fine taking.[4]

HARRIET If your friend Mr. Dorimant were but here now, that she might find me talking with him!

YOUNG BELLAIR She does not know him but dreads him, I hear, of all mankind.

HARRIET She concludes if he does but speak to a woman, she's undone[5]—is on her knees every day to pray heav'n defend me from him.

YOUNG BELLAIR You do not apprehend him so much as she does?

HARRIET I never saw anything in him that was frightful.

YOUNG BELLAIR On the contrary, have you not observed something extreme delightful in his wit and person?

HARRIET He's agreeable and pleasant, I must own, but he does so much affect being so, he displeases me.

YOUNG BELLAIR Lord, madam, all he does and says is so easy and so natural.

HARRIET Some men's verses seem so to the unskilful; but labor i' the one and affectation in the other to the judicious plainly appear.

---

8. To stum wine is to refreshen it by mixing it with half-fermented grapes: Dorimant implies that Fopling only appears to sparkle.
9. Passes off.
1. Adulterated, tricked-out.

2. Whim.
3. The reign of Charles I.
4. Temper.
5. Her virtue and reputation are lost.

YOUNG BELLAIR I never heard him accused of affectation before.

[*Enter Dorimant and stares upon her.*]

HARRIET It passes on the easy town, who are favorably pleased in him to call it humor. [*Exeunt Young Bellair and Harriet.*]

DORIMANT 'Tis she! It must be she—that lovely hair, that easy shape, those wanton eyes, and all those melting charms about her mouth which Medley spoke of. I'll follow the lottery and put in for a prize with my friend Bellair.

[*Exit Dorimant, repeating:*]

"In love the victors from the vanquished fly;
They fly that wound, and they pursue that die."[6]

[*Enter Young Bellair and Harriet; and after them Dorimant, standing at a distance.*]

YOUNG BELLAIR Most people prefer High Park[7] to this place.

HARRIET It has the better reputation, I confess; but I abominate the dull diversions there—the formal bows, the affected smiles, the silly by-words and amorous tweers[8] in passing. Here one meets with a little conversation now and then.

YOUNG BELLAIR These conversations have been fatal to some of your sex, madam.

HARRIET It may be so. Because some who want temper[9] have been undone by gaming, must others who have it wholly deny themselves the pleasure of play?

DORIMANT [*coming up gently and bowing to her*] Trust me, it were unreasonable, madam.

[*She starts and looks grave.*]

HARRIET Lord, who's this?

YOUNG BELLAIR Dorimant.

DORIMANT Is this the woman your father would have you marry?

YOUNG BELLAIR It is.

DORIMANT Her name?

YOUNG BELLAIR Harriet.

DORIMANT [*aside*] I am not mistaken.—She's handsome.

YOUNG BELLAIR Talk to her; her wit is better than her face. We were wishing for you but now.

DORIMANT [*to Harriet*] Overcast with seriousness o' the sudden! A thousand smiles were shining in that face but now. I never saw so quick a change of weather.

HARRIET [*aside*] I feel as great a change within, but he shall never know it.

DORIMANT You were talking of play, madam. Pray, what may be your stint?[1]

HARRIET A little harmless discourse in public walks or at most an appointment in a box, barefaced, at the playhouse. You are for masks and private meetings, where women engage[2] for all they are worth, I hear.

DORIMANT I have been used to deep play, but I can make one at[3] small game when I like my gamester well.

HARRIET And be so unconcerned you'll ha' no pleasure in't.

DORIMANT Where there is a considerable sum to be won, the hope of drawing people in makes every trifle considerable.

HARRIET The sordidness of men's natures, I know, makes 'em willing to flatter and comply with the rich, though they are sure never to be the better for 'em.

---

6. Lines from Waller's *To a Friend, of the Different Success of their Loves.*
7. Hyde Park.
8. Leers.

9. Self-control.
1. Upper limit.
2. Gamble.
3. Join in.

DORIMANT 'Tis in their power to do us good, and we despair not but at some time or other they may be willing.

HARRIET To men who have fared in this town like you, 'twould be a great mortification to live on hope. Could you keep a Lent for a mistress?

DORIMANT In expectation of a happy Easter; and though time be very precious, think forty days well lost to gain your favor.

HARRIET Mr. Bellair! Let us walk, 'tis time to leave him. Men grow dull when they begin to be particular.[4]

DORIMANT Y'are mistaken: flattery will not ensue, though I know y'are greedy of the praises of the whole Mail.

HARRIET You do me wrong.

DORIMANT I do not. As I followed you, I observed how you were pleased when the fops cried, "She's handsome, very handsome, by God she is!" and whispered aloud your name—the thousand several forms you put your face into; then, to make yourself more agreeable, how wantonly you played with your head, flung back your locks, and looked smilingly over your shoulder at 'em.

HARRIET I do not go begging the men's, as you do the ladies' good liking, with a sly softness in your looks and a gentle slowness in your bows as you pass by 'em. As thus, sir. [Acts him.] Is not this like you?

[Enter Lady Woodvill and Busy.]

YOUNG BELLAIR Your mother, madam!

[Pulls Harriet. She composes herself.]

LADY WOODVILL Ah, my dear child Harriet!

BUSY [aside] Now is she so pleased with finding her again, she cannot chide her.

LADY WOODVILL Come away!

DORIMANT 'Tis now but high Mail,[5] madam—the most entertaining time of all the evening.

HARRIET I would fain see that Dorimant, mother, you so cry out of for a monster. He's in the Mail, I hear.

LADY WOODVILL Come away, then! The plague is here, and you should dread the infection.

YOUNG BELLAIR You may be misinformed of the gentleman.

LADY WOODVILL Oh, no! I hope you do not know him. He is the prince of all the devils in the town—delights in nothing but in rapes and riots.

DORIMANT If you did but hear him speak, madam—

LADY WOODVILL Oh, he has a tongue, they say, would tempt the angels to a second fall.

[Enter Sir Fopling with his equipage, six footmen, and a page.]

SIR FOPLING Hey, Champagne, Norman, La Rose, La Fleur, La Tour, La Verdure![6]—Dorimant!—

LADY WOODVILL Here, here he is among this rout![7] He names him! Come away, Harriet, come away!

[Exeunt Lady Woodvill, Harriet, Busy, and Young Bellair.]

DORIMANT This fool's coming has spoiled all: she's gone. But she has left a pleasing image of herself behind that wanders in my soul. It must not settle there.

---

4. Marked in their flattery.
5. The hours when the most people strolled the walk.
6. The names of Sir Fopling's footmen echo those of ser-

vants in Moliere's *Les Précieuses Ridicules* (1659).
7. Disorderly crowd.

SIR FOPLING What reverie is this? Speak, man.

DORIMANT "Snatched from myself, how far behind
        Already I behold the shore!"[8]

[Enter Medley.]

MEDLEY Dorimant, a discovery! I met with Bellair—

DORIMANT You can tell me no news, sir. I know all.

MEDLEY How do you like the daughter?

DORIMANT You never came so near truth in your life as you did in her description.

MEDLEY What think you of the mother?

DORIMANT Whatever I think of her, she thinks very well of me, I find.

MEDLEY Did she know you?

DORIMANT She did not. Whether she does now or no, I know not. Here was a
    pleasant scene towards,[9] when in came Sir Fopling, mustering up his equipage,
    and at the latter end named me and frighted her away.

MEDLEY Loveit and Bellinda are not far off. I saw 'em alight at St. James's.

DORIMANT Sir Fopling, hark you, a word or two. [Whispers.] Look you do not want
    assurance.

SIR FOPLING I never do on these occasions.

DORIMANT Walk on; we must not be seen together. Make your advantage of what
    I have told you. The next turn[1] you will meet the lady.

SIR FOPLING Hey! Follow me all.   [Exeunt Sir Fopling and his equipage.]

DORIMANT Medley, you shall see good sport anon between Loveit and this Fopling.

MEDLEY I thought there was something toward, by that whisper.

DORIMANT You know a worthy principle of hers?

MEDLEY Not to be so much as civil to a man who speaks to her in the presence of
    him she professes to love.

DORIMANT I have encouraged Fopling to talk to her tonight.

MEDLEY Now you are here, she will go nigh to beat him.

DORIMANT In the humor she's in, her love will make her do some very extravagant
    thing, doubtless.

MEDLEY What was Bellinda's business with you at my Lady Townley's?

DORIMANT To get me to meet Loveit here in order to an *éclaircissement*.[2] I made
    some difficulty of it and have prepared this rencounter to make good my jealousy.

    [Enter Mrs. Loveit, Bellinda, and Pert.]

MEDLEY Here they come.

DORIMANT I'll meet her and provoke her with a deal of dumb civility in passing by,
    then turn short and be behind her when Sir Fopling sets upon her.

                [Bows to Mrs. Loveit.]

            "See how unregarded now
            That piece of beauty passes."[3]

                [Exeunt Dorimant and Medley.]

BELLINDA How wonderful respectfully he bowed!

PERT He's always over-mannerly when he has done a mischief.

BELLINDA Methoughts, indeed, at the same time he had a strange, despising
    countenance.

---

8. Lines from Waller's *Of Loving at First Sight*.
9. At hand, about to happen.
1. Next circuit around the Mall.

2. In order to clarify the situation.
3. Lines from *Sonnet I* by Sir John Suckling (1609–1642).

PERT The unlucky look he thinks becomes him.

BELLINDA I was afraid you would have spoke to him, my dear.

MRS. LOVEIT I would have died first. He shall no more find me the loving fool he has done.

BELLINDA You love him still!

MRS. LOVEIT No.

PERT I wish you did not.

MRS. LOVEIT I do not, and I will have you think so!—What made you hale[4] me to this odious place, Bellinda?

BELLINDA I hate to be hulched up[5] in a coach. Walking is much better.

MRS. LOVEIT Would we could meet Sir Fopling now!

BELLINDA Lord, would you not avoid him?

MRS. LOVEIT I would make him all the advances that may be.

BELLINDA That would confirm Dorimant's suspicion, my dear.

MRS. LOVEIT He is not jealous; but I will make him so, and be revenged a way he little thinks on.

BELLINDA [aside] If she should make him jealous, that may make him fond of her again. I must dissuade her from it.—Lord, my dear, this will certainly make him hate you.

MRS. LOVEIT 'Twill make him uneasy, though he does not care for me. I know the effects of jealousy on men of his proud temper.

BELLINDA 'Tis a fantastic remedy: its operations are dangerous and uncertain.

MRS. LOVEIT 'Tis the strongest cordial[6] we can give to dying love. It often brings it back when there's no sign of life remaining. But I design not so much the reviving his, as my revenge.

[Enter Sir Fopling and his equipage.]

SIR FOPLING Hey! Bid the coachman send home four of his horses and bring the coach to Whitehall.[7] I'll walk over the Park. [To Mrs. Loveit.] Madam, the honor of kissing your fair hands is a happiness I missed this afternoon at my Lady Townley's.

MRS. LOVEIT You were very obliging, Sir Fopling, the last time I saw you there.

SIR FOPLING The preference was due to your wit and beauty. [To Bellinda.] Madam, your servant. There never was so sweet an evening.

BELLINDA 'T has drawn all the rabble of the town hither.

SIR FOPLING 'Tis pity there's not an order made that none but the beau monde[8] should walk here.

MRS. LOVEIT 'Twould add much to the beauty of the place. See what a sort of nasty fellows are coming!

[Enter four ill-fashioned fellows singing:]

"'Tis not for kisses alone, etc."[9]

MRS. LOVEIT Foh! Their periwigs are scented with tobacco so strong—

SIR FOPLING —It overcomes our pulvilio.[1] Methinks I smell the coffeehouse they come from.

FIRST MAN Dorimant's convenient,[2] Madam Loveit.

4. Drag.
5. Doubled up.
6. Medicine to stimulate the heart.
7. The royal palace, situated across St. James's Park from the Mall.
8. Beautiful world: fashionable members of the upper class.
9. From an anonymous song, Tell me no more you love, published in 1676.
1. Scented powder.
2. Mistress.

SECOND MAN I like the oily buttock[3] with her.

THIRD MAN [*pointing to Sir Fopling*] What spruce prig[4] is that?

FIRST MAN A caravan,[5] lately come from Paris.

SECOND MAN Peace, they smoke![6]   [*All of them coughing; exeunt singing:*]
    "There's something else to be done, etc."[7]
                    [*Enter Dorimant and Medley.*]

DORIMANT They're engaged.

MEDLEY She entertains him as if she liked him.

DORIMANT Let us go forward, seem earnest in discourse, and show ourselves. Then
    you shall see how she'll use him.

BELLINDA Yonder's Dorimant, my dear.

MRS. LOVEIT I see him. [*Aside.*] He comes insulting, but I will disappoint him in
    his expectations. [*To Sir Fopling.*] I like this pretty, nice humor of yours, Sir
    Fopling. [*To Bellinda.*] With what a loathing eye he looked upon those fellows!

SIR FOPLING I sat near one of 'em at a play today and was almost poisoned with a
    pair of cordovan[8] gloves he wears.

MRS. LOVEIT Oh, filthy cordovan! How I hate the smell!

                    [*Laughs in a loud, affected way.*]

SIR FOPLING Did you observe, madam, how their cravats hung loose an inch from
    their neck, and what a frightful air it gave 'em?

MRS. LOVEIT Oh! I took particular notice of one that is always spruced up with a
    deal of dirty, sky-colored ribbon.

BELLINDA That's one of the walking flageolets[9] who haunt the Mail o' nights.

MRS. LOVEIT Oh, I remember him. H' has a hollow tooth,[1] enough to spoil the
    sweetness of an evening.

SIR FOPLING I have seen the tallest walk the streets with a dainty pair of boxes,[2]
    neatly buckled on.

MRS. LOVEIT And a little footboy at his heels, pocket-high, with a flat cap, a dirty face—

SIR FOPLING —And a snotty nose.

MRS. LOVEIT Oh, odious! There's many of my own sex, with that Holborn
    equipage,[3] trig to Gray's Inn Walks,[4] and now and then travel hither on a Sunday.

MEDLEY [*to Dorimant*] She takes no notice of you.

DORIMANT Damn her! I am jealous of a counterplot.

MRS. LOVEIT Your liveries[5] are the finest, Sir Fopling. Oh, that page! That page is
    the prettily'st dressed. They are all Frenchmen?

SIR FOPLING There's one damned English blockhead among 'em. You may know
    him by his mien.[6]

MRS. LOVEIT Oh, that's he, that's he! What do you call him?

SIR FOPLING [*calling Footman*] Hey!—I know not what to call him.

MRS. LOVEIT What's your name?

FOOTMAN John Trott, madam.

SIR FOPLING Oh, insufferable! Trott, Trott, Trott! There's nothing so barbarous as
    the names of our English servants. What countryman are you,[7] sirrah?

---

3. Slang for "whore."
4. Showy, conceited man.
5. Someone ripe to be cheated of money (thieves' cant).
6. Smoke us out: notice us.
7. Another line from *Tell me no more you love.*
8. Spanish leather.
9. Small wind instruments.

1. I.e., he *is* a hollow (or rotten) tooth.
2. Clumsy overshoes, usually of wood.
3. Merchant's Retinue.
4. Gardens notorious for secret meetings. Trig: hasten.
5. Footmen's costumes.
6. Look, bearing.
7. What county are you from?

FOOTMAN Hampshire, sir.

SIR FOPLING Then Hampshire be your name. Hey, Hampshire!

MRS. LOVEIT Oh, that sound! That sound becomes the mouth of a man of quality.

MEDLEY Dorimant, you look a little bashful on the matter.

DORIMANT She dissembles better than I thought she could have done.

MEDLEY You have tempted her with too luscious a bait. She bites at the coxcomb.

DORIMANT She cannot fall from loving me to that?

MEDLEY You begin to be jealous in earnest.

DORIMANT Of one I do not love?

MEDLEY You did love her.

DORIMANT The fit has long been over.

MEDLEY But I have known men fall into dangerous relapses when they have found a woman inclining to another.

DORIMANT [to himself] He guesses the secret of my heart. I am concerned but dare not show it, lest Bellinda should mistrust all I have done to gain her.

BELLINDA [aside] I have watched his look and find no alteration there. Did he love her, some signs of jealousy would have appeared.

DORIMANT [to Mrs. Loveit] I hope this happy evening, madam, has reconciled you to the scandalous Mail. We shall have you now hankering[8] here again.

MRS. LOVEIT Sir Fopling, will you walk?

SIR FOPLING I am all obedience, madam.

MRS. LOVEIT Come along then, and let's agree to be malicious on all the ill-fashioned things we meet.

SIR FOPLING We'll make a critique on the whole Mail, madam.

MRS. LOVEIT Bellinda, you shall engage.[9]

BELLINDA To the reserve of[1] our friends, my dear.

MRS. LOVEIT No! No exceptions.

SIR FOPLING We'll sacrifice all to our diversion.

MRS. LOVEIT All, all.

SIR FOPLING All!

BELLINDA All? Then let it be.

[Exeunt Sir Fopling, Mrs. Loveit, Bellinda, and Pert, laughing.]

MEDLEY Would you had brought some more of your friends, Dorimant, to have been witnesses of Sir Fopling's disgrace and your triumph!

DORIMANT 'Twere unreasonable to desire you not to laugh at me; but pray do not expose me to the town this day or two.

MEDLEY By that time you hope to have regained your credit?

DORIMANT I know she hates Fopling and only makes use of him in hope to work me on again. Had it not been for some powerful considerations which will be removed tomorrow morning, I had made her pluck off this mask and show the passion that lies panting under.

[Enter a Footman.]

MEDLEY Here comes a man from Bellair, with news of your last adventure.

DORIMANT I am glad he sent him. I long to know the consequence of our parting.

FOOTMAN Sir, my master desires you to come to my Lady Townley's presently and bring Mr. Medley with you. My Lady Woodvill and her daughter are there.

8. Lingering.
9. Join in.

1. Except for.

MEDLEY Then all's well, Dorimant.

FOOTMAN They have sent for the fiddles and mean to dance. He bid me tell you, sir, the old lady does not know you; and would have you own yourself to be Mr. Courtage. They are all prepared to receive you by that name.

DORIMANT That foppish admirer of quality, who flatters the very meat at honorable tables and never offers love to a woman below a lady-grandmother!

MEDLEY You know the character you are to act, I see.

DORIMANT This is Harriet's contrivance—wild, witty, lovesome, beautiful, and young.—Come along, Medley.

MEDLEY This new woman would well supply[2] the loss of Loveit.

DORIMANT That business must not end so. Before tomorrow sun is set, I will revenge and clear it.

> And you and Loveit, to her cost, shall find
I fathom all the depths of womankind.   [Exeunt.]

A c t I V

Scene 1

[Lady Townley's. The scene opens with the fiddles playing a country dance. Enter Dorimant and Lady Woodvill, Young Bellair and Mrs. Harriet, Old Bellair and Emilia, Mr. Medley and Lady Townley, as having just ended the dance.]

OLD BELLAIR So, so, so! A smart bout, a very smart bout,[1] adod!

LADY TOWNLEY How do you like Emilia's dancing, brother?

OLD BELLAIR Not at all, not at all!

LADY TOWNLEY You speak not what you think, I am sure.

OLD BELLAIR No matter for that; go, bid her dance no more. It don't become her, it don't become her. Tell her I say so. [*Aside.*] Adod, I love her.

DORIMANT [*to Lady Woodvill*] All people mingle nowadays, madam. And in public places women of quality have the least respect showed 'em.

LADY WOODVILL I protest you say the truth, Mr. Courtage.

DORIMANT Forms and ceremonies, the only things that uphold quality and greatness, are now shamefully laid aside and neglected.

LADY WOODVILL Well, this is not the women's age, let 'em think what they will. Lewdness is the business now; love was the business in my time.

DORIMANT The women, indeed, are little beholding[2] to the young men of this age. They're generally only dull admirers of themselves and make their court to nothing but their periwigs and their cravats—and would be more concerned for the disordering of 'em, though on a good occasion,[3] than a young maid would be for the tumbling of her head or handkercher.

LADY WOODVILL I protest you hit 'em.

DORIMANT They are very assiduous to show themselves at court, well-dressed, to the women of quality; but their business is with the stale mistresses of the town, who are prepared to receive their lazy addresses by industrious old lovers who have cast 'em off and made 'em easy.

HARRIET [*to Medley*] He fits my mother's humor so well, a little more and she'll dance a kissing dance with him anon.

MEDLEY Dutifully observed, madam.

---

2. Make up for.
1. A "round" of exercise.

2. Indebted.
3. For a good reason.

DORIMANT They pretend to be great critics in beauty—by their talk you would think they liked no face—and yet can dote on an ill one if it belong to a laundress or a tailor's daughter. They cry a woman's past her prime at twenty, decayed at four-and-twenty, old and insufferable at thirty.

LADY WOODVILL Insufferable at thirty! That they are in the wrong, Mr. Courtage, at five-and-thirty there are living proofs enough to convince 'em.

DORIMANT Ay, madam; there's Mrs. Setlooks, Mrs. Droplip, and my Lady Loud. Show me among all our opening buds a face that promises so much beauty as the remains of theirs.

LADY WOODVILL The depraved appetite of this vicious age tastes[4] nothing but green fruit and loathes it when 'tis kindly ripened.

DORIMANT Else so many deserving women, madam, would not be so untimely neglected.

LADY WOODVILL I protest, Mr. Courtage, a dozen such good men as you would be enough to atone for that wicked Dorimant and all the under-debauchees of the town.

[Harriet, Emilia, Young Bellair, Medley, and Lady Townley break out into a laughter.] What's the matter there?

MEDLEY A pleasant mistake, madam, that a lady has made occasions a little laughter.

OLD BELLAIR [to Dorimant and Lady Woodvill] Come, come, you keep 'em idle! They are impatient till the fiddles play again.

DORIMANT You are not weary, madam?

LADY WOODVILL One dance more. I cannot refuse you, Mr. Courtage.

[They dance. After the dance, Old Bellair singing and dancing up to Emilia.]

EMILIA You are very active, sir.

OLD BELLAIR Adod, sirrah, when I was a young fellow, I could ha' capered up to my woman's gorget.[5]

DORIMANT [to Lady Woodvill] You are willing to rest yourself, madam?

LADY TOWNLEY [to Dorimant and Lady Woodvill] We'll walk into my chamber and sit down.

MEDLEY Leave us Mr. Courtage; he's a dancer, and the young ladies are not weary yet.

LADY WOODVILL We'll send him out again.

HARRIET If you do not quickly, I know where to send for Mr. Dorimant.

LADY WOODVILL This girl's head, Mr. Courtage, is ever running on that wild fellow.

DORIMANT 'Tis well you have got her a good husband, madam. That will settle it.

[Exeunt Lady Townley, Lady Woodvill, and Dorimant.]

OLD BELLAIR [to Emilia] Adod, sweetheart, be advised and do not throw thyself away on a young idle fellow.

EMILIA I have no such intention, sir.

OLD BELLAIR Have a little patience! Thou shalt have the man I spake of. Adod, he loves thee and will make a good husband. But no words—

EMILIA But, sir—

OLD BELLAIR No answer, out a pize! Peace, and think on't.

[Enter Dorimant.]

DORIMANT Your company is desired within, sir.

OLD BELLAIR I go, I go! Good Mr. Courtage, fare you well. [To Emilia.] Go, I'll see you no more!

EMILIA What have I done, sir?

---

4. Likes.   5. Kicked as high as my partner's collar.

OLD BELLAIR You are ugly, you are ugly!—Is she not, Mr. Courtage?

EMILIA Better words, or I shan't abide you!

OLD BELLAIR Out a pize! Adod, what does she say?—Hit her a pat for me there.

[Exit Old Bellair.]

MEDLEY *[to Dorimant]* You have charms for the whole family.

DORIMANT You'll spoil all with some unseasonable jest, Medley.

MEDLEY You see I confine my tongue and am content to be a bare spectator, much contrary to my nature.

EMILIA Methinks, Mr. Dorimant, my Lady Woodvill is a little fond of you.

DORIMANT Would her daughter were.

MEDLEY It may be you may find her so. Try her. You have an opportunity.

DORIMANT And I will not lose it.—Bellair, here's a lady has something to say to you.

YOUNG BELLAIR I wait upon her.—Mr. Medley, we have both business with you.

DORIMANT Get you all together, then.

[He bows to Harriet; she curtsies.]

[To Harriet.] That demure curtsy is not amiss in jest, but do not think in earnest it becomes you.

HARRIET Affectation is catching, I find. From your grave bow I got it.

DORIMANT Where had you all that scorn and coldness in your look?

HARRIET From nature, sir; pardon my want of art. I have not learnt those softnesses and languishings which now in faces are so much in fashion.

DORIMANT You need 'em not. You have a sweetness of your own, if you would but calm your frowns and let it settle.

HARRIET My eyes are wild and wand'ring like my passions, and cannot yet be tied to rules of charming.

DORIMANT Women, indeed, have commonly a method of managing those messengers of love. Now they will look as if they would kill, and anon they will look as if they were dying. They point and rebate[6] their glances, the better to invite us.

HARRIET I like this variety well enough, but hate the set face that always looks as it would say, "Come love me"—a woman who at plays makes the *doux yeux* to[7] a whole audience and at home cannot forbear 'em to her monkey.

DORIMANT Put on a gentle smile and let me see how well it will become you.

HARRIET I am sorry my face does not please you as it is; but I shall not be complaisant and change it.

DORIMANT Though you are obstinate, I know 'tis capable of improvement, and shall do you justice, madam, if I chance to be at court when the critics of the circle[8] pass their judgment; for thither you must come.

HARRIET And expect to be taken in pieces, have all my features examined, every motion censured, and on the whole be condemned to be but pretty—or a beauty of the lowest rate. What think you?

DORIMANT The women—nay, the very lovers who belong to the drawing room—will maliciously allow you more than that. They always grant what is apparent, that they may the better be believed when they name concealed faults they cannot easily be disproved in.

HARRIET Beauty runs as great a risk exposed at court as wit does on the stage, where the ugly and the foolish all are free to censure.

---

6. Heat up and then damp down.
7. Makes eyes at.

8. The influential group of wits to which Etherege himself belonged.

DORIMANT [aside] I love her and dare not let her know it. I fear sh'as an ascendant o'er me and may revenge the wrongs I have done her sex. [To her.] Think of making a party,[9] madam; love will engage.

HARRIET You make me start. I did not think to have heard of love from you.

DORIMANT I never knew what 'twas to have a settled ague[1] yet, but now and then have had irregular fits.

HARRIET Take heed; sickness after long health is commonly more violent and dangerous.

DORIMANT [aside] I have took the infection from her and feel the disease now spreading in me. [To her.] Is the name of love so frightful that you dare not stand it?

HARRIET 'Twill do little execution[2] out of your mouth on me, I am sure.

DORIMANT It has been fatal—

HARRIET To some easy women, but we are not all born to one destiny. I was informed you use to laugh at love, and not make it.

DORIMANT The time has been, but now I must speak.

HARRIET If it be on that idle subject, I will put on my serious look, turn my head carelessly from you, drop my lip, let my eyelids fall and hang half o'er my eyes— thus, while you buzz a speech of an hour long in my ear and I answer never a word. Why do you not begin?

DORIMANT That the company may take notice how passionately I made advances of love and how disdainfully you receive 'em.

HARRIET When your love's grown strong enough to make you bear being laughed at, I'll give you leave to trouble me with it. Till then, pray forbear, sir.

[Enter Sir Fopling and others in masks.]

DORIMANT What's here—masquerades?

HARRIET I thought that foppery had been left off, and people might have been in private with a fiddle.

DORIMANT 'Tis endeavored to be kept on foot still by some who find themselves the more acceptable, the less they are known.

YOUNG BELLAIR This must be Sir Fopling.

MEDLEY That extraordinary habit[3] shows it.

YOUNG BELLAIR What are the rest?

MEDLEY A company of French rascals whom he picked up in Paris and has brought over to be his dancing equipage on these occasions. Make him own[4] himself; a fool is very troublesome when he presumes he is incognito.

SIR FOPLING [to Harriet]. Do you know me?

HARRIET Ten to one but I guess at you.

SIR FOPLING Are you women as fond of a vizard as we men are?

HARRIET I am very fond of a vizard that covers a face I do not like, sir.

YOUNG BELLAIR Here are no masks, you see, sir, but those which came with you. This was intended a private meeting; but because you look like a gentleman, if you will discover yourself and we know you to be such, you shall be welcome.

SIR FOPLING [pulling off his mask] Dear Bellair.

MEDLEY Sir Fopling! How came you hither?

SIR FOPLING Faith, as I was coming late from Whitehall, after the King's couchée,[5] one of my people told me he had heard fiddles at my Lady Townley's, and—

9. Making up an army (to defend beauty with the help of love).
1. Lasting fit (of love).
2. Inflict little damage.

3. Outfit.
4. Reveal.
5. Evening reception.

DORIMANT You need not say any more, sir.

SIR FOPLING Dorimant, let me kiss thee.

DORIMANT Hark you, Sir Fopling—[*Whispers.*]

SIR FOPLING Enough, enough, Courtage.—[*Glancing at Harriet.*] A pretty kind of young woman that, Medley. I observed her in the Mail, more *éveillée*[6] than our English women commonly are. Prithee, what is she?

MEDLEY The most noted *coquette*[7] in town. Beware of her.

SIR FOPLING Let her be what she will, I know how to take my measures.[8] In Paris the mode is to flatter the *prude*, laugh at the *faux-prude*,[9] make serious love to the *demi-prude*,[1] and only rally with the *coquette*. Medley, what think you?

MEDLEY That for all this smattering of the mathematics, you may be out in your judgment at tennis.

SIR FOPLING What a *coq-à-l'âne*[2] is this? I talk of women, and thou answer'st tennis.

MEDLEY Mistakes will be, for want of apprehension.

SIR FOPLING I am very glad of the acquaintance I have with this family.

MEDLEY My lady truly is a good woman.

SIR FOPLING Ah, Dorimant—Courtage, I would say—would thou hadst spent the last winter in Paris with me. When thou wert there, La Corneus and Sallyes[3] were the only habitudes[4] we had; a comedian would have been a *bonne fortune*.[5] No stranger ever passed his time so well as I did some months before I came over. I was well received in a dozen families, where all the women of quality used to visit. I have intrigues to tell thee more pleasant than ever thou read'st in a novel.

HARRIET Write 'em, sir, and oblige us women. Our language wants such little stories.

SIR FOPLING Writing, madam, 's a mechanic[6] part of wit. A gentleman should never go beyond a song or a *billet*.[7]

HARRIET Bussy[8] was a gentleman.

SIR FOPLING Who, d'Ambois?[9]

MEDLEY [*aside*] Was there ever such a brisk blockhead?

HARRIET Not d'Ambois, sir, but Rabutin: he who writ the *Loves of France*.

SIR FOPLING That may be, madam; many gentlemen do things that are below 'em.—Damn your authors, Courtage. Women are the prettiest things we can fool away our time with.

HARRIET I hope ye have wearied yourself tonight at court, sir, and will not think of fooling with anybody here.

SIR FOPLING I cannot complain of my fortune there, madam.—Dorimant—

DORIMANT Again!

SIR FOPLING Courtage, a pox on't! I have something to tell thee. When I had made my court within, I came out and flung myself upon the mat under the state[1] i' th' outward room, i' th' midst of half a dozen beauties who were withdrawn to jeer among themselves, as they called it.

DORIMANT Did you know 'em?

6. Wide-awake, sprightly.
7. Flirt.
8. Form an estimate.
9. False prude.
1. Half prude.
2. Nonsense.
3. Fashionable Parisians.
4. Acquaintances.
5. Stroke of good luck.
6. Base, low.

7. Billet-doux, or love letter.
8. Roger de Rabutin, Comte de Bussy (1618–1693), author of *Histoire Amoureuse des Gaules* (*The Loves of France*), a gossipy account of love affairs among French aristocrats.
9. Sir Fopling has heard only of Louis de Clermont d'Amboise, Sieur de Bussy (1549–1579), an adventurer whose story had been made into a popular play.
1. Canopy.

SIR FOPLING Not one of 'em, by heav'ns, not I! But they were all your friends.

DORIMANT How are you sure of that?

SIR FOPLING Why, we laughed at all the town—spared nobody but yourself. They found me a man for their purpose.

DORIMANT I know you are malicious to[2] your power.

SIR FOPLING And, faith, I had occasion to show it; for I never saw more gaping fools at a ball or on a Birthday.[3]

DORIMANT You learned who the women were?

SIR FOPLING No matter; they frequent the drawing room.

DORIMANT And entertain themselves at the expense of all the fops who come there.

SIR FOPLING That's their bus'ness. Faith, I sifted[4] 'em and find they have a sort of wit among them.

[Pinches a tallow candle.]

Ah, filthy!

DORIMANT Look, he has been pinching the tallow candle.

SIR FOPLING How can you breathe in a room where there's grease frying? Dorimant, thou art intimate with my lady: advise her, for her own sake and the good company that comes hither, to burn wax lights.

HARRIET What are these masquerades who stand so obsequiously at a distance?

SIR FOPLING A set of balladines, whom I picked out of the best in France and brought over with a flûte douce or two—my servants. They shall entertain you.

HARRIET I had rather see you dance yourself, Sir Fopling.

SIR FOPLING And I had rather do it—all the company knows it. But, madam—

MEDLEY Come, come, no excuses, Sir Fopling!

SIR FOPLING By heav'ns, Medley

MEDLEY Like a woman I find you must be struggled with before one brings you to what you desire.

HARRIET [aside] Can he dance?

EMILIA And fence and sing too, if you'll believe him.

DORIMANT He has no more excellence in his heels than in his head. He went to Paris a plain, bashful English blockhead and is returned a fine, undertaking[5] French fop.

MEDLEY [to Harriet] I cannot prevail.

SIR FOPLING Do not think it want of complaisance, madam.

HARRIET You are too well-bred to want that, Sir Fopling. I think it want of power.

SIR FOPLING By heav'ns, and so it is! I have sat up so damned late and drunk so cursed hard since I came to this lewd town that I am fit for nothing but low dancing now—a courante, a bourrée, or a menuet.[6] But St. André[7] tells me, if I will but be regular, in one month I shall rise again.

[Endeavors at a caper.]

Pox on this debauchery!

EMILIA I have heard your dancing much commended.

SIR FOPLING It had the good fortune to please in Paris. I was judged to rise within an inch as high as the Basque[8] in an entry[9] I danced there.

---

2. To the extent of.

3. I.e., at one of the King's birthday celebrations.

4. Appraised.

5. Enterprising.

6. Three dances that require no high capers.

7. French dance master who performed in England in

1675.

8. Probably a reference to "le Basque Sauteur," a French dancer mentioned by Bussy in La France Galante.

9. Dance performed between the acts of a play or other entertainment.

HARRIET [*to Emilia*] I am mightily taken with this fool. Let us sit.—Here's a seat, Sir Fopling.

SIR FOPLING At your feet, madam. I can be nowhere so much at ease.—By your leave, gown.[1]   [*Sits.*]

HARRIET. EMILIA Ah, you'll spoil it!

SIR FOPLING No matter, my clothes are my creatures. I make 'em to make my court to you ladies.—Hey, *qu'on commence!*[2]

[*Dance.*]

To an English dancer, English motions! I was forced to entertain[3] this fellow [*pointing to John Trott*], one of my set miscarrying.[4]—Oh, horrid! Leave your damned manner of dancing and put on the French air. Have you not a pattern before you?—Pretty well! Imitation in time may bring him to something.

[*After the dance, enter Old Bellair, Lady Woodvill, and Lady Townley.*]

OLD BELLAIR Hey, adod, what have we here? A mumming?[5]

LADY WOODVILL Where's my daughter?—Harriet!

DORIMANT Here, here, madam. I know not but under these disguises there may be dangerous sparks. I gave the lady warning.

LADY WOODVILL Lord, I am so obliged to you, Mr. Courtage.

HARRIET Lord, how you admire this man!

LADY WOODVILL What have you to except against him?

HARRIET He's a fop.

LADY WOODVILL He's not a Dorimant, a wild, extravagant fellow of the times.

HARRIET He's a man made up of forms and commonplaces, sucked out of the remaining lees[6] of the last age.

LADY WOODVILL He's so good a man that were you not engaged—

LADY TOWNLEY You'll have but little night to sleep in.

LADY WOODVILL Lord, 'tis perfect day!

DORIMANT [*aside*] The hour is almost come I appointed Bellinda, and I am not so foppishly in love here to forget. I am flesh and blood yet.

LADY TOWNLEY I am very sensible, madam.

LADY WOODVILL Lord, madam—

HARRIET Look, in what a struggle is my poor mother yonder!

YOUNG BELLAIR She has much ado to bring out the compliment.

DORIMANT She strains hard for it.

HARRIET See, see—her head tottering, her eyes staring, and her underlip trembling.

DORIMANT Now, now she's in the very convulsions of her civility. [*Aside.*] 'Sdeath, I shall lose Bellinda! I must fright her hence. She'll be an hour in this fit of good manners else. [*To Lady Woodvill.*] Do you not know Sir Fopling, madam?

LADY WOODVILL I have seen that face. Oh heav'n, 'tis the same we met in the Mail! How came he here?

DORIMANT A fiddle in this town is a kind of fop-call. No sooner it strikes up, but the house is besieged with an army of masquerades straight.

LADY WOODVILL Lord, I tremble, Mr. Courtage. For certain Dorimant is in the company.

DORIMANT I cannot confidently say he is not. You had best begone; I will wait upon you. Your daughter is in the hands of Mr. Bellair.

---

1. He addresses his own suit of clothing.
2. Let's begin!
3. Hire.

4. Leaving my service.
5. A play performed in fancy folk costume.
6. Dregs (as in wine).

LADY WOODVILL I'll see her before me.—Harriet, come away!
  [*Exeunt Lady Woodvill and Harriet.*]
YOUNG BELLAIR Lights, lights!
LADY TOWNLEY Light, down there!
OLD BELLAIR Adod, it needs not—
  [*Exeunt Lady Townley and Young Bellair.*]
DORIMANT [*calling to the servants outside*] Call my Lady Woodvill's coach to the
  door! Quickly!   [*Exit Dorimant.*]
OLD BELLAIR Stay, Mr. Medley; let the young fellows do that duty. We will drink
  a glass of wine together. 'Tis good after dancing. [*Looks at Sir Fopling.*] What mum-
  ming spark is that?
MEDLEY He is not to be comprehended in few words.
SIR FOPLING Hey, La Tour!
MEDLEY Whither away, Sir Fopling?
SIR FOPLING I have business with Courtage.
MEDLEY He'll but put the ladies into their coach and come up again.
OLD BELLAIR In the meantime I'll call for a bottle. [*Exit Old Bellair.*]
                  [*Enter Young Bellair.*]
MEDLEY Where's Dorimant?
YOUNG BELLAIR Stolen home. He has had business waiting for him there all this
  night, I believe, by an impatience I observed in him.
MEDLEY Very likely. 'Tis but dissembling drunkenness, railing at his friends, and the
  kind soul will embrace the blessing and forget the tedious expectation.[7]
SIR FOPLING I must speak with him before I sleep.
YOUNG BELLAIR [*to Medley*] Emilia and I are resolved on that business.
MEDLEY Peace, here's your father.
            [*Enter Old Bellair and a butler with a bottle of wine.*]
OLD BELLAIR The women are all gone to bed.—Fill, boy!—Mr. Medley, begin a
  health.
MEDLEY [*whispers*] To Emilia.
OLD BELLAIR Out a pize! She's a rogue, and I'll not pledge you.[8]
MEDLEY I know you will.
OLD BELLAIR Adod, drink it, then!
SIR FOPLING Let us have the new bachique.
OLD BELLAIR Adod, that is a hard word! What does it mean, sir?
MEDLEY A catch or drinking song.
OLD BELLAIR Let us have it, then.
SIR FOPLING Fill the glasses round, and draw up in a body.—Hey, music!
  [*They sing.*]

>   The pleasures of love and the joys of good wine,
>   To perfect our happiness wisely we join.
>   We to beauty all day
>   Give the sovereign sway
>   And her favorite nymphs devoutly obey;
>   At the plays we are constantly making our court,
>   And when they are ended, we follow the sport

---

7. On arriving home Dorimant will blame his friends for
his late arrival and his lover will embrace him and forget

the time she has spent waiting.
8. I'll not second you in your toast.

To the Mail and the Park,
Where we love till 'tis dark.
Then sparkling champagne
Puts an end to their reign:
It quickly recovers
Poor languishing lovers,
Makes us frolic and gay, and drowns all our sorrow;
But alas, we relapse again on the morrow.
Let every man stand
With his glass in his hand,
And briskly discharge at the word of command.
Here's a health to all those
Whom tonight we depose.
Wine and beauty by turns great souls should inspire;
Present all together;[9] and now, boys, give fire!

[*They drink.*]

OLD BELLAIR Adod, a pretty business and very merry!

SIR FOPLING Hark you, Medley, let you and I take the fiddles and go waken Dorimant.

MEDLEY We shall do him a courtesy, if it be as I guess. For after the fatigue of this night, he'll quickly have his belly full and be glad of an occasion to cry, "Take away, Handy!"

YOUNG BELLAIR I'll go with you; and there we'll consult about affairs, Medley.

OLD BELLAIR [*looks on his watch*] Adod, 'tis six o'clock!

SIR FOPLING Let's away, then.

OLD BELLAIR Mr. Medley, my sister tells me you are an honest man. And, adod, I love you.—Few words and hearty, that's the way with old Harry, old Harry.

SIR FOPLING [*to his servants*] Light your flambeaux![1] Hey!

OLD BELLAIR What does the man mean?

MEDLEY 'Tis day, Sir Fopling.

SIR FOPLING No matter; our serenade will look the greater.   [*Exeunt omnes.*]

Scene 2

[*Dorimant's lodging; a table, a candle, a toilet, etc. Handy tying up linen.[2] Enter Dorimant in his gown, and Bellinda.*]

DORIMANT Why will you be gone so soon?

BELLINDA Why did you stay out so late?

DORIMANT Call a chair, Handy. [*Exit Handy.*] What makes you tremble so?

BELLINDA I have a thousand fears about me. Have I not been seen, think you?

DORIMANT By nobody but myself and trusty Handy.

BELLINDA Where are all your people?

DORIMANT I have dispersed 'em on sleeveless[3] errands. What does that sigh mean?

BELLINDA Can you be so unkind to ask me? Well [*sighs*], were it to do again—

DORIMANT We should do it, should we not?

BELLINDA I think we should: the wickeder man you, to make me love so well. Will you be discreet now?

---

9. Raise your glasses together.
1. Torches.

2. The dirty bed sheets.
3. Useless.

DORIMANT I will.

BELLINDA You cannot.

DORIMANT Never doubt it.

BELLINDA I will not expect it.

DORIMANT You do me wrong.

BELLINDA You have no more power to keep the secret than I had not to trust you with it.

DORIMANT By all the joys I have had and those you keep in store—

BELLINDA —You'll do for my sake what you never did before.

DORIMANT By that truth thou hast spoken, a wife shall sooner betray herself to her husband.

BELLINDA Yet I had rather you should be false in this than in another thing you promised me.

DORIMANT What's that?

BELLINDA That you would never see Loveit more but in public places—in the Park, at court and plays.

DORIMANT 'Tis not likely a man should be fond of seeing a damned old play when there is a new one acted.

BELLINDA I dare not trust your promise.

DORIMANT You may.

BELLINDA This does not satisfy me. You shall swear you never will see her more.

DORIMANT I will, a thousand oaths. By all—

BELLINDA Hold! You shall not, now I think on't better.

DORIMANT I will swear!

BELLINDA I shall grow jealous of the oath and think I owe your truth to that, not to your love.

DORIMANT Then, by my love! No other oath I'll swear.

[Enter Handy.]

HANDY Here's a chair.

BELLINDA Let me go.

DORIMANT I cannot.

BELLINDA Too willingly, I fear.

DORIMANT Too unkindly feared. When will you promise me again?

BELLINDA Not this fortnight.

DORIMANT You will be better than your word.

BELLINDA I think I shall. Will it not make you love me less?

[Fiddles without.]

[Starting.] Hark, what fiddles are these?

DORIMANT Look out, Handy.   [Exit Handy and returns.]

HANDY Mr. Medley, Mr. Bellair, and Sir Fopling. They are coming up.

DORIMANT How got they in?

HANDY The door was open for the chair.

BELLINDA Lord, let me fly!

DORIMANT Here, here, down the back stairs. I'll see you into your chair.

BELLINDA No, no, stay and receive 'em. And be sure you keep your word and never see Loveit more. Let it be a proof of your kindness.

DORIMANT It shall.—Handy, direct her.—[Kissing her hand.] Everlasting love go along with thee.

[Exeunt Bellinda and Handy.]
[Enter Young Bellair, Medley, and Sir Fopling, with his page.]

YOUNG BELLAIR Not abed yet?

MEDLEY You have had an irregular fit, Dorimant.

DORIMANT I have.

YOUNG BELLAIR And is it off already?

DORIMANT Nature has done her part, gentlemen. When she falls kindly to work, great cures are effected in little time, you know.

SIR FOPLING We thought there was a wench in the case, by the chair that waited. Prithee, make us a *confidence*.

DORIMANT Excuse me.

SIR FOPLING *Le sage*[4] Dorimant. Was she pretty?

DORIMANT So pretty she may come to keep her coach and pay parish duties,[5] if the good humor of the age continue.

MEDLEY And be of the number of the ladies kept by public-spirited men for the good of the whole town.

SIR FOPLING Well said, Medley.

[*Sir Fopling dancing by himself.*]

YOUNG BELLAIR See Sir Fopling dancing.

DORIMANT You are practicing and have a mind to recover, I see.

SIR FOPLING Prithee, Dorimant, why hast not thou a glass hung up here? A room is the dullest thing without one.

YOUNG BELLAIR Here is company to entertain you.

SIR FOPLING But I mean in case of being alone. In a glass a man may entertain himself—

DORIMANT The shadow of himself, indeed.

SIR FOPLING —Correct the errors of his motions and his dress.

MEDLEY I find, Sir Fopling, in your solitude you remember the saying of the wise man, and study yourself.[6]

SIR FOPLING 'Tis the best diversion in our retirements. Dorimant, thou art a pretty fellow and wear'st thy clothes well, but I never saw thee have a handsome cravat. Were they made up like mine, they'd give another air to thy face. Prithee, let me send my man to dress thee but one day. By heav'ns, an Englishman cannot tie a ribbon!

DORIMANT They are something clumsy-fisted.

SIR FOPLING I have brought over the prettiest fellow that ever spread a toilet. He served some time under Merille,[7] the greatest genie in the world for a *valet de chambre*.[8]

DORIMANT What, he who formerly belonged to the Duke of Candle?

SIR FOPLING The same, and got him his immortal reputation.

DORIMANT Y' have a very fine brandenburgh[9] on, Sir Fopling.

SIR FOPLING It serves to wrap me up, after the fatigue of a ball.

MEDLEY I see you often in it, with your periwig tied up.

SIR FOPLING We should not always be in a set dress. 'Tis more *en cavalier*[1] to appear now and then in a *déshabillé*.

MEDLEY Pray, how goes your business with Loveit?

4. Discreet.

5. Dorimant's comment that his lover may soon be paying taxes (parish duties) suggests that he was with a prostitute—either a sign of his discretion in terms of Bellinda, or a scornful estimate of her future.

6. Ironic: Socrates actually says "know thyself."

7. A valet currently in the service of the Duc d'Orléans.

8. Gentleman's personal attendant.

9. Morning gown.

1. Dashing, stylish.

SIR FOPLING You might have answered yourself in the Mail last night.—Dorimant, did you not see the advances she made me? I have been endeavoring at a song.

DORIMANT Already?

SIR FOPLING 'Tis my *coup d'essai*[2] in English. I would fain have thy opinion of it.

DORIMANT Let's see it.

SIR FOPLING Hey, page, give me my song.—Bellair, here. Thou hast a pretty voice; sing it.

YOUNG BELLAIR Sing it yourself, Sir Fopling.

SIR FOPLING Excuse me.

YOUNG BELLAIR You learnt to sing in Paris.

SIR FOPLING I did—of Lambert,[3] the greatest master in the world; but I have his own fault, a weak voice, and care not to sing out of a *ruelle*.[4]

DORIMANT A *ruelle* is a pretty cage for a singing fop, indeed.

[*Young Bellair reads the song.*]

How charming Phillis is, how fair!
    Ah, that she were as willing
To ease my wounded heart of care,
    And make her eyes less killing.
I sigh, I sigh, I languish now,
    And love will not let me rest;
I drive about the Park and bow,
    Still as[5] I meet my dearest.

SIR FOPLING Sing it, sing it, man! It goes to a pretty new tune which I am confident was made by Baptiste.[6]

MEDLEY Sing it yourself, Sir Fopling. He does not know the tune.

SIR FOPLING I'll venture.

[*Sir Fopling sings.*]

DORIMANT Ay, marry, now 'tis something. I shall not flatter you, Sir Fopling: there is not much thought in't, but 'tis passionate and well-turned.

MEDLEY After the French way.

SIR FOPLING That I aimed at. Does it not give you a lively image of the thing? Slap, down goes the glass,[7] and thus we are at it.

[*He bows and grimaces.*]

DORIMANT It does indeed. I perceive, Sir Fopling, you'll be the very head of the sparks who are lucky in compositions of this nature.

[*Enter Sir Fopling's Footman.*]

SIR FOPLING La Tour, is the bath ready?

FOOTMAN Yes, sir.

SIR FOPLING *Adieu donc, mes chers.*[8]

[*Exit Sir Fopling with his Footman and Page.*]

MEDLEY When have you your revenge on Loveit, Dorimant?

DORIMANT I will but change my linen[9] and about it.

MEDLEY The powerful considerations which hindered have been removed, then?

---

2. First attempt.
3. Michel Lambert (1610–1696), master of chamber music to Louis XIV.
4. A lady's bedroom, used in France for morning receptions.
5. Whenever.

6. Jean-Baptiste Lully (1638–1687), composer of Court music to Louis XIV.
7. The coach window.
8. Farewell then, my dears.
9. Undergarments.

DORIMANT Most luckily, this morning. You must along with me; my reputation lies at stake there.

MEDLEY I am engaged to Bellair.

DORIMANT What's your business?

MEDLEY Ma—tri—mony,[1] an't like you.

DORIMANT It does not, sir.

YOUNG BELLAIR It may in time, Dorimant. What think you of Mrs. Harriet?

DORIMANT What does she think of me?

YOUNG BELLAIR I am confident she loves you.

DORIMANT How does it appear?

YOUNG BELLAIR Why, she's never well but when she's talking of you, but then she finds all the faults in you she can. She laughs at all who commend you; but then she speaks ill of all who do not.

DORIMANT Women of her temper betray themselves by their over-cunning. I had once a growing love with a lady who would always quarrel with me when I came to see her, and yet was never quiet if I stayed a day from her.

YOUNG BELLAIR My father is in love with Emilia.

DORIMANT That is a good warrant for your proceedings. Go on and prosper; I must to Loveit.—Medley, I am sorry you cannot be a witness.

MEDLEY Make her meet Sir Fopling again in the same place and use him ill before me.

DORIMANT That may be brought about, I think.—I'll be at your aunt's anon and give you joy, Mr. Bellair.

YOUNG BELLAIR You had best not think of Mrs. Harriet too much. Without church security, there's no taking up there.[2]

DORIMANT I may fall into the snare, too. But,

> The wise will find a difference in our fate:
> You wed a woman, I a good estate.   [*Exeunt*.]

Scene 3

[*The Mail; in front of Mrs. Loveit's. Enter the chair with Bellinda; the men set it down and open it. Bellinda starting.*]

BELLINDA [*surprised*] Lord, where am I? In the Mail! Whither have you brought me?

FIRST CHAIRMAN You gave us no directions, madam.

BELLINDA [*aside*] The fright I was in made me forget it.

FIRST CHAIRMAN We use to carry a lady from the squire's hither.

BELLINDA [*aside*] This is Loveit! I am undone if she sees me.—Quickly, carry me away!

FIRST CHAIRMAN Whither, an't like your honor?

BELLINDA Ask no questions!

[*Enter Mrs. Loveit's Footman.*]

FOOTMAN Have you seen my lady, madam?

BELLINDA I am just come to wait upon her.

FOOTMAN She will be glad to see you, madam. She sent me to you this morning to desire your company, and I was told you went out by five o'clock.

BELLINDA [*aside*] More and more unlucky!

FOOTMAN Will you walk in, madam?

BELLINDA I'll discharge my chair and follow. Tell your mistress I am here.

[*Exit Footman.*]

---

1. Medley drawls in imitation of tradesmen's speech (since Dorimant asked about "business").   2. Possibility of having her.

[*Bellinda gives the Chairmen money.*]

Take this; and if ever you should be examined, be sure you say you took me up in the Strand, over against the Exchange—as you will answer it to Mr. Dorimant.

CHAIRMEN We will, an't like your honor.   [*Exeunt Chairmen.*]

BELLINDA Now to come off,[3] I must on:
                    In confidence and lies some hope is left;
                    'Twere hard to be found out in the first theft.   [*Exit.*]

Act V

Scene 1

[*Mrs. Loveit's. Enter Mrs. Loveit and Pert, her woman.*]

PERT Well! In my eyes, Sir Fopling is no such despicable person.

MRS. LOVEIT You are an excellent judge.

PERT He's as handsome a man as Mr. Dorimant, and as great a gallant.

MRS. LOVEIT Intolerable! Is't not enough I submit to his impertinences, but must I be plagued with yours too?

PERT Indeed, madam—

MRS. LOVEIT 'Tis false, mercenary malice—

[*Enter her Footman.*]

FOOTMAN Mrs. Bellinda, madam.

MRS. LOVEIT What of her?

FOOTMAN She's below.

MRS. LOVEIT How came she?

FOOTMAN In a chair; ambling Harry brought her.

MRS. LOVEIT [*aside*]. He bring her! His chair stands near Dorimant's door and always brings me from thence.—Run and ask him where he took her up. Go!

[*Exit Footman.*]

There is no truth in friendship neither. Women as well as men, all are false, or all are so to me at least.

PERT You are jealous of her too?

MRS. LOVEIT You had best tell her I am. 'Twill become the liberty you take of late. [*Aside.*] This fellow's bringing of her, her going out by five o'clock—I know not what to think.

[*Enter Bellinda.*]

Bellinda, you are grown an early riser, I hear.

BELLINDA Do you not wonder, my dear, what made me abroad so soon?

MRS. LOVEIT You do not use to be so.

BELLINDA The country gentlewomen I told you of—Lord, they have the oddest diversions—would never let me rest till I promised to go with them to the markets this morning to eat fruit and buy nosegays.[1]

MRS. LOVEIT Are they so fond of a filthy nosegay?

BELLINDA They complain of the stinks of the town and are never well but when they have their noses in one.

MRS. LOVEIT There are essences and sweet waters.[2]

BELLINDA Oh, they cry out upon perfumes, they are unwholesome. One of 'em was falling into a fit with the smell of these *narolii*.[3]

3. Escape, without blame.
1. Bunches of flowers.
2. Perfumes, scents.

3. Bellinda's gloves are scented with "neroli," or oil of the bitter orange.

MRS. LOVEIT Methinks, in complaisance you should have had a nosegay too.

BELLINDA Do you think, my dear, I could be so loathsome to trick myself up with carnations and stock-gillyflowers? I begged their pardon and told them I never wore anything but orange-flowers and tuberose.[4] That which made me willing to go was a strange desire I had to eat some fresh nectarines.

MRS. LOVEIT And had you any?

BELLINDA The best I ever tasted.

MRS. LOVEIT Whence came you now?

BELLINDA From their lodgings, where I crowded out of a coach and took a chair to come and see you, my dear.

MRS. LOVEIT Whither did you send for that chair?

BELLINDA 'Twas going by empty.

MRS. LOVEIT Where do these country gentlewomen lodge, I pray?

BELLINDA In the Strand, over against the Exchange.

PERT That place is never without a nest of 'em. They are always, as one goes by, fleering in balconies or staring out of windows.

[Enter Footman.]

MRS. LOVEIT *[to the Footman]* Come hither. *[Whispers.]*

BELLINDA *[aside]* This fellow by her order has been questioning the chairmen. I threatened 'em with the name of Dorimant. If they should have told truth, I am lost forever.

MRS. LOVEIT In the Strand, said you?

FOOTMAN Yes, madam, over against the Exchange.   *[Exit Footman.]*

MRS. LOVEIT She's innocent, and I am much to blame.

BELLINDA *[aside]* I am so frighted, my countenance will betray me.

MRS. LOVEIT Bellinda, what makes you look so pale?

BELLINDA Want of my usual rest and jolting up and down so long in an odious hackney.

[Footman returns]

FOOTMAN Madam, Mr. Dorimant.   *[Exit Footman.]*

MRS. LOVEIT What makes him here?

BELLINDA *[aside]* Then I am betrayed indeed. H' has broke his word, and I love a man that does not care for me.

MRS. LOVEIT Lord, you faint, Bellinda.

BELLINDA I think I shall—such an oppression[5] here on the sudden.

PERT She has eaten too much fruit, I warrant you.

MRS. LOVEIT Not unlikely.

PERT 'Tis that lies heavy on her stomach.

MRS. LOVEIT Have her into my chamber, give her some surfeit-water,[6] and let her lie down a little.

PERT Come, madam. I was a strange[7] devourer of fruit when I was young—so ravenous.

[Exeunt Bellinda and Pert, leading her off.]

MRS. LOVEIT Oh, that my love would be but calm awhile, that I might receive this man with all the scorn and indignation he deserves!

[Enter Dorimant.]

---

4. A white tropical flower.
5. Pain.
6. Distilled medicine.
7. Extraordinary.

DORIMANT Now for a touch of Sir Fopling to begin with.—Hey, page! Give positive order that none of my people stir. Let the *canaille*[8] wait, as they should do.— Since noise and nonsense have such pow'rful charms,

> "I, that I may successful prove,
> Transform myself to what you love."[9]

MRS. LOVEIT If that would do, you need not change from what you are: you can be vain and loud enough.

DORIMANT But not with so good a grace as Sir Fopling.—"Hey, Hampshire!"—Oh, that sound! That sound becomes the mouth of a man of quality.

MRS. LOVEIT Is there a thing so hateful as a senseless mimic?

DORIMANT He's a great grievance, indeed, to all who—like yourself, madam—love to play the fool in quiet.

MRS. LOVEIT A ridiculous animal, who has more of the ape than the ape has of the man in him.

DORIMANT I have as mean an opinion of a sheer mimic as yourself; yet were he all ape, I should prefer him to the gay, the giddy, brisk, insipid, noisy fool you dote on.

MRS. LOVEIT Those noisy fools, however you despise 'em, have good qualities which weigh more (or ought, at least) with us women than all the pernicious wit you have to boast of.

DORIMANT That I may hereafter have a just value for their merit, pray do me the favor to name 'em.

MRS. LOVEIT You'll despise 'em as the dull effects of ignorance and vanity, yet I care not if I mention some. First, they really admire us, while you at best but flatter us well.

DORIMANT Take heed; fools can dissemble too.

MRS. LOVEIT They may—but not so artificially as you. There is no fear they should deceive us. Then, they are assiduous, sir. They are ever offering us their service and always waiting on our will.

DORIMANT You owe that to their excessive idleness. They know not how to entertain themselves at home, and find so little welcome abroad, they are fain to fly to you who countenance 'em, as a refuge against the solitude they would be otherwise condemned to.

MRS. LOVEIT Their conversation, too, diverts us better.

DORIMANT Playing with your fan, smelling to[1] your gloves, commending your hair, and taking notice how 'tis cut and shaded after the new way—

MRS. LOVEIT Were it sillier than you can make it, you must allow 'tis pleasanter to laugh at others than to be laughed at ourselves, though never so wittily. Then, though they want skill to flatter us, they flatter themselves so well, they save us the labor. We need not take that care and pains to satisfy 'em of our love, which we so often lose on you.

DORIMANT They commonly, indeed, believe too well of themselves—and always better of you than you deserve.

MRS. LOVEIT You are in the right: they have an implicit faith in us, which keeps 'em from prying narrowly into our secrets and saves us the vexatious trouble of clearing doubts which your subtle and causeless jealousies every moment raise.

---

8. Riff-raff.
9. Lines from Waller's *To the Mutable Fair*.

1. Sniffing.

DORIMANT There is an inbred falsehood in women which inclines 'em still to them whom they may most easily deceive.

MRS. LOVEIT The man who loves above his quality[2] does not suffer more from the insolent impertinence of his mistress than the woman who loves above her understanding does from the arrogant presumptions of her friend.

DORIMANT You mistake the use of fools: they are designed for properties[3] and not for friends. You have an indifferent stock of reputation left yet. Lose it all like a frank gamester on the square.[4] 'Twill then be time enough to turn rook[5] and cheat it up again on a good, substantial bubble.[6]

MRS. LOVEIT The old and the ill-favored are only fit for properties, indeed; but young and handsome fools have met with kinder fortunes.

DORIMANT They have, to the shame of your sex be it spoken. 'Twas this, the thought of this, made me by a timely jealousy endeavor to prevent the good fortune you are providing for Sir Fopling. But against a woman's frailty all our care is vain.

MRS. LOVEIT Had I not with a dear experience bought the knowledge of your falsehood, you might have fooled me yet. This is not the first jealousy you have feigned to make a quarrel with me, and get a week to throw away on some such unknown, inconsiderable slut as you have been lately lurking with at plays.

DORIMANT Women, when they would break off with a man, never want th'address[7] to turn the fault on him.

MRS. LOVEIT You take a pride of late in using of me ill, that the town may know the power you have over me, which now (as unreasonably as yourself) expects that I, do me all the injuries you can, must love you still.

DORIMANT I am so far from expecting that you should, I begin to think you never did love me.

MRS. LOVEIT Would the memory of it were so wholly worn out in me that I did doubt it too. What made you come to disturb my growing quiet?

DORIMANT To give you joy of your growing infamy.

MRS. LOVEIT Insupportable! Insulting devil! This from you, the only author of my shame! This from another had been justice; but from you, 'tis a hellish and inhuman outrage. What have I done?

DORIMANT A thing that puts you below my scorn and makes my anger as ridiculous as you have made my love.

MRS. LOVEIT I walked last night with Sir Fopling.

DORIMANT You did, madam; and you talked and laughed aloud, "Ha, ha, ha." Oh, that laugh! That laugh becomes the confidence of a woman of quality.

MRS. LOVEIT You, who have more pleasure in the ruin of a woman's reputation than in the endearments of her love, reproach me not with yourself and I defy you to name the man can lay a blemish on my fame.

DORIMANT To be seen publicly so transported with the vain follies of that notorious fop, to me is an infamy below the sin of prostitution with another man.

MRS. LOVEIT Rail on! I am satisfied in the justice of what I did: you had provoked me to it.

DORIMANT What I did was the effect of a passion whose extravagancies you have been willing to forgive.

---

2. Above his rank.
3. As tools.
4. Without trickery.
5. Turn swindler.

6. Save your reputation by getting married to a prosperous fool.
7. The verbal skill.

MRS. LOVEIT And what I did was the effect of a passion you may forgive if you think fit.

DORIMANT Are you so indifferent grown?

MRS. LOVEIT I am.

DORIMANT Nay, then 'tis time to part. I'll send you back your letters you have so often asked for. [Looks in his pockets.] I have two or three of 'em about me.

MRS. LOVEIT Give 'em me.

DORIMANT You snatch as if you thought I would not.

[Gives her the letters.]

There. And may the perjuries in 'em be mine if e'er I see you more.

[Offers to go; she catches him.]

MRS. LOVEIT Stay!

DORIMANT I will not.

MRS. LOVEIT You shall!

DORIMANT What have you to say?

MRS. LOVEIT I cannot speak it yet.

DORIMANT Something more in commendation of the fool. Death, I want patience! Let me go.

MRS. LOVEIT I cannot. [Aside.] I can sooner part with the limbs that hold him.—I hate that nauseous fool, you know I do.

DORIMANT Was it the scandal you were fond of, then?

MRS. LOVEIT Y' had raised my anger equal to my love, a thing you ne'er could do before; and in revenge I did—I know not what I did. Would you would not think on't any more.

DORIMANT Should I be willing to forget it, I shall be daily minded of it. 'Twill be a commonplace for all the town to laugh at me, and Medley, when he is rhetorically drunk, will ever be declaiming on it in my ears.

MRS. LOVEIT 'Twill be believed a jealous spite. Come, forget it.

DORIMANT Let me consult my reputation; You are too careless of it. [Pauses.] You shall meet Sir Fopling in the Mail again tonight.

MRS. LOVEIT What mean you?

DORIMANT I have thought on it, and you must. 'Tis necessary to justify my love to the world. You can handle a coxcomb as he deserves when you are not out of humor, madam.

MRS. LOVEIT Public satisfaction for the wrong I have done you? This is some new device to make me more ridiculous.

DORIMANT Hear me.

MRS. LOVEIT I will not.

DORIMANT You will be persuaded.

MRS. LOVIET Never!

DORIMANT Are you so obstinate?

MRS. LOVEIT Are you so base?

DORIMANT You will not satisfy my love?

MRS. LOVEIT I would die to satisfy that; but I will not, to save you from a thousand racks, do a shameless thing to please your vanity.

DORIMANT Farewell, false woman.

MRS. LOVEIT Do! Go!

DORIMANT You will call me back again.

MRS. LOVEIT Exquisite fiend! I knew you came but to torment me.

[*Enter Bellinda and Pert.*]

DORIMANT [*surprised*] Bellinda here!

BELLINDA [*aside*] He starts and looks pale. The sight of me has touched his guilty soul.

PERT 'Twas but a qualm, as I said, a little indigestion. The surfeit-water did it, madam, mixed with a little mirabilis.[8]

DORIMANT [*aside*] I am confounded, and cannot guess how she came hither.

MRS. LOVEIT 'Tis your fortune, Bellinda, ever to be here when I am abused by this prodigy of ill nature.

BELLINDA I am amazed to find him here. How has he the face to come near you?

DORIMANT [*aside*] Here is fine work towards! I never was at such a loss before.

BELLINDA One who makes a public profession of breach of faith and ingratitude—I loathe the sight of him.

DORIMANT [*aside*] There is no remedy. I must submit to their tongues now and some other time bring myself off as well as I can.

BELLINDA Other men are wicked, but then they have some sense of shame. He is never well but when he triumphs—nay, glories—to a woman's face in his villainies.

MRS. LOVEIT You are in the right, Bellinda; but methinks your kindness for me makes you concern yourself too much with him.

BELLINDA It does indeed, my dear. His barbarous carriage to you yesterday made me hope you ne'er would see him more, and the very next day to find him here again provokes me strangely. But because I know you love him, I have done.

DORIMANT You have reproached me handsomely, and I deserve it for coming hither, but—

PERT You must expect it, sir. All women will hate you for my lady's sake.

DORIMANT [*aside*] Nay, if she begins too, 'tis time to fly. I shall be scolded to death, else. [*To Bellinda.*] I am to blame in some circumstances, I confess; but as to the main, I am not so guilty as you imagine. [*Aloud.*] I shall seek a more convenient time to clear myself.

MRS. LOVEIT Do it now! What impediments are here?

DORIMANT I want time, and you want temper.

MRS. LOVEIT These are weak pretenses.

DORIMANT You were never more mistaken in your life; and so farewell.

[*Dorimant flings off.*]

MRS. LOVEIT Call a footman, Pert. Quickly! I will have him dogged.

PERT I wish you would not, for my quiet and your own.

MRS. LOVEIT I'll find out the infamous cause of all our quarrels, pluck her mask off, and expose her bare-faced to the world!

[*Exit Pert.*]

BELLINDA [*aside*] Let me but escape this time, I'll never venture more.[9]

MRS. LOVEIT Bellinda, you shall go with me.

BELLINDA I have such a heaviness hangs on me with what I did this morning, I would fain go home and sleep, my dear.

MRS. LOVEIT Death and eternal darkness! I shall never sleep again. Raging fevers seize the world and make mankind as restless all as I am!   [*Exit Mrs. Loveit.*]

BELLINDA I knew him false and helped to make him so. Was not her ruin enough to fright me from the danger? It should have been, but love can take no warning.

[*Exit Bellinda.*]

---

8. Medicinal spiced wine.   9. Risk it again.

Scene 2

[*Lady Townley's house. Enter Medley, Young Bellair, Lady Townley, Emilia, and Smirk, a chaplain.*]

MEDLEY Bear up, Bellair, and do not let us see that repentance in thine we daily do in married faces.

LADY TOWNLEY This wedding will strangely surprise my brother when he knows it.

MEDLEY Your nephew ought to conceal it for a time, madam. Since marriage has lost its good name, prudent men seldom expose their own reputations till 'tis convenient to justify their wives'.

OLD BELLAIR [*without*] Where are you all there? Out, adod, will nobody hear?

LADY TOWNLEY My brother! Quickly, Mr. Smirk, into this closet.[1] You must not be seen yet.

[*Smirk goes into the closet.*]

[*Enter Old Bellair and Lady Townley's Page.*]

OLD BELLAIR [*to Page*] Desire Mr. Fourbe to walk into the lower parlor. I will be with him presently.   [*Exit Page.*]

[*To Young Bellair.*] Where have you been, sir, you could not wait on me today?

YOUNG BELLAIR About a business.

OLD BELLAIR Are you so good at business? Adod, I have a business too, you shall dispatch out of hand, sir.—Send for a parson, sister. My Lady Woodvill and her daughter are coming.

LADY TOWNLEY What need you huddle up things[2] thus?

OLD BELLAIR Out a pize! Youth is apt to play the fool, and 'tis not good it should be in their power.

LADY TOWNLEY You need not fear your son.

OLD BELLAIR H' has been idling this morning, and adod, I do not like him. [*To Emilia.*] How dost thou do, sweetheart?

EMILIA You are very severe, sir. Married in such haste!

OLD BELLAIR Go to, thou'rt a rogue, and I will talk with thee anon.

[*Enter Lady Woodvill, Harriet, and Busy.*]

Here's my Lady Woodvill come.—Welcome, madam. Mr. Fourbe's below with the writings.[3]

LADY WOODVILL Let us down and make an end, then.

OLD BELLAIR Sister, show the way. [*To Young Bellair, who is talking to Harriet.*] Harry, your business lies not there yet.—Excuse him till we have done, lady, and then, adod, he shall be for thee.—Mr. Medley, we must trouble you to be a witness.

MEDLEY I luckily came for that purpose, sir.

[*Exeunt Old Bellair, Medley, Young Bellair, Lady Townley, and Lady Woodvill.*]

BUSY [*to Harriet*] What will you do, madam?

HARRIET Be carried back and mewed up[4] in the country again, run away here— anything rather than be married to a man I do not care for.—Dear Emilia, do thou advise me.

EMILIA Mr. Bellair is engaged, you know.

HARRIET I do, but know not what the fear of losing an estate may fright him to.

EMILIA In the desp'rate condition you are in, you should consult with some judicious man. What think you of Mr. Dorimant?

---

1. Small inner room.
2. Hustle things.

3. Legal documents concerning the marriage settlement.
4. Cooped up.

HARRIET I do not think of him at all.

BUSY [aside] She thinks of nothing else, I am sure.

EMILIA How fond your mother was of Mr. Courtage.

HARRIET Because I contrived the mistake to make a little mirth, you believe I like the man.

EMILIA Mr. Bellair believes you love him.

HARRIET Men are seldom in the right when they guess at a woman's mind. Would she whom he loves loved him no better!

BUSY [aside] That's e'en well enough, on all conscience.

EMILIA Mr. Dorimant has a great deal of wit.

HARRIET And takes a great deal of pains to show it.

EMILIA He's extremely well-fashioned.

HARRIET Affectedly grave, or ridiculously wild and apish.

BUSY You defend him still against your mother.

HARRIET I would not, were he justly rallied; but I cannot hear anyone undeservedly railed at.

EMILIA Has your woman learnt the song you were so taken with?

HARRIET I was fond of a new thing. 'Tis dull at second hearing.

EMILIA Mr. Dorimant made it.

BUSY She knows it, madam, and has made me sing it at least a dozen times this morning.

HARRIET Thy tongue is as impertinent as thy fingers.

EMILIA [to Busy] You have provoked her.

BUSY 'Tis but singing the song and I shall appease her.

EMILIA Prithee, do.

HARRIET She has a voice will grate your ears worse than a catcall, and dresses[5] so ill she's scarce fit to trick up a yeoman's daughter on a holiday.

[Busy sings.]

Song, by Sir C. S.[6]

As Amoret with Phillis sat
    One evening on the plain,
And saw the charming Strephon wait
    To tell the nymph his pain,

The threat'ning danger to remove,
    She whispered in her ear,
"Ah, Phillis, if you would not love,
    This shepherd do not hear:

"None ever had so strange an art,
    His passion to convey
Into a list'ning virgin's heart
    And steal her soul away.

"Fly, fly betimes, for fear you give
    Occasion for your fate."
"In vain," said she, "in vain I strive.
    Alas, 'tis now too late."

---

5. Dresses her mistress.

6. Busy's song was probably written by Sir Car Scroope, author of the Prologue.

[*Enter Dorimant.*]

DORIMANT "Music so softens and disarms the mind—"

HARRIET "That not one arrow does resistance find."[7]

DORIMANT Let us make use of the lucky minute, then.

HARRIET [*aside, turning from Dorimant*] My love springs with my blood into my face. I dare not look upon him yet.

DORIMANT What have we here—the picture of a celebrated beauty giving audience in public to a declared lover?

HARRIET Play the dying fop and make the piece complete, sir.

DORIMANT What think you if the hint were well improved[8]—the whole mystery of making love pleasantly designed and wrought in a suit of hangings?[9]

HARRIET 'Twere needless to execute[1] fools in effigy who suffer daily in their own persons.

DORIMANT [*to Emilia, aside*] Mrs. Bride, for such I know this happy day has made you—

EMILIA Defer the formal joy you are to give me, and mind your business with her. [*Aloud.*] Here are dreadful preparations, Mr. Dorimant—writings sealing, and a parson sent for.

DORIMANT To marry this lady?

BUSY Condemned she is; and what will become of her I know not, without you generously engage in a rescue.

DORIMANT In this sad condition, madam, I can do no less than offer you my service.

HARRIET The obligation is not great: you are the common sanctuary for all young women who run from their relations.

DORIMANT I have always my arms open to receive the distressed. But I will open my heart and receive you where none yet did ever enter. You have filled it with a secret, might I but let you know it.

HARRIET Do not speak it if you would have me believe it. Your tongue is so famed for falsehood, 'twill do the truth an injury. [*Turns away her head.*]

DORIMANT Turn not away, then, but look on me and guess it.

HARRIET Did you not tell me there was no credit to be given to faces—that women nowadays have their passions as much at will as they have their complexions, and put on joy and sadness, scorn and kindness, with the same ease they do their paint and patches? Are they the only counterfeits?

DORIMANT You wrong your own while you suspect my eyes. By all the hope I have in you, the inimitable color in your cheeks is not more free from art than are the sighs I offer.

HARRIET In men who have been long hardened in sin, we have reason to mistrust the first signs of repentance.

DORIMANT The prospect of such a heav'n will make me persevere and give you marks that are infallible.

HARRIET What are those?

DORIMANT I will renounce all the joys I have in friendship and in wine, sacrifice to you all the interest I have in other women—

HARRIET Hold! Though I wish you devout, I would not have you turn fanatic. Could you neglect these a while and make a journey into the country?

DORIMANT To be with you, I could live there and never send one thought to London.

---

7. Lines from Waller's *Of My Lady Isabella, Playing on the Lute*.
8. Used to best advantage.

9. Set of tapestries.
1. Depict.

HARRIET Whate'er you say, I know all beyond High Park's a desert to you, and that no gallantry can draw you farther.

DORIMANT That has been the utmost limit of my love; but now my passion knows no bounds, and there's no measure to be taken of what I'll do for you from anything I ever did before.

HARRIET When I hear you talk thus in Hampshire, I shall begin to think there may be some little truth enlarged upon.[2]

DORIMANT Is this all? Will you not promise me—

HARRIET I hate to promise. What we do then is expected from us and wants much of the welcome it finds when it surprises.

DORIMANT May I not hope?

HARRIET That depends on you and not on me; and 'tis to no purpose to forbid it. [*Turns to Busy.*]

BUSY Faith, madam, now I perceive the gentleman loves you too. E'en let him know your mind, and torment yourselves no longer.

HARRIET Dost think I have no sense of modesty?

BUSY Think, if you lose this, you may never have another opportunity.

HARRIET May he hate me—a curse that frights me when I speak it—if ever I do a thing against the rules of decency and honor.

DORIMANT [*to Emilia*] I am beholding to you for your good intentions, madam.

EMILIA I thought the concealing of our marriage from her might have done you better service.

DORIMANT Try her again.

EMILIA [*to Harriet*] What have you resolved, madam? The time draws near.

HARRIET To be obstinate and protest against this marriage.
  [*Enter Lady Townley in haste.*]

LADY TOWNLEY [*to Emilia*] Quickly, quickly, let Mr. Smirk out of the closet!
  [*Smirk comes out of the closet.*]

HARRIET A parson! [*To Dorimant.*] Had you laid him in here?

DORIMANT I knew nothing of him.

HARRIET Should it appear you did, your opinion of my easiness may cost you dear.
  [*Enter Old Bellair, Young Bellair, Medley, and Lady Woodvill.*]

OLD BELLAIR Out a pize, the canonical hour[3] is almost past! Sister, is the man of God come?

LADY TOWNLEY [*indicating Smirk*] He waits your leisure.

OLD BELLAIR [*to Smirk*] By your favor, sir.—Adod, a pretty spruce fellow. What may we call him?

LADY TOWNLEY Mr. Smirk—my Lady Biggot's chaplain.

OLD BELLAIR A wise woman, adod she is; the man will serve for the flesh as well as the spirit.—Please you, sir, to commission a young couple to go to bed together in God's name?—Harry!

YOUNG BELLAIR Here, sir.

OLD BELLAIR Out a pize! Without your mistress in your hand?

SMIRK Is this the gentleman?

OLD BELLAIR Yes, sir.

---

2. In what you say.

3. Legally, marriages could only be performed between 8 A.M. and noon.

SMIRK Are you not mistaken, sir?

OLD BELLAIR Adod, I think not, sir!

SMIRK Sure you are, sir.

OLD BELLAIR You look as if you would forbid the banns,[4] Mr. Smirk. I hope you have no pretension to the lady.

SMIRK Wish him joy, sir. I have done him the good office today already.

OLD BELLAIR Out a pize! What do I hear?

LADY TOWNLEY Never storm, brother. The truth is out.

OLD BELLAIR How say you, sir? Is this your wedding day?

YOUNG BELLAIR It is, sir.

OLD BELLAIR And, adod, it shall be mine too. [To Emilia.] Give me thy hand, sweetheart. [She refuses.] What dost thou mean? Give me thy hand, I say!

[Emilia kneels and Young Bellair.]

LADY TOWNLEY Come, come, give her your blessing. This is the woman your son loved and is married to.

OLD BELLAIR Ha! Cheated! Cozened![5] And by your contrivance, sister!

LADY TOWNLEY What would you do with her? She's a rogue, and you can't abide her.

MEDLEY Shall I hit her a pat for you, sir?

OLD BELLAIR Adod, you are all rogues, and I never will forgive you.

[Flings away, as if to exit.]

LADY TOWNLEY Whither? Whither away?

MEDLEY Let him go and cool awhile.

LADY WOODVILL [to Dorimant] Here's a business broke out[6] now, Mr. Courtage. I am made a fine fool of.

DORIMANT You see the old gentleman knew nothing of it.

LADY WOODVILL I find he did not. I shall have some trick put upon me, if I stay in this wicked town any longer.—Harriet, dear child, where art thou? I'll into the country straight.

OLD BELLAIR Adod, madam, you shall hear me first.

[Enter Mrs. Loveit and Bellinda.]

MRS. LOVEIT Hither my man dogged him.

BELLINDA Yonder he stands, my dear.

MRS. LOVEIT I see him, [aside] and with him the face that has undone me. Oh, that I were but where I might throw out the anguish of my heart! Here it must rage within and break it.

LADY TOWNLEY Mrs. Loveit! Are you afraid to come forward?

MRS. LOVEIT I was amazed to see so much company here in a morning. The occasion sure is extraordinary.

DORIMANT [aside] Loveit and Bellinda! The devil owes me a shame today, and I think never will have done paying it.

MRS. LOVEIT Married! Dear Emilia, how am I transported with the news!

HARRIET [to Dorimant] I little thought Emilia was the woman Mr. Bellair was in love with. I'll chide her for not trusting me with the secret.

DORIMANT How do you like Mrs. Loveit?

4. Raise an objection to the marriage.   6. Revealed.
5. Swindled!

HARRIET She's a famed mistress of yours, I hear.

DORIMANT She has been, on occasion.

OLD BELLAIR [to Lady Woodvill] Adod, madam, I cannot help it.

LADY WOODVILL You need make no more apologies, sir.

EMILIA [to Mrs. Loveit] The old gentleman's excusing himself to my Lady Woodvill.

MRS. LOVEIT Ha, ha, ha! I never heard of anything so pleasant.

HARRIET [to Dorimant] She's extremely overjoyed at something.

DORIMANT At nothing. She is one of those hoiting[7] ladies who gaily fling themselves about and force a laugh when their aching hearts are full of discontent and malice.

MRS. LOVEIT Oh heav'n, I was never so near killing myself with laughing.—Mr. Dorimant, are you a brideman?

LADY WOODVILL Mr. Dorimant! Is this Mr. Dorimant, madam?

MRS. LOVEIT If you doubt it, your daughter can resolve you, I suppose.

LADY WOODVILL I am cheated too, basely cheated!

OLD BELLAIR Out a pize, what's here? More knavery yet?

LADY WOODVILL Harriet! On my blessing, come away, I charge you.

HARRIET Dear mother, do but stay and hear me.

LADY WOODVILL I am betrayed! And thou art undone, I fear.

HARRIET Do not fear it. I have not, nor never will, do anything against my duty. Believe me, dear mother, do!

DORIMANT [to Mrs. Loveit] I had trusted you with this secret but that I knew the violence of your nature would ruin my fortune—as now unluckily it has. I thank you, madam.

MRS. LOVEIT She's an heiress, I know, and very rich.

DORIMANT To satisfy you, I must give up my interest wholly to my love. Had you been a reasonable woman, I might have secured 'em both and been happy.

MRS. LOVEIT You might have trusted me with anything of this kind; you know you might. Why did you go under a wrong name?

DORIMANT The story is too long to tell you now. Be satisfied; this is the business, this is the mask has kept me from you.

BELLINDA [aside] He's tender of my honor, though he's cruel to my love.

MRS. LOVEIT Was it no idle mistress, then?

DORIMANT Believe me—a wife, to repair the ruins of my estate that needs it.

MRS. LOVEIT The knowledge of this makes my grief hang lighter on my soul, but I shall never more be happy.

DORIMANT Bellinda—

BELLINDA Do not think of clearing yourself with me. It is impossible. Do all men break their words thus?

DORIMANT Th'extravagant words they speak in love. 'Tis as unreasonable to expect we should perform all we promise then, as do all we threaten when we are angry. When I see you next—

BELLINDA Take no notice of me, and I shall not hate you.

DORIMANT How came you to Mrs. Loveit?

BELLINDA By a mistake the chairmen made for want of my giving them directions.

DORIMANT 'Twas a pleasant one. We must meet again.

BELLINDA Never.

7. Giddy, strident.

DORIMANT Never?

BELLINDA When we do, may I be as infamous as you are false.

LADY TOWNLEY [to Lady Woodvill] Men of Mr. Dorimant's character always suffer in the general opinion of the world.

MEDLEY You can make no judgment of a witty man from common fame, considering the prevailing faction,[8] madam.

OLD BELLAIR Adod, he's in the right.

MEDLEY Besides, 'tis a common error among women to believe too well of them they know and too ill of them they don't.

OLD BELLAIR Adod, he observes well.

LADY TOWNLEY Believe me, madam, you will find Mr. Dorimant as civil a gentleman as you thought Mr. Courtage.

HARRIET If you would but know him better—

LADY WOODVILL You have a mind to know him better? Come away! You shall never see him more.

HARRIET Dear mother, stay!

LADY WOODVILL I would not be consenting to your ruin.

HARRIET Were my fortune in your power—

LADY WOODVILL Your person is.

HARRIET Could I be disobedient, I might take it out of yours and put it into his.

LADY WOODVILL 'Tis that you would be at! You would marry this Dorimant!

HARRIET I cannot deny it. I would, and never will marry any other man.

LADY WOODVILL Is this the duty that you promised?

HARRIET But I will never marry him against your will.

LADY WOODVILL [aside] She knows the way to melt my heart. [To Harriet.] Upon yourself light your undoing.

MEDLEY [to Old Bellair] Come, sir, you have not the heart any longer to refuse your blessing.

OLD BELLAIR Adod, I ha' not.—Rise, and God bless you both. Make much of her, Harry; she deserves thy kindness. [To Emilia.] Adod, sirrah, I did not think it had been in thee.

[Enter Sir Fopling and his Page.]

SIR FOPLING 'Tis a damned windy day. Hey, page! Is my periwig right?

PAGE A little out of order, sir.

SIR FOPLING Pox o' this apartment! It wants an antechamber to adjust oneself in. [To Mrs. Loveit.] Madam, I came from your house, and your servants directed me hither.

MRS. LOVEIT I will give order hereafter they shall direct you better.

SIR FOPLING The great satisfaction I had in the Mail last night has given me much disquiet since.

MRS. LOVEIT 'Tis likely to give me more than I desire.

SIR FOPLING [aside] What the devil makes her so reserved? Am I guilty of an indiscretion, madam?

MRS. LOVEIT You will be of a great one, if you continue your mistake, sir.

SIR FOPLING Something puts you out of humor.

MRS. LOVEIT The most foolish, inconsiderable thing that ever did.

8. I.e., the quality of the people who condemn the "wits."

SIR FOPLING Is it in my power?

MRS. LOVEIT To hang or drown it. Do one of 'em, and trouble me no more.

SIR FOPLING So *fière?*[9] *Serviteur,*[1] madam.—Medley, where's Dorimant?

MEDLEY Methinks the lady has not made you those advances today she did last night, Sir Fopling.

SIR FOPLING Prithee, do not talk of her.

MEDLEY She would be a *bonne fortune.*

SIR FOPLING Not to me at present.

MEDLEY How so?

SIR FOPLING An intrigue now would be but a temptation to me to throw away that vigor on one which I mean shall shortly make my court to the whole sex in a ballet.

MEDLEY Wisely considered, Sir Fopling.

SIR FOPLING No one woman is worth the loss of a cut in a caper.[2]

MEDLEY Not when 'tis so universally designed.[3]

LADY WOODVILL Mr. Dorimant, everyone has spoke so much in your behalf that I can no longer doubt but I was in the wrong.

MRS. LOVEIT [*to Bellinda*] There's nothing but falsehood and impertinence in this world. All men are villains or fools. Take example from my misfortunes. Bellinda, if thou wouldst be happy, give thyself wholly up to goodness.

HARRIET [*to Mrs. Loveit*] Mr. Dorimant has been your God almighty long enough. 'Tis time to think of another.

MRS. LOVEIT [*to Bellinda*] Jeered by her! I will lock myself up in my house and never see the world again.

HARRIET A nunnery is the more fashionable place for such a retreat and has been the fatal consequence of many a *belle passion.*

MRS. LOVEIT [*aside*] Hold, heart, till I get home! Should I answer, 'twould make her triumph greater.   [*Is going out.*]

DORIMANT Your hand, Sir Fopling—

SIR FOPLING Shall I wait upon you, madam?

MRS. LOVEIT Legion of fools, as many devils take thee!

[*Exit Mrs. Loveit.*]

MEDLEY Dorimant, I pronounce thy reputation clear; and henceforward, when I would know anything of woman, I will consult no other oracle.

SIR FOPLING Stark mad, by all that's handsome!—Dorimant, thou hast engaged me in a pretty business.

DORIMANT I have not leisure now to talk about it.

OLD BELLAIR Out a pize, what does this man of mode do here again?

LADY TOWNLEY He'll be an excellent entertainment within, brother, and is luckily come to raise the mirth of the company.

LADY WOODVILL Madam, I take my leave of you.

LADY TOWNLEY What do you mean, madam?

LADY WOODVILL To go this afternoon part of my way to Hartly.[4]

OLD BELLAIR Adod, you shall stay and dine first! Come, we will all be good friends; and you shall give Mr. Dorimant leave to wait upon you and your daughter in the country.

---

9. Proud.
1. Your servant.
2. A leap in dancing.

3. Not when the leap might please so many at one time.
4. The location of Lady Woodvill's country house in Hampshire.

LADY WOODVILL If his occasions[5] bring him that way, I have now so good an opinion of him, he shall be welcome.

HARRIET To a great, rambling, lone house that looks as it were not inhabited, the family's so small. There you'll find my mother, an old lame aunt, and myself, sir, perched up on chairs at a distance in a large parlor, sitting moping like three or four melancholy birds in a spacious volary.[6] Does not this stagger your resolution?

DORIMANT Not at all, madam. The first time I saw you, you left me with the pangs of love upon me; and this day my soul has quite given up her liberty.

HARRIET This is more dismal than the country.—Emilia, pity me who am going to that sad place. Methinks I hear the hateful noise of rooks[7] already—kaw, kaw, kaw. There's music in the worst cry[8] in London. "My dill and cucumbers to pickle."

OLD BELLAIR Sister, knowing of this matter, I hope you have provided us some good cheer.

LADY TOWNLEY I have, brother, and the fiddles too.

OLD BELLAIR Let 'em strike up then. The young lady shall have a dance before she departs.

[Dance.]

[After the dance.] So now we'll in, and make this an arrant[9] wedding day.

[To the pit.]

And if these honest gentlemen rejoice,
Adod, the boy has made a happy choice.

[Exeunt omnes.]

The Epilogue

BY MR. DRYDEN[1]

Most modern wits such monstrous fools have shown,
They seemed not of heav'n's making, but their own.
Those nauseous harlequins° in farce may pass,   *clowns*
But there goes more to a substantial ass;
5   Something of man must be exposed to view,
That, gallants, it may more resemble you.
Sir Fopling is a fool so nicely writ,
The ladies would mistake him for a wit
And when he sings, talks loud, and cocks,° would cry: *struts*
10   "Ay, now methinks he's pretty company—
So brisk, so gay, so traveled, so refined,
As he took pains to graft upon his kind."[2]
True fops help nature's work, and go to school
To file and finish God a'mighty's fool.
15   Yet none Sir Fopling him, or him, can call:

---

5. Business affairs.
6. Bird cage.
7. Crows.
8. Street vendor's shout.
9. Genuine; but "arrant" also carried the pejorative con-

notation "notorious."
1. The playwright and poet John Dryden was a friend of Etherege's.
2. Add to his own natural properties.

He's knight of th' shire³ and represents ye all.
From each he meets, he culls whate'er he can;
Legion's his name, a people in a man.
His bulky folly gathers as it goes,
20   And, rolling o'er you, like a snowball grows.
His various modes from various fathers follow;
One taught the toss,⁴ and one the new French wallow.°   *rolling walk*
His sword-knot,⁵ this; his cravat, this designed;
And this, the yard-long snake⁶ he twirls behind.
25   From one, the sacred periwig he gained,
Which wind ne'er blew, nor touch of hat prophaned;
Another's diving bow he did adore,
Which with a shog° casts all the hair before,   *shake*
Till he with full decorum brings it back
30   And rises with a water spaniel shake.
As for his songs (the ladies' dear delight),
Those sure he took from most of you who write.
Yet every man is safe from what he feared,
For no one fool is hunted from the herd.

FINIS

THE MAN OF MODE IN CONTEXT
The Collier Controversy

The Man of Mode was often revived in the half-century following its debut; during the same period, it sustained a second life as a recurrent test case in a long-running critical controversy about the nature of comedy, and about the viability of theater as a moral force in the lives of its audiences. Jeremy Collier, a clergyman who initiated the controversy in 1698 with his caustic *Short View of the Immorality and Profaneness of the English Stage*, wrote in the hope of eliminating theaters altogether. By portraying wickedness in ways that give delight, he argued, contemporary plays cultivated in their audience the vices of their characters. Since "nothing can be more disserviceable to probity and religion than the management of the stage," he concluded, the stage should be not merely censored but abolished. Thirteen years later the essayist and playwright Richard Steele, writing in the pages of his spectacularly successful periodical *The Spectator*, recapitulated many of Collier's arguments, using *The Man of Mode* as his chief exhibit of what a comedy should not do. His intent, though, differed strikingly from Collier's: as a practitioner in the theater, he wrote not to eliminate but to reform it, and to pave the way for the sentimental, moralizing comedy of which he was himself a pioneer. The playwright and critic John Dennis remained active throughout the two decades of the controversy. In the 1690s, he had appeared as Collier's most articulate antagonist; in the 1720s, he took up arms against Collier's quasi-successor Steele. In his *Defense of Sir Fopling Flutter*, he confronted the charges against Etherege levelled by the *Spectator*. On the very eve of Steele's definitive theatrical triumph (with the sentimental play *The Conscious Lovers*), Dennis fought a rearguard action in favor of the Restoration comedy that he had learned to love in his youth and (unlike many in the culture) had neither outgrown nor renounced.

---

3. Member of Parliament for a county.
4. I.e., of the head.

5. Ribbon tied to a sword hilt.
6. Long curl or pigtail attached to a wig.

Jeremy Collier[1]
from *A Short View of the Immorality and Profaneness
of the English Stage*

To sum up the evidence.[2] A fine gentleman is a fine whoring, swearing, smutty, atheistical man. These qualifications, it seems, complete the idea of honor. They are the top improvements of fortune, and the distinguishing glories of birth and breeding! This is the stage-test for quality, and those that can't stand it ought to be disclaimed. The restraints of conscience and the pedantry of virtue are unbecoming a cavalier: future securities and reaching beyond life are vulgar provisions. If he falls a-thinking at this rate, he forfeits his honor; for his head was only made to run against a post! Here you have a man of breeding and figure that burlesques the Bible, swears and talks smut to ladies, speaks ill of his friend behind his back, and betrays his interest. A fine gentleman that has neither honesty nor honor, conscience nor manners, good nature nor civil hypocrisy:[3] fine only in the insignificancy of life, the abuse of religion, and the scandals of conversation. These worshipful things are the poet's favorites: they appear at the head of the fashion, and shine in character and equipage. If there is any sense stirring, they must have it,[4] though the rest of the stage suffer never so much by the partiality. And what can be the meaning of this wretched distribution of honor? Is it not to give credit and countenance to vice, and to shame young people out of all pretense to conscience and regularity? They seem forced to turn lewd in their own defense: they can't otherwise justify themselves to the fashion, nor keep up the character of gentlemen. Thus people not well furnished with thought and experience are debauched both in practice and principle. And thus religion grows uncreditable, and passes for ill education. The stage seldom gives quarter to anything that's serviceable or significant, but persecutes worth and goodness under every appearance. He that would be safe from their satire must take care to disguise himself in vice, and hang out the colors of debauchery. How often is learning, industry, and frugality ridiculed in comedy? The rich citizens are often misers and cuckolds, and the universities, schools of pedantry upon this score. In short, libertinism and profaneness, dressing, idleness, and gallantry are the only valuable qualities. As if people were not apt enough of themselves to be lazy, lewd, and extravagant, unless they were pricked forward and provoked by glory and reputation. Thus the marks of honor and infamy are misapplied, and the ideas of virtue and vice confounded. Thus monstrousness goes for proportion, and the blemishes of human nature make up the beauties of it.

The fine ladies are of the same cut with the gentlemen. Moraima is scandalously rude to her father, helps him to a beating, and runs away with Antonio.[5] Angelica talks saucily to her uncle,[6] and Belinda confesses her inclination for a gallant.[7] And

---

1. "Contest was his delight," Samuel Johnson wrote of Collier (1650–1726); that predilection often got the clergyman in trouble. As a vociferous opponent of William and Mary's "bloodless revolution" and Whig government, Collier spent time both in prison and in hiding, from charges that he had publicly granted absolution to two men about to be executed for plotting to assassinate the king. In his *Short View,* Collier made the theater a stalking horse for his political agenda, attacking the perceived licentiousness of the Whig regime while aligning himself with the widespread movement for reform of morals and of manners (which the monarchs themselves had in fact repeatedly endorsed). After the *Short View* appeared, some playwrights were prosecuted, some actors fined, and

Collier himself was prompted to produce many sequels, in which he carried on the combat with his detractors.
2. At this point, Collier has just finished a survey of Restoration comedies in which (as he declares in the title of the present chapter) the playwrights "make their principal persons vicious, and reward them at the end of the play."
3. I.e., he does not even tell white lies.
4. If there is any intelligence displayed, it is given to the leads, who are all dissolute gentlemen.
5. In Dryden's *Don Sebastian* (1689).
6. In William Congreve's *Love for Love* (1695).
7. In John Vanbrugh's *The Provoked Wife* (1697).

as I have observed already, the topping[8] ladies in the *Mock Astrologer, Spanish Friar, Country Wife, Old Bachelor, Orphan, Double Dealer,* and *Love Triumphant* are smutty, and sometimes profane. * * *

Indeed, to make delight the main business of comedy is an unreasonable and dangerous principle: it opens the way to all licentiousness, and confounds the distinction between mirth and madness. For if diversion is the chief end, it must be had at any price. No serviceable expedient must be refused, though never so scandalous. And thus the worst things are said, and the best abused; religion is insulted, and the most serious matters turned into ridicule! As if the blind side of an audience ought to be caressed, and their folly and atheism entertained in the first place. Yes, if the palate is pleased, no matter though the body is poisoned! For can one die of an easier disease than diversion? But raillery[9] apart, certainly mirth and laughing without respect to the cause are not such supreme satisfactions! A man has sometimes pleasure in losing his wits. Frenzy and possession will shake the lungs and brighten the face; and yet I suppose they are not much to be coveted. However, now we know the reason of the profaneness and obscenity of the stage, of their hellish cursing and swearing, and in short of their great industry to make God and goodness contemptible: 'tis all to satisfy the company, and make people laugh! A most admirable justification! What can be more engaging to an audience than to see a poet thus atheistically brave? To see him charge up to the cannon's mouth, and defy the vengeance of Heaven to serve them? Besides, there may be somewhat of convenience in the case. To fetch diversion out of innocence is no such easy matter. There's no succeeding, it may be, in this method without sweat and drudging. Clean wit, inoffensive humor, and handsome contrivance require time and thought. And who would be at this expense, when the purchase is so cheap another way? 'Tis possible a poet may not always have sense enough by him for such an occasion. And since we are upon supposals, it may be the audience is not to be gained without straining a point, and giving a loose to[1] conscience. And when people are sick, are they not to be humored? In fine, we must make them laugh, right or wrong, for "delight" is the "chief end of comedy."[2] Delight! He should have said debauchery: that's the English of the word, and the consequence of the practice. But the original design of comedy was otherwise. And granting 'twas not so, what then? If the ends of things are naught, they must be mended. Mischief is the chief end of malice; would it be then a blemish in ill nature to change temper, and relent into goodness? The chief end of a madman it may be is to fire a house; must we not therefore bind him in his bed? To conclude. If delight without restraint or distinction, without conscience or shame, is the supreme law of comedy, 'twere well if we had less on't. Arbitrary pleasure is more dangerous than arbitrary power. Nothing is more brutal than to be abandoned to appetite; and nothing more wretched than to serve in such a design. The Mock-Astrologer, to clear himself of this imputation, is glad to give up his principle at last. "Lest any man should think" (says he) "that I write this to make libertinism amiable, or that I cared not to debate the end and institution of comedy" (it seems then delight is not the chief end) "I must further declare that we make not vicious persons happy, but only as Heaven makes sinners so, etc." If this will hold all's well. But

---

8. Distinguished, fine.
9. Good-humored ridicule.
1. Entirely letting go of.
2. Here and below, Collier quotes and rebuts John Dry-

den's preface to his comedy *An Evening's Love: or, The Mock Astrologer* (produced 1668, published 1671). In his preface, Dryden defended his work against charges of immorality.

Heaven does not forgive without repentance. Let us see then what satisfaction he requires from his Wild-Blood, and what discipline he puts him under. Why, he helps him to his mistress, he marries him to a lady of birth and fortune. And now do you think he has not made him an example, and punished him to some purpose! These are frightful severities! Who would be vicious when such terrors hang over his head? And does "Heaven make sinners happy" upon these conditions? Sure some people have a good opinion of vice, or a very ill one of marriage, otherwise they would have charged the penance a little more. But I have nothing further with the Mock-Astrologer. * * *

1698   1698

Richard Steele[1]
The Spectator, No. 65

Tuesday, May 15, 1711

> *. . . Demetri, teque, Tigell;*
> *Discipularum inter Jubeo plorare cathedras.*
>
> *Hor.*[2]

After having at large explained what wit is, and described the false appearances of it, all that labor seems but an useless inquiry, without some time be spent in considering the application of it. The seat of wit, when one speaks as a man of the town and the world, is the playhouse; I shall therefore fill this paper with reflections upon the use of it in that place. The application of wit in the theater has as strong an effect upon the manners of our gentlemen, as the taste of it has upon the writings of our authors. It may, perhaps, look like a very presumptuous work, though not foreign from the duty of a Spectator, to tax the writings of such as have long had the general applause of a nation: but I shall always make reason, truth, and nature the measures of praise and dispraise; if those are for me, the generality of opinion is of no consequence against me; if they are against me, the general opinion cannot long support me.

Without further preface, I am going to look into some of our most applauded plays, and see whether they deserve the figure[3] they at present bear in the imaginations of men, or not.

In reflecting upon these works, I shall chiefly dwell upon that for which each respective play is most celebrated. The present paper shall be employed upon *Sir Fopling Flutter*. The received character of this play is, that it is the pattern of genteel[4] comedy. Dorimant and Harriet are the characters of greatest consequence,[5] and if these are low and mean, the reputation of the play is very unjust.

---

1. Impressed by Collier's arguments but devoted to the theater, the playwright, journalist, and essayist Richard Steele (1672–1729) began in the early 1700s to experiment with a new kind of comedy, one populated by paragons rather than by reprobates, "which might" (as he put it) "be no improper entertainment in a Christian commonwealth." His *Spectator* papers on *The Man of Mode* (Nos. 65 and 75) were partly propaganda for this endeavor. In No. 65 Steele picks up on one of Collier's key phrases—"the fine gentleman"—and turns it to his own account. Where Collier uses the phrase sarcastically, to describe the stage rakes of Restoration comedy, Steele finds it full of redemptive possibility: the stage (like the periodical page) might present the reader with models of

people authentically "fine." A few years later, Steele made *The Fine Gentleman* the working title for the play that would bring him his greatest success in the new comic mode, *The Conscious Lovers* (1722).

2. The ancient Roman poet, Horace (65–8 B.C.): "Demetrius and Tigellius, know your place; / Go hence, and whine among the schoolboy race" (*Satires*, Book 1, 10.90).

3. Admired position.

4. Characteristic of persons of quality (those who are well bred).

5. Importance (as romantic leads); also rank, social distinction.

I will take for granted, that a fine gentleman should be honest in his actions, and refined in his language. Instead of this, our hero, in this piece, is a direct knave in his designs, and a clown in his language. Bellair is his admirer and friend, in return for which, because he is forsooth a greater wit than his said friend, he thinks it reasonable to persuade him to marry a young lady whose virtue, he thinks, will last no longer than 'till she is a wife, and then she cannot but fall to his share, as he is an irresistible fine gentleman. The falsehood to Mrs. Loveit, and the barbarity of triumphing over her anguish for losing him, is another instance of his honesty as well as his good nature. As to his fine language: he calls the Orange-Woman, who, it seems, is inclined to grow fat, "an over-grown jade, with a flasket of guts before her"; and salutes her with a pretty phrase of, "How now, double tripe?" Upon the mention of a country gentlewoman, whom he knows nothing of (no one can imagine why), he "will lay his life she is some awkward, ill-fashioned country toad, who not having above four dozen of hairs on her head, has adorned her baldness with a large white fruz, that she may look sparkishly in the forefront of the King's box at an old play." Unnatural mixture of senseless common place![6]

As to the generosity of his temper, he tells his poor footman, if he did not wait better he would turn him away, in the insolent phrase of, "I'll uncase you."

Now for Mrs. Harriet: she laughs at obedience to an absent mother, whose tenderness Busy describes to be very exquisite, for "that she is so pleased with finding Harriet again that she cannot chide her for being out of the way." This witty daughter, and fine lady, has so little respect for this good woman that she ridicules her air in taking leave, and cries, "In what struggle is my poor mother yonder? See, see, her head tottering, her eyes staring, and her underlip trembling." But all this is atoned for, because "she has more wit than is usual in her sex, and as much malice, though she is as wild as you would wish her, and has a demureness in her looks that makes it so surprising!" Then to recommend her as a fit spouse for his hero, the poet makes her speak her sense of marriage very ingeniously. "I think," says she, "I might be brought to endure him, and that is all a reasonable woman should expect in a husband." It is, methinks, unnatural that we are not made to understand how she that was bred under a silly pious old mother, that would never trust her out of her sight, came to be so polite.

It cannot be denied, but that the negligence of everything, which engages the attention of the sober and valuable part of mankind, appears very well drawn in this piece: but it is denied, that it is necessary to the character of a fine gentleman that he should in that manner trample upon all order and decency. As for the character of Dorimant, it is more of a coxcomb[7] than that of Fopling. He says of one of his companions that a good correspondence between them is their mutual interest. Speaking of that friend, he declares, their being much together "makes the women think the better of his understanding, and judge more favorably of my reputation. It makes him pass upon some for a man of very good sense, and me upon others for a very civil person."

This whole celebrated piece is a perfect contradiction to good manners, good sense, and common honesty; and as there is nothing in it but what is built upon the ruin of virtue and innocence, according to the notion of merit in this comedy, I take the Shoemaker to be, in reality, the fine gentleman of the play: for it seems he is an

---

6. Trite phrases.   7. A vain, conceited fop.

atheist, if we may depend upon his character as given by the Orange-Woman, who is herself far from being the lowest in the play. She says of a fine man, who is Dorimant's companion, there "is not such another heathen in the town, except the Shoemaker." His pretension[8] to be the hero of the drama appears still more in his own description of his way of living with his lady. "There is," says he, "never a man in town lives more like a gentleman with his wife than I do; I never mind her motions; she never inquires into mine. We speak to one another civilly, hate one another heartily; and because it is vulgar to lie and soak together, we have each of us our several settle-bed." That of "soaking together" is as good as if Dorimant had spoken it himself; and, I think, since he puts human nature in as ugly a form as the circumstance will bear, and is a staunch unbeliever, he is very much wronged in having no part of the good fortune bestowed in the last act.

To speak plainly of this whole work, I think nothing but being lost to a sense of innocence and virtue can make anyone see this comedy, without observing more frequent occasion to move sorrow and indignation, than mirth and laughter. At the same time I allow it to be nature, but it is nature in its utmost corruption and degeneracy.

John Dennis[1]
from *A Defense of "Sir Fopling Flutter,"*
A Comedy Written by Sir George Etherege

A certain knight, who has employed so much of his empty labor in extolling the weak performances of some living authors, has scurrilously and inhumanly in the sixty-fifth *Spectator* attacked one of the most entertaining comedies of the last age, written by a most ingenious gentleman, who perfectly understood the world, the Court, and the town, and whose reputation has now for near thirty years together survived his person, and will, in all probability, survive it as long as comedy shall be in vogue; by which proceeding, this worthy knight has incurred the double censure that Olivia in *The Plain Dealer* has cast upon a certain coxcomb, "who rather," says she, "than not flatter, will flatter the poets of the age, whom none will flatter; and rather than not rail, will rail at the dead, at whom none besides will rail."[2] * * *

What the knight falsely and impudently says of the comedy, may be justly said of the criticism, and of the whole sixty-fifth *Spectator*, that 'tis a perfect contradiction to good manners and good sense. He allows this comedy, he says, to be in nature, but 'tis nature in its utmost corruption and degeneracy.

Suppose this were true, I would feign know where he learnt that nature in its utmost corruption and degeneracy, is not the proper subject of comedy? Is not this a merry person, who, after he has been writing what he calls comedy for twenty years

8. Claim.

1. Son of a London saddler, born on the verge of the Restoration, John Dennis (1658–1734) was early enamored of the world of wits and gallants that Etherege depicted in *The Man of Mode*. He sought a way into it by ingratiating himself among its leading writers. When the Jacobite Collier launched his attack on the immorality of the theater, the Whig Dennis retorted by upholding "the usefulness of the stage" in a book so titled (1698) that procured him some fame. Twenty-two years later, in his *Defense of "Sir Fopling Flutter,"* Dennis expanded on some of his earlier arguments, but with a purpose at once more personal and particular. He was now countering not Collier but Steele, whom he suspected of having caused the failure of his most recent play at Drury Lane. Dennis timed his pamphlet to coincide with the opening of Steele's long-prepared, much-publicized sentimental comedy *The Conscious Lovers*. With the success of Steele's play, a new mode of comedy firmly supplanted the old, despite Dennis's spirited *Defense*.

2. Loosely quoted from William Wycherley's *The Plain Dealer* (1676) (2.1.126–129).

together, shows plainly to all the world that he knows nothing of the nature of true comedy, and that he has not learnt the very first rudiments of an art which he pretends to teach? I must confess, the ridicule in *Sir Fopling Flutter* is an imitation of corrupt and degenerate nature, but not the most corrupt and the most degenerate; for there is neither adultery, murder, nor sodomy in it. But can anything but corrupt and degenerate nature be the proper subject of ridicule? And can anything but ridicule be the proper subject of comedy? Has not Aristotle told us in the fifth chapter of his *Poetics* that comedy is an imitation of the very worst of men? Not the worst, says he, in every sort of vice, but the worst in the ridicule. And has not Horace, in the fourth satire of his first book, reminded us that the old Athenian comic poets made it their business to bring all sorts of villains upon the stage, adulterers, cheats, thieves, murderers? But then they always took care, says a modern critic, that those several villainies should be enveloped in the ridicule which alone, says he, could make them the proper subjects of comedy. If this facetious knight had formerly lived at Lacedaemon[3] with the same wrong-turned noddle[4] that he has now among us, would he not, do you think, have inveighed against that people, for showing their drunken slaves to their children?[5] Would he not have represented it as a thing of most pernicious example? What the Lacedaemonians did by drunkenness, the comic poet does by that and all other vices. He exposes them to the view of his fellow subjects, for no other reason than to render them ridiculous and contemptible.

But the criticism of the knight in the foresaid *Spectator* is as contrary to good manners as it is to good sense. What Aristotle and his interpreters say of tragedy, that 'tis infallibly good when it pleases both the judges and the people, is certainly as true of comedy; for the judges are equally qualified to judge of both, and the people may be supposed to be better judges of comedy than they are of tragedy, because comedy is nothing but a picture of common life, and a representation of their own humors[6] and manners. Now this comedy of *Sir Fopling Flutter* has not been only well received, and believed by the people of England to be a most agreeable comedy for about half a century, but the judges have been still more pleased with it than the people. They have justly believed (I speak of the judges) that the characters, and especially the principal characters, are admirably drawn to answer the two ends of comedy, pleasure and instruction; and that the dialogue is the most charming that has been writ by the moderns: that with purity and simplicity, it has art and elegance; and with force and vivacity, the utmost grace and delicacy. This, I know very well, was the opinion of the most eminent writers, and of the best judges contemporary with the author; and of the whole court of King Charles the Second, a court the most polite that ever England saw.

Now, after this comedy has passed with the whole people of England, the knowing as well as the ignorant, for a most entertaining and most instructive comedy, for fifty years together, after that long time comes a two-penny author, who has given a thousand proofs through the course of his rhapsodies that he understands not a tittle[7] of all this matter; this author comes and impudently declares that this whole celebrated piece, that has for half a century been admired by the whole people of Great

---

3. Sparta, ancient Greek city-state known for bravery and rectitude.
4. Empty head.
5. As examples of how not to behave.
6. Traits.
7. Bit.

Britain, is "a perfect contradiction to good sense, to good manners, and to common honesty." *O Tempora! O Mores!*[8]

The knight certainly wrote the forementioned *Spectator*, though it has been writ these ten years, on purpose to make way for his fine gentlemen,[9] and therefore he endeavors to prove that *Sir Fopling* is not that genteel comedy, which the world allows it to be. * * *

To prove that this comedy is not a genteel one, he endeavors to prove that one of the principal characters, is not a fine gentleman. I appeal to every impartial man if, when he says that a man or a woman are genteel, he means anything more than that they are agreeable in their air, graceful in their motions, and polite in their conversation. But when he endeavors to prove that Dorimant is not a fine gentleman, he says no more to the purpose than he said before, when he affirmed that the comedy is not a genteel comedy; for either the author designed in Dorimant a fine gentleman, or he did not. If he did not, the character is ne'er the less excellent on that account, because Dorimant is an admirable picture of a courtier in the court of King Charles the Second. But if Dorimant was designed for a fine gentleman by the author, he was obliged to accommodate himself to that notion of a fine gentleman, which the Court and the town both had at the time of the writing of this comedy. 'Tis reasonable to believe, that he did so, and we see that he succeeded accordingly. For Dorimant not only passed for a fine gentleman with the court of King Charles the Second, but he has passed for such with all the world, for fifty years together. And what indeed can anyone mean, when he speaks of a fine gentleman, but one who is qualified in conversation, to please the best company of either sex? * * *

How little do they know of the nature of true comedy, who believe that its proper business is to set us patterns for imitation: for all such patterns are serious things, and laughter is the life, and the very soul of comedy. 'Tis its proper business to expose persons to our view, whose views we may shun, and whose follies we may despise; and by showing us what is done upon the comic stage, to show us what ought never to be done upon the stage of the world.

All the characters in *Sir Fopling Flutter*, and especially the principal characters, are admirably drawn, both to please and to instruct. First, they are drawn to please, because they are drawn in the truth of Nature; but to be drawn in the truth of Nature, they must be drawn with those qualities that are proper to each respective season of life.

* * * The characters in *Sir Fopling* are admirably contrived to please, and more particularly the principal ones, because we find in those characters, a true resemblance of the persons both in Court and town, who lived at the time when that comedy was writ: for Rapin[1] tells us with a great deal of judgment, that "comedy is as it ought to be, when an audience is apt to imagine, that instead of being in the pit and boxes, they are in some assembly of the neighborhood, or in some family meeting, and that we see nothing done in it, but what is done in the world. For it is," says he, "not worth one farthing, if we do not discover ourselves in it, and do not

8. "What times! What manners!" (Cicero, *Against Catiline* 1.1).
9. Steele had been at work on *The Conscious Lovers* (initially titled *The Fine Gentleman*) for several years (though probably not as far back as when he wrote *The Spectator*).
1. René Rapin, a 17th-century French critic whose commentary on Aristotle had appeared in English as *Reflections on Aristotle's Poesie* (London, 1716).

find in it both our own manners, and those of the persons with whom we live and converse."[2]

The reason of this rule is manifest: for as 'tis the business of a comic poet to cure his spectators of vice and folly, by the apprehension of being laughed at, 'tis plain that his business must be with the reigning follies and vices. The violent passions, which are the subjects of tragedy, are the same in every age, and appear with the same face; but those vices and follies which are the subjects of comedy, are seen to vary continually: some of those that belonged to our ancestors, have no relation to us, and can no more come under the cognizance[3] of our present comic poets, than the sweating and sneezing sickness[4] can come under the practice of our contemporary physicians. What vices and follies may infect those who are to come after us, we know not; 'tis the present, the reigning vices and follies, that must be the subjects of our present comedy: the comic poet therefore must take characters from such persons as are his contemporaries, and are infected with the foresaid follies and vices. * * *

Now I remember very well, that upon the first acting this comedy, it was generally believed to be an agreeable representation of the persons of condition of both sexes, both in Court and town; and that all the world was charmed with Dorimant; and that it was unanimously agreed, that he had in him several of the qualities of Wilmot, Earl of Rochester,[5] as, his wit, his spirit, his amorous temper, the charms that he had for the fair sex, his falsehood, and his inconstancy; the agreeable manner of his chiding his servants, which the late Bishop of Salisbury takes notice of in his *Life*;[6] and lastly, his repeating, on every occasion, the verses of Waller,[7] for whom that noble lord had a very particular esteem. * * *

But the characters in this comedy are very well formed to instruct as well as to please, especially those of Dorimant and of Loveit; and they instruct by the same qualities to which the knight has taken so much whimsical exception; as Dorimant instructs by his insulting, and his perfidiousness, and Loveit by the violence of her resentment and her anguish. For Loveit has youth, beauty, quality, wit, and spirit. And it was depending upon these, that she reposed so dangerous a trust in Dorimant, which is a just caution to the fair sex, never to be so conceited of the power of their charms, or their other extraordinary qualities, as to believe they can engage a man to be true to them, to whom they grant the best favor, without the only sure engagement, without which they can never be certain, that they shall not be hated and despised by that very person whom they have done everything to oblige.

To conclude with one general observation: that comedy may be qualified in a powerful manner both to instruct and to please, the very constitution of its subject ought always to be ridiculous. Comedy, says Rapin, is an image of common life, and its end is to expose upon the stage the defects of particular persons, in order to cure the defects of the public, and to correct and amend the people, by the fear of being laughed at. That therefore, says he, which is most essential to comedy, is certainly the ridicule.[8]

---

2. *Reflections* 2.25.

3. Knowledge gained by observation.

4. An epidemic of unknown origin that struck England between 1485 and 1578, causing many deaths.

5. John Wilmot (1647–1680), poet, libertine, and wit.

6. *Some Passages in the Life and Death of Rochester* (1705), by Gilbert Burnet.

7. Edmund Waller (1606–1687), famous for his elaborate, lyric praise poems and eulogies.

8. *Reflections* 2.25.

Every poem is qualified to instruct, and to please most powerfully by that very quality which makes the fort[9] and the characteristic of it, and which distinguishes it from all other kinds of poems. As tragedy is qualified to instruct and to please, by terror and compassion, which two passions ought always to be predominant in it, and to distinguish it from all other poems; epic poetry pleases and instructs chiefly by admiration, which reigns throughout it, and distinguishes it from poems of every other kind. Thus comedy instructs and pleases most powerfully by the ridicule, because that is the quality which distinguishes it from every other poem. The subject therefore of every comedy ought to be ridiculous by its constitution; the ridicule ought to be of the very nature and essence of it. Where there is none of that, there can be no comedy. It ought to reign both in the incidents and in the characters, and especially in the principal characters, which ought to be ridiculous in themselves, or so contrived, as to show and expose the ridicule of others. In all the masterpieces of Ben Jonson, the principal character has the ridicule in himself, as Morose in *The Silent Woman,* Volpone in *The Fox,* and Subtle and Face in *The Alchemist:* And the very ground and foundation of all these comedies is ridiculous. * * *

'Tis by the ridicule that there is in the character of Sir Fopling, which is one of the principal ones of this comedy, and from which it takes its name, that he is so very well qualified to please and to instruct. What true Englishman is there, but must be pleased to see this ridiculous knight made the jest and the scorn of all the other characters, for showing, by his foolish aping foreign customs and manners, that he prefers another country to his own? And of what important instruction must it be to all our youth who travel, to show them that if they so far forget the love of their country as to declare by their espousing foreign customs and manners that they prefer France or Italy to Great Britain, at their return, they must justly expect to be the jest and the scorn of their own countrymen.

Thus, I hope, I have convinced the reader that this comical knight, Sir Fopling, has been justly formed by the knight his father, to instruct and please, whatever may be the opinion to the contrary of the knight his brother.[1]

Whenever *The Fine Gentleman* of the latter comes upon the stage, I shall be glad to see that it has all the shining qualities which recommended *Sir Fopling,* that his characters are always drawn in Nature, and that he never gives to a young man the qualities of a middle-aged man, or an old one; that they are the just images of our contemporaries, and of what we everyday see in the world; that instead of setting us patterns for our imitation, which is not the proper business of comedy, he makes those follies and vices ridiculous, which we ought to shun and despise; that the subject of his comedy is comical by its constitution; and that the ridicule is particularly in the grand incidents, and in the principal characters.[2] For a true comic poet is a philosopher, who, like old Democritus,[3] always instructs us laughing.

1722   1722

---

9. Its strongest point.

1. The "father" is Sir George Etherege; the "brother," Sir Richard Steele.

2. Dennis was enraged by the immediate success of Steele's play; in 1723 he published a pamphlet attacking

the implausibility of both the characters and the plot.

3. The Greek thinker (460–c.370 B.C.), dubbed "the laughing philosopher" because of his amusement at human failings, and because his ethical system posited cheerfulness as the ultimate good.

Mary Astell
1666–1731

The pioneering feminist Mary Astell was born in Newcastle to a merchant who dealt in coal, and she was tutored early by an uncle who immersed himself in literature and philosophy. From him she absorbed a lifelong affinity for the ideas of the Cambridge Platonists, who held that reason was the sole route to truth and to the proper love of God; out of this conviction she developed her defiant argument that, despite centuries of cultural practice to the contrary, women's powers of reason were as worth cultivating as men's. At age twenty Astell moved to London, where eight years later she published the book that made her fame. In A Serious Proposal to the Ladies (1694), Astell argued for the founding of an all-female academy, where unmarried women might develop their reason, deepen their knowledge, and nurture their faith free from the distractions imposed by social conventions. Astell's idea for such a school exerted a lasting influence: Daniel Defoe enthusiastically revived it in his Essay upon Projects (1697), Samuel Johnson wove it into his philosophical tale Rasselas (1759), and Sarah Scott made it the premise of her feminist novel Millenium Hall (1762). More important, perhaps, was the Proposal's immediate effect on contemporary women writers and thinkers (Ladies Mary Chudleigh and Mary Wortley Montagu among them), who found in it a template and an endorsement for their own most cherished pursuits and for their sense of possibilities.

Dwelling abstemiously in the Thames-side town of Chelsea, Astell began to enjoy the consequences of celebrity. She received tributes and visits from admiring readers, and she assembled a circle of women like herself—well-educated, pious, unmarried—whose friendships she deeply valued and with whose help she later founded a charity school for girls. Still, the Proposal itself was never implemented in her time, in part because the imagined academy for women sounded too much like a Catholic convent to find ready acceptance in Protestant England, and in part because the argument's point—that women could find intellectual, moral, and spiritual self-sufficiency outside marriage—was so unsettling as to rouse energetic opposition.

Astell pushed the argument further in Some Reflections upon Marriage (1700), a hundred-page tract written, she reported, in the white heat of an angry and inspired afternoon. Starting from a conservative premise—that as the monarch rightfully possesses absolute authority over the state, so does the husband over his wife—Astell develops a breathtakingly skeptical line of inquiry: why, then, would a woman wish to enter into so self-immolating a contract as marriage in the first place? The question ultimately brings her back to the theme of the Serious Proposal: the importance for women of a good education, one that will enable them to see their choices clearly, to make those choices discerningly, and to lead, whether married or not, a Christian life grounded in the cultivation of their own intellect and faith (though Astell strongly implies that within marriage female virtue will produce a grim martyrdom; outside marriage, a richer fulfillment). In limning the alternatives, Astell deploys the directness, the sarcasm, and the urgency that made her famous in her own day and again in ours. She was, as her biographer Ruth Perry notes, "probably the first person to consider the rights and duties of women as a political question"; the prose in which she couched the question gave it an often hypnotic pugnacity.

from Some Reflections upon Marriage

But how can a man respect his wife when he has a contemptible opinion of her and her sex? When from his own elevation he looks down on them as void of understanding, and full of ignorance and passion, so that folly and a woman are equivalent terms with him? Can he think there is any gratitude due to her whose utmost services he exacts as strict duty? Because she was made to be a slave to his will, and has no higher end than to serve and obey him? Perhaps we arrogate too much to ourselves when we say this material world was made for our sakes; that its glorious maker has given us the use of it is certain, but when we suppose that over which we have dominion to be made purely for our sakes, we draw a false conclusion, as he who should say the people were made for the prince who is set over them, would be thought to be out of his senses as well as his politics. Yet even allowing that He who made everything in number, weight and measure, who never acts but for some great and glorious end, an end agreeable to His majesty, allowing that He created such a number of rational spirits merely to serve their fellow creatures, yet how are these lords and masters helped by the contempt they show of their poor humble vassals? Is it not rather an hindrance to that service they expect, as being undeniable and constant proof how unworthy they are to receive it?

None of God's creatures absolutely considered are in their own nature contemptible; the meanest fly, the poorest insect has its use and virtue. Contempt is scarce a human passion; one may venture to say it was not in innocent man, for till sin came into the world, there was nothing in it to be condemned. But pride, which makes everything serve its purposes, wrested this passion from its only use, so that instead of being an antidote against sin, it is become a grand promoter of it, nothing making us more worthy of that contempt we show, than when (poor, weak, dependent creatures as we are!) we look down with scorn and disdain on others.

There is not a surer sign of a noble mind, a mind very far advanced towards perfection, than the being able to bear contempt and an unjust treatment from one's superiors evenly and patiently. For inward worth and real excellency are the true ground of superiority, and one person is not in reality better than another, but as he is more wise and good. But this world being a place of trial and governed by general laws, just retributions being reserved for hereafter, respect and obedience many times become due for order's sake to those who don't otherwise deserve them. Now though humility keeps us from over-valuing ourselves or viewing our merit through a false and magnifying medium, yet it does not put out our eyes; it does not, it ought not to deprive us of that pleasing sentiment which attends our acting as we ought to act, which is as it were a foretaste of heaven, our present reward for doing what is just and fit. And when a superior does a mean and unjust thing, as all contempt of one's neighbor is, and yet this does not provoke his inferiors to refuse that observance which their stations in the world require, they cannot but have an inward sense of their own real superiority, the other having no pretense to it, at the same time that they pay him an outward respect and deference, which is such a flagrant testimony of the sincerest love of order as proves their souls to be of the highest and noblest rank.

A man therefore for his own sake, and to give evidence that he has a right to those prerogatives he assumes, should treat women with a little more humanity and regard than is usually paid them. Your whiffling wits may scoff at them, and what then? It matters not, for they rally[1] everything though ever so sacred, and rail at the women commonly in very good company. Religion, its priests, and these its most constant and regular professors, are the usual subjects of their manly, mannerly, and surprising jests. Surprising indeed! not for the newness of the thought, the brightness of the fancy, or nobleness of expression, but for the good assurance with which such threadbare jests are again and again repeated. But that your grave dons, your learned men, and which is more your men of sense as they would be thought, should stoop so

1. Mock.

low as to make invectives against the women, forget themselves so much as to jest with their slaves, who have neither liberty nor ingenuity to make reprisals! that they should waste their time and debase their good sense which fits them for the most weighty affairs, such as are suitable to their profound wisdoms and exalted understandings! to render those poor wretches more ridiculous and odious who are already in their opinion sufficiently contemptible, and find no better exercise of their wit and satire than such as are not worth their pains, though it were possible to reform them—this, this indeed may justly be wondered at!

I know not whether or no women are allowed to have souls. If they have, perhaps it is not prudent to provoke them too much, lest silly as they are, they at last recriminate, and then what polite and well-bred gentleman, though himself is concerned, can forbear taking that lawful pleasure which all who understand raillery must taste, when they find his jests who insolently began to peck at his neighbor, returned with interest upon his own head? And indeed men are too humane, too wise to venture at it did they not hope for this effect, and expect the pleasure of finding their wit turn to such account; for if it be lawful to reveal a secret, this is without doubt the whole design of those fine discourses which have been made against the women from our great forefathers to this present time. Generous man has too much bravery, he is too just and too good to assault a defenseless enemy, and if he did inveigh against the women it was only to do them service. For since neither his care of their education, his hearty endeavors to improve their minds, his wholesome precepts, nor great example could do them good, as his last and kindest essay he resolved to try what contempt would do, and chose rather to expose himself by a seeming want of justice, equity, ingenuity, and good nature, than suffer women to remain such vain and insignificant creatures as they have hitherto been reckoned. And truly women are some degrees beneath what I have thus far thought them, if they do not make the best use of his kindness, improve themselves, and like Christians return it.

Let us see then what is their part, what must they do to make the matrimonial yoke tolerable to themselves as well as pleasing to their lords and masters? That the world is an empty and deceitful thing, that those enjoyments which appear so desirable at a distance, which raised our hopes and expectations to such a mighty pitch, which we so passionately coveted and so eagerly pursued, vanish at our first approach, leaving nothing behind them but the folly of delusion, and the pain of disappointed hopes, is a common outcry; and yet as common as it is, though we complain of being deceived this instant, we do not fail of contributing to the cheat the very next. Though in reality it is not the world that abuses us, 'tis we abuse ourselves, it is not the emptiness of that, but our own false judgments, our unreasonable desires and expectations that torment us; for he who exerts his whole strength to lift a straw, ought not to complain of the burden but of his own disproportionate endeavor which gives him the pain he feels. The world affords us all that pleasure a sound judgment can expect from it, and answers all those ends and purposes for which it was designed. Let us expect no more than is reasonable, and then we shall not fail of our expectations.

It is even so in the case before us: a woman who has been taught to think marriage her only preferment, the sum-total of her endeavors, the completion of all her hopes, that which must settle and make her happy in this world, and very few, in their youth especially, carry a thought steadily to a greater distance; she who has seen a lover dying at her feet, and can't therefore imagine that he who professes to receive all his happiness from her can have any other design or desire than to please her; whose eyes have been dazzled with all the glitter and pomp of a wedding, and who hears of nothing but joy and congratulation; who is transported with the pleasure of being out of pupillage, and mistress not only of herself but of a family too; she who is either so simple or so vain as to take her lover at his word either as to the praises he gave her, or the promises he made for himself. In sum, she whose expectation has been raised by courtship, by all the fine things that her lover, her governess, and domestic flatterers say, will find a terrible disappointment when the hurry is over, and when she comes calmly to consider her condition, and views it no more under a false appearance, but as it truly is.

I doubt in such a view it will not appear over-desirable if she regards only the present state of things. Hereafter may make amends for what she must be prepared to suffer here; then will be her reward, this is her time of trial, the season of exercising and improving her virtues. A woman that is not mistress of her passions, that cannot patiently submit even when reason suffers with her, who does not practice passive obedience[2] to the utmost, will never be acceptable to such an absolute sovereign as a husband. Wisdom ought to govern without contradiction, but strength however will be obeyed. There are but few of those wise persons who can be content to be made yet wiser by contradiction; the most will have their will, and it is right because it is theirs. Such is the vanity of human nature that nothing pleases like an entire subjection; what imperfections won't a man overlook where this is not wanting! Though we live like brutes, we would have incense offered us that is only due to heaven itself, would have an absolute and blind obedience paid us by all over whom we pretend authority. We were not made to idolize one another, yet the whole strain of courtship is little less than rank idolatry. But does a man intend to give and not receive his share in this religious worship? No such matter; pride and vanity and self-love have their designs, and if the lover is so condescending as to set a pattern in the time of his addresses, he is so just as to expect his wife should strictly copy after it all the rest of her life.

But how can a woman scruple entire subjection, how can she forbear to admire the worth and excellency of the superior sex, if she at all considers it? Have not all the great actions that have been performed in the world been done by them? Have not they founded empires and overturned them? Do not they make laws and continually repeal them and amend them? Their vast minds lay kingdoms waste; no bounds or measures can be prescribed to their desires. War and peace depend on them, they form cabals[3] and have the wisdom and courage to get over all these rubs[4] which may lie in the way of their desired grandeur. What is it they cannot do? They make worlds and ruin them, form systems of universal nature and dispute eternally about them, their pen gives worth to the most trifling controversy, nor can a fray be inconsiderable if they have drawn their swords in't. All that the wise man pronounces is an oracle, and every word the witty speaks a jest. It is a woman's happiness to hear, admire, and praise them, especially if a little ill-nature keeps them at anytime from bestowing due applause on each other. And if she aspires no further she is thought to be in her proper sphere of action; she is as wise and as good as can be expected from her.

She then who marries ought to lay it down for an indisputable maxim, that her husband must govern absolutely and entirely, and that she has nothing else to do but to please and obey. She must not attempt to divide his authority, or so much as dispute it (to struggle with her yoke will only make it gall the more) but must believe him wise and good and in all respects the best, at least he must be so to her. She who can't do this is no way fit to be a wife; she may set up for that peculiar coronet the

---

2. The term denoted the Tory policy of obeying Whig monarchs and of refraining from rebellion despite their "usurpation" of the Stuart throne, on the principle that rebellion itself would run contrary to divine and human law.

3. Small, secretive groups formed to wield power.
4. Obstacles.

ancient fathers talked of, but is not qualified to receive that great reward,[5] which attends the eminent exercise of humility and self-denial, patience and resignation—the duties that a wife is called to.

But some refractory woman perhaps will say how can this be? Is it possible for her to believe him wise and good who by a thousand demonstrations convinces her and all the world of the contrary? Did the bare name of husband confer sense on a man, and the mere being in authority infallibly qualify him for government, much might be done. But since a wise man and a husband are not terms convertible, and how loath soever one is to own it, matter of fact won't allow us to deny that the head many times stands in need of the inferior's brains to manage it, she must beg leave to be excused from such high thoughts of her sovereign, and if she submits to his power, it is not so much reason as necessity that compels her.

Now of how little force soever this objection may be in other respects, methinks it is strong enough to prove the necessity of a good education, and that men never mistake their true interest more than when they endeavor to keep women in ignorance. Could they indeed deprive them of their natural good sense at the same time they deny them the due improvement of it, they might compass their end; otherwise natural sense unassisted may run into a false track, and serve only to punish him justly, who would not allow it to be useful to himself or others. If man's authority be justly established, the more sense a woman has the more reason she will find to submit to it; if according to the tradition of our fathers (who having had *possession* of the pen, thought they had also the best *right* to it), women's understanding is but small, and men's partiality adds no weight to the observation, ought not the more care to be taken to improve them? How it agrees with the justice of men we inquire not, but certainly Heaven is abundantly more equitable than to enjoin women the hardest task and give them the least strength to perform it. And if men, learned, wise, and discreet as they are, who have as is said all the advantages of nature, and without controversy have or may have all the assistance of art, are so far from acquitting themselves as they ought, from living according to that reason and excellent understanding they so much boast of, can it be expected that a woman who is reckoned silly enough in herself, at least comparatively, and whom men take care to make yet more so, can it be expected that she should constantly perform so difficult a duty as entire subjection, to which corrupt nature is so averse?

If the great and wise Cato,[6] a *man*, a man of no ordinary firmness and strength of mind, a man who was esteemed as an oracle, and by the philosophers and great men of his nation equaled even to the gods themselves; if he with all his stoical principles was not able to bear the sight of a triumphant conqueror (who perhaps would have insulted and perhaps would not), but out of a cowardly fear of an insult, ran to death to secure him from it; can it be thought that an ignorant weak woman should have patience to bear a continual outrage and insolence all the days of her life? Unless you will suppose her a very ass, but then remember what the Italians say, to quote them once more, since being very husbands they may be presumed to have some authority in this case: *L'asino pur pigro, stimulato tira quelche calcio;* an ass though slow if provoked will kick.

---

5. Salvation. The "peculiar coronet" is that of martyrdom, often imaged as a crown in the writings of early Christian theologians.
6. Cato of Utica (95–46 B.C.), Stoic Roman senator and commander, whose devotion to the ideal of a Republic prompted him to commit suicide rather than accede to the growing power of Julius Caesar; his death was traditionally represented as heroic.

We never see or perhaps make sport with the ill effects of a bad education, till it come to touch us home in the ill conduct of a sister, a daughter, or wife. Then the women must be blamed, their folly is exclaimed against, when all this while it was the wise man's fault who did not set a better guard on those who according to him stand in so much need of one. A young gentleman, as a celebrated author tells us, ought above all things to be acquainted with the state of the world, the ways and humors, the follies, the cheats, the faults of the age he is fallen into; he should by degrees be informed of the vice of fashion, and warned of the application and design of those who will make it their business to corrupt him, should be told the arts they use and the trains they lay, be prepared to be shocked by some and caressed by others; warned who are like to oppose, who to mislead; who to undermine and who to serve him. He should be instructed how to know and distinguish them, where he should let them see, and when dissemble the knowledge of them and their aims and workings. Our author is much in the right, and not to disparage any other accomplishments which are useful in their kind, this will turn to more account than any language or philosophy, art or science, or any other piece of good-breeding and fine education that can be taught him, which are no otherwise excellent than as they contribute to this, as this does above all things to the making him a wise, virtuous, and useful man.

And it is not less necessary that a young lady should receive the like instructions; whether or no her temptations be fewer, her reputation and honor however are to be more nicely preserved; they may be ruined by a little ignorance or indiscretion, and then though she has kept her innocence, and so is secured as to the next world, yet she is in a great measure lost to this. A woman cannot be too watchful, too apprehensive of her danger, nor keep at too great a distance from it, since man, whose wisdom and ingenuity is so much superior to hers, condescends for his interest sometimes, and sometimes by way of diversion, to lay snares for her. For though men are virtuous, philosophers and politicians in comparison of the ignorant and illiterate women, yet they don't all pretend to be saints, and 'tis no great matter to them if women, who were born to be their slaves, be now and then ruined for their entertainment.

But according to the rate that young women are educated; according to the way their time is spent; they are destined to folly and impertinence, to say no worse, and which is yet more inhuman, they are blamed for that ill conduct they are not suffered to avoid, and reproached for those faults they are in a manner forced into; so that if heaven has bestowed any sense on them, no other use is made of it than to leave them without excuse. So much and no more of the world is shown them, as serves to weaken and corrupt their minds, to give them wrong notions, and busy them in mean pursuits; to disturb, not to regulate their passions, to make them timorous and dependent, and in a word, fit for nothing else but to act a farce for the diversion of their governors.

Even men themselves improve no otherwise than according to the aim they take, and the end they propose; and he whose designs are but little and mean, will be the same himself. Though ambition, as 'tis usually understood, is a foolish, not to say a base and pitiful vice, yet the aspirings of the soul after true glory are so much its nature, that it seems to have forgot itself and to degenerate, if it can forbear; and perhaps the great secret of education lies in affecting the soul with a lively sense of what is truly its perfection, and exciting the most ardent desires after it.

But, alas! what poor woman is ever taught that she should have a higher design than to get her a husband? Heaven will fall in of course; and if she make but an obedient and dutiful wife, she cannot miss of it. A husband indeed is thought by both sexes so very valuable, that scarce a man who can keep himself clean and make a bow, but thinks he is good enough to pretend to any woman, no matter for the difference of birth or fortune, a *husband* is such a wonder-working name as to make an equality, or something more, whenever it is pronounced. * * *

To wind up this matter, if a woman were duly principled and taught to know the world, especially the true sentiments that men have of her, and the traps they lay for her under so many gilded compliments, and such a seemingly great respect, that disgrace would be prevented which is brought upon too many families, women would marry more discreetly, and demean[7] themselves better in a married state than some people say they do. The foundation indeed ought to be laid deep and strong: she should be made a good Christian, and understand why she is so, and then she will be everything else that is good. Men need keep no spies on a woman's conduct, need have no fear of her virtue, or so much as of her prudence and caution, were but a due sense of true honor and virtue awakened in her, were her reason excited and prepared to consider the sophistry of those temptations which would persuade her from her duty, and were she put in a way to know that it is both her wisdom and interest to observe it. She would then duly examine and weigh all the circumstances, the good and evil of a married state, and not be surprised with unforeseen inconveniences, and either never consent to be a wife, or make a good one when she does. This would show her what human nature *is*, as well as what it *ought* to be, and teach her not only what she may justly expect, but what she must be content with; would enable her to cure some faults, and patiently to suffer what she cannot cure.

Indeed nothing can assure obedience, and render it what it ought to be, but the confidence of duty, the paying it for God's sake. Superiors don't rightly understand their own interest when they attempt to put out their subjects' eyes to keep them obedient. A blind obedience is what a rational creature should never pay, nor would such an one receive it did he rightly understand its nature. For human actions are no otherwise valuable than as they are conformable to reason, but blind obedience is an obeying *without reason*, for ought we know, *against it*. God himself does not require our obedience at this rate; He lays before us the goodness and reasonableness of His laws, and were there anything in them whose equity we could not readily comprehend, yet we have this clear and sufficient reason on which to found our obedience, that nothing but what's just and fit can be enjoined by a just, a wise, and gracious God. But this is a reason will never hold in respect of men's commands unless they can prove themselves infallible, and consequently impeccable too.

It is therefore very much a man's interest that women should be good Christians, in this as in every other instance; he who does his duty finds his own account[8] in it. Duty and true interest are one and the same thing, and he who thinks otherwise is to be pitied for being so much in the wrong; but what can be more the duty of the head, than to instruct and improve those who are under government? She will freely leave him the quiet dominion of this world whose thoughts and expectations are placed on the next. A prospect of heaven, and that only, will cure that ambition which all generous minds are filled with, not by taking it away but by placing it on a right object. She will discern a time when her sex shall be no bar to the best employments, the highest honor; a time when that distinction, now so much used to her prejudice, shall be no more, but provided she is not wanting to herself, her soul shall shine as bright as the greatest hero's. This is a true, and indeed the only consolation, this

7. Behave (though the meaning "to lower herself" was also current).   8. I.e., is amply compensated.

makes her a sufficient compensation for all the neglect and contempt the ill-grounded customs of the world throw on her, for all the injuries brutal power may do her, and is a sufficient cordial to support her spirits, be her lot in this world what it may.

But some sage persons may perhaps object that were women allowed to improve themselves, and not amongst other discouragements driven back by those wise jests and scoffs that are put upon a woman of sense or learning, a philosophical lady as she is called by way of ridicule, they would be too wise and too good for the men. I grant it, for vicious and foolish men. Nor is it to be wondered that he is afraid he should not be able to govern them were their understandings improved, who is resolved not to take too much pains with his own. But these 'tis to be hoped are no very considerable number, the foolish at least; and therefore this is so far from being an argument against their improvement, that it is a strong one for it, if we do but suppose the men to be as capable of improvement as the women, but much more if according to tradition we believe they have greater capacities. This, if anything, would stir them up to be what they ought, not permit them to waste their time and abuse their faculties in the service of their irregular appetites and unreasonable desires, and to let poor contemptible women who have been their slaves excel them in all that is truly excellent. This would make them blush at employing an immoral mind no better than in making provision for the flesh to fulfill the lusts thereof, since women by a wiser conduct have brought themselves to such a reach of thought, to such exactness of judgment, such clearness and strength of reasoning, such purity and elevation of mind, such command of their passions, such regularity of will and affection, and in a word to such a pitch of perfection as the human soul is capable of attaining even in this life by the grace of God, such true wisdom, such real greatness, as though it does not qualify them to make a noise in this world, to found or overturn empires, yet it qualifies them for what is infinitely better, a kingdom that cannot be moved, an incorruptible crown of glory.

Besides, it were ridiculous to suppose that a woman, were she ever so much improved, could come near the topping genius of men, and therefore why should they envy or discourage her? Strength of mind goes along with strength of body, and 'tis only for some odd accidents which philosophers have not yet thought worthwhile to inquire into, that the sturdiest porter is not the wisest man. As therefore the men have the power in their hands, so there's no dispute of their having the brains to manage it. There is no such thing as good judgment and sense upon earth, if it is not to be found among them. Do not they generally speaking do all the great actions and considerable business of this world, and leave that of the next to the women? Their subtlety in forming cabals and laying deep designs, their courage and conduct in breaking through all ties sacred and civil to effect them, not only advances them to the post of honor and keeps them securely in it for twenty or thirty years, but gets them a name, and conveys it down to posterity for some hundreds, and who would look any further? Justice and injustice are administered by their hands; courts and schools are filled with these sages; 'tis men who dispute for truth as well as men who argue against it; histories are writ by them, they recount each others' great exploits, and have always done so. All famous arts have their original from men, even from the invention of guns to the mystery of good eating. And to show that nothing is beneath their care, any more than above their reach, they have brought *gaming*[9] to an art and science, and a more profitable and honorable one too, than any of those that

9. Gambling.

used to be called *liberal*. Indeed what is it they can't perform, when they attempt it? This strength of their brains shall be every whit as conspicuous at their cups as in a Senate house, and when they please they can make it pass for as sure a mark of wisdom to drink deep as to reason profoundly; a greater proof of courage and consequently of understanding to dare the vengeance of heaven itself than to stand the raillery of some of the worst of their fellow creatures!

Again, it may be said, if a wife's case be as it is here represented, it is not good for a woman to marry, and so there's an end of human race. But this is no fair consequence, for all that can justly be inferred from hence is that a woman has no mighty obligations to the man who makes love to her, she has no reason to be fond of being a wife, or to reckon it a piece of preferment when she is taken to be a man's upper-servant; it is no advantage to her in this world, if rightly managed it may prove one as to the next. For she who marries purely to do good, to educate souls for heaven, who can be so truly mortified as to lay aside her own will and desires, to pay such an entire submission for life, to one whom she cannot be sure will always deserve it, does certainly perform a more heroic action than all the famous masculine heroes can boast of; she suffers a continual martyrdom to bring glory to God and benefit to mankind, which consideration indeed may carry her though all difficulties, I know not what else can, and engage her to love him who proves perhaps so much more worse than a brute, as to make this condition yet more grievous than it needed to be. She has need of a strong reason, of a truly Christian and well-tempered spirit, of all the assistance the best education can give her, and ought to have some good assistance of her own firmness and virtue, who ventures on such a trial; and for this reason 'tis less to be wondered at that women marry off in haste, for perhaps if they took time to consider and reflect upon it, they seldom would.

To conclude, perhaps I've said more than most men will thank me for; I cannot help it, for how much soever I may be their friend and humble servant, I am more a friend to truth. Truth is strong, and some time or other will prevail; nor is it for their honor, and therefore one would think not for their interest, to be partial to themselves and unjust to others. They may fancy I have made some discoveries which like *arcana imperii*[1] ought to be kept secret, but in good earnest I do them more honor than to suppose their lawful prerogatives need any mean arts to support them. If they have usurped, I love justice too much to wish success and continuance to usurpations, which though submitted to out of prudence and for quietness' sake, yet leave everybody free to regain their lawful right whenever they have power and opportunity. I don't say that tyranny *ought*, but we find in *fact*, that it provokes the oppressed to throw off even a lawful yoke that fits too heavy. And if he who is freely elected, after all his fair promises and the fine hopes he raised, proves a tyrant, the consideration that he was one's own choice will not render more submissive and patient, but I fear more refractory. For though it is very unreasonable, yet we see 'tis the course of the world not only to return injury for injury, but crime for crime; both parties indeed are guilty, but the aggressors have a double guilt; they have not only their own, but their neighbor's ruin to answer for.

As to the female reader, I hope she will allow I've endeavored to do her justice, nor betrayed her cause as her advocates usually do, under pretense of defending it: a practice too mean for any to be guilty of who have the least sense of honor, and who do any more than merely pretend to it. I think I have held the balance even, and not

1. The secrets of power.

being conscious of partiality I ask no pardon for it. To plead for the oppressed and to defend the weak seemed to me a generous undertaking; for though it may be secure, 'tis not always honorable to run over to the strongest party. And if she infers from what has been said that marriage is a very happy state for men, if they think fit to make it so; that they govern the world, they have prescription on their side, women are too weak to dispute it with them, therefore they, as all other governors, are most, if not only, accountable for what's amiss. For whether other governments in their original were or were not conferred according to the merit of the person, yet certainly in this case Heaven would not have allotted the man to govern, but because he was best qualified for it. So far I agree with him. But if she goes on to infer, that therefore he has not these qualifications, where is his right? If he misemploys, does he not abuse it? And if he abuses, according to modern deduction, he forfeits it; I must leave her there. A peaceable woman indeed will not carry it so far, she will neither question her husband's right nor his fitness to govern, but how? Not as an absolute lord and master, with an arbitrary and tyrannical sway, but as reason governs and conducts a man, by proposing what is just and fit. And the man who acts according to that wisdom he assumes, who would have that superiority he pretends to acknowledged just, will receive no injury by anything that has been offered here. A woman will value him the more who is so wise and good, when she discerns how much he excels the rest of his noble sex; the less he requires, the more will he merit that esteem and deference, which those who are so forward to exact seem conscious they don't deserve. So then the man's prerogative is not at all infringed, whilst the woman's privileges are secured; and if any woman think herself injured, she has a remedy in reserve which few men will envy or endeavor to rob her of, the exercise and improvement of her virtue here, and the reward of it hereafter.

1700   1700

Daniel Defoe
1660–1731

At the age of fifty-two, Daniel Defoe summed up his life in a couplet:

> No man has tasted differing fortunes more,
> And thirteen times I have been rich or poor.

Vicissitude marked his career until the very end, and money, though a constant preoccupation, was not the only medium of change. Deeply engaged in politics, and phenomenally skilled at promoting causes with his pen, Defoe switched allegiances several times among the most conspicuous factions of his day. What's more, since he was prized by each side in turn for his efficiency as a secret agent, his political work often required him to present himself—in person and in print—as someone or something he was not, to incur hostilities from the very factions he was secretly working to support. His accomplishments, late in life, as a pioneer of English fiction partly originate in the fictions he manipulated as a consummate political journalist and spy obliged to "taste" in imagination and performance the "differing fortunes" of the person he pretended, for one purpose or another, to be. Out of all these oscillations— financial, political, imaginative—came one of the most prolific and inventive careers in British literature.

Defoe was born in the City of London in the year of the Restoration to a family whose fortunes were on the rise. His father James Foe manufactured and sold candles, and over the ensuing decades attained positions of increasing eminence in his trade (Defoe himself later added the French prefix to his family surname). Under the influence of their pastor, the Foes left the Church of England to become Dissenters, at a time when to do so was to incur certain exclusion—from attending universities, from holding public office—and possible persecution (violence, imprisonment). At around the age of ten, shortly after his mother's early death, Defoe began a decade in the schools of the Dissenters. The curriculum, underplaying the Greek and Latin of conventional Anglican education, focused instead on new science and philosophy, on clear argument and public speaking, as well as on two forms of thought and composition that cultivated the student's ability to imagine "differing fortunes": prose impersonation, where the student was asked to "play" a given figure (for example, a secretary of state) in a particular situation, and to write a letter or give a speech suitable to the occasion; and casuistry, a kind of moral and theological game of "What if?": if I were to find myself in such and such a predicament, such a dilemma, what should I do? The question recurs, explicitly and implicitly, throughout Defoe's prose.

As Defoe entered his twenties, the question became personally pressing. Many of his classmates were preparing for the ministry; he opted instead to enter his father's world of trade, though with a taste for range and risk that his prudent forebear had never displayed. Defoe dealt at one time or another in men's clothing, tobacco, wine; opened and operated a brick and tile factory, and invested capital so audaciously and ill-advisedly that in 1692 he was forced to declare bankruptcy, having incurred the enormous debt of £17,000. "The God that gave me brains will give me bread," Defoe remarked at one point, with characteristic confidence in both the deity and himself. From his late thirties onward, he used those brains to earn bread, for himself and his large family, by writing. He worked with astonishing speed and efficiency, producing by his life's end more than 500 separate works, as well as several periodical series that he wrote (at the rate of two or three essays a week) over the course of many years. Nonetheless, he never quite escaped the financial distresses that had first pushed him into print.

His pen's other impetus was politics. As a Whig and a Dissenter eager to end the reign of the Catholic James II, Defoe had fought as soldier in the abortive Monmouth Rebellion of 1685, and in 1688 celebrated the advent of the Glorious Revolution and William III. He served his new king as secret agent and as author, publishing the phenomenally popular poem *The True-Born Englishman* (1701), whose title sarcastically identifies those "natives" hostile to William on the grounds of his foreign birth (the poem argues, among other things, that their own lineage is far more complex and corrupt than they admit). Defoe's powers as a political advocate were now near full stride, and his knack for irony soon brought him trouble. In his parodic pamphlet *The Shortest Way with Dissenters*, published anonymously in 1702 at the height of Tory hopes for a new assault on Nonconformists, Defoe impersonates a rabid Tory eager to mete out extravagant punishments on the Nonconformists (to whom Defoe himself had felt a lifelong loyalty and tenderness). Neither faction appreciated the joke. After four months in hiding, Defoe was arrested, convicted of libel, and sentenced to prison and to three separate sessions in the pillory, where the crowds (to his surprise) celebrated him as a hero, pelting him with fresh flowers rather than rotten vegetables. The episode initiated a sea change in his affiliations. Disillusioned with Whigs and Dissenters, Defoe secretly aligned himself with the ambitious Tory politician Robert Harley, who in an inspired move had arranged to pay some of Defoe's fines and debts after his release from jail. Commissioned by Harley to create and manage a kind of personal secret service, Defoe traveled extensively, often under assumed names, advocating Tory causes (most notably the Union with Scotland) and reporting on the opposition; he also wrote the widely read *Review* (1704–1713), a thrice-weekly periodical essay intricately calculated to further Harley's interests. After the fall of the Tories, the intricacy deepened. Under threat of punishment by the new Whig government, Defoe agreed to work as double agent for *them*, by moving among Tory journalists and contributing to Tory papers, but in such ways as to undermine the Tory cause. For the seasoned ironist and impersonator this was irony enough: having worked brilliantly for years to devise Tory propaganda, he was now at pains to dilute it.

At the age of fifty-nine, Defoe hit upon a new way to make impersonation pay. His book *The Strange, Surprising Adventures of Robinson Crusoe* (1719) was the first in a series of long fictions that present themselves as historical fact, as the written reminiscences of people who had actually lived the extraordinary experiences they relate, in books that often bear their fictive names as titles: *Captain Singleton* (1720); *Moll Flanders* (1722); *Colonel Jack* (1722); *Roxana* (1724). In creating these memoirists, Defoe drew on his decades as a journalist. He saturated his stories with particulars (clothing, furniture, tools); his memoirists write a prose that often reads like talk—digressive, fervent, improvisatory. By such strategies he made his tales persuasive. As a genre, the novel has no one inventor, because it absorbs so much (and so variously) from other kinds of texts: newspapers, essays, diaries, financial accounts, religious devotions, conduct manuals. Defoe, though, was perhaps the most astute early orchestrator of such absorptions. Having written in most of his culture's modes, he melded them into a form of fiction that still seems (in keeping with the genre's name) new.

Vicissitude persisted. Having written his last long fiction (*Roxana*) in 1724, Defoe turned his hand to another project. In his *Tour through the Whole Island of Great Britain* (three volumes, 1724–1726), and in other late works, he celebrated British trade as a source of present prosperity and a seedbed of future empire. He died while hiding out from his creditors in the neighborhood of his birth, once again on the run from debt and cut off from his contentious family. The ending feels emblematic. In many ways the most communicative of writers, Defoe often used his powers to study solitude. "Between thee and me there is a great gulf fixed," remarks Robinson Crusoe on his island, quoting scripture: "thee" is the whole world, from which he finds himself definitively sundered. But the phrase might be invoked by almost any speaker in Defoe—characters talking to characters, ghosts to the living, narrators to readers— as they survey the landscape of their own isolation, even in crowded cities. Defoe devoted his writing life to mapping these "great gulfs," to chronicling the energies—political, social, and commercial—by which the mortals of his time and place tried to bridge them, and to seeking out the work of God and Providence in all these prolific, troubled transactions.

A True Relation of the Apparition of One Mrs. Veal
the Next Day after Her Death
to One Mrs. Bargrave at Canterbury
the 8th of September, 1705[1]
The Preface

This relation is matter of fact, and attended with such circumstances as may induce any reasonable man to believe it. It was sent by a gentleman, a Justice of Peace at Maidstone in Kent and a very intelligent person, to his friend in London, as it is here worded. Which discourse is attested by a very sober and understanding gentlewoman, a kinswoman of the said gentleman's, who lives in Canterbury within a few doors of the house in which the within named Mrs. Bargrave lives; who believes his

---

1. This narrative was long thought to be Defoe's earliest foray into pure fiction; it was then discovered to have a firm basis in fact. Nevertheless, in the way he mingles "matter of fact" (a recurrent phrase) with matters of mystery, Defoe here manages (as Leslie Stephen once remarked) to embody "in a few lines all the essential particularities of his art."

kinswoman to be of so discerning a spirit, as not to be put upon by any fallacy. And who positively assured him that the whole matter, as it is here related and laid down, is what is really true, and what she herself had in the same words (as near as may be) from Mrs. Bargrave's own mouth, who she knows had no reason to invent and publish such a story, nor any design to forge and tell a lie, being a woman of much honesty and virtue, and her whole life a course as it were of piety. The use which we ought to make of it is to consider that there is a life to come after this, and a just God who will retribute to everyone according to the deeds done in the body; and therefore, to reflect upon our past course of life we have led in the world, that our time is short and uncertain, and that if we would escape the punishment of the ungodly and receive the reward of the righteous, which is the laying hold of eternal life, we ought for the time to come to turn to God by a speedy repentance, ceasing to do evil and learning to do well: to seek after God early, if happily he may be found of us, and lead such lives for the future as may be well pleasing in his sight.

A Relation of the Apparition of Mrs. Veal

This thing is so rare in all its circumstances, and on so good authority, that my reading and conversation has not given me anything like it; it is fit to gratify the most ingenious and serious inquirer. Mrs. Bargrave is the person to whom Mrs. Veal appeared after her death. She is my intimate friend, and I can avouch for her reputation for these last fifteen or sixteen years on my own knowledge; and I can confirm the good character she had from her youth, to the time of my acquaintance. Though since this relation she is calumniated by some people that are friends to the brother of Mrs. Veal who appeared, who think the relation of this appearance to be a reflection,[2] and endeavor what they can to blast Mrs. Bargrave's reputation and to laugh the story out of countenance. But the circumstances thereof, and the cheerful disposition of Mrs. Bargrave, notwithstanding the unheard of ill usage of a very wicked husband, there is not the least sign of dejection in her face; nor did I ever hear her let fall a desponding or murmuring expression; nay, not when actually under her husband's barbarity, which I have been witness to, and several other persons of undoubted reputation.[3]

Now you must know that Mrs. Veal was a maiden gentlewoman[4] of about thirty years of age, and for some years last past had been troubled with fits, which were perceived coming on her by her leaving off from her discourse very abruptly to some impertinence.[5] She was maintained by an only brother, and kept his house in Dover. She was a very pious woman, and her brother a very sober man to all appearance. But now he does all he can to null or quash the story. Mrs. Veal was intimately acquainted with Mrs. Bargrave from her childhood. Mrs. Veal's circumstances were then mean; her father did not take care of his children as he ought, so that they were exposed to hardships. And Mrs. Bargrave in those days had as unkind a father, though she wanted for neither food nor clothing, whilst Mrs. Veal wanted for both. So that it was in the power of Mrs. Bargrave to be very much her friend in several instances, which mightily endeared Mrs. Veal; insomuch that she would often say, "Mrs. Bargrave, you are not only the best, but the only friend I have in the world, and no circumstances of life shall ever dissolve my friendship." They would often

---

2. I.e., injurious to the family's reputation.
3. The sentence is grammatically incomplete (Defoe supplies no verb for the initial subject "the circumstances").

4. "Mrs." (pronounced "Mistress") designated any adult woman, married or unmarried.
5. Irrelevance; digression.

condole each other's adverse fortunes, and read together *Drelincourt upon Death*[6] and other good books. And so like two Christian friends they comforted each other under their sorrow.

Sometime after, Mr. Veal's friends got him a place in the custom house at Dover, which occasioned Mrs. Veal by little and little to fall off from her intimacy with Mrs. Bargrave, though there was never any such thing as a quarrel; but an indifferency came on by degrees, till at last Mrs. Bargrave had not seen her in two years and a half; though above a twelve month of the time Mrs. Bargrave had been absent from Dover, and this last half year has been in Canterbury about two months of the time, dwelling in a house of her own.

In this house, on the eighth of September last, viz. 1705, she was sitting alone in the forenoon, thinking over her unfortunate life and arguing herself into a due resignation to Providence, though her condition seemed hard. And said she, "I have been provided for hitherto, and doubt not but I shall be still, and am well satisfied that my afflictions shall end when it is most fit for me." And then took up her sewing work, which she had no sooner done but she hears a knocking at the door. She went to see who it was there, and this proved to be Mrs. Veal, her old friend, who was in a riding habit. At that moment of time, the clock struck twelve at noon.

"Madam," says Mrs. Bargrave, "I am surprised to see you, you have been so long a stranger," but told her she was glad to see her and offered to salute[7] her, which Mrs. Veal complied with till their lips almost touched, and then Mrs. Veal drew her hand cross her own eyes and said, "I am not very well," and so waived it. She told Mrs. Bargrave she was going a journey, and had a great mind to see her first. "But," says Mrs. Bargrave, "how came you to take a journey alone? I am amazed at it, because I know you have so fond a brother." "O!" says Mrs. Veal, "I gave my brother the slip and came away, because I had so great a mind to see you before I took my journey." So Mrs. Bargrave went in with her, into another room within the first, and Mrs. Veal sat herself down in an elbow-chair, in which Mrs. Bargrave was sitting when she heard Mrs. Veal knock. Then says Mrs. Veal, "My dear friend, I am come to renew our old friendship again, and to beg your pardon for my breach of it, and if you can forgive me you are one of the best of women." "O!" says Mrs. Bargrave, "don't mention such a thing. I have not had an uneasy thought about it; I can easily forgive it." "What did you think of me?" says Mrs. Veal. Says Mrs. Bargrave, "I thought you were like the rest of the world, and that prosperity had made you forget yourself and me." Then Mrs. Veal reminded Mrs. Bargrave of the many friendly offices she did her in former days, and much of the conversation they had with each other in the time of their adversity: what books they read, and what comfort in particular they received from *Drelincourt's Book of Death*, which was the best, she said, on that subject ever wrote. She also mentioned Dr. Sherlock,[8] and two Dutch books which were translated, wrote upon death, and several others. But Drelincourt, she said, had the clearest notions of death and of the future state of any who have handled that subject. Then she asked Mrs. Bargrave whether she had Drelincourt. She said, "Yes." Says Mrs. Veal, "Fetch it," and so Mrs. Bargrave goes upstairs and brings it down. Says Mrs. Veal, "Dear Mrs. Bargrave, if the eyes of our faith were as open as the eyes of our

---

6. I.e., *The Christian's Defense against the Fears of Death*, by Charles Drelincourt, a French Protestant pastor and prolific devotional writer who published the book in 1651; the first English translation appeared in 1675.

7. Kiss.

8. William Sherlock, Protestant divine and author of the widely read *Practical Discourse upon Death* (1689).

body, we should see numbers of angels about us for our guard. The notions we have of Heaven now are nothing like what it is, as Drelincourt says. Therefore be comforted under your afflictions, and believe that the Almighty has a particular regard to you, and that your afflictions are marks of God's favor. And when they have done the business they were sent for, they shall be removed from you. And believe me, my dear friend, believe what I say to you, one minute of future happiness will infinitely reward you for all your sufferings. For I can never believe" (and claps her hand upon her knee, with a great deal of earnestness, which indeed ran through all her discourse) "that ever God will suffer you to spend all your days in this afflicted state. But be assured that your afflictions shall leave you, or you them, in a short time." She spake in that pathetical and heavenly manner, that Mrs. Bargrave wept several times, she was so deeply affected with it. Then Mrs. Veal mentioned Dr. Horneck's *Ascetic*,[9] at the end of which he gives an account of the lives of the primitive Christians. Their pattern she recommended to our imitation, and said their conversation was not like this of our age. "For now" (says she) "there is nothing but frothy vain discourse, which is far different from theirs. Theirs was to edification, and to build one another up in the faith. So that they were not as we are, nor are we as they are. But," said she, "we might do as they did. There was a hearty friendship among them, but where is it now to be found?" Says Mrs. Bargrave, " 'Tis hard indeed to find a true friend in these days." Says Mrs. Veal, "Mr. Norris[1] has a fine copy of verses called *Friendship in Perfection*, which I wonderfully admire. Have you seen the book?" says Mrs. Veal. "No," says Mrs. Bargrave, "but I have the verses of my own writing out." "Have you?" says Mrs. Veal, "then fetch them." Which she did from above stairs, and offered them to Mrs. Veal to read, who refused, and waived the thing, saying holding down her head would make it ache, and then desired Mrs. Bargrave to read them to her, which she did. As they were admiring friendship, Mrs. Veal said, "Dear Mrs. Bargrave, I shall love you forever. In the verses, there is twice used the word Elysium. Ah!" says Mrs. Veal, "these poets have such names for heaven." She would often draw her hand cross her own eyes, and say, "Mrs. Bargrave, don't you think I am mightily impaired by my fits?" "No," says Mrs. Bargrave, "I think you look as well as ever I knew you."

After all this discourse, which the apparition put in words much finer than Mrs. Bargrave said she could pretend to, and was much more than she can remember (for it cannot be thought that an hour and three quarters' conversation could all be retained, though the main of it she thinks she does). She said to Mrs. Bargrave she would have her write a letter to her brother, and tell him she would have him give rings to such and such, and that there was a purse of gold in her cabinet, and that she would have two broad pieces given to her cousin Watson. Talking at this rate, Mrs. Bargrave thought that a fit was coming upon her,[2] and so placed herself in a chair just before her knees, to keep her from falling to the ground if her fits should occasion it; for the elbow chair she thought would keep her from falling on either side. And to divert Mrs. Veal, as she thought, she took hold of her gown sleeve several times, and commended it. Mrs. Veal told her it was a scoured[3] silk, and newly made up. But for all this Mrs. Veal persisted in her request, and told Mrs. Bargrave she must not deny her. And she would have her tell her brother all their conversation, when she had an opportunity. "Dear Mrs. Veal," says Mrs. Bargrave, "this seems so impertinent that I

---

9. Anthony Horneck, clergyman and author of *The Happy Ascetic* (1681).
1. John Norris, a clergyman, philosopher, and poet.

2. I.e., Mrs. Veal.
3. Polished; cleaned with detergent.

cannot tell how to comply with it; and what a mortifying story will our conversation be to a young gentleman?" "Well," says Mrs. Veal, "I must not be denied." "Why," says Mrs. Bargrave, "'tis much better methinks to do it yourself." "No," says Mrs. Veal, "though it seems impertinent to you now, you will see more reason for it hereafter." Mrs. Bargrave then, to satisfy her importunity, was going to fetch a pen and ink; but Mrs. Veal said, "Let it alone now, and do it when I am gone; but you must be sure to do it." Which was one of the last things she enjoined her at parting; and so she promised her.

Then Mrs. Veal asked for Mrs. Bargrave's daughter. She said she was not at home. "But if you have a mind to see her," says Mrs. Bargrave, "I'll send for her." "Do," says Mrs. Veal. On which she left her, and went to a neighbor's to send for her. And by the time Mrs. Bargrave was returning, Mrs. Veal was got without the door in the street, in the face of the beast-market on a Saturday (which is market day), and stood ready to part as soon as Mrs. Bargrave came to her. She asked her why she was in such haste. She said she must be going, though perhaps she might not go her journey till Monday. And told Mrs. Bargrave she hoped she should see her again at her cousin Watson's before she went whither she was a-going. Then she said she would take her leave of her, and walked from Mrs. Bargrave in her view till a turning interrupted the sight of her, which was three quarters after one in the afternoon.

Mrs. Veal died the 7th of September at 12 o'clock at noon, of her fits, and had not above four hours' senses before her death, in which time she received the sacrament. The next day after Mrs. Veal's appearing being Sunday, Mrs. Bargrave was mightily indisposed with a cold and a sore throat, that she could not go out that day. But on Monday morning she sends a person to Captain Watson's to know if Mrs. Veal were there. They wondered at Mrs. Bargrave's inquiry, and sent her word that she was not there, nor was she expected. At this answer Mrs. Bargrave told the maid she had certainly mistook the name, or made some blunder. And though she was ill, she put on her hood and went herself to Captain Watson's, though she knew none of the family, to see if Mrs. Veal was there or not. They said they wondered at her asking, for that she had not been in town; they were sure, if she had, she would have been there. Says Mrs. Bargrave, "I am sure she was with me on Saturday almost two hours." They said it was impossible, for they must have seen her if she had. In comes Captain Watson, while they were in dispute, and said that Mrs. Veal was certainly dead, and her escutcheons were making.[4] This strangely surprised Mrs. Bargrave, who went to the person immediately who had the care of them, and found it true. Then she related the whole story to Captain Watson's family, and what gown she had on, and how striped. And that Mrs. Veal told her it was scoured. Then Mrs. Watson cried out, "You have seen her indeed, for none knew but Mrs. Veal and myself that the gown was scoured." And Mrs. Watson owned that she described the gown exactly; "for," said she, "I helped her to make it up." This, Mrs. Watson blazed all about the town, and avouched the demonstration of the truth of Mrs. Bargrave's seeing Mrs. Veal's apparition. And Captain Watson carried two gentlemen immediately to Mrs. Bargrave's house, to hear the relation from her own mouth. And then it spread so fast that gentlemen and persons of quality, the judicious and skeptical part of the world, flocked in upon her, which at last became such a task that she was forced to go out of the way. For they were, in general, extremely satisfied of the truth of the thing,

4. Funeral ornaments were being prepared.

and plainly saw that Mrs. Bargrave was no hypochondriac, for she always appears with such a cheerful air and pleasing mien that she has gained the favor and esteem of all the gentry. And it's thought a great favor if they can but get the relation from her own mouth. I should have told you before that Mrs. Veal told Mrs. Bargrave that her sister and brother-in-law were just come down from London to see her. Says Mrs. Bargrave, "How came you to order matters so strangely?" "It could not be helped," said Mrs. Veal. And her sister and brother did come to see her, and entered the town of Dover just as Mrs. Veal was expiring. Mrs. Bargrave asked her whether she would drink some tea. Says Mrs. Veal, "I do not care if I do. But I'll warrant this mad fellow" (meaning Mrs. Bargrave's husband) "has broke all your trinkets." "But," says Mrs. Bargrave, "I'll get something to drink in for all that." But Mrs. Veal waived it, and said, "It is no matter, let it alone," and so it passed.

All the time I sat with Mrs. Bargrave, which was some hours, she recollected fresh sayings of Mrs. Veal. And one material thing more she told Mrs. Bargrave, that old Mr. Breton allowed Mrs. Veal ten pounds a year, which was a secret, and unknown to Mrs. Bargrave till Mrs. Veal told it her. Mrs. Bargrave never varies in her story, which puzzles those who doubt of the truth, or are unwilling to believe it. A servant in a neighbor's yard adjoining to Mrs. Bargrave's house heard her talking to somebody an hour of the time Mrs. Veal was with her. Mrs. Bargrave went out to her next neighbors the very moment she parted with Mrs. Veal, and told her what ravishing conversation she had with an old friend, and told the whole of it. *Drelincourt's Book of Death* is, since this happened, bought up strangely. And it is to be observed that notwithstanding all this trouble and fatigue Mrs. Bargrave has undergone upon this account, she never took the value of a farthing, nor suffered her daughter to take anything of anybody, and therefore can have no interest in telling the story.

But Mr. Veal does what he can to stifle the matter, and said he would see Mrs. Bargrave. But yet it is certain matter fact that he has been at Captain Watson's since the death of his sister, and yet never went near Mrs. Bargrave. And some of his friends report her to be a great liar, and that she knew of Mr. Breton's ten pounds a year. But the person who pretends to say so has the reputation of a notorious liar among persons which I know to be of undoubted repute. Now Mr. Veal is more a gentleman than to say she lies, but says a bad husband has crazed her. But she needs only to present herself, and it will effectually confute that pretense. Mr. Veal says he asked his sister on her deathbed whether she had a mind to dispose of anything, and she said, "No." Now, what the things which Mrs. Veal's apparition would have disposed of were so trifling, and nothing of justice aimed at in their disposal, that the design of it appears to me to be only in order to make Mrs. Bargrave, so to demonstrate the truth of her appearance as to satisfy the world of the reality thereof, as to what she had seen and heard, and to secure her reputation among the reasonable and understanding part of mankind. And then again, Mr. Veal owns that there was a purse of gold; but it was not found in her cabinet, but in a comb box. This looks improbable, for that Mrs. Watson owned that Mrs. Veal was so very careful of the key of her cabinet that she would trust nobody with it. And if so, no doubt she would not trust her gold out of it. And Mrs. Veal's often drawing her hand over her eyes, and asking Mrs. Bargrave whether her fits had not impaired her, looks to me as if she did it on purpose to remind Mrs. Bargrave of her fits, to prepare her not to think it strange that she should put her upon writing to her brother to dispose of rings and gold, which looked so much like a dying person's bequest. And it took accordingly with Mrs. Bargrave, as the effect of her fits coming upon her, and was one of the many instances of her wonderful love to her, and care of her, that she should not be affrighted. Which indeed appears in her whole management; particularly in her coming to her in the daytime, waiving the salutation, and when she was alone; and then the manner of her parting, to prevent a second attempt to salute her.

Now, why Mr. Veal should think this relation a reflection (as 'tis plain he does by his endeavoring to stifle it), I can't imagine, because the generality believe her to be a good spirit, her discourse was so heavenly. Her two great errands were to comfort Mrs. Bargrave in her affliction and to ask her forgiveness for her breach of friendship, and with a pious discourse to encourage her. So that after all, to suppose that Mrs. Bargrave could hatch such an invention as this from Friday noon till Saturday noon (supposing that she knew of Mrs. Veal's death the very first moment) without jumbling circumstances, and without any interest too—she must be more witty, fortunate, and wicked too than any indifferent person, I dare say, will allow. I asked Mrs. Bargrave several times if she was sure she felt the gown. She answered modestly, "If my senses be to be relied on, I am sure of it." I asked her if she heard a sound when she clapped her hand upon her knee. She said she did not remember she did. And she said, "She appeared to be as much a substance as I did, who talked with her. And I may," said she, "be as soon persuaded that your apparition is talking to me now, as that I did not really see her. For I was under no manner of fear; I received her as a friend, and parted with her as such. I would not," says she, "give one farthing to make anyone believe it. I have no interest in it; nothing but trouble is entailed upon me for a long time for aught that I know. And had it not come to light by accident, it would never have been made public." But now, she says, she will make her own private use of it, and keep herself out of the way as much as she can. And so she has done since. She says she had a gentleman who came thirty miles to her to hear the relation, and that she had told it to a room full of people at a time. Several particular gentlemen have had the story from Mrs. Bargrave's own mouth.

This thing has very much affected me, and I am as well satisfied as I am of the best grounded matter of fact. And why should we dispute matter of fact, because we cannot solve things of which we can have no certain or demonstrative notions, seems strange to me. Mrs. Bargrave's authority and sincerity alone would have been undoubted in any other case.

A *TRUE RELATION* IN CONTEXT
Parallel Accounts

A True Relation was published anonymously; Defoe was not identified as author until 1790. For most of the nineteenth century it was assumed that he had made up the entire story, possibly as publicity for Charles Drelincourt's *Defense against the Fears of Death,* the book that the ghost of Mrs. Veal repeatedly recommends to her friend. Shortly after the *Apparition's* first appearance as a pamphlet, in fact, Defoe's text and Drelincourt's were combined into a single, popular volume which went through many printings. In 1895 the Defoe scholar George Aitken published the first independent evidence for the authenticity of the story, if not of the ghost: a Latin memorandum from 1714 recorded an interview with the actual Mrs. Bargrave, who adhered (and added) to her narrative nearly a decade after it took place. Other contemporary accounts of her and her story have since been discovered. Defoe, then, was practicing

not fiction but journalism, sifting, selecting, and arranging testimony then in circulation, presenting it in the voice of Mrs. Bargrave's "intimate friend," the "very intelligent" justice of the peace who repeats her story (his own status, whether as historical
person or as fabricated narrator, has never been determined). Below are three other
accounts, in different social and intellectual registers: one from a Canterbury woman
writing to appease her aunt; another from an informant writing to satisfy the curiosity of one of the chief scientists of the day; and finally, the memorandum that first
suggested that Defoe's *Relation* was in some sense *True*.

L. Lukyn
Letter to her Aunt

[Canterbury, 9 October 1705]

Honored Aunt,

You may very well complain of our negligence in not writing to you, but hope
you have a better opinion of me than to think I have quite forgot I have such a relation as an aunt, and to show that I have not, do write, though I have very little to
say, without I tell you a long story of an apparition that appeared to one Mrs. Bargrove here at Canterbury at noonday. What I sent[1] you I had from Mrs. Bargrove herself. Last Saturday, was five or six weeks ago, Mrs. Bargrove was in a low room in her
own house, and somebody knocked at the door, and it was one Mrs. Veal of Dover,
who she was very intimately acquainted with when she lived at Dover, but had not
seen her these two years and a half, for so long Mrs. B. has lived in Canterbury. This
gentlewoman was much overjoyed at the sight of Mrs. Veal, and went to salute her,
but she rushed by her and sat herself down in a great armed chair, and fell into discourse of several things that had happened when they lived together at Dover. Mrs.
B. asked Mrs. Veal if she would drink any coffee or tea. She told her that if she talked
of eating or drinking she would be gone. That Mrs. Veal was subject to fits and was
never trusted alone anywhere without a servant with her, for which reason Mrs. B.
asked her how she ventured to come alone. She told her she gave them the slip, for
she had a mind to see her alone. She told Mrs. B. she was going a long journey, and
she was minded to tell her some things before she went. She desired Mrs. B. if she
should die to tell her brother that she would have Mrs. Margaret Watson have a suit
of mourning, if not her best gown and petticoat and several other things she had in a
cabinet. Captain Watson is this Mrs. Veal's uncle. Mrs. Veal told Mrs. B. that her
brother and sister Hazelwood were coming to Dover, but they would not come till
she was gone her journey, and it was true as she said, for when they came into Dover,
the bell was ringing for her; she was just dead. That was the day after she died, she
appeared to Mrs. B. She desired Mrs. B. to write down what she said but Mrs. B. [said]
'twas more proper for her to write it. She told her no, she was not well and could not.
But Mrs. B. there lay a book in the room where they were which had like to have
thrown down;[2] Mrs. Veal asked her what book it was. She told her it was somebody's
consolations against the fears of death (but I have forgot the man's name that writ
it). Says Mrs. Veal, "The things of the other world are not as we here think them."
She says, "You know that book tells us so." And upon that they had a great deal of
very heavenly talk. Mrs. B. said Mrs. Veal did not care she should look her in the
face, but would rub her hand over it. She asked Mrs. B. if she did not think her fits

---

1. Send.   2. Perhaps "had been dropped there."

had mightily impaired her. She told her she thought she looked a little pale, and Mrs. B. says she had the strangest blackness about her eyes she ever saw. She stayed two hours and at last seemed uneasy to be gone, and did rise up two or three times and sit down again. She desired she might see Mrs. B.'s little girl who boards with Mrs. Frances Casibon. She went to the next door to get somebody to send for the child, and when she came again Mrs. Veal was in the street as far from Mrs. B.'s door as from our house to Mr. Oughton's. So Mrs. B. went after her, and asked her if she would not stay and see the child. She told her no, she could not stay; she was going to her Uncle Watson's, and would have had Mrs. B. agone[3] with her. But she could not then but promised to come to her the next day. And so she had, but she has so sad a husband, and he came home in a cross drunkenness and shut her out of doors, and made her lay in a wet wash-house[4] all night, which hindered her going to Captain Watson's. But a[5] Monday morning she sent there to know if Mrs. Veal was gone her journey. Mrs. Watson wondered what the woman meant; there had been no Mrs. Veal. So when the messenger came to Mrs. B. she fancies she had mistook the message, and so Mrs. B. went herself to Mrs. Watson's, and while they were disputing the matter there came in news of the death of Mrs. Veal, which Mrs. B. and all present were very much surprised at as much a[6] more as she.

Mrs. Veal lay but a day ill; she was taken a-Wednesday and died a-Friday. I have writ you a long epistle and think it high time to conclude with all the duty, love, and service from whom it's due, dear aunt.

Your dutiful niece,
L. Lukyn

Stephen Gray
Letter to John Flamsteed[1]

Canterbury, November 15, 1705

Reverend Sir,

Yours of the third instant[2] I have received and have according to the utmost of my ability endeavored to fulfill your request. I have not only made inquiry into Mrs. Bargrave's character from persons which were most likely to give a just account of her, but have been and conversed with her myself, so that if I have not answered your queries concerning her to your satisfaction you will impute it to my weakness and not to a want of will to serve you. For indeed my temper is very averse to conversation, yet I must strive what I can to overcome my inclinations when they are any wise obstructive to the obedience due to your commands.

Sir, I have taken the account I have had of Mrs. Bargrave's character from persons that are esteemed qualified in all things as you direct,[3] from those that have known her conversation, both when she lived at Dover and here in Canterbury, as well of the clergy as others, and all give her the character of a religious, discreet, witty, and well-accomplished gentlewoman. She was bred up in the

---

3. Go.
4. A shed used for laundry.
5. On.
6. Or.
1. Flamsteed (1646–1719) was the astronomer-royal, charged with producing newly precise charts of the heavens. His informant Stephen Gray may be the person of

the same name (d. 1736) who later distinguished himself as a very early student of electricity.
2. November 3.
3. Flamsteed's "direction" possesses Royal Society resonance, prizing the testimony of those best "qualified" (by intelligence, reputation, rank) to assess the evidence.

Church of England; her father, who was Mr. Lodowick, was in his lifetime minister of the church at Dover, and she is seen often to frequent the divine service of the church. And as she herself told me, she was once beaten by her husband for being so silly (as he called it) as to receive the sacrament. This in answer to your first query. As to your second, I cannot find but she is a serious person not given to anything of levity. * * * 'Tis now become difficult to get an account of Mrs. Bargrave's relation of her conversation with Mrs. Veal. Mr. Veal, her brother at Dover, and his relations and friends that live here at Canterbury, being willing to have it forgotten, do all they can to stifle it. But I, happening to go to a gentleman's house whose wife I had heard was well acquainted with Mrs. Bargrave at a time when she was there, I acquainted him with the design of my coming. He so far interceded for me that I were the next day sent for to hear Mrs. Bargrave relate her whole story. But I must own that her narrative of it was so very long, and my memory so weak, that I began to despair of giving you a tolerable account of it, had I not been assisted with a copy of it as it was written by an ingenious gentleman who had it from her own mouth before several gentlemen. And as far as I can remember, 'tis very agreeable to what I heard her say.

Mrs. Bargrave, the wife of Mr. Bargrave, an attorney, who formerly lived in Dover, now in Canterbury, had when in Dover contracted a very intimate friendship with one Mrs. Veal, a maiden gentlewoman. But upon Mrs. Bargrave's coming to Canterbury, their friendly conversation had been discontinued for some time. Mrs. Veal died Friday, September 7th, at Dover, but visited Mrs. Bargrave on Saturday the 8th. She conversed with her two hours, viz. from 12 till 2 in the afternoon. Mrs. Bargrave in the forenoon had been weeping and bewailing herself upon the account of her afflicted condition, but had pretty well composed herself when about 12 o'clock she heard somebody knock at the door. Being alone, she went to the door herself to see who it was, and found it to be Mrs. Veal, her former friend, in a traveling habit. Being very joyful to see her, asked her how she came to find her out in that old hole. To whom Mrs. Veal replied that she would find her out wherever she was. Then Mrs. B. told her she was glad to see her, but wondered she came alone; she, being subject to fits, used not to go but with somebody to attend her. She replied that she had given her friends at her Uncle Watson's the slip. Then Mrs. Bargrave asked her to come in, and offered to salute her, upon which she sat herself down in a chair, saying she was very weary. Then Mrs. Bargrave sat down beside her and told Mrs. Veal she had been in a sad humor just before she came in. "Yes," said Mrs. Veal, "I perceived it by your eyes. Is it no better with you and your husband than it used to be?" To which Mrs. Bargrave replying, "No," Mrs. Veal thereupon undertook to comfort her by giving her hope that in a little time it would be otherwise, and then fell into some religious discourses and exhortations. And seeing a book lie in the window, asked Mrs. Bargrave what book it was. She said it was a book they two had taken great delight in reading in at Dover; it was Drelincourt's discourse *Against the Fear of Death*. Mrs. Veal replied it was an excellent book and full of truth. Mrs. Bargrave answered she preferred it to any she had seen on that subject. "Yes," said Mrs. Veal, "but death and eternity are much other things than the world takes them to be." Mrs. Bargrave, being much pleased with her friend's conversation, began a discourse on friendship and some things past, of the cause of the decay of it in them, and asked her if she had read any of Mr. Norris his works. Mrs. Veal replied she had read some of his letters of divine love. Mrs. Bargrave asked her if she had read a copy of verses of his on friendship. Mrs. Veal said no, and asked Mrs. Bargrave if she had that book, who said no, but she had written them out in another book and would fetch them down and show them to her if she pleased. To which she consented, and Mrs. Bargrave fetched them and offered them to her to read, but she refused, saying she could not read them, but desired Mrs. Bargrave to read them. Which she did, and seemed much affected with them, but told Mrs. Bargrave that friendship was much better and more perfect in the other world than in this. And in discourse she spent some time, to Mrs. Bargrave's great satisfaction. Mrs. Bargrave asked Mrs. Veal if she would drink any tea. To which she replied, "Now but if I would you have no fire to make it." To which she replied that she would soon have her fire. "Nay," said Mrs. Veal, "if you talk of drinking I am gone." Mrs. Veal, perceiving Mrs. Bargrave to look pretty earnestly upon her, endeavored to cover her face with her hand, and asked Mrs. Bargrave if her fits have not somewhat altered her. Mrs. Bargrave, being fearful of discouraging her, endeavored to mitigate.[5] Then Mrs. Veal made as if she was rising to be gone, but sat down again and told Mrs. Bargrave she had almost forgot a main thing she came to her about; and that was that she being to go a journey would desire her to tell her brother some things from her. "What," said Mrs. Bargrave, "you are going your old journey," meaning to Bath or Wells, where she knew she was wont frequently to go. To which Mrs. Veal made little or no reply, but went on to tell Mrs. Bargrave what she would have her tell her brother about a tombstone, saying her brother said he would have a tombstone made for her mother but had not done it, so she would now have him make one large enough to contain them both. And told her some things she had in her cabinet, and of a suit of clothes which she would have given to her cousin, Mrs. Margaret Watson, with some other things which Mrs. Bargrave will relate to none but Mrs. Veal's brother. Mrs. Bargrave thought this might be the effect of her head's being disturbed by some approaching fit that was coming upon her, went to divert her by some discourse about her gown, taking it in her hand, saying, "This is very pretty stuff, madam." Mrs. Veal replied, "It is an old gown I have had scoured and newly made up, but you do this to divert me. But I will not be diverted." Then Mrs. Bargrave would have fetched a pen and ink, that Mrs. Veal might have written what she would have her brother know, but she said she could not write then. Mrs. Bargrave asked her why she did not tell her brother before she came out of Dover, or tell her Uncle Watson now, as one that would sooner be believed. She replied no, and would not be satisfied without a promise from her to do it, which, after some reluctancy, she did. Then Mrs. Veal asked Mrs. Bargrave if she knew her sister who married a clergyman, Mr.——, that lives somewhere in Southwark. Mrs. Bargrave said it was about 20 years ago since she saw her at Dover. "Yes," says Mrs. Veal, "'tis above 25 years since," and told her that her sister, brother, and children were now coming to Dover, "and all things were provided for them just as I were going my journey." Then Mrs. Bargrave asked Mrs. Veal if she would see her little girl, who was at school, but she would send for her if she pleased, and went out of the door to see for a neighbor to call her. But looking back, saw Mrs. Veal was come to the door. Then said Mrs. Bargrave, "Then you will be going?" "Yes," says Mrs. Veal, "I cannot stay." Says Mrs. Bargrave, "I hope you do not go out of town tonight." "No," says Mrs. Veal, "I am going to my uncle Captain Watson's, and shall be there till Monday morning." And asked Mrs. Bargrave if she would not go with her. She said no, she could not go with her,

5. To reassure her.

because her husband was not at home, but would come tomorrow and see her before she went her journey; but would walk a little way with her. Which she did, and then they parted. And Mrs. Bargrave saw Mrs. Veal going towards Captain Watson's house for several rods,[6] and then before she went into her own house stepped into a neighbor's, who asked her what made her look so cheerful. Mrs. Bargrave replied that she had had two hours' conversation with an old friend of hers which was come to renew her friendship. Next day in the evening she went to Captain Watson's to inquire for Mrs. Veal, but they said she had not been there. When she came home, her husband told her that her old friend Mrs. Veal was dead. She said nothing to him till next morning; then asked him how he knew it, telling him what had happened. Being greatly surprised, went again to Captain Watson's and described her gown, which Mrs. Watson's daughter knew to be one which Mrs. Veal was wont to wear. But this not satisfying her, she went to the party that brought the news to Canterbury, who told her that Mrs. Veal died on Friday in the afternoon, and that her brother and sister was coming into Dover as the bell was ringing for her. There is this further observable, that the next neighbor's maid, as she was at work in the yard, heard somebody talking very pleasantly with Mrs. Bargrave, and when she came in told her Mrs. so, who said Mrs. Bargrave's husband does not use to be[7] so pleasant with her. Upon which the maid said no, that it was both women's voices she heard, but was not near enough to distinguish their words.

This, Sir, is the substance of Mrs. Bargrave's relation. Most of the sober men of our city do believe it, but there are some that do not. Their chief objections are that Mrs. Bargrave mentions some things in the cabinet that Mr. Veal, when he opened it, could not find there, though he opened it in the presence of several persons whom he called as witnesses. And 'tis likewise said that nobody saw Mrs. Bargrave in the street at that time when she says she walked with her Mrs. Veal. And it's reported of Mrs. Bargrave that she is wont to report the houses wherein she has lived to be haunted, as you have heard. How far this is true, you have heard, in part already heard, but I have received a fuller information of this chatter than Mrs. Veal's[8] modesty would permit her to give me, though consonant enough to what she told me. Mr. Bargrave one day rode a-hunting with some gentlemen. And when they had done, towards night went to a public house about nine miles from Canterbury, where he got drunk and lay there not only that night but some days after. His wife, hearing where he was, went after him, to see if she could get him home (for she is very careful of him, notwithstanding his severity to her). It happened she came at a time when her husband was in the company of a whore. They were, it seems, together in the house of ease.[9] Mrs. Bargrave, when she came in, asked for her husband. They told her he was without in the garden, whither she went. The whore, it seems, saw her, and for fear of being discovered fled immediately; and before she was got over the wall Mrs. Bargrave saw her, and, when her husband came to her, told him that she had seen somewhat getting over the wall which she thought was an apparition. Which he seemed willing to believe, being glad of the opportunity of so pretty a delusion to conceal his roguery. And this Mr. Bargrave has been heard to relate himself long before the apparition of Mrs. Veal to Mrs. Bargrave. Upon the whole consideration of all circumstances, I cannot say those that do not believe Mrs. Bargrave's relation to be true are altogether without reason. Yet I think the arguments for the truth

---

6. A rod is 16.5 feet.
7. Is not ordinarily.

8. A slip for "Mrs. Bargrave."
9. The outhouse.

of it are of much greater validity than those against it, and am inclined to believe that Mrs. Bargrave did really converse with the apparition of her deceased friend; but shall leave you, Sir, to consider and weigh the arguments for the credibility or incredibility of it and to determine as you in your incomparably more mature judgment shall think fit to. I asked Mrs. Bargrave if she were willing to take her oath of her relation of this her conversation with Mrs. Veal. She answered, "Not without the consent of Mr. Veal," and that it should be before the Archbishop of Canterbury and some others of the chief ministers of state. Then I told her it would as soon be credited if it were given before two Justices of the Peace. She replied she did not care whether it were believed or not; she knew it to be true, and her word was as good as her oath. And added that it was no article of our faith; we may be saved without it. Besides, those that will not believe the Scriptures will not believe her upon her oath, and that she has no advantage by it, but a great deal of trouble, by multitudes of people coming to her or sending for her almost daily, so that she has had little rest since.

Sir, this is all that I can collect that may either confirm or contradict the credibility of Mrs. Veal's apparition to Mrs. Bargrave. I could have wished the task had been on others that was more capable of it, and then you might have had a more satisfactory account than I fear this will be to you.

This time of the year we are in the greatest hurry of our business, so that I have very little time, and am so fatigued that I can make but few astronomical observations. I do now and then get time to make a few hasty observations of the spots in the sun, and shall observe some of the eclipses of Jupiter's satellites that happen in convenient times; but I will assure you, Sir, tis not without some regret that I must tell you I am afraid I shall not have so many as you may expect, and therefore would not have you so far depend on my observations as not to get what you can observed by others. Though I shall endeavor to serve you in all things to the very extremity of my power.

Sir, your most humble servant,
Stephen Gray

An Interview with Mrs. Bargrave[1]

On May 21, 1714, I asked Mrs. Bargrave whether the matters contained in this narrative are true. To which she replied that she had neither written the printed narrative nor published it, nor did she know the editor;[2] all things contained in it, however, were true as regards the event itself or matters of importance; but one or two circumstances relating to the affair were not described with perfect accuracy by the editor. The editor, no doubt, learned all particulars by word of mouth from Mrs. Bargrave,[3] and then published them without her knowledge. Whatever is changed for the better in this copy[4] is derived from Mrs. Bargrave herself.

Something was also mentioned in this conversation of the former times when the Dissenters were persecuted by King Charles II. At which says Mrs. Veal, "People should not persecute one another whilst they all are upon the road to eternity."

---

1. This account was found written in Latin in a copy of the fourth edition of Defoe's *A True Relation*. The writer has not been identified; it is presented in the translation by George Aitken, the scholar who discovered and published it in his edition of *The Romances and Narratives of Daniel Defoe* (1895), 15.xix.

2. Defoe (whose identity as author/"editor" of the narrative was not yet known).
3. The writer here appears either to forget or to disbelieve Mrs. Bargrave's assertion in the previous sentence.
4. I.e., the fourth edition, in a copy of which these memoranda are inscribed.

from A Journal of the Plague Year

*Being Observations or Memorials of the Most Remarkable Occurrences,
as Well Public as Private, Which Happened in London during
the Last Great Visitation in 1665*[1]

[AT THE BURIAL PIT]

I went all the first part of the time freely about the streets, though not so freely as to
run myself into apparent danger, except when they dug the great pit in the churchyard of our parish of Aldgate; a terrible pit it was, and I could not resist my curiosity
to go and see it. As near as I may judge, it was about 40 foot in length, and about 15
or 16 foot broad; and at the time I first looked at it, about nine foot deep; but it was
said they dug it near 20 foot deep afterwards, in one part of it, till they could go no
deeper for the water: for they had, it seems, dug several large pits before this, for
though the plague was long a-coming to our parish, yet when it did come, there was
no parish in or about London where it raged with such violence as in the two parishes of Aldgate and Whitechapel.

I say they had dug several pits in another ground, when the distemper began to
spread in our parish, and especially when the dead carts began to go about, which was
not in our parish till the beginning of August. Into these pits they had put perhaps 50
or 60 bodies each; then they made larger holes, wherein they buried all that the cart
brought in a week, which by the middle to the end of August, came to from 200 to
400 a week; and they could not well dig them larger, because of the order of the magistrates, confining them to leave no bodies within six foot of the surface; and the
water coming on, at about 17 or 18 foot, they could not well, I say, put more in one
pit; but now at the beginning of September, the plague raging in a dreadful manner,
and the number of burials in our parish increasing to more than was ever buried in
any parish about London of no larger extent, they ordered this dreadful gulf to be
dug; for such it was, rather than a pit.

They had supposed this pit would have supplied them for a month or more,
when they dug it, and some blamed the church wardens for suffering such a frightful
thing, telling them they were making preparations to bury the whole parish, and the
like; but time made it appear, the church wardens knew the condition of the parish
better than they did; for the pit being finished the 4th of September, I think, they
began to bury in it the 6th, and by the 20th, which was just two weeks, they had
thrown into it 1,114 bodies, when they were obliged to fill it up, the bodies being
then come to lie within six foot of the surface: I doubt not but there may be some
ancient persons alive in the parish, who can justify the fact of this, and are able to
show even in what part of the churchyard the pit lay, better than I can; the mark of
it also was many years to be seen in the churchyard on the surface lying in length,
parallel with the passage which goes by the west wall of the churchyard, out of
Houndsditch, and turns east again into Whitechapel, coming out near the Three
Nuns Inn.

---

1. In the early 1720s, London found itself once again
threatened with the prospect of bubonic plague. Defoe
responded with two long pieces of prose: a manual of preventive measures called *Due Preparations for the Plague*
(1720), and a historical fiction thoroughly researched
and deeply grounded in historical facts. The text's purported narrator—already dead by the time his book is
published—presents himself as recasting in retrospect the
journal entries he wrote during that terrible year, in the
hope that they may benefit future generations. Designated only by his initials, "H. F.," he is probably modeled in
part on the author's uncle Henry Foe, who like "H. F."
was a London saddler who lived in the parish of Aldgate.

It was about the 10th of September, that my curiosity led, or rather drove me to go and see this pit again, when there had been near 400 people buried in it; and I was not content to see it in the daytime, as I had done before; for then there would have been nothing to have been seen but the loose earth; for all the bodies that were thrown in were immediately covered with earth, by those they called the buriers, which at other times were called bearers;[2] but I resolved to go in the night and see some of them thrown in.

There was a strict order to prevent people coming to those pits, and that was only to prevent infection: but after some time, that order was more necessary, for people that were infected, and near their end, and delirious also, would run to those pits wrapped in blankets or rugs and throw themselves in and, as they said, bury themselves: I cannot say that the officers suffered any willingly to lie there; but I have heard that in a great pit in Finsbury, in the parish of Cripplegate, it lying open then to the fields (for it was not then walled about) came and threw themselves in, and expired there, before they threw any earth upon them; and that when they came to bury others, and found them there, they were quite dead, though not cold.

This may serve a little to describe the dreadful condition of that day, though it is impossible to say anything that is able to give a true idea of it to those who did not see it, other than this; that it was indeed *very, very, very* dreadful, and such as no tongue can express.

I got admittance into the churchyard by being acquainted with the sexton[3] who attended, who though he did not refuse me at all, yet earnestly persuaded me not to go; telling me very seriously, for he was a good religious and sensible man, that it was indeed their business and duty to venture, and to run all hazards; and that in it they might hope to be preserved; but that I had no apparent call to it, but my own curiosity, which, he said, he believed I would not pretend was sufficient to justify my running that hazard. I told him I had been pressed in my mind to go, and that perhaps it might be an instructing sight that might not be without its uses. "Nay," says the good man, "if you will venture upon that score, *'Name of God go in;* for depend upon it, 'twill be a sermon to you, it may be, the best that ever you heard in your life. 'Tis a speaking sight," says he, "and has a voice with it, and a loud one, to call us all to repentance." And with that he opened the door and said, "Go, if you will."

His discourse had shocked my resolution a little, and I stood wavering for a good while; but just at that interval I saw two links[4] come over from the end of the Minories,[5] and heard the bellman,[6] and then appeared a dead cart, as they called it, coming over the streets so I could no longer resist my desire of seeing it, and went in: there was nobody, as I could perceive at first, in the churchyard or going into it, but the buriers and the fellow that drove the cart, or rather led the horse and cart; but when they came up to the pit, they saw a man go to and again, muffled up in a brown cloak and making motions with his hands, under his cloak, as if

---

2. H.F. combines two categories: the buriers put the dead bodies into the pits, arranging them in order to conserve space, and covering them with lime in order to quicken decomposition. The bearers, by contrast, handled bodies living and dead: during the day they delivered the infected to the plague-hospitals; by night they collected corpses for the pits.

3. Caretaker of the church and graveyard.

4. I.e., boys carrying torches ("links"), who for a fee led people through the streets at night.

5. A street.

6. In ordinary times, the bellman announced the time and weather as he made his way through the streets at night; in plague time, he rang his bell to alert people that the cart burying the dead was approaching.

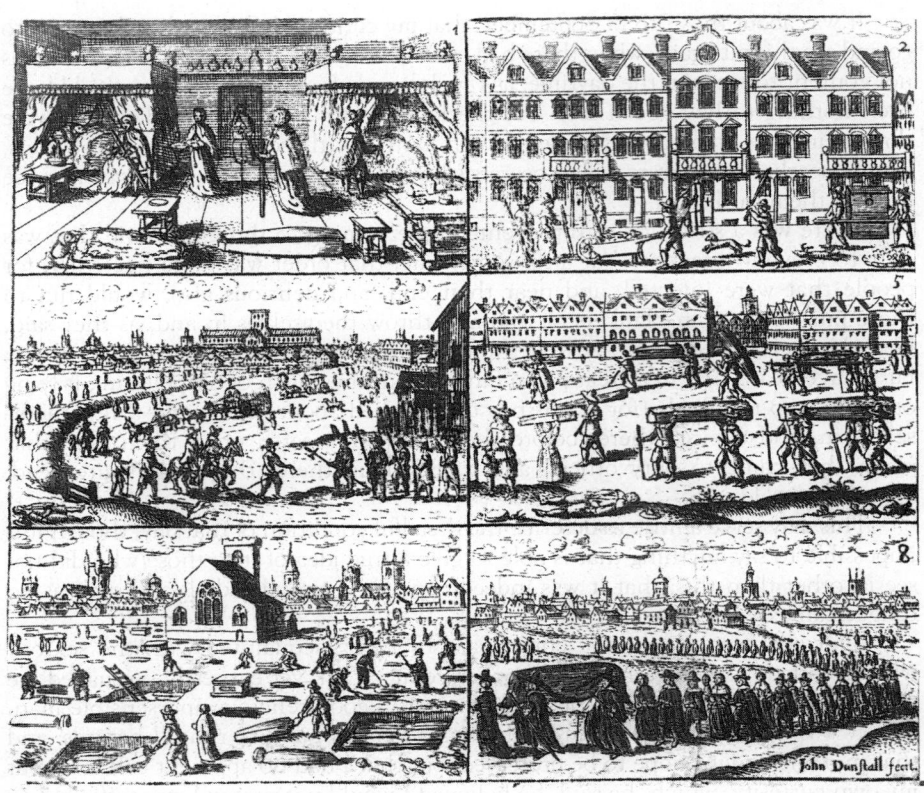

John Dunſtall fecit.

he was in a great agony; and the buriers immediately gathered about him, supposing he was one of those poor delirious or desperate creatures that used to pretend,[7] as I have said, to bury themselves. He said nothing as he walked about, but two or three times groaned very deeply, and loud, and sighed as he would break his heart.

When the buriers came up to him they soon found he was neither a person infected and desperate, as I have observed above, or a person distempered in mind, but one oppressed with a dreadful weight of grief indeed, having his wife and several of his children, all in the cart that was just come in with him, and he followed in an agony and excess of sorrow. He mourned heartily, as it was easy to see, but with a kind of masculine grief that could not give itself vent by tears, and calmly desiring the buriers to let him alone, said he would only see the bodies thrown in, and go away, so they left importuning him; but no sooner was the cart turned round, and the bodies shot into the pit promiscuously, which was a surprise to him, for he at least expected they would have been decently laid in, though

7. Attempt.

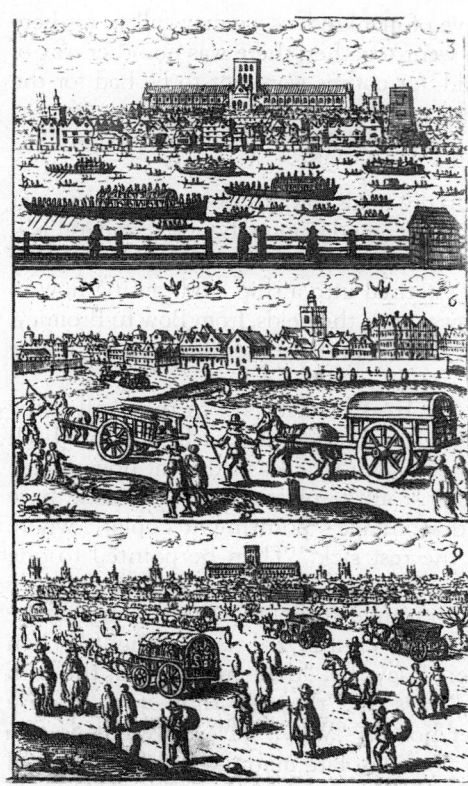

John Dunstall. *Scenes from the Plague in London.* 1665. The sequence tracks the course of corpses, from death within the city to burial in the plague-pits outside the city's walls.

indeed he was afterwards convinced that was impractible; I say, no sooner did he see the sight, but he cried out aloud unable to contain himself; I could not hear what he said, but he went backward two or three steps, and fell down in a swoon: the buriers ran to him and took him up, and in a little while he came to himself, and they led him away to the Pye Tavern over-against the end of Houndsditch, where, it seems, the man was known, and where they took care of him. He looked into the pit again, as he went away, but the buriers had covered the bodies so immediately with throwing in earth that, though there was light enough, for there were lanterns and candles in them placed all night round the sides of the pit, upon the heaps of earth, seven or eight, or perhaps more, yet nothing could be seen.

This was a mournful scene indeed, and affected me almost as much as the rest; but the other was awful, and full of terror. The cart had in it sixteen or seventeen bodies; some were wrapped up in linen sheets, some in rugs, some little other than naked, or so loose that what covering they had fell from them in the shooting out of the cart, and they fell quite naked among the rest; but the matter was not much to them, or the indecency much to anyone else, seeing they were all dead, and were to be huddled together into the common grave of mankind, as we may call it, for here was no difference made, but poor and rich went together; there was no other way of burials, neither was it possible there should, for coffins were not to be had for the prodigious numbers that fell in such a calamity as this.

[ENCOUNTER WITH A WATERMAN]

Much about the same time I walked out into the fields towards Bow; for I had a great mind to see how things were managed in the river, and among the ships; and as I had some concern in shipping, I had a notion that it had been one of the best ways of securing oneself from the infection to have retired into a ship, and musing how to satisfy my curiosity in that point, I turned away over the fields, from Bow to Bromley, and down to Blackwall, to the Stairs, which are there for landing or taking water.[1]

Here I saw a poor man walking on the bank, or seawall, as they call it, by himself. I walked a while also about, seeing the houses all shut up;[2] at last I fell into some talk, at a distance, with this poor man; first I asked him, how people did thereabouts? "Alas, Sir!" says he, "almost all desolate; all dead or sick: here are very few families in this part, or in that village," pointing at Poplar, "where half of them are not dead already, and the rest sick." Then he pointed to one house. "There they are all dead," said he, "and the house stands open; nobody dares go into it. A poor thief," says he, "ventured in to steal something, but he paid dear for his theft; for he was carried to the churchyard too last night." Then he pointed to several other houses. "There," says he, "they are all dead; the man and his wife, and five children. There," says he, "they are shut up; you see a watchman at the door," and so of other houses. "Why," says I, "What do you here all alone?" "Why," says he, "I am a poor desolate man; it has pleased God I am not yet visited,[3] though my family is, and one of my children dead." "How do you mean then," said I, "that you are not visited?" "Why," says he, "that's my house," pointing to a very little low boarded house, "and there my poor wife and two children live," said he, "if they may be said to live; for my wife and one of the children are visited, but I do not come at them." And with that word I saw the tears run very plentifully down his face; and so they did down mine too, I assure you.

But said I, "Why do you not come at them? How can you abandon your own flesh, and blood?" "Oh, Sir!" says he, "the Lord forbid; I do not abandon them; I work for them as much as I am able, and blessed be the Lord, I keep them from want," and with that I observed, he lifted up his eyes to Heaven, with a countenance that presently told me, I had happened on a man that was no hypocrite, but a serious, religious good man, and his ejaculation was an expression of thankfulness, that in such a condition as he was in, he should be able to say his family did not want. "Well," says I, "honest man, that is a great mercy as things go now with the poor: but how do you live then, and how are you kept from the dreadful calamity that is now upon us all?" "Why Sir," says he, "I am a waterman,[4] and there's my boat," says he, "and the boat serves me for a house; I work in it in the day, and I sleep in it in the night; and what I get, I lay down upon that stone," says he, showing me a broad stone on the other side of the street, a good way from his house, "and then," says he, "I halloo, and call to them till I make them hear; and they come and fetch it."

"Well friend," says I, "but how can you get any money as a waterman? Does anybody go by water these times?" "Yes Sir," says he, "in the way I am employed there does. Do you see there," says he, "five ships lie at anchor," pointing down the river, a good way below the town, "and do you see," says he, "eight or ten ships lie at the chain, there, and at anchor yonder," pointing above the town. "All those ships have families on board, of their merchants and owners, and such like, who have locked themselves up, and live on board, close shut in, for fear of the infection; and I tend on them to fetch things for them, carry letters, and do what is absolutely necessary, that they may not be obliged to come on shore; and every night I fasten my boat on board one of the ship's boats, and there I sleep by myself, and blessed be God, I am preserved hitherto."

"Well," said I, "friend, but will they let you come on board, after you have been on shore here, when this is such a terrible place, and so infected as it is?"

"Why, as to that," said he, "I very seldom go up the ship side, but deliver what I bring to their boat, or lie by the side, and they hoist it on board; if I did, I think they are in no danger from me, for I never go into any house on shore, or touch anybody, no, not of my own family; but I fetch provisions for them."

"Nay," says I, "but that may be worse, for you must have those provisions of somebody or other; and since all this part of the town is so infected, it is dangerous so much as to speak with anybody; for this village," said I, "is as it were, the beginning of London, though it be at some distance from it."

"That is true," added he, "but you do not understand me right, I do not buy provisions for them here; I row up to Greenwich and buy fresh meat there, and sometimes I row down the river to Woolwich and buy there; then I go to single farm houses on the Kentish side, where I am known, and buy fowls and eggs and butter, and bring to the ships, as they direct me, sometimes one, sometimes the other; I seldom come on shore here; and I came now only to call to my wife, and hear how my little family do, and give them a little money, which I received last night."

"Poor man!" said I, "and how much hast thou gotten for them?"

"I have gotten four shillings," said he, "which is a great sum, as things go now with poor men; but they have given me a bag of bread too, and a salt fish and some flesh; so all helps out."

"Well," said I, "and have you given it them yet?"

"No," said he, "but I have called, and my wife has answered, that she cannot come out yet, but in half an hour she hopes to come, and I am waiting for her: poor woman!" says he, "she is brought sadly down; she has a swelling, and it is broke, and I hope she will recover;[5] but I fear the child will die; but *it is the Lord!*"—Here he stopped, and wept very much.

---

5. The plague afflicted its victims with painful swellings ("buboes"); if the swelling broke open, it was thought to presage recovery.

"Well, honest friend," said I, "thou hast a sure comforter, if thou hast brought thyself to be resigned to the will of God; He is dealing with us all in judgment."

"Oh, Sir," says he, "it is infinite mercy, if any of us are spared; and who am I to repine!"

"Sayest thou so," said I, "and how much less is my faith than thine?" And here my heart smote me, suggesting how much better this poor man's foundation was, on which he stayed in the danger, than mine; that he had nowhere to fly; that he had a family to bind him to attendance, which I had not; and mine was mere presumption, his a true dependence, and a courage resting on God: and yet, that he used all possible caution for his safety.

I turned a little way from the man, while these thoughts engaged me, for indeed, I could no more refrain from tears than he.

At length, after some farther talk, the poor woman opened the door, and called, "Robert, Robert." He answered and bid her stay a few moments, and he would come; so he ran down the common stairs to his boat, and fetched up a sack in which was the provisions he had brought from the ships; and when he returned, he hallooed again; then he went to the great stone which he showed me, and emptied the sack, and laid all out, everything by themselves, and then retired; and his wife came with a little boy to fetch them away; and he called, and said, such a captain had sent such a thing, and such a captain such a thing, and at the end adds, "God has sent it all, give thanks to Him." When the poor woman had taken up all, she was so weak, she could not carry it at once in, *though the weight was not much neither;* so she left the biscuit which was in a little bag and left a little boy to watch it till she came again.

"Well, but," says I to him, "did you leave her the four shillings too, which you said was your week's pay?"

"YES, YES," says he, "you shall hear her own it." So he calls again, "Rachel, Rachel,"[6] which it seems was her name, "did you take up the money?" "YES," said she. "How much was it?" said he. "Four shillings and a groat," said she. "Well, well," says he, "the Lord keep you all"; and so he turned to go away.

As I could not refrain contributing tears to this man's story, so neither could I refrain my charity for his assistance; so I called him. "Hark thee friend," said I, "come hither; for I believe thou art in health, that I may venture thee." So I pulled out my hand, which was in my pocket before. "Here," says I, "go and call thy Rachel once more, and give her a little more comfort from me. God will never forsake a family that trust in him as thou dost." So I gave him four other shillings, and bade him go lay them on the stone and call his wife.

I have not words to express the poor man's thankfulness, neither could he express it himself, but by tears running down his face; he called his wife, and told her God had moved the heart of a stranger, upon hearing their condition, to give them all that money; and a great deal more such as that he said to her. The woman too made signs of the like thankfulness, as well to Heaven, as to me, and joyfully picked it up; and I parted with no money all that year that I thought better bestowed.

1722

6. The name evokes Jeremiah 31.15: "Rachel weeping for her children refused to be comforted."

PERSPECTIVES

Reading Papers

Shakespeare never read a newspaper. In the early seventeenth century, the news was purveyed irregularly and improvisatorily. A breaking story or a sensational event might
prompt a spate of ballads, broadsides, and bulletins, which would then abate until the next
big thing hove into view. The news periodical, nascent on the Continent during Shakespeare's lifetime, arrived in England in 1620 in the form of English-language news sheets
dispatched from Amsterdam. London publishers quickly took up the enterprise, to their
considerable profit. Shakespeare's caustic contemporary Ben Jonson lived to witness their
innovation; he promptly forecast an imminent glut of cheap and worthless information—
fearing, with reason, that the new medium would supplant the theater as the public's
favored oracle.

Even Jonson, though, could not have foreseen the quantities of print that would pour
from presses decades later during the Civil Wars, when the instability of authority allowed
innumerable newsbooks to appear, supporting every party in the conflict. During the Interregnum and Restoration, government tried through strict licensing laws to limit the flow and
narrow the range of newsprint, but whenever those laws lapsed, innovations abounded: the
first daily reports on proceedings in the House of Commons (1680), the first English newspaper outside London (1701), the first daily newspaper (1702), the first weekly journals (1713),
melding the news with a miscellany of other departments. At the centennial of Shakespeare's
death, London was producing some sixteen newspapers; a century later Britain possessed
more than 350, in addition to legions of other periodicals purveying opinion and advice. The
newspaper, the periodical essay, and the magazine had become confirmed habits in the lives
of almost everyone who could read, and even of many who could not, since the papers were
often read aloud, their contents discussed and debated, in public gathering places and household circles.

The periodical was a creature of the seventeenth century and a staple of the eighteenth. It punctuated the calendar with a new print pulse, and imparted to its readership a
new sense of moving together in synchrony, in a rhythm that paradoxically combined the
solitary and the social, the private and the public. The "mass ceremony" of reading the
newspaper is generally performed (as the historian Benedict Anderson has observed) in
"privacy, in the lair of the skull. Yet each communicant is well aware that the ceremony
he performs is being replicated simultaneously by thousands (or millions) of others, of
whose existence he is confident, yet of whose identity he has not the slightest notion."
The periodical press, then, gave its readers a new way of seeing the world, and of seeing
themselves in the world, as private beings and public entities; it prompted them (in
Anderson's phrase) to imagine themselves as a community.

Monarchs and politicians tried hard to control the press, to dictate its views and to contain its criticisms, but in Britain the phenomenon proved too large for such arrant limitation.
The news sheets and the essays helped create a new arena of political thought and action, separate from the older power centers of Court and Parliament, a public sphere of newly engaged
readers who increasingly valued and deployed their own capacity to form collective opinions,
and who increasingly expected their opinions to affect events. The freedom and copiousness of
the press became a national boast, and abetted Britons in a conviction they were already cultivating: that they were participants in an ongoing narrative of commerce and taste, politeness,
politics, and empire, protagonists in a story with numberless installments and no foreseeable
end, unfolding at the center of the world.

Each newspaper in this section is introduced at its first appearance.

━•━ ≊⧩≋ ⊹━•━

News and Comment

If the seventeenth century gave birth to the seething enterprise of print journalism, it also ushered in still-lingering distinctions and confusions as to what newspapers ought to be, and do. Most papers proudly declared their objectivity, yet at the same time they plainly manifested their partisan sympathies in their reportage and their prose. The division between news and opinion was rarely sharp, but in the early 1700s, opinion found fuller expression in periodicals like Defoe's *Review* (which more or less took for granted that readers had gathered their news elsewhere, and offered instead a running commentary on events), and in weekly journals like the *Craftsman*, which included ordinary news but which began each number with a long, fervently partisan political essay. Such essays anticipated the op-ed pages of today's newspapers, the closing meditations of news broadcasters.

Mercurius Publicus (1660–1663)

During the Civil Wars, journalism gave voice to different factions; afterwards, it became the instrument of consolidated power. During the Interregnum, Cromwell controlled the news through his chief journalist Marchamont Nedham; strict licensing laws ensured that Nedham's *Public Intelligencer* (published every Monday) and *Mercurius Politicus* (every Thursday) were virtually the sole print sources for fresh information. (Mercury, the speedy messenger-god, remained throughout the century the favorite titular deity of the English press; more than a hundred periodicals bore his name). In 1660 the chief architects of the Restoration dismissed Nedham and supplanted him with their own advocate, Henry Muddiman (1629–1692). Taking over Nedham's newsbooks (now pointedly renamed the *Kingdom's Intelligencer* and *Mercurius Publicus*), Muddiman denounced the old regime and heralded the new with the zeal that would maintain him for nearly three decades, despite stiff competition from rival newsmen, as a favored journalist with the House of Stuart, right up to its fall from power in the 1688 Revolution.

from Mercurius Publicus
24–31 January 1661
[Anniversary of the Regicide]

London

   This day January 30 (we need say no more but name the day of the month) was doubly observed, not only by a solemn fast, sermons, and prayers at every parish church, for the precious blood of our late pious sovereign King Charles the First, of ever glorious memory; but also by public dragging of those odious carcasses of Oliver Cromwell, Henry Ireton, and John Bradshaw to Tyburn.[1] On Monday night Cromwell and Ireton in two several carts were drawn to Holborn from Westminster, after they were digged up on Saturday last, and the next morning Bradshaw; today they were drawn upon sledges to Tyburn, all the way (as before from Westminster) the outcry of the people went along with them. When these their carcasses were at Tyburn, they were pulled out of their coffins and hanged at the several angles of the triple tree,[2] where they hung till the sun was set; after which they were taken down,

---

1. Ireton (1611–1651) and Bradshaw (1602–1659) had played key roles in the trial, condemnation, and execution of Charles I. Tyburn had been for nearly three centuries the site for the public execution of common criminals (Charles had been dispatched on the grounds of the royal palace at Whitehall).

2. Tyburn's notorious "triangular gallows," whose three long horizontal beams could support as many as 21 hangings at a time.

their heads cut off, and their loathsome trunks thrown into a deep hole under the gallows. And now we cannot forget how at Cambridge when Cromwell first set up for a rebel, he rode under the gallows where, his horse just curvetting,[3] threw his cursed Highness out of the saddle just under the gallows (as if he had been turned off[4] the ladder), the spectators then observing the place, and rather presaging the present work of this day, than the monstrous villainies of this day twelve years.[5] But he is now again thrown under the gallows (never more to be digged up) and there we leave him.

London Gazette (1665–present)

New media are often modeled on old. In its first decades, English print journalism took the shape of a newsbook (actually a pamphlet) because that was a format with which printers and consumers had been long familiar. The London Gazette was something visibly different: the first newspaper, a single sheet printed in double columns. Containment was the paper's whole point, not only in format but in content. Published twice weekly, "by authority" (as it proclaimed on its masthead), it remained for thirteen years the only printed news source the English were legally permitted to read, and it presented only that news which its government masters deemed fit for wide publication: full accounts of Continental politics, carefully trimmed treatments of domestic doings, all couched in a dry prose that deliberately eschewed the popular (and sometimes rabble-rousing) effects of the paper's midcentury forebears. The Gazette broke briefly from its self-constraints in the number for 10 September 1666, when the Great Fire of London had forced the printer to set up his press in the open air, and the correspondents reported very local events with considerable accuracy and unaccustomed fervor.

from The London Gazette
10 September 1666

[THE FIRE OF LONDON[1]]

Whitehall, September 8

The ordinary course of this paper having been interrupted by a sad and lamentable accident of fire lately happened in the City of London, it hath been thought fit for satisfying the minds of so many of His Majesty's good subjects, who must needs be concerned for the issue of so great an accident, to give this short, but true account of it.

On the second instant[2] at one of the clock in the morning there happened to break out a sad and deplorable fire, in Pudding Lane near New Fish Street, which falling out at that hour of the night, and in a quarter of the town so close-built with wooden pitched[3] houses, spread itself so far before day, and with such distraction to the inhabitants and neighbors, that care was not taken for the timely preventing the further diffusion of it by pulling down houses, as ought to have been; so that this lamentable fire in a short time became too big to be mastered by any engines or working near it. It fell out most unhappily too, that a violent easterly wind fomented it, and kept it burning all that day, and the night following spreading itself up to Gracechurch Street, and downwards from Cannon Street to the waterside as far as the Three Cranes in the Vintry.

---

3. Leaping, frisking.
4. Dropped from.
5. Ago. I.e., they foresaw that he would eventually be hung, but not that he would accomplish the regicide of 30 January 1649.

1. Compare the accounts of Pepys (page 2014) and Evelyn (page 2018).
2. 2 September.
3. Covered with pitch (distilled tar) in order to keep out water.

The people in all parts about it distracted by the vastness of it, and their particular care to carry away their goods, many attempts were made to prevent the spreading of it, by pulling down houses, and making great intervals, but all in vain, the fire seizing upon the timber and rubbish, and so continuing itself, even through those spaces, and raging in a bright flame all Monday and Tuesday, notwithstanding His Majesty's own, and his Royal Highness's[4] indefatigable and personal pains to apply all possible remedies to prevent it, calling upon and helping the people with their Guards;[5] and a great number of nobility and gentry unweariedly assisting therein, for which they were requited with a thousand blessings from the poor distressed people. * * *

And we cannot but observe, to the confutation of all His Majesty's enemies, who endeavor to persuade the world abroad of great parties and disaffection at home against His Majesty's government, that a greater instance of the affections of this City could never be given than hath been now given in this sad and deplorable accident, when if at any time disorder might have been expected from the losses, distraction, and almost desperation of some persons in their private fortunes, thousands of people not having had habitations to cover them. And yet in all this time it hath been so far from any appearance of designs or attempts against His Majesty's government, that His Majesty and his royal brother, out of their care to stop and prevent the fire, frequently exposing their persons with very small attendance in all parts of the town, sometimes even to be intermixed with those who labored in the business, yet nevertheless there hath not been observed so much as a murmuring word to fall from any, but on the contrary, even those persons whose losses rendered their conditions most desperate, and to be fit objects of other prayers, beholding those frequent instances of His Majesty's care of this people, forgot their own misery, and filled the streets with their prayers for His Majesty, whose trouble they seemed to compassionate before their own.

The Daily Courant (1702–1735)

The *Daily Courant's* title announced its innovation. Its editor-publisher, Samuel Buckley (d. 1741), was the first in England to put out a paper every day (except for Sunday, which had no paper of its own until the 1770s); before now, papers had appeared thrice weekly at most. In his opening number, Buckley made clear both his dependence on "foreign prints" (newspapers from the Continent) and his distrust of them; his faith in his readers' capacity to winnow bias and interpret information; and his perhaps defensive condescension to his journalistic rivals as he embarked on the audacious enterprise of a daily paper.

from The Daily Courant No. 1
Wednesday, 11 March 1702

[EDITORIAL POLICY]

It will be found from the foreign prints, which from time to time, as occasion offers, will be mentioned in this paper, that the author has taken care to be duly furnished with all that comes from abroad in any language. And for an assurance that he will not, under pretense of having private intelligence, impose any additions of feigned circumstances to an action, but give his extracts fairly and impartially, at the beginning of each article he will quote the foreign paper from whence 'tis taken, that the

---

4. The king's brother James, Duke of York.
5. The royal brothers deployed their soldiers to aid the

fire's victims.

public, seeing from what country a piece of news comes with the allowance of that government, may be better able to judge of the credibility and fairness of the relation. Nor will he take upon him to give any comments or conjectures of his own, but will relate only matter of fact, supposing other people to have sense enough to make reflections for themselves.

The *Courant* (as the title shows) will be published daily, being designed to give all the material[1] news as soon as every post arrives; and is confined to half the compass,[2] to save the public at least half the impertinences[3] of ordinary news-papers.

A Review of the State of the British Nation (1704–1713)

Of the periodical commentators on the news, none was more formidable than Daniel Defoe, who single-handedly wrote his *Review* twice and sometimes thrice a week for nine years. The paper changed its name, its format, and its ostensible focus several times during its long run, but its general purposes remained the same throughout. Defoe wrote to celebrate trade, and to propose strategies for its improvement; to teach a rigorous piety and morality to a readership he saw as lax; and to advance by adroit advocacy the favorite programs of the paper's secret sponsor, Secretary of State Robert Harley (1661–1724). One of these was the Treaty of Union, whereby Scotland would merge under a single government with England and Wales to form the new national entity of Great Britain. Advocates of the measure construed it as a fair exchange, providing expanded trade for Scotland, enhanced security for England. In support of the cause, Defoe not only wrote copiously (pamphlets and essays as well as *Reviews*), he also persuaded Harley to send him to Scotland (where the prospect of Union was far from popular) to serve as chief strategist and propagandist. There, he argued energetically and successfully for passage of the treaty, while keeping his affiliation with Harley a close secret. When the Treaty of Union was ratified, the *Review* indulged in a moment of exultation, in the characteristic voice its creator had devised during his sustained periodic enterprise: that of a writer enmeshed in actual and volatile circumstance, deeply engaged with the politics, conduct, and commerce of the real world, sometimes embattled, often exasperated, occasionally exhausted, but ultimately indefatigable.

For more about Defoe, see his principal listing on page 2289.

Daniel Defoe: *from* A Review of the State of the British Nation, Vol. 4, No. 21
Saturday, 29 March 1707

[THE NEW UNION]

I have a long time dwelt on the subject of a Union; I have happily seen it transacted in the kingdom of Scotland; I have seen it carried on there through innumerable oppositions, both public and private, peaceable and unpeaceable; I have seen it perfected there, and ratified, sent up to England, debated, opposed, and at last passed in both houses, and having obtained the royal assent, I have the pleasure, just while I am writing these lines, to hear the guns proclaiming the happy conjunction from Edinburgh Castle. And though it brings an unsatisfying childish custom in play, and exposes me to a vain and truly ridiculous saying in England, "as the fool thinks, etc.,"

---

1. Relevant.
2. Space. Most newspapers printed on both sides of the sheet. At first, Buckley printed on only one side, unsure

that his sources would supply him with enough matter to fill two sides daily (they soon did).
3. Irrelevancies; filler.

yet 'tis impossible to put the lively sound of the cannon just now firing into any other note to my ear than the articulate expression of Union, Union. Strange power of imagination, strange incoherence of circumstances that fills the mind so with the thing that it makes even the thunder of warlike engines cry peace; and what is made to divide and destroy, speaks out the language of this glorious conjunction!

I have hardly room to introduce the various contemplations of the consequences of this mighty transaction; 'tis a sea of universal improvement, every day it discovers new mines of treasure, and when I launch out in the bark of my own imagination, I every minute discover new success, new advantages, and the approaching happiness of both kingdoms. Nor am I an idle spectator here; I have told Scotland of improvements in trade, wealth, and shipping that shall accrue to them on the happy conclusion of this affair, and I am pleased double with this, that I am like to be one of the first men that shall give them the pleasure of the experiment. I have told them of the improvement of their coal trade, and 'tis their own fault if they do not particularly engage 20 or 25 sail of ships immediately from England on that work. I have told them of the improvement of their salt, and I am now contracting for English merchants for Scots salt to the value of about ten thousand pounds per annum. I have told them of linen manufactures, and I have now above 100 poor families at work, by my procuring and direction, for the making such sorts of linen, and in such manner as never was made here before, and as no person in the trade will believe could be made here, till they see it.

This has been my employment in Scotland, and this my endeavor to do that nation service, and convince them by the practice that what I have said of the Union has more weight in it than some have endeavored to persuade them. Those that have charged me with missions and commissions from neither they nor I know who, shall blush at their rashness, and be ashamed for reflecting on a man come hither on purpose to do them good.[1] Have I had a hand in the Union, have I been maltreated by the tongues of the violent, threatened to be murdered, and insulted, because I have pleaded for it and pressed you to it—gentlemen, in Scotland, I refer you to Her Majesty's speech; there's my claim, and you do me too much honor to entitle me to a share in what Her Majesty says shall be their due that have done so. Hearken to the words of your sovereign: "I make no doubt but it will be remembered and spoke of hereafter to the honor of those that have been instrumental to bring it to such an happy conclusion." (Queen's Speech to the Parliament, 6 March 1707.)

Pray, gentlemen, have a care how you charge me with having any hand in bringing forward this matter *to such an happy conclusion*, lest you build that monument upon me which Her Majesty has foretold, and honor the man you would debase. I plead no merit, I do not raise the value of what I have done; and I know some that are gone to London to solicit the reward of what they have had no hand in—I might have said, are gone to claim the merit of what I have been the single author of—but as this has been the constant way of the world with me, so I have no repinings on that account. Nor am I pleading any other merit than that I may have it wrote on my grave that I did my duty in promoting the Union, and consequently the happiness of these nations. * * *

The Craftsman (1726–1750)

From 1721 to 1742, Sir Robert Walpole served George I and George II as First Lord of the Treasury, and, in effect, as prime minister. Walpole refined the techniques of earlier ministers.

---

1. In both England and Scotland, Defoe had been accused (with reason) of conducting a kind of espionage on behalf of Harley and the Union.

He used his control of the royal purse to build up a following in the House of Commons by means of pensions and lucrative government positions as reward for loyal service; he sought to shape public opinion by imposing strict libel laws against his critics, and by controlling prominent papers (the *London Journal*, the *Free Briton*, and others, as well as the government's long-running *London Gazette*) through adroitly managed patronage. He also enriched himself in the process, building a stately mansion at Houghton, and becoming an avid collector of art. Such brazen abuse of power prompted a two-party coalition in Parliament consisting of members opposed to Walpole's policies.

Many journals and periodicals contributed to the opposition to Walpole, but none was as feared or as popular as the *Craftsman*. In part, this was because no other journal could boast as compelling an array of writing talent. Edited by Nicholas Amhurst (1697–1742), an expelled student and hack writer from Oxford University, the journal derived its political philosophy and character from two politicians: William Pulteney (later Earl of Bath) and Henry St. John (Viscount Bolingbroke). As the respective leaders of the Whig and Tory factions of the Walpole opposition, Pulteney (1684–1764) and Bolingbroke (1678–1751) were in a unique position to coordinate parliamentary attacks on Walpole, as well as to generate public support for their criticisms of the ministry. Thus, from its first appearance in December 1726, the journal dedicated itself to exposing the "mystery of state-craft" in Walpole's ministry, a ministry which it regarded as the "grand fountain of corruption."

Hampered by the libel laws from attacking Walpole outright, the authors of the *Craftsman*, writing under the pseudonym "Caleb D'Anvers," pioneered new techniques of innuendo and allusion that allowed them to attack the ministry without actually breaking the law and incurring its penalties. The following number, for example, pretends to mediate an argument that took place at a party attended by Caleb D'Anvers. It takes advantage of the English interest in "prodigies"—monstrous births, strange apparitions, and vampires—to generate a stinging attack on Walpole as the great "bloodsucker." In so doing, this particular number of the *Craftsman* relies heavily on the pun implicit in the phrase "body politic."

from **The Craftsman No. 307**
Saturday, 20 May 1732

[Vampires in Britain]

Non missura cutem, nisi plena cruoris hirudo.[1]

One evening last week I called to see a friend, and met a company of gentlemen and ladies engaged in a dispute about prodigies, occasioned by a very remarkable event which hath lately happened in Hungary. The account of this affair, as it is given in the *London Journal* of March the 11th, is of so extraordinary a nature, that it will be difficult to give my readers any just conception of it, without quoting it at large.

Extract of a private letter from Vienna:

> We have received certain advice of a sort of prodigy lately discovered in Hungary, at a place called Heyducken, situate on the other side of the Tibiscus, or Teys; namely, of dead bodies sucking, as it were, the blood of the living; for the latter visibly dry up, while the former are filled with blood. The fact at first sight seems to be impossible and even ridiculous; but the following is a true copy of a relation attested by unexceptionable witnesses, and sent to the imperial council of war.

---

1. "A leech that will not let the skin go, unless gorged with blood" (Horace, *Ars Poetica* 476), referring to mad poets who insist on reading their worthless verses to everyone.

Medreyga in Hungary, Jan. 7, 1732.

Upon a current report, that in the village of Medreyga certain dead bodies (called here Vampyres) had killed several persons, by sucking out all their blood, the present inquiry was made by the honorable commander in chief; and Capt. Goschutz of the company of Stallater, the Hadnagi Bariacrar, and the senior Heyduke of the village were severally examined; who unanimously declared that about five years ago a certain Heyduke, named Arnold Paul, was killed by the overturning of a cartload of hay, who in his lifetime was often heard to say, he had been tormented near Caschaw, and upon the borders of Turkish Serbia, by a vampyre; and that to extricate himself, he had eaten some of the earth of the vampyres' graves, and rubbed himself with their blood.

That 20 or 30 days after the decease of the said Arnold Paul, several persons complained that they were tormented, and that, in short, he had taken away the lives of four persons. In order, therefore, to put a stop to such a calamity, the inhabitants of the place, after having consulted their Hadnagi, caused the body of the said Arnold Paul to be taken up, 40 days after he had been dead, and found the same to be fresh and free from all manner of corruption; that he bled at the nose, mouth and ears, as pure and florid blood as was ever seen; and that his shroud and winding sheet were all over bloody; and lastly his finger and toe nails were fallen off, and new ones grown in their room.

As they observed from all these circumstances that he was a vampyre, they according to custom drove a stake through his heart; at which he gave a horrid groan, and lost a great deal of blood. Afterwards they burnt his body to ashes the same day, and threw them into his grave.

These good men say farther that all such as have been tormented or killed by the vampyres become vampyres when they are dead; and therefore they served several other dead bodies as they had done Arnold Paul's, for tormenting the living.

Signed,
Batruer, first lieutenant of the regiment of Alexander.
Flickhenger, surgeon major to the regiment of Furstemburch.
—three other surgeons.
Gurschitz, Captain at Stallath.

I shall now proceed to give my readers the substance of our conversation upon this extraordinary narrative.

The brunt of the dispute, upon my entering the room, lay between a grave doctor of physic and a beautiful young lady, who was a great admirer of strange and wonderful occurrences. The doctor endeavored to ridicule such romantic stories, by treating them as the common artifices of newswriters to fill up their papers at a dead season, for want of other intelligence. The young lady confessed, with a good deal of modesty and candor, that she believed such things were frequently done; but still insisted on the truth of this relation, which stood attested by such unexceptionable witnesses. She observed that the time, the place, and the names of the persons concerned in this affair were particularly mentioned; that an authentic account of it appears to have been transmitted to the court of Vienna, signed by no less than six persons; four of whom were surgeons, and the other two officers of the army; that such gentlemen must be supposed to have too much skill to be imposed upon themselves in such a matter, and too much honor to impose upon others. To this the doctor replied, with some disdain, that all the surgeons and soldiers in the universe should never make him believe that a dead body, whose animal powers were totally extinguished, could torment the living, by sucking their blood, or performing any other active and operative functions. He added, that it was contrary to all the principles of philosophy, as well as the laws of nature; and, in my opinion, urged the point somewhat too far against a young, female opponent; who, by the color in her cheeks, appeared to be a little nettled and, with a scornful smile, returned; "Well, well, doctor, you may say what you please; but as wise as you pretend to be now, it is not long ago that you endeavored to make us believe a fact equally ridiculous and absurd. Surely, doctor," said she, "you cannot have forgot the famous Rabbit-Woman of Godalmin."[2]—The smartness of this reply produced an hearty laugh on the lady's side, and put the doctor somewhat out of countenance. Then turning to me with an air of triumph and satisfaction, "I am sure," said she, "Mr. D'Anvers, that you are of my opinion, and believe there may be such things as vampyres."—A man, who hath any degree of complaisance, is loathe to contradict a pretty girl, who forestalls his judgment in so agreeable a manner. I desired therefore to read over the account very attentively before I gave my opinion upon it; and, clapping on my political spectacles, I soon discovered a secret meaning in it, which I was in hopes would moderate the dispute. I perceived the whole company waited with impatience for my answer; so that having unsaddled my nose, and composed my muscles into a becoming gravity for such an occasion, I delivered myself to them in the following manner.

Gentlemen and ladies,
I think this dispute may be easily compromised without any reproach, or disgrace to either side. I must agree with the learned doctor that an inanimate corpse cannot possibly perform any vital functions; and yet I am firmly persuaded, with the young lady, that there are vampyres, or dead bodies, which afflict and torment the living. In order to explain myself the more clearly on this head, I must desire you to reflect that the account, now before us, comes from the eastern part of the world, which hath always been remarkable for writing in the allegorical style.[3] Besides, it deserves our consideration that the states of Hungary are, at present, under the subjection of the Turks, or the Germans, and governed by them with a pretty hard rein; which obliges them to couch all their complaints under types, figures, and parables. I believe you will make no doubt that this relation of the vampyres is a piece of that kind, and contains a secret satire upon the administration of those countries, when you consider the following particulars.

You see that the method, by which these vampyres are said to torment and kill the living, is by sucking out all their blood; and what, I pray, is a more common phrase for a ravenous minister, even in this part of the world, than a leech, or a bloodsucker, who preys upon human gore, and fattens himself upon the vitals of his country?

Now, if you admit of this interpretation, which I think far from being strained, the whole mystery of the vampyres will unfold itself of course; for a plundering minister carries his oppressions beyond the grave, and continues to torment those whom he leaves behind him by anticipating the public revenues, and entailing a perpetuity of taxes and gabels[4] upon the people, which must drain the body politic by degrees of all its blood and spirit.

2. Mary Tofts, of Godalming in Surrey, reportedly gave birth to a litter of rabbits in the winter of 1726. For a time, this famous fraud deceived many physicians.
3. "Eastern," or Oriental, tales included a wide variety of fables, tall tales, mythical representations, and stories of wonder. Samuel Johnson's *Rasselas* (1759) is perhaps the most famous example of this broad genre.
4. A form of interest or rent due on land.

It is farther said, in the narrative, that all such as have been tormented, or killed by the vampyres, become vampyres, when they are dead.—This likewise is perfectly agreeable to my system; for those persons who groan under the burdens of such a minister are often obliged to sell or mortgage their estates, and therefore may be said, in a proper sense, to torment their unhappy posterity in the same manner.

Whether this Arnold Paul, or Paul Arnold, mentioned in the narrative, was a person in any office, or employment in the administration, which gave him a power of oppressing the people, either as a tax-layer or a tax-gatherer, I am not able to determine without farther inquiry. He is said, indeed, to have been a Heyduke, which I take to be a character of some consequence in those countries; but, perhaps, he might have been employed only as a ministerial tool, or instrument of oppression, under some great bloodsucker of state. For my own part, I am inclined to this opinion; because it is said that he had killed only four persons; whereas if he had been a vampyre of any considerable rank, we should in all probability have heard of his thousands and his ten thousands.[5] * * *

Having finished my speech, which was honored with the strictest attention, I was very much pleased to find it produce the desired effect, by putting an end to the dispute, which occasioned it. The doctor only nodded his head and told me, with a smile, that I had a political turn for every thing. The young lady expressed her satisfaction in the most obliging terms, and was pleased to say that my solution of this prodigy would make a very good *Craftsman*. She was immediately seconded by the whole company, who pressed me with so much importunity to print it in my next paper, that I could not in good manners refuse their request; and I hope my loving readers will excuse me, on that account, for troubling them this week with a loose, unpremeditated piece of conversation.

Having afterwards smoked my pipe, and spent the evening very agreeably, I took my leave at eleven o'clock, which hath been, for many years, my constant hour. The young lady followed me to the door, and, pulling me by the sleeve, "Pray, Mr. D'Anvers," said she, "don't forget the paper upon the vampyres."

———— ❧◆❧ ————

Periodical Personae

In print journalism it was primarily the news that sold the paper; in the periodical essay it was the voice: the idiosyncratic mix of assertion and deference, comedy and charisma, with which author addressed audience. Political writers had long known the advantages of using a mask or *persona*—a pen name, a fictitious character—as a means of both concealing their identity and expanding the appeal of their controversial arguments. In the early 1700s, the inventors of the periodical essay extended the tactic of the fictitious self into new territory. While collaborating on *The Tatler* and *The Spectator*, Richard Steele and Joseph Addison devised strategies for making the unreal author a real arbitrator in the culture, a teacher of taste and conduct, manners and morality, someone whom readers found it pleasurable to learn from, to identify with, even to "believe in," despite (and because of) his comically exaggerated quirks, his patent nonexistence. Working behind their carefully crafted masks, Addison and Steele sold so many papers and impressed so many readers that their mark became indelible. For the rest of the century, the periodical essayist's first task was to devise a persona unusual enough to define the paper, and engaging enough to sustain it.

5. An allusion to Saul, who had "slain his thousands," and David, "his ten thousands" (1 Samuel 21.11). D'Anvers goes on to explain that certain private citizens ("sharpers, usurers, stock-jobbers") pursue an economic vampirism as skillfully as do the public officials.

The Tatler (1709–1711)

At age thirty-five, after a checkered career as soldier, poet, playwright, popular moralist, and Whig propagandist, Captain Richard Steele (1672–1729) was appointed editor of the *London Gazette*, the government's long-running newspaper. Evidently even this task did not sufficiently absorb his energies. Two years later, while still supervising the *Gazette*, he launched *The Tatler*, a periodical of his own that outstripped all its predecessors in commercial success and enduring appeal. It appeared three times a week, ran for two years and 271 numbers, spawned many imitators, and continued to sell (in a four-volume collected edition) for the rest of the century. The *Tatler*'s appeal derived in large measure from its putative author, Isaac Bickerstaff, Esquire, whose name Steele had borrowed from one of Swift's satires, but whose character he elaborated into that of a genial, perceptive, and comically self-congratulatory old man. The paper's commodious structure mirrored the gregariousness of its "author." Bickerstaff datelined his dispatches from the coffeehouses around London where papers were distributed, read, and discussed; he included letters (fictitious and authentic) from readers all over the country. The *Tatler*'s audience thus found itself absorbed into the paper several ways: they were its constant topic, they sometimes supplied its text, they constituted both its origin and its endpoint, and they gave it their unprecedented devotion. Steele soon made further discoveries of form under the influence of his school friend Joseph Addison (1672–1729), whom he had brought in (so one contemporary put it) as his "great and constant assistant." Addison and Steele found that Bickerstaff's private musings, dispatched "From my Own Apartment," were the most pleasing items of all, and so they often devoted whole papers to reprinting what their character was pleased to call his "lucubrations" (meditations by candlelight, late at night). John Gay summed up the strategy's success. Coffeehouse owners, Gay reported, "began to be sensible that the Esquire's lucubrations alone had brought them more customers than all their other newspapers put together." Bickerstaff's other "departments" diminished or disappeared, and "the Esquire's lucubrations," now running the full length of the paper, created the format and the fashion for the periodical essay, a unified piece on a single topic as opposed to the fragmentary "miscellany" from which Steele had started. By the time he stopped *The Tatler* (probably because of political pressures following the Whigs' fall from power), he and Addison had devised means and achieved ends with which they would experiment anew in the *Spectator*: ways of creating community shot through with solitude, of mixing sociability and meditation, morality and mirth.

Richard Steele: *from* Tatler No. 1
Tuesday, 12 April 1709

[INTRODUCING MR. BICKERSTAFF]

Quicquid agunt homines nostri farrago libelli.[1]

Though the other papers which are published for the use of the good people of England have certainly very wholesome effects, and are laudable in their particular kinds, they do not seem to come up to the main design of such narrations, which, I humbly presume, should be principally intended for the use of politic persons, who are so public-spirited as to neglect their own affairs to look into transactions of state. Now these gentlemen, for the most part, being persons of strong zeal and weak intellects,[2] it is both a charitable and necessary work to offer something whereby such worthy and well-affected members of the commonwealth may be instructed, after their reading, *what to think*: which shall be the end and purpose of this my paper, wherein I shall

---

1. "Whatever people do [will furnish] the variety of our little book"; or (in the freer and more apt 18th-century translation by Thomas Percy) "Whate'er men do, or say, or think, or dream, / Our motley paper seizes for its theme" (Juvenal, *Satires* 1.85–86).

2. Bickerstaff mocks that category of men known as the "coffeehouse politicians," who spent long hours together discussing news. For a more sustained satire of them, see *Tatler* No. 155 (pages 2328–2330).

from time to time report and consider all matters of what kind soever that shall occur to me, and publish such my advices and reflections every Tuesday, Thursday, and Saturday in the week, for the convenience of the post.[3] I resolve also to have something which may be of entertainment to the fair sex, in honor of whom I have invented the title of this paper. I therefore earnestly desire all persons, without distinction, to take it in for the present *gratis*,[4] and hereafter at the price of one penny, forbidding all hawkers to take more for it at their peril. And I desire all persons to consider, that I am at a very great charge for proper materials for this work, as well as that before I resolved upon it, I had settled a correspondence in all parts of the known and knowing world. And forasmuch as this globe is not trodden upon by mere drudges of business only, but that men of spirit and genius are justly to be esteemed as considerable agents in it, we shall not upon a dearth of news present you with musty foreign edicts, or dull proclamations, but shall divide our relations of the passages which occur in action or discourse throughout this town, as well as elsewhere, under such dates of places as may prepare you for the matter you are to expect, in the following manner.

All accounts of gallantry,[5] pleasure, and entertainment shall be under the article of White's Chocolate House; poetry, under that of Will's Coffeehouse; learning, under the title of Grecian; foreign and domestic news you will have from St. James's Coffeehouse; and what else I have to offer on any other subject, shall be dated from my own apartment.[6]

I once more desire my reader to consider, that as I cannot keep an ingenious man to go daily to Will's, under two-pence each day merely for his charges; to White's, under sixpence; nor to the Grecian, without allowing him some Plain Spanish,[7] to be as able as others at the learned table; and that a good observer cannot speak with even Kidney[8] at St. James's without clean linen. I say, these considerations will, I hope, make all persons willing to comply with my humble request (when my *gratis* stock is exhausted) of a penny apiece; especially since they are sure of some proper amusement, and that it is impossible for me to want means to entertain 'em, having, besides the force of my own parts, the power of divination, and that I can, by casting a figure, tell you all that will happen before it comes to pass.[9]

But this last faculty I shall use very sparingly, and speak but of few things 'till they are passed, for fear of divulging matters which may offend our superiors.[1] * * *

From my own apartment

I am sorry I am obliged to trouble the public with so much discourse, upon a matter which I at the very first mentioned as a trifle, *viz.* the death of Mr. Partridge, under whose name there is an almanac come out for the year 1709.[2] In one page of which, it is asserted by the said John Partridge, that he is still living, and not only so, but that he was also living some time before, and even at the instant when I writ of his death.

---

3. These were the days on which the postal system carried mail from London to the provinces.
4. Steele distributed his first four numbers free, as a way of attracting readers.
5. Flirtation and self-display.
6. Steele exploits associations between topic and venue long familiar to his readers. Each of the coffeehouses he names catered to a clientele "specializing" in the pursuits he names. A journalist himself, Steele parodies the newspaper format that headed each item by the name of its (usually foreign) city of origin.
7. A kind of snuff, used as a stimulant to induce sneezing.
8. A waiter.
9. To "cast a figure" is to work out a horoscope, an ability that the *Tatler*'s first readers would readily associate with

the character "Isaac Bickerstaff." Jonathan Swift had originally created the character (in a series of pamphlets in 1708), as a way of satirizing the fashion for astrological almanacs, which purported to foretell the important events of the coming year. In Swift's first pamphlet, the fictitious astrologer Isaac Bickerstaff forecast the imminent death of the real (and very successful) astrologer John Partridge; in the second pamphlet, Bickerstaff declared blithely that his prophecy had come to pass. Partridge's subsequent, frantic protestations added relish to the joke.
1. Bickerstaff proceeds to supply first dispatches from White's, Will's, and St. James's coffeehouses.
2. In the 1709 issue of his annual almanac *Merlinus Liberatus*, Partridge had insisted that he was "still alive."

I have in another place, and in a paper by itself, sufficiently convinced this man that he is dead, and if he has any shame, I don't doubt but that by this time he owns it to all his acquaintance: for though the legs and arms, and whole body, of that man may still appear and perform their animal functions; yet since, as I have elsewhere observed, his art is gone, the man is gone. I am, as I said, concerned that this little matter should make so much noise; but since I am engaged, I take myself obliged in honor to go on in my lucubrations, and by the help of these arts of which I am master, as well as my skill in astrological speculations, I shall, as I see occasion, proceed to confute other dead men, who pretend to be in being, that they are actually deceased. I therefore give all men fair warning to mend their manners, for I shall from time to time print bills of mortality; and I beg the pardon of all such who shall be named therein, if they who are good for nothing shall find themselves in the number of the deceased.

The Spectator (1711–1713)

In the weeks of the *Spectator*'s first appearance, readers marveled at both its contents and its pace. "We had at first . . . no manner of notion," the wit John Gay reported from London, "how a diurnal paper could be continued in the spirit and style of our present *Spectators*; but to our no small surprise we find them still rising upon us, and can only wonder from whence so prodigious a run of wit and learning can proceed." It proceeded (as Gay guessed) from the minds and pens of the same two writers who had shut down the *Tatler* just a few months before. For their second periodical collaboration, Addison and Steele considerably upped the ante. Not only did they undertake to publish a new number every day (something no essayist had hitherto attempted), they also devised a new persona, intricately linked with their triumphant earlier creation Isaac Bickerstaff. Where the *Tatler* had begun in gregariousness and modulated towards solitude (at "my own apartment"), the new paper started from an even farther remove, in the eccentric silence of Mr. Spectator, who declares at the outset that he has not spoken "three sentences together" since birth. Mr. Spectator carries his "own apartment"—his state of psychological apartness—with him, not at his residence but in his head; "the working of my own mind," he announces early on, "is the chief entertainment of my life."

In his focused interiority, Mr. Spectator played out the principles of psychology that John Locke had propounded, but his extreme self-possession turned out to possess enormous rhetorical impact and commercial cachet as well. More than any other periodical persona, Mr. Spectator managed to embody and to allegorize the operations of the paper he inhabited. Like the paper he was everywhere, at once silent and articulate, fictitious in substance but impressive in effect, observant and absorbent of the culture, able to move into his readers' minds by the mysterious osmosis of reading itself, and to remain there, a disembodied monitor with a rapidly growing portfolio of daily essays. An anonymous pamphleteer reproached Mr. Spectator for the presumptuous "tyranny" of his surveillance, but the paper's tactics of reform remained in power for most of the century. It was read (and imitated) on the Continent, in the American colonies, and in remoter outposts like Sumatra, from whence a British trader wrote home to his daughter in London, admonishing her "to study the *Spectators*, especially those which relate to religion and domestic life. Next to the Bible you cannot read any writings so much to your purpose for the improvement of your mind and the conduct of your actions." The *Spectator*, Gay noted soon after the paper's debut, "is in everyone's hands, and a constant topic for our morning conversation at tea tables and coffeehouses." More than sixty years later, the Scots rhetorician Hugh Blair could only echo and elaborate on Gay's phrasing, in accordance with the paper's now long-established place in the British canon: "The *Spectator* . . . is a book which is in the hands of everyone, and which cannot be praised too highly. The good sense, and good writing, the useful morality, and the admirable vein of humor which abound in it, render it one of those standard books which have done the greatest honor to the English nation."

Joseph Addison: *from* Spectator No. 1
Thursday, 1 March 1711

[INTRODUCING MR. SPECTATOR]

Non fumum ex fulgore, sed ex fumo dare lucem
Cogitat, ut speciosa debinc miracula promat.[1]

I have observed, that a reader seldom peruses a book with pleasure 'till he knows whether the writer of it be a black or a fair man,[2] of a mild or choleric disposition, married or a bachelor, with other particulars of the like nature, that conduce very much to the right understanding of an author. To gratify this curiosity, which is so natural to a reader, I design this paper, and my next, as prefatory discourses to my following writings, and shall give some account in them of the several persons that are engaged in this work. As the chief trouble of compiling, digesting, and correcting will fall to my share, I must do myself the justice to open the work with my own history.

I was born to a small hereditary estate, which, according to the tradition of the village where it lies, was bounded by the same hedges and ditches in William the Conqueror's time[3] that it is at present, and has been delivered down from father to son whole and entire, without the loss or acquisition of a single field or meadow, during the space of six hundred years. There runs a story in the family, that when my mother was gone with child of me about three months, she dreamt that she was brought to bed of[4] a judge. Whether this might proceed from a lawsuit which was then depending in the family, or my father's being a justice of the peace, I cannot determine; for I am not so vain as to think it presaged any dignity that I should arrive at in my future life, though that was the interpretation which the neighborhood put upon it. The gravity of my behavior at my very first appearance in the world, and all the time that I sucked, seemed to favor my mother's dream: for, as she has often told me, I threw away my rattle before I was two months old, and would not make use of my coral[5] 'till they had taken away the bells from it.

As for the rest of my infancy, there being nothing in it remarkable, I shall pass it over in silence. I find that, during my nonage,[6] I had the reputation of a very sullen youth, but was always a favorite of my schoolmaster, who used to say, *that my parts were solid and would wear well.* I had not been long at the university before I distinguished myself by a most profound silence: for during the space of eight years, excepting in the public exercises of the college, I scarce uttered the quantity of an hundred words; and indeed do not remember that I ever spoke three sentences together in my whole life. Whilst I was in this learned body I applied myself with so much diligence to my studies that there are very few celebrated books, either in the learned or the modern tongues, which I am not acquainted with.

Upon the death of my father I was resolved to travel into foreign countries, and therefore left the university, with the character[7] of an odd unaccountable fellow that had a great deal of learning, if I would but show it. An insatiable thirst after knowledge carried me into all the countries of Europe, in which there was anything

---

1. "He intends to produce not smoke from fire, but light from smoke, so that he may then put forth striking and amazing things" (Horace, *Ars Poetica* 143–144).
2. Of dark or light complexion.
3. The late 11th century, when William ruled as king of England.

4. Had given birth to. The silence of judges was proverbial.
5. Another sound maker for infants.
6. Childhood.
7. Reputation.

new or strange to be seen; nay, to such a degree was my curiosity raised, that having read the controversies of some great men concerning the antiquities of Egypt, I made a voyage to Grand Cairo, on purpose to take the measure of a pyramid; and as soon as I had set myself right in that particular, returned to my native country with great satisfaction.

I have passed my latter years in this city, where I am frequently seen in most public places, though there are not above half a dozen of my select friends that know me; of whom my next paper shall give a more particular account. There is no place of general resort, wherein I do not often make my appearance.[8] Sometimes I am seen thrusting my head into a round of politicians at Will's, and listening with great attention to the narratives that are made in those little circular audiences. Sometimes I smoke a pipe at Child's; and whilst I seem attentive to nothing but the *Post-Man*,[9] overhear the conversation of every table in the room. I appear on Sunday nights at St. James's Coffeehouse, and sometimes join the little committee of politics in the inner-room, as one who comes there to hear and improve. My face is likewise very well known at the Grecian, the Cocoa Tree, and in the theaters both of Drury Lane, and the Haymarket. I have been taken for a merchant upon the Exchange[1] for above these ten years, and sometimes pass for a Jew in the assembly of stock-jobbers at Jonathan's.[2] In short, wherever I see a cluster of people I always mix with them, though I never open my lips but in my own club.

Thus I live in the world, rather as a spectator of mankind than as one of the species; by which means I have made myself a speculative statesman, soldier, merchant, and artisan, without ever meddling with any practical part in life. I am very well versed in the theory of an husband or a father, and can discern the errors in the economy, business, and diversion of others, better than those who are engaged in them; as standers-by discover blots,[3] which are apt to escape those who are in the game. I never espoused any party with violence, and am resolved to observe an exact neutrality between the Whigs and Tories,[4] unless I shall be forced to declare myself by the hostilities of either side. In short, I have acted in all the parts of my life as a looker-on, which is the character I intend to preserve in this paper.

I have given the reader just so much of my history and character as to let him see I am not altogether unqualified for the business I have undertaken. As for other particulars in my life and adventures, I shall insert them in following papers as I shall see occasion. In the mean time, when I consider how much I have seen, read, and heard, I begin to blame my own taciturnity; and since I have neither time nor inclination to communicate the fullness of my heart in speech, I am resolved to do it in writing; and to print my self out, if possible, before I die. I have been often told by my friends that it is pity so many useful discoveries which I have made should be in the possession of a silent man. For this reason therefore, I shall publish a sheet-full of thoughts every morning, for the benefit of my contemporaries; and if I can any way contribute to the

8. With a conspicuous openness to all parties and pursuits, Mr. Spectator distributes his visitations among some of London's favorite meeting places, including ones popular with Whigs (St. James's), Tories (the Cocoa Tree), authors (Child's), lawyers (the Grecian), and the news-obsessives he calls "politicians" (Will's).
9. A thrice-weekly newspaper, favored by Whigs.
1. The Royal Exchange was a large building containing many shops and serving as a meeting place for merchants. (For Addison's paean to the place, see *Spectator* No. 69,

page 2334).
2. Jonathan's coffeehouse, near the Royal Exchange, was a principal meeting place of merchants and stockbrokers ("stock-jobbers").
3. In backgammon, a blot is a piece whose position puts it at risk of being taken.
4. Addison and Steele maintained "neutrality" more strictly in the *Spectator* than they had in the *Tatler*, which had incurred much controversy by its Whig partisanship.

diversion or improvement of the country in which I live, I shall leave it, when I am summoned out of it, with the secret satisfaction of thinking that I have not lived in vain. * * *

The Female Spectator (April 1744–May 1746)

The Female Spectator was the first periodical written by a woman for women. Its author, Eliza Haywood (c. 1693–1756), had been an actress, a playwright, and the writer of some sixty romances, novels, and other narratives, many of them scandalous and some of them wildly successful. In the mid-1740s, after a long eclipse prompted in part by Alexander Pope's derision of her in the *Dunciad*, Haywood emerged in a new guise: no longer a purveyor of exotic thrills, she set up instead as a teacher of morality. *The Female Spectator* differed from its namesake in calendar (monthly rather than daily) and format: a pamphlet and not a sheet, each number presented an essay focused on a single topic with several illustrative fictional stories interspersed. The biggest difference, though, was in the new paper's point of view. Mr. Spectator had observed, described, and instructed "the fair sex" from without, as supremely self-confident male mentor. Haywood offered instead a running report from the interior of women's lives. Her vantage point proved popular. *The Female Spectator* continued to sell, in a four-volume collected edition, for more than two decades after its periodical run had ceased.

from Female Spectator Vol. 1, No. 1
[THE AUTHOR'S INTENT]

It is very much by the choice we make of subjects for our entertainment that the refined taste distinguishes itself from the vulgar and more gross. Reading is universally allowed to be one of the most improving as well as agreeable amusements; but then to render it so, one should, among the number of books which are perpetually issuing from the press, endeavor to single out such as promise to be most conducive to those ends. In order to be as little deceived as possible, I, for my own part, love to get as well acquainted as I can with an author, before I run the risk of losing my time in perusing his work; and as I doubt not but most people are of this way of thinking, I shall, in imitation of my learned brother of ever precious memory,[1] give some account of what I am, and those concerned with me in this undertaking; and likewise of the chief intent of the lucubrations[2] hereafter communicated, that the reader, on casting his eye over the four or five first pages, may judge how far the book may or may not be qualified to entertain him, and either accept or throw it aside as he thinks proper. And here I promise that in the pictures I shall give of myself and associates, I will draw no flattering lines, assume no perfection that we are not in reality possessed of, nor attempt to shadow over any defect with an artificial gloss.

As a proof of my sincerity, I shall in the first place assure him that for my own part I never was a beauty, and am now very far from being young (a confession he will find few of my sex ready to make). I shall also acknowledge that I have run through as many scenes of vanity and folly as the greatest coquette of them all. Dress, equipage,[3] and flattery were the idols of my heart. I should have thought that day lost which did not present me with some new opportunity of showing myself. My life, for some years, was a continued round of what I then called pleasure, and my whole time engrossed by a hurry of promiscuous diversions. But whatever inconveniences such a manner of conduct has brought upon myself, I have this consolation, to think that

---

1. Addison and Steele's Mr. Spectator.
2. Writings by candlelight; Haywood pointedly picks up

Isaac Bickerstaff's catchword for his essays in the *Tatler*.
3. Fancy carriages, servants, and furniture.

the public may reap some benefit from it. The company I kept was not, indeed, always so well chosen as it ought to have been, for the sake of my own interest or reputation; but then it was general, and by consequence furnished me not only with the knowledge of many occurrences, which otherwise I had been ignorant of, but also enabled me, when the too great vivacity of my nature became tempered with reflection, to see into the secret springs which gave rise to the actions I had either heard or been witness of—to judge of the various passions of the human mind, and distinguish those imperceptible degrees by which they become masters of the heart, and attain the dominion over reason. A thousand odd adventures, which at the time they happened made slight impression on me, and seemed to dwell no longer on my mind than the wonder they occasioned, now rise fresh to my remembrance, with this advantage, that the mystery I then, for want of attention, imagined they contained, is entirely vanished, and I find it easy to account for the cause by the consequence.

With this experience, added to a genius[4] tolerably extensive, and an education more liberal than is ordinarily allowed to persons of my sex, I flattered myself that it might be in my power to be in some measure both useful and entertaining to the public; and this thought was so soothing to those remains of vanity not yet wholly extinguished in me, that I resolved to pursue it, and immediately began to consider by what method I should be most likely to succeed. To confine myself to any one subject, I knew could please but one kind of taste, and my ambition was to be as universally read as possible. From my observations of human nature, I found that curiosity had more or less a share in every breast; and my business, therefore, was to hit this reigning humor in such a manner as that the gratification it should receive from being made acquainted with other people's affairs should at the same time teach every one to regulate their own.

Having agreed within myself on this important point, I commenced author, by setting down many things which, being pleasing to myself, I imagined would be so to others; but on examining them the next day, I found an infinite deficiency both in matter and style, and that there was an absolute necessity for me to call in to my assistance such of my acquaintance as were qulaified for that purpose. The first that occurred to me, I shall distinguish by the name of Mira, a lady descended from a family to which wit seems hereditary, married to a gentleman every way worthy of so excellent a wife, and with whom she lives in so perfect a harmony, that having nothing to ruffle the composure of her soul, or disturb those sparkling ideas she received from nature and education, left me no room to doubt if what she favored me with would be acceptable to the public. The next is a widow of quality, who not having buried her vivacity in the tomb of her lord, continues to make one in all the modish diversions of the times, so far, I mean, as she finds them consistent with innocence and honor; and as she is far from having the least austerity in her behavior, nor is rigid to the failings she is wholly free from herself, those of her acquaintance who had been less circumspect scruple not to make her the confidante of secrets they conceal from all the world beside. The third is the daughter of a wealthy merchant, charming as an angel, but endued with so many accomplishments that to those who know her truly, her beauty is the least distinguished part of her. This fine young creature I shall call Euphrosyne, since she has all the cheerfulness and sweetness ascribed to that goddess.[5]

---

4. Talent, ability.
5. Euphrosyne is one of the three Graces, sister goddesses

in Greek mythology who possess (and bestow) the gift of beauty.

These three approved my design, assured me of all the help they could afford, and soon gave a proof of it in bringing their several essays; but as the reader, provided the entertainment be agreeable, will not be interested from which quarter it comes, whatever productions I shall be favored with from these ladies, or any others I may hereafter correspond with, will be exhibited under the general title of *The Female Spectator*, and how many contributors soever there may happen to be to the work, they are to be considered only as several members of one body, of which I am the mouth. * * *

Richard Steele: *from* Tatler No. 18
21 May 1709

[THE NEWS WRITERS IN DANGER[1]]

St. James's Coffeehouse, May 20.

* * * It being therefore visible, that our society[2] will be greater sufferers by the peace than the soldiery itself; insomuch, that the *Daily Courant* is in danger of being broken, my friend Dyer of being reformed,[3] and the very best of the whole band of being reduced to half-pay; might I presume to offer anything in the behalf of my distressed brethren, I would humbly move, that an appendix of proper apartments furnished with pen, ink, and paper, and other necessaries of life should be added to the Hospital of Chelsea,[4] for the relief of such decayed news writers as have served their country in the wars; and that for their exercise, they should compile the annals of their brother-veterans, who have been engaged in the same service, and are still obliged to do duty after the same manner.

I cannot be thought to speak this out of an eye to any private interest; for, as my chief scenes of action are coffeehouses, playhouses, and my own apartment, I am in no need of camps, fortifications, and fields of battle, to support me; I don't call out for heroes and generals to my assistance. Though the officers are broken, and the armies disbanded, I shall still be safe as long as there are men or women, or politicians, or lovers, or poets, or nymphs, or swains, or cits,[5] or courtiers, in being.

Joseph Addison: *from* Tatler No. 155
Thursday, 6 April 1710

[THE POLITICAL UPHOLSTERER]

—Aliena negotia curat
Excussus propriis.[1]

1. Papers often defined themselves by contrasting their methods and achievements with those of their rivals. For the essayists, the newspapers afforded the readiest foil. Steele was a seasoned journalist, but he and Addison devised many ways of mocking the vacuity of the newsmongers, and of flattering those readers who preferred essays to mere journalism. In this early *Tatler*, Bickerstaff announces that England will soon be victorious in its foreign wars, observes that "the approach of peace strikes a panic through our armies," who will have nowhere left to fight, and worries that peace will prove even more costly to the journalists, who will have nothing left to write about.
2. I.e., the "brotherhood" of news writers.
3. John Dyer's fervently Tory newsletter often denounced the Whigs for (among other things) mismanaging the wars abroad.
4. Where disabled soldiers were given care and lodging.
5. City dwellers, tradespeople.
1. "He minds others' concerns, since he has lost his own" (Horace, *Satires* 2.3.19–20).

From My Own Apartment, April 5

There lived some years since within my neighborhood a very grave person, an upholsterer, who seemed a man of more than ordinary application to business. He was a very early riser, and was often abroad two or three hours before any of his neighbors. He had a particular carefulness in the knitting of his brows, and a kind of impatience in all his motions, that plainly discovered he was always intent on matters of importance. Upon my enquiry into his life and conversation, I found him to be the greatest newsmonger in our quarter;[2] that he rose before day to read the *Post-Man;*[3] and that he would take two or three turns to the other end of the town before his neighbors were up, to see if there were any Dutch mails[4] come in. He had a wife and several children; but was much more inquisitive to know what passed in Poland than in his own family, and was in greater pain and anxiety of mind for King Augustus's[5] welfare than that of his nearest relations. He looked extremely thin in a dearth of news, and never enjoyed himself in a westerly wind.[6] This indefatigable kind of life was the ruin of his shop; for about the time that his favorite prince left the crown of Poland, he broke and disappeared.

This man and his affairs had been long out of my mind, till about three days ago, as I was walking in St. James's Park, I heard somebody at a distance hemming after me: and who should it be but my old neighbor the upholsterer? I saw he was reduced to extreme poverty, by certain shabby superfluities in his dress: for notwithstanding that it was a very sultry day for the time of the year, he wore a loose great coat and a muff, with a long campaign-wig out of curl;[7] to which he had added the ornament of a pair of black garters buckled under the knee. Upon his coming up to me, I was going to inquire into his present circumstances; but was prevented by his asking me, with a whisper, whether the last letters brought any accounts that one might rely upon from Bender?[8] I told him, none that I heard of; and asked him, whether he had yet married his eldest daughter? He told me, No. But pray, says he, tell me sincerely, what are your thoughts of the King of Sweden? For though his wife and children were starving, I found his chief concern at present was for this great monarch. I told him, that I looked upon him as one of the first heroes of the age. But pray, says he, do you think there is anything in the story of his wound? And finding me surprised at the question, Nay, says he, I only propose it to you. I answered, that I thought there was no reason to doubt of it. But why in the heel, says he, more than in any other part of the body? Because, says I, the bullet chanced to light there. * * *

We were now got to the upper end of the Mall,[9] where were three or four very odd fellows sitting together upon the bench. These I found were all of them politicians, who used to sun themselves in that place every day about dinner time.[1] * * *

I at length took my leave of the company, and was going away; but had not been gone thirty yards before the upholsterer hemmed again after me. Upon his advancing towards me, with a whisper, I expected to hear some secret piece of news,

---

2. "Monger" not because he sells news but because he tells it, to anyone who will listen; Addison's news-addicted upholsterer became one of the *Tatler*'s most popular comic creations, reappearing in several later numbers.
3. The leading Whig newspaper (1695–1730).
4. Mailboats from the Netherlands, bringing fresh news.
5. Frederick Augustus I of Poland, whose loss and recovery of power had filled the papers for several years.
6. Which prevented the arrival of the "Dutch mails."
7. A "campaign wig" was used when traveling and was remarkable for its decorative curls (here flattened and

disordered).
8. A town in modern Bessarabia, where Charles XII of Sweden (1682–1718) had sought refuge after a long string of military victories and a final catastrophic defeat (see Samuel Johnson, *The Vanity of Human Wishes*, lines 191–222, pages 2696–2697).
9. The public walk in St. James's Park, near the royal residence.
1. Bickerstaff proceeds to eavesdrop, astonished, on the conversation of these news-obsessives.

which he had not thought fit to communicate to the bench; but instead of that, he desired me in my ear to lend him half a crown. In compassion to so needy a statesman, and to dissipate the confusion I found he was in, I told him, if he pleased, I would give him five shillings, to receive five pounds of him when the Great Turk was driven out of Constantinople; which he very readily accepted, but not before he had laid down to me the impossibility of such an event, as the affairs of Europe now stand.

This paper I design for the particular benefit of those worthy citizens who live more in a coffeehouse than in their shops, and whose thoughts are so taken up with the affairs of the Allies, that they forget their customers.

from Joseph Addison: Spectator No. 10
Monday, 12 March 1711

[THE SPECTATOR AND ITS READERS[1]]

Non aliter quam qui adverso vix flumine lembum
Remigiis subigit: si brachia forte remisit,
Atque illum in praeceps prono rapit alveus amni.[2]

It is with much satisfaction that I hear this great city inquiring day by day after these my papers, and receiving my morning lectures with a becoming seriousness and attention. My publisher tells me, that there are already three thousand of them distributed every day: so that if I allow twenty readers to every paper, which I look upon as a modest computation, I may reckon about three-score thousand disciples in London and Westminster, who I hope will take care to distinguish themselves from the thoughtless herd of their ignorant and inattentive brethren. Since I have raised to myself so great an audience, I shall spare no pains to make their instruction agreeable, and their diversion useful. For which reasons I shall endeavor to enliven morality with wit, and to temper wit with morality, that my readers may, if possible, both ways find their account in the speculation of the day. And to the end that their virtue and discretion may not be short transient intermitting starts of thought, I have resolved to refresh their memories from day to day, till I have recovered them out of that desperate state of vice and folly into which the age is fallen. The mind that lies fallow but a single day sprouts up in follies that are only to be killed by a constant and assiduous culture. It was said of Socrates, that he brought philosophy down from heaven, to inhabit among men;[3] and I shall be ambitious to have it said of me, that I have brought philosophy out of closets and libraries, schools and colleges, to dwell in clubs and assemblies, at tea tables, and in coffeehouses.

I would therefore in a very particular manner recommend these my speculations to all well-regulated families, that set apart an hour in every morning for tea and bread and butter; and would earnestly advise them for their good to order this

---

1. The *Spectator* bore a close resemblance to the *Daily Courant:* both papers were a single sheet produced by the same printer (Samuel Buckley) for the same price (a penny), and both appeared every day except Sunday. In this number, Addison elaborates on the ways in which his new essay—less than two weeks old and already very successful—is *not* a newspaper.

2. "As if one, whose oars can scarce force his skiff against the stream, should by chance slacken his arms, and lo! headlong down the current the channel sweeps it away" (Virgil, *Georgics* 1.201–203).
3. Addison paraphrases a remark by the Roman orator Cicero (*Tusculan Disputations* 5.4.10).

paper to be punctually served up, and to be looked upon as a part of the tea equipage.

Sir Francis Bacon observes that a well-written book, compared with its rivals and antagonists, is like Moses's serpent, that immediately swallowed up and devoured those of the Egyptians.[4] I shall not be so vain as to think that where the *Spectator* appears, the other public prints will vanish; but shall leave it to my readers' consideration whether, is it not much better to be let into the knowledge of oneself, than to hear what passes in Muscovy[5] or Poland; and to amuse ourselves with such writings as tend to the wearing out of ignorance, passion, and prejudice, than such as naturally conduce to inflame hatreds and make enmities irreconcilable?

In the next place, I would recommend this paper to the daily perusal of those gentlemen whom I cannot but consider as my good brothers and allies, I mean the fraternity of spectators who live in the world without having anything to do in it; and either by the affluence of their fortunes, or laziness of their dispositions, have no other business with the rest of mankind but to look upon them. Under this class of men are comprehended all contemplative tradesmen, titular physicians, Fellows of the Royal Society,[6] Templers[7] that are not given to be contentious, and statesmen that are out of business. In short, everyone that considers the world as a theater, and desires to form a right judgment of those who are the actors on it.

There is another set of men that I must likewise lay a claim to, whom I have lately called the Blanks of society, as being altogether unfurnished with ideas, till the business and conversation of the day has supplied them. I have often considered these poor souls with an eye of great commiseration, when I have heard them asking the first man they have met with, whether there was any news stirring? and by that means gathering together materials for thinking. These needy persons do not know what to talk of, till about twelve a clock in the morning; for by that time they are pretty good judges of the weather, know which way the wind sits, and whether the Dutch mail[8] be come in. As they lie at the mercy of the first man they meet, and are grave or impertinent all the day long, according to the notions which they have imbibed in the morning, I would earnestly entreat them not to stir out of their chambers till they have read this paper, and do promise them that I will daily instill into them such sound and wholesome sentiments as shall have a good effect on their conversation for the ensuing twelve hours.

But there are none to whom this paper will be more useful than to the female world. I have often thought there has not been sufficient pains taken in finding out proper employments and diversions for the fair ones. Their amusements seem contrived for them rather as they are women, than as they are reasonable creatures; and are more adapted to the sex, than to the species. The toilet[9] is their great scene of business, and the right adjusting of their hair the principal employment of their lives. The sorting of a suit of ribbons is reckoned a very good morning's work; and if they

4. Bacon makes this point in his *Advancement of Learning* (2.14), alluding to Exodus 7.10–12
5. A territory in west-central Russia (Moscow was its capital).
6. The London group chartered in the 1660s for the advancement of scientific inquiry.
7. Lawyers.
8. The boat bearing letters and newspapers from Holland.
9. Dressing tables.

make an excursion to a mercer's[1] or a toy shop,[2] so great a fatigue makes them unfit for anything else all the day after. Their more serious occupations are sewing and embroidery, and their greatest drudgery the preparation of jellies and sweetmeats. This, I say, is the state of ordinary women; though I know there are multitudes of those of a more elevated life and conversation, that move in an exalted sphere of knowledge and virtue, that join all the beauties of the mind to the ornaments of dress, and inspire a kind of awe and respect, as well as love, into their male beholders. I hope to increase the number of these by publishing this daily paper, which I shall always endeavor to make an innocent if not an improving entertainment, and by that means at least divert the minds of my female readers from greater trifles. At the same time, as I would fain give some finishing touches to those which are already the most beautiful pieces in human nature, I shall endeavor to point out all those imperfections that are the blemishes, as well as those virtues which are the embellishments, of the sex. In the meanwhile I hope these my gentle readers, who have so much time on their hands, will not grudge throwing away a quarter of an hour in a day on this paper, since they may do it without any hindrance to business.

I know several of my friends and well-wishers are in great pain for me, lest I should not be able to keep up the spirit of a paper which I oblige myself to furnish every day: but to make them easy in this particular, I will promise them faithfully to give it over as soon as I grow dull. This I know will be matter of great raillery to the small wits; who will frequently put me in mind of my promise, desire me to keep my word, assure me that it is high time to give over, with many other little pleasantries of the like nature, which men of a little smart genius cannot forbear throwing out against their best friends, when they have such a handle given them of being witty. But let them remember, that I do hereby enter my caveat against this piece of raillery.

⊢━⊰◆⊱━⊣

Getting, Spending, Speculating

The periodical essay was one commodity among many, in an economy whose energies were evident almost everywhere: in shops stocked with new (often exotic) goods; at outposts in remote countries where trade was gradually being transmuted into empire; at London banks, where the apparatus of transaction (loans, bills, draughts) was rapidly being refined; in nearby coffeehouses, where the agents and accumulators of wealth paused during busy days to absorb substances imported from abroad (coffee, tobacco, chocolate) as well as that home-crafted item of consumption, the periodical essay itself. The essayists often construed their audience as though it consisted *primarily* of merchants, shopkeepers, and customers—of people profoundly concerned with the course of commerce, whatever their gender or occupation. Defoe, Addison, and Steele all wrote to celebrate trade (its new profusions and possibilities), but also to regularize it, to render it respectable, to reconcile it with notions of human excellence originating in an earlier culture centered on aristocracy. The *Review*, the *Tatler*, and the *Spectator* all undertook (as the historian J. G. A. Pocock has elegantly argued) to redefine the idea of "virtue," to shift its focus of application from the classically defined obligations of the hereditary landowner to the prudent calculation of the urban merchant, alert to realities and probabilities in an economy awash with speculation and controlled by credit, where "what one owned was promises": promises by entrepreneurs in search of capital; by stock-jobbers selling

---

1. Fabric sellers.

2. Where they might buy ornamental accessories—fans, silks, ribbons, laces—as well as playthings.

The *Gentleman's Magazine*:

St JOHN's GATE.

Lond. Gazette
Lond. Journ
Fog's Journ.
Applebee's : :
Read's : : : :
Craftsman : :
P. Spectator
Lit Courier of
Grubstreet
Hyp-Docra
Daily-Post
D. Advertiser
St James's Eb.
Whitehall Eb
Lond. Eveni
Weekly Misc
General Evc.
Old Whig
D. Gazetteer
Lon. D. Post
Com. Sense

Foreign News
Dublin 5 : :
Edinburgh 2
Bristol : : : :
Norwich 2
Exeter 2 : : :
Worcester
Northampton
Glocester : :
Stamford : :
Nottingham
Bury Journ.
Chester ditto
Derby ditto
Ipswich do.
Reading do.
Leeds Merc:
Newcastle C.
Canterbury
Durham
Kendal
Boston : : ¶
Barbados :
Jamaica &c

For **JANUARY**, 1738.

CONTAINING,

(More in Quantity, and greater Variety, than any Book of the kind and Price).

I.   ORIGINAL ESSAYS, Moral : The Character of a *Good Man*, by a late illustrious Lady. Of the Magistrate's Right to punish by Death. Prescience consistent with Liberty. Whether Heaven and Hell be Local.
II. —— PHILOLOGICAL : Essay on Tragedy, with *Horace's* four Rules for ⸐ Drama. Answers to Biblical Questions.
III. —— MATHEMATICKS : A new Astronomical Equation, discover'd by Mr *Facio*. A Method to find the Longitude and Latitude at Sea.
IV. —— THE Lady's Adventure, and Love Letters from a Protestant Gent. to a Catholic Lady.
V.   ESSAYS from the Weekly Papers, *The Literary Courier of Grub-street*. Characters of News-Papers. Advice to Ladies on their Return to *London*. *Zenger's* Tryal for printing a Libel. Rules

of Physiognomy in chusing Husbands. The Widow describ'd. The Character of a Prince Royal, *&c.*
VI. POETRY. A Poem, inscrib'd to the *Dublin* Society, by Mr *Arbuckle*. Ode on the Death of P. *George of Denmark*, by the celebrated Mr *Alsop*. Prologue to *Venice preserv'd*, by a Person of Quality. The Blind Boy, with the Musick correct. Songs, Epigrams, Ænigmas, &c.
VII. HISTORICAL. The King's Speech; Addresses of the Lords and Commons. The Secrets of Free-Masonry.
VIII. LISTS of Births, Mariages, and Deaths, *&c.*
IX. FOREIGN AFFAIRS.   Match of Don *Carlos* with the Princess Royal of *Poland*, &c. Caution to Mariners.
X.   Price of Stocks. Bill of Mortality.
XI. Register of Books.
XII. TABLE of Contents.

By SYLVANUS URBAN, Gent.

LONDON: Printed by E. CAVE at St JOHN's GATE, and Sold by the Booksellers of Town and Country ; of whom may be had any former Month.

Where the *Review, Tatler,* and *Spectator* defined themselves *against* their print contemporaries, other periodicals took a different tack. With so much information, instruction, and entertainment flowing from so many sources, a desire developed for a digest that might organize it all. No one catered more adroitly to this new market than did Edward Cave, founder and editor of *Gentleman's Magazine,* a monthly pamphlet whose title coined a pivotal new term for print. "Magazine" meant a military storehouse of provisions and artillery; the *Gentleman's Magazine* promised an intellectual storehouse similarly well stocked. Cave promised "more in quantity, and greater variety, than any book of the kind and price." He delivered on the promise by publishing extracts and abstracts from many periodicals, but he soon cultivated a stable of his own writers (including the young Samuel Johnson) who furnished his readers with an ever-widening range of fresh materials: biographies, poetry, parliamentary debates. The *Magazine*'s logo presents it as a compendium of other papers, but Cave had in fact produced a true original, "one of the most successful and lucrative pamphlets" (wrote Johnson, whose observation still holds true) "which literary history has upon record." The title page depicts the 200 year-old gatehouse where the *Gentleman's Magazine* was composed, printed, and sold (the building's fortress-like appearance may entail a visual pun, conjuring up the military meaning of "magazine"). The building is flanked by the names of papers that the *Magazine* has incorporated, one way or another, into its own pages (London papers on the left, provincial and foreign ones on the right). The fictitious name "Sylvanus Urban" conjures up both countryside (*sylvanus,* "wooded") and city; as the bottom lines make clear, Cave aimed his appeal at audiences in both domains.

hopes of future prosperity; by the government whose operations depended on intricately structured loans from its own citizens. One central concern of the periodicals was how to commute promise into actual prosperity, rather than mere air.

In the selections in this section, Addison rejoices in the commercial and cultural confluence at the Royal Exchange (London's shopping center). In a more sentimental vein, Steele tracks the consequences of foreign trade in the lives and feelings of two lovers. Defoe, by contrast, is harder-headed, more closely analytic. Unlike the authors of the *Spectator*, he had spent years in business, making and losing fortunes. Surveying the shops of London, Defoe declares (as in virtually every *Review*) his passion for trade, but he asks what prospects the *present* patterns of consumption actually hold forth.

Joseph Addison: Spectator No. 69
Saturday, 19 May 1711

[ROYAL EXCHANGE[1]]

Hic segetes, illic veniunt felicius uvae:
Arborei foetus alibi, atque injussa virescunt
Gramina. Nonne vides, croceos ut Tmolus odores,
India mittit ebur, molles sua thura Sabaei?
At Chalybes nudi ferrum, virosaque Pontus
Castorea, Eliadum palmas Epirus equarum?
Continuo has leges aeternaque foedera certis
Imposuit Natura locis . . . [2]

There is no place in the town which I so much love to frequent as the Royal Exchange. It gives me a secret satisfaction, and in some measure gratifies my vanity, as I am an Englishman, to see so rich an assembly of countrymen and foreigners consulting together upon the private business of mankind, and making this metropolis a kind of emporium for the whole earth. I must confess I look upon high-change[3] to be a great council, in which all considerable nations have their representatives. Factors[4] in the trading world are what ambassadors are in the politic world; they negotiate affairs, conclude treaties, and maintain a good correspondence between those wealthy societies of men that are divided from one another by seas and oceans, or live on the different extremities of a continent. I have often been pleased to hear disputes adjusted between an inhabitant of Japan and an alderman of London, or to see a subject of the Great Mogul[5] entering into a league with one of the Czar of Muscovy.[6] I am infinitely delighted in mixing with these several ministers of commerce, as they are distinguished by their different walks and different languages. Sometimes

1. The Exchange, a quadrangle of arcades and shops surrounding a huge courtyard, had functioned as a crucial site of London commerce since its creation in 1570. Destroyed in the Great Fire, it was rebuilt from a new design in 1669. The illustration on page 2335 depicts both the original building by Thomas Gresham (upper right corner) and the later structure with its more intricate, Baroque ornamentation. Statues of English kings occupy the second-floor arches. At the center of the courtyard, the statue of Charles II in the garb of a Roman emperor enacts that favored comparison (echoed by Addison in his essay's epigraph from Virgil) between contemporary Britain and the ancient Roman Empire.
2. "Corn grows more plentifully here, grapes there. In other places grow trees laden with fruit, and grasses

unbidden. Do you not see how Tmolus sends us its saffron perfumes; India her ivory; the soft Sabaens their frankincense; but the naked Chalybes send us iron, the Pontus pungent beaver-oil, and Epirus prize-winning Olympic horses? These perpetual laws and eternal covenants Nature has imposed on certain places" (Virgil, *Georgics* 1.54–61).
3. In addition to housing shops, the Exchange was a central meeting place for international merchants, who frequently closed deals in the courtyard. "High change" was that period when trading was at its peak.
4. Commercial agents.
5. The Indian emperor.
6. A territory in west-central Russia (Moscow was its capital).

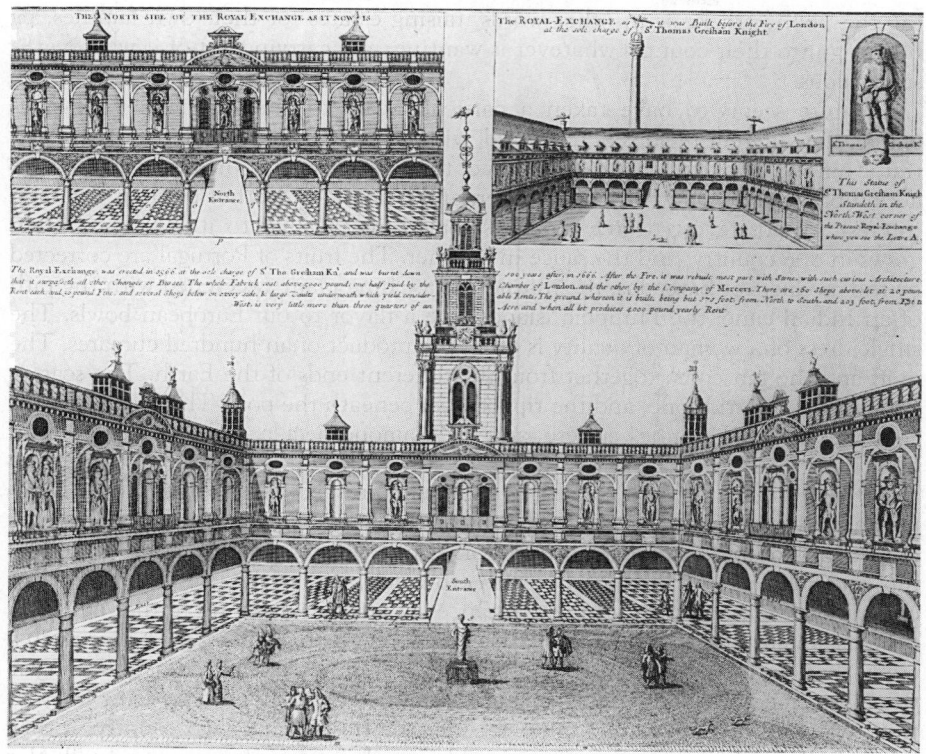

Sutton Nicholls. *The Royal Exchange*. 1712

I am jostled among a body of Armenians: sometimes I am lost in a crowd of Jews, and sometimes make one in a group of Dutchmen. I am a Dane, Swede, or Frenchman at different times, or rather fancy myself like the old philosopher,[7] who upon being asked what countryman he was, replied that he was a citizen of the world.

Though I very frequently visit this busy multitude of people, I am known to nobody there but my friend, Sir Andrew,[8] who often smiles upon me as he sees me bustling in the crowd, but at the same time connives at my presence without taking any further notice of me. There is indeed a merchant of Egypt, who just knows me by sight, having formerly remitted me some money to Grand Cairo;[9] but as I am not versed in the modern Coptic, our conferences go no further than a bow and a grimace.[1]

This grand scene of business gives me an infinite variety of solid and substantial entertainments. As I am a great lover of mankind, my heart naturally overflows with pleasure at the sight of a prosperous and happy multitude, insomuch that at many public solemnities I cannot forbear expressing my joy with tears that have stolen down my cheeks. For this reason I am wonderfully delighted to see such a body of men thriving in their own private fortunes, and at the same time promot-

7. Diogenes the Cynic, credited for developing the concept of "cosmopolitanism"(citizenship in the universe), in which all beings are parts of a single whole.
8. Sir Andrew Freeport, a member of Mr. Spectator's club: Whig merchant and ardent advocate (as his name

implies) of free trade.
9. Where Mr. Spectator spent some time as a young man (see *Spectator* No. 1, page 2325).
1. The word denoted an expression of politeness.

ing the public stock; or in other words, raising estates for their own families, by bringing into their country whatever is wanting, and carrying out of it whatever is superfluous.

Nature seems to have taken a particular care to disseminate her blessings among the different regions of the world, with an eye to this mutual intercourse and traffic among mankind, that the natives of the several parts of the globe might have a kind of dependence upon one another, and be united together by their common interest. Almost every degree produces something peculiar to it. The food often grows in one country, and the sauce in another. The fruits of Portugal are corrected by the products of Barbados; the infusion of a China plant sweetened with the pith of an Indian cane; the Philippic islands give a flavor to our European bowls. The single dress of a woman of quality is often the product of an hundred climates. The muff and the fan come together from the different ends of the Earth. The scarf is sent from the torrid zone, and the tippet from beneath the pole. The brocade petticoat rises out of the mines of Peru, and the diamond necklace out of the bowels of Indostan.

If we consider our own country in its natural prospect, without any of the benefits and advantages of commerce, what a barren uncomfortable spot of earth falls to our share! Natural historians tell us that no fruit grows originally among us, besides hips and haws, acorns and pig-nuts, with other delicacies of the like nature; that our climate of itself, and without the assistances of art, can make no further advances towards a plum than to a sloe,[2] and carries an apple to no greater a perfection than a crab;[3] that our melons, our peaches, our figs, our apricots, and cherries, are strangers among us, imported in different ages, and naturalized in our English gardens; and that they would all degenerate and fall away into the trash of our own country, if they were wholly neglected by the planter, and left to the mercy of our sun and soil. Nor has traffic more enriched our vegetable world, than it has improved the whole face of nature among us. Our ships are laden with the harvest of every climate; our tables are stored with spices, and oils, and wines; our rooms are filled with pyramids of China, and adorned with the workmanship of Japan; our morning's draught[4] comes to us from the remotest corners of the earth; we repair our bodies by the drugs of America, and repose ourselves under Indian canopies. My friend Sir Andrew calls the vineyards of France our gardens; the Spice Islands[5] our hotbeds; the Persians our silk weavers, and the Chinese our potters. Nature indeed furnishes us with the bare necessaries of life, but traffic gives us a great variety of what is useful, and at the same time supplies us with everything that is convenient and ornamental. Nor is it the least part of this our happiness, that whilst we enjoy the remotest products of the north and south, we are free from those extremities of weather which give them birth; that our eyes are refreshed with the green fields of Britain, at the same time that our palates are feasted with fruits that rise between the tropics.

For these reasons there are not more useful members in a commonwealth than merchants. They knit mankind together in a mutual intercourse of good offices, distribute the gifts of nature, find work for the poor, add wealth to the rich, and magnificence to the great. Our English merchant converts the tin of his own country into gold, and exchanges his wool for rubies. The Mahometans are clothed in our British manufacture, and the inhabitants of the frozen zone warmed with the fleeces of our sheep.

---

2. The berry of the blackthorn.
3. Crabapple.

4. Drink.
5. A cluster of islands in modern Indonesia.

When I have been upon the 'Change, I have often fancied one of our old kings[6] standing in person, where he is represented in effigy, and looking down upon the wealthy concourse of people with which that place is every day filled. In this case, how would he be surprised to hear all the languages of Europe spoken in this little spot of his former dominions, and to see so many private men, who in his time would have been the vassals of some powerful baron, negotiating like princes for greater sums of money than were formerly to be met with in the Royal Treasury! Trade, without enlarging the British territories, has given us a kind of additional empire: it has multiplied the number of the rich, made our landed estates infinitely more valuable than they were formerly, and added to them an accession of other estates as valuable as the lands themselves.

Richard Steele: Spectator No. 11
Tuesday, 13 March 1711

[INKLE AND YARICO[1]]

Dat veniam corvis, vexat censura columbas.[2]

Arietta is visited by all persons of both sexes who have any pretense to wit and gallantry. She is in that time of life which is neither affected with the follies of youth or infirmities of age; and her conversation is so mixed with gaiety and prudence that she is agreeable both to the young and the old. Her behavior is very frank, without being in the least blameable; and as she is out of the tract of any amorous or ambitious pursuits of her own, her visitants entertain her with accounts of themselves very freely, whether they concern their passions or their interests. I made her a visit this afternoon, having been formerly introduced to the honor of her acquaintance by my friend Will. Honeycomb,[3] who has prevailed upon her to admit me sometimes into her assembly, as a civil, inoffensive man. I found her accompanied with one person only, a commonplace talker who, upon my entrance, rose, and after a very slight civility sat down again; then turning to Arietta, pursued his discourse, which I found was upon the old topic of constancy in love. He went on with great facility in repeating what he talks every day of his life; and with the ornaments of insignificant laughs and gestures, enforced his arguments by quotations out of plays and songs, which allude to the perjuries of the fair, and the general levity[4] of women. Methought he strove to shine more than ordinarily in his talkative way, that he might insult my silence, and distinguish himself before a woman of Arietta's taste and understanding. She had often an inclination to interrupt him, but could find no opportunity, 'till the larum[5] ceased of itself; which it did not 'till he had repeated and murdered the celebrated story of the Ephesian matron.[6]

Arietta seemed to regard this piece of raillery as an outrage done to her sex, as indeed I have always observed that women, whether out of a nicer[7] regard to their

6. As depicted in the statues on the second story (see illustration on page 2335).

1. Steele here elaborates on a 60-year-old traveler's tale, in such a way as to combine two of the *Spectator*'s central concerns: the transactions of love and power between men and women, and the impact of commerce on human conduct.

2. "Their verdict goes easy on the raven, but is severe on the dove" (Juvenal, *Satires* 2.63). The speaker, a woman, is complaining of how leniently men assess themselves, and how harshly they criticize women.

3. An aged member of Mr. Spectator's club, proud of his long-ago days as a Restoration rake, and still deeply interested in matters of the heart.

4. Lightness, fickleness.

5. The long-ringing alarm bell (of his talk).

6. The Roman story (told in Petronius's *Satyricon*, part 2) of a widow who, while mourning at the tomb of her newly deceased husband, succumbs to the attractions of a soldier standing nearby, and makes love with him on her husband's tomb.

7. More precise.

honor, or what other reason I cannot tell, are more sensibly touched with those general aspersions which are cast upon their sex, than men are by what is said of theirs.

When she had a little recovered herself from the serious anger she was in, she replied in the following manner.

"Sir, when I consider, how perfectly new all you have said on this subject is, and that the story you have given us is not quite two thousand years old, I cannot but think it a piece of presumption to dispute with you: but your quotations put me in mind of the fable of the lion and the man.[8] The man, walking with that noble animal, showed him, in the ostentation of human superiority, a sign of a man killing a lion. Upon which the lion said very justly, 'We lions are none of us painters, else we could show a hundred men killed by lions, for one lion killed by a man.' You men are writers, and can represent us women as unbecoming as you please in your works, while we are unable to return the injury. You have twice or thrice observed in your discourse that hypocrisy is the very foundation of our education; and that an ability to dissemble our affections is a professed part of our breeding. These, and such other reflections, are sprinkled up and down the writings of all ages, by authors who leave behind them memorials of their resentment against the scorn of particular women, in invectives against the whole sex. Such a writer, I doubt not, was the celebrated Petronius, who invented the pleasant aggravations of the frailty of the Ephesian lady; but when we consider this question between the sexes, which has been either a point of dispute or raillery ever since there were men and women, let us take facts from plain people, and from such as have not either ambition or capacity to embellish their narrations with any beauties of imagination. I was the other day amusing myself with Ligon's *Account of Barbados*; and, in answer to your well-wrought tale, I will give you (as it dwells upon my memory) out of that honest traveler, in his fifty-fifth page, the History of Inkle and Yarico.[9]

"Mr. Thomas Inkle[1] of London, aged 20 years, embarked in the Downs[2] on the good ship called the Achilles, bound for the West Indies, on the 16th of June 1647, in order to improve his fortune by trade and merchandise. Our adventurer was the third son of an eminent citizen, who had taken particular care to instill into his mind an early love of gain, by making him a perfect master of numbers, and consequently giving him a quick view of loss and advantage, and preventing the natural impulses of his passions, by prepossession towards his interests. With a mind thus turned, young Inkle had a person every way agreeable, a ruddy vigor in his countenance, strength in his limbs, with ringlets of fair hair loosely flowing on his shoulders. It happened, in the course of the voyage, that the Achilles, in some distress, put into a creek on the main of America, in search of provisions. The youth, who is the hero of my story, among others, went ashore on this occasion. From their first landing they were observed by a party of Indians, who hid themselves in the woods for that purpose. The English unadvisedly marched a great distance from the shore into the country, and were intercepted by the natives, who slew the greatest number of them. Our adventurer escaped among others, by flying

8. In Aesop's *Fables* (No. 219).
9. Richard Ligon's *True and Exact History of the Island of Barbados* (1657) includes a paragraph on a slave named Yarico and her misadventures in love, which Steele elaborates into the tale that follows.

1. Steele invents the name for this character; it means (perhaps prophetically) "linen tape," a common commodity.
2. A harbor on the southeastern coast of England.

into a forest. Upon his coming into a remote and pathless part of the wood, he threw himself, tired and breathless, on a little hillock, when an Indian maid rushed from a thicket behind him. After the first surprise, they appeared mutually agreeable to each other. If the European was highly charmed with the limbs, features, and wild graces of the naked American, the American was no less taken with the dress, complexion, and shape of an European, covered from head to foot. The Indian grew immediately enamored of him, and consequently solicitous for his preservation. She therefore conveyed him to a cave, where she gave him a delicious repast of fruits, and led him to a stream to slake his thirst. In the midst of these good offices, she would sometimes play with his hair, and delight in the opposition of its color to that of her fingers; then open his bosom, then laugh at him for covering it. She was, it seems, a person of distinction, for she every day came to him in a different dress, of the most beautiful shells, bugles, and bredes.[3] She likewise brought him a great many spoils, which her other lovers had presented to her; so that his cave was richly adorned with all the spotted skins of beasts, and most parti-colored feathers of fowls, which that world afforded. To make his confinement more tolerable, she would carry him in the dusk of the evening, or by the favor of moonlight, to unfrequented groves and solitudes, and show him where to lie down in safety, and sleep amidst the falls of waters, and melody of nightingales. Her part was to watch and hold him in her arms, for fear of her countrymen, and wake him on occasions to consult his safety. In this manner did the lovers pass away their time, till they had learned a language of their own, in which the voyager communicated to his mistress, how happy he should be to have her in his country, where she should be clothed in such silks as his waistcoat was made of, and be carried in houses drawn by horses, without being exposed to wind or weather. All this he promised her the enjoyment of, without such fears and alarms as they were there tormented with. In this tender correspondence these lovers lived for several months, when Yarico, instructed by her lover, discovered a vessel on the coast, to which she made signals, and in the night, with the utmost joy and satisfaction accompanied him to a ship's crew of his countrymen, bound for Barbados. When a vessel from the main arrives in that island, it seems the planters come down to the shore, where there is an immediate market of the Indians and other slaves, as with us of horses and oxen.

"To be short, Mr. Thomas Inkle, now coming into English territories, began seriously to reflect upon his loss of time, and to weigh with himself how many days' interest of his money he had lost during his stay with Yarico. This thought made the young man very pensive, and careful what account he should be able to give his friends of his voyage. Upon which considerations, the prudent and frugal young man sold Yarico to a Barbadian merchant; notwithstanding that the poor girl, to incline him to commiserate her condition, told him that she was with child by him; but he only made use of that information, to rise in his demands upon the purchaser."

I was so touched with this story, (which I think should be always a counterpart to the Ephesian matron) that I left the room with tears in my eyes; which a woman of Arietta's good sense did, I am sure, take for greater applause, than any compliments I could make her.

---

3. Tube-shaped glass beads and braiding.

Daniel Defoe: *from* **A Review of the State of the British Nation,**
Vol. 1, No. 43
Thursday, 8 January 1713
[WEAK FOUNDATIONS]

The subject of trade which I am now entered upon has this one excellency in it, for the benefit of the author, that really it can never be exhausted. * * * I remember some time ago I gave you a hint about the mighty alteration in the face of trade in this city; I cannot but touch it again on this occasion, because it relates to what I am upon. Let any man who remembers the glorious state of our trade about thirty or forty years past view but the streets of this opulent city and even the Exchange of London—nay, even our courts of law. It must of necessity put him in mind of Ezra 3.12, where the ancient men who had seen the old temple wept when they saw the weak foundations of the new.

However, to go on as I began and examine our new increase of commerce which we so must boast of: let me note a little to you with what mighty advantages the chasms, gaps, and breaches of our trade are filled up of late, and let us see it, I say, in the streets. Here, in the room of a trifling banker, or goldsmith, we are supplied with a most eminent brandy shop (Cheapside). There in the room of ditto you have a flaming shop[1] for white tea pots and luted earthen mugs (Cornhill), the most excellent offspring of that most valuable manufacture of earthenware. It is impossible that coffee, tea, and chocolate can be so advanced in their consumption without an eminent increase of those trades that attend them; whence we see the most noble shops in the city taken up with the valuable utensils of the tea table. The china warehouses are little marts within themselves (and by the way, are newly become markets of clandestine trade, of which I shall say more very quickly), and the eminent corner houses in the chief streets of London are chosen out by the town tinkers to furnish us with tea kettles and chocolate pots—vide Catherine Street and Bedford Buildings. Two thousand pound is reckoned a small stock in copper pots and lacquered kettles, and the very fitting up one of these brazen people's shops with fine sashes,[2] etc., to set forth his ware, costs above 500£ sterling, which is more by half than the best draper or mercer's shop in London requires.

This certainly shows the increase of our trade. Brass locks for our chambers and parlors, brass knockers for our doors, and the like add to the luster of those shops, of which hereafter. And the same sash works, only finer and larger, are now used to range[3] your brass and copper, that the goldsmiths had always to set out their less valuable silver and gold plate. From hence, be pleased to look upon the druggists of the town who are the merchants of these things. Bucklers-Bury and Little Lombard Street were the places which a few years ago held the whole number, a very few excepted, of that difficult nice employment, whose number is now spread over the whole town and with the most capital stocks, whose whole employ is the furnishing us by wholesale and retail with these most valuable of all drugs, coffee, tea, and chocolate—the general furniture of a druggist's shop being now three bales of coffee, twelve boxes of chocolate, six large canisters of tea, and an hundred and fifty empty gilded boxes. In like manner the rest of the town—how gloriously it is supplied! How

---

1. A shop with a kiln for making earthenware.
2. Windows made up of two sliding frames (common now, new and fancy at this time).
3. Display.

do pastry cooks and periwig makers, brandy shops and toy shops, succeed linen drapers, mercers, upholsterers, and the like. A hundred pounds to rent for a house to sell jellies and apple pies; two hundred pounds to fit up a brandy shop, and afterwards not a hundred pound stock to put into it. These I can show many instances of.

Look, gentlemen, upon the particular parts of your town, formerly eminent for the best of tradesmen! View the famous churchyard of St. Paul's where so many aldermen and lord mayors have been raised by the trade of broadcloth and mere woolen manufactures,[4] and on whose trades so many families of poor always depended, that Sir William Turner used to say his shop alone employed 50,000 poor people! What succeeds him? A most noble, and to be sure, a much more valuable vintner's warehouse, *Anglice*,[5] a tavern, more vulgarly a bawdyhouse. And the next draper's shop, a coffee house; what takes up the whole row there? and supplies the place of eighteen or nineteen topping drapers? Who can but observe it! Cane chair makers, gilders of leather, looking-glass shops, and peddlers or toy shops—manifold improvements of trade! and an eminent instance of the growth of our manufactures! * * *

Advertisements from the *Spectator*[1]

At the Lace Chamber on Ludgate Hill, kept by Mary Parsons, is a great quantity of Flanders lace, lately come over, to be sold off at great pennyworths[2] by wholesale or retail. She bought them there herself. [No. 200; Friday, 19 October 1711]

This day is published *The Court and City Vagaries*, being some late (and real) intrigues of several gentlemen and ladies. Written by one of the fair sex, price 6d. Sold by J. Baker in Paternoster Row. [No. 255; Saturday, 22 December 1711]

The famous Italian water, for dying red and grey hairs of the head and eyebrows into a lasting brown or black; at 1, 2, or 4s. the bottle, with printed directions for the use of it. To be had at Mrs. Hannam's toyshop, at the sign of the Three Angels near the Half-Moon Tavern in Cheapside. [Vol. 8, No. 634; Friday, 17 December 1714]

The ladies that called at Mr. Charles Lillie's at the corner of Beauford Buildings,[3] in a hackney coach on Wednesday night, the 6th of this instant, about 10 o'clock, are desired to let him know where to direct to them, he being now able to give a particular account of what they enquired after. [No. 305; Tuesday, 19 February 1712]

A Bubbler's Medley

In a culture preoccupied with commerce, sensational economic developments not only filled the columns of the regular newspapers and periodical essays; they also produced reams of "occasional" print—satires and songs, broadsides and commentaries catering to

---

4. The trade in textiles had provided the foundation for many family fortunes and (hence) political careers.
5. In English.
1. Periodicals did not merely comment on commerce, they participated in it, earning much of their revenue from the advertisements that they printed at the conclusion of their main editorial matter.

2. At a terrific bargain.
3. Charles Lillie, a close associate of Addison's and Steele's, owned a perfume shop in the Strand. He had been one of the publishers and distributors of the *Tatler*, and sold the *Spectator* at his shop, where he also accepted advertisements for inclusion in the paper.

readers tremulously concerned about the fate of their nation's fortunes and their own. In the early eighteenth century, no such event worried more readers, and produced more print, than the South Sea Bubble, an investment scheme whose origin was intricate and outcome catastrophic. (For a picture of the profusion, see the frontispiece to this section opposite page 1979).

The wars Britain fought during William III's and Anne's reigns had a lingering effect. In order to finance expensive military ventures on the Continent, the British relied on a complex system of annuities, lotteries, and loans. Of these methods, the annuities caused the most strain in subsequent years. This was because the holders of the annuities had loaned the government money at a time of great crisis, and were guaranteed a fixed income for the rest of their lives as well as their children's lives. The interest on these loans varied from 7 percent to 9 percent. Moreover, these particular loans often were irredeemable, that is, the principal could not be paid off without the holder's consent.

In the fall of 1719, the South Sea Company, a concern holding monopoly rights to trade in South America and the Pacific, offered to take over the government's burdensome debt (about £51,000,000). Its plan was as follows: the company would assume the national debt and receive interest at the rate of 5 percent till 1727, when the rate would fall to 4 percent. For this right, it would pay the government a one-time fee of £7,567,000. The company hoped to persuade annuitants to exchange their annuities for stock. The only way the company could make money from this scheme was if its stock rapidly inflated in value. With the connivance of the government and a series of public relations moves designed to foster confidence, the company's stock rose steadily throughout the spring of 1720, hitting a high of 1000 (from a starting point near 100).

The whole scheme oddly mirrored the rise and fall of a similar plan in France in 1719. John Law (1671–1729), a Scottish emigrant and financier, had begun his rise to economic preeminence in 1715. By 1719, he controlled the finances of France, and attempted to incorporate the national debt of France into a trading company known as the Mississippi Company. By a similar inflation of company stock, he managed for a time to redeem much of the national debt, but by March 1720—at the same moment that Britain's plan was being put into operation—his scheme fell apart and he was discredited.

Despite the obvious warnings Law's failure presented, the rise of South Sea stock touched off an investment mania. Companies came into being overnight, often with little more than a name and a crazy idea to recommend them, and were bought into by investors hungry to reap the seemingly endless profit promised by speculating. The government attempted (with little success) to limit the more scandalous of these companies in June, but the speculative fever continued unabated. By the fall of 1720, stocks of all kinds had begun to fall. Fortunes on paper disappeared overnight, and people suffered disastrous losses. Popular resentment threatened to overthrow the government. Sir Robert Walpole (1676–1745), an early opponent of the scheme, came to the rescue of the government, proposing a series of measures to restore public credit and stabilize the financing of the national debt. Many of the South Sea directors had their assets seized, but several of the worst malefactors, including Secretary of State Charles Spencer, Third Earl of Sunderland, were screened from retribution (though Sunderland did lose office). From this crisis one can date the ascendancy of Walpole, which continued until 1742.

The Bubble ruined numberless investors, and sold a lot of papers. Popular feeling about the crisis exploded in pamphlets, poems, plays, broadsides, and prose satires. The following selection represents a cross-section of genres and a miscellany of reactions to the expansion and the explosion of the South Sea Bubble.

from **Historical Register for the Year 1720**[1]

His Lordship was backed by the Duke of W_____n,[2] who endeavored chiefly to evince, "that the South Sea Project might prove of infinite disadvantage to the nation; first, as it gave foreigners an opportunity to double and treble the vast sums they had in our public funds, which could not but tempt them to withdraw their capital stock, with their immense gains, to other countries, which might drain Great Britain of a considerable part of its gold and silver. Secondly, that the artificial and prodigious rise of the South Sea stock was a dangerous bait, which might decoy many unwary people to their ruin, and allure them by false prospect of gain, to part with what they had got by their labor and industry, to purchase imaginary riches. And, in the third place, that the addition of above thirty millions new capital, would give such a vast power to the South Sea company, as might endanger the liberties of the nation, and, in time, subvert our excellent constitution; since by their extensive interest they might influence most, if not all, the elections of the members, and consequently overrule the resolutions of the House of Commons." Earl C____per[3] spoke also against the bill, and said "that like the Trojan Horse, it was ushered in, and received with great pomp and acclamations of joy; but was contrived for treachery and destruction." His lordship urged in particular, "that in all public bargains, it is a duty incumbent on them who are entrusted with the administration, to take care that the same be more advantageous to the state than to private persons; but that a quite contrary method seemed to have been followed in the contract made with the South Sea Company." * * *

But the Earl of S_____d[4] answered most of their objections; and, among other things, said, "that they who encouraged and countenanced the scheme of the South Sea company, had nothing in their view, but the easing the nation of part of that heavy load of debt it labors under. That on the other hand, the managers of that company had, undoubtedly, a prospect of private gain, either to themselves, or to their corporation; but that, when that scheme was accepted, neither the one nor the other could foresee that the stocks would have risen to the price they were now advanced. That if they had continued as they were at that time, the public would have had the far greater share of the advantage accruing from that scheme; and if the stocks were kept up to the price they had been raised to, which was not unlikely, it was but reasonable that the South Sea company should enjoy the profits procured to it by the wise management and industry of its directors, which would enable it both to make large dividends among its members, and thereby to compass the ends intended by this scheme." After this the question for committing the bill being put, it was carried in the affirmative, by a majority of 83 voices to 17.

---

1. The *Historical Register* was a periodical publication that described recent proceedings in the House of Lords and the House of Commons, as well as foreign negotiations, treaties, etc. This excerpt summarizes some speeches delivered in April 1720, for and against the South Sea plan.
2. Philip, first Duke of Wharton. Famous libertine, staunch opponent of the South Sea scheme, author of the anti-Walpole journal *The True Briton* (1723–1724) following that minister's ascent in 1721, and, in his final years, a Jacobite.

3. William, first Earl of Cowper, served George I as Chancellor from 1714 to 1718, when he resigned over the ministry's religious policy but remained on good terms with the court. As an outsider to the Stanhope-Sunderland ministry in good standing with the king, his words against the scheme carried weight.
4. Charles Spencer, third Earl of Sunderland; junior partner in Stanhope's ministry (1718–1721), Secretary of State for the north, and chief ministerial proponent of the South Sea scheme.

Anne Finch: A Song on the South Sea[1]

Ombre and basset[2] laid aside,
  New games employ the fair;
And brokers all those hours divide
  Which lovers used to share.

5 The court, the park, the foreign song
  And harlequin's grimace,[3]
Forlorn; amidst the city throng
  Behold each blooming face.

With Jews and Gentiles undismayed
  Young tender virgins mix,
10 Of whiskers nor of beards afraid,
  Nor all the cozening tricks.

Bright jewels, polished once to deck
  The fair one's rising breast,
15 Or sparkle round her ivory neck,
  Lie pawned in iron chest.

The gayer passions of the mind
  How avarice controls!
Even love does now no longer find
20 A place in female souls.

Thomas D'Urfey: The Hubble Bubbles
[A Ballad to the tune of "Over the Hills and Far Away"][1]

Ye circum, and uncircumcised,[2]
Come hear my song and be advised.
Sell all your lands, sell all your flocks,
Put your money in the stocks,
5 Hubble bubble, bubble hubble now's in play,
Come buy our hubble bubble whilst may;
For there's hubble bubble, bubble hubble, night and day,
  At Jonathan's and Garraway.[3]

Come all who would by fishing gain,[4]
10 Venture like gamesters on the main,°   *the ocean*
Whate'er you lose projectors[5] get,

---

1. This poem by Anne Finch, Countess of Winchilsea (1661–1720) appeared posthumously in 1724 (for other poems by Finch, see pages 2141–2145). Since she died in August 1720, she must have written the poem during the height of the Bubble mania. The poem reflects a fact sometimes obscured by all the pamphleteering and satire surrounding the scheme: namely, that it enabled women, for the first time in English history, to indulge in financial speculation and trade at a level nearly equal with men.
2. Popular card games.
3. Either the popular masquerade costume (at least one writer praised the Bubble of 1720 for putting a temporary end to licentious masquerades) or a reference to the

vogue for harlequin plays on stage in London.
1. Printed ballads, providing commentary on the news set to familiar tunes, remained a popular commodity from the Elizabethan era well into the 18th century. The playwright and poet, Thomas D'Urfey (1653–1723) produced many of them.
2. I.e., Jews and gentiles.
3. Two coffeehouses located in Exchange Alley, where shares and stocks were often traded.
4. This stanza alludes to one of the many new companies that sprung up in the wake of the South Sea stock rise; specifically, one of several fishing companies offering stock in 1720.
5. The devisers of the investment scheme.

For you're the gudgeons[6] in the net.
Hubble bubble, bubble hubble . . .

Come all ye nymphs of gay desire,
15   Insure your house and selves from fire.[7]
A house insured brings better rent.
Come then insure your tenement.
Hubble bubble, bubble hubble . . .

A bubble is blown up with air,
20   In which fine prospects do appear.
The Bubble breaks, the prospect's lost.
Yet must some bubble° pay the cost,   *fool*
Hubble bubble, bubble hubble . . .

1720

Thomas Read: *from* The Weekly Journal
Saturday, 24 September 1720[1]

Mr. Journalman,

I am a farmer in this neighborhood, and by my industry have scraped about £700 together. Not long ago a gentleman of a small estate offered me his sister in wedlock, and she having the name of a good huswife, while she kept her brother's house, I courted, and married her. 'Tis now about five years since, and I am father by her of a boy and girl, and we have lived as contented and happily together, though I say it, as ever a couple in Essex. But a plague of all chances, within this three or four months some of her relations, who used frequently before to walk over afoot to see us, have come a-visiting in their chariots and berlins, fine equipage and liveries,[2] so that they have set my poor wife, one of the best wives in the world before, so agog, that nothing would serve her but must up to town, and try my fortune in the South Sea, where I might get, she said, more by one lucky hit, than by following my plough all my life. I drove her off as long as I could. "Prithee, Honey," said I, "consider that we thrive in the world already, we live contented, which is a kingdom in itself, and bustle and noise is what I hate dreadfully. I am going to put what little money I have upon a mortgage, and that will be gathering with my other honest-got means, till I may be able to purchase the farm I now rent." But all this availed nothing, she said; she had rather see me taken quite off my slavery, and as they had a topping uncle in the South Sea, who had helped other relations, I should venture. I carried up a letter to him, he called me cousin very kindly, subscribed £500 for me, and bought me 100 capital, so that in the compass of a month or six week, I have lost above one half of

6. A kind of fish; the word was often applied to gullible people.

7. Among the new companies in 1720 were those offering insurance on anything from houses to horses.

1. Thomas Read's *Weekly Journal* advertised itself as "Being the Freshest Advices Foreign or Domestick" and largely lived up to its billing. Following the foreign notices (this particular number carried information from Malaga, Madrid, Genoa, Vienna, Copenhagen, Stock-

holm, Geneva, and The Hague), the journal would recount the activities of English lords, gentlemen, and, in 1720, businessmen. Each number also included letters purportedly written by readers on a wide variety of topics. Toward the end of 1720, more and more of these letters included tales of woe. "William Wheatsheaf's" letter from Rumford is just such a cautionary story, and demonstrates how deeply Bubble mania penetrated English society.

2. All four terms refer to fancy carriages.

what I was worth.[3] I was for selling out in time, crying the first loss was the best; but I am still teased to death to venture at all. These disputes are grown up into a family quarrel, and we who never had any words in our lives before, are every day at daggers drawing. So that in short I have even agreed to let her go to town, and manage stocks there, whilst I take care of my stock at home, and we shall see in the end, which of us shall come to the best market, I at Rumford or she in Change Alley. In the meantime I wish Sir, for we usually read your journal at home, that you would put in a word or two between us, which may be of service.

I am your humble servant
and constant reader,
William Wheatsheaf

Nicholas Amhurst: *from* The Craftsman No. 47
Saturday, 27 May 1727

[USBECK TO RICA AT ISPAHAN[1]]

Among the Christians, with whom I reside, there are a peculiar sort called stock-jobbers. * * * [They] grow rich very unaccountably, not by traffic, not by arts, or science, or industry, or labor, or mechanics, or navigation, or warfare, or any other business of use or advantage to mankind; but, I will tell thee, Rica, their commerce is lying, political lying; and though each man knows the other to deal in this commodity, yet no one day passes, in which some of these strange fellows do not grow rich, and others are undone, as they out-lie one another, or as the lie of the one gains more credit than that of another. They call the chief nominal commodity which they deal in *South Sea stock*; this is worth more or less in idea only, as the lie of the day takes or does not take. Thou wilt think I rave, that I talk idly, when I tell thee here are many people, whom I have conversed with and who appear in other particulars to be men of reason, and yet, on the first mention of these syllables *South Sea stock*, lose at once all reflection and comparison. They told me that in the year 1720, they carried this ideal value of their stock so high, that what, in the beginning of the year, was not valued above 1000 piasters, mounted to more than 10,000 in less than the space of seven moons; that is, every man had agreed to call himself exceeding rich. At that time indeed the malady was almost epidemical, and the few among the people who retained their reason and their original substance, and would not agree to call it more than what it was intrinsically worth, were grown by the madness of their countrymen very poor on the sudden, and found themselves at once from a plentiful substance, on the point of wanting the common necessaries of life. So dangerous is it for a man to keep his understanding in a general frenzy! But at last, as I have said, at the close of six or seven moons, the people awoke from their golden dreams, and a little time after condescended to call their estates by their real values; though some of them are still as mad as ever. * * *

---

3. This indicates that Wheatsheaf bought his £100 worth of South Sea stock when it was at 500, that is, at half its highest value (£1000) and falling fast.
1. For the *Craftsman*, see page 2316. In this particular "letter," the *Craftsman* borrows the form and parodic strategies of Charles-Louis Montesquieu's hugely successful *Persian Letters* (1721), in which Usbek, a traveler from Persia, moves through Europe, reporting home on the customs of the various peoples encountered. The *Craftsman* letter suggests how, with the passage of time, many English people came to the whimsical conclusion that the South Sea obsession was a form of temporary mass insanity.

Women and Men, Manners and Marriage

When Isaac Bickerstaff, in his first *Tatler*, undertook to teach his readers "what to think," politics was apparently what he most expected them to think about. Soon, though, he found a second focus: that cluster of questions today grouped under the rubric "gender." Bickerstaff, his imitators, and his successors strove constantly to instruct men and women as to who they were, what they should become, how they differed from each other, how they ought to interact, and how they might most happily merge in love and marriage. The *Tatler*, the *Review*, and the *Spectator* all urged men to supplant aggression with morality and grace; women to cultivate sound sense over mere caprice; and both sexes to ground their marriages in reciprocity, love, and reason, rather than financial gain or impulsive passion.

The essayists' instruction, though, was far from even-handed. "I will not meddle with the *Spectator*," Jonathan Swift wrote scornfully to Stella in 1711. "Let him *fair-sex* it to the world's end." Addison and Steele had used that phrase obsessively to describe, address, and instruct their female readers; it had by now become a kind of shorthand for a variable blend of courtesy and condescension endemic to the periodicals, almost all of which were written by men and directed at an audience in which males possessed a barely questioned sway. Nonetheless, women had for more than a decade occupied an important (albeit elusive) place in the periodical scheme of things, as purchasers, as readers, as participants. In the early 1690s, when John Dunton launched the first "question and answer" periodical, he quickly discovered that queries submitted by women were abundant, popular, and profitable. In the wake of his *Athenian Mercury*, almost all important periodicals devised strategies for incorporating "the fair sex" into their texts and even into their titles: Mr. Spectator sketched lines of identification between his silent, self-contained conduct, and the proper demeanor of the women whom he proposed to instruct; the *Tatler* proposed to "honor" (but also mocked) its female audience by its choice of title; many periodicals bore titles pitched even more explicitly at women: the *Female Tatler*, the *Ladies' Almanac*, the *Ladies' Magazine*, etc.

Such "inclusion" entailed obvious control. If the periodicals took up women's questions, they almost invariably supplied men's answers (even the *Ladies'* titles were mostly run by men). Eliza Haywood's *Female Spectator*, written not only for women but by a woman, offered something different. Far more fascinated with women's predicaments than with men's opinions, it helped foster a tradition of women's writing that grew richer and more various (encompassing novels and tracts as well as periodicals) as the century progressed.

Richard Steele: *from* Tatler No. 25

Tuesday, 7 June 1709

[DUELLISTS]

White's Chocolate-house, June 6

A letter from a young lady, written in the most passionate terms (wherein she laments the misfortune of a gentleman, her lover, who was lately wounded in a duel) has turned my thoughts to that subject, and inclined me to examine into the causes which precipitate men into so fatal a folly. And as it has been proposed to treat of subjects of gallantry[1] in the article from hence,[2] and no one point in nature is more proper to be considered by the company who frequent this place, than that of duels, it is worth our consideration to examine into this chimerical groundless humor, and to lay every other thought aside, till we have stripped it of all its false pretenses to credit and reputation amongst men.

But I must confess, when I consider what I am going about, and run over in my imagination all the endless crowd of men of honor who will be offended at such a discourse, I am undertaking, methinks, a work worthy an invulnerable hero in Romance, rather than a private gentleman with a single rapier. But as I am pretty well acquainted by great opportunities with the nature of man, and know of a truth, that all men fight *against their will*, the danger vanishes, and resolution rises upon this subject. For this reason I shall talk very freely on a custom which all men wish exploded, though no man has courage enough to resist it.

But there is one unintelligible word which I fear will extremely perplex my dissertation, and I confess to you I find very hard to explain, which is, the term *satisfaction*. An honest country gentleman had the misfortune to fall into company with two or three modern men of honor, where he happened to be very ill treated; and one of the company being conscious of his offense, sends a note to him in the morning, and tells him, he was ready to give him satisfaction. This is fine doing (says the plain fellow): last night he sent me away cursedly out of humor, and this morning he fancies it would be a satisfaction to be run through the body.

As the matter at present stands, it is not to do handsome actions denominates a man of honor; it is enough if he dares to defend ill ones. Thus you often see a common sharper[3] in competition with a gentleman of the first rank; though all mankind is convinced, that a fighting gamester is only a pickpocket with the courage of an highwayman. One cannot with any patience reflect on the unaccountable jumble of persons and things in this town and nation, which occasions very frequently, that a brave man falls by a hand below that of the common hangman, and yet his executioner escapes the clutches of the hangman for doing it. I shall therefore hereafter consider, how the bravest men in other ages and nations have behaved themselves upon such incidents as we decide by combat; and show, from their practice, that this resentment neither has its foundation from true reason, or solid fame; but is an imposture, made up of cowardice, falsehood, and want of understanding. For this work, a good history of quarrels would be very edifying to the public, and I apply myself to the town for particulars and circumstances within their knowledge, which may serve to embellish the dissertation with proper cuts. Most of the quarrels I have ever known, have proceeded from some valiant coxcomb's persisting in the wrong, to defend some prevailing folly, and preserve himself from the ingenuity of owning a mistake.

By this means it is called, "giving a man satisfaction," to urge your offense against him with your sword; which puts me in mind of Peter's order to the keeper, in *The Tale of a Tub*: "If you neglect to do all this, damn you and your generation forever; and so we bid you heartily farewell."[4] If the contradiction in the very terms of one of our challenges were as well explained, and turned into downright English, would it not run after this manner?

---

1. Social conduct, particularly that having to do with courtship and self-display.
2. From White's.
3. Trickster.
4. Steele paraphrases this fervent curse from Jonathan Swift's intricate satire *A Tale of a Tub* (1704), section 4.

Sir,

Your extraordinary behavior last night, and the liberty you were pleased to take with me, makes me this morning give you this, to tell you, because you are an ill-bred puppy, I will meet you in Hyde Park an hour hence; and because you want both breeding and humanity, I desire you would come with a pistol in your hand, on horseback, and endeavor to shoot me through the head, to teach you more manners. If you fail of doing me this pleasure, I shall say, you are a rascal on every post in town: and so, Sir, if you will not injure me more, I shall never forgive what you have done already. Pray Sir, do not fail of getting everything ready, and you will infinitely oblige,

Sir,

Your most obedient
humble servant, &c.

Daniel Defoe: *from* A Review of the State of the British Nation, Vol. 9, No. 34
Saturday, 29 November 1712

[A DUELLIST'S CONSCIENCE]

I have in one *Review* lately taken the liberty to mention that so exploded, rejected thing called peace among ourselves. I confess I see no room to expect good usage among you when I touch so ungrateful a subject, but I look for all sides to fall upon me as upon one prompting them to what they are resolved against.

I look upon the present feuds and outrageous party quarrelling which we are all embarked in to be the worst war we could ever engage in; and I think it was never so lively represented as by the late wretched unhappy duel between the Lord M[ohu]n and Duke H[amilto]n, wherein, both enraged, both desperately bent to ruin and destroy one another, both draw their swords in an unjust, needless, and dishonorable quarrel, and both die in the engagement.[1] I call the quarrel unjust and dishonorable not as to the cause of quarrel, which I have nothing to do with, but as to the manner of duelling, which I undertake to be unjust and dishonorable, because illegal and unchristian. * * *

I cannot but observe * * * what some public papers pretend about His Grace Duke H[amilto]n, viz., that he spent all the night before the action in his closet, retired pensive; and, says another author, in his devotion. I have nothing to say to the fact in this, for I do not believe it to be true. But for the sake of the surviving part of mankind, let us speak to this ridiculous newsmonger a little. Pray, sir, what devotion could you rationally suppose the Duke to be passing the time in? I cannot but think His Grace was a better Christian, at least I am sure he knew better, than to be praying to God for success upon what he was going about. Let all the men in England but tell me, what could the Duke say? Could anything of a Christian bring him in saying thus, with his eyes up to heaven: "Lord, thou knowest I will affront thy justice tomorrow by taking my cause into my own hand, and executing that vengeance which thou hast forbid me, and reserved to thyself. Lord, give me thy blessing to this wicked and willful action, and grant me success that I may kill my enemy, and

---

1. The duel, between James Douglas, Duke of Hamilton (1658–1712), and Charles Mohun (1675?–1712), had taken place two weeks earlier, on November 15.

become a murderer of my neighbor, etc." If he could not say this, let anyone tell me what he could pray. Can they think he would say thus? "Lord, I am going to commit a most grievous wickedness, and I am resolved to do it in spite of its being abhorred and forbidden by thee. But I WILL do it; however, I desire thou wilt pardon the sin and assist me to increase it by my murdering my adversary." This must be the devotion, the wretched devotion of such a retreat, and for that reason I will not so far affront the memory of Duke H[amilto]n to say he employed that time in devotion. If I might guess at the perturbation of thoughts which took up those few, or such unhappy hours; I say, if I may guess at them *by my own unhappy experience*, and may appeal to others who know what it is, I am of the opinion such times are taken up in the rolling of the passions, the boiling of the blood, the furious agitation of the animal spirits moved by the violence of the provocation. If conscience presumes to give a pinch in the dark, or put in a word, the inflamed organ answers: "Come what will, I cannot go back, I cannot live; I had better be run a thousand times through the body, I can die but once; but to bear this, is to be stabbed every day, to be insulted at the corner of every street, be posted, caned, and the Devil; I cannot bear it, I cannot help it." If the mind retreats a little and looks in through a very, very little bit, it occurs thus: "You are mad, you give up your reason, you are a murderer if you fall not in the action, you are a lost man forever. You know it is not a lawful action." All this is stopped thus: "What! Can I bear to be called COWARD! Had I not better be out of the world! I cannot go off, I must do it, all is at stake, I must, I cannot go from it, die or be damned, or anything is all one, I must do it." And so in the morning away he goes to be undone; goes to lay in a store for repentance; goes to take away his neighbor's life, and lay at stake his own, and sometimes, as in this case, to lose both.

Those people who would send the late Duke to his closet to prayers to prepare for his next day's work, I believe know little what fighting a duel is, or what temper the mind is in when such an appointment is upon their hands; I rather believe His Grace was fighting with my Lord M[ohu]n all night; many a silent pass was made that night in imagination, I doubt not; not that I believe the Duke was weak enough to act by himself the postures or motions of fighting; but I believe it was impossible to suppose that a mind possessed with such views and such resolutions as he then had could refrain from fixing the ideas of the action itself in its thoughts.

But to talk of devotion, let that jest be laid by. I can take upon me to say, God hears no such prayers, nor can any man who is in his right senses have the face to look up to his Maker in such a case as that was.

The Athenian Mercury (1691–1697)

In *The Athenian Mercury* (initially titled the *Athenian Gazette*, until the *London Gazette* clamped down), the eccentric and ingenious entrepreneur John Dunton (1659–1732) performed a bold and experiment in interactive media. "All persons whatever," announced the paper's first number, "may be resolved *gratis* in any question that their own satisfaction or curiosity shall prompt them to, if they send [in] their questions by a penny-post letter." Inquiring readers, Dunton promised, would soon see their questions in print, accompanied by knowledgable and thoughtful answers from a society of "Athenians"—actually a quartet of learned but not particularly eminent men (including the editor himself), whose identities Dunton both cloaked and burnished by that elegant cover name, which connoted both ancient wisdom and university education. The paper succeeded so well that he promptly expanded his operation, adding more "members" to the Athenian Society (including Daniel Defoe) and pages to the publication in order to absorb the multitude of questions that kept pouring in. The paper prided itself on its range of topics, but announced in its eighteenth number a particular area of specialization: "Whereas the questions we receive from the *fair sex* are both *pressing* and *numerous*, we being willing to oblige 'em, as knowing they have a very *strong party* in the world, resolve to set apart the first Tuesday in every month on purpose to satisfy questions of that nature"; the recurrent special issue proved so popular that it was soon appearing biweekly, then weekly. Its pages included questions from both men and women on those subjects construed as particularly "feminine" (love, courtship, marriage); the letters often took the form of short but expressive autobiographies—a mode Steele, Addison, and numberless others imitated and developed during the following decades. Dunton claimed to have conceived his "question project" (as he affectionately termed it) in the course of an afternoon's walk. Its influence has lasted centuries, and is still plain to see in columns of advice and information. Dunton taught the periodical press an irresistibly simple and enduringly successful way of mirroring its readers, making them part of (and hence committed to) the papers they read.

from The Athenian Mercury[1]

QUEST. Whether it is lawful for a man to beat his wife?

ANSW. The affirmative would be very disobliging to that sex, without adding any more to it. Therefore we ought to be as cautious and tender as may be in asserting such an ill-natured position. We allow a wife to be[2] naturalized into, and part of her husband, and yet nature sometimes wars against part of itself, in ejecting by sweat, urine, etc. what otherwise would be destructive to its very frame; nay, sometimes there is occasion of greater violence, as lancing,[3] burning, dismembering, etc., which the patient submits to as his interest. Now if a man may thus cruelly treat himself, and be an accessory to his own torture, he may legally chastise his wife, who is no nearer to him than he is to himself, but yet (for I am not covetous of the fate of Orpheus[4]) as none but doctors are proper judges of seasonable violences to nature, so there are but few husbands that know how to correct a wife. To do it in a passion, and pretend justice, is ridiculous, because that passion incapacitates the judgment from its office; and to do it when one is pleased is a harder task; so that we conclude, as the legality is unquestionable, so the time and measure are generally too critical[5] for a calculation. When a wife goes astray, it is safe to use a sympathetic remedy, as the rebuke of a kiss; the antipathetic[6] may prove worse than the disease.

QUEST. Whether since it is your opinion that if a man be a discreet and prudent man, he may correct the misbehavior of his wife by beating, *vice versa*, a wife being so qualified, and having a sot to her husband, whether she may not (if able) beat her husband?

ANSW. The power was at first vested in man specifically,[7] without provisions, distinctions, or limitations of sot, foolish, weak, etc. Therefore these altering not his species by consequence, cannot annul his prerogative.

---

1. The following questions and answers are taken from Volume 1, nos. 1 and 2 (1691); Volume 2, no. 15 (1691); and Volume 14, no. 23 (1694).
2. Agree that a wife is.
3. Pricking, for medical purposes.
4. The musician of Greek myth, torn apart by raging

women, votaries of Bacchus.
5. Complicated.
6. Remedy.
7. Refers to God's "curse" upon Eve for eating the forbidden fruit: "Thy desire shall be to thy husband, and he shall rule over thee" (Genesis 3.12).

QUEST. Whether it be lawful for a young lady to pray for a husband, and if lawful, in what form?

ANSW. He must renounce humanity, and confess himself a sort of an aggressor upon the privileges of nature, that would not make it as immortal as possible, which is only honorably effected by marriage, whereby we survive in our children. Misery without a friend to bear a part is very afflicting, and happiness without communication is tedious, and (as Seneca[8] has observed) sometimes inclines us to make a voluntary choice of misery for novelty. We should be vagrant sort of animals without marriage, as if nature were ashamed of our converse. We should contribute to the destruction of states, condemn the wisdom of the first Institutor and censure the edicts of such commonwealths who have upon very good grounds discountenanced and punished celibacy. Nay, supposing all the miseries that marriage-haters suggest should fall upon us, it is our own fault, if with Socrates we don't learn more by a scolding wife than by all the precepts of philosophers.[9]

Now if it be lawful to marry, it is lawful for ladies to pray for good husbands, if they find their inclination, concerns in the world, or other motives (which they are to be judges of) consistent with the ends of such society. As to the form of prayer required, they may, if they please, use the following, if they are not better furnished already:

From a profane libertine, from one affectedly pious, from a profuse almoner,[1] from an uncharitable wretch, from a wavering religioso,[2] and an injudicious zealot—deliver me!

From one of a starched gravity, or of ridiculous levity, from an ambitious statesman, from a restless projector,[3] from one that loves anything besides me, but what is very just and honorable—deliver me!

From an ecstasied poet, from a modern wit, from a base coward and a rash fool, from a pad[4] and a pauper—deliver me!

From a Venus's darling, from a Bacchus's proselyte,[5] from a traveling half,[6] from a domestic animal, from all masculine plagues not yet recounted—deliver me!

Give me one whose love has more of judgment than passion, who is master of himself, or at least an indefatigable scholar in such a study, who has an equal flame, that as two tallies[7] we may appear more perfect by union.

Give me one of as genteel an education as a little expense of time will permit, with an indifferent fortune, rather independent of the servile fate of palaces, and yet one whose retirement is not so much from the public as into himself. One (if possible) above all flattery and affronts, and yet as careful in preventing the injury as able to repair it. One, the beauty of whose mind exceeds that of his face, yet not deformed so as to be distinguishable from others even unto a ridicule.

---

8. Stoic philosopher and tragic playwright.
9. A misogynist tradition held that the philosopher Socrates's wife Xanthippe berated him constantly, and thereby taught him skill in argument.
1. Charity-giver.
2. One who changes his faith.
3. Scientist; deviser of grand plans and schemes.
4. Thief.

5. From a rake, from a drunk.
6. Perhaps suggesting a passive, mute companion.
7. A "tally" was originally a tool used to record a debt or payment. A wooden rod, notched several times crosswise (to indicate the amount of money transferred) was then cut lengthwise. Creditor and debtor each retained one of the halves, whose "match" with each other constituted legal proof of the transaction.

Give me one that has learnt to live much in a little time, one that is no great familiar in converse with the world, nor no little one with himself. One (if two such happinesses may be granted at one time to our sex) who with these uncommon endowments of mind may (naturally) have a sweet, mild, easy disposition, or at least one who by his practice and frequent habit has made himself so before he is made mine. But as the master-perfection and chiefest draught,[8] let him be truly virtuous and pious; that is to say, let me be truly happy in my choice. * * *

QUEST. It was my fortune about four years since to be for some time in a family,[9] and a son of the family addressed himself to me. I told him his parents would not like it, my fortune being much inferior to his, and that I feared he would incur his father's displeasure, if he knew he loved me. He said he loved no woman upon the earth but me, and assured me it was for my sake he rejected a very advantageous match that was offered him at that time. All his actions persuaded me his intentions were real. I found myself inclinable to love him. He urged me to make him a promise, that then he would be contented to live so until it should please God to take his good father, who, if he could possibly, he would not disoblige. Now I do love him not for his estate, I take God to witness; for if he had not six pence in the world I could love him as I do, which is far beyond what I am able to say. There was a mutual vow made between us; we called God to witness. He added that if ever he falsified the least tittle of what he had promised, that God's just curse might light on him. Gentlemen, he is twelve years older than I. He is a scholar, and very well qualified. And to show you it was not done rashly, since we were parted (which was as soon as they had any suspicion of our love), he has repeated the same promises in several letters to me. Some time before I went from him, I was told he was married to a gentlewoman that he had a child by. I told him of it; he protested it was false, and that the child was not his, nor did he ever converse with the person since; it was at least twelve years ago that the child was born. He invited me lately to see his house, where I observed some of the goods marked with the gentlewoman's name. It made me very uneasy. He quickly found the reason, and assured me there was nothing at all in it; but I since found a letter that came with those goods from that very person. At the reading it I thought I should have died, and I have scarce been myself ever since. She tells him she loves him before her life, and subscribes herself thus, "No more at present from your truest of lovers," and the two first letters of her own name to it. I showed him the letter, and then he said it was things he took for a debt of a relation of hers. Gentlemen, pray, as soon as you can possible, advise me in this thing, for there's not one creature upon the earth that knows it; nor can I confide in any person to ask their advice.

ANSW. We'd not willingly either injure an innocent gentleman, nor mislead you who desire our advice. But if the letter you found was worded as you relate it, his excuse is too weak to clear him. For the writer of it must at least be more than an ordinary friend or acquaintance; and he a very ill man to endeavor to deceive you both, which we should think would go a good way towards taking off your love from him, and settling it on a more worthy object, that neither will nor can deceive or abuse you.

---

8. I.e., feature of the portrait.

9. As a servant ("family" meant "household").

Richard Steele: *from* Tatler No. 104
Thursday, 8 December 1709

[JENNY DISTAFF NEWLY MARRIED[1]]

—*Garrit aniles*
Ex re Fabellas.—[2]

From My Own Apartment, December 7

My brother[3] Tranquillus being gone out of town for some days, my sister Jenny sent me word she would come and dine with me, and therefore desired me to have no other company. I took care accordingly, and was not a little pleased to see her enter the room with a decent and matronlike behavior, which I thought very much became her. I saw she had a great deal to say to me, and easily discovered in her eyes, and the air of her countenance, that she had abundance of satisfaction in her heart, which she longed to communicate. However, I was resolved to let her break into her discourse her own way, and reduced her to a thousand little devices and intimations to bring me to the mention of her husband. But finding I was resolved not to name him, she began of her own accord; my husband (said she) gives his humble service to you: to which I only answered, I hope he is well; and without waiting for a reply, fell into other subjects. She at last was out of all patience, and said (with a smile and manner that I thought had more beauty and spirit than I had ever observed before in her) I did not think, Brother, you had been so ill-natured. You have seen ever since I came in, that I had a mind to talk of my husband, and you won't be so kind as to give me an occasion. I did not know (said I) but it might be a disagreeable subject to you. You do not take me for so old-fashioned a fellow as to think of entertaining a young lady with the discourse of her husband. I know, nothing is more acceptable than to speak of one who is to be so; but to speak of one who is so! Indeed, Jenny, I am a better bred man than you think me. She showed a little dislike at my raillery; and by her bridling up, I perceived she expected to be treated hereafter not as Jenny Distaff, but Mrs. Tranquillus. I was very well pleased with this change in her humor; and upon talking with her on several subjects, I could not but fancy that I saw a great deal of her husband's way and manner in her remarks, her phrases, the tone of her voice, and the very air of her countenance. This gave me an unspeakable satisfaction, not only because I had found her an husband, from whom she could learn many things that were laudable, but also because I looked upon her imitation of him as an infallible sign that she entirely loved him. This is an observation that I never knew fail, though I do not remember that any other has made it. The natural shyness of her sex hindered her from telling me the greatness of her own passion; but I easily collected it, from the representation she gave me of his. I have everything, says she, in Tranquillus that I can wish for; and enjoy in him (what indeed you have told me were to be met with in a good husband) the fondness of a lover, the tenderness of a parent, and the intimacy of a friend. It transported me to see her eyes swimming in tears of affection when she spoke. And is there not, Dear Sister, said I, more pleasure in the pos-

1. Jenny Distaff is Isaac Bickerstaff's half-sister. In some earlier *Tatlers* (Nos. 10 and 33), she appeared as an essayist in her own right, composing pieces for the paper whenever her brother was out of town. In more recent numbers (75, 79), Bickerstaff had told the story of arranging her marriage to "Tranquillus" ("the calm one"), which he described as "a domestic affair of great importance, . . . no less than the disposal of my sister Jenny for life."

2. "He tells an old wives' tale very pertinently" (Horace, *Satires* 2.6.77–78).

3. Brother-in-law.

session of such a man, than in all the little impertinencies[4] of balls, assemblies, and equipage, which it cost me so much pains to make you condemn? She answered, smiling, Tranquillus has made me a sincere convert in a few weeks, though I am afraid you could not have done it in your whole life. To tell you truly, I have only one fear hanging upon me, which is apt to give me trouble in the midst of all my satisfactions: I am afraid, you must know, that I shall not always make the same amiable appearance in his eye that I do at present. You know, Brother Bickerstaff, that you have the reputation of a conjurer; and if you have any one secret in your art to make your sister always beautiful, I should be happier than if I were mistress of all the worlds you have shown me in a starry night. Jenny (said I) without having recourse to magic, I shall give you one plain rule, that will not fail of making you always amiable to a man who has so great a passion for you, and is of so equal and reasonable a temper as Tranquillus. Endeavor to please, and you must please; be always in the same disposition as you are when you ask for this secret, and, you may take my word, you will never want it. An inviolable fidelity, good humor, and complacency of temper, outlive all the charms of a fine face, and make the decays of it invisible.

We discoursed very long upon this head, which was equally agreeable to us both; for I must confess, (as I tenderly love her) I take as much pleasure in giving her instructions for her welfare, as she herself does in receiving them. * * *

Joseph Addison: Spectator No. 128
Friday, 27 July 1711

[VARIETY OF TEMPER[1]]

. . . *Concordia discors.*[2]

Women in their nature are much more gay and joyous than men; whether it be that their blood is more refined, their fibers more delicate, and their animal spirits more light and volatile; or whether, as some have imagined, there may not be a kind of sex in the very soul,[3] I shall not pretend to determine. As vivacity is the gift of women, gravity is that of men. They should each of them therefore keep a watch upon the particular bias which nature has fixed in their minds, that it may not draw too much, and lead them out of the paths of reason. This will certainly happen, if the one in every word and action affects the character of being rigid and severe, and the other of being brisk and airy. Men should beware of being captivated by a kind of savage philosophy, women by a thoughtless gallantry. Where these precautions are not observed, the man often degenerates into a cynic, the woman into a coquette; the man grows sullen and morose, the woman impertinent and fantastical.[4]

By what I have said we may conclude, men and women were made as counterparts to one another, that the pains and anxieties of the husband might be relieved by the sprightliness and good humor of the wife. When these are rightly tempered, care and cheerfulness go hand in hand; and the family, like a ship that is duly trimmed, wants neither sail nor ballast.

---

4. Irrelevancies, distractions.
1. Lady Mary Wortley Montagu praised this essay in a letter written to her husband shortly after it appeared: "One of the *Spectators* is very just, that says a man ought always to be on his guard against spleen and too severe a philosophy; a woman against levity and coquetry."

2. "Discordant concord" (i.e., harmony arising from difference; Lucan, *Pharsalia* 1.98).
3. In *Tatler* No. 172, Steele had asserted that "there is a sort of sex in souls" (i.e., an essential difference between men and women).
4. Irrelevant in her talk, preposterous in her thought.

Natural historians observe (for whilst I am in the country I must fetch my allusions from thence[5]) that only the male birds have voices; that their songs begin a little before feeding-time, and end a little after; that whilst the hen is covering her eggs, the male generally takes his stand upon a neighboring bough within her hearing; and by that means amuses and diverts her with his songs during the whole time of her sitting.

This contract among birds lasts no longer than till a brood of young ones arises from it; so that in the feathered kind, the cares and fatigues of the married state, if I may so call it, lie principally upon the female. On the contrary, as in our species the man and woman are joined together for life, and the main burden rests upon the former, nature has given all the little arts of soothing and blandishment to the female, that she may cheer and animate her companion in a constant and assiduous application to the making a provision for his family, and the educating of their common children. This however is not to be taken so strictly, as if the same duties were not often reciprocal, and incumbent on both parties; but only to set forth what seems to have been the general intention of Nature, in the different inclinations and endowments which are bestowed on the different sexes.

But whatever was the reason that man and woman were made with this variety of temper, if we observe the conduct of the fair sex, we find that they choose rather to associate themselves with a person who resembles them in that light and volatile humor which is natural to them, than to such as are qualified to moderate and counterbalance it. It has been an old complaint, that the coxcomb carries it[6] with them before the man of sense. When we see a fellow loud and talkative, full of insipid life and laughter, we may venture to pronounce him a female favorite. Noise and flutter are such accomplishments as they cannot withstand. To be short, the passion of an ordinary woman for a man, is nothing else but self-love diverted upon another object: she would have the lover a woman in every thing but the sex. I do not know a finer piece of satire on this part of womankind than those lines of Mr. Dryden,

> Our thoughtless sex is caught by outward form
> And empty noise, and loves itself in man.[7]

This is a source of infinite calamities to the sex, as it frequently joins them to men who in their own thoughts are as fine creatures as themselves; or if they chance to be good-humored, serve only to dissipate their fortunes, inflame their follies, and aggravate their indiscretions.

The same female levity is no less fatal to them after marriage than before. It represents to their imaginations the faithful prudent husband as an honest tractable and domestic animal, and turns their thoughts upon the fine gay gentleman that laughs, sings, and dresses so much more agreeably.

As this irregular vivacity of temper leads astray the hearts of ordinary women in the choice of their lovers and the treatment of their husbands, it operates with the same pernicious influence towards their children, who are taught to accomplish themselves in all those sublime perfections that appear captivating in the eye of their mother. She admires in her son what she loved in her gallant; and by that means contributes all she can to perpetuate herself in a worthless progeny.

The younger Faustina[8] was a lively instance of this sort of women. Notwithstanding she was married to Marcus Aurelius, one of the greatest, wisest, and best of

---

5. Mr. Spectator is visiting the country estate of his friend and club fellow, Sir Roger de Coverley.
6. Succeeds.
7. From John Dryden's tragedy *Oedipus* (1.1).

8. Annia Galeria Faustina (d. A.D. 175), wife of Marcus Aurelius (A.D. 121–180), cherished by her husband but dispraised by ancient writers as an unfaithful wife.

the Roman emperors, she thought a common gladiator much the prettier gentleman; and had taken such care to accomplish[9] her son Commodus according to her own notions of a fine man, that when he ascended the throne of his father, he became the most foolish and abandoned tyrant that was ever placed at the head of the Roman Empire, signalizing himself in nothing but the fighting of prizes, and knocking out men's brains. As he had no taste of true glory, we see him in several medals and statues which are still extant of him, equipped like an Hercules with a club and a lion's skin.

I have been led into this speculation by the characters I have heard of a country gentleman and his lady, who do not live many miles from Sir Roger. The wife is an old coquette, that is always hankering after the diversions of the town; the husband is a morose rustic, that frowns and frets at the name of it; the wife is overrun with affectation, the husband sunk into brutality. The lady cannot bear the noise of the larks and nightingales, hates your tedious summer days, and is sick at the sight of shady woods and purling streams; the husband wonders how any one can be pleased with the fooleries of plays and operas, and rails from morning to night at essenced[1] fops and tawdry courtiers. The children are educated in these different notions of their parents. The sons follow the father about his grounds, while the daughters read volumes of love letters and romances to their mother. By this means it comes to pass, that the girls look upon their father as a clown, and the boys think their mother no better than she should be.

How different are the lives of Aristus and Aspatia? The innocent vivacity of the one is tempered and composed by the cheerful gravity of the other. The wife grows wise by the discourses of the husband, and the husband good-humored by the conversations of the wife. Aristus would not be so amiable were it not for his Aspatia, nor Aspatia so much to be esteemed were it not for her Aristus. Their virtues are blended in their children, and diffuse through the whole family a perpetual spirit of benevolence, complacency, and satisfaction.

Eliza Haywood: *from* The Female Spectator, Vol. 1, No. 1
April 1744

[SEOMANTHE'S ELOPEMENT[1]]

Seomanthe, to her misfortune, was brought up under the tuition of her aunt Negratia,[2] a woman extremely sour by nature, but rendered yet more so by age and infirmity. Past all the joys of life herself, she looked with a malicious eye on every one who partook of them, censured the most innocent diversions in the severest manner, and the least complaisance between persons of different sexes was, with her, scandalous to the last degree. Her character was so well known that none but prudes, whose deformity was an antidote to desire (worn-out, superannuated rakes, who had outlived all sense of pleasure) and canting zealots,[3] whose bread depended on their hypocrisy, frequented her house. To this sort of company was the young, beautiful, and naturally gay Seomanthe condemned. She heard nothing but railing against that way of life she knew was enjoyed by others of equal rank and fortune with herself,

9. Educate.
1. Perfumed.
1. Haywood tells this story to illustrate her point that it is sometimes wrong to blame young women for marrying unwisely; parents and other authorities "are sometimes,

by an over-caution, guilty of forcing them into things, which otherwise would be far distant from their thoughts."
2. The name means "unpleasing."
3. People pretending to fanatic piety.

and which she had too much good sense to look upon as criminal. She thought people might be perfectly innocent, yet indulge themselves in sometimes going to a play
or opera; nor could be brought to believe the court such a bugbear[4] as she was told it
was: a laced coat and a toupee wig had double charms for her, as they were every day
so much preached against; and she never saw a coach pass, wherein were gentlemen
and ladies, but she wished to be among them, or a well-dressed beau, with whom she
did not languish to be acquainted.

At length her desires were fulfilled. Close as she was kept, the report that Negratia had a young lady in her house, who was mistress of a large fortune on the day of
marriage, reached the ears of one of those harpies who purchase to themselves a
wretched sustenance, by decoying the unwary into everlasting ruin. This creature,
who had been employed by one so far a gentleman as to be bred to no business, and
whose whole estate was laid out on his back,[5] in hopes of appearing charming in the
eyes of some moneyed woman, too truly guessed she had found in Seomanthe what
she sought. She came to the house under the pretense of offering some lace, holland,[6]
and fine tea, extraordinary cheap. Negratia being what is called a good housewife,
and a great lover of bargains, readily admitted her; and while she was examining
some of the goods at a small distance off, the artful woman put a letter into Seomanthe's hand, telling her it came from the finest gentleman in the world, who she was
sure would die, if she did not favor him with an answer. The young lady took it,
blushed, and put it in her bosom, but had not time to make any reply to the woman,
Negratia that instant coming towards them. As nobody understood her business better, she managed it so that she was ordered to come again the next day, when she said
she should have greater variety to show their ladyships. While she was packing up
her bundles, she winked on Seomanthe, and at the same time gave her the most
beseeching look; the meaning of which, young and unexperienced as she was, the
destined victim but too well comprehended, and was, perhaps, no less impatient for
the success of an adventure, the beginning of which afforded her infinite satisfaction.

She ran immediately to her chamber, shut herself in, and broke open her billet,[7]
which she found stuffed with flames, darts, wounds, love, and death; the highest
encomiums on her beauty, and the most vehement imprecations of not outliving his
hope of obtaining her favor—expressions which would have excited only the laughter of a woman who knew the world, but drew tears into the eyes of the innocent
Seomanthe. She imagined he had seen her either at church or looking out of the
window, for she was permitted to show herself in no other place; and doubted not but
all he had wrote to her of his love and despair, was no less true than what she had
heard delivered from the pulpit. She looked upon herself as too much obliged by the
passion he had for her, not to write an answer full of complaisance, and very dexter-
ously gave it to the woman, on her coming the next day.

On the ensuing Sunday she saw a strange gentleman in the next pew to her; by
the glances he stole at her every time he could do it without being taken notice of,
she fancied him the person who had declared himself her lover, and was convinced
her conjecture had not deceived her, when being kneeled down at her devotions, he
found means, while everyone had their fans before their faces, to drop a letter on the

---

4. Danger (with the illusory connotation of "boogey-
man").
5. Spent on clothing.

6. Imported fabric.
7. Letter.

bench she leaned upon. She was not so much taken up with the business she was employed about, as not to see it immediately, and throwing her handkerchief over it, clapped it into her pocket. The looks that passed between them afterwards, during the time of divine service, confirmed her in the opinion that he was no less charmed with her than he said he was; and him, that the sight of him had not destroyed the impression his letter by the old woman had made on her.

Both thought they had reason to be highly satisfied with this interview; but poor Seomanthe was up to the head and ears in love. The person of the man was agreeable enough, and, compared to those Negratia had suffered her to converse with, angelic. The prepossession she had for him, at least, rendered him so in her eyes, and she thought every moment an age till she got home to read this second billet, the contents of which were of the same nature with the former, only a postscript added, entreating she would contrive some means to let him entertain her with his passion, by word of mouth. He mentioned the woman who sold the things, and by whose means he at first made a discovery of it,[8] and gave the directions where she lived; begged a meeting there, if possible; at least an answer, whether he might be so happy or not; which, he told her, he would wait for himself early the next morning under her window, if she would be so good as to throw it out.

She sighed at reading it; thought her fate very hard that it was not in her power to comply with the first part of his request, but hesitated not in the least if she ought to grant the other. She snatched the first opportunity she could lay hold on to prepare a letter, in which she let him know how impossible it was for her to come out; but expressed such a regret at not being able to do so, as showed it would be no difficult matter to prevail on her to run the greatest lengths.

By the help of his adviser, he carried on a correspondence with her, which ended in her consenting to quit Negratia forever, and put herself under his protection. In fine, she packed up all her clothes and jewels, threw the former from the window to the woman, who stood ready to receive them on an appointed night; and having put the other into her pocket, exchanged one scene of hypocrisy for another, and flew from a life irksome for the present, to enter into one of lasting misery.

Early in the morning they were married, and it is possible passed some days in the usual transports of a bridal state. But when their place of abode was discovered by the friends and kindred of Seomanthe, who, distracted at her elopement, had searched the whole town, in how wretched a manner was she found! The villain had drawn her whole fortune out of the bank, robbed her of all her jewels and the best of her apparel, had shipped everything off, and was himself embarked she knew not to what place. The people of the house where they lodged, perceiving him, whom they expected to have been their paymaster, gone, seized on the few trifles he had left behind, as satisfaction for the rent, and were going to turn the unfortunate Seomanthe out of doors.

Not the sight of her distress, nor the lamentations she made, which were pitiful enough to have softened the most rugged hearts, had any effect on that of Negratia, who thought no punishment too severe for a person who had deceived her caution. But some others were of a more compassionate disposition. They took her home with them, and comforted her as well as they were able. She still lives with them a dependent on their courtesy, which she is obliged to purchase

---

8. I.e., had revealed his passion.

Reading Papers

the continuance of, by rendering herself subservient to all their humors.[9] No news is yet arrived what course her wicked husband took; but it is supposed he is retired either to France or Holland, being almost as much in debt here, as all he wronged Seomanthe of would discharge; so that there is little probability of his ever returning, or if he did, that it would be at all to the satisfaction of his unhappy wife.

I was going on to recite some other instances of the mischiefs, which, for the most part, are the consequence of laying young people under too great a restraint, when Mira[1] came in, and seeing what I was about, took the pen out of my hand, and told me I had already said enough; if I proceeded to expatiate any farther on that head, I should be in danger of being understood to countenance an extreme on the other side,[2] which was much more frequently fatal to our sex.

I yielded to her superior judgment, and needed but few arguments to be convinced, that if unbridled youth were indulged in all the liberties it would take, we should scarce see anything but unhappy objects before maturity arrived.

Eliza Haywood: *from The Female Specatator,* Vol. 2, No. 10

February 1745

[WOMEN'S EDUCATION]

We[1] were beginning to lament the misfortunes our sex frequently fall into through the want of those improvements we are doubtless capable of, when a letter, left for us at our publisher's, was brought in which happened to be on that subject, and cannot anywhere be more properly inserted than in this place.

To the Female Spectator

Ladies,

Permit me to thank you for the kind and generous task you have undertaken in endeavoring to improve the minds and manners of our unthinking sex. It is the noblest act of charity you could exercise in an age like ours, where the sense of good and evil is almost extinguished, and people desire to appear more vicious than they really are, that so they may be less unfashionable. This humor, which is too prevalent in the female sex, is the true occasion of the many evils and dangers to which they are daily exposed. No wonder the men of sense disregard us! and the dissolute triumph over that virtue they ought to protect!

Yet I think it would be cruel to charge the ladies with all the errors they commit; it is most commonly the fault of a wrong education, which makes them frequently do amiss, while they think they act not only innocently but uprightly. It is therefore only the men—and the men of understanding, too—who, in effect, merit the blame of this, and are answerable for all the misconduct we are guilty of. Why do they call us silly women, and not endeavor to make us otherwise? God and Nature has endued them with means, and custom has established them in the power of rendering our minds such as they ought to be. How highly ungenerous is it then to give us a wrong turn, and then despise us for it!

---

9. Whims, moods.
1. One of the Female Spectator's collaborators.

2. I.e., in favor of leniency.
1. The Female Spectator and her collaborators.

The Mahometans indeed enslave their women, but then they teach them to believe their inferiority will extend to eternity. But our case is even worse than this; for while we live in a free country, and are assured from our excellent Christian principles that we are capable of those refined pleasures which last to immortality, our minds, our better parts, are wholly left uncultivated, and, like a rich soil neglected, bring forth nothing but noxious weeds.

There are, undoubtedly, no sexes in souls; and we are as able to receive and practice the impressions, not only of virtue and religion, but also of those sciences which the men engross to themselves, as they can be. Surely our bodies were not formed by the great Creator out of the finest mold, that our souls might be neglected like the coarsest of the clay?

O! would too imperious and too tenacious man be so just to the world as to be more careful of the education of those females to whom they are parents or guardians! Would they convince them in their infancy, that dress and show are not the essentials of a fine lady, and that true beauty is seated in the mind; how soon should we see our sex retrieve the many virtues which false taste has buried in oblivion! Strange infatuation! to refuse us what would so much contribute to their own felicity! Would not themselves reap the benefit of our amendment? Should we not be more obedient daughters, more faithful wives, more tender mothers, more sincere friends, and more valuable in every other station of life?

But, I find, I have let my pen run a much greater length than I at first intended. If I have said anything worthy your notice, or what you think the truth of the case, I hope you will mention this subject in some of your future essays; or if you find I have any way erred in my judgment, to set me right will be the greatest favor you can confer on,

Ladies,

Your constant reader,

And humble servant,

CLEORA

Hampton Court,
January 12, 1744–45

After thanking this lady for the favor of her obliging letter, we think it our duty to congratulate her on being one of those happy few who have been blessed with that sort of education which she so pathetically laments the want of in the greatest part of our sex.

Those men are certainly guilty of a great deal of injustice who think that all the learning becoming in a woman is confined to the management of her family; that is, to give orders concerning the table, take care of her children in their infancy, and observe that her servants do not neglect their business. All this, no doubt, is very necessary; but would it not be better if she performs those duties more through principle than custom? And will she be less punctual in her observance of them after she becomes a wife, for being perfectly convinced, before she is so, of the reasonableness of them, and why they are expected from her?

Many women have not been inspired with the least notion of even those requisites in a wife, and when they become so, continue the same loitering, lolloping, idle creatures they were before; and then the men are ready enough to condemn those who had the care of their education. * * *

[END OF PERSPECTIVES: READING PAPERS]

━━━━ ≈✧≈ ━━━━

Jonathan Swift

1667–1745

Arguably the greatest prose satirist in the history of English literature, Jonathan Swift was born in Dublin, the only son of English parents, seven months after his father died. In his infancy he was kidnapped by his nurse and did not see his mother for three years. With the future dramatist William Congreve he attended the Kilkenny School (Ireland's best), and in 1682 he began six years of study at Trinity College, Dublin. He received his B.A. degree in 1686. From 1689, Swift served as secretary to Sir William Temple (1628–1699), a retired diplomat whose father had befriended Swift's family. Swift worked at Temple's estate at Moor Park in Surrey for most of the next ten years. It was at Moor Park that Swift first experienced the vertigo, nausea, and hearing impairment of Ménière's syndrome, a disturbance of the inner ear that would plague him for the rest of his life and sometimes wrongly led him (and others) to question his mental stability. While working for Temple, Swift also wrote his first poems, undistinguished compositions that do not presage the literary acclaim that was to come.

Not content with his station in life, Swift took an M.A. degree from Oxford University in 1692; three years later, he was ordained a priest in the (Anglican) Church of Ireland and appointed to the undesirable prebendary of Kilroot, where he found the local Presbyterians unsympathetic and the salary meager. Added to professional discontent was personal disappointment: Swift was rejected in his marriage proposal to Jane "Varina" Waring, the daughter of an Anglican clergyman. Swift returned to Moor Park in 1696, and, after Temple died in 1699, held a series of ecclesiastical posts in Ireland, none of which fulfilled his ambition for an important position in England. In 1702 he was made Doctor of Divinity by his alma mater, Trinity College, Dublin.

While at Moor Park, Swift began to tutor an eight-year-old girl, Esther "Stella" Johnson, daughter of Sir William's late steward. Though she was nearly fourteen years Swift's junior, "Stella" would in time become his beloved companion and his most trusted friend. When she was eighteen, Swift described her as "one of the most beautiful, graceful, and agreeable young women in London." In 1701, at Swift's request, Stella and Sir William's spinster cousin, Rebecca Dingley, moved to Dublin, where they remained for the rest of their lives. Swift and Stella met regularly, but never alone. Although there has been much debate about the nature of their relationship, it is clear that Swift and Stella loved, trusted, and valued each other, whether or not they were ever secretly married (the evidence suggests they were not). Swift's *Journal to Stella* (composed 1710 to 1713) and the series of poems he composed for her birthdays reveal a playful intimacy and affection not seen in his more public writings.

Moor Park not only led him to Stella but was also the cradle of Swift's first major literary work: *A Tale of a Tub* (composed 1697 to 1698, published 1704), a brilliant satire on "corruptions in religion and learning," published with *The Battle of the Books,* Swift's mock-epic salvo in the debate between the Ancients and the Moderns. Like most of his subsequent works, *A Tale of a Tub* did not appear under Swift's name, though its ironic treatment of the church subsequently damaged his prospects for ecclesiastical preferment when his authorship became widely known.

In the first decade of the new century Swift placed his hopes for preferment with the Whigs, then in power, and became associated with the Whig writers Joseph Addison and Richard Steele, founder of the *Tatler,* a London periodical in which two of Swift's important early poems, *A Description of the Morning* (1709) and *A Description of a City Shower* (1710), first appeared. Swift's career as a political polemicist began when he rose to the defense of three Whig lords facing impeachment with his allegorical *Discourse of the Contests and Dissentions between the Nobles and Commons in Athens and Rome* (1701). His *Bickerstaff Papers*

(1708–1709), witty parodies of the cobbler-turned-astrologer John Partridge, occasioned much laughter regardless of party allegiances. More importantly, Swift began to write a series of pamphlets on church affairs, including his ironical *Argument against Abolishing Christianity* (1708) and *A Letter . . . Concerning the Sacramental Test* (1709), which damaged his relationship with the Whigs.

While in London as an emissary for the Irish clergy in 1708, Swift met Esther "Vanessa" Vanhomrigh (pronounced "Vanummry") and, as with "Stella," acted as her mentor. Although his feelings for this attractive young woman (twenty-one years younger than he) clearly became more than paternal, Swift was eventually put off by her declaration of "inexpressible passion" and wrote *Cadenus and Vanessa* (composed 1713, published 1726) to cool the relationship.

Vehemently disagreeing with the Whig policies supporting the Dissenters (Protestants who were not members of the established church), because he feared they would weaken the Anglican church, Swift shifted his allegiance to the Tories in 1710 and soon became their principal spokesman and propagandist, taking charge of their weekly periodical the *Examiner* (1710–1711) and producing a series of highly effective political pamphlets, such as *The Conduct of the Allies* (1712), which called for an end to the War of Spanish Succession (1701–1713). Swift's years in London from 1710 to 1714, when he was an important lobbyist for the Church of Ireland and an influential agent of the Tory government, were the most exciting of his life.

In 1713 Swift was installed as Dean of Saint Patrick's Cathedral, Dublin—a prestigious appointment, but far short of the English bishopric he felt he deserved. Returning quickly to London, Swift became a vital presence in the Scriblerus Club—with Alexander Pope, John Arbuthnot, John Gay, Thomas Parnell, and Robert Harley, Earl of Oxford—which met in 1714. The influence of this group, with its love of parody, literary hoaxes, and the ridicule of false learning, is evident in *Gulliver's Travels*. Upon the death of Queen Anne in 1714 and the resultant fall of the Tory Ministry, Swift's hopes for further advancement were dashed, and he took up permanent residence in Ireland, where he conscientiously carried out his duties as Dean.

When Swift successfully defended Irish interests by writing *The Drapier's Letters* (1724–1725)—attacking a government plan to impose a new coin, "Wood's halfpence," that would devalue Ireland's currency and seriously damage the economy—he became a national hero. Thereafter, the people lit bonfires on his birthday and hailed him as a champion of Irish liberty, though he never ceased to regard Ireland as the land of his exile. From Dublin, he corresponded with Pope, Gay, Arbuthnot, and Henry St. John, Lord Bolingbroke; he enjoyed a long visit with his friends in England in 1726. While there, he encouraged Gay's *The Beggar's Opera* and Pope's *The Dunciad,* and arranged for the publication of his own masterpiece, *Gulliver's Travels* (1726).

When the death of George I the following year briefly created hopes of unseating "Prime Minister" Robert Walpole, Swift paid his final visit to England, where he assisted Pope in editing their joint *Miscellanies* in three volumes (1727, 1728, 1732). The years that followed in Dublin saw the production of many of Swift's finest poems, including *The Lady's Dressing Room* (1732), *A Beautiful Young Nymph Going to Bed* (1734), and *Verses on the Death of Dr. Swift* (composed 1731–1732, published 1739), his most celebrated poem. Swift continued to champion the cause of Irish political and economic freedom; with his like-minded friend Thomas Sheridan, he conducted a weekly periodical, the *Intelligencer* (1728). In 1729, he published his most famous essay, *A Modest Proposal.* Some years later, he supervised the publication of the first four volumes of his *Works* (1735) by the Dublin publisher George Faulkner.

When Swift reached his early seventies, his infirmities made him incapable of carrying out his clerical duties at Saint Patrick's; at seventy-five, he was found "of unsound mind and memory," and guardians were appointed to manage his affairs. In addition to ongoing debilities from Ménière's syndrome, he suffered from arteriosclerosis, aphasia, memory loss, and other diseases of old age; he was not insane, however, as many of his contemporaries believed. A devoted clergyman, Swift practiced the Christian charity he preached, giving more than half of his income to the needy; the founding of Ireland's first mental hospital through a generous provision in his will was the most famous of Swift's many benefactions.

Voltaire hailed Swift as the "English Rabelais," while Henry Fielding lauded him as the "English Lucian." Although the more delicate sensibilities of the nineteenth century eschewed his writings for their coarseness and truculence, twentieth-century readers have prized Swift's work for its intelligence, wit, and inventiveness. A committed champion of social justice and an untiring enemy of pride, Swift was a brilliant satirist in part because he was a thoroughgoing humanist.

A Description of the Morning

Introducing this poem in the ninth number of his new periodical, the *Tatler* (for 30 April 1709), Richard Steele wrote that Swift, "has . . . run into a way [of writing] perfectly new, and described things exactly as they happen." *A Description of the Morning* is an early and important example of the "town eclogue," or urban pastoral, a poetic style further popularized by John Gay's *Trivia, or The Art of Walking the Streets of London* (1716). Traditionally, the eclogue—Virgil's bucolic poems are the most famous example—has no appreciable action or characterization, but depends on the thorough and evocative depiction of a pastoral scene. Swift's *Morning* imitates the conventions of pastoral description, not to portray the idealized natural harmony of Arcadia but rather to present the reality of social disorder masquerading under the appearance of order as day breaks over London. Remarkably, Alexander Pope's *Pastorals*, his first published poems, went on sale in the same week that Swift's pioneering mock-pastoral appeared, though the two future friends would not meet for several years.

A Description of the Morning

	Now hardly° here and there a hackney coach[1]	*harshly*
	Appearing, showed the ruddy morn's approach.	
	Now Betty[2] from her master's bed has flown,	
	And softly stole to discompose her own.	
5	The slipshod 'prentice from his master's door	
	Had pared° the dirt, and sprinkled round the floor.[3]	*reduced*
	Now Moll had whirled her mop with dexterous airs,	
	Prepared to scrub the entry and the stairs.	
	The youth with broomy stumps began to trace	
10	The kennel edge, where wheels had worn the place.[4]	
	The smallcoal man was heard with cadence deep;[5]	
	Till drowned in shriller notes of chimney sweep.	
	Duns° at his Lordship's gate began to meet;	*creditors*
	And brickdust[6] Moll had screamed through half a street.	
15	The turnkey now his flock returning sees,	
	Duly let out a-nights to steal for fees.[7]	

1. A hired coach, drawn by two horses and seating six people; here, equated with the chariot of Phoebus Apollo, Greek god of the sun.
2. Like "Moll" (line 7), a typical maidservant's name.
3. Fresh sawdust was used to absorb mud.
4. Scavenging in the gutters (kennels) "to find old nails" [Swift's note] was common.
5. Small pieces of coal or charcoal used to light fires; like many other products and services, they were sold by street vendors who advertised, or "cried," their wares by calling or singing as they walked the streets. The smallcoal man has a deep voice; sweeps were always small boys.
6. An abrasive, used for cleaning or for sharpening knives.
7. As prisoners had to pay the jailer for food and for other comforts, the jailer has let them out over night to steal.

The watchful bailiffs take their silent stands;
And schoolboys lag with satchels in their hands.[8]

1709   1709

A Description of a City Shower

"They say 'tis the best thing I ever writ, and I think so too," boasted Swift of his *Description of a City Shower* in 1710. It was first published in the *Tatler*, No. 238, on 17 October 1710, soon after its composition. Swift's closely observed rendering of London street life playfully mocks the English imitators of Virgil, especially John Dryden and his celebrated translation, *The Works of Virgil* (1697). We see, for example, Swift's mock-heroic effects based on Virgil's *Aeneid* (29–19 B.C.), most notably in comparing the timorous "beau" trapped in his sedan chair to the fierce Greek warriors hiding inside the Trojan Horse, and in calling to mind the storm that led to Queen Dido's seduction and eventual ruin (Dryden's translation 4.231–238). More importantly, just as Swift invoked the mock-pastoral in *A Description of the Morning*, so too does he create a mock-georgic mode in his *City Shower*. The division of the poem into portents, preliminaries, and deluge closely parallels the tempest scene in Virgil's *Georgics* (36–29 B.C.; book 1, 431–458, 483–538 in Dryden), so that Swift uses structural and verbal elements from a classical poem extolling the virtues of agriculture and rural life to depict the teeming diversity of the contemporary urban scene.

A Description of a City Shower

Careful observers may foretell the hour
(By sure prognostics) when to dread a shower.
While rain depends,° the pensive cat gives o'er   *is impending*
Her frolics, and pursues her tail no more.
5   Returning home at night you find the sink[1]
Strike your offended sense with double stink.
If you be wise, then go not far to dine,
You spend in coach-hire more than save in wine.
A coming shower your shooting corns[2] presage,
10   Old aches[3] throb, your hollow tooth will rage:
Sauntering in coffee-house is Dulman seen;
He damns the climate, and complains of spleen.[4]

Meanwhile the South,° rising with dabbled° wings,   *south wind/muddy*
A sable cloud athwart the welkin° flings;   *sky*
15   That swilled more liquor than it could contain,
And like a drunkard gives it up again.
Brisk Susan whips her linen from the rope,[5]
While the first drizzling shower is borne aslope:°   *at a slant*
Such is that sprinkling which some careless quean°   *hussy*
20   Flirts° on you from her mop, but not so clean: *flicks*

---

8. Cf. the second "age of man" in Shakespeare's *As You Like It*: "Then the whining schoolboy, with his satchel / And shining morning face, creeping like snail / Unwillingly to school" (2.7.145–47).
1. Sewer. The poem is built upon Swift's experiences in London: on November 8, 1710, Swift wrote to his beloved Stella (Esther Johnson) that "I will give ten shillings a week for my lodging; for I am almost stunk out of this with the sink, and it helps me to verses in my

Shower." The parsimonious Swift normally spent around half this amount for lodgings.
2. The shooting pain in your corns.
3. Pronounced "aitches."
4. Dulman (a descriptive name) complains of melancholy or depression, then attributed to the spleen.
5. The typically named maid brings in her washing from the line.

You fly, invoke the gods; then turning, stop
To rail; she singing, still whirls on her mop.
Nor yet the dust had shunned th' unequal strife,
But aided by the wind, fought still for life;
25 And wafted with its foe by violent gust,
'Twas doubtful which was rain, and which was dust.[6]
Ah! Where must needy poet seek for aid,
When dust and rain at once his coat invade?
Sole coat, where dust cemented by the rain
30 Erects the nap, and leaves a cloudy stain.
    Now in contiguous drops the flood comes down,
Threatening with deluge this devoted° town.   doomed
To shops in crowds the daggled° females fly,   muddied
Pretend to cheapen° goods, but nothing buy.   bargain for
35 The Templer spruce,[7] while every spout's abroach,[8]
Stays till 'tis fair, yet seems to call a coach.
The tucked-up seamstress walks with hasty strides,
While streams run down her oiled umbrella's sides.
Here various kinds by various fortunes led,
40 Commence acquaintance underneath a shed.°   shelter
Triumphant Tories, and desponding Whigs,[9]
Forget their feuds, and join to save their wigs.
Boxed° in a chair[1] the beau impatient sits,   confined
While spouts run clattering o'er the roof by fits;
45 And ever and anon with frightful din
The leather sounds; he trembles from within.
So when Troy chairmen bore the wooden steed,
Pregnant with Greeks, impatient to be freed;
(Those bully Greeks, who, as the moderns do,
50 Instead of paying chairmen, run them through[2])
Laocoon struck the outside with his spear,
And each imprisoned hero quaked for fear.[3]

    Now from all parts the swelling kennels[4] flow,
And bear their trophies with them as they go:
55 Filths of all hues and odors, seem to tell
What streets they sailed from, by the sight and smell.
They, as each torrent drives with rapid force
From Smithfield, or St. Pulchre's shape their course;[5]
And in huge confluent join at Snow Hill ridge,
60 Fall from the conduit prone to Holborn Bridge.[6]

---

6. Swift here parallels a line from Samuel Garth's popular satirical poem, *The Dispensary* (1699): "'Tis doubtful which is sea, and which is sky" (5.176).
7. Well-dressed lawyer.
8. Drainpipe pouring water.
9. 1710, the year this poem was written, was the first year of the Tory ministry under Queen Anne.
1. A sedan chair, carried by two men; this one has a leather roof.
2. With their swords.
3. When the Trojans carried the Greek's wooden horse

into Troy, thinking that the opposing army had given up their siege, the priest Laocoon was suspicious, and struck the horse. See *Aeneid* 2.50–53.
4. Gutters, which were also open sewers.
5. Respectively, the cattle market and the parish west of the Newgate prison.
6. Snow Hill ridge extended down to Holborn Bridge, which spanned Fleet ditch, used as an open sewer; from 1343, local butchers had been given permission to dump entrails in the Fleet.

Sweepings from butchers' stalls, dung, guts, and blood,
Drowned puppies, stinking sprats,° all drenched in mud,   } *small fish*
Dead cats and turnip tops come tumbling down the flood.[7]

1710   1710

Stella's Birthday

Between 1719 and 1727 Swift wrote seven birthday poems to "Stella," his dear Esther Johnson. The two reprinted here are his first and last. Swift's earliest use of the name "Stella" in verse was in the first of this series of celebratory verses, which play on the obligation of the Poet Laureate to write an official "birthday ode" for the monarch every year. Placing himself in the role of her laureate, Swift may have chosen the name "Stella" to highlight the difference between his own uncontrived expressions of affection and those of the courtly Sir Philip Sidney in *Astrophel and Stella* (1591). Like Shakespeare's Sonnet 130 ("My mistress' eyes are nothing like the sun"), Swift's first poem on Stella's birthday violates the traditions of the conventional love lyric by calling attention to his beloved's considerable weight and age, only to suggest that his admiration of her lies in her deeper virtues. In his last birthday poem, Swift attempts to escape from the prospect of Stella's impending death, first by humor and then by the power of reason; when these fail, he tenderly acknowledges how much she means to him. Swift was to sail for England less than a month after he gave those verses to her—both knew that they might never see each other again. Though more formal than the *Journal to Stella*, Swift's birthday verses were written primarily for Stella's enjoyment and for the entertainment of their small circle of intimate friends. Despite the private nature of these poems, Swift nevertheless authorized their publication in the third and last volume of the Pope-Swift *Miscellanies*, which appeared in March 1728.

Stella's Birthday, 1719

WRITTEN IN THE YEAR 1718/9[1]

Stella this day is thirty-four,[2]
(We shan't dispute a year or more):
However, Stella, be not troubled,
Although thy size and years are doubled,
5   Since first I saw thee at sixteen,[3]
The brightest virgin on the green.[4]
So little is thy form° declined;   *figure*
Made up° so largely in thy mind.   *compensated*

    Oh, would it please the gods to *split*
10   Thy beauty, size, and years, and wit,
No age could furnish out a pair
Of nymphs so graceful, wise, and fair:

---

7. These last three lines were intended against the licentious manner of modern poets, in making three rhymes together, which they call *Triplets*; and the last of the three was two, or sometimes more syllables longer, called an *Alexandrian*. These *Triplets* and *Alexandrians* were brought in by Dryden, and other poets in the reign of Charles II. They were the mere effect of haste, idleness, and want of money, and have been wholly avoided by the best poets since these verses were written [Swift's note].
1. Until the calendar was reformed in 1751, the new year legally began on the Feast of the Annunciation (sometimes called "Lady Day") on March 25th, though January 1st was also commonly recognized as the start of the new

year. Therefore, to avoid confusion, it was a widely accepted practice to write dates between January 1 and March 24 according to both methods of reckoning: 1718/19. Since Swift's poem was composed in February or March, we would say it was written in 1719.
2. Stella (Esther Johnson) actually celebrated her thirty-eighth birthday on 13 March 1719.
3. Swift first met Stella when she was eight years old; he may have "seen" her only when she grew from child to woman.
4. The village green, or common land, here implies a pastoral simplicity that suggests the natural innocence of their relationship.

With half the luster of your eyes,
With half your wit, your years, and size:
15   And then before it grew too late,
How should I beg of gentle fate,
(That either nymph might have her swain),
To split my worship too in twain.

1719   1728

Stella's Birthday, 1727

This day, whate'er the fates decree,
Shall still be kept with joy by me:
This day then, let us not be told,
That you are sick, and I grown old,
5   Nor think on our approaching ills,
And talk of spectacles and pills.
Tomorrow will be time enough
To hear such mortifying stuff.[1]
Yet, since from reason may be brought
10   A better and more pleasing thought,
Which can in spite of all decays,
Support a few remaining days:
From not the gravest of divines,°   clergymen
Accept for once some serious lines.

15   Although we now can form no more
Long schemes of life, as heretofore;
Yet you, while time is running fast,
Can look with joy on what is past.

          Were future happiness and pain[2]
20   A mere contrivance of the brain,
As atheists argue, to entice
And fit their proselytes° for vice   converts
(The only comfort they propose,
To have companions in their woes);
25   Grant this the case, yet sure 'tis hard,
That virtue, styled its own reward,
And by all sages understood
To be the chief of human good,
Should acting, die, nor leave behind
30   Some lasting pleasure in the mind;
Which by remembrance will assuage
Grief, sickness, poverty, and age;
And strongly shoot a radiant dart
To shine through life's declining part.

35   Say, Stella, feel you no content,
Reflecting on a life well spent?
Your skillful hand employed to save

---

1. Both humbling and leading to death. Stella died less   2. I.e., heaven and hell.
than a year later.

Despairing wretches from the grave;[3]
And then supporting with your store,
40   Those whom you dragged from death before
(So Providence on mortals waits,
Preserving what it first creates);
Your generous boldness to defend
An innocent and absent friend;
45   That courage which can make you just,
To merit humbled in the dust;
The detestation you express
For vice in all its glittering dress;
That patience under torturing pain,
50   Where stubborn Stoics would complain.

      Shall these like empty shadows pass,
Or forms reflected from a glass?
Or mere chimeras° in the mind,   *imaginary creatures or notions*
That fly and leave no marks behind?
50   Does not the body thrive and grow
By food of twenty years ago?
And had it not been still supplied,
It must a thousand times have died.
Then, who with reason can maintain
60   That no effects of food remain?
And is not virtue in mankind
The nutriment that feeds the mind?
Upheld by each good action past,
And still continued by the last:
65   Then who with reason can pretend,
That all effects of virtue end?

      Believe me, Stella, when you show
That true contempt for things below,
Nor prize your life for other ends
70   Than merely to oblige your friends;
Your former actions claim their part,
And join to fortify your heart.
For Virtue in her daily race,
Like Janus[4] bears a double face;
75   Looks back with joy where she has gone,
And therefore goes with courage on.
She at your sickly couch will wait,
And guide you to a better state.

      O then, whatever Heaven intends,
80   Take pity on your pitying friends;
Nor let your ills affect your mind,
To fancy they can be unkind.
Me, surely me, you ought to spare,

---

3. Swift often praised Stella's charity, not only for nursing him in his bouts of illness, but also for attending to the poor in her neighborhood.

4. The god of doorways and of the rising and setting sun, whose two-faced head looks forward and backward, and after whom the month of January is named.

Who gladly would your sufferings share;
85 Or give my scrap of life to you,
And think it far beneath your due;
You, to whose care so oft I owe
That I'm alive to tell you so.

1727   1728

The Lady's Dressing Room

The first of Swift's so-called scatological poems, which have attracted much critical attention and amateur psychoanalysis, these verses enjoyed considerable popularity in Swift's lifetime, though some contemporaries condemned them as "deficient in point of delicacy, even to the highest degree." One of Swift's friends recorded in her memoirs that *The Lady's Dressing Room* made her mother "instantly" lose her lunch. Sir Walter Scott found in this poem (and other pieces by Swift) "the marks of an incipient disorder of the mind, which induced the author to dwell on degrading and disgusting subjects." If Pope's *The Rape of the Lock* describes Belinda at the "altar" of her dressing table undergoing "the sacred rites of pride" as she and her maid apply all manner of cosmetics to make her a beautiful "goddess" and arm her for the battle of the sexes, then *The Lady's Dressing Room* reveals the coarse realities of Celia's embodiment—a humorous and disturbing corrective to the pretense and false appearances on which her glorification depends. Although Swift assails the social and literary conventions that celebrate women for their superficial qualities, there is also a misogynistic quality to the poem, which may be attributable to his anger and disappointment over his beloved Stella's death in January 1728. Nevertheless, Strephon is ridiculed for being so naively idealistic about his lover and so easily deceived by appearances; once his secret investigations free him from his illusions, Strephon's permanent revulsion and rejection of all women show his inability to follow a middle course by appreciating women in their complex reality.

The Lady's Dressing Room

Five hours (and who can do it less in?)
By haughty Celia spent in dressing;
The goddess from her chamber issues,
Arrayed in lace, brocade, and tissues:
5   Strephon,[1] who found the room was void,
And Betty[2] otherwise employed,
Stole in, and took a strict survey,
Of all the litter as it lay:
Whereof, to make the matter clear,
10   An *inventory* follows here.

And first, a dirty smock appeared,
Beneath the arm-pits well besmeared;
Strephon, the rogue, displayed it wide,
And turned it round on every side.
15   In such a case few words are best,
And Strephon bids us guess the rest;
But swears how damnably the men lie,
In calling Celia sweet and cleanly.

---

1. Strephon and Celia are names usually associated with pastoral poetry, and are therefore used mockingly here.

2. A typical maidservant's name.

Now listen while he next produces
20 The various combs for various uses,
Filled up with dirt so closely fixed,
No brush could force a way betwixt;
A paste of composition rare,
Sweat, dandruff, powder, lead,[3] and hair,
25 A forehead cloth with oil upon't
To smooth the wrinkles on her front;
Here alum flour[4] to stop the steams,
Exhaled from sour, unsavory streams;
There night-gloves made of Tripsy's[5] hide,
30 Bequeathed by Tripsy when she died;
With puppy water,[6] beauty's help,
Distilled from Tripsy's darling whelp.
Here gallipots° and vials placed,   *ointment jars*
Some filled with washes, some with paste;
35 Some with pomatum,° paints, and slops,   *hair ointment*
And ointments good for scabby chops.°   *lips or cheeks*
Hard° by a filthy basin stands,   *close*
Fouled with the scouring of her hands;
The basin takes whatever comes,
40 The scrapings of her teeth and gums,
A nasty compound of all hues,
For here she spits, and here she spews.

But oh! it turned poor Strephon's bowels,
When he beheld and smelt the towels;
45 Begummed, bemattered, and beslimed;
With dirt, and sweat, and ear-wax grimed.
No object Strephon's eye escapes,
Here, petticoats in frowzy° heaps;   *unkempt*
Nor be the handkerchiefs forgot,
50 All varnished o'er with snuff[7] and snot.
The stockings why should I expose,
Stained with the moisture of her toes;
Or greasy coifs and pinners° reeking,   *night caps*
Which Celia slept at least a week in?
55 A pair of tweezers next he found
To pluck her brows in arches round,
Or hairs that sink the forehead low,
Or on her chin like bristles grow.

The virtues we must not let pass
60 Of Celia's magnifying glass;
When frighted Strephon cast his eye on't,

It showed the visage of a giant:[8]
A glass that can to sight disclose
The smallest worm in Celia's nose,
65   And faithfully direct her nail
To squeeze it out from head to tail;
For catch it nicely by the head,
It must come out alive or dead.

Why, Strephon, will you tell the rest?
70   And must you needs describe the chest?
That careless wench! no creature warn her
To move it out from yonder corner,
But leave it standing full in sight,
For you to exercise your spite!
75   In vain the workman showed his wit
With rings and hinges counterfeit
To make it seem in this disguise
A cabinet to vulgar eyes;
Which Strephon ventured to look in,
80   Resolved to go through *thick and thin*;
He lifts the lid: there need no more,
He smelt it all the time before.

As, from within Pandora's box,
When Epimethus oped the locks,
85   A sudden universal crew
Of human evils upward flew;[9]
He still was comforted to find
That hope at last remained behind.

So, Strephon, lifting up the lid,
90   To view what in the chest was hid,
The vapors flew from out the vent,
But Strephon cautious never meant
The bottom of the pan to grope,
And foul his hands in search of hope.

95   O! ne'er may such a vile machine°   construction
Be once in Celia's chamber seen!
O! may she better learn to keep
"Those secrets of the hoary deep."[1]

As mutton cutlets, prime of meat,
100   Which though with art you salt and beat
As laws of cookery require,
And roast them at the clearest fire;
If from adown the hopeful chops

---

8. Cf. *Gulliver's Travels*, Part 2, "A Voyage to Brobding-nag," ch. 1: "This made me reflect upon the fair skins of our *English* ladies, who appear so beautiful to us, only because they are of our own size, and their defects not to be seen but through magnifying glass, where we find by experiment that the smoothest and whitest skins look rough and coarse, and ill colored."

9. In Greek mythology, Epimethus, acting against advice, opened the box Jove had given his wife Pandora, and all the evils and vices of the world flew out, leaving only hope in the box.
1. Quoting Milton's *Paradise Lost* 2.891, in which Sin is unleashing the chaotic forces of her infernal realm.

The fat upon a cinder drops,
105 To stinking smoke it turns the flame
Poisoning the flesh from whence it came;
And up exhales a greasy stench
For which you curse the careless wench:
So things which must not be expressed,
110 When *plumped*° into the reeking chest,   *dropped*
Send up an excremental smell
To taint the parts from which they fell:
The petticoats and gown perfume,
And waft a stink round every room.

115   Thus finishing his grand survey,
The swain disgusted slunk away,
Repeating in his amorous fits,
"Oh! Celia, Celia, Celia shits!"

      But Vengeance, goddess never sleeping,
120 Soon punished Strephon for his peeping.
His foul imagination links
Each dame he sees with all her stinks:
And if unsavory odors fly,
Conceives a lady standing by:
125 All women his description fits,
And both ideas jump° like wits   *join together*
By vicious fancy coupled fast,
And still appearing in contrast.

      I pity wretched Strephon, blind
130 To all the charms of womankind;
Should I the queen of love refuse,
Because she rose from stinking ooze?[2]
To him that looks behind the scene,
Statira's but some pocky quean.[3]

135   When Celia in her glory shows,
If Strephon would but stop his nose,
Who now so impiously blasphemes
Her ointments, daubs, and paints and creams;
Her washes, slops, and every clout,[4]
140 With which she makes so foul a rout;[5]
He soon would learn to think like me,
And bless his ravished eyes to see
Such order from confusion sprung,
Such gaudy *tulips* raised from *dung*.

c. 1730   1732

---

2. Venus, Roman goddess of sexual love and physical
beauty, rose from the sea.
3. One of the heroines of Nathaniel Lee's highly popular
tragedy *The Rival Queens* (1677); Swift's common slat-
tern (quean) has had either smallpox or venereal disease.

4. Washes were either treated water used for the complexion or stale urine used as a detergent; clouts were
rags.
5. Both of her skin and, presumably, of the men.

Verses on the Death of Dr. Swift

"I have been several months writing near five hundred lines on a pleasant subject," wrote Swift to his friend John Gay in December 1731, "only to tell what my friends and enemies will say on me after I am dead." Swift completed what was to become his most celebrated poem by adding explanatory notes in the early months of 1732. It seems that Swift intended the *Verses* to be published after his death but showed the poem in manuscript to various friends. When the reputation of his *Verses* spread, Swift used the opportunity to publish a different autobiographical poem, *The Life and Genuine Character of Dr. Swift* (1733), which would satisfy public demand and make the eventual appearance of the *Verses* all the more surprising. Six years later, believing they were doing their friend a service, Alexander Pope and William King (1685–1763) published a version of the poem in which they edited out some of Swift's most self-aggrandizing and controversial lines. Swift was "much dissatisfied" with this London edition and responded by supervising the speedy publication of an unexpurgated text of the work in Dublin, though even he had the prudence to leave blank spaces for some of the names in his poem. Among the most controversial elements in the *Verses* were its direct attack on Prime Minister Robert Walpole and his government; the unflattering depiction of the court and singling out of Lady Suffolk and Queen Caroline for ridicule; and Swift's praise of Bolingbroke and Pulteney, leading opposition politicians. Swift's jaunty tetrameter carries an admixture of self-fashioning for posterity and moral instruction, a spirited apologia for his life and writings, and an idealized account of the principles by which he strove to live. *Verses on the Death of Dr. Swift* reveals its subject as a champion of liberty and embattled self-promoter, a humanistic preacher and an unsparing satirist.

Verses on the Death of Dr. Swift, D.S.P.D.[1]
Occasioned by Reading a Maxim in Rochefoucauld

*Dans l'adversité de nos meilleurs amis nous trouvons quelque
chose, qui ne nous deplaist pas.*[2]

"In the adversity of our best friends, we find something that
doth not displease us."

As Rochefoucauld his maxims drew	
From Nature, I believe 'em true:	
They argue° no corrupted mind	suggest
In him; the fault is in mankind.	
5 This maxim more than all the rest	
Is thought too base for human breast;	
"In all distresses of our friends	
We first consult our private ends,	
While Nature kindly bent to ease us,	
10 Points out some circumstance to please us."	
If this perhaps your patience move°	strains
Let reason and experience prove.	
We all behold with envious eyes,	
Our equal raised above our size;	
15 Who would not at a crowded show,	

---

1. Dean of St. Patrick's, Dublin.
2. François, duc de La Rochefoucauld, *Réflexions ou Sen-* *tences et Maximes Morales* ("Reflections or Moral Aphorisms and Maxims," 1665).

Stand high himself, keep others low?
I love my friend as well as you,
But would not have him stop my view;
Then let me have the higher post;
20 I ask but for an inch at most.

    If in a battle you should find,
One, whom you love of all mankind,
Had some heroic action done,
A champion killed, or trophy won;
25 Rather than thus be overtopped,
Would you not wish his laurels[3] cropped?

    Dear honest Ned is in the gout,[4]
Lies racked with pain, and you without:[5]
How patiently you hear him groan!
30 How glad the case is not your own!

    What poet would not grieve to see,
His brethren write as well as he?
But rather than they should excel,
He'd wish his rivals all in Hell.

35   Her end when emulation misses,
She turns to envy, stings, and hisses:
The strongest friendship yields to pride,
Unless the odds be on our side.

    Vain humankind! Fantastic race!
40 Thy various follies, who can trace?
Self-love, ambition, envy, pride,
Their empire in our hearts divide:
Give others riches, power, and station,
'Tis all on me a usurpation.
45 I have no title to aspire;
Yet, when you sink, I seem the higher.
In Pope,[6] I cannot read a line,
But with a sigh, I wish it mine:
When he can in one couplet fix
More sense than I can do in six:
It gives me such a jealous fit,
I cry, "Pox take him, and his wit."

    Why must I be outdone by Gay,[7]
In my own humorous, biting way?

55   Arbuthnot[8] is no more my friend,
Who dares to irony pretend;

---

3. In ancient times, laurel wreaths were given to poets, athletes, and war heroes to signify their preeminence.
4. A disease characterized by an inflammation of small joints, especially in the feet and hands.
5. Outside his room.
6. Alexander Pope, poet, satirist, and friend of Swift.

7. John Gay, poet and playwright, author of *The Beggar's Opera* (1728), friend of Swift, Pope, and Arbuthnot.
8. John Arbuthnot (1667–1735), physician to Queen Anne and member of Scriblerus Club along with Swift, Pope, and Gay; he was the principal author of *Memoirs of . . . Martinus Scriblerus* (1741).

Which I was born to introduce,
Refined it first, and showed its use.

St. John, as well as Pulteney[9] knows,
60   That I had some repute for prose;
And till they drove me out of date,
Could maul a minister of state:
If they have mortified my pride,
And made me throw my pen aside;
65   If with such talents Heaven hath blest 'em,
Have I not reason to detest 'em?

To all my foes, dear fortune, send
Thy gifts, but never to my friend:
I tamely can endure the first,
70   But, this with envy makes me burst.

Thus much may serve by way of proem,°   *preface*
Proceed we therefore to our poem.

The time is not remote, when I
Must by the course of nature die:
75   When I foresee my special friends,
Will try to find their private ends:
Though it is hardly understood,[1]
Which way my death can do them good;
Yet, thus methinks, I hear 'em speak;
80   "See, how the Dean begins to break:°   *weaken*
Poor gentleman, he droops apace,°   *quickly*
You plainly find it in his face:
That old vertigo in his head
Will never leave him, till he's dead:
85   Besides, his memory decays,
He recollects not what he says;
He cannot call his friends to mind;
Forgets the place where last he dined:
Plies you with stories o'er and o'er,
90   He told them fifty times before.
How does he fancy we can sit
To hear his out-of-fashioned wit?
But he takes up with younger folks,
Who for his wine will bear his jokes:
95   Faith,° he must make his stories shorter,   *in truth*
Or change his comrades once a quarter:
In half the time, he talks them round;[2]
There must another set be found.

"For poetry, he's past his prime,
100 He takes an hour to find a rhyme:

9. Henry St. John Bolingbroke (1678–1751) and William Pulteney; both politicians—one a Tory, the other a Whig—were united in their opposition to Robert Walpole. See Swift's notes to lines 194 and 196.

1. Hard to understand.
2. Runs through his stock of stories and has to begin again.

His fire° is out, his wit decayed,   *creative fire*
His fancy sunk, his muse a jade.[3]
I'd have him throw away his pen;
But there's no talking to some men."

105   And then their tenderness appears,
By adding largely to my years:
"He's older than he would be reckoned,
And well remembers Charles the Second."[4]

        "He hardly° drinks a pint of wine;   *barely*
110   And that, I doubt,° is no good sign.   *suspect*
His stomach° too begins to fail: *appetite*
Last year we thought him strong and hale;
But now, he's quite another thing;
I wish he may hold out till spring."

115   Then hug themselves, and reason thus:
"It is not yet so bad with us."

        In such a case they talk in tropes,°   *figuratively*
And by their fears express their hopes:
Some great misfortune to portend,°   *predict*
120   No enemy can match a friend;
With all the kindness they profess,
The merit of a lucky guess
(When daily "Howd'y's"[5] come of course,°   *routinely*
And servants answer: "Worse and worse")
25   Would please 'em better than to tell
That, God be praised, the Dean is well.
Then he who prophesied the best,
Approves° his foresight to the rest: *confirms*
"You know, I always feared the worst,
130   And often told you so at first":
He'd rather choose that I should die
Than his prediction prove a lie.
No one foretells I shall recover;
But, all agree to give me over.°   *give up hope*

135   Yet should some neighbor feel a pain
Just in the parts where I complain;
How many a message would he send?
What hearty prayers that I should mend?
Inquire what regimen[6] I kept;
140   What gave me ease, and how I slept?
And more lament, when I was dead,
Than all the snivellers round my bed.

        My good companions, never fear,
For though you may mistake a year;

---

3. The poet's muse—his inspiration (always female)—is here a worn-out horse or a disreputable or shrewish woman.

4. King Charles II died in 1685, when Swift was 18.
5. How does [is] he?
6. Prescribed pattern of living, exercising, and eating.

145 Though your prognostics run too fast,
They must be verified at last.

"Behold the fatal day arrive!
How is the Dean? He's just alive.
Now the departing prayer is read:
150 He hardly breathes. The Dean is dead.
Before the passing bell[7] begun,
The news through half the town has run.
O, may we all for death prepare!
What has he left? And who's his heir?
155 I know no more than what the news is,
'Tis all bequeathed to public uses.[8]
To public use! A perfect whim!
What had the public done for him?
Mere envy, avarice, and pride!
160 He gave it all.—But first he died.
And had the Dean, in all the nation,
No worthy friend, no poor relation?
So ready to do strangers good,
Forgetting his own flesh and blood?"

165 Now Grub Street wits[9] are all employed;
With elegies, the town is cloyed:
Some paragraph in every paper,
To curse the Dean, or bless the Drapier.[1]

The doctors tender of their fame,
170 Wisely on me lay all the blame:
"We must confess his case was nice,°   *difficult*
But he would never take advice;
Had he been ruled, for aught appears,
He might have lived these twenty years:
175 For when we opened him we found
That all his vital parts were sound."

From Dublin soon to London spread,[2]
'Tis told at court, the Dean is dead.

Kind Lady Suffolk[3] in the spleen,[4]
180 Runs laughing up to tell the Queen.
The Queen, so gracious, mild, and good,

7. Death bell, rung to obtain prayers for the passing soul.
8. In fact, when Swift died he left a number of small personal bequests in addition to his large gifts to public charities.
9. Hack writers, paid to produce (often libelous) materials for London journals.
1. The Author imagines, that the Scribblers of the prevailing Party, which he always opposed, will libel him after his Death; but that others will remember him with gratitude, who consider the service he had done to Ireland, under the name of M. B. Drapier [Swift's note, referring to *The Drapier's Letters* (1724–1725), a series of essays he wrote to defend Ireland from the the British government's plan to impose a new coin, "Wood's half-

pence," that would have devastated Ireland's economy].
2. The Dean supposeth himself to die in Ireland [Swift's note]; he did.
3. Mrs. Howard, afterwards Countess of Suffolk, then of the Bedchamber to the Queen, professed much friendship for the Dean. The Queen, then Princess, sent a dozen times to the Dean (then in London) with her command to attend her; which at last he did, by advice of all his friends. She often sent for him afterwards, and always treated him very graciously. He taxed her with a present worth ten pounds, which she promised before he should return to Ireland, but on his taking leave, the medals were not ready" [Swift's note].
4. The 18th-century equivalent of "depression."

Cries, "Is he gone? 'Tis time he should.
He's dead you say, why let him rot;
I'm glad the medals were forgot.[5]
185   I promised them, I own;° but when?   *admit*
I only was a princess then;
But now as consort of the King,
You know 'tis quite a different thing."

Now, Chartres[6] at Sir Robert's levee,[7]
190   Tells, with a sneer, the tidings heavy:
"Why, is he dead without his shoes?"[8]
(Cries Bob)[9] "I'm sorry for the news;
Oh, were the wretch but living still,
And in his place my good friend Will;[1]
195   Or had a miter° on his head,   *bishop's hat*
Provided Bolingbroke[2] were dead."

Now Curll his shop from rubbish drains:
Three genuine tomes of Swift's remains.[3]
And then to make them pass the glibber,°   *sell better*
200   Revised by Tibbalds, Moore, and Cibber.[4]
He'll treat me as he does my betters:
Publish my will, my life, my letters,[5]
Revive the libels born to die;
Which Pope must bear, as well as I.

205   Here shift the scene, to represent
How those I love, my death lament.
Poor Pope will grieve a month; and Gay
A week; and Arbuthnot a day.

---

5. The medals were to be sent to the Dean in four months, but she forgot them, or thought them too dear [expensive]. The Dean, being in Ireland, sent Mrs. Howard a piece of Indian plaid made in that kingdom [Ireland]: which the Queen seeing took from her, and wore it herself, and sent to the Dean for as much as would clothe herself and her children, desiring he would send charge of it. He did the former. It cost thirty-five pounds, but he said he would have nothing except the medals. He was the summer following in England, was treated as usual, and she being then Queen, the Dean was promised a settlement in England, but returned as he went, and, instead of favor or medals, hath been ever since under her Majesty's displeasure [Swift's note].

6. Chartres is a most infamous, vile scoundrel, grown from a foot-boy, or worse, to a prodigious fortune [Swift's note]. Francis Charteris was convicted of rape, and pardoned by the prime minister, Robert Walpole, in 1730.

7. A morning audience held in the bedchamber of a person of distinction before or after rising.

8. I.e., in his bed, rather than meeting a violent death or being hanged.

9. Sir Robert Walpole, Chief Minister of State, treated the Dean, in 1726, with great distinction, invited him to dinner at Chelsea, with the Dean's friends chosen on purpose; appointed an hour to talk with him of Ireland, to which kingdom and people the Dean found him no great friend. . . . The Dean would see him no more [Swift's note].

1. Mr. William Pulteney, from being Mr. Walpole's inti-

mate friend, detesting his Administration, opposed his measures, and joined with my Lord Bolingbroke, to represent his conduct in an excellent paper, called the *Craftsman*, which is still continued [Swift's note].

2. Henry St. John, Lord Viscount Bolingbroke, Secretary of State to Queen Anne of blessed memory. He is reckoned the most universal genius in Europe; Walpole dreading his abilities, treated him most injuriously, working with King George, who forgot his promise of restoring the said Lord, upon the restless importunity of Walpole [Swift's note].

3. Edmund Curll hath been the most infamous bookseller of any age or country: his character in part may be found in Mr. Pope's *Dunciad*. He published three volumes all charged on [i.e., attributed to] the Dean, who never writ three pages of them: he hath used many of the Dean's friends in almost as vile a manner [Swift's note].

4. Three stupid verse writers in London, the last to the shame of the Court, and the highest disgrace to wit and learning, was made Laureate [Swift's note]. Lewis Theobald (1688–1744), Shakespearean scholar and poet; James Moore Smythe (1702–1734), playwright whom Pope accused of plagiarism; Colley Cibber (1671–1757), actor and playwright. All three men are satirized in Pope's *Dunciad*.

5. Curll is notoriously infamous for publishing the lives, letters, and last Wills and Testaments of the nobility and ministers of State, as well as of all the rogues who are hanged at Tyburn [Swift's note].

St. John himself will scarce forbear
210 To bite his pen, and drop a tear.
The rest will give a shrug and cry
"I'm sorry; but we all must die."
Indifference clad in wisdom's guise
All fortitude of mind supplies:
215 For how can stony bowels melt,[6]
In those who never pity felt;
When *we* are lashed, *they* kiss the rod,[7]
Resigning to the will of God.

The fools, my juniors by a year,
220 Are tortured with suspense and fear—
Who wisely thought my age a screen,
When death approached, to stand between:
The screen removed, their hearts are trembling,
They mourn for me without dissembling.

225 My female friends, whose tender hearts
Have better learnt to act their parts,
Receive the news in doleful dumps,
"The Dean is dead (*and what is trumps?*),
Then Lord have mercy on his soul.
230 (*Ladies, I'll venture for the vole.*[8])
Six deans they say must bear the pall.
(*I wish I knew which king to call.*)"
"Madam, your husband will attend
The funeral of so good a friend."
235 "No madam, 'tis a shocking sight,
And he's engaged tomorrow night!
My Lady Club would take it ill,
If he should fail her at quadrille.
He loved the Dean. (*I lead a heart.*)
240 But dearest friends, they say, must part.
His time was come, he ran his race;
We hope he's in a better place."

Why do we grieve that friends should die?
No loss more easy to supply.
245 One year is past; a different scene;
No further mention of the Dean;
Who now, alas, no more is missed
Than if he never did exist.
Where's now this fav'rite of Apollo?[9]
250 Departed; and his works must follow:
Must undergo the common fate;
His kind of wit is out of date.
Some country squire to Lintot[1] goes,

6. I.e., how can one feel compassion.
7. Accept chastisement submissively; kissing a monarch's
scepter or a state official's staff was a ritual of submission
to authority.
8. All the tricks in the highly popular four-handed card

game, quadrille.
9. Patron of poets.
1. Bernard Lintot (1675–1736), London publisher of
Pope, Gay, and Steele, among others.

Inquires for Swift in verse and prose:
255 Says Lintot, "I have heard the name:
He died a year ago." "The same."
He searcheth all his shop in vain;
"Sir, you may find them in Duck Lane:[2]
I sent them with a load of books
260 Last Monday to the pastry-cook's.[3]
To fancy they could live a year!
I find you're but a stranger here.
The Dean was famous in his time
And had a kind of knack at rhyme
265 His way of writing now is past;
The town hath got a better taste:
I keep no antiquated stuff;
But, spick and span I have enough.
Pray, do but give me leave to show 'em;
270 Here's Colley Cibber's birthday poem.[4]
This ode you never yet have seen
By Stephen Duck,[5] upon the Queen.
Then, here's a letter finely penned,
Against the *Craftsman*[6] and his friend;
275 It clearly shows that all reflection
On ministers, is disaffection.
Next, here's Sir Robert's vindication,[7]
And Mr Henley's last oration:[8]
The hawkers° have not got 'em yet,   *street sellers*
280 Your Honor please to buy a set?

"Here's Woolston's tracts,[9] the twelfth edition;
'Tis read by every politician:
The country members,[1] when in town,
To all their boroughs send them down:
285 You never met a thing so smart;
The courtiers have them all by heart:
Those maids of honor (who can read)
Are taught to use them for their creed.
The reverend author's good intention

2. A place in London where old [i.e., remaindered] books are sold [Swift's note].
3. Wastepaper from unsold books was used to line baking tins. Cf. Dryden's *MacFlecknoe* (1682), who notes similar uses for old texts: "Martyrs of pies and relics of the bum" (line 101).
4. The Poet Laureate was required to write an ode for the monarch's birthday each year. Cibber's appointment as Laureate in 1730 was based on politics, not literary merit.
5. Stephen Duck (1705–1756), known as "the thresher poet," was a laborer whose poetry won him Queen Caroline's favor; Swift made fun of him in *On Stephen Duck, the Thresher, and Favorite Poet, A Quibbling Epigram* (1730).
6. From 1726, the principal periodical written in opposition to Robert Walpole's government. Its title was meant to indicate that Walpole was "a man of craft" (i.e., scheming and deceptive).

7. Walpole hires a set of Party scribblers, who do nothing else but write in his defense [Swift's note].
8. John Henley (1692–1756), known as "Orator Henley" for the Oratory he founded where "at set times, he delivereth strange speeches compiled by himself and his associates. . . . He is an absolute dunce, but generally reputed crazy" [Swift's note].
9. Woolston was a clergyman, but for want of bread, hath in several treatises, in the most blasphemous manner, attempted to turn our Savior and his miracles into ridicule. He is much caressed by many great courtiers, and by all the infidels, and his books read generally by the Court ladies [Swift's note]. Swift appears to conflate the identities of two contemporary clergymen: Thomas Woolston (1670–1733), a notorious Deist, and William Woollaston (1660–1724).
1. Members of Parliament from rural boroughs.

290   Hath been rewarded with a pension:
           He doth an honor to his gown,
           By bravely running priestcraft down:
           He shows, as sure as God's in Gloucester,[2]
           That Jesus was a grand impostor:
295   That all his miracles were cheats,
           Performed as jugglers do their feats;
           The church had never such a writer:
           A shame he hath not got a miter!"

           Suppose me dead; and then suppose
300   A club assembled at the Rose;[3]
           Where from discourse of this and that,
           I grow the subject of their chat:
           And while they toss my name about,
           With favor some, and some without;
305   One quite indifferent in the cause
           My character impartial draws:

           "The Dean, if we believe report,
           Was never ill received at court;
           As for his works in verse and prose,
310   I own myself no judge of those:
           Nor can I tell what critics thought 'em;
           But this I know, all people bought 'em;
           As with a moral view designed
           To cure the vices of mankind:
315   His vein, ironically grave,
           Exposed the fool, and lashed the knave:
           To steal a hint was never known,
           But what he writ was all his own.[4]

           "He never thought an honor done him,
320   Because a duke was proud to own him:
           Would rather slip aside, and choose
           To talk with wits in dirty shoes:
           Despised the fools with stars and garters,[5]
           So often seen caressing Chartres:
325   He never courted men in station,
           Nor persons had in admiration;°   *was in awe of*
           Of no man's greatness was afraid,
           Because he sought for no man's aid.
           Though trusted long in great affairs,
330   He gave himself no haughty airs;
           Without regarding private ends,
           Spent all his credit for his friends,
           And only chose the wise and good;

---

2. A proverb derived from the number of monasteries there once were in that county.

3. The Rose Tavern, near Drury Lane Theatre, and therefore popular with playgoers.

4. Swift is here having fun with the reader, since this line claiming Swift's originality is stolen from Sir John Denham's elegy *On Mr. Abraham Cowley*: "To him no author was unknown / Yet what he wrote was all his own."

5. Worn by Knights of the Garter.

No flatt'rers; no allies in blood;°   *relatives*
335   But succored virtue in distress,
And seldom failed of good success;
As numbers in their hearts must own,
Who, but for him, had been unknown.

"With princes kept a due decorum,
340   But never stood in awe before 'em:
And to her Majesty, God bless her,
Would speak as free as to her dresser,[6]
She thought it his peculiar whim,
Nor took it ill as come from him.
345   He followed David's lesson just,
"In princes never put thy trust."[7]
And, would you make him truly sour,
Provoke him with a slave in power:
The Irish senate, if you named,
350   With what impatience he declaimed!
Fair LIBERTY was all his cry;
For her he stood prepared to die;
For her he boldly stood alone;
For her he oft exposed his own.
355   Two kingdoms, just as factions led,
Had set a price upon his head;
But not a traitor could be found,
To sell him for six hundred pound.[8]

"Had he but spared his tongue and pen,
360   He might have rose like other men:
But power was never in his thought,
And wealth he valued not a groat;
Ingratitude he often found,
And pitied those who meant the wound;
365   But kept the tenor° of his mind,   *prevailing course*
To merit well of humankind;
Nor made a sacrifice of those
Who still° were true, to please his foes.   *always*
He labored many a fruitless hour
370   To reconcile his friends in power;
Saw mischief by a faction brewing,
While they pursued each other's ruin.
But finding vain was all his care,
He left the Court in mere° despair.[9]   *total*

375   "And, oh! how short are human schemes!
Here ended all our golden dreams.

6. Queen Caroline and Lady Suffolk, one of the Ladies of Her Majesty's bedchamber.
7. Psalm 146.3.
8. Two rewards of £300 each were offered in 1713 and 1724 for the revelation of the author of *The Public Spirit of the Whigs* and *The Drapier's Fourth Letter*, respectively, "but in neither kingdoms was the Dean discovered" [Swift's note].
9. Under Queen Anne's Tory ministry, Swift tried to resolve differences between the Chancellor, Simon Harcourt (1661–1727), Lord Bolingbroke, and the Earl of Oxford, but was unsuccessful, and left London shortly before the collapse of their government.

What St. John's skill in state affairs,
What Ormonde's valor,[1] Oxford's cares,
To save their sinking country lent,
380 Was all destroyed by one event.
Too soon that precious life was ended,[2]
On which alone our weal° depended.   *well-being*
When up a dangerous faction starts,[3]
With wrath and vengeance in their hearts:
385 By *solemn league and covenant bound*,[4]
To ruin, slaughter, and confound;
To turn religion to a fable,
And make the government a Babel:
Pervert the law, disgrace the gown,
390 Corrupt the senate, rob the crown;
To sacrifice old England's glory,
And make her infamous in story.
When such a tempest shook the land,
How could unguarded virtue stand?

395   "With horror, grief, despair the Dean
Beheld the dire destructive scene:
His friends in exile, or the Tower,[5]
Himself within the frown of power;
Pursued by base, envenomed pens,[6]
400 Far to the land of slaves and fens;°   *Ireland*
A servile race in folly nursed,
Who truckle° most, when treated worst.   *cringe obsequiously*

          "By innocence and resolution,
He bore continual persecution;
405 While numbers to preferment[7] rose;
Whose merits were, to be his foes.
When, *ev'n his own familiar*° *friends*   *close*
Intent upon their private ends,
Like renegadoes now he feels,
410 *Against him lifting up their heels*.[8]

          "The Dean did by his pen defeat
An infamous, destructive cheat,[9]
Taught fools their interest to know,

1. James Butler (1665–1745), second Earl of Ormonde, succeeded Marlborough as commander in chief of the allied forces in 1712.
2. In the height of the quarrel between the ministers, the Queen [Anne] died [Swift's note].
3. When Queen Anne died, the Whigs were restored to power, "which they exercised with the utmost rage and revenge" [Swift's note]. Swift initially feared for his own safety, and considered emigrating to the island of Guernsey.
4. Alluding to the establishment of Scottish Presbyterianism in 1643, which Swift (as an Anglican) regretted.
5. The Tower of London, where convicted (or suspected) traitors were held.
6. Upon the Queen's death, the Dean returned to live in

Dublin . . . numberless libels were writ against him in England, as a Jacobite; he was insulted in the street, and at nights was forced to be attended by his servants armed [Swift's note].
7. Places at the Court or in the church hierarchy, especially bishoprics.
8. From Psalm 41.9: "Yea, mine own familiar friend, in whom I trusted, which did eat of my bread, hath lifted up his heel against me."
9. One Wood, a Hardware-man from England, had a patent for coining copper halfpence in Ireland, to the sum of £108,000, which in the consequence, must leave the kingdom without gold or silver [Swift's note]. Swift responded with *The Drapier's Letters* (1724–1725).

And gave them arms to ward the blow.°   *defend themselves*
415   Envy hath owned it was his doing
      To save that helpless land from ruin,
      While they who at the steerage[1] stood,
      And reaped the profit, sought his blood.

      "To save them from their evil fate,
420   In him was held a crime of state.
      A wicked monster on the bench,[2]
      Whose fury blood could never quench;
      As vile and profligate a villain,
      As modern Scroggs, or old Tresilian;[3]
425   Who long all justice had discarded,
      Nor feared he God, nor man regarded;[4]
      Vowed on the Dean his rage to vent,
      And make him of his zeal repent;
      But heaven his innocence defends,
430   The grateful people stand his friends;
      Not strains of law, nor judges' frown,
      Nor topics° brought to please the crown,   *charges*
      Nor witness hired, nor jury picked,
      Prevail to bring him in convict.

435   "In exile[5] with a steady heart,
      He spent his life's declining part;
      Where folly, pride, and faction sway,
      Remote from St. John, Pope, and Gay.

           "His friendship there to few confined,
440   Were always of the middling kind:[6]
      No fools of rank, a mongrel breed,
      Who fain would pass for lords indeed:
      Where titles give no right or power,
      And peerage is a withered flower,[7]
445   He would have held it a disgrace,
      If such a wretch had known his face.
      On rural squires, that kingdom's bane,
      He vented oft his wrath in vain:
      Biennial squires,[8] to market brought,

1. The helm (of the ship of state).
2. One Whitshed was then Chief Justice: he had some years before prosecuted a printer for a pamphlet writ by the Dean, to persuade the people of Ireland to wear their own manufactures. . . . He sat as Judge afterwards on the trial of the printer of the Drapier's Fourth Letter; but the Jury, against all he could say or swear, threw out the Bill [Swift's note].
3. Scroggs was Chief Justice under King Charles the Second: his judgment always varied in State trials, according to directions from the [royal] Court. Tresilian was a wicked Judge, hanged above three hundred years ago [Swift's note].
4. Cf. Luke 18.2: "There was in a city a judge, which feared not God, neither regarded man."
5. In Ireland, which he had reason to call a place of exile;

to which country nothing could have driven him, but the Queen's death, who had determined to fix him in England [Swift's note].
6. The Dean was not acquainted with one single Lord spiritual or temporal. He only conversed with private gentlemen of the clergy or laity, and but a small number of either [Swift's note]; not entirely true.
7. The peers of Ireland lost a great part of their jurisdiction by one single Act [of 1720], and tamely submitted to this infamous mark of slavery without the least resentment, or remonstrance [Swift's note].
8. The Parliament (as they call it) in Ireland meet but once in two years; and after giving five times more than they can afford, return home to reimburse themselves by all country jobs and oppressions, of which some few only are here mentioned [Swift's note].

450 Who sell their souls and votes for naught;
     The nation stripped, go joyful back,
     To rob the church, their tenants rack,⁹
     Go snacks° with thieves and rapparees,¹   *divide the spoils*
     And keep the peace,² to pick up fees:
455 In every job³ to have a share,
     A jail or barrack⁴ to repair;
     And turn the tax for public roads
     Commodious to their own abodes.⁵

       "Perhaps I may allow the Dean
460 Had too much satire in his vein;
     And seemed determined not to starve it,
     Because no age could more deserve it.
     Yet, malice never was his aim;
     He lashed the vice but spared the name.⁶
465 No individual could resent,
     Where thousands equally were meant.
     His satire points at no defect,
     But what all mortals may correct;
     For he abhorred that senseless tribe,
470 Who call it humor when they jibe;
     He spared a hump or crooked nose,
     Whose owners set not up for beaux.
     True, genuine dullness moved his pity,
     Unless it offered to be witty.
475 Those who their ignorance confessed,
     He ne'er offended with a jest;
     But laughed to hear an idiot quote,
     A verse from Horace, learned by rote.

       "He knew an hundred pleasant stories,
480 With all the turns of Whigs and Tories:
     Was cheerful to his dying day,
     And friends would let him have his way.

       "He gave the little wealth he had
     To build a house for fools and mad:⁷
485 And showed by one satiric touch,
     No nation wanted it so much:
     That kingdom he hath left his debtor,
     I wish it soon may have a better."

1731–1732   1739

---

9. I.e., torture by extortionate rent; "rack-rent" was an
excessive rent nearly equal to the full value of the land.
1. The highwaymen in Ireland are, since the late wars
there, usually called rapparees, which was a name given
to those Irish soldiers who in small parties used, at that
time, to plunder the Protestants [Swift's note].
2. Act as magistrates.
3. Implying a business racket.
4. The army in Ireland is lodged in barracks, the building
and repairing whereof, and other charges, have cost a

prodigious sum to that unhappy kingdom [Swift's note].
5. There were complaints that the new system of public
turnpike roads, then being established in England and in
Ireland, was manipulated by estate owners so that the
roads ran directly to their own properties.
6. Swift is being ironic, since the poem explicitly identifies many targets of his satire.
7. In his will, Swift made a large bequest to build a mental
institution (the first in Ireland), St. Patrick's Hospital,
which was opened in 1757.

Journal to Stella

In 1710, Swift was sent from Dublin to London by his patron, Archbishop King, with an important commission—to petition the Queen's Bounty (via the government and the Court) for the remission of the Irish "first fruits," the British monarch's tax on the revenues of clergymen in the Church of Ireland. Swift saw the campaign to repeal the "first fruits"—and his contribution to its success—as his passport to fame and preferment. Though Swift did not yet realize it, these were to be the greatest years of his career, a time when he routinely mixed with the most powerful men of his day, when he was courted for his considerable influence, and when he established himself as the most brilliant and successful of the Tory pamphleteers. He was heavily involved in the intricacies of party politics on his country's behalf and for his own advancement; his prospects for success on both fronts were highly promising. Swift never intended to publish the diary-like letters he wrote to his beloved Esther Johnson and her companion, Rebecca Dingley, during the first three years of his extended sojourn in London from 1710 to 1714. He wrote them, as Virginia Woolf keenly observed in *The Common Reader*, because "the reserved, the powerful, the admired, have the most need of such a refuge." After Esther Johnson's death in 1728, Swift preserved this highly personal "journal" probably both for sentimental reasons and for its historical importance, since it provided a unique insider's view of political affairs and Court intrigues—in addition to social gossip and immediate reactions to important public events—in the final years of Queen Anne's reign. Some of these letters were published in the 1750s and 1760s, in collections of Swift's correspondence and works; the entire sequence first appeared, as *Dr. Swift's Journal to Stella*, in 1784.

from Journal to Stella

from *Letter 10*

[SATURDAY]   London, Nov. 25, 1710

I'll tell you something that's plaguy[1] silly: I had forgot to say on the 23d in my last, where I dined, and because I had done it constantly, I thought it was a great omission, and was going to interline it;[2] but at last the silliness of it made me cry, "Pshaw," and I let it alone. I was today to see the Parliament meet; but only saw a great crowd: and Ford[3] and I went to see the tombs at Westminster,[4] and sauntered so long I was forced to go to an eating house for my dinner. Bromley is chosen speaker,[5] *nemine contradicente:*[6] Do you understand those two words? And Pompey, Colonel Hill's[7] black, designs to stand speaker for the footmen.[8] I am engaged to use my interest for him, and have spoken to Patrick[9] to get him some votes. We are now all impatient for the Queen's speech, what she will say about removing the ministry, &c.[1] I have got a cold, and I don't know how; but got it I have, and am hoarse: I don't know whether it will grow better or worse. What's that to you? I won't answer your letter

---

1. Annoyingly, exceedingly.
2. Write it in between the lines he had already written.
3. Charles Ford (1682–1741), an Anglo-Irish friend of Swift's living in London, with whom he corresponded (on and off) for nearly 30 years.
4. Royalty and other members of the aristocracy were buried at Westminster Abbey.
5. William Bromley (1664–1732), high churchman and Member of Parliament for Oxford University from 1702, was chosen speaker of the House of Commons on this day.
6. Nobody voting against.
7. John Hill (d. 1735), major general; like his sister Mrs. Masham, Hill was a favorite of Queen Anne.

8. The footmen to Members of Parliament sometimes held their own unofficial "parliament" and debated the issues of the day while their masters were legislating inside the House.
9. Swift's manservant.
1. Following the trial of the high churchman Dr. Henry Sacheverell (c. 1674–1724) in 1710 for a contentious sermon he had given, there was such strong feeling against the Whig Ministry's apparent oppression of the established Church that the Queen dismissed the Ministry, dissolving Parliament on 21 September 1710. When the new Parliament opened in November, a Tory administration was given control of the government.

to-night. I'll keep you a little longer in suspense: I can't send it. Your mother's cakes are very good, and one of them serves me for a breakfast, and so I'll go sleep like a good boy.

26. I have got a cruel cold, and stayed within all this day in my nightgown, and dined on six pennyworth of victuals, and read and writ, and was denied to everybody.[2] Dr. Raymond[3] called often, and I was denied; and at last, when I was weary, I let him come up, and asked him, without consequence, "How Patrick denied me, and whether he had the art of it?" So by this means he shall be used to have me denied to him;[4] otherwise he would be a plaguy trouble and hindrance to me: he has sat with me two hours, and drank a pint of ale cost me five pence, and smoked his pipe, and 'tis now past eleven that he is just gone. Well, my eighth is with you now, young women, and your seventh to me is somewhere in a postboy's bag; and so go to your gang of Deans, and Stoytes, and Walls, and lose your money;[5] go, sauce-boxes, and so goodnight and be happy, dear rogues. Oh, but your box was sent to Dr. Hawkshaw by Sterne, and you will have it with Hawkshaw, and spectacles, &c. &c.

27.[6] To-day Mr. Harley[7] met me in the court of requests,[8] and whispered me to dine with him. At dinner I told him what those bishops had done, and the difficulty I was under.[9] He bid me never trouble myself; he would tell the Duke of Ormonde the business was done, and that he need not concern himself about it. So now I am easy, and they may hang themselves for a parcel of insolent ungrateful rascals. I suppose I told you in my last, how they sent an address to the Duke of Ormonde, and a letter to Southwell, to call on me for the papers, after the thing was over, but they had not received my letter; though the Archbishop might, by what I writ to him, have expected it would be done. Well, there's an end of that; and in a little time the Queen will send them notice, &c. And so the methods will be settled; and then I shall think of returning, although the baseness of those bishops makes me love Ireland less than I did.

28. Lord Halifax[1] sent to invite me to dinner, where I stayed till six, and crossed him in all his Whig talk, and made him often come over to me.[2] I know he makes court to the new men, although he affects to talk like a Whig. I had a letter today from the Bishop of Clogher;[3] but I writ to him lately, that I would obey his com-

---

2. I.e., visitors were not allowed to see him.

3. Rev. Anthony Raymond (c. 1675–1726), rector of Trim, and neighbor of Swift's.

4. I.e., Swift let Raymond know that he would not always be admitted on demand.

5. Stella played cards—and often gambled for small stakes—with a circle of friends, including Dean Sterne, Alderman Stoyte, his wife and her sister, and Archdeacon Walls and his wife.

6. Parliament was formally opened by the queen on this day (Swift does not mention it).

7. Swift cultivated friendships with Robert Harley (1661–1724), first Earl of Oxford, and Henry St. John, first Viscount Bolingbroke (1678–1751), as it became clear that they would rule the new Tory Ministry, in the hope, no doubt, of various favors.

8. A court of equity, actually abolished in 1641; it seems the room at Whitehall retained its name long after losing its function.

9. Swift was concerned to receive due recognition for his part in the success of the "first fruits" scheme: Harley had by this time told Swift that the Queen had accepted his proposal, but enjoined him to secrecy until it could be

made public. While Harley eventually allowed Swift to report some limited success to Archbishop King, the politician procrastinated on making the matter more widely known. The Queen, meanwhile, appointed a new Governor of Ireland (Ormonde), and the Irish bishops who had commissioned Swift naturally felt it would be politically expedient to hand Swift's petition over to the Secretary of State for Ireland, Edward Southwell, especially since they still saw Swift as a Whig. When the letter patent was eventually granted, in July 1711 (though dated 17 February 1711), no mention of Swift was made.

1. Charles Montague, Earl of Halifax (1661–1715), a senior Whig statesman; on 2 October 1710, Swift noted in the *Journal* that he had refused to join Halifax in toasting the revival of Whig fortunes: "I told him he was the only Whig in England I loved."

2. I.e., Swift argued against Halifax, and persuaded him to his point of view.

3. St. George Ashe (c. 1658–1718), successively Bishop of Cloyne, of Clogher, and of Derry, and Swift's tutor at Trinity College, Dublin; obviously he was writing to Swift about the "first fruits" question.

mands to the Duke of Ormonde. He says I bid him read the *London Shaver*, and that
you both swore it was *Shaver*, and not *Shower*.[4] You all lie, and you are puppies, and
can't read Presto's hand.[5] The Bishop is out entirely in his conjectures of my share in
the *Tatlers*.[6]—I have other things to mind, and of much greater importance,[7] else I
have little to do to be acquainted with a new ministry, who consider me a little more
than Irish bishops do.

29. Now for your saucy good dear letter: let me see, what does it say? Come
then. I dined today with Ford, and went home early; he debauched me to his chamber again with a bottle of wine till twelve: so goodnight. I can't write an answer now,
you rogues.

30. Today I have been visiting, which I had long neglected; and I dined with
Mrs. Barton[8] alone; and sauntered at the coffeehouse till past eight, and have been
busy till eleven, and now I'll answer your letter, sauce-box. Well, let me see now
again. My wax candle's almost out, but however I'll begin. Well then, don't be so
tedious, Mr. Presto; what can you say to MD's letter?[9] Make haste, have done with
your preambles—Why, I say I am glad you are so often abroad; your mother thinks it
is want of exercise hurts you, and so do I. (She called here tonight, but I was not
within, that's by the bye.) Sure you don't deceive me, Stella, when you say you are in
better health than you were these three weeks; for Dr. Raymond told me yesterday,
that Smyth[1] of the Blind Quay had been telling Mr. Leigh, that he left you extremely ill; and in short, spoke so, that he almost put poor Leigh into tears, and would have
made me run distracted; though your letter is dated the 11th instant, and I saw
Smyth in the city above a fortnight ago, as I passed by in a coach. Pray, pray, don't
write, Stella, until you are mighty, mighty, mighty, mighty well in your eyes, and are
sure it won't do you the least hurt. Or come, I'll tell you what; you, mistress Stella,
shall write your share at five or six sittings, one sitting a day; and then comes Dingley
all together, and then Stella a little crumb towards the end, to let us see she remembers Presto; and then conclude with something handsome and genteel, as your most
humblecumdumble, or, &c. O Lord! does Patrick write word of my not coming till
spring? Insolent man! he know my secrets? No; as my Lord Mayor said, No; if I
thought my shirt knew, &c.[2] Faith, I will come as soon as it is any way proper for me
to come; but, to say the truth, I am at present a little involved with the present ministry in some certain things (which I tell you as a secret) and soon as ever I can clear
my hands, I will stay no longer: for I hope the first-fruit business will be soon over in
all its forms. But, to say the truth, the present ministry have a difficult task, and want
me, &c. Perhaps they may be just as grateful as others: but, according to the best
judgment I have, they are pursuing the true interest of the public; and therefore I am

4. Stella and Mrs. Dingley have persuaded the bishop
that he should read "shaver" for "shower" in Swift's
Description of a City Shower; the verses first appeared in
the *Tatler*, No. 238 (17 October 1710). Swift was
extremely proud of this poem; he mentions it in several
letters to Stella.

5. After the Duchess of Shrewsbury called him "Dr.
Presto" (a pun on "Swift"), Swift adopted this name
throughout his *Journal*.

6. The *Tatler*, founded by Swift's sometime friend
Richard Steele, ran from 12 April 1709 to 2 January
1711; Swift contributed to several early numbers.

7. At the request of Harley, Swift took control of the
Examiner between November 1710 and June 1711 (Nos.

14–46), a weekly Tory periodical founded by Bolingbroke in August 1710.

8. Catherine Barton (1679–1740), niece of Sir Isaac
Newton, and a noted beauty who, despite her Whig affil-
iations and argumentative ability, remained one of
Swift's favorites.

9. MD/Md (my dears?) refers to both Esther Johnson and
Rebecca Dingley, though Swift is chiefly directing his
thoughts to Esther.

1. "Smyth" may be John Smith, one of Swift's booksellers.

2. Patrick is not as close to Swift as his shirt, and even his
shirt does not know.

glad to contribute what is in my power. For God's sake, not a word of this to any alive.—Your chancellor?[3] Why, madam, I can tell you he has been dead this fortnight. Faith, I could hardly forbear our little language about a nasty dead chancellor, as you may see by the blot.[4] Ploughing? A pox plough them; they'll plough me to nothing. But have you got your money, both the ten pounds? How durst he pay you the second so soon? Pray be good huswives.—Aye, well, and Joe;[5] why, I had a letter lately from Joe, desiring I would take some care of their poor town, who, he says, will lose their liberties. To which I desired Dr. Raymond would return answer; that the town had behaved themselves so ill to me, so little regarded the advice I gave them, and disagreed so much among themselves, that I was resolved never to have more to do with them; but that whatever personal kindness I could do to Joe, should be done. Pray, when you happen to see Joe, tell him this, lest Raymond should have blundered or forgotten.—Poor Mrs. Wesley—Why these poligyes[6] for being abroad?[7] Why should you be at home at all, until Stella is quite well?—So, here is mistress Stella again with her two eggs, &c. My *Shower* admired with you; why, the Bishop of Clogher says, he has seen something of mine of the same sort, better than the *Shower*. I suppose he means *The Morning*;[8] but it is not half so good. I want your judgment of things, and not your country's. How does MD like it? and do they taste it *all*? &c.[9] I am glad Dean Bolton has paid the twenty pounds.[1] Why should not I chide the Bishop of Clogher for writing to the Archbishop of Cashel, without sending the letter first to me?[2] It does not signify a ——; for he has no credit at court. Stuff—they are all puppies. I'll break your head in good earnest, young woman, for your nasty jest about Mrs. Barton. Unlucky sluttikin, what a word is there? Faith, I was thinking yesterday, when I was with her, whether she could break them or no,[3] and it quite spoiled my imagination. Mrs. Walls, does Stella win as she pretends? No indeed, *doctor*; she loses always, and will play so *ventursomely*, how can she win? See here now; an't you an impudent lying slut? Do, open Domville's[4] letter; what does it signify, if you have a mind? Yes, faith, you write smartly with your eyes shut; all was well but the w. See how I can do it; *Madam Stella, your humble servant.*[5] O, but one may look whether one goes crooked or no, and so write on. I'll tell you what you may do; you may write with your eyes half shut, just as when one is going to sleep: I have done so for two or three lines now; 'tis but just seeing enough to go straight.—Now, madam Dingley, I think I bid you tell Mr. Walls, that in case there be occasion, I will serve

3. Richard Freeman, a Whig, appointed Lord Chancellor of Ireland in 1707, apparently on the basis of his politics, not his abilities.

4. To make this intelligible, it is necessary to observe, that the words "this fortnight" in the preceding sentence, were first written in what he calls their little language, and afterwards scratched out and written plain. It must be confessed this little language, which passed current between Swift and Stella, had occasioned infinite trouble in the revisal of theses papers [Deane Swift's note]. In 1768, Deane Swift (1706–1783), the son of Swift's cousin and a favorite relation of Jonathan Swift published a selection of his famous relation's correspondence with his own annotations, including some of the letters to Esther Johnson and Rebecca Dingley that comprise the *Journal*.

5. Joseph Beaumont (d. 1731), a linen draper from Trim and Swift's business agent.

6. Apologies.

7. Leaving the house.

8. *A Description of the Morning*, which appeared in the *Tatler*, No. 9 (30 April 1709).

9. I.e., do they understand and appreciate it?

1. John Bolton (c. 1656–1724), Dean of Derry.

2. William Palliser (1646–1726), Archbishop of Cashel since 1694, and a signatory of Swift's commission to petition on behalf of the Irish "first fruits" proposal.

3. This jest is lost, whatever it was, for want of MD's letter [Deane Swift's note].

4. William Domville (born c. 1686), Irishman living in London, and grandson of the attorney general, whom Swift called "perfectly as fine a gentleman as I know" (*Journal*, 27 November 1711).

5. Here he writ with his eyes shut, and the writing is somewhat crooked, although as well in other respects as if his eyes had been open [Deane Swift's note]. Swift had expressed concern about Stella straining her eyes in an earlier letter (7), and suggested that "if you will write, shut your eyes, and write just a line, and no more."

his friend as far as I can; but I hope there will be none.[6] Yet I believe you will have a new Parliament; but I care not whether you have or no a better.[7] You are mistaken in all your conjectures about the *Tatlers*. I have given him one or two hints, and you have heard me talk about the *Shilling*.[8] Faith, these answering letters are very long ones: you have taken up almost the room of a week in journals; and I'll tell you what, I saw fellows wearing crosses today,[9] and I wondered what was the matter; but just this minute I recollect it is little Presto's birthday;[1] and I was resolved these three days to remember it when it came, but could not. Pray, drink my health today at dinner; do, you rogues. Do you like *Sid Hamet's Rod?*[2] Do you understand it all? Well, now at last I have done with your letter, and so I'll lay me down to sleep, and about fair maids; and I hope merry maids all. * * *

1768

Gulliver's Travels

Travels into Several Remote Nations of the World. In Four Parts. By Lemuel Gulliver—better known as *Gulliver's Travels*—was first published in late October 1726 and enjoyed instant success. One contemporary observer noted that "several thousands sold in a week," and Swift's London friends wrote to him in Dublin to say that everyone was reading and talking about Gulliver (see *Companion Reading* on page 2448). Readers continue to be fascinated by Swift's masterpiece: since 1945, more than 500 books and scholarly articles have been devoted to *Gulliver's Travels*. Variously classified as an early novel, an imaginary voyage, a moral and political allegory, and even a children's story, Lemuel Gulliver's four journeys, representing the four directions of the globe, comprise a survey of the human condition: a comic, ironic, and sometimes harrowing answer to the question, "What does it mean to be a human being?"

In the first voyage, the diminutive citizens of Lilliput represent human small-mindedness and petty ambitions. Filled with self-importance, the Lilliputians are cruel, treacherous, malicious, and destructive. The perspective is reversed in the second voyage to Brobdingnag, land of giants, where Gulliver has the stature of a Lilliputian. He is humbled by his own helplessness and, finding the huge bodies of the Brobdingnagians grotesque, he realizes how repulsive the Lilliputians must have found him. When Gulliver gives the wise king an account of the political affairs of England—which manifest hypocrisy, avarice, and hatred—the enlightened monarch concludes that most of the country's inhabitants must be "the most pernicious race of little odious vermin that Nature ever suffered to crawl upon the surface of the earth." In the third voyage (which was written last), Gulliver visits the flying island of Laputa and the metropolis of Lagado, on an adjacent continent, where he encounters the misuse of human reason. In Laputa, those who are supposedly "wise" lack all common sense and practical ability; at Lagado, the Academy of Projectors is staffed by professors who waste both money and intelligence on absurd endeavors. Swift aims his satire at so-called intellectuals—especially the "virtuosi," or amateur scientists of the Royal Society—who live in the world of their own speculations and so fail to use their gifts for the common good. Throughout *Gulliver's Travels* that which is admirable is held up to expose corruption in the reader's world, and that which is

---

6. Rev. Thomas Wall's friend was Captain John Pratt (born c. 1670), Deputy Vice-Treasurer of Ireland and younger brother of Benjamin Pratt, Provost of Trinity College, Dublin; his place in Parliament was in jeopardy. He later embezzled large sums of Swift's (and Ireland's) cash.

7. The Irish House of Commons was adjourned on 28

August 1710 and reassembled on 9 July 1711.

8. Discussion of John Philips's *The Splendid Shilling* (1701) appeared in the *Tatler*, No. 249 (11 November 1710).

9. For St. Andrew's Day.

1. I.e., his own birthday.

2. Swift's *The Virtues of Sid Hamet the Magician's Rod* (1710), a satire on Sidney Godolphin.

deplorable is identified with the institutions and practices associated with contemporary Europe, particularly Britain.

Gulliver's fourth voyage (printed in its entirety below) finds him on the island of the Houyhnhnms, horses endowed with reason, whose highly rational and well-ordered (though emotionally sterile) society is contrasted with the violence, selfishness, and brutality of the Yahoos, irrational beasts who bear a disconcerting resemblance to humans. In his foolish pride, Gulliver believes that he can escape the human condition and live as a stoical Houyhnhnm, even when he returns to his family in England. Of course, Gulliver is neither Houyhnhnm nor Yahoo, but a man. His time in Houyhnhnm-land does not teach him to be more rational or compassionate, but makes him more foolish, derelict in his duties as husband, father, and citizen. Instead of seeking to become a better man, Gulliver strives to become what he is not— with results that are both tragic and farcical. Although the poet Edward Young charged Swift with having "blasphemed a nature little lower than that of the angels" in satirizing the follies of humankind, *Gulliver's Travels* reveals the Dean of Saint Patrick's to be more a humanist than a misanthrope. With brilliantly modulated ironic self-awareness, Swift's painful comedy of exposure to the truth of human frailty demonstrates that there is no room for the distortions of human pride in a world where our practices are so evidently at variance with our principles. Swift advances no program of social reform, but provokes a new recognition—literally, a rethinking—of our own humanity.

from Gulliver's Travels
from Part 3. A Voyage to Laputa
CHAPTER 5

The author permitted to see the grand Academy of Lagado. The Academy largely[1] described. The arts wherein the professors employ themselves.

This Academy is not an entire single building, but a continuation of several houses on both sides of a street, which growing waste,[2] was purchased and applied to that use.

I was received very kindly by the Warden, and went for many days to the Academy. Every room has in it one or more projectors,[3] and I believe I could not be[4] in fewer than five hundred rooms.

The first man I saw was of a meager aspect, with sooty hands and face, his hair and beard long, ragged and singed in several places. His clothes, shirt, and skin were all of the same color. He had been eight years upon a project for extracting sunbeams out of cucumbers,[5] which were to be put into vials hermetically sealed, and let out to warm the air in raw, inclement summers. He told me, he did not doubt in eight years more, that he should be able to supply the Governor's gardens with sunshine at a reasonable rate; but he complained that his stock was low, and entreated me to give him something as an encouragement to ingenuity,[6] especially since this had been a very dear season for cucumbers. I made him a small present, for my Lord[7] had furnished

1. In general. The academy is a satire of the Royal Society, founded in 1662 for the purpose of scientific experimentation (see Perspectives: The Royal Society and the New Science, page 2039). Though many of its members made major contributions to science, the Society had a reputation for bizarre speculation. Swift had visited the Society in 1710 and here parodies actual experiments recorded in its *Philosophical Transactions;* he is also parodying the description of "Solomon's House," an academy of science in Francis Bacon's *New Atlantis* (1626).

2. Falling into disuse.
3. Those people undertaking the project.
4. Could not have been.
5. Stephen Hales (1677–1761), English botanist and physiologist, had recently investigated sunlight's agency in plant respiration. This and other studies were published in his *Vegetable Staticks* (1726).
6. His investigative powers.
7. The warden of the Academy.

me with money on purpose, because he knew their practice of begging from all who go to see them.

I went into another chamber, but was ready to hasten back, being almost overcome with a horrible stink. My conductor pressed me forward, conjuring me in a whisper to give no offense, which would be highly resented, and therefore I durst not so much as stop my nose. The projector of this cell was the most ancient student of the Academy. His face and beard were of a pale yellow; his hands and clothes daubed over with filth. When I was presented to him, he gave me a very close embrace (a compliment I could well have excused). His employment from his first coming into the Academy was an operation to reduce human excrement to its original food, by separating the several parts, removing the tincture which it receives from the gall, making the odor exhale, and scumming off the saliva. He had a weekly allowance from the Society of a vessel filled with human ordure,[8] about the bigness of a Bristol barrel.[9]

I saw another at work to calcine[1] ice into gunpowder, who likewise showed me a treatise he had written concerning the malleability of fire,[2] which he intended to publish.

There was a most ingenious architect who had contrived a new method for building houses, by beginning at the roof and working downwards to the foundation, which he justified to me by the like practice of those two prudent insects, the bee and the spider.

There was a man born blind, who had several apprentices in his own condition: their employment was to mix colors for painters, which their master taught them to distinguish by feeling and smelling.[3] It was indeed my misfortune to find them at that time not very perfect in their lessons, and the professor himself happened to be generally mistaken: this artist is much encouraged and esteemed by the whole fraternity.

In another apartment I was highly pleased with a projector, who had found a device of ploughing the ground with hogs, to save the charges of ploughs, cattle, and labor. The method is this; in an acre of ground you bury, at six inches distance, and eight deep, a quantity of acorns, dates, chestnuts, and other mast[4] or vegetables whereof these animals are fondest: then you drive six hundred or more of them into the field, where in a few days they will root up the whole ground in search of their food, and make it fit for sowing, at the same time manuring it with their dung; it is true upon experiment they found the charge and trouble very great, and they had little or no crop. However, it is not doubted that this invention may be capable of great improvement.

I went into another room, where the walls and ceiling were all hung round with cobwebs, except a narrow passage for the artist[5] to go in and out. At my entrance he called aloud to me not to disturb his webs. He lamented the fatal mistake the world had been so long in of using silkworms, while we had such plenty of domestic insects, who infinitely excelled the former, because they understood how to weave as well as spin. And he proposed farther, that by employing spiders, the charge[6] of dyeing silks

8. Excrement.
9. A medium-size barrel, holding about 37 gallons.
1. Desiccate.
2. Cf. Rabelais, *Gargantua and Pantagruel* (1532–1564), bk. 5, ch. 22: "Others were cutting fire with a knife, and drawing water up in a net."
3. Based on Robert Boyle's account in *Experiments and Observations Upon Colors* (1665), of a blind man who

could distinguish colors.
4. Nuts.
5. Modeled on both the Frenchman M. Bon, who believed silk could be made from cobwebs, and Dr. Wall, who suggested that the excreta of ants fed on plant sap could be used as dye; both suggestions were published in the *Transactions of the Royal Society*.
6. Expense.

would be wholly saved, whereof I was fully convinced when he showed me a vast number of flies most beautifully colored, wherewith he fed his spiders, assuring us, that the webs would take a tincture from them; and as he had them of all hues, he hoped to fit everybody's fancy, as soon as he could find proper food for the flies, of certain gums, oils, and other glutinous matter to give a strength and consistence to the threads.

There was an astronomer who had undertaken to place a sundial upon the great weathercock on the Town House,[7] by adjusting the annual and diurnal motions of the earth and sun, so as to answer and coincide with all accidental turnings of the wind.

I was complaining of a small fit of the colic, upon which my conductor led me into a room, where a great physician resided, who was famous for curing that disease by contrary operations from the same instrument. He had a large pair of bellows with a long slender muzzle of ivory. This he conveyed eight inches up the anus, and drawing in the wind, he affirmed he could make the guts as lank as a dried bladder. But when the disease was more stubborn and violent, he let in the muzzle while the bellows was full of wind, which he discharged into the body of the patient, then withdrew the instrument to replenish it, clapping his thumb strongly against the orifice of the fundament; and this being repeated three or four times, the adventitious wind would rush out, bringing the noxious along with it (like water put into a pump) and the patient recover. I saw him try both experiments upon a dog, but could not discern any effect from the former. After the latter, the animal was ready to burst, and made so violent a discharge, as was very offensive to me and my companions. The dog died on the spot, and we left the doctor endeavoring to recover him by the same operation.[8]

I visited many other apartments, but shall not trouble my reader with all the curiosities I observed, being studious of brevity.

I had hitherto seen only one side of the Academy, the other being appropriated to the advancers of speculative learning, of whom I shall say something when I have mentioned one illustrious person more, who is called among them *the universal artist.*[9] He told us he had been thirty years employing his thoughts for the improvement of human life. He had two large rooms full of wonderful curiosities, and fifty men at work. Some were condensing air into a dry, tangible substance, by extracting the niter,[1] and letting the aqueous or fluid particles percolate; others softening marble for pillows and pincushions; others petrifying the hoofs of a living horse to preserve them from foundering. The artist himself was at that time busy upon two great designs: the first, to sow land with chaff, wherein he affirmed the true seminal virtue to be contained, as he demonstrated by several experiments which I was not skillful enough to comprehend. The other was, by a certain composition of gums, minerals, and vegetables outwardly applied, to prevent the growth of wool upon two young lambs; and he hoped in a reasonable time to propagate the breed of naked sheep all over the kingdom.

We crossed a walk to the other part of the Academy, where, as I have already said, the projectors in speculative learning resided.

The first professor I saw was in a very large room, with forty pupils about him. After salutation, observing me to look earnestly upon a frame, which took up the

---

7. Town Hall.
8. Robert Hooke (1635–1703) produced artificial respiration in a dog (1667) by blowing air into its windpipe with a pair of bellows.

9. Possibly Robert Boyle (1627–1691), whose many scientific experiments investigated the nature of air, marble, petrifaction, agriculture, and sheep breeding.
1. Air was believed to contain nitrous matter.

greatest part of both the length and breadth of the room, he said perhaps I might wonder to see him employed in a project for improving speculative knowledge by practical and mechanical operations. But the world would soon be sensible[2] of its usefulness, and he flattered himself that a more noble exalted thought never sprang in any other man's head. Everyone knew how laborious the usual method is of attaining to arts and sciences; whereas by his contrivance, the most ignorant person at a reasonable charge, and with a little bodily labor, may write books in philosophy, poetry, politics, law, mathematics, and theology, without the least assistance from genius or study. He then led me to the frame, about the sides whereof all his pupils stood in ranks. It was twenty foot square, placed in the middle of the room. The superficies[3] was composed of several bits of wood, about the bigness of a die,[4] but some larger than others. They were all linked together by slender wires. These bits of wood were covered on every square with papers pasted on them, and on these papers were written all the words of their language in their several moods, tenses, and declensions, but without any order. The professor then desired me to observe, for he was going to set his engine[5] at work. The pupils at his command took each of them hold of an iron handle, whereof there were forty fixed round the edges of the frame, and giving them a sudden turn, the whole disposition of the words was entirely changed. He then commanded six and thirty of the lads to read the several lines softly as they appeared upon the frame; and where they found three or four words together that might make part of a sentence, they dictated to the four remaining boys who were scribes. This work was repeated three or four times, and at every turn the engine was so contrived, that the words shifted into new places, as the square bits of wood moved upside down.

Six hours a day the young students were employed in this labor, and the professor showed me several volumes in large folio already collected, of broken sentences, which he intended to piece together, and out of those rich materials to give the world a complete body of all arts and sciences; which however might be still improved, and much expedited, if the public would raise a fund for making and employing five hundred such frames in Lagado, and oblige the managers to contribute in common their several[6] collections.

He assured me, that this invention had employed all his thoughts from his youth, that he had emptied the whole vocabulary into his frame, and made the strictest computation of the general proportion there is in books between the numbers of particles, nouns, and verbs, and other parts of speech.

I made my humblest acknowledgments to this illustrious person for his great communicativeness, and promised if ever I had the good fortune to return to my native country, that I would do him justice, as the sole inventor of this wonderful machine; the form and contrivance of which I desired leave to delineate upon paper as in the figure here annexed. I told him, although it were the custom of our learned in Europe to steal inventions from each other,[7] who had thereby at least this advantage, that it became a controversy which was the right owner, yet I would take such caution, that he should have the honor entire without a rival.

---

2. Aware.
3. Surface.
4. Singular of dice.
5. Machine.
6. Individual.

7. No international patent agreement existed at this time, and the theft of inventions was common as nations competed in developing technology for commercial manufacturing and navigation on the open seas.

We next went to the school of languages, where three professors sat in consultation upon improving that of their own country.[8]

The first project was to shorten discourse by cutting polysyllables into one, and leaving out verbs and participles, because in reality all things imaginable are but nouns.

The other project was a scheme for entirely abolishing all words whatsoever; and this was urged as a great advantage in point of health as well as brevity. For, it is plain, that every word we speak is in some degree a diminution of our lungs by corrosion, and consequently contributes to the shortening of our lives. An expedient was therefore offered, that since words are only names for *things*, it would be more convenient for all men to carry about them such *things* as were necessary to express the particular business they are to discourse on.[9] And this invention would certainly have taken place, to the great ease as well as health of the subject,[1] if the women in conjunction with the vulgar and illiterate had not threatened to raise a rebellion, unless they might be allowed the liberty to speak with their tongues, after the manner of their forefathers; such constant irreconcilable enemies to science are the common people. However, many of the most learned and wise adhere to the new scheme of expressing themselves by *things*, which hath only this inconvenience attending it, that if a man's business be very great, and of various kinds, he must be obliged in proportion to carry a greater bundle of *things* upon his back, unless he can afford one or two strong servants to attend him. I have often beheld two of those sages almost sinking under the weight of their packs, like peddlers among us; who when they met in the streets would lay down their loads, open their sacks, and hold conversation for an hour together; then put up their implements, help each other to resume their burdens, and take their leave.

But for short conversations a man may carry implements in his pockets and under his arms, enough to supply him, and in his house he cannot be at a loss; therefore the room where company meet who practice this art, is full of all *things* ready at hand, requisite to furnish matter for this kind of artificial converse.[2]

Another great advantage proposed by this invention, was that it would serve as a universal language to be understood in all civilized nations, whose goods and utensils are generally of the same kind, or nearly resembling, so that their uses might easily be comprehended. And thus, ambassadors would be qualified to treat with foreign princes or ministers of state, to whose tongues they were utter strangers.

I was at the mathematical school, where the master taught his pupils after a method scarce imaginable to us in Europe. The proposition and demonstration were fairly written on a thin wafer, with ink composed of a cephalic[3] tincture. This the student was to swallow upon a fasting stomach, and for three days following eat noth-

---

8. The first secretary to the Royal Society, Thomas Spratt, in his *History* (1667) of that institution, recommended that such an Academy be founded, as the new style of science writing should strive to describe "so many *things* in an equal number of words." Although Swift burlesques this notion, he himself had published *Proposals for Correcting, Improving and Ascertaining the English Tongue* (1712), in which he suggested that an Academy be established with the aim of preserving culture and "fixing our language for ever."

9. The growth of scientific knowledge about the nature of the material world had encouraged suggestions that language should be made less abstract. In satirizing the projector, Swift alludes to John Locke's theory of language in Book 3 of *An Essay Concerning Human Understanding* (1690), where Locke argues that words stand for things only indirectly.

1. Both the individual practitioner and the people of the nation as a whole.

2. A reference to the Royal Society's attempt to collect one specimen or example of every thing in the world.

3. Of or for the head.

ing but bread and water. As the wafer digested, the tincture mounted to his brain, bearing the proposition along with it. But the success has not hitherto been answerable, partly by some error in the *quantum* or composition, and partly by the perverseness of lads, to whom this bolus[4] is so nauseous that they generally steal aside, and discharge it upwards before it can operate; neither have they been yet persuaded to use so long an abstinence as the prescription requires.

CHAPTER 10

The Luggnaggians commended. A particular description of the Struldbruggs, with many conversations between the author and some eminent persons upon that subject.[1]

The Luggnaggians are a polite and generous people, and although they are not without some share of that pride which is peculiar to all Eastern countries, yet they show themselves courteous to strangers, especially such who are countenanced by the Court. I had many acquaintance among persons of the best fashion, and being always attended by my interpreter, the conversation we had was not disagreeable.

One day in much good company, I was asked by a person of quality, whether I had seen any of their Struldbruggs or Immortals. I said I had not, and desired he would explain to me what he meant by such an appellation applied to a mortal creature. He told me, that sometimes, though very rarely, a child happened to be born in a family with a red circular spot in the forehead, directly over the left eyebrow, which was an infallible mark that it should never die. The spot, as he described it, was about the compass of a silver threepence, but in the course of time grew larger, and changed its color; for at twelve years old it became green, so continued till five and twenty, then turned to a deep blue; at five and forty it grew coal black, and as large as an English shilling, but never admitted any farther alteration. He said these births were so rare, that he did not believe there could be above eleven hundred Struldbruggs of both sexes in the whole kingdom, of which he computed about fifty in the metropolis, and among the rest a young girl born about three years ago. That these productions were not peculiar to any family, but a mere effect of chance, and the children of the Struldbruggs themselves, were equally mortal with the rest of the people.

I freely own myself to have been struck with inexpressible delight upon hearing this account: and the person who gave it me happening to understand the Balnibarbian language, which I spoke very well, I could not forbear breaking out into expressions perhaps a little too extravagant. I cried out as in a rapture: Happy nation where every child hath at least a chance for being immortal! Happy people who enjoy so many living examples of ancient virtue, and have masters ready to instruct them in the wisdom of all former ages! But, happiest beyond all comparison are those excellent Struldbruggs, who being born exempt from that universal calamity of human nature, have their minds free and disengaged, without the weight and depression of spirits caused by the continual apprehension of death. I discovered my admiration[2] that I had not observed any of these illustrious persons at Court, the black spot on

4. Mass of chewed food.
1. In order to return to England, Gulliver sails west on the Pacific from Balnibarbi (the country of which Lagado

is the capital) to Japan, stopping en route at the island of "Luggnagg," where he makes the following observations.
2. Expressed my surprise.

the forehead being so remarkable a distinction, that I could not have easily overlooked it; and it was impossible that his Majesty, a most judicious prince, should not provide himself with a good number of such wise and able counselors. Yet perhaps the virtue of those reverend sages was too strict for the corrupt and libertine manners of a Court. And we often find by experience that young men are too opinionative and volatile to be guided by the sober dictates of their seniors. However, since the King was pleased to allow me access to his royal person, I was resolved upon the very first occasion to deliver my opinion to him on this matter freely, and at large, by the help of my interpreter; and whether he would please to take my advice or no, yet in one thing I was determined, that his Majesty having frequently offered me an establishment in this country, I would with great thankfulness accept the favor, and pass my life here in the conversation of those superior beings the Struldbruggs, if they would please to admit me.

The gentleman to whom I addressed my discourse, because (as I have already observed) he spoke the language of Balnibarbi, said to me with a sort of a smile, which usually ariseth from pity to the ignorant, that he was glad of any occasion to keep me among them, and desired my permission to explain to the company what I had spoke. He did so, and they talked together for some time in their own language, whereof I understood not a syllable, neither could I observe by their countenances what impression my discourse had made on them. After a short silence the same person told me, that his friends and mine (so he thought fit to express himself) were very much pleased with the judicious remarks I had made on the great happiness and advantages of immortal life, and they were desirous to know in a particular manner, what scheme of living I should have formed to myself, if it had fallen to my lot to have been born a Struldbrugg.

I answered, it was easy to be eloquent on so copious and delightful a subject, especially to me who have been often apt to amuse myself with visions of what I should do if I were a king, a general, or a great lord; and upon this very case I had frequently run over the whole system how I should employ myself, and pass the time if I were sure to live for ever.

That, if it had been my good fortune to come into the world a Struldbrugg, as soon as I could discover my own happiness by understanding the difference between life and death, I would first resolve by all arts and methods whatsoever to procure myself riches. In the pursuit of which by thrift and management, I might reasonably expect in about two hundred years, to be the wealthiest man in the kingdom. In the second place, I would from my earliest youth apply myself to the study of arts and sciences, by which I should arrive in time to excel all others in learning. Lastly I would carefully record every action and event of consequence that happened in the public,[3] impartially draw the characters of the several successions of princes, and great ministers of state, with my own observations on every point. I would exactly set down the several changes in customs, language, fashions of dress, diet and diversions. By all which acquirements, I should be a living treasury of knowledge and wisdom, and certainly become the oracle of the nation.

I would never marry after threescore, but live in an hospitable manner, yet still on the saving side. I would entertain myself in forming and directing the minds of hopeful young men, by convincing them from my own remembrance, experience,

3. The state (from Latin *res publica*, the "public thing," from which derives the word *republic*).

and observation, fortified by numerous examples, of the usefulness of virtue in public and private life. But, my choice and constant companions should be a set of my own immortal brotherhood, among whom I would elect a dozen from the most ancient down to my own contemporaries. Where any of these wanted[4] fortunes, I would provide them with convenient lodges round my own estate, and have some of them always at my table, only mingling a few of the most valuable among you mortals, whom length of time would harden me to lose with little or no reluctance, and treat your posterity after the same manner, just as a man diverts himself with the annual succession of pinks and tulips in his garden, without regretting the loss of those which withered the preceding year.

These Struldbruggs and I would mutually communicate our observations and memorials through the course of time, remark the several gradations by which corruption steals into the world, and oppose it in every step, by giving perpetual warning and instruction to mankind; which, added to the strong influence of our own example, would probably prevent that continual degeneracy of human nature so justly complained of in all ages.

Add to all this, the pleasure of seeing the various revolutions of states and empires, the changes in the lower and upper world,[5] ancient cities in ruins, and obscure villages become the seats of kings. Famous rivers lessening into shallow brooks, the ocean leaving one coast dry, and overwhelming another, the discovery of many countries yet unknown. Barbarity overrunning the politest nations, and the most barbarous becoming civilized. I should then see the discovery of the longitude, the perpetual motion, the universal medicine,[6] and many other great inventions brought to the utmost perfection.

What wonderful discoveries should we make in astronomy, by outliving and confirming our own predictions, by observing the progress and returns of comets, with the changes of motion in the sun, moon, and stars.

I enlarged upon many other topics, which the natural desire of endless life and sublunary[7] happiness could easily furnish me with. When I had ended, and the sum of my discourse had been interpreted as before, to the rest of the company, there was a good deal of talk among them in the language of the country, not without some laughter at my expense. At last the same gentleman who had been my interpreter said, he was desired by the rest to set me right in a few mistakes, which I had fallen into through the common imbecility of human nature, and upon that allowance was less answerable for them. That, this breed of Struldbruggs was peculiar to their country, for there were no such people either in Balnibarbi or Japan, where he had the honor to be ambassador from his Majesty, and found the natives in both those kingdoms very hard to believe[8] that the fact was possible, and it appeared from my astonishment when he first mentioned the matter to me, that I received it as a thing wholly new, and scarcely to be credited. That in the two kingdoms above-mentioned, where during his residence he had conversed very much, he observed long life to be the universal desire and wish of mankind. That whoever had one foot in the grave, was sure to hold back the other as strongly as he could. That the oldest had still hopes of living one day longer, and looked on death as the greatest evil, from which nature always prompted him to retreat; only in this island of Luggnagg, the appetite

4. Lacked.
5. On the earth and in the heavens.
6. As at Lagado, Gulliver enumerates scientific quests Swift scoffed at: for a method of determining the longitude of a ship at sea, for a perpetual motion machine, for one drug sufficient to cure all ills.
7. Earthly.
8. To convince.

for living was not so eager, from the continual example of the Struldbruggs before their eyes.

That the system of living contrived by me was unreasonable and unjust, because it supposed a perpetuity of youth, health, and vigor, which no man could be so foolish to hope, however extravagant he may be in his wishes. That the question therefore was not whether a man would choose to be always in the prime of youth, attended with prosperity and health, but how he would pass a perpetual life under all the usual disadvantages which old age brings along with it. For although few men will avow their desires of being immortal upon such hard conditions, yet in the two kingdoms before-mentioned of Balnibarbi and Japan, he observed that every man desired to put off death for some time longer, let it approach ever so late, and he rarely heard of any man who died willingly, except he were incited by the extremity of grief or torture. And he appealed to me whether in those countries I had traveled, as well as my own, I had not observed the same general disposition.

After this preface he gave me a particular account of the Struldbruggs among them. He said they commonly acted like mortals, till about thirty years old, after which by degrees they grew melancholy and dejected, increasing in both till they came to fourscore. This he learned from their own confession; for otherwise there not being above two or three of that species born in an age, they were too few to form a general observation by. When they came to fourscore years, which is reckoned the extremity of living in this country, they had not only all the follies and infirmities of other old men, but many more which arose from the dreadful prospect of never dying. They were not only opinionative, peevish, covetous, morose, vain, talkative, but uncapable of friendship, and dead to all natural affection, which never descended below their grandchildren. Envy and impotent desires are their prevailing passions. But those objects against which their envy seems principally directed, are the vices of the younger sort, and the deaths of the old. By reflecting on the former, they find themselves cut off from all possibility of pleasure; and whenever they see a funeral, they lament and repine that others have gone to an harbor of rest, to which they themselves never can hope to arrive. They have no remembrance of anything but what they learned and observed in their youth and middle age, and even that is very imperfect. And for the truth or particulars of any fact, it is safer to depend on common traditions than upon their best recollections. The least miserable among them appear to be those who turn to dotage, and entirely lose their memories; these meet with more pity and assistance, because they want many bad qualities which abound in others.

If a Struldbrugg happen to marry one of his own kind, the marriage is dissolved of course by the courtesy of the kingdom, as soon as the younger of the two comes to be fourscore. For the law thinks it a reasonable indulgence, that those who are condemned without any fault of their own to a perpetual continuance in the world, should not have their misery doubled by the load of a wife.[9]

As soon as they have completed the term of eighty years, they are looked on as dead in law; their heirs immediately succeed to their estates, only a small pittance is reserved for their support, and the poor ones are maintained at the public charge. After that period they are held incapable of any employment of trust or profit, they cannot purchase lands or take leases, neither are they allowed to be witnesses in any cause, either civil or criminal, not even for the decision of meres[1] and bounds.

---

9. Swift himself never married.   1. Property lines (at issue in property disputes).

At ninety they lose their teeth and hair, they have at that age no distinction of taste, but eat and drink whatever they can get, without relish or appetite. The diseases they were subject to, still continue without increasing or diminishing. In talking they forget the common appellation of things, and the names of persons, even of those who are their nearest friends and relations. For the same reason they never can amuse themselves with reading, because their memory will not serve to carry them from the beginning of a sentence to the end; and by this defect they are deprived of the only entertainment whereof they might otherwise be capable.

The language of this country being always upon the flux, the Struldbruggs of one age do not understand those of another, neither are they able after two hundred years to hold any conversation (farther than by a few general words) with their neighbors the mortals, and thus they lie under the disadvantage of living like foreigners in their own country. This was the account given me of the Struldbruggs, as near as I can remember. I afterwards saw five or six of different ages, the youngest not above two hundred years old, who were brought to me at several times by some of my friends; but although they were told that I was a great traveler, and had seen all the world, they had not the least curiosity to ask me a question; only desired I would give them *slumskudask*, or a token of remembrance, which is a modest way of begging, to avoid the law that strictly forbids it, because they are provided for by the public, although indeed with a very scanty allowance.

They are despised and hated by all sorts of people; when one of them is born, it is reckoned ominous, and their birth is recorded very particularly; so that you may know their age by consulting the registry, which however hath not been kept above a thousand years past, or at least hath been destroyed by time or public disturbances. But the usual way of computing how old they are, is, by asking them what kings or great persons they can remember, and then consulting history, for infallibly the last prince in their mind did not begin his reign after they were fourscore years old.

They were the most mortifying sight I ever beheld, and the women more horrible than the men. Besides the usual deformities in extreme old age, they acquired an additional ghastliness in proportion to their number of years, which is not to be described, and among half a dozen I soon distinguished which was the eldest, although there were not above a century or two between them.

The reader will easily believe, that from what I had heard and seen, my keen appetite for perpetuity of life was much abated. I grew heartily ashamed of the pleasing visions I had formed, and thought no tyrant could invent a death into which I would not run with pleasure from such a life. The king heard of all that had passed between me and my friends upon this occasion, and rallied me very pleasantly, wishing I would send a couple of Struldbruggs to my own country, to arm our people against the fear of death; but this it seems is forbidden by the fundamental laws of the kingdom, or else I should have been well content with the trouble and expense of transporting them.

I could not but agree that the laws of this kingdom, relating to the Struldbruggs, were founded upon the strongest reasons, and such as any other country would be under the necessity of enacting in the like circumstances. Otherwise, as avarice is the necessary consequent of old age, those Immortals would in time become proprietors of the whole nation, and engross the civil power, which, for want of abilities to manage, must end in the ruin of the public.

Part 4. A Voyage to the Country of the Houyhnhnms[1]

CHAPTER 1

The author sets out as Captain of a ship. His men conspire against him, confine him a long time to his cabin, set him on shore in an unknown land. He travels up into the country. The Yahoos,[2] a strange sort of animal, described. The author meets two Houyhnhnms.

I continued at home with my wife and children about five months in a very happy condition, if I could have learned the lesson of knowing when I was well. I left my poor wife big with child, and accepted an advantageous offer made me to be Captain of the *Adventure*,[3] a stout merchantman of 350 tons: for I understood navigation well, and being grown weary of a surgeon's employment at sea, which however I could exercise upon occasion, I took a skillful young man of that calling, one Robert Purefoy,[4] into my ship. We set sail from Portsmouth upon the seventh day of September, 1710; on the fourteenth, we met with Captain Pocock[5] of Bristol, at Teneriffe,[6] who was going to the bay of Campeche, to cut logwood. On the sixteenth, he was parted from us by a storm; I heard since my return, that his ship foundered, and none escaped, but one cabin boy. He was an honest man, and a good sailor, but a little too positive in his own opinions, which was the cause of his destruction, as it hath been of several others. For if he had followed my advice, he might at this time have been safe at home with his family as well as myself.

I had several men died in my ship of calentures,[7] so that I was forced to get recruits out of Barbados, and the Leeward Islands, where I touched by[8] the direction of the merchants who employed me, which I had soon too much cause to repent; for I found afterwards that most of them had been buccaneers. I had fifty hands on board, and my orders were, that I should trade with the Indians in the South Sea, and make what discoveries I could. These rogues whom I had picked up debauched my other men, and they all formed a conspiracy to seize the ship and secure me; which they did one morning, rushing into my cabin, and binding me hand and foot, threatening to throw me overboard, if I offered to stir. I told them, I was their prisoner, and would submit. This they made me swear to do, and then unbound me, only fastening one of my legs with a chain near my bed, and placed a sentry at my door with his piece charged,[9] who was commanded to shoot me dead, if I attempted my liberty. They sent me down victuals and drink, and took the government of the ship to themselves. Their design was to turn pirates, and plunder the Spaniards, which they could not do till they got more men. But first they resolved to sell the goods in the ship, and then go to Madagascar[1] for recruits, several among them having died since my confine-

1. Pronounced "whinnims," to mimic the sound of a horse's whinny, though some scholars have offered more complex interpretations of this name. With characteristic irony, Swift probably chose horses to represent rational creatures because the philosopher John Locke (1632–1704) and Bishop Edward Stillingfleet (1635–1699) had argued extensively about how one might distinguish man as a rational animal from an evidently irrational animal, such as a horse.
2. The name may be derived from similarly titled African or Guianan tribes. The animals represent sinful, fallen humanity, and their juxtaposition with the Houyhnhnms is designed to question belief in the innate rationality of humankind and the superiority of humans over other creatures.
3. The name of two ships of the notorious pirate Captain

William Kidd (d. 1701). Kidd, originally commissioned to capture pirates, was also subject to a mutiny.
4. "Pure faith," associating Gulliver with the overzealous Puritans.
5. Probably modeled on the dogmatic Captain Dampier (1652–1715), who had spent three years logcutting around the Campeche Bay, on the Yucatan Peninsula, in the Gulf of Mexico. His violent disagreements with his lieutenant led to a court martial.
6. One of the Canary Islands, off the northwestern coast of Africa.
7. Tropical fevers.
8. Landed according to.
9. Gun loaded.
1. A popular meeting place for pirates.

ment. They sailed many weeks, and traded with the Indians, but I knew not what course they took, being kept close prisoner in my cabin, and expecting nothing less than to be murdered, as they often threatened me.

Upon the ninth day of May, 1711, one James Welch came down to my cabin; and said he had orders from the Captain to set me ashore. I expostulated with him, but in vain; neither would he so much as tell me who their new captain was. They forced me into the longboat, letting me put on my best suit of clothes, which were good as new, and a small bundle of linen, but no arms except my hanger;[2] and they were so civil as not to search my pockets, into which I conveyed what money I had, with some other little necessaries. They rowed about a league; and then set me down on a strand.[3] I desired them to tell me what country it was. They all swore, they knew no more than myself, but said, that the Captain (as they called him) was resolved, after they had sold the lading,[4] to get rid of me in the first place where they discovered land. They pushed off immediately, advising me to make haste, for fear of being overtaken by the tide, and bade me farewell.

In this desolate condition I advanced forward, and soon got upon firm ground, where I sat down on a bank to rest myself, and consider what I had best to do. When I was a little refreshed, I went up into the country, resolving to deliver myself to the first savages I should meet, and purchase my life from them by some bracelets, glass rings, and other toys,[5] which sailors usually provide themselves with in those voyages, and whereof I had some about me: the land was divided by long rows of trees, not regularly planted, but naturally growing; there was great plenty of grass, and several fields of oats. I walked very circumspectly for fear of being surprised, or suddenly shot with an arrow from behind or on either side. I fell into a beaten road, where I saw many tracks of human feet, and some of cows, but most of horses. At last I beheld several animals in a field, and one or two of the same kind sitting in trees. Their shape was very singular, and deformed, which a little discomposed me, so that I lay down behind a thicket to observe them better. Some of them coming forward near the place where I lay, gave me an opportunity of distinctly marking[6] their form. Their heads and breasts were covered with a thick hair, some frizzled and others lank; they had beards like goats, and a long ridge of hair down their backs, and the foreparts of their legs and feet, but the rest of their bodies were bare, so that I might see their skins, which were of a brown buff color. They had no tails, nor any hair at all on their buttocks, except about the anus; which, I presume, Nature had placed there to defend them as they sat on the ground; for this posture they used, as well as lying down, and often stood on their hind feet. They climbed high trees, as nimbly as a squirrel, for they had strong extended claws before and behind, terminating in sharp points, and hooked. They would often spring, and bound, and leap with prodigious agility. The females were not so large as the males; they had long lank hair on their heads, and only a sort of down on the rest of their bodies, except about the anus, and pudenda.[7] Their dugs[8] hung between their forefeet, and often reached almost to the ground as they walked. The hair of both sexes was of several colors, brown, red, black, and yellow. Upon the whole, I never beheld in all my travels so disagreeable an animal, nor one against which I naturally conceived so strong an antipathy. So that thinking I had seen enough, full of contempt and aversion, I got up and pursued

---

2. A short sword, typically hung from the belt.
3. The shore; in this context, apparently a spit extending into the sea.
4. Cargo.

5. Trinkets.
6. Observing.
7. Genitals.
8. Breasts.

the beaten road, hoping it might direct me to the cabin of some Indian. I had not gone far when I met one of these creatures full in my way, and coming up directly to me. The ugly monster, when he saw me, distorted several ways every feature of his visage, and stared as at an object he had never seen before; then approaching nearer, lifted up his forepaw, whether out of curiosity or mischief, I could not tell. But I drew my hanger, and gave him a good blow with the flat side of it; for I durst not strike him with the edge, fearing the inhabitants might be provoked against me, if they should come to know, that I had killed or maimed any of their cattle. When the beast felt the smart, he drew back, and roared so loud, that a herd of at least forty came flocking about me from the next field, howling and making odious faces; but I ran to the body of a tree, and leaning my back against it, kept them off, by waving my hanger. Several of this cursed brood getting hold of the branches behind leaped up into the tree, from whence they began to discharge their excrements on my head: however, I escaped pretty well, by sticking close to the stem of the tree, but was almost stifled with the filth, which fell about me on every side.

In the midst of this distress, I observed them all to run away on a sudden as fast as they could, at which I ventured to leave the tree, and pursue the road, wondering what it was that could put them into this flight. But looking on my left hand, I saw a horse walking softly in the field, which my persecutors having sooner discovered, was the cause of their flight. The horse started a little when he came near me, but soon recovering himself, looked full in my face with manifest tokens of wonder: he viewed my hands and feet, walking round me several times. I would have pursued my journey, but he placed himself directly in the way, yet looking with a very mild aspect, never offering the least violence. We stood gazing at each other for some time; at last I took the boldness to reach my hand towards his neck, with a design to stroke it, using the common style and whistle of jockeys when they are going to handle a strange horse. But this animal, seeming to receive my civilities with disdain, shook his head, and bent his brows, softly raising up his left forefoot to remove my hand. Then he neighed three or four times, but in so different a cadence, that I almost began to think he was speaking to himself in some language of his own.

While he and I were thus employed, another horse came up; who applying[9] himself to the first in a very formal manner, they gently struck each other's right hoof before, neighing several times by turns, and varying the sound, which seemed to be almost articulate. They went some paces off, as if it were to confer together, walking side by side, backward and forward, like persons deliberating upon some affair of weight, but often turning their eyes towards me, as it were to watch that I might not escape. I was amazed to see such actions and behavior in brute beasts, and concluded with myself, that if the inhabitants of this country were endued with a proportionable degree of reason, they must needs be the wisest people upon earth. This thought gave me so much comfort, that I resolved to go forward until I could discover some house or village, or meet with any of the natives, leaving the two horses to discourse together as they pleased. But the first, who was a dapple-grey, observing me to steal off, neighed after me in so expressive a tone, that I fancied myself to understand what he meant; whereupon I turned back, and came near him, to expect[1] his farther commands. But concealing my fear as much as I could, for I began to be in some pain,[2] how this adventure might terminate; and the reader will easily believe I did not much like my present situation.

9. Addressing.
1. Await.

2. Began to be worried.

The two horses came up close to me, looking with great earnestness upon my face and hands. The grey steed rubbed my hat all round with his right forehoof, and discomposed it so much, that I was forced to adjust it better, by taking it off, and settling it again; whereat both he and his companion (who was a brown bay) appeared to be much surprised; the latter felt the lappet[3] of my coat, and finding it to hang loose about me, they both looked with new signs of wonder. He stroked my right hand, seeming to admire the softness, and color; but he squeezed it so hard between his hoof and his pastern,[4] that I was forced to roar; after which they both touched me with all possible tenderness. They were under great perplexity about my shoes and stockings, which they felt very often, neighing to each other, and using various gestures, not unlike those of a philosopher,[5] when he would attempt to solve some new and difficult phenomenon.

Upon the whole, the behavior of these animals was so orderly and rational, so acute and judicious, that I at last concluded, they must needs be magicians, who had thus metamorphosed themselves upon some design, and seeing a stranger in the way, were resolved to divert themselves with him; or perhaps were really amazed at the sight of a man so very different in habit, feature, and complexion from those who might probably live in so remote a climate.[6] Upon the strength of this reasoning, I ventured to address them in the following manner: Gentlemen, if you be conjurers, as I have good cause to believe, you can understand any language; therefore I make bold to let your Worships know, that I am a poor distressed Englishman, driven by his misfortunes upon your coast, and I entreat one of you, to let me ride upon his back, as if he were a real horse, to some house or village, where I can be relieved. In return of which favor, I will make you a present of this knife and bracelet (taking them out of my pocket). The two creatures stood silent while I spoke, seeming to listen with great attention; and when I had ended, they neighed frequently towards each other, as if they were engaged in serious conversation. I plainly observed that their language expressed the passions[7] very well, and the words might with little pains be resolved into an alphabet more easily than the Chinese.

I could frequently distinguish the word *Yahoo*, which was repeated by each of them several times; and although it were impossible for me to conjecture what it meant, yet while the two horses were busy in conversation, I endeavored to practice this word upon my tongue; and as soon as they were silent, I boldly pronounced *Yahoo* in a loud voice, imitating, at the same time, as near as I could, the neighing of a horse; at which they were both visibly surprised, and the grey repeated the same word twice, as if he meant to teach me the right accent, wherein I spoke after him as well as I could, and found myself perceivably to improve every time, although very far from any degree of perfection. Then the bay tried me with a second word, much harder to be pronounced; but reducing it to the English *orthography*,[8] may be spelled thus, *Houyhnhnm*. I did not succeed in this so well as the former, but after two or three farther trials, I had better fortune; and they both appeared amazed at my capacity.

After some farther discourse, which I then conjectured might relate to me, the two friends took their leaves, with the same compliment of striking each other's hoof; and the grey made me signs that I should walk before him; wherein I thought it prudent to comply, till I could find a better director. When I offered to slacken my pace,

---

3. Lapel.
4. Part of a horse's foot between the fetlock (a projection of the lower leg) and the hoof.
5. Scientist.

6. Region.
7. Emotions.
8. Spelling.

he would cry *Hhuun, Hhuun;* I guessed his meaning, and gave him to understand, as well as I could, that I was weary, and not able to walk faster; upon which, he would stand a while to let me rest.

CHAPTER 2

The author conducted by a Houyhnhnm to his house. The house described. The author's reception. The food of the Houyhnhnms. The author in distress for want of meat, is at last relieved. His manner of feeding in that country.

Having traveled about three miles, we came to a long kind of building, made of timber stuck in the ground, and wattled across;[9] the roof was low, and covered with straw. I now began to be a little comforted, and took out some toys, which travelers usually carry for presents to the savage Indians of America and other parts, in hopes the people of the house would be thereby encouraged to receive me kindly. The horse made me a sign to go in first; it was a large room with a smooth, clay floor, and a rack[1] and manger extending the whole length on one side. There were three nags,[2] and two mares, not eating, but some of them sitting down upon their hams,[3] which I very much wondered at; but wondered more to see the rest employed in domestic business. The last seemed but ordinary cattle; however, this confirmed my first opinion, that a people who could so far civilize brute animals, must needs excel in wisdom all the nations of the world. The grey came in just after, and thereby prevented any ill treatment, which the others might have given me. He neighed to them several times in a style of authority, and received answers.

Beyond this room there were three others, reaching the length of the house, to which you passed through three doors, opposite to each other, in the manner of a vista;[4] we went through the second room towards the third; here the grey walked in first, beckoning me to attend:[5] I waited in the second room, and got ready my presents, for the master and mistress of the house: they were two knives, three bracelets of false pearl, a small looking glass, and a bead necklace. The horse neighed three or four times, and I waited to hear some answers in a human voice, but I heard no other returns than in the same dialect, only one or two a little shriller than his. I began to think that this house must belong to some person of great note among them, because there appeared so much ceremony before I could gain admittance. But, that a man of quality should be served all by horses, was beyond my comprehension. I feared my brain was disturbed by my sufferings and misfortunes: I roused myself, and looked about me in the room where I was left alone; this was furnished as the first, only after a more elegant manner. I rubbed mine eyes often, but the same objects still occurred. I pinched my arms and sides, to awake myself, hoping I might be in a dream. I then absolutely concluded, that all these appearances could be nothing else but necromancy[6] and magic. But I had no time to pursue these reflections; for the grey horse came to the door, and made me a sign to follow him into the third room, where I saw a very comely mare, together with a colt and foal, sitting on their haunches, upon mats of straw, not unartfully made, and perfectly neat and clean.

The mare, soon after my entrance, rose from her mat, and coming up close, after having nicely[7] observed my hands and face, gave me a most contemptuous look; then turning to the horse, I heard the word *Yahoo* often repeated betwixt them; the meaning of which word I could not then comprehend, although it were the first I had learned to pronounce; but I was soon better informed, to my everlasting mortification: for the horse beckoning to me with his head, and repeating the word *Hhuun, Hhuun*, as he did upon the road, which I understood was to attend him, led me out into a kind of court, where was another building at some distance from the house. Here we entered, and I saw three of those detestable creatures, which I first met after my landing, feeding upon roots, and the flesh of some animals, which I afterwards found to be that of asses and dogs, and now and then a cow dead by accident or disease.[8] They were all tied by the neck with strong withes,[9] fastened to a beam; they held their food between the claws of their forefeet, and tore it with their teeth.

The master horse ordered a sorrel nag, one of his servants, to untie the largest of these animals, and take him into the yard. The beast and I were brought close together, and our countenances diligently compared, both by master and servant, who thereupon repeated several times the word *Yahoo*. My horror and astonishment are not to be described, when I observed, in this abominable animal, a perfect human figure; the face of it indeed was flat and broad, the nose depressed, the lips large, and the mouth wide. But these differences are common to all savage nations, where the lineaments of the countenance are distorted by the natives suffering[1] their infants to lie groveling on the earth, or by carrying them on their backs, nuzzling with their face against the mother's shoulders. The forefeet of the Yahoo differed from my hands in nothing else but the length of the nails, the coarseness and brownness of the palms, and the hairiness on the backs. There was the same resemblance between our feet, with the same differences, which I knew very well, though the horses did not, because of my shoes and stockings; the same in every part of our bodies, except as to hairiness and color, which I have already described.

The great difficulty that seemed to stick with the two horses, was, to see the rest of my body so very different from that of a Yahoo, for which I was obliged to my clothes, whereof they had no conception: the sorrel nag offered me a root, which he held (after their manner, as we shall describe in its proper place) between his hoof and pastern; I took it in my hand, and having smelt it, returned it to him as civilly as I could. He brought out of the Yahoo's kennel a piece of ass's flesh, but it smelt so offensively that I turned from it with loathing; he then threw it to the Yahoo, by whom it was greedily devoured. He afterwards showed me a wisp of hay, and a fetlock full of oats; but I shook my head, to signify, that neither of these were food for me. And indeed, I now apprehended, that I must absolutely starve, if I did not get to some of my own species: for as to those filthy Yahoos, although there were few greater lovers of mankind, at that time, than myself; yet I confess I never saw any sensitive[2] being so detestable on all accounts; and the more I came near them, the more hateful they grew, while I stayed in that country. This the master horse observed by my behavior, and therefore sent the Yahoo back to his kennel. He then put his forehoof to his mouth, at which I was much surprised, although he

---

7. Closely.
8. The Yahoos eat food listed in Leviticus (11.3, 27, 39–40) as unclean, suggesting that they exemplify the human condition distorted and debased by sin.

9. Leashes.
1. Allowing.
2. "Having sense or perception, but not reason" (Johnson's *Dictionary*).

did it with ease, and with a motion that appeared perfectly natural, and made other signs to know what I would eat; but I could not return him such an answer as he was able to apprehend; and if he had understood me, I did not see how it was possible to contrive any way for finding myself nourishment. While we were thus engaged, I observed a cow passing by, whereupon I pointed to her, and expressed a desire to let me go and milk her. This had its effect; for he led me back into the house, and ordered a mare-servant to open a room, where a good store of milk lay in earthen and wooden vessels, after a very orderly and cleanly manner. She gave me a large bowl full, of which I drank very heartily, and found myself well refreshed.

About noon I saw coming towards the house a kind of vehicle drawn like a sledge by four Yahoos. There was in it an old steed, who seemed to be of quality; he alighted with his hind feet forward, having by accident got a hurt in his left forefoot. He came to dine with our horse, who received him with great civility. They dined in the best room, and had oats boiled in milk for the second course, which the old horse ate warm, but the rest cold. Their mangers were placed circular in the middle of the room, and divided into several partitions, round which they sat on their haunches upon bosses[3] of straw. In the middle was a large rack with angles answering to every partition of the manger. So that each horse and mare ate their own hay, and their own mash of oats and milk, with much decency and regularity. The behavior of the young colt and foal appeared very modest, and that of the master and mistress extremely cheerful and complaisant[4] to their guest. The grey ordered me to stand by him, and much discourse passed between him and his friend concerning me, as I found by the stranger's often looking on me, and the frequent repetition of the word Yahoo.

I happened to wear my gloves, which the master grey observing, seemed perplexed, discovering signs of wonder what I had done to my forefeet; he put his hoof three or four times to them, as if he would signify, that I should reduce them to their former shape, which I presently did, pulling off both my gloves, and putting them into my pocket. This occasioned farther talk, and I saw the company was pleased with my behavior, whereof I soon found the good effects. I was ordered to speak the few words I understood, and while they were at dinner, the master taught me the names for oats, milk, fire, water, and some others; which I could readily pronounce after him, having from my youth a great facility in learning languages.

When dinner was done, the master horse took me aside, and by signs and words made me understand the concern he was in, that I had nothing to eat. Oats in their tongue are called *hlunnh*. This word I pronounced two or three times; for although I had refused them at first, yet upon second thoughts, I considered that I could contrive to make of them a kind of bread, which might be sufficient with milk to keep me alive, till I could make my escape to some other country, and to creatures of my own species. The horse immediately ordered a white mare-servant of his family to bring me a good quantity of oats in a sort of wooden tray. These I heated before the fire as well as I could, and rubbed them till the husks came off, which I made a shift[5] to winnow from the grain; I ground and beat them between two stones, then took water, and made them into a paste or cake, which I toasted at the fire, and ate warm with milk. It was at first a very insipid diet, although common enough in many parts of Europe, but grew tolerable by time; and having been often reduced to hard fare in

3. Piles or seats.
4. Courteous.

5. Attempted.

my life, this was not the first experiment I had made how easily nature is satisfied.[6] And I cannot but observe, that I never had one hour's sickness, while I stayed in this island. 'Tis true, I sometimes made a shift to catch a rabbit, or bird, by springes[7] made of Yahoos' hairs, and I often gathered wholesome herbs, which I boiled, or ate as salads with my bread, and now and then, for a rarity, I made a little butter, and drank the whey. I was at first at a great loss for salt; but custom soon reconciled the want of it; and I am confident that the frequent use of salt among us is an effect of luxury, and was first introduced only as a provocative to drink; except where it is necessary for preserving of flesh in long voyages, or in places remote from great markets. For we observe no animal to be fond of it but man:[8] and as to myself, when I left this country, it was a great while before I could endure the taste of it in anything that I ate.

This is enough to say upon the subject of my diet, wherewith other travelers fill their books, as if the readers were personally concerned whether we fared[9] well or ill. However, it was necessary to mention this matter, lest the world should think it impossible that I could find sustenance for three years in such a country, and among such inhabitants.

When it grew towards evening, the master horse ordered a place for me to lodge in; it was but six yards from the house, and separated from the stable of the Yahoos. Here I got some straw, and covering myself with my own clothes, slept very sound. But I was in a short time better accommodated, as the reader shall know hereafter, when I come to treat more particularly about my way of living.

CHAPTER 3

The author studious to learn the language, the Houyhnhnm his master assists in teaching him. The language described. Several Houyhnhnms of quality come out of curiosity to see the author. He gives his master a short account of his voyage.

My principal endeavor was to learn the language, which my master (for so I shall henceforth call him) and his children, and every servant of his house were desirous to teach me. For they looked upon it as a prodigy that a brute animal should discover[1] such marks of a rational creature. I pointed to everything, and inquired the name of it, which I wrote down in my journal book when I was alone, and corrected my bad accent, by desiring those of the family to pronounce it often. In this employment, a sorrel nag, one of the under servants, was very ready to assist me.

In speaking, they pronounce through the nose and throat, and their language approaches nearest to the High Dutch or German, of any I know in Europe; but is much more graceful and significant.[2] The Emperor Charles V made almost the same observation, when he said, that if he were to speak to his horse, it should be in High Dutch.[3]

The curiosity and impatience of my master were so great, that he spent many hours of his leisure to instruct me. He was convinced (as he afterwards told me) that I must be a Yahoo, but my teachableness, civility, and cleanliness astonished him; which were qualities altogether so opposite to those animals. He was most perplexed

---

6. A commonplace idea in ancient satire; Swift may here be mocking it.
7. Snares.
8. This is, of course, untrue, but Gulliver's subsequent dislike of salt indicates his dislike of human society in general.

9. A pun on "fare," meaning both food and "to get along."
1. Display.
2. Expressive.
3. I.e., German; Charles V of Spain (1500–1551) was believed to have said that he would address his God in Spanish, his mistress in Italian, and his horse in German.

about my clothes, reasoning sometimes with himself, whether they were a part of my body; for I never pulled them off till the family were asleep, and got them on before they waked in the morning. My master was eager to learn from whence I came, how I acquired those appearances of reason, which I discovered in all my actions, and to know my story from my own mouth, which he hoped he should soon do by the great proficiency I made in learning and pronouncing their words and sentences. To help my memory, I formed all I learned into the English alphabet, and writ the words down with the translations. This last, after some time, I ventured to do in my master's presence. It cost me much trouble to explain to him what I was doing; for the inhabitants have not the least idea of books or literature.

In about ten weeks' time I was able to understand most of his questions, and in three months could give him some tolerable answers. He was extremely curious to know from what part of the country I came, and how I was taught to imitate a rational creature, because the Yahoos (whom he saw I exactly resembled in my head, hands, and face, that were only visible), with some appearance of cunning, and the strongest disposition to mischief, were observed to be the most unteachable of all brutes. I answered, that I came over the sea, from a far place, with many others of my own kind, in a great hollow vessel made of the bodies of trees. That my companions forced me to land on this coast, and then left me to shift for myself. It was with some difficulty, and by the help of many signs, that I brought him to understand me. He replied, that I must needs be mistaken, or that I *said the thing which was not*. (For they have no word in their language to express lying or falsehood.) He knew it was impossible[4] that there could be a country beyond the sea, or that a parcel of brutes could move a wooden vessel whither they pleased upon water. He was sure no Houyhnhnm alive could make such a vessel, or would trust Yahoos to manage it.

The word *Houyhnhnm*, in their tongue, signifies a *horse*, and in its etymology, the *Perfection of Nature*. I told my master, that I was at a loss for expression, but would improve as fast as I could; and hoped in a short time I should be able to tell him wonders: he was pleased to direct his own mare, his colt and foal, and the servants of the family to take all opportunities of instructing me, and every day for two or three hours, he was at the same pains himself: several horses and mares of quality in the neighborhood came often to our house upon the report spread of a wonderful Yahoo, that could speak like a Houyhnhnm, and seemed in his words and actions to discover some glimmerings of reason. These delighted to converse with me; they put many questions, and received such answers as I was able to return. By all which advantages, I made so great a progress, that in five months from my arrival, I understood whatever was spoke, and could express myself tolerably well.

The Houyhnhnms who came to visit my master, out of a design of seeing and talking with me, could hardly believe me to be a right[5] Yahoo, because my body had a different covering from others of my kind. They were astonished to observe me without the usual hair or skin, except on my head, face, and hands; but I discovered that secret to my master, upon an accident, which happened about a fortnight before.

I have already told the reader, that every night when the family were gone to bed, it was my custom to strip and cover myself with my clothes: it happened one morning early, that my master sent for me, by the sorrel nag, who was his valet; when he came, I was fast asleep, my clothes fallen off on one side, and my shirt above my waist. I awaked at the noise he made, and observed him to deliver his message in some disorder; after which he went to my master, and in a great fright gave him a very confused account of what he had seen: this I presently discovered; for going as soon as I was dressed, to pay my attendance upon his Honor, he asked me the meaning of what his servant had reported, that I was not the same thing when I slept as I appeared to be at other times; that his valet assured him, some part of me was white, some yellow, at least not so white, and some brown.

I had hitherto concealed the secret of my dress, in order to distinguish myself as much as possible, from that cursed race of Yahoos; but now I found it in vain to do so any longer. Besides, I considered that my clothes and shoes would soon wear out, which already were in a declining condition, and must be supplied by some contrivance from the hides of Yahoos or other brutes; whereby the whole secret would be known: I therefore told my master, that in the country from whence I came, those of my kind always covered their bodies with the hairs of certain animals prepared by art, as well for decency, as to avoid inclemencies of air both hot and cold; of which, as to my own person, I would give him immediate conviction, if he pleased to command me; only desiring his excuse, if I did not expose those parts that Nature taught us to conceal. He said my discourse was all very strange, but especially the last part; for he could not understand why Nature should teach us to conceal what Nature had given. That neither himself nor family were ashamed of any parts of their bodies; but however I might do as I pleased. Whereupon, I first unbuttoned my coat, and pulled it off. I did the same with my waistcoat;[6] I drew off my shoes, stockings, and breeches. I let my shirt down to my waist, and drew up the bottom, fastening it like a girdle about my middle to hide my nakedness.

My master observed the whole performance with great signs of curiosity and admiration. He took up all my clothes in his pastern, one piece after another, and examined them diligently; he then stroked my body very gently, and looked round me several times, after which he said, it was plain I must be a perfect Yahoo; but that I differed very much from the rest of my species, in the softness, and whiteness, and smoothness of my skin, my want of hair in several parts of my body, the shape and shortness of my claws behind and before, and my affectation of walking continually on my two hinder feet. He desired to see no more, and gave me leave to put on my clothes again, for I was shuddering with cold.

I expressed my uneasiness at his giving me so often the appellation of *Yahoo*, an odious animal, for which I had so utter an hatred and contempt; I begged he would forbear applying that word to me, and take the same order in his family, and among his friends whom he suffered to see me. I requested likewise, that the secret of my having a false covering to my body might be known to none but himself, at least as long as my present clothing should last; for, as to what the sorrel nag his valet had observed, his Honor might command him to conceal it.

All this my master very graciously consented to,[7] and thus the secret was kept till my clothes began to wear out, which I was forced to supply by several contrivances, that shall hereafter be mentioned. In the meantime, he desired I would go on with my utmost diligence to learn their language, because he was more astonished at my

6. Vest.

7. The Houyhnhnms may have no word for "lying," but they can hide the truth.

capacity for speech and reason, than at the figure of my body, whether it were covered or no; adding, that he waited with some impatience to hear the wonders which I promised to tell him.

From thenceforward he doubled the pains he had been at to instruct me; he brought me into all company, and made them treat me with civility, because, as he told them privately, this would put me into good humor, and make me more diverting.

Every day when I waited on him, beside the trouble he was at in teaching, he would ask me several questions concerning myself, which I answered as well as I could; and by those means he had already received some general ideas, though very imperfect. It would be tedious to relate the several steps, by which I advanced to a more regular conversation: but the first account I gave of myself in any order and length, was to this purpose:

That, I came from a very far country, as I already had attempted to tell him, with about fifty more of my own species; that we traveled upon the seas, in a great hollow vessel made of wood, and larger than his Honor's house. I described the ship to him in the best terms I could, and explained by the help of my handkerchief displayed, how it was driven forward by the wind. That upon a quarrel among us, I was set on shore on this coast, where I walked forward without knowing whither, till he delivered me from the persecution of those execrable Yahoos. He asked me, who made the ship, and how it was possible that the Houyhnhnms of my country would leave it to the management of brutes? My answer was, that I durst proceed no farther in my relation, unless he would give me his word and honor that he would not be offended, and then I would tell him the wonders I had so often promised. He agreed; and I went on by assuring him, that the ship was made by creatures like myself, who in all the countries I had traveled, as well as in my own, were the only governing, rational animals; and that upon my arrival hither, I was as much astonished to see the Houyhnhnms act like rational beings, as he or his friends could be in finding some marks of reason in a creature he was pleased to call a Yahoo, to which I owned my resemblance in every part, but could not account for their degenerate and brutal nature. I said farther, that if good fortune ever restored me to my native country, to relate my travels hither, as I resolved to do, everybody would believe that I *said the thing which was not*; that I invented the story out of my own head; and with all possible respect to himself, his family, and friends, and under his promise of not being offended, our countrymen would hardly think it probable, that a Houyhnhnm should be the presiding creature of a nation, and a Yahoo the brute.

CHAPTER 4

The Houyhnhnms' notion of truth and falsehood. The author's discourse disapproved by his master. The author gives a more particular account of himself, and the accidents of his voyage.

My master heard me with great appearances of uneasiness in his countenance, because *doubting* or *not believing*, are so little known in this country, that the inhabitants cannot tell how to behave themselves under such circumstances. And I remember in frequent discourses with my master concerning the nature of manhood,[8] in other parts of the world, having occasion to talk of *lying*, and *false representation*, it was with much difficulty that he comprehended what I meant, although he

8. Human nature.

had otherwise a most acute judgment. For he argued thus: that the use of speech was to make us understand one another, and to receive information of facts; now if any one *said the thing which was not*, these ends were defeated; because I cannot properly be said to understand him, and I am so far from receiving information, that he leaves me worse than in ignorance, for I am led to believe a thing *black* when it is *white*, and *short* when it is *long*. And these were all the notions he had concerning that faculty of *lying*, so perfectly well understood, and so universally practiced among human creatures.

To return from this digression; when I asserted that the Yahoos were the only governing animal in my country, which my master said was altogether past his conception, he desired to know, whether we had Houyhnhnms among us, and what was their employment: I told him, we had great numbers, that in summer they grazed in the fields, and in winter were kept in houses, with hay and oats, where Yahoo servants were employed to rub their skins smooth, comb their manes, pick their feet, serve them with food, and make their beds. I understand you well, said my master; it is now very plain, from all you have spoken, that whatever share of reason the Yahoos pretend to, the Houyhnhnms are your masters;[9] I heartily wish our Yahoos would be so tractable. I begged his Honor would please to excuse me from proceeding any farther, because I was very certain that the account he expected from me would be highly displeasing. But he insisted in commanding me to let him know the best and the worst: I told him, he should be obeyed. I owned, that the Houyhnhnms among us, whom we called *horses*, were the most generous and comely animal we had, that they excelled in strength and swiftness; and when they belonged to persons of quality, employed in traveling, racing, or drawing chariots, they were treated with much kindness and care, till they fell into diseases, or became foundered in the feet;[1] but then they were sold, and used to all kind of drudgery till they died; after which their skins were stripped and sold for what they were worth, and their bodies left to be devoured by dogs and birds of prey.[2] But the common race of horses had not so good fortune, being kept by farmers and carriers and other mean people, who put them to greater labor, and fed them worse. I described as well as I could, our way of riding, the shape and use of a bridle, a saddle, a spur, and a whip, of harness and wheels. I added, that we fastened plates of a certain hard substance called *iron* at the bottom of their feet, to preserve their hoofs from being broken by the stony ways on which we often traveled.

My master, after some expressions of great indignation, wondered how we dared to venture upon a Houyhnhnm's back, for he was sure that the weakest servant in his house would be able to shake off the strongest Yahoo, or by lying down, and rolling upon his back, squeeze the brute to death. I answered, that our horses were trained up from three or four years old to the several uses we intended them for; that if any of them proved intolerably vicious, they were employed for carriages; that they were severely beaten while they were young, for any mischievous tricks; that the males, designed for the common use of riding or draft, were generally *castrated* about two years after their birth, to take down their spirits, and make them more tame and gentle; that they were indeed sensible of rewards and punishments; but his Honor would please to consider, that they had not the least tincture of reason any more than the Yahoos in this country.

---

9. Possibly a satire on the English love of horses.
1. Until their feet give in from overwork.
2. Swift mockingly paraphrases the *Iliad* 1.4–6: "The souls of mighty Chiefs untimely slain; / Whose limbs unburied on the naked shore, / Devouring dogs and hungry vultures tore" (Pope's translation).

It put me to the pains of many circumlocutions to give my master a right idea of what I spoke; for their language doth not abound in variety of words, because their wants and passions are fewer than among us. But it is impossible to express his noble resentment at our savage treatment of the Houyhnhnm race, particularly after I had explained the manner and use of *castrating* horses among us, to hinder them from propagating their kind, and to render them more servile. He said, if it were possible there could be any country where Yahoos alone were endued with reason, they certainly must be the governing animal, because reason will in time always prevail against brutal strength. But, considering the frame of our bodies, and especially of mine, he thought no creature of equal bulk was so ill-contrived for employing that reason in the common offices of life; whereupon he desired to know whether those among whom I lived, resembled me or the Yahoos of his country. I assured him, that I was as well shaped as most of my age, but the younger and the females were much more soft and tender, and the skins of the latter generally as white as milk. He said, I differed indeed from other Yahoos, being much more cleanly, and not altogether so deformed, but in point of real advantage, he thought I differed for the worse. That my nails were of no use either to my fore or hinder feet; as to my forefeet, he could not properly call them by that name, for he never observed me to walk upon them; that they were too soft to bear the ground; that I generally went with them uncovered, neither was the covering I sometimes wore on them of the same shape, or so strong as that on my feet behind. That I could not walk with any security, for if either of my hinder feet slipped, I must inevitably fall. He then began to find fault with other parts of my body, the flatness of my face, the prominence of my nose, mine eyes placed directly in front, so that I could not look on either side without turning my head, that I was not able to feed myself, without lifting one of my forefeet to my mouth, and therefore Nature had placed those joints to answer that necessity. He knew not what could be the use of those several clefts and divisions in my feet behind; that these were too soft to bear the hardness and sharpness of stones without a covering made from the skin of some other brute; that my whole body wanted a fence against heat and cold, which I was forced to put on and off every day with tediousness and trouble. And lastly, that he observed every animal in this country naturally to abhor the Yahoos, whom the weaker avoided, and the stronger drove from them. So that supposing us to have the gift of reason, he could not see how it were possible to cure that natural antipathy which every creature discovered[3] against us; nor consequently, how we could tame and render them serviceable. However, he would (as he said) debate that matter no farther, because he was more desirous to know my own story, the country where I was born, and the several actions and events of my life before I came hither.

I assured him, how extremely desirous I was that he should be satisfied in every point; but I doubted much, whether it would be possible for me to explain myself on several subjects whereof his Honor could have no conception, because I saw nothing in his country to which I could resemble[4] them. That, however, I would do my best, and strive to express myself by similitudes, humbly desiring his assistance when I wanted proper words; which he was pleased to promise me.

I said, my birth was of honest parents, in an island called England, which was remote from this country, as many days' journey as the strongest of his Honor's servants could travel in the annual course of the sun. That I was bred a surgeon, whose

---

3. Displayed.   4. Compare.

trade it is to cure wounds and hurts in the body, got by accident or violence; that my country was governed by a female man, whom we called a *Queen*. That I left it to get riches,[5] whereby I might maintain myself and family when I should return. That in my last voyage, I was commander of the ship, and had about fifty Yahoos under me, many of which died at sea, and I was forced to supply[6] them by others picked out from several nations. That our ship was twice in danger of being sunk; the first time by a great storm, and the second, by striking against a rock. Here my master interposed, by asking me, how I could persuade strangers out of different countries to venture with me, after the losses I had sustained, and the hazards I had run. I said, they were fellows of desperate fortunes, forced to fly from the places of their birth, on account of their poverty or their crimes. Some were undone by lawsuits; others spent all they had in drinking, whoring, and gaming; others fled for treason; many for murder, theft, poisoning, robbery, perjury, forgery, coining false money, for committing rapes or sodomy, for flying from their colors,[7] or deserting to the enemy, and most of them had broken prison; none of these durst return to their native countries for fear of being hanged, or of starving in a jail; and therefore were under a necessity of seeking a livelihood in other places.

During this discourse, my master was pleased often to interrupt me. I had made use of many circumlocutions in describing to him the nature of the several crimes, for which most of our crew had been forced to fly their country. This labor took up several days' conversation before he was able to comprehend me. He was wholly at a loss to know what could be the use or necessity of practicing those vices. To clear up which I endeavored to give him some ideas of the desire of power and riches, of the terrible effects of lust, intemperance, malice, and envy. All this I was forced to define and describe by putting of cases, and making suppositions. After which, like one whose imagination was struck with something never seen or heard of before, he would lift up his eyes with amazement and indignation. Power, government, war, law, punishment, and a thousand other things had no terms, wherein that language could express them, which made the difficulty almost insuperable to give my master any conception of what I meant. But being of an excellent understanding, much improved by contemplation and converse, he at last arrived at a competent knowledge of what human nature in our parts of the world is capable to perform, and desired I would give him some particular account of that land, which we call Europe, but especially, of my own country.

CHAPTER 5

The author at his master's commands informs him of the state of England. The causes of war among the princes of Europe. The author begins to explain the English Constitution.

The reader may please to observe, that the following extract of many conversations I had with my master, contains a summary of the most material points, which were discoursed at several times for above two years; his Honor often desiring fuller satisfaction[8] as I farther improved in the Houyhnhnm tongue. I laid before him, as well as I could, the whole state of Europe; I discoursed of trade and manufactures, of arts and sciences; and the answers I gave to all the questions he made, as they arose upon several subjects, were a fund of conversation not to be exhausted. But I shall here only

---

5. Gulliver originally stated that he undertook his second and third voyages out of a desire to travel: he now reads all human motivation in the worst possible light.

6. Replace.
7. Deserting their regiment in the army.
8. Better explanation.

set down the substance of what passed between us concerning my own country, reducing it into order as well as I can, without any regard to time or other circumstances, while I strictly adhere to truth. My only concern is, that I shall hardly be able to do justice to my master's arguments and expressions, which must needs suffer by my want of capacity, as well as by a translation into our barbarous English.[9]

In obedience therefore to his Honor's commands, I related to him the Revolution under the Prince of Orange,[1] the long war with France[2] entered into by the said Prince, and renewed by his successor the present Queen, wherein the greatest powers of Christendom were engaged, and which still continued: I computed, at his request, that about a million of Yahoos might have been killed in the whole progress of it, and perhaps a hundred or more cities taken, and five times as many ships burnt or sunk.

He asked me what were the usual causes or motives that made one country go to war with another. I answered they were innumerable, but I should only mention a few of the chief. Sometimes the ambition of princes, who never think they have land or people enough to govern; sometimes the corruption of ministers, who engage their master in a war in order to stifle or divert the clamor of the subjects against their evil administration. Difference in opinions[3] hath cost many millions of lives: for instance, whether *flesh* be *bread*, or *bread* be *flesh*; whether the juice of a certain *berry* be *blood* or *wine*; whether *whistling* be a vice or a virtue; whether it be better to *kiss a post*, or throw it into the fire; what is the best color for a *coat*, whether *black, white, red*, or *grey*; and whether it should be *long* or *short, narrow* or *wide, dirty* or *clean*, with many more. Neither are any wars so furious and bloody, or of so long continuance, as those occasioned by difference in opinion, especially if it be in things indifferent.[4]

Sometimes the quarrel between two princes is to decide which of them shall dispossess a third of his dominions, where neither of them pretend to any right. Sometimes one prince quarrels with another, for fear the other should quarrel with him. Sometimes a war is entered upon, because the enemy is too *strong*, and sometimes because he is too *weak*. Sometimes our neighbors *want* the *things* which we *have*, or *have* the *things* which we *want*; and we both fight, till they take ours or give us theirs. It is a very justifiable cause of war to invade a country after the people have been wasted by famine, destroyed by pestilence, or embroiled by factions amongst themselves.[5] It is justifiable to enter into a war against our nearest ally, when one of his towns lies convenient for us, or a territory of land, that would render our dominions round and compact. If a prince send forces into a nation where the people are poor and ignorant, he may lawfully put half of them to death, and make slaves of the rest, in order to civilize and reduce[6] them from their barbarous way of living. It is a very kingly, honorable, and frequent practice, when one prince desires the assistance of another to secure him against an invasion, that the assistant, when he hath driven out the invader, should seize on the dominions himself, and kill, imprison, or banish the prince he came to relieve. Alliance by blood or marriage is a sufficient cause of war between princes, and the nearer the kindred is, the greater is their disposition to

9. Presumably "barbarous," because English both lacks appropriate words to express Houyhnhnm concepts and has concepts (e.g., of lust, malice, envy) for which the other language has no words.
1. The Glorious Revolution of 1688 by which William of Orange, and his wife, Mary Stuart, ascended to the English throne in 1689.
2. The War of the League of Augsburg (1689–1697) and the War of the Spanish Succession (1701–1713), which

Swift (as a good Tory) opposed.
3. Religious controversies, over the doctrine of transubstantiation, the place of music (whistling) and images (the post) in church, and the color and style of liturgical vestments.
4. Of no importance either way.
5. Probably a reference to the English Civil War of 1642–1646, 1648.
6. Convert.

quarrel: *poor* nations are *hungry*, and *rich* nations are *proud*, and pride and hunger will ever be at variance. For these reasons, the trade of a *soldier* is held the most honorable of all others: because a *soldier* is a Yahoo hired to kill in cold blood as many of his own species, who have never offended him, as possibly he can.

There is likewise a kind of beggarly princes in Europe, not able to make war by themselves, who hire out their troops to richer nations, for so much a day to each man; of which they keep three fourths to themselves, and it is the best part of their maintenance; such are those in Germany and other northern parts of Europe.[7]

What you have told me (said my master), upon the subject of war, doth indeed discover most admirably the effects of that reason you pretend to: however, it is happy that the *shame* is greater than the *danger;* and that Nature hath left you utterly uncapable of doing much mischief. For your mouths lying flat with your faces, you can hardly bite each other to any purpose, unless by consent. Then as to the claws upon your feet before and behind, they are so short and tender, that one of our Yahoos would drive a dozen of yours before him. And therefore in recounting the numbers of those who have been killed in battle, I cannot but think that you have *said the thing which is not.*

I could not forbear shaking my head and smiling a little at his ignorance. And, being no stranger to the art of war, I gave him a description of cannons, culverins,[8] muskets, carabines,[9] pistols, bullets, powder, swords, bayonets, battles, sieges, retreats, attacks, undermines, countermines,[1] bombardments, seafights; ships sunk with a thousand men, twenty thousand killed on each side; dying groans, limbs flying in the air, smoke, noise, confusion, trampling to death under horses' feet; flight, pursuit, victory; fields strewed with carcasses left for food to dogs, and wolves, and birds of prey; plundering, stripping, ravishing, burning, and destroying. And to set forth the valor of my own dear countrymen, I assured him, that I had seen them blow up a hundred enemies at once in a siege, and as many in a ship, and beheld the dead bodies drop down in pieces from the clouds, to the great diversion of all the spectators.

I was going on to more particulars, when my master commanded me silence. He said, whoever understood the nature of Yahoos might easily believe it possible for so vile an animal to be capable of every action I had named, if their strength and cunning equaled their malice. But as my discourse had increased his abhorrence of the whole species, so he found it gave him a disturbance in his mind, to which he was wholly a stranger before. He thought his ears being used to such abominable words, might by degrees admit them with less detestation. That although he hated the Yahoos of this country, yet he no more blamed them for their odious qualities, than he did a *gnnayh* (a bird of prey) for its cruelty, or a sharp stone for cutting his hoof. But when a creature pretending to reason could be capable of such enormities, he dreaded lest[2] the corruption of that faculty might be worse than brutality itself. He seemed therefore confident, that instead of reason, we were only possessed of some quality fitted to increase our natural vices; as the reflection from a troubled stream returns the image of an ill-shapen body, not only *larger*, but more *distorted.*

He added, that he had heard too much upon the subject of war, both in this, and some former discourses. There was another point which a little perplexed him at present. I had said, that some of our crew left their country on account of being ruined

---

7. George I employed German mercenaries in his defense of Hanover.
8. Large cannons.
9. Short firearms.

1. Digging under fortification walls, and counter-digging by those inside the fort to stop the besiegers.
2. Worried that.

by *law*; that I had already explained the meaning of the word; but he was at a loss how it should come to pass, that the *law* which was intended for *every* man's preservation, should be any man's ruin. Therefore he desired to be farther satisfied what I meant by *law*, and the dispensers thereof, according to the present practice in my own country; because he thought Nature and reason were sufficient guides for a reasonable animal, as we pretended to be, in showing us what we ought to do, and what to avoid.

I assured his Honor, that law was a science wherein I had not much conversed,[3] further than by employing advocates in vain, upon some injustices that had been done me; however, I would give him all the satisfaction I was able.

I said there was a society of men among us, bred up from their youth in the art of proving by words multiplied for the purpose, that white is black, and black is white, according as they are paid.[4] To this society all the rest of the people are slaves. For example, if my neighbor hath a mind to my cow, he hires a lawyer to prove that he ought to have my cow from me. I must then hire another to defend my right, it being against all rules of law that any man should be allowed to speak for himself.[5] Now in this case, I who am the true owner lie under two great disadvantages. First, my lawyer, being practiced almost from his cradle in defending falsehood, is quite out of his element when he would be an advocate for justice, which as an office unnatural, he always attempts with great awkwardness, if not with ill will. The second disadvantage is, that my lawyer must proceed with great caution, or else he will be reprimanded by the judges, and abhorred by his brethren, as one who would lessen the practice[6] of the law. And therefore I have but two methods to preserve my cow. The first is to gain over my adversary's lawyer with a double fee, who will then betray his client by insinuating that he hath justice on his side. The second way is for my lawyer to make my cause appear as unjust as he can, by allowing the cow to belong to my adversary; and this if it be skillfully done will certainly bespeak[7] the favor of the Bench.

Now, your Honor is to know that these judges are persons appointed to decide all controversies of property, as well as for the trial of criminals, and picked out from the most dexterous lawyers who are grown old or lazy, and having been biased all their lives against truth and equity, lie under such a fatal necessity of favoring fraud, perjury, and oppression, that I have known several of them refuse a large bribe from the side where justice lay, rather than injure the *Faculty*[8] by doing anything unbecoming their nature or their office.

It is a maxim among these lawyers, that whatever hath been done before, may legally be done again; and therefore they take special care to record all the decisions formerly made against common justice and the general reason of mankind. These, under the name of *precedents*, they produce as authorities to justify the most iniquitous opinions; and the judges never fail of directing accordingly.

---

3. Had not had much instruction.
4. Swift's satirical treatment of lawyers probably stems from his dislike of Lord Chief Justice Whitehead, who tried to force juries to give verdicts against Swift and the printer of two of his political pamphlets.
5. One of Swift's many references to Thomas More's *Utopia* (1516) in this discussion of the ideals of human and Houyhnhnm society. *Utopia* suggests that it is "better for each man to plead for his own cause, and tell the judge the same story he'd otherwise tell his lawyer." Other important sources for *Gulliver* include Lucian's *True*

History (mid-second century A.D.); Cyrano de Bergerac's *Histoire comique des états et empires de la lune* (1656); William Temple's essay *Of Heroick Virtue* (in *Miscellanea*, pt. 2, 1692); William Dampier's *New Voyage Round the World* (1697); and Lionel Wafer's *A New Voyage and Description of the Isthmus of America* (1699), which includes descriptions of monkeys Swift may have used for the Yahoos.
6. Both profession, and morally questionable dealing.
7. Gain.
8. Legal profession.

In pleading, they studiously avoid entering into the *merits* of the cause; but are loud, violent, and tedious in dwelling upon all *circumstances* which are not to the purpose. For instance, in the case already mentioned; they never desire to know what claim or title my adversary hath to my cow, but whether the said cow were red or black, her horns long or short, whether the field I graze her in be round or square, whether she were milked at home or abroad, what diseases she is subject to, and the like; after which they consult *precedents*, adjourn the cause from time to time, and in ten, twenty, or thirty years come to an issue.

It is likewise to be observed that this society hath a peculiar cant[9] and jargon of their own, that no other mortal can understand, and wherein all their laws are written, which they take special care to multiply; whereby they have wholly confounded the very essence of truth and falsehood, of right and wrong; so that it will take thirty years to decide whether the field, left me by my ancestors for six generations, belong to me or to a stranger three hundred miles off.

In the trial of persons accused for crimes against the state the method is much more short and commendable: the judge first sends to sound the disposition of those in power, after which he can easily hang or save the criminal, strictly preserving all the forms of law.

Here my master, interposing, said it was a pity, that creatures endowed with such prodigious abilities of mind as these lawyers, by the description I gave of them, must certainly be, were not rather encouraged to be instructors of others in wisdom and knowledge. In answer to which, I assured his Honor, that in all points out of their own trade they were usually the most ignorant and stupid generation among us, the most despicable in common conversation, avowed enemies to all knowledge and learning, and equally disposed to pervert the general reason of mankind in every other subject of discourse, as in that of their own profession.

CHAPTER 6

A continuation of the state of England. The character of a first Minister.[1]

My master was yet wholly at a loss to understand what motives could incite this race of lawyers to perplex, disquiet, and weary themselves by engaging in a confederacy of injustice, merely for the sake of injuring their fellow animals; neither could he comprehend what I meant in saying they did it for *hire*. Whereupon I was at much pains to describe to him the use of *money*, the materials it was made of, and the value of the metals; that when a Yahoo had got a great store of this precious substance, he was able to purchase whatever he had a mind to, the finest clothing, the noblest houses, great tracts of land, the most costly meats and drinks, and have his choice of the most beautiful females. Therefore since *money* alone was able to perform all these feats, our Yahoos thought they could never have enough of it to spend or to save, as they found themselves inclined from their natural bent either to profusion or avarice. That the rich man enjoyed the fruit of the poor man's labor, and the latter were a thousand to one in proportion to the former.[2] That the bulk of our people was forced to live miserably, by laboring every day for small wages to make a few live plentifully. I enlarged

---

9. Both insincere and specialist language.

1. Swift's first printer/publisher, Benjamin Motte, prudently added "under Queen Anne" and "in the Courts of Europe" at the end of these two sentences, respectively, to remove some of the sting from this satire on George I's reign.

2. A theme of Thomas More's *Utopia* (1516).

myself[3] much on these and many other particulars to the same purpose: but his Honor was still to seek:[4] for he went upon a supposition that all animals had a title to their share in the productions of the earth, and especially those[5] who presided over the rest. Therefore he desired I would let him know, what these costly meats were, and how any of us happened to want them. Whereupon I enumerated as many sorts as came into my head, with the various methods of dressing them, which could not be done without sending vessels by sea to every part of the world, as well for liquors to drink, as for sauces, and innumerable other conveniencies. I assured him, that this whole globe of earth must be at least three times gone round, before one of our better female Yahoos could get her breakfast, or a cup to put it in.[6] He said, that must needs be a miserable country which cannot furnish food for its own inhabitants. But what he chiefly wondered at was how such vast tracts of ground as I described should be wholly without *fresh water*, and the people put to the necessity of sending over the sea for drink. I replied, that England (the dear place of my nativity) was computed to produce three times the quantity of food more than its inhabitants are able to consume, as well as liquors extracted from grain, or pressed out of the fruit of certain trees, which made excellent drink, and the same proportion in every other convenience of life. But in order to feed the luxury and intemperance of the males, and the vanity of the females, we sent away the greatest part of our necessary things to other countries, from whence in return we brought the materials of diseases, folly, and vice, to spend among ourselves. Hence it follows of necessity, that vast numbers of our people are compelled to seek their livelihood by begging, robbing, stealing, cheating, pimping, forswearing,[7] flattering, suborning,[8] forging, gaming, lying, fawning, hectoring,[9] voting, scribbling, stargazing,[1] poisoning, whoring, canting,[2] libeling, freethinking,[3] and the like occupations: every one of which terms, I was at much pains to make him understand.

That *wine* was not imported among us from foreign countries to supply the want of water or other drinks, but because it was a sort of liquid which made us merry, by putting us out of our senses; diverted all melancholy thoughts, begat wild extravagant imaginations in the brain, raised our hopes, and banished our fears, suspended every office of reason for a time, and deprived us of the use of our limbs, till we fell into a profound sleep; although it must be confessed, that we always awaked sick and dispirited, and that the use of this liquor filled us with diseases, which made our lives uncomfortable and short.[4]

But beside all this, the bulk of our people supported themselves by furnishing the necessities or conveniencies of life to the rich, and to each other. For instance, when I am at home and dressed as I ought to be, I carry on my body the workmanship of an hundred tradesmen; the building and furniture of my house employ as many more, and five times the number to adorn my wife.

I was going on to tell him of another sort of people, who get their livelihood by attending the sick, having upon some occasions informed his Honor that many of my crew had died of diseases. But here it was with the utmost difficulty that I brought him to apprehend what I meant. He could easily conceive, that a Houyhnhnm grew

---

3. Explained myself further.
4. Unable to understand.
5. The ruling species.
6. Coffee, tea, and chocolate were relatively new (and highly fashionable) drinks; chinaware was also imported.
7. Perjury.
8. Inducing through bribery.

9. Bullying.
1. Sensationalist popular astrology of the type Swift mocked when writing as "Isaac Bickerstaff" in 1708.
2. Using jargon, often for deceit.
3. Freethinkers rejected religious authority and dogma in favor of rational inquiry and speculation.
4. Swift, however, was a great wine drinker.

weak and heavy a few days before his death, or by some accident might hurt a limb. But that Nature, who worketh all things to perfection, should suffer any pains to breed in our bodies, he thought impossible, and desired to know the reason of so unaccountable an evil. I told him, we fed on a thousand things which operated contrary to each other; that we ate when we were not hungry, and drank without the provocation of thirst; that we sat whole nights drinking strong liquors without eating a bit, which disposed us to sloth, inflamed our bodies, and precipitated or prevented digestion. That prostitute female Yahoos acquired a certain malady, which bred rottenness in the bones of those who fell into their embraces; that this and many other diseases were propagated from father to son, so that great numbers come into the world with complicated maladies upon them; that it would be endless to give him a catalog of all diseases incident to human bodies; for they could not be fewer than five or six hundred, spread over every limb, and joint; in short, every part, external and intestine, having diseases appropriated to each. To remedy which, there was a sort of people bred up among us, in the profession or pretense of curing the sick. And because I had some skill in the faculty, I would, in gratitude to his Honor, let him know the whole mystery[5] and method by which they proceed.

Their fundamental is, that all diseases arise from *repletion*, from whence they conclude, that a great *evacuation* of the body is necessary, either through the natural passage, or upwards at the mouth. Their next business is, from herbs, minerals, gums, oils, shells, salts, juices, seaweed, excrements, barks of trees, serpents, toads, frogs, spiders, dead men's flesh and bones, birds, beasts and fishes, to form a composition for smell and taste the most abominable, nauseous, and detestable that they can possibly contrive, which the stomach immediately rejects with loathing; and this they call a *vomit*;[6] or else from the same storehouse, with some other poisonous additions, they command us to take in at the orifice *above* or *below* (just as the physician then happens to be disposed), a medicine equally annoying and disgustful to the bowels, which, relaxing the belly, drives down all before it; and this they call a *purge*, or a *clyster*.[7] For Nature (as the physicians allege) having intended the superior anterior orifice[8] only for the *intromission* of solids and liquids, and the inferior posterior for ejection, these artists ingeniously considering that in all diseases Nature is forced out of her seat; therefore to replace her in it, the body must be treated in a manner directly contrary, by interchanging the use of each orifice, forcing solids and liquids in at the anus, and making evacuations at the mouth.

But, besides real diseases, we are subject to many that are only imaginary, for which the physicians have invented imaginary cures; these have their several names, and so have the drugs that are proper for them, and with these our female Yahoos are always infested.

One great excellency in this tribe is their skill at *prognostics*, wherein they seldom fail; their predictions in real diseases, when they rise to any degree of malignity, generally portending *death*, which is always in their power, when recovery is not: and therefore, upon any unexpected signs of amendment, after they have pronounced their sentence, rather than be accused as false prophets, they know how to approve their sagacity to the world by a seasonable dose.[9]

---

5. Medical secrets.
6. Dr. John Woodward (1665–1728), a leading member of the Royal Society, was noted for believing this method a cure for virtually all ills.
7. Enema.

8. The mouth.
9. Cf. *Verses on the Death of Dr. Swift*, lines 131–132: "He'd rather choose that I should die / Than his prediction prove a lie" (page 2377).

They are likewise of special use to husbands and wives who are grown weary of their mates, to eldest sons, to great ministers of state, and often to princes.[1]

I had formerly upon occasion discoursed with my master upon the nature of *government* in general, and particularly of our own *excellent Constitution*, deservedly the wonder and envy of the whole world. But having here accidentally mentioned a *Minister of State*, he commanded me some time after to inform him, what species of Yahoo I particularly meant by that appellation.

I told him, that a *First* or *Chief Minister of State*,[2] whom I intended to describe, was a creature wholly exempt from joy and grief, love and hatred, pity and anger; at least made use of no other passions but a violent desire of wealth, power, and titles; that he applies his words to all uses, except to the indication of his mind;[3] that he never tells a *truth*, but with an intent that you should take it for a *lie*; nor a *lie*, but with a design that you should take it for a *truth*; that those he speaks worst of behind their backs are in the surest way to preferment;[4] and whenever he begins to praise you to others or to yourself, you are from that day forlorn.[5] The worst mark you can receive is a *promise*, especially when it is confirmed with an oath; after which every wise man retires, and gives over all hopes.

There are three methods by which a man may rise to be Chief Minister: the first is, by knowing how with prudence to dispose of a wife, a daughter, or a sister; the second, by betraying or undermining his predecessor; and the third is, by a *furious zeal* in public assemblies against the corruptions of the Court. But a wise prince would rather choose to employ those who practice the last of these methods; because such zealots prove always the most obsequious and subservient to the will and passions of their master. That the *Ministers* having all employments[6] at their disposal, preserve themselves in power by bribing the majority of a senate or great council; and at last, by an expedient called an *Act of Indemnity*[7] (whereof I described the nature to him) they secure themselves from after-reckonings, and retire from the public, laden with the spoils of the nation.

The palace of a *Chief Minister* is a seminary to breed up others in his own trade: the pages, lackeys, and porter, by imitating their master, become *Ministers of State* in their several districts, and learn to excel in the three principal *ingredients*, of *insolence, lying*, and *bribery*. Accordingly, they have a *subaltern*[8] court paid to them by persons of the best rank, and sometimes by the force of dexterity and impudence arrive through several gradations to be successors to their lord.

He is usually governed by a decayed wench[9] or favorite footman, who are the tunnels[1] through which all graces[2] are conveyed, and may properly be called, *in the last resort*, the governors of the kingdom.

One day my master, having heard me mention the *nobility* of my country, was pleased to make me a compliment which I could not pretend to deserve: that he was sure I must have been born of some noble family, because I far exceeded in shape,

---

1. The references are to Queen Caroline, Prince Frederick, and Walpole.
2. A satire on Robert Walpole, then the First Minister or "Prime Minister."
3. Real thoughts or intentions.
4. Most likely to receive a government position or promotion.
5. Forsaken, ruined.
6. Government positions.
7. Swift here suggests that corrupt government ministers make themselves secure from any future legal prosecution

for their illegal dealings. He refers to the Act of Indemnity and Oblivion of 1660, which pardoned almost all those who had taken part in the English Civil War (1642–1646, 1648), or the subsequent Commonwealth government (1649–1660).
8. Lower-ranking
9. The government Minister's mistress is "decayed" either in age or in morals.
1. Routes or conduits.
2. Favors.

color, and cleanliness, all the Yahoos of his nation, although I seemed to fail in strength and agility, which must be imputed to my different way of living from those other brutes; and besides, I was not only endowed with a faculty of speech, but likewise with some rudiments of reason, to a degree, that with all his acquaintance I passed for a prodigy.

He made me observe, that among the Houyhnhnms, the white, the *sorrel*, and the *iron-grey* were not so exactly shaped as the *bay*, the *dapple-grey*, and the *black*; nor born with equal talents of mind, or a capacity to improve them; and therefore continued always in the condition of servants, without ever aspiring to match[3] out of their own race, which in that country would be reckoned monstrous and unnatural.

I made his Honor my most humble acknowledgments for the good opinion he was pleased to conceive of me; but assured him at the same time, that my birth was of the lower sort, having been born of plain, honest parents, who were just able to give me a tolerable education; that *nobility* among us was altogether a different thing from the idea he had of it; that our young *noblemen* are bred from their childhood in idleness and luxury; that as soon as years will permit, they consume their vigor and contract odious diseases among lewd females; and when their fortunes are almost ruined, they marry some woman of mean birth, disagreeable person, and unsound constitution, merely for the sake of money, whom they hate and despise. That the productions of such marriages are generally scrofulous,[4] rickety,[5] or deformed children, by which means the family seldom continues above three generations, unless the wife take care to provide a healthy father among her neighbors or domestics, in order to improve and continue the breed. That a weak diseased body, a meager countenance, and sallow complexion are the true marks of *noble blood*; and a healthy robust appearance is so disgraceful in a man of quality, that the world concludes his real father to have been a groom, or a coachman. The imperfections of his mind run parallel with those of his body, being a composition of spleen, dullness, ignorance, caprice, sensuality, and pride.

Without the consent of this *illustrious body* no law can be enacted, repealed, or altered, and these nobles have likewise the decision of all our possessions without appeal.[6]

CHAPTER 7

The author's great love of his native country. His master's observations upon the Constitution and Administration of England, as described by the author, with parallel cases and comparisons. His master's observations upon human nature.

The reader may be disposed to wonder how I could prevail on myself to give so free a representation of my own species, among a race of mortals who were already too apt to conceive the vilest opinion of humankind from that entire congruity betwixt me and their Yahoos. But I must freely confess, that the many virtues of those excellent *quadrupeds*, placed in opposite view to human corruptions, had so far opened mine eyes and enlarged my understanding, that I began to view the actions and passions of man in a very different light, and to think the honor of my own kind not worth managing;[7] which, besides, it was impossible for me to do before a person of so acute a

---

3. Mate.
4. Tubercular.
5. Feeble, weak-jointed.
6. Swift here refers to the House of Lords, the upper

house of Parliament and the highest law court in the land.
7. Maintaining.

judgment as my master, who daily convinced me of a thousand faults in myself, whereof I had not the least perception before, and which with us would never be numbered even among human infirmities. I had likewise learned from his example an utter detestation of all falsehood or disguise; and *truth* appeared so amiable to me, that I determined upon sacrificing everything to it.

Let me deal so candidly with the reader, as to confess, that there was yet a much stronger motive for the freedom I took in my representation of things. I had not been a year in this country before I contracted such a love and veneration for the inhabitants, that I entered on a firm resolution never to return to humankind, but to pass the rest of my life among these admirable Houyhnhnms in the contemplation and practice of every virtue; where I could have no example or incitement to vice. But it was decreed by Fortune, my perpetual enemy, that so great a felicity should not fall to my share. However, it is now some comfort to reflect, that in what I said of my countrymen, I *extenuated* their faults as much as I durst before so strict an examiner, and upon every article gave as *favorable* a turn as the matter would bear. For, indeed, who is there alive that will not be swayed by his bias and partiality to the place of his birth?

I have related the substance of several conversations I had with my master, during the greatest part of the time I had the honor to be in his service, but have indeed for brevity sake omitted much more than is here set down.

When I had answered all his questions, and his curiosity seemed to be fully satisfied, he sent for me one morning early, and commanding me to sit down at some distance (an honor which he had never before conferred upon me), he said, he had been very seriously considering my whole story, as far as it related both to myself and my country: that he looked upon us as a sort of animals to whose share, by what accident he could not conjecture, some small pittance of *reason* had fallen, whereof we made no other use than by its assistance to aggravate our *natural* corruptions, and to acquire new ones which Nature had not given us. That we disarmed ourselves of the few abilities she had bestowed, had been very successful in multiplying our original wants, and seemed to spend our whole lives in vain endeavors to supply them by our own inventions. That as to myself, it was manifest I had neither the strength or agility of a common Yahoo, that I walked infirmly on my hinder feet, had found out a contrivance to make my claws of no use or defense, and to remove the hair from my chin, which was intended as a shelter from the sun and the weather. Lastly, that I could neither run with speed, nor climb trees like my *brethren* (as he called them) the Yahoos in this country.

That our institutions of *government* and *law* were plainly owing to our gross defects in *reason*, and by consequence, in *virtue*; because *reason* alone is sufficient to govern a *rational* creature; which was therefore a character we had no pretense to challenge,[8] even from the account I had given of my own people, although he manifestly perceived, that in order to favor them I had concealed many particulars, and often *said the thing which was not*.

He was the more confirmed in this opinion, because he observed, that as I agreed in every feature of my body with other Yahoos, except where it was to my real disadvantage in point of strength, speed, and activity, the shortness of my claws, and some other particulars where Nature had no part; so from the representation I had given him of our lives, our manners, and our actions, he found as near a resemblance in the disposition of our minds. He said the Yahoos were known to hate one another more than they did any different species of animals; and the reason usually assigned, was,

---

8. We had no right to claim to be rational creatures.

the odiousness of their own shapes, which all could see in the rest, but not in themselves. He had therefore begun to think it not unwise in us to *cover* our bodies, and, by that invention, conceal many of our deformities from each other, which would else be hardly supportable. But, he now found he had been mistaken, and that the dissensions of those brutes in his country were owing to the same cause with ours, as I had described them. For if (said he) you throw among five Yahoos as much food as would be sufficient for fifty, they will, instead of eating peaceably, fall together by the ears, each single one impatient to *have all to itself;* and therefore a servant was usually employed to stand by while they were feeding abroad, and those kept at home were tied at a distance from each other; that if a cow died of age or accident, before a Houyhnhnm could secure it for his own Yahoos, those in the neighborhood would come in herds to seize it, and then would ensue such a battle as I had described, with terrible wounds made by their claws on both sides, although they seldom were able to kill one another, for want of such convenient instruments of death as we had invented. At other times the like battles have been fought between the Yahoos of several neighborhoods without any visible cause: those of one district watching all opportunities to surprise the next before they are prepared. But if they find their project hath miscarried, they return home, and for want of enemies, engage in what I call a civil war among themselves.

That in some fields of his country there are certain *shining stones* of several colors, whereof the Yahoos are violently fond, and when part of these *stones* are fixed in the earth, as it sometimes happens, they will dig with their claws for whole days to get them out, and carry them away, and hide them by heaps in their kennels; but still looking round with great caution, for fear their comrades should find out their treasure. My master said, he could never discover the reason of this unnatural appetite, or how these *stones* could be of any use to a Yahoo; but now he believed it might proceed from the same principle of *avarice* which I had ascribed to mankind; that he had once, by way of experiment, privately removed a heap of these *stones* from the place where one of his Yahoos had buried it: whereupon, the sordid animal, missing his treasure, by his loud lamenting brought the whole herd to the place, there miserably howled, then fell to biting and tearing the rest, began to pine away, would neither eat, nor sleep, nor work, till he ordered a servant privately to convey the *stones* into the same hole, and hide them as before; which when his Yahoo had found, he presently recovered his spirits and good humor, but took care to remove them to a better hiding place, and hath ever since been a very serviceable brute.

My master farther assured me, which I also observed myself, that in the fields where these *shining stones* abound, the fiercest and most frequent battles are fought, occasioned by perpetual inroads of the neighboring Yahoos.[9]

He said, it was common, when two Yahoos discovered such a *stone* in a field, and were contending which of them should be the proprietor, a third would take the advantage,[1] and carry it away from them both; which my master would needs contend to have some resemblance with our *suits at law;* wherein I thought it for our credit not to undeceive him; since the decision he mentioned was much more equitable than many decrees among us: because the plaintiff and defendant there lost nothing beside the *stone* they contended for, whereas our *Courts of Equity*[2] would never have dismissed the cause while either of them had anything left.

---

9. Neighboring Yahoos attempt invasions to steal these stones.
1. Opportunity.

2. Courts that decide on general (rather than common) principles of law. Swift ironically plays on the name of the court.

My master, continuing his discourse, said, there was nothing that rendered the Yahoos more odious, than their undistinguishing appetite to devour everything that came in their way, whether herbs, roots, berries, the corrupted flesh of animals, or all mingled together; and it was peculiar in their temper, that they were fonder of what they could get by rapine or stealth at a greater distance, than much better food provided for them at home. If their prey held out, they would eat till they were ready to burst, after which Nature had pointed out to them a certain *root* that gave them a general evacuation.

There was also another kind of *root* very *juicy*, but something rare and difficult to be found, which the Yahoos sought for with much eagerness, and would suck it with great delight; and it produced in them the same effects that wine hath upon us. It would make them sometimes hug, and sometimes tear one another; they would howl and grin, and chatter, and reel, and tumble, and then fall asleep in the mud.

I did indeed observe, that the Yahoos were the only animals in this country subject to any diseases; which, however, were much fewer than horses have among us, and contracted not by any ill treatment they meet with, but by the nastiness and greediness of that sordid brute. Neither has their language any more than a general appellation for those maladies, which is borrowed from the name of the beast, and called *hnea-Yahoo*, or the *Yahoo's-evil*, and the cure prescribed is a mixture of *their own dung* and *urine* forcibly put down the Yahoo's throat. This I have since often known to have been taken with success, and do here freely recommend it to my countrymen, for the public good, as an admirable specific against all diseases produced by repletion.[3]

As to learning, government, arts, manufactures, and the like, my master confessed he could find little or no resemblance between the Yahoos of that country and those in ours. For, he only meant to observe what parity there was in our natures. He had heard indeed some curious Houyhnhnms observe, that in most herds there was a sort of ruling Yahoo (as among us there is generally some leading or principal stag in a park), who was always more *deformed* in body, and *mischievous* in *disposition*, than any of the rest. That this *leader* had usually a favorite as *like himself* as he could get, whose employment was to *lick his master's feet and posteriors, and drive the female Yahoos to his kennel;* for which he was now and then rewarded with a piece of ass's flesh. This *favorite* is hated by the whole herd, and therefore to protect himself, keeps always *near the person of his leader.* He usually continues in office till a worse can be found; but the very moment he is discarded, his successor, at the head of all the Yahoos in that district, young and old, male and female, come in a body, and discharge their excrements upon him from head to foot. But how far this might be applicable to our *Courts* and *favorites,* and *Ministers of State,* my master said I could best determine.

I durst make no return to this malicious insinuation, which debased human understanding below the sagacity of a common *hound,* who hath judgment enough to distinguish and follow the cry of the *ablest dog in the pack,* without being ever mistaken.

My master told me, there were some qualities remarkable in the Yahoos, which he had not observed me to mention, or at least very slightly, in the accounts I had given him of humankind: he said, those animals, like other brutes, had their females in common;[4] but in this they differed, that the she-Yahoo would admit the male

---

3. Overeating.   4. Implying that English society did the same.

while she was pregnant, and that the hes[5] would quarrel and fight with the females as fiercely as with each other. Both which practices were such degrees of infamous brutality, that no other sensitive[6] creature ever arrived at.

Another thing he wondered at in the Yahoos, was their strange disposition to nastiness and dirt, whereas there appears to be a natural love of cleanliness in all other animals. As to the two former accusations, I was glad to let them pass without any reply, because I had not a word to offer upon them in defense of my species, which otherwise I certainly had done from my own inclinations. But I could have easily vindicated humankind from the imputation of singularity upon the last article, if there had been any *swine* in that country (as unluckily for me there were not), which although it may be a *sweeter quadruped* than a Yahoo, cannot, I humbly conceive, in justice pretend to more cleanliness; and so his Honor himself must have owned, if he had seen their filthy way of feeding, and their custom of wallowing and sleeping in the mud.

My master likewise mentioned another quality which his servants had discovered in several Yahoos, and to him was wholly unaccountable. He said, a fancy would sometimes take a Yahoo to retire into a corner, to lie down and howl, and groan, and spurn away all that came near him, although he were young and fat, and wanted neither food nor water; nor did the servants imagine what could possibly ail him. And the only remedy they found was to set him to hard work, after which he would infallibly come to himself. To this I was silent out of partiality to my own kind; yet here I could plainly discover the true seeds of *spleen*,[7] which only seizeth on the *lazy*, the *luxurious*, and the *rich*; who, if they were forced to undergo the *same regimen*, I would undertake for[8] the cure.

His Honor had farther observed, that a female Yahoo would often stand behind a bank or a bush, to gaze on the young males passing by, and then appear, and hide, using many antic gestures and grimaces, at which time it was observed, that she had a most *offensive smell*; and when any of the males advanced, would slowly retire, looking often back, and with a counterfeit show of fear, run off into some convenient place where she knew the male would follow her.[9]

At other times if a female stranger came among them, three or four of her own sex would get about her, and stare and chatter, and grin, and smell her all over, and then turn off with gestures that seemed to express contempt and disdain.

Perhaps my master might refine a little in these speculations, which he had drawn from what he observed himself, or had been told him by others; however, I could not reflect without some amazement, and much sorrow, that the rudiments of *lewdness*, *coquetry*, *censure*, and *scandal*, should have place by instinct in womankind.

I expected every moment that my master would accuse the Yahoos of those unnatural appetites in both sexes, so common among us. But Nature it seems hath not been so expert a schoolmistress; and these politer pleasures are entirely the productions of art and reason, on our side of the globe.

CHAPTER 8

The author relateth several particulars of the Yahoos. The great virtues of the Houyhnhnms. The education and exercise of their youth. Their general Assembly.

5. The males.
6. Sensible, thinking.
7. Depression.

8. Guarantee.
9. The sort of seduction tactics used by female characters in literary pastoral.

As I ought to have understood human nature much better than I supposed it possible for my master to do, so it was easy to apply the character he gave of the Yahoos to myself and my countrymen, and I believed I could yet make farther discoveries from my own observation. I therefore often begged his Honor to let me go among the herds of Yahoos in the neighborhood, to which he always very graciously consented, being perfectly convinced that the hatred I bore those brutes would never suffer me to be corrupted by them; and his Honor ordered one of his servants, a strong sorrel nag, very honest and good-natured, to be my guard, without whose protection I durst not undertake such adventures. For I have already told the reader how much I was pestered by those odious animals upon my first arrival. I afterwards failed very narrowly three or four times of falling into their clutches, when I happened to stray at any distance without my hanger. And I have reason to believe they had some imagination that I was of their own species, which I often assisted myself, by stripping up my sleeves, and showing my naked arms and breast in their sight, when my protector was with me. At which times they would approach as near as they durst, and imitate my actions after the manner of monkeys, but ever with great signs of hatred, as a tame *jackdaw*,[1] with cap and stockings, is always persecuted by the wild ones, when he happens to be got among them.

They are prodigiously nimble from their infancy; however, I once caught a young male of three years old, and endeavored by all marks of tenderness to make it quiet; but the little imp fell a squalling, and scratching, and biting with such violence, that I was forced to let it go, and it was high time, for a whole troop of old ones came about us at the noise, but finding the cub was safe (for away it ran), and my sorrel nag being by, they durst not venture near us. I observed the young animal's flesh to smell very rank, and the stink was somewhat between a *weasel* and a *fox*, but much more disagreeable. I forgot another circumstance (and perhaps I might have the reader's pardon, if it were wholly omitted), that while I held the odious vermin in my hands, it voided its filthy excrements of a yellow liquid substance all over my clothes; but by good fortune there was a small brook hard by, where I washed myself as clean as I could, although I durst not come into my master's presence, until I were sufficiently aired.

By what I could discover, the Yahoos appear to be the most unteachable of all animals, their capacities never reaching higher than to draw or carry burdens. Yet I am of opinion this defect ariseth chiefly from a perverse, restive[2] disposition. For they are cunning, malicious, treacherous, and revengeful. They are strong and hardy, but of a cowardly spirit, and by consequence insolent, abject, and cruel. It is observed, that the *red-haired* of both sexes are more libidinous and mischievous than the rest, whom yet they much exceed in strength and activity.[3]

The Houyhnhnms keep the Yahoos for present[4] use in huts not far from the house; but the rest are sent abroad to certain fields, where they dig up roots, eat several kinds of herbs, and search about for carrion, or sometimes catch weasels and *luhimuhs* (a sort of wild rat), which they greedily devour. Nature hath taught them to dig deep holes with their nails on the side of a rising ground, wherein they lie by themselves, only the kennels of the females are larger, sufficient to hold two or three cubs.

They swim from their infancy like frogs, and are able to continue long under water, where they often take fish, which the females carry home to their young. And upon this occasion, I hope the reader will pardon my relating an odd adventure.

---

1. Small crow, often kept as a pet.
2. Stubborn.

3. A prejudice dating back to medieval times.
4. Daily.

Being one day abroad with my protector the sorrel nag, and the weather exceeding hot, I entreated him to let me bathe in a river that was near. He consented, and I immediately stripped myself stark naked, and went down softly into the stream. It happened that a young female Yahoo, standing behind a bank, saw the whole proceeding, and inflamed by desire, as the nag and I conjectured, came running with all speed, and leaped into the water within five yards of the place where I bathed. I was never in my life so terribly frighted; the nag was grazing at some distance, not suspecting any harm. She embraced me after a most fulsome manner; I roared as loud as I could, and the nag came galloping towards me, whereupon she quitted her grasp, with the utmost reluctancy, and leaped upon the opposite bank, where she stood gazing and howling all the time I was putting on my clothes.

This was matter of diversion to my master and his family, as well as of mortification to myself. For now I could no longer deny, that I was a real Yahoo in every limb and feature, since the females had a natural propensity to me as one of their own species; neither was the hair of this brute of a red color (which might have been some excuse for an appetite a little irregular) but black as a sloe,[5] and her countenance did not make an appearance altogether so hideous as the rest of the kind; for, I think, she could not be above eleven years old.[6]

Having already lived three years in this country, the reader I suppose will expect that I should, like other travelers, give him some account of the manners and customs of its inhabitants, which it was indeed my principal study to learn.

As these noble Houyhnhnms are endowed by Nature with a general disposition to all virtues, and have no conceptions or ideas of what is evil in a rational creature, so their grand maxim is, to cultivate *Reason*, and to be wholly governed by it. Neither is *Reason* among them a point problematical as with us, where men can argue with plausibility on both sides of a question, but strikes you with immediate conviction, as it must needs do where it is not mingled, obscured, or discolored by passion and interest.[7] I remember it was with extreme difficulty that I could bring my master to understand the meaning of the word opinion, or how a point could be disputable, because *Reason* taught us to affirm or deny only where we are certain, and beyond our knowledge we cannot do either.[8] So that controversies, wranglings, disputes, and positiveness[9] in false or dubious propositions are evils unknown among the Houyhnhnms. In the like manner, when I used to explain to him our several systems of *natural philosophy*, he would laugh that a creature pretending to *Reason* should value itself upon the knowledge of other people's conjectures, and in things where that knowledge, if it were certain, could be of no use. Wherein he agreed entirely with the sentiments of Socrates, as Plato delivers them;[1] which I mention as the highest honor I can do that prince of philosophers. I have often since reflected what destruction such a doctrine would make in the libraries of Europe, and how many paths to fame would be then shut up in the learned world.

Friendship and benevolence are the two principal virtues among the Houyhnhnms, and these not confined to particular objects,[2] but universal to the whole race. For a stranger from the remotest part is equally treated with the nearest

---

5. A wild berry.
6. The disparity in age between Gulliver and the Yahoo may suggest a grotesque parody of Esther Vanhomrigh's pursuit of Swift, she being 21 years his junior.
7. Prejudice based on interest in personal benefit. Both Descartes (*Discourse on Method*) and Locke (*Essay Concerning Human Understanding*) wrote of the intuitive nature of some knowledge.
8. Gulliver's master has clearly expressed "opinion" (i.e.,

prejudice) himself, however.
9. Assertiveness.
1. I.e., that ethics (human nature) is worth studying, while the physical world is not, as we can never have certain knowledge of it: "Socrates: I am a friend of learning—the trees and the countryside won't teach me anything, but the people in the city do" *Phaedrus* (230d3–5).
2. To other, particular Houyhnhnms.

neighbor, and wherever he goes, looks upon himself as at home. They preserve *decency* and *civility* in the highest degrees, but are altogether ignorant of *ceremo-ny*.[3] They have no fondness for their colts or foals, but the care they take in educating them proceedeth entirely from the dictates of *Reason*. And I observed my master to show the same affection to his neighbor's issue that he had for his own.[4] They will have it that *Nature* teaches them to love the whole species, and it is *Reason* only that maketh a distinction of persons, where there is a superior degree of virtue.

When the matron Houyhnhnms have produced one of each sex, they no longer accompany with[5] their consorts, except they lose one of their issue by some casualty, which very seldom happens: but in such a case they meet again. Or when the like accident befalls a person,[6] whose wife is past bearing, some other couple bestow him one of their own colts, and then go together a second time, till the mother be pregnant. This caution is necessary to prevent the country from being overburdened with numbers.[7] But the race of inferior Houyhnhnms bred up to be servants is not so strictly limited upon this article; these are allowed to produce three of each sex, to be domestics in the noble families.

In their marriages they are exactly careful to choose such colors as will not make any disagreeable mixture in the breed.[8] *Strength* is chiefly valued in the male, and *comeliness* in the female, not upon the account of *love*, but to preserve the race from degenerating; for where a female happens to excel in *strength*, a consort is chosen with regard to *comeliness*. Courtship, love, presents, jointures,[9] settlements, have no place in their thoughts, or terms whereby to express them in their language. The young couple meet and are joined, merely because it is the determination of their parents and friends: it is what they see done every day, and they look upon it as one of the necessary actions in a reasonable being. But the violation of marriage, or any other unchastity, was never heard of, and the married pair pass their lives with the same friendship, and mutual benevolence that they bear to others of the same species who come in their way; without jealousy, fondness, quarreling, or discontent.

In educating the youth of both sexes, their method is admirable, and highly deserveth our imitation. These are not suffered to taste a grain of *oats*, except upon certain days, till eighteen years old; nor *milk*, but very rarely; and in summer they graze two hours in the morning, and as many in the evening, which their parents likewise observe, but the servants are not allowed above half that time, and a great part of their grass is brought home, which they eat at the most convenient hours, when they can be best spared from work.

Temperance, industry, exercise, and *cleanliness,* are the lessons equally enjoined to the young ones of both sexes, and my master thought it monstrous in us to give the females a different kind of education from the males, except in some articles of domestic management;[1] whereby as he truly observed, one half of our natives were good for nothing but bringing children into the world, and to trust the care of their children to such useless animals, he said, was yet a greater instance of brutality.

---

3. As are the Utopians.
4. As do men in Plato's *Republic* (461d).
5. Have sex with.
6. A male Houyhnhnm.
7. The Utopians are under no such restriction, knowing (as the Houyhnhnms do not) of other lands to which they can send their excess population.
8. In Plato's *Republic* (458d–461e), eugenic principles

also control mating.
9. Marriage settlements for wives, should they survive their husbands.
1. In both Plato's *Republic* (451e6–7) and *Utopia,* the sexes receive the same education; Swift also began (but never completed) an essay entitled *Of the Education of Ladies* (c. 1728).

But the Houyhnhnms train up their youth to strength, speed, and hardiness, by exercising them in running races up and down steep hills, or over hard stony grounds, and when they are all in a sweat, they are ordered to leap over head and ears into a pond or a river. Four times a year the youth of certain districts meet to show their proficiency in running, and leaping, and other feats of strength or agility, where the victor is rewarded with a song made in his or her praise. On this festival the servants drive a herd of Yahoos into the field, laden with hay, and oats, and milk for a repast to the Houyhnhnms; after which, these brutes are immediately driven back again, for fear of being noisome to the assembly.

Every fourth year, at the *vernal equinox*, there is a Representative Council of the whole nation, which meets in a plain about twenty miles from our house, and continueth about five or six days. Here they inquire into the state and condition of the several districts, whether they abound or be deficient in hay or oats, or cows or Yahoos? And wherever there is any want (which is but seldom) it is immediately supplied by unanimous consent and contribution. Here likewise the regulation of children is settled: as for instance, if a Houyhnhnm hath two males, he changeth one of them with another who hath two females: and when a child hath been lost by any casualty, where the mother is past breeding, it is determined what family in the district shall breed another to supply the loss.

CHAPTER 9

A grand debate at the general Assembly of the Houyhnhnms, and how it was determined. The learning of the Houyhnhnms. Their buildings. Their manner of burials. The defectiveness of their language.

One of these grand Assemblies was held in my time, about three months before my departure, whither my master went as the Representative of our district. In this Council was resumed their old debate, and indeed, the only debate that ever happened in their country; whereof my master after his return gave me a very particular account.

The question to be debated, was, whether the Yahoos should be exterminated from the face of the earth. One of the *members* for the affirmative offered several arguments of great strength and weight, alleging, that as the Yahoos were the most filthy, noisome, and deformed animal which Nature ever produced, so they were the most restive and indocible,[2] mischievous, and malicious: they would privately suck the teats of the Houyhnhnms' cows, kill and devour their cats, trample down their oats and grass, if they were not continually watched, and commit a thousand other extravagancies. He took notice of a general tradition, that Yahoos had not been always in their country, but, that many ages ago, two of these brutes appeared together upon a mountain,[3] whether produced by the heat of the sun upon corrupted mud and slime, or from the ooze and froth of the sea, was never known.[4] That these Yahoos engendered, and their brood in a short time grew so numerous as to overrun and infest the whole nation. That the Houyhnhnms, to get rid of this evil, made a general hunting, and at last enclosed the whole herd; and destroying the elder, every Houyhnhnm kept two young ones in a kennel, and brought them to such a degree of tameness, as an animal so savage by nature can be capable of acquiring; using them

---

2. Unteachable.
3. Probably Milton's "steep savage Hill," the garden of Eden (*Paradise Lost*, 4.172).
4. Humans are supposed to be of divine origin, but the

Yahoos represent such a degraded form of humanity that they (like, it was believed, insects on the Nile's banks) were formed from the action of the sun on mud.

for draft and carriage. That there seemed to be much truth in this tradition, and that those creatures could not be *ylnhniamshy* (or *aborigines* of the land) because of the violent hatred the Houyhnhnms, as well as all other animals, bore them; which although their evil disposition sufficiently deserved, could never have arrived at so high a degree, if they had been *aborigines*, or else they would have long since been rooted out. That the inhabitants taking a fancy to use the service of the Yahoos, had very imprudently neglected to cultivate the breed of *asses*, which were a comely animal, easily kept, more tame and orderly, without any offensive smell, strong enough for labor, although they yield to the other in agility of body; and if their braying be no agreeable sound, it is far preferable to the horrible howlings of the Yahoos.[5]

Several others declared their sentiments to the same purpose, when my master proposed an expedient to the assembly, whereof he had indeed borrowed the hint from me. He approved of the tradition, mentioned by the Honorable Member who spoke before, and affirmed, that the two Yahoos said to be first seen among them had been driven thither over the sea; that coming to land, and being forsaken by their companions, they retired to the mountains, and degenerating by degrees, became in process of time, much more savage than those of their own species in the country from whence these two originals came. The reason of his assertion was, that he had now in his possession a certain wonderful[6] Yahoo (meaning myself), which most of them had heard of, and many of them had seen. He then related to them, how he first found me: that my body was all covered with an artificial composure of the skins and hairs of other animals; that I spoke in a language of my own, and had thoroughly learned theirs; that I had related to him the accidents which brought me thither; that when he saw me without my covering, I was an exact Yahoo in every part, only of a whiter color, less hairy, and with shorter claws. He added, how I had endeavored to persuade him, that in my own and other countries the Yahoos acted as the governing, rational animal, and held the Houyhnhnms in servitude; that he observed in me all the qualities of a Yahoo, only a little more civilized by some tincture of reason, which however was in a degree as far inferior to the Houyhnhnm race, as the Yahoos of their country were to me;[7] that, among other things, I mentioned a custom we had of *castrating* Houyhnhnms when they were young, in order to render them tame; that the operation was easy and safe; that it was no shame to learn wisdom from brutes, as industry is taught by the ant, and building by the swallow. (For so I translate the word *lyhannh*, although it be a much larger fowl.) That this invention might be practiced upon the younger Yahoos here, which, besides rendering them tractable and fitter for use, would in an age put an end to the whole species without destroying life. That, in the meantime the Houyhnhnms should be exhorted to cultivate the breed of asses, which, as they are in all respects more valuable brutes, so they have this advantage, to be fit for service at five years old, which the others are not till twelve.

This was all my master thought fit to tell me at that time, of what passed in the grand Council. But he was pleased to conceal[8] one particular, which related personally to myself, whereof I soon felt the unhappy effect, as the reader will know in its proper place, and from whence I date all the succeeding misfortunes of my life.

---

5. The commonplace comparison of humans to asses was one Swift had previously used in *A Tale of a Tub* (1704) and *The Battle of the Books* (1704).
6. Amazing, unusual.
7. Gulliver falls between the Houyhnhnms and the Yahoos in reason, as he did between the Lilliputians and the Brobdingnagians in size.
8. Another indication that the Houyhnhnms are not completely honest or candid.

The Houyhnhnms have no letters, and consequently their knowledge is all traditional. But there happening few events of any moment among a people so well united, naturally disposed to every virtue, wholly governed by reason, and cut off from all commerce with other nations, the historical part is easily preserved without burdening their memories. I have already observed, that they are subject to no diseases, and therefore can have no need of physicians. However, they have excellent medicines composed of herbs, to cure accidental bruises and cuts in the pastern or frog of the foot by sharp stones, as well as other maims and hurts in the several parts of the body.

They calculate the year by the revolution of the sun and the moon, but use no subdivisions into weeks. They are well enough acquainted with the motions of those two luminaries, and understand the nature of eclipses; and this is the utmost progress of their astronomy.

In poetry they must be allowed to excel all other mortals; wherein the justness of their similes, and the minuteness, as well as exactness of their descriptions, are indeed inimitable. Their verses abound very much in both of these, and usually contain either some exalted notions of friendship and benevolence, or the praises of those who were victors in races, and other bodily exercises.[9] Their buildings, although very rude and simple, are not inconvenient, but well contrived to defend them from all injuries of cold and heat. They have a kind of tree, which at forty years old loosens in the root, and falls with the first storm; it grows very straight, and being pointed like stakes with a sharp stone (for the Houyhnhnms know not the use of iron), they stick them erect in the ground about ten inches asunder,[1] and then weave in oat-straw, or sometimes wattles betwixt them. The roof is made after the same manner, and so are the doors.

The Houyhnhnms use the hollow part between the pastern and the hoof of their forefeet as we do our hands, and this with greater dexterity than I could at first imagine. I have seen a white mare of our family thread a needle (which I lent her on purpose) with that joint. They milk their cows, reap their oats, and do all the work which requires hands, in the same manner. They have a kind of hard flints, which by grinding against other stones, they form into instruments, that serve instead of wedges, axes, and hammers. With tools made of these flints they likewise cut their hay, and reap their oats, which there groweth naturally in several fields: the Yahoos draw home the sheaves in carriages, and the servants tread them in certain covered huts, to get out the grain, which is kept in stores. They make a rude kind of earthen and wooden vessels, and bake the former in the sun.

If they can avoid casualties, they die only of old age, and are buried in the obscurest places that can be found, their friends and relations expressing neither joy nor grief at their departure; nor does the dying person discover the least regret that he is leaving the world, any more than if he were upon returning[2] home from a visit to one of his neighbors;[3] I remember, my master having once made an appointment with a friend and his family to come to his house upon some affair of importance, on the day fixed, the mistress and her two children came very late; she made two excuses, first for her husband, who, as she said, happened that very morning to *lhnuwnh*. The word is strongly expressive in their language, but not easily rendered into English; it signifies, *to retire to his first mother*. Her excuse for not coming sooner, was, that

---

9. The type of poetry advocated in Plato's *Republic* (390d1–3) and practiced in Sparta.
1. Apart.

2. About to return.
3. This attitude toward death is characteristic of both the Stoics, and the Utopians.

her husband dying late in the morning, she was a good while consulting her servants about a convenient place where his body should be laid; and I observed she behaved herself at our house as cheerfully as the rest; she died about three months after.

They live generally to seventy or seventy-five years, very seldom to fourscore; some weeks before their death they feel a gradual decay, but without pain. During this time they are much visited by their friends, because they cannot go abroad with their usual ease and satisfaction. However, about ten days before their death, which they seldom fail in computing, they return the visits that have been made them by those who are nearest in the neighborhood, being carried in a convenient sledge drawn by Yahoos, which vehicle they use, not only upon this occasion, but when they grow old, upon long journeys, or when they are lamed by an accident. And therefore when the dying Houyhnhnms return those visits, they take a solemn leave of their friends, as if they were going to some remote part of the country, where they designed to pass the rest of their lives.

I know not whether it may be worth observing, that the Houyhnhnms have no word in their language to express anything that is *evil*, except what they borrow from the deformities or ill qualities of the Yahoos. Thus they denote the folly of a servant, an omission of a child, a stone that cuts their feet, a continuance of foul or unseasonable weather, and the like, by adding to each the epithet of *yahoo*. For instance, *hhnm yahoo*, *whnaholm yahoo*, *ynlhmnawihlma yahoo*, and an ill-contrived house, *ynholmhnmrohlnw yahoo*.

I could with great pleasure enlarge farther upon the manners and virtues of this excellent people; but intending in a short time to publish a volume by itself expressly upon that subject, I refer the reader thither. And in the meantime, proceed to relate my own sad catastrophe.

CHAPTER 10

The author's economy[4] and happy life among the Houyhnhnms. His great improvement in virtue, by conversing with them. Their conversations. The author hath notice given him by his master that he must depart from the country. He falls into a swoon for grief, but submits. He contrives and finishes a canoe, by the help of a fellow servant, and puts to sea at a venture.[5]

I had settled my little economy to my own heart's content. My master had ordered a room to be made for me after their manner, about six yards from the house, the sides and floors of which I plastered with clay, and covered with rush mats of my own contriving; I had beaten hemp, which there grows wild, and made of it a sort of ticking;[6] this I filled with the feathers of several birds I had taken with springes made of Yahoos' hairs, and were excellent food. I had worked[7] two chairs with my knife, the sorrel nag helping me in the grosser[8] and more laborious part. When my clothes were worn to rags, I made myself others with the skins of rabbits, and of a certain beautiful animal about the same size, called *nnuhnoh*, the skin of which is covered with a fine down. Of these I likewise made very tolerable stockings. I soled my shoes with wood which I cut from a tree, and fitted to the upper leather, and when this was worn out, I supplied it with the skins of Yahoos dried in the sun. I often got honey out of hollow

4. Method of living.
5. Without further planning.
6. Sturdy material used for making mattress covering.
7. Made.
8. Heavier, larger.

trees, which I mingled with water,[9] or ate it with my bread. No man could more verify the truth of these two maxims, *That nature is very easily satisfied;* and, *That necessity is the mother of invention.* I enjoyed perfect health of body and tranquillity of mind; I did not feel the treachery or inconstancy of a friend, nor the injuries of a secret or open enemy. I had no occasion of bribing, flattering, or pimping, to procure the favor of any great man or of his minion. I wanted no fence[1] against fraud or oppression; here was neither physician to destroy my body, nor lawyer to ruin my fortune; no informer to watch my words and actions, or forge accusations against me for hire; here were no jibers, censurers, backbiters, pickpockets, highwaymen, housebreakers, attorneys, bawds, buffoons, gamesters, politicians, wits, splenetics, tedious talkers, controvertists, ravishers, murderers, robbers, virtuosos;[2] no leaders or followers of party and faction; no encouragers to vice, by seducement or examples; no dungeon, axes, gibbets, whipping posts, or pillories; no cheating shopkeepers or mechanics;[3] no pride, vanity, or affectation; no fops, bullies, drunkards, strolling whores, or poxes;[4] no ranting, lewd, expensive wives; no stupid, proud pendants; no importunate, overbearing, quarrelsome, noisy, roaring, empty, conceited, swearing companions; no scoundrels, raised from the dust upon the merit of their vices, or nobility thrown into it on account of their virtues; no lords, fiddlers, judges, or dancing masters.[5]

I had the favor of being admitted to[6] several Houyhnhnms, who came to visit or dine with my master; where his Honor graciously suffered me to wait in the room, and listen to their discourse. Both he and his company would often descend to ask me questions, and receive my answers. I had also sometimes the honor of attending my master in his visits to others. I never presumed to speak, except in answer to a question, and then I did it with inward regret, because it was a loss of so much time for improving myself; but I was infinitely delighted with the station of a humble auditor in such conversations, where nothing passed but what was useful, expressed in the fewest and most significant words; where (as I have already said) the greatest *decency* was observed, without the least degree of ceremony; where no person spoke without being pleased himself, and pleasing his companions; where there was no interruption, tediousness, heat,[7] or difference of sentiments. They have a notion, that when people are met together, a short silence doth much improve conversation: this I found to be true, for during those little intermissions of talk, new ideas would arise in their minds, which very much enlivened the discourse. Their subjects are generally on friendship and benevolence, or order and economy, sometimes upon the visible operations of Nature, or ancient traditions, upon the bounds and limits of virtue, upon the unerring rules of reason, or upon some determinations to be taken at the next great Assembly, and often upon the various excellencies of *poetry.* I may add without vanity, that my presence often gave them sufficient matter for discourse, because it afforded my master an occasion of letting his friends into the history of me and my country, upon which they were all pleased to descant in a manner not very advantageous to humankind; and for that reason I shall not repeat what they said: only I may be allowed to observe, that his Honor, to my great admiration, appeared to understand the nature of Yahoos much better than myself. He went through all our vices and follies, and discovered many which I had never mentioned to him, by only supposing

9. Honey-sweetened water was a Utopian drink.
1. Defense.
2. One knowledgeable or interested in apparently trivial "scientific" pursuits.
3. Laborers.
4. Venereal diseases.

5. That necessary tutor for the socially aspiring, the dancing master (usually French), was a particular figure of fun; he usually accompanied himself on the fiddle.
6. Allowed to meet.
7. Heat of argument.

what qualities a Yahoo of their country, with a small proportion of reason, might be capable of exerting; and concluded, with too much probability, how vile as well as miserable such a creature must be.

I freely confess, that all the little knowledge I have of any value, was acquired by the lectures I received from my master, and from hearing the discourses of him and his friends; to which I should be prouder to listen, than to dictate to the greatest and wisest assembly in Europe. I admired the strength, comeliness, and speed of the inhabitants; and such a constellation of virtues in such amiable persons produced in me the highest veneration. At first, indeed, I did not feel that natural awe which the Yahoos and all other animals bear towards them, but it grew upon me by degrees, much sooner than I imagined, and was mingled with a respectful love and gratitude, that they would condescend to distinguish me from the rest of my species.

When I thought of my family, my friends, my countrymen, or human race in general, I considered them as they really were, Yahoos in shape and disposition, perhaps a little more civilized, and qualified with the gift of speech, but making no other use of reason, than to improve and multiply those vices, whereof their brethren in this country had only the share that Nature allotted them. When I happened to behold the reflection of my own form in a lake or a fountain, I turned away my face in horror and detestation of myself,[8] and could better endure the sight of a common Yahoo, than of my own person. By conversing with the Houyhnhnms, and looking upon them with delight, I fell to imitate their gait and gesture, which is now grown into a habit, and my friends often tell me in a blunt way, that I *trot like a horse*; which, however, I take for a great compliment; neither shall I disown, that in speaking I am apt to fall into the voice and manner of the Houyhnhnms, and hear myself ridiculed on that account without the least mortification.

In the midst of all this happiness, when I looked upon myself to be fully settled for life, my master sent for me one morning a little earlier than his usual hour. I observed by his countenance that he was in some perplexity, and at a loss how to begin what he had to speak. After a short silence, he told me, he did not know how I would take what he was going to say; that in the last general Assembly, when the affair of the Yahoos was entered upon, the representatives had taken offense at his keeping a Yahoo (meaning myself) in his family more like a Houyhnhnm, than a brute animal. That he was known frequently to converse with me, as if he could receive some advantage or pleasure in my company; that such a practice was not agreeable to reason or Nature, or a thing ever heard of before among them. The Assembly did therefore *exhort* him, either to employ me like the rest of my species, or command me to swim back to the place from whence I came. That the first of these expedients was utterly rejected by all the Houyhnhnms who had ever seen me at his house or their own, for they alleged, that because I had some rudiments of reason, added to the natural pravity[9] of those animals, it was to be feared, I might be able to seduce them into the woody and mountainous parts of the country, and bring them in troops by night to destroy the Houyhnhnms' cattle, as being naturally of the ravenous[1] kind, and averse from labor.

My master added, that he was daily pressed by the Houyhnhnms of the neighborhood to have the Assembly's *exhortation* executed, which he could not put off much longer. He doubted[2] it would be impossible for me to swim to another country, and

---

8. A mocking reversal both of a common pattern in pastoral love poetry and of the Greek myth of Narcissus.
9. Depravity.

1. Rapacious, predatory, or greedy.
2. Feared.

therefore wished I would contrive some sort of vehicle resembling those I had described to him, that might carry me on the sea, in which work I should have the assistance of his own servants, as well as those of his neighbors. He concluded, that for his own part he could have been content to keep me in his service as long as I lived, because he found I had cured myself of some bad habits and dispositions, by endeavoring, as far as my inferior nature was capable, to imitate the Houyhnhnms.

I should here observe to the reader, that a decree of the general Assembly in this country is expressed by the word *hnhloayn*, which signifies an *exhortation*, as near as I can render it, for they have no conception how a rational creature can be *compelled*, but only advised, or *exhorted*, because no person can disobey reason, without giving up his claim to be a rational creature.

I was struck with the utmost grief and despair at my master's discourse, and being unable to support the agonies I was under, I fell into a swoon at his feet; when I came to myself, he told me, that he concluded I had been dead. (For these people are subject to no such imbecilities of nature.) I answered, in a faint voice, that death would have been too great an happiness; that although I could not blame the Assembly's *exhortation*, or the urgency[3] of his friends, yet in my weak and corrupt judgment, I thought it might consist[4] with reason to have been less rigorous. That I could not swim a league, and probably the nearest land to theirs might be distant above a hundred; that many materials, necessary for making a small vessel to carry me off, were wholly wanting in this country, which, however, I would attempt in obedience and gratitude to his Honor, although I concluded the thing to be impossible, and therefore looked on myself as already devoted to destruction. That the certain prospect of an unnatural death was the least of my evils: for, supposing I should escape with life by some strange adventure, how could I think with temper[5] of passing my days among Yahoos, and relapsing into my old corruptions, for want of examples to lead and keep me within the paths of virtue? That I knew too well upon what solid reasons all the determinations of the wise Houyhnhnms were founded, not to be shaken by arguments of mine, a miserable Yahoo; and therefore after presenting him with my humble thanks for the offer of his servants' assistance in making a vessel, and desiring a reasonable time for so difficult a work, I told him I would endeavor to preserve a wretched being; and, if ever I returned to England, was not without hopes of being useful to my own species, by celebrating the praises of the renowned Houyhnhnms, and proposing their virtues to the imitation of mankind.

My master in a few words made me a very gracious reply, allowed me the space of two *months* to finish my boat; and ordered the sorrel nag, my fellow servant (for so at this distance I may presume to call him) to follow my instructions, because I told my master, that his help would be sufficient, and I knew he had a tenderness for me.

In his company my first business was to go to that part of the coast, where my rebellious crew had ordered me to be set on shore. I got upon a height, and looking on every side into the sea, fancied I saw a small island, towards the northeast: I took out my pocket glass, and could then clearly distinguish it about five leagues off, as I computed; but it appeared to the sorrel nag to be only a blue cloud: for, as he had no conception of any country beside his own, so he could not be as expert in distinguishing remote objects at sea, as we who so much converse[6] in that element.

After I had discovered this island, I considered no farther; but resolved it should, if possible, be the first place of my banishment, leaving the consequence to Fortune.

3. Urging.
4. Be consistent.

5. Calmness.
6. Are familiar with.

I returned home, and consulting with the sorrel nag, we went into a copse at some distance, where I with my knife, and he with a sharp flint fastened very artificially, after their manner, to a wooden handle, cut down several oak wattles about the thickness of a walking staff, and some larger pieces. But I shall not trouble the reader with a particular description of my own mechanics; let it suffice to say, that in six weeks' time, with the help of the sorrel nag, who performed the parts that required most labor, I finished a sort of Indian canoe, but much larger, covering it with the skins of Yahoos well stitched together, with hempen threads of my own making. My sail was likewise composed of the skins of the same animal; but I made use of the youngest I could get, the older being too tough and thick, and I likewise provided myself with four paddles. I laid in a stock of boiled flesh, of rabbits and fowls, and took with me two vessels, one filled with milk, and the other with water.

I tried my canoe in a large pond near my master's house, and then corrected in it what was amiss; stopping all the chinks with Yahoos' tallow, till I found it staunch,[7] and able to bear me and my freight. And when it was as complete as I could possibly make it, I had it drawn on a carriage very gently by Yahoos, to the seaside, under the conduct of the sorrel nag, and another servant.

When all was ready, and the day came for my departure, I took leave of my master and lady, and the whole family, mine eyes flowing with tears, and my heart quite sunk with grief. But his Honor, out of curiosity, and perhaps (if I may speak it without vanity) partly out of kindness, was determined to see me in my canoe, and got several of his neighboring friends to accompany him. I was forced to wait above an hour for the tide, and then observing the wind very fortunately bearing towards the island, to which I intended to steer my course, I took a second leave of my master, but as I was going to prostrate myself to kiss his hoof, he did me the honor to raise it gently to my mouth. I am not ignorant how much I have been censured for mentioning this last particular. For my detractors are pleased to think it improbable, that so illustrious a person should descend to give so great a mark of distinction to a creature so inferior as I. Neither have I forgot, how apt some travelers are to boast of extraordinary favors they have received.[8] But if these censurers were better acquainted with the noble and courteous disposition of the Houyhnhnms, they would soon change their opinion.

I paid my respects to the rest of the Houyhnhnms in his Honor's company; then getting into my canoe, I pushed off from shore.

CHAPTER 11

The author's dangerous voyage. He arrives at New Holland, hoping to settle there. Is wounded with an arrow by one of the natives. Is seized and carried by force into a Portuguese ship. The great civilities of the captain. The author arrives at England.

I began this desperate voyage on February 15, 1715, at 9 o'clock in the morning. The wind was very favorable; however, I made use at first only of my paddles, but considering I should soon be weary, and that the wind might probably chop about,[9] I ventured to set up my little sail; and thus, with the help of the tide, I went at the rate of a league and a half an hour, as near as I could guess. My master and his friends continued[1] on the shore, till I was almost out of sight; and I often heard the sorrel nag (who always loved me) crying out, *Hnuy illa nyha maiah Yahoo*, Take care of thyself, gentle Yahoo.

7. Watertight.
8. Swift heightens the absurdity of Gulliver's action, and draws attention to his later misanthropy.

9. Change direction.
1. Stayed.

My design was, if possible, to discover some small island uninhabited, yet sufficient by my labor to furnish me with the necessaries of life, which I would have thought a greater happiness than to be first minister in the politest court of Europe; so horrible was the idea I conceived of returning to live in the society and under the government of Yahoos. For in such a solitude as I desired, I could at least enjoy my own thoughts, and reflect with delight on the virtues of those inimitable Houyhnhnms, without any opportunity of degenerating into the vices and corruptions of my own species.

The reader may remember what I related when my crew conspired against me, and confined me to my cabin. How I continued there several weeks, without knowing what course we took, and when I was put ashore in the longboat, how the sailors told me with oaths, whether true or false, that they knew not in what part of the world we were. However, I did then believe us to be about ten degrees southward of the Cape of Good Hope, or about 45 degrees southern latitude, as I gathered from some general words I overheard among them, being I supposed to the southeast in their intended voyage to Madagascar. And although this were but little better than conjecture, yet I resolved to steer my course eastward, hoping to reach the southwest coast of New Holland, and perhaps some such island as I desired, lying westward of it. The wind was full west, and by six in the evening I computed I had gone eastward at least eighteen leagues, when I spied a very small island about half a league off, which I soon reached. It was nothing but a rock, with one creek, naturally arched by the force of tempests. Here I put in my canoe, and climbing a part of the rock, I could plainly discover[2] land to the east, extending from south to north. I lay all night in my canoe, and repeating my voyage early in the morning, I arrived in seven hours to the southwest point of New Holland.[3] This confirmed me in the opinion I have long entertained, that the maps and charts place this country at least three degrees more to the east than it really is;[4] which thought I communicated many years ago to my worthy friend Mr. Herman Moll, and gave him my reasons for it, although he hath rather chosen to follow other authors.[5]

I saw no inhabitants in the place where I landed, and being unarmed, I was afraid of venturing far into the country. I found some shellfish on the shore, and ate them raw, not daring to kindle a fire, for fear of being discovered by the natives. I continued three days feeding on oysters and limpets,[6] to save my own provisions, and I fortunately found a brook of excellent water, which gave me great relief.

On the fourth day, venturing out early a little too far, I saw twenty or thirty natives upon a height, not above five hundred yards from me. They were stark naked, men, women, and children, round a fire, as I could discover by the smoke. One of them spied me, and gave notice to the rest; five of them advanced towards me, leaving the women and children at the fire. I made what haste I could to the shore, and getting into my canoe, shoved off: the savages observing me retreat, ran after me; and before I could get far enough into the sea, discharged an arrow, which wounded me deeply on the inside of my left knee (I shall carry the mark to my grave). I apprehended the arrow might be poisoned, and paddling out of the reach of their darts (being a calm day) I made a shift to suck the wound, and dress it as well as I could.

---

2. Discern.
3. New Holland was the name the explorer Abel Tasman originally gave to the western coast of Australia. Gulliver seems to place the land of the Houyhnhnms west of southwestern Australia, in which case the distance he covers to reach New Holland is improbable (1,500 to 2,000 nautical miles in 16 hours). It is possible, however, that Gulliver is meant to have landed on Tasmania, thus putting the Houyhnhnms a short distance west of this island.
4. Dampier claimed that he had found New Holland further west than indicated in Tasman's charts.
5. This geographer's *New and Correct Map of the Whole World* (1719) was probably the basis for Swift's geography in *Gulliver's Travels*.
6. Small mollusks that attach themselves to rocks.

I was at a loss what to do, for I durst not return to the same landing place, but stood[7] to the north, and was forced to paddle; for the wind though very gentle was against me, blowing northwest. As I was looking about for a secure landing place, I saw a sail to the north-north-east, which appearing every minute more visible, I was in some doubt, whether I should wait for them or no; but at last my detestation of the Yahoo race prevailed, and turning my canoe, I sailed and paddled together to the south, and got into the same creek from whence I set out in the morning, choosing rather to trust myself among these *barbarians*, than live with European Yahoos. I drew up my canoe as close as I could to the shore, and hid myself behind a stone by the little brook, which, as I have already said, was excellent water.

The ship came within a half a league of this creek, and sent out her longboat with vessels to take in fresh water (for the place it seems was very well known) but I did not observe it till the boat was almost on shore, and it was too late to seek another hiding place. The seamen at their landing observed my canoe, and rummaging it all over, easily conjectured that the owner could not be far off. Four of them well armed searched every cranny and lurking hole, till at last they found me flat on my face behind the stone. They gazed a while in admiration[8] at my strange uncouth dress, my coat made of skins, my wooden-soled shoes, and my furred stockings; from whence, however, they concluded I was not a native of the place, who all go naked. One of the seamen in Portuguese bid me rise, and asked who I was. I understood that language very well, and getting upon my feet, said, I was a poor Yahoo, banished from the Houyhnhnms, and desired they would please to let me depart. They admired to hear me answer them in their own tongue, and saw by my complexion I must be a European; but were at a loss to know what I meant by Yahoos and Houyhnhnms, and at the same time fell a laughing at my strange tone in speaking, which resembled the neighing of a horse. I trembled all the while betwixt fear and hatred: I again desired leave to depart, and was gently moving to my canoe; but they laid hold on me, desiring to know, what country I was of? whence I came? with many other questions. I told them, I was born in England, from whence I came about five years ago, and then their country and ours were at peace. I therefore hoped they would not treat me as an enemy, since I meant them no harm, but was a poor Yahoo, seeking some desolate place where to pass the remainder of his unfortunate life.

When they began to talk, I thought I never heard or saw anything so unnatural; for it appeared to me as monstrous as if a dog or a cow should speak in England, or a Yahoo in Houyhnhnmland. The honest Portuguese were equally amazed at my strange dress, and the odd manner of delivering my words, which however they understood very well. They spoke to me with great humanity, and said they were sure their captain would carry me *gratis* to Lisbon, from whence I might return to my own country; that two of the seamen would go back to the ship, to inform the captain of what they had seen, and receive his orders; in the meantime, unless I would give my solemn oath not to fly,[9] they would secure me by force. I thought it best to comply with their proposal. They were very curious to know my story, but I gave them very little satisfaction; and they all conjectured, that my misfortunes had impaired my reason. In two hours the boat, which went loaden with vessels of water, returned with the captain's commands to fetch me on board. I fell on my knees to

7. Steered.
8. Wonder, amazement.

9. Attempt to escape.

preserve my liberty; but all was in vain, and the men having tied me with cords, heaved me into the boat, from whence I was taken into the ship, and from thence into the captain's cabin.

His name was Pedro de Mendez; he was a very courteous and generous person; he entreated me to give some account of myself, and desired to know what I would eat or drink; said, I should be used as well as himself, and spoke so many obliging things, that I wondered to find such civilities from a Yahoo. However, I remained silent and sullen; I was ready to faint at the very smell of him and his men. At last I desired something to eat out of my own canoe; but he ordered me a chicken and some excellent wine, and then directed that I should be put to bed in a very clean cabin. I would not undress myself, but lay on the bed clothes, and in half an hour stole out, when I thought the crew was at dinner, and getting to the side of the ship was going to leap into the sea, and swim for my life, rather than continue among Yahoos. But one of the seamen prevented me, and having informed the captain, I was chained to my cabin.

After dinner Don Pedro came to me, and desired to know my reason for so desperate an attempt: assured me he only meant to do me all the service he was able, and spoke so very movingly, that at last I descended[1] to treat him like an animal which had some little portion of reason. I gave him a very short relation of my voyage, of the conspiracy against me by my own men, of the country where they set me on shore, and of my three years' residence there. All which he looked upon as if it were a dream or a vision; whereat I took great offense; for I had quite forgot the faculty of lying, so peculiar to Yahoos in all countries where they preside, and consequently the disposition of suspecting truth in others of their own species. I asked him, whether it were the custom of his country to *say the thing that was not?* I assured him I had almost forgot what he meant by falsehood, and if I had lived a thousand years in Houyhnhnmland, I should never have heard a lie from the meanest servant; that I was altogether indifferent whether he believed me or no; but however, in return for his favors, I would give so much allowance to the corruption of his nature, as to answer any objection he would please to make, and then he might easily discover the truth.

The captain, a wise man, after many endeavors to catch me tripping in some part of my story, at last began to have a better opinion of my veracity.[2] But he added, that since I professed so inviolable an attachment to truth, I must give him my word of honor to bear him company in this voyage without attempting anything against my life, or else he would continue[3] me a prisoner till we arrived at Lisbon. I gave him the promise he required; but at the same time protested that I would suffer the greatest hardships rather than return to live among Yahoos.

Our voyage passed without any considerable accident.[4] In gratitude to the captain I sometimes sat with him at his earnest request, and strove to conceal my antipathy against human kind, although it often broke out, which he suffered to pass without observation. But the greatest part of the day, I confined myself to my cabin, to avoid seeing any of the crew. The captain had often entreated me to strip myself of

---

1. Condescended.
2. In the first edition, the sentence continues: "and the rather, because he confessed, he met with a Dutch Skipper, who pretended to have landed with five others of his crew upon a certain island or continent south of New Holland, where they went for fresh water, and observed a horse driving before him several animals exactly resembling those I had described under the name of Yahoos,

with some other particulars, which the captain said he had forgot, because he then concluded them all to be lies." In 1735 Swift's Dublin publisher, George Faulkener, omitted these lines, probably because they contradicted Gulliver's later statement that no other European had visited this land.
3. Keep.
4. Incident.

my savage dress, and offered to lend me the best suit of clothes he had. This I would not be prevailed on to accept, abhorring to cover myself with anything that had been on the back of a Yahoo. I only desired he would lend me two clean shirts, which having been washed since he wore them, I believed would not so much defile me. These I changed every second day, and washed them myself.

We arrived at Lisbon, Nov. 5, 1715. At our landing the captain forced me to cover myself with his cloak, to prevent the rabble from crowding about me. I was conveyed to his own house, and at my earnest request, he led me up to the highest room backwards.[5] I conjured[6] him to conceal from all persons what I had told him of the Houyhnhnms, because the least hint of such a story would not only draw numbers of people to see me, but probably put me in danger of being imprisoned, or burnt by the Inquisition.[7] The captain persuaded me to accept a suit of clothes newly made, but I would not suffer the tailor to take my measure; however, Don Pedro being almost of my size, they fitted me well enough. He accoutered[8] me with other necessaries all new, which I aired for twenty-four hours before I would use them.

The captain had no wife, nor above three servants, none of which were suffered to attend at meals, and his whole deportment was so obliging, added to very good *human* understanding, that I really began to tolerate his company. He gained so far upon me, that I ventured to look out of the back window. By degrees I was brought into another room, from whence I peeped into the street, but drew my head back in a fright. In a week's time he seduced me down to the door. I found my terror gradually lessened, but my hatred and contempt seemed to increase. I was at last bold enough to walk the street in his company, but kept my nose well stopped with rue,[9] or sometimes with tobacco.

In ten days Don Pedro, to whom I had given some account of my domestic affairs, put it upon me as a point of honor and conscience, that I ought to return to my native country, and live at home with my wife and children. He told me, there was an English ship in the port just ready to sail, and he would furnish me with all things necessary. It would be tedious to repeat his arguments, and my contradictions. He said, it was altogether impossible to find such a solitary island as I had desired to live in; but I might command in my own house, and pass my time in a manner as recluse as I pleased.

I complied at last, finding I could not do better. I left Lisbon the 24th day of November, in an English merchantman, but who was the master I never inquired. Don Pedro accompanied me to the ship, and lent me twenty pounds. He took kind leave of me, and embraced me at parting, which I bore as well as I could. During this last voyage I had no commerce[1] with the master or any of his men, but pretending I was sick kept close in my cabin. On the fifth of December, 1715, we cast anchor in the Downs[2] about nine in the morning, and at three in the afternoon I got safe to my house at Redriff.

My wife and family received me with great surprise and joy, because they concluded me certainly dead; but I must freely confess the sight of them filled me only with hatred, disgust, and contempt, and the more by reflecting on the near alliance I

5. At the back of the house.
6. Appealed earnestly to.
7. Either because the Houyhnhnm hierarchy contradicted Genesis, in which man has dominion over the earth, or because Gulliver had been associating with diabolical powers, who could make humans appear to be horses (as

Gulliver himself had first believed).
8. Attired.
9. Strong-smelling shrub, used for medicinal purposes.
1. Interaction.
2. The sea off the North Downs in East Kent.

had to them. For, although since my unfortunate exile from the Houyhnhnm country, I had compelled myself to tolerate the sight of Yahoos, and to converse with Don Pedro de Mendez, yet my memory and imaginations were perpetually filled with the virtues and ideas of those exalted Houyhnhnms. And when I began to consider, that by copulating with one of the Yahoo species, I had become a parent of more, it struck me with the utmost shame, confusion, and horror.

As soon as I entered the house, my wife took me in her arms, and kissed me, at which, having not been used to the touch of that odious animal for so many years, I fell in a swoon for almost an hour. At the time I am writing it is five years since my last return to England: during the first year I could not endure my wife or children in my presence, the very smell of them was intolerable, much less could I suffer them to eat in the same room. To this hour they dare not presume to touch my bread, or drink out of the same cup, neither was I ever able to let one of them take me by the hand.[3] The first money I laid out was to buy two young stone-horses,[4] which I keep in a good stable, and next to them the groom is my greatest favorite; for I feel my spirits revived by the smell he contracts in the stable. My horses understand me tolerably well; I converse with them at least four hours every day. They are strangers to bridle or saddle, they live in great amity with me, and friendship to each other.

CHAPTER 12

The author's veracity. His design in publishing this work. His censure of those travelers who swerve from the truth. The author clears himself from any sinister ends in writing. An objection answered. The method of planting Colonies. His native country commended. The right of the Crown to those countries described by the author is justified. The difficulty of conquering them. The author takes his last leave of the reader, proposeth his manner of living for the future, gives good advice, and concludeth.

Thus, gentle reader,[5] I have given thee a faithful history of my travels for sixteen years, and above seven months, wherein I have not been so studious of ornament as of truth. I could perhaps like others have astonished thee with strange improbable tales; but I rather chose to relate plain matter of fact in the simplest manner and style, because my principal design was to inform, and not to amuse thee.

It is easy for us who travel into remote countries, which are seldom visited by Englishmen or other Europeans, to form descriptions of wonderful animals both at sea and land. Whereas a traveler's chief aim should be to make men wiser and better, and to improve their minds by the bad as well as good example of what they deliver concerning foreign places.[6]

I could heartily wish a law were enacted, that every traveler, before he were permitted to publish his voyages, should be obliged to make oath before the Lord High Chancellor that all he intended to print was absolutely true to the best of his knowledge; for then the world would no longer be deceived as it usually is, while some writers, to make their works pass the better upon the public, impose the grossest falsities on the unwary reader. I have perused several books of travels with great delight in my younger days; but having since gone over most parts of the globe, and been able to

---

3. Gulliver's unwillingness to share his bread or cup with his wife or children emphasizes his unchristian behavior.
4. Stallions.
5. Highly ironic, since the "gentle" readers must be Yahoos.
6. More's *Utopia* also argues that accounts of distant travels should provide useful lessons rather than fabulous tales.

contradict many fabulous accounts from my own observation, it hath given me a great disgust against this part of reading, and some indignation to see the credulity of mankind so impudently abused. Therefore since my acquaintance were pleased to think my poor endeavors might not be unacceptable to my country, I imposed on myself as a maxim, never to be swerved from, that I would *strictly adhere to truth*; neither indeed can I be ever under the least temptation to vary from it, while I retain in my mind the lectures and example of my noble master, and the other illustrious Houyhnhnms, of whom I had so long the honor to be an humble hearer.

> —*Nec si miserum Fortuna Sinonem*
> *Finxit, vanum etiam mendacemque improba finget.*[7]

I know very well how little reputation is to be got by writings which require neither genius nor learning, nor indeed any other talent, except a good memory or an exact journal. I know likewise, that writers of travels, like dictionary-makers, are sunk into oblivion by the weight and bulk of those who come last, and therefore lie uppermost.[8] And it is highly probable, that such travelers who shall hereafter visit the countries described in this work of mine, may, by detecting my errors (if there be any), and adding many new discoveries of their own, jostle me out of vogue, and stand in my place, making the world forget that ever I was an author. This indeed would be too great a mortification if I wrote for fame; but, as my sole intention was the PUBLIC GOOD,[9] I cannot be altogether disappointed. For who can read of the virtues I have mentioned in the glorious Houyhnhnms, without being ashamed of his own vices, when he considers himself as the reasoning, governing animal of his country? I shall say nothing of those remote nations where Yahoos preside, amongst which the least corrupted are the Brobdingnagians, whose wise maxims in morality and government it would be our happiness to observe. But I forbear descanting further, and rather leave the judicious reader to his own remarks and applications.

I am not a little pleased that this work of mine can possibly meet with no[1] censurers: for what objections can be made against a writer who relates only plain facts that happened in such distant countries, where we have not the least interest with respect either to trade or negotiations? I have carefully avoided every fault with which common writers of travels are often too justly charged. Besides, I meddle not the least with any *party*, but write without passion, prejudice, or ill-will against any man or number of men whatsoever. I write for the noblest end, to inform and instruct mankind, over whom I may, without breach of modesty, pretend to some superiority from the advantages I received by conversing so long among the most accomplished Houyhnhnms. I write without any view towards profit or praise. I never suffer a word to pass that may look like reflection,[2] or possibly give the least offense even to those who are most ready to take it. So that I hope I may with justice pronounce myself an author perfectly blameless, against whom the tribe of answerers, considerers, observers, reflecters, detecters, remarkers, will never be able to find matter for exercising their talents.[3]

---

7. "Nor, if cruel Fortune has made Sinon miserable, shall he also make him false and deceitful" (Virgil, *Aeneid* 2. 79–80). Swift cleverly employs the words that the Greek Sinon, the most famous liar in antiquity, used in the fraudulent tale he told to fool the Trojans into accepting *his* (wooden) horse.

8. The most current dictionary is the one most frequently used.

9. The English buccaneer and navigator William Dampi-
er professes a similar aim in the dedication to his *New Voyage Round the World* (1697).

1. Cannot possibly encounter any.

2. Criticism.

3. At this time it was common for historical and fictional accounts to be "applied" to contemporary situations or persons; by having Gulliver deny at such length that he is doing this, Swift draws attention to the possibility of making such connections.

I confess, it was whispered to me, that I was bound in duty as a subject of England, to have given in a memorial to a Secretary of State, at my first coming over; because, whatever lands are discovered by a subject belong to the Crown. But I doubt whether our conquests in the countries I treat of, would be as easy as those of Ferdinando Cortez over the naked Americans.[4] The Lilliputians, I think, are hardly worth the charge of a fleet and army to reduce them, and I question whether it might be prudent or safe to attempt the Brobdingnagians. Or whether an English army would be much at their ease with the Flying Island over their heads.[5] The Houyhnhnms, indeed, appear not to be so well prepared for war, a science to which they are perfect strangers, and especially against missive weapons.[6] However, supposing myself to be a minister of State, I could never give my advice for invading them. Their prudence, unanimity, unacquaintedness with fear, and their love of their country would amply supply all defects in the military art. Imagine twenty thousand of them breaking into the midst of an European army, confounding the ranks, overturning the carriages, battering the warriors' faces into mummy,[7] by terrible yerks[8] from their hinder hoofs. For they would well deserve the character given to Augustus; *Recalcitrat undique tutus.*[9] But instead of proposals for conquering that magnanimous nation, I rather wish they were in a capacity or disposition to send a sufficient number of their inhabitants for civilizing Europe, by teaching us the first principles of honor, justice, truth, temperance, public spirit, fortitude, chastity, friendship, benevolence, and fidelity. The *names* of all which virtues are still retained among us in most languages, and are to be met with in modern as well as ancient authors; which I am able to assert from my own small reading.

But I had another reason which made me less forward[1] to enlarge his Majesty's dominions by my discoveries. To say the truth, I had conceived a few scruples with relation to the distributive justice[2] of princes upon those occasions. For instance, a crew of pirates[3] are driven by a storm they know not whither, at length a boy discovers land from the topmast, they go on shore to rob and plunder; they see a harmless people, are entertained with kindness, they give the country a new name, they take formal possession of it for the king, they set up a rotten plank or a stone for a memorial, they murder two or three dozen of the natives, bring away a couple more by force for a sample, return home, and get their pardon. Here commences a new dominion acquired with a title by *divine right*. Ships are sent with the first opportunity, the natives driven out or destroyed, their princes tortured to discover their gold;[4] a free license given to all acts of inhumanity and lust, the earth reeking with the blood of its inhabitants; and this execrable crew of butchers employed in so pious an expedition, is a *modern colony* sent to convert and civilize an idolatrous and barbarous people.

---

4. In the 1520s, Cortés and 400 soldiers rapidly conquered the Aztec empire in Mexico.
5. These sentences refer to Gulliver's other travels: in Lilliput he encountered a miniature people; in Brobdingnag he met with giants; and in Laputa he encountered the Flying Island (able to force inhabitants below to submit either through starving them by blocking out the sun or by crushing them).
6. Anything thrown or shot through the air.
7. Pulp.
8. Kicks.
9. "He kicks back, well protected on every side" (Horace, *Satires* 2.i.20). While Gulliver refers admiringly to the horse's ability to defend itself, Swift recalls the context

for Horace's decision to use satire (rather than praise) when writing about Augustus: according to Horace, Augustus would kick out like a horse if he sensed servile flattery, so flattery was pointless. Gulliver's lavish praise of the Houyhnhnms backfires on him, not because the Houyhnhnms disliked it, but because his uncritical identification with them leaves him unable to cope with human society.
1. Eager.
2. Fairness with regard to the rights of the native people.
3. Referring to the first Spanish colonizers of America.
4. Montezuma was tortured by Cortés, and the Incan emperor Atahuallpa by Pizarro (1533).

But this description, I confess, doth by no means affect the British nation, who may be an example to the whole world for their wisdom, care, and justice in planting colonies;[5] their liberal endowments for the advancement of religion and learning; their choice of devout and able pastors to propagate Christianity; their caution in stocking their provinces with people of sober lives and conversations from this the mother kingdom;[6] their strict regard to the distribution of justice, in supplying the civil administration through all their colonies with officers of the greatest abilities, utter strangers to corruption; and to crown all, by sending the most vigilant and virtuous governors, who have no other views than the happiness of the people over whom they preside, and the honor of the King their master.

But, as those countries which I have described do not appear to have any desire of being conquered, and enslaved, murdered, or driven out by colonies, nor abound either in gold, silver, sugar, or tobacco; I did humbly conceive they were by no means proper objects of our zeal, our valor, or our interest. However, if those whom it more concerns, think fit to be of another opinion, I am ready to depose, when I shall be lawfully called, that no European did ever visit those countries before me. I mean, if the inhabitants ought to be believed.[7]

But as to the formality of taking possession in my Sovereign's name, it never came once into my thoughts; and if it had, yet as my affairs then stood, I should perhaps in point of prudence and self-preservation, have put it off to a better opportunity.

Having thus answered the *only* objection that can ever be raised against me as a traveler, I here take a final leave of my courteous readers, and return to enjoy my own speculations in my little garden at Redriff, to apply those excellent lessons of virtue which I learned among the Houyhnhnms, to instruct the Yahoos of my own family as far as I shall find them docible[8] animals, to behold my figure often in a glass, and thus if possible habituate myself by time to tolerate the sight of a human creature, to lament the brutality of Houyhnhnms in my own country, but always treat their persons with respect, for the sake of my noble master, his family, his friends, and the whole Houyhnhnm race, whom these of ours[9] have the honor to resemble in all their lineaments, however their intellectuals[1] came to degenerate.

I began last week to permit my wife to sit at dinner with me, at the farthest end of a long table, and to answer (but with the utmost brevity) the few questions I ask her. Yet the smell of a Yahoo continuing very offensive, I always keep my nose well stopped with rue, lavender, or tobacco leaves. And although it be hard for a man late in life to remove old habits, I am not altogether out of hopes in some time to suffer a neighbor Yahoo in my company, without the apprehensions I am yet under of his teeth or his claws.

My reconcilement to the Yahoo-kind in general might not be so difficult if they would be content with those vices and follies only, which Nature hath entitled them to. I am not in the least provoked at the sight of a lawyer, a pickpocket, a colonel, a fool, a lord, a gamester, a politician, a whoremonger, a physician, an evidence,[2] a suborner,[3] an attorney, a traitor, or the like: this is all according to the due course of

---

5. Intended ironically.
6. Felons were commonly given a sentence of mandatory "transportation" to Britain's colonies.
7. The first edition continued: "unless a dispute may arise about the two Yahoos, said to have been seen many Ages ago on a mountain in Houyhnhnm-land, from whence the opinion is, that the race of those brutes hath descended; and these, for anything I know, may have been English, which indeed I was apt to suspect from the linea-

ments of their posterity's countenances, although very much defaced. But how far that will go to make out a title, I leave to the learned in colony law." Faulkener omitted this passage in the 1735 edition.
8. Teachable.
9. I.e., horses.
1. Intellects.
2. A (false) witness.
3. One who bribes another to commit a misdeed.

things; but when I behold a lump of deformity and diseases both in body and mind, smitten with *pride,* it immediately breaks all the measures of my patience; neither shall I be ever able to comprehend how such an animal and such a vice could tally together. The wise and virtuous Houyhnhnms, who abound in all excellencies that can adorn a rational creature, have no name for this vice in their language, which hath no terms to express anything that is evil, except those whereby they describe the detestable qualities of their Yahoos, among which they were not able to distinguish this of pride, for want of thoroughly understanding human nature, as it showeth itself in other countries, where that animal presides. But I, who had more experience, could plainly observe some rudiments of it among the wild Yahoos.

But the Houyhnhnms, who live under the government of Reason, are no more proud of the good qualities they possess, than I should be for not wanting a leg or an arm, which no man in his wits would boast of, although he must be miserable without them. I dwell the longer upon this subject from the desire I have to make the society of an English Yahoo by any means not insupportable, and therefore I here entreat those who have any tincture of this absurd vice, that they will not presume to appear in my sight.[4]

FINIS

c. 1721–1725   1726

COMPANION READINGS[1]

from Letters on *Gulliver's Travels*
Jonathan Swift to Alexander Pope

29 Sep[tember] 1725

Sir, * * * I have employed my time (besides ditching)[2] in finishing correcting, amending, and transcribing my *Travels,* in four parts complete newly augmented, and intended for the press when the world shall deserve them, or rather when a printer shall be found brave enough to venture his ears.[3] I like your schemes of our meeting after distresses and dispersions, but the chief end I propose to myself in all my labors is to vex the world rather than divert it; and if I could compass that design[4] without hurting my own person or fortune, I would be the most indefatigable writer you have ever seen without reading.[5] I am exceedingly pleased that you have done with translations. Lord Treasurer Oxford[6] often lamented that a rascally world should lay you under a necessity of misemploying your genius for so long a time.[7] But since you will now be so much better employed, when you think of the world give it one lash the more at my request. I have ever hated all nations, professions, and communities and all my love is towards individuals. For instance, I hate the tribe of lawyers, but I love Councilor Such-a-one, Judge Such-a-one, for so with physicians (I will not speak of my own trade), soldiers, English, Scotch, French, and the rest. But principally I hate

---

4. Gulliver thus falls into pride, the very vice he rejects.
1. The following five letters to and from Jonathan Swift were written over a period of nearly 18 months and span the progress of *Gulliver's Travels* from Swift's corrections of the manuscript to reports on the reactions of London readers. The celebratory letters from his old friends Pope and Gay are valuable in chronicling the reception of *Gulliver,* and the three letters from Swift himself are particularly interesting, revealing a playfulness, warmth, and gift for friendship not ordinarily associated with the common misconception of Swift as darkly misanthropic and sarcastic.
2. Digging ditches or doing one's daily labor.

3. In earlier times printers could have their ears cut off as punishment for printing seditious material. Since the legal penalty had lapsed, the idea of venturing one's ears more generally meant being willing to risk punishment or make a sacrifice.
4. Achieve that end.
5. Education; Swift ironically deprecates his own learning.
6. Robert Harley (1661–1724), first Earl of Oxford; a Tory statesman and member of the Scriblerus Club, he was a mutual friend of Pope and of Swift.
7. Pope spent 12 years (1713–1725) translating Homer's *Iliad* and *Odyssey.*

and detest that animal called man, although I heartily love John, Peter, Thomas, and so forth. This is the system upon which I have governed myself many years (but do not tell), and so I shall go on till I have done with them. I have got materials towards a treatise proving the falsity of that definition *animal rationale* and to show it should be only *rationis capax*.[8] Upon this great foundation of misanthropy (though not Timon's manner[9]), the whole building of my *Travels* is erected, and I never will have peace of mind till all honest men are of my opinion. By consequence you are to embrace it immediately and procure that all who deserve my esteem may do so too. The matter is so clear that it will admit little dispute. Nay, I will hold a hundred pounds that you and I agree in the point. * * *

Alexander Pope to Jonathan Swift

November 16, 1726

I have resolved to take time, and in spite of all misfortunes and demurs, which sickness, lameness, or disability of any kind can throw in my way, to write you (at intervals) a long letter. My two least fingers of one hand hang impediments to the others, like useless dependents, who only take up room, and never are active or assistant to our wants: I shall never be much the better for 'em.[1] I congratulate you first upon what you call your cousin's wonderful book,[2] which is *publica trita manu*[3] at present, and I prophesy will be in future the admiration of all men. That countenance[4] with which it is received by some statesmen is delightful; I wish I could tell you how every single man looks upon it, to observe which has been my whole diversion this fortnight. I've never been a night in London since you left me,[5] till now for this very end, and indeed it has fully answered my expectations.

I find no considerable man very angry at the book: some indeed think it rather too bold, and too general a satire, but none that I hear of accuse it of particular reflections[6] (I mean no persons of consequence, or good judgment; the mob of critics, you know, always are desirous to apply satire to those that they envy for being above them), so that you needed not to have been so secret upon this head. Motte[7] received the copy (he tells me) he knew not from whence, nor from whom, dropped at his house in the dark from a hackney coach; by computing the time, I found it was after you left England, so for my part, I suspend my judgment.[8] * * *

John Gay to Jonathan Swift

Nov. 17. 1726

About ten days ago a book was published here of the travels of one Gulliver, which hath been the conversation of the whole town ever since. The whole impression[9] sold in a week, and nothing is more diverting than to hear the different opin-

---

8. Humans are not automatically rational animals, as Aristotle had said, but rather only *rationis capax*—capable of reasoning.
9. Timon, a nobleman of Athens who, after losing his riches and receiving no help from his wealthy friends, lived a life of solitary misanthropy in a cave outside the city.
1. In September the tendons of Pope's two fingers had been severed when his hand was cut in a near-fatal coach accident.
2. The manuscript for *Gulliver's Travels* was submitted to the London publisher Benjamin Motte, by "Richard

Sympson," the imaginary cousin of Gulliver.
3. Passed from hand to hand.
4. Both the expression on the face and general composure of temperament.
5. Swift had been visiting friends in London from mid-March to mid-August this year and stayed mainly at Pope's house at Twickenham.
6. Direct satire of contemporary people or affairs.
7. Benjamin Motte (d. 1738), bookseller and printer.
8. Pope had assisted his friend in getting *Gulliver* published anonymously.
9. Print run.

ions people give of it, though all agree in liking it extremely. 'Tis generally said that you are the author, but I am told, the bookseller declares he knows not from what hand it came.[1] From the highest to the lowest it is universally read, from the Cabinet council to the nursery. The politicians to a man agree that it is free from particular reflections, but that the satire on general societies of men is too severe. Not but we now and then meet with people of greater perspicuity, who are in search for particular applications in every leaf; and it is highly probable we shall have keys[2] published to give light into Gulliver's design. Your Lord ———[3] is the person who least approves it, blaming it as a design of evil consequence to depreciate human nature, at which it cannot be wondered that he takes most offense, being himself the most accomplished of his species, and so losing more than any other of that praise which is due both to the dignity and virtue of a man. Your friend, my Lord Harcourt,[4] commends it very much, though he thinks in some places the matter too far carried. The Duchess Dowager of Marlborough[5] is in raptures at it; she says she can dream of nothing else since she read it; she declares, that she hath now found out that her whole life hath been lost in caressing the worst part of mankind and treating the best as her foes, and that if she knew Gulliver, though he had been the worst enemy she ever had, she would give up all her present acquaintance for his friendship. You may see by this, that you are not much injured by being supposed the author of this piece. If you are, you have disobliged us, and two or three of your best friends, in not giving us the least hint of it while you were with us, and in particular Dr. Arbuthnot, who says it is ten thousand pities he had not known it, he could have added such abundance of things upon every subject.[6] Among lady critics, some have found out that Mr. Gulliver had a particular malice to maids of honor.[7] Those of them who frequent the church say his design is impious, and that it is an insult on Providence, by depreciating the works of the Creator. Notwithstanding, I am told the Princess hath read it with great pleasure. As to other critics, they think the flying island is the least entertaining,[8] and so great an opinion the town have of the impossibility of Gulliver's writing at all below himself, that 'tis agreed that part was not writ by the same hand, though this hath its defenders too. It hath passed Lords and Commons, *nemine contradicente*;[9] and the whole town, men, women, and children are quite full of it.

Perhaps I may all this time be talking to you of a book you have never seen, and which hath not yet reached Ireland; if it hath not, I believe what we have said will be sufficient to recommend it to your reading, and that you order me to send it to you.

But it will be much better to come over yourself, and read it here. * * *

---

1. Gay had copied out Swift's original letter to the publisher (signing it "Richard Sympson," Gulliver's alleged cousin), in order to assist Swift in hiding his authorship of *Gulliver* from his publisher, and, thus, from the general public.

2. The publication of "keys," which helped readers unlock the contemporary application of satires, was highly popular at this time; a "key" to Gay's *Beggar's Opera* was published after its success, in 1728. Alexander Pope took advantage of this trend by publishing a pamphlet entitled *A Key to the Lock. Or, A Treatise proving . . . the dangerous Tendency of a late Poem, The Rape of the Lock, To Government and Religion* (1715).

3. Bolingbroke.

4. Simon Harcourt, first Viscount (1667–1727), an old friend of Swift's, one of the few who managed to do well under the new Whig government without losing touch

with his old friends.

5. Sarah Churchill (1660–1744), a favorite of Queen Anne's.

6. Gay here feigns complete ignorance of *Gulliver's* authorship partly in jest, partly because both men knew that the letters of those hostile to the government were routinely opened and read by officials in the post office.

7. Companions to the queen. Swift's references to the maids of honor in Lilliput and Brobdingnag involved incidents that were indelicate and, by implication, potentially embarrassing to the women of rank at the English Court; see, for example, "A Voyage to Brobdingnag," chapter 5, in which the maids of honor use the diminutive Gulliver to titillate their breasts.

8. "A Voyage to Laputa."

9. Nobody voting against.

Jonathan Swift to Alexander Pope

Dublin, Nov. [27] 1726

I am just come from answering a letter of Mrs. Howard's writ in such mystical terms that I should never have found out the meaning,[1] if a book had not been sent me called *Gulliver's Travels*, of which you say so much in yours.[2] I read the book over, and in the second volume observe several passages which appear to be patched and altered, and the style of a different sort (unless I am much mistaken).[3] Dr. Arbuthnot likes the projectors least; others you tell me, the flying island; some think it wrong to be so hard upon whole bodies or corporations.[4] Yet the general opinion is that reflections on particular persons are most to be blamed, so that in these cases, I think the best method is to let censure and opinion take their course. A Bishop here said, that book was full of improbable lies, and for his part, he hardly believed a word of it; and so much for Gulliver. ***

"The Prince of Lilliput" to Stella[5]

[11 March 1727]

†**††*[6]

In *European* characters and *English* thus;

The high and mighty prince EGROEGO[7] born to the most puissant[8] empire of the *East*,

Unto STELLA, the most resplendent glory of the *Western* hemisphere, sendeth health and happiness.

BRIGHTEST PRINCESS,

That invincible hero, the MAN MOUNTAIN,[9] fortunately arriving at our coasts some years ago, delivered us from ruin by conquering the fleets and armies of our enemies, and gave us hopes of a durable peace and happiness. But now the martial people of *Blefuscu*, encouraged from his absence, have renewed the war,[1] to revenge upon us the loss and disgrace they suffered by our valiant champion.

The fame of your superexcellent person and virtue, and the huge esteem which that great general has for you, urged us in this our second distress to sue for[2] your favor. In order to which we have sent our able and trusty Nardac[3] KOORB-NILOB,[4] requesting, that if our general does yet tread upon the terrestrial globe, you, in compassion for us, would prevail upon him to take another voyage for our deliverance.

And, lest any apprehensions of famine amongst us, should render Nardac MOUNTAIN averse to the undertaking, we signify to you, that we have stored our folds, our coops, our granaries, and cellars with plenty of provision for a long supply of the wastes to be made by his capacious stomach.

---

1. A letter of 17 November, to which Swift replied in tones of mock-mystification.
2. His letter of 17 November.
3. Fearful of the law, Swift's publisher Benjamin Motte made several alterations to the *Travels*.
4. Professions or groups, all from "A Voyage to Laputa."
5. Esther Johnson (1681–1728), Swift's beloved and most valued friend.
6. Here we have a parcel of characters formed at random, by way of the address in the *Lilliputian* tongue [Swift's

note].
7. I.e., O'George (an anagram).
8. Powerful.
9. Gulliver, later also called "that great general."
1. Spain had besieged Gibraltar in February.
2. Ask for.
3. The "highest title of honor" among the Lilliputians; see "A Voyage to Lilliput," chapter 5, in which Gulliver is created a Nardac for his service to the nation.
4. An anagram: Bolinbrook, i.e., the Tory politician.

And furthermore, because as we hear you are not so well as we could wish, we beg you would complete our happiness by venturing your most valuable person along with him into our country; where, by the salubrity[5] of our finer air and diet, you will soon recover your health and stomach.[6]

In full assurance of your complying goodness, we have sent you some provision for your voyage, and we shall with impatience wait for your safe arrival in our kingdom. Most illustrious lady, farewell. Prince EGROEGO.

Dated the 11th day of the 6th Moon, in the
2001 year of the *Lilliputian* era.

A Modest Proposal

In a letter written to Alexander Pope in August 1729, Swift described the condition of Ireland: "There have been three terrible years' dearth of corn [i.e., wheat], and every place strewn with beggars, but dearths are common in better climates, and our evils lie much deeper. Imagine a nation the two-thirds of whose revenues are spent out of it, and who are not permitted [by Britain] to trade with the other third, and where the pride of the women will not suffer them to wear their own manufactures even where they excel what come from abroad." Two months later, Swift published what is today his most famous political essay: *A Modest Proposal*. Swift had previously written a dozen or more tracts to help free Ireland from its desperate social, economic, and political plight. In *A Modest Proposal*, however, Swift wielded two favorite weapons from his armory of satirical techniques— irony and parody—with devastating effect. In creating a persona who combines a mixture of calculating rationality and misplaced compassion but does not comprehend the enormity of his plan, Swift aims his satire not only at the political arithmeticians (forerunners of today's social engineers and economic planners) and the exploitative and predatory absentee landlords living in England but at the Irish people as well. Believing Ireland to be its own worst enemy, Swift delineates a program of commercial cannibalism that institutionalizes the country's own self-destructive tendencies. Preserving a nation through the consumption of its children is self-defeating, however demographically logical, because it undermines the understanding of humanity upon which civil society depends. Swift thus highlights the futility of financial improvement unaccompanied by social and moral reform.

A Modest Proposal

*FOR PREVENTING THE CHILDREN OF POOR PEOPLE IN IRELAND
FROM BEING A BURDEN TO THEIR PARENTS OR COUNTRY,
AND FOR MAKING THEM BENEFICIAL TO THE PUBLIC*

It is a melancholy object to those who walk through this great town,[1] or travel in the country, when they see the streets, the roads, and cabin doors crowded with beggars of the female sex, followed by three, four, or six children, *all in rags,* and importuning every passenger[2] for an alms. These mothers, instead of being able to work for their honest livelihood, are forced to employ all their time in strolling,[3] to beg sustenance

---

5. Healthfulness.
6. Appetite. Stella had been in declining health for some time. Swift's playful letter was obviously meant to cheer her.

1. Dublin.
2. Passerby.
3. Wandering aimlessly.

for their helpless infants, who, as they grow up, either turn thieves for want of work, or leave their dear native country to fight for the Pretender in Spain,[4] or sell themselves to the Barbados.[5]

I think it is agreed by all parties that this prodigious number of children, in the arms, or on the backs, or at the heels of their mothers, and frequently of their fathers, is in the present deplorable state of the kingdom a very great additional grievance; and therefore whoever could find out a fair, cheap, and easy method of making these children sound, useful members of the commonwealth would deserve so well of the public, as to have his statue set up for a preserver of the nation.

But my intention is very far from being confined to provide only for the children of professed beggars; it is of a much greater extent, and shall take in the whole number of infants at a certain age who are born of parents in effect as little able to support them as those who demand our charity in the streets.

As to my own part, having turned my thoughts for many years upon this important subject, and maturely weighed the several schemes of other projectors,[6] I have always found them grossly mistaken in their computation. It is true a child just dropped from its dam may be supported by her milk for a solar year with little other nourishment, at most not above the value of two shillings, which the mother may certainly get, or the value in scraps, by her lawful occupation of begging, and it is exactly at one year old that I propose to provide for them, in such a manner as instead of being a charge upon their parents or the parish, or wanting food and raiment for the rest of their lives, they shall, on the contrary, contribute to the feeding and partly to the clothing of many thousands.

There is likewise another great advantage in my scheme, that it will prevent those voluntary abortions, and that horrid practice of women murdering their bastard children, alas, too frequent among us, sacrificing the poor innocent babes, I doubt[7] more to avoid the expense than the shame, which would move tears and pity in the most savage and inhuman breast.

The number of souls in this kingdom being usually reckoned one million and a half, of these I calculate there may be about two hundred thousand couple whose wives are breeders, from which number I subtract thirty thousand couple who are able to maintain their own children, although I apprehend there cannot be so many under the present distresses of the kingdom; but this being granted, there will remain an hundred and seventy thousand breeders. I again subtract fifty thousand for those women who miscarry, or whose children die by accident or disease within the year.[8] There only remain a hundred and twenty thousand children of poor parents annually born: the question therefore is how this number shall be reared and provided for, which, as I have already said, under the present situation of affairs, is utterly impossible by all the methods hitherto proposed: for we can neither employ them in handicraft, or agriculture; we neither build houses (I mean in the country) nor cultivate land;[9] they can very seldom pick up a livelihood by stealing till they arrive at six years old, except where they are of towardly parts,[1] although, I confess they learn the

---

4. Catholic Ireland was loyal to the Pretender, James Francis Edward Stuart (1688–1766), son of James II, who was deposed from the English throne in 1688 because of his Catholicism. Religious ties also made the Irish ideal recruits for France and Spain in their wars against England.
5. The impoverished Irish emigrated to the West Indies in large numbers, buying their passage by selling their labor in advance to the sugar plantations.

6. Devisers of new "projects," usually of doubtful value.
7. Believe.
8. It is telling that Swift here projects an infant mortality rate of approximately 30 percent in a child's first year.
9. The vast estates of English absentee landlords, and British retention of Irish land for grazing sheep, rather than agriculture, contributed to Ireland's poverty.
1. Precocious.

rudiments much earlier, during which time they can however be properly looked upon only as *probationers*, as I have been informed by a principal gentleman in the County of Cavan, who protested to me, that he never knew above one or two instances under the age of six, even in a part of the kingdom so renowned for the quickest proficiency in that art.

I am assured by our merchants that a boy or a girl, before twelve years old, is no salable commodity, and even when they come to this age, they will not yield above three pounds, or three pounds and half-a-crown at most on the Exchange,[2] which cannot turn to account[3] either to the parents or kingdom, the charge of nutriment and rags having been at least four times that value.

I shall now therefore humbly propose my own thoughts, which I hope will not be liable to the least objection.

I have been assured by a very knowing American[4] of my acquaintance in London, that a young healthy child well nursed is at a year old a most delicious, nourishing, and wholesome food, whether stewed, roasted, baked, or boiled, and I make no doubt that it will equally serve in a fricassee or ragout.[5]

I do therefore humbly offer it to public consideration, that of the hundred and twenty thousand children already computed, twenty thousand may be reserved for breed, whereof only one fourth part to be males, which is more than we allow to sheep, black cattle, or swine, and my reason is that these children are seldom the fruits of marriage, a circumstance not much regarded by our savages, therefore one male will be sufficient to serve four females. That the remaining hundred thousand may at a year old be offered in sale to the persons of quality and fortune through the kingdom, always advising the mother to let them suck plentifully in the last month, so as to render them plump, and fat for a good table. A child will make two dishes at an entertainment for friends, and when the family dines alone, the fore or hind quarter will make a reasonable dish, and seasoned with a little pepper or salt will be very good boiled on the fourth day, especially in winter.

I have reckoned upon a medium, that a child just born will weigh 12 pounds, and in a solar year if tolerably nursed increaseth to 28 pounds.

I grant this food will be somewhat dear,[6] and therefore very proper for landlords, who, as they have already devoured most of the parents, seem to have the best title to the children.

Infants' flesh will be in season throughout the year, but more plentiful in March, and a little before and after, for we are told by a grave author,[7] an eminent French physician, that fish being a prolific diet,[8] there are more children born in Roman Catholic countries about nine months after Lent than at any other season; therefore reckoning a year after Lent, the markets will be more glutted than usual, because the number of Popish infants is at least three to one in this kingdom, and therefore it will have one other collateral advantage by lessening the number of Papists among us.

I have already computed the charge of nursing a beggar's child (in which list I reckon all cottagers,[9] laborers, and four-fifths of the farmers) to be about two shillings *per annum*, rags included, and I believe no gentleman would repine to give ten

---

2. At the market.
3. Be of value.
4. Some of the British believed that the harsh living conditions in America made the colonists adopt "savage" practices.
5. A fricassee is meat stewed in gravy, a ragout is a highly seasoned French stew; such foreign dishes were becoming

increasingly popular with fashionable Britons.
6. Both expensive and, of course, beloved.
7. The satirist François Rabelais, in *Gargantua and Pantagruel* (1532–1564), book 5, ch. 29.
8. One increasing fertility.
9. Tenant farmers.

shillings for the carcass of a good fat child, which, as I have said, will make four dishes of excellent nutritive meat, when he hath only some particular friend or his own family to dine with him. Thus the Squire will learn to be a good landlord and grow popular among his tenants, the mother will have eight shillings net profit, and be fit for work till she produces another child.

Those who are more thrifty (as I must confess the times require) may flay the carcass, the skin of which, artificially[1] dressed, will make admirable gloves for ladies and summer boots for fine gentlemen.

As to our City of Dublin, shambles[2] may be appointed for this purpose in the most convenient parts of it, and butchers we may be assured will not be wanting, although I rather recommend buying the children alive and dressing them hot from the knife,[3] as we do roasting pigs.

A very worthy person, a true lover of his country, and whose virtues I highly esteem, was lately pleased, in discoursing on this matter, to offer a refinement upon my scheme. He said that many gentlemen of this kingdom, having of late destroyed their deer, he conceived that the want of venison might be well supplied by the bodies of young lads and maidens, not exceeding fourteen years of age nor under twelve, so great a number of both sexes in every country being now ready to starve for want of work and service;[4] and these to be disposed of by their parents if alive, or otherwise by their nearest relations. But with due deference to so excellent a friend and so deserving a patriot, I cannot be altogether in his sentiments; for as to the males, my American acquaintance assured me from frequent experience that their flesh was generally tough and lean, like that of our schoolboys, by continual exercise, and their taste disagreeable, and to fatten them would not answer the charge. Then as to the females, it would, I think with humble submission, be a loss to the public, because they soon would become breeders themselves; and besides, it is not improbable that some scrupulous people might be apt to censure such a practice (although indeed very unjustly) as a little bordering upon cruelty which, I confess, hath always been with me the strongest objection against any project, however so well intended.

But in order to justify my friend, he confessed that this expedient was put into his head by the famous Psalmanazar,[5] a native of the island Formosa, who came from thence to London above twenty years ago, and in conversation told my friend that in his country when any young person happened to be put to death, the executioner sold the carcass to persons of quality as a prime dainty, and that, in his time, the body of a plump girl of fifteen, who was crucified for an attempt to poison the emperor, was sold to his Imperial Majesty's Prime Minister of State[6] and other great Mandarins of the Court, in joints from the gibbet,[7] at four hundred crowns. Neither indeed can I deny that if the same use were made of several plump young girls in this town, who, without one single groat[8] to their fortunes, cannot stir abroad without a chair,[9] and appear at the playhouse and assemblies[1] in foreign fineries which they never will pay for, the kingdom would not be the worse.

Some persons of a desponding spirit are in great concern about that vast number of poor people who are aged, diseased, or maimed, and I have been desired to employ my thoughts what course may be taken to ease the nation of so grievous an

---

1. Skillfully.
2. Places where meat is slaughtered and sold.
3. Skinning and gutting them immediately after killing.
4. Positions as servants.
5. George Psalmanazar, a Frenchman who pretended to be from Formosa (now Taiwan), wrote a book about its customs, the *Historical and Geographical Description of For-*

mosa (1704), which was quickly exposed as fraudulent.
6. A reference to Robert Walpole.
7. Gallows.
8. Silver coin (issued 1351–1662) equal to four pennies.
9. A sedan chair, carried by two men.
1. Social gatherings.

encumbrance. But I am not in the least pain upon that matter, because it is very well known that they are every day dying, and rotting, by cold, and famine, and filth, and vermin, as fast as can be reasonably expected. And as to the younger laborers they are now in almost as hopeful a condition. They cannot get work, and consequently pine away for want of nourishment, to a degree that if at any time they are accidentally hired to common labor, they have not strength to perform it; and thus the country and themselves are in a fair way of being soon delivered from the evils to come.

I have too long digressed, and therefore shall return to my subject. I think the advantages by the proposal which I have made are obvious and many, as well as of the highest importance.

For first, as I have already observed, it would greatly lessen the number of Papists, with whom we are yearly overrun, being the principal breeders of the nation as well as our most dangerous enemies, and who stay at home on purpose with a design to deliver the kingdom to the Pretender, hoping to take their advantage by the absence of so many good Protestants, who have chosen rather to leave their country than stay at home, and pay tithes against their conscience, to an Episcopal curate.[2]

Secondly, the poorer tenants will have something valuable of their own, which by law may be made liable to distress,[3] and help to pay their landlords rent, their corn and cattle being already seized, and *money a thing unknown*.

Thirdly, whereas the maintenance of a hundred thousand children from two years old and upwards cannot be computed at less than ten shillings a piece *per annum*, the nation's stock will be thereby increased fifty thousand pounds *per annum*, besides the profit of a new dish introduced to the tables of all gentlemen of fortune in the kingdom who have any refinement in taste, and the money will circulate among ourselves, the goods being entirely of our own growth and manufacture.

Fourthly, the constant breeders, besides the gain of eight shillings sterling *per annum* by the sale of their children, will be rid of the charge of maintaining them after the first year.

Fifthly, this food would likewise bring great custom to taverns, where the vintners will certainly be so prudent as to procure the best receipts[4] for dressing it to perfection, and consequently have their houses frequented by all the fine gentlemen, who justly value themselves upon their knowledge in good eating; and a skillful cook who understands how to oblige his guests will contrive to make it as expensive as they please.

Sixthly, this would be a great inducement to marriage, which all wise nations have either encouraged by rewards or enforced by laws and penalties. It would increase the care and tenderness of mothers toward their children, when they were sure of a settlement for life to the poor babes, provided in some sort by the public to their annual profit instead of expense. We should see an honest emulation[5] among the married women, which of them could bring the fattest child to the market; men would become as fond of their wives, during the time of their pregnancy, as they are now of their mares in foal, their cows in calf, or sows when they are ready to farrow,[6] nor offer to beat or kick them (as it is too frequent a practice) for fear of a miscarriage.

---

2. The tithes, or ecclesiastical taxes, that supported the Church were avoided by the many "good" Protestants who absented themselves from Ireland on the grounds—spurious, Swift implies—of "conscience."

3. Seizure for debt.
4. Recipes.
5. Competition.
6. Give birth.

Many other advantages might be enumerated: for instance, the addition of some thousand carcasses in our exportation of barreled beef;[7] the propagation of swine's flesh, and improvement in the art of making good bacon, so much wanted among us by the great destruction of pigs, too frequent at our tables, which are no way comparable in taste or magnificence to a well-grown, fat yearling child, which roasted whole will make a considerable figure at a Lord Mayor's feast or any other public entertainment. But this and many others I omit, being studious of brevity.

Supposing that one thousand families in this city would be constant customers for infants' flesh, besides others who might have it at merry-meetings, particularly weddings and christenings, I compute that Dublin would take off annually about twenty thousand carcasses, and the rest of the kingdom (where probably they will be sold somewhat cheaper) the remaining eighty thousand.

I can think of no one objection that will possibly be raised against this proposal, unless it should be urged that the number of people will be thereby much lessened in the kingdom. This I freely own, and was indeed one principal design in offering it to the world. I desire the reader will observe that I calculate my remedy *for this one individual Kingdom of Ireland, and for no other that ever was, is, or, I think, ever can be upon earth.* Therefore let no man talk to me of other expedients:[8] *Of taxing our absentees at five shillings a pound; of using neither clothes nor household furniture, except what is of our own growth and manufacture; of utterly rejecting the materials and instruments that promote foreign luxury; of curing the expensiveness of pride, vanity, idleness, and gaming in our women; of introducing a vein of parsimony, prudence, and temperance; of learning to love our country, wherein we differ even from* LAPLANDERS, *and the inhabitants of* TOP-INAMBOO;[9] *of quitting our animosities and factions, nor act any longer like the Jews, who were murdering one another at the very moment their city was taken;*[1] *of being a little cautious not to sell our country and consciences for nothing; of teaching landlords to have at least one degree of mercy toward their tenants. Lastly, of putting a spirit of honesty, industry, and skill into our shopkeepers, who, if a resolution could now be taken to buy our native goods, would immediately unite to cheat and exact upon us in the price, the measure, and the goodness, nor could ever yet be brought to make one fair proposal of just dealing, though often and earnestly invited to it.*

Therefore I repeat, let no man talk to me of these and the like expedients till he hath at least some glimpse of hope that there will ever be some hearty and sincere attempt to put them in practice.

But as to myself, having been wearied out for many years with offering vain, idle, visionary thoughts, and at length utterly despairing of success, I fortunately fell upon this proposal, which as it is wholly new, so it hath something solid and real, of no expense and little trouble, full in our own power, and whereby we can incur no danger in *disobliging* ENGLAND. For this kind of commodity will not bear exportation, the flesh being of too tender a consistence, to admit a long continuance in salt, *although perhaps I could name a country*[2] *which would be glad to eat up our whole nation without it.*

---

7. Pickled beef.
8. The kind of proposals Swift himself had made in earnest for remedying the poverty of Ireland; his *Proposal for the Universal Use of Irish Manufacture in Cloaths and Furniture . . . Utterly Rejecting and Renouncing Everything Wearable that Comes from England* (1720) is a typical example.
9. The inhabitants of the most hostile environments—

the frozen north or the Brazilian jungle—love their countries more than the Irish.
1. According to one historian, when Jerusalem was besieged and captured by the Emperor Titus in A.D. 70, factional fighting inside the city contributed to its destruction.
2. England.

After all I am not so violently bent upon my own opinion as to reject any offer proposed by wise men, which shall be found equally innocent, cheap, easy, and effectual. But before something of that kind shall be advanced in contradiction to my scheme and offering a better, I desire the author or authors will be pleased maturely to consider two points. First, as things now stand, how they will be able to find food and raiment for an hundred thousand useless mouths and backs. And secondly, there being a round million of creatures in human figure throughout this kingdom whose whole subsistence put into a common stock would leave them in debt two millions of pounds sterling; adding those who are beggars by profession to the bulk of farmers, cottagers, and laborers with their wives and children, who are beggars in effect; I desire those politicians who dislike my overture, and may perhaps be so bold to attempt an answer, that they will first ask the parents of these mortals whether they would not at this day think it a great happiness to have been sold for food at a year old, in the manner I prescribe, and thereby have avoided such a perpetual scene of misfortunes as they have since gone through, by the oppression of landlords, the impossibility of paying rent without money or trade, the want of common sustenance, with neither house nor clothes to cover them from the inclemencies of the weather, and the most inevitable prospect of entailing[3] the like or greater miseries upon their breed forever.

I profess in the sincerity of my heart that I have not the least personal interest in endeavoring to promote this necessary work, having no other motive than the *public good of my country, by advancing our trade, providing for infants, relieving the poor, and giving some pleasure to the rich.* I have no children by which I can propose to get a single penny; the youngest being nine years old, and my wife past child-bearing.

1729   1729

COMPANION READING

William Petty: from Political Arithmetic[1]

from *Chapter 4. How to enable the people of England and Ireland to spend 5 millions worth of commodities more than now; and how to raise the present value of the lands and goods of Ireland from 2 to 3.*

This is to be done: 1. By bringing one million of the present 1,300 thousand of the people out of Ireland into England, though at the expense of a million of money. 2. That the remaining three hundred thousand left behind be all herdsmen and dairy women, servants to the owners of the lands and stock transplanted into England, all aged between 16 and 60 years, and to quit all other trades, but that of cattle, and to import nothing but salt and tobacco. Neglecting all housing, but what is fittest for these 300 thousand people, and this trade, though to the loss of 2 millions-worth of houses. Now

---

3. Bequeathing.

1. William Petty (1623–1687) represents the type of Englishman Swift had in mind in his implicit criticism of English rapaciousness in Ireland in *A Modest Proposal*. Petty, the son of a London clothier and weaver, was an extraordinary scholar and anatomist, and a charter member of the Royal Society. Appointed physician-general to the parliamentary army in Ireland in 1652, he obtained considerable property holdings in Ireland through his additional task of surveying lands forfeited by Roman Catholics. His new-found fortune enabled him to devote

his attention to his economic writings and to the Royal Society in London, though he was less than solicitous of his tenants in Ireland. Swift's friendship with Petty's children, Lord Shelburne and Lady Kerry, did not prevent him parodying Petty's *Political Arithmetic* (1691) in *A Modest Proposal*. Petty's suggestion that Ireland be turned into one huge farm to supply England by removing all the Irish was only one of many "political arithmetic" projects published during the Restoration and 18th century, reflecting English interest in "scientific" programs for social "improvement."

if a million of people be worth 70 pounds per head one with another, the whole are worth 70 millions; then the said people, reckoned as money at 5 percent interest, will yield 3 millions and a half per annum. 3. And if Ireland send into England 1 million and a half worth of effects (receiving nothing back), then England will be enriched from Ireland, and otherwise, 5 millions per annum more than now, which, at 20 year's purchase, is worth one hundred millions of pounds sterling, as was propounded. * * *

Postscript

If in this jealous age this essay should be taxed of an evil design to waste and dispeople Ireland, we say that the author of it intends not to be *Felo de se*,[4] and propound something quite contrary, by saying it is naturally possible in about 25 years to double the inhabitants of Great Britain and Ireland and make the people full as many as the territory of those kingdoms can with tolerable labor afford a competent livelihood unto, which I prove thus, (viz.)

1. The sixth part of the people are teeming women[5] of between 18 and 44 years old.
2. It is found by observation that but 1/3 part or between 30 and 40 of the teeming women are married.
3. That a teeming woman, at a medium, bear a child every two years and a half.
4. That in mankind at London, there are 14 males for 13 females, and because males are prolific[6] 40 years, and females but 25, there are in effect 560 males for 325 females.
5. That out of the mass of mankind there dies one out of 30 per annum.
6. That at Paris, where the christenings and the births are the same in number, the christenings are above 18,000 per annum, and consequently the births at London, which far exceed the christenings there, cannot be less than 19,000 where the burials are above 23,000.

As for Example

Of 600 people, the sixth part (viz. 100) are teeming women, which (if they were all married) might bear 40 children per annum (viz.) 20 more than do die out of 600, at the rate of one out of 30; and consequently in 16 years the increase will be 320, making the whole 920. And by the same reason, in the next 9 years, the said 920 will be 280 more, in all 1,200, viz. double of the original number of 600.

Upon these principles, if there be about 19,000 births per annum at London, the number of the married teeming women must be above 38,000; and of the whole stock of the teeming women must be above 114,000, and of the whole people six times as many viz. 684,000; which agrees well enough with 69,6000, which they have been elsewhere computed to be.

To conclude it is naturally possible, that all teeming women may be married, since there are in effect 560 males to 325 females; and since Great Britain and Ireland can with moderate labor, food, and other necessaries to near double the present people or to about 20 millions of heads, as shall when occasion requires it, be demonstrated. * * *   1691

---

4. Self-murder; literally, "felon of (one)self."   6. Capable of procreation.
5. Women capable of breeding.

Alexander Pope
1688–1744

"The life of a wit is a warfare upon earth; and the present spirit of the learned world is such, that to serve it . . . one must have the constancy of a martyr, and a resolution to suffer for its sake." Though still in his twenties when he wrote these words, Alexander Pope knew from painful experience their bitter truth. As a Roman Catholic, he could not vote, inherit or purchase land, attend a "public" school or a university, live within ten miles of London, hold public office, or openly practice his religion. He was obliged to pay double taxes. Such civil disenfranchisement barred him from receiving the literary patronage most talented writers depended upon for their livelihood. No wonder Pope wrote of "certain laws, by suff'rers thought unjust," by which he was "denied all posts of profit or of trust" (*Imitations of Horace, Epistle 2. 2.* 60–61). Despite whatever patriotism or loyalty to their country they may have felt, Catholics were widely regarded as alien and seditious. Pope's resentment of this attitude is evident in the *Epistle to Bathurst* (1733) when he calls the London Monument, which bears an inscription blaming the Great Fire of 1666 on a Papist conspiracy to destroy the capital, "a tall bully" who "lies."

Religion was not Pope's greatest impediment to success, however. When he was twelve, he contracted tuberculosis of the spine (Pott's disease), a condition that stunted his growth and left him humpbacked and deformed. At four feet six inches, he could not sit at an ordinary table with other adults unless his seat was raised. His constitution was so weakened that he frequently suffered from migraine headaches, asthma, nausea, and fevers. For much of his life, he could not hold his body upright without the help of stays, and he was unable to bathe, dress or undress, rise or go to bed by himself. Pope summarized his condition most succinctly in *An Epistle to Dr. Arbuthnot* (1735), when he wrote of "this long disease, my life."

Pope was born in London in 1688, the only child of his parents' marriage. Pope's *Epistle to Dr. Arbuthnot* includes a tribute to his father's equanimity and goodness; his mother is praised as "a noble wife." At the age of nine, Pope was sent to a school for Catholic boys but was expelled in his first year for writing a satire on his schoolmaster—a sign of things to come. When he was twelve, his family moved from the environs of London to Binfield, in the royal forest of Windsor; the effect of Windsor's "green retreats" on Pope's youthful imagination is apparent in the *Pastorals* (1709) and in *Windsor-Forest* (1713). At Binfield, he began to teach himself Greek and Latin with great determination, though the rigors of his studies made his sickness worse. Refusing to yield to his infirmity, he began, at fifteen, to journey into London to learn French and Italian. Pope spoke of these adolescent years as his "great reading period" when he "went through all the best critics, almost all the English, French, and Latin poets of any name . . . [and] Homer and some other of the Greek poets in the original." During this time Pope met his great friend John Caryll, at whose request he would write *The Rape of the Lock,* and Martha Blount, who was to become his lifelong intimate companion and to whom he addressed *Of the Characters of Women: An Epistle to a Lady* (1735).

Pope claimed that "as yet a child . . . I lisp'd in numbers [i.e., meter]." Certainly he was a precocious poet and his early efforts were encouraged by many, including the playwrights William Wycherley and William Congreve, to whom Pope dedicated his *Iliad* (1715–1720). If Pope had encouraging friends, he soon had detracting enemies as well. His first publication, the *Pastorals* (1709), occasioned a rivalry between Pope's Tory supporters and the Whig partisans of Ambrose Philips, whose *Pastorals* appeared in the same volume. Pope's next important poem, *An Essay on Criticism* (1711), brought a barrage of vituperative abuse from the critic John Dennis, who called Pope "a hunch-backed toad" and argued that his deformity was merely the outward sign of mental and moral ugliness. Undaunted, Pope continued to publish: the

Messiah (1712), *The Rape of the Lock* (1712, substantially enlarged in 1714), *Windsor-Forest* (1713), and *The Temple of Fame* (1715). With the publication of his *Works* (1717), Pope had proved himself master of a dazzling repertoire of poetic modes: pastoral and georgic, didactic, eclogue, mock-epic, allegorical dream-vision, heroic, and elegiac. No other living poet could display such dazzling versatility and comprehensive control.

There was still another area, however, in which Pope was proving the breathtaking range of his poetic gifts. Between 1713 and 1726, Pope devoted much of his creative energy to translating Homer's epics, the *Iliad* and the *Odyssey*, into heroic couplets. "Pope's Homer" not only won for him financial independence so that he could "live and thrive, / Indebted to no Prince or Peer alive" (*Imitations of Horace, Epistle 2. 2*), it also confirmed his reputation as the presiding poetic genius of his time. While he was working on the *Odyssey*, Pope produced a six-volume edition of Shakespeare's works (1725), which, though it contained some valuable insights, was very much an amateur effort. When Lewis Theobald, the leading Shakespeare scholar of the time, rather pedantically highlighted Pope's many editorial shortcomings in *Shakespeare Restored, or, a Specimen of the Many Errors Committed . . . by Mr. Pope* (1726), Pope's revenge was not far off: two years later, he published *The Dunciad*, a savagely satirical assault on Pope's critics and the bankrupt cultural values they embodied.

In the seventeen years between Dennis's attack and the publication of *The Dunciad*, Pope's appearance, talent, and character had been assailed in print more than fifty times. His enemies accused him of being obscene, seditious, duplicitous, venal, vain, blasphemous, libelous, ignorant, and a bad poet. Theobald's rebuke was the last straw, perhaps because it was the most justified. Pope's style of comic social criticism owed much to his membership in the Scriblerus Club with John Gay, Jonathan Swift, Dr. John Arbuthnot, Thomas Parnell, and Robert Harley, Earl of Oxford. The Scriblerians originally planned to produce a series entitled *The Works of the Unlearned;* although the group regularly met only for a short while in 1714, its members remained in contact. In addition to *The Dunciad*, the fruit of their exchanges may be seen in Swift's *Gulliver's Travels* (1726), Gay's *The Beggar's Opera* (1728), Pope's *Peri Bathous: Or, the Art of Sinking in Poetry* (1728), and Arbuthnot's and Pope's *Memoirs of the Extraordinary Life, Works, and Discoveries of Martinus Scriblerus* (1741).

An Essay on Man (1733–1734) showcased Pope's talent for philosophical poetry. This work and four *Moral Essays* (1731–1735) were originally intended to form part of a long poetic sequence on the nature of humankind that Pope had hoped would be his greatest work, though the project was abandoned. Between 1733 and 1738, Pope published more than a dozen *Imitations of Horace*. In these loose adaptations of Horace's epistles and satires, Pope invested his modern social criticism with the classical authority of a revered Roman poet. The *Moral Essays*, or "Epistles to Several Persons" as Pope called them, also show Pope assuming the mantle of Horace by using the familiar epistle as a vehicle for social commentary. Pope's Horatian poems are his most mature, elegant, and self-assured works.

In 1737, he published an authorized version of his letters, which he doctored to improve his reputation. His last years were a time of retirement at his villa at Twickenham, famous for its grotto of "Friendship and Liberty" and for the five-acre landscape garden Pope had designed. In *The New Dunciad* (1742), Pope shifted his attack from hack writers and low culture to all forms of hypocrisy and pretense. It was his final triumph. He worked with William Warburton on a new edition of his *Works* (1751), even as his many illnesses became still more overwhelming. Though he was a self-confessed "fool to Fame" (*Arbuthnot*), he told those gathered around his deathbed: "There is nothing that is meritorious but virtue and friendship." He was, as his enemies claimed, bellicose, self-indulgent, and self-aggrandizing. He was morally and physically courageous and had a great gift for friendship. Although it is no longer fashionable to call the first half of the eighteenth century the "Age of Pope," many of his contemporaries saw him as the predominant literary genius of his time. Today, most literary historians agree that the greatest English poet between John Milton and William Wordsworth was Alexander Pope.

An Essay on Criticism

Pope was only twenty-one years old when he wrote *An Essay on Criticism*, which was published anonymously in 1711. This aesthetic manifesto in heroic couplets is written in the tradition of Horace's *Ars Poetica* (c. 19 B.C.), Boileau's *Art poétique* (1674), and other verse essays delineating poetic principles and practices. Pope's chief contributions to the genre are his ringing epigrams and the playful ease with which he satirizes contemporary critics who lack genuine poetic understanding. The *Essay on Criticism* is divided into three parts: the first examines the rules of taste, their relationship to Nature, and the authority of classical authors. The second section (lines 201–559) considers the impediments preventing the attainment of the classical ideals outlined in part one. In the third part, Pope proposes an aesthetic and moral reformation to restore wit, sense, and taste to their former glory. While acknowledging the importance of precepts, Pope asserts the primacy of poetic genius and the power of imagination.

An Essay on Criticism

'Tis hard to say, if greater want of skill
Appear in writing or in judging ill;
But, of the two, less dangerous is th' offense,
To tire our patience, than mislead our sense:°   *judgment*
5 Some few in that, but numbers err in this,
Ten censure wrong for one who writes amiss;
A fool might once himself alone expose,
Now one in verse makes many more in prose.[1]
    'Tis with our judgments as our watches, none
10 Go just alike, yet each believes his own.
In poets as true genius is but rare,
True taste as seldom is the critic's share;
Both must alike from Heav'n derive their light,
These born to judge, as well as those to write.
15 Let such teach others who themselves excel,
And censure freely who have written well.
Authors are partial to their wit,[2] 'tis true,
But are not critics to their judgment too?
    Yet if we look more closely, we shall find
20 Most have the seeds of judgment in their mind;
Nature affords at least a glimm'ring light;
The lines, though touched but faintly, are drawn right.
But as the slightest sketch, if justly traced,
Is by ill coloring but the more disgraced,
25 So by false learning is good sense defaced;
Some are bewildered in the maze of Schools,[3]
And some made coxcombs[4] Nature meant but fools.
In search of wit these lose their common sense,
And then turn critics in their own defense.
30 Each burns alike, who can, or cannot write,
Or° with a rival's or an eunuch's spite.[5]   *either*

---

1. I.e., many bad critics respond to one bad poet.
2. Both their writings and their (fancied) ability to write well.
3. Schools of criticism.

4. Conceited show-offs.
5. I.e., they either seek to compete or, knowing themselves sterile, criticize out of envy.

<table>
<tr><td></td><td>All fools have still° an itching to deride,[6]</td><td>continually</td></tr>
<tr><td></td><td>And fain° would be upon the laughing side:</td><td>gladly</td></tr>
<tr><td></td><td>If Maevius scribble in Apollo's spite,[7]</td><td></td></tr>
<tr><td>35</td><td>There are, who judge still worse than he can write.</td><td></td></tr>
<tr><td></td><td>   Some have at first for wits,° then poets past,</td><td>intellectuals</td></tr>
<tr><td></td><td>Turned critics next, and proved plain fools at last;</td><td></td></tr>
<tr><td></td><td>Some neither can for wits nor critics pass,</td><td></td></tr>
<tr><td></td><td>As heavy mules are neither horse nor ass.</td><td></td></tr>
<tr><td>40</td><td>Those half-learned witlings, num'rous in our isle,</td><td></td></tr>
<tr><td></td><td>As half-formed insects on the banks of Nile;</td><td></td></tr>
<tr><td></td><td>Unfinished things, one knows not what to call,</td><td></td></tr>
<tr><td></td><td>Their generation's so equivocal:[8]</td><td></td></tr>
<tr><td></td><td>To tell° 'em, would a hundred tongues require,</td><td>count</td></tr>
<tr><td>45</td><td>Or one vain wit's, that might a hundred tire.</td><td></td></tr>
<tr><td></td><td>   But you who seek to give and merit° fame,</td><td>deserve</td></tr>
<tr><td></td><td>And justly bear a critic's noble name,</td><td></td></tr>
<tr><td></td><td>Be sure yourself and your own reach° to know,</td><td>ability</td></tr>
<tr><td></td><td>How far your genius, taste, and learning go;</td><td></td></tr>
<tr><td>50</td><td>Launch not beyond your depth, but be discrete,</td><td></td></tr>
<tr><td></td><td>And mark° that point where sense and dullness meet.</td><td>note</td></tr>
<tr><td></td><td>   Nature to all things fixed the limits fit,</td><td></td></tr>
<tr><td></td><td>And wisely curbed proud man's pretending° wit:</td><td>aspiring</td></tr>
<tr><td></td><td>As on the land while here the ocean gains,</td><td></td></tr>
<tr><td>55</td><td>In other parts it leaves wide sandy plains;</td><td></td></tr>
<tr><td></td><td>Thus in the soul while memory prevails,</td><td></td></tr>
<tr><td></td><td>The solid power of understanding fails;</td><td></td></tr>
<tr><td></td><td>Where beams of warm imagination play,</td><td></td></tr>
<tr><td></td><td>The memory's soft figures melt away.</td><td></td></tr>
<tr><td>60</td><td>One science only will one genius fit;[9]</td><td></td></tr>
<tr><td></td><td>So vast is Art, so narrow human wit;°</td><td>understanding</td></tr>
<tr><td></td><td>Not only bounded to peculiar° arts,</td><td>particular</td></tr>
<tr><td></td><td>But oft in those, confined to single parts.</td><td></td></tr>
<tr><td></td><td>Like kings we lose the conquests gained before,</td><td></td></tr>
<tr><td>65</td><td>By vain ambition still to make them more:</td><td></td></tr>
<tr><td></td><td>Each might his several province well command,</td><td></td></tr>
<tr><td></td><td>Would all but stoop to what they understand.</td><td></td></tr>
<tr><td></td><td>   First follow NATURE, and your judgment frame</td><td></td></tr>
<tr><td></td><td>By her just standard, which is still° the same:</td><td>always</td></tr>
<tr><td>70</td><td>Unerring Nature, still divinely bright,</td><td></td></tr>
<tr><td></td><td>One clear, unchanged, and universal light,</td><td></td></tr>
<tr><td></td><td>Life, force, and beauty, must to all impart,</td><td></td></tr>
<tr><td></td><td>At once the source, and end, and test of art.</td><td></td></tr>
<tr><td></td><td>Art from that fund each just supply provides,</td><td></td></tr>
<tr><td>75</td><td>Works without show,[1] and without pomp presides:</td><td></td></tr>
<tr><td></td><td>In some fair body thus th' informing soul[2]</td><td></td></tr>
</table>

---

6. The fool's perpetual itching suggests disease.
7. Maevius, a third-rate Roman poet, is set against Apollo, patron of good poetry.
8. Like the generation of insects on the banks of the Nile, thought to occur spontaneously, through the action of sun on mud.

9. The artist can hope only to succeed in one subject area or object of study.
1. The suggestion that art should mask its presence came from Horace.
2. The force that animates.

　　　　With spirits feeds, with vigor fills the whole,
　　　　Each motion guides, and every nerve sustains;
　　　　Itself unseen, but in th' effects, remains.
80　　 Some, to whom Heav'n in wit has been profuse,
　　　　Want° as much more, to turn it to its use;　　　　　　　　　　*need*
　　　　For wit and judgment often are at strife,
　　　　Though meant each other's aid, like man and wife.
　　　　'Tis more to guide than spur the Muse's steed;[3]
85　　 Restrain his fury, than provoke his speed;
　　　　The winged courser,° like a gen'rous horse,　　　　　　*swift horse*
　　　　Shows most true mettle° when you check his course.　　　　*spirit*
　　　　　　Those RULES of old discovered, not devised,
　　　　Are Nature still, but Nature *methodized*;
90　　 Nature, like Liberty, is but restrained
　　　　By the same laws which first herself ordained.
　　　　　　Hear how learn'd Greece her useful rules indites,°　　*composes*
　　　　When to repress, and when indulge our flights:
　　　　High on Parnassus'[4] top her sons she showed,
95　　 And pointed out° those arduous paths they trod,　　　　　*appointed*
　　　　Held from afar, aloft, th' immortal prize,
　　　　And urged the rest by equal steps to rise;
　　　　Just precepts thus from great examples giv'n,
　　　　She drew from them what they derived from Heav'n.
100　 The gen'rous critic fanned the poet's fire,
　　　　And taught the world, with reason to admire.
　　　　Then criticism the Muse's handmaid proved,
　　　　To dress her charms,[5] and make her more beloved;
　　　　But following wits from that intention strayed;
105　 Who could not win the mistress, wooed the maid;
　　　　Against the poets their own arms they turned,
　　　　Sure to hate most the men from whom they learned.
　　　　So modern 'pothecaries,° taught the art　　　　　　　　　*druggists*
　　　　By doctors' bills° to play the doctor's part,　　　　　　*prescriptions*
110　 Bold in the practice of mistaken° rules,　　　　　　　　　*misunderstood*
　　　　Prescribe, apply, and call their masters fools.
　　　　Some on the leaves of ancient authors prey,[6]
　　　　Nor time nor moths e'er spoiled so much as they:
　　　　Some dryly plain, without invention's° aid,　　　　　　*imagination's*
115　 Write dull receipts° how poems may be made:　　　　　　*recipes*
　　　　These leave the sense, their learning to display,
　　　　And those explain the meaning quite away.
　　　　　　You then whose judgment the right course would steer,
　　　　Know well each ANCIENT'S proper character,[7]
120　 His fable,° subject, scope° in every page,　　　　　　　　*plot/intention*
　　　　Religion, country, genius of his age:
　　　　Without all these at once before your eyes,

---

3. Pegasus, the winged horse.
4. Mount Parnassus in Greece was sacred to the Muses.
5. Both dress and address, i.e., both interpret and adjust.
6. Textual commentators, depicted as literal bookworms

in continuation of the earlier insect metaphor.
7. An interest in the historical method in criticism was
on the rise.

Cavil° you may, but never criticize.   *quibble*
Be Homer's works your study, and delight,
125 Read them by day, and meditate by night,
Thence form your judgment, thence your maxims bring,
And trace the Muses upward to their spring;
Still with itself compared, his text peruse;
And let your comment be the Mantuan Muse.[8]
130   When first young Maro° in his boundless mind   *Virgil*
A work t' outlast immortal Rome designed,
Perhaps he seemed° above the critic's law,   *thought himself*
And but from Nature's fountains scorned to draw:
But when t' examine every part he came,
135 Nature and Homer were, he found, the same:
Convinced, amazed, he checks the bold design, ⎤
And rules as strict his labored work confine,   ⎬
As if the Stagyrite[9] o'erlooked each line.   ⎦
Learn hence for ancient rules a just esteem;
140 To copy Nature is to copy them.
     Some beauties yet, no precepts can declare,[1]
For there's a happiness as well as care.
Music resembles poetry, in each   ⎤
Are nameless graces which no methods teach,   ⎬
145 And which a master-hand alone can reach.   ⎦
If, where the rules not far enough extend,
(Since rules were made but to promote their end)
Some lucky license° answers to the full   *deviation*
Th' intent proposed, that license is a rule.
150 Thus Pegasus, a nearer way to take,
May boldly deviate from the common track.
Great wits sometimes may gloriously offend,
And rise to faults true critics dare not mend;
From vulgar bounds with brave disorder part,
155 And snatch a grace beyond the reach of Art,
Which, without passing through the judgment, gains
The heart, and all its end at once attains.
In prospects,[2] thus, some objects please our eyes, ⎤
Which out of Nature's common order rise,   ⎬
160 The shapeless rock, or hanging precipice.   ⎦
But though the Ancients thus their rules invade,
(As kings dispense with laws themselves have made)
Moderns, beware! Or if you must offend
Against the precept, ne'er transgress its end,
165 Let it be seldom, and compelled by need,
And have, at least, their precedent to plead.
The critic else proceeds without remorse,

---

8. Virgil (born near Mantua) and his *Aeneid*, which took
Homer's epics as models and was the best commentary on
them.
9. Aristotle, whose *Poetics* provided the basis for later
rules on poetry and epic writing.
1. Pope's belief that true poetic genius consisted not of

rigid adherence to rules but of "brave disorder" and "grace
beyond the reach of art" had earlier been expressed in the
treatise *On the Sublime*, attributed to the Greek rhetorician Longinus (210?–273).
2. Views of an extensive landscape.

Seizes your fame, and puts his laws in force.
   I know there are, to whose presumptuous thoughts
170   Those freer beauties, ev'n in them, seem faults:[3]
Some figures[4] monstrous and misshaped appear,
Considered singly, or beheld too near,
Which, but proportioned to their light, or place,
Due distance reconciles to form and grace.
175   A prudent chief not always must display
His pow'rs in equal ranks, and fair array,
But with th' occasion and the place comply,
Conceal his force, nay seem sometimes to fly.
Those oft are stratagems which errors seem,
180   Nor is it Homer nods, but we that dream.
   Still green with bays[5] each ancient altar[6] stands,
Above the reach of sacrilegious hands,
Secure from flames, from envy's fiercer rage,
Destructive war, and all-involving age.
185   See, from each clime the learn'd their incense bring;
Hear, in all tongues consenting paeans° ring!   *songs of praise*
In praise so just, let every voice be joined,
And fill the gen'ral chorus of mankind!
Hail bards triumphant! born in happier days;
190   Immortal heirs of universal praise!
Whose honors with increase of Ages grow,
As streams roll down, enlarging as they flow!
Nations unborn your mighty names shall sound,
And worlds applaud that must not yet be found!
195   Oh may some spark of your celestial fire
The last, the meanest of your sons inspire,[7]
(That on weak wings, from far, pursues your flights;
Glows while he reads, but trembles as he writes)
To teach vain wits° a science little known,   *would-be critics*
200   T' admire superior sense, and doubt their own!

   Of all the causes which conspire to blind
Man's erring judgment, and misguide the mind,
What the weak head with strongest bias[8] rules,
Is pride, the never-failing vice of fools.
205   Whatever Nature has in worth denied,
She gives in large recruits° of needful° pride;   *supplies/needed*
For as in bodies, thus in souls, we find
What wants° in blood and spirits, swelled with wind;   *is lacking*
Pride, where wit fails, steps in to our defense,
210   And fills up all the mighty void of sense!
If once right reason drives that cloud away,
Truth breaks upon us with resistless day;

---

3. I.e., there are critics to whom even the Ancients' occasional "glorious offense" is unforgivable.
4. Both figures in the landscape and rhetorical figures or literary style.
5. Laurels, used to crown both poets and military heroes.

6. The works of each ancient author.
7. Pope himself, who follows tradition in writing about writing.
8. Not only prejudice but a kind of bowling ball. (In bowls, the bias ball is one weighted to roll obliquely.)

Trust not yourself; but your defects to know,
Make use of every friend—and every foe.
215 A little learning is a dang'rous thing;
Drink deep, or taste not the Pierian spring:[9]
There shallow draughts[1] intoxicate the brain,
And drinking largely sobers us again.
Fired at first sight with what the Muse imparts,
220 In fearless youth we tempt° the heights of Arts,   *attempt*
While from the bounded° level of our mind,   *limited*
Short views we take, nor see the lengths behind,
But more advanced, behold with strange surprise
New, distant scenes of endless science[2] rise!
225 So pleased at first, the towering Alps we try,
Mount o'er the vales, and seem to tread the sky;
Th' eternal snows appear already past,
And the first clouds and mountains seem the last:
But those attained, we tremble to survey
230 The growing labors of the lengthened way,
Th' increasing prospect tires our wandering eyes,
Hills peep o'er hills, and Alps on Alps arise!
  A perfect judge will read each work of wit
With the same spirit that its author writ,
235 Survey the whole, nor seek slight faults to find,
Where Nature moves, and rapture warms the mind;
Nor lose, for that malignant dull delight,
The gen'rous pleasure to be charmed with wit.
But in such lays° as neither ebb, nor flow,   *poems*
240 Correctly cold, and regularly low,
That shunning faults, one quiet tenor° keep;   *tone*
We cannot blame indeed—but we may sleep.
In wit, as Nature, what affects our hearts
Is not th' exactness of peculiar° parts;   *particular*
245 'Tis not a lip, or eye, we beauty call,
But the joint force and full result of all.
Thus when we view some well-proportioned dome,[3]
(The world's just wonder, and even thine O Rome!)
No single parts unequally surprise;
250 All comes united to th' admiring eyes;
No monstrous height, or breadth, or length appear;
The whole at once is bold, and regular.°   *well-proportioned*
  Whoever thinks a faultless piece to see,
Thinks what ne'er was, nor is, nor e'er shall be.
255 In every work regard the writer's end,
Since none can compass° more than they intend;   *encompass*
And if the means be just, the conduct° true,   *execution*
Applause, in spite of trivial faults, is due.
As men of breeding,[4] sometimes men of wit,

---

9. Hippocrene, the stream associated with the Muses.
1. I.e., drinking small amounts.
2. Knowledge, subjects requiring study.

3. Any large and stately building, but those of a classical design are particularly implied.
4. Good breeding (in both birth and upbringing).

260   T' avoid great errors, must the less commit,
       Neglect the rules each verbal critic lays,[5]
       For not to know some trifles, is a praise.
       Most critics, fond of some subservient art,
       Still make the whole depend upon a part,
265   They talk of principles, but notions° prize,   *prejudices*
       And all to one loved folly sacrifice.
           Once on a time, La Mancha's Knight,[6] they say,
       A certain bard encountering on the way,
       Discoursed in terms as just, with looks as sage,
270   As e'er could Dennis,[7] of the Grecian stage;
       Concluding all were desp'rate sots and fools,
       Who durst depart from Aristotle's rules.
       Our author, happy in a judge so nice,
       Produced his play, and begged the Knight's advice,
275   Made him observe the subject and the plot,
       The manners, passions, unities,[8] what not?
       All which, exact to rule were brought about,
       Were but a combat in the lists[9] left out.
       "What! leave the combat out?" exclaims the Knight;
280   Yes, or we must renounce the Stagyrite.°   *Aristotle*
       "Not so by Heav'n" (he answers in a rage)
       "Knights, squires, and steeds, must enter on the stage."
       So vast a throng the stage can ne'er contain.
       "Then build a new, or act it in a plain."
285   Thus critics, of less judgment than caprice,
       Curious,° not knowing, not exact, but nice,°   *picky/fussy*
       Form short ideas; and offend in arts
       (As most in manners) by a love to parts.[1]
       Some to conceit[2] alone their taste confine,
290   And glitt'ring thoughts struck out at every line;
       Pleased with a work where nothing's just or fit;
       One glaring chaos and wild heap of wit:
       Poets like painters, thus, unskilled to trace
       The naked Nature and the living grace,
295   With gold and jewels cover every part,
       And hide with ornaments their want° of art.   *lack*
       True wit is Nature to advantage dressed,
       What oft was thought, but ne'er so well expressed,
       Something, whose truth convinced at sight we find,
300   That gives us back the image of our mind:
       As shades° more sweetly recommend the light,   *shadows*
       So modest plainness sets off sprightly wit:
       For works may have more wit than does 'em good,

---

5. Lays down. A verbal critic is one concerned with linguistic detail rather than literary whole.
6. Don Quixote, Cervantes's foolish knight errant. This episode comes from part two of *Don Quixote* (1615), bk. 3, ch. 10.
7. John Dennis (1657–1734), an eminent critic but not one in Pope's favor.

8. The three unities of plot (one story), time (one day), and place (one location) were thought to have been the Greek playwrights' structuring principles, recommended by Aristotle.
9. The field of combat in medieval jousting tournaments.
1. Individual talents.
2. Extravagant use of metaphor.

As bodies perish through excess of blood.[3]
305   Others for language all their care express,
And value books, as women men, for dress:
Their praise is still—The style is excellent:
The sense, they humbly take upon content.°   *trust*
Words are like leaves; and where they most abound,
310 Much fruit of sense beneath is rarely found.
False eloquence, like the prismatic glass,
Its gaudy colors spreads on every place;
The face of Nature we no more survey,°   *observe*
All glares alike, without distinction gay:
315 But true expression, like th' unchanging sun, ⎤
Clears, and improves whate'er it shines upon, ⎬
It gilds all objects, but it alters none. ⎦
Expression is the dress of thought,[4] and still
Appears more decent° as more suitable;   *correct*
320 A vile conceit° in pompous words expressed,   *idea*
Is like a clown° in regal purple dressed;   *peasant*
For different styles with different subjects sort,°   *belong*
As several garbs with Country, Town, and Court.[5]
Some by old words to fame have made pretense;[6]
325 Ancients in phrase, mere Moderns in their sense!
Such labored nothings, in so strange a style,
Amaze the unlearn'd, and make the learned smile.
Unlucky, as Fungoso in the play,[7] ⎤
These sparks[8] with awkward vanity display ⎬
330 What the fine gentleman wore yesterday! ⎦
And but so mimic ancient wits at best,
As apes our grandsires in their doublets[9] dressed.
In words, as fashions, the same rule will hold;
Alike fantastic, if too new, or old;
335 Be not the first by whom the new are tried,
Nor yet the last to lay the old aside.
     But most by numbers[1] judge a poet's song,
And smooth or rough, with them, is right or wrong;
In the bright Muse though thousand charms conspire,° *work together*
340 Her voice is all these tuneful fools admire,
Who haunt Parnassus but to please their ear, ⎤
Not mend their minds; as some to church repair, ⎬
Not for the doctrine, but the music there. ⎦
These equal syllables alone require,
345 Though oft the ear the open vowels tire,[2]
While expletives their feeble aid do join,

---

3. Apoplexy, it was thought, was caused by such an excess.
4. It was generally held that a person's appearance reflected his or her inner self.
5. As various styles of dress suit country, mercantile, and courtly life.
6. Made a claim. Deliberately archaic language was used by Spenser and by a number of his 18th-century imitators.

7. In Ben Jonson's *Every Man Out of His Humor* (1599), this student lagged behind the fashions.
8. Hot-blooded young men, aspiring to fame and romantic conquest.
9. Close-fitting garment for the upper body.
1. Meter of verse, patterns of sound.
2. This line, like the couplets that follow, illustrates the fault it criticizes.

And ten low words oft creep in one dull line,
While they ring round the same unvaried chimes,
With sure returns of still expected rhymes.

350   Where-e'er you find the cooling western breeze,
In the next line, it whispers through the trees;
If crystal streams with pleasing murmurs creep,
The reader's threatened (not in vain) with sleep.
Then, at the last, and only couplet fraught

355   With some unmeaning thing they call a thought,
A needless Alexandrine[3] ends the song,
That like a wounded snake, drags its slow length along.
Leave such to tune their own dull rhymes, and know
What's roundly smooth, or languishingly slow;

360   And praise the easy vigor of a line,
Where Denham's strength, and Waller's sweetness join.[4]
True ease in writing comes from art, not chance,
As those move easiest who have learned to dance.
'Tis not enough no harshness gives offense,

365   The sound must seem an echo to the sense.[5]
Soft is the strain when Zephyr° gently blows,   *the west wind*
And the smooth stream in smoother numbers flows;
But when loud surges lash the sounding shore,
The hoarse, rough verse should like the torrent roar.

370   When Ajax[6] strives, some rock's vast weight to throw,
The line too labors, and the words move slow;
Not so, when swift Camilla[7] scours the plain,
Flies o'er th' unbending corn, and skims along the main.°   *sea*
Hear how Timotheus'[8] varied lays surprise,

375   And bid alternate passions fall and rise!
While, at each change, the son of Lybian Jove[9]
Now burns with glory, and then melts with love;
Now his fierce eyes with sparkling fury glow;
Now sighs steal out, and tears begin to flow:

380   Persians and Greeks like turns of nature[1] found,
And the world's victor stood subdued by sound!
The pow'rs of music all our hearts allow;°   *admit to*
And what Timotheus was, is Dryden now.

    Avoid extremes; and shun the fault of such,
385   Who still are pleased too little, or too much.
At every trifle scorn to take offense,
That always shows great pride, or little sense;
Those heads as stomachs are not sure the best
Which nauseate° all, and nothing can digest.   *feel sick at*

---

3. The 12 syllables and six stresses of an Alexandrine are illustrated in the next line.
4. Pope follows Dryden in his stylistic characterization of John Denham (1615–1669) and Edmund Waller (1606–1687), two poets greatly respected by writers of the early 18th century, especially for their work in heroic couplets.
5. The following nine lines exemplify the rule laid down

here.
6. The fabulously strong Greek hero in Homer's *Iliad*.
7. An Amazon warrior in Virgil's *Aeneid*.
8. Musician to Alexander the Great, as portrayed in Dryden's *Alexander's Feast* (1697).
9. Alexander the Great.
1. Similar changes of emotion.

390	Yet let not each gay turn° thy rapture move,
	For fools admire,[2] but men of sense approve;
	As things seem large which we through mists descry,°
	Dullness is ever apt to magnify.
	Some foreign writers, some our own despise;
395	The Ancients only, or the Moderns prize:
	(Thus wit, like faith, by each man is applied
	To one small sect, and all are damned beside.)
	Meanly they seek the blessing to confine,
	And force that sun but on a part to shine;
400	Which not alone the southern wit sublimes,°
	But ripens spirits in cold northern climes;
	Which from the first has shone on Ages past,
	Enlights the present, and shall warm the last:
	(Though each may feel increases and decays,
405	And see now clearer and now darker days)
	Regard not then if wit be old or new,
	But blame the false, and value still the true.
	Some ne'er advance a judgment of their own,
	But catch the spreading notion° of the Town;[3]
410	They reason and conclude by precedent,
	And own° stale nonsense which they ne'er invent.
	Some judge of authors' names, not works, and then
	Nor° praise nor blame the writings, but the men.
	Of all this servile herd the worst is he
415	That in proud dullness joins with Quality,[4]
	A constant critic at the great man's board,[5]
	To fetch and carry nonsense for my Lord.
	What woeful stuff this madrigal would be,
	In some starved Hackney sonneteer,[6] or me?
420	But let a Lord once own[7] the happy lines,
	How the wit brightens! How the style refines!
	Before his sacred name flies every fault,
	And each exalted stanza teems with thought!
	The vulgar thus through imitation err;
425	As oft the learned by being singular;
	So much they scorn the crowd, that if the throng
	By chance go right, they purposely go wrong;
	So Schismatics[8] the plain believers quit,
	And are but damned for having too much wit.
430	Some praise at morning what they blame at night;
	But always think the last° opinion right.
	A Muse by these is like a mistress used,
	This hour she's idolized, the next abused,

Right margin glosses:
- *phrase* (line 390)
- *see* (line 392)
- *exalts* (line 400)
- *fashion* (line 409)
- *express* (line 411)
- *neither* (line 413)
- *latest* (line 431)

---

2. Wonder at the poetry, while "men of sense" deliberate before reaching favorable judgment.
3. The fashionable members of the city; the term was commonly used for fashionable London society.
4. The nobility, people of quality.
5. Dining table; i.e., he always eats there.
6. Like the horses from Hackney, in Middlesex, this

poet's services are readily for hire. The designation "sonneteer" indicates one who writes poor poetry. Pope, who made a point of refusing to sell his services, includes himself here perhaps because of his youth when the *Essay* was written.
7. Own up to, admit that they are his.
8. Religious sectarians.

While their weak heads, like towns unfortified,

435   'Twixt sense and nonsense daily change their side.

Ask them the cause; they're "wiser still," they say;

And still tomorrow's wiser than today.

We think our fathers fools, so wise we grow;

Our wiser sons, no doubt, will think us so.

440   Once School-Divines[9] this zealous Isle o'erspread;

Who knew most sentences[1] was deepest read;

Faith, gospel, all, seemed made to be disputed,

And none had sense enough to be confuted.°   *disproved*

Scotists and Thomists,[2] now, in peace remain,

445   Amidst their kindred cobwebs in Duck Lane.[3]

If faith itself has diff'rent dresses worn,

What wonder modes in wit should take their turn?

Oft, leaving what is natural and fit,

The current folly proves the ready wit,[4]

450   And authors think their reputation safe,

Which lives as long as fools are pleased to laugh.

    Some valuing those of their own side,[5] or mind,

Still make themselves the measure of mankind;

Fondly we think we honor merit then,

455   When we but praise ourselves in other men.

Parties in wit attend on those of state,

And public faction doubles private hate.

Pride, malice, folly, against Dryden rose,

In various shapes of parsons, critics, beaus;[6]

460   But sense survived, when merry jests were past;

For rising merit will buoy up at last.

Might he return, and bless once more our eyes,

New Blackmores and new Milbourns must arise;

Nay should great Homer lift his awful head,

465   Zoilus[7] again would start up from the dead.

Envy will merit as its shade° pursue,   *shadow*

But like a shadow, proves the substance true;

For envied wit, like Sol° eclipsed, makes known   *the sun*

Th' opposing body's grossness,° not its own.   *ponderousness*

470   When first that sun too powerful beams displays,

It draws up vapors which obscure its rays;

But ev'n those clouds at last adorn its way,

Reflect new glories, and augment the day.

    Be thou the first true merit to befriend;

---

9. Theologians who followed the highly formal Scholastic method.

1. The *sententiae*, or sayings of the Church Fathers, presented and explained for the student in works like Peter Lombard's *Book of Sentences* (1148–1151).

2. The schools of medieval philosophy formed by followers of Duns Scotus and Thomas Aquinas.

3. A street in London where old and secondhand books were sold.

4. Current folly allows ready wit to show itself.

5. Political persuasion.

6. The parsons: Jeremy Collier, *A Short View of the Profaneness and Immorality of the English Stage* (1698); Luke Milbourne, *Notes on Dryden's Virgil* (1698). The critics: Thomas Shadwell (1642?–1692); Elkanah Settle (1648–1724); Gerard Langbaine (1656–1692), *An Account of the English Dramatic Poets;* Richard Blackmore (1654–1729). Among the beaus: George Villiers, Second Duke of Buckingham, who co-authored *The Rehearsal* (1671); John Wilmot, Second Earl of Rochester, *An Allusion to Horace The 10th Satyr of the 1st Book* (1680).

7. A critic of Homer's, of the fourth century B.C.

475   His praise is lost, who stays till all commend;
        Short is the date,° alas, of modern rhymes;   *life*
        And 'tis but just to let 'em live betimes.°   *awhile*
        No longer now that Golden Age appears,
        When Patriarch-Wits survived a thousand years;
480   Now length of fame (our second life) is lost,
        And bare threescore is all ev'n that can boast:
        Our sons their fathers' failing language see,
        And such as Chaucer[8] is, shall Dryden be.
        So when the faithful pencil has designed
485   Some bright idea of the master's mind,
        Where a new world leaps out at his command,
        And ready Nature waits upon his hand;
        When the ripe colors soften and unite,
        And sweetly melt into just shade and light,
490   When mellowing years their full perfection give,
        And each bold figure just begins to live;
        The treach'rous colors the fair art betray,
        And all the bright creation fades away!
            Unhappy wit, like most mistaken° things,   *misunderstood*
495   Atones not for that envy which it brings.
        In youth alone its empty praise we boast,
        But soon the short-lived vanity is lost!
        Like some fair flow'r the early spring supplies,
        That gaily blooms, but ev'n in blooming dies.
500   What is this wit which must our cares employ?
        The owner's wife, that other men enjoy,
        Then most our trouble still when most admired,
        And still the more we give, the more required;
        Whose fame with pains we guard, but lose with ease,
505   Sure some to vex, but never all to please;
        'Tis what the vicious° fear, the virtuous shun;   *wicked*
        By fools 'tis hated, and by knaves undone!
            If wit so much from ign'rance undergo,
        Ah, let not learning too commence° its foe!   *start to be*
510   Of old, those met rewards who could excel,
        And such were praised who but endeavored well:
        Though triumphs were to gen'rals only due,
        Crowns were reserved to grace the soldiers too.[9]
        Now, they who reached Parnassus' lofty crown,
515   Employ their plans to spurn some others down;
        And while self-love each jealous writer rules,
        Contending wits become the sport of fools:
        But still the worst with most regret commend,
        For each ill author is as bad a friend.
520   To what base ends, and by what abject ways,
        Are mortals urged through sacred° lust of praise!   *accursed*

---

8. Chaucer was admired but seen as quaint and arcane, his language unintelligible. It was common to complain of the transience of the English language at this time.
9. Soldiers who had distinguished themselves in the field received crowns. Unlike those soldiers rewarded for assisting one another, the poets in the following lines achieve their crowns, then turn on their fellow writers.

Ah, ne'er so dire a thirst of glory boast,
Nor in the critic let the man be lost!
Good nature and good sense must ever join;
525 To err is human; to forgive, divine.
     But if in noble minds some dregs remain,
Not yet purged off, of spleen° and sour disdain,   *bad temper*
Discharge that rage on more provoking crimes,
Nor fear a dearth in these flagitious° times.   *corrupt*
530 No pardon vile obscenity should find,
Though wit and art conspire to move your mind;
But dullness with obscenity must prove
As shameful sure as impotence in love.
In the fat Age of pleasure, wealth, and ease,
535 Sprung the rank weed, and thrived with large increase;
When love was all an easy monarch's[1] care;
Seldom at council, never in a war:[2]
Jilts ruled the State, and statesmen farces writ;[3]
Nay wits had pensions,° and young Lords had wit: *government salaries*
540 The fair sat panting at a courtier's play,
And not a Mask[4] went unimproved away:
The modest fan was lifted up no more,
And virgins smiled at what they blushed before—
The following license of a foreign reign[5]
545 Did all the dregs of bold Socinus[6] drain;
Then unbelieving priests reformed the nation,
And taught more pleasant methods of salvation;
Where Heav'ns free subjects might their rights dispute,
Lest God himself should seem too absolute.
550 Pulpits their sacred satire learned to spare,
And vice admired° to find a flatt'rer there!   *was surprised*
Encouraged thus, wit's Titans[7] braved the skies,
And the press groaned with licensed blasphemies[8]—
These monsters, critics! with your darts engage,
555 Here point your thunder, and exhaust your rage!
Yet shun their fault, who, scandalously nice,°   *fastidious*
Will needs mistake an author into vice;
All seems infected that th' infected spy,°   *see*
As all looks yellow to the jaundiced eye.
560 LEARN then what MORALS critics ought to show,
For 'tis but half a judge's task, to know.
'Tis not enough, taste, judgment, learning, join;

1. Charles II (1630–1685). Ease was a much-prized social grace in the late 17th and early 18th centuries.
2. Charles had commanded an army defeated at the Battle of Worcester in 1651.
3. "Jilts" were whores, a reference to Charles's many mistresses. The statesmen were the Duke of Buckingham, *The Rehearsal* (1671); Sir Charles Sedley, *The Mulberry Garden* (1668); Sir George Etherege (1634–1691), a number of plays.
4. Masks were initially worn by noblewomen attending plays, but the potential for concealment meant that they came to be particularly associated with prostitutes.

5. That of William III (1650–1702), from the Netherlands, who introduced policies of increased religious toleration.
6. Laelius Socinus (1525–1562) and Faustus Socinus (1539–1604), two Italian theologians who sponsored various heresies, including denying the divinity of Christ.
7. This reference compares the deistic writers to the classical giants, the Titans, who attempted to conquer heaven, and were severely punished as a result.
8. The Licensing Act lapsed in 1663, allowing books to be published that Pope and others found blasphemous.

In all you speak, let truth and candor shine;
That not alone what to your sense is due,
565   All may allow; but seek your friendship too.
        Be silent always when you doubt your sense;
And speak, though sure, with seeming diffidence:
Some positive persisting fops we know,
Who, if once wrong, will needs be always so;
570   But you, with pleasure own your errors past,
And make each day a critic on° the last.   *assessment of*
        'Tis not enough your counsel still be true;
Blunt truths more mischief than nice° falsehoods do.   *delicate*
Men must be taught as if you taught them not;
575   And things unknown proposed as things forgot:
Without good breeding, truth is disapproved;
That only makes superior sense belov'd.
        Be niggards of advice on no pretense;[9]
For the worse avarice is that of sense:
580   With mean complacence ne'er betray your trust,[1]
Nor be so civil as to prove unjust;
Fear not the anger of the wise to raise;
Those best can bear reproof, who merit praise.
        'Twere well, might critics still this freedom take;
585   But Appius[2] reddens at each word you speak,
And stares, tremendous![3] with a threatening eye,
Like some fierce tyrant in old tapestry!
Fear most to tax an honorable fool,
Whose right it is, uncensured to be dull;
590   Such without wit are poets when they please,
As without learning they can take degrees.[4]
Leave dang'rous truths to unsuccessful satires,
And flattery to fulsome dedicators,
Whom, when they praise, the world believes no more,
595   Than when they promise to give scribbling o'er.
'Tis best sometimes your censure to restrain,
And charitably let the dull be vain:
Your silence there is better than your spite,
For who can rail so long as they can write?
600   Still humming on, their drowsy course they keep,
And lashed so long, like tops,° are lashed asleep.   *spinning tops*
False steps but help them to renew the race,
As after stumbling, jades° will mend their pace.   *ruined horses*
What crowds of these, impenitently bold,
605   In sounds and jingling syllables grown old,
Still run on poets in a raging vein,
Ev'n to the dregs and squeezings of the brain;
Strain out the last, dull droppings of their sense,

And rhyme with all the rage of impotence!
610 Such shameless bards we have; and yet 'tis true,
There are as mad, abandoned critics too.
The bookful blockhead, ignorantly read,
With loads of learned lumber in his head,
With his own tongue still edifies his ears,
615 And always listening to himself appears.
All books he reads, and all he reads assails,
From Dryden's Fables down to Durfey's Tales.[5]
With him, most authors steal their works, or buy;
Garth did not write his own Dispensary.[6]
620 Name a new play, and he's the poet's friend,
Nay showed his faults—but when would poets mend?
No place so sacred from such fops is barred,
Nor is Paul's church more safe than Paul's churchyard:[7]
Nay, fly to altars; there they'll talk you dead;
625 For fools rush in where angels fear to tread.
Distrustful sense with modest caution speaks; ⎫
It still looks home, and short excursions makes; ⎬
But rattling nonsense in full volleys breaks; ⎭
And never shocked, and never turned aside,
630 Bursts out, resistless, with a thundering tide!
  But where's the man, who counsel can bestow,
Still pleased to teach, and yet not proud to know?°   *of knowing*
Unbiased, or° by favor or by spite;   *either*
Not dully prepossessed, nor blindly right;
635 Though learn'd, well-bred; and though well-bred, sincere;
Modestly bold, and humanly severe?
Who to a friend his faults can freely show,
And gladly praise the merit of a foe?
Blest with a taste exact, yet unconfined;
640 A knowledge both of books and humankind;
Generous converse;[8] a soul exempt from pride;
And love to praise, with reason on his side?
  Such once were critics, such the happy few,
Athens and Rome in better Ages knew.
645 The mighty Stagyrite° first left the shore,   *Aristotle*
Spread all his sails, and durst the deeps explore;
He steered securely, and discovered far,
Led by the light of the Maeonian star.°   *Homer*
Poets, a race long unconfined and free,
650 Still fond and proud of savage liberty,
Received his laws,[9] and stood convinced 'twas fit
Who conquered Nature,[1] should preside o'er wit.
  Horace still charms with graceful negligence,

---

5. Dryden, *Fables Ancient and Modern* (1700); Thomas D'Urfey, *Tales Tragical and Comical* (1704). D'Urfey, a popular playwright and singer, is best known for the ballad collection *Pills to Purge Melancholy*, to which his name was attached.
6. The report that Pope's friend Samuel Garth had plagiarized his popular mock-heroic work *The Dispensary*

(1699) was, according to William Warburton, "a common slander at that time."
7. Booksellers kept stalls in St. Paul's churchyard.
8. Good conversation and well-mannered behavior.
9. Aristotle's *Poetics* set rules for poetic composition.
1. Aristotle was also noted for his study of the physical world.

And without method talks us into sense,
655   Will like a friend familiarly convey
The truest notions in the easiest way.
He, who supreme in judgment, as in wit,
Might boldly censure, as he boldly writ,
Yet judged with coolness though he sung with fire;
660   His precepts teach but what his works inspire.
Our critics take a contrary extreme,
They judge with fury, but they write with phlegm:[2]
Nor suffers Horace more in wrong translations
By wits, than critics in as wrong quotations.
665   See Dionysius[3] Homer's thoughts refine,
And call new beauties forth from ev'ry line!
    Fancy and art in gay Petronius[4] please,
The Scholar's learning, with the courtier's ease.
    In grave Quintilian's copious work[5] we find
670   The justest rules, and clearest method joined;
Thus useful arms in magazines we place,
All ranged in order, and disposed with grace,
But less to please the eye, than arm the hand,
Still fit for use, and ready at command.
675   Thee, bold Longinus![6] all the Nine° inspire,   *the Muses*
And bless their critic with a poet's fire.
    And ardent judge, who zealous in his trust,
With warmth gives sentence, yet is always just;
Whose own example strengthens all his laws,
680   And is himself that great sublime he draws.
    Thus long succeeding critics justly reigned,
License repressed, and useful laws ordained;
Learning and Rome alike in Empire grew,
And Arts still followed where her eagles[7] flew;
685   From the same foes, at last, both felt their doom,
And the same Age saw learning fall, and Rome.
With tyranny, then superstition joined,
As that the body, this enslaved the mind;
Much was believed, but little understood,
690   And to be dull was construed to be good;
A second deluge learning thus o'er-run,
And the monks finished what the Goths begun.
    At length, Erasmus, that great, injured name,
(The glory of the priesthood, and the shame!)[8]
695   Stemmed the wild torrent of a barb'rous age,
And drove those holy vandals off the stage.

---

2. Under the humoral understanding of the body, an excess of phlegm caused disease, and so the term came to mean coolness, dullness, or apathy.
3. Dionysius of Halicarnassus, a Roman critic contemporary with Horace.
4. Petronius Arbiter (d. A.D. 66) judged on matters of taste in Nero's court.
5. Quintilian (c. 35–c. 99 A.D.) was a Latin rhetorician, whose *Institutio Oratoria* Pope knew well.

6. Longinus (210?–273) was a Greek rhetorician, to whom was attributed the enormously influential treatise *On the Sublime*.
7. The emblem of the Roman Empire.
8. Erasmus (c. 1466–1536), the Dutch humanist who influenced the course of the Reformation; the "glory of the priesthood" because of his learning, Erasmus was its "shame" both because he criticized priests and because he was persecuted for his outspokenness.

But see! each Muse, in Leo's[9] golden days,
Starts from her trance, and trims her withered bays!
Rome's ancient Genius,° o'er its ruins spread,   *guardian spirit*
700 Shakes off the dust, and rears his rev'rend head!
Then Sculpture and her sister Arts revive;
Stones leaped to form, and rocks began to live;
With sweeter notes each rising temple rung;
A Raphael painted, and a Vida sung![1]
705 Immortal Vida! on whose honored brow
The Poet's bays and critic's ivy[2] grow:
Cremona now shall ever boast thy name,
As next in place to Mantua, next in fame![3]
But soon by impious arms from Latium[4] chased,
710 Their ancient bounds the banished Muses passed;
Thence Arts o'er all the northern world advance;
But critic Learning flourished most in France.
The rules, a nation born to serve,[5] obeys,
And Boileau[6] still in right of Horace sways.
715 But we, brave Britons, foreign laws despised,
And kept unconquered, and uncivilized,
Fierce for the liberties of wit, and bold,
We still defied the Romans, as of old.
Yet some there were, among the sounder few
720 Of those who less presumed, and better knew,
Who durst° assert the juster ancient cause,   *dared to*
And here restored wit's fundamental laws.
Such was the Muse, whose rules and practice tell,
Nature's chief Master-piece is writing well.[7]
725 Such was Roscommon[8]—not more learn'd than good,
With manners gen'rous as his noble blood;
To him the wit of Greece and Rome was known,
And ev'ry author's merit, but his own.
Such late was Walsh,[9]—the Muse's judge and friend,
730 Who justly knew° to blame or to commend;   *knew when to*
To failings mild, but zealous for desert;
The clearest head, and the sincerest heart.
This humble praise, lamented shade!° receive,   *spirit*
This praise at least a grateful Muse may give!
735 The Muse, whose early voice you taught to sing,
Prescribed her heights, and pruned° her tender wing,   *groomed*
(Her guide now lost) no more attempts to rise,
But in low numbers° short excursions tries: *lowly verses*

9. Pope Leo X (1475–1521), patron of letters and arts.
1. Raphael (1483–1520) was considered the greatest of painters; Girolamo Vida (c. 1485–1566), Italian poet.
2. Ivy was associated with poets (and with Bacchus), but also with learning.
3. Cremona and Mantua were the birthplaces of Vida and Virgil, respectively.
4. Italy; Rome was conquered by the Holy Roman Empire in 1527.
5. A reference to the despotic reign of Louis XIV.

6. Nicolas Boileau-Despréaux (1636–1711) wrote much that was praised in England.
7. This line is quoted from the then well-known *Essay on Poetry* (1682) by John Sheffield, third Earl of Mulgrave and later first Duke of Buckingham.
8. Wentworth Dillon (c. 1630–1685), fourth Earl of Roscommon; poet, critic, didactic writer.
9. William Walsh (1663–1708), friend and mentor of Pope.

Content, if hence th' unlearn'd their wants° may view,   *lacks*
740   The learn'd reflect on what before they knew:
Careless of censure, nor too fond of fame,
Still pleased to praise, yet not afraid to blame,
Averse alike to flatter, or offend,
Not free from faults, nor yet too vain to mend.

c. 1709   1711

Windsor-Forest

"Mr. Pope has published a fine poem called Windsor Forest," wrote Jonathan Swift to his beloved
Stella; "read it," he urged her in a letter sent just two days after the poem went on sale. Pope wrote
Windsor-Forest in two distinct stages: the first part (lines 1–290) was composed in 1704–1705, but
the remaining lines celebrating the imminent Peace of Utrecht (1713) that formally ended the
long War of Spanish Succession were penned in late 1712 and early 1713. The Peace—a great triumph for the ruling Tory party and the last Stuart monarch, Queen Anne—recognized Great
Britain as the world's leading naval power and greatly augmented its colonial and commercial
empire at the expense of Spain and France. It would be wrong, however, to imagine that *Windsor-
Forest* is half pastoral idyll and half Tory political propaganda; it is, rather, a thoroughgoing synthesis of the topographical, the moral, and the political. Pope's sources for *Windsor-Forest* include
Virgil's *Eclogues* and *Georgics*, Ovid's *Metamorphoses*, the Bible, Spenser's *Faerie Queene*, Milton's
Paradise Lost, Edmund Waller's *On St. James's Park* (1661), and Thomas Otway's *Windsor Castle*
(1685). It is, however, Pope's comment on "the distinguishing excellence" of John Denham's
Cooper's Hill (1642) that best explains Pope's own imaginative procedure in *Windsor-Forest*: "the
descriptions of places, and images raised by the poet, are still [i.e., continually] tending to some
hint, or leading into some reflection, upon moral life or political institution" (*Iliad* 16.466n).
Windsor was the ideal setting for a political poem in which landscape evoked England's proud
heritage: from William the Conqueror, who first established a royal residence at Windsor, to
"great ANNA" (line 327), who made Windsor Castle her chief residence and frequently rode and
hunted in the forest, this was a place suffused with English history. From this enclave of natural
beauty and political tradition—the home of monarchs and the haven of Muses—Pope's mythmaking genius created a triumphant vision of peace and prosperity, the dawning of a Golden Age.

Windsor-Forest
To the Right Honorable George Lord Lansdowne[1]

Non injussa cano: te nostrae, Vare, myricae
Te nemus omne canet; nec Phoebo gratior ulla est
Quam sibi quae Vari praescripsit pagina nomen. [2]

Thy forests, Windsor! and thy green retreats,
At once the monarch's and the Muse's seats,[3]
Invite my lays.° Be present, sylvan maids![4]   *prompt my poetry*

---

1. George Granville (1667–1735), Baron Lansdowne,
was himself a poet and playwright. A Tory politician
close to Queen Anne, he became Secretary of War in
1710 and so was partly responsible both for British victory and for the peace that followed. Lord Lansdowne
greatly admired Pope's poetry and encouraged him to
publish a poem on the Peace.
2. Adapted from Virgil's sixth *Eclogue*, lines 9–12, in
which the poet dedicates his pastoral poem to his friend
Varus (like Lansdowne a prominent military figure): "I do

not sing without purpose: our tamarisks, Varus, every
grove will sing of you; nor is any page more pleasing to
Apollo than one that begins with the name of Varus."
3. Windsor Forest, seat (country home) of Britain's monarchs since Norman times (and even fabled to be the site
of the legendary King Arthur's court), in Pope's view was
also home to the Muses because the 17th-century poets
Sir John Denham and Abraham Cowley had lived nearby.
4. Dryads and naiads, spirits of the trees and water.

Unlock your springs, and open all your shades.
5   Granville commands: Your aid O Muses bring!
What Muse for Granville can refuse to sing?
     The groves of Eden, vanished now so long,
Live in description, and look green in song:[5]
These, were my breast inspired with equal flame,
10   Like them in beauty, should be like in fame.
Here hills and vales, the woodland and the plain,
Here earth and water seem to strive again,
Not chaos-like together crushed and bruised,
But as the world, harmoniously confused:
15   Where order in variety we see,
And where, though all things differ, all agree.
Here waving groves a checkered scene display,
And part admit and part exclude the day;
As some coy nymph her lover's warm address
20   Nor° quite indulges, nor can quite repress.   neither
There, interspersed in lawns° and opening glades,   clearings
Thin trees arise that shun each other's shades.
Here in full light the russet plains extend;
There wrapped in clouds the blueish hills ascend:
25   Ev'n the wild heath displays her purple dyes,[6]
And 'midst the desert° fruitful fields arise,   uncultivated land
That crowned with tufted trees[7] and springing corn,
Like verdant isles the sable waste adorn.
Let India boast her plants, nor envy we
30   The weeping amber or the balmy tree,
While by our oaks the precious loads are born,[8]
And realms commanded which those trees adorn.
Not proud Olympus[9] yields a nobler sight,
Though gods assembled grace his tow'ring height,
35   Than what more humble mountains offer here,
Where, in their blessings, all those gods appear.
See Pan with flocks, and fruits Pomona crowned,
Here blushing Flora[1] paints th' enameled ground,[2]
Here Ceres' gifts° in waving prospect stand,   grain crops
40   And nodding tempt the joyful reaper's hand,
Rich Industry sits smiling on the plains,
And Peace and Plenty tell, a STUART reigns.[3]
     Not thus the land appeared in ages past,[4]
A dreary desert and a gloomy waste,

---

5. The Garden of Eden in Genesis was made "green in song" in Milton's (relatively) recent *Paradise Lost*.
6. Heather's purple blooms cover open moorland in late summer.
7. A cluster of trees; Pope borrowed the phrase from Milton's *L'Allegro* (1632).
8. British ships made of oak allowed Britain both to conquer distant countries and to carry goods from them.
9. The mountain home of the Greek gods.
1. Three deities of natural abundance: Pan presides over shepherds and sheep; Pomona over fruits; Flora over flowers.

2. The enameling of metal to allow for over-layers of intricate painted designs was commonly used as a metaphor for nature.
3. Queen Anne (reigned 1702–1714), last of the Stuart monarchs.
4. Pope's history of the landscape begins with William the Conqueror's creation of the New Forest as a hunting ground reserved for royalty, and chronicles the disastrous impact of this appropriation on his successors and the ordinary people.

45   To savage beasts and savage laws a prey,[5]
      And kings more furious and severe than they:
      Who claimed the skies, dispeopled° air and floods,   *depopulated*
      The lonely lords of empty wilds and woods.
      Cities laid waste, they stormed the dens and caves,
50   (For wiser brutes were backward° to be slaves.)   *unwilling*
      What could be free, when lawless beasts obeyed,
      And ev'n the elements[6] a tyrant swayed?
      In vain kind seasons swelled the teeming grain,
      Soft show'rs distilled, and suns grew warm in vain;
55   The swain with tears his frustrate labor yields,
      And famished dies amidst his ripened fields.[7]
      What wonder then, a beast or subject slain
      Were equal crimes in a despotic reign;
      Both doomed alike for sportive tyrants bled,
60   But while the subject starved, the beast was fed.
      Proud Nimrod[8] first the bloody chase began,
      A mighty hunter, and his prey was man.
      Our haughty Norman boasts that barb'rous name,
      And makes his trembling slaves the royal game.
65   The fields are ravished from th' industrious swains,
      From men their cities, and from gods their fanes:[9]
      The leveled towns with weeds lie covered o'er,
      The hollow winds through naked temples roar;
      Round broken columns clasping ivy twined;
70   O'er heaps of ruin stalked the stately hind;°   *female deer*
      The fox obscene° to gaping tombs retires,   *loathsome*
      And savage howlings till the sacred quires.[1]
      Awed by his nobles, by his commons° cursed,   *commoners*
      The oppressor ruled tyrannic where he durst,
75   Stretched o'er the poor, and church, his iron rod,
      And served alike his vassals and his God.
      Whom ev'n the Saxon spared, and bloody Dane,
      The wanton victims of his sport remain.
      But see the man who spacious regions gave
80   A waste for beasts, himself denied a grave![2]
      Stretched on the lawn his second hope[3] survey,
      At once the chaser and at once the prey.
      Lo Rufus, tugging at the deadly dart,
      Bleeds in the forest, like a wounded hart.[4]

---

5. The Forest Laws had imposed harsh penalties on those caught stealing the king's game.
6. Through controlling the animals, they effectively controlled their "elements."
7. Because the produce is being cultivated for the game animals, and not for humans.
8. In Genesis 10.9, Nimrod is described as a mighty hunter, but he was also seen as a tyrant, as he founded the kingdoms of Babylon and Assyria.
9. Temples; William I destroyed many villages and churches in creating the New Forest. He was sharply criticized for demolishing God's houses to make dens for wild beasts.
1. Choir stalls; Pope deliberately uses archaic spelling.

His description of "quires," "broken columns," and "temples" also suggests grander buildings than the parish churches of this time, calling to mind the destruction of the abbeys during the Reformation.
2. Apparently, at William I's funeral, a knight had tried to stop the King from being buried in land he claimed to own. Pope suggests that this incident and the several royal deaths related to hunting in the forest (depicted in the following four lines) were divine vengeance.
3. Richard, second son of William the Conqueror [Pope's note].
4. William Rufus was accidentally killed by a friend's arrow while out hunting; a hart is a male deer.

85   Succeeding monarchs heard the subjects' cries,
    Nor saw displeased the peaceful cottage rise.
    Then gath'ring flocks on unknown° mountains fed,   *unfamiliar*
    O'er sandy wilds were yellow harvests spread,
    The forests wondered at th' unusual grain,
90   And secret transport touched the conscious swain.[5]
    Fair Liberty, Britannia's goddess, rears
    Her cheerful head, and leads the golden years.
       Ye vig'rous swains! while youth ferments your blood,[6]
    And purer spirits swell the sprightly flood,
95   Now range the hills, the gameful woods beset,
    Wind° the shrill horn, or spread the waving net.   *blow*
    When milder Autumn Summer's heat succeeds,
    And in the new-shorn field the partridge feeds,
    Before his lord the ready spaniel bounds,
100   Panting with hope, he tries the furrowed grounds,
    But when the tainted[7] gales the game betray,
    Couched close[8] he lies, and meditates the prey;
    Secure they trust th' unfaithful field, beset,
    Till hov'ring o'er 'em sweeps the swelling net.
105   Thus (if small things we may with great compare)
    When Albion° sends her eager sons to war,   *England*
    Some thoughtless town, with ease and plenty blessed,
    Near, and more near, the closing lines invest;°   *surround*
    Sudden they seize th' amazed, defenseless prize,
110   And high in air Britannia's standard flies.
       See! from the brake° the whirring pheasant springs,   *bushes*
    And mounts exulting on triumphant wings;
    Short is his joy! he feels the fiery wound,
    Flutters in blood, and panting beats the ground.
115   Ah! what avail his glossy, varying dyes,
    His purple crest, and scarlet-circled eyes,
    The vivid green his shining plumes unfold;
    His painted wings, and breast that flames with gold?
       Nor yet, when moist Arcturus[9] clouds the sky,
120   The woods and fields their pleasing toils deny.
    To plains with well-breathed beagles we repair,
    And trace the mazes of the circling hare.
    (Beasts, urged by us, their fellow beasts pursue,
    And learn of Man each other to undo.)
125   With slaught'ring guns th' unwearied fowler roves,
    When frosts have whitened all the naked groves;
    Where doves in flocks the leafless trees o'ershade,
    And lonely woodcocks haunt the watry glade.
    He lifts the tube, and levels with his eye;
130   Straight° a short thunder breaks the frozen sky.   *immediately*

---

5. Joy moves the peasant, well aware of what he has gained; this is a fairly new use of this sense of "conscious."
6. The blood is quickened by the animal spirits supposed to move in it.
7. With the animal's scent.

8. Crouching close to the ground.
9. One of the stars in the Great Bear constellation; in antiquity, its rise with the sun in September was associated with bad weather.

Oft, as in airy rings they skim the heath,
The clam'rous lapwings feel the leaden death:
Oft as the mounting larks their notes prepare,
They fall, and leave their little lives in air.
135   In genial Spring, beneath the quiv'ring shade
Where cooling vapors breathe along the mead,
The patient fisher takes his silent stand
Intent, his angle trembling in his hand;
With looks unmoved, he hopes the scaly breed,
140   And eyes the dancing cork and bending reed.
Our plenteous streams a various race supply;
The bright-eyed perch with fins of Tyrian° dye,   *purple*
The silver eel, in shining volumes° rolled,   *coils*
The yellow carp, in scales bedropped with gold,
145   Swift trouts, diversified with crimson stains,
And pikes, the tyrants of the watry plains.
Now Cancer glows with Phoebus' fiery car;[1]
The youth rush eager to the sylvan war;
Swarm o'er the lawns, the forest walks surround,
150   Rouse°the fleet hart, and cheer the opening° hound.   *flush out/baying*
Th' impatient courser° pants in ev'ry vein,   *fast horse*
And pawing, seems to beat the distant plain,
Hills, vales, and floods appear already crossed,
And ere he starts, a thousand steps are lost.
155   See! the bold youth strain up the threatening steep,
Rush through the thickets, down the valleys sweep,
Hang o'er their coursers' heads with eager speed,
And earth rolls back beneath the flying steed.
Let old Arcadia boast her ample plain,
160   Th' immortal Huntress, and her virgin train;
Nor envy, Windsor! since thy shades have seen
As bright a goddess, and as chaste a Queen;
Whose care, like hers, protects the sylvan reign,[2]
The earth's fair light, and empress of the main.[3]
165   Here too, 'tis sung, of old Diana strayed,
And Cynthus' top[4] forsook for Windsor shade;
Here was she seen o'er airy wastes to rove,
Seek the clear spring, or haunt the pathless grove;
Here armed with silver bows, in early dawn,
170   Her buskined° virgins traced the dewy lawn.   *boot-wearing*
Above the rest a rural nymph was famed,
Thy offspring, Thames! the fair Lodona named
(Lodona's fate, in long oblivion cast,
The Muse shall sing, and what she sings shall last),
175   Scarce could the goddess from her nymph be known,
But by the crescent° and the golden zone,°   *moon/belt*
She scorned the praise of beauty, and the care;

1. The sun (Phoebus's chariot) enters the constellation of
Cancer, the crab, on June 22.
2. Queen Anne is compared both to the "immortal
Huntress" Diana, goddess of chastity, and to Anne's illustrious forebear, the "virgin queen" Elizabeth I.

3. Like Diana, the moon goddess, who governed the tides,
Britannia ruled the seas.
4. The mountain on which Diana was said to have been
born.

A belt her waist, a fillet° binds her hair,   *headband*
A painted quiver on her shoulder sounds,
180 And with her dart the flying deer she wounds.
It chanced, as eager of the chase the maid
Beyond the forest's verdant limits strayed,
Pan saw and loved, and burning with desire
Pursued her flight; her flight increased his fire.
185 Not half so swift the trembling doves can fly,
When the fierce eagle cleaves the liquid° sky;   *transparent*
Not half so swiftly the fierce eagle moves,
When through the clouds he drives the trembling doves;
As from the god she flew with furious pace,
190 Or as the god, more furious, urged the chase.
Now fainting, sinking, pale, the nymph appears;
Now close behind his sounding steps she hears;
And now his shadow reached her as she run,
(His shadow lengthened by the setting sun)
195 And now his shorter breath with sultry air
Pants on her neck, and fans her parting hair.
In vain on Father Thames she calls for aid,
Nor could Diana help her injured maid.
Faint, breathless, thus she prayed, nor prayed in vain:
200 "Ah Cynthia! ah—though banished from thy train,
Let me, O let me, to the shades repair,
My native shades—there weep, and murmur there."
She said, and melting as in tears she lay,
In a soft, silver stream dissolved away.
205 The silver stream her virgin coldness keeps,
Forever murmurs, and forever weeps;
Still bears the name the hapless virgin bore,[5]
And bathes the forest where she ranged before.
In her chaste current oft the goddess laves,°   *bathes*
210 And with celestial tears augments the waves.
Oft in her glass the musing shepherd spies
The headlong mountains and the downward skies,
The watry landscape of the pendant[6] woods,
And absent° trees that tremble in the floods;   *illusory*
215 In the clear azure gleam the flocks are seen,
And floating forests paint the waves with green.
Through the fair scene roll slow the lingering streams,
Then foaming pour along, and rush into the Thames.
      Thou too, great father° of the British floods!   *the Thames*
220 With joyful pride survey'st our lofty woods,
Where tow'ring oaks their growing honors rear,
And future navies on thy shores appear.
Not Neptune's self from all his streams receives
A wealthier tribute, than to thine he gives.
225 No seas so rich, so gay no banks appear,
No lake so gentle, and no spring so clear.

---

5. I.e., Loddon, a river that runs through Windsor Forest
and into the Thames.

6. Hanging; the woods both hang over the stream and, in
the stream's reflection, appear to stand upside down.

Nor Po so swells the fabling poets' lays,[7]
While led along the skies his current strays,
As thine, which visits Windsor's famed abodes,
230   To grace the mansion of our earthly gods.
Nor all his stars above a luster show,
Like the bright beauties on thy banks below;
Where Jove, subdued by mortal passion still,
Might change Olympus for a nobler hill.
235   Happy the man whom this bright court approves,
His sov'reign favors, and his country loves;
Happy next him who to these shades retires,
Whom Nature charms, and whom the Muse inspires,
Whom humbler joys of home-felt quiet please,
240   Successive study, exercise and ease.
He gathers health from herbs the forest yields,
And of their fragrant physic° spoils° the fields: medicines / despoils
With chemic art[8] exalts° the min'ral pow'rs,   distills
And draws° the aromatic souls of flow'rs.   extracts
245   Now marks the course of rolling orbs on high;
O'er figured worlds[9] now travels with his eye.
Of ancient writ unlocks the learned store,
Consults the dead, and lives past ages o'er.
Or wand'ring thoughtful in the silent wood,
250   Attends the duties of the wise and good,
T' observe a mean,[1] be to himself a friend,
To follow Nature, and regard his end.
Or looks on Heav'n with more than mortal eyes,
Bids his free soul expatiate in the skies,
255   Amid her kindred stars familiar roam,
Survey the region, and confess her home!
Such was the life great Scipio[2] once admired,
Thus Atticus,[3] and Trumbull[4] thus retired.
        Ye sacred Nine![5] that all my soul possess,
260   Whose Raptures fire me, and whose visions bless,
Bear me, oh bear me to sequestered scenes,
The bow'ry mazes and surrounding greens;
To Thames's banks which fragrant breezes fill,
Or where ye Muses sport on Cooper's Hill.
265   (On Cooper's Hill eternal wreaths shall grow,[6]
While lasts the mountain, or while Thames shall flow)
I seem through consecrated walks to rove,

7. Both Virgil and Ovid compared the Po, a river in Italy,
to the winding constellation Eridanus, named for a river
in Greek mythology.
8. The skills of the chemist.
9. The earth or possibly the zodiac portrayed on a globe.
1. To maintain a steady, balanced course through life;
according to Aristotle, wisdom lay in following the "gold-
en mean," or middle way.
2. Scipio Africanus, the Roman general who defeated
Hannibal and the Carthaginians in 202 B.C. but declined
political office, choosing eventually to retire to the country.

3. Titus Pomponius (109–32 B.C.), despite his friendship
and correspondence with Cicero, refused to become
involved in politics; he was called Atticus because he
spent much time studying in Athens, which lies in the
region of Attica.
4. Sir William Trumbull (1639–1716), Pope's elderly
friend.
5. The Nine Muses, daughters of Mnemosyne (goddess of
memory) and Zeus, each of whom presided over a different art or science.
6. Because commemorated in Sir John Denham's poem
Cooper's Hill (1642).

I hear soft music die along the grove;
Led by the sound I roam from shade to shade,
270 By god-like poets venerable made:
Here his first lays majestic Denham sung;[7]
There the last numbers flowed from Cowley's tongue.[8]
O early lost![9] what tears the river shed
When the sad pomp along his banks was led?
275 His drooping swans on ev'ry note expire,
And on his willows[1] hung each Muse's lyre.
 Since Fate relentless stopped their heav'nly voice,
No more the forests ring, or groves rejoice;
Who now shall charm the shades where Cowley strung
280 His living harp, and lofty Denham sung?
But hark! the groves rejoice, the forest rings!
Are these revived? Or is it Granville sings?
 'Tis yours, my Lord, to bless our soft retreats,
And call the Muses to their ancient seats,
285 To paint anew the flow'ry sylvan scenes,
To crown the forests with immortal greens,
Make Windsor hills in lofty numbers rise,
And lift her turrets nearer to the skies;
To sing those honors you deserve to wear,
290 And add new luster to her silver star.[2]
 Here noble Surrey[3] felt the sacred rage,
Surrey, the Granville of a former age:
Matchless his pen, victorious was his lance;
Bold in the lists, and graceful in the dance:
295 In the same shades the Cupids tuned his lyre,
To the same notes of love, and soft desire:
Fair Geraldine,[4] bright object of his vow,
Then filled the groves, as heav'nly Myra[5] now.
 Oh wouldst thou sing what heroes Windsor bore,
300 What kings first breathed upon her winding shore,[6]
Or raise old warriors whose adored remains
In weeping vaults[7] her hallowed earth contains!
With Edward's[8] acts adorn the shining page,
Stretch his long triumphs down through ev'ry age,
305 Draw monarchs chained, and Cressi's glorious field,[9]
The lilies[1] blazing on the regal shield.

7. Denham, described as "majestic" because of the (then unusual) style of the couplets in *Cooper's Hill*, lived near Windsor before the Civil War.
8. Mr. [Abraham] Cowley died at Chertsey, on the borders of the Forest, and was from thence conveyed to Westminster [Pope's note], where he was buried in state.
9. Cowley died at age 49.
1. Emblems of sorrow.
2. The star worn by members inducted into the highly prestigious Order of the Garter, founded by Edward III in Windsor Castle's Chapel of St. George.
3. Henry Howard, Earl of Surrey, one of the first refiners of the English poetry; famous in the time of Henry VIIIth for his sonnets, the scene of many of which is laid at Windsor [Pope's note].

4. Lady Elizabeth Fitzgerald (1528?–1589) to whom Surrey was thought to have directed his love poems.
5. The poetic name Granville used for his female addressee.
6. Suggesting the etymological meaning of "Windsor."
7. Because of the seepage of water through the walls; similar natural phenomena explain the conceits in lines 307 and 313.
8. Edward III. born here [Pope's note].
9. The village in northern France where Edward III defeated the French; English triumph over the French (and other nations) was the theme of many of these paintings.
1. Emblem of France, but added to the English crest of arms.

Then, from her roofs when Verrio's colors fall,
And leave inanimate the naked wall;[2]
Still in thy song should vanquished France appear,
310   And bleed forever under Britain's spear.
        Let softer strains ill-fated Henry[3] mourn,
And palms eternal flourish round his urn.
Here o'er the martyr-king the marble weeps,
And fast beside him, once-feared Edward[4] sleeps;
315   Whom not th' extended Albion could contain,
From old Belerium[5] to the northern main,
The grave unites; where ev'n the great find rest,
And blended lie th' oppressor and th' oppressed!
        Make sacred Charles's tomb forever known,[6]
320   (Obscure the place, and uninscribed the stone)
Oh fact° accursed! What tears has Albion shed,   deed
Heav'ns! what new wounds, and how her old have bled?
She saw her sons with purple deaths[7] expire,
Her sacred domes° involved in rolling fire,   stately buildings
325   A dreadful series of intestine wars,[8]
Inglorious triumphs, and dishonest° scars.   shameful
At length great ANNA° said—"Let discord cease!"   Queen Anne
She said, the world obeyed, and all was peace!
        In that blessed moment, from his oozy bed
330   Old Father Thames advanced his rev'rend head.
His tresses dropped with dews, and o'er the stream
His shining horns[9] diffused a golden gleam:
Graved on his urn appeared the moon, that guides
His swelling waters, and alternate tides;
335   The figured streams in waves of silver rolled,
And on their banks Augusta° rose in gold.[1]   London
Around his throne the sea-born brothers[2] stood,
Who swell with tributary urns his flood.
First the famed authors of his ancient name,
340   The winding Isis and the fruitful Thame:[3]
The Kennet swift, for silver eels renowned;
The Loddon slow, with verdant alders crowned:
Cole, whose dark streams his flow'ry islands lave;

2. In ceiling paintings at Windsor Castle, the artist Antonio Verrio (1639–1707) had depicted the surrender of
France in 1356 to Edward the Black Prince, son of
Edward III; the paintings were now starting to disinte-
grate.
3. Henry VI, murdered in 1471, was looked upon by some
in northern Britain (where he lived for some time as a
fugitive) as a saint; the "palms" in line 32 are emblems of
martyrdom.
4. Edward IV, responsible for Henry VI's murder, was
buried in St. George's Chapel, Windsor, where Henry
was later re-interred.
5. Land's End in Cornwall, the south-westernmost point
in England.
6. Charles I, executed by the Puritans in 1649 and consequently considered by many a Christian and political
martyr, was buried in St. George's Chapel without any
service; his tomb remained unidentified until 1813.

7. Death from the Great Plague in 1665; this event, like
the Great Fire of London (1666) and the 1688 Revolution alluded to in the following lines, was viewed by
many as a result of God's wrath, possibly (as Pope here
implies) visited on the nation as a result of Charles I's
murder.
8. The civil wars during the reigns of Charles I, Cromwell
(in Ireland), James II, and William III (in Ireland).
9. River gods often had bulls' horns, representing their
strength, noisiness, and importance for agriculture.
1. A reference to Dryden's description of London's
rebuilding after the Great Fire (in brick and white Port-
land stone) in Annus Mirabilis (1667), to which work the
rest of this poem is indebted.
2. According to myth, all rivers were children of the sea
gods Oceanus and Thethys.
3. The Thames was seen as the son of the Thame and the
Isis rivers.

And chalky Wey, that rolls a milky wave:
345 The blue, transparent Vandalis° appears;   *the Wandle*
The gulphy Lee his sedgy tresses rears:
And sullen Mole, that hides his diving flood;
And silent Darent, stained with Danish blood.[4]
          High in the midst, upon his urn reclined,
350 (His sea-green mantle waving with the wind)
The god appeared; he turned his azure eyes
Where Windsor domes and pompous turrets rise,
Then bowed and spoke; the winds forget to roar,
And the hushed waves glide softly to the shore.
355   Hail sacred peace![5] hail long-expected days,
That Thames's glory to the stars shall raise!
Though Tiber's streams immortal Rome behold,
Though foaming Hermus[6] swells with tides of gold,
From Heav'n itself though sev'nfold Nilus[7] flows,
360 And harvests on a hundred realms bestows;
These now no more shall be the Muse's themes,
Lost in my fame, as in the sea their streams.
Let Volga's banks[8] with iron squadrons° shine,   *cavalry*
And groves of lances glitter on the Rhine,
365 Let barb'rous Ganges[9] arm a servile train;
Be mine the blessings of a peaceful reign.
No more my sons shall dye with British blood
Red Iber's[1] sands, or Ister's[2] foaming flood;
Safe on my shore each unmolested swain
370 Shall tend the flocks, or reap the bearded grain;
The shady empire shall retain no trace
Of war or blood, but in the sylvan chase,
The trumpets sleep, while cheerful horns are blown,
And arms employed on birds and beasts alone.
375 Behold! th' ascending villas[3] on my side
Project long shadows o'er the crystal tide.
Behold! Augusta's glitt'ring spires increase,
And temples rise,[4] the beauteous works of peace.
I see, I see where two fair cities[5] bend
380 Their ample bow,° a new Whitehall[6] ascend!   *riverbend*
There mighty nations shall inquire their doom,[7]
The world's great oracle in times to come;

4. The Danes were defeated at Otford, on the Darent, in 1016.
5. The war of the Spanish Succession had begun in 1701; peace treaties were signed at London in 1711, and at Utrecht in 1713.
6. An Italian river distinguished by Virgil.
7. Because of its delta, Ovid called the Nile *septemfluus*.
8. An allusion to the defeat of Charles XII of Sweden by the Russians in 1709 (though the battle did not take place near the Volga).
9. Alluding to the Mogul Emperor Aurangzeb's recent wars in India.
1. The Ebro in Spain, where the Allies had gained victory in 1710.
2. The Danube, where Marlborough achieved his famous

victory at Blenheim in 1704.
3. Many new private country homes were being built along the Thames up from London at this time.
4. The fifty new churches [Pope's note], built on the queen's orders to meet the requirements of a growing London.
5. London and Westminster, separated by the Thames, were still distinct cities at this time.
6. There were plans afoot to rebuild the palace of Whitehall, which had largely burnt down in the fires of 1691 and 1697.
7. Fate or destiny. In lines 381–422 Pope makes extensive use of Isaiah chapter 60, which forecasts Zion's future glory.

There kings shall sue, and suppliant states be seen
Once more to bend before a British QUEEN.
385   Thy trees, fair Windsor! now shall leave their woods,
And half thy forests rush into my floods,
Bear Britain's thunder, and her cross[8] display,
To the bright regions of the rising day;
Tempt° icy seas, where scarce the waters roll,   *attempt*
390 Where clearer flames glow round the frozen pole;
Or under southern skies exalt° their sails,   *raise*
Led by new stars, and born by spicy gales!
For me the balm[9] shall bleed, and amber flow,
The coral redden, and the ruby glow,
395 The pearly shell its lucid globe infold,
And Phoebus warm the ripening ore to gold.[1]
The time shall come, when free as seas or wind
Unbounded Thames[2] shall flow for all mankind,
Whole nations enter with each swelling tide,
400 And seas but join the regions they divide;
Earth's distant ends our glory shall behold,
And the new world launch forth to seek the old.
Then ships of uncouth form shall stem the tide,
And feathered people crowd my wealthy side,[3]
405 And naked youths and painted chiefs admire
Our speech, our color, and our strange attire!
Oh stretch thy reign, fair Peace! from shore to shore,
Till conquest cease, and slav'ry be no more:
Till the freed[4] Indians in their native groves
410 Reap their own fruits and woo their sable loves,
Peru once more a race of kings behold,
And other Mexicos be roofed with gold.
Exiled by thee from earth to deepest hell,
In brazen bonds shall barb'rous Discord dwell:
415 Gigantic Pride, pale Terror, gloomy Care,
And mad Ambition, shall attend her there.
There purple Vengeance bathed in gore retires,
Her weapons blunted, and extinct her fires:
There hateful Envy her own snakes shall feel,
420 And Persecution mourn her broken wheel:[5]
There Faction roar, Rebellion bite her chain,
And gasping Furies thirst for blood in vain.
    Here cease thy flight, nor with unhallowed lays
Touch the fair fame of Albion's golden days.

---

8. St. George's cross which, with the cross of St. Andrew, made the new Union flag of Great Britain; Pope may also allude to recent British missionary work overseas.
9. Tree sap, often having soothing or healing properties.
1. Phoebus Apollo, god of the sun and patron of poets, was commonly believed to ripen metal into gold with his rays.
2. A wish that London may be made a FREE PORT [Pope's

note]; many merchants proposed that customs duties be abolished to make Britain more open to international trade.
3. Four Iroquois Indian chiefs visited England in 1710, causing a sensation.
4. From Spanish oppression.
5. An instrument of torture.

425   The thoughts of gods let Granville's verse recite,
       And bring the scenes of opening fate to light.
       My humble Muse, in unambitious strains,
       Paints the green forests and the flow'ry plains,
       Where Peace descending bids her olives spring,
430   And scatters blessings from her dove-like wing.
       Ev'n I more sweetly pass my careless days,
       Pleased in the silent shade with empty praise;
       Enough for me, that to the list'ning swains
       First in these fields I sung the sylvan strains.

1704–13   1713

The Rape of the Lock

"New things are made familiar, and familiar things are made new," wrote Samuel Johnson about the most accomplished poem of Pope's younger years. "The whole detail of a female day is brought before us invested with so much art of decoration that, though nothing is disguised, everything is striking."

Only a poet with formidable imaginative powers could have made a great mock-heroic poem out of such unpromising materials. When Robert, Lord Petre, cut a love-lock from the head of Arabella Fermor without her permission, the two young people, both in their early twenties, quarreled bitterly. Their families, leading members of the Roman Catholic gentry once on the friendliest terms, became seriously estranged. Pope's friend John Caryll, who saw himself as a mediator among the group, asked him "to write a poem to make a jest of it, and laugh them together."

Pope's first effort was a poem in two cantos, *The Rape of the Locke*, printed in 1712 with some of his other pieces and the work of other poets. Two years later, Pope separately published *The Rape of the Lock*, enlarged to five cantos by the addition of the "machinery" of the sylphs and gnomes, and by the game of Ombre. The poem reached its final form in 1717 when Pope added the moralizing declamation of Clarissa (5.7–35), a parody of the speech of Sarpedon to Glaucus in the *Iliad*. The mock-epic tenor of the five-canto poem was clearly influenced by Pope's translation of the *Iliad*, his main project while most of *The Rape of the Lock* was being composed. Other influences were Homer's *Odyssey*, Virgil's *Aeneid*, Milton's *Paradise Lost*, and Boileau's *Le Lutrin* (1674, 1683), a mock-heroic satire on clerical infighting over the placement of a lectern. Yoking together the mundanely trivial and the mythically heroic as he follows the course of Belinda's day, Pope produced a vivid, yet affectionate, mockery of the fashions and sexual mores common in his own social circle.

The arming of the champion for war became the application of Belinda's (i.e., Arabella's) make-up for the battle of the sexes; the larger-than-life gods of classical mythology became miniature cartoon-like sylphs; Aeneas' voyage up the Tiber became Belinda's progress up the Thames; the depiction of Achilles' shield became the description of Belinda's petticoat; the test of single combat became the game of cards; the hero's journey to the underworld became the gnome's adventure in the Cave of Spleen; and the rape of Helen that started the Trojan War became the "rape" (stealing) of Belinda's hair that began an unpleasant social squabble. All the trappings of classical epic are here: the divine messenger appearing to the hero in a dream, the sacrifice to the gods, the inspirational speech to the troops before battle, the epic feast, the violent melee, and the final triumphant apotheosis. Throughout the poem, the enormous distance between the trivial *matter* and the heroic *manner* produces brilliantly comic results.

The Rape of the Lock

An Heroi-Comical Poem in Five Cantos

Nolueram, Belinda, tuos violare capillos,
Sed juvat hoc precibus me tribuisse tuis.

Martial[1]

To Mrs. Arabella Fermor
    Madam,
    It will be in vain to deny that I have some regard for this piece, since I dedicate it to you. Yet you may bear me witness, it was intended only to divert a few young ladies, who have good sense and good humor enough, to laugh not only at their sex's little unguarded follies, but at their own.[2] But as it was communicated with the air of a secret, it soon found its way into the world. An imperfect copy having been offered to a bookseller, you had the good nature for my sake to consent to the publication of one more correct; this I was forced to before I had executed half my design, for the *machinery* was entirely wanting to complete it.

    The *machinery*, Madam, is a term invented by the critics, to signify that part which the deities, angels, or demons, are made to act in a poem; for the ancient poets are in one respect like many modern ladies: let an action be never so trivial in itself, they always make it appear of the utmost importance. These machines I determined to raise on a very new and odd foundation, the Rosicrucian[3] doctrine of spirits.

    I know how disagreeable it is to make use of hard words before a lady; but 'tis so much the concern of a poet to have his works understood, and particularly by your sex, that you must give me leave to explain two or three difficult terms.

    The Rosicrucians are a people I must bring you acquainted with. The best account I know of them is in a French book called *Le Comte de Gabalis*,[4] which both in its title and size is so like a novel, that many of the fair sex have read it for one by mistake. According to these gentlemen, the four elements are inhabited by spirits, which they call Sylphs, Gnomes, Nymphs, and Salamanders.[5] The Gnomes, or Demons of Earth, delight in mischief; but the Sylphs, whose habitation is in the air, are the best-conditioned[6] creatures imaginable. For they say, any mortals may enjoy the most intimate familiarities with these gentle spirits, upon a condition very easy to all true adepts, an inviolate preservation of chastity.

    As to the following cantos, all the passages of them are as fabulous,[7] as the vision at the beginning, or the transformation at the end (except the loss of your hair, which I always mention with reverence). The human persons are as fictitious as the airy ones; and the character of Belinda, as it is now managed, resembles you in nothing but in beauty.

    If this poem had as many graces as there are in your person, or in your mind, yet I could never hope it should pass through the world half so uncensured as you have done. But let its fortune be what it will, mine is happy enough, to have given me this occasion of assuring you that I am, with the truest esteem,

Madam,
Your most obedient
humble servant.
A. Pope

1. "I did not wish, [Belinda,] to violate your locks, but I rejoice to have yielded this to your wishes" (Martial, *Epigrams* 12.84). Pope has substituted "Belinda" for Martial's "Polytimus."
2. I.e., at their own individual follies as well.
3. A secret society of the 17th and 18th centuries, devoted to the study of ancient religious, philosophical, and mystical doctrines.

4. Written in 1670 by the Abbé de Monfaucon de Villars, its approach to Rosicrucian philosophy was lighthearted. It was printed in duodecimo, a small "pocketbook" size common to many inexpensive novels.
5. Elemental spirits living in fire.
6. Best natured, having the best character.
7. Fictional.

CANTO 1

What dire offense from am'rous causes springs,
What mighty contests rise from trivial things,
I sing[8]—This verse to Caryll, Muse! is due;
This, ev'n Belinda may vouchsafe to view:
5 Slight is the subject, but not so the praise,
If she inspire, and he approve my lays.°   *verses*
   Say what strange motive, Goddess!° could compel   *his Muse*
A well-bred lord t' assault a gentle belle?
Oh say what stranger cause, yet unexplored,
10 Could make a gentle belle reject a lord?
In tasks so bold, can little men engage,
And in soft bosoms dwells such mighty rage?
   Sol through white curtains shot a tim'rous ray,
And op'd those eyes that must eclipse the day;
15 Now lapdogs[9] give themselves the rousing shake,
And sleepless lovers, just at twelve, awake:
Thrice rung the bell, the slipper knocked the ground,[1]
And the pressed watch returned a silver sound.[2]
Belinda still her downy pillow pressed,
20 Her guardian Sylph prolonged the balmy rest.
'Twas he had summoned to her silent bed
The morning dream that hovered o'er her head.
A youth more glitt'ring than a birthnight beau,[3]
(That ev'n in slumber caused her cheek to glow)
25 Seemed to her ear his winning lips to lay,
And thus in whispers said, or seemed to say:[4]
   "Fairest of mortals, thou distinguished care
Of thousand bright inhabitants of air!
If e'er one vision touched thy infant thought,
30 Of all the nurse and all the priest have taught,[5]
Of airy elves by moonlight shadows seen,
The silver token, and the circled green,[6]
Or virgins visited by angel pow'rs,[7]
With golden crowns and wreaths of heav'nly flow'rs,
35 Hear and believe! thy own importance know,
Nor bound thy narrow views to things below.
Some secret truths from learned pride concealed,
To maids alone and children are revealed:
What though no credit doubting wits may give?[8]
40 The fair and innocent shall still believe.
Know then, unnumbered spirits round thee fly,

8. Pope begins with the ancient epic formula of "proposition" of the work as a whole, and "invocation" of the gods' assistance, continuing with the traditional epic questions.
9. Small dogs imported from Asia were highly fashionable ladies' pets at this time.
1. Belinda rings the bell and then finally bangs her slipper on the floor to call her maid.
2. The popular "pressed watch" chimed the hour and quarter hours when its stem was pressed, saving its owner from striking a match to see the time.

3. On a royal birthday, courtiers' clothes were particularly extravagant.
4. His whispering recalls the serpent's temptation of Eve in Milton.
5. The nurse and priest were seen as two standard sources of superstition.
6. Withered circles in the grass and silver coins were supposed to be signs of fairies' presence.
7. Belinda is reminded of the many virgin saints, and particularly the Annunciation to the Virgin Mary.
8. Religious skepticism was on the increase.

The light militia of the lower sky;
These, though unseen, are ever on the wing,
Hang o'er the box, and hover round the ring.[9]
45   Think what an equipage[1] thou hast in air,
And view with scorn two pages and a chair.[2]
As now your own, our beings were of old,
And once enclosed in woman's beauteous mold;
Thence, by a soft transition, we repair
50   From earthly vehicles[3] to these of air.
Think not, when woman's transient breath is fled,
That all her vanities at once are dead:
Succeeding vanities she still regards,
And though she plays no more, o'erlooks the cards.
55   Her joy in gilded chariots, when alive,
And love of Ombre,[4] after death survive.
For when the fair in all their pride expire,
To their first elements[5] their souls retire:
The sprites of fiery termagants° in flame   *scolding women*
60   Mount up, and take a salamander's name.
Soft yielding minds to water glide away,
And sip with Nymphs, their elemental tea.
The graver prude sinks downward to a Gnome,
In search of mischief still on earth to roam.
65   The light coquettes in Sylphs aloft repair,
And sport and flutter in the fields of air.
      "Know farther yet; whoever fair and chaste
Rejects mankind, is by some Sylph embraced:
For spirits, freed from mortal laws, with ease
70   Assume what sexes and what shapes they please.[6]
What guards the purity of melting maids,[7]
In courtly balls, and midnight masquerades,
Safe from the treach'rous friend, the daring spark,[8]
The glance by day, the whisper in the dark;
75   When kind occasion prompts their warm desires,
When music softens, and when dancing fires?
'Tis but their Sylph, the wise celestials know,
Though *Honor* is the word with men below.
      "Some nymphs there are, too conscious of their face,
80   For life predestined to the Gnomes' embrace.
These swell their prospects and exalt their pride,
When offers are disdained, and love denied.

9. The theater box and the equally fashionable drive round Hyde Park.
1. Carriage, horses, and attendants.
2. A sedan chair, carried by two chairmen.
3. Both the carriage, and the physical body.
4. Ombre (pronounced Omber) was an elaborate card game, introduced into England in the 17th century and highly fashionable in the early 18th century. Given the general tenor of the poem, Pope may also be punning on the origin of the word "Ombre," from the Spanish *hom-*

bre, meaning "man."
5. The four elements of fire, water, earth, and air were thought to make up all things; so an individual's character was determined by whichever element dominated his or her soul.
6. Cf. *Paradise Lost*, "For spirits when they please / Can either sex assume, or both" (1.423–424).
7. I.e., the chastity of weakening virgins.
8. A bold, brash, and showy young man.

Then gay ideas crowd the vacant brain;
While peers° and dukes, and all their sweeping train,   *aristocrats*
85   And garters, stars, and coronets⁹ appear,
And in soft sounds, "your Grace"¹ salutes their ear.
'Tis these that early taint the female soul,
Instruct the eyes of young coquettes to roll,
Teach infant cheeks a bidden° blush to know,   *deliberate*
90   And little hearts to flutter at a beau.
     "Oft when the world imagine women stray,
The Sylphs through mystic mazes guide their way,
Through all the giddy circle they pursue,
And old impertinence° expel by new.   *frivolity*
95   What tender maid but must a victim fall
To one man's treat, but for another's ball?
When Florio speaks, what virgin could withstand,
If gentle Damon did not squeeze her hand?
With varying vanities, from ev'ry part,
100 They shift the moving toy shop² of their heart;
Where wigs with wigs, with sword knots sword knots strive,³
Beaus banish beaus, and coaches coaches drive.⁴
This erring mortals levity may call,
Oh blind to truth! the Sylphs contrive it all.
105   "Of these am I, who thy protection claim,
A watchful sprite, and Ariel is my name.
Late, as I ranged the crystal wilds of air,
In the clear mirror of thy ruling star
I saw, alas! some dread event impend,
110 Ere to the main° this morning sun descend.   *sea*
But Heav'n reveals not what, or how, or where:
Warned by thy Sylph, oh pious maid beware!
This to disclose is all thy guardian can.
Beware of all, but most beware of man!"
115   He said; when Shock,⁵ who thought she slept too long,
Leapt up, and waked his mistress with his tongue.
'Twas then Belinda! if report say true,
Thy eyes first opened on a *billet-doux*;°   *love letter*
Wounds, charms, and ardors, were no sooner read,
120 But all the vision vanished from thy head.
     And now, unveiled, the toilet° stands displayed,   *dressing table*
Each silver vase in mystic order laid.
First, robed in white, the nymph intent adores
With head uncovered, the cosmetic pow'rs.
125 A heav'nly image⁶ in the glass appears,
To that she bends, to that her eyes she rears;°   *raises*

---

9. Emblems of noble rank.
1. Form of address for a duke or a duchess.
2. Where toys and trinkets are sold; "moving" here means easily changed, unstable.
3. Most men wore wigs in public; formally dressed men tied ribbons to the hilt of their swords.

4. In word order and versification, these two lines mimic both Homer's and Ovid's description of heroic combat.
5. The shock or shough, a long-haired Icelandic poodle, fashionable as a lapdog.
6. I.e., Belinda herself.

Th' inferior priestess,[7] at her altar's side,
Trembling, begins the sacred rites of pride.
Unnumbered treasures ope at once, and here
130   The various off'rings of the world appear;
From each she nicely culls with curious° toil,   careful
And decks the goddess with the glitt'ring spoil.
This casket India's glowing gems unlocks,
And all Arabia° breathes from yonder box.   eastern perfume
135   The tortoise here and elephant unite,
Transformed to combs, the speckled and the white.[8]
Here files of pins extend their shining rows,
Puffs, powders, patches, Bibles,[9] *billet-doux.*
Now awful° beauty puts on all its arms;   awe-inspiring
140   The fair each moment rises in her charms,
Repairs her smiles, awakens ev'ry grace,
And calls forth all the wonders of her face;
Sees by degrees a purer blush[1] arise,
And keener lightnings[2] quicken in her eyes.
145   The busy Sylphs surround their darling care;
These set the head, and those divide the hair,
Some fold the sleeve, whilst others plait the gown;
And Betty's praised for labors not her own.

Canto 2

Not with more glories, in th' ethereal plain,°   sky
The sun first rises o'er the purpled main,
Than issuing forth, the rival of his beams
Launched on the bosom of the silver Thames.[1]
5   Fair nymphs, and well-dressed youths around her shone,
But ev'ry eye was fixed on her alone.
On her white breast a sparkling cross she wore,
Which Jews might kiss, and infidels adore.[2]
Her lively looks a sprightly mind disclose,
10   Quick as her eyes, and as unfixed as those:
Favors to none, to all she smiles extends,
Oft she rejects, but never once offends.
Bright as the sun, her eyes the gazers strike,
And, like the sun, they shine on all alike.
15   Yet graceful ease, and sweetness void of pride,
Might hide her faults, if belles had faults to hide:
If to her share some female errors fall,
Look on her face, and you'll forget 'em all.
This nymph, to the destruction of mankind,
20   Nourished two locks which graceful hung behind

---

7. Belinda's maid, Betty.
8. Tortoise-shell and ivory.
9. Patches were small beauty spots of black silk, pasted
onto the face to make the skin appear whiter. It was fashionable to own Bibles in very small format.
1. The even, artificial blush of rouge.
2. Caused by drops of belladonna (deadly nightshade),

which dilates the pupils.
1. Belinda takes a boat from London to Hampton Court,
avoiding the dirt and squalor of the streets; her voyage
compares with Aeneas's up the Tiber (*Aeneid* 7), or,
alternatively, Cleopatra's up the Nile (*Antony and
Cleopatra* 2.2).
2. Kissing the cross was the sign of religious conversion.

In equal curls, and well conspired to deck
With shining ringlets the smooth iv'ry neck.
Love in these labyrinths his slaves detains,
And mighty hearts are held in slender chains.

25 With hairy springes° we the birds betray,   *noose traps*
    Slight lines° of hair surprise the finny prey,   *fishing lines*
    Fair tresses man's imperial race ensnare,
    And beauty draws us with a single hair.
         Th' adventurous Baron[3] the bright locks admired,
30 He saw, he wished, and to the prize aspired:
    Resolved to win, he meditates the way,
    By force to ravish, or by fraud betray;
    For when success a lover's toil attends,
    Few ask, if fraud or force attained his ends.
35   For this, ere Phoebus rose, he had implored
    Propitious Heav'n, and ev'ry pow'r adored,°   *worshipped*
    But chiefly *Love*—to *Love* an altar built,
    Of twelve vast French romances, neatly gilt.
    There lay three garters, half a pair of gloves;
40 And all the trophies of his former loves.
    With tender *billet-doux* he lights the pyre,
    And breathes three am'rous sighs to raise the fire.
    Then prostrate falls, and begs with ardent eyes
    Soon to obtain, and long possess the prize:
45 The pow'rs gave ear, and granted half his pray'r,
    The rest the winds dispersed in empty air.[4]
         But now secure the painted vessel glides,
    The sunbeams trembling on the floating tides,
    While melting music steals upon the sky,
50 And softened sounds along the waters die.
    Smooth flow the waves, the zephyrs° gently play,   *breezes*
    Belinda smiled, and all the world was gay.
    All but the Sylph—with careful° thoughts oppressed,   *worried*
    Th' impending woe sat heavy on his breast.
55 He summons strait his denizens[5] of air;
    The lucid squadrons round the sails repair:
    Soft o'er the shrouds° aerial whispers breathe,   *ropes*
    That seemed but zephyrs to the train beneath.
    Some to the sun their insect wings unfold,
60 Waft on the breeze, or sink in clouds of gold.
    Transparent forms, too fine for mortal sight,
    Their fluid bodies half dissolved in light,
    Loose to the wind their airy garments flew,
    Thin glitt'ring textures of the filmy dew;
65 Dipped in the richest tincture of the skies,
    Where light disports in ever-mingling dyes,
    While ev'ry beam new transient colors flings,

---

3. Robert, Lord Petre (1690–1713), responsible for the
original incident.
4. Cf. *The Aeneid* 2.794–795, which Dryden translated:

"Apollo heard, and granting half his pray'r, / Shuffled in
winds the rest, and toss'd in empty air."
5. Naturalized foreigner.

Colors that change whene'er they wave their wings.
Amid the circle, on the gilded mast,
70 Superior by the head, was Ariel placed;[6]
His purple pinions opening to the sun,
He raised his azure wand, and thus begun:
    "Ye Sylphs and Sylphids,° to your chief give ear,   *female Sylphs*
Fays, Fairies, Genii, Elves, and Demons hear!
75 Ye know the spheres and various tasks assigned,
By laws eternal to th' aerial kind.
Some in the fields of purest ether[7] play,
And bask and whiten in the blaze of day.
Some guide the course of wandering orbs° on high,   *comets*
80 Or roll the planets through the boundless sky.
Some less refined, beneath the moon's pale light
Pursue the stars that shoot athwart the night,
Or suck the mists in grosser° air below,   *heavier*
Or dip their pinions in the painted bow,°   *rainbow*
85 Or brew fierce tempests on the wintry main,
Or o'er the glebe° distill the kindly rain.   *farmland*
Others on earth o'er human race preside,
Watch all their ways, and all their actions guide:
Of these the chief the care of nations own,
90 And guard with arms divine the British throne.
    "Our humbler province is to tend the fair,
Not a less pleasing, though less glorious care.
To save the powder from too rude° a gale,   *rough*
Nor let th' imprisoned essences° exhale,   *perfumes*
95 To draw fresh colors from the vernal flow'rs,
To steal from rainbows ere they drop in show'rs
A brighter wash;[8] to curl their waving hairs,
Assist their blushes, and inspire their airs;
Nay oft, in dreams, invention we bestow,
100 To change a flounce, or add a furbelow.°   *fringe*
    "This day, black omens threat the brightest fair
That e'er deserved a watchful spirit's care;
Some dire disaster, or° by force or sleight,°   *either/trick*
But what, or where, the fates have wrapped in night.
105 Whether the nymph shall break Diana's law,°   *virginity*
Or some frail China jar receive a flaw,
Or stain her honor, or her new brocade,
Forget her pray'rs, or miss a masquerade,
Or lose her heart, or necklace, at a ball;
110 Or whether Heav'n has doomed that Shock must fall.
Haste then ye spirits! to your charge° repair;   *duty*
The flutt'ring fan be Zephyretta's care;
The drops° to thee, Brillante, we consign;   *earrings*
And, Momentilla, let the watch be thine;
115 Do thou, Crispissa,[9] tend her fav'rite lock;

---

6. Heroes of epics were typically taller than their men.
7. Air beyond the moon.
8. A cosmetic rinse.
9. The Latin *crispere* means "to curl."

Ariel himself shall be the guard of Shock.
"To fifty chosen Sylphs, of special note,
We trust th' important charge, the petticoat:
Oft have we known that sev'nfold fence[1] to fail,
120   Though stiff with hoops, and armed with ribs of whale.
Form a strong line about the silver bound,
And guard the wide circumference around.
"Whatever spirit, careless of his charge,
His post neglects, or leaves the fair at large,
125   Shall feel sharp vengeance soon o'ertake his sins,
Be stopped in vials, or transfixed with pins;
Or plunged in lakes of bitter washes lie,
Or wedged whole ages in a bodkin's[2] eye:
Gums and pomatums° shall his flight restrain,   ointments
130   While clogged he beats his silken wings in vain;
Or alum styptics[3] with contracting power
Shrink his thin essence like a rivelled° flower.   shriveled
Or as Ixion[4] fixed, the wretch shall feel
The giddy motion of the whirling mill,[5]
135   In fumes of burning chocolate shall glow,
And tremble at the sea that froths below!"
He spoke; the spirits from the sails descend;
Some, orb in orb, around the nymph extend,
Some thrid° the mazy ringlets of her hair,   slid through
140   Some hang upon the pendants of her ear;
With beating hearts the dire event they wait,
Anxious, and trembling for the birth of fate.

Canto 3

Close by those meads forever crowned with flow'rs,
Where Thames with pride surveys his rising tow'rs,
There stands a structure of majestic frame,
Which from the neighb'ring Hampton takes its name.[1]
5   Here Britain's statesmen oft the fall foredoom
Of foreign tyrants, and of nymphs at home;
Here thou, great Anna! whom three realms obey,[2]
Dost sometimes counsel take—and sometimes tea.
Hither the heroes and the nymphs resort,
10   To taste awhile the pleasures of a court;
In various talk th' instructive hours they passed,
Who gave the ball, or paid the visit last:
One speaks the glory of the British Queen,
And one describes a charming Indian screen;

1. Serving Belinda like the epic warrior's shield, her petticoat has seven layers bound together with a silver band (cf. *Iliad* 18 or *Aeneid* 8).
2. Blunt, thick needle; the Sylph, like the camel in Matthew 19.24, has difficulty getting through. Pope later plays on the various meanings of "bodkin," which also include a hair ornament and a dagger.
3. Astringents that stopped bleeding.
4. Having tried the chastity of Hera, Ixion was punished

by being tied to a revolving wheel of fire.
5. For beating chocolate, a new and highly fashionable drink.
1. Hampton Court, about 15 miles upriver from London, was built in the 16th century by Cardinal Wolsey, and by Queen Anne's day was associated with wits as well as with statesmen.
2. The English Crown still maintained its ancient claim to rule France as well as Great Britain and Ireland.

15   A third interprets motions, looks, and eyes;
  At ev'ry word a reputation dies.
  Snuff, or the fan, supply each pause of chat,
  With singing, laughing, ogling, and all that.
   Meanwhile declining from the noon of day,
20   The sun obliquely shoots his burning ray;
  The hungry judges soon the sentence sign,
  And wretches hang that jurymen may dine;
  The merchant from th' Exchange° returns in peace,   *market*
  And the long labors of the toilette cease—
25   Belinda now, whom thirst of fame invites,
  Burns to encounter two advent'rous knights,
  At Ombre³ singly to decide their doom;
  And swells her breast with conquests yet to come.
  Straight the three bands prepare in arms to join,
30   Each band the number of the Sacred Nine.⁴
  Soon as she spreads her hand, th' aerial guard
  Descend, and sit on each important card:
  First Ariel perched upon a Matador,⁵
  Then each, according to the rank they bore;
35   For Sylphs, yet mindful of their ancient race,
  Are, as when women, wondrous fond of place.°   *rank*
   Behold, four kings in majesty revered,
  With hoary whiskers⁶ and a forky beard;
  And four fair queens whose hands sustain° a flow'r,   *hold*
40   Th' expressive emblem of their softer pow'r;
  Four knaves in garbs succinct,° a trusty band,   *girded up*
  Caps on their heads, and halberds in their hand;
  And particolored troops, a shining train,
  Draw forth to combat on the velvet plain.⁷
45   The skillful nymph reviews her force with care;
  "Let spades be trumps!" she said, and trumps they were.⁸
   Now move to war her sable Matadors,
  In show like leaders of the swarthy moors.
  Spadillio first, unconquerable lord!
50   Led off two captive trumps, and swept the board.
  As many more Manillio forced to yield,
  And marched a victor from the verdant field.
  Him Basto followed, but his fate more hard
  Gained but one trump and one plebeian card.
55   With his broad saber next, a chief in years,
  The hoary majesty of spades appears;
  Puts forth one manly leg, to sight revealed;

---

3. A card game played with 40 cards, similar to modern bridge: three players hold nine cards each and bid for tricks, with the highest bidder becoming the "ombre" (man) and choosing trumps.
4. Pope links the nine Muses to the nine cards each player holds.
5. The Matadores are the three cards of highest value; Belinda holds all three: when trumps are black, they are the Spadillio (ace of spades), Manillio (deuce of spades),

and Basto (ace of clubs).
6. Gray mustache. The royal figures on the cards now conduct a mock-epic review of their forces, and the whole game is described as an epic battle, with the characters appearing as on the cards.
7. The green velvet card table.
8. Cf. Genesis 1.3, "Then God said, 'Let there be light'; and there was light."

The rest his many-colored robe concealed.
The rebel knave who dares his prince engage,
60   Proves the just victim of his royal rage.
Ev'n mighty Pam[9] that kings and queens o'erthrew,
And mowed down armies in the fights of Lu,
Sad chance of war! now, destitute of aid,
Falls undistinguished by the victor spade!
65   Thus far both armies to Belinda yield;
Now to the Baron fate inclines the field.
His warlike amazon her host invades,
Th' imperial consort of the crown of spades.
The club's black tyrant first her victim died,
70   Spite of his haughty mien and barb'rous pride:
What boots the regal circle on his head,
His giant limbs in state unwieldy spread?
That long behind he trails his pompous robe,
And of all monarchs only grasps the globe?
75   The Baron now his diamonds pours apace;
Th' embroidered king who shows but half his face,
And his refulgent queen, with pow'rs combined,
Of broken troops an easy conquest find.
Clubs, diamonds, hearts, in wild disorder seen,
80   With throngs promiscuous strew the level green.
Thus when dispersed a routed army runs,
Of Asia's troops and Afric's sable sons,
With like confusion different nations fly,
Of various habit and of various dye,
85   The pierced battalions disunited fall,
In heaps on heaps; one fate o'erwhelms them all.
     The knave of diamonds tries his wily arts,
And wins (oh shameful chance!) the queen of hearts.
At this, the blood the virgin's cheek forsook,
90   A livid paleness spreads o'er all her look;
She sees, and trembles at th' approaching ill,
Just in the jaws of ruin, and codille.[1]
And now (as oft in some distempered state)
On one nice trick[2] depends the gen'ral fate.
95   An ace of hearts steps forth: the king[3] unseen
Lurked in her hand, and mourned his captive queen.
He springs to vengeance with an eager pace,
And falls like thunder on the prostrate ace.
The nymph exulting fills with shouts the sky,
100   The walls, the woods, and long canals reply.
     Oh thoughtless mortals! ever blind to fate,
Too soon dejected, and too soon elate!
Sudden these honors shall be snatched away,
And cursed forever this victorious day.

---

9. The knave or jack of clubs, which took precedence over all trumps in the game of Lu, or Loo.
1. Literally "elbow": the defeat suffered by the ombre if another player wins more tricks.

2. Trick applies in both its technical and general senses as Belinda makes this careful maneuver.
3. The King of Hearts.

105   For lo! the board with cups and spoons is crowned,
        The berries crackle, and the Mill turns round.[4]
        On shining altars of Japan[5] they raise
        The silver lamp; the fiery spirits blaze.
        From silver spouts the grateful° liquors glide,   *pleasing*
110   While China's earth receives the smoking tide.
        At once they gratify their scent and taste,
        And frequent cups prolong the rich repast.
        Straight° hover round the fair her airy band;   *immediately*
        Some, as she sipped, the fuming liquor fanned,
115   Some o'er her lap their careful plumes displayed,
        Trembling, and conscious of the rich brocade.
        Coffee (which makes the politician wise,
        And see through all things with his half-shut eyes)
        Sent up in vapors[6] to the Baron's brain
120   New stratagems, the radiant lock to gain.
        Ah cease rash youth! desist ere 'tis too late,
        Fear the just gods, and think of Scylla's fate![7]
        Changed to a bird, and sent to flit in air,
        She dearly pays for Nisus' injured hair!
            But when to mischief mortals bend their will,
125   How soon they find fit instruments of ill!
        Just then, Clarissa drew with tempting grace
        A two-edged weapon from her shining case;
        So ladies in romance assist their knight,
130   Present the spear, and arm him for the fight.
        He takes the gift with rev'rence, and extends
        The little engine° on his fingers' ends,   *instrument*
        This just behind Belinda's neck he spread,
        As o'er the fragrant steams she bends her head:
135   Swift to the lock a thousand sprites repair,
        A thousand wings, by turns, blow back the hair,
        And thrice they twitched the diamond in her ear,
        Thrice she looked back, and thrice the foe drew near.
        Just in that instant, anxious Ariel sought
140   The close recesses of the virgin's thought;
        As on the nosegay in her breast reclined,
        He watched th' ideas rising in her mind,
        Sudden he viewed, in spite of all her art,
        An earthly lover° lurking at her heart.   *Lord Petre*
145   Amazed, confused, he found his pow'r expired,
        Resigned to fate, and with a sigh retired.
            The peer now spreads the glitt'ring forefx° wide,   *scissors*
        T' enclose the lock; now joins it, to divide.
        Ev'n then, before the fatal engine closed,
150   A wretched Sylph too fondly interposed;
        Fate urged the shears, and cut the Sylph in twain

4. Grinding coffee beans.
5. Lacquered tables ("Japan" was a type of varnish originating in that country).
6. Both steam and vain imaginations.

7. Scylla plucked purple hair from the head of her father,
King Nisus, to offer to her lover, Minos, so destroying her
father's power. Minos rejected her impiety, and Scylla
was transformed into a bird.

(But airy substance soon unites again)[8]
The meeting points the sacred hair dissever
From the fair head, forever and forever!
155   Then flashed the living lightning from her eyes,
And screams of horror rend th' affrighted skies.
Not louder shrieks to pitying Heav'n are cast,
When husbands or when lapdogs breathe their last,
Or when rich china vessels, fall'n from high,
160 In glitt'ring dust and painted fragments lie!
    Let wreaths of triumph now my temples twine,
(The victor cried) the glorious prize is mine!
While fish in streams, or birds delight in air,
Or in a coach and six[9] the British fair,
165 As long as *Atalantis*[1] shall be read,
Or the small pillow grace a lady's bed,[2]
While visits shall be paid on solemn days,
When numerous wax lights[3] in bright order blaze,
While nymphs take treats, or assignations give,
170 So long my honor, name, and praise shall live!
    What time would spare, from steel receives its date,°   *end*
And monuments, like men, submit to fate!
Steel could the labor of the gods destroy,
And strike to dust th' imperial tow'rs of Troy;[4]
175 Steel could the works of mortal pride confound,
And hew triumphal arches to the ground.
What wonder then, fair nymph! thy hairs should feel
The conqu'ring force of unresisted steel?

CANTO 4

But anxious cares the pensive nymph oppressed,
And secret passions labored in her breast.
Not youthful kings in battle seized alive,
Not scornful virgins who their charms survive,
5 Not ardent lovers robbed of all their bliss,
Not ancient ladies when refused a kiss,
Not tyrants fierce that unrepenting die,
Not Cynthia when her manteau's° pinned awry,   *gown's*
E'er felt such rage, resentment, and despair,
10 As thou, sad virgin! for thy ravished hair.
    For, that sad moment, when the Sylphs withdrew,
And Ariel weeping from Belinda flew,
Umbriel, a dusky melancholy sprite
As ever sullied the fair face of light,
15 Down to the central earth, his proper scene,

8. *Milton* lib. 6 [Pope's note], citing *Paradise Lost*
6.329–331, "The girding sword with discontinuous
wound / Passed through him, but the ethereal substance
closed / Not long divisible . . . ."
9. A carriage drawn by six horses; a symbol of wealth and
prestige.
1. The scandalous *Atalantis: Secret Memoirs and Manners
of Several Persons of Quality* (1709), by Mary Delarivière

Manley.
2. Said to be a place where ladies hid romance novels and
other contraband.
3. Candles made of wax, rather than the cheaper tallow.
Evening social visits were an essential part of the fashionable woman's routine.
4. Even Troy, fabled to have been built by Apollo and
Poseidon, was destroyed by arms.

Repaired to search the gloomy Cave of Spleen.[1]
 Swift on his sooty pinions flits the Gnome,
And in a vapor[2] reached the dismal dome.
No cheerful breeze this sullen region knows,
20 The dreaded east[3] is all the wind that blows.
Here, in a grotto, sheltered close from air,
And screened in shades° from day's detested glare,   *shadows*
She sighs forever on her pensive bed,
Pain at her side, and Megrim° at her head.   *migraine*
25 Two handmaids wait the throne: alike in place,
But diff'ring far in figure and in face.
Here stood Ill-Nature like an ancient maid,
Her wrinkled form in black and white arrayed;
With store of pray'rs, for mornings, nights, and noons,
30 Her hand is filled; her bosom with lampoons.
  There Affectation with a sickly mien
Shows in her cheek the roses of eighteen,
Practiced to lisp, and hang the head aside,
Faints into airs, and languishes with pride;
35 On the rich quilt sinks with becoming woe,
Wrapped in a gown, for sickness, and for show.
The fair ones feel such maladies as these,
When each new nightdress gives a new disease.
40 A constant vapor o'er the palace flies;
Strange phantoms rising as the mists arise;
Dreadful, as hermit's dreams in haunted shades,
Or bright as visions of expiring maids.[4]
Now glaring fiends, and snakes on rolling spires,°   *coils*
Pale specters, gaping tombs, and purple fires:
45 Now lakes of liquid gold, Elysian scenes,[5]
And crystal domes, and angels in machines.
  Unnumbered throngs on ev'ry side are seen
Of bodies changed to various forms by Spleen.[6]
Here living teapots stand, one arm held out,
50 One bent; the handle this, and that the spout:
A pipkin[7] there like Homer's tripod walks;
Here sighs a jar, and there a goose pie[8] talks;
Men prove with child, as pow'rful fancy works,
And maids turned bottles, call aloud for corks.
55 Safe passed the Gnome through this fantastic band,
A branch of healing spleenwort[9] in his hand.
Then thus addressed the pow'r—"Hail, wayward Queen!

1. Named after the bodily organ, "spleen" was the current name for the fashionable affliction of melancholy or ill-humor. Umbriel's descent into the womb-like Cave of Spleen suggests the epic commonplace of the journey to the underworld.
2. "The spleen" was also called "the vapors."
3. The east wind was supposed to induce fits of spleen.
4. Religious visions of hell and heaven.
5. Elysium was the classical paradise, but this also recalls contemporary theater, which made much of scenic spectacle and the use of machinery.
6. Hallucinations similar to those described in the following lines were common to those afflicted with spleen.
7. Small pot or pan. Hephaistos's "walking" tripods are described in the *Iliad* 18.439ff.
8. Alludes to a real fact, a Lady of distinction imagin'd herself in this condition [Pope's note].
9. Pope changes the golden bough that protected Aeneas on his trip through the underworld into a herb that was supposed to be good for the spleen.

Who rule the sex to fifty from fifteen,
Parent of vapors and of female wit,
60 Who give th' hysteric or poetic fit,
On various tempers act by various ways,
Make some take physic,° others scribble plays;[1]   *medicine*
Who cause the proud their visits to delay,
And send the godly in a pet° to pray.   *ill-humor*
65 A nymph there is that all thy pow'r disdains,
And thousands more in equal mirth maintains.
But oh! if e'er thy Gnome could spoil a grace,
Or raise a pimple on a beauteous face,
Like citron-waters° matrons' cheeks inflame,   *flavored brandy*
70 Or change complexions at a losing game;
If e'er with airy horns[2] I planted heads,
Or rumpled petticoats, or tumbled beds,
Or caused suspicion when no soul was rude,
Or discomposed the headdress of a prude,
75 Or e'er to costive° lapdog gave disease,   *constipated*
Which not the tears of brightest eyes could ease:
Hear me, and touch Belinda with chagrin;
That single act gives half the world the spleen."
          The goddess with a discontented air
80 Seems to reject him, though she grants his pray'r.
A wondrous bag with both her hands she binds,
Like that where once Ulysses held the winds;[3]
There she collects the force of female lungs,
Sighs, sobs, and passions, and the war of tongues.
85 A vial next she fills with fainting fears,
Soft sorrows, melting griefs, and flowing tears.
The Gnome rejoicing bears her gifts away,
Spreads his black wings, and slowly mounts to day.
          Sunk in Thalestris'[4] arms the nymph he found,
90 Her eyes dejected and her hair unbound.
Full o'er their heads the swelling bag he rent,
And all the furies issued at the vent.
Belinda burns with more than mortal ire,
And fierce Thalestris fans the rising fire.
95 "O wretched maid!" she spread her hands, and cried,
(While Hampton's echoes "Wretched maid!" replied)
"Was it for this you took such constant care
The bodkin, comb, and essence to prepare;
For this your locks in paper durance° bound,   *curling papers*
100 For this with tort'ring irons wreathed around?
For this with fillets[5] strained your tender head,
And bravely bore the double loads of lead?°   *wire supports*
Gods! shall the ravisher display your hair,

---

1. Melancholy was associated with artistic creativity.
2. A sign that a husband had been cuckolded.
3. Given to him by the wind god Aeolus (*Odyssey* 10.19ff.).

4. A queen of the Amazons; here Mrs. Morley, Arabella's second cousin.
5. Headbands, with reference to priestesses in the *Aeneid*.

While the fops envy, and the ladies stare!
105　Honor forbid! at whose unrivaled shrine
Ease, pleasure, virtue, all, our sex resign.
Methinks already I your tears survey,
Already hear the horrid things they say,
Already see you a degraded toast,[6]
110　And all your honor in a whisper lost!
How shall I, then, your helpless fame defend?
'Twill then be infamy to seem your friend!
And shall this prize, th' inestimable prize,
Exposed through crystal to the gazing eyes,
115　And heightened by the diamond's circling rays,
On that rapacious hand forever blaze?[7]
Sooner shall grass in Hyde Park Circus grow,[8]
And wits take lodgings in the sound of Bow;[9]
Sooner let earth, air, sea, to Chaos fall,
120　Men, monkeys, lapdogs, parrots, perish all!"
　　She said; then raging to Sir Plume[1] repairs,
And bids her beau demand the precious hairs:
(Sir Plume, of amber snuffbox justly vain,
And the nice conduct of a clouded cane[2])
125　With earnest eyes, and round unthinking face,
He first the snuffbox opened, then the case,
And thus broke out—"My Lord, why, what the devil?
Z—ds![3] damn the lock! 'fore Gad, you must be civil!
Plague on't! 'tis past a jest—nay prithee, Pox!
130　Give her the hair"—he spoke, and rapped his box.
　　"It grieves me much" (replied the Peer again)
"Who speaks so well should ever speak in vain.
But by this lock, this sacred lock I swear
(Which never more shall join its parted hair,
135　Which never more its honors shall renew,
Clipped from the lovely head where late it grew)
That while my nostrils draw the vital air,
This hand which won it shall forever wear."
He spoke, and speaking, in proud triumph spread
140　The long-contended honors[4] of her head.
　　But Umbriel, hateful Gnome! forbears not so;
He breaks the vial whence the sorrows flow.
Then see! the nymph in beauteous grief appears,
Her eyes half-languishing, half-drowned in tears;
145　On her heaved bosom hung her drooping head,
Which, with a sigh, she raised; and thus she said:
　　"Forever cursed be this detested day,[5]

---

6. A woman whose toast is often drunk, and who by
implication is all too well known to her (male) toasters:
(cf. Canto 5.10, and Fielding's *Tom Jones*, where Sophia
is not pleased by reports that she has been Tom's toast,
bk. 13, ch. 11).
7. I.e., mounted in a ring.
8. The fashion for driving coaches around Hyde Park prevented grass from growing there.

9. A commercial area around St. Mary-le-Bow, and not at
all fashionable.
1. Sir George Browne, cousin of Arabella's mother.
2. Skilled use of a cane with a head of dark polished stone.
3. Zounds, a corruption of "God's wounds," a mild oath.
4. Her beautiful hair.
5. Echoing Achilles' lament for his slain friend Patroclus
(*Iliad* 18.107ff.).

Which snatched my best, my fav'rite curl away!
Happy! ah ten times happy, had I been,
150 If Hampton Court these eyes had never seen!
Yet am not I the first mistaken maid,
By love of courts to num'rous ills betrayed.
Oh had I rather unadmired remained
In some lone isle, or distant northern land;
155 Where the gilt chariot never marks the way,
Where none learn Ombre, none e'er taste bohea!°   tea
There kept my charms concealed from mortal eye,
Like roses that in deserts bloom and die.
What moved my mind with youthful lords to roam?
160 O had I stayed, and said my pray'rs at home!
'Twas this, the morning omens seemed to tell;
Thrice from my trembling hand the patch box fell;
The tott'ring china shook without a wind,
Nay, Poll° sat mute, and Shock was most unkind!   her parrot
165 A Sylph too warned me of the threats of fate,
In mystic visions, now believed too late!
See the poor remnants of these slighted hairs!
My hands shall rend what ev'n thy rapine spares:
These, in two sable ringlets taught to break,°   divide
170 Once gave new beauties to the snowy neck.
The sister lock now sits uncouth, alone,
And in its fellow's fate foresees its own;
Uncurled it hangs, the fatal shears demands;
And tempts once more thy sacrilegious hands.
175 Oh hadst thou, cruel! been content to seize
Hairs less in sight, or any hairs but these!"

CANTO 5

She said: the pitying audience melt in tears,
But Fate and Jove had stopped the Baron's ears.
In vain Thalestris with reproach assails,
For who can move when fair Belinda fails?
5 Not half so fixed the Trojan[1] could remain,
While Anna begged and Dido raged in vain.
Then grave Clarissa[2] graceful waved her fan;
Silence ensued, and thus the nymph began.
    "Say, why are beauties praised and honored most,
10 The wise man's passion, and the vain man's toast?
Why decked with all that land and sea afford,
Why angels called, and angel-like adored?
Why round our coaches crowd the white-gloved beaus,
Why bows the side box from its inmost rows?[3]
15 How vain are all these glories, all our pains,

1. Aeneas, fixed on his decision to leave Carthage and abandon Dido despite her pleas and those of her sister Anna (*Aeneid* 4.269–449).
2. A new character introduced . . . to open more clearly the moral of the poem, in a parody of the speech of Sarpedon to Glaucus in Homer [Pope's note in the 1717 edition]. Sarpedon's speech (*Iliad* 12) is a famous reflection on glory: see page 2511 for Pope's translation of the speech.
3. At the theater, gentlemen sat in the side boxes, ladies in the front boxes facing the stage.

Unless good sense preserve what beauty gains:
That men may say when we the front box grace,
Behold the first in virtue as in face!
Oh! if to dance all night, and dress all day,
20   Charmed the smallpox,[4] or chased old age away;
Who would not scorn what housewife's cares produce,
Or who would learn one earthly thing of use?
To patch, nay ogle, might become a saint,
Nor could it sure be such a sin to paint.
25   But since, alas! frail beauty must decay,
Curled or uncurled, since locks will turn to gray,
Since painted or not painted, all shall fade,
And she who scorns a man, must die a maid;
What then remains, but well our pow'r to use,
30   And keep good humor still whate'er we lose?
And trust me, dear! good humor can prevail,
When airs, and flights, and screams, and scolding fail.
Beauties in vain their pretty eyes may roll;
Charms strike the sight, but merit wins the soul."
35   So spoke the dame, but no applause ensued;
Belinda frowned, Thalestris called her prude.
"To arms, to arms!" the fierce virago[5] cries,
And swift as lightning to the combat flies.
All side in parties, and begin th' attack;
40   Fans clap, silks rustle, and tough whalebones crack;
Heroes' and heroines' shouts confus'dly rise,
And bass and treble voices strike the skies.
No common weapons in their hands are found,
Like gods they fight, nor dread a mortal wound.
45   So when bold Homer makes the gods engage,
And heav'nly breasts with human passions rage;
'Gainst Pallas,° Mars; Latona,[6] Hermes arms;   *Athena*
And all Olympus rings with loud alarms.
Jove's thunder roars, Heav'n trembles all around;
50   Blue Neptune storms, the bellowing deeps resound;
Earth shakes her nodding tow'rs, the ground gives way;
And the pale ghosts start at the flash of day!
     Triumphant Umbriel on a sconce's[7] height
Clapped his glad wings, and sat to view the fight:
55   Propped on their bodkin spears, the sprites survey
The growing combat, or assist the fray.
     While through the press enraged Thalestris flies,
And scatters deaths around from both her eyes,
A beau and witling° perished in the throng,   *little wit*
60   One died in metaphor, and one in song.
"O cruel Nymph! a living death I bear,"
Cried Dapperwit, and sunk beside his chair.
A mournful glance Sir Fopling upwards cast,

---

4. A common disease, which frequently left permanent facial scars.
5. Woman who behaves like a man.

6. Mother of Diana and Apollo.
7. Candlestick attached to the wall.

"Those eyes are made so killing"[8]—was his last:
65   Thus on Meander's flow'ry margin lies
Th' expiring swan, and as he sings he dies.[9]
　　　　When bold Sir Plume had drawn Clarissa down,
Chloe stepped in, and killed him with a frown;
She smiled to see the doughty hero slain,
70   But at her smile the beau revived again.
　　　　Now Jove suspends his golden scales in air,[1]
Weighs the men's wits against the lady's hair;
The doubtful beam long nods from side to side;
At length the wits mount up, the hairs subside.
75   　　　See fierce Belinda on the Baron flies,
With more than usual lightning in her eyes;
Nor feared the chief th' unequal fight to try,
Who sought no more than on his foe to die.[2]
But this bold lord, with manly strength indued,
80   She with one finger and a thumb subdued:
Just where the breath of life his nostrils drew,
A charge of snuff the wily virgin threw;
The Gnomes direct, to ev'ry atom just,
The pungent grains of titillating dust.
85   Sudden, with starting tears each eye o'erflows,
And the high dome re-echoes to his nose.[3]
　　　　"Now meet thy fate," incensed Belinda cried,
And drew a deadly bodkin from her side.
(The same, his ancient personage to deck,
90   Her great–great–grandsire wore about his neck
In three seal rings; which after, melted down,
Formed a vast buckle for his widow's gown:
Her infant grandame's° whistle next it grew,　　　　　　　　grandmother's
The bells she jingled, and the whistle blew;
95   Then in a bodkin[4] graced her mother's hairs,
Which long she wore, and now Belinda wears.)
　　　　"Boast not my fall" (he cried) "insulting foe!
Thou by some other shalt be laid as low.
Nor think, to die dejects my lofty mind;
100   All that I dread is leaving you behind!
Rather than so, ah let me still survive,
And burn in Cupid's flames—but burn alive."
　　　　"Restore the lock!" she cries; and all around
"Restore the lock!" the vaulted roofs rebound.
105   Not fierce Othello in so loud a strain
Roared for the handkerchief that caused his pain.
But see how oft ambitious aims are crossed,
And chiefs contend 'till all the prize is lost!
The lock, obtained with guilt, and kept with pain,

---

8. A line from Giovanni Bononcini's opera, *Camilla* (1696), which at this time was popular in London.
9. Meander: a river in Asia Minor. Swans were popularly believed to sing only on their death. This simile refers to Ovid's *Heroides*, 7, a lament from Dido to Aeneas.

1. To determine victory in battle; a convention found in both Homer and Virgil.
2. A standard metaphor for sexual climax.
3. Cf. his boast, 4.133–138.
4. A decorative pin, shaped like a dagger.

110　　In ev'ry place is sought, but sought in vain:
　　　　With such a prize no mortal must be blest,
　　　　So Heav'n decrees! with Heav'n who can contest?
　　　　　　Some thought it mounted to the lunar sphere,[5]
　　　　Since all things lost on earth are treasured there.
115　　There heroes' wits are kept in ponderous vases,
　　　　And beaus' in snuffboxes and tweezer cases.
　　　　There broken vows and deathbed alms are found,
　　　　And lovers' hearts with ends of riband bound;
　　　　The courtier's promises, and sick man's pray'rs,
120　　The smiles of harlots, and the tears of heirs,
　　　　Cages for gnats, and chains to yoke a flea;
　　　　Dried butterflies, and tomes of casuistry.[6]
　　　　　　But trust the Muse—she saw it upward rise,
　　　　Though marked by none but quick poetic eyes:
125　　(So Rome's great founder to the heav'ns withdrew,
　　　　To Proculus alone confessed in view.[7])
　　　　A sudden star, it shot through liquid air,
　　　　And drew behind a radiant trail of hair.
　　　　Not Berenice's locks first rose so bright,[8]
130　　The heav'ns bespangling with disheveled light.
　　　　The Sylphs behold it kindling as it flies,
　　　　And pleased pursue its progress through the skies.
　　　　　　This the beau monde shall from the Mall[9] survey,
　　　　And hail with music its propitious ray.
135　　This, the blest lover shall for Venus° take,　　　　　*the planet*
　　　　And send up vows from Rosamonda's Lake.[1]
　　　　This Partridge[2] soon shall view in cloudless skies,
　　　　When next he looks through Galileo's eyes;[3]
　　　　And hence th' egregious wizard shall foredoom
140　　The fate of Louis, and the fall of Rome.
　　　　　　Then cease, bright nymph! to mourn thy ravished hair
　　　　Which adds new glory to the shining sphere!
　　　　Not all the tresses that fair head can boast
　　　　Shall draw such envy as the lock you lost.
145　　For, after all the murders of your eye,
　　　　When, after millions slain, yourself shall die;
　　　　When those fair suns[4] shall set, as set they must,
　　　　And all those tresses shall be laid in dust;
　　　　This lock, the Muse shall consecrate to fame,
150　　And mid'st the stars inscribe Belinda's name!

1711–1717　　　　　　　　　　　　　　　　　1712; 1714; 1717

---

5. Cf. Ariosto's *Orlando Furioso* (1516–1532), in which Orlando's lost wits are sought on the moon. See also *Paradise Lost* 3.444ff.

6. Subtle reasoning (often used of arguments justifying immoral conduct).

7. When Romulus was killed mysteriously, Proculus soothed popular grief by asserting that he had been taken up to heaven.

8. The Egyptian queen Berenice made an offering of her hair after her husband returned victorious from the wars;

when it disappeared from the temple, the court astronomer claimed it had been made into a new constellation.

9. A fashionable walk in St. James's Park.

1. Where lovers met in St. James's Park.

2. John Partridge was a ridiculous star-gazer, who in his almanacs every year, never failed to predict the downfall of the Pope and the King of France, then at war with the English [Pope's note].

3. I.e., a telescope.

4. I.e., her eyes

The Iliad

"In the beginning of my translating the *Iliad* I wished anybody would hang me, a hundred times," Pope confided to his friend Joseph Spence, "it sat so heavily on my mind at first that I often used to dream of it, and so do sometimes still." Pope spent nearly seven years (1713–1720) translating the *Iliad* and writing critical notes to accompany his text. His work was an outstanding commercial and literary success; for his labors Pope made about £5,000, more than a hundred times the annual earnings of a skilled craftsman or a shop owner in Pope's day. Samuel Johnson called Pope's *Iliad* "the noblest version [translation] of poetry which the world has ever seen"; Samuel Taylor Coleridge said Pope's poem was "an astonishing product of matchless talent and ingenuity."

Pope's *Preface* to the translation is an important statement of his poetic values and his ideas on translation. A sample of the translation itself follows, taken from Book 12. In the passage, Sarpedon, king of the Lycians who were allied with the Trojans against the Greeks, exhorts his lieutenant Glaucus to fight bravely. This was the first passage of the *Iliad* that Pope published; it appeared in 1709 with the *Pastorals* as the *Episode of Sarpedon*. Eight years later, Pope's final addition to *The Rape of the Lock* (1717) was a parody of the warrior's famous speech, spoken by Clarissa at the beginning of Canto 5. Pope's own comment reveals his thoughts about Sarpedon's great exhortation: "In former times, kings were looked upon as the generals of armies, who to return the honors that were done to them, were obliged to expose themselves first in battle, and be an example to their soldiers. Upon this Sarpedon grounds his discourse, which is full of generosity and nobleness. We are, says he, honored like gods, and what can be more unjust than not to behave ourselves like men? He ought to be superior in virtue, who is superior in dignity. What strength is there and what greatness in that thought! It includes justice, gratitude, and magnanimity: justice, in that he scorns to enjoy what he does not merit; gratitude, because he would endeavor to recompense his obligations to his subjects; and magnanimity, because he despises death, and thinks of nothing but glory."

from The Iliad

from Preface

[ON TRANSLATION]

Having now spoken of the beauties and defects of the original, it remains to treat of the translation, with the same view to the chief characteristic. As far as that is seen in the main parts of the poem, such as the fable, manners, and sentiments, no translator can prejudice it but by willful omissions or contractions. As it also breaks out in every particular image, description, and simile, whoever lessens or too much softens those takes off from this chief character. It is the first grand duty of an interpreter to give his author entire and unmaimed; and for the rest, the diction and versification only are his proper province, since these must be his own, but the others he is to take as he finds them.

It should then be considered what methods may afford some equivalent in our language for the graces of these in the Greek. It is certain no literal translation can be just to an excellent original in a superior language, but it is a great mistake to imagine (as many have done) that a rash paraphrase can make amends for this general defect, which is no less in danger to lose the spirit of an Ancient, by deviating into the modern manners of expression. If there be sometimes a *darkness*, there is often a *light* in antiquity which nothing better preserves than a version almost literal. I know no liberties one ought to take, but those which are necessary for transfusing the spirit of the original, and supporting the poetical style of the translation; and I will venture to say, there have not been more men misled in former times by a servile dull adherence to the letter, than have been deluded in ours by a chimerical[1] insolent hope of raising and improving their author. It is not to be doubted that the *fire* of the poem is what a translator should principally regard, as it is most likely to expire in his managing; however, it is his safest way to be content with preserving this to his utmost in the whole, without endeavoring to be more than he finds his author is in any particular place. 'Tis a great secret in writing to know when to be plain, and when poetical and figurative, and it is what Homer will teach us if we will but follow modestly in his footsteps. Where his diction is bold and lofty, let us raise ours as high as we can; but where his is plain and humble, we ought not to be deterred from imitating him by the fear of incurring the censure of a mere English critic. Nothing that belongs to Homer seems to have been more commonly mistaken than the just pitch of his style: some of his translators having swelled into fustian[2] in a proud confidence of the sublime; others sunk into flatness in a cold and timorous notion of simplicity. Methinks I see these different followers of Homer, some sweating and straining after him by violent leaps and bounds (the certain signs of false mettle), others slowly and servilely creeping in his train, while the poet himself is all the time proceeding with an unaffected and equal[3] majesty before them. However, of the two extremes one could sooner pardon frenzy than frigidity: no author is to be envied for such commendations as he may gain by that character of style which his friends must agree together to call simplicity, and the rest of the world will call dullness. There is a graceful and dignified simplicity, as well as a bald and sordid one, which differ as much from each other as the air of a plain man from that of a sloven: 'tis one thing to be tricked up,[4] and another not to be dressed at all. Simplicity is the mean between ostentation and rusticity.

This pure and noble simplicity is nowhere in such perfection as in the Scripture and our author. One may affirm with all respect to the inspired writings, that the divine spirit made use of no other words but what were intelligible and common to men at that time, and in that part of the world; and as Homer is the author nearest to those, his style must of course bear a greater resemblance to the sacred books than that of any other writer. This consideration (together with what has been observed of the parity of some of his thoughts) may, methinks, induce a translator on the one hand to give in to several of those general phrases and manners of expression, which have attained a veneration even in our language from being used in the Old Testament, as on the other, to avoid those which have been appropriated to the divinity, and in a manner consigned to mystery and religion.

For a farther preservation of this air of simplicity, a particular care should be taken to express with all plainness those moral sentences and proverbial speeches which are so numerous in this poet. They have something venerable, and as I may say oracular, in that unadorned gravity and shortness with which they are delivered, a grace which would be utterly lost by endeavoring to give them what we call a more ingenious (that is a more modern) turn in the paraphrase.

Perhaps the mixture of some Graecisms and old words after the manner of Milton, if done without too much affectation, might not have an ill effect in a version of this particular work, which most of any other seems to require a venerable antique cast. But certainly the use of modern terms of war and government, such as platoon,

---

1. Fanciful.
2. Bombast; high-flown language.

3. Consistent
4. Overdressed.

campaign, junto, or the like (into which some of his translators have fallen) cannot be allowable; those only excepted, without which it is impossible to treat the subjects in any living language.

* * *

It only remains to speak of the versification. Homer (as has been said) is perpetually applying the sound to the sense, and varying it on every new subject. This is indeed one of the most exquisite beauties of poetry, and attainable by very few: I know only of Homer eminent for it in the Greek, and Virgil in Latin. I am sensible it is what may sometimes happen by chance, when a writer is warm, and fully possessed of his image: however it may be reasonably believed they designed this, in whose verse it so manifestly appears in a superior degree to all others. Few readers have the ear to be judges of it, but those who have will see I have endeavored at this beauty.

Upon the whole, I must confess myself utterly incapable of doing justice to Homer. I attempt him in no other hope but that which one may entertain without much vanity, of giving a more tolerable copy of him than any entire translation in verse has yet done.

* * *

1715   1715

from *Book 12*

[SARPEDON'S SPEECH]

    Resolved alike, divine Sarpedon[1] glows
    With gen'rous rage that drives him on the foes.
    He views the tow'rs, and meditates° their fall,   *plans*
    To sure destruction dooms th' aspiring° wall;   *high*
5   Then casting on his friend an ardent look,
    Fir'd with the thirst of glory, thus he spoke.
      "Why boast we, Glaucus! our extended reign,
    Where Xanthus' streams[2] enrich the Lycian plain,
    Our num'rous herds that range the fruitful field,
10   And hills where vines their purple harvest yield,
    Our foaming bowls with purer nectar[3] crowned,
    Our feasts enhanced with music's sprightly° sound?   *lively*
    Why on those shores° are we with joy surveyed,°   *of Greece/observed*
    Admired as heroes, and as gods obeyed?
15   Unless great acts superior merit prove,
    And vindicate the bount'ous pow'rs above.[4]
    'Tis ours, the dignity they give, to grace;
    The first in valor, as the first in place.[5]
    That when with wond'ring eyes our martial bands
20   Behold our deeds transcending our commands,[6]
    Such, they may cry, deserve the sov'reign state,°   *role*

---

1. Sarpedon's father was Zeus, the supreme Olympian deity; his mother was Laodemia, a mortal.
2. The Xanthus is the principal river flowing through Lycia, a mountainous country in southwestern Asia Minor.
3. Perhaps mead, which is made from fermented honey, but probably any drink.

4. I.e., the gods' blessings on us.
5. I.e., we must justify our position of authority over the people (which the gods have bestowed) through valor.
6. I.e., we set an example for our troops, rather than commanding from the rear.

Whom those that envy, dare not imitate!
Could all our care elude the gloomy° grave,[7]   *dark*
Which claims no less the fearful than the brave,
25   For lust of fame I should not vainly dare
In fighting fields, nor urge thy soul to war.
But since, alas! ignoble age must come,
Disease, and death's inexorable doom;°   *fate*
The life which others pay, let us bestow,
30   And give to Fame what we to Nature owe;
Brave though we fall, and honored if we live,
Or° let us glory gain, or glory give!"   *either*
He said;° his words the list'ning chief inspire   *spoke*
With equal warmth, and rouse the warrior's fire;
35   The troops pursue their leaders with delight,
Rush to the foe, and claim the promised fight.

c. 1707   1709

Eloisa to Abelard

Peter Abelard (1079–1142), a great French philosopher and theologian, was tutor to the young Heloise (Eloisa). They fell in love, had a son, and secretly married. When the affair became known, Heloise was forced to enter a convent and Abelard was castrated by a gang of thugs hired by Heloise's enraged uncle. Abelard became a Benedictine monk, founding the monastery of the Paraclete, or Holy Spirit. After many years of living respectable and success-ful lives devoted to God, the two former lovers exchanged a series of epistles in Latin. These austere letters were made more romantic and psychologically complex when they were loosely translated into French in the later seventeenth century. In 1713 Pope's friend John Hughes translated the silently "improved" French version into English; this became the source for Pope's poem, which he chose to conclude his 1717 *Works*. Modeled upon Ovid's *Heroides*, *Eloisa to Abelard* is a *heroic epistle*, a dramatic expression of a lover's feelings in a verse letter addressed to an absent loved one. Alternately erotic and pious, gothic and tender, Pope's intensely passionate and penetratingly psychological portrait of Eloisa's conflicting feelings was one of his most widely admired works, particularly among eighteenth-century women readers.

Eloisa to Abelard
The Argument

Abelard and Eloisa flourished in the twelfth century; they were two of the most dis-tinguished persons of their age in learning and beauty, but for nothing more famous than for their unfortunate passion. After a long course of calamities, they retired each to a several[1] convent, and consecrated the remainder of their days to religion. It was many years after this separation, that a letter of Abelard's to a friend which con-tained the history of his misfortune, fell into the hands of Eloisa. This awakening all

---

7. There is not a more forcible argument than this, to make all men condemn dangers, and seek glory by brave actions. Immortality with eternal youth is certainly preferable to glory purchased with the loss of life; but glo-ry is certainly better than an ignominious life, which at last, though perhaps late, must end. It is ordained that all men shall die, nor can our escaping danger secure us immortality; it can only give us a longer continuance in

disgrace, and even that continuance will be but short, though the infamy everlasting. This is incontestable, and whoever weighs his actions in these scales, can never hes-itate in his choice; but what is most remarkable is that Homer does not put this in the mouth of an ordinary per-son, but ascribes it to the son of Jupiter [Pope's note].
1. Different.

her tenderness, occasioned those celebrated letters (out of which the following is partly extracted) which give so lively a picture of the struggles of grace and nature, virtue and passion.

> In these deep solitudes and awful° cells,   *awe-inspiring*
> Where heav'nly-pensive, contemplation dwells,
> And ever-musing melancholy reigns;
> What means this tumult in a vestal's[2] veins?
> 5   Why rove my thoughts beyond this last retreat?
> Why feels my heart its long-forgotten heat?
> Yet, yet[3] I love!—From Abelard it came,
> And Eloisa yet must kiss the name.
>   Dear fatal name! rest ever unrevealed,
> 10   Nor pass these lips in holy silence sealed.
> Hide it, my heart, within that close disguise,
> Where, mixed with God's, his loved idea° lies.   *image*
> Oh write it not, my hand—the name appears
> Already written—wash it out, my tears!
> 15   In vain lost Eloisa weeps and prays,
> Her heart still dictates, and her hand obeys.
>   Relentless walls! whose darksome round contains
> Repentant sighs, and voluntary pains;
> Ye rugged rocks! which holy knees have worn;
> 20   Ye grots° and caverns shagged with horrid° thorn!   *grottos / bristling*
> Shrines! where their vigils pale-eyed virgins keep,
> And pitying saints, whose statues learn to weep![4]
> Though cold like you, unmoved, and silent grown,
> I have not yet forgot myself to stone.[5]
> 25   All is not Heav'n's while Abelard has part,
> Still rebel nature holds out half my heart;
> Nor pray'rs nor fast its stubborn pulse restrain,
> Nor tears, for ages, taught to flow in vain.
>   Soon as thy letters trembling I unclose,
> 30   That well-known name awakens all my woes.
> Oh name forever sad! forever dear!
> Still breathed in sighs, still ushered with a tear.
> I tremble too where'er my own I find,
> Some dire misfortune follows close behind.
> 35   Line after line my gushing eyes o'erflow,
> Led through a sad variety of woe:
> Now warm in love, now with'ring in thy bloom,
> Lost in a convent's° solitary gloom!   *monastery's*
> There stern religion quenched th' unwilling flame,
> 40   There died the best of passions, love and fame.
>   Yet write, or write me all, that I may join
> Griefs to thy griefs, and echo sighs to thine.

---

2. Virgin bound to the service of the Roman goddess Vesta. As a nun Eloisa, like the vestals, was now set aside for service to the divine.

3. In the sense of both "but" and "still."

4. Through condensation that ran down the statues.

5. This metaphor comes from Hughes's translation of the *Letters of Abelard and Heloise:* "O Vows! O Convent! I have not lost my humanity under your inexorable discipline! You have not made me marble by changing my habit" (129). See also Milton, *Il Penseroso,* line 42, page 1735.

Nor foes nor fortune take this pow'r away.
And is my Abelard less kind than they?
45   Tears still are mine, and those I need not spare,
Love but demands what else were shed in pray'r;
No happier task these faded eyes pursue,
To read and weep is all they now can do.
    Then share thy pain, allow that sad relief;
50   Ah more than share it! give me all thy grief.
Heav'n first taught letters for some wretch's aid,
Some banished lover, or some captive maid;
They live, they speak, they breathe what love inspires,
Warm from the soul, and faithful to its fires,
55   The virgin's wish without her fears impart,
Excuse[6] the blush, and pour out all the heart,
Speed the soft intercourse from soul to soul,
And waft a sigh from Indus[7] to the Pole.
    Thou know'st how guiltless first I met thy flame,
60   When love approached me under friendship's name;
My fancy formed thee of angelic kind,
Some emanation of th' all-beauteous Mind.°   *God*
Those smiling eyes, attemp'ring° ev'ry ray,   *softening*
Shone sweetly lambent° with celestial day: *radiant*
65   Guiltless I gazed; Heav'n listened while you sung;
And truths divine came mended from that tongue.[8]
From lips like those what precept failed to move?
Too soon they taught me 'twas no sin to love.
Back through the paths of pleasing sense I ran,
70   Nor wished an angel whom I loved a man.[9]
Dim and remote the joys of saints I see,
Nor envy them, that Heav'n I lose for thee.
    How oft, when pressed to marriage, have I said,
Curse on all laws but those which love has made!
75   Love, free as air, at sight of human ties
Spreads his light wings, and in a moment flies.
Let wealth, let honor, wait the wedded dame,
August her deed, and sacred be her fame;
Before true passion all those views remove,°   *disperse*
80   Fame, wealth, and honor! what are you to love?
The jealous god,° when we profane his fires,   *Cupid*
Those restless passions in revenge inspires;
And bids them make mistaken mortals groan,
Who seek in love for ought but love alone.
85   Should at my feet the world's great master fall,
Himself, his throne, his world, I'd scorn 'em all:
Not Caesar's empress would I deign to prove;
No, make me mistress to the man I love;
If there be yet another name more free,

---

6. Release from the need for.
7. A southern constellation far distant from the northern
Polestar
8. He was her preceptor in philosophy and divinity

[Pope's note].
9. Having thought you an angel, I now return to my senses, and happily accept you as human.

90   More fond° than mistress, make me that to thee!   *beloved*
     Oh happy state! when souls each other draw,
     When love is liberty, and nature, law:
     All then is full, possessing, and possessed,
     No craving void left aching in the breast:
95   Ev'n thought meets thought ere from the lips it part,
     And each warm wish springs mutual from the heart.
     This sure is bliss (if bliss on earth there be)
     And once the lot of Abelard and me.
          Alas how changed! what sudden horrors rise!
100 A naked lover bound and bleeding lies!
     Where, where was Eloise? her voice, her hand,
     Her poniard, had opposed the dire command.
     Barbarian stay! that bloody stroke restrain;
     The crime was common, common be the pain.[1]
105 I can no more; by shame, by rage suppressed,
     Let tears and burning blushes speak the rest.
          Canst thou forget that sad, that solemn day,
     When victims at yon altar's foot we lay?
     Canst thou forget what tears that moment fell,
110 When, warm in youth, I bade the world farewell?
     As with cold lips I kissed the sacred veil,
     The shrines all trembled, and the lamps grew pale:
     Heav'n scarce believed the conquest it surveyed,
     And saints with wonder heard the vows I made.
115 Yet then, to those dread altars as I drew,
     Not on the Cross my eyes were fixed, but you;
     Not grace, or zeal, love only was my call,
     And if I lose thy love, I lose my all.
     Come! with thy looks, thy words, relieve my woe;
120 Those still at least are left thee to bestow.
     Still on that breast enamored let me lie,
     Still drink delicious poison from thy eye,
     Pant on thy lip, and to thy heart be pressed;
     Give all thou canst—and let me dream the rest.
125 Ah no! instruct me other joys to prize,
     With other beauties charm my partial° eyes,   *fondly biased*
     Full in my view set all the bright abode,
     And make my soul quit Abelard for God.
          Ah think at least thy flock deserves thy care,
130 Plants of thy hand, and children of thy pray'r.
     From the false world in early youth they fled,
     By thee to mountains, wilds, and deserts led.
     You raised these hallowed walls;[2] the desert smiled,
     And paradise was opened in the wild.
135 No weeping orphan saw his father's stores
     Our shrines irradiate, or emblaze the floors;[3]
     No silver saints, by dying misers giv'n,

---

1. The crime was shared, so also should have been the
penalty.
2. He founded the monastery [Pope's note].

3. "Irradiate" and "emblaze," meaning "adorn gloriously,"
both come from Milton.

Here bribed the rage of ill-requited Heav'n:
But such plain roofs as piety could raise,
140   And only vocal with the Maker's[4] praise.
In these lone walls (their day's eternal bound)
These moss-grown domes° with spiry turrets crowned,   *buildings*
Where awful arches make a noon-day night,
And the dim windows shed a solemn light;
145   Thy eyes diffused a reconciling ray,
And gleams of glory brightened all the day.
But now no face divine contentment wears,
'Tis all blank sadness, or continual tears.
See how the force of others' pray'rs I try
150   (Oh pious fraud of am'rous charity!)
But why should I on others' pray'rs depend?
Come thou, my father, brother,[5] husband, friend!
Ah let thy handmaid, sister, daughter, move,
And, all those tender names in one, thy love!
155   The darksome pines that o'er yon rocks reclined
Wave high, and murmur to the hollow wind,
The wandering streams that shine between the hills,
The grots that echo to the tinkling rills,
The dying gales that pant upon the trees,
160   The lakes that quiver to the curling breeze;
No more these scenes my meditation aid,
Or lull to rest the visionary maid:[6]
But o'er the twilight groves, and dusky caves,
Long-sounding isles, and intermingled graves,
165   Black Melancholy sits, and round her throws
A death-like silence, and a dread repose:
Her gloomy presence saddens all the scene,
Shades ev'ry flow'r, and darkens ev'ry green,
Deepens the murmur of the falling floods,
170   And breathes a browner horror on the woods.
     Yet here forever, ever must I stay;
Sad proof how well a lover can obey!
Death, only death, can break the lasting chain;
And here ev'n then, shall my cold dust remain,
175   Here all its frailties, all its flames resign,
And wait, till 'tis no sin to mix with thine.
     Ah wretch! believed the spouse of God in vain,
Confessed within the slave of love and man.
Assist me Heav'n! but whence arose that pray'r?
180   Sprung it from piety, or from despair?
Ev'n here, where frozen chastity retires,
Love finds an altar for forbidden fires.
I ought to grieve, but cannot what I ought;
I mourn the lover, not lament the fault;

---

4. The satirical tone of the previous lines prompts us to ask whether the "Maker" is God or Abelard.
5. "Father" and "brother" in the ecclesiastical, as well as emotional, sense. This also applies for "handmaid," "sister," and "daughter" in the following line.
6. One prone to visions.

185   I view my crime, but kindle at the view,
       Repent old pleasures, and solicit new:
       Now turned to Heav'n, I weep my past offense,
       Now think of thee, and curse my innocence.[7]
       Of all affliction taught a lover yet,
190   'Tis sure the hardest science° to forget!   knowledge
       How shall I lose the sin, yet keep the sense,
       And love th' offender, yet detest th' offense?
       How the dear object from the crime remove,
       Or how distinguish penitence from love?
195   Unequal task! a passion to resign,
       For hearts so touched, so pierced, so lost as mine.
       Ere such a soul regains its peaceful state,
       How often must it love, how often hate!
       How often, hope, despair, resent, regret,
200   Conceal, disdain—do all things but forget.
       But let Heav'n seize it, all at once 'tis fir'd,
       Not° touched, but rapt, not wakened, but inspired!   not only
       Oh come! oh teach me nature to subdue,
       Renounce my love, my life, myself—and you.
205   Fill my fond heart with God alone, for he
       Alone can rival, can succeed to thee.
           How happy is the blameless vestal's lot!
       The world forgetting, by the world forgot.
       Eternal sunshine of the spotless mind!
210   Each pray'r accepted, and each wish resigned;
       Labor and rest, that equal periods keep;
       "Obedient slumbers that can wake and weep";[8]
       Desires composed, affections ever ev'n,
       Tears that delight, and sighs that waft to Heav'n.
215   Grace shines around her with serenest beams,
       And whisp'ring angels prompt her golden dreams.
       For her th' unfading rose of Eden blooms,
       And wings of seraphs shed divine perfumes;
       For her the Spouse° prepares the bridal ring,   Christ
220   For her white virgins hymenaeals° sing;   wedding songs
       To sounds of heav'nly harps, she dies away,
       And melts in visions of eternal day.
           Far other dreams my erring soul employ,
       Far other raptures, of unholy joy:
225   When at the close of each sad, sorrowing day,
       Fancy restores what vengeance snatched away,
       Then conscience sleeps, and leaving nature free,
       All my loose soul unbounded springs to thee.
       O cursed, dear horrors of all-conscious° night!   all-knowing
230   How glowing guilt exalts the keen delight!

---

7. Cf. *Letters of Abelard and Heloise:* "Among those who
are wedded to God I serve a man. . . . I am here, I confess,
a sinner, but one who far from weeping for her sins, weeps
only for her lover. . . . Every object brings to my mind
what I ought to forget. . . . Even into the holy places
before the altar I carry with me the memory of our guilty
loves" (trans. Hughes, 120–124).
8. Line 16 from *Description of a Religious House,* by
Richard Crashaw (1612–1649).

Provoking demons all restraint remove,
And stir within me ev'ry source of love.
I hear thee, view thee, gaze o'er all thy charms,
And round thy phantom glue my clasping arms.
235   I wake—no more I hear, no more I view,
The phantom flies me, as unkind as you,
I call aloud; it hears not what I say;
I stretch my empty arms; it glides away:
To dream once more I close my willing eyes;
240   Ye soft illusions, dear deceits, arise!
Alas no more!—methinks we wandering go
Through dreary wastes, and weep each other's woe;
Where round some mold'ring tow'r pale ivy creeps,
And low-browed rocks hang nodding o'er the deeps.
245   Sudden you mount! you beckon from the skies;
Clouds interpose, waves roar, and winds arise.
I shriek, start up, the same sad prospect find,
And wake to all the griefs I left behind.[9]
       For thee the fates, severely kind, ordain
250   A cool suspense from pleasure and from pain;
Thy life a long, dead calm of fixed repose;
No pulse that riots, and no blood that glows.
Still as the sea, ere winds were taught to blow,
Or moving spirit bade the waters flow;
255   Soft as the slumbers of a saint forgiv'n,
And mild as opening gleams of promised Heaven.
       Come Abelard! for what hast thou to dread?
The torch of Venus burns not for the dead;
Nature stands checked; religion disapproves;
260   Ev'n thou art cold—yet Eloisa loves.
Ah hopeless, lasting flames! like those that burn
To light the dead, and warm th' unfruitful urn.[1]
       What scenes appear where'er I turn my view!
The dear ideas, where I fly, pursue,
265   Rise in the grove, before the altar rise,
Stain all my soul, and wanton in my eyes!
I waste the matin[2] lamp in sighs for thee,
Thy image steals between my God and me,
Thy voice I seem in ev'ry hymn to hear,
270   With ev'ry bead I drop too soft a tear.[3]
When from the censer clouds of fragrance roll,
And swelling organs lift the rising soul;
One thought of thee puts all the pomp to flight,
Priests, tapers, temples, swim before my sight:
275   In seas of flame my plunging soul is drowned,
While altars blaze, and angels tremble round.
       While prostrate here in humble grief I lie,

---

9. Cf. Pope's comic *Epistle to Miss Blount.*
1. The Romans attempted to supply tombs with inextin-
guishable fires.

2. Morning; Matins are the psalms sung at dawn.
3. Tears of love, not repentance.

Kind, virtuous drops just gath'ring in my eye,
While praying, trembling, in the dust I roll,
280 And dawning grace is opening on my soul:
Come, thou dar'st, all charming as thou art!
Oppose thyself to Heav'n; dispute° my heart;   *compete for*
Come, with one glance of those deluding eyes,
Blot out each bright idea of the skies.
285 Take back that grace, those sorrows, and those tears,
Take back my fruitless penitence and pray'rs,
Snatch me, just mounting, from the blest abode,
Assist the fiends and tear me from my God!
      No, fly me, fly me! far as Pole from Pole;
290 Rise Alps between us! and whole oceans roll!
Ah come not, write not, think not once of me,
Nor share one pang of all I felt for thee.
Thy oaths I quit,° thy memory resign,   *absolve*
Forget, renounce me, hate whate'er was mine.
295 Fair eyes, and tempting looks (which yet I view!)
Long loved, adored ideas! all adieu!
O grace serene! oh virtue heav'nly fair!
Divine oblivion of low-thoughted care!
Fresh blooming hope, gay daughter of the sky!
300 And faith, our early immortality![4]
Enter each mild, each amicable guest;
Receive, and wrap me in eternal rest!
      See in her cell sad Eloisa spread,
Propped on some tomb, a neighbor of the dead!
305 In each low wind methinks a spirit calls,
And more than echoes talk along the walls.
Here, as I watched the dying lamps around,
From yonder shrine I heard a hollow sound.
"Come, sister come!" (it said, or seemed to say)
310 "Thy place is here, sad sister come away!
Once like thy self, I trembled, wept, and prayed,
Love's victim then, though now a sainted maid:
But all is calm in this eternal sleep;
Here grief forgets to groan, and love to weep,
315 Ev'n superstition loses ev'ry fear:
For God, not man, absolves our frailties here."
      I come, I come! prepare your roseate bow'rs,
Celestial palms, and ever-blooming flow'rs.
Thither, where sinners may have rest, I go,
320 Where flames refined in breasts seraphic glow.
Thou, Abelard! the last sad office pay,
And smooth my passage to the realms of day:
See my lips tremble, and my eyeballs roll,
Suck my last breath, and catch my flying soul!
325 Ah no—in sacred vestments may'st thou stand,
The hallowed taper trembling in thy hand,

4. Faith seen as a foretaste of immortality.

Present the Cross before my lifted eye,
Teach me at once, and learn of° me to die.   *from*
Ah then, thy once-loved Eloisa see!
330   It will be then no crime to gaze on me.
See from my cheek the transient roses fly!
See the last sparkle languish in my eye!
Till ev'ry motion, pulse, and breath, be o'er;
And ev'n my Abelard be loved no more.
335   O death all-eloquent! you only prove
What dust we dote on, when 'tis man we love.
      Then too, when fate shall thy fair frame destroy,
(That cause of all my guilt, and all my joy)
In trance ecstatic may thy pangs be drowned,
340   Bright clouds descend, and angels watch thee round,
From opening skies may streaming glories shine,
And saints embrace thee with a love like mine.
      May one kind grave unite each hapless name,[5]
And graft my love immortal on thy fame.
345   Then, ages hence, when all my woes are o'er,
When this rebellious heart shall beat no more;
If ever chance two wandering lovers brings
To Paraclete's white walls, and silver springs,
O'er the pale marble shall they join their heads,
350   And drink the falling tears each other sheds,
Then sadly say, with mutual pity moved,
Oh may we never love as these have loved!
From the full choir when loud Hosanna's rise,
And swell the pomp of dreadful sacrifice,[6]
355   Amid that scene, if some relenting eye
Glance on the stone where our cold relics lie,
Devotion's self shall steal a thought from Heav'n,
One human tear shall drop, and be forgiv'n.
And sure if fate some future bard[7] shall join
360   In sad similitude of griefs to mine,
Condemned whole years in absence to deplore,
And image charms he must behold no more,
Such if there be, who loves so long, so well;
Let him our sad, our tender story tell;
365   The well-sung woes will soothe my pensive ghost;
He best can paint 'em, who shall feel 'em most.
c. 1716   1717

Epistle to Burlington

For years Pope planned to write a magnum opus, a "system of ethics in the Horatian way."
Though this ambitious project was never completed, some of its parts were written, including a
set of four verse letters that were intended to conclude the work. Pope himself called the

---

5. Abelard and Eloisa were interred in the same grave, or
in monuments adjoining, in the Monastery of the Paraclete [Pope's note].
6. The Mass, in which Christ's saving sacrifice is ritually

reenacted.
7. Pope himself; he probably refers to Lady Mary Wortley
Montagu, then traveling in the Middle East, with whom
he later quarreled and became estranged.

poems *Epistles to Several Persons*; a later editor dubbed them *Moral Essays*. Each work is a familiar letter in verse addressed to someone he knew well and admired. Richard Boyle, third Earl of Burlington (1695–1753), was a connoisseur and patron of the arts, and a capable architect who became a highly influential arbiter of polite taste in English building and landscape design. When first published in 1731, the poem declared on its title page that it was "occasioned by [Burlington's] publishing Palladio's designs of the baths, arches, theaters etc. of Ancient Rome." Burlington was partly responsible for leading an English revival of architecture modeled upon the designs of Andrea Palladio (1508–1580), and his house at Chiswick was a masterful example of the Palladian style. Pope contrasts Burlington's wise and discerning stewardship with the foolish prodigality of "Lord Timon," an emblem of bad taste and extravagant wastefulness. Though there has been much debate about the identity of Lord Timon and the real-life model for his gaudy estate, Timon (and his infamous villa) are most probably composite sketches of, among others, the Duke of Chandos (at Cannons), the Duke of Devonshire (at Chatsworth), and Robert Walpole (at Houghton)—all known for lavish displays of wealth more redolent of vulgar ostentation than aesthetic acumen.

Epistle 4. To Richard Boyle, Earl of Burlington

ARGUMENT

Of the use of riches. The vanity of expense in people of wealth and quality. The abuse of the word "taste," verse 13. That the first principle and foundation in this as in everything else is good sense, v. 40. The chief proof of it is to follow Nature, even in works of mere luxury and elegance. Instanced in architecture and gardening, where all must be adapted to the genius[1] and use of the place, and the beauties not forced into it, but resulting from it, v. 50. How men are disappointed in their most expensive undertakings, for want of this true foundation, without which nothing can please long, if at all, and the best examples and rules will but be perverted into something burdensome or ridiculous, v. 65, etc. to 92. A description of the false taste of magnificence, the first grand error of which is to imagine that greatness consists in the *size* and *dimension*,[2] instead of the *proportion* and *harmony* of the whole, v. 97, and the second, either in joining together parts incoherent, or too minutely resembling, or in the repetition of the same too frequently, v. 105, etc. A word or two of false taste in books, in music, in painting, even in preaching and prayer, and lastly in entertainments, v. 133, etc. Yet PROVIDENCE is justified in giving wealth to be squandered in this manner, since it is dispersed to the poor and laborious part of mankind, v. 169. [Recurring to what is laid down in the first book, Ep. 2[3] and in the Epistle preceding this, v. 159, etc.[4]] What are the proper objects of magnificence, and a proper field for the expense[5] of great men, v. 177, etc., and finally, the great and public works which become a prince, v. 191, to the end.

> 'Tis strange, the miser should his cares employ,
> To gain those riches he can ne'er enjoy:
> Is it less strange, the prodigal should waste
> His wealth, to purchase what he ne'er can taste?
> 5   Not for himself he sees, or hears, or eats:
> Artists must choose his pictures, music, meats:
> He buys for Topham[6] drawings and designs,

---

1. Character.
2. Extent.
3. Epistle 2 of Pope's *Essay on Man*.
4. Epistle 3, to Allen Lord Bathurst (1685–1775), *Of the Use of Riches*. Epistle 4 to Burlington was also sometimes

given this subtitle.
5. Expenditure.
6. Richard Topham (d. 1735), who was a "gentleman famous for a judicious collection of drawings" [Pope's note].

For Pembroke[7] statues, dirty gods,[8] and coins;
Rare monkish manuscripts for Hearne[9] alone,
10   And books for Mead, and butterflies for Sloane.[1]
Think we all these are for himself? no more
Than his fine wife, alas! or finer whore.
        For what has Virro[2] painted, built, and planted?
Only to show, how many tastes he wanted.
15   What brought Sir Visto's[3] ill got wealth to waste?
Some demon whispered, "Visto! have a taste."
Heav'n visits with a taste the wealthy fool,
And needs no rod but Ripley with a rule.[4]
See! sportive fate, to punish awkward pride,
20   Bids Bubo[5] build, and sends him such a guide:
A standing sermon,[6] at each year's expense,
That never coxcomb[7] reached magnificence!
        You[8] show us Rome was glorious, not profuse,
And pompous buildings once were things of use.
25   Yet shall (my Lord) your just, your noble rules
Fill half the land with imitating fools;
Who random drawings from your sheets shall take,
And of one beauty many blunders make;
Load some vain church with old theatric state,[9]
30   Turn arcs of triumph to a garden gate;
Reverse your ornaments, and hang them all
On some patched dog hole eked° with ends of wall,   °added to
Then clap four slices of pilaster[1] on't,
That, laced with bits of rustic,[2] makes a front.
35   Or call the winds through long arcades to roar,
Proud to catch cold at a venetian door;[3]
Conscious they act a true Palladian part,
And if they starve,[4] they starve by rules of art.
        Oft have you hinted to your brother peer,
40   A certain truth, which many buy too dear:
Something there is more needful than expense,
And something previous ev'n to taste—'tis sense:
Good sense, which only is the gift of Heav'n,
And though no science, fairly worth the sev'n:[5]

7. Thomas Herbert, eighth Earl of Pembroke (1656–1733).
8. Renaissance pseudo-antiquities.
9. Thomas Hearne (1678–1735), eminent medievalist.
1. Richard Mead (1673–1754) and Sir Hans Sloane (1660–1753), both eminent physicians; the former had a library of around 30,000 books, while the latter had "the finest collection in Europe of natural curiosities" [Pope's note].
2. The wealthy but despicable patron in Juvenal's Fifth Satire.
3. Vista: long, narrow view between rows of trees.
4. Thomas Ripley (d. 1758), "a carpenter employed by a First Minister [Robert Walpole], who raised him into an architect without any genius in the art" [Pope's note]; he worked on Walpole's hall at Houghton. His carpenter's "rule," or ruler, is also a principle which, if misapplied, would become a rod for the foolish Visto's back.
5. George Bubb Dodington (1691–1762); his mansion at Eastbury, Dorset, designed by Sir John Vanbrugh (whose

work Pope disliked), cost £140,000 to complete. "Bubo" is Latin for "owl."
6. The building silently instructs the viewer in gaudy taste.
7. Conceited fool.
8. Burlington, then publishing Palladio's *Antiquities of Rome*, and *The Designs of Inigo Jones*.
9. Design details from classical Roman amphitheaters.
1. Column joined to a wall.
2. A roughened, stone-like surface. The "front" is the entrance to the building.
3. The key unit of Palladio's design: a door with an arched top, framed by two smaller rectangular openings.
4. Both because of the cost of the building and the impractical way in which it is laid out.
5. The seven fields of knowledge since medieval times were grammar, rhetoric, logic (the Trivium), arithmetic, geometry, astronomy, and music (the Quadrivium).

45　　　A light, which in yourself you must perceive;
　　　　Jones and Le Nôtre[6] have it not to give.
　　　　　　To build, to plant, whatever you intend,
　　　　To rear the column, or the arch to bend,
　　　　To swell the terrace, or to sink the grot;[7]
50　　　In all, let Nature never be forgot.
　　　　But treat the goddess like a modest fair,
　　　　Nor° overdress, nor leave her wholly bare;　　　　　　　*neither*
　　　　Let not each beauty ev'rywhere be spied,
　　　　Where half the skill is decently° to hide.　　　　　　　*suitably*
55　　　He gains all points, who pleasingly confounds,
　　　　Surprises, varies, and conceals the bounds.
　　　　　　Consult the genius of the place[8] in all;
　　　　That tells the waters or° to rise, or fall,　　　　　　　*either*
　　　　Or helps th' ambitious hill the heav'n to scale,
60　　　Or scoops in circling theaters° the vale,　　　　　　*amphitheaters*
　　　　Calls in the country, catches opening glades,
　　　　Joins willing woods, and varies shades from shades,
　　　　Now breaks or now directs, th' intending lines;[9]
　　　　Paints as you plant, and, as you work, designs.
65　　　　　Still follow sense, of ev'ry art the soul,
　　　　Parts answ'ring parts shall slide into a whole,
　　　　Spontaneous beauties all around advance,
　　　　Start ev'n from difficulty, strike from chance;
　　　　Nature shall join you, time shall make it grow
70　　　A Work to wonder at—perhaps a Stowe.[1]
　　　　　　Without it, proud Versailles![2] thy glory falls;
　　　　And Nero's terraces desert their walls:[3]
　　　　The vast parterres° a thousand hands shall make,　　　*terraces*
　　　　Lo! COBHAM comes, and floats° them with a lake:　　　*floods*
75　　　Or cut wide views through mountains to the plain,
　　　　You'll wish your hill or sheltered seat again.
　　　　Ev'n in an ornament its place remark,°　　　　　　*consider*
　　　　Nor in an Hermitage set Dr. Clarke.[4]
　　　　　　Behold Villario's ten years' toil complete;
80　　　His quincunx darkens, his espaliers meet,[5]
　　　　The wood supports the plain, the parts unite,
　　　　And strength of shade contends with strength of light;
　　　　A waving glow his bloomy beds display,
　　　　Blushing in bright diversities of day,
85　　　With silver-quiv'ring rills meandered o'er—
　　　　Enjoy them, you! Villario can no more;
　　　　Tir'd of the scene parterres and fountains yield,
　　　　He finds at last he better likes a field.

6. Inigo Jones (1573–1652), the architect; André Le Nôtre (1613–1700), great French garden designer.
7. Grotto: an artificial cavern.
8. Both the classical guardian spirit and the character of the particular setting.
9. Lines that direct the viewer's eye.
1. The seat and gardens of Richard Temple, Viscount Cobham (1675–1749), highly praised in its day.
2. Louis XIV's palace, which had the most celebrated gardens in Europe until the advent of landscape gardening.
3. The Golden House of Nero, in Rome.
4. Samuel Clarke (1675–1729) was a distinguished philosopher and theologian. Queen Caroline's ornamental and frivolous "hermitage" in Richmond Park contained a bust of Clarke, among others.
5. Quincunx: group of five trees; espaliers: trees trained on latticework, against walls.

Through his young woods how pleased Sabinus strayed,
90   Or sat delighted in the thick'ning shade
With annual joy the red'ning shoots to greet,
Or see the stretching branches long to meet!
His Son's fine taste an op'ner vista loves,
Foe to the dryads° of his father's groves,   *wood nymphs*
95   One boundless green, or flourished carpet views,[6]
With all the mournful family of yews;[7]
The thriving plants ignoble broomsticks made,
Now sweep those alleys they were born to shade.
    At Timon's villa let us pass a day,
100   Where all cry out, "What sums are thrown away!"
So proud, so grand, of that stupendous air,
Soft and agreeable come never there.
Greatness, with Timon, dwells in such a draught
As brings all Brobdignag[8] before your thought.
105   To compass this, his building is a town,
His pond an ocean, his parterre a down:[9]
Who but must laugh, the master when he sees,
A puny insect, shiv'ring at a breeze!
Lo, what huge heaps of littleness around!
110   The whole, a labored quarry above ground.
Two cupids squirt before: a lake behind
Improves the keenness of the northern wind.[1]
His gardens next your admiration call,
On ev'ry side you look, behold the wall!
115   No pleasing intricacies intervene,
No artful wildness to perplex the scene;
Grove nods at grove, each alley has a brother,
And half the platform just reflects the other.
The suff'ring eye inverted Nature sees,
120   Trees cut to statues,[2] statues thick as trees,
With here a fountain, never to be played,
And there a summerhouse, that knows no shade;
Here Amphitrite[3] sails through myrtle[4] bow'rs;
There gladiators fight, or die, in flow'rs;
125   Unwatered see the drooping sea-horse mourn,
And swallows roost in Nilus' dusty urn.[5]
    My Lord advances with majestic mien,
Smit° with the mighty pleasure, to be seen: *struck*
But soft—by regular approach—not yet—
130   First through the length of yon hot terrace sweat,
And when up ten steep slopes you've dragged your thighs,
Just at his study door he'll bless your eyes.
    His study! with what authors is it stored?

6. The two extremes in parterres, which are equally faulty [Pope's note], the "boundless green" being a virtual field, while the "flourished carpet" is overladen with ornamental flowerbeds.
7. Trees usually planted in cemeteries; Pope's objection is that these evergreens are favored to the exclusion of "the nobler forest trees," now used for brooms.
8. The land of giants in Swift's *Gulliver's Travels*, filled with items too large to be used by normal humans.
9. Open uplands of southern England.
1. I.e., the landscaping has worsened, rather than mitigated, natural problems.
2. Cut into ornamental shapes.
3. A sea nymph, Poseidon's wife.
4. Myrtle was associated with Venus, goddess of love.
5. The river god's urn should obviously be pouring water.

parchment

In books, not authors, curious is my Lord;[6]
135   To all their dated backs[7] he turns you round,
These Aldus printed, those Du Suëil has bound.[8]
Lo some are vellum,° and the rest as good
For all his Lordship knows, but they are wood.
For Locke or Milton 'tis in vain to look,
140   These shelves admit not any modern book.
       And now the chapel's silver bell you hear,
That summons you to all the pride of pray'r:
Light quirks of music, broken and uneven,
Make the soul dance upon a jig to Heaven.
145   On painted ceilings you devoutly stare,
Where sprawl the saints of Verrio or Laguerre,[9]
On gilded clouds in fair expansion lie,
And bring all paradise before your eye.
To rest, the cushion and soft dean invite,
150   Who never mentions Hell to ears polite.[1]
       But hark! the chiming clocks to dinner call;
A hundred footsteps scrape the marble hall:
The rich buffet well-colored serpents grace,
And gaping Tritons[2] spew to wash your face.[3]

welcoming
ritual sacrifice

155   Is this a dinner? this a genial° room?
No, 'tis a temple, and a hecatomb.°
A solemn sacrifice, performed in state,
You drink by measure, and to minutes eat.
So quick retires each flying course, you'd swear
160   Sancho's dread doctor and his wand were there.[4]
Between each act the trembling salvers ring,
From soup to sweet-wine, and God bless the King.[5]
In plenty starving, tantalized in state,
And complaisantly helped to all I hate,
165   Treated, caressed, and tir'd, I take my leave,
Sick of his civil pride from morn to eve;
I curse such lavish cost, and little skill,
And swear no day was ever passed so ill.
       Yet hence the poor are clothed, the hungry fed;
170   Health to himself, and to his infants bread
The lab'rer bears: what his hard heart denies,
His charitable vanity supplies.
       Another age shall see the golden ear
Imbrown the slope, and nod on the parterre,

---

6. I.e., he is fussy about having books to decorate his shelves but does not care what the books contain.
7. Many delight chiefly in the elegance of the print or the binding [Pope's note]: some collected rare editions with "dated backs" stamped in gold, others, books in languages they could not read, while some simply painted books onto the upper shelves.
8. Aldus Manutius (1450–1515), Venetian printer; Augustin Desueil (1673–1746), Parisian bookbinder.
9. Antonio Verrio (1639–1707) and Louis Laguerre (1663–1721) had painted many ceilings in castles and stately homes.
1. This is a fact: a reverend Dean preaching at Court, threat-

ened the sinner with punishment in "a place he thought it not decent to name in so polite an assembly" [Pope's note].
2. Half human, half fish.
3. Taxes the incongruity of ornaments . . . where an open mouth ejects the water into a fountain, or where shocking images of serpents, etc. are introduced into grottos or buffets [Pope's note].
4. In Cervante's *Don Quixote* vol. 2, book 3, ch. 15, a doctor whisks food away before Sancho can eat it. The similarity to pantomime's conjuring tricks is reinforced by the equation of courses with "acts" in line 161.
5. Soup begins the meal, port wine ends it, with the traditional toast to the king.

175 Deep harvests bury all his pride has planned,
     And laughing Ceres[6] reassume the land.
     Who then shall grace, or who improve the soil?
     Who plants like BATHURST,[7] or who builds like BOYLE.[8]
     'Tis use alone that sanctifies expense,
180 And splendor borrows all her rays from sense.
        His Father's acres who enjoys in peace,
     Or makes his neighbors glad, if he increase;
     Whose cheerful tenants bless their yearly toil,
     Yet to their Lord owe more than to the soil;
185 Whose ample lawns are not ashamed to feed
     The milky heifer and deserving steed;
     Whose rising forests, not for pride or show,
     But future buildings, future navies grow:
     Let his plantations stretch from down to down,
190 First shade a country, and then raise a town.
        You too proceed! make falling arts your care,
     Erect new wonders, and the old repair,
     Jones and Palladio to themselves restore,
     And be whate'er Vitruvius[9] was before:
195 Till kings call forth th' idea's of your mind,
     Proud to accomplish what such hands designed,
     Bid harbors open, public ways extend,
     Bid temples,[1] worthier of the God, ascend;
     Bid the broad arch the dang'rous flood contain,
200 The mole projected break the roaring main;[2]
     Back to his bounds their subject sea command,
     And roll obedient rivers through the land;
     These honors, peace to happy Britain brings,
     These are imperial works, and worthy kings.

1730–1731   1731

from An Essay on Man

In Four Epistles to Henry St. John, Lord Bolingbroke[1]
Epistle 1

TO THE READER

As the epistolary way of writing hath prevailed much of late, we have ventured to
publish this piece composed some time since, and whose author chose this manner,

---

6. Roman goddess of agriculture.
7. Allen, Lord Bathurst, to whom Epistle 3, *Of the Use of
Riches*, is addressed.
8. Richard Boyle, Lord Burlington.
9. Marcus Vitruvius Pollio (1st century B.C.), whose book
on architecture was highly influential.
1. This poem was published in the year 1732, when some
of the new-built churches, by the Act of Queen Anne,
were ready to fall, being founded in boggy land . . . others
were vilely executed [i.e., built; Pope's note].
2. Burlington eventually helped oversee the building of
Westminster Bridge over the Thames, the design of
which had originally been left to "the carpenter [Ripley]
who would have made it a wooden one" [Pope's note].
1. "I believe," wrote Pope to his friend John Caryll, "that
there is not in the whole course of the Scripture any pre-

cept so often and so strongly inculcated, as the trust and
eternal dependence we ought to repose in that Supreme
Being who is our constant preserver and benefactor."
This is the theme of Pope's didactic and exhortatory
Essay on Man, whose four epistles were published anonymously over eleven months in 1733–1734. For Pope, "to
reason right is to submit" (line 164), not least because
humankind occupies a middle ground—between angels
and beasts—in a divinely ordered universe. Pope had
intended the *Essay on Man* and the four *Moral Essays*
(1731–1735) to be the first and last parts of a great poetic
sequence on the nature of humankind, though he never
completed the project. The *Essay* is addressed to Henry
St. John, first Viscount Bolingbroke (1678–1751), a leading Tory statesman and political writer whom Pope
described as "my guide, philosopher, and friend."

notwithstanding his subject was high and of dignity, because of its being mixed with argument which of its nature approacheth to prose. This,[2] which we first give the reader, treats of the Nature and State of MAN, with respect to the UNIVERSAL SYSTEM;[3] the rest will treat of him with respect to his OWN SYSTEM, as an individual, and as a member of society, under one or other of which heads all ethics are included.

As he imitates no man, so he would be thought to vie with no man in these Epistles, particularly with the noted author of two lately published;[4] but this he may most surely say: that the matter of them is such as is of importance to all in general, and of offense to none in particular.

THE DESIGN

Having proposed to write some pieces on human life and manners, such as (to use my lord Bacon's expression) "come home to men's business and bosoms,"[5] I thought it more satisfactory to begin with considering Man in the abstract, his Nature and his State, since, to prove any moral duty, to enforce any moral precept, or to examine the perfection or imperfection of any creature whatsoever, it is necessary first to know what condition and relation it is placed in, and what is the proper end and purpose of its being.

The science[6] of human nature is, like all other sciences, reduced to a few clear points: there are not many *certain truths* in this world. It is therefore in the anatomy of the mind as in that of the body: more good will accrue to mankind by attending to the large, open, and perceptible parts, than by studying too much such finer nerves and vessels, the conformations and uses of which will forever escape our observation. The disputes are all upon these last, and, I will venture to say, they have less sharpened the wits than the hearts of men against each other, and have diminished the practice more than advanced the theory of morality. If I could flatter myself that this Essay has any merit, it is in steering betwixt the extremes of doctrines seemingly opposite, in passing over terms utterly unintelligible, and in forming a temperate yet not inconsistent, and a short yet not imperfect system of ethics.

This I might have done in prose, but I chose verse, and even rhyme, for two reasons. The one will appear obvious: that principles, maxims, or precepts so written, both strike the reader more strongly at first, and are more easily retained by him afterwards. The other may seem odd, but is true: I found I could express them more shortly this way than in prose itself; and nothing is more certain, than that much of the force as well as grace of arguments or instructions depends on their conciseness. I was unable to treat this part of my subject more in detail without becoming dry and tedious, or more poetically, without sacrificing perspicuity to ornament, without wandering from the precision, or breaking the chain of reasoning. If any man can unite all these without diminution of any of them, I freely confess he will compass a thing above my capacity.

What is now published, is only to be considered as a general map of MAN, marking out no more than the greater parts, their extent, their limits, and their connection, but leaving the particular to be more fully delineated in the charts which are to follow. Consequently, these Epistles in their progress (if I have health and leisure to

---

2. I.e., the first Epistle.
3. I.e., within the cosmic order, ordained by God.
4. I.e., Pope himself, whose *Epistle to Bathurst* (1733) and the first *Imitation of Horace* (1733) had recently been published. The *Essay on Man* was published anonymously; Pope uses his little address to the reader both to adver-

tise his own work and to confuse his enemies about the identity of the poem's author.
5. From Bacon's Dedicatory Epistle in the collected edition of the *Essays* (1625).
6. Knowledge.

make any progress) will be less dry, and more susceptible of poetical ornament. I am here only opening the fountains, and clearing the passage. To deduce the rivers, to follow them in their course, and to observe their effects, may be a task more agreeable.

ARGUMENT

Of the Nature and State of Man, with respect to the UNIVERSE.

Of Man in the abstract.—I. That we can judge only with regard to our own system, being ignorant of the relations of systems and things, verses 17, etc. II. That Man is not to be deemed imperfect, but a being suited to his place and rank in the creation, agreeable to the general order of things, and conformable to ends and relations to him unknown, ver. 35, etc. III. That it is partly upon his ignorance of future events, and partly upon the hope of a future state, that all his happiness in the present depends, ver. 77, etc. IV. The pride of aiming at more knowledge, and pretending to more perfection, the cause of man's error and misery. The impiety of putting himself in the place of God, and judging of the fitness or unfitness, perfection or imperfection, justice or injustice of his dispensations, Ver. 113, etc. V. The absurdity of conceiting himself the final cause of the creation, or expecting that perfection in the *moral* world, which is not in the *natural*, Ver. 131, etc. VI. The unreasonableness of his complaints against Providence, while on the one hand he demands the perfections of the angels, and on the other the bodily qualifications of the brutes; though, to possess any of the sensitive faculties in a higher degree, would render him miserable, Ver. 173, etc. VII. That throughout the whole visible world, an universal order and gradation in the sensual and mental faculties is observed, which causes a subordination of creature to creature, and of all creatures to Man. The gradations of sense, instinct, thought, reflection, reason; that reason alone countervails all the other faculties, Ver. 207. VIII. How much farther this order and subordination of living creatures may extend, above and below us; were any part of which broken, not that part only, but the whole connected creation must be destroyed. Ver. 233. IX. The extravagance, madness, and pride of such a desire, Ver. 259. X. The consequence of all the absolute submission due to providence, both as to our present and future state, Ver. 281, etc. to the end.

Awake, my St. JOHN! leave all meaner° things   *base*
To low ambition, and the pride of kings.
Let us (since life can little more supply
Than just to look about us and to die)
5   Expatiate free[7] o'er all this scene of man;
A mighty maze! but not without a plan;
A wild, where weeds and flow'rs promiscuous° shoot,   *randomly mixed*
Or garden, tempting with forbidden fruit.
Together let us beat[8] this ample field,
10   Try what the open, what the covert yield;
The latent tracts, the giddy heights explore
Of all who blindly creep, or sightless soar;[9]
Eye nature's walks,° shoot folly as it flies,   *behaviors*
And catch the manners living as they rise;

---

7. Wander or speak unrestrainedly.
8. "Beat," "open," "covert" are all hunting terms: Pope imagines them to be searching out game by walking back

and forth across open and wooded land.
9. There is a middle way appropriate to man between ignorance and presumption.

15   Laugh where we must, be candid° where we can;   *generous*
      But vindicate the ways of God to Man.[1]

      1. Say first, of God above, or Man below,
      What can we reason, but from what we know?
      Of Man what see we, but his station here,
20   From which to reason, or to which refer?
      Through worlds unnumbered though the God be known,
      'Tis ours to trace him only in our own.
      He, who through vast immensity can pierce,
      See worlds on worlds compose one universe,
25   Observe how system into system runs,
      What other planets circle other suns,
      What varied being peoples° ev'ry star,   *inhabits*
      May tell why Heav'n has made us as we are.
      But of this frame the bearings, and the ties,
30   The strong connections, nice dependencies,
      Gradations just,[2] has thy° pervading soul   *the reader's*
      Looked through? or can a part contain the whole?
      Is the great chain,[3] that draws all to agree,
      And drawn supports, upheld by God, or thee?

35   2. Presumptuous Man! the reason wouldst thou find,
      Why formed so weak, so little, and so blind!
      First, if thou canst, the harder reason guess,
      Why formed no weaker, blinder, and no less!
      Ask of thy mother earth, why oaks are made
40   Taller or stronger than the weeds they shade?
      Or ask of yonder argent fields above,
      Why Jove's satellites[4] are less than Jove?
      Of systems possible, if 'tis confest
      That wisdom infinite must form the best,
45   Where all must full or not coherent be,[5]
      And all that rises, rise in due degree;
      Then, in the scale of reas'ning life, 'tis plain
      There must be, somewhere, such a rank as Man;
      And all the question (wrangle e'er so long)
50   Is only this, if God has placed him wrong?
      Respecting Man, whatever wrong we call,
      May, must be right, as relative to all.
      In human works, though labored on with pain,
      A thousand movements scarce one purpose gain;
55   In God's, one single can its end produce;
      Yet serves to second too some other use.
      So Man, who here seems principal alone,
      Perhaps acts second to some sphere unknown,
      Touches some wheel, or verges to some goal;

1. Cf. *Paradise Lost*, 1.24–26: "That to the highth of this great argument / I may assert eternal providence, / And justify the ways of God to men." Pope's mention of the "garden, tempting with forbidden fruit" (line 8) also calls to mind the opening lines of Milton's epic.
2. "Connections," "dependencies," and "gradations" were

key terms of the new sciences.
3. The Great Chain of Being linked all levels of creation, at the same time maintaining a fixed hierarchy.
4. Jupiter's moons. "Satellites" here has four syllables.
5. The Great Chain of Being could not be broken at any point.

'Tis but a part we see, and not a whole.
60
        When the proud steed shall know why Man restrains
    His fiery course, or drives him o'er the plains;
    When the dull ox, why now he breaks the clod,
    Is now a victim, and now Egypt's god:[6]
65 Then shall Man's pride and dullness comprehend
    His actions', passions', being's, use and end;
    Why doing, suff'ring, checked, impelled; and why
    This hour a slave, the next a deity.
        Then say not Man's imperfect, Heav'n in fault;
70 Say rather, Man's as perfect as he ought;
    His knowledge measured to his state and place,
    His time a moment, and a point his space.
    If to be perfect in a certain sphere,°   *area of influence*
    What matter, soon or late, or here or there?
75 The blest today is as completely so,
    As who began a thousand years ago.

        3. Heav'n from all creatures hides the book of fate,
    All but the page prescribed, their present state;
    From brutes what men, from men what spirits° know: *angels*
80 Or who could suffer being here below?
    The lamb thy riot° dooms to bleed today,   *extravagance*
    Had he thy reason, would he skip and play?
    Pleased to the last, he crops the flow'ry food,
    And licks the hand just raised to shed his blood.
85 Oh blindness to the future! kindly giv'n,
    That each may fill the circle marked by Heav'n;
    Who sees with equal eye, as God of all,
    A hero perish, or a sparrow fall,
    Atoms or systems° into ruin hurled,   *solar systems*
90 And now a bubble burst, and now a world.
        Hope humbly then; with trembling pinions soar;
    Wait the great teacher death, and God adore!
    What future bliss, he gives not thee to know,
    But gives that hope to be thy blessing now.
95 Hope springs eternal in the human breast:
    Man never *is*, but always to *be* blest:
    The soul, uneasy and confined from home,[7]
    Rests and expatiates in a life to come.
        Lo! the poor Indian, whose untutored mind
100 Sees God in clouds, or hears him in the wind;
    His soul proud science never taught to stray
    Far as the solar walk, or milky way;
    Yet simple nature to his hope has giv'n,
    Behind the cloud-topped hill, an humbler Heav'n;
105 Some safer world in depth of woods embraced,
    Some happier island in the watry waste,
    Where slaves once more their native land behold,

---

6. Apis, sacred bull of Memphis.   7. Away from its heavenly origin.

No fiends torment, no Christians thirst for gold![8]
To be, contents his natural desire,
110 He asks no angel's wing, no seraph's fire;[9]
But thinks, admitted to that equal sky,
His faithful dog shall bear him company.

    4. Go, wiser thou! and in thy scale of sense
Weigh thy opinion against providence;
115 Call imperfection what thou fancy'st such,
Say, here he gives too little, there too much;
Destroy all creatures for thy sport or gust,°   *appetite*
Yet cry, If Man's unhappy, God's unjust;
If Man alone engross not Heav'n's high care,
120 Alone made perfect here, immortal there:
Snatch from his hand the balance and the rod,
Rejudge his justice, be the God of God!
    In pride, in reas'ning pride, our error lies;
All quit their sphere, and rush into the skies.
125 Pride still is aiming at the blest abodes,
Men would be angels, angels would be gods.
Aspiring to be gods, if angels fell,
Aspiring to be angels, men rebel;
And who but wishes to invert the laws
130 Of ORDER, sins against th' Eternal Cause.

    5. Ask for what end th' heav'nly bodies shine,
Earth for whose use? Pride answers, "'Tis for mine:
For me kind Nature wakes her genial° pow'r,   *generating*
Suckles each herb, and spreads out ev'ry flow'r;
135 Annual for me, the grape, the rose renew
The juice nectareous, and the balmy dew;
For me, the mine a thousand treasures brings;
For me, health gushes from a thousand springs;
Seas roll to waft me, suns to light me rise;
140 My foot-stool earth, my canopy the skies."
    But errs not Nature from this gracious end,
From burning suns when livid deaths descend,
When earthquakes swallow, or when tempests sweep
Towns to one grave, whole nations to the deep?
145 "No" ('tis replied) "the first Almighty cause[1]
Acts not by partial, but by gen'ral laws;
Th' exceptions few; some change since all began,
And what created perfect?"—Why then Man?
If the great end be human happiness,
150 Then Nature deviates; and can Man do less?
As much that end a constant course requires
Of show'rs and sunshine, as of Man's desires;
As much eternal springs and cloudless skies,
As men for ever temp'rate, calm, and wise.

8. The Christian is meant to "thirst for God" (Psalm 42.2).

9. Seraphs were traditionally thought of as fiery.
1. God the Creator.

155   If plagues or earthquakes break not Heav'n's design,
        Why then a Borgia, or a Catiline?[2]
        Who knows but he, whose hand the light'ning forms,
        Who heaves old ocean, and who wings the storms,
        Pours fierce ambition in a Caesar's mind,
160   Or turns young Ammon[3] loose to scourge mankind?
        From pride, from pride, our very reas'ning springs;
        Account for moral as for nat'ral things:
        Why charge we Heav'n in those, in these acquit?
        In both, to reason right is to submit.
165   Better for us, perhaps, it might appear,
        Were there all harmony, all virtue here;
        That never air or ocean felt the wind;
        That never passion discomposed the mind:
        But all subsists by elemental strife;
170   And passions are the elements of life.
        The gen'ral ORDER, since the whole began,
        Is kept in Nature, and is kept in Man.

          6. What would this Man? Now upward will he soar,
        And little less than angel, would be more;
175   Now looking downwards, just as grieved appears
        To want the strength of bulls, the fur of bears.
        Made for his use all creatures if he call,
        Say what their use, had he the pow'rs of all?
        Nature to these, without profusion kind,
180   The proper organs, proper pow'rs assigned;
        Each seeming want compensated of course,[4]
        Here with degrees of swiftness, there of force;
        All in exact proportion to the state;
        Nothing to add, and nothing to abate.
185   Each beast, each insect, happy in its own;
        Is Heav'n unkind to Man, and Man alone?
        Shall he alone, whom rational we call,
        Be pleased with nothing, if not blessed with all?
          The bliss of Man (could pride that blessing find)
190   Is not to act or think beyond mankind;
        No pow'rs of body or of soul to share,
        But what his nature and his state can bear.
        Why has not Man a microscopic eye?
        For this plain reason, Man is not a fly.
195   Say what the use, were finer optics giv'n,
        T' inspect a mite, not comprehend the Heav'n?[5]
        Or touch, if tremblingly alive all o'er,
        To smart and agonize at ev'ry pore?
        Or quick effluvia[6] darting through the brain,

---

2. Cesare Borgia (1476–1507), an Italian duke from a notoriously ruthless family. Lucius Sergius Catiline (d. 62 B.C.) plotted unsuccessfully against the Roman state.
3. Alexander the Great, King of Macedonia (336–323 B.C.) and conqueror of Asia Minor, Syria, Egypt, Babylonia, and Persia.

4. As is fitting, in the normal course of events.
5. It was commonly believed that man alone of all the animals was able to look up to Heaven.
6. Epicurus (c.370–270 B.C.) and others believed that sensations reached the brain from the pores via streams of invisible particles.

200   Die of a rose in aromatic pain?
         If Nature thundered in his op'ning ears,
         And stunned him with the music of the spheres,
         How would he wish that Heav'n had left him still
         The whisp'ring zephyr,° and the purling rill?   *breeze*
205   Who finds not providence all good and wise,
         Alike in what it gives, and what denies?

       7. Far as creation's ample range extends,
         The scale of sensual, mental pow'rs ascends:
         Mark how it mounts, to Man's imperial race,
210   From the green myriads in the peopled grass:
         What modes of sight betwixt each wide extreme,
         The mole's dim curtain, and the lynx's beam:
         Of smell, the headlong lioness[7] between,
         And hound sagacious on the tainted[8] green:
215   Of hearing, from the life that fills the flood,
         To that which warbles through the vernal wood:
         The spider's touch, how exquisitely fine!
         Feels at each thread, and lives along the line:
         In the nice bee, what sense so subtly true
220   From pois'nous herbs extracts the healing dew:[9]
         How instinct varies in the grov'ling swine,
         Compared, half-reas'ning elephant, with thine:
         'Twixt that, and reason, what a nice barrier;[1]
         Forever sep'rate, yet forever near!
225   Remembrance and reflection how allied;
         What thin partitions sense from thought divide:
         And middle natures, how they long to join,
         Yet never pass th' insuperable line!
         Without this just gradation, could they be
230   Subjected these to those, or all to thee?
         The pow'rs of all subdued by thee alone,
         Is not thy reason all these pow'rs in one?

       8. See, through this air, this ocean, and this earth,
         All matter quick,° and bursting into birth.   *living*
235   Above, how high progressive life may go!
         Around, how wide! how deep extend below!
         Vast chain of being, which from God began,
         Natures ethereal, human, angel, Man,
         Beast, bird, fish, insect! what no eye can see,
240   No glass° can reach! from infinite to thee,   *magnifying glass*
         From thee to nothing!—On superior pow'rs
         Were we to press, inferior might on ours:
         Or in the full creation leave a void,
         Where, one step broken, the great scale's destroyed:
245   From nature's chain whatever link you strike,

---

7. Lions were, according to Pope, believed to hunt "by the ear, and not by the nostril."

8. Sagacious: of acute perception; tainted: i.e., with the smell of the hunted animal.

9. Honey had been thought to fall on flowers as dew and was used for medicinal purposes.

1. Fine distinction. "Barrier" is pronounced "bar-REAR."

Tenth or ten thousandth, breaks the chain alike.
　　And if each system in gradation roll,
Alike essential to th' amazing whole;
The least confusion but in one, not all
250　That system only, but the whole must fall.
Let earth unbalanced from her orbit fly,[2]
Planets and suns run lawless through the sky,
Let ruling angels from their spheres be hurled,[3]
Being on being wrecked, and world on world,
255　Heav'n's whole foundations to their center nod,
And Nature tremble to the throne of God:
All this dread ORDER break—for whom? for thee?
Vile worm!—oh madness, pride, impiety!

　　9. What if the foot, ordained the dust to tread,
260　Or hand to toil, aspired to be the head?
What if the head, the eye, or ear repined
To serve mere engines to the ruling mind?
Just as absurd for any part to claim
To be another, in this gen'ral frame:
265　Just as absurd, to mourn the tasks or pains
The great directing MIND of ALL ordains.
　　All are but parts of one stupendous whole,
Whose body, Nature is, and God the soul;
That, changed through all, and yet in all the same,
270　Great in the earth, as in th' ethereal frame,
Warms in the sun, refreshes in the breeze,
Glows in the stars, and blossoms in the trees,
Lives through all life, extends through all extent,
Spreads undivided, operates unspent,
275　Breathes in our soul, informs° our mortal part,　　　　　*permeates*
As full, as perfect, in a hair as heart;
As full, as perfect, in vile Man that mourns,
As the rapt seraph that adores and burns;
To him no high, no low, no great, no small;
280　He fills, he bounds, connects, and equals all.

　　10. Cease then, nor ORDER imperfection name:[4]
Our proper bliss depends on what we blame.
Know thy own point: This kind, this due degree
Of blindness, weakness, Heav'n bestows on thee.
285　Submit—In this, or any other sphere,
Secure to be as blest as thou canst bear:
Safe in the hand of one disposing Pow'r,
Or° in the natal, or the mortal hour.　　　　　　　　　　*either*
All nature is but art, unknown to thee;
290　All chance, direction, which thou canst not see;
All discord, harmony, not understood;[5]

---

2. Cf. *Paradise Lost* 7.242, where "Earth, self-balanced, on her center hung."
3. According to Thomas Aquinas (c.1225–1274), a sign of the end of the world.

4. I.e., do not call order imperfection.
5. Here, as earlier in the poem, Pope invokes the Horatian principle of *concordia discors* (Horace, *Epistles* 1.12.19), a harmony of opposites.

All partial evil, universal good:[6]
And, spite of pride, in erring reason's spite,
One truth is clear, "Whatever IS, is RIGHT."

1733

An Epistle from Mr. Pope, to Dr. Arbuthnot

The *Epistle to Dr. Arbuthnot*, perhaps the most relaxed and engaging of all Pope's verse letters, is addressed to John Arbuthnot (1667–1735), who was physician to Queen Anne, a close friend of Pope and Swift, a valued member of the Scriblerus Club, and principal author of the *Memoirs of the Extraordinary Life, Works, and Discoveries of Martinus Scriblerus*, published with Pope's *Works* in 1741. Samuel Johnson described Arbuthnot as "the most universal genius," for he was a fine satirist, a skillful physician, an amateur mathematician, and a capable poet. Pope's epistle is an apology both for himself and for the satirist's art, written against those who had attacked his "person, morals, and family." He asserts the social role of the poet, includes moving autobiographical passages, and powerfully assails his enemies. This Horatian epistle, to the friend whose satires had delighted Pope and whose care had helped preserve and prolong Pope's own frail health, was published just seven weeks before the doctor died.

An Epistle from Mr. Pope, to Dr. Arbuthnot

Neque sermonibus vulgi dederis te, nec in Praemiis humanis spem posueris rerum tuarum: suis te oportet illecebris ipsa virtus trahat ad verum decus. Quid de te alii loquantur, ipsi videant, sed loquentur tamen.[1]

Tully

Advertisement

This paper is a sort of Bill of Complaint, begun many years since, and drawn up by snatches, as the several occasions offered. I had no thoughts of publishing it, till it pleased some persons of rank and fortune [the authors of *Verses to the Imitator of Horace*, and of an *Epistle to a Doctor of Divinity from a Nobleman at Hampton Court*][2] to attack in a very extraordinary manner, not only my writings (of which being public the public judge) but my person, morals, and family, whereof to those who know me not, a truer information may be requisite. Being divided between the necessity to say something of myself, and my own laziness to undertake so awkward a task, I thought it the shortest way to put the last hand to this Epistle. If it have anything pleasing, it will be that by which I am most desirous to please, the *truth* and the *sentiment*; and if anything offensive, it will be only to those I am least sorry to offend, the *vicious* or the *ungenerous*.

Many will know their own pictures in it, there being not a circumstance but what is true; but I have, for the most part spared their *names*, and they may escape being laughed at, if they please.

I would have some of them know, it was owing to the request of the learned and candid friend to whom it is inscribed, that I make not as free use of theirs as they have done of mine. However, I shall have this advantage, and honor, on my side,

---

6. In a letter to John Caryll in 1718, Pope wrote that "true piety would make us know, that all misfortunes may as well be blessings."
1. You will not give yourself up to the flattery of the vulgar, nor hope for success in your affairs from mortal

hands; virtue herself will lead to true honor; see that you follow her guidance. What others see fit to say of you let them say (Cicero, *De Re Publica* 6.23).
2. Lady Mary Wortley Montagu (1689–1762) and John Hervey (1696–1743), Baron Hervey of Ickworth.

that whereas by their proceeding, any abuse may be directed at any man, no injury can possibly be done by mine, since a nameless character can never be found out, but by its *truth* and *likeness*.[3]

Shut, shut the door, good John![4] fatigued I said,
Tie up the knocker, say I'm sick, I'm dead,
The Dog-star[5] rages! nay 'tis past a doubt,
All Bedlam, or Parnassus,[6] is let out:
5   Fire in each eye, and papers in each hand,
They rave, recite, and madden[7] round the land.
　　What walls can guard me, or what shades can hide?
They pierce my thickets, through my grot[8] they glide,
By land, by water,[9] they renew the charge,
10   They stop the chariot, and they board the barge.
No place is sacred, not the church is free,
Ev'n Sunday shines no Sabbath-day to me:
Then from the Mint[1] walks forth the man of rhyme,
Happy! to catch me, just at dinner time.
15   　　Is here a parson, much bemused in beer,[2]
A maudlin poetess, a rhyming peer,
A clerk, foredoomed his father's soul to cross,
Who pens a stanza when he should engross?°   *copy documents*
Is there, who locked from ink and paper, scrawls
20   With desp'rate charcoal round his darkened walls?
All fly to Twit'nam,° and in humble strain   *Twickenham*
Apply to me, to keep them mad or vain.
Arthur,[3] whose giddy son neglects the laws,
Imputes to me and my damned works the cause:
25   Poor Cornus° sees his frantic wife elope,   *cuckold*
And curses wit, and poetry, and Pope.[4]
　　Friend to my life, (which did not you prolong,
The world had wanted many an idle Song)
What drop or nostrum° can this plague remove?   *medicines*
30   Or which must end me, a fool's wrath or love?
A dire dilemma! either way I'm sped,°   *hurried toward death*
If foes, they write, if friends, they read me dead.
Seized and tied down to judge, how wretched I!
Who can't be silent, and who will not lie;
35   To laugh were want of goodness and of grace,
And to be grave exceeds all pow'r of face.
I sit with sad civility, I read
With honest anguish, and an aching head;

---

3. I.e., its similarity to the original.
4. Pope's servant, John Serle.
5. Sirius, which appears in the heat of summer; Pope was finishing the poem in August 1734. The late summer was also the time for reciting poetry in classical Rome.
6. Bedlam (Bethlehem Hospital) was a London "lunatic" asylum; Parnassus was the mountain of the Muses.
7. A word Pope invented.
8. Pope's artificial grotto or cavern, his retreat, at Twickenham.
9. Pope's house at Twickenham was on the river Thames,

and could be reached by boat from London.
1. Debtors were safe from the law in Southwark, London; on Sunday there were no arrests anywhere.
2. Laurence Eusden (1688–1730), Poet Laureate and parson given to drink.
3. Arthur Moore; his son James Moore-Smythe had plagiarized from Pope's works.
4. Both the Pope and the author: as a nation, the British were preoccupied with the threat of Roman Catholicism without (from France and Spain) and within (from Catholics like Pope).

And drop at last, but in unwilling ears,
40   This saving counsel, "Keep your piece nine years."[5]
     Nine years! cries he, who high in Drury Lane[6]
Lulled by soft zephyrs° through the broken pane,   *breezes*
Rhymes ere he wakes, and prints before term ends,[7]
Obliged by hunger and request of friends:[8]
45   "The piece you think is incorrect: why take it,
I'm all submission, what you'd have it, make it."
     Three things another's modest wishes bound,°   *encompass*
My friendship, and a prologue,[9] and ten pound.
     Pitholeon[1] sends to me: "You know his Grace,
50   I want a patron; ask him for a place."°   *paid position*
Pitholeon libeled me—"but here's a letter
Informs you, sir, 'twas when he knew no better.
Dare you refuse him? Curl[2] invites to dine,
He'll write a Journal, or he'll turn divine."[3]
55   Bless me! a packet.—"'Tis a stranger sues,
A virgin tragedy, an orphan Muse."
If I dislike it, "Furies, death and rage!"
If I approve, "Commend it to the stage."
There (thank my stars) my whole commission ends,
60   The play'rs and I are, luckily, no friends.
Fired that the house° reject him, "'Sdeath I'll print it   *theater*
And shame the fools—your int'rest, sir, with Lintot."[4]
Lintot, dull rogue! will think your price too much.
"Not Sir, if you revise it, and retouch."
65   All my demurs but double his attacks,
At last he whispers "Do, and we go snacks."[5]
Glad of a quarrel, straight° I clap the door,   *immediately*
Sir, let me see your works and you no more.
     'Tis sung, when Midas' ears began to spring,[6]
70   Midas, a sacred person and a King),
His very Minister who spied them first,
(Some say his Queen) was forced to speak, or burst.
And is not mine, my friend, a sorer case,
When every coxcomb° perks° them in my face?   *fool / shoves*
75   "Good friend forbear! you deal in dang'rous things,
I'd never name Queens, Ministers, or Kings;
Keep close to ears,° and those let asses prick,[7]   *whisper it*
Tis nothing"—Nothing? if they bite and kick?
Out with it, Dunciad! let the secret pass,

---

5. Horace's advice to a poet eager to publish (*Ars Poetica*, lines 386–389).
6. A bad neighborhood where writers lived in garrets.
7. Law court terms were the preferred publishing seasons.
8. It is the second reason, rather than the first, that the aspiring poet gives in his prefaces.
9. To a play of his: a good way to show the public who your friends were.
1. The name taken from a foolish Poet at Rhodes [Pope's note].
2. Edmund Curll (1675–1747), a publisher notorious for commissioning hacks to write libelous journals, full of

"news and scandal."
3. Pope may have meant Leonard Welsted (1688–1747), who was planning a religious work.
4. Bernard Lintot (1675–1736), who published for Pope.
5. Share the profits.
6. King Midas grew ass's ears when he preferred Pan to Apollo in their music contest. One of those closest to him whispered the story to the earth, and it was in turn told by the reeds. Pope was also referring to that contemporary artistic dunce King George II, his wife Queen Caroline, and first minister Robert Walpole.
7. Presumably, their ears, as well as the poet.

80   That secret to each fool, that he's an ass:
      The truth once told (and wherefore should we lie?),
      The Queen of Midas slept, and so may I.
          You think this cruel? take it for a rule,
      No creature smarts so little as a fool.
85   Let peals of laughter, Codrus![8] round thee break,
      Thou unconcerned canst hear the mighty crack.[9]
      Pit, box and gall'ry in convulsions hurled,
      Thou stand'st unshook amidst a bursting world.
      Who shames a scribbler? break one cobweb through,
90   He spins the slight, self-pleasing thread anew;
      Destroy his fib, or sophistry; in vain,
      The creature's at his dirty work again;
      Throned in the center of his thin designs;
      Proud of a vast extent of flimsy lines.
95   Whom have I hurt? has poet yet, or peer,
      Lost the arched eyebrow, or Parnassian sneer?
      And has not Colley[1] still his Lord, and whore?
      His butchers Henley, his Freemasons Moore?[2]
      Does not one table Bavius[3] still admit?
100   Still to one bishop Philips[4] seem a wit?
      Still Sappho[5]—"Hold! for God's sake—you'll offend:
      No names—be calm—learn prudence of a friend:
      I too could write, and I am twice as tall,
      But foes like these!"—One flatt'rer's worse than all;
105   Of all mad creatures, if the learn'd are right,
      It is the slaver kills, and not the bite.
      A fool quite angry is quite innocent;
      Alas! 'tis ten times worse when they *repent*.

          One dedicates, in high heroic prose,
110   And ridicules beyond a hundred foes;
      One from all Grub Street[6] will my fame defend,
      And, more abusive, calls himself my friend.
      This prints my letters,[7] that expects a bribe,
      And others roar aloud, "Subscribe, subscribe."
115   There are, who to my person pay their court,
      I cough like Horace, and though lean, am short,
      Ammon's great son[8] one shoulder had too high,
      Such Ovid's nose, and "Sir! you have an eye—"
      Go on, obliging creatures, make me see

8. A poet, perhaps fictional, ridiculed by Virgil and Juvenal.
9. "Mighty crack" was a phrase used by Addison to describe the collapse of the world; Pope showed how inadequate he thought it both in *Peri Bathous* and here, where it signals the failure of a play.
1. Colley Cibber (1671–1757), actor, playwright, Poet Laureate; he replaced Lewis Theobald as the "hero" of *The Dunciad*, from where the "Parnassian sneer" comes.
2. John "Orator" Henley (1692–1756), a popular and unusual preacher, had set up an "oratory" in Newport Market, one of London's principal meat markets, causing enemies to claim that his audiences consisted only of ignorant butchers. James Moore-Smythe was a Freemason.
3. A bad poet who had attacked Virgil and Horace.
4. Ambrose Philips (c. 1675–1749), poet and secretary to the Bishop of Armagh.
5. Lady Mary Wortley Montagu, whom Pope had attacked previously under the name of this Greek lyric poet; from Arbuthnot's interjection, Pope seems to be implying that she was under Walpole's protection.
6. Home of literary hacks.
7. Forged or stolen (as Curll had in 1726).
8. Alexander the Great.

120 All that disgraced my betters, met in me:
Say for my comfort, languishing in bed,
"Just so immortal Maro° held his head:"   *Virgil*
And when I die, be sure you let me know
Great Homer died three thousand years ago.

125 Why did I write? what sin to me unknown
Dipped me in ink, my parents', or my own?
As yet a child, nor yet a fool to fame,
I lisped in numbers,° for the numbers came.   *verse, meter*
I left no calling for this idle trade,
130 No duty broke, no father disobeyed.
The Muse but served to ease some friend, not wife,
To help me through this long disease, my life,
To second, Arbuthnot! thy art and care,
And teach the being you preserved to bear.

135 But why then publish? Granville[9] the polite,
And knowing Walsh, would tell me I could write;
Well-natured Garth inflamed with early praise,
And Congreve loved, and Swift endured my lays;
The courtly Talbot, Somers, Sheffield read,
140 Ev'n mitered Rochester would nod the head,
And St. John's self (great Dryden's friends before)
With open arms received one poet more.
Happy my studies, when by these approved!
Happier their author, when by these beloved!
145 From these the world will judge of men and books,
Not from the Burnets, Oldmixons, and Cookes.[1]
  Soft were my numbers, who could take offense
While pure description held the place of sense?
Like gentle Fanny's[2] was my flow'ry theme,
150 A painted mistress, or a purling stream.
Yet then did Gildon[3] draw his venal quill;
I wished the man a dinner, and sat still:
Yet then did Dennis rave in furious fret;[4]
I never answered, I was not in debt:
155 If want provoked, or madness made them print,
I waged no war with Bedlam or the Mint.
  Did some more sober critic come abroad?
If wrong, I smiled; if right, I kissed the rod.[5]
Pains, reading, study, are their just pretense,

9. Pope associates himself (and Dryden) with a number of important figures, friends, and patrons: George Granville, Baron Lansdowne (1666–1735); William Walsh (1663–1708); Sir Samuel Garth (1661–1719); William Congreve; Jonathan Swift; Charles Talbot, Duke of Shrewsbury (1660–1718); John Lord Somers (1651–1721); Francis Atterbury, Bishop of Rochester (1662–1732); Henry St. John, Viscount Bolingbroke (1678–1751).
1. Thomas Burnet, John Oldmixon, and Thomas Cooke: "authors of secret and scandalous history" [Pope's note]; Pope is comparing the greatness of his friends with the small-mindedness of those who attacked him.

2. Lord Hervey, court Vice Chamberlain, whom Pope thought effeminate, and later satirizes as Sporus (lines 305ff.).
3. Charles Gildon (1665–1724) had attacked *The Rape of the Lock.* Pope insinuates that Gildon writes to keep poverty at bay.
4. John Dennis (1657–1734), had attacked Pope; both, Gildon and Dennis, Pope thought, had acted at the instigation of Addison.
5. Accepted their criticism; kissing a monarch's scepter or an official's staff was a ritual of submission to authority.

160   And all they want is spirit, taste, and sense.
  Commas and points they set exactly right,
  And 'twere a sin to rob them of their mite.
  Yet ne'er one sprig of laurel graced these ribalds,[6]
  From slashing Bentley down to piddling Tibalds.[7]
165   Each wight who reads not, and but scans and spells,
  Each word-catcher that lives on syllables,
  Ev'n such small critics some regard may claim,
  Preserved in Milton's or in Shakespeare's name.
  Pretty! in amber to observe the forms
170   Of hairs, or straws, or dirt, or grubs, or worms;
  The things, we know, are neither rich nor rare,
  But wonder how the devil they got there?
   Were others angry? I excused them too;
  Well might they rage; I gave them but their due.
175   A man's true merit 'tis not hard to find,
  But each man's secret standard in his mind,
  That casting-weight[8] pride adds to emptiness,
  This, who can gratify? for who can *guess*?
  The Bard[9] whom pilf'red pastorals renown,
180   Who turns a Persian tale for half a crown,[1]
  Just writes to make his barrenness appear,
  And strains from hard-bound brains eight lines a year:
  He, who still wanting though he lives on theft,
  Steals much, spends little, yet has nothing left:
185   And he, who now to sense, now nonsense leaning,
  Means not, but blunders round about a meaning:
  And he, whose fustian's° so sublimely bad,   *bombastic style*
  It is not poetry, but prose run mad:
  All these, my modest satire bad translate,
190   And owned, that nine such poets made a Tate.[2]
  How did they fume, and stamp, and roar, and chafe?
  And swear, not Addison himself was safe.
   Peace to all such! but were there one[3] whose fires
  True genius kindles, and fair fame inspires,
195   Blest with each talent and each art to please,
  And born to write, converse, and live with ease:
  Should such a man, too fond to rule° alone,   *of ruling*
  Bear, like the Turk, no brother near the throne,[4]
  View him with scornful, yet with jealous eyes,
200   And hate for arts that caused himself to rise;
  Damn with faint praise,[5] assent with civil leer,

6. Laurel: the poet's crown; ribalds: foolish jesters.
7. Richard Bentley (1662–1742), a classical scholar of great learning and bad temper, earned ridicule for his "corrected" edition of *Paradise Lost* (1732), while Lewis Theobald (1688–1744), sometime "hero" of *The Dunciad*, criticized Pope's edition of Shakespeare in his *Shakespeare Restored* (1726).
8. The weight that tips the balance.
9. Ambrose Philips wrote pastoral poems in imitation of Spenser and translated a book of *Persian Tales*. The fact that, in 1709, his pastorals were published in the same volume as Pope's occasioned a rivalry between the two poets.
1. A standard prostitute's charge.
2. Nahum Tate (1652–1715), playwright and poet.
3. Joseph Addison, here portrayed as Atticus, friend of Cicero. Pope respected Addison's abilities as a writer but did not like him or his politics.
4. Turkish rulers killed close relatives who might be potential rivals.
5. Cf. William Wycherley's prologue to *The Plain Dealer* (1677): "And, with faint praises, one another damn."

And without sneering, teach the rest to sneer;
Willing to wound, and yet afraid to strike,
Just hint a fault, and hesitate dislike;
205 Alike reserved to blame, or to commend,
A tim'rous foe, and a suspicious friend,
Dreading ev'n fools, by flatterers besieged,
And so obliging that he ne'er obliged;
Like Cato, give his little Senate laws,[6]
210 And sit attentive to his own applause;
While wits and templars° ev'ry sentence raise,   *young lawyers*
And wonder with a foolish face of praise.
Who but must laugh, if such a man there be?
Who would not weep, if Atticus were he!
215   What though my name stood rubric on the walls?
Or plastered posts, with claps in capitals?[7]
Or smoking forth, a hundred hawkers[8] load,
On wings of winds came flying all abroad?
I sought no homage from the race that write;
220 I kept, like Asian monarchs, from their sight:
Poems I heeded (now berhymed so long)
No more than thou, great George! a birthday song.[9]
I ne'er with wits or witlings passed my days,
To spread about the itch of verse and praise;
225 Nor like a puppy daggled° through the town,   *wandered*
To fetch and carry singsong up and down;
Nor at rehearsals sweat, and mouthed, and cried,
With handkerchief and orange[1] at my side:
But sick of fops, and poetry, and prate,
230 To Bufo left the whole Castalian State.[2]
    Proud, as Apollo on his forked hill,
Sat full-blown Bufo, puffed by ev'ry quill;
Fed with soft dedication all day long,
Horace and he went hand in hand in song.[3]
235 His library (where busts of poets dead
And a true Pindar stood without a head)[4]
Received of wits an undistinguished race,
Who first his judgment asked, and then a place:
Much they extolled his pictures, much his seat,°   *estate*
240 And flattered ev'ry day, and some days eat;
Till grown more frugal in his riper days,
He paid some bards with port, and some with praise,
To some a dry rehearsal was assigned,

6. Pope's prologue to Addison's play *Cato* (1713) included a version of this line. Now Pope turns the tables, and the noble Roman senator becomes the petty Addison, the senate, his coffeehouse clique.
7. Red lettering, or rubric, was often used by Lintot, Pope's publisher; "claps" were placards, pasted up around the city by booksellers.
8. Hawking by street criers was another way to publicize new works.
9. The Poet Laureate's official ode to the king.
1. Sold in the theaters for eating or throwing.

2. Poetry is the "Castalian State," named for the spring sacred to the Muses on Parnassus (the "forked hill"); it is left to "Bufo," a patron whose name derives from the Latin for toad and who was probably George Bubb Dodington (1691–1762).
3. Dodington, a patron of literature, had been given the place of Maecenas, patron of Virgil and Horace, in a recent translation from Horace's *Odes*.
4. In *Peri Bathous* (1728), Pope ridiculed those antiquaries who exhibited headless statues, claiming they were busts of great poets.

And others (harder still) he paid in kind.[5]
245   Dryden alone (what wonder?) came not nigh,
      Dryden alone escaped this judging eye:
      But still the great have kindness in reserve,
      He helped to bury whom he helped to starve.[6]
          May some choice patron bless each gray goose quill!
250   May ev'ry Bavius have his Bufo still!
      So, when a statesman wants a day's defense,
      Or envy holds a whole week's war with sense,
      Or simple pride for flatt'ry makes demands;
      May dunce by dunce be whistled off my hands!
255   Blest be the Great! for those they take away,
      And those they left me—For they left me Gay,[7]
      Left me to see neglected genius bloom,
      Neglected die! and tell it on his tomb;
      Of all thy blameless life the sole return
260   My verse, and Queensb'ry[8] weeping o'er thy urn!
      Oh let me live my own! and die so too!
      ("To live and die is all I have to do"):[9]
      Maintain a poet's dignity and ease,
      And see what friends, and read what books I please.
265   Above a patron, though I condescend
      Sometimes to call a minister my friend:
      I was not born for courts or great affairs,
      I pay my debts, believe, and say my pray'rs,
      Can sleep without a poem in my head,
270   Nor know, if Dennis be alive or dead.
          Why am I asked, what next shall see the light?
      Heav'ns! was I born for nothing but to write?
      Has life no joys for me? or (to be grave)
      Have I no friend to serve, no soul to save?
275   "I found him close with Swift"—"Indeed? no doubt"
      (Cries prating Balbus[1]) "something will come out."
      'Tis all in vain, deny it as I will.
      "No, such a genius never can lie still,"
      And then for mine obligingly mistakes
280   The first Lampoon Sir Will. or Bubo[2] makes.
      Poor guiltless I! and can I choose but smile,
      When ev'ry coxcomb knows me by my *style*?
          Cursed be the verse, how well soe'er it flow,
      That tends to make one worthy man my foe,
285   Give virtue scandal, innocence a fear,
      Or from the soft-eyed virgin steal a tear!
      But he, who hurts a harmless neighbor's peace,

5. I.e., he read or gave them his own poetry.
6. Mr. Dryden, after having liv'd in exigencies, had a magnificent funeral bestow'd upon him by the contributions of several persons of quality [Pope's note].
7. John Gay, poet, playwright, and friend of Pope; it was apparently his failure to win patronage that prompted him to write The Beggar's Opera (1728).

8. The Duke and Duchess of Queensberry were Gay's patrons.
9. Slightly adapted from Of Prudence (1668) by Sir John Denham.
1. A Roman lawyer.
2. Sir William Yonge (d. 1755) and Dodington.

Insults fall'n worth, or beauty in distress,
Who loves a lie, lame slander helps about,
290   Who writes a libel, or who copies out:
That fop whose pride affects a patron's name,
Yet absent, wounds an author's honest fame;
Who can your merit selfishly approve,
And show the sense of it, without the love;
295   Who has the vanity to call you friend,
Yet wants the honor injured to defend;[3]
Who tells whate'er you think, whate'er you say,
And, if he lie not, must at least betray:
Who to the Dean and silver bell can swear,
300   And sees at Cannons what was never there:[4]
Who reads but with a lust to misapply,
Make satire a lampoon, and fiction, lie.
A lash like mine no honest man shall dread,
But all such babbling blockheads in his stead.
305   Let Sporus[5] tremble—"What? that thing of silk,
Sporus, that mere white curd of ass's milk?
Satire or sense alas! can Sporus feel?
Who breaks a butterfly upon a wheel?"[6]
Yet let me flap this bug with gilded wings,
310   This painted child of dirt that stinks and stings;
Whose buzz the witty and the fair annoys,
Yet wit ne'er tastes, and beauty ne'er enjoys,
So well-bred spaniels civilly delight
In mumbling of the game they dare not bite.
315   Eternal smiles his emptiness betray,
As shallow streams run dimpling all the way.
Whether in florid impotence he speaks,
And, as the prompter breathes, the puppet squeaks;
Or at the ear of Eve,[7] familiar toad,
320   Half froth, half venom, spits himself abroad,
In puns, or politics, or tales, or lies,
Or spite, or smut, or rhymes, or blasphemies.
His wit all seesaw between that and this,
Now high, now low, now master up, now miss,
325   And he himself one vile antithesis.
Amphibious Thing! that acting either part,
The trifling head, or the corrupted heart!
Fop at the toilet,[8] flatt'rer at the board,°   *dining table*
Now trips a Lady, and now struts a Lord.
330   Eve's tempter thus the Rabbins° have expressed,   *Jewish scholars*
A cherub's face, a reptile all the rest;

---

3. I.e., lacks the honor when you are injured to defend
you.
4. I.e., who misapplies satirical references in Pope's *Epistle
to Burlington*. Pope was upset by the willful misreading of
"Timon's villa" in the poem as Cannons, estate of the
Duke of Chandos.
5. A boy, Nero's favorite sexual partner; here, Lord Her-

vey, confidante of Queen Caroline.
6. The rack, an instrument of torture.
7. In the fourth book of Milton [*Paradise Lost* 4.800] the
devil is represented in this posture [Pope's note]. "Eve" is
Queen Caroline, with whom Hervey is both familiar and
a familiar (a witch's pet).
8. Dressing table.

Beauty that shocks you, parts that none will trust,
Wit that can creep, and pride that licks the dust.
    Not fortune's worshipper, nor fashion's fool,
335 Not lucre's madman, nor ambition's tool,
Not proud, nor servile, be one poet's praise
That, if he pleased, he pleased by manly ways;
That flatt'ry, ev'n to kings, he held a shame,
And thought a lie in verse or prose the same:
340 That not in fancy's maze he wandered long,
But stooped° to truth, and moralized his song: *pounced upon*
That not for fame, but virtue's better end,
He stood° the furious foe, the timid friend,   *withstood*
The damning critic, half-approving wit,
345 The coxcomb hit, or fearing to be hit;
Laughed at the loss of friends he never had,
The dull, the proud, the wicked, and the mad;
The distant threats of vengeance on his head,
The blow unfelt, the tear he never shed;[9]
350 The tale revived, the lie so oft o'erthrown;
Th' imputed trash, and dullness not his own;
The morals blackened when the writings 'scape;
The libeled person, and the pictured shape;[1]
Abuse on all he loved, or loved him, spread,
355 A friend in exile, or a father, dead;
The whisper that to greatness still too near,
Perhaps, yet vibrates on his Sovereign's ear—
Welcome for thee, fair virtue! all the past:
For thee, fair virtue! welcome ev'n the last!
360   "But why insult the poor, affront the great?"
A knave's a knave, to me, in ev'ry state,
Alike my scorn, if he succeed or fail,
Sporus at court, or Japhet[2] in a jail,
A hireling scribbler, or a hireling peer,
365 Knight of the post[3] corrupt, or of the shire,
If on a pillory, or near a throne,
He gain his prince's ear, or lose his own.
    Yet soft by nature, more a dupe than wit,
Sappho[4] can tell you how this man was bit°   *deceived*
370 This dreaded sat'rist Dennis will confess
Foe to his pride, but friend to his distress:[5]
So humble, he has knocked at Tibbald's door,
Has drunk with Cibber, nay has rhymed for Moore.[6]
Full ten years slandered, did he once reply?
375 Three thousand suns went down on Welsted's lie:
To please a mistress, one aspersed his life;

---

9. *A Pop upon Pope* (1728) tried to humiliate Pope by pretending he had been whipped.
1. Pope was frequently vilified in print by his enemies. His deformity and Roman Catholicism were often mocked—he was even caricatured as a hunchbacked ape wearing the papal crown.
2. Japhet Crook, a forger.

3. A person who supported himself by giving false evidence.
4. Lady Mary Wortley Montagu hurt Pope, who had been very close to her, by switching loyalties to Hervey.
5. In Dennis's old age, Pope had publicly supported his work.
6. Or rather, Moore-Smythe plagiarized from him.

He lashed him not, but let her be his wife:
Let Budgell[7] charge low Grubstreet on his quill,
And write whate'er he pleased, except his will;
380 Let the two Curlls[8] of town and court, abuse
His father, mother, body, soul, and Muse.
Yet why? that father held it for a rule
It was a sin to call our neighbor fool,
That harmless mother thought no wife a whore,—
385 Hear this! and spare his family, James Moore!
Unspotted names! and memorable long,
If there be force in virtue, or in song.
    Of gentle blood (part shed in honor's cause,
While yet in Britain honor had applause)
390 Each parent sprung—"What Fortune, pray?"—Their own,
And better got than Bestia's[9] from the throne.
Born to no pride, inheriting no strife,
Nor marrying discord in a noble wife,
Stranger to civil and religious rage,
395 The good man walked innoxious through his Age.
No courts he saw, no suits would ever try,
Nor dared an oath, nor hazarded a lie:[1]
Unlearn'd, he knew no schoolman's subtle art,
No language, but the language of the heart.
400 By nature honest, by experience wise,
Healthy by temp'rance and by exercise:
His life, though long, to sickness past unknown,
His death was instant, and without a groan.
Oh grant me thus to live, and thus to die!
405 Who sprung from kings shall know less joy than I.
    O Friend!° may each domestic bliss be thine!   Arbuthnot
Be no unpleasing melancholy mine:
Me, let the tender office long engage
To rock the cradle of reposing age,
410 With lenient arts extend a mother's breath,[2]
Make languor smile, and smooth the bed of death,
Explore the thought, explain the asking eye,
And keep a while one parent from the sky!
On cares like these if length of days attend,
415 May Heav'n, to bless those days, preserve my friend,
Preserve him social, cheerful, and serene,
And just as rich as when he served a Queen![3]
Whether that blessing be denied, or giv'n,
Thus far was right, the rest belongs to Heav'n.
1731–1734   1735

7. Eustace Budgell (1686–1737); the *Grub Street Journal* accused him of forging the will of Dr. Matthew Tindal to make himself inheritor.
8. Pope uses Edmund Curll's name as a derogatory epithet for Hervey. Curll, an unscrupulous publisher, is attacked in *The Dunciad* and in Swift's *Verses on the Death of Dr. Swift.*
9. A Roman consul who accepted bribes for peace, sug-

gesting the Duke of Marlborough's rewards from Queen Anne.
1. Pope's father refused to take oaths against the Pope, which would have helped him avoid anti-Catholic measures.
2. Pope's mother died two years before the poem was published, but he retained these lines, written in 1731.
3. Arbuthnot had been physician to Queen Anne.

The Dunciad

Encouraged by Jonathan Swift, who spent some months with him at Twickenham in 1726, Pope produced two satires against "Dulness," bad writing, and the stupidity of "Dunces." *Peri Bathous, or the Art of Sinking in Poetry*, a prose treatise about how to write bad poetry, illustrated with many examples from Pope's contemporaries, was first published in 1728. Just two months later there appeared Pope's comic masterpiece, *The Dunciad*, in three books. Pope's pseudo-scholarly edition, *The Dunciad Variorum* (1729), intensified his attack on the hack writers of Grub Street and the proliferation of popular culture. In *The New Dunciad* (1742), the focus of Pope's contempt expand-ed from Grub Street to the pretentious, the ponderous, and the pedantic in its many forms. In 1743 Pope issued *The Dunciad in Four Books*, incorporating *The New Dunciad* as Book 4 of the poem, adding further mock-scholarly trappings, and transferring the conclusion of the three-book *Dunciad* to the end of Book 4; the "hero" of Books 1–3, Lewis Theobald (1688–1744), a minor writer and editor of Shakespeare, is replaced by the self-aggrandizing playwright and Poet Laureate Colly Cibber (1671–1757). In Book 4, the hero does nothing, and the climax of the poem is the goddess Dulness's infectious yawn which sends all the world into darkness and primeval chaos. For the reader, the actions of Dulness and her sychophants engender not sleep, but laughter.

from The Dunciad
from *Book the Fourth*

ARGUMENT

The poet being, in this book, to declare the completion of the prophecies mentioned at the end of the former,[1] makes a new invocation, as the greater poets are wont, when some high and worthy matter is to be sung. He shows the Goddess coming in her majesty, to destroy *Order* and *Science*,[2] and to substitute the *Kingdom of the Dull* upon earth. How she leads captive the Sciences, and silenceth the Muses; and what they be who succeed in their stead. All her children, by a wonderful attraction, are drawn about her, and bear along with them divers others, who promote her empire by connivance, weak resistance, or discouragement of arts, such as half-wits, tasteless admirers, vain pretenders, the flatterers of dunces, or the patrons of them. All these crowd round her; one of them offering to approach her, is driven back by a rival, but she commends and encourages both. The first who speak in form[3] are the geniuses[4] of the schools, who assure her of their care to advance her cause, by confining youth to words, and keeping them out of the way of real knowledge. Their address, and her gracious answer, with her charge[5] to them and the universities. The universities appear by their proper deputies, and assure her that the same method is observed in the progress of education; the speech of Aristarchus[6] on this subject. They are driven off by a band of young gentlemen returned from travel with their tutors, one of whom delivers to the Goddess, in a polite oration, an account of the whole conduct and fruits of their travels, presenting to her at the same time a young nobleman perfectly accomplished. She receives him graciously, and indues him with the happy quality of *want of shame*. She sees loitering about her a number of indolent persons abandoning

---

1. Book 3 of *The Dunciad* concludes with an oracle fore-telling that the goddess Dulness and her sons shall tri-umph in the theaters, the court, and the universities.
2. Knowledge.
3. Formally.
4. Guardian deities.
5. Commission, instruction of duties.

6. Aristarchus of Samothrace (c. 217–145 B.C.), a scholar who "corrected" the poems of Homer; he represents a severe and short-sighted critic. In a preface added to *The Dunciad in Four Books* (1743), he is named "Richard Aristarchus" and clearly represents Richard Bentley, the scholar and critic who, in 1732, published a disastrous "corrected" version of Milton's *Paradise Lost*.

all business and duty, and dying with laziness; to these approaches the antiquary Annius,[7] entreating her to make them virtuosos,[8] and assign them over to him. But Mummius,[9] another antiquary, complaining of his fraudulent proceeding, she finds a method to reconcile their difference. Then enter a troop of people fantastically adorned, offering her strange and exotic presents. Amongst them, one stands forth and demands justice on another, who had deprived him of one of the greatest curiosities in Nature; but he justifies himself so well, that the Goddess gives them both her approbation. She recommends to them to find proper employment for the indolents before-mentioned, in the study of butterflies, shells, birds' nests, moss, etc. but with particular caution not to proceed beyond trifles, to any useful or extensive views of Nature, or of the Author of Nature. Against the last of these apprehensions, she is secured by a hearty address from the Minute Philosophers and Freethinkers,[1] one of whom speaks in the name of the rest. The youth thus instructed and principled are delivered to her in a body, by the hands of Silenus, and then admitted to taste the cup of the Magus her high priest, which causes a total oblivion of all obligations, divine, civil, moral, or rational. To these her adepts she sends priests, attendants, and comforters, of various kinds; confers on them Orders and Degrees; and then dismissing them with a speech, confirming to each his privileges[2] and telling what she expects from each, concludes with a yawn of extraordinary virtue,[3] the progress and effects whereof on all orders of men, and the consummation of all, in the restoration of night and chaos, conclude the poem.

[THE GODDESS COMING IN HER MAJESTY]

Yet, yet a moment, one dim ray of light
Indulge, dread chaos, and eternal night!
Of darkness visible[4] so much be lent,
As half[5] to show, half veil the deep intent.
5   Ye pow'rs! whose mysteries restored I sing,
To whom Time bears me on his rapid wing,
Suspend a while your force inertly strong,
Then take at once the poet and the song.
     Now flamed the Dog-star's unpropitious ray,[6]
10 Smote ev'ry brain, and withered ev'ry bay;[7]
Sick was the sun, the owl forsook his bow'r,
The moon-struck prophet felt the madding hour:
Then rose the seed of chaos, and of night,
To blot out order, and extinguish light,
15 Of dull and venal a new world to mold,
And bring Saturnian days[8] of lead and gold.

---

7. A monk, famous for his forgeries.
8. Men knowledgeable in trivial subjects or antique curiosities.
9. A Roman general, who burned Corinth.
1. Petty philosophers and those who rejected orthodox religious dogma in favor of rational inquiry.
2. From this point, the rest of the Argument was added in 1743, describing the new ending added at the same time.
3. Power.
4. Cf. Milton's description of Hell in *Paradise Lost* 1.62–65: "yet from those flames / No light, but rather darkness visible / Served only to discover sights of woe, / Regions of sorrow."

5. This is a great propriety, for a dull poet can never express himself otherwise than by halves or imperfectly [Pope's note].
6. Sirius, the Dog-star, is most visible at the end of summer, the time at which poetry recitals used to take place in classical Rome.
7. The laurel leaves symbolic of poetic success.
8. Saturn's many associations are played on here: Saturnalia was the Roman festival of misrule; while the age of Saturn was the Golden Age, Saturn also symbolized lead, these two metals respectively representing venality (corruption) and dullness.

She mounts the throne: her head a cloud concealed,
In broad effulgence all below revealed[9]
('Tis thus aspiring Dulness ever shines)
20   Soft on her lap her laureate son reclines.
Beneath her footstool, Science groans in chains,
And Wit dreads exile, penalties, and pains.
There foamed rebellious Logic, gagged and bound,
There, stripped, fair Rhet'ric languished on the ground;
25   His blunted arms by Sophistry are born,[1]
And shameless Billingsgate her robes adorn.
Morality, by her false guardians drawn,
Chicane in furs, and Casuistry in lawn,[2]
Gasps, as they straiten° at each end the cord,   *tighten*
30   And dies, when Dulness gives her Page[3] the word.

[THE GENIUSES OF THE SCHOOLS]

135   Now crowds on crowds around the Goddess press,
Each eager to present the first address.[4]
Dunce scorning dunce beholds the next advance,
But fop shows fop superior complaisance.
When lo! a specter[5] rose, whose index hand
140   Held forth the virtue of the dreadful wand;
His beavered brow° a birchen garland wears,   *beaver hat*
Dropping with infant's blood, and mother's tears.[6]
O'er ev'ry vein a shudd'ring horror runs;
Eton and Winton[7] shake through all their sons.
145   All flesh is humbled, Westminster's bold race[8]
Shrink, and confess the genius° of the place: *guardian deity*
The pale boy-senator[9] yet tingling stands,
And holds his breeches close with both his hands.
Then thus: "Since man from beast by words is known,
150   Words are man's province, words we teach alone.
When reason doubtful, like the Samian letter,[1]
Points him two ways, the narrower is the better.
Placed at the door of learning, youth to guide,
We never suffer it to stand too wide.
155   To ask, to guess, to know, as they commence,
As fancy opens the quick springs of sense,
We ply the memory, we load the brain,
Bind rebel wit, and double chain on chain,

---

9. Pope glosses this line: "The higher you climb, the more you show your arse."
1. The quibbling reasoning of Sophistry replaces Logic, while Billingsgate (the slang of fish sellers) replaces Rhetoric.
2. Legal trickery wears a judge's ermine robes, while the moral quibbler wears a bishop's fine linen.
3. Sir Francis Page, the "hanging judge," is linked with "Mutes or Pages" given the task of "strangling state criminals in Turkey" [Pope's note].
4. Written congratulations.
5. Dr. Richard Busby (1605–1695), headmaster of Westminster School, famed for instilling discipline as well as

learning: the "dreadful wand" is his birch cane.
6. Cf. *Paradise Lost* 1.392–393. "First Moloch, horrid king besmeared with blood / Of human sacrifice, and parents' tears. " In the Ancient Near East, the cult of Moloch practiced child sacrifice.
7. Eton and Winchester, two schools influenced by Busby.
8. The many graduates of the top schools who went on to be parliamentarians (at Westminster).
9. Young member of Parliament.
1. The letter "Y", emblem of the choice between the paths of virtue and vice.

160
Confine the thought, to exercise the breath;[2]
And keep them in the pale of words[3] till death.
Whate'er the talents, or howe'er designed,
We hang one jingling padlock on the mind:[4]
A poet the first day, he dips his quill;
And what the last? a very poet still.

165
Pity! the charm works only in our wall,
Lost, lost too soon in yonder House or Hall."[5]

[YOUNG GENTLEMEN RETURNED FROM TRAVEL]

275
In flowed at once a gay embroidered race,
And titt'ring pushed the pedants off the place:
Some would have spoken, but the voice was drowned
By the French horn, or by the op'ning° hound.   *baying*
The first came forwards, with as easy mien,

280
As if he saw St. James's° and the Queen.   *the palace*
When thus th' attendant orator[6] begun.
"Receive, great Empress! thy accomplished son:
Thine from the birth, and sacred° from the rod,   *spared*
A dauntless infant! never scared with God.

285
The sire saw, one by one, his virtues wake:
The mother begged the blessing of a rake.[7]
Thou gav'st that ripeness, which so soon began,
And ceased so soon, he ne'er was boy, nor man.
Through school and college, thy kind cloud o'ercast,

290
Safe and unseen the young Aeneas past:[8]
Thence bursting glorious, all at once let down,°   *released*
Stunned with his giddy larum° half the town.   *noise*
Intrepid then, o'er seas and lands he flew:
Europe he saw, and Europe saw him too.

295
There all thy gifts and graces we display,
Thou, only thou, directing all our way!
To where the Seine, obsequious as she runs,
Pours at great Bourbon's feet her silken sons;[9]
Or Tiber, now no longer Roman, rolls,

300
Vain of Italian arts, Italian souls:[1]
To happy convents, bosomed deep in vines,
Where slumber abbots, purple as their wines:
To isles of fragrance, lily-silvered vales,
Diffusing languor in the panting gales:°   *light winds*

---

2. By obliging them to get the classic poets by heart, which furnishes them with endless matter for conversation, and verbal amusement for their whole lives [Pope's note].

3. I.e., within the boundaries of pedantic learning.

4. For youth being used like packhorses and beaten on under a heavy load of words, lest they should tire, their instructors contrive to make the words jingle in rhyme and meter [Pope's note].

5. They can no longer compose once they leave the school for the parliamentary or legal professions, in the House of Commons or Westminster Hall.

6. The "lac'd governor from France" who had entered earlier with "whore" and "pupil" (line 272).

7. She hoped he would become a rake (an arrogant young libertine).

8. Aeneas was hidden in a cloud by Venus when entering Carthage.

9. Bourbon: Louis XIV, so absolute a monarch that even the rivers are "obsequious" (servile).

1. The poetic and martial might of the Roman Empire had degenerated into the effeminacy and shallowness of the Italian states.

305   To lands of singing, or of dancing slaves,
       Love-whisp'ring woods, and lute-resounding waves.
       But chief her shrine where naked Venus keeps,
       And cupids ride the Lion of the Deeps;[2]
       Where, eased of fleets, the Adriatic main°   sea
310   Wafts the smooth eunuch and enamored swain.
       Led by my hand, he sauntered Europe round,
       And gathered ev'ry vice on Christian ground;
       Saw ev'ry court, heard ev'ry king declare
       His royal sense, of op'ra's or the fair;[3]
315   The stews° and palace equally explored,   brothels
       Intrigued with glory, and with spirit whored;
       Tried all *hors d'oeuvres*, all *liqueurs* defined,
       Judicious drank, and greatly-daring dined;
       Dropped the dull lumber of the Latin store,[4]
320   Spoiled his own language, and acquired no more;
       All classic learning lost on classic ground;
       And last turned *Air*, the echo of a sound![5]
       See now, half-cured, and perfectly well-bred,
       With nothing but a solo in his head;
325   As much estate, and principle, and wit,
       As Jansen, Fleetwood, Cibber[6] shall think fit;
       Stol'n from a duel, followed by a nun,
       And, if a borough choose him, not undone;[7]
       See, to my country happy I restore
330   This glorious youth, and add one Venus[8] more.
       Her too receive (for her my soul adores)
       So may the sons of sons of sons of whores
       Prop thine, O Empress! like each neighbor throne,
       And make a long posterity thy own."
335   Pleased, she accepts the hero, and the dame,
       Wraps in her veil, and frees from sense of shame.

[THE MINUTE PHILOSOPHERS AND THE CONSUMMATION OF ALL]

       Then thick as locusts black'ning all the ground,
       A tribe, with weeds and shells fantastic crowned,
       Each with some wond'rous gift approached the Pow'r,
400   A nest, a toad, a fungus, or a flow'r.
       But far the foremost, two, with earnest zeal,
       And aspect ardent to the throne appeal.
           The first thus opened: "Hear thy suppliant's call,
       Great Queen, and common mother of us all!

---

2. The winged lion of Venice, a city-state known previously for its naval and trading might, known now as "the brothel of Europe."
3. Britain's king, George II, was notorious for his interest in women and song.
4. His classical learning.
5. Yet less a body than Echo itself; for Echo reflects sense or words at least, this gentleman only airs and tunes [Pope's note].

6. Three very eminent persons, all managers of plays [the first at gambling, the latter two in the theater], who, though not [school] governors by profession, had, each in his way, concerned themselves in the education of youth . . . [Pope's note].
7. If elected to Parliament, he could not be arrested for debt.
8. A prostitute he brings back with him.

405 Fair from its humble bed I reared this flow'r,[9]
Suckled, and cheered, with air, and sun, and show'r,
Soft on the paper ruff its leaves I spread,
Bright with the gilded button tipped its head,
Then throned in glass, and named it CAROLINE:[1]
410 Each maid cried, charming! and each youth, divine!
Did Nature's pencil ever blend such rays,
Such varied light in one promiscuous blaze?
Now prostrate! dead! behold that Caroline:
No maid cries, charming! and no youth, divine!
415 And lo the wretch! whose vile, whose insect lust
Laid this gay daughter of the spring in dust.
Oh punish him, or to th' Elysian shades[2]
Dismiss my soul, where no carnation fades."[3]
     He ceased, and wept. With innocence of mein,
420 Th' accused stood forth, and thus addressed the Queen.
     "Of all th' enameled race,° whose silv'ry wing   *butterflies*
Waves to the tepid zephyrs° of the spring,   *breezes*
Or swims along the fluid atmosphere,
Once brightest shined this child of heat and air.
425 I saw, and started from its vernal bow'r
The rising game,[4] and chased from flow'r to flow'r.
It fled, I followed; now in hope, now pain;
It stopped, I stopped; it moved, I moved again.[5]
At last it fixed, 'twas on what plant it pleased,
430 And where it fixed, the beauteous bird° I seized: *winged thing*
Rose or carnation was below by care;
I meddle, Goddess! only in my sphere.
I tell the naked fact without disguise,
And to excuse it need but show the prize;
435 Whose spoils this paper[6] offers to your eye,
Fair ev'n in death! this peerless *butterfly*."
     "My sons!" (she answered) "both have done your parts:
Live happy both, and long promote our arts.
But hear a mother, when she recommends
440 To your fraternal care, our sleeping friends.[7]
The common soul, of heav'n's more frugal make,
Serves but to keep fools pert, and knaves awake:
A drowsy watchman, that just gives a knock,
And breaks our rest, to tell us what's a clock.
445 Yet by some object every brain is stirred;

9. The attempt to produce the perfect carnation was a contemporary obsession among amateur scientists (or "virtuosi") and compulsive gardeners.
1. Queen Caroline, wife of George II, patron of gardeners and artists. Pope relates that "one ambitious Gardner at Hammersmith . . . caused his favorite [bloom] to be painted on his sign, with this inscription, 'This is My Queen Caroline.'"
2. The classical paradise.
3. Cf. 1 Peter 1.4: for the believer, there is "an inheritance incorruptible, and undefiled, and that fadeth not

away, reserved in heaven."
4. As would a hunter of bigger game.
5. Pope here alludes to *Paradise Lost* 4.462–63, in which Eve becomes fascinated with her own reflection, a passage that in turn alludes to the story of Narcissus in Ovid's *Metamorphoses*. Pope thus obliquely comments on the insubstantial character and self-absorption of the butterfly hunter.
6. On which the butterfly is mounted.
7. The other inhabitants of Dulness's court.

The dull may waken to a hummingbird;
The most recluse, discreetly opened find
Congenial matter in the cockle kind;
The mind, in metaphysics at a loss,
450   May wander in a wilderness of moss;[8]
The head that turns° at superlunar things,   *turns away*
Poised with a tail, may steer on Wilkins' wings.[9]
       "O! would the sons of men once think their eyes
And reason giv'n them but to study *flies?*
455   See Nature in some partial narrow shape,
And let the author of the whole escape:
Learn but to trifle; or, who most observe,
To wonder at their maker, not to serve."
       "Be that my task" (replies a gloomy clerk,[1]
460   Sworn foe to myst'ry,[2] yet divinely dark;
Whose pious hope aspires to see the day
When moral evidence[3] shall quite decay,
And damns implicit faith, and holy lies,
Prompt to impose, and fond to dogmatize):
465   "Let others creep by timid steps, and slow,
On plain experience lay foundations low,
By common sense to common knowledge bred,
And last, to Nature's cause through Nature led.
All-seeing in thy mists, we want no guide,
470   Mother of arrogance, and source of pride!
We nobly take the high priori road,[4]
And reason downward, till we doubt of God:
Make Nature still encroach upon his plan;
And shove him off as far as e'er we can:
475   Thrust some mechanic cause into his place;
Or bind in matter, or diffuse in space.[5]
Or, at one bound o'er-leaping all his laws,
Make God man's image, man, the final cause,[6]
Find virtue local, all relation scorn,[7]
480   See all in *Self*, and but for self be born:
Of nought so certain as our *Reason* still,
Of nought so doubtful as of *Soul* and *Will*.
Oh hide the God still more! and make us see
Such as Lucretius[8] drew, a God like thee:

---

8. Of which the naturalists count above three hundred species [Pope's note].

9. John Wilkins (1614–1672), bishop and first secretary of the Royal Society; he "entertain'd the extravagant hope of a possibility to fly to the Moon; which has put some volatile geniuses upon making wings for that purpose" [Pope's note].

1. Pope may be punning on the word clerk (pronounced "clark" and meaning one in holy orders) to refer to Samuel Clarke (1675–1729), an Anglican theologian who could not accept the mystery of the Trinity (though otherwise he was orthodox). Pope sees him as an exponent of rational theology: it is his religious skepticism that makes him "gloomy."

2. Religious mystery requiring faith.

3. Evidence able to be assessed by reason or common sense.

4. Arguing *a priori*, from a prior or assumed truth: here, a conception of God that will not stand up to testing in the real, natural world, which instead takes over his role.

5. The first of these follies is that of Descartes; the second of Hobbes; the third of some succeeding philosophers [Pope's note].

6. Human pride in being God's final, perfect creation leads man to put his desires over God's plan.

7. Without God's absolute order, moral relativism rules relations between cultures and individuals.

8. Materialist Roman philosopher, 1st century B.C.; the next two lines are adapted from his *De Rerum Natura*, 2. 646ff.

485 Wrapped up in self, a God without a thought,
Regardless of our merit or default.
Or that bright image to our fancy draw,
Which Theocles[9] in raptured vision saw,
While through poetic scenes the genius roves,
490 Or wanders wild in academic groves;
That NATURE our society adores,
Where Tindal dictates, and Silenus snores."[1]
        Roused at his name, up rose the bousy° sire,   *drowsy*
And shook from out his pipe the seeds of fire;[2]
495 Then snapped his box,° and stroked his belly down: *snuffbox*
Rosy and rev'rend, though without a gown.[3]
Bland and familiar to the throne he came,
Led up the youth, and called the Goddess "Dame."
Then thus. "From priestcraft happily set free,
500 Lo! ev'ry finished son returns to thee:
First slave to words, then vassal to a name,[4]
Then dupe to party; child and man the same;
Bounded by nature, narrowed still by art,
A trifling head, and a contracted heart.
505 Thus bred, thus taught, how many have I seen,
Smiling on all, and smiled on by a Queen.
Marked out for honors, honored for their birth,
To thee the most rebellious things on earth:
Now to thy gentle shadow all are shrunk,
510 All melted down, in pension, or in punk![5]
So K * so B * * sneaked into the grave,[6]
A monarch's half, and half a harlot's slave.
Poor W * * nipped in folly's broadest bloom,[7]
Who praises now? his chaplain on his tomb.
515 Then take them all, oh take them to thy breast!
Thy magus,[8] Goddess! shall perform the rest."
        With that, a WIZARD OLD his cup extends;
Which who so tastes, forgets his former friends,
Sire, ancestors, himself. One casts his eyes
520 Up to a star, and like Endymion dies:[9]

9. A philosopher featured in Shaftesbury's *The Moralists* (1709), who here worships his "genius," nature.
1. Matthew Tindal (1657–1733), a famous deist (i.e., one who bases belief in God solely upon reason, rejecting revelation). Silenus: "an Epicurean philosopher [who] sings the principles of that philosophy in his drink" [Pope's note], associated with Thomas Gordon, Commissioner of the Wine for Walpole's government.
2. In Epicurean language, atoms.
3. Silenus wears no priest's gown because he is usually naked.
4. A recapitulation of the whole course of modern education described in this book, which confines youth to the study of words only in schools, subjects them to the authority of systems in the universities, and deludes them with the names of party distinctions in the world. All equally concurring to narrow the understanding, and establish slavery and error in literature, philosophy, and politics. The whole finished in modern free-thinking; the completion of whatever is vain, wrong, and destructive to the happiness of mankind, as it establishes self-love for the sole principle of action [Pope's note].
5. Paid to keep quiet by Walpole's government, or interested only in whoring.
6. Possibly the Duke of Kent and Earl of Berkeley, both honored as Knights of the Garter, though Pope's joke here is that these "honor'd" men cannot be identified with certainty.
7. Possibly the dissolute young Earl of Warwick, though the obscurity of the reference is again part of Pope's point.
8. The high priest or wizard of the goddess Dulness may be Walpole.
9. The star and feather were insignia of Knights of the Garter; the star was also worn by Knights of the Bath. Loved by the Moon, Endymion was kept in endless slumber by her.

A feather shooting from another's head,
Extracts his brain, and principle is fled,
Lost is his God, his country, ev'rything;
And nothing left but homage to a king!
525   The vulgar herd turn off to roll with hogs,[1]
To run with horses, or to hunt with dogs;
But, sad example! never to escape
Their infamy, still keep the human shape.

But she, good Goddess, sent to ev'ry child
530   Firm impudence, or stupefaction mild;
And straight succeeded, leaving shame no room,
Cibberian forehead, or Cimmerian gloom.[2]

Kind self-conceit to some her glass° applies,   *mirror*
Which no one looks in with another's eyes:
535   But as the flatt'rer or dependant paint,
Beholds himself a patriot, chief, or saint.

On others int'rest her gay liv'ry° flings,   *servants' uniform*
Int'rest, that waves on party-colored[3] wings:
Turned to the sun, she casts a thousand dyes,
540   And, as she turns, the colors fall or rise.

Others the Siren Sisters[4] warble round,
And empty heads console with empty sound.
No more, alas! the voice of fame they hear,
The balm of Dulness trickling in their ear.
545   Great C**, H**, P**, R**, K*,[5]
Why all your toils? your sons have learned to sing.
How quick ambition hastes to ridicule!
The sire is made a peer, the son a fool.

On some, a priest succinct in amice white[6]
550   Attends; all flesh is nothing in his sight!
Beeves, at his touch, at once to jelly turn,[7]
And the huge boar is shrunk into an urn:
The board with specious miracles he loads,
Turns hares to larks, and pigeons into toads.
555   Another (for in all what one can shine?)
Explains the *seve* and *verdeur* of the vine.[8]
What cannot copious sacrifice atone?[9]
Thy truffles, Perigord! thy hams, Bayonne!
With French libation, and Italian strain,

---

1. The wizard's cup has the transformative powers of the witch Circe; but while she changed men to beasts and left them their minds, here the minds are changed while the bodies remain human.
2. The Cimmerians lived in Homer's far-western land of darkness, where Odysseus entered the underworld.
3. Meaning both multicolored, and colored according to party political allegiance.
4. Italian opera singers.
5. Although possible identifications have been made for these men, Pope's joke is that their sons, despite having

the advantages of birth, earned no place for themselves in history, causing the "great" family names to fall into obscurity.
6. The priest's amice (a linen vestment) becomes the cook's apron.
7. The chef performs priestly miracles, turning beef to jelly and carving meat into odd shapes.
8. Different qualities of wine.
9. French regional foods are sacrificed to the goddess, accompanied by Italian singing.

560 Wash Bladen white, and expiate Hays's stain.
　　Knight lifts the head,[1] for what are crowds undone
　　To three essential partridges in one?[2]
　　Gone ev'ry blush, and silent all reproach,
　　Contending princes mount them in their coach.
565 　　Next bidding all draw near on bended knees,
　　The Queen confers her *Titles* and *Degrees*.
　　Her children first of more distinguished sort,
　　Who study Shakespeare at the Inns of Court,[3]
　　Impale a glowworm, or vertù[4] profess,
570 Shine in the dignity of F. R. S.[5]
　　Some, deep Freemasons,[6] join the silent race
　　Worthy to fill Pythagoras's place:
　　Some botanists, or florists at the least,
　　Or issue members of an annual feast.
575 Nor past the meanest unregarded, one
　　Rose a Gregorian, one a Gormogon.[7]
　　The last, not least in honor or applause,
　　Isis and Cam made Doctors of her Laws.[8]
　　　Then blessing all, "Go children of my care!
580 To practice now from theory repair.
　　All my commands are easy, short, and full:
　　My sons! be proud, be selfish, and be dull.
　　Guard my prerogative, assert my throne:
　　This nod confirms each privilege your own.
585 The cap and switch[9] be sacred to his Grace;
　　With staff and pumps[1] the Marquis lead the race;
　　From stage to stage the licensed Earl may run,[2]
　　Paired with his fellow charioteer the sun;
　　The learned Baron butterflies design,°　　　　　　　　　*sketch*
590 Or draw to silk arachne's subtle line;[3]
　　The Judge to dance his brother Sergeant[4] call;
　　The Senator at cricket urge the ball;
　　The Bishop stow (pontific luxury!)
　　An hundred souls of turkeys in a pie;[5]

---

1. Bladen and Hays were gamblers; Robert Knight, cashier of the South Sea Company, fled England when the company collapsed in 1720, leaving many ruined. All three "lived with the utmost magnificence at Paris, and kept open tables, frequented by persons of the first quality of England, and even by Princes of the blood of France" [Pope's note].
2. Two partridges were used to make the sauce for the third; alluding to the mystery of the Trinity.
3. When they should be studying law.
4. An interest in antiquities and artistic curios; hence "virtuoso."
5. Fellow of the Royal Society, as many noble virtuosos were.
6. Where taciturnity is the only essential qualification, as it was one of the chief of the disciples of Pythagoras

[Pope's note]. The Freemasons were often deists and free-thinkers, who adapted religious rituals in meetings devoted to secular fellowship and philsophical inquiry.
7. Societies founded in ridicule of the Freemasons.
8. Oxford and Cambridge gave honorary degrees.
9. Jockeys' equipment, awarded here to followers of racing.
1. These footman's items were popular with young gentlemen.
2. The Earl of Salisbury had a license to drive a stage-coach.
3. Making stockings out of spider's webs had been attempted.
4. The barrister; the call of sergeants involved pompous, dancelike ceremony.
5. As did the Bishop of Durham.

595   The sturdy Squire to Gallic masters stoop,[6]
    And drown his lands and manors in a soup.
    Others import yet nobler arts from France,
    Teach kings to fiddle, and make Senates dance.[7]
    Perhaps more high some daring son[8] may soar,
600   Proud to my list to add one monarch more;
    And nobly conscious, princes are but things
    Born for first ministers, as slaves for kings,
    Tyrant supreme! shall three estates command,[9]
    And MAKE ONE MIGHTY DUNCIAD OF THE LAND!"
605   More she had spoke, but yawned—all nature nods:
    What Mortal can resist the yawn of gods?[1]
    Churches and chapels instantly it reached;
    (St. James's first, for leaden Gilbert[2] preached)
    Then catched the schools; the Hall scarce kept awake;
610   The Convocation[3] gaped, but could not speak:
    Lost was the nation's sense,[4] nor could be found,
    While the long solemn unison went round:
    Wide, and more wide, it spread o'er all the realm;
    Ev'n Palinurus[5] nodded at the helm:
615   The vapor mild o'er each committee crept;
    Unfinished treaties in each office slept;
    And chiefless armies dozed out the campaign;
    And navies yawned for orders on the main.[6]
      O Muse! relate (for you can tell alone,
620   Wits have short memories, and dunces none)
    Relate, who first, who last resigned to rest;
    Whose heads she partly, whose completely blest;
    What charms could faction, what ambition dull,
    The venal quiet, and entrance the dull;
625   'Till drowned was sense, and shame, and right, and wrong—
    O sing, and hush the nations with thy song![7]
* *
    In vain, in vain,—the all-composing hour
    Resistless falls: The Muse obeys the pow'r.
    She comes! she comes! the sable throne behold
630   Of Night Primaeval, and of Chaos old!
    Before her, Fancy's gilded clouds decay,
    And all its varying rainbows die away.

---

6. Even the traditionally conservative country Squires bowed to French fashions, like eating soup.
7. After their prince [Pope's note], as Lilliputian courtiers had to in *Gulliver's Travels* 1.3.
8. Walpole, whose unprecedented post of "first minister" gave him virtual control of the country from 1721 till he was ousted in 1742.
9. The three estates of nobility, clergy, and commoners, all of which Walpole controlled by various means.
1. This verse is truly Homerical, as is the conclusion of the Action, where the great Mother composes all, in the same manner at the period of the Odyssey [Pope's note].
2. Dr. John Gilbert, Dean of Exeter.
3. Assembly of the clergy.
4. The House of Commons, "justly called the sense of the

nation" [Pope's note].
5. Aeneas's helmsman, who falls asleep and drowns; here Robert Walpole, steering the state aimlessly.
6. The sea; referring to governmental delays during the war with Spain.
7. To this couplet, which concluded *The New Dunciad* (1742), Pope added a final note: "It is impossible to lament sufficiently the loss of the rest of this poem, just at the opening of so fair a scene as the invocation seems to promise. It is to be hoped however that the poet completed it, and that it will not be lost to posterity. . . ." The thirty lines of the poem which follow were moved from the ending of the three-book *Dunciad* (1728) to *The Dunciad, In Four Books* (1743).

Wit shoots in vain its momentary fires,
The meteor drops, and in a flash expires.
635 As one by one, at dread Medea's strain,[8]
The sick'ning stars fade off th' ethereal plain;
As Argus' eyes by Hermes' wand oppressed,[9]
Closed one by one to everlasting rest;
Thus at her felt approach, and secret might,
640 Art after Art goes out, and all is night.
See skulking Truth to her old cavern fled,
Mountains of casuistry° heaped o'er her head!   *false reasoning*
Philosophy, that leaned on Heav'n before,
Shrinks to her second cause,[1] and is no more.
645 Physic of Metaphysic begs defense,
And Metaphysic calls for aid on Sense![2]
See Mystery to Mathematics fly![3]
In vain! they gaze, turn giddy, rave, and die.
Religion blushing veils her sacred fires,
650 And unawares Morality expires.
Nor public flame, nor private, dares to shine;
Nor human spark is left, nor glimpse divine!
Lo! thy dread empire, CHAOS! is restored;
Light dies before thy uncreating word:[4]
655 Thy hand, great Anarch![5] lets the curtain fall;
And Universal Darkness buries All.

c. 1741   1742

+→ ⊰✦⊱ ←+

Lady Mary Wortley Montagu
1689–1762

In learning, literature, and travel, Lady Mary Wortley Montagu outdistanced virtually all of her contemporaries. Born Mary Pierrepont, she acquired her title at age one (when her father became an earl), lost her mother at age three, and immersed herself throughout her youth in the Roman classics, fervently pursuing a plan of self-education at odds with the conventional domesticating agenda (dancing, drawing, social graces) laid out for young women of her rank. For a time in her teens she aspired to implement the idea set forth by the feminist Mary Astell, of founding a convent consecrated to women's learning. In 1712 she married, against her father's wishes, a Whig Member of Parliament named Edward Wortley Montagu, after conducting with him a wary, carefully reasoned courtship mostly by means of letters. When he was appointed Ambassador to Turkey four years later, she accompanied him, and was fascinated by

---

8. In Seneca's play *Medea*, the witch attempts to revenge herself for Jason's desertion by causing stars to fall and the sun to halt in its course.
9. Argus had a hundred eyes, enabling him to guard Io against Jupiter's advances. Jupiter, however, sent Mercury (Hermes) to charm Argus to sleep and kill him.
1. The world is now explained by natural causes.
2. Natural science turns to theoretical philosophy, which in turn looks back to empiricism.

3. Divine revelation is threatened by "certain defenders of religion [who] attempted to show that the mysteries of religion may be mathematically demonstrated" [Pope's note].
4. Reversing the order of the creation of the world in Genesis, and restoring chaos.
5. A ruler with no political authority; one who promotes disorder and confusion.

what she saw: by the Turkish practice of inoculating against smallpox, which (having survived the disease herself) she successfully championed in England at her return; by the gaps and continuities between British and Turkish culture, on which she reported eloquently in missives home. Her *Turkish Embassy Letters*, which she compiled from her writings during this sojourn for publication after her death, remain the foundation of her fame.

Her life as a writer yielded other riches, just now beginning to be explored. She wrote essays, including a *Spectator* for Addison and Steele and a later periodical series of her own (1737–1738). She produced short fiction and a comedy but worked more steadily at verse, collaborating with Alexander Pope on some poems and combating him in others, after their friendship had disintegrated into a round of bitter, witty recriminations. Most plentifully she wrote letters, sharp and searching, adroitly tailored to please her wide array of correspondents.

Montagu's spate of accomplishment made her alert to the constrictions of gender. "There is hardly a character in the world," she wrote at age twenty, "more liable to universal ridicule than that of a Learned Woman." Women, she counseled, should know much but hide their knowledge, lest they lose out on the comforts of love, marriage, and social ease. Deeply attentive to the burdens imposed on women and the tactics available to them, Montagu's idiosyncratic feminism earned esteem from her predecessor Astell, and from many who came after.

Idiosyncrasy exacted costs, in the form of that "ridicule" she had early anticipated, and in the breakdown of important relationships. Her marriage failed, as did a passionate love affair (again largely epistolary) with the bisexual Italian writer Francesco Algarotti. Montagu lived her last twenty-five years mostly in Italy. In retrospect, her self-removal looks like part of a lifelong strategy. Montagu had always held it crucial to keep some distance from her culture's assumptions in order to see them clearly, to critique them, to change or expunge their operations in herself and in the world. The title she chose for her periodical series, *The Nonsense of Common Sense*, encapsulates her lifelong conviction. By the eccentricity of her self-education, the remoteness of her travels and her residences, the originality of her thought and conduct, the amused acerbity of her style, Montagu kept her distance and found her voice.

from The Turkish Embassy Letters[1]
To Lady ———[2]
[ON THE TURKISH BATHS]

Adrianople, 1 April 1717

I am now got into a new world where everything I see appears to me a change of scene, and I write to your Ladyship with some content of mind, hoping at least that you will find the charm of novelty in my letters and no longer reproach me that I tell you nothing extraordinary. I won't trouble you with a relation of our tedious journey, but I must not omit what I saw remarkable at Sophia, one of the most beautiful towns in the Turkish Empire and famous for its hot baths that are resorted to both for diversion and health. I stopped here one day on purpose to see them. Designing to go

---

1. The text of the *Turkish Embassy Letters* comes not from the actual letters Montagu sent while on her travels but from two manuscript books in which she combined portions of her letters and travel journals with new prose to produce a hybrid account of the trip, which she intended for posthumous publication. In 1724 Montagu lent the volumes to Mary Astell, who inscribed into the second a preface addressed to future readers: ". . . I confess I am malicious enough to desire that the world should see to how much better purpose the *ladies* travel than their

lords, and that whilst it is surfeited with male travels [i.e., travel-books], all in the same tone and stuffed with the same trifles, a *lady* has the skill to strike out a new path and to embellish a worn out subject with variety of fresh and elegant entertainment . . . Let us freely own the superiority of this sublime genius as I do in sincerity of my soul, pleased that a *woman* triumphs, and proud to follow in her train."

2. In the manuscript, Montagu supplies no name for this person, who may be a fictive "recipient."

incognito, I hired a Turkish coach. These *voitures* are not at all like ours, but much more convenient for the country, the heat being so great that glasses[3] would be very troublesome. They are made a good deal in the manner of the Dutch coaches, having wooden lattices painted and gilded, the inside being painted with baskets and nosegays of flowers, intermixed commonly with little poetical mottoes. They are covered all over with scarlet cloth, lined with silk and very often richly embroidered and fringed. This covering entirely hides the persons in them, but may be thrown back at pleasure and the ladies peep through the lattices. They hold four people very conveniently, seated on cushions, but not raised.

In one of these covered wagons I went to the bagnio[4] about ten o'clock. It was already full of women. It is built of stone in the shape of a dome with no windows but in the roof, which gives light enough. There was five of these domes joined together, the outmost being less than the rest and serving only as a hall where the porteress stood at the door. Ladies of quality generally give this woman the value of a crown or ten shillings, and I did not forget that ceremony. The next room is a very large one, paved with marble, and all round it raised two sofas of marble, one above another. There were four fountains of cold water in this room, falling first into marble basins and then running on the floor in little channels made for that purpose, which carried the streams into the next room, something less than this, with the same sort of marble sofas, but so hot with steams of sulphur proceeding from the baths joining to it, 'twas impossible to stay there with one's clothes on. The two other domes were the hot baths, one of which had cocks of cold water turning into it to temper it to what degree of warmth the bathers have a mind to.

I was in my traveling habit, which is a riding dress, and certainly appeared very extraordinary to them, yet there was not one of 'em that showed the least surprise or impertinent curiosity, but received me with all the obliging civility possible. I know of no European court where the ladies would have behaved themselves in so polite a manner to a stranger.

I believe in the whole there were two hundred women, and yet none of those disdainful smiles or satiric whispers that never fail in our asemblies when anybody appears that is not dressed exactly in fashion. They repeated over and over to me, *uzelle, pek uzelle*, which is nothing but "charming, very charming." The first sofas were covered with cushioned and rich carpets, on which sat the ladies, and on the second their slaves behind 'em, but without any distinction of rank by their dress, all being in the state of nature, that is, in plain English, stark naked, without any beauty or defect concealed, yet there was not the least wanton smile or immodest gesture amongst 'em. They walked and moved with the same majestic grace which Milton describes of our "general mother."[5] There were many amongst them as exactly proportioned as ever any goddess was drawn by the pencil of Guido or Titian,[6] and most of their skins shiningly white, only adorned by their beautiful hair divided into many tresses hanging on their shoulders, braided either with pearl or riband,[7] perfectly representing the figures of the Graces.[8] I was here convinced of the truth of a reflection that I had often made, that if 'twas the fashion to go naked, the face would be hardly observed. I perceived that the ladies with the finest skins and most delicate shapes had the greatest share of my admiration, though their faces were sometimes less beau-

---

3. Glass windows (which the Turkish coaches lacked).
4. The bath.
5. Eve (*Paradise Lost* 4.304–318).
6. Artists of the Italian Renaissance.

7. Ribbon.
8. Resembling the three sister divinities who (in Greek mythology) embody and endow grace and beauty.

tiful than those of their companions. To tell you the truth, I had wickedness enough to wish secretly that Mr. Gervase could have been there invisible.[9] I fancy it would have very much improved his art to see so many fine women naked in different postures, some in conversation, some working, others drinking coffee or sherbet, and many negligently lying on their cushions while their slaves (generally pretty girls of seventeen or eighteen) were employed in braiding their hair in several pretty manners. In short, 'tis the women's coffee-house, where all the news of the town is told, scandal invented, etc. They generally take this diversion once a week, and stay there at least four or five hours without getting cold by immediate coming out of the hot bath into the cool room, which was very surprising to me. The lady that seemed the most considerable amongst them entreated me to sit by her and would fain have undressed me for the bath. I excused myself with some difficulty, they being all so earnest in persuading me. I was at last forced to open my skirt and show them my stays,[1] which satisfied them very well, for I saw they believed I was so locked up in that machine that it was not in my own power to open it, which contrivance they attributed to my husband. I was charmed with their civility and beauty, and should have been very glad to pass more time with them, but Mr. W[2] resolving to pursue his journey the next morning early, I was in haste to see the ruins of Justinian's church,[3] which did not afford me so agreeable a prospect as I had left, being little more than a heap of stones.

Adieu, Madam. I am sure I have now entertained you with an account of such a sight as you never saw in your life and that no book of travels could inform you of. 'Tis no less than death for a man to be found in one of those places.

To *Lady Mar*[1]

[On Turkish Dress]

Adrianople, 1 April 1717

I wish to God (dear Sister) that you was as regular in letting me have the pleasure of knowing what passes on your side of the globe as I am careful in endeavoring to amuse you by the account of all I see that I think you care to hear of. You content yourself with telling me over and over that the town is very dull. It may possibly be dull to you when every day does not present you with something new, but for me that am in arrear at least two months' news, all that seems very stale with you would be fresh and sweet here; pray let me into more particulars. I will try to awaken your gratitude by giving you a full and true relation of the novelties of this place, none of which would surprise you more than a sight of my person as I am now in my Turkish habit, though I believe you would be of my opinion that 'tis admirably becoming. I intend to send you my picture; in the meantime accept of it here.

The first piece of my dress is a pair of drawers, very full, that reach to my shoes and conceal the legs more modestly than your petticoats. They are of a thin rose-color damask brocaded with silver flowers, my shoes of white kid leather embroidered

9. Charles Jervas (c. 1675–1739), a successful portraitist who had once painted Montagu as a shepherdess. The French painter Jean Auguste Dominique Ingres (1780–1867) later took up the hint implicit in Montagu's "fancy" here. Having transcribed portions of this letter from a French edition (1805), he made use of Montagu's descriptions in his painting *Le Bain Turc* (The Turkish Bath, 1862).
1. A tightly laced undergarment, stiffened with whalebone, extending from breast to thigh.
2. Her husband, Edward Wortley Montagu.
3. The Church of St. Sofia, built during the reign of the Byzantine Emperor Justinian (483–565).
1. Montagu's sister Frances (1690–1761), who had married the Earl of Mar.

with gold. Over this hangs my smock of a fine white silk gauze edged with embroidery. This smock has wide sleeves hanging half way down the arm and is closed at the neck with a diamond button, but the shape and color of the bosom very well to be distinguished through it. The *antery* is a waistcoat[2] made close to the shape, of white and gold damask, with very long sleeves falling back and fringed with deep gold fringe, and should have diamond or pearl buttons. My caftan, of the same stuff with my drawers, is a robe exactly fitted to my shape and reaching to my feet, with very long straight falling sleeves. Over this is the girdle of about four fingers broad, which all that can afford have entirely of diamonds or other precious stones. Those that will not be at that expense have it of exquisite embroidery on satin, but it must be fastened before with a clasp of diamonds. The *curdée* is a loose robe they throw off or put on according to the weather, being of a rich brocade (mine is green and gold) either lined with ermine or sables; the sleeves reach very little below the shoulders. The headdress is composed of a cap called *talpock,* which is in winter of fine velvet embroidered with pearls or diamonds and in summer of a light shining silver stuff. This is fixed on one side of the head, hanging a little way down with a gold tassel and bound on either with a circle of diamonds (as I have seen several) or a rich embroidered handkerchief. On the other side of the head the hair is laid flat, and here the ladies are at liberty to show their fancies, some putting flowers, others a plume of heron's feathers, and, in short, what they please, but the most general fashion is a large bouquet of jewels made like natural flowers, that is, the buds of pearl, the roses of different colored rubies, the jasmines of diamonds, jonquils of topazes, etc., so well set and enameled 'tis hard to imagine anything of that kind so beautiful. The hair hangs at its full length behind, divided into tresses braided with pearl or riband, which is always in great quantity.

I never saw in my Life so many fine heads of hair. I have counted 110 of these tresses of one lady's, all natural; but it must be owned that every beauty is more common here than with us. 'Tis surprising to see a young woman that is not very handsome. They have naturally the most beautiful complexions in the world and generally large black eyes. I can assure you with great truth that the Court of England (though I believe it the fairest in Christendom) cannot show so many beauties as are under our protection here. They generally shape their eyebrows, and the Greeks and Turks have a custom of putting round their eyes on the inside a black tincture that, at a distance or by candlelight, adds very much to the blackness of them. I fancy many of our ladies would be overjoyed to know this secret, but 'tis too visible by day. They dye their nails rose color; I own I cannot enough accustom myself to this fashion to find any beauty in it.

As to their morality or good conduct, I can say like Arlequin, 'tis just as 'tis with you,[3] and the Turkish ladies don't commit one sin the less for not being Christians. Now I am a little acquainted with their ways, I cannot forbear admiring either the exemplary discretion or extreme stupidity of all the writers that have given accounts of 'em.[4] 'Tis very easy to see they have more liberty than we have, no woman of what rank soever being permitted to go in the streets without two muslins, one that covers her face all but her eyes and another that hides the whole

---

2. A vest.
3. A paraphrase (and misattribution) of a line from Aphra Behn's comedy *The Emperor of the Moon* (1687): the prankster Harlequin, pretending to be an ambassador from the moon, describes the corrupt social customs of

his world to a gullible listener, who repeatedly exclaims that morality there is "just as 'tis here" (3.2).
4. Many (though not all) writers on Turkey had emphasized the strict confinement and chastity of the women there.

dress of her head and hangs half way down her back; and their shapes are wholly concealed by a thing they call a *ferigée*, which no woman of any sort appears without. This has straight sleeves that reaches to their fingers' ends and it laps all round 'em, not unlike a riding hood. In winter 'tis of cloth, and in summer, plain stuff or silk. You may guess how effectually this disguises them, that there is no distinguishing the great lady from her slave, and 'tis impossible for the most jealous husband to know his wife when he meets her, and no man dare either touch or follow a woman in the street.

This perpetual masquerade gives them entire liberty of following their inclinations without danger of discovery. The most usual method of intrigue is to send an appointment to the lover to meet the lady at a Jew's shop,[5] which are as notoriously convenient as our Indian houses,[6] and yet even those that don't make that use of 'em do not scruple to go to buy pennorths and tumble over[7] rich goods, which are chiefly to be found amongst that sort of people.[8] The great ladies seldom let their gallants[9] know who they are, and 'tis so difficult to find it out that they can very seldom guess at her name they have corresponded with above half a year together. You may easily imagine the number of faithful wives very small in a country where they have nothing to fear from their lovers' indiscretion, since we see so many that have the courage to expose themselves to that in this world and all the threatened punishment of the next, which is never preached to the Turkish damsels. Neither have they much to apprehend from the resentment of their husbands, those ladies that are rich having all their money in their own hands, which they take with 'em upon a divorce with an addition which he is obliged to give 'em. Upon the whole, I look upon the Turkish women as the only free people in the Empire. The very *Divan*[1] pays a respect to 'em, and the *Grand Signor* himself, when a *Bassa*[2] is executed, never violates the privileges of the harem (or women's apartment), which remains unsearched entire to the widow. They are queens of their slaves, which the husband has no permission so much as to look upon, except it be an old woman or two that his lady chooses. 'Tis true their law permits them four wives, but there is no instance of a man of quality that makes use of this liberty, or of a woman of rank that would suffer it. When a husband happens to be inconstant (as those things will happen) he keeps his mistress in a house apart and visits her as privately as he can, just as 'tis with you. Amongst all the great men here I only know the *Tefterdar* (i.e. treasurer) that keeps a number of she slaves for his own use (that is, on his own side of the house, for a slave once given to serve a lady is entirely at her disposal) and he is spoke of as a libertine, or what we should call a rake, and his wife won't see him, though she continues to live in his house.

Thus you see, dear Sister, the manners of mankind do not differ so widely as our voyage writers would make us believe. Perhaps it would be more entertaining to add a few surprising customs of my own invention, but nothing seems to me so agreeable as truth, and I believe nothing so acceptable to you. I conclude with repeating the great truth of my being, dear Sister, etc.

---

5. Jewish women sometimes helped arrange these assignations; being permitted to enter the harems, they could transmit secret messages.
6. London shops selling goods imported from India.
7. Penny-worths: good bargains; tumble over: browse

through.
8. Jews.
9. Lovers.
1. A governmental official.
2. *Pasha*: a high official.

Letter to Lady Bute[1]

[ON HER GRANDDAUGHTER]

28 January 1753

Dear Child,

You have given me a great deal of satisfaction by your account of your eldest daughter. I am particularly pleased to hear she is a good arithmetician; it is the best proof of understanding. The knowledge of numbers is one of the chief distinctions between us and brutes. If there is anything in blood, you may reasonably expect your children should be endowed with an uncommon share of good sense. Mr. Wortley's[2] family and mine have both produced some of the greatest Men that have been born in England. I mean Admiral Sandwich,[3] and my great grandfather who was distinguished by the name of Wise William.[4] I have heard Lord Bute's father mentioned as an extraordinary genius (though he had not many opportunities of showing it), and his uncle the present Duke of Argyll has one of the best heads I ever knew.

I will therefore speak to you as supposing Lady Mary not only capable but desirous of learning. In that case, by all means let her be indulged in it. You will tell me, I did not make it a part of your education. Your prospect was very different from hers, as you had no defect either in mind or person to hinder, and much in your circumstances to attract, the highest offers. It seemed your business to learn how to live in the world, as it is hers to know how to be easy out of it. It is the common error of builders and parents to follow some plan they think beautiful (and perhaps is so) without considering that nothing is beautiful that is misplaced. Hence we see so many edifices raised that the raisers can never inhabit, being too large for their fortunes. Vistas are laid open over barren heaths, and apartments contrived for a coolness very agreeable in Italy but killing in the north of Britain. Thus every woman endeavors to breed her daughter a fine lady, qualifying her for a station in which she will never appear, and at the same time incapacitating her for that retirement to which she is destined. Learning (if she has a real taste for it) will not only make her contented but happy in it. No entertainment is so cheap as reading, nor any pleasure so lasting. She will not want new fashions nor regret the loss of expensive diversions or variety of company if she can be amused with an author in her closet. To render this amusement extensive, she should be permitted to learn the languages. I have heard it lamented that boys lose so many years in mere learning of words. This is no objection to a girl, whose time is not so precious. She cannot advance herself in any profession, and has therefore more hours to spare; and as you say her memory is good, she will be very agreeably employed this way.

There are two cautions to be given on this subject: first, not to think herself learned when she can read Latin or even Greek. Languages are more properly to be called vehicles of learning than learning itself, as may be observed in many schoolmasters, who though perhaps critics in grammar are the most ignorant fellows upon earth. True knowledge consists in knowing things, not words. I would wish her no farther a linguist than to enable her to read books in their originals, that are often

---

1. Montagu's only daughter, Mary (1718–1794), had in 1736 married John Stuart, third Earl of Bute. At the time this letter was written, Montagu had been long separated from her husband and was living in Italy.
2. Her estranged husband, Edward Wortley Montagu.

3. Edward Montagu (1625–1672), first Earl of Sandwich (and Samuel Pepys's patron), was Wortley's grandfather.
4. The Hon. William Pierrepont (1608–1678) was a prominent politician.

corrupted and always injured by translations. Two hours' application every morning will bring this about much sooner than you can imagine, and she will have leisure enough beside to run over the English poetry, which is a more important part of a woman's education than it is generally supposed. Many a young damsel has been ruined by a fine copy of verses, which she would have laughed at if she had known it had been stolen from Mr. Waller.[5] I remember when I was a girl I saved one of my companions from destruction, who communicated to me an epistle she was quite charmed with. As she had a natural good taste, she observed the lines were not so smooth as Prior's[6] or Pope's, but had more thought and spirit than any of theirs. She was wonderfully delighted with such a demonstration of her lover's sense and passion, and not a little pleased with her own charms, that had force enough to inspire such elegancies. In the midst of this triumph, I showed her they were taken from Randolph's poems,[7] and the unfortunate transcriber was dismissed with the scorn he deserved. To say truth, the poor plagiary was very unlucky to fall into my hands; that author, being no longer in fashion, would have escaped anyone of less universal reading than myself. You should encourage your daughter to talk over with you what she reads, and as you are very capable of distinguishing, take care she does not mistake pert folly for wit and humor, or rhyme for poetry, which are the common errors of young people, and have a train of ill consequences.

The second caution to be given her (and which is most absolutely necessary) is to conceal whatever learning she attains, with as much solicitude as she would hide crookedness or lameness. The parade of it can only serve to draw on her the envy, and consequently the most inveterate hatred, of all he and she fools, which will certainly be at least three parts in four of all her acquaintance. The use of knowledge in our sex (beside the amusement of solitude) is to moderate the passions and learn to be contented with a small expense, which are the certain effects of a studious life and, it may be, preferable even to that fame which men have engrossed to themselves and will not suffer us to share. You will tell me I have not observed this rule myself, but you are mistaken; it is only inevitable accident that has given me any reputation that way. I have always carefully avoided it, and ever thought it a misfortune.

The explanation of this paragraph would occasion a long digression, which I will not trouble you with, it being my present design only to say what I think useful for the instruction of my granddaughter, which I have much at heart. If she has the same inclination (I should say passion) for learning that I was born with, history, geography, and philosophy will furnish her with materials to pass away cheerfully a longer life than is allotted to mortals. I believe there are few heads capable of making Sir I. Newton's[8] calculations, but the result of them is not difficult to be understood by a moderate capacity. Do not fear this should make her affect the character of Lady ———, or Lady ———, or Mrs.———.[9] Those women are ridiculous, not because they have learning but because they have it not. One thinks herself a complete historian after reading Eachard's *Roman History*,[1] another a profound philosopher having got by heart some of Pope's unintelligible essays,[2] and a third an able divine on the strength of Whitfield's sermons.[3] Thus you hear them screaming politics and controversy. It is a saying

5. Edmund Waller (1606–1687), love poet frequently quoted (or plagiarized) by amorous wooers.
6. Matthew Prior (1664–1721), like Alexander Pope a celebrated poet.
7. The minor writer Thomas Randolph (1605–1635), whose collected *Poems* were published in 1638.
8. Isaac Newton, mathematician and scientist, author of *Principia Mathematica* (1687).

9. The names, which Montagu omitted in her manuscript, have not been recovered.
1. Lawrence Echard, *The Roman History* (1695–1698).
2. Probably his *Essay on Man* (1733–1734) in four epistles, published long after the friendship between him and Montagu had ended.
3. George Whitfield (1714–1770), Methodist preacher.

of Thucydides, ignorance is bold, and knowledge reserved.[4] Indeed it is impossible to be far advanced in it without being more humbled by a conviction of human ignorance than elated by learning.

At the same time I recommend books, I neither exclude work nor drawing. I think it as scandalous for a woman not to know how to use a needle, as for a man not to know how to use a sword. I was once extreme fond of my pencil, and it was a great mortification to me when my father turned off[5] my master, having made a considerable progress for the short time I learnt. My over eagerness in the pursuit of it had brought a weakness on my eyes that made it necessary to leave it off, and all the advantage I got was the improvement of my hand. I see by hers that practice will make her a ready writer. She may attain it by serving you for a secretary when your health or affairs make it troublesome to you to write yourself, and custom will make it an agreeable amusement to her. She cannot have too many for that station of life which will probably be her fate. The ultimate end of your education was to make you a good wife (and I have the comfort to hear that you are one); hers ought to be, to make her happy in a virgin state. I will not say it is happier, but it is undoubtedly safer than any marriage. In a lottery where there is (at the lowest computation) ten thousand blanks to a prize, it is the most prudent choice not to venture.

I have always been so thoroughly persuaded of this truth that, notwithstanding the flattering views I had for you (as I never intended you a sacrifice to my vanity), I thought I owed you the justice to lay before you all the hazards attending matrimony. You may recollect I did so in the strongest manner. Perhaps you may have more success in the instructing your daughter. She has so much company at home she will not need seeking it abroad, and will more readily take the notions you think fit to give her. As you were alone in my family, it would have been thought a great cruelty to suffer you no companions of your own age, especially having so many near relations, and I do not wonder their opinions influenced yours. I was not sorry to see you not determined on a single life, knowing it was not your father's intention, and contented myself with endeavoring to make your home so easy that you might not be in haste to leave it.

I am afraid you will think this a very long and insignificant letter. I hope the kindness of the design will excuse it, being willing to give you every proof in my power that I am your most affectionate Mother,

M. Wortley.

Epistle from Mrs. Yonge to her Husband[1]

Think not this paper comes with vain pretense
To move your pity, or to mourn th' offence.
Too well I know that hard obdurate heart;
No soft'ning mercy there will take my part,
5   Nor can a woman's arguments prevail,
When even your patron's wise example fails,[2]

4. Thucydides (5th–4th centuries B.C.), Greek historian of the Peloponnesian War; Montagu paraphrases his assertion that "boldness means ignorance and reflection brings hesitation" (*History* 2.40.3).
5. Dismissed.
1. In 1724 the heiress Mary Yonge became embroiled in a highly publicized divorce from her notorious, womanizing husband William, who accused her (accurately) of adultery committed during the couple's separation. Public

sympathy was on her side, but the king approved a divorce that allowed her husband to retain most of her fortune. Montagu's poem remained in manuscript throughout her life.
2. I.e., Robert Walpole's. William Yonge was a devoted adherent of the powerful minister, who carried on open adulteries himself but also (unlike Yonge) permitted them to his wife.

But this last privilege I still retain,
Th' oppressed and injured always may complain.
    Too, too severely laws of honor bind
10   The weak submissive sex of womankind.
If sighs have gained or force compelled our hand,
Deceived by art, or urged by stern command,
Whatever motive binds the fatal tie,
The judging world expects our constancy.
15   Just Heaven! (for sure in heaven does justice reign
Though tricks below that sacred name profane)
To you appealing I submit my cause
Nor fear a judgment from impartial laws.
All bargains but conditional are made;
20   The purchase void, the creditor unpaid,
Defrauded servants are from service free;
A wounded slave regains his liberty.
For wives ill used no remedy remains,
To daily racks condemned, and to eternal chains.
25   From whence is this unjust distinction grown?
Are we not formed with passions like your own?
Nature with equal fire our souls endued,
Our minds as haughty, and as warm our blood;
O're the wide world your pleasures you pursue, ⎫
30   The change is justified by something new; ⎬
But we must sigh in silence—and be true. ⎭
Our sex's weakness you expose and blame
(Of every prattling fop the common theme),
Yet from this weakness you suppose is due
35   Sublimer virtue than your Cato[3] knew.
Had Heaven designed us trials so severe,
It would have formed our tempers then to bear.
    And I have borne (O what have I not borne!)
The pang of jealousy, th' insults of scorn.
40   Wearied at length, I from your sight remove,
And place my future hopes in secret love.
In the gay bloom of glowing youth retired,
I quit the woman's joy to be admired,
With that small pension your hard heart allows,
45   Renounce your fortune, and release your vows.
To custom (though unjust) so much is due;
I hide my frailty from the public view.
My conscience clear, yet sensible of shame,
My life I hazard, to preserve my fame.
50   And I prefer this low inglorious state, ⎫
To vile dependence on the thing I hate— ⎬
But you pursue me to this last retreat. ⎭
Dragged into light, my tender crime is shown
And every circumstance of fondness known.

3. Marcus Porcius Cato of Utica (B.C. 95–46), champion of the Roman Republic, whose name had become a byword for integrity.

55 Beneath the shelter of the law you stand,
And urge my ruin with a cruel hand.
While to my fault thus rigidly severe,
Tamely submissive to the man you fear.
    This wretched outcast, this abandoned wife,
60 Has yet this joy to sweeten shameful life,
By your mean conduct, infamously loose,
You are at once my accuser, and excuse.
Let me be damned by the censorious prude
(Stupidly dull, or spiritually lewd),
65 My hapless case will surely pity find
From every just and reasonable mind,
When to the final sentence I submit;
The lips condemn me, but their souls acquit.
    No more my husband, to your pleasures go,
70 The sweets of your recovered freedom know;
Go; court the brittle friendship of the great,
Smile at his board, or at his levée[4] wait
And when dismissed, to Madam's toilet° fly,   dressing room
More than her chambermaids, or glasses,° lie,   mirrors
75 Tell her how young she looks, how heavenly fair,
Admire the lilies and the roses there;
Your high ambition may be gratified,
Some cousin of her own be made your bride,
And you the father of a glorious race
80 Endowed with Ch——l's strength and Low——r's face.[5]
1724   1972

The Lover: A Ballad

1

At length, by so much importunity pressed,
Take (Molly[1]) at once the inside of my breast;
This stupid indifference so often you blame
Is not owing to nature, to fear, or to shame;
5 I am not as cold as a virgin in lead,
Nor is Sunday's sermon so strong in my head;
I know but too well how time flies along,
That we live but few years and yet fewer are young.

2

But I hate to be cheated, and never will buy
10 Long years of repentance for moments of joy.
Oh was there a man (but where shall I find
Good sense, and good nature so equally joined?)
Would value his pleasure, contribute to mine,
Not meanly would boast, nor lewdly design,

---

4. Social assemblies at the homes of the "great," often crowded with petitioners, opportunists, and sycophants.
5. The line implies that the adulterous William Yonge will himself be supplanted in his next wife's bed by fel-

low-libertines: Charles Churchill (c. 1679–1745) and Antony Lowther (d. 1741).
1. Probably Maria ("Molly") Skerrett (1702–1738), Montagu's friend and Robert Walpole's mistress.

15 Not over severe, yet not stupidly vain,
    For I would have the power though not give the pain.

                        3

    No pedant yet learned, not rakehelly gay
    Or laughing because he has nothing to say,
    To all my whole sex obliging and free,
20 Yet never be fond of any but me.
    In public preserve the decorums are just
    And show in his eyes he is true to his trust,
    Then rarely approach, and respectfully bow,
    Yet not fulsomely pert, nor yet foppishly low.

                        4

25 But when the long hours of public are past
    And we meet with champagne and a chicken at last,
    May every fond pleasure that hour endear,
    Be banished afar both discretion and fear,
    Forgetting or scorning the airs of the crowd
30 He may cease to be formal, and I to be proud,
    Till lost in the joy, we confess that we live
    And he may be rude, and yet I may forgive.

                        5

    And that my delight may be solidly fixed
    Let the friend and the lover be handsomely mixed,
35 In whose tender bosom my soul might confide,
    Whose kindness can soothe me, whose counsel could guide;
    From such a dear lover as here I describe
    No danger should fright me, no millions should bribe,
    But till this astonishing creature I know
40 As I long have lived chaste I will keep myself so.

                        6

    I never will share with the wanton coquette,
    Or be caught by a vain affectation of wit.
    The toasters and songsters may try all their art
    But never shall enter the pass of my heart;
45 I loath the lewd rake, the dressed fopling despise,
    Before such pursuers the nice virgin flies;
    And as Ovid has sweetly in parables told
    We harden like trees, and like rivers are cold.[2]

c. 1721–1725   1747

The Reasons that Induced Dr. S. to write a Poem called
The Lady's Dressing Room[1]

    The Doctor in a clean starched band,
    His golden snuff box in his hand,
    With care his diamond ring displays

---

2. In his *Metamorphoses*, Ovid tells stories of virgins who
are transformed into a laurel tree (Daphne) or a fountain
(Arethusa), rather than succumb to the importunities of
a pursuing god (1.452–567; 5.572–641).

1. For Jonathan Swift's poem, see page 2370. In her
riposte, Montagu mimics Swift's iambic tetrameter and
other mannerisms.

And artful shows its various rays,
5   While grave he stalks down —— street
His dearest Betty —— to meet.[2]
    Long had he waited for this hour,
Nor gained admittance to the bower,
Had joked and punned, and swore and writ,
10   Tried all his gallantry and wit,[3]
Had told her oft what part he bore
In Oxford's schemes in days of yore,[4]
But bawdy,° politics, nor satire   obscenity
Could move this dull hard hearted creature.
15   Jenny her maid could taste° a rhyme   enjoy
And, grieved to see him lose his time,
Had kindly whispered in his ear,
"For twice two pound you enter here;
My lady vows without that sum
20   It is in vain you write or come."
    The destined offering now he brought,
And in a paradise of thought,
With a low bow approached the dame,
Who smiling heard him preach his flame.
25   His gold she takes (such proofs as these
Convince most unbelieving shes)
And in her trunk rose up to lock it
(Too wise to trust it in her pocket)
And then, returned with blushing grace,
30   Expects the doctor's warm embrace.
    But now this is the proper place
Where morals stare me in the face,
And for the sake of fine expression
I'm forced to make a small digression.
35   Alas for wretched humankind,
With learning mad, with wisdom blind!
The ox thinks he's for saddle fit
(As long ago friend Horace writ[5])
And men their talents still mistaking,
40   The stutterer fancies his is speaking.
With admiration oft we see
Hard features heightened by toupée,
The beau affects° the politician,   pretends to be
Wit is the citizen's ambition,
45   Poor Pope philosophy displays on
With so much rhyme and little reason,
And though he argues ne'er so long

---

2. In Swift's poem, Betty is the maid's name, Celia, the
mistress's.
3. Montagu echoes Swift's poem *Cadenus and Vanessa*,
where the clumsy lover "Had sighed and languished,
vowed, and writ, / For pastime, or to show his wit"
(542–543).

4. Swift had collaborated closely in the political
schemes of Robert Harley, first Earl of Oxford
(1661–1724).
5. "The ox desires the saddle" (Horace, *Epistles* 1.14.43).

That all is right, his head is wrong.[6]
   None strive to know their proper merit
50   But strain for wisdom, beauty, spirit,
And lose the praise that is their due
While they've th' impossible in view.
So have I seen the injudicious heir
To add one window the whole house impair.
55   Instinct the hound does better teach,
Who never undertook to preach;
The frighted hare from dogs does run
But not attempts to bear a gun.
Here many noble thoughts occur
60   But I prolixity abhor,
And will pursue th' instructive tale
To show the wise in some things fail.
   The reverend lover with surprise ⎤
Peeps in her bubbies, and her eyes, ⎬
65   And kisses both, and tries—and tries. ⎦
The evening in this hellish play,
Beside his guineas thrown away,
Provoked the priest to that degree
He swore, "The fault is not in me.
70   Your damned close stool° so near my nose,   *chamber pot*
Your dirty smock, and stinking toes
Would make a Hercules as tame
As any beau that you can name."
   The nymph grown furious roared, "By God
75   The blame lies all in sixty odd,"[7]
And scornful pointing to the door
Cried, "Fumbler, see my face no more."
"With all my heart I'll go away,
But nothing done, I'll nothing pay.
80   Give back the money." "How," cried she,
"Would you palm such a cheat on me!
For poor four pound to roar and bellow—
Why sure you want some new Prunella?"[8]
"I'll be revenged, you saucy quean"°   *whore*
85   (Replies the disappointed Dean)
"I'll so describe your dressing room
The very Irish shall not come."
She answered short, "I'm glad you'll write.
You'll furnish paper when I shite."[9]

1734

6. Montagu ridicules Pope's conclusion to *An Essay on Man:* "Whatever IS, is RIGHT." See page 2535.
7. I.e., Swift's impotence derives not from her odors but from his age (65 at the time the poem was written).
8. "Prunella" is both a fabric used in clergy vestments (Swift was a clergyman), and the name of the promiscuous, low-born heroine in Richard Estcourt's comic interlude *Prunella* (1708).
9. Compare line 118 of Swift's poem, page 2373.

John Gay
1685–1732

John Gay was born to hardworking, pious tradespeople in Barnstaple, a busy port town in southwestern England. Educated well but orphaned early, he moved at age eighteen to London, where he tried trade for a time, gave it up for literature, and made himself a master of the mock, at a moment when the mock mattered most.

In the early eighteenth century, the "mock" was not just a gesture of derision but an intricate art form, in which scenes of contemporary life, appropriated from streets, stables, salons, and other ordinary sites were represented in grand styles first crafted for the actions of ancient heroes. In his mock-pastoral *Description of a City Shower* (1709), for example, Swift depicted the muddy chaos of an urban rainstorm in the language Virgil had devised to render the rural delights of a Golden Age; in his mock-epic *Rape of the Lock* (1712), Pope portrayed the trivial agitations of London beaux and belles in formulations absorbed from Homer. Befriended by Pope and Swift, Gay became perhaps the most supple and assiduous practitioner in their mock-heroic vein. In his early successes, he showed himself adept at devising new combinations of mode and topic, new ways of savoring both high styles and low subjects even while making fun of them. In *The Shepherd's Week* (1714), he took on both Virgil's idealism and also the ungainly "realism" attempted by some of that Roman poet's eighteenth-century imitators. He endowed his shepherds with preposterously "rustic" names (Bumkinet, Hobnelia, Bowzybeus) and a ludicrously hybrid language, alternately high-flying and homespun. But he gave them also a grace and good nature that survive the mock. The poem's closing image of a drunken swain sleeping out the sunset ("ruddy, like his face, the sun descends") reads like the poet's own benediction. In his next big work, *Trivia, or the Art of Walking the Streets of London* (1716), Gay's grandiloquent Virgilian instruction makes city walking seem not just a "trivial" chore but an "art," comic, challenging, alternately appalling and attractive.

Gay built his life as he made his art, by improvising. He earned money by his plays and poems; he lost money in that evanescent investment scheme the South Sea Bubble; he served as Commissioner of Lotteries, and as secretary, steward, and companion to several members of the nobility; and he sought for years to secure steady patronage at court, by means of flattering verse and ingratiating conduct. His frustration peaked when he published a virtuosic set of *Fables* (1727) for the four-year-old Prince William and received as reward a royal appointment as attendant to the prince's two-year-old sister. The aristocrats he courted valued him for his compliant temper and beguiling company, but they patronized him in both senses of the word.

Gay refused the royal appointment, staking his hopes instead on his new project for the stage, *The Beggar's Opera* (1728). The initial notion for the piece had come from Swift, who suggested a "Newgate pastoral"—that is, a mixture in which the "whores and thieves" who inhabited Newgate prison and its neighborhood would supplant the nymphs and shepherds frolicking on Arcadian hillsides. Swift's hint is an ordinary mock recipe: two worlds collide, one real, one fictitious. Gay built from it an intricate hall of mirrors, where many more worlds met. For his thieves he drew on two real-life models, recently executed: Jonathan Wild and Jack Sheppard. Wild had run a large criminal organization which profited him two ways: he collected money from the resale of goods stolen by his subordinates; and he collected rewards from the government for turning in his associates and rivals whenever they became too troublesome. Sheppard had acquired fame as Wild's most high-spirited and elusive prey; a brilliant thief in his own right, he had often managed to escape the prisons and predicaments into which Wild had betrayed him. In *The Beggar's Opera*, Gay resurrects the two late criminals as Mr. Peachum, who like Wild manages a lucrative double life, and Captain Macheath, who like Sheppard proves susceptible of capture and gifted at escape. Here the worlds begin to multiply. Developing a comparison then current in the political press, Gay made his criminals conjure up the most powerful politician alive: Robert Walpole, the Whig prime minister who ran his political machine (so the *Opera* insists) with the efficiency of Peachum and the self-indulgence of Macheath.

The *Beggar's Opera* mixed low with high in form as well as content. Like "Newgate pastoral," the phrase "beggar's opera" fuses opposites. Italian opera was the most expensive, exotic, and fashionable entertainment in London. Gay's theatrical game was to replay opera's intricacies using beggars' means. He supplanted the elaborate arias of foreign composers with the simpler tunes of British street songs; he replaced the original words to those tunes with new lyrics that voiced his characters' strong emotions; he even re-enacted a recent, much-publicized rivalry between two high-paid prima donnas, at war for the allegiance of their audience, in the contest he stages between Peachum's daughter Polly and the jailer's daughter Lucy Lockit for the devotion of fickle Captain Macheath. On Gay's stage, worlds converge with a density even Swift could not have foreseen. Opera house and street corner; Whitehall and Newgate; art and commerce; politics, business, and crime: all of these turn out to operate on the same principles of self-interest.

Reading the new piece before its premiere, Gay's well-wishers hedged their bets as to its success. "It would either take greatly," the playwright William Congreve predicted, "or be damned confoundedly." In the event, it did both. The triumph of the opening night is the stuff of theatrical legend, but it provoked a counter-chorus of condemnation from critics who saw the play as endangering opera, glorifying thieves, traducing government. Amidst the debate, the play enjoyed a long run, entrancing an audience made up of the very people it mocked (including Walpole himself, who reportedly conducted an extra chorus of the play's most satiric song, "When you censure the age"). The *Beggar's Opera* offered theatergoers simple pleasures (deft performances, comic reversals, well-loved tunes) and intricate ones too: the often ironic play of Gay's new lyrics against the original words that the auditors had already in their heads; the debunking of love and marriage in sharp dialogue and the glorifying of it in sentimental song; the volatile charisma of the mock-hero Macheath, who for many observers came to seem utterly heroic by evening's end; the arresting alchemy by which Gay transmuted (as the Romantic essayist William Hazlitt later expressed it) "this motley group" of "highwaymen, turnkeys, their mistresses, wives, or daughters . . . into a set of fine gentlemen and ladies, satirists and philosophers." In his painting of the opening night, William Hogarth suggests how these transformations came to include the spectators as well. Occupying the sides of the stage, an audience of aristocrats, politicians, and theater people (Gay himself among them) observe the play in progress; they are encompassed by the same prison walls wherein Macheath and his pursuers play out their intricate transactions, in which everything and everyone—goods, votes, spouses—had become commodities, items of exchange, reckoned in account books as profit and as loss.

The *Beggar's Opera* brought Gay prosperity and celebrity but not security. Walpole evicted him from his subsidized lodgings and banned production of the *Opera*'s much-anticipated sequel *Polly*. When Gay died less than five years after his fabled first night, however, he was buried with elaborate ceremony in the Poet's Corner of Westminster Abbey. Friends commended the appropriateness of the site but marvelled at the incongruity of the pomp. Incongruity, though, had been Gay's stock in trade, and nowhere more so than in his greatest hit. Its long run continues in theaters around the world. It spawned numberless short-lived imitations in its own time and a more durable descendant in the twentieth century: *Die Dreigroschenoper* (*The Threepenny Opera*, 1928), in which Bertolt Brecht and Kurt Weill adapted Gay's characters, plot, and critique of commerce to produce their own dark and gleeful Marxist assault on contemporary capitalism. By routes less direct, Gay's work has infused both the modern musical theater (which continues to combine operatic and popular modes) and pop culture in general—where, for example, Brecht and Weill's sardonic "Ballad of Mack the Knife" became a pop hit of the early 1960s. The *Beggar's Opera* grabbed attention first—and sustains it still—for the ironic dexterity with which it mixed things up, in full mock mode.

William Hogarth. *The Beggar's Opera, Act 3, scene 9.* 1729.

The Beggar's Opera

Nos haec novimus esse nihil.[1]

Dramatis Personae[2]

Men

Peachum
Lockit
Macheath
Filch
Jemmy Twitcher
Crook-fingered Jack
Wat Dreary
Robin of Bagshot   } Macheath's Gang
Nimming Ned
Harry Padington
Matt of the Mint
Ben Budge
Beggar
Player
Constables, Drawer, Turnkey, etc.

---

1. We know these things to be nothing (Martial, *Epigrams* 13.2.8).
2. Many of these names reflect the characters' low-life habits: to "peach" is to inform on, to filch is to steal, twitchers are pickpockets, nimmers are thieves, and trulls and doxies are prostitutes.

Women

Mrs. Peachum
Polly Peachum
Lucy Lockit
Diana Trapes
Mrs. Coaxer
Dolly Trull
Mrs. Vixen   } *Women of the Town*
Betty Doxy
Jenny Diver
Mrs. Slammekin
Suky Tawdry
Molly Brazen

Introduction

Beggar, Player

BEGGAR If poverty be a title[3] to poetry, I am sure nobody can dispute mine. I own myself of the Company of Beggars; and I make one at their weekly festivals at St. Giles's.[4] I have a small yearly salary for my catches,[5] and am welcome to a mock laureate dinner there whenever I please, which is more than most poets can say.

PLAYER As we live by the Muses, 'tis but gratitude in us to encourage poetical merit wherever we find it. The Muses, contrary to all other ladies, pay no distinction to dress, and never partially[6] mistake the pertness of embroidery for wit, nor the modesty of want for dullness. Be the author who he will, we push his play as far as it will go. So (though you are in want) I wish you success heartily.

BEGGAR This piece I own was originally writ for the celebrating the marriage of James Chanter and Moll Lay, two most excellent ballad singers. I have introduced the similes that are in all your celebrated operas: the swallow, the moth, the bee, the ship, the flower, etc. Besides, I have a prison scene which the ladies always reckon charmingly pathetic. As to the parts, I have observed such a nice impartiality to our two ladies, that it is impossible for either of them to take offense.[7] I hope I may be forgiven, that I have not made my opera throughout unnatural, like those in vogue; for I have no recitative.[8] Excepting this, as I have consented to have neither prologue nor epilogue, it must be allowed an opera in all its forms. The piece indeed hath been heretofore frequently represented by ourselves in our great room at St. Giles's, so that I cannot too often acknowledge your charity in bringing it now on the stage.

PLAYER But I see 'tis time for us to withdraw; the actors are preparing to begin. Play away the overture.   [*Exeunt.*]

Act 1

Scene 1. Peachum's House

Peachum sitting at a table with a large book of accounts before him.

---

3. Deed of ownership.
4. An almshouse near the parish of St.-Giles, patron saint of lepers and beggars.
5. Rounds, songs for two or more voices in which each voice starts the same melody at a different time. The form was very popular; enthusiasts assembled in "catch clubs" for whole evenings of singing.

6. In a prejudiced way.
7. The Beggar alludes to recent rivalries between leading ladies in Italian operas.
8. Sung speech, an operatic convention. The Beggar promises that here, by contrast, dialog will be spoken naturally.

Air 1. An old woman clothed in gray, etc.[9]

Through all the employments of life
  Each neighbor abuses his brother;
Whore and rogue they call husband and wife:
  All professions be-rogue one another.
The priest calls the lawyer a cheat,
  The lawyer be-knaves the divine;
And the statesman, because he's so great,[1]
  Thinks his trade as honest as mine.

A lawyer is an honest employment, so is mine. Like me too he acts in a double capacity, both against rogues and for 'em; for 'tis but fitting that we should protect and encourage cheats, since we live by them.

Scene 2

Peachum, Filch

FILCH Sir, Black Moll hath sent word her trial comes on in the afternoon, and she hopes you will order matters so as to bring her off.

PEACHUM Why, she may plead her belly at worst;[2] to my knowledge she hath taken care of that security. But as the wench is very active and industrious, you may satisfy her that I'll soften the evidence.

FILCH Tom Gagg, Sir, is found guilty.

PEACHUM A lazy dog! When I took him the time before, I told him what he would come to if he did not mend his hand. This is death without reprieve. I may venture to book him.[3] [*Writes.*] For Tom Gagg, forty pounds. Let Betty Sly know that I'll save her from transportation,[4] for I can get more by her staying in England.

FILCH Betty hath brought more goods into our lock to-year than any five of the gang; and in truth, 'tis a pity to lose so good a customer.

PEACHUM If none of the gang take her off, she may, in the common course of business, live a twelve-month longer. I love to let women scape. A good sportsman always lets the hen partridges fly, because the breed of the game depends upon them. Besides, here the law allows us no reward; there is nothing to be got by the death of woman—except our wives.[5]

FILCH Without dispute, she is a fine woman! 'Twas to her I was obliged for my education, and (to say a bold word) she hath trained up more young fellows to the business than the gaming-table.

PEACHUM Truly, Filch, thy observation is right. We and the surgeons[6] are more beholden to women than all the professions besides.

Air 2. The bonny gray-eyed morn, etc.

FILCH *'Tis woman that seduces all mankind,*
  By her we first were taught the wheedling arts:
Her very eyes can cheat; when most she's kind,
  She tricks us of our money with our hearts.

---

9. I.e., this air is to be sung to the familiar ballad tune, *An Old Woman Clothed in Gray.*
1. The word "great" was often attached to the Whig Prime Minister Robert Walpole, whom Gay's Tory party opposed vigorously in the 1720s and 1730s.

2. A pregnant woman could not be hanged.
3. I.e., enter in the books the reward for "peaching" him.
4. Convicts were often transported to the colonies.
5. Husbands inherited their wives' property.
6. Who treat venereal diseases.

> For her, like wolves by night we roam for prey,
>   And practice ev'ry fraud to bribe her charms;
> For suits of love, like law, are won by pay,
>   And beauty must be fee'd into our arms.

PEACHUM But make haste to Newgate,[7] boy, and let my friends know what I intend; for I love to make them easy one way or other.

FILCH When a gentleman is long kept in suspense, penitence may break his spirit ever after. Besides, certainty gives a man a good air upon his trial, and makes him risk another without fear or scruple. But I'll away, for 'tis a pleasure to be the messenger of comfort to friends in affliction.

Scene 3

Peachum

But 'tis now high time to look about me for a decent execution against next Sessions.[8] I hate a lazy rogue, by whom one can get nothing 'till he is hanged. A register of the gang, [reading] Crook-fingered Jack. A year and a half in the service; Let me see how much the stock owes to his industry; one, two, three, four, five gold watches, and seven silver ones. A mighty clean-handed fellow! Sixteen snuffboxes, five of them of true gold. Six dozen of handkerchiefs, four silver-hilted swords, half a dozen of shirts, three tie-perriwigs, and a piece of broad cloth. Considering these are only the fruits of his leisure hours, I don't know a prettier fellow, for no man alive hath a more engaging presence of mind upon the road. Wat Dreary, alias Brown Will, an irregular dog, who hath an underhand way of disposing of his goods. I'll try him[9] only for a Sessions or two longer upon his good behavior. Harry Padington, a poor petty-larceny rascal, without the least genius; that fellow, though he were to live these six months, will never come to the gallows with any credit. Slippery Sam; he goes off the next Sessions, for the villain hath the impudence to have views of following his trade as a tailor, which he calls an honest employment. Mat of the Mint; lifted[1] not above a month ago, a promising sturdy fellow, and diligent in his way; somewhat too bold and hasty, and may raise good contributions on[2] the public, if he does not cut himself short by murder. Tom. Tipple, a guzzling soaking sot, who is always too drunk to stand himself, or to make others stand. A cart[3] is absolutely necessary for him. Robin of Bagshot, alias Gorgon, alias Bluff Bob, alias Carbuncle, alias Bob Booty.[4]

Scene 4

Peachum, Mrs. Peachum

MRS. PEACHUM What of Bob Booty, husband? I hope nothing bad hath betided him. You know, my dear, he's a favorite customer of mine. 'Twas he made me a present of this ring.

PEACHUM I have set his name down in the blacklist, that's all, my dear; he spends his life among women, and as soon as his money is gone, one or other of the ladies will hang him for the reward, and there's forty pound lost to us forever.

---

7. London's main prison.
8. Of the criminal court.
9. Keep him on.
1. Enlisted.

2. From.
3. A condemned prisoner rode in a cart to his execution.
4. All names referring to the prime minister, Robert Walpole.

MRS. PEACHUM You know, my dear, I never meddle in matters of death; I always leave those affairs to you. Women indeed are bitter bad judges in these cases, for they are so partial to the brave that they think every man handsome who is going to the camp[5] or the gallows.

Air 3. Cold and raw, etc.

> If any wench Venus's girdle wear,
>> Though she be never so ugly;
> Lilies and roses will quickly appear,
>> And her face look wond'rous smugly.
> Beneath the left ear so fit but a cord
>> (A rope so charming a zone[6] is!),
> The youth in his cart hath the air of a lord,
>> And we cry, There dies an Adonis!

But really, husband, you should not be too hardhearted, for you never had a finer, braver set of men than at present. We have not had a murder among them all, these seven months. And truly, my dear, that is a great blessing.

PEACHUM What a dickens is the woman always a whimpering about murder for? No gentleman is ever looked upon the worse for killing a man in his own defense; and if business cannot be carried on without it, what would you have a gentleman do?

MRS. PEACHUM If I am in the wrong, my dear, you must excuse me, for nobody can help the frailty of an over-scrupulous conscience.

PEACHUM Murder is as fashionable a crime as a man can be guilty of. How many fine gentlemen have we in Newgate every year, purely upon that article! If they have wherewithal to persuade the jury to bring it in[7] manslaughter, what are they the worse for it? So, my dear, have done upon this subject. Was Captain Macheath here this morning, for the bank-notes[8] he left with you last week?

MRS. PEACHUM Yes, my dear; and though the bank hath stopped payment, he was so cheerful and so agreeable! Sure there is not a finer gentleman upon the road than the Captain! If he comes from Bagshot[9] at any reasonable hour he hath promised to make one this evening with Polly and me, and Bob Booty, at a party of quadrille.[1] Pray, my dear, is the Captain rich?

PEACHUM The Captain keeps too good company ever to grow rich. Marybone and the chocolate-houses[2] are his undoing. The man that proposes to get money by "play" should have the education of a fine gentleman, and be trained up to it from his youth.

MRS. PEACHUM Really, I am sorry upon Polly's account the Captain hath not more discretion. What business hath he to keep company with lords and gentlemen? He should leave them to prey upon one another.

PEACHUM Upon Polly's account! What, a plague, does the woman mean? Upon Polly's account!

MRS. PEACHUM Captain Macheath is very fond of the girl.

PEACHUM And what then?

---

5. To war.
6. Belt.
7. Reduce it to.
8. Bankers' checks.

9. Bagshot Heath, west of London, where many highwaymen plied their trade.
1. A fashionable card game for four.
2. Both sites of gambling.

MRS. PEACHUM If I have any skill in the ways of women, I am sure Polly thinks him a very pretty man.

PEACHUM And what then? You would not be so mad to have the wench marry him! Gamesters and highwaymen are generally very good to their whores, but they are very devils to their wives.

MRS. PEACHUM But if Polly should be in love, how should we help her, or how can she help herself? Poor girl, I am in the utmost concern about her.

Air 4. Why is your faithful slave disdained? etc.

If love the virgin's heart invade,
How, like a moth, the simple maid
Still plays about the flame!
If soon she be not made a wife;
Her honor's singed, and then for life,
She's—what I dare not name.

PEACHUM Look ye, wife. A handsome wench in our way of business is as profitable as at the bar of a Temple coffeehouse, who looks upon it as her livelihood to grant every liberty but one. You see I would indulge the girl as far as prudently we can. In anything, but marriage! After that, my dear, how shall we be safe? Are we not then in her husband's power? For a husband hath the absolute power over all a wife's secrets but her own. If the girl had the discretion of a court lady, who can have a dozen young fellows at her ear without complying with one, I should not matter it; but Polly is tinder, and a spark will at once set her on a flame. Married! If the wench does not know her own profit, sure she knows her own pleasure better than to make herself a property! My daughter to me should be, like a court lady to a minister of state, a key to the whole gang. Married! If the affair is not already done, I'll terrify her from it, by the example of our neighbors.

MRS. PEACHUM Mayhap, my dear, you may injure the girl. She loves to imitate the fine ladies, and she may only allow the Captain liberties in the view of interest.[3]

PEACHUM But 'tis your duty, my dear, to warn the girl against her ruin, and to instruct her how to make the most of her beauty. I'll go to her this moment, and sift[4] her. In the meantime, wife, rip out the coronets and marks[5] of these dozen of cambric handkerchiefs, for I can dispose of them this afternoon to a chap in the city.

Scene 5

Mrs. Peachum

Never was a man more out of the way[6] in an argument than my husband! Why must our Polly, forsooth, differ from her sex, and love only her husband? And why must Polly's marriage, contrary to all observation, make her the less followed by other men? All men are thieves in love, and like a woman the better for being another's property.

Air 5. Of all the simple things we do, etc.

A maid is like the golden oar,[7]
Which hath guineas intrinsical in't,

---

3. Self-interest, profit.
4. Question.
5. The embroidered marks of the handkerchiefs' aristocratic owners.

6. In the wrong.
7. Ore.

> *Whose worth is never known, before*
> *It is tried and imprest*[8] *in the Mint.*
> *A wife's like a guinea in gold,*
> *Stamped with the name of her spouse;*
> *Now here, now there; is bought, or is sold;*
> *And is current in every house.*

Scene 6

Mrs. Peachum, Filch

MRS. PEACHUM Come hither Filch. I am as fond of this child, as though my mind misgave me[9] he were my own. He hath as fine a hand at picking a pocket as a woman, and is as nimble fingered as a juggler. If an unlucky Session does not cut the rope of thy life, I pronounce, boy, thou wilt be a great man[1] in history. Where was your post last night, my boy?

FILCH I plyed at the opera, Madam; and considering 'twas neither dark nor rainy, so that there was no great hurry in getting chairs and coaches, made a tolerable hand on't. These seven handkerchiefs, Madam.

MRS. PEACHUM Colored ones, I see. They are of sure sale from our warehouse at Redriff among the seamen.

FILCH And this snuffbox.

MRS. PEACHUM Set in gold! A pretty encouragement this to a young beginner.

FILCH I had a fair tug at a charming gold watch. Pox take the tailors for making the fobs[2] so deep and narrow! It stuck by the way, and I was forced to make my escape under a coach. Really, Madam, I fear I shall be cut off in the flower of my youth, so that every now and then (since I was pumped[3]) I have thoughts of taking up[4] and going to sea.

MRS. PEACHUM You should go to Hockley in the Hole,[5] and to Marybone, child, to learn valor. These are the schools that have bred so many brave men. I thought, boy, by this time, thou hadst lost fear as well as shame. Poor lad! How little does he know as yet of the Old Baily![6] For the first fact I'll insure thee from being hanged; and going to sea, Filch, will come time enough upon a sentence of transportation. But now, since you have nothing better to do, ev'n go to your book, and learn your catechism;[7] for really a man makes but an ill figure in the ordinary's paper,[8] who cannot give a satisfactory answer to his questions. But, hark you, my lad. Don't tell me a lie; for you know I hate a liar. Do you know of anything that hath passed between Captain Macheath and our Polly?

FILCH I beg you, Madam, don't ask me; for I must either tell a lie to you or to Miss Polly; for I promised her I would not tell.

MRS. PEACHUM But when the honor of our family is concerned—

FILCH I shall lead a sad life with Miss Polly, if ever she come to know that I told you. Besides, I would not willingly forfeit my own honor by betraying anybody.

MRS. PEACHUM Yonder comes my husband and Polly. Come Filch, you shall go with me into my own room, and tell me the whole story. I'll give thee a glass of a most delicious cordial that I keep for my own drinking.

---

8. Smelted and stamped.
9. Suspected.
1. Another jab at the prime minister, Robert Walpole.
2. Watch-pockets.
3. Half-drowned under a pump (a punishment for pickpockets).

4. Reforming.
5. A site of boxing and bear-baiting.
6. London's main trial court.
7. Religious instruction.
8. The chaplain of Newgate (the Ordinary) often published the confessions of recently executed prisoners.

Scene 7

Peachum, Polly

POLLY I know as well as any of the fine ladies how to make the most of myself and of my man too. A woman knows how to be mercenary, though she hath never been in a court or at an assembly.[9] We have it in our natures, Papa. If I allow Captain Macheath some trifling liberties, I have this watch and other visible marks of his favor to show for it. A girl who cannot grant some things, and refuse what is most material, will make but a poor hand of her beauty, and soon be thrown upon the common.

Air 6. What shall I do to show how much I love her, etc.

Virgins are like the fair flower in its luster,
    Which in the garden enamels the ground;
Near it the bees in play flutter and cluster,
    And gaudy butterflies frolic around.
But, when once plucked, 'tis no longer alluring,
    To Covent Garden[1] 'tis sent (as yet sweet),
There fades, and shrinks, and grows past all enduring,
    Rots, stinks, and dies, and is trod under feet.

PEACHUM You know, Polly, I am not against your toying and trifling with a customer in the way of business, or to get out a secret, or so. But if I find out that you have played the fool and are married, you jade you, I'll cut your throat, hussy. Now you know my mind.

Scene 8

Peachum, Polly, Mrs. Peachum

Air 7. Oh London is a fine town.

Mrs. Peachum, in a very great passion.

Our Polly is a sad slut! nor heeds what we have taught her.
I wonder any man alive will ever rear a daughter!
For she must have both hoods and gowns, and hoops to swell her pride,
With scarves and stays,[2] and gloves and lace; and she will have men beside;
And when she's dressed with care and cost, all tempting, fine and gay,
As men should serve a cowcumber,[3] she flings herself away.
Our Polly is a sad slut, etc.

You baggage! You hussy! You inconsiderate jade! Had you been hanged, it would not have vexed me, for that might have been your misfortune; but to do such a mad thing by choice! The wench is married, husband.

PEACHUM Married! The Captain is a bold man, and will risk anything for money; to be sure he believes her a fortune. Do you think your mother and I should have lived comfortably so long together, if ever we had been married? Baggage!

---

9. A fashionable social gathering.
1. A London market for flowers, fruits, and vegetables; also a haunt of prostitutes.

2. Corsets.
3. A (worthless) cucumber.

MRS. PEACHUM I knew she was always a proud slut; and now the wench hath played the fool and married, because forsooth she would do like the gentry. Can you support the expense of a husband, hussy, in gaming, drinking, and whoring? Have you money enough to carry on the daily quarrels of man and wife about who shall squander most? There are not many husbands and wives who can bear the charges[4] of plaguing one another in a handsome way. If you must be married, could you introduce nobody into our family but a highwayman? Why, thou foolish jade, thou wilt be as ill-used, and as much neglected, as if thou hadst married a lord!

PEACHUM Let not your anger, my dear, break through the rules of decency, for the Captain looks upon himself in the military capacity, as a gentleman by his profession. Besides what he hath already, I know he is in a fair way of getting, or of dying;[5] and both these ways, let me tell you, are most excellent chances for a wife. Tell me hussy, are you ruined or no?

MRS. PEACHUM With Polly's fortune, she might very well have gone off to a person of distinction. Yes, that you might, you pouting slut!

PEACHUM What, is the wench dumb? Speak, or I'll make you plead by squeezing out an answer from you.[6] Are you really bound wife to him, or are you only upon liking? [Pinches her.]

POLLY Oh! [Screaming.]

MRS. PEACHUM How the mother is to be pitied who hath handsome daughters! Locks, bolts, bars, and lectures of morality are nothing to them. They break through them all. They have as much pleasure in cheating a father and mother, as in cheating at cards.

PEACHUM Why, Polly, I shall soon know if you are married, by Macheath's keeping from[7] our house.

Air 8. Grim king of the ghosts, etc.

POLLY Can love be controlled by advice?
    Will Cupid our mothers obey?
    Though my heart were as frozen as ice,
      At his flame 'twould have melted away.

    When he kissed me so closely he pressed,
      'Twas so sweet that I must have complied;
    So I thought it both safest and best
      To marry, for fear you should chide.

MRS. PEACHUM Then all the hopes of our family are gone forever and ever!

PEACHUM And Macheath may hang his father and mother-in-law, in hope to get into their daughter's fortune.

POLLY I did not marry him (as 'tis the fashion) coolly and deliberately for honor and money. But, I love him.

MRS. PEACHUM Love him! worse and worse! I thought the girl had been better bred. Oh husband, husband! Her folly makes me mad! My head swims! I'm distracted! I can't support myself—Oh! [Faints.]

PEACHUM See, wench, to what a condition you have reduced your poor mother! A glass of cordial, this instant. How the poor woman takes it to heart!

---

4. Expense.
5. He is likely to make more or to die trying.

6. Confessions were sometimes extracted by pressing with weights.
7. Staying away from.

[*Polly goes out, and returns with it.*]

Ah, hussy, now this is the only comfort your mother has left!

POLLY Give her another glass, Sir; my mama drinks double the quantity whenever she is out of order. This, you see, fetches[8] her.

MRS. PEACHUM The girl shows such a readiness, and so much concern, that I could almost find in my heart to forgive her.

Air 9. O Jenny, O Jenny, where hast thou been.

O Polly, you might have toyed and kissed.
By keeping men off, you keep them on.

POLLY *But he so teased me,*
        And he so pleased me,
    What I did, you must have done.

MRS. PEACHUM Not with a highwayman.—You sorry slut!

PEACHUM A word with you, wife. 'Tis no new thing for a wench to take man without consent of parents. You know 'tis the frailty of woman, my dear.

MRS. PEACHUM Yes, indeed, the sex is frail. But the first time a woman is frail, she should be somewhat nice[9] methinks, for then or never is the time to make her fortune. After that, she hath nothing to do but guard herself from being found out, and she may do what she pleases.

PEACHUM Make yourself a little easy; I have a thought shall soon set all matters again to rights. Why so melancholy, Polly? Since what is done cannot be undone, we must all endeavor to make the best of it.

MRS. PEACHUM Well, Polly, as far as one woman can forgive another, I forgive thee. Your father is too fond of you, hussy.

POLLY Then all my sorrows are at an end.

MRS. PEACHUM A mighty likely speech in troth, for a wench who is just married!

Air 10. Thomas, I cannot, etc.

POLLY *I, like a ship in storms, was tossed;*
        Yet afraid to put into land;
        For seized in the port the vessel's lost,
        Whose treasure is contraband.
            The waves are laid,[1]
            My duty's paid.
        O joy beyond expression!
            Thus, safe a-shore,
            I ask no more,
        My all is in my possession.

PEACHUM I hear customers in t'other room; Go, talk with 'em, Polly; but come to us again, as soon as they are gone. But, hark ye, child, if 'tis the gentleman who was here yesterday about the repeating-watch,[2] say you believe we can't get intelligence of it till tomorrow. For I lent it to Suky Straddle, to make a figure with it

8. Revives.
9. Careful, fastidious.
1. Have subsided.

2. An especially valuable timepiece: it announced the current hour and quarter-hour by a series of bells that rang at the push of a button.

tonight at a tavern in Drury Lane.[3] If t'other gentleman calls for the silver-hilted sword; you know beetle-browed Jemmy hath it on, and he doth not come from Tunbridge till Tuesday night; so that it cannot be had till then.

Scene 9

Peachum, Mrs. Peachum

PEACHUM Dear wife, be a little pacified. Don't let your passion run away with your senses. Polly, I grant you, hath done a rash thing.

MRS. PEACHUM If she had had only an intrigue with the fellow, why the very best families have excused and huddled up a frailty of that sort. 'Tis marriage, husband, that makes it a blemish.

PEACHUM But money, wife, is the true fuller's earth[4] for reputations, there is not a spot or a stain but what it can take out. A rich rogue nowadays is fit company for any gentleman; and the world, my dear, hath not such a contempt for roguery as you imagine. I tell you, wife, I can make this match turn to our advantage.

MRS. PEACHUM I am very sensible,[5] husband, that Captain Macheath is worth money, but I am in doubt whether he hath not two or three wives already, and then if he should die in a Session or two, Polly's dower would come into dispute.

PEACHUM That, indeed, is a point which ought to be considered.

Air 11. A soldier and a sailor.

> *A fox may steal your hens, Sir,*
> *A whore your health and pence, Sir,*
> *Your daughter rob your chest, Sir,*
> *Your wife may steal your rest, Sir,*
>   *A thief your goods and plate.[6]*
> *But this is all but picking,*
> *With rest, pence, chest, and chicken;*
> *It ever was decreed, Sir,*
> *If lawyer's hand is fee'd, Sir,*
>   *He steals your whole estate.*

The lawyers are bitter enemies to those in our way.[7] They *don't care*[8] that anybody should get a clandestine livelihood but themselves.

Scene 10

Mrs. Peachum, Peachum, Polly

POLLY 'Twas only Nimming Ned. He brought in a damask window curtain, a hoop petticoat, a pair of silver candlesticks, a periwig, and one silk stocking from the fire that happened last night.

PEACHUM There is not a fellow that is cleverer in his way, and saves more goods out of the fire than Ned. But now, Polly, to your affair; for matters must not be left as they are. You are married then, it seems?

POLLY Yes, Sir.

---

3. Another haunt of prostitutes; also the location of the rival theater.
4. A mineral used as a cleaning solvent.
5. Well aware.

6. Utensils plated with silver or gold.
7. In our line of work.
8. Want.

PEACHUM And how do you propose to live, child?

POLLY Like other women, Sir, upon the industry of my husband.

MRS. PEACHUM What, is the wench turned fool? A highwayman's wife, like a soldier's, hath as little of his pay as of his company.

PEACHUM And had not you the common views of a gentlewoman in your marriage, Polly?

POLLY I don't know what you mean, Sir.

PEACHUM Of a jointure,[9] and of being a widow.

POLLY But I love him, Sir: how then could I have thoughts of parting with him?

PEACHUM Parting with him! Why, that is the whole scheme and intention of all marriage articles. The comfortable estate of widowhood is the only hope that keeps up a wife's spirits. Where is the woman who would scruple to be a wife, if she had it in her power to be a widow whenever she pleased? If you have any views of this sort, Polly, I shall think the match not so very unreasonable.

POLLY How I dread to hear your advice! Yet I must beg you to explain yourself.

PEACHUM Secure what he hath got, have him peached the next Sessions, and then at once you are made a rich widow.

POLLY What, murder the man I love! The blood runs cold at my heart with the very thought of it.

PEACHUM Fie, Polly! What hath murder to do in the affair? Since the thing sooner or later must happen, I dare say, the Captain himself would like that we should get the reward for his death sooner than a stranger. Why, Polly, the Captain knows, that as 'tis his employment to rob, so 'tis ours to take robbers; every man in his business. So that there is no malice in the case.

MRS. PEACHUM Ay, husband, now you have nicked the matter. To have him peached is the only thing could ever make me forgive her.

Air 12. Now ponder well, ye parents dear.

POLLY *Oh, ponder well! be not severe;*
So save a wretched wife!
For on the rope that hangs my dear
Depends poor Polly's life.

MRS. PEACHUM But your duty to your parents, hussy, obliges you to hang him. What would many a wife give for such an opportunity!

POLLY What is a jointure, what is widowhood to me? I know my heart. I cannot survive him.

Air 13. Le printemps rappelle aux armes.[1]

The turtle[2] thus with plaintive crying,
Her lover dying,
The turtle thus with plaintive crying,
Laments her dove.
Down she drops quite spent with sighing,
Paired in death, as paired in love.

Thus, Sir, it will happen to your poor Polly.

MRS. PEACHUM What, is the fool in love in earnest then? I hate thee for being particular.[3] Why, wench, thou art a shame to thy very sex.

9. "Estate settled on a wife to be enjoyed after her husband's decease" (Johnson's *Dictionary*).
1. Spring calls to arms.
2. Turtledove.
3. Odd, exceptional.

POLLY But hear me, Mother. If you ever loved—

MRS. PEACHUM Those cursed playbooks she reads have been her ruin. One word more, hussy, and I shall knock your brains out, if you have any.

PEACHUM Keep out of the way, Polly, for fear of mischief, and consider of what is proposed to you.

MRS. PEACHUM Away, hussy. Hang your husband, and be dutiful.

Scene 11

Mrs. Peachum, Peachum

[Polly listening.]

MRS. PEACHUM The thing, husband, must and shall be done. For the sake of intelligence[4] we must take other measures, and have him peached the next Session without her consent. If she will not know her duty, we know ours.

PEACHUM But really, my dear, it grieves one's heart to take off a great man. When I consider his personal bravery, his fine stratagem, how much we have already got by him, and how much more we may get, methinks I can't find in my heart to have a hand in his death. I wish you could have made Polly undertake it.

MRS. PEACHUM But in a case of necessity—our own lives are in danger.

PEACHUM Then, indeed, we must comply with the customs of the world, and make gratitude give way to interest. He shall be taken off.

MRS. PEACHUM I'll undertake to manage Polly.

PEACHUM And I'll prepare matters for the Old Baily.

Scene 12

Polly

Now I'm a wretch, indeed. Methinks I see him already in the cart, sweeter and more lovely than the nosegay[5] in his hand! I hear the crowd extolling his resolution and intrepidity! What volleys of sighs are sent from the windows of Holborn,[6] that so comely a youth should be brought to disgrace! I see him at the tree![7] The whole circle are in tears! Even butchers weep! Jack Ketch[8] himself hesitates to perform his duty, and would be glad to lose his fee, by a reprieve. What then will become of Polly! As yet I may inform him of their design, and aid him in his escape. It shall be so. But then he flies, absents himself, and I bar myself from his dear dear conversation! That too will distract me.[9] If he keep out of the way, my Papa and Mama may in time relent, and we may be happy. If he stays, he is hanged, and then he is lost forever! He intended to lie concealed in my room, 'till the dusk of the evening: If they are abroad, I'll this instant let him out, lest some accident should prevent him. [Exit, and returns.]

Scene 13

Polly, Macheath

Air 14. Pretty Parrot, say—

MACHEATH   Pretty Polly, say,
                   When I was away,

4. "Account of things distant or secret" (Johnson's Dictionary).
5. Bouquet, often carried by condemned prisoners.
6. The road from Newgate to Tyburn, where criminals were hanged.
7. The gallows ("Tyburn tree").
8. England's most famous hangman (d. 1686); thereafter, any hangman.
9. Make me crazy.

> *Did your fancy never stray*
> *To some newer lover?*

POLLY   *Without disguise,*
> *Heaving sighs,*
> *Doting eyes,*
> *My constant heart discover.[1]*
> *Fondly let me loll!*

MACHEATH *O pretty, pretty Poll.*

POLLY And are *you* as fond as ever, my dear?

MACHEATH Suspect my honor, my courage, suspect anything but my love. May my pistols miss fire, and my mare slip her shoulder while I am pursued, if I ever forsake thee!

POLLY Nay, my dear, I have no reason to doubt you, for I find in the romance you lent me, none of the great heroes were ever false in love.

Air 15. Pray, fair one, be kind.

MACHEATH *My heart was so free,*
> *It roved like the bee,*
> *'Till Polly my passion requited;*
> *I sipped each flower,*
> *I changed ev'ry hour,*
> *But here ev'ry flower is united.*

POLLY Were you sentenced to transportation, sure, my dear, you could not leave me behind you—could you?

MACHEATH Is there any power, any force that could tear me from thee? You might sooner tear a pension out of the hands of a courtier, a fee from a lawyer, a pretty woman from a looking glass, or any woman from quadrille. But to tear me from thee is impossible!

Air 16. Over the hills and far away.

> *Were I laid on Greenland's coast,*
> *And in my arms embraced my lass;*
> *Warm amidst eternal frost,*
> *Too soon the half year's night[2] would pass.*

POLLY *Were I sold on Indian soil,*
> *Soon as the burning day was closed,*
> *I could mock the sultry toil,*
> *When on my charmer's breast reposed.*

MACHEATH *And I would love you all the day,*
POLLY   *Every night would kiss and play,*
MACHEATH *If with me you'd fondly stray*
POLLY   *Over the hills and far away.*

POLLY Yes, I would go with thee. But oh!—how shall I speak it? I must be torn from thee. We must part.

MACHEATH How! Part!

---

1. Reveal, uncover.   2. The long dark winter of the polar regions.

POLLY We must, we must. My Papa and Mama are set against thy life. They now, even now are in search after thee. They are preparing evidence against thee. Thy life depends upon a moment.

Air 17. Gin thou wert mine awn thing—

O what pain it is to part!
    Can I leave thee, can I leave thee?
O what pain it is to part!
    Can thy Polly ever leave thee?
But lest death my love should thwart,
    And bring thee to the fatal cart,
Thus I tear thee from my bleeding heart!
    Fly hence, and let me leave thee.

One kiss and then—one kiss—begone—farewell.

MACHEATH My hand, my heart, my dear, is so riveted to thine, that I cannot unloose my hold.

POLLY But my Papa may intercept thee, and then I should lose the very glimmering of hope. A few weeks, perhaps, may reconcile us all. Shall thy Polly hear from thee?

MACHEATH Must I then go?

POLLY And will not absence change your love?

MACHEATH If you doubt it, let me stay—and be hanged.

POLLY O how I fear! How I tremble! Go—but when safety will give you leave, you will be sure to see me again; for 'till then Polly is wretched.

Air 18. O the broom, etc.

[Parting, and looking back at each other with fondness; he at one door, she at the other.]

MACHEATH The miser thus a shilling sees,
    Which he's obliged to pay,
With sighs resigns it by degrees,
    And fears 'tis gone for aye.[3]

POLLY The boy, thus, when his sparrow's flown,
    The bird in silence eyes;
But soon as out of sight 'tis gone,
    Whines, whimpers, sobs, and cries.

Act 2

Scene 1. A Tavern near Newgate

Jemmy Twitcher, Crook-fingered Jack, Wat Dreary, Robin of Bagshot, Nimming Ned, Henry Padington, Matt of the Mint, Ben Budge, and the rest of the gang, at the table, with wine, brandy, and tobacco.

BEN But prithee, Matt, what is become of thy brother Tom? I have not seen him since my return from transportation.

MATT Poor brother Tom had an accident this time twelvemonth, and so clever a made fellow he was, that I could not save him from those fleaing[4] rascals the surgeons; and now, poor man, he is among the otamys[5] at Surgeon's Hall.

BEN So it seems, his time was come.

---

3. Forever.
4. Flaying, robbing.

5. Skeletons (from "anatomies"). The corpses of executed criminals were often used in medical studies.

JEMMY But the present time is ours, and nobody alive hath more. Why are the laws leveled at us? Are we more dishonest than the rest of mankind? What we win, gentlemen, is our own by the law of arms, and the right of conquest.

CROOK-FINGERED JACK Where shall we find such another set of practical philosophers, who to a man are above the fear of death?

WAT Sound men, and true!

ROBIN Of tried courage, and indefatigable industry!

NED Who is there here that would not die for his friend?

HARRY Who is there here that would betray him for his interest?

MATT Show me a gang of courtiers that can say as much.

BEN We are for a just partition of the world, for every man hath a right to enjoy life.

MATT We retrench⁶ the superfluities of mankind. The world is avaricious, and I hate avarice. A covetous fellow, like a jackdaw, steals what he was never made to enjoy, for the sake of hiding it. These are the robbers of mankind, for money was made for the free-hearted and generous, and where is the injury of taking from another, what he hath not the heart to make use of?

JEMMY Our several stations⁷ for the day are fixed. Good luck attend us all. Fill the glasses.

Air 19. Fill ev'ry glass, etc.

MATT   *Fill ev'ry glass, for wine inspires us,*
        And fires us
    With courage, love, and joy.
    Women and wine should life employ.
    Is there aught else on earth desirous?

CHORUS *Fill ev'ry glass, etc.*

Scene 2

To them enter Macheath.

MACHEATH Gentlemen, well met. My heart hath been with you this hour; but an unexpected affair hath detained me. No ceremony, I beg you.

MATT We were just breaking up to go upon duty. Am I to have the honor of taking the air with you, Sir, this evening upon the heath? I drink a dram now and then with the stage-coachmen in the way of friendship and intelligence; and I know that about this time there will be passengers upon the Western Road,⁸ who are worth speaking with.

MACHEATH I was to have been of that party—but—

MATT But what, Sir?

MACHEATH Is there any man who suspects my courage?

MATT We have all been witnesses of it.

MACHEATH My honor and truth to the gang?

MATT I'll be answerable for it.

MACHEATH In the division of our booty, have I ever shown the least marks of avarice or injustice?

MATT By these questions something seems to have ruffled you. Are any of us suspected?

MACHEATH I have a fixed confidence, gentlemen, in you all, as men of honor, and as such I value and respect you. Peachum is a man that is useful to us.

---

6. Cut back, economize.   8. Through Bagshot Heath, west of London.
7. Our respective jobs.

MATT Is he about to play us any foul play? I'll shoot him through the head.

MACHEATH I beg you, gentlemen, act with conduct and discretion. A pistol is your last resort.

MATT He knows nothing of this meeting.

MACHEATH Business cannot go on without him. He is a man who knows the world, and is a necessary agent to us. We have had a slight difference, and till it is accommodated I shall be obliged to keep out of his way. Any private dispute of mine shall be of no ill consequence to my friends. You must continue to act under his direction, for the moment we break loose from him, our gang is ruined.

MATT As a bawd[9] to a whore, I grant you, he is to us of great convenience.

MACHEATH Make him believe I have quitted the gang, which I can never do but with life.[1] At our private quarters I will continue to meet you. A week or so will probably reconcile us.

MATT Your instructions shall be observed. 'Tis now high time for us to repair to our several duties; so till the evening at our quarters in Moor-fields[2] we bid you farewell.

MACHEATH I shall wish myself with you. Success attend you.

[Sits down melancholy at the table.]

Air 20. March in Rinaldo, with drums and trumpets.

MATT   Let us take the road.
    Hark! I hear the sound of coaches!
    The hour of attack approaches,
To your arms, brave boys, and load.
    See the ball I hold!
    Let the chemists[3] toil like asses,
    Our fire their fire surpasses,
    And turns all our lead to gold.

[The gang, ranged in the front of the stage, load their pistols, and stick them under their girdles,[4] then go off singing the first part in chorus.]

Scene 3

Macheath, Drawer[5]

MACHEATH What a fool is a fond wench! Polly is most confoundedly bit.[6] I love the sex. And a man who loves money might as well be contended with one guinea, as I with one woman. The town perhaps hath been as much obliged to me, for recruiting it with free-hearted ladies, as to any recruiting officer in the army. If it were not for us and the other gentlemen of the sword, Drury Lane would be uninhabited.

Air 21. Would you have a young virgin, etc.

If the heart of a man is depressed with cares,
    The mist is dispelled when a woman appears;
Like the notes of a fiddle, she sweetly, sweetly
Raises the spirits, and charms our ears,
    Roses and lilies her cheeks disclose,

---

9. Pimp.
1. I.e., I will quit the gang only when I quit my life.
2. Just outside the old City wall.
3. Alchemists, who sought to turn base metals into gold.

4. Belts.
5. Bartender.
6. Ensnared.

> *But her ripe lips are more sweet than those.*
> *Press her,*
> *Caress her*
> *With blisses,*
> *Her kisses*
> *Dissolve us in pleasure, and soft repose.*

I must have women. There is nothing unbends[7] the mind like them. Money is not so strong a cordial for the time. Drawer! [*Enter Drawer.*] Is the porter gone for all the ladies, according to my directions?

DRAWER I expect him back every minute. But you know, Sir, you sent him as far as Hockley in the Hole, for three of the ladies, for one in Vinegar Yard, and for the rest of them somewhere about Lewkner's Lane.[8] Sure some of them are below, for I hear the bar bell. As they come I will show them up. Coming, coming!

Scene 4

Macheath, Mrs. Coaxer, Dolly Trull, Mrs. Vixen, Betty Doxy, Jenny Diver, Mrs. Slammekin, Suky Tawdry, and Molly Brazen.

MACHEATH Dear Mrs. Coaxer, you are welcome. You look charmingly today. I hope you don't want the repairs of quality, and lay on paint.[9]—Dolly Trull! Kiss me, you slut; are you as amorous as ever, hussy? You are always so taken up with stealing hearts, that you don't allow yourself time to steal anything else. Ah Dolly, thou wilt ever be a coquette!—Mrs. Vixen, I'm yours, I always loved a woman of wit and spirit; they make charming mistresses, but plaguy wives.—Betty Doxy! Come hither, hussy. Do you drink as hard as ever? You had better stick to good wholesome beer; for in troth, Betty, strong waters[1] will in time ruin your constitution. You should leave those to your betters.—What! And my pretty Jenny Diver too! As prim and demure as ever! There is not any prude, though ever so high bred, hath a more sanctified look, with a more mischievous heart. Ah! Thou art a dear artful hypocrite.—Mrs. Slammekin! As careless and genteel as ever! All you fine ladies, who know your own beauty, affect an undress.—But see, here's Suky Tawdry come to contradict what I was saying. Everything she gets one way she lays out upon her back. Why, Suky, you must keep at least a dozen tallymen.[2]— Molly Brazen! [*She kisses him.*] That's well done. I love a free-hearted wench. Thou hast a most agreeable assurance, girl, and art as willing as a turtle. But hark! I hear music. The harper is at the door. "If music be the food of love, play on."[3] Ere you seat yourselves, ladies, what think you of a dance? Come in. [*Enter Harper.*] Play the French tune, that Mrs. Slammekin was so fond of.

[*A dance a la ronde[4] in the French manner; near the end of it this song and chorus.*]

Air 22. Cotillon.

> *Youth's the season made for joys,*
>   *Love is then our duty,*
> *She alone who that employs,*
>   *Well deserves her beauty.*

---

7. Relaxes.
8. Both in Drury Lane.
9. I hope you do not need to paint your face as women of quality do.

1. Hard liquor.
2. Merchants who provide goods on credit.
3. The opening line of Shakespeare's *Twelfth Night*.
4. A circular dance.

> Let's be gay,
>> While we may,
> Beauty's a flower, despised in decay.
> Youth's the season etc.
>
>> Let us drink and sport today,
>>> Ours is not tomorrow.
>> Love with youth flies swift away,
>>> Age is nought but sorrow.
>>>> Dance and sing,
>>>> Time's on the wing,
>> Life never knows the return of spring.

CHORUS *Let us drink, etc.*

MACHEATH Now, pray ladies, take your places. Here fellow. [*Pays the Harper.*] Bid the Drawer bring us more wine. [*Exit Harper.*] If any of the ladies choose gin, I hope they will be so free to call for it.

JENNY. You look as if you meant me. Wine is strong enough for me. Indeed, Sir, I never drink strong waters, but when I have the cholic.

MACHEATH Just the excuse of the fine ladies! Why, a lady of quality is never without the cholic. I hope, Mrs. Coaxer, you have had good success of late in your visits among the mercers.[5]

COAXER We have so many interlopers—yet with industry, one may still have a little picking. I carried a silver-flowered lutestring, and a piece of black padesoy[6] to Mr. Peachum's lock but last week.

VIXEN There's Molly Brazen hath the ogle of a rattlesnake. She riveted a linen-draper's eye so fast upon her, that he was nicked[7] of three pieces of cambric before he could look off.

BRAZEN Oh dear, Madam! But sure nothing can come up to your handling of laces! And then you have such a sweet deluding tongue! To cheat a man is nothing; but the woman must have fine parts indeed who cheats a woman!

VIXEN Lace, Madam, lies in a small compass, and is of easy conveyance. But you are apt, Madam, to think too well of your friends.

COAXER If any woman hath more art than another, to be sure, 'tis Jenny Diver. Though her fellow be never so agreeable, she can pick his pocket as coolly, as if money were her only pleasure. Now that is a command of the passions uncommon in a woman!

JENNY I never go to the tavern with a man, but in the view of business. I have other hours, and other sort of men for my pleasure. But had I your address,[8] Madam—

MACHEATH Have done with your compliments, ladies; and drink about: You are not so fond of me, Jenny, as you use to be.

JENNY 'Tis not convenient, Sir, to show my fondness among so many rivals. 'Tis your own choice, and not the warmth of my inclination that will determine you.[9]

Air 23. All in a misty morning, etc.

> Before the barn door crowing,
>> The cock by hens attended,

---

5. Dealers in textiles.
6. Types of silk fabric.
7. Robbed.

8. Polished manner.
9. Make up your mind.

His eyes around him throwing,
  Stands for a while suspended.
Then one he singles from the crew,
  And cheers the happy hen;
With how do you do, and how do you do,
  And how do you do again.

MACHEATH Ah Jenny! Thou art a dear slut.

TRULL Pray, Madam, were you ever in keeping?[1]

TAWDRY I hope, Madam, I ha'nt been so long upon the town, but I have met with some good fortunes as well as my neighbors.

TRULL Pardon me, Madam, I meant no harm by the question; 'twas only in the way of conversation.

TAWDRY Indeed, Madam, if I had not been a fool, I might have lived very handsomely with my last friend. But upon his missing five guineas, he turned me off. Now I never suspected he had counted them.

SLAMMEKIN Who do you look upon, Madam, as your best sort of keepers?

TRULL That, Madam, is thereafter as they be.[2]

SLAMMEKIN I, Madam, was once kept by a Jew; and bating[3] their religion, to women they are a good sort of people.

TAWDRY Now for my part, I own I like an old fellow: for we always make them pay for what they can't do.

VIXEN A spruce prentice, let me tell you, ladies, is no ill thing, they bleed[4] freely. I have sent at least two or three dozen of them in my time to the plantations.[5]

JENNY But to be sure, Sir, with so much good fortune as you have had upon the road, you must be grown immensely rich.

MACHEATH The road, indeed, hath done me justice, but the gaming table hath been my ruin.

Air 24. When once I lay with another man's wife, etc.

JENNY *The gamesters and lawyers are jugglers[6] alike,*
  If they meddle your all is in danger.
Like gypsies, if once they can finger a souse,[7]
  Your pockets they pick, and they pilfer your house,
  And give your estate to a stranger.

A man of courage should never put anything to the risk, but his life. These are the tools of a man of honor. Cards and dice are only fit for cowardly cheats, who prey upon their friends. [*She takes up his pistol. Tawdry takes up the other.*]

TAWDRY This, Sir, is fitter for your hand. Besides your loss of money, 'tis a loss to the ladies. Gaming takes you off from women. How fond could I be of you! But before company, 'tis ill bred.

MACHEATH Wanton hussies!

JENNY I must and will have a kiss to give my wine a zest.

---

1. A kept mistress of a wealthy gentleman.
2. It depends how they treat me.
3. Apart from.
4. Spend.

5. I.e., incited them to steal and thereby caused them to be transported to the colonies.
6. Sleight-of-hand artists.
7. Get their hands on a sou (a French penny).

[*They take him about the neck, and make signs to Peachum and the constables, who rush in upon him.*]

Scene 5

To them, Peachum and constables.

PEACHUM I seize you, Sir, as my prisoner.

MACHEATH Was this well done, Jenny? Women are decoy ducks; who can trust them! Beasts, jades, jilts, harpies, furies, whores!

PEACHUM Your case, Mr. Macheath, is not particular. The greatest heroes have been ruined by women. But, to do them justice, I must own they are a pretty sort of creatures, if we could trust them. You must now, Sir, take your leave of the ladies, and if they have a mind to make you a visit, they will be sure to find you at home. The gentleman, ladies, lodges in Newgate. Constables, wait upon the Captain to his lodgings.

Air 25. When first I laid siege to my Chloris, etc.

MACHEATH *At the tree I shall suffer with pleasure,*
At the tree I shall suffer with pleasure,
Let me go where I will,
In all kinds of ill,
I shall find no such furies as these are.

PEACHUM Ladies, I'll take care the reckoning shall be discharged.[8]
[*Exit Macheath, guarded with Peachum and constables.*]

Scene 6

The women remain.

VIXEN Look ye, Mrs. Jenny, though Mr. Peachum may have made a private bargain with you and Suky Tawdry for betraying the Captain, as we were all assisting, we ought all to share alike.

COAXER I think, Mr. Peachum, after so long an acquaintance, might have trusted me as well as Jenny Diver.

SLAMMEKIN I am sure at least three men of his hanging, and in a year's time too (if he did me justice) should be set down to my account.[9]

TRULL Mrs. Slammekin, that is not fair. For you know one of them was taken in bed with me.

JENNY As far as a bowl of punch or a treat, I believe Mrs. Suky will join with me. As for anything else, ladies, you cannot in conscience expect it.

SLAMMEKIN Dear Madam—

TRULL I would not for the world—

SLAMMEKIN 'Tis impossible for me—

TRULL As I hope to be saved, Madam—

SLAMMEKIN Nay, then I must stay here all night—

TRULL Since you command me.

[*Exit with great ceremony.*]

8. The bill shall be paid.

9. I.e., I deserve the credit for at least three men that Peachum has had hanged.

Scene 7. Newgate

Lockit, Turnkeys,[1] Macheath, Constables.

LOCKIT Noble Captain, you are welcome. You have not been a lodger of mine this year and half. You know the custom, Sir. Garnish,[2] Captain, garnish. Hand me down those fetters there.

MACHEATH Those, Mr. Lockit, seem to be the heaviest of the whole set. With your leave, I should like the further pair better.

LOCKIT Look ye, Captain, we know what is fittest for our prisoners. When a gentleman uses me with civility, I always do the best I can to please him. Hand them down I say. We have them of all prices, from one guinea to ten, and 'tis fitting every gentleman should please himself.

MACHEATH I understand you, Sir. [*Gives money.*] The fees here are so many, and so exorbitant, that few fortunes can bear the expense of getting off[3] handsomely, or of dying like a gentleman.

LOCKIT Those, I see, will fit the Captain better. Take down the further pair. Do but examine them, Sir. Never was better work. How genteelly they are made! They will sit as easy as a glove, and the nicest[4] man in England might not be ashamed to wear them. [*He puts on the chains.*] If I had the best gentleman in the land in my custody I could not equip him more handsomely. And so, Sir, I now leave you to your private meditations.

Scene 8

Macheath

Air 26. Courtiers, courtiers think it no harm, etc.

Man may escape from rope and gun;
Nay, some have outlived the doctor's pill:
Who takes a woman must be undone,
That basilisk[5] is sure to kill.
The fly that sips treacle is lost in the sweets,
So he that tastes woman, woman, woman,
He that tastes woman, ruin meets.

To what a woeful plight have I brought myself! Here must I (all day long, 'till I am hanged) be confined to hear the reproaches of a wench who lays her ruin at my door. I am in the custody of her father, and to be sure if he knows of the matter, I shall have a fine time on't betwixt this[6] and my execution. But I promised the wench marriage. What signifies a promise to a woman? Does not man in marriage itself promise a hundred things that he never means to perform? Do all we can, women will believe us; for they look upon a promise as an excuse for following their own inclinations. But here comes Lucy, and I cannot get from her. Would I were deaf!

---

1. Jailers.
2. Pay the jailer the customary bribe.
3. Escaping punishment.
4. Most discerning.

5. Mythical serpent which killed by its breath or its glance.
6. This moment.

Scene 9

Macheath, Lucy

LUCY You base man you, how can you look me in the face after what hath passed between us? See here, perfidious wretch, how I am forced to bear about the load of infamy you have laid upon me.[7] O Macheath! Thou hast robbed me of my quiet. To see thee tortured would give me pleasure.

Air 27. A lovely lass to a friar came, etc.

> *Thus when a good housewife sees a rat*
> *In her trap in the morning taken,*
> *With pleasure her heart goes pit a pat,*
> *In revenge for her loss of bacon.*
> *Then she throws him*
> *To the dog or cat,*
> *To be worried, crushed, and shaken.*

MACHEATH Have you no bowels,[8] no tenderness, my dear Lucy, to see a husband in these circumstances?

LUCY A husband!

MACHEATH In every respect but the form, and that, my dear, may be said over us at any time. Friends should not insist upon ceremonies. From a man of honor, his word is as good as his bond.

LUCY 'Tis the pleasure of all you fine men to insult the women you have ruined.

Air 28. 'Twas when the sea was roaring, etc.

> *How cruel are the traitors,*
> *Who lie and swear in jest,*
> *To cheat unguarded creatures*
> *Of virtue, fame, and rest!*
> *Whoever steals a shilling,*
> *Through shame the guilt conceals:*
> *In love the perjured villain*
> *With boasts the theft reveals.*

MACHEATH The very first opportunity, my dear (have but patience), you shall be my wife in whatever manner you please.

LUCY Insinuating monster! And so you think I know nothing of the affair of Miss Polly Peachum. I could tear thy eyes out!

HEATH Sure Lucy, you can't be such a fool as to be jealous of Polly!

LUCY Are you not married to her, you brute you?

MACHEATH Married! Very good. The wench gives it out only to vex thee, and to ruin me in thy good opinion. 'Tis true, I go to the house; I chat with the girl, I kiss her, I say a thousand things to her (as all gentlemen do) that mean nothing, to divert myself; and now the silly jade hath set it about that I am married to her, to let me know what she would be at. Indeed, my dear Lucy, these violent passions may be of ill consequence to a woman in your condition.

LUCY Come, come, Captain, for all your assurance, you know that Miss Polly hath put it out of your power to do me the justice you promised me.

---

7. I.e., she is pregnant.   8. The bodily seat of tenderness, pity.

MACHEATH A jealous woman believes everything her passion suggests. To convince you of my sincerity, if we can find the ordinary,[9] I shall have no scruples of making you my wife; and I know the consequence of having two at a time.

LUCY That you are only to be hanged, and so get rid of them both.

MACHEATH I am ready, my dear Lucy, to give you satisfaction—if you think there is any in marriage. What can a man of honor say more?

LUCY So then it seems, you are not married to Miss Polly.

MACHEATH You know, Lucy, the girl is prodigiously conceited. No man can say a civil thing to her, but (like other fine ladies) her vanity makes her think he's her own for ever and ever.

Air 29. The sun had loosed his weary teams, etc.

> *The first time at the lookingglass*
> *The mother sets her daughter,*
> *The image strikes the smiling lass*
> *With self-love ever after.*
> *Each time she looks, she, fonder grown,*
> *Thinks ev'ry charm grows stronger.*
> *But alas, vain maid, all eyes but your own*
> *Can see you are not younger.*

When women consider their own beauties, they are all alike unreasonable in their demands; for they expect their lovers should like them as long as they like themselves.

LUCY Yonder is my father—perhaps this way we may light upon the ordinary, who shall try if you will be as good as your word. For I long to be made an honest woman.

Scene 10

Peachum, Lockit with an account book

LOCKIT In this last affair, Brother Peachum, we are agreed. You have consented to go halves in Macheath.

PEACHUM We shall never fall out about an execution. But as to that article, pray how stands our last year's account?

LOCKIT If you will run your eye over it, you'll find 'tis fair and clearly stated.

PEACHUM This long arrear[1] of the government is very hard upon us! Can it be expected that we should hang our acquaintance for nothing, when our betters will hardly save theirs without being paid for it. Unless the people in employment pay better, I promise them for the future, I shall let other rogues live besides their own.

LOCKIT Perhaps, Brother, they are afraid these matters may be carried too far. We are treated too by them with contempt, as if our profession was not reputable.

PEACHUM In one respect indeed, our employment may be reckoned dishonest, because like great statesmen, we encourage those who betray their friends.

LOCKIT Such language, Brother, anywhere else, might turn to your prejudice.[2] Learn to be more guarded, I beg you.

Air 30. How happy are we, etc.

> *When you censure the age,*
> *Be cautious and sage,*
> *Lest the courtiers offended should be:*

---

9. The prison chaplain.
1. Lateness in the payment of debts.

2. Be used against you.

> *If you mention vice or bribe,*
> *'Tis so pat[3] to all the tribe;*
> *Each cries, "That was leveled at me!"*

PEACHUM Here's poor Ned Clincher's name, I see. Sure, Brother Lockit, there was a little unfair proceeding in Ned's case: for he told me in the condemned hold,[4] that for value received, you had promised him a Session or two longer without molestation.

LOCKIT Mr. Peachum, this is the first time my honor was ever called in question.

PEACHUM Business is at an end if once we act dishonorably.

LOCKIT Who accuses me?

PEACHUM You are warm,[5] Brother.

LOCKIT He that attacks my honor, attacks my livelihood. And this usage, Sir, is not to be borne.

PEACHUM Since you provoke me to speak, I must tell you too, that Mrs. Coaxer charges you with defrauding her of her information money[6] for the apprehending of curl-pated Hugh. Indeed, indeed, Brother, we must punctually pay our spies, or we shall have no information.

LOCKIT Is this language to me, Sirrah, who have saved you from the gallows, Sirrah!

[*Collaring each other.*]

PEACHUM If I am hanged, it shall be for ridding the world of an arrant rascal.

LOCKIT This hand shall do the office of the halter[7] you deserve, and throttle you— you dog!—

PEACHUM Brother, Brother, we are both in the wrong. We shall be both losers in the dispute—for you know we have it in our power to hang each other. You should not be so passionate.

LOCKIT Nor you so provoking.

PEACHUM 'Tis our mutual interest; 'tis for the interest of the world we should agree. If I said anything, Brother, to the prejudice of your character, I ask pardon.

LOCKIT Brother Peachum, I can forgive as well as resent. Give me your hand. Suspicion does not become a friend.

PEACHUM I only meant to give you occasion to justify yourself. But I must now step home, for I expect the gentleman about this snuffbox that Filch nimmed two nights ago in the park. I appointed him at this hour.

Scene 11

Lockit, Lucy

LOCKIT Whence come you, hussy?

LUCY My tears might answer that question.

LOCKIT You have then been whimpering and fondling, like a spaniel, over the fellow that hath abused you.

LUCY One can't help love; one can't cure it. 'Tis not in my power to obey you, and hate him.

LOCKIT Learn to bear your husband's death like a reasonable woman. 'Tis not the fashion, nowadays, so much as to affect sorrow upon these occasions. No woman would ever marry, if she had not the chance of mortality for a release. Act like a woman of spirit, hussy, and thank your father for what he is doing.

---

3. Suitable.
4. Death row.
5. Angry.

6. Reward for informing on someone.
7. Noose.

Air 31. Of a noble race was Shenkin.

LUCY   Is then his fate decreed, Sir?
        Such a man can I think of quitting?
        When first we met, so moves me yet,
        O see how my heart is splitting!

LOCKIT Look ye, Lucy, there is no saving him. So, I think, you must do like other
widows: buy yourself weeds,[8] and be cheerful.

Air 32

        You'll think ere many days ensue
            This sentence not severe;
        I hang your husband, child, 'tis true,
            But with him hang your care.
                Twang dang dillo dee.

Like a good wife, go moan over your dying husband. That, child, is your duty.
Consider, girl, you can't have the man and the money too—so make yourself as
easy as you can, by getting all you can from him.

Scene 12

Lucy, Macheath

LUCY Though the ordinary was out of the way today, I hope, my dear, you will, upon
the first opportunity, quiet my scruples. Oh, Sir! My father's hard heart is not to
be softened, and I am in the utmost despair.

MACHEATH But if I could raise a small sum—would not twenty guineas, think you,
move him? Of all the arguments in the way of business, the perquisite[9] is the most
prevailing. Your father's perquisites for the escape of prisoners must amount to a
considerable sum in the year. Money well timed, and properly applied, will do
anything.

Air 33. London ladies.

        If you at an office solicit your due,[1]
            And would not have matters neglected;
        You must quicken the clerk with the perquisite too,
            To do what his duty directed.
        Or would you the frowns of a lady prevent,
            She too has this palpable failing,
        The perquisite softens her into consent;
            That reason with all is prevailing.

LUCY What love or money can do shall be done: for all my comfort depends upon
your safety.

Scene 13

Lucy, Macheath, Polly

POLLY Where is my dear husband? Was a rope ever intended for this neck! O let me
throw my arms about it, and throttle thee with love! Why dost thou turn away
from me? 'Tis thy Polly. 'Tis thy wife.

8. A widow's mourning clothes.   1. Seek what is due to you.
9. Tip.

MACHEATH Was ever such an unfortunate rascal as I am!

LUCY Was there ever such another villain!

POLLY O Macheath! Was it for this we parted? Taken! Imprisoned! Tried! Hanged! Cruel reflection! I'll stay with thee 'till death. No force shall tear thy dear wife from thee now. What means my love? Not one kind word! Not one kind look! Think what thy Polly suffers to see thee in this condition.

Air 34. All in the downs, etc.

> *Thus when the swallow, seeking prey,*
> *Within the sash[2] is closely pent,*
> *His comfort, with bemoaning lay,[3]*
> *Without sits pining for th' event.*
> *Her chatt'ring lovers all around her skim;*
> *She heeds them not (poor bird!) her soul's with him.*

MACHEATH I must disown her. [*Aside.*] The wench is distracted.

LUCY Am I then bilked of my virtue? Can I have no reparation? Sure men were born to lie, and women to believe them! O villain! Villain!

POLLY Am I not thy wife? Thy neglect of me, thy aversion to me too severely proves it. Look on me. Tell me, am I not thy wife?

LUCY Perfidious wretch!

POLLY Barbarous husband!

LUCY Hadst thou been hanged five months ago, I had been happy.

POLLY And I too. If you had been kind to me 'till death, it would not have vexed me. And that's no very unreasonable request (though from a wife) to a man who hath not above seven or eight days to live.

LUCY Art thou then married to another? Hast thou two wives, monster?

MACHEATH If women's tongues can cease for an answer—hear me.

LUCY I won't. Flesh and blood can't bear my usage.

POLLY Shall I not claim my own? Justice bids me speak.

Air 35. Have you heard of a frolicsome ditty, etc.

MACHEATH *How happy could I be with either,*
> *Were t' other dear charmer away!*
> *But while you thus tease me together,*
> *To neither a word will I say;*
> *But tol de rol, etc.*

POLLY Sure, my dear, there ought to be some preference shown to a wife! At least she may claim the appearance of it. He must be distracted with his misfortunes, or he could not use me thus!

LUCY O villain, villain! Thou hast deceived me. I could even inform against thee with pleasure. Not a prude wishes more heartily to have facts against her intimate acquaintance, than I now wish to have facts against thee. I would have her satisfaction, and they should all out.

Air 36. Irish trot.

POLLY *I'm bubbled.[4]*

---

2. Window frame.
3. Plaintive song.

4. Cheated, fooled.

LUCY   *I'm bubbled.*

POLLY   *Oh how I am troubled!*

LUCY *Bamboozled, and bit!*

POLLY   *My distresses are doubled.*

LUCY *When you come to the tree, should the hangman refuse,*
            These fingers, with pleasure, could fasten the noose.

POLLY *I'm bubbled, etc.*

MACHEATH Be pacified, my dear Lucy. This is all a fetch[5] of Polly's, to make me desperate with[6] you in case I get off. If I am hanged, she would fain[7] the credit of being thought my widow. Really, Polly, this is no time for a dispute of this sort; for whenever you are talking of marriage, I am thinking of hanging.

POLLY And hast thou the heart to persist in disowning me?

MACHEATH And hast thou the heart to persist in persuading me that I am married? Why, Polly, dost thou seek to aggravate my misfortunes?

LUCY Really, Miss Peachum, you but expose yourself. Besides, 'tis barbarous in you to worry a gentleman in his circumstances.

Air 37

POLLY   *Cease your funning;*
            Force or cunning
            Never shall my heart trapan.[8]
            All these sallies
            Are but malice
            To seduce my constant man.
              'Tis most certain,
              By their flirting
            Women oft, have envy shown;
              Pleased, to ruin
              Others' wooing;
            Never happy in their own!

POLLY Decency, Madam, methinks might teach you to behave yourself with some reserve with the husband, while his wife is present.

MACHEATH But seriously, Polly, this is carrying the joke a little too far.

LUCY If you are determined, Madam, to raise a disturbance in the prison, I shall be obliged to send for the turnkey to show you the door. I am sorry, Madam, you force me to be so ill-bred.

POLLY Give me leave to tell you, Madam. These forward airs don't become you in the least, Madam. And my duty, Madam, obliges me to stay with my husband, Madam.

Air 38. Good-morrow, gossip Joan.

LUCY   *Why how now, Madam Flirt?*
            If you thus must chatter;
            And are for flinging dirt,
            Let's try who best can spatter;
                    Madam Flirt!

5. Trick.   7. Would like.
6. Ruin my hopes of having.   8. Esnare.

POLLY   *Why how now, saucy jade;*
       Sure the wench is tipsy!
 [*To him.*] *How can you see me made*
       The scoff of such a gypsy?
 [*To her.*] *Saucy jade!*

Scene 14

Lucy, Macheath, Polly, Peachum.

PEACHUM Where's my wench? Ah, hussy! Hussy! Come you home, you slut; and
  when your fellow is hanged, hang yourself, to make your family some amends.

POLLY Dear, dear father, do not tear me from him—I must speak; I have more to say
  to him. Oh! Twist thy fetters about me, that he may not haul me from thee!

PEACHUM Sure all women are alike! If ever they commit the folly, they are sure to
  commit another by exposing themselves. Away—not a word more. You are my
  prisoner now, hussy.

Air 39. Irish howl.

POLLY *No power on earth can e'er divide*
   The knot that sacred love hath tied.
   When parents draw against our mind,[9]
   The true-love's knot they faster bind.
    Oh, oh ray, oh Amborah, oh, oh, etc.

          [*Holding Macheath, Peachum pulling her.*]

Scene 15

Lucy, Macheath

MACHEATH I am naturally compassionate, wife, so that I could not use the wench as
  she deserved, which made you at first suspect there was something in what she said.

LUCY Indeed, my dear, I was strangely puzzled.

MACHEATH If that had been the case, her father would never have brought me
  into this circumstance. No, Lucy, I had rather die than be false to thee.

LUCY How happy am I, if you say this from your heart! For I love thee so, that I
  could sooner bear to see thee hanged than in the arms of another.

MACHEATH But couldst thou bear to see me hanged?

LUCY O, Macheath, I can never live to see that day.

MACHEATH You see, Lucy, in the account of love you are in my debt, and you must
  now be convinced, that I rather choose to die than be another's. Make me, if possible, love thee more, and let me owe my life to thee. If you refuse to assist me,
  Peachum and your father will immediately put me beyond all means of escape.

LUCY My father, I know, hath been drinking hard with the prisoners, and I fancy he
  is now taking his nap in his own room. If I can procure the keys, shall I go off with
  thee, my dear?

MACHEATH If we are together, 'twill be impossible to lie concealed. As soon as
  the search begins to be a little cool, I will send to thee. 'Till then my heart is thy
  prisoner.

9. Pull against our wishes.

LUCY Come then, my dear husband, owe thy life to me, and though you love me not, be grateful. But that Polly runs in my head strangely.

MACHEATH A moment of time may make us unhappy forever.

Air 40. The lass of Patie's mill, etc.

LUCY   I like the fox shall grieve,
    Whose mate hath left her side.
    Whom hounds, from morn to eve,
    Chase o'er the country wide.
    Where can my lover hide?
    Where cheat the weary pack?
    If love be not his guide,
    He never will come back!

Act 3

Scene 1. Newgate

Lockit, Lucy

LOCKIT To be sure, wench, you must have been aiding and abetting to help him to this escape.

LUCY Sir, here hath been Peachum and his daughter Polly, and to be sure they know the ways of Newgate as well as if they had been born and bred in the place all their lives. Why must all your suspicion light upon me?

LOCKIT Lucy, Lucy, I will have none of these shuffling answers.

LUCY Well then, if I know anything of him I wish I may be burnt!

LOCKIT Keep your temper, Lucy, or I shall pronounce you guilty.

LUCY Keep yours, Sir, I do wish I may be burned. I do—and what can I say more to convince you?

LOCKIT Did he tip handsomely? How much did he come down with? Come hussy, don't cheat your father; and I shall not be angry with you. Perhaps you have made a better bargain with him than I could have done. How much, my good girl?

LUCY You know, Sir, I am fond of him, and would have given money to have kept him with me.

LOCKIT Ah, Lucy! Thy education might have put thee more upon thy guard; for a girl in the bar of an alehouse is always besieged.

LUCY Dear Sir, mention not my education—for 'twas to that I owe my ruin.

Air 41. If love's a sweet passion, etc.

When young at the bar you first taught me to score,[1]
And bid me be free of my lips, and no more;
I was kissed by the parson, the squire, and the sot.
When the guest was departed, the kiss was forgot.
But his kiss was so sweet, and so closely he pressed,
That I languished and pined till I granted the rest.

If you can forgive me, Sir, I will make a fair confession, for to be sure he hath been a most barbarous villain to me.

LOCKIT And so you have let him escape, hussy? Have you?

---

1. Tally, keep an account.

LUCY When a woman loves, a kind look, a tender word can persuade her to anything, and I could ask no other bribe.

LOCKIT Thou wilt always be a vulgar[2] slut, Lucy. If you would not be looked upon as a fool, you should never do anything but upon the foot of[3] interest. Those that act otherwise are their own bubbles.[4]

LUCY But love, Sir, is a misfortune that may happen to the most discreet woman, and in love we are all fools alike. Notwithstanding all he swore, I am now fully convinced that Polly Peachum is actually his wife. Did I let him escape (fool that I was!) to go to her? Polly will wheedle herself into his money, and then Peachum will hang him, and cheat us both.

LOCKIT So I am to be ruined, because, forsooth, you must be in love! A very pretty excuse!

LUCY I could murder that impudent happy strumpet. I gave him his life, and that creature enjoys the sweets of it. Ungrateful Macheath!

Air 42. South Sea ballad.

> *My love is all madness and folly,*
>   *Alone I lie,*
>   *Toss, tumble, and cry,*
> *What a happy creature is Polly!*
> *Was e'er such a wretch as I!*
> *With rage I redden like scarlet,*
> *That my dear inconstant varlet,*
>   *Stark blind to my charms,*
>   *Is lost in the arms*
> *Of that jilt, that inveigling harlot!*
>   *Stark blind to my charms,*
>   *Is lost in the arms*
> *Of that jilt, that inveigling harlot!*
> *This, this my resentment alarms.*

LOCKIT And so, after all this mischief, I must stay here to be entertained with your caterwauling, Mistress Puss! Out of my sight, wanton strumpet! You shall fast and mortify yourself into reason, with now and then a little handsome discipline[5] to bring you to your senses. Go.

Scene 2

Lockit

LOCKIT Peachum then intends to outwit me in this affair; but I'll be even with him. The dog is leaky in his liquor,[6] so I'll ply him that way, get the secret from him, and turn this affair to my own advantage. Lions, wolves, and vultures don't live together in herds, droves, or flocks. Of all animals of prey, man is the only sociable one. Every one of us preys upon his neighbor, and yet we herd together. Peachum is my companion, my friend. According to the custom of the world, indeed, he may quote thousands of precedents for cheating me. And shall not I make use of the privilege of friendship to make him a return?

---

2. Common.
3. For the sake of.
4. Cheat themselves.

5. A beating.
6. Talkative when drunk.

Air 43. Packington's Pound.

Thus gamesters united in friendship are found,
Though they know that their industry all is a cheat;
They flock to their prey at the dicebox's sound,
And join to promote one another's deceit.
　　But if by mishap
　　They fail of a chap,[7]
To keep in their hands, they each other entrap.
Like pikes, lank with hunger, who miss of their ends,[8]
They bite their companions, and prey on their friends.

Now, Peachum, you and I, like honest tradesmen, are to have a fair trial which of us two can overreach the other.—Lucy! [*Enter Lucy.*] Are there any of Peachum's people now in the house?

LUCY Filch, Sir, is drinking a quartern[9] of strong waters in the next room with Black Moll.

LOCKIT Bid him come to me.

Scene 3

Lockit, Filch

LOCKIT Why, boy, thou lookest as if thou wert half starved, like a shotten herring.[1]

FILCH One had need have the constitution of a horse to go through the business. Since the favorite child-getter[2] was disabled by a mishap, I have picked up a little money by helping the ladies to a pregnancy against their being called down to sentence. But if a man cannot get an honest livelihood any easier way, I am sure, 'tis what I can't undertake for another Session.

LOCKIT Truly, if that great man should tip off,[3] 'twould be an irreparable loss. The vigor and prowess of a knight-errant never saved half the ladies in distress that he hath done. But, boy, can'st thou tell me where thy master is to be found?

FILCH At his lock,[4] Sir, at the Crooked Billet.

LOCKIT Very well. I have nothing more with you.

[*Exit Filch.*]

I'll go to him there, for I have many important affairs to settle with him; and in the way of those transactions, I'll artfully get into his secret. So that Macheath shall not remain a day longer out of my clutches.

Scene 4. A Gaming House.

Macheath in a fine tarnished coat, Ben Budge, Matt of the Mint.

MACHEATH I am sorry, gentlemen, the road was so barren of money. When my friends are in difficulties, I am always glad that my fortune can be serviceable to them. [*Gives them money.*] You see, gentlemen, I am not a mere Court friend, who professes everything and will do nothing.

Air 44. Lillibullero.

The modes of the Court so common are grown,
　　That a true friend can hardly be met;

---

7. Cannot get a customer (prey).
8. Fail to catch their prey.
9. Quarter-pint.
1. A herring that has spawned.

2. Begetter (i.e., Macheath).
3. Die.
4. A cant word signifying a warehouse where stolen goods are deposited [Gay's note].

Friendship for interest is but a loan,
　Which they let out for what they can get.
　　'Tis true, you find
　　Some friends so kind,
Who will give you good counsel themselves to defend.
　　In sorrowful ditty,
　　They promise, they pity,
But shift you[5] for money, from friend to friend.

But we, gentlemen, have still honor enough to break through the corruptions of the world. And while I can serve you, you may command me.

BEN It grieves my heart that so generous a man should be involved in such difficulties, as oblige him to live with such ill company, and herd with gamesters.

MATT See the partiality of mankind! One man may steal a horse, better than another look over a hedge.[6] Of all mechanics,[7] of all servile handicraftsmen, a gamester is the vilest. But yet, as many of the quality[8] are of the profession, he is admitted amongst the politest company. I wonder we are not more respected.

MACHEATH There will be deep play tonight at Marybone, and consequently money may be picked up upon the road. Meet me there, and I'll give you the hint who is worth setting.[9]

MATT The fellow with a brown coat with a narrow gold binding, I am told, is never without money.

MACHEATH What do you mean, Matt? Sure you will not think of meddling with him! He's a good honest kind of a fellow, and one of us.

BEN To be sure, Sir, we will put ourselves under your direction.

MACHEATH Have an eye upon the moneylenders. A rouleau,[1] or two, would prove a pretty sort of an expedition. I hate extortion.

MATT Those rouleaus are very pretty things. I hate your bank bills. There is such a hazard in putting them off.[2]

MACHEATH There is a certain man of distinction, who in his time hath nicked me out of a great deal of the ready. He is in my cash,[3] Ben; I'll point him out to you this evening, and you shall draw upon him for the debt. The company are met; I hear the dicebox in the other room. So, gentlemen, your servant. You'll meet me at Marybone.

Scene 5. Peachum's Lock

A table with wine, brandy, pipes, and tobacco.
Peachum, Lockit

LOCKIT The coronation account,[4] Brother Peachum, is of so intricate a nature, that I believe it will never be settled.

PEACHUM It consists indeed of a great variety of articles. It was worth to our people, in fees of different kinds, above ten installments.[5] This is part of the account, Brother, that lies open before us.

---

5. Put you off.
6. I.e., one man is permitted to steal a horse, though another is not permitted even to look at one; proverbial.
7. Tradesmen.
8. The people of quality (gentry).
9. Setting upon, robbing.
1. A packet of gold coins.
2. Getting rid of them, passing them off.

3. Owes me money.
4. A manuscript inventory of items stolen during the coronation of George II; Peachum "keeps books" like an ordinary businessman.
5. I.e., the thieves have found a single coronation more than ten times as profitable as the annual installment of the new Lord Mayor.

LOCKIT A lady's tail[6] of rich brocade—that, I see, is disposed of.

PEACHUM To Mrs. Diana Trapes, the tallywoman,[7] and she will make a good hand[8] on't in shoes and slippers, to trick out young ladies, upon their going into keeping.

LOCKIT But I don't see any article of the jewels.

PEACHUM Those are so well known, that they must be sent abroad. You'll find them entered under the article of exportation. As for the snuffboxes, watches, swords, etc., I thought it best to enter them under their several heads.

LOCKIT Seven and twenty women's pockets[9] complete; with the several things therein contained; all sealed, numbered, and entered.

PEACHUM But, Brother, it is impossible for us now to enter upon this affair. We should have the whole day before us. Besides, the account of the last half year's plate is in a book by itself, which lies at the other office.

LOCKIT Bring us then more liquor. Today shall be for pleasure, tomorrow for business. Ah, Brother, those daughters of ours are two slippery hussies. Keep a watchful eye upon Polly, and Macheath in a day or two shall be our own again.

Air 45. Down in the north country, etc.

LOCKIT *What gudgeons[1] are we men!*
  Ev'ry woman's easy prey.
  Though we have felt the hook, again
   We bite and they betray.
  The bird that hath been trapped,
   When he hears his calling mate,
  To her he flies, again he's clapped
   Within the wiry grate.

PEACHUM But what signifies catching the bird, if your daughter Lucy will set open the door of the cage?

LOCKIT If men were answerable for the follies and frailties of their wives and daughters, no friends could keep a good correspondence together for two days. This is unkind of you, Brother; for among good friends, what they say or do goes for nothing.
[Enter a servant.]

SERVANT Sir, here's Mrs. Diana Trapes wants to speak with you.

PEACHUM Shall we admit her, Brother Lockit?

LOCKIT By all means. She's a good customer, and a fine-spoken woman. And a woman who drinks and talks so freely will enliven the conversation.

PEACHUM Desire her to walk in.   [Exit servant.]

Scene 6

Peachum, Lockit, Mrs. Trapes

PEACHUM Dear Mrs. Dye, your servant. One may know by your kiss, that your gin is excellent.

TRAPES I was always very curious[2] in my liquors.

LOCKIT There is no perfumed breath like it. I have been long acquainted with the flavor of those lips. Han't I, Mrs. Dye?

---

6. Train (of a woman's dress).
7. One who provides goods on credit.
8. Profit.
9. A pocket was a detachable bag worn outside the woman's dress.

1. "A small fish . . . easily caught, and therefore made a proverbial name for a man easily cheated" (Johnson's *Dictionary*).
2. Fastidious.

TRAPES Fill it up. I take as large draughts of liquor, as I did of love. I hate a flincher in either.

Air 46. A shepherd kept sheep, etc.

In the days of my youth I could bill like a dove, fa, la, la, etc.
Like a sparrow at all times was ready for love, fa, la, la, etc.
The life of all mortals in kissing should pass,
Lip to lip while we're young—then the lip to the glass, fa, la, la, etc.

But now, Mr. Peachum, to our business. If you have blacks[3] of any kind, brought in of late: mantoes,[4] velvet scarves, petticoats—let it be what it will—I am your chap, for all my ladies are very fond of mourning.

PEACHUM Why, look ye, Mrs. Dye, you deal so hard with us, that we can afford to give the gentlemen, who venture their lives for the goods, little or nothing.

TRAPES The hard times oblige me to go very near[5] in my dealing. To be sure, of late years I have been a great sufferer by the Parliament. Three thousand pounds would hardly make me amends. The act for destroying the Mint[6] was a severe cut upon our business. 'Till then, if a customer[7] stepped out of the way, we knew where to have her. No doubt you know Mrs. Coaxer. There's a wench now (till today) with a good suit of clothes of mine upon her back, and I could never set eyes upon her for three months together. Since the act too against imprisonment for small sums,[8] my loss there too hath been very considerable, and it must be so, when a lady can borrow a handsome petticoat, or a clean gown, and I not have the least hank[9] upon her! And, o' my conscience, now-a-days most ladies take a delight in cheating, when they can do it with safety.

PEACHUM Madam, you had a handsome gold watch of us t'other day for seven guineas. Considering we must have our profit, to a gentleman upon the road, a gold watch will be scarce worth the taking.

TRAPES Consider, Mr. Peachum, that watch was remarkable, and not of very safe sale. If you have any black velvet scarves—they are a handsome winter wear; and take with most gentlemen who deal with my customers. 'Tis I that put the ladies upon a good foot. 'Tis not youth or beauty that fixes their price. The gentlemen always pay according to their dress, from half a crown to two guineas; and yet those hussies make nothing of bilking of me. Then too, allowing for accidents. I have eleven fine customers now down under the surgeon's hands[1]—what with fees and other expenses, there are great goings-out, and no comings-in, and not a farthing to pay for at least a month's clothing. We run great risks—great risks indeed.

PEACHUM As I remember, you said something just now of Mrs. Coaxer.

TRAPES Yes, Sir. To be sure I stripped her of a suit of my own clothes about two hours ago; and have left her as she should be, in her shift, with a lover of hers at my house. She called him upstairs, as he was going to Marybone in a hackney coach. And I hope, for her own sake and mine, she will persuade the Captain to redeem[2] her, for the Captain is very generous to the ladies.

---

3. Black clothing.
4. Loose robes (French: *manteaux*).
5. To pay as little as possible.
6. The Mint was a safe haven for debtors, and hence a gathering place for disreputable characters. The act (10 October 1723) made it much harder to feign bankruptcy, and thereby to take refuge in the Mint.
7. Prostitute.

8. 24 June 1726: "An Act to Prevent Frivolous and Vexatious Arrests"; "small sums" meant ten pounds if a Superior court matter, or 40 shillings if an Inferior.
9. Hold.
1. For treatment of venereal disease.
2. I.e., will help her to buy back (as at a pawn shop) her "suit of . . . clothes."

LOCKIT What Captain?

TRAPES He thought I did not know him. An intimate acquaintance of yours, Mr. Peachum—only Captain Macheath—as fine as a lord.

PEACHUM Tomorrow, dear Mrs. Dye, you shall set your own price upon any of the goods you like. We have at least half a dozen velvet scarves, and all at your service. Will you give me leave to make you a present of this suit of nightclothes for your own wearing? But are you sure it is Captain Macheath?

TRAPES Though he thinks I have forgot him, nobody knows him better. I have taken a great deal of the Captain's money in my time at second hand, for he always loved to have his ladies well dressed.

PEACHUM Mr. Lockit and I have a little business with the Captain—you understand me—and we will satisfy you for Mrs. Coaxer's debt.

LOCKIT Depend upon it. We will deal like men of honor.

TRAPES I don't inquire after your affairs—so whatever happens, I wash my hands on't. It hath always been my maxim, that one friend should assist another. But if you please, I'll take one of the scarves home with me. 'Tis always good to have something in hand.

Scene 7. Newgate

Lucy

LUCY Jealousy, rage, love, and fear are at once tearing me to pieces. How I am weather-beaten and shattered with distresses!

Air 47. One evening, having lost my way, etc.

> *I'm like a skiff on the ocean tossed,*
>   *Now high, now low, with each billow born,*
> *With her rudder broke, and her anchor lost,*
>   *Deserted and all forlorn.*
> *While thus I lie rolling and tossing all night,*
> *That Polly lies sporting on seas of delight!*
>   *Revenge, revenge, revenge,*
> *Shall appease my restless sprite.*

I have the ratsbane[3] ready. I run no risk; for I can lay her death upon the gin, and so many die of that naturally that I shall never be called in question. But say I were to be hanged—I never could be hanged for anything that would give me greater comfort than the poisoning that slut.

[*Enter Filch.*]

FILCH Madam, here's our Miss Polly come to wait upon you.

LUCY Show her in.

Scene 8

Lucy, Polly

LUCY Dear Madam, your servant. I hope you will pardon my passion, when I was so happy to see you last. I was so overrun with the spleen,[4] that I was perfectly out of myself. And really when one hath the spleen, everything is to be excused by a friend.

---

3. Rat poison.
4. Generally, ill temper; more specifically, a fashionable

disease resembling hypochondria, also known as "the vapors."

Air 48. Now Roger, I'll tell thee, because thou'rt my son.

> *When a wife's in her pout,*
> *(As she's sometimes, no doubt)*
>   *The good husband as meek as a lamb,*
>   *Her vapors to still,*
>   *First grants her her will,*
>   *And the quieting draught is a dram.*[5]
> *Poor man! And the quieting draught is a dram.*

I wish all our quarrels might have so comfortable a reconciliation.

POLLY I have no excuse for my own behavior, Madam, but my misfortunes. And really, Madam, I suffer too upon your account.

LUCY But, Miss Polly, in the way of friendship, will you give me leave to propose a glass of cordial to you?

POLLY Strong waters are apt to give me the headache. I hope, Madam, you will excuse me.

LUCY Not the greatest lady in the land could have better in her closet, for her own private drinking. You seem mighty low in spirits, my dear.

POLLY I am sorry, Madam, my health will not allow me to accept of your offer. I should not have left you in the rude manner I did when we met last, Madam, had not my Papa hauled me away so unexpectedly. I was indeed somewhat provoked, and perhaps might use some expressions that were disrespectful. But really, Madam, the Captain treated me with so much contempt and cruelty, that I deserved your pity, rather than your resentment.

LUCY But since his escape, no doubt all matters are made up again. Ah Polly! Polly! 'Tis I am the unhappy wife; and he loves you as if you were only his mistress.

POLLY Sure, Madam, you cannot think me so happy as to be the object of your jealousy. A man is always afraid of a woman who loves him too well—so that I must expect to be neglected and avoided.

LUCY Then our cases, my dear Polly, are exactly alike. Both of us indeed have been too fond.

Air 49. O Bessy Bell.

POLLY   *A curse attends that woman's love,*
      Who always would be pleasing.
LUCY   *The pertness of the billing dove,*
      Like tickling, is but teasing.
POLLY   *What then in love can woman do?*
LUCY   *If we grow fond they shun us.*
POLLY   *And when we fly them, they pursue.*
LUCY   *But leave us when they've won us.*

LUCY Love is so very whimsical in both sexes, that it is impossible to be lasting. But my heart is particular,[6] and contradicts my own observation.

POLLY But really, Mistress Lucy, by his last behavior, I think I ought to envy you. When I was forced from him, he did not show the least tenderness. But perhaps, he hath a heart not capable of it.

---

5. A shot of alcohol.
6. In two senses: (1) preoccupied with one person (Macheath), and therefore (2) idiosyncratic—an exception to the rule she has just pronounced.

Air 50. Would fate to me Belinda give.

Among the men, coquettes we find,
Who court by turns all womankind;
And we grant all their hearts desired,
When they are flattered, and admired.

The coquettes of both sexes are self-lovers, and that is a love no other whatever can dispossess. I fear, my dear Lucy, our husband is one of those.

LUCY   Away with these melancholy reflections; indeed, my dear Polly, we are both of us a cup too low.[7] Let me prevail upon you, to accept of my offer.

Air 51. Come, sweet lass, etc.

Come, sweet lass,
Let's banish sorrow
Till tomorrow;
Come, sweet lass,
Let's take a chirping[8] glass.
Wine can clear
The vapors of despair;
And make us light as air;
Then drink, and banish care.

I can't bear, child, to see you in such low spirits. And I must persuade you to what I know will do you good. [*Aside.*] I shall now soon be even with the hypocritical strumpet.   [*Exit.*]

Scene 9.

Polly

All this wheedling of Lucy cannot be for nothing. At this time too! When I know she hates me! The dissembling of a woman is always the forerunner of mischief. By pouring strong waters down my throat, she thinks to pump some secrets out of me. I'll be upon my guard, and won't taste a drop of her liquor, I'm resolved.

Scene 10

Lucy, with strong waters; Polly

LUCY   Come, Miss Polly.

POLLY   Indeed, child, you have given yourself trouble to no purpose. You must, my dear, excuse me.

LUCY   Really, Miss Polly, you are so squeamishly affected about taking a cup of strong waters as a lady before company. I vow, Polly, I shall take it monstrously ill if you refuse me. Brandy and men (though women love them never so well)[9] are always taken by us with some reluctance—unless 'tis in private.

POLLY   I protest, Madam, it goes against me. What do I see! Macheath again in custody! Now every glimmering of happiness is lost. [*Drops the glass of liquor on the ground.*]

LUCY   [*Aside.*] Since things are thus, I'm glad the wench hath escaped: for by this event, 'tis plain, she was not happy enough to deserve to be poisoned.

---

7. I.e, needing a drink.
8. Cheering.

9. However much women may love them.

Scene 11

Lockit, Macheath, Peachum, Lucy, Polly

LOCKIT Set your heart to rest, Captain. You have neither the chance of love or money for another escape, for you are ordered to be called down upon your trial immediately.

PEACHUM Away, hussies! This is not a time for a man to be hampered with his wives. You see, the gentleman is in chains already.

LUCY O husband, husband, my heart longed to see thee; but to see thee thus distracts me!

POLLY Will not my dear husband look upon his Polly? Why hadst thou not flown to me for protection? With me thou hadst been safe.

Air 52. The last time I went o'er the moor.

POLLY *Hither, dear husband, turn your eyes.*
LUCY *Bestow one glance to cheer me.*
POLLY *Think with that look, thy Polly dies.*
LUCY *O shun me not—but hear me.*
POLLY *'Tis Polly sues.*
LUCY   *'Tis Lucy speaks.*
POLLY *Is thus true love requited?*
LUCY *My heart is bursting.*
POLLY   *Mine too breaks.*
LUCY *Must I—*
POLLY   *Must I be slighted?*

MACHEATH What would you have me say, ladies? You see, this affair will soon be at an end, without my disobliging either of you.

PEACHUM But the settling this point, Captain, might prevent a lawsuit between your two widows.

Air 53. Tom Tinker's my true love.

MACHEATH *Which way shall I turn me? How can I decide?*
        Wives, the day of our death, are as fond as a bride.
        One wife is too much for most husbands to hear,
        But two at a time there's no mortal can bear.
        This way, and that way, and which way I will,
        What would comfort the one, t'other wife would take ill.

POLLY But if his own misfortunes have made him insensible to mine—A father sure will be more compassionate. Dear, dear Sir, sink[1] the material evidence, and bring him off at his trial. Polly upon her knees begs it of you.

Air 54. I am a poor shepherd undone.

When my hero in court appears,
    And stands arraigned for his life;
Then think of poor Polly's tears;
    For Ah! Poor Polly's his wife.

1. Suppress.

> Like the sailor he holds up his hand,
>   Distressed on the dashing wave.
> To die a dry death at land,
>   Is as bad as a wat'ry grave.
> And alas, poor Polly!
> Alack, and well-a-day!
> Before I was in love,
>   Oh! Every month was May.

LUCY If Peachum's heart is hardened, sure you, Sir, will have more compassion on a daughter. I know the evidence is in your power. How then can you be a tyrant to me? [Kneeling.]

Air 55. Ianthe the lovely, etc.

> When he holds up his hand arraigned for his life,
> O think of your daughter, and think I'm his wife!
> What are cannons, or bombs, or clashing of swords?
> For death is more certain by witness's words.
> Then nail up their lips; that dread thunder allay;
> And each month of my life will hereafter be May.

LOCKIT Macheath's time is come, Lucy. We know our own affairs, therefore let us have no more whimpering or whining.

Air 56. A cobbler there was, etc.

> Ourselves, like the great, to secure a retreat,
> When matters require it, must give up our gang:
>   And good reason why,
>   Or, instead of the fry,[2]
>   Ev'n Peachum and I,
> Like poor petty rascals, might hang, hang;
> Like poor petty rascals, might hang.

PEACHUM Set your heart at rest, Polly. Your husband is to die today. Therefore, if you are not already provided, 'tis high time to look about for another. There's comfort for you, you slut.

LOCKIT We are ready, Sir, to conduct you to the Old Bailey.

Air 57. Bonny Dundee.

MACHEATH The charge is prepared; the lawyers are met,
> The judges all ranged (a terrible show!).
> I go undismayed, for death is a debt—
> A debt on demand—so take what I owe.
> Then farewell my love. Dear charmers, adieu.
> Contented I die—'tis the better for you.
> Here ends all dispute the rest of our lives,
> For this way at once I please all my wives.

Now, gentlemen, I am ready to attend you.

---

2. Small fish.

Scene 12

Lucy, Polly, Filch

POLLY Follow them, Filch, to the court. And when the trial is over, bring me a particular account of his behavior, and of everything that happened. You'll find me here with Miss Lucy. [*Exit Filch.*] But why is all this music?

LUCY The prisoners, whose trials are put off till next Session, are diverting themselves.

POLLY Sure there is nothing so charming as music! I'm fond of it to distraction! But alas! Now, all mirth seems an insult upon my affliction. Let us retire, my dear Lucy, and indulge our sorrows. The noisy crew, you see, are coming upon us.

[*Exit.*]

[*A dance of prisoners in chains, etc.*]

Scene 13. The Condemned Hold

Macheath, in a melancholy posture.

Air 58. Happy Groves.

O cruel, cruel, cruel case!
Must I suffer this disgrace?

Air 59. Of all the girls that are so smart.

Of all the friends in time of grief,
When threatening death looks grimmer,
Not one so sure can bring relief,
As this best friend, a brimmer.[3]   [*Drinks.*]

Air 60. Britons strike home.

Since I must swing, I scorn, I scorn to wince or whine.   [*Rises.*]

Air 61. Chevy Chase.

But now again my spirits sink;
I'll raise them high with wine.

[*Drinks a glass of wine.*]

Air 62. To old Sir Simon the king.

But valor the stronger grows,
The stronger liquor we're drinking.
And how can we feel our woes,
When we've lost the trouble of thinking?   [*Drinks.*]

Air 63. Joy to great Caesar.

If thus—A man can die
Much bolder with brandy.   [*Pours out a bumper of brandy.*]

---

3. A cup filled to the brim.

Air 64. There was an old woman.

So I drink off this bumper. And now I can stand the test.
And my comrades shall see, that I die as brave as the best.

[*Drinks.*]

Air 65. Did you ever hear of a gallant sailor.

But can I leave my pretty hussies,
Without one tear, or tender sigh?

Air 66. Why are mine eyes still flowing.

Their eyes, their lips, their busses[4]
Recall my love—Ah must I die?

Air 67. Green Sleeves.

Since laws were made for ev'ry degree,
To curb vice in others, as well as me,
I wonder we ha'n't better company,
     Upon Tyburn tree!
But gold from law can take out the sting;
And if rich men like us were to swing,
'Twould thin the land, such numbers to string
     Upon Tyburn tree!

JAILER Some friends of yours, Captain, desire to be admitted. I leave you together.

Scene 14

Macheath, Ben Budge, Matt of the Mint

MACHEATH For my having broke[5] prison, you see, gentlemen, I am ordered immediate execution. The sheriff's officers, I believe, are now at the door. That Jemmy Twitcher should peach me, I own surprised me! 'Tis a plain proof that the world is all alike, and that even our gang can no more trust one another than other people. Therefore, I beg you, gentlemen, look well to yourselves, for in all probability you may live some months longer.

MATT We are heartily sorry, Captain, for your misfortune. But 'tis what we must all come to.

MACHEATH Peachum and Lockit, you know, are infamous scoundrels. Their lives are as much in your power, as yours are in theirs. Remember your dying friend. 'Tis my last request. Bring those villains to the gallows before you, and I am satisfied.

MATT We'll do't.

JAILER Miss Polly and Miss Lucy entreat a word with you.

MACHEATH Gentlemen, adieu.

Scene 15

Lucy, Macheath, Polly

MACHEATH My dear Lucy—my dear Polly—whatsoever hath passed between us is now at an end. If you are fond of marrying again, the best advice I can give you is

4. Kisses.   5. Broken out of.

to ship yourselves off for the West Indies, where you'll have a fair chance of getting a husband apiece; or by good luck, two or three, as you like best.

POLLY How can I support this sight!

LUCY There is nothing moves one so much as a great man in distress.

Air 68. All you that must take a leap, etc.

LUCY *Would I might be hanged!*

POLLY   *And I would so too!*

LUCY *To be hanged with you.*

POLLY   *My dear, with you.*

MACHEATH *O leave me to thought! I fear! I doubt!*
       I tremble! I droop! See, my courage is out.

[*Turns up the empty bottle.*]

POLLY *No token of love?*

MACHEATH   *See, my courage is out.*

[*Turns up the empty pot.*]

LUCY *No token of love?*

POLLY   *Adieu!*

LUCY   *Farewell!*

MACHEATH *But hark! I hear the toll of the bell.*

CHORUS *Tol de rol lol, etc.*

JAILER Four women more, Captain, with a child a-piece! See, here they come.
    [*Enter women and children.*]

MACHEATH What—four wives more! This is too much. Here—tell the sheriff's officers I am ready.

[*Exit Macheath guarded.*]

Scene 16
To them, enter Player and Beggar.

PLAYER But, honest friend, I hope you don't intend that Macheath shall be really executed.

BEGGAR Most certainly, Sir. To make the piece perfect, I was for doing strict poetical justice. Macheath is to be hanged; and for the other personages of the drama, the audience must have supposed they were all either hanged or transported.

PLAYER Why then, friend, this is a downright deep tragedy. The catastrophe is manifestly wrong, for an opera must end happily.

BEGGAR Your objection, Sir, is very just; and is easily removed. For you must allow, that in this kind of drama, 'tis no matter how absurdly things are brought about. So—you rabble there—run and cry a reprieve—let the prisoner be brought back to his wives in triumph.

PLAYER All this we must do, to comply with the taste of the town.[6]

BEGGAR Through the whole piece you may observe such a similitude of manners in high and low life, that it is difficult to determine whether (in the fashionable vices) the fine gentlemen imitate the gentlemen of the road, or the gentlemen of

6. The fashionable audience.

the road the fine gentlemen. Had the play remained, as I at first intended, it would have carried a most excellent moral. 'Twould have shown that the lower sort of people have their vices in a degree as well as the rich, and that they are punished for them.

Scene 17

To them, Macheath with rabble, etc.

MACHEATH So, it seems, I am not left to my choice, but must have a wife at last. Look ye, my dears, we will have no controversy now. Let us give this day to mirth, and I am sure she who thinks herself my wife will testify her joy by a dance.

ALL Come, a dance, a dance.

MACHEATH Ladies, I hope you will give me leave to present a partner to each of you. And (if I may without offense) for this time, I take Polly for mine. [*To Polly.*] And for life, you slut, for we were really married. As for the rest—But at present keep your own secret.

A Dance.

Air 69. Lumps of pudding, etc.

Thus I stand like the Turk, with his doxies around;[7]
From all sides their glances his passion confound;
For black, brown, and fair, his inconstancy burns,
And the different beauties subdue him by turns:
Each calls forth her charms, to provoke his desires:
Though willing to all; with but one he retires.
But think of this maxim, and put off your sorrow,
The wretch of today, may be happy tomorrow.

CHORUS *But think of this maxim, etc.*

FINIS.

1727   1728

◆━━ ⚏ ━━◆

William Hogarth
1697–1764

"I had naturally a good eye," William Hogarth remembered near his life's end. "Shows of all sorts gave me uncommon pleasure when an infant." The "shows" (spectacles) that filled his eye in the turbulent London neighborhood of Smithfield where he grew up suffused his art for life: the antics of actors and the raucousness of audiences at Bartholomew Fair; the chicanery and pathos of prostitutes and thieves; the casual injustice of constables and magistrates. Above

---

7. Like a Sultan in a harem.

all, he watched his father fail. Richard Hogarth, a classical scholar, spent four years as a prisoner for debt, when his coffeehouse (catering to learned men and specializing in Latin conversation) failed to cover its own expenses. The debtor's family was effectually imprisoned too, and Hogarth, in his early teens during the ordeal, never forgot. "The emphasis throughout his work" (notes his biographer Ronald Paulson) "is on prisons, real and metaphorical. Even when he is not dealing with people who are in a prison . . . he portrays rooms that are more like prison cells than boudoirs or parlors."

At age seventeen, Hogarth was apprenticed to a silver engraver, ornamenting platters, rings, tableware, and the like. Finding the work dull, he switched to copper engraving, the technique by which book illustrators and printmakers created and reproduced their pictures. Late in his twenties he commenced his career as painter. His first great successes combined both craft and art. Hogarth produced the series of six pictures that make up *A Harlot's Progress* first as a set of paintings in oil, then as a sequence of copper engravings aimed at wider distribution. If *A Harlot's Progress* launched his popularity, *A Rake's Progress* (engraved in 1735 from canvases painted the year before) clinched his reputation as Britain's most masterly, mocking delineator of contemporary vice and folly. Though he continued for a while to nurture conventional ambitions as a painter of portraits and historical subjects catering to aristocratic tastes, Hogarth came gradually to recognize the originality, force, and commercial viability of his satrical engravings. As he later expressed it (in his own idiosyncratic syntax), he had discovered a style pitched between "the sublime and the grotesque," and had devised "a more new way of proceeding, viz. painting and engraving modern moral subjects, a field unbroke up in any country or any age. . . . Provided I could strike the passions, and by small sums from many, by means of prints which I could engrave from my pictures myself, I could secure my property to myself." Hogarth managed to "strike the passions" both ways: by depicting them vividly in the countenance of his characters, and by igniting them in his audience. He also managed, better than any predecessor, to "secure his property to himself." He petitioned Parliament to pass the Engraver's Copyright Act (often called "Hogarth's Act"), which protected printmakers from the then rampant piratical reproduction of their work, and which thereby (in Hogarth's proud words) "made prints a considerable article and trade in this country, there being more business of that kind done in this town than in Paris or anywhere else." The engravings of *A Rake's Progress* were first published, pointedly, the day after Hogarth's Act became the law of the land.

Early in his career, Hogarth had been praised as a "Shakespeare in painting," and admirers noted repeatedly the literary force of his graphic art; only he, wrote one, could "teach pictures to speak and to think." Hogarth had appropriated the very idea of an instructive moral "progress" from John Bunyan's phenomenally popular religious narrative *Pilgrim's Progress*, but he made the journey at once darker and more satiric. Bunyan's Mr. Christian progresses through Vanity Fair and other dangers toward the Celestial City; Hogarth's protagonists remain mired within the Vanity Fair of contemporary London; their "progress" takes them downward to degradation and death. His art also helped shape a newer form of narrative, the novel. Like the novel, Hogarth's sequences abound in suggestive subplots, telling asides, and startling revelations, played out in the tiniest details carefully placed. Novelists as different from one another as Samuel Richardson, Henry Fielding, and Laurence Sterne valued him as a friend, sought him as a collaborator, and embraced him as a past master in their own moral and narrative mode. "I almost dare affirm," wrote Fielding, "that those two works of his, which he calls *The Rake's* and *The Harlot's Progress*, are calculated more to serve the cause of virtue, and for the preservation of mankind, than all the folios of morality which have ever been written."

A Rake's Progress

Plate 1: Tom Rakewell's father (depicted in the portrait above the mantle) has recently died. The old man was miserly: he wore a coat and fur hat indoors so as not to incur the costs of a fire; he saved broken junk (in the open chest); he nearly starved his housecat (lower left). The young man is profligate: he has torn open doors and cabinets in search of sequestered wealth; he is being measured for new and ostentatious clothes; he is trying to pay off the raging mother of Sarah Young, the weeping woman (at right) whom he has made pregnant.

Plate 2: Nearly unrecognizable in his new elegance, Rakewell (the tallest figure in the picture) surrounds himself with instructors and tradespeople eager to sell their services. In the foreground (from left to right) are a composer, a fencing master, a dance teacher (with fiddle), a hired killer (in black; the note in Tom's hand, from "William Stab," vouches for the assassin as "a man of honor"); a huntsman (with horn); and a jockey, whose trophy cup bears the suggestive name of the winning horse: "Silly Tom." The two moping Englishmen at the back may be miffed to find themselves supplanted by the fashionable foreigners in front of them. The painting above the mantle depicts the Judgment of Paris, that indolent princeling whose unrestrained desires precipitated the catastrophe of the Trojan War.

Plate 3: Rakewell (sprawled at left) has bought himself an orgy. All the Roman portraits in the upper right corner have been defaced, except that of the emperor Nero, who looks out over the havoc like some patron saint of vandalism (his reputed incendarism is re-enacted by the woman standing at the back near the shattered mirror, holding a candle flame to the map of the world). One prostitute caresses Tom while conveying away his watch; in the foreground opposite, a woman disrobes in preparation for an obscene dance that will likely involve the reflective platter and large candle held by the cross-eyed lackey in the doorway. Admonitions to the orgiasts lie at hand, in the form of the chicken's carcass (lower right corner), stripped and forked; and in the person of the ballad singer, tattered, pregnant, and ignored, whose song bears the telling title "Black Joke."

Plate 4: Carried in his sedan chair to a night of gaming at White's Chocolate House and gambling club (rear left), Tom is stopped by a bailiff who serves him with a notice of arrest for debt. He receives aid not from the revellers in the distance but from Sarah Young, the abandoned woman whose mother he tried to buy off in Plate 1. Reversing that gesture, she seeks to secure his release by offering the money she has earned by making ribbons and caps (sample wares hang at her side). On a ladder a lamplighter, distracted by the goings-on, carelessly (and emblematically) spills his flammable fluid onto Rakewell's head.

Plate 5: Intent on wealth, not the love Sarah offers, Rakewell weds an old woman in a dim, disintegrating church where light and faith are in scant supply. On the left, the "Poor's Box," receptacle of charity, has long been shut (a cobweb covers its lid); on the right wall, the table of commandments is cracked. The one-eyed bride appears to wink at the grim parson; Rakewell proffers her the ring while eying her maid. On the floor, a canine couple parodies the human ceremony; in the back, a woman with churchkeys flailing tries to prevent the intrusion of Sarah Young, holding the child Rakewell has sired; Sarah's mother does vigorous but unavailing battle.

Plate 6: During a night of gambling, Rakewell has evidently lost the fortune he acquired by his calculating marriage. Wigless, frantic, he falls to one knee and curses his lot; his rage is replicated (as were his nuptials) by a dog on the floor to his right. The croupier at rear center, carrying the candles, echoes the "world-burning" woman in Plate 3. This time, though, the building is actually on fire. The lantern-bearing watchman at left has come to give warning. Most of the gamblers are too immersed in their own operations to notice either Rakewell's anguish or their own danger.

Plate 7: In the wake of his losses, Rakewell has at last been imprisoned for debt, unable to pay the "garnish" (or customary bribe) that the jailer behind him expects, or even the cost of a beer. The note on the table—"I have read your play and find it will not do"—rejects his last poor, literary attempt at solvency. His wife rails, Sarah faints, his daughter tugs at Sarah's skirts, and his cellmates embody futilities even more preposterous than his own playwriting. The impoverished man at left has devised "a new scheme for paying the debts of the nation." The man seated at the stove is an alchemist, vainly trying to transmute base metals into gold; before his imprisonment, he also built himself a pair of wings (upper left), but they, like Rakewell's upward aspirations, have produced only debt and confinement, not flight and freedom.

Plate 8: Rakewell has been moved from debtor's prison to Bethlehem Royal Hospital (better known as Bedlam), London's asylum for the insane. Grinning outright for the first time in the series, Tom claws at his head while guards restrain him. Sarah Young, weeping, has come to give him comfort. The other two women are here to amuse themselves (at the cost of two pence per visit, Bedlam had become one of London's most popular entertainments). Some inmates display lunatic religious zeal; others have gone mad in pursuit of science. The man drawing the world on the wall seeks a solution to the longitude, the navigational problem that had obsessed Britons for many decades. Behind the open door of the central cell, a naked madman sits and thinks he's king. In a later revision (1763), Hogarth superimposed upon the longitudinist's globe an emblem of Britannia, as though empire and madhouse were now one.

Mind and God

Nature, and Nature's Laws lay hid in Night.
God said, *Let Newton be!* and All was *Light*.

So wrote Alexander Pope, capturing in a couplet the awe with which many of his contemporaries regarded the accomplishments of Isaac Newton. The lines, intended for Newton's tomb, compass his whole career. Pope's last word evokes one of the scientist's early breakthroughs: the discovery that sunlight, for all its seeming "whiteness," teemed with colors, whose operations could be mathematically described. Later, in his masterwork *Naturalis Philosophiae Principia Mathematica* (The Mathematical Principles of Natural Philosophy, 1687), Newton had expounded "Nature's Laws" on a scale and with a precision heretofore unmatched, pinpointing, in compact mathematical formulas, the laws governing gravity and motion, both on earth and throughout the heavens. In Pope's replaying of Genesis, Newton himself becomes a principle, not merely the interpreter of Creation but virtually synonomous with it: God's luminous word, from which revelation follows. For numberless admirers, the name of Newton figured forth not only the intricate simplicities of "Nature's Laws," but also the astonishing, hitherto unsuspected capacity of the human mind to shed light upon the works of God.

The human mind itself promptly became the object of new investigation, Newtonian in its ambitions and its methods. Two years after the *Principia* appeared, John Locke published his *Essay Concerning Human Understanding* (1689), a work comparably influential, in which he sought answers to key questions of epistemology: what do we know? and by what means do we come to know it? Locke, like Newton, brought luster to the scientific approach championed by the Royal Society (of which both men were members): empiricism, the conviction that truth could be attained solely through experiment and experience. The intimate interplay of those two crucial elements is nicely registered in Albert Einstein's account of the way that Newton did his work: "The conceptions which he used to reduce the material of experience to order seemed to flow spontaneously from experience itself, from the beautiful experiments which he ranged in order like playthings and describes with an affectionate wealth of detail." Locke imported empiricism from the physical sciences into the realms of philosophy and psychology. Striving to found a science of mind, to make sense of the running encounter between the material world and human perception, Locke and his successors found in experience both a method for investigating epistemological problems and the core of their solution: for these thinkers, experience is how we know, it is what we know, and it is how we can learn more about the processes of our knowing. The human mind is intrinsically (though not methodically) empiricist in its ways of gathering its "wealth of detail" about the world.

Under the mind's new scrutinies, God's place and primacy fell open to new questions. Empiricism itself was seen to cut two ways. On the one hand, as Newton and the vast majority of his followers delightedly proclaimed, experimental observation was revealing a universal architecture so exquisite as to prove both the existence and the matchless artistry of God the architect; this route from reason to religious faith became known as the "argument from design." On the other hand, discovery was beginning to conjure up alternative possibilities unsettling to faith: of a God not wholly supreme but subject to nature's inexorable laws; or of laws so efficiently self-sustaining that they needed no God to enforce them. In some of its modes, empiricism itself could be seen to imperil faith, since direct experience or demonstration of the divine proved elusive in a science that limited itself to the observation of material, mechanical causes and effects. For Newton, Locke, and countless other inquirers, empiricism promised to explain the ways of God; but they had begun a process which, in other hands, might threaten to explain God away.

The clash between science and theology gathered force in the mid-nineteenth century, when discoveries in geology (the age of the Earth) and biology (evolution) rendered Scripture strongly suspect. But contention between faith and science was manifest much earlier. At the start of the nineteenth century, William Blake briefly sketched the lines of struggle in his private notebook. "Newton's particles of light," he wrote

> Are sands upon the Red sea shore,
> Where Israel's tents do shine so bright.

Against the arrogance of inquiry, Blake insists upon humility and awe; biblical revelation trumps all the small advancements of human knowledge. Pope had gestured in this direction some seven decades earlier. He suggested, in his *Essay on Man*, that for "superior beings" (angels, God), the sight of Newton unfolding "all Nature's law" might provide the same kind of amazement and amusement that we mortals derive from the antics of a performing ape—a creature who knows more than we might expect, but far less than we ourselves. So great (Pope argues) is the difference between human and divine capacities. Throughout the eighteenth century, in works suffused by the concepts of Newton and of Locke, the relations between mind and God were brilliantly explicated and newly contested, as poets and philosophers undertook, from varying vantages and factions, to sing God's praise, to parse his ways, to work toward him by reason or (in rare instances) to reason him out of existence altogether.

✦

Isaac Newton
1642–1727

Albert Einstein summed up Newton's abilities as follows: "In one person, he combined the experimenter, the theorist, the mechanic, and, not least, the artist in exposition." Einstein praises magnificently, and omits much. Newton also combined in his one person a supreme mathematician, an obsessive alchemist, a forceful administrator, and (perhaps most importantly, in his own view) an ardent theologian, eager to discover and expound the place of God in his creation. His voluminous, unorthodox writings on the subject remained unpublished in his lifetime. By denying the full divinity of Christ, Newton accorded God *more* authority than did conventional Anglicanism. His views, if known, would have toppled him from the public eminences he enjoyed: as Lucasian Professor of Mathematics at Cambridge, as Master of the Mint in London, as President of the Royal Society. Still, Newton's first admirers found in his scientific work exhilarating support for a more mainstream theology: the strongest foundation yet for the argument from design. It was the business of natural philosophy, Newton repeatedly insisted, "to deduce causes from effects, until we come to the First Cause, which is certainly not mechanical." Newton's own scientific revelations gave rise to a passionate interest in "natural religion"—a faith in God's existence and benevolence, grounded in the orderliness and beauty of the natural world. One of that faith's adherents was the ambitious young classicist and clergyman Richard Bentley (1662–1742), who, having been been commissioned to deliver a series of lectures defending Christianity against atheism, found in Newton's recently published *Principia* abundant new evidence for his own arguments about the divine "origin and frame of the universe." While preparing his lectures for the press, Bentley sent Newton a set of questions, in order to make sure that he was correctly understanding and deploying the *Principia*. Newton's four replies (the first is excerpted here) map the convergence that interests him most, between the discoveries of science and the majesty of God.

from **Letter to Richard Bentley**

10 December 1692

Sir,

When I wrote my treatise about our system, I had an eye upon such principles as might work with considering men for the belief of a Deity, and nothing can rejoice me more than to find it useful for that purpose. But if I have done the public any service this way, 'tis due to nothing but industry and a patient thought.

As to your first query, it seems to me, that if the matter of our sun and planets and all the matter in the universe was evenly scattered throughout all the heavens, and every particle had an innate gravity towards all the rest,[1] and the whole space throughout which this matter was scattered was but finite, the matter on the outside of this space would by its gravity tend towards all the matter on the inside, and by consequence fall down to the middle of the whole space, and there compose one great spherical mass. But if the matter was evenly diffused through an infinite space, it would never convene into one mass, but some of it convene into one mass and some into another so as to make an infinite number of great masses scattered at great distances from one to another throughout all that infinite space. And thus might the sun and fixed stars be formed, supposing the matter were of a lucid[2] nature. But how the matter should divide itself into two sorts, and that part of it which is fit to compose a shining body should fall down into one mass and make a sun, and the rest which is fit to compose an opaque body should coalesce not into one great body like the shining matter but into many little ones; or, if the sun was at first an opaque body like the planets, or the planets lucid bodies like the sun, how he alone should be changed into a shining body whilst all they continue opaque, or all they be changed into opaque ones whilst he remains unchanged, I do not think explicable by mere natural causes but am forced to ascribe it to the counsel[3] and contrivance of a voluntary agent. The same power, whether natural or supernatural, which placed the sun in the center of the orbs[4] of the six primary planets, placed Saturn in the center of the orbs of his five secondary planets,[5] and Jupiter in the center of the orbs of his four secondary ones, and the Earth in the center of the moon's orb; and therefore, had this cause been a blind one without contrivance and design, the sun would have been a body of the same kind with Saturn, Jupiter and the Earth; that is without light and heat. Why there is one body in our system qualified to give light and heat to all the rest I know no reason but because the author of the system thought it convenient, and why there is but one body of this kind I know no reason but because one was sufficient to warm and enlighten all the rest. For the Cartesian hypothesis[6] of suns losing their light and then turning into comets and comets into planets can have no place in my system and is plainly erroneous, because it's certain that comets as often as they appear to us descend into the system of our planets lower than the orb of Jupiter and sometimes lower than the orbs of Venus and Mercury, and yet never stay here but always return from the sun with the same degrees of motion by which they approached him.

1. Newton did not endorse this premise. "You sometimes speak," he wrote Bentley in his second letter, "of gravity as essential and inherent to matter: pray do not ascribe that notion to me, for the cause of gravity is what I do not pretend to know."
2. Light-producing.
3. Deliberate design.

4. Orbits.
5. I.e., Saturn's moons; Newton states the numbers of planets and their moons then known.
6. A theory put forth by the French mathematician and philosopher René Descartes (1596–1650) in his highly influential treatises on physics, which Newton's *Principia* had challenged.

To your second query I answer that the motions which the planets now have could not spring from any natural cause alone but were impressed by an intelligent agent. For since comets descend into the region of our planets and here move all manner of ways, going sometimes the same way with the planets, sometimes the contrary way, and sometimes in cross ways in planes inclined to the plane of the ecliptic at all kinds of angles, it's plain that there is no natural cause which could determine all the planets both primary and secondary to move the same way and in the same plane without any considerable variation.[7] This must have been the effect of counsel. Nor is there any natural cause which could give the planets those just degrees of velocity in proportion to their distances from the sun and other central bodies about which they move and to the quantity of matter contained in those bodies, which were requisite to make them move in concentric orbs about those bodies. Had the planets been as swift as comets in proportion to their distances from the sun (as they would have been, had their motions been caused by their gravity, whereby the matter at the first formation of the planets might fall from the remotest regions towards the sun), they would not move in concentric orbs but in such eccentric ones as the comets move in. Were all the planets as swift as Mercury or as slow as Saturn or his satellites, or were their several velocities otherwise much greater or less than they are (as they might have been had they arose from any other cause than their gravity), or had their distances from the centers about which they move been greater or less than they are with the same velocities; or had the quantity of matter in the sun or in Saturn, Jupiter, and the Earth and by consequence their gravitating power been greater or less than it is, the primary planets could not have revolved about the sun nor the secondary ones about Saturn, Jupiter and the Earth in concentric circles as they do, but would have moved in hyperbolas or parabolas or in ellipses very eccentric. To make this system therefore, with all its motions, required a cause which understood and compared together the quantities of matter in the several bodies of the sun and planets and the gravitating powers resulting from thence, the several distances of the primary planets from the sun and secondary ones from Saturn, Jupiter, and the Earth, and the velocities with which these planets could revolve at those distances about those quantities of matter in the central bodies. And to compare and adjust all these things together in so great a variety of bodies argues that cause to be not blind and fortuitous, but very well skilled in mechanics and geometry.

To your third query I answer that it may be represented that the sun may, by heating those planets most which are nearest to him, cause them to be better concocted[8] and more condensed by concoction. But when I consider that our Earth is much more heated in its bowels below the upper crust by subterraneous fermentations of mineral bodies than by the sun, I see not why the interior parts of Jupiter and Saturn might not be as much heated, concocted, and coagulated by those fermentations as our Earth is, and therefore this various density should have some other cause than the various distances of the planets from the sun; and I am confirmed in this

7. Newton oversimplifies: the planes of the planets actually incline to each other by as much as five degrees. Newton's arguments in this letter, suggests his biographer Richard Westfall, "reveal above all a determination to find God in nature," even to impose God upon nature. All the phenomena that Newton here attributes to the intervention of divine "counsel" and "skill" were explained scientifically over the course of the next centu-

ry by physicists applying and extending Newton's own system, so that (as the most brilliant of the extenders, Pierre Simon Laplace, is said to have remarked to Napoleon) the hypothesis of divine intervention was no longer necessary.

8. Purified by heat (and hence made denser by the absence of the extraneous matter that the heat has annihilated).

opinion by considering that the planets of Jupiter and Saturn, as they are rarer[9] than the rest, so they are vastly greater and contain a far greater quantity of matter and have many satellites about them, which qualifications surely arose not from their being placed at so great a distance from the sun, but were rather the cause why the Creator placed them at that great distance. For by their gravitating powers they disturb one another's motions very sensibly, as I find by some late observations of Mr. Flamsteed,[1] and had they been placed much nearer to the sun and to one another they would by the same powers have caused a considerable disturbance in the whole system. * * *

Lastly, I see nothing extraordinary in the inclination of the Earth's axis for proving a Deity unless you will urge it as a contrivance for winter and summer and for making the Earth habitable towards the poles, and that the diurnal rotations of the sun and planets, as they could hardly arise from any cause purely mechanical, so by being determined all the same way with the annual and menstrual[2] motions they seem to make up that harmony in the system which (as I explained above) was the effect of choice rather than of chance.

There is yet another argument for a Deity which I take to be a very strong one, but till the principles on which 'tis grounded be better received I think it more advisable to let it sleep. I am

Your most humble servant to command
IS. NEWTON

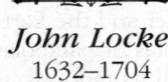

John Locke
1632–1704

In the preface to his *Essay Concerning Human Understanding*, Locke depicts "the incomparable Mr. Newton" as one of the "master builders" of the new science, and himself as a mere "under-laborer," busy "clearing the ground a little, and removing some of the rubbish that lies in the way to knowledge." The eighteenth century, though, tended to venerate the two thinkers equally, Newton as master explicator of the cosmos, Locke as master inquirer into the mind. Starting from the claim that "simple ideas," acquired early, constituted the building blocks of thought, Locke constructed a system of the mind of comparable in intricacy with Newton's universe, but of greater idiosyncrasy (since the content of consciousness differed from person to person, and indeed determined individual identity). Part of Locke's appeal lay in the comparative accessibility of his empiricism. His experiments, unlike Newton's, required neither telescope nor prism, calculus nor genius: readers could perform them (as Locke repeatedly suggested) in the laboratories of their minds, using their own perceptions and memories as raw material. More than any other text, Locke's *Essay* spurred that fascination with the first person which suffuses so much eighteenth-century writing: autobiographies, essays, diaries, travel journals, philosophic treatises, novels. Locke described the workings of the mind so persuasively that in effect he changed them too, prompting an analytic self-consciousness that had not obtained in the same kind and to the same degree before his book appeared.

9. Less dense.
1. John Flamsteed (1646–1719), astronomer and director of the Royal Greenwich Observatory, had recently supplied Newton with these data; the two men later quar-

relled bitterly over Flamsteed's reluctance to make available the immense, precise, and urgently needed records of his celestial observations.
2. Monthly.

from An Essay Concerning Human Understanding

[ON IDEAS[1]]

Every man being conscious to himself that he thinks, and that which his mind is employed about whilst thinking being the *ideas* that are there, 'tis past doubt, that men have in their minds several *ideas*, such as are those expressed by the words *whiteness, hardness, sweetness, thinking, motion, man, elephant, army, drunkenness*, and others. It is in the first place then to be inquired, how he comes by them? I know it is a received doctrine, that men have native *ideas* and original characters[2] stamped upon their minds, in their very first being. This opinion I have at large examined already, and I suppose what I have said in the foregoing book[3] will be much more easily admitted, when I have shown whence the understanding may get all the *ideas* it has, and by what ways and degrees they may come into the mind; for which I shall appeal to everyone's own observation and experience.

Let us then suppose the mind to be, as we say, white paper, void of all characters, without any *ideas*. How comes it to be furnished? Whence comes it by that vast store, which the busy and boundless fancy of man has painted on it, with an almost endless variety? Whence has it all the materials of reason and knowledge? To this I answer, in one word, from *experience*. In that, all our knowledge is founded, and from that it ultimately derives itself. Our observation employed either about *external, sensible objects, or about the internal operations of our minds, perceived and reflected on by ourselves, is that which supplies our understandings with all the materials of thinking.* These two are the fountains of knowledge, from whence all the *ideas* we have, or can naturally have, do spring.

First, *our senses*, conversant about particular sensible objects, do *convey into the mind*, several distinct *perceptions* of things, according to those various ways, wherein those objects do affect them; and thus we come by those *ideas* we have of *yellow, white, heat, cold, soft, hard, bitter, sweet*, and all those which we call sensible qualities, which when I say the senses convey into the mind, I mean, they from external objects convey into the mind what produces there those *perceptions*. This great source of most of the *ideas* we have, depending wholly upon our senses and derived by them to the understanding, I call SENSATION.

Secondly, the other fountain from which experience furnisheth the understanding with *ideas* is the *perception of the operations of our own minds* within us, as it is employed about the *ideas* it has got; which operations, when the soul comes to reflect on, and consider, do furnish the understanding with another set of *ideas*, which could not be had from things without; and such are *perception, thinking, doubting, believing, reasoning, knowing, willing*, and all the different actings of our own minds; which we being conscious of, and observing in ourselves, do from these receive into our understandings, as distinct *ideas*, as we do from bodies affecting our senses. This source of *ideas* every man has wholly in himself. And though it be not sense, as having nothing to do with external objects, yet it is very like it, and might properly enough be called internal sense. But as I call the other *sensation*, so I call this REFLECTION, the *ideas* it affords being such only, as the mind gets by reflecting on its own operations within itself. By REFLECTION then, in the following part of this discourse, I would be understood to mean, that notice which the mind takes of its own operations, and the man-

---

1. All selections are from Book 2, "Of Ideas"; chapter and section numbers follow each section, in brackets. Most of Locke's italics have been retained.

2. Inscriptions.
3. In which Locke denied the existence of "innate principles," received by the soul "in its very first being" (1.2.1).

ner of them, by reason whereof there come to be *ideas* of these operations in the understanding. These two, I say, *viz.* external, material things, as the objects of SEN-SATION, and the operations of our own minds within, as the objects of REFLECTION, are, to me, the only originals,[4] from whence all our *ideas* take their beginnings. The term *operations* here I use in a large sense, as comprehending not barely the actions of the mind about its *ideas*, but some sort of passions arising sometimes from them, such as is the satisfaction or uneasiness arising from any thought.

The understanding seems to me not to have the least glimmering of any *ideas*, which it doth not receive from one of these two. *External objects furnish the mind with the* ideas *of sensible qualities*, which are all those different perceptions they produce in us; and the *mind furnishes the understanding with* ideas *of its own operations*.

These, when we have taken a full survey of them, and their several modes, combinations, and relations, we shall find to contain all our whole stock of *ideas*; and that we have nothing in our minds which did not come in one of these two ways. Let anyone examine his own thoughts, and thoroughly search into his understanding, and then let him tell me, whether all the original *ideas* he has there are any other than of the objects of his *senses*, or of the operations of his mind, considered as objects of his *reflection*; and how great a mass of knowledge soever he imagines to be lodged there, he will, upon taking a strict view, see that he has *not any* idea *in his mind, but what one of these two have imprinted*; though, perhaps, with infinite variety compounded and enlarged by the understanding, as we shall see hereafter.

He that attentively considers the state of a *child*, at his first coming into the world, will have little reason to think him stored with plenty of *ideas*, that are to be the matter of his future knowledge. 'Tis by degrees he comes to be furnished with them. And though the *ideas* of obvious and familiar qualities imprint themselves before the memory begins to keep a register of time and order, yet 'tis often so late, before some unusual qualities come in the way, that there are few men that cannot recollect the beginning of their acquaintance with them; and if it were worthwhile, no doubt a child might be so ordered as to have but a very few, even of the ordinary *ideas*, till he were grown up to a man. But all that are born into the world being surrounded with bodies that perpetually and diversely affect them, variety of *ideas*, whether care be taken about it or no, are imprinted on the minds of children. *Light* and *colors* are busy at hand everywhere, when the eye is but open; *sounds* and some *tangible qualities* fail not to solicit their proper senses, and force an entrance to the mind; but yet, I think, it will be granted easily, that if a child were kept in a place where he never saw any other but black and white till he were a man, he would have no more *ideas* of scarlet or green, than he that from his childhood never tasted an oyster, or a pineapple, has of those particular relishes.

Men then come to be furnished with fewer or more simple *ideas* from without, according as the *objects* they converse with[5] afford greater or less variety; and from the operation of their minds within, according as they more or less *reflect* on them. For, though he that contemplates the operations of his mind cannot but have plain and clear *ideas* of them; yet unless he turn his thoughts that way, and considers them *attentively*, he will no more have clear and distinct *ideas* of all the *operations of his mind*, and all that may be observed therein, than he will have all the particular *ideas* of any landscape, or of the parts and motions of a clock, who will not turn his eyes to it, and with attention heed all the parts of it. The picture or clock may be so placed

---

4. Origins.   5. Encounter.

that they may come in his way every day; but yet he will have but a confused *idea* of all the parts they are made up of, till he *applies himself with attention*, to consider them each in particular. [1.1–7]

* * *

But to return to the matter in hand, the *ideas* we have of substances, and the ways we come by them; I say *our specific* ideas *of substances* are nothing else but *a collection of a certain number of simple* ideas, *considered as united in one thing*. These *ideas* of substances, though they are commonly called simple apprehensions, and the names of them simple terms, yet in effect, are complex and compounded. Thus the *idea* which an *Englishman* signifies by the name *swan* is white color, long neck, red beak, black legs, and whole feet, and all these of a certain size, with a power of swimming in the water, and making a certain kind of noise, and, perhaps, to a man who has long observed those kind of birds, some other properties, which all terminate in sensible simple *ideas*, all united in one common subject.

Besides the complex *ideas* we have of material sensible substances, of which I have last spoken, by the simple *ideas* we have taken from those operations of our own minds, which we experiment[6] daily in ourselves, as thinking, understanding, willing, knowing, and power of beginning motion, etc. co-existing in some substance, we are able to frame *the complex* idea *of an immaterial spirit*. And thus by putting together the *ideas* of thinking, perceiving, liberty, and power of moving themselves and other things, we have as clear a perception and notion of immaterial substances, as we have of material. For putting together the *ideas* of thinking and willing, or the power of moving or quieting corporeal motion, joined to substance, of which we have no distinct *idea*, we have the *idea* of an immaterial spirit; and by putting together the *ideas* of coherent solid parts, and a power of being moved, joined with substance, of which likewise we have no positive *idea*, we have the *idea* of matter. The one is as clear and distinct an *idea*, as the other: the *idea* of thinking, and moving a body, being as clear and distinct *ideas*, as the *ideas* of extension, solidity, and being moved. [23.14–15]

* * *

If we examine the *idea* we have of the incomprehensible Supreme Being, we shall find that we come by it the same way; and that the complex *ideas* we have both of God, and separate spirits, are made up of the simple *ideas* we receive from *reflection; v.g.* having, from what we experiment in ourselves, got the *ideas* of existence and duration; of knowledge and power; of pleasure and happiness; and of several other qualities and powers, which it is better to have than to be without; when we would frame an *idea* the most suitable we can to the Supreme Being, we enlarge every one of these with our *idea* of infinity; and so putting them together, make our complex *idea* of God. For that the mind has such a power of enlarging some of its *ideas*, received from sensation and reflection, has been already showed. [23.33]

[ON IDENTITY]

Personal identity consists, not in the identity of substance, but, as I have said, in the identity of *consciousness*, wherein, if Socrates and the present Mayor of Queenborough agree, they are the same person. If the same Socrates waking and sleeping do not partake of the same *consciousness*, Socrates waking and sleeping is not the same person. And to punish Socrates waking, for what sleeping Socrates thought, and

6. Experience.

waking Socrates was never conscious of, would be no more of right, than to punish one twin for what his brother-twin did, whereof he knew nothing, because their outsides were so like that they could not be distinguished; for such twins have been seen.

But yet possibly it will still be objected, suppose I wholly lose the memory of some parts of my life, beyond a possibility of retrieving them, so that perhaps I shall never be conscious of them again; yet am I not the same person that did those actions, had those thoughts, that I was once conscious of, though I have now forgot them? To which I answer, that we must here take notice what the word *I* is applied to, which in this case is the man only. And the same man being presumed to be the same person, *I* is easily here supposed to stand also for the same person. But if it be possible for the same man to have distinct incommunicable consciousness at different times, it is past doubt the same man would at different times make different persons; which, we see, is the sense of mankind in the solemnest declaration of their opinions, human laws not punishing the *mad man* for the *sober man's* actions, nor the *sober man* for what the *mad man* did, thereby making them two persons; which is somewhat explained by our way of speaking in *English,* when we say such an one *is not himself,* or is *besides himself;* in which phrases it is insinuated, as if those who now, or, at least, first used them, thought, that *self* was changed, the *self* same person was no longer in that man.

But yet 'tis hard to conceive that Socrates the same individual man should be two persons. To help us a little in this, we must consider what is meant by *Socrates,* or the same individual *man.*

First, it must be either the same individual, immaterial, thinking substance: in short, the same numerical soul, and nothing else.

Secondly, or the same animal,[7] without any regard to an immaterial soul.

Thirdly, or the same immaterial spirit united to the same animal.

Now take which of these suppositions you please, it is impossible to make personal identity to consist in anything but consciousness, or reach any farther than that does.

For by the first of them, it must be allowed possible that a man born of different women, and in distant times, may be the same man. A way of speaking, which whoever admits, must allow it possible for the same man to be two distinct persons, as any two that have lived in different ages without the knowledge of one another's thoughts.

By the second and third, Socrates in this life, and after it, cannot be the same man any way, but by the same consciousness; and so making *human identity* to consist in the same thing wherein we place *personal identity,* there will be no difficulty to allow the same man to be the same person. But then they who place *human identity* in consciousness only, and not in something else, must consider how they will make the infant Socrates the same man with Socrates after the resurrection. But whatsoever to some men makes a *man,* and consequently the same individual man, wherein perhaps few are agreed, personal identity can by us be placed in nothing but consciousness (which is that alone which makes what we call *self*) without involving us in great absurdities.

But is not a man drunk and sober the same person? Why else is he punished for the fact[8] he commits when drunk, though he be never afterwards conscious of it? Just as much the same person, as a man that walks, and does other things in his sleep, is

7. Physical, living body.   8. Deed.

the same person, and is answerable for any mischief he shall do in it. Human laws punish both with a justice suitable to their way of knowledge: because in these cases, they cannot distinguish certainly what is real, what counterfeit; and so the ignorance in drunkeness or sleep is not admitted as a plea. For though punishment be annexed to personality, and personality to consciousness, and the drunkard perhaps be not conscious of what he did, yet human judicatures justly punish him; because the fact is proved against him, but what of consciousness cannot be proved for him. But in the great day,[9] wherein the secrets of all hearts shall be laid open, it may be reasonable to think, no one shall be made to answer for what he knows nothing of; but shall receive his doom, his conscience accusing or excusing him. [27.19–22]

1671–1689   1689

Isaac Watts
1674–1748

"As his mind was capacious, his curiosity excursive, and his industry continual," wrote Samuel Johnson in praise of the dissenting minister Isaac Watts, "his writings are very numerous." Watts produced books of poetry, logic, theology, philosophy, and science, but the writings that have mattered most are the hymns and psalm translations (about seven hundred in all) that he began composing in his early twenties. In his philosophical writings, Watts worked hard to absorb the innovations of Newton's physics and Locke's psychology; in his hymns, an older structure of piety prevails. One of empiricism's chief effects was to entangle truth with time, to make knowledge a consequence of *process* (a series of experiments, a sequence of ideas). In Watts's hymns, truth is eternal; the mind's chief tasks are to register God's greatness and to praise it aright. The singing of hymns, and of psalms awkwardly translated from the Hebrew, had been a practice of long standing in Protestant congregations. Watts brought to these forms a new clarity and grace, in verses he carefully crafted, week after week, for the immediate use and pleasure of his congregants. He sought (he once explained) to achieve an "ease of numbers [i.e., meter] and smoothness of sound, and . . . to make the sense plain and obvious." In print, the simplicity of his style gradually won a wider attention, extending far beyond local circles of dissent. As the religious historian and poet Donald Davie has pointed out, Watts's hymns and psalms probably touched more minds (and certainly resounded in more throats) over the course of the eighteenth century than any of the texts we now deem greater hits: *Gulliver's Travels*, Johnson's *Dictionary*, Thomson's *Seasons*. In his lifetime and for more than a century after, Watts was reckoned the English, Christian successor to that ancient king of Israel traditionally credited with creating the Psalms. "Were David to speak English," Watts's brother once remarked to him, "he would choose to make use of your style."

A Prospect of Heaven Makes Death Easy[1]

There is a land of pure delight
    Where saints immortal reign;
Infinite day excludes the night,
    And pleasures banish pain.

5   There everlasting spring abides,
    And never-withering flowers:

---

9. I.e., Judgment Day.

1. From *Hymns and Spiritual Songs* (1707).

Death like a narrow sea divides
        This heav'nly land from ours.

Sweet fields beyond the swelling flood
10   Stand dressed in living green:
So to the Jews old Canaan stood,
        While Jordan rolled between.[2]

But timorous mortals start° and shrink   *tremble*
        To cross this narrow sea,
15   And linger shivering on the brink,
        And fear to launch away.

O! could we make our doubts remove,°   *withdraw*
        Those gloomy doubts that rise,
And see the Canaan that we love,
20   With unbeclouded eyes:

Could we but climb where Moses stood,[3]
        And view the landskip° o'er,   *landscape*
Not Jordan's stream, nor death's cold flood
        Should fright us from the shore.

                                                                    1707

The Hurry of the Spirits, in a Fever and Nervous Disorders[1]

My frame of nature is a ruffled sea,
And my disease the tempest. Nature feels
A strange commotion to her inmost center;
The throne of reason shakes. "Be still, my thoughts;
5   Peace and be still." In vain my reason gives
The peaceful word, my spirit strives in vain
To calm the tumult and command my thoughts.
This flesh, this circling blood, these brutal powers
Made to obey, turn rebels to the mind,
10   Nor hear its laws. The engine° rules the man.   *body*
Unhappy change! When nature's meaner springs,
Fired to impetuous ferments, break all order;
When little restless atoms rise and reign
Tyrants in sovereign uproar, and impose
15   Ideas on the mind; confused ideas
Of non-existents and impossibles,
Who can describe them? Fragments of old dreams,
Borrowed from midnight, torn from fairy fields
And fairy skies, and regions of the dead,
20   Abrupt, ill-sorted. O 'tis all confusion!
If I but close my eyes, strange images

---

2. In Joshua 3, the children of Israel, at the end of their
40-year journey in the desert, see the promised land of
Canaan across the River Jordan.
3. Having led the Israelites to the end of their desert journey, Moses on his last day of life climbed the mountain of
Nebo, and surveyed the entire promised land (Deuteron-

omy 34.1–4).
1. Not a hymn but an autobiographical poem, the first in
a sequence entitled *Thoughts and Meditations in a Long
Sickness, 1712 and 1713*, published decades later in
Watts' *Reliquiae Juveniles* (writings in youth).

In thousand forms and thousand colors rise,
Stars, rainbows, moons, green dragons, bears and ghosts,
An endless medley rush upon the stage
25   And dance and riot wild in reason's court
Above control. I'm in a raging storm,
Where seas and skies are blended, while my soul
Like some light worthless chip of floating cork
Is tossed from wave to wave: now overwhelmed
30   With breaking floods, I drown, and seem to lose
All being; now high-mounted on the ridge
Of tall foaming surge, I'm all at once
Caught up into the storm, and ride the wind,
The whistling wind; unmanageable steed,
35   And feeble rider! Hurried many a league
Over the rising hills of roaring brine,
Through airy wilds unknown, with dreadful speed
And infinite surprise, till some few minutes
Have spent the blast, and then perhaps I drop
40   Near to the peaceful coast. Some friendly billow
Lodges me on the beach, and I find rest.
Short rest I find; for the next rolling wave
Snatches me back again; then ebbing far
Sets me adrift, and I am borne off to sea,
45   Helpless, amidst the bluster of the winds,
Beyond the ken of shore.

Ah, when will these tumultuous scenes be gone?
When shall this weary spirit, tossed with tempests,
Harassed and broken, reach the ports of rest,
50   And hold it firm? When shall this wayward flesh
With all th' irregular springs of vital movement
Ungovernable, return to sacred order,
And pay their duties to the ruling mind?

1712   1734

Against Idleness and Mischief[1]

How doth the little busy bee
    Improve each shining hour,
And gather honey all the day
    From every opening flower!

5   How skillfully she builds her cell!
    How neat she spreads the wax!
And labors hard to store it well
    With the sweet food she makes.

In works of labor, or of skill,
10   I would be busy too;

---

1. From *Divine Songs Attempted in Easy Language, for the Use of Children*. The poems in this durable little collection were memorized by numberless children in the 18th and 19th centuries, including Lewis Carroll's Alice. Wandering through Wonderland, she is commanded by its inhabitants (as she doubtless was in school) to recite these verses, and discovers to her dismay that the lines come out all wrong.

For Satan finds some mischief still°   *always*
    For idle hands to do.

In books, or work, or healthful play,
    Let my first years be passed.
15   That I may give for every day
       Some good account at last.

                                      1715

Man Frail, and God Eternal[1]

Our God, our help in ages past,
    Our hope for years to come,
Our shelter from the stormy blast,
    And our eternal home.

5   Under the shadow of thy throne
       Thy saints have dwelt secure.
Sufficient is thine arm alone,
       And our defense is sure.

Before the hills in order stood,
10   Or earth received her frame,
From everlasting thou art God,
       To endless years the same.

Thy word commands our flesh to dust,
    Return, ye sons of men.
15   All nations rose from earth at first,
       And turn to earth again.

A thousand ages in thy sight
    Are like an evening gone;
Short as the watch that ends the night,
20   Before the rising sun.

The busy tribes of flesh and blood
    With all their lives and cares
Are carried downwards by thy flood,
    And lost in following years.

25   Time, like an ever-rolling stream
       Bears all its sons away.
They fly forgotten, as a dream
       Dies at the opening day.

Like flowery fields the nations stand
30   Pleased with the morning light.
The flowers beneath the mower's hand
       Lie withering ere 'tis night.

---

1. An imitation of Psalm 90, lines 1–6. This and the next poem are from *The Psalms of David Imitated in the Language of the New Testament, and Applied to the Christian State and Worship*. As the title indicates, Watts intended not merely to translate the Psalms, but to recast them. In his preface, he declares himself "the first who hath brought down the royal author [King David] into the common affairs of the Christian life, and let the psalmist of Israel into the Church of Christ, without anything of a Jew about him."

Our God, our help in ages past,
Our hope for years to come,
35 Be thou our guard while troubles last,
And our eternal home.

1719

Miracles Attending Israel's Journey[1]

When Israel, freed from Pharaoh's hand,
Left the proud tyrant and his land,
The tribes with cheerful homage own[2]
Their king, and Judah[3] was his throne.

5   Across the deep[4] their journey lay;
The deep divides to make them way.
Jordan beheld their march, and fled
With backward current to his head.[5]

The mountains shook like frighted sheep.
10 Like lambs the little hillocks leap.[6]
Not Sinai[7] on her base could stand,
Conscious of sovereign power at hand.

What power could make the deep divide?
Make Jordan backward roll his tide?
15 Why did ye leap, ye little hills?
And whence the fright that Sinai feels?

Let every mountain, every flood,
Retire, and know th'approaching God,
The king of Israel. See him here.
20 Tremble thou earth, adore, and fear.

He thunders, and all nature mourns.
The rock to standing pool he turns.
Flints spring with fountains at his word,[8]
And fires and seas confess the Lord.

1719

1. An imitation of Psalm 114. In 1712, Watts sent a version of this poem to the *Spectator*, where it appeared (No. 461, Tuesday, 19 August 1712) along with a letter from the poet explaining a discovery he had made while translating: "As I was describing the journey of Israel from Egypt, and added the Divine Presence amongst them, I perceived a beauty in the Psalm which was entirely new to me, and which I was going to lose; and that is, that the poet utterly conceals the presence of God in the beginning of it. . . . The reason now seems evident, and this conduct necessary. For if God had appeared before [i.e., at the start of the poem], there could be no wonder why the mountains should leap and the sea retire; therefore that this convulsion of nature may be brought in with due surprise, his name is not mentioned till afterward, and then with a very agreeable turn of thought God is introduced at once in all his majesty."
2. Acknowledged (God as their king).
3. A portion of the land promised by God to the Israelites; here the name is used to designate the entire promised land.
4. The Red Sea, whose miraculous parting made possible the Israelites' escape from Egypt (Exodus 14.21–31).
5. Alludes to a second, similar miracle later in the journey: God makes the waters of the river Jordan "stand upon an heap," so that the Israelites can pass "clean over" dry ground, into the promised land (Joshua 3.14–17).
6. Lines 9–10 may refer (in the original Psalm) to the hills and mountains of the promised land, the dwelling places of local gods who tremble at Israel's advent.
7. The sacred mountain on which Moses received from the Lord the Ten Commandments. At the Lord's approach, "the whole mount quaked greatly" (Exodus 19.18).
8. In the Book of Numbers (20.8–11), God miraculously produces water from rock in order to sustain the Israelites during their journey.

—→ ⊱✦⊰ ←—

Joseph Addison
1672–1719

The ideas of Newton and Locke became widely known not through their own writings (which were voluminous and often dense, but through various popularizations: lectures, demonstrations, explanatory handbooks, the popular press. One of the chief disseminators was the *Spectator*, the phenomenally successful series of daily essays composed by Joseph Addison and Richard Steele (for more on the *Spectator*, see page 2323). Addison in particular undertook to inculcate the ideas of Newton and Locke, sometimes directly by quotation and commentary, but more often indirectly, by absorption and a kind of tacit transmission. "The working of my own mind," Mr. Spectator announces early on, "is the general entertainment of my life," and he recommends this notably Lockean "entertainment" to his readers too; his own name honors Locke's reckoning of sight as the mind's chief instrument for the gathering of ideas. In the following extract, Addison pays comparably implicit homage to Newton, in an ode that quickly became one of the touchstones of eighteenth-century devotion. Though Addison places his poem in a tradition that combines Aristotle with the Psalms, Newton is powerfully present too, in the depiction of a heaven whose silent motions proclaim to human reason the perfection of God's design.

from Spectator No. 465
Saturday, 23 August 1712[1]

* * * The last method which I shall mention for the giving life to a man's faith is frequent retirement from the world, accompanied with religious meditation. When a man thinks of any thing in the darkness of the night, whatever deep impressions it may make in his mind, they are apt to vanish as soon as the day breaks about him. The light and noise of the day, which are perpetually soliciting his senses and calling off his attention, wear out of his mind the thoughts that imprinted themselves in it with so much strength during the silence and darkness of the night. A man finds the same difference as to himself in a crowd and in a solitude; the mind is stunned and dazzled amidst that variety of objects which press upon her in a great city: she cannot apply herself to the consideration of those things which are of the utmost concern to her. The cares or pleasures of the world strike in with every thought, and a multitude of vicious examples give a kind of justification to our folly. In our retirements everything disposes us to be serious. In courts and cities we are entertained with the works of men, in the country with those of God. One is the province of art, the other of nature. Faith and devotion naturally grow in the mind of every reasonable man, who sees the impressions of divine power and wisdom in every object on which he casts his eye. The Supreme Being has made the best arguments for his own existence, in the formation of the heavens and the earth, and these are arguments which a man of sense cannot forbear attending to, who is out of the noise and hurry of human affairs. Aristotle says,[2] that should a man live under ground, and there converse with works of art and mechanism, and should afterwards be brought up into the open day, and see the several glories of the heaven and earth, he would immediately pronounce

---

1. Addison often set Saturdays aside for particularly serious topics, as a way of preparing his readers for the religious solemnities of Sunday (the only day on which the *Spectator* did not appear). He devotes the present paper to

"the proper means of strengthening and confirming" Christian faith.
2. Addison paraphrases lines quoted by Cicero from *De Philosophia*, a work of Aristotle's long lost.

them the works of such a being as we define God to be. The Psalmist has very beautiful strokes of poetry to this purpose, in that exalted strain, "The heavens declare the
glory of God: and the firmament showeth his handiwork. One day telleth another:
and one night certifieth another. There is neither speech nor language: but their
voices are heard among them. Their sound is gone out into all lands: and their words
into the ends of the world."[3] As such a bold and sublime manner of thinking furnishes very noble matter for an ode, the reader may see it wrought into the following
one.[4]

1

The spacious firmament on high,
With all the blue ethereal sky,
And spangled heav'ns, a shining frame,
Their great original proclaim:
5   Th' unwearied sun, from day to day,
Does his Creator's power display,
And publishes to every land
The works of an almighty hand.

2

Soon as the evening shades prevail,
10   The moon takes up the wondrous tale,
And nightly to the list'ning earth
Repeats the story of her birth:
Whilst all the stars that round her burn,
And all the planets, in their turn,
15   Confirm the tidings as they roll,
And spread the truth from pole to pole.

3

What though, in solemn silence, all
Move round the dark terrestrial ball?
What though nor real voice nor sound
20   Amid their radiant orbs be found?
In reason's ear they all rejoice,
And utter forth a glorious voice,
For ever singing, as they shine,
"The hand that made us is divine."

George Berkeley
1685–1753

For Locke, "ideas" are formed in the mind out of its ongoing encounter with the very real
world outside it, where swans swim and elephants plod. For George Berkeley—clergyman,
poet, traveler, and philosopher—ideas are all there is. *Esse est percipi*, he argues throughout his
philosophical writings: to be is to be perceived. "All those bodies which compose the mighty

3. Psalm 19.1–4.
4. Addison may have published this ode partly as a
response to Watts's imitation of Psalm 114, which had

appeared in the *Spectator* just four days earlier (see page
2639).

frame of the world, have not any subsistence without a mind"—a mind engaged in the act of perceiving them. What, then, accounts for the apparent independence and continuity of real objects (trees, to take one of Berkeley's recurrent examples), which seem to remain in place even when no mortal observes them? Berkeley's answer: one mind *is* perpetually engaged in perceiving them. The mind of God creates the ideas, sustains them, renders them consistent with themselves and independent of our intermittent human perceptions. In Berkeley's argument, this divine activity both constitutes proof of God's existence (since such an "infinite mind" is necessary to explain why the world appears to us as it does), and lies at the core of God's benevolence. Berkeley expounded his theory of "immaterialism" in his *Essay Towards a New Theory of Vision* (1709) and *Treatise Concerning the Principles of Human Knowledge* (1710), before recasting it in the more compact, accessible, and popular format of *Three Dialogues Between Hylas and Philonous*. Philonous ("Lover of mind") voices Berkeley's views, while Hylas ("Wooden") expresses the bemused incredulity with which Berkeley's readers continued to greet the philosopher's radical unmaking and reweaving of the fabric of everyday life. Scoffers tended to overlook the solution Berkeley was proffering to an abiding theological problem. Newton's cosmology had given rise (despite his own piety) to the unsettling image of the Clockmaker God, who having made the universe a perfectly efficient mechanism, could now let it run without further intervention. Newton addressed this problem in part by insisting that God had to intervene at intervals in order to adjust his system. Berkeley's God, by contrast, is no clockmaker at all; having authored the world in the beginning, he continues to make it anew at every moment by the creative act of his continual perception.

from Three Dialogues Between Hylas and Philonous

HYLAS But do you in earnest think, the real existence of sensible things consists in their being actually perceived? If so, how comes it that all mankind distinguish between them? Ask the first man you meet, and he shall tell you, *to be perceived* is one thing, and *to exist* is another.

PHILONOUS I am content, Hylas, to appeal to the common sense of the world for the truth of my notion. Ask the gardener why he thinks yonder cherry tree exists in the garden, and he shall tell you, because he sees and feels it; in a word, because he perceives it by his senses. Ask him why he thinks an orange tree not to be there, and he shall tell you, because he does not perceive it. What he perceives by sense, that he terms a real being, and saith it *is*, or *exists*; but that which is not perceivable, the same, he saith, hath no being.

HYLAS Yes, Philonous, I grant the existence of a sensible thing consists in being perceivable, but not in being actually perceived.

PHILONOUS And what is perceivable but an idea? And can an idea exist without being actually perceived? These are points long since agreed between us.

HYLAS But be your opinion never so true, yet surely you will not deny it is shocking, and contrary to the common sense of men. Ask the fellow whether yonder tree hath an existence out of his mind: what answer think you he would make?

PHILONOUS The same that I should myself, to wit, that it doth exist out of his mind. But then to a Christian it cannot surely be shocking to say, the real tree existing without his mind is truly known and comprehended by (that is, *exists in*) the infinite mind of God. Probably he may not at first glance be aware of the direct and immediate proof there is of this, inasmuch as the very being of a tree, or any other sensible thing, implies a mind wherein it is. But the point itself he cannot deny. The question between the materialists[1] and me is not whether things have a real

---

1. Those who assert the existence of matter, independent of perception.

existence out of the mind of this or that person, but whether they have an absolute existence, distinct from being perceived by God, and exterior to all minds. This indeed some heathens and philosophers have affirmed, but whoever entertains notions of the Deity suitable to the Holy Scriptures will be of another opinion.

HYLAS But according to your notions, what difference is there between real things, and chimeras formed by the imagination, or the visions of a dream, since they are all equally in the mind?

PHILONOUS The ideas formed by the imagination are faint and indistinct; they have besides an entire dependence on the will. But the ideas perceived by sense, that is, real things, are more vivid and clear, and being imprinted on the mind by a spirit distinct from us, have not a like dependence on our will. There is therefore no danger of confounding these with the foregoing: and there is as little of confounding them with the visions of a dream, which are dim, irregular, and confused. And though they should happen to be never so lively and natural, yet by their not being connected, and of a piece with the preceding and subsequent transactions of our lives, they might easily be distinguished from realities. In short, by whatever method you distinguish *things* from *chimeras* on your own scheme, the same, it is evident, will hold also upon mine. For it must be, I presume, by some perceived difference, and I am not for depriving you of any one thing that you perceive.

HYLAS But still, Philonous, you hold, there is nothing in the world but spirits and ideas. And this, you must needs acknowledge, sounds very oddly.

PHILONOUS I own the word *idea*, not being commonly used for *thing*, sounds something out of the way. My reason for using it was, because a necessary relation to the mind is understood to be implied by that term; and it is now commonly used by philosophers to denote the immediate objects of the understanding. But however oddly the proposition may sound in words, yet it includes nothing so very strange or shocking in its sense, which in effect amounts to no more than this, to wit, that there are only things perceiving, and things perceived; or that every unthinking being is necessarily, and from the very nature of its existence, perceived by some mind; if not by any finite created mind, yet certainly by the infinite mind of God, in whom "we live, and move, and have our being."[2] Is this as strange as to say, the sensible qualities are not on the objects, or that we cannot be sure of the existence of things, or know anything of their real natures, though we both see and feel them, and perceive them by all our senses?

HYLAS And in consequence of this, must we not think there are no such things as physical or corporeal causes but that a spirit is the immediate cause of all the phenomena in nature? Can there be anything more extravagant than this?

PHILONOUS Yes, it is infinitely more extravagant to say, a thing which is inert, operates on the mind, and which is unperceiving, is the cause of our perceptions. Besides, that which to you, I know not for what reason, seems so extravagant, is no more than the Holy Scriptures assert in a hundred places. In them God is represented as the sole and immediate author of all those effects which some heathens and philosophers are wont to ascribe to nature, matter, fate, or the like unthinking principle. This is so much the constant language of Scripture, that it were needless to confirm it by citations. * * *

1713

---

2. Acts 17.28.

━━ ◆◇◈ ━━

David Hume
1711–1776

As he lay dying at home in his native city of Edinburgh, David Hume entertained a visitor by conjuring up, with characteristic cheerfulness, a scenario in the afterlife. He imagined himself begging the fatal ferryman Charon for a little more time: "Have a little patience, good Charon, I have been endeavoring to open the eyes of the public. If I live a few years longer, I may have the satisfaction of seeing the downfall of some of the prevailing systems of superstition." The "prevailing system" which Hume had become most notorious for attacking was the Christian religion, whose favorite tenets—providence, miracles, the argument from design, the afterlife itself—he had called into question, with increasing audacity, over the course of his work. But he had also done much damage to newer systems of thought, notably Locke's. Locke had regarded personal identity as coherent and continuous, the consequence of lifelong experiences and ideas accumulated in the memory. Hume, in his early, massive *Treatise of Human Nature* (1739–1740), waived all this away as an arrant fiction—though perhaps a necessary one, since empiricism properly pursued reveals so radical an incoherence in mortal minds that empiricists themselves must intermittently abandon philosophy in order to go about their daily lives. Like many of his empiric predecessors Hume argued that knowledge of the real world "must be founded entirely on experience"; more than any predecessor he was willing to entertain (and to entertain with) the doubts and demolitions arising from that premise. In his own lifetime, his skepticism did not prove as contagious as he had hoped. The *Treatise*, he recalled wryly, "fell *deadborn from the press*, without reaching such distinction as even to excite a murmur among the zealots." Though his attempt to recast his chief arguments more succinctly in *An Enquiry Concerning Human Understanding* (1748) prompted a somewhat livelier response, he eventually made his fortune not as a philosopher but as author of the highly successful *History of England* (1754–1763). He faced the general indifference or hostility to his arguments as blithely as he later greeted death, continually refining his views and revising his prose. He knew himself out of sync with his times. When, in his fantasy, he forecasts to Charon the imminent downfall of superstition, the ferryman responds, "You loitering rogue, that will not happen these many hundred years. Do you fancy I will grant you a lease for so long a term? Get into the boat this instant, you lazy loitering rogue." More than two hundred years later, the artful mischief of Hume's work has secured him some such lease. His writings, lucid and elusive, forthright and sly, demand (and receive) continual reassessment; his skepticism has proven more powerful than his contemporaries suspected, and he figures as perhaps the wittiest and most self-possessed philosophical troublemaker since Socrates.

from A Treatise of Human Nature
[THE MIND AS THEATER[1]]

There are some philosophers,[2] who imagine we are every moment intimately conscious of what we call our *self*; that we feel its existence and its continuance in existence; and are certain, beyond the evidence of a demonstration, both of its perfect identity and simplicity. The strongest sensation, the most violent passion, say they, instead of distracting us from this view, only fix it the more intensely, and make us consider their influence on *self* either by their pain or pleasure. To attempt a farther

---

1. From Book 1, section 6, "Of Personal Identity."
2. Notably Joseph Butler, an Anglican bishop who argued in *The Analogy of Religion* (1736) that the existence of the

self is a truth of which every person is continually (and correctly) certain.

proof of this were to weaken its evidence; since no proof can be derived from any fact, of which we are so intimately conscious; nor is there anything of which we can be certain, if we doubt of this.

Unluckily all these positive assertions are contrary to that very experience which is pleaded for them, nor have we any idea of *self,* after the manner it is here explained. For from what impression could this idea be derived? This question 'tis impossible to answer without a manifest contradiction and absurdity; and yet 'tis a question, which must necessarily be answered, if we would have the idea of self pass for clear and intelligible. It must be some one impression, that gives rise to every real idea. But self or person is not any one impression, but that to which our several impressions and ideas are supposed to have a reference. If any impression gives rise to the idea of self, that impression must continue invariably the same through the whole course of our lives, since self is supposed to exist after that manner. But there is no impression constant and invariable. Pain and pleasure, grief and joy, passions and sensations succeed each other, and never all exist at the same time. It cannot, therefore, be from any of these impressions, or from any other, that the idea of self is derived; and consequently there is no such idea.

But farther, what must become of all our particular perceptions upon this hypothesis? All these are different, and distinguishable, and separable from each other, and may be separately considered, and may exist separately, and have no need of anything to support their existence. After what manner, therefore, do they belong to self; and how are they connected with it? For my part, when I enter most intimately into what I call *myself,* I always stumble on some particular perception or other, of heat or cold, light or shade, love or hatred, pain or pleasure. I never can catch *myself* at any time without a perception, and never can observe anything but the perception. When my perceptions are removed for any time, as by sound sleep, so long am I insensible of *myself,* and may truly be said not to exist. And were all my perceptions removed by death, and could I neither think, nor feel, nor see, nor love, nor hate after the dissolution of my body, I should be entirely annihilated, nor do I conceive what is farther requisite to make me a perfect nonentity. If anyone upon serious and unprejudiced reflection, thinks he has a different notion of *himself,* I must confess I can reason no longer with him. All I can allow him is, that he may be in the right as well as I, and that we are essentially different in this particular. He may, perhaps, perceive something simple and continued, which he calls *himself;* though I am certain there is no such principle in me.

But setting aside some metaphysicians of this kind, I may venture to affirm of the rest of mankind, that they are nothing but a bundle or collection of different perceptions, which succeed each other with an inconceivable rapidity, and are in a perpetual flux and movement. Our eyes cannot turn in their sockets without varying our perceptions. Our thought is still more variable than our sight; and all our other senses and faculties contribute to this change; nor is there any single power of the soul which remains unalterably the same, perhaps for one moment. The mind is a kind of theater, where several perceptions successively make their appearance: pass, re-pass, glide away, and mingle in an infinite variety of postures and situations. There is properly no *simplicity* in it at one time, nor *identity* in different; whatever natural propension we may have to imagine that simplicity and identity. The comparison of the theater must not mislead us. They are the successive perceptions only, that constitute the mind; nor have we the most distant notion of the place where these scenes are represented, or of the materials, of which it is composed. * * *

[PHILOSOPHY AND COMMON LIFE³]

But what have I here said, that reflections very refined and metaphysical have little or no influence upon us? This opinion I can scarce forbear retracting, and condemning from my present feeling and experience. The *intense* view of these manifold contradictions and imperfections in human reason has so wrought upon me, and heated my brain, that I am ready to reject all belief and reasoning, and can look upon no opinion even as more probable or likely than another. Where am I, or what? From what causes do I derive my existence, and to what condition shall I return? Whose favor shall I court, and whose anger must I dread? What beings surround me? and on whom have I any influence, or who have any influence on me? I am confounded with all these questions, and begin to fancy myself in the most deplorable condition imaginable, environed with the deepest darkness, and utterly deprived of the use of every member and faculty.

Most fortunately it happens, that since reason is incapable of dispelling these clouds, nature herself suffices to that purpose, and cures me of this philosophical melancholy and delirium, either by relaxing this bent of mind, or by some avocation and lively impression of my senses, which obliterate all these chimeras. I dine, I play a game of backgammon, I converse, and am merry with my friends; and when after three or four hour's amusement, I would return to these speculations, they appear so cold, and strained, and ridiculous, that I cannot find in my heart to enter into them any farther.

Here then I find myself absolutely and necessarily determined to live, and talk, and act like other people in the common affairs of life. But notwithstanding that my natural propensity, and the course of my animal spirits and passions reduce me to this indolent belief in the general maxims of the world, I still feel such remains of my former disposition, that I am ready to throw all my books and papers into the fire, and resolve never more to renounce the pleasures of life for the sake of reasoning and philosophy. For these are my sentiments in that splenetic⁴ humor, which governs me at present. I may, nay I must yield to the current of nature, in submitting to my senses and understanding; and in this blind submission I show most perfectly my skeptical disposition and principles. But does it follow, that I must strive against the current of nature, which leads me to indolence and pleasure; that I must seclude myself, in some measure, from the commerce and society of men, which is so agreeable; and that I must torture my brain with subtleties and sophistries, at the very time that I cannot satisfy myself concerning the reasonableness of so painful an application, nor have any tolerable prospect of arriving by its means at truth and certainty? Under what obligation do I lie of making such an abuse of time? And to what end can it serve either for the service of mankind, or for my own private interest? No: if I must be a fool, as well as those who reason or believe anything *certainly* are, my follies shall at least be natural and agreeable. Where I strive against my inclination, I shall have a good reason for my resistance; and will no more be led a wandering into such dreary solitudes, and rough passages, as I have hitherto met with.

---

3. From Book 1, section 7: "Conclusion of This Book." The first book of the *Treatise* serves as a long prelude to the whole; in concluding it, Hume considers the "manifest contradictions" between the assumptions on which ordinary people lead their lives, and the volatile questions raised by "refined reasoning" (rigorous philosophic inquiry). Pinpointing these contradictions in himself, he contemplates the precariousness of his enterprise, and the intricacy of his motives for undertaking it.

4. Depressive, irritable.

There are the sentiments of my spleen[5] and indolence; and indeed I must confess, that philosophy has nothing to oppose to them, and expects a victory more from the returns of a serious good-humored disposition, than from the force of reason and conviction. In all the incidents of life we ought still to preserve our skepticism. If we believe, that fire warms, or water refreshes, 'tis only because it costs us too much pains to think otherwise. Nay if we are philosophers, it ought only to be upon skeptical principles, and from an inclination, which we feel to the employing ourselves after that manner. Where reason is lively, and mixes itself with some propensity, it ought to be assented to. Where it does not, it never can have any title to operate upon us.

At the time, therefore, that I am tired with amusement and company, and have indulged a *reverie* in my chamber, or in a solitary walk by a riverside, I feel my mind all collected within itself, and am naturally *inclined* to carry my view into all those subjects, about which I have met with so many disputes in the course of my reading and conversation.[6] I cannot forbear having a curiosity to be acquainted with the principles of moral good and evil, the nature and foundation of government, and the cause of those several passions and inclinations, which actuate and govern me. I am uneasy to think I approve of one object, and disapprove of another; call one thing beautiful, and another deformed; decide concerning truth and falsehood, reason and folly, without knowing upon what principles I proceed. I am concerned for the condition of the learned world, which lies under such a deplorable ignorance in all these particulars. I feel an ambition to arise in me of contributing to the instruction of mankind, and of acquiring a name by my inventions and discoveries. These sentiments spring up naturally in my present disposition; and should I endeavor to banish them, by attaching myself to any other business or diversion, I *feel* I should be a loser in point of pleasure; and this is the origin of my philosophy.

1734–1737   1739–1740

from An Enquiry Concerning Human Understanding[1]
from *Section 10: Of Miracles*

A miracle is a violation of the laws of nature; and as a firm and unalterable experience has established these laws, the proof against a miracle, from the very nature of the fact, is as entire as any argument from experience can possibly be imagined. Why is it more than probable that all men must die; that lead cannot, of itself, remain suspended in the air; that fire consumes wood, and is extinguished by water; unless it be, that these events are found agreeable to the laws of nature, and there is required a violation of these laws, or in other words, a miracle to prevent them? Nothing is esteemed a miracle, if it ever happen in the common course of nature. It is no miracle that a man, seemingly in good health, should die on a sudden; because such a kind of death, though more unusual than any other, has yet been frequently observed to happen. But it is a miracle that a dead man should come to life; because that has never been observed in any age or country. There must, therefore, be a uniform experience against every miraculous event, otherwise the event would not merit that appella-

---

5. Despondency.
6. In the list that follows, Hume names many of the topics he will take up later in the *Treatise*.
1. Hume wrote this essay in the mid-1730s, intending to include it in his *Treatise*; conscious of its volatility, he withheld it for a dozen years, publishing it for the first

time in his *Philosophical Essays Concerning Human Understanding* (1748); ten years later a revised version of the work appeared, under the new title *An Enquiry. . . .* The essay proved at least as explosive as he had anticipated, prompting a spate of refutations; for Samuel Johnson's and James Boswell's views, see pages 2815 and 2805).

tion. And as a uniform experience amounts to a proof, there is here a direct and full *proof*, from the nature of the fact, against the existence of any miracle; nor can such a proof be destroyed, or the miracle rendered credible, but by an opposite proof, which is superior.

The plain consequence is (and it is a general maxim worthy of our attention), "That no testimony is sufficient to establish a miracle, unless the testimony be of such a kind, that its falsehood would be more miraculous than the fact which it endeavors to establish; and even in that case there is a mutual destruction of arguments, and the superior only gives us an assurance suitable to that degree of force which remains after deducting the inferior." When anyone tells me, that he saw a dead man restored to life, I immediately consider with myself, whether it be more probable, that this person should either deceive or be deceived, or that the fact, which he relates, should really have happened. I weigh the one miracle against the other; and according to the superiority which I discover, I pronounce my decision, and always reject the greater miracle. If the falsehood of his testimony would be more miraculous than the event which he relates, then, and not till then, can he pretend to command my belief or opinion.

In the foregoing reasoning we have supposed, that the testimony, upon which a miracle is founded, may possibly amount to an entire proof, and that the falsehood of that testimony would be a real prodigy. But it is easy to show that we have been a great deal too liberal in our concession, and that there never was a miraculous event established on so full an evidence.

For *first*, there is not to be found, in all history, any miracle attested by a sufficient number of men, of such unquestioned good sense, education, and learning, as to secure us against all delusion in themselves; of such undoubted integrity, as to place them beyond all suspicion of any design to deceive others; of such credit and reputation in the eyes of mankind, as to have a great deal to lose in case of their being detected in any falsehood; and at the same time, attesting facts performed in such a public manner and in so celebrated a part of the world, as to render the detection unavoidable. All which circumstances are requisite to give us a full assurance in the testimony of men.

Secondly. We may observe in human nature a principle which, if strictly examined, will be found to diminish extremely the assurance which we might, from human testimony, have, in any kind of prodigy. The maxim by which we commonly conduct ourselves in our reasonings is that the objects of which we have no experience resemble those of which we have; that what we have found to be most usual is always most probable; and that where there is an opposition of arguments, we ought to give the preference to such as are founded on the greatest number of past observations. But though, in proceeding by this rule, we readily reject any fact which is unusual and incredible in an ordinary degree; yet in advancing farther, the mind observes not always the same rule; but when anything is affirmed utterly absurd and miraculous, it rather the more readily admits of such a fact, upon account of that very circumstance which ought to destroy all its authority. The passion of *surprise* and *wonder*, arising from miracles, being an agreeable emotion, gives a sensible tendency towards the belief of those events from which it is derived. And this goes so far, that even those who cannot enjoy this pleasure immediately, nor can believe those miraculous events, of which they are informed, yet love to partake of the satisfaction at second-hand or by rebound, and place a pride and delight in exciting the admiration of others.

With what greediness are the miraculous accounts of travelers received, their descriptions of sea and land monsters, their relations of wonderful adventures, strange men, and uncouth manners? But if the spirit of religion join itself to the love of wonder, there is an end of common sense; and human testimony, in these circumstances, loses all pretensions to authority. A religionist may be an enthusiast,[2] and imagine he sees what has no reality. He may know his narrative to be false, and yet persevere in it, with the best intentions in the world, for the sake of promoting so holy a cause; or even where this delusion has not place, vanity, excited by so strong a temptation, operates on him more powerfully than on the rest of mankind in any other circumstances; and self-interest with equal force. His auditors may not have, and commonly have not, sufficient judgment to canvass his evidence. What judgment they have, they renounce by principle, in these sublime and mysterious subjects; or if they were ever so willing to employ it, passion and a heated imagination disturb the regularity of its operations. Their credulity increases his impudence; and his impudence overpowers their credulity. * * *

Thirdly. It forms a strong presumption against all supernatural and miraculous relations, that they are observed chiefly to abound among ignorant and barbarous nations; or if a civilized people has ever given admission to any of them, that people will be found to have received them from ignorant and barbarous ancestors, who transmitted them with that inviolable sanction and authority, which always attend received opinions. When we peruse the first histories of all nations, we are apt to imagine ourselves transported into some new world, where the whole frame of nature is disjointed, and every element performs its operations in a different manner from what it does at present. Battles, revolutions, pestilence, famine, and death are never the effect of those natural causes which we experience. Prodigies, omens, oracles, judgments, quite obscure the few natural events that are intermingled with them. But as the former grow thinner every page, in proportion as we advance nearer the enlightened ages, we soon learn that there is nothing mysterious or supernatural in the case, but that all proceeds from the usual propensity of mankind towards the marvelous, and that, though this inclination may at intervals receive a check from sense and learning, it can never be thoroughly extirpated from human nature. * * *

Upon the whole, then, it appears that no testimony for any kind of miracle has ever amounted to a probability, much less to a proof; and that, even supposing it amounted to a proof, it would be opposed by another proof; derived from the very nature of the fact, which it would endeavor to establish. It is experience only which gives authority to human testimony; and it is the same experience which assures us of the laws of nature. When, therefore, these two kinds of experience are contrary, we have nothing to do but subtract the one from the other, and embrace an opinion, either on one side or the other, with that assurance which arises from the remainder. But according to the principle here explained, this subtraction, with regard to all popular religions, amounts to an entire annihilation; and therefore we may establish it as a maxim, that no human testimony can have such force as to prove a miracle, and make it a just foundation for any such system of religion. * * *

What we have said of miracles may be applied, without any variation, to prophecies; and indeed, all prophecies are real miracles, and as such only can be admitted as proofs of any revelation. If it did not exceed the capacity of human nature to foretell

---

2. Fanatic.

future events, it would be absurd to employ any prophecy as an argument for a divine mission or authority from heaven. So that, upon the whole, we may conclude, that the *Christian religion* not only was at first attended with miracles, but even at this day cannot be believed by any reasonable person without one. Mere reason is insufficient to convince us of its veracity. And whoever is moved by *faith* to assent to it, is conscious of a continued miracle in his own person, which subverts all the principles of his understanding, and gives him a determination to believe what is most contrary to custom and experience.

c. 1736   1748

+→ ⇌◆⇌ ←+

Christopher Smart
1722–1771

"Newton . . . is more of error than of the truth, but I am of the Word of God," wrote Christopher Smart in his astonishing poem *Jubilate Agno* ("Rejoice in the Lamb"). For Smart, as for a growing number of Christians in the century's second half, the Newtonian "error" consisted in a commitment to materialist science, to an empiricism which investigated the physical world and sought its seeming system, rather than submitting to faith in a God who worked by will and sometimes by miracle, free of any fixed laws of nature. Smart composed *Jubilate Agno* in his late thirties, while confined in a madhouse; after a brilliant career as a classical scholar at Cambridge, and an auspicious start in London as a literary adventurer (poet, editor, translator, essayist), he suffered a derangement whose chief symptom was his compulsion to pray spontaneously in public places (he was too much "of the Word of God" to be socially acceptable). Released from the asylum after five years, Smart recast much material from the *Jubilate Agno* in his *Song of David* (1763); following Watts's precedent, he published a translation of the Psalms (1767) and (while imprisoned for debt at the very end of his life) a book of *Hymns for the Amusement of Children* (1771). *Jubilate Agno* remained in manuscript and unknown for a century and a half after the poet's death. Smart called it "my Magnificat," *magnificat* being the title of the liturgical hymn first uttered by the Virgin Mary upon learning that she would conceive a son: "My Soul doth magnify the Lord" (Luke 1.46–55). Structured like a responsive prayer, Smart's poem moves rapidly across a wide range of reference, from the scriptural and mystical to the local and the homely ("God be gracious to Baumgarden"—a London bassoon player). But Smart returns repeatedly to a preoccupation touched on in the poem's title: to the animal world as emblem and embodiment of God's grace and greatness (in Smart's time natural history was among the branches of knowledge least touched by the new science, and most inflected by faith and folklore). In the excerpts below, Smart punningly pinpoints the animal essences of languages ancient and modern, then depicts the feline who kept him company during his years of confinement, singing Jeoffry's praises with such exuberance as to make *magnificat* seem a latent, sacred, and affectionate pun.

from Jubilate Agno
[ANIMALS IN LANGUAGE[1]]

625   For the power of some animal is predominant in every language.
           For the power and spirit of a CAT is in the Greek.

---

1. These selections come from Fragment B of Smart's manuscript. Some pages of Smart's manuscript contain long sequences of lines beginning "Let"; other pages contain lines beginning "For," with clear enough indications that the "Let" and "For" lines were meant to be dovetailed and read alternately, in the form of responsive prayer. For the two excerpts printed here, though, lines beginning "Let" have not been found—and may never have been written.

For the sound of a cat is in the most useful preposition κατ' ευχην.[2]

For the pleasantry of a cat at pranks is in the language ten thousand times over.[3]

For JACK UPON PRANCK is in the performance of περι together or separate.[4]

630   For Clapperclaw[5] is in the grappling of the words upon one another in all the modes of versification.

For the sleekness of a Cat is in his αγλαιηφι.[6]

For the Greek is thrown from heaven and falls upon its feet.[7]

For the Greek when distracted from the line is sooner restored to rank and rallied into some form than any other.

For the purring of a Cat is his τρυζει.[8]

635   For his cry is in ουαι,[9] which I am sorry for.

For the Mouse (*Mus*) prevails in the Latin.[1]

For *Edi-mus, bibi-mus, vivi-mus—ore-mus*.[2]

For the Mouse is a creature of great personal valor.

For—this is a true case—Cat takes female mouse from the company of male—male mouse will not depart, but stands threat'ning and daring.

640   For this is as much as to challenge, if you will let her go, I will engage you, as prodigious a creature as you are.

For the Mouse is of an hospitable disposition.

For bravery and hospitality were said and done by the Romans rather than others.

For two creatures the Bull and the Dog prevail in the English.

For all the words ending in -ble are in the creature. Invisi-ble, Incompre-hensi-ble, ineffa-ble, A-ble.

645   For the Greek and Latin are not dead languages, but taken up and accepted for the sake of him that spoke them.

For can is (*canis*[3]) is cause and effect a dog.

For the English is concise and strong. Dog and Bull again.

For Newton's notion of colors is αλογος,[4] unphilosophical.

[MY CAT JEOFFRY]

695   For I will consider my Cat Jeoffry.

For he is the servant of the Living God duly and daily serving him.

For at the first glance of the glory of God in the East he worships in his way.

For is this done by wreathing his body seven times round with elegant quickness.

For then he leaps up to catch the musk, which is the blessing of God upon his prayer.

700   For he rolls upon prank to work it in.

For having done duty and received blessing he begins to consider himself.

For this he performs in ten degrees.

For first he looks upon his fore-paws to see if they are clean.

For secondly he kicks up behind to clear away there.

---

2. Greek *kat' euchen:* "according to prayer."
3. The syllable *kat* appears in many word forms.
4. Greek *perikato* means "upside down" (as, probably, does "Jack Upon Pranck").
5. To claw, scratch.
6. *Aglaiefi:* "beauty."
7. Perhaps an allusion to the Greek poetic term *catalexis,* the shortening or omission of a "foot" from a line of verse; the prefix *cata-* means "down."

8. *Truzei:* "murmur."
9. *Ouai:* exclamation of lament ("ah!").
1. Partly because (as Smart illustrates in line 637), the syllable *mus* means "mouse" and is also the suffix for first person plural present-tense conjugations.
2. "We eat, we drink, we live—let us pray."
3. Latin: dog.
4. *Alogos:* literally, "without the Word."

705   For thirdly he works it upon stretch with the fore-paws extended.
        For fourthly he sharpens his paws by wood.
        For fifthly he washes himself.
        For sixthly he rolls upon wash.
        For seventhly he fleas himself, that he may not be interrupted upon the beat.
710   For eighthly he rubs himself against a post.
        For ninthly he looks up for his instructions.
        For tenthly he goes in quest of food.
        For having considered God and himself he will consider his neighbor.
        For if he meets another cat he will kiss her in kindness.
715   For when he takes his prey he plays with it to give it chance.
        For one mouse in seven escapes by his dallying.
        For when his day's work is done his business more properly begins.
        For he keeps the Lord's watch in the night against the adversary.
        For he counteracts the powers of darkness by his electrical skin and glar-
            ing eyes.
720   For he counteracts the Devil, who is death, by brisking about the life.
        For in his morning orisons he loves the sun and the sun loves him.
        For he is of the tribe of Tiger.
        For the Cherub Cat is a term of the Angel Tiger.
        For he has the subtlety and hissing of a serpent, which in goodness he
            suppresses.
725   For he will not do destruction, if he is well-fed, neither will he spit without
            provocation.
        For he purrs in thankfulness, when God tells him he's a good Cat.
        For he is an instrument for the children to learn benevolence upon.
        For every house is incomplete without him and a blessing is lacking in
            the spirit.
        For the Lord commanded Moses concerning the cats at the departure of the
            Children of Israel from Egypt.[5]
730   For every family had one cat at least in the bag.
        For the English Cats are the best in Europe.
        For he is the cleanest in the use of his fore-paws of any quadrupede.
        For the dexterity of his defense is an instance of the love of God to him
            exceedingly.
        For he is the quickest to his mark of any creature.
735   For he is tenacious of his point.
        For he is a mixture of gravity and waggery.
        For he knows that God is his Savior.
        For there is nothing sweeter than his peace when at rest.
        For there is nothing brisker than his life when in motion.
740   For he is of the Lord's poor and so indeed is he called by benevolence per-
            petually—Poor Jeoffry! poor Jeoffry! the rat has bit thy throat.
        For I bless the name of the Lord Jesus that Jeoffry is better.
        For the divine spirit comes about his body to sustain it in complete cat.
        For his tongue is exceeding pure so that it has in purity what it wants in music.
        For he is docile and can learn certain things.
745   For he can set up with gravity which is patience upon approbation.

___

5. "Take your flocks and your herds," says the Egyptian Pharaoh when demanding the Israelites' departure (Exodus 12.32); Smart adds the Lord and the cats.

For he can fetch and carry, which is patience in employment.
For he can jump over a stick which is patience upon proof positive.
For he can spraggle° upon waggle at the word of command.   *sprawl*
For he can jump from an eminence into his master's bosom.
750 For he can catch the cork and toss it again.
For he is hated by the hypocrite and miser.
For the former is afraid of detection.
For the latter refuses the charge.
For he camels his back to bear the first notion of business.
755 For he is good to think on, if a man would express himself neatly.
For he made a great figure in Egypt for his signal services.
For he killed the Ichneumon-rat° very pernicious by land.   *mongoose*
For his ears are so acute that they sting again.
For from this proceeds the passing quickness of his attention.
760 For by stroking of him I have found out electricity.
For I perceived God's light about him both wax and fire.
For the Electrical fire is the spiritual substance, which God sends from
   heaven to sustain the bodies both of man and beast.
For God has blessed him in the variety of his movements.
For, though he cannot fly, he is an excellent clamberer.
765 For his motions upon the face of the earth are more than any other
   quadrupede.
For he can tread to all the measures upon the music.
For he can swim for life.
For he can creep.

c. 1758–1763   1939

———— ⊰✦⊱ ————

William Cowper
1731–1800

Like Christopher Smart, William Cowper suffered madness, loved animals, wrote hymns, and invented capacious new structures for religious verse. But where Smart wrote to celebrate his sure salvation, Cowper wrote out of the certainty that he was damned—unworthy of redemption and predestined for hellfire. The conviction first took hold in 1763, when a paralyzing panic cut him off from impending attachments (to a new job he was about to secure, a beloved woman he was soon to marry) and prompted several attempts at suicide. The course of recovery took him first to an asylum, then through a conversion to Calvinism, then to the household of Mary Unwin, who loved and looked after him for the next four decades, and finally into partnership with Unwin's neighbor, the austere hymn-writer John Newton, with whom Cowper collaborated for years on a new collection of religious song, the *Olney Hymns* (it included, along with several of Cowper's still-sung texts, Newton's perdurable *Amazing Grace*). A second, sharper attack of madness, ten years after the first, deepened Cowper's conviction of his doom but also ushered in years of plentiful poetic composition. Seizing any small occasion (a fish dinner, the death of a pet bird) to produce a short, often comic piece of verse, Cowper wrote poems to hold terror at bay. As his output increased, his ambition did too. *The Task*, a massive mock-epic grounded in the comforts of Cowper's rural retirement (sofa, garden, seasons) but ranging satirically over the whole wide world, surprised even its author by its scope and popularity. Spurred by its success, Cowper undertook to translate Homer's epics, hoping to surpass Pope's attempts earlier in the century. In a passage near the midpoint of the poem (printed here), Newton appears briefly as the embodiment of Cowper's deepest hope, that the mind might merge with God through a science immersed in faith—"philosophy baptized." In his last, autobiographical poem, *The Cast-away,* Cowper draws a darker picture, of a mind sundered from its maker by distance and despair.

Light Shining out of Darkness[1]

God moves in a mysterious way,
    His wonders to perform;
He plants his footsteps in the sea,
    And rides upon the storm.

5   Deep in unfathomable mines
        Of never-failing skill,
He treasures up his bright designs,
    And works his sov'reign will.

Ye fearful saints[2] fresh courage take,
10   The clouds ye so much dread
Are big with mercy, and shall break
    In blessings on your head.

Judge not the Lord by feeble sense,
    But trust him for his grace;
15   Behind a frowning providence,
    He hides a smiling face.

His purposes will ripen fast,
    Unfolding every hour;
The bud may have a bitter taste,
20   But sweet will be the flower.

Blind unbelief is sure to err,
    And scan his work in vain;
God is his own interpreter,
    And he will make it plain.

c. 1773   1774

from **The Task**

["PHILOSOPHY BAPTIZED"[1]]

God never meant that man should scale the heav'ns
By strides of human wisdom. In his works
Though wond'rous, he commands us in his word
To seek *him* rather, where his mercy shines.
225   The mind indeed enlightened from above
Views him in all. Ascribes to the grand cause
The grand effect. Acknowledges with joy
His manner, and with rapture tastes his style.
But never yet did philosophic° tube   *scientific*

---

1. Written and first published during the period of Cowper's collaboration with John Newton; later included in their *Olney Hymns* (1779).
2. Cowper addresses those who (according to Calvinist theology) are predestined for salvation.

1. From Book 3, The Garden. (For more of *The Task,* see pages 2674–2677).

230　That brings the planets home into the eye
　　Of observation, and discovers, else°　　　　　　　　　　*otherwise*
　　Not visible, his family of worlds,
　　Discover him that rules them; such a veil
　　Hangs over mortal eyes, blind from the birth
235　And dark in things divine. Full often too
　　Our wayward intellect, the more we learn
　　Of nature, overlooks her author more,
　　From instrumental causes proud to draw
　　Conclusions retrograde and mad mistake.
240　But if his word once teach us, shoot a ray
　　Through all the heart's dark chambers, and reveal
　　Truths undiscerned but by that holy light,
　　Then all is plain. Philosophy baptized
　　In the pure fountain of eternal love
245　Has eyes indeed; and viewing all she sees
　　As meant to indicate a God to man,
　　Gives *him* his praise, and forfeits not her own.
　　Learning has borne such fruit in other days
　　On all her branches. Piety has found
250　Friends in the friends of science, and true prayer
　　Has flowed from lips wet with Castalian dews.[2]
　　Such was thy wisdom, Newton, childlike sage!
　　Sagacious reader of the works of God,
　　And in his word sagacious. * * *

1783–1785　　　　　　　　　　　　　　　　　　　　　　　　1785

The Cast-away[1]

　　Obscurest night involved° the sky,　　　　　　　　　　*encompassed*
　　　　Th' Atlantic billows roared,
　　When such a destined° wretch as I　　　　　　　　　　*doomed*
　　　　Washed headlong from on board
5　　Of friends, of hope, of all bereft,
　　　　His floating home for ever left.

　　No braver chief[2] could Albion° boast　　　　　　　　*Britain*
　　　　Than he with whom he went,
　　Nor ever ship left Albion's coast
10　　　With warmer wishes sent.
　　He loved them both, but both in vain,
　　Nor him beheld, nor her again.

　　Not long beneath the whelming brine
　　　　Expert to swim, he lay,

2. I.e., from poets (who have drunk of the inspirational Castalian spring on the mountain of the Muses).
1. Cowper based this poem on a mariner's account, in a popular travel book, of having watched helplessly as a shipmate was hurled overboard during a storm: "We were the more grieved at his unhappy fate, as we . . . conceived from the manner in which he swam that he might continue sensible, for a considerable time longer, of the hor-

ror attending his irretrievable situation." Cowper collates the doomed man's situation with his own, which he conceived as also "irretrievable"; the poem, left in manuscript at his death, is his last surviving original poem in English.
2. George Anson, commander of the naval squadron in which the sailor was lost.

15   Nor soon he felt his strength decline
        Or courage die away;
    But waged with Death a lasting strife
        Supported by despair of life.

    He shouted, nor his friends had failed
20   To check the vessel's course,
    But so the furious blast prevailed
        That, pitiless perforce,
    They left their outcast mate behind,
    And scudded still before the wind.

25   Some succor yet they could afford,
        And, such as storms allow,
    The cask, the coop, the floated cord
        Delayed not to bestow;
    But he, they knew, nor ship nor shore,
30   Whate'er they gave, should visit more.

    Nor, cruel as it seemed, could he
        Their haste, himself, condemn,
    Aware that flight, in such a sea,
        Alone could rescue them;
35   Yet bitter felt it still to die
    Deserted, and his friends so nigh.

    He long survives who lives an hour
        In ocean, self-upheld,
    And so long he, with unspent power,
40   His destiny repelled,
    And ever, as the minutes flew,
    Entreated help, or cried, Adieu!

    At length, his transient respite past,
        His comrades, who before
45   Had heard his voice in every blast,
        Could catch the sound no more;
    For then, by toil subdued, he drank
    The stifling wave, and then he sank.

    No poet wept him: but the page
50   Of narrative[3] sincere
    That tells his name, his worth,° his age,   *rank*
        Is wet with Anson's tear,
    And tears by bards or heroes shed
    Alike immortalize the dead.

55   I therefore purpose not or dream,
        Descanting on his fate,
    To give the melancholy theme
        A more enduring date,

---

3. The log book of the ship from which he fell.

But misery still delights to trace
60   Its semblance in another's case.

No voice divine the storm allayed,
    No light propitious shone,
When, snatched from all effectual aid,
    We perished, each, alone;
65   But I beneath a rougher sea,
And whelmed in deeper gulphs than he.

1799   1804

[END OF PERSPECTIVES: MIND AND GOD]

James Thomson
1700–1748

"Nature delights me in every form," James Thomson declared in a letter at age twenty-five. "I am just now painting her in her most lugubrious dress; for my own amusement describing winter as it presents itself." Though he may not have known it yet, he was "just now" embarking on his life's central work. In his long poem *The Seasons* (of which this piece on winter was the earliest installment), Thomson sought to develop a poetic structure capacious enough to compass the varied forms of nature in which he took so much delight.

Thomson wrote his letter in London, where he had recently arrived, to a friend in his native Scotland, where he would never return. The winters he remembered were those of the terrain where he had spent his first fifteen years, in a village near the border with England. When Thomson was seven, geographical proximity became political reality. The Act of Union, energetically endorsed by the poet's Whig neighbors, linked Scotland with England and Wales to form the new entity of Great Britain; that event resonates throughout the poet's life and work, in his depictions of nature (which remain centered in Scotland even as they span the globe), in his passionate advocacy of the politics he'd absorbed in youth, in his celebration of the incipient British empire.

Born to a Presbyterian minister praised for his "diligence," and to a mother noted for her "imagination," "warmth," and enthusiastic piety, Thomson felt toward both parents a lifelong affection. In deference to their wishes, and despite an early inclination to poetry, he initially planned to follow his father into the ministry. But Edinburgh, where he went at age fifteen to study divinity, abounded in literary aspirants, endeavors, publications, and societies. During his ten years there, Thomson gradually found that the attractions of poetry outflanked those of professional piety. Like many ambitious Scotsmen of the time, Thomson headed for London, along the route the Union had made smooth. There, aided and encouraged by new literary friends (Pope and Gay among them), he launched the poem of nature that he describes in his letter home. *Winter* (1726) was followed by *Summer* and *Spring* (both 1727); *The Seasons* (1730) brought the cycle to completion, with the new piece on *Autumn* added to the three earlier sections, now much expanded and revised. The work struck readers and reviewers as something altogether new, and quickly established the poet's fame. The following years produced another long poem, equally ambitious but less successful (*Liberty*, 1735–1736), a series of verse tragedies, and a plenitude of distractions. Thomson engaged exuberantly in politics and in the pleasures of food and drink, cherished his friends, and fell in love with women who did not love him back. The years also brought recurrent returns of *The Seasons*: the poem reappeared, in a greatly enlarged and altered edition, in 1744, and in yet another incarnation two years later. In *The Castle of Indolence* (1748), Thomson produced an allegory, by turns serious and comic, on that very propensity toward imaginative idleness that had both generated his poetry and prevented his producing more. The poem, deeply autobiographical, proved valedictory as well. Four months after its publication the poet died, mourned by his many friends as "our old, tried, amiable, open, and honest-hearted Thomson," and by a wider world of readers as the writer who had newly transmuted nature into language, in the century's single most popular poem.

The Seasons often gave rise to a measure of puzzlement commingled with its popularity. Thomson had set so much going in the poem that familiar conventions of artistic order and containment seemed overthrown. "The great defect of *The Seasons*," Samuel Johnson opined, "is its want of method"—its lack of a self-evident logical structure. Still, reader after reader (including Johnson) discovered that this seeming defect correlated mysteriously with the poem's many pleasures: its comprehensiveness, its range of tones and modes, its contagious "enthusiasm," whereby (in Johnson's account) "our thoughts expand with [Thomson's] imagery and kindle with his sentiments." Expansiveness had marked the poem's making as well as its impact. During two decades of creation and revision, Thomson kept nature at the center of his scrutiny, but made it the repository for his many preoccupations: Whig politics, imperial expansion, ancient history, Christian faith, modern science. The poem links and navigates all these topics not so much by "method" as by the restless motion of the maker's mind. In this innovative arrangement, the physical world becomes a medium of meditation, a mirror of mind and culture, the meeting place where human inquiry most fully encounters divine display, in order to discern and to wonder at the ways of both self and God. Like his idol Isaac Newton, whose discoveries pervade the poem, Thomson was reading and representing God's Book of Nature in new, immensely influential terms. "Enthusiasm" itself means immersion "in the God," possession by the divine. Thomson makes good on the term when he declares at the poem's close that the seasons "are but the varied God," phenomena that mortals must inhabit and observe with deep discernment, proper awe. Thomson's own enthusiasm proved contagious across boundaries of space, time, and medium. His poem was translated and ardently imitated in most of the languages of Europe; the composer Franz Haydn set its sentiments to music, and draughtsmen depicted its scenes so often that it remained for a hundred years the most illustrated work in English. For writers of many nations and several generations, *The Seasons* served as almost inexhaustible sourcebook, as supplementary Scripture.

from Winter. A Poem[1]

[AUTUMN EVENING AND NIGHT]

> See! Winter comes, to rule the varied year,
> Sullen and sad; with all his rising train,
> Vapors, and clouds, and storms. Be these my theme,
> These, that exalt the soul to solemn thought,
> 5   And heavenly musing. Welcome kindred glooms!
> Wished, wintery horrors, hail! With frequent foot,
> Pleased have I, in my cheerful morn of life,
> When nursed by careless solitude I lived,
> And sung of Nature with unceasing joy,
> 10   Pleased have I wandered through your rough domains;
> Trod the pure, virgin-snows, myself as pure;

1. This was the earliest version Thomson published; for some of his subsequent revisions, see the selection from *Autumn* on pages 2662–2666.

Heard the winds roar, and the big torrent burst;
Or seen the deep-fermenting tempest brewed
In the red evening sky. Thus passed the time
15 Till, through the opening chambers of the south,[2]
Looked out the joyous Spring, looked out, and smiled.

Thee too, inspirer of the toiling swain!
Fair Autumn, yellow robed! I'll sing of thee,
Of thy last, tempered days and sunny calms;
20 When all the golden hours are on the wing,
Attending thy retreat, and round thy wain,°   chariot
Slow-rolling, onward to the southern sky.

Behold![3] the well-poised hornet, hovering, hangs
With quivering pinions in the genial blaze;
25 Flies off in airy circles; then returns
And hums and dances to the beating ray.
Nor shall the man that, musing, walks alone,
And, heedless, strays within his radiant lists,°   boundaries
Go unchastised away. Sometimes a fleece
30 Of clouds, wide-scattering, with a lucid[4] veil,
Soft, shadow o'er th' unruffled face of heaven;
And, through their dewy sluices,° shed the sun,   floodgates
With tempered influence down. Then is the time,
For those, whom Wisdom, and whom Nature charm,
35 To steal themselves from the degenerate crowd,
And soar above this little scene of things:
To tread low-thoughted Vice beneath their feet:
To lay their passions in a gentle calm,
And woo lone Quiet, in her silent walks.

40 Now solitary, and in pensive guise,
Oft let me wander o'er the russet mead,°   meadow
Or through the pining grove, where scarce is heard
One dying strain, to cheer the woodman's toil.
Sad Philomel,[5] perchance, pours forth her plaint
45 Far through the withering copse.° Meanwhile the leaves, woods
That late the forest clad with lively green,
Nipped by the drizzly night, and sallow-hued,
Fall wavering through the air; or shower amain,°   fiercely
Urged by the breeze, that sobs amid the boughs.
50 Then listening hares forsake the rustling woods,
And, starting at the frequent noise, escape
To the rough stubble, and the rushy fen.°   marsh
Then woodcocks o'er the fluctuating main
That glimmers to the glimpses of the moon
55 Stretch their long voyage to the woodland glade;
Where, wheeling with uncertain flight, they mock

---

2. The southern sky, "opening" as clouds dissipate.
3. In *The Seasons*, Thomson transferred this passage (lines 23–79), extensively revised, to *Autumn* (lines 955–1036; see page 2662).

4. The adjective meant both "shining" and "transparent."
5. The nightingale. In Greek myth, the Athenian princess Philomela, raped by her brother-in-law Tereus, is transformed into a bird and nightly laments her fate.

The nimble fowler's° aim. Now Nature droops;   *bird hunter's*
Languish the living herbs, with pale decay:
And all the various family of flowers
60   Their sunny robes resign. The falling fruits,
Through the still night, forsake the parent bough
That in the first gray glances of the dawn,
Looks wild, and wonders at the wintry waste.

The year, yet pleasing, but declining fast,
65   Soft, o'er the secret soul, in gentle gales,
A philosophic melancholy breathes,
And bears the swelling thought aloft to heaven.
Then forming fancy rouses to conceive,
What never mingled with the vulgar's° dream: *common people's*
70   Then wake the tender pang, the pitying tear,
The sigh for suffering worth, the wish preferred°   *offered up*
For humankind, the joy to see them blessed,
And all the social offspring of the heart!

Oh! bear me then to high embowering shades;
75   To twilight groves and visionary vales;
To weeping grottos and to hoary caves;
Where angel forms are seen, and voices heard,
Sighed in low whispers that abstract the soul
From outward sense far into worlds remote.

80   Now,[6] when the western sun withdraws the day,
And humid evening, gliding o'er the sky,
In her chill progress checks the straggling beams,
And robs them of their gathered, vapory prey,
Where marshes stagnate, and where rivers wind,
85   Cluster the rolling fogs, and swim along   *open ground*
The dusky-mantled lawn:° then slow descend,
Once more to mingle with their watery friends.
The vivid stars shine out, in radiant files;
And boundless ether[7] glows; till the fair moon
90   Shows her broad visage, in the crimsoned east;
Now, stooping, seems to kiss the passing cloud:
Now, o'er the pure cerulean,[8] rides sublime.
Wide the pale deluge floats, with silver waves,
O'er the skied° mountain, to the low-laid vale;   *sky-high*
95   From the white rocks, with dim reflection, gleams,
And faintly glitters through the waving shades.

All night, abundant dews, unnoted, fall,
And, at return of morning, silver o'er
The face of Mother Earth; from every branch
100   Depending,° tremble the translucent gems,   *hanging*
And, quivering, seem to fall away, yet cling,

6. In *The Seasons*, this passage (lines 80–103) appeared, revised, in *Autumn* (lines 1082–1102; see page 2665).
7. "An element more fine and subtle than air" (Johnson's *Dictionary*); it was assumed to fill the highest regions above the earth.
8. Deep blue (of the evening sky).

And sparkle in the sun, whose rising eye,
With fogs bedimmed, portends a beauteous day.

* * *

[WINTER NIGHT]

Now, all amid the rigors of the year,
In the wild depth of winter, while without
255　　The ceaseless winds blow keen, be my retreat
A rural, sheltered, solitary scene;
Where ruddy fire and beaming tapers join
To chase the cheerless gloom. There let me sit,
And hold high converse with the mighty dead—
260　　Sages of ancient time, as gods revered,
As gods beneficent, who blessed mankind
With arts and arms, and humanized a world.
Roused at th' inspiring thought, I throw aside
The long-lived volume[9] and, deep-musing, hail
265　　The sacred shades that slowly rising pass
Before my wondering eyes. First Socrates,[1]
Truth's early champion, martyr for his God;
Solon[2] the next, who built his commonweal
On equity's firm base. Lycurgus[3] then,
270　　Severely good; and him of rugged Rome,
Numa,[4] who softened her rapacious sons.
Cimon sweet-souled, and Aristides[5] just.
Unconquered Cato,[6] virtuous in extreme;
With that attempered hero,[7] mild and firm,
275　　Who wept the brother while the tyrant bled.
Scipio[8] the humane warrior, gently brave,
Fair learning's friend, who early sought the shade,
To dwell, with innocence, and truth, retired.
And, equal to the best, the Theban,[9] he
280　　Who, single, raised his country into fame.
Thousands behind, the boast of Greece and Rome,
Whom virtue owns, the tribute of a verse
Demand, but who can count the stars of heaven?
Who sing their influence on this lower world?
285　　But see who yonder comes! nor comes alone,

9. Plutarch's Lives: biographies of eminent Greeks and Romans—composed by the Greek historian and philosopher (c. A.D. 46–120).
1. Socrates (469–399 B.C.), Athenian philospher, condemned to death for his teachings.
2. Solon (639–558 B.C.), Athenian statesman who introduced a newly humane system of laws.
3. Legendary Spartan lawgiver.
4. Rome's legendary second king, deemed a better ruler than the founder Romulus because his long reign was peaceful and enlightened.
5. Cimon (c.510–449 B.C.) and Aristeides (d. 468 B.C.), military leaders and statesmen noted for their victorious strategies in the Persian Wars and for their rectitude in government.

6. Marcus Porcius Cato (96–46 B.C), Roman champion of republican government; he chose to commit suicide rather than surrender himself to Julius Caesar, whose imperial ambitions he had resisted in the Roman civil wars.
7. Timoleon, a Corinthian who, alarmed at the tyrannical aspirations of his brother Timophanes, conspired in his assassination (365 B.C.), during which he wept for the kin he had helped to kill.
8. Scipio Africanus (236–183 B.C.), charismatic Roman general, conqueror of Spain and defeater of Hannibal.
9. Eiter Pelopidas (c.410–364 B.C.) or Epaminondas (d. 362 B.C.), military tacticians who led Thebes to victory over Sparta.

With sober state, and of majestic mien,
The Sister-Muses in his train. 'Tis he!
Maro![1] the best of poets, and of men!
Great Homer too appears, of daring wing!
290   Parent of song! and equal by this side,
The British Muse,[2] joined hand in hand, they walk
Darkling,[3] nor miss their way to fame's ascent.

    Society divine! Immortal minds!
Still visit thus my nights, for you reserved,
295   And mount my soaring soul to deeds like yours.
Silence! thou lonely power! the door be thine:
See, on the hallowed hour, that none intrude,
Save Lycidas,[4] the friend, with sense refined,
Learning digested well, exalted faith,
300   Unstudied wit, and humor ever gay.
1725–1726   1726

from The Seasons

from *Autumn*

[NIGHTFALL AND NIGHT[1]]

950   But see the fading many-colored woods,
Shade deepening over shade, the country round
Imbrown; a crowded umbrage,° dusk and dun.   shade
Of every hue from wan declining green
To sooty dark. These now the lonesome Muse,
955   Low-whispering, lead into their leaf-strewn walks,
And give the season in its latest view.[2]
    Meantime,[3] light shadowing all, a sober calm
Fleeces unbound ether; whose least wave
Stands tremulous, uncertain where to turn
960   The gentle current; while, illumined wide,
The dewy-skirted clouds imbibe the sun,
And through their lucid veil his softened force
Shed o'er the peaceful world. Then is the time
For those whom Wisdom and whom Nature charm
965   To steal themselves from the degenerate° crowd,   unworthy
And soar above this little scene of things—
To tread low-thoughted Vice beneath their feet,
To soothe the throbbing passions into peace,
And woo lone Quiet in her silent walks.

---

1. Virgil (Publius Virgilius Maro, 70–19 B.C.), Roman poet, author of the *Aeneid*.
2. John Milton.
3. In the dark (Milton was blind, and Homer was traditionally thought to have been so).
4. Thomson takes the name (and its connotation of learned companion) from Milton's pastoral elegy (1638) lamenting the death of his college friend Edward King.
1. The original version of *Winter* begins with the description of an evening in late autumn; later, Thomson revised this description and transferred it to the section on autumn, which made its first appearance in *The Seasons* (1730). Thomson repeatedly revised the poem in the years that followed; the text here is taken from the last edition he produced (1746).
2. The colors display the very end of autumn.
3. For Thomson's earlier version of this passage (lines 955–1036), see *Winter*, lines 23–79, page 2659.

970   Thus solitary, and in pensive guise,
      Oft let me wander o'er the russet mead,
      And through the saddened grove, where scarce is heard
      One dying strain to cheer the woodman's toil.
      Haply some widowed songster pours his plaint
975   Far in faint warblings through the tawny copse;
      While congregated thrushes, linnets, larks,
      And each wild throat whose artless strains so late
      Swelled all the music of the swarming shades,
      Robbed of their tuneful souls, now shivering sit
980   On the dead tree, a dull despondent flock,
      With not a brightness waving o'er their plumes,
      And naught save chattering discord in their note.
      Oh, let not, aimed from some inhuman eye,
      The gun the music of the coming year
985   Destroy, and harmless, unsuspecting harm,
      Lay the weak tribes, a miserable prey!
      In mingled murder fluttering on the ground!
          The pale descending year, yet pleasing still,
      A gentler mood inspires; for now the leaf
990   Incessant rustles from the mournful grove,
      Oft startling such as, studious, walk below,
      And slowly circles through the waving air.
      But should a quicker breeze amid the boughs
      Sob, o'er the sky the leafy deluge streams;
995   Till choked, and matted with the dreary shower,
      The forest-walks, at every rising gale,
      Roll wide the withered waste, and whistle bleak.
      Fled is the blasted verdure of the fields;
      And, shrunk into their beds, the flowery race
1000 Their sunny robes resign. Even what remained
      Of bolder fruits falls from the naked tree;
      And woods, fields, gardens, orchards, all around
      The desolated prospect thrills the soul.
          He comes! he comes! in every breeze the power
1005 Of Philosophic Melancholy comes!
      His near approach the sudden-starting tear,
      The glowing cheek, the mild dejected air,
      The softened feature, and the beating heart,
      Pierced deep with many a virtuous pang, declare.
1010 O'er all the soul his sacred influence breathes;
      Inflames imagination; through the breast
      Infuses every tenderness; and far
      Beyond dim earth exalts the swelling thought.
      Ten thousand thousand fleet° ideas, such   rapid
1015 As never mingled with the vulgar dream,
      Crowd fast into the mind's creative eye.
      As fast the correspondent passions rise,
      As varied, and as high—devotion raised
      To rapture, and divine astonishment;
1020 The love of nature unconfined, and, chief,

Of human race; the large ambitious wish,
To make them blest; the sigh for suffering worth,
Lost in obscurity; the noble scorn,
Of tyrant pride; the fearless great resolve;
1025 The wonder which the dying patriot draws,
Inspiring glory through remotest time;
The awakened throb for virtue, and for fame;
The sympathies of love, and friendship dear;
With all the social offspring of the heart.
1030   Oh! bear me then to vast embowering shades,
To twilight groves, and visionary vales![4]
To weeping grottoes, and prophetic glooms!
Where angel forms athwart the solemn dusk,
Tremendous sweep, or seem to sweep along;
1035 And voices more than human, through the void
Deep-sounding, seize the enthusiastic ear.
     Or is this gloom too much?[5] Then lead, ye powers,
That o'er the garden and the rural seat
Preside, which shining through the cheerful land
1040 In countless numbers blest Britannia sees;
O lead me to the wide-extended walks,
The fair majestic paradise of Stowe![6]
Not Persian Cyrus,[7] on Ionia's shore,
E'er saw such sylvan scenes; such various art
1045 By genius fired, such ardent genius tamed
By cool judicious art; that, in the strife,
All-beauteous Nature fears to be outdone.
And there, O Pitt,[8] thy country's early boast,
There let me sit beneath the sheltered slopes,
1050 Or in that Temple[9] where, in future times,
Thou well shalt merit a distinguished name;
And, with thy converse blest, catch the last smiles
Of Autumn beaming o'er the yellow woods.
While there with thee the enchanted round I walk,
1055 The regulated wild, gay Fancy° then   *imagination*
Will tread in thought the groves of Attic land;[1]
Will from thy standard taste refine her own,[2]
Correct her pencil to the purest truth
Of Nature, or, the unimpassioned shades
1060 Forsaking, raise it to the human mind.
O if hereafter she, with juster hand,

---

4. Valleys where I may see visions.
5. Thomson added lines 1036–1081 in his revision of 1744.
6. Stowe, the Buckinghamshire estate of Sir Richard Temple, Viscount Cobham (1669–1749), had been laid out and reworked by a long series of distinguished architects and landscapers; the garden was among the most celebrated of the 18th century (see Pope, *Epistle to Burlington*, lines 57–70, page 2523).
7. Cyrus the Younger (d. 401 B.C.), a Persian prince, designed and planted a famous garden at Sardis (on "Ionia's shore," the coast of Asia Minor).

8. The statesman and orator William Pitt (1708–1778) was esteemed by Thomson and Cobham as a leading voice among those Whigs opposed to the still-dominant party faction led by Robert Walpole; Pitt later became Secretary of State and Prime Minister.
9. The Temple of Virtue in Stowe Gardens [Thomson's note]; this monument to ancient heroes was one of the gardens' most celebrated buildings.
1. Ancient Greece (Attica was the countryside surrounding Athens).
2. Influenced by your standard of taste, Fancy will refine hers.

Shall draw the tragic scene, instruct her thou,
To mark the varied movements of the heart,
What every decent[3] character requires,
1065 And every passion speaks. O through her strain°   *song, style*
Breathe thy pathetic eloquence! that molds
Th' attentive senate, charms, persuades, exalts,
Of honest zeal th' indignant lightning throws,
And shakes corruption on her venal throne.
1070 While thus we talk, and through Elysian vales[4]
Delighted rove, perhaps a sigh escapes.
What pity, Cobham, thou thy verdant files
Of ordered trees shouldst here inglorious range,
Instead of squadrons flaming o'er the field,
1075 And long-embattled hosts![5] When the proud foe
The faithless vain disturber of mankind,
Insulting Gaul, has roused the world to war;
When keen, once more, within their bounds to press[6]
Those polished robbers, those ambitious slaves,
1080 The British youth would hail thy wise command,
They tempered ardor and thy veteran skill.[7]

The western sun withdraws the shortened day;[8]
And humid evening, gliding o'er the sky,
In her chill progress, to the ground condensed
1085 The vapors throws. Where creeping waters ooze,
Where marshes stagnate, and where rivers wind,
Cluster the rolling fogs, and swim along
The dusky-mantled lawn. Meanwhile the moon,
Full-orbed and breaking through the scattered clouds,
1090 Shows her broad visage in the crimsoned east.
Turned to the sun direct, her spotted disk
(Where mountains rise, umbrageous dales descend,
And oceans roll, as optic tube° descries)   *telescope*
A smaller earth, gives all his blaze again,
1095 Void of its flame, and sheds a softer day.
Now through the passing cloud she seems to stoop,
Now up the pure cerulean rides sublime.
Wide the pale deluge floats, and streaming mild
O'er the skied° mountain to the shadowy vale,   *sky-high*
1100 While rocks and floods reflect the quivering gleam,
The whole air whitens with a boundless tide
Of silver radiance, trembling round the world.
But when, half-blotted from the sky, her light,

---

3. Appropriate (Thomson, who wrote several tragedies, here asks Pitt for guidance in suiting his language to his characers and their emotions).
4. The Elysian Fields at Stowe (named for Elysium, Greek myth's paradise for heroes) were the most wild and natural area of the gardens.
5. Cobham left the Walpole government in 1733; thereafter he worked on his gardens and formed a group of opposition Whigs known as "Cobham's Cubs." Here Thomson wishes that Cobham, an accomplished soldier,

might deploy his gifts as military leader rather than as shaper of landscapes.
6. I.e., contain within their own borders.
7. Thomson here imagines how effective Cobham would be as a leader in the War of the Austrian Succession (1740–1748), England's current conflict with France ("insulting Gaul," "polished robbers," "ambitious slaves").
8. Compare the earlier version of these lines in *Winter* (lines 80–96 on page 2660).

Fainting, permits the starry fires to burn,
1105   With keener luster through the depth of heaven;
Or quite extinct her deadened orb appears,
And scarce appears, of sickly beamless white;
Oft in this season, silent from the north
A blaze of meteors shoots[9]—ensweeping first
1110   The lower skies, they all at once converge
High to the crown of heaven, and all at once
Relapsing quick as quickly reascend,
And mix, and thwart,° extinguish, and renew,   cross
All ether coursing in a maze of light.
1115   From look to look, contagious through the crowd,
The panic runs, and into wondrous shapes
Th' appearance throws—armies in meet array,
Thronged with aërial spears, and steeds of fire;
Till the long lines of full-extended war
1120   In bleeding fight commixed, the sanguine flood
Rolls a broad slaughter o'er the plains of heaven.
As thus they scan the visionary scene,
On all sides swells the superstitious din,
Incontinent;° and busy frenzy talks   unrestrained
1125   Of blood and battle; cities overturned,
And late at night in swallowing earthquake sunk,
Or hideous wrapped in fierce ascending flame;
Of sallow famine, inundation, storm;
Of pestilence, and every great distress;
1130   Empires subversed, when ruling fate has struck
The unalterable hour: even Nature's self
Is deemed to totter on the brink of time.
Not so the man of philosophic eye,
And inspect sage;° the waving brightness he   wise insight
1135   Curious surveys, inquisitive to know
The causes, and materials, yet unfixed,[1]
Of this appearance beautiful, and new. * * *

1726–1746   1746

Rule, Britannia[1]

When Britain first, at Heaven's command,
    Arose from out the azure main;°   sea
This was the charter of the land,

9. The aurora borealis, or northern lights.
1. Unaccounted for (by science).
1. Thomson wrote several longer poems of impassioned patriotism (*Britannia*, 1729; *Liberty*, 1735–1736) but his convictions found their most enduring expression in this short piece, first performed as the climactic song of *Alfred*, a patriotic masque on the subject of the Saxon king (848–899). Defeated by the Danes, the monarch receives comfort from a "venerable bard," who expresses with uncanny prescience the 18th-century appetite for naval conquest and expanding empire. The masque was created by Thomson in collaboration with his fellow

Scots expatriate David Mallet (?1705–1765) and the composer Thomas Arne (1710–1778), as part of an entertainment commissioned by Frederick, Prince of Wales, to celebrate his daughter's third birthday and the anniversary of his German grandfather's accession to the English throne. Thomson's ode outlasted its occasion, gradually acquiring the status of an alternate national anthem (just behind *God Save the King*). While the Empire endured, Thomson's song proffered for many Britons a stirring account of their national origins, essence, and destiny.

And guardian angels sung this strain:
5   "Rule, Britannia, rule the waves;
       "Britons never will be slaves."

The nations, not so blest as thee,
       Must, in their turns, to tyrants fall:
While thou shalt flourish great and free,
10   The dread and envy of them all.
       "Rule," etc.

Still more majestic shalt thou rise,
       More dreadful, from each foreign stroke:
As the loud blast that tears the skies,
15   Serves but to root thy native oak.
       "Rule," etc.

Thee haughty tyrants ne'er shall tame:
       All their attempts to bend thee down
Will but arouse thy generous flame;
20   But work their woe, and thy renown.
       "Rule," etc.

To thee belongs the rural reign;
       Thy cities shall with commerce shine:
All thine shall be the subject main,
25   And every shore it circles thine.
       "Rule," etc.

The Muses, still[2] with freedom found,
       Shall to thy happy coast repair:
Blest isle! with matchless beauty crowned,
30   And manly hearts to guard the fair.
       "Rule, Britannia, rule the waves;
       "Britons never will be slaves."

1740   1740

THE SEASONS IN CONTEXT
Poems of Nightfall and Night

The aubade, or dawn-song, was a favorite form in the Middle Ages and the Renaissance: poets from Chaucer to Donne portrayed lovers entwined abed, lamenting the intrusive rising of the sun. In eighteenth-century England, poets were more preoccupied with the night piece, as a medium not for amorous pairings but for meditative solitude. In a culture marked by the intensified noise, density, and busyness of the cities, privacy was an experience newly construed and prized; in the scene of nightfall (particularly *country* nightfall), poets found an ideal setting for its enactment. Anne Finch opens her *Nocturnal Reverie* with a key line from one of Shakespeare's dialogues between lovers, but she transmutes conversation into soliloquy. William Collins, in his most famous ode, addresses the Evening as a "maid composed," a "nymph reserved," whose quietude facilitates his solitary thought; in his poem on the death of his friend James Thomson, Collins renders his sense of loss by images of encroaching dark. The

---

2. The word meant both "always" and "as yet."

other selections here come from larger works—Edward Young's *Night Thoughts* and William Cowper's *The Task*—which participate in the tradition that Thomson's *Seasons* had commenced: copious blank-verse description and meditation, produced, expanded, and revised over the course of years, mingling widely various materials and modes in a new, purportedly improvisatory way. "The method pursued," Young explained of his long poem, "was rather *imposed*, by what spontaneously arose in the author's mind on that occasion, than *meditated* or *designed*"; Cowper, more simply, attributed the expansion of *The Task* to the unexpected directions dictated by his own "train of thought." Drawing on darkness as resource and backdrop, Thomson, Young, and Cowper were working toward a new mode: the epic of the solitary mind in action. From them the lines of influence run long and clear, through the Gothic fiction of the late eighteenth century, through Wordsworth's meditative excursions, into the stream of consciousness in Joyce's *Ulysses* and the nocturnal dreamspeak of *Finnegans Wake*.

Anne Finch
A Nocturnal Reverie[1]

	In such a night,[2] when every louder wind	
	Is to its distant cavern safe confined;	
	And only gentle Zephyr° fans his wings,	*the west wind*
	And lonely Philomel,° still waking, sings;	*the nightingale*
5	Or from some tree, famed for the owl's delight,	
	She, hollowing clear, directs the wanderer right:	
	In such a night, when passing clouds give place,	
	Or thinly veil the heavens' mysterious face;	
	When in some river, overhung with green,	
10	The waving moon and trembling leaves are seen;	
	When freshened grass now bears itself upright,	
	And makes cool banks to pleasing rest invite,	
	Whence springs the woodbind, and the bramble-rose,	
	And where the sleepy cowslip sheltered grows;	
15	Whilst now a paler hue the foxglove takes,	
	Yet checkers still with red the dusky brakes:°	*thickets*
	When scattered glow-worms, but in twilight fine,	
	Show trivial beauties, watch their hour to shine;	
	Whilst Salisbury[3] stands the test of every light,	
20	In perfect charms, and perfect virtue bright;	
	When odors, which declined repelling day,	
	Through temperate air uninterrupted stray;	
	When darkened groves their softest shadows wear,	
	And falling waters we distinctly hear;	
25	When through the gloom more venerable shows	
	Some ancient fabric,° awful in repose,	*building*
	While sunburnt hills their swarthy looks conceal,	
	And swelling haycocks thicken up the vale;	
	When the loosed horse now, as his pasture leads,	
30	Comes slowly grazing through th' adjoining meads,	
	Whose stealing pace, and lengthened shade we fear,	
	Till torn up forage in his teeth we hear;	

---

1. For Anne Finch, see page 2141.
2. Finch takes her opening words from the evocation of night in Shakespeare's *Merchant of Venice* (5.1.1–21), where the lovers Lorenzo and Jessica speak the phrase repeatedly to each other, as they retell old tales of nocturnal passion and betrayal.
3. Anne Tufton, Countess of Salisbury, daughter of one of Finch's close friends.

When nibbling sheep at large pursue their food,
And unmolested kine rechew the cud;
35 When curlews cry beneath the village-walls,
And to her straggling brood the partridge calls;
Their short-lived jubilee the creatures keep,
Which but endures, whilst tyrant-man does sleep;
When a sedate content the spirit feels,
40 And no fierce light disturbs, whilst it reveals;
But silent musings urge the mind to seek
Something, too high for syllables to speak;
Till the free soul to a compos'dness charmed,
Finding the elements of rage disarmed,
45 O'er all below a solemn quiet grown,
Joys in th' inferior° world, and thinks it like her own: *lower*
In such a night let me abroad remain,
Till morning breaks, and all's confused again;
Our cares, our toils, our clamors are renewed,
50 Or pleasures, seldom reached, again pursued.

1713

Edward Young[1]
from *The Complaint*
or Night Thoughts on Life, Death, and Immortality

Tired Nature's sweet restorer, balmy Sleep!
He, like the world, his ready visit pays
Where Fortune smiles; the wretched he forsakes:
Swift on his downy pinion° flies from woe,   *wing*
5 And lights on lids unsullied with a tear.
    From short (as usual) and disturbed repose,
I wake. How happy they, who wake no more!
Yet that were vain, if dreams infest the grave.
I wake, emerging from a sea of dreams
10 Tumultuous; where my wrecked, desponding thought
From wave to wave of fancied misery,
At random drove, her helm of reason lost.
Though now restored, 'tis only change of pain,
(A bitter change!) severer for severe.
15 The day too short for my distress! and Night,
Even in the zenith of her dark domain,
Is sunshine, to the color of my fate.
    Night, sable goddess! from her ebon° throne,   *black*
In rayless majesty, now stretches forth
20 Her leaden scepter o'er a slumb'ring world.

1. After a frustrating London career as poet and playwright in frantic pursuit of political advancement, Edward Young (1683–1765) took holy orders, withdrew to a small village, and at age 59 commenced a set of poems that brought him sudden, staggering success. In *The Complaint*, a sequence of nine night pieces (and more than 9,000 lines) published serially over the course of three years, Young mixed morbid melancholy, Gothic dread, and Christian solace. The combination appealed powerfully to a vast number and variety of readers, in Britain and on the Continent. In its meditative blank verse and its capacious, fluid form, *Night Thoughts* was plainly influenced by Thomson's *Seasons;* well into the 19th century, the two works were often packaged (along with *Paradise Lost*) in a single, highly saleable volume. Both poems pervaded the century's consciousness, and later figured as principle forebears of Romantic thought and writing. This excerpt is from *Night 1*.

Silence, how dead! and darkness, how profound!
Nor eye, nor list'ning ear an object finds;
Creation sleeps. 'Tis as° the general pulse   *as if*
Of life stood still, and Nature made a pause;
25   An awful pause! prophetic of her end.
And let her prophecy be soon fulfilled;
Fate! drop the curtain; I can lose no more.
    Silence, and Darkness! Solemn sisters! Twins
From ancient Night, who nurse the tender thought
30   To reason, and on reason build resolve
(That column of true majesty in man),
Assist me: I will thank you in the grave;
The grave, your kingdom. There this frame shall fall
A victim sacred to your dreary shrine.
35   But what are ye? Thou,[2] who didst put to flight
Primeval Silence, when the morning stars,
Exulting, shouted o'er the rising ball;
O Thou! whose word from solid darkness struck
That spark, the sun; strike wisdom from my soul;
40   My soul, which flies to Thee, her trust, her treasure,
As misers to their gold, while others rest.
    Through this opaque of nature, and of soul,
This double night, transmit one pitying ray,
To lighten, and to cheer. O lead my mind,
45   (A mind that fain would wander from its woe)
Lead it through various scenes of life and death;
And from each scene the noblest truths inspire.
Nor less inspire my conduct than my song;
Teach my best reason reason; my best will
Teach rectitude; and fix my firm resolve
50   Wisdom to wed, and pay her long arrear:°   *old debt*
Nor let the phial of Thy vengeance, poured
On this devoted head, be poured in vain.
    The bell strikes one. We take no note of time
But from its loss. To give it then a tongue,
55   Is wise in man. As if an angel spoke,
I feel the solemn sound. If heard aright,
It is the knell of my departed hours:
Where are they? With the years beyond the flood.
It is the signal that demands dispatch;
60   How much is to be done? my hopes and fears
Start up alarmed, and o'er life's narrow verge
Look down—on what? A fathomless abyss;
A dread eternity! how surely mine!
And can eternity belong to me,
65   Poor pensioner on the bounties of an hour?
    How poor, how rich, how abject, how august,
How complicate, how wonderful, is man?
How passing wonder He, who made him such?

---

2. Young here shifts addressees, from the plural "ye" (Silence and Darkness) to the singular "Thou" (God, imagined at the moment of Creation).

Who centered in our make such strange extremes?
From different natures marvelously mixed,
70   Connection exquisite of distant worlds!
Distinguished link in being's endless chain!
Midway from nothing to the deity!
A beam ethereal sullied and absorbed!
Though sullied and dishonored, still divine!
75   Dim miniature of greatness absolute!
An heir of glory! a frail child of dust!
Helpless immortal! Insect infinite!
A worm! a God! I tremble at myself,
And in myself am lost! At home a stranger,
80   Thought wanders up and down, surprised, aghast,
And wondering at her own. How reason reels!
O what a miracle to man is man,
Triumphantly distressed! what joy, what dread!
Alternately transported and alarmed!
85   What can preserve my life? or what destroy?
An angel's arm can't snatch me from the grave;
Legions of angels can't confine me there.
'Tis past conjecture; all things rise in proof:
While o'er my limbs sleep's soft dominion spread,
90   What, though my soul fantastic measures trod
O'er fairy fields; or mourned along the gloom
Of pathless woods; or down the craggy steep
Hurled headlong, swam with pain the mantled pool;
Or scaled the cliff; or danced on hollow winds,
95   With antic shapes, wild natives of the brain?
Her ceaseless flight, though devious, speaks her nature
Of subtler essence than the trodden clod;
Active, aërial, towering, unconfined,
Unfettered with her gross companion's fall.
100 Even silent night proclaims my soul immortal:
Even silent night proclaims eternal day.
For human weal, Heaven husbands all events,
Dull sleep instructs, nor sport vain dreams in vain.

1742   1742, 1750

William Collins[1]
Ode to Evening

If aught of oaten stop,[2] or pastoral song,
May hope, chaste Eve, to soothe thy modest ear,

---

1. As a student at Oxford, William Collins (1721–1759) secured some distinction, published a few poems, and promptly left for London and the life (as his friend Samuel Johnson described it) of "a literary adventurer." While amusing himself at the city's pleasure gardens and playhouses, amid a spritely circle of actors and writers, Collins planned a number of books. He published only one, a small collection entitled *Odes on Several Descriptive and Allegorical Subjects* (1747); its failure to attract notice prompted him to burn the many copies that had gone unsold. In his late 20s, the poet fell prey to a manic depression verging on madness, which disabled him the rest of his life. His odes, neglected in his time, appealed strongly to tastes that came into vogue just after his death: for sentiment and the sublime, for the expression of overpowering emotions, of disruptive experiences, and of visionary intensities beyond the familiar, civic, human scale.

2. If any music played on an oat-reed pipe (Collins uses the pastoral-archaic idiom associated with Spenser and Milton).

Like thy own solemn springs,
Thy springs, and dying gales,
5   O nymph reserved, while now the bright-haired sun
Sits in yon western tent, whose cloudy skirts,
With brede° ethereal wove,   braid
O'erhang his wavy bed:
Now air is hushed, save where the weak-eyed bat,
10   With short shrill shriek flits by on leathern wing,
Or where the beetle winds°   blows
His small but sullen horn,
As oft he rises 'midst the twilight path,
Against the pilgrim borne in heedless hum:
15   Now teach me, maid composed,
To breathe some softened strain,°   song
Whose numbers° stealing through thy darkening vale,   verses
May not unseemly with its stillness suit,
As musing slow, I hail
20   Thy genial loved return!
For when thy folding star arising shows
His paly circlet, at his warning lamp
The fragrant Hours, and elves
Who slept in flowers the day,
25   And many a nymph who wreathes her brows with sedge,
And sheds the freshening dew, and lovelier still,
The pensive Pleasures sweet
Prepare thy shadowy car.°   chariot
Then lead, calm vot'ress,[3] where some sheety lake
30   Cheers the lone heath, or some time-hallowed pile,°   building
Or upland fallows[4] gray
Reflect its last cool gleam.
But when chill blustering winds, or driving rain,
Forbid my willing feet, be mine the hut,
35   That from the mountain's side,
Views wilds, and swelling floods,
And hamlets brown, and dim-discovered spires,
And hears their simple bell, and marks o'er all
Thy dewy fingers draw
40   The gradual dusky veil.
While Spring shall pour his showers, as oft he wont,[5]
And bathe thy breathing tresses, meekest Eve!
While Summer loves to sport,
Beneath thy lingering light;
45   While sallow Autumn fills thy lap with leaves;
Or Winter, yelling through the troublous air,
Affrights thy shrinking train,
And rudely rends thy robes;
So long, sure-found beneath the sylvan shed,
50   Shall Fancy, Friendship, Science, rose-lipped Health,

---

3. "A woman devoted to . . . worship" (Johnson's *Dictio-*
nary).

4. Fields ploughed but unplanted.
5. Is accustomed to do.

Thy gentlest influence own,
And hymn thy favorite name!

1746   1746, 1748

William Collins
Ode Occasioned by the Death of Mr. Thomson

The scene of the following stanzas is supposed to lie on the Thames near Richmond.[1]

*Haec tibi semper erunt, et cum solennia vota
reddemus Nymphis, et cum lustrabimus agros.*

———— ————*Amavit nos quoque Daphnis.*[2]

1

In yonder grave a Druid[3] lies,
    Where slowly winds the stealing wave!
The year's best sweets shall duteous rise
    To deck its poet's sylvan grave!

2

5   In yon deep bed of whispering reeds
    His airy harp[4] shall now be laid,
That he, whose heart in sorrow bleeds,
    May love through life the soothing shade.

3

Then maids and youths shall linger here,
10   And, while its sounds at distance swell,
Shall sadly seem in Pity's ear
    To hear the woodland pilgrim's[5] knell.

4

Remembrance oft shall haunt the shore
    When Thames in summer wreaths is dressed,
15 And oft suspend the dashing oar
    To bid his gentle spirit rest!

5

And oft as Ease and Health retire
    To breezy lawn or forest deep,

1. A scenic riverside village nine miles from London's center; Thomson had lived there in his last years, and was buried in the parish churchyard. Collins, who had dwelt there too, in close friendship with Thomson, here invokes the local geography quite specifically. His ode compasses two motions: in space, as the speaker moves past Richmond up the river; in time, as day modulates into night. Collins's poem was praised by a contemporary for the "dirge-like melancholy it breathes, and the warmth of affection that seems to have dictated it"; it has long enjoyed a print intimacy with the poet whom it eulogizes. Thomson's editors have often presented it as a preface to his works; his biographers have reprinted it as a coda to his life, a summation of his worth.

2. "These rites shall be thine forever, both when we pay our yearly vows to the Nymphs, and when we purify our fields . . . Daphnis loved us too" (Virgil, *Eclogues* 5.74–75, 52). In the pastoral tradition, the legendary Daphnis is

credited as the first shepherd to have made music, the inventor of bucolic song; in Virgil's lines, one of Daphnis's followers mourns his master's "cruel death" and promises perpetual homage.

3. The Druids were the priest-magicians of ancient Britain. In the 18th century they were thought to have possessed extraordinary intimacy with, and power over, the forces of nature.

4. "The harp of Aeolus" [Collins's note], an instrument whose strings make sounds when the breezes play upon them (Aeolus was the mythological Greek monarch of the winds). Thomson, the first to invoke this instrument in English verse, had made it a figure for poetic responsiveness to inspiration; many poets since have taken up the trope.

5. I.e., Thomson's, whose love of forest walks Collins here recalls.

The friend shall view yon whitening spire,[6]
20   And mid the varied landscape weep.

6

But thou, who own'st that earthy bed,
          Ah! what will every dirge avail?
Or tears, which Love and Pity shed
          That mourn beneath the gliding sail![7]

7

25   Yet lives there one, whose heedless eye
          Shall scorn thy pale shrine glimmering near?
With him, sweet bard, may Fancy die,
          And Joy desert the blooming year.

8

But thou, lorn stream,[8] whose sullen tide
30   No sedge-crowned Sisters now attend,
Now waft me from the green hill's side,
          Whose cold turf hides the buried friend!

9

And see, the fairy valleys fade,
          Dun Night has veiled the solemn view![9]
35   —Yet once again, dear parted shade,
          Meek Nature's child, again adieu!

10

The genial meads,° assigned to bless   *meadows*
          Thy life, shall mourn thy early doom,
Their hinds° and shepherd-girls shall dress   *shepherds*
40   With simple hands thy rural tomb.

11

Long, long, thy stone and pointed clay[1]
          Shall melt the musing Briton's eyes:
"O! vales and wild woods," shall he say,
          "In yonder grave your Druid lies!"

1748–1749   1749

William Cowper
from *The Task*[1]

FROM BOOK 4. THE WINTER EVENING
[READING THE NEWSPAPER]

Now stir the fire, and close the shutters fast,
Let fall the curtains, wheel the sofa round,

---

6. Of the parish church where Thomson was buried.
7. Of the boat moving down the Thames (see line 15).
8. The Thames, forlorn because it is no longer inhabited by the leaf-adorned river nymphs ("sedge-crowned Sisters") who dwelt there during Thomson's lifetime.
9. Collins echoes Thomson's *Autumn* lines 950–952 (see page 2662).
1. I.e., the poet's churchyard monument.
1. For William Cowper, see page 2653. As preface to *The Task*, Cowper offered the following brief "history": "A lady, fond of blank verse, demanded a poem of that kind from the author, and gave him the SOFA for a subject. He obeyed; and having much leisure, connected another subject with it; and pursuing the train of thought to which

his situation and turn of mind led him, brought forth at length, instead of the trifle which he at first intended, a serious affair—a volume." The modulation from triviality to seriousness (and back again) is intrinsic not only to the history of the poem but to its substance too. In six epic "Books" bearing markedly domestic titles (*The Sofa, The Time-Piece, The Garden, The Winter Evening, The Winter Morning Walk, The Winter Walk at Noon*), Cowper savors rural pleasures and satirizes the life of cities. Mingling grand diction with cozy fact ("I sing the Sofa," the poem begins), Cowper revels in their seeming disparity, as a resource both for comic self-deprecation and for earnest affirmation. These domestic delights, *The Task* implies, deserve this scale of celebration.

And while the bubbling and loud-hissing urn
Throws up a steamy column, and the cups°   *of tea*
40 That cheer but not inebriate, wait on each,
So let us welcome peaceful evening in.
Not such his ev'ning, who with shining face
Sweats in the crowded theater, and squeezed
And bored with elbow-points through both his sides,
45 Out-scolds the ranting actor on the stage.
Nor his, who patient stands till his feet throb,
And his head thumps, to feed upon the breath
Of patriots[2] bursting with heroic rage,
Or placemen,[3] all tranquility and smiles.
50 This folio of four pages,° happy work!   *the newspaper*
Which not ev'n critics criticize, that holds
Inquisitive attention while I read,
Fast bound in chains of silence, which the fair,[4]
Though eloquent themselves, yet fear to break,
55 What is it, but a map of busy life,
Its fluctuations and its vast concerns?
Here runs the mountainous and craggy ridge
That tempts ambition. On the summit, see,
The seals of office glitter in his eyes;
60 He climbs, he pants, he grasps them. At his heels,
Close at his heels a demagogue ascends,
And with a dext'rous jerk soon twists him down
And wins them, but to lose them in his turn.
Here rills of oily eloquence in soft
65 Meanders lubricate the course they take;
The modest speaker is ashamed and grieved
T' engross a moment's notice, and yet begs,
Begs a propitious ear for his poor thoughts,
However trivial all that he conceives.
70 Sweet bashfulness! it claims, at last, this praise:
The dearth of information and good sense
That it foretells us, always comes to pass.
Cataracts of declamation thunder here,
There forests of no-meaning spread the page
75 In which all comprehension wanders lost;
While fields of pleasantry amuse us there,
With merry descants° on a nation's woes.   *commentaries*
The rest[5] appears a wilderness of strange
But gay confusion: roses for the cheeks,
80 And lilies for the brows of faded age,
Teeth for the toothless, ringlets for the bald,
Heaven, earth, and ocean plundered of their sweets,
Nectareous essences, Olympian dews,
Sermons and city feasts and favorite airs,[6]
85 Aetherial journies,[7] submarine exploits,[8]

---

2. Political zealots.
3. Office-holders, bureaucrats.
4. The women of the house.
5. I.e., the newspaper's advertisements.

6. Popular melodies (sold as sheet music).
7. In hot-air balloons; the first flight had taken place in 1783.
8. In diving bells, which had been in use for more than a century.

And Katterfelto[9] with his hair on end
At his own wonders, wond'ring for his bread.
     'Tis pleasant through the loop-holes of retreat
To peep at such a world. To see the stir
90   Of the great Babel[1] and not feel the crowd.
To hear the roar she sends through all her gates
At a safe distance, where the dying sound
Falls a soft murmur on th' uninjured ear.
Thus sitting and surveying thus at ease
95   The globe and its concerns, I seem advanced
To some secure and more than mortal height,
That lib'rates and exempts me from them all.
It turns submitted to my view, turns round
With all its generations; I behold
100 The tumult and am still. The sound of war
Has lost its terrors ere it reaches me;
Grieves but alarms me not. I mourn the pride
And avarice that make man a wolf to man,
Hear the faint echo of those brazen throats
105 By which he speaks the language of his heart,
And sigh, but never tremble at the sound.
He travels and expatiates, as the bee
From flow'r to flow'r, so he from land to land;
The manners, customs, policy of all
110 Pay contribution to the store he gleans,
He sucks intelligence in every clime,
And spreads the honey of his deep research
At his return, a rich repast for me.
He travels and I too. I tread his deck,
115 Ascend his topmast, through his peering eyes
Discover countries, with a kindred heart
Suffer his woes, and share in his escapes,
While fancy, like the finger of a clock,
Runs the great circuit, and is still at home.

[THE INVOCATION]

Come Ev'ning once again,[1] season of peace
Return sweet Ev'ning, and continue long!
245 Methinks I see thee in the streaky west,
With matron-step slow-moving, while the night
Treads on thy sweeping train; one hand employed
In letting fall the curtain of repose
On bird and beast, the other charged for man
250 With sweet oblivion of the cares of day;

---

9. Gustave Katterfelto, a magician whose performances were advertised under the rubric "Wonders, Wonders, Wonders."
1. The biblical Tower of Babel (Genesis 11.1–9), whose construction God prevented by making the builders speak different languages ("babble"); Cowper here uses

the word for its long-established association with "Babylon," meaning any great city.
1. Cowper's invocation in the ensuing lines echoes both Milton's *Paradise Lost* (4.568–609) and Collin's *Ode to Evening* (page 2671).

Not sumptuously adorned, nor needing aid
Like homely featured Night, of clust'ring gems,
A star or two just twinkling on thy brow
Suffices thee; save that the moon is thine
255 No less than hers, not worn indeed on high
With ostentatious pageantry, but set
With modest grandeur in thy purple zone,°   belt
Resplendent less, but of an ampler round.
Come then, and thou shalt find thy vot'ry° calm   worshipper
260 Or make me so. Composure is thy gift.
And whether I devote thy gentle hours
To books, to music, or the poet's toil,
To weaving nets for bird-alluring fruit;
Or twining silken threads round ivory reels.
265 When they° command whom man was born to please,   women
I slight thee not, but make thee welcome still.
1783–1785   1785

+‑‑≍✦≍‑‑+

Thomas Gray
1716–1771

Toward the end of his most famous poem, *Elegy Written in a Country Churchyard*, Thomas Gray
commends the quietude with which the villagers have led their ordinary lives:

> Along the cool sequestered vale of life
> They kept the noiseless tenor of their way.

Tenor here means "course," and the line incorporates a notable revision: Gray had originally
written "silent tenor," and then written the new adjective "noiseless" above the old, without
crossing out "silent." In retrospect, this manuscript moment of alternate possibilities looks
emblematic. Sickly, shy, and melancholic, Gray was often drawn toward silence but never settled there. Words—in ancient literature and in modern history, in talk and in correspondence
with his friends, in the varied idioms of his own compelling poems—exerted too strong a fascination. The fascination started early. At age nine, having weathered a bleak childhood in the
troubled London household of his irascible father and doting mother, he entered the privileged
precincts of Eton College, where his uncles worked and where he hit upon the satisfactions
that would fill his life: passionate reading (in the classics first and foremost) and passionate
friendships, with three schoolmates in particular: Richard West, Thomas Ashton, and Horace
Walpole, son of the notorious prime minister Robert Walpole. Dubbing themselves the
Quadruple Alliance, the four friends piqued themselves on a collective erudition, refinement,
and wit that set them off from their contemporaries. The links among them mattered enormously in Gray's life of writing: West inspired his poems; Walpole sponsored their publication;
and all Gray's friendships, at Eton and beyond, drew from Gray a steady flow of virtuosic letters, in which the voice of the "Alliance," at once antic and vulnerable, never abated. "His letters," remarked Walpole (whose own letters have evoked similar praise), "were the best I ever
saw, and had more novelty and wit." Gray's affections took form and motion partly from their
containment. He was homosexual; yet there is no evidence that he ever physically consummated the great passions of his life—for Walpole, for West, and, in his last years, for the young
Swiss scion Charles-Victor de Bonstatten.

After nine years at Eton, Gray was admitted to Cambridge. He found university life far less pleasing, with its drudgeries, pressures, and solitudes, but Cambridge ultimately afforded him a few new friendships and a permanent sanctuary. After a Grand Tour of Europe, undertaken in Walpole's company (the two men quarreled en route, after which they were estranged for five years), Gray returned to the university, ostensibly to learn law, but in fact to pursue his own private program of study. He read widely, copiously, and systematically in many subjects (botany, zoology, and music, as well as literature and history), making himself one of the most learned scholars alive, and eventually becoming (in 1768) Regius Professor of Modern History. He never delivered a lecture, and continued to spend much of his time alone reading, but thoroughgoing privacy had long ceased to be an option. In his late thirties, Gray had stumbled, reluctantly, into enormous poetic fame. He had written Latin verse when young; in 1742, the year his beloved West died of tuberculosis, he commenced English poetry in earnest. Some of his labor's early fruits bespeak an insistent sense of loss: a sonnet on West's death (never printed during the poet's lifetime); the *Ode on a Distant Prospect of Eton College*, in which the distance is one of time as well as space; and the *Elegy*, whose completion took five years or more and whose publication in 1751 (a "distress" the poet had hoped to avoid) brought upon Gray an instantaneous, massive, and baffling celebrity. As if in recoil, he veered onto an alternate poetic path, carefully crafting over the ensuing years a set of intricate Pindaric odes, including *The Bard* and *The Progress of Poesy*; the two poems were printed, on Walpole's own press, in 1754. They provoked both admiration, as a new embodiment of poetic sublimity, and derision, as gratuitously labored, showily obscure. In the years following their murky reception, Gray wrote only a few poems, and published none. He pursued other studies (including Norse literature); fell in love one final time; and died abruptly, mourned deeply by his friends and widely by a public whose thoughts and feelings about death itself he had done much to shape. In one early version of the *Elegy* the line about silence appears as an admonition addressed by the poet to himself: "Pursue the silent tenor of thy doom." In his letters (published posthumously) and in his poems, Gray worked for that doom a delicate but decisive reversal.

LETTERS
To Horace Walpole, 16 April 1734[1]

I believe by your not making me happy in a longer letter than that I have just received, you had a design to prevent my tiring you with a tedious one; but in revenge for your neglect I'm resolved to send you one five times as long. Sir, do you think that I'll be fobbed off with eleven lines and a half?[2] After waiting this week in continual expectation, and proposing to myself all the pleasure that you, if you would, might give me; Gadsbud! I am provoked into a fermentation! when I see you next, I'll firk you, I'll rattle you with a *certiorari*.[3] Let me tell you, I am at present as full of wrath and choler as—as—you are of wit and good-nature; though I begin to doubt your title to the last of them, since you have balked me in this manner: what an excuse do you make with your Passion-week and fiddle-faddle, as if you could ever be at a loss what to say; why, I that am in the country could give you a full and true account of half a dozen intrigues, between a boar and a sow, people of very good fashion, that come to an assignation and squeak like ten masquerades; I have a great

---

1. This is Gray's earliest extant letter, written during Eton College's Easter holidays, when Gray and Walpole were both away from school.
2. Gray echoes Shakespeare's tavern-hostess Mrs. Quickly, complaining that Sir John Falstaff constantly postpones the payment of his debts: "I . . . have been fubbed off, and fubbed off, and fubbed off, . . . that it is a shame

to be thought on." (*Henry IV, Part 2*, 2.1).
3. From William Congreve's comedy *The Double Dealer*, where Sir Paul Plyant, "provoked into a fermentation" by fear of his wife's infidelity, vows vengeance on her wooer: "I'll rattle him up, I warrant you, I'll firk him with a *certiorari!*" (punish with a legal writ establishing his claim) (2.4).

mind to make you hear the whole progress of the affair, together with the humors of Miss Pigsnies,[4] the lady's confidante; but you will perhaps think I invent it, and so I shall let it alone. But I wonder you are not ashamed of yourself; in town, and not able to furnish out an epistle as long as a cow's tail! (excuse the rusticity of my simile). In short, I have tried and condemned you in my mind; all that you can allege to save yourself won't do; for I find by your excuses you are brought to your *derniere chemise;*[5] and as you stand guilty, I adjudge you to be drawn to the place of execution, your chamber, where taking pen in hand, you shall write a letter as long as this, to him, who is nothing, when not

Your sincere friend and most devoted humble servant,
T. Gray

To Richard West, December 1736[6]

You must know that I do not take degrees,[7] and, after this term, shall have nothing more of college impertinencies to undergo, which I trust will be some pleasure to you, as it is a great one to me. I have endured lectures daily and hourly since I came last, supported by the hopes of being shortly at full liberty to give myself up to my friends and classical companions,[8] who, poor souls! though I see them fallen into great contempt with most people here, yet I cannot help sticking to them, and out of a spirit of obstinacy (I think) love them the better for it; and indeed what can I do else? Must I plunge into metaphysics? Alas, I cannot see in the dark; nature has not furnished me with the optics of a cat. Must I pore upon mathematics? Alas, I cannot see in too much light; I am no eagle. It is very possible that two and two make four, but I would not give four farthings to demonstrate this ever so clearly; and if these be the profits of life, give me the amusements of it. The people I behold all around me, it seems, know all this and more, and yet I do not know one of them who inspires me with any ambition of being like him. Surely it was of this place, now Cambridge, but formerly known by the name of Babylon, that the prophet spoke when he said, "the wild beasts of the desert shall dwell there, and their houses shall be full of doleful creatures, and owls shall build there, and satyrs shall dance there; their forts and towers shall be a den forever, a joy of wild asses; there shall the great owl make her nest, and lay and hatch and gather under her shadow; it shall be a court of dragons; the screech owl also shall rest there, and find for herself a place of rest."[9] You see here is a pretty collection of desolate animals, which is verified in this town to a tittle, and perhaps it may also allude to your habitation, for you know all types may be taken by abundance of handles;[1] however, I defy your owls to match mine.

If the default of your spirits and nerves be nothing but the effect of the hyp,[2] I have not more to say. We all must submit to that wayward queen; I too in no small degree own her sway,

---

4. I.e., "Miss Darling" (from Middle English *piggesnye*—"pig's eye"—a term of endearment).

5. Gray echoes the title of Colley Cibber's popular comedy *Love's Last Shift* (French: *La Dernière Chemise de l'Amour*), with a pun on "shift": as petticoat (Fr.: *chemise*) and as stratagem or trick.

6. Gray writes from Peterhouse, Cambridge, to West at Christ Church, Oxford.

7. Having decided (for the time being) to enroll in the legal training program at the Inner Temple, London, with a view to becoming a barrister, Gray no longer needed to obtain a Cambridge degree.

8. I.e., the ancient Greek and Roman authors; the

requirements for his degree had obliged him to neglect these in favor of logic, philosophy ("metaphysics"), and mathematics.

9. Gray quotes passages from Isaiah (chapters 13, 33, and 34), prophesying ruin to sinful cities (Babylon among them).

1. "Types" are biblical motifs, re-echoed through history (animals in ancient Babylon are equated to scholars in present Cambridge); in the religious and allusive 18th century, the ways of applying them (of making them into "handles") were indeed many and varied.

2. Short for *hypochondria*, the standard 18th-century term for melancholy, depression.

I feel her influence while I speak her power.

But if it be a real distemper, pray take more care of your health, if not for your own at least for our sakes, and do not be so soon weary of this little world: I do not know what refined friendships you may have contracted in the other, but pray do not be in a hurry to see your acquaintance above; among your terrestrial familiars, however, though I say it that should not say it, there positively is not one that has a greater esteem for you than

Yours most sincerely, etc.

To Horace Walpole, 12 June 1750[3]

Dear Sir,

As I live in a place where even the ordinary tattle of the town arrives not till it is stale, and which produces no events of its own, you will not desire any excuse from me for writing so seldom, especially as of all people living I know you are the least a friend to letters spun out of one's own brains, with all the toil and constraint that accompanies sentimental productions. I have been here at Stoke a few days (where I shall continue good part of the summer); and having put an end to a thing, whose beginning you have seen long ago, I immediately send it you.[4] You will, I hope, look upon it in the light of a *thing with an end to it*; a merit that most of my writings have wanted,[5] and are like to want, but which this epistle I am determined shall not want, when it tells you that I am ever

Yours,

T. Gray

Not that I have done yet; but who could avoid the temptation of finishing so roundly and so cleverly in the manner of good queen Anne's days?[6] Now I have talked of writings, I have seen a book, which is by this time in the press, against Middleton (though without naming him), by Ashton.[7] As far as I can judge from a very hasty reading, there are things in it new and ingenious, but rather too prolix, and the style here and there savoring too strongly of sermon. I imagine it will do him credit. So much for other people, now to *self* again. You are desired to tell me your opinion, if you can take the pains, of these lines.[8] I am once more

Ever Yours.

To Horace Walpole, 11 February 1751[9]

My dear Sir,

As you have brought me into a little sort of distress, you must assist me, I believe, to get out of it, as well as I can. Yesterday I had the misfortune of receiving a letter from certain gentlemen (as their bookseller expresses it) who have taken the *Maga-*

---

3. Gray writes to Walpole (in London) from Stoke Poges, the village where his mother and aunt (once partners in a London millinery shop) had retired following the death of his father; Gray often paid long visits there.
4. The "thing" is Gray's poem, eventually published as *Elegy Written in a Country Churchyard.* Walpole noted later that he had seen "the twelve or more first lines" of the poem about four years before the date of this letter.
5. Lacked. (Gray and his friends were bemused by his disinclination to complete and publish most of his projects.)
6. Queen Anne's reign (1702–1714) was famed for the letter-writing of witty authors, notably Swift and Pope.

7. In the book, a work of theological controversy, Thomas Ashton, Walpole's and Gray's old comrade in the Quadruple Alliance, had attacked Walpole's late friend Conyers Middleton (1683–1750); Walpole chose to break off relations with Ashton and to "forbid him my house."
8. Walpole admired the poem enormously and promoted it enthusiastically, circulating manuscript copies among his London friends.
9. In this and the following letter, Gray writes from Cambridge to Walpole in London.

zine of Magazines into their hands.[1] They tell me, that an *ingenious* poem, called *Reflections* in a Country Churchyard, has been communicated to them, which they are printing forthwith: that they are informed, that the *excellent* author of it is I by name, and that they beg not only his *indulgence,* but the *honor of his correspondence,* etc. As I am not at all disposed to be either so indulgent, or so correspondent, as they desire, I have but one bad way left to escape the honor they would inflict upon me and am therefore obliged to desire you would make Dodsley print it immediately (which may be done in less than a week's time[2]) from your copy, but without my name, in what form is most convenient for him, but in his best paper and character.[3] He must correct the press himself, and print it without any interval between the stanzas,[4] because the sense is in some places continued beyond them; and the title must be, "Elegy, wrote in a Country Church-yard." If he would add a line or two to say it came into his hands by accident, I should like it better.[5] If you think fit, the 102nd line may be read "Awake, and faithful to her wonted fires," but if this be worse than before, it must go as it was. In the 126th, for *ancient* Thorn, read *aged*.[6]

If you behold the *Mag: of Mag:* in the light that I do, you will not refuse to give yourself this trouble on my account, which you have taken of your own accord before now. Adieu, Sir, I am

Yours ever,

TG

If Dodsley don't do this immediately, he may as well let it alone.[7]

from To Horace Walpole, 20 February 1751

My dear Sir,

You have indeed conducted with great decency my little *misfortune:* you have taken a paternal care of it, and expressed much more kindness than could have been expected from so near a relation. But we are all frail; and I hope to do as much for you another time. Nurse Dodsley has given it a pinch or two in the cradle,[8] that (I doubt) it will bear the marks of as long as it lives. But no matter: we have ourselves suffered under her hands before now; and besides, it will only look the more careless, and by *accident* as it were.[9] I thank you for your advertisement, which saves my honor, and in a manner *bien flatteuse pour moi,*[1] who should be put to it[2] even to make myself a compliment in good English. * * *

I am ever yours,

T. Gray

---

1. Both Walpole and Gray despised the monthly magazines (including this comparative newcomer) as cynically exploitative, gathering any text they could use to their advantage, and printing it (sloppily) without compensating the author. In this case, though, as the letter notes, Walpole is partly (and perhaps deliberately) responsible for Gray's "distress": once the poem started circulating in manuscript, it became inevitable that some editor would get hold of it.
2. The thriving publisher Robert Dodsley (1704–1764) worked even faster than expected, producing a pamphlet edition of the *Elegy* four days after the date of this letter.
3. Typeface.
4. Gray later changed his mind about this, separating each quatrain with space before and after.
5. Walpole devised an "Advertisement," published in the first edition: "The following poem came into my hands by

accident, if the general approbation with which this little piece has been spread may be called by so slight a term as accident. It is this approbation which makes it unnecessary for me to make any apology but to the author; as he cannot but feel some satisfaction in having pleased so many readers already, I flatter myself he will forgive my communicating that pleasure to many more."
6. Gray miscounted the poem's lines; the revisions proposed here apply to lines 92 and 116 (Gray later removed the comma after "Awake").
7. Dodsley did it in the nick of time; a day after his edition appeared, the *Magazine of Magazines* published the poem and (unlike Dodsley) named Gray as its author.
8. Misprints.
9. Gray echoes Walpole's "Advertisement" (see note 5).
1. French: very flattering for me.
2. Should find it difficult.

Sonnet on the Death of Mr. Richard West[1]

In vain to me the smiling mornings shine,
And redd'ning Phoebus lifts his golden fire:
The birds in vain their amorous descant join,
Or cheerful fields resume their green attire:
5   These ears, alas! for other notes repine,
A different object do these eyes require.
My lonely anguish melts no heart but mine;
And in my breast the imperfect joys expire.
Yet morning smiles the busy race to cheer,
10   And new-born pleasure brings to happier men;
The fields to all their wonted tribute bear;
To warm their little loves the birds complain.
I fruitless mourn to him that cannot hear,
And weep the more because I weep in vain.

1742   1775

Ode on a Distant Prospect of Eton College[1]

Ye distant spires, ye antique towers,
That crown the wat'ry glade,
Where grateful Science° still adores   knowledge
Her Henry's holy shade;[2]
5   And ye, that from the stately brow
Of Windsor's heights[3] th' expanse below
Of grove, of lawn, of mead survey,
Whose turf, whose shade, whose flowers among
Wanders the hoary Thames along
10   His silver-winding way.

Ah happy hills, ah, pleasing shade,
Ah, fields beloved in vain,
Where once my careless childhood strayed,
A stranger yet to pain!
15   I feel the gales, that from ye blow,
A momentary bliss bestow,
As waving fresh their gladsome wing,
My weary soul they seem to soothe,
And, redolent of joy and youth,
20   To breathe a second spring.

Say, Father Thames, for thou hast seen
Full many a sprightly race
Disporting on thy margent° green   margin
The paths of pleasure trace,
25   Who foremost now delight to cleave

1. West had died of tuberculosis on 1 June 1742, at age 25. Gray composed this sonnet the following August, and in the same month wrote the ode that follows.
1. One of England's oldest and most eminent schools for boys (founded 1440); Gray had attended from 1725

to 1734.
2. The ghost ("shade") of Henry VI (1421–1471), the school's founder.
3. The college is located within the borough of Windsor, on the river Thames.

With pliant arm thy glassy wave?
The captive linnet which enthrall?
What idle progeny succeed
To chase the rolling circle's speed,[4]
30   Or urge the flying ball?

    While some on earnest business bent
Their murm'ring labors ply
'Gainst graver hours, that bring constraint
To sweeten liberty:
35   Some bold adventurers disdain
The limits of their little reign,
And unknown regions dare descry:
Still as they run they look behind,
They hear a voice in every wind,
40   And snatch a fearful joy.

    Gay hope is theirs by fancy fed,
Less pleasing when possessed;
The tear forgot as soon as shed,
The sunshine of the breast:
45   Theirs buxom° health of rosy hue,   *lively*
Wild wit, invention ever-new,
And lively cheer of vigor born;
The thoughtless day, the easy night,
The spirits pure, the slumbers light,
50   That fly th' approach of morn.

    Alas, regardless of their doom,
The little victims play!
No sense have they of ills to come,
Nor care beyond today:
55   Yet see how all around 'em wait
The ministers of human fate,
And black Misfortune's baleful train!°   *attendants*
Ah, shew them where in ambush stand
To seize their prey the murth'rous° band!   *murderous*
60   Ah, tell them, they are men!

    These shall the fury Passions tear,
The vultures of the mind,
Disdainful Anger, pallid Fear,
And Shame that skulks behind;
65   Or pining Love shall waste their youth,
Or Jealousy with rankling tooth,
That inly gnaws the secret heart,
And Envy wan, and faded Care,
Grim-visaged comfortless Despair,
70   And Sorrow's piercing dart.

    Ambition this shall tempt to rise,
Then whirl the wretch from high,

4. A children's game involving a hoop.

To bitter Scorn a sacrifice,
And grinning Infamy.
75   The stings of Falsehood those shall try,
And hard Unkindness' altered eye,
That mocks the tear it forced to flow;
And keen Remorse with blood defiled,
And moody Madness laughing wild
80   Amid severest woe.

Lo, in the vale of years beneath
A grisly troop are seen,
The painful family of Death,
More hideous than their Queen:
85   This racks the joints, this fires the veins,
That every laboring sinew strains,
Those in the deeper vitals rage:
Lo, Poverty, to fill the band,
That numbs the soul with icy hand,
90   And slow-consuming Age.

To each his suff'rings: all are men,
Condemned alike to groan;
The tender for another's pain;
Th' unfeeling for his own.
95   Yet ah! why should they know their fate?
Since sorrow never comes too late,
And happiness too swiftly flies.
Thought would destroy their paradise.
No more; where ignorance is bliss,
100   'Tis folly to be wise.
1742   1747

Ode on the Death of a Favorite Cat, Drowned in a Tub of Gold Fishes[1]

'Twas on a lofty vase's side,
Where China's gayest art had dyed
    The azure flowers, that blow°;   blossom
Demurest of the tabby kind,
5   The pensive Selima reclined,
    Gazed on the lake below.

Her conscious tail her joy declared;
The fair round face, the snowy beard,
    The velvet of her paws,
10   Her coat, that with the tortoise vies,
Her ears of jet, and emerald eyes,
    She saw; and purred applause.

---

1. The cat had belonged to Walpole, who asked Gray to write her an epitaph. Gray sent something more substantial: "There's a poem for you; it is rather too long for an epitaph." Walpole admired the ode so much that he saw to its publication and had the first stanza inscribed on the "tub" itself—actually a china vase, which Walpole enshrined on a pedestal and displayed at his home, Strawberry Hill, where it still stands.

Still had she gazed; but 'midst the tide
Two angel forms were seen to glide,
15   The genii° of the stream: *protective deities*
Their scaly armor's Tyrian hue²
Through richest purple to the view
    Betrayed a golden gleam.

The hapless nymph with wonder saw:
20 A whisker first and then a claw,
    With many an ardent wish,
She stretched in vain to reach the prize.
What female heart can gold despise?
    What cat's averse to fish?

25 Presumptuous maid! with looks intent
Again she stretched, again she bent,
    Nor knew the gulf between.
(Malignant Fate sat by and smiled)
The slippery verge her feet beguiled,
30   She tumbled headlong in.

Eight times emerging from the flood
She mewed to ev'ry wat'ry God,
    Some speedy aid to send.
No dolphin came,³ no Nereid° stirred: *water-nymph*
35 Nor cruel Tom, nor Susan heard.
    A favorite has no friend!

From hence, ye beauties, undeceived,
Know, one false step is ne'er retrieved,
    And be with caution bold.
40 Not all that tempts your wandering eyes
And heedless hearts, is lawful prize;
    Nor all that glisters,° gold.   *glitters*
1747   1748

Elegy Written in a Country Churchyard

The curfew tolls the knell of parting day,
The lowing herd wind slowly o'er the lea,
The plowman homeward plods his weary way,
And leaves the world to darkness and to me.

5 Now fades the glimmering landscape on the sight,
And all the air a solemn stillness holds,
Save where the beetle wheels his droning flight,
And drowsy tinklings lull the distant folds;

Save that from yonder ivy-mantled tower
10 The moping owl does to the moon complain
Of such as, wand'ring near her secret bower,
Molest her ancient solitary reign.

2. A deep purple dye made from mollusks, prized by the ancients as a mark of luxury.

3. As did the dolphin who, in Greek mythology, rescued the drowning poet Arion.

Beneath those rugged elms, that yew-tree's shade,
Where heaves the turf in many a mouldering heap,
15   Each in his narrow cell for ever laid,
The rude forefathers of the hamlet sleep.

The breezy call of incense-breathing morn,
The swallow twitt'ring from the straw-built shed,
The cock's shrill clarion, or the echoing horn,
20   No more shall rouse them from their lowly bed.

For them no more the blazing hearth shall burn,
Or busy housewife ply her evening care:
No children run to lisp their sire's return,
Or climb his knees the envied kiss to share.

25   Oft did the harvest to their sickle yield,
Their furrow oft the stubborn glebe° has broke;   clod of earth
How jocund did they drive their team afield!
How bowed the woods beneath their sturdy stroke!

Let not Ambition mock their useful toil,
30   Their homely joys, and destiny obscure;
Nor Grandeur hear, with a disdainful smile,
The short and simple annals of the poor.

The boast of heraldry, the pomp of power,
And all that beauty, all that wealth e'er gave,
35   Awaits alike th' inevitable hour.
The paths of glory lead but to the grave.

Nor you, ye Proud, impute to these the fault,
If Mem'ry o'er their tomb no trophies raise,
Where through the long-drawn isle and fretted vault
40   The pealing anthem swells the note of praise.

Can storied urn or animated bust
Back to its mansion call the fleeting breath?
Can Honor's voice provoke the silent dust,
Or Flatt'ry soothe the dull cold ear of Death?

45   Perhaps in this neglected spot is laid
Some heart once pregnant with celestial fire;
Hands, that the rod of empire might have swayed,
Or waked to ecstasy the living lyre.

But Knowledge to their eyes her ample page
50   Rich with the spoils of time did ne'er unroll;
Chill Penury repressed their noble rage,
And froze the genial current of the soul.

Full many a gem of purest ray serene,
The dark unfathomed caves of ocean bear:
55   Full many a flower is born to blush unseen,
And waste its sweetness on the desert air.

Some village-Hampden[1] that with dauntless breast
The little tyrant of his fields withstood;
Some mute inglorious Milton here may rest,
60 Some Cromwell guiltless of his country's blood.

Th' applause of listening senates to command,
The threats of pain and ruin to despise,
To scatter plenty o'er a smiling land,
And read their hist'ry in a nation's eyes,

65 Their lot forbade: nor circumscribed alone
Their growing virtues, but their crimes confined;
Forbade to wade through slaughter to a throne,
And shut the gates of mercy on mankind,

The struggling pangs of conscious truth to hide,
70 To quench the blushes of ingenuous shame,
Or heap the shrine of Luxury and Pride
With incense kindled at the Muse's flame.[2]

Far from the madding crowd's ignoble strife,
Their sober wishes never learned to stray;
75 Along the cool sequestered vale of life
They kept the noiseless tenor of their way.

Yet ev'n these bones from insult to protect
Some frail memorial still erected nigh,
With uncouth rhymes and shapeless sculpture decked,
80 Implores the passing tribute of a sigh.

Their name, their years, spelt by th' unlettered muse,
The place of fame and elegy supply:
And many a holy text around she strews,
That teach the rustic moralist to die.

85 For who to dumb Forgetfulness a prey,
This pleasing anxious being e'er resigned,
Left the warm precincts of the cheerful day,
Nor cast one longing ling'ring look behind?

On some fond breast the parting soul relies,
90 Some pious drops the closing eye requires;
Ev'n from the tomb the voice of nature cries,
Ev'n in our ashes live their wonted fires.

---

1. John Hampden (1594–1643), Parliamentary statesman
and general in the Civil Wars, famed for his firm defiance
of Charles I.
2. According to Gray's friend William Mason, the poem
originally concluded at this juncture with the following
four stanzas, preserved in a manuscript at Eton College:

The thoughtless world to majesty may bow
Exalt the brave, and idolize success,
But more to innocence their safety owe
Than power and genius e'er conspired to bless.

And thou, who mindful of the unhonored dead
Dost in these notes their artless tale relate

By night and lonely contemplation led
To linger in the gloomy walks of fate,

Hark how the sacred calm, that broods around
Bids ev'ry fierce tumultuous passion cease
In still small accents whisp'ring from the ground
A grateful earnest of eternal peace.

No more with reason and thyself at strife;
Give anxious cares and endless wishes room
But through the cool sequestered vale of life
Pursue the silent tenor of thy doom.

For thee, who mindful of th' unhonored dead
Dost in these lines their artless tale relate;
95   If chance, by lonely Contemplation led,
Some kindred spirit shall inquire thy fate,

Haply some hoary-headed swain may say,
"Oft have we seen him at the peep of dawn
Brushing with hasty steps the dews away
100   To meet the sun upon the upland lawn.

"There at the foot of yonder nodding beech
That wreathes its old fantastic roots so high,
His listless length at noontide would he stretch,
And pore upon the brook that babbles by.

105   "Hard by yon wood, now smiling as in scorn,
Mutt'ring his wayward fancies he would rove,
Now drooping, woeful wan, like one forlorn,
Or crazed with care, or crossed in hopeless love.

"One morn I missed him on the 'customed hill,
110   Along the heath and near his favorite tree;
Another came; nor yet beside the rill,
Nor up the lawn, nor at the wood was he;

"The next with dirges due in sad array
Slow through the church-way path we saw him borne.
115   Approach and read (for thou can'st read) the lay,
Graved on the stone beneath yon aged thorn."

The Epitaph

Here rests his head upon the lap of earth
A youth to fortune and to fame unknown.
Fair Science frowned not on his humble birth,
120   *And Melancholy marked him for her own.*

Large was his bounty, and his soul sincere,
Heaven did a recompense as largely send:
He gave to Mis'ry all he had, a tear,
He gained from Heav'n ('twas all he wished) a friend.

125   *No farther seek his merits to disclose,*
Or draw his frailties from their dread abode,
(There they alike in trembling hope repose)
The bosom of his Father and his God.

1746–1750   1751

Samuel Johnson
1709–1784

Samuel Johnson was born among books—his father sold them, not very successfully, at the family's combined home and shop in the market town of Lichfield. The son went on to create some of the most celebrated books of his age: an entire *Dictionary*, an edition of Shakespeare, a travel book, philosophical fictions, two eminent series of essays, a thick cluster of biographies. Despite his output, Johnson suffered from a chronic sense that he was underusing his talent, and throughout his *oeuvre* he wrote about "human unsuccess" (in W. H. Auden's phrase) with an empathy and acuity that few have matched before or since.

Johnson's struggles began early. An infection in infancy, followed by an attack of scrofula at age two, left his face scarred and his sight and hearing permanently impaired; by the age of eight a nervous disorder, probably Tourette's syndrome, brought on the compulsive gesticulations and intermittent muttering that would afflict him throughout his life, making him appear bizarre or even repellent at first encounter—until (as many testified) the stunning moment when he would begin to speak. His impressiveness had begun early, too. In childhood, the speed with which he acquired knowledge and the force with which he retained it astonished classmates and teachers, and also his parents, whose desire to show off his attainments often made him miserable. Johnson found more congenial mentors in his cousin, the rakish but learned young clergyman Cornelius Ford, at whose home he spent about half a year at age sixteen, and in Gilbert Walmesley, a middle-aged Lichfield lawyer, who welcomed Johnson often to his ample table and to the intelligent, disputatious company there assembled. Under Ford's and Walmesley's influence, Johnson undertook an intense but improvisatory program of reading, mostly in his father's shop. He read with a ferocious concentration that locked the texts into lifelong memory. "In this irregular manner," he later recalled, "I had looked into a great many books, which were not commonly known at the university, where they seldom read any books but what are put into their hands by their tutors; so that when I came to Oxford, Dr. Adams, now master of Pembroke College, told me, I was the best qualified for the university that he had ever known come there."

Despite such qualifications, Johnson's time at Oxford ushered in not triumph but frustration, and an oppressive sense of failure. Though he continued to be admired for his reading, and began to be noted for his writing, Johnson left the university after only thirteen months, "miserably poor" and unable to pay the fees, unbearably depressed and incapable of envisioning a viable future. After a melancholy year at home, during which his father died in debt, Johnson tried his hand at a variety of jobs beneath his earlier expectations: as assistant at a grammar school (he applied for three such positions, secured one, and left it in disgust after six months), and as occasional contributor to *The Birmingham Journal*. At Birmingham, he befriended the merchant Harry Porter and his wife Elizabeth ("Tetty"); she saw past his awkwardness at their first encounter, remarking to her daughter, "This is the most sensible man that I ever saw in my life." In 1735, ten months after her husband's death, she and Johnson married, despite wariness in both families at their difference in age (she was twenty years his senior). The new husband and wife tried to start a country boarding school, but it attracted only a handful of students. Early in 1737, Johnson decided to try something new: the life of a freelance writer in London.

The generic term for such a life was "Grub Street": it identified both an actual London street where some writers lived and plied their trade, and also the painful state of mind in which almost all of them did so, eking out precarious incomes from whatever assignments they could drum up. From the first, Johnson fared a little better than most. He attached himself immediately to Edward Cave, founder of the flourishing *Gentleman's Magazine*, in which Johnson's writing appeared plentifully over the next decade: essays, poems, short biographies, reviews, and voluminous, ingeniously fictionalized reports of debates in Parliament (authentic transcriptions were prohibited by law). The work provided some security but no prosperity: Johnson and his wife lived in poverty for many years. The struggle fueled articulate rage: in his poem *London* (1738), Johnson inveighed against the corruption of Robert Walpole's Whig government and the cruelties of the city. Among his Grub Street colleagues he found a friend who, far more than himself, had made a sense of injury the basis of both life and art. The poet Richard Savage, generous, brilliant, and unstable, believed himself the abandoned offspring of a wealthy countess, and squandered much of his short life in the vain pursuit of recognition and redress. In *The Life of Richard Savage* (1744), published soon after his friend's early death, Johnson for the first time orchestrated many of the elements that would make his own work great: a commitment to biographical precision rather than routine panegyric; an analysis of expectation, self-delusion, and disappointment; a deep sympathy combined with nuanced judgment.

Savage was a memoir of Grub Street, but not yet for Johnson a valedictory. For two more years he continued his life of anonymous publication, narrow income, and declining spirits— "lost," as a friend lamented, "both to himself and the world." Then a new project found him. In 1746, the bookseller Robert Dodsley, struck by the erudition evident in Johnson's unsigned pieces, persuaded him to create a new dictionary of English, and assembled a consortium of publishers to finance (and profit from) the enormous undertaking. Johnson and his wife promptly moved from cramped and squalid quarters to a three-story house complete with a well-lit garret. There, with the help of six part-time assistants, Johnson made his lexicon, compiling word lists, tracking shifts and gradations of meaning, devising definitions, and illustrating them with quotations culled from the authors he most admired. The writer who (as Adam Smith later testified) "knew more books than any man alive" now decanted them discriminatingly into the two folio volumes of his *Dictionary* (1755), so as to make the work not only a standard reference for the language but also a compendium of its literature and its learning. The task took Johnson longer than he'd anticipated—seven years, not three—but during this span he had busied himself in other ways as well: publishing *The Vanity of Human Wishes* (1749), a long poem on the pain of disillusion; witnessing the long-postponed production of his tragedy *Irene* (which brought him welcome added income); and composing, twice a week for two years, the periodical essay called *The Rambler* (1750–1752), the most formidable and famous instance of the genre since Addison and Steele had set down the *Spectator* forty years before. Johnson had embarked on the *Dictionary* as a virtual unknown; he emerged from the project with lasting fame, and a double measure of celebratory sobriquets: he was widely known as "Dictionary Johnson," and was sometimes referred to simply (without surname) as "the Rambler."

As an epitome of his character the second label was perhaps more apt. A restlessness closely connected with loneliness had marked Johnson's mind since childhood. During the years of the *Dictionary*'s making, the loneliness had deepened. In 1752 Tetty died, and despite the strains in a marriage that had been differently difficult for both of them, Johnson mourned her obsessively for the rest of his days. He also contrived new sources of companionship, at home and in the wider world. He housed under his roof a group of eccentric, often difficult characters, including the ungainly man of medicine Robert Levet; the Jamaican servant Francis Barber; the blind Anna Williams, who waited up late every night to keep him company in his final cup of tea, often after he had spent long hours in more elevated society. He established what amounted to a second residence in the more polished household of the brewer Henry Thrale and his witty wife Hester, who welcomed and pampered not only Johnson but also the accomplished people who now rejoiced to rotate in his orbit: the actor David Garrick (who had been his pupil in the failed school and his companion on the road to London); the painter Joshua Reynolds; the politician and orator Edmund Burke; the writer Oliver Goldsmith; and Johnson's ardent young protégé and future biographer James Boswell. At the Thrales' country seat, and at the London clubs he formed to stave off solitude, Johnson sat surrounded by luminaries, savoring and often dominating the conversation. He talked (as Boswell noted) "for victory," and he generally secured it by a kind of surprise attack, a witty demolition of his companions' most familiar premises and casual assumptions. He won his listeners over by texture as well as text: by the spontaneous clarity and force of his utterance (as lexicographer he had defined every word he spoke); by the depth and energy of his voice.

Writing was by contrast largely solitary. Johnson's work pattern in the decade after the *Dictionary* recapitulated that of the one before: one ambitious, overarching project—this time an edition of all Shakespeare's plays (1665)—punctuated by shorter writings of lasting significance: a new periodical essay called *The Idler* (1758–1760); the philosophical tale *Rasselas, Prince of Abyssinia* (1759). In 1762 Johnson received a royal pension from George III in recognition of the *Dictionary*, assuring him an income of £300 a year for the remainder of his life. The pension brought Johnson a new security, along with the occasional accusation that his subsequent political pamphlets, generally favorable to the regime, amounted to paid propaganda. In fact, Johnson's politics throughout his life correlated fairly well with the views he implicitly espoused in the distinction he once drew for Boswell: "The prejudice of the Tory is for establishment; the prejudice of the Whig is for innovation." Born into a world where Whigs had long prevailed, Johnson early committed himself to Tory ways of thought: he cherished precedent, defended "subordination" (social hierarchy), and opposed Whiggish innovation with seriocomic fervor. What remained most notable about his politics was their compassion. "From first to last," John Wain remarks, Johnson "rooted his life among the poor and outcast"; in his work he argued the causes of prostitutes and slaves, of anyone sunk by the "want of necessaries" into "motionless despondence."

In the wake of his pension, Johnson's writing grew sparser, and markedly more social, compassing gestures to and for people he valued. He continued an ingrained habit of churning out prose for his friends to use under their own names: dictating law briefs for lawyers, composing sermons for preachers. He carried on an abundant and affectionate correspondence with Hester Thrale. With Boswell as companion, he traveled to the Scottish Highlands, and on his return published his account of that gregarious trip, *A Journey to the Western Islands* (1775). His final large work was social in a different sense. He accepted a commission to provide *Prefaces Biographical and Critical* for an anthology of English poets of the past hundred and fifty years. These included predecessors who had influenced him, contemporaries he had known, successors he regarded with admiration or alarm. To write their biographies, to analyze their works, was in a sense to live over his own literary life, and to reenter, at length and for the last time, the world of reading and of writing in which he'd now made his way for almost seven decades.

"Our social comforts drop away," Johnson lamented when his friend Levet died in 1782; his own last years were marred by loss. Successive deaths shrunk his contentious household; his friendship with Hester Thrale disintegrated under the pressure of her passion for a man of whom Johnson disapproved; a stroke temporarily deprived him of speech and ushered in his final difficult illness. At his death, an admirer remarked that Johnson had left "a chasm, which not only nothing can fill up, but which nothing has a tendency to fill up. Johnson is dead. Let us go to the next best:—there is nobody: no man can be said to put you in mind of Johnson." Biographers rushed in to fill the chasm, with the testimony of friends and of detractors, and with transcriptions of the hypnotic talk that many of them (notably Boswell and Thrale) had begun to record decades before. For most of the nineteenth century the fame of Johnson's talk far surpassed that of his writing. In recent decades scholars and readers have redressed the balance, finding in Johnson's prose and verse the richest repositories of his thought. Throughout a life of arduous struggle, prodigious accomplishment, and (in the end) near-matchless celebrity, Johnson wrote most eloquently and most feelingly—even in the *Dictionary*, even in literary criticism—of human vulnerabilities: to hope and disappointment, suffering and loss.

The Vanity of Human Wishes

In his *Life of Pope,* Johnson defines the imitation, a poetic form much in vogue during the late seventeenth and early eighteenth centuries, as a "mode . . . in which the ancients are familiarized by adapting their sentiments to modern topics. . . . It is a kind of middle composition between translation and original design, which pleases when the thoughts are unexpectedly applicable and the parallels lucky." *The Vanity of Human Wishes* is Johnson's most sustained and successful endeavor in the mode. In the second century A.D., the Roman poet Juvenal had written an enduring satire on human ambition and failure, drawing vivid instances from history and from contemporary life. Johnson does the same, replacing the Roman's ancient examples with modern ones, supplanting his Stoic "sentiments" with a Christian credo. Johnson produced his imitation quickly, composing the whole of it in his mind before writing any of it down. It was the first work to appear under his own name, after more than a decade of abundant but anonymous publications. Its title and text sound themes that would preoccupy him for the remainder of his writing life: the dangers of desire, the inevitability of disappointment, the necessity of faith. *The Vanity of Human Wishes* is Johnson's signature poem in more ways than one.

The Vanity of Human Wishes
The Tenth Satire of Juvenal Imitated

Let Observation, with extensive view,
Survey mankind, from China to Peru;
Remark each anxious toil, each eager strife,
And watch the busy scenes of crowded life;
5   Then say how hope and fear, desire and hate,
O'erspread with snares the clouded maze of fate,
Where wav'ring man, betrayed by vent'rous pride,
To tread the dreary paths without a guide,
As treach'rous phantoms in the mist delude,
10   Shuns fancied ills, or chases airy[1] good;
How rarely reason guides the stubborn choice,
Rules the bold hand, or prompts the suppliant voice;
How nations sink, by darling schemes oppressed,
When vengeance listens to the fool's request.
15   Fate wings with every wish th' afflictive dart,
Each gift of nature, and each grace of art,
With fatal heat impetuous courage glows,
With fatal sweetness elocution flows,
Impeachment stops the speaker's pow'rful breath,
20   And restless fire precipitates on death.
     But scarce observed, the knowing and the bold
Fall in the gen'ral massacre of gold;
Wide-wasting pest! that rages unconfined,
And crowds with crimes the records of mankind;
25   For gold his sword the hireling ruffian draws,
For gold the hireling judge distorts the laws;
Wealth heaped on wealth, nor truth nor safety buys,
The dangers gather as the treasures rise.

---

1. "Wanting reality; having no steady foundation in truth or nature" (Johnson's *Dictionary*).

Let hist'ry tell where rival kings command,
30   And dubious title shakes the madded land,
When statutes° glean the refuse of the sword,   *tax laws*
How much more safe the vassal than the lord;
Low skulks the hind° beneath the rage of pow'r,   *rural laborer*
And leaves the wealthy traitor in the Tow'r,[2]
35   Untouched his cottage, and his slumbers sound,
Though confiscation's vultures hover round.
The needy traveler, secure and gay,
Walks the wild heath, and sings his toil away.
Does envy seize thee? crush th' upbraiding joy,
40   Increase his riches and his peace destroy;
Now fears in dire vicissitude invade,
The rustling brake° alarms, and quiv'ring shade,   *thicket*
Nor light nor darkness bring his pain relief,
One shows the plunder, and one hides the thief.
45   Yet still one gen'ral cry the skies assails,
And gain and grandeur load the tainted gales;
Few know the toiling statesman's fear or care,
Th' insidious rival and the gaping heir.
Once more, Democritus,[3] arise on earth,
50   With cheerful wisdom and instructive mirth,
See motley[4] life in modern trappings dressed,
And feed with varied fools th' eternal jest:
Thou who couldst laugh where want enchained caprice,
Toil crushed conceit, and man was of a piece;
55   Where wealth unloved without a mourner died,
And scarce a sycophant was fed by pride;
Where ne'er was known the form of mock debate,
Or seen a new-made mayor's unwieldy state;
Where change of fav'rites made no change of laws,
60   And senates heard before they judged a cause;
How wouldst thou shake at Britain's modish tribe,
Dart the quick taunt, and edge the piercing gibe?
Attentive truth and nature to descry,°   *discern*
And pierce each scene with philosophic eye.
65   To thee were solemn toys or empty show,
The robes of pleasure and the veils of woe:
All aid the farce, and all thy mirth maintain,
Whose joys are causeless, or whose griefs are vain.
Such was the scorn that filled the sage's mind,
70   Renewed at ev'ry glance on humankind;
How just that scorn ere yet thy voice declare,
Search every state, and canvass every prayer.
Unnumbered suppliants crowd Preferment's gate,
Athirst for wealth, and burning to be great;
75   Delusive Fortune hears th' incessant call,
They mount, they shine, evaporate, and fall.[5]

---

2. The Tower of London.
3. Ancient Greek philosopher who laughed at the follies
of humanity.

4. Multicolored clothes worn by jesters.
5. The image is that of Fortune's wheel.

On every stage the foes of peace attend,
Hate dogs their flight, and insult mocks their end.
Love ends with hope, the sinking statesman's door
80 Pours in the morning worshiper no more;
For growing names the weekly scribbler lies,
To growing wealth the dedicator flies,
From ev'ry room descends the painted face,
That hung the bright Palladium[6] of the place,
85 And smoked in kitchens, or in auctions sold,
To better features yields the frame of gold;
For now no more we trace in ev'ry line
Heroic worth, benevolence divine:
The form distorted justifies the fall,
90 And detestation rids th' indignant wall.
     But will not Britain hear the last appeal,
Sign her foes' doom, or guard her fav'rites' zeal?
Through Freedom's sons no more remonstrance rings,
Degrading nobles and controlling kings;
95 Our supple tribes° repress their patriot throats,   *of voters*
And ask no questions but the price of votes;
With weekly libels and septennial ale,[7]
Their wish is full to riot and to rail.
     In full-blown dignity, see Wolsey[8] stand,
100 Law in his voice, and fortune in his hand:
To him the church, the realm, their pow'rs consign,
Through him the rays of regal bounty shine,
Turned by his nod the stream of honor flows,
His smile alone security bestows:
105 Still to new heights his restless wishes tow'r,
Claim leads to claim, and pow'r advances pow'r;
Till conquest unresisted ceased to please,
And rights submitted, left him none to seize.
At length his sov'reign frowns—the train of state
110 Mark the keen glance, and watch the sign to hate.
Wheree'er he turns he meets a stranger's eye,
His suppliants scorn him, and his followers fly;
At once is lost the pride of awful state,
The golden canopy, the glitt'ring plate,
115 The regal palace, the luxurious board,
The liv'ried army, and the menial lord.
With age, with cares, with maladies oppressed,
He seeks the refuge of monastic rest.
Grief aids disease, remembered folly stings,
120 And his last sighs reproach the faith of kings.
     Speak thou, whose thoughts at humble peace repine,
Shall Wolsey's wealth, with Wolsey's end be thine?
Or liv'st thou now, with safer pride content,

---

6. A statue of Pallas Athene, guardian of Troy.
7. Drink offered to voters as bribes during campaigns for Parliament, held every seven years.

8. Cardinal Wolsey (1475–1530), Henry VIII's Lord Chancellor, who was dismissed and imprisoned for failing to procure the King a divorce from Catherine of Aragon.

The wisest justice on the banks of Trent?[9]
125   For why did Wolsey near the steeps° of fate,   *precipices*
      On weak foundations raise th' enormous weight?
      Why but to sink beneath misfortune's blow,
      With louder ruin to the gulfs below?
          What gave great Villiers[1] to th' assassin's knife,
130   And fixed disease on Harley's[2] closing life?
      What murdered Wentworth, and what exiled Hyde,[3]
      By kings protected, and to kings allied?
      What but their wish indulged in courts to shine,
      And pow'r too great to keep, or to resign?
135   When first the college rolls receive his name,
      The young enthusiast[4] quits his ease for fame;
      Through all his veins the fever of renown
      Burns from the strong contagion of the gown;[5]
      O'er Bodley's dome[6] his future labors spread,
140   And Bacon's mansion[7] trembles o'er his head.
      Are these thy views? proceed, illustrious youth,
      And virtue guard thee to the throne of Truth!
      Yet should thy soul indulge the gen'rous heat,
      Till captive Science° yields her last retreat;   *knowledge*
145   Should Reason guide thee with her brightest ray,
      And pour on misty Doubt resistless day;
      Should no false Kindness lure to loose delight,
      Nor Praise relax, nor Difficulty fright;
      Should tempting Novelty thy cell refrain,
150   And Sloth effuse her opiate fumes in vain;
      Should Beauty blunt on fops her fatal dart,
      Nor claim the triumph of a lettered heart;
      Should no disease thy torpid veins invade,
      Nor Melancholy's phantoms haunt thy shade;
155   Yet hope not life from grief or danger free,
      Nor think the doom of man reversed for thee:
      Deign on the passing world to turn thine eyes,
      And pause awhile from letters, to be wise;
      There mark what ills the scholar's life assail,
160   Toil, envy, want, the patron,[8] and the jail.
      See nations slowly wise, and meanly just,
      To buried merit raise the tardy bust.
      If dreams yet flatter, once again attend,

9. The river that divides northern from southern England; it is near Lichfield, Johnson's birthplace.
1. George Villiers (1592–1628), first Duke of Buckingham and a favorite of James I, was stabbed to death.
2. Robert Harley (1661–1724), first Earl of Oxford and leading statesman during the reign of Queen Anne, was impeached when George I succeeded to the throne in 1714.
3. Thomas Wentworth (1593–1641), first Earl of Strafford and adviser to Charles I, was executed at the beginning of the English Civil War. Edward Hyde (1609–1674), first Earl of Clarendon, served Charles II but then

fell from favor.
4. "One of hot imagination" (Johnson's *Dictionary*).
5. Scholastic dress (but also a reference to the poisoned garment that killed Hercules).
6. The Bodleian Library, Oxford.
7. "There is a tradition, that the study of friar Bacon [Roger Bacon, a medieval philosopher] built an arch over the bridge, will fall, when a man greater than Bacon shall pass under it" [Johnson's note].
8. Johnson originally wrote "garret," but changed it to "patron" after enduring the neglect of Lord Chesterfield (see his letter to Chesterfield, page 2792).

Hear Lydiat's life, and Galileo's end.[9]
165 Nor deem, when learning her last prize bestows,
The glitt'ring eminence exempt from foes;
See when the vulgar 'scape, despised or awed,
Rebellion's vengeful talons seize on Laud.[1]
From meaner minds, though smaller fines content,
170 The plundered palace or sequestered rent;
Marked out by dangerous parts° he meets the shock,   *abilities*
And fatal Learning leads him to the block:
Around his tomb let Art and Genius weep,
But hear his death, ye blockheads, hear and sleep.
175 The festal blazes, the triumphal show,
The ravished standard, and the captive foe,
The senate's thanks, the gazette's pompous tale,
With force resistless o'er the brave prevail.
Such bribes the rapid Greek[2] o'er Asia whirled,
180 For such the steady Romans shook the world;
For such in distant lands the Britons shine,
And stain with blood the Danube or the Rhine;
This pow'r has praise, that virtue scarce can warm,
Till fame supplies the universal charm.
185 Yet Reason frowns on War's unequal game,
Where wasted nations raise a single name,
And mortgaged states their grandsires' wreaths[3] regret,
From age to age in everlasting debt;
Wreaths which at last the dear-bought right convey
190 To rust on medals, or on stones decay.
On what foundation stands the warrior's pride,
How just his hopes let Swedish Charles[4] decide;
A frame of adamant, a soul of fire,
No dangers fright him, and no labors tire;
195 O'er love, o'er fear, extends his wide domain,
Unconquered lord of pleasure and of pain;
No joys to him pacific scepters yield,
War sounds the trump, he rushes to the field;
Behold surrounding kings their pow'r combine,
200 And one capitulate, and one resign;
Peace courts his hand, but spreads her charms in vain;
"Think nothing gained," he cries, "till nought remain,
On Moscow's walls till Gothic standards fly,
And all be mine beneath the polar sky."
205 The march begins in military state,
And nations on his eye suspended wait;
Stern Famine guards the solitary coast,
And Winter barricades the realms of Frost;

9. Thomas Lydiat (1572–1646) was a distinguished but impoverished mathematician. The astronomer Galileo Galilei (1564–1642) was silenced by the Inquisition.
1. William Laud (1572–1645), Archbishop of Canterbury under Charles I, was beheaded by the Parliamentarians.
2. Alexander the Great.

3. Garlands of victory.
4. Charles XII of Sweden, whose precarious military career ended at the Battle of Pultowa (1709). After his defeat by the Russians, Charles attempted to forge an alliance with the Turks.

He comes, not want and cold his course delay—
210   Hide, blushing Glory, hide Pultowa's day:
The vanquished hero leaves his broken bands,
And shows his miseries in distant lands;
Condemned a needy supplicant to wait,
While ladies interpose, and slaves debate.
215   But did not Chance at length her error mend?
Did no subverted empire mark his end?
Did rival monarchs give the fatal wound?
Or hostile millions press him to the ground?
His fall was destined to a barren strand,
220   A petty fortress, and a dubious hand;[5]
He left the name, at which the world grew pale,
To point a moral, or adorn a tale.
       All times their scenes of pompous woes afford,
From Persia's tyrant[6] to Bavaria's lord.[7]
225   In gay hostility, and barb'rous pride,
With half mankind embattled at his side,
Great Xerxes comes to seize the certain prey,
And starves exhausted regions in his way;
Attendant Flattery counts his myriads o'er,
230   Till counted myriads soothe his pride no more;
Fresh praise is tried till madness fires his mind,
The waves he lashes, and enchains the wind;
New pow'rs are claimed, new pow'rs are still bestowed,
Till rude resistance lops the spreading god;
235   The daring Greeks deride the martial show,
And heap their valleys with the gaudy foe;
Th' insulted sea with humbler thoughts he gains,
A single skiff to speed his flight remains;
Th' encumbered oar scarce leaves the dreaded coast
240   Through purple billows and a floating host.
       The bold Bavarian, in a luckless hour,
Tries the dread summits of Cesarean power,
With unexpected legions bursts away,
And sees defenseless realms receive his sway;
245   Short sway! fair Austria spreads her mournful charms,
The queen, the beauty, sets the world in arms;
From hill to hill the beacon's rousing blaze
Spreads wide the hope of plunder and of praise;
The fierce Croatian, and the wild Hussar,
250   And all the sons of ravage crowd the war;
The baffled prince in honor's flattering bloom
Of hasty greatness finds the fatal doom,

5. Charles XII of Sweden was thought to have been killed by one of his own officers during a siege of little military consequence.
6. Xerxes (?519–465 B.C.) invaded Greece with a large army and navy. In order to transport his troops, he built a bridge of boats across the Hellespont. When a storm broke up this bridge, Xerxes ordered the wind and water to be punished. The Persian army was defeated at the Battle of Plataea, the navy at the Battle of Salamis.
7. Charles Albert (1697–1745), Elector of Bavaria, was defeated by Empress Maria Theresa, whose army included Austrian colonists from Croatia and Hungarian cavalry called "jussars."

His foes' derision, and his subjects' blame,
And steals to death from anguish and from shame.
255   Enlarge my life with multitude of days,
In health, in sickness, thus the suppliant prays;
Hides from himself his state, and shuns to know,
That life protracted is protracted woe.
Time hovers o'er, impatient to destroy,
260   And shuts up all the passages of joy:
In vain their gifts the bounteous seasons pour,
The fruit autumnal, and the vernal flow'r,
With listless eyes the dotard views the store,
He views, and wonders that they please no more;
265   Now pall the tasteless meats, and joyless wines,
And Luxury° with sighs her slave resigns.   *voluptuousness*
Approach, ye minstrels, try the soothing strain,
Diffuse the tuneful lenitives[8] of pain:
No sounds alas would touch th' impervious ear,
270   Though dancing mountains witnessed Orpheus[9] near;
Nor lute nor lyre his feeble pow'rs attend,
Nor sweeter music of a virtuous friend,
But everlasting dictates crowd his tongue,
Perversely grave, or positively wrong.
275   The still returning tale, and ling'ring jest,
Perplex the fawning niece and pampered guest,
While growing hopes scarce awe the gathering sneer,
And scarce a legacy can bribe to hear;
The watchful guests still hint the last° offense,   *latest*
280   The daughter's petulance, the son's expense,
Improve his heady rage with treach'rous skill,
And mold his passions till they make his will.
      Unnumbered maladies his joints invade,
Lay siege to life and press the dire blockade;
285   But unextinguished Avarice still remains,
And dreaded losses aggravate his pains;
He turns, with anxious heart and crippled hands,
His bonds of debt, and mortgages of lands;
Or views his coffers with suspicious eyes,
290   Unlocks his gold, and counts it till he dies.
      But grant, the virtues of a temp'rate prime
Bless with an age exempt from scorn or crime;
An age that melts with unperceived decay,
And glides in modest innocence away;
295   Whose peaceful day Benevolence endears,
Whose night congratulating Conscience cheers;
The gen'ral favorite as the gen'ral friend:
Such age there is, and who shall wish its end?
      Yet ev'n on this her load Misfortune flings,
300   To press the weary minutes' flagging wings:

8. "Anything medicinally applied to ease pain" (Johnson's *Dictionary*).

9. In Greek mythology, the musician Orpheus charmed wild beasts and moved mountains.

New sorrow rises as the day returns,
A sister sickens, or a daughter mourns.
Now kindred Merit fills the sable bier,
Now lacerated Friendship claims a tear.
305 Year chases year, decay pursues decay,
Still drops some joy from with'ring life away;
New forms arise, and different views engage,
Superfluous lags the vet'ran on the stage,
Till pitying Nature signs the last release,
310 And bids afflicted worth retire to peace.
     But few there are whom hours like these await,
Who set unclouded in the gulfs of fate.
From Lydia's monarch should the search descend,
By Solon cautioned to regard his end,[1]
315 In life's last scene what prodigies surprise,
Fears of the brave, and follies of the wise?
From Marlborough's eyes the streams of dotage flow,[2]
And Swift expires a driveler and a show.[3]
     The teeming mother, anxious for her race,
320 Begs for each birth the fortune of a face:
Yet Vane could tell what ills from beauty spring;
And Sedley cursed the form that pleased a king.[4]
Ye nymphs of rosy lips and radiant eyes,
Whom Pleasure keeps too busy to be wise,
325 Whom Joys with soft varieties invite,
By day the frolic, and the dance by night,
Who frown with vanity, who smile with art,
And ask the latest fashion of the heart,
What care, what rules your heedless charms shall save,
330 Each nymph your rival, and each youth your slave?
Against your fame with fondness hate combines,
The rival batters, and the lover mines.
With distant voice neglected Virtue calls,
Less heard and less, the faint remonstrance falls;
335 Tired with contempt, she quits the slipp'ry reign,
And Pride and Prudence take her seat in vain.
In crowd at once, where none the pass defend,
The harmless Freedom, and the private Friend.
The guardians yield, by force superior plied;
340 By Interest, Prudence; and by Flattery, Pride.
Now beauty falls betrayed, despised, distressed,
And hissing Infamy proclaims the rest.
     Where then shall Hope and Fear their objects find?
Must dull Suspense corrupt the stagnant mind?
345 Must helpless man, in ignorance sedate,°   calm

---

1. Solon, Greek philosopher and legislator, warned the wealthy King Croesus of Lydia that no one should count himself happy until reaching the end of life.
2. John Churchill (1650–1722), first Duke of Marlborough, hero of the War of the Spanish Succession, lived for six years after suffering two paralytic strokes.

3. Jonathan Swift, who declined into senility, was thought to have been exhibited by his servant for money.
4. Anne Vane (1705–1736) was the mistress of the Prince of Wales, Catherine Sedley (1657–1717) of James II.

Roll darkling° down the torrent of his fate?   *in the dark*
Must no dislike alarm, no wishes rise,
No cries attempt the mercies of the skies?
Inquirer, cease, petitions yet remain,
350   Which Heav'n may hear, nor deem religion vain.
Still raise for good the supplicating voice,
But leave to Heav'n the measure and the choice,
Safe in his power, whose eyes discern afar
The secret ambush of a specious prayer.
355   Implore his aid, in his decisions rest,
Secure whate'er he gives, he gives the best.
Yet when the sense of sacred presence fires,
And strong devotion to the skies aspires,
Pour forth thy fervors for a healthful mind,
360   Obedient passions, and a will resigned;
For love, which scarce collective man can fill;
For patience sov'reign o'er transmuted ill;
For faith, that panting for a happier seat,
Counts death kind Nature's signal of retreat:
365   These goods for man the laws of Heav'n ordain,
These goods he grants, who grants the power to gain;
With these celestial wisdom calms the mind,
And makes the happiness she does not find.

1748   1749

A Short Song of Congratulation[1]

Long expected one and twenty
    Ling'ring year at last is flown,
Pomp and pleasure, pride and plenty,
    Great Sir John, are all your own.

5   Loosened from the minor's tether,
    Free to mortgage or to sell,
Wild as wind, and light as feather
    Bid the slaves of thrift farewell.[2]

Call the Bettys, Kates, and Jennys
10   Ev'ry name that laughs at care,
Lavish of your grandsire's guineas,
    Show the spirit of an heir.

All that prey on vice and folly
    Joy to see their quarry fly,
15   Here the gamester light and jolly
    There the lender grave and sly.

Wealth, Sir John, was made to wander,
    Let it wander as it will;

---

1. Written for Sir John Lade (1759–1838), the nephew of
Johnson's close friend Henry Thrale.
2. Sir John fulfilled Johnson's predictions: he made a
scandalous marriage and then squandered his inheritance.

See the jockey, see the pander,
20   Bid them come, and take their fill.

When the bonny blade carouses,
    Pockets full, and spirits high,
What are acres? What are houses?
    Only dirt, or wet or dry.

25 If the guardian or the mother
    Tell the woes of willful waste,
Scorn their counsel and their pother,
    You can hang or drown at last.

1780   1794

On the Death of Dr. Robert Levet[1]

Condemned to Hope's delusive mine,
    As on we toil from day to day,
By sudden blasts, or slow decline,
    Our social comforts drop away.

5   Well tried through many a varying year,
    See Levet to the grave descend;
Officious,[2] innocent, sincere,
    Of ev'ry friendless name the friend.

Yet still he fills Affection's eye,
10   Obscurely° wise, and coarsely kind;   *privately*
Nor, lettered Arrogance, deny
    Thy praise to merit unrefined.

When fainting Nature called for aid,
    And hov'ring Death prepared the blow,
15 His vig'rous remedy displayed
    The power of art without the show.

In Misery's darkest caverns known,
    His useful care was ever nigh,
Where hopeless Anguish poured his groan,
20   And lonely Want retired to die.

No summons mocked by chill delay,
    No petty gain disdained by pride,
The modest wants of ev'ry day
    The toil of ev'ry day supplied.

25 His virtues walked their narrow round,
    Nor made a pause, nor left a void;
And sure th' Eternal Master found
    The single talent well employed.[3]

1. Robert Levet (1705–1782), a friend and dependent of Johnson, had acquired a modicum of medical training while working as a waiter in Paris; he put this training to use by caring for the poorest of the London poor ("Dr." was an honorific title). Many of Johnson's friends wondered why he admired and supported a man whom Boswell described as "an obscure practiser in physick amongst the lower people." Johnson's elegy answers that question.
2. "Kind; doing good offices" (Johnson's *Dictionary*).
3. A reference to Jesus' Parable of the Talents (Matthew 25.14–30), which haunted Johnson throughout his adult life.

The busy day, the peaceful night,
30   Unfelt, uncounted, glided by;
His frame was firm, his pow'rs were bright,
    Though now his eightieth year was nigh.

Then with no throbbing fiery pain,
    No cold gradations of decay,
35 Death broke at once the vital chain,
    And freed his soul the nearest way.

1782   1783

The Rambler

In the midst of working on his *Dictionary*, Johnson took on an ambitious additional task: he wrote *The Rambler*, a twice-weekly periodical essay which he sustained for two full years (1750–1752). The project brought him needed income and also a useful respite from the strains of lexicography. *The Rambler*'s most famous antecedent was Addison and Steele's the *Spectator* (1711–1713), and though Johnson would later praise Addison's prose as a "model of the middle style . . . always equable and always easy," he chose for his own essays a mode more astringent: a large, often Latinate vocabulary, intricately balanced sentences, a steady alertness to the human propensity for self-delusion, a willingness to confront rather than ingratiate. Pressures of production could run high (Johnson later claimed that he sometimes wrote his essay with the printer's messenger standing at his side, waiting to take the text to the press), and speed of output may have helped shape the results. Many *Ramblers*, with their formidably wrought prose and surprising turns of thought, manage to seem imposing and improvisatory at the same time. Free to choose his topics, working under relentlessly recurrent deadlines, Johnson drew on four decades dense with reading and thought, during which (in the words of his biographer John Hawkins) he had "accumulated a fund of moral science that was more than sufficient for such an undertaking," and had become "in a very eminent degree qualified for the office of an instructor of mankind in their greatest and most important concerns." Readers proved eager for the instruction. More than any of his earlier writings, *The Rambler* established Johnson's style, his substance, and his fame.

Rambler No. 4
[ON FICTION]

Saturday, 31 March 1750

Simul et jucunda et idonea dicere vitae.

Horace, *Ars Poetica* 1.334

And join both profit and delight in one.

Creech

The works of fiction with which the present generation seems more particularly delighted are such as exhibit life in its true state, diversified only by accidents that daily happen in the world, and influenced by passions and qualities which are really to be found in conversing with mankind.

This kind of writing may be termed not improperly the comedy of romance, and is to be conducted nearly by the rules of comic poetry. Its province is to bring about natural events by easy means, and to keep up curiosity without the help of wonder: it is therefore precluded from the machines[1] and expedients of the heroic romance, and can neither employ giants to snatch away a lady from the nuptial rites, nor knights to bring her back from captivity; it can neither bewilder its personages in deserts, nor lodge them in imaginary castles.

I remember a remark made by Scaliger upon Pontanus,[2] that all his writings are filled with the same images; and that if you take from him his lillies and his roses, his satyrs and his dryads, he will have nothing left that can be called poetry. In like manner, almost all the fictions of the last age will vanish, if you deprive them of a hermit and a wood, a battle and a shipwreck.

Why this wild strain of imagination found reception so long, in polite and learned ages, it is not easy to conceive; but we cannot wonder that, while readers could be procured, the authors were willing to continue it: for when a man had by practice gained some fluency of language, he had no further care than to retire to his closet,[3] let loose his invention, and heat his mind with incredibilities; a book was thus produced without fear of criticism, without the toil of study, without knowledge of nature, or acquaintance with life.

The task of our present writers is very different; it requires, together with that learning which is to be gained from books, that experience which can never be attained by solitary diligence, but must arise from general converse, and accurate observation of the living world. Their performances have, as Horace expresses it, *plus oneris quantum veniae minus*, little indulgence, and therefore more difficulty.[4] They are engaged in portraits of which every one knows the original, and can detect any deviation from exactness of resemblance. Other writings are safe, except from the malice of learning, but these are in danger from every common reader; as the slipper ill executed was censured by a shoemaker who happened to stop in his way at the Venus of Apelles.[5]

But the fear of not being approved as just copiers of human manners, is not the most important concern that an author of this sort ought to have before him. These books are written chiefly to the young, the ignorant, and the idle, to whom they serve as lectures of conduct, and introductions into life. They are the entertainment of minds unfurnished with ideas, and therefore easily susceptible of impressions; not fixed by principles, and therefore easily following the current of fancy; not informed by experience, and consequently open to every false suggestion and partial account.

That the highest degree of reverence should be paid to youth, and that nothing indecent should be suffered to approach their eyes or ears, are precepts extorted by sense and virtue from an ancient writer, by no means eminent for chastity of thought.[6] The same kind, though not the same degree of caution, is required in every thing which is laid before them, to secure them from unjust prejudices, perverse opinions, and incongruous combinations of images.

In the romances formerly written, every transaction and sentiment was so remote from all that passes among men, that the reader was in very little danger of making any applications to himself; the virtues and crimes were equally beyond his sphere of

1. "Supernatural agency in poems" (Johnson's *Dictionary*).
2. The Renaissance humanist Julius Caesar Scaliger (1484–1558) criticized the poetry of Giovanni Pontano (1426–1503).
3. Study.

4. Horace, *Epistles* 2.1.170.
5. In his *Natural History*, Pliny the Elder tells this story of the famous painter Apelles.
6. Johnson refers to the opening lines of Juvenal's fourteenth satire.

activity; and he amused himself with heroes and with traitors, deliverers and persecutors, as with beings of another species, whose actions were regulated upon motives of their own, and who had neither faults nor excellencies in common with himself.

But when an adventurer is leveled with the rest of the world, and acts in such scenes of the universal drama, as may be the lot of any other man, young spectators fix their eyes upon him with closer attention, and hope by observing his behavior and success to regulate their own practices, when they shall be engaged in the like part.

For this reason these familiar histories may perhaps be made of greater use than the solemnities of professed morality, and convey the knowledge of vice and virtue with more efficacy than axioms and definitions. But if the power of example is so great, as to take possession of the memory by a kind of violence, and produce effects almost without the intervention of the will, care ought to be taken that, when the choice is unrestrained, the best examples only should be exhibited; and that which is likely to operate so strongly, should not be mischievous or uncertain in its effects.

The chief advantage which these fictions have over real life is, that their authors are at liberty, though not to invent, yet to select objects, and to cull from the mass of mankind those individuals upon which the attention ought most to be employed; as a diamond, though it cannot be made, may be polished by art, and placed in such a situation as to display that lustre which before was buried among common stones.

It is justly considered as the greatest excellency of art, to imitate nature; but it is necessary to distinguish those parts of nature, which are most proper for imitation: greater care is still required in representing life, which is so often discolored by passion, or deformed by wickedness. If the world be promiscuously[7] described, I cannot see of what use it can be to read the account; or why it may not be as safe to turn the eye immediately upon mankind, as upon a mirror which shows all that presents itself without discrimination.

It is therefore not a sufficient vindication of a character, that it is drawn as it appears, for many characters ought never to be drawn; nor of a narrative, that the train of events is agreeable to observation and experience, for that observation which is called knowledge of the world will be found much more frequently to make men cunning than good. The purpose of these writings is surely not only to show mankind, but to provide that they may be seen hereafter with less hazard; to teach the means of avoiding the snares which are laid by Treachery for Innocence, without infusing any wish for that superiority with which the betrayer flatters his vanity; to give the power of counteracting fraud, without the temptation to practice it; to initiate youth by mock encounters in the art of necessary defense, and to increase prudence without impairing virtue.

Many writers, for the sake of following nature, so mingle good and bad qualities in their principal personages, that they are both equally conspicuous; and as we accompany them through their adventures with delight, and are led by degrees to interest ourselves in their favor, we lose the abhorrence of their faults, because they do not hinder our pleasure, or, perhaps, regard them with some kindness for being united with so much merit.

There have been men indeed splendidly wicked, whose endowments threw a brightness on their crimes, and whom scarce any villainy made perfectly detestable, because they never could be wholly divested of their excellencies; but such have been in all ages the great corrupters of the world, and their resemblance ought no more to be preserved, than the art of murdering without pain.

---

7. Indiscriminately.

Some have advanced, without due attention to the consequences of this notion, that certain virtues have their correspondent faults, and therefore that to exhibit either apart is to deviate from probability. Thus men are observed by Swift to be "grateful in the same degree as they are resentful."[8] This principle, with others of the same kind, supposes man to act from a brute impulse, and pursue a certain degree of inclination, without any choice of the object; for otherwise, though it should be allowed that gratitude and resentment arise from the same constitution of the passions, it follows not that they will be equally indulged when reason is consulted; yet unless that consequence be admitted, this sagacious maxim becomes an empty sound, without any relation to practice or to life.

Nor is it evident, that even the first motions to these effects are always in the same proportion. For pride, which produces quickness of resentment, will obstruct gratitude, by unwillingness to admit that inferiority which obligation implies; and it is very unlikely that he who cannot think he receives a favor will acknowledge or repay it.

It is of the utmost importance to mankind that positions of this tendency should be laid open and confuted; for while men consider good and evil as springing from the same root, they will spare the one for the sake of the other, and in judging, if not of others at least of themselves, will be apt to estimate their virtues by their vices. To this fatal error all those will contribute, who confound the colors of right and wrong, and instead of helping to settle their boundaries, mix them with so much art, that no common mind is able to disunite them.

In narratives where historical veracity has no place, I cannot discover why there should not be exhibited the most perfect idea of virtue; of virtue not angelical, nor above probability, for what we cannot credit we shall never imitate, but the highest and purest that humanity can reach, which, exercised in such trials as the various revolutions of things shall bring upon it, may, by conquering some calamities, and enduring others, teach us what we may hope, and what we can perform. Vice, for vice is necessary to be shown, should always disgust; nor should the graces of gaiety, or the dignity of courage, be so united with it, as to reconcile it to the mind. Wherever it appears, it should raise hatred by the malignity of its practices, and contempt by the meanness of its stratagems; for while it is supported by either parts[9] or spirit, it will be seldom heartily abhorred. The Roman tyrant was content to be hated, if he was but feared;[1] and there are thousands of the readers of romances willing to be thought wicked, if they may be allowed to be wits. It is therefore to be steadily inculcated, that virtue is the highest proof of understanding, and the only solid basis of greatness; and that vice is the natural consequence of narrow thoughts, that it begins in mistake, and ends in ignominy.

Rambler No. 5

[ON SPRING]

Tuesday, 3 April 1750

Et nunc omnis ager, nunc omnis parturit arbos,
   Nunc frondent silvae, nunc formosissimus annus.

Virgil, *Eclogues* 3.56–57

---

8. In fact, it was Pope who made this observation, in the *Miscellanies* he coauthored with Swift.
9. Abilities.

1. The Roman historian Suetonius reports this of the emperor Caligula.

> Now every field, now every tree is green;
> Now genial nature's fairest face is seen.

> Elphinston

Every man is sufficiently discontented with some circumstances of his present state, to suffer his imagination to range more or less in quest of future happiness, and to fix upon some point of time, in which, by the removal of the inconvenience which now perplexes him, or acquisition of the advantage which he at present wants,[1] he shall find the condition of his life very much improved.

When this time, which is too often expected with great impatience, at last arrives, it generally comes without the blessing for which it was desired; but we solace ourselves with some new prospect, and press forward again with equal eagerness.

It is lucky for a man, in whom this temper prevails, when he turns his hopes upon things wholly out of his own power; since he forbears then to precipitate his affairs, for the sake of the great event that is to complete his felicity, and waits for the blissful hour, with less neglect of the measures necessary to be taken in the mean time.

I have long known a person of this temper, who indulged his dream of happiness with less hurt to himself than such chimerical wishes commonly produce, and adjusted his scheme with such address, that his hopes were in full bloom three parts of the year, and in the other part never wholly blasted. Many, perhaps, would be desirous of learning by what means he procured to himself such a cheap and lasting satisfaction. It was gained by a constant practice of referring the removal of all his uneasiness to the coming of the next spring; if his health was impaired, the spring would restore it; if what he wanted was at a high price, it would fall its value in the spring.

The spring, indeed, did often come without any of these effects, but he was always certain that the next would be more propitious; nor was ever convinced that the present spring would fail him before the middle of summer; for he always talked of the spring as coming 'till it was past, and when it was once past, everyone agreed with him that it was coming.

By long converse with this man, I am, perhaps, brought to feel immoderate pleasure in the contemplation of this delightful season; but I have the satisfaction of finding many, whom it can be no shame to resemble, infected with the same enthusiasm;[2] for there is, I believe, scarce any poet of eminence, who has not left some testimony of his fondness for the flowers, the zephyrs, and the warblers of the spring. Nor has the most luxuriant imagination been able to describe the serenity and happiness of the golden age, otherwise than by giving a perpetual spring, as the highest reward of uncorrupted innocence.

There is, indeed, something inexpressibly pleasing, in the annual renovation of the world, and the new display of the treasures of nature. The cold and darkness of winter, with the naked deformity of every object on which we turn our eyes, make us rejoice at the succeeding season, as well for what we have escaped, as for what we may enjoy; and every budding flower, which a warm situation brings early to our view, is considered by us as a messenger to notify the approach of more joyous days.

---

1. Lacks.

2. "Elevation of fancy; exaltation of ideas" (Johnson's *Dictionary*).

The spring affords to a mind, so free from the disturbance of cares or passions as to be vacant to calm amusements, almost every thing that our present state makes us capable of enjoying. The variegated verdure of the fields and woods, the succession of grateful odors, the voice of pleasure pouring out its notes on every side, with the gladness apparently conceived by every animal, from the growth of his food, and the clemency of the weather, throw over the whole earth an air of gaiety, significantly expressed by the smile of nature.

Yet there are men to whom these scenes are able to give no delight, and who hurry away from all the varieties of rural beauty, to lose their hours, and divert their thoughts by cards, or assemblies, a tavern dinner, or the prattle of the day.

It may be laid down as a position which will seldom deceive, that when a man cannot bear his own company there is something wrong. He must fly from himself, either because he feels a tediousness in life from the equipoise of an empty mind, which, having no tendency to one motion more than another but as it is impelled by some external power, must always have recourse to foreign objects; or he must be afraid of the intrusion of some unpleasing ideas, and, perhaps, is struggling to escape from the remembrance of a loss, the fear of a calamity, or some other thought of greater horror.

Those whom sorrow incapacitates to enjoy the pleasures of contemplation, may properly apply to such diversions, provided they are innocent, as lay strong hold on the attention; and those, whom fear of any future affliction chains down to misery, must endeavor to obviate the danger.

My considerations shall, on this occasion, be turned on such as are burdensome to themselves merely because they want subjects for reflection, and to whom the volume of nature is thrown open, without affording them pleasure or instruction, because they never learned to read the characters.

A French author has advanced this seeming paradox, that "very few men know how to take a walk"; and, indeed, it is true, that few know how to take a walk with a prospect of any other pleasure, than the same company would have afforded them at home.

There are animals that borrow their color from the neighboring body, and, consequently, vary their hue as they happen to change their place. In like manner it ought to be the endeavor of every man to derive his reflections from the objects about him; for it is to no purpose that he alters his position, if his attention continues fixed to the same point. The mind should be kept open to the access of every new idea, and so far disengaged from the predominance of particular thoughts, as easily to accommodate itself to occasional entertainment.

A man that has formed this habit of turning every new object to his entertainment, finds in the productions of nature an inexhaustible stock of materials upon which he can employ himself, without any temptations to envy or malevolence; faults, perhaps, seldom totally avoided by those, whose judgment is much exercised upon the works of art. He has always a certain prospect of discovering new reasons for adoring the sovereign author of the universe, and probable hopes of making some discovery of benefit to others, or of profit to himself. There is no doubt but many vegetables and animals have qualities that might be of great use, to the knowledge of which there is not required much force of penetration, or fatigue of study, but only frequent experiments, and close attention. What is said by the chemists of their darling mercury, is, perhaps, true of every body through the whole creation, that, if a thousand lives should be spent upon it, all its properties would not be found out.

Mankind must necessarily be diversified by various tastes, since life affords and requires such multiplicity of employments, and a nation of naturalists is neither to be hoped, or desired; but it is surely not improper to point out a fresh amusement to those who languish in health, and repine in plenty, for want of some source of diversion that may be less easily exhausted, and to inform the multitudes of both sexes, who are burdened with every new day, that there are many shows which they have not seen.

He that enlarges his curiosity after the works of nature, demonstrably multiplies the inlets to happiness; and, therefore, the younger part of my readers, to whom I dedicate this vernal speculation, must excuse me for calling upon them, to make use at once of the spring of the year, and the spring of life; to acquire, while their minds may be yet impressed with new images, a love of innocent pleasures, and an ardor for useful knowledge; and to remember, that a blighted spring makes a barren year, and that the vernal flowers, however beautiful and gay, are only intended by nature as preparatives to autumnal fruits.

Rambler No. 60

[ON BIOGRAPHY]

Saturday, 13 October 1750

—Quid sit pulchrum, quid turpe, quid utile, quid non,
Plenius et melius Chrysippo et Crantore dicit.

Horace, *Epistles*, 1.2.3–4.

Whose works the beautiful and base contain;
Of vice and virtue more instructive rules,
Than all the sober sages of the schools.

Francis

All joy or sorrow for the happiness or calamities of others is produced by an act of the imagination, that realizes the event however fictitious, or approximates[1] it however remote, by placing us, for a time, in the condition of him whose fortune we contemplate; so that we feel, while the deception lasts, whatever motions would be excited by the same good or evil happening to ourselves.

Our passions are therefore more strongly moved, in proportion as we can more readily adopt the pains or pleasures proposed to our minds, by recognizing them as once our own, or considering them as naturally incident to our state of life. It is not easy for the most artful writer to give us an interest in happiness or misery, which we think ourselves never likely to feel, and with which we have never yet been made acquainted. Histories of the downfall of kingdoms, and revolutions of empires, are read with great tranquility; the imperial tragedy pleases common auditors only by its pomp of ornament, and grandeur of ideas; and the man whose faculties have been engrossed by business, and whose heart never fluttered but at the rise or fall of stocks, wonders how the attention can be seized, or the affections agitated by a tale of love.

Those parallel circumstances, and kindred images, to which we readily conform our minds, are, above all other writings, to be found in narratives of the lives of particular persons; and therefore no species of writing seems more worthy of cultivation

1. Bring close.

than biography, since none can be more delightful or more useful, none can more certainly enchain the heart by irresistible interest, or more widely diffuse instruction to every diversity of condition.

The general and rapid narratives of history, which involve a thousand fortunes in the business of a day, and complicate innumerable incidents in one great transaction, afford few lessons applicable to private life, which derives its comforts and its wretchedness from the right or wrong management of things which nothing but their frequency makes considerable, *parva, si non fiant quotidie*, says Pliny,[2] and which can have no place in those relations which never descend below the consultation of senates, the motions of armies, and the schemes of conspirators.

I have often thought that there has rarely passed a life of which a judicious and faithful narrative would not be useful. For, not only every man has, in the mighty mass of the world, great numbers in the same condition with himself, to whom his mistakes and miscarriages, escapes and expedients, would be of immediate and apparent use; but there is such an uniformity in the state of man, considered apart from adventitious and separable decorations and disguises, that there is scarce any possibility of good or ill, but is common to humankind. A great part of the time of those who are placed at the greatest distance by fortune, or by temper, must unavoidably pass in the same manner; and though, when the claims of nature are satisfied, caprice, and vanity, and accident, begin to produce discriminations and peculiarities, yet the eye is not very heedful, or quick, which cannot discover the same causes still terminating their influence in the same effects, though sometimes accelerated, sometimes retarded, or perplexed by multiplied combinations. We are all prompted by the same motives, all deceived by the same fallacies, all animated by hope, obstructed by danger, entangled by desire, and seduced by pleasure.

It is frequently objected to relations of particular lives, that they are not distinguished by any striking or wonderful vicissitudes. The scholar who passed his life among his books, the merchant who conducted only his own affairs, the priest, whose sphere of action was not extended beyond that of his duty, are considered as no proper objects of public regard, however they might have excelled in their several stations, whatever might have been their learning, integrity, and piety. But this notion arises from false measures of excellence and dignity, and must be eradicated by considering that, in the esteem of uncorrupted reason, what is of most use is of most value.

It is, indeed, not improper to take honest advantages of prejudice, and to gain attention by a celebrated name; but the business of the biographer is often to pass slightly over those performances and incidents, which produce vulgar greatness, to lead the thoughts into domestic privacies, and display the minute details of daily life, where exterior appendages are cast aside, and men excel each other only by prudence and by virtue. The account of Thuanus is, with great propriety, said by its author to have been written, that it might lay open to posterity the private and familiar character of that man, *cujus ingenium et candorem ex ipsius scriptis sunt olim semper miraturi*,[3] whose candor and genius will to the end of time be by his writings preserved in admiration.

There are many invisible circumstances which, whether we read as inquirers after natural or moral knowledge, whether we intend to enlarge our science,[4] or increase our virtue, are more important than public occurrences. Thus Sallust, the

2. "Matters which would be trivial were they not part of a daily routine" (Pliny the Younger, *Epistles* 3.1).
3. Johnson quotes from a commentary affixed by Nicolas Rigault to the *History of His Own Time* by the French historian Jacques-Auguste de Thou (1553–1617). The Latin is translated by the words that follow.
4. Knowledge.

great master of nature, has not forgot, in his account of Catiline, to remark that "his walk was now quick, and again slow," as an indication of a mind revolving something with violent commotion.[5] Thus the story of Melancthon[6] affords a striking lecture on the value of time, by informing us, that when he made an appointment, he expected not only the hour, but the minute to be fixed, that the day might not run out in the idleness of suspense; and all the plans and enterprises of De Witt are now of less importance to the world, than that part of his personal character which represents him as "careful of his health, and negligent of his life."[7]

But biography has often been allotted to writers who seem very little acquainted with the nature of their task, or very negligent about the performance. They rarely afford any other account than might be collected from public papers, but imagine themselves writing a life when they exhibit a chronological series of actions or preferments; and so little regard the manners or behavior of their heroes, that more knowledge may be gained of a man's real character, by a short conversation with one of his servants, than from a formal and studied narrative, begun with his pedigree, and ended with his funeral.

If now and then they condescend to inform the world of particular facts, they are not always so happy as to select the most important. I know not well what advantage posterity can receive from the only circumstance by which Tickell has distinguished Addison from the rest of mankind, the irregularity of his pulse:[8] nor can I think myself overpaid for the time spent in reading the life of Malherb,[9] by being enabled to relate, after the learned biographer, that Malherb had two predominant opinions; one, that the looseness of a single woman might destroy all her boast of ancient descent; the other, that the French beggars made use very improperly and barbarously of the phrase "noble gentleman," because either word included the sense of both.

There are, indeed, some natural reasons why these narratives are often written by such as were not likely to give much instruction or delight, and why most accounts of particular persons are barren and useless. If a life be delayed till interest and envy are at an end, we may hope for impartiality, but must expect little intelligence; for the incidents which give excellence to biography are of a volatile and evanescent kind, such as soon escape the memory, and are rarely transmitted by tradition. We know how few can portray a living acquaintance, except by his most prominent and observable particularities, and the grosser features of his mind; and it may be easily imagined how much of this little knowledge may be lost in imparting it, and how soon a succession of copies will lose all resemblance of the original.

If the biographer writes from personal knowledge, and makes haste to gratify the public curiosity, there is danger lest his interest, his fear, his gratitude, or his tenderness, overpower his fidelity, and tempt him to conceal, if not to invent. There are many who think it an act of piety to hide the faults or failings of their friends, even when they can no longer suffer by their detection; we therefore see whole ranks of characters adorned with uniform panegyric, and not to be known from one another, but by extrinsic and casual circumstances. "Let me remember," says Hale, "when I

5. Johnson quotes from an account by the Roman historian Sallust of Catiline's conspiracy against Rome.
6. Johnson quotes from a biography of the Protestant theologian Philip Melancthon (1497–1560) by Joachim Camerarius.
7. Johnson quotes the essayist Sir William Temple's verdict on the Dutch statesman Jan de Witt (1625–1672).
8. Thomas Tickell prefixed a biography of Joseph Addison to his edition of Addison's Works (1721).
9. Johnson refers to the biography of the French poet Francois de Malherbe (1555–1628) by the Marquis de Racan.

find myself inclined to pity a criminal, that there is likewise a pity due to the country."[1] If we owe regard to the memory of the dead, there is yet more respect to be paid to knowledge, to virtue, and to truth.

Rambler No. 170

[On Misella, a Prostitute][1]

Saturday, 2 November 1751

Confiteor; si quid prodest delicta fateri.

Ovid, *Amores*, 2.4.3

I grant the charge; forgive the fault confess'd.

TO THE RAMBLER

SIR,

I am one of those beings, from whom many, that melt at the sight of all other misery, think it meritorious to withhold relief; one whom the rigor of virtuous indignation dooms to suffer without complaint, and perish without regard; and whom I myself have formerly insulted in the pride of reputation and security of innocence.

I am of a good family, but my father was burdened with more children than he could decently support. A wealthy relation, as he traveled from London to his country seat, condescending to make him a visit, was touched with compassion of his narrow fortune, and resolved to ease him of part of his charge, by taking the care of a child upon himself. Distress on one side and ambition on the other, were too powerful for parental fondness, and the little family passed in review before him, that he might make his choice. I was then ten years old, and without knowing for what purpose, I was called to my great cousin, endeavored to recommend myself by my best courtesy, sung him my prettiest song, told the last story that I had read, and so much endeared myself by my innocence, that he declared his resolution to adopt me, and to educate me with his own daughters.

My parents felt the common struggles at the thought of parting, and "some natural tears they dropped, but wiped them soon."[2] They considered, not without that false estimation of the value of wealth which poverty long continued always produces, that I was raised to higher rank than they could give me, and to hopes of more ample fortune than they could bequeath. My mother sold some of her ornaments to dress me in such a manner as might secure me from contempt at my first arrival; and when she dismissed me, pressed me to her bosom with an embrace that I still feel, gave me some precepts of piety which, however neglected, I have not forgotten, and uttered prayers for my final happiness, of which I have not yet ceased to hope, that they will at last be granted.

My sisters envied my new finery, and seemed not much to regret our separation; my father conducted me to the stagecoach with a kind of cheerful tenderness; and in a very short time, I was transported to splendid apartments, and a luxurious table, and grew familiar to show, noise and gaiety.

1. Johnson quotes from the biography of Sir Matthew Hale (1609–1676), eminent jurist and religious writer, by Gilbert Burnet.

1. Deriving from Latin, Misella means literally "wretched little one."

2. Milton, *Paradise Lost* 12.645, describing Adam and Eve's emotions on leaving Eden.

In three years my mother died, having implored a blessing on her family with her last breath. I had little opportunity to indulge a sorrow, which there was none to partake with me, and therefore soon ceased to reflect much upon my loss. My father turned all his care upon his other children, whom some fortunate adventures and unexpected legacies enabled him, when he died four years after my mother, to leave in a condition above their expectations.

I should have shared the increase of his fortune, and had once a portion assigned me in his will; but my cousin assuring him that all care for me was needless, since he had resolved to place me happily in the world, directed him to divide my part amongst my sisters.

Thus I was thrown upon dependence without resource. Being now at an age in which young women are initiated in company, I was no longer to be supported in my former character but at considerable expense; so that partly lest I should waste money, and partly lest my appearance might draw too many compliments and assiduities, I was insensibly degraded from my equality, and enjoyed few privileges above the head servant, but that of receiving no wages.

I felt every indignity, but knew that resentment would precipitate my fall. I therefore endeavored to continue my importance by little services and active officiousness,[3] and for a time preserved myself from neglect, by withdrawing all pretenses to competition, and studying to please rather than to shine. But my interest, notwithstanding this expedient, hourly declined, and my cousin's favorite maid began to exchange repartees with me, and consult me about the alterations of a cast gown.

I was now completely depressed, and though I had seen mankind enough to know the necessity of outward cheerfulness, I often withdrew to my chamber to vent my grief, or turn my condition in my mind, and examine by what means I might escape from perpetual mortification. At last, my schemes and sorrows were interrupted by a sudden change of my relation's behavior, who one day took an occasion when we were left together in a room, to bid me suffer myself no longer to be insulted, but assume the place which he always intended me to hold in the family. He assured me, that his wife's preference of her own daughters should never hurt me; and, accompanying his professions with a purse of gold, ordered me to bespeak a rich suit at the mercer's,[4] and to apply privately to him for money when I wanted it, and insinuate that my other friends supplied me, which he would take care to confirm.

By this stratagem, which I did not then understand, he filled me with tenderness and gratitude, compelled me to repose on him as my only support, and produced a necessity of private conversation. He often appointed interviews at the house of an acquaintance, and sometimes called on me with a coach, and carried me abroad. My sense of his favor, and the desire of retaining it, disposed me to unlimited complaisance, and though I saw his kindness grow every day more fond, I did not suffer any suspicion to enter my thoughts. At last the wretch took advantage of the familiarity which he enjoyed as my relation, and the submission which he exacted as my benefactor, to complete the ruin of an orphan whom his own promises had made indigent, whom his indulgence had melted, and his authority subdued.

I know not why it should afford subject of exultation, to overpower on any terms the resolution, or surprise the caution of a girl; but of all the boasters that deck themselves in the spoils of innocence and beauty, they surely have the least pretensions to triumph, who submit to owe their success to some casual influence. They neither employ the graces of fancy, nor the force of understanding, in their attempts; they

---

3. Dutiful behavior.   4. Dealer in fabrics.

cannot please their vanity with the art of their approaches, the delicacy of their adulations, the elegance of their address, or the efficacy of their eloquence; nor applaud themselves as possessed of any qualities, by which affection is attracted. They surmount no obstacles, they defeat no rivals, but attack only those who cannot resist, and are often content to possess the body without any solicitude to gain the heart.

Many of these despicable wretches does my present acquaintance with infamy and wickedness enable me to number among the heroes of debauchery. Reptiles whom their own servants would have despised, had they not been their servants, and with whom beggary would have disdained intercourse, had she not been allured by hopes of relief. Many of the beings which are now rioting in taverns, or shivering in the streets, have been corrupted not by arts of gallantry which stole gradually upon the affections and laid prudence asleep, but by the fear of losing benefits which were never intended, or of incurring resentment which they could not escape; some have been frighted by masters, and some awed by guardians into ruin.

Our crime had its usual consequence, and he soon perceived that I could not long continue in his family. I was distracted at the thought of the reproach which I now believed inevitable. He comforted me with hopes of eluding all discovery, and often upbraided me with the anxiety, which perhaps none but himself saw in my countenance; but at last mingled his assurances of protection and maintenance with menaces of total desertion, if in the moments of perturbation I should suffer his secret to escape, or endeavor to throw on him any part of my infamy.

Thus passed the dismal hours till my retreat could no longer be delayed. It was pretended that my relations had sent for me to a distant county, and I entered upon a state which shall be described in my next letter.

I am, Sir, &c.
MISELLA

Rambler No. 171

[MISELLA CONTINUES]

Tuesday, 5 November 1751

Taedet coeli convexa tueri.

Virgil, *Aeneid*, 4.451

Dark is the sun, and loathsome is the day.

TO THE RAMBLER

SIR,

Misella now sits down to continue her narrative. I am convinced that nothing would more powerfully preserve youth from irregularity, or guard inexperience from seduction, than a just description of the condition into which the wanton plunges herself, and therefore hope that my letter may be a sufficient antidote to my example.

After the distraction, hesitation and delays which the timidity of guilt naturally produces, I was removed to lodgings in a distant part of the town, under one of the characters commonly assumed upon such occasions. Here being, by my circumstances, condemned to solitude, I passed most of my hours in bitterness and anguish. The conversation of the people with whom I was placed, was not at all capable of engaging my attention or dispossessing the reigning ideas. The books which I carried to my retreat were such as heightened my abhorrence of myself; for I was not so far abandoned as to sink voluntarily into corruption, or endeavor to conceal from my own mind the enormity of my crime.

My relation remitted none of his fondness, but visited me so often that I was sometimes afraid lest his assiduity should expose him to suspicion. Whenever he came he found me weeping, and was therefore less delightfully entertained than he expected. After frequent expostulations upon the unreasonableness of my sorrow, and innumerable protestations of everlasting regard, he at last found that I was more affected with the loss of my innocence, than the danger of my fame,[1] and that he might not be disturbed by my remorse, began to lull my conscience with the opiates of irreligion. His arguments were such as my course of life has since exposed me often to the necessity of hearing, vulgar, empty and fallacious; yet they at first confounded me by their novelty, filled me with doubt and perplexity, and interrupted that peace which I began to feel from the sincerity of my repentance, without substituting any other support. I listened a while to his impious gabble, but its influence was soon overpowered by natural reason and early education, and the convictions which this new attempt gave me of his baseness completed my abhorrence. I have heard of barbarians, who, when tempests drive ships upon their coast, decoy them to the rocks that they may plunder their lading, and have always thought that wretches thus merciless in their depredations, ought to be destroyed by a general insurrection of all social beings; yet how light is this guilt to the crime of him, who in the agitations of remorse cuts away the anchor of piety, and when he has drawn aside credulity from the paths of virtue, hides the light of heaven which would direct her to return. I had hitherto considered him as a man equally betrayed with myself by the concurrence of appetite and opportunity; but I now saw with horror that he was contriving to perpetuate his gratification, and was desirous to fit me to his purpose by complete and radical corruption.

To escape, however, was not yet in my power. I could support the expenses of my condition, only by the continuance of his favor. He provided all that was necessary, and in a few weeks, congratulated me upon my escape from the danger which we had both expected with so much anxiety. I then began to remind him of his promise to restore me with my fame uninjured to the world. He promised me in general terms, that nothing should be wanting which his power could add to my happiness, but forbore to release me from my confinement. I knew how much my reception in the world depended upon my speedy return, and was therefore outrageously impatient of his delays, which I now perceived to be only artifices of lewdness. He told me, at last, with an appearance of sorrow, that all hopes of restoration to my former state were forever precluded; that chance had discovered my secret, and malice divulged it; and that nothing now remained, but to seek a retreat more private, where curiosity or hatred could never find us.

The rage, anguish, and resentment, which I felt at this account, are not to be expressed. I was in so much dread of reproach and infamy, which he represented as pursuing me with full cry, that I yielded myself implicitly to his disposal, and was removed with a thousand studied precautions through by-ways and dark passages, to another house, where I harassed him with perpetual solicitations for a small annuity, that might enable me to live in the country with obscurity and innocence.

This demand he at first evaded with ardent professions, but in time appeared offended at my importunity and distrust; and having one day endeavored to soothe me with uncommon expressions of tenderness, when he found my discontent immovable, left me with some inarticulate murmurs of anger. I was pleased that he was at last roused to sensibility, and expecting that at his next visit, he would comply

1. Reputation.

with my request, lived with great tranquility upon the money in my hands, and was so much pleased with this pause of persecution, that I did not reflect how much his absence had exceeded the usual intervals, till I was alarmed with the danger of wanting subsistence. I then suddenly contracted my expenses, but was unwilling to supplicate for assistance. Necessity, however, soon overcame my modesty or my pride, and I applied to him by a letter, but had no answer. I writ in terms more pressing, but without effect. I then sent an agent to inquire after him, who informed me, that he had quitted his house, and was gone with his family to reside for some time upon his estate in Ireland.

However shocked at this abrupt departure, I was yet unwilling to believe that he could wholly abandon me, and therefore by the sale of my clothes I supported myself, expecting that every post would bring me relief. Thus I passed seven months between hope and dejection, in a gradual approach to poverty and distress, emaciated with discontent and bewildered with uncertainty. At last, my landlady, after many hints of the necessity of a new lover, took the opportunity of my absence to search my boxes, and missing some of my apparel, seized the remainder for rent, and led me to the door.

To remonstrate against legal cruelty, was vain; to supplicate obdurate brutality, was hopeless. I went away I knew not whither, and wandered about without any settled purpose, unacquainted with the usual expedients of misery, unqualified for laborious offices, afraid to meet an eye that had seen me before, and hopeless of relief from those who were strangers to my former condition. Night came on in the midst of my distraction, and I still continued to wander till the menaces of the watch obliged me to shelter myself in a covered passage.

Next day, I procured a lodging in the backward garret of a mean house, and employed my landlady to inquire for a service. My applications were generally rejected for want of a character.[2] At length, I was received at a draper's; but when it was known to my mistress that I had only one gown, and that of silk, she was of opinion, that I looked like a thief, and without warning, hurried me away. I then tried to support myself by my needle, and by my landlady's recommendation, obtained a little work from a shop, and for three weeks lived without repining; but when my punctuality had gained me so much reputation, that I was trusted to make up a head[3] of some value, one of my fellow-lodgers stole the lace, and I was obliged to fly from a prosecution.

Thus driven again into the streets, I lived upon the least that could support me, and at night accommodated myself under penthouses[4] as well as I could. At length I became absolutely penniless; and having strolled all day without sustenance, was at the close of evening accosted by an elderly man, with an invitation to a tavern. I refused him with hesitation; he seized me by the hand, and drew me into a neighboring house, where when he saw my face pale with hunger, and my eyes swelling with tears, he spurned me from him, and bad me cant and whine in some other place; he for his part would take care of his pockets.

I still continued to stand in the way, having scarcely strength to walk farther, when another soon addressed me in the same manner. When he saw the same tokens of calamity, he considered that I might be obtained at a cheap rate, and therefore quickly made overtures, which I had no longer firmness to reject. By this man I was maintained four months in penurious wickedness, and then abandoned to my former condition, from which I was delivered by another keeper.

2. Letter of reference.   4. Eaves of houses.
3. Headdress.

In this abject state I have now passed four years, the drudge of extortion and the sport of drunkenness; sometimes the property of one man, and sometimes the common prey of accidental lewdness; at one time tricked up for sale by the mistress of a brothel, at another begging in the streets to be relieved from hunger by wickedness; without any hope in the day but of finding some whom folly or excess may expose to my allurements, and without any reflections at night, but such as guilt and terror impress upon me.

If those who pass their days in plenty and security, could visit for an hour the dismal receptacles to which the prostitute retires from her nocturnal excursions, and see the wretches that lie crowded together, mad with intemperance, ghastly with famine, nauseous with filth, and noisome with disease; it would not be easy for any degree of abhorrence to harden them against compassion, or to repress the desire which they must immediately feel to rescue such numbers of human beings from a state so dreadful.

It is said that in France they annually evacuate their streets, and ship their prostitutes and vagabonds to their colonies. If the women that infest this city had the same opportunity of escaping from their miseries, I believe very little force would be necessary; for who among them can dread any change? Many of us indeed are wholly unqualified for any but the most servile employments, and those perhaps would require the care of a magistrate to hinder them from following the same practices in another country; but others are only precluded by infamy from reformation, and would gladly be delivered on any terms from the necessity of guilt and the tyranny of chance. No place but a populous city can afford opportunities for open prostitution, and where the eye of justice can attend to individuals, those who cannot be made good may be restrained from mischief. For my part I should exult at the privilege of banishment, and think myself happy in any region that should restore me once again to honesty and peace.

I am, Sir, &c.

MISELLA

Rambler No. 207

[Beginnings, Middles, and Ends]

Tuesday, 10 March 1752

Solve senescentem mature sanus equum, ne
Peccet ad extremum ridendus.

Horace, *Epistles* 1.1.8–9

The voice of reason cries with winning force,
Loose from the rapid car your aged horse,
Lest, in the race derided, left behind,
He drag his jaded limbs and burst his wind.

Francis

Such is the emptiness of human enjoyment, that we are always impatient of the present. Attainment is followed by neglect, and possession by disgust; and the malicious remark of the Greek epigrammatist on marriage may be applied to every other course of life, that its two days of happiness are the first and the last.[1]

---

1. Johnson paraphrases the poet Palladas, whose epigrams appear in the *Greek Anthology* (11.381).

Few moments are more pleasing than those in which the mind is concerting measures for a new undertaking. From the first hint that wakens the fancy, till the hour of actual execution, all is improvement and progress, triumph and felicity. Every hour brings additions to the original scheme, suggests some new expedient to secure success, or discovers consequential advantages not hitherto foreseen. While preparations are made, and materials accumulated, day glides after day through elysian prospects, and the heart dances to the song of hope.

Such is the pleasure of projecting, that many content themselves with a succession of visionary schemes, and wear out their allotted time in the calm amusement of contriving what they never attempt or hope to execute.

Others, not able to feast their imagination with pure ideas, advance somewhat nearer to the grossness of action, with great diligence collect whatever is requisite to their design, and, after a thousand researches and consultations, are snatched away by death, as they stand in *procinctu*[2] waiting for a proper opportunity to begin.

If there were no other end of life, than to find some adequate solace for every day, I know not whether any condition could be preferred to that of the man who involves himself in his own thoughts, and never suffers experience to show him the vanity of speculation; for no sooner are notions reduced to practice, than tranquility and confidence forsake the breast; every day brings its task, and often without bringing abilities to perform it: difficulties embarrass, uncertainty perplexes, opposition retards, censure exasperates, or neglect depresses. We proceed, because we have begun; we complete our design, that the labor already spent may not be vain: but as expectation gradually dies away, the gay smile of alacrity disappears, we are compelled to implore severer powers, and trust the event to patience and constancy.

When once our labor has begun, the comfort that enables us to endure it is the prospect of its end; for though in every long work there are some joyous intervals of self-applause, when the attention is recreated by unexpected facility, and the imagination soothed by incidental excellencies; yet the toil with which performance struggles after idea, is so irksome and disgusting,[3] and so frequent is the necessity of resting below that perfection which we imagined within our reach, that seldom any man obtains more from his endeavors than a painful conviction of his defects, and a continual resuscitation of desires which he feels himself unable to gratify.

So certainly is weariness the concomitant of our undertakings, that every man, in whatever he is engaged, consoles himself with the hope of change; if he has made his way by assiduity to public employment, he talks among his friends of the delight of retreat; if by the necessity of solitary application he is secluded from the world, he listens with a beating heart to distant noises, longs to mingle with living beings, and resolves to take hereafter his fill of diversions, or display his abilities on the universal theatre, and enjoy the pleasure of distinction and applause.

Every desire, however innocent, grows dangerous, as by long indulgence it becomes ascendant in the mind. When we have been much accustomed to consider any thing as capable of giving happiness, it is not easy to restrain our ardor, or to forbear some precipitation in our advances, and irregularity in our pursuits. He that has cultivated the tree, watched the swelling bud and opening blossom, and pleased himself with computing how much every sun and shower add to its growth, scarcely stays till the fruit has obtained its maturity, but defeats his own cares by eagerness to

2. Under arms, ready for action.   3. Distasteful.

reward them. When we have diligently labored for any purpose, we are willing to believe that we have attained it, and, because we have already done much, too suddenly conclude that no more is to be done.

All attraction is increased by the approach of the attracting body. We never find ourselves so desirous to finish, as in the latter part of our work, or so impatient of delay, as when we know that delay cannot be long. This unseasonable importunity of discontent may be partly imputed to languor and weariness, which must always oppress those more whose toil has been longer continued; but the greater part usually proceeds from frequent contemplation of that ease which is now considered as within reach, and which, when it has once flattered our hopes, we cannot suffer to be withheld.

In some of the noblest compositions of wit, the conclusion falls below the vigor and spirit of the first books; and as a genius is not to be degraded by the imputation of human failings, the cause of this declension is commonly sought in the structure of the work, and plausible reasons are given why in the defective part less ornament was necessary, or less could be admitted. But, perhaps, the author would have confessed, that his fancy was tired, and his perseverance broken; that he knew his design to be unfinished, but that, when he saw the end so near, he could no longer refuse to be at rest.

Against the instillations of this frigid opiate, the heart should be secured by all the considerations which once concurred to kindle the ardor of enterprise. Whatever motive first incited action, has still greater force to stimulate perseverance; since he that might have lain still at first in blameless obscurity, cannot afterwards desist but with infamy and reproach. He, whom a doubtful promise of distant good, could encourage to set difficulties at defiance, ought not to remit his vigor, when he has almost obtained his recompense. To faint or loiter, when only the last efforts are required, is to steer the ship through tempests, and abandon it to the winds in sight of land; it is to break the ground and scatter the seed, and at last to neglect the harvest.

The masters of rhetoric direct, that the most forcible arguments be produced in the latter part of an oration, lest they should be effaced or perplexed by supervenient images. This precept may be justly extended to the series of life: nothing is ended with honor, which does not conclude better than it begun. It is not sufficient to maintain the first vigor; for excellence loses its effect upon the mind by custom, as light after a time ceases to dazzle. Admiration must be continued by that novelty which first produced it, and how much soever is given, there must always be reason to imagine that more remains.

We not only are most sensible of the last impressions, but such is the unwillingness of mankind to admit transcendent merit, that, though it be difficult to obliterate the reproach of miscarriages by any subsequent achievement, however illustrious, yet the reputation raised by a long train of success, may be finally ruined by a single failure, for weakness or error will be always remembered by that malice and envy which it gratifies.

For the prevention of that disgrace, which lassitude and negligence may bring at last upon the greatest performances, it is necessary to proportion carefully our labor to our strength. If the design comprises many parts, equally essential, and therefore not to be separated, the only time for caution is before we engage; the powers of the mind must be then impartially estimated, and it must be remembered, that not to complete the plan, is not to have begun it; and, that nothing is done, while any thing is omitted.

But, if the task consists in the repetition of single acts, no one of which derives its efficacy from the rest, it may be attempted with less scruple, because there is always opportunity to retreat with honor. The danger is only lest we expect from the world the indulgence with which most are disposed to treat themselves; and in the hour of listlessness imagine, that the diligence of one day will atone for the idleness of another, and that applause begun by approbation will be continued by habit.

He that is himself weary will soon weary the public. Let him therefore lay down his employment, whatever it be, who can no longer exert his former activity or attention; let him not endeavor to struggle with censure, or obstinately infest the stage till a general hiss commands him to depart.[4]

from A Review of Soame Jenyns' *A Free Inquiry into the Nature and Origin of Evil*[1]

This is a treatise, consisting of six letters, upon a very difficult and important question, which, I am afraid, this author's endeavors will not free from the perplexity which has entangled the speculatists of all ages, and which must always continue while *we see* but *in part*. He calls it a *free* inquiry, and indeed his freedom is, I think, greater than his modesty. Though he is far from the contemptible arrogance or the impious licentiousness of Bolingbroke,[2] yet he decides too easily upon questions out of the reach of human determination, with too little consideration of mortal weakness, and with too much vivacity for the necessary caution.

* * *

We are next entertained with Pope's alleviations of those evils which we are doomed to suffer:

> Poverty, or the want of riches, is generally compensated by having more hopes and fewer fears, by a greater share of health, and a more exquisite relish of the smallest enjoyments, than those who possess them are usually blessed with. The want of taste and genius, with all the pleasures that arise from them, are commonly recompensed by a more useful kind of common sense, together with a wonderful delight, as well as success, in the busy pursuits of a scrambling world. The sufferings of the sick are greatly relieved by many trifling gratifications imperceptible to others, and sometimes almost repaid by the inconceivable transports occasioned by the return of health and vigor. Folly cannot be very grievous, because imperceptible; and I doubt not but there is some truth in that rant of a mad poet, that there is a pleasure in being mad which none but madmen know. Ignorance, or the want of knowledge and literature, the appointed lot of all born to poverty and the drudgeries of life, is the only opiate capable of infusing that insensibility which can enable them to endure the miseries of the one, and the fatigues of the other. It is a cordial administered by the gracious hand of providence, of which they ought never to be deprived by an ill-judged and improper education. It is the basis of all subordination, the support of

4. With his next essay (*Rambler* No. 208), Johnson brought the series to a close.
1. Soame Jenyns (1704–1787), a wealthy dilettante who dabbled in literature, politics, and theology, published his *Free Inquiry* early in 1757; Johnson's review appeared in the *Literary Magazine* a few months later. Much of what Jenyns has to say in his theodicy (or vindication of the justice and goodness of God) is derived from Pope's *Essay on Man* (for Johnson's opinion of the *Essay*, see page 2787). Central to both Pope's poem and Jenyns's treatise

is the doctrine of the Great Chain of Being, which models the universe as a hierarchical scale or continuum. This continuum stretches from God down through angels, humans, animals, and inanimate nature. Like Pope, Jenyns concludes that the cosmos is formed on principles of a "just subordination."
2. Henry St. John (1678–1751), Viscount Bolingbroke, politician and political theorist, whose *Reflections Concerning Innate Moral Principles* Johnson considered dangerous in its deism.

society, and the privilege of individuals: and I have ever thought it a most remarkable instance of the divine wisdom that whereas in all animals, whose individuals rise little above the rest of their species, knowledge is instinctive, in man, whose individuals are so widely different, it is acquired by education, by which means the prince and the laborer, the philosopher and the peasant, are in some measure fitted for their respective situations.

Much of these positions is perhaps true, and the whole paragraph might well pass without censure, were not objections necessary to the establishment of knowledge. *Poverty* is very gently paraphrased by *want of riches*. In that sense almost every man may in his own opinion be poor. But there is another poverty which is *want of competence*, of all that can soften the miseries of life, of all that diversify attention, or delight imagination. There is yet another poverty which is *want of necessaries*, a species of poverty which no care of the public, no charity of particulars,[3] can preserve many from feeling openly, and many secretly.

That hope and fear are inseparably or very frequently connected with poverty and riches my surveys of life have not informed me. The milder degrees of poverty are sometimes supported by hope, but the more severe often sink down in motionless despondence. Life must be seen before it can be known. This author and Pope perhaps never saw the miseries which they imagine thus easy to be borne. The poor indeed are insensible of many little vexations which sometimes embitter the possessions and pollute the enjoyment of the rich. They are not pained by casual incivility, or mortified by the mutilation of a compliment; but this happiness is like that of a malefactor who ceases to feel the cords that bind him when the pincers are tearing his flesh.

That want of taste for one enjoyment is supplied by the pleasures of some other may be fairly allowed. But the compensations of sickness I have never found near to equivalence, and the transports of recovery only prove the intenseness of the pain.

With folly no man is willing to confess himself very intimately acquainted, and therefore its pains and pleasures are kept secret. But what the author says of its happiness seems applicable only to fatuity, or gross dullness, for that inferiority of understanding which makes one man without any other reason the slave, or tool, or property of another, which makes him sometimes useless, and sometimes ridiculous, is often felt with very quick sensibility. On the happiness of madmen, as the case is not very frequent, it is not necessary to raise a disquisition, but I cannot forbear to observe that I never yet knew disorders of mind increase felicity: every madman is either arrogant and irascible, or gloomy and suspicious, or possessed by some passion or notion destructive to his quiet. He has always discontent in his look, and malignity in his bosom. And, if we had the power of choice, he would soon repent, who should resign his reason to secure his peace.

Concerning the portion of ignorance necessary to make the condition of the lower classes of mankind safe to the public and tolerable to themselves, both morals and policy exact a nicer[4] inquiry than will be very soon or very easily made. There is undoubtedly a degree of knowledge which will direct a man to refer all to providence, and to acquiesce in the condition which omniscient goodness has determined to allot him; to consider this world as a phantom that must soon glide from before his eyes, and the distresses and vexations that encompass him as dust scattered in his path, as a blast that chills him for a moment, and passes off forever.

---

3. Particular individuals.

4. More discriminating.

Such wisdom, arising from the comparison of part with the whole of our existence, those that want[5] it most cannot possibly obtain from philosophy, nor, unless the method of education and the general tenor of life are changed, will very easily receive it from religion. The bulk of mankind is not likely to be very wise or very good: and I know not whether there are not many states of life in which all knowledge less than the highest wisdom will produce discontent and danger. I believe it may be sometimes found that a *little learning* is to a poor man a *dangerous thing*.[6] But such is the condition of humanity that we easily see, or quickly feel the wrong, but cannot always distinguish the right. Whatever knowledge is superfluous, in irremediable poverty, is hurtful, but the difficulty is to determine when poverty is irremediable, and at what point superfluity begins. Gross ignorance every man has found equally dangerous with perverted knowledge. Men left wholly to their appetites and their instincts, with little sense of moral or religious obligation, and with very faint distinctions of right and wrong, can never be safely employed or confidently trusted: they can be honest only by obstinacy, and diligent only by compulsion or caprice. Some instruction, therefore, is necessary, and much, perhaps, may be dangerous.

Though it should be granted that those who are *born to poverty and drudgery* should not be *deprived* by an *improper education* of the *opiate of ignorance*, even this concession will not be of much use to direct our practice, unless it be determined who are those that are *born to poverty*. To entail irreversible poverty upon generation after generation only because the ancestor happened to be poor is in itself cruel, if not unjust, and is wholly contrary to the maxims of a commercial nation, which always suppose and promote a rotation of property, and offer every individual a chance of mending his condition by his diligence. Those who communicate literature to the son of a poor man consider him as one not born to poverty, but to the necessity of deriving a better fortune from himself. In this attempt, as in others, many fail, and many succeed. Those that fail will feel their misery more acutely; but since poverty is now confessed to be such a calamity as cannot be borne without the opiate of insensibility, I hope the happiness of those whom education enables to escape from it may turn the balance against that exacerbation which the others suffer.

I am always afraid of determining on the side of envy or cruelty. The privileges of education may sometimes be improperly bestowed, but I shall always fear to withhold them, lest I should be yielding to the suggestions of pride, while I persuade myself that I am following the maxims of policy; and under the appearance of salutary restraints, should be indulging the lust of dominion, and that malevolence which delights in seeing others depressed.

Pope's doctrine is at last exhibited in a comparison which, like other proofs of the same kind, is better adapted to delight the fancy than convince the reason:

> Thus the universe resembles a large and well-regulated family, in which all the officers and servants, and even the domestic animals, are subservient to each other in a proper subordination: each enjoys the privileges and perquisites peculiar to his place, and at the same time contributes by that just subordination to the magnificence and happiness of the whole.

---

5. Lack.

6. "A little learning is a dangerous thing" (Pope, *Essay on Criticism*, line 215).

The magnificence of a house is of use or pleasure to the master, and sometimes to the domestics. But the magnificence of the universe adds nothing to the supreme Being; for any part of its inhabitants with which human knowledge is acquainted, an universe much less spacious or splendid would have been sufficient; and of happiness it does not appear that any is communicated from the beings of a lower world to those of a higher. * * *

Having thus dispatched the consideration of particular evils, he comes at last to a general reason for which *evil* may be said to be *our good*. He is of opinion that there is some inconceivable benefit in pain abstractedly considered; that pain however inflicted, or wherever felt, communicates some good to the general system of being, and that every animal is some way or other the better for the pain of every other animal. This opinion he carries so far as to suppose that there passes some principle of union through all animal life, as attraction is communicated to all corporeal nature, and that the evils suffered on this globe may by some inconceivable means contribute to the felicity of the inhabitants of the remotest planet.

How the origin of evil is brought nearer to human conception by any *inconceivable* means, I am not able to discover. We believed that the present system of creation was right, though we could not explain the adaptation of one part to the other, or for the whole succession of causes and consequences. Where has this inquirer added to the little knowledge that we had before? He has told us of the benefits of evil, which no man feels, and relations between distant parts of the universe, which he cannot himself conceive. There was enough in this question inconceivable before, and we have little advantage from a new inconceivable solution.

I do not mean to reproach this author for not knowing what is equally hidden from learning and from ignorance. The shame is to impose words for ideas upon ourselves or others. To imagine that we are going forward when we are only turning round. To think that there is any difference between him that gives no reason, and him that gives a reason which by his own confession cannot be conceived.

But that he may not be thought to conceive nothing but things inconceivable, he has at last thought on a way by which human sufferings may produce good effects. He imagines that as we have not only animals for food, but choose some for our diversion, the same privilege may be allowed to some beings above us, *who may deceive, torment, or destroy us for the ends only of their own pleasure or utility.* This he again finds impossible to be conceived, *but that impossibility lessens not the probability of the conjecture, which by analogy is so strongly confirmed.*

I cannot resist the temptation of contemplating this analogy, which I think he might have carried further very much to the advantage of his argument. He might have shown that these *hunters whose game is man* have many sports analogous to our own. As we drown whelps and kittens, they amuse themselves now and then with sinking a ship, and stand round the fields of Blenheim or the walls of Prague,[7] as we encircle a cockpit.[8] As we shoot a bird flying, they take a man in the midst of his business or pleasure, and knock him down with an apoplexy. Some of them, perhaps, are virtuosi, and delight in the operations of an asthma, as a human philosopher[9] in

7. Johnson refers to famous, and famously bloody, battles.
8. The arena in which cocks equipped with spurs fought

each other, often to the death.
9. Scientist.

the effects of the air pump.[1] To swell a man with a tympany[2] is as good sport as to blow a frog. Many a merry bout have these frolic beings at the vicissitudes of an ague,[3] and good sport it is to see a man tumble with an epilepsy, and revive and tumble again, and all this he knows not why. As they are wiser and more powerful than we, they have more exquisite diversions, for we have no way of procuring any sport so brisk and so lasting as the paroxysms of the gout and stone,[4] which undoubtedly must make high mirth, especially if the play be a little diversified with the blunders and puzzles of the blind and deaf. We know not how far their sphere of observation may extend. Perhaps now and then a merry being may place himself in such a situation as to enjoy at once all the varieties of an epidemical disease, or amuse his leisure with the tossings and contortions of every possible pain exhibited together.

One sport the merry malice of these beings has found means of enjoying to which we have nothing equal or similar. They now and then catch a mortal proud of his parts,[5] and flattered either by the submission of those who court his kindness, or the notice of those who suffer him to court theirs. A head thus prepared for the reception of false opinions, and the projection of vain designs, they easily fill with idle notions, till in time they make their plaything an author; their first diversion commonly begins with an ode or an epistle, then rises perhaps to a political irony, and is at last brought to its height by a treatise of philosophy. Then begins the poor animal to entangle himself in sophisms, and flounder in absurdity, to talk confidently of the scale of being, and to give solutions which himself confesses impossible to be understood. Sometimes, however, it happens that their pleasure is without much mischief. The author feels no pain, but while they are wondering at the extravagance of his opinion, and pointing him out to one another as a new example of human folly, he is enjoying his own applause, and that of his companions, and perhaps is elevated with the hope of standing at the head of a new sect.

Many of the books which now crowd the world may be justly suspected to be written for the sake of some invisible order of beings, for surely they are of no use to any of the corporeal inhabitants of the world. Of the productions of the last bounteous year, how many can be said to serve any purpose of use or pleasure? The only end of writing is to enable the readers better to enjoy life, or better to endure it; and how will either of those be put more in our power by him who tells us that we are puppets, of which some creature not much wiser than ourselves manages the wires? That a set of beings unseen and unheard are hovering about us, trying experiments upon our sensibility, putting us in agonies to see our limbs quiver, torturing us to madness that they may laugh at our vagaries; sometimes obstructing the bile that they may see how a man looks when he is yellow; sometimes breaking a traveler's bones to try how he will get home; sometimes wasting a man to a skeleton, and sometimes killing him fat for the greater elegance of his hide?

This is an account of natural evil which though, like the rest, not quite new, is very entertaining, though I know not how much it may contribute to patience. The only reason why we should contemplate evil is that we may bear it better; and I am afraid nothing is much more placidly endured for the sake of making others sport. * * *

1757   1757

---

1. A vacuum pump used in experiments concerning air to deprive animals of oxygen.
2. "A kind of obstructed flatulence that swells the body like a drum" (Johnson's *Dictionary*).
3. Fever.
4. Kidney or gall stone.
5. Abilities.

Idler No. 31[1]

[ON IDLENESS]

Saturday, 18 November 1758

Many moralists have remarked, that pride has of all human vices the widest dominion, appears in the greatest multiplicity of forms, and lies hid under the greatest variety of disguises; of disguises, which, like the moon's "veil of brightness," are both its "luster and its shade,"[2] and betray it to others, though they hide it from ourselves.

It is not my intention to degrade pride from this pre-eminence of mischief, yet I know not whether idleness may not maintain a very doubtful and obstinate competition.

There are some that profess idleness in its full dignity, who call themselves the Idle, as Busiris in the play "calls himself the Proud";[3] who boast that they do nothing, and thank their stars that they have nothing to do; who sleep every night till they can sleep no longer, and rise only that exercise may enable them to sleep again; who prolong the reign of darkness by double curtains, and never see the sun but to "tell him how they hate his beams";[4] whose whole labor is to vary the postures of indulgence, and whose day differs from their night but as a couch or chair differs from a bed.

These are the true and open votaries of idleness, for whom she weaves the garlands of poppies, and into whose cup she pours the waters of oblivion; who exist in a state of unruffled stupidity,[5] forgetting and forgotten; who have long ceased to live, and at whose death the survivors can only say, that they have ceased to breathe.

But idleness predominates in many lives where it is not suspected, for being a vice which terminates in itself, it may be enjoyed without injury to others, and is therefore not watched like fraud, which endangers property, or like pride, which naturally seeks its gratifications in another's inferiority. Idleness is a silent and peaceful quality, that neither raises envy by ostentation, nor hatred by opposition; and therefore nobody is busy to censure or detect it.

As pride sometimes is hid under humility, idleness is often covered by turbulence and hurry. He that neglects his known duty and real employment, naturally endeavors to crowd his mind with something that may bar out the remembrance of his own folly, and does any thing but what he ought to do with eager diligence, that he may keep himself in his own favor.

Some are always in a state of preparation, occupied in previous measures, forming plans, accumulating materials, and providing for the main affair. These are certainly under the secret power of idleness. Nothing is to be expected from the workman whose tools are forever to be sought. I was once told by a great master, that no man ever excelled in painting, who was eminently curious[6] about pencils[7] and colors.

1. *The Idler* (1758–1760) bears a more self-deprecating title than *The Rambler*; other circumstances, too, suggest that Johnson intended a less imposing performance in this series of periodical essay than in its predecessor. The new pieces appeared not twice but once a week, and not as an independent sheet but as a department within a weekly newspaper called *The Universal Chronicle* (which achieved little eminence apart from Johnson's contribution). The *Idlers* were shorter than the *Ramblers*, and dealt more often in light topics and comic touches. Boswell opined that the second series had "less body and

more spirit . . . more variety of real life, and greater facility of language." His judgment is hardly definitive; the comparison has been assayed, with varying results, many times since.
2. Both quotations come from Samuel Butler's poem *Hudibras* (1663–1678), 2.1.905 and 908.
3. *Busiris* (1719) by Edward Young.
4. Milton, *Paradise Lost* 4.37.
5. Stupor.
6. "Difficult to please" (Johnson's *Dictionary*).
7. Brushes.

There are others to whom idleness dictates another expedient, by which life may be passed unprofitably away without the tediousness of many vacant hours. The art is, to fill the day with petty business, to have always something in hand which may raise curiosity, but not solicitude, and keep the mind in a state of action, but not of labor.

This art has for many years been practiced by my old friend Sober,[8] with wonderful success. Sober is a man of strong desires and quick imagination, so exactly balanced by the love of ease, that they can seldom stimulate him to any difficult undertaking; they have, however, so much power, that they will not suffer him to lie quite at rest, and though they do not make him sufficiently useful to others, they make him at least weary of himself.

Mr. Sober's chief pleasure is conversation; there is no end of his talk or his attention; to speak or to hear is equally pleasing; for he still fancies that he is teaching or learning something, and is free for the time from his own reproaches.

But there is one time at night when he must go home, that his friends may sleep; and another time in the morning, when all the world agrees to shut out interruption. These are the moments of which poor Sober trembles at the thought. But the misery of these tiresome intervals, he has many means of alleviating. He has persuaded himself that the manual arts are undeservedly overlooked; he has observed in many trades the effects of close thought, and just ratiocination. From speculation he proceeded to practice, and supplied himself with the tools of a carpenter, with which he mended his coal-box very successfully, and which he still continues to employ, as he finds occasion.

He has attempted at other times the crafts of the shoemaker, tinman, plumber, and potter; in all these arts he has failed, and resolves to qualify himself for them by better information. But his daily amusement is chemistry. He has a small furnace, which he employs in distillation, and which has long been the solace of his life. He draws oils and waters, and essences and spirits, which he knows to be of no use; sits and counts the drops as they come from his retort, and forgets that, while a drop is falling, a moment flies away.

Poor Sober! I have often teased him with reproof, and he has often promised reformation; for no man is so much open to conviction as the idler, but there is none on whom it operates so little. What will be the effect of this paper I know not; perhaps he will read it and laugh, and light the fire in his furnace; but my hope is that he will quit his trifles, and betake himself to rational and useful diligence.

Idler No. 32

[ON SLEEP]

Saturday, 25 November 1758

Among the innumerable mortifications that waylay human arrogance on every side may well be reckoned our ignorance of the most common objects and effects, a defect of which we become more sensible by every attempt to supply it. Vulgar and inactive minds confound familiarity with knowledge, and conceive themselves informed of the whole nature of things when they are shown their form or told their use; but the speculatist, who is not content with superficial views, harasses himself with fruitless curiosity, and still as he inquires more perceives only that he knows less.

8. Johnson's friends believed that the portrait of Sober was autobiographical.

Sleep is a state in which a great part of every life is passed. No animal has been yet discovered, whose existence is not varied with intervals of insensibility; and some late philosophers have extended the empire of sleep over the vegetable world.

Yet of this change so frequent, so great, so general, and so necessary, no searcher has yet found either the efficient or final cause; or can tell by what power the mind and body are thus chained down in irresistible stupefaction; or what benefits the animal receives from this alternate suspension of its active powers.

Whatever may be the multiplicity or contrariety of opinions upon this subject, nature has taken sufficient care that theory shall have little influence on practice. The most diligent inquirer is not able long to keep his eyes open; the most eager disputant will begin about midnight to desert his argument, and once in four and twenty hours, the gay and the gloomy, the witty and the dull, the clamorous and the silent, the busy and the idle, are all overpowered by the gentle tyrant, and all lie down in the equality of sleep.

Philosophy has often attempted to repress insolence by asserting that all conditions are leveled by death; a position which, however it may deject the happy, will seldom afford much comfort to the wretched. It is far more pleasing to consider that sleep is equally a leveler with death; that the time is never at a great distance, when the balm of rest shall be effused alike upon every head, when the diversities of life shall stop their operation, and the high and the low shall lie down together.

It is somewhere recorded of Alexander, that in the pride of conquests, and intoxication of flattery, he declared that he only perceived himself to be a man by the necessity of sleep. Whether he considered sleep as necessary to his mind or body it was indeed a sufficient evidence of human infirmity; the body which required such frequency of renovation gave but faint promises of immortality; and the mind which, from time to time, sunk gladly into insensibility had made no very near approaches to the felicity of the supreme and self-sufficient nature.

I know not what can tend more to repress all the passions that disturb the peace of the world than the consideration that there is no height of happiness or honor from which man does not eagerly descend to a state of unconscious repose; that the best condition of life is such that we contentedly quit its good to be disentangled from its evils; that in a few hours splendor fades before the eye and praise itself deadens in the ear; the senses withdraw from their objects, and reason favors the retreat.

What then are the hopes and prospects of covetousness, ambition and rapacity? Let him that desires most have all his desires gratified, he never shall attain a state which he can, for a day and a night, contemplate with satisfaction, or from which, if he had the power of perpetual vigilance, he would not long for periodical separations.

All envy would be extinguished if it were universally known that there are none to be envied, and surely none can be much envied who are not pleased with themselves. There is reason to suspect that the distinctions of mankind have more show than value when it is found that all agree to be weary alike of pleasures and of cares, that the powerful and the weak, the celebrated and obscure, join in one common wish, and implore from nature's hand the nectar of oblivion.

Such is our desire of abstraction from ourselves that very few are satisfied with the quantity of stupefaction which the needs of the body force upon the mind. Alexander himself added intemperance to sleep, and solaced with the fumes of wine the sovereignty of the world. And almost every man has some art by which he steals his thoughts away from his present state.

It is not much of life that is spent in close attention to any important duty. Many hours of every day are suffered to fly away without any traces left upon the intellects. We suffer phantoms to rise up before us, and amuse ourselves with the dance of airy images, which after a time we dismiss forever, and know not how we have been busied.

Many have no happier moments than those that they pass in solitude, abandoned to their own imagination, which sometimes puts sceptres in their hands or mitres on their heads, shifts the scene of pleasure with endless variety, bids all the forms of beauty sparkle before them, and gluts them with every change of visionary luxury.

It is easy in these semi-slumbers to collect all the possibilities of happiness, to alter the course of the sun, to bring back the past, and anticipate the future, to unite all the beauties of all seasons, and all the blessings of all climates, to receive and bestow felicity, and forget that misery is the lot of man. All this is a voluntary dream, a temporary recession from the realities of life to airy fictions; an habitual subjection of reason to fancy.

Others are afraid to be alone, and amuse themselves by a perpetual succession of companions, but the difference is not great; in solitude we have our dreams to ourselves, and in company we agree to dream in concert. The end sought in both is forgetfulness of ourselves.

Idler No. 84

[ON AUTOBIOGRAPHY]

Saturday, 24 November 1759

Biography is, of the various kinds of narrative writing, that which is most eagerly read, and most easily applied to the purposes of life.

In romances, when the wild field of possibility lies open to invention, the incidents may easily be made more numerous, the vicissitudes more sudden, and the events more wonderful; but from the time of life when fancy begins to be overruled by reason and corrected by experience, the most artful tale raises little curiosity when it is known to be false; though it may, perhaps, be sometimes read as a model of a neat or elegant style, not for the sake of knowing what it contains, but how it is written; or those that are weary of themselves, may have recourse to it as a pleasing dream, of which, when they awake, they voluntarily dismiss the images from their minds.

The examples and events of history press, indeed, upon the mind with the weight of truth; but when they are reposited in the memory, they are oftener employed for show than use, and rather diversify conversation than regulate life. Few are engaged in such scenes as give them opportunities of growing wiser by the downfall of statesmen or the defeat of generals. The stratagems of war, and the intrigues of courts, are read by far the greater part of mankind with the same indifference as the adventures of fabled heroes, or the revolutions of a fairy region. Between falsehood and useless truth there is little difference. As gold which he cannot spend will make no man rich, so knowledge which he cannot apply will make no man wise.

The mischievous consequences of vice and folly, of irregular desires and predominant passions, are best discovered by those relations which are leveled with the general surface of life, which tell not how any man became great, but how he was made happy; not how he lost the favor of his prince, but how he became discontented with himself.

Those relations are therefore commonly of most value in which the writer tells his own story. He that recounts the life of another, commonly dwells most upon conspicuous events, lessens the familiarity of his tale to increase its dignity, shows his favorite at a distance decorated and magnified like the ancient actors in their tragic dress, and endeavors to hide the man that he may produce a hero.

But if it be true which was said by a French prince, "that no man was a hero to the servants of his chamber," it is equally true that every man is yet less a hero to himself. He that is most elevated above the crowd by the importance of his employments or the reputation of his genius, feels himself affected by fame or business but as they influence his domestic life. The high and low, as they have the same faculties and the same senses, have no less similitude in their pains and pleasures. The sensations are the same in all, though produced by very different occasions. The prince feels the same pain when an invader seizes a province, as the farmer when a thief drives away his cow. Men thus equal in themselves will appear equal in honest and impartial biography; and those whom fortune or nature place at the greatest distance may afford instruction to each other.

The writer of his own life has at least the first qualification of an historian, the knowledge of the truth; and though it may be plausibly objected that his temptations to disguise it are equal to his opportunities of knowing it, yet I cannot but think that impartiality may be expected with equal confidence from him that relates the passages of his own life, as from him that delivers the transactions of another.

Certainty of knowledge not only excludes mistake but fortifies veracity. What we collect by conjecture, and by conjecture only can one man judge of another's motives or sentiments, is easily modified by fancy or by desire; as objects imperfectly discerned take forms from the hope or fear of the beholder. But that which is fully known cannot be falsified but with reluctance of understanding, and alarm of conscience; of understanding, the lover of truth; of conscience, the sentinel of virtue.

He that writes the life of another is either his friend or his enemy, and wishes either to exalt his praise or aggravate his infamy; many temptations to falsehood will occur in the disguise of passions, too specious[1] to fear much resistance. Love of virtue will animate panegyric, and hatred of wickedness embitter censure. The zeal of gratitude, the ardor of patriotism, fondness for an opinion, or fidelity to a party, may easily overpower the vigilance of a mind habitually well disposed, and prevail over unassisted and unfriended veracity.

But he that speaks of himself has no motive to falsehood or partiality except self-love, by which all have so often been betrayed, that all are on the watch against its artifices. He that writes an apology for[2] a single action, to confute an accusation, or recommend himself to favor, is indeed always to be suspected of favoring his own cause; but he that sits down calmly and voluntarily to review his life for the admonition of posterity, or to amuse himself, and leaves this account unpublished, may be commonly presumed to tell truth, since falsehood cannot appease his own mind, and fame will not be heard beneath the tomb.

---

1. "Plausible; superficially, not solidly right" (Johnson's   2. Defense of.
Dictionary).

Idler No. 97

[ON TRAVEL WRITING]

Saturday, 23 February 1760

It may, I think, be justly observed, that few books disappoint their readers more than the narrations of travelers. One part of mankind is naturally curious to learn the sentiments, manners, and condition of the rest; and every mind that has leisure or power to extend its views, must be desirous of knowing in what proportion Providence has distributed the blessings of nature or the advantages of art, among the several nations of the earth.

This general desire easily procures readers to every book from which it can expect gratification. The adventurer upon unknown coasts, and the describer of distant regions, is always welcomed as a man who has labored for the pleasure of others, and who is able to enlarge our knowledge and rectify our opinions; but when the volume is opened, nothing is found but such general accounts as leave no distinct idea behind them, or such minute enumerations as few can read with either profit or delight.

Every writer of travels should consider that, like all other authors, he undertakes either to instruct or please, or to mingle pleasure with instruction. He that instructs must offer to the mind something to be imitated or something to be avoided; he that pleases must offer new images to his reader, and enable him to form a tacit comparison of his own state with that of others.

The greater part of travelers tell nothing, because their method of traveling supplies them with nothing to be told. He that enters a town at night and surveys it in the morning, and then hastens away to another place, and guesses at the manners of the inhabitants by the entertainment which his inn afforded him, may please himself for a time with a hasty change of scenes, and a confused remembrance of palaces and churches; he may gratify his eye with variety of landscapes; and regale his palate with a succession of vintages; but let him be contented to please himself without endeavor to disturb others. Why should he record excursions by which nothing could be learned, or wish to make a show of knowledge which, without some power of intuition unknown to other mortals, he never could attain.

Of those who crowd the world with their itineraries,[1] some have no other purpose than to describe the face of the country; those who sit idle at home, and are curious to know what is done or suffered in distant countries, may be informed by one of these wanderers, that on a certain day he set out early with the caravan, and in the first hour's march saw, towards the south, a hill covered with trees, then passed over a stream which ran northward with a swift course, but which is probably dry in the summer months; that an hour after he saw something to the right which looked at a distance like a castle with towers, but which he discovered afterwards to be a craggy rock; that he then entered a valley in which he saw several trees tall and flourishing, watered by a rivulet not marked in the maps, of which he was not able to learn the name; that the road afterward grew stony, and the country uneven, where he observed among the hills many hollows worn by torrents, and was told that the road was passable only part of the year: that going on they found the remains of a building, once perhaps a fortress to secure the pass, or to restrain the robbers, of which the present inhabitants can give no other account than that it is haunted by fairies; that

1. Travel books.

they went to dine at the foot of a rock, and traveled the rest of the day along the banks of a river, from which the road turned aside towards evening, and brought them within sight of a village, which was once a considerable town, but which afforded them neither good victuals nor commodious lodging.

Thus he conducts his reader through wet and dry, over rough and smooth, without incidents, without reflection; and, if he obtains his company for another day, will dismiss him again at night equally fatigued with a like succession of rocks and streams, mountains and ruins.

This is the common style of those sons of enterprise, who visit savage countries, and range through solitude and desolation; who pass a desert, and tell that it is sandy; who cross a valley, and find that it is green. There are others of more delicate sensibility, that visit only the realms of elegance and softness; that wander through Italian palaces, and amuse the gentle reader with catalogues of pictures; that hear masses in magnificent churches, and recount the number of the pillars or variegations of the pavement. And there are yet others who, in disdain of trifles, copy inscriptions elegant and rude, ancient and modern; and transcribe into their book the walls of every edifice, sacred or civil. He that reads these books must consider his labor as its own reward; for he will find nothing on which attention can fix, or which memory can retain.

He that would travel for the entertainment of others should remember that the great object of remark is human life. Every nation has something peculiar in its manufactures, its works of genius, its medicines, its agriculture, its customs, and its policy. He only is a useful traveler who brings home something by which his country may be benefited; who procures some supply of want or some mitigation of evil, which may enable his readers to compare their condition with that of others, to improve it whenever it is worse, and whenever it is better to enjoy it.

A Dictionary of the English Language

Johnson's *Dictionary* struck its first readers as a nearly superhuman accomplishment; it seems one still. "A dictionary of the English language," observed one early reviewer, had never before "been attempted with the least degree of success"; the closest antecedents to Johnson's project were the national dictionaries of France and Italy, and these had been composed by whole academies of scholars, working collectively over the course of decades. Here, by contrast, was the seven years' labor of a single author (aided only by six part-time amanuenses): 40,000 words defined with unprecedented exactitude, and illustrated with more than 114,000 passages drawn from English prose and poetry of the previous 250 years. Ninety years earlier, members of the newly founded Royal Society for Improving Natural Knowledge had dreamed of such a resource; Johnson produced it by empirical methods much like the ones they promulgated. He spent his first years on the project accumulating data, rereading the English writers he valued most, marking any passage that strikingly illuminated the workings of a particular word. He then worked from this heap of collected evidence to the fine-honed, sharply distinguished conclusions of his definitions. The results have been variously and accurately described as the first standard English dictionary; as one of the final fruits of Renaissance humanism; as a commonplace-book (or database) of important English writing from Sidney to Pope; as a massive map of its author's mind. The key to that map resides in the *Dictionary*'s Preface, where Johnson measures the grandeur of his aspirations against the limitations of his achievement. In this mix of personal memoir and linguistic meditation, lexicography becomes a local instance of the vanity of human wishes. Human language, massive, metamorphic, and intractable, overmatches the human desire to codify and contain it, to fix it once and for all.

from A Dictionary of the English Language
from *Preface*
[ON METHOD]

It is the fate of those who toil at the lower employments of life to be rather driven by the fear of evil than attracted by the prospect of good; to be exposed to censure, without hope of praise; to be disgraced by miscarriage or punished for neglect, where success would have been without applause and diligence without reward.

Among these unhappy mortals is the writer of dictionaries; whom mankind have considered not as the pupil but the slave of science, the pioneer[1] of literature, doomed only to remove rubbish and clear obstructions from the paths through which learning and genius press forward to conquest and glory, without bestowing a smile on the humble drudge that facilitates their progress. Every other author may aspire to praise; the lexicographer can only hope to escape reproach, and even this negative recompense has been yet granted to very few.

I have, notwithstanding this discouragement, attempted a dictionary of the English language which, while it was employed in the cultivation of every species of literature, has itself been hitherto neglected; suffered to spread, under the direction of chance, into wild exuberance; resigned to the tyranny of time and fashion; and exposed to the corruptions of ignorance, and caprices of innovation.

When I took the first survey of my undertaking, I found our speech copious without order, and energetic without rules: wherever I turned my view, there was perplexity to be disentangled and confusion to be regulated; choice was to be made out of boundless variety, without any established principle of selection; adulterations were to be detected without a settled test of purity; and modes of expression to be rejected or received without the suffrages[2] of any writers of classical reputation or acknowledged authority.

Having therefore no assistance but from general grammar, I applied myself to the perusal of our writers; and, noting whatever might be of use to ascertain or illustrate any word or phrase, accumulated in time the materials of a dictionary, which, by degrees, I reduced to method, establishing to myself in the progress of the work such rules as experience and analogy suggested to me; experience, which practice and observation were continually increasing; and analogy, which, though in some words obscure, was evident in others.

[ON DEFINITIONS AND EXAMPLES]

That part of my work on which I expect malignity most frequently to fasten is the explanation; in which I cannot hope to satisfy those who are perhaps not inclined to be pleased, since I have not always been able to satisfy myself. To interpret a language by itself is very difficult; many words cannot be explained by synonyms because the idea signified by them has not more than one appellation; nor by paraphrase, because simple ideas cannot be described. When the nature of things is unknown, or the notion unsettled and indefinite, and various in various minds, the words by which such notions are conveyed or such things denoted will be ambiguous and perplexed. And such is the fate of hapless lexicography that not only darkness, but light,

---

1. "One whose business is to level the road, throw up works, or sink mines in military operations" (Johnson's *Dictionary*).   2. Votes, testimonies.

impedes and distresses it; things may be not only too little, but too much known, to be happily illustrated. To explain requires the use of terms less abstruse than that which is to be explained, and such terms cannot always be found; for as nothing can be proved but by supposing something intuitively known and evident without proof, so nothing can be defined but by the use of words too plain to admit a definition.

Other words there are, of which the sense is too subtle and evanescent to be fixed in a paraphrase; such are all those which are by the grammarians termed expletives, and, in dead languages, are suffered to pass for empty sounds, of no other use than to fill a verse or to modulate a period,[1] but which are easily perceived in living tongues to have power and emphasis, though it be sometimes such as no other form of expression can convey. * * *

The solution of all difficulties and the supply of all defects must be sought in the examples subjoined to the various senses of each word, and ranged according to the time of their authors.

When first I collected these authorities, I was desirous that every quotation should be useful to some other end than the illustration of a word; I therefore extracted from philosophers principles of science; from historians remarkable facts; from chemists complete processes; from divines striking exhortations; and from poets beautiful descriptions. Such is design while it is yet at a distance from execution. When the time called upon me to range this accumulation of elegance and wisdom into an alphabetical series, I soon discovered that the bulk of my volumes would fright away the student, and was forced to depart from my scheme of including all that was pleasing or useful in English literature, and reduce my transcripts very often to clusters of words in which scarcely any meaning is retained; thus to the weariness of copying, I was condemned to add the vexation of expunging. Some passages I have yet spared which may relieve the labor of verbal searches, and intersperse with verdure and flowers the dusty deserts of barren philology.

The examples, thus mutilated, are no longer to be considered as conveying the sentiments or doctrine of their authors; the word for the sake of which they are inserted, with all its appendant clauses, has been carefully preserved; but it may sometimes happen, by hasty detruncation, that the general tendency of the sentence may be changed: the divine may desert his tenets, or the philosopher his system.

Some of the examples have been taken from writers who were never mentioned as masters of elegance or models of style; but words must be sought where they are used; and in what pages, eminent for purity, can terms of manufacture or agriculture be found? Many quotations serve no other purpose than that of proving the bare existence of words, and are therefore selected with less scrupulousness than those which are to teach their structures and relations.

My purpose was to admit no testimony of living authors, that I might not be misled by partiality, and that none of my cotemporaries might have reason to complain; nor have I departed from this resolution but when some performance of uncommon excellence excited my veneration, when my memory supplied me, from late books, with an example that was wanting, or when my heart, in the tenderness of friendship, solicited admission for a favorite name.

So far have I been from any care to grace my pages with modern decorations that I have studiously endeavored to collect examples and authorities from the writers before the Restoration, whose works I regard as "the wells of English undefiled,"[2] as

---

1. Clause or sentence.

2. Johnson quotes Spenser's praise of Chaucer in *The Faerie Queene* (4.2.2).

the pure sources of genuine diction. Our language, for almost a century, has, by the concurrence of many causes, been gradually departing from its original Teutonic character, and deviating towards a Gallic structure and phraseology, from which it ought to be our endeavor to recall it by making our ancient volumes the groundwork of style, admitting among the additions of later times only such as may supply real deficiencies, such as are readily adopted by the genius[3] of our tongue, and incorporate easily with our native idioms.

But as every language has a time of rudeness[4] antecedent to perfection, as well as of false refinement and declension, I have been cautious lest my zeal for antiquity might drive me into times too remote and crowd my book with words now no longer understood. I have fixed Sidney's work for the boundary beyond which I make few excursions. From the authors which rose in the time of Elizabeth, a speech might be formed adequate to all the purposes of use and elegance. If the language of theology were extracted from Hooker and the translation of the Bible; the terms of natural knowledge[5] from Bacon; the phrases of policy, war, and navigation from Raleigh; the dialect of poetry and fiction from Spenser and Sidney; and the diction of common life from Shakespeare, few ideas would be lost to mankind for want of English words in which they might be expressed.

It is not sufficient that a word is found unless it be so combined as that its meaning is apparently[6] determined by the tract[7] and tenor of the sentence; such passages I have therefore chosen, and when it happened that any author gave a definition of a term or such an explanation as is equivalent to a definition, I have placed his authority as a supplement to my own, without regard to the chronological order that is otherwise observed.

Some words, indeed, stand unsupported by any authority, but they are commonly derivative nouns or adverbs, formed from their primitives by regular and constant analogy, or names of things seldom occurring in books, or words of which I have reason to doubt the existence.

There is more danger of censure from the multiplicity than paucity of examples; authorities will sometimes seem to have been accumulated without necessity or use, and perhaps some will be found which might, without loss, have been omitted. But a work of this kind is not hastily to be charged with superfluities: those quotations which to careless or unskillful perusers appear only to repeat the same sense will often exhibit to a more accurate examiner diversities of signification or, at least, afford different shades of the same meaning: one will show the word applied to persons, another to things; one will express an ill, another a good, and a third a neutral sense; one will prove the expression genuine from an ancient author; another will show it elegant from a modern: a doubtful authority is corroborated by another of more credit; an ambiguous sentence is ascertained by a passage clear and determinate; the word, how often soever repeated, appears with new associates and in different combinations, and every quotation contributes something to the stability or enlargement of the language. * * *

I have sometimes, though rarely, yielded to the temptation of exhibiting a genealogy of sentiments, by showing how one author copied the thoughts and diction of another: such quotations are indeed little more than repetitions which might justly be censured, did they not gratify the mind by affording a kind of intellectual history.

---

3. Native spirit.
4. Barbarism.
5. Science.

6. Clearly.
7. "Continuity; course; manner of process" (Johnson's *Dictionary*).

[CONCLUSION]

A large work is difficult because it is large, even though all its parts might singly be performed with facility; where there are many things to be done, each must be allowed its share of time and labor in the proportion only which it bears to the whole; nor can it be expected that the stones which form the dome of a temple should be squared and polished like the diamond of a ring.

Of the event of this work, for which, having labored it with so much application, I cannot but have some degree of parental fondness, it is natural to form conjectures. Those who have been persuaded to think well of my design will require that it should fix our language and put a stop to those alterations which time and chance have hitherto been suffered to make in it without opposition. With this consequence I will confess that I flattered myself for a while; but now begin to fear that I have indulged expectation which neither reason nor experience can justify. When we see men grow old and die at a certain time one after another, from century to century, we laugh at the elixir that promises to prolong life to a thousand years; and with equal justice may the lexicographer be derided, who being able to produce no example of a nation that has preserved their words and phrases from mutability, shall imagine that his dictionary can embalm his language and secure it from corruption and decay, that it is in his power to change sublunary nature, and clear the world at once from folly, vanity, and affectation.

With this hope, however, academies have been instituted to guard the avenues of their languages, to retain fugitives and repulse intruders; but their vigilance and activity have hitherto been vain; sounds are too volatile and subtle for legal restraints; to enchain syllables and to lash the wind are equally the undertakings of pride, unwilling to measure its desires by its strength. The French language has visibly changed under the inspection of the Academy,[1] the style of Amelot's translation of Father Paul is observed by Le Courayer to be *un peu passé;*[2] and no Italian will maintain that the diction of any modern writer is not perceptibly different from that of Boccace, Machiavel, or Caro.[3]

Total and sudden transformations of a language seldom happen; conquests and migrations are now very rare; but there are other causes of change which, though slow in their operation, and invisible in their progress, are perhaps as much superior to human resistance, as the revolutions of the sky, or intumescence of the tide. Commerce, however necessary, however lucrative, as it depraves the manners, corrupts the language; they that have frequent intercourse with strangers, to whom they endeavor to accommodate themselves, must in time learn a mingled dialect, like the jargon which serves the traffickers[4] on the Mediterranean and Indian coasts. This will not always be confined to the exchange, the warehouse, or the port, but will be communicated by degrees to other ranks of the people, and be at last incorporated with the current speech.

There are likewise internal causes equally forcible. The language most likely to continue long without alteration would be that of a nation raised a little, and but a little, above barbarity, secluded from strangers, and totally employed in procuring the

---

1. The French Academy, founded in 1635, undertook to preserve the purity of the language.
2. When in the 1730s Le Courayer retranslated Father Paolo Sarpi's *History of the Council of Trent,* he criticized his predecessor Amelot's version (1683) as "a little outdated."

3. Johnson refers to Giovanni Boccaccio (1313–1375), author of *The Decameron;* Niccolo Machiavelli (1469–1527), author of *The Prince;* and Annibale Caro (1507–1566), author of pastoral romances.
4. Merchants.

conveniences of life; either without books or, like some of the Mahometan countries, with very few: men thus busied and unlearned, having only such words as common use requires, would perhaps long continue to express the same notions by the same signs. But no such constancy can be expected in a people polished by arts and classed by subordination, where one part of the community is sustained and accommodated by the labor of the other. Those who have much leisure to think will always be enlarging the stock of ideas, and every increase of knowledge, whether real or fancied, will produce new words or combinations of words. When the mind is unchained from necessity, it will range after convenience; when it is left at large in the fields of speculation, it will shift opinions; as any custom is disused, the words that expressed it must perish with it; as any opinion grows popular, it will innovate speech in the same proportion as it alters practice.

As by the cultivation of various sciences a language is amplified, it will be more furnished with words deflected from their original sense; the geometrician will talk of a courtier's zenith, or the eccentric[5] virtue of a wild hero, and the physician of sanguine expectations and phlegmatic delays.[6] Copiousness of speech will give opportunities to capricious choice, by which some words will be preferred and others degraded; vicissitudes of fashion will enforce the use of new or extend the signification of known terms. The tropes of poetry will make hourly encroachments, and the metaphorical will become the current sense: pronunciation will be varied by levity or ignorance, and the pen must at length comply with the tongue; illiterate writers will at one time or other, by public infatuation, rise into renown, who, not knowing the original import of words, will use them with colloquial licentiousness, confound distinction, and forget propriety. As politeness increases, some expressions will be considered as too gross and vulgar for the delicate, others as too formal and ceremonious for the gay and airy; new phrases are therefore adopted, which must for the same reasons be in time dismissed. Swift, in his petty[7] treatise on the English language,[8] allows that new words must sometimes be introduced, but proposes that none should be suffered to become obsolete. But what makes a word obsolete more than general agreement to forbear it? and how shall it be continued when it conveys an offensive idea, or recalled again into the mouths of mankind when it has once become unfamiliar by disuse and unpleasing by unfamiliarity?

There is another cause of alteration more prevalent than any other, which yet in the present state of the world cannot be obviated. A mixture of two languages will produce a third distinct from both, and they will always be mixed where the chief part of education, and the most conspicuous accomplishment, is skill in ancient or in foreign tongues. He that has long cultivated another language will find its words and combinations crowd upon his memory; and haste or negligence, refinement or affectation, will obtrude borrowed terms and exotic expressions.

The great pest of speech is frequency of translation. No book was ever turned from one language into another without imparting something of its native idiom; this is the most mischievous and comprehensive innovation; single words may enter by thousands and the fabric of the tongue continue the same, but new phraseology changes much at once; it alters not the single stones of the building but the order of the columns.[9] If an academy should be established for the cultivation of our style, which I,

5. "Deviating from the center" (Johnson's *Dictionary*).
6. "Sanguine" and "phlegmatic" are medical terms relating to the doctrine of the four humors. Those in whom blood predominates are "sanguine" or optimistic, those ruled by phlegm are dull and sluggish.
7. Little.
8. *A Proposal for Correcting, Improving, and Ascertaining the English Tongue* (1712).
9. In classical architecture, the five "orders" are Doric, Ionic, Corinthian, Tuscan, and Composite.

who can never wish to see dependence multiplied, hope the spirit of English liberty will hinder or destroy, let them, instead of compiling grammars and dictionaries, endeavor, with all their influence, to stop the license of translators, whose idleness and ignorance, if it be suffered to proceed, will reduce us to babble a dialect of France.

If the changes that we fear be thus irresistible, what remains but to acquiesce with silence, as in the other insurmountable distresses of humanity? It remains that we retard what we cannot repel, that we palliate what we cannot cure. Life may be lengthened by care, though death cannot be ultimately defeated: tongues, like governments, have a natural tendency to degeneration; we have long preserved our constitution, let us make some struggles for our language.

In hope of giving longevity to that which its own nature forbids to be immortal, I have devoted this book, the labor of years, to the honor of my country, that we may no longer yield the palm[1] of philology without a contest to the nations of the Continent. The chief glory of every people arises from its authors: whether I shall add anything by my own writings to the reputation of English literature must be left to time: much of my life has been lost under the pressures of disease; much has been trifled away; and much has always been spent in provision for the day that was passing over me; but I shall not think my employment useless or ignoble if by my assistance foreign nations and distant ages gain access to the propagators of knowledge, and understand the teachers of truth; if my labors afford light to the repositories of science, and add celebrity to Bacon, to Hooker, to Milton, and to Boyle.

When I am animated by this wish, I look with pleasure on my book, however defective, and deliver it to the world with the spirit of a man that has endeavored well. That it will immediately become popular I have not promised to myself: a few wild blunders and risible absurdities, from which no work of such multiplicity was ever free, may for a time furnish folly with laughter, and harden ignorance in contempt; but useful diligence will at last prevail, and there never can be wanting some who distinguish desert,[2] who will consider that no dictionary of a living tongue ever can be perfect, since while it is hastening to publication some words are budding and some falling away; that a whole life cannot be spent upon syntax and etymology, and that even a whole life would not be sufficient; that he whose design includes whatever language can express, must often speak of what he does not understand; that a writer will sometimes be hurried by eagerness to the end, and sometimes faint with weariness under a task, which Scaliger compares to the labors of the anvil and the mine;[3] that what is obvious is not always known, and what is known is not always present; that sudden fits of inadvertency will surprise vigilance, slight avocations will seduce attention, and casual eclipses of the mind will darken learning; and that the writer shall often in vain trace his memory at the moment of need for that which yesterday he knew with intuitive readiness, and which will come uncalled into his thoughts tomorrow.

In this work, when it shall be found that much is omitted, let it not be forgotten that much likewise is performed; and though no book was ever spared out of tenderness to the author, and the world is little solicitous to know whence proceeded the faults of that which it condemns; yet it may gratify curiosity to inform it, that the *English Dictionary* was written with little assistance of the learned, and without any

---

1. Crown (symbol of victory).
2. Merit.
3. Johnson refers to a poem, *Against the Compilers of the*

Lexicons, by the great Renaissance scholar Joseph Justus Scaliger.

patronage of the great; not in the soft obscurities of retirement or under the shelter of academic bowers, but amidst inconvenience and distraction, in sickness and in sorrow. It may repress the triumph of malignant criticism to observe that if our language is not here fully displayed, I have only failed in an attempt which no human powers have hitherto completed. If the lexicons of ancient tongues, now immutably fixed and comprised in a few volumes, are yet, after the toil of successive ages, inadequate and delusive; if the aggregated knowledge, and cooperating diligence of the Italian academicians did not secure them from the censure of Beni;[4] if the embodied critics of France, when fifty years had been spent upon their work, were obliged to change its economy and give their second edition another form, I may surely be contented without the praise of perfection, which, if I could obtain, in this gloom of solitude, what would it avail me? I have protracted my work till most of those whom I wished to please have sunk into the grave, and success and miscarriage are empty sounds: I therefore dismiss it with frigid tranquility, having little to fear or hope from censure or from praise.

[SOME ENTRIES][1]

FUNK. n.s. A stink. A low word.

FÚNNEL. n.s. [*infundibulum*, Latin; whence *fundible*, *fundle*, *funnel*.]

1. An inverted hollow cone with a pipe descending from it, through which liquors are poured into vessels with narrow mouths; a tundish.

    If you pour a glut of water upon a bottle, it receives little of it; but with a *funnel*, and by degrees, you shall fill many of them.

    —Ben. Jonson's *Discoveries*

    Some the long *funnel*'s curious mouth extend,
    Through which ingested meats with ease descend.

    —Blackmore

    The outward ear or auricula is made hollow, and contracted by degrees, to draw the sound inward, to take in as much as may be of it, as we use a *funnel* to pour liquor into any vessel.

    —Ray on the Creation

2. A pipe or passage of communication.

    Towards the middle are two large *funnels*, bored through the roof of the grotto, to let in light or fresh air.

    —Addison

FÚTURE. n.s. [from the adjective.] Time to come; somewhat to happen hereafter.

    Thy letters have transported me beyond
    This ign'rant present time; and I feel now
    The *future* in the instant.

    —Shakespeare's *Macbeth*

---

4. Paolo Beni criticized the Italian dictionary published in 1612 by the Accademia della Crusca.
1. All entries are from the fourth edition of Johnson's *Dictionary* (1773), the last which Johnson prepared. Each entry is presented complete, with etymology, definitions, illustrations.

The mind, once jaded by an attempt above its power, either is disabled for the *future*, or else checks at any vigorous undertaking ever after.

—Locke

IMAGINÁTION. n.s. [*imaginatio*, Lat. *imagination*, Fr. from *imagine*.]

1. Fancy; the power of forming ideal pictures; the power of representing things absent to one's self or others.

> *Imagination* I understand to be the representation of an individual thought. Imagination is of three kinds: joined with belief of that which is to come; joined with memory of that which is past; and of things present, or as if they were present: for I comprehend in this imagination feigned and at pleasure, as if one should imagine such a man to be in the vestments of a pope, or to have wings.
>
> —Bacon

> Our simple apprehension of corporal objects, if present, is sense; if absent, *imagination:* when we would perceive a material object, our fancies present us with its idea.
>
> —Glanville

> O whither shall I run, or which way fly
> The sight of this so horrid spectacle,
> Which erst my eyes beheld, and yet behold!
> For dire *imagination* still pursues me.
>
> —Milton

> Where beams of warm *imagination* play,
> The memory's soft figures melt away.
>
> —Pope

2. Conception; image in the mind; idea.

> Sometimes despair darkens all her *imaginations;* sometimes the active passion of love cheers and clears her invention.
>
> —Sidney

> Princes have but their titles for their glories,
> An outward honor for an inward toil;
> And, for unfelt *imaginations,*
> They often feel a world of restless cares.
>
> —Shakespeare, *Richard III*

> Better I were distract,
> So should my thoughts be severed from my griefs;
> And woes, by wrong *imaginations,* lose
> The knowledge of themselves.
>
> —Shakespeare, *King Lear*

> His *imaginations* were often as just as they were bold and strong.
>
> —Dennis

3. Contrivance; scheme.

> Thou hast seen all their vengeance, and all their *imaginations* against me.
>
> —Bible (Lamentations 3.60)

4. An unsolid or fanciful opinion.

We are apt to think that space, in itself, is actually boundless; to which *imagination*, the idea of space, of itself leads us.

—Locke

JÚDGMENT. n.s. [*jugement*, Fr.]

1. The power of discerning the relations between one term or one proposition and another.

> O *judgment!* thou art fled to brutish beasts,
> And men have lost their reason.

—Shakespeare, *Julius Caesar*

> The faculty, which God has given man to supply the want of certain knowledge, is *judgment*, whereby the mind takes any proposition to be true or false, without perceiving a demonstrative evidence in the proofs.

—Locke

> *Judgment* is that whereby we join ideas together by affirmation or negation; so, this tree is high.

—Watts

2. Doom; the right or power of passing judgment.

> If my suspect be false, forgive me, God;
> For *judgment* only doth belong to thee.

—Shakespeare, *Henry VI*

3. The act of exercising judicature; judicatory.

> They gave *judgment* upon him.

—Bible (2 Kings)

> When thou, O Lord, shalt stand disclosed
> In majesty severe,
> And sit in *judgment* on my soul,
> O how shall I appear?

—Addison's *Spectator*

4. Determination; decision.

> Where distinctions or identities are purely material, the *judgment* is made by the imagination, otherwise by the understanding.

—Glanville's *Scepsis*

> We shall make a certain *judgment* what kind of dissolution that earth was capable of.

—Burnet's *Theory*

> Reason ought to accompany the exercise of our senses, whenever we would form a just *judgment* of things proposed to our inquiry.

—Watts

5. The quality of distinguishing propriety and impropriety; criticism.

> *Judgment*, a cool and slow faculty, attends not a man in the rapture of poetical composition.

—Dennis

> 'Tis with our *judgments* as our watches, none
> Go just alike; yet each believes his own.

—Pope

6. Opinion; notion.

> I see men's *judgments* are
> A parcel of their fortunes, and things outward
> Draw the inward quality after them,
> To suffer all alike.
>
> —Shakespeare, *Antony and Cleopatra*

> When she did think my master loved her well,
> She, in my *judgment*, was as fair as you.
>
> —Shakespeare

7. Sentence against a criminal.

> When he was brought again to th' bar, to hear
> His knell rung out, his *judgment*, he was stirred
> With agony.
>
> —Shakespeare, *Henry VIII*

> The chief priests informed me, desiring to have *judgment* against him.
>
> —Bible (Acts 25.15)

> On Adam last this *judgment* he pronounced.
>
> —Milton

8. Condemnation. This is a theological use.

> The *judgment* was by one to condemnation; but the free gift is of many offenses unto justification.
>
> —Bible (Romans 5.16)

> The precepts, promises, and threatenings of the Gospel will rise up in *judgment* against us, and the articles of our faith will be so many articles of accusation.
>
> —Tillotson

9. Punishment inflicted by Providence, with reference to some particular crime.

> This *judgment* of the heavens that makes us tremble,
> Touches us not with pity.
>
> —Shakespeare, *King Lear*

> We cannot be guilty of greater uncharitableness, than to interpret afflictions as punishments and *judgments*: it aggravates the evil to him who suffers, when he looks upon himself as the mark of divine vengeance.
>
> —Addison's *Spectator*

10. Distribution of justice.

> The Jews made insurrection against Paul, and brought him to the *judgment* seat.
>
> —Bible (Acts 18.12)

> Your dishonor
> Mangles true *judgment*, and bereaves the state
> Of that integrity which should become it.
>
> —Shakespeare's *Coriolanus*

> In *judgments* between rich and poor, consider not what the poor man needs, but what is his own.
>
> —Taylor

> A bold and wise petitioner goes strait to the throne and *judgment* seat of the monarch.
>
> —Arbuthnot and Pope

11. Judiciary law; statute.

> If ye hearken to these *judgments,* and keep and do them, the Lord thy God shall keep unto thee the covenant.
>
> —Bible (Deuteronomy)

12. The last doom.

> The dreadful *judgment* day
> So dreadful will not be as was his sight.
>
> —Shakespeare's *Henry VI*

KNACK. n.s.

1. A little machine; a petty contrivance; a toy.

> When I was young, I was wont
> To load my she with *knacks:* I would have ransacked
> The peddler's silken treasury, and have poured it
> To her acceptance.
>
> —Shakespeare's *Winter's Tale*

> For thee, fond boy,
> If I may ever know thou dost but sigh
> That thou no more shalt see this *knack,* as never
> I mean thou shalt, we'll bar thee from success.
>
> —Shakespeare

> This cap was moulded on a porringer,
> A velvet dish; fie, fie, 'tis lewd and filthy:
> Why 'tis a cockle, or a walnut shell,
> A *knack,* a toy, a trick, a baby's cap.
>
> —Shakespeare

> But is't not presumption to write verse to you,
> Who make the better poems of the two?
> For all these pretty *knacks* that you compose,
> Alas! what are they but poems in prose!
>
> —Denham

> He expounded both his pockets,
> And found a watch, with rings and lockets;
> A copper-plate, with almanacks
> Engraved upon't, with other *knacks*.
>
> —Hudibras

2. A readiness; an habitual facility; a lucky dexterity.

> I'll teach you the *knacks*
> Of eating of flax,
> And out of their noses
> Draw ribbands and posies.
>
> —Ben. Jonson's *Gypsies*

The *knack* of fast and loose passes with foolish people for a turn of wit; but they are not aware all this while of the desperate consequences of an ill habit.

—L'Estrange

There is a certain *knack* in conversation that gives a good grace by the manner and address.

—L'Estrange

Knaves, who in full assemblies have the *knack*
Of turning truth to lies, and white to black.

—Dryden

My author has a great *knack* at remarks: in the end he makes another, about our refining in controversy, and coming nearer and nearer to the church of Rome.

—Atterbury

The dean was famous in his time,
And had a kind of *knack* at rhyme.

—Swift

3. A nice trick.

For how should equal colors do the *knack*?
Chameleons who can paint in white and black?

—Pope

LEXICÓGRAPHER. n.s. [λεξικον and γραφειν; *lexicographe*, Fr.] A writer of dictionaries; a harmless drudge, that busies himself in tracing the original, and detailing the signification of words.

Commentators and *lexicographers* acquainted with the Syriac language, have given these hints in their writings on scripture.

—Watt's *Improvement of the Mind*

SÚBSTANCE. n.s. [*substance*, Fr.; *substantia*, Lat.]

1. Being; something existing; something of which we can say that it is.

Since then the soul works by herself alone,
Springs not from sense, nor humors well agreeing,
Her nature is peculiar, and her own;
She is a *substance*, and a perfect being.

—Davies

The strength of gods,
And this empyreal *substance* cannot fail.

—Milton

2. That which supports accidents.

What creatures there inhabit, of what mold,
And *substance*.

—Milton

Every being is considered as subsisting in and by itself, and then it is called a *substance*; or it subsists in and by another, and then it is called a mode or manner of being.

—Watts

3. The essential part.

> It will serve our turn to comprehend the *substance*, without confining ourselves to scrupulous exactness in form.
>
> —Digby

> This edition is the same in *substance* with the Latin.
>
> —Burn

> They are the best epitomes, and let you see with one cast of the eye the *substance* of a hundred pages.
>
> —Addison

4. Something real, not imaginary; something solid, not empty.

> Shadows tonight
> Have struck more terror to the soul of Richard,
> Than can the *substance* of ten thousand soldiers
> Armed in proof and led by shallow Richmond.
>
> —Shakespeare

> He the future evil shall no less
> In apprehension than in *substance* feel.
>
> —Milton

> Heroic virtue did his actions guide,
> And he the *substance*, not th' appearance chose:
> To rescue one such friend he took more pride,
> Than to destroy whole thousands of such foes.
>
> —Dryden

> God is no longer to be worshipped and believed in as a god foreshowing and assuring by types, but as a god who has performed the *substance* of what he promised.
>
> —Nelson

5. Body; corporeal nature.

> Between the parts of opaque and colored bodies are many spaces, either empty or replenished with mediums of other densities; as water between the tinging corpuscles wherewith any liquor is impregnated, air between the aqueous globules that constitute clouds or mists, and for the most part spaces void of both air and water; but yet perhaps not wholly void of all *substance* between the parts of hard bodies.
>
> —Newton

> The qualities of plants are more various than those of animal *substances*.
>
> —Arbuthnot on Aliments

> There may be a great and constant cough, with an extraordinary discharge of phlegmatic matter, while, notwithstanding, the *substance* of the lungs remains sound.
>
> —Blackmore

6. Wealth; means of life.

> He hath eaten me out of house and home, and hath put all my *substance* into that fat belly of his, but I will have some of it out again.
>
> —Shakespeare's *Henry IV*

We are destroying many thousand lives, and exhausting our *substance*, but not for our own interest.

—Swift

VACÚITY. n.s. [*vacuitas*; from *vacuus*, Lat. *vacuité*, Fr.]

1. Emptiness; state of being unfilled.

Hunger is such a state of *vacuity*, as to require a fresh supply of aliment.

—Arbuthnot

2. Space unfilled; space unoccupied.

In filling up *vacuities*, turning out shadows and ceremonies, by explicit prescription of substantial duties, which those shadows did obscurely represent.

—Hammond's *Fund*

He, that seat soon failing, meets
A vast *vacuity*.

—Milton

Body and space are quite different things, and a *vacuity* is interspersed among the particles of matter.

—Bentley

God, who alone can answer all our longings, and fill every *vacuity* of our soul, should entirely possess our heart.

—Rogers

Redeeming still at night these *vacuities* of the day.

—Fell

3. Inanity; want of reality.

The soul is seen, like other things, in the mirror of its effects: but if they'll run behind the glass to catch at it, their expectations will meet with *vacuity* and emptiness.

—Glanville

The History of Rasselas, Prince of Abyssinia

Johnson wrote *Rasselas* with his customary speed but under particular pressures. He composed the tale probably in late January 1759, possibly (as Boswell reports) during the "evenings of one week." This was the month of his mother's death; he may have made the book in order to help defray expenses and to articulate loss. His friend the painter Sir Joshua Reynolds later praised *Rasselas* for compassing within its few pages as much wisdom as though it had been written "by an angel or some superior being, whose comprehensive faculties could develop and lay open the inmost recesses of the human mind," and who could convey "in a few hours the experience of ages." The experience that *Rasselas* imparts, Johnson had expressed in other forms before. Rasselas is a prince born to a life of ease within the Happy Valley, a sequestered utopia of limitless luxuries; he suffers, though, from an oppressive sense of dissatisfaction, or (in a favorite Johnsonian term) "vacuity." Tantalized by his conviction that true happiness must lie elsewhere, he escapes the valley accompanied by his sister Nekayah and his mentor Imlac, only to find his own propensity for misplaced hopes, unfulfilled plans, and ineffectual wishes mirrored in the unhappy lives of nearly every mortal he meets with. Early in the tale, just before effecting his escape, Rasselas asks Imlac to tell the story of his own life, lived mostly in the larger world. In his reminiscences, Imlac gently sketches the cycles of desire and disillusion that the prince and princess will shortly experience for themselves.

from The History of Rasselas, Prince of Abyssinia
Chapter 8. The History of Imlac

The close of the day is, in the regions of the torrid zone, the only season of diversion and entertainment, and it was therefore mid-night before the music ceased, and the princesses retired. Rasselas then called for his companion and required him to begin the story of his life.

"Sir," said Imlac, "my history will not be long: the life that is devoted to knowledge passes silently away, and is very little diversified by events. To talk in public, to think in solitude, to read and to hear, to inquire, and answer inquiries, is the business of a scholar. He wanders about the world without pomp or terror, and is neither known nor valued but by men like himself.

"I was born in the kingdom of Goiama, at no great distance from the fountain of the Nile. My father was a wealthy merchant, who traded between the inland countries of Africk and the ports of the Red Sea. He was honest, frugal and diligent, but of mean sentiments, and narrow comprehension: he desired only to be rich, and to conceal his riches, lest he should be spoiled[1] by the governors of the province."

"Surely," said the prince, "my father must be negligent of his charge, if any man in his dominions dares take that which belongs to another. Does he not know that kings are accountable for injustice permitted as well as done? If I were emperor, not the meanest of my subjects should be oppressed with impunity. My blood boils when I am told that a merchant durst not enjoy his honest gains for fear of losing them by the rapacity of power. Name the governor who robbed the people, that I may declare his crimes to the emperor."

"Sir," said Imlac, "your ardor is the natural effect of virtue animated by youth: the time will come when you will acquit your father, and perhaps hear with less impatience of the governor. Oppression is, in the Abyssinian dominions, neither frequent nor tolerated; but no form of government has been yet discovered, by which cruelty can be wholly prevented. Subordination supposes power on one part and subjection on the other; and if power be in the hands of men, it will sometimes be abused. The vigilance of the supreme magistrate may do much, but much will still remain undone. He can never know all the crimes that are committed, and can seldom punish all that he knows."

"This," said the prince, "I do not understand, but I had rather hear thee than dispute. Continue thy narration."

"My father," proceeded Imlac, "originally intended that I should have no other education, than such as might qualify me for commerce; and discovering in me great strength of memory, and quickness of apprehension, often declared his hope that I should be some time the richest man in Abyssinia."

"Why," said the prince, "did thy father desire the increase of his wealth, when it was already greater than he durst discover or enjoy? I am unwilling to doubt thy veracity, yet inconsistencies cannot both be true."

"Inconsistencies," answered Imlac, "cannot both be right, but, imputed to man, they may both be true. Yet diversity is not inconsistency. My father might expect a time of greater security. However, some desire is necessary to keep life in motion, and he, whose real wants are supplied, must admit those of fancy."

"This," said the prince, "I can in some measure conceive. I repent that I interrupted thee."

1. Plundered.

"With this hope," proceeded Imlac, "he sent me to school; but when I had once found the delight of knowledge, and felt the pleasure of intelligence and the pride of invention, I began silently to despise riches, and determined to disappoint the purpose of my father, whose grossness of conception raised my pity. I was twenty years old before his tenderness would expose me to the fatigue of travel, in which time I had been instructed, by successive masters, in all the literature[2] of my native country. As every hour taught me something new, I lived in a continual course of gratifications; but, as I advanced towards manhood, I lost much of the reverence with which I had been used to look on my instructors; because, when the lesson was ended, I did not find them wiser or better than common men.

"At length my father resolved to initiate me in commerce, and, opening one of his subterranean treasuries, counted out ten thousand pieces of gold. 'This, young man,' said he, 'is the stock with which you must negotiate. I began with less than the fifth part, and you see how diligence and parsimony have increased it. This is your own to waste or to improve. If you squander it by negligence or caprice, you must wait for my death before you will be rich: if, in four years, you double your stock, we will thenceforward let subordination cease, and live together as friends and partners; for he shall always be equal with me, who is equally skilled in the art of growing rich.'

"We laid our money upon camels, concealed in bales of cheap goods, and traveled to the shore of the Red Sea. When I cast my eye on the expanse of waters my heart bounded like that of a prisoner escaped. I felt an unextinguishable curiosity kindle in my mind, and resolved to snatch this opportunity of seeing the manners of other nations, and of learning sciences[3] unknown in Abyssinia.

"I remembered that my father had obliged me to the improvement of my stock, not by a promise which I ought not to violate, but by a penalty which I was at liberty to incur, and therefore determined to gratify my predominant desire, and by drinking at the fountains of knowledge, to quench the thirst of curiosity.

"As I was supposed to trade without connection with my father, it was easy for me to become acquainted with the master of a ship, and procure a passage to some other country. I had no motives of choice to regulate my voyage; it was sufficient for me that, wherever I wandered, I should see a country which I had not seen before. I therefore entered a ship bound for Surat, having left a letter for my father declaring my intention.

Chapter 9. The History of Imlac Continued.

"When I first entered upon the world of waters, and lost sight of land, I looked round about me with pleasing terror, and thinking my soul enlarged by the boundless prospect, imagined that I could gaze round for ever without satiety; but, in a short time, I grew weary of looking on barren uniformity, where I could only see again what I had already seen. I then descended into the ship, and doubted for a while whether all my future pleasures would not end like this in disgust and disappointment. 'Yet, surely,' said I, 'the ocean and the land are very different; the only variety of water is rest and motion, but the earth has mountains and valleys, deserts and cities: it is inhabited by men of different customs and contrary opinions; and I may hope to find variety in life, though I should miss it in nature.'

2. "Learning; skill in letters" (Johnson's *Dictionary*).   3. Modes of knowledge.

"With this thought I quieted my mind, and amused myself during the voyage; sometimes by learning from the sailors the art of navigation, which I have never practiced, and sometimes by forming schemes for my conduct in different situations, in not one of which I have been ever placed.

"I was almost weary of my naval amusements when we landed safely at Surat. I secured my money, and purchasing some commodities for show, joined myself to a caravan that was passing into the inland country. My companions, for some reason or other, conjecturing that I was rich, and, by my inquiries and admiration,[4] finding that I was ignorant, considered me as a novice whom they had a right to cheat, and who was to learn at the usual expense the art of fraud. They exposed me to the theft of servants, and the exaction of officers, and saw me plundered upon false pretenses, without any advantage to themselves, but that of rejoicing in the superiority of their own knowledge."

"Stop a moment," said the prince. "Is there such depravity in man, as that he should injure another without benefit to himself? I can easily conceive that all are pleased with superiority; but your ignorance was merely accidental, which, being neither your crime nor your folly, could afford them no reason to applaud themselves; and the knowledge which they had, and which you wanted, they might as effectually have shown by warning, as betraying you."

"Pride," said Imlac, "is seldom delicate, it will please itself with very mean advantages; and envy feels not its own happiness, but when it may be compared with the misery of others. They were my enemies because they grieved to think me rich, and my oppressors because they delighted to find me weak."

"Proceed," said the prince. "I doubt not of the facts which you relate, but imagine that you impute them to mistaken motives."

"In this company," said Imlac, "I arrived at Agra, the capital of Indostan, the city in which the great Mogul commonly resides. I applied myself to the language of the country, and in a few months was able to converse with the learned men; some of whom I found morose and reserved, and others easy and communicative; some were unwilling to teach another what they had with difficulty learned themselves; and some showed that the end of their studies was to gain the dignity of instructing.

"To the tutor of the young princes I recommended myself so much, that I was presented to the emperor as a man of uncommon knowledge. The emperor asked me many questions concerning my country and my travels; and though I cannot now recollect any thing that he uttered above the power of a common man, he dismissed me astonished at his wisdom, and enamored of his goodness.

"My credit was now so high, that the merchants, with whom I had traveled, applied to me for recommendations to the ladies of the court. I was surprised at their confidence of solicitation, and gently reproached them with their practices on the road. They heard me with cold indifference, and showed no tokens of shame or sorrow.

"They then urged their request with the offer of a bribe; but what I would not do for kindness I would not do for money; and refused them, not because they had injured me, but because I would not enable them to injure others; for I knew they would have made use of my credit to cheat those who should buy their wares.

4. "Wonder; the act of admiring or wondering" (Johnson's *Dictionary*).

"Having resided at Agra, till there was no more to be learned, I traveled into Persia, where I saw many remains of ancient magnificence, and observed many new accommodations[5] of life. The Persians are a nation eminently social, and their assemblies afforded me daily opportunities of remarking characters and manners, and of tracing human nature through all its variations.

"From Persia I passed into Arabia, where I saw a nation at once pastoral and warlike; who live without any settled habitation; whose only wealth is their flocks and herds; and who have yet carried on, through all ages, an hereditary war with all mankind, though they neither covet nor envy their possessions.

Chapter 10. Imlac's History Continued.
A Dissertation upon Poetry.

"Wherever I went, I found that poetry was considered as the highest learning, and regarded with a veneration somewhat approaching to that which man would pay to the angelic nature. And it yet fills me with wonder, that, in almost all countries, the most ancient poets are considered as the best: whether it be that every other kind of knowledge is an acquisition gradually attained, and poetry is a gift conferred at once; or that the first poetry of every nation surprised them as a novelty, and retained the credit by consent which it received by accident at first: or whether, as the province of poetry is to describe nature and passion,[6] which are always the same, the first writers took possession of the most striking objects for description, and the most probable occurrences for fiction, and left nothing to those that followed them, but transcription of the same events, and new combinations of the same images. Whatever be the reason, it is commonly observed that the early writers are in possession of nature, and their followers of art: that the first excel in strength and invention, and the latter in elegance and refinement.

"I was desirous to add my name to this illustrious fraternity. I read all the poets of Persia and Arabia, and was able to repeat by memory the volumes that are suspended in the mosque of Mecca. But I soon found that no man was ever great by imitation. My desire of excellence impelled me to transfer my attention to nature and to life. Nature was to be my subject, and men to be my auditors: I could never describe what I had not seen: I could not hope to move those with delight or terror, whose interests and opinions I did not understand.

"Being now resolved to be a poet, I saw every thing with a new purpose; my sphere of attention was suddenly magnified: no kind of knowledge was to be overlooked. I ranged mountains and deserts for images and resemblances, and pictured upon my mind every tree of the forest and flower of the valley. I observed with equal care the crags of the rock and the pinnacles of the palace. Sometimes I wandered along the mazes of the rivulet, and sometimes watched the changes of the summer clouds. To a poet nothing can be useless. Whatever is beautiful, and whatever is dreadful, must be familiar to his imagination: he must be conversant with all that is awfully[7] vast or elegantly little. The plants of the garden, the animals of the wood, the minerals of the earth, and meteors of the sky, must all concur to store his mind

5. "Conveniences, things requisite to ease or refreshment" (Johnson's *Dictionary*).
6. Nature: "the constitution and appearance of things"

(Johnson's *Dictionary*); Passion: "violent commotion of the mind" (Johnson's *Dictionary*).
7. Solemnly.

with inexhaustible variety: for every idea is useful for the enforcement or decoration of moral or religious truth; and he who knows most will have most power of diversifying his scenes, and of gratifying his reader with remote allusions and unexpected instruction.

"All the appearances of nature I was therefore careful to study, and every country which I have surveyed has contributed something to my poetical powers."

"In so wide a survey," said the prince, "you must surely have left much unobserved. I have lived, till now, within the circuit of these mountains, and yet cannot walk abroad without the sight of something which I had never beheld before, or never heeded."

"The business of a poet," said Imlac, "is to examine, not the individual, but the species; to remark general properties and large appearances: he does not number the streaks of the tulip, or describe the different shades in the verdure of the forest. He is to exhibit in his portraits of nature such prominent and striking features, as recall the original to every mind; and must neglect the minuter discriminations, which one may have remarked, and another have neglected, for those characteristics which are alike obvious to vigilance and carelessness.

"But the knowledge of nature is only half the task of a poet; he must be acquainted likewise with all the modes of life. His character requires that he estimate the happiness and misery of every condition; observe the power of all the passions in all their combinations, and trace the changes of the human mind as they are modified by various institutions and accidental influences of climate or custom, from the sprightliness of infancy to the despondence of decrepitude. He must divest himself of the prejudices of his age or country; he must consider right and wrong in their abstracted and invariable state; he must disregard present laws and opinions, and rise to general and transcendental truths, which will always be the same: he must therefore content himself with the slow progress of his name; condemn the applause of his own time, and commit his claims to the justice of posterity. He must write as the interpreter of nature, and the legislator of mankind, and consider himself as presiding over the thoughts and manners of future generations; as a being superior to time and place.

"His labor is not yet at an end: he must know many languages and many sciences; and, that his style may be worthy of his thoughts, must, by incessant practice, familiarize to himself every delicacy of speech and grace of harmony."

Chapter 11. Imlac's Narrative Continued. A Hint on Pilgrimage.

Imlac now felt the enthusiastic[8] fit, and was proceeding to aggrandize his own profession, when the prince cried out, "Enough! Thou hast convinced me, that no human being can ever be a poet. Proceed with thy narration."

"To be a poet," said Imlac, "is indeed very difficult." "So difficult," returned the prince, "that I will at present hear no more of his labors. Tell me whither you went when you had seen Persia."

"From Persia," said the poet, "I traveled through Syria, and for three years resided in Palestine, where I conversed with great numbers of the northern and western nations of Europe; the nations which are now in possession of all power and all

---

8. "Vehemently hot in any cause" (Johnson's *Dictionary*).

knowledge; whose armies are irresistible, and whose fleets command the remotest parts of the globe. When I compared these men with the natives of our own kingdom, and those that surround us, they appeared almost another order of beings. In their countries it is difficult to wish for any thing that may not be obtained: a thousand arts, of which we never heard, are continually laboring for their convenience and pleasure; and whatever their own climate has denied them is supplied by their commerce."

"By what means," said the prince, "are the Europeans thus powerful? or why, since they can so easily visit Asia and Africa for trade or conquest, cannot the Asiatics and Africans invade their coasts, plant colonies in their ports, and give laws to their natural princes? The same wind that carries them back would bring us thither."

"They are more powerful, Sir, than we," answered Imlac, "because they are wiser; knowledge will always predominate over ignorance, as man governs the other animals. But why their knowledge is more than ours, I know not what reason can be given, but the unsearchable will of the Supreme Being."

"When," said the prince with a sigh, "shall I be able to visit Palestine, and mingle with this mighty confluence of nations? Till that happy moment shall arrive, let me fill up the time with such representations as thou canst give me. I am not ignorant of the motive that assembles such numbers in that place, and cannot but consider it as the center of wisdom and piety, to which the best and wisest men of every land must be continually resorting."

"There are some nations," said Imlac, "that send few visitants[9] to Palestine; for many numerous and learned sects in Europe concur to censure pilgrimage as superstitious, or deride it as ridiculous."

"You know," said the prince, "how little my life has made me acquainted with diversity of opinions: it will be too long to hear the arguments on both sides; you, that have considered them, tell me the result."

"Pilgrimage," said Imlac, "like many other acts of piety, may be reasonable or superstitious, according to the principles upon which it is performed. Long journeys in search of truth are not commanded. Truth, such as is necessary to the regulation of life, is always found where it is honestly sought. Change of place is no natural cause of the increase of piety, for it inevitably produces dissipation of mind. Yet, since men go every day to view the fields where great actions have been performed, and return with stronger impressions of the event, curiosity of the same kind may naturally dispose us to view that country whence our religion had its beginning; and I believe no man surveys those awful scenes without some confirmation of holy resolutions. That the Supreme Being may be more easily propitiated in one place than in another, is the dream of idle superstition; but that some places may operate upon our own minds in an uncommon manner, is an opinion which hourly experience will justify. He who supposes that his vices may be more successfully combated in Palestine, will, perhaps, find himself mistaken, yet he may go thither without folly: he who thinks they will be more freely pardoned, dishonors at once his reason and religion."

"These," said the prince, "are European distinctions. I will consider them another time. What have you found to be the effect of knowledge? Are those nations happier than we?"

9. Pilgrims.

"There is so much infelicity," said the poet, "in the world, that scarce any man has leisure from his own distresses to estimate the comparative happiness of others. Knowledge is certainly one of the means of pleasure, as is confessed by the natural desire which every mind feels of increasing its ideas. Ignorance is mere privation, by which nothing can be produced: it is a vacuity in which the soul sits motionless and torpid for want of attraction; and, without knowing why, we always rejoice when we learn, and grieve when we forget. I am therefore inclined to conclude that, if nothing counteracts the natural consequence of learning, we grow more happy as our minds take a wider range.

"In enumerating the particular comforts of life we shall find many advantages on the side of the Europeans. They cure wounds and diseases with which we languish and perish. We suffer inclemencies of weather which they can obviate. They have engines for the dispatch of many laborious works, which we must perform by manual industry. There is such communication between distant places, that one friend can hardly be said to be absent from another. Their policy removes all public inconveniences: they have roads cut through their mountains, and bridges laid upon their rivers. And, if we descend to the privacies of life, their habitations are more commodious, and their possessions are more secure."

"They are surely happy," said the prince, "who have all these conveniences, of which I envy none so much as the facility with which separated friends interchange their thoughts."

"The Europeans," answered Imlac, "are less unhappy than we, but they are not happy. Human life is every where a state in which much is to be endured, and little to be enjoyed."

Chapter 12. The Story of Imlac Continued.

"I am not yet willing," said the prince, "to suppose that happiness is so parsimoniously distributed to mortals; nor can believe but that, if I had the choice of life, I should be able to fill every day with pleasure. I would injure no man, and should provoke no resentment: I would relieve every distress, and should enjoy the benedictions of gratitude. I would choose my friends among the wise, and my wife among the virtuous; and therefore should be in no danger from treachery, or unkindness. My children should, by my care, be learned and pious, and would repay to my age what their childhood had received. What would dare to molest him who might call on every side to thousands enriched by his bounty, or assisted by his power? And why should not life glide quietly away in the soft reciprocation of protection and reverence? All this may be done without the help of European refinements, which appear by their effects to be rather specious[1] than useful. Let us leave them and pursue our journey."

"From Palestine," said Imlac, "I passed through many regions of Asia; in the more civilized kingdoms as a trader, and among the barbarians of the mountains as a pilgrim. At last I began to long for my native country, that I might repose after my travels, and fatigues, in the places where I had spent my earliest years, and gladden my old companions with the recital of my adventures. Often did I figure to myself those, with whom I had sported away the gay hours of dawning life, sitting round me in its evening, wondering at my tales, and listening to my counsels.

1. "Showy; pleasing to the view" (Johnson's *Dictionary*).

"When this thought had taken possession of my mind, I considered every moment as wasted which did not bring me nearer to Abyssinia. I hastened into Egypt, and, notwithstanding my impatience, was detained ten months in the contemplation of its ancient magnificence, and in enquiries after the remains of its ancient learning. I found in Cairo a mixture of all nations; some brought thither by the love of knowledge, some by the hope of gain, and many by the desire of living after their own manner without observation, and of lying hid in the obscurity of multitudes: for, in a city, populous as Cairo, it is possible to obtain at the same time the gratifications of society, and the secrecy of solitude.

"From Cairo I traveled to Suez, and embarked on the Red Sea, passing along the coast till I arrived at the port from which I had departed twenty years before. Here I joined myself to a caravan and re-entered my native country.

"I now expected the caresses of my kinsmen, and the congratulations of my friends, and was not without hope that my father, whatever value he had set upon riches, would own with gladness and pride a son who was able to add to the felicity and honor of the nation. But I was soon convinced that my thoughts were vain. My father had been dead fourteen years, having divided his wealth among my brothers, who were removed to some other provinces. Of my companions the greater part was in the grave, of the rest some could with difficulty remember me, and some considered me as one corrupted by foreign manners.

"A man used to vicissitudes is not easily dejected. I forgot, after a time, my disappointment, and endeavored to recommend myself to the nobles of the kingdom: they admitted me to their tables, heard my story, and dismissed me. I opened a school, and was prohibited to teach. I then resolved to sit down in the quiet of domestic life, and addressed a lady that was fond of my conversation, but rejected my suit, because my father was a merchant.

"Wearied at last with solicitation and repulses, I resolved to hide myself for ever from the world, and depend no longer on the opinion or caprice of others. I waited for the time when the gate of the Happy Valley should open, that I might bid farewell to hope and fear: the day came; my performance was distinguished with favor, and I resigned myself with joy to perpetual confinement."

"Hast thou here found happiness at last?" said Rasselas. "Tell me without reserve; art thou content with thy condition? or, dost thou wish to be again wandering and inquiring? All the inhabitants of this valley celebrate their lot, and, at the annual visit of the emperor, invite others to partake of their felicity."

"Great prince," said Imlac, "I shall speak the truth: I know not one of all your attendants who does not lament the hour when he entered this retreat. I am less unhappy than the rest, because I have a mind replete with images, which I can vary and combine at pleasure. I can amuse my solitude by the renovation of the knowledge which begins to fade from my memory, and by recollection of the accidents of my past life. Yet all this ends in the sorrowful consideration, that my acquirements are now useless, and that none of my pleasures can be again enjoyed. The rest, whose minds have no impression but of the present moment, are either corroded by malignant passions, or sit stupid in the gloom of perpetual vacancy."

"What passions can infest those," said the prince, "who have no rivals? We are in a place where impotence precludes malice, and where all envy is repressed by community of enjoyments."

"There may be community," said Imlac, "of material possessions, but there can never be community of love or of esteem. It must happen that one will please more than another; he that knows himself despised will always be envious; and still more envious and malevolent, if he is condemned to live in the presence of those who despise him. The invitations, by which they allure others to a state which they feel to be wretched, proceed from the natural malignity of hopeless misery. They are weary of themselves, and of each other, and expect to find relief in new companions. They envy the liberty which their folly has forfeited, and would gladly see all mankind imprisoned like themselves.

"From this crime, however, I am wholly free. No man can say that he is wretched by my persuasion. I look with pity on the crowds who are annually soliciting admission to captivity, and wish that it were lawful for me to warn them of their danger."

"My dear Imlac," said the prince, "I will open to thee my whole heart. I have long meditated an escape from the Happy Valley. I have examined the mountains on every side, but find myself insuperably barred: teach me the way to break my prison; thou shalt be the companion of my flight, the guide of my rambles, the partner of my fortune, and my sole director in the *choice of life*."

"Sir," answered the poet, "your escape will be difficult, and, perhaps, you may soon repent your curiosity. The world, which you figure to yourself smooth and quiet as the lake in the valley, you will find a sea foaming with tempests, and boiling with whirlpools: you will be sometimes overwhelmed by the waves of violence, and sometimes dashed against the rocks of treachery. Amidst wrongs and frauds, competitions and anxieties, you will wish a thousand times for these seats of quiet, and willingly quit hope to be free from fear."

"Do not seek to deter me from my purpose," said the prince: "I am impatient to see what thou hast seen; and, since thou art thyself weary of the valley, it is evident, that thy former state was better than this. Whatever be the consequence of my experiment, I am resolved to judge with my own eyes of the various conditions of men, and then to make deliberately my *choice of life*."

"I am afraid," said Imlac, "you are hindered by stronger restraints than my persuasions; yet, if your determination is fixed, I do not counsel you to despair. Few things are impossible to diligence and skill."

1759   1759

The Plays of William Shakespeare

Johnson first proposed a new edition of Shakespeare's plays, without success, in 1745; he finally published one twenty tears later. In the intervening decades, his work on the *Dictionary* had made him (in Bertrand Bronson's phrase) "the greatest living authority on Shakespeare's diction," and had secured him such fame that the booksellers greeted his renewed Shakespeare proposal with enthusiasm rather than indifference. Even so, he found the work slow going; he promised completion in eighteen months and took nine years. Five major editions had appeared since the start of the century, and Johnson was alert to their many inadequacies. Earlier editors displayed a passion for emendation, for finding "printer's errors" everywhere in the text, and replacing them with overconfident conjectures as to what Shakespeare had really "meant" and wrote. Johnson opted more often to let things be: to take a passage as given, to discover its intention, to explain its success, or to analyze its failure. The same kind of scrutiny suffuses his Preface, in which he investigates how plays really operate upon their audience. In the process, he demolishes the critical criteria by which Shakespeare had long been deemed an inferior crafter of drama (albeit an inimitably inspired poet). Johnson's *Shakespeare* is distinctive for the energy of its thought and of its feeling; for the intensity of its grappling with the impact of tiny passages and of towering genius.

from *Preface*

["JUST REPRESENTATIONS OF GENERAL NATURE"]

That praises are without reason lavished on the dead, and that the honors due only to excellence are paid to antiquity, is a complaint likely to be always continued by those who, being able to add nothing to truth, hope for eminence from the heresies of paradox; or those who, being forced by disappointment upon consolatory expedients, are willing to hope from posterity what the present age refuses and flatter themselves that the regard which is yet denied by envy will be at last bestowed by time.

Antiquity, like every other quality that attracts the notice of mankind, has undoubtedly votaries that reverence it not from reason, but from prejudice. Some seem to admire indiscriminately whatever has been long preserved, without considering that time has sometimes cooperated with chance; all perhaps are more willing to honor past than present excellence; and the mind contemplates genius through the shades of age, as the eye surveys the sun through artificial opacity. The great contention of criticism is to find the faults of the moderns and the beauties of the ancients. While an author is yet living, we estimate his powers by his worst performance; and when he is dead, we rate them by his best.

To works, however, of which the excellence is not absolute and definite, but gradual and comparative; to works not raised upon principles demonstrative and scientific but appealing wholly to observation and experience, no other test can be applied than length of duration and continuance of esteem. What mankind have long possessed they have often examined and compared; and if they persist to value the possession, it is because frequent comparisons have confirmed opinion in its favor. As among the works of nature no man can properly call a river deep or a mountain high, without the knowledge of many mountains and many rivers; so, in the productions of genius, nothing can be styled excellent till it has been compared with other works of the same kind. Demonstration immediately displays its power and has nothing to hope or fear from the flux of years; but works tentative and experimental must be estimated by their proportion to the general and collective ability of man, as it is discovered in a long succession of endeavors. Of the first building that was raised, it might be with certainty determined that it was round or square, but whether it was spacious or lofty must have been referred to time. The Pythagorean scale of numbers was at once discovered to be perfect; but the poems of Homer we yet know not to transcend the common limits of human intelligence but by remarking that nation after nation, and century after century, has been able to do little more than transpose his incidents, new-name his characters, and paraphrase his sentiments.

The reverence due to writings that have long subsisted arises, therefore, not from any credulous confidence in the superior wisdom of past ages or gloomy persuasion of the degeneracy of mankind, but is the consequence of acknowledged and indubitable positions that what has been longest known has been most considered, and what is most considered is best understood.

The poet of whose works I have undertaken the revision[1] may now begin to assume the dignity of an ancient and claim the privilege of established fame and prescriptive veneration. He has long outlived his century, the term commonly fixed as the test of literary merit. Whatever advantages he might once derive from personal allusions, local customs, or temporary opinions have for many years been lost; and every topic of merriment or motive of sorrow which the modes of artificial[2] life afforded him now only obscure the scenes which they once illuminated. The effects of favor and competition are at an end; the tradition of his friendships and his enmities have perished; his works support no opinion with arguments nor supply any faction with invectives; they can neither indulge vanity nor gratify malignity, but are read without any other reason than the desire of pleasure and are therefore praised only as pleasure is obtained; yet, thus unassisted by interest or passion, they have passed through variations of taste and changes of manners, and, as they devolved from one generation to another, have received new honors at every transmission.

But because human judgment, though it be gradually gaining upon certainty, never becomes infallible; and approbation, though long continued, may yet be only the approbation of prejudice or fashion; it is proper to inquire by what peculiarities of excellence Shakespeare has gained and kept the favor of his countrymen.

Nothing can please many, and please long, but just representations of general nature. Particular manners can be known to few, and therefore few only can judge how nearly they are copied. The irregular combinations of fanciful invention may delight awhile by that novelty of which the common satiety of life sends us all in quest; but the pleasures of sudden wonder are soon exhausted, and the mind can only repose on the stability of truth.

Shakespeare is, above all writers, at least above all modern writers, the poet of nature, the poet that holds up to his readers a faithful mirror of manners and of life. His characters are not modified by the customs of particular places, unpracticed by the rest of the world; by the peculiarities of studies or professions which can operate but upon small numbers; or by the accidents of transient fashions or temporary opinions: they are the genuine progeny of common humanity, such as the world will always supply, and observation will always find. His persons act and speak by the influence of those general passions and principles by which all minds are agitated and the whole system of life is continued in motion. In the writings of other poets a character is too often an individual; in those of Shakespeare it is commonly a species.

It is from this wide extension of design that so much instruction is derived. It is this which fills the plays of Shakespeare with practical axioms and domestic wisdom. It was said of Euripides that every verse was a precept;[3] and it may be said of Shakespeare that from his works may be collected a system of civil and economical prudence.[4] Yet his real power is not shown in the splendor of particular

---

1. Edition.
2. "Made by art; not natural" (Johnson's *Dictionary*).
3. This observation was made by Cicero in his *Familiar*

Letters (16.8).
4. Public and private duty.

passages, but by the progress of his fable and the tenor of his dialogue; and he that tries to recommend him by select quotations will succeed like the pedant in Hierocles,[5] who, when he offered his house for sale, carried a brick in his pocket as a specimen.

It will not easily be imagined how much Shakespeare excels in accommodating his sentiments to real life but by comparing him with other authors. It was observed of the ancient schools of declamation that the more diligently they were frequented, the more was the student disqualified for the world, because he found nothing there which he should ever meet in any other place. The same remark may be applied to every stage but that of Shakespeare. The theater, when it is under any other direction, is peopled by such characters as were never seen, conversing in a language which was never heard, upon topics which will never arise in the commerce of mankind. But the dialogue of this author is often so evidently determined by the incident which produces it, and is pursued with so much ease and simplicity, that it seems scarcely to claim the merit of fiction, but to have been gleaned by diligent selection out of common conversation and common occurrences.

Upon every other stage the universal agent is love, by whose power all good and evil is distributed and every action quickened or retarded. To bring a lover, a lady, and a rival into the fable; to entangle them in contradictory obligations, perplex them with oppositions of interest, and harass them with violence of desires inconsistent with each other; to make them meet in rapture and part in agony, to fill their mouths with hyperbolical joy and outrageous sorrow, to distress them as nothing human ever was distressed, to deliver them as nothing human ever was delivered, is the business of a modern dramatist. For this, probability is violated, life is misrepresented, and language is depraved. But love is only one of many passions; and as it has no great influence upon the sum of life, it has little operation in the dramas of a poet who caught his ideas from the living world and exhibited only what he saw before him. He knew that any other passion, as it was regular or exorbitant, was a cause of happiness or calamity.

Characters thus ample and general were not easily discriminated and preserved, yet perhaps no poet ever kept his personages more distinct from each other. I will not say with Pope that every speech may be assigned to the proper speaker, because many speeches there are which have nothing characteristical; but, perhaps, though some may be equally adapted to every person, it will be difficult to find any that can be properly transferred from the present possessor to another claimant. The choice is right, when there is reason for choice.

Other dramatists can only gain attention by hyperbolical or aggravated[6] characters, by fabulous and unexampled excellence or depravity, as the writers of barbarous romances invigorated the reader by a giant and a dwarf; and he that should form his expectations of human affairs from the play, or from the tale, would be equally deceived. Shakespeare has no heroes; his scenes are occupied only by men, who act and speak as the reader thinks that he should himself have spoken or acted on the same occasion. Even where the agency is supernatural, the dialogue is level with life. Other writers disguise the most natural passions and most frequent incidents, so that he who contemplates them in the book will not know them in the world. Shakespeare approximates the remote and familiarizes the wonderful; the event which he

---

5. The critic Hierocles, writing in the 5th century A.D., tells this story in his commentary on Pythagoras.   6. Exaggerated.

represents will not happen but, if it were possible, its effects would probably be such as he has assigned; and it may be said that he has not only shown human nature as it acts in real exigences, but as it would be found in trials to which it cannot be exposed.

This, therefore, is the praise of Shakespeare, that his drama is the mirror of life; that he who has mazed his imagination in following the phantoms which other writers raise up before him may here be cured of his delirious ecstasies by reading human sentiments in human language, by scenes from which a hermit may estimate the transactions of the world and a confessor predict the progress of the passions.

[FAULTS; THE UNITIES]

Shakespeare with his excellencies has likewise faults, and faults sufficient to obscure and overwhelm any other merit. I shall show them in the proportion in which they appear to me, without envious malignity or superstitious veneration. No question can be more innocently discussed than a dead poet's pretensions to renown; and little regard is due to that bigotry which sets candor[1] higher than truth.

His first defect is that to which may be imputed most of the evil in books or in men. He sacrifices virtue to convenience and is so much more careful to please than to instruct that he seems to write without any moral purpose. From his writings indeed a system of social duty may be selected, for he that thinks reasonably must think morally; but his precepts and axioms drop casually from him; he makes no just distribution of good or evil, nor is always careful to show in the virtuous a disapprobation of the wicked; he carries his persons indifferently through right and wrong and at the close dismisses them without further care and leaves their examples to operate by chance. This fault the barbarity of his age cannot extenuate; for it is always a writer's duty to make the world better, and justice is a virtue independent on time or place.

The plots are often so loosely formed that a very slight consideration may improve them, and so carelessly pursued that he seems not always to comprehend his own design. He omits opportunities of instructing or delighting which the train of his story seems to force upon him, and apparently rejects those exhibitions which would be more affecting, for the sake of those which are more easy.

It may be observed that in many of his plays the latter part is evidently neglected. When he found himself near the end of his work and in view of his reward, he shortened the labor to snatch the profit. He therefore remits his efforts where he should most vigorously exert them, and his catastrophe is improbably produced or imperfectly represented.

He had no regard to distinction of time or place but gives to one age or nation, without scruple, the customs, institutions, and opinions of another, at the expense not only of likelihood but of possibility. These faults Pope has endeavored, with more zeal than judgment, to transfer to his imagined interpolators. We need not wonder to find Hector quoting Aristotle,[2] when we see the loves of Theseus and Hippolyta combined with the Gothic mythology of fairies.[3] Shakespeare, indeed, was not the only violator of chronology, for in the same age Sidney, who wanted not[4] the advantages of learning, has, in his Arcadia, confounded the pastoral with the feudal times, the days of innocence, quiet, and security, with those of turbulence, violence, and adventure.

---

1. "Sweetness of temper; kindness" (Johnson's *Dictionary*).
2. *Troilus and Cressida* 2.2.166–67.

3. This combination occurs in *A Midsummer Night's Dream*.
4. Did not lack.

In his comic scenes he is seldom very successful when he engages his characters in reciprocations of smartness and contests of sarcasm; their jests are commonly gross and their pleasantry licentious; neither his gentlemen nor his ladies have much delicacy nor are sufficiently distinguished from his clowns by any appearance of refined manners. Whether he represented the real conversation of his time is not easy to determine. The reign of Elizabeth is commonly supposed to have been a time of stateliness, formality, and reserve; yet perhaps the relaxations of that severity were not very elegant. There must, however, have been always some modes of gaiety preferable to others, and a writer ought to choose the best.

In tragedy his performance seems constantly to be worse as his labor is more. The effusions of passion which exigence forces out are for the most part striking and energetic; but whenever he solicits his invention or strains his faculties, the offspring of his throes is tumor, meanness, tediousness, and obscurity.

In narration he affects a disproportionate pomp of diction and a wearisome train of circumlocution and tells the incident imperfectly in many words which might have been more plainly delivered in few. Narration in dramatic poetry is naturally tedious, as it is unanimated and inactive and obstructs the progress of the action; it should therefore always be rapid and enlivened by frequent interruption. Shakespeare found it an encumbrance and, instead of lightening it by brevity, endeavored to recommend it by dignity and splendor.

His declamations or set speeches are commonly cold and weak, for his power was the power of nature; when he endeavored, like other tragic writers, to catch opportunities of amplification and, instead of inquiring what the occasion demanded, to show how much his stores of knowledge could supply, he seldom escapes without the pity or resentment of his reader.

It is incident to him to be now and then entangled with an unwieldy sentiment, which he cannot well express and will not reject; he struggles with it awhile and, if it continues stubborn, comprises it in words such as occur and leaves it to be disentangled and evolved by those who have more leisure to bestow upon it.

Not that always where the language is intricate the thought is subtle, or the image always great where the line is bulky; the equality of words to things is very often neglected, and trivial sentiments and vulgar ideas disappoint the attention to which they are recommended by sonorous epithets and swelling figures.[5]

But the admirers of this great poet have most reason to complain when he approaches nearest to his highest excellence and seems fully resolved to sink them in dejection and mollify them with tender emotions by the fall of greatness, the danger of innocence, or the crosses[6] of love. What he does best, he soon ceases to do. He is not long soft and pathetic without some idle conceit[7] or contemptible equivocation. He no sooner begins to move than he counteracts himself; and terror and pity, as they are rising in the mind, are checked and blasted by sudden frigidity.

A quibble[8] is to Shakespeare what luminous vapors are to the traveler; he follows it at all adventures; it is sure to lead him out of his way and sure to engulf him in the mire. It has some malignant power over his mind, and its fascinations are irresistible. Whatever be the dignity or profundity of his disquisition, whether he be enlarging knowledge or exalting affection, whether he be amusing attention with incidents or enchaining it in suspense, let but a quibble spring up before him and he leaves his

---

5. Figures of speech.
6. Obstacles, vexations.

7. Play on words.
8. Pun.

work unfinished. A quibble is the golden apple for which he will always turn aside from his career or stoop from his elevation.[9] A quibble, poor and barren as it is, gave him such delight that he was content to purchase it by the sacrifice of reason, propriety, and truth. A quibble was to him the fatal Cleopatra for which he lost the world and was content to lose it.

It will be thought strange that in enumerating the defects of this writer I have not yet mentioned his neglect of the unities, his violation of those laws which have been instituted and established by the joint authority of poets and critics.

For his other deviations from the art of writing, I resign him to critical justice without making any other demand in his favor than that which must be indulged to all human excellence: that his virtues be rated with his failings. But from the censure which this irregularity may bring upon him, I shall, with due reverence to that learning which I must oppose, adventure to try how I can defend him.

His histories, being neither tragedies nor comedies, are not subject to any of their laws; nothing more is necessary to all the praise which they expect than that the changes of action be so prepared as to be understood, that the incidents be various and affecting, and the characters consistent, natural, and distinct. No other unity is intended, and therefore none is to be sought.

In his other works he has well enough preserved the unity of action. He has not, indeed, an intrigue regularly perplexed and regularly unraveled; he does not endeavor to hide his design only to discover it, for this is seldom the order of real events, and Shakespeare is the poet of nature; but his plan has commonly, what Aristotle requires,[1] a beginning, a middle, and an end, one event is concatenated with another, and the conclusion follows by easy consequence. There are perhaps some incidents that might be spared, as in other poets there is much talk that only fills up time upon the stage; but the general system makes gradual advances, and the end of the play is the end of expectation.

To the unities of time and place he has shown no regard; and perhaps a nearer view of the principles on which they stand will diminish their value and withdraw from them the veneration which, from the time of Corneille,[2] they have very generally received, by discovering that they have given more trouble to the poet than pleasure to the auditor.

The necessity of observing the unities of time and place arises from the supposed necessity of making the drama credible. The critics hold it impossible that an action of months or years can be possibly believed to pass in three hours; or that the spectator can suppose himself to sit in the theater while ambassadors go and return between distant kings, while armies are levied and towns besieged, while an exile wanders and returns, or till he whom they saw courting his mistress shall lament the untimely fall of his son. The mind revolts from evident falsehood, and fiction loses its force when it departs from the resemblance of reality.

From the narrow limitation of time necessarily arises the contraction of place. The spectator, who knows that he saw the first act at Alexandria, cannot suppose that he sees the next at Rome, at a distance to which not the dragons of Medea[3] could, in so short a time, have transported him; he knows with certainty that he has not changed his place; and he knows that place cannot change itself; that what was a house cannot become a plain; that what was Thebes can never be Persepolis.

9. Johnson alludes to the story of the runner Atalanta, who lost a race because she was distracted by golden apples tossed in her path.
1. Aristotle, *Poetics*, chapter 8.
2. The French neoclassical dramatist Pierre Corneille

published his influential *Essay on the Three Unities* in 1660.
3. After killing her rival and her children, Medea eluded pursuit in a chariot drawn by dragons.

Such is the triumphant language with which a critic exults over the misery of an irregular poet and exults commonly without resistance or reply. It is time, therefore, to tell him by the authority of Shakespeare, that he assumes, as an unquestionable principle, a position which, while his breath is forming it into words, his understanding pronounces to be false. It is false, that any representation is mistaken for reality; that any dramatic fable in its materiality was ever credible, or, for a single moment, was ever credited.

The objection arising from the impossibility of passing the first hour at Alexandria and the next at Rome supposes that when the play opens the spectator really imagines himself at Alexandria and believes that his walk to the theater has been a voyage to Egypt, and that he lives in the days of Antony and Cleopatra. Surely he that imagines this may imagine more. He that can take the stage at one time for the palace of the Ptolemies may take it in half an hour for the promontory of Actium. Delusion, if delusion be admitted, has no certain limitation; if the spectator can be once persuaded that his old acquaintance are Alexander and Caesar, that a room illuminated with candles is the plain of Pharsalia or the bank of Granicus,[4] he is in a state of elevation above the reach of reason or of truth, and from the heights of empyrean poetry may despise the circumscriptions of terrestrial nature. There is no reason why a mind thus wandering in ecstasy should count the clock, or why an hour should not be a century in that calenture[5] of the brains that can make the stage a field.

The truth is that the spectators are always in their senses and know from the first act to the last that the stage is only a stage, and that the players are only players. They come to hear a certain number of lines recited with just gesture and elegant modulation. The lines relate to some action, and an action must be in some place; but the different actions that complete a story may be in places very remote from each other; and where is the absurdity of allowing that space to represent first Athens and then Sicily which was always known to be neither Sicily nor Athens, but a modern theater?

By supposition, as place is introduced, time may be extended; the time required by the fable elapses for the most part between the acts; for, of so much of the action as is represented, the real and poetical duration is the same. If in the first act preparations for war against Mithridates are represented to be made in Rome, the event of the war may, without absurdity, be represented in the catastrophe as happening in Pontus; we know that there is neither war nor preparation for war; we know that we are neither in Rome nor Pontus; that neither Mithridates nor Lucullus are before us. The drama exhibits successive imitations of successive actions; and why may not the second imitation represent an action that happened years after the first if it be so connected with it that nothing but time can be supposed to intervene? Time is, of all modes of existence, most obsequious to the imagination; a lapse of years is as easily conceived as a passage of hours. In contemplation we easily contract the time of real actions and therefore willingly permit it to be contracted when we only see their imitation.

It will be asked how the drama moves if it is not credited. It is credited with all the credit due to a drama. It is credited, whenever it moves, as a just picture of a real original; as representing to the auditor what he would himself feel if he were to do or suffer what is there feigned to be suffered or to be done. The reflection that strikes

4. Johnson refers to the site of battles fought by Julius   5. Fever.
Caesar and Alexander the Great.

the heart is not that the evils before us are real evils, but that they are evils to which we ourselves may be exposed. If there be any fallacy, it is not that we fancy the players, but that we fancy ourselves unhappy for a moment; but we rather lament the possibility than suppose the presence of misery, as a mother weeps over her babe when she remembers that death may take it from her. The delight of tragedy proceeds from our consciousness of fiction; if we thought murders and treasons real, they would please no more.

　　Imitations produce pain or pleasure not because they are mistaken for realities, but because they bring realities to mind. When the imagination is recreated[6] by a painted landscape, the trees are not supposed capable to give us shade, or the fountains coolness; but we consider how we should be pleased with such fountains playing beside us and such woods waving over us. We are agitated in reading the history of _Henry the Fifth_, yet no man takes his book for the field of Agincourt. A dramatic exhibition is a book recited with concomitants that increase or diminish its effect. Familiar[7] comedy is often more powerful in the theater than on the page; imperial tragedy is always less. The humor of Petruchio[8] may be heightened by grimace; but what voice or what gesture can hope to add dignity or force to the soliloquy of Cato?[9]

　　A play read affects the mind like a play acted. It is therefore evident that the action is not supposed to be real; and it follows that between the acts a longer or shorter time may be allowed to pass, and that no more account of space or duration is to be taken by the auditor of a drama than by the reader of a narrative, before whom may pass in an hour the life of a hero or the revolutions of an empire.

　　Whether Shakespeare knew the unities and rejected them by design, or deviated from them by happy ignorance, it is, I think, impossible to decide and useless to inquire. We may reasonably suppose that when he rose to notice, he did not want the counsels and admonitions of scholars and critics, and that he at last deliberately persisted in a practice which he might have begun by chance. As nothing is essential to the fable but unity of action, and as the unities of time and place arise evidently from false assumptions, and, by circumscribing the extent of the drama, lessen its variety, I cannot think it much to be lamented that they were not known by him, or not observed; nor, if such another poet could arise, should I very vehemently reproach him that his first act passed at Venice and his next in Cyprus.[1] Such violations of rules merely positive become the comprehensive genius of Shakespeare, and such censures are suitable to the minute and slender criticism of Voltaire:

> Non usque adeo permiscuit imis
> Longus summa dies, ut non, si voce Metelli
> Serventur leges, malint a Caesare tolli.[2]

　　Yet when I speak thus slightly of dramatic rules, I cannot but recollect how much wit and learning may be produced against me; before such authorities I am afraid to stand, not that I think the present question one of those that are to be decided by mere authority, but because it is to be suspected that these precepts have not been so easily received but for better reasons than I have yet been able to find.

---

6. "Delighted, gratified" (Johnson's _Dictionary_).
7. Domestic.
8. The hero of _The Taming of the Shrew_.
9. The protagonist of Addison's tragedy, _Cato_ (1713), soliloquizes at the beginning of the final act.
1. Johnson refers to _Othello_.

2. Johnson quotes from the epic poem _Pharsalia_ by Lucan: "Things are not yet so confused that / If the laws were preserved by the voice of Metellus, / They would not prefer to be suppressed by Caesar." Johnson aligns Metellus, a politician of negligible importance, with Voltaire; Caesar correlates with Shakespeare.

The result of my inquiries, in which it would be ludicrous to boast of impartiality, is that the unities of time and place are not essential to a just drama; that, though they may sometimes conduce to pleasure, they are always to be sacrificed to the nobler beauties of variety and instruction; and that a play written with nice observation of critical rules is to be contemplated as an elaborate curiosity, as the product of superfluous and ostentatious art, by which is shown rather what is possible than what is necessary.

He that, without diminution of any other excellence, shall preserve all the unities unbroken deserves the like applause with the architect who shall display all the orders of architecture[3] in a citadel without any deduction from its strength; but the principal beauty of a citadel is to exclude the enemy, and the greatest graces of a play are to copy nature and instruct life. * * *

[SELECTED NOTES ON OTHELLO]

> OTHELLO Wherein of antres vast, and deserts idle,
> Rough quarries, rocks, and hills, whose heads touch heaven . . . (1.3.141–42)

Whoever ridicules this account of the progress of love,[1] shows his ignorance, not only of history, but of nature and manners. It is no wonder that, in any age, or in any nation, a lady, recluse, timorous, and delicate, should desire to hear of events and scenes which she could never see, and should admire the man who had endured dangers, and performed actions, which, however great, were yet magnified by her timidity.

Every mind is liable to absence and inadvertency, else Pope could never have rejected a word so poetically beautiful.[2] "Idle" is an epithet used to express the infertility of the chaotic state, in the Saxon translation of the Pentateuch.

> DESDEMONA That I did love the Moor to live with him,
> My downright violence and storm of fortunes
> May trumpet to the world. (1.3.249–51)

There is no need of this emendation.[3] "Violence" is not "violence suffered," but "violence acted." Breach of common rules and obligations. The old quarto has, "scorn" of fortune, which is perhaps the true reading.

> DESDEMONA I saw Othello's visage in his mind,
> And to his honors and his valiant parts
> Did I my soul and fortunes consecrate. (1.3.253–55)

It must raise no wonder, that I loved a man of an appearance so little engaging; I saw his face only in his mind; the greatness of his character reconciled me to his form.

> OTHELLO Excellent wretch![4] (3.3.91)

---

3. The five classical styles of architecture.
1. As had Thomas Rymer in his *Short View of Tragedy* (1692).
2. In his edition of Shakespeare's works (1725), Alexander Pope had emended "deserts idle" to "deserts wild."

3. A prior editor had emended "violence and storm of fortunes" to "violence to forms, my fortunes."
4. In his edition of Shakespeare's works (1733–1734), Lewis Theobald had emended "wretch" to "wench."

The meaning of the word "wretch," is not generally understood. It is now, in some parts of England, a term of the softest and fondest tenderness. It expresses the utmost degree of amiableness, joined with an idea, which perhaps all tenderness includes, of feebleness, softness, and want of protection. Othello, considering Desdemona as excelling in beauty and virtue, soft and timorous by her sex, and by her situation absolutely in his power, calls her "excellent wretch." It may be expressed: "Dear, harmless, helpless excellence."

> OTHELLO   when I love thee not,
> Chaos is come again. (3.3.91–2)

When my love is for a moment suspended by suspicion, I have nothing in my mind but discord, tumult, perturbation, and confusion.

> IAGO She did deceive her father, marrying you;
> And when she seemed to shake and fear your looks,
> She loved them most. (3.3.206–8)

This and the following argument of Iago ought to be deeply impressed on every reader. Deceit and falsehood, whatever conveniences they may for a time promise or produce, are, in the sum of life, obstacles to happiness. Those who profit by the cheat, distrust the deceiver, and the act by which kindness was sought, puts an end to confidence.

The same objection may be made with a lower degree of strength against the imprudent generosity of disproportionate marriages. When the first heat of passion is over, it is easily succeeded by suspicion, that the same violence of inclination which caused one irregularity, may stimulate to another; and those who have shown, that their passions are too powerful for their prudence, will, with very slight appearances against them, be censured, as not very likely to restrain them by their virtue.

> EMILIA 'Tis not a year or two shows us a man. (3.4.97)

From this line it may be conjectured, that the author intended the action of this play to be considered as longer than is marked by any note of time. Since their arrival at Cyprus, to which they were hurried on their wedding-night, the fable seems to have been in one continual progress, nor can I see any vacuity into which a "year or two," or even a month or two, could be put. On the night of Othello's arrival, a feast was proclaimed; at that feast Cassio was degraded, and immediately applies to Desdemona to get him restored. Iago indeed advises Othello to hold him off a while, but there is no reason to think, that he has been held off long. A little longer interval would increase the probability of the story, though it might violate the rules of the drama. See Act 5, Scene 2.

> OTHELLO It is the cause, it is the cause, my soul.
> Let me not name it to you, you chaste stars!
> It is the cause. (5.2.1–3)

The abruptness of this soliloquy makes it obscure. The meaning I think is this. "I am here," says Othello in his mind, "overwhelmed with horror. What is the reason of this perturbation? Is it want of resolution to do justice? Is it the dread of shedding blood? No; it is not the action that shocks me, but 'it is the cause, it is the cause, my soul; let me not name it to you, ye chaste stars! it is the cause.'"

> OTHELLO   This sorrow's heavenly;
> It strikes where it doth love. (5.2.21–2)

This tenderness, with which I lament the punishment which justice compels me to inflict, is a holy passion.

I wish these two lines could be honestly ejected. It is the fate of Shakespeare to counteract his own pathos.

> OTHELLO Oh perjured woman! thou dost stone my heart,
> And mak'st me call, what I intend to do,
> A murder, which I thought a sacrifice. (5.2.67–69)

This line is difficult. "Thou hast hardened my heart, and makest me" kill thee with the rage of a "murderer," when "I thought to have sacrificed" thee to justice with the calmness of a priest striking a victim.

It must not be omitted, that one of the elder quartos reads, "thou dost stone *thy* heart"; which I suspect to be genuine. The meaning then will be, "thou forcest me" to dismiss thee from the world in the state of the "murdered" without preparation for death, "when I intended" that thy punishment should have been "a sacrifice" atoning for thy crime.

I am glad that I have ended my revisal of this dreadful scene. It is not to be endured.

The beauties of this play impress themselves so strongly upon the attention of the reader, that they can draw no aid from critical illustration. The fiery openness of Othello, magnanimous, artless, and credulous, boundless in his confidence, ardent in his affection, inflexible in his resolution, and obdurate in his revenge; the cool malignity of Iago, silent in his resentment, subtle in his designs, and studious at once of his interest and his vengeance; the soft simplicity of Desdemona, confident of merit, and conscious of innocence, her artless perseverance in her suit, and her slowness to suspect that she can be suspected, are such proofs of Shakespeare's skill in human nature, as, I suppose, it is vain to seek in any modern writer. The gradual progress which Iago makes in the Moor's conviction, and the circumstances which he employs to inflame him, are so artfully natural, that, though it will perhaps not be said of him as he says of himself, that he is "a man not easily jealous," yet we cannot but pity him when at last we find him "perplexed in the extreme."

There is always danger lest wickedness conjoined with abilities should steal upon esteem, though it misses of approbation; but the character of Iago is so conducted, that he is from the first scene to the last hated and despised.

Even the inferior characters of this play would be very conspicuous in any other piece, not only for their justness but their strength. Cassio is brave, benevolent, and honest, ruined only by his want of stubbornness to resist an insidious invitation. Roderigo's suspicious credulity, and impatient submission to the cheats which he sees practiced upon him, and which by persuasion he suffers to be repeated, exhibit a strong picture of a weak mind betrayed by unlawful desires, to a false friend; and the virtue of Emilia is such as we often find, worn loosely, but not cast off, easy to commit small crimes, but quickened and alarmed at atrocious villanies.

The scenes from the beginning to the end are busy, varied by happy interchanges, and regularly promoting the progression of the story; and the narrative in the end, though it tells but what is known already, yet is necessary to produce the death of Othello.

Had the scene opened in Cyprus, and the preceding incidents been occasionally related, there had been little wanting to a drama of the most exact and scrupulous regularity.[5]

TRAVEL WRITING

In the late eighteenth century, travel books were among the most popular genres on the market; they appear to have outsold novels many times over. In a 1770 letter to Hester Thrale, Johnson offered a simple explanation for why so many were so bad: "Those whose lot it is to ramble can seldom write, and those who know how to write very seldom ramble." Three years later, a journey with his friend James Boswell, to the Hebridean islands of northwest Scotland, gave Johnson an opportunity to show that he could do both. Writing plentiful notes and letters *en route*, and a book shortly after his return, Johnson clearly saw himself as participating in his century's new passion for anthropological exploration, transporting hard data from the islands of Scotland as Captain James Cook (for example) was doing from those of the South Pacific. Though the 1707 Act of Union had officially made Scotland one with England in the new national entity Great Britain, it had actually exacerbated difference rather than erased it: in the Jacobite uprisings of the ensuing half century, Scots rebels fiercely resisted assimilation, while English armies and politicians ever more ruthlessly enforced it. Nowhere were the costs of both resistance and defeat so available for scrutiny as in the Hebrides, the home of the Highland clans that had waged the rebellion against huge odds, and were now being systematically stripped of the cultural practices that had set them apart from centuries. In their predicament Johnson found new matter for old preoccupations: in their glorification of their past he saw the persistent human tendency to distract itself with delusion when truth is too hard to bear; in the paucity of natural resources and the disintegration of the culture he found fresh evidence that (in the words of *Rasselas*) "human life is everywhere a state in which much is to be endured, and little to be enjoyed." For many Scots readers of the *Journey*, Johnson's interpretation of their culture seemed too narrow to be forgiven. They claimed that as a prejudiced Englishman he had failed to appreciate the fertility of their history, the abundance of their resources, the plenitude of their prospects. What Johnson constructed as empathetic but empiric inquiry, they dismissed as bigoted opacity. The *Journey* excited controversy at its first appearance, and does so still; it remains nonetheless one of the eighteenth century's richest documents of cultural encounter.

Letter to Hester Thrale[1]

Dearest Madam: Skye, Sep. 21, 1773

I am so vexed at the necessity of sending yesterday so short a letter, that I purpose to get a long letter beforehand by writing something every day, which I may the more easily do, as a cold makes me now too deaf to take the usual pleasure in conversation. Lady Macleod[2] is very kind to me, and the place at which we now are, is equal in strength of situation, in the wildness of the adjacent country, and in the plenty and elegance of the domestic entertainment, to a castle in gothic romances. The sea with a little island is before us, cascades play within view. Close to the house is the formidable skeleton of an old castle probably Danish; and the whole mass of building stands upon a protuberance of rock, inaccessible till of late but by a pair of stairs on the sea side, and secure in ancient times against any enemy that was likely to invade the kingdom of Skye. Macleod has offered me an island, if it were not too far off I

5. I.e., according to the rules of the "unities," which Johnson rejects in the Preface.
1. Writer, and wife of the properous brewer Henry Thrale; she was one of Johnson's dearest friends and favorite correspondents. For more on her life and writings, see page 2829. In this letter Johnson narrates rough-

ly the same stretch of days covered in the selections below from Johnson's *Journey* (pages 2770–2778) and Boswell's *Journal* (pages 2809–2813).
2. Johnson's hostess at Dunvegan, a Macleod family seat on the island of Skye and the oldest continuously inhabited castle in Scotland.

should hardly refuse it; my island would be pleasanter than Brighthelmston,[3] if You and Master[4] could come to it, but I cannot think it pleasant to live quite alone. *Oblitusque meorum, obliviscendus et illis*.[5] That I should be elated by the dominion of an Island to forgetfulness of my friends at Streatham,[6] and I hope never to deserve that they should be willing to forget me.

It has happened that I have been often recognized in my journey where I did not expect it. At Aberdeen I found one of my acquaintance a professor of physic. Turning aside to dine with a country gentleman, I was owned at table by one who had seen me at a philosophical lecture. At Macdonald's[7] I was claimed by a naturalist, who wanders about the Islands to pick up curiosities, and I had once in London attracted the notice of Lady Macleod. I will now go on with my account.

The Highland girl made tea, and looked and talked not inelegantly. Her father was by no means an ignorant or a weak man. There were books in the cottage, among which were some volumes of Prideaux's *Connection*.[8] This man's conversation we were glad of while we stayed. He had been out as they call it, in forty five,[9] and still retained his old opinions. He was going to America, because his rent was raised beyond what he thought himself able to pay.

At night our beds were made, but we had some difficulty in persuading ourselves to lie down in them, though we had put on our own sheets. At last we ventured, and I slept very soundly, in the vale called Glenmorison amidst the rocks and mountains. Next morning our landlord liked us so well, that he walked some miles with us for our company through a country so wild and barren that the proprietor does not with all his pressure upon his tenants raise more than four hundred a year from near an hundred square miles, or sixty thousand acres. He let us know that he had forty head of black cattle, an hundred goats, and an hundred sheep upon a farm which he remembered let at five pounds a year, but for which he now paid twenty. He told us some stories of their march into England. At last he left us, and we went forward, winding among mountains sometimes green and sometimes naked, commonly so steep as not easily to be climbed by the greatest vigor and activity. Our way was often crossed by little rivulets, and we were entertained with small streams trickling from the rocks, which after heavy rains must be tremendous torrents.

About noon, we came to a small glen, so they call a valley, which compared with other places appeared rich and fertile. Here our guides desired us to stop that the horses might graze, for the journey was very laborious, and no more grass would be found. We made no difficulty of compliance, and I sat down to make notes on a green bank, with a small stream running at my feet, in the midst of savage solitude, with mountains before me, and on either hand covered with heath. I looked round me, and wondered that I was not more affected, but the mind is not at all times equally ready to be put in motion. If my Mistress, and Master, and Queeny[1] had been there we should have produced some reflections among us either poetical or philosophical, for though *solitude be the nurse of woe*,[2] conversation is often the parent of remarks and discoveries.

3. Johnson compares the island of Isa (in the gift of Norman Macleod, chief of the Macleods of Dunvegan) to the Thrales' retreat at the sea resort of Brighton ("Brighthelmston").
4. Johnson's nickname for Hester Thrale's husband Henry.
5. Yet there would I live, forgetting my friends and by them forgotten (Horace, *Epistles* 1.11.8–9).
6. The Thrales' principal residence outside of London.
7. The home of Allan Macdonald at Kingsburgh, where Johnson had stayed before going to Dunvegan.

8. *The Old and New Testaments Connected* (1716–1718) by Humphrey Prideaux.
9. The Jacobite Rebellion of 1745–1746, which ended when the army of Prince Charles Edward Stuart ("Bonnie Prince Charlie") was defeated at the Battle of Culloden.
1. Hester and Henry Thrale, and their eldest daughter Hester Maria, whose family nickname was "Queeny."
2. "The silent heart . . . learns to know / That solitude's the nurse of woe" (Thomas Parnell, *Hymn to Contentment*, lines 19, 23–24).

In about an hour we remounted, and pursued our journey. The lake by which we had traveled from some time ended in a river, which we passed by a bridge and came to another glen with a collection of huts, called Auknasheals, the huts were generally built of clods of earth held together by the intertexture of vegetable fibers, of which earth there are great levels in Scotland which they call mosses. Moss in Scotland, is bog in Ireland, and mosstrooper is bogtrotter. There was however one hut built of loose stones piled up with great thickness into a strong though not solid wall. From this house we obtained some great pails of milk, and having brought bread with us, were very liberally regaled. The inhabitants, a very coarse tribe, ignorant of any language but Earse,[3] gathered so fast about us, that if we had not had Highlanders with us, they might have caused more alarm than pleasure. They are called the clan of Macrae.

We had been told that nothing gratified the Highlanders so much as snuff and tobacco, and had accordingly stowed ourselves with both at Fort Augustus. Boswell opened his treasure and gave them each a piece of tobacco roll. We had more bread than we could eat for the present, and were more liberal than provident. Boswell cut it in slices and gave each of them an opportunity of tasting wheaten bread for the first time. I then got some halfpence for a shilling and made up the deficiencies of Boswell's distribution, who had given some money among the children. We then directed that the mistress of the stone house should be asked what we must pay her, she who perhaps had never sold anything but cattle before, knew not, I believe, well what to ask, and referred herself to us. We obliged her to make some demand, and our Highlanders settled the account with her at a shilling. One of the men advised her, with the cunning that clowns[4] never can be without, to ask more but she said that a shilling was enough. We gave her half a crown[5] and she offered part of it again. The Macraes were so well pleased with our behavior, that they declared it the best day they had seen since the time of the old Laird of MacLeod, who I suppose, like us, stopped in their valley, as he was travelling to Skye.

We were mentioning this view of the Highlander's life at Macdonald's, and mentioning the Macraes with some degree of pity, when a Highland lady informed us, that we might spare our tenderness, for she doubted not, but the woman who supplied us with milk, was mistress of thirteen or fourteen milch cows.

I cannot forbear to interrupt my narrative. Boswell, with some of his troublesome kindness, has informed this family, and reminded me that the eighteenth of September is my birthday. The return of my birthday, if I remember it, fills me with thoughts which it seems to be the general care of humanity to escape. I can now look back upon threescore and four years, in which little has been done, and little has been enjoyed, a life diversified by misery, spent part in the sluggishness of penury, and part under the violence of pain, in gloomy discontent, or importunate distress. But perhaps I am better than I should have been, if I had been less afflicted. With this I will try to be content.

In proportion as there is less pleasure in retrospective considerations the mind is more disposed to wander forward into futurity, but at sixty four what promises, however liberal of imaginary good, can futurity venture to make? Yet something will be always promised, and some promises will always be credited. I am hoping, and I am praying that I may live better in the time to come, whether long or short, than I have yet lived, and in the solace of that hope endeavor to repose. Dear Queeney's day is next, I hope, she at sixty four will have less to regret.

---

3. The form of Gaelic spoken in Scotland.   5. A crown was worth five shillings.
4. Yokels.

I will now complain no more, but tell my Mistress of my travels.

After we left the Macraes, we traveled on through a country like that which we passed in the morning, the highlands are very uniform, for there is little variety in universal barrenness. The rocks however are not all naked, some have grass on their sides, and birches and alders on their tops, and in the valleys are often broad and clear streams which have little depth, and commonly run very quick. The channels are made by the violence of wintry floods, the quickness of the stream is in proportion to the declivity of the descent, and the breadth of the channel makes the water shallow in a dry season.

There are red deer and roebucks in the mountains, but we found only goats in the road, and had very little entertainment as we traveled either for the eye or ear. There are, I fancy, no singing birds in the Highlands.

Towards night we came to a very formidable hill named Ratiken, which we climbed with more difficulty than we had yet experienced, and at last came to Glenelg a place on the seaside opposite to Skye. We were by this time weary and disgusted, nor was our humor much mended, by an inn, which, though it was built with lime and slate, the Highlander's description of a house which he thinks magnificent, had neither wine, bread, eggs, nor anything that we could eat or drink. When we were taken up stairs, a dirty fellow bounced out of the bed in which one of us was to lie. Boswell blustered, but nothing could he get. At last a gentleman in the neighborhood who heard of our arrival sent us rum and white sugar. Boswell was now provided for in part, and the landlord prepared some mutton chops, which we could not eat, and killed two hens, of which Boswell made his servant broil a limb, with what effect I know not. We had a lemon, and a piece of bread, which supplied me with my supper.

When the repast was ended, we began to deliberate upon bed. Mrs. Boswell had warned us that we should *catch something,* and had given us sheets for our security; for Sir Alexander and Lady Macdonald, she said, came back from Skye, so scratching themselves———. I thought sheets a slender defense, against the confederacy with which we were threatened, and by this time our Highlanders had found a place where they could get some hay; I ordered hay to be laid thick upon the bed, and slept upon it in my great coat. Boswell laid sheets upon his hay, and reposed in linen like a gentleman. The horses were turned out to grass, with a man to watch them. The hill Ratiken, and the inn at Glenelg, are the only things of which we or travelers yet more delicate, could find any pretensions to complain.

Sept. 2. I rose rustling from the hay, and went to tea, which I forget whether we found or brought. We saw the Isle of Skye before us darkening the horizon with its rocky coast. A boat was procured, and we launched into one of the Straits of the Atlantic Ocean. We had a passage of about twelve miles to the point where Sir Alexander resided, having come from his seat in the midland part, to a small house on the shore, as we believe, that he might with less reproach entertain us meanly. If he aspired to meanness[6] his retrograde ambition was completely gratified, but he did not succeed equally in escaping reproach. He had no cook, nor, I suppose, much provision, nor had the Lady the common decencies of her tea table. We picked up our sugar with our fingers. Boswell was very angry, and reproached him with his improper parsimony. I did not much reflect upon the conduct of a man with whom I was not likely to converse as long at any other time.

---

6. Lack of generosity.

You will now expect that I should give you some account of the Isle of Skye, of which though I have been twelve days upon it, I have little to say. It is an island perhaps fifty miles long, so much indented by inlets of the sea, that there is no part of it removed from the water more than six miles. No part that I have seen is plain, you are always climbing or descending, and every step is upon rock or mire. A walk upon plowed ground in England is a dance upon carpets, compared to the toilsome drudgery of wandering in Skye. There is neither town nor village in the island, nor have I seen any house but Macleod's, that is not much below your habitation at Brighthelmston. In the mountains there are stags and roebucks, but no hares and few rabbits, nor have I seen any thing that interested me, as zoologist, except an otter, bigger than I thought an otter could have been.

You are perhaps imagining that I am withdrawn from the gay and the busy world into regions of peace and pastoral felicity, and am enjoying the relics of the golden age; that I am surveying Nature's magnificence from a mountain, or remarking her minuter beauties on the flowery bank of a winding rivulet, that I am invigorating myself in the sunshine, or delighting my imagination with being hidden from the invasion of human evils and human passions in the darkness of a thicket, that I am busy in gathering shells and pebbles on the shore, or contemplative on a rock, from which I look upon the water and consider how many waves are rolling between me and Streatham.

The use of traveling is to regulate imagination by reality, and instead of thinking how things may be, to see them as they are. Here are mountains which I should once have climbed, but to climb steeps is now very laborious, and to descend them dangerous, and I am now content with knowing that by a scrambling up a rock, I shall only see other rocks, and a wider circuit of barren desolation. Of streams we have here a sufficient number, but they murmur not upon pebbles but upon rocks; of flowers, if Chloris[7] herself were here, I could present her only with the bloom of heath. Of lawns and thickets, he must read, that would know them, for here is little sun and no shade. On the sea I look from my window, but am not much tempted to the shore for since I came to this island, almost every breath of air has been a storm, and what is worse, a storm with all its severity, but without its magnificence, for the sea is here so broken into channels, that there is not a sufficient volume of water either for lofty surges, or loud roar.

On Sept. 6 we left Macdonald, to visit Raarsa, the island which I have already mentioned. We were to cross part of Skye on horseback, a mode of traveling very uncomfortable, for the road is so narrow, where any road can be found, that only one can go, and so craggy that the attention can never be remitted. It allows therefore neither the gaiety of conversation nor the laxity of solitude, nor has it in itself the amusement of much variety, as it affords only all the possible transpositions of bog, rock, and rivulet. Twelve miles, by computation, make a reasonable journey for a day.

At night we came to a tenant's house of the first rank of tenants where we were entertained better than the landlords. There were books, both English and Latin. Company gathered about us, and we heard some talk of the second sight and some talk of the events of forty five, a year which will not soon be forgotten among the islanders. The next day we were confined by a storm, the company, I think, increased and our entertainment was not only hospitable but elegant. At night, a minister's sister in very fine brocade sung Earse songs. I wished to know the meaning, but the Highlanders are not much used to scholastic questions, and no translation could be obtained.

7. Goddess of flowers.

Next day, Sept. 8, the weather allowed us to depart, a good boat was provided us, and we went to Raarsa, under the conduct of Mr. Malcolm Macleod, a gentleman who conducted Prince Charles through the mountains in his distresses.[8] The prince, he says, was more active than himself, they were at least one night, without any shelter.

The wind blew enough to give the boat a kind of dancing agitation, and in about three or four hours we arrived at Raarsa, where we were met by the Laird and his friends upon the shore. Raarsa, for such is his title, is master of two islands, upon the smaller of which, called Rona, he has only flocks and herds. Rona gives title to his eldest son. The money which he raises by rent from all his dominions, which contain at least fifty thousand acres, is not believed to exceed two hundred and fifty pounds, but as he keeps a large farm in his own hands, he sells every year great numbers of cattle which he adds to his revenue, and, his table is furnished from the farm and from the sea with very little expense, except for those things this country does not produce, and of these he is very liberal. The wine circulates vigorously, and the tea and chocolate[9] and coffee, however they are got are always at hand. I am, Madam, Your most obedient servant,

SAM. JOHNSON

We are this morning trying to get out of Skye.

from A Journey to the Western Islands of Scotland
Anoch

Early in the afternoon we came to Anoch, a village in Glenmollison of three huts, one of which is distinguished by a chimney. Here we were to dine and lodge, and were conducted through the first room, that had the chimney, into another lighted by a small glass window. The landlord attended us with great civility, and told us what he could give us to eat and drink. I found some books on a shelf, among which were a volume or more of Prideaux's *Connection*.

This I mentioned as something unexpected, and perceived that I did not please him: I praised the propriety of his language, and was answered that I need not wonder, for he had learned it by grammar.[1]

By subsequent opportunities of observation, I found that my host's diction had nothing peculiar. Those Highlanders that can speak English, commonly speak it well, with few of the words, and little of the tone by which a Scotchman is distinguished. Their language seems to have been learned in the army or the navy, or by some communication with those who could give them good examples of accent and pronunciation. By their Lowland neighbors they would not willingly be taught; for they have long considered them as a mean and degenerate race. These prejudices are wearing fast away; but so much of them still remains, that when I asked a very learned minister in the islands, which they considered as their most savage clans: "Those," said he, "that live next the Lowlands."

As we came hither early in the day, we had time sufficient to survey the place. The house was built like other huts of loose stones, but the part in which we dined and slept was lined with turf and wattled with twigs, which kept the earth from falling. Near it was a garden of turnips and a field of potatoes. It stands in a glen, or valley, pleasantly watered by a winding river. But this country, however it may

---

8. After the Battle of Culloden (see note 9 on page 2840), Bonnie Prince Charlie escaped capture with difficulty; his adventures as a fugitive in the Highlands and the Hebrides became legendary.

9. Hot chocolate.

1. Through study of Latin grammar.

delight the gazer or amuse the naturalist, is of no great advantage to its owners. Our landlord told us of a gentleman, who possesses lands, eighteen Scotch miles[2] in length, and three in breadth; a space containing at least a hundred square English miles. He has raised his rents, to the danger of depopulating his farms, and he sells his timber, and by exerting every art of augmentation, has obtained an yearly revenue of four hundred pounds, which for a hundred square miles is three halfpence an acre.

Some time after dinner we were surprised by the entrance of a young woman, not inelegant either in mien or dress, who asked us whether we would have tea. We found that she was the daughter of our host, and desired her to make it. Her conversation, like her appearance, was gentle and pleasing. We knew that the girls of the Highlands are all gentlewomen, and treated her with great respect, which she received as customary and due, and was neither elated by it, nor confused, but repaid my civilities without embarrassment, and told me how much I honored her country by coming to survey it.

She had been at Inverness to gain the common female qualifications, and had, like her father, the English pronunciation. I presented her with a book,[3] which I happened to have about me, and should not be pleased to think that she forgets me.

In the evening the soldiers, whom we had passed on the road, came to spend at our inn the little money that we had given them. They had the true military impatience of coin in their pockets, and had marched at least six miles to find the first place where liquor could be bought. Having never been before in a place so wild and unfrequented, I was glad of their arrival, because I knew that we had made them friends, and to gain still more of their good will, we went to them, where they were carousing in the barn, and added something to our former gift. All that we gave was not much, but it detained them in the barn, either merry or quarreling, the whole night, and in the morning they went back to their work, with great indignation at the bad qualities of whiskey.

We had gained so much the favor of our host, that, when we left his house in the morning, he walked by us a great way, and entertained us with conversation both on his own condition, and that of the country. His life seemed to be merely pastoral, except that he differed from some of the ancient Nomads in having a settled dwelling. His wealth consists of one hundred sheep, as many goats, twelve milk-cows, and twenty-eight beeves[4] ready for the drover.

From him we first heard of the general dissatisfaction, which is now driving the Highlanders into the other hemisphere;[5] and when I asked him whether they would stay at home, if they were well treated, he answered with indignation, that no man willingly left his native country. Of the farm, which he himself occupied, the rent had, in twenty-five years, been advanced from five to twenty pounds, which he found himself so little able to pay, that he would be glad to try his fortune in some other place. Yet he owned the reasonableness of raising the Highland rents in a certain degree, and declared himself willing to pay ten pounds for the ground which he had formerly had for five.

Our host having amused us for a time, resigned us to our guides. The journey of this day was long, not that the distance was great, but that the way was difficult. We were now in the bosom of the Highlands, with full leisure to contemplate the appearance and properties of mountainous regions, such as have been, in many countries, the last shelters of national distress, and are everywhere the scenes of adventures, stratagems, surprises and escapes.

---

2. Longer than English miles.
3. A treatise on arithmetic by Edward Cocker. Johnson later defended his choice to Boswell: "Why, sir, if you are to have but one book with you upon a journey, let it be a book of science. . . . a book of science is inexhaustible."
4. Oxen.
5. At this time, increasing numbers of impoverished Scots farmers were emigrating to America.

Mountainous countries are not passed but with difficulty, not merely from the labor of climbing, for to climb is not always necessary, but because that which is not mountain is commonly bog, through which the way must be picked with caution. Where there are hills, there is much rain, and the torrents pouring down into the intermediate spaces, seldom find so ready an outlet, as not to stagnate, till they have broken the texture of the ground.

Of the hills, which our journey offered to the view on either side, we did not take the height, nor did we see any that astonished us with their loftiness. Towards the summit of one, there was a white spot, which I should have called a naked rock, but the guides, who had better eyes, and were acquainted with the phenomena of the country, declared it to be snow. It had already lasted to the end of August, and was likely to maintain its contest with the sun, till it should be reinforced by winter.

The height of mountains philosophically considered is properly computed from the surface of the next sea; but as it affects the eye or imagination of the passenger, as it makes either a spectacle or an obstruction, it must be reckoned from the place where the rise begins to make a considerable angle with the plain. In extensive continents the land may, by gradual elevation, attain great height, without any other appearance than that of a plane gently inclined, and if a hill placed upon such raised ground be described, as having its altitude equal to the whole space above the sea, the representation will be fallacious.

These mountains may be properly enough measured from the inland base; for it is not much above the sea. As we advanced at evening towards the western coast, I did not observe the declivity to be greater than is necessary for the discharge of the inland waters.

We passed many rivers and rivulets, which commonly ran with a clear shallow stream over a hard pebbly bottom. These channels, which seem so much wider than the water that they convey would naturally require, are formed by the violence of wintry floods, produced by the accumulation of innumerable streams that fall in rainy weather from the hills, and bursting away with resistless impetuosity, make themselves a passage proportionate to their mass.

Such capricious and temporary waters cannot be expected to produce many fish. The rapidity of the wintry deluge sweeps them away, and the scantiness of the summer stream would hardly sustain them above the ground. This is the reason why in fording the northern rivers, no fishes are seen, as in England, wandering in the water.

Of the hills many may be called with Homer's Ida "abundant in springs," but few can deserve the epithet which he bestows upon Pelion by "waving their leaves."[6] They exhibit very little variety; being almost wholly covered with dark heath, and even that seems to be checked in its growth. What is not heath is nakedness, a little diversified by now and then a stream rushing down the steep. An eye accustomed to flowery pastures and waving harvests is astonished and repelled by this wide extent of hopeless sterility. The appearance is that of matter incapable of form or usefulness, dismissed by nature from her care and disinherited of her favors, left in its original elemental state, or quickened only with one sullen power of useless vegetation.

It will very readily occur, that this uniformity of barrenness can afford very little amusement to the traveler; that it is easy to sit at home and conceive rocks and heath, and waterfalls; and that these journeys are useless labors, which neither impregnate the imagination, nor enlarge the understanding. It is true that of far the

---

6. Mount Ida and Mount Pelion are thus described in Homer's *Iliad*.

greater part of things, we must content ourselves with such knowledge as description may exhibit, or analogy supply; but it is true likewise, that these ideas are always incomplete, and that, at least till we have compared them with realities, we do not know them to be just. As we see more, we become possessed of more certainties, and consequently gain more principles of reasoning, and found a wider basis of analogy.

Regions mountainous and wild, thinly inhabited, and little cultivated, make a great part of the earth, and he that has never seen them, must live unacquainted with much of the face of nature, and with one of the great scenes of human existence.

As the day advanced towards noon, we entered a narrow valley not very flowery, but sufficiently verdant. Our guides told us, that the horses could not travel all day without rest or meat, and entreated us to stop here, because no grass would be found in any other place. The request was reasonable and the argument cogent. We therefore willingly dismounted and diverted ourselves as the place gave us opportunity.

I sat down on a bank, such as a writer of romance might have delighted to feign. I had indeed no trees to whisper over my head, but a clear rivulet streamed at my feet. The day was calm, the air soft, and all was rudeness, silence, and solitude. Before me, and on either side, were high hills, which by hindering the eye from ranging, forced the mind to find entertainment for itself. Whether I spent the hour well I know not; for here I first conceived the thought of this narration.

We were in this place at ease and by choice, and had no evils to suffer or to fear; yet the imaginations excited by the view of an unknown and untraveled wilderness are not such as arise in the artificial solitude of parks and gardens: a flattering notion of self-sufficiency, a placid indulgence of voluntary delusions, a secure expansion of the fancy, or a cool concentration of the mental powers. The phantoms which haunt a desert are want, and misery, and danger; the evils of dereliction rush upon the thoughts; man is made unwillingly acquainted with his own weakness, and meditation shows him only how little he can sustain, and how little he can perform. There were no traces of inhabitants, except perhaps a rude pile of clods called a summer hut, in which a herdsman had rested in the favorable seasons. Whoever had been in the place where I then sat, unprovided with provisions and ignorant of the country, might, at least before the roads were made, have wandered among the rocks, till he had perished with hardship, before he could have found either food or shelter. Yet what are these hillocks to the ridges of Taurus, or these spots of wildness to the deserts of America?

It was not long before we were invited to mount, and continued our journey along the side of a lough, kept full by many streams, which with more or less rapidity and noise crossed the road from the hills on the other hand. These currents, in their diminished state, after several dry months, afford, to one who has always lived in level countries, an unusual and delightful spectacle; but in the rainy season, such as every winter may be expected to bring, must precipitate an impetuous and tremendous flood. I suppose the way by which we went is at that time impassable.

Glensheals

The lough at last ended in a river broad and shallow like the rest, but that it may be passed when it is deeper, there is a bridge over it. Beyond it is a valley called Glensheals, inhabited by the clan of Macrae. Here we found a village called Auknasheals, consisting of many huts, perhaps twenty, built all of "dry-stone," that is, stones piled up without mortar.

We had, by the direction of the officers at Fort Augustus, taken bread for ourselves, and tobacco for those Highlanders who might show us any kindness. We were now at a place where we could obtain milk, but must have wanted[7] bread if we had not brought it. The people of this valley did not appear to know any English, and our guides now became doubly necessary as interpreters. A woman, whose hut was distinguished by greater spaciousness and better architecture, brought out some pails of milk. The villagers gathered about us in considerable numbers, I believe without any evil intention, but with a very savage wildness of aspect and manner. When our meal was over, Mr. Boswell sliced the bread, and divided it amongst them, as he supposed them never to have tasted a wheaten loaf before. He then gave them little pieces of twisted tobacco, and among the children we distributed a small handful of halfpence, which they received with great eagerness. Yet I have been since told, that the people of that valley are not indigent; and when we mentioned them afterwards as needy and pitiable, a Highland lady let us know, that we might spare our commiseration; for the dame whose milk we drank had probably more than a dozen milk-cows. She seemed unwilling to take any price, but being pressed to make a demand, at last named a shilling. Honesty is not greater where elegance is less. One of the bystanders, as we were told afterwards, advised her to ask more, but she said a shilling was enough. We gave her half a crown, and I hope got some credit by our behavior; for the company said, if our interpreters did not flatter us, that they had not seen such a day since the old Laird of Macleod passed through their country.

The Macraes, as we heard afterwards in the Hebrides, were originally an indigent and subordinate clan, and having no farms nor stock, were in great numbers servants to the Maclellans, who, in the war of Charles the First, took arms at the call of the heroic Montrose,[8] and were, in one of his battles, almost all destroyed. The women that were left at home, being thus deprived of their husbands, like the Scythian ladies of old, married their servants,[9] and the Macraes became a considerable race.

The Highlands

As we continued our journey, we were at leisure to extend our speculations, and to investigate the reason of those peculiarities by which such rugged regions as these before us are generally distinguished.

Mountainous countries commonly contain the original, at least the oldest race of inhabitants, for they are not easily conquered, because they must be entered by narrow ways, exposed to every power of mischief from those that occupy the heights; and every new ridge is a new fortress, where the defendants have again the same advantages. If the assailants either force the strait, or storm the summit, they gain only so much ground; their enemies are fled to take possession of the next rock, and the pursuers stand at gaze, knowing neither where the ways of escape wind among the steeps, nor where the bog has firmness to sustain them: besides that, mountaineers have an agility in climbing and descending distinct from strength or courage, and attainable only by use.

If the war be not soon concluded, the invaders are dislodged by hunger; for in those anxious and toilsome marches, provisions cannot easily be carried, and are never to be found. The wealth of mountains is cattle, which, while the men stand in the

7. Lacked.
8. James Graham (1612–1650), Marquis of Montrose, fought the Parliamentarians in a doomed attempt to

restore the Stuart monarchy.
9. The Greek historian Herodotus tells this story in his *Histories* (4.2).

passes, the women drive away. Such lands at last cannot repay the expense of conquest, and therefore perhaps have not been so often invaded by the mere ambition of dominion; as by resentment of robberies and insults, or the desire of enjoying in security the more fruitful provinces.

As mountains are long before they are conquered, they are likewise long before they are civilized. Men are softened by intercourse mutually profitable, and instructed by comparing their own notions with those of others. Thus Caesar found the maritime parts of Britain made less barbarous by their commerce with the Gauls.[1] Into a barren and rough tract no stranger is brought either by the hope of gain or of pleasure. The inhabitants having neither commodities for sale, nor money for purchase, seldom visit more polished places, or if they do visit them, seldom return.

It sometimes happens that by conquest, intermixture, or gradual refinement, the cultivated parts of a country change their language. The mountaineers then become a distinct nation, cut off by dissimilitude of speech from conversation with their neighbors. Thus in Biscay, the original Cantabrian,[2] and in Dalecarlia, the old Swedish still subsists.[3] Thus Wales and the Highlands speak the tongue of the first inhabitants of Britain, while the other parts have received first the Saxon, and in some degree afterwards the French, and then formed a third language between them.

That the primitive manners are continued where the primitive language is spoken, no nation will desire me to suppose, for the manners of mountaineers are commonly savage, but they are rather produced by their situation than derived from their ancestors.

Such seems to be the disposition of man, that whatever makes a distinction produces rivalry. England, before other causes of enmity were found, was disturbed for some centuries by the contests of the northern and southern counties; so that at Oxford, the peace of study could for a long time be preserved only by choosing annually one of the Proctors from each side of the Trent.[4] A tract intersected by many ridges of mountains, naturally divides its inhabitants into petty nations, which are made by a thousand causes enemies to each other. Each will exalt its own chiefs, each will boast the valor of its men, or the beauty of its women, and every claim of superiority irritates competition; injuries will sometimes be done, and be more injuriously defended; retaliation will sometimes be attempted, and the debt exacted with too much interest.

In the Highlands it was a law, that if a robber was sheltered from justice, any man of the same clan might be taken in his place. This was a kind of irregular justice, which, though necessary in savage times, could hardly fail to end in a feud, and a feud once kindled among an idle people with no variety of pursuits to divert their thoughts, burned on for ages either sullenly glowing in secret mischief, or openly blazing into public violence. Of the effects of this violent judicature, there are not wanting memorials. The cave is now to be seen to which one of the Campbells, who had injured the Macdonalds, retired with a body of his own clan. The Macdonalds required the offender, and being refused, made a fire at the mouth of the cave, by which he and his adherents were suffocated together.

---

1. In his *De Bello Gallico* (5.14.1), Julius Caesar describes the civilizing effects of commerce on English ports along the southern coast.
2. The Romans called the northern province of Spain "Cantabria"; Johnson's name for the same region is "Biscay."

3. Dalecarlia was a province in southern Sweden.
4. A river that forms the traditional boundary between northern and southern England.

Mountaineers are warlike, because by their feuds and competitions they consider themselves as surrounded with enemies, and are always prepared to repel incursions, or to make them. Like the Greeks in their unpolished state, described by Thucydides,[5] the Highlanders, till lately, went always armed, and carried their weapons to visits, and to church.[6]

Mountaineers are thievish, because they are poor, and having neither manufactures nor commerce, can grow richer only by robbery. They regularly plunder their neighbors, for their neighbors are commonly their enemies; and having lost that reverence for property, by which the order of civil life is preserved, soon consider all as enemies, whom they do not reckon as friends, and think themselves licensed to invade whatever they are not obliged to protect.

By a strict administration of the laws, since the laws have been introduced into the Highlands, this disposition to thievery is very much repressed. Thirty years ago no herd had ever been conducted through the mountains, without paying tribute in the night, to some of the clans; but cattle are now driven, and passengers travel without danger, fear, or molestation.

Among a warlike people, the quality of highest esteem is personal courage, and with the ostentatious display of courage are closely connected promptitude of offense and quickness of resentment. The Highlanders, before they were disarmed, were so addicted to quarrels, that the boys used to follow any public procession or ceremony, however festive, or however solemn, in expectation of the battle, which was sure to happen before the company dispersed.

Mountainous regions are sometimes so remote from the seat of government, and so difficult of access, that they are very little under the influence of the sovereign, or within the reach of national justice. Law is nothing without power; and the sentence of a distant court could not be easily executed, nor perhaps very safely promulgated, among men ignorantly proud and habitually violent, unconnected with the general system, and accustomed to reverence only their own lords. It has therefore been necessary to erect many particular jurisdictions, and commit the punishment of crimes, and the decision of right to the proprietors of the country who could enforce their own decrees. It immediately appears that such judges will be often ignorant, and often partial;[7] but in the immaturity of political establishments no better expedient could be found. As government advances towards perfection, provincial judicature is perhaps in every empire gradually abolished.

Those who had thus the dispensation of law, were by consequence themselves lawless. Their vassals had no shelter from outrages and oppressions; but were condemned to endure, without resistance, the caprices of wantonness, and the rage of cruelty.

In the Highlands, some great lords had an hereditary jurisdiction over counties; and some chieftains over their own lands; till the final conquest of the Highlands afforded an opportunity of crushing all the local courts, and of extending the general benefits of equal law to the low and the high, in the deepest recesses and obscurest corners.

While the chiefs had this resemblance of royalty, they had little inclination to appeal, on any question, to superior judicatures. A claim of lands between two powerful lairds was decided like a contest for dominion between sovereign powers. They drew their forces into the field, and right attended on the strongest. This was, in ruder times, the common practice, which the kings of Scotland could seldom control.

---

5. In his history of the Peloponnesian War (1.6.3).
6. After crushing the Jacobite Rebellion of 1745–1746, the English attempted to stamp out future revolts by

enacting a series of repressive laws, one of which forbade Highlanders to carry arms.
7. Prejudiced.

Even so lately as in the last years of King William,[8] a battle was fought at Mull Roy, on a plain a few miles to the south of Inverness, between the clans of Mackintosh and Macdonald of Keppoch. Col. Macdonald, the head of a small clan, refused to pay the dues demanded from him by Mackintosh, as his superior lord. They disdained the interposition of judges and laws, and calling each his followers to maintain the dignity of the clan, fought a formal battle, in which several considerable men fell on the side of Mackintosh, without a complete victory to either. This is said to have been the last open war made between the clans by their own authority.

The Highland lords made treaties, and formed alliances, of which some traces may still be found, and some consequences still remain as lasting evidences of petty regality. The terms of one of these confederacies were, that each should support the other in the right, or in the wrong, except against the king.

The inhabitants of mountains form distinct races, and are careful to preserve their genealogies. Men in a small district necessarily mingle blood by intermarriages, and combine at last into one family, with a common interest in the honor and disgrace of every individual. Then begins that union of affections, and cooperation of endeavors, that constitute a clan. They who consider themselves as ennobled by their family, will think highly of their progenitors, and they who through successive generations live always together in the same place, will preserve local stories and hereditary prejudices. Thus every Highlander can talk of his ancestors, and recount the outrages which they suffered from the wicked inhabitants of the next valley.

Such are the effects of habitation among mountains, and such were the qualities of the Highlanders, while their rocks secluded them from the rest of mankind, and kept them an unaltered and discriminated race. They are now losing their distinction, and hastening to mingle with the general community.

Glenelg

We left Auknasheals and the Macraes in the afternoon, and in the evening came to Ratiken, a high hill on which a road is cut, but so steep and narrow, that it is very difficult. There is now a design of making another way round the bottom. Upon one of the precipices, my horse, weary with the steepness of the rise, staggered a little, and I called in haste to the Highlander to hold him. This was the only moment of my journey, in which I thought myself endangered.

Having surmounted the hill at last, we were told that at Glenelg, on the sea-side, we should come to a house of lime and slate and glass. This image of magnificence raised our expectation. At last we came to our inn weary and peevish, and began to inquire for meat and beds.

Of the provisions the negative catalogue was very copious. Here was no meat, no milk, no bread, no eggs, no wine. We did not express much satisfaction. Here however we were to stay. Whisky we might have, and I believe at last they caught a fowl and killed it. We had some bread, and with that we prepared ourselves to be contented, when we had a very eminent proof of Highland hospitality. Along some miles of the way, in the evening, a gentleman's servant had kept us company on foot with very little notice on our part. He left us near Glenelg, and we thought on him no more till he came to us again, in about two hours, with a present from his master of rum and sugar. The man had mentioned his company, and the gentleman, whose

8. William III ruled from 1689 to 1702.

name, I think, is Gordon, well knowing the penury of the place, had this attention to two men, whose names perhaps he had not heard, by whom his kindness was not likely to be ever repaid, and who could be recommended to him only by their necessities.

We were now to examine our lodging. Out of one of the beds, on which we were to repose, started up, at our entrance, a man black as a Cyclops from the forge.[9] Other circumstances of no elegant recital concurred to disgust us. We had been frighted by a lady at Edinburgh, with discouraging representations of Highland lodgings. Sleep, however, was necessary. Our Highlanders had at last found some hay, with which the inn could not supply them. I directed them to bring a bundle into the room, and slept upon it in my riding coat. Mr. Boswell being more delicate, laid himself sheets with hay over and under him, and lay in linen like a gentleman.

from *Skye. Armidel*

In the morning, September the second, we found ourselves on the edge of the sea. Having procured a boat, we dismissed our Highlanders, whom I would recommend to the service of any future travelers, and were ferried over to the Isle of Sky. We landed at Armidel, where we were met on the sands by Sir Alexander Macdonald, who was at that time there with his lady, preparing to leave the island and reside at Edinburgh.

Armidel is a neat house, built where the Macdonalds had once a seat, which was burned in the commotions that followed the Revolution.[1] The walled orchard, which belonged to the former house, still remains. It is well shaded by tall ash trees, of a species, as Mr. Janes the fossilist[2] informed me, uncommonly valuable. This plantation is very properly mentioned by Dr. Campbell, in his new account of the state of Britain,[3] and deserves attention; because it proves that the present nakedness of the Hebrides is not wholly the fault of Nature. * * *

1773–1774   1775

Lives of the Poets

In March 1777, a consortium of booksellers persuaded Johnson to undertake a new endeavor. "I am engaged," he informed Boswell, "to write little Lives and little Prefaces, to a little edition of the English Poets" of the past century and a half. In the end, he produced fifty-two *Prefaces Biographical and Critical*, now better known as *Lives of the Poets*. Some of the lives remained "little" (the booksellers had selected the poets, and Johnson did not consider all of them worthy of sustained attention); but many of them expanded in range and interest far beyond Johnson's initial expectation. As Boswell later observed, Johnson pursued the project "with peculiar delight" because he knew this literary territory so very well. In the longest *Lives* (of Milton, Dryden, Addison, and Pope), Johnson paid complex tribute to the predecessors who had mattered most to him as models in his youth—who had shaped the literary world in which he had now found his own place. The three-part structure in which Johnson cast most of the prefaces was well calculated to display the powers and precepts accumulated over a lifetime. In the first part, an account of the poet's life, he fulfilled his own dictum (in *Rambler* No. 60) that biography is most useful when it deals in the "minute details" and "domestic privacies" of the subject's daily life; in the second part, an assessment of the poet's character, he implemented his own conviction that the biographer (unlike the eulogist) should forgo pure

---

9. In classical literature, the Cyclops were often described as blacksmiths, who forged weapons for the gods in an underground workshop.

1. The "Glorious Revolution" of 1688–1689, when the Stuart monarch James II was replaced by William and

Mary.

2. The mineralogist John Jeans.

3. Johnson refers to John Campbell's *Political Survey of Britain* (1774).

praise in favor of complex truth; in the third section, a critical review of the poet's work, he found full scope for the close analysis of literary cause and effect that had always informed his reading. "The biographical part of literature," he had once remarked, "is what I love the most." The *Lives* were that love's last labor. In them, the fusion of a favorite genre with a deeply familiar subject produced, in John Wain's words, "the greatest masterpiece of English eighteenth-century criticism."

from Lives of the Poets
from The Life of Milton

[ON *PARADISE LOST*]

Whatever be his subject he never fails to fill the imagination. But his images and descriptions of the scenes or operations of nature do not seem to be always copied from original form, nor to have the freshness, raciness,[1] and energy of immediate observation. He saw nature, as Dryden expresses it, "through the spectacles of books"; and on most occasions calls learning to his assistance. The garden of Eden brings to his mind the vale of Enna, where Proserpine was gathering flowers. Satan makes his way through fighting elements, like Argo between the Cyanean rocks, or Ulysses between the two Sicilian whirlpools, when he shunned Charybdis "on the larboard." The mythological allusions have been justly censured, as not being always used with notice of their vanity; but they contribute variety to the narration, and produce an alternate exercise of the memory and the fancy.

His similes are less numerous and more various than those of his predecessors. But he does not confine himself within the limits of rigorous comparison: his great excellence is amplitude, and he expands the adventitious[2] image beyond the dimensions which the occasion required. Thus, comparing the shield of Satan to the orb of the moon, he crowds the imagination with the discovery of the telescope and all the wonders which the telescope discovers.

Of his moral sentiments it is hardly praise to affirm that they excel those of all other poets; for this superiority he was indebted to his acquaintance with the sacred writings. The ancient epic poets, wanting the light of Revelation, were very unskillful teachers of virtue: their principal characters may be great, but they are not amiable. The reader may rise from their works with a greater degree of active or passive fortitude, and sometimes of prudence; but he will be able to carry away few precepts of justice, and none of mercy. * * *

In Milton every line breathes sanctity of thought and purity of manners, except when the train of the narration requires the introduction of the rebellious spirits; and even they are compelled to acknowledge their subjection to God in such a manner as excites reverence and confirms piety.

Of human beings there are but two; but those two are the parents of mankind, venerable before their fall for dignity and innocence, and amiable after it for repentance and submission. In their first state their affection is tender without weakness, and their piety sublime without presumption. When they have sinned they show how discord begins in mutual frailty, and how it ought to cease in mutual forbearance; how confidence of the divine favor is forfeited by sin, and how hope of pardon may be obtained by penitence and prayer. A state of innocence we can only conceive, if indeed in our present misery it be possible to conceive it; but the sentiments and worship proper to a fallen and offending being we have all to learn, as we have all to practice.

---

1. "Strong; flavorous; tasting of the soil" (Johnson's *Dictionary*). 2. Accidental.

The poet whatever be done is always great. Our progenitors in their first state conversed with angels; even when folly and sin had degraded them they had not in their humiliation "the port of mean suitors"; and they rise again to reverential regard when we find that their prayers were heard.

As human passions did not enter the world before the Fall, there is in the *Paradise Lost* little opportunity for the pathetic;[3] but what little there is has not been lost. That passion which is peculiar to rational nature, the anguish arising from the consciousness of transgression and the horrors attending the sense of the Divine Displeasure, are very justly described and forcibly impressed. But the passions are moved only on one occasion; sublimity is the general and prevailing quality in this poem— sublimity variously modified, sometimes descriptive, sometimes argumentative.

The defects and faults of *Paradise Lost*, for faults and defects every work of man must have, it is the business of impartial criticism to discover. As in displaying the excellence of Milton I have not made long quotations, because of selecting beauties there had been no end, I shall in the same general manner mention that which seems to deserve censure; for what Englishman can take delight in transcribing passages, which, if they lessen the reputation of Milton, diminish in some degree the honor of our country?

The generality of my scheme does not admit the frequent notice of verbal inaccuracies which Bentley,[4] perhaps better skilled in grammar than in poetry, has often found, though he sometimes made them, and which he imputed to the obtrusions of a reviser whom the author's blindness obliged him to employ. A supposition rash and groundless, if he thought it true; and vile and pernicious, if, as is said, he in private allowed it to be false.

The plan of *Paradise Lost* has this inconvenience, that it comprises neither human actions nor human manners. The man and woman who act and suffer are in a state which no other man or woman can ever know. The reader finds no transaction in which he can be engaged, beholds no condition in which he can by any effort of imagination place himself; he has, therefore, little natural curiosity or sympathy.

We all, indeed, feel the effects of Adam's disobedience; we all sin like Adam, and like him must all bewail our offenses; we have restless and insidious enemies in the fallen angels, and in the blessed spirits we have guardians and friends; in the Redemption of mankind we hope to be included: in the description of heaven and hell we are surely interested, as we are all to reside hereafter either in the regions of horror or of bliss.

But these truths are too important to be new: they have been taught to our infancy; they have mingled with our solitary thoughts and familiar conversation, and are habitually interwoven with the whole texture of life. Being therefore not new they raise no unaccustomed emotion in the mind: what we knew before we cannot learn; what is not unexpected, cannot surprise.

Of the ideas suggested by these awful scenes, from some we recede with reverence, except when stated hours require their association; and from others we shrink with horror, or admit them only as salutary inflictions, as counterpoises to our interests and passions. Such images rather obstruct the career of fancy than incite it.

---

3. "Affecting the passions" (Johnson's *Dictionary*).
4. Richard Bentley, a distinguished classical scholar

whose edition of *Paradise Lost* (1732) incorporates numerous misguided "corrections."

Pleasure and terror are indeed the genuine sources of poetry; but poetical pleasure must be such as human imagination can at least conceive, and poetical terror such as human strength and fortitude may combat. The good and evil of Eternity are too ponderous for the wings of wit; the mind sinks under them in passive helplessness, content with calm belief and humble adoration.

Known truths however may take a different appearance, and be conveyed to the mind by a new train of intermediate images. This Milton has undertaken, and performed with pregnancy and vigor of mind peculiar to himself. Whoever considers the few radical[5] positions which the Scriptures afforded him will wonder by what energetic operations he expanded them to such extent and ramified them to so much variety, restrained as he was by religious reverence from licentiousness of fiction.

Here is a full display of the united force of study and genius; of a great accumulation of materials, with judgment to digest and fancy to combine them: Milton was able to select from nature or from story, from ancient fable or from modern science, whatever could illustrate or adorn his thoughts. An accumulation of knowledge impregnated his mind, fermented by study and exalted by imagination.

It has been therefore said without an indecent hyperbole by one of his encomiasts, that in reading *Paradise Lost* we read a book of universal knowledge.

But original deficience cannot be supplied. The want of human interest is always felt. *Paradise Lost* is one of the books which the reader admires and lays down, and forgets to take up again. None ever wished it longer than it is. Its perusal is a duty rather than a pleasure. We read Milton for instruction, retire harassed and overburdened, and look elsewhere for recreation; we desert our master, and seek for companions.

from *The Life of Pope*

[TRANSLATING THE *ILIAD*]

The next year (1713) produced a bolder attempt, by which profit was sought as well as praise. The poems which he had hitherto written, however they might have diffused his name, had made very little addition to his fortune. The allowance which his father made him, though, proportioned to what he had, it might be liberal, could not be large; his religion hindered him from the occupation of any civil employment,[1] and he complained that he wanted even money to buy books.

He therefore resolved to try how far the favor of the public extended, by soliciting a subscription to a version of the *Iliad*, with large notes.

To print by subscription[2] was, for some time, a practice peculiar to the English. The first considerable work for which this expedient was employed is said to have been Dryden's *Virgil*, and it had been tried again with great success when *The Tatlers* were collected into volumes.

There was reason to believe that Pope's attempt would be successful. He was in the full bloom of reputation, and was personally known to almost all whom dignity of employment or splendor of reputation had made eminent; he conversed indifferently[3] with both parties, and never disturbed the public with his political opinions; and it might be naturally expected, as each faction then boasted its literary zeal, that

5. Original.
1. As a Roman Catholic, Pope was prohibited from holding public office or from entering such professions as the law and medicine.

2. A method of publication in which customers subsidized the cost of printing a book by paying all or part of the price in advance.
3. Impartially.

the great men, who on other occasions practiced all the violence of opposition, would emulate each other in their encouragement of a poet who had delighted all, and by whom none had been offended.

With those hopes, he offered an English *Iliad* to subscribers, in six volumes in quarto,[4] for six guineas; a sum, according to the value of money at that time, by no means inconsiderable, and greater than I believe to have been ever asked before. His proposal, however, was very favorably received, and the patrons of literature were busy to recommend his undertaking, and promote his interest. Lord Oxford,[5] indeed, lamented that such a genius should be wasted upon a work not original; but proposed no means by which he might live without it. Addison recommended caution and moderation, and advised him not to be content with the praise of half the nation, when he might be universally favored.

The greatness of the design, the popularity of the author, and the attention of the literary world, naturally raised such expectations of the future sale, that the booksellers[6] made their offers with great eagerness; but the highest bidder was Bernard Lintot, who became proprietor on condition of supplying, at his own expense, all the copies which were to be delivered to subscribers, or presented to friends, and paying two hundred pounds for every volume.

Of the quartos it was, I believe, stipulated that none should be printed but for the author, that the subscription might not be depreciated; but Lintot impressed the same pages upon a small folio, and paper perhaps a little thinner; and sold exactly at half the price, for half a guinea each volume, books so little inferior to the quartos, that, by a fraud of trade, those folios, being afterwards shortened by cutting away the top and bottom, were sold as copies printed for the subscribers.

Lintot printed two hundred and fifty on royal paper in folio for two guineas a volume; of the small folio, having printed seventeen hundred and fifty copies of the first volume, he reduced the number in the other volumes to a thousand.

It is unpleasant to relate that the bookseller, after all his hopes and all his liberality, was, by a very unjust and illegal action, defrauded of his profit. An edition of the English *Iliad* was printed in Holland in duodecimo, and imported clandestinely for the gratification of those who were impatient to read what they could not yet afford to buy. This fraud could only be counteracted by an edition equally cheap and more commodious; and Lintot was compelled to contract his folio at once into a duodecimo, and lose the advantage of an intermediate gradation.[7] The notes, which in the Dutch copies were placed at the end of each book, as they had been in the large volumes, were now subjoined to the text in the same page, and are therefore more easily consulted. Of this edition two thousand five hundred were first printed, and five thousand a few weeks afterwards; but indeed great numbers were necessary to produce considerable profit.

Pope, having now emitted his proposals, and engaged not only his own reputation, but in some degree that of his friends who patronized his subscription, began to be frighted at his own undertaking; and finding himself at first embarrassed with difficulties, which retarded and oppressed him, he was for a time timorous and uneasy; had his nights disturbed by dreams of long journeys through unknown ways, and wished, as he said, "that somebody would hang him."

---

4. A book consisting of printed sheets that have been folded twice; typically, a quarto is smaller than a folio, whose sheets have been folded only once.
5. Robert Harley, first Earl of Oxford, was head of the Tory ministry that held power from 1710 to 1714.

6. Publishers.
7. Lintot had to forgo publication in the larger and more profitable quarto or octavo formats for a smaller duodecimo edition. This format was commonly adopted for inexpensive books designed for a popular audience.

This misery, however, was not of long continuance; he grew by degrees more acquainted with Homer's images and expressions, and practice increased his facility of versification. In a short time he represents himself as dispatching regularly fifty verses a day, which would show him by an easy computation the termination of his labor.

His own diffidence was not his only vexation. He that asks a subscription soon finds that he has enemies. All who do not encourage him defame him. He that wants money will rather be thought angry than poor, and he that wishes to save his money conceals his avarice by his malice. Addison had hinted his suspicion that Pope was too much a Tory; and some of the Tories suspected his principles because he had contributed to *The Guardian*, which was carried on by Steele.[8]

To those who censured his politics were added enemies yet more dangerous, who called in question his knowledge of Greek, and his qualifications for a translator of Homer. To these he made no public opposition, but in one of his letters escapes from them as well as he can. At an age like his, for he was not more than twenty-five, with an irregular education, and a course of life of which much seems to have passed in conversation, it is not very likely that he overflowed with Greek. But when he felt himself deficient he sought assistance; and what man of learning would refuse to help him? Minute enquiries into the force of words are less necessary in translating Homer than other poets, because his positions are general, and his representations natural, with very little dependence on local or temporary customs, on those changeable scenes of artificial life, which, by mingling original with accidental notions, and crowding the mind with images which time effaces, produce ambiguity in diction, and obscurity in books. To this open display of unadulterated nature it must be ascribed, that Homer has fewer passages of doubtful meaning than any other poet either in the learned or in modern languages. I have read of a man, who being, by his ignorance of Greek, compelled to gratify his curiosity with the Latin printed on the opposite page, declared that from the rude simplicity of the lines literally rendered, he formed nobler ideas of the Homeric majesty than from the labored elegance of polished versions.

Those literal translations were always at hand, and from them he could easily obtain his author's sense with sufficient certainty; and among the readers of Homer the number is very small of those who find much in the Greek more than in the Latin, except the music of the numbers.[9]

If more help was wanting, he had the poetical translation of Eobanus Hessus, an unwearied writer of Latin verses; he had the French *Homers* of La Valterie and Dacier, and the English of Chapman,[1] Hobbes, and Ogylby. With Chapman, whose work, though now totally neglected, seems to have been popular almost to the end of the last century, he had very frequent consultations, and perhaps never translated any passage till he had read his version, which indeed he has been sometimes suspected of using instead of the original.

Notes were likewise to be provided; for the six volumes would have been very little more than six pamphlets without them. What the mere perusal of the text could suggest, Pope wanted no assistance to collect or methodize; but more was necessary; many pages were to be filled, and learning must supply materials to wit and judgment.

8. Three months after *The Spectator* was brought to a close, Richard Steele started *The Guardian*, which appeared every weekday for seven months. Unlike its predecessor, this new periodical had a partisan (Whig) political cast.

9. Poetic meter.

1. George Chapman's translation of *The Iliad* appeared in 1611.

Something might be gathered from Dacier;[2] but no man loves to be indebted to his contemporaries, and Dacier was accessible to common readers. Eustathius[3] was therefore necessarily consulted. To read Eustathius, of whose work there was then no Latin version, I suspect Pope, if he had been willing, not to have been able; some other was therefore to be found, who had leisure as well as abilities, and he was doubtless most readily employed who would do much work for little money.

The history of the notes has never been traced. Broome, in his preface to his poems, declares himself the commentator "in part upon the *Iliad*"; and it appears from Fenton's letter, preserved in the Museum, that Broome was at first engaged in consulting Eustathius; but that after a time, whatever was the reason, he desisted; another man of Cambridge was then employed, who soon grew weary of the work; and a third, that was recommended by Thirlby, is now discovered to have been Jortin, a man since well known to the learned world, who complained that Pope, having accepted and approved his performance, never testified any curiosity to see him, and who professed to have forgotten the terms on which he worked.[4] The terms which Fenton uses are very mercantile: "I think at first sight that his performance is very commendable, and have sent word for him to finish the 17th book, and to send it with his demands for his trouble. I have here enclosed the specimen; if the rest come before the return, I will keep them till I receive your orders."

Broome then offered his service a second time, which was probably accepted, as they had afterwards a closer correspondence. Parnell[5] contributed the *Life of Homer*, which Pope found so harsh, that he took great pains in correcting it; and by his own diligence, with such help as kindness or money could procure him, in somewhat more than five years he completed his version of the *Iliad*, with the notes. He began it in 1712, his twenty-fifth year, and concluded it in 1718, his thirtieth year.

When we find him translating fifty lines a day, it is natural to suppose that he would have brought his work to a more speedy conclusion. The *Iliad*, containing less than sixteen thousand verses, might have been dispatched in less than three hundred and twenty days by fifty verses in a day. The notes, compiled with the assistance of his mercenaries, could not be supposed to require more time than the text. According to this calculation, the progress of Pope may seem to have been slow; but the distance is commonly very great between actual performances and speculative possibility. It is natural to suppose, that as much as has been done today may be done tomorrow; but on the morrow some difficulty emerges, or some external impediment obstructs. Indolence, interruption, business, and pleasure, all take their turns of retardation; and every long work is lengthened by a thousand causes that can, and ten thousand that cannot, be recounted. Perhaps no extensive and multifarious performance was ever effected within the term originally fixed in the undertaker's mind. He that runs against Time, has an antagonist not subject to casualties.

The encouragement given to this translation, though report seems to have overrated it, was such as the world has not often seen. The subscribers were five hundred and seventy-five. The copies for which subscriptions were given were six hundred and fifty-four; and only six hundred and sixty were printed. For those copies Pope had

---

2. The annotated French version of the *Iliad* by Anne Dacier (1654–1720) had been translated into English in 1712.
3. A 12-century Byzantine commentator on Homer.
4. Because Pope's knowledge of Greek was uncertain, he depended on others to help him translate Eustathius. These assistants included the scholars William Broome and John Jortin; Jortin had been recommended by his Cambridge tutor, Styan Thirlby. Broome and Elijah Fenton went on to assist Pope in his translation of *The Odyssey*.
5. Thomas Parnell (1679–1718), Irish poet and friend of Pope and of Swift.

nothing to pay; he therefore received, including the two hundred pounds a volume, five thousand three hundred and twenty pounds four shillings, without deduction, as the books were supplied by Lintot.

By the success of his subscription Pope was relieved from those pecuniary distresses with which, notwithstanding his popularity, he had hitherto struggled. Lord Oxford had often lamented his disqualification for public employment, but never proposed a pension. While the translation of Homer was in its progress, Mr. Craggs, then secretary of state, offered to procure him a pension, which, at least during his ministry, might be enjoyed with secrecy. This was not accepted by Pope, who told him, however, that, if he should be pressed with want of money, he would send to him for occasional supplies. Craggs was not long in power, and was never solicited for money by Pope, who disdained to beg what he did not want.

With the product of this subscription, which he had too much discretion to squander, he secured his future life from want, by considerable annuities. The estate of the Duke of Buckingham was found to have been charged with five hundred pounds a year, payable to Pope, which doubtless his translation enabled him to purchase.

It cannot be unwelcome to literary curiosity, that I deduce thus minutely the history of the English *Iliad*. It is certainly the noblest version of poetry which the world has ever seen; and its publication must therefore be considered as one of the great events in the annals of learning.

[POPE AND DRYDEN]

In acquired knowledge the superiority must be allowed to Dryden, whose education was more scholastic, and who before he became an author had been allowed more time for study, with better means of information. His mind has a larger range, and he collects his images and illustrations from a more extensive circumference of science. Dryden knew more of man in his general nature, and Pope in his local manners. The notions of Dryden were formed by comprehensive speculation, and those of Pope by minute attention. There is more dignity in the knowledge of Dryden, and more certainty in that of Pope.

Poetry was not the sole praise of either, for both excelled likewise in prose; but Pope did not borrow his prose from his predecessor. The style of Dryden is capricious and varied, that of Pope is cautious and uniform; Dryden obeys the motions of his own mind, Pope constrains his mind to his own rules of composition. Dryden is sometimes vehement and rapid; Pope is always smooth, uniform, and gentle. Dryden's page is a natural field, rising into inequalities, and diversified by the varied exuberance of abundant vegetation; Pope's is a velvet lawn, shaven by the scythe, and leveled by the roller.

Of genius, that power which constitutes a poet; that quality without which judgment is cold and knowledge is inert; that energy which collects, combines, amplifies, and animates—the superiority must, with some hesitation, be allowed to Dryden. It is not to be inferred that of this poetical vigor Pope had only a little, because Dryden had more, for every other writer since Milton must give place to Pope; and even of Dryden it must be said that if he has brighter paragraphs, he has not better poems. Dryden's performances were always hasty, either excited by some external occasion, or extorted by domestic necessity; he composed without consideration, and published without correction. What his mind could supply at call, or gather in one excursion, was all that he sought, and all that he gave. The dilatory caution of Pope enabled him to condense his sentiments, to multiply his images, and to accumulate all that study might produce, or chance might supply. If the flights of Dryden therefore are higher, Pope continues longer on the wing. If of Dryden's fire the blaze is brighter, of Pope's the heat is more regular and constant. Dryden often surpasses expectation, and Pope never falls below it. Dryden is read with frequent astonishment, and Pope with perpetual delight.

This parallel will, I hope, when it is well considered, be found just; and if the reader should suspect me, as I suspect myself, of some partial fondness for the memory of Dryden, let him not too hastily condemn me; for meditation and enquiry may, perhaps, show him the reasonableness of my determination.

[ON *THE RAPE OF THE LOCK*]

To the praises which have been accumulated on *The Rape of the Lock* by readers of every class, from the critic to the waiting-maid, it is difficult to make any addition. Of that which is universally allowed to be the most attractive of all ludicrous compositions, let it rather be now inquired from what sources the power of pleasing is derived.

Dr. Warburton, who excelled in critical perspicacity, has remarked that the preternatural agents are very happily adapted to the purposes of the poem. The heathen deities can no longer gain attention: we should have turned away from a contest between Venus and Diana. The employment of allegorical persons always excites conviction of its own absurdity: they may produce effects, but cannot conduct actions; when the phantom is put in motion, it dissolves; thus Discord may raise a mutiny, but Discord cannot conduct a march, nor besiege a town. Pope brought into view a new race of Beings, with powers and passions proportionate to their operation. The sylphs and gnomes act at the toilet[1] and the tea-table, what more terrific and more powerful phantoms perform on the stormy ocean or the field of battle; they give their proper help, and do their proper mischief. * * *

In this work are exhibited in a very high degree the two most engaging powers of an author: new things are made familiar, and familiar things are made new. A race of aerial people never heard of before is presented to us in a manner so clear and easy, that the reader seeks for no further information, but immediately mingles with his new acquaintance, adopts their interests and attends their pursuits, loves a sylph and detests a gnome.

That familiar things are made new every paragraph will prove. The subject of the poem is an event below the common incidents of common life; nothing real is introduced that is not seen so often as to be no longer regarded, yet the whole detail of a female-day is here brought before us invested with so much art of decoration that, though nothing is disguised, every thing is striking, and we feel all the appetite of curiosity for that from which we have a thousand times turned fastidiously away.

[ON *ELOISA TO ABELARD*]

The *Epistle of Eloisa to Abelard* is one of the most happy productions of human wit: the subject is so judiciously chosen that it would be difficult, in turning over the annals of the world, to find another which so many circumstances concur to recommend. We regularly interest ourselves most in the fortune of those who most deserve our notice. Abelard and Eloisa were conspicuous in their days for eminence of merit.

---

1. Dressing table.

The heart naturally loves truth. The adventures and misfortunes of this illustrious pair are known from undisputed history. Their fate does not leave the mind in hopeless dejection; for they both found quiet and consolation in retirement and piety. So new and so affecting is their story that it supersedes invention, and imagination ranges at full liberty without straggling into scenes of fable.

The story thus skillfully adopted has been diligently improved. Pope has left nothing behind him which seems more the effect of studious perseverance and laborious revisal. Here is particularly observable the *curiosa felicitas*,[1] a fruitful soil, and careful cultivation. Here is no crudeness of sense, nor asperity of language.

[On An Essay on Man]

The *Essay on Man* was a work of great labor and long consideration, but certainly not the happiest of Pope's performances. The subject is perhaps not very proper for poetry, and the poet was not sufficiently master of his subject; metaphysical morality was to him a new study, he was proud of his acquisitions, and, supposing himself master of great secrets, was in haste to teach what he had not learned. Thus he tells us, in the first Epistle, that from the nature of the Supreme Being may be deduced an order of beings such as mankind, because Infinite Excellence can do only what is best. He finds out that these beings must be "somewhere," and that "all the question is whether man be in a wrong place." Surely if, according to the poet's Leibnitzian reasoning,[1] we may infer that man ought to be only because he is, we may allow that his place is the right place, because he has it. Supreme Wisdom is not less infallible in disposing than in creating. But what is meant by "somewhere" and "place" and "wrong place" it had been vain to ask Pope, who probably had never asked himself.

Having exalted himself into the chair of wisdom he tells us much that every man knows, and much that he does not know himself; that we see but little, and that the order of the universe is beyond our comprehension, and opinion not very uncommon; and that there is a chain of subordinate beings "from infinite to nothing," of which himself and his readers are equally ignorant. But he gives us one comfort which, without his help, he supposes unattainable, in the position "that though we are fools, yet God is wise."

This *Essay* affords an egregious instance of the predominance of genius, the dazzling splendor of imagery, and the seductive powers of eloquence. Never were penury of knowledge and vulgarity of sentiment so happily disguised. The reader feels his mind full, though he learns nothing; and when he meets it in its new array no longer knows the talk of his mother and his nurse. When these wonder-working sounds sink into sense, and the doctrine of the *Essay*, disrobed of its ornaments, is left to the powers of its naked excellence, what shall we discover? That we are, in comparison with our Creator, very weak and ignorant; that we do not uphold the chain of existence; and that we could not make one another with more skill than we are made. We may learn yet more: that the arts of human life were copied from the instinctive operations of other animals; that if the world be made for man, it may be said that man was made for geese. To these profound principles of natural knowledge are added some moral instructions equally new: that self-interest well understood will produce social

---

1. Studied inspiration.
1. Johnson believed that Pope had been influenced by the deterministic philosophy of Gottfried Wilhelm von Leibnitz (1646–1716).

concord; that men are mutual gainers by mutual benefits; that evil is sometimes balanced by good; that human advantages are unstable and fallacious, of uncertain duration and doubtful effect; that our true honor is not to have a great part, but to act it well; that virtue only is our own; and that happiness is always in our power.

Surely a man of no very comprehensive search may venture to say that he has heard all this before, but it was never till now recommended by such a blaze of embellishment or such sweetness of melody. The vigorous contraction of some thoughts, the luxuriant amplification of others, the incidental illustrations, and sometimes the dignity, sometimes the softness of the verses, enchain philosophy, suspend criticism, and oppress judgment by overpowering pleasure.

This is true of many paragraphs; yet if I had undertaken to exemplify Pope's felicity of composition before a rigid critic I should not select the *Essay on Man*, for it contains more lines unsuccessfully labored, more harshness of diction, more thoughts imperfectly expressed, more levity without elegance, and more heaviness without strength, than will easily be found in all his other works.

from Annals[1]

[INFANCY AND CHILDHOOD]

1. 1709-10

Sept. 7,[2] 1709, I was born at Lichfield. My mother had a very difficult and dangerous labor, and was assisted by George Hector, a man-midwife of great reputation. I was born almost dead, and could not cry for some time. When he had me in his arms, he said, "Here is a brave boy."

In a few weeks an inflammation was discovered on my buttock, which was at first, I think, taken for a burn; but soon appeared to be a natural disorder. It swelled, broke, and healed.

My father being that year Sheriff of Lichfield, and to ride the circuit of the County next day, which was a ceremony then performed with great pomp; he was asked by my mother, "Whom he would invite to the Riding?" and answered, "All the town now." He feasted the citizens with uncommon magnificence, and was the last but one that maintained the splendor of the riding.

I was, by my father's persuasion, put to one Marclew, commonly called Bellison, the servant, or wife of a servant of my father, to be nursed in George Lane, where I used to call when I was a bigger boy, and eat fruit in the garden, which was full of trees. Here it was discovered that my eyes were bad; and an issue[3] was cut in my left arm, of which I took no great notice, as I think my mother has told me, having my little hand in a custard. How long this issue was continued I do not remember. I believe it was suffered to dry when I was about six years old.

---

1. Johnson often recommended that his friends keep records of their lives—in diaries, in autobiography—but he generally regarded the practice as intrinsically private. Just before his death, he burned two large volumes of his own diaries that Boswell in particular had longed to consult for his planned biography. Boswell never knew about another manuscript, titled *Annals*, which had partly survived the deathbed purge (though Johnson managed to destroy 32 pages of it). This account, of Johnson's early years, was first published in 1805; the original is now lost. Johnson apparently began writing it in his middle fifties, perhaps with the intention of producing a full autobiography, but perhaps also to investigate the origin of conditions of mind and of body that had affected him his whole life.

2. "18, in the present style" (Johnson's note). Britain's shift to the Gregorian calendar in 1752 "advanced" all previous bithdays and other anniversaries by eleven days.

3. An incision designed to drain off the scrofular infection. Johnson assumed that his ailment, which deprived him of all but peripheral vision in one eye, was caused by the scrofula (or tuberculosis of the lymph glands) that left his face and neck permanently scarred. In fact, the eye ailment occurred when he was only a few weeks old, whereas he contracted scrofula when he was two.

It is observable, that, having been told of this operation, I always imagined that I remembered it, but I laid the scene in the wrong house. Such confusions of memory I suspect to be common.

My mother visited me every day, and used to go different ways, that her assiduity might not expose her to ridicule; and often left her fan or glove behind her, that she might have a pretense to come back unexpected; but she never discovered any token of neglect. Dr. Swinfen told me, that the scrofulous sores which afflicted me proceeded from the bad humors[4] of the nurse, whose son had the same distemper, and was likewise short-sighted, but both in a less degree. My mother thought my diseases derived from her family.

In ten weeks I was taken home, a poor, diseased infant, almost blind.

I remember my aunt Nath. Ford told me, when I was about . . . years old, that she would not have picked such a poor creature up in the street.

In . . . 67, when I was at Lichfield, I went to look for my nurse's house; and, inquiring somewhat obscurely, was told "this is the house in which you were nursed." I saw my nurse's son, to whose milk I succeeded, reading a large Bible,[5] which my nurse had bought, as I was then told, some time before her death.

Dr. Swinfen used to say, that he never knew any child reared with so much difficulty.

2. 1710–11

In the second year I know not what happened to me. I believe it was then that my mother carried me to Trysul,[6] to consult Dr. Atwood, an oculist of Worcester. My father and Mrs. Harriots, I think, never had much kindness for each other. She was my mother's relation; and he had none so high to whom he could send any of his family. He saw her seldom himself, and willingly disgusted her, by sending his horses from home on Sunday; which she considered, and with reason, as a breach of duty. My father had much vanity, which his adversity hindered from being fully exerted. I remember that, mentioning her legacy in the humility of distress, he called her *our good Cousin Harriots*. My mother had no value for his relations; those indeed whom we knew of were much lower than hers. This contempt began, I know not on which side, very early: but, as my father was little at home, it had not much effect.

My father and mother had not much happiness from each other. They seldom conversed; for my father could not bear to talk of his affairs; and my mother, being unacquainted with books, cared not to talk of any thing else. Had my mother been more literate, they had been better companions. She might have sometimes introduced her unwelcome topic with more success, if she could have diversified her conversation. Of business she had no distinct conception; and therefore her discourse was composed only of complaint, fear, and suspicion. Neither of them ever tried to calculate the profits of trade, or the expenses of living. My mother concluded that we were poor, because we lost by some of our trades; but the truth was, that my father, having in the early part of his life contracted debts, never had trade sufficient to enable him to pay them, and maintain his family; he got something, but not enough.

It was not till about 1768 that I thought to calculate the returns of my father's trade, and by that estimate his probable profits. This, I believe, my parents never did.

---

4. Infectious tendencies (Johnson's nurse was thought to be a carrier of scrofula).
5. He needed a large-print Bible because he was almost blind.
6. Near Wolverhampton, Staffordshire, the home of Mrs. Johnson's first cousin, Elizabeth Harriots.

3. 1711-12

This year, in Lent—12, I was taken to London, to be touched for the evil by Queen Anne.[7] My mother was at Nicholson's, the famous bookseller, in Little Britain. My mother, then with child, concealed her pregnancy, that she might not be hindered from the journey. I always retained some memory of this journey, though I was then but thirty months old. I remembered a little dark room behind the kitchen, where the jack-weight[8] fell through a hole in the floor, into which I once slipped my leg. I seem to remember, that I played with a string and a bell, which my cousin Isaac Johnson gave me; and that there was a cat with a white collar, and a dog, called Chops, that leaped over a stick: but I know not whether I remember the thing, or the talk of it.

I remember a boy crying at the palace when I went to be touched. Being asked "on which side of the shop was the counter?" I answered, "on the left from the entrance," many years after, and spoke, not by guess, but by memory. We went in the stage-coach, and returned in the wagon, as my mother said, because my cough was violent. The hope of saving a few shillings was no slight motive; for she, not having been accustomed to money, was afraid of such expenses as now seem very small. She sewed two guineas in her petticoat, lest she should be robbed.

We were troublesome to the passengers; but to suffer such inconveniences in the stage-coach was common in those days to persons in much higher rank. I was sick; one woman fondled me, the other was disgusted. She bought me a small silver cup and spoon, marked SAM. I. lest if they had been marked S. I. which was her name, they should, upon her death, have been taken from me. She bought me a speckled linen frock, which I knew afterwards by the name of my London frock. The cup was one of the last pieces of plate which dear Tetty[9] sold in our distress. I have now the spoon. She bought at the same time two teaspoons, and till my manhood she had no more.

My father considered tea as very expensive, and discouraged my mother from keeping company with the neighbors, and from paying visits or receiving them. She lived to say, many years after, that, if the time were to pass again, she would not comply with such unsocial injunctions.

I suppose that in this year I was first informed of a future state. I remember, that being in bed with my mother one morning, I was told by her of the two places to which the inhabitants of this world were received after death; one a fine place filled with happiness, called Heaven; the other a sad place, called Hell. That this account much affected my imagination, I do not remember. When I was risen, my mother bade me repeat what she had told me to Thomas Jackson.[1] When I told this afterwards to my mother, she seemed to wonder that she should begin such talk so late as that the first time could be remembered. * * *

On Saturday, as on Thursday, we were examined. We were sometimes, on one of those days, asked our Catechism,[2] but with no regularity or constancy. G. Hector never had been taught his Catechism.

The progress of examination was this. When we learned *Propria quae Maribus*, we were examined in the Accidence;[3] particularly we formed verbs, that is, went through the same person in all the moods and tenses. This was very difficult to me; and I was once

---

7. It was widely believed that the monarch had the power to cure scrofula through "the royal touch."
8. Part of the mechanism that turned the spit upon which meat was roasted.
9. Elizabeth, Johnson's wife ("Tetty" was a provincial diminutive of Elizabeth).

1. A family retainer.
2. The essentials of Christianity set down in question-and-answer form.
3. Johnson refers to sections from William Lily's *Short Introduction of Grammar*, which had served as a basic textbook since the mid-16th century.

very anxious about the next day, when this exercise was to be performed, in which I had failed till I was discouraged. My mother encouraged me, and I proceeded better. When I told her of my good escape, "We often," said she, dear mother! "come off best, when we are most afraid." She told me that once, when she asked me about forming verbs, I said, "I did not form them in an ugly shape." "You could not," said she, "speak plain; and I was proud that I had a boy who was forming verbs." These little memorials soothe my mind. Of the parts of Corderius or Aesop,[4] which we learned to repeat, I have not the least recollection, except of a passage in one of the Morals, where it is said of some man, that, when he hated another, he made him rich; this I repeated emphatically in my mother's hearing, who could never conceive that riches could bring any evil. She remarked it, as I expected.

I had the curiosity, two or three years ago, to look over Garretson's *Exercises*, Willymot's *Particles*, and Walker's *Exercises*;[5] and found very few sentences that I should have recollected if I had found them in any other books. That which is read without pleasure is not often recollected nor infixed by conversation, and therefore in a great measure drops from the memory. Thus it happens that those who are taken early from school, commonly lose all that they had learned. ＊ ＊ ＊

The whole week before we broke up, and the part of the week in which we broke up, were spent wholly, I know not why, in examination; and were therefore easy to both us and the master. The two nights before the vacation were free from exercise.

This was the course of the school, which I remember with pleasure; for I was indulged and caressed by my master, and, I think, really excelled the rest.

I was with Hawkins[6] but two years, and perhaps four months. The time, till I had computed it, appeared much longer by the multitude of novelties which it supplied, and of incidents, then in my thoughts important, it produced. Perhaps it is not possible that any other period can make the same impression on the memory.

10. 1719

In the Spring of 1719, our class consisting of eleven, the number was always fixed in my memory, but one of the names I have forgotten, was removed to the upper school, and put under Holbrook,[7] a peevish and ill-tempered man. We were removed sooner than had been the custom; for the head-master, intent upon his boarders, left the town-boys long in the lower school. Our removal was caused by a reproof from the town clerk; and Hawkins complained that he had lost half his profit. At this removal I cried. The rest were indifferent. My exercise in Garretson was somewhere about the gerunds. Our places in Aesop and Helvicus I have totally forgotten.

At Whitsuntide[8] Mrs. Longworth brought me a "Hermes Garretsoni," of which I do not remember that I ever could make much use. It was afterwards lost, or stolen at school. My exercise was then in the end of the syntax. Hermes furnished me with the word *inliciturus*, which I did not understand, but used it.

This task was very troublesome to me; I made all the twenty-five exercises, others made but sixteen. I never showed all mine; five lay long after in a drawer in the shop. I made an exercise in a little time, and showed it my mother; but the task being long upon me, she said, "Though you could make an exercise in so short a time, I thought you would find it difficult to make them all as soon as you should."

This Whitsuntide, I and my brother were sent to pass some time at Birmingham; I believe, a fortnight. Why such boys were sent to trouble other houses, I cannot tell. My

---

4. Central to the grammar school curriculum were the fables of Aesop and the dialogues of the Renaissance scholar Mathurin Corderius.
5. Grammatical textbooks.

6. Humphrey Hawkins, a Lichfield schoolmaster.
7. The Reverend Edward Holbrooke, clergyman and schoolmaster.
8. The week beginning on the seventh Sunday after Easter.

mother had some opinion that much improvement was to be had by changing the mode of life. My uncle Harrison was a widower; and his house was kept by Sally Ford, a young woman of such sweetness of temper, that I used to say she had no fault. We lived most at uncle Ford's, being much caressed by my aunt, a good-natured, coarse woman, easy of converse, but willing to find something to censure in the absent. My uncle Harrison did not much like us, nor did we like him. He was a very mean and vulgar man, drunk every night, but drunk with little drink, very peevish, very proud, very ostentatious, but, luckily, not rich. At my aunt Ford's I eat so much of a boiled leg of mutton, that she used to talk of it. My mother, who had lived in a narrow sphere, and was then affected by little things, told me seriously that it would hardly ever be forgotten. Her mind, I think, was afterwards much enlarged, or greater evils wore out the care of less.

I stayed after the vacation was over some days; and remember, when I wrote home, that I desired the horses to come on Thursday of the first school week; and then, and not till then, they should be welcome to go. I was much pleased with a rattle to my whip, and wrote of it to my mother.

When my father came to fetch us home, he told the ostler,[9] that he had twelve miles home, and two boys under his care. This offended me. He had then a watch, which he returned when he was to pay for it.

In making, I think, the first exercise under Holbrook, I perceived the power of continuity of attention, of application not suffered to wander or to pause. I was writing at the kitchen windows, as I thought, alone, and turning my head saw Sally dancing. I went on without notice, and had finished almost without perceiving that any time had elapsed. This close attention I have seldom in my whole life obtained. * * *

LETTERS

To Lord Chesterfield[1]

My Lord: 7 February 1755

I have been lately informed by the proprietor of *The World* that two papers in which my Dictionary is recommended to the public were written by your Lordship.[2] To be so distinguished is an honor which, being very little accustomed to favors from the great, I know not well how to receive, or in what terms to acknowledge.

When upon some slight encouragement I first visited your Lordship I was overpowered like the rest of mankind by the enchantment of your adress, and could not forbear to wish that I might boast myself *le vainqueur du vainqueur de la terre*,[3] that I might obtain that regard for which I saw the world contending; but I found my attendance so little encouraged, that neither pride nor modesty would suffer me to continue it. When I had once adressed your Lordship in public, I had exhausted all the art of pleasing which a retired and uncourtly scholar can possess. I had done all that I could, and no man is well pleased to have his all neglected, be it ever so little.

Seven years, my lord, have now passed since I waited in your outward rooms or was repulsed from your door, during which time I have been pushing on my work through difficulties of which it is useless to complain, and have brought it at last to the

9. Stableman.
1. Philip Dormer Stanhope (1694–1773), fourth Earl of Chesterfield, a politician and man of letters renowned for his elegant manners and his knowledge of the polite world. In 1747 Johnson had dedicated his *Plan of a Dictionary* to Chesterfield but had received neither financial nor moral support from him during the long years of labor

on the *Dictionary*.
2. Chesterfield had contributed two essays to Robert Dodsley's periodical *The World*. In these essays he praised the forthcoming *Dictionary* in such a way as to imply that he had been its enlightened sponsor.
3. "The conqueror of the world's conqueror" (the opening line of the epic *Alaric*, by Georges de Scudéry).

verge of publication without one act of assistance, one word of encouragement, or one smile of favor. Such treatment I did not expect, for I never had a patron before.

The shepherd in Virgil grew at last acquainted with Love, and found him a native of the rocks.[4] Is not a patron, my lord, one who looks with unconcern on a man struggling for life in the water and when he has reached ground encumbers him with help?[5] The notice which you have been pleased to take of my labors, had it been early, had been kind; but it has been delayed till I am indifferent and cannot enjoy it, till I am solitary and cannot impart it, till I am known and do not want it.

I hope it is no very cynical asperity not to confess obligation where no benefit has been received, or to be unwilling that the public should consider me as owing that to a patron, which providence has enabled me to do for myself.

Having carried on my work thus far with so little obligation to any favorer of learning I shall not be disappointed though I should conclude it, if less be possible, with less, for I have been long wakened from that dream of hope, in which I once boasted myself with so much exultation, my Lord, your Lordship's most humble, most obedient servant,

S.J.

To Hester Thrale

Dear Madam: Bolt Court, Fleetstreet, June 19, 1783

I am sitting down in no cheerful solitude to write a narrative which would once have affected you with tenderness and sorrow, but which you will perhaps pass over now with the careless glance of frigid indifference.[1] For this diminution of regard however, I know not whether I ought to blame you, who may have reasons which I cannot know, and I do not blame myself who have for a great part of human life done you what good I could, and have never done you evil.

I had been disordered in the usual way, and had been relieved by the usual methods, by opium and cathartics,[2] but had rather lessened my dose of opium.

On Monday the 16 I sat for my picture,[3] and walked a considerable way with little inconvenience. In the afternoon and evening I felt myself light and easy, and began to plan schemes of life. Thus I went to bed, and in a short time waked and sat up as has been long my custom when I felt a confusion and indistinctness in my head which lasted, I suppose about half a minute. I was alarmed and prayed God, that however he might afflict my body he would spare my understanding. This prayer, that I might try the integrity of my faculties, I made in Latin verse. The lines were not very good, but I knew them not to be very good, I made them easily, and concluded myself to be unimpaired in my faculties.

Soon after I perceived that I had suffered a paralytic stroke, and that my speech was taken from me. I had no pain, and so little dejection in this dreadful state that I wondered at my own apathy, and considered that perhaps death itself when it should come, would excite less horror than seems now to attend it.

In order to rouse the vocal organs I took two drams. Wine has been celebrated for the production of eloquence; I put myself into violent motion, and, I think, repeated it.

---

4. Johnson alludes to a pastoral poem by Virgil (*Eclogue* 8), in which Love is described as coming from a land of "flinty crags."
5. In his *Dictionary*, Johnson defines "patron" as "commonly a wretch who supports with insolence, and is paid with flattery."
1. As she became more and more attached to Gabriel Piozzi, an Italian musician, Hester Thrale (correctly sens-

ing how angry Johnson would be) began to disengage from their close friendship. Though he knew something had gone wrong, Johnson did not learn of the love affair until a year later, when Mrs. Thrale wrote to inform him of her marriage.
2. Purgatives.
3. Johnson's portrait was being painted.

But all was vain; I then went to bed, and, strange as it may seem, I think, slept. When I saw light, it was time to contrive what I should do. Though God stopped my speech he left me my hand, I enjoyed a mercy which was not granted to my Dear Friend Lawrence,[4] who now perhaps overlooks me as I am writing and rejoices that I have what he wanted.[5] My first note was necessarily to my servant, who came in talking, and could not immediately comprehend why he should read what I put into his hands.

I then wrote a card to Mr. Allen,[6] that I might have a discreet friend at hand to act as occasion should require. In penning this note I had some difficulty, my hand, I know not how nor why, made wrong letters. I then wrote to Dr. Taylor[7] to come to me, and bring Dr. Heberden, and I sent to Dr. Brocklesby, who is my neighbor. My physicians are very friendly and very disinterested; and give me great hopes, but you may imagine my situation. I have so far recovered my vocal powers, as to repeat the Lord's Prayer with no very imperfect articulation. My memory, I hope, yet remains as it was. But such an attack produces solicitude for the safety of every faculty.

How this will be received by you, I know not, I hope you will sympathize with me, but perhaps

> My Mistress gracious, mild, and good,
> Cries, Is he dumb? 'tis time he should.[8]

But can this be possible, I hope it cannot. I hope that what, when I could speak, I spoke of You, and to You, will be in a sober and serious hour remembered by You, and surely it cannot be remembered but with some degree of kindness. I have loved You with virtuous affection, I have honoured You with sincere esteem. Let not all our endearment be forgotten, but let me have in this great distress your pity and your prayers. You see I yet turn to You with my complaints as a settled and unalienable friend, do not, do not drive me from You, for I have not deserved either neglect or hatred.

To the girls,[9] who do not write often, for Susy has written only once, and Miss Thrale owes me a letter, I earnestly recommend as their guardian and friend, that they remember their Creator in the days of their youth.[1]

I suppose You may wish to know how my disease is treated by the physicians. They put a blister upon my back, and two from my ear to my throat, one on a side. The blister on the back has done little, and those on the throat have not risen. I bullied, and bounced, (it sticks to our last sand)[2] and compelled the apothecary to make his salve according to the Edinburgh dispensatory[3] that it might adhere better. I have two on now of my own prescription. They likewise give me salt of hartshorn, which I take with no great confidence, but am satisfied that what can be done, is done for me.

O God, give me comfort and confidence in Thee, forgive my sins, and if it be thy good pleasure, relieve my diseases for Jesus Christ's sake. Amen.

I am almost ashamed of this querulous letter, but now it is written, let it go. I am Madam, Your most humble servant,

SAM. JOHNSON

---

4. Johnson's favorite physician, Dr. Thomas Lawrence, had died earlier that month after suffering a stroke.
5. Lacked.
6. Johnson's printer and neighbor, Edmund Allen.
7. The clergyman John Taylor, one of Johnson's oldest and closest friends.
8. Johnson adapts a couplet from Swift's *Verses on the Death of Dr. Swift*: "The Queen, so gracious, mild and good, / Cries, 'Is he gone? 'Tis time he should'" (lines 181–182).

9. Hester Thrale's four surviving daughters: Hester Maria ("Miss Thrale"), Susanna ("Susy"), Sophia, and Cecilia.
1. "Remember now thy Creator in the days of thy youth, while the evil days come not" (Ecclesiastes 12.1).
2. "Time, that on all things lays his lenient hand, / Yet tames not this; it sticks to our last sand" (Pope, *Epistle to Cobham*, lines 224–225).
3. Medical manual.

To Hester Thrale Piozzi

Madam: July 2, 1784

If I interpret your letter right, You are ignominiously married,[1] if it is yet undone, let us once talk together. If You have abandoned your children and your religion, God forgive your wickedness; if You have forfeited your fame, and your country, may your folly do no further mischief.[2]

If the last act is yet to do, I, who have loved you, esteemed you, reverenced you, and served you, I who long thought You the first of humankind, entreat that before your fate is irrevocable, I may once more see You. I was, I once was, Madam, most truly yours,

SAM. JOHNSON

I will come down if you permit it.

To Hester Thrale Piozzi

Dear Madam: London, July 8, 1784

What You have done, however I may lament it, I have no pretense to resent, as it has not been injurious to me. I therefore breathe out one sigh more of tenderness perhaps useless, but at least sincere.

I wish that God may grant You every blessing, that you may be happy in this world for its short continuance, and eternally happy in a better state. And whatever I can contribute to your happiness, I am very ready to repay for that kindness which soothed twenty years of a life radically wretched.

Do not think slightly of the advice which I now presume to offer. Prevail upon Mr. Piozzi to settle in England. You may live here with more dignity than in Italy, and with more security. Your rank will be higher, and your fortune more under your own eye. I desire not to detail all my reasons; but every argument of prudence and interest is for England, and only some phantoms of imagination seduce you to Italy.

I am afraid, however, that my counsel is vain, yet I have eased my heart by giving it.

When Queen Mary took the resolution of sheltering herself in England, the Archbishop of St. Andrew's attempting to dissuade her,[1] attended on her journey and when they came to the irremeable[2] stream that separated the two kingdoms, walked by her side into the water, in the middle of which he seized her bridle, and with earnestness proportioned to her danger and his own affection, pressed her to return. The Queen went forward.—If the parallel reaches thus far; may it go no further. The tears stand in my eyes.

I am going into Derbyshire,[3] and hope to be followed by your good wishes, for I am with great affection, Your most humble servant,

SAM. JOHNSON

Any letters that come for me hither, will be sent me.

---

1. Hester Thrale had written on June 30 to inform Johnson of her marriage to Gabriel Piozzi.
2. Johnson's objections to Gabriel Piozzi include the fact that he is a musician (and therefore socially inferior), a Catholic, and an Italian.
1. Johnson draws on a semifictional account of Mary Queen of Scots' fateful decision to take refuge in England. According to this version, she crossed the river on horseback, attended by John Hamilton, Archbishop of St. Andrews.
2. "Admitting no return" (Johnson's *Dictionary*).
3. The home of John Taylor.

James Boswell
1740–1795

"I have discovered," James Boswell announced at age twenty-two in the journal he had just commenced, "that we may be in some degree whatever character we choose." The possibilities opened up by this discovery both exhilarated and troubled him. Neither the "choosing" nor the "being" turned out to be as simple as he expected, in part because some alternate choice always beckoned. In the pages of his journal, Boswell performed his excited choices and anxious reconsiderations. The oscillation did much to drive the intricate comedy and intermittent pathos, the energetic posing and fervent self-scrutiny of the diaries he kept all his adult life, and of the published books he crafted from them.

Boswell's parents had chosen their own characters early, and had stuck to them assiduously. His father was a Scots laird—heir to an ancient family and a landed estate—and a distinguished jurist, serving as justice on Scotland's highest courts. His mother was an impassioned Calvinist, who numbered among her many strictures an abhorrence of the theater; the actors' freedom of character-choice, which made the playhouse for her a place of sinful deception, would make it the site of a lifelong enchantment for her son. Boswell's parents had chosen firmly for their first-born too. James was to become, like his father, an eminent lawyer and respectable landowner.

Boswell chafed at the narrowness of the scheme. Struggling (he later recalled) "against paternal affection, ambition, interest," he ran away to London for a short spell at age eighteen and returned there at twenty-two, seeking a commission as a soldier with the king's personal bodyguard, a post that would have secured him lifelong residence in the city, flashy uniforms, and ample opportunities to display himself in them. While Boswell waited for this prospect to materialize (it never did), he found his real calling. He started to keep a copious journal, narrating each day in succession, dispatching the text in weekly packets to his friend John Johnston back home in Scotland. Here too was self-display, intricately contrived. Boswell managed his journal as a kind of manuscript theater—often written as a play text, complete with dialogue and stage directions—for an audience of one (the performance of his journal texts for a wider reading public would later become his literary life's work). London, the theatrical city, teemed with "characters" living and dead, real and fictional, whom Boswell by turns and in combinations strove to "be": Addison, Steele, and their imaginary paragon of self-possession Mr. Spectator; Captain Macheath from *The Beggar's Opera* (on whose adventures Boswell modeled many of his own sexual exploits); the actors Thomas Sheridan and David Garrick; and most importantly, Garrick's old teacher Samuel Johnson, whose writings had provided Boswell with a model of moral firmness more attractive than his father's, and who befriended the young diarist six months into his London stay.

The friendship with Johnson gave Boswell's journal a new purpose (to record the conversations of this dazzling talker) and his life a new direction. Reconciled to his father's plan, Boswell studied law in Holland and, as reward for his painfully diligent endeavors, made the Grand Tour of Europe, where he collected the conversation and the counsel of further celebrities: the French iconoclasts Voltaire and Rousseau, and the Corsican rebel leader Pasquale Paoli, then fighting to free his island from foreign domination. Returning to Scotland in 1766, Boswell took up the life his father had mapped for him, settling in Edinburgh, and becoming (as he haughtily informed his disreputable friend John Wilkes) "a Scottish lawyer, a Scottish laird, and a Scottish married man." In each of these roles, though, he repeatedly broke character. He went down to London almost every spring, ostensibly to cultivate his legal practice but really to renew his old absorptions: in theater, in sexual adventure, in the spellbinding company of Johnson and the group of artists, writers, and thinkers who surrounded him.

Boswell yearned to join their number not merely as admirer but as eminent author, and he soon did. Over the ensuing years, he produced much journalism and some verse, as well as three books in which he explored with increasing audacity the potential of his own diary as a public text—as a vehicle of entertainment, instruction, profit, and fame. He pursued for the journal form a print authority it had not previously possessed, devising ways for it to encroach upon, even to colonize, territory and tasks traditionally reserved to other genres: travel book, "character" sketch, biography. In his first attempt, *An Account of Corsica . . . and Memoirs of Pascal Paoli* (1769), he recast his original travel journal (rearranging the entries, dropping the dates) to produce a heroic portrait of his friend the liberator. In his second experiment, *A Journal of a Tour to the Hebrides with Samuel Johnson* (1785), which appeared the year after Johnson's death, the imperative to portraiture was even more pronounced. The public craved accounts of the lost titan, and this time Boswell met that demand a different way. He presented his journal *as* a journal, with scrupulously dated, plentifully narrated consecutive entries rich in the "minute details of daily life" that Johnson himself had stipulated as the criteria for good biography. The book struck readers as startlingly new. Some mocked it for its minutiae ("How are we all with rapture touched," exclaimed one versifier, "to see / Where, when, and at what hour, you swallowed tea!"), while many praised its veracity and abundance.

There was much more where that came from. In *The Life of Samuel Johnson, LL.D.* (1791), Boswell deployed the *Tour*'s techniques on a massive scale. Drawing on his diaries, and on years of arduous research among Johnson's many acquaintances, Boswell built a thousand-page biography that is largely a book of talk, of conversations diligently recorded and deftly dramatized, the culmination of the textual theater that Boswell had long practiced in manuscript. Johnson's capacious mind and imposing presence find embodiment in a text dense with accumulated time, told and retold over the span of almost three decades that stretches from Boswell's first Johnsonian journal entry to the biography's publication. Pleased with the book's commercial success, stung by charges that he had been either too partial to Johnson or too critical of him, Boswell worked at two further editions (in which his footnotes swelled with new information and rebuttals). He died at fifty-five, unmade by alcoholism, by venereal disease, and by the violent depressions that accompanied his ongoing uncertainty as to what he might "be" and had become.

His books sustained his fame, though ever since the *Life*'s first appearance, readers have debated the degree of its accuracy and the merits of its portraiture. Two centuries later, Boswell's biography has become a touchstone text for the problem of the "documentary"—the question of how art and "fact" should merge in representations of historical events. Over the past eighty years the debate has been deepened by the unexpected recovery of Boswell's original papers, including the diaries that he drew on and boasted of in his published books. The papers had long been given up for lost, but masses of them had actually been stashed and forgotten by various descendants in odd receptacles (cabinet, croquet box, grain loft) on estates scattered across Scotland and Ireland. The papers' recovery took more than twenty years; the process of their publication continues. Taken together, Boswell's papers and his published works make it possible to trace the intricate course by which the flux of his energetic, agitated life became fixed in text.

from London Journal

[A Scot in London]

Wednesday, 1 December [1762]. * * * On Tuesday I wanted to have a silver-hilted sword, but upon examining my pockets as I walked up the Strand,[1] I found that I had left the most of my guineas at home and had not enough to pay for it with me.

---

1. A major commercial street in the West End of London.

I determined to make a trial of the civility of my fellow-creatures, and what effect my external appearance and address would have. I accordingly went to the shop of Mr. Jefferys, sword-cutter to his Majesty, looked at a number of his swords, and at last picked out a very handsome one at five guineas. "Mr. Jefferys," said I, "I have not money here to pay for it. Will you trust me?" "Upon my word, Sir," said he, "you must excuse me. It is a thing we never do to a stranger." I bowed genteelly and said, "Indeed, Sir, I believe it is not right." However, I stood and looked at him, and he looked at me. "Come, Sir," cried he, "I will trust you." "Sir," said I, "if you had not trusted me, I should not have bought it from you." He asked my name and place of abode, which I told him. I then chose a belt, put the sword on, told him I would call and pay it tomorrow, and walked off. I called this day and paid him. "Mr. Jefferys," said I, "there is your money. You paid me a very great compliment. I am much obliged to you. But pray don't do such a thing again. It is dangerous." "Sir," said he, "we know our men. I would have trusted you with the value of a hundred pounds." This I think was a good adventure and much to my honor.

* * *

This afternoon I was surprised with the arrival of Lady Betty Macfarlane, Lady Anne Erskine, Captain Erskine, and Miss Dempster, who were come to the Red Lion Inn at Charing Cross. It seems Lady Betty had written to the laird that if he would not come down, she would come up; and upon his giving her an indolent answer, like a woman of spirit, she put her resolution in practice. I immediately went to them.[2]

To tell the plain truth, I was vexed at their coming. For to see just the plain *hamely*[3] Fife family hurt my grand ideas of London. Besides, I was now upon a plan of studying polite reserved behavior, which is the only way to keep up dignity of character. And as I have a good share of pride, which I think is very proper and even noble, I am hurt with the taunts of ridicule and am unsatisfied if I do not feel myself something of a superior animal. This has always been my favorite idea in my best moments. Indeed, I have been obliged to deviate from it by a variety of circumstances. After my wild expedition to London in the year 1760, after I got rid of the load of serious reflection which then burthened me, by being always in Lord Eglinton's company, very fond of him, and much caressed by him, I became dissipated and thoughtless.[4] When my father forced me down to Scotland, I was at first very low-spirited, although to appearance very high. I afterwards from my natural vivacity endeavored to make myself easy; and like a man who takes to drinking to banish care, I threw myself loose as a heedless, dissipated, rattling fellow who might say or do every ridiculous thing. This made me sought after by everybody for the present hour, but I found myself a very inferior being; and I found many people presuming to treat me as such, which notwithstanding of my appearance of undiscerning gaiety, gave me much pain. I was, in short, a character very different from what God intended me and I myself chose. I remember my friend Johnston[5] told me one day after my return from London that I had turned out different from what he imagined, as he thought I would resemble Mr. Addi-

---

2. With the exception of Miss Dempster, the sister of his friend George, Boswell refers to the daughters and son of the Fifth Earl of Kellie ("the laird"). The family came from Fife, a county in eastern Scotland.

3. Scots dialect for "homely," home-like.

4. At the age of 18, Boswell had run away to London,

where he impulsively converted to Catholicism. The tenth Earl of Eglinton, a charming and generous rake, weaned him from religion by turning him into a libertine.

5. John Johnston of Grange, Boswell's close friend, to whom he was sending the journal in weekly installments.

son.[6] I laughed and threw out some loud sally of humor, but the observation struck deep. Indeed, I must do myself the justice to say that I always resolved to be such a man whenever my affairs were made easy and I got upon my own footing. For as I despaired of that, I endeavored to lower my views and just to be a good-humored comical being, well liked either as a waiter, a common soldier, a clerk in Jamaica, or some other odd out-of-the-way sphere. Now, when my father at last put me into an independent situation, I felt my mind regain its native dignity. I felt strong dispositions to be a Mr. Addison. Indeed, I had accustomed myself so much to laugh at everything that it required time to render my imagination solid and give me just notions of real life and of religion. But I hoped by degrees to attain to some degree of propriety. Mr. Addison's character in sentiment, mixed with a little of the gaiety of Sir Richard Steele and the manners of Mr. Digges,[7] were the ideas which I aimed to realize.

Indeed, I must say that Digges has more or as much of the deportment of a man of fashion as anybody I ever saw; and he keeps up this so well that he never once lessened upon me even on an intimate acquaintance, although he is now and then somewhat melancholy, under which it is very difficult to preserve dignity; and this I think is particularly to be admired in Mr. Digges. Indeed, he and I never came to familiarity, which is justly said to beget contempt. The great art of living easy and happy in society is to study proper behavior, and even with our most intimate friends to observe politeness; otherwise we will insensibly treat each other with a degree of rudeness, and each will find himself despised in some measure by the other. As I was therefore pursuing this laudable plan, I was vexed at the arrival of the Kellie family, with whom when in Scotland I had been in the greatest familiarity. Had they not come for a twelvemonth, I should have been somewhat established in my address, but as I had been but a fortnight from them, I could not without the appearance of strong affectation appear much different from what they had seen me. I accordingly was very free, but rather more silent, which they imputed to my dullness, and roasted me about London's not being agreeable to me. I bore it pretty well, and left them.

* * *

Wednesday, 15 December [1762]. The enemies of the people of England who would have them considered in the worst light represent them as selfish, beef-eaters, and cruel. In this view I resolved today to be a true-born Old Englishman. I went into the City[8] to Dolly's Steak-house in Paternoster Row and swallowed my dinner by myself to fulfill the charge of selfishness; I had a large fat beefsteak to fulfill the charge of beef-eating; and I went at five o'clock to the Royal Cockpit in St. James's Park and saw cockfighting for about five hours to fulfill the charge of cruelty.

A beefsteak house is a most excellent place to dine at. You come in there to a warm, comfortable, large room, where a number of people are sitting at table. You take whatever place you find empty; call for what you like, which you get well and cleverly dressed. You may either chat or not as you like. Nobody minds you, and you pay very reasonably. My dinner (beef, bread and beer and waiter) was only a shilling. The waiters make a great deal of money by these pennies.[9] Indeed, I admire the English for attending to small sums, as many smalls make a great, according to the proverb.

---

6. Joseph Addison, author, with Sir Richard Steele, of the *Tatler* and *Spectator* papers. Addison was particularly identified with the character of the silent, all-seeing Mr. Spectator.
7. West Digges, an actor in Edinburgh, particularly known

for his portrayal of Macheath in *The Beggar's Opera*.
8. The older, eastern half of London, which included the centers of finance, law, and journalism.
9. The waiter's tip was one of the 12 pence that made up a shilling.

At five I filled my pockets with gingerbread and apples (quite the method), put on my old clothes and laced hat, laid by my watch, purse, and pocketbook, and with oaken stick in my hand sallied to the pit. I was too soon there. So I went into a low inn, sat down amongst a parcel of arrant blackguards, and drank some beer. The sentry near the house had been very civil in showing me the way. It was very cold. I bethought myself of the poor fellow, so I carried out a pint of beer myself to him. He was very thankful and drank my health cordially. He told me his name was Hobard, that he was a watchmaker but in distress for debt, and enlisted that his creditors might not touch him.

I then went to the Cockpit, which is a circular room in the middle of which the cocks fight. It is seated round with rows gradually rising. The pit and the seats are all covered with mat. The cocks, nicely cut and dressed and armed with silver heels, are set down and fight with amazing bitterness and resolution. Some of them were quickly dispatched. One pair fought three quarters of an hour. The uproar and noise of betting is prodigious. A great deal of money made a very quick circulation from hand to hand. There was a number of professed gamblers there. An old cunning dog whose face I had seen at Newmarket[1] sat by me a while. I told him I knew nothing of the matter.[2] "Sir," said he, "you have as good a chance as anybody." He thought I would be a good subject for him. I was young-like. But he found himself balked. I was shocked to see the distraction and anxiety of the betters. I was sorry for the poor cocks. I looked round to see if any of the spectators pitied them when mangled and torn in a most cruel manner, but I could not observe the smallest relenting sign in any countenance. I was therefore not ill pleased to see them endure mental torment. Thus did I complete my true English day, and came home pretty much fatigued and pretty much confounded at the strange turn of this people.

[LOUISA][1]

Wednesday, 12 January [1763]. Louisa and I agreed that at eight at night she would meet me in the piazzas of Covent Garden.[2] I was quite elevated, and felt myself able and undaunted to engage in the wars of the Paphian Queen.[3]

I dined at Sheridan's[4] very heartily. He showed to my conviction that Garrick[5] did not play the great scene in the Second Part of King Henry[6] with propriety. "People," said he, "in this age know when particular lines or even speeches are well spoke; but they do not study character, which is a matter of the utmost moment, as people of different characters feel and express their feelings very differently. For want of a knowledge of this, Mr. Barry[7] acted the distress of Othello, the Moorish warrior whose stubborn soul was hard to bend, and that of Castalio, the gentle lover who was all tenderness, in the self-same way. Now Mr. Garrick in that famous scene whines most piteously when he ought to upbraid. Shakespeare has discovered[8] there a most intimate knowledge of human nature. He shows you the King worn out with sickness

1. A town in Suffolk famous for horse racing.
2. About betting on cockfighting.
1. An actress at Covent Garden Theater, whose real name was Mrs. Lewis.
2. The arcades along the northern perimeter of the square, designed by Inigo Jones and popularly known as "piazzas," were a famous trysting place.
3. Venus.
4. Thomas Sheridan, Irish actor and teacher of elocution;

father of Richard Brinsley Sheridan, author of The School for Scandal.
5. David Garrick (1717–1779), the most celebrated actor-manager of his age.
6. Shakespeare's 2 Henry IV 4.5.
7. Spranger Barry, a well-known actor who played the protagonist in Shakespeare's Othello and in Otway's The Orphan.
8. Revealed.

and so weak that he faints. He had usurped the crown by the force of arms and was convinced that it must be held with spirit. He saw his son given up to low debauchery. He was anxious and vexed to think of the anarchy that would ensue at his death. Upon discovering that the Prince had taken the crown from his pillow, and concluding him desirous of his death, he is fired with rage. He starts up. He cries, 'Go chide him hither!' His anger animates him so much that he throws aside his distemper. Nature furnishes all her strength for one last effort. He is for a moment renewed. He is for a moment the spirited Henry the Fourth. He upbraids him with bitter sarcasm and bold figures. And then what a beautiful variety is there, when, upon young Harry's contrition, he falls on his neck and melts into parental tenderness."

I yielded this point to Sheridan candidly. But upon his attacking Garrick as a tragedian in his usual way, I opposed him keenly, and declared he was prejudiced; because the world thought him a good tragic actor. "So do I, Sir," said he; "I think him the best I ever saw." BOSWELL: "Except yourself, Mr. Sheridan. But come, we shall take this for granted. The world then think him near equal or as good as you in what you excel in." SHERIDAN: "Sir, I am not a bit prejudiced. I don't value acting. I shall suppose that I was the greatest actor that ever lived and universally acknowledged so, I would not choose that it should be remembered. I would have it erased out of the anecdotes of my life. Acting is a poor thing in the present state of the stage. For my own part, I engaged in it merely as a step to something greater, a just notion of eloquence." This was in a good measure true. But he certainly talked too extravagantly.

An old Irish maid, or rather an Irish old maid (O most hideous character!) dined with us. She was indeed a terrible Joy.[9] She was a woman of knowledge and criticism and correct taste. But there came to tea a Miss Mowat who played once on the stage here for a winter or two, a lovely girl. Many an amorous glance did I exchange with her. I was this day quite flashy with love. We often addressed our discourse to each other. I hope to see her again; and yet what have I to do with anybody but dear Louisa?

At the appointed hour of eight I went to the piazzas, where I sauntered up and down for a while in a sort of trembling suspense, I knew not why. At last my charming companion appeared, and I immediately conducted her to a hackney coach which I had ready waiting, pulled up the blinds, and away we drove to the destined scene of delight. We contrived to seem as if we had come off a journey, and carried in a bundle our nightclothes, handkerchiefs, and other little things. We also had with us some almond biscuits, or as they call them in London, macaroons, which looked like provision on the road. On our arrival at Hayward's[1] we were shown into the parlor, in the same manner that any decent couple would be. I here thought proper to conceal my own name (which the people of the house had never heard), and assumed the name of Mr. Digges. We were shown up to the very room where he slept. I said my cousin, as I called him, was very well. That Ceres and Bacchus might in moderation lend their assistance to Venus,[2] I ordered a genteel supper and some wine.

Louisa told me she had two aunts who carried her over to France when she was a girl, and that she could once speak French as fluently as English. We talked a little in it, and agreed that we would improve ourselves by reading and speaking it every day.

---

9. Irishwoman.
1. Fleet Street inn, recommended to Boswell by Digges.
2. Deities of grain, wine, and love, respectively. Boswell

refers to the proverb, "without Ceres and Bacchus, Venus grows cold."

I asked her if we did not just look like man and wife. "No," said she, "we are too fond for married people." No wonder that she may have a bad idea of that union, considering how bad it was for her. She has contrived a pretty device for a seal.[3] A heart is gently warmed by Cupid's flame, and Hymen[4] comes with his rude torch and extinguishes it. She said she found herself quite in a flutter. "Why, really," said I, "reason sometimes has no power. We have no occasion to be frightened, and yet we are both a little so. Indeed, I preserve a tolerable presence of mind." I rose and kissed her, and conscious that I had no occasion to doubt my qualifications as a gallant,[5] I joked about it: "How curious would it be if I should be so frightened that we should rise as we lay down." She reproved my wanton language by a look of modesty. The bells of St. Bride's church rung their merry chimes hard by. I said that the bells in Cupid's court would be this night set a-ringing for joy at our union.

We supped cheerfully and agreeably and drank a few glasses, and then the maid came and put the sheets, well aired, upon the bed. I now contemplated my fair prize. Louisa is just twenty-four, of a tall rather than short figure, finely made in person, with a handsome face and an enchanting languish in her eyes. She dresses with taste. She has sense, good humour, and vivacity, and looks quite a woman in genteel life. As I mused on this elevating subject, I could not help being somehow pleasingly confounded to think that so fine a woman was at this moment in my possession, that without any motives of interest[6] she had come with me to an inn, agreed to be my intimate companion, as to be my bedfellow all night, and to permit me the full enjoyment of her person.

When the servant left the room, I embraced her warmly and begged that she would not now delay my felicity. She declined to undress before me, and begged I would retire and send her one of the maids. I did so, gravely desiring the girl to go up to Mrs. Digges. I then took a candle in my hand and walked out to the yard. The night was very dark and very cold. I experienced for some minutes the rigors of the season, and called into my mind many terrible ideas of hardships, that I might make a transition from such dreary thoughts to the most gay and delicious feelings. I then caused make a bowl of negus,[7] very rich of the fruit, which I caused be set in the room as a reviving cordial.

I came softly into the room, and in a sweet delirium slipped into bed and was immediately clasped in her snowy arms and pressed to her milk-white bosom. Good heavens, what a loose[8] did we give to amorous dalliance! The friendly curtain of darkness concealed our blushes. In a moment I felt myself animated with the strongest powers of love, and, from my dearest creature's kindness, had a most luscious feast. Proud of my godlike vigor, I soon resumed the noble game. I was in full glow of health. Sobriety had preserved me from effeminacy[9] and weakness, and my bounding blood beat quick and high alarms. A more voluptuous night I never enjoyed. Five times was I fairly lost in supreme rapture. Louisa was madly fond of me; she declared I was a prodigy, and asked me if this was not extraordinary for human nature. I said twice as much might be, but this was not, although in my own mind I was somewhat proud of my performance. She said it was what there was no just reason to be proud of. But I

---

3. A personal emblem or insignia, which would be impressed on the wax sealing a letter.
4. God of marriage, who traditionally carries a torch.
5. A lover; Boswell jokes that, were he anxious, he might lose his erection, in which case the couple would "rise" from the bed, without consummation.
6. Mercenary motives.
7. A drink of wine and hot water, sweetened and flavored.
8. What freedom.
9. Impotence.

told her I could not help it. She said it was what we had in common with the beasts. I said no. For we had it highly improved by the pleasures of sentiment.[1] I asked her what she thought enough. She gently chid me for asking such questions, but said two times. I mentioned the Sunday's assignation,[2] when I was in such bad spirits, told her in what agony of mind I was, and asked her if she would not have despised me for my imbecility. She declared she would not, as it was what people had not in their own power.

She often insisted that we should compose ourselves to sleep before I would consent to it. At last I sunk to rest in her arms and she in mine. I found the negus, which had a fine flavor, very refreshing to me. Louisa had an exquisite mixture of delicacy and wantonness that made me enjoy her with more relish. Indeed I could not help roving in fancy to the embraces of some other ladies which my lively imagination strongly pictured. I don't know if that was altogether fair. However, Louisa had all the advantage. She said she was quite fatigued and could neither stir leg nor arm. She begged I would not despise her, and hoped my love would not be altogether transient. I have painted this night as well as I could. The description is faint; but I surely may be styled a Man of Pleasure.

Thursday, 20 January [1763][3] * * * I then went to Louisa. With excellent address did I carry on this interview, as the following scene, I trust, will make appear:

LOUISA My dear Sir! I hope you are well today.

BOSWELL Excessively well, I thank you. I hope I find you so.

LOUISA No, really, Sir. I am distressed with a thousand things. (Cunning jade, her circumstances![4]) I really don't know what to do.

BOSWELL Do you know that I have been very unhappy since I saw you?

LOUISA How so, Sir?

BOSWELL Why, I am afraid that you don't love me so well, nor have not such a regard for me, as I thought you had.

LOUISA Nay, dear Sir! [Seeming unconcerned.]

BOSWELL Pray, Madam, have I no reason?

LOUISA No, indeed, Sir, you have not.

BOSWELL Have I no reason, Madam? Pray think.

LOUISA Sir!

BOSWELL Pray, Madam, in what state of health have you been in for some time?

LOUISA Sir, you amaze me.

BOSWELL I have but too strong, too plain reason to doubt of your regard. I have for some days observed the symptoms of disease, but was unwilling to believe you so very ungenerous. But now, Madam, I am thoroughly convinced.

LOUISA Sir, you have terrified me. I protest I know nothing of the matter.

BOSWELL Madam, I have had no connection with any woman but you these two months. I was with my surgeon this morning, who declared I had got a strong infection, and that she from whom I had it could not be ignorant of it. Madam, such a thing in this case is worse than from a woman of the town,[5] as from her you may expect it. You have used me very ill. I did not deserve it. You know you said

1. Feelings of affection.
2. During an assignation ten days earlier, Boswell had attempted—unsuccessfully—to consummate the relationship.
3. The day before, Boswell had observed in himself the unmistakable signs of venereal disease: "Too, too plain

was Signor Gonorrhoea!" He then visited his doctor, who confirmed the diagnosis and asserted "that the woman who gave it me could not but know about it."
4. During the course of the relationship, Louisa had talked often about her debts, and Boswell had made her a loan.
5. Prostitute.

where there was no confidence, there was no breach of trust. But surely I placed some confidence in you. I am sorry that I was mistaken.

LOUISA Sir, I will confess to you that about three years ago I was very bad.[6] But for these fifteen months I have been quite well. I appeal to God Almighty that I am speaking true; and for these six months I have had to do with no man but yourself.

BOSWELL But by G–d, Madam, I have been with none but you, and here am I very bad.

LOUISA Well, Sir, by the same solemn oath I protest that I was ignorant of it.

BOSWELL Madam, I wish much to believe you. But I own I cannot upon this occasion believe a miracle.

LOUISA Sir, I cannot say more to you. But you will leave me in the greatest misery. I shall lose your esteem. I shall be hurt in the opinion of everybody, and in my circumstances.

BOSWELL [to himself] What the devil does the confounded jilt mean by being hurt in her circumstances? This is the grossest cunning. But I won't take notice of that at all. —Madam, as to the opinion of everybody, you need not be afraid. I was going to joke and say that I never boast of a lady's *favors*. But I give you my word of honor that you shall not be discovered.

LOUISA Sir, this is being more generous than I could expect.

BOSWELL I hope, Madam, you will own that since I have been with you I have always behaved like a man of honor.

LOUISA You have indeed, Sir.

BOSWELL [rising] Madam, your most obedient servant.

During all this conversation I really behaved with a manly composure and polite dignity that could not fail to inspire an awe, and she was pale as ashes and trembled and faltered. Thrice did she insist on my staying a little longer, as it was probably the last time that I should be with her. She could say nothing to the purpose. And I sat silent. As I was going, said she, "I hope, Sir, you will give me leave to inquire after your health." "Madam," said I, archly, "I fancy it will be needless for some weeks." She again renewed her request. But unwilling to be plagued any more with her, I put her off by saying I might perhaps go to the country, and left her. I was really confounded at her behavior. There is scarcely a possibility that she could be innocent of the crime of horrid imposition. And yet her positive asseverations really stunned me. She is in all probability a most consummate dissembling whore.

Thus ended my intrigue with the fair Louisa, which I flattered myself so much with, and from which I expected at least a winter's safe copulation. It is indeed very hard. I cannot say, like young fellows who get themselves clapped in a bawdy house,[7] that I will take better care again. For I really did take care. However, since I am fairly trapped, let me make the best of it. I have not got it from imprudence. It is merely the chance of war.

I then called at Drury Lane for Mr. Garrick. He was vastly good to me. "Sir," said he, "you will be a very great man. And when you are so, remember the year 1763. I want to contribute my part towards saving you. And pray, will you fix a day when I shall have the pleasure of treating you with tea?" I fixed next day. "Then, Sir," said he, "the cups shall dance and the saucers skip."

What he meant by my being a great man I can understand. For really, to speak seriously, I think there is a blossom about me of something more distinguished than

6. Severely infected.   7. Acquire gonorrhea in a brothel.

the generality of mankind. But I am much afraid that this blossom will never swell into fruit, but will be nipped and destroyed by many a blighting heat and chilling frost. Indeed, I sometimes indulge noble reveries of having a regiment, of getting into Parliament, making a figure, and becoming a man of consequence in the state. But these are checked by dispiriting reflections on my melancholy temper and imbecility of mind. Yet I may probably become sounder and stronger as I grow up. Heaven knows. I am resigned. I trust to Providence. I was quite in raptures with Garrick's kindness—the man whom from a boy I used to adore and look upon as a heathen god—to find him paying me so much respect! How amiable is he in comparison of Sheridan! I was this day with him what the French call un étourdi [a scatterbrain]. I gave free vent to my feelings. Love[8] was by, to whom I cried, "This, Sir, is the real scene." And taking Mr. Garrick cordially by the hand, "Thou greatest of men," said I, "I cannot express how happy you make me." This, upon my soul, was no flattery. He saw it was not. And the dear great man was truly pleased with it. This scene gave me a charming flutter of spirits and dispelled my former gloom. * * *

[FIRST MEETING WITH JOHNSON]

Monday, 16 May [1763]. Temple[1] and his brother breakfasted with me. I went to Love's to try to recover some of the money which he owes me. But, alas, a single guinea was all I could get. He was just going to dinner, so I stayed and eat a bit, though I was angry at myself afterwards. I drank tea at Davies's[2] in Russell Street, and about seven came in the great Mr. Samuel Johnson, whom I have so long wished to see. Mr. Davies introduced me to him. As I knew his mortal antipathy at the Scotch, I cried to Davies, "Don't tell where I come from." However, he said, "From Scotland." "Mr. Johnson," said I, "indeed I come from Scotland, but I cannot help it." "Sir," replied he, "that, I find, is what a very great many of your countrymen cannot help." Mr. Johnson is a man of a most dreadful appearance. He is a very big man, is troubled with sore eyes, the palsy, and the king's evil.[3] He is very slovenly in his dress and speaks with a most uncouth voice. Yet his great knowledge and strength of expression command vast respect and render him very excellent company. He has great humor and is a worthy man. But his dogmatical roughness of manners is disagreeable. I shall mark what I remember of his conversation. * * *
1762–1763   1950

An Account of My Last Interview with David Hume, Esq.
Partly recorded in my Journal, partly enlarged from my memory,
3 March 1777[1]

On Sunday forenoon the 7 of July 1776, being too late for church, I went to see Mr. David Hume, who was returned from London and Bath,[2] just a-dying. I found him alone, in a reclining posture in his drawing room. He was lean, ghastly, and quite of an earthy appearance. He was dressed in a suit of gray cloth with white metal but-

8. James Love, actor and longtime friend of Boswell.
1. William Johnson Temple, Boswell's most intimate and upstanding friend.
2. Thomas Davies, actor and bookseller.
3. Scrofula, a form of tuberculosis that the king's touch was believed to cure.
1. Boswell was terrified of death, preoccupied with the question of an afterlife, and in doubt as to the sturdiness of his own Christian faith. All these agitations converged at the deathbed of the "infidel" Scots philosopher David

Hume (1711–1776), whom he had known (and intermittently exasperated) for about 15 years. Boswell first wrote this account three weeks after the event, and revisited it twice, altering and expanding it in March of the following year, and adding a postscript ten months later. For David Hume, see Perspectives: Mind and God (page 2644), and the conversations recorded in the Life of Johnson (page 2815).
2. To his house in Edinburgh.

tons, and a kind of scratch wig. He was quite different from the plump figure which he used to present. He had before him Dr. Campbell's *Philosophy of Rhetoric*.[3] He seemed to be placid and even cheerful. He said he was just approaching to his end. I think these were his words. I know not how I contrived to get the subject of immortality introduced. He said he never had entertained any belief in religion since he began to read Locke and Clarke. I asked him if he was not religious when he was young. He said he was, and he used to read *The Whole Duty of Man*;[4] that he made an abstract from the catalogue of vices at the end of it, and examined himself by this, leaving out murder and theft and such vices as he had no chance of committing, having no inclination to commit them. This, he said, was strange work; for instance, to try if, notwithstanding his excelling his schoolfellows, he had no pride or vanity. He smiled in ridicule of this as absurd and contrary to fixed principles and necessary consequences, not adverting that religious discipline does not mean to extinguish, but to moderate, the passions; and certainly an excess of pride or vanity is dangerous and generally hurtful. He then said flatly that the morality of every religion was bad, and, I really thought, was not jocular when he said that when he heard a man was religious, he concluded he was a rascal, though he had known some instances of very good men being religious. This was just an extravagant reverse of the common remark as to infidels.

I had a strong curiosity to be satisfied if he persisted in disbelieving a future state even when he had death before his eyes. I was persuaded from what he now said, and from his manner of saying it, that he did persist. I asked him if it was not possible that there might be a future state. He answered it was possible that a piece of coal put upon the fire would not burn; and he added that it was a most unreasonable fancy that we should exist forever. That immortality, if it were at all, must be general; that a great proportion of the human race has hardly any intellectual qualities; that a great proportion dies in infancy before being possessed of reason; yet all these must be immortal; that a porter who gets drunk by ten o'clock with gin must be immortal; that the trash of every age must be preserved, and that new universes must be created to contain such infinite numbers. This appeared to me an unphilosophical objection, and I said, "Mr. Hume, you know spirit does not take up space."

I may illustrate what he last said by mentioning that in a former conversation with me on this subject he used pretty much the same mode of reasoning, and urged that Wilkes[5] and his mob must be immortal. One night last May as I was coming up King Street, Westminster, I met Wilkes, who carried me into Parliament Street to see a curious procession pass: the funeral of a lamplighter attended by some hundreds of his fraternity with torches. Wilkes, who either is, or affects to be, an infidel, was rattling away, "I think there's an end of that fellow. I think he won't rise again." I very calmly said to him, "You bring into my mind the strongest argument that ever I heard against a future state"; and then told him David Hume's objection that Wilkes and his mob must be immortal. It seemed to make a proper impression, for he grinned abashment, as a Negro grows whiter when he blushes. But to return to my last interview with Mr. Hume.

---

3. George Campbell (1719–1796), a Scots clergyman, had made his philosophical reputation by a book-length rebuttal to Hume's essay *Of Miracles,* but he cheerfully acknowledged Hume's influence on his thought, and the two men sustained an affectionate relationship. *The Philosophy of Rhetoric*, which would become Campbell's most successful work, was now newly published.
4. A massively popular work of uncertain authorship, first published in 1658, which prescribed a rigorous code of Christian conduct.
5. John Wilkes (1725–1797), radical politician.

I asked him if the thought of annihilation never gave him any uneasiness. He said not the least; no more than the thought that he had not been, as Lucretius observes.[6] "Well," said I, "Mr. Hume, I hope to triumph over you when I meet you in a future state; and remember you are not to pretend that you was joking with all this infidelity." "No, no," said he. "But I shall have been so long there before you come that it will be nothing new." In this style of good humor and levity did I conduct the conversation. Perhaps it was wrong on so awful[7] a subject. But as nobody was present, I thought it could have no bad effect. I however felt a degree of horror, mixed with a sort of wild, strange, hurrying recollection of my excellent mother's pious instructions, of Dr. Johnson's noble lessons, and of my religious sentiments and affections during the course of my life. I was like a man in sudden danger eagerly seeking his defensive arms; and I could not but be assailed by momentary doubts while I had actually before me a man of such strong abilities and extensive inquiry dying in the persuasion of being annihilated. But I maintained my faith. I told him that I believed the Christian religion as I believed history. Said he: "You do not believe it as you believe the Revolution."[8] "Yes," said I; "but the difference is that I am not so much interested in the truth of the Revolution; otherwise I should have anxious doubts concerning it. A man who is in love has doubts of the affection of his mistress, without cause." I mentioned Soame Jenyns's little book in defense of Christianity, which was just published but which I had not yet read.[9] Mr. Hume said, "I am told there is nothing of his usual spirit in it."

He had once said to me, on a forenoon while the sun was shining bright, that he did not wish to be immortal. This was a most wonderful[1] thought. The reason he gave was that he was very well in this state of being, and that the chances were very much against his being so well in another state; and he would rather not be more than be worse. I answered that it was reasonable to hope he would be better; that there would be a progressive improvement. I tried him at this interview with that topic, saying that a future state was surely a pleasing idea. He said no, for that it was always seen through a gloomy medium; there was always a Phlegethon[2] or a hell. "But," said I, "would it not be agreeable to have hopes of seeing our friends again?" and I mentioned three men lately deceased, for whom I knew he had a high value: Ambassador Keith, Lord Alemoor, and Baron Mure. He owned it would be agreeable, but added that none of them entertained such a notion. I believe he said, such a foolish, or such an absurd, notion; for he was indecently[3] and impolitely positive in incredulity. "Yes," said I, "Lord Alemoor was a believer." David acknowledged that *he* had *some* belief.

I somehow or other brought Dr. Johnson's name into our conversation. I had often heard him speak of that great man in a very illiberal manner. He said upon this occasion, "Johnson should be pleased with my *History*."[4] Nettled by Hume's frequent attacks upon my revered friend in former conversations, I told him now that Dr. Johnson did not allow him much credit; for he said, "Sir, the fellow is a Tory by

---

6. Titus Lucretius Carus, Roman philosopher and poet; Hume's observation appears to echo more closely an observation by the Stoic philosopher Seneca: "Death is non-existence. What that may be I already know. What shall be after me is what was before me" (*Epistolae* 54.4).
7. Solemn.
8. The "Glorious Revolution" of 1688–1689, when the Stuart monarch James I was replaced by William and Mary.
9. Soame Jenyns (1704–1787) had published *A View of*

the *Internal Evidence of the Christian Religion*; for Johnson's review of his earlier *Free Inquiry*, see page 2719.
1. Astonishing.
2. In Greek mythology, a river in Hades.
3. In his first version, Boswell had written the milder "improperly."
4. The six-volume *History of Great Britain* (1754–1762); Hume was now revising it, and had noted that his alterations to the portion on the "two first Stuarts" were "invariably to the Tory side" (the view favored by Johnson).

chance."[5] I am sorry that I mentioned this at such a time. I was off my guard; for the truth is that Mr. Hume's pleasantry was such that there was no solemnity in the scene; and death for the time did not seem dismal. It surprised me to find him talking of different matters with a tranquility of mind and a clearness of head which few men posses at any time. Two particulars I remember: Smith's *Wealth of Nations*, which he commended much, and Monboddo's *Origin of Language*, which he treated contemptuously.[6] I said, "If I were you, I should regret annihilation. Had I written such an admirable history, I should be sorry to leave it." He said, "I shall leave that history, of which you are pleased to speak so favorably, as perfect as I can."[7] He said, too, that all the great abilities with which men had ever been endowed were relative to this world. He said he became a greater friend to the Stuart family as he advanced in studying for his history; and he hoped he had vindicated the two first of them so effectually that they would never again be attacked.

Mr. Lauder, his surgeon, came in for a little, and Mr. Mure, the Baron's son, for another small interval. He was, as far as I could judge, quite easy with both. He said he had no pain, but was wasting away. I left him with impressions which disturbed me for some time.

(Additions from memory, 22 January 1778) Speaking of his singular notion that men of religion were generally bad men, he said, "One of the men" (or "The man"—I am not sure which) "of the greatest honor that I ever knew is my Lord Marischal,[8] who is a downright atheist. I remember I once hinted something as if I believed in the being of a God, and he would not speak to me for a week." He said this with his usual grunting pleasantry, with that thick breath which fatness had rendered habitual to him, and that smile of simplicity which his good humor constantly produced.

When he spoke against Monboddo, I told him that Monboddo said to me that he believed the abusive criticism upon his book in *The Edinburgh Magazine and Review* was written by Mr. Hume's direction. David seemed irritated, and said, "Does the *scoundrel*" (I am sure either *that* or "*rascal*") "say so?" He then told me that he had observed to one of the Faculty of Advocates that Monboddo was wrong in his observation that ———— and gave as a proof the line in Milton. When the review came out, he found this very remark in it, and said to that advocate, "Oho! I have discovered you"—reminding him of the circumstance.[9]

It was amazing to find him so keen in such a state. I must add one other circumstance which is material, as it shows that he perhaps was not without some hope of a future state, and that his spirits were supported by a consciousness (or at least a notion) that his conduct had been virtuous. He said, "If there were a future state, Mr. Boswell, I think I could give as good an account of my life as most people."

1776–1778   1970

5. "As being a Scotchman," Johnson had gone on to explain, "but not upon a principle of duty; for he has no principle."

6. *The Wealth of Nations* (1776), by Hume's friend Adam Smith, is the foundation text of modern economics; in *The Origin and Progress of Language* (1773), James Burnett, Lord Monboddo, argued (among other things) that humans and orangutans are of the same species.

7. Once, to entertain Adam Smith, Hume pretended that these revisions might furnish him with an excuse for living longer: "'Allow me a little time,'" he imagined himself saying to the mythic ferryman who conveyed the dead to Hades, "'that I may see how the public receives the alterations.' But Charon would answer, 'When you have seen the effect of these, you will be for making other alterations. There will be no end to such excuses; so, honest friend, please step into the boat.'"

8. George Keith, tenth Earl Marischal of Scotland, a renowned Jacobite who as an old man had befriended the young Boswell and accompanied him on the German portion of his Grand Tour.

9. The details of the dispute remain obscure; Boswell never filled in the blank or identified the "line in Milton."

from A Journal of a Tour to the Hebrides with Dr. Samuel Johnson[1]

Tuesday, August 31 [1773] * * * We had tea in the afternoon, and our landlord's daughter, a modest civil girl, very neatly dressed, made it for us. She told us, she had been a year at Inverness, and learned reading and writing, sewing, knotting, working lace, and pastry. Dr. Johnson made her a present of a book which he had bought at Inverness.

The room had some deals laid across the joists,[2] as a kind of ceiling. There were two beds in the room, and a woman's gown was hung on a rope to make a curtain of separation between them. Joseph[3] had sheets, which my wife had sent with us, laid on them. We had much hesitation, whether to undress, or lie down with our clothes on. I said at last, "I'll plunge in! There will be less harbor for vermin about me, when I am stripped!" Dr. Johnson said, he was like one hesitating whether to go into the cold bath. At last he resolved too. I observed he might serve a campaign.[4] JOHNSON: "I could do all that can be done by patience: whether I should have strength enough, I know not." He was in excellent humor. To see the Rambler[5] as I saw him tonight was really an amusement. I yesterday told him I was thinking of writing a poetical letter to him, on his return from Scotland, in the style of Swift's humorous epistle[6] in the character of Mary Gulliver to her husband, Captain Lemuel Gulliver, on his return to England from the country of the Houyhnhums:—

> At early morn I to the market haste,
> Studious in ev'ry thing to please thy taste.
> A curious fowl and sparagrass I chose;
> (For I remember you were fond of those).
> Three shillings cost the first, the last sev'n groats;
> Sullen you turn from both, and call for *oats:*

He laughed, and asked in whose name I would write it. I said, in Mrs. Thrale's.[7] He was angry. "Sir, if you have any sense of decency or delicacy, you won't do that!" BOSWELL: "Then let it be in Cole's, the landlord of the Mitre Tavern; where we have so often sat together." JOHNSON: "Ay, that may do."

After we had offered up our private devotions, and had chatted a little from our beds, Dr. Johnson said, "God bless us both, for Jesus Christ's sake! Good night!" I pronounced "Amen." He fell asleep immediately. I was not so fortunate for a long time. I fancied myself bit by innumerable vermin under the clothes; and that a spider was traveling from the wainscot towards my mouth. At last I fell into insensibility.

Wednesday, September 1. I awaked very early. I began to imagine that the landlord, being about to emigrate, might murder us to get our money, and lay it upon the soldiers in the barn. Such groundless fears will arise in the mind before it has resumed its vigor after sleep! Dr. Johnson had had the same kind of ideas; for he told me after-

---

1. In the fall of 1773, Boswell fulfilled his long-held ambition of accompanying Johnson on a journey through Scotland. Throughout the tour he kept a copious journal, which Johnson read in progress. Eleven years later, in the months following Johnson's death, Boswell revised the journal, with much help from their mutual friend the Shakespearean scholar Edmond Malone, and published it as a "good prelude"—foretaste and trial balloon—for the full *Life* that he and Johnson had long known he would write. For parallel accounts by Johnson of the days that Boswell narrates here, see the selections from his letters to Hester Thrale (page 2765) and his *Journey to the West-*

ern *Islands of Scotland* (page 2770).
2. Planks laid across roof beams.
3. Boswell's servant, Joseph Ritter.
4. A military campaign.
5. The title of Johnson's biweekly periodical essay (1750–1752) had become a kind of shorthand for the author at his most learned and magisterial.
6. This poem was actually written by Alexander Pope. It first appeared in *Several Copies of Verses on Occasion of Mr. Gulliver's Travels* (1727).
7. Johnson's close friend and favorite correspondent.

wards, that he considered so many soldiers, having seen us, would be witnesses, should any harm be done, and that circumstance, I suppose, he considered as a security. When I got up, I found him sound asleep in his miserable stye,[8] as I may call it, with a colored handkerchief tied round his head. With difficulty could I awaken him. It reminded me of Henry the Fourth's fine soliloquy on sleep; for there was here as uneasy a pallet as the poet's imagination could possibly conceive.[9]

A redcoat of the 15th regiment, whether officer or only sergeant, I could not be sure, came to the house on his way to the mountains to shoot deer, which it seems the Laird of Glenmorison does not hinder anybody to do. Few, indeed, can do them harm. We had him to breakfast with us. We got away about eight. M'Queen[1] walked some miles to give us a convoy. He had, in 1745, joined the Highland army at Fort Augustus, and continued in it till after the battle of Culloden. As he narrated the particulars of that ill-advised but brave attempt,[2] I could not refrain from tears. There is a certain association of ideas in my mind upon that subject, by which I am strongly affected. The very Highland names, or the sound of a bagpipe, will stir my blood, and fill me with a mixture of melancholy and respect for courage; with pity for an unfortunate and superstitious regard for antiquity, and thoughtless inclination for war; in short, with a crowd of sensations with which sober rationality has nothing to do.

We passed through Glensheal, with prodigious mountains on each side. We saw where the battle was fought in the year 1719.[3] Dr. Johnson owned he was now in a scene of as wild nature as he could see; but he corrected me sometimes in my inaccurate observations. "There, (said I) is a mountain like a cone." JOHNSON: "No, Sir. It would be called so in a book; and when a man comes to look at it, he sees it is not so. It is indeed pointed at the top; but one side of it is larger than the other." Another mountain I called immense. JOHNSON: "No; it is no more than a considerable protuberance."

We came to a rich green valley, comparatively speaking, and stopped awhile to let our horses rest and eat grass. We soon afterwards came to Auchnasheal, a kind of rural village, a number of cottages being built together, as we saw all along in the Highlands. We passed many miles this day without seeing a house, but only little summer huts, called *shielings*. Evan Campbell, servant to Mr. Murchison, factor[4] to the Laird of Macleod in Glenelg, ran along with us today. He was a very obliging fellow. At Auchnasheal, we sat down on a green turf seat at the end of a house; they brought us out two wooden dishes of milk, which we tasted. One of them was frothed like a syllabub.[5] I saw a woman preparing it with such a stick as is used for chocolate, and in the same manner. We had a considerable circle about us, men, women, and children, all M'Craas, Lord Seaforth's people. Not one of them could speak English.[6] I observed to Dr. Johnson, it was much the same as being with a tribe of Indians. JOHNSON: "Yes, Sir; but not so terrifying." I gave all who chose it, snuff and tobacco. Governor Trapaud had made us buy a quantity at Fort Augustus, and put them up in

---

8. Pig pen.
9. In Shakespeare's *2 Henry IV*, the wakeful king muses that sleep comes more readily to "the uneasy pallets" of the poor than to the bed of the monarch (3.1.4–31).
1. The keeper of the inn at Glenmoriston.
2. Originating in the Highlands of Scotland, the 1745 rebellion was an unsuccessful attempt to restore "Bonny Prince Charlie" (Charles Stuart, grandson of the deposed James II) to the throne of England and Scotland. The

Jacobite forces were finally subdued at the battle of Culloden, and this defeat (as well as the restrictive measures enforced by the British afterward) meant the end of the old way of life for the once-powerful clans.
3. On 10 June 1719 a combined army of Spaniards and Highlanders was crushed by the British.
4. Estate manager.
5. A drink of milk, curdled, sweetened, and whipped.
6. They spoke Erse, the Gaelic dialect of the Highlands.

small parcels. I also gave each person a bit of wheat bread, which they had never tasted before. I then gave a penny apiece to each child. I told Dr. Johnson of this; upon which he called to Joseph and our guides, for change for a shilling, and declared that he would distribute among the children. Upon this being announced in Erse, there was a great stir; not only did some children come running down from neighboring huts, but I observed one black-haired man, who had been with us all along, had gone off, and returned, bringing a very young child. My fellow traveler then ordered the children to be drawn up in a row; and he dealt about[7] his copper, and made them and their parents all happy. The poor M'Craas,[8] whatever may be their present state, were of considerable estimation in the year 1715, when there was a line in a song,

> And aw[9] the brave M'Craas are coming.

There was great diversity in the faces of the circle around us: some were as black and wild in their appearance as any American savages whatever. One woman was as comely almost as the figure of Sappho,[1] as we see it painted. We asked the old woman, the mistress of the house where we had the milk, (which by the bye, Dr. Johnson told me, for I did not observe it myself, was built not of turf, but of stone) what we should pay. She said, what we pleased. One of our guides asked her in Erse if a shilling was enough. She said, "Yes." But some of the men bade her ask more. This vexed me; because it showed a desire to impose upon strangers, as they knew that even a shilling was high payment. The woman, however, honestly persisted in her first price; so I gave her half a crown. Thus we had one good scene of life uncommon to us. The people were very much pleased, gave us many blessings, and said they had not had such a day since the old Laird of Macleod's time.

Dr. Johnson was much refreshed by this repast. He was pleased when I told him he would make a good chief. He said, "Were I a chief, I would dress my servants better than myself, and knock a fellow down if he looked saucy to a Macdonald in rags: but I would not treat men as brutes. I would let them know why all of my clan were to have attention paid to them. I would tell my upper servants why, and make them tell the others."

We rode on well, till we came to the high mountain called the Rattakin, by which time both Dr. Johnson and the horses were a good deal fatigued. It is a terrible steep to climb, notwithstanding the road is formed slanting along it; however, we made it out. On the top of it we met Captain M'Leod of Balmenoch (a Dutch officer[2] who had come from Skye) riding with his sword slung across him. He asked, "Is this Mr. Boswell?" which was a proof that we were expected. Going down the hill on the other side was no easy task. As Dr. Johnson was a great weight, the two guides agreed that he should ride the horses alternately. Hay's were the two best, and the Doctor would not ride but upon one or other of them, a black or a brown. But as Hay complained much after ascending the Rattakin, the Doctor was prevailed with to mount one of Vass's greys.[3] As he rode upon it downhill, it did not go well; and he grumbled. I walked on a little before, but was excessively entertained with the method taken to keep him in good humor. Hay led the horse's head, talk-

---

7. Handed out.
8. This clan played an important part in the Jacobite rebellion of 1715.
9. All (in Scots dialect).

1. Ancient Greek poet.
2. A mercenary in the Dutch army.
3. John Hay and Lauchlan Vass were Highland guides employed by Boswell.

ing to Dr. Johnson as much as he could; and (having heard him, in the forenoon, express a pastoral pleasure on seeing the goats browsing) just when the Doctor was uttering his displeasure, the fellow cried, with a very Highland accent, "See, such pretty goats!" Then he whistled, *whu!* and made them jump. Little did he conceive what Dr. Johnson was. Here now was a common ignorant Highland clown, imagining that he could divert, as one does a child, *Dr. Samuel Johnson!* The ludicrousness, absurdity, and extraordinary contrast between what the fellow fancied, and the reality, was truly comic.

It grew dusky; and we had a very tedious ride for what was called five miles, but I am sure would measure ten. We had no conversation. I was riding forward to the inn at Glenelg, on the shore opposite to Skye, that I might take proper measures, before Dr. Johnson, who was now advancing in dreary silence, Hay leading his horse, should arrive. Vass also walked by the side of his horse, and Joseph followed behind: as therefore he was thus attended, and seemed to be in deep meditation, I thought there could be no harm in leaving him for a little while. He called me back with a tremendous shout, and was really in a passion with me for leaving him. I told him my intentions, but he was not satisfied, and said, "Do you know, I should as soon have thought of picking a pocket, as doing so?" BOSWELL: "I am diverted with you, Sir." JOHNSON: "Sir, I could never be diverted with incivility. Doing such a thing, makes one lose confidence in him who has done it, as one cannot tell what he may do next." His extraordinary warmth confounded me so much, that I justified myself but lamely to him; yet my intentions were not improper. I wished to get on, to see how we were to be lodged, and how we were to get a boat; all which I thought I could best settle myself, without his having any trouble. To apply his great mind to minute particulars is wrong: it is like taking an immense balance, such as is kept on quays for weighing cargoes of ships, to weigh a guinea. I knew I had neat little scales, which would do better: and that his attention to everything which falls in his way, and his uncommon desire to be always in the right, would make him weigh, if he knew of the particulars: it was right therefore for me to weigh them, and let him have them only in effect. I however continued to ride by him, finding he wished I should do so.

As we passed the barracks at Bernéra, I looked at them wishfully, as soldiers have always everything in the best order: but there was only a sergeant and a few men there. We came on to the inn at Glenelg. There was no provender for our horses; so they were sent to grass,[4] with a man to watch them. A maid showed us up stairs into a room damp and dirty, with bare walls, a variety of bad smells, a coarse black greasy fir table, and forms of the same kind; and out of a wretched bed started a fellow from his sleep, like Edgar in *King Lear*, "Poor Tom's a cold."[5]

This inn was furnished with not a single article that we could either eat or drink; but Mr. Murchison, factor to the Laird of Macleod in Glenelg, sent us a bottle of rum and some sugar, with a polite message to acquaint us that he was very sorry that he did not hear of us till we had passed his house, otherwise he should have insisted on our sleeping there that night; and that, if he were not obliged to set out for Inverness early next morning, he would have waited upon us. Such extraordinary attention from this gentleman, to entire strangers, deserves the most honorable commemoration.

---

4. Graze.

5. The frequent refrain of Edgar (disguised as the beggar Poor Tom) in Shakespeare's *King Lear*.

Our bad accommodation here made me uneasy, and almost fretful. Dr. Johnson was calm. I said, he was so from vanity. JOHNSON: "No, Sir, it is from philosophy." It pleased me to see that the Rambler could practice so well his own lessons.

I resumed the subject of my leaving him on the road, and endeavored to defend it better. He was still violent upon that head, and said, "Sir, had you gone on, I was thinking that I should have returned with you to Edinburgh, and then have parted from you, and never spoken to you more."

I sent for fresh hay, with which we made beds for ourselves, each in a room equally miserable. Like Wolfe, we had a "choice of difficulties."[6] Dr. Johnson made things easier by comparison. At M'Queen's, last night, he observed that few were so well lodged in a ship. Tonight he said, we were better than if we had been upon the hill. He lay down buttoned up in his great coat.[7] I had my sheets spread on the hay, and my clothes and great coat laid over me, by way of blankets.

Thursday, September 2. I had slept ill. Dr. Johnson's anger had affected me much. I considered that, without any bad intention, I might suddenly forfeit his friendship; and was impatient to see him this morning. I told him how uneasy he had made me by what he had said, and reminded him of his own remark at Aberdeen, upon old friendships being hastily broken off. He owned he had spoken to me in passion; that he would not have done what he threatened; and that, if he had, he should have been ten times worse than I; that forming intimacies, would indeed be "limning the water,"[8] were they liable to such sudden dissolution; and he added, "Let's think no more on't." BOSWELL: "Well, then, Sir, I shall be easy. Remember, I am to have fair warning in case of any quarrel. You are never to spring[9] a mine upon me. It was absurd in me to believe you." JOHNSON: "You deserved about as much, as to believe me from night to morning." * * *

1773   1785

The Life of Samuel Johnson, LL.D.

[INTRODUCTION; BOSWELL'S METHOD]

To write the Life of him who excelled all mankind in writing the lives of others, and who, whether we consider his extraordinary endowments or his various works, has been equaled by few in any age, is an arduous, and may be reckoned in me a presumptuous task.

Had Dr. Johnson written his own life, in conformity with the opinion which he has given, that every man's life may be best written by himself;[1] had he employed in the preservation of his own history, that clearness of narration and elegance of language in which he has embalmed so many eminent persons, the world would probably have had the most perfect example of biography that was ever exhibited. But although he at different times, in a desultory manner, committed to writing many particulars of the progress of his mind and fortunes, he never had preserving diligence enough to form them into a regular composition. Of these memorials a few have been preserved; but the greater part was consigned by him to the flames, a few days before his death.

---

6. General James Wolfe, who died fighting the French in Canada in 1759. Describing his campaign against Quebec, Wolfe wrote, "In this situation there is such a choice of difficulties that I own myself at a loss how to determine."
7. Overcoat.

8. A quotation from an epigram by Francis Bacon: "Who then to frail mortality shall trust, / But limns [paints] the water, or but writes in dust."
9. Explode.
1. In *Idler* No. 84.

As I had the honor and happiness of enjoying his friendship for upwards of twenty years; as I had the scheme of writing his life constantly in view; as he was well apprised of this circumstance, and from time to time obligingly satisfied my inquiries, by communicating to me the incidents of his early years; as I acquired a facility in recollecting, and was very assiduous in recording, his conversation, of which the extraordinary vigor and vivacity constituted one of the first features of his character; and as I have spared no pains in obtaining materials concerning him, from every quarter where I could discover that they were to be found, and have been favored with the most liberal communications by his friends; I flatter myself that few biographers have entered upon such a work as this with more advantages; independent of literary abilities, in which I am not vain enough to compare myself with some great names who have gone before me in this kind of writing. * * *

Instead of melting down my materials into one mass, and constantly speaking in my own person, by which I might have appeared to have more merit in the execution of the work, I have resolved to adopt and enlarge upon the excellent plan of Mr. Mason, in his *Memoirs* of Gray.[2] Wherever narrative is necessary to explain, connect, and supply, I furnish it to the best of my abilities; but in the chronological series of Johnson's life, which I trace as distinctly as I can, year by year, I produce, wherever it is in my power, his own minutes,[3] letters, or conversation, being convinced that this mode is more lively, and will make my readers better acquainted with him, than even most of those were who actually knew him, but could know him only partially; whereas there is here an accumulation of intelligence from various points, by which his character is more fully understood and illustrated.

Indeed I cannot conceive a more perfect mode of writing any man's life than not only relating all the most important events of it in their order, but interweaving what he privately wrote, and said, and thought; by which mankind are enabled as it were to see him live, and to "live o'er each scene"[4] with him, as he actually advanced through the several stages of his life. Had his other friends been as diligent and ardent as I was, he might have been almost entirely preserved. As it is, I will venture to say that he will be seen in this work more completely than any man who has ever yet lived.

And he will be seen as he really was; for I profess to write, not his panegyric, which must be all praise, but his Life; which, great and good as he was, must not be supposed to be entirely perfect. To be as he was, is indeed subject of panegyric enough to any man in this state of being; but in every picture there should be shade as well as light, and when I delineate him without reserve, I do what he himself recommended, both by his precept[5] and his example. * * *

What I consider as the peculiar value of the following work is the quantity that it contains of Johnson's conversation; which is universally acknowledged to have been eminently instructive and entertaining; and of which the specimens that I have given upon a former occasion have been received with so much approbation that I have good grounds for supposing that the world will not be indifferent to more ample communications of a similar nature. * * *

---

2. William Mason constructed his *Memoirs* of Thomas Gray (1775) around a selection of the poet's letters.
3. Memoranda.
4. "To wake the soul by tender strokes of art, / To raise the genius, and to mend the heart, / To make mankind in conscious virtue bold, / Live o'er each scene, and be what

they behold" (lines 1–4 of Pope's prologue to Addison's *Cato*).
5. Boswell proceeds to quote from *Rambler* No. 60 (see page 2708) in which Johnson articulates his biographical principles.

I am fully aware of the objections which may be made to the minuteness on some occasions of my detail of Johnson's conversation, and how happily it is adapted for the petty exercise of ridicule, by men of superficial understanding and ludicrous fancy;[6] but I remain firm and confident in my opinion, that minute particulars are frequently characteristic,[7] and always amusing, when they relate to a distinguished man. I am therefore exceedingly unwilling that anything, however slight, which my illustrious friend thought it worth his while to express, with any degree of point,[8] should perish. * * *

Of one thing I am certain, that considering how highly the small portion which we have of the table talk and other anecdotes of our celebrated writers[9] is valued, and how earnestly it is regretted that we have not more, I am justified in preserving rather too many of Johnson's sayings than too few; especially as from the diversity of dispositions it cannot be known with certainty beforehand, whether what may seem trifling to some, and perhaps to the collector himself, may not be most agreeable to many; and the greater number that an author can please in any degree, the more pleasure does there arise to a benevolent mind.

To those who are weak enough to think this a degrading task, and the time and labor which have been devoted to it misemployed, I shall content myself with opposing the authority of the greatest man of any age, Julius Caesar, of whom Bacon observes, that "in his book of Apothegms which he collected, we see that he esteemed it more honor to make himself but a pair of tables, to take the wise and pithy words of others, than to have every word of his own to be made an apothegm or an oracle."

Having said thus much by way of introduction, I commit the following pages to the candor of the Public.

[CONVERSATIONS ABOUT HUME]

[21 July 1763] Next morning I found him alone, and have preserved the following fragments of his conversation. Of a gentleman[1] who was mentioned, he said, "I have not met with any man for a long time who has given me such general displeasure. He is totally unfixed in his principles, and wants to puzzle other people." I said his principles had been poisoned by a noted infidel writer,[2] but that he was, nevertheless, a benevolent good man. JOHNSON: "We can have no dependence upon that instinctive, that constitutional goodness which is not founded upon principle. I grant you that such a man may be a very amiable member of society. I can conceive him placed in such a situation that he is not much tempted to deviate from what is right; and as every man prefers virtue, when there is not some strong incitement to transgress its precepts, I can conceive him doing nothing wrong. But if such a man stood in need of money, I should not like to trust him; and I should certainly not trust him with young ladies, for *there* there is always temptation. Hume and other skeptical innovators are vain men, and will gratify themselves at any expense. Truth will not afford sufficient food to their vanity; so they have betaken themselves to error. Truth, Sir, is a cow which will yield such people no more milk, and so they are gone to milk the bull. If I could have allowed myself to gratify my vanity at the expense of truth, what

6. Boswell's Hebridean journal had already been parodied in print for its "minuteness" and "detail."
7. Revealing of character.
8. "Remarkable turn of words or thought" (Johnson's *Dictionary*).
9. E.g., Joseph Spence's *Anecdotes, Observations and Char-*

acters of Books and Men, Collected from the Conversation of Mr. Pope, which (though unpublished until 1820) Johnson drew on for his *Life of Pope*.
1. Boswell's friend George Dempster.
2. The skeptical philosopher David Hume.

fame might I have acquired. Everything which Hume has advanced against Christianity had passed through my mind long before he wrote. Always remember this, that after a system is well settled upon positive evidence, a few partial objections ought not to shake it. The human mind is so limited that it cannot take in all the parts of a subject, so that there may be objections raised against anything. There are objections against a *plenum*, and objections against a *vacuum*;[3] yet one of them must certainly be true."

I mentioned Hume's argument against the belief of miracles, that it is more probable that the witnesses to the truth of them are mistaken, or speak falsely, than that the miracles should be true. JOHNSON: "Why, Sir, the great difficulty of proving miracles should make us very cautious in believing them. But let us consider; although God has made Nature to operate by certain fixed laws, yet it is not unreasonable to think that he may suspend those laws, in order to establish a system highly advantageous to mankind. Now the Christian religion is a most beneficial system, as it gives us light and certainty where we were before in darkness and doubt. The miracles which prove it are attested by men who had no interest in deceiving us; but who, on the contrary, were told that they should suffer persecution, and did actually lay down their lives in confirmation of the truth of the facts which they asserted. Indeed, for some centuries the heathens did not pretend to deny the miracles; but said they were performed by the aid of evil spirits. This is a circumstance of great weight. Then, Sir, when we take the proofs derived from prophecies which have been so exactly fulfilled, we have most satisfactory evidence. Supposing a miracle possible, as to which, in my opinion, there can be no doubt, we have as strong evidence for the miracles in support of Christianity, as the nature of the thing admits."

At night Mr. Johnson and I supped in a private room at the Turk's Head coffeehouse, in the Strand. "I encourage this house (said he); for the mistress of it is a good civil woman, and has not much business."

"Sir, I love the acquaintance of young people; because, in the first place, I don't like to think myself growing old. In the next place, young acquaintances must last longest, if they do last; and then, Sir, young men have more virtue than old men; they have more generous sentiments in every respect. I love the young dogs of this age: they have more wit and humor and knowledge of life than we had; but then the dogs are not so good scholars. Sir, in my early years I read very hard. It is a sad reflection, but a true one, that I knew almost as much at eighteen as I do now. My judgment, to be sure, was not so good; but I had all the facts. I remember very well, when I was at Oxford, an old gentleman said to me, 'Young man, ply your book diligently now, and acquire a stock of knowledge; for when years come upon you, you will find that poring upon books will be but an irksome task.'"

* * *

[26 October 1769] When we were alone, I introduced the subject of death, and endeavored to maintain that the fear of it might be got over. I told him that David Hume said to me, he was no more uneasy to think he should *not be* after this life, than that he *had not been* before he began to exist. JOHNSON: "Sir, if he really thinks so, his perceptions are disturbed; he is mad: if he does not think so, he lies. He may tell you, he holds his finger in the flame of a candle, without feeling pain; would you

3. According to the scientific theory of the *plenum*, all space is full (*plenus*) of matter; the opposing theory postulated that there are parts of space that are empty (*vacuus*) of matter.

believe him? When he dies, he at least gives up all he has." BOSWELL: "Foote,[4] Sir, told me, that when he was very ill he was not afraid to die." JOHNSON: "It is not true, Sir. Hold a pistol to Foote's breast, or to Hume's breast, and threaten to kill them, and you'll see how they behave." BOSWELL: "But may we not fortify our minds for the approach of death?" Here I am sensible I was in the wrong, to bring before his view what he ever looked upon with horror; for although when in a celestial frame, in his *Vanity of Human Wishes*,[5] he has supposed death to be "kind Nature's signal for retreat," from this state of being to "a happier seat," his thoughts upon this awful change were in general full of dismal apprehensions. His mind resembled the vast amphitheater, the Colosseum at Rome. In the center stood his judgment, which, like a mighty gladiator, combated those apprehensions that, like the wild beasts of the Arena, were all around in cells, ready to be let out upon him. After a conflict, he drove them back into their dens; but not killing them, they were still assailing him. To my question, whether we might not fortify our minds for the approach of death, he answered, in a passion, "No, Sir, let it alone. It matters not how a man dies, but how he lives. The act of dying is not of importance, it lasts so short a time." He added (with an earnest look), "A man knows it must be so, and submits. It will do him no good to whine."

I attempted to continue the conversation. He was so provoked that he said, "Give us no more of this"; and was thrown into such a state of agitation, that he expressed himself in a way that alarmed and distressed me, showed an impatience that I should leave him, and when I was going away, called to me sternly, "Don't let us meet tomorrow."

I went home exceedingly uneasy. All the harsh observations which I had ever heard made upon his character crowded into my mind; and I seemed to myself like the man who had put his head into the lion's mouth a great many times with perfect safety, but at last had it bit off.

[DINNER WITH WILKES]

[May 1776] I am now to record a very curious incident in Dr. Johnson's life, which fell under my own observation; of which *pars magna fui*,[1] and which I am persuaded will, with the liberal-minded, be much to his credit.

My desire of being acquainted with celebrated men of every description had made me, much about the same time, obtain an introduction to Dr. Samuel Johnson and to John Wilkes, Esq.[2] Two men more different could perhaps not be selected out of all mankind. They had even attacked one another with some asperity in their writings; yet I lived in habits of friendship with both. I could fully relish the excellence of each; for I have ever delighted in that intellectual chemistry which can separate good qualities from evil in the same person.

Sir John Pringle,[3] "mine own friend and my Father's friend," between whom and Dr. Johnson I in vain wished to establish an acquaintance, as I respected and lived in intimacy with both of them, observed to me once, very ingeniously, "It is not in

---

4. Samuel Foote (1721–1771), actor, playwright, and theatrical manager.
5. Johnson's imitation of Juvenal's tenth satire, lines 363–4 (see page 2700).
1. "I was no small part." (Virgil, *Aeneid* 2.5).
2. John Wilkes (1727–1797), libertine, satirist, and radical politician, had been expelled from Parliament for

blasphemous and seditious libel. Johnson considered Wilkes an unprincipled philanderer and demagogue.
3. John Pringle (1707–1782), distinguished physician and president of the Royal Society. Johnson disliked Pringle's freethinking religious views and his pro-American political convictions.

friendship as in mathematics, where two things, each equal to a third, are equal between themselves. You agree with Johnson as a middle quality, and you agree with me as a middle quality; but Johnson and I should not agree." Sir John was not sufficiently flexible, so I desisted, knowing, indeed, that the repulsion was equally strong on the part of Johnson, who, I know not from what cause, unless his being a Scotchman, had formed a very erroneous opinion of Sir John. But I conceived an irresistible wish, if possible, to bring Dr. Johnson and Mr. Wilkes together. How to manage it was a nice[4] and difficult matter.

My worthy booksellers[5] and friends, Messieurs Dilly in the Poultry, at whose hospitable and well-covered table I have seen a greater number of literary men than at any other, except that of Sir Joshua Reynolds, had invited me to meet Mr. Wilkes and some more gentlemen on Wednesday, May 15. "Pray," said I, "let us have Dr. Johnson."—"What, with Mr. Wilkes? not for the world," said Mr. Edward Dilly, "Dr. Johnson would never forgive me."—"Come," said I, "if you'll let me negotiate for you, I will be answerable that all shall go well." DILLY: "Nay, if you will take it upon you, I am sure I shall be very happy to see them both here."

Notwithstanding the high veneration which I entertained for Dr. Johnson, I was sensible that he was sometimes a little actuated by the spirit of contradiction, and by means of that I hoped I should gain my point. I was persuaded that if I had come upon him with a direct proposal, "Sir, will you dine in company with Jack Wilkes?" he would have flown into a passion, and would probably have answered, "Dine with Jack Wilkes, Sir! I'd as soon dine with Jack Ketch."[6] I therefore, while we were sitting quietly by ourselves at his house in an evening, took occasion to open my plan thus:—"Mr. Dilly, Sir, sends his respectful compliments to you, and would be happy if you would do him the honor to dine with him on Wednesday next along with me, as I must soon go to Scotland." JOHNSON: "Sir, I am obliged to Mr. Dilly. I will wait upon him:" BOSWELL: "Provided, Sir, I suppose, that the company which he is to have is agreeable to you." JOHNSON: "What do you mean, Sir? What do you take me for? Do you think I am so ignorant of the world, as to imagine that I am to prescribe to a gentleman what company he is to have at his table?" BOSWELL: "I beg your pardon, Sir, for wishing to prevent you from meeting people whom you might not like. Perhaps he may have some of what he calls his patriotic[7] friends with him." JOHNSON: "Well, Sir, and what then? What care I for his *patriotic friends*? Poh!" BOSWELL: "I should not be surprised to find Jack Wilkes there." JOHNSON: "And if Jack Wilkes *should* be there, what is that to *me*, Sir? My dear friend, let us have no more of this. I am sorry to be angry with you; but really it is treating me strangely to talk to me as if I could not meet any company whatever, occasionally." BOSWELL: "Pray forgive me, Sir. I meant well. But you shall meet whoever comes, for me." Thus I secured him, and told Dilly that he would find him very well pleased to be one of his guests on the day appointed.

Upon the much-expected Wednesday, I called on him about half an hour before dinner, as I often did when we were to dine out together, to see that he was ready in time, and to accompany him. I found him buffeting[8] his books, as upon a former occasion, covered with dust and making no preparation for going abroad. "How is

---

4. Delicate.
5. Publishers.
6. Famous 17th-century hangman.
7. Those in favor of diminishing the power of the monarch and supporting the rights of the American

colonists. Johnson had recently written a political tract called *The Patriot* (1774) in which he attacked Wilkes and his supporters.
8. Vigorously cleaning.

this, Sir?" said I. "Don't you recollect that you are to dine at Mr. Dilly's?" JOHNSON: "Sir, I did not think of going to Dilly's: it went out of my head. I have ordered dinner at home with Mrs. Williams."[9] BOSWELL: "But, my dear Sir, you know you were engaged to Mr. Dilly, and I told him so. He will expect you, and will be much disappointed if you don't come." JOHNSON: "You must talk to Mrs. Williams about this."

Here was a sad dilemma. I feared that what I was so confident I had secured would yet be frustrated. He had accustomed himself to show Mrs. Williams such a degree of humane attention, as frequently imposed some restraint upon him; and I knew that if she should be obstinate, he would not stir. I hastened downstairs to the blind lady's room and told her I was in great uneasiness, for Dr. Johnson had engaged to me to dine this day at Mr. Dilly's, but that he had told me he had forgotten his engagement, and had ordered dinner at home. "Yes, Sir," said she, pretty peevishly, "Dr. Johnson is to dine at home." "Madam," said I "his respect for you is such that I know he will not leave you unless you absolutely desire it. But as you have so much of his company, I hope you will be good enough to forgo it for a day; as Mr. Dilly is a very worthy man, has frequently had agreeable parties at his house for Dr. Johnson, and will be vexed if the Doctor neglects him today. And then, Madam, be pleased to consider my situation; I carried the message, and I assured Mr. Dilly that Dr. Johnson was to come, and no doubt he has made a dinner, and invited a company, and boasted of the honor he expected to have. I shall be quite disgraced if the Doctor is not there." She gradually softened to my solicitations, which were certainly as earnest as most entreaties to ladies upon any occasion, and was graciously pleased to empower me to tell Dr. Johnson, "That all things considered, she thought he should certainly go." I flew back to him, still in dust, and careless of what should be the event,[1] "indifferent in his choice to go or stay";[2] but as soon as I had announced to him Mrs. Williams's consent, he roared, "Frank, a clean shirt," and was very soon dressed. When I had him fairly[3] seated in a hackney coach with me, I exulted as much as a fortune hunter who has got an heiress into a post chaise with him to set out for Gretna Green.[4]

When we entered Mr. Dilly's drawing room, he found himself in the midst of a company he did not know. I kept myself snug and silent, watching how he would conduct himself. I observed him whispering to Mr. Dilly, "Who is that gentleman, Sir?"—"Mr. Arthur Lee."—JOHNSON: "Too, too, too" (under his breath), which was one of his habitual mutterings. Mr. Arthur Lee could not but be very obnoxious to Johnson, for he was not only a *patriot* but an *American*. He was afterwards minister from the United States at the court of Madrid. "And who is the gentleman in lace?"—"Mr. Wilkes, Sir." This information confounded him still more; he had some difficulty to restrain himself, and taking up a book, sat down upon a window seat and read, or at least kept his eye upon it intently for some time, till he composed himself. His feelings, I dare say, were awkward enough. But he no doubt recollected his having rated[5] me for supposing that he could be at all disconcerted by any company, and he, therefore, resolutely set himself to behave quite as an easy man of the world, who could adapt himself at once to the disposition and manners of those whom he might chance to meet.

---

9. An elderly blind woman who lived in Johnson's house as one of several dependents.
1. Not caring how the matter turned out.
2. Boswell adapts a line from Addison's *Cato:* "Indiff'rent in his choice to sleep or die" (5.1).
3. Securely.

4. A village just across the border in Scotland; it was the common destination of eloping couples who could thereby bypass the formalities and restrictions of the Anglican Church.
5. Chided.

The cheering sound of "Dinner is upon the table" dissolved his reverie, and we *all* sat down without any symptom of ill humor. There were present, besides Mr. Wilkes, and Mr. Arthur Lee, who was an old companion of mine when he studied physics at Edinburgh, Mr. (now Sir John) Miller, Dr. Lettsom, and Mr. Slater, the druggist. Mr. Wilkes placed himself next to Dr. Johnson and behaved to him with so much attention and politeness that he gained upon him insensibly.[6] No man eat[7] more heartily than Johnson, or loved better what was nice and delicate. Mr. Wilkes was very assiduous in helping him to some fine veal. "Pray give me leave, Sir—It is better here—A little of the brown—Some fat, Sir—A little of the stuffing—Some gravy—Let me have the pleasure of giving you some butter—Allow me to recommend a squeeze of this orange, or the lemon, perhaps, may have more zest."—"Sir, Sir, I am obliged to you, Sir," cried Johnson, bowing, and turning his head to him with a look for some time of "surly virtue,"[8] but, in a short while, of complacency.

Foote being mentioned, Johnson said, "He is not a good mimic." One of the company added, "A merry Andrew, a buffoon." JOHNSON: "But he has wit[9] too, and is not deficient in ideas, or in fertility and variety of imagery, and not empty of reading;[1] he has knowledge enough to fill up his part. One species of wit he has in an eminent degree, that of escape. You drive him into a corner with both hands; but he's gone, Sir, when you think you have got him—like an animal that jumps over your head. Then he has a great range for his wit; he never lets truth stand between him and a jest, and he is sometimes mighty coarse. Garrick is under many restraints from which Foote is free." WILKES: "Garrick's wit is more like Lord Chesterfield's." JOHNSON: "The first time I was in company with Foote was at Fitzherbert's.[2] Having no good opinion of the fellow, I was resolved not to be pleased; and it is very difficult to please a man against his will. I went on eating my dinner pretty sullenly, affecting not to mind him. But the dog was so very comical, that I was obliged to lay down my knife and fork, throw myself back upon my chair, and fairly laugh it out. No, Sir, he was irresistible. He upon one occasion experienced, in an extraordinary degree, the efficacy of his powers of entertaining. Amongst the many and various modes which he tried of getting money, he became a partner with a small-beer brewer, and he was to have a share of the profits for procuring customers amongst his numerous acquaintance. Fitzherbert was one who took his small beer;[3] but it was so bad that the servants resolved not to drink it. They were at some loss how to notify[4] their resolution, being afraid of offending their master, who they knew liked Foote much as a companion. At last they fixed upon a little black boy, who was rather a favorite, to be their deputy and deliver their remonstrance; and having invested him with the whole authority of the kitchen, he was to inform Mr. Fitzherbert, in all their names, upon a certain day, that they would drink Foote's small beer no longer. On that day Foote happened to dine at Fitzherbert's, and this boy served at table; he was so delighted with Foote's stories, and merriment, and grimace,[5] that when he went downstairs, he told them, 'This is the finest man I have ever seen. I will not deliver your message. I will drink his small beer.'"

---

6. Imperceptibly.
7. Ate (pronounced "ett").
8. Boswell quotes from Johnson's poem *London*.
9. Intelligence, cleverness.
1. Devoid of learning.
2. William Fitzherbert (1712–1772), landowner and politician.
3. Weak beer.
4. Express.
5. Exaggerated facial expressions (Foote specialized in caricatures of his contemporaries).

Somebody observed that Garrick could not have done this. WILKES: "Garrick would have made the small beer still smaller. He is now leaving the stage; but he will play Scrub[6] all his life." I knew that Johnson would let nobody attack Garrick but himself, as Garrick once said to me, and I had heard him praise his liberality; so to bring out his commendation of his celebrated pupil, I said, loudly, "I have heard Garrick is liberal." JOHNSON: "Yes, Sir, I know that Garrick has given away more money than any man in England that I am acquainted with, and that not from ostentatious views. Garrick was very poor when he began life; so when he came to have money, he probably was very unskillful in giving away, and saved when he should not. But Garrick began to be liberal as soon as he could; and I am of opinion, the reputation of avarice which he has had, has been very lucky for him and prevented his having many enemies. You despise a man for avarice, but do not hate him. Garrick might have been much better attacked for living with more splendor than is suitable to a player: if they had had the wit to have assaulted him in that quarter, they might have galled him more. But they have kept clamoring about his avarice, which has rescued him from much obloquy and envy."

Talking of the great difficulty of obtaining authentic information for biography, Johnson told us, "When I was a young fellow I wanted to write the *Life of Dryden*, and in order to get materials, I applied to the only two persons then alive who had seen him; these were old Swinney, and old Cibber.[7] Swinney's information was no more than this, "That at Will's coffeehouse Dryden had a particular chair for himself, which was set by the fire in winter, and was then called his winter-chair; and that it was carried out for him to the balcony in summer, and was then called his summer-chair." Cibber could tell no more but "that he remembered him a decent old man, arbiter of critical disputes at Will's." You are to consider that Cibber was then at a great distance from Dryden, had perhaps one leg only in the room, and durst not draw in the other." BOSWELL: "Yet Cibber was a man of observation?" JOHNSON: "I think not." BOSWELL: "You will allow his *Apology* to be well done." JOHNSON: "Very well done, to be sure, Sir. That book is a striking proof of the justice of Pope's remark:

> Each might his several province well command,
> Would all but stoop to what they understand."[8]

BOSWELL: "And his plays are good." JOHNSON: "Yes; but that was his trade; *l'esprit du corps:* he had been all his life among players and play-writers. I wondered that he had so little to say in conversation, for he had kept the best company, and learnt all that can be got by the ear. He abused Pindar[9] to me, and then showed me an ode of his own, with an absurd couplet, making a linnet soar on an eagle's wing. I told him that when the ancients made a simile, they always made it like something real."

Mr. Wilkes remarked, that "among all the bold flights of Shakespeare's imagination, the boldest was making Birnam Wood march to Dunsinane,[1] creating a wood where there never was a shrub; a wood in Scotland! ha! ha! ha!" And he also

---

6. A character in George Farquhar's comedy, *The Beaux' Stratagem*.

7. Owen Mac Swiney and Colley Cibber, actors from the first half of the 18th century. Cibber was also a poet, playwright, and the author of a widely read autobiography (his *Apology*).

8. Pope, *Essay on Criticism*, lines 66–67.

9. Spoke disparagingly of the ancient Greek poet Pindar, famous for his odes.

1. In Act 5 of *Macbeth*. In his *Journey to the Western Islands* (1775), Johnson had commented repeatedly on the treelessness of Scotland.

observed that "the clannish slavery of the Highlands of Scotland was the single exception to Milton's remark[2] of 'The mountain nymph, sweet Liberty,' being worshipped in all hilly countries." "When I was at Inverary," said he, "on a visit to my old friend, Archibald, Duke of Argyle, his dependents congratulated me on being such a favorite of his Grace. I said, 'It is then, gentlemen, truly lucky for me; for if I had displeased the Duke, and he had wished it, there is not a Campbell among you but would have been ready to bring John Wilkes's head to him in a charger. It would have been only

Off with his head! So much for Aylesbury.'[3]

I was then member[4] for Aylesbury." * * *

Mr. Arthur Lee mentioned some Scotch who had taken possession of a barren part of America, and wondered why they should choose it. JOHNSON: "Why, Sir, all barrenness is comparative. The *Scotch* would not know it to be barren." BOSWELL: "Come, come, he is flattering the English. You have now been in Scotland, Sir, and say if you did not see meat and drink enough there." JOHNSON: "Why yes, Sir; meat and drink enough to give the inhabitants sufficient strength to run away from home." All these quick and lively sallies were said sportively, quite in jest, and with a smile, which showed that he meant only wit. Upon this topic he and Mr. Wilkes could perfectly assimilate; here was a bond of union between them, and I was conscious that as both of them had visited Caledonia,[5] both were fully satisfied of the strange narrow ignorance of those who imagine that it is a land of famine. But they amused themselves with persevering in the old jokes. When I claimed a superiority for Scotland over England in one respect, that no man can be arrested there for a debt merely because another swears it against him; but there must first be the judgment of a court of law ascertaining its justice; and that a seizure of the person, before judgment is obtained, can take place only if his creditor should swear that he is about to fly from the country, or, as it is technically expressed, is *in meditatione fugae.* WILKES: "That, I should think, may be safely sworn of all the Scotch nation." JOHNSON (to Mr. Wilkes): "You must know, Sir, I lately took my friend Boswell and showed him genuine civilized life in an English provincial town. I turned him loose at Lichfield, my native city, that he might see for once real civility: for you know he lives among savages in Scotland, and among rakes in London." WILKES: "Except when he is with grave, sober, decent people like you and me." JOHNSON (smiling): "And we ashamed of him."

They were quite frank and easy. Johnson told the story of his asking Mrs. Macaulay[6] to allow her footman to sit down with them, to prove the ridiculousness of the argument for the equality of mankind; and he said to me afterwards, with a nod of satisfaction, "You saw Mr. Wilkes acquiesced." Wilkes talked with all imaginable freedom of the ludicrous title given to the Attorney General, *Diabolus Regis,*[7] adding, "I have reason to know something about that officer; for I was prosecuted for a libel."[8]

---

2. In his poem *L'Allegro* (36).
3. Wilkes adapts Colley Cibber's popular version of Shakespeare's *Richard III,* which contains the line, "Off with his head. So much for Buckingham."
4. Of Parliament.
5. Scotland (from the Roman name for North Britain).
6. Catherine Macaulay, author of a controversial *History*

of England (1763–1783). In order to test her egalitarian principles, Johnson had proposed that she invite her footman to join them at dinner. "I thus, Sir, showed her the absurdity of the levelling doctrine," he told Boswell. "She has never liked me since."
7. The King's Devil.
8. See n. 2, page 2817.

Johnson, who many people would have supposed must have been furiously angry at hearing this talked of so lightly, said not a word. He was now, *indeed,* "a good-humored fellow."

After dinner we had an accession[9] of Mrs. Knowles, the Quaker lady, well known for her various talents, and of Mr. Alderman Lee. Amidst some patriotic groans, somebody (I think the Alderman) said, "Poor old England is lost." JOHNSON: "Sir, it is not so much to be lamented that Old England is lost, as that the Scotch have found it."[1] WILKES: "Had Lord Bute governed Scotland only, I should not have taken the trouble to write his eulogy, and dedicate *Mortimer* to him."[2]

Mr. Wilkes held a candle to show a fine print of a beautiful female figure which hung in the room, and pointed out the elegant contour of the bosom with the finger of an arch connoisseur. He afterwards, in a conversation with me, waggishly insisted that all the time Johnson showed visible signs of a fervent admiration of the corresponding charms of the fair Quaker.

This record, though by no means so perfect as I could wish, will serve to give a notion of a very curious interview, which was not only pleasing at the time, but had the agreeable and benignant effect of reconciling any animosity, and sweetening any acidity, which in the various bustle of political contest, had been produced in the minds of two men, who though widely different, had so many things in common—classical learning, modern literature, wit, and humor, and ready repartee—that it would have been much to be regretted if they had been forever at a distance from each other.

Mr. Burke gave me much credit for this successful *negotiation* and pleasantly said that "there was nothing to equal it in the whole history of the *Corps Diplomatique.*"

I attended Dr. Johnson home, and had the satisfaction to hear him tell Mrs. Williams how much he had been pleased with Mr. Wilkes's company, and what an agreeable day he had passed.

[CONVERSATIONS AT STREATHAM AND THE CLUB][1]

[30 March 1778] I mentioned that I had in my possession the Life of Sir Robert Sibbald, the celebrated Scottish antiquary, and founder of the Royal College of Physicians at Edinburgh, in the original manuscript in his own handwriting; and that it was I believed the most natural and candid account of himself that ever was given by any man. As an instance, he tells that the Duke of Perth, then Chancellor of Scotland, pressed him very much to come over to the Roman Catholic faith; that he resisted all his Grace's arguments for a considerable time, till one day he felt himself, as it were, instantaneously convinced, and with tears in his eyes ran into the Duke's arms, and embraced the ancient religion; that he continued very steady in it for some time, and accompanied his Grace to London one winter, and lived in his household; that there he found the rigid fasting prescribed by the church very severe upon him; that this disposed him to reconsider the controversy, and having then seen that he was in the

9. I.e., these additional guests arrived: Mary Morris Knowles (1733–1807), a highly accomplished needlewoman whose "sutile pictures" Johnson praised in a letter to Mrs. Thrale; and William Lee (1739–1795), merchant, diplomat, and the only American ever elected an alderman of London.
1. Soon after succeeding to the throne in 1760, George III made his former tutor, the Scottish Earl of Bute, Prime Minister of Britain. The appointment unleashed a flood of anti-Scottish propaganda.

2. As part of a sustained campaign against Bute's government, Wilkes had chosen to reprint a 1731 play called *The Fall of Mortimer* and had prefaced it with a mock-respectful dedication to the prime minister.
1. These were two of Johnson's favorite venues of conversation. Streatham was the country estate of Henry and Hester Thrale, where Johnson and his friends were often guests. The Club was a group of distinguished thinkers, writers, artists, and statesman that met weekly.

wrong, he returned to Protestantism. I talked of some time or other publishing this curious life. MRS. THRALE: "I think you had as well let alone that publication. To discover[2] such weakness exposes a man when he is gone." JOHNSON: "Nay, it is an honest picture of human nature. How often are the primary motives of our greatest actions as small as Sibbald's, for his re-conversion." MRS. THRALE: "But may they not as well be forgotten?" JOHNSON: "No, Madam, a man loves to review his own mind. That is the use of a diary, or journal." LORD TRIMLESTOWN: "True, Sir. As the ladies love to see themselves in a glass, so a man likes to see himself in his journal." BOSWELL: "A very pretty allusion." JOHNSON: "Yes, indeed." BOSWELL: "And as a lady adjusts her dress before a mirror, a man adjusts his character by looking at his journal." I next year found the very same thought in Atterbury's *Funeral Sermon on Lady Cutts,* where, having mentioned her *Diary,* he says, "In this glass she every day dressed her mind." This is a proof of coincidence, and not of plagiarism; for I had never read that sermon before.

Next morning, while we were at breakfast, Johnson gave a very earnest recommendation of what he himself practiced with the utmost conscientiousness: I mean a strict attention to truth, even in the most minute particulars. "Accustom your children," said he, "constantly to this; if a thing happened at one window, and they, when relating it, say that it happened at another, do not let it pass, but instantly check them; you do not know where deviation from truth will end." BOSWELL: "It may come to the door: and when once an account is at all varied in one circumstance, it may by degrees be varied so as to be totally different from what really happened." Our lively hostess, whose fancy was impatient of the rein,[3] fidgeted at this, and ventured to say, "Nay, this is too much. If Mr. Johnson should forbid me to drink tea, I would comply, as I should feel the restraint only twice a day; but little variations in narrative must happen a thousand times a day, if one is not perpetually watching." JOHNSON: "Well, Madam, and you *ought* to be perpetually watching. It is more from carelessness about truth than from intentional lying, that there is so much falsehood in the world."

In his review of Dr. Warton's *Essay on the Writings and Genius of Pope,* Johnson has given the following salutary caution upon this subject:

"Nothing but experience could evince[4] the freqency of false information, or enable any man to conceive that so many groundless reports should be propagated, as every man of eminence may hear of himself. Some men relate what they think, as what they know; some men of confused memories and habitual inaccuracy ascribe to one man what belongs to another; and some talk on, without thought or care. A few men are sufficient to broach falsehoods, which are afterwards innocently diffused by successive relaters."

Had he lived to read what Sir John Hawkins and Mrs. Piozzi have related concerning himself[5] how much would he have found his observation illustrated. He was indeed so much impressed with the prevalence of falsehood, voluntary or unintentional, that I never knew any person who upon hearing an extraordinary circumstance told, discovered more of the *incredulus odi*.[6] He would say, with a significant look and decisive tone, "It is not so. Do not tell this again." He inculcated upon all his friends the importance of perpetual vigilance against the slightest degrees of falsehood; the effect of which, as Sir Joshua Reynolds observed to me, has been, that all

---

2. Reveal.
3. Whose imagination did not like to be restrained.
4. Prove, serve as evidence of.
5. Boswell refers to the two rival biographies, Sir John

Hawkins's *Life of Samuel Johnson LL.D.* (1787) and Hester Thrale Piozzi's *Anecdotes of the Late Samuel Johnson LL.D.* (1786).
6. Hostile incredulity.

who were of his *school* are distinguished for a love of truth and accuracy, which they would not have possessed in the same degree, if they had not been acquainted with Johnson.

Talking of ghosts, he said, "It is wonderful that five thousand years have now elapsed since the creation of the world, and still it is undecided whether or not there has ever been an instance of the spirit of any person appearing after death. All argument is against it; but all belief is for it."

He said, "John Wesley's[7] conversation is good, but he is never at leisure. He is always obliged to go at a certain hour. This is very disagreeable to a man who loves to fold his legs and have out his talk, as I do."

On Friday, April 3, I dined with him in London, in a company where were present several eminent men, whom I shall not name, but distinguish their parts in the conversation by different letters.[8]

F: "I have been looking at this famous antique marble dog of Mr. Jennings, valued at a thousand guineas, said to be Alcibiades's dog."[9] JOHNSON: "His tail then must be docked.[1] That was the mark of Alcibiades's dog." E: "A thousand guineas! The representation of no animal whatever is worth so much. At this rate a dead dog would indeed be better than a living lion." JOHNSON: "Sir, it is not the worth of the thing, but of the skill in forming it which is so highly estimated. Everything that enlarges the sphere of human powers, that shows man he can do what he thought he could not do, is valuable. The first man who balanced a straw upon his nose; Johnson,[2] who rode upon three horses at a time; in short, all such men deserved the applause of mankind, not on account of the use of what they did, but of the dexterity which they exhibited." BOSWELL: "Yet a misapplication of time and assiduity is not to be encouraged. Addison, in one of his *Spectators*, commends the judgment of a king, who, as a suitable reward to a man that by long perseverance had attained to the art of throwing a barleycorn through the eye of a needle, gave him a bushel of barley." JOHNSON: "He must have been a king of Scotland, where barley is scarce." F: "One of the most remarkable antique figures of an animal is the boar at Florence." JOHNSON: "The first boar that is well made in marble should be preserved as a wonder. When men arrive at a facility of making boars well, then the workmanship is not of such value, but they should however be preserved as examples, and as a greater security for the restoration of the art, should it be lost."

E: "We hear prodigious complaints at present of emigration. I am convinced that emigration makes a country more populous." J: "That sounds very much like a paradox." E: "Exportation of men, like exportation of all other commodities, makes more be produced." JOHNSON: "But there would be more people were there not emigration, provided there were food for more." E: "No; leave a few breeders, and you'll have more people than if there were no emigration." JOHNSON: "Nay, Sir, it is plain there will be more people, if there are more breeders. Thirty cows in good pasture will produce more calves than ten cows, provided they have good bulls." E: "There are bulls enough in Ireland."[3] JOHNSON (smiling): "So, Sir, I should think from your

7. Co-founder (1703–1791) of the Methodist movement.
8. "F" stands for John Fitzpatrick, Earl of Upper Ossory, an Irish nobleman; "E" for Edmund Burke, statesman and political theorist; "R" for Richard Brinsley Sheridan, playwright; "C" or George Fordyce, a chemist; "P" for Sir Joshua Reynolds ("Painter").

9. A marble statue purchased in Rome by the collector Henry Jennings, it was called after an antique sculpture in the Uffizi, Florence.
1. Clipped.
2. An acrobatic rider (no relation).
3. An "Irish bull" was a foolish blunder.

argument." BOSWELL: "You said, exportation of men, like exportation of other commodities, makes more be produced. But a bounty is given to encourage the exportation of corn, and no bounty is given for the exportation of men, though, indeed, those who go, gain by it." R: "But the bounty on the exportation of corn is paid at home." E: "That's the same thing." JOHNSON: "No, Sir." R: "A man who stays at home gains nothing by his neighbors emigrating." BOSWELL: "I can understand that emigration may be the cause that more people may be produced in a country; but the country will not therefore be the more populous, for the people issue from it. It can only be said that there is a flow of people. It is an encouragement to have children, to know that they can get a living by emigration." R: "Yes, if there were an emigration of children under six years of age. But they don't emigrate till they could earn their livelihood in some way at home." C: "It is remarkable that the most unhealthy countries, where there are the most destructive diseases, such as Egypt and Bengal, are the most populous." JOHNSON: "Countries which are the most populous have the most destructive diseases. *That* is the true state of the proposition." C: "Holland is very unhealthy, yet it is exceedingly populous." JOHNSON: "I know not that Holland is unhealthy. But its populousness is owing to an influx of people from all other countries. Disease cannot be the cause of populousness, for it not only carries off a great proportion of the people, but those who are left are weakened and unfit for the purposes of increase."

R: "Mr. E., I don't mean to flatter, but when posterity reads one of your speeches in Parliament, it will be difficult to believe that you took so much pains, knowing with certainty that it could produce no effect, that not one vote would be gained by it." E. "Waiving your compliment to me, I shall say in general, that it is very well worthwhile for a man to take pains to speak well in Parliament. A man, who has vanity, speaks to display his talents; and if a man speaks well, he gradually establishes a certain reputation and consequence[4] in the general opinion, which sooner or later will have its political reward. Besides, though not one vote is gained, a good speech has its effect. Though an act which has been ably opposed passes into a law, yet in its progress it is modeled, it is softened in such a manner that we see plainly the Minister[5] has been told that the Members attached to him are so sensible of its injustice or absurdity from what they have heard that it must be altered." JOHNSON: "And, Sir, there is a gratification of pride. Though we cannot out-vote them we will out-argue them. They shall not do wrong without its being shown both to themselves and to the world." E: "The House of Commons is a mixed body. (I except the Minority, which I hold to be pure [smiling][6] but I take the whole House.) It is a mass by no means pure; but neither is it wholly corrupt, though there is a large proportion of corruption in it. There are many members who generally go with the Minister, who will not go all lengths. There are many honest well-meaning country gentlemen who are in Parliament only to keep up the consequence of their families. Upon most of these a good speech will have influence." JOHNSON: "We are all more or less governed by interest.[7] But interest will not make us do everything. In a case which admits of doubt, we try to think on the side which is for our interest, and generally bring ourselves to act accordingly. But the subject must admit of diversity of coloring;[8] it must receive a color on that side." * * * In the House of Commons there are

---

4. Importance, social standing.
5. Prime minister.
6. The party to which Burke belonged was out of power.
7. Self-interest.
8. Legitimately have two sides to it.

members enough who will not vote what is grossly unjust or absurd. No, Sir, there must always be right enough, or appearance of right, to keep wrong in countenance." BOSWELL: "There is surely always a majority in Parliament who have places, or who want to have them, and who therefore will be generally ready to support government without requiring any pretext." E: "True, Sir; that majority will always follow

Quo clamor vocat et turba faventium."[9]

BOSWELL: "Well now, let us take the common phrase, Place-hunters.[1] I thought they had hunted without regard to anything, just as their huntsmen, the Minister, leads, looking only to the prey." J: "But taking your metaphor, you know that in hunting there are few so desperately keen as to follow without reserve. Some do not choose to leap ditches and hedges and risk their necks, or gallop over steeps, or even to dirty themselves in bogs and mire." BOSWELL: "I am glad there are some good, quiet, moderate political hunters." E: "I believe, in any body of men in England, I should have been in the Minority; I have always been in the Minority." P: "The House of Commons resembles a private company. How seldom is any man convinced by another's argument; passion and pride rise against it." R: "What would be the consequence, if a Minister, sure of a majority in the House of Commons, should resolve that there should be no speaking at all upon his side." E: "He must soon go out. That has been tried; but it was found it would not do."

E: "The Irish language is not primitive; it is Teutonic, a mixture of the northern tongues: it has much English in it." JOHNSON: "It may have been radically Teutonic; but English and High Dutch have no similarity to the eye, though radically the same. Once, when looking into Low Dutch, I found, in a whole page, only one word similar to English; *stroem*, like *stream*, and it signified *tide*." E: "I remember having seen a Dutch sonnet, in which I found this word, *roesnopies*. Nobody would at first think that this could be English; but, when we inquire, we find *roes*, rose, and *nopie*, knob; so we have *rosebuds*."

JOHNSON: "I have been reading Thicknesse's travels, which I think are entertaining." BOSWELL: "What, Sir, a good book?" JOHNSON: "Yes, Sir, to read once; I do not say you are to make a study of it and digest it; and I believe it to be a true book in his intention. All travelers generally mean to tell truth; though Thicknesse observes, upon Smollett's account[2] of his alarming a whole town in France by firing a blunderbuss, and frightening a French nobleman till he made him tie on his portmanteau, that he would be loath to say Smollett had told two lies in one page; but he had found the only town in France where these things could have happened. Travelers must often be mistaken. In everything, except where mensuration can be applied, they may honestly differ. There has been, of late, a strange turn in travelers to be displeased."

E: "From the experience which I have had—and I have had a great deal—I have learnt to think *better* of mankind." JOHNSON: "From my experience I have found them worse in commercial dealings, more disposed to cheat, than I had any notion of; but more disposed to do one another good than I had conceived." J:

---

9. Amid the plaudits of the noisy crowd (Horace, *Odes* 3.24.46).
1. Those who sought political sinecures ("places").

2. Philip Thicknesse, *A Year's Journey through France and Spain* (1777); Tobias Smollett, *Travels in France and Italy* (1766).

"Less just and more beneficent." JOHNSON: "And really it is wonderful, considering how much attention is necessary for men to take care of themselves, and ward off immediate evils which press upon them, it is wonderful how much they do for others. As it is said of the greatest liar, that he tells more truth than falsehood; so it may be said of the worst man, that he does more good than evil." BOSWELL: "Perhaps from experience men may be found *happier* than we suppose." JOHNSON: "No, Sir; the more we inquire, we shall find men the less happy." P: "As to thinking better or worse of mankind from experience, some cunning people will not be satisfied unless they have put men to the test, as they think. There is a very good story told of Sir Godfrey Kneller, in his character of a justice of the peace. A gentleman brought his servant before him, upon an accusation of having stolen some money from him; but it having come out that he had laid it purposely in the servant's way, in order to try his honesty, Sir Godfrey sent the master to prison." JOHNSON: "To resist temptation once is not a sufficient proof of honesty. If a servant, indeed, were to resist the continued temptation of silver lying in a window, as some people let it lie, when he is sure his master does not know how much there is of it, he would give a strong proof of honesty. But this is a proof to which you have no right to put a man. You know, humanly speaking, there is a certain degree of temptation which will overcome any virtue. Now, in so far as you approach temptation to a man, you do him an injury; and, if he is overcome, you share his guilt." P: "And, when once overcome, it is easier for him to be got the better of again." BOSWELL: "Yes, you are his seducer; you have debauched him. I have known a man resolve to put friendship to the test by asking a friend to lend him money merely with that view, when he did not want it." JOHNSON: "That is very wrong, Sir. Your friend may be a narrow man, and yet have many good qualities: narrowness may be his only fault. Now you are trying his general character as a friend, by one particular singly, in which he happens to be defective, when, in truth, his character is composed of many particulars."

E: "I understand the hogshead[3] of claret, which this society was favored with by our friend the Dean, is nearly out; I think he should be written to, to send another of the same kind. Let the request be made with a happy ambiguity of expression, so that we may have the chance of his sending *it* also as a present." JOHNSON: "I am willing to offer my services as secretary on this occasion." P: "As many as are for Dr. Johnson being secretary hold up your hands.—Carried unanimously." BOSWELL: "He will be our Dictator." JOHNSON: "No, the company is to dictate to me. I am only to write for wine; and I am quite disinterested, as I drink none; I shall not be suspected of having forged the application. I am no more than humble *scribe*." E: "Then you shall *prescribe*." BOSWELL: "Very well. The first play of words today." J: "No, no; the *bulls* in Ireland." JOHNSON: "Were I your Dictator you should have no wine. It would be my business *cavere ne quid detrimenti Respublica caperet*,[4] and wine is dangerous. Rome was ruined by luxury" (smiling). E: "If you allow no wine as Dictator, you shall not have me for your master of horse."[5]

1791

3. A large barrel.
4. "To ensure that no harm befall the republic." Johnson quotes from the *Senatus Consultum Ultimum*, a declaration of public emergency by the Roman senate. This declaration suspended ordinary laws and appointed a dictator for the duration of the emergency.
5. Under the emergency decree, the master of the horse served as second in command to the dictator.

Hester Salusbury Thrale Piozzi
1740–1821

Hester Salusbury Thrale Piozzi: the litany of last names tells some of her story. She was born to the Salusburys, an aristocratic and in some branches wealthy Welsh family; both her parents could claim the bloodline, neither of them the wealth. So she was wed at age twenty-three to Henry Thrale, a successful English brewer twelve years her senior, for whom she neither felt nor feigned love. She accepted his proposal in order to secure for her family a large bequest that hinged on her being married. Nonetheless, she threw herself with a will into domestic life at Streatham, Henry's estate six miles outside London. She bore twelve children and mourned eight of them, dead in infancy or childhood. She worked hard helping her husband to advance his endless commercial and political aspirations. And she hosted frequent gatherings of eminent houseguests, with Samuel Johnson the most frequent and most eminent of them all. Johnson had met the Thrales in 1765 and valued them both, Henry for his affability, Hester for her wide curiosity, sharp conversation, and attentive care. For nearly two decades she made Streatham Johnson's second home, and a center of British intellectual life.

Hester Thrale had always read and written plentifully, and in her early twenties had published some short verse in newspapers. During her marriage to Thrale her writing remained mostly a matter of manuscript—occasional poems, innumerable letters, and two sustained autobiographical documents: *The Family Book,* in which she recorded the progress of her offspring, and *Thraliana,* a text more her own, in which she recorded talk, thought, experience, feeling, "and in fine, every thing that struck me at the time." Johnson had recommended the practice, and her husband had given her the handsomely bound blank books in which to pursue it. In those volumes she detailed (among many other things) her intricate connection and her frequent exasperation with both men.

At Henry's death in 1781, much changed. Helped by Johnson, Hester Thrale managed and then sold the brewery. Despite objections by Johnson, and by almost all her family and friends, she fell deeply in love for the only time in her life, with the Italian musician Gabriel Piozzi. Foreign, Roman Catholic, irascible, and not rich, Piozzi combined traits that alienated virtually everyone in Thrale's once cohesive world. Friends marveled at the sudden prevalence of passion in a woman who had once been, as one of them lamented, "the best mother, the best wife, the best friend, the most amiable member of society. . . . I am myself convinced that the poor woman is mad." So were many others, but in the summer of 1784, the "poor woman" married her beloved and departed with him for Italy, leaving in her wake a cacophony, in gossip and newsprint, of scandal and scorn.

In her new marriage and new country, Hester Piozzi launched her career as published author. She produced *Anecdotes of the Late Samuel Johnson* (1786), culled from *Thraliana;* a collection of Johnson's *Letters* (1788); *Observations and Reflections* (1789), reworked from her journal of a tour through Europe; and *British Synonymy* (1794), an anecdotal survey of the overlapping meanings of English words. Piozzi's books brought her equivocal fame at best, heavily mixed with retrospectives on her history as celebrated hostess and social renegade. She spent her last decades in England, Wales, and (after Piozzi's death) at Bath, where she once reported with amusement that a tourist had "brought his son here, that he might see the *first woman in England.* So I am now grown one of the curiosities of Bath, it seems, and *one of the Antiquities.*" Her writing, though, has too much edge to pass as harmless "curiosity." When her *Anecdotes of Johnson* first appeared, Horace Walpole voiced a common complaint: "Her panegyric is loud in praise of her hero; and almost every fact she relates disgraces him." Walpole exaggerates, but the push-pull that he points to is one aspect that makes her work still fascinating. Again and again she immerses herself energetically in the conventional roles assigned to women ("best mother," "best wife," "best friend"), then steps aside to examine them askance, to question, to debunk, even to renounce them. Vibrating between acquiescence and anger, sentimentality and acerbity, Hester Salusbury Thrale Piozzi struck a note of her own, making for herself an interesting life, and a various and idiosyncratic body of work.

from The Family Book

[ON HER DAUGHTER'S PROGRESS]

Hester Maria Thrale born on the 17th September 1764 at her father's house, Southwark.[1]

This is to serve as a memorandum of her corporeal and mental powers at the age of two years, to which she is arrived this 17 September 1766. She can walk and run alone up and down all smooth places though pretty steep, and though the backstring[2] is still kept on it is no longer of use. She is perfectly healthy, of a lax constitution, and is strong enough to carry a hound-puppy two months old quite across the lawn at Streatham; also to carry a bowl[3] such as are used on bowling greens up the mount to the tubs.[4] She is neither remarkably big nor tall, being just 34 inches high, but eminently pretty. She can speak most words and speak them plain enough too, but is no great talker. She repeats the Pater Noster,[5] the three Christian virtues[6] and the signs of the zodiac in Watt's verses;[7] she likewise knows them on the globe perfectly well. She can tell all her letters great and small and spell little words as D,o,g, Dog, C,a,t, Cat etc. She knows her nine figures and the simplest combinations of 'em as 3, 4, 34; 6, 8, 68; but none beyond a hundred. She knows all the heathen deities by their attributes and counts 20 without missing one. Signed—H. L. Thrale.

Sponsors[8] to H. M. T.: Mrs. Salusbury, Mrs. Nesbitt, and Sir John Lade.

* * *

Hester Maria Thrale,   London 17 March 1767.

Six months have now elapsed since I wrote down an account of what she could do; the following is for a record of the amazing improvements made in this last half year; her person has however undergone no visible change. She cannot read at all, but knows the compass as perfectly as any mariner upon the seas; is mistress of the solar system, can trace the orbits, and tell the arbitrary marks of the planets as readily as Dr. Bradley.[9] The comets she knows at sight when represented upon paper, and all the chief constellations on the celestial globe. The signs of the zodiac she is thoroughly acquainted with, as also the difference between the ecliptic and equator. She has too by the help of the dissected maps acquired so nice a knowledge of geography as to be well able to describe not only the four quarters of the world, but almost, nay, I do think every nation on the terrestrial globe, and all the principal islands in all parts of the world. These—with the most remarkable seas, gulfs, straits, etc.—she has so full an acquaintance with, that she discovers them colored, or penciled, separate or together in any scale small or great, map or globe. She can repeat likewise the names of all the capital cities in Europe besides those of Persia and India—China I mean; also the 3 Christian virtues in English, the 4 cardinal ones in Latin[1], the 1st page of Lily's Grammar[2] to the bottom, the seven days of the week, the 12 months of

---

1. In this borough across the river from London, the Thrales owned a city home adjacent to their brewery.
2. A cord at the back of the pinafore, sometimes held like a leash to keep the infant from harm.
3. A bowling ball.
4. Watering troughs.
5. The Lord's Prayer.

6. Faith, hope, and charity (1 Corinthians 13.13).
7. Isaac Watts, poet and hymnist whose *Divine Songs for the Use of Children* (1715) includes a poem on the zodiac.
8. Godparents.
9. James Bradley (1693–1762), eminent astronomer.
1. Prudence, temperance, fortitude, and justice.
2. A Latin textbook.

the Year, the twos of the multiplication table, the four points of the compass, the four quarters of the world, the Pater Noster, the Nicene Creed and the Decalogue;[3] the responses of the church catechism to the end of the duty to our neighbor, and the names of the richest, wisest, and meekest man, etc. She has also in these last six months learned to distinguish colors, and to name them; as also to tell a little story with some grace and emphasis, as the story of the Fall of Man, of Perseus and Andromeda, of the Judgment of Paris, and two or three more. These are certainly uncommon performances of a baby 2 years and 6 months only; but they are most strictly true. She cannot however read at all. * * *

17 September 1767. A little blue-cover book will now best show the further acquisitions of Hester M. Thrale who has this day completed the second and begun the third[4] year of her life by repeating all the responses in that book by heart—this 17 September 1767 at Brighthelmstone.[5] She is yet a miserable poor speller, and can scarce read a word.

* * *

17 December 1768. Hester Maria Thrale is this day four years and a quarter old. I have made her up a little red book to which I must appeal for her progress in improvements. She went through it this day quite well. The astronomical part is the hardest. She can now read tolerably, but not at sight, and has a manner of reading that is perfectly agreeable, free from tone or accent. At 3 years and a half however she wrote some cards to her friends with a print taken from the picture which Zoffany[6] drew of her at 20 months old; but as I lay in[7] soon after, the writing was totally forgotten, and is now all to begin again. She has this day repeated her catechism quite through, her Latin grammar to the end of the 5 declensions, a fable in Phaedrus, an epigram in Martial,[8] the revolutions, diameters, and distance of the planets. She is come vastly forward in sense and expression and once more I appeal to her little red book. With regard to her person, it is accounted exquisitely pretty. Her hair is sandy, her eyes of a very dark blue, and their luster particularly fine; her complexion delicate, and her carriage[9] uncommonly genteel. Her temper is not so good; reserved to all, insolent where she is free, and sullen to those who teach or dress or do anything towards her. Never in a passion, but obstinate to that uncommon degree that no punishment except severe smart[1] can prevail on her to beg pardon if she has offended.

[ON THE DEATH OF HER SON]

[March 1776] On Thursday the 21st they all[1] rose well and lively, and Queeney went with me to fetch her sister from school for a week. She seemed sullen all the way there and back but not sick, so I huffed her and we got home in good time to dress for dinner, when we expected Sir Robert Cotton and the Davenants.[2] Harry however had seen a play of his friend Murphy's[3] advertised, and teased me so to let him see it that I could not resist his importunity, and treated one of our principle clerks to go

3. The Ten Commandments.
4. I.e., completed the third and begun the fourth.
5. Brighton, a popular seaside resort, where the Thrales kept a house for use each autumn.
6. John Zoffany (1733–1810), a portraitist much in demand by royal, aristocratic, and merchant families (see his portrait of Queen Charlotte and her children, page 1992).
7. Gave birth (to her fourth child) and convalesced.
8. Phaedrus translated Aesop's *Fables* from Greek into Latin; Martial was a Roman poet celebrated for his short, witty verses.

9. Bearing
1. I.e., a whipping (with a rod that was kept on the nursery mantle).
1. I.e., the three children now at home: Hester ("Queeney"), Henry (the only son, now nine years old), and Sophy (four); the sister at school was Susan (five).
2. Cousins of Hester Thrale.
3. Arthur Murphy (1727–1805), Irish actor, playwright, and friend of the family.

with him. He came home at 12 o'clock half mad with delight, and in such spirits, health, and happiness that nothing ever exceeded. Queeney however drooped all afternoon, complained of the headache, and Mr. Thrale was so cross at my giving Harry leave to go to the play, instead of showing him to Sir Robert, that I passed an uneasy time of it, and could not enjoy the praises given to Susan, I was so fretted about the two eldest. When Harry came home so happy, however, all was forgotten, and he went to rest in perfect tranquility. Queeney however felt hot, and I was not at all pleased with her, but on Friday morning the boy rose quite cheerful and did our little business with great alacrity. Count Manucci[4] came to breakfast by appointment. We were all to go show him the Tower[5] forsooth, so Queeney made light of her illness and pressed me to take her too. There was one of the ships bound for Boston now in the river with our beer aboard.[6] Harry ran to see the blaze in the morning and coming back to the counting-house, "I see," he says to our first clerk, "I see your porter[7] is good, Mr. Perkins, for it *burns* special well." Well by this time we set out for the Tower, Papa and Manucci and the children and I. Queeney was not half well, but Harry continued in high spirits both among the lions and the arms, repeating passages from the English history, examining the artillery and getting into every mortar[8] till he was as black as the ground. Count Manucci observed his pranks, and said he must be a soldier with him; but Harry would not fight for the Grand Duke of Tuscany because he was a Papist, and "Look here," said he, showing the instruments of torture to the Count, "what those Spanish Papists intended for *us*." From the place we drove to Moore's Carpet Manufactory, where the boy was still active, attentive, and lively. But as Queeney's looks betrayed the sickness she would fain have concealed, we drove homewards, taking in our way Brooke's Menagerie, where I just stopped to speak about my peafowl. Here Harry was happy again with a lion intended for a show who was remarkably tame, and a monkey so beautiful and gentle, that I was as much pleased with him as the children. Here we met a Mr. Hervey who took notice of the boy how *well* he looked. "Yes," said I, "if the dirt were scraped off him." It was now time to get home, and Harry after saying how hungry he was, instantly "pounced" as he called it on a piece of cold mutton and spent the afternoon among us all recounting the pleasures of the day. He went to bed that night as perfectly well as ever I saw man, woman, or child in my life. Queeney however took some rhubarb, and went on drooping and felt feverish. I looked at her two or three times in the night too, and found her hot and feverish, but her dear brother slept as cool and comfortable as possible, and on the morning of the next fatal day, Saturday 23rd of March 1776, he rose in perfect health, went to the baker for his roll and watched the drawing it out of the oven, carried it to *Bachelor's Hall,* as he called it where the young clerks live down the brewhouse yard; there he got butter, and cooked a merry breakfast among them. After this he returned with two penny cakes he had bought for the little girls, and distributed them between them in his pleasant manner for[9] minuets that he made them dance. I was all this while waiting on Queeney, who seemed far from well, and I was once very impatient at the noise the maids and children made in the nursery, by laughing excessively at his antic tricks. By this time I came down to my dressing room to tutor Sophy till the clock struck ten which is my regular breakfast hour. I had scarce made the tea when Moll came to tell me Queeney was better, and Harry

---

4. A Florentine nobleman whom the Thrales had first met in Paris.
5. Of London.
6. Carrying a cargo of beer from the Thrale brewery; while in the river, the ship had caught fire.
7. Dark beer.
8. Canon.
9. In exchange for.

making a figure of 5:10,[1] so we always called his manner of twisitng about when any-thing ailed him. When I got to the nursery, there was Harry crying as if he had been whipped instead of ill, so I reproved him for making such a bustle about nothing, and said, "See how differently your sister behaves," who though in earnest far from well, had begged to make breakfast for Papa and Mr. Baretti,[2] while I was employed above. The next thing I did was to send for Mr. Lawrence of York Buildings, to whom Nurse was always partial.[3] My note expressed to him that both the eldest children were ill, but Hetty *worst*. Presently, however, finding the boy inclined to vomit, I adminis-tered a large wine glass of emetic wine, which however did nothing *any way*, though he drank small liquids with avidity. And now, seeing his sickness increase, and his countenance begin to alter, I sent out Sam with orders not to come back without *some* physician—Jebb, Bromfield, Pinkstan, or Lawrence of Essex Street, whichever he could find. In the mean time I plunged Harry into water as hot as could easily be borne, up to his middle, and had just taken him out of the tub and laid him in a warm bed, when Jebb came, and gave him first hot wine, then usquebaugh,[4] then Daffy's Elixir,[5] so fast that it alarmed me, though I had not notion of *Death* having seen him so perfectly well at 9 o'clock. He then had poultices made with mustard put to his feet, and strong broth and wine clysters[6] injected, but we could get no evacuation *any* way, and the inclination to vomit still continuing, Jebb gave him five grains of ipecacuanha[7] and then drove away to call Heberden's help.[8] The child all this while spoke well and brisk, sat upright to talk with the doctors, and said he had no pain now but his breath was short. This I attributed to the hot things he had taken, and thought Jebb in my heart far more officious than wise. I was however all confusion, distress, and perplexity, and Mr. Thrale bid me not cry so, for I should look like a hag when I went to Court next day. He often saw Harry in the course of the morning, and apprehended no danger at all. No more did Baretti, who said he should be whipped for frighting his mother for nothing. Queeney had for some time been laid down on her own bed, and got up fancying herself better. But soon a universal shriek called us all together to Harry's bedside, where he struggled a moment—thrusting his finger down his throat to excite vomiting—and then, turning to Nurse, said very dis-tinctly, "Don't scream so—I *know* I must die."

This however I did not hear. Lady Lade, who I believe had been here half the morning watching the event, asked me kindly what she should do for me. I replied, "Oh take me these two little girls away—they distract me." She accordingly then car-ried them off and set 'em safe at Kensington, where they are still. This most dreadful of all our misfortunes, which they say happened about 3 o'clock or 4, on the 23rd day of March 1776, had such an effect on poor Queeney that I expected her to follow him. Jebb however did something for her, and advising speedy change of scene, I rose in the morning of the 30th after a sleepless night, and in a sort of desperation drove away with her to Bath, which little journey did her infinite service. Baretti kindly offered to go with me, so he conducted the troop and diverted Queeney's melancholy with all the tricks he could think on. She is now—though not recovered—yet I hope out of danger (as the phrase is). I saw the little girls at Kensington yesterday as I came home. This is the 9th of April 1776.

---

1. I.e., bent in half, with knees pulled in to the chest.
2. Giuseppe Baretti (1719–1789), Italian scholar and author, a close friend of Henry Thrale.
3. Herbert Lawrence was a local physician; "Nurse" took care of the Thrale children.
4. Whiskey.

5. A laxative.
6. Enemas.
7. A purgative.
8. William Heberden, one of the best physicians in Lon-don.

[On Her Marriage and Household]

25 September 1778. My eldest daughter Hester Maria was measured, and found of a pleasing and sufficient height. She was this last birthday, 17 September 1778, fourteen years old. She is very pretty still, but is of a pale complection. Her person, mind, and temper have never indeed suffered any considerable changes. Her face and figure are very lovely, her mind very highly cultivated, and her temper haughty and contemptuous. She is blue-eyed, fair-haired, has a good set of teeth, good shape, and the carriage of a girl of fashion. Books are her delight, and she chooses her own studies now for me, who do not interfere much—nor would she suffer[1] me. She is my Mistress completely, but has I think no great influence over her Papa. We kept her birthday merrily, gave old Nurse money, and she treated the servants with a dance. If my Master's mad management does not bereave us all of all our property,[2] she stands foremost now to inherit our possessions, and *mine* thank God are entailed.[3] Little as they are, and greatly as Mr. Thrale despises them, they may become our best friends, and he will take the swiftest methods to make them so, by feeding the brew house with its own flesh till it perishes with a sudden and dreadful ruin.

* * *

This is the last day of the year 1778. My children are all about me and my house is full of friends. Susan and I read two acts of Molière's *Bourgeois*[4] today. She understands it to a miracle, and translates with some idea even of giving an English turn to the idiom, or an English idiom to the phrase. Sophy reads English narrative to amuse herself perfectly well without any tone or drawl; they both work well, and write very prettily, spelling as exactly as myself. Sue can do sums in the three first rules of arithmetic; pounds, shillings, and pence quite readily, and pretends to tinkle the harpsichord, but I think she has for that affair neither ear nor fingers. Susan's geographical and grammatical knowledge amazes even me, but she never will dance I think. When Sophy gets a good master[5] she will be eminent in that art. Hester is well—and beautiful, Susan is a pretty girl as need be, Cecilia is much liked, and Harriett quite a cherubim. Sophy is much the plainest as to countenance but her form is most complete and her temper enchanting. Hester and Susan are touchy, moody, and capricious.

Mr. Thrale is once more happy in his mind, and at leisure to be so in love with S.S.[6] that it is comical. She is a charming young creature; everybody must love her. We have her, and F. Browne and Murphy and Seward and the Davenants and Johnson here, besides Tom Cotton and occasional comers in.

I think I am again pregnant, I think I am; then let us conclude the old year with humble thanks to almighty God for all his mercies through Jesus Christ our Lord, and most of all for the health of my dear children, and for the boon I hope I have obtained by my prayers and tears—that I shall never follow any more of my offspring to the grave—Amen Lord Jesus!

Amen!

if so—I will not fret about this rival this S.S. no I won't.[7]

1766–1778   1976

---

1. Allow.
2. "My Master" is Henry Thrale, who often spent more capital than his brewery could afford, in an obsessive attempt to surpass his competitors.
3. Secured by law to be inherited by her husband and children. She is mistaken here, and later reclaimed the property for herself and her second husband.
4. The comedy *Le Bourgeois Gentilhomme* (1671) by the French playwright Molière.
5. Teacher.
6. Sophia Streatfield (1754–1835); noted for her beauty and for her accomplished Greek scholarship, she had become a family friend, a godparent to Henrietta, and an obsession of Henry Thrale's.
7. The Family Book ends here.

from **Thraliana**

[FIRST ENTRIES]

It is many years since Doctor Samuel Johnson advised me to get a little book, and write in it all the little anecdotes which might come to my knowledge, all the observations I might make or hear; all the verses never likely to be published, and in fine every thing which struck me at the time. Mr. Thrale has now treated me with a repository, and provided it with the pompous title of Thraliana.[1] I must endeavor to fill it with nonsense new and old. 15 September 1776.

Bob Lloyd[2] used to say that a parent or other person devoted to the care and instruction of youth, led the life of a finger post, still fixed to one disagreeable spot himself, while his whole business was only to direct others in the way.

An old man's child, says Johnson, leads much the same sort of life as a child's dog, teased like that with fondness through folly, and exhibited like that to every company, through idle and empty vanity.

I have heard Johnson observe that as education is often compared to agriculture, so it resembles it chiefly in this: that though no one can tell whether the crop may answer the culture,[3] yet if nothing be sowed, we all see that no crop can be obtained.

* * *

[Brighton, July–August 1780] I have picked up Piozzi[4] here, the great Italian singer; he shall teach Hester. She will have some powers in the musical way I believe. Her voice though not strong is sweet and flexible, her taste correct, and her expression pleasing. The other two girls leave me tomorrow; they will do very well; Susan is three parts a Beauty, and quite a Scholar for ten Years old. * * *

I dread the general election more than ever. Mr. Thrale is now well enough to canvass in person, and 'twill kill him.[5] Had it happened when he *could not absolutely* have stirred, we would have done it for him, but now! Well! One should not however anticipate misfortunes, they will come time enough.

* * *

[8 August 1780] Piozzi is become a prodigious favorite with me. He is so intelligent a creature, so discerning, one can't help wishing for his good opinion. His singing surpasses everybody's for taste, tenderness, and true elegance. His hand on the fortepiano too is so soft, so sweet, so delicate, every tone goes to one's heart I think, and fills the mind with emotions one would not be without, though inconvenient enough sometimes. I made him sing yesterday, and though he says his voice is gone, I cannot somehow or other get it out of my ears—odd enough!

These were the Verses he sung to me.

> Amor—non sò che sia,
>> Ma sò che è un traditor;
> Cosa è la gelosia?
>> Non l'hò provato ancor.
>
> La donna mi vien detto
>> Fà molto sospirar;

---

1. He had given his wife six leather-bound blank volumes, each displaying the "pompous title" on its cover, on a red label stamped with gold lettering.
2. A poet.
3. I.e., will prove worth the care expended on it.
4. "He is amazingly like my father" [Thrale's note]. Born near Venice, Gabriel Piozzi (1740–1809) had now lived in England for about four years, giving concerts and teaching voice.
5. Henry Thrale was running for Parliament; he ended up finishing third in a field of three.

>   Ed Io poveretto,
>   Men' voglio innamorar.

I instantly translated them for him, and made him sing them in English thus all'Improviso.

>   For Love—I can't abide it,
>   The treacherous rogue I know;
>   Distrust!—I never tried it
>   Whether t'would sting or no.
>
>   For Flavia many sighs are,
>   Sent up by sad despair.
>   And yet poor simple I Sir
>   Am hasting to the snare.

[October–November 1780] Here is Sophy Streatfield again, handsomer than ever, and flushed with new conquests: the Bishop of Chester feels her power I am sure. She showed me a letter from him that was as tender, and had all the *tokens* upon it as strong as ever I remember to have seen 'em. I repeated to her out of Pope's Homer. "Very well Sophy," says I,

>   "Range undisturbed among the hostile crew,
>   But touch not *Hinchliffe*, Hinchliffe is *my* due."[6]

"Miss Streatfield," says my Master, "could have quoted these lines *in the Greek*." His saying so piqued me; and piqued me because it was true. I wish I understood Greek! Mr. Thrale's preference of her to me never vexed me so much as my consciousness—or fear at least—that he had *reason* for his preference. She has ten times my beauty, and five times my scholarship. Wit and knowledge has she none.

How fond some people are of riding in a carriage! Those most I think who had from beginning least chance of keeping one. Johnson dotes on a coach; so do many people indeed. I never get into any vehicle, but for the sake of being conveyed to some place, or some person. The motion is unpleasing to me in itself, and the straitness[7] of the room makes it inconvenient. Conversation too is almost wholly precluded, the grinding of the wheels hinders one from hearing, and the necessity of raising one's voice makes it less comfortable to talk. A book is better than a friend in a carriage—and a carriage is the only place where it is so.

* * *

[10 December 1780] We have got a sort of literary curiosity amongst us; the foul copy of Pope's Homer,[8] with all his old intended verses, sketches, emendations etc. Strange that a man should keep such things! Stranger still that a woman should write such a book as this; put down every occurrence of her life, every emotion of her heart, and call it a *Thraliana* forsooth—but then I mean to destroy it.

All wood and wire behind the scenes[9] sure enough! One sees that Pope labored as hard—

---

6. "Rage uncontrolled through all the hostile crew / But touch not Hector; Hector is my due"; Achilles's instructions to Patroclus in Pope's translation of Homer's *Iliad* (16.113). John Hinchliffe was Bishop of Peterborough and a friend of the family.

7. Narrowness

8. The manuscript draft of Pope's translation of the *Iliad* (see page 2509). Johnson was consulting it for his biography of Pope (see page 2781).

9. I.e., backstage at a theater.

as if the Stagyrite o'erlooked each line[1]

indeed, and how very little effect those glorious verses at the end of the 8th book of the *Iliad* have upon one, when one sees 'em all in their cradles and clouts;[2] and "light" changed for "bright"—and then the whole altered again, and the line must end with "night"—and Oh Dear! thus—*torturing one poor word a thousand ways.*[3]

Johnson says 'tis pleasant to see the progress of such a mind. True; but 'tis a malicious pleasure, such as men feel when they watch a woman at her toilet[4] and

see by degrees a purer blush arise, *etc.*[5]

Wood and wire once more! Wood and wire!—

* * *

[January 1781] What an odd partiality I have for a rough character! and even for the hard parts of a soft one! Fanny Burney[6] has secured my heart. I now love her with a fond and firm affection, besides my esteem of her parts,[7] and my regard for her father. Her lofty spirit—dear Creature!—has quite subdued mine; and I adore her for the pride which once revolted me. There is no true affection, no friendship in the sneakers and fawners. 'Tis not for obsequious civility that I delight in Johnson or Hinchliffe, Sir Richard Jebb or Piozzi, who has as much spirit *in his way* as the best of them—great solidity of mind too I think, some sarcasm, and wonderful discernment in that rough Italian. I will do him all the service I can.

[10 January 1781] I will now write out the Characters of the people who are intended to have their portraits hung up in the Library here at Streatham.[8] * * *

My own and my eldest daughter's portraits in one picture come next, and are to be placed over the chimney.[9]

> In features so placid, so smooth, so serene,
> What trace of the wit or the Welsh-woman's seen?
> Of the temper sarcastic, the flattering tongue,
> The sentiment right—with th' occasion still wrong.
> What trace of the tender, the rough, the refined,
> The soul in which all contrarieties joined?
> Where though merriment loves over method to rule,
> Religion resides, and the virtues keep school;
> Till when tired we condemn her dogmatical air,
> Like a rocket she rises, and leaves us to stare.
> To such contradictions d'ye wish for a clue?
> Keep vanity still—that vile passion—in view.
> For 'tis thus the slow miner his fortune to make,
> Of arsenic thin scattered pursues the pale track;
> Secure where that poison pollutes the rich ground,
> That it points to the soil where some silver is found.

1. Pope's *Essay on Criticism* (line 138). The "Stagyrite" is Aristotle, the Greek philosopher Pope here invokes as the ultimate arbiter of literary judgment.
2. Diapers.
3. Dryden, *Mac Flecknoe* (line 208).
4. Dressing table.
5. From Pope's description of Belinda in *The Rape of the Lock* (1.143).
6. Daughter of the musicologist Charles Burney, and author of the novel *Evelina, or a Young Lady's Entrance*

into the World (1778), which brought her to the attention and admiration of the Streatham circle.
7. Intellect.
8. The 13 paintings, by Sir Joshua Reynolds, had been commissioned by Henry Thrale. They depicted his wife, daughter, and distinguished friends, including Johnson, Burke, Baretti, and Reynolds himself. A "character" is a word portrait; Hester Thrale wrote one in verse for each person Reynolds depicted.
9. Her verse self-portrait follows.

The portrait of my eldest daughter deserves better lines than these which follow. She is a valuable girl.

> Of a virgin so tender the face or the fame,
> Alike would be injured by praise or by blame.
> To the world's fiery trial too early consigned,
> She soon shall experience it, cruel or kind.
>
> His concern thus the anxious enameller hides,
> And his well finished work to the furnace confides;
> But jocund resumes it secure from decay,
> If the colors stand firm on the dangerous day.

* * *

One Page more I see ends the 3d Volume of Thraliana! strange farrago as it is of sense, nonsense, public, private follies—but chiefly my own—and *I* the little Hero etc. Well! but who should be the Hero of an *Ana?* Let me vindicate my own vanity if it be with my last pen. This volume will be finished at Streatham and be left there—where I may never more return to dwell!

Mr. Thrale *may* die,[1] and not leave me sufficient to keep Streatham open as it has been kept, and I shall hate to live in it with more thought about expenses than I have done. I *may* indeed be left sole mistress of the brewhouse to manage for my girls, but that I hardly think will be the case; and if not so, why Farewell pretty Streatham, where I have spent many a merry hour, and many a sad one.

My poor little old Aunt at Bath is dying too, and I am dolt enough to be sincerely sorry, the more as her past kindnesses claim that personal attendance from me, which Mr. Thrale will not permit me to pay her—poor, little, old, insipid, useless creature! May God Almighty in his mercy, pity, receive and bless her, as a most inoffensive atom of humanity—for whom his only Son consented to be crucified, and among whose flock she has most innocently fed for sixty or seventy years.—

Here closes the third volume

Streatham
Monday 29 January 1781.

[THE DEATH OF HENRY THRALE; MARRIAGE TO GABRIEL PIOZZI]

[Sunday 18 March 1781] Well! Now I have experienced the delights of a London winter spent in the bosom of flattery, gaiety, and Grosvenor Square. 'Tis a poor thing however, and leaves a void in the mind; but I have had my compting-house[2] duties to attend, my sick Master to watch, my little children to look after—and how much good have I done in any way? Not a scrap as I can see. The pecuniary affairs have gone on perversely: how should they choose when the sole proprietor is incapable of giving orders, yet not so far incapable as to be set aside! Distress, fraud, folly meet me at every turn, and I am not able to fight against them all, though endued with an iron constitution which shakes not by sleepless nights, or days severely fretted. Mr. Thrale talks now of going to Spa and Italy again. How shall we drag him thither? A man who cannot keep awake four hours at a stroke, who can scarce retain the Feces etc. Well! This will indeed be a trial of one's patience; and who must go with us on this

---

1. He had suffered a series of strokes.
2. Bookkeeping. During her husband's final illness,

Thrale was helping to manage the brewery.

expedition? Mr. Johnson! He will indeed be the only happy person of the party. He values nothing under heaven but his own mind, which is a spark *from* Heaven; and *that* will be invigorated by the addition of new ideas. If Mr. Thrale dies on the road, Johnson will console himself by learning *how it is* to travel with a corpse—and after all, such reasoning is the true philosophy—one's heart is a mere encumbrance. Would I could leave mine behind. The children shall go to their sisters at Kensington. Mrs. Cumyns[3] may take care of 'em all. God grant us a happy Meeting! Some *where* and some *time!*

Baretti should attend I think. There is no man who has so much of *every* language, and can manage so well with Johnson, and is so tidy on the road, so active too to obtain good accommodations. He is the man in the world I think whom I most abhor, and who hates, and professes to hate me the most. But what does that signify? He will be careful of Mr. Thrale and Hester whom he *does* love—and he won't strangle me I suppose. It will be very convenient to have him. Somebody we must have. Croza would court our Daughter, and Piozzi could not talk to Johnson, nor I suppose do one any good, but sing to one—and how should we sing *songs in a strange land?* Baretti must be the man, and I will beg it of him as a favor. Oh the triumph he will have! and the lies that he will tell!

If I die abroad I shall leave all my papers in charge with Fanny Burney. I have at length conquered all her scruples, and won her confidence and her heart. 'Tis the most valuable conquest I ever *did* make, and dearly, very dearly, do I love my little *Tayo,* so the people at Otaheite[4] call a *bosom friend.* She is now satisfied of my affection, and has no reserves, no ill opinion, no further notion I shall insult her sweetness. I now respect her caution, and esteem her above all living women. Mrs. Byron will half break her heart at my going. Mrs. Lambart is going herself.[5]

No danger of all these distresses it seems. Mr. Thrale died on the 4th of April 1781.[6]

* * *

[20 September 1782] Now! That little dear discerning creature Fanny Burney says I'm in love with Piozzi—very likely! He is so amiable, so honorable, so much above his situation by his abilities, that if

> Fate hadn't fast bound her
> With Styx nine times round her
> Sure Music and Love were victorious.[7]

But if he is ever so worthy, ever so lovely, he is *below me* forsooth. In what is he below me? In virtue—I would I were above him. In understanding—I would mine were from this instant under the guardianship of his. In birth—to be sure, he is below me in birth, and so is almost every man I know, or have a chance to know. But he is below me in fortune—is mine sufficient for us both? More than amply so. Does he deserve it by his conduct in which he has always united warm notions of honor with cool attention to economy, the spirit of a gentleman with the talents of a professor? How shall any man deserve fortune if he does not? But I am the guardian of five

---

3. A childhood friend, who now ran a school which Sophia and Susan Thrale attended.
4. Tahiti, where Burney's brother James had traveled on one of Captain James Cook's expeditions.
5. Sophia Byron and Elizabeth Lambart were Thrale's close friends and frequent correspondents.

6. Thrale set down these two sentences at the center of a blank page.
7. Pope, *Ode for Music, on St. Cecelia's Day* (lines 90–92). The passage describes Eurydice, momentarily freed from her imprisonment in the underworld by the enchanting music of her lover Orpheus.

daughters by Mr. Thrale, and must not disgrace their name and family. Was then the man my mother chose for me of higher extraction than him I have chosen for myself? No. But his fortune was higher. I wanted fortune then perhaps, do I want it now? Not at all. But I am not to think about myself. I married the first time to please my mother, I must marry the second time to please my daughter.[8] I have always sacrificed my own choice to that of others, so I must sacrifice it again. But why? Oh because I am a woman of superior understanding, and must not for the world degrade myself from my situation in life. But if I have superior understanding, let me at least make use of it for once, and rise to the rank of a human being conscious of its own power to discern good from ill. The person who has uniformly acted by the will of others, has hardly that dignity to boast. * * *

[4 November 1782] Sir Richard Musgrave[9] has sent me proposals of marriage from Ireland. His wife is dying at least if not dead, and he is in haste for a better. He will get *me* to be sure!! a likely matter! when my head is full of nothing but my children—my heart of my beloved Piozzi! * * *

[Brighthelmstone, Saturday, 16 November 1782] For him I have been contented to reverse the laws of Nature, and request of my child that concurrence which at my age (and a widow) I am not required either by divine or human institutions to ask even of a parent. The life I gave her she may now more than repay, only by agreeing to what she will with difficulty prevent, and which if she does prevent, will give her lasting remorse—for those who stab *me* shall hear me groan—whereas if she will—but how can she?—gracefully, or even compassionately consent, if she will go abroad with me upon the chance of his death or mine preventing our union, and live with me till she is of age—perhaps there is no heart so callous by avarice, no soul so poisoned by prejudice, no head so feathered by foppery, that will forbear to excuse her when she returns to the rich and the gay, for having saved the life of a mother through compliance extorted by anguish, contrary to the received opinions of the world.

[Brighthelmstone, 19 November 1782] What is above written, though intended only to unload my heart by writing it, I showed in a transport of passion to Queeney and to Burney. Sweet Fanny Burney cried herself half blind over it, said there was no resisting such pathetic eloquence, and that if she was the daughter instead of the friend, she should be even tempted to attend me to the altar. But that while she possessed her reason, nothing should seduce her to approve what reason itself would condemn: that children, religion, situation, country and character—besides the diminution of fortune by the certain loss of £800 a year were too much to sacrifice to any *one* man. If however I were resolved to make the sacrifice, *à la bonne heure!*[1] It was an astonishing proof of an attachment, very difficult for mortal man to repay.

I will talk no more of it.

* * *

[29 January 1783] Adieu to all that's dear, to all that's lovely. I am parted from my Life, my Soul! my Piozzi: *Sposo promesso! Amante adorato! Amico senza equale.*[2] If I can get health and strength to write my story here, 'tis all I wish for now! Oh Misery!

The cold dislike of my eldest daughter I thought might wear away by familiarity with his merit, and that we might live tolerably together or at least part friends, but no. Her aversion increased daily, and she communicated it to the others. They treat-

---

8. Queeney, who objected vehemently to the prospect of her mother's marriage to Piozzi.
9. Irish baronet and member of Parliament, whom Thrale

had met at Bath in 1776.
1. Fine! Good for you! (French.)
2. Promised husband, adored lover, friend without equal.

ed *me* insolently, and *him* very strangely—running away whenever he came as if they saw a serpent, and plotting with their governess, a cunning Italian, how to invent lies to make me hate him, and twenty such narrow tricks. By these means the notion of my partiality took air—and whether Miss Thrale sent him word slyly, or not I cannot tell; but on the 25 January 1783 Mr. Crutchley[3] came hither to *conjure* me not to go to Italy: he had heard *such* things he said, and by *means* next to *miraculous*. The next day, Sunday 26, Fanny Burney came, said I must marry him instantly, or give him up; that my reputation would be lost else. I actually groaned with anguish, threw myself on the bed in an agony which my fair daughter beheld with frigid indifference. She had indeed never by one tender word endeavored to dissuade me from the match, but said coldly that if I *would* abandon my children, I *must*; that their father had not deserved such treatment from me; that I should be punished by Piozzi's neglect, for that she knew he hated me, and that I turned out my offspring to chance for his sake like puppies in a pond to swim or drown according as Providence pleased; that for her part she must look herself out a place like the other servants, for my face would she never see more. "Nor write to me?" said I. "I shall not Madam," replied she with a cold sneer, "easily find *out your address*, for you are going you know not whither I believe." Susan and Sophy said nothing at all, but they taught the two little ones to cry, "Where are you going Mama? Will you leave us, and die as our poor papa did?" There was no standing *that*, so I wrote my lover word that my mind was all distraction, and bid him come to me the next morning my birthday, 27 January. Mean time I took a vomit, and spent the Sunday night in torture not to be described. My falsehood to my Piozzi, my strong affection for him, the incapacity I felt in myself to resign the man I so adored, the hopes I had so cherished, inclined me strongly to set them all at defiance, and go with him to Church to sanctify the promises I had so often made him, while the idea of abandoning the children of my first husband, who left me so nobly provided for, and who depended on my attachment to his offspring, awakened the voice of conscience, and threw me on my knees to pray for *his* direction who was hereafter to judge my conduct.

His grace illuminated me, his power strengthened me; and I flew to my daughter's bed in the morning and told, told her my resolution to resign my own, my dear, my favorite purposes; and to prefer my children's interest to my love. She questioned my ability to make the sacrifice; said one word from him would undo all my[4] * * *

[27 June 1784] My daughters parted with me at last prettily enough *considering* (as the phrase is). We shall perhaps be still better friends apart than together. Promises of correspondence and kindness were very sweetly reciprocated, and the eldest wished for Piozzi's safe return obligingly.[5]

I fancy two days more will absolutely bring him to Bath—The present moments are critical and dreadful, and would shake stronger nerves than mine. Oh Lord strengthen me to do thy will I pray.

[28 June] I am not *yet* sure of seeing him again—not *sure* he lives, not *sure* he loves me, *yet*. Should any thing happen *now*!! Oh I will not trust myself with such a fancy—it will either kill me, or drive me distracted.

3. Jeremiah Crutchley, one of the executors of Henry Thrale's will.
4. The remainder of the entry is lost, because the next page is missing. Informed of Thrale's decision, Piozzi left for Italy. Negotiations between mother and daughter continued for another year, until Queeney finally capitu-

lated on the grounds that Thrale's agitation was endangering her health. The daughters were to remain in England, looked after by the trustees of their father's estate; the mother would reside with her new husband in Italy.
5. He was now returning from Italy to England.

[2 July] The happiest day of my whole life I think. Yes, *quite* the happiest.[6] My Piozzi came home yesterday and dined with me. But my spirits were too much agitated, my heart too much dilated, I was too painfully happy *then*. My sensations are more quiet today, and my felicity less tumultuous. I have spent the night as I ought in prayer and Thanksgiving. Could I have slept, I had not deserved such blessings. May the Almighty but preserve them to me! He lodges at our old house on the South Parade. His companion Mecci[7] is a faithless treacherous fellow—but no matter! 'Tis all over now.

[Bath, 25 July] I am returned from church the happy wife of my lovely, my faithful Piozzi, subject of my prayers, object of my wishes, my sighs, my reverence, my esteem.

His nerves have been horribly shaken, but he lives, he loves me, and will be mine *for ever*. He has sworn it in the face of God and the whole Christian Church: Catholics, Protestants, all are witnesses. May he who has preserved us thus long for each other give us a long life together—and so I hope and trust he will through the merits of Jesus Christ. Amen.

[3 September] Wellbeck Street, Cavendish Square, London] I have now been six weeks married, and enjoyed greater and longer felicity than I ever yet experienced. To crown all, my dear daughters Susanna and Sophia have spent the day with myself and my amiable husband. We part in peace, and love, and harmony, and tomorrow I set off for the finest country in the world, in company with the most excellent man in it.

Some natural tears they dropped, but wiped 'em soon.   Milton.[8]

* * *

[THE DEATH OF JOHNSON]

[Milan, January 1785] The new year is begun. May God prosper it to my husband, my children, and myself. I went to church and prayed most fervently for their happiness.

My Piozzi is not well. He has no disorder though that shortens life, notwithstanding the uneasiness it occasions him. Strong fibers with weak nerves produce all his sufferings, and add to his natural irritability. The constant complaints too which he makes of his health take off from the envy his situation would otherwise provoke, but he is best on a journey. I shall like to go to Venice in the spring—if nothing prevents me, *which I should like still better*. Praying for children is wrong however, and I will do it no more. I used to weary Heaven with requests for pregnancy, and now!! all I begged for are in the grave almost, and those that are left, love not *me*.

I had letters the other day indeed of which I ought not to complain. Susan and Sophy's kindness *should* compensate for the frigidity of their elder sister, and Mr. Cator says all of them are well.

Oh poor Dr. Johnson!!![9]

[25 January 1785] I have recovered myself sufficiently to think what will be the consequence to me of Johnson's death, but must wait the event as all thoughts on the future in this world are vain.

---

6. For Johnson's admonitory letter on this same date, see page 2795.
7. Francesco Mecci, a teacher of Italian, whom Thrale apparently suspected of trying to prevent the marriage.

8. From the description of Adam and Eve as they prepare to depart from paradise (*Paradise Lost* 12.645).
9. He had died 13 December 1785.

Six people have already undertaken to write his life I hear, of which Sir John Hawkins, Mr. Boswell, Tom Davies, and Dr. Kippis are four. Piozzi says he would have me add to the number, and so I would; but that I think my anecdotes too few, and am afraid of saucy answers if I send to England for others. The saucy answers I should disregard, but my heart is made vulnerable by my late marriage, and I am certain that to spite me, they would insult my husband. Poor Johnson! I see they will leave *nothing untold* that I labored so long to keep secret; and I was so very delicate in trying to conceal his fancied insanity,[1] that I retained no proofs of it—or hardly any—nor ever mentioned it in these books, lest by dying first *they* might be printed and the secret (for such I thought it) discovered.

I used to tell him in jest that his biographers would be at a loss concerning some orange peel he used to keep in his pocket,[2] and many a joke we had about the Lives that would be published. "Rescue me out of all their hands, my dear, and do it *yourself*," said he. "Taylor, Adams, and Hector[3] will furnish you with juvenile anecdotes, and Baretti will give you all the rest that you have not already—for I think Baretti is a liar only when he speaks of himself." "Oh!" said I, "Baretti told me yesterday that you got by heart six pages of Machiavel's *History*[4] once, and repeated 'em thirty years afterwards word for word." "O why this indeed is a *gross* lie," says Johnson. "I never read the book at all." "Baretti too told me of *you*" (said I) "that you once kept sixteen cats in your chamber, and yet they scratched your legs to such a degree, you were forced to use mercurial plasters[5] for some time after." "Why this" (replied Johnson) "is an unprovoked lie indeed. I thought the fellow would not have broken through divine and human laws thus, to make Puss his heroine. But I see I was mistaken."
1776–1808   1951

⭑ ⬦ ⭑

Oliver Goldsmith
1730–1774

Goldsmith's cluster of famous friends never tired of describing and diagnosing what they saw as the baffling discrepancy between his success in writing and his oddity in conversation. Samuel Johnson put the problem succinctly: "No man was more foolish when he had not a pen in his hand, or more wise when he had." The actor David Garrick compacted the same paradox into the second line of an imaginary epitaph, composed while its outraged subject was present in the room: "Here lies Nolly Goldsmith, for shortness called Noll, / Who wrote like an angel, and talked like poor Poll"—that is, like a parrot, noisily spouting verbiage mimicked from minds better furnished than his own. Always quick to take offense, Goldsmith took so much at this that he devoted the remaining months of his short life to a *Retaliation* in which he took vengeance, in the form of caustic verse epitaphs, on the many people from whom he thought he had suffered slights.

Goldsmith's awkwardness, competitiveness, and defensiveness arose partly from discomfort as to humble origins and scattershot education. Born in Ireland to an eccentric curate, he had come to London in 1756 after a checkered academic career spent in Dublin, Edinburgh,

---

1. Johnson had confided to her more than to others how deeply and how often he feared the loss of his faculties.
2. He used it as a laxative.
3. Johnson's childhood friends.

4. Niccolò Machiavelli's history of Florence, *Storie Fiorentine* (1520–1525).
5. Bandages soaked in mercury.

and on the Continent, half-heartedly pursuing degrees (never obtained) in divinity and medicine. Upon arriving in London, Goldsmith took a series of odd jobs (druggist, physician, school custodian) before establishing himself as a reviewer, translator, essayist, and editor. His work brought him to the attention of the eminent, in whose company he launched that precarious social strategy which his closest friend, the painter Joshua Reynolds, later analyzed: "He had a very strong desire, which I believe nobody will think very peculiar, to be liked, to have his company sought after by his friends. To this end, for it was a system, he abandoned his respectable character as a writer or a man of observation to that of a character [in whose presence] nobody was afraid of being humiliated." As Reynolds acknowledges, the "system" often backfired, because Goldsmith wanted desperately to be impressive as well as "liked." Friends found his mystery worth probing because of the almost palpable preponderance of his merits: alongside irascibility, Goldsmith possessed a compelling charm and generosity; and an amazing *feeling* (Reynolds's emphatic term) for what made writing work.

To support spendthrift habits and a love of gambling, Goldsmith undertook much compendious hackwork—*A History of England* (1764); *Roman History* (1769); *Grecian History* (1774); and a *History of the Earth, and Animated Nature* (1774). At the same time, he managed to score more successes in more genres than almost any of his contemporaries save Johnson: periodical essay (*The Citizen of the World*, 1760–1761); biography (*The Life of Richard Nash*, 1762); novel (*The Vicar of Wakefield*, 1766); stage comedy (*The Good Natured Man*, 1768; *She Stoops to Conquer*, 1773); and poetry (*The Traveller*, 1764; and *The Deserted Village*, 1770). *The Deserted Village* was the work most celebrated in his own lifetime. Two years in the making, the poem recasts an argument Goldsmith had voiced earlier in an essay against the acquisition of rural acreage by merchants who, having acquired their wealth by the commerce of empire and the trade in luxuries, were now bent on converting their new-bought lands from productive communal pasture into pretty pleasure grounds: "In almost every part of the kingdom the laborious husbandman [farmer] has been reduced, and the lands are now either occupied by some general undertaker, or turned into enclosures destined for the purposes of amusement or luxury." Such encroachment, Goldsmith contended, was driving farm families from their villages and annihilating centuries of graceful country tradition. In his poem, Goldsmith mingled nostalgia for a rural past with dread of a commercial future. Contemporary critics promptly ushered *The Deserted Village* into the poetic canon by sundering those elements Goldsmith had worked hard to fuse: they dismissed the poem's economic doctrine and praised its imaginative power. Like the poet's friends, the poem's readers are left to sort out and savor Goldsmith's characteristic complexity: a "sentimental radicalism" (the phrase is John Barrell's) whereby the conservative defense of old values produces a new and volatile empathy with the plight of the poor.

The Deserted Village

To Sir Joshua Reynolds[1]

Dear Sir,

I can have no expectations in an address of this kind, either to add to your reputation, or to establish my own. You can gain nothing from my admiration, as I am ignorant of that art in which you are said to excel; and I may lose much by the severity of your judgment, as few have a juster taste in poetry than you. Setting interest therefore aside, to which I never paid much attention, I must be indulged at present in following my affections. The only dedication I ever made was to my brother,[2] because I loved him better than most other men. He is since dead. Permit me to inscribe this poem to you.

---

1. Reynolds (1723–1792) was one of England's leading portrait painters and first president of the Royal Academy; his close friendship with Goldsmith had begun in the mid-1760s.

2. Goldsmith had dedicated his previous long poem, *The Traveller* (1764), to his brother Henry, who died in 1768.

How far you may be pleased with the versification and mere mechanical parts of this attempt, I don't pretend to inquire; but I know you will object (and indeed several of our best and wisest friends concur in the opinion) that the depopulation it deplores is nowhere to be seen, and the disorders it laments are only to be found in the poet's own imagination. To this I can scarce make any other answer than that I sincerely believe what I have written; that I have taken all possible pains, in my country excursions, for these four or five years past, to be certain of what I allege; and that all my views and inquiries have led me to believe those miseries real, which I here attempt to display. But this is not the place to enter into an inquiry, whether the country be depopulating, or not; the discussion would take up much room, and I should prove myself, at best, an indifferent politician, to tire the reader with a long preface, when I want his unfatigued attention to a long poem.

In regretting the depopulation of the country, I inveigh against the increase of our luxuries; and here also I expect the shout of modern politicians against me. For twenty or thirty years past, it has been the fashion to consider luxury as one of the greatest national advantages; and all the wisdom of antiquity in that particular, as erroneous.[3] Still however, I must remain a professed ancient on that head, and continue to think those luxuries prejudicial to states, by which so many vices are introduced, and so many kingdoms have been undone. Indeed so much has been poured out of late on the other side of the question, that, merely for the sake of novelty and variety, one would sometimes wish to be in the right.

> I am,
> Dear Sir,
> Your sincere friend,
> and ardent admirer,
> OLIVER GOLDSMITH.

Sweet Auburn, loveliest village of the plain,[4]
Where health and plenty cheered the laboring swain,
Where smiling spring its earliest visit paid,
And parting summer's lingering blooms delayed:
5   Dear lovely bowers of innocence and ease,
Seats of my youth, when every sport could please,
How often have I loitered o'er thy green,
Where humble happiness endeared each scene;
How often have I paused on every charm,
10 The sheltered cot,° the cultivated farm,   cottage
The never-failing brook, the busy mill,
The decent church that topped the neighboring hill,
The hawthorn bush, with seats beneath the shade,
For talking age and whispering lovers made.
15 How often have I blessed the coming day,
When toil remitting lent its turn to play,
And all the village train, from labor free,
Led up their sports beneath the spreading tree,
While many a pastime circled in the shade,
20 The young contending as the old surveyed;

3. A long line of ancient authors—Horace, Seneca, and Pliny among them—had warned that the traffic in luxuries was sapping Rome's health, and had urged moderation.

4. "Auburn" is fictitious; it may be based in part on the Irish village of Lissoy, Goldsmith's childhood home.

And many a gambol frolicked o'er the ground,
And sleights of art and feats of strength went round.
And still as each repeated pleasure tired,
Succeeding sports the mirthful band inspired;
25   The dancing pair that simply sought renown
By holding out to tire each other down;
The swain mistrustless of his smutted face,
While secret laughter tittered round the place;
The bashful virgin's sidelong looks of love,
30   The matron's glance that would those looks reprove.
These were thy charms, sweet village; sports like these,
With sweet succession, taught even toil to please;
These round thy bowers their cheerful influence shed,
These were thy charms—But all these charms are fled.

35   Sweet smiling village, loveliest of the lawn,
Thy sports are fled, and all thy charms withdrawn;
Amidst thy bowers the tyrant's hand is seen,
And desolation saddens all thy green:
One only master grasps the whole domain,
40   And half a tillage⁵ stints° thy smiling plain;   *sets limits to*
No more thy glassy brook reflects the day,
But choked with sedges, works its weedy way.
Along thy glades, a solitary guest,
The hollow sounding bittern guards its nest;
45   Amidst thy desert walks the lapwing flies,
And tires their echoes with unvaried cries.
Sunk are thy bowers, in shapeless ruin all,
And the long grass o'ertops the mouldering wall,
And trembling, shrinking from the spoiler's hand,
50   Far, far away thy children leave the land.

        Ill fares the land, to hastening ills a prey,
Where wealth accumulates and men decay:
Princes and lords may flourish or may fade;
A breath can make them, as a breath has made;
55   But a bold peasantry, their country's pride,
When once destroyed, can never be supplied.

        A time there was, ere England's griefs began,
When every rood° of ground maintained its man;   *quarter acre*
For him light labor spread her wholesome store,
60   Just gave what life required, but gave no more:
His best companions, innocence and health;
And his best riches, ignorance of wealth.

        But times are altered; trade's unfeeling train
Usurp the land and dispossess the swain;
65   Along the lawn,° where scattered hamlets rose,   *open countryside*
Unwieldy wealth and cumbrous pomp repose;
And every want to opulence allied,

5. Piece of tilled land.

And every pang that folly pays to pride.
These gentle hours that plenty bade to bloom,
70   Those calm desires that asked but little room,
Those healthful sports that graced the peaceful scene,
Lived in each look, and brightened all the green;
These far departing seek a kinder shore,
And rural mirth and manners are no more.

75   Sweet Auburn! parent of the blissful hour,
Thy glades forlorn confess the tyrant's power.
Here as I take my solitary rounds,
Amidst thy tangling walks, and ruined grounds,
And, many a year elapsed, return to view
80   Where once the cottage stood, the hawthorn grew,
Remembrance wakes with all her busy train,
Swells at my breast, and turns the past to pain.

In all my wanderings round this world of care,
In all my griefs—and God has given my share—
85   I still had hopes my latest hours to crown,
Amidst these humble bowers to lay me down;
To husband out life's taper[6] at the close,
And keep the flame from wasting by repose.
I still had hopes, for pride attends us still,
90   Amidst the swains to show my book-learned skill,
Around my fire an evening group to draw,
And tell of all I felt, and all I saw;
And, as an hare whom hounds and horns pursue,
Pants to the place from whence at first she flew,
95   I still had hopes, my long vexations past,
Here to return—and die at home at last.

O blest retirement, friend to life's decline,
Retreats from care that never must be mine,
How happy he who crowns in shades like these
100   A youth of labor with an age of ease;
Who quits a world where strong temptations try,
And, since 'tis hard to combat, learns to fly.
For him no wretches, born to work and weep,
Explore the mine, or tempt the dangerous deep;
105   No surly porter stands in guilty state
To spurn imploring famine from the gate,
But on he moves to meet his latter end,
Angels around befriending virtue's friend;
Bends to the grave with unperceived decay,
110   While resignation gently slopes the way;
And, all his prospects brightening to the last,
His Heaven commences ere the world be past!

Sweet was the sound when oft at evening's close
Up yonder hill the village murmur rose;

---

6. Candle. "To husband out" means to maintain something thriftily, so that it lasts long.

115   There as I passed with careless steps and slow,
The mingling notes came softened from below;
The swain responsive as the milkmaid sung,
The sober herd that lowed to meet their young,
The noisy geese that gabbled o'er the pool,
120   The playful children just let loose from school,
The watchdog's voice that bayed the whispering wind,
And the loud laugh that spoke the vacant° mind,   *carefree*
These all in sweet confusion sought the shade,
And filled each pause the nightingale had made.
125   But now the sounds of population fail,
No cheerful murmurs fluctuate in the gale,
No busy steps the grass-grown footway tread,
For all the bloomy flush of life is fled.
All but yon widowed, solitary thing
130   That feebly bends beside the plashy[7] spring;
She, wretched matron, forced, in age, for bread,
To strip the brook with mantling° cresses[8] spread,   *growing*
To pick her wintry faggot° from the thorn,   *firewood*
To seek her nightly shed, and weep till morn;
135   She only left of all the harmless train,
The sad historian of the pensive plain.

    Near yonder copse, where once the garden smiled,
And still where many a garden flower grows wild;
There, where a few torn shrubs the place disclose,
140   The village preacher's modest mansion rose.
A man he was, to all the country dear,
And passing rich with forty pounds a year;
Remote from towns he ran his godly race,
Nor e'er had changed, nor wished to change his place;
145   Unpracticed he to fawn, or seek for power,
By doctrines fashioned to the varying hour;
Far other aims his heart had learned to prize,
More skilled to raise the wretched than to rise.
His house was known to all the vagrant train,
150   He chid their wanderings, but relieved their pain;
The long remembered beggar was his guest,
Whose beard descending swept his aged breast;
The ruined spendthrift, now no longer proud,
Claimed kindred there, and had his claims allowed;
155   The broken soldier, kindly bade to stay,
Sat by his fire, and talked the night away;
Wept o'er his wounds, or tales of sorrow done,
Shouldered his crutch, and showed how fields were won.
Pleased with his guests, the good man learned to glow,
160   And quite forgot their vices in their woe;
Careless their merits or their faults to scan,
His pity gave ere charity began.

---

7. Abounding in pools.   8. Leafy, edible plants.

Thus to relieve the wretched was his pride,
And even his failings leaned to virtue's side;
165   But in his duty prompt at every call,
He watched and wept, he prayed and felt, for all.
And, as a bird each fond endearment tries,
To tempt its new fledged offspring to the skies,
He tried each art, reproved each dull delay,
170   Allured to brighter worlds, and led the way.

Beside the bed where parting life was laid,
And sorrow, guilt, and pain by turns dismayed,
The reverend champion stood. At his control,
Despair and anguish fled the struggling soul;
175   Comfort came down the trembling wretch to raise,
And his last faltering accents whispered praise.

At church, with meek and unaffected grace,
His looks adorned the venerable place;
Truth from his lips prevailed with double sway,
180   And fools, who came to scoff, remained to pray.
The service past, around the pious man,
With steady zeal each honest rustic ran;
Even children followed with endearing wile,
And plucked his gown, to share the good man's smile.
185   His ready smile a parent's warmth expressed,
Their welfare pleased him, and their cares distressed;
To them his heart, his love, his griefs were given,
But all his serious thoughts had rest in Heaven.
As some tall cliff that lifts its awful form,
190   Swells from the vale, and midway leaves the storm,
Though round its breast the rolling clouds are spread,
Eternal sunshine settles on its head.

Beside yon straggling fence that skirts the way,
With blossomed furze° unprofitably gay,   *thorny bushes*
195   There, in his noisy mansion, skilled to rule,
The village master taught his little school;
A man severe he was, and stern to view,
I knew him well, and every truant knew;
Well had the boding tremblers learned to trace
200   The day's disasters in his morning face;
Full well they laughed with counterfeited glee,
At all his jokes, for many a joke had he;
Full well the busy whisper circling round,
Conveyed the dismal tidings when he frowned;
205   Yet he was kind, or if severe in aught,
The love he bore to learning was in fault;
The village all declared how much he knew;
'Twas certain he could write, and cipher too;
Lands he could measure, terms and tides presage,[9]

---

9. "Terms" were the days when payments of rents and wages were due; "tides" were holidays like Easter that shifted date from year to year; information on both was readily available in the annual almanacs.

210 And even the story ran that he could gauge.[1]
    In arguing too, the parson owned° his skill,   *acknowledged*
    For even though vanquished, he could argue still;
    While words of learned length, and thundering sound,
    Amazed the gazing rustics ranged around;
215 And still they gazed, and still the wonder grew,
    That one small head could carry all he knew.

        But past is all his fame. The very spot,
    Where many a time he triumphed, is forgot.
    Near yonder thorn, that lifts its head on high,
220 Where once the signpost caught the passing eye,
    Low lies that house where nut-brown draughts° inspired,   *drinks*
    Where gray-beard mirth and smiling toil retired,
    Where village statesmen talked with looks profound,
    And news much older than their ale went round.
225 Imagination fondly stoops to trace
    The parlor splendors of that festive place;
    The whitewashed wall, the nicely sanded floor,
    The varnished clock that clicked behind the door;
    The chest contrived a double debt to pay,
230 A bed by night, a chest of drawers by day;
    The pictures placed for ornament and use,
    The twelve good rules,[2] the royal game of goose;[3]
    The hearth, except when winter chilled the day,
    With aspen boughs, and flowers, and fennel gay,
235 While broken teacups, wisely kept for show,
    Ranged o'er the chimney, glistened in a row.

        Vain transitory splendors! Could not all
    Reprieve the tottering mansion from its fall!
    Obscure it sinks, nor shall it more impart
240 An hour's importance to the poor man's heart;
    Thither no more the peasant shall repair
    To sweet oblivion of his daily care;
    No more the farmer's news, the barber's tale,
    No more the woodman's ballad shall prevail;
245 No more the smith his dusky brow shall clear,
    Relax his ponderous strength, and lean to hear;
    The host himself no longer shall be found
    Careful to see the mantling° bliss go round;   *foaming*
    Nor the coy maid, half willing to be pressed,
250 Shall kiss the cup to pass it to the rest.

        Yes! let the rich deride, the proud disdain,
    These simple blessings of the lowly train;
    To me more dear, congenial to my heart,
    One native charm, than all the gloss of art;

---

1. Calculate the capacity of barrels and other containers.
2. This list of simple life lessons ("Keep no bad company"; "Encourage no vice"), supposedly compiled by Charles I, was displayed, beneath a picture of his execution, in many country inns and houses.
3. A game in which dice determine the movement of the pieces across the board.

255 Spontaneous joys, where nature has its play,
 The soul adopts, and owns their first born sway;
 Lightly they frolic o'er the vacant mind,
 Unenvied, unmolested, unconfined.
 But the long pomp, the midnight masquerade,
260 With all the freaks of wanton wealth arrayed,
 In these, ere triflers half their wish obtain,
 The toiling pleasure sickens into pain;
 And, even while fashion's brightest arts decoy,
 The heart distrusting asks, if this be joy.

265 Ye friends to truth, ye statesmen, who survey
 The rich man's joys increase, the poor's decay,
 'Tis yours to judge, how wide the limits stand
 Between a splendid and an happy land.
 Proud swells the tide with loads of freighted ore,
270 And shouting Folly hails them from her shore;
 Hoards, even beyond the miser's wish abound,
 And rich men flock from all the world around.
 Yet count our gains. This wealth is but a name
 That leaves our useful products still the same.
275 Not so the loss. The man of wealth and pride
 Takes up a space that many poor supplied;
 Space for his lake, his park's extended bounds,
 Space for his horses, equipage, and hounds;
 The robe that wraps his limbs in silken sloth
280 Has robbed the neighboring fields of half their growth;
 His seat, where solitary sports are seen,
 Indignant spurns the cottage from the green;
 Around the world each needful product flies,
 For all the luxuries the world supplies.
285 While thus the land adorned for pleasure all
 In barren splendor feebly waits the fall.

  As some fair female unadorned and plain,
 Secure to please while youth confirms her reign,
 Slights every borrowed charm that dress supplies,
290 Nor shares with art the triumph of her eyes;
 But when those charms are past, for charms are frail,
 When time advances, and when lovers fail,
 She then shines forth, solicitous to bless,
 In all the glaring impotence of dress.
295 Thus fares the land, by luxury betrayed;
 In nature's simplest charms at first arrayed;
 But verging to decline, its splendors rise,
 Its vistas strike, its palaces surprise;
 While scourged by famine from the smiling land,
300 The mournful peasant leads his humble band;
 And while he sinks without one arm to save,
 The country blooms—a garden, and a grave.

  Where then, ah where, shall poverty reside,
 To scape the pressure of contiguous pride?

305 If to some common's[4] fenceless limits strayed,
He drives his flock to pick the scanty blade,
Those fenceless fields the sons of wealth divide,
And even the bare-worn common is denied.

If to the city sped—What waits him there?
310 To see profusion that he must not share;
To see ten thousand baneful arts combined
To pamper luxury, and thin mankind;
To see those joys the sons of pleasure know
Extorted from his fellow-creature's woe.
315 Here, while the courtier glitters in brocade,
There the pale artist° plies the sickly trade;   *artisan*
Here, while the proud their long-drawn pomps display,
There the black gibbet glooms beside the way.
The dome° where Pleasure holds her midnight reign,   *lavish house*
320 Here, richly decked, admits the gorgeous train;
Tumultuous grandeur crowds the blazing square,
The rattling chariots clash, the torches glare.
Sure scenes like these no troubles e'er annoy!
Sure these denote one universal joy!
325 Are these thy serious thoughts?—Ah, turn thine eyes
Where the poor houseless shivering female lies.
She once, perhaps, in village plenty blest,
Has wept at tales of innocence distressed;
Her modest looks the cottage might adorn,
330 Sweet as the primrose peeps beneath the thorn;
Now lost to all; her friends, her virtue fled,
Near her betrayer's door she lays her head,
And pinched with cold, and shrinking from the shower,
With heavy heart deplores that luckless hour
335 When idly first, ambitious of the town,
She left her wheel and robes of country brown.

Do thine, sweet Auburn, thine, the loveliest train,
Do thy fair tribes participate° her pain?   *partake of*
Even now, perhaps, by cold and hunger led,
340 At proud men's doors they ask a little bread!

Ah, no. To distant climes, a dreary scene,
Where half the convex world intrudes between,
Through torrid tracts with fainting steps they go,
Where wild Altama[5] murmurs to their woe.
345 Far different there from all that charmed before,
The various terrors of that horrid shore;
Those blazing suns that dart a downward ray,
And fiercely shed intolerable day;
Those matted woods where birds forget to sing,
350 But silent bats in drowsy clusters cling,
Those poisonous fields with rank luxuriance crowned,

4. Grazing land once shared by all the villagers.   5. The Altamaha River, in Georgia (then a colony).

Where the dark scorpion gathers death around;
Where at each step the stranger fears to wake
The rattling terrors of the vengeful snake;
355   Where crouching tigers wait their hapless prey,
And savage men, more murderous still than they;
While oft in whirls the mad tornado flies,
Mingling the ravaged landscape with the skies.
Far different these from every former scene,
360   The cooling brook, the grassy vested green,
The breezy covert of the warbling grove,
That only sheltered thefts of harmless love.

    Good Heaven! what sorrows gloomed that parting day,
That called them from their native walks away;
365   When the poor exiles, every pleasure past,
Hung round their bowers, and fondly looked their last,
And took a long farewell, and wished in vain
For seats like these beyond the western main;
And shuddering still to face the distant deep,
370   Returned and wept, and still returned to weep.
The good old sire the first prepared to go
To new-found worlds, and wept for others' woe.
But for himself, in conscious virtue brave,
He only wished for worlds beyond the grave.
375   His lovely daughter, lovelier in her tears,
The fond companion of his helpless years,
Silent went next, neglectful of her charms,
And left a lover's for a father's arms.
With louder plaints the mother spoke her woes,
380   And blessed the cot° where every pleasure rose;   *cottage*
And kissed her thoughtless babes with many a tear,
And clasped them close in sorrow doubly dear;
Whilst her fond husband strove to lend relief
In all the silent manliness of grief.

385   O luxury! Thou curst by Heaven's decree,
How ill exchanged are things like these for thee!
How do thy potions, with insidious joy,
Diffuse their pleasures only to destroy!
Kingdoms, by thee to sickly greatness grown,
390   Boast of a florid vigor not their own;
At every draught more large and large they grow,
A bloated mass of rank unwieldy woe;
Till sapped their strength, and every part unsound,
Down, down they sink, and spread a ruin round.

395   Even now the devastation is begun,
And half the business of destruction done;
Even now, methinks, as pondering here I stand,
I see the rural virtues leave the land.
Down where yon anchoring vessel spreads the sail,
400   That idly waiting flaps with every gale,
Downward they move, a melancholy band,

Pass from the shore, and darken all the strand.
Contented toil, and hospitable care,
And kind connubial tenderness are there;
405 And piety, with wishes placed above,
And steady loyalty, and faithful love:
And thou, sweet Poetry, thou loveliest maid,
Still first to fly where sensual joys invade;
Unfit, in these degenerate times of shame,
410 To catch the heart, or strike for honest fame;
Dear charming nymph, neglected and decried,
My shame in crowds, my solitary pride;
Thou source of all my bliss, and all my woe,
That found'st me poor at first, and keep'st me so;
415 Thou guide by which the nobler arts excel,
Thou nurse of every virtue, fare thee well.
Farewell, and O where'er thy voice be tried,
On Torno's[6] cliffs, or Pambamarca's[7] side,
Whether where equinoctial fervors[8] glow,
420 Or winter wraps the polar world in snow,
Still let thy voice, prevailing over time,
Redress the rigors of the inclement clime;
Aid slighted truth, with thy persuasive strain
Teach erring man to spurn the rage of gain;
425 Teach him that states of native strength possessed,
Though very poor, may still be very blest;
That trade's proud empire hastes to swift decay,
As ocean sweeps the labored mole° away;   breakwater
While self-dependent power can time defy,
430 As rocks resist the billows and the sky.[9]

1770

COMPANION READINGS

George Crabbe:[1] from *The Village*

The village life, and every care that reigns
O'er youthful peasants and declining swains;
What labor yields, and what, that labor past,
Age, in its hour of languor, finds at last;
5 What forms the real picture of the poor,
Demand a song—the Muse can give no more.

* * *

I grant indeed that fields and flocks have charms

---

6. The Tornio, a river in Sweden.
7. A mountain in Ecuador.
8. Equatorial heat.
9. Samuel Johnson supplied the poem's last two couplets.
1. Physician, clergyman, poet (1754–1832). Reacting against Goldsmith's poetic nostalgia in *The Deserted Village*, and against the larger tradition of pastoral poetry which conceived the countryside as an Arcadia abounding in simple pleasures, Crabbe tried to depict realistical-

ly the benighted lives of the rural poor. Within the long compass of his own lifetime, his work found favor among readers of widely divergent convictions and generations, across the cusp of centuries and revolutions. Johnson, Reynolds, and Burke encouraged him early; Jane Austen reckoned him her favorite poet; Lord Byron praised him as "Nature's sternest painter yet the best." The first three excerpts given here are from Book 1 of *The Village*.

Thomas Gainsborough. *Cottage Door with Children Playing,* c. 1788. As the critic John Barrell has pointed out, Gainsborough's painting mingles two different perceptions of the rural poor: the gracious women and boisterous children basking in the day's last light conjure up Goldmith's sentimental idealization of pastoral joys; Crabbe's contrapuntal insistence on the misery of the laborer's lot is figured in the form of the returning husband at bottom left, bent with his burden of firewood and nearly buried by the shadows.

40	For him that grazes or for him that farms;
	But when amid such pleasing scenes I trace
	The poor laborious natives of the place,
	And see the midday sun, with fervid ray,
	On their bare heads and dewy temples play;
45	While some, with feebler heads and fainter hearts,
	Deplore their fortune, yet sustain their parts,
	Then shall I dare these real ills to hide
	In tinsel trappings of poetic pride?

* * *

	Ye gentle souls who dream of rural ease,
	Whom the smooth stream and smoother sonnet please;
	Go! if the peaceful cot your praises share,
175	Go, look within, and ask if peace be there;
	If peace be his—that drooping weary fire,
	Or theirs, that offspring round their feeble sire,
	Or hers, that matron pale, whose trembling hand
	Turns on the wretched hearth th' expiring brand.

* * *

See the stout churl, in drunken fury great,
Strike the bare bosom of his teeming mate![2]
35   His naked vices, rude and unrefined,
Exert their open empire o'er the mind;
But can we less the senseless rage despise,
Because the savage acts without disguise?

* * *

And hark! the riots of the green begin,
That sprang at first from yonder noisy inn;
65   What time° the weekly pay was vanished all,   *once*
And the slow hostess scored the threatening wall;[3]
What time they asked, their friendly feast to close,
A final cup, and that will make them foes;
When blows ensue that break the arm of toil,
70   And rustic battle ends the boobies' broil.

* * *

Yet why, you ask, these humble crimes relate,
Why make the poor as guilty as the great?
90   To show the great, those mightier sons of Pride,
How near in vice the lowest are allied;
Such are their natures and their passions such,
But these disguise too little, those too much:
So shall the man of power and pleasure see
95   In his own slave as vile a wretch as he;
In his luxurious lord the servant find
His own low pleasures and degenerate mind;
And each in all the kindred vices trace
Of a poor, blind, bewildered, erring race;
100 Who, a short time in varied fortune past,
Die, and are equal in the dust at last.

1780–1783   1783

George Crabbe: from *The Parish Register*

The year revolves, and I again explore
The simple annals of my parish poor;[1]
What infant members in my flock appear,
What pairs I blessed in the departed year;
5   And who, of old or young, of nymphs or swains,
Are lost to life, its pleasures and its pains.
        No Muse I ask, before my view to bring
The humble actions of the swains I sing.—
How passed the youthful, how the old their days;
10   Who sank in sloth, and who aspired to praise;
Their tempers, manners, morals, customs, arts,
What parts° they had, and how they employed their parts;   *talents*
By what elated, soothed, seduced, depressed,

---

2. From Book 2. In this section of *The Village* Crabbe is describing (according to rubrics he published with the poem) "the repose and pleasure of a summer Sabbath, interrupted by intoxication and dispute"; in the next excerpt he proceeds to "the evening riots."

3. At taverns, the running debts of the drinkers were often recorded by means of marks ("scores") on the wall. Compare Goldsmith's description of the village tavern (*Deserted Village* 217–220).
1. The speaker is a parish priest.

Full well I know—these records give the rest.
15   Is there a place, save one the poet sees,
A land of love, of liberty and ease,
Where labor wearies not, nor cares suppress
Th' eternal flow of rustic happiness;
Where no proud mansion frowns in awful state,
20   Or keeps the sunshine from the cottage gate;
Where young and old, intent on pleasure, throng,
And half man's life is holiday and song?
Vain search for scenes like these! no view appears,
By sighs unruffled or unstained by tears;
25   Since vice the world subdued and waters drowned,
Auburn and Eden can no more be found.

c. 1802–1806   1807

PERSPECTIVES

Landscape, Pleasure, Power

The pieces in this section trace a shift in the history of perception, in how observers made meaning out of the landscapes that they looked at. In *Cooper's Hill*, a widely praised poem of the mid-1600s, John Denham reads into a local landscape the history of English monarchic power. A century later, observers influenced by Edmund Burke's *Philosophical Enquiry* sought in landscape not distant history but immediate sensation, an overwhelming and gratifying grandeur. In Denham's poem landscape figures power. In Burke's *Enquiry* and the works that it influenced landscape exerts power: the right vista, rightly observed, can leave the seer speechless. Over the course of a hundred years, the perception and description of landscape modulated from the overtly political to the emphatically aesthetic.

This seeming de-politicization was political in itself, intimately bound up with the distribution of power, the management of possessions, and the manifestation of those national "liberties" which (to the patriotic mind) set the Protestant British apart from (and above) their slavish, Catholic, European contemporaries. The paradoxes of power that attended these developments were nowhere more evident than in a major object of eighteenth-century English passion, the landscape garden: a stretch of terrain whose owner (with his attendant designers) pursued an elusive, barely calculable balance between the accomplishments of art and the effects of nature. Seventeenth-century English gardens, imitating Continental models, had pursued no such balance. In them, elaborate symmetrical arrangements and ubiquitous topiary (bushes and trees painstakingly sculpted in the forms of cones, cubes, birds, etc.) had asserted the primacy of human intervention, the gardener's capacity to improve on nature. By contrast, eighteenth-century "gardenists" (a new-coined term) saw themselves as engaged in a sustained submission to nature, a liberating of the landscape's natural propensities. They sought to make manifest the "genius of the place," a presiding spirit supposedly intrinsic to the site before human incursion. In their designs, the tyrannic (French) symmetries of the preceding century gave way to proud English irregularity (that word, too, became a nearly sacred term of art). Straight lines gave way to serpentine curves; high surrounding walls disappeared in favor of the "ha-ha," a low boundary line (usually a dry moat or trench) that allowed occupants of the garden to view the vistas of the surrounding countryside.

The very word "ha-ha" was meant to express the pleased surprise (*aha!*) of the observer, gratified by the designer's strategies of concealment and revelation. The new landscaper, wrote Stephen Switzer (one of the style's first advocates), "will endeavor to diversify his views, always striving that they may be so intermixed as not to be all discovered at once; but that there should be, as much as possible, something appearing new and diverting, while the whole should correspond together by the natural error [i.e., wandering] of its natural avenues and meanders." Contradictions clustered fairly thick around such schemes. These surrenders to nature, these assertions of liberty, required considerable contrivance and a great deal of ready cash. The proponents and practitioners of the landscape garden were for the most part Whig landowners, made secure by a long season of political power and rich by the overseas trade they so ardently championed. The capacity to shape landscape, even to see it correctly, was an expression of power and position (a point that the Tory Oliver Goldsmith ruefully elaborated in his poem *The Deserted Village*; see page 2844). The landscape garden asserted its makers' eminence another way as well: by century's end, *le jardin anglais* had (as the French phrase implies) established a pattern for gardens far beyond the British Isles, in both Europe and America. Having defied the Continental model in the name of native liberty, the English gardenists could now witness the international dominion of their own.

Seventy years earlier, the Whig Joseph Addison had laid out much of the gardenists' agenda. Every landowner, he urged, might implement an aesthetic program, might make "a pretty landskip of his own possessions." The phrase points deliberately in two directions: *landskip* then (like *landscape* now) could denote either a real prospect (composed of air, earth, light, leafage) or a painting. Over the course of the century, sightseers and aestheticians became increasingly interested in the pictorial possibility. In 1792 Arthur Young, traveling among the Alps, reported that "in several places the view is picturesque and pleasing: enclosures [private estates] seem hung against the mountain sides as a picture is suspended to the wall of a room." Young's adjective, "picturesque," had already become a noun to conjure with. "The picturesque" named an aesthetic outlook in which landscape proved more "pleasing" the more it resembled a well-made painting, both in its barely verbalizable grace (the convergences of curves and colors) and in its susceptibility of being aesthetically possessed (hung on the mind's wall) by the properly informed and appreciative viewer. The pursuit of the picturesque arose in part as a way of accommodating, perhaps even of taming, a more unsettling aesthetic argument, which Burke had announced in his *Enquiry* just after mid-century. There Burke asserted that our highest delight derives not from the beautiful but from the sublime: from precisely those objects which we cannot own or control, which by their formidable scale threaten us with intimations of pain or terror, and so establish their power over us. In the wake of the *Enquiry*, travelers sought out the sublime in cliffs and crags, cataracts and caverns. Their interest in the pleasure of *surrender* to nature's power persisted into the next century and beyond. The sublime mattered hugely to the Romantics, who recalculated its meanings and workings; it matters still, in the ways we behold buildings and landscapes, in our taste for terror in all kinds of texts (fiction, movies, news), and in our propensity to regard pleasure as a matter of being overpowered by what we hear or see.

——◦━✠━◦——

Sir John Denham
1615–1669

In *Cooper's Hill*, wrote Samuel Johnson, John Denham attained "the rank and dignity of an original author. He seems to have been, at least among us, the author [i.e., inventor] of a species of composition that may be denominated *local poetry*, of which the fundamental subject is some particular landscape, to be poetically described, with the addition of such embellishments as may be supplied by historical retrospection, or incidental meditation." Denham, a devout and active Royalist, embellishes his description of the vistas from Cooper's Hill with monarchic history, making them expressive both of England's expansive power—its commerce, its wealth—and of its turmoils past, passing, and to come: the Reformation, the Civil Wars. The vantage of Denham's "historical retrospection" shifted over the long course of the poem's making: when *Cooper's Hill* first appeared in a pirated text in 1642, Denham's friend Charles I was on the throne and the Civil Wars were not begun; when Denham published his own text, in 1655, Charles had been executed and Cromwell ruled; when he produced his last revision (1668), Charles II sat on the throne. The poem exerted an influence commensurate with its vistas. Dryden praised its lyric "sweetness" and asserted that the poem "for the majesty of its style is and ever will be the standard of exact writing." Pope appropriated both its site and themes for one his earliest successes, *Windsor-Forest* (see page 2478), in which again the contours of landscape mirrored the political and economic potentialities of the nation. Throughout the eighteenth century, as the "local poetry" that Denham had pioneered became a dominant genre, *Cooper's Hill* remained a touchstone, quoted and imitated so often that Swift once wrote a mock-injunction (spoken by Apollo, god of poets) forbidding writers to "show their skill / In aping lines from *Cooper's Hill.*"

Cooper's Hill[1]

Sure there are poets which did never dream
Upon Parnassus, nor did taste the stream
Of Helicon;[2] we therefore may suppose
Those made not poets, but the poets those.
5   And as courts make not kings, but kings the court,
So where the Muses and their train resort,
Parnassus stands; if I can be to thee[3]
A poet, thou Parnassus art to me.
Nor wonder, if (advantaged in my flight,
10   By taking wing from thy auspicious height)
Through untraced ways, and aery paths I fly,
More boundless in my fancy than my eye:
My eye, which swift as thought contracts the space
That lies between, and first salutes the place
15   Crowned with that sacred pile,[4] so vast, so high,
That whether 'tis a part of earth, or sky,
Uncertain seems, and may be thought a proud
Aspiring mountain, or descending cloud,
Paul's, the late theme of such a Muse whose flight
20   Has bravely reached and soared above thy height:[5]
Now shalt thou stand, though sword, or time, or fire,
Or zeal more fierce than they thy fall conspire,
Secure, whilst thee the best of poets sings,
Preserved from ruin by the best of kings.°   *Charles I*
25   Under his proud survey the city lies,
And like a mist beneath a hill doth rise;
Whose state and wealth, the business and the crowd,
Seems at this distance but a darker cloud;
And is to him who rightly things esteems,

1. Cooper's Hill, 18 miles west of London, afforded views of London and of Windsor Castle. At the time he began work on the poem, Denham lived nearby.
2. The Greek mountains Parnassus and Helicon were both held sacred to the Muses; the springs ("stream") on Helicon were thought to imbue with poetic inspiration

those who drank from them.
3. I.e., to Cooper's Hill.
4. St. Paul's Cathedral, the largest building in London.
5. Denham here praises the "Muse" of Edmund Waller (1606–1687), who had published a poem *Upon His Majesty's Repairing of Paul's* (1645).

30   No other in effect than what it seems;
        Where with like haste, though several ways, they run,
        Some to undo, and some to be undone;
        While luxury and wealth, like war and peace,
        Are each the other's ruin, and increase;
35   As rivers lost in seas some secret vein
        Thence reconveys, there to be lost again.
        Oh happiness of sweet retired content!
        To be at once secure, and innocent.
            Windsor[6] the next (where Mars with Venus dwells,
40   Beauty with strength) above the valley swells
        Into my eye, and doth itself present
        With such an easy and unforced ascent,
        That no stupendious precipice denies
        Access, no horror turns away our eyes;
45   But such a rise, as doth at once invite
        A pleasure, and a reverence from the sight.
        Thy mighty master's emblem, in whose face
        Sat meekness, heightened with majestic grace
        Such seems thy gentle height, made only proud
50   To be the basis of that pompous load,
        Than which a nobler weight no mountain bears,
        But Atlas[7] only that supports the spheres.
        When Nature's hand this ground did thus advance,
        'Twas guided by a wiser power than chance;
55   Marked out for such a use, as if 'twere meant
        To invite the builder, and his choice prevent.°   *anticipate*
        Nor can we call it choice, when what we choose,
        Folly or blindness only could refuse.
        A crown of such majestic towers doth grace
60   The gods' great mother,[8] when her heavenly race
        Do homage to her, yet she cannot boast
        Amongst that numerous and celestial host,
        More heroes than can Windsor, nor doth Fame's
        Immortal book record more noble names.
65   Not to look back so far, to whom this isle
        Owes the first glory of so brave a pile,
        Whether to Caesar, Albanact, or Brute,[9]
        The British Arthur, or the Danish Knute[1]
        (Though this of old no less contest did move,
70   Than when for Homer's birth[2] seven cities strove)
        (Like him in birth, thou should'st be like in fame,
        As thine his fate, if mine had been his flame)
        But whosoe'er it was, Nature designed
        First a brave place, and then as brave a mind.

6. A borough on the Thames, some 21 miles west of London; site of Windsor Castle, the royal residence.
7. The ancient divinity whose task is to hold up the heavens.
8. Cybele, goddess of nature and of fertility.
9. Julius Caesar (100–44 B.C.) was (erroneously) thought to have built some of Britain's loftiest structures; the mythical Brutus, grandson of the Trojan hero Aeneas,

was traditionally regarded as London's founder; his son Albanact was thought to have ruled Scotland.
1. Canute (995?–1035), king of England, Norway, and Denmark.
2. I.e., for the honor of being identified as birthplace of the epic poet.

75   Not to recount those several kings, to whom
      It gave a cradle, or to whom a tomb,
      But thee (great Edward) and thy greater son
      (The lilies which his father wore, he won),
      And thy Bellona, who the consort came
80   Not only to thy bed, but to thy fame,
      She to thy triumph led one captive king,
      And brought that son, which did the second bring.[3]
      Then didst thou found that order[4] (whither love
      Or victory thy royal thoughts did move),
85   Each was a noble cause, and nothing less
      Than the design has been the great success—
      Which foreign kings and emperors esteem
      The second honor to their diadem.
      Had thy great destiny but given thee skill,
90   To know as well, as power to act her will,
      That from those kings, who then thy captives were,
      In after-times should spring a royal pair[5]
      Who should possess all that thy mighty power,
      Or thy desires more mighty, did devour;
95   To whom their better fate reserves whate'er
      The victor hopes for, or the vanquished fear;
      That blood, which thou and thy great grandsire shed,
      And all that since these sister nations[6] bled,
      Had been unspilt, had happy Edward known
100   That all the blood he spilt had been his own.
      When he that patron[7] chose, in whom are joined
      Soldier and martyr, and his arms confined
      Within the azure circle,[8] he did seem
      But to foretell, and prophesy of him,[9]
105   Who to his realms that azure round hath joined,
      Which Nature for their bound at first designed.
      That bound, which to the world's extremest ends,
      Endless itself, its liquid arms extends;
      Nor doth he need those emblems which we paint,
110   But is himself the soldier and the saint.
      Here should my wonder dwell, and here my praise,
      But my fixed thoughts my wandering eye betrays,
      Viewing a neighboring hill,[1] whose top of late

3. "Edward" is Edward III (1312–1377); "Bellona" (the Roman goddess of war) is Denhamn's designation for Edward's wife Phillipa of Hainault (1314–1369), whose speech to the troops before a famous battle helped spur them to take as "captive king" David II of Scotland; the "greater son" is Edward's and Phillipa's eldest son Edward the Black Prince (1330–1376), the accomplished soldier who briefly conquered France (land of "lilies") and took captive its king, John II (1319–1364).
4. The Order of the Garter, created in 1344 by Edward III to honor military valor, in fulfillment of a vow he had made to reinstate the Arthurian Round Table.
5. Charles I and his queen consort Henrietta Maria (1606–1669), daughter of the French king Henri IV. Denham fudges the geneaology here: neither Charles nor

his queen could claim direct descent from Edward III's "captive kings."
6. Scotland (where Edward's "grandsire" Edward I shed much blood) and France. Charles I was Scots; his wife was French.
7. St. George, patron saint of England.
8. The emblem of the Order of the Garter depicts St. George's red cross surrounded by the "azure circle" of the blue garter.
9. Charles I, whose realm conjoins Scotland and England, surrounded by the natural "azure circle" of the sea.
1. St. Anne's Hill, where had once stood an abbey and chapel, destroyed by Henry VIII as part of his campaign to render England independent of the Roman Catholic Church.

A chapel crowned, till in the common fate,
115   The adjoining abbey fell (may no such storm
Fall on our times, where ruin must reform).
Tell me (my Muse) what monstrous dire offense,
What crime could any Christian king incense
To such a rage? Was't luxury, or lust?
120   Was he so temperate, so chaste, so just?
Were these[2] their crimes? They were his own much more:
But wealth is crime enough to him that's poor,
Who having spent the treasures of his crown,
Condemns their luxury to feed his own.
125   And yet this act, to varnish o'er the shame
Of sacrilege, must bear devotion's name.
No crime so bold, but would be understood
A real, or at least a seeming good.
Who fears not to do ill, yet fears the name,
130   And free from conscience, is a slave to fame.
Thus he the Church at once protects, and spoils:
But princes' swords are sharper than their styles.[3]
And thus to th' ages past he makes amends,
Their charity destroys, their faith defends.
135   Then did religion in a lazy cell,
In empty, airy contemplations dwell;
And like the block, unmoved lay: but ours,
As much too active, like the stork devours.[4]
Is there no temperate region can be known,
140   Betwixt their frigid, and our torrid zone?
Could we not wake from that lethargic dream,
But to be restless in a worse extreme?
And for that lethargy was there no cure,
But to be cast into a calenture?°   fever
145   Can knowledge have no bound, but must advance
So far, to make us wish for ignorance?
And rather in the dark to grope our way,
Than led by a false guide to err by day?
Who sees these dismal heaps, but would demand
150   What barbarous invader sacked the land?
But when he hears° no Goth, no Turk did bring   hears that
This desolation, but a Christian king;
When nothing but the name of zeal appears
'Twixt our best actions and the worst of theirs,
155   What does he think our sacrilege would spare,
When such th' effects of our devotions are?
Parting from thence 'twixt anger, shame, and fear,
Those for what's past, and this for what's too near,
My eye, descending from the hill, surveys
160   Where Thames amongst the wanton valleys strays.

2. I.e., "luxury" and "lust."
3. Their pens. Before defying Rome himself, Henry VIII
had written an attack on Martin Luther, for which the
Pope awarded him the title Defender of the Faith.

4. Denham refers to the fable in which Jupiter sends a log
to serve as ruler over a nation of frogs that craves a king;
when the frogs complain that the log does nothing,
Jupiter replaces it with a stork which eats them all.

Thames, the most loved of all the Ocean's sons,
By his old sire to his embraces runs,
Hasting to pay his tribute to the sea,
Like mortal life to meet eternity.

165 Though with those streams he no resemblance hold,
Whose foam is amber, and their gravel gold,[5]
His genuine, and less guilty wealth t' explore,
Search not his bottom, but survey his shore,
O'er which he kindly spreads his spacious wing,

170 And hatches plenty for th' ensuing spring.
Nor then destroys it with too fond a stay,
Like mothers which their infants overlay.
Nor with a sudden and impetuous wave,
Like profuse kings, resumes the wealth he gave.

175 No unexpected inundations spoil
The mower's hopes, nor mock the plowman's toil;
But God-like his unwearied bounty flows;
First loves to do, then loves the good he does.
Nor are his blessings to his banks confined,

180 But free, and common, as the sea or wind;
When he to boast, or to disperse his stores
Full of the tributes of his grateful shores,
Visits the world, and in his flying towers
Brings home to us, and makes both Indies ours;

185 Finds wealth where 'tis, bestows it where it wants
Cities in deserts, woods in cities plants.
So that to us no thing, no place is strange,
While his fair bosom is the world's exchange.
O could I flow like thee, and make thy stream

190 My great example, as it is my theme!
Though deep, yet clear, though gentle, yet not dull,
Strong without rage, without o'er-flowing full.
Heaven her Eridanus[6] no more shall boast,
Whose fame in thine, like lesser currents lost,

195 Thy nobler streams shall visit Jove's abodes,
To shine amongst the stars, and bathe the gods.
Here Nature, whether more intent to please
Us or herself, with strange varieties
(For things of wonder give no less delight

200 To the wise maker's, than beholder's sight.
Though these delights from several causes move;
For so our children, thus our friends we love),[7]
Wisely she knew° the harmony of things,   knew that
As well as that of sounds, from discords springs.

205 Such was the discord, which did first disperse
Form, order, beauty through the universe;

---

5. Referring to the Po River, where trees were thought to drip amber into the flowing waters, and the Pactolus River, whose sands contain gold (supposedly because King Midas once washed his hands there).
6. A mythical river (sometimes identified with the Po in

Italy, sometimes with a stream in Athens), into which the presumptuous Greek divinity Phaethon fell after driving the sun's chariot too near the earth.
7. As "makers" we love our children; as "beholders" our friends.

While dryness moisture, coldness heat resists,
All that we have, and that we are, subsists.
While the steep horrid roughness of the wood
210 Strives with the gentle calmness of the flood.
Such huge extremes when Nature doth unite,
Wonder from thence results, from thence delight.
The stream is so transparent, pure, and clear,
That had the self-enamored youth[8] gazed here,
215 So fatally deceived he had not been,
While he the bottom, not his face had seen.
But his proud head the aery mountain hides[9]
Among the clouds; his shoulders, and his sides
A shady mantle clothes; his curled brows
220 Frown on the gentle stream, which calmly flows,
While winds and storms his lofty forehead beat:
The common fate of all that's high or great.
Low at his foot a spacious plain is placed,
Between the mountain and the stream embraced;
225 Which shade and shelter from the hill derives,
While the kind river wealth and beauty gives;
And in the mixture of all these appears
Variety, which all the rest endears.
This scene had some bold Greek, or British bard
230 Beheld of old, what stories had we heard,
Of fairies, satyrs, and the nymphs their dames,
Their feasts, their revels, and their amorous flames.
'Tis still the same, although their aery shape
All but a quick poetic sight escape.
235 There Faunus and Sylvanus° keep their courts,   woodland gods
And thither all the horned host resorts,
To graze the ranker mead, that noble herd
On whose sublime and shady fronts is reared
Nature's great masterpiece; to show how soon
240 Great things are made, but sooner are undone.
Here have I seen the King, when great affairs
Give leave to slacken, and unbend his cares,
Attended to the chase by all the flower
Of youth, whose hopes a nobler prey devour:
245 Pleasure with praise, and danger, they would buy,
And wish a foe that would not only fly.
The stag now conscious of his fatal growth,
At once indulgent to his fear and sloth,
To some dark covert his retreat had made,
250 Where nor man's eye, nor heaven's should invade
His soft repose; when th' unexpected sound
Of dogs, and men, his wakeful ear doth wound.
Roused with the noise, he scarce believes his ear,
Willing to think th' illusions of his fear

---

8. Narcissus, who saw his reflection in water, and fell in
love with himself.

9. The mountain hides its own head (not Narcissus's).

255   Had given this false alarm, but straight his view
      Confirms, that more than all he fears is true.
      Betrayed in all his strengths, the wood beset,
      All instruments, all arts of ruin met;
      He calls to mind his strength, and then his speed,
260   His winged heels, and then his armed head;
      With these t' avoid, with that his fate to meet.
      But fear prevails, and bids him trust his feet.
      So fast he flies, that his reviewing eye
      Has lost the chasers, and his ear the cry;
265   Exulting, till he finds, their nobler sense
      Their disproportioned speed does recompense.
      Then curses his conspiring feet, whose scent
      Betrays that safety which their swiftness lent.
      Then tries his friends among the baser herd,
270   Where he so lately was obeyed, and feared,
      His safety seeks: the herd, unkindly wise,
      Or° chases him from thence, or from him flies.   *either*
      Like a declining statesman, left forlorn
      To his friends' pity, and pursuers' scorn,
275   With shame remembers, while himself was one
      Of the same herd, himself the same had done.
      Thence to the coverts, and the conscious groves,
      The scenes of his past triumphs, and his loves;
      Sadly surveying where he ranged alone
280   Prince of the soil, and all the herd his own;
      And like a bold knight errant did proclaim
      Combat to all, and bore away the dame;
      And taught the woods to echo to the stream
      His dreadful challenge, and his clashing beam.[1]
285   Yet faintly now declines the fatal strife;
      So much his love was dearer than his life.
      Now every leaf, and every moving breath
      Presents a foe, and every foe a death.
      Wearied, forsaken, and pursued, at last
290   All safety in despair of safety placed,
      Courage he thence resumes, resolved to bear
      All their assaults, since 'tis in vain to fear.
      And now too late he wishes for the fight
      That strength he wasted in ignoble flight;
295   But when he sees the eager chase renewed,
      Himself by dogs, the dogs by men pursued,
      He straight revokes his bold resolve, and more
      Repents his courage, than his fear before;
      Finds that uncertain ways unsafest are,
300   And doubt a greater mischief than despair.
      Then to the stream, when neither friends, nor force,
      Nor speed, nor art avail, he shapes his course;
      Thinks not their rage so desperate t' assay

---

1. The central portion of the stag's horns.

An element more merciless than they.
305　But fearless they pursue, nor can the flood
　　Quench their dire thirst; alas, they thirst for blood.
　　So towards a ship the oarefined° galleys ply,　　　　　*oar-equipped*
　　Which wanting sea to ride, or wind to fly,
　　Stands but to fall revenged on those that dare
310　Tempt the last fury of extreme despair.
　　So fares the stag among th' enraged hounds,
　　Repels their force, and wounds returns for wounds.
　　And as a hero, whom his baser foes
　　In troops surround, now these assails, now those,
315　Though prodigal of life, disdains to die
　　By common hands; but if he can descry
　　Some nobler foe's approach, to him he calls,
　　And begs his fate, and then contented falls.
　　So when the King a mortal shaft lets fly
320　From his unerring hand, then glad to die,
　　Proud of the wound, to it resigns his blood,
　　And stains the crystal with a purple flood.
　　This a more innocent, and happy chase,
　　Than when of old, but in the self-same place,[2]
325　Fair liberty pursued, and meant a prey
　　To lawless power, here turned, and stood at bay.
　　When in that remedy all hope was placed
　　Which was, or should have been at least, the last.
　　Here was that charter sealed, wherein the Crown
330　All marks of arbitrary power lays down:
　　Tyrant and slave, those names of hate and fear,
　　The happier style of king and subject bear:
　　Happy, when both to the same center move,
　　When kings give liberty, and subjects love.
335　Therefore not long in force this charter stood;
　　Wanting that seal,[3] it must be sealed in blood.
　　The subjects armed, the more their princes gave,
　　Th' advantage only took the more to crave.
　　Till kings by giving, give themselves away,
340　And even that power, that should deny, betray.
　　"Who gives constrained, but his own fear reviles
　　Not thanked, but scorned; nor are they gifts, but spoils."[4]
　　Thus kings, by grasping more than they could hold,
　　First made their subjects by oppression bold:
345　And popular sway, by forcing kings to give
　　More than was fit for subjects to receive,
　　Ran to the same extremes; and one excess
　　Made both, by striving to be greater, less.
　　When a calm river raised with sudden rains,
350　Or snows dissolved, o'erflows th' adjoining plains,

---

2. Runnymede, the Thames-side meadow where the stag hunt takes place, is also the site where King John (the unpopular embodiment of "lawless power") is traditionally thought to have signed the Magna Carta (the Great Charter), limiting his power and increasing the liberties of his subjects.

3. Lacking that basis (in reciprocal "liberty" and "love").

4. The source of this quotation has not been identified.

The husbandmen with high-raised banks secure
Their greedy hopes, and this he can endure.
But if with bays and dams they strive to force
His channel to a new, or narrow course;
355   No longer then within his banks he dwells,
First to a torrent, then a deluge swells:
Stronger, and fiercer by restraint he roars,
And knows no bound, but makes his power his shores.

1642, 1655, 1668

━━◄══◆══►━━

Joseph Addison
1672–1719

By its very title, the best-selling periodical called *The Spectator* privileged the eye and preached its power (for more on the paper's history, see page 2323). The paper's two authors, Joseph Addison and Richard Steele, never tired of advising their readers that to observe any object with intelligence and taste was to acquire a "kind of property" in it; that spectatorship conferred automatic and vicarious possession. The idea held enormous appeal for the paper's mainly middle-class readership, eager to improve their standing, cultivate their taste, and increase their holdings. Addison set forth the powers of spectatorship most fully in the sequence of papers dubbed the "Pleasures of the Imagination," a serial essay he may have begun much earlier, while still a student at Oxford, and which he expanded for publication during the *Spectator*'s second year. The twelve essays appeared over the course of two weeks; their influence on aesthetics persisted throughout the century. In his definitions and demonstrations of such terms as "greatness," "novelty," and "imagination" (by which he meant our capacity both to form images in our mind of things we are actually witnessing, and to envision objects not present before us), Addison established criteria that were widely absorbed and repeatedly taken up by later thinkers (Burke among them). He paid particular attention to landscape as a focal point of both pleasure and power; and in *Spectator* No. 414 he produced an early manifesto for those new artificers in earth and seed, the landscape gardenists.

from **Spectator No. 412**
Monday, 23 June 1712

[THE GREAT, THE UNCOMMON, THE BEAUTIFUL]

. . . Divisum sic breve fiet opus.[1]

I shall first consider those pleasures of the imagination which arise from the actual view and survey of outward objects: And these, I think, all proceed from the sight of what is *great, uncommon,* or *beautiful.* There may, indeed, be something so terrible or offensive, that the horror or loathsomeness of an object may overbear the pleasure which results from its *greatness, novelty,* or *beauty;* but still there will be such a mixture of delight in the very disgust it gives us, as any of these three qualifications are most conspicuous and prevailing.

---

1. "The work thus divided will become brief" (Martial, *Epigrams* 4.82.8).

By *greatness*, I do not only mean the bulk of any single object, but the largeness of a whole view, considered as one entire piece. Such are the prospects of an open champian[2] country, a vast uncultivated desert, of huge heaps of mountains, high rocks and precipices, or a wide expanse of waters, where we are not struck with the novelty or beauty of the sight, but with that rude kind of magnificence which appears in many of these stupendous works of nature. Our imagination loves to be filled with an object, or to grasp at anything that is too big for its capacity. We are flung into a pleasing astonishment at such unbounded views, and feel a delightful stillness and amazement in the soul at the apprehension of them. The mind of man naturally hates everything that looks like a restraint upon it, and is apt to fancy itself under a sort of confinement, when the sight is pent up in a narrow compass, and shortened on every side by the neighborhood of walls or mountains. On the contrary, a spacious horizon is an image of liberty, where the eye has room to range abroad, to expatiate at large on the immensity of its views, and to lose itself amidst the variety of objects that offer themselves to its observation. Such wide and undetermined prospects are as pleasing to the fancy, as the speculations of eternity or infinitude are to the understanding. But if there be a beauty or uncommonness joined with this grandeur, as in a troubled ocean, a heaven adorned with stars and meteors, or a spacious landscape cut out into rivers, woods, rocks, and meadows, the pleasure still grows upon us, as it arises from more than a single principle.

Everything that is *new* or *uncommon* raises a pleasure in the imagination, because it fills the soul with an agreeable surprise, gratifies its curiosity, and gives it an idea of which it was not before possessed. We are, indeed, so often conversant with one set of objects, and tired out with so many repeated shows of the same things, that whatever is *new* or *uncommon* contributes a little to vary human life, and to divert our minds, for a while, with the strangeness of its appearance. It serves us for a kind of refreshment, and takes off from that satiety we are apt to complain of in our usual and ordinary entertainments. It is this that bestows charms on a monster, and makes even the imperfections of nature please us. It is this that recommends variety, where the mind is every instant called off to something new, and the attention not suffered to dwell too long, and waste itself on any particular object. It is this, likewise, that improves what is great or beautiful, and makes it afford the mind a double entertainment. Groves, fields, and meadows are at any season of the year pleasant to look upon, but never so much as in the opening of the spring, when they are all new and fresh, with their first gloss upon them, and not yet too much accustomed and familiar to the eye. For this reason there is nothing that more enlivens a prospect than rivers, jetties, or falls of water, where the scene is perpetually shifting, and entertaining the sight every moment with something that is new. We are quickly tired with looking upon hills and valleys, where everything continues fixed and settled in the same place and posture, but find our thoughts a little agitated and relieved at the sight of such objects as are ever in motion, and sliding away from beneath the eye of the beholder.

But there is nothing that makes its way more directly to the soul than *beauty*, which immediately diffuses a secret satisfaction and complacency through the imagination, and gives a finishing to anything that is great or uncommon. The very first discovery of it strikes the mind with an inward joy, and spreads a cheerfulness and delight through all its faculties. There is not perhaps any real beauty or deformity

---

2. I.e., *champaign*: "A flat open country" (Johnson's *Dictionary*).

more in one piece of matter than another, because we might have been so made, that whatsoever now appears loathsome to us, might have shown itself agreeable; but we find by experience that there are several modifications of matter which the mind, without any previous consideration, pronounces at first sight beautiful or deformed. Thus we see that every different species of sensible creatures has its different notions of beauty, and that each of them is most affected with the beauties of its own kind.

* * *

There is a second kind of *beauty* that we find in the several products of art and nature, which does not work in the imagination with that warmth and violence as the beauty that appears in our proper species, but is apt however to raise in us a secret delight, and a kind of fondness for the places or objects in which we discover it. This consists either in the gaiety or variety of colors, in the symmetry and proportion of parts, in the arrangement and disposition of bodies, or in a just mixture and concurrence of all together. Among these several kinds of beauty the eye takes most delight in colors. We nowhere meet with a more glorious or pleasing show in nature, than what appears in the heavens at the rising and setting of the sun, which is wholly made up of those different stains of light that show themselves in clouds of a different situation. For this reason we find the poets, who are always addressing themselves to the imagination, borrowing more of their epithets from colors than from any other topic.

As the fancy delights in everything that is great, strange, or beautiful, and is still more pleased the more it finds of these perfections in the same object, so is it capable of receiving a new satisfaction by the assistance of another sense. Thus any continued sound, as the music of birds, or a fall of water, awakens every moment the mind of the beholder, and makes him more attentive to the several beauties of the place that lie before him. Thus if there arises a fragrancy of smells or perfumes, they heighten the pleasures of the imagination, and make even the colors and verdure of the landscape appear more agreeable; for the ideas of both senses recommend each other, and are pleasanter together than when they enter the mind separately; as the different colors of a picture, when they are well disposed, set off one another, and receive an additional beauty from the advantage of their situation.

Spectator No. 414
Wednesday, 25 June 1712

[NATURE, ART, GARDENS]

> . . . *Alterius sic*
> *Altera poscit opem res et conjurat amice.*[1]

> Hor.

If we consider the works of *nature* and *art*, as they are qualified to entertain the imagination, we shall find the last very defective, in comparison of the former; for though they may sometimes appear as beautiful or strange, they can have nothing in them of that vastness and immensity which afford so great an entertainment to the mind of the beholder. The one may be as polite and delicate as the other, but can never show herself so august and magnificent in the design. There is some-

---

1. "Each by itself is vain, I'm sure, but joined, / Their force is strong, each proves the other's friend" (Horace, *Ars Poetica* 410–411; translation by Thomas Creech).

thing more bold and masterly in the rough careless strokes of nature, than in the nice touches and embellishments of art. The beauties of the most stately garden or palace lie in a narrow compass, the imagination immediately runs them over, and requires something else to gratify her; but, in the wide fields of nature, the sight wanders up and down without confinement, and is fed with an infinite variety of images, without any certain stint or number. For this reason we always find the poet in love with a country life, where nature appears in the greatest perfection, and furnishes out all those scenes that are most apt to delight the imagination.

> *Scriptorum chorus omnis amat nemus et fugit urbes.*[2]
>
> Hor.

> *Hic secura quies, et nescia fallere vita,*
> *Dives opum variarum; hic latis otia fundis,*
> *Speluncae, vivique lacus, hic frigida tempe,*
> *Mugitusque boum, mollesque sub arbore somni.*[3]
>
> Vir.

But though there are several of these wild scenes that are more delightful than any artificial shows, yet we find the works of nature still more pleasant, the more they resemble those of art. For in this case our pleasure arises from a double principle; from the agreeableness of the objects to the eye, and from their similitude to other objects: We are pleased as well with comparing their beauties as with surveying them, and can represent them to our minds either as copies or originals. Hence it is that we take delight in a prospect which is well laid out, and diversified with fields and meadows, woods and rivers, in those accidental landskips of trees, clouds and cities, that are sometimes found in the veins of marble, in the curious fret-work of rocks and grottos, and, in a word, in anything that hath such a variety or regularity as may seem the effect of design, in what we call the works of chance.

If the products of nature rise in value, according as they more or less resemble those of art, we may be sure that artificial works receive a greater advantage from their resemblance of such as are natural; because here the similitude is not only pleasant, but the pattern more perfect. The prettiest landskip I ever saw, was one drawn on the walls of a dark room, which stood opposite on one side to a navigable river, and on the other to a park.[4] The experiment is very common in optics. Here you might discover the waves and fluctuations of the water in strong and proper colors, with the picture of a ship entering at one end, and sailing by degrees through the whole piece. On another there appeared the green shadows of trees, waving to and fro with the wind, and herds of deer among them in miniature, leaping about upon the wall. I must confess, the novelty of such a sight may be one occasion of its pleasantness to the imagination, but certainly the chief reason is its near resemblance to

---

2. "Each writer hates the town and woods approves" (Horace, *Epistles* 2.2.77; translation by Thomas Creech).
3. Unvexed with quarrels, undisturbed with noise,
   The country king his peaceful realm enjoys:
   Cool grots, and living lakes, the flow'ry pride
   Of meads, and streams that through the valley glide,
   And shady groves that easy sleep invite,
   And after toilsome days, a soft repose at night.
(Virgil, *Georgics* 2.467–470; Dryden's translation).

4. The room was a *camera obscura*, literally a "dark chamber," in which light reflected from objects outside the chamber is projected onto the chamber walls, producing images of the objects. A *camera obscura* such as Addison describes (with a park on one side and the river on the other) was located in Greenwich Park. For another Thames-side instance, see Pope's description of his grotto (page 2872).

nature, as it does not only, like other pictures, give the color and figure, but the motion of the things it represents.

We have before observed that there is generally in nature something more grand and august than what we meet with in the curiosities of art. When, therefore, we see this imitated in any measure, it gives us a nobler and more exalted kind of pleasure than what we receive from the nicer and more accurate productions of art. On this account our English gardens are not so entertaining to the fancy as those in France and Italy, where we see a large extent of ground covered over with an agreeable mixture of garden and forest, which represent everywhere an artificial rudeness, much more charming than that neatness and elegancy which we meet with in those of our own country. It might, indeed, be of ill consequence to the public, as well as unprofitable to private persons, to alienate so much ground from pasturage and the plow,[5] in many parts of a country that is so well peopled, and cultivated to a far greater advantage. But why may not a whole estate be thrown into a kind of garden by frequent plantations, that may turn as much to the profit, as the pleasure of the owner? A marsh overgrown with willows, or a mountain shaded with oaks, are not only more beautiful, but more beneficial, than when they lie bare and unadorned. Fields of corn make a pleasant prospect, and if the walks were a little taken care of that lie between them, if the natural embroidery of the meadows were helped and improved by some small additions of art, and the several rows of hedges set off by trees and flowers that the soil was capable of receiving, a man might make a pretty landskip[6] of his own possessions.

Writers who have given us an account of China tell us the inhabitants of that country laugh at the plantations of our Europeans, which are laid out by the rule and line; because, they say, any one may place trees in equal rows and uniform figures. They choose rather to show a genius in works of this nature, and therefore always conceal the art by which they direct themselves. They have a word, it seems, in their language, by which they express the particular beauty of a plantation that thus strikes the imagination at first sight, without discovering what it is that has so agreeable an effect. Our British gardeners, on the contrary, instead of humoring nature, love to deviate from it as much as possible. Our trees rise in cones, globes, and pyramids. We see the marks of the scissors upon every plant and bush. I do not know whether I am singular in my opinion, but, for my own part, I would rather look upon a tree in all its luxuriancy and diffusion of boughs and branches, than when it is thus cut and trimmed into a mathematical figure; and cannot but fancy that an orchard in flower looks infinitely more delightful than all the little labyrinths of the most finished parterre.[7] But as our great modelers of gardens have their magazines[8] of plants to dispose of, it is very natural for them to tear up all the beautiful plantations of fruit trees, and contrive a plan that may most turn to their own profit, in taking off[9] their evergreens, and the like moveable plants, with which their shops are plentifully stocked.

＋＊ ⊰⊱ ＊＋

Alexander Pope
1688–1744

The most celebrated poet of his age, Alexander Pope was for several decades both the preeminent publicist for the new landscape garden, and one of the form's most ingenious, indefatigable practitioners. "Of all his works," wrote Horace Walpole in praiseful retrospect, "he was most proud of his garden." Pope's written works related to his garden in several ways. They set forth its principles; they recorded its particulars and effects; but first and foremost, they financed it. In 1718, newly prosperous with the profits from his translation of Homer's *Iliad*, the poet bought a small riverside estate in the village of Twickenham, a few miles west of London. Here he began to implement the ideas of gardening that he had first propounded in an essay for Steele's paper *The Guardian*, and that he would later elaborate in his *Epistle to Burlington* (see page 2521): "I believe it is no wrong observation, that persons of genius, and those who are most capable of art, are always most fond of nature, as such are chiefly sensible that all art consists in the imitation and study of nature." What impressed visitors about Pope's own garden was the delicate success with which his art both shaped and followed nature. Walpole again: "It was a singular effort of art and taste to impress as much variety and scenery on a spot of five acres. The passing through the gloom from the grotto to the opening day, the retiring and again assembling shades, the dusky groves, the larger lawn . . . are managed with exquisite judgment." The play of openness and enclosure, of light and shadow, suffused another feature of the estate: Pope's cherished grotto. The grotto had originated in necessity. Pope's property was split in two by a busy public road that led to London; on one side of the road lay the river and the poet's house, on the other side lay the gardens proper. The grotto was a tunnel that passed, under the ground and under the road, from the riverbank to the garden, in such a way that an observer situated on either side could savor the vista of the other. For reasons that he sketches in the letter below, Pope came to regard the grotto as a microcosm of all that he valued in his property and in his poetry—as "the best imitation of nature" he had ever produced. Friends concurred. Swift commended Pope for having "turned a blunder into a beauty which is a piece of *ars poetica* [poetic art]"; William Warburton later remarked that in the grotto at Twickenham, "the beauty of [Pope's] poetic genius . . . appears to as much advantage as in his best contrived poems."

from **Letter to Edward Blount**[1]
[GROTTO AND GARDEN]

2 June 1725

* * * Let the young ladies[2] be assured I make nothing new in my gardens without wishing to see the print of their fairy steps in every part of 'em. I have put the last hand to my works of this kind,[3] in happily finishing the subterraneous way and grotto; I there found a spring of the clearest water, which falls in a perpetual rill, that echoes through the cavern day and night. From the river Thames, you see through my arch up a walk of the wilderness to a kind of open temple, wholly composed of shells in the rustic manner; and from that distance[4] under the temple you look down through a sloping arcade of trees, and see the sails on the river passing suddenly and vanishing, as through a perspective glass. When you shut the doors of this grotto, it

---

1. Patriarch of an eminent Roman Catholic family, Edward Blount was a friend of Pope's, and the father of Martha (1690–1762), with whom the poet carried on an ardent, playful, and sustained friendship and correspondence.

2. Blount's daughters, Martha and Teresa.

3. Despite frequent announcements to this effect, Pope's work on and "revision" of his garden continued to the end of his life.

4. I.e., from that vantage point: from within the garden, looking back through the temple and grotto out onto the river.

William Kent. A sketch of Pope's garden, fancifully embellished, c. 1725–1730. The low central arch opens into the grotto and onto the Thames, where a passing boat can be seen.

becomes on the instant, from a luminous room, a *camera obscura*; on the walls of which all the objects of the river, hills, woods, and boats, are forming a moving picture in their visible radiations. And when you have a mind to light it up, it affords you a very different scene: it is finished with shells interspersed with pieces of looking glass in angular forms; and in the ceiling is a star of the same material, at which when a lamp (of an orbicular figure of thin alabaster) is hung in the middle, a thousand pointed rays glitter and are reflected over the place. There are connected to this grotto by a narrower passage two porches, with niches and seats; one toward the river, of smooth stones, full of light and open; the other toward the arch of trees, rough with shells, flints, and iron ore. The bottom is paved with simple pebble, as the adjoining walk up the wilderness to the temple is to be cockleshells, in the natural taste, agreeing not ill with the little dripping murmur, and the aquatic idea of the whole place. It wants nothing to complete it but a good statue with an inscription, like that beautiful antique one which you know I am so fond of,

> *Huius Nympha loci, sacri, custodia fontis,*
> *Dormio, dum blandae sentio murmur aquae.*
> *Parce meum, quisquis tangis cava marmora somnum*
> *Rumpere, seu bibas, sive lavere, tace.*

> Nymph of the grot, these sacred springs I keep,
> And to the murmur of these waters sleep;
> Whoe'er thou art, ah gently tread the cave,
> Ah bathe in silence, or in silence lave.

You'll think I have been very poetical in this description, but it is pretty near the truth. I wish you were here to bear testimony how little it owes to art, either the place itself, or the image I give of it.

⊷ ⇌♦⇋ ⊶

Horace Walpole
1717–1797

In 1747, three years after Pope's death, Horace Walpole, devoted son of the late, cunning, and notoriously powerful Whig prime minister Robert (whom Pope had utterly detested), moved into the neighborhood of Twickenham, acquiring (and soon expanding) a five-acre estate he named Strawberry Hill. There he spent half a century, collecting and cataloguing artworks and curiosities, writing scholarly tracts and deft, gossipy letters, printing works by himself and others on his private press, and developing and implementing his own notions in architecture and landscape. As a builder, Walpole cultivated his fascination with the Gothic—with castles, battlements, arches, windows of colored glass; this passion produced literary consequences in his novella *The Castle of Otranto* (1764), whose success initiated the long-running fashion for Gothic fiction. As a "gardenist" (he was the one who coined the term), Walpole extended the innovations in openness and deception that he had admired in predecessors like Pope. In the letter excerpted here, he describes the grounds of his estate. He went on to write the first scholarly account of the landscape garden, his brief *History of the Modern Taste in Gardening* (1780). There he celebrated the "ha-ha," that "sunk fence" which freed the garden from sequestration and opened it onto its surroundings (this, he said, was the "capital stroke, the leading step to all that has followed"); and he sung the praises of its purported inventor, William Kent (1685–1748), as the presiding genius of many places, made beautiful by his key discovery: "He leaped the fence, and saw that all nature was a garden."

from Letter to Sir Horace Mann[1]
[THE GARDEN AT STRAWBERRY HILL]

12 June 1753

I could not rest any longer with the thought of your having no idea of a place of which you hear so much, and therefore desired Mr. Bentley[2] to draw you as much idea of it, as the post would be persuaded to carry from Twickenham to Florence. The enclosed enchanted little landscape then is Strawberry Hill; and I will try to explain so much of it to you as will help to let you know whereabouts we are, when we are talking to you, for it is uncomfortable in so intimate a correspondence as ours, not to be exactly master of every spot where one another is writing or reading or sauntering. This view of the castle is what I have just finished, and is the only side that will be at all regular. Directly before it is an open grove, through which you see a field which is bounded by a serpentine wood of all kind of trees and flowering shrubs and flowers. The lawn before the house is situated on the top of a small hill, from whence to the left you see the town and church of Twickenham encircling a turn of the river, that looks exactly like a seaport in miniature. The opposite shore is a most delicious

---

1. Horace Mann (1701–1786) was the British envoy at Florence, where Walpole met him in 1739; the two corresponded abundantly, but never met again.
2. Richard Bentley (1708–1782), artist, was a close friend of Walpole's and of Thomas Gray's (whose poems he illustrated). He designed many interior elements of the Strawberry Hill house.

meadow, bounded by Richmond Hill, which loses itself in the noble woods of the park to the end of the prospect on the right, where is another turn of the river and the suburbs of Kingston, as luckily placed as Twickenham is on the left; and a natural terrace on the brow of my hill, with meadows of my own down to the river, commands both extremities. Is not this a tolerable prospect? You must figure that all this is perpetually enlivened by a navigation of boats and barges, and by a road below my terrace, with coaches, post chaises, wagons and horsemen constantly in motion, and the fields speckled with cows, horses and sheep. * * *

+→ ≡◊≡ ←+

Edmund Burke
1729–1797

Later celebrated as orator, statesman, and political theorist, the Dublin-born Edmund Burke first achieved fame as an aesthetician. In 1757 he published *A Philosophical Enquiry into the Origin of Our Ideas of the Sublime and Beautiful*, a comparatively short work with a long gestation: he had begun it some ten years earlier, while a student at Trinity College. Burke's arguments about beauty took their starting point in ideas familiar from the work of earlier thinkers (Addison among them). What struck his first reviewers and readers as new, somewhat dubious, and utterly arresting was his elaboration on the sublime, his argument that our strongest emotion, and hence our keenest delight, originates not in objects merely beautiful, but in those that "at certain distances" instill in us ideas of fear and pain. In the course of his *Enquiry*, Burke looks at landscape only intermittently, but others readily elaborated his aesthetics into terms of terrain. "What are the scenes of nature," asked the Scots rhetorician Hugh Blair, "that elevate the mind in the highest degree, and produce the sublime sensation? Not the gay landscape, the flowery field, or the flourishing city; but the hoary mountain, and the solitary lake; the aged forest, and the torrent falling over the rock." Beginning with Burke's *Enquiry*, the search for "sublime sensation," in landscapes and in literature, took on high purpose and strong momentum.

from A Philosophical Enquiry into the Origin of Our Ideas of the Sublime and the Beautiful

OF THE SUBLIME[1]

Whatever is fitted in any sort to excite the ideas of pain and danger, that is to say, whatever is in any sort terrible, or is conversant about terrible objects, or operates in a manner analogous to terror, is a source of the *sublime*; that is, it is productive of the strongest emotion which the mind is capable of feeling. I say the strongest emotion, because I am satisfied the ideas of pain are much more powerful than those which enter on the part of pleasure. Without all doubt, the torments which we may be made to suffer, are much greater in their effect on the body and mind, than any pleasures which the most learned voluptuary could suggest, or than the liveliest imagination, and the most sound and exquisitely sensible body could enjoy. Nay I am in great doubt, whether any man could be found who would earn a life of the most perfect satisfaction, at the price of ending it in the torments which justice inflicted in a few hours on the late unfortunate regicide in France.[2] But as pain is stronger in its operation than pleasure, so death is in general a much more affecting idea than pain;

1. Part 1, Section 7.
2. For his failed attempt to murder Louis XV, Robert

Francis Damiens (1714–1757) was elaborately tortured, then executed.

because there are very few pains, however exquisite, which are not preferred to death; nay, what generally makes pain itself, if I may say so, more painful, is, that it is considered as an emissary of this king of terrors. When danger or pain press too nearly, they are incapable of giving any delight, and are simply terrible; but at certain distances, and with certain modifications, they may be, and they are delightful, as we every day experience. The cause of this I shall endeavor to investigate hereafter.

OF THE PASSION CAUSED BY THE SUBLIME[3]

The passion caused by the great and sublime in *nature*, when those causes operate most powerfully, is Astonishment; and astonishment is that state of the soul, in which all its motions are suspended, with some degree of horror. In this case the mind is so entirely filled with its object, that it cannot entertain any other, nor by consequence reason on that object which employs it. Hence arises the great power of the sublime, that far from being produced by them, it anticipates our reasonings, and hurries us on by an irresistible force. Astonishment, as I have said, is the effect of the sublime in its highest degree; the inferior effects are admiration, reverence, and respect.

from POWER[4]

Besides these things which *directly* suggest the idea of danger, and those which produce a similar effect from a mechanical cause, I know of nothing sublime which is not some modification of power. And this branch rises as naturally as the other two branches, from terror, the common stock of everything that is sublime. The idea of power at first view seems of the class of these indifferent ones, which may equally belong to pain or to pleasure. But in reality, the affection arising from the idea of vast power is extremely remote from that neutral character. For first, we must remember that the idea of pain, in its highest degree, is much stronger than the highest degree of pleasure; and that it preserves the same superiority through all the subordinate gradations. From hence it is, that where the chances for equal degrees of suffering or enjoyment are in any sort equal, the idea of the suffering must always be prevalent. And indeed the ideas of pain, and above all of death, are so very affecting, that whilst we remain in the presence of whatever is supposed to have the power of inflicting either, it is impossible to be perfectly free from terror. Again, we know by experience that for the enjoyment of pleasure, no great efforts of power are at all necessary; nay we know that such efforts would go a great way towards destroying our satisfaction: for pleasure must be stolen, and not forced upon us; pleasure follows the will; and therefore we are generally affected with it by many things of a force greatly inferior to our own. But pain is always inflicted by a power in some way superior, because we never submit to pain willingly. So that strength, violence, pain, and terror are ideas that rush in upon the mind together. Look at a man, or any other animal of prodigious strength, and what is your idea before reflection? Is it that this strength will be subservient to you, to your ease, to your pleasure, to your interest in any sense? No; the emotion you feel is, lest this enormous strength should be employed to the purposes of rapine and destruction. That power derives all its sublimity from the terror with which it is generally accompanied, will appear evidently from its effect in the very few cases in which it may be possible to strip a considerable degree of strength of

---

3. Part 2, Section 1.   4. From Part 2, Section 5.

its ability to hurt. When you do this, you spoil it of everything sublime, and it immediately becomes contemptible. An ox is a creature of vast strength; but he is an innocent creature, extremely serviceable, and not at all dangerous; for which reason the idea of an ox is by no means grand. A bull is strong too; but his strength is of another kind; often very destructive, seldom (at least amongst us) of any use in our business; the idea of a bull is therefore great, and it has frequently a place in sublime descriptions, and elevating comparisons. Let us look at another strong animal in the two distinct lights in which we may consider him. The horse in the light of an useful beast, fit for the plow, the road, the draft, in every social useful light the horse has nothing of the sublime; but is it thus that we are affected with him, *whose neck is clothed with thunder, the glory of whose nostrils is terrible, who swalloweth the ground with fierceness and rage, neither believeth that it is the sound of the trumpet?*[5] In this description the useful character of the horse entirely disappears, and the terrible and sublime blaze out together. We have continually about us animals of a strength that is considerable, but not pernicious. Amongst these we never look for the sublime: it comes upon us in the gloomy forest, and in the howling wilderness, in the form of the lion, the tiger, the panther, or rhinoceros. Whenever strength is only useful, and employed for our benefit or our pleasure, then it is never sublime; for nothing can act agreeably to us that does not act in conformity to our will; but to act agreeably to our will, it must be subject to us; and therefore can never be the cause of a grand and commanding conception. The description of the wild ass, in Job, is worked up into no small sublimity, merely by insisting on his freedom, and his setting mankind at defiance; otherwise the description of such an animal could have had nothing noble in it. *Who hath loosed* (says he) *the bands of the wild ass? whose house I have made the wilderness, and the barren land his dwellings. He scorneth the multitude of the city, neither regardeth he the voice of the driver. The range of the mountains is his pasture.*[6] The magnificent description of the unicorn and of leviathan in the same book, is full of the same heightening circumstances. *Will the unicorn be willing to serve thee? canst thou bind the unicorn with his band in the furrow? wilt thou trust him because his strength is great?—Canst thou draw out leviathan with an hook? will he make a covenant with thee? wilt thou take him for a servant forever? shall not one be cast down even at the sight of him?*[7] In short, wheresoever we find strength, and in what light soever we look upon power, we shall all along observe the sublime the concomitant of terror, and contempt the attendant on a strength that is subservient and innoxious. * * *

from VASTNESS[8]

Greatness of dimension is a powerful cause of the sublime. This is too evident, and the observation too common, to need any illustration; it is not so common to consider in what ways greatness of dimension, vastness of extent, or quantity, has the most striking effect. For certainly there are ways and modes wherein the same quantity of extension shall produce greater effects than it is found to do in others. Extension is either in length, height, or depth. Of these the length strikes least; an hundred yards of even ground will never work such an effect as a tower an hundred yards high, or a rock or mountain of that altitude. I am apt to imagine likewise, that

---

5. Job 39.19,20,24. Here and in several ensuing biblical passages, Burke, working from memory and for his own rhetorical purposes, slightly misquotes the Authorized Version.

6. Job 39.5–8.
7. Job 39.9,10,11; 41.1,4,9.
8. Part 2, Section 7.

height is less grand than depth; and that we are more struck at looking down from a precipice, than at looking up at an object of equal height, but of that I am not very positive. A perpendicular has more force in forming the sublime than an inclined plane; and the effects of a rugged and broken surface seem stronger than where it is smooth and polished. It would carry us out of our way to enter in this place into the cause of these appearances, but certain is it they afford a large and fruitful field of speculation. * * *

from INFINITY[9]

Another source of the sublime is *infinity;* if it does not rather belong to the last. Infinity has a tendency to fill the mind with that sort of delightful horror which is the most genuine effect, and truest test of the sublime. There are scarce any things which can become the objects of our senses that are really and in their own nature infinite. But the eye not being able to perceive the bounds of many things, they seem to be infinite, and they produce the same effects as if they were really so. * * *

DIFFICULTY[1]

Another source of greatness is *difficulty.* When any work seems to have required immense force and labor to effect it, the idea is grand. Stonehenge, neither for disposition nor ornament, has anything admirable; but those huge rude masses of stone, set on end, and piled each on other, turn the mind on the immense force necessary for such a work. Nay the rudeness of the work increases this cause of grandeur, as it excludes the idea of art, and contrivance; for dexterity produces another sort of effect, which is different enough from this.

THE SUBLIME AND BEAUTIFUL COMPARED[2]

On closing this general view of beauty, it naturally occurs, that we should compare it with the sublime; and in this comparison there appears a remarkable contrast. For sublime objects are vast in their dimensions, beautiful ones comparatively small; beauty should be smooth, and polished; the great, rugged and negligent; beauty should shun the right line, yet deviate from it insensibly; the great in many cases loves the right line, and when it deviates, it often makes a strong deviation; beauty should not be obscure; the great ought to be dark and gloomy; beauty should be light and delicate; the great ought to be solid, and even massive. They are indeed ideas of a very different nature, one being founded on pain, the other on pleasure; and however they may vary afterwards from the direct nature of their causes, yet these causes keep up an eternal distinction between them, a distinction never to be forgotten by any whose business it is to affect the passions. In the infinite variety of natural combinations we must expect to find the qualities of things the most remote imaginable from each other united in the same object. We must expect also to find combinations of the same kind in the works of art. But when we consider the power of an object upon our passions, we must know that when anything is intended to affect the mind by the force of some predominant property, the affection produced is like to be the more uniform and perfect if all the other properties or qualities of the object be of the same nature, and tending to the same design as the principal;

9. Part 2, Section 8.   2. Part 3, Section 27.
1. Part 2, Section 12.

If black and white blend, soften, and unite,
  A thousand ways, are there no black and white?[3]

If the qualities of the sublime and beautiful are sometimes found united, does this prove that they are the same, does it prove, that they are any way allied, does it prove even that they are not opposite and contradictory? Black and white may soften, may blend, but they are not therefore the same. Nor when they are so softened and blended with each other, or with different colors, is the power of black as black, or of white as white, so strong as when each stands uniform and distinguished.

HOW PAIN CAN BE A CAUSE OF DELIGHT[4]

Providence has so ordered it, that a state of rest and inaction, however it may flatter our indolence, should be productive of many inconveniencies; that it should generate such disorders as may force us to have recourse to some labor, as a thing absolutely requisite to make us pass our lives with tolerable satisfaction; for the nature of rest is to suffer all the parts of our bodies to fall into a relaxation that not only disables the members from performing their functions, but takes away the vigorous tone of fiber which is requisite for carrying on the natural and necessary secretions. At the same time, that in this languid inactive state, the nerves are more liable to the most horrid convulsions than when they are sufficiently braced and strengthened. Melancholy, dejection, despair, and often self-murder, is the consequence of the gloomy view we take of things in this relaxed state of body. The best remedy for all these evils is exercise or *labor*; and labor is a surmounting of *difficulties*, an exertion of the contracting power of the muscles; and as such resembles pain, which consists in tension or contraction, in everything but degree. Labor is not only requisite to preserve the coarser organs in a state fit for their functions, but it is equally necessary to these finer and more delicate organs on which, and by which, the imagination and perhaps the other mental powers act. Since it is probable that not only the inferior parts of the soul, as the passions are called, but the understanding itself makes use of some fine corporeal instruments in its operation; though what they are, and where they are, may be somewhat hard to settle: but that it does make use of such, appears from hence; that a long exercise of the mental powers induces a remarkable lassitude of the whole body; and on the other hand, that great bodily labor, or pain, weakens, and sometimes actually destroys the mental faculties. Now, as a due exercise is essential to the coarse muscular parts of the constitution, and that without this rousing they would become languid, and diseased, the very same rule holds with regard to those finer parts we have mentioned; to have them in proper order, they must be shaken and worked to a proper degree.

WHY VISUAL OBJECTS OF GREAT DIMENSIONS ARE SUBLIME[5]

Vision is performed by having a picture formed by the rays of light which are reflected from the object, painted in one piece, instantaneously, on the retina, or last nervous part of the eye. Or, according to others, there is but one point of any object painted on the eye in such a manner as to be perceived at once; but by moving the eye, we gather up with great celerity the several parts of the object, so as to

---

3. Alexander Pope, *Essay on Man* 2.213–214 (Pope wrote
is rather than *are*).

4. Part 4, Section 6.
5. Part 4, Section 9.

form one uniform piece. If the former opinion be allowed, it will be considered, that though all the light reflected from a large body should strike the eye in one instant; yet we must suppose that the body itself is formed of a vast number of distinct points, every one of which, or the ray from every one, makes an impression on the retina. So that, though the image of one point should cause but a small tension of this membrane, another, and another, and another stroke must in their progress cause a very great one, until it arrives at last to the highest degree; and the whole capacity of the eye, vibrating in all its parts, must approach near to the nature of what causes pain, and consequently must produce an idea of the sublime. Again, if we take it that one point only of an object is distinguishable at once, the matter will amount nearly to the same thing, or rather it will make the origin of the sublime from greatness of dimension yet clearer. For if but one point is observed at once, the eye must traverse the vast space of such bodies with great quickness, and consequently the fine nerves and muscles destined to the motion of that part must be very much strained; and their great sensibility must make them highly affected by this straining. Besides, it signifies just nothing to the effect produced, whether a body has its parts connected and makes its impression at once; or making but one impression of a point at a time, it causes a succession of the same, or others, so quickly, as to make them seem united; as is evident from the common effect of whirling about a lighted torch or piece of wood; which if done with celerity, seems a circle of fire.

How Words Influence the Passions[6]

Now, as words affect, not by any original power, but by representation, it might be supposed that their influence over the passions should be but light; yet it is quite otherwise; for we find by experience that eloquence and poetry are as capable, nay indeed much more capable of making deep and lively impressions than any other arts, and even than nature itself in very many cases. And this arises chiefly from these three causes. First, that we take an extraordinary part in the passions of others, and that we are easily affected and brought into sympathy by any tokens which are shown of them; and there are no tokens which can express all the circumstances of most passions so fully as words; so that if a person speaks upon any subject, he can not only convey the subject to you, but likewise the manner in which he is himself affected by it. Certain it is, that the influence of most things on our passions is not so much from the things themselves, as from our opinions concerning them; and these again depend very much on the opinions of other men, conveyable for the most part by words only. Secondly, there are many things of a very affecting nature, which can seldom occur in the reality, but the words which represent them often do; and thus they have an opportunity of making a deep impression and taking root in the mind, whilst the idea of the reality was transient; and to some perhaps never really occurred in any shape, to whom it is notwithstanding very affecting, as war, death, famine, etc. Besides, many ideas have never been at all presented to the senses of any men but by words, as God, angels, devils, heaven and hell, all of which have however a great influence over the passions. Thirdly, by words we have it in our power to make such *combinations* as we cannot possibly do otherwise. By this power of combining we are able, by

6. Part 5, section 7; this is the final section of the *Enquiry*.

the addition of well-chosen circumstances, to give a new life and force to the simple object. In painting we may represent any fine figure we please; but we never can give it those enlivening touches which it may receive from words. To represent an angel in a picture, you can only draw a beautiful young man winged; but what painting can furnish out anything so grand as the addition of one word, "the angel of the *Lord*"? It is true, I have here no clear idea, but these words affect the mind more than the sensible image did, which is all I contend for. A picture of Priam[7] dragged to the altar's foot, and there murdered, if it were well executed would undoubtedly be very moving; but there are very aggravating circumstances which it could never represent.

> *Sanguine foedantem quos ipse sacraverat ignes.*[8]

As a further instance, let us consider those lines of Milton, where he describes the travels of the fallen angels through their dismal habitation,

> —O'er many a dark and dreary vale
> They pass'd, and many a region dolorous;
> O'er many a frozen, many a fiery Alp;
> Rocks, caves, lakes, fens, bogs, dens and shade of death,
> A universe of death.[9]

Here is displayed the force of union in

> Rocks, caves, lakes, dens, bogs, fens and shades;

which yet would lose the greatest part of their effect, if they were not the

> Rocks, caves, lakes, dens, bogs, fens and shades—
> —of death.

This idea or this affection caused by a word, which nothing but a word could annex to the others, raises a very great degree of the sublime; and this sublime is raised yet higher by what follows, a *universe of death.* Here are again two ideas not presentable but by language; and an union of them great and amazing beyond conception; if they may properly be called ideas, which present no distinct image to the mind— but still it will be difficult to conceive how words can move the passions which belong to real objects, without representing these objects clearly. This is difficult to us, because we do not sufficiently distinguish, in our observations upon language, between a clear expression, and a strong expression. These are frequently confounded with each other, though they are in reality extremely different. The former regards the understanding; the latter belongs to the passions. The one describes a thing as it is; the other describes it as it is felt. Now, as there is a moving tone of voice, an impassioned countenance, an agitated gesture, which affect independently of the things about which they are exerted, so there are words, and certain dispositions of words, which being peculiarly devoted to passionate subjects, and always used by those who are under the influence of any passion, they touch and move us more than those which far more clearly and distinctly express the subject matter. We yield to sympathy what we refuse to description. The truth is, all verbal description, merely as naked description, though never so exact, conveys so poor and insuf-

---

7. King of Troy, slain during the Greek invasion of the city.
8. "Fires which he had sanctified with his own blood"
(Virgil, *Aeneid* 2.502).
9. *Paradise Lost* 2.618–622.

ficient an idea of the thing described, that it could scarcely have the smallest effect, if the speaker did not call in to his aid those modes of speech that mark a strong and lively feeling in himself. Then, by the contagion of our passions, we catch a fire already kindled in another, which probably might never have been struck out by the object described. Words, by strongly conveying the passions, by those means which we have already mentioned, fully compensate for their weakness in other respects. It may be observed that very polished languages, and such as are praised for their superior clearness and perspicuity, are generally deficient in strength. The French language has that perfection, and that defect. Whereas the Oriental tongues, and in general the languages of most unpolished people, have a great force and energy of expression; and this is but natural. Uncultivated people are but ordinary observers of things, and not critical in distinguishing them; but, for that reason, they admire more, and are more affected with what they see, and therefore express themselves in a warmer and more passionate manner. If the affection be well conveyed, it will work its effect without any clear idea; often without any idea at all of the thing which has originally given rise to it.

It might be expected from the fertility of the subject, that I should consider poetry as it regards the sublime and beautiful more at large; but it must be observed that in this light it has been often and well handled already. It was not my design to enter into the criticism of the sublime and beautiful in any art, but to attempt to lay down such principles as may tend to ascertain, to distinguish, and to form a sort of standard for them; which purposes I thought might be best effected by an enquiry into the properties of such things in nature as raise love and astonishment in us; and by showing in what manner they operated to produce these passions. Words were only so far to be considered, as to show upon what principle they were capable of being the representatives of these natural things, and by what powers they were able to affect us often as strongly as the things they represent, and sometimes much more strongly.

1747–1754   1757

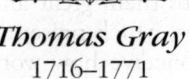

Thomas Gray
1716–1771

Having first found fame for meditations purportedly generated within the close confines of a country churchyard (see page 2685), Thomas Gray went on to set new precedents for the observation and description of larger landscapes, broader vistas. During a tour of the Lake District, Gray wrote and dispatched a continuous travel journal to his friend Thomas Wharton, who had been prevented by illness from accompanying him. The text of the journal first appeared (much garbled) in the collection of Gray's poems and letters compiled by his friend William Mason four years after the poet's death. Once it made its way into print, Gray's journal did much to establish the fashion for picturesque travel, to model new ways in which landscapes (and the Lake District in particular) might be looked on, wondered at, written up.

from A Journal-Letter to Thomas Wharton
[THE SUBLIME AND THE BEAUTIFUL IN THE LAKE DISTRICT]

3 October [1769]: * * * In the evening walked alone down to the lake by the side of Crow Park after sunset and saw the solemn coloring of night draw on, the last gleam of sunshine fading away on the hilltops, the deep serene of the waters, and the long shad-

ows of the mountains thrown across them, till they nearly touched the hithermost shore. At distance heard the murmur of many waterfalls not audible in the daytime. Wished for the moon, but she was *dark to me and silent, hid in her vacant interlunar cave*.[1]

4 October: Wind east; clouds and sunshine, and in the course of the day a few drops of rain. Walked to Crow Park, now a rough pasture, once a glade of ancient oaks, whose large roots still remain on the ground, but nothing has sprung from them. If one single tree had remained, this would have been an unparalleled spot, and Smith[2] judged right, when he took his print of the lake from hence, for it is a gentle eminence, not too high, on the very margin of the water and commanding it from end to end, looking full into the gorge of Borodale. I prefer it even to Cockshut Hill, which lies beside it, and to which I walked in the afternoon. It is covered with young trees both sown and planted, oak, spruce, scotch-fir, etc., all which thrive wonderfully. There is an easy ascent to the top, and the view far preferable to that on Castle Hill (which you remember) because this is lower and nearer to the Lake: for I find all points, that are much elevated, spoil the beauty of the valley, and make its parts (which are not large) look poor and diminutive.[3] While I was here, a little shower fell, red clouds came marching up the hills from the east, and part of a bright rainbow seemed to rise along the side of Castle Hill.

From hence I got to the parsonage a little before sunset, and saw in my glass[4] a picture, that if I could transmit to you, and fix it in all the softness of its living colors, would fairly sell for a thousand pounds. This is the sweetest scene I can yet discover in point of pastoral beauty. The rest are in a sublimer style. (to be continued *without end*.[5])

1775

◆━━◆◆◆━━◆

William Gilpin
1724–1804

William Gilpin was a vicar by vocation; scrupulous and generous, he founded a poorhouse and a school for the people of his parish. By avocation, he was one of the pioneers of the picturesque. He defined the term anew, in his *Essay on Prints* (1768), as "that kind of beauty which would look well in a picture." Before now, the word had referred (like our "graphic") to qualities within pictures; now it named an attribute of the natural world, to be recognized and savored by the well-instructed viewer. Gilpin went on to provide the instruction, in five books of *Observations* culled during travels to the most picturesque parts of Britain, among them the New Forest, the Scottish Highlands, and the Lake District. In his books, Gilpin described, drew, and analyzed many vistas, suggesting how they should be seen, and prompting unprecedented numbers of people to go and see them. Approaching old age, Gilpin reverted from

1. Gray echoes the blind hero of Milton's *Samson Agonistes*, unable to see the moon (86–89).
2. Thomas Smith (d. 1767), landscape painter, one of the earliest to specialize in the depiction of English vistas.
3. Gray's editor Mason appended this note: "The *picturesque point* is always thus low in all prospects—a truth which, though the landscape painter knows, he cannot always observe; since the patron who employs him to take a view of his place usually carries him to some elevation for that purpose."

4. This was a "Claude glass," so named for the influential French landscape painter Claude Lorrain (1600–1682); it consisted (in Mason's words) of a "convex mirror of about four inches in diameter on a black foil, and bound up like a pocket-book." The purpose and pleasure of the instrument consisted in placing the mirror so that its reflection displayed the landscape as a picture, a fleeting approximation of a painted image.
5. Gray refers jokingly to the journal itself, in terms that echo the "infinite" of Burke's sublime.

practice to theory. In the essay on travel excerpted here, he attempts to place the picturesque among Burke's categories, to restate its underlying principles, and to describe the emotions by which it will reward its dedicated pursuers.

from On Picturesque Travel[1]

That we may examine picturesque objects with more ease, it may be useful to class them into the *sublime* and the *beautiful*; though in fact, this distinction is rather inaccurate. Sublimity alone cannot make an object picturesque. However grand the mountain or the rock may be, it has no claim to this epithet, unless its form, its color, or its accompaniments have *some degree of beauty*. Nothing can be more sublime than the ocean; but wholly unaccompanied, it has little of the picturesque. When we talk therefore of a sublime object, we always understand, that it is also beautiful: and we call it sublime, or beautiful, only as the ideas of sublimity, or of simple beauty, prevail. * * *

The first source of amusement[2] to the picturesque traveler is the pursuit of his object—the expectation of new scenes continually opening, and arising to his view. We suppose the country to have been unexplored. Under this circumstance the mind is kept constantly in an agreeable suspense. The love of novelty is the foundation of this pleasure. Every distant horizon promises something new; and with this pleasing expectation we follow nature through all her walks. We pursue her from hill to dale, and hunt after those various beauties, with which she everywhere abounds.

The pleasures of the chase are universal. A hare started before dogs is enough to set a whole country in an uproar. The plow and the spade are deserted. Care is left behind; and every human faculty is dilated with joy.

And shall we suppose it a greater pleasure to the sportsman to pursue a trivial animal, than it is to the man of taste to pursue the beauties of nature? to follow her through all her recesses? to obtain a sudden glance, as she flits past him in some airy shape? to trace her through the mazes of the cover? to wind after her along the vale? or along the reaches of the river?

After the pursuit we are gratified with the *attainment* of the object. Our amusement, on this head, arises from the employment of the mind in examining the beautiful scenes we have found. Sometimes we examine them under the idea of a *whole*: we admire the composition, the coloring, and the light, in one *comprehensive view*. When we are fortunate enough to fall in with scenes of this kind, we are highly delighted. But as we have less frequent opportunities of being thus gratified, we are more commonly employed in analyzing the *parts of scenes*, which may be exquisitely beautiful, though unable to produce a whole. We examine what would amend the composition; how little is wanting to reduce it to the rules of our art; what a trifling circumstance sometimes forms the limit between beauty and deformity. Or we compare the objects before us with other objects of the same kind—or perhaps we compare them with the imitations of art. From all these operations of the mind results great amusement.

But it is not from this *scientifical* employment that we derive our chief pleasure. We are most delighted when some grand scene, though perhaps of incorrect composition, rising before the eye, strikes us beyond the power of thought—when the *vox faucibus haeret*,[3] and every mental operation is suspended. In this pause of intellect;

1. This is the second of Gilpin's *Three Essays* (*On Picturesque Beauty*, *On Picturesque Travel*, and *On Sketching Landscapes*).
2. The word meant "entertainment," but without the lat-

er connotation of comedy.
3. "The voice sticks in the throat." Gilpin echoes a line from Virgil's *Aeneid* (12.868) in which the warrior Turnus is overcome by terror.

this *deliquirium*[4] of the soul, an enthusiastic sensation of pleasure overspreads it, previous to any examination by the rules of art. The general idea of the scene makes an impression, before any appeal is made to the judgment. We rather *feel*, than *survey* it.

1792

[END OF PERSPECTIVES: LANDSCAPE, PLEASURE, POWER]

4. Dissolution; melting away.

POLITICAL AND RELIGIOUS ORDERS

One political order that cannot be ignored by readers of British literature and history is the monarchy, since it provides the terms by which historical periods are even today divided up. Thus much of the nineteenth century is often spoken of as the "Victorian" age or period, after Queen Victoria (reigned 1837–1901), and the writing of the period is given the name Victorian literature. By the same token, writing of the period 1559–1603 is often called "Elizabethan" after Elizabeth I, and that of 1901–1910 "Edwardian" after Edward VII. This system however is based more on convention than logic, since few would call the history (or literature) of late twentieth-century Britain "Elizabethan" any more than they would call the history and literature of the eighteenth century "Georgian," though four king Georges reigned between 1714 and 1820. Where other, better terms exist these are generally adopted.

As these notes suggest, however, it is still common to think of British history in terms of the dates of the reigning monarch, even though the political influence of the monarchy has been strictly limited since the seventeenth century. Thus, where an outstanding political figure has emerged it is he or she who tends to name the period of a decade or longer; for the British, for example, the 1980s was the decade of "Thatcherism" as for Americans it was the period of "Reaganomics." The monarchy, though, still provides a point of common reference and has up to now shown a remarkable historical persistence, transforming itself as occasion dictates to fit new social circumstances. Thus, while most of the other European monarchies disappeared early in the twentieth century, if they had not already done so, the British institution managed to transform itself from imperial monarchy, a role adopted in the nineteenth century, to become the head of a welfare state and member of the European Union. Few of the titles gathered by Queen Victoria, such as Empress of India, remain to Elizabeth II (reigns 1952–), whose responsibilities now extend only to the British Isles with some vestigial role in Australia, Canada, and New Zealand among other places.

The monarchy's political power, like that of the aristocracy, has been successively diminished over the past several centuries, with the result that today both monarch and aristocracy have only formal authority. This withered state of today's institutions, however, should not blind us to the very real power they wielded in earlier centuries. Though the medieval monarch King John had famously been obliged to recognize the rule of law by signing the Magna Carta ("Great Charter") in 1215, thus ending arbitrary rule, the sixteenth- and seventeenth-century English monarchs still officially ruled by "divine right" and were under no obligation to attend to the wishes of Parliament. Charles I in the 1630s reigned mostly without summoning a parliament, and the concept of a "constitutional monarchy," being one whose powers were formally bound by statute, was introduced only when King William agreed to the Declaration of Right in 1689. This document, together with the contemporaneous Bill of Rights, while recognizing that sovereignty still rests in the monarch, formally transferred executive and legislative powers to Parliament. Bills still have to receive Royal Assent, though this was last denied by Queen Anne in 1707; the monarch still holds "prerogative" powers, though these, which include the appointment of certain officials, the dissolution of Parliament and so on, are, in practice wielded by the prime minister. Further information on the political character of various historical periods can be found in the period introductions.

Political power in Britain is thus held by the prime minister and his or her cabinet, members of which are also members of the governing party in the House of Commons. As long as the government is able to command a majority in the House of Commons, sometimes by a coalition of several parties but more usually by the absolute majority of one, it both makes the laws and carries them out. The situation is therefore very different from the American doctrine of the "Separation of Powers," in which Congress is independent of the President and can even be controlled by the opposing party. The British state of affairs has led to the office of prime minister being compared to that of an "elected dictatorship" with surprising frequency over the past several hundred years.

British government is bicameral, having both an upper and a lower house. Unlike other bicameral systems, however, the upper house, the House of Lords, is not elected, its membership being largely hereditary. Membership can come about in four main ways: (1) by birth, (2) by appointment by the current prime minister often in consultation with the Leader of the Opposition, (3) by virtue of holding a senior position in the judiciary, and (4) by being a bishop of the Established Church (the Church of England). In the House of Commons, the lower house, the particular features of the British electoral system have meant that there are never more than two large parties, one of which is in power. These are, together, "Her Majesty's Government and Opposition." Local conditions in Northern Ireland and Scotland have meant that these areas sometimes send members to Parliament in London who are members neither of the Conservative nor of the Labour parties; in general, however, the only other group in the Commons is the small Liberal Party.

Taking these categories in turn, all members of the hereditary aristocracy (the "peerage") have a seat in the House of Lords. The British aristocracy, unlike those of other European countries, was never formally dispossessed of political power (for example by a revolution), and though their influence is now limited, nevertheless all holders of hereditary title—dukes, marquesses, earls, viscounts and barons, in that order of precedence—sit in the Lords. Some continue to do political work and may be members of the Government or of the Opposition, though today it would be considered unusual for a senior member of government to sit in the House of Lords. The presence of the hereditary element in the Lords tends to give the institution a conservative tone, though the presence of the other members ensures this is by no means always the case. Secondly there are "life peers," who are created by the monarch on the prime minister's recommendation under legislation dating from 1958. They are generally individuals who have distinguished themselves in one field or another; retiring senior politicians from the Commons are generally elevated to the Lords, for example, as are some senior civil servants, diplomats, business and trade union leaders, academics, figures in the arts, retiring archbishops, and members of the military. Some of these take on formal political responsibilities and others do not. Finally, senior members of the judiciary sit in the Lords as Law Lords, while senior members of the Church of England hierarchy also sit in the Lords and frequently intervene in political matters. It has been a matter of some controversy whether senior members of other religious denominations, or religions, should also sit in the House of Lords. Within the constitution (by the Parliament Act of 1911 and other acts) the powers of the House of Lords are limited mostly to the amendment and delay of legislation; from time to time the question of its reform or abolition is raised.

In addition, there are minor orders of nobility that should be mentioned. A baronet is a holder of a hereditary title, but he is not a member of the peerage; the style is Sir (followed by his first and last names), Baronet (usually abbreviated as Bart. or Bt.). A knight is a member of one of the various orders of British knighthood, the oldest of which dates back to the Middle Ages (the Order of the Garter), the majority to the eighteenth or nineteenth centuries (the Order of the Thistle, the Bath, Saint Michael, and Saint George, etc.). The title is nonhereditary and is given for various services; it is marked by various initials coming after the name. K.C.B., for example, stands for "Knight Commander of the Bath," and there are many others.

In the House of Commons itself, the outstanding feature is the dominance of the party system. Party labels, such as "Whigs" and "Tories," were first used from the late seventeenth century, when groups of members began to form opposing factions in a Parliament now freed of much of the power of the king. The "Tories," for example, a name now used to refer to the modern Conservative Party, were originally members of that faction that supported James II (exiled in 1689); the word "Tory" comes from the Irish (Gaelic) for outlaw or thief. The "Whigs," on the other hand, supported the constitutional reforms associated with the 1689 Glorious Revolution; the word "whig" is obscurely related to the idea of regicide. The Whig faction largely dominated the political history of the eighteenth century, though the electorate was too small, and politics too controlled by the patronage of the great aristocratic families, for much of a party system to develop. It was only in the middle decades of the nineteenth century that the familiar party system in parliament and the associated electioneering organization in the country at large came into being. The Whigs were replaced by the Liberal Party around the mid-century, as the Liberals were to be replaced by the Labour Party in the early decades of the twentieth century; the Tories had become firm Conservatives by the time of Lord Derby's administrations in the mid-nineteenth century.

The party system has always been fertile ground for a certain amount of parliamentary theater, and it has fostered the emergence of some powerful personalities. Whereas the eighteenth-century Whig prime minister Sir Robert Walpole owed his authority to a mixture of personal patronage and the power made available through the alliances of powerful families, nineteenth-century figures such as Benjamin Disraeli (Conservative prime minister 1868, 1874–1880) and William Ewart Gladstone (Liberal prime minister 1868–1874; 1880–1885; 1885; 1892–1894), were at the apex of their respective party machines. Disraeli, theatrical, personable and with a keen eye for publicity (he was, among other things, a close personal friend of Queen Victoria), formed a great contrast to the massive moral appeals of his parliamentary opponent Gladstone. One earlier figure, William Pitt (1759–1806), prime minister at twenty-four and leader of the country during the French Revolution and earlier Napoleonic wars, stands comparison with these in the historical record; of twentieth-century political figures, David Lloyd-George, Liberal prime minister during World War I, and Winston Churchill, Conservative, during World War II, deserve special mention.

Though political power in the United Kingdom now rests with Parliament at Westminster in London, this has not always been the only case. Wales, which is now formally a principality within the political construction "England and Wales," was conquered by the English toward the end of the thirteenth century—too early for indigenous representative institutions to have fallen into place. Scotland, on the other hand, which from 1603 was linked with England under a joint monarchy but only became part of the same political entity with the Act of Union in 1707, did develop discrete institutions. Recent votes in both Scotland and Wales are leading toward greater local legislative control over domestic issues in both Scotland and Wales. Many Scottish institutions—for example, the legal and educational systems—are substantially different from those of England, which is not true in the case of Wales. The Church of Scotland in particular has no link with the Church of England, having been separately established in 1690 on a Presbyterian basis; this means that authority in the Scottish church is vested in elected pastors and lay elders and not in an ecclesiastical hierarchy of priests and bishops. But the most vexed of the relationships within the union has undoubtedly been that between England and Ireland.

There has been an English presence in Ireland from the Middle Ages on, and this became dominant in the later sixteenth century when English policy was deliberately to conquer and colonize the rest of the country. The consequence of this policy, however, was that an Irish Protestant "Ascendancy" came to rule over a largely dispossessed Catholic Irish peasantry; in 1689 at the Battle of the Boyne this state of affairs was made permanent, as Irish Catholic support for the exiled and Catholic-sympathizing James II was routed by the invading troops of the new Protestant king, William III. An Irish parliament met in Dublin, but this was restricted to Protestants; the Church of Ireland was the established Protestant church in a country where most of the population was Catholic. Irish political representation was shifted to Westminster by Pitt in 1800 under the formal Act of Union with Ireland; the Church of Ireland was disestablished by Gladstone later in the century. In the twentieth century, continuing agitation in the Catholic south of the country first for Home Rule and subsequently for independence from Britain—agitation that had been a feature of almost the whole nineteenth century at greater or lesser levels of intensity—led to the establishment first of the Irish Free State (1922) and later of the Republic (1948). In the Protestant North of the country, a local parliament met from 1922 within the common framework of the United Kingdom, but this was suspended in 1972 and representation returned to Westminster, as renewed violence in the province threatened local institutions. In Northern Ireland several hundred years of conflict between Protestants, who form the majority of the population in the province, and Catholics have led to continuing political problems.

Since the Reformation in the sixteenth century Britain has officially been a Protestant country with a national church headed by the monarch. This "Established Church," the Church of England or Anglican Church, has its own body of doctrine in the Thirty-Nine Articles and elsewhere, its own order of services in the Book of Common Prayer, and its own translation of the Bible (the "Authorized Version"), commissioned by James I (reigned 1603–1625) as Head of the Church. There is an extensive ecclesiastical hierarchy and a worldwide communion that includes the American Episcopalian Church.

The Reformation in England was not an easy business, and it has certain negative consequences even today. Some of these have been touched upon above in the case of Ireland. Those professing Roman Catholicism were excluded from political office and suffered other penalties until 1829, and a Catholic hierarchy parallel to that of the Church of England only came into being in Britain in the later nineteenth century. Though many of the restrictions on Roman Catholics enacted by Act of Parliament at the end of the seventeenth century were considerably softened in the course of the eighteenth, nevertheless they were very real.

English Protestantism, however, is far from being all of a piece. As early as the sixteenth century, many saw the substitution of the King's authority and that of the national ecclesiastical hierarchy for that of the Pope to be no genuine Protestant Reformation, which they thought demanded local autonomy and individual judgment. In the seventeenth century many "dissenting" or "Non-Conformist" Protestant sects thus grew up or gathered strength (many becoming "Puritans"), and these rejected the authority of the national church and its bishops and so the authority of the king. They had a brief moment of freedom during the Civil War and the Commonwealth (1649–1660) following the execution of Charles I, when there was a flowering of sects from Baptists and Quakers, which still exist today, to Ranters, Shakers, Anabaptists, Muggletonians, etc., which in the main do not (except for some sects in the United States). The monarchy and the Church were decisively reestablished in 1660, but subsequent legislation, most importantly the Act of Toleration (1689), suspended laws against dissenters on certain conditions.

Religious dissent or nonconformity remained powerful social movements over the following centuries and received new stimulus from the "New Dissenting" revivalist movements of the eighteenth century (particularly Methodism, though there was also a growth in the Congregationalist and Baptist churches). By the nineteenth century, the social character and geographical pattern of English dissent had been established: religious nonconformity was a feature of the new working classes brought into being by the Industrial Revolution in the towns of the Midlands and North of England. Anglicanism, which was associated with the pre-industrial traditional order, was rejected also by many among the rising bourgeoisie and lower middle classes; almost every major English novel of the mid-nineteenth century and beyond is written against a background of religious nonconformity or dissent, which had complex social and political meanings. Nonconformity was also a particular feature of Welsh society.

Under legislation enacted by Edward I in 1290, the Jews were expelled from England, and there were few of them in the country until the end of the seventeenth century, when well-established Jewish communities began to appear in London (the medieval legislation was repealed under the Commonwealth in the 1650s). Restrictions on Jews holding public office continued until the mid-nineteenth century, and at the end of the century large Jewish communities were formed in many English cities by refugees from Central and Eastern European anti-Semitism.

Britain today is a multicultural country and significant proportions of the population, many of whom came to Britain from former British Empire territories, profess Hinduism or Islam, among other religions. The United Kingdom has been a member of the European Union since the early 1970s, and this has further loosened ties between Britain and former empire territories or dominions, many of which are still linked to Britain by virtue of the fact that the British monarch is Head of the "Commonwealth," an organization to which many of them belong. In some cases, the British monarch is also Head of State. Most importantly, however, British membership of the European Union has meant that powers formerly held by the national parliament have been transferred either to the European Parliament in Strasbourg, France, or to the European Commission, the executive agency in Brussels, Belgium, or, in the case of judicial review and appeal, to the European Court of Justice. This process seems set to generate tensions in Britain for some years to come.

David Tresilian

ENGLISH MONARCHS

Before the Norman conquest (1066), these included:

Alfred the Great	871–899
Edmund I	940–946
Ethelred the Unready	948–1016
Edward the Confessor	1042–1066
Harold II	1066

The following monarchs are divided by the dynasty ("House") to which they belong:

Normandy

William I the Conqueror	1066–1087
William II, Rufus	1087–1100
Henry I	1100–1135

Blois

Stephen	1135–1154

Plantagenet

Henry II	1154–1189
Richard I "Coeur de Lion"	1189–1199
John	1199–1216
Henry III	1216–1272
Edward I	1272–1307
Edward II	1307–1327
Edward III	1327–1377
Richard II	1377–1400

Lancaster

Henry IV	1399–1413
Henry V	1413–1422
Henry VI	1422–1471

York

Edward IV	1461–1483
Edward V	1483
Richard III	1483–1485

Tudor

Henry VII	1485–1509
Henry VIII	1509–1547
Edward VI	1547–1553
Mary I	1553–1558
Elizabeth I	1558–1603

Kings of England and of Scotland:
Stuart

James I (James VI of Scotland)	1603–1625
Charles I	1625–1649

Commonwealth (Republic)

Council of State	1649–1653
Oliver Cromwell, Lord Protector	1653–1658
Richard Cromwell	1658–1660

Stuart

Charles II	1660–1685
James II	1685–1688
(Interregnum 1688–1689)	
William III and Mary II	1685–1701 (Mary dies 1694)
Anne	1702–1714

Hanover

George I	1714–1727
George II	1727–1760
George III	1760–1820
George IV	1820–1830
William IV	1830–1837
Victoria	1837–1901

Saxe-Coburg and Gotha

Edward VII	1901–1910

Windsor

George V	1910–1936
Edward VIII	1936
George VI	1936–1952
Elizabeth II	1952–

LITERARY AND CULTURAL TERMS[*]

Absolutism. In criticism, the belief in irreducible, unchanging values of form and content that underlie the tastes of individuals and periods and arise from the stability of an absolute hierarchical order.

Accent. Stress or emphasis on a syllable, as opposed to the syllable's length of duration, its quantity. *Metrical accent* denotes the metrical pattern ($\smile$ –) to which writers fit and adjust accented words and rhetorical emphases, keeping the meter as they substitute word-accented feet and tune their rhetoric.

Accentual Verse. Verse with lines established by counting accents only, without regard to the number of unstressed syllables. This was the dominant form of verse in English until the time of Chaucer.

Acrostic. Words arranged, frequently in a poem or puzzle, to disclose a hidden word or message when the correct combination of letters is read in sequence.

Aestheticism. Devotion to beauty. The term applies particularly to a 19th-century literary and artistic movement celebrating beauty as independent from morality, and praising form above content; art for art's sake.

Aesthetics. The study of the beautiful; the branch of philosophy concerned with defining the nature of art and establishing criteria of judgment.

Alexandrine. A six-foot iambic pentameter line.

Allegorical Meaning. A secondary meaning of a narrative in addition to its primary meaning or literal meaning.

Allegory. A story that suggests another story. The first part of this word comes from the Greek *allos*, "other." An allegory is present in literature whenever it is clear that the author is saying, "By this I also mean that." In practice, allegory appears when a progression of events or images suggests a translation of them into conceptual language. Allegory is thus a technique of aligning imaginative constructs, mythological or poetic, with conceptual or moral models. During the Romantic era a distinction arose between allegory and symbol. With Coleridge, symbol took precedence: "an allegory is but a translation of abstract notions into picture-language," but "a symbol always partakes of the reality which it makes intelligible."

Alliteration. "Adding letters" (Latin *ad* + *littera*, "letter"). Two or more words, or accented syllables, chime on the same initial letter (*l*ost *l*ove *a*lone; *a*fter *a*pple-picking) or repeat the same consonant.

Alliterative Revival. The outburst of alliterative verse that occurred in the second half of the 14th century in west and northwest England.

Alliterative Verse. Verse using alliteration on stressed syllables for its fundamental structure.

Allusion. A meaningful reference, direct or indirect, as when William Butler Yeats writes, "Another Troy must rise and set," calling to mind the whole tragic history of Troy.

Amplification. A restatement of something more fully and in more detail, especially in oratory, poetry, and music.

Analogy. A comparison between things similar in a number of ways; frequently used to explain the unfamiliar by the familiar.

Anapest. A metrical foot: $\smile \smile$ –.

Anaphora. The technique of beginning successive clauses or lines with the same word.

[*]Adapted from *The Harper Handbook to Literature* by Northrop Frye, Sheridan Baker, George Perkins, and Barbara M. Perkins, 2d edition (Longman, 1997).

Anatomy. Greek for "a cutting up": a dissection, analysis, or systematic study. The term was popular in titles in the 16th and 17th centuries.

Anglo-Norman (Language). The language of upper-class England after the Norman Conquest in 1066.

Anglo-Saxon. The people, culture, and language of three neighboring tribes—Jutes, Angles, and Saxons—who invaded England, beginning in 449, from the lower part of Denmark's Jutland Peninsula. The Angles, settling along the eastern seaboard of central and northern England, developed the first literate culture of any Germanic people. Hence England (Angle-land) became the dominant term.

Antagonist. In Greek drama, the character who opposes the protagonist, or hero: therefore, any character who opposes another. In some works, the antagonist is clearly the villain (Iago in *Othello*), but in strict terminology an antagonist is merely an opponent and may be in the right.

Anthropomorphism. The practice of giving human attributes to animals, plants, rivers, winds, and the like, or to such entities as Grecian urns and abstract ideas.

Antithesis. (1) A direct contrast or opposition. (2) The second phase of dialectical argument, which considers the opposition—the three steps being *thesis, antithesis, synthesis*. (3) A rhetorical figure sharply contrasting ideas in balanced parallel structures.

Aphorism. A pithy saying of known authorship, as distinguished from a folk proverb.

Apology. A justification, as in Sir Philip Sidney's *The Apology for Poetry* (1595).

Apostrophe. (Greek, "a turning away"). An address to an absent or imaginary person, a thing, or a personified abstraction.

Archaism. An archaic or old-fashioned word or expression—for example, *o'er, ere,* or *darkling*.

Archetype. (1) The first of a genre, like Homer's *Iliad*, the first heroic epic. (2) A natural symbol imprinted in human consciousness by experience and literature, like dawn symbolizing hope or an awakening; night, death or repose.

Assonance. Repetition of middle vowel sounds: *fight, hive; pane, make*. Assonance, most effective on stressed syllables, is often found within a line of poetry; less frequently it substitutes for end rhyme.

Aubade. Dawn song, from French *aube*, for dawn. The aubade originated in the Middle Ages as a song sung by a lover greeting the dawn, ordinarily expressing regret that morning means parting.

Avant-Garde. Experimental, innovative, at the forefront of a literary or artistic trend or movement. The term is French for *vanguard*, the advance unit of an army. It frequently suggests a struggle with tradition and convention.

Ballad. A narrative poem in short stanzas, with or without music. The term derives by way of French *ballade* from Latin *ballare*, "to dance," and once meant a simple song of any kind, lyric or narrative, especially one to accompany a dance. As ballads evolved, most lost their association with dance, although they kept their strong rhythms. Modern usage distinguishes three major kinds: the anonymous *traditional ballad* (popular ballad or *folk ballad*), transmitted orally; the *broadside ballad*, printed and sold on single sheets; and the *literary ballad* (or art ballad), a sophisticated imitation of the traditional ballad.

Ballad Stanza. The name for common meter as found in ballads: a quatrain in iambic meter, alternating tetrameter and trimeter lines, usually rhyming *abcb*.

Bard. An ancient Celtic singer of the culture's lore in epic form; a poetic term for any poet.

Baroque. (1) A richly ornamented style in architecture and art. Founded in Rome by Frederigo Barocci about 1550, and characterized by swirling allegorical frescoes on ceilings and walls, it flourished throughout Europe until 1700. (2) A chromatic musical style with strict forms containing similar exuberant ornamentation, flourishing from 1600 to 1750. In literature, Richard Crashaw's bizarre imagery and the conceits and rhythms of John Donne and other metaphysical poets are sometimes called baroque, sometimes mannerist.

Some literary historians designate a Baroque Age from 1580 to 1680, between the Renaissance and the Enlightenment.

Bathos. (1) A sudden slippage from the sublime to the ridiculous. (2) Any anticlimax. (3) Sentimental pathos. (4) Triteness or dullness.

Blank Verse. Unrhymed iambic pentameter. *See also* Meter. In the 1540s Henry Howard, earl of Surrey, seems to have originated it in English as the equivalent of Virgil's unrhymed dactylic hexameter. In *Gorboduc* (1561), Thomas Sackville and Thomas Norton introduced blank verse into the drama, whence it soared with Marlowe and Shakespeare in the 1590s. Milton forged it anew for the epic in *Paradise Lost* (1667).

Bloomsbury Group. An informal social and intellectual group associated with Bloomsbury, a London residential district near the British Museum, from about 1904 until the outbreak of World War II. Virginia Woolf was a principal member. With her husband, Leonard Woolf, she established the Hogarth Press, which published works by many of their friends. The group was loosely knit, but famed, especially in the 1920s, for its exclusiveness, aestheticism, and social and political freethinking.

Broadside. A sheet of paper printed on one side only. Broadsides containing a ballad, a tract, a criminal's gallows speech, a scurrilous satire, and the like were once commonly sold on the streets like newspapers.

Burden. (1) A refrain or set phrase repeated at intervals throughout a song or poem. (2) A bass accompaniment, the "load" carried by the melody, the origin of the term.

Burlesque. (1) A ridicule, especially on the stage, treating the lofty in low style, or the low in grandiose style. (2) A bawdy vaudeville, with obscene clowning and stripteasing.

Caesura. A pause in a metrical line, indicated by punctuation, momentarily suspending the beat (from Latin "a cutting off"). Caesuras are *masculine* at the end of a foot, and *feminine* in mid-foot.

Canon. The writings accepted as forming a part of the Bible, of the works of an author, or of a body of literature. Shakespeare's canon consists of works he wrote, which may be distinguished from works attributed to him but written by others. The word derives from Greek *kanon*, "rod" or "rule," and suggests authority. Canonical authors and texts are those taught most frequently, noncanonical are those rarely taught, and in between are disputed degrees of canonicity for authors considered minor or marginalized.

Canto. A major division in a long poem. The Italian expression is from Latin *cantus*, "song," a section singable in one sitting.

Caricature. Literary cartooning, depicting characters with exaggerated physical traits such as huge noses and bellies, short stature, squints, tics, humped backs, and so forth. Sir Thomas Browne seems to have introduced the term into English in 1682 from the Italian *caricatura*.

Catalog. In literature, an enumeration of ancestors, of ships, of warriors, of a woman's beauties, and the like; a standard feature of the classical epic.

Celtic Revival. In the 18th century, a groundswell of the Romantic movement in discovering the power in ancient, primitive poetry, particularly Welsh and Scottish Gaelic, as distinct from that of the classics.

Chiasmus. A rhetorical balance created by the inversion of one of two parallel phrases or clauses; from the Greek for a "placing crosswise," as in the Greek letter χ (chi).

Chronicle. A kind of history, with the emphasis on *time* (Greek *chronos*). Events are described in order as they occurred. The chronicles of the Middle Ages provided material for later writers and serve now as important sources of knowledge about the period. Raphael Holinshed's *Chronicle* (1577) is especially famous as the immediate source of much of Shakespeare's knowledge of English history.

Chronicle Play. A play dramatizing historical events, as from a chronicle. Chronicle plays tend to stress time order, presenting the reign of a king, for example, with much emphasis on pageantry and little on the unity of action and dramatic conflict necessary for a tragedy.

Classical Literature. (1) The literature of ancient Greece and Rome. (2) Later literature reflecting the qualities of classical Greece or Rome. *See also,* Classicism; Neoclassicism. (3) The classic literature of any time or place, as, for example, classical American literature or classical Japanese literature.

Classicism. A principle in art and conduct reflecting the ethos of ancient Greece and Rome: balance, form, proportion, propriety, dignity, simplicity, objectivity, rationality, restraint, unity rather than diversity. In English literature, classicism emerged with Erasmus (1466–1536) and his fellow humanists. In the Restoration and 18th century, classicism, or neoclassicism, expressed society's deep need for balance and restraint after the shattering Civil War and Puritan commonwealth. Classicism continued in the 19th century, after the Romantic period, particularly in the work of Matthew Arnold. T. E. Hulme, Ezra Pound, and T. S. Eliot expressed it for the 20th century.

Cliché. An overused expression, once clever or metaphorical but now trite and timeworn.

Closed Couplet. The heroic couplet, especially when the thought and grammar are complete in the two iambic pentameter lines.

Closet Drama. A play written for reading in the "closet," or private study. Closet dramas were usually in verse, like Percy Shelley's *Prometheus Unbound* (1820) and Robert Browning's *Pippa Passes* (1841).

Cockney. A native of the East End of central London. The term originally meant "cocks' eggs," a rural term of contempt for city softies and fools. Cockneys are London's ingenious street peddlers, speaking a dialect rich with an inventive rhyming slang, dropping and adding aitches.

Comedy. One of the typical literary structures, originating as a form of drama and later extending into prose fiction and other genres as well. Comedy, as Susanne Langer says, is the image of Fortune; tragedy, the image of Fate. Each sorts out for attention the different facts of life. Comedy sorts its pleasures. It pleases our egos and endows our dreams, stirring at once two opposing impulses, our vindictive lust for superiority and our wishful drive for success and happiness ever after. The dark impulse stirs the pleasure of laughter; the light, the pleasure of wish fulfillment.

Comedy of Humors. Comedy based on the ancient physiological theory that a predominance of one of the body's four fluids (humors) produces a comically unbalanced personality: (1) blood—sanguine, hearty, cheerful, amorous; (2) phlegm—phlegmatic, sluggish; (3) choler (yellow bile)—angry, touchy; (4) black bile—melancholic.

Comedy of Manners. Suave, witty, and risqué, satire of upper-class manners and immorals, particularly that of Restoration masters like George Etherege and William Congreve.

Common Meter. The ballad stanza as found in hymns and other poems: a quatrain (four-line stanza) in iambic meter, alternating tetrameter and trimeter, rhyming *abcb* or *abab*.

Complaint. A lyric poem, popular in the Middle Ages and the Renaissance, complaining of unrequited love, a personal situation, or the state of the world.

Conceit. Any fanciful, ingenious expression or idea, but especially one in the form of an extended metaphor.

Concordia Discors. "Discordant harmony," a phrase expressing for the 18th century the harmonious diversity of nature, a pleasing balance of opposites.

Concrete Poetry. Poetry that attempts a concrete embodiment of its idea, expressing itself physically apart from the meaning of the words. A recent relative of the much older *shaped poem,* the concrete poem places heavy emphasis on the picture and less on the words, so that the visual experience may be more interesting than the linguistic.

Connotation. The ideas, attitudes, or emotions associated with a word in the mind of speaker or listener, writer or reader. It is contrasted with the *denotation,* the thing the word stands for, the dictionary definition, an objective concept without emotional coloring.

Consonance. (1) Repetition of inner or end consonant sounds, as, for example, the *r* and *s* sounds from Gerard Manley Hopkins's *God's Grandeur*: "broods with warm breast." (2) In a broader sense, a generally pleasing combination of sounds or ideas; things that sound well together.

Couplet. A pair of rhymed metrical lines, usually in iambic tetrameter or pentameter. Sometimes the two lines are of different length.

Covenanters. Scottish Presbyterians who signed a covenant in 1557 as a "godly band" to stand together to resist the Anglican church and the English establishment.

Cynghanedd. A complex medieval Welsh system of rhyme, alliteration, and consonance, to which Gerard Manley Hopkins alluded to describe his interplay of euphonious sounds, actually to be heard in any rich poet, as in the Welsh Dylan Thomas: "The force that through the green fuse drives the flower / Drives my green age."

Dactyl. A three-syllable metrical foot: $-\smile\smile$. It is the basic foot of dactylic hexameter, the six-foot line of Greek and Roman epic poetry.

Dactylic Hexameter. The classical or heroic line of the epic. A line based on six dactylic feet, with spondees substituted, and always ending $-\smile\smile \mid --$.

Dead Metaphor. A metaphor accepted without its figurative picture: "a jacket," for the paper around a book, with no mental picture of the human coat that prompted the original metaphor.

Decasyllabic. Having ten syllables. An iambic pentameter line is decasyllabic.

Deconstruction. The critical dissection of a literary text's statements, ambiguities, and structure to expose its hidden contradictions, implications, and fundamental instability of meaning. Jacques Derrida originated deconstruction in *Of Grammatology* (1967) and *Writing and Difference* (1967). Because no understanding of any text is stable, as each new reading is subject to the deconstruction of any meaning it appears to have established, it follows that criticism can be a kind of game, either playful or serious, as each critic ingeniously deconstructs the meanings established by others.

Decorum. Propriety, fitness, the quality of being appropriate. George Puttenham, in his *Arte of English Poesie* (1589), chides a translator of Virgil for his indecorum of having Aeneas "trudge," like a beggar, from Troy.

Defamiliarization. Turning the familiar to the strange by disrupting habitual ways of perceiving things. Derived from the thought of Victor Shklovsky and other Russian formalists, the idea is that art forces us to see things differently as we view them through the artist's sensibility, not our own.

Deism. A rational philosophy of religion, beginning with the theories of Lord Herbert of Cherbury, the "Father of Deism," in his *De Veritate* (1624). Deists generally held that God, the supreme Artisan, created a perfect clock of a universe, withdrew, and left it running, not to return to intervene in its natural works or the life of humankind; that the Bible is a moral guide, but neither historically accurate nor divinely authentic; and that reason guides human beings to virtuous conduct.

Denotation. The thing that a word stands for, the dictionary definition, an objective concept without emotional coloring. It is contrasted with the *connotation*, ideas, attitudes, or emotions associated with the word in the mind of user or hearer.

Dénouement. French for "unknotting": the unraveling of plot threads toward the end of a play, novel, or other narrative.

Determinism. The philosophical belief that events are shaped by forces beyond the control of human beings.

Dialect. A variety of language belonging to a particular time, place, or social group, as, for example, an 18th-century cockney dialect, a New England dialect, or a coal miner's dialect. A language other than one's own is for the most part unintelligible without study or translation; a dialect other than one's own can generally be understood, although pronunciation, vocabulary, and syntax seem strange.

Dialogue. Conversation between two or more persons, as represented in prose fiction, drama, or essays, as opposed to *monologue*, the speech of one person. Good dialogue characterizes each speaker by idiom and attitude as it advances the dramatic conflict. The dialogue as a form of speculative exposition, or dialectical argument, is often less careful to distinguish the diction and character of the speakers.

Diatribe. Greek for "a wearing away": a bitter and abusive criticism or invective, often lengthy, directed against a person, institution, or work.

Diction. Word choice in speech or writing, an important element of style.

Didactic. Greek for "teaching": instructive, or having the qualities of a teacher. Since ancient times, literature has been assumed to have two functions, instruction and entertainment, with sometimes one and sometimes the other dominant. Literature intended primarily for instruction or containing an important moralistic element is didactic.

Dirge. A lamenting funeral song.

Discourse. (1) A formal discussion of a subject. (2) The conventions of communication associated with specific areas, in usages such as "poetic discourse," "the discourse of the novel," or "historical discourse."

Dissenter. A term arising in the 1640s for a member of the clergy or a follower who dissented from the forms of the established Anglican church, particularly Puritans. Dissenters generally came from the lower middle classes, merchants who disapproved of aristocratic frivolity and ecclesiastical pomp.

Dissonance. (1) Harsh and jarring sound; discord. It is frequently an intentional effect, as in the poems of Robert Browning. (2) Occasionally a term for half rhyme or slant rhyme.

Distich. A couplet, or pair of rhymed metrical lines.

Dithyramb. A frenzied choral song and dance to honor Dionysus, Greek god of wine and the power of fertility. Any irregular, impassioned poetry may be called *dithyrambic*. The irregular ode also evolved from the dithyramb.

Doggerel. (1) Trivial verse clumsily aiming at meter, usually tetrameter. (2) Any verse facetiously low and loose in meter and rhyme.

Domesday Book. The recorded census and survey of landholders that William the Conqueror ordered in 1085; from "Doomsday," the Last Judgment.

Dramatic Irony. A character in drama or fiction unknowingly says or does something in ironic contrast to what the audience or reader knows or will learn.

Dramatic Monologue. A monologue in verse. A speaker addresses a silent listener, revealing, in dramatic irony, things about himself or herself of which the speaker is unaware.

Eclogue. A short poem, usually a pastoral, and often in the form of a dialogue or soliloquy. During the Renaissance, in the works of Spenser and others, the eclogue became a major form of verse, with shepherds exchanging verses of love, lament, or eulogy.

Edition. The form in which a book is published, including its physical qualities and its content. A *first edition* is the first form of a book, printed and bound; a *second edition* is a later form, usually with substantial changes in content. Between the two, there may be more than one printing or impression of the first edition, sometimes with minor corrections. The term *edition* also refers to the format of a book. For example, an *illustrated edition* or a *two-volume edition* may be identical in verbal content to one without pictures or bound in a single volume.

Edwardian Period (1901–1914). From the death of Queen Victoria to the outbreak of World War I, named for the reign of Victoria's son, Edward VII (1901–1910), a period generally reacting against Victorian propriety and convention.

Elegiac Stanza. An iambic pentameter quatrain rhyming *abab*. Taking its name from Thomas Gray's *Elegy Written in a Country Churchyard* (1751), it is identical to the heroic quatrain.

Elegy. Greek for "lament": a poem on death or on a serious loss; characteristically a sustained meditation expressing sorrow and, frequently, an explicit or implied consolation.

Elision. Latin for "striking out": the omission or slurring of an unstressed vowel at the end of a word to bring a line of poetry closer to a prescribed metrical pattern, as in John Milton's *Lycidas*: "Tempered to th'oaten flute." *See also* Meter; Syncope.

Elizabethan Drama. English drama of the reign of Elizabeth I (1558–1603). Strictly speaking, drama from the reign of James I (1603–1625) belongs to the Jacobean period and that from the reign of Charles I (1625–1642) to the Caroline period, but the term *Elizabethan* is sometimes extended to include works of later reigns, before the closing of the theaters in 1642.

Elizabethan Period (1558–1603). The years marked by the reign of Elizabeth I; the "Golden Age of English Literature," especially as exemplified by the lyric poetry and dramas of Christopher Marlowe, Edmund Spenser, Sir Philip Sidney, and William Shakespeare, as well as the early Ben Jonson and John Donne.

Ellipsis. The omission of words for rhetorical effect: "*Drop dead*" for "You drop dead."

Emblem. (1) A didactic pictorial and literary form consisting of a word or phrase (*mot* or *motto*), a symbolic woodcut or engraving, and a brief moralistic poem (*explicatio*). Collections of emblems in book form were popular in the 16th and 17th centuries. (2) A type or symbol.

Emendation. A change made in a literary text to remove faults that have appeared through tampering or by errors in reading, transcription, or printing from the manuscript.

Empathy. Greek for "feeling with": identification with the feelings or passions of another person, natural creature, or even an inanimate object conceived of as possessing human attributes. Empathy suggests emotional identification, whereas sympathy may be largely an intellectual appreciation of another's situation.

Emphasis. Stress placed on words, phrases, or ideas to show their importance, by *italics*, **bold-face,** and punctuation "!!!"; by figurative language, meter, and rhyme; or by strategies of rhetoric, like climactic order, contrast, repetition, and position.

Empiricism. Greek for "experience": the belief that all knowledge comes from experience, that human understanding of general truth can be founded only on observation of particulars. Empiricism is basic to the scientific method and to literary naturalism. It is opposed to rationalism, which discovers truth through reason alone, without regard to experience.

Enclosed Rhyme. A couplet, or pair of rhyming lines, enclosed in rhyming lines to give the pattern *abba*.

Encomium. Originally a Greek choral song in praise of a hero; later, any formal expression of praise, in verse or prose.

End Rhyme. Rhyme at the end of a line of verse (the usual placement), as distinguished from *initial rhyme*, at the beginning, or *internal rhyme*, within the line.

Enjambment. Run-on lines in which grammatical sense runs from one line of poetry to the next without pause or punctuation. The opposite of an end-stopped line.

Enlightenment. A philosophical movement in the 17th and 18th centuries, particularly in France, characterized by the conviction that reason could achieve all knowledge, supplant organized religion, and ensure progress toward happiness and perfection.

Envoy (or **Envoi**). A concluding stanza, generally shorter than the earlier stanzas of a poem, giving a brief summary of theme, address to a prince or patron, or return to a refrain.

Epic. A long narrative poem, typically a recounting of history or legend or of the deeds of a national hero. During the Renaissance, critical theory emphasized two assumptions: (1) the encyclopedic knowledge needed for major poetry, and (2) an aristocracy of genres, according to which epic and tragedy, because they deal with heroes and ruling-class figures, were reserved for major poets. Romanticism revived both the long mythological poem and the verse romance, but the prestige of the encyclopedic epic still lingered. In his autobiographical poem *The Prelude,* Wordsworth self-consciously internalized the heroic argument of the epic.

Epic Simile. Sometimes called a *Homeric simile*: an extended simile, comparing one thing with another by lengthy description of the second, often beginning with "as when" and concluding with "so" or "such."

Epicurean. Often meaning hedonistic (*see also* Hedonism), devoted to sensual pleasure and ease. Actually, Epicurus (c. 341–270 B.C.) was a kind of puritanical Stoic, recommending detachment from pleasure and pain to avoid life's inevitable suffering, hence advocating serenity as the highest happiness, intellect over the senses.

Epigram. (1) A brief poetic and witty couching of a home truth. (2) An equivalent statement in prose.

Epigraph. (1) An inscription on a monument or building. (2) A quotation or motto heading a book or chapter.

Epilogue. (1) A poetic address to the audience at the end of a play. (2) The actor performing the address. (3) Any similar appendage to a literary work, usually describing what happens to the characters in the future.

Epiphany. In religious tradition, the revelation of a divinity. James Joyce adapted the term to signify a moment of profound or spiritual revelation, when even the stroke of a clock or a noise in the street brings sudden illumination, and "its soul, its whatness leaps to us from the vestment of its appearance." For Joyce, art was an epiphany.

Episode. An incident in a play or novel; a continuous event in action and dialogue. Originally the term referred to a section in Greek tragedy between two choric songs.

Episodic Structure. In narration, the incidental stringing of one episode upon another, as in *Don Quixote* or *Moll Flanders,* in which one episode follows another with no necessary causal connection or plot.

Epistle. (1) A letter, usually a formal or artistic one, like Saint Paul's Epistles in the New Testament, or Horace's verse *Epistles,* widely imitated in the late 17th and 18th centuries, most notably by Alexander Pope. (2) A dedication in a prefatory epistle to a play or book.

Epitaph. (1) An inscription on a tombstone or monument memorializing the person, or persons, buried there. (2) A literary epigram or brief poem epitomizing the dead.

Epithalamium (or **Epithalamion**). A lyric ode honoring a bride and groom.

Epithet. A term characterizing a person or thing: e.g., *Richard the Lion-Hearted.*

Epitome. (1) A summary, an abridgment, an abstract. (2) One that supremely represents an entire class.

Essay. A literary composition on a single subject; usually short, in prose, and nonexhaustive. The word derives from French *essai* "an attempt," first used in the modern sense by Michel de Montaigne, whose *Essais* (1580–1588) are classics of the genre. Francis Bacon's *Essays* (1597) brought the term and form to English.

Estates. The "three estates of the realm," recognized from feudal times onward: the clergy (Lords Spiritual), the nobility (Lords Temporal), and the burghers (the Commons). In *Heroes and Hero-Worship,* Thomas Carlyle says that Edmund Burke (member of Parliament from 1766 to 1794) added to Parliament's three estates "the Reporters' Gallery" where "sat a fourth Estate more important than they all" (Lecture V). The Fourth Estate is now the press and other media.

Eulogy. A speech or composition of praise, especially of a deceased person.

Euphemism. Greek for "good speech": an attractive substitute for a harsh or unpleasant word or concept; figurative language or circumlocution substituting an indirect or oblique reference for a direct one.

Euphony. Melodious sound, the opposite of cacophony. A major feature of verse, but also a consideration in prose, euphony results from smooth-flowing meter or sentence rhythm as well as attractive sounds.

Euphuism. An artificial, highly elaborate affected style that takes its name from John Lyly's *Euphues: The Anatomy of Wit* (1578). Euphuism is characterized by the heavy use of rhetorical devices such as balance and antithesis, by much attention to alliteration and other sound patterns, and by learned allusion.

Excursus. (1) A lengthy discussion of a point, appended to a literary work. (2) A long digression.

Exegesis. (1) A detailed analysis, explanation, and interpretation of a difficult text, especially the Bible. (2) A rhetorical figure, also called *explicatio*, which clarifies a thought.

Exemplum. Latin for "example": a story used to illustrate a moral point. *Exempla* were a characteristic feature of medieval sermons. Chaucer's *Pardoner's Tale* and *Nun's Priest's Tale* are famous secular examples.

Existentialism. A philosophy centered on individual existence as unique and unrepeatable, hence rejecting the past for present existence and its unique dilemmas. Existentialism rose to prominence in the 1930s and 1940s, particularly in France after World War II in the work of Jean-Paul Sartre.

Expressionism. An early 20th-century movement in art and literature, best understood as a reaction against conventional realism and naturalism, and especially as a revolt against conventional society. The expressionist looked inward for images, expressing in paint, on stage, or in prose or verse a distorted, nightmarish version of reality, things dreamed about rather than actually existing.

Eye Rhyme. A rhyme of words that look but do not sound the same: *one, stone; word, lord; teak, break.*

Fable. (1) A short, allegorical story in verse or prose, frequently of animals, told to illustrate a moral. (2) The story line or plot of a narrative or drama. (3) Loosely, any legendary or fabulous account.

Falling Meter. A meter beginning with a stress, running from heavy to light.

Farce. A wildly comic play, mocking dramatic and social conventions, frequently with satiric intent.

Feminine Ending. An extra unstressed syllable at the end of a metrical line, usually iambic.

Feminine Rhyme. A rhyme of both the stressed and the unstressed syllables of one feminine ending with another.

Feudalism. The political and social system prevailing in Europe from the ninth century until the 1400s. It was a system of independent holdings (*feud* is Germanic for "estate") in which autonomous lords pledged fealty and service to those more powerful in exchange for protection, as did villagers to the neighboring lord of the manor.

Fiction. An imagined creation in verse, drama, or prose. Fiction is a thing made, an invention. It is distinguished from nonfiction by its essentially imaginative nature, but elements of fiction appear in fundamentally nonfictional constructions such as essays, biographies, autobiographies, and histories. Fictional anecdotes and illustrations abound in the works of politicians, business leaders, the clergy, philosophers, and scientists. Although any invented person, place, event, or condition is a fiction, the term is now most frequently used to mean "prose fiction," as distinct from verse or drama.

Figurative Language. Language that is not literal, being either metaphorical or rhetorically patterned.

Figure of Speech. An expression extending language beyond its literal meaning, either pictorially through metaphor, simile, allusion, and the like, or rhetorically through repetition, balance, antithesis, and the like. A figure of speech is also called a *trope*.

Fin de Siècle. "The end of the century," especially the last decade of the 19th. The term, acquired with the French influence of the symbolists Stéphane Mallarmé and Charles Baudelaire, connotes preciosity and decadence.

First-Person Narration. Narration by a character involved in a story.

Flyting. Scottish for "scolding": a form of invective, or violent verbal assault, in verse; traditional in Scottish literature, possibly Celtic in origin. Typically, two poets exchange scurrilous and often exhaustive abuse.

Folio. From Latin for "leaf." (1) A sheet of paper, folded once. (2) The largest of the book sizes, made from standard printing sheets, folded once before trimming and binding.

Folk Song. A song forming part of the folklore of a community. Like the folktale and the legend, a folk song is a traditional creative expression, characteristically shaped by oral tradition into the form in which it is later recorded in manuscript or print.

Folktale. A story forming part of the folklore of a community, generally less serious than the stories called *myths*. In preliterate societies, virtually all narratives were either myths or folktales: oral histories of real wars, kings, heroes, great families, and the like accumulating large amounts of legendary material.

Foot. The metrical unit; in English, an accented syllable with accompanying light syllable or syllables.

Foreshadowing. The technique of suggesting or prefiguring a development in a literary work before it occurs.

Formula. A plot outline or set of characteristic ingredients used in the construction of a literary work or applied to a portion of one. Formula fiction is written to the requirements of a particular market, usually undistinguished by much imagination or originality in applying the formula.

Foul Copy. A manuscript that has been used for printing, bearing the marks of the proofreader, editor, and printer, as well as, frequently, the author's queries and comments.

Four Elements. In ancient and medieval cosmology, earth, air, fire, and water—the four ultimate, exclusive, and eternal constituents that, according to Empedocles (c. 493–c. 433 B.C.) made up the world.

Four Senses of Interpretation. A mode of medieval criticism in which a work is examined for four kinds of meaning. The *literal meaning* is related to fact or history. The *moral* or *tropological meaning* is the lesson of the work as applied to individual behavior. The *allegorical meaning* is the particular story in its application to people generally, with emphasis on their beliefs. The *anagogical meaning* is its spiritual or mystical truth, its universal significance. After the literal, each of the others represents a broader form of what is usually called allegory, moving from individual morality to social organization to God.

Fourteeners. Lines of 14 syllables—7 iambic feet, popular with the Elizabethans.

Frame Narrative. A narrative enclosing one or more separate stories. Characteristically, the frame narrative is created as a vehicle for the stories it contains.

Free Verse. French *vers libre*; poetry free of traditional metrical and stanzaic patterns.

Genre. A term often applied loosely to the larger forms of literary convention, roughly analogous to "species" in biology. The Greeks spoke of three main genres of poetry—lyric, epic, and drama. Within each major genre, there are subgenres. In written forms dominated by prose, for example, there is a broad distinction between works of fiction (e.g., the novel) and thematic works (e.g., the essay). Within the fictional category, we note a distinction between novel and romance, and other forms such as satire and confession. The object of making these distinctions in literary tradition is not simply to classify but to judge authors in terms of the conventions they themselves chose.

Georgian. (1) Pertaining to the reigns of the four Georges—1714–1830, particularly the reigns of the first three, up to the close of the 18th century. (2) The literature written during the early years (1910–1914) of the reign of George V.

Georgic. A poem about farming and annual rural labors, after Virgil's *Georgics*.

Gloss. An explanation (from Greek *glossa* "tongue, language"); originally, Latin synonyms in the margins of Greek manuscripts and vernacular synonyms in later manuscripts as scribes gave the reader some help.

Glossary. A list of words, with explanations or definitions. A glossary is ordinarily a partial dictionary, appended to the end of a book to explain technical or unfamiliar terms.

Gothic. Originally, pertaining to the Goths, then to any Germanic people. Because the Goths began warring with the Roman empire in the 3rd century A.D., eventually sacking Rome itself, the term later became a synonym for "barbaric," which the 18th century next applied to anything medieval, of the Dark Ages.

Gothic Novel. A type of fiction introduced and named by Horace Walpole's *Castle of Otranto, A Gothic Story* (1764). Walpole introduced supernatural terror, with a huge mysterious helmet, portraits that walk abroad, and statues with nosebleeds. Matthew Gregory Lewis, "Monk Lewis," added sexual depravity to the murderous supernatural mix (*The Monk*, 1796). Mary Shelley's *Frankenstein* (1818) transformed the Gothic into moral science fiction.

Grotesque. Anything unnaturally distorted, ugly, ludicrous, fanciful, or bizarre; especially, in the 19th century, literature exploiting the abnormal.

Hedonism. A philosophy that sees pleasure as the highest good.

Hegelianism. The philosophy of G. W. F. Hegel (1770–1831), who developed the system of thought known as Hegelian dialectic, in which a given concept, or *thesis*, generates its opposite, or *antithesis*, and from the interaction of the two arises a *synthesis*. The synthesis then forms a thesis for a new cycle. Hegelian dialectic suggests that history is not static but contains a rational progression, an idea influential on many later thinkers.

Heroic Couplet. The closed and balanced iambic pentameter couplet typical of the heroic plays of John Dryden; hence, any closed couplet.

Heroic Quatrain. A stanza in four lines of iambic pentameter, rhyming *abab* (*see also* Meter). Also known as the *heroic stanza* and the *elegiac stanza*.

Hexameter. Six-foot lines.

Historicism. (1) Historical relativism. (2) An approach to literature that emphasizes its historical environment, the climate of ideas, belief, and literary conventions surrounding and influencing the writer.

Homily. A religious discourse or sermon, especially one emphasizing practical spiritual or moral advice.

Hubris. From Greek *hybris*, "pride": prideful arrogance or insolence of the kind that causes the tragic hero to ignore the warnings that might turn aside the action that leads to disaster.

Humors. The *cardinal humors* of ancient medical theory: blood, phlegm, yellow bile (choler), black bile (melancholy). From ancient times until the 19th century, the humors were believed largely responsible for health and disposition. Hippocrates (c. 460–c. 370 B.C.) thought an imbalance produced illness. Galen (c. A.D. 130–300) suggested that character types are produced by dominance of fluids: *sanguine*, or kindly, cheerful, amorous; *phlegmatic*, or sluggish, unresponsive; *choleric*, or quick-tempered; and *melancholic*, or brooding, dejected. In literature, especially during the early modern period, characters were portrayed according to the humors that dominated them, as in the comedy of humors.

Hyperbole. Overstatement to make a point, as when a parent tells a child "I've told you a thousand times."

Iambus (or **Iamb**). A metrical foot: ˘ ‒ .

Idealism. (1) In philosophy and ethics, an emphasis on ideas and ideals, as opposed to the sensory emphasis of materialism. (2) Literary idealism follows from philosophical precepts, emphasizing a world in which the most important reality is a spiritual or transcendent truth not always reflected in the world of sense perception.

Idyll. A short poem of rustic pastoral serenity.

Image. A concrete picture, either literally descriptive, as in "Red roses covered the white wall," or figurative, as in "She is a rose," each carrying a sensual and emotive connotation. A figurative image may be an analogy, metaphor, simile, personification, or the like.

Impressionism. A literary style conveying subjective impressions rather than objective reality, taking its name from the movement in French painting in the mid-19th century, notably in the works of Manet, Monet, and Renoir. The Imagists represented impressionism in poetry; in fiction, writers like Virginia Woolf and James Joyce.

Industrial Revolution. The accelerated change, beginning in the 1760s, from an agricultural-shopkeeping society, using hand tools, to an industrial-mechanized one.

Influence. The apparent effect of literary works on subsequent writers and their work, as in Robert Browning's influence on T. S. Eliot.

Innuendo. An indirect remark or gesture, especially one implying something derogatory; an insinuation.

Interlocking Rhyme. Rhyme between stanzas; a word unrhymed in one stanza is used as a rhyme for the next, as in terza rima: *aba bcb cdc* and so on.

Internal Rhyme. Rhyme within a line, rather than at the beginning (*initial rhyme*) or end (*end rhyme*); also, rhyme matching sounds in the middle of a line with sounds at the end.

Intertextuality. (1) The relations between one literary text and others it evokes through such means as quotation, paraphrase, allusion, parody, and revision. (2) More broadly, the relations between a given text and all other texts, the potentially infinite sum of knowledge within which any text has its meaning.

Inversion. A reversal of sequence or position, as when the normal order of elements within a sentence is inverted for poetic or rhetorical effect.

Irony. In general, irony is the perception of a clash between appearance and reality, between *seems* and *is*, or between *ought* and *is*. The myriad shadings of irony seem to fall into three categories: (1) *Verbal irony*—saying something contrary to what it means; the appearance is what the words say, the reality is their contrary meaning. (2) *Dramatic irony*—saying or doing something while unaware of its ironic contrast with the whole truth; named for its frequency in drama, dramatic irony is a verbal irony with the speaker's awareness erased. (3) *Situational irony*—events turning to the opposite of what is expected or what should be. The ironic situation turns the speaker's unknowing words ironic. Situational irony is the essence of both comedy and tragedy: the young lovers run into the worst possible luck, until everything clears up happily; the most noble spirits go to their death, while the featherheads survive.

Italian Sonnet (or **Petrarchan Sonnet**). A sonnet composed of an octave and sestet, rhyming *abbaabba cdecde* (or *cdcdcd* or some variant, without a closing couplet).

Italic (or **Italics**). Type slanting upward to the right. *This sentence is italic.*

Jacobean Period (1603–1625). The reign of James I, *Jacobus* being the Latin for "James." A certain skepticism and even cynicism seeped into Elizabethan joy. The Puritans and the court party, the Cavaliers, grew more antagonistic. But it was in the Jacobean period that Shakespeare wrote his greatest tragedies and tragi-comedies, and Ben Jonson did his major work.

Jargon. (1) Language peculiar to a trade or calling, as, for example, the jargon of astronauts, lawyers, or literary critics. (2) Confused or confusing language. This kind of jargon does not communicate to anybody.

Jeremiad. A lament or complaint, especially one enumerating transgressions and predicting destruction of a people, of the kind found in the Book of Jeremiah.

Juvenilia. Youthful literary products.

Kenning. A compound figurative metaphor, a circumlocution, in Old English and Old Norse poetry: hronrād, "whale-road," for the sea.

Lament. A grieving poem, an elegy, in Anglo-Saxon or Renaissance times. *Deor's Lament* (c. 980) records the actual grief of a scop, or court poet, at being displaced in his lord's hall.

Lampoon. A satirical, personal ridicule in verse or prose. The term probably derives from the French *lampons*, "Let's guzzle," a refrain in 17th-century drinking songs.

Lay (or **Lai**). (1) A ballad or related metrical romance originating with the Breton lay of French Brittany and retaining some of its Celtic magic and folklore.

Lexicon. A word list, a vocabulary, a dictionary.

Libretto. "The little book" (Italian): the text of an opera, cantata, or other musical drama.

Iambic Pentameter

Love's not | Time's fool, | though ros- | y lips | and cheeks |
Within | his bend- | ing sick- | le's com- | pass come |

William Shakespeare, Sonnet 116

When to | the ses- | sions of | sweet si- | lent thought |

William Shakespeare, Sonnet 30

Anapestic Tetrameter
(trochees substituted)
The pop- | lars are felled; | farewell | to the shade |
And the whis- | pering sound | of the cool | colonnade |

William Cowper, "The Popular Field"

Trochaic Tetrameter
Tell me | not in | mournful | numbers |

Henry Wadsworth Longfellow, "A Psalm of Life"

Dactylic Hexameter
This is the | forest prim- | eval. The | murmuring | pines and the | hemlocks |
Bearded with | moss . . . .

Henry Wadsworth Longfellow, "Evangeline"

Metonymy. "Substitute naming." A figure of speech in which an associated idea stands in for the actual item: "The *pen* is mightier than the *sword*" for "Literature and propaganda accomplish more and survive longer than warfare," or "The *White House* announced" for "The President announced." *See also* synecdoche.

Metrics. The analysis and description of meter; also called *prosody*.

Middle English. The language of England from the middle of the 12th century to approximately 1500. English began to lose its inflectional endings and accepted many French words into its vocabulary, especially terms associated with the new social, legal, and governmental structures (*baron, judge, jury, marshal, parliament, prince*), and those in common use by the French upper classes (*mansion, chamber, veal, beef*).

Mimesis. A term meaning "imitation." It has been central to literary criticism since Aristotle's *Poetics*. The ordinary meaning of *imitation* as creating a resemblance to something else is clearly involved in Aristotle's definition of dramatic plot as *mimesis praxeos*, the imitation of an action. But there are many things that a work of literature may imitate, and hence many contexts of imitation. Works of literature may imitate other works of literature: this is the aspect of literature that comes into such conceptions as convention and genre. In a larger sense, every work of literature imitates, or finds its identity in, the entire "world of words," in Wallace Stevens's phrase, the sense of the whole of reality as potentially literary, as finding its end in a book, as Stéphane Mallarmé says.

Miracle Play. A medieval play based on a saint's life or story from the Bible.

Miscellany. A collection of various things. A literary miscellany is therefore a book collecting varied works, usually poems by different authors, a kind of anthology. The term is applied especially to the many books of this kind that appeared in the Elizabethan period.

Mock Epic. A poem in epic form and manner ludicrously elevating some trivial subject to epic grandeur.

Modernism. A collective term, generally associated with the first half of the 20th century, for various aesthetic and cultural attempts to place a "modern" face on experience. Modernism arose from a sense that the old ways were worn out. The new century opened with broad social, philosophical, religious, and cultural discussion and reform. For creative artists, the challenges of the new present meant that art became subject to change in every way, that the content, forms, and techniques inherited from the 19th century existed to be challenged, broken apart, and re-formed.

Monodrama. (1) A play with one character. (2) A closet drama or dramatic monologue.

Monody. (1) A Greek ode for one voice. (2) An elegiac lament, a dirge, in poetic soliloquy.

Monologue. (1) A poem or story in the form of a soliloquy. (2) Any extended speech.

Motif (or **Motive**). (1) A recurrent thematic element—word, image, symbol, object, phrase, action. (2) A conventional incident, situation, or device like the unknown knight of mysterious origin and low degree in the romance, or the baffling riddle in fairy tales.

Muse. The inspirer of poetry, on whom the poet calls for assistance. In Greek mythology the Muses were the nine daughters of Zeus and Mnemosyne ("Memory") presiding over the arts and sciences.

Mystery Play. Medieval religious drama; eventually performed in elaborate cycles of plays acted on pageant wagons or stages throughout city streets, with different guilds of artisans and merchants responsible for each.

Mysticism. A spiritual discipline in which sensory experience is expunged and the mind is devoted to deep contemplation and the reaching of a transcendental union with God.

Myth. From Greek *mythos*, "plot" or "narrative." The verbal culture of most if not all human societies began with stories, and certain stories have achieved a distinctive importance as being connected with what the society feels it most needs to know: stories illustrating the society's religion, history, class structure, or the origin of peculiar features of the natural environment.

Narrative Poem. One that tells a story, particularly the epic, metrical romance, and shorter narratives, like the ballad.

Naturalism. (1) Broadly, according to nature. In this sense, naturalism is opposed to idealism, emphasizing things accessible to the senses in this world in contrast to permanent or spiritual truths presumed to lie outside it. (2) More specifically, a literary movement of the late 19th century; an extension of realism, naturalism was a reaction against the restrictions inherent in the realistic emphasis on the ordinary, as naturalists insisted that the extraordinary is real, too.

Neoclassical Period. Generally, the span of time from the restoration of Charles II to his father's throne in 1660 until the publication of William Wordsworth and Samuel Taylor Coleridge's *Lyrical Ballads* (1798). Writers hoped to revive something like the classical Pax Romana, an era of peace and literary excellence.

Neologism. A word newly coined or introduced into a language, or a new meaning given to an old word.

New Criticism. An approach to criticism prominent in the United States after the publication of John Crowe Ransom's *New Criticism* (1941). Generally, the New Critics were agreed that a poem or story should be considered an organic unit, with each part working to support the whole. They worked by close analysis, considering the text as the final authority, and were distrustful, though not wholly neglectful, of considerations brought from outside the text, as, for example, from biography or history.

New Historicism. A cross-disciplinary approach fostered by the rise of feminist and multicultural studies as well as a renewed emphasis on historical perspective. Associated in particular with work on the early modern and the romantic periods in the United States and England, the approach emphasizes analysis of the relationship between history and literature, viewing writings in both fields as "texts" for study. New Historicism has tended to note political influences on literary and historical texts, to illuminate the role of the writer against the backdrop of social customs and assumptions, and to view history as changeable and interconnected instead of as a linear progressive evolution.

Nocturne. A night piece; writing evocative of evening or night.

Nominalism. In the Middle Ages, the belief that universals have no real being, but are only names, their existence limited to their presence in the minds and language of humans. This belief was opposed to the beliefs of medieval realists, who held that universals have an independent existence, at least in the mind of God.

Norman Conquest. The period of English history in which the Normans consolidated their hold on England after the defeat of the Saxon King Harold by William, Duke of Normandy, in 1066. French became the court language and Norman lords gained control of English lands, but Anglo-Saxon administrative and judicial systems remained largely in place.

Novel. The extended prose fiction that arose in the 18th century to become a major literary expression of the modern world. The term comes from the Italian *novella*, the short "new" tale of intrigue and moral comeuppance most eminently disseminated by Boccaccio's *Decameron* (1348–1353). The terms *novel* and *romance*, from the French *roman*, competed interchangeably for most of the 18th century.

Novella. (1) Originally, a short tale. (2) In modern usage, a term sometimes used interchangeably with short novel or for a fiction of middle length, between a short story and a novel. See Novel, above.

Octave. (1) The first unit in an Italian sonnet: eight lines of iambic pentameter, rhyming *abbaabba*. *See also* Meter. (2) A stanza in eight lines.

Octavo (Abbreviated 8vo). A book made from sheets folded to give signatures of eight leaves (16 pages), a book of average size.

Octet. An octastich or octave.

Octosyllabic. Eight-syllable.

Ode. A long, stately lyric poem in stanzas of varied metrical pattern.

Old English. The language brought to England, beginning in 449, by the Jute, Angle, and Saxon invaders from Denmark; the language base from which modern English evolved.

Old English Literature. The literature of England from the Anglo-Saxon invasion of the mid-5th century until the beginning of the Middle English period in the mid-12th century.

Omniscient Narrative. A narrative account untrammeled by constraints of time or space. An omniscient narrator perspective knows about the external and internal realities of characters as well as incidents unknown to them, and can interpret motivation and meaning.

Onomatopoeia. The use of words formed or sounding like what they signify—*buzz, crack, smack, whinny*—especially in an extensive capturing of sense by sound.

Orientalism. A term denoting Western portrayals of Oriental culture. In literature it refers to a varied body of work beginning in the 18th century that described for Western readers the history, language, politics, and culture of the area east of the Mediterranean.

Oxford Movement. A 19th-century movement to reform the Anglican church according to the high-church and more nearly Catholic ideals and rituals of the later 17th-century church.

Oxymoron. A pointed stupidity: *oxy*, "sharp," plus *moron*. One of the great ironic figures of speech—for example, "a fearful joy," or Milton's "darkness visible."

Paleography. The study and interpretation of ancient handwriting and manuscript styles.

Palimpsest. A piece of writing on secondhand vellum, parchment, or other surface carrying traces of erased previous writings.

Panegyric. A piece of writing in praise of a person, thing, or achievement.

Pantheism. A belief that God and the universe are identical, from the Greek words *pan* ("all") and *theos* ("god"). God is all; all is God.

Pantomime. A form of drama presented without words, in a dumb show.

Parable. (1) A short tale, such as those of Jesus in the gospels, encapsulating a moral or religious lesson. (2) Any saying, figure of speech, or narrative in which one thing is expressed in terms of another.

Paradox. An apparently untrue or self-contradictory statement or circumstance that proves true upon reflection or when examined in another light.

Paraphrase. A rendering in other words of the sense of a text or passage, as of a poem, essay, short story, or other writing.

Parody. Originally, "a song sung beside" another. From this idea of juxtaposition arose the two basic elements of parody, comedy and criticism. As comedy, parody exaggerates or distorts the prominent features of style or content in a work. As criticism, it mimics the work, borrowing words or phrases or characteristic turns of thought in order to highlight weaknesses of conception or expression.

Passion Play. Originally a play based on Christ's Passion; later, one including both Passion and Resurrection. Such plays began in the Middle Ages, performed from the 13th century onward, often as part of the pageants presented for the feast of Corpus Christi.

Pastiche. A literary or other artistic work created by assembling bits and pieces from other works.

Pastoral. From Latin *pastor,* a shepherd. The first pastoral poet was Theocritus, a Greek of the 3rd century B.C. The pastoral was especially popular in Europe from the 14th through the 18th centuries, with some fine examples still written in England in the 19th century. The pastoral mode is self-reflexive. Typically the poet echoes the conventions of earlier pastorals in order to put "the complex into the simple," as William Empson observed in *Some Versions of Pastoral* (1935). The poem is not really about shepherds, but about the complex society the poet and readers inhabit.

Pathetic Fallacy. The attribution of animate or human characteristics to nature, as, for example, when rocks, trees, or weather are portrayed as reacting in sympathy to human feelings or events.

Pathos. The feeling of pity, sympathy, tenderness, compassion, or sorrow evoked by someone or something that is helpless.

Pedantry. Ostentatious book learning: an accusation frequently hurled in scholarly disagreements.

Pentameter. A line of five metrical feet. (*See* Meter.)

Peripeteia (or **Peripetia, Peripety**). A sudden change in situation in a drama or fiction, a reversal of luck for good or ill.

Periphrasis. The practice of talking around the point; a wordy restatement; a circumlocution.

Peroration. (1) The summative conclusion of a formal oration. (2) Loosely, a grandiloquent speech.

Persona. A mask (in Latin); in poetry and fiction, the projected speaker or narrator of the work—that is, a mask for the actual author.

Personification. The technique of treating abstractions, things, or animals as persons. A kind of metaphor, personification turns abstract ideas, like love, into a physical beauty named Venus, or conversely, makes dumb animals speak and act like humans.

Petrarchan Sonnet. Another name for an Italian sonnet.

Philology. The study of ancient languages and literatures; also more broadly interpreted from its basic meaning, "love of the word," to include all literary studies. In the 19th century, the field of historical linguistics.

Phoneme. In linguistics, the smallest distinguishable unit of sound. Different for each language, phonemes are defined by determining which differences in sound function to signal a difference in meaning.

Phonetics. (1) The study of speech sounds and their production, transmission, and reception. (2) The phonetic system of a particular language. (3) Symbols used to represent speech sounds.

Picaresque Novel. A novel chronicling the adventures of a rogue (Spanish: *picaro*), typically presented as an autobiography, episodic in structure and panoramic in its coverage of time and place.

Picturesque, The. A quality in landscape, and in idealized landscape painting, admired in the second half of the 18th century and featuring crags, flaring and blasted trees, a torrent or winding stream, ruins, and perhaps a quiet cottage and cart, with contrasting light and shadow. It was considered an aesthetic mean between the poles of Edmund Burke's *A Philosophical Inquiry into the Sublime and the Beautiful* (1756).

Plagiarism. Literary kidnapping (Latin *plagiarius*, "kidnapper")—the seizing and presenting as one's own the ideas or writings of another.

Plain Style. The straightforward, unembellished style of preaching favored by 17th-century Puritans as well as by reformers within the Anglican church, as speaking God's word directly from the inspired heart as opposed to the high style of aristocratic oratory and courtliness, the vehicle of subterfuge. Plain style was simultaneously advocated for scientific accuracy by the Royal Society.

Platonism. Any reflection of Plato's philosophy, particularly the belief in the eternal reality of ideal forms, of which the diversities of the physical world are but transitory shadows.

Poetics. The theory, art, or science of poetry. Poetics is concerned with the nature and function of poetry and with identifying and explaining its types, forms, and techniques.

Poet Laureate. Since the 17th century, a title conferred by the monarch on English poets. At first, the laureate was required to write poems to commemorate special occasions, such as royal birthdays, national celebrations, and the like, but since the early 19th century the appointment has been for the most part honorary.

Poetry. Imaginatively intense language, usually in verse. Poetry is a form of fiction—"the supreme fiction," said Wallace Stevens. It is distinguished from other fictions by the compression resulting from its heavier use of figures of speech and allusion and, usually, by the music of its patterns of sounds.

Postmodernism. A term first used in relation to literature in the late 1940s by Randall Jarrell and John Berryman to proclaim a new sensibility arising to challenge the reigning assumptions and practices of modernism. The attitudes and literary devices of the modernists—stream of consciousness, for example—had taken on the patina of tradition. For many of the postmodernists, disillusionment seemed to have reached its fullest measure. Life had little meaning, art less, and a neat closure to expectations raised by the artist seemed impossible. Intruding into one's own fiction to ponder its powers became a hallmark of the 1960s and 1970s.

Poststructuralism. A mode of literary criticism and thought centered on Jacques Derrida's concept of deconstruction. Structuralists see language as the paradigm for all structures. Poststructuralists see language as based on differences—hence the analytical deconstruction of what seemed an immutable system. What language expresses is already absent. Poststructuralism challenges the New Criticism, which seeks a truth fixed within the "verbal icon," the text, in W. K. Wimsatt's term. Poststructuralism invites interpretations through the spaces left by the way words operate.

Pragmatism. In philosophy, the idea that the value of a belief is best judged by the acts that follow from it—its practical results.

Preciosity. Since the 19th century, a term for an affected or overingenious refinement of language.

Predestination. The belief that an omniscient God, at the Creation, destined all subsequent events, particularly, in Calvinist belief, the election for salvation and the damnation of individual souls.

Pre-Raphaelite. Characteristic of a small but influential group of mid-19th-century painters who hoped to recapture the spiritual vividness they saw in medieval painting before Raphael (1483–1520).

Presbyterianism. John Calvin's organization of ecclesiastical governance not by bishops representing the pope but by elders representing the congregation.

Proscenium. Originally, in Greece, the whole acting area ("in front of the scenery"); now, that part of the stage projecting in front of the curtain.

Prose. Ordinary writing patterned on speech, as distinct from verse.

Prose Poetry. Prose rich in cadenced and poetic effects like alliteration, assonance, consonance, and the like, and in imagery.

Prosody. The analysis and description of meters; metrics (*see also* Meter). Linguists apply the term to the study of patterns of accent in a language.

Protagonist. The leading character in a play or story; originally the leader of the chorus in the agon ("contest") of Greek drama, faced with the antagonist, the opposition.

Pseudonym. A fictitious name adopted by an author for public use, like George Eliot (Mary Ann/Marian Evans), and George Orwell (Eric Arthur Blair).

Psychoanalytic Criticism. A form of criticism that uses the insights of Freudian psychology to illuminate a work.

Ptolemaic Universe. The universe as perceived by Ptolemy, a Greco-Egyptian astronomer of the 2nd century A.D., whose theories were dominant until the Renaissance produced the Copernican universe. In Ptolemy's system, the universe was world-centered, with the sun, moon, planets, and stars understood as rotating around the earth in a series of concentric spheres, producing as they revolved the harmonious "music of the spheres."

Puritanism. A Protestant movement arising in the mid-16th century with the Reformation in England. Theocracy—the individual and the congregation governed directly under God through Christ—became primary, reflected in the centrality of the Scriptures and their exposition, direct confession through prayer and public confession to the congregation rather than through priests, and the direct individual experience of God's grace.

Quadrivium. The more advanced four of the seven liberal arts as studied in medieval universities: arithmetic, geometry, astronomy, and music.

Quantitative Verse. Verse that takes account of the quantity of the syllables (whether they take a long or short time to pronounce) rather than their stress patterns.

Quarto (Abbreviated 4to, 4o). A book made from sheets folded twice, giving signatures of four leaves (eight pages). Many of Shakespeare's plays were first printed individually in quarto editions, designated First Quarto, Second Quarto, etc.

Quatrain. A stanza of four lines, rhymed or unrhymed. With its many variations, it is the most common stanzaic form in English.

Rationalism. The theory that reason, rather than revelation or authority, provides knowledge, truth, the choice of good over evil, and an adequate understanding of God and the universe.

Reader-Response Theory. A form of criticism that arose during the 1970s; it postulates the essential active involvement of the reader with the text and focuses on the effect of the process of reading on the mind.

Realism (in literature). The faithful representation of life. Realism carries the conviction of true reports of phenomena observable by others.

Realism (in philosophy). (1) In the Middle Ages, the belief that universal concepts possess real existence apart from particular things and the human mind. They exist either as entities like Platonic forms or as concepts in the mind of God. Medieval realism was opposed to nominalism. (2) In later epistemology, the belief that things exist apart from our perception of them. In this sense, realism is opposed to idealism, which locates all reality in our minds.

Recension. (1) A process of editorial revision based on an examination of the various versions and sources of a literary text. (2) The text produced as a result of reconciling variant readings.

Recto. The right-hand page of an open book; the front of a leaf as opposed to the *verso* or back of a leaf.

Redaction. (1) A revised version. (2) A rewriting or condensing of an older work.

Refrain. A set phrase, or chorus, recurring throughout a song or poem, usually at the end of a stanza or other regular interval.

Relativism. The philosophical belief that nothing is absolute, that values are relative to circumstances. In criticism, relativism is either personal or historical.

Revenge Tragedy. The popular Elizabethan mode, initiated by Thomas Kyd's *Spanish Tragedy* (c. 1586), wherein the hero must revenge a ruler's murder of father, son, or lover.

Reversal. The thrilling change of luck for the protagonist at the last moment in comedy or tragedy—the *peripeteia*, which Aristotle first described in his *Poetics*, along with the discovery that usually sparks it.

Rhetoric. From Greek *rhetor*, "orator": the art of persuasion in speaking or writing. Since ancient times, rhetoric has been understood by some as a system of persuasive devices divorced from considerations of the merits of the case argued.

Rhetorical Figure. A figure of speech employing stylized patterns of word order or meaning for purposes of ornamentation or persuasion.

Rhetorical Question. A question posed for rhetorical effect, usually with a self-evident answer.

Rhyme (sometimes **Rime,** an older spelling). The effect created by matching sounds at the ends of words. The functions of rhyme are essentially four: pleasurable, mnemonic, structural, and rhetorical. Like meter and figurative language, rhyme provides a pleasure derived from fulfillment of a basic human desire to see similarity in dissimilarity, likeness with a difference.

Rhyme Royal. A stanza of seven lines of iambic pentameter, rhyming *ababbcc* (*see also* Meter).

Rhythm. The measured flow of repeated sound patterns, as, for example, the heavy stresses of accentual verse, the long and short syllables of quantitative verse, the balanced syntactical arrangements of parallelism in either verse or prose.

Romance. A continuous narrative in which the emphasis is on what happens in the plot, rather than on what is reflected from ordinary life or experience. Thus a central element in romance is adventure; at its most primitive, romance is an endless sequence of adventures.

Romanticism. A term describing qualities that colored most elements of European and American intellectual life in the late 18th and early 19th centuries, from literature, art, and music, through architecture, landscape gardening, philosophy, and politics. Within the social, political, and intellectual structures of society, the Romantics stressed the separateness of the person, celebrated individual perception and imagination, and embraced nature as a model for harmony in society and art. Their view was an egalitarian one, stressing the value of expressive abilities common to all, inborn rather than developed through training.

Roundheads. Adherents of the Parliamentary, or Puritan, party in the English Civil War, so called from their short haircuts, as opposed to the fashionable long wigs of the Cavaliers, supporters of King Charles I.

Rubric. From Latin *rubrica*, "red earth" (for coloring): in a book or manuscript, a heading, marginal notation, or other section distinguished for special attention by being printed in red ink or in distinctive type.

Run-on Line. A line of poetry whose sense does not stop at the end, with punctuation, but runs on to the next line.

Satire. Poking corrective ridicule at persons, types, actions, follies, mores, and beliefs.

Scop. An Anglo-Saxon bard, or court poet, a kind of poet laureate.

Semiotics. In anthropology, sociology, and linguistics, the study of signs, including words, other sounds, gestures, facial expressions, music, pictures, and other signals used in communication.

Senecan Tragedy. The bloody and bombastic tragedies of revenge inspired by Seneca's nine closet dramas, which had been discovered in Italy in the mid-16th century and soon thereafter translated into English.

Sensibility. Sensitive feeling, emotion. The term arose early in the 18th century to denote the tender undercurrent of feeling in the neoclassical period, continuing through Jane Austen's *Sense and Sensibility* (1811) and afterward.

Sequel. A literary work that explores later events in the lives of characters introduced elsewhere.

Serial. A narration presented in segments separated by time. Novels by Charles Dickens and other 19th-century writers were first serialized in magazines.

Seven Liberal Arts. The subjects studied in medieval universities, consisting of the *trivium* (grammar, logic, and rhetoric), for the B.A., and the *quadrivium* (arithmetic, geometry, astronomy, and music), for the M.A.

Shakespearean Sonnet (or English Sonnet). A sonnet in three quatrains and a couplet, rhyming *abab cdcd efef gg*.

Signified, Signifier. In structural linguistics, the *signified* is the idea in mind when a word is used, an entity separate from the *signifier*, the word itself.

Simile. A metaphor stating the comparison by use of *like*, *as*, or *as if*.

Slang. The special vocabulary of a class or group of people (as, for example, truck drivers, jazz musicians, salespeople, drug dealers), generally considered substandard, low, or offensive when measured against formal, educated usage.

Sonnet. A verse form of 14 lines, in English characteristically in iambic pentameter and most often in one of two rhyme schemes: the *Italian* (or *Petrarchan*) or *Shakespearean* (or *English*). An Italian sonnet is composed of an octave, rhyming *abbaabba*, and a sestet, rhyming *cdecde* or *cdcdcd*, or in some variant pattern, but with no closing couplet. A Shakespearean sonnet has three quatrains and a couplet, and rhymes *abab cdcd efef gg*. In both types, the content tends to follow the formal outline suggested by rhyme linkage, giving two divisions to the thought of an Italian sonnet and four to a Shakespearean one.

Sonnet Sequence. A group of sonnets thematically unified to create a longer work, although generally, unlike the stanza, each sonnet so connected can also be read as a meaningful separate unit.

Spondee. A metrical foot of two long, or stressed, syllables: – –.

Sprung Rhythm. Gerard Manley Hopkins's term to describe his variations of iambic meter to avoid the "same and tame." His feet, he said, vary from one to four syllables, with one stress per foot, on the first syllable.

Stanza. A term derived from an Italian word for "room" or "stopping place" and used, loosely, to designate any grouping of lines in a separate unit in a poem: a verse paragraph. More strictly, a stanza is a grouping of a prescribed number of lines in a given meter, usually with a particular rhyme scheme, repeated as a unit of structure. Poems in stanzas provide an instance of the aesthetic pleasure in repetition with a difference that also underlies the metrical and rhyming elements of poetry.

Stereotype. A character representing generalized racial or social traits repeated as typical from work to work, with no individualizing traits.

Stichomythia. Dialogue in alternate lines, favored in Greek tragedy and by Seneca and his imitators among the Elizabethans—including William Shakespeare.

Stock Characters. Familiar types repeated in literature to become symbolic of a particular genre, like the strong, silent hero of the western or the hard-boiled hero of the detective story.

Stoicism. (1) Generally, fortitude, repression of feeling, indifference to pleasure or pain. (2) Specifically, the philosophy of the Stoics, who, cultivating endurance and self-control, restrain passions such as joy and grief that place them in conflict with nature's dictates.

Stress. In poetry, the accent or emphasis given to certain syllables, indicated in scansion by a *macron* (–). In a trochee, for example, the stress falls on the first syllable: *sŭmmĕr*. *See also* Meter.

Structuralism. The study of social organizations and myths, of language, and of literature as structures. Each part is significant only as it relates to others in the total structure, with nothing meaningful by itself.

Structural Linguistics. Analysis and description of the grammatical structures of a spoken language.

Sublime. In literature, a quality attributed to lofty or noble ideas, grand or elevated expression, or (the ideal of sublimity) an inspiring combination of thought and language. In nature or art, it is a quality, as in a landscape or painting, that inspires awe or reverence.

Subplot. A sequence of events subordinate to the main story in a narrative or dramatic work.

Syllabic Verse. Poetry in which meter has been set aside and the line is controlled by a set number of syllables, regardless of stress.

Symbol. Something standing for its natural qualities in another context, with human meaning added: an eagle, standing for the soaring imperious dominance of Rome.

Symbolism. Any use of symbols, especially with a theoretical commitment, as when the French Symbolists of the 1880s and 1890s stressed, in Stéphane Mallarmé's words, not the thing but the effect, the subjective emotion implied by the surface rendering.

Snycopation. The effect produced in verse or music when two stress patterns play off against one another.

Synecdoche. The understanding of one thing by another—a kind of metaphor in which a part stands for the whole, or the whole for a part: *a hired hand* meaning "a laborer."

Synesthesia. Greek for "perceiving together": close association or confusion of sense impressions. The result is essentially a metaphor, transferring qualities of one sense to another, as in common phrases like "blue note" and "cold eye."

Synonyms. Words in the same language denoting the same thing, usually with different connotations: *female, woman, lady, dame; male, masculine, macho.*

Synopsis. A summary of a play, a narrative, or an argument.

Tenor and **Vehicle.** I. A. Richards's terms for the two aspects of metaphor, *tenor* being the actual thing projected figuratively in the *vehicle*. "She [tenor] is a rose [vehicle]."

Tercet (or **Triplet**). A verse unit of three lines, sometimes rhymed, sometimes not.

Terza Rima. A verse form composed of tercets with interlocking rhyme (*aba bcb cdc*, and so on), usually in iambic pentameter. Invented by Dante for his *Divine Comedy*.

Third-Person Narration. A method of storytelling in which someone who is not involved in the story, but stands somewhere outside it in space and time, tells of the events.

Topos. A commonplace, from Greek *topos* (plural *topoi*), "place." (1) A topic for argument, remembered by the classical system of placing it, in the mind's eye, in a place within a building and then proceeding mentally from one place to the next. (2) A rhetorical device, similarly remembered as a commonplace.

Tragedy. Fundamentally, a serious fiction involving the downfall of a hero or heroine. As a literary form, a basic mode of drama. Tragedy often involves the theme of isolation, in which a hero, a character of greater than ordinary human importance, becomes isolated from the community. Then there is the theme of the violation and reestablishment of order, in which the neutralizing of the violent act may take the form of revenge. Finally, a character may embody a passion too great for the cosmic order to tolerate, such as the passion of sexual love. Renaissance tragedy seems to be essentially a mixture of the heroic and the ironic. It tends to center on heroes who, though they cannot be of divine parentage in Christianized Western Europe, are still of titanic importance, with an articulate-ness and social authority beyond anything in our normal experience.

Tragic Irony. The essence of tragedy, in which the most noble and most deserving person, because of the very grounds of his or her excellence, dies in defeat. *See also* Irony.

Tragicomedy. (1) A tragedy with happy ending, frequently with penitent villain and roman-tic setting, disguises, and discoveries.

Travesty. Literally a "cross-dressing": a literary work so clothed, or presented, as to appear ludicrous; a grotesque image or likeness.

Trivium. The first three of the seven liberal arts as studied in medieval universities: grammar, logic, and rhetoric (including oratory).

Trochee. A metrical foot going – ⌣.

Trope. Greek *tropos* for "a turn": a word or phrase turned from its usual meaning to an unusu-al one; hence, a figure of speech, or an expression turned beyond its literal meaning.

Type. (1) A literary genre. (2) One of the type characters. (3) A symbol or emblem. (4) In theology and literary criticism, an event in early Scriptures or literatures that is seen as prefiguring an event in later Scriptures or in history or literature generally.

Type Characters. Individuals endowed with traits that mark them more distinctly as repre-sentatives of a type or class than as standing apart from a type: the typical doctor or rakish aristocrat, for example. Type characters are the opposite of individualized characters.

Typology. The study of types. Typology springs from a theory of literature or history that rec-ognizes events as duplicated in time.

Utopia. A word from two Greek roots (*outopia*, meaning "no place," and *eutopia*, meaning "good place"), pointing to the idea that a utopia is a nonexistent land of social perfection.

Verisimilitude (*vraisemblance* in French). The appearance of actuality.

Verso. The left-hand page of an open book; the back of a leaf of paper.

Vice. A stock character from the medieval morality play, a mischief-making tempter.

Vignette. (1) A brief, subtle, and intimate literary portrait, named for *vignette* portraiture, which is unbordered, shading off into the surrounding color at the edges, with features delicately rendered. (2) A short essay, sketch, or story, usually fewer than five hundred words.

Villanelle. One of the French verse forms, in five tercets, all rhyming *aba*, and a quatrain, rhyming *abaa*. The entire first and third lines are repeated alternately as the final lines of tercets 2, 3, 4, and 5, and together to conclude the quatrain.

Virgule. A "little rod"—the diagonal mark or slash used to indicate line ends in poetry print-ed continuously in running prose.

Vulgate. (1) A people's common vernacular language (Latin *vulgus*, "common people"). (2) The Vulgate Bible, translated by St. Jerome c. 383–405; the official Roman Catholic Bible.

Wit and Humor. *Wit* is intellectual acuity; *humor*, an amused indulgence of human deficien-cies. Wit now denotes the acuity that produces laughter. It originally meant mere under-standing, then quickness of understanding, then, beginning in the 17th century, quick perception coupled with creative fancy. Humor (British *humour*, from the four bodily humors) was simply a disposition, usually eccentric. In the 18th century, *humour* came to mean a laughable eccentricity and then a kindly amusement at such eccentricity.

Zeugma. The technique of using one word to yoke two or more others for ironic or amusing effect, achieved when at least one of the yoked is a misfit, as in Alexander Pope's "lose her Heart, or Necklace, at a Ball."

BIBLIOGRAPHIES
The Middle Ages

Dictionaries, Encyclopedias • Miranda Green, ed., *Dictionary of Celtic Mythology*, 1992. • Hans Kurath et al., eds., *The Middle English Dictionary*, 1952–. • Norris J. Lacy, ed., *The New Arthurian Encyclopedia*, 1991. • Joseph Strayer, gen. ed., *The Dictionary of the Middle Ages*, 13 vols., 1982–1989.

Journals • *Celtica* • *Exemplaria: A Journal of Theory in Medieval and Renaissance Studies* • *Medium Aevum* • *Speculum*, vol. 1–64 (1926–1989); available on-line through JS-TOR ("Journal Storage"): http://www.jstor.org

On-Line Sources • BARD (Bodleian Access to Remote Databases) online Chaucer Bibliography: http://www.bodley.ox.ac.uk/bardhtml/descriptions/ chaucer.html • *Beowulf* manuscript in color facsimile: http://www.uky.edu/~kiernan/BL/kportico.html • Images from medieval manuscripts can be viewed at http://acs1.byu.edu/7Ehurlbutj/dscriptorium/dscriptorium.html • French art of Chaucer's time, arranged by theme, can be viewed at an archive maintained by the Bibliothèque Nationale in Paris: http://www.bnf.fr/enluminures/accueil.htm • *The Labyrinth*, developed by Prof. Martin Irvine and Prof. Deborah Everhart, a clearing house for access to other, more specialized sites; a good starting point: http://www/georgetown.edu/labyrinth/ • Especially useful in *The Labyrinth* is "Daedalus' Guide to the Web," which surveys directories, search engines, and other resources: http://www.georgetown.edu/labyrinth/general/general.html • *The Piers Plowman Electronic Archive*: http://jefferson.village.virginia.edu/piers/archive.goals.html • For further primary texts that may be unavailable in some libraries, consult the University of Virginia's Electronic Text Center, accessible via *The Labyrinth* or at http://etext.lib.virginia.edu/

The British Isles Before the Norman Conquest • D. A. Binchy, *Celtic and Anglo-Saxon Kingship*, 1970. • Peter Hunter Blair, *Roman Britain and Early England, 55 B.C.–A.D. 871*, 1963. • Peter Hunter Blair, *Introduction to Anglo-Saxon England*, 2nd ed., 1977. • H. M. Chadwick, *The Heroic Age*, 1912. • Nora K. Chadwick, *The Celts*, 1970. • Liam de Paor, *The Peoples of Ireland*, 1986. • Myles Dillon and Nora K. Chadwick, *The Celtic Realms*, 1972. • *English Historical Documents*, vol. I, c. 500–1042, ed. Dorothy Whitelock, 1953. [Primary sources in English translation; introductions provide excellent context.] • Nicholas Howe, *Migration and Mythmaking in Anglo-Saxon England*, 1989. • Hugh A. MacDougall, *Racial Myth in English History: Trojans, Teutons, and Anglo-Saxons*, 1982. • Nerys Patterson, *Cattle Lords and Clansmen: The Social Structure of Early Ireland*, 2nd ed., 1996. • Frank M. Stenton, "Anglo-Saxon England," *The Oxford History of England*, vol. 2, 1971. • Dorothy Whitelock, *The Beginnings of English Society*, 1952. • David M. Wilson, *The Anglo-Saxons*, 1960.

The Norman Conquest and Its Impact • Jonathan Alexander and Paul Binski, *Age of Chivalry: Art in Plantagenet England 1200–1400*, 1987. • Christopher Brooke, *From Alfred to Henry III, 871–1272*, 1961. • R. Allen Brown, *The Normans*, 1984. • *English Historical Documents*, vol. II, *1042–1189*, eds. David C. Douglas and George W. Greenaway, 1953; vol. III, *1189–1327*, ed. Harry Rothwell, 1975. • Elizabeth Hallam, *Plantagenet Chronicles*, 1986. Chronicle sources, fine illustrations. • H. W. Koch, *Medieval Warfare*, 1978. • A. L. Poole, *From Domesday Book to Magna Carta*, The Oxford History of England, 1955. • F. M. Powicke, "The Thirteenth Century, 1216–1307," *The Oxford History of England*, vol. 4, 1953. • Pauline Stafford, *Unification and Conquest: A Political and Social History of England in the Tenth and Eleventh Centuries*, 1989. • Philip Warner, *The Medieval Castle*, 1971.

Continental and Insular Cultures • Judson B. Allen, *The Friar as Critic: Literary Attitudes in the Later Middle Ages*, 1971. • Erich Auerbach, *Mimesis: The Representation of Reality in Western Literature*, trans. Willard R. Trask, 1957. • William Calin, *The French Tradition and the Literature of Medieval England*, 1994. • Marcia Colish, *The Mirror of Language*, rev. ed., 1983. • Ernst Robert Curtius, *European Literature* and the Latin Middle Ages, trans. Willard R. Trask, 1953. • Peter Dronke, Medieval Latin and the Rise of the European Love Lyric, 2nd ed., 2 vols., 1968. • Robert W. Hanning, The Individual in Twelfth-Century Romance, 1978. • Johan Huizinga, The Autumn of the Middle Ages, trans. Rodney J. Payton and Ulrich Mammitzsch, 1996. • W. P. Ker, Epic and Romance, 1957. • C. S. Lewis, The Discarded Image: An Introduction to Medieval and Renaissance Literature, 1964. • A. J. Minnis, Medieval Theory of Authorship: Scholastic Literary Attitudes in the Later Middle Ages, 2nd ed., 1988. • Nigel Saul, ed., England in Europe 1066–1453, 1994. • Rosamund Tuve, Allegorical Imagery: Some Medieval Books and their Posterity, 1966.

Politics and Society in the Fourteenth and Fifteenth Centuries • David Aers, ed., Culture and History, 1350–1600, 1992. • R. B. Dobson, The Peasants' Revolt of 1381, 2nd ed., 1983. • English Historical Documents, vol. IV, 1327–1485, ed. A. R. Myers, 1969. • Rodney H. Hilton, Bond Men Made Free: Medieval Peasant Movements and the English Rising of 1381, 1973. • Ernest F. Jacob, "The Fifteenth Century," The Oxford History of England, vol. 6, 1961. • Maurice Keen, English Society in the Later Middle Ages, 1990. • Gordon Leff, The Dissolution of the Medieval Outlook: An Essay on Intellectual and Spiritual Change in the Fourteenth Century, 1976. • Gervase Matthew, The Court of Richard II, 1968. • May McKisack, The Fourteenth Century, 1307–1399, 1959. • Colin Platt, The English Medieval Town, 1976. • Juliet Vale, Edward III and Chivalry: Chivalric Society and Its Context 1270–1350, 1982. • David Wallace, Bodies and Disciplines: Intersections of Literature and History in Fifteenth-Century England, 1996. • Scott L. Waugh, England in the Reign of Edward III, 1991. [Extensive and helpful bibliography.]

Religious Institutions and Cultures • Margaret Aston, Lollards and Reformers, 1994. • Renate Blumenfeld-Kosinski and Timea Szell, eds., Images of Sainthood in Medieval Europe, 1991. • Janet Burton, Monastic and Religious Orders in Britain, 1000–1300, 1994. • M. D. Chenu, Nature, Man, and Society in the Twelfth Century, eds. and trans. Jerome Taylor and Lester K. Little, 1968. • Ronald C. Finucane, Miracles and Pilgrims: Popular Beliefs in Medieval England, 1977. • Thomas Heffernan, Sacred Biography: Saints and Their Biographers in the Middle Ages, 1988. • Anne Hudson, The Pre-mature Reformation: Wycliffite Texts and Lollard History, 1988. • W. A. Pantin, The English Church in the Fourteenth Century, 1980.

Gender, Sexuality, Courtliness, Marriage • John Boswell, Christianity, Social Tolerance, and Homosexuality: Gay People in Western Europe from the Beginning of the Christian Era to the Fourteenth Century, 1980. • Christopher Brooke, The Medieval Idea of Marriage, 1989. • Susan Crane, Insular Romance: Politics, Faith, and Culture in Anglo-Norman and Middle English Literature, 1986. • Georges Duby, The Knight, the Lady, and the Priest: The Making of Modern Marriage in Medieval France, trans. Barbara Bray, 1983. • Frances and Joseph Gies, Marriage and the Family in the Middle Ages, 1987. • Henry A. Kelly, Love and Marriage in the Age of Chaucer, 1975. • Clare A. Lees, ed., Medieval Masculinities: Regarding Men in the Middle Ages, 1994. • C. S. Lewis, The Allegory of Love, 1938. • V. J. Scattergood and J. W. Sherborne, eds., English Court Culture in the Later Middle Ages, 1983.

Women, Work, and Religion • Judith Bennett, Women in the Medieval English Countryside, 1986. • Caroline Walker Bynum, Holy Feast and Holy Fast: The Religious Significance of Food to Medieval Women, 1987. • Sharon Elkins, Holy Women of Twelfth Century England, 1988. • Mary Erler and Maryanne Kowaleski, eds., Women and Power in the Middle Ages, 1988. • Christine Fell, Women in Anglo-Saxon England, 1986. • Penny Schine Gold, The Lady and the Virgin: Image, Attitude, and Experience in Twelfth-Century France, 1985. • Barbara Hanawalt, ed., Women and Work in Preindustrial Europe, 1986. • Martha Howell, Women, Production and Patriarchy in Late Medieval Cities, 1986. • C. E. Meek and M. K. Simms, eds., The Fragility of Her Sex? Medieval Irish Women in Their European Context, 1995. • Barbara Newman, From Virile Woman to Woman Christ: Studies in Medieval Religion and Literature, 1995. • Pauline Stafford, Queens, Concubines, and Dowagers: The King's Wife in the Early Middle Ages, 1983. • Ulrike Wiethaus, ed., Maps of Flesh and Light: The Religious Experience of Medieval Women Mystics, 1993.

Modes of Transmission: Orality, Literacy, Manuscripts, Languages • Janet Backhouse, Books of Hours, 1985. • Mary Carruthers, The Book of Memory: A Study of Memory in Medieval Culture, 1990. • Roger Chartier, ed., The Culture of Print: Power and the Uses of Print in

Early Modern Europe, 1989. • M. T. Clanchy, From Memory to Written Record: England, 1066–1307, 2nd ed., 1993. • Janet Coleman, Medieval Readers and Writers, 1350–1400, 1981. • Joyce Coleman, Public Reading and the Reading Public in Late Medieval England and France, 1996. • John H. Fisher, The Emergence of Standard English, 1996. • John Miles Foley, The Theory of Oral Composition: History and Methodology, 1988. • Christopher de Hamel, A History of Illuminated Manuscripts, 1986. • Seth Lerer, Literacy and Power in Anglo-Saxon England, 1991. • Jeff Opland, Anglo-Saxon Oral Poetry: A Study of the Traditions, 1979. • Nicholas Orme, From Childhood to Chivalry: The Education of the English Kings and Aristocracy 1066–1530, 1984.

Old English Literature • Journals. • Anglo-Saxon England • Old English Newsletter

Bibliography. • Stanley B. Greenfield and Fred C. Robinson, Bibliography of Publications on Old English Literature, 1980.

Studies and Guides. • Michael Alexander, Old English Literature, 1983. • Jess B. Bessinger and Stanley J. Kahrl, eds., Essential Articles for the Study of Old English Poetry, 1968. • Jane Chance, Woman as Hero in Old English Literature, 1986. • Helen Damico and Alexandra Hennessey Olsen, eds., New Readings on Women in Old English Literature, 1990. • Allen J. Franzten, The Desire for Origins: New Language, Old English, and Teaching the Tradition, 1990. • Allen J. Franzten, ed., Speaking Two Languages: Traditional Disciplines and Contemporary Theory in Medieval Studies, 1991. • Malcolm Godden and Michael Lapidge, eds., The Cambridge Companion to Old English Literature, 1991. • Stanley B. Greenfield, Hero and Exile: The Art of Old English Poetry, 1989. • Stanley B. Greenfield and Daniel G. Calder, A New Critical History of Old English Literature, 1986. • Britton J. Harwood and Gillian Overing, eds., Class and Gender in Early English Literature: Intersections, 1994. • Katherine O'Brien O'Keeffe, ed., Old English Shorter Poems: Basic Readings, 1994. • Charles D. Wright, The Irish Tradition in Old English Literature, 1993.

Middle English Language and Literature • Middle English Grammar. • John A. Burrow and Thorlac Turville-Petre, A Book of Middle English, 1996. • Joseph Wright and Elizabeth Mary Wright, An Elementary Middle English Grammar, 1979.

Studies. • David Aers, Community, Gender, and Individual Identity: English Writing 1360–1430, 1988. • H. S. Bennett, "Chaucer and the Fifteenth Century," The Oxford History of English Literature, vol. 2, part 1, 1947. • J. A. W. Bennett and Douglas Gray, "Middle English Literature," The Oxford History of English Literature, vol. 1, part 2, 1986. • J. A. Burrow, Ricardian Poetry: Chaucer, Gower, Langland, and the Gawain, 1971. • E. K. Chambers, "English Literature at the Close of the Middle Ages," The Oxford History of English Literature, vol. 2, part 2, 1961. • Laurie A. Finke and Martin B. Schichtman, eds., Medieval Texts and Contemporary Readers, 1987. • Boris Ford, Medieval Literature: Chaucer and the Alliterative Tradition, 1982. • Stephen Justice, Writing and Rebellion: England in 1381, 1994. • Charles Muscatine, Poetry and Crisis in the Age of Chaucer, 1972. • Glending Olson, Literature as Recreation in the Later Middle Ages, 1982. • Lee Patterson, ed., Literary Practice and Social Change in Britain, 1380–1530, 1990. • Lee Patterson, Negotiating the Past: The Historical Understanding of Medieval Literature, 1987. • Larry Scanlon, Narrative, Authority, and Power: The Medieval Exemplum and the Chaucerian Tradition, 1994. • A. C. Spearing, Readings in Medieval Poetry, 1987. • Paul Strohm, Hochon's Arrow: The Social Imagination of Fourteenth-Century Texts, 1992. • Thorlac Turville-Petre, The Alliterative Revival, 1977.

Celtic Culture and Literature • Bibliography. • Rachel Bromwich, Medieval Celtic Literature: A Select Bibliography, 1974.

Studies. • Miranda J. Green, ed., Celtic Goddesses: Warriors, Virgins, and Mothers, 1995. • Miranda J. Green, ed., The Celtic World, 1995.

Irish Culture and Literature • Translations. • James Carney, Medieval Irish Lyrics with "The Irish Bardic Poet," 1985. • Tom Peete Cross and Clark Harris Slover, eds., Ancient Irish Tales, 1936; repr. with updated bibliography, 1969. • Kenneth Hurlstone Jackson, A Celtic Miscellany: Translations from the Celtic Literatures, 1951. • Kuno Meyer, trans., Ancient Irish Poetry, 1994. • Frank O'Connor, trans., Kings, Lords, and Commons: An Anthology from the Irish, 1959.

Studies. • James Carney, Studies in Irish Literature and History, 1979. • Doris Edel, ed., Cultural Identity and Cultural Integration: Ireland

and Europe in the Early Middle Ages, 1995. • Jeffrey Gantz, Early Irish Myths and Sagas, 1981. • Kim McKone, Pagan Past and Christian Present in Early Irish Literature, 1990. • Nerys Patterson, Cattle Lords and Clansmen: The Social Structure of Early Ireland, 2nd ed., 1996. • Alwyn Rees and Brinley Rees, Celtic Heritage, 1961. • J. E. Caerwyn Williams and Patrick K. Ford, The Irish Literary Tradition, 1992.

Welsh Culture and Literature • Translations. • Joseph Clancy, The Earliest Welsh Poetry, 1970. • Anthony Conran, The Penguin Book of Welsh Verse, 1967. • D. Johnston, ed. and trans., Medieval Welsh Erotic Poetry, 1991.

Bibliography. • Rachel Bromwich, Medieval Celtic Literature: A Select Bibliography, 1974.

Studies. • Stephen S. Evans, The Heroic Poetry of Dark-Age Britain, 1997. • Kenneth Jackson, Language and History in Early Britain, 1953. • A. O. H. Jarman, The Cynfeirdd: Early Welsh Poets and Poetry, 1981. • A. O. H. Jarman and Gwilym Rees Hughes, eds., A Guide to Welsh Literature, vol. I, 1976. • Jenny Rowland, Early Welsh Saga Poetry, 1990. • Sir Ifor Williams, The Beginnings of Welsh Poetry: Studies, 1980.

Perspectives: Arthurian Myth in the History of Britain • Translations. • Geoffrey of Monmouth, History of the Kings of Britain, trans. Lewis Thorpe, 1966. • Gerald of Wales, The Journey through Wales and The Description of Wales, trans. L. Thorpe, 1978. • E. L. G. Stones, ed. and trans., Anglo-Scottish Relations 1174–1328: Some Selected Documents, 1965.

Studies. • Christopher Brooke, "Geoffrey of Monmouth as a Historian," in C. Brooke et al., eds., Church and Government in the Middle Ages, 1976. • Michael J. Curley, Geoffrey of Monmouth, 1994. • John Gillingham, "The Context and Purposes of Geoffrey of Monmouth's History of the Kings of Britain," Anglo-Norman Studies vol. 13, 1990. • Robert W. Hanning, The Vision of History in Early Britain: From Gildas to Geoffrey of Monmouth, 1966. • R. William Leckie, Jr., The Passage of Dominion: Geoffrey of Monmouth and the Periodization of Insular History in the Twelfth Century, 1981. • Roger Sherman Loomis, ed., Arthurian Literature in the Middle Ages, 1959. • Monika Otter, Inventiones: Fiction and Referentiality in Twelfth-Century Historical Writing, 1996. • Michael Prestwich, Edward the First, 1988. •

E. L. G. Stones, Edward I, 1968. • J. S. P. Tatlock, The Legendary History of Britain, 1950.

Arthurian Romance • Bibliography. • Norris J. Lacy, ed., Medieval Arthurian Literature: A Guide to Recent Research, 1996.

Encyclopedia. • Norris J. Lacy, ed., The New Arthurian Encyclopedia, 1991.

Journal. • Arthurian Literature

Studies. • John Darrah, Paganism in Arthurian Romance, 1994. • Thelma Fenster, ed., Arthurian Women: A Casebook, 1996. • Maureen Fries and Jeanie Watson, eds., Approaches to Teaching the Arthurian Tradition, 1992. • Edward D. Kennedy, ed., King Arthur: A Casebook, 1996. • Stephen Knight, Arthurian Literature and Society, 1983. • Roger Sherman Loomis, ed., Arthurian Literature in the Middle Ages: A Collaborative History, 1969. • Martin Schichtman and James Carley, eds., Culture and the King: the Social Implications of the Arthurian Legend, 1994. • Eugene Vinaver, The Rise of Romance, 1984.

Middle Scots Poetry • Walter Scheps and J. Anna Looney, eds., Middle Scots Poets: A Reference Guide to James I of Scotland, Robert Henryson, William Dunbar, and Gavin Douglas, 1986.

Mystical Writings • Bibliography. • Michael E. Sawyer, A Bibliographical Index of Five English Mystics: Richard Rolle, Julian of Norwich, the Author of The Cloud of Unknowing, Walter Hilton, Margery Kempe, 1978.

General Studies. • David Aers and Lynn Staley, The Powers of the Holy: Religion, Politics, and Gender in Late Medieval English Culture, 1996. • Sarah Beckwith, Christ's Body: Identity, Culture, and Society in Late Medieval Writings, 1993. • Frances Beer, Women and Mystical Experience in the Middle Ages, 1992. • Marion Glasscoe, ed., The Medieval Mystical Tradition in England, Exeter Symposium, vols. 1–5, 1980–1992. • Wolfgang Riehle, The Middle English Mystics, trans. Bernard Standring, 1981. • Paul Szarmach, ed., An Introduction to the Medieval Mystics of Europe, 1984. • A. K. Warren, Anchorites and their Patrons in Medieval England, 1985.

Travel • Studies. • A. L. Binns, Viking Voyages, 1980. • Mary B. Campbell, The Witness and the Other World: Exotic European Travel Writing, 400–1600, 1988. • Donald R. Howard, Writers and Pilgrims: Medieval Pilgrimage Narra-

tives and their Posterity, 1980. • Scott D. Westrem, ed., *Discovering New Worlds: Essays on Medieval Exploration and Imagination*, 1991.

King Alfred and Asser's *Life of Alfred* • Translations. • Kevin Crossley-Holland, ed., *The Anglo-Saxon World: An Anthology*, 1983. [translation used] • L. C. Jane, trans., *Asser's Life of King Alfred*, 1926. [translation used] • Simon Keynes and Michael Lapidge, trans., *Alfred the Great: Asser's Life of King Alfred and Other Contemporary Sources*, 1983.

Studies. • Alfred P. Smyth, *King Alfred the Great*, 1995. • David J. Sturdy, *Alfred the Great*, 1995. • Dorothy Whitelock, *The Genuine Asser*, 1968.

The Anglo-Saxon Chronicle • Translation. • Anne Savage, trans., *The Anglo-Saxon Chronicles*, 1982.

Study. • Stephen Morillo, ed., *The Battle of Hastings: Sources and Interpretations*, 1996.

Bede • Translation. • Bertram Colgrave and R. A. B. Mynors., eds. and trans., *Bede's Ecclesiastical History of the English People*, 1969.

Studies. • Peter Hunter Blair, *The World of Bede*, 1970. • George H. Brown, *Bede, the Venerable*, 1987. • Robert T. Farrell, ed., *Bede and Anglo-Saxon England*, 1978. • J. M. Wallace-Hadrill, *Bede's Ecclesiastical History of the English People: A Historical Commentary*, 1993. • Benedicta Ward, *The Venerable Bede*, 1990.

Beowulf • Edition. • Frederick Klaeber, ed., *Beowulf and the Fight at Finnsburg*, rev. W. F. Bolton, 1973. [standard edition]

Translations. • Kevin Crossley-Holland, trans., *Beowulf*, 1968. [translation used] • E. T. Donaldson, trans., *Beowulf*, ed. Joseph F. Tuso, 1975. [Norton Critical Edition] • Howell D. Chickering, Jr., trans., Beowulf: *A Dual-Language Edition*, 1977.

Bibliography. • Robert J. Hasenfratz, *Beowulf Scholarship: An Annotated Bibliography, 1979–1990*, 1993.

Studies. • Peter S. Baker, *Beowulf: Basic Readings*, 1995. • Adrien Bonjour, *The Digressions in Beowulf*, 1950. • R. W. Chambers, *Beowulf: An Introduction to the Study of the Poem*, 3rd ed., suppl. C. L. Wrenn, 1959. • George Clark, *Beowulf*, 1990. • John Miles Foley, *Traditional Oral Epic: The Odyssey, Beowulf, and the Serbo-Croatian Return Song*, 1990. •

Donald K. Fry, ed. *The Beowulf Poet*, 1968. • R. D. Fulk, ed., *Interpretations of Beowulf: A Critical Anthology*, 1991. • Edward B. Irving, Jr., *Rereading Beowulf*, 1989. • J. D. A. Ogilvy and Donald C. Baker, *Reading Beowulf: An Introduction to the Poem, Its Background, and Its Style*, 1983. • Gillian Overing, *Language, Sign, and Gender in Beowulf*, 1990. • Fred C. Robinson, Beowulf *and the Appositive Style*, 1985. • J. R. R. Tolkien, Beowulf, *the Monsters, and the Critics*, 1937.

Chaucer • Editions. • E. Talbot Donaldson, ed., *Chaucer's Poetry*, 1957. [edition used] • Larry D. Benson, gen. ed., *The Riverside Chaucer*, 3rd ed., 1987. [standard edition] • V. A. Kolve and Glending Olson, eds., The Canterbury Tales: *Nine Tales and the "General Prologe,"* 1989. [Norton Critical Edition] • Peter G. Beidler, ed., *Geoffrey Chaucer: "The Wife of Bath": Complete, Authoritative Text with Biographical and Historical Context, Critical History, and Essays from Five Contemporary Critical Perspectives*, 1996.

Electronic Editions. • *Chaucer: Life and Times*, CD-ROM, Primary Sources Media 1995. [With full text from *The Riverside Chaucer*; notes and glosses in pull-down windows.] • Peter Robinson, ed., *The Wife of Bath's Prologue*, Cambridge University Press 1996. [Challenging format, but complete survey of manuscripts.]

Biographies. • Martin M. Crow and C. Olson, eds., *Chaucer Life-Records*, 1966. • Donald R. Howard, *Chaucer: His Life, His Works, His World*, 1987.

Bibliography. • John Leyerle and Anne Quick, *Chaucer: A Bibliographical Introduction*, 1986. • BARD (Bodleian Access to Remote Databases) online Chaucer Bibliography: http://www.ox. ac.uk/bardhtml/descriptions/chaucer.html

Journals. • *Studies in the Age of Chaucer* • *Chaucer Review* • *Chaucer Yearbook: A Journal of Late Medieval Studies*

Handbooks and Source Collections. • Larry D. Benson and Theodore Anderson, eds., *The Literary Context of Chaucer's Fabliaux*, 1971. • Piero Boitani and Jill Mann, eds., *Cambridge Chaucer Companion*, 1986. • Robert P. Miller, ed., *Chaucer: Sources and Backgrounds*, 1977. • Beryl Rowland, ed., *Companion to Chaucer Studies*, 2nd ed., rev. 1979.

General Studies. • Susan Crane, *Gender and Romance in Chaucer's Canterbury Tales*, 1994.

• Alfred David, *The Strumpet Muse: Art and Morals in Chaucer's Poetry*, 1976. • Carolyn Dinshaw, *Chaucer's Sexual Poetics*, 1989. • E. Talbot Donaldson, *Speaking of Chaucer*, 1970. • John M. Fyler, *Chaucer and Ovid*, 1979. • Peggy Knapp, *Chaucer and the Social Contest*, 1990. • Stephen Knight, *Geoffrey Chaucer*, 1986. • V. A. Kolve, *Chaucer and the Imagery of Narrative*, 1984. • Charles Muscatine, *Chaucer and the French Tradition*, 1957. • Lee Patterson, *Chaucer and the Subject of History*, 1991. • D. W. Robertson Jr., *Chaucer's London*, 1968. • D. W. Robertson Jr., *A Preface to Chaucer*, 1962. • Donald M. Rose, ed., *New Perspectives in Chaucer Criticism*, 1981. • Paul Strohm, *Social Chaucer*, 1989. • David Wallace, *Chaucerian Polity: Absolutist Lineages and Associational Forms in England and Italy*, 1997.

Studies, *Parliament of Fowls*. • Jerome Mitchell and William Provost, eds., *Chaucer the Love Poet*, 1973. • Robert O. Payne, *The Key of Remembrance*, 1963. • Winthrop Wetherbee, *Platonism and Poetry in the Twelfth Century: The Literary Influence of the School of Chartres*, 1972.

Studies, *Canterbury Tales*. • C. David Benson, *Chaucer's Drama of Style: Poetic Variety and Contrast in The Canterbury Tales*, 1986. • Muriel Bowden, *A Commentary on the General Prologue to The Canterbury Tales*, 1948. • Donald R. Howard, *The Idea of The Canterbury Tales*, 1976. • H. Marshall Leicester Jr., *The Disenchanted Self: Representing the Subject in The Canterbury Tales*, 1990. • Carl Lindahl, *Earnest Games: Folkloric Patterns in The Canterbury Tales*, 1987. • Jill Mann, *Chaucer and the Medieval Estates Satire*, 1973. • Paul A. Olson, *The Canterbury Tales and the Good Society*, 1986. • Winthrop Wetherbee, *Geoffrey Chaucer: The Canterbury Tales*, 1989.

The Cloud of Unknowing • Translation. • *The Cloud of Unknowing*, trans. Clifton Wolters, 1978.

Edition. • *The Cloud of Unknowing*, ed. James Walsh, 1981.

Study. • A. J. Burrow, "Fantasy and Language in *The Cloud of Unknowing*," *Essays in Criticism*, vol. 27, 1977.

Dayfydd ap Gwilym • Translations. • Rolfe Humphries, trans., *Nine Thorny Thickets: Selected Poems by Dafydd ap Gwilym in New Arrangements by Jon Roush*, 1969. [edition used] • Rachel Bromwich, trans., *Dafydd ap Gwilym: A Selection of Poems*, 1982. • Richard Morgan Loomis, trans., *Dafydd ap Gwilym: The Poems*, 1982.

Studies. • Rachel Bromwich, *Aspects of the Poetry of Dafydd ap Gwilym: Collected Papers*, 1986. • Helen Fulton, *Dafydd ap Gwilym and the European Context*, 1989.

The Dream of the Rood • Edition. • *The Dream of the Rood*, ed. Michael Swanton, 1970.

Translation. • Kevin Crossley-Holland, ed., *The Anglo-Saxon World: An Anthology*, 1983.

Studies. • Martin Irvine, "Anglo-Saxon Literary Theory Exemplified in Old English Poems: Interpreting the Cross in *The Dream of the Rood* and *Elene*," *Old English Shorter Poems*, ed. Katherine O'Brien O'Keeffe, 1994. • Rosemary Woolf, "Doctrinal Influences in *The Dream of the Rood*," *Medium Aevum*, vol. 27, 1958.

William Dunbar • Edition. • *William Dunbar: Poems*, ed. James Kinsley, 1958.

Studies. • Priscilla Bawcutt, *Dunbar the Maker*, 1992. • Edmund Reiss, *William Dunbar*, 1978. • Florence Ridley, "Studies in Dunbar and Henryson: The Present Situation," *Fifteenth-Century Studies: Recent Essays*, ed. Robert F. Yeager, 1984.

Marie de France • Translations. • Glyn S. Burgess and Keith Busby, trans., *The Lais of Marie de France*, 1986. • Robert Hanning and Joan Ferrante, *The Lais of Marie de France*, 1978. [translation used]

Bibliography. • Glyn S. Burgess, *Marie de France: An Analytical Bibliography*, 1977; suppl. no. 1, 1986.

Studies. • Margaret M. Boland, *Architectural Structure in the Lais of Marie de France*, 1995. • Glyn S. Burgess, *The Lais of Marie de France: Text and Context*, 1987. • Paula M. Clifford, *Marie de France, Lais*, 1982. • Emanuel J. Mickel, *Marie de France*, 1974.

Robert Henryson • Edition. • *Robert Henryson: Poems*, ed. Charles Elliott, 1963.

Critical Study. • Robert L. Kindrick, *Robert Henryson*, 1974.

Judith • Edition. • *Judith*, ed. B. J. Timmer, 1966.

Translation. • S. A. J. Bradley, trans., *Anglo-Saxon Poetry*, 1982.

Studies. • Karma Lochrie, "Gender, Sexual Violence, and the Politics of War in the Old English *Judith*," *Class and Gender in Early English Literature*, eds. Britton J. Harwood and Gillian Overing, 1994. • Helen Damico, "The Valkyrie Reflex in Old English Literature," *New Readings on Women in Old English Literature*, eds. Helen Damico and Alexandra Hennessey Olsen.

Julian of Norwich • Translation. • *Showings*, trans. Edmund Colledge and James Walsh, 1978.

Study. • Denise Nowakowski Baker, *Julian of Norwich's Showings: From Vision to Book*, 1994.

Margery Kempe • Translation. • *The Book of Margery Kempe*, trans. B. A. Windeatt, 1985.

Studies. • Clarissa W. Atkinson, *Mystic and Pilgrim: The Book and the World of Margery Kempe*, 1983. • Karma Lochrie, *Margery Kempe and Translations of the Flesh*, 1991. • Sandra McEntire, ed., *Margery Kempe: A Book of Essays*, 1992. • Lynn Staley, *Margery Kempe's Dissenting Fictions*, 1994.

William Langland, *Piers Plowman* • Editions. • Derek Pearsall, ed., Piers Plowman *by William Langland: An Edition of the C-Text*, 1979. • A. V. C. Schmidt, ed., Piers Plowman: *A Parallel-Text Edition of the A, B, C, and Z Versions*, 2 vols., 1995.

Translations. • E. T. Donaldson, trans., Piers Ploughman: *An Alliterative Verse Translation*, 1990. [translation used] • J. F. Goodridge, trans., *Langland: Piers the Ploughman*, rev. 1966.

Bibliography. • Anthony J. Colaianne, Piers Plowman: *An Annotated Bibliography of Editions and Criticism 1550–1977*, 1978.

Studies. • David Aers, *Chaucer, Langland, and the Creative Imagination*, 1980. • John A. Alford, *A Companion to Piers Plowman*, 1988. • Anna Baldwin, *The Theme of Government in Piers Plowman*, 1981. • J. A. Burrow, *Langland's Fictions*, 1993. • F. R. H. DuBoulay, *The England of Piers Plowman*, 1991. • S. S. Hussey, ed., Piers Plowman: *Critical Approaches*, 1969. • Steven Justice and Kathryn Kerby-Fulton, eds., *Written Work: Langland, Labor, and Authorship*, 1997. • Kathryn Kerby-Fulton, *Reformist Apocalypticism and* Piers Plowman, 1990. • Jeanne Krochalis and Edward Peters, *The World of* Piers Plowman,

1975. • Elizabeth Salter, Piers Plowman: *An Introduction*, 1962. • James Simpson, Piers Plowman: *An Introduction to the B-Text*, 1990.

***Piers Plowman* in Context** • Editions. • R. B. Dobson, *The Peasants' Revolt of 1381*, 1970. • Rossell Hope Robbins, ed., *Historical Poems of the XIVth and XVth Centuries*, 1959. • Eric W. Stockton, trans., *The Major Latin Works of John Gower*, 1962.

Studies. • David Aers, *Community, Gender, and Individual Identity: English Writing 1360–1430*, 1988. • Allen Frantzen, ed., *The Work of Work: Servitude, Slavery, and Work in Medieval England*, 1994. • Jesse Gellrich, *Discourse and Dominion in the Fourteenth Century*, 1995. • Barbara Hanawalt, ed., *Chaucer's England: Literature in Historical Context*, 1992. • Stephen Justice, *Writing and Rebellion: England in 1381*, 1994.

Second Play of the Shepherds • Editions. • Peter Happ, *English Mystery Plays: A Selection*, 1975. [edition used] • David Bevington, ed., *Medieval Drama*, 1975. • Martin Stevens and A. C. Cawley, eds., *The Townley Plays*, 2 vols., 1994.

Bibliography. • Sidney E. Berger, ed., *Medieval English Drama: An Annotated Bibliography of Recent Criticism*, 1990.

Studies and Guides. • Richard Beadle, ed., *The Cambridge Companion to Medieval English Theatre*, 1994. • Richard K. Emmerson, ed., and V. A. Kolve, intro., *Approaches to Teaching Medieval English Drama*, 1990. • O. B. Hardison Jr., *Christian Rite and Christian Drama in the Middle Ages*, 1965. • V. A. Kolve, *The Play Called Corpus Christi*, 1966. • Martin Stevens, *Four Middle English Mystery Cycles: Textual, Contextual, and Critical Interpretations*, 1987.

The Mabinogi • Translation. • Patrick Ford, trans., *The Mabinogi and Other Medieval Welsh Tales*, 1977. [translation used] • Gwyn and Thomas Jones, trans., *The Mabinogion*, 1949.

Studies. • W. J. Gruffyd, *Folklore and Myth in The Mabinogion*, 1994. • Sioned Davies, *The Four Branches of The Mabinogi*, 1993. • Proinsias MacCana, *The Mabinogi*, 1992. • Caitlin Matthews, *Mabon and the Mysteries of Britain: An Exploration of The Mabinogion*, 1987.

Sir Thomas Malory • Editions. • Thomas Malory, *Le Morte d'Arthur*, ed. Janet Cowen, intro.

John Lawlor, 2 vols., 1969. • Thomas Malory, *King Arthur and his Knights: Selected Tales*, ed. E. Vinaver, 1975. [edition used] • *The Works of Sir Thomas Malory*, ed. Eugene Vinaver, 1977.

Guides and Studies. • Elizabeth Archibald and A. S. G. Edwards, *A Companion to Malory*, 1996. • Larry D. Benson, *Malory's Morte Darthur*, 1976. • Burt Dillon, *A Malory Handbook*, 1978. • P. J. C. Field, *The Life and Times of Sir Thomas Malory*, 1993. • Beverly Kennedy, *Knighthood in the Morte d'Arthur*, 1985. • Terence McCarthy, *An Introduction to Malory*, rev. ed., 1991. • William Matthews, *The Ill-Framed Knight: A Skeptical Inquiry into the Identity of Sir Thomas Malory*, 1966. • Charles Moorman, *The Book of Kyng Arthur: The Unity of Malory's Morte Darthur*, 1965. • Felicity Riddy, *Sir Thomas Malory*, 1987. • Toshiyuki Takamiya and Derek Brewer, eds., *Aspects of Malory*, 1981. • Muriel Whitaker, *Arthur's Kingdom of Adventure: The World of Malory's Morte Darthur*, 1984.

Sir John Mandeville • Translation. • *The Travels of Sir John Mandeville*, trans. C. W. R. D. Moseley, 1983.

Studies. • Iain Higgins, *Writing East: The Travels of Sir John Mandeville*, 1997. • Josef Krasa, ed., The Travels of Sir John Mandeville: *A Manuscript in the British Library*, 1983.

Middle English Lyrics • Editions. • Maxwell S. Luria and Richard L. Hoffman, eds., *Middle English Lyrics*, 1974. [Norton Critical Edition; edition used] • R. T. Davies, *Medieval English Lyrics: A Critical Anthology*, 1963. [edition used] • Theodore Silverstein, ed., *English Lyrics Before 1500*, 1971. • Celia Sisam and Kenneth Sisam, eds., *The Oxford Book of Medieval English Verse*, 1970.

Translations. • Frederick Goldin, trans., *The Lyrics of the Troubadours and Trouvères: Original Texts, with Translations and Introductions*, 1973. • James J. Wilhelm, *Medieval Song: An Anthology of Hymns and Lyrics*, 1971.

Studies. • Peter Dronke, *The Medieval Lyric*, 3rd ed., 1996. • John F. Plummer, ed., *Vox Feminae: Studies in Medieval Woman's Song*, 1981. • Douglas Gray, *Themes and Images in the Medieval English Religious Lyric*, 1972. • Rosemary Woolf, *The English Religious Lyric in the Middle Ages*, 1968.

Ohthere's Journey • Translation and Study. • Niels Lund, ed., and Christine Fell, trans.,

Two Voyagers at the Court of King Alfred: The Ventures of Ohthere and Wulfstan, 1984.

Riddles • Edition. • Frederick Tupper Jr., ed., *The Riddles of the Exeter Book*, repr. 1968.

Translations. • Michael J. Alexander, trans. *Old English Riddles from the Exeter Book*, 1980. [translation used] • James Hall Pitman, ed. and trans., *The Riddles of Aldhelm: Text and Verse Translation*, 1925. [translation used] • Craig Williamson, trans., *A Feast of Creatures: Anglo-Saxon Riddle Songs*, 1982.

Study. • Nancy Porter Stork, *Through a Gloss Darkly: Aldhelm's Riddles in the British Library*, ms. Royal 12.c.xxiii, 1990.

Richard Rolle • Translation. • *The Fire of Love*, trans. Clifton Wolters, 1972.

Study. • Nicholas Watson, *Richard Rolle and the Invention of Authority*, 1992.

Sir Gawain and the Green Knight • Translations. • Marie Borroff, trans., *Sir Gawain and the Green Knight*, 1967. [translation used] • W. R. J. Barron, ed. and trans., *Sir Gawain and the Green Knight*, 1974.

Bibliography. • Malcolm Andrew, *The Gawain-Poet: An Annotated Bibliography, 1839–1977*, 1979.

Guides and Studies. • Ross Arthur, *Medieval Sign Theory and Sir Gawain and the Green Knight*, 1987. • Larry D. Benson, *Art and Tradition in Sir Gawain and the Green Knight*, 1965. • Robert J. Blanch et al., eds., *Text and Matter: New Critical Perspectives of the Pearl-Poet*, 1991. • Robert J. Blanch and Julian Wasserman, *From Pearl to Gawain: Forme to Fynisment*, 1995. • Marie Borroff, *Sir Gawain and the Green Knight: A Stylistic and Metrical Study*, 1973. • Derek Brewer and Jonathan Gibson, eds., *A Companion to the Gawain-Poet*, 1997. • Elisabeth Brewer, comp., *Sir Gawain and the Green Knight: Sources and Analogues*, 1992. • John Burrow, *A Reading of Sir Gawain and the Green Knight*, 1966. • Wendy Clein, *Concepts of Chivalry in Sir Gawain and the Green Knight*, 1987. • Lynn Staley Johnson, *The Voice of the Gawain-Poet*, 1984. • Sandra Pierson Prior, *The Pearl Poet Revisited*, 1994. • Ad Putter, *An Introduction to the Gawain-Poet*, 1996. • Allen Shoaf, *The Poem as Green Girdle: Commercium in Sir Gawain and the Green Knight*, 1984. • A. C. Spearing, *The Gawain-Poet: a Critical Study*, 1970. • Meg Stainsby,

Sir Gawain and the Green Knight: *An Annotated Bibliography, 1978–1989*, 1992.

The Táin • Translations. • Cecile O'Rahilly, ed. and trans., *Táin bó Cúalnge from the Book of Leinster*, 1967. [translation used] • Thomas Kinsella, trans., *The Tain*, 1985. [A powerful translation, assembled and slightly rearranged from several Old Irish versions.]

Studies. • Kenneth H. Jackson, *The Oldest Irish Tradition: A Window on the Iron Age*, 1964. • J. P. Mallory, ed., *Aspects of* The Tain, 1992.

Taliesin • Translation. • Ifor and J. Caerwyn Williams, trans., *The Poems of Taliesin*, 1968.

Study. • J. E. Caerwyn Williams, *The Poets of the Welsh Princes*, 1994.

The Voyage of St. Brendan • Translation. • J. F. Webb, trans., *Lives of the Saints*, 1965.

Studies. • Geoffrey Ashe, *Land to the West: St. Brendan's Voyage to America*, 1962. • Frederick Buechner, *Brendan*, 1987.

The Wanderer • Editions. • T. P. Dunning and A. J. Bliss, eds., *The Wanderer*, 1969. • Anne L. Klinck, *The Old English Elegies: A Critical Edition and Genre Study*, 1992.

Translation. • Kevin Crossley-Holland, ed., *The Anglo-Saxon World: An Anthology*, 1983.

Study. • Martin Green, ed., *The Old English Elegies: New Essays in Criticism and Research*, 1983.

The Wife's Lament • Edition. • Anne L. Klinck, *The Old English Elegies: A Critical Edition and Genre Study*, 1992.

Translation. • Kevin Crossley-Holland, ed., *The Anglo-Saxon World: An Anthology*, 1983.

Studies. • Helen T. Bennett, "Exile and the Semiosis of Gender in Old English Elegies," *Class and Gender in Early English Literature*, eds. Britton J. Harwood and Gillian Overing, 1994. • Ruth Barrie Strauss, "Women's Words as Weapons in The Wife's Lament," *Old English Shorter Poems*, ed. Katharine O'Brien O'Keeffe, 1994.

Wulf and Eadwacer • Edition. • Anne L. Klinck, *The Old English Elegies: A Critical Edition and Genre Study*, 1992.

Translation. • Kevin Crossley-Holland, ed., *The Anglo-Saxon World: An Anthology*, 1983.

Studies. • Helen T. Bennett, "Exile and the Semiosis of Gender in Old English Elegies" *Class and Gender in Early English Literature*, ed. Britton J. Harwood and Gillian Overing, 1994. • Pat Bellanoff, "Women's Songs, Women's Language: *Wulf and Eadwacer* and *The Wife's Lament*," *New Readings on Women in Old English Literature*, eds. Helen Damico and Alexandra Hennessey Olsen, 1990. • Marilyn Desmond, "The Voice of Exile: Feminist Literary History and the Anonymous Anglo-Saxon Elegy," *Critical Inquiry*, vol. 16, 1990.

Early Modern Period

Bibliographies • *English Literary Renaissance*, 1971 to present. • Alfred Harbage, ed., S. Schoenbaum rev., *Annals of English Drama, 975–1700*, 3 vols. • *New Cambridge Bibliography of English Literature, 600–1600*, 1969. • S. A. and D. R. Tannenbaum, eds., *Elizabethan Bibliographies*, 10 vols., 1967.

Guides to Research • A. R. Braunmuller and Michael Hattaway, *The Cambridge Companion to English Renaissance Drama*, 1990. • Douglas Bush, *English Literature in the Earlier Seventeenth Century 1600–1660*, 1962. • C. S. Lewis, *English Literature in the Sixteenth Century*, 1954. • A. W. Ward and A. R. Waller, eds., *The Cambridge History of English Literature*, 15 vols., vols. 3–6, 1909.

Drama, Poetry, and Prose • David Bevington, *Tudor Drama and Politics*, 1968. • Rebecca Bushnell, *Tragedies of Tyrants*, 1990. • Jonathan Dollimore, *Radical Tragedy. Religion, Ideology and Power in the Drama of Shakespeare and His Contemporaries*, 1985. • Martin Elsky, *Authorizing Words: Speech, Writing and Print in the Renaissance*, 1989. • Anne Ferry, *"The Inward Language": Sonnets of Wyatt, Sidney, Shakespeare and Donne*, 1983. • Ernest B. Gilman, *Iconoclasm and Poetry in the English Reformation*, 1986. • Stephen Greenblatt, *Renaissance Self-*

Fashioning, 1980. • Thomas M. Greene, The Light in Troy: Imitation and Discovery in Renaissance Poetry, 1982. • Andrew Gurr, Playgoing in Shakespeare's London, 1987. • Peter Herman, ed., Rethinking the Henrician Age: Essays on Early Tudor Texts and Contexts, 1994. • John King, English Reformation Literature: The Tudor Origins of the Protestant Tradition, 1982. • Janel Mueller, The Native Tongue and the Word: Developments in English Prose Style, 1380–1580, 1984. • Steven Mullaney, The Place of the Stage: License, Place and Power in Renaissance England, 1988. • David Norbrook, Poetry and Politics in the English Renaissance, 1984. • Stephen Orgel, The Illusion of Power: Political Theater in the English Renaissance, 1971. • Patricia Parker, Inescapable Romance, 1979. • David Quint, Epic and Empire, 1993. • Wayne Rebhorn, The Emperor of Men's Minds: Literature and the Renaissance Discourse of Rhetoric, 1995. • Rosemund Tuve, Elizabethan and Metaphysical Imagery, 1947.

History, Religion, and Political Thought • Glenn Burgess, Absolute Monarchy and the Stuart Constitution, 1996. • Patrick Collinson, The Elizabethan Puritan Movement, 1967. • John Guy, Tudor England, 1988. • Richard Helgerson, Forms of Nationhood: The Elizabethan Writing of England, 1992. • F. J. Levy, Tudor Historical Thought, 1967. • Annabel Patterson, Reading Holinshed's Cronicles, 1994. • Linda Levy Peck, ed., The Mental World of the Jacobean Court, 1991. • Conrad Russell, The Crisis of Parliaments: English History 1509–1660, 1971. • Quentin Skinner, The Foundations of Modern Political Thought, 2 vols., 1978. • J. P. Sommerville, Politics and Ideology in England, 1608–1640, 1986. • D. W. Woolf, The Idea of History in Early Stuart England, 1990.

Humanism • Douglas Bush, The Renaissance and English Humanism, 1939. • William Kerrigan and Gordon Braden, The Idea of the Renaissance, 1989. • Arthur Kinney, Humanist Poetics, 1986. • Charles Schmitt and Quentin Skinner, eds., The Cambridge History of Renaissance Philosophy, 1988.

Science and Exploration • David Cressy, Coming Over: Migration and Communication between England and New England in the Seventeenth Century, 1987. • Stephen Greenblatt, Marvelous Possessions: The Wonder of the New World, 1991. • Stephen Greenblatt, ed., New World Encounters, 1993. • Jeffrey Knapp, An Empire Nowhere: England, America, and Literature from Utopia to The Tempest, 1995. • Thomas Laqueur, Making Sex: Body and Gender from the Greeks to Freud, 1990. • Frank Lestrigant, Mapping the Renaissance World, 1991. • Wayne Shumaker, The Occult Sciences in the Renaissance, 1972. • Nancy G. Siraisi, Medieval and Early Renaissance Science, 1990. • Keith Thomas, Religion and the Decline of Magic, 1971.

Social Settings and Gender Roles • Susan Dwyer Amussen, An Ordered Society: Gender and Class in Early Modern England, 1988. • Elaine V. Beilin, Redeeming Eve: Women Writers of the English Renaissance, 1987. • Alan Bray, Homosexuality in Renaissance England, 1982. • Anthony Fletcher, Gender, Sex, and Subordination in England, 1500–1800, 1995. • Kim F. Hall, Things of Darkness: Economies of Race and Gender in Early Modern England, 1995. • Margo Hendricks and Patricia Parker, eds., Women, "Race" and Writing in the Early Modern Period, 1994. • Daniel Javitch, Poetry and Courtliness in Renaissance England, 1976. • Constance Jordan, Renaissance Feminism: Literary Texts and Political Models, 1990. • Peter Laslett, The World We Have Lost—Further Explored, 1983. • Barbara Kiefer Lewalski, Writing Women in Jacobean England, 1993. • Ian Maclean, The Renaissance Notion of Woman, 1980. • Lawrence Manley, Literature and Culture in Early Modern London, 1995. • Steve Rappaport, Worlds within Worlds: Structures of Life in Sixteenth-Century London, 1989. • Bruce R. Smith, Homosexual Desire in Shakespeare's England: A Cultural Poetics, 1991. • Lawrence Stone, The Family, Sex, and Marriage, 1500–1800, 1965. • Linda Woodbridge, Women and the English Renaissance: Literature and the Nature of Womankind, 1540–1640, 1984.

Perspectives: The Civil War, or the Wars of Three Kingdoms • Texts. • Thomas Carlyle, ed., Oliver Cromwell's Letters and Speeches: With Elucidations, 2 vols., 1904. • Pádraig De Brún, Breandán O Buachalla, and Tomás O Concheanainn, eds., Nua-Dhuanaire, vol. 1., 1971. • "John O'Dwyer of the Glenn" in Irish Mistrelsy or the Bardic Remains of Ireland, ed. James Hardiman, 2 vols., 1831. • Philip A. Knachel, ed., Eikon Basilike, 1966. • John Lilburne, Englands New Chains Discoverd. The Leveller Tracts, 1647–1653, ed. Godfrey Davies Haller, 1944. • W. Dunn Macray, ed., History of the Rebellion and Civil Wars in England: Begun in the Year 1641 by Edward, Earl of Clarendon, 1888. • "The Petition of the Gentlewomen and Tradesmen's Wives" in *English Women's Voices 1540–1700*, ed. Charlotte F. Otten, 1992.

Criticism and History. • Martyn Bennett, *The Civil Wars in Britain and Ireland: 1638–1651*, 1997. • Martyn Bennett, *The English Civil War: 1640–1649*, 1995. • Christopher Hill, *The World Turned Upside Down: Radical Ideas During the English Revolution*, 1972. • Jane Ohlmeyer, ed., *Ireland from Independence to Occupation, 1641–1660*, 1995. • Nigel Smith, *Literature and Revolution in England, 1640–1660*, 1994. • Keith Thomas, "Women and the Civil War Sects," *Past and Present*, 1958.

Perspectives: Emblem, Style, and Metaphor • Editions. • Giordano Bruno, *De Imaginum, Signorum & Idearum Compositione*, 1591. • Dick Higgins, ed., Giordano Bruno, *On the Composition of Images, Signs and Ideas*, trans. Charles Doria, 1991. • L. C. Martin, ed., *The Poems English, Latin and Greek of Richard Crashaw*, 1927. • Henry Green, ed., A Choice of Emblemes by Geoffrey Whitney, 1967. • Ezio Raimondi, ed., *Emanuele Tesauro, Il Cannocchiale Aristotelico*, 1978. • James D. Redwine, ed., *Ben Jonson's Literary Criticism*, 1970.

Criticism. • Michael Bath, *Speaking Pictures: English Emblem Books and Renaissance Culture*, 1993. • Joan F. Bennett, *Five Metaphysical Poets: Donne, Herbert, Vaughan, Crashaw, Marvell*, 1964. • Michel Foucault, "The Prose of the World," in *The Order of Things*, 1970. • Rosemary Freeman, *English Emblem Books*, 1948. • John Manning, "Whitney's *Choice of Emblemes*: A Reassessment," *Renaissance Studies*, vol. 4, no. 2, 1990. • Mario Praz, *The Flaming Heart*, 1958. • Ezio Raimondi, *Letteratura Barocca*, 1961. • John R. Roberts, *New Perspectives on the Life and Art of Richard Crashaw*, 1990. • George Walton Williams, *Image and Symbol in the Sacred Poetry of Richard Crashaw*, 1963. • Frances Yates, *Giordano Bruno and the Hermetic Tradition*, 1964.

Perspectives: Government and Self-Government • Editions. • Roger Ascham, *The Schoolmaster*, 1570, ed. Lawrence Ryan. • Baldassare Castiglione, *The Book of the Courtier*, trans. Sir Thomas Hoby, 1966. • Sir Thomas Elyot, *The Book Named the Governor*, ed. S. E. Lehmberg, 1963. • Sir Thomas Elyot, *The Defence of Good Women*, ed. Edwin Johnson Howard, 1940. • John Foxe, *The Acts and Monuments of John Foxe*, ed. Stephen Cattley, 8 vols., 1843–1847, repr. 1965. •

Richard Hooker, *The Folger Library Edition of the Works of Richard Hooker*, ed. W. Speed Hill, 8 vols, 1977. • James VI and I, *Political Writings*, ed. Johann P. Sommerville, 1994. • Richard Mulcaster, *Elementarie*, ed. E. T. Compagnac, 1925. • Thomas Russell, ed., *The Works of the English Reformers: William Tyndale and John Frith*, 3 vols., 1831. • Juan Luis Vives, *The Instruction of a Christen Woman*, trans. Richard Hyrde, 1540.

Perspectives: Spiritual Self-Reckonings • Editions. • John Bunyan, *The Pilgrim's Progress*, ed. J. B. Wharey, 1928. • Daniel Defoe, *The Life and Strange and Surprizing Adventures of Robinson Crusoe of York*, ed. Donald Crowley, 1972. • Margaret Ferguson and Barry Weller, eds., *The Tragedy of Mariam: The Fair Queen of Jewry with The Lady Falkland: Her Life by One of Her Daughters*, 1994. • Alan MacFarlane, ed., *The Diary of Ralph Josselin*, 1976. • Charlotte F. Otten, ed., *English Women's Voices 1540–1700*, 1992.

Criticism. • Paul Delany, *British Autobiography in the Seventeenth Century*, 1969. • Thomas H. Luxon, *Literal Figures: Puritan Allegory and the Reformation Crisis in Representation*, 1995. • Phyllis Mack, "Women as Prophets During the English Civil War," *Feminist Studies*, vol. 8 (Spring), 1982. • Mary Beth Rose, "Gender, Genre, and History: Seventeenth-Century English Women and the Art of Autobiography," in *Women in the Middle Ages and Renaissance: Literary and Historical Perspectives*, ed. Mary Beth Rose, 1986. • Sandra Sherman, *Finance and Fictionality in the Early Eighteenth Century: Accounting for Defoe*, 1996. • Stuart Sherman, *Telling Time: Clocks and Calendars, Secrecy and Self Recording in English Diurnal Form*, 1997.

Perspectives: Tracts on Women and Gender • Editions. • Desiderius Erasmus, *A Ryght Frutefull Epistle Devised in Laude and Praise of Matrimony*, trans. Richard Tavernour, 1534. • *Haec Vir: Or, The Womanish Man*, 1620. • *Hic Mulier: Or The Man-Woman*, 1620. • Barbara Kiefer Lewalski, ed., *The Polemics and Poems of Rachel Speght*, 1996. • Randall Martin, *Women Writers in Renaissance England*, 1997. • Charlotte F. Otten, ed., *English Women's Voices, 1540–1700*, 1992. • Barnabe Riche, *My Ladies Looking-Glasse*, 1616. • Simon Shepherd, ed., *The Women's Sharp Revenge: Five Women's Pamphlets from the Renaissance*, 1985. • Esther Soweram, *Ester Hath Hang'd Haman*, 1617. • Rachel Speght, *A Mouzell for*

Melastomus, 1617. • Joseph Swetnam, *The Araignment of Lewde, Idle, Froward, and Unconstant Women*, 1615. • Betty Travitsky, ed., *The Paradise of Women: Writings by Englishwomen of the Renaissance*, 1981. • Margaret Tyler, *The Mirrour of Princely Deedes and Knighthood, Book I*, 1578.

Criticism. • Elaine Beilin, *Redeeming Eve: Women Writers of the English Renaissance*, 1987. • Ann Rosalind Jones, "Counterattacks on 'the Bayter of Women': Three Pamphleteers of the Early Seventeenth Century," in *The Renaissance Englishwoman in Print*, eds. Anne Hazelcorn and Betty Travitsky, 1990. • Constance Jordan, *Renaissance Feminism: Literary Texts and Political Models*, 1990. • Barbara Kiefer Lewalski, *Writing Women in Jacobean England*, 1993. • R. Valerie Lucas, "Hic Mulier: The Female Transvestite in Early Modern England," *Renaissance and Reformation*, vol. XXIV, no. 1, 1988. • Megan Matchinske, "Legislating 'Middle-Class' Morality in the Marriage Market: Ester Sowernam's, *Ester Hath Hang'd Haman*," *English Literary Renaissance*, vol. 24, no. 1, 1994. • Linda Woodbridge, *Women and the English Renaissance: Literature and the Nature of Womankind, 1540–1620*, 1986.

Francis Bacon • Editions. • John Pitcher, ed., *The Essays*, 1985. • Robert Leslie Ellis Spedding and Douglas Denon Heath, eds., *The Works of Francis Bacon (English and Latin)*, 14 vols., 1857–1874. • Brian Vickers, ed., *Selections*, 1996. • Sidney Warhaft, ed., *Selections*, 1986.

Biography. • Catherine Drinker Bowen, *Francis Bacon: The Temper of a Man*, 1963. • Jonathan L. Marwil, *The Trials of Counsel: Francis Bacon in 1621*, 1976. • Anthony Quinton, *Francis Bacon*, 1980. • Charles Williams, *Bacon*, 1933.

Criticism. • John C. Briggs, *Francis Bacon and the Rhetoric of Nature*, 1989. • Lisa Jardine, *Francis Bacon: Discovery and the Art of Discourse*, 1974. • Brian Vickers, *Francis Bacon and Renaissance Prose*, 1968.

Our Text. • Robert Leslie Ellis Spedding and Douglas Denon Heath, eds., *The Works of Francis Bacon (English and Latin)*, 14 vols., 1857–1874.

Richard Barnfield • Editions. • George Klawitter, ed., *Complete Poems*, 1990.

Criticism. • Alan Bray, *Homosexual Desire in Shakespeare's England*, 1982. • Gregory W.

Bredbeck, *Sodomy and Interpretation: Marlowe to Milton*, 1991. • Bruce R. Smith, *Homosexual Desire in Shakespeare's England: A Cultural Poetics*, 1991.

The King James Bible • Elizabeth W. Cleaveland, *A Study of Tindale's Genesis, Compared with the Genesis of Coverdale and of the Authorized Version*, 1911, repr. 1972. • S. L. Greenslade, ed., *The Cambridge History of the Bible*, vol. 3, *The West from the Reformation to the Present Day*, 1963. • John Ray Knott, *The Sword of the Spirit: Puritan Responses to the Bible*, 1980. • David Norton, *A History of the Bible as Literature*, 1993. • H. Wheeler Robinson, *The Bible in Its Ancient and English Versions*, 1954.

Sir Thomas Browne • Editions. • L. C. Martin, ed., Religio Medici *and Other Works*, 1964. • C. A. Patrides, ed., *Thomas Browne: The Major Works*, 1977. • Robin Robbins, ed., *Pseudodoxia Epidemica*, 1981. • James Winny, ed., *Religio Medici*, 1963.

Biography. • Joan Bennett, *Sir Thomas Browne*, 1962. • Dennis G. Donovan, *Sir Thomas Browne and Robert Burton: A Reference Guide*, 1981. • Frank L. Huntley, *Sir Thomas Browne: A Biographical and Critical Study*, 1962. • Jonathan F. S. Post, *Sir Thomas Browne*, 1987.

Criticism. • Roberta F. Brinkley, ed., *Coleridge on the Seventeenth Century*, 1955. • Howard Marchitello, *Narrative and Meaning in Early Modern England: Browne's Skull and Other Histories*, 1997. • Leonard Nathanson, *The Strategy of Truth*, 1967. • C. A. Patrides, ed., *Approaches to Sir Thomas Browne: The Ann Arbor Tercentenary Lectures and Essays*, 1982. • Sharon Cadman Seelig, *Generating Texts: The Progeny of Seventeenth-Century Prose*, 1996. • Victoria Silver, "Liberal Theology and Sir Thomas Browne's 'Soft and Flexible Discourse'," *English Literary Renaissance*, vol. 20, no. 1 (Winter), 1990.

Robert Burton • Editions. • Thomas C. Faulkner, Nicholas K. Kiessling, and Rhonda L. Blair, eds., *The Anatomy of Melancholy*, 1989. • Holbrook Jackson, ed., *Anatomy of Melancholy*, 1932.

Biography. • Michael O'Connell, *Robert Burton*, 1986.

Criticism. • Lawrence Babb, *Sanity in Bedlam*, 1959. • Ruth A. Fox, *The Tangled Chain: The*

Structure of Disorder in The Anatomy of Melancholy, 1976. • Martin Heusser, *The Gilded Pill: A Study of the Reader-Writer Relationship in Robert Burton's* Anatomy of Melancholy, 1987. • Devon Hodges, *Renaissance Fictions of Anatomy*, 1985. • Raymond Klibanksy, Erwin Panofksky, and Fritz Saxl, *Saturn and Melancholy*, 1964. • Patricia Vicari, *The View from Minerva's Tower: Learning and Imagination in* The Anatomy of Melancholy, 1989.

Our Text. • Floyd Dell and Paul Jordan-Smith, eds., The Anatomy of Melancholy: *Now for the First Time with the Latin Given Completely in an All-English Text*, 1927.

Elizabeth Cary, Lady Falkland • Editions. • A. C. Dunstan and W. W. Greg, eds., *Elizabeth Cary*. The Tragedy of Mariam. *Facsimile of the 1613 Edition*, 1914. • Margaret Ferguson and Barry Weller, eds., The Tragedy of Mariam: The Fair Queen of Jewry *with* The Lady Falkland: Her Life by One of Her Daughters, 1994.

Biography. • Virginia Blain, Patricia Clements, and Isobel Grundy, eds., *The Feminist Companion to Literature in English: Women Writers from the Middle Ages to the Present*, 1990. • Kenneth Murdock, *The Sun at Noon: Three Biographical Sketches*, 1939.

Criticism. • Elaine Beilin, "Elizabeth Cary and *The Tragedie of Mariam*," *Papers on Language and Literature*, vol. 16, no. 1 (Winter), 1980. • Dympna Callaghan, "Re-reading, The Tragedie of Mariam, the Faire Queene of Jewry," in *Women, "Race," Writing in the Early Modern Period*, eds. Margo Hendricks and Patricia Parker, 1994. • Margaret Ferguson, "Running on With Almost Public Voice: The Case of 'E.C.'," *Tradition and the Talents of Women*, ed. Florence Howe, 1991. • Margaret Ferguson, "The Spectre of Resistance," *Staging the Renaissance: Reinterpretations of Elizabethan and Jacobean Drama*, eds. David Kastan and Peter Stallybrass, 1991. • Tina Krontiris, *Oppositional Voices: Women as Writers and Translators of Literature in the English Renaissance*, 1992. • Maureen Quilligan, "Staging Gender: William Shakespeare and Elizabeth Cary," *Sexuality and Gender in Early Modern Europe: Institutions, Texts, Images*, ed. James Grantham Turner, 1993. • Laurie J. Shannon, "*The Tragedie of Mariam*: Cary's Critique of the Terms of Founding Social Discourses," *English Literary Renaissance*, vol. 24, no. 1 (Winter), 1994. • Betty Travitsky, "The *Feme Covert* in Elizabeth Cary's *Mariam*," *Ambiguous Realities:*

Women in the Middle Ages and Renaissance, eds. Carole Levin and Jeanie Watson, 1987.

Our Text. • A. C. Dunstan and W. W. Greg, eds., *Elizabeth Cary*. The Tragedy of Mariam. *Facsimile of the 1613 Edition*, 1914.

Thomas Dekker and Thomas Middleton • Editions. • Fredson Bowers, ed., *The Dramatic Works of Thomas Dekker*, 1953–1961. • A. H. Bullen, ed., *Works*, 1885–1886. • Havelock Ellis, ed., *Thomas Middleton*, 1887–1890. • Paul Mulholland, ed., *The Roaring Girl*, 1987.

Biography. • Doris Ray Adler, *Thomas Dekker: A Reference Guide*, 1983. • Norman A. Brittin, *Thomas Middleton*, 1972. • George R. Price, *Thomas Dekker*, 1969. • Sara Jayne Steen, *Thomas Middleton: A Reference Guide*, 1984.

Criticism. • Jane Baston, "Rehabilitating Moll's Subversion in *The Roaring Girl*," *Studies in English Literature*, vol. 37, no. 2 (Spring), 1997. • Swapan Chakravorty, *Society and Politics in the Plays of Thomas Middleton*, 1996. • Larry Champion, *Thomas Dekker and the Traditions of English Drama*, 1985. • Viviana Comensoli, "Play-Making, Domestic Conduct, and the Multiple Plot in *The Roaring Girl*," *Studies in English Literature*, vol. 27, no. 2 (Spring), 1987. • Marjorie Garber, "The Logic of the Transvestite: *The Roaring Girl*," in *Staging the Renaissance: Reinterpretations of Elizabethan and Jacobean Drama*, David Scott Kastan and Peter Stallybrass, eds., 1991. • David M. Holmes, *The Art of Thomas Middleton*, 1970. • Jo E. Miller, "Women and the Market in *The Roaring Girl*," *Renaissance and Reformation*, vol. 14, no. 1 (Winter), 1990. • Mary Beth Rose, "Women in Men's Clothing: Apparel and Social Stability in *The Roaring Girl*," *English Literary Renaissance*, vol. 14, no. 3 (Autumn), 1984. • Paul Edward Yachnin, *Stage-Wrights: Shakespeare, Jonson, Middleton and the Making of Theatrical Value*, 1997. • Susan Zimmerman, ed., *Erotic Politics: Desire on the Renaissance Stage*, 1992.

Our Text. • A. H. Bullen, ed., *Works*, 1885–1886.

***The Roaring Girl* in Context: City Life** • Editions. • James Craigie and Alexander Law, eds., *Minor Prose Works of King James VI and I*, 1982. • Robert Greene, *A Notable Discovery of Cosenage*, 1591, ed. G. B. Harrison, 1923. • Arthur Kinney, ed., *Rogues, Vagabonds, and Sturdy Beggars: A New Gallery of Tudor and*

Early Stuart Rogue Literature, 1990. • Francis Oscar Mann, ed., *The Works of Thomas Deloney,* 1912. • E. D. Pendry, ed., *Thomas Dekker: The Wonderful Year; The Gulls's Horn-Book; Penny-Wise and Pound Foolish: English Villainies Discovered by Lantern and Candlelight and Selected Writings,* 1967. • Barnabe Riche, *My Ladies Looking-Glasse,* 1616. • Stanley Wells, ed., *Thomas Nashe: Selected Writings,* 1964. • F. P. Wilson, ed., *The Works of Thomas Nashe, Edited from the Original Texts by Ronald B. McKerrow,* 1958.

Criticism. • Lorna Hutson, *Thomas Nashe in Context,* 1989. • Virginia L. MacDonald, "Robert Greene's Innovative Contributions to Prose Fiction in *A Notable Discovery,*" *Shakespeare-Jarbuch,* vol. 117, 1981. • David Margolies, *Novel and Society in Elizabethan England,* 1985. • John Simons, *Realistic Romance: The Prose Fiction of Thomas Deloney,* 1983. • David L. Smith, Richard Strier, and David Bevington, eds., *The Theatrical City: Culture, Theatre, and Politics in London,* 1995. • Frederick Oswin Waage, *Thomas Dekker's Pamphlets, 1603–1609, and Jacobean Popular Literature,* 1977.

John Donne • Editions. • John Carey, ed., *John Donne: Selected Poetry,* 1996. • Helen Gardner, ed., *John Donne: The Divine Poems,* 1952. • Helen Gardner, ed., *John Donne: The Elegies and The Songs and Sonnets,* 1965. • H. J. C. Grierson, ed., *The Poems of John Donne,* 1912. • G. R. Peter and Evelyn Simpson, eds., *Sermons,* 10 vols., 1953–1962. • Neil Rhodes, ed., *Prose Works: Selections,* 1987. • A. J. Smith, ed., *John Donne: The Complete English Poems,* 1971. • Gary A. Stringer, ed., *The Variorum Edition of the Poetry of John Donne,* 1995.

Biography. • R. C. Bald, *John Donne: A Life.* 1970. • John Carey, *John Donne: Life, Mind and Art,* 1981. • Izaac Walton, *Life of Dr. John Donne,* ed. G. Saintsbury, 1927. • Frank J. Warnke, *John Donne,* 1987.

Criticism. • James S. Baumlin, *John Donne and the Rhetorics of Renaissance Discourse,* 1991. • Harold Bloom, ed., *John Donne and the Seventeenth-Century Metaphysical Poets,* 1986. • Cleanth Brooks, *The Well Wrought Urn,* 1949. • Meg Lotta Brown, *Donne and the Politics of Conscience,* 1995. • Naresh Chandra, *John Donne and Metaphysical Poetry,* 1990. • Denis Flynn, *John Donne and the Ancient Catholic Nobility,* 1995. • T. S. Eliot, *The Varieties of Metaphysical Poetry,* ed. Ronald Schuchard, 1993. • Barbara L. Estrin, *Laura:*

Uncovering Gender and Genre in Wyatt, Donne, and Marvell, 1994. • Pierre Legouis, *Donne the Craftsman,* 1928. • Arthur F. Marotti, ed., *Critical Essays on John Donne,* 1994. • Arthur Marotti, *John Donne, a Coterie Poet,* 1986. • Murray Roston, *The Soul of Wit,* 1974. • A. J. Smith, ed., *John Donne: The Critical Heritage,* 1975–1996. • A. J. Smith, ed., *John Donne: Essays in Celebration,* 1972. • Helen Wilcox, Richard Todd, and Alasdair MacDonald, eds., *Sacred and Profane: Secular and Devotional Interplay in Early Modern British Literature,* 1996. • William Zunder, *The Poetry of John Donne: Literature and Culture in the Elizabethan and Jacobean Period,* 1982.

Our Texts. • Helen Gardner, ed., *John Donne: The Divine Poems,* 1952. • H. J. C. Grierson, ed., *The Poems of John Donne,* 1912. • G. R. Peter and Evelyn Simpson, eds., *Sermons,* 10 vols., 1953–1962. • J. Sparrow, ed., *Devotions Upon Emergent Occasions,* 1923.

Queen Elizabeth I • Editions. • Leicester Bradner, ed., *The Poems of Elizabeth I,* 1964. • Caroline Pemberton, ed., *Queen Elizabeth's Englishings of Boethius, De Consolatione Philosophiae, A.D. 1593,* 1889, repr. 1973.

Biography. • Christopher Haigh, *Elizabeth I,* 1988. • Christopher Hibbert, *Elizabeth I: Genius of the Golden Age,* 1991. • Wallace MacCaffrey, *Elizabeth I,* 1993. • J. E. Neale, *Queen Elizabeth I,* 1934. • Maria Perry, *The Word of a Prince: The Life of Elizabeth from Contemporary Documents,* 1990.

Criticism. • Marie Axton, *The Queen's Two Bodies: Drama and Elizabethan Succession,* 1977. • Philippa Berry, *Of Chastity and Power: Elizabethan Literature and the Unmarried Queen,* 1989. • Susan Frye, *Elizabeth I: The Competition for Representation,* 1993. • Helen Hackett, *Virgin Mother, Maiden Queen: Elizabeth I and the Cult of the Virgin Mary,* 1995. • Lisa Hopkins, *Queen Elizabeth and Her Court,* 1990. • J. E. Neale, *Elizabeth and Her Parliaments,* 2 vols., 1953 • Frances Yates, *Astraea: The Imperial Theme,* 1973.

George Gascoigne • Editions. • John Cunliffe, ed., *The Complete Works,* 2 vols., 1907, 1910. • C. T. Prouty, ed., *A Hundreth Sundrie Flowres,* 1942.

Biography. • Ronald Johnson, *George Gascoigne,* 1972.

Criticism. • E. Jane Hedley, "Allegoria: Gascoigne's Master Trope," *English Literary Renais-*

sance, vol. 11, 1981. • Richard Helgerson, *Elizabethan Prodigals*, 1976. • Richard C. McCoy, "Gascoigne's 'Poemata Castrata': The Wages of Courtly Success." *Criticism*, vol. 27, 1985. • C. T. Prouty, *George Gascoigne, Elizabethan Courtier, Soldier, and Poet*, 1942, repr. 1966.

Edmund Spenser • Editions. • Edwin A. Greenlaw et al., eds., *The Works of Edmund Spenser, a Variorum Edition*, 10 vols., 1932–1949. • A. C. Hamilton, ed., *The Faerie Queene*, 1980. • William Oram et al., eds., *The Yale Edition of the Shorter Poems of Edmund Spenser*, 1989. • Thomas P. Roche, Jr. and C. Patrick O'Donell, eds., *Edmund Spenser: The Faerie Queene*, 1981. • J. C. Smith and E. De Selincourt, eds., *Complete Poetical Works*, 1970.

Biography. • Judith H. Anderson, Donald Cheney, and David A. Richardson, eds., *Spenser's Life and the Subject of Biography*, 1996. • Patrick Cheney, *Spenser's Famous Flight: A Renaissance Idea of a Literary Career*, 1993. • Richard Rambuss, *Spenser's Secret Career*, 1993.

Criticism. • Paul Alpers, *The Poetry of The Faerie Queene*, 1967. • Harry Berger, *The Allegorical Temper*, 1957. • Harry Berger, *Revisionary Play: Studies in the Spenserian Dynamics*, 1988. • Patricia Coughlan, ed., *Spenser and Ireland: An Interdisciplinary Perspective*, 1989. • Jonathan Goldberg, *Endlesse Worke: Spenser and the Structures of Discourse*, 1981. • Kenneth Gross, *Spenserian Poetics: Idolatry, Iconoclasm, and Magic*, 1985. • John Guillory, *Poetic Authority: Spenser, Milton, and Literary History*, 1983. • A .C. Hamilton, *The Spenser Encyclopedia*, 1990. • John N. King, *Spenser's Poetry and the Reformation Tradition*, 1990. • Theresa M. Krier, *Gazing on Secret Sights: Spenser, Classical Imitation, and the Decorums of Vision*, 1990. • Isabel G. MacCaffrey, *Spenser's Allegory: The Anatomy of the Imagination*, 1976. • David Lee Miller, *The Poem's Two Bodies: The Poetics of the 1590 Faerie Queene*, 1988. • James Nohrnberg, *The Analogy of The Faerie Queene*, 1976. • Thomas P. Roche, Jr., *The Kindly Flame: A Study of the Third and Fourth Books of Spenser's* Faerie Queene, 1964. • John Rooks, *Love's Courtly Ethic in* The Faerie Queene: *From Garden to Wilderness*, 1992. • David R. Shore, *Spenser and the Poetics of Pastoral*, 1985. • Kathleen Williams, *Spenser's World of Glass: A Reading of* The Faerie Queene, 1966.

George Herbert • Editions. • Mario Di Cesare, ed., *George Herbert and the Seventeenth-Century*

Religious Poets, 1978. • F. E. Hutchinson, ed., *The Works of George Herbert*, 1941. • C. A. Patrides, ed., *The English Poems of George Herbert*, 1974.

Biography. • Amy M. Charles, *Life of George Herbert*, 1977. • Stanley Stewart, *George Herbert*, 1986.

Criticism. • Stanley Fish, *The Living Temple: George Herbert and Catechizing*, 1978. • Barbara Leah Harman, *Costly Monuments: Representations of the Self in George Herbert's Poetry*, 1982. • Seamus Heaney, *The Redress of Poetry*, 1990. • Christopher Hodgkins, *Authority, Church, and Society in George Herbert: Return to the Middle Way*, 1993 • C. A. Patrides, ed., *George Herbert: The Critical Heritage*, 1983. • Terry Sherwood, *Herbert's Prayerful Art*, 1989. • Marion White Singleton, *God's Courtier: Configuring a Different Grace in George Herbert's Temple*, 1987. • J. H. Summers, *George Herbert: His Religion and Art*, 1954. • Rosemond Tuve, *A Reading of George Herbert*, 1952. • Helen Vendler, *The Poetry of George Herbert*, 1975.

Mary Herbert, Countess of Pembroke • Editions. • J. C. A. Rathmell, *The Psalms of Sir Philip Sidney and the Countess of Pembroke*, 1963. • G. F. Waller, *Poems, etc.*, 1977.

Biography. • Margaret P. Hannay, *Philip's Phoenix*, 1990.

Criticism. • Anne M. Haselkorn and Betty Travitsky, eds., *The Renaissance Englishwoman in Print: Counterbalancing the Canon*, 1990. • Mary Ellen Lamb, *Gender and Authorship in the Sidney Circle*, 1990. • Gary Waller, *Mary Sidney, Countess of Pembroke: A Critical Study of Her Writings and Literary Milieu*, 1979.

Robert Herrick • Editions. • L. C. Martin, ed., *Poetical Works*, 1956. • J. Max Patrick, ed., *Complete Poetry*, 1963.

Biography. • Roger B. Rollin, *Robert Herrick*, 1966. • George Walton Scott, *Robert Herrick*, 1974.

Criticism. • Robert Deming, *Ceremony and Art*, 1974. • A. Leigh Deneef, "This Poetick Liturgy": *Robert Herrick's Ceremonial Mode*, 1974. • Leah Marcus, *The Politics of Mirth: Jonson, Herrick, Milton, Marvell, and the Defense of Old Holiday Pastimes*, 1986. • Roger B. Rollin and J. Max Patrick, eds., "Trust To Good Verses": *Herrick Tercentenary Essays*,

1978. • L. E. Semler, "Robert Herrick, the Human Figure, and the English Mannerist Aesthetic," *Studies in English Literature*, vol. 35, no. 1 (Winter), 1995.

Thomas Hobbes • Editions. • C. P. MacPherson, ed., *Hobbes:* Leviathan, 1968. • Sir William Molesworth, ed., *Thomas Hobbes: English Works*, 11 vols., 1839–1845.

Biography. • Miriam Reik, *The Golden Lands of Thomas Hobbes*, 1977. • Arnold Rogow, *Thomas Hobbes: Radical in the Service of Reaction*, 1986.

Criticism. • Charles Cantalupo, *A Literary Leviathan*: Thomas Hobbes' Masterpiece of Language, 1991. • R. G. Collingwood, The New Leviathan *or Man, Civilization, and Barbarism*, ed. David Boucher. 1992. • David Johnston, *The Rhetoric of* Leviathan: *Thomas Hobbes and the Politics of Cultural Transformation*, 1986. • Samuel I. Mintz, *The Hunting of* Leviathan: *Seventeenth-Century Reaction to the Materialism and Moral Philosophy of Thomas Hobbes*, 1962. • Michael Oakeshott, *Hobbes on Civil Association*, 1975.

Henry Howard, Earl of Surrey • Editions. • Emrys Jones, ed., *Henry Howard, Earl of Surrey: Poems*, 1964.

Biography. • William Sessions, *Henry Howard, Earl of Surrey*, 1986.

Criticism. • Leonard Forster, *The Icy Fire: Five Studies in European Petrarchanism*, 1969. • Susanne Woods, *Natural Emphasis: English Versification from Chaucer to Dryden*, 1984, c1985.

Ben Jonson • Editions. • Robert Adams, ed., *Ben Jonson's Plays and Masques*, 1979. • Ian Donaldson, ed., *Ben Jonson*, 1985. • C. H. Herford, Percy Simspon, and Evelyn Simpson, eds., *The Works of Ben Jonson*, 11 vols., 1925–1952. • Stephen Orgel, ed., *Complete Masques*, 1969. • Helen Ostovich, ed., *Jonson, Four Comedies*, 1997.

Biography. • David Riggs, *Ben Jonson: A Life*, 1989. • George E. Rowe, *Distinguishing Jonson*, 1988.

Criticism. • Richard Burt, *Licensed by Authority: Ben Jonson and the Discourses of Censorship*, 1993. • Ian Donaldson, *The World Upside Down*, 1970. • Jonathan Haynes, *The Social Relations of Jonson's Theater*, 1992. • Richard Helgerson, *Self-Crowned Laureates*, 1983. •

James Hirsh, ed., *New Perspectives on Ben Jonson*, 1997. • G. B. Jackson, *Vision and Judgment in Ben Jonson's Drama*, 1968. • Alexander Leggatt, *Ben Jonson, His Vision and His Art*, 1981. • Katharine Eisaman Maus, *Ben Jonson and the Roman Frame of Mind*, 1984. • David C. McPherson, *Shakespeare, Jonson and the Myth of Venice*, 1990. • Rosalind Miles, *Ben Jonson, His Craft and Art*, 1990. • Stephen Orgel, *The Jonsonian Masque*, 1965. • Stephen Orgel and Roy Strong, *Inigo Jones: The Theatre of the Stuart Court*, 1973. • E. B. Patridge, *The Broken Compass*, 1958. • William W. E. Slights, *Ben Jonson and the Art of Secrecy*, 1994. John Gordon Sweeney, *Jonson and the Psychology of the Public Theater*, 1985. • Robert N. Watson, *Ben Jonson's Parodic Strategy*, 1987. • Don E. Wayne, *Penshurst: The Semiotics of Place and the Poetics of History*, 1984.

Our Text. • C. H. Herford, Percy Simspon, and Eveyln Simpson, eds., *The Works of Ben Jonson*, 11 vols., 1925–1952.

Aemilia Lanyer • Editions. • A. L. Rowse, ed., *The Poems of Shakespeare's Dark Lady: Salve Deus Rex Judaeorum*, 1979. • Susanne Woods, ed., *The Poems of Aemilia Lanyer: Salve Deus Rex Judaeorum*, 1993.

Criticism. • Barbara Kiefer Lewalski, *Writing Women in Jacobean England*, 1993. • Lisa Schnell, "'So Great a Diffrence Is There in Degree': Aemilia Lanyer and the Aims of Feminist Criticism," *Modern Language Quarterly*, vol. 57, no. 1, 1996.

Richard Lovelace • Editions. • C. H. Wilkinson, ed., *The Poems of Richard Lovelace*, 1925.

Biography. • Manfred Weidhorn, *Richard Lovelace*, 1970.

Criticism. • Raymond A. Anselment, "'Stone Walls' and 'Iron Bars': Richard Lovelace and the Conventions of Seventeenth-Century Prison Literature," *Renaissance and Reformation*, vol. 17, no. 1 (Winter), 1993. • Cyril Hughes Hartmann, *The Cavalier Spirit and Its Influence on the Life and Work of Richard Lovelace*, 1970. • Earl Miner, *The Cavalier Mode from Jonson to Cotton*, 1971. • Sharon Cadman Seelig, "My Curious Hand or Eye: The Wit of Richard Lovelace," *The Wit of Seventeenth-Century Poetry*, eds. Claude J. Summers and Ted-Larry Pebworth, 1995. • Claude J. Summers and Ted-Larry Pebworth, eds., *Classic and Cavalier: Essays on Jonson and the*

Sons of Ben, 1982. • Geoffrey Walton, "The Cavalier Poets," *The New Pelican Guide to English Literature III: From Donne to Marvell*, ed. Boris Ford, 1982.

Our Text. • C. H. Wilkinson, ed., *The Poems of Richard Lovelace*, 1925.

Andrew Marvell • Editions. • Elizabeth Story Donno, ed., *The Complete Poems*, 1985. • Frank Kermode and Keith Walker, eds., *Poems. Selections*, 1994. • M. Margoliouth, ed., *Poems and Letters*, 1927, rev. Pierre Legouis and E. E. Duncan-Jones, 1971.

Biography. • John Dixon Hunt, *Andrew Marvell: His Life and Writings*, 1978. • Patsy Griffin, *The Modest Ambition of Andrew Marvell: A Study of Marvell and His Relation to Lovelace, Fairfax, Cromwell, and Milton*, 1995. • Thomas Wheeler, *Andrew Marvell Revisited*, 1996.

Criticism. • Philip Brockbank, *Approaches to Marvell*, ed. C. A. Patrides, 1978. • Warren L. Chernaik, *The Poet's Time: Politics and Religion in the Work of Andrew Marvell*, 1983. • Rosalie Colie, *My Echoing Song*, 1970. • Conal Condren and A. D. Cousins, eds., *The Political Identity of Andrew Marvell*, 1990. • Patrick Cullen, *Spenser, Marvell, and Renaissance Pastoral*, 1970. • E. S. Donno, ed., *Andrew Marvell: The Critical Heritage*, 1978. • Annabel Patterson, *Marvell and the Civic Crown*, 1978. • Allan Pritchard, "Marvell's 'The Garden': A Restoration Poem?" *Studies in English Literature*, vol. 23, no. 3 (Summer), 1983. • Robert Wilcher, *Andrew Marvell*, 1985.

Our Text. • M. Margoliouth, ed., *Poems and Letters*, 1927.

Christopher Marlowe • Editions. • David Bevington and Eric Rasmussen, eds., Doctor Faustus *A-and B-Texts (1604, 1616): Christopher Marlowe and his Collaborator and Revisers*, 1993. • Fredson Bowers, *The Complete Works of Christopher Marlowe*, 2 vols., 1981. • Stephen Orgel, *The Complete Poems and Translations of Christopher Marlowe*, 1971.

Biography. • John Bakeless, *The Tragicall History of Christopher Marlowe*, 2 vols., 1942. • Charles Nicholl, *The Reckoning: The Murder of Christopher Marlowe*, 1992.

Criticism. • C. L. Barber, *Creating Elizabethan Tragedy: The Theater of Marlowe and Kyd*, 1988. • Douglas Cole, *Suffering and Evil in the*

Plays of Christopher Marlowe, 1962. • Roma Gill, *The Plays of Christopher Marlowe*, 1971. • Darryll Grantley and Peter Roberts, eds., *Christopher Marlowe and English Renaissance Culture*, 1996. • Clark Hulse, *Metamorphic Verse: The Elizabethan Minor Epic*, 1981. • William Keach, *Elizabethan Erotic Narratives*, 1977. • Harry Levin, *The Overreacher: A Study of Christopher Marlowe*, 1952. • Simon Shepherd, *Marlowe and the Politics of Elizabethan Theater*, 1986. • Vivien Thomas and William Tydeman, eds., *Christopher Marlowe: The Plays and Their Sources*, 1994.

John Milton • Editions. • John Carey and Alastair Fowler, eds., *The Poems of John Milton*, 1968. • Alastair Fowler, ed., *John Milton: Paradise Lost*, 1968. • Merrit Y. Hughes, ed., *Complete Poetry and Major Prose*, 1957. • C. A. Patrides, ed., *John Milton: Selected Prose*, 1985. • F. A. Patterson et al., eds., *The Works of John Milton*, 1931–1938. • Don M. Wolfe, ed., *The Complete Prose Works of John Milton*, 1953–1982.

Biography. • Douglas Bush, *John Milton*, 1964. • Joseph M. French, *The Life Records of John Milton*, 1949–1958. • W. R. Parker, *Milton: A Biography*, 1968. • A. N. Wilson, *The Life of John Milton*, 1983.

Criticism. • Arthur Barker, *Milton and the Puritan Dilemma, 1641–1660*, 1942. • Joan S. Bennett, *Reviving Liberty: Radical Christian Humanism in Milton's Great Poems*, 1989. • Lana Cable, *Carnal Rhetoric: Milton's Iconoclasm and the Poetics of Desire*, 1995. • Dennis Danielson, ed., *The Cambridge Companion to Milton*, 1989. • Mario Di Cesare, ed., *Milton in Italy*, 1991. • William Empson, *Milton's God*, 1965. • Stanley Fish, *Surprised by Sin: The Argument of* Paradise Lost, 1971. • Christopher Hill, *Milton and the English Revolution*, 1977. • Frank Kermode, *The Living Milton*, 1960. • Barbara K. Lewalski, Paradise Lost *and the Rhetoric of Literary Forms*, 1985. • C. S. Lewis, *A Preface to* Paradise Lost, 1942. • David Lowenstein and James Grantham Turner, *Politics, Poetics, and Hermeneutics in Milton's Prose*, 1990. • Kristin McColgan and Charles Durham, eds., *Arenas of Conflict: Milton and the Unfettered Mind*, 1996. • Marjorie Nicolson, *John Milton: A Reader's Guide to His Poetry*, 1963. • Mary Nyquist and Margaret Ferguson, eds., *Remembering Milton: Essays on the Texts and Traditions*, 1988. • W. R. Parker, *Milton's Debt to Greek Tragedy in Samson Ago-*

nistes, 1937. • Annabel Patterson, ed., *John Milton*, 1992. • Maureen Quilligan, *Milton's Spenser: The Politics of Reading*, 1983. • Mary Ann Radzinowicz, *Toward Samson Agonistes*, 1978. • B. Rajan, Paradise Lost *and the Seventeenth-Century Reader*, 1962. • John Rogers, *The Matter of Revolution: Science, Poetry and Politics in the Age of Milton*, 1996. • John P. Rumrich, *Milton Unbound: Controversy and Reinterpretation*, 1996. • John T. Shawcross, *John Milton: The Self and the World*, 1993. • John Steadman, *Epic and Tragic Structure in* Paradise Lost, 1976. • Paul Stevens, *Imagination and the Presence of Shakespeare in* Paradise Lost, 1985. • Joseph Summers, *The Muse's Method: An Introduction to* Paradise Lost, 1962. • Joseph Wittreich, *Interpreting* Samson Agonistes, 1986.

Our Text. • Merrit Y. Hughes, ed., *Complete Poetry and Major Prose*, 1957.

Annotations Based On. • John Carey and Alastair Fowler, eds., *The Poems of John Milton*, 1968. • Alastair Fowler, ed., *John Milton: Paradise Lost*, 1968.

Sir Thomas More • Editions. • *The Yale Edition of the Complete Works of St. Thomas More*, vols. 2–6, 8–15, 1963–1984. • George M. Logan and Robert M. Adams, eds., *Utopia*, 1989. • Edward Surtz and J. H. Hexter, eds., *Utopia*, 1964.

Biography. • Alistair Fox, *Thomas More: History and Providence*, 1983. • Richard Marius, *Thomas More: A Biography*, 1984. • Louis L. Martz, *Thomas More: The Search for the Inner Man*, 1990.

Criticism. • Alistair Fox, Utopia: *An Elusive Vision*, 1993. • J. H. Hexter, *More's* Utopia: *Biography of an Idea*, 1952, rev. 1965. • Robbin S. Johnson, *More's* Utopia: *Ideal and Illusion*, 1969. • George M. Logan, *The Meaning of More's* Utopia, 1983.

Katherine Philips • Editions. • George Saintsbury, ed., *Minor Poets of the Caroline Period*, 1905. • Patrick Thomas, ed., *The Collected Works of Katherine Philips: The Matchless Orinda*, 1993.

Biography. • Philip Webster Souers, *The Matchless Orinda*, 1931. • Patrick Thomas, *Katherine Philips* (Orinda), 1988.

Criticism. • Harriette Andreadis, "The Sapphic-Platonics of Katherine Philips,

1632–1664," *Signs*, vol. 15, no. 1 (Autumn), 1989. • Celia A. Easton, "Excusing the Breach of Nature's Laws: The Discourse of Denial and Disguise in Katherine Philips' Friendship Poetry," *Restoration Studies in English Literary Culture, 1660–1700*, vol. 14, no. 1 (Spring), 1990. • Elizabeth Hageman, "Katherine Philips: *The Matchless Orinda*," in Katharina M. Wilson, ed., *Women Writers of the Renaissance and Reformation*, 1987. • Claudia A. Limbert, "The Poetry of Katherine Philips: Holographs, Manuscripts, and Early Printed Texts," *Philological Quarterly*, vol. 70, no. 2 (Spring), 1991. • Dorothy Mermin, "Women Becoming Poets: Katherine Philips, Aphra Behn, Anne Finch," *English Literary History*, vol. 57, no. 2 (Summer), 1990. • Ellen Moody, "Orinda, Rosania, Lucasia et Aliae: Towards a New Edition of the Works of Katherine Philips," *Philological Quarterly*, vol. 66, no. 3 (Summer), 1987. • Arlene Stiebel, "Subversive Sexuality: Masking the Erotic in Poems by Katherine Philips and Aphra Behn," *Renaissance Discourses of Desire*, eds. Claude J. Summers and Ted Larry Pebworth, 1993.

Our Text. • Katherine Philips, *Poems by the Most Deservedly Admired Mrs. Katherine Philips The Matchless Orinda*, 1669.

Sir Walter Raleigh • Editions. • A. M. C. Latham, ed., *Poems*, 1950. • William Oldys and Thomas Birch, eds., *The Works of Sir Walter Raleigh*, 8 vols., 1829, repr. 1968.

Biography. • Willard Wallace, *Sir Walter Raleigh*, 1959.

Criticism. • Philip Edwards, *Sir Walter Ralegh*, 1953, repr. 1976. • Stephen J. Greenblatt, *Sir Walter Ralegh: The Renaissance Man and His Roles*, 1973. • David B. Quinn, *Ralegh and the British Empire*, 1947, repr. 1962. • E. A. Strathmann, *Sir Walter Ralegh: A Study in Elizabethan Skepticism*, 1951.

The Discovery in Context: Voyage Literature • Editions. • Arthur Barlow, in Richard Hakluyt, *The Principal Navigations, Voyages, Traffiques, and Discoveries of the English Nation*, 8 vols., 1907. • Richard Hakluyt, *Divers Voyages Touching the Discoverie of America*, 1580. • Thomas Hariot, *Briefe and True Report of the Newfoundland Land of Virginia*, 1580; facs., 1931. • René Landonnière in Richard Hakluyt, *The Principal Navigations, Voyages, Traffiques, and Discoveries of the English Nation*, 8 vols., 1907. • Michel de Montaigne, *Essays*, trans. John Florio, 3 vols., 1910, repr. 1928.

William Shakespeare, Othello • Editions. • David Bevington, ed., *The Complete Works of Shakespeare*, 1992. • Alvin Kernan, ed., *The Tragedy of Othello, the Moor of Venice*, 1965. • Norman Sanders, *Othello*, 1984. • Alice Walker and John Dover Wilson, eds., *Othello*, 1969.

Criticism. • Jane Adamson, *Othello as Tragedy: Some Problems of Judgment and Feeling*, 1980. • James R. Aubrey, "Race and the Spectacle of the Monstrous in *Othello*," *Clio*, vol. 22, no. 3 (Spring), 1993. • John Bayley, "Love and Identity," *The Characters of Love: A Study in the Literature of Personality*, 1960. • Anthony Gerard Barthelemy, ed., *Critical Essays on Shakespeare's Othello*, 1994. • Lynda E. Boose, "Othello's Handkerchief: 'The Recognizance and Pledge of Love'," *English Literary Renaissance*, vol. 5, 1975. • A. C. Bradley, "*Othello*," in *Shakespearean Tragedy*, 1904. • Stanley Cavell, "Literature as Knowledge of the Outsider," *The Claim of Reason: Wittgenstein, Scepticism, Morality and Tragedy*, 1979. • Helen Gardner, "The Noble Moor," *Proceedings of the British Academy*, vol. 41, 1956 (for 1955). • Harley Granville-Barker, "Preface to *Othello*," *Prefaces to Shakespeare*, vol. II, 1946–1947. • Stephen Greenblatt, "The Improvisation of Power," *Renaissance Self-Fashioning*, 1980. • Kim Hall, "Beauty and the Beast of Whiteness: Teaching Race and Gender," *Shakespeare Quarterly*, vol. 47, no. 4 (Winter), 1996. • Margo Hendricks and Patricia Parker, eds., *Women, "Race," and Writing in the Early Modern Period*, 1994. • Eldred Jones, *Othello's Countrymen: The African in English Renaissance Drama*, 1965. • Carol Thomas Neely, "Women and Men in *Othello*: 'What Should Such a Fool / Do With So Good a Woman?'" in *The Woman's Part: Feminist Criticism of Shakespeare*, eds. Carolyn Ruth Swift Lenz, Gayle Greene, and Carol Thomas Neely, 1980. • Martin Orkin, "*Othello* and the 'Plain Face' of Racism," *Shakespeare Quarterly*, vol. 38, 1987. • Marvin Rosenberg, *The Masks of Othello: The Search for the Identity of Othello, Iago and Desdemona by Three Centuries of Actors and Critics*, 1961. • Virginia Mason Vaughan, *Othello: A Contextual History*, 1994.

Our Text. • David Bevington, ed., *The Complete Works of Shakespeare*, 1992.

***Othello* in Context: Ethnography and the Literature of Travel and Colonization** • Editions. • Edward Arber, ed., *The First Three English Books on America*, 1885, repr. 1971. • Richard Eden, *The Decades of the New World … Written in … Latin … by Peter Martyr*, 1555. • Robert Brown, ed., *The History and Description of Africa … Written by Al-Hassan Ibn-Mohammed Al Wezaz Al-Fasi … Done into English in the Year 1600, by John Pory*, 3 vols., 1896. • Henry Morley, ed., *Ireland Under Elizabeth and James the First, Described by Edmund Spenser, Sir John Davies and Fynes Moryson*, 1890. • Andrew Hadfield and Willy Maley, eds., *A View of the State of Ireland: From the First Printed Edition (1633)*, 1997. • Pliny the younger, *The History of the World. Commonly Called the Naturall Historie of C. Plinius Secundus. Translated into English by Philemon Holland*, 1601. • Philip L. Barbour, ed., *The Complete Works of Captain John Smith*, 1986.

Criticism. • Emily C. Bartels, "Making More of the Moor: Aaron, Othello, and Renaissance Refashioning of Race," *Shakespeare Quarterly*, vol. 41, no. 4 (Winter), 1990. • Rosalind R. Johnson, "The African Presence in Shakespearean Drama: Parallels Between Othello and the Historical Leo Africanus," *Journal of African Civilizations*, vol. 7, no. 2, 1985. • Eldred D. Jones, *The Elizabethan Image of Africa*, 1971.

Sir Philip Sidney • Editions. • Katherine Duncan-Jones, ed., *The Countess of Pembroke's Arcadia (The Old Arcadia)*, 1985. • Katherine Duncan-Jones and Jan van Dorsten, eds., *Miscellaneous Prose of Sir Philip Sidney*, 1973. • Maurice Evans, ed., *The Countess of Pembroke's Arcadia*, 1977. • Albert Feuillerat, ed., *The Complete Works*, 4 vols., 1922–1926. • Robert Kimbrough, ed., *Sir Philip Sidney: Selected Prose and Poetry*, 1983. • William Ringler, ed., *Poetry*, 1962. • Jean Robertson, *The Countess of Pembroke's Arcadia (The Old Arcadia)*, 1973. • J. A Van Dorsten, ed., *A Defence of Poetry*, 1966.

Biography. • John Buxton, *Sir Philip Sidney and the English Renaissance*, 1964. • Katharine Duncan-Jones, *Sir Philip Sidney, Courtier Poet*, 1991. • A. C. Hamilton, *Sir Philip Sidney: A Study of His Life and Works*, 1977. • James M. Osborn, *Young Philip Sidney, 1572–1577*, 1972.

Criticism. • Dorothy Connell, *Sir Philip Sidney: The Maker's Mind*, 1977. • David Kalstone, *Sidney's Poetry: Contexts and Interpretations*, 1965. • Dennis Kay, ed., *Sir Philip*

Sidney: An Anthology of Modern Criticism, 1987. • Arthur F. Kinney, ed., *Sidney in Retrospect: Selections from English Literary Renaissance,* 1988. • Jon S. Lawry, *Sidney's Two Arcadias; Pattern and Proceeding,* 1972. • Richard C. McCoy, *Sir Philip Sidney: Rebellion in Arcadia,* 1978. • Gary F. Waller and Michael D. Moore, *Sir Philip Sidney and the Interpretation of Renaissance Culture: A Collection of Critical and Scholarly Essays,* 1984. • Andrew D. Weiner, *Sir Philip Sidney and the Poetics of Protestantism: A Study of Contexts,* 1978.

The Apology in Context: The Art of Poetry • Editions. • Samuel Daniel, *A Defence of Ryme,* ed. G. B. Harrison, 1966. • George Gascoigne, *The Complete Works,* ed. John Cunliffe, 2 vols., 1907, 1910. • Stephen Gosson, *The School of Abuse,* ed. Edward Arber, 1869. • George Puttenham, *The Arte of English Poesie,* eds. Gladys Dodge Willcock and Alice Walker, 1970.

Criticism. • Peter C. Herman, *Squitter-Wits and Muse-Haters: Sidney, Spenser, Milton and Renaissance Antipoetic Sentiment,* 1996.

John Skelton • Editions. • Robert S. Kinsman, ed., *Poems,* 1969. • John Scattergood, ed., *Complete English Poems,* 1983.

Biography. • Nan Cooke Carpenter, *John Skelton,* 1967.

Criticism. • Stanley Fish, *John Skelton's Poetry,* 1965. • Richard Halpern, *The Poetics of Primitive Accumulation: English Renaissance Culture and the Genealogy of Capital,* 1991. • Arthur F. Kinney, *John Skelton: Priest as Poet, Seasons of Discovery,* 1987. • Greg Walker, *John Skelton and the Politics of the 1520s,* 1988.

Henry Vaughan • Editions. • French Fogle, ed., *The Complete Poetry of Henry Vaughan,* 1964. • Alan Rudrum, ed., *The Complete Poems of Henry Vaughan,* 1976.

Biography. • F. E. Hutchinson, *Henry Vaughan, a Life and Interpretation,* 1947.

Criticism. • Thomas O. Calhoun, *Henry Vaughan: The Achievement of Silex Scintillans,* 1981. • Elizabeth Holmes, *Henry Vaughan and the Hermetic Philosophy,* 1932. • E. C. Pettet, *Of Paradise and Light,* 1960. • Jonathan Post, *The Unfolding Vision,* 1982. • Alan Rudrum, *Essential Articles for the Study of Henry Vaughan,* 1987. • Noel K. Thomas, *Henry Vaughan: Poet of Revelation,* 1986.

Our Text. • L. C. Martin, *Works,* 1957.

Isabella Whitney • Editions. • Michael David Felder, *The Poems of Isabella Whitney: A Critical Edition.*

Criticism. • Elaine V. Beilin, "Writing Public Poetry: Humanism and the Woman Writer," *Modern Language Quarterly,* vol. 51, 1990. • Ann Rosalind Jones, "Nets and Bridles: Early Modern Conduct Books and Sixteenth-Century Women's Lyrics," *The Ideology of Conduct: Essays on Literature and the History of Sexuality,* eds. Nancy Armstrong and Leonard Tennenhouse, 1987. • Wendy Wall, "Isabella Whitney and the Female Legacy," *English Literary History,* vol. 58, 1991.

Lady Mary Wroth • Editions. • R. E. Pritchard, ed., *Poems: A Modernized Edition,* 1996. • Josephine A. Roberts, ed., *The Poems of Lady Mary Wroth,* 1983. • Josephine A. Roberts, ed., *The First Part of the Countess of Montgomery's Urania by Lady Mary Wroth,* 1995. • G. F. Waller, ed., *Pamphilia to Amphilanthus,* 1977.

Biography. • Kim Walker, *Women Writers of the English Renaissance,* 1996.

Criticism. • Naomi J. Miller, *Changing the Subject: Mary Wroth and the Figurations of Gender in Early Modern England,* 1996. • Naomi J. Miller and Gary Waller, eds., *Reading Mary Wroth: Representing Alternatives in Early Modern England,* 1991. • May Nelson Paulissen, *The Love Sonnets of Lady Mary Wroth: A Critical Introduction,* 1982. • Gary Waller, *The Sidney Family Romance: Mary Wroth, William Herbert, and the Early Modern Construction of Gender,* 1993. • Anne Hazelcorn and Betty Travitsky, eds., *The Renaissance Englishwoman in Print,* 1990.

Sir Thomas Wyatt • Editions. • Kenneth Muir and Patricia Thomson, *Collected Poems of Sir Thomas Wyatt,* 1693. • Richard Harrier, *The Canon of Sir Thomas Wyatt's Poetry,* 1975.

Biography. • Stephen Foley, *Sir Thomas Wyatt,* 1990.

Criticism. • Jonathan Crewe, *Trials of Authorship: Anterior Forms and Poetic Reconstruction from Wyatt to Shakespeare,* 1990. • Barbara Estrin, *Laura: Uncovering Gender and Genre in Wyatt, Donne and Marvell,* 1994. • Thomas M. Greene, *The Light in Troy: Imitation and Discovery in Renaissance Poetry,* 1982.

The Restoration and the Eighteenth Century

Bibliographies and Guides to Research • Robin Alston et al., *The Eighteenth-Century Short-Title Catalogue (ESTC)*, online and on CD-ROM. • Margaret M. Duggan, *English Literature and Backgrounds, 1660–1700: A Selective Critical Guide*, 2 vols., 1990. • *The Eighteenth Century: A Current Bibliography for [1925–]*, annual. The bibliographies for 1925–1970 have been reprinted as *English Literature, 1660–1800: A Bibliography of Modern Studies, 1950–1972.* • Waldo Sumner Glock, *Eighteenth-Century English Literary Studies: A Bibliography*, 1984. • Roger D. Lund, *Restoration and Early Eighteenth-Century English Literature, 1660–1740: A Selected Bibliography of Resource Materials*, 1980. • R. D. Spector, *Backgrounds to Restoration and Eighteenth-Century English Literature: An Annotated Bibliographical Guide to Modern Scholarship*, 1989. • *Studies in English Literature*, Annual review of "Recent Studies in the Restoration and Eighteenth Century" (Summer issue), 1961–. • George Watson, *The New Cambridge Bibliography of English Literature*, vol. 2, 1660–1800, 1971.

Online Resources • *Eighteenth-Century Threads and Tapestries*: http://www.sunysb.edu/english/18thcentury/texts.htm • Alan Liu et al., eds., *Voice of the Shuttle: Restoration and Eighteenth Century*: http://humanitas.ucsb.edu/shuttle/eng-18th.html • Jack Lynch, ed., *Eighteenth-Century Resources*: http://www.english.upenn.edu/~jlynch/18th/

Cultural and Intellectual Background • John Brewer, *The Pleasures of the Imagination: English Culture in the Eighteenth Century*, 1997. • James Engell, *The Creative Imagination: Enlightenment to Romanticism*, 1981. • James Engell, *Forming the Critical Mind: Dryden to Coleridge*, 1989. • Northrop Frye, "Towards Defining an Age of Sensibility," *English Literary History*, vol. 23, 1956; repr. in *Backgrounds to Eighteenth-Century Literature*, ed. Kathleen Williams, 1971. • Donald Greene, *The Age of Exuberance: Backgrounds to Eighteenth-Century English Literature*, 1970. • Jürgen Habermas, *The Structural Transformation of the Public Sphere*, 1962; trans., 1989. • Jean H. Hagstrum, *Sex and Sensibility: Ideal and Erotic Love from Milton to Mozart*, 1980. • Tim Har-

ris, *Popular Culture in Restoration England, c. 1500–1800*, 1995. • Lawrence Lipking, *The Ordering of the Arts in Eighteenth-Century England*, 1970. • Gerald MacLean, ed., *Culture and Society in the Stuart Restoration: Literature, Drama, History*, 1995. • C. A. Moore, *Backgrounds of English Literature, 1700–1760*, 1953. • Ronald Paulson, *Breaking and Remaking: Aesthetic Practice in England, 1700–1820*, 1989. • Pat Rogers, ed., *The Context of English Literature: The Eighteenth Century*, 1978. • Pat Rogers, *Grub Street: Studies in a Subculture*, 1972. • James Sambrook, *The Eighteenth Century: The Intellectual and Cultural Context of English Literature, 1700–1789*, 2nd ed., 1993. • J. W. Yolton et al., eds., *The Blackwell Companion to the Enlightenment*, 1991. • Steven N. Zwicker, *The Cambridge Companion to English Literature, 1650–1740*, 1998.

History, Religion, and Political Thought • Jeremy Black, *An Illustrated History of Eighteenth-Century Britain*, 1996. • John Brewer, *The Sinews of Power: War, Money, and the English State, 1688–1783*, 1989. • J. C. D. Clark, *English Society, 1688–1832*, 1985. • Linda Colley, *Britons: Forging the Nation, 1707–1837*, 1992. • Peter Earle, *The Making of the English Middle Class*, 1989. • Tim Harris, *Politics Under the Later Stuarts*, 1993. • Tim Harris, *The Politics of Religion in Restoration England*, 1990. • T. W. Heyck, *The Peoples of the British Isles*, vol. 2, 1688–1870, 1992. • Ronald Hutton, *Charles II*, 1989. • Ronald Hutton, *The Restoration*, 1985. • J. P. Kenyon, *The Stuart Constitution*, 2nd ed., 1986. • Mark Kishlansky, *A Monarchy Transformed: Britain 1603–1714*, 1996. • Paul Langford, *A Polite and Commercial People: England 1727–1783*, 1989. • Dorothy Marshall, *Eighteenth Century England*, 2nd. ed., 1962. • Neil McKendrick, John Brewer, and J. H. Plumb, *The Birth of a Consumer Society: The Commercialization of Eighteenth-Century Britain*, 1982. • J. H. Plumb, *England in the Eighteenth Century*, 1972. • J. G. A. Pocock, *Politics, Language, and Time: Essays on Political Thought and History*, 1989. • J. G. A. Pocock, *Virtue, Commerce, and History*, 1985. • Roy Porter, *English Society in the Eighteenth Century*, rev. ed., 1990. • Isabel Rivers, *Reason, Grace, and Sentiment:*

A Study of the Language of Religion and Ethics in England, 1660–1780, vol. 1, Whichcote to Wesley, 1991. • Richard B. Schwartz, Daily Life in Johnson's London, 1983. • W. A. Speck, Stability and Strife: England, 1714–1760, 1977. • John Spurr, The Restoration Church of England, 1991. • E. P. Thompson, Albion's Fatal Tree: Crime and Society in Eighteenth-Century England, 1976. • E. P. Thompson, Customs in Common, 1991.

Women, Writing, Politics, and Culture • George Ballard, Memoirs of Several Ladies of Great Britain Who Have Been Celebrated for Their Writings or Skill in the Learned Languages, Arts, and Sciences, 1752; ed. Ruth Perry, 1985. • Margaret J. M. Ezell, Writing Women's Literary History, 1993. • Catherine Gallagher, Nobody's Story: The Vanishing Acts of Women Writers in the Marketplace, 1670–1820, 1994. • Isobel Grundy and Susan Wiseman, eds., Women, Writing, and History: 1640–1799, 1992. • Bridget Hill, Eighteenth-Century Women: An Anthology, 1984. • Bridget Hill, Women, Work, and Sexual Politics in Eigtheenth-Century England, 1989. • Sylvia Meyers, The Bluestocking Circle, 1990. • Myra Reynolds, The Learned Lady in England, 1650–1760, 1920. • Mona Scheuermann, Her Bread to Earn: Women, Money, and Society from Defoe to Austen, 1993. • Hilda Smith, Reason's Disciples: Seventeenth-Century English Feminists, 1982. • Susan Staves, Married Women's Separate Property in England, 1660–1833, 1990. • Beth Fawkes Tobin, History, Gender, and Eighteenth-Century Literature, 1994. • Janet Todd, ed., A Dictionary of British and American Women Writers, 1660–1800, 1985. • Janet Todd, The Sign of Angellica: Women, Writing, and Fiction, 1660–1800, 1989. • Katherine Wilson and Frank J. Warnke, eds., Women Writers of the Seventeenth Century, 1989.

General Literature • Martin C. Battestin, The Providence of Wit: Aspects of Form in Augustan Literature and the Arts, 1974. • John Butt and Geoffrey Carnall, English Literature in the Mid-Eighteenth Century, 1979. • James L. Clifford, ed., Eighteenth-Century English Literature: Modern Essays in Criticism, 1959. • Leopold Damrosch Jr., ed., Modern Essays on Eighteenth-Century Literature, 1988. • Bonamy Dobrée, English Literature in the Early Eighteenth Century, 1700–1740, 1959. • Paul Fussell, The Rhetorical World of Augustan Humanism, 1965. • Roger Lonsdale, ed., The Sphere History of

Literature, vol. 4, Dryden to Johnson, rev. ed., 1987. • Felicity Nussbaum and Laura Brown, eds., The New Eighteenth Century: Theory, Politics, English Literature, 1987. • Ronald Paulson, Popular and Polite Art in the Age of Hogarth and Fielding, 1979. • Martin Price, To the Palace of Wisdom: Studies in Order and Energy from Dryden to Blake, 1964. • Isabel Rivers, ed., Books and Their Readers in Eighteenth-Century England, 1982. • John Sitter, Literary Loneliness in Mid-Eighteenth-Century England, 1982. • James Sutherland, English Literature of the Late Seventeenth Century, 1969. • Howard Weinbrot, Britannia's Issue: The Rise of British Literature from Dryden to Ossian, 1993. • Steven N. Zwicker, Lines of Authority: Politics and English Literary Culture, 1649–1689, 1993.

Drama • R. W. Bevis, English Drama: Restoration and Eighteenth Century, 1660–1789, 1988. • J. Douglas Canfield and Deborah C. Payne, eds., Cultural Readings of Restoration and Eighteenth-Century English Theater, 1995. • T. W. Craik et al., eds., The Revels History of Drama in English, vol. 5, 1660–1750. • Pat Gill, Interpreting Ladies: Women, Wit, and Morality in the Restoration Comedy of Manners, 1994. • John T. Harwood, Critics, Values, and Restoration Comedy, 1982. • Robert D. Hume, The Development of English Drama in the Late Seventeenth Century, 1976. • Robert D. Hume, The Rakish Stage: Studies in English Drama, 1660–1800, 1983. • John Loftis, ed., Restoration Drama, 1966. • Earl Miner, ed., Restoration Dramatists, 1966. • Allardyce Nicoll, A History of English Drama, 1660–1900, vols. 1–3 (1660–1800), 1952. • David Roberts, The Ladies: Female Patronage of Restoration Drama, 1660–1700, 1989.

Fiction • Nancy Armstrong, Desire and Domestic Fiction, 1989. • Jerry C. Beasley, English Fiction, 1660–1800: A Guide to Information Sources, 1978. • John Bender, Imagining the Penitentiary, 1987. • Terry Castle, Masquerade and Civilization, 1986. • Leopold Damrosch, God's Plot and Man's Stories, 1985. • Lennard J. Davis, Factual Fictions: The Origins of the English Novel, 1983. • Margaret Anne Doody, The True Story of the Novel, 1996. • J. Paul Hunter, Before Novels, 1990. • Michael McKeon, The Origins of the English Novel, 1660–1740, 1987. • John Richetti, ed., The Cambridge Companion to the Eighteenth-Century Novel, 1996. • John Richetti, Popular Fiction Before Richardson, 1969. • Paul Salzman, English Prose Fiction,

1558–1700: A Critical History, 1985. • Mary Ann Schofield and Cecelia Macheski, *Fetter'd or Free? British Women Novelists, 1670–1815*, 1986. • Jane Spencer, *The Rise of the Woman Novelist*, 1986. • Ian Watt, *The Rise of the Novel: Studies in Defoe, Richardson, and Fielding*, 1957.

Poetry • Carol Barash, *English Women's Poetry, 1649–1714: Politics, Community, and Linguistic Authority*, 1997. • Margaret Doody, *The Daring Muse: Augustan Poetry Reconsidered*, 1985. • Germaine Greer et al., eds., *Kissing the Rod: An Anthology of Seventeenth-Century Women's Verse*, 1988. • Jean Hagstrum, *The Sister Arts: The Tradition of Literary Pictorialism and English Poetry from Dryden to Gray*, 1958. • Ian Jack, *Augustan Satire: Intention and Idiom in English Poetry, 1660–1750*, 1952. • Donna Landry, *The Muses of Resistance: Laboring-Class Women's Poetry in Britain, 1739–1796*, 1990. • Roger Lonsdale, ed., *The New Oxford Book of Eighteenth-Century Verse*, 1984. • Roger Lonsdale, ed., *Eighteenth-Century Women Poets*, 1990. • Eric Rothstein, *Restoration and Eighteenth-Century Poetry, 1660–1800*, 1981. • Patricia Spacks, *The Poetry of Vision*, 1967. • James Sutherland, *A Preface to Eighteenth-Century Poetry*, 1948. • Howard Weinbrot, *The Formal Strain: Studies in Augustan Imitation and Satire*, 1969.

Satire • Ronald Paulson, *The Fictions of Satire*, 1967. • Claude Rawson, ed., *English Satire and the Satiric Tradition*, 1984. • Claude Rawson, *Order from Confusion Sprung*, 1985. • Michael Seidel, *Satiric Inheritance: Rabelais to Sterne*, 1979.

Letters, Diaries, Autobiography, Biography • Howard Anderson, Philip B. Daghlian, and Irvin Ehrenpreis, eds., *The Familiar Letter in the Eighteenth Century*, 1966. • William Epstein, *Recognizing Biography*, 1987. • Felicity Nussbaum, *The Autobiographical Subject: Gender and Ideology in Eighteenth-Century England*, 1989. • Bruce Redford, *The Converse of the Pen: Acts of Intimacy in the Eighteenth-Century Familiar Letter*, 1987. • Stuart Sherman, *Telling Time: Clocks, Diaries, and English Diurnal Form, 1660–1785*, 1996. • Patricia Meyer Spacks, *Imagining a Self: Autobiography and Novel in Eighteenth-Century England*, 1976. • Richard Wendorf, *The Elements of Life: Biography and Portrait Painting in Stuart and Georgian England*, 1990.

Perspectives: Landscape, Pleasure, Power • Peter de Bolla, *The Discourse of the Sublime*,

1989. • John Dixon Hunt, *The Figure in the Landscape: Poetry, Painting, and Gardening During the Eighteenth Century*, 1976. • John Dixon Hunt and Peter Willis, eds., *The Genius of Place: the English Landscape Garden, 1620–1820*, 1988. • W. J. T. Mitchell, *Iconology: Image, Text, Ideology*, 1986. • Samuel H. Monk, *The Sublime*, 1960. • Ronald Paulson, *Breaking and Remaking: Aesthetic Practice in England, 1700–1820*, 1989. • Sidney K. Robinson, *Inquiry into the Picturesque*, 1991. • David Watkin, *The English Vision: the Picturesque in Architecture, Landscape, and Garden Design*, 1982.

Perspectives: Mind and God (See also "Cultural and Intellectual Backgrounds") • Jonathan Bennett, *Locke, Berkeley, Hume: Central Themes*, 1971. • James Collins, *The British Empiricists*, 1967. • Peter Gay, ed., *The Enlightenment: A Comprehensive Anthology*, 1973. • John J. Richetti, *Philosophical Writing: Locke, Berkeley, Hume*, 1983. • Keith Thomas, ed., *The British Empiricists*, 1992. • Richard S. Westfall, *Science and Religion in Seventeenth-Century England*, 1958. • R. S. Woolhouse, *The Empiricists*, 1988. • John W. Yolton, *Perception and Reality: A History from Descartes to Kant*, 1996. • John W. Yolton, ed., *Philosophy, Religion, and Science in the Seventeenth and Eighteenth Centuries*, 1990.

Perspectives: Reading Papers • Jeremy Black, *The English Press in the Eighteenth Century*, 1986. • Donovan H. Bond and W. Reynolds McLeod, eds., *Newsletters to Newspapers: Eighteenth-Century Journalism*, 1977. • Richmond P. Bond, ed., *Studies in the Early English Periodical*, 1957. • C. L. Carlson, *The First Magazine: A History of The Gentleman's Magazine*, 1938. • J. A. Downie and Thomas N. Corns, eds., *Telling People What to Think: Early Eighteenth-Century Periodicals from The Review to The Rambler*, 1993. • Walter Graham, *English Literary Periodicals*, 1930. • Kathryn Shevelow, *Women and Print Culture: The Construction of Femininity in the Early Periodical*, 1989. • James Sutherland, *The Restoration Newspaper and its Development*, 1986. • Katherine K. Weed and Richmond P. Bond, *Studies of British Newspapers and Periodicals from Their Beginning to 1800: A Bibliography*, 1946.

Perspectives: The Royal Society and the New Science • I. Bernard Cohen with K. E. Duffin and Stuart Strickland, eds., *Puritanism and the*

Rise of Modern Science: The Merton Thesis, 1990. • Michael Hunter, *Science and Society in Restoration England*, 1981. • Michael Hunter, *Science and the Shape of Orthodoxy: Intellectual Change in Late Seventeenth-Century Britain*, 1995. • Michael Hunter, *The Royal Society and Its Fellows, 1660–1700: The Morphology of an Early Scientific Institution*, 2nd ed., 1994. • Londa Schiebinger, *The Mind Has No Sex?: Women in the Origins of Modern Science*, 1989. • Londa Schiebinger, *Nature's Body: Gender in the Making of Modern Science*, 1993. • Steven Shapin and Simon Schaffer, *Leviathan and the Air-Pump: Hobbes, Boyle, and the Experimental Life*, 1985. • Steven Shapin, *The Scientific Revolution*, 1996. • Steven Shapin, *A Social History of Truth: Civility and Science in Seventeenth-Century England*, 1994. • Larry R. Stewart, *The Rise of Public Science: Rhetoric, Technology and Natural Philosophy in Newtonian Britain, 1660–1750*, 1992. • Geoffrey V. Sutton, *Science for a Polite Society: Gender, Culture, and the Demonstration of Enlightenment*, 1995. • Catherine Wilson, *The Invisible World: Early Modern Philosophy and the Invention of the Microscope*, 1995. • John W. Yolton, ed., *Philosophy, Religion, and Science in the Seventeenth and Eighteenth Centuries*, 1990.

Joseph Addison and Richard Steele • Editions. Donald F. Bond, ed., *The Spectator*, 5 vols., 1965. • Donald F. Bond, ed., *The Tatler*, 3 vols., 1987. • Erin Mackie, ed., *The Commerce of Everyday Life: Selections from* The Tatler *and* The Spectator, 1998. • Angus Ross, ed., *Selections from* The Tatler *and* The Spectator, 1988.

Biographies. • George A. Aitken, *The Life of Richard Steele*, 2 vols., 1889. • Peter Smithers, *The Life of Joseph Addison*, 1954. • Calhoun Winton, *Captain Steele: The Early Career of Richard Steele*, 1964. • Calhoun Winton, *Sir Richard Steele M.P.: The Later Career*, 1970.

Criticism. • Edward A. Bloom and Lillian D. Bloom, eds., *Addison and Steele, the Critical Heritage*, 1980. • Edward A. Bloom, *Joseph Addison's Sociable Animal*, 1971. • Michael G. Ketcham, *Transparent Designs: Reading, Performance and Form in the Spectator Papers*, 1985. • Erin Mackie, *Market à la Mode: Fashion, Commodity, and Gender in* The Tatler *and* The Spectator, 1997.

Mary Astell • Editions. • Bridget Hill, ed., *The First English Feminist: Reflections upon Mar-* riage *and Other Writings by Mary Astell*, 1986. • Patricia Springborg, ed., *Political Writings*, 1996. • Patricia Springborg, ed., *A Serious Proposal to the Ladies*, parts I and II, 1997.

Biography. • Ruth Perry, *The Celebrated Mary Astell: An Early English Feminist*, 1986.

Criticism. • Catherine Gallagher, "Embracing the Absolute: The Politics of the Female Subject in Seventeenth-Century England," *Gender*, vol. 1, 1988.

John Aubrey • Editions. • Andrew Clark, ed., *"Brief Lives," Chiefly of Contemporaries, Set Down by John Aubrey, Between the Years 1669 & 1696*, 2 vols., 1898. • Oliver Lawson Dick, ed., *Aubrey's Brief Lives*, 1949.

Biographies. • Anthony Powell, *John Aubrey and His Friends*, 1988. • David Tylden-Wright, *John Aubrey: A Life*, 1991.

Criticism. • Michael Hunter, *John Aubrey and the Realm of Learning*, 1975.

Aphra Behn • Editions. • Joanna Lipking, ed., *Oroonoko: An Authoritative Text, Historical Backgrounds, Criticism*, 1997. • Janet Todd, ed., *Oronooko, The Rover, and other Works*, 1992. • Janet Todd, ed., *The Works of Aphra Behn*, 7 vols., 1992– .

Biography. • Janet Todd, *The Secret Life of Aphra Behn*, 1997.

Criticism. • Laura Brown, "The Romance of Empire: Oroonoko and the Trade in Slaves," *The New Eighteenth Century*, eds. Felicity Nussbaum and Laura Brown, 1987. • Margaret W. Ferguson, "Juggling the Categories of Race, Class and Gender: Aphra Behn's Oroonoko," *Women's Studies*, vol. 19, 1991. • Catherine Gallagher, "The Author-Monarch and the Royal Slave: *Oroonoko* and the Blackness of Representation," *Nobody's Story: The Vanishing Acts of Women Writers in the Marketplace, 1670–1820*, 1994. • Heidi Hutner, ed., *Rereading Aphra Behn*, 1993. • Sara Heller Mendelson, *The Mental World of Stuart Women: Three Studies*, 1987. • Mary Ann O'Donnell, *Aphra Behn: An Annotated Bibliography*, 1986. • Janet Todd, ed., *Aphra Behn Studies*, 1996.

George Berkeley • Editions. • M. R. Ayers, ed., *Philosophical Works, Including the Works on Vision*, rev. ed., 1980 • A. A. Luce and T. E. Jessop, eds., *The Works of George Berkeley, Bishop of Cloyne*, 9 vols., 1948–1952.

Biography. • A. A. Luce, *The Life of George Berkeley, Bishop of Cloyne*, 1949.

Criticism. • David Berman, ed., *George Berkeley: Eighteenth-Century Responses*, 2 vols., 1989. • Jonathan Dancy, *Berkeley, an Introduction*, 1987. • A. C. Grayling, *Berkeley: The Central Arguments*, 1986. • K. P. Winkler, *Berkeley: An Interpretation*, 1989.

James Boswell • Editions. • R. W. Chapman, ed., *Life of Johnson*, rev. J. D. Fleeman. 1970. • G. B. Hill and L. F. Powell, eds., *Boswell's Life of Johnson*, 6 vols., 1934–1964. • Frederick A. Pottle, et al., eds., *The Yale Editions of the Private Papers of James Boswell*, 1950–. • Frederick A. Pottle, ed., *Boswell's London Journal, 1762–1763*, 1950. • Frederick A. Pottle and Charles H. Bennett, eds., *Boswell's Journal of a Tour to the Hebrides with Samuel Johnson, 1773*, 1963. • John Wain, ed., *The Journals of James Boswell, 1762–1795*, 1991.

Biographies. • Frank Brady, *James Boswell, the Later Years, 1769–1795*, 1984. • Mary Hyde, *The Impossible Friendship: Boswell and Mrs. Thrale*, 1972. • Frederick A. Pottle, *James Boswell, the Earlier Years, 1740–1769*, 1985. • Frederick A. Pottle, *The Literary Career of James Boswell*, 1929.

Criticism. (See Also the Listings of Criticism on Samuel Johnson). • Hamilton Cochrane, *Boswell's Literary Art: An Annotated Bibliography of Critical Studies*, 1992. • James L. Clifford, ed., *Twentieth Century Interpretations of Boswell's Life of Johnson*, 1970. • Greg Clingham, ed., *New Light on Boswell: Critical and Historical Essays on the Occasion of the Bicentenary of The Life of Johnson*, 1991. • Irma S. Lustig, ed., *Boswell: Citizen of the World, Man of Letters*, 1995. • John A. Vance, ed., *Boswell's Life of Johnson: New Questions, New Answers*, 1995.

Edmund Burke • Editions. • J. T. Boulton, ed., *A Philosophical Enquiry into the Origin of Our Ideas of the Sublime and Beautiful*, 1958. • Adam Phillips, ed., *A Philosophical Enquiry into the Origin of Our Ideas of the Sublime and Beautiful*, 1990.

Biographies. • Stanley Ayling, *Edmund Burke: His Life and Opinions*, 1988. • Conor Cruise O'Brien, *The Great Melody: A Thematic Biography and Commented Anthology of Edmund Burke*, 1992. • Isaac Kramnick, *The Rage of Edmund Burke: Portrait of an Ambivalent Conservative*, 1977.

Criticism. • Geoffrey Hartmann, *The Fate of Reading and Other Essays*, 1975. • E. J. Clery, "The Pleasure of Terror: Paradox in Edmund Burke's Theory of the Sublime," *Pleasure in the Eighteenth Century*, eds. Roy Porter and Marie Mulvey Roberts, 1986. • C. B. MacPherson, *Burke*, 1980.

Mary Carleton • Edition. • Janet Todd and Elizabeth Spearing, eds., "The Case of Madam Mary Carleton," *Counterfeit Ladies: The Life and Death of Moll Cutpurse, The Case of Mary Carleton*, 1994.

Criticism. • Hero Chalmers, "The Person I Am, or What They Made Me To Be: The Construction of the Feminine Subject in the Autobiographies of Mary Carleton," *Women, Texts and Histories 1575–1760*, eds. Clare Brant and Diane Purkiss, 1992. • Mihoko Suzuki, "The Case of Mary Carleton: Representing the Female Subject, 1663–1673," *Tulsa Studies in Women's Literature*, vol. 12, no. 1, 1993.

Margaret Lucas Cavendish, Duchess of Newcastle • Editions. • Kate Lilley, ed., *The Blazing World and Other Writings*, 1994. • Paul Salzman, ed. *The Blazing World, An Anthology of Seventeenth-Century Fiction*, 1991.

Biography. • Kathleen Jones, *A Glorious Fame: The Life of Margaret Cavendish, Duchess of Newcastle*, 1988.

Criticism. • Catherine Gallagher, "Embracing the Absolute: The Politics of the Female Subject in Seventeenth-Century England," *Genders*, vol. 1, 1988. • Rosemary Kegl, "The World I Have Made: Margaret Cavendish, Feminism, and the Blazing World," *Feminist Readings of Early Modern Culture*, eds. Valerie Traub, M. Lindsay Kaplan, and Dympna Callaghan, 1996. • Eve Keller, "Producing Petty Gods: Margaret Cavendish's Critique of Experimental Science," *English Literary History*, vol. 64, no. 2, 1997. • Sara Heller Mendelson, *The Mental World of Stuart Women: Three Studies*, 1987. • John Rogers, *The Matter of Revolution: Science, Poetry, and Politics in the Age of Milton*, 1996.

Mary, Lady Chudleigh • Edition. • Margaret J. M. Ezell, ed., *The Poems and Prose of Mary, Lady Chudleigh*, 1993.

Criticism. • Carol Barash, "*The Native Liberty.*"

Jeremy Collier • Edition. • Benjamin Hellinger, ed., *A Short View of the Immorality and Profaneness of the English Stage*, 1987.

Criticism. • Rose Anthony, *The Jeremy Collier Stage Controversy 1698–1726*, 1937.

William Collins • Editions. • Roger Lonsdale, ed., *The Poems of Gray, Collins and Goldsmith*, 1969. • Richard Wendorf and Charles Ryskamp, eds., *The Works of William Collins*, 1979.

Biography. • Edward Gay Ainsworth, *Poor Collins: His Life, His Art, and His Influence*, 1937. • P. L. Carver, *The Life of a Poet: A Biographical Sketch of William Collins*, 1967.

Criticism. • Richard Wendorf, *William Collins and Eighteenth-Century English Poetry*, 1981.

William Cowper • Editions. • John D. Baird and Charles Ryskamp, eds., *The Poems of William Cowper*, 3 vols., 1980–1995. • James King and Charles Ryskamp, eds., *The Letters and Prose Writings of William Cowper*, 5 vols., 1979–1986. • James Sambrook, ed., *"The Task" and Selected Other Poems*, 1994.

Biography. • James King, *William Cowper: A Biography*, 1986. • Charles Ryskamp, *William Cowper of the Inner Temple, Esq.*, 1959.

Criticism. • Morris Golden, *In Search of Stability: The Poetry of William Cowper*, 1960. • Vincent Newey, *Cowper's Poetry: A Critical Study and Reassessment*, 1982.

George Crabbe • Edition. • Norma Dalrymple-Champneys and Arthur Pollard, *George Crabbe: The Complete Poetical Works*, 3 vols., 1988.

Biography. • George Crabbe, *The Life of George Crabbe by His Son*, introd. Edmund Blunden, 1947.

Criticism. • Jerome McGann, "The Anachronism of George Crabbe," *English Literary History*, vol. 48, no. 3, 1981. • Peter New, *George Crabbe's Poetry*, 1976. • Mark Storey, "George Crabbe (1754–1832)," in *A Handbook to English Romanticism*, eds. Jean Raimond and J. R. Watson, 1992. • Frank Whitehead, "Crabbe, 'Realism', and Poetic Truth," *Essays in Criticism*, vol. 39, no. 1, 1989.

Daniel Defoe • Editions. • Paula Backscheider, ed., *A Journal of the Plague Year*, 1992. • P. N. Furbank and W. R. Owens, eds., The True-Born Englishman *and Other Writings*, 1997. • Louis Landa and David Roberts, eds., A Journal of the Plague Year: *Text, Backgrounds, Criticism*, 1990. • William L. Payne, ed., *The Best of Defoe's Review: An Anthology*, 1951. • Manuel Schonhorn, *Accounts of the Apparition of Mrs. Veal*, 1965.

Biography. • Paula R. Backscheider, *Daniel Defoe: His Life*, 1989.

Criticism. • Paula R. Backscheider, *Daniel Defoe: Ambition and Innovation*, 1986. • Rodney Baine, *Daniel Defoe and the Supernatural*, 1979. • David Blewett, *Defoe's Art of Fiction*, 1979. • Lincoln B. Faller, *Crime and Defoe: A New Kind of Writing*, 1993. • P. N. Furbank and W. R. Owens, *The Canonisation of Daniel Defoe*, 1988. • J. Paul Hunter, *The Reluctant Pilgrim: Defoe's Emblematic Method and Quest for Form in Robinson Crusoe*, 1966. • Roger D. Lund, ed., *Critical Essays on Daniel Defoe*, 1997. • Watson Nicholson, *The Historical Sources of Defoe's Journal of the Plague Year*, 1919. • Watson Nicholson, *Realism, Myth and History in Defoe's Fiction*, 1983. • Maximilian E. Novak, *Economics and the Fiction of Daniel Defoe*, 1962. • Maximilian E. Novak, *Realism, Myth, and History in Defoe's Fiction*, 1983. • William Payne, *Mr. Review: Daniel Defoe as the Author of the Review*, 1961. • John J. Richetti, *Daniel Defoe*, 1987. • John J. Richetti, *Defoe's Narratives*, 1975. • Pat Rogers, ed., *Defoe, the Critical Heritage*, 1972.

John Denham • Editions. • Theodore Howard Banks, ed., *The Poetical Works of Sir John Denham*, 2nd ed., 1969. • Brendan O'Hehir, ed., *Expans'd Hieroglyphicks: A Critical Edition of Sir John Denham's Coopers Hill*, 1969.

Biography. • Brendan O'Hehir, *Harmony from Discord: A Life of Sir John Denham*, 1968.

Criticism. • David Hill Radcliffe, "These Delights from Several Causes Move: Heterogeneity and Genre in *Coopers Hill*," *Papers on Language and Literature*, vol. 22, no. 2, 1986. • William Rockett, "'Courts Make Not Kings, but Kings the Court': *Coopers Hill* and the Constitutional Crisis of 1642," *Restoration*, vol. 17, no. 1, 1993. • Earl R. Wasserman, "Denham: *Coopers Hill*," *The Subtler Language: Critical Readings of Neoclassic and Romantic Poems*, 1959.

John Dryden • Editions. • Paul Hammond, *The Poems of John Dryden*, 1995–. • James Kinsley, ed., *The Poems and Fables of John Dryden*, 1962. • H. T. Swedenberg Jr. and Edward Niles Hooker, eds., *Works*, 20 vols., 1961–. • Keith Walker, ed., *John Dryden*, 1987. • George Watson, ed., *"Of Dramatick Poesy" and Other Critical Essays*, 2 vols., 1962.

Biographies. • Paul Hammond, *John Dryden: A Literary Life*, 1991. • James Anderson Winn, *John Dryden and His World*, 1987.

Criticism. • Reuben Brower, "An Allusion to Europe: Dryden and Poetic Tradition," *English Literary History*, vol. 19, 1952. • David A. Bywaters, *Dryden in Revolutionary England*, 1991. • Phillip Harth, *Contexts of Dryden's Thought*, 1968. • Geoffrey Hill, *The Enemy's Country*, 1991. • David Hopkins, *John Dryden*, 1986. • Robert Hume, *Dryden's Criticism*, 1970. • James and Helen Kinsley, *Dryden: The Critical Heritage*, 1971. • Earl Miner, *Dryden's Poetry*, 1967. • Earl Miner, ed., *John Dryden*, 1972. • H. T. Swedenborg, ed., *Essential Articles for the Study of John Dryden*, 1966. • James A. Winn, ed., *Critical Essays on John Dryden*, 1997. • David Wykes, *A Preface to Dryden*, 1977. • Steven N. Zwicker, *Dryden's Political Poetry: The Typology of King and Nation*, 1972. • Steven N. Zwicker, *Politics and Language in Dryden's Poetry: The Arts of Disguise*, 1984.

Sir George Etherege • Editions. • John Barnard, ed., *The Man of Mode*, 1979. • W. B. Carnochan, ed., *The Man of Mode*, 1966. • Michael Cordner, ed., *The Plays of Sir George Etherege*, 1982.

Biography. • Arthur R. Huseboe, *Sir George Etherege*, 1987.

Criticism. • Norman N. Holland, *The First Modern Comedies: The Significance of Etherege, Wycherley and Congreve*, 1959. • Robert Markley, *Two-Edg'd Weapons: Style and Ideology in the Comedies of Etherege, Wycherley and Congreve*, 1988. • Jeffrey Plank, "Augustan Conversion of Pastoral: Waller, Denham, and Etherege's *The Man of Mode*," *Essays in Literature*, vol. 12, no. 2, 1985. • Dale Underwood, *Etherege and the Seventeenth-Century Comedy of Manners*, 1957.

John Evelyn • Editions. • John Bowie, *The Diary of John Evelyn*, 1983. • E. S. de Beer, *The Diary of John Evelyn*, 6 vols., 1955.

Biography. • John Bowie, *John Evelyn and His World*, 1981.

Anne Finch, Countess of Winchilsea • Editions. • Myra Reynolds, ed., *The Poems of Anne, Countess of Winchilsea*, 1903. • Katherine M. Rogers, ed., *Selected Poems of Anne Finch, Countess of Winchilsea*, 1979.

Biography. • Barbara McGovern, *Anne Finch and Her Poetry: A Critical Biography*, 1992.

Criticism. • Charles H. Hinnant, *The Poetry of Anne Finch*, 1994.

John Gay • Editions. • Vinton A. Dearing and Charles Beckwith, eds., *John Gay: Poetry and Prose*, 2 vols., 1974. • John Fuller, *John Gay: Dramatic Works*, 2 vols., 1983. • Bryan Loughery and T. O. Treadwell, eds., *The Beggar's Opera*, 1987. • Edgar V. Roberts, ed., *The Beggar's Opera*, 1969.

Biography. • David Nokes, *John Gay: A Profession of Friendship*, 1995.

Criticism. • Sven Armens, *John Gay, Social Critic*, 1954. • William Empson, "The Beggar's Opera: Mock-Pastoral as the Cult of Independence," *Some Versions of Pastoral*, 1935. • Peter Elfed Lewis, *John Gay: The Beggar's Opera*, 1976. • Peter Lewis and Nigel Wood, eds., *John Gay and the Scriblerians*, 1988. • Yvonne Noble, ed., *Twentieth-Century Interpretations of The Beggar's Opera: A Collection of Critical Essays*, 1975. • Calhoun Winton, *John Gay and the London Theatre*, 1993.

Oliver Goldsmith • Editions. • Arthur Friedman, ed., *Collected Works of Oliver Goldsmith*, 5 vols., 1966. • Roger Lonsdale, ed., *The Poems of Gray, Collins and Goldsmith*, 1969.

Biography. • Ralph M. Wardle, *Oliver Goldsmith*, 1957.

Criticism. • John Barrell, *The Dark Side of the Landscape: The Rural Poor in English Painting, 1730–1840*, 1980. • Howard J. Bell, Jr., "The Deserted Village and Goldsmith's Social Doctrines," *PMLA*, vol. 59, 1944. • Peter Dixon, *Oliver Goldsmith Revisited*, 1991. • Alfred Lutz, "The Deserted Village, and the Politics of Genre," *Modern Language Quarterly*, vol. 55, no. 2, 1994. • G. S. Rousseau, ed., *Goldsmith, the Critical Heritage*, 1974. • Andrew Swarbrick, ed., *The Art of Oliver Goldsmith*, 1984.

Thomas Gray • Editions. • Roger Lonsdale, ed., *The Poems of Gray, Collins and Goldsmith*, 1969. • Alastair Macdonald, ed., *An Elegy Wrote in a Country Church Yard*, 1976. • H.

W. Starr and J. R. Hendrickson, eds., *The Complete Poems of Thomas Gray: English, Latin and Greek*, 1966. • Paget Toynbee and Leonard Whibley, eds., *The Correspondence of Thomas Gray*, rev. ed., 1971.

Biography. • R. W. Ketton-Cremer, *Thomas Gray*, 1955.

Criticism. • F. W. Hilles and Harold Bloom, eds., *From Sensibility to Romanticism*, 1965. • James Downey and Ben Jones, eds., *Fearful Joy: Papers from the Thomas Gray Bicentenary Conference*, 1974. • Robert F. Gleckner, *Gray Agonistes: Thomas Gray and Masculine Friendship*, 1997. • Morris Golden, *Thomas Gray*, 1988. • W. B. Hutchings and William Ruddick, eds., *Thomas Gray: Contemporary Essays*, 1993. • Suvir Kaul, *Thomas Gray and Literary Authority: A Study in Ideology and Poetics*, 1992. • Vincent Newey, "The Selving of Thomas Gray," *Centring the Self: Subjectivity, Society, and Reading from Thomas Gray to Thomas Hardy*, 1995. • Herbert W. Starr, *Twentieth-Century Interpretations of Gray's Elegy*, 1968. • Frank A. Vaughan, *Again to the Life of Eternity: William Blake's Illustrations of the Poems of Thomas Gray*, 1995. • Henry Winefield, *The Poet Without a Name: Gray's Elegy and the Problem of History*, 1991.

Eliza Haywood • Editions. • *The Female Spectator*, 1745–1746. • Gabrielle M. Firmager, ed., The Female Spectator: *Being Selections from Mrs. Eliza Haywood's Periodical, First Published in Monthly Parts (1744–6)*, 1993. • Mary Priestley, The Female Spectator: *Being Selections from Mrs. Eliza Haywood's Periodical*, 1929.

Biography. • Mary Anne Schofield, *Eliza Haywood*, 1985.

Criticism. • James Hodges, "The Female Spectator: A Courtesy Periodical," *Studies in the Early English Periodical*, ed. Richmond Bond, 1957. • Helene Koon, "Eliza Haywood and The Female Spectator," *Huntington Library Quarterly*, vol. 42, 1978–1979. • Kathryn Shevelow, "Re-Writing the Moral Essay: Eliza Haywood's *Female Spectator*," *Reader*, vol. 13, 1985.

William Hogarth • Editions. • Ronald Paulson, ed., *The Analysis of Beauty*, 1998. • Ronald Paulson, ed., *Hogarth's Graphic Works*, 3rd ed., 1989. • Sean Shesgreen, ed., *Engravings by Hogarth*, 1973.

Biographies. • Ronald Paulson, *Hogarth*, 3 vols., 1991–1993. • Jenny Uglow, *Hogarth: A Life and a World*, 1997.

Criticism. • David Bindman, *Hogarth*, 1981. • David Dabydeen, *Hogarth, Walpole, and Commercial Britain*, 1987. • Ronald Paulson, *The Art of Hogarth*, 1975.

Robert Hooke • Criticism. • Ellen Tan Drake, *Restless Genius: Robert Hooke and his Earthly Thoughts*, 1996. • Michael Hunter Hunter and Simon Schaffer, eds., *Robert Hooke: New Studies*, 1989.

David Hume • Editions. • Antony Flew, ed., *An Enquiry Concerning Human Understanding*, 1988. • Selby-Bigge and P. H. Nidditch, eds., *Enquiries Concerning Human Understanding and Concerning the Principles of Morals*, 3rd ed., 1975. • Selby-Bigge and P. H. Nidditch, eds., *A Treatise of Human Nature*, 2nd ed., 1978.

Biography. • E. E. Mossner, *The Life of David Hume*, 1954.

Criticism. • A. J. Ayer, *Hume*, 1980. • John Bricke, *Hume's Philosophy of Mind*, 1980. • V. C. Chappell, ed., *Hume*, 1966. • Jerome Christensen, *Practicing Enlightenment: Hume and the Formation of a Literary Career*, 1987. • Antony Flew, *David Hume, Philosopher of Moral Science*, 1986. • J. C. A. Gaskin, *Hume's Philosophy of Religion*, rev. ed. 1988. • Norman Kemp Smith, *The Philosophy of David Hume*, 1941. • David Fate Norton, ed., *The Cambridge Companion to Hume*, 1993.

Samuel Johnson • Editions. • Frank Brady and W. K. Wimsatt, eds., *Selected Poetry and Prose*, 1977. • J. D. Fleeman, *A Journey to the Western Islands of Scotland*, 1985. • Donald Greene, ed., *Samuel Johnson*, 1984. • G. B. Hill, ed., *Johnson's Lives of the English Poets*, 3 vols., 1905. • Peter Levi, *A Journey to the Western Islands of Scotland and The Journal of a Tour to the Hebrides*, 1984. • E. L. McAdam Jr. and George Milne, *Johnson's Dictionary: A Modern Selection*, 1963. • E. L. McAdam Jr. et al., eds., *The Yale Edition of the Works of Samuel Johnson*, 14 vols., 1958–. • Anne McDermott, ed., *A Dictionary of the English Language* on CD-ROM [computer file], 1996. • Bruce Redford, ed., *The Letters of Samuel Johnson*, 5 vols., 1992–1994. • Pat Rogers, *Johnson and Boswell in Scotland: A Journey to the Hebrides*, 1993.

Biographies. • Walter Jackson Bate, *Samuel Johnson*, 1977. • James Boswell, *Boswell's Life* of Johnson, eds. G. B. Hill and L. F. Powell, 6 vols., 1934–1964. • O. M. Brack Jr. and Robert E. Kelley, *The Early Biographies of Samuel Johnson*, 1974. • James L. Clifford, *Dictionary Johnson: The Middle Years of Samuel Johnson*, 1979. • James L. Clifford, *Young Sam Johnson*, 1955. • Robert DeMaria Jr., *The Life of Samuel Johnson: A Critical Biography*, 1993. • John Hawkins, *The Life of Samuel Johnson, LL.D.*, ed. Bertram Davis, 1961. • G. B. Hill, ed., *Johnsonian Miscellanies*, 2 vols., 1897. • Thomas Kaminski, *The Early Career of Samuel Johnson*, 1987. • John Wain, *Samuel Johnson*, 1974.

Criticism. • Walter Jackson Bate, *The Achievement of Samuel Johnson*, 1955. • Harold Bloom, ed., *Modern Critical Views: Dr. Samuel Johnson and James Boswell*, 1986. • James T. Boulton, ed., *Johnson, the Critical Heritage*, 1971. • James L. Clifford and Donald Greene, *Johnsonian Studies, 1887–1950: A Survey and Bibliography*, 1951. • Greg Clingham, *The Cambridge Companion to Samuel Johnson*, 1997. • Leopold Damrosch, *The Uses of Johnson's Criticism*, 1976. • Philip Davis, *In Mind of Johnson: A Study of Johnson the Rambler*, 1989. • Robert DeMaria Jr., *Johnson's, Dictionary, and the Language of Learning*, 1986. • Robert DeMaria Jr., *Samuel Johnson and the Life of Reading*, 1997. • Robert Folkenflik, *Samuel Johnson, Biographer*, 1978. • Paul Fussell, *Samuel Johnson and the Life of Writing*, 1971. • Donald Greene, *The Politics of Samuel Johnson*, 2nd ed., 1990. • Donald Greene and John A. Vance, *A Bibliography of Johnsonian Studies, 1970–1985*, 1987. • Isobel Grundy, ed., *Samuel Johnson: New Critical Essays*, 1984. • Jean H. Hagstrum, *Samuel Johnson's Literary Criticism*, 1967. • Nicholas Hudson, *Samuel Johnson and Eighteenth-Century Thought*, 1988. • Paul J. Korshin, ed., *Johnson after Two Hundred Years*, 1986. • G. F. Parker, *Johnson's Shakespeare*, 1989. • Allen Reddick, *The Making of Johnson's Dictionary, 1746–1773*, 1996. • Pat Rogers, *Johnson and Boswell: The Transit of Caledonia*, 1995. • Pat Rogers, *The Samuel Johnson Encyclopedia*, 1996. • Arthur Sherbo, *Samuel Johnson's Critical Opinions: A Reexamination*, 1995. • James H. Sledd and Gwin J. Kolb, *Dr. Johnson's Dictionary: Essays in the Biography of a Book*, 1955. • Robert D. Spector, *Samuel Johnson and the Essay*, 1997. • David Wheeler, ed., *Domestick Privacies*, 1987. • William K. Wimsatt, *Philosophic Words: A Study of Style and Meaning in the Rambler and Dictionary of Samuel Johnson*, 1948. • William

K. Wimsatt, *The Prose Style of Samuel Johnson*, 1941. • Thomas M. Woodman, *A Preface to Samuel Johnson*, 1993.

Mary Leapor • Biography and Criticism. • Richard Greene, *Mary Leapor: A Study in Eighteenth-Century Women's Poetry*, 1993.

John Locke • Editions. • Peter H. Nidditch, ed., *An Essay Concerning Human Understanding*, 1975. • J. W. Yolton, *The Locke Reader*, 1977.

Criticism. • R. I. Aaron, *John Locke*, rev. ed., 1955. • Vere Chappell, ed., *The Cambridge Companion to Locke*, 1994. • John Dunn, *Locke*, 1984. • Christopher Fox, *Locke and the Scriblerians: Identity and Consciousness in Early Eighteenth-Century Britain*, 1988. • W. M. Spellman, *John Locke*, 1997. • John W. Yolton, *Locke: An Introduction*, 1985.

Lady Mary Wortley Montagu • Editions. • Robert Halsband, ed., *The Complete Letters of Lady Mary Wortley Montagu*, 1965–1967. • Robert Halsband and Isobel Grundy, eds., *Essays and Poems and Simplicity, a Comedy*, 1977. • Malcolm Jack, ed., *Turkish Embassy Letters*, 1993.

Biography. • Robert Halsband, *The Life of Lady Mary Wortley Montagu*, 1956.

Criticism. • Jill Campbell, "Lady Mary Wortley Montagu and the Historical Machinery of Female Identity," *History, Gender, and Eighteenth-Century Literature*, ed. Beth Fawkes Tobin, 1994. • Cynthia Lowenthal, *Lady Mary Wortley Montagu and the Eighteenth-Century Familiar Letter*, 1994. • Ruth Bernard Yeazell, "Public Baths and Private Harems: Lady Mary Wortley Montagu and the Origins of Ingres's *Bain Turc*," *Yale Journal of Criticism*, vol. 7, no. 1, 1994.

Sir Isaac Newton • Editions. • I. Bernard Cohen and Richard S. Westfall, eds., *Newton: Texts, Backgrounds, Commentaries*, 1995. • H. W. Turnbull, *The Correspondence of Isaac Newton*, 7 vols., 1959–1977.

Biography. • Richard S. Westfall, *Never at Rest*, 1980.

Criticism. • D. Gjertsen, *The Newton Handbook*, 1986. • F. E. Manuel, *The Religion of Isaac Newton*, 1974. • Marjorie Hope Nicolson, *Newton Demands the Muse: Newton's Opticks and the Eighteenth-Century Poets*, 1946.

Samuel Pepys • Editions. • Robert Latham, ed., *The Illustrated Pepys*, 1983. • Robert Latham, ed., *The Shorter Pepys*, 1985. • Robert Latham and William Matthews, eds., *The Diary of Samuel Pepys*, 11 vols., 1970–1983.

Biographies. • Arthur Bryant, *Samuel Pepys*, 3 vols., 3rd ed., 1967. • Richard Ollard, *Pepys: A Biography*, 1975. • J. R. Tanner, *Samuel Pepys and the Royal Navy*, 1920.

Criticism. • Francis Barker, *The Tremulous Private Body: Essays on Subjection*, rev. ed., 1995. • Marjorie Hope Nicolson, *Pepys' Diary and the New Science*, 1965. • Robert Louis Stevenson, "Samuel Pepys," *Familiar Studies of Men and Books*, 1895. • Stuart Sherman, "'In the Fullness of Time': Pepys and His Predecessors" and "'With My Minute Wach in My Hand': The Diary as Timekeeper," *Telling Time: Clocks, Diaries, and English Diurnal Form, 1660–1785*, 1996. • James Grantham Turner, "Pepys and the Private Parts of Monarchy," in *Culture and Society in the Restoration*, ed. Gerald MacLean, 1995.

Hester Lynch Thrale Piozzi • Editions. • Katherine C. Balderston, ed., *Thraliana; the Diary of Mrs. Hester Lynch Thrale (later Mrs. Piozzi) 1776–1809*, 2nd ed., 1951. • Edward A. Bloom and Lillian D. Bloom, eds., *The Piozzi Letters*, 1989–. • A. Hayward, ed., *Autobiography, Letters and Literary Remains of Mrs. Piozzi (Thrale)*, 2 vols., 1975. • Mary Hyde, ed., *The Thrales of Streatham Park*, 1977.

Biographies. • James L. Clifford, *Hester Lynch Piozzi (Mrs. Thrale)*, rev. ed., 1968. • William McCarthy, *Hester Thrale Piozzi, Portrait of a Literary Woman*, 1985.

Criticism. • Martine Watson Brownely, "Eighteenth-Century Women's Images and Roles: The Case of Hester Thrale Piozzi," *Biography*, vol. 3, 1980. • Felicity A. Nussbaum, "Managing Women: Thrale's *Family Book* and *Thraliana*," *The Autobiographical Subject: Gender and Ideology in Eighteenth-Century England*, 1989. • John Riely, "Johnson and Mrs. Thrale: The Beginning and the End," *Johnson and His Age*, ed. James Engell, 1984. • Judy Simons, "The Unfixed Text: Narrative and Identity in Women's Private Writings," *The Representation of the Self in Women's Autobiography*, eds. Vita Fortunati and Gabriella Morisco, 1993.

Alexander Pope • Editions. • John Butt et al., eds., *The Twickenham Edition of the Poems of Alexander Pope*, 11 vols., 1940–1969. • John Butt, ed., *The Poems of Alexander Pope*, 1963. • George Sherburn, ed., *The Correspondence of Alexander Pope*, 5 vols., 1956. • Cynthia Wall, ed., *The Rape of the Lock*, 1998. • Aubrey Williams, ed., *Poetry and Prose of Alexander Pope*, 1969.

Biographies. • Maynard Mack, *Alexander Pope: A Life*, 1985. • George Sherburn, *The Early Career of Alexander Pope*, 1934. • Joseph Spence, *Observations, Anecdotes, and Characters of Books and Men*, ed. James M. Osborn, 2 vols., 1966.

Criticism. • Reuben Brower, *Alexander Pope: The Poetry of Allusion*, 1959. • Laura Brown, *Alexander Pope*, 1985. • Morris Brownell, *Alexander Pope and the Arts of Georgian England*, 1978. • Helen Deutsch, *Resemblance and Disgrace: Alexander Pope and the Deformation of Culture*, 1996. • H. H. Erskine-Hill, *The Social Milieu of Alexander Pope*, 1978. • David Fairer, ed., *Pope: New Contexts*, 1990. • David Fairer, *Pope's Imagination*, 1984. • David F. Foxon, *Pope and the Eighteenth-Century Book Trade*, 1991. • Bertrand A. Goldgar, *Literary Criticism of Alexander Pope*, 1965. • Dustin Griffin, *Alexander Pope: The Poet in the Poems*, 1978. • Brean Hammond, ed., *Longman Critical Readers: Pope*, 1966. • J. Paul Hunter, "Pope and the Ideology of the Couplet," *Ideas*, vol. 4, no. 1, 1996. • Maynard Mack, *The Garden and the City: Retirement and Politics in the Later Poetry of Pope*, 1969. • Maynard Mack, ed., *Essential Articles for the Study of Alexander Pope*, 1968. • Maynard Mack and James Winn, eds., *Pope: Recent Essays by Several Hands*, 1980. • David B. Morris, *Alexander Pope: The Genius of Sense*, 1984. • Marjorie Hope Nicolson and G. S. Rousseau, *"This Long Disease, My Life": Alexander Pope and the Sciences*, 1968. • Valerie Rumbold, *Women's Place in Pope's World*, 1989. • Geoffrey Tillotson, *On the Poetry of Pope*, 2nd. ed., 1950. • Howard Weinbrot, *Alexander Pope and the Tradition of Formal Verse Satire*, 1982. • Aubrey L. Williams, *Pope's Dunciad: A Study of Its Meaning*, 1955.

Christopher Smart • Editions. • Karina Williamson, ed., *The Poetical Works of Christopher Smart*, 5 vols., 1980–1996. • Karina Williamson and Marcus Walsh, eds., *Selected Poems*, 1990.

Biographies. • Christopher Devlin, *Poor Kit Smart*, 1961. • Arthur Sherbo, *Christopher Smart, Scholar of the University*, 1967.

Criticism. • Moira Dearnely, *The Poetry of Christopher Smart*, 1967. • Harriet Guest, *A Form of Sound Words: The Religious Poetry of Christopher Smart*, 1989. • Geoffrey H. Hartmann, "Christopher Smart's, 'Magnificat', : Towards a Theory of Representation," *English Literary History*, vol. 41, 1974. • Clement Hawes, *Mania and Literary Style: The Rhetoric of Enthusiasm from the Ranters to Christopher Smart*, 1996.

Jonathan Swift • Editions. • Herbert Davis, ed., *The Prose Works of Jonathan Swift*, 14 vols., 1939–1968. • Christopher Fox, ed., *Gulliver's Travels: Complete, Authoritative Text with Biographical and Historical Contexts, Critical History, and Essays from Five Contemporary Critical Perspectives*, 1995. • A. C. Guthkelch and D. Nichol Smith, eds., *"A Tale of a Tub," to Which Is Added "The Battle of the Books," and the "Mechanical Operation of the Spirit,"* 2nd ed., 1958. • Pat Rogers, ed., *The Complete Poems*, 1983. • Harold Williams, ed., *The Correspondence of Jonathan Swift*, 5 vols., 1963–1965. • Harold Williams, ed., *Journal to Stella*, 2 vols., 1948. • Harold Williams, ed., *The Poems of Jonathan Swift*, 2nd ed., 3 vols., 1958.

Biographies. • Irvin Ehrenpreis, *Swift: The Man, His Works, and the Age*, 3 vols., 1962–1983. • David Nokes, *Jonathan Swift, A Hypocrite Reversed: A Critical Biography*, 1985.

Criticism. • J. A. Downie, *Jonathan Swift: Political Writer*, 1985. • Irvin Ehrenpreis, "The Meaning of Gulliver's Last Voyage," *Review of English Literature* [later, *Ariel*], vol. 3, no. 3, 1962. • Irvin Ehrenpreis, "The Origin of Gulliver's Travels," *PMLA*, vol. 72, 1957. • Robert C. Elliott, *The Power of Satire: Magic, Ritual, Art*, 1960. • Howard Erskine-Hill, *Gulliver's Travels*, 1993. • Oliver W. Ferguson, *Jonathan Swift and Ireland*, 1962. • H. J. Real Fischer and J. Wooley, eds., *Swift and His Contexts*, 1989. • John Irwin Fischer and Donald C. Mell Jr., eds., *Contemporary Studies of Swift's Poetry*, 1980. • Carol Houlihan Flynn, *The Body in Swift and Defoe*, 1990. • Christopher Fox, ed., *Walking Naboth's Vineyard: New Studies of Swift*, 1995. • Nora Crow Jaffe, *The Poet Swift*, 1977. • F. P. Lock, *The Politics of Gulliver's Travels*, 1980. • Marjorie Hope Nicolson and Nora M. Moehler, "The Scientific Background of Swift's *Voyage to Laputa*," *Science and Imagination*, 1956. • Ellen Pollak, *The Poetics of Sexual Myth: Gender and Ideology in the Verse of Swift and Pope*, 1985. • Martin

Price, *Swift's Rhetorical Art: A Study in Structure and Meaning*, 1953. • C. J. Rawson, *Gulliver and the Gentle Reader*, 1973. • C. J. Rawson, ed., *The Character of Swift's Satire*, 1983. • Richard H. Rodino, *Swift Studies, 1965–1980: An Annotated Bibliography*, 1984. • Edward W. Rosenheim, *Swift and the Satirist's Art*, 1963. • Edward W. Said, "Swift as Intellectual" and "Swift's Tory Anarchy," *The World, the Text, and the Critic*, 1983. • Brian Vickers, ed., *The World of Jonathan Swift: Essays for the Tercentenary*, 1968. • David M. Vieth, *Swift's Poetry 1900–1980: An Annotated Bibliography of Studies*, 1982. • Kathleen Williams, ed., *Swift: The Critical Heritage*, 1970.

James Thomson • Editions. • James Sambrook, ed., *"Liberty," "The Castle of Indolence," and Other Poems*, 1986. • James Sambrook, ed., *The Seasons*, 1981. • James Sambrook, ed., *The Seasons and "The Castle of Indolence"*, 1972.

Biographies. • A. D. McKillop, *James Thomson: Letters and Documents*, 1958. • James Sambrook, *James Thomson, 1700–1748: A Life*, 1991. • Mary Jane W. Scott, *James Thomson, Anglo-Scot*, 1988.

Criticism. • John Barrell, *English Literature in History, 1730–1780*, 1983. • Ralph Cohen, *The Art of Discrimination: Thomson's The Seasons and the Language of Criticism*, 1964. • Ralph Cohen, *The Unfolding of The Seasons*, 1970. • Patricia Meyer Spacks, *The Varied God*, 1959.

Horace Walpole • Editions. • Isabel Wakelin Urban Chase, *Horace Walpole: Gardenist*, 1943. • W. S. Lewis, ed., *The Yale Edition of Horace Walpole's Correspondence*, 48 vols., 1937–1983.

Biography. • Tim Mowl, *Horace Walpole: The Great Outsider*, 1996.

Isaac Watts • Editions. • Bennett A. Brockman, ed., *Divine Songs Attempted in an Easy Language for the Use of Children*, 1978. • Bennett A. Brockman, *The Psalms and Hymns of Isaac Watts: With All the Additional Hymns and Complete Indexes*, 1997.

Biography. • Arthur Paul Davis, *Isaac Watts: His Life and Work*, 1943.

Criticism. • Donald Davie, *The Eighteenth-Century Hymn in England*, 1993. • Madeleine Forell Marshall and Janet Todd, *English Con-*

gregational Hymns in the Eighteenth Century, 1982. • J. R. Watson, *The English Hymn: A Critical and Historical Study*, 1997.

John Wilmot, Earl of Rochester • Editions. • Frank H. Ellis, ed., *The Complete Works*, 1994. • Jeremy Treglown, *The Letters of John Wilmot, Earl of Rochester*, 1980. • David M. Vieth, ed., *The Complete Poems of John Wilmot, Earl of Rochester*, 1968. • Keith Walker, ed., *The Poems of John Wilmot, Earl of Rochester*, 1984.

Biographies. • John Adlard, *The Debt to Pleasure*, 1974. • Graham Greene, *Lord Rochester's Monkey; Being the Life of John Wilmot, Second Earl of Rochester*, 1974. • Jeremy Lamb, *So Idle a Rogue: The Life and Death of Lord Rochester*, 1993. • Vivian de Sola Pinto, *Enthusiast in Wit: A Portrait of John Wilmot, Earl of Rochester*, 1962.

Criticism. • David Farley-Hills, *Rochester's Poetry*, 1978. • David Farley-Hills, ed., *Rochester: The Critical Heritage*, 1972. • Dustin Griffin, *Satires Against Man: The Poems of Rochester*, 1973. • Marianne Thormählen, *Rochester: The Poems in Context*, 1993. • Jeremy Treglown, ed., *Spirit of Wit: Reconsiderations of Rochester*, 1982. • David M. Vieth, ed., *John Wilmot, Earl of Rochester: Critical Essays*, 1988.

Edward Young • Edition. • Stephen Cornford, *Edward Young: Night Thoughts*, 1989.

Biography. • Isabel St. John Bliss, *Edward Young*, 1969.

Criticism. • Vincent Newey, "Edward Young," in *A Handbook to English Romanticism*, eds. Jean Raimond and J. R. Watson, 1992.

CREDITS

Shakespeare, William: Notes for "Othello" from THE COMPLETE WORKS OF SHAKESPEARE edited by David Bevington, 4/E. Copyright © 1992 by HarperCollins Publishers, Inc.

Sir Gawain and the Green Knight: from SIR GAWAIN AND THE GREEN KNIGHT: A NEW VERSE TRANSLATION by Marie Boroff, translator. Copyright © 1967 by W. W. Norton & Company, Inc. Reprinted by permission of W. W. Norton & Company, Inc.

Stones, E. L. G.: ANGLO-SAXON RELATIONS, 1174-1328. London: Thomas Nelson and Sons Ltd., 1965, pp. 97-114.

Tain bo Cualnge: Excerpt from TÁIN BÓ CÚALNGE FROM THE BOOK OF LEINSTER edited by Cecile O'Rahilly. Reprinted by permission of The Governing Board of the School of Celtic Studies of the Dublin Institute for Advanced Studies.

Taliesin: "The Tale of Taliesin" from THE MABINOGI AND OTHER MEDIEVAL WELSH TALES, translated by Patrick K. Ford. Copyright © 1977 by The Regents of the University of California. Reprinted by permission of the University of California Press. "The War-Band's Return" from THE EARLIEST WELSH POETRY by Joseph P. Clancy. Copyright © 1970 by Joseph P. Clancy. Reprinted by permission of the author. "Urien Yechwydd" translated by Saunders Lewis. Reprinted by permission of Mair Saunders. "The Battle of Aargoed Llwyfain" translated by Anthony Conran. Reprinted by permission of Anthony Conran. "Lament For Owain Son of Urien" translated by Anthony Conran. Reprinted by permission of Anthony Conran.

Thrale, Hester Lynch: Excerpt from THRALIANA: THE DIARY OF MRS. HESTER LYNCH THRALE edited by Katharine C. Balderston. Copyright 1951 Oxford University Press. Reprinted by permission of Oxford University Press.

The Voyage of Saint Brendan: "The Voyage of St. Brendan" from LIVES OF THE SAINTS trans. by J. F. Webb. Penguin Classics, 1965. Copyright © 1965 J. F. Webb. Reprinted by permission of Penguin Books Ltd., England.

Whitelock, Dorothy, and David Douglas: Excerpts from THE ANGLO-SAXON CHRONICLE. London: Eyre & Spottiswoode, 1961.

Wroth, Lady Mary: THE POEMS OF LADY MARY WROTH, edited, with and Introduction and Notes, by Josephine A. Roberts. Copyright © 1983 by Louisiana State University Press. Reprinted by permission of Louisiana State University Press.

ILLUSTRATION CREDITS

Cover: Reproduced with the permission of the Board of Trinity College, Dublin/Bridgeman Art Library, London/New York. Front endpaper: Jan Baptist Vrients, map of Britain, 1606. Back endpaper: Sutton Nichols. Prospect of London. 1723. Copyright © The British Museum. Page 2: © Durham University Library. Page 4: © British Library. Page 11: © The Board of Trinity College, Dublin. Page 12: © British Library. Page 14: The Conway Library, Courtauld Institute of Art/The Master & Fellows of Corpus Cristi College, Cambridge. Page 18: © The Bodleian Library, Oxford MS Douce366, fol. 147 verso. Page 19: © British Library. Page 37: © Conway Librarian/Courtauld Institute of Art. Page 95: © National Museum of Ireland. Page 121: © Dept. of Archeology, University of Durham; photograph T. Middlemass. Page 212: © British Library. Page 213: © British Library. Page 273: The Huntington Library Art Collections and Botanical Gardens, San Marino, California/ Superstock. Page 402: © British Library. Page 415: © British Library. Page 479: © British Library. Page 481: © Giraudon/Art Resource. Page 522: © British Library. Page 568: By permission of the Folger Shakespeare Library. Page 572: By permission of the National Portrait Gallery, London. Page 573: Copyright © The British Museum. Page 580: Stock Montage. Page 587: The British Library. Page 707: Rare Book Collection, Cornell University Library, Ithaca, NY. Pages 1022–1023: Sherborne Castle Estate. Page 1067: British Library. Page 1097: Victoria & Albert Museum, London/Art Resource, NY. Page 1262: Devonshire Collection, Chatsworth. Reproduced by permission of the Chatsworth Settlement Trustees. Page 1329: By permission of the Folger Shakespeare Library. Page 1426–1427: Copyright © The British Museum. Page 1598: The British Library. Page 1599: By permission of the Folger Shakespeare Library. Page 1698: National Portrait Gallery. Page 1700: The National Gallery, London. Page 1978: Copyright © The British Museum. Page 1986: © Her Majesty Queen Elizabeth II. Page 1992: © Her Majesty Queen Elizabeth II. Page 2051: © Rare Books Division, The New York Public Library; Astor, Lenox and Tilden Foundations. Page 2053: © Rare Books Division, The New York Public Library; Astor, Lenox and Tilden Foundations. Page 2306: ©Museum of London. Page 2307: ©Museum of London. Page 2333: Courtesy of Washington University Libraries. Page 2335: Guildhall Library, Corporation of London. Page 2855: © Given in honor of Mr. and Mrs. Charles F. Williams by their children/Cincinnati Art Museum. Page 2874: Copyright © The British Museum. Page 2618-2625: © The Metropolitan Museum of Art, Harris Brisbane Dick Fund, 1932. [32.35 (28), (29), (30), (31), (32), (33), (34), (35)]. Page 2573: © Yale Center for British Art, Paul Mellon Collection. Page 2002: © Yale Center for British Art, Paul Mellon Collection, Page 1607. Columbia University Library.

INDEX

A broken altar, Lord, thy servant rears, 1584

Absalom and Achitophel: A Poem, 2076

Abuse of Women, 525

Account of My Last Interview with David Hume, Esq., An, 2805

Across North Wales, 557

Adam Lay Ibounden, 530

Adam scrivain, if evere it thee bifalle, 392

Addison, Joseph, 2867, 2324, 2328, 2330, 2355, 2640

A, dere God, what I am fayn, 528

Admonition by the Author, The, 998

Advice to Sophronia, 2147

Affectionate Shepherd, The, 1079

Affliction (1), 1587

Against Constancy, 2194

Against Idleness and Mischief, 2637

Ah no; nor I myself: though my pure love, 1097

Air and Angels, 1555

Alas, So All Things Now Do Hold Their Peace, 631

Aldhelm, 150

Alexander's Feast, 2114

Alfred, King, 134

Alisoun, 523

All human things are subject to decay, 2103

All were too little for the merchant's hand, 730

Alphabet, 150

Altar, The, 1584

Amhurst, Nicholas, 2346

Am I thus conquered? Have I lost the powers, 1573

Amor, che nel penser mio vive et regna, 621

Amoretti, 898

A moth devoured words. When I heard, 151

An Apology for Writing So Much upon This Book, 2060

Anatomy of Melancholy, The, 1690

And every year a world my will did deem, 729

An enemy ended my life, took away, 151

Anglo-Saxon Chronicle, The, 138

Annals, 2788

Anna Trapnel's Report and Plea, 1954

Anne Finch: A Song on the South Sea, 2344

Anonimalle Chronicle, The, 426

Apology for Poetry, The, 913

Arcadia, The, 954

Areopagitica, 1746

Argument of His Book, The, 1578

Arraignment of Lewd, Idle, Forward, and Inconstant Women, The, 1336

Art of English Poesie, The, 948

Ascham, Roger, 724

As close as you your wedding kept, 994

As due by many titles I resign, 1564

As Rochefoucauld his maxims drew, 2374

Asser, Bishop, 131

As some brave admiral, in former war, 2195

Astell, Mary, 2280

Astrophil and Stella, 987

As virtuous men pass mildly away, 1559

A sweet disorder in the dress, 1579

As when the glorious magazine of light, 1649

As You Came from the Holy Land, 1049

At court I met it, in clothes brave enough, 1531

Athenian Mercury, The, 2351

At length, by so much importunity pressed, 2567

At the round earth's imagined corners, blow, 1565

Aubade, 551

Aubrey, John, 2054

Aurelia, when your zeal makes known, 2145

Author's Epitaph, Made by Himself, The, 1049

Avenge O Lord thy slaughtered saints, whose bones, 1745

A ward, and still in bonds, one day, 1615

A woman's face with Nature's own hand painted, 1170

A yard she had with pales enclosed about, 2127

Ay me, to whom shall I my case complain, 1019

Bacon, Francis, 1655

Ballad to Mrs. Catherine Fleming in London from Malshanger Farm in Hampshire, A, 2143

Barlow, Arthur, 1067

Barnfield, Richard, 1078

Batter my heart, three-personed God; for, you, 1567

Battle of Argoed Llwyfain, The, 141

Because you have thrown off your prelate Lord, 1743

Bede, 126

Before mine eye to feed my greedy will, 729

Beggar's Opera, The, 2573

Behn, Aphra, 2129

Beowulf, 27

Berkeley, George, 2641

Bermudas, 1624

Betwixt two ridges of plowed land sat Wat, 2060

Bitwerne Mersh and Averil, 523

Blame Not My Lute, 625

Blithe the bright dawn found me, 1722

Book Named the Governor, The, 711

Book of Margery Kempe, The, 502

Book of Martyrs, The, 716

Book of Remembrances, 1961

Book of Showings, A, 448

Book of the Courtier, The, 723

Boswell, James, 2796

Brave infant of Saguntum, clear, 1538

Break of Day, 1555

Brendan, Saint, 482

Brief and True Report of the New-found Land of Virginia, A, 1071

Brief Lives, 2055

Browne, Sir Thomas, 1673

Bruno, Giordano, 1604

Bubblers' Medley, A, 2341

Bunyan, John, 1968

Burke, Edmund, 2875

Burton, Robert, 1690

Busy old fool, unruly Sun, 1552

But see the fading many-colored woods, 2662

By that the Manciple hadde his tale al ended, 388

Canonization, The, 1554

Canting Song, A, 1432

Careful Complaint by the Unfortunate Author, A, 1001

Careful observers may foretell the hour, 2365

Carleton, Mary, 2030

Cary, Elizabeth, 1275

Case of Madam Mary Carleton, The, 2030

Cast-away, The, 2655

Castiglione, Baldassare, 722
Cavendish, Margaret, Duchess of Newcastle, 2058
Caxton, William, 243
Certain Notes of Instruction, 950
Charles II, 2101
Chaucer, Geoffrey, 272
Chudleigh, Lady Mary, 2139
Church Monuments, 1589
City, The, 1425
Cloud of Unknowing, The, 445
Cock and the Fox, The, 2127
Collar, The, 1593
Collier, Jeremy, 2271
Collins, William, 2671, 2673
Come live with me, and be my love, 1098
Come, Madam, come, all rest my powers defy, 1563
Come sleep, O sleep, the certain knot of peace, 988
Come, sons of summer, by whose toil, 1581
Complaint, The, or Night Thoughts on Life, Death, and Immortality, 2669
Complaint to His Purse, 393
Condemned to Hope's delusive mine, 2701
Condemn me not, I make so much ado, 2060
Contempt of the World, 535
Cooper's Hill, 2859
Corinna's Going A-Maying, 1579
Coronet, The, 1624
Counterblast to Tobacco, A, 1441
Countess of Montgomery's Urania, The, 1666
Course of Revolt, The, 432
Coverdale, Miles, 1018
Cowper, William, 2653, 2674
Crabbe, George, 2854
Craftsman No. 47, 2346
Craftsman No. 307, 2317
Crashaw, Richard, 1607
Cromwell, Oliver, 1718
Cromwell, our chief of men, who through a cloud, 1744
Crown of Sonnets Dedicated to Love, A, 1576
Cuckoo Song, The, 522
Cuddie, for shame hold up thy heavye head, 737

Dafydd ap Gwilym, 549
Daily Courant, No. 1, The, 2314
Daniel, Samuel, 952
Daphnis, because I am your debtor, 2136
Dearly beloved Cousin, these, 2149
Death be not proud, though some have called thee, 1566
Decades of the New World, 1263
Defence of Good Women, The, 712

Defense of Rhyme, A, 952
Defense of "Sir Fopling Flutter," A, 2275
Definition of Love, The, 1629
Defoe, Daniel, 2289, 1966, 2315, 2340, 2349
Dekker, Thomas, 1355, 1429
Delight in Disorder, 1579
Deloney, Thomas, 1432
Denham, Sir John, 2858
Denial, 1590
Dennis, John, 2275
Description of a City Shower, A, 2365
Description of Cookham, The, 1036
Description of the Morning, A, 2364
Description of a New, Blazing World, The, 2070
Deserted Village, The, 2844
Devotions Upon Emergent Occasions, 1568
Diana (on a time) walking the wood, 1096
Diary (Josselin), 1965
Diary, The (Pepys), 2004
Dictionary of the English Language, A, 2730
Did I my lines intend for public view, 2141
Dim clouds, 1026
Disabled Debauchee, The, 2195
Disappointment, The, 2130
Discovery of the Large, Rich and Beautiful Empire of Guiana, The, 1055
Doleful Lay of Clorinda, The, 1019
Done Is a Battell, 562
Donne, John, 1549
Donne, the delight of Phoebus, and each Muse, 1532
Doubt of Future Foes, The, 1024
Dream of the Rood, The, 120
Drink to me only with thine eyes, 1535
Dryden, John, 2074
Dunbar, William, 559
Dunciad, The, 2546

Easter, 1585
Easter Wings, 1586
Ecclesiastical History of the English People, An, 126
Ecstasy, The, 1560
Edi be thu, Hevene Quene, 531
Edward I, 167
Eikon Basilike, 1702
Eikonoklastes, 1705
Elegy 19: To His Mistress Going to Bed, 1563
Elegy Written in a Country Churchyard, 2685
Elizabeth I, 1021

Eloisa to Abelard, 2512
Elyot, Sir Thomas, 710
England's New Chains Discovered, 1715
Enquiry Concerning Human Understanding, An, 2647
Epistle from Mr. Pope, to Dr. Arbuthnot, An, 2535
Epistle from Mrs. Yonge to her Husband, 2565
Epistle of Deborah Dough, The, 2149
Epistle 4. To Richard Boyle, Earl of Burlington, 2521
Epithalamion, 901
Erasmus, Desiderius, 1330
Essay Concerning Human Understanding, An, 2631
Essay on Criticism, An, 2461
Essay on Man, An, 2526
Essay on Woman, An, 2147
Esther Hath Hanged Haman, 1344
Etherege, George, 2204
Evelyn, John, 2018
Even Now That Care, 1010
Experience, though noon auctoritee, 330

Fables Ancient and Modern, 2119
Faerie Queene, The, 740
Fair lovely Lady, whose angelic eyes, 1079
Fair lovely maid, or if that title be, 2138
False hope which feeds but to destroy, and spill, 1575
Family Book, The, 2830
Farewell (sweet Cookham) where I first obtained, 1036
Farewell! Thou art too dear for my possessing, 1174
Farewell, thou child of my right hand, and joy, 1532
Farewell, too little and too lately known, 2109
Father, part of his double interest, 1568
Female Spectator, Vol. 1, No. 1, The, 2326, 2357
Female Spectator, Vol. 2, No. 10, The, 2360
Finch, Anne, Countess of Winchilsea, 2141, 2668
Fire of Love, The, 438
First Part of the Elementary, The, 726
First Voyage Made to the Coasts of America, The, 1067
Five hours (and who can do it less in?), 2370
Five Old English Riddles, 150
Flea, The, 1557
Fools that true faith yet never had, 1025
Forerunners, The, 1595

Forget Not Yet, 624
For God's sake hold your tongue,
    and let me love, 1554
Forsaken Maiden's Lament, A,
    527
For the power of some animal is
    predominant in every lan-
    guage, 2650
For why? the gains doth seldom
    quit the charge, 730
Fowls in the Frith, 525
Foxe, John, 715
*Friendship Between Ephelia and
    Ardelia*, 2143
Friendship in Emblem, 1647
From fairest creatures we desire
    increase, 1169
From me, who whilom sung the
    town, 2143
Full many a glorious morning
    have I seen, 1171
Funeral, The, 1562

Garden, The, 1631
Gascoigne, George, 728, 950
Gather ye rosebuds while ye may,
    1581
Gauden, John, 1701
Gay, John, 2571
General History of Virginia, The,
    1273
General Prologue, The, 294
Geoffrey of Monmouth, 153
Gerald of Wales, 165
Get up, get up for shame! the
    blooming morn, 1579
Gilpin, William, 2883
Girls of Llanbadarn, The, 553
Go, and catch a falling star, 1551
God, consider the soul's need,
    143
God moves in a mysterious way,
    2654
God never meant that man
    should scale the heavens,
    2654
Golden Speech, The, 1034
Goldsmith, Oliver, 2843
Good Dido stint thy tears, 1001
Good Morrow, The, 1550
Gosson, Stephen, 946
Grasshopper, The, 1610
Gray, Stephen, 2299
Gray, Thomas, 2677, 2882
Greene, Robert, 1428
Gulliver's Travels, 2391

Had we but world enough, and
    time, 1628
Haec Vir, 1347
Happy those early days! when I,
    1617
Happy ye leaves when as those
    lilly hands, 898
Hariot, Thomas, 1071

Hateful Husband, The, 556
Having been tenant long to a
    rich lord, 1585
Haywood, Eliza, 2357
Headache, The. To Aurelia, 2145
Hence loathèd Melancholy, 1731
Hence vain deluding joys, 1734
Henryson, Robert, 564
Herbert, George, 1583
**Herbert, Mary, Countess of
    Pembroke**, 1010
Here lies to each her parents'
    ruth, 1531
Hero and Leander, 1100
Herrick, Robert, 1578
Hic Mulier, 1347
His Majesty's Declaration, 2101
His Prayer to Ben Jonson, 1582
*Historical Register for the Year
    1720*, 2343
*History and Description of Africa,
    The*, 1266
*History of Rasselas, Prince of
    Abyssinia*, 2744
History of the Kings of Britain, 155
*History of the Royal Society of Lon-
    don, The*, 2042
History of the World, The, 1265
Hobbes, Thomas, 1670
*Hock-Cart, or Harvest Home,
    The*, 1581
Hogarth, William, 2616
Holy Sonnets, 1564
Hooke, Robert, 2047
Hooker, Richard, 718
"Ho!" quod the Knight, "good
    sire, namore of this, 372
*Horatian Ode Upon Cromwell's
    Return from Ireland, An*,
    1643
Howard, Henry, Earl of Surrey,
    629
How blessed be they then, who
    his favors prove, 1577
How doth the little busy bee,
    2637
How Soon Hath Time, 1743
How vainly men themselves
    amaze, 1631
Hume, David, 2644
Hunting of the Hare, The, 2060
*Hurry of the Spirits, in a Fever and
    Nervous Disorders, The*,
    2636
**Hyde, Edward, Earl of Claren-
    don**, 1725
Hydriotaphia, Urn Burial, 1680

I am one of passion's asses, 553
I can love both fair and brown,
    1553
Ich am of Irlaunde, 527
I did not live until this time,
    1652
Idler No. 31, 2724

Idler No. 32, 2725
Idler No. 84, 2727
Idler No. 97, 2729
I draw these words from my deep
    sadness, 148
If all the world and love were
    young, 1099
If aught of oaten stop, or pastoral
    song, 2671
If ever Love had force in human
    breast?, 1575
If my dear love were but the
    child of state, 1176
If poisonous minerals, and if that
    tree, 1566
I grieve and dare not show my
    discontent, 1024
I Have a Noble Cock, 525
I have done one braver thing,
    1552
I have examined, and do find,
    1651
Iliad, The, 2509
Il Penseroso, 1734
I'm a strange creature, for I satisfy
    women, 150
Imperfect Enjoyment, The, 2196
In a grove most rich of shade,
    990
In a summer season when the sun
    was mild, 396
In Context
    Aphra Behn: Coterie Writing,
        2139
    *Discovery, The: Voyage litera-
        ture*, 1066
    *Man of Mode, The: The Collier
        Controversy*, 2270
    *Othello: Ethnography in the
        Literature of Travel and
        Colonization*, 1261
    *Piers Plowman: The Rising of
        1381*, 425
    Roaring Girl, The: The City,
        1425
    *Seasons, The: Poems of Night-
        fall and Night*, 2667
    *True Relation, A: Parallel
        Accounts*, 2297
Indifferent, The, 1553
In Flandres whilom was a com-
    paignye, 361
In haste, post haste, when first
    my wand'ring mind, 728
In Laude and Praise of Matrimony,
    1331
In loving thee thou know'st I am
    forsworn, 1178
In pious times, ere priestcraft did
    begin, 2078
In pool when Phoebus with reddy
    wain, 1027
In Praise of Mary, 531
In Secreit Place This Hyndir Nycht,
    563

Instruction of a Christian Woman, 709

Instruction of Princes, The, 165

In such a night, when every louder wind, 2668

Interview with Mrs. Bargrave, An, 2303

In that proud port, which her so goodly graceth, 898

In the nativity of time, 1612

In these deep solitudes and awful cells, 2513

In this strange labyrinth how shall I turn?, 1576

In th'olde days of the King Arthour, 348

Introduction, The, 2141

In vain to me the smiling mornings shine, 2682

Inviting a Friend to Supper, 1532

In yonder grave a Druid lies, 2673

Iohan the mullere hath y-grounde smal, smal, smal, 432

Irish Dancer, The, 527

I sank roots first of all, stood, 151

I saw eternity the other night, 1618

I shall tell you the adventure of another *lai,* 172

I Sing of a Maiden, 530

I sing of brooks, of blossoms, birds, and bowers, 1578

I struck the board, and cried, No more, 1593

I that in heill wes and gladnes, 559

I think not on the state, nor am concerned, 1648

It is reported of fair Thetis' son, 1095

It seemed as if we did not sleep, 551

It was too much, ye gods, to see and hear, 2135

I watched four curious creatures, 151

I whole in body, and in mind, 1003

I wonder by my troth, what thou, and I, 1550

I. W. To Her Unconstant Lover, 994

James I, 720, 1441

Jesu Christ, my lemmon swete, 535

Jesus, My Sweet Lover, 535

John Ball's First Letter, 431

John Ball's Second Letter, 431

John Gower, 434

John O'Dwyer of the Glenn, 1722

Johnson, Samuel, 2689

Jolly Jankin, 528

Jonson, Ben, 1443, 1600

Jordan (1), 1588

Jordan (2), 1592

Josselin, Ralph, 1965

Journal-Letter to Thomas Wharton, A, 2882

Journal of a Tour to the Hebrides with Dr. Samuel Johnson, A, 2809

Journal of the Plague Year, A, 2304

Journal to Stella, 2387

Journey to the Western Islands of Scotland, A, 2770

Jubilate Agno, 2650

Judith, 114

Julian of Norwich, 447

Kalendarium, 2018

Kempe, Margery, 500

King James Bible, The, 1663

"Kyrie," so "Kyrie," 528

Lady Falkland: Her Life, The, 1946

Lady's Dressing Room, The, 2370

Lais, Prologue, 171

L'Allegro, 1731

Lament for Owain Son of Urien, 143

Lament for the Makers, 559

Landonnière, René, 1074

Langland, William, 394

Lantern and Candlelight, 1429

Lanval, 172

Lanyer, Aemilia, 1036

Laws of Ecclesiastical Polity, The, 718

Leapor, Mary, 2145

Lenten is come with love to toune, 523

Leo Africanus, 1265

Let me not to the marriage of true minds, 1176

Let me pour forth, 1556

Let Observation, with extensive view, 2692

Letter sent to the Papal Court, 167

Letters from Ireland, 1719

Letters
  on Gullivers Travels, 2447
  to Hester Thrale, 2793
  to Hester Thrale Piozzi, 2795
  to Horace Walpole, 16 April 1734, 2678
  to Horace Walpole, 11 February 1751, 2680
  to Horace Walpole, 20 February 1751, 2681
  to Horace Walpole, 12 June 1750, 2680
  to Lord Chesterfield, 2792
  to Richard West, December 1736, 2679
  to Edward Blount, 2872
  to her Aunt (Lukyn), 2298

  to Hester Thralet, 2765
  to John Flamsteed (Gray), 2299
  to Lady Bute, 2563
  to Mr. Creech at Oxford, A, 2136
  to Richard Bentley, 2628
  to Sir Horace Mann, 2874

Leviathan, 1670

Life and Strange and Surprising Adventures of Robinson Crusoe, of York, Mariner, The, 1967

Life of King Alfred, The, 132

Life of Milton, The, 2779

Life of Pope, The, 2781

Life of Samuel Johnson, L.L.D., 2813

Light Shining out of Darkness, 2654

Like as the waves make towards the pebbled shore, 1172

Like dancers on the ropes poor poets fare, 2206

Like to a fever's pulse my heart doth beat, 2060

Lilburne, John, 1715

Listen! I will describe the best of dreams, 120

Listen! The fame of Danish kings, 30

Lives of the Poets, 2778

Locke, John, 2630

Lo I the man, whose Muse whilome did maske, 744

London Gazette, The, 2313

London, Hast Thou Accused Me, 633

London Journal, 2797

Long expected one and twenty, 2700

Long Love, That in My Thought Doth Harbor, The, 620

Lord, how can man preach thy eternal word?, 1589

Lord, who createdst man in wealth and store?, 1586

Love (3), 1596

Love a child is ever crying, 1576

Love a woman? You're an ass!, 2196

Love bade me welcome: yet my soul drew back, 1596

Lovelace, Richard, 1609

Love Made in the First Age: To Chloris, 1612

Lover: A Ballad, The, 2567

Love's Alchemy, 1557

Love That Doth Reign and Live within My Thought, 630

Loving in truth, and fain in verse my love to show, 987

Lucks, My Fair Falcon, and Your Fellows All, 626

Lukyn, L., 2298

Luxurious man, to bring his vice in use, 1630
Lycidas, 1738

Mac Flecknoe, 2103
Madam, As in a triumph conquerors admit, 1650
Malory, Sir Thomas, 242
Man, 1591
Mandeville, Sir John, 492
Man Frail, and God Eternal, 2638
Manner of Her Will, The, 1002
Man of Mode, The, or Sir Fopling Flutter, 2205
Marie de France, 170
Mark but this flea, and mark in this, 1557
Marlowe, Christopher, 1098
Martyr, Peter, 1261
Marvell, Andrew, 1622
Mary Is with Child, 532
Meeting with time, "Slack thing," said I, 1593
Mercurius Publicus, 2312
Methought I Saw My Late Espoused Saint, 1746
Metres of Boethius's Consolation of Philosophy, The, 1025
Micrographia, 2048
Middleton, Thomas, 1355
Miller's Tale, The, 313
Milton, John, 1704, 1729
Mine Own John Poyns, 627
Miracles Attending Israel's Journey, 2639
Modest Proposal, A, 2451
Montagu, Lady Mary Wortley, 2557
Montaigne, Michel de, 1077
More, Sir Thomas, 636
Morte Darthur, 243
Most glorious Lord of lyfe that on this day, 900
Mower Against Gardens, The, 1630
Mower's Song, The, 1631
Much suspected by me, 1023
Mulcaster, Richard, 726
Muzzle for Melastomus, A, 1339
My frame of nature is a ruffled sea, 2636
My Galley, 622
My God, I heard this day, 1591
My Lady's Looking Glass, 1332, 1427
My Lefe is Faren in a Lond, 525
My Love is of a birth as rare, 1629
My Lute, Awake!, 623
My mind was once the true survey, 1631
My mistress' eyes are nothing like the sun, 1177
My muse now happy, lay thyself to rest, 1577

My pain, still smothered in my grièved breast, 1576
My Radcliffe, When Thy Reckless Youth Offends, 636
My worthy Lord, I pray you wonder not, 731

Naked she lay, clasped in my longing arms, 2196
Nashe, Thomas, 1439
Nature That Washed Her Hands in Milk, 1047
Newton, Isaac, 2627
New yeare forth looking out of Janus gate, 898
Next morning when the golden sun was risen, 1085
Night, The, 1621
Nocturnal Reverie, A, 2668
No haste but good, where wisdom makes the way, 730
No more be grieved at that which thou hast done, 1172
Notable Discovery of Cosenage, A, 1428
Notable History Containing Four Voyages Made to Florida, A, 1074
Nothing but a hovel now, 558
Nothing! thou elder brother even to Shade, 2198
No, Time, thou shalt not boast that I do change, 1176
Not marble nor the gilded monuments, 1172
Not mine own fears nor the prophetic soul, 1175
Nowel! nowel! nowel!, 532
Now gins this goodly frame of Temperance, 879
Now Goeth Sun under Wood, 534
Now hardly here and there a hackney coach, 2364
Now raygneth pride in price, 431
Now stir the fire, and close the shutters fast, 2674
Now thou art dead, no eye shall ever see, 1583
Nun's Priest's Prologue and Tale, The, 372
Nymph Complaining for the Death of Her Fawn, The, 1625
Nymph's Reply to the Shepherd, The, 1099

O absent presence, Stella is not here, 993
Obedience of a Christian Man, The, 708
Obscurest night involved the sky, 2655
Observations upon Experimental Philosophy, 2068

Ode Occasioned by the Death of Mr. Thomson, 2673
Ode on a Distant Prospect of Eton College, 2682
Ode on the Death of a Favorite Cat, Drowned in a Tub of Gold Fishes, 2684
Ode to Evening, 2671
Ode to Mrs. Anne Killigrew, 2109
Of all creatures women be best, 525
Of Cannibals, 1077
Of honey-laden bees I first was born, 150
Of Man's First Disobedience, and the Fruit, 1757
Of Marriage and Single Life, 1657
Of Plantations, 1659
Of Studies (1597), 1661
Of Studies (1625), 1662
Of Superstition, 1658
Often the wanderer pleads for pity, 144
Of Truth, 1656
Oh fortune, thy wresting wavering state, 1024
Oh my black soul! Now that art summoned, 1565
O, how I faint when I of you do write, 1173
Ohthere's Journeys, 135
O in how headlong depth the drowned mind is dim!, 1025
Ombre and basset laid aside, 2344
One day I wrote her name upon the strand, 901
One day the amorous Lysander, 2130
One Saving Place, 552
On Hellespont, guilty of true love's blood, 1100
Only joy, now here you are, 989
On Marriage, 1027
On Mary, Queen of Scots, 1028
On Mary's Execution, 1031
On Monsieur's Departure, 1024
On My First Daughter, 1531
On My First Son, 1532
On Picturesque Travel, 2884
On Something, That Walks Somewhere, 1531
On the Composition of Images, Signs, and Ideas, 1604
On the Death of Dr. Robert Levet, 2701
On thee, my trust is grounded, 1015
On the Late Massacre in Piedmont, 1745
On the Life of Man, 1049
On the New Forcers of Conscience Under the Long Parliament, 1743
On the Third of September, 1651, 1649

Or che 'l ciel et la terra e 'l vento
      tace, 631
Oroonoko, 2150
Othello, 1179
O thou, my lonely boy, who in
      thy power, 1177
O thou that swing'st upon the
      waving hair, 1610
Oure Hoste gan to swere as he
      were wood, 357
Our God, our help in ages past,
      2638
Our passions are most like to
      floods and streams, 1048

Pamphilia to Amphilanthus, 1573
Paradise Lost, 1755
Pardoner's Prologue and Tale, The,
      357
Parish Register, The, 2856
Parliament of Fowls, The, 276
Parson's Tale, The, 387
Passionate Shepherd to His Love,
      The, 1098
Pen, 150
Pepys, Samuel, 2003
Permit Marissa in an artless lay,
      2140
Perspectives
      Arthurian Myth in the History
            of Britain, 152
      The Civil War, or the Wars of
            Three Kingdoms, 1698
      Emblem, Style, and Metaphor,
            1596
      Ethnic and Religious Encoun-
            ters, 124
      Government and Self-Govern-
            ment, 707
      Landscape, Pleasure, Power,
            2857
      Mind and God, 2626
      Reading Papers, 2311
      The Royal Society and the
            New Science, 2039
      Spiritual Self-Reckonings,
            1946
      Tracts on Women and Gen-
            der, 1329
Petition of Gentlewomen and
      Tradesmen's Wives, The,
      1711
Petrarch, Sonnet 140, 621
Petrarch, Sonnet 164, 631
Petrarch, Sonnet 190, 622
Petty, William, 2457
Philips, Katherine, 1646
Philip Sparrow, 590
Philosophical Enquiry into the Ori-
      gin of Our Ideas of the Sub-
      lime and the Beautiful, A,
      2875
Philosophical Transactions, 2044
Pierce Penniless, 1439
Piers Plowman, 396

Pilgrim's Progress from This World
      to That Which Is to Come,
      The, 1968
Piozzi, Hester Salusbury
      Thrale, 2829
Plays of William Shakespeare, The,
      2753
Pleasure Reconciled to Virtue,
      1541
Pliny the Elder, 1265
Poetress's Hasty Resolution, The,
      2059
Poetress's Petition, The, 2060
Political Arithmetic, 2457
Ponet, John, 713
Pope, Alexander, 2459, 2872
Prayer (1), 1588
Prayer the church's banquet;
      angel's age, 1588
Preface to Saint Gregory's Pastoral
      Care, 134
Preface to The First Part of the
      Mirror of Princely Deeds,
      1334
Prey, it's as if my people have
      been handed prey, 147
Prospect of Heaven Makes Death
      Easy, A, 2635
Psalm 13, 1025
Psalm 71: In Te Domini Speravi,
      1015
Psalm 121: Levavi Oculos, 1018
Pseudodoxia Epidemica, 1678
Pulley, The, 1594
Puttenham, George, 948

Queen and Huntress, 1536
Queen and huntress, chaste and
      fair, 1536

Rake's Progress, A, 2618
Raleigh, Sir Walter, 1046,
      1099
Rambler No. 4, 2702
Rambler No. 5, 2705
Rambler No. 60, 2708
Rambler No. 170, 2711
Rambler No. 171, 2713
Rambler No. 207, 2716
Rape of the Lock, The, 2489
Reading my verses, I liked them
      so well, 2059
Read, Thomas, 2345
Reasons that Induced Dr. S. to
      write a Poem called The
      Lady's Dressing Room, The,
      2568
Redemption, 1585
Regeneration, 1615
Relic, The, 1562
Religio Medici, 1674
Report to Edward I, A, 169
Resolved alike, divine Sarpedon
      glows, 2511
Retreat, The, 1617

Review of Soames Jenyns' A Free
      Inquiry into the Nature and
      Origin of Evil, A, 2719
Review of the State of the British
      Nation, Vol. 1, No. 43, A,
      2340
Review of the State of the British
      Nation, Vol. 4, No. 21, A,
      2315
Review of the State of the British
      Nation, Vol. 9, No. 34, A,
      2349
Riche, Barnabe, 1332, 1427
Rise heart, thy Lord is risen. Sing
      his praise, 1585
Roaring Girl, The, 1357
Robene and Makyne, 565
Robene sat on gud grene hill,
      565
Rolle, Richard, 438
Room, room, make room for the
      bouncing belly, 1542
Ruin, The, 558
Rule, Britannia, 2666

Salve Deus Rex Judaeorum, 1041
Samson Agonistes, 1905
Satyr Against Reason and
      Mankind, A, 2199
Scarce had the morning star hid
      from the light, 1079
Schoolmaster, The, 724
School of Abuse, The, 946
Seasons, The, 2662
Second Booke of the Faerie
      Queene, The, 879
Second Play of the Shepherds, The,
      461
See! Winter comes, to rule the
      varied year, 2658
Sermon Preached to the Honorable
      Company of the Virginia
      Plantation, A, 1569
Set Me Whereas the Sun Doth
      Parch the Green, 630
Seven Sonnets to Alexander
      Neville, 728
Shakespeare, William, 1166
Shall I compare thee to a sum-
      mer's day?, 1170
Shepheardes Calender, The, 736
... She was suspicious of gifts in
      this wide world, 115
Short Song of Congratulation, A,
      2700
Short Treatise of Political Power,
      A, 713
Short View of the Immorality and
      Profaneness of the English
      Stage, A, 2271
Sidney, Sir Philip, 911, 954
Sighing, and sadly sitting by my
      love, 1096
Silence, and Stealth of Days,
      1618

Since the siege and the assault was eased at Troy, 187
Sir Gawain and the Green Knight, 185
Sith *Cynthia* is ascended to that rest, 1042
Skelton, John, 589
Smart, Christopher, 2650
Smith, Sir John, 1273
So Cruel Prison, 632
Some Reflections upon Marriage, 2280
Some that have deeper digged love's mine than I, 1557
Some Time I Fled the Fire, 623
Song (Donne), 1551
Song to Celia, 1535
Song (Wilmot), 2196
Song (Wroth), 1574, 1576
Sonnet on the Death of Mr. Richard West, 2682
Sonnets from Cynthia, 1095
Sonnets (Shakespeare), 1169
Soote Season, The, 631
So shall I live, supposing thou art true, 1174
Sowernam, Esther, 1344
Speak, Echo, tell; how my I call my love?, 1096
Spectator, 2323, 2341
Spectator No. 1, 2324
Spectator No. 10, 2330
Spectator No. 11, 2337
Spectator No. 65, 2273
Spectator No. 69, 2334
Spectator No. 128, 2355
Spectator No. 412, 2867
Spectator No. 414, 2869
Spectator No. 465, 2640
Speght, Rachel, 1338
Spenser, Edmund, 735, 1271
Spit in my face ye Jews, and pierce my side, 1566
Sporting at fancy, setting light by love, 1095
Sprat, Thomas, 2041
Spring, 523
Stand Whoso List, 626
Steele, Richard, 2273, 2321, 2328, 2337, 2347, 2354
Stella oft sees the very face of woe, 988
Stella's Birthday, 1719, 2367
Stella's Birthday, 1727, 2368
Stella this day is thirty-four, 2367
Story of Alexander Agnew, The; or Jock of Broad Scotland, 1724
Sufficeth to you, my joys interred, 1051
Sumer is icumen in, 522
Sun Rising, The, 1552
Sure there are poets which did never dream, 2859

Sweet Auburn, loveliest village of the plain, 2845
Sweet day, so cool, so calm, so bright, 1591
Sweetest love, return again, 1574
Sweet Jesus, King of Bliss, 533
Swetnam, Joseph, 1335
Swift, Jonathan, 2362, 2447

Tagus, Farewell, 624
Táin Bó Cuailnge, The, 95
Take back that heart you with such caution give, 2133
Take heed mine eyes, how you your looks do cast, 1575
Tale of a Wayside Inn, 554
Tale of Taliesin, The, 536
Taliesin, 139
Task, The, 2654, 2674
Tatler, 2320
Tatler No. 1, 2321
Tatler No. 18, 2328
Tatler No. 25, 2347
Tatler No. 104, 2354
Tatler No. 155, 2328
Tell me no more of constancy, 2194
Tell me not, sweet, I am unkind, 1610
Tesauro, Conte Emmanuele, 1605
Th'Assyrians' King, in Peace with Foul Desire, 630
That time of year thou mayst in me behold, 1173
The curfew tolls the knell of parting day, 2685
The Devil take the Constable's head!, 1432
The Doctor in a clean starched band, 2568
The doubt which ye misdeeme, fayre love, is vaine, 899
The forward youth that would appear, 1643
The harbingers are come: see, see their mark, 1595
The hearts thus intermixèd speak, 1647
The lif so short, the craft so long to lerne, 277
"The Prince of Lilliput" to Stella, 2450
There is a land of pure delight, 2635
There was a great battle Saturday morning, 141
The Ruffian cly the nab of the harman beck!, 1432
The shining pelican, whose yawning throat, 150
The spacious firmament on high, 2641
The taxe hath tened vs alle, 432

The time is come I must depart, 1002
The wanton troopers riding by, 1625
The weary yeare his race now having run, 899
They Are All Gone into the World of Light!, 1620
The year revolves, and I again explore, 2856
They Flee from Me, 623
Think not this paper comes with vain pretense, 2565
This day, whate'er the fates decree, 2368
This holy season fit to fast and pray, 899
This is my play's last scene, here heavens appoint, 1565
Thomas D'Urfey: The Hubble Bubbles, 2344
Thomas of Reading, 1432
Thomson, James, 2657
Thornton, Alice, 1961
Thou art not, Penshurst, built to envious show, 1533
Thou youngest virgin-daughter of the skies, 2110
Thraliana, 2835
Three Anglo-Latin Riddles by Aldhelm, 150
Three Dialogues Between Hylas and Philonous, 2642
Through a single year, 141
Through that pure virgin-shrine, 1621
Through the Lens of Aristotle, 1606
Thus Englished, 1432
Thy bosom is endearèd with all hearts, 1171
Thy forests, Windsor! and thy green retreats, 2478
Timber: or Discoveries, 1600
Time, 1593
Tired Nature's sweet restorer, balmy Sleep!, 2669
'Tis hard to say, if greater want of skill, 2461
'Tis sorrow and pain, 556
'Tis true, 'tis day; what though it be?, 1555
To Alexander Pope (Swift), 2450
To all those happy blessings which ye have, 900
To Almystrea, 2140
To Althea, from Prison, 1612
To draw no envy, Shakespeare, on thy name, 1536
To His Coy Mistress, 1628
To His Scribe Adam, 392
To John Donne, 1532
To Lucasta, Going to the Wars, 1610
To Lysander at the Music-Meeting, 2135

To Lysander, on Some Verses He Writ, 2133

To me, fair friend, you never can be old, 1175

To Mrs. Mary Awbrey at Parting, 1651

To My Excellent Lucasia, on Our Friendship, 1652

Tonight, grave sir, both my poor house and I, 1532

To Penshurst, 1533

To prink me up and make me higher placed, 729

To the English Troops at Tilbury, 1033

To Thee Pure Sprite, 1013

To the Fair Clarinda, Who Made Love to Me, Imagined More than Woman, 2138

To the Immortal Memory, and Friendship of that Noble Pair, Sir Lucius Cary and Sir H. Morison, 1538

To the Ladies, 2139

To the Lord General Cromwell, 1744

To the Memory of Mr. Oldham, 2109

To the Memory of My Beloved, the Author, Mr. William Shakespeare, and What He Hath Left Us, 1536

To the Noblest and best of Ladies, the Countess of Denbigh, 1608

To the Queen, 1048

To the Truly Noble, and Obliging Mrs. Anne Owen, 1650

To the Virgins, to Make Much of Time, 1581

To you, my purs, and to noon other wight, 393

Tragedy of Mariam, the Fair Queen of Jewry, The, 1277

Tragical History of Dr. Faustus, The, 1117

Trapnel, Anna, 1954

Travels of Sir John Mandeville, The, 493

Treatise on Human Nature, A, 2644

True Historical Narrative of the Rebellion, 1726

True Law of Free Monarchies, The, 721

True Relation of my Birth, Breeding, and Life, A, 2063

True Relation of the Apparition of One Mrs. Veal, A, 2291

Truly poor Night thou welcome art to me, 1573

Turkish Embassy Letters, The, 2558

'Twas at the royal feast, for Persia won, 2114

'Twas on a lofty vase's side, 2684

21st and Last Book of the Ocean to Cynthia, The, 1051

Twice or thrice had I loved thee, 1555

Two loves I have, of comfort and despair, 1178

Tyler, Margaret, 1333

Tyndale, William, 708

Una candida cerva sopra l'erba, 622

Undertaking, The, 1552

Unto the hills, I now will bend, 1018

Upon Appleton House, 1633

Upon His Spaniel Tracie, 1583

Upon Julia's Clothes, 1583

Upon Nothing, 2198

Upon the Double Murder of King Charles, 1648

Urien Yrechwydd, 140

Utopia, 637

Valediction: Forbidden Mourning, A, 1559

Valediction: of Weeping, A, 1556

Vanity of Human Wishes, The, 2692

Vaughan, Henry, 1614

Verses on the Death of Dr. Swift, D.S.P.D., 2374

View of the Present State of Ireland, A, 1271

Village, The, 2854

Virtue, 1591

Vives, Juan Luis, 709

Voice of One Crying, The, 434

Volpone; or, The Fox, 1444

Voyage of Saint Brendan, The, 482

Walpole, Horace, 2873

Wanderer, The, 143

War-Band's Return, The, 141

Was it the proud full sail of his great verse, 1173

Watts, Isaac, 2635

Weekly Journal, The, 2345

We falsely think it due unto our friends, 1653

Were it undo that is ido, 527

Were I (who to my cost already am), 2199

We seventeen sisters, voiceless all, declare, 150

Whan that April with his showres soote, 294

Whan that the Knight hadde thus his tale ytold, 314

What dire offense from am'rous causes spring, 2491

What friendship is, Ardelia, show, 2143

What heaven-entreated heart is this?, 1608

What if this present were the world's last night?, 1567

What is our life? A play of passion, 1049

What wooer ever walked through frost and snow, 552

When as in silks my Julia goes, 1583

When at the first I took my pen in hand, 1968

When Britain first, at heaven's command, 2666

When everyone to pleasing pastime hies, 1574

When first my lines of heav'nly joys made mention, 1592

When first thou didst entice to thee my heart, 1587

When for the thorns with which I long, too long, 1624

When God at first made man, 1594

When I a verse shall make, 1582

When I consider every thing that grows, 1170

When I Consider How My Light Is Spent, 1745

When I do count the clock that tells the time, 1169

When, in disgrace with fortune and men's eyes, 1171

When in the chronicle of wasted time, 1175

When Israel, freed from Pharaoh's hand, 2639

When love with unconfined wings, 1612

When my devotions could not pierce, 1590

When my good Angel guides me to the place, 988

When my grave is broke up again, 1562

When my love swears that she is made of truth, 1178

When night's black mantle could most darkness prove, 1573

When sorrow (using mine own fire's might), 993

When the remote Bermudas ride, 1624

When youth and charms have taken their wanton flight, 2147

Where beth they biforen us weren?, 535

Where, like a pillow on a bed, 1560

While that my soul repairs to her devotion, 1589

Whitney, Geoffrey, 1599

Whitney, Isabella, 994

Whoever comes to shroud me, do not harm, 1562

Whoever has received knowledge, 171

Who says that fictions only and false hair, 1588
Whoso List to Hunt, 621
Who will in fairest book of Nature know, 989
Why are we by all creatures waited on?, 1567
Wife and servant are the same, 2139
Wife of Bath's Prologue, The, 330
Wife of Bath's Tale, The, 348
Wife's Lament, The, 146
Wilmot, John, Earl of Rochester, 2193
Wilt thou love God, as he thee? Then digest, 1568
Wily Clerk, The, 528
Windows, The, 1589

Windsor-Forest, 2478
Winter. A Poem, 2658
Winter, The, 557
With how sad steps, O Moon, thou climb'st the skies, 987
Within this sober frame expect, 1633
With one servant, I went down, 554
Woman, a pleasing but a short-lived flower, 2147
Woodmanship, 731
World, The, 1618, 1653
Writing Tablets, 150
Written on a Wall at Woodstock, 1024
Written with a Diamond on Her Window at Woodstock, 1023

Wroth, Lady Mary, 1571, 1666
Wulf and Eadwacer, 146
Wyatt Resteth Here, 635
Wyatt, Sir Thomas, 619

Ye circum, and uncircumcised, 2344
Ye distant spires, ye antique towers, 2682
Ye learned sisters which have oftentimes, 901
Yet once more, O ye laurels, and once more, 1739
Yet, yet a moment, one dim ray of light, 2547
Ye virgins that from Cupid's tents, 998
Young, Edward, 2669